Who's Who in the East

**Biographical Reference Works
Published by Marquis Who's Who**

Who's Who in America

Who Was Who in America

  Historical Volume (1607-1896)

  Volume I (1897-1942)

  Volume II (1943-1950)

  Volume III (1951-1960)

  Volume IV (1961-1968)

  Volume V (1969-1973)

  Volume VI (1974-1976)

Who Was Who in American History—Arts and Letters

Who Was Who in American History—The Military

Who Was Who in American History—Science and Technology

Who's Who in the Midwest

Who's Who in the East

Who's Who in the South and Southwest

Who's Who in the West

Who's Who of American Women

Who's Who in Government

Who's Who in Finance and Industry

Who's Who in Religion

Who's Who in American Law

Who's Who in the World

Who's Who Biographical Record—Child Development Professionals

Who's Who Biographical Record—School District Officials

World Who's Who in Science

Directory of Medical Specialists

Marquis Who's Who Publications/Index to All Books

Travelers' Guide to U.S. Certified Doctors Abroad

Who's Who in the East ®

Including Connecticut, Delaware, the District of Columbia,
Maine, Maryland, Massachusetts, New Hampshire, New
Jersey, New York, Pennsylvania, Rhode Island, Vermont,
and in Canada, the provinces of New Brunswick,
Newfoundland, Nova Scotia, Prince Edward Island,
Quebec, and the eastern half of Ontario.

17th edition
1979-1980

MARQUIS
Who's Who

Marquis Who's Who, Inc.
200 East Ohio Street
Chicago, Illinois 60611 U.S.A.

Library of Congress Catalog Card Number 43-18522
International Standard Book Number 0-8379-0617-2
Product Code Number 030220

Distributed in the United Kingdom by
George Prior Associated Publishers
37-41 Bedford Row
London WC 1, England

Manufactured in the United States of America

Table of Contents

Preface

The constant and dramatic development of the eastern United States and Canadian regions—in business, the professions and the arts; in urban, suburban and rural progress—requires close vigilance from the editors of *Who's Who in the East.* Only through such vigilance can the editors identify those eastern men and women who are of the most outstanding and frequent reference interest in that region.

This seventeenth edition of *Who's Who in the East* represents the latest effort to identify and provide accurate biographical data on those individuals of regional importance.

Assiduously reviewed, revised, and amended, the seventeenth edition offers up-to-the-minute coverage of a broad range of Easterners based on position or individual achievement. Our editors have made every effort to present a balanced picture of achievement in the East. To assure such balance in the compilation of the volume, a list of essential names is made up of those men and women who are so eminent that their omission would fault the usefulness of this book. In the great majority of cases these individuals have furnished their own data, thus assuring a high degree of accuracy. In some cases where individuals have failed to supply information, Marquis staff members compile the data through careful and independent research. Sketches compiled in this manner are denoted by an asterisk. As in previous editions, biographees are given the opportunity to review prepublication proofs of their sketches to make sure they are correct.

Marquis Who's Who editors exercise the utmost care in preparing each biographical sketch for publication. Occasionally, however, errors do occur despite all precautions taken to minimize such occurrences. All users of this directory are requested to draw the attention of the publisher to any errors found, so that corrections can be made in a later edition.

The seventeenth edition contains approximately 19,000 names from the region embracing Connecticut, Delaware, Maine, Maryland, Massachusetts, New Hampshire, New Jersey, New York, Pennsylvania, Rhode Island, Vermont, Washington, D.C. . . . and in Canada, the provinces of New Brunswick, Newfoundland, Nova Scotia, Prince Edward Island, Quebec, and eastern Ontario.

The persons sketched in this volume represent a broad spectrum of achievement in virtually every significant field of endeavor. Included are executives and officials in government, business, education, religion, the press, civic affairs, the arts, cultural affairs, law and other fields. This edition also includes significant contributors in such fields as contemporary art, music, and science.

The question is often asked, "How do people get into a Who's Who volume?" Name selection is based on one fundamental principle: reference value.

Biographees of *Who's Who in the East* can be classified into two basic categories: (1) Persons who are of regional reference importance to colleagues, librarians, researchers, scholars, the press, historians, biographers, participants in business and civic affairs, and others with specific or general inquiry needs; (2) Individuals of national reference interest who are also of such regional or local importance that their inclusion in the book is essential to its serviceability. With these names there is a minimum of duplication between this volume and *Who's Who in America.*

In recognition of the complementary relationship between these two Marquis publications, however, this seventeenth edition of *Who's Who in the East* contains a listing of all those biographees of the Eastern region whose sketches appear in the fortieth edition of *Who's Who in America.*

In the editorial evaluation that resulted in the ultimate selection of the names in this directory, an individual's desire to be listed was not sufficient reason for inclusion; rather it was the individual's demonstrated merit that ruled. Similarly wealth or social position was not a criterion; only occupational stature or achievement in some field affecting the development of the Eastern region of North America influenced selection. Indeed, many of the biographees are engaged in fields marked far more by service than by monetary reward. And, of course, this volume lists individuals regardless of their race or ethnic origin.

Thus this seventeenth edition of *Who's Who in the East* carries on the tradition of excellence established in 1899 with the publication of the first edition of *Who's Who in America.* The essence of that tradition is reflected in our continuing effort to produce reference works that are responsive to the needs of their users throughout the world.

Standards of Admission

The foremost consideration in determining possible biographees of *Who's Who in the East* is the extent of an individual's reference interest. Such reference interest is judged on either of two factors: (1) The position of responsibility held, or (2) The level of significant achievement attained.

Admissions based on the factor of position include:

Members of the U.S. Congress

Federal judges

Governors of states covered by this volume

Premiers of Canadian provinces covered by this volume

State attorneys general

Judges of state and territorial courts of highest appellate jurisdiction

Mayors of major cities

Heads of the major universities and colleges

Heads of leading philanthropic, educational, cultural, and scientific institutions and associations

Chief ecclesiastics of the principal religious denominations

Principal officers of national and international businesses

Others chosen because of incumbency, authorship, or membership

Admission based on individual achievement, on the other hand, must be decided by a judicious process of evaluating qualitative factors. To be selected on this basis, a person must have accomplished some conspicuous achievement—something that distinguishes him from the vast majority of his contemporaries. He or she may scarcely be known in the local community, but may be widely recognized in some special field of endeavor. Such a person often is one whose work is better known than his/her name.

Key to Information in this Directory

❶ KILLBROOK, WALTER BOSTON, **❷** lawyer; **❸** b. Topeka, Kans., Aug. 3, 1922; **❹** s. Samuel Taylor and Bertha (Hanson) K.; **❺** B.A., Pa. State U., 1943; J.D., Syracuse U., 1948; **❻** m. Nancy Roudebush, June 20, 1943; **❼** children—Marilyn, Barbara Anne, Eugene Maurice. **❽** Admitted to N.Y. bar, 1948; asso. firm Prine, Belden and Coates, Rochester, N.Y., 1948-55; mem. firm Johnson, Randolph, Sikes and Bord, Rochester, 1955—, partner, 1961—; legal cons. Rochester Urban League, 1968—. **❾** Commr., Monroe County Park Dist., 1967-68; mem. planning com. Genesee-Crossroads Redevel. Project, Rochester, 1970—; bd. dirs. Eastman Sch. Music, 1973—. **❿** Served with U.S. Army, 1944-45. **⓫** Named Man of Year, Rochester Times-Union, 1969. **⓬** Mem. Am. Bar Assn., N.Y. Bar Assn., Rochester Bar Assn., Am. Judicature Soc., Order of Coif. **⓭** Democrat. **⓮** Episcopalian. **⓯** Clubs: Rochester Country, Tuesday Luncheon, Lions. **⓰** Author: Urban Renewal and the Law, 1969. **⓱** Home: 3080 Grant St Rochester NY 14650 **⓲** Office: 10 St Paul St Rochester NY 14604

Key

- ❶ Name
- ❷ Occupation
- ❸ Vital Statistics
- ❹ Parents
- ❺ Education
- ❻ Marriage
- ❼ Children
- ❽ Career
- ❾ Civic and Political Activities
- ❿ Military Record
- ⓫ Awards and Certifications
- ⓬ Professional and Association Memberships
- ⓭ Political Affiliation
- ⓮ Religion
- ⓯ Clubs (including lodges)
- ⓰ Writings and Special Achievements
- ⓱ Home Address
- ⓲ Office Address

The biographical listings in *Who's Who in the East* are arranged in alphabetical order according to the first letter of the biographee's last name. Each sketch is presented in a uniform order as in the sample sketch above. The many abbreviations used in the sketches are explained in the Table of Abbreviations.

Table of Abbreviations

The following abbreviations and symbols are frequently used in this Directory

✻ (An asterisk) following a sketch indicates that it was researched by the Marquis Who's Who editorial staff and has not been verified by the biographee.

A.A. Associate in Arts
AAAL American Academy of Arts and Letters
AAAS American Association for the Advancement of Science
AAHPER Alliance for Health, Physical Education and Recreation
A. and M. Agricultural and Mechanical
AAU Amateur Athletic Union
AAUP American Association of University Professors
AAUW American Association of University Women
A.B. Arts, Bachelor of
AB Alberta
ABC American Broadcasting Company
AC Air Corps
acad. academy, academic
acct. accountant
acctg. accounting
ACDA Arms Control and Disarmament Agency
ACLU American Civil Liberties Union
A.C.P. American College of Physicians
A.C.S. American College of Surgeons
ADA American Dental Association
a.d.c. aide-de-camp
adj. adjunct, adjutant
adj. gen. adjutant general
adm. admiral
adminstr. administrator
adminstrn. administration
adminstrv. administrative
adv. advocate, advisory, adviser
advt. advertising
A.E. Agricultural Engineeer
A.E. and P., AEP Ambassador Extraordinary and Plenipotentiary
AEC Atomic Energy Commission
aero. aeronautical, aeronautic
aerodyn. aerodynamic
AFB Air Force Base
AFL-CIO American Federation of Labor and Congress of Industrial Organizations
AFTRA American Federation TV and Radio Artists
agr. agriculture
agrl. agricultural
agt. agent
AGVA American Guild of Variety Artists
agy. agency
A&I Agricultural and Industrial
AIA American Institute of Architects
AIAA American Institute of Aeronautics Astronautics
AID Agency for International Development
AIEE American Institute of Electrical Engineers
AIM American Institute of Management
AIME American Institute of Mining, Metallurgy, and Petroleum Engineers
AK Alaska
AL Alabama
ALA American Library Association
Ala. Alabama
alt. alternate
Alta. Alberta
A&M Agricultural and Mechanical
A.M. Arts, Master of
Am. American, America
AMA American Medical Association

A.M.E. African Methodist Episcopal
Amtrak National Railroad Passenger Corporation
AMVETS American Veterans of World War II, Korea, Vietnam
anat. anatomical
ann. annual
ANTA American National Theatre and Academy
anthrop. anthropological
AP Associated Press
APO Army Post Office
apptd. appointed
apt. apartment
AR Arkansas
ARC American Red Cross
archeol. archeological
archtl. architectural
Ariz. Arizona
Ark. Arkansas
Arts D. Arts, Doctor of
arty. artillery
ASCAP American Society of Composers, Authors and Publishers
ASCE American Society of Civil Engineers
ASHRAE American Society of Heating, Refrigeration, and Air Conditioning Engineers
ASME American Society of Mechanical Engineers
assn. association
asso. associate
asst. assistant
ASTM American Society for Testing and Materials
astron. astronomical
astrophys. astrophysical
ATSC Air Technical Service Command
AT&T American Telephone & Telegraph Company
atty. attorney
AUS Army of the United States
aux. auxiliary
Ave. Avenue
AVMA American Veterinary Medical Association
AZ Arizona

B. Bachelor
b. born
B.A. Bachelor of Arts
B. Agr. Bachelor of Agriculture
Balt. Baltimore
Bapt. Baptist
B.Arch. Bachelor of Architecture
B.A.S. Bachelor of Agricultural Science
B.B.A. Bachelor of Business Administration
BBC British Broadcasting Corporation
B.C.,BC British Columbia
B.C.E. Bachelor of Civil Engineering
B.Chir. Bachelor of Surgery
B.C.L. Bachelor of Civil Law
B.C.S. Bachelor of Commerical Science
B.D. Bachelor of Divinity
bd. board
B.E. Bachelor of Education
B.E.E. Bachelor of Electrical Engineering
B.F.A. Bachelor of Fine Arts
bibl. biblical
bibliog. bibliographical
biog. biographical
biol. biological
B.J. Bachelor of Journalism
Bklyn. Brooklyn
B.L. Bachelor of Letters
bldg. building
B.L.S. Bachelor of Library Science

Blvd. Boulevard
bn. battalion
B.&O.R.R. Baltimore & Ohio Railroad
bot. botanical
B.P.E. Bachelor of Physical Education
br. branch
B.R.E. Bachelor of Religious Education
brig. gen. brigadier general
Brit. British, Britannica
Bros. Brothers
B.S. Bachelor of Science
B.S.A. Bachelor of Agricultural Science
B.S.D. Bachelor of Didactic Science
B.S.T. Bachelor of Sacred Theology
B.Th. Bachelor of Theology
bull. bulletin
bur. bureau
bus. business
B.W.I. British West Indies

CA California
CAA Civil Aeronautics Administration
CAB Civil Aeronautics Board
Calif. California
C.Am. Central America
Can. Canada, Canadian
CAP Civil Air Patrol
capt. captain
CARE Cooperative American Relief Everywhere
Cath. Catholic
cav. cavalry
CBC Canadian Broadcasting Company
CBI China, Burma, India Theatre of Operations
CBS Columbia Broadcasting System
CCC Commodity Credit Corporation
CCNY City College of New York
CCU Cardiac Care Unit
CD Civil Defense
C.E. Corps of Engineers, Civil Engineer
CENTO Central Treaty Organization
CERN European Organization of Nuclear Research
cert. certificate, certification, certified
CETA Comprehensive Employment Training Act
CFL Canadian Football League
ch. church
Ch.D. Doctor of Chemistry
chem. chemical
Chem. E. Chemical Engineer
Chgo. Chicago
chirurg. chirurgical
chmn. chairman
chpt. chapter
CIA Central Intelligence Agency
CIC Counter Intelligence Corps
Cin. Cincinnati
Cleve. Cleveland
climatol. climatological
clin. clinical
clk. clerk
C.L.U. Chartered Life Underwriter
C.M. Master in Surgery
C.& N.W.Ry. Chicago & Northwestern Railway
CO Colorado
Co. Company
COF Catholic Order of Foresters
C. of C. Chamber of Commerce
col. colonel
coll. college
Colo. Colorado
com. committee
comd. commanded
comdg. commanding

comdr. commander
comdt. commandant
commd. commissioned
comml. commercial
commn. commission
commr. commissioner
condr. conductor
Conf. Conference
Congl. Congregational
Conglist. Congregationalist
Conn. Connecticut
cons. consultant, consulting
consol. consolidated
constl. constitutional
constn. constitution
constrn. construction
contbd. contributed
contbg. contributing
contbn. contribution
contbr. contributor
Conv. Convention
coop., co-op. cooperative
CORDS Civil Operations and Revolutionary
  Development Support
CORE Congress of Racial Equality
corp. corporation, corporate
corr. correspondent, corresponding,
  correspondence
C.&O.Ry. Chesapeake & Ohio Railway
C.P.A. Certified Public Accountant
C.P.C.U. Chartered property and casualty
  underwriter
C.P.H. Certificate of Public Health
cpl. corporal
CPR Cardiac Pulmonary Resuscitation
C.P.Ry. Canadian Pacific Railway
C.S. Christian Science
C.S.B. Bachelor of Christian Science
CSC Civil Service Commission
C.S.D. Doctor of Christian Science
CT Connecticut
ct. Court
CWS Chemical Warfare Service
C.Z. Canal Zone

d. daughter
D. Doctor
D.Agr. Doctor of Agriculture
DAR Daughters of the American Revolution
dau. daughter
DAV Disabled American Veterans
D.C., DC District of Columbia
D.C.L. Doctor of Civil Law
D.C.S. Doctor of Commercial Science
D.D. Doctor of Divinity
D.D.S. Doctor of Dental Surgery
DE Delaware
dec. deceased
def. defense
Del. Delaware
del. delegate, delegation
Dem. Democrat, Democratic
D.Eng. Doctor of Engineering
denom. denomination, denominational
dep. deputy
dept. department
dermatol. dermatological
desc. descendant
devel. development, developmental
D.F.A. Doctor of Fine Arts
D.F.C. Distinguished Flying Cross
D.H.L. Doctor of Hebrew Literature
dir. director
dist. district
distbg. distributing
distbn. distribution

distbr. distributor
disting. distinguished
div. division, divinity, divorce
D.Litt. Doctor of Literature
D.M.D. Doctor of Medical Dentistry
D.M.S. Doctor of Medical Science
D.O. Doctor of Osteopathy
D.P.H. Diploma in Public Health
D.R. Daughters of the Revolution
Dr. Drive
D.R.E. Doctor of Religious Education
Dr.P.H. Doctor of Public Health, Doctor
  of Public Hygiene
D.S.C. Distinguished Service Cross
D.Sc. Doctor of Science
D.S.M. Distinguished Service Medal
D.S.T. Doctor of Sacred Theology
D.T.M. Doctor of Tropical Medicine
D.V.M. Doctor of Veterinary Medicine
D.V.S. Doctor of Veterinary Surgery

E. East
E. and P. Extraordinary and Plenipotentiary
Eccles. Ecclesiastical
ecol. ecology, ecological
econ. economic
ECOSOC Economic and Social Council
  (of the UN)
E.D. Doctor of Engineering
ed. educated
Ed.B. Bachelor of Education
Ed.D. Doctor of Education
edit. edition
Ed.M. Master of Education
edn. education
ednl. educational
EDP electronic data processing
Ed.S. Specialist in Education
E.E. Electrical Engineer
E.E. and M.P. Envoy Extraordinary and
  Minister Plenipotentiary
EEC European Economic Community
EEG electroencephalogram
EEO Equal Employment Opportunity
EKG electrocardiogram
E.Ger. German Democratic Republic
elec. electrical
electrochem. electrochemical
electrophys. electrophysical
elem. elementary
E.M. Engineer of Mines
ency. encyclopedia
Eng. England
engr. engineer
engring. engineering
entomol. entomological
environ. environmental, environment
EPA Environmental Protection Agency
epidemiol. epidemiological
Episc. Episcopalian
ERA Equal Rights Amendment
ERDA Energy Research and Development
  Administration
ESEA Elementary and Secondary Education Act
ESSA Environmental Science Services
  Administration
ethnol. ethnological
ETO European Theatre of Operations
Evang. Evangelical
exam. examination, examining
exec. executive
exhbn. exhibition
expdn. expedition
expn. exposition
expt. experiment
exptl. experimental

F.A. Field Artillery
FAA Federal Aviation Administration
FAO Food and Agriculture Organization
  (of the UN)
FBI Federal Bureau of Investigation
FCA Farm Credit Administration
FCC Federal Communication Commission
FCDA Federal Civil Defense Administration
FDA Food and Drug Administration
FDIA Federal Deposit Insurance Administration
FDIC Federal Deposit Insurance Corporation
F.E. Forest Engineer
FEA Federal Energy Administration
fed. federal
fedn. federation
fgn. foreign
FHA Federal Housing Administration
fin. financial, finance
FL Florida
Fla. Florida
FMC Federal Maritime Commission
FOA Foreign Operations Administration
found. foundation
FPC Federal Power Commission
FPO Fleet Post Office
frat. fraternity
FRS Federal Reserve System
FSA Federal Security Agency
Ft. Fort
FTC Federal Trade Commission

G-1 (or other number) Division of General Staff
Ga., GA Georgia
GAO General Accounting Office
gastroent. gastroenterological
GATT General Agreement of Tariff and Trades
gen. general
geneal. genealogical
geod. geodetic
geog. geographic, geographical
geol. geological
geophys. geophysical
gerontol. gerontological
G.H.Q. General Headquarters
G.N.Ry. Great Northern Railway
gov. governor
govt. government
govtl. governmental
GPO Government Printing Office
grad. graduate, graduated
GSA General Services Administration
Gt. Great
GU Guam
gynecol. gynecological

hdqrs. headquarters
HEW Department of Health, Education and
  Welfare
H.H.D. Doctor of Humanities
HHFA Housing and Home Finance Agency
HI Hawaii
hist. historical, historic
H.M. Master of Humanics
homeo. homeopathic
hon. honorary, honorable
Ho. of Dels. House of Delegates
Ho. of Reps. House of Representatives
hort. horticultural
hosp. hospital
HUD Department of Housing and Urban Develop-
  ment
Hwy. Highway
hydrog. hydrographic

IA Iowa
IAEA International Atomic Energy Agency
IBM International Business Machines Corporation
IBRD International Bank for Reconstruction and Development
ICA International Cooperation Administration
ICC Interstate Commerce Commission
ICU Intensive Care Unit
ID Idaho
IEEE Institute of Electrical and Electronics Engineers
IFC International Finance Corporation
IGY International Geophysical Year
IL Illinois
Ill. Illinois
illus. illustrated
ILO International Labor Organization
IMF International Monetary Fund
IN Indiana
Inc. Incorporated
ind. independent
Ind. Indiana
Indpls. Indianapolis
indsl. industrial
inf. infantry
info. information
ins. insurance
insp. inspector
insp. gen. inspector general
inst. institute
instl. institutional
instn. institution
instr. instructor
instrn. instruction
internat. international
intro. introduction
IRE Institute of Radio Engineers
IRS Internal Revenue Service
ITT International Telephone & Telegraph Corporation

J.B. Jurum Baccolaureus
J.C.B. Juris Canonici Bachelor
J.C.L. Juris Canonici Lector
J.D. Juris Doctor
j.g. junior grade
jour. journal
jr. junior
J.S.D. Jurum Scientiae Doctor
J.U.D. Juris Utriusque Doctor
Judge Adv. Gen. Judge Advocate General

Kans. Kansas
K.C. Knights of Columbus
K.P. Knights of Pythias
KS Kansas
K.T. Knight Templar
Ky., KY Kentucky

La., LA Louisiana
lab. laboratory
lang. language
laryngol. laryngological
LB Labrador
lectr. lecturer
legis. legislation, legislative
L.H.D. Doctor of Humane Letters
L.I. Long Island
lic. licensed, license
L.I.R.R. Long Island Railroad
lit. literary, literature
Litt. B. Bachelor of Letters

Litt. D. Doctor of Letters
LL.B. Bachelor of Laws
LL.D. Doctor of Laws
LL.M. Master of Laws
Ln. Lane
L.&N.R.R. Louisville & Nashville Railroad
L.S. Library Science (in degree)
lt. lieutenant
Ltd. Limited
Luth. Lutheran
LWV League of Women Voters

m. married
M. Master
M.A. Master of Arts
MA Massachusetts
mag. magazine
M.Agr. Master of Agriculture
maj. major
Man. Manitoba
M.Arch. Master in Architecture
Mass. Massachusetts
math. mathematics, mathematical
MATS Military Air Transport Service
M.B. Bachelor of Medicine
MB Manitoba
M.B.A. Master of Business Administration
MBS Mutual Broadcasting System
M.C. Medical Corps
M.C.E. Master of Civil Engineering
mcht. merchant
mcpl. municipal
M.C.S. Master of Commercial Science
M.D. Doctor of Medicine
Md., MD Maryland
M.Dip. Master in Diplomacy
mdse. merchandise
M.D.V. Doctor of Veterinary Medicine
M.E. Mechanical Engineer
ME Maine
M.E. Ch. Methodist Episcopal Church
mech. mechanical
M.Ed. Master of Education
med. medical
M.E.E. Master of Electrical Engineering
mem. member
meml. memorial
merc. mercantile
met. metropolitan
metall. metallurgical
Met. E. Metallurgical Engineer
meteorol. meteorological
Meth. Methodist
Mex. Mexico
M.F. Master of Forestry
M.F.A. Master of Fine Arts
mfg. manufacturing
mfr. manufacturer
mgmt. management
mgr. manager
M.H.A. Master of Hospital Administration
M.I. Military Intelligence
MI Michigan
Mich. Michigan
micros. microscopic, microscopical
mil. military
Milw. Milwaukee
mineral. mineralogical
Minn. Minnesota
Miss. Mississippi
M.I.T. Massachusetts Institute of Technology
mktg. marketing
M.L. Master of Laws
MLA Modern Language Association
M.L.D. Magister Legnum Diplomatic

M.Litt. Master of Literature
M.L.S. Master of Library Science
M.M.E. Master of Mechanical Engineering
MN Minnesota
mng. managing
Mo., MO Missouri
moblzn. mobilization
Mont. Montana
M.P. Member of Parliament
M.P.E. Master of Physical Education
M.P.H. Master of Public Health
M.P.L. Master of Patent Law
Mpls. Minneapolis
M.R.E. Master of Religious Education
M.S. Master of Science
MS Mississippi
M.Sc. Master of Science
M.S.F. Master of Science of Forestry
M.S.T. Master of Sacred Theology
M.S.W. Master of Social Work
MT Montana
Mt. Mount
MTO Mediterranean Theatre of Operations
mus. museum, musical
Mus.B. Bachelor of Music
Mus.D. Doctor of Music
Mus.M. Master of Music
mut. mutual
mycol. mycological

N. North
NAACP National Association for the Advancement of Colored People
NACA National Advisory Committee for Aeronautics
NAD National Academy of Design
N.Am. North America
NAM National Association of Manufacturers
NAPA National Association of Performing Artists
NAREB National Association of Real Estate Boards
NARS National Archives and Record Service
NASA National Aeronautics and Space Administration
nat. national
NATO North Atlantic Treaty Organization
NATOUSA North African Theatre of Operations
nav. navigation
N.B., NB New Brunswick
NBC National Broadcasting Company
N.C., NC North Carolina
NCCJ National Conference of Christians and Jews
N.D., ND North Dakota
NDEA National Defense Education Act
NE Nebraska
N.E. Northeast
NEA National Education Association
Nebr. Nebraska
neurol. neurological
Nev. Nevada
NF Newfoundland
NFL National Football League
Nfld. Newfoundland
N.G. National Guard
N.H., NH New Hampshire
NHL National Hockey League
NIH National Institutes of Health
NIMH National Institute of Mental Health
N.J., NJ New Jersey
NLRB National Labor Relations Board
NM New Mexico
N.Mex. New Mexico
No. Northern

NOAA National Oceanographic and Atmospheric Administration
NORAD North American Air Defense
NOW National Organization for Women
N.P. Ry. Northern Pacific Railway
nr. near
NRC National Research Council
N.S., NS Nova Scotia
NSC National Security Council
NSF National Science Foundation
N.T. New Testament
NT Northwest Territories
numis. numismatic
NV Nevada
NW Northwest
N.W.T. Northwest Territories
N.Y., NY New York
N.Y.C. New York City
N.Z. New Zealand

OAS Organization of American States
Ob-Gyn obstetrics-gynecology
obs. observatory
O.D. Doctor of Optometry
OECD Organization of European Cooperation and Development
OEEC Organization of European Economic Cooperation
OEO Office of Economic Opportunity
ofcl. official
OH Ohio
OK Oklahoma
Okla. Oklahoma
ON Ontario
Ont. Ontario
ophthal. ophthalmological
ops. operations
OR Oregon
orch. orchestra
Oreg. Oregon
orgn. organization
ornithol. ornithological
OSRD Office of Scientific Research and Development
OSS Office of Strategic Services
osteo. osteopathic
otol. otological
otolaryn. otolaryngological

Pa., PA Pennsylvania
P.A. Professional Association
paleontol. paleontological
path. pathological
P.C. Professional Corporation
PE Prince Edward Island
P.E. Professional Engineer
P.E.I. Prince Edward Island
PEN Poets, Playwrights, Editors, Essayists and Novelists (international association)
penol. penological
P.E.O. women's organization (full name not disclosed)
pfc. private first class
PHA Public Housing Administration
pharm. Pharmaceutical
Pharm.D. Doctor of Pharmacy
Pharm.M. Master of Pharmacy
Ph.B. Bachelor of Philosophy
Ph.D. Doctor of Philosophy
Phila. Philadelphia
philharm. philharmonic
philol. philological
philos. philosophical
photog. photographic

phys. physical
physiol. physiological
Pitts. Pittsburgh
Pkwy. Parkway
Pl. Place
P.&L.E.R.R. Pittsburgh & Lake Erie Railroad
P.O. Post Office
PO Box Post Office Box
polit. political
poly. polytechnic, polytechnical
P.Q. Province of Quebec
P.R., PR Puerto Rico
prep. preparatory
pres. president
Presbyn. Presbyterian
presdl. presidential
prin. principal
proc. proceedings
prod. produced (play production)
prof. professor
profl. professional
prog. progressive
propr. proprietor
pros. atty. prosecuting attorney
pro tem pro tempore
PSRO Professional Services Review Organization
psychiat. psychiatric
psychol. psychological
PTA Parent-Teachers Association
PTO Pacific Theatre of Operations
pub. publisher, publishing, published
publ. publication
pvt. private

quar. quarterly
q.m. quartermaster
Q.M.C. Quartermaster Corps
Que. Quebec

radiol. radiological
RAF Royal Air Force
RCA Radio Corporation of America
RCAF Royal Canadian Air Force
R.D. Rural Delivery
Rd. Road
REA Rural Electrification Administration
rec. recording
ref. reformed
regt. regiment
regtl. regimental
rehab. rehabilitation
rep. representative
Rep. Republican
Res. Reserve
ret. retired
rev. review, revised
RFC Reconstruction Finance Corporation
R.F.D. Rural Free Delivery
rhinol. rhinological
R.I., RI Rhode Island
R.N. Registered Nurse
roentgenol. roentgenological
ROTC Reserve Officers Training Corps
R.R. Railroad
Ry. Railway

s. son
S. South
SAC Strategic Air Command
SALT Strategic Arms Limitation Talks
S.Am. South America
san sanitary
SAR Sons of the American Revolution

Sask. Saskatchewan
savs. savings
S.B. Bachelor of Science
SBA Small Business Administration
S.C., SC South Carolina
SCAP Supreme Command Allies Pacific
Sc.B. Bachelor of Science
S.C.D. Doctor of Commercial Science
Sc.D. Doctor of Science
sch. school
sci. science, scientific
SCLC Southern Christian Leadership Conference
SCV Sons of Confederate Veterans
S.D., SD South Dakota
SE Southeast
SEATO Southeast Asia Treaty Organization
sec. secretary
SEC Securities and Exchange Commission
sect. section
seismol. seismological
sem. seminary
sgt. sergeant
SHAEF Supreme Headquarters Allied Expeditionary Forces
SHAPE Supreme Headquarters Allied Powers in Europe
S.I. Staten Island
S.J. Society of Jesus (Jesuit)
S.J.D. Scientiae Juridicae Doctor
SK Saskatchewan
S.M. Master of Science
So. Southern
soc. society
sociol. sociological
S.P. Co. Southern Pacific Company
spl. special
splty. specialty
Sq. Square
sr. senior
S.R. Sons of the Revolution
S.S. Steamship
SSS Selective Service System
St. Saint
St. Street
sta. station
statis. statistical
stats. statistics
S.T.B. Bachelor of Sacred Theology
stblzn. stabilization
S.T.D. Doctor of Sacred Theology
subs. subsidiary
SUNY State University of New York
supr. supervisor
supt. superintendent
surg. surgical
SW Southwest

TAPPI Technical Association of Pulp and Paper Industry
Tb Tuberculosis
tchr. teacher
tech. technical, technology
technol. technological
Tel.&Tel. Telephone & Telegraph
temp. temporary
Tenn. Tennessee
Ter. Territory
Terr. Terrace
TESL Teaching English as a Second Language
Tex. Texas
Th.D. Doctor of Theology
theol. theological
Th.M. Master of Theology
TN Tennessee
tng. training

topog. topographical
trans. transaction, transferred
transl. translation, translated
transp. transportation
treas. treasurer
TV television
TVA Tennessee Valley Authority
twp. township
TX Texas
typog. typographical

U. University
UAW United Auto Workers
UCLA University of California at Los Angeles
UDC United Daughters of the Confederacy
U.K. United Kingdom
UN United Nations
UNESCO United Nations Educational, Scientific and Cultural Organization
UNICEF United Nations International Children's Emergency Fund
univ. university
UNRRA United Nations Relief and Rehabilitation Administration
UPI United Press International
U.P.R.R. Union Pacific Railroad
urol. urological
U.S. United States
U.S.A. United States of America
USAAF United States Army Air Force
USAF United States Air Force

USAFR United States Air Force Reserve
USAR United States Army Reserve
USCG United States Coast Guard
USCGR United States Coast Guard Reserve
USES United States Employment Service
USIA United States Information Agency
USIS United States Information Service
USMC United States Marine Corps
USMCR United States Marine Corps Reserve
USN United States Navy
USNG United States National Guard
USNR United States Naval Reserve
USO United Service Organizations
USPHS United States Public Health Service
U.S.S. United States Ship
USSR Union of the Soviet Socialist Republics
USV United States Volunteers
UT Utah

VA Veterans' Administration
Va., VA Virginia
vet. veteran, veterinary
VFW Veterans of Foreign Wars
V.I., VI Virgin Islands
vice pres. vice president
vis. visiting
VISTA Volunteers in Service to America
VITA Volunteers in Technical Service
vocat. vocational
vol. volunteer, volume

v.p. vice president
vs. versus
VT., VT Vermont

W. West
WA Washington
WAC Women's Army Corps
Wash. Washington
WAVES Women's Reserve, U.S. Naval Reserve
WCTU Women's Christian Temperance Union
W. Ger. Germany, Federal Republic of
WHO World Health Organization
WI Wisconsin
Wis. Wisconsin
WSB Wage Stabilization Board
WV West Virginia
W. VA. West Virginia
WY Wyoming
Wyo. Wyoming

YK Yukon
YMCA Young Men's Christian Association
YMHA Young Men's Hebrew Association
YM & YWHA Young Men's and Young Women's Hebrew Association
YWCA Young Women's Christian Association
yr. year

zool. zoological

Alphabetical Practices

Names are arranged alphabetically according to the surnames, and under identical surnames according to the first given name. If both surname and first given name are identical, names are arranged alphabetically according to the second given name. Where full names are identical, they are arranged in order of age—those of the elder being put first.

Surnames beginning with De, Des, Du, etc., however capitalized or spaced, are recorded with the prefix preceding the surname and arranged alphabetically, under the letter D.

Surnames beginning with Mac are arranged alphabetically under M. This likewise holds for names beginning with Mc; that is, all names beginning Mc will be found in alphabetical order after those beginning Mac.

Surnames beginning with Saint or St. all appear after names that would begin Sains, and such surnames are arranged according to the second part of the name, e.g., St. Clair would come before Saint Dennis.

Surnames beginning with prefix Van are arranged alphabetically under letter V.

Surnames containing the prefix Von or von are usually arranged alphabetically under letter V; any exceptions are noted by cross references (Von Kleinsmid, Rufus Bernhard; see Kleinsmid, Rufus Bernhard von).

Compound hyphenated surnames are arranged according to the first member of the compound.

Compound unhyphenated surnames common in Spanish are not rearranged but are treated as hyphenated names.

Since Chinese names have the family name first, they are so arranged, but without comma between family name and given name (as Lin Yutang).

Parentheses used in connection with a name indicate which part of the full name is usually deleted in common usage. Hence Abbott, W(illiam) Lewis indicates that the usual form of the given name is W. Lewis. In alphabetizing this type name, the parentheses are not considered. However if the name is recorded Abbott, (William) Lewis, signifying that the entire name William is not commonly used, the alphabetizing would be arranged as though the name were Abbott, Lewis.

Who'sWho in the East

AAGRE, CURT, mfg. co. exec.; b. Grimstad, Norway, Oct. 11, 1909; s. George and Tecla (Nilsen) A.; student Columbia, 1927-28, N.Y.U., 1929-30; grad. Pace Inst., 1933; postgrad. Harvard, 1948; m. Helen Winter, Oct. 19, 1946; children—Phyllis Kim, Carol Dee. Various positions to asst. div. sales mgr. Corn Products Refining Co., N.Y.C., 1926-40, fgn. rep., Mexico, 1947-48, Europe, 1949-52; asst. sales mgr. Hubinger Co., N.Y.C., 1953-59; sales mgr. Connell Rice & Sugar Co., Westfield, N.J., 1960-63; sales mgr. nat. accounts Olavarria & Co., N.Y.C., 1963; asst. v.p. Lamborn & Co., Inc., N.Y.C., 1964-69, v.p., mgr. diversification program, 1969-73; asso. broker B.W. Dyer Co., N.Y.C.; pres. Curt Aagre Co., food ingredients broker. Served to maj. (acting col.) AUS, 1941-46. Decorated D.S.M. Mem. Harvard Assn., AIM, Nat. Confectioners Salesmen Assn., N.Y. Preservers Assn., Sales Exec. Club, Candy Exec. Club. Presbyn. Home: 858 Boulevard Westfield NJ 07090 Office: Box 201 Westfield NJ 07090

AARON, ARNOLD, dental products co. exec.; b. Bklyn., Jan. 31, 1930; s. Harry and Ida (Rosenblum) A.; student N.Y.U., 1946-50, Ohio State U., 1950-52; m. Sydell Herman, Dec. 20, 1953; children—Clifford Bradley, Mindy Lynn, Amy Lisa. Teaching fellow N.Y.U., 1952-55; chemist J.F. Jelenko & Co., N.Y.C., 1958-62, chief chemist and purchasing agt., 1962-68; chemist J.F. Jelenko & Co. div. Pennwalt Corp., New Rochelle, N.Y., 1968-74, asst. to pres., 1974-75, v.p., 1975—. Pres., Jewish Community Center, 1975-77; chmn. United Jewish Appeal, Rockland County, N.Y., 1977. Served with USNR, 1955-57. Recipient Man of Year award Jewish Community Center, Spring Valley, 1968, David Ben-Gurion award, 1976. Fellow Am. Inst. Chemists; mem. Am. Chem. Soc., Internat. Assn. Dental Research, AAAS, Internat. Precious Metals Inst. (dir.), Alpha Epsilon Pi. Jewish. Clubs: K.P., B'nai B'rith. Home: 108 W Maple Ave Monsey NY 10952 Office: 170 Petersville Rd New Rochelle NY 10801

AARON, EVALYN WILHELMINA KEISLER (MRS. PAUL AARON), artist; b. N.Y.C.; d. John J. and Anna (Horowitz) Keisler; student Art Students League; pvt. student in watercolor and Sumi-e; m. Paul Aaron, Nov. 14, 1937; children—L. Neil, Barry. One-woman show Unitarian Ch., Plandome, N.Y., 1968, Port Washington, N.Y., 1976, Mirage Gallery, N.Y.C., 1978; exhibited in juried shows Nippon Club N.Y., Japan Soc., Internat. Platform Assn., Sumi-e Soc. shows, 1963-68, 70-76, Community Synagogue, Sands Point, N.Y., 1966-72, North Shore Community Arts Center, 1976, Port Washington Library, 1976; represented in permanent collections; pres. Workshops for Art, Port Washington, N.Y., 1967-75; instr. fine arts Arrandale Sch., Gt. Neck, N.Y., 1964-74; sec. Gallery Soho-7 Ltd., Great Neck, N.Y.; lectr., demonstrator Sumi-e art before civic and ch. groups. Recipient 1st prize for Sumi-e Nippon Club exhibit, 1964; cup Consul Gen. Japan, 1966; 1st prize Sumi-e Soc. Show, 1970, also others. Mem. Sumi-e Soc. Am. (a founder, pres.), Water Color Soc. Am. (asso.), Japan Soc. (asso., past coordinator, adminstr. service program for Japanese students in U.S.), Nat. Women's Com. Brandeis U., Am. Jewish Congress, Internat. Platform Assn. (art com.), Art League Nassau County, Artist Equity Assn. N.Y. Home: 60 Richards Rd Port Washington NY 11050 Office: Workshops for Art 301 Main St Port Washington NY 11050

AARON, ROBERT SAUL, physician; b. N.Y.C., Jan. 11, 1924; s. George W. and Sarah (Cohen) A.; student Northwestern U., 1943; M.D., L.I. Coll. Medicine, 1946; m. Norma Schilder, Mar. 23, 1946; children—Andrew Lewis, Daniel David, Robin Myra. Intern Montefiore Hosp., Bronx, N.Y., 1946-47; resident Kings County Hosp., Bklyn., 1949-50; resident Montefiore Hosp., Bronx, N.Y., 1950-51, fellow in cardiology, 1951-52; practice medicine specializing in internal medicine and cardiology, Gt. Neck; N.Y., 1952—; attending staff L.I. Jewish Hosp., North Shore Hosp.; dir. consultation and diagnostic center L.I. Jewish Med. Center; asst. prof. clin. medicine State U. N.Y. Sch. Medicine at Stonybrook, Cornell U. Med. Center. Served with USNR, 1947. Diplomate Am. Bd. Internal Medicine. Fellow A.C.P., Am. Coll. Cardiology; mem. Am. Heart Assn. Contbr. articles to profl. jours. Home: 18 Grassfield Rd Great Neck NY 11024 Office: 29 Barstow Rd Great Neck NY 11021

AARONSON, WARREN DAVID, educator; b. Phila., July 6, 1948; s. Samuel and Fae (Katz) A.; B.S. in Psychology, Pa. State U., 1970; M.A. in Counseling, Glassboro State Coll., 1976; m. Fern Rochelle Friedlander, Dec. 22, 1974. Tchr. Catto Opportunity Sch. for Emotionally Disturbed and Socially Maladjusted Children, Camden, N.J., 1970-76; tchr. educably retarded adolescents Woodrow Wilson High Sch., Camden, 1976—; instr. psychology Phila. Community Coll., 1976—; vol. probation counselor. Recipient certificate of appreciation Supreme Ct. N.J., 1976. Mem. Am. Personnel and Guidance Assn., Am. Sch. Counselor Assn., NEA, N.J., Camden edn. assns., Camden County Council of Edn. Assns., Camden City Tchrs. Assn. (mem. exec., negotiating coms), Pi Lambda Phi Alumni Assn. (pres. Omega Gamma br., certificate of merit 1975). Home: 223 Woodbine Dr Marlton NJ 08053 Office: 3100 Federal St Camden NJ 08105

AASEN, LAWRENCE OBERT, assn. exec.; b. Gardner, N.D., Dec. 5, 1922; s. Theodore and Clara Olina (Brenden) A.; Ph.B. in Journalism, U. N.D., 1947; M.S. in Pub. Relations, Boston U., 1949; m. Martha Ann McMullan, Nov. 25, 1954; children—David Lawrence, Susan Clare. Asst. editor McGraw Hill Pub. Co., N.Y.C., 1952-54; asst. v.p. N.Y. Life Ins. Co., N.Y.C., 1954-67; exec. sec. pub. relations Better Vision Inst., N.Y.C., 1967—. Justice of peace, Westport, Conn., 1973—; dist. leader Dem. Com., Westport, 1971—. Served with USAAF, 1943-45. Recipient Sioux award U. N.D., 1969. Mem. Pub. Relations Soc. Am., Am. Soc. Assn. Execs., Blue Key, Sigma Delta Chi, Tau Kappa Epsilon. Conglist. (deacon 1966). Home: 31 Ellery Ln Westport CT 06880 Office: 230 Park Ave New York City NY 10017

AASKOV, CHARLES EDWARD, microbiologist b. Portland, Maine, Aug. 9, 1938; s. Edward Wadsworth and Emma Mae (Milligan) A.; grad. U.S. Navy Clin. Lab. and Blood Bank Sch., 1960; m. Linda Rae Zeaman, Oct. 14, 1956; children—Michael, Tanya. Lab. supr. Profl. Assos., Sanford, Maine, 1965—. Vice pres. YMCA, Bar Harbor, 1971-73, mem. state exec. com., 1970—, bd. dirs., 1968-73. Served with USN, 1956-65. Mem. Am. Med Technologists (state soc. v.p. 1972—), Am. Soc Microbiology. Mason. Home: Pine Springs Lake Shapleigh ME 04073 Office: 29 June St Sanford ME 04073

ABADIR, ADEL RAMSEY, physician; b. Cairo, Egypt, Apr. 15, 1935; s. Ramsey E. and Victoria S. (Shefik) A.; M.D., Alexandria Med. Sch., 1957; m. Dale M. Garlick, Dec. 21, 1969; 1 dau., Tanya; children by previous marriage—Michelle Christine, Adel Ramsey. Came to U.S., 1958, naturalized, 1966. Intern, Alexandria U. Hosp., 1957-58; rotating intern Misericordia Hosp., 1958-59; resident N.Y. U. Hosp., 1959-61, from clin. instr. to clin. prof. medicine N.Y. U., 1962-72; attending physician Univ. Hosp., N.Y.C., 1971—, acting dir., 1972; acting asso. dir. Bellevue Hosp., N.Y.C., 1972-73; dir. Brookdale Hosp. Med. Center, Bklyn., 1973—; prof. anesthesia N.Y. U. Med. Sch., 1972—. Diplomate Am. Bd. Anesthesiology. Fellow Am. Soc. Anesthesiologists; mem. Am., N.Y. State socs. anesthesiologists, Am. Soc. Abdominal Surgeons, Soc. Neurosurg. Anesthesia and Neurologic Supportive Care, N.Y. Acad. Sci., N.Y. Acad. Medicine. Club: N.Y. Athletic. Contbr. articles to profl. jours. Home: 1045 Constable Dr Mamaroneck NY 10543 Office: Brookdale Hosp Center Brooklyn NY 11212

ABADIR, DALE MAREE, physician; b. Sydney, Australia, Oct. 14, 1944; d. Hubert Warren Moss and Gladys Mary (Crawford) Garlick; M.D., U. Sydney, 1967; m. Adel Ramsey Abadir, Dec. 21, 1969; children—Michelle Christine, Ramsey Adel, Tanya Irene. Resident in dermatology N.Y. U. Med. Center, 1969-72; practice medicine specializing in dermatology and dermatologic surgery, New Rochelle, N.Y., 1973—; asst. clin. prof. Albert Einstein Med. Center, N.Y.C., 1973—. Diplomate Am. Bd. Dermatology. Mem. Am. Acad. Dermatology, Westchester, New Rochelle med. socs., Am. Assn. Dermatologic Surgery, Dermatology Soc. Greater N.Y. Office: 150 Lockwood Ave New Rochelle NY 10801

ABATE, VINCENZO, physician; b. Naples, Italy, Sept. 20, 1931; s. Genneroso and Flora (Valle) A.; came to U.S., 1954; naturalized, 1960; M.D., U. Naples, 1954; m. Lola Rose Nicolazzo, Oct. 13, 1956; children—Marisa, Vincent, Mario, Flora. Rotating intern Mother Cabrini Meml. Hosp., N.Y.C., 1955-56; resident in obstetrics and gynecology N.Y. Polyclinic Med. Sch. and Hosp., 1956-59; clin. instr., 1962-67; resident St. Joseph Hosp., Paterson, N.J., 1959-60; practice medicine specializing in obstetrics and gynecology, Paterson, 1957-60; sr. attending physician Montefibre-Morrisania Hosp. Assn., 1961-67. Diplomate Am. Bd. Obstetrics and Gynecology. Mem. AMA, N.J. Obstetrics and Gynecology Assn., Am. Soc. Abdominal Surgeons, Am. Fertility Soc., Pan Am. Cytology Soc., Internat. Family Planning, Royal Soc. Medicine. Roman Catholic. Contbr. numerous articles to med. jours. Home and office: 152 Butler St Paterson NJ 07524

ABAZA, NABIL ABDEL-AZIZ, dentist; b. Meet-Gumr, Egypt, July 12, 1935; s. Abdel-Aziz Mohamed and Aziza Ismail (Shoukry) A.; came to U.S., 1960, naturalized, 1975; P.N.S., Sch. Sci. and Dentistry, Cairo, Egypt, 1954, B.Ch.D., 1958; M.S., U. Pitts., 1963, Ph.D., 1973; D.M.D., U. Pa., 1975; m. Ann Marie Iglesias, Sept. 14, 1963; children—Mona, Sharif. Instr. oral surgery Cairo U., 1958-60; teaching fellow oral surgery Sch. Dental Medicine, U. Pitts., 1960-62; resident in oral surgery Sch. Dental Medicine, U. Pitts.-Magee Women's Hosp., 1960-62, Allegheny Gen. Hosp., Pitts., 1962-63; practice oral surgery, also asst. prof. oral surgery Cairo U., 1963-66; instr. oral pathology Sch. Dental Medicine, U. Pitts., 1967-68, jr. instr. pathology Sch. Medicine, 1970-71; instr. pathology Med. Coll. Pa., Phila., 1971-72, asst. prof., 1972-76, asso. prof., 1976—; asso. oral surgery Sch. Dental Medicine, U. Pa., 1977—. Licensed dentist, Pa., N.Y., Egypt. Mem. Egyptian Dental Assn., ADA, Internat. Assn. Oral Surgeons, Internat. Assn. Dental Research, AAAS, Internat. Coll. Dentists, Pathology Soc. Phila., Pa., Delaware Valley socs. oral and maxillofacial surgeons, Tissue Culture Assn., Am. Assn. Dental Schs. Contbr. articles to dental and med. jours. Home: 13 Downs Circle Wynnewood PA 19096 Office: 3300 Henry Ave Philadelphia PA 19129

ABBAGNARO, LOUIS ANTHONY, acoustical engr.; b. New Haven, Conn., Nov. 7, 1942; s. Louis and Josephine Mary (DeFelice) A.; B.S. in Elec. Engring., Yale U., 1964; M.S. in Mech. Engring., U. Bridgeport, 1970, M.S. in Elec. Engring., 1974; m. Joan Carol Spiers, Oct. 9, 1965; children—Michael, Marc, Karin. Project engr. CBS Labs., Stamford, Conn., 1964-68, sect. head acoustical transducers, 1968-72, mgr. acoustical research, 1972-75, dir. sound tech. CBS Tech. Center, 1975—. Fellow Audio Engring. Soc.; mem. Acoustical Soc. Am., Am. Inst. Physics. Contbr. articles to profl. jours. Patentee in field. Home: 14 Lily Ln Huntington CT 06484 Office: 227 High Ridge Rd Stamford CT 06905

ABBAS, MIAN MOHAMMAD, space scientist; b. Nawanshehr, India, June 22, 1933; s. Ataullah and Iasha (Begum) Mian; came to U.S., 1962, naturalized, 1974; B.S., W. Pakistan U. Engring. and Tech., 1955; M.S., Laval (Que.) U., 1960; Ph.D., U. R.I., 1968; m. Adiba Haq, July 24, 1960; children—Hamid, Rashida, Sarah Sheerin. Electronics engr. Canadair, Montreal, Que., Can., 1960-62; teaching fellow U. Calif., Berkeley, 1962-64; asst. prof. fields and plasma physics Ohio U., 1968-70; asso. prof. U. Ky., 1970-74; sr. research asso. infrared astronomy Nat. Acad. Scis. and U. Md. Dept. Astronomy, NASA-Goddard Space Flight Center, Greenbelt, Md., 1974—. Mem. IEEE, Am. Geophys. Union, Sigma Xi. Moslem. Contbr. articles to profl. jours. Home: 12200 Remington Dr Silver Spring MD 20902 Office: 693 NASA-Goddard Space Flight Center Greenbelt MD 20701

ABBASI, ASLAM, systems engr.; b. Karachi, Pakistan, Nov. 30, 1936; s. Usif M. and Saida B. (Ibrahim) A.; came to U.S., 1954, naturalized, 1964; B.S. in Elec. Engring., 1957; M.S. in Elec. Engring., U. Pa., 1963; m. Gael MacFarlan, Jan. 10, 1967; 1 son, Usif. With dept. elec. engring. Milw. Sch. Engring., 1957-59; mem. faculty Villanova U., 1959-73; systems program engr. U.S. Naval Air Devel. Center, Warminster, Pa., 1968—, chmn. equal employment opportunity Subcom. on skill utilizations and upward mobility programs, 1977. Treas. Berwyn (Pa.) Sch. PTA, 1976; soccer referee Chester Gt. Valley Soccer Assn., 1978. Recipient duPont award, 1961, Lindback award, 1973. Ford Found., 1962, NSF, fellow, 1963. Mem. IEEE, Am. Inst. Aeros. and Astronautics, Am. Def. Preparedness Assn., Sigma Xi, Eta Kappa Nu, Tau Beta Pi, Tau Omega Mu. Contbr. articles to profl. jours Home: 7 Devon Rd Malvern PA 19355 Office: Naval Air Devel Center Street Rd Warminster PA 18974

ABBETT, ROBERT KENNEDY, artist; b. Hammond, Ind., Jan. 5, 1926; s. Clarence Coredon and Vere (Kennedy) A.; B.S., Purdue U., 1946; B.A., U. Mo., 1948; student Chgo. Acad. Fine Art, 1948-50, Am. Acad. Art, Chgo., 1949; m. Marilyn Kay Smith, Mar. 1, 1952; children—Robert S., Linda J. Artist, writer K.E. Shepard Advt. Co., Chgo. 1947; illustrator Stevens-Gross Studios, Chgo., 1948-52, Bielefeld Studios, Chgo., 1952-54, Chaite Studios, N.Y.C., 1955-56; free-lance illustrator, N.Y.C., 1957-70; exhibited in group shows at Nat. Acad. Western Art, Oklahoma City, 1974, 75, Soc. Animal Artists, N.Y.C., 1974-79; represented in permanent collections including Parker Collection, Tulsa, Dangerfield Collection, Ardmore, Okla., Sporting Art Collection, Genesee County Mus., Rochester, N.Y., works include: Portrait of Mrs. Roy Larsen, 1973, Portrait of Jimmy Stewart, 1975, Portrait of Silver, 1977; artist mem. Grand Central Galleries, N.Y.C.; pres. Westport Artists, 1964-65; mem. faculty Silvermine Coll., 1959-61, Washington (Conn.) Art Assn., 1977. Served with USN, 1943-45. Recipient Outstanding Work award Artists and Books Exhibit, N.Y.C., 1965; 1st prize Salmagundi Summer Exhibit, 1973. Mem. Soc. Animal Artists, Soc. Illustrators (Merit citation 1966). Contbr. art to books: Great Lives—Great Deeds, 1965; Western Art Today, 1975; subject of book: Outdoor Paintings of Robert K. Abbett, 1976. Home and office: Oakdale Farm Bridgewater CT 06752

ABBEY, ALBERT ASHER, dermatologist; b. N.Y.C., Mar. 8, 1939; s. Maurice A. and Sylvia A.; A.B., cum laude, Harvard Coll., 1960; M.D., cum laude Tufts U., 1964; m. Joan E. Stein, Sept. 5, 1965; children—Jonathan, Joshua, Seth. Intern Boston City Hosp., 1964-65, resident internal medicine, 1965-66; resident internal medicine L.I. Jewish Hosp., New Hyde Park, N.Y., 1968-69, dermatology N.Y. Hosp., Cornell Med. Center, N.Y.C., 1969-72; practice medicine specializing in dermatology, West Orange, N.J., 1972—; clin. instr. Cornell U. Med. Sch., N.Y.C., 1972-73, Coll. Medicine and Dentistry N.J., Newark, 1972—; asso. attending physician Newark Beth Israel Med. Center, 1973—, N.Y. Hosp., N.Y.C., 1973-75, St. Barnabas Med. Center, Livingston, N.J., 1973—; cons. VA Hosp., East Orange, N.J., 1972—. Served with U.S. Army, 1966-68; decorated Bronze Star; USPHS fellow, 1969-70; diplomate Am. Bd. Dermatology, Nat. Bd. Med. Examiners. Fellow Am. Acad. Dermatology; mem. AMA, Med. Soc. N.J., Essex County Med. Soc., Internat. Soc. for Tropical Dermatology, N.J. Dermatol. Soc. (pres. 1977-78). Office: 769 Northfield Ave West Orange NJ 07052

ABBEY, LELAND RUSSELL, physician; b. N.Y.C., Dec. 18, 1945; s. Solomon and Bettina (Zipper) A.; A.B., Drew U., Madison, N.J., 1967; M.D., Hahneman Med. Coll., 1971. Intern, then resident in internal medicine Mt. Sinai Hosp., N.Y.C., 1971-74, fellow in rheumatology, 1974-76; staff physician Bronx (N.Y.) VA Hosp., 1976-78, chief rheumatology sect., 1978—; mem. attending staff Mt. Sinai Hosp.; instr. Mt. Sinai Sch. Medicine. Diplomate Am. Bd. Internal Medicine, Am. Bd. Rheumatology. Mem. AMA, Am. Rheumatism Assn. Office: Bronx VA Hosp 130 W Kingsbridge Rd Bronx NY 10468

ABBOTT, ANTON DWIGHT, aero. engr.; b. Indpls., Aug. 28, 1936; s. Horace Emerson and Evelyn (Goff) A.; B.S., Purdue U., 1958, M.S., 1965; m. Janet Kyseth, June 27, 1964; children—Steven Dwight, Douglas Duane. Mgr. systems definition weapons systems div. Aerospace Corp., San Bernardino, Calif., 1965-68, dir. advanced projects devel. planning div., El Segundo, Calif., 1968-75, group dir. environment and energy conservation div., Germantown, Md., 1975—. Mem. AAAS, Am. Inst. Aeros. and Astronatuics, Am. Fedn. Scientists. Patentee in field. Home: 9108 Shad Ln Potomac MD 20854 Office: 20030 Century Blvd Germantown MD 20767

ABBOTT, EDWARD LEROY, ins. co. exec.; b. Dayton, Ohio, Dec. 18, 1930; s. Roy Edward and Mildred Eileen (Filler) A.; A.B., Wittenberg U., 1952; postgrad. Ohio State U., 1952-53; m. Elizabeth Joan Grahame, June 8, 1957; children—Jay Edward, Julie Beth. Various positions Northwestern Mut. Life Ins. Co., Columbus, Ohio, 1956-64, asst. regional mgr., Dallas, 1964-68, mortgage loan regional mgr., Columbus, 1968-70, Washington, 1970-73; v.p. real estate Acacia Mut. Life Ins. Co., Washington, 1973-74, fin. v.p., 1974-78, exec. v.p., 1978—, treas., 1974—; dir. Acacia Fin. Corp., Acacia Equity Sales Corp.; fin. v.p., treas., dir. Acacia Nat. Life Ins. Co. Served with U.S. Army, 1954-55. Mem. Washington Bd. Trade, Am., D.C. mortgage bankers assns., Am. Council Life Ins., Internat. Platform Assn., Friends of Kennedy Center, Alpha Tau Omega. Republican. Home: 6605 Goldsboro Rd Falls Church VA 22042 Office: 51 Louisiana Ave NW Washington DC 20001

ABBOTT, JAMES ALLEN, psychiatrist; b. Detroit, Nov. 6, 1920; s. Arthur James and Florence Eulalia (Allen) A.; student Kalamazoo Coll., 1939-42; M.D., U. Mich., 1945; m. Margaret Jane Olmstead, Aug. 31, 1949; children—James Allen, Thomas Michael, Stephen Charles, Mark Weldon. Rotating intern Butterworth Hosp., Grand Rapids, Mich., 1945-46; hosp. physician Pontiac (Mich.) State Hosp., 1946-54; clin. dir., 1954-55; psychiatrist VA Outpatient Clinic, Detroit, 1955-60, Allen Park VA Hosp., 1960-76; practice medicine specializing in psychiatry, Detroit, 1956-73; psychiatrist VA Outpatient Clinic, Rochester, 1976; chief, 1977—; clin. asst. prof. psychiatry U. Rochester, 1977—. Diplomate Am. Bd. Psychiatry and Neurology. Fellow Am. Psychiat. Assn. Office: 100 State St Rochester NY 14614

ABBOTT, JOSEPH ALOYSIUS, public relations exec.; b. Paterson, N.J., June 19, 1905; s. Henry Augustus and Mary (Rogiers) A.; B.S., Notre Dame U., 1930; m. Alice M. Hughes, Aug. 30, 1930; 1 son, Joseph A. With ITT, Nutley, N.J., 1942—, asst. personnel mgr., 1942-48, dir. personnel and labor relations, 1948-55, dir. pub. relations, 1955-66, dir. pub. relations def. space group, 1966-74, dir. pub. relations and advt., aerospace, electronics, components and energy group, 1975-78, dir. pub. relations and advt. ITT Telecommunications and Electronics Group-N.Am., 1978—; dir. Fed. Electric Corp. Chmn. N.J. Little Hoover Commn., 1968-69; pres. Passaic Valley Water Commn., Clifton, N.J., 1962-66. Bd. dirs. St. Mary's Hosp., Passaic, N.J., 1961—, Jr. Achievement, Passaic-Clifton area, 1959—. Recipient Boys' Club medallion Boys' Club Am., Clifton, 1963. Mem. Assn. U.S. Army (life), Air Force Assn. (life), Navy League U.S. (life), N.J. Press Assn. (hon. life mem., dir. 1969—), Pub. Relations Soc. Am., Clifton C. of C. (pres. 1972), Notre Dame Alumni Assn. of N.J. Clubs: Nat. Press, Pica (hon. life). Home

25 E 40th St Apt 2G Paterson NJ 07514 Office: 500 Washington Ave Nutley NJ 07110

ABBOTT, LORETTA A., dance instr.; d. Alfred and Agatha (Alexander) Bruce-Abbott. Mem., soloist Donald McKayle Dance Co., 1969, Louis Johnson Dance Co., 1969; dancer, actress, singer world tour Alvin Ailey Am. Dance Theatre; appeared in Peer Gynt, N.Y. Shakespeare Festival, 1969; appeared in Broadway prodn. La Strada, N.Y.C., 1969, also dance capt., appeared in Broadway prodns. Purlie, 1970-71, Two Gentlemen of Verona, 1971-72; featured dancer-singer Broadway prodn. Raisin, 1973-76; guest artist Harkness Ballet Co., Robert de Cormier Chorale, Contemporary Ballet Co. N.Y.; appeared in TV spl. Seven Deadly Sins, Stockholm, Sweden; dancer, singer (with Liza Minnelli) on TV Show Liza With A "Z"; off-Broadway actress, dancer, singer Holy Moses and The Top Ten, 1978, Miss Truth, 1978; asst. choreographer The Vampire and the Dentist, 1978; appeared in film The Wiz, 1977, Voices, 1978; guest instr., tchr. master classes, Scarsdale, Hofstra U., Nyacak (N.Y.) Acad. Classical Ballet, Am. U. Wolf Trap Acad., Washington, Choreographer The Rent Party Story TV Show Good Times.

ABBOTT, WILBURN LYNN, computer pub. cons.; b. Seymour, Tex., July 14, 1929; s. Wilburn Barton and Johnnie Ladelle (Chilcoat) A.; student San Angelo (Tex.) State Coll., 1952-54; B.S. in Journalism, Calif. State Coll. at Los Angeles, 1962; m. Joyce Verniele Buckner, June 17, 1967; children—Vicki Lynn, Robert Alan, Jean Lorraine, Mauri Jon, Wesley Scott, Gregory Martin. Apprentice compositor San Angelo Standard Times, 1952-55; compositor Los Angeles Times, 1955-62, programmer, 1962-64, mgr. pub. systems, 1964-65, systems mgr., 1965-69; asst. prodn. mgr. N.Y. Times, N.Y.C., 1970-72, data processing mgr., 1972-76, dir. computer research, 1976-77; computer pub. cons., 1977—. Served with USN, 1948-52. Home and office: 54 Van Rensselaer Ave Stamford CT 06902

ABBOTT, WILLIAM SAUNDERS, lawyer; b. Medford, Mass., June 2, 1938; s. Charles Theodoric and Evelyn Gertrude (Saunders) A.; A.B. magna cum laude (Harvard Nat. scholar, John Harvard scholar), Harvard, 1960, LL.B. magna cum laude, 1966; m. Susan Shaw, June 24, 1961; children—Cathryn, Stephen, David. Admitted to Mass. bar, 1967; dir. U.S. Agrl. Food Programs for Asia, State Dept., Washington, 1967-68; v.p., gen. counsel Cabot, Cabot & Forbes Co., real estate devel., Boston, 1968-77; v.p., gen. counsel Cabot, Cabot & Forbes Land Trust, 1971-73; practice law, Boston, 1977—. Pres., Found. to Improve TV, 1969—; Mass. commr., Edn. Commn. of States, 1969-75. Chmn., Bd. Selectman Arlington (Mass.), 1970-72. Bd. dirs. World Affairs Council Boston. Served to lt. USNR, 1960-63. White House fellow, 1966-67. Mem. Phi Beta Kappa. Home: Herring Way RFD 6 Plymouth MA 02360 Office: 50 Congress St Boston MA 02109

ABDALIAN, ARBAK ARSHAK, structural engr.; b. Teheran, Iran, May 12, 1920; s. Arshak M. and Anna (Khosrovian) A.; B.S.C., Am. Coll. Teheran, 1939; diploma engring. within industry London, Eng., 1949; m. Suzane Kadimian, Nov. 22, 1943; children—Arbak Anthony, Arline, Adriene, Alexandra. Came to U.S., 1950, naturalized, 1955. Asst. chief engr. Societe Baziar, Teheran, 1940-41; engr. Anglo-Iranian Oil Co., Abadan, Iran, 1941-42, dep. supt., 1942-49; office engr. 3d Mil. Service, U.S. Army, 1945-46; dep. chief engr. Custom Engring. Co., N.Y.C., 1951-52; cons. engr., N.Y.C., 1952—, Newark, 1957—, Los Angeles, 1962—; sr. v.p., dir. structural and civil engring. Welton Becket Assos., N.Y.C., Los Angeles, Houston, Atlanta, Chgo., San Francisco; dir. Iran Becket. Cons., Marist Coll., Poughkeepsie, N.Y., 1952—. Recipient concrete industry award for best design and conception of concrete structure; Merit award Concrete Industry Bd., 1972, Silver prize L.I. Assn. Commerce and Industry, 1972. Registered profl. structural engr., Iran, N.Y., N.J., Conn., Mass., D.C., Calif., Nev., Ohio, Fla. Fellow ASCE; mem. Am. Concrete Inst., Iranian Armenian Soc. (hon.). Democrat. Club: Presidential (N.Y.C.). Designer: Cantiague Park Stadium, L.I., N.Y., Armenian Cathedral, N.Y.C., Champagniat Hall, Marist Coll. Home: 47-27 243d St Douglaston NY 11362 Office: 110 E 59th St New York City 10022

ABDOU, HAMED M., chemist; b. Cairo, Egypt, Feb. 2, 1941; s. Mahmoud A. and Fatima S. (Noman) A.; came to U.S., 1969, naturalized, 1974; B.S. in Pharmacy and Pharm. Chemistry, Cairo U., 1961, M.S. in Pharm. Sci., 1966; Ph.D., Rutgers U., 1977; m. Fe Abdou, July 18, 1970; 1 child, Nyier H. Analytical chemist Elkahira Pharm. Inc., Cairo, 1962-67, head dept. solid dosage forms, 1967-69; analytic research chemist E.R. Squibb & Sons, Inc., New Brunswick, N.J., 1969-77, sr. research chemist, 1977-78, sect. head quality control, 1978—. Mem. Am. Chem. Soc., Am. Pharm. Assn. Rho Chi. Home: 1620 Platte Ave North Brunswick NJ 09802 Office: ER Squibb and Sons Inc Georges Rd New Brunswick NJ 08903

ABDUL, RAOUL, author; b. Cleve., Nov. 7, 1929; s. Hamid and Etta Beatrice (Shreve) A.; grad. Vienna Acad. Music and Dramatic Art, 1962; student New Sch. Social Research, Mannes Coll. Music, Harvard Summer Sch., N.Y. Coll. Music, Cleve. Inst. Music. Mem. Karamu Theatre, 1950-52; vocal concerts German songs, Germany, Austria, Netherlands, Hungary, 1959-62; tours U.S. and Can., 1962-67; N.Y. debut at Carnegie Hall, 1967; dir. Coffee Concerts in Harlem, N.Y.C., 1958-63; author: Famous Black Entertainers of Today, 1974; Blacks in Classical Music, 1977; editor (with Alan Lomax) Three Thousand Years of Black Poetry, 1970; editor The Magic of Black Poetry, 1972; music critic N.Y. Amsterdam News, 1975—; program annotator Symphony of the New World, 1977—; mem. Harold Jackman Meml. Com., 1973—. Mem. NAACP, Nat. Urban League, Nat. Assn. Negro Musicians, Music Critics Assn. Home: 360 W 22d St New York City NY 10011

ABDUL-SHAHID, LATIF, debit mgr., ins. cons.; b. Abba, Saudi Arabia, Jan. 19, 1950; came to U.S., 1950, naturalized, 1950; B.A., Ky. State U., 1972; student U. Tenn. at Chattanooga, 1972-73, Entrepreneur Devl. and Tng. Sch., 1978. Ins. cons. Met. Life Ins. Co., Chattanooga, 1972-73; agt. N.C. Mut. Life Ins. Co., Phila., 1973-74, ins. cons., 1975-76, debit mgr., 1976—, asst. sales mgr., 1978—. Active mem. Phila. United Way fund drs.; sec. Esquires Soc. Club, 1968. Recipient 2d pl. trophy for Nat. Ins. Week, N.C. Mut. Life Ins. Co., 1975. Mem. Internat. Graphoanalysis Soc., Phila. Ins. Mgrs. Council, Ins. Workers Internat. Union, Nat. Assn. Life Underwriters. Democrat. Afro-Am. Islamic Umma. Contbr. articles in field and on religions of Middle East to jours. Home: PO Box 13301 Philadelphia PA 19101 Office: 1501 N Broad St Philadelphia PA 19122

ABEL, ROBERT, JR., ophthalmologist; b. Phila., Nov. 10, 1943; s. Robert and Ruth R. A.; B.A., Wesleyan U., 1965; M.D., Thomas Jefferson U., 1969; m. Kathie Buchsbaum, Mar. 2, 1968; children—Ari, Adam. Intern, Temple U. Hosp., Phila., 1969-70; resident Mt. Sinai Hosp., N.Y.C., 1970-73; fellow U. Fla., Gainesville, 1973-74; practice medicine specializing in ophthalmology, Wilmington, Del., 1974—; mem. staffs Wilmington Med. Center, St. Francis Hosp., Temple U. Hosp., Jefferson U. Hosp., Wills Eye Hosp., St. Christopher's Hosp.; adj. clin. prof. Temple U. Hosp., 1975—, dir. cornea service, 1976—; mem. exec. bd. Kutz Nursing Home, Wilmington, 1978—, DELRO. Recipient Practice Prize in Medicine, 1969; William H. Hoppin award, 1973; diplomate Am. Bd. Ophthalmology. Fellow A.C.S.; mem. Am. Assn. Ophthalmology (state del.), Del. Acad. Ophthalmology, Del. Acad. Medicine (exec. bd.), Del., New Castle County med. socs., Am. Assn. Clin. Pharmacology, Assn. for Research in Ophthalmology and Vision, Castroviejo Corneal Soc., Ocular Immunology and Microbiology Soc., Mensa. Jewish. Club: Odd Fellows. Contbr. articles, chpts. to med. jours., texts. Home: 2119 Dunhill Dr Brandywood Wilmington DE 19810 Office: 1300 Harrison St Wilmington DE 19806

ABELES, ERNEST D., orthopaedic surgeon; b. Munich, Germany, Aug. 31, 1935; s. Otto and Ilse (Straus) A.; came to U.S., 1939, naturalized, 1944; B.A. with honors in Chemistry, Cornell U., 1956; M.D., N.Y.U., 1960; m. Francine Forte, Dec. 29, 1957; children—Edward, Jennifer Evelyn. Intern surgery Bellevue Hosp., N.Y.C., 1960-61; asst. resident gen. surgery Manhattan VA Hosp., N.Y.C., 1963-64; resident orthopaedic surgery Bklyn. Jewish Hosp., 1964-67; practice medicine specializing in orthopaedic surgery, N.Y.C., 1967—; attending in charge orthopaedics Greenpoint Hosp., 1967-73; dir. div. orthopedic surgery L.I. Coll. Hosp., 1975-77; attending orthopaedic surgeon Jewish Hosp. and Med. Center of Bklyn., Bklyn. Cumberland Med. Center, L.I. Coll. Hosp.; asst. attending orthopaedic surgeon Beth Israel Hosp., N.Y.C., N.Y. Infirmary, Cabrini Med. Center; clin. instr. Downstate Med. Center, N.Y.C., 1967—. Served as capt. M.C., AUS, 1961-63. Diplomate Am. Bd. Orthopaedic Surgery. Fellow A.C.S., Am. Acad. Orthopedic Surgeons; mem. Phi Beta Kappa, Phi Delta Epsilon. Office: 193 3d Ave New York City NY 10003 also 175 Adams St Brooklyn NY 11201

ABEND, KENNETH, elec. engr.; b. N.Y.C., Jan. 14, 1936; s. Isadore and Sadie (Abend) A.; B.E.E. cum laude, Coll. City N.Y., 1958; M.S. in Elec. Engring., U. Pa., 1963, Ph.D. (Grad. Sch. fellow), 1966; m. Judith Segal, June 26, 1966; children—Cary Brian, Illysa Susan, Debra Lyn, Lori Jan. Jr. engr. Philco Research Lab., Phila., 1958-59, engr., 1959-62, sr. research engr., 1963-64, project engr., 1964-67, engring. research specialist, 1967-68; sr. engring. specialist Aeronutronic Ford Corp. (formerly Philco-Ford Corp.), Willow Grove, Pa., 1968-76; prin. mem. engring. staff RCA, Moorestown, N.J., 1976—; instr. grad. courses in elec. engring. Lehigh U., Bethlehem, Pa., 1970, Pa. State U., King of Prussia, 1967—, U. Pa., Phila., 1972—. Bd. dirs. Welcome House Adoptive Parents Group, Doylestown, Pa. Recipient Outstanding Young Engr. award City Univ. N.Y., 1969. Mem. IEEE (mem. info. theory group 1959—), Inst. Math. Statistics, Sigma Xi, Eta Kappa Nu. Mem. B'nai B'rith. Jewish. Contbr. articles on signal processing, communications theory to profl. jours. Home: 623 Killdeer Ln Huntingdon Valley PA 19006 Office: RCA 108-210 Moorestown NJ 08057

ABER, JOHN WILLIAM, finance specialist, educator; b. Canonsburg, Pa., Sept. 9, 1937; s. John William and Rose (Lauda) A.; B.S., Pa. State U., 1959; M.B.A. (McKinsey scholar), Columbia, 1965; D.B.A. (Bus. Sch. Leadership fellow, Bus. Sch. div. research fellow), Harvard, 1972; m. Cynthia Louise Sousa, Nov. 24, 1962; children—John Jarrett, Valerie Susan, Alexander Jude. Research asso. Harvard Bus. Sch., Boston, 1967-69; asst. prof. fin. Ga. State U., Atlanta, 1971-72; asst. prof. fin. Boston U., 1972-78, asso. prof. fin., 1978—, research grantee, 1975, dir. mgmt. program, 1977—. Author: Beta Coefficients and Models of Security Return, 1973. Office: Boston Univ 212 Bay State Rd Boston MA 02215

ABER, WILLIAM MCKEE, clergyman; b. Pitts., July 29, 1929; s. William Clarence and Jean (McKee) A.; B.A., Coll. of Wooster, 1951; M.Div. (Sylvester S. Marvin fellow) Western Theol. Sem., 1956; M.Ed., U. Pitts., 1956; D.Min., Pitts. Theol. Sem., 1976; D.D. (hon.), Westminister Coll., 1967; m. Sarah Katherine Sterrett, Feb. 4, 1952; children—Katherine Aber Gaylor, John Preston, James McKee, Ann Sloan. Ordained to ministry, Presbyterian Ch., 1956; pastor Gibsonia Presbyn. Ch., Pitts., 1956-59; sr. pastor First United Presyn. Ch., Oil City, Pa., 1959-64, Hiland Presbyn. Ch., Pitts., 1964-72; exec. presbyter Redstone Presbytery, Greensburg, Pa., 1972—. Mem. exec. com. of council Christian Assos. of S.W. Pa., 1972—; mem. Presbytery and Synod Gen. Councils; teaching pastor Pitts. Sem., 1968-69; dean Synod Leadership Sch., 1970-72; mem. Drug Abuse Council, 1967-72; mem. policy council Westmoreland County OEO, 1976—; mem. corporate bd. North Hills Passavant Hosp., 1966-72; bd. dirs. Lutheran Service Soc., 1973—; adv. council on discipleship and worship United Presbyn. Ch.; pres.'s roundtable Pitts. Theol. Sem. Served to 1st lt. USMC, 1951-53. Mem. Witherspoon Soc., Alpha Tau Epsilon. Democrat. Clubs: Four Winds, Teutonia Moenmercher. Author: The Gap, 1971; Avenues of Advent, 1972; A Lenten Zoo, 1973; Behind the Begats, 1977. Home: 211 Walnut Ave Greensburg PA 15601 Office: 107 W 2d St Greensburg PA 15601

ABERMAN, HUGH MAURICE, educator; b. Phila., May 24, 1938; s. Joseph W. and Sylvia (Polakoff) A.; B.A., U. Pa., 1960, M.A. (Nat. Def. fellow), 1962; Ed.D., Temple U., 1969; m. Kathryn A. Katz, June 19, 1966. Adminstrv. asst., faculty club Temple U., Phila., 1964-65, teaching asso., 1965-69; asso. prof. Shippensburg (Pa.) State Coll., 1969-72, prof. psychology, 1972—. Ednl. cons. Thomas Jefferson U., 1968—, Health Career Guidance Clinic. Mem. adult edn. adv. bd., coordinator health career student clinic Carlisle (Pa.) High Schs., 1970—; bd. dirs. YMCA, 1974—, chmn. profl. div. membership drive, 1974, v.p. bd. dirs., 1976, pres., 1976—. Recipient Elmahlah prize U. Pa., 1960, Benjamin Rush award Cumberland County Med. Soc., 1972; named Citizen of the Yr., Lions Club, 1978. Mem. Am., Eastern, Pa. psychol. assns., Am. Ednl. Research Assn., AAUP, Phi Delta Kappa. Office: Dept Psychology Shippensburg State Coll Shippensburg PA 17257

ABERNATHY, JAMES LOGAN, broadcasting exec.; b. Kansas City, Mo., Jan. 23, 1941; s. James Logan and Caryl (Nicolson) A.; ed. Hackley Sch., 1959, Brown U., 1964; Dir. corporate info., asso. dir. investor relations CBS, N.Y.C., 1967-72; v.p. investor relations Warner Communications, Inc., N.Y.C., 1972-74; v.p. ABC, Inc., N.Y.C., 1974—. Served with USMCR, 1959-65. Mem. Investor Relations Assn. (exec. com.), Nat. Investor Relations Inst. Clubs: Metropolitan, Coffee House, Rockaway Hunting. Home: 40 Central Park S New York City NY 10019 Office: ABC 1330 Ave of Americas New York City NY 10019

ABEYATUNGE, LAMBERT RAJENDRA, surgeon; b. Sri Lanka, Nov. 17, 1940; s. Morren and Lizzie Pumawathie A.; came to U.S., 1971, naturalized, 1974; M.B.B.S., U. Ceylon, Colombo, 1965; m. Irene Ann Mancini, Nov. 10, 1970; children—Ranji, Krishan. Intern, Gen. Hosp., Colombo, Ceylon, 1965-66; resident Nat. Health Service, U.K., 1966-69, surg. registrar, 1970-71; intern French Hosp., N.Y.C., 1969-70; surg. resident Coney Island Hosp. and Maimonides Med. Center, Bklyn., 1971-75; attending surgeon Schuyler Hosp., Montour Falls, N.Y., 1975—; attending surgeon Arnot-Ogden Meml. Hosp., Elmira, N.Y., 1975—, chief surgery, 1978—. Recipient Best Chief Resident award Coney Island Hosp., 1975. Diplomate Am. Bd. Surgery. Fellow Royal Coll. Surgeons Eng., Canadian Coll. Surgeons, A.C.S.; mem. AMA, N.Y. State, Schuyler County med. socs. Home: 122 Presidential Dr Horseheads NY 14845 Office: Rollin O Baker Med Arts Montour Falls NY 14865

ABRAHAM, CARL JOEL, tech. cons., engr., educator; b. N.Y.C., Dec. 31, 1937; s. Sol and Mildred (Siegal) A.; B.S., Hofstra U., 1959, postgrad., 1972; M.S., U. Pacific, 1961; Ph.D., U. N.C., 1963, Open U., 1975; postgrad. U. Oreg., 1959-60, Hofstra U., 1972, Walden U., 1974; children—Carl Joel, Elizabeth Jean, Carrie Anne. Research engr. Aeorjet Gen. Corp., Sacramento, 1961, research engr. and chemist, 1963-65; materials specialist, corporate research lab. J.P. Stevens & Co., Inc., Garfield, N.J., 1965-66; dir. research and devel. Mansol Ceramics Co., Belleville, N.J., 1966-68; v.p., tech. dir. Polyphase Chem. Service, Inc., West Hempstead, N.Y., 1968-69; chmn. bd., pres. C.J.A. Industries, Inc., Copiague, N.Y., 1968-71; tech. dir. Inter-City Testing & Cons. Corp., Great Neck, N.Y., Kew Gardens and Plantation, Fla., 1971—; prof. chemistry Nassau Community Coll., Garden City, N.Y., 1973-75, adj. faculty physics Empire State Coll., Old Westbury, N.Y., 1975—; adj. faculty engring. Hofstra U., 1974—; lectr. continuing edn. programs. Mem. ch. council North Shore Unitarian Soc., Plandome, N.Y., 1974-75. Recipient Civilian award for Outstanding Police Assistance, Police Dept. County of Nassau, 1974. Certified tchr. U. State N.Y.; certified in food tech. and processing N.Y.C. Dept. Health; registered profl. engr. Fellow Royal Inst. Chemistry; mem. Am. Chem. Soc., AAAS, ANSI, Am. Acad. Law and Medicine, Systems Safety Soc., ASTM, Alpha Chi Sigma. Club: Elks. Contbr. articles to profl. jours. Patentee high temperature carbonaceous and siliceous materials. Home: 609 Middle Neck Rd PO Drawer O Great Neck NY 11023 Office: Drawer O Great Neck NY 11023 also 8225 NW 13th St Plantation FL 33522

ABRAHAM, MILTON EDWARD, cons. engring. firm partner; b. N.Y.C., Mar. 3, 1921; s. Jacob and Johanna (Goetz) A.; B.Chem. Engring., City U. N.Y., 1942; M.Chem. Engring., Poly. Inst. Bklyn., 1953, Ph.D., 1966; m. Ernestine Gelblum, June 19, 1964; children—Joyce E. (Mrs. Eugene Reed), Ellen (Mrs. Richard Lebeaux), David, Joanne. Chief devel. engr. pharms. Warner Lambert Co., Harriman, N.Y., 1952-59; mgr. research and devel. pharms. Reheis Co., Inc., Berkeley Heights, N.J., 1959-61; supt. Celanese Fibers Co., Cumberland, Md., 1961-71; partner R.B. MacMullin Assos., Niagara Falls, N.Y., 1971—. Lay mem. accreditation task force Allegany Community Coll., 1961-65; pres. bd. trustees Temple Beth El. Served with USN, 1942-44; PTO. Registered profl. engr., Ohio, N.Y. Fellow Am. Inst. Chemists; mem. Niagara Falls C. of C. (chmn. water pollution subcom. 1973—, v.p.), Am. Chem. Soc. (editor Western N.Y. local sect. 1972-75, mem. exec. com. 1971—, 1st vice chmn. 1976-77, chmn. 1977—), AAAS (life), N.Y. Acad. Scis. (life), Am. Inst. Chem. Engrs., Phi Lambda Upsilon, Omega Chi Epsilon. Contbr. articles to profl. jours. Patentee. Home: 368 Brentwood Dr Youngstown NY 14174 Office: 826 Pine Ave Niagara Falls NY 14301

ABRAHAM, MORRIS, architect; b. N.Y.C., July 18, 1921; s. Moreno and Dora (Levy) A.; m. Esther Shaloum, Apr. 3, 1949; children—Judith (Mrs. Allan J. Press), Marc. Project dir. Isadore Rosenfield, architect, N.Y.C., 1946-54; chief hosp. planning Ferrenz and Taylor, architects, N.Y.C., 1954-70, design program coordinator, 1970-78, v.p., dir., 1978—. Archtl. cons. in hosp. design. Served with USAAF, 1942-45. Mem. A.I.A. (com. hosp., health), N.Y. Soc. Architects, Nat. Council Archtl. Registration Bds., Am. Assn. for Hosp. Planning. Prin. archtl. works include: St. Clare's Hosp. and Health Center, Dobbs Ferry Hosp., Westchester Sq. Hosp., Harlem Hosp., Cumberland Hosp., Center for Mental Retardation, N.Y. Med. Coll., Mt. Vernon Hosp. nurses residence, L.I. Coll. Hosp. Community Health Center Maryknoll Nursing Home (all N.Y.), numerous hosps. in N.J. Home: 226-51 77th Ave Flushing NY 11364 Office: 810 7th Ave New York City NY 10019

ABRAHAM, POLACHIRAKAL VARKEY, surgeon; b. Alleppey, India, Sept. 18, 1933; s. P. Abraham and Annamma Varkey; M.B.B.S., Kasturba Med. Coll., India, 1961; m. Sarah Kuruvilla Omana, Dec. 28, 1961; 4 children. Rotating intern St. Luke's Hosp., Milw., 1963-64, resident in surgery, 1964-65; resident in surgery Stamford (Conn.) Hosp., 1965-67; chief resident in surgery Newark City Hosp., 1967-68; preceptor and asso. in surgery St. Clare's Hosp., Schenectady, 1968-72, emergency room physician, 1972-73; staff surgeon Tioga Gen. Hosp., Waverly, N.Y., 1973-77, chief surgery, 1978—. Diplomate Am. Bd. Surgery. Fellow A.C.S., Royal Coll. Physicians Surgeons (Can.); mem. Med. Soc. N.Y., Am. Cancer Soc. (dir. Tioga County, N.Y.). Address: 37 N Chemong St Waverly NY 14892

ABRAHAM, RAJENDER, toxicologist; b. Hyderabad, India, May 26, 1932; s. Alexander Clement and Evangeline Lila (Cornelius) A.; B.Sc., Nizam Coll., 1952; M.Sc., Osmania U., Hyderabad, 1954, Ph.D., 1957; m. K. Janakidevi, July 9, 1958; 1 dau., Malini. Lectr. zoology Osmania U., 1958-62; research asso. U. Mass., 1962-64, Tufts Med. Coll., Boston, 1964-66; sr. scientist Brit. Biol. Research Assn., Carshalton, Surrey, Eng., 1966-69; research prof. toxicology Albany (N.Y.) Med. Coll., 1969—; dir. Toxicology Tng. Program, Nat. Inst. Environ. Health Scis., 1978—. Recipient Career Research award, 1973—; Cystic Fibrosis Summer fellow, 1976-77. Fellow Royal Microscopic Soc.; mem. Soc. Toxicology, Soc. for Study Reproduction, Pathol. Soc. Gt. Britain and Ireland, Soc. Exptl. Biology and Medicine, Reticuloendothelial Soc. Anglican. Editor: Ecotoxicology and Environmental Safety, 1977. Contbr. articles to profl. jours. Office: Albany Med Coll 47 New Scotland Ave Albany NY 12208

ABRAHAMS, ROBERT ALAN, med. products co. exec.; b. Bklyn., Dec. 30, 1942; s. Maurice and Sophie Hannah (Weingast) A.; B.S., Queens Coll., 1963; Ph.D., Poly. Inst. Bklyn., 1970; M.B.A. with distinction, Fordham U., 1975; m. Myra Riskin, Aug. 29, 1965; children—Lauren, Stephanie, Eric. Instr. chemistry Poly. Inst. Bklyn., 1969-70; research chemist Johns-Manville Corp., Manville, N.J., 1970-72; sr. research chemist Hydro Med. Sci. div. Nat. Patent Devel. Corp., New Brunswick, N.J., 1972-74, project leader, 1974-76, tech. dir. Med. Products div., 1976-77, product mgr. Hydron burn dressing, Burron Med. div., Bethlehem, Pa., 1977; dir. mktg. NPD Dental Systems div., Melville, N.Y., 1978, v.p. sales and mktg., 1978—. Named Alumnus of Yr., Queens Coll., 1978; NASA research trainee, 1965-68. Mem. AAAS, Am. Burn Assn., Am. Chem. Soc., Assn. M.B.A. Execs., Internat. Soc. Burn Injuries, N.Y. Acad. Scis., Soc. Biomaterials, Sigma Xi, Phi Lambda Upsilon, Beta Delta Chi. Jewish. Contbr. articles to profl. publs.; patentee Hydron burn dressing. Home: 10 Bender Ct Dix Hills NY 11746 Office: 3 Huntington Quadrangle Melville NY 11746

ABRAMO, RALPH JOHN, plastics cons.; b. Atlantic City, N.J., Mar. 15, 1935; s. Louis and Catherine A.; Asso. in Engring., Stevens Inst. Tech., 1961; B.A., Northeastern U., 1968; m. Gail Verna Warker, Feb. 22, 1956; children—Ralph, Mark, Scott. Designer, Atlantic City Electric Co., 1956-66; mgr. tech. services Wheaton Plastics Co., Mays Landing, N.J., 1966-72; v.p., dir. mfg. Ilikon Corp., Natick, Mass., 1972; pres. R.J. Abramo Assos., Inc., Holliston, Mass., 1972—; instr. extension mgmt. services N.Y. U., 1973-74. Served with U.S. Navy, 1957-58. Recipient Speak Up award Jaycees, 1962; Jaycee of the Year award, 1966. Mem. Soc. Plastic Engrs., Nat. Soc. Profl. Engrs., Holliston Business men Assn. (dir.). Roman Catholic. Club: Holliston Fathers. Patentee process for molding multi layer articles. Home: 72 Alden Rd Holliston MA 01746 Office: 140 Lowland St Holliston MA 01746

ABRAMOVITZ, MAX, architect; b. Chgo., May 23, 1908; s. Benjamin and Sophia (Maimon) A.; B.S., U. Ill., 1929; D.F.A. (hon.), 1970; M.S., Columbia, 1931; grad. study Ecole des Beaux Arts, 1932-34; D.F.A. (hon.), U. Pitts., 1961; m. Anne Marie Causey, Sept. 4, 1937 (div.); children—Michael John, Katherine Paul (Mrs. John E. Coleman); m. 2d, Anita Zeltner Brooks, Feb. 29, 1964. Partner, Harrison, Fouilhoux & Abramovitz, architects, 1940, Harrison & Abramovitz, N.Y.C., 1945-77, Abramovits-Harris-Kingsland, 1977—; asso. prof. Sch. Fine Arts, Yale, 1939-42; dep. dir. UN Hdqrs. Planning Office, 1947-52. Cons., U. Pitts., Brandeis U. Trustee Mt. Sinai Hosp., N.Y.C., Served with C.E., AUS, 1942-45; col., 1950-52. Decorated Legion of Merit; recipient Achievement award U. Ill. Alumni Assn., 1963. Fellow Brandeis U., 1963. Fellow A.I.A.; mem. Am. Soc. C.E., Regional Plan Assn. (chmn. bd. 1966-68, dir. 1968—), Archtl. League N.Y., N.Y. Bldg. Congress (gov. 1957-64). Club: Century Assn. Prin works include: Assembly Hall, U. Ill., Urbana, also Krannert Center for Performing Arts; 3 chapels Brandeis U.; U.S. Steel Bldg., Pitts.; Hilles Library, Radcliffe Coll.; Columbia U. Law Sch. and Library, N.Y.C.; Alcoa Bldg., Pitts.; La Banque Rothschild, Paris, France; Philharmonic Hall, Lincoln Center, N.Y.C. Home: 418 E 50th St New York City NY 10022 Office: 630 Fifth Ave New York City NY 10020

ABRAMOWITZ, SOL, pulmonary physiologist; b. N.Y.C., Sept. 10, 1922; s. Isadore and Minnie (Beiser) A.; student Va. Mil. Inst., 1943-44, Yale U., 1944; B.A., Bklyn. Coll., 1947; postgrad. Siena Coll., 1951-53; m. Charlotte Hoch, Feb. 27, 1954; children—Jodi Susan, Bess Shira. Chief cardiopulmonary lab. Halloran Hosp., S.I., 1948-51, Albany (N.Y.) VA Hosp., 1951-54, East Orange (N.J.) VA Hosp., 1954—; research asso. N.J. Coll. Medicine, 1967—. Served with U.S. Army, 1943-46. Mem. Nat. Soc. Cardiopulmonary Technologists, AAAS. Contbr. articles in field to profl. jours. Home: 364 Leslie St Newark NJ 07112 Office: VA Hosp East Orange NJ 07019

ABRAMS, CHARLES ROBERT, aerospace engr.; b. N.Y.C., Jan. 16, 1925; s. Louis and Hannah (Pekarsky) A.; A.A., El Camino Coll., 1956; B.S. in Aerospace Engring., U. Colo., 1958; M.S., Mass. Inst. Tech., 1960; M.S., Princeton U., 1968; m. Anne Mask, July 13, 1958; children—Lori, Lance, Lynne, Lane, Lise. With U.S. Naval Air Devel. Center, Warminster, Pa., 1958—, program mgr. advanced flight control systems, 1970—; guest lectr. on flight control systems Weizmann Inst. Served with U.S. Army, 1950-54. Mem. Soc. Automotive Engrs. (aerospace guidance and control systems com.). Contbr. articles in field to profl. jours. Home: 200 Kingsley Ct Mount Laurel NJ 08054 Office: US Navy Air Devel Center Street and Jacksonville Rd Warminster PA 18974

ABRAMS, FLOYD, lawyer; b. N.Y.C., July 9, 1936; s. Isadore and Rae (Eberlin) A.; B.A., Cornell U., 1956; LL.B., Yale, 1960; m. Efrat Surasky, Dec. 25, 1963; children—Daniel, Ronnie. Admitted to N.Y. bar, 1961; research asst. dept. of politics Princeton, 1960-61; law clk. Hon. Paul Leahy, U.S. Dist. Ct., Wilmington, Del., 1961-63; asso. firm Cahill Gordon & Reindel, 1963—, partner, 1970—. Vis. lectr. Yale, 1974—. Bd. dirs. Mexican Am. Legal Def. and Ednl. Fund, Dalton Sch. Recipient Ross essay prize Am. Bar Assn., 1967, First amendment award Am. Jewish Congress, 1978. Mem. Am. Bar Assn (vice chmn. rights of expression com., litigation sec. 1974—, chmn. freedom of speech and press com. individual rights sect. 1977—), Assn. Bar City N.Y. Home: 1136 Fifth Ave New York City NY 10028 Office: 80 Pine St New York City NY 10005

ABRAMS, JEROME, obstetrician, gynecologist; b. Plainfield, N.J., Apr. 8, 1925; s. Hyman and Leah (Canter) A.; A.B., Swarthmore Coll., 1947; M.A., Columbia U., 1948; M.D., Jefferson Med. Coll., 1953; m. Rosalyn Yaskin, Dec. 28, 1952; children—Alan Thomas Yaskin, Joseph Yaskin. Intern Jefferson Hosp., Phila., 1953-54, resident, 1954-58; dir. Plainfield (N.J.) Cytology Lab., Inc., 1959—; dep. chief, dept. obstetrics and gynecology Muhlenberg Hosp., Plainfield, 1973—; clin. asst. prof. obstetrics and gynecology Rutgers Med. Sch., New Brunswick, N.J., 1974—; cons. in obstetrics and gynecology for Somerset County, 1977—; cons. United Family and Children's Soc., 1963—; mem. N.J. Bd. Med. Examiners; chmn. med. adv. com. for Planned Parenthood, Union County, 1965-68, 72-74. Served to ensign USNR, 1944-46. Diplomate Am. Bd. Obstetrics and Gynecology. Mem. Am. Cytology Soc. (certified), Am. Coll. Obstetricians and Gynecologists, N.J. Obstet. and Gynecol. Soc., AMA, Med. Soc. N.J., Union County Med. Soc., Jerusalem Acad. Medicine. Club: B'nai B'rith. Book reviewer Jour. Med. Soc. N.J., 1972—, mem. manuscript rev. bd., 1977—; contbr. articles to profl. publs., papers to confs. U.S., Austria, Israel, Sweden, Venezuela, Yugoslavia. Home: 323 W 9th St Plainfield NJ 07060 Office: 190 Greenbrook Rd North Plainfield NJ 07060

ABRAMS, JULES CLINTON, psychologist; b. Phila., June 4, 1927; s. Abraham and Sara (Rubinoff) A.; student La Salle Coll., 1944-45; A.B., Temple U., 1948, M.A., 1949, Ph.D., 1955; student U. Toronto, 1949-50; m. Ellen Shuman, Aug. 7, 1955; children—Richard, Robbi, Larry, Nancy. Psychologist, Sklar Sch., Phila., 1956-60; dir. Reading Improvement Inst., Pa., 1955-64; prof. psychiatry, head sect. psychology, dir. Inst. for Learning, dir. grad. edn. in psychology. Hahnemann Med. Coll., Phila., 1968—; prof. Johns Hopkins, 1975—. Pres., Parkway Day Sch., Phila., 1966-76. Fellow Am. Psychol. Assn.; mem. Assn. for Child Psychoanalysis, AAAS, Internat. Reading Assn., N.Y. Acad. Sci., Council for Exceptional Children, Sigma Xi. Contbr. numerous articles to profl. jours. Home: 1505 Paper Mill Rd Philadelphia PA 19118 Office: 230 N Broad St Philadelphia PA 19102

ABRAMS, JULIUS, engr.; b. Butrimantzi, Lithuania, Oct. 27, 1902; s. Harry Isaac and Etta (Ginsberg) A.; brought to U.S., 1903; B.C.E., Northeastern U., 1925, D.Eng. (hon.), 1973, m. Eva Hodess, June 2, 1926; children—Fay Rosalind (Mrs. Louis Wilgoren), Benjamin Emanuel, Phillip. Civil and constrn. engr. Gleason Engring Corp., Wellesley, Mass., 1932-39; chief engr. B. A. Gardett Corp., 1936-40; civil engr., supt. J. Slotnik Co., Boston, 1940-45; engr. Joseph Bennett Co., Boston, 1945; pres. Poley-Abrams Corp., engrs.-constructors, Brookline, Mass., 1945—, J. Abrams Constrn. Co. Inc., 1975—; dir., past pres. Asso. Gen. Contractors of Mass. Chmn., Brookline Bldg. Dept. Bd. Examiners, 1972-76; mem. Commn. of Mass. Designers Selection Bd. Corporator Lesley Coll.; mem. corp. dir., past chmn. nat. council, chmn. Hillel adv. com. Northeastern U. Registered profl. engr., Mass. Mem. Nat. Soc. Profl. Engrs., Am. Soc. Engring. Edn., Am. Inst. Constructors, Am. Arbitration Assn., Am. Council Constrn. Edn. (nat. standard com.), Alpha Epsilon Pi. Republican. Mason; mem. B'nai B'rith (past pres. architects-engrs. lodge). Home: 171 Shaw Rd Brookline MA 02167 Office: 45 Bartlett Crescent Brookline MA 02146

ABRAMS, PHILIP, constrn. co. exec.; b. Boston, Nov. 13, 1939; s. Julius and Eva (Hodess) A.; B.A., Williams Coll., 1961; m. Rosalyn Merle Heifetz, Aug. 23, 1970; children—Mark Solomon, Jonathan Samuel, Daniel Jason. Supt., project mgr. Poley-Abrams Corp., Brookline, Mass., 1961, 65-66; partner, treas. Abreen Corp., Needham Heights, Mass., 1966—. Mem. local bd. SSS, 1970-74; mem. Gov. Sargeant's Adv. Com. on Constrn. Industry, 1971-72; mem. Brookline Redevel. Authority, 1971-74; mem. Nat. Def. Exec. Res., 1978—. Served to lt. USNR, 1961-65. Mem. Asso. Gen. Contractors, Am. Inst. Constructors, Asso. Builders and Contractors (pres. 1975), Nat. Constrn. Industry Council (chmn. 1976-77). Republican. Jewish. Clubs: B'nai B'rith, Masons. Home: 32 Pickwick Rd West Newton MA 02165 Office: 140 Gould St Needham Heights MA 02194

ABRAMS, ROBERT, state ofcl.; b. Bronx, N.Y., July 4, 1938; s. Benjamin and Dorothy (Kaplan) A.; B.A., Columbia Coll., 1960; J.D., N.Y. U., 1963; m. Diane Blossom Schulder, Sept. 15, 1974; 1 dau., Rachel Schulder. Mem. N.Y. State Assembly, 1965-69; pres. Borough of Bronx, 1970-78; atty. gen. State of N.Y., 1979—; past chmn. Greater N.Y. Council on Soviet Jewry. Recipient Interfaith award Council Chs. N.Y.C.; Brotherhood award B'nai B'rith; Man of Year award NAACP; Cardozo award for legal excellence, Man of Year award N.Y. State Fedn. Italian Orgns.; Man of Year award Irish No. Aid Com.; Adam Clayton Powell award for public service O.I.C.; Maccabean award N.Y. Bd. Rabbis; others. Democrat. Jewish. Office: 2 World Trade Center New York NY 10047

ABRAMS, ROSALIE SILBER, state legislator; b. Balt., June 2, 1916; d. Isaac and Dora (Rodbell) Silber; grad. with honors, Sinai Hosp. Sch. Nursing, 1938; B.S., Johns Hopkins, 1963, M.A. in Polit. Sci., 1969; m. William Abrams, Oct. 14, 1953; 1 dau., Elizabeth Joan. Instr., supr. operating room Sinai Hosp., Balt., 1938-40; pub. health nurse Balt. City Dept. Edn., 1941-45; bus. mgr. Sequoia Med. Group, Redwood City, Calif., 1946-47; asst. bus. mgr. Silber's Bakery, Inc., Balt., 1947-53. Mem. health com. Md. Conf. Social Welfare, 1968-69; founder, dir. Cross Country Improvement Assn., 1969—; dir. Md. Food Com., Inc., 1969—; mem. adv. com. cost containment Hosp. Cost Analysis Service, Inc., 1969-76; bd. dirs. Sinai Hosp., 1971—; mem. exec. com. Md. Health Maintenenace Orgn., 1971-73. Mem. Md. Ho. of Dels., 1967-69, Md. Senate, 1970—, mem. senate finance com., 1970-74; mem. Mayor's Health Services Adv. and Planning Council, 1968; mem. comprehensive health planning com. Balt. Regional Planning Council, 1967—; mem. Gov.'s Adv. Council Comprehensive Health Planning, 1968-75, Md. Commn. on Status Women, 1968—; chmn. legislative com. Balt. Area Council Alcoholism, 1970-75; mem. Md. Humane Practices Commn., 1971—, chmn., 1974—; mem. Md. adv. com. Traffic Safety and Alcoholism Project, 1970-77; vice chmn. human resources and urban affairs com. So. Legis. Conf., Council State Govts., 1975—; mem. Gov.'s Task Force on Mental Health Support Systems, 1978; pres. Md. Order Women Legislators, 1973-74. Bd. dirs. Safety First Club Md., Sinai Hosp. Served as ensign USNR, 1945-46. Recipient Louise Waterman Wise community service award Am. Jewish Congress, 1969; award for health legislation Am. Assn. for Comprehensive Health Planning, 1971; Safety Crusader plaque Safety First Club Md., 1971; Jewish Nat. Fund award, 1975; Ann London Scott meml. award for legis. excellence, 1975, others. Home: 6205 Wirt Ave Baltimore MD 21215

ABRAMS, WARREN ELLIOTT, paper co. exec.; b. Bklyn., Oct. 27, 1928; s. Joseph D. and Ann (Weidenbaum) A.; B.S., Va. Poly. Inst., 1950; postgrad. U. Maine, 1952-53; m. Roberta Nathanson, Aug. 26, 1952; children—Alan, Michael, Carolyn. Indsl. engr. Lewyt Corp., Bklyn., 1950-52; with Hudson Pulp & Paper Corp., N.Y.C., 1953—, sr. v.p. indsl. products, 1970-73, exec. v.p., 1973—; also dir. Chmn. L.I. unit United Jewish Appeal, 1969-74; chmn. joint purchasing com. Fedn. Jewish Philanthropies, 1971-76. Served to capt. AUS, 1950-62. Mem. Paper Bag Inst. (pres. 1971-73), Gummed Industries Assn. (pres. 1969-70). Home: 860 UN Plaza New York City NY 10017 Office: 477 Madison Ave New York City NY 10022

ABRAMSON, ARTHUR HARRIS, textile co. exec.; b. Syracuse, N.Y., Oct. 5, 1918; s. Moses Brockway and Lillian (Egerl) A.; student Syracuse U., 1936-38; B.S. in Accounting, U. Ill., 1940; m. Naomi Shirley Gilbert, Sept. 16, 1943; children—Richard, Kenneth, Bonnie. Partner Stillman's, Syracuse, 1946-59; pres. Wilson-Ranger Inc., Syracuse, 1959-68; v.p., dir. Gladding Corp., Syracuse, 1968—; dir. Syracuse Safety Service. Served with AUS, 1941-46. Mason. Home: 204 Hurlburt Rd Syracuse NY 13224 Office: 1224 W Genesee St Syracuse NY 13201

ABRAMSON, EDWIN DONALD, accountant; b. Newark, Mar. 3, 1934; s. Jacob C. and H. Cecelia (Landersman) A.; B.S. in Econs., U. Pa., 1956; m. Sondra Stone, Sept. 15, 1957. Staff accountant J. C. Abramson & Co., West Orange, N.J., 1956-64; partner Abramson, Quittner & Abramson, West Orange, 1964—; v.p., acting pres. Essex County State Bank, 1971-73; dir. Internat. Career Consultants, Inc., Creative Film Enterprise Inc., Piel Industria, Inc. of P.R. Active Civilian Def., Music and Performing Arts Lodge of B'nai B'rith. C.P.A., N.J., N.Y. State. Clubs: Cedar Hill Country (trustee), Jaycees (senator). Home: 4 Shadowlawn Dr Livingston NJ 07039 Office: 59 Main St West Orange NJ 07052

ABRAMSON, MICHAEL, photojournalist, author; b. Plainfield, N.J., July 5, 1944; s. Philip and Frieda (Belsky) A.; A.B. in History cum laude, Kenyon Coll., Gambier, Ohio, 1966; M.A. in History of Culture (Woodrow Wilson fellow), U. Chgo., 1968. Freelance photojournalist, 1969—; author, photographer: Palante, 1970; photographer: Our Portion of Hell, 1971, Inside Las Vegas, 1977; (anthology with others) The Eye of Conscience, 1973; one-man exhbns. include Berengo-Gardin Gallery, Milan, Italy, 1972, Modernage Discovery Gallery, N.Y.C., 1973, Soho Photo Gallery, N.Y.C., 1973, O.K. Harris Gallery, N.Y.C., 1978; represented in group exhbns. U.S. and abroad. Grantee N.Y. State Creative Artists Pub. Service Program, 1974-75. Mem. Am. Soc. Mag. Photographers. Address: 84 University Pl New York City NY 10003

ABRAMSON, SAMUEL ROBERT, indsl. psychologist; b. Phila., June 8, 1943; s. Louis R. and Sara Abramson; B.A., Rutgers U., 1965; M.A., U. Del., 1969; Ph.D., Stevens Inst. Tech., Hoboken, N.J., 1974. Cons. psychologist Project Head Start, N.J., 1966; research psychologist, mgmt. sci. dept. Stevens Inst. Tech., 1969-73; sr. project specialist corp. tng. devel. Citicorp., N.Y.C., 1973-75; dir. human resources and tng. Travelers Cheque and Money Order div. Am. Express Co., N.Y.C., 1975-79; asst. v.p. organizational devel. Am. Express Internat. Banking Corp., N.Y.C., 1979—. NASA fellow, 1966; research fellow U. Del., 1967. Mem. Am. Psychol. Assn., Am. Mgmt. Assn., Am. Soc. Tng. and Devel., Met. Assn. Applied Psychology, Psi Chi. Address: Amexco Plaza 125 Broad St New York NY 10004

ABRAVANEL, DIANE (MRS. BEN DON ABRAVANEL), hosp. adminstr.; b. Pitts., Aug. 26, 1921; d. Nicholas W. and Etta (Hazin) Rosenberg; student Bus. Tng. Coll., Pitts., 1938-39, U. Pitts., 1971-74; m. Ben Don Abravanel, Sept. 29, 1946; children—Lynn, Nicki Ann. Asst. to pub. relations dir. United Jewish Fedn. Pitts., 1956-57; pub. relations and advt. firm account exec. William H. Mazefsky Assos., Pitts., 1957-62; dir. pub. relations Montefiore Hosp., Pitts., 1962-75, asst. adminstr., 1975—. Mem. Pub. Relations Soc. Health Care Orgns. (pres. 1967-68), Pub. Relations Soc. Am. (dir. Pitts. chpt. 1971-72, 2d v.p. 1973, 1st v.p., 1974, pres. 1975, dir. 1976-79), Pub. Relations Soc. of Hosp. Assn. Pa. (chmn. edn. com. 1971), Assn. Am. Med. Colls. (pub. relations sect.), Am. Soc. Hosp. Pub. Relations, Montefiore Hosp. Ladies Hosp. Aid Soc., Nat. Council Jewish Women, Women's Am. Orgn. for Rehab. Through Tng., Ladies Aux. Jewish Home and Hosp. for the Aged, Women's Aux. Am. Cancer Soc. Jewish (mem. Rodef Shalum temple sisterhood). Clubs: Pittsburgh Press; Hadassah (Pitts. chpt.). Home: 2770 Fernwald Rd Pittsburgh PA 15217 Office: 3459 5th Ave Pittsburgh PA 15213

ABT, CLARK CLAUS, social and econ. research and devel. co. exec.; b. Cologne, Germany, Aug. 31, 1929; came to U.S., 1937, naturalized, 1945; B.S., Mass. Inst. Tech., 1951, postgrad., 1961-65, Ph.D., 1965; M.A., John Hopkins, 1952; m. Wendy Peter, Nov. 3, 1972; children—Thomas, Emily. Research asst. social sci. Mass. Inst. Tech., 1950-51; instr. humanities Johns Hopkins, 1951-52; sr. staff engr. ops. analysis Raytheon Co., 1957-59, mgr. preliminary systems design Missile and Space div., 1960-61, mgr. Strategic Studies dept., 1962-63, mgr. advanced systems dept., 1964; pres., founder Abt Asso., Inc., Cambridge, Mass., 1965—; mem. council on urban devel. Inst. Human Sci., Boston Coll., 1969; mem. core curriculum panel dept. city and regional planning Harvard U., 1974; vis. prof. State U. N.Y., 1976; mem. adv. bd. M.S. in Accounting program Bentley Coll., 1974; mem. vis. com. sociology dept. Harvard U.; pres., dir. Council Applied Social Research, Washington, 1978-79; pub. scholarly books. Bd. dirs. League Sch. of Boston, Inc., 1969, Theatre Co. of Boston, 1972. Served to capt. USAF, 1952-57. Recipient Grand prize Thoreau award, 1975. Author: Serious Games, 1970, The Social Audit for Management, 1977; editor: The Evaluation of Social Programs, 1977, Costs and Benefits of Applied Social Research, 1978; contbr. articles in field to profl. jours. Office: 55 Wheeler St Cambridge MA 02138

ABT, VICKI, educator; b. N.Y.C., Dec. 9, 1944; d. Harold and Sylvia (Marcus) Abt; student Mich. State U., 1960-61; B.A., Hofstra U., 1963; M.A., Pa. State U., 1966; Ph.D., Temple U., 1972; 1 dau., Andrea Abt Jones. Caseworker, N.Y. Dept. Welfare, N.Y.C., 1964; faculty Pa. State U., University Park, 1964-66, asso. prof. sociology, 1971—; faculty Temple U., Phila., 1967-71; lectr. women's issues. Pres., Judson Meadow Civic Assn., 1973-75; mem. Bucks County Citizens Com., 1975—; mem. Phila. Mental Health Task Force, 1979—. Pa. State U. teaching fellow, 1964-66; Temple U. fellow, 1967-71; research grantee NIMH, 1971-73; Pa. State U. grantee, 1978. Mem. Am. Sociol. Assn., Am. Psychol. Assn., Soc. for Psychol. Study of Social Issues, Eastern, Pa. sociol. socs., NOW. Jewish. Author: Symbolic Social Interaction, 1973. Home: 1369 Abbey Way Cornwells Heights PA 19020 Office: Pa State Univ Ogontz Campus Abington PA 19001

ABU-MOUSTAFA, ADEL H., ednl. adminstr.; b. Cairo, Egypt, Nov. 18, 1939; s. Abdel Hamid and Zenab A. (Ayaad) A.; B.S. in Geology, U. Cairo, 1960; M.A. in Geology, Harvard U., 1964; Ph.D. in Geology, Boston U., 1969; m. Magda Ismail, Sept. 4, 1962; children—Howayda, Sally, Sharief. Demonstrator Cairo U., 1960-62; research asst. Harvard U., Cambridge, Mass., 1963-64; teaching fellow Boston U., 1964-66; lectr., researcher Boston Coll., 1964-67; asst. prof. Salem (Mass.) State Coll., 1967-69, asso. prof., 1969-70, prof., 1971—, dir. summer session, 1971, dean undergrad. studies, 1972-76, acting acad. dean, 1974-76, dean acad. services, 1976—. Recipient Baraka prize Cairo U., 1960; univ. scholarship Egyptian Govt., 1962-68; presdl. medal Egypt, 1960; staff scholarship Boston U., 1964-66. Mem. Mass. Tchrs. Assn., Geol. Soc. Am., Mineral. Soc. Am., Sigma Xi. Author various geol. articles. Home: 51 Paul Revere Rd Lexington MA 02173 Office: Salem State Coll Lafayette St Salem MA 01970

ABUSCH, SIDNEY, accountant; b. Bklyn., Mar. 11, 1941; s. Joseph Jerome and Bessie (Schwartz) A.; B.B.A., CCNY, 1962; diploma N.Y. Inst. Fin., 1968; m. Ann Berman, June 13, 1964; children—Lynn, Steven, Karen. Sr. acct. Siegel Seltzer & Co., C.P.A.'s, N.Y.C., 1964-67; v.p. A.T. Brod & Co. and TPO Inc., N.Y.C., 1968-70; v.p., controller, dir. Pennco Enterprises, 1971-72; pres., dir. Galaxy Industries Inc., Kings Park, N.Y., 1972—; chmn. bd., dirs. Videoscope Inc., Realty TV Previews. Served with AUS, 1962-63. C.P.A., N.Y. Mem. Am. Inst. C.P.A.'s, N.Y. State Soc. C.P.A.'s, Nat. Assn. Accts., L.I. Bd. Realtors, Huntington C. of C. Democrat. Jewish. Club: Commack-Kings Park Rotary (treas. 1974—). Home: 29 Meadowrue Ln East Northport NY 11731 Office: 16 Henry St Kings Park NY 11754

ABUSH, RONNIE, educator; b. N.Y.C., Aug. 19, 1949; s. Joseph and Gertrude (Berfield) A.; B.A., City U. N.Y., 1970; M.Ed., Boston U., 1972. Tchr., Martin Luther King Sch., Boston, 1971-73; guidance counselor Boston Pub. Schs., 1973—. Mem. exec. bd. Boston Sc. dist. council Office for Children, Commonwealth of Mass., 1976—, chmn., 1978—, statewide advisory council del., 1977—. Mem. Am., Mass., Boston personnel and guidance assns., Am. Sch. Counselors Assn. Home: 10 Wave Ave Boston MA 02125

ABZUG, BELLA SAVITZKY (MRS. MARTIN ABZUG), former congresswoman, lawyer; b. N.Y.C., July 24, 1920; d. Emanuel and Esther Savitzky; B.A., Hunter Coll., 1942; LL.B., Columbia; m. Martin Abzug, June 4, 1944; children—Eve Gail, Isobel Jo. Admitted to N.Y. State bar, 1947, practice law, N.Y.C., 1944-70; legislative dir. Women's Strike for Peace, 1961-70; mem. 92d-94th congresses from 20th N.Y. Dist.; presiding officer Nat. Commn. Observance Internat. Women's Year, 1977; presided Nat. Women's Conf., Houston, 1977; co-chmn. Nat. Advisory Com. Women, 1978—. Candidate U.S. Senate, 1976, mayor N.Y.C., 1977, U.S. Congress, 1978. Mem. Women's Strike for Peace, NOW, Nat. Women's Polit. Caucus, Women's Action Alliance, Urban League, Women's Prison Assn., Mems. Congress for Peace Through Law, Dem. Study Group, ACLU, UN Assn., Hadassah. Mem. B'nai B'rith. Home: 37 Bank St New York City NY 10011

ACCARDO, SALVATORE FRANCIS, investment analysis exec.; b. Newark, Dec. 30, 1937; s. Settimo and Teresa (Mineo) A.; B.E.E., Cornell U., 1961; M.B.A. with distinction, N.Y. U., 1963; m. Kathleen Marie O'Shea, Oct. 4, 1969. Bus. planner, market researcher Gen. Electric Co., N.Y.C., 1963-67; with William D. Witter, Inc., N.Y.C., 1969-76, v.p., 1971-76; v.p. Drexel Burnham & Lambert Group, N.Y.C., 1976-77; v.p. Kidder, Peabody & Co., 1977—. Bd. dirs. 93d St. Park-Lexington Assn. Served with USAF, 1968. Named Instl. Investor All-Star Analyst, 1975-76, 78. Mem. N.Y. Elec. and Electronics Analysts Group, N.Y. Soc. Security Analysts. Club: Univ. Home: 956 Fifth Ave New York City NY 10021 Office: Kidder Peabody & Co 10 Hanover Sq New York City NY 10005

ACCETTOLA, ALBERT BERNARD, physician; b. N.Y.C., Feb. 4, 1918; s. Vincent and Rose (Andriola) A.; B.S., Wagner Coll., 1941; M.D., Boston U., 1944; m. Rose Galasso, Mar. 14, 1943; children—Albert Bernard, Paul E., Judith A. Intern, S.I. (N.Y.) Hosp., 1944-45, coordinator intern and resident edn., 1949-55, attending orthopedic surgeon, 1951—, pres. med. bd. 1968-69; resident in orthopedic surgery Bellevue Hosp., N.Y.C., 1945-47, asso. vis. orthopedic surgeon, 1964—; resident fracture service Milw. County Hosp., 1948; asst. orthopedic surgery Sch. Medicine, Milw., 1948; practice medicine specializing in orthopedic surgery, S.I., 1948—; asso. clin. prof. orthopedic surgery Sch. Medicine, N.Y. U., 1964—; surgeon collegiate athletics Wagner Coll., S.I., 1949—; asso. staff mem., orthopedic surgeon Hunterdon Med. Center, Flemington, N.J., 1953-77; chmn. pub. health forums Richmond County Med. Soc., S.I. Advance, 1953-54; mem. community adv. bd. USPHS Hosp., S.I., 1965-68; chmn. med. adv. bd. Vis. Nurse Assn., S.I., 1967-68. Trustee

Staten Island Hosp., 1973-76. Served with M.C., AUS, 1944. Recipient service award Wagner Coll., 1957, Achievement award, 1973. Diplomate Am. Bd. Orthopedic Surgery, Nat. Bd. Med. Examiners. Fellow A.C.S., Am. Acad. Orthopedic Surgeons; mem. Richmond County (pres. elect 1963-64, pres. 1964-65), N.Y State (chmn. med. -legal and workmen's compensation sect. 1974) med. socs., AMA. Home: 51 Springhill Ave Staten Island NY 10301 Office: 100 Central Ave Staten Island NY 10301

ACETO, VINCENT JOHN, librarian, educator; b. Schenectady, Feb. 5, 1932; s. Henry and Gilda (Maietta) A.; A.B., State U. N.Y., 1953, M.A., 1953, M.L.S., 1959; postgrad. Western Res. U., 1959, 62, 65-66; m. Jean Louise Rasey, Aug. 27, 1955 (div. 1974); children—David, Paul, Andrew; m. 2d, Virginia Marie Borys, May 11, 1974. Tchr., Scotia (N.Y.)-Glenville Central Schs., 1956-57; high sch. librarian Burnt Hills (N.Y.)-Ballston Lake Central Schs., 1957-59; library dir. Town Ballston Pub. Library, Burnt Hills, 1958-60; Fulbright lectr. U. Dacca, East Pakistan, 1964-65; asst. prof. Sch. Library Sci., State U. N.Y., Albany, 1959-62, asso. prof. library sci., 1963-69, prof., 1969—. Pres., Filmdex, Inc., 1973—; library cons. various pub. schs., N.Y. State Edn. Dept.; dir. U.S. Office Edn. insts. and traineeships Sch. Libraries, State U. N.Y., Albany, 1965, 68, 69, 74. Bd. dirs. Schenectady Citizens League, 1963-64; bd. dirs. Freedom Forum, Schenectady, 1970—, chmn., 1976—. Served with AUS, 1954-56. Mem. Am., Pakistan, East Pakistan, N.Y., Hudson-Mohawk (v.p. 1964-66) library assns., NEA, Idaka Forum, Kappa Phi Kappa, Phi Delta Kappa. Democrat. Unitarian. Joint editor Film Lit. Index. Contbr. articles to profl. jours. Home: 950 Madison Ave Albany NY 12208 Office: Sch Library and Information Sci State U NY Albany NY 12222

ACHESON, PATRICIA LOUISE, counselor; b. Pitts., July 3, 1928; d. William Edward and Louise Seymour (White) Marshall; B.A., Westminster Coll., 1949; postgrad. Pa. State U., 1950; M.Ed. in Rehab. Counseling, U. Pitts., 1973; m. Willard Phillips Acheson, Aug. 26, 1949; children—Louise S., Ann L., Amy J. Matron, tchr. boarding sch., Asyut, Egypt, 1950-51; tchr. Pressley Meml. Inst., Asyut, 1951-52; nurse Am. Mission Hosp., Asyut, Egypt, 1952-53; corrections counselor Bur. Corrections, Pa. Dept. Justice, Pitts., 1973—. Certified rehab. counselor, Pa. Mem. Nat. Rehab. Assn., Nat. Rehab. Counseling Assn., Am. Personnel and Guidance Assn., Internat. Half-way House Assn., Am. Assn. Correctional Psychologists, Pub. Offender Counselor Assn. Presbyterian. Home: 806 Heberton St Pittsburgh PA 15206

ACHEY, DOROTHY MAIE, former textile co. exec.; b. Bethlehem, Pa., Oct. 8, 1914; d. William C. and Sadie (Stine) Achey; grad. high sch. Lab. technician, clk. Queen City Textile Co., Allentown, Pa., 1933-39; supt. dyeing Blue Ridge Textile Co., Bangor, Pa., 1939-49, supt. dyeing and finishing, 1949-56, exec. asst., 1956-59; tech. dir., tech. asst. to pres. Blue Ridge-Winkler Textiles div. Lehigh Valley Industries Inc., Bangor, 1959-66, product mgr. automotive and indsl., 1966-71; supt. dyeing and finishing Timme Fabrics, Inc., Rio Grande, N.J., 1971-74, supt. tech. services, 1974; plant mgr. dyeing and finishing Travis Mills Corp., Lititz, Pa., 1975-76; dyeing supt. Redmond Finishing Co., East Stroudsburg, Pa., 1976-78, ret., 1978. Mem. Am. Assn. Textile Colorists & Chemists. Home: 3045 Center St Bethlehem PA 18017

ACHOR, WILLIAM THOMAS, educator; b. Birmingham, Ala., June 18, 1929; s. David Thomas and Helen (Neill) A.; B.S., Ala. Poly. Inst., 1952; M.S., Vanderbilt U., 1954, Ph.D., 1958; m. Dorothy Carol Whipple, Aug. 9, 1958; children—Kathleen, Alison. Instr. physics Western Res. U., Cleve., 1957-59; mem. tech. staff RCA Labs., Princeton, N.J., 1959-62; asst. prof. physics Earlham Coll., Richmond, Ind., 1963-65; prof., dept. head physics Western Md. Coll., Westminster, 1965—; cons. Carroll County Bd. Edn., 1977-78; vis. prof. acoustic research Pa. State U., 1978-79. Pres. West End Sch. PTA, 1969-70. AEC radiol. physics fellow, 1952-54, Ford fellow, 1954-56. Mem. Am. Assn. Physics Tchrs. (chmn. Balt. area 1966-67, 77-78, v.p. Chesapeake sect. 1967-68, pres. Chesapeake sec. 1968-69), AAUP (v.p. Md. conf., 1970-73), Sigma Xi. Democrat. Mem. Ch. of Brethren. Home: 64 Ridge Rd Westminster MD 21157

ACHTENTUCH, HERBERT, accountant; b. Vienna, Austria, Sept. 9, 1922; s. Herman and Paula (Kohn) A.; came to U.S., 1938, naturalized, 1944; B.B.A magna cum laude, City Coll. N.Y., 1946; m. Marion Rosenbaum, Nov. 26, 1961; children—Jeanne Sharon, Harriet Rose. Owner Herbert Achtentuch, C.P.A., N.Y.C., 1949—; partner Haft & Achtentuch, C.P.A.'s, 1972—. Cons. to pub. and pvt. cos. and founds. C.P.A., N.Y. Mem. N.Y. State Soc. C.P.A.'s, Am. Inst. C.P.A.'s, Inst. C.P.A.'s Israel (asso. internat. mem.), Beta Gamma Sigma. Home: 2 Middlemay Circle Forest Hills Gardens NY 11375 Office: 635 Madison Ave New York City NY 10022

ACKER, JACK LILLY, dietitian; b. Venango, Pa., Apr. 19, 1925; s. George David and Mildred Marie (Lilly) A.; B.S., Pa. State Coll., 1949. Chief dietitian Scotland (Pa.) Sch. Vets. Children, 1949-51; asst. dietitian Mayview (Pa.) State Hosp. for Mentally Ill, 1951-57; chief dietitian Farview State Hosp. for Criminally Insane Men, Waymart, Pa., 1957-59; food service mgr. Woodville State Hosp. for Mentally Ill, Carnegie, Pa., 1959—; chmn. Food Service Dirs. Western Region Pa., 1977—. Served with AUS, 1943-44. Registered dietitian. Mem. Am. (chmn. survey nutritional standards 1969-71), Pa., Pitts. dietetic assns., Am. Legion, Western Pa. Kennel Assn., Appaloosa Horse Assn., Internat. Sundance 500 Horse Club, Col. Rangerbred Horse Club, Am. Hunter and Jumper Horse Assn., Australian Shepherd Dog Club, Lutheran. Clubs: Midway Lions, Grange, Masons. Home: Route 1 Box 156 Bulger PA 15019 Office: Woodville State Hosp Carnegie PA 15106

ACKER, SHERRON NAY, educator; b. Lusk, Wyo., Sept. 12, 1941; d. Walton Haynes and Zella Mae (Humphreys) Nay; B.A., Colo. State Coll., 1963; M.A., U. Colo., 1969; postgrad. Rutgers U., 1975—; m. Edward Richard Acker, Mar. 27, 1976. Tchr. history Wasson High Sch., Colorado Springs, 1963-68; instr. dept. history Chadron (Nebr.) State Coll., 1969-70; tchr. Tappan Zee High Sch., Orangeburg, N.Y., 1972-74; instr. dept. history Pace U., Pleasantville, N.Y., 1976—. Democratic committeewoman, Nyack, N.Y., 1977—. Mem. Am. Hist. Assn., Mid-Atlantic Slavic Assn., Am. Assn. for Advancement Slavic Studies. Home: 26 6th Ave Nyack NY 10960 Office: Pace Univ Pleasantville NY 10570

ACKERBERG, ROBERT CYRIL, educator, chem. engr.; b. Mpls., Sept. 14, 1934; s. David and Eva (Fefercorn) A.; B.S. in Chem. Engring., Mass. Inst. Tech., 1956; M.S.Engring., U. Mich., 1957; M.A., Harvard, 1960, Ph.D. in Applied Mathematics, 1963; m. Sylvia Kent Healy, May 19, 1963; children—Daniel, Anna. Sr. research asso. Raytheon Corp., Waltham, Mass., 1962-63; asst. prof. aerospace engring. Poly. Inst. Bklyn. (name changed to Poly. Inst. N.Y. 1973), 1963-66, asso. prof., 1966-72, asso. prof. chem. engring., 1972-73; prof., 1973—. NSF fellow, 1956-59; NSF grantee, 1971-72, 74—; Sci. Research Council Gt. Britain grantee, 1971-72. Mem. Am. Inst. Chem. Engring., Soc. Indsl. and Applied Mathematics, Tau Beta Pi, Phi Lambda Upsilon, Sigma Gamma Tau, Omega Xi Epsilon. Contbr. articles in field to profl. jours. Home: 70 Cherokee St Massapequa NY 11758 Office: Polytechnic Inst New York Long Island Center Route 110 Farmingdale NY 11735 also Polytechnic Inst New York 333 Jay St Brooklyn NY 11201

ACKERMAN, JACOB LEWIS, ophthalmic surgeon; b. Berlin, July 22, 1947; s. Joseph and Pearl A.; M.D., Albert Einstein Coll. Medicine, 1971; m. Elaine Marcia Horowitz, Aug. 10, 1969; children—Rita Lynne, Karen Tracy, Steven Charles, Julie Gail. Intern, Brookdale Hosp. Med. Center, Bklyn., 1971-72; resident in ophthalmology L.I.-Hillside Med. Center, New Hyde Park, N.Y., 1972-75; attending surgeon, also coordinator residency tng. dept. ophthalmology Brookdale Hosp. Med. Center, 1975—; dir. ophthalmology Empire Med. Center, Bklyn., 1977—; vis. prof. ophthalmology Touro Coll., N.Y.C., 1977—; asso. clin. prof. ophthalmology Downstate Med. Center, Bklyn.; cons. in field. Chmn. blood dr. Greater N.Y. Blood Bank, Woodmere, N.Y.C. Served to capt., U.S. Army, 1971-77. Brownstone Meml. scholar, 1967-71. Diplomate Am. Bd. Ophthalmology. Fellow A.C.S.; mem. AMA, Internat. Glaucoma Congress, Am. Assn. Ophthalmology, Am. Acad. Ophthalmology, Am. Physicians Fellowship, Contact Lens Assn. Am., Kings County, N.Y. State med. socs., N.Y. Acad. Sci., Bklyn. Ophthalmol. Soc., Mensa. Club: Fabulous Fifth of Fifth Congressional Dist. Office: Dept Ophthalmology Brookdale Hosp Med Center Linden Blvd at Rockaway Pkwy Brooklyn NY 11212

ACLIN, JOHN JOSEPH, chemist; b. N.Y.C., Jan. 8, 1928; s. John and Vitina (Gioia) A.; B.A., Adelphi U., 1952; student Bklyn. Poly. Inst., 1953-55, Newark Coll. Engring., 1955-57; m. Anne C. Barr, Dec. 4, 1949; children—Elizabeth Anne, John Joseph, Debra June, Keith Andrew. Sr. polymer chemist Nopco, Harrison, N.Y., 1952-57; tech. service chemist Celanese Corp., Linden, N.J., 1957-59; project mgr. Olin Chem. Corp., New Haven, 1959-61, research and devel. supr., Ordill, Ill., 1961-63; individual contbr. Gen. Electric Co., Coshocton, Ohio, 1963-67; v.p., tech. dir. Parkwood Laminates, Lowell, Mass., 1968-76; sales mgr., tech. mgr., asst. v.p. Polychrome Corp., Clark, N.J., 1976—. Served with USN, 1946-48. Mem. Am. Chem. Soc., Soc. Photog. Scientists and Engrs. Methodist. Home: 138 Meridian Dr Bricktown NJ 08723 Office: 160 Terminal Ave Clark NJ 07066

ACOCELLA, ANTHONY FRANK, nutritionist, pharmacist; b. Elizabeth, N.J., Feb. 1, 1932; s. Angelo and Carmella (Nocera) A.; B.S., St. John's U., 1960; B.A., 1977; postgrad. Thomas Edison Coll., 1976; M.S., Calif. Western U., 1976, Ph.D., 1977; m. Violet Mazzucca, May 30, 1958; children—Marisa, Anthony, Dina, David. Pharm. chemist Intcom, Elizabeth, N.J., 1956-60; pharmacist Oak Tree Pharmacy, Woodbridge, N.J., 1961-73; staff A/C Labs., Carteret, N.J., 1973-76, S&W Med. Service, Carteret, 1975-76; owner, operator Nutritional Center Pharmacy, Scotch Plains, N.J., 1976—; cons., lectr. nutrition. Served with USAF, 1949-53. Mem. Am. Inst. Chemists, Nat. Assn. Nutrition, Fla., N.J. pharm. socs., Acad. Nutrition Consultants. Roman Catholic. Club: Lions (asso.). Home: 14 Round Hill Rd Scotch Plains NJ 07076 Office: 1812 E 2d St Scotch Plains NJ 07076

ACOCELLA, LOUIS CARMINE, ednl. adminstr.; b. Newark, Mar. 28, 1938; married, 3 children. B.A. in Gen. Elementary Edn., Kean Coll., Union, N.J., 1964, M.A. in Adminstrn. and Supervision, 1966, postgrad. in sch. adminstrn. Asst. prin. Lincoln Sch., Roselle, N.J., 1967-68; prin., Robert Morris Sch., S. Boundbrook, N.J., 1968-71, Park Ave. Sch., Orange (N.J.) Bd. Edn., 1971-72; adminstrv. prin. Moonachie (N.J.) Bd. Edn., 1972-73; supt. Riverdale (N.J.) Pub. Schs., 1973—. Trustee, v.p. Bloomfield Pub. Library, 1970—, chmn. Riverdale Juvenile Conf. com., 1974—. Mem. Am., N.J., Morris County assns. sch. adminstrs. Certified as tchr., prin., supr., sch. adminstr., N.J. Home: 69 Willard Ave Bloomfield NJ 07003 Office: 52 Newark Pompton Turnpike Riverdale NJ 07457

ACQUAVIVA, SAMUEL JOSEPH, research engr.; b. Boston, Jan. 25, 1921; s. Daniel and Anna (Settana) A.; B.S., Purdue U., 1949; m. Margaret Corbett, June 21, 1952; children—Daniel, Donna, David, Denise. Materials engr. Watertown Arsenal (Mass.), 1949-55, Mass. Inst. Tech. Lincoln Lab., 1955-60, Army Materials Research Center, Watertown, Mass., 1960—, sr. materials research engr., 1974—. Served with USAF, 1942-45. Decorated D.F.C., Air medal; registered profl. engr., Mass. Mem. ASTM, ASME, Soc. Exper-Stress Analysis. Roman Catholic. Club: K.C. Editor: Structural Ceramics and Testing of Brittle Materials 1967; Structural Ceramics and Design, 1968. Home: 18 Rosemary Rd Dedham MA 02026 Office: Army Materials Research Center Watertown MA 02172

ACTON, CONSTANCE FOSTER, metall. exec.; b. Fall River, Mass., July 12, 1947; d. Foster Southworth and Constance Norton (McIntyre) A.; B.S. with honor, Mich. Technol. U., 1968; Ph.D., U. Pa., 1973; postdoctoral fellow Yale U., 1974; postgrad. in environ. engring. U. Conn., 1973-74. Chem. metallurgist Handy & Harman, Fairfield, Conn., 1973-74; research staff scientist Yale U., New Haven, 1974-75; asst. prof. chem. metallurgy Mich. Technol. U., Houghton, 1975-76; sr. research metallurgist Olin Metals Research Labs., New Haven, 1976-78; dir. research Jensen Industries, Inc., North Haven, Conn., 1978—; reviewer research grant proposals NSF, 1975-77; cons. EPA, 1974; judge Delaware Valley Sci. Fair, 1970-72; moderator Women in Sci. and Engring. Conf., Yale U., 1977; vis. scientist speaker Alcoa Research Center (Pa.), 1976. Am. Soc. Metals scholar, 1965, 68; NDEA fellow, 1971; NSF grantee, 1975. Mem. Am. Inst. Mining, Metall. and Petroleum Engrs., Internat. Assn. Pollution Control, Am. Soc. Metals (tchr.), ACLU, Tau Beta Pi, Am. Chem. Soc., Electrochem. Soc., Soc. Women Engrs., Nat. Assn. Corrosion Engrs., AAAS, Am. Inst. Chem. Engrs., New Eng. AAU, Finnish Am. Marathon Assn. Sleeping Giant Pacers Track Club, Alpha Sigma Mu. Democrat. Contbr. articles in field to profl. jours. Recipient Silver medal Hennesey Cross-Country Ski Marathon, Brandon, Vt., 1978; 1st pl. Hartford 10 km AAU Road Race, 1977, Milford, Conn. 7 mile AAU Road Race, 1977; 1st pl. woman 50 mile ultramarathon, Lake Waramang, Conn., 1978; 3d pl. 100 km RRCA nat. championship, Miami, 1979; nationally ranked woman marathoner and ultramarathoner. Home: 36 Hallmark Dr Wallingford CT 06492 Office: 417 Washington Ave North Haven CT 06473

ACTON, WINSER PAUL, paper product co. exec., chemist; b. Salem, Oreg., Aug. 8, 1925; s. Paul Hobart and Serena (Philips) A.; B.S., Willamette U., 1947; M.S., Pa. State U., 1949, Ph.D. (Am. Petroleum Inst. fellow), 1952; m. Betty Louise Sinkola, Dec. 27, 1947 (div. 1974); 1 dau., Catherine Lynn; m. 2d, Caroline Sue Kast, Sept. 14, 1974. With Hercules, Inc., Wilmington, Del., 1951-62, sr. tech. rep., 1961-62; mktg. mgr., v.p. E.B. and A.C. Whiting Co., Burlington, Vt., 1962-66; sr. project mgr. Monsanto Co., St. Louis, 1966-67; tech. service rep. ITT Rayonier Inc., N.Y.C., 1967-74, asst. mgr. N.Am. sales, 1975-77, mgr., 1977—. Vice chmn. English in Action, N.Y.C., 1971-75. Served to ensign USNR, 1943-46. Mem. AAAS, Am. Chem. Soc., Am. Forestry Assn., TAPPI, Nat. Arts Club. Democrat. Episcopalian (vestryman, parish treas.). Patentee in purification of pentaerythritol by ion exchange resins. Home: 201 E 25th St New York City NY 10010 Office: 605 3d Ave New York City NY 10017

ADAM, RICHARD SCHOFER, counselor, educator; b. Reading, Pa., Sept. 29, 1947; s. Kermit Fegely and Pauline Ellen (Schofer) A.; B.S., Kutztown State Coll., 1969; M.Ed., Lehigh U., 1973; m. Mary Frances Troilo, May 31, 1969; children—Gina, Gian, Luis, Liesel. Tchr. spl. edn. Parkland Sch. Dist., Allentown, Pa., 1969-70; tchr. sr. high sch. spl. edn. Fleetwood (Pa.) High Sch., 1970-73, elementary sch. counselor, 1973-77, tchr. exptl. open edn., 1977—. Active ARC. Mem. NEA, Pa. Edn. Assn., Am. Personnel and Guidance Assn., Am. Sch. Counselors Assn. Democrat. Lutheran. Home: 10 W High St Topton PA 19562 Office: Box 4026 Richmond Elementary Sch Fleetwood PA 19522

ADAMO, JOSEPH ALBERT, biologist, educator; b. Hoboken, N.J., Oct. 22, 1938; s. Anthony and Helen Annamarie (Hornfeck) A.; B.A., Jersey City State Coll., 1964; M.S. (Univ. fellow), Fairleigh Dickinson U., 1967; postgrad. (Fulbright-Hayes fellow) U. Philippines, Los Baños, 1973-74; Ph.D., Rutgers U., 1975; children—Thomas Anthony, Jo Anne, Samantha. Instr. botany Fairleigh Dickinson U., 1965-66; asst. prof. biology Jersey City State Coll., 1966-67; prof. Ocean County Coll., 1967—, co-dir. auto-tutorial units in biology, 1968—, dir. Environ. Center, 1978—. Fulbright-Hays fellbw Internat. Rice Research Inst., Los Bañs, 1973-74. Served with USAF, 1955-59. Recipient Hammond Sci. award Jersey City State Coll., 1964. Mem. Am. Microbiol. Soc., Soc. Nematologists, Am., Internat., Philippine phytopathol. socs., AAUP, Iota Mu Pi, Phi Theta Kappa, Phi Sigma. Democrat. Roman Catholic. Home: 185 Maple Ave Island Heights NJ 08732 Office: Dept of Biology Ocean County Coll Toms River NJ 08753

ADAMS, A(LFRED) JOHN, pub. affairs cons.; b. Liverpool, Eng., Nov. 22, 1931; s. Wilfrid and Francine Sophia (Bertrand) A.; came to U.S., 1962, naturalized, 1971; student pvt. schs., Eng., France, Germany; m. Vibeke Dinsen, June 3, 1963 (div. 1975); m. 2d, Judith Ann Duff, Oct. 15, 1978. Correspondent, London Daily Telegraph, 1952-56; editor, bureau chief, asst. dir. news Radio Free Europe, Bonn and Munich, W.Ger., 1956-62; Africa corr. ABC News, 1963; writer CBS News, N.Y.C., 1964-70; dir. pub. affairs U.S. Price Commn., Washington, 1972-73; pres. John Adams Assos., Inc., Washington, 1973—. Bd. dirs. Psychiat. Inst. Found., Washington, 1974—; exec. dir. Environ. Industry Council, 1975—; advisory bd. Gallaudet Coll. for the Deaf, Washington, 1977—. Served to lt. King's Shropshire Light Inf., 1951-52; Korea. Recipient Distinguished Service award, U.S. Price Commn., 1973. Mem. Inst. of Journalists (London), Overseas Press Club (N.Y.), Pub. Relations Soc. Am. (Silver anvil award 1978), Georgetown Citizens Assn. Club: Fed. City. Co-author: (with J.M. Burke) Civil Rights: A Current Guide to the People, Organizations and Events, 1970; editor: Energy Policy: Industry Perspectives, 1975. Home: 1003 Abbey Way McLean VA 22101 Office: 1825 K St NW Washington DC 20006

ADAMS, ARLON TAYLOR, elec. engr., educator; b. Bottineau, N.D., Apr. 26, 1931; s. Arlon Taylor and Ruth Iola (McFall) A.; B.A., Harvard U., 1953; M.S., U. Mich., 1961, Ph.D., 1964; m. Judith May Schettler, Aug. 29, 1958; children—Robert Daniel, Catherine McFall, Margarethe Ann, David Benjamin. Engr., Sperry Gyroscope Co., Great Neck, N.Y., 1957-59; research asso. U. Mich., Ann Arbor, 1959-63; asst. prof. elec. engring. Syracuse (N.Y.) U., 1963-68, asso. prof., 1968-74, prof., 1974—. Cons., Hughes Aircraft Co., Syracuse U. Research Corp. Served with USNR, 1953-57. Mem. IEEE, (achievement award 1973), AAUP, Phi Kappa Phi, Eta Kappa Nu. Episcopalian. Author: Electromagnetics for Engineers, 1971; (with W. Everett and J. Perini) Topics in Intra System Electromagnetic Compatibility, 1972. Contbr. numerous articles on antennas to profl. publs. Home: 102 Kensington Rd Syracuse NY 13210

ADAMS, BENJAMIN HEDGES, JR., clergyman; b. Bridgeport, Conn., Nov. 24, 1925; s. Benjamin Hedges and Georgia (Lazenby) A.; B.A., U. Pa., 1949; M.Div., Princeton Sem., 1952; D.Ministry, Andover Newton Theol. Sch., 1974; m. Jane Elizabeth Kirkner, Aug. 24, 1957; children—Pamela, John. Ordained to ministry Presbyn. Ch., 1952; pastor United Presbyn. Chs., N.J., 1955-65; founder Presbytery Counseling Center, Rutherford, N.J., 1965, exec. dir. and pastoral psychotherapist 1965—; exec. dir. Palisades Counseling Center, Rutherford, 1965—; staff mem. Westchester Inst. for Psychotherapy, Rye, N.Y., 1969-74; faculty Seton Hall U., 1977—. Served with USAF, 1943-45; served to maj. USAF, 1944-45. Decorated Air medal. Licensed marriage counselor, N.J. Diplomate Am. Assn. Pastoral Counselors. Fellow Am. Assn. Social Psychiatrists; mem. Am. Assn. Marriage Counselors (supr. 1971—), Inst. Existential Analysis, Assn. Applied Psychoanalysis, Am. Acad. Psychotherapists, Am. Psychol. Assn. Club: Polytopic (pres. Rutherford 1973-74). Home: 47 Meadowbrook Rd Randolph NJ 07801 Office: 2 E Passaic St Rutherford NJ 07070

ADAMS, BROCKMAN, sec. transp.; b. Atlanta, Jan. 13, 1927; s. Charles Leslie and Vera (Beemer) A.; B.A. in Econs. summa cum laude, U. Wash., 1949; J.D., Harvard, 1952; m. Mary Elizabeth Scott, Aug. 16, 1952; children—Scott, Dean, Katherine, Aleen. Admitted to Wash. bar, 1952, practiced in Seattle, 1952-61; with firm Little, LeSourd, Palmer, Scott & Slemmons, 1952-60; partner firm LeSourd, Patten & Adams, 1960-61; U.S. atty. for western Wash., Seattle, 1961-64; mem. 89th to 94th congresses from 7th Wash. Dist.; mem. Interstate and Fgn. Commerce Com., mem. Transp. and Aeronautics Subcom.; chmn. Budget Com.; sec. U.S. Dept. Transp., Washington, 1977—; instr. Am. Inst. Banking, Seattle, 1954-60. Pres., Neighborhood Settlement House, Seattle, 1958. Served with USNR, 1944-46. Recipient Distinguished Ser. award Seattle Jaycees, 1960. Mem. Am., Wash., Fed. bar assns., Phi Beta Kappa. Episcopalian. Office: Dept Transp 400 7th St SW Washington DC 20590

ADAMS, CARLYLE, clergyman; b. Monticello, Ohio, Aug. 14, 1906; s. Selden Connor and Iva May (Bedell) A.; student Ohio State U., 1923-25, George Washington U., 1927-29; B.R.E., Auburn Sch. Religious Edn., 1931; B.D., Auburn Theol. Sem., 1934; spl. student in psychiatry Syracuse U., 1931; Litt.D., Waynesburg Coll., 1945; m. Mary York Critchley, June 26, 1935; children—Martha Elizabeth (Mrs. Marc Drogin), Ruth Kathryn (Mrs. George Wilson); m. 2d, Kathleen Hutter Manzella, Aug. 7, 1954. Newspaper reporter, Clarksburg, W.Va., Canton, Ohio, 1920-23; sch. editor Columbus (Ohio) Dispatch, 1923-25; edn. reporter U.S. Daily, Washington, 1926; dir. pub. relations NEA, Washington, 1927-29; instr. psychology Auburn Theol. Sem., 1930-34; ordained to ministry Presbyn. Ch., 1934; pastorates in Oswego, Rome and Utica, N.Y., 1936-42; chaplain, prof. religion Park Coll., 1942-45; editor Presbyn. Tribune, 1940-48; pastor Madison Av. Ch., Albany, N.Y., 1948-52; lectr. philosophy, religion Russell Sage Coll., 1952; pastor First Presbyn. Ch., Rensselaer, N.Y., 1952-71, emeritus, 1971—. Vis. lectr. theology St. Michael's (Vt.) Coll., 1967. moderator, Presbytery of Albany, 1956-57, stated clerk, 1960-75; religion editor Albany Times-Union, 1951-72; commr. Presbyn. Gen. Assembly, 1952, 58, 66; chmn. com. on Christian year Nat. Council of Chs., 1956-64; journalistic observer II Vatican Council, 1963-65. Mem. City Planning Commn., Rensselaer, 1964-71. Hon. pres. bd. Rensselaer Girls Club, 1968—; trustee LaSalle Sch., Albany. Decorated Cross of Constantinople, 1972. Mem. Hymn Soc. Am. (v.p. 1946-48), Capital Area Council Chs. (pres. 1958-60), NEA (life), N.Am. Acad. Ecumenists, Kappa Phi Kappa. Clubs: Albany Torch (pres. 1963-64), Kiwanis. Author: My Secret Prayer, 1956; syndicated newspaper column Our Religions. Home: 64 Summit Ave Albany NY 12209 Office: POB 9034 Albany NY 12209

ADAMS, CAROLE C., research co. exec.; b. N.Y.C., Oct. 29, 1940; d. David and Yetta (Halpern) Frankel; grad. Sandy Lane Sch. Music, 1954; student Washington Sch. Art, 1971-73; m. David M. Fleischer, June 18, 1960 (div. Dec. 1977); 1 son, Adam. Asst., Mfrs. Trust Co., N.Y.C., 1958-59; asst. Standard Factors Inc., N.Y.C., 1959-61; field supr. market research dept. Storm II Inc., N.Y.C., 1971-73; v.p., prin. Reliable Research Inc., market research, Bklyn., 1973—. Recipient Spl. award Certificate for outstanding and meritorious performance Carnegie Hall, 1953. Mem. Market Research Assn., Am. Mktg. Assn. Office: 2600 Flatbush Ave Brooklyn NY 11236

ADAMS, CLARENCE LANCELOT, JR., psychologist; b. N.Y.C.; s. Clarence Lancelot and Ernesta Clarissa (Larrier) A.; B.S., L.I. U., 1950; M.A. (N.Y. State scholar), N.Y. U., 1952; Ed.D., Yeshiva U., 1972. Pvt. practice clin. psychology, N.Y.C., 1958—; sch. psychologist Bur. Guild Guidance, N.Y.C. Bd. Edn., 1967-68, research cons. psychologist, 1970-73, diagnostician learning and reading disabilities, 1976—; chief supr. counseling and psychol. services, dept. academic skills Hunter Coll., City U. N.Y., N.Y.C., 1968-70; asso. prof. psychology Bronx Community Coll., City U. N.Y., 1973-76; cons. in clin. and sch. psychology, mental retardation mgmt. Certified psychologist, N.Y.; nat. registered health service provider in psychology. Mem. Am., N.Y. State psychol. assns., N.Y. Soc. Clin. Psychologists, Assn. Black Psychologists, Am. Soc. Group Psychol. Therapy, Soc. Study Group Tensions, Am. Ortho-psychol. Assn. Address: 200 W 90th St New York City NY 10024

ADAMS, CLYDE BRUCE, ornithologist; b. N.Y.C., Oct. 16, 1936; s. Clyde and Evelyn Murray (Queen) A.; student U. Vt., 1957-60. Computer operator McGraw-Hill, Inc., Hightstown, N.J., 1970—. Served with Army N.G., 1960-66, USAF Res., 1977—. Mem. Am. Ornithologists Union, Brit. Ornithologists Union, Wilson, Cooper ornithol. socs., Eastern, Northeastern bird banding assns. Episcopalian. Club: Explorer's. Contbr. articles and papers to ornithological jours.; inventer bird trap, 1959; developer techniques trapping and banding birds for sci. research. Home: 271 Edgerstoune Rd Princeton NJ 08540 Office: McGraw-Hill Inc Hightstown Rd Hightstown NJ 08520

ADAMS, DONALD KENDRICK, educator; b. North Berwick, Maine, Feb. 21, 1925; s. Howard Franklin and Amy Francis (Welch) A.; B.S., U. N.H., 1949; M.A., U. Conn., 1956, Ph.D., 1956; m. Janet Cabe, June 1, 1961 children—Lance Howard, Amy Louise. Asst. prof. George Peabody Coll., Nashville, Tenn., 1958-62; asso. prof. Syracuse U., 1962-66, prof., chmn. cultural founds. edn., 1966-69; prof. edn., econ. and social devel., chmn. div. ednl. studies U. Pitts., 1969-75. Cons. U.S. AID, Peace Corps, Ford Found., U.S. Office Edn., GE-Tempo, David McKay and Longman Inc. Pubs. scholar-in-residence East-West Center, Hawaii, 1965-67. Pres. Eastmont PTA, 1972-73; chmn. citizens' com. edn. Churchill Area Schs., 1972-73. Served to lt. USAC, 1943-45; served to 1st lt., USAF, 1950-51. Recipient Book Distinction award N.E.A., 1965, Nat. Book award Pi Lambda Theta, 1970. Mem. Internat. Soc. Ednl. Planners (pres. 1973-74), Comparative Edn. Soc. (pres. 1965-66, bd. dirs. 1966-69), Soc. Internat. Devel. (mem. research com. 1960-62), Am. Assn. Pub. Adminstrn. (mem. internat. research com. comparative adminstrv. group 1960-63). Editor: Educational Plnning, 1965; Introduction to Education: A Comparative Analysis, 1966; Education and National Development, 1971; Planning Policy and Theory in Education, Author: (with I.N. Thut) Patterns of Education in Contemporary Societies, 1964; (with Robert Bjork) Education in Developing Areas, 1970; Education and Social Change in Modern America, 1972; also several book chpts., numerous articles. Cons. editor Comparative Edn. Rev., 1961—, Ednl. Studies, 1969—. Home: 1106 Gilchrest Dr Pittsburgh PA 15235

ADAMS, FRANCIS VINCENT, physician, educator; b. N.Y.C., July 31, 1946; s. Vincent Joseph and Rose (Rudin) A.; B.A. cum laude, Georgetown U., 1967; M.D., Cornell U., Ithaca, N.Y., 1971; m. Laurel S. Haring, May 24, 1972. Intern Georgetown U. Hosp., 1971-72, resident in medicine, 1972-73; pulmonary fellow Bellevue Hosp., N.Y.C., 1973-75, clin. asst. attending physician chest service, 1975—; staff physician pulmonary div. VA Hosp., N.Y.C., 1975—; instr. medicine N.Y. U., 1975-78, asst. prof. clin. medicine, 1978—; clin. asst. attending physician N.Y. U. Med. Center, 1975—. Recipient Physician Recognition award AMA, 1974—. Diplomate Am. Bd. Internal Medicine. Mem. Am. Thoracic Soc., N.Y. Trudeau Soc., Phi Beta Kappa, Alpha Sigma Nu. Roman Catholic. Home: 333 E 34th St Apt 12F New York City NY 10016 Office: VA Hosp 1st Ave and 24th St New York City NY 10010

ADAMS, FRANK ANTHONY, lawyer, service co. exec.; b. Balt., Sept. 26, 1945; s. Patrick Anthony and Eleanor Lucille (Lombardo) A.; B.S. in Indsl. Mgmt., U. Balt., 1967, J.D., 1973; Certified in Fin. Mgmt., Stanford U., 1977; Certified in Computer Mgmt., Harvard U., 1978; m. Sunny Leigh Dixon, Oct. 27, 1967; children—Michelle Marie, Jennifer Leigh, Ashley. Sr. analyst mgmt. compensation Westinghouse Electric Corp., Balt., 1967, supr. wage and salary, 1968, supr. labor relations, 1969-71, mgr. indsl. relations, 1971-73; admitted to Pa. bar, 1973, Md. bar, 1978; v.p. labor counsel Matlack, Inc., Phila., 1973, regional v.p., 1974, v.p. indsl. relations, corporate counsel, 1975-77; dir. human resources PHH Group, Inc., Balt., 1976, v.p. adminstrn., 1978—; individual practice law, Phila., 1973-78, Balt., 1978—; chmn. Eastern Labor Advisory Assn. Bd. dirs., pres. Summer Hill Improvement Assn.; corporate chmn. United Fund Central Md., mem. allocation com. Mem. Pa., Am. (labor law, adminstrv. law, corporate law, gen. practice sects.) bar assns. Author: DOT Compliance Through An Incentive Plan, 1975. Home: 13606 Summer Hill St Phoenix MD 21131 Office: PO Box 2174 Baltimore MD 21203

ADAMS, HUGH WHITE, economist; b. N.Y.C., Feb. 15, 1925; s. Hugh White and Mary Morris (Ostrander) A.; A.B. in Polit. Sci., Princeton, 1946; m. Anne Mechelina Scheerder, Jan. 26, 1957. Tng. adminstr. Nat. Tb Assn., 1956-61; exec. dir. N.W. Area Tb and Health Assn., N.J., 1961-63; research asso. Fairleigh Dickinson U., 1967-68; economist Office Econ. Devel., City Newark, 1968-73, Newark Econ. Devel. Corp., 1974. Mem. adv. bd. Morristown (N.J.) Salvation Army, 1965—; bd. dirs. Morris County Soc. Crippled Children and Adults. Served with AUS, 1943-46. Mem. Washington Assn. N.J. (pres. 1966-74), Ralston Hist. Assn. (pres. 1963-67). Clubs: Exchange (pres. Morristown 1966-67); Mendham (N.J.) Wranglers. Home: Spring Hollow Route 1 Box 128 Califon NJ 07830

ADAMS, JOHN LAURENCE, acctg. exec.; b. Reading, Pa., Feb. 24, 1943; s. Charles Anthony and Edith May (Frame) A.; B.S., Lehigh U., 1965, M.B.A., 1978; m. Georgia Brown, May 25, 1968; children—Catherine Patricia, Lauren Elizabeth. Data processing trainee IBM, Bethlehem, Pa., 1966-67, mktg. rep. data processing div., 1967-72, adv. mktg. rep., 1973-76, internat. account mgr., 1976—. Pres. St. Elmo Corp. of Lehigh (Pa.), 1974-76. Served with U.S. Army, 1965-71. Mem. Data Processing Mgmt. Assn. Republican. Roman Catholic. Home: 1410 Princeton Dr Bethlehem PA 18017 Office: 1770 Bathgate Rd Bethlehem PA 18018

ADAMS, JOHN OLLIE, psychologist; b. Sussex County, Del., Aug. 17, 1928; s. Isaac John and Phoebe Harriet (Parker) A.; B.S., U. Md., 1967; M.Ed., U. Del., 1972; m. Florence Anita Pettyjohn, Oct. 21, 1950; children—Isaac John, Derek Karl, Eric Kurt. Enlisted in USAF, 1946, advanced through grades to capt., 1957, pilot, 1952-62, avionics officer, 1963-67, ret., 1967; electroplater and computerized drill operator Litton Industries, Smyrna, Del., 1967-68; dealer sales rep. Sherwin-Williams Co., Dover, Del., 1968-70; counselor Selbyville (Del.) Middle Sch., 1970-73; sch. psychologist Seaford (Del.) Sch. Dist., 1973—. Certified flight instr. Mem. Nat. Assn. Sch. Psychologists, Nat. Council Exceptional Children, NEA, Am. Personnel and Guidance Assn. Mem. Ch. Jesus Christ of Latter-day Saints. Club: Indian River Yacht. Home: Route 1 Box 76-F River Bend Dagsboro DE 19939 Office: Delaware Pl Seaford DE 19973

ADAMS, JOHN OSCAR, lawyer, aircraft co. exec.; b. Chattanooga, Tenn., Apr. 3, 1937; s. John M. and Queen M. (Smith) A.; B.S., Wayne State U., 1962; J.D., Loyola U., Los Angeles, 1970. Tchr., Detroit Pub. Schs., 1962-64; with IBM Corp., Los Angeles, 1964-70; admitted to Calif. bar, 1971; atty. IBM Corp., Armonk, N.Y., 1970-72, San Jose, Calif., 1971; chief Republican counsel Small Bus. Com., U.S. Senate, Washington, 1972-75; dep. city atty., Los Angeles, 1975; individual practice law, Los Angeles, 1975—; chmn. bd. Adams Industries, Inc., Los Angeles, 1977—; asst. to pres. Wallace & Wallace Enterprises, Washington, 1975—, N.Y.C., 1975—; co-founder The Pendulum, Inc. of Capitol Hill, Washington, 1972, chmn., 1972-73. Bd. dirs. Green Power Found., Los Angeles. Served with USN, 1958-62. Recipient Spl. Contbns. award Los Angeles Urban League, 1968, Mgrs. award IBM, 1969. Mem. Am., Fed., Nat., Washington, N.Y., Calif. bar assns., Am. Judicature Soc., Potomac Fiscal Soc., Nat. Assn. of Black Mfrs. Author: Notes of an Afro-Saxon, 1977. Home: 8880 Appian Way Los Angeles CA 90046 Office: 910 16th St NW Washington DC 20006

ADAMS, LAURENCE JOHN, neurosurgeon; b. Norwalk, Conn., Jan. 24, 1927; s. Lorenzo Victor and Margaret (Fagan) A.; B.S., Va. Mil. Inst., 1949; M.D., Georgetown U., 1953; m. Marguerite Thatcher Swartz, Jan. 20, 1968; children—Laurence John, Patricia, James, Dennis, Brian, Mary Colleen, Missy, John. Intern, Brooke Army Hosp., San Antonio, 1953-54; resident in neurosurgery Duke U. Hosp., 1955-56, Jefferson Med. Coll. Hosp., 1956-60; practice medicine specializing in neurosurgery, Lancaster and Ephrata, Pa., 1960—; mem. staff St. Joseph Hosp., Lancaster Osteopathic, Lancaster Gen. hosps., Ephrata Community Hosp.; instr. neurosurgery Jefferson Med. Coll., 1960-61; edn. dir. Lancaster County Multiple Sclerosis Soc. Served with USAAF, 1944-45, USAF, 1953-55, 60. Mem. Am. Assn. Neurol. Surgeons. Republican. Roman Catholic. Club: Sertoma. Home: 1960 Melody Ln Lancaster PA 17601 Office: 822 Marietta Ave Lancaster PA 17603 also 208 W Main St Ephrata PA 17522

ADAMS, MIRIAM, communications specialist; b. N.Y.C., July 8, 1941; d. Joseph Vincent and Rose Sandra (Zeichner) Mazzola; B.A., Coll. City N.Y., 1963; m. William Stapleton Howland, Feb. 14, 1974. Account exec. Jay DeBow & Partners, Inc., N.Y.C., 1963-66; asst. dir. pub. affairs Meml. Sloan-Kettering Cancer Center, N.Y.C., 1966-75, dir. office of cancer communications, 1975—; cons. N.Y. State Soc. Anesthesiologists. Mem. exec. com. Coalition on Critical Health Issues N.Y. State; mem. edn. com. L.I. Cancer Council; mem. cancer control advisory council Sidney Farber Cancer Center; mem. Citywide Advisory Council Sch. Health. Mem. Am. Med. Writers Assn., Internat. Communication Assn., Hosp. Pub. Relations Soc. Greater N.Y. Clubs: Sitzmark Golf and Tennis; Griffis Faculty, Cornell U. Home: 345 E 68th St New York City NY 10021 Office: 1275 York Ave New York City NY 10021

ADAMS, RALPH ELLISON, electronic engr.; b. Phila., Jan. 22, 1927; s. Ralph Snyder and Louisa Ellison (Kriebel) A.; student W.Va. U., 1944-45; B.A., Ohio Wesleyan U., 1952; postgrad. Monmouth Coll., 1953-57, George Washington U., 1963-64, m. Marie Kaptein, June 22, 1957; children—Louisa-Marie, Johanna Lynellen Marie. Radar instr. U.S. Civil Service, Ft. Monmouth, N.J., 1952-57; electronic engr. Datamatic div. Honeywell, Inc., Newton Highlands, Mass., 1957-62; system analyst Vitro Labs., div. Automation Industries, Inc., Silver Spring, Md., 1962—. Mem. advisory council Montgomery County (Md.) Bd. Edn., 1968-69; v.p. Walden's Landing Community Assn. Served with USAAF, 1945-46. Mem. Assn. Computer Programmers and Analysts (chpt. v.p. 1974-75, dir. 1977—, treas. 1978—), Full Gospel Business Men's Fellowship Internat. (chpt. v.p. 1977—), Theta Alpha Phi, Kappa Delta Pi, Phi Mu Alpha, Tau Kappa Epsilon. Republican. Mem. United Ch. of Christ. Home: 5663 Phelps Luck Dr Columbia MD 21045 Office: 14000 Georgia Ave Silver Spring MD 20910

ADAMS, THEODORE RICHARD, assn. exec.; b. Mohawk, N.Y., Nov. 25, 1934; s. Donald Burgess and Isabel Veronica (Pettit) A.; grad. Herkimer County Community Coll., 1975. Asst. collection mgr. Universal C.I.T. Credit Corp., Rochester, N.Y., 1957-60; N.Y. State sales mgr. F. O'Connor Sport Goods Co., Buffalo, 1960-62; mgr. Winn's Furniture Store, Herkimer, N.Y., 1962-67; asst. credit mgr. Sears Roebuck, Elmira, N.Y. 1967-70; dir. membership Herkimer County C. of C., Mohawk, N.Y., 1971-72, exec. dir., 1972—. Mem. Mohawk Valley Econ. Devel. Dist., 1972—, Herkimer County Area Devel. Corp., Mohawk, 1972—, Congl. Task Force on Tourism for Mohawk Valley, 1973—; pres. Nat. Council Alcoholism of Oneida County, 1978—; bd. dirs. N.Y. State Travel and Vacation Assn., 1976—, Leather Stocking Country N.Y., 1976—; bd. dirs., founder Sr. Citizen Adv. Com. Herkimer County, 1972—. Served with USAF, 1953-56; mem. Res. Mem. Mohawk Valley Indsl. Mgmt. Club, Herkimer County Community Coll. Accounting Soc., Herkimer County Hist. Soc., SR, Internat. Platform Assn., Internat. Biog. Assn. Home: 205 Henry St Herkimer NY 13350 Office: 19 W Main St Mohawk NY 13407

ADAMS, WILLARD DALE, dentist; b. Indian Head, Pa., Nov. 12, 1923; s. John Wilson and Goldie Caroline (Knopsnyder) A.; student St. Vincent's Coll., 1942-43, Villanova U., 1943-44; D.D.S., Temple U., 1948; m. Halene Marietta Roach, Nov. 18, 1972; children—Sarah, Katherine; children by previous marriage—Diane, Michael. Gen. practice dentistry, North Huntingdon, Pa., 1948—; mem. staff H.C. Frick Community Hosp., Mt. Pleasant, Pa., 1956—, Connellsville (Pa.) State Gen. Hosp., 1975—, Somerset (Pa.) Community Hosp., 1975—; pres. Laurel Highland Meadowlands, Inc. Served with Dental Corps, U.S. Navy, 1950-52. Licensed dentist, Pa. Mem. Acad. Gen. Dentistry, Acad. Dentistry for Handicapped, Am. Legion, Omicron Kappa Upsilon, Xi Psi Phi. Mem. Ch. of Brethren. Clubs: Masons, Shriners. Home: 670 Brush Hill Rd Irwin PA 15642 Office: 11345 Route 30 North Huntingdon PA 15642

ADAMSKI, JOSEPH ALEXANDER, metall. engr.; b. Exeter, N.H., Mar. 20, 1925; s. Ignacy John and Margaret Frances (Nowak) A.; student N.H. Tech. Inst., 1949-51, Lincoln Coll., 1966-67, Mass. Inst. Tech., 1968; m. Margaret Lauretta Ciccola, Sept. 4, 1948; children—Carleen, Robin. Electronic technician, adminstrv. asst. Mass. Inst. Tech. Lincoln Lab., Lexington, Mass., 1953-57; adminstrv. asst., asso. engr., Ewen-Knight Corp., Natick, Mass., 1957-60; co-founder, project engr. Solid State Materials Corp., Natick, 1960-62; scientist Am. Sci. & Engring. Inc., Cambridge, Mass., 1962-65, now cons.; engr. Hdqrs. Rome Air Devel. Center, dept. for electronic tech. Hanscom AFB, Mass., 1965—; cons. Perkin Elmer Corp., Wilton, Conn. Served with USN, 1943-46, 51-53. Registered profl. engr., Mass. Mem. Profl. Engrs. of Commonwealth of Mass., Am. Assn. for Crystal Growth. Roman Catholic. Contbr. articles to profl. jours. Patentee in field. Home: 468 Central St Framingham MA 01701 Office: RADC/ESM Hanscomb AFB MA 01731

ADANALIAN, ALICE ARAXIE, research scientist; b. Turkey; d. Garabed and Vartouhie (Manisalian) Adanalian; came to U.S., 1920, naturalized, 1927; student U. Pa., 1926-28; B.A., Northwestern U., 1930; M.A., Columbia, 1935; post-grad. Johns Hopkins, 1954, 57. Exec. sec. Bus. and Profl. Women's Program YWCA, Yonkers, N.Y., 1930-37; dir. Cleve. Guidance Service, 1937-39; exec. sec. group work-recreation employment-guidance div. Welfare Council N.Y., 1939-44; welfare specialist Middle East mission UNRRA, Egypt, Italy, 1944-45; chief liaison officer UN mission, Austria, 1946-47; head leaders and specialist div. Inst. Internat. Edn., 1948-51; Africa-Middle East specialist U.S. Govt., Washington, 1951-67; dep. chief Middle East Africa br. Center Research of Social Systems, Am. U., Washington, 1967-69; cons. Am. Inst. for Research, 1969—. Sec. exec. com. Community Chest, Yonkers, 1936-37; mem. program planning bd. Nat. Youth Adminstrn., Yonkers, 1936-37; sec. Fair Employment Practice Com. N.Y., 1943-44; chmn. Human Rights Task Force UNA-CAD. Bd. missions Meth. Ch., 1960-68. Mem. Nat. Vocational Guidance Assn. (chmn. internat. relations com. 1949-51), Am. Personnel and Guidance Assn., Africa Studies Assn., Johns Hopkins Alumni Assn., Columbia Tchrs. Coll. Alumni Assn., Am. Polit. and Social Sci. Assn., Nat. Capital Area Councilors Assn. (dir.), Acad. Am. Polit. and Social Scis. Contbr. articles to profl. jours. Home: 4600 Connecticut Ave NW Washington DC 20008

ADANIEL, TINDALO ROGELIO AGANA, surgeon; b. President Roxas, Capiz, Philippines, Sept. 17, 1941; s. Juan L. and Maria A. Adaniel; came to U.S., 1965; M.D., U. Santo Tomas, Manila, Philippines, 1964. Intern St. Clare's Hosp., N.Y.C., 1965-66; resident, 1967-70; resident Coney Island (N.Y.) Hosp., 1967; practice medicine specializing in surgery, N.Y.C., 1972—; asst. attending surgeon French Hosp.; clin. instr. surgery N.Y. Med. Coll. Exec. v.p. KAHIRUP, U.S.A., 1975—. Diplomate Am. Bd. Surgery. Fellow A.C.S.; mem. John L. Madden Surg. Soc. (sec.-treas.), N.Y. State Med. Soc., Philippine Med. Assn. in Am. Roman Catholic. Home: 330 W 45th St New York City NY 10036 Office: 310 W 56th St New York City NY 10019

ADDABBO, JOSEPH PATRICK, lawyer, congressman; b. Queens County, N.Y., Mar. 17, 1925; s. Dominick and Anna A.; student Coll. City N.Y.; LL.B., St. John's Law Sch.; m. Grace Salamone, June 12, 1949; children—Dominic, Dina, Joseph. Gen. practice law, Ozone Park, N.Y.; mem. 87th Congress from 5th N.Y. Dist., mem. 88th-95th congresses from 7th N.Y. Congl. Dist. Formerly pres. Ozone Park Men's Assn., Ferrini Welfare League Catholic Charities; mem. bldg. com. Ozone Park Jewish Center; regional chmn. bishop's diocesan drive for high sch. and old age home; mem. Mayor's Scholastic Achievement Award Com. Mem. Queens County Bar Assn. Democrat. Kiwanian, Elk. Home: 132-43 86th St Ozone Park NY 11417 Office: 96-11 101st Ave Ozone Park NY 11416 also House Office Bldg Washington DC 20515

ADDEI, KWABENA ADUTWUM, surgeon; b. Kumasi, Ghana, June 12, 1940; s. Kwadwo Adutwum and Akua (Adaa) A.; came to U.S., 1959, naturalized, 1978; diploma Cambridge U. (Eng.), 1958; B.S., Columbia U., 1964; M.D., N.Y. Med. Coll., 1968; m. Arthella Harris, Nov. 28, 1970. Intern, resident, now asso. attending surgeon Nassau Hosp., Mineola, N.Y.; practice medicine specializing in surgery, Mineola; med. advisor Eagle Scouts, Mineola, 1972-73; med. cons. Sickle Cell Clinic of Nassau Hosps., N.Y.C.; asst. prof. clin. surgery State U. N.Y., Stony Brook, also coordinator univ. residency program in surg. edn. at Nassau Hosp.; lectr. in field. Recipient Physician Recognition award AMA, 1971, 73, 76, 78; Community Recognition award Westbury Mother's Group, 1972; Community Service award Nat. Assn. for Study Black History and Life, 1974. Fellow A.C.S. (co-chmn. sci. and continuing med. edn. com. Bklyn.-L.I. chpt.); mem. AMA, Nassau County Med. Soc., Nassau Surg. Soc., Nat. Soc. Pub. Poets. Address: Nassau Profl Bldg 222 Front St Mineola NY 11501

ADDELSTON, LORRAINE WALLENSTEIN (MRS. AARON ADDELSTON), ret. ednl. adminstr.; b. N.Y.C., July 4, 1913; d. Samuel and Etta (Levin) Wallenstein; B.A., Hunter Coll., 1932; M.A., Columbia, 1934; m. Aaron Addelston, Dec. 26, 1935; 1 son, Jonathan. Research asst. Inst. Ednl. Research, 1932-34; tchr. math. N.Y.C. Schs., 1934-42, 46-49, asst. prin., 1949-52, elementary sch. prin., 1952-56; jr. high sch. prin., 1956-76. Ednl. cons. L.I. area NCCJ, 1976—; bd. dirs. spl. com. on judiciary League Women Voters of N.Y.C., 1978—. Served with WAVES, 1942-45. Mem. Jr. High Sch. Prins. Assn. N.Y.C. (pres. 1968-69), Council Suprs. and Adminstrs. N.Y.C. (exec. v.p. 1969-70), N.Y. Acad. Pub. Edn., Phi Beta Kappa. Author: Mathematics at Your Service, 1939. Home: 42-24 147th St Flushing NY 11355

ADDISON, ANNE SIMONE POMEX (MRS. JOHN ADDISON), television exec.; b. Antwerp, Belgium, Dec. 2, 1927; d. Eli and Mary Deborah (Rubinstein) Cleeman; B.A., Barnard Coll., 1947; M.A., Columbia U., 1952; m. Joseph B. Pomex, Mar. 6, 1947 (div. Apr. 1954); 1 son, Steven M.; m. 2d, John Addison, Sept. 1, 1966. Instr., Columbia, 1947-48; circulation dir. Ford Found., N.Y.C., 1952-58; asso. dir. Broadcasting Found. Am., radio, N.Y.C., 1958-60; dir. NET (WNET-13) TV internat. dir., 1960—; cons. cultural dept. Dept. State, Washington, 1961. Bd. dirs. Coll. Skills, Inc., N.Y.C. Recipient awards, medals for fostering understanding and cultural cooperation, Austria, Belgium, Holland, Israel, Italy, Brazil. Mem. Am. Women Radio and TV (1st v.p. 1972—), Advt. Club Am., Am. Women in Communications. Contbr. articles to profl. jours. Home: 1035 Fifth Ave New York City NY 10028 Office: 356 W 58th St New York City NY 10019

ADDY, JOHN KEITH, educator; b. Sheffield, Eng., June 30, 1937; s. John Arthur and Gladys (Powell) A.; B.S., Kings Coll. U. London, 1958; Ph.D., U. Southampton (Eng.), 1962; m. Jean Elizabeth Branagan, July 27, 1963; children—John David, June Elizabeth. Came to U.S., 1966. Postdoctoral research asso. U. Oreg., Eugene, 1962-63; lectr. John Dalton Coll., Manchester, Eng., 1963-66; asso. prof. chemistry Wagner Coll., Staten Island, N.Y., 1966-74, prof., 1974—. Fellow Royal Inst. Chemistry London; mem. Am. Chem. Soc. (dir., nat. councillor 1973-76, 79—, asst. treas. 1972-76). Mem. Evang. Free Ch. Rotarian. Contbr. articles to profl. jours. Home: 166 Chelsea St Staten Island NY 10307

ADELMAN, MARTIN HARRIS, instrument co. exec.; b. N.Y.C., Nov. 5, 1935; s. Sam G. and Pauline (Kletter) A.; B.S., Queens Coll., 1957; M.S., St. Josephs Coll., 1962; m. Glenda Sorsher, Sept. 6, 1958; children—Jill, Beth, Charles, Steven. Mktg. mgr. environ. sci. Technicon Corp., Tarrytown, N.Y., 1966-72; div. mgr. CEA Instruments, Stamford, Conn., 1972-77; pres., sales mgr., 1977—. Mgr., Little League; officer. N.J. Soc. Prevention Cruelty to Animals; trustee Temple Beth Sholom, also mem. sch. bd. Mem. Instrument Soc. Am. (sr.), ASTM, Air Pollution Control Assn., Mfrs. Agts. Nat. Assn., Am. Indsl. Hygiene Assn. Contbr. articles to profl. jours. Home:

58 Ralph Ave Hillsdale NJ 07642 Office: 15 Charles St Westwood NJ 07675

ADELSBERG, HARVEY, hosp. adminstr.; b. Bronx, N.Y., Aug. 5, 1931; s. Joseph and Becky (Rindner) A.; B.A., N.Y. U., 1953, M.P.A., 1960, postgrad., 1960-65; m. Miriam Levine, June 20, 1964; children—Jonathan, Risa, Seth. Adminstrv. resident Beth David Hosp., N.Y.C., 1953-54; adminstrv. asst. Met. Jewish Geriatric Center, Bklyn., 1954-58; asst. dir. Kingsbrook Jewish Med. Center, Bklyn., 1958-61; asst. dir. Hosp. for Joint Diseases, N.Y.C., 1961-64; exec. dir. Theresa Grotta Center for Restorative Services, Caldwell, N.J., 1964-70; asst. dir. Mount Sinai Hosp., N.Y.C., 1970-72; cons. med. care and services to aged Fedn. Jewish Philanthropies, N.Y.C., 1972-74; exec. dir. Daus. of Miriam Center for Aged, Clifton, N.J., 1974-76, exec. v.p., 1977—; adj. asst. prof. health care adminstrn., Bernard M. Baruch Coll., Mt. Sinai Sch. Medicine, City U. N.Y., 1973—; mem. adv. com. Rutgers U., 1969—; mem. N.J. Licensing Bd. for Nursing Home Adminstrs., 1969—, vice chmn., 1969-77; mem. Adv. Council on Aging, Livingston, N.J., 1977—. Trustee Hospital and Council Met. N.J., 1967-70, Health and Hosp. Council So. N.Y., 1972-74, N.J. Assn. Non-Profit Homes for Aging, 1976—, Jewish Community Housing Corp., Paterson, N.J., 1975—, Solomon Schechter Day Sch. of Essex and Union, 1977—; bd. govs. Greater N.Y. Hosp. Assn., 1972-74. Fellow Am. Coll. Hosp. Adminstrs., Am. Coll. Nursing Home Adminstrs., Am. Geriatric Soc., Am. Pub. Health Assn.; mem. Am., N.J. hosp. assns., Hosp. Exec. Club. Jewish (v.p. 1970, 71, 73, trustee 1968-70, 75—). Mem. B'nai B'rith (v.p. 1960-64). Home: 27 Tuxedo Dr Livingston NJ 07039 Office: 155 Hazel St Clifton NJ 07015

ADELSON, JERRY JACOB, dentist; b. N.Y.C., Dec. 3, 1924; s. Samuel and Augusta (Kassman) A.; B.S. in Biochemistry, U. Pa., 1944; D.D.S., N.Y. U., 1951; Ed.D., Yeshiva U., 1959; children—David, Amy. Tchr. exceptional children, 1944-45, 46-47; intern Polyclinic Hosp., N.Y.C., 1951-52; practice dentistry ltd. to dentistry with gen. anesthesia, N.Y.C., 1952—; mem. faculty N.Y.U. Coll. Dentistry, 1952-54; chief dental cons. clinic for retarded patients Flower and Fifth Ave. Hosps., 1953—, dir. dentistry, mental retardation clinic Flower Med. Sch.; asst. clin. prof. Columbia U. Coll. Dentistry, 1955-61, vis. lectr., 1977—; chmn. dental service for handicapped patients Jewish Meml. Hosp., N.Y.C., 1955—, attending anesthesiologist, 1959-61; chief childrens dentistry Mt. Sinai Hosp., N.Y.C., 1957-58; mem. faculty 1st Dist. Dental Soc. Postgrad. Sch., N.Y.C., 1957—, supr. postgrad. edn. program, 1962-69; attending and chief of clinic for handicapped individuals Polyclinic Med. Sch., 1968—; adj. prof. spl. edn. Yeshiva U. Grad. Sch. Edn., 1959-60; chief clinic for handicapped patients Grand Central Hosp., 1961-68; mem. adv. com. Soc. for Children with Emotional Disturbances, 1965; mem. govt. com. on dental care for mentally retarded children HEW, 1964-65. Mem. profl. adv. bd. United Cerebral Palsy of N.Y. State, 1959—. Bd. dirs. N.Am. Riding for Handicapped Assn. Served with USAAF, 1944-46; ETO. Recipient Bausch & Lomb medal for outstanding work in biol. research, 1956, Distinguished Service award Jewish Meml. Hosp. Fellow Am. Assn. Mental Deficiency, Am. Coll. Dentists, Internat., N.Y. colls. dentists, Am. Dental Soc. Anesthesiology; mem. ADA (gen. chmn. ann. conv. 1969, 3d v.p. 1969-70, dir. 1970—), Midtown Dental Soc. (pres. 1960), Omicron Kappa Upsilon. Contbr. numerous articles to profl. jours. Address: 200 Central Park S New York City NY 10019

ADELSON, WARREN JAY, art dealer; b. Cambridge, Mass., Jan. 4, 1942; s. Harry and Beatrice (Gellar) A.; certificate U. Florence (Italy), 1962; A.B., Boston U., 1963, A.M., 1964; m. La Trelle Brewster, Dec. 16, 1966; 1 son, Harry. Pres., Adelson Galleries, Inc., art co., Boston, 1964-71; head Am. dept. M Knoedler & Co., art co., N.Y.C., 1972-73; v.p. Coe Kerr Gallery Inc., N.Y.C., 1974—, also dir. Mem. Art Dealers Assn. Author art catalogs. Home: 21 E 66th St New York City NY 10028 Office: 49 E 82d St New York City NY 10028

ADES, CHARLES DOUGLAS, bank exec.; b. Pomona, Calif., Sept. 3, 1942; s. Elvin Earl and Miriam Bernice (Hull) A.; B.A., U. Redlands, Calif., 1966; M.Div., Union Theol. Sem., 1969; m. Susan Blanchard Jacobson, Feb. 10, 1972; children—Shannon Douglas; stepchildren—Amy Fonda, Marc Weisgal. Adminstr., IBM Corp., Riverside, Calif., 1961-63; dir. edn. Peoples Narcotics Rehab. Program, Harlem, N.Y., 1967-68; asst. dir. Harlem Domestic Peace Corps, 1968-69, asst. in ministry Jazz Musicians of N.Y.C., St. Peters Luth. Ch., 1966-67; youth minister, United Ch. of Christ Congregational, Manhasset, N.Y., 1967-69; v.p., dir. corp. social policy Chem. Bank, N.Y., 1969—. Co-founder, Downtown Wall St. Narcotics Center; mem. Greater N.Y. Fund's Spl. Allocations Com.; founder Intergroup Fellowship House; bd. dirs. Fortune Soc.; chmn. bd. Antioch U.; trustee New Lincoln Sch. Recipient award for outstanding service Bronx C. of C.; Rockefeller fellow. Mem. N.Y. C. of C., N.Y. State Bankers Assn. Office: 20 Pine St New York City NY 10005

ADIE, CHARLES LESLIE, educator; b. Lowell, Mass., Dec. 25, 1936; s. Charles Leslie and Anna Marie (Michalik) A.; B.S., U. Notre Dame, 1958; M.A., Boston Coll., 1966; m. Joanne Faith Jean, Apr. 15, 1961; children—John, Jean, Judith. Tchr. sci. pub. schs., Wilmington, Mass., 1958-59; tchr. math. pub. schs., Nashua, N.H., 1959-60, Lowell, Mass., 1960-67; asso. prof. math. No. Essex Community Coll., Haverhill, Mass., 1967—, vice chmn. acad. council, 1973—. Vis. prof. math. N.H. Tech. Inst., Manchester, 1967; guidance counselor Nashua (N.H.) Bus. Coll., 1969; chmn. faculty adv. body Mass. Regional Bd. Community Colls., 1974-75. NSF grantee, Boston Coll., 1961-66, Oberlin Coll., 1968. Mem. Math. Assn. Am., Nat. Council Tchrs. Math., Am. Assn. U. Profs., Math. Assn. Two Year Colls., New Eng. Assn. Tchrs. Math. (mem. exec. council 1972-73), Mass. Regional Community Coll. Faculty Assn. Home: 6 Miami St Nashua NH 03060 Office: 100 Elliot St Haverhill MA 01830

ADISMAN, IRWIN KENNETH, dentist; b. N.Y.C., Aug. 3, 1919; s. Joseph and Frances (Gertz) A.; student Mich. State Coll., 1935-37; D.D.S., U. Buffalo, 1940; M.S., N.Y.U., 1960; m. Joan Sugarman, Aug. 27, 1957; children—Leslie, Kathryn. Intern, Beth Israel Hosp., 1940-41; resident in prosthodontics Home Sons and Daus. Israel, 1941-42; individual practice dentistry, 1946-48; faculty prosthodontics N.Y.U. Coll. Dentistry, 1948-60; Attending dentist N.Y.U. Med. Center, Univ. Hosp., N.Y.C., 1970—, Meml. Hosp., N.Y.C., 1976—; prof., chmn. dept. removable prosthodontics N.Y.U. Dental Center, N.Y.C., 1978—. Served to maj. Dental Corps, AUS, 1942-46. Diplomate Am. Bd. Prosthodontics (v.p., examiner). Fellow Acad. Denture Prosthetics; mem. Am. Acad. Maxillofcaial Prosthetics (asso. editor jour. 1967-78), Am., Internat. colls. dentists, Greater N.Y. Acad. Prosthodontics (v.p.), N.Y. Acad. Dentistry. Clubs: Harmonie, Century. Sect. editor Jour. Prosthetic Dentistry, 1974—. Home: 40 E 66th St New York City NY 10021 Office: 100 Central Park S New York City NY 10019

ADKINS, GEORGE BOZEMAN, JR., technical adviser; b. Ft. Worth, July 30, 1921; s. George Bozeman and Ethel (Hough) A.; B.S., U. Mo., 1950, M.A., 1951; grad. Naval War Coll., Newport, R.I., 1972; m. Edith G. Mercer, Aug. 16, 1958; 1 dau., Virginia Ann. Chief statistician Gen. Motors Corp., Kansas City, Kan., 1951-53, Dept. Air Force, Kansas City, Mo., 1952-54, Dept. Def., 1953-56 chief math. statistics br. AEC, Washington, 1956-60; chief operation and intelligence br. Strategy and Tactics Analysis Group, Dept. Army, 1960-62; charge operations research group FAA, Washington, 1962-66; chief Vulnerability Damage Assessment div. Def. Communication Agy., 1966—. Served with USN, 1940-46. Recipient Outstanding award Navy Dept., 1955, Superior Performance award, 1955, Outstanding award Def. Communication Agy., 1974. Mem. A.A.A.S., Inst. Math. Statistics. Author: (with others) The Management of Nuclear Materials, 1960; Operational Evaluation of Flight Inspections of Instrument Landing Systems, 1968. Research in electronics, ship propulsion, nuclear materials mgmt. Home: 4801 Kenmore Ave Alexandria VA 22304 Office: Pentagon Washington DC 20301

ADLER, CARL GEORGE, automotive products co. exec.; b. Buffalo, Nov. 12, 1912; s. William Henry and Margaret Theresa (Corcoran) A.; B.S. in Chemistry, Canisius Coll., 1936, postgrad., 1936-38; postgrad. Notre Dame U., 1937; m. Mary Elizabeth McGarry, Nov. 24, 1938; children—Carl G., Gary J. With engring. dept. Exolon Co., Blasedell, N.Y., 1938-41; metallurgist Vanadium Corp. Am., Niagara Falls, N.Y., 1941-46, supervising metallurgist, 1947-50, plant metallurgist, 1950, furnace reduction supr., 1950-51, prodn. supr., 1954-73; plant mgr. Foote Mineral Co., New Haven, W.Va., 1974—. Asst. to pres. Garry Labs., Tonawanda, N.Y., 1958-73. Trustee Pleasant Valley Hosp., Point Pleasant, W.Va. Mem. Am. Chem. Soc., Am. Inst. M.E., Am. Soc. for Metals, W.Va. C. of C. Moose. Clubs: Press, Edgewood Country (Charleston, W.Va.); Pleasant Valley Country (Point Pleasant). Home: 85 Oakbrook Dr Williamsville NY 14221 Office: 260 Creekside Dr Tonawanda NY 14150

ADLER, CHARLES, inventor; b. Balt., June 20, 1899; s. Harry and Carolyn (Frank) A.; student John Hopkins, 1917-20; m. Alene Steiger, June 10, 1925; children—Amalie Carol, Harry. Inventor rotating stop-sign, r.r.-highway crossing signal, Adler flasher relay, traffic sonic detector, Adler double filament incandescent lamps for r.r. signals, traffic signals and airplane navigation lights, speed control highway signal systems, aircraft anticollision light, aircraft flashing position-light system, aircraft studded reflector tail-light, and aircraft reflector lamp, aircraft proximity indicator, traffic actuated traffic signal, automobile spaceometer, aircraft height light, fail-safe, streamlined reflectorized aircraft anti-collision light, and others. Bd. dirs. Balt.-Washington Internat. Airport, 1960-66; mem. State Aviation Commn. Md., 1953-59, Md. Traffic Safety Commn. Recipient awards Am. Legion, CAA, USAF, USN, Nat. Aero. Assn., Aircraft Owners and Pilots Assn.; named Engr. of Yr., Balt. Engring. Council, 1976; licensed profl. airplane pilot. Mem. Nat. Aeros. Assn. (life, nat. councillor Md.), Inst. Transp. Engrs. (award), Soc. Automotive Engrs., Airways Engring. Soc. Guest appearances on TV. Contbr. to nat. mags. Office: 1506 Sutton Pl Apts Baltimore MD 21201

ADLER, CHARLES HENRY, former candy mfg. co. exec.; b. Germany, May 17, 1927; s. Victor and Bessie (Stern) A.; came to U.S., 1938, naturalized, 1944; student Coll. City N.Y., 1945, 47-51; m. Edwina Joan Evans, Feb. 3, 1969; children—Cary Lee, Alan David, Melody Susan. With Estee Corp., Parsippany, N.J., 1946-78, gen. mgr., 1954-59, chmn. 1959-76, pres., chief exec. officer, 1976-78. Mason. Home: 228 Fox Ledge Rd Smoke Rise NJ

ADLER, DAVID, physicist, educator; b. Bronx, N.Y., Apr. 13, 1935; s. Saul and Betty (Kopelman) A.; B.A., Rensselaer Poly. Inst., 1956; A.M. (Leeds and Northrup fellow), Harvard, 1958, Ph.D. (NSF Coop. Grad. fellow), 1964; m. Alice Joan Salzman, June 8, 1958; children—Kyle, Andrew, Carrie. Research asso. U.K. Atomic Energy Research Establishment, Harwell, Eng., 1964-65; research asso. Mass. Inst. Tech., 1965-67, asst. prof. elec. engring., 1967-69, asso. prof., 1969-75, prof., 1975—; lectr. Franco-Russian Summer Sch., Grenoble, France, 1971, Queens Coll., Kingston, Ont., 1975, Latin Am. Sch. Physics, Venezuela, 1976, U. Campinas (Brazil), 1976, McMaster U., Hamilton, Ont., 1977; chmn. Solar Photovoltaic Panel, Solar Energy Workshop, 1975; mem. com. basic research NRC, 1973-76; judge Mass. Sci. Fair, 1973—. Treas., Community Nursery Sch., Lexington, Mass., 1971-73, Maria Hastings PTA, Lexington, 1974-75. Recipient McKinney prize Rensselaer Poly. Inst., 1954, Gold medal Soc. Actuaries, 1955. Fellow Am. Phys. Soc. (exec. com. div. solid state physics 1976—); mem. IEEE (sr.), Am. Vacuum Soc. (sr.). Author: Amorphous Semiconductors, 1971; editorial bd. Jour. Nonmetals, 1971-76, Semicondrs. and Insulators, 1976—. Home: 10 Nickerson Rd Lexington MA 02173 Office: 77 Massachusetts Ave Room 13-3050 Cambridge MA 02139

ADLER, FREDA, criminologist, educator; b. Phila., Nov. 21, 1934; d. David and Lucia Green (De Wolfson) Schaffer; B.A., U. Pa., 1956, M.A., 1968, Ph.D., 1971; m. Gerhard O.W. Mueller, Feb. 29, 1976; children by previous marriage—Mark, Jill, Nancy. Teaching fellow sociology U. Pa., 1967-68, research asst., 1968-69; instr. psychiatry, research coordinator Addiction Scis. Center, Temple U., Phila., 1971-72; research dir. sect. drug and alcohol abuse asst. prof. psychiatry, Med. Coll. Pa., 1972-74; asso. prof. criminal justice Rutgers U., Newark, 1974—; mem. faculty Nat. Coll. State Judiciary at U. Nev., 1973—. Bd. dirs., v.p. Inst. for Continuous Study of Man; female criminality cons. UN; cons. Nat. Commn. Marijuana and Drug Abuse, also N.Y.U. Sch. Law; rep. UN for Internat. Prisoners Aid Assn., 1975. Mem. advisory com. Hands Up, Gen. Fedn. Women's Clubs. Mem. Am. Soc. Criminology (exec. counselor, Herbert Bloch award 1972), Am. Sociol. Assn., Internat. Assn. Penal Law, U. Pa. Alumnae Assn., Chi Omega. Author: Medical Lollipop, 1974; Sisters in Crime, 1975; (with others) A Systems Approach to Drug Treatment, 1975; The Criminology of Deviant Women, 1978. Editor: (with others) Revue Internationale de Droit Penal, 1974; Crime and the International Scene, 1972; asso. editor LAE Jour., 1977—; mem. editorial bd. of Criminology, 1972-73. Contbr. articles to profl. jours. Home: 30 Waterside Plaza Apt 37J New York City NY 10010 Office: 15 Washington St Newark NJ 07102

ADLER, HYMAN HENRY, surgeon; b. N.Y.C., June 19, 1910; s. Peter and Rose Adler; B.S., Coll. City N.Y., 1931; M.A., Columbia U., 1932; M.D., U. Vienna (Austria), 1937; m. Geraldine Koeppel, Dec. 15, 1946; children—Edward Andrew Koeppel, Alyson Koeppel. Intern, French Hosp., N.Y.C., 1938-39; practice medicine specializing in ear, nose, and throat surgery, Great Neck, N.Y., 1951—. Served to maj. M.C., U.S. Army, 1941-46. Fellow Am. Acad. Ophthalmology and Otolaryngology, Am. Acad. Facial Plastic and Reconstructive Surgery, Internat. Acad. Cosmetic Surgery; mem. N.Y. State, Nassau County med. socs., Nassau Acad. Medicine. Office: 150 Middle Neck Rd Great Neck NY 11024

ADLER, JACK FRANKLIN, accountant; b. Norfolk, Va., Nov. 13, 1911; s. Isaac and Jennie (Selig) A.; B.S., U. Va., 1932; m. Jean Anathan, Nov. 28, 1935; children—Jack F., Judy A. (Mrs. Nathan Elitzky). Staff Goldsmith's Accountants, Phila. 1931-35, partner, 1936-52; sr. partner Adler, Faunce & Co., Phila., 1953-57, Adler, Faunce & Leonard Co., Phila., 1958-67; sr. partner Touche Ross & Co., Phila., 1967-72, partner in charge Phila. office, 1972—. Mem. exec. com., bd. dirs. United Fund, Phila., 1968—, Abington YMCA, Phila., 1965-68, Assn. Jewish Children, Phila.; 1968—; v.p. Fedn. Jewish Agys., Phila., 1966-69, now bd. dirs., mem. cabinet, exec. com.; fund raising chmn. Study Mission, United Jewish Appeal, 1967, now nat. campaign cabinet; v.p. Albert Einstein Med. Center, Phila.; asso. chmn. bd. govs. Phila. com. State of Israel Bonds; bd. dirs. World Affairs Council; v.p. Am. Jewish Com. C.P.A., Pa. Mem. Am., Pa. insts. C.P.A.s Clubs: Philmont Country (past pres.), Locust (past chmn. bd.) (Phila.). Home: 406 B Elkins Park House Elkins Park PA 19117 Office: 1700 Market St Philadelphia PA 19103

ADLER, KURT, psychoanalyst; b. Nieder Florstadt, Germany, Apr. 10, 1907; s. Herman and Augusta (Seligman) A.; M.D., Frankfurt, Germany, 1931; m. Edna Mae Mannion, Sept. 30, 1939; children—Karen Adler Evans, Constance Adrienne, Audrey Lynn; came to U.S., 1937, naturalized, 1941. Intern, Mcpl. Hosp., Munich, Germany, 1931-32; resident Univ. Psychiat. Hosp., Heidelberg, Germany, 1932-33, Salpêtrière, Paris, 1933-34; instr., research asst. Path. Inst. U. Istanbul (Turkey), 1934-36; practice neurology and psychiatry, N.Y.C., 1937-42, Jamaica, N.Y., 1946—, psychoanalysis, 1953—; mem. staff Queens Gen., Triboro hosps., 1946-67; cons. Queens Hosp. Center, 1967—; cons. psychiatry Jamaica Hosp., 1952—. Served to lt. col. AUS, 1942-46. Diplomate Am. Bd. Psychiatry and Neurology. Fellow Am. Psychiat. Assn. (life), Am. Acad. Psychoanalysis, AAAS; mem. Am. Acad. Neurology, N.Y. Acad. Scis. Home: RD 1 Pine Valley Rd Oyster Bay NY 11771 Office: 119-36 80th Rd Kew Gardens NY 11415

ADLER, LOIS, actress; b. Nyack, N.Y., Sept. 17, 1929; d. Barnett and Treva (Simon) Blumenson; B.A., N.Y. U., 1951, M.A., 1967; student Paul Mann at Actor's Workshop, 1956-60, Etienne Decroux, 1960-61; m. June 1, 1952. Actress, coach, dir., N.Y.C., 1958-72; chairperson speech/theatre dept. Manhattan Community Coll., 1973-77, asso. prof. theatre dept., 1976—. Rep. to Democratic County Com. from N.Y.C., 1974-76. Mem. Am. Theatre Assn., Profl. Staff Congress, Am. Soc. for Theatre Research. Club: Community Free Democrats. Contbr. articles to theater jours. Home: 120 Riverside Dr New York City NY 10024 Office: 1633 Broadway New York City NY 10019

ADLER, MYRIL (MRS. JACK ADLER), artist, art tchr., printmaker; b. Vitebsk, Russia, Sept. 22, 1920; came to U.S., 1923; d. Sam and Sarah (Pakul) Stangen; student Art Students League, N.Y.C., 1937-38, Theatre Arts Workshop, N.Y.C., 1938-39, Atelier Moi Solotaroff, 1939-44, Pratt Graphics Center, N.Y.C., 1960-64; m. Jack Adler, Oct. 18, 1941; children—David, Sharon. Exhibited in one person shows at Gallerie Bernheim Jeune, Paris, 1950, Casa Municipale, Merano, Italy, 1952, Royal Athena II Gallery, N.Y.C., 1964, Katonah Gallery, N.Y.C., 1972, 76, Hudson River Mus., Yonkers, N.Y., 1972, 74, Westbroadway Gallery, N.Y.C., 1973, 74, 76; exhibited in group shows at Salon de Mai, Salon des Femmes Peintres, Paris, 1950, USIS traveling exhbn., France, Germany, N. Africa, 1950, 51, Pan Am. Bldg., N.Y.C., Salute to 1965, Internat. Miniature Print Show, Audubon Artists, N.Y.C., 1970, 71; represented in permanent collections at Mus. Modern Art, Caracas, Venezuela, U. Calif. at Berkeley, U. R.I., Hudson River Mus., N.Y. Pub. Library; organizer, dir. art program Hawthorne (N.Y.) Cedar Knolls Sch., 1953-56; tchr. art for children and adults, Briarcliff Manor, N.Y., 1956—; organizer monthly exhibits internat. graphic artists Briarcliff Pub. Library, 1963-67; chmn. local com. Rescue Italian Art, 1967; condr. workshops for tchrs. chmn., Citizens Com. Recreation, Briarcliff Manor, 1960; adv. com. Pratt Graphic Center, 1967. Recipient 1st prize graphics and sculpture Artists No. Westchester Juried Ann., 1968, 1st prize, 1969; Claude Gallery award, purchase award Yonkers Art Assn., 1970, Camhi Graphics award, 1971. Mem. Westchester Art Soc. (dir. 1969-71), Yonkers Art Assn., Nat. Assn. Women Artists. Home: 266 Dalmeny Rd Briarcliff Manor NY 10510

ADLER, RENEE, career counselor; b. N.Y.C., Dec. 7, 1927; d. Max and Francis (Baum) Bloksberg; B.A., Bklyn., Coll., 1948; certificate human relations New Sch. Social Research, 1970; M.S. in Edn., C.W. Post Coll., L.I. U., 1978; m. Marvin Adler, June 20, 1948; children—Marlene, Jack, Freda. Tchr. in Bklyn., 1948-52, L.I., 1960-65; intern C.W. Post Coll. Career Service Center, 1977; conducts career-planning workshop high schs., 1977—; with personnel dept. Abraham and Straus, N.Y.C., 1978—. Chmn. drama dept. Five Towns Music and Arts Found., 1973-76, corr. sec., 1976—. Mem. Am., N.Y. State personnel and guidance assns., Am. Mental Health Counselors Assn., Women's Am. Orgn. for Rehab., Nat. Council Jewish Women. Democrat. Address: 864 Oliver Ave North Woodmere NY 11581

ADLER, ROBERT IRA, ophthalmologist; b. Bklyn., Jan. 20, 1941; s. Nathan Ralph and Lillian (Mushkin) A.; B.A., Columbia Coll., 1962; M.D., N.Y. U., 1966; m. Bonnie Edith Bolker, Oct. 23, 1965; 1 son, Kevin Edward. Intern Downstate Med. Center-Kings County Hosp., Bklyn., 1966-67, resident in ophthalmology, 1969-72; instr. ophthalmology Downstate Med. Center, State U. N.Y., Bklyn., 1969-74, fellow, 1972-74; now engaged in practice medicine specializing in ophthalmology, Plattsburgh, N.Y.; mem. staff CVPH Med. Center. Served as sr. surgeon USPHS, 1967-69. Diplomate Nat. Bd. Med. Examiners, Am. Bd. Ophthalmology. Fellow Am. Acad. Ophthalmology and Otolaryngology, A.C.S., Internat. Coll. Surgeons, Am. Geriatric Soc.; mem. AMA, Soc. Eye Surgeons, Contact Lens Assn. Ophthalmologists, Internat. Phacoemulsification and Cataract Methodology Soc., Am. Assn. Ophthalmology, Am. Assn. for Contemporary Ophthalmology, Ophthal. Assn. in Research to Prevent Blindness, Undersea Med. Soc., Pan Am. Ophthal. Found., N.Y. State, Bklyn. ophthalmology socs., Clinton County Med. Soc. Jewish. Home: 48 Cumberland Ave Plattsburgh NY 12901 Office: 210 Cornelia St Suite 302 Plattsburgh NY 12901

ADLER, SAMUEL HANS, educator, composer; b. Mannheim, Germany, Mar. 4, 1928; s. Hugo Chaim and Selma (Rothschild) A.; came to U.S., 1939, naturalized, 1945; Mus.B., Boston U., 1948; M.A., Harvard, 1950; Dr.Mus. (hon.), So. Meth. U., 1969; m. Carol E. Stalker, Feb. 14, 1960; children—Deborah Ruth, Naomi Leah. Faculty composition N. Tex. State U., Denton, 1958-66; prof. composition Eastman Sch. Music U. Rochester (N.Y.), 1966—, chmn. dept., 1973—. Instr. fine arts Hockaday Sch., Dallas, 1957-66; organizer, condr. Dallas Chorale, 1954-56; condr. Dallas Lyric Theater, 1955-57; Eastern regional dir. contemporary music project Music Educators Nat. Conf./Ford Found., 1967-69. Served with AUS, 1950-52. Decorated Medal of Honor. Recipient Dallas Symphony prize U. Tex., 1953; 1st prize Tex. Composers guild, 1955, 57-63, Lazare Saminsky Meml. award, 1959; Southwestern Coll. Band Masters award, 1964; Charles Ives Meml. award U. Houston, 1963; Lillian Fairchild award U. Rochester, 1969, also ASCAP awards. Rockefeller grantee, Ford Found. grantee, 1965; comms. throughout country. Mem. ASCAP, Nat. Assn. Am. Composers and Condrs., Am. Music Center, Am. Choral Condrs., Am. Choral Found. Music Tchrs. Nat. Assn., Music Educators Nat. Conf., Phi Mu Alpha. Author: Anthology for the Teaching of Choral Conducting, 1972; "Sightsinging", Pitch Interval Rhythm, 1979. Composer 5 symphonies, 4 operas, chamber and choral works. Contbr. articles to profl. jours. Home: 54 Railroad Mills Rd Pittsford NY 14534 Office: 26 Gibbs St Rochester NY 14604

ADLER, STEPHEN FRED, chemist; b. Berlin, Germany, Sept. 27, 1930; s. Alfred Max and Ilse Johanna (Liepmann) A.; B.S. (Sidney Hillman scholar), Roosevelt U., 1951; M.S. (Sinclair Research fellow), Northwestern U., 1953, Ph.D., 1954; m. Judith Regina Weinberg, Dec. 23, 1951; children—Deborah Jeanne, Barbara Gail. Research chemist Am. Cyanamid Co., Stamford, Conn., 1954-59, sr. research chemist, 1959-60, group leader, 1960-69; mgr. inorganic research sect. Stauffer Chem. Co., Dobbs Ferry, N.Y., 1969-70, mgr. chems. dept., 1970—, asst. dir. Eastern Research Center, 1976—. Pres., Brookside Community Assn., Norwalk, Conn., 1963-65. Mem. Am. Chem. Soc. Jewish (chmn. adult edn. com. 1968-72). Patentee in field. Home: 16 Grey Hollow Rd Norwalk CT 06850 Office: Livingstone St Dobbs Ferry NY 10522

ADNOPOZ, DOROTHY JEAN, program coordinator; b. New Haven, Oct. 15, 1932; d. Abner Arthur and Hannah (Schwartz) Alderman; B.A., Wellesley Coll., 1954; m. Robert Adnopoz, June 29, 1954; children—Stephen, Sally. Adminstrv. vol. children's services, health care, pres. Yale-New Haven Hosp. Aux., 1970-73, bd. dirs., 1973—, chmn. hosp. com. on community health needs, 1976-78; pres. Children's Center, Hamden, Conn., 1974-78; pres. Conn. Child Welfare Assn., 1971-74, 76-77; now chief adminstr. Coordinating Com. for Children in Crisis, Inc.; vice chmn. council on govt. relations Conn. Hosp. Assn., 1976-78, vice chmn. Assn., 1978—; community coordinator Yale Child Study Center; dir. Nat. Savs. Bank. Bd. dirs. Shirley Frank Found. for Alcoholism, 1976—; acting chmn. regional advisory com. Dept. Children and Youth Services Conn., 1976-77, chmn., 1977—; vice chmn. bd. Yale-New Haven Hosp., 1979—; chmn. adv. com. Conn. Mental Health Center, 1976—; bd. dirs. New Haven Symphony Orch., 1970-76, v.p. aux., 1976-78, pres. aux., 1978—; chmn. United Way Conf. Agency Lay Leaders, 1976-78. Recipient Ira Hiscock award for consumer service Conn. Pub. Health Assn., 1978. Democrat. Jewish. Clubs: Lawn, New Haven, Country, Wellesley (past pres.) (New Haven). Home: 1085 Ridge Rd Hamden CT 06517 Office: Children's Center 1400 Whitney Ave Hamden CT 06517

ADOLFI, ROBERT JOSEPH, real estate exec.; b. Rome, N.Y., Feb. 3, 1934; s. Nazie and Josephine (Casale) A.; student in bus. adminstrn. Utica (N.Y.) Coll., 1952-55; m. RoseMary Healy, May 25, 1956; children—R. Scott, Steven M., Christopher P., Patrick T. With Adolfi Oil Co., Rome, 1958-67; salesman Henry Real Estate, Rome, 1967-72; owner, pres. Adolfi Realty, Rome, 1972—; pres. Beer Parlor Inc. County legislator, 1978—. Served with AUS, 1956-58. Mem. Rome C. of C. (dir.), N.Y. State Realtors, Nat. Assn. Realtors, Grad. Realtors Inst., Rome Bd. Realtors (sec. 1976-77). Republican. Roman Catholic. Clubs: Rome, Kiwanis, K.C., Elks. Home: 207 W Sycamore St Rome NY 13440 Office: 225 N Washington St Rome NY 13440

ADORIAN, STEPHEN JOHN, retail and comml. phone systems co. exec.; b. Washington, June 28, 1940; s. Stephen John and Kathryn (Grissinger) A.; B.A., Lafayette Coll., 1962; M.A., Ohio U., 1966; Ph.D., State U. N.Y., 1974; m. Suzanne Burch Darneille, Aug. 29, 1964; children—Donna Lynn, Stephen Bruce. Field sec. Phi Gamma Delta, Washington, 1962-63; regional mgr. Univ. Program of People-to-People, Inc., Kansas City, Mo., 1963-64; resident dir. Ohio U., Athens, 1964-66; asst. dir. housing, dir. housing State Univ. Coll. N.Y., Fredonia, 1966-68; dir. housing State U. Coll. N.Y., Buffalo, 1968-70; dir. residence life Canisius Coll., Buffalo, 1970-72; asst. dir. admissions Daemen Coll., Amherst, N.Y., 1972-75; sr. job developer, exec. dir. Comprehensive Employment Tng. Act, Project Upgrade, Buffalo, 1975-77; communications cons. Phone World, Inc., Buffalo, 1977—. Served with AUS, 1958-62. Mem. Nat. Assn. Student Personnel Adminstrs., Am., N.Y., Western N.Y. (pres. 1971-72) personnel and guidance assns., Nat. Alliance Businessmen, Nat. Vocat. Guidance Assn. Methodist. Club: Masons. Home: 146 Robert Dr Lancaster NY 14086 Office: 4239 Transit Rd Williamsville NY 14221

AEBI, ERNST WALTER, artist; b. Zurich, Switzerland, Mar. 25, 1938; s. Walter and Marie (Giger) A.; came to U.S., 1967, naturalized, 1977; Diploma Elektronik, Gewerbeschule, Zurich, 1958; Diploma Matura C, Akademikergemeinschaft, Zurich, 1960; postgrad. Grande Chaumiere, Paris, 1962, Chester (Eng.) Coll., 1963; Diplome I and II, Alliance Française, Paris, 1964; diploma in polit. sci. Zurich U., 1965; children—Tania Sabina, Nina Rahel, Anthony Walter, Jade Michelle. One man shows; At Arakawa, Tokyo, 1960, Carter Galleries, West Nyack, N.Y., 1966, Bognar Gallery, Los Angeles, 1967, Lowitz Galleries, Palm Springs, Calif., 1967, Gallerie Haudenschild und Laubscher, Bern, Switzerland, 1968, Verzyl Gallery, Northport, N.Y., 1969, Haudenschild und Laubscher, Bern, 1969, Ly Goldbach Gallery, Frankfort, Germany, 1970, Aqueduct Raceway Gallery, N.Y.C., 1970, Verzyl Gallery, 1970, 71, 72, Swiss Center Gallery, N.Y.C., 1972, James Yu Gallery, N.Y.C., 1976, N.Y. U., 1976, Gallerie Boesch, Zurich, 1976, Saratoga Gallery, (N.Y.), 1976, Hubris Gallery, 1978; group shows include: Moucheiber Studio, Beirut, 1960, Gallerie Verlaine, Paris, 1963, Montmartre Gallery, Palm Beach, Fla., 1967, Huntington Art League, L.I., N.Y., 1967, Virginia Beach (Va.) Art Festival, 1967, Fisher Galleries, Washington, 1967, Southampton Parrish Mus., L.I., N.Y., 1967, Little Gallery, Phila., 1968, Bklyn. Mus., 1968, Adriance Mus., N.Y.C., 1968, Bklyn. Mus. Community Gallery, 1968, Gallery 12, Livingston, N.J., 1969, Schweizerkunst in Prague, 1969, Studio Gallery, N.Y.C., 1970, Pulitzer Gallery, London, 1970, Kasser Found. Show, Montclair, N.J., 1971, Union Carbide Gallery, N.Y.C., 1972, M. Elson Gallery, N.Y.C., 1976; executed mural Roosevelt Raceway, Westbury, 1969; illustrator N.Y. Times, 1976; appeared TV shows The World of Ernst Aebi, 1975, Exploring the Works of Ernst Aebi, 1975. Served with Swiss Army, 1958. Recipient art awards. Mem. Nat. Soc. Pub. Poets. Address: 478 W Broadway New York City NY 10012

AFFLECK, JOHN HARVEY, III, physicist; b. Kansas City, Mo., Sept. 1, 1923; s. John Harvey Jr. and Alma Blanche (Stone) A.; B.S., Rockhurst Coll., 1945; M.A., U. Mo., 1948; m. Louise E. Youngdoff, Sept. 10, 1947; children—Mary Kathleen, Michael Francis, Anne Therese, Joan Clare, John Robert. Research asst. Midwest Research Inst., Kansas City, Mo., 1945-46, U. Mo., Columbia, 1946-54; research physicist Cin. Milling Machine Co., 1954-55; research physicist Gen. Electric Co., Schenectady, 1955-66, mgr. materials and reliability engring., 1966—. Adult leader Boy Scouts Am., 1958-76; mem. adv. bd. Notre Dame High Sch., Schenectady, 1965-66. Mem. Am. Phys. Soc., Electrochem. Soc., ASTM, Gen. Electric Engring. Assn., Sigma Xi. Republican. Roman Catholic. Contbr. articles to profl. jours.; patentee in field. Home: 604 Granger Rd Syracuse NY 13219 Office: Electronics Park Syracuse NY 13201

AGARWAL, BAL KRISHAN, physician; b. Bikaner, India, Aug. 15, 1941; s. Ghansham D. and Champa (Agarwal) A.; came to U.S., 1969, naturalized, 1972; M.D., S.M.S. Med. Coll. (India), 1963; m. Brij L. Agarwal, Jan. 16, 1967; children—Bhawna, Manish. Intern, P.B.M. Group of Hosps., Bikaner, Rajasthan, India; resident S.M.S. Med. Coll. and Hosp., Jaipur, Rajasthan, 1964-66, Jersey City Med. Center, Beth Israel Med. Center, Newark, and Maimonides Med. Center, Bklyn., 1970-73; practice medicine specializing in cardiology, Salisbury, Md., 1974—; mem. staff Peninsula Gen. Hosp. and Med. Center, 1974—. Fellow A.C.P., Am. Coll. Angiology; mem. Am. Soc. Internal Medicine, Wicomico County Med. Soc., Med. and Chirurgical Faculty of Md. Hindu. Contbr. articles in field to med. jours. Home: 1405 Woodland Rd Salisbury MD 21801 Office: 237 Florida Ave Salisbury MD 21801

AGBAN, GALAA M., plastic surgeon; b. Alexandria, Egypt, June 4, 1934; s. Agban and Liza B. (Raphael) B.; M.B., Ch.B., U. Alexandria, 1959; m. Gene Marie Wegman, June 7, 1969; children—Liza Marie, Amy Ann, Julie Ann. Intern, Hamilton (Ont.) Civic Hosp., 1965-66; resident in surgery St. Mary's Hosp., Rochester, N.Y., 1966-70; fellow in plastic surgery Albany (N.Y.) Med. Center, Union U., 1970-72; asst. instr., instr. plastic surgery Albany Med. Coll., Union U., 1970-72; practice medicine specializing in plastic surgery, Rochester, N.Y., 1972—; attending physician Highland Hosp., Park Ridge Hosp., Rochester, 1972—; sr. attending physician Genesee Hosp., Rochester, 1974—; chmn. plastic surgery div. St. Mary's Hosp., 1975—; asst. clin. prof. U. Rochester Sch. Medicine and Dentistry, 1978—. Diplomate Am. Bd. Surgery, Am. Bd. Plastic Surgery. Fellow A.C.S., Internat. Coll. Surgeons; mem. Internat. Acad. Cosmetic Surgery, Internat. Soc. Burn Injuries, Am. Soc. Plastic and Reconstructive Surgeons, Am. Burn Assn., AMA, Am. Assn. Hand Surgery, Am. Trauma Soc., Am. Cleft Palate Assn., Am. Soc. Aesthetic Plastic Surgery, Soc. Plastic Surgery Upstate N.Y., Am., Empire med. polit. action coms., Am. Physicians Art Assn., Am. Soc. History of Medicine. Roman Catholic. Club: Oak Hill Country. Contbr. chpts. to med. textbook. Office: 1651 Chili Ave Rochester NY 14624

AGHA, FAROOQ PERVIAZ, physician; b. Lahore, Pakistan, Feb. 8, 1943; s. Ahmad Hussain and Nasrin (Asghari) A.; came to U.S., 1968, naturalized, 1972; M.B.B.S., King Edward Med. Coll. (Pakistan), 1965; m. Alice Lorraine Devita, 1969; children—Marisa, Vanessa. Intern, Bronx Lebanon Hosp., N.Y.C., 1968; resident Flower-Fifth Ave. Met. Hosp. Center, 1968-71; instr. radiology N.Y. Med. Coll., N.Y.C., 1971-72, asst. prof. radiology, 1972-76; dir. radiology and nuclear medicine Jones Meml. Hosp., Wellsville, 1976-78; practice medicine specializing in radiology and nuclear medicine, South Charleston, W.Va., 1978—; cons. radiologist Grassland Hosp., Valhalla, N.Y., 1972-76, W. Side Med. group, N.Y.C., 1971-76; cons. Fifth Ave. Radiology Assos., N.Y.C., 1972-76, St. Clares Hosp., N.Y.C., 1975-76; mem. staff Herbert J. Thomas Meml. Hosp., St. Francis Hosp., Kanawka Valley Meml. Hosp., Picks Hosp., Staats Hosp. Chmn. profl. edn. com. Am. Cancer Soc., 1976—, bd. dirs., 1976-78. Recipient Physicians Recognition award AMA, 1972, 75, 78; diplomate Am. Bd. Radiology, Am. Bd. Nuclear Medicine. Fellow N.Y. Acad. Medicine, Royal Soc. Medicine; mem. AMA, Med. Soc. State N.Y., Am. Coll. Radiology, A.C.S., Soc. Nuclear Medicine, Am. Roentgen Ray Soc., Radiol. Soc. N.Am., Assn. Univ. Radiologists, Rochester Roentgen Ray Soc., Radiol. Soc. of N.Y. Med. Coll., Med. Soc. County Allegany. Contbr. articles to med. jours. Home: 2204 Weberwood Dr South Charleston WV 25303 Office: 4620 McCorkle Ave South Charleston WV 25303

AGID, STEVEN JAY, communications co. exec.; b. Bklyn., May 9, 1952; s. Jack and Marion (Popick) A.; B.S., Fla. Inst. Tech., 1974. Sci. writer TWA, NASA, Kennedy Space Center tours, 1973-74; spacecraft controller Vernon Valley Earth Sta., RCA Am. Communication. Mem. Am. Inst. Aeronautics and Astronautics (exec. bd.), Nat. Space Inst., Aerial Phenomena Research Orgn., Smithsonian Assos. Author: The Ups and Downs of Scientific Exploration, 1977. Home: Sussex Hills Manor Apt 8B 3 Wilson Rd Sussex NJ 07461 Office: RCA Am Communications Vernon Valley Earth Sta Rural Delivery #2 Edsall Rd Sussex NJ 07462

AGNES, SISTER MARY (ROSEMARY AGNES O'BRIEN), librarian; b. N.Y.C.; d. William P. and Mary (Boyce) O'Brien; entered Sisters of Charity of St. Vincent de Paul, 1923; A.B., Coll. Mt. St. Vincent, 1932; M.A., Columbia, 1936; B.S., 1944; Ph.D., 1949. Tchr. St. Peter's High Sch., S.I., 1926-32, Blessed Sacrament High Sch., N.Y.C., 1932-43; librarian Cathedral High Sch., N.Y.C., 1943-47, Coll. of Mt. St. Vincent, 1947-51, Elizabeth Seton Sch., Yonkers, N.Y., 1951-59, St. Gabriel High Sch., New Rochelle, N.Y., 1959-67, St. Barnabas High Sch., Bronx, N.Y., 1967-72, Cathedral Prep. Sem., N.Y.C., 1972—. Mem. selections com. Catholic Children's Book Club, 1947-51; mem. adv. bd. Catholic Supplement to Standard Catalog for High Sch. Libraries, 1947-77. Mem. Am., Catholic (chmn. Greater N.Y. 1956—) library assns., Nat. Catholic Edn. Assn., Nat. Council Tchrs. English. Home: 450 W 51st St New York City NY 10019 Office: 555 West End Ave New York City NY 10024

AGNEW, DONALD BURNS, govt. ofcl.; b. Ogden, Ill., 10, 1922; s. Theodore Lee and Agnes (Faris) A.; B. (Sears Roebuck scholar 1938-1940), U. Ill., 1941; postgrad. Am. U., 1955, U. Md., 1957-65; m. Virginia L. Penn, Feb. 14, 1946 (div. June 1966); children—Donald Burns Lee, Melissa Louise; m. 2d, Joan Lee Parker, June 28, 1969; 1 dau., Leslye Ann. Began career as research asst. econ. entomology Ill. Natural History Survey, Urbana, 1940-41; economist Bur. Land Mgmt., U.S. Interior Dept., Cheyenne, Wyo., also Washington, 1946-48; with U.S. Dept. Agr., 1948—, economist Agrl. Mktg. Service, also Prodn. and Mktg. Adminstrn., 1948-62, eocnomist Econ. Research Service, Washington, 1962—; dir. Spl. Econ. Surveys, Washington, 1954-58; econ. cons. U.S. AID Mission in Panama, 1972, in Chile, 1976; cons. on food irradiation studies to AEC and food industry; lectr. various univs., dairy and livestock industry meetings; instr. econs. U. Md., 1969-73. Served with inf. AUS, 1941-46; PTO. Recipient citation for meritorious research U.S. Dept. Agr., 1952, 72, 73; commendation Nat. Commn. Food Mktg., 1966. Mem. AAAS, Am. Agrl. Econ. Assn., Northeastern Agrl. Econ. Council, Am. Mktg. Assn., Western Farm Econs. Assn., Anteaters Assn., Internat. Assn. Agrl. Economists, Orgn. Profl. Employees Dept. Agr., Alpha Zeta. Contbr. to Readings in Agricultural Marketing, 1954; also articles to profl. jours. Compiler: Readings in Linear Programming: Applications to Agricultural Problems, 1956. Home: 6108 Rivanna Dr Springfield VA 22150 Office: South Agriculture bldg 14th and C Sts SW Washington DC 20250 also 500 C St SW Washington DC

AGRESTA, ANTHONY JOHN, SR., ednl. adminstr.; b. Jersey City, Apr. 8, 1933; s. Charles and Pauline (Truncellito) A.; B.S., Fairleigh Dickinson U., 1955; M.S. (N.J. State scholar), William Paterson Coll., 1959; certificate in sch. counseling Rutgers U., 1966; Ph.D., U. Am., 1975; m. Evangeline Presutti, Oct. 30, 1976; children by previous marriage—Lisane, Suzanne, Anthony; 1 stepson, Brian Biedinger. Tchr. English and social studies Dumont (N.J.) Pub. Schs., 1955-57; tchr. math. and English, Rochelle Park (N.J.) Pub. Schs., 1957-62; elementary guidance dir., acting adminstrv. prin., 1962-63; guidance coordinator Wallington (N.J.) High Sch., 1963-64, prin. elementary schs., dir. remedial services Wallington Pub. Schs., 1965-70, prin. Wallington High Sch., 1971—, coordinator State T and E programs, 1976—. Recipient citation Republic of Korea, 1966. Fellow Internat. Inst. Community Service, Leonardo DaVinci Soc.; mem. Brookchester Community Assn. (N.J.) (pres.), Rochelle Park Tchrs. Assn. (pres. 1959-61), Alpha Psi Omega (nat. advisory bd. dirs.). Roman Catholic. Contbr. poems to Jour. Contemporary Poets, Quaderni Di Poesia and other jours. Home: 39 Maple Ln Emerson NJ 07630

AHLGREN, MILDRED CARLSON, club woman, lectr., writer, pub. relations cons.; b. Chgo.; d. August John and Hilda Sophia (Peterson) Carlson; student Columbia Coll., U. Chgo.; m. Oscar Alexander Ahlgren, June 6, 1923; 1 dau., Adrienne Ahlgren Haeuser. Spl. corr. Hammond (Ind.) Times 1935-52. Pres. Ind. Fedn. Women's Club, 1941-44; dean of dirs., mem. exec. com. Gen. Fedn. Women's Clubs, 1943-44, rec. sec., 1944-47, 2d v.p., 1947-50, 1st v.p., 1950-52, pres., 1952-54; nat. sponsoring com. Allied Youth; nat. adv. com., pub. relations panel Savs. Bonds, U.S. Treasury; mem. Planning Commn. Indiana State, 1941-43. Personnel Bd., 1943-46; chmn. women's div. Ind. War Finance Com., 1940-46; chmn. women's com. Ind. War History Commn., 1945-48; mem. Ind. com. George Foster Peabody radio awards; mem. Govs. Com. of Children and Youth. Chmn. Women's Nat. Com. Savs. Bonds; mem. nat. planning com. White House Conf. on Edn., 1953-54; asst. to dir. U.S. Savs. Bonds Div., Treas. Dept., 1955-57; pub. relations cons.; observer food gift program FOA Austria, 1953; ruling elder Nat. Presbyn. Ch. Trustee Ind. State Employes Retirement Fund, 1949-52, Ind. State Tchrs. Colls., 1952-58; bd. Ind. Inst. Psychiat. Research; trustee Radio Liberty Com.; v.p. All Am. Conf. Nat. co-chmn. Women for Nixon and Lodge, 1960. Recipient Royal Order of Vasa (Sweden), 1954, George Washington medal Freedoms Found., 1954, 70, Hoosier Halo, Hammond Newspaper Guild, 1953; numerous other honors and awards; named Ind. woman of year Theta Sigma Phi, 1952. Mem. Nat. Fedn. Press Women, Nat. League Am. Penwomen, Bus. and Profl. Women's Am. Legion Aux., Am. Women in Radio and TV, Women in Communications, Scandinavian Found. (hon.), League Women Voters, P.E.O., Alpha Delta Pi, Phi Beta, Beta Gamma Epsilon. Republican. Presbyn. Clubs: San Antonio Breakfast: Chautauqua (N.Y.) Woman's: Ind. Harbor (Ind.) Women's (hon.); Ind. Women's Press; Whiting (Ind.) Woman's (hon. life, dir.); Nat. Press (Washington); Lake Hills Country; Am. Newspaper Women's (Washington); Washington. Research on status of women, S.Am., 1950, W.I. and Alaska, 1953, Russia, 1956, 71. Home: Dupont East 1545 18th St NW Washington DC 20036 Office: 1734 N St NW Washington DC 20036

AHLGREN, ROY BERTIL, art educator, printmaker; b. Erie, Pa., July 6, 1927; s. Agnar and Annie Pauline (Lovendahl) A.; M.E. in Vocat. Edn., U. Pitts., 1975; m. Martha Ann Nemeth, June 28, 1952; children—Deborah Sue, Alan Roy, David Bruce, Brian Douglas. Artist, designer Louis Marx Toy Co., Erie, 1959-70; asst. partner, asso. dir. Galerie 8, Erie, 1968-75; tchr. art Tech. Meml. High Sch., Erie, 1970—; prof. printmaking Edinboro (Pa.) State Coll., spring 1974; one man shows include Del Mar Coll., Corpus Christi, Tex., 1973, Okla. Art Center, 1974, Chautaugua Art Center, 1978; exhibited traveling shows Library of Congress, 1969-71, St. Paul Art Center, 1969-70, No. Ill. U., 1970, Boston Printmakers, 1973-75, USIA, Europe and Asia, 1971-74; exhibited 7th Internat. Print Biennale, Cracow, Poland, 1978, Intergrafia 78, Katowice, Poland, 1978; represented in permanent collections Butler Art Inst., Youngstown, Ohio, Minn. Mus. Art, St. Paul, Seattle Art Mus., Meml. Art Gallery, Rochester, N.Y., Tex. Tech U., Lubbock, USIA, Washington, Potsdam (N.Y.) U., also numerous pvt. collections; serigraphs (prints) include: Homage to the Cross, 1968, Desert Icon, 1968, Spatial Concept, 1969, Exatopia, 1970, Olympian, 1972, Extrinsic, 1974, Portals, 1976, Concert, 1977, Seabird, 1978. Served with USN, 1944-46. Recipient 1st prize for best print 11th R.I. Arts Festival, 1968. Mem. Phila. Watercolor Club, Boston Printmakers, Phila. Print Club, Erie Art Center (dir. 1972—), N.H. Graphics Soc., Los Angeles Printmaking Soc., NW Pa. Artists Assn. Republican. Lutheran. Home: 1012 Boyer Rd Erie PA 16511 Office: 3325 Cherry St Erie PA 16508

AHMAD, SARFARAZ, physician; b. Delhi, Nov. 29, 1940; s. Israr and Khurshid M.; M.B.B.S., Dow Med. Coll., Karachi, Pakistan, 1964; m. Raafat Ahmad, Mar. 9, 1969; children—Suhail, Indillah. Intern, Nazareth Hosp., Phila., 1966-68; resident in surgery St. Francis Med. Center, Trenton, N.J., 1969-72; practice medicine specializing in surgery, Trenton, 1972—; mem. staff St. Francis, Hamilton hosps.; sr. instr. Hahnemann Med. Coll. and Hosp., Phila. Diplomate Am. Bd. Surgery. Fellow A.C.S.; mem. AMA, Am. Soc. Abdominal Surgeons, N.J. State, Mercer County med. socs. Republican. Muslim. Home: 1017 Lafayette Dr Yardley PA 19067 Office: 717 Hamilton Ave Trenton NJ 08629

AHMAD, SYED IFTIKHAR, chem. engr.; b. Saharanpur, India, Sept. 20, 1943; s. Syed Gulzar Ahmad and Zubeda Khatoon; came to U.S., 1973, naturalized, 1978; B.S., Agra U., 1961; M.S., Aligarh U., 1963; Ph.D. in Chemistry (fellow), U. of Roorkee, 1966; Ph.D. in Chem. Engring (fellow), I.I.Sc. Banglore (India), 1970; m. Tanwir Khanam, Oct. 13, 1969; 1 child—Sumbul. Scientist, Swedish Inst. for Surface Chemistry, Stockholm, 1970-73; research asso. Sch. of Pharmacy, U. Wis., Madison, 1973; adj. asst. prof. chem. engring. Va. Poly. Inst. and State U., Blacksburg, 1973-75; sr. scientist Technicon Instruments Corp., Tarrytown, N.Y., 1975—. NIH fellow, 1973-75. Mem. Chem. Engring. Assn. Bangalore (sec. 1967-68), Am. Chem. Soc. (fellowship 1973), Indian Inst. Chem. Engrs., Am. Assn. Clin. Chemistry. Inventor catalysis by reversed miscelles and liquid crystals; contbr. over 35 research articles in field. Home: Diplomat Gardens Piermont NY 10968 Office: Technicon Corp 511 Benedict Ave Tarrytown NY 10591

AHMED, PERVEZ ALI, cardiologist; b. Shillong, India, Dec. 24, 1948; s. Fakhruddin Ali and Abida (Haider) A.; came to U.S., 1972, naturalized, 1975; M.B., B.S., Armed Forces Med. Coll., Poona, India, 1970; m. Anjum Ali Agha, Mar. 22, 1973; 1 dau., Talaiya. Intern, Brookdale Hosp. Med. Center, Bklyn., 1972-73, resident in medicine, 1973-75, fellow in cardiology, 1975-77, dir. med. intensive care unit, 1977—. Diplomate Am. Bd. Internal Medicine. Mem. AMA, N.Y. Cardiological Soc. Office: Brookdale Hospital Medical Center Linden Blvd Brooklyn NY 11212

AHN, DON, artist, taichi master; b. Seoul, Korea, Jan. 9, 1937; s. Kun Soo and Chunsu Ahn; came to U.S., 1962, naturalized, 1965; B.F.A., Seoul U., 1960; M.F.A., Pratt Inst., 1964; certificate Taichichuan Assn., 1970; divorced; 1 child, Tai Young. Adj. instr. art Cooper Union, 1965-70; asst. prof. N.Y. Inst. Tech., 1965-75; adj. instr. C.W. Post Coll., 1964-68; instr. Hunter Coll., N.Y.C., 1974; taichi master Ahn Taichi Studio, N.Y.C., 1970—; dir. Lotus Gallery, N.Y.C., 1973—; represented in permanent collection Mus. Modern Art, N.Y.C., Dayton (Ohio) Mus., Evansville (Ind.) Mus. Recipient numerous awards for print making and painting. Taoist. Address: PO Box 301 Canal St Station New York City NY 10013

AHNER, RUSSEL OLIVER, geophys. researcher; b. Ouaquaga, N.Y., Jan. 19, 1936; s. Russel Oliver and Thelma Elizabeth (Park) A.; B.A. in Statistics, Am. U., 1971; m. Linda Rae Stage, Aug. 21, 1959; children—Joanne Loraine, Russel Oliver III, Sandra Rae. Teletype operator, data analyst Bendix Radio, Ft. Myers (Fla.) Radio Tracking Facility 1960-61; seismic field team leader Geotech Co., Garland, Tex., 1961-62, electronics tech., 1962; sr. seismic date analyst Uintah Basin Seismol. Obs., Vernal, Utah, 1963-66; research Seismic Data Lab., Alexandria, Va., 1966-71, research asso., 1971-74; research asso. Marine Scis. Inst., U. Conn., Groton, 1974-76; cons. Weston (Mass.) Obs., Boston Coll., 1976, research asso., 1976—. Served with USAF, 1955-59. Mem. Am. Geophys, Union. Republican. Methodist. Author and co-author 13 Teledyne research reports, 1966-74. Home: 15 Main St Acton MA 01720 Office: Weston Obs Concord Rd Weston MA 02193

AHR, GEORGE W(ILLIAM), bishop; b. Newark, June 23, 1904; s. George and Mary (Mueller) A.; student St. Vincent's Coll., 1918-23, Seton Hall Coll., 1923-25, N.Am. Coll., Rome, 1925-29; A.B., A.M., S.T.D. Ordained priest Roman Catholic Ch., 1928; asst. St. Mary's Ch., Jersey City, 1929, St. Venantius Ch., Orange, N.J., 1929-30; faculty mem. Seton Hall Coll., South Orange, N.J., 1930-33; faculty mem. Immaculate Conception Sem., Darlington, N.J., 1933-47, rector, 1947-50; bishop Roman Catholic Diocese of Trenton (N.J.), 1950—. Home: 901 W State St Trenton NJ 08618 Office: 701 Lawrenceville Rd Trenton NJ 08638*

AHSEN, AKHTER, psychologist; b. Sialkot, Pakistan, Jan. 28, 1931; s. Sufi Mohammad and Noor (Zainab) Shafi; came to U.S., 1966; naturalized, 1978; B.A. with honors, Punjab U., 1952, M.A., 1954, Ph.D., 1972. Mem. Inter-Services Selection Bd., Pakistan, 1955-66; chief psychologist Central Superior Services Commn., Pakistan, 1959-60; dir. Eidetic Psychotherapy Inst., Phila., 1966-69; dir. research and tng. Eidetic Analysis Inst., Yonkers, N.Y., 1969—; practice psychology, Yonkers, 1969—; mem. editorial bd. Jour. Mental Imagery, 1977—. Mem. Am. Psychol. Assn. Author: Eidetic Psychotherapy, a Short Introduction, 1965; Basic Concepts in Eidetic Psychotherapy, 1968; Eidetic Parents Test and Analysis, 1972; Psycheye: Self-Analytic Consciousness, 1977. Home and Office: 22 Edgecliff Terr Yonkers NY 10705

AIDINOFF, M(ERTON) BERNARD, lawyer; b. Newport, R.I., Feb. 2, 1929; s. Simon and Esther (Miller) A.; B.A., U. Mich., 1950; LL.B., Harvard U., 1953; m. Celia Spiro, May 30, 1956; children—Seth G., Gail M. Admitted to N.Y. bar, 1954; law clk. to Judge Learned Hand, U.S. Ct. of Appeals, N.Y.C., 1955-56; with firm Sullivan & Cromwell, N.Y.C., 1956—, partner, 1963—; dir. Gibbs & Cox, Inc. Trustee Spence Sch.; mem. vis. com. Harvard Law Sch. Served as 1st lt. JAG, AUS, 1953-55. Mem. Am. (vice chmn. taxation sect. 1974-77), N.Y. State bar assns., Assn. Bar City N.Y. (exec. com. 1974-78, v.p. 1978—), Am. Law Inst. (cons. subchpt. C and K income tax project), Council on Fgn. Relations, India House, Phi Beta Kappa. Editor-in-chief Tax Lawyer, 1974-77. Home: 1120 Fifth Ave New York City NY 10028 Office: 125 Broad St New York City NY 10005

AIELLO, ROBERT JAMES, advt. agy. exec.; b. Sewickley, Pa., Sept. 24, 1937; s. James Vincent and Christine Cecilia (Knott) A.; B.A., Duquesne U., 1960; grad. program for mgmt. devel. Grad. Sch. Bus., Harvard U., 1978. Pub. relations dir. Goodwill Industries of Pitts., 1960-61; advt. mgr. Wilkinsburg Gazette, Pitts., 1961-62; account exec. Ralph Klinefelter & Assos., Pitts., 1962-64; v.p. pub. relations dept. Ketchum, MacLeod & Grove, Pitts., 1964—. Recipient Honor award Pa. Newspaper Pubs. Assn., 1960. Mem. Pub. Relations Soc. Am. (dir. Pitts. chpt. 1975—, accreditation chmn. Pitts. chpt. 1975-77, pres.-elect 1978-79), Harvard Bus. Sch. Assn. Pitts. Club: Pitts. Press. Home: 10 Allegheny Center Pittsburgh PA 15212 Office: 4 Gateway Center Pittsburgh PA 15222

AIKMAN, ROBERT HOWARD, physician; b. N.Y.C., Aug. 12, 1940; s. Edward Percival and Jet (Black) A.; B.Sc. with honors, McGill U., 1962, M.D.C.M., 1966; m. Jane Christy Owen, July 16, 1963; children—Jennifer Lynn, Laurie Kathleen, David Scott. Intern Montreal (Que., Can.) Gen. Hosp., 1966-67; resident in obstetrics and gynecology McGill U., 1966-71, lectr., 1971-76, asst. prof., 1976—; practice medicine specializing in obstetrics and gynecology, Montreal, 1971—; dir. adolescent gynecology unit Montreal Children's Hosp., 1971—; asso. obstetrician and gynecologist Montreal Gen. and Royal Victoria Hosp. Family life coordinator Mt. Royal United Ch., 1974—. Fellow Royal Coll. Physicians and Surgeons Can., Am. Coll. Obstetrics and Gynecology; mem. Soc. Adolescent Medicine, Can. Med. Assn., Co. Mil. Historians. Mem. United Ch. of Can. Home: 155 Dobie Ave Montreal PQ H3A 1S3 Canada Office: 300 Leo Pariseau Suite 1007 Montreal PQ H2W 2N1 Canada

AILEY, ALVIN, dancer; b. Rogers, Tex., Jan. 5, 1931; s. Alvin and Lula E. (Cliff) A.; student U. Calif. at Los Angeles, 1949-50, Los Angeles City Coll., 1950-51, San Francisco State Coll., 1952-53, Lester Horton Dance Theater, Los Angeles, 1949-51, 53, with Hanya Holm, N.Y.C., 1954-55, with Martha Graham, 1956, others; acting student with Stella Adler, 1960-62, with Milton Katselas, 1961. Choreographer, Lester Horton Dance Theater, 1953—; formed Alvin Ailey Am. Dance Theater, 1958, now dir., perfomred numerous festivals, 1959—. Australian, S.E. Asian tour, 1962; actor, 1961—; choreographer, dancer TV, 1954—; also motion pictures. Performances include House of Flowers, 1954, Sing, Man, Sing, 1956, Jamaica, 1957, Carmen Jones, 1959, Call Me by My Rightful Name, 1961, My People, 1963. Address: Alvin Ailey City Center Dance Theater 229 E 59th St New York City NY 10022*

AILLONI-CHARAS, DAN, business exec.; b. Ploiesti, May 22, 1930; s. Max and Felicia (Lupescu) C.; A.B. with honors, U. Calif. at Berkeley, 1952, M.A., 1953; Ph.D. (Univ. honors scholar), N.Y. U., 1968; m. Miriam C. Taytelbaum, Oct. 8, 1957; children—Ethan Benjamin, Orrin, Adam. Project dir. Marplan div. Communications Affiliates, Inc., N.Y.C., 1958-60; supr. advt. studies NBC, N.Y.C., 1960-62; dir. consumer and communications research Forbes Research, Inc., N.Y.C., 1962; mgr. market research Chesebrough-Pond's, Inc., N.Y.C., 1963-64, new products mgr., 1964-68, mgr. internat. marketing services dept., 1968-69; pres. Stratmar Systems, Inc., N.Y.C., 1969—. Adj. asst. prof. marketing Pace U. Grad. Sch. Bus. Adminstrn., from 1963, now adj. prof. Bd. dirs. Young Men's Bd. Trade, 1960-61, 62-63, Philharmonic Symphony Westchester, 1977—; trustee Inst. Advanced Mktg. Studies, 1965-66; bd. advisers Ad Expo, 1978. Mem. Am. Mktg. Assn. (pres. N.Y. chpt. 1965-66, nat. v.p. 1970—), N.Am. Soc. for Corp. Planning (dir. 1970-72), AAUP, N.Y. State Jaycees (dir. 1962-63), Sigma Delta Chi, Phi Sigma Alpha. Editor: Marketing Rev., 1960-63; Proc. 1st Ann. Conf. on Research Design, 1964; New Directions in Research Design, 2d Conf., 1965, Planning, 1968-71. Home: Woodland Dr Town of Rye NY 10573 Office: 385 Madison Ave New York City NY 10017

AIRD, JOHN BLACK, lawyer; b. Toronto, Ont., Can., May 5, 1923; s. Hugh Reston and May (Black) A.; B.A., Trinity Coll., 1946; LL.B., Osgoode Hall Law Sch., Toronto; LL.D. (hon.), Wilfrid Laurier U., 1975; m. Lucille Jane Housser, July 27, 1944; children—Lucille Elizabeth Aird Menear, Jane Victoria Aird Blackmore, Hugh Housser, Katherine Black. Called to Ont. bar, 1949, apptd. queen's counsel, 1960; asso. firm Wilton & Edison, 1949-53; partner firm Edison Aird & Berlis, Toronto, 1953-74, Aird, Zimmerman & Berlis, Toronto, 1974-78; chmn. bd., dir. Reed Stenhouse Cos., Algoma Central Ry.; dir. AMAX, Inc., Bank of N.S., Can. Tungsten Mining Corp., Ltd., Nat. Life Assurance Co. Can., Domglas Ltd., Consol.-Bathurst Ltd., Econ. Investment Trust Ltd., Molson Cos. Ltd., All Canadian-Am. Investments Ltd., Rolland Paper Co. Ltd., Petro-Can., Famous Players Ltd.; mem. Senate of Can., 1964-74; chmn. Canadian sect. Can.-U.S. Permanent Joint Bd. on Def., 1971—; mem. Com. of Nine, 1973; chancellor Wilfrid Laurier U., 1977. Chmn. Inst. Research on Pub. Policy, 1974—; bd. govs. Lester B. Pearson Coll. Pacific, Victoria, B.C.; mem. nat. adv. bd. Canadian Mental Health Assn. Served to lt. Royal Canadian Navy, 1942-45. Named officer Order of Can., 1976. Mem. Canadian Bar Assn., Law Soc. Upper Can., Alpha Delta Phi. Liberal. Anglican. Clubs: York, Toronto, Toronto Golf, Granite. Home: 2 Glenallan Rd Toronto ON M4N 1G7 Canada Office: 145 King St W Toronto ON M5H 2J3 Canada

AITCHISON, IAN ALEXANDER, chartered surveyor; b. Edinburgh, Scotland, Aug. 6, 1935; s. Alexander Fairley and Lucille Wilhelmena Page (Gillon) A.; grad. Leith Acad. Sch., 1953; grad. Heriot Watt Tech. U., 1958; diploma Royal Instn. Chartered Surveyors, 1960; m. Nan Reed, Apr. 29, 1961; children—Mark Jonathan, Clive Jeremey. Apprentice quantity surveyor James D. Gibson & Simpson, Edinburgh, 1953-59; asst. quantity surveyor Sir William Baird & Partners, Edinburgh. 1959-60; sr. cost cons. G.A. Hanscomb Partnership, London, 1960-62, mgr. Nigerian offices, Ibadan and Lagos, 1962-66; sr. partner Hanscomb, Roy Assos., Toronto, Ont., Can., 1966—, chmn., 1974-76; pres. Hanscomb, Roy Assos. Ltd.; v.p., chmn. CEREC Group Ltd. (Can.); v.p. Constrn. Data Systems Ltd. (Can.), Dunbar Realty Ltd. (Can.), Hanscomb Assos. Inc. (U.S.A.), Constrn. Mgmt. Services Ltd. (Nigeria); partner Hanscomb Partnership (U.K.); pres. Hanscomb Roy Internat. Ltd. (Bermuda); cons., lectr. constrn. econs. registration course Ont. Assn. Architects. Elder, Armour Heights Presbyn. Ch., chmn. bd. mgrs., 1968-70; vice chmn. bd. govs. YMCA, Toronto. Certified cost engr. Fellow Royal Instn. Chartered Surveyors; mem. Can. Inst. Quantity Surveyros (treas. 1975-76), Ont. Assn. Land Economists, Arbitrators Inst. Can., Inst. Arbitrators U.K. (asso.), Ont. Assn. Cons. Quantity Surveyros (pres. 1975-76), Am. Assn. Cost Engrs., Bd. Trade Met. Toronto, Fitness Inst. Club: Empire. Contbr. articles to profl. jours. Home: 176 Forest Hill Rd Toronto ON M5P 2N4 Canada Office: Suite 2301 2 Bloor St W Toronto ON M4W 3E2 Canada

AITKEN, ROBERT PETERS, mktg. cons.; b. Mpls.; s. Robert Arthur and Rose (Peters) A.; B.C.S., Drake U., 1934; M.S., Columbia, 1936; m. Marjorie Dorothea Jackson, Apr. 24, 1943; children—Robert G., Bruce E., Gerald T. Indsl. engr. Johns Mansville Corp., N.Y.C., 1936-41; market analyst Supple Wills Jones Co., Phila., 1941-51; dir. market research Eastern div. Sealtest Foods, Inc., Phila., 1951-54, nat. dir. market research Sealtest div. Kraft Inc., N.Y.C., 1954-72; pres. RPA MKtg. & Cons. Services, Walden, N.Y., 1972—; instr. statistics Temple U., Phila., 1946-49; mem. adv. com. U.S. Bur. Census, 1972, 73; auditor Warminster Twp., Bucks County, Pa., 1948. Served to lt. (s.g.) USNR, 1943-45. Mem. Am. Mktg. Assn., Montgomery C. of C., Am. Legion, Mil. Order World Wars. Club: Sales Execs. N.Y. Home: 75F Lake Osiris Rd Walden NY 12586 Office: Box 453 Walden NY 12586

AJELLO, CARL RICHARD, atty. gen. State of Conn.; b. Ansonia, Conn., Aug. 22, 1932; s. Carl Richard and Kathryn (Flanigan) A.; B.S., U. Conn., 1953; LL.B., J.D., N.Y. U., 1956; m. Jacqueline Culmo, June 11, 1956; children—Michele, Carl Richard III. Admitted to Conn. bar, 1956; mem. firm Ajello, Hoyle & Sponheimer, Ansonia, 1956—; justice of peace City of Ansonia, 1960-62, corp. counsel, 1965-68; mem. Conn. Ho. of Reps., 1963-74, asst. majority leader, 1967-69, majority leader, 1969-73, minority leader, 1973-74; atty. gen. State of Conn., Hartford, 1975—; corporator Savs. Bank Ansonia. Mem. Ansonia Charter Revision Commn., 1974-75; mem. Conn. Gov.'s Adv. Commn. Adult Edn., 1974—; mem. NE Regional Forest Fire Protection Compact, 1973—; bd. dirs. Julia Day Nursery Inc., Ansonia; corporator Griffin Hosp., Derby, Conn.; mem. Lower Naugatuck Valley Mental Health Planning Council. Served to capt. U.S. Army, 1957-60. Recipient Distinguished Service award Ansonia Jaycees, 1965; Outstanding Alumnus award U. Conn., 1976; Gold medal Hartford Italian-Am. Home, 1976; Distinguished Service award New Haven Football Found., 1977. Mem. Nat. Legis. Conf., Am., Conn., Naugutuck Valley (pres. 1965-66) bar assns., Am. Trial Lawyers Assn., N.Y. U. Alumni Assn., Nat. Assn. Attys. Gen. Democrat. Roman Catholic. Clubs: Central Subalpi, Lions, Elks, Racebrook Country, Woodbridge, Officers Conn. Home: Pulaski Hwy Ansonia CT 06401 Office: 290 Main St Ansonia CT 06401

AJELLO, DOMINICK ARNOLD, ophthalmologist; b. Bklyn., Oct. 24, 1908; s. Vincent and Concetta Maria (Riccio) A.; grad. Columbia, 1928; M.D., U. Geneva (Switzerland), 1953; m. Bridget Andreozzi, June 28, 1934; children—Ronald V., Lawrence R., Irene M., Lisa J. Intern, Broad St. Hosp., N.Y.C., 1933-34; resident physician City Home for Dependents, City Island, N.Y., 1934-37; chief surgeon Bklyn. Eye and Ear Hosp., 1974—. Mem. pres's. council Monmouth Coll., West Long Branch, N.J. Diplomate Am. Bd. Ophthalmology. Fellow A.C.S., Am. Acad. Ophthalmology and Otolaryngology; mem. AMA, King's County Med. Soc. (head ophthalmic com. 1970), Bklyn. Ophthal. Soc. (pres. 1974). Clubs: Deal (N.J.) Golf and Country, Channel of Monmouth Beach (N.J.). Home: 27 Milan Pl Deal NJ 07723 Office: 1 Hanson Pl Brooklyn NY 11243

AKALIN, MAZHAR ALI, physician; b. Eskisehir, Turkey, Mar. 10, 1927; s. Hafiz Hasan and Rukiye Nernin (Soydan) A.; came to Can., 1961, naturalized, 1966; M.D., Istanbul Med. Sch., 1951; m. Nihal Timocin, Dec. 29, 1964; 1 dau., Nur. Resident in internal medicine, Istanbul, 1951-56; house physician hosp., Que., Can., 1961-67; gen. practice medicine, Laval, Que., 1967—. Served with Turkish Army, 1956-58. Mem. Assn. Med. de Langue Francaise du Can., L'Assn. des Medecins Omnipracticiens de Montreal, Turkish Cultural Assn. Can. (pres. 1976). Muslim. Home: 914 D'Alencon St Chomedey Laval PQ Canada Office: 4361 Notre Dame St Chomedey Laval PQ Canada

AKE, H(ARRY) WORTH, ins. co. exec.; b. Chgo., Feb. 7, 1923; s. Harry Fulton and Mabelle (Welwood) A.; student N.Y.C. Coll. Ins., 1947-51, C.W. Post Coll., 1961-62, St. Peters Coll., 1967, N.Y. U., 1976; m. Regina A. Downes, Sept. 7, 1946; children—Jean-Marie, Worth Gerard. Underwriter, Mass. Bonding & Ins. Co., N.Y.C., 1941-43, 46-50; underwriting supr. U.S. Fidelity & Guaranty Co., N.Y.C., 1950-53, 56-65, personnel supt., 1961-63; sales agt. Nationwide Mut. Ins. Co., Trenton, N.J., 1953-55, sales mgr., 1955-56; with Gen. Fire & Casualty Co., Carle Place, L.I., N.Y., 1963-74, asst. sec., 1968-70, v.p., 1970-74; v.p. Compass Ins. Co., Carle Place, 1970-73; pres., dir. All Statewide Inc. Agy., Jersey City, 1974—. Cons. ins., cities, truck and bus lines; sports historian Amityville (N.Y.) High Sch., Williamsburg (Pa.) High Schs., Wagner (S.I., N.Y.) Coll., C.W. Post Coll., L.I., 1955—; feature columnist Drum Corps World, Denver, 1973—. Chmn. fund raising N.Y. ins. cos., A.R.C., United Fund, 1960-63. Served with Signal Corps, AUS, 1942-45; PTO. Mem. Nat. Judges Assn. Drum and Bugle Corps, N.Y. Casualty Mgrs. Assn., N.Y.C. Auto Underwriters Assn. K.C. (3 deg.). Asst. editor Drum Corps News, Boston, 1970—. Home: 11 Reservoir Ave Jersey City NJ 07307 Office: 2184 JFK Blvd Jersey City NJ 07305

AKELEY, JOHN WILDER, design engr.; b. Coudersport, Pa., May 23, 1920; s. Archibald Paul and Doris Elizabeth (Heymann) A.; student Norwich U., 1938; B.S., Lock Haven State Coll., 1943; m. Rose Minnie Probst, Sept. 21, 1943; children—Wendalee, Doris Jane, Nancy E., James P. Tool designer Piper Aircraft. Corp., Lock Haven, Pa., 1941-47; indsl. engr., pulp mill supt. N.Y. & Pa. Co., Lock Haven, 1947-59; instrument and project engr. Koppers Co., Lock Haven, 1959-64; engr. interior design, human factors Pipers Aircraft Corp., 1964—. Pres. Millbrook Playhouse, 1960-71, v.p., 1971—, trustee United Methodist Ch. Lock Haven, 1967—. Served with Ordnance Corps, U.S. Army, 1943-46. Mem. Bald Eagle Tourist Assn., Lock Haven State Coll. Alumni Assn., Human Factors Soc., Alpha Psi Omega. Clubs: Masons, Area Suprs. (pres. 1961-62). Researcher aircraft crashworthiness. Home: 110 6th St Lock Haven PA 17745 Office: Piper Aircraft Corp Lock Haven PA 17745

AKERBERG, AKE, psychiatrist; b. Borga, Finland, May 6, 1917; s. Henrik Ivar and Alma Maria (Eriksson) A.; came to U.S., 1955, naturalized, 1961; B.A., U. Helsinki (Finland), 1941, M.D., 1946; m. Elizabeth J. Karlson, June 9, 1943; children—Fred Gordon, Frank Edgar, Mark Joel. Resident in psychiatry U. Vt., Burlington, 1968-71; missionary physician Methodist Ch., Belgian Congo, 1948-55; gen. practice medicine, South Paris, Maine, 1956-68; attending psychiatrist Maine Med. Center, Portland, 1971-73; chief of psychiatry St. Mary's Med. Center, Lewiston, Maine, 1975—; chief of psychiatry Central Maine Gen. Hosp., Lewiston, Maine, 1975—, instr. of psychiatry in gen. practice residency program, 1973—. Served as 1st lt. Finnish Army, 1941-44. Mem. Androscoggin County (Maine) Med. Soc., Maine Med. Assn., Am. Psychiat. Assn. Home and office: 487 Main St Lewiston ME 04240

AKERS, CAROLYN, ins. co. exec.; b. Goshen, N.Y., Aug. 6, 1946; d. Leslie and Catherine (Tuthill) A.; A.S., Becker Jr. Coll., 1966. Cost analyst Pratt & Whitney Aircraft Corp., East Hartford, Conn., 1966-68; sr. equities adminstr. Travelers Equities Sales Inc., Hartford, Conn., 1968-72; ops. mgr. CG Investment Mgmt. Co., Hartford, Conn., 1972-76, controller, 1976—; fin. mgr. common stock div. Conn. Gen. Life Ins. Co., Hartford, 1978—, controller Group of Mut. Funds, 1979—. Mem. adv. bd. Investment Co. Inst., Washington, 1976—; mem. zoning bd. appeals Town of Granby, Conn., 1974—, mem. Democratic Town Com., 1977—. Methodist. Office: 950 Cottage Grove Rd Bloomfield CT 06002

AKINS, LEROY BURTON, JR., county ofcl., educator; b. Glens Falls, N.Y., Dec. 26, 1941; s. LeRoy Burton and Agnes Cecelia (Beaudin) A.; ed. USN Electronics Sch., Great Lakes, Ill., 1961; m. Phyllis Norton, June 4, 1966; children—Sean, LeRoy Burton III, Sabrina. Freelance radio personality WWSC Radio, Glens Falls, 1956-60; communications dep. sheriff Warren County Sheriff's Dept., 1964; radio producer, engr. WFIL Radio, Phila., 1964-71; salesman No. Homes, Hudson Falls, N.Y., 1972-73; instr. radio broadcasting Adirondack Community Coll., Glens Falls, 1973-77; publicity, tourism dir. Warren County, 1976—. Served with USN, 1962-64. Recipient several civic awards from various groups. Home: 26 W Notre Dame St Glens Falls NY 12801 Office: Municipal Center Lake George NY 12845

AKIYAMA, TOSHIO, physician, educator, researcher; b. Shizuoka, Japan, Mar. 10, 1941; s. Senkichi and Kimiko A.; M.D., Kyoto Prefectural U. Medicine, Japan, 1966; came to U.S., 1968; m. Akiko Okamura, Aug. 31, 1969; children—Naoko, Sachiko. Asso. resident in medicine Strong Meml. Hosp., Rochester, N.Y., 1970-71; fellow in cardiology Emory U. Sch. Medicine, Atlanta, 1971-72; fellow in cardiology U. Rochester Sch. Medicine, 1972-73, asst. prof. medicine, 1975—; research asso. and fellow in cardiology U. Chgo. Sch. Medicine, 1973-75. Diplomate Am. Bd. Internal Medicine, Am. Bd. Cardiovascular Diseases. Fellow Am. Coll. Cardiology, councils on clin. cardiology and basic sci. Am. Heart Assn. Contbr. articles to med. jours. Home: 50 Boniface Dr Rochester NY 14620 Office: 601 Elmwood Ave Rochester NY 14642

AKSNES, KAARE, astronomer; b. Kvam, Norway, Mar. 25, 1938; s. Olav Larson and Magnhild Olava (Westreng) A.; B.S., U. Bergen (Norway), 1960; M.S., U. Oslo (Norway), 1963; Ph.D. (NATO sci. fellow), Yale U., 1969; m. Liv Kristin Maroy, Sept. 19, 1959; children—Kjersti, Astrid, Hallgjerd. Research asst. U. Oslo, 1961-63, 64-65; mathematician Smithsonian Astrophys. Obs., Cambridge, Mass., 1965-67; sr. engr. Jet Propulsion Lab., Pasadena, Calif., 1969-71; celestial mechanician Smithsonian Astrophys. Obs., asso. Harvard Obs., Cambridge, 1971—; vis. astronomer Tokyo Astron. Obs., 1976. Mem. outer planets grand tour imaging sci. team NASA, 1971-72. Served with Norwegian Navy, 1963-64. Recipient Dirk Brouwer Meml. prize Yale U., 1969. Fellow Royal Astron. Soc. Engring.; mem. Am. Astron. Soc., Internat. Astron. Union, Sigma Xi. Contbr. articles to profl. jours. Home: 6 Peachtree Rd Lexington MA 02173 Office: 60 Garden St Cambridge MA 02138

ALASIA, ALFRED VICTOR, photographer; b. N.Y.C., Jan. 28, 1925; s. Cesare and Caterina (Roccati) A.; student Iona Coll., 1943, N.Y. U., 1951, N.Y. Inst. Photography, 1946, Coll. City N.Y., 1953; m. Eleanor Babich, Feb. 22, 1949; children—Denise, JoAnn, Audrey, Nanette, Alfred, Thomas. Head film dept. Television Workshop N.Y., 1951-54, Cambridge Sch. Broadcasting, 1954-55; staff instr. N.Y. Inst. Photography, 1955; owner Al Victor Studio, Whitestone, N.Y., 1953—; product devel. mgr., research div. Brit.-Am. Bank Note Ltd., Ottawa, Ont., Can. Served with inf. AUS, 1943-46. Decorated Bronze Star. Mem. Soc. Motion Picture and Television Engrs., L.I. Profl. Photographers Assn. Research in autostereoscopic photography. Patentee 3-dimensional camera, maximum security printing system; designer one piece stereo speaker system. Home: 146-07 13th Ave Whitestone NY 11357 Office: 49 Bryant Ave Roslyn NY 11576

ALATIS, JAMES EFSTATHIOS, univ. dean; b. Weirton, W.Va., July 13, 1926; s. Efstathios and Vasiliki (Galanoudis) A.; B.A., W.Va. U., 1948; M.A., Ohio State U., 1953; Ph.D., 1966; m. Penelope Mastorides, Dec. 30, 1951; children—William, Stephen, Anthony. Fulbright lectr. English, U. Athens, 1955-57; English testing and teaching specialist Dept. State, 1959-61; specialist for lang. research U.S. Office Edn., 1961-65, chief lang. sect., 1965-66; asso. dean Sch. Langs. and Linguistics, Georgetown U., Washington, 1966-73, dean, 1973—, asso. prof. linguistics, 1966-75, prof., 1975—; exec. sec. Tchrs. of English to Speakers of Other Langs., 1966—; prin. investigator team to evaluate English as second lang. programs Navajo Area Schs., Bur. Indian Affairs, 1969-70. Mem. adv. council ERIC Clearinghouse on Linguistics, 1966-71; bd. dirs. CONPASS, 1966-70. Served with USNR, 1944-46. Recipient Mary Glide Goethe prize Am. Name Soc., 1954. Am. Council Learned Socs. study grantee in linguistics U. Mich., 1954. Fellow AAAS, mem. Am. Council on Teaching Fgn. Langs. (adv. assembly), Linguistic Soc. Am. (del. 1966-69), Nat. Council Tchrs. English, Modern Lang. Assn. Am., Nat. Assn. Fgn. Student Affairs (dir. 1965-66), Fedn. Internationale des Professeurs de Langues Vivantes (exec. com.), Phi Beta Kappa. Editor: Studies in Honor of Albert H. Marckwardt, 1972. Contbr. articles to profl. jours. Home: 5108 Sutton Pl Alexandria VA 22304 Office: Sch Langs and Linguistics Georgetown U Washington DC 20057

ALBANO, D. JOHN, wastewater treatment co. exec.; b. Bronx, N.Y., Dec. 9, 1927; s. Dominick I. and Millie (Prinelli) A.; B.S. in Mech. Engring., Newark Coll. Engring., 1956, M.S., 1960; m. Virginia A. Lommatzsch, Nov. 26, 1950; children—Thomas, Virginia, Michael. Regional sales mgr. Ralph B. Carter Co., Hackensack, N.J., 1960-75; v.p., gen. mgr., partner Atara Inc., Paramus, N.J., 1975—. Mem. ASME, Water Pollution Control Fedn., Water and Wastewater Equipment Mfrs. Assn. Roman Catholic. Clubs: Lions, K.C., City Island Yacht. Author tech. papers. Office: 299 Forest Ave Paramus NJ 07652

ALBEE, EDWARD FRANKLIN, author, playwright; b. Mar. 12, 1928. Plays wirtten include The Zoo Story, 1958, The Death of Bessie Smith, 1959, The Sandbox, 1959, The American Dream, 1960, Who's Afraid of Virginia Woolf?, 1961-62, The Ballad of the Sad Cafe (adaptation of Carson McCullers' novella), 1963, Tiny Alice, 1964, Malcolm, 1966, A Delicate Balance, 1966 (Pulitzer Prize winner 1967), Everything in the Garden, 1968, Box, Quotations from Chairman Mao, 1970, All Over, 1971, Seascape, 1977, Counting the Ways, 1976, Listening, 1977, The Lady from Dubuque, 1978. Bd. dirs. Montauk Writers' Colony. Recipient Pulitzer prize, 1975. Mem. Nat. Inst. Arts and Letters. Address: 14 Hannison St New York City NY 10013

ALBERS, HARRY ROBERT, coll. adminstr.; b. Jersey City, Mar. 6, 1938; s. Harry Robert and Lee (Vetreno) A.; B.S., U. Pitts., 1961; M.S. (Univ. fellow 1961-63), Cornell U., 1963; postgrad. Boston U., 1968-69; M.B.A., George Washington U., 1971-72; m. Jean Ellen Cherry, Jan. 26, 1963; children—Harry Robert, Robert Steaphan, Steaphan Harry. Mgr. satellite tracking program Smithsonian Astrophys. Obs., Cambridge, Mass., 1963-68; dir. adminstrn. Assn. Univs. for Research in Astronomy, Tucson, 1972-76; bus. mgr. Smithsonian Instn., Washington, 1968-72, also exec. dir. Smithsonian Research Found.; v.p. for adminstrn. Barnard Coll., Columbia U., N.Y.C., 1976—; cons. NSF, Smithsonian Instn., Tonka Corp., Mpls. Chmn. Skyline Belair Swim Team. Recipient Leadership award Am. Legion, 1956. Mem. Nat. Assn. Coll. and Univ. Bus. Officers, Soc. Research Adminstrs., Am. Assn. Museums, Profl. Assn. Diving Instrs. Contbr. articles to profl. jours. Home: 24 Chamberlain Rd Hupatcong NJ 07843 Office: Barnard College Columbia Univ New York City NY 10027

ALBERT, GERALD, psychologist, educator; b. N.Y.C., Nov. 13, 1917; s. Andrew and Eleanor (Walder) A.; B.A. cum laude, Coll. City N.Y., 1938; M.A., New Sch. Social Research, 1958; Ed.D., Columbia, 1964; m. Debrah Shanna Fineberg, May 24, 1970; m. Myra Leventhal, Dec. 25, 1940 (div. Feb. 1970); children—Jay Harvey, Laurie Ellen (Mrs. Christopher Moxham). Asst. editor, asso. pub. Vulcan Pub. Corp., N.Y.C., 1939-42; editor Creston Pub. Corp., N.Y.C., 1942-45; dir. advt. and psychol. services Edn. div. Universal Pictures, N.Y.C., 1945-50; pres. Advt. Enterprises, Inc., N.Y.C., 1950-62; exec. dir. Consumer Research Continental Research Inst., N.Y.C., 1962-64; pvt. practice psychotherapy, N.Y.C., 1958-72; dir. counseling C.W. Post Coll., L.I. U., Brookville, 1964-70, asst. prof. Grad. Sch. Edn., 1964-67, asso. prof., 1967-74, prof. ednl. psychology and psychol. counseling, 1974—; pvt. practice ind., marriage and family psychotherapy, Port Washington, N.Y., 1972—; exec. coordinator Inst. Testing and Guidance, Forest Hills, N.Y., 1966—; co-dir., supr. psychologist L.I. Cons. Center, Forest Hills, N.Y., 1974—, clin. dir., 1975—; asst. dir. L.I. Inst. Mental Health, 1977—; diagnostic cons. psychologist Probation div. Queens (N.Y.) Family Ct., 1973; fellow psychotherapy tng. program L.I. Cons. Center, 1962-64, dir. Dropout Prevention Scholarship Program, 1966-68; workshop leader family counseling L.I. Counselors Ann. Conf., 1973; workshop leader NCCJ, 1965; panel chmn. 16th Ann. Conf., League Parent Edn., 1964. Licensed sch. psychologist, also clin. and counseling psychologist. Mem. Am. Psychol. Assn., Am., L.I. personnel and guidance assns., AAAS, Am. Assn. Marriage and Family Counselors, N.Y. Soc. Clin. Psychologists. Author: Choosing and Keeping a Marriage Partner, 1971; Mate Selection Check List, 1971; I-Am Marriage Counseling Sentence Completion Test, 1971; Children's Sentence Completion Test, 1974. Asso. editor Jour. Contemporary Psychotherapy, 1967—. Contbr. articles to profl. jours. Office: Grad Sch Edn CW Post Center LI U Greenvale NY 11548

ALBERTA, WILLIAM NEIL, coll. adminstr., counselor; b. Waterbury, Vt., Jan. 29, 1946; s. Neil William and Pauline Elaine A.; B.S., State U. N.Y. Coll., Oswego, 1969; postgrad. Northeastern U.; M.S., Cornell U., 1977. Asst. purchasing agt. Binghamton (N.Y.) Savs. Bank, 1964-65; instr. indsl. arts. Roscoe (N.Y.) Central Sch., 1969-74; research asst. Cornell U., Ithaca, N.Y., 1974-76; asst. dean, career counselor Herkimer (N.Y.) Community Coll., 1976—. Chmn. bd. edn. United Ch. Roscoe, 1971-73; pres. Roscoe Tchrs. Assn., 1973-74; active Boy Scouts Am., 1973-74. Mem. Am. Personnel and Guidance Assn., Mid-Atlantic Career Counselors Assn., State U. N.Y. Career Devel. Officers Assn. Democrat. Home: Sands Creek Rd Hancock NY 13783 Office: Herkimer Community Coll Reservoir Rd Herkimer NY 13350

ALBERTIAN, ALICE NAZENIG, banker; b. Istanbul, Turkey, July 13, 1922; d. John Vagharshag and Zivart (Destenian) Albertian; came to the U.S., 1924, naturalized, 1932; student Am. Inst. Banking, 1947. With State Street Trust Co., Boston, 1942—, bookkeeper, 1942-47, gen. banking supr., 1950-65, asst. mgr., 1966-68, asst. treas., 1968—. Adviser, Jr. Achievement of Boston, 1967-71. Mem. Nat. Assn. Armenian Studies and Research (exec. com. 1970-71), Am. Inst. Banking, Bank Officers Assn., Nat. Assn. Bank Women (group treas. 1971-72), Fanewil Bus. and Profl. Women's Club. Club: Zonta Internat. (dir. Boston 1976—). Home: 56 Bigelow Ave #16 Watertown MA 02172 Office: 225 Franklin St Boston MA 02110

ALBERTS, DONALD ALLAN, oil co. exec.; b. Cleve., Mar. 29, 1932; s. Milton Charles and Ruth Louise (Graves) A.; B.A. in Bus. Adminstrn., Bowling Green U., 1968; LL.D., LaSalle U., 1971; m. Shirley Ethel Tripp, Mar. 25, 1952; children—Donald, Beverly Ann, Keith, Dawn. Served with U.S. Coast Guard, 1949-73; with Texaco Inc., Beacon, N.Y., 1973—, sr. environ. specialist, 1978—. Mem. Internat. Assn. Pollution Control, Am. Standards and Testing Assn., Am. Petroleum Inst. Roman Catholic. Home: Rural Delivery 3 Box 223 Longhill Rd Hopewell Junction NY 12533 Office: Texaco Inc PO Box 509 Beacon NY 12533

ALBERTS, ROBERT LOUIS, advt. agy. exec.; b. Richmond, Va., Dec. 18, 1898; s. David Louis and Elizabeth (Von Zimmerman) A.; student U.S. and fgn. schs.; m. Evelyn Mansfield Brown, May 29, 1926; children—Arnold Edward, David Leo. Mech. engr. Am. Machine Tool Corp., N.Y.C., CLeve., Cin.; profl. portrait painter, 1912—; chmn. bd., Allied Bus. Ads Inc., Westbury, N.Y. Decorated Sovereign Order of St. George, Order Croix de Lorraine (France); Order of St. Dennis, Order of St. Stephen (Greece); others; recipient Freedom award Order Lafayette, 1965. Mem. C. of C. (past pres.), Am. Order of Croix de Guerre (past pres.), Am. Legion, Soc. Am. Wars, Verdun-Meuse-Argonne Veterans Assn. Club: Masons. Author: Anyone Can Paint, 1924. Contbr. articles to various art mags. Home: 101 Harbor Ln Massapequa Park NY 11762

ALBERTSON, CHRISTIERN GUNNAR, broadcaster, writer; b. Reykjavik, Iceland, Oct. 18, 1931; s. Thordur and Yvonne (Broberg) A.; came to U.S., 1957, naturalized, 1963; student Kent Coll., Canterbury, Eng., 1947-49; grad. Royal Acad. Art, Copenhagen, Denmark, 1952; m. Hanne Elisabeth Christensen, 1954 (div. 1958). Gen. mgr. Storyville Club, Copenhagen, 1952-54; producer, writer U.S. Armed Forces Radio and TV, Iceland, 1954-57, WCAU radio, Phila., 1957-58; disc jockey WHAT-FM, Phila., 1958-60; producer Riverside Records, N.Y.C., 1960-62; continuity dir. WNEW radio, N.Y.C., 1963-64; gen. mgr. WBAI-FM, N.Y.C., 1964-66; dir. BBC programs Hartwest Prodns., N.Y.C., 1966-67; co-producer, host weekly TV series The Jazz Set, PBS Network, 1972-73; pres. Video One, Inc., 1976—; producer, co-host weekly cable TV series Doin' It, 1976-77; entertainment editor Beauty Trade mag., 1978—; asso. producer, cons. film Bessie, 1974; music cons. film Buddy Can You Spare A Dime, 1974. Producer Bessie Smith blues series Columbia Records, 1970; U.S. jazz reporter Danish TV, 1972-75; U.S. music corr. Berlingske Tidende, Copenhagen, 1960-64; talent cons. Dupont Show of Week, 1961. Adv. bd. N.Y. Jazz Mus., 1972-75. Recipient Grand Prix du Disque, Montreal Jazz Festival, 1971, Trendsetter of Year award Billboard, 1971. Mem. Nat. Acad. Rec. Arts and Scis. (Grammy award 1971, Trustees award 1971, Grammy nomination 1977). Author: Bessie-The Life of Bessie Smith, 1972; Empress of the Blues, 1974. Contbg. editor Stereo Review, 1973—, Routes mag., 1978—. Contbr. articles to Down Beat, Saturday Rev., Rolling Stone, N.Y. Times, Jazz Forum, others. Address: 444 Central Park W New York City NY 10025

ALBERTSON, DEAN, educator; b. Denver, Aug. 22, 1920; s. George Howard and Vinnie (Robinson) A.; B.A., U. Calif. at Berkeley, 1942, M.A., 1947; Ph.D., Columbia, 1955; m. Johnnie Leinbach, Mar. 6, 1954 (div. Dec. 1968); children—Mark Nevins, Constant Kathryn. Asst. dir. oral history project Columbia, 1948-55; exec. asst. Com. Internat. Exchange Persons, 1956-59; instr. history Bklyn. Coll., 1959-61, asst. prof. history, 1961-64, asso. prof. history, 1965; prof. history U. Mass., Amherst, 1965—, dir. Nat. Def. Edn. Act Insts. History, 1966, 67, 68. Served to lt. (j.g.) USNR, 1943-45. Decorated Air medal with 3 clusters; recipient Research grant Am. Council Learned Socs., Social Sci. Research Council, Am. Philos. Soc., 1962-64. Mem. Am. Hist. Assn., Orgn. Am. Historians, Oral History Assn. (sec. 1968-69). Democrat. Author: Roosevelt's Farmer, 1961; Eisenhower as President, 1963; (with Howard H. Quint and Milton Cantor) Main Problems in American History, 1964, rev. edits., 1968, 72, 78; Am. History Visually, 1969; Rebels or Revolutionaries, Student Movements of the 1960's, 1975. Office: Dept History U Mass Amherst MA 01002

ALBERTSON, MURRAY GRIEVE, civil engr.; b. Oradell, N.J., Apr. 4, 1925; s. John Gilbert and Jess Cameron (Richmond) A.; B.S. in Civil Engring., Swarthmore (Pa.) Coll., 1949; student N.Y. U. Grad. Sch. Bus., 1958; m. Marjorie Helen Erickson, May 1, 1954; children—Thomas, Bonnie, Lisa. Instr., U. B.C., Vancouver, Can., 1949-50; engr. Bowe, Albertson & Assos., N.Y.C., 1950-54; sales engr. Dorr Oliver, Inc., Stamford, Conn., 1954-56, Richard Dudgeon, Inc., Bklyn., 1956-58; mgr. san. engring. dept. Pease Co., Stamford, 1958-61; founder, pres. Albertson, Sharp & Ewing, Inc., Norwalk, Conn., 1961—; dir. Norwalk YMCA, 1963-68, chmn. bldg. addition com., 1964, trustee, 1968—; treas. Rowayton Sch. PTA, Norwalk, 1962-64. Served with USNR, 1943-46. Registered profl. engr., Conn. Mem. Conn. Soc. Profl. Engrs., Water Pollution Control Fedn., ASME. Republican. Congregationalist. Clubs: Norwalk Rotary (pres. 1965-66); New Canaan Field, Winter. Home: 519 Weed St New Canaan CT 06840 Office: 83 East Ave Norwalk CT 06851

ALBOND, HARVEY NEUMAN, city ofcl.; b. Duluth, Minn., June 2, 1928; s. Isadore and Frances (Rosenfield) A.; B.A., U. Minn., 1950; m. Evelyn Karen Snyder, Nov. 25, 1959; 1 dau., Roxane Cheryl. Dir. research Iowa Planning Commn., Des Moines, 1958-60, John Child & Co., Honolulu, 1960-61, Australia, 1961-64; planning economist DeLeuw, Cather & Co., Chgo., 1964-65; prin. planner City of Mpls., Minn. Planning Commn., 1965-66; dir. research Harland Bartholomew & Assos., Memphis, 1966-67; dir. planning and devel. City of Niagara Falls, 1967-78, acting city mgr., 1978-79, city mgr., 1979—, chmn. Niagara Frontier Transp. Study, 1974-75; prof. transp. planning Niagara U. 1972—; cons. Niagara Falls Sch. Bd., Niagara Falls Housing Authority; founding mem. Niagara Coalition, 1968-74; cons. mem. nat. housing com. AIA, 1970-71; panelist Inst. Environ. Design, Nat. Assn. Home Builders, Washington, 1971. Served with USNR, 1946-48, to capt. USAFR, 1950-53. Mem. Am. Inst. Planners (depts. planning and mgmt., transp. planning), Am. Soc. Planning Ofcls., Nat. Assn. Housing and Redevel. Ofcls., Am. Statis. Assn. (past pres. Iowa chpt.). Democrat. Jewish. Clubs: Rotary, B'nai B'rith. Presented papers at profl. confs.; author: Retail Plan for Canberra, 1961. Home: 4816 Penn St Niagara Falls NY 14305 Office: City Hall 745 Main St Niagara Falls NY 14302

ALBRITTAIN, MARY KATHERINE, guidance specialist; b. Leonardtown, Md., June 2, 1929; d. Thomas Wright and Anna (Swann) Wills; B.A., Western Md.Coll., 1951; M.A., George Washington U., Washington, 1967; m. William Miles, Oct. 13, 1951; children—William, Marianna, James, Kathryn, Thomas. Specialist guidance, coordinator career edn. Charles County (Md.) Bd. Edn., 1976—. Recipient merit award Md. Personnel and Guidance Assn., 1976. Mem. task forces Md. Dept. Edn., also advisory bds., coms.; co-chairperson Charles County Counselors Accountibility Com., 1972—. Mem. Charles County Edn. Assn. (sec. legis. com. 1950—), Md. Tchrs. Assn., So. Md. (pres. 1970-71), Am. Personnel and Guidance Assn., Md. (pres. 1977-78), Am. (Md. del. nat.conv. 1974-76) sch. counselor assns., Md. Assn. Non-White Concerns, other orgns. Home: Box 66 Popes Creek Rd Faulkner MD 20632 Office: Box D Charles County Bd Edn La Plata MD 20646

ALBUM, MANUEL MOSES, pedodontist; b. Phila., Nov. 20, 1919; s. Leon and Amelia (Sobel) A.; D.D.S., Temple U., 1943, postgrad., 1947, 50; postgrad. N.Y. U., 1946, U. Pa., 1949, U. Mich., 1956; m. Shirley E. Israel, Jan. 14, 1951; children—Michael Jeffrey, Fredlyn Jo. Pvt. practice dentistry as pedodontist, Jenkintown, Pa., 1950—; asst. surgeon Abington (Pa.) Hosp., 1950—; dental staff Grad. Hosp., Phila., 1963—; cons. Phila. Gen. Hosp., 1965—; prof. pediatric dentistry, dir. spl. patient clinic U. Pa. Sch. Dental Medicine, 1960-72; dir. dental services Children's Hosp. Phila., 1970-78. Vice pres. Camp Council for Underprivileged Children Phila., 1970—. Recipient Bronze medal Cannes (France) Film Festival, 1956. Served to maj. USAAF, 1943-46. Diplomate Am. Bd. Pedodontics. Fellow Am. Acad. Pedodontics, Internat. Coll. Dentists, Acad. Cerebral Palsy, Acad. Dentistry for Handicapped (pres. 1952-56), Am. Pub. Health Assn., Am. Coll. Dentists; mem. Nat. Soc. Crippled Children and Adults (dental cons. 1960-66), Nat. Assn. Retarded Children (mem. pub. health com. 1966-68), Internat. Assn. Dentistry for Children (pres.-elect 1977), Am. Soc. Dentistry for Children (pres. 1968-69), Alpha Omega. Club: Variety Tent 13 (Phila.). Contbr. to textbook on dentistry for children, also articles to profl. jours. Home: Develon Rd Melrose Park PA 19126 Office: Med Arts Bldg Jenkintown PA 19046

ALBURY, GEORGE DANIEL, accountant; b. Harbour Island, Bahamas, Mar. 18, 1948; s. Charles Curtis and Muriel Evandeline (Sweeting) A.; naturalized, 1970; B.S., Thomas S. Clarkson Coll. Tech., 1973; m. LaVerne Antoinette Dowdell, June 30, 1973; 1 dau., Tamara Vera-Nicole. Telephone sales rep. British Airways, Bahamas, 1965-67; cost clk. South Mall Assos., Albany, Summers, 1970-72; accountant Peat, Marwick, Mitchell & Co., N.Y.C., 1973—, supervising sr. accountant, 1978—. Ser ved with AUS, 1967-69. Decorated Bronze Star. Mem. Urban Bankers Coalition, Nat. Assn. Black Accountants, Omega Psi Phi. Mason. Home: 83-60 118th St Kew Gardens NY 11415 Office: 345 Park Ave New York City NY 10022

ALCABES, JOSEPH, hosp. adminstr.; b. N.Y.C., Mar. 16, 1931; s. Haim and Rebecca (Eskenazi) A.; B.C.E., City Coll. N.Y., 1952; M.B.A., Bernard Baruch Coll., 1958; m. Devorah Almeleh, Sept. 12, 1954; children—Howard, Philip. Engr., Bechtel Corp., N.Y.C., 1956-60; mgr. estimating, cost and scheduling div. Stone & Webster, Garden City, N.Y., 1960-69; dir. engring. planning L.I. Jewish Med. Center, New Hyde Park, N.Y., 1969-74; dir. planning Lincoln Med. Center, Bronx, N.Y., 1974-75, dir. adminstrv. services, 1976—; asst. v.p. Bronx-Lebanon Hosp. Center, 1978—; lectr. in field. Vice-pres., membership chmn. Morton Civic Assn., 1971-76; citizens adv. coms. budget and facility disposal Franklin Sq. Sch. Dist., 1968—; tech. adviser Franklin Sq. Citizens Assn., 1969-70. Registered profl. engr. N.Y., S.C. Mem. Greater N.Y. Hosp. Assn. (chmn. engring. adv. com. 1976-77), Am. Assn. Cost Engrs. (certified cost engr., dir. 1973-75), Am. Coll. Hosp. Adminstrs., Nat. Soc. Profl. Engrs., Am. Hosp. Assn. Hosp. Mgmt. Systems Soc., Hosp. Exec. Engrs. Assn. Greater N.Y., Am. Soc. Hosp. Engrs., Alumni Assn. City Coll. N.Y., Engrs. Joint Council, K.P. (chancelor 1966-67). Contbr. articles to profl. publs. Home: 483 Steven Ave West Hempstead NY 11552 Office: 234 E 149th St Bronx NY 10451

ALCALA, RAMON L., JR., obstetrician, gynecologist; b. Philippines, Nov. 27, 1937; s. Ramon U. Alcala and Abundia Loterte; M.D., U. of the East, 1963; m. Narcisa C. Pablo, M.D., Jan. 8, 1967; children—Ramon III, Ronald, Robert. Rotating intern St. John's Riverside Hosp., Yonkers, N.Y., 1964-65; resident in obstetrics, gynecology French Hosp., N.Y.C., 1965-66, Bklyn. Cumberland Med. Center, Bklyn., 1966-69, fellow in gynecologic oncology, 1969-70; practice medicine specializing in obstetrics, gynecology, Ramsey, N.J., 1974—; asst. attending obstetrician, gynecologist Bklyn. Cumberland Med. Center and Maimonides Hosp., Bklyn., 1972-74; attending obstetrician, gynecologist Valley Hosp., Ridgewood, N.J., Good Samaritan Hosp., Suffern N.Y., 1974—; clin. instr. obstetrics, gynecology State U. N.Y., Downstate Med. Center, Bklyn., 1972-74. Diplomate Am. Bd. Obstetrics and Gynecology. Mem. Am. Coll. Obstetricians and Gynecologists, N.J. State, Bergen County med. socs., Am. Assn. Gynecol. Laparoscopists. Office: 246 N Franklin Turnpike Ramsey NJ 07446

ALCAMO, FRANK PAUL, educator; b. South Fork, Pa., May 25, 1920; s. Carmelo and Antonia (Trifiro) A.; student Johnstown Coll., 1938-39; B.S., Indiana U. Pa., 1942; M.Ed., Pa. State U., 1954; m. Josephine Giusto, June 22, 1944; 1 dau., Antoinette. Math. and sci. tchr. Wilmore (Pa.) High Sch., 1942-54, Beaverdale (Pa.)-Wilmore High Sch., 1954-56; math. tchr. South Fork (Pa.)-Croyle High Sch., 1956-61, Triangle Area High Sch., Sidman, Pa., 1961-62; asst. prin. Windber (Pa.) Area High Sch., 1962-63, prin., 1963—. Treas., Windber Summer Playground Assn., 1963; chmn. Windber Police Civil Service Commn., 1964—. Bd. dirs. Johnstown Motor Club, Cambria County Sch. Fed. Credit Union, Windber Indsl. Devel. Assn.; v.p. Windber Pub. Library, 1976—; bd. dirs. Windber Recreation Assn., treas., 1974—. Served to lt. (j.g.) USNR, 1944-46. Mem. Pa. Edn. Assn. (local br. com. 1966-70, dept. adminstrn. pres. 1971-75, pres. Windber 1965-66), Somerset County Secondary Prins. Assn. (pres. 1965-66), NEA (life), Pa. Council Tchrs. Math., Am. Legion, Windber Sportsmen's Assn., Nat., Pa. assns. secondary sch. prins., PIAA (dist. treas. 1970—), Sons of Italy, Pa. Soc., Holy Name Soc., Phi Delta Kappa, Sigma Tau Gamma. Democrat. Roman Catholic. Rotarian. (dir. Windber 1964-69, 77—, pres. 1968-69). Home: 1011 Cambria Ave Windber PA 15963 Office: 23d St Windber PA 15963

ALDAN, DAVID RICHARD, bath fixtures mfg. co. exec.; b. New Castle, Pa., May 6, 1946; s. Traean Richard and Dorothy Jean (Thompson) A.; student Youngstown State Coll., 1965-68; m. Cynthia Luann Leicht, June 28, 1969; children—Erika Lyn, Brandon Todd. Laborer, D.D. Davis Constrn. Co., Youngstown, Ohio, 1968-71; moldmaker helper Universal-Rundle Corp., New Castle, Pa., 1972-75, research asst. fiberglass div., 1975-77, research asst. china div., 1977—. Co-chmn. indsl. dr. Lawrence County chpt. Am. Heart Assn., 1978; active United Fund, Easter Seal Soc. Mem. Am. Mgmt. Assn., Indsl. Mgmt. Club. Republican. Club: Eagles. Home: 25 West Mill St Mount Jackson PA 16102 Office: Bolt and Power Sts New Castle PA 16102

ALDERMAN, DONALD BRUCE, vascular surgeon; b. New Haven, Feb. 26, 1922; s. Sydney William and Anna Gertrude (Isacoff) A.; B.A., Yale, 1943; M.D., State U. N.Y., Downstate Med. Center, N.Y.C., 1946; m. Betsy G. Betzes, Dec. 24, 1944; children—Jeffrey A., Lawrence D., Cathie E. Intern, Montefiore Hosp., 1946-47; resident in surgery Newington (Conn.) VA Hosp., and Yale-New Haven Hosp., 1949-53; extern peripheral vascular surgery Mass. Gen. Hosp., Boston, Presbyn. Hosp., N.Y.C., Meth. Hosp., Houston, 1954-55; pvt. practice medicine specializing in vascular surgery, New Haven, 1955—; asst. clin. prof. surgery Yale, surgeon dept. univ. health, 1952-67; acting chief surgery U.S. Marine Hosp., Savannah, Ga., 1948-49; attending surgeon VA Hosp., West Haven, Conn., 1951-58, Yale-New Haven Med. Center, 1958—, Hosp. St. Raphael, 1957—; cons. surgeon Bradley Meml. Hosp., Southington, Conn., 1955—;. Served with USPHS, 1947-49. Diplomate Am. Bd. Surgery. Fellow A.C.S.; mem. Internat. Coll. Angiology, Internat. Soc. Chirurgy, AMA, Conn., New Haven, New Haven County med. socs., Am. Diabetes Assn., Am. Geriatrics Assn., Assn. Mil. Surgeons, Am. Coll. Angiology, Peripheral Vascular Soc. Am. (past pres.), Pan. Am. Med. Assn. Contbr. articles to profl. jours. Home: 19 Inwood Rd Woodbridge CT 06525 Office: 1423 Chapel St New Haven CT 06511

ALDIERI, MICHAEL JAMES, real estate appraiser; b. Bristol, Conn., May 8, 1933; s. Charles J. and Antoinette (Cassella) A.; student Hillyer Coll., 1956-58; m. Doris Laprise, Feb. 16, 1957; children—Sharon, Doreen, Michael, David. With Valuation Assos., Bridgeport, Conn., 1952-60, FHA, 1961-67; zone valuation advisor Michael J. Aldieri & Assos., Bristol, Conn., 1967-71; owner Aldieri-Heberger Assos., Inc., Bristol, Conn., 1971—; chmn. bd. N. Am. Bank, Wolcott-Bristol. Mem. Am. Inst. Real Estate Appraisers, Soc. Real Estate Appraisers. Club: Rotary (Bristol). Home: 22 Glenview Dr Bristol CT 06010 Office: PO Box 796 Bristol CT 06010

ALDIN, PETER, psychiatrist; b. Schwerin, Ger., Oct. 29, 1932; s. Otto and Elly (Meyerhoff) A.; came to U.S., 1952, naturalized, 1957; Baccalaureat en Philosophie, U. Paris, 1952; B.A. cum laude, Coll. City N.Y., 1954, M.A. in Psychology, 1955; M.D., Boston U., 1964; Ph.D. in Clin. Psychology, Clark U., 1967; m. Rosemarie Bersch, 1959; children—Michele, Kenneth. Psychology trainee Boston VA Hosp., 1958-60; intern Maimonides Hosp., Bklyn., 1964-65; resident in psychiatry Hillside Hosp., Glen Oaks, N.Y., 1965-68; practice medicine specializing in psychiatry, N.Y.C., 1968—; mem. staff Columbia U. Sch. Medicine, 1969—, St. Luke's Hosp., N.Y.C., 1969—; cons. in field. Diplomate Am. Bd. Neurology and Psychiatry. Mem. Am. (chmn.), N.Y. County (interprofl. relations com., legis. com.) psychiat. assns., AMA, N.Y. County Med. Soc. Address: 524 E 87th St New York City NY 10028

ALDRICH, ALTON PARKER, ret. educator, lectr.; b. East Killingly, Conn., July 13, 1904; s. James Prescot and Betsey (Owen) A.; grad. Putnam State Tech. Sch., 1922; B.S., Central Conn. State Coll., 1948; M.S., Cornell U., 1952; m. Bertha Lauf, Aug. 30, 1930 (dec. Dec.

1971). Journeyman electrician, 1922-26; instr. indsl. arts and indsl. electricity Conn. Dept. Edn., Danbury, 1926-54; asst. dir. Eli Whitney Tech. Sch., Hamden, Conn., 1954-56; asst. dir. to dir. Putnam Tech. Sch., 1956-59; dir. Harvard H. Ellis Tech. Sch., Danielson, Conn., 1959-74, ret., 1974; now lectr. Corporator, Bklyn. Savs. Bank. Mem. Killingly Parking Authority. Trustee Almond M. Paine Meml. Trust Fund; bd. dirs. Bapt. Homes, Inc., Putnam, Conn. Mem. Am., Conn. vocational assns., Am. Tech. Edn. Assn., Conn. Tech. Sch. Adminstrs. Assn., Orleans County (Vt.), Killingly (Conn.) hist. socs., Slater Mill Hist. Assn., Phi Delta Kappa. Baptist. Mason. Home: Bear Hill Rd PO Box 81 East Killingly CT 06243

ALDRICH, FRANK NATHAN, banker; b. Jackson, Mich., June 8, 1923; s. Frank Nathan and Marion (Butterfield) A.; student U. Md., summer 1943; A.B. in Govt., Dartmouth Coll., 1948; postgrad. Harvard U., summer 1948; m. Edna Dora DeJan, Nov. 21, 1956; children—Marion Dolores, Clinton Pershing. Sub-mgr. First Nat. Bank of Boston, Havana, Cuba, 1949-60, Rio de Janeiro, Brazil, 1961-62, sub-mgr., Sao Paulo, Brazil, 1963-64, mgr., 1965, exec. mgr., Rio de Janeiro, 1966, v.p. Brazilian brs., 1966-69, v.p. overseas ops., Boston, 1969-70, v.p. Latin Am.-Asia-Africa-Middle East div., Boston, 1970-72, sr. v.p. Latin Am. div., Boston, 1973—; exec. v.p., dir. Boston Overseas Financial Corp., Boston; chmn. bd. Caribbean Am. Service Investment & Finance Co. Ltd., Cayman Islands, Bank of Boston Trust Co., (Bahamas) Ltd., Nassau, dir. Corporacion Financiera de Boston, S.A., La Paz, Bolivia, Corporacion Internacional de Boston S.A., San Jose, Costa Rica, Sociedad Anonima Servicios e Inversiones, Buenos Aires, Boston S.A. Administracao e Empreendimentos, Sao Paulo, Brazil, Arrendadora Industrial Venezolana C.A., Caracas, Venezuela, Banco de Boston Dominicano S.A., Santo Domingo, Dominican Republic, Bank of Boston Internat., N.Y.C., Los Angeles and Miami. Served with USAAF, 1943-46. Decorated Air medal with 4 oak leaf clusters, D.F.C. (U.S.); medalha Marechal Candido Mariano da Silva Rondon (Brazil). Mem. Air Force Assn., Res. Officers Assn., Inst. Navigation, Royal Astron. Soc. Canada, Brit. Interplanetary Soc., Md. Hist. Soc., Am. C. of C. Rio de Janeiro, Am. C. of C. Sao Paulo, Sphinx Soc., Beta Theta Pi. Clubs: Masons, Shriners, Internat. (Washington); Yale, Dartmouth Coll. (N.Y.C.); American (Miami, Fla.); Harvard (Boston). Home: 3 Indian Spring Rd Dover MA 02030 Office: 100 Federal St Boston MA 02106

ALEKSANDROWICZ, LENA IORIO (BROWN), nursing adminstr.; b. Phila., Dec. 9, 1927; d. Louis and Anne (Iorio) Petrini; R.N., Meth. Hosp., Phila., 1949; B.S. in Nursing and Edn., Johns Hopkins U., 1964, M.Ed. in Counseling, 1967; postgrad. health care adminstrn., George Washington U., 1973; m. Edward A. Aleksandrowicz, Apr. 20, 1974; children—Carolyn Brown, Philip Brown. Staff nurse post-partum Meth. Hosp., Phila., 1951-52; head psychiat. nurse Crownsville (Md.) State Hosp., 1953-54; head med. surg. nurse Meth. Hosp., Phila., 1954-55; staff nurse cancer USPHS Hosp., Balt., 1956-57; head pediatrics nurse Sinai Hosp., Balt., 1957-62; instr. medicine surgery Union Meml. Hosp., Balt., 1962-65; clin. dir., asst. dir. medicine surgery Greater Balt. Med. Center, 1965-67; dir. nurses, asst. adminstr. Happy Hills Hosp., Balt., 1967-71; asst. adminstr. patient services Montgomery Gen. Hosp., Olney, Md., 1971-74; dir. maternal and child health nursing U. Md. Hosp., Balt., 1975-76, asso. dir. hosp. nursing services, 1976—. Advisory com. March of Dimes; trustee Md. Hosp. Edn. Inst., 1976—; chmn. nursing advisory com. Howard Community Coll., 1972-76. Mem. Am., Md. nurses assns., Meth. Hosp., Johns Hopkins U. alumnae assns., Phi Delta Gamma, Pi Lambda Theta. Home: 438 Park Creek Rd Pasadena MD 21122 Office: 22 S Green St Baltimore MD 21201

ALERS, JOSE OSCAR, sociologist; b. N.Y.C., Apr. 15, 1933; s. Jose Oscar and Paulina (Irizarry) A.; A.B. (sociol. research fellow), Coll. City N.Y., 1955; A.M. Harvard U., 1959; Ph.D., Cornell U., 1966; m. Miriam Elaine Schwartz, July 14, 1956; children—Neil Franklin, Scott Martin. Asst. prof. indsl. and labor relations Cornell U., Ithaca, 1965-68; asso. prof. sociology Boston Coll., 1968-71; staff asso. Population Council, N.Y.C., 1971-75; research dir. Puerto Rican Inst. Social Research, Flushing, N.Y., 1975-76; coordinator Puerto Rican Migration Research Consortium, N.Y.C., 1976—. New Eng. coordinator Peru Earthquake Relief Com., 1970; chmn. Puerto Rican Com. on 1980 Census, 1975—. Served with U.S. Army, 1955-57. Fellow Cornell U., 1961-63. Mem. Am. Sociol. Assn., Eastern Sociol. Soc., Population Assn. Am., Latin Am. Studies Assn., City Coll. Alumni Assn. Author: Dominacion y Cambios en el Peru Rural, 1969; Population Growth in Thailand, 1972; Family Planning in Thailand, 1972; The Thai Family Planning Statistics System, 1974; Continuation of Contraceptive Practice in Thailand, 1974; Puerto Ricans and Health: Findings from New York City, 1978; contbr. to profl. jours. Home: 1 Summit St Tarrytown NY 10591 Office: 205 Lexington Ave 12th Floor New York City NY 10016

ALEX, RALPH PAUL, aerospace cons. co. exec.; b. Brockton, Mass., Dec. 19, 1916; s. William J. and Christine C. A.; m. Louise A. Pesanelli, 1942; children—Paula A., Paul A. Aero. engr. Bell Aircraft Corp., Buffalo, 1937-39, Republic Aviation Corp., Farmingdale, N.Y., 1939-40, Wallace-Martin Aircraft Corp., Long Island City, N.Y., 1940-41; project engr., sr. product design engr., head product components design, asst. chief design and devel. Sikorsky Aircraft div. United Technologies, Stratford, Conn., after 1941, chief mktg. research and devel.; now pres. Ralph P. Alex & Assos., Inc., Fairfield, Conn.; aero. cons. Investment Trust Co., N.Y.C., 1938; tech. adviser NRC, USAAF Volcano Expdn., Uruapan, Mexico, 1945; cons. FAA, 1954—; lectr. helicopter tech. Recipient certificate of merit aerospace vehicle com. Am. Inst. Aeros. and Astronautics, 1963; Pioneer award Helicopter Assn. Am., 1973; Yuri Gagarin award USSR Sporting Aviation Club, 1977. Mem. Am. Helicopter Soc. (pres. 1943-44, 59-60, certificate of merit 1947, chmn. bd. 1960, hon. fellow 1964, chmn. nat. heliport com. 1965-67, chmn. Helicopter Ops. Forum 1973, v.p. internat. affairs 1970—, v.p. NE region: Alexander Klemin award 1977), Soc. Automotive Engrs., Air Force Assn., Am. Def. Preparedness Assn. (chpt. pres. 1977-78), Nat. Aeros. Assn. (dir. 1959-62), Army Aviation Assn. Am., Fedn. Aeronautique Internat. (pres. internat. helicopter com. 1961—, chief juror 1st, 2d and 3d World Helicopter competitions), Internat. Order Characters, 1st Calvary Div. Assn. (life). Club: Milford (Conn.) Yacht. Contbr. to Helicopter Section Science and Technology, 1968, Weapons Systems Acquisition Process, 1970; contbr. articles to tech. jours. and news media. Patentee in field. Home and Office: 1037 Stratfield Rd Fairfield CT 06432

ALEXANDER, CHRISTINA LILLIAN, pharmacist; b. N.Y.C., Dec. 25, 1942; d. Stanley Urich and Roselyn Helen (Joseph) A.; B.S. in Pharmacy, Fordham U., 1965; M.S. in Pharmacology, St. John's U., Jamaica, N.Y., 1977. Pharm. intern St. Vincent's Hosp. and Med. Center, N.Y.C., 1965-66; chief pharmacist Holy Family Hosp., Bklyn., 1966; asst. chief pharmacist N.Y. Polyclinic Hosp., N.Y.C., 1967-69; pharmacist Mt. Sinai Hosp. Med. Center, N.Y.C., 1969; night pharamcist Maimonides Med. Center, N.Y.C., 1969-71; pharamacist N.Y. U. Hosp. and Med. Center, 1971-72; night pharamacist, drug info. specialist Brookdale (N.Y.) Med. Center and Hosp., 1972—; clin. instr. in pharmacy Rutgers' U., New Brunswick, N.J., 1975, clin. cons. Coll. Pharmacy, 1977—; sec. internat. advisory council Am. Bd. Pharmacy, Internat. Recipient Scholarship Incentive award N.Y. State, 1960-65. Mem. Am. Museum Natural History (life), Am. Bd. Diplomates in Pharmacy, Internat., Federation Internationale Pharmaceutique, Fedn. Am. Scientists, AAAS, Am. Pharm. Assn., Am. Soc. Hosp. Pharmacists, Fordham U. Coll. Pharmacy Alumni Fedn. (dir.), Rho Chi. Democrat. Roman Catholic. Clubs: Nevisians Am. (treas. N.Y. chpt. 1977), Fordham of N.Y., Cornell of N.Y. (asso.). Home: 3333 F Henry Hudson Pkwy Riverdale NY 10463

ALEXANDER, GABRIEL ALEXANDER, economist; b. Cambridge, Mass.; s. Alexander Gabriel and Varsenig L. A.; B.S., Tufts U., 1950; M.A., Trinity Coll., 1957; m. Sonia Etmekdjian, Mar. 22, 1959; children—Mark Gabriel, Carol Elaine, Patricia Anne. With Raytheon Co., Lexington, Mass., 1957-64; cons. Non Ferrous Metals and Natural Gas Industry, 1964-68; mgr. econometrics and industry analysis United Technologies Corp., Hartford, Conn., 1968—. Active bd. Jr. Achievement; mem. adminstrv. bd., commn. chmn. United Methodist Ch. of New Canaan; chmn. bd. dirs. Planners League. Mem. Nat. Assn. Bus. Economists, Am. Mktg. Assn., Am. Rocket Soc., N. Am. Soc. for Corp. Planning. Home: 154 Fieldcrest Rd New Canaan CT 06840 Office: United Technologies Corp 1 Financial Plaza Hartford CT 06101

ALEXANDER, HAROLD, bioengr., educator; b. N.Y.C., Nov. 12, 1940; s. Jack and Freda (Koltun) A.; B.S., N.Y. U., 1962, M.S., 1963, Ph.D., 1967; m. Sheila M. Eisner, Dec. 20, 1964; children—Robin, Andrea. Asst. research scientist N.Y. U., Bronx, 1966-67, asso. research scientist, 1967-68; asst. prof. Stevens Inst. Tech., Hoboken, N.J., 1968-71, asso. prof., 1971-77, co-dir. med. engring. lab., 1973-77, head lab. balloon tech., 1968-74; asso. prof. dept. surgery, dir. biomechanics lab. N.J. Med. Sch., Newark, 1977—; lectr. in pediatrics Mt. Sinai Sch. of Medicine, N.Y.C., 1975-77; cons. Johnson & Johnson Research Labs., New Brunswick, N.J., 1975-76; vis. prof. Coll. Engring., Rutgers U., 1975-76; adviser on fabrication of balloons USAF, 1968-74; v.p. C.A.S., Inc., 1974—. NSF travel grantee, 1975. Mem. ASME, Soc. for Biomaterials, N.J. Orthopedic Soc. Contbr. articles on applications of mechanics and engring. to medicine; contbr. chpts. on balloon research to books; research in cardiovascular bioengring.; instrumental for development of new system in measurement of infant blood pressure. Home: 47 Elmwood Pl Short Hills NJ 07078 Office: 100 Bergen St G-574 Newark NJ 07103

ALEXANDER, JON, educator; b. Carbondale, Ill., Jan. 2, 1940; s. Orville Burris and Ola (Anderson) A.; B.A., So. Ill., U., 1960, M.A., 1961; Ph.D., U. Kans., 1966; m. Linda Marie Tripp, Sept. 5, 1962; children—Jon Burris, Gern. Asst. prof. polit. sci. and internat. affairs Carleton U., Ottawa, 1967—; vis. scholar Center Study Democratic Instns., Santa Barbara, 1965-66; vis. asst. prof. Emory U., Atlanta, 1966-67, Columbia U., summer 1967; sci. adviser Sci. Council Can., 1974. Precinct committeeman Democratic Party, Lawrence, Kans., 1964; bd. dirs. West End Coop. Nursery Sch., Ottawa, 1975-77, Center for Devel. Community Resources, 1972-75, Ottawa Valley Home Builders Coop., 1976—, Ottawa Country Lot Devel. Corp., 1976—. Francis Drown Found. fellow, 1965. Mem. Am., Internat. polit. sci. assns., Internat. Studies Assn., Candian Assn. Univ. Tchrs. Presbyterian. Editorial bd. Survival mag., 1974. Home: Route 1 Osgoode ON K0A 2W0 Canada Office: Dept Political Science Carleton Univ Ottawa K1S 5B6 Canada

ALEXANDER, LEE, mayor; b. Jersey City, May 18, 1927; s. Peter and Rita (Rovatcos) A.; B.A., Syracuse U., 1950, J.D., 1955; m. Elizabeth Strates, May 12, 1957; children—James Matthew, Rita, Stacy. Admitted to N.Y. bar, 1955; practiced in Syracuse, 1955-69; mayor City of Syracuse, 1969—; mem. adv. bd. U.S. Conf. Mayors, 1971-76, v.p., 1976, pres., 1977-78, mem. legislative action com., 1971-76. Councilman-at-large, Syracuse, 1966-69; nat. chmn. Cyprus Relief Fund, Inc., Cyprus Children's Fund Am., Inc., 1975—; trustee Syracuse U., Everson Mus.; pres.'s asso. LeMoyne Coll. Sereed with AUS, 1944-46. Mem. Nat. League Cities (adv. bd. 1971—, chmn. community devel. com. 1970-73). Democrat. Mem. Greek Orthodox Ch. (archon dep.). Home: 314 Summit Ave Syracuse NY 13207 Office: 201 City Hall Syracuse NY 13202

ALEXANDER, LUCILLE DILLINGER, musician, educator; b. Edina, Mo., Oct. 4, 1921; d. James Marion and Bernice Lucille (Brown) Dillinger; student U. Mo., 1939-41; B.S. in Edn., N.E. Mo. State Coll., 1942, M.A., Columbia, 1946, postgrad. Tchrs. Coll., 1955-76; m. Robert Sherwin Alexander, Mar. 22, 1959; children—Michael, Mark, Jennifer; children by previous marriage—Jan Edward Helfeld, Thomas Helfeld. Band and orch. dir. pub. schs., Berkeley City, Mo., 1942, Memphis, Mo., 1943, Moravia, Iowa, 1943, Guilford, Conn., 1946-48, San Juan, Puerto Rico, 1950-54; choral dir. pub. schs. West Hempstead, N.Y., 1955, Brentwood, N.Y., 1956-58, Yonkers, N.Y., 1959; band dir. pub. schs., N.Y.C., 1963, Kinnelon, N.J., 1964-66, Wayne, N.J., 1966—; tchr. dancing Dales Studios, N.Y.C., 1944-46, Fred Astaire Studios, N.Y.C., 1954-55. Precinct worker Democratic Party, Hannibal, Mo., 1939-40, New Haven, 1946-48, N.Y.C., 1958-64; committeewoman, Manhattan County Dem. Com., 1963-64, Passaic County Dem. Com., 1975—. Served as pilot in WASP, 1943. Mem. Music Educators Nat. Conf., Mensa, Nat. Assn. Jazz Educators, Am. String Tchrs. Assn., N.J. Sch. Music Assn., Nat. Sch. Orch. Assn., NOW, Nat. Band Assn., Women Band Dirs. Nat. Assn., Montclair Operetta Club (bd. govs. 1975—), Packanack Players. Arranger pub. band, orch. and choral music, 1970-75. Home: 56 Chestnut Dr Wayne NJ 07470 Office: Board Office Nellis Drive Wayne NJ 07470

ALEXANDER, MYRNA B., counselor, psychotherapist, educator; b. Phila., Apr. 13, 1949; d. Max and Mildred (Ethridge) Bock; B.A. with honors, U. Md., 1971, M.A., 1972; postgrad. George Washington U., 1976—. Tchr., Prince George's County (Md.) Bd. Edn., 1971-72; rehab. counselor Kensington (Md.) Workshop for the Handicapped, 1972, Area D Community Mental Health Center, Washington, 1972; mental health counselor Melwood Tng. Center for the Mentally Retarded, Upper Marlboro, Md., 1973, Learning Disability Center, Clinton, Md., 1973; pvt. practice mental health counseling College Park, Md., 1973—; mental health counselor Prince George's Gen. Hosp., Cheverly, Md., 1974—; therapeutic social program dir. Walden Resource, Inc., Kensington, Md., 1974; guest lectr. Women's Homemakers Group, Landover, Md., 1976, Women's Referral Service, Adelphi, Md., 1977; designer crisis intervention tng. program Prince George's Community Coll., Md., 1975-78; guest lectr. dept. of community devel. and family mgmt. U. Md., 1976, 77. Certified marriage and family counselor, rehab. counselor. Mem. Am. Rehab. Counseling Assn., Am. Personnel and Guidance Assn., Am. Soc. for Tng. and Devel., Am. Assn. Marriage and Family Therapists, Am. Assn. Sex Educators, Counselors and Therapists, Phi Kappa Phi, Kappa Delta Pi. Contbr. articles on counseling and human devel. to profl. jours. Home: 3801 Kenilworth Ave Apt 316 E Bladensburg MD 20710 Office: Emergency Psychiatric Service Prince George's General Hosp Cheverly MD 20785

ALEXANDER, RAYMOND DANIEL, JR., wire co. rep.; b. Darby, Pa., Dec. 31, 1947; s. Raymond Daniel and Mary Jane (Gordon) A.; B.S. in Communications, Emerson Coll., 1970; m. Judith Ann Russo, Sept. 16, 1972. Asso. dir. NBC, N.Y.C., 1971-73; regional sales and marketing mgr. Ullrich Copper Co., Inc., Kenilworth, N.J., 1973-78; regional account mgr. Essex Group div. United Technologies, South Hackensack, N.J., 1978—. News and sports announcer/writer Sta. WCTC and WMGQ-FM, New Brunswick, N.J., 1973—, talk show host, 1974-76. Recipient Peabody award, 1972, 73. Home: 296 Carlton Club Dr Piscataway NJ 08854 Office: State and Congress Dr South Hackensack NJ 07602

ALEXANDER, ROBERT WILLIAM, radiologist; b. Reading, Pa., May 30, 1924; s. Robert Mackey and Jessie Forbes (Smith) A.; student Swarthmore Coll., 1942-44; M.D., Jefferson Med. Coll., 1948; m. Nancy Ann Wetty, June 19, 1964; children—William, Heather. Intern, Phila. Gen. Hosp., 1948-49, resident in radiology, 1950-52; radiologist San Antonio Med. and Surg. Clinic, 1954, Hamburg (Pa.) Hosp., 1965—; individual practice medicine specializing in radiology, Reading, 1955—; cons. VA Hosp., Lebanon, Pa. Bd. dirs. Vis. Nurse Assn. Reading, 1959—, Reading chpt. Am. Lung Assn., 1960—; chmn. profl. div. United Fund Reading, 1968; bd. dirs. Reading chpt. ARC, 1970-76; pres. Berks County Tb Soc., 1970—. Served with U.S. Army, 1952-54; PTO. Nat. Cancer Inst. fellow, 1952-53; diplomate Am. Bd. Radiology. Fellow Am. Coll. Radiology; mem. Berks County (pres. 1964), Pa. (chmn. council govtl. relations 1977—) med. socs., AMA (del. 1974—), Pa., N. Am., Phila., Blockly radiol. socs., Reading-Berks C. of C. (dir. 1966-73). Republican. Presbyterian. Clubs: Kiwanis (pres. Reading 1966), Berkshire Country (dir. 1964-69) (life). Contbr. articles to profl. publs., 1948-55. Home: 1417 Old Mill Rd Wyomissing PA 19610 Office: 544 Elm St Reading PA 19601

ALEXANDER, THERON, psychologist, writer; s. Theron and Mary Helen (Jones) A.; Ph.D. U. Chgo., 1949; m. Marie Bailey; children—Thomas Alexander, Mary (Mrs. George Zerwas). Research prof. Community Studies Center of Temple U., 1966-68, dir. Child Devel. Research Center, 1966-69, prof. human devel. and ednl. psychology, 1966—; lectr., Sao Paulo, Brazil, 1977. Served with USNR, World War II; PTO. Fellow Am. Psychol. Assn.; mem. Eastern Psychol. Assn., Sigma Xi. Author: Psychotherapy in Our Society, 1963; Children and Adolescents, 1969; Human Development in an Urban Age, 1973.

ALEXANDRU, RENE SIMIONESCU, civil engr.; b. Romania, June 3, 1939; s. Neculai and Eugenia (Buturca) S.; diploma civil engring. Inst. Constrn., Bucharest, Romania, 1960; m. Marie Molineaux, Mar. 31, 1973; 1 dau., Sarah Jocelyn. Project engr. comml. bldgs. Ants P. Leemets, Constrn. Engrs., N.Y.C., 1970-71; sr. design engr., structural engr. Aggra (Brazil) Nuclear Power Plant, Gibbs & Hills Inc., N.Y.C., 1971-73; prin. civil engr. Ebasco Services, Inc., N.Y.C., 1973—, lead engr. nuclear power plants Conn. (Millstone 1), Tex. (Allen's Creek). Registered profl. engr., N.Y. Mem. Am. Concrete Inst., ASCE. Research in Mark III containment concept for boiling water nuclear plants. Home: 233 E 69th St Apt 15 N New York NY 10021 Office: 19 Rector St New York NY 10006

ALEXY, CORNELIUS G. LOUIS, ultrasonic equipment co. exec.; b. N.Y.C., Dec. 9, 1943; s. Bela C. and Pauline (Wirth) A.; m. Sharon Mary Adams, Sept. 30, 1967; children—James Louis, Jeremiah Adam, Joseph David. Electronic technician Branson Inst., Inc., Stamford, Conn., 1961-63, field sales and service, 1964-66, mgr. service dept., 1966, supr. electronic testing, 1966-68, supr. mfg. spl. systems, 1968-73; owner, gen. mgr. Alexy Assos., sales and mfg. ultrasonic equipment, Georgetown, Conn., 1973—. Lutheran. Clubs: Masons. Home: Maple St Weston CT 06883 Office: Alexy Assos Georgetown CT 06829

ALFANO, BLAISE FRANCIS, surgeon; b. Boston, Sept. 14, 1923; s. Frank and Frances M. (Palopoli) A.; A.B., Harvard, 1946; M.D., Tufts U., 1950; m. Virginia Forte, Sept. 19, 1953; children—Blaise Francis (dec.), Kathryn, Mark, Stephen, Paul. Intern Cambridge (Mass.) City Hosp., 1950-51, resident surgery, 1951-54; sr. surg. staff Melrose-Wakefield Hosp., Melrose, Mass., 1954—, New Eng. San. and Hosp., Stoneham, Mass., 1954—, Winchester (Mass.) Hosp., 1954—; mem. surg. teaching staff Cambridge Hosp., 1954-64. Mem. adv. bd. Middlesex County (Mass.) Nat. Bank, 1966—, chmn., 1969-76, now dir.; dir. Bay Bank of Middlesex. Diplomate Am. Bd. Abdominal Surgery (sec. 1958—). Fellow Am. Geriatrics Soc.; mem. AMA, Mass., Middlesex East Dist. med. socs., Am. Soc. Abdominal Surgeons (exec. sec. 1959—), AAAS, Assn. Med. and Applied Publs., Inst. Advancement Med. Communication, Am. Med. Writers Assn., Med. Soc. Execs. Assn., Clin. Congress Abdominal Surgeons, Phi Beta Phi. Home: 22 Everett Ave Winchester MA 01890 Office: 675 Main St Melrose MA 02176

ALFONSO, ANTONIO ESCOLAR, surgeon; b. Manila, Philippines, Nov. 25, 1943; s. Ricardo Lagdameo and Marita (Escolar) A.; came to U.S., 1968; A.B. cum laude, Ateneo U., 1963; M.D. cum laude, Univ. of the Philippines, 1968; m. Teresita Nazareno, Apr. 25, 1970; children—Margaretta, Roberto. Intern., U. Philippines-Philippine Gen. Hosp., 1967-68; instr. surgery Temple U., Phila., 1968-72; sr. fellow surg. oncology Meml. Sloan Kettering Cancer Center, N.Y.C., 1972-74; fellow surgery Cornell U. Med. Center, N.Y.C., 1972-74; dir. head and neck surgery service Downstate Med. Center, Bklyn., 1974—, asso. dir. div. surg. oncolongy, 1974—; asst. prof. surgery, 1974-77, asso. prof. surgery, 1977—; cons. head and neck surgery Bklyn. VA Hosp., 1974—. Recipient research essay prize, N.Y. Colon and Rectal Surg. Soc., 1973; Am. Cancer Soc. grantee, 1978; diplomate Am. Bd. Surgery. Mem. Assn. of Academic Surgeons, Am. Soc. of Clin. Oncology, Am. Assn. for Cancer Edn., Soc. of Head and Neck Surgeons, A.C.S., N.Y., Bklyn. surg. socs., N.Y. Cancer Soc., Soc. Surg. Oncology, N.Y. Soc. of Colon and Rectal Surgeons, Phi Kappa Phi. Roman Catholic. Contbr. articles in field to profl. jours. and chpts. to textbooks. Home: 69-03 112th St Forest Hills NY 11375 Office: Box 40 450 Clarkson Ave Brooklyn NY 11203

ALFULTIS, RICHARD JOSEPH, ofcl. Transp. Dept.; b. Oran, Mo., June 29, 1928; s. Henry Owen and Sarah Carolyn (Barnhill) A.; B.S., S.E. Mo. U., 1951; M.P.A., St. Louis U., 1959; m. Janet Marie Baronowsky, May 30, 1953; children—Lisa Jo, Gail Ann. With CSC, St. Louis, 1952-62; chief employment br. FAA, Washington, 1962-66, personnel officer, Honolulu, 1966-70; dep. dir. Office Adminstrv. Ops., Office Sec. Transp., Washington, 1970-71; asst. dir. adminstrn. Cost of Living Council, Washington, 1971-73; dir. personnel and tng. Dept. Transp., Washington, 1973-77, dep. asst. sec. for adminstrn., 1977—. Served with USMC, 1946-48, 50-51. Office: 400 7th St SW Washington DC 20590

ALI, MAJID, pathologist, lab. dir.; b. Sheikhura, Pakistan, June 27, 1940; s. Azam and Skina (Begum) A.; came to U.S., 1966, naturalized, 1977; M.B., B.S., King Edward Med. Coll., Lahore, Pakistan, 1963; m. Talat Ali, Apt. 1, 1966; children—Sarah, Omar, Amir. Resident in surgery Princess Margaret Hosp., Swindon, Eng., 1966; resident in pathology Holy Name Hosp., Teaneck, N.J., 1968, pathologist, 1972-74, dir. labs., 1974—; resident in pathology Columbia Presbyn. Hosp., N.Y.C., 1972; adj. asst. prof. pathology Columbia U., N.Y.C., 1975—. Treas. Ahmadiyya Movement in Islam, Teaneck, 1976-77. Fellow Am. Coll. Pathologists, Royal Coll. Surgeons (Eng.); mem. Am. Soc. Clin. Pathologists, AMA. Prin. author: Pathology Review,

6th edit. 1978; Surgical Pathology, Case Studies, 1978; research immunochemistry. Home: 19 Edgemont Pl Teaneck NJ 07666

ALI, SYED WAJED, engr.; b. Bangladesh, Oct. 1, 1939; s. Syed Shahed and Ajimon Nessa (Begum) A.; came to U.S., 1974; diploma mech. engring. Dacca Poly. Inst., 1961; Asso. Mech. Engring. Quality Tech., Poly. S. Bank, London, 1969; m. Aganesh Ali, Aug. 12, 1967; children—Syed Omar, Anjana. Engr. quality control Internat. Computers Ltd., London, 1968-71; mgr. quality control Oliver Pell Control Ltd., London, 1971-74; technician quality control Syntech Corp., Rockville, Md., 1974—. Mem. Am. Soc. Quality Control (certified quality technician), Inst. Quality Assurance London (corporate). Home: 14318 Astrodome Dr Silver Spring MD 20906 Office: 11810 Parklawn Dr Rockville MD 20852

ALIANO, RICHARD ANTHONY, educator; b. N.Y.C., Oct. 26, 1946; s. Albert Anthony and Ann (Barbera) A.; B.A. magna cum laude, Queens Coll., 1968, M.A., 1969; Ph.D., City U. N.Y., 1973. Lectr. polit. sci. Queens Coll., N.Y.C., 1969-73, asst. prof., 1973—. Served with Army NG, 1969-75. N.Y. State Regents teaching fellow, 1969-70; teaching fellow, 1969-70. Mem. Am., N.E. polit. sci. assns., AAUP, Assn. Italian Am. Faculty City U., Phi Beta Kappa. Republican. Roman Catholic. Author: American Defense Policy from Eisenhower to Kennedy, 1975; The Crime of World Power, 1978. Home: 75-08 249th St Bellerose NY 11426

ALIHAN, MILLA, indsl. psychologist and sociologist, mgmt. counsel; b. Vladikavkas, Russia; d. Alexander and Maria Sidamon (Tolpar) A.; M.A., Smith Coll.; Ph.D., Columbia; m. Bertram Cecil Eskell, July 16, 1938 (dec.). Lectr. sociology Smith Coll., Barnard Coll., Columbia; editorial advisor Can. Forum publ.; editorial writer Good Housekeeping mag.; pub. relations exec. transp., housing and welfare sects. N.Y. World's Fair; publicity dir. Beekman Downtown Hosp., Bldg. and Maintenance Fund, 1941-42; simultaneous interpreter Nurenberg trials, U.S. War Dept., 1946; pres. Milla Alihan Assos., 1945—; cons. Kollsman Instrument Corp., 1945-59, Paul Kollsman Labs., 1947-50, Walter Kidde & Co., Inc., 1953-65, Walter Kidde Constructors, Inc., 1953-58, Avien, Inc., 1956-63, Colvin Labs. Socony-Mobil, McKinsey & Co., Inc., 1959-65, Genesco Inc., Seaboard World Airlines, Inc., Eastern Air Lines, others; faculty Internat. Grad. U., Switzerland, Internat. Grad. Sch. Behavioral Sci. Fla. Inst. Tech.; lectr. in field profl. orgns., hosps., univs., civic and ednl. groups; trustee, mem. supervisory psychol. staff Morton Prince Clinic for Hypnotherapy, N.Y.C. Named one of state's outstanding women N.J. Tercentenary Com. Fellow Am. Sociol. Soc.; mem. Am. Psychol. Assn., Am. Mgmt. Assn., Am. Acad. Psychotherapists, Internat. Soc. Clin. and Exptl. Hypnosis, Inst. Research in Hypnosis (dir.), Mensa, Internat. Platform Assn., Aviation Writers Assn., Caucasion Soc. Allaverdy. Author synchronized Eng. script: Wait for Me, 1944; author: Social Ecology, 1938, 2d edit., 1964; Corporate Etiquette, 1970, German edit. 1970, Portuguese edit. 1971, paperback edit., 1974, German paperback edit., 1976. Editor: America, 1944; Illustrated America, 1944. Contbr. articles, brochures in field. Home: 15 Litchfield Rd Port Washington Long Island NY 11050 Office: 25 E 83d St New York City NY 10028

ALILUNAS, LEO JOHN, educator; b. DeKalb, Ill., Apr. 4, 1912; s. John and Marian (Kasarskis) A.; B.J., U. Mo., 1933, M.A., 1938; Ph.D., U. Mich., 1946; m. Wilma Kleive, June 17, 1939; children—John Kleive, Kristine Horne. Instr. pub. schs., Davis, Ill., 1935-37; tchr. Kemper Mil. Sch., Boonville, Mo., 1938-40, Dearborn (Mich.) High Sch., 1940-43, Ann Arbor (Mich.) Pub. Schs., 1944-45; prof. edn. State U. of N.Y. Coll., Fredonia, 1946—; vis. prof. edn. U. Mich., summer 1950, U. Vt., summer 1956, Mich. State U., summers 1960-65. Cons. religion and social sci. Tchr. Edn. and Religion Project, 1953-57; mem. citizens adv. com. Dunkirk (N.Y.) Urban Renewal Project, 1966-73. Recipient prize for best hist. research publ. Jour. Negro History, 1940; Research Found. State U. N.Y. research grantee, 1962-63, 70-71. Mem. Am. Sociol. Hist of Edn. Soc., AAUP, Nat. Soc. Coll. Tchr. Edn., Nat. Council Social Studies, Phi Kappa Phi, Phi Delta Kappa. Presbyn. (elder 1957—). Author: (with J.W. Sayre) Youth Faces American Citizenship, 1970. Compiler, editor: Lithuanians in the United States: Selected Studies, 1978. Contbr. articles to profl. jours. Home: 29 Birchwood Dr Fredonia NY 14063

ALINSANGAN, HERMENEGILDO ALIGAEN, pathologist; b. Alimodian, Iloilo, Philippines, June 19, 1931; s. Juan A. and Soledad (Aligaen) A.; M.D., U. Santo Tomas, Manila, 1957; m. Joyce Lorraine Brinson, Nov. 27, 1974; children—Nancy Soledad, Heather Priscilla. Intern, South Shore Hosp., Chgo., 1959; resident in pathology Community Hosp. Glen Cove, N.Y., 1964; resident pathologist Jewish Hosp. Montreal, Que., Can., 1964-65, Reddy Meml. Hosp., Montreal, 1965-66, Jewish Hosp., Montreal, 1966-68; pathologist, dir. labs. James Paton Meml. Hosp., Gander, Nfld., Can., 1968—. Diplomate Am. Bd. Pathology. Mem. Coll. Am. Pathologists, Canadian Med. Assn., Nfld. Med. Assn. Roman Catholic. Home: 65 Memorial Dr Gander NF Canada Office: James Paton Meml Hosp Gander NF A1V 1A5 Canada

ALIO, IVAN STAMENITOV, ofcl. Peace Corps; b. Sofia, Bulgaria, May 26, 1921; s. Peter and Elizabeth (Alio) S.; came to U.S., 1954, naturalized, 1958; D.M., Sofia Gymnasium, 1940; M.D., U. Tubingen (Ger.), 1945; M.P.H., Johns Hopkins, 1955; Dr. Pub. Health Epidemiology, Columbia, 1968; hon. prof. Sch. Chinese Medicine, Seoul, Korea, 1958; m. Geraldine Riley, July 1, 1955; children—Elizabeth, John, Richard, Jamila. Intern, Alexander Hosp., Sofia, 1946-47; practice medicine, Bulgaria and Italy, 1947-49; med. officer jungle dispensary, Burzual de Apure, Venezuela, 1949-50; dir. floating health center along Orinoco River, Venezuela, 1950-53; phys. malariologist 10th Internat. Course Metaxenic Diseases, Maracay, Venezuela, 1953-54; chief preventive medicine, Ft. Chaffee, Ark., 1954-56; resident in family practice Ireland Army Hosp., Ft. Knox, 1957-58; preventive medicine adviser to Surgeon Gen. Korean Army, 1958-60; phys. epidemiologist Dhahran (Saudi Arabia) Health Center, 1960-69; cons. WHO, 1970; tech. specialist Peace Corps, Washington, 1970-73, med. dir., 1973—. Served to maj. AUS, 1955-60. Recipient Physician Recognition award AMA, 1969. Fellow Am. Pub. Health Assn., Royal Soc. Tropical Medicine and Hygiene; mem. Am. Soc. Tropical Medicine and Hygiene, Assn. Mil. Surgeons U.S., Res. Officers Assn., 38th Parallel, Gulf med. socs., Tri-dist., Lebanon med. assns., Am. Assn. Fgn. Med. Grads., Soc. Epidemiol. Research, Med. Soc. D.C., . Interagy. Com. Nutrition Edn., Epidemiol. Working Group, Smithsonian Assos., Internat. Health Soc. Home: 43 McPherson Rd Annapolis MD 21401 Office: Peace Corps 806 Connecticut Ave Washington DC 20525

ALISON, DARCY WILLIAM, retail co. exec.; b. Galt, Ont., Can., Apr. 22, 1925; s. Thomas Joseph and Edith Margaret (Cooper) A.; student pvt. schs.; m. Jeanne Shirley Willson, Apr. 30, 1949; children—Ford Thomas, Timothy James. Asst. mfg. mgr. Kawneer Can., Toronto, Ont., 1957-61, asst. to sec. treas., 1963-66; mgr. systems and services Becker Milk Co., Toronto, 1967—; systems cons. Ont. Ministry Colls. and Univs., 1974—. Mem. Assn. for Systems Mgmt. (internat. dir., achievement award), Canadian Info. Processing Soc. Author: Basic Systems Course-Association for Systems Mgmt., 1974. Home. 3 Ashgrove Pl Don Mills ON M3B 2Y9 Canada Office: 671 Warden Ave Scarborough ON M1L 3Z7 Canada

ALL, FRANK EDWARD, devel. engr.; b. Grand Gorge, N.Y., June 26, 1941; s. Lambert W. and Zada M. (Lutz) A.; A.A., Delhi Tech. Inst., 1961; B.S., U. Ga., 1963; m. Bonny Lynn Kaufman, July 5, 1964; children—Darrin, Karen. Tech. service rep. Am. Can Co., Union, N.J., 1966-71; retail mcht., Hazlet, N.J., 1971-75; sr. devel. engr. Mobil Chem. Co., Macedon, N.Y., 1976—. Little League coach, Middletown, N.J., 1968-70; mem. Middletown (N.J.) Youth Athletic Assn. Served to capt. USMC, 1963-66. Mem. Am. Dairy Sci. Assn., Am. Chem. Soc. Republican. Methodist. Club: Kiwanis (Middletown). Home: RD 3 Box 291 Newark NY 14513 Office: Tech Center Mobil Chem Co Macedon NY 14513

ALLAIRE, ROYAL PHILLIP, electronic co. exec.; b. Northampton, Mass., Sept. 12, 1915; s. Ovila and Agnes L. (Rogers) A.; B.S., U. Mass., 1938; M.S., U. Notre Dame, 1940; M.B.A., Northeastern U., 1959; Ph.D., Walden U., 1978. Dept. head physics and math. St. Bede Jr. Coll., Peru, Ill., 1940-42; staff mem. Mass. Inst. Tech., Cambridge, 1942-45; with Raytheon Co., Waltham, Mass., 1945—, mgr. microwave and power tube div. facilities, 1968—. Registered profl. engr., Calif., Mass.; certified mfg. engr., certified plant engr. Mem. Am. Phys. Soc., Raytheon Employees Credit Union (dir., v.p. 1955—), Soc. Mfg. Engrs., Internat. Mgmt. by Objectives Inst., Sigma Xi. Home: 19 Pearson Dr Warwick RI 02888 Office: Foundry Ave Waltham MA 02154

ALLAN, HUGH DAVID, pump corp. exec.; b. Toronto, Ont., Can., Feb. 25, 1925; s. Arthur Alexander and Gladys (Gurney) A.; A.B. in Sci., U. Toronto, 1946; m. Susan Mary Barclay, May 17, 1947; children—H. Michael, Barbara S., David G. Estimator, John Inglis Co., Ltd., Toronto, Ont., Can., 1946-47, sales engr., dept. mgr., 1947-55; asst. to gen. mgr. Worthington (Can.) Ltd., 1956-57, gen. sales mgr., 1957-60, v.p., gen. mgr., 1960-65, pres., gen. mgr., 1965-74, chmn., pres., gen. mgr., 1974-76; group v.p. corp. devel. Worthington Pump Inc., Mountainside, N.J., 1976—. Mem. Assn. Profl. Engrs. Ont. Mem. United Church of Canada. Clubs: Rosedale Golf (Toronto), Badminton and Racquet (Toronto). Home: 6 Cleveland Rd Summit NJ 07901 Office: 270 Sheffield St Mountainside NJ 07092

ALLAN, JAMES DAVIS, surgeon; b. Newark, July 14, 1924; s. Robert Williamson and Florence Isabell (Blake) A.; A.B., Cornell U., 1947, M.D., 1951; m. Katharine Jane Thiffault, Sept. 27, 1951; children—Leslie Allan Mullane, James Davis, Scott W., Andrea. Intern, Newark City Hosp., 1951-52; resident in surgery N.Y.U.-Bellevue Med. Center, 1952-53, Martland Med. Center, N.J., 1953-56; surgeon Douglas Clinic, Westfield, Mass., 1956-59; practice medicine specializing in surgery, West Springfield, Mass., 1959—; sr. examiner FAA; med. staff Providence Hosp., Holyoke, Mass.; dir. Blue Shield Mass., Inc. Chmn. Baystate Physicians Polit. Action Com., 1971-73; mem. adv. bd. Mass. Registry Motor Vehicles, 1974—. Served to 1st lt. USAAF, 1942-45, to maj. M.C., USAF, 1951-61. Decorated D.F.C., 6 Air Medals, Purple Heart. Diplomate Am. Bd. Surgery. Fellow A.C.S.; mem. Mass. (chmn. bylaws), Hampden Dist. med. socs., AMA, Am. Cancer Soc. Roman Catholic. Asso. editor Hampden Hippocrat, 1971-75. Contbr. articles to profl. jours. Office: 75 Van Deene Ave West Springfield MA 01089

ALLARD, PIERRE, educator, psychologist; b. Quebec City, Que., Can., Nov. 9, 1938; s. Napoleon and Antoinette (Olivier) A.; B.A., Marist Coll. (Mass.), 1961; B.Ped., U. Laval (Can.), 1962, diploma Ecole Normale Supérieure, 1968; B.Th., U. Ottawa (Can.), 1964, M.A., 1966; Ph.D., U. Mich., 1972; Ph.D., Heed U., 1976. Educator, Inst. St. Georges, Chicoutimi, Que., 1962-63, dir. clin. services, 1966-69; prof. psycho-edn. Bon-Pasteur, Chicoutimi, 1967-68; prof. psychology Cardinal Bégin Tchrs. Coll., Chicoutimi, 1968-69; prof. psychology Sem. Saint Augustin, Cap Rouge, Que., 1973—, head dept. psychology, 1974—; pvt. practice psychology, Cap Rouge, part-time 1973—. Mem. Can., Am. psychol. assns., Corp. Psychologists Province of Que. Contbr. articles to profl. jours. Home: Pères Maristes Cap-Rouge PQ G0A 1K0 Canada

ALLARD, SERGE BRUNO, librarian; b. Sherbrooke, Que., Can., June 3, 1931; s. Omer and Colette (Bruneau) A.; B.A., U. Ottawa, 1953, B.Ph., 1954, L.Ph., 1955, L.Th., 1960, B.Edn., 1961, B.L.S., 1964. Tchr., Coll. de Rouyn (Que.), 1961-64, chief librarian, 1964—, chief librarian U. Quebec, 1970—. Mem. Am., Can. library assns., Assn. pour l'Avancement Scis. et Tecniques Documentation. Home: 515 Cuddihy St Rouyn PQ J9X 5C6 Canada Office: PO Box 8000 Rouyn PQ J9X 5M5 Canada

ALLEMAN, G(ELLERT) S(PENCER), educator; b. Swarthmore, Pa., June 24, 1913; s. Gellert and Katharine Constable (Spencer) A.; B.A., Lehigh U., 1934; M.A., U. Pa., 1937, Ph.D., 1942; m. Anita Lucille Lange, Dec. 19, 1953; 1 dau., Anne Katharine. Instr. English, Lehigh U., 1938-40, 42-47; asst. prof. English, Newark Coll. Arts and Scis., Rutgers U., 1947-56; asso. prof. English, 1956-61, prof., 1961—, chmn. dept. 1962-66. Served with AUS, USAAF, 1942-46. Mem. Bibliog. Soc. U. Va., Modern Lang. Assn., Modern Humanities Research Assn., Nat. Council Tchrs. English, Coll. English Assn., Nat. Rifle Assn., Phi Beta Kappa, Phi Eta Sigma. Contbr. articles to profl. jours. Home: 86 Vreeland Ave Nutley NJ 07110

ALLEMAN, RAYMOND ARTHUR, electronics co. exec.; b. Mercersburg, Pa., Sept. 18, 1923; s. Paul K. and Myra E. Alleman; B.S., Pa. State U., 1950; m. Isabell Elaine Erzen, Aug. 1, 1953; children—Raymond Arthur, Charles Richard, Robert Wayne. Project engr. Baldwin-Lima-Hamilton Corp., Eddystone, Pa., 1950-56; engr. equipment devel. RCA, Lancaster, Pa., 1956-59, engring. leader equipment devel. and engring., 1959-77, leader tech. staff, 1977—; cons. in field. Served with F.A., U.S. Army, 1943-45; ETO. Registered profl. engr., Pa. Mem. ASME, Soc. Advancement Mgmt. Lutheran. Patentee in field. Office: RCA New Holland Ave Lancaster PA 17604

ALLEN, ANGELENE ELLIOTT, coll. ofcl.; b. Fayetteville, N.C., July 4, 1936; d. Booker Washington and Mary Magdalene (Matthews) Elliott; A.B., Johnson C. Smith U., 1958; M.A., Montclair State Coll., 1973; m. James Henry Allen, Aug. 29, 1959; children—James Henry, Anita, Edward. Tchr., Huntington High Sch., Newport News, Va., 1958-60, Jersey City Bd. Edn., 1963, Paterson (N.J.) Bd. Edn., 1964; employment counselor N.J. Employment Service, Newark 1964-66, Paterson, 1967-70; head counselor Bergen Community Coll., Hackensack, N.J., 1970—. Sec., League Women Voters, 1977—; active Girl Scouts U.S.A.; treas. YWCA, Hacksenack 1974—. Mem. Am. Personnel and Guidance Assn., Nat. Employment Counselors Assn., Nat. Vocat. Guidance Assn., Assn. for Counselor Edn. and Supervision, NEA, N.J., Bergen County edn. assns., NAACP, Nat. Council Negro Women. Baptist. Home: 495 E 29th St Paterson NJ 07514 Office: 295 Main St Hackensack NJ 07601

ALLEN, B. MARC, med. assn. exec.; b. Balt.; s. Ralph A. and Frona B. A.; B.A., U. Balt., 1967, J.D., 1971; m. Judy E. Luray, Jan. 24, 1967; children—Lara Ann, Mason Luray. Mgr. med. affairs Md. Blue Cross, Balt., 1967-73; cons. Am. Health Systems, Boston, 1973-74; dir. field ops. Bay State PSRO, Boston, 1974-75; exec. dir. Essex Physicians' Review Orgn., South Orange, N.J., 1975—; cons. in field; guest lectr. health policy Rutgers U. Active Selective Service Systems, 1972-73, New Democratic Coalition, 1969-70. Mem. Nat. Health Lawyers Assn., Am. Assn. PSROs. Office: 15 Village Plaza South Orange NJ 07079

ALLEN, COURTNEY KEITH, profl. hockey team exec.; b. Saskatoon, Sask., Can., Aug. 21, 1923; s. Courtney Bliss and Gertrude Marguerite (Armitage) A.; came to U.S., 1941; m. Joyce Adele Webster, Apr. 21, 1948; children—Bradford Keith, Traci Jo, Blake Patrick. Hockey player with Buffalo Bison, Springfield Indians, Detroit Red Wings, Edmonton Flyers, Regina Capitals, Brandon Regals, Seattle Americans, 1942-57; gen. mgr., coach Seattle Americans, also Seattle Totems, 1956-66; coach, then asst. gen. mgr. Phila. Flyers Profl. Hockey Club, 1967-68, v.p., gen. mgr., 1968—. Served with Canadian Navy, 1943-45. Club: Overbrook Country (Radnor, Pa.). Office: The Sprectrum Broad and Pattison Sts Philadelphia PA 19148*

ALLEN, EDGARD YAN, pharm. chemist; b. Riga, Latvia, Oct. 18, 1914; s. Andrew Jacob and Josephine (von Reimann) A.; brought to U.S., 1916, naturalized, 1943; B.S. in Pharmacy, Fordham U., 1939; M.S. (pharmacognosy asst.), Phila. Coll. Pharmacy and Sci., 1942. Pharm. chemist (control) E.R. Squibb Corp., New Brunswick, N.J., 1943-69, environmental control chemist, 1970-78. Life corporate mem. Phila. Coll. Pharmacy and Sci., 1974—. Fellow Royal Soc. Health (Gt. Britain) (life), Am. Inst. Chemists, AAAS; mem. Am. Pharm. Assn., Am. Chem. Soc., Am. Assn. Hosp. Pharmacists (asso.), Am. Soc. Econ. Botany, New Eng. Assn. Chemistry Tchrs., Am. Soc. Pharmacognosy, Fedn. Internat. Pharmaceutique (The Hague, Netherlands). Roman Catholic. K.C. Contbr. to profl. jours.; investigater new sources for drugs and essential raw materials, World War II. Home: 8 Paulus Blvd New Brunswick NJ 08901

ALLEN, EMIL WILLIAM, JR., librarian; b. Raymond, N.H., Mar. 4, 1926; s. Emil William and Thelma Mae (Brown) A.; A.B., Bowdoin Coll., 1950; M.L.S., Pratt Inst., 1952; m. Anna Marilyn Coviello, Feb. 12, 1955; children—Mark Vincent, Megan Elizabeth, Rachel Ann. With sci. div. Bklyn. Pub. Library, 1952-53, stack curator, 1953-54; chief bus. and industry div. Ferguson Library, Stamford, Conn., 1955-56; asst. state librarian N.H. Library, Concord, 1956-64, state librarian, 1964—. Sec. N.H. Library Commn., 1964—; chmn. New Eng. Interstate Library Compact Bd., 1967-72, treas., 1972—; cons. S.C. State Library, 1970. Dir. Saban Electric Co. Mem. Warner Town budget com., 1962-68, 70-72, chmn., 1966-68; mem. Kearsarge Coop. Sch. Dist. planning bd., 1964-66, Kearsarge Regional Sch. Bd., 1966-69; treas. New Eng. Library Bd., 1972—, New Eng. Document Conservation Center, 1972—; mem. Warner Cemetery Commn., 1970—; precinct commr. Warner Village Fire Dist., 1971-72. Trustee Concord Hosp.; exec. bd. New Eng. Library Information Network, 1972-73; bd. dirs. Concord Mental Health Center, 1969-71. Served with AUS, 1944-46, USAF, 1950-51. Mem. Am. Soc. Pub. Adminstrn., Am. (council 1965-69), New Eng. (pres. 1965-66), N.H. library assns., Am. Library Trustees Assn. (v.p. 1969-70), N.H. Library Council, Audubon Soc. N.H., Warner Hist. Soc., Soc. Protection N.H. Forests, N.H. Hist. Assn., ACLU, N.H. Meml. Soc. (pres. 1967-69). Republican. Unitarian. Clubs: Kiwanis (pres. Concord 1962), Bowdoin of N.H. Home: RFD 2 Warner NH 03278 Office: NH State Libary Concord NH 03301

ALLEN, EUGENE MURRAY, chemist, educator; b. Newark, Nov. 7, 1916; s. Mitchell and Celia (Schnitter) Kaplan; B.A., Columbia U., 1938; M.S., Stevens Inst. Tech., 1944; Ph.D., Rutgers U., 1952; m. Beatrice Hyman, Jan. 23, 1937; children—Marlene (Mrs. Jean Louis Galzin), Julian. Research chemist United Color & Pigment Co., Newark, 1939-41, E.R. Squibb & Sons, Bklyn., 1941-42, Picatinny Arsenal, Dover, N.J., 1942-45; research chemist Am. Cyanamid Co., Bound Brook, N.J., 1945-63, research asso., 1963-65, research fellow, 1965-67; prof. chemistry, dir. color sci. lab. Lehigh U., Bethlehem, Pa., 1967—. Mem. Am. com., cons. Internat. Commn. on Illumination, 1967—. Recipient Research award Am. Cyanamid Co., 1958. Mem. Am. Chem. Soc., Optical Soc. Am., Am. Assn. Textile Chemists and Colorists (chmn. color tech. com. 1965), Inter-Soc. Color Council (chmn. fluorescent subcom. 1952-67, dir. 1974-76), Consortium for Color Tech. (dir. 1973—), Sigma Xi. Asso. editor Color Engring., 1965-71, Jour. Color and Appearance, 1971-74; mem. editorial bd. Color Research and Application, 1975-78. Contbr. numerous articles on optics, color and analytical chemistry to sci. jours. Home: 2100 Main St Bethlehem PA 18017

ALLEN, GEORGE FERGUSON, hosp. adminstr.; b. Lewiston, Maine, May 24, 1923; s. Shirley Burbank and Marion Evelyn (Ferguson) A.; B.A., Bates Coll., 1950; M.Ed., Boston U., 1953; M.A. in Hosp. Adminstrn., State U. Iowa, 1960; m. Judith Margaret Hawkins, Aug. 14, 1949; children—Douglas Ferguson, Carolyn Diane, David VanNuys, Donald Brown, Dorothy Elizabeth, Derek Fraser. Intelligence specialist USAAF, ETO, 1943-46, non-commd. officer USAF Med. Service, 1950-51; commd. 2d lt. U.S. Air Force, 1951, advanced through grades to maj., 1964; med. adminstrv. officer, psychologist, 1951-67, ret., 1967; exec. dir. Corning (N.Y.) Hosp., after 1967; now dir. hosp. and med. care div. Conn. State Dept. Health, Hartford. Instr. Macdill AFB campus Fla. So. Coll., 1953-54; lectr. psychology Ramey AFB (P.R.) campus Fla. State U., 1954-57; prof. hosp. mgmt. Ga. State Coll., Atlanta, 1964-65; active numerous local, area, regional and state orgns. devoted to health planning and delivery, mental health, environ. health, pub. info. and health orgn. relationship to state, fed. legis. reps. Mem. Air Force Assn., Am. Coll. Hosp. Adminstrn., N.Y. State Hosp. Assn. (mem. com. mgmt. engring. 1970-74), Am. Hosp. Assn. Presbyterian. Mason. Home: PH15E 500 Cold Spring Rocky Hill CT 06067 Office: Room 412 79 Elm St Hartford CT 06115

ALLEN, GEORGE HOWARD, pub. exec.; b. Boston, June 1, 1914; s. Albert Hacker and Myrtie A. (Lawton) A.; B.S., U. Mass., 1936, LL.D., 1967; M.B.A., Harvard U., 1938; m. Virginia Russell, Sept. 7, 1940; children—Russell Lawton, Douglas Winslow (dec.). Asst. to pres. Nat. Theatre Supply Co., N.Y.C., 1938-40; research mgr. radio sta. WOR, 1941, asst. dir. promotion and research, 1942-43; radio cons. U.S. Treasury Dept., 1943-45; gen. mgr., sec. bd. Coop. Analysis of Broadcasting, N.Y.C., 1944-46; N.E. sales mgr. N.Y. Herald Tribune, 1946, promotion mgr., 1947-50; chmn. 20th Nat. Bus. Conf., Harvard, 1950; dir. sales promotion McCall's mag., 1950-57, asst. pub., gen. mgr., 1957-60; pub. Better Living mag., 1956; v.p. Mass. Markets Publs., Inc., 1953-54, pres., 1954-55, dir., 1953-55; spl. asst. to pres. Meredith Pub. Co., N.Y.C., 1960-61, v.p., 1961-66, dir., 1965-66, gen. mgr. mag. pub. div., Des Moines, 1962-66; pub. Better Homes and Gardens, Successful Farming mags., 1964-66; chmn. bd. Nat. Plan Service, Chgo., 1965-66; pub. v.p. Fawcett Publs., Inc., N.Y.C., 1966-72, exec. v.p., 1972—. Mem. panel Pres.'s White House Conf. on Food and Nutrition, 1969. Bd. dirs. Internat. Exchange Program, Ann Arbor, Advt. Council. Recipient leadership award Am. Legion, 1932; Young Advt. Man of Year, 1956; Achievement award Wash. Ad Club, 1956; Silver Anvil award, Am. Pub. Relations Assn., 1957; Bell Ringer award, Salt Lake City Ad Club, 1957; Pub. Relations News award, 1957; Mgmt. Man of Year, 1965. Mem. Am. Mktg. Assn. (pres. N.Y. 1946), N.A.M. (dir. 1965-66), Mag. Pubs. Assn. (dir., sec. 1974-75, vice chmn. 1976, chmn. 1977-79), Advt. Fedn. Am. (dir. 1965-67), U.S. C. of C. (edn. com. 1964-66), Advt. Research Found. (dir. 1965, sec.-treas. 1971, vice chmn. 1972, chmn., 1974-75), U. Mass. Alumni (v.p.), Harvard Bus. Sch. Assn. (pres. 1967), Pubs.

Info. Bur. (dir. 1966, vice chmn. 1974), Harvard Alumni Assn. (dir. 1958-59), Sales Promotion Execs. Assn. (mem. nat. bd. 1958), Pub. Relations Soc. Am., Newcomen Soc., Lambda Chi Alpha, Adelphia. Congregationalist. Clubs: Harvard, Canadian, Economic, Dutch Treat, Sky (N.Y.C.), International (Chgo.). Author: Individual Initiative in Business. Contbr. artilces profl. mags. Home: 112 Pear Tree Point Rd Darien CT 06820 Office: Fawcett Publs Inc 1515 Broadway New York City NY 10036*

ALLEN, GERALD GORDON, utility exec.; b. Massena, N.Y., Nov. 11, 1944; s. Gordon Newell and Ruth Elizabeth (Smith) A.; B.S.E.E., Clarkson Coll. Tech., 1966, M.S.E.E., 1979; m. Phyllis Jesmer, May 26, 1973; 1 dau., Karen Elizabeth. Project engr. Niagara Mohawk Power Corp., Syracuse, N.Y., 1966-69, scheduling engr., 1970-72, supr. engring. schedules and budgets, 1972—; research asst. elec. engring. Clarkson Coll. Tech., Potsdam, N.Y., 1969-70. Niagara Mohawk Research fellow, 1969. Mem. Project Mgmt. Inst., Eta Kappa Nu. Republican. Roman Catholic. Home: 43 Carousel Ln Baldwinsville NY 13027 Office: 300 Erie Blvd W Syracuse NY 13202

ALLEN, HENRY JOSEPH, aircraft parts co. exec.; b. Passaic, N.J., Sept. 6, 1931; s. Edward J. and Mary B. A.; student Fairleigh Dickinson U., 1950-52, Am. Grad. U., 1975—; m. Clare B. Reardon, Jan. 21, 1956; children—Patricia Ann, Mark Terrence. Service engr. Curtiss-Wright Corp., Woodridge, N.J., 1952-56, customer service rep, 1956-60, mil. salesman, 1960-64, sr. sales engr., 1964-66, mgr. mktg., 1966-77, dir. mil.-govt. mktg., 1977—. Served with U.S. Army, 1952-55. Mem. Tech. Mktg. Soc. Am., Am. Boat and Yacht Council, Assn. U.S. Army, Am. Mktg. Assn., Remotely Piloted Vehicle Assn., Am. Def. Preparedness Assn. Republican. Roman Catholic. Home: 21 Roosevelt Ave Elmwood Pk NJ 07407 Office: Curtiss-Wright Corp 1 Rotary Dr Woodridge NJ 07075

ALLEN, JAMES P., banker; b. Morristown, N.J., June 21, 1937; s. Patrick and Mary (Feeney) A.; B.A., Fairleigh Dickinson U., 1962; postgrad. U. Okla. Sch. Exec. Devel., 1977-78; m. Geraldine A. Donattello, Apr. 18, 1964; children—James Patrick, John Joseph, Kathleen A., Patrick P., Michael J. U.S. attaché, Rome, Italy, 1957-60; with Beneficial Mgmt. Corp., Morristown, N.J., 1960-65, Comml. Investment Trust, N.Y.C., 1965-66, Suburban Fin., Newark, 1966-74; pres. City Fed. Savs. subs., Elizabeth, N.J., 1974—; mem. N.J. Savs. League sr. mgmt. seminar Columbia U., 1978—. Mayor, Morris Twp., N.J., 1973-76; mem. Morris County Park Commn., 1976—. Served with USMC, 1955-61. Mem. Consumer Bankers Assn., Columbia U. Grad. Sch. Bus. Alumni Assn. Club: Springbrook Country. Home: South Rd Chester NJ 07930 Office: North Ave at Newark Elizabeth NJ 07208

ALLEN, JOHN JOSEPH, social worker; b. N.Y.C., Oct. 12, 1922; s. John M. and Ellen (Flynn) A.; B.S., Fordham U., 1947; M.S., Columbia, 1957; m. Dorothy G. Siller, Aug. 23, 1947; children—Patricia Ann (Mrs. Stephen Nickerson), Kathleen Marie, John Kevin, Maureen Ellen. Caseworker, Westchester County Dept. Social Services, White Plains, N.Y., 1948-54, supr. casework, 1954-62, asst. commr., 1963-67; chief social worker Westchester County Community Mental Health Bd., White Plains, 1962-63; dir. social services div. Social Services, White Plains, 1967—. Lectr., Columbia Sch. Pub. Health and Adminstrv. Medicine, 1965; mem. Cortland Youth Bd., 1965-69; Active Boy Scouts Am., 1965-68. Served with USAAF, 1943-46. Mem. Nat. Assn. Social Workers (exec. com. 1957—), Am. Soc. for Pub. Adminstrn., Lake Allandale Home Owners Assn. Lion, Elk, K.C. Contbr. articles to profl. jours. Home: 189 Frederick St Peekskill NY 10566 Office: Room 633 150 Grand St White Plains NY 10601

ALLEN, KATHERINE, ret. editor-writer; b. Williamstown, Mass.; d. George E. and Katherine (Wallace) Allen; student N.Y. U., A.B. cum laude, Bklyn. Coll., 1961. Editor-writer U.S. Mission to UN, N.Y.C., 1948-78. Recipient Meritorious Honor award Dept. State.

ALLEN, KRISTIN LLOYD, naval officer; b. Richmond, Va., Aug. 6, 1949; s. Lloyd Simmons and Lois Jacqueline (Phillips) A.; B.S. in Nuclear Engring. summa cum laude, U. Va., 1972; M.S. in Physics, U.S. Naval Postgrad. Sch., 1973; m. Sarah McCulloch Dils, June 10, 1972; 1 dau., Rebekah Marion. Commd. ensign U.S. Navy, 1972, advanced through grades to lt., 1976; nuclear power tng., Vallejo, Calif., 1973-74; submarine officers indoctrination course, New London, Conn., 1974; asst. engr. officer U.S.S. Lapon, Norfolk, Va., 1974-77; instr. U.S. Naval Acad., Annapolis, Md., 1977—. Deacon Christian Ch., 1976-77; pres. Christian Men's Fellowship, 1976-77. Mem. U.S. Naval Inst., Am. Nurclear Soc., Sigma Xi, Tau Beta Pi. Club: Commd. Officers and Faculty (U.S. Naval Acad.). Home: 12A Sellers Rd Annapolis MD 21402 Office: 315 Rickover Hall Naval System Engring US Naval Academy Annapolis MD 21402

ALLEN, LEE THOMAS, criminologist; b. N.Y.C., Jan. 20, 1945; s. Lee T. and Mary Louise A.; Ph.D., U. Eastern Fla., 1972; LL.B., Blackstone Sch. Law, 1970. Pres., W.H.I.P.S. Protective Services, Inc., Bronx, N.Y., 1974—, Alarm and Security Guard Co., Bronx, 1974—; cons. in field. Mem. Internat. Assn. Criminology, Am. Law Enforcement Assn. Democrat. Home: 1412 Harrod Ave Bronx NY 10472 Office: 1408 Harrod Ave Bronx NY 10472

ALLEN, LOMA MOYER (MRS. DELESLIE ALLEN), ednl. adminstr.; b. Niagara Falls, N.Y., May 16, 1913; d. Arnold R. and Edyth (Hawkins) Moyer; student Wheelock Coll., 1930-31; m. DeLeslie Allen, Feb. 24, 1934 (dec. Nov. 1973); children—Loma Joy (Mrs. Rush Clarke III), Leslie Cornelia Hays. Dir. Assn. Jr. Leagues of Am., 1948-50, sec., 1950-52, pres., 1952-54; sec., mem. exec. com. Nat. Social Welfare Assembly, 1954-68; dir. Am. Social Health Assn., 1955-67, exec. bd., 1956-67; past dir., past mem. adv. council Am. br. Internat. Social Service; formerly dir. community relations Rochester Inst. Tech., asst. to pres., 1974—; vice chmn. social welfare com. Nat. Council of Chs., 1960-66; incorporator Family Life Found., 1957-60; v.p. Nat. Family Life Found.; bd. dirs. Rochester Area Council Chs., 1962-65; v.p. Nat. Fedn. Settlements and Neighborhood Centers, 1962-66, pres., 1966-68; past mem. Rochester Housing Authority; past mem. Rochester and Monroe County Youth Bd.; past chmn. adv. com. Rochester Careers in Social Work; mem. Nat. Assembly for Social Policy and Devel., 1968-73; mem. Rochester Met. Housing Study Com., 1967-70; mem. adv. com. 1970 White House Conf. on Children and Youth; mem. exec. com. N.Y. State Welfare Conf., Inc., 1975—; bd. dirs. Rochester Family Service Assn., 1955-60; bd. dirs. Baden St. Settlement, Rochester, 1954-72, hon. bd. dirs., 1972—, sec. 1956-57, pres., 1964-66; mem. adv. council welfare services HEW, 1964-66; bd. dirs. United Community Chest Greater Rochester, 1977—. Formerly trustee The Harley Sch. Recipient Ethel H. Wise Spl. Merit award Columbia U. Sch. Social Work, 1967; Distinguished Service award Nat. Conf. on Social Welfare; Forman Flair award for outstanding community service, 1971; Community Chest citation, 1977. Mem. Buffalo and Erie County Council of Social Agys. (dir. 1947-53), Buffalo YWCA (dir. 1948-50), Buffalo City Planning Assn. (dir. 1947-50), Planned Parenthood League (sec. 1960), Jr. League of Buffalo, Inc. (hon.), Am. Social Health Assn. (v.p. 1962-67), Urban League of Rochester (v.p. 1965-70). Home: 22 Barrington Park Rochester NY 14607

ALLEN, MARSHA LYNN, bus. machine mfg. co. exec.; b. Atlantic City, Nov. 28, 1952; d. John C. and Marsielle A.; B.A., U. Pa., 1974; M.B.A., Harvard U., 1976. Intern, Mayor City of Newark, 1973-74; admissions counselor Harvard Bus. Sch., 1975-76; mktg. rep. IBM, N.Y.C., 1976—. Recipient Wall St. Jour. Student Achievement award, 1976. Cogme fellow, 1974-76. Mem. Am. Mgmt. Bus. Assn., Nat. Black Harvard Alumni Assn. (nat. dir. recruiting), Harvard Bus. Club. Home: 143 Hoyt St Apt 1D Stamford CT 06905 Office: 2 Penn Plaza New York NY 10001

ALLEN, PHILIP DILLON, investment co. exec.; b. N.Y.C., Oct. 31, 1938; s. Philip Elsworth and Dorothy Anne (Dillon) A.; B.A., Am. U., 1961; m. Elisabeth Horne Fell, July 29, 1967; children—Alexandra, Christopher, Andrew, Nicholas. With Dillon Read & Co. Inc., N.Y.C., 1965-71; with Trainer Wortham & Co. Inc., N.Y.C., 1972-75, asst. v.p., 1973-75; dir. U.S. and Fgn. Securities Corp., N.Y.C.; v.p., dir. Bedminster Fund, N.Y.C. Trustee Am. U., Washington, Morristown (N.J.) Hosp. Served with AUS, 1962-64. Clubs: Racquet and Tennis, Knickerbocker (N.Y.C.); Essex Hunt (Peapack, N.J.); Somerset Hills Country (Bernardsville, N.J.); Tarratine (Dark Harbor, Maine). Home and Office: Box 597 Far Hills NJ 07931

ALLEN, RALEIGH HOWELL, JR., ednl. adminstr.; b. Seffner, Fla., May 24, 1924; s. Raleigh Howell and Thelma Hortense (Greenier) A.; B.S., Fla. A&M U., 1948; D.V.M., Tuskegee Inst., 1956; m. Minnie Bumpers, Feb. 20, 1954; children—Hollianne Yvonne, Renee Francene. Vets. tchr. agr., Sumter County, Fla., 1948; vocat. agr. tchr., Orange County, Fla., 1951; veterinarian pathology dept. Tuskegee Inst. (Ala.), 1956; pvt. practice vet. medicine, N.D., 1957-62, Tampa, Fla., 1962-66; veterinarian USDA, Washington, 1966-72; dean Sch. Agr. and Natural Resources, Washington Tech. Inst., 1972-75; dean acad. affairs U. D.C. Van Ness Campus, Washington, 1975—. Mem. adv. bd. to supt. pub. instrn. Hillsborough County, Fla., 1962-66, mem. county adv. bd. on Headstart programs, 1963-66, interracial adv. coms., 1958-70. Served with USNR, 1942-45. Mem. Am. Vet. Med. Assn., Nat. Assn. Fed. Veterinarians, Am. Assn. Avian Pathologists, U.S. Animal Health Assn., Vet. Assn. Am. Hygienists. Research and publs. on Western strain equine encephalomyelits. Home: 1794 Verbena St NW Washington DC 20012

ALLEN, REGINALD BENJAMIN, govt. drug treatment program ofcl.; b. N.Y.C., Apr. 14, 1931; s. Reginald Beemer and Thelma Ann (Hart) A.; B.A. in Sociology, City Coll. N.Y.; m. Alicia Corpus, Oct. 9, 1965. Mgr., Mut. Employment Agency, N.Y.C., 1960-63; fed. corrections officer Fed. Detention Hdqrs., N.Y.C., 1966-67; asst. intake supr. Addiction Research and Treatment Corp., Bklyn., 1970-72; dir., cons., adviser Operation Rap Neighborhood Patrol Team 77th precinct N.Y.C. Police Dept., 1971-72; sr. ct. liaison officer, supervising addiction specialist ct. referral project Addiction Services Agency, City of New York, Bklyn., 1972-73, evaluator, addiction specialist, N.Y.C., 1973—; income maintenance specialist Dept. Social Services, N.Y.C., 1976—; lectr. Met. Tng. Inst. Drug Abuse Treatment Queens Coll., 1973; alcohol, drug abuse counselor U.S. Marine Corps Reserves. Served with USMC, 1952-54. Mem. Assn. Alcoholism Counselors, Nat. Fedn. Concerned Drug Abuse Workers, Recovered Alcoholics in the Professions, Correctional Assn. N.Y., NAACP, Am. Legion, Marine Corps Assn., Noncommissioned Officers Assn., Mil. Order Devil Dogs, Naval Enlisted Reserve Assn., Nat. Rifle Assn., Am. Mgmt. Assn., City Coll. Alumni Assn., Omega Psi Phi. Mormon. Club: Chelsea Gun. Home: 164 Somers St Brooklyn NY 11233 Office: 103 Clinton St Brooklyn NY 11201

ALLEN, RICHARD PUTNAM, psychologist; b. Waterloo, Iowa, Sept. 6, 1938; s. Dean H. and Gretchen R. (Putnam) A.; B.S. (Alumni scholar), Mass. Inst. Tech., 1961, postgrad. in psychology, 1961-62; Ph.D. (Ford student) Churchill Coll., U. Cambridge (Eng.), 1967; m. Patricia Randle, Dec. 13, 1969; children—Heidi, Richard. Asst. prof. Johns Hopkins U., 1969—; chief psychology Balt. City Hosps., 1969—, dir. alcoholism services, 1973—; prof. U. Balt., 1970—, U. Md., Balt. County, 1971-73; cons. Balt. County Sch. Child Mental Health, 1970—. Served with AUS, 1967-69. Recipient Nat. Merit certificate of Honor, 1956. Mem. Am., Md. psychol. assns., Soc. Psychophysiol. Research. Author sci. publs. Home: 1403 Park Ave Baltimore MD 21217 Office: Dept Psychology Balt City Hosps Baltimore MD 21224

ALLEN, ROBERT ERWIN, physiologist; b. Lufkin, Tex., Oct. 9, 1941; s. John Franklin and Bonnie Mae (Smith) A.; B.A., Stephen F. Austin State Coll., 1963; Ph.D., Vanderbilt Med. Sch., 1969; m. Roma Leah Trobaugh, Oct. 18, 1970; 1 dau., Jennifer Kay. With NASA Marshall Space Flight Center, Huntsville, Ala., 1969—, chief biometrics, 1972-74, chief biotech. br., 1975-76; spl. asst. to v.p. U. Ala. Med. Sch. System, 1976; exec. sec. Nat. Inst. Health, Bethesda, 1976-78; spl. asst. to dir. med. research service VA, Washington, 1978—. Home: 5001 Aurora Dr Kensington MD 20795 Office: Central Office VA Washington DC 20420

ALLEN, ROCELIA J., elementary tchr.; b. Cin., Oct. 19, 1924; married, 1 child. B. in Instrumental Mus., Chgo. Conservatory zzusic, 1948; M.Ed. in Spl. Edn., U. Del., Newark, 1966; Ph.D., Union Grad. Sch., 1979. Tchr. exceptional children DeLa Warr Sch. Dist., New Castle, Del., from 1960; now chmn. spl. edn. dept George Read Sch., Area IV, New Castle County, Del.; asst. prof. English and reading spltys. Del. Tech. Community Coll., Stanton, 1974—. Mem. NEA, Del., De La Warr edn. assns., Nat., Del. music educators assns., Council Exceptional Children, Nat. Assn. Univ. Women, Phi Delta Kappa, Zeta Phi Beta. Certified in spl. and elementary edn., music, Del.; specialist in lang. arts, using the operatta to teach lang. arts to educable mentally retarded. Home: 712 S Harmony Rd Tanglewood Newark DE 19713 Office: George Read Sch New Castle DE 19720

ALLEN, THOMAS ELMER, obstetrician, gynecologist, educator; b. Bairdford, Pa., July 2, 1919; s. Emerson Ray and Lillie Mabel (McIntyre) A.; B.S., M.D., U. Pitts., 1943; m. Ruth Jenkins, June 18, 1943; children—Catherine, Christine, Cynthia, Carolyn, Thomas Jenkins, Candace. Rotating intern U. Pitts., 1944; teaching fellow and resident in obstetrics and gynecology Magee Womens Hosp., Pitts., 1944-45, 48-51; practice medicine specializing in obstetrics and gynecology, pres. Dr. Thomas E. Allen & Assos., Pitts., 1962—; asso. clin. prof. obstetrics gynecology U. Pitts., 1976—; med. dir. Women Health Services, Inc., Pitts., 1973—. Served from 1st lt. to capt. M.C., U.S. Army, 1945-47. Diplomate Am. Bd. Obstetrics and Gynecology. Fellow A.C.S., Am. Coll. Obstetics Gynecology; mem. Med. Soc. Pa., AMA. Democrat. Home: 386 California Ave Oakmont PA 15139 Office: 204 Craft Ave Pittsburgh PA 15213

ALLEN, WILBERT, city ofcl.; b. Newark, Nov. 17, 1946; s. Gilbert and Carrie Bell (Martin) A.; B.Arch., Hampton Inst., 1969; M.Urban and Regional Planning (Urban fellow 1969-71), U. Ill., 1971; certificates in real estate appraisal, real estate devel., fed. income tax N.Y. U., 1977; postgrad. (Loeb fellow) Harvard U., 1977-78; m. Barbara A. Tate, Aug. 21, 1971; 1 son, Kenyan Faustyn. Architect/urban designer Community Adovacy Depot, Urbana/Champaign, Ill., 1969-71; urban designer Newark Div. City Planning, 1971-74; cons. Regional Planning Assn., N.Y.C., 1975; instr. Essex County Coll., Newark, 1973-76; city planning dir. City of Newark, 1974-78, exec. dir. Mayor's Policy and Devel. Office, 1978—. Mem. City of Newark Real Estate Commn., 1974—, Landmarks and Preservation Commn., 1974—; mem. capital budget com. S. 13th St. Block Club, 1974-75. Mem. Am. Inst. Planners, Council Urban Econ. Devel., Am. Soc. Pub. Ofcls., Urban Land Inst. Methodist. Home: 381 Broad St A-2015 Newark NJ 07104 Office: City Hall Room 218 Newark NJ 07102

ALLEN, WILLIAM ARTHUR, author, photographer; b. Colchester, Vt., Apr. 28, 1947; s. Julius Chapman and Chalcib Elizabeth (Warner) A.; student USCG Acad., 1965-66; m. Clara Elena Fernandez, June 20, 1973 (div. 1977). Asst. exec. dir. Soaring Soc. Am., Santa Monica, Calif., 1970-72; pub. relations dir. Eipper-Formance, Inc., Carson, Calif., 1973; asst. editor Ground Skimmer, U.S. Hang Gliding Assn., Los Angeles, 1973-74, editor, 1974, bd. dirs. assn., 1977; freelance author, photographer, 1972—. Served with AUS, 1966-70. Decorated Bronze Star. Mem. Aviation/Space Writers Assn., Nat. Assn. Sci. Writers. Home and Office: Star Route (Rogers) Alstead NH 03602

ALLEN-CLAIBORNE, JOYCE G., clin. psychologist; b. Columbus, Ga., Feb. 23, 1948; d. Homer W. and Berneda C. Allen, Jr.; B.A. cum laude, Spelman Coll., 1970; M.S., U. Pitts., 1972, Ph.D., 1975; m. Andrew J. Claiborne, Nov. 20, 1976. Psychology intern U. Tex., VA Hosp., Dallas, 1974-75; cons. on racialism La Roche Coll., Pitts., 1976-77; research asso. U. Pitts., 1975-77; clin. psychologist Hillcrest Children's Center, Washington, 1977-78; psychologist Region IV, D.C. pub. schs., 1979—. Spelman Coll. Acad. scholar, 1966-69; teaching fellow, U. Pitts., 1972; pub. health fellow NIMH, 1972-74; VA trainee, 1970-72; recipient Ludie Andrews prize, 1969. Licensed clin. psychologist, D.C. Mem. Am. Psychol. Assn. Baptist. Contbr. articles to profl. jours.

ALLEY, FREDERICK DON, med. center exec.; b. Detroit, May 27, 1940; s. William and Rita A.; B.S. in Commerce, Ferris State Coll., 1962; M.S., Sch. Pub. Health and Adminstrv. Medicine, Columbia U., 1965; m. Joann Kathleen O'Hara, May 20, 1960; children—Kirk, Nicole. Adminstrv. aide Hackensack (N.J.) Hosp. Assn., 1962, adminstrv. resident, 1963-64, adminstrv. asst., 1964-65, asst. dir., 1965-68; asst. dir., Bklyn. Hosp., 1964-65, asso. dir., 1969-77, exec. dir., 1977—; lectr., Columbia U.; preceptor in health adminstrn., cons. N.Y. State Civil Service Dept. Recipient awards Citizens Adv. Urban Renewal Com., 1967, Community Planning Bd. #2, 1977, Cumberland Hosp. Community Bd., 1977, Health Systems Agency and Pub. Health Assn. N.Y.C., 1977. Fellow Am. Coll. Hosp. Adminstrs.; mem. Am., N.Y. State, Greater N.Y. hosp. assns. Club: Brooklyn. Contbr. articles to profl. publs. Home: 5 Cathy Rd Hillsdale NJ 07642 Office: Brooklyn Hospital 121 De Kalb Ave Brooklyn NY 11201

ALLGEYER, FERNAND EDWARD, ins. agt.; b. Bklyn., Sept. 24, 1930; s. Fernand F. and Jeanette L. (Moeglin) A.; grad. high sch.; m. Vita Vaccaro, Sept. 24, 1950; children—Steven, Robert, Jacqueline and Joann (twins). Salesman, Markel's Inc., Jamaica, N.Y., 1948-52, 54-56; shop mgr. Internat. Typog. Union at John A. Livingstone Co., Atlantic City, 1956-70; salesman Prudential Ins. Co., Atlantic City, 1970—. Active Boy Scouts Am.; mem. zoning bd. City of Port Republic (N.J.), 1958-69, mem. planning bd., 1969-75, councilman, 1971-72; founder Taxpayers Assn. Port Republic, 1969-73. Served with USMC, 1952-54, USMCR, 1954-56. Mem. Am. Legion (past comdr. Galloway Twp.), Marine Corps League, Ins. Workers Am. (treas. 1972-73). Roman Catholic. Clubs: K.C., Moose. Home: 247 Allgeyer Ln Port Republic NJ 08241 Office: 1337 Tilton Rd Northfield NJ 08225

ALLIET, DAVID FREDERICK, chemist; b. Rochester, N.Y., May 9, 1938; s. Albert Jerome and Irene Florence (Alcock) A.; B.S. with honors, Rochester Inst. Tech., 1967; m. Diane Louise Kingston, Aug. 27, 1960; children—Robert, Karen, Janet. Research technician Xerox Corp., Rochester, 1960-65, research chemist, 1965-70, project mgr., 1970—. Cubmaster Boy Scouts Am., 1970-73, scoutmaster, 1974—, Dist. award Merit, 1974. Fellow Am. Inst. Chemists (certified), Am. Chem. Soc., Fine Particle Soc. Republican. Contbr. articles in field to sci. jours. Home: 6 Cypress Circle Fairport NY 14450 Office: 800 Phillips Rd Webster NY 14580

ALLIN, JOHN MAURY, bishop; b. Helena, Ark., Apr. 22, 1921; s. Richard and Dura (Harper) A.; A.B., U. of South, 1943, M.Div., 1945, D.D., 1962; M.Ed. Miss Coll., 1960; m. Frances Ann Kelly, Oct. 18, 1949; children—Martha May, Kelly Ann and John Maury (twins), Frances Elizabeth. Ordained to ministry Episcopal Ch., 1944; vicar St. Peter's Ch., Conway, Ark., 1945-49; surage St. Andrew's Ch., New Orleans, 1950-51; chaplain to Episcopal students and institutions, New Orleans, 1950-52; rector Grace Ch., Monroe, La., 1952-58; rector, pres. All Saints Jr. Coll., Vicksburg, Miss., 1958-61; bishop coadjutor Diocese of Miss., P.E. Ch., Jackson, 1961-66, bishop, from Examining chaplain Diocese of La., 1952-61; mem. com. on pastoral counseling House of Bishops, 1966—; mem. Joint Commn. on Ecumenical Relations, 1964—; chmn. com. on councils of chs., Consultation, 1967—; mem. exec. council Episcopal Ch., 1970—, mem. steering com. of exec. council, 1970—, chmn. program adv. com. on communications, 1970—, mem. ecumenical standing com., 1970—; v.p. Province IV of Episcopal Ch., 1971—; now presiding bishop Episcopal Ch. U.S.A.; mem. Miss. Religious Leadership Con., 1969—, chmn. 1972-73. Mem. exec. bd. County Health Improvement Project, 1968—. Trustee, All Saints Episcopal Sch., Vicksburg, 1961—, Episcopal Radio-TV Found., 1963-69; trustee U. of South, 1961—, bd. regents, 1965-71, chancellor, 1973—. Mem. Jackson C. of C. Home: 338 Round Hill Rd Greenwich CT 06830 Office: 815 2d Ave New York City NY 10017

ALLING, WILBUR MERWIN, accounting co. exec.; b. N.Y.C., Nov. 9, 1942; s. Wilbur M. and June Wood (Meder) A.; B.S., Yale, 1964; M.B.A., Dartmouth, 1966; m. Katherine Ann Pantlind, Sept. 9, 1967; children—Carolyn Meder, Andrew Pantlind, Sarah Thomson. Staff, Hurdman and Cranstoun, C.P.A.'s, N.Y.C., 1966-70, Syracuse, N.Y., 1970-77, partner mgmt. adv. services, 1975-77; gen. practices partner, Boston, 1978—. Active United Way Central N.Y., 1974-75, Landmark Assn. Central N.Y., 1974—; trustee Kiwanis Found., Syracuse, 1975-77. C.P.A. Mem. Am. Inst. C.P.A.'s, N.Y. State, Mass. socs. C.P.A.'s. Clubs: Yale, Harvard, Fed. (Boston); Wellesley Country. Office: Hurdman and Cranstoun 236 Lewis Wharf Boston MA 02110

ALLISON, DAVID ARTHUR, ret. steel co. exec.; b. Hillside, Pa., May 5, 1905; s. Elmer Ellsworth and Laura (Schultz) A.; grad. LeSalle Extension U., 1928, student U. Pitts. Extension, 1930; m. Margaret Harshey Kerr, June 29, 1935. With Latrobe Steel Co., Pa., 1925-71, chief accountant, credit mgr., 1947-58, exec. asst., finance and gen. credit mgr., 1958-70, also dir.; dir. Derry Bldg. & Loan Assn., 1941—, v.p., 1946—, sec., 1950—; treas., dir. Water Savers Systems, Inc., Farmington, 1966-73; dir. Sun Steel Treating Corp., Farmington, 1960-73, sec., 1965-73. Life mem. Muscular Dystrophy Research Center Hosp., N.Y.C., 1959—; bd. dirs., treas. Lesco Employees' Relief Soc., 1955—; pres. bd. dirs., chmn. mems. Coles Cemetery Assn., Derry, Pa., 1948—; trustee, treas. Latrobe Masonic Bldg. Trust, 1945—. Mem. Office Mgmt. Assn. Pitts. (past pres., recipient merit key and scroll 1951, adv. council 1948-71), Nat. Assn. Accountants (pres. Westmoreland chpt. 1946-48), Nat. Assn. Credit Men (life). Methodist (pres. bd. trustees 1958-73, pres. congregation 1958-73). Mason (Shriner, 32 deg., past supreme scribe), Rotarian. Contbr. articles to office equipment mags. Home: 168 3d St Derry PA 15627

ALLISON, JOHN R., business cons.; b. 1913; student Northwestern U., Am. Inst. Banking, Sophia U.; m. Asst. to treas. Norton Co., 1951-54; treas., dir. Norton Behr Manning Overseas Inc., 1954-59; v.p. internat., controller Richardson-Merrell, Inc., 1959-63; v.p., treas. PepsiCo Inc., 1963-65, v.p., controller, chief accounting officer, 1965-67; pres., chief exec. officer PepsiCo Service Industries, 1967-70; sr. v.p., treas. Raytheon Co., Lexington, Mass., 1970-73; adminstrv. partner Cons. Partners Inc., N.Y.C., 1973—; cons., profl. dir. Served to 1st lt. U.S. Army, 1943-45. Office: 143 Chestnut Circle Lincoln MA 01773

ALLISON, JONATHAN, lawyer; b. Washington, Pa., Apr. 17, 1916; s. Albert Johnson and Etta (Tucker) A.; B.S., Washington and Jefferson Coll., 1937; J.D., U. Pa., 1940; postgrad. Harvard Grad. Sch. Bus. Adminstrn., 1940-41. Admitted to Pa. bar, 1942; practiced in Washington, 1946—; partner firm Schmidt & Allison, and predecessors, 1949—. Served from pvt. to maj., AUS, 1941-46. Mem. Am., Pa., Washington County bar assns. Republican. Presbyn. Club: Duquesne (Pitts.). Home: 331 E Wheeling St Washington PA 15301 Office: 438 Washington Trust Bldg Washington PA 15301

ALLMAN, MARGO HUTZ, artist; b. N.Y.C., Feb. 23, 1933; d. Werner Herbert and Avis (Newcomb) Hutz; student Smith Coll., 1950-51, Moore Coll. Art, 1952-54, Hans Hofman Sch. Art, 1953, U. Del., 1967-70; m. William B. Allman, Feb. 19, 1954; children—Avis Louise, David Drue. Exhibited one-person shows Wallingford (Pa.) Art Center, 1964, Windham Coll., Putney, Vt., 1974, Bloomsburg (Pa.) State Coll., 1976, 77, others; group shows Phila. Art Alliance, 1954, U. Del., Newark, 1958, Print Club Phila., 1959, Del. Art Mus., 1967, 77, others; juried shows Pa. Acad. Fine Art, 1964, Phila. Mus. Art, 1962, Del. Art Mus., 1956-76, others; invited shows N.J., Pa., Del.; represented in permanent collections Del. Art Mus., Phila. Mus., others. lectr. in field. Active Del. Art Mus., 1967-70. Recipient Mildred Boericke prize Print Club Phila., 1958, ann. show drawing prize Del. Art Mus., 1965, landscape prize Wilmington (Del.) Trust Bank, 1969. Mem. Nat. League Am. Pen Women (art chmn. 1968-69), Phila. Print Club (dir. 1961-63), Am. Craft Council, Moore Coll. Art Alumnae Assn. Unitarian. Ferro cement sculpture Tidewater Pub. Co., Centerville, Md., 1975; crocheted sculpture Herculon, Hercules Inc., Wilmington, 1975. Home: Rose Hill Manor RD 1 Box 45B West Grove PA 19390

ALLSHOUSE, FRANK, textile machinery mfg. co. exec.; b. York, Pa., Sept. 29, 1924; s. Frank Pierce and Minnie Catherine (Files) A.; A.A., Monmouth Coll., 1943; student Phila. Coll. Textiles, 1943-49; m. Arline Ethel Walker, June 1, 1946; children—Bruce Alan, Craig Arlen, Randy Lee. Supervisory positions A & M Karagheusian Co., Freehold, N.J., 1941-53, Beattie Mfg. Co., Little Falls, N.J., 1953-56; various positions service engring., sales, pres. Tubular Textile Machinery Corp., Woodside, N.Y., 1956-69, v.p., 1969-78, pres., 1978—; cons. in field. Served with USNR, 1942-46, 51-53. Mem. Am. Assn. Textile Colorists and Chemists, Internat. Textile Club, Sales Exec. Club, Am. Legion. Republican. Club: Elks. Home: 68 Elm Ave Hackensack NJ 07601 Office: 33-61 54th St Woodside NY 11377

ALLUKIAN, MYRON, JR., dental adminstr.; b. Cambridge, Mass., Jan. 6, 1939; s. Myron and Mary (Nahabedian) A.; B.S. in Psychology, Tufts U., 1960; D.D.S., U. Pa., 1964; M.P.H., Harvard, 1967; m. Ruth F. Losco. Resident in dental pub. health Mass. Dept. Health and Harvard Sch. Dental Medicine, 1967-68; research fellow ecol. dentistry Harvard Sch. Dental Medicine, 1968-69; chief dental services Bunker Hill Health Center, Mass. Gen. Hosp., 1969-77; dir. community dental health Boston Dept. Health and Hosps., 1970-71; asst. dep. commr., dir. community dental programs, 1971—. Dental cons. Tng. Center for Comprehensive Care, 1967-69; lectr. Forsyth Sch. Dental Hygiene, 1969—; asst. clin. prof. Harvard Sch. Dental Medicine, 1971-77, asso. clin. prof. medicine, 1978—; instr. Tufts Sch. Dental Medicine, 1971—; lectr. Boston U. Sch. Grad. Dentistry, 1977—; chmn. ambulatory com. Statewide Health Coordinating Council Mass., 1977—; regional dental cons. Job Corps, U.S. Dept. Labor, 1973—, also Region I, HEW; mem. Mass. Bd. Registration in Dentistry, 1978—. Bd. dirs. Mass. Citizens Com. for Dental Health, S. Boston Community Health Center, 1977-78; corp. mem. Mass. Dental Service Corp., Boston Young Men's Christian Union (hon. mem. Barbell Club). Served to lt. USNR, 1964-66. Diplomate Am. Bd. Dental Pub. Health. Fellow Am. Acad. Dental Sci., Internat. Coll. Dentists; mem. ADA (certificate of commendation 1978), Mass. Dental Soc., Mass. (v.p. 1975, pres. 1977, James M. Dunning award 1977, Alfred Frechette award 1978), Am. (chmn. dental health sect. 1977-78, governing council 1978—) pub. health assns., Am. Assn. Pub. Health Dentists, Omicron Kappa Upsilon. Home: 76 Haynes Rd Newton Center MA 02159 Office: 818 Harrison Ave Boston MA 02118

ALLYN, JAMES LYMAN, microbiologist; b. Gowen, Okla., Nov. 25, 1930; s. Charles Lyman and Barbara M (Hague) A.; certificate Payne Hall Sch. for Lab. Technicians, 1951, St. Simmonds Sch. Lab. Tech., 1952; B.S., Fairleigh Dickinson U., 1964; m. Katy Stickelmayer, Oct. 4, 1954; children—Barbara, Linda, Cindy. Bacteriology technician St. Joseph Hosp., Paterson, N.J., 1952; med. technician Valley Hosp., Ridgewood, N.J., 1957-60; technician in biochemistry Lederle Lab., Pearl River, N.Y., 1960-64, analytical microbiologist, 1964-67, specifications writer, lab. supr. quality control, 1970-75, asst. adminstr., new product evaluator pharm. research and devel.-stability group, 1975—; v.p., treas. Lenrow Allergy, Inc., Passaic, N.J., 1955-68; buyer, seller antiques, Hawthorne, N.J., 1950-60. Served with N.J. Nat. Guard, 1950-52, AUS, 1952-54. Mem. Am. Soc. Microbiologists. Democrat. Home: 84 Garden Ave Hawthorne NJ 07506 Office: Lederle Lab N Middletown Rd Pearl River NY 10965

ALMOND, PAUL, film producer, dir.; b. Montreal, Que., Can., Apr. 26, 1931; s. Eric and Irene Clarice (Gray) A.; student Bishops Coll. Sch., 1944-48, McGill U., 1948-49; B.A., M.A., Balliol. Coll., Oxford, 1949-52; m. Joan Elkins, Sept. 11, 1976; 1 son, Matthew James Almond. TV producer, dir. Canadian Broadcasting Corp., Toronto, Ont., 1953-67; pres. Quest Film Productions Ltd., Montreal, 1968—, writer, producer, dir. feature films Isabel, 1968, Act of the Heart ("Etrog" best dir. award), 1970, Journey, 1972. Mem. Dirs.' Guild Can., Am., Canadian Assn. Motion Picture Producers, Royal Canadian Acad. Arts. Anglican. Home: 1272 Redpath Crescent Montreal PQ H3G 2K1 Canada

ALMY, RYDIA EUSTACE, bacteriologist; b. Newport, R.I., Oct. 13, 1935; d. Gideon Wilcox and Rydia Eustace (Champion) Almy; B.A., Salve Regina Coll., 1957. Asso. bacteriologist N.Y. State Dept. Health, Albany, 1958—. Roman Catholic. Contbr. articles in field to profl. jours. Office: New York State Health Dept Division Labs and Research Empire State Plaza Albany NY 12201

ALOISIO, MARY, hosp. exec.; b. N.Y.C., Oct. 5, 1924; d. Joseph and Domenica (Galeano) Papale; Accounting certificate Queens Coll., 1944; m. John Aloisio, Apr. 5, 1947; children—Elizabeth, John Joseph, Mary Anne. Statis. typist U.S. Dept. Agr., N.Y.C., 1943-48; sec. Booth Meml. Med. Center, Flushing, N.Y., 1957-59, jr. buyer, 1960-62, adminstrv. buyer, 1962-64, dir. purchasing, 1964—. Certified purchasing mgr. Mem. Hosp. Purchasing Agts. Assn. (pres. 1974-75), Nat. Assn. Purchasing Mgmt., Am. Soc. for Hosp. Purchasing Agts. Home: 134-33 57th Rd Flushing NY 11355 Office: 56-45 Main St Flushing NY 11355

ALOSSO, JOHN, loss prevention co. exec.; b. Somerville, Mass., May 31, 1953; s. Thomas William and Angela Stella (Fazio) A.; B.S., Boston State Coll., 1976; m. Kathleen Ann Mullen, June 20, 1976. Chief security investigator Lechmere Sales Co., Cambridge, Mass., 1969-74; cons. N. Am. Security Services, Boston, 1975-76; loss prevention regional mgr. Mammoth Mart, Inc., W. Bridgewater, Mass., 1976-77; cons. Asset Mgmt. Cons., Boston, 1977-78; loss prevention regional mgr. Marshall's Inc., Woburn, Mass., 1978—; lectr. North Shore Community Coll., Beverly, Mass. Mem. Internat. Acad. Criminology, Internat. Narcotic Enforcement Officers Assn., Am. Judicature Soc., Am. Soc. Indsl. Security. Home: 54 Arlington St Tewksbury MA 01876 Office: 83 Commerce Way Woburn MA 01801

ALOTTA, ROBERT IGNATIUS, author, historian; b. Phila., Feb. 26, 1937; s. Peter Philip and Jean (Sacchetti) A.; B.A., LaSalle Coll., Phila., 1959; m. Alice Danley, Oct. 1, 1960; children—Peter Anthony, Amy Louise. With Triangle Publs., Phila., 1959-67, mdsg. mgr. Inquirer div., 1959-63; mgr. customer service Inquir-Daily News, 1963-66; new bus. coordinator Daily News, 1966-67; mgr. spl. projects Penn Central Transp. Co., 1967-72; dir. pub. info. Phila. Housing Authority, 1972—; tchr. creative writing Holmesburg Prison; author: Street Names of Philadelphia, 1975; Stop the Evil, 1978; (radio series) Past/Prolog, 1976; Old Names and New Places, 1970; also articles; narrator own radio series A Minute of Your Time, 1977—; scriptwriter for radio and TV. Mem. Phila. Area Council Tourism, 1975—, chmn., 1978—; mem. Friends of Free Library Phila., 1976—; bd. dirs. Wheels, Inc., 1978—, Council Internat. Visitors, 1975—; pres. Shackamaxon Soc., 1967—; mem. pres. council LaSalle Coll., 1976—. Served with U.S. Army Security Agy., 1960-61. Recipient Legion of Honor award Chapel 4 Chaplains, 1975; Americanism award County Detectives Assn. Pa., 1977; award Freedoms Found. at Valley Forge, 1970, 73, 74, 76, Colonial Dames, 1976, DAR, 1976. Mem. Am. Name Soc., Council Abandoned Mil. Posts (chpt. pres. 1970—), Co. Mil. Historians (chpt. treas. 1976—), Hist. Soc. Pa., Cross Keys, Tau Alpha Pi, Alpha Phi Omega. Clubs: Vesper; Nat. Press (Washington). Home: 315 S 12th St Philadelphia PA 19107

ALPER, ALLEN MYRON, elec. mfg. co. exec.; b. N.Y.C., Oct. 23, 1932; s. Joseph and Pauline (Frohlich) A.; B.S., Bklyn. Coll., 1954; Ph.D., Columbia (Univ. fellow, Dyckman Inst. Scholar, Univ. pres.'s scholar), 1957; m. Barbara Marshall, Dec. 20, 1959; children—Allen Myron, Andrew Marshall. Sr. mineralogist Corning Glass Works (N.Y.), 1957-59, research mineralogist, 1959-62, mgr. ceramic research, also sr. research asso., 1962-69; with GTE Sylvania Inc., Towanda, Pa., 1969—, chief engr., 1971-72, dir. research and engring., 1972—, 75, dir. research and engring., mgr. aperture mask prodn., 1975—. Mem. Pa. Gov.'s Adv. Panel on Materials, 1971—. Grantee N.M. Bur. Mines, 1954-57. Fellow Am. Ceramic Soc., Geol. Soc. Am., Am. Inst. Chemists; mem. British Ceramic Soc., Am. Soc. Metals, Geophy. Union, Am. Chem. Soc., Sigma Xi. Presbyterian. Mason. Clubs: Mariners, Towanda Country, Lake Wesauking Assn. Patentee in field. Contbr. to profl. jours. Editor: Phase Diagrams: Materials Science and Technology, 4 vols., 1976; High Temperature Oxides, 4 parts, 1970-71. Editorial bd. High Temperature Sci. jour., 1969—, High Temperature Chemistry, 1973—, Materials Handbook, 1974—; editor Materials Sci. and Tech. Series, Acad. Press, 1972—. Contbr. articles to profl. jours. Home: 4 3d St Towanda PA 18848 Office: GTE Sylvania Towanda PA 18848

ALPER, CARL, med. analytical lab. dir.; b. Hoboken, N.J., May 28, 1920; s. Max and Sonia (Feldman) A.; B.A., Drew U., 1941; M.S., Tulane U., 1943, Ph.D., 1947; m. Freda Panter, June 5, 1949; children—Seth, Steven, Naomi, Marilyn. Instr. chemistry Tulane U., New Orleans, 1943-46; chemist protein nutrition and immunochemistry E.R. Squibb and Sons, New Brunswick, N.J., 1947-49; asst. prof. biochemistry Hahnemann Med. Coll. and Hosp., Phila., 1949-54, asso. prof., 1954-66, dir. lab. clin. biochemistry, 1962-66; asso. prof. biochemistry, dir. dept. clin. biochemistry Temple U., Phila., 1966-70; dir. Phila. br. Bio-Sci. Labs., 1970—; lectr. biochemistry St. Joseph's Coll., Phila., 1957-59; lectr. sci. Rutgers U., Camden, 1959-63; adj. prof. biochemistry St. Christopher's Hosp., Temple U., 1975—. Fellow Phila. Coll. Physicians; mem. Am. Assn. Clin. Chemistry, Acad. Clin. Lab. Physicians and Scientists, Am. Chem. Soc., Am. Inst. Nutrition, Assn. Clin. Biochemists Gt. Britain, Can. Soc. Clin. Chemistry, Nat. Registry Clin. Chemistry, Am. Soc. Clin. Pathology (asso.). Jewish religion. Contbr. articles to profl. jours. Home: 1126 S Park Ave Haddon Heights NJ 08035 Office: 114 S 18th St Philadelphia PA 19103

ALPER, M(AX) VICTOR, educator, writer; b. Wilkes-Barre, Pa., Mar. 23, 1944; s. Samuel and Hannah (Robin) A.; A.B., Boston U., 1964, M.A., 1967; Ph.D., N.Y. U., 1972; postgrad. Harvard. Instr., N.Y. U., 1969-73; asst. prof. humanities Montclair (N.J.) State Coll., 1973-77; exec. asst. to exec. v.p. Rutgers U., New Brunswick, N.J., 1977—; participant N.Y. U.'s Art Critics in Residence Program, 1972; contbg. editor to Arts Mag., N.Y.C., 1970-74; lectr. N.Y.C. museums; researcher art exhibits; author catalogues; cons. to Newsweek, 1975, Marriott Corp., 1977; guest lectr. U. Mass., Rutgers U.; vis. prof. City U. N.Y.; participant Internat. Conf. on Subsidy of Arts, N.Y.C., 1975, confs. Am. Council on Edn., 1977-78; mem. TV and radio programs for bicentennial and hist. activities, 1976; host weekly radio series Historic Sites of Am., WGBH, Boston, 1976; author; books include America's Freedom Trail, 1976; America's Heritage Trail, 1976. Bd. dirs. Am. History Photo Archives, N.Y.C., 1975-77. Mem. AAUP, Modern Lang. Assn., N.Y. State English Council (editorial bd.), Nat. Acad. TV Arts and Scis. (mem. Emmy nomination com. 1970, Acad. council 1977), Am. Fedn. Arts, Soc. Am. Historians, Nat. Trust Hist. Preservation. Contbr. to Ency. English Lit., also numerous articles and revs. to jours. and mags. Home: 145 W 79th St 11C New York City NY 10024 Office: Box 1773 86 Bayard St New Brunswick NJ 08903

ALPER, MELVIN GUSTAVUS, ophthalmologist; b. Balt., Nov. 13, 1921; s. Saul and Fannie Esther (Sollod) A.; B.A., U. Va., 1942, M.D., 1945; postgrad. Harvard Med. Sch., 1950-51; m. Jane Roslyn Liebling, Aug. 23, 1957; children—Nancy Lynn, John Liebling. Intern Phila. Gen. Hosp., 1945-46; resident in surgery Emergency Hosp., Washington, 1948-50; resident in ophthalmology Hosp. U. Pa., Phila., 1951-54; practice medicine specializing in ophthalmology, 1954—; clin. instr. ophthalmology George Washington U. Med. Sch., 1954-60, asst. prof., 1960-68, prof., acting chmn. dept. ophthalmology, 1969-70, clin. prof. ophthalmology and neurol. surgery, 1970—; cons. to surgeon gens. U.S. Army, USN; chmn. dept. ophthalmology Washington Hosp. Center, 1973-75, pres. med. and dental staffs, 1975-77. Served with M.C., U.S. Army, 1946-48. Diplomate Am. Bd. Ophthalmology. Mem. Am. Acad. Ophthalmology and Otolaryngology (prize sci. exhibit 1969), Cushing Soc., Am. Radiol. Soc. (prize sci. exhibit 1969), AMA, So., Pan-Am. med. assns., D.C. Med. Soc. (prize sci. exhibits 1968), Am. Ophthal. Soc., Phi Beta Kappa, Alpha Omega Alpha. Democrat. Jewish. Clubs: Cosmos, Edgemoor Tennis; Woodmont Country; Coral Beach and Tennis, Belmont Golf and Country (Bermuda); Masons. Contbr. chpts. to books and ophthalmic lit. Home: 5309 Edgemoor Ln Bethesda MD 20014 Office: 5454 Wisconsin Ave Chevy Chase MD 20015

ALPERIN, IRWIN EPHRAIM, clothing co. exec.; b. Scranton, Pa., Apr. 29, 1925; s. Louis I. and Bessie (Wickner) A.; B.S. in Indsl. Engring., Lehigh U., 1947; certificate mech. engring. Pa. State U., 1945; m. Francine Leah Friedman, Dec. 5, 1948; children—Barbara Joy, Jane Leslie. Mgmt. trainee Mayflower Mfg. Co., Scranton, 1947-49, sec., 1952—; with Triple A Trouser Mfg. Co., Inc., Scranton, 1952, v.p., treas., 1958—; with Gold Star Mfg. Co., Inc., Scranton, 1956, pres., 1956—; an organizer Astro Warehousing, Inc., Scranton, 1962, sec., 1962—; sec.-treas. Bondeal, Inc., Scranton, 1977—. Vice pres. Econ. Devel. Council N.E. Pa., Avoca, Pa., 1978—; bd. dirs. ARC, Scranton, 1968—, Jewish Home N.E. Pa., Scranton, 1970—, Jewish Community Center, Scranton, 1971—, Community Services Pa., 1973-78, Scranton Mental Health/Mental Retardation Center 1975-78; pres. Planning Council Social Services Lackawanna County, 1972-74, Jewish Fedn. Lackawanna County, 1967-70; v.p. United Way Lackawanna County, 1974-78; pres. Alperin Found., Scranton, 1962—; treas. Scranton-Lackawanna Jewish Council, 1973-74. Served with C.E., AUS, 1944-46. Named Man of Year Jewish Community Center, 1973. Mem. Am. Inst. Indsl. Engrs. (sr.). Jewish religion (temple pres. 1969-71). Mason (Shriner), Elk; mem. B'nai B'rith. Club: Glen Oak Country (Clarks Summit, Pa.). Home: 600 Colfax Ave Scranton PA 18510 Office: Meadow and Maple Sts PO Box 470 Scranton PA 18503

ALPERIN, RICHARD JUNIUS, biologist, educator; b. Phila., Dec. 16, 1941; s. Norman and Dorothy Edythe (Gross) A.; A.B., U. Pa., 1963, Ph.D. (fellow), 1969. Asso. prof. biology Community Coll., Phila., 1969-77, prof., 1977—, chmn. faculty senate, 1975-76; postdoctoral fellow in anatomy U. Pa., 1969-74, lectr. electron microscopy and cytochemistry, dept. animal biology, 1970-74; guest lectr. Chestnut Hill Coll.; designer NASA Spacelab 1 expt. Mem. health care com. Phila. council AFL-CIO, also ofcl. del. to Phila. council; mem. Congregation B'nai Abraham; v.p. Congregation Mikveh Israel. Recipient Pro Mundi Beneficio medal Brazilian Acad. Humanities, award Phila. Citizens Commn. on Pub. Edn., 1975. Mem. Am. Fedn. Tchrs. (pres. 1971-72, 75-76), N.Y. Acad. Scis., Am. Soc. Zoologists, Am. Micros. Soc., Biol. Photog. Assn., ASTM (officer, surg. implants com.), N.Y. Acad. Scis., Internat. Platform Assn., Union Concerned Scientists, Hubrecht Embryological Lab., Fedn. Am. Scientists, German Soc. Herpetology and Vivarium Sci., Pattern Recognition Soc., Soc. Devel. Biology, Phila. Bot. Club, Phila. Electronmicroscopy Club, Phila. Devel. Biologists. Club: Explorers. Research on submicroscopic cytochemistry of nucleic acids in vivo during metaplasia and determination in embryos. Home: 842 Lombard St Philadelphia PA 19147

ALPERN, ANDREW, architect; b. N.Y.C., Nov. 1, 1938; s. Dwight K. and Grace M. (Michelman) A.; B.Arch., Columbia, 1964; Sc.D. (hon.), London (Eng.) Coll. Applied Sci., 1971. With Haines Lundberg Waehler, architects, N.Y.C., 1962-67; project dir. Saphier, Lerner, Schindler, Environetics, space planning and design, N.Y.C., 1968-72; v.p., dir. arch. Environmental Research & Devel., Inc., Space Planning and Design, N.Y.C., 1972-75; dir. research Corporate Planners and Coordinators, real estate, N.Y.C., 1974-75; project mgr. Hellmuth, Obata & Kassabaum, architects, engrs. and planners, N.Y.C., 1977-78; mgr. facilities planning Coopers & Lybrand, N.Y.C.; pvt. practice residential architecture, interior design, shopping center planning, N.Y.C., 1964—. Cons. urban real estate and architecture, 1967—. Mem. adv. bd. Inst. Applied Psychotherapy, 1969-72, therapist, cons. state-funded program drug abuse prevention, 1970-72, mem. nat. panel arbitrators Am. Arbitration Assn., 1971—; lectr. City U. N.Y., Inst. Architecture and Urban Studies, Grolier Club. Registered architect, N.Y., Pa., Calif., W.Va., D.C. Mem. A.I.A., Soc. Archtl. Historians, L.I., N.Y. hist. socs., Nat. Trust Historic Preservation, Municipal Art Soc., N.Y. State Assn. Architects, Met. Assn. Urban Designers and Environmental Planners, Assn. Collegiate Schs. Architecture, Real Estate Bd. N.Y. Author: Apartments for the Affluent: A Historical Survey of Buildings in New York, 1975; Garret Ellis Winants: 1813-1890, 1976; Handbook of Specialty Elements in Architecture, 1979; The Architect's Vade Mecum, 1979. Editor-in-chief: Legal Briefs for Architects, Engineers and Contractors, 1978—. Address: 315 8th Ave New York City NY 10001

ALPERN, MILTON, cons. civil engr.; b. N.Y.C., June 25, 1925; s. Nathan and Rae (Kraft) A.; B.C.E., Cooper Union, 1945; M.S. in Civil Engring., Columbia, 1951; postgrad. Poly. Inst. Bklyn., 1957-63; m. Beverly Katzman, May 30, 1946; children—Warren Deems, Barbara Lynn. Test engr. Edo Aircraft Co., Flushing, N.Y., 1945; design engr. Frederick Snare Corp., N.Y.C., 1947-49; asst. prof. civil engring. Cooper Union, N.Y.C., 1948-60; prin. Milton Alpern cons. engr., Wantagh, N.Y., 1960-71, Alpern & Soifer, cons. engrs., Massapequa, N.Y., 1971—; mem. N.Y. State Bd. Engring. and Land Surveying, 1978; adj. asso. prof. Structures N.Y. Inst. Tech., 1978—. Chmn. bldg. com. Union Free Sch. Dist. 5, Nassau County, 1955-56; pres. Wantagh Oaks Civic Assn., 1957; mem. steering com. Am. Cancer Soc. Theatre Party, 1968-76. Served with C.E., AUS, 1945-47. Registered profl. engr., N.Y., N.J., Pa., Conn., Mass., Ill., Tex., Ky., Mo.; also nat. certification. Recipient Engr. of Year award Nassau County Profl. Engring. Soc., 1972; Lincoln Arc Welding Design awards, 1961, 69. Fellow ASCE (Engr. of Yr. award L.I. chpt. 1974); mem. N.Y. State (pres. 1972-73), Nat. (dir. 1967-77) socs. profl. engrs., Am. Concrete Inst., Prestressed Concrete Inst., Constrn. Specifications Inst., N.Y. Cons. Engrs. Council (pres. L.I. chpt. 1970-71, chmn. edn. and long range planning coms. 1965-69), Am. Arbitration Assn., Internat. Assn. Bridge and Structural Engrs., Am. Soc. Testing and Materials, Soc. Am. Mil. Engrs., Am. Welding Soc., Chi Epsilon. Odd Fellow. Contbr. articles to profl. jours. Home: 153 Biltmore Blvd Massapequa NY 11758 Office: 18 Unqua Rd Massapequa NY 11758

ALPERT, GEORGE, media exec.; b. Bklyn., Apr. 3, 1922; s. Samuel and Rose (Wendorf) A.; student N.Y.U., 1940, N.C. State Coll., 1941, Inst. Seven Arts, 1945-46; m. Elizabeth Heinz, Apr. 15, 1967; children—Steven, Joseph. Pres., George Alpert Co., merchandising and advt. cons., N.Y.C., 1947-55; Dorothy Lamour, Inc., cosmetics, N.Y.C., 1959-62; advt. and mktg. cons., N.Y.C., 1962-73; pres. Broadcast Mktg. Corp., N.Y.C., 1973. Exhibited photographs at Everson Mus. Art, 1974, Il Diafragmma, Milan, Italy, 1975, Neikrug Gallery, 1971-72; mem. faculty New Sch. for Social Research, N.Y.C., 1975—. Bd. dirs. Project Return, drug rehab. program for adolescents; bd. dirs., pres. Soho Photo Found.; bd. dirs. Alfred Stieglitz Gallery. Served with AUS, 1942-44. Mem. Am. Soc. Mag. Photographers. Author: The Queens, 1974; Second Chance to Live: The Suicide Syndrome, 1976. Home: 79 W 12th St New York City NY 10011 Office: 4 E 52d St New York City NY 10022

ALPERT, GRACE KENNISON, psychologist; b. Providence, Sept. 18, 1929; d. Samuel I. and Bertha (Sherman) Kennison; A.B. cum laude, Brown U., 1951; Ed.M., Boston U., 1959; m. Wesley Simon Alpert, May 10, 1968. Psychol. staff R.I. Mental Hygiene Services, Providence, 1955-58, 59-72, psychometrist, 1955-58, 59-60, clin. psychologist, 1960-72, cons. R.I. Tng. Sch. for Girls, 1967-68, supr., 1968-72; pvt. practice clin. psychology, Providence, 1970—; clin. psychologist-cons. Project Grow, Providence Sch. Dept., 1973-74. Bd. dirs. Providence chpt. Brandeis U. Nat. Women's Com., 1972—, corr. sec., 1972-75; bd. dirs. dist. 1, Nat. Fedn. Temple Sisterhoods, 1973-76, regional chmn. Youth, Edn. and Sisterhood Fund, 1973-76; v.p., chmn. dept. human relations Sisterhood of Temple Beth-El, Providence, 1975-77; chmn. Mid-Atlantic region Central Scholarship Com., Pembroke Coll., Brown U., 1970-72, treas. class, 1976—; bd. dirs. Nat. Council Jewish Women, 1975—; mem. advisory com. Jewish Fedn. R.I., 1978—. Mem. Am., Eastern, New Eng., R.I. psychol. assns., Bradley, Butler, Miriam hosp. auxs., Pi Lambda Theta. Jewish. Clubs: Pembroke Coll., Ledgemont Country, Faculty Brown U. Home: 53 Wingate Rd Providence RI 02906

ALPERT, HERMAN SAUL, psychiatrist; b. Potsdam, N.Y., Jan. 17, 1913; s. Israel Noah and Sarah Leah (Lehrman) A.; A.B., U. Rochester, 1934; M.D., Eclectic Med. Coll., Med. Coll., Cin., 1938; m. Eileen Rita Picker, Mar. 31, 1946 (dec. Sept. 1970); children—Cheryl Lynne Alpert Sofer, Jeffrey Neal; m. 2d, Harriet M. Lesnik, Nov. 7, 1971; stepchildren—Margery P. Karp, Peter J. Lesnik. Gen. rotating intern Rockaway Beach Hosp., 1938-39; resident Letchworth Village Hosp., Thiells, N.Y., 1939-42; supervising psychiatrist State Hosp., Marcy, N.Y., 1946-47, clin. asst., 1947-56; sr. clin. asst. Mt. Sinai Hosp., N.Y.C., 1956-62, asst. attending psychiatrist, 1962-73, asso. attending psychiatrist, 1973—; asst. clin. prof. psychiatry Mt. Sinai Sch. Medicine, N.Y.C., 1966—; lectr. Inst. Pastoral Psychiatry, Mt. Sinai Hosp., N.Y.C., 1955-60. Acting chmn. exec. com. Mt. Sinai Music Soc. Orch., 1970—. Served to maj. M.C., AUS, 1942-46; ETO. Diplomate Am. Bd. Psychiatry and Neurology. Fellow AMA (physicians recognition award 1972, 75), Am. Psychiat. Assn. (life), Am. Assn. Mental Deficiency (life), Am. Group Psychotherapy Assn.; mem. Internat. Assn. Social Psychiatry, AAAS, Assn. Advancement Psychotherapy, Pan Am. Med. Assn., AAUP. Democrat. Jewish. Club: B'nai B'rith. Home: 360 E 72d St Apt B-1610 New York City NY 10021 Office: 993 Park Ave New York City NY 10028

ALPERT, JOEL JACOBS, physician, educator; b. New Haven, May 9, 1930; s. Herman H. and Alice (Jacobs) A.; A.B. with high honors, Yale U., 1952; M.D., Harvard U., 1956; m. Barbara E. Wasserstrom, July 13, 1957; children—Norman, Mark, Deborah. Intern Children's Hosp. Med. Center, Boston, 1956-57, jr. asst. resident in medicine, 1957-58; sr. registrar St. Mary's Hosp. Med. Sch., London, 1958-59; chief resident for ambulatory services Children's Hosp. Med. Center, Boston, 1961-62, also fellow in medicine, 1961-62, asst. dir. family health care program, 1962-63, asst. in medicine, 1963-64, asso. in medicine, 1964-66, chief Family and Child Health Div., 1964-72, sr. asso. in medicine, 1966-73, cons. in child and family medicine, 1972—; research fellow in pediatrics Harvard Med. Sch., Boston, 1962-63; practice medicine specializing in pediatrics, Boston, 1964—, asst. dir. Family Health Care Programs, Harvard Med. Sch., Boston, 1962-64; instr. in pediatrics, 1963-66, asso. in pediatrics, 1966-68, med. dir. Family Health Care Program, 1963-72, asst. prof. pediatrics, 1968-69, asso. prof. pediatrics, 1969-72, lectr. in pediatrics, 1972—; asso. in medicine Beth Israel Hosp., Boston, 1964-73; asso. pediatrician Boston Hosp. for Women, 1966—; lectr. in medicine Simmons Coll., Boston, 1964-72; prof., chmn. dept. pediatrics Boston U. Sch. Medicine, 1972—, prof. dept. socio-med. sci., 1976—, dir. pediatric service Boston City Hosp., 1972—; vis. lectr. health services Harvard Sch. Pub. Health, 1976—, cons. pediatrics Joseph P. Kennedy Meml. Hosp., 1972—, Carney Hosp., 1972—; mem. health services research study sect. HEW, 1968-72, cons. Bur. Health Services, 1972—; vis. research asso. dept. econs. Northeastern U., 1975—; chmn. exec. com. Boston Poison Info. Center, 1976-78. Mem. Advisory Com. Spl. Edn., Winchester, Mass., 1969—; mem. exec. com. Mass. Commn. on Children and Youth, 1972—. Served as capt. M.C., U.S. Army, 1959-61. USPHS Spl. fellow, 1972. Diplomate Am. Bd. Pediatrics. Mem. Inst. Medicine of Nat. Acad. Scis., Am. Pediatric Soc., Soc. Pediatric Research, New Eng. Pediatric Soc., Soc. Research in Child Devel., Am. Acad. Pediatrics (mem. sect. on child devel. 1966—), AAAS, Am. Pub. Health Assn., Soc. Tchrs. Family Medicine, Mass. Med. Soc., Ambulatory Pediatric Assn. (pres. 1969), Am. Assn. Poison Control Centers (dir. 1965-68). Clubs: Aesculapian, Yale of Boston. Author: (with F.H. Lovejoy, Jr.) A Handbook for Acute Childhood Poisoning, 1971; (with E. Charney) The Education of Physicians for Primary Care, 1973, (with others) Towards Changing the Medicial Care System, 1974. Contbr. numerous articles on poisoning, med. edn. and pediatrics to med. jours. Home: 6 Partridge Ln Winchester MA 01890 Office: 818 Harrison Ave Boston MA 02118

AL-SAKKAL, SAAD, physician; b. Aleppo, Syria, Nov. 5, 1947; s. Lotfi and Dorie (Katib) A.; came to U.S., 1972; P.C.B., Damascus U., 1966, M.D., 1972. Intern, Luth. Med. Center, Bklyn., 1972-73; resident medicine St. Joseph's Hosp., Paterson, N.J., 1973-74, Phila. Gen. Hosp., 1974-75; chief resident medicine Conemaugh Valley Meml. Hosp., Johnstown, Pa., 1975-76; fellow in endocrinology, asst. in medicine George Washington U. Med. Center, Washington, 1976—. Diplomate Am. Bd. Internal Medicine, subsplty. endocrinology and metabolism. Mem. A.C.P. Recipient Physician's Recognition award AMA. Home: 1301 20th St NW Apt 607 Washington DC 20036 Office: Grad Program Dept Physiology George Washington U Washington DC 20037

ALSHUK, THOMAS JOHN, machinery mfg. co. exec.; b. Waterbury, Conn., Aug. 4, 1949; s. Thomas and Zenobia Phyllis (Neminski) A.; B.S., Cornell U., 1973; M.S. in Engring. Sci., Rensselaer Poly. Inst., 1976; diploma in intermediate Russian, Vidil-Rock Sch. Modern Langs., 1976; m. Rebecca Kay Crossley Coyle, Mar. 26, 1977. Engr.-systems analyst Waterbury Farrel Co. div. Textron Inc., 1969-71; ind. cons. computer hardware, software, systems, 1971-73; mgr. control systems Fenn Mfg. Co. div. AMCA Inc., Newington, Conn., 1973—. Mem. bd. advisers (Russian) Vidil-Rock Sch. Modern Langs., 1976—. Registered profl. engr., Conn.; certified in data processing. Mem. Am. Nat. Standards Inst., Nat. Machine Tool Builders Assn., Conn. Soc. Profl. Engrs. (Young Engr. of Year award 1976, sec. state bd. dirs. 1978—, chpt. v.p. profl. engrs. in industry sect. 1978—), IEEE, Assn. for Computing Machinery. Democrat. Roman Catholic/Russian Orthodox. Patentee in field. Home: 7 Wilcox St Old Wethersfield CT 06109 Office: 300 Fenn Rd Newington CT 06111

ALSON, ALLAN LESTER, editor; b. Phila., Dec. 13, 1947; s. Milton C. and Rosalie B. (Lester) A.; B.A., Hamline U., St. Paul, 1969; M.Ed., Temple U., 1971; Ed.D., Boston U., 1978. Tchr. math. Sayre Jr. High Sch., Phila., 1969-72, Mass. Exptl. Sch. System, Middle and High Schs., Dorchester, 1972-75; mng. editor Jour. of Edn., Boston, 1975—; instr. social psychology of edn. Boston U., 1976, instr. urban edn., 1978; coordinator ednl. programs Dist. I-Boston U. Collaborative, 1976—, dep. dir. desegregation project, 1977; creator, dir. Project Give a Damn motivational tutorial program St. Paul Inner City Schs., 1968-69. Mem. Am. Fedn. Tchrs., Hamline U. Medalist Soc. Home: 84 Brooks St Brighton MA 02135 Office: 704 Commonwealth Ave Boston MA 02215

ALSPAUGH, ROBERT ODO, mgmt. cons.; b. Cuyahoga Falls, Ohio, Jan. 30, 1912; s. Odo and Lea (Case) A.; student U. Akron, 1931-32, Case Western Res. U., 1933; m. Jane M. Bradner, Dec. 6, 1941; 1 dau., Jane M. Bradner. Asst. to comml. research dir. Forest City Pub. Co., 1934-37; mgmt., cons., 1938-41; mem. staff Office Chief Ordnance U.S. Army, Washington, 1941-45; chmn. Alspaugh & Co., mgmt. cons., 1946—; pres. Alspaugh Assos., engring. cons., 1946—; mng. dir. Ipham A.G., Zurich, Switzerland, Franfurt, Germany, Athens, Greece, Stockholm, Sweden, Helsinki, Finland, and Innsbruck, Austria; ltd. partner Sterling Grace & Co., N.Y.C. Dep. auditor Cuyahoga County, Ohio, 1965-66. Served to maj. AUS, 1942-45. Decorated Legion of Merit. Mem. Am. Def. Preparedness Assn., Newcomen Soc., Cleve. C. of C. Episcopalian. Clubs: Country, Union, Bratenahl (Cleve.); Racquet and Tennis, River, India House (N.Y.C.); American, Annabels (London). Home: 2952 Fairmount Blvd Cleveland Heights OH 44118 also 160 E 65th St New York City NY 10017 Office: Union Commerce Bldg PO Box 18620 Cleveland OH also 39 Broadway New York City NY 10006

ALSTON, CASCO, physician; b. Phila., Sept. 23, 1911; s. Casco N. and Alberta A.; B.A., U.Pa., 1936; M.D., Howard U., 1942; m. Marjorie Poysky Terrasa, June 2, 1962; children—Christofer, Angela, Gwen. Trainee juvenile delinquency studies Wharton Settlement, 1935; actor, play design WPA theater, New Theatre, Hedgerow Theatre, 1936; intern, Met. Gen. Hosp., Cleve., 1942-43, resident in internal medicine, 1943-47, asst. supt. medicine, 1947-48; lectr. medicine Case Western Res. U., Cleve., 1945-47; asst. prof. clin. medicine N.Y. U., N.Y.C., 1955-65; dir. medicine Sydenham Hosp., N.Y.C., 1965-75; asst. clin. prof. medicine Columbia U., N.Y.C., 1965—; asst. attending in medicine Columbia-Presbyn. Med. Centre, 1952—; asst. to dir. diagnostic center, N.Y.C. Dept. Health, 1952-65. Chmn. med. bd. N.Y.C. Employees Retirement, 1969—; med. bd. Dept. Corrections N.Y.C., 1960-65. Mem. AAAS, Am. Heart Assn., Am. Geriatric Soc., N.Y. State Med. Soc., Royal Inst. Anthropology. Home: 7 W 96th St New York City NY 10025 Office: 1865 Amsterdam Ave New York City NY 10031

ALSTON, GWENDOLYN YVONNE, counselor; b. Phila., Aug. 16, 1948; d. Jesse Lee Alston and Mozelle Alston McKay; student Cheyney State Coll., 1966-68; B.S., Temple U., 1970, postgrad. 1974—; M.S., Troy State U., 1973. Dir. counseling services Phila. Center for Health Careers, 1974-75; program adminstr. for aged Family Service of Phila., 1975-76; vocat. counselor Remedial Edn. and Diagnostic Services, Inc., Phila., 1976-77; vocat. and career specialist Learning Plus of Phila. Child Guidance Clinic, 1977—. Served with USAF, 1970-73, capt. Res., 1973—. Mem. Am., Phila., Pa. personnel and guidance assns., Nat. Vocat. Guidance Assn., Assn. Counselor Edn. and Supervision, Airmans Caucus, Zeta Phi Beta. Mem. Order Eastern Star. Office: 121 Broad St N Philadelphia PA 19107

ALTABE, JOAN BERG (MRS. DAVID ALTABE), muralist, illustrator, painter; b. N.Y.C., Apr. 27, 1935; d. Harold and Evelyn (Cooperman) Berg; B.A., Hunter Coll., 1956, postgrad., 1957; m. David Fintz Altabe, Sept. 28, 1958; children—Richard Jonathan, Madeline Nissa. Sculpture instr. N.Y. Lighthouse for Blind, 1949-55; art coordinator Croton-on-Hudson Sch. System, 1957; tech. drafting tchr. Haaren High Sch., N.Y.C., 1958-59; art tchr. jr. high schs., N.Y.C., 1959-72; art dir., partner Regina Pub. Co., 1973-78; partner Fintzenberg Pubs., 1978—; one-woman show Caravan House Gallery, N.Y.C., 1979; Bicentennial exhbn. dir. Long Beach Mus.; murals include stained glass N.Y. Synagogue, Bicentennial flag design for Smithsonian Instn. exhibited at Mus. Modern Art; prodn. mgr. trade mag. Am. Hairdresser, 1956-57. Mem. Nat. Soc. Mural Painters (treas.), Artists Equity Assn. N.Y. Editor: Nat. Drawing Anthology, 1974; contbr. illustrated articles to pubs. Home and Studio: 421 W Olive St Long Beach NY 11561

ALTBACH, PHILIP G., educator; b. Chgo., May 3, 1941; s. Milton S. and Josephine (Huebsch) A.; B.A., U. Chgo., 1960, M.A., 1962, Ph.D., 1966; m. Edith Hoshino, June 16, 1962; children—Eric, Fredrick. Lectr. edn. Harvard, 1966-67; research asso. Center for Internat. Affairs, 1967; asst. prof. edn. U. Wis., Madison, 1968-69, asso. prof. ednl. policy studies and S. Asian studies, 1970-74; Fulbright vis. prof. U. Bombay (India), 1969; prof. founds. edn. and higher edn. State U. N.Y at Buffalo, 1975—, chmn. dept. founds. of edn., 1978—, dir. Comparative Edn. Center, 1977—; dir. research and reference service Internat. Council Ednl. Devel., 1974-76; bd. dirs. Wil-Mar Neighborhood Center, Madison, 1970-73. NSF fellow, India, 1977. Mem. Comparative Edn. Soc., Assn. Profs. Higher Edn., Am. Ednl. Studies Assn. (dir. 1968-69). Author: Student Politics in America, 1974; Students in Revolt, 1970; Comparative Higher Education, 1973; American Students, 1973; University Reform, 1974; Perspectives on Publishing, 1976; Indian Publishing, 1975; Colonialism and Education, 1977; N.Am. editor Higher Edn., 1974—; book rev. editor Comparative Edn. Rev., 1968-71, chief editor, 1979—; contbr. articles to profl. pubs. Home: 172 Woodward Ave Buffalo NY 14214 Office: Baldy Hall State U NY at Buffalo Buffalo NY 14261

ALTCHEK, EDGAR DAVID, plastic surgeon; b. N.Y.C., Feb. 4, 1940; s. Emanuel and Beatrice (Davidoff) A.; A.B., Columbia, 1961; M.D., N.Y. Med. Coll., 1965; m. Leah Wertheim, Feb. 3, 1974; 1 son, Daniel. Intern, Beth Israel Hosp., N.Y.C., 1965-66, resident in surgery, 1966-69; resident in plastic surgery Mt. Sinai Hosp., N.Y.C., 1969-72; asst. attending surgeon Beth Israel Hosp., 1972-76; asst. attending surgeon Mt. Sinai Hosp., also asst. clin. prof. surgery Mt. Sinai Hosp. Sch. Medicine, 1972—; practice medicine specializing in plastic surgery, N.Y.C., 1972—. Diplomate Am. Bd. Plastic Surgery. Fellow A.C.S.; N.Y. Acad. Medicine; mem. Am. Soc. Plastic and Reconstructive Surgeons, AMA. Office: 102 E 78th St New York City NY 10021

ALTEMOSE, JAMES LEON, constrn. co. exec.; b. Whitehaven, Pa., Aug. 21, 1939; student in mech. engring. and real estate Pa. State U., 1959-61; m. Carol Lee Clemson, Sept. 22, 1963; children—Lynn, Lance. Pres., Altemose Cos., Center Square, 1962—; dir. Bank of King of Prussia (Pa.). Former sec., pres. Merit Shop Def. Fund; mem. Montgomery County (Pa.) Republican Com. Served with N.G., 1962-65. Recipient Freedoms Found. George Washington Honor medal, 1973; Engring. News Record Mag. Man of Year award, 1973; Everett M. Dirksen Meml. Employer of Year award Pennsylvanians for Right to Work, 1974, named Ky. col., 1973, licensed real estate broker, Pa. Mem. Montgomery County Realtors Assn., Young Pres.'s Orgn., Nat. Home Builders Assn., Asso. Builders and Contractors (spl. award of merit 1975), Pa. Jr. C. of C. Lutheran. Home: Box 292 S Whitehorse Rd RD 1 Malvern PA 19355 Office: 1166 DeKalb Pike Center Square PA 19432

ALTENBERN, ROBERT ALLEN, microbiologist; b. Junction City, Kans., June 12, 1923; s. Albert Wesley and Eleanor Mary (Hitchcock) A.; B.S., U. N.H., 1943; M.S., U. Ill., 1947, Ph.D., 1949; m. Audrey Louise Blank, Nov. 17, 1950; children—James A., Robert W., Barbara Ann. Microbiologist, med. bacteriology div. Dept. Army, Ft. Detrick, Frederick, Md., 1949—. Med. microbiologist Frederick Meml. Hosp., 1956-70. Served with USNR, 1944-46. Recipient U.S. Army Meritorious Civilian Service award, 1969, Leroy D. Fothergill Research award, 1970. Mem. Am. Soc. Microbiology, Soc. for Gen. Microbiology, Sigma Xi. Contbr. articles on microbiology to sci. jours. Home: Route 8 Frederick MD 21701 Office: Pathology Div USAMRIID Fort Detrick Frederick MD 21701

ALTIMARI, FRANK XAVIER, judge, educator; b. Mineola, N.Y., Sept. 4, 1928; s. Antonio and Elvira (Stumpo) A.; student St. Francis Coll., 1946-48; LL.B., Bklyn. Law Sch., 1951; LL.D., St. Francis Coll., 1967; m. Angela Scavuzzo, Sept. 23, 1951; children—Anthony Francis, Nicholas Stephen, Elvira Anne, Michael Joseph. Admitted to N.Y. State bar, 1951; asso. firm Austin & Du Pont, Jamaica, N.Y., 1951-55; partner firm Hoffmann & Altimari, Esquires, Mineola, 1956-65; judge Dist. Ct., Nassau County, Mineola, 1966-70; judge County Ct., Nassau County, 1970-73, adminstrv. judge, 1973; justice 10th jud. dist. N.Y. State Supreme Ct., 1974—; lectr. law St. Francis Coll., Bklyn., 1954-59, lectr., asst. prof., 1959-64, lectr., asso. prof., 1964-70, prof., 1970—. Gen. counsel, mem. Westbury (N.Y.) Bd. Edn., 1962-65. Dist. chmn. Cerebral Palsy, 1962-63, Am. Cancer Soc., 1964. Recipient citation St. Francis Coll., 1961; Pax et Bonum medal, 1967; Albert J. Conway award, 1973; Norman F. Lent Meml. award Criminal Cts. Bar Assn. Nassau County, 1976. Mem. N.Y., Nassau County bar assns. Club: Jamaica Lawyers (past pres.). Office: Chambers Supreme Ct Mineola NY 11501

ALTMAN, ALLAN, lawyer; b. Holyoke, Mass., Sept. 4, 1929; s. Leo and Elsie Eleanor (Siegel) A.; A.B., Bklyn. Coll., 1951; LL.B., Bklyn. Law Sch., 1956; m. Marcia Ann Edelman, Dec. 6, 1959; children—Steven Lawrence, Michael Jay. Asst. mng. clk. Messrs. Cravath, Swaine & Moore, N.Y.C., 1953-56; admitted to N.Y. bar, 1957, since practiced in N.Y.C.; asso. firm Henry F. Dressel, Esq., 1957-65; partner firm Dressel & Altman, 1965—. Trustee, Temple Beth Elohim. Served with USMC, 1951-53. Mem. Assn. Bar City N.Y., N.Y. County Lawyers Assn., Am., N.Y. bar assns., Am. Judicature Soc. Home: 19 Faulkner Ln Dix Hills NY 11746 Office: 150 Broadway New York City NY 10038

ALTMAN, BARRY LAYTON, urologist; b. Bklyn., May 30, 1933; s. Louis and Beatrice Marilyn (Miller) A.; B.S., Muhlenberg Coll., 1954; M.D., Jefferson Med. Coll., 1958; m. Rhoda Sara Weinstein, June 16, 1957; children—Jon Mitchell, Mara Beth, Pamela Dawn. Intern, Newark Beth Israel Hosp., 1958-59; resident VA Hosp., East Orange, N.J., 1959-60, 62-65, Met. Hosp., N.Y.C., 1963; practice medicine specializing in urology, Wayne N.J., 1965—; mem. staffs Chilton Meml. Hosp., St. Joseph's Hosp., Montclair Community Hosp., St. Vincent's Hosp.; chmn. urology dept. Chilton Meml. Hosp., Pompton Plains, N.J., 1972—; cons. urologist VA Hosp., East Orange, 1965-70; clin. instr. N.J. Coll. Medicine, Newark, 1969—. Served to capt. M.C., U.S. Army, 1960-62. Diplomate Am. Bd. Urology. Fellow A.C.S., Acad. Medicine N.J.; mem. Am. Urol. Assn., Am. Fertility Soc., N.J. State, Passaic County med. socs. Jewish. Contbr. articles in field to profl. jours. Office: 1777 Hamburg Turnpike Wayne NJ 07470

ALTMAN, LAWRENCE KIMBALL, physician, med. journalist; b. Quincy, Mass., June 19, 1937; s. William S. and Esther E. (Kimball) A.; grad. Milton Acad., 1954; A.B. cum laude in Govt., Harvard, 1958; M.D., Tufts U., 1962. Intern, Mt. Zion Med. Center, San Francisco, 1962-63; resident in internal medicine U. Wash. Affiliated Hosps., Seattle, 1966-68, sr. fellow dept. medicine, 1968-69, vis. scientist dept. medicine, 1971; sr. asst. in medicine U. Wash., Seattle, 1966-69; staff med. corr. N.Y. Times, N.Y.C., 1969—; clin. asst. prof. N.Y.U. Med. Sch., 1970—; cons. to med. schs. Served to lt. comdr. USPHS, 1963-66. Recipient Claude Bernard award Nat. Soc. for Med. Research, 1971, 75. Fellow A.C.P., N.Y. Acad. Medicine; mem. Soc. for Epidemiol. Research, Am. Soc. Tropical Medicine and Hygiene. Clubs: Harvard (N.Y. and Boston). Home: 140 West End Ave New York City NY 10023 Office: 229 W 43d St New York City NY 10036

ALTMAN, STUART HAROLD, univ. adminstr.; b. N.Y.C., Aug. 8, 1937; s. Sidney and Florence A.; B.B.A., CCNY; M.A. in Econs., Ph.D., UCLA; m. Diane Kleinsberg, June 7, 1959; children—Beth, Renee, Heather. Dept. asst. sec. for health planning and evaluation HEW, Washington, 1971-76; dep. dir. health Cost of Living Council, Washington, 1973-74; asso. prof. econs. Brown U., 1966-71; now dean Florence Heller Grad. Sch., Brandeis U., Waltham, Mass., chmn. bd. United Health Policy Consortium, Heller Sch.; mem. Inst. Medicine, Nat. Acad. Scis., 1978—; bd. clin. scholars Robert Wood Johnson Found., 1977—. Mem. Am. Public Health Assn. Home: 11 Bakers Hill Rd Weston MA 02193*

ALTSCHULER, ROBERT ALEXANDER, JR., ret. ins. agy. exec.; b. Summit, N.J., Feb. 10, 1917; s. Robert Alexander and Beatrice Elaine (Stoutenburgh) A.; student Lafayette Coll., 1936-38, N.Y. U., 1939; m. Adelaide S. Raynolds, Oct. 11, 1940; children—Gary Robert, Bruce Charles. Owner ins. agy., Hackensack, N.J., 1940-44; underwriter, v.p., dir. Internat. Fidelity Ins. Co., 1946-64; with Internat. Securities Co., 1960-64; owner Altschuler Agy., 1964-70; v.p. Martz-Altschuler & Assos., Inc., Madison, N.J., 1970-75, ret., 1975. Active Boy Scouts Am., 1951-54, ARC, 1950-53; mem. Convent Station Homeowners Assn. Served with AUS, 1944-46; ETO. Mem. Delta Kappa Epsilon. Republican. Presbyn. Mason. Club: Maroon (Lafayette Coll.). Home: 25 Canfield Rd Convent Station NJ 07961

ALTURA, BURTON MYRON, physiologist, educator; b. N.Y.C., Apr. 9, 1936; s. Barney and Frances (Dorfman) A.; B.A., Hofstra U., 1957; M.S., N.Y. U., 1961, Ph.D., 1964; m. Bella Tabak, Dec. 27, 1961; 1 dau., Rachel Allison. Teaching fellow in biology N.Y. U., N.Y.C., 1960-61, instr. exptl. anesthesiology Sch. Medicine, 1964-65, asst. prof., 1965-66; asst. prof. physiology and anesthesiology Albert Einstein Coll. Medicine, N.Y.C., 1967-70, asso. prof., 1970-74, vis. prof., 1974—; prof. physiology State U. N.Y. Downstate Med. Center, 1974—; research fellow Bronx Municipal Hosp. Center, 1967-76; mem. spl. study sect. on toxicology Nat. Inst. Environ. Health Scis., 1977—; cons. NSF, Nat. Heart, Lung and Blood Inst., U. City N.Y., Upjohn Co. Recipient research grants NIH, 1968—, NIMH, 1974—, predoctoral fellowship USPHS, 1962-64, Research Career Devel. award USPHS, 1968-72, travel award NIH, 1968, travel award Am. Soc. Pharm. and Exptl. Therapeutics, 1969. Fellow Am. Heart Assn. (mem. council on stroke 1973—, council basic sci. 1969—, council on thrombosis 1971—, council on circulation 1978—, council on high blood pressure 1978—), Am. Coll. Nutrition; mem. Microcirculatory Soc. (past mem. exec. council, mem. nominating com. 1973-74), Am. Physiol. Soc. (mem. circulation group 1971—), Soc. Exptl. Biology and Medicine (editorial bd. 1976—), AAUP, Am. Pub. Health Assn., Am. Chem. Soc. (div. medicinal chemistry), Am. Soc. Pharm. and Exptl. Therapeutics, Endocrine Soc., Harvey Soc., Am. Coll. Toxicology, Research Soc. on Alcoholism, Shock Soc. (founding), Am. Fedn. Clin. Research, AAAS, European Conf. Microcirculation, Internat. Soc. Thrombosis and Haemostasis, Internat. Soc. Biorheology, Reticuloendothelial Soc., Am. Inst. Biol. Sci., Assn. Gnotobiotics, Am. Micro. Soc., Am. Soc. Zoologists, Am. Soc. Cell Biology, Soc. Protozoologists, N.Y. Acad. Scis., N.Y. Heart Assn., Sigma Xi. Author: Microcirculation, 3 vols., 1976-78; Vascular Endothelium and Basement Membranes, 1978. Editor-in-chief

Physiology and Patho-physiology Series, 1976—; mem. editorial bd. Jour. Circulatory Shock, 1973—, Jour. Artery, 1974—, Recent Advances in Microcirculation, 1976—, Jour. Cardiovascular Pharmacology, 1977—, Prostaglandins and Medicine, 1978—. Office: 450 Clarkson Ave Brooklyn NY 11203

ALTVATER, WILLIAM CALDWELL, sales exec.; b. Aspinwall, Pa., Feb. 6, 1909; s. Fred Louis and Emilie (Daub) A.; student pub. schs., Shadyside Acad.; m. Mary Elizabeth Fullman, Aug. 5, 1935; 1 dau., Jo-Anna. Vice pres. sales, dir. Pitts. and Shawmut Coal Co., Kittanning, Pa., 1944-63; pres., chmn. bd. Allegheny & Eastern Coal Co., 1963-77; pres. Allegheny & Eastern Coal Sales, Inc., 1977—; receiver for Maple Hill Coal Co., 1968-70. Mem. Kittanning Union Sch. Bd., 1955-61; pres. Kittanning Area Joint School Bd., Armstrong County Sch. Bd.; chmn. operating com. Kittanning Area Schs., dir. Kittanning Union Sch. Dist., 1965-71; mem. Applewold (Pa.) Boro Council, 1978-1982. Mem. Pa. Coal Mining Assn. (v.p., dir. 1965—, chmn. bd. dirs. 1971-73), Engrs. Soc. Western Pa. (life). Clubs: Traffic (life) (Pitts.); Pa. Conservation Assn. (dir.). Home and Office: 328 Allegheny Ave Kittanning PA 16201

ALUISE, ROBERT RICHARD, civil engr.; b. Carlim, Pa., Aug. 2, 1905; s. Joseph and Joanna (Galano) A.; B.S., Pa. State U., 1929; m. Catherine E. Dalesio, May 17, 1930; children—Dolores R., Jacqueline C. (Mrs. W. Gordon), Joseph R. Bridge draftsman Pa. Dept. Hwys., Hollidaysburg, 1929-33, sr. bridge draftsman, 1933-37; structural engr. Pangborn Corp., Hagerstown, Md., 1937-39; bridge designer head Pa. Turnpike Commn., Everett, 1939-40; asst. engr., naval architect Puget Sound Naval Shipyard, Bremerton, Wash., 1940-41; asst. engr., naval architect Navy Dept., Washington, 1941, asso. engr., naval architect, 1941-45, engr., naval architect, 1945-46; underwriting supr., engr. architect FHA, Washington, 1946-47; engr. architect U.S. Army Office Chief Engrs., 1947-49; contrn. engr. Bur. Indian Affairs, Dept. Interior, Washington, 1949-52; gen. engr. research and devel. facilities dept. def. U.S. Army Ordnance, 1952-53; missile system engr. Vitro Corp. Am., Silver Spring, Md., 1953-73, project supr., 1958-73; now cons. civil, archtl., mech. and naval engr.; v.p. engring. Metro Truck & Tractor Leasing Inc., Beltsville, Md. Registered profl. engr., D.C. Fellow ASCE; mem. Constrn. Specification Inst., Washington Soc. Engrs., Pa. State U. Engrs. Assn., Am. Ordnance Assn., Pa. State U. Alumni Assn. K.C. Patentee in field. Home: 2901 Plyers Mill Rd Silver Spring MD 20902 Office: 2901 Plyers Mill Rd Silver Spring MD 20902

ALVARADO, ALFREDO, physician; b. Bogota, Colombia, May 9, 1931; s. Ciro Antonio and Maria J. (Barrera) A.; came to U.S., 1964; B.A., Nat. Coll., Bogota, 1950; M.D., Nat. U., Bogota, 1956; m. Salesia Burbano, July 3, 1964; children—Ciro, Lorena, Salesita, Natalia. Intern, Charleston (W.Va.) Gen. Hosp., 1964; resident Good Samaritan Hosp., Cin., 1965-66, Orange Meml. Hosp., Orlando, Fla., 1966-67; Nazareth Hosp., Phila., 1968-69, Temple U. Hosp., Phila., 1968-69, Episcopal Hosp., Phila., 1969-70; attending in gen. and thoracic surgery Nazareth Hosp., Phila., 1971—, St. Mary's Hosp., Langhorne, Pa., 1973—, Frankford Hosp., Phila., 1978—; clin. instr. surgery Temple U., Phila., 1973—. Served with Colombian Navy, 1957-64. Diplomate Am. Bd. Surgery. Mem. Phila. County Med. Assn., Pa. Med. Soc. Roman Catholic. Contbr. articles to med. jours. Home: 9114 Dale Rd Philadelphia PA 19115 Office: Northeast Med Center Welsh Rd and Roosevelt Blvd Philadelphia PA 19114

ALVAREZ, MANUEL, chemist; b. New Brunswick, N.J., July 30, 1937; s. Joseph and Rose (Vasquez) A.; B.S., Rutgers U., 1959, B.A. in Math., 1964, M.S. in Chemistry, 1970, postgrad., 1971-78; m. Antigone Kuklakis, June 19, 1960; children—Deborah, Emanuel, Michael. Chemist, chem. research and devel. center FMC Corp., 1959-64, research chemist, 1964-70, sr. research chemist, 1970—. Mem. E. Brunswick (N.J.) Zoning Bd. Mem. Am. Chem. Soc. Roman Catholic. Club: Kiwanis (pres. 1977-78, lt. gov. 1978-79). Patentee. Home: 37 Gates Ave East Brunswick NJ 08816 Office: FMC Corp PO Box 8 Princeton NJ 08540

ALVES, JOSEPH THOMAS, clergyman, mental health clinic exec.; b. Boston, Oct. 4, 1921; s. Joseph Francis and Mary (McDermott) A.; A.B., Boston Coll., 1944, M.S.W., 1948; M.A., St. John's Sem., 1953, M.Div., 1977; Dr. Social Work, Catholic U. Am., 1959. Asso. dir. Pittsfield (Mass.) Community Chest and Berkshire County Council Social Agys., 1948-49; ordained priest Roman Catholic Ch., 1953; parish priest, Everett, Mass., 1953-56; elevated to domestic prelate by Pope, 1965; exec. dir. Family Counseling and Guidance Centers Inc., Boston, 1958—; pres. Samaritans, Inc., 1977—. Bd. dirs. Nat. Council on Aging, 1969—, chmn. membership com., 1974-77, v.p., 1978—; bd. dirs. Pastoral Service Commn., Mass. Council Chs., 1971-75; del. White House Conf. on Aging, 1961; mem. adv. com. on services Mass. Dept. Pub. Welfare; mem. Health Planning Council for Greater Boston; chmn. adv. council for Community Mental Health Center Constrn.; bd. dirs. Assn. Psychiat. Outpatient Centers Am., 1978—, Nat. Conf. Cath. Charities, 1959—. Served as 1st lt., pilot USAAF, 1943-46. Decorated D.F.C., Air medal with oak leaf clusters. Mem. Nat. Assn. Social Workers (chmn. social policy and action com. Eastern Mass. chpt. 1967—), Acad. Religion and Mental Health, Gerontol. Soc. Inc., Nat. Council on Family Relations, Mass. Conf. on Social Welfare, Council Social Work Edn., Nat. Conf. Social Welfare, Nat. Conf. Catholic Charities, Am. Acad. Clin. Sociologists, Inst. Soc., Ethics and Life Scis., Internat. Council Social Welfare (U.S. Com.), Am. Sociol. Assn., Am. Acad. Polit. and Social Sci., Boston Soc. Gerontol. Psychiatry, Citizens for Decent Housing, Soc. Family Therapy and Research, Internat. Soc. Existential Psychology and Psychiatry, AAAS, Mass. Pub. Welfare Council, Am. Acad. Psychotherapists, Am. Arbitration Assn. (nat. panel arbitrators), AAAS, Mass. Assn. to Advance Human Scis., Boston Latin Sch. Assn., South Shore C. of C., New Directions, Common Cause, World Federalist Assn. Clubs: St. Botolph, Plymouth Country, K.C. Author: Confidentiality in Social Work, 1959. Contbr. articles to profl. and popular jours. and mags. Home: 55 W Broadway South Boston MA 02127 Office: 49 Franklin St Boston MA 02110

ALYEA, FREDERICK NEWCOMBE, atmospheric physicist; b. Glen Ridge, N.J., Oct. 3, 1935; s. Hubert Newcombe and Evelyn (Shields) A.; A.B. in Chemistry, Princeton, 1957; Ph.D. in Chem. Engring. (Dow Chem. Co. fellow, Univ. Merit fellow), Stanford, 1962; m. Retha Lois Ballard, June 8, 1963; 1 dau., Sara. Research scientist LTV Research Center, Dallas, 1962-65; mem. staff, space scis. lab. Gen. Electric Co., Valley Forge, Pa., 1965—, project leader, 1971—; cons. Inst. Def. Analysis, Washington, 1972-73. Mem. Am. Chem. Soc., Sigma Xi. Republican. Presbyn. Home: 251 W DeKalb Pike A-616 King of Prussia PA 19406 Office: Gen Electric Co SSL PO Box 8555 Philadelphia PA 19101

AMAN, MOHAMMED MOHAMMED, educator; b. Alexandria, Egypt, Jan. 3, 1940; s. Mohammed Aman and Fathia Ali (al-Maghrabi) Mohammed; came to U.S., 1963, naturalized, 1975; B.A. with honors, Cairo (Egypt) U., 1961; M.S., Columbia, 1965; Ph.D., U. Pitts., 1968; m. Mary Jo Parker, Sept. 15, 1972; 1 son, David. Reference librarian, bibliographer Egyptian Nat. Library, Cairo, 1961-63; reference librarian, instr. library sci. Duquesne U., Pitts., 1965-68; asst. prof. library sci. Pratt Inst., N.Y.C., 1968-69; asst. prof. library and info. sci. St. John's U., N.Y.C., 1969-71, asso. prof., 1971-74, prof., 1974—, dir. div., 1973-76; dean Palmer Grad. Library Sch., C.W. Post Center, L.I. U., 1976—; cons. in field; UNESCO expert to Bahrain, 1976; adviser to pres. Kuwait U., 1977—; examiner N.Y. State Edn. Dept., 1974. Mem. ALA, Am. Soc. Info. Sci., Middle East Studies Assn., AAUP, Am. Assn. Library Schs., Egyptian Am. Scholars Assn. Moslem. Clubs: Archons of Colophon, Melvil Dui Marching and Chowder Assn. Author: Analysis of Form and Structure of Arabic Subject Headings, 1969; Arab States Author Headings, 1973; Librarianship and the Third World, 1977. Editor Leads, 1974-76. Contbr. articles to profl. publs. Home: 137-47 228th St Laurelton NY 11413 Office: CW Post Center LI U Greenvale Long Island NY 11548

AMATO, PETER ROBERT, gastroenterologist; b. Boston, Nov. 2, 1935; s. Peter and Grace (Rinaldi) A.; A.B. cum laude, Harvard U., 1957; M.D., Tufts U., 1961; m. Clementine A. Costello, June 27, 1959; children—Lisa Marie, Lynore Grace, Peter Robert. Intern, Hartford (Conn.) Hosp., 1961-62; resident in medicine Jackson Meml. Hosp., Miami, Fla., 1962-63, VA Hosp., East Orange, N.J., 1965-67; fellow in gastroenterology Yale U. Affiliated Program, New Haven, 1967-68; practice medicine specializing in gastroenterology, Hartford, 1968—; dir. gastroenterology St. Francis Hosp., Hartford; asst. clin. prof. U. Conn. Med. Sch., Farmington. Served to capt. M.C., U.S. Army, 1963-65. Mem. AMA, Conn. State, Hartford County med. socs. Roman Catholic. Home: 8 Timrod Ln West Hartford CT 06107 Office: 1000 Asylum Ave Hartford CT 06105

AMBER, EUGENE LEWIS, ins. co. exec.; b. Buffalo, Mar. 8, 1923; s. Harrison L. and Emma (Cobb) A.; B.A., Cornell U., 1948; m. Katherine M. Midgette, Nov. 17, 1945; children—Lisa K., Deborah A., John L., Gilbert H. Underwriting trainee Hartford Accident & Indemnity, Hartford, Conn., 1948-51, spl. agt., 1951-53; securities analyst Berkshire Life Ins. Co., Pittsfield, Mass., 1953-56, asst. treas., 1956-59, investment officer, 1959-62, 1st v.p. investments, 1962-63, sr. vice pres. investments, 1963—; pres., dir. Berkshire Mgmt. & Research Corp., Pittsfield, 1968—; dir. Mass. Bus. Devel. Corp., Boston, Pittsfield Nat. Bank; trustee Guardian Mortgage Investors. Chmn. investment com., mem. finance com. Berkshire County Home for Aged Women, 1959—; pres. Berkshire County Soc. for Care of Crippled and Deformed Children, 1956—; treas. Pittsfield Boys Club, 1963—; bd. dirs. Berkshire Rehab. Center, 1964—. Served with USMC, 1942-46. Decorated Air medal. Mem. Investment Co. Inst., N.Y. Soc. Security Analysts, Newcomen Soc. N. Am. Congregationalist. Club: Country (Pittsfield). Home: 152 Main St Dalton MA 01226 Office: 700 South St Pittsfield MA 01201

AMBERSON, J(AMES) BURNS, physician; b. Waynesboro, Pa., June 8, 1890; s. James Burns and Katherine (Good) A.; Ph.B., Lafayette Coll., 1913, Sc.D. 1944; M.D., Johns Hopkins, 1917; Sc.D., U. Pa., 1953; m. Rebecca T. Steen, Jan. 1, 1919 (dec. Aug. 1969); children—James Burns III, Mrs. Mary Priscilla Adsit; m. 2d, Margaret T. Goldsmith, Nov. 27, 1971. Asst. and asso. physician, Loomis Sanatorium, 1917-26, physician in chief, 1927-29; vis. physician Herman Kiefer Hosp., Detroit, and William H. Maybury Sanatorium, Northville, Mich., 1926-27; vis. physician chest service Bellevue Hosp., 1927-38, vis. physician in charge, 1938-55, cons., 1955—; cons. physician N.Y. State Tb hosps., 1935-67. Grassland Hosp., 1939—; cons. Presbyn. Hosp. Asst. prof. and prof. clin. medicine Coll. Phys. & Surg., Columbia, 1927-38, prof. medicine, 1938-55, prof. emeritus, 1955—. Recipient plaque N.Y. Acad. Medicine, 1970. Master A.C.P.; mem. Am. Lung Assn. (pres. 1942, Trudeau medal 1952, hon.), Brit. (hon.), Am. (hon.; lectr.; pres. 1940) thoracic socs., N.Y. Lung Assn. (pres. 1941-46; gen. dir. 1955-65), Am. Clin. and Climatol. Assn., Assn. Am. Physicians, AAAS, AMA, Harvey Soc., N.Y. Acad. Medicine (v.p. 1945-47, 55, Acad. plaque 1970), Sigma Xi, Alpha Omega Alpha (hon.). Home: 16 Sherwood Dr Hillsdale NY 07642

AMBLER, E(DWARD) CURTIS, mech. engr.; b. South Norwalk, Conn., Feb. 16, 1920; s. Tracy Bell and Ethel (Wurtzbach) A.; B.S. in Mech. Engring., Worcester Poly. Inst., 1942; m. M. Jacqueline Palmer, Oct. 3, 1942 (dec.); m. 2d, Mary L. McClure, Nov. 27, 1970; children—Curtis P., Tracy B., Rosalind; stepchildren—William McClure, Martha McClure Patterson. Lab. engr. Landers, Frary & Clark, New Britain, Conn., 1946-50, chief engr., 1952-60; sr. engr.-computer Veeder-Root Inc., Hartford, Conn., 1961-67; engr. mgr., corp. research, devel. mgr., chief engr. tech. services The Stanley Works, New Britain, 1967-77, v.p. research and product engring. Stanley Indsl. Hardware div., 1978—. Chmn. Town Plan Commn., Newington, Conn., 1961-66; mem. Newington Town Council, 1971-77; bd. dirs. Newington Children's Hosp., 1968—; officer Vol. Fire Dept., 1946—; ch. officer, 1949-72. Served to lt. comdr. USN, 1942-46, 50-52. Recipient Jaycee's Distinguished Pub. Servant award. Mem. ASME. Republican. Mason. Patentee in field. Home: 72 Centerwood Rd Newington CT 06111 Office: The Stanley Laboratory 1309 Corbin Ave New Britain CT 06053

AMBRO, JEROME A., JR., congressman; children—Cathleen, David, Richard. Mem. Suffolk County (N.Y.) Bd. Suprs., 1968-70; supr. Town of Huntington (N.Y.), 1968-75; mem. 94th-96th Congresses from 3d N.Y. Dist. Served with M.P., AUS. Recipient Torch of Liberty award B'nai B'rith, 1967, Distinguished Service award N.Y. State VFW, Ednl. award SCOPE, award N.Y. State Recreation and Parks Assn., Outstanding Public Service award IEEE. Roman Catholic. Home: 15 Harvest Time Ct Huntington Station NY 11746 Office: 236 Cannon House Office Bldg Washington DC 20505

AMBROSE, FREDERICK HALSEY, JR., neurosurgeon; b. Grand Forks, N.D., Dec. 13, 1919; s. Frederick Halsey and Edna (Morrill) A.; A.B., Cornell Coll., 1941; B.S., U. N.D., 1944; M.D., Temple U., 1946; m. Jeane Marie Adams, Nov. 3, 1946; children—Frederick Halsey 3d, Stacey M., Kevin B., Shawn M., Brian P. Intern, Jersey City Med. Center, 1946-47; resident St. Thomas Hosp., Akron, Ohio, 1947-48, Bellevue Hosp. Center, 1955-58; practice medicine specializing in neurosurgery, 1958—; mem. staffs Elizabeth City Hosp., St. Elizabeth Hosp., Alexian Bros. Hosp., Rahway (N.J.) Hosp., J.F. Kennedy Hosp., Edison, N.J., Meml. Hosp., Union, N.J.; asst. clin. prof. neurosurgery N.J. Sch. Medicine, 1953-55. Served with U.S. Army, 1943-45, with USNR, 1952-54. Diplomate Am. Bd. Neurosurgery. Mem. N.J. Neurosurgical Soc. (sec. 1973, pres. 1974), Med. Soc. N.J., Internat. Congress Neurol. Surgery, Congress Neurol. Surgeons. Republican. Methodist. Home: 401 Kenli Ln Brielle NJ 08730 Office: 701 Newark Ave Elizabeth NJ 07208

AMBROSE, JOSEPH M., lawyer, army officer; b. Arlington, Mass., May 10, 1921; s. Joseph Patrick and Julia (Walsh) A.; A.B. cum laude, Harvard, 1942, LL.B., 1948. Admitted to Mass. bar, 1948; practiced in Boston, 1948-53; supr., atty. Mass. Div. Youth Service, 1953-64; adj. gen. State of Mass., 1964-69; exec. sec. Mass. Council Juvenile Behavior, 1970-73; U.S. property and fiscal officer for Mass., U.S. Army, Natick, 1973—. Mem. Town Meeting, Danvers, Mass. 1946-50, 52-54, mem. finance com., 1950-52. Pres. Mass. Half-way Houses, Inc.; bd. visitors New Eng. Mil. Sch. Served to capt. AUS, 1942-46, to maj. gen. Mass. N.G., 1946-69. Decorated Legion of Merit. Mem. Am. Legion, Ancient and Hon. Arty. Co. Roman Catholic. K.C. Clubs: North Shore Harvard, Dugout. Home: 114 Howe St Framingham MA 01701 Office: USPFO 143 Speen St Natick MA 01760

AMBROSIO, THOMAS JAMES, pharm. research scientist; b. Bklyn., Apr. 20, 1932; s. Pasquale and Fortunata Fetura (Annunziata) A.; B.S. in Pharmacy, L.I. U., 1954; M.S. in Pharm. Sci., Rutgers U., 1966, Ph.D., 1970; m. Antonina Marie Bilello, June 26, 1954; children—Patrick James, Donna Marie. Pharmacist, Katz Drug, N.Y.C., 1954-57; research pharmacist Ortho Research Found., Raritan, N.J., 1957-70, Schering Pharm., Bloomfield, N.J., 1970—; chmn. steering com. Packaging Sci. and Engring. Program, Rutgers U., also guest lectr. Coll. Pharmacy and Grad. Sch.; continuing edn. lectr. pharm., packaging sci. Mem. Somerset County (N.J.) Republican Com., 1966-68. Served with AUS, 1955-57. Recipient award Am. Legion, 1947; Schering research fellow, 1970-71. Mem. Am., N.J. pharm. assns., Acad. Pharm. Sci., Packaging Inst., ASTM, Sigma Xi, Rho Chi. Republican. Roman Catholic. Contbr. articles to profl. jours. Home: 15 W Cliff St Somerville NJ 08876 Office: 86 Orange St Bloomfield NJ 07003

AMBS, WILLIAM JOSEPH, chemist; b. Phila., Dec. 3, 1929; s. Herman Joseph and Geraldine Rosalita (Kenny) A.; B.S. (R.A. Foley Merit scholar), Villanova U., 1952; M.S., Stevens Inst. Tech., 1954; Ph.D., Cath. U. Am., 1961; m. Edith Marie McCoy, June 22, 1957; 1 dau., Caroline Marie. Research chemist Nat. Bur. Standards, Washington, 1957-63; research chemist Houdry div. Air Products & Chems., Inc., Marcus Hook, Pa., 1963-71, sr. research chemist, 1971-77, group leader fluid cracking catalyst research group, 1977—. Mem. Am. Chem. Soc., Nat. Catalysis Soc., Sigma Xi. Club: Phila. Catalysis. Author: Deep Water, 1977. Contbr. articles to sci. jours. Office: Houdry Div Air Products and Chems Inc PO Box 427 Marcus Hook PA 19061

AMENT, RICHARD, anesthesiologist; b. N.Y.C., Jan. 27, 1919; B.A., U. Buffalo, 1938, M.D., 1942; m. Esther Abrams, Apr. 18, 1943; children—Sara Lauren Ament Baron, David S., Robert H., Victor C. Mem. faculty U. Buffalo Med. Sch., 1949—, clin. prof. anesthesiology, 1971—; attending anesthesiologist Buffalo Gen. Hosp., 1963—; courtesy staff Buffalo Children's Hosp., 1974—; mem. Comprehensive Health Planning Council Erie County, 1972-74; dir. ednl. programs dept. anesthesiology State U. N.Y. at Buffalo, 1978—; vis. prof. med. schs. univs. Md., Tex., N.Y., Colo., Wash. Pres. Jewish Center Greater Buffalo, 1970-72, 74-75, Temple Beth Zion, Buffalo, 1971-73; bd. govd. Jewish Fedn Greater Buffalo, 1977—, chmn. social planning com., 1968-69. Served to capt. M.C., USAAF, 1943-46. Diplomate Nat. Bd. Med. Examiners, Am. Bd. Anesthesiology (sr. examiner 1969—). Mem. Am. Coll. Anesthesiologist (gov. 1972-75), Am. (pres. 1977, past dir., chmn. com. fin.), N.Y. State (pres. 1967) socs. anesthesiologists, N.Y. State (past com. chmn.), Erie County (past com. chmn.) med. socsl. Address: 22 Lake Ledge Dr Williamsville NY 14221

AMENTA, PETER SEBASTIAN, educator, researcher; b. Cromwell, Conn., Mar. 26, 1927; s. Peter and Mary (DeMauro) A.; student Conn. Wesleyan U., 1947-49; B.S., Fairfield U., 1952; M.S., Marquette U., 1954; Ph.D., U. Chgo., 1958; m. Rose Phyllis Russo, June 20, 1953; children—Mary Vincenza, Rosemarie. Undergrad. asst. Fairfield U., 1949-52; grad. asst. Marquette U., 1952-54; grad. asst. U. Chgo., 1955-58; instr., ind. investigator Marine Biol. Lab., Woods Hole, Mass., summer 1956; instr. anatomy Hahnemann Med. Coll., 1958-60, asst. prof. anatomy, 1960-63, asso. prof., 1963-71, prof., 1971—, acting chmn. dept., 1973-75, chmn. dept., 1975—, head miscroscopic anatomy, 1968-75, treas. exec. faculty, 1970-73, dir. div. electron microscopy, 1970-75; vis. prof. cytology Rome U., 1966, 76, Estacao Agronomica National, Oeiras, Portugal, 1970, Edinburg (Scotland) U., 1972; instr. Trenton Diocese High Sch. Religion, 1967-72; lectr. N.J. Right to Life Com., 1969-73, Am. Cancer Soc., 1969—, Continuing Edn. Program, Roxborough Hosp., Phila., 1970—; pres. Humanities Gifts Registry, U. Pa., 1976—. Twp. chmn. Burlington County Juvenile Conf. Com., 1967-70; mem. Trenton Diocesan Pastoral Council, 1968-73, vice chmn., 1970-72; dir. St. Joan of Arc Choir; mem. Palmyra String Band. Served with AUS, 1946-47. Named Man of Year, Fairfield U., 1962; Distinguished Alumnus, Am. Jesuit U., 1967. Fellow AAAS; mem. Am. Assn. Anatomists, Assn. Anatomy Chairmen, Albertus Magnus Guild of Catholic Scientists, AMA, N.Y. Acad. Scis., Am. Inst. Biol. Scis., Tissue Culture Assn., Am. Soc. Photobiology, Internat. Congress Photobiology, Am. Soc. Zoologists, Hahnemann Alumni Assn. (hon.), Sigma Xi, Phi Sigma. Office: 230 N Broad St Philadelphia PA 19102

AMERSHEK, KATHLEEN, educator; b. Johnstown, Pa., Dec. 1, 1929; d. Rudie J. and Helen (McKernan) Amershek; B.S., Western Pa. State Coll., 1951; M.Ed., Pa. State U., 1957; Ph.D., U. Minn., 1966; m. E.P. McLoone, 1973. Tchr., Westmont-Upper Yoder Sch. Dist., Johnstown, 1951-56; grad. asst. Pa. State U., 1956-57; supr. State U. N.Y. at Brockport, 1957-60; instr. U. Minn., 1960-63; asso. prof. State U. N.Y. at Buffalo, 1963-66; asso. prof. early childhood and elementary edn. U. Md., College Park, 1966—; cons. Student Vol. Programs of Catholic Student Center, Pa. Dept. Pub. Health. Mem. Md. Com. Early Childhood Edn., 1969—. Mem. Tri-state Assn. Student Teaching (past rec. sec. Minn.), Md. Tchrs. Assn. (pres. higher edn. council 1973-75), Am. Ednl. Research Assn., Assn. Student Teaching, Pi Lambda Theta. Contbr. to Ency. Research in Edn. Home: 4602 Clemson Rd College Park MD 20740 Office: College of Education University of Maryland College Park MD 10742

AMES, BERNARD GARETH, bookstore exec.; b. N.Y.C., Feb. 9, 1925; s. Benjamin and Sarah (Jacobowitz) Abramowitz; student U. Hawaii, 1945, Kahaliu Coll., Maui, Hawaii, 1945; m. Patricia Alice Nugent, May 22, 1966; 1 son, Richard Keith. Pres., Womrath County Bookshop, Hempstead, N.Y., 1956—, Hobbymasters, 1970—, Gareth Ames Enterprises, Hempstead, 1972—, Hobbymaster Internat., 1973—, Civil Service Books, 1975—. Served with USNR, 1942-46, 50-51. Mem. Am. Book Sellers Assn., 8th Regiment Vets. Assn. (v.p. 1971—), Am. Fedn. Small Bus., Am. Security Council (asso.), Am. Def. Council. Home: 36 Cathedral Ave Hempstead NY 11550 Office: 229 Fulton Ave Hempstead NY 11550

AMES, LINCOLN, investment co. exec.; b. Glen Ridge, N.J., Aug. 8, 1932; s. Wyllys P. and Anna (Lincoln) A.; B.S., Yale U., 1954; M.B.A., Harvard U., 1960; m. Aubin Wells Zabriskie, Nov. 26, 1960; children—Hyla Lincoln, Mark Zabriskie, David Wyllys. Sr. v.p., dir. Blyth & Co., Inc., N.Y.C., 1960-72; exec. v.p., nat. dir. investment banking, dir. Dean Witter Reynolds, Inc., N.Y.C., 1972—. Trustee, Mountainside Hosp., Montclair, N.J. Served with USNR, 1954-58. Mem. N.Y. Soc. Security Analysts, N.Y. Bond Club. Republican. Presbyterian. Clubs: City Midday, Montclair Golf, The Brook, Hartwood. Office: Dean Witter Reynolds Inc 130 Liberty St New York City NY 10006

AMES, RICHARD ALLEN, physician; b. Moultonboro, N.H., Dec. 2, 1933; s. Harold Burleigh and Charlotte Elvira (Wakefield) A.; B.A., Dartmouth Coll., 1955; M.D., Tufts U., 1959. Med. intern, Chelsea (Mass.) Naval Hosp., 1959-60; individual practice medicine, gen. practice, Center Sandwich, N.H., 1963-65, specializing in dermatology, South Weymouth, Mass., 1968-72, Laconia, N.H., 1972—; resident in dermatology Columbia Presbyn. Hosp., N.Y.C.,

1965-68; mem. staff Lake Regions Gen. Hosp., Laconia, South Shore Hosp., S. Weymouth, Mass., 1968-72. Diplomate Am. Bd. Dermatology. Mem. AMA (physician's recognition award 1977), N.H., Belknap County (pres. 1977) med. socs., N.H. Soc. Dermatology (sec.-treas. 1973—), Am. Acad. Dermatology, New Eng. Dermatol. Soc., N.H. Med. Soc., Boston Dermatology Club. Home: Center Harbor NH 03226 Office: One Mill Plaza Laconia NH 03246

AMES, THOMAS-ROBERT HOWLAND, psychotherapist, educator; b. Daytona Beach, Fla., Feb. 22, 1930; s. Orris Kingsley and Helen Margaret (Reed) A.; A.A. in Liberal Arts, U. Fla., 1951, B.A. in Social Scis., 1952; M.A. in Rehab. Counseling, N.Y. U., 1960; postgrad., 1960—. Program coordinator Eastern Sch., Inc., N.Y.C., 1960-66; program dir. Young Adult Inst. and Workshop, Inc., N.Y.C., 1966-67, exec. dir., 1967-71; asst. prof. Manhattan Community Coll., City U. N.Y., N.Y.C., 1970—, coordinator community mental health curriculum, 1973-76; dir. T.R.Y.A. Hostel for Developmentally Disabled Adults, Nassau County chpt. Assn. Children Learning Disabilities, 1974—. Day camp dir. Mental Retardation Inst. N.Y. Med. Coll., N.Y.C., 1971; founding pres. Life Adjustment Cons. Center, Inc., N.Y.C., 1972—; cons. Joint Commn. Mental Health Children, Inc., Chevy Chase, Md., 1968, Nat. Assn. Mental Health, N.Y.C., 1968-70, Assn. Advancement Mentally Handicapped, Princeton, Opengate, Inc., Sumers, N.Y., 1969-71, Burt Center, Inc., San Francisco, Adams Sch., Inc., N.Y.C. Transitional Services Nassau County, Wantaugh, N.Y., Mem. N.Y.C. Mayor's Com. Mental Retardation, 1967-68; mem. steering com. Lower Manhattan Mental Retardation Region, N.Y.C., 1969-71. Recipient Leadership and Service awards Young Adult Inst., 1972, N.Y. Met. Rehab. Counseling Assn., 1974, Community Mental Health Soc. Manhattan Community Coll., 1976; Meritorious Service award Northeast Region Nat. Rehab. Assn., 1973, certified rehab. counselor, sex therapist, sex educator. Fellow Am. Assn. Mental Deficiency (chmn. region X adminstrn., exec. bd. 1973-74), Royal Soc. Health, Am. Soc. Group Psychotherapy and Psychodrama, Nat. Rehab. Counseling Assn.; mem. Assn. for Children with Retarded Mental Devel. (mem. adv. bd. 1967—), Assn. Adminstrs. Mental Health and Mental Retardation Facilities (mem. exec. bd. 1970-71), N.Y. Met. (pres. 1974, permanent ex-officio mem. exec. bd.), Nat. (edn. com. 1974-75, council profl. devel. 1976), N.E. (mem. exec. bd. 1973-74) rehab. counseling assns., Am. Psychol. Assn., Am. Orthopsychiat. Assn., Am. Assn. Spl. Educators, Am. Assn. Sex Educators, Counselors and Therapists, Phi Kappa Phi, Phi Alpha Theta, Phi Eta Sigma. Contbr. articles and chpts. to various publs. Office: Manhattan Community Coll City U NY 1633 Broadway New York City NY 10019

AMICK, CAROL CAMPBELL, state legislator; b. Cleve., June 17, 1945; d. Charles Lorayne and Janet Robertson Gilchrist (Campbell) Amick; B.S., Iowa State U., 1968; m. William Stevenson Moonan. Reporter radio-TV news WOI-AM-FM-TV, Ames, Iowa, 1967-68; asst. editor Belmont (Mass.) Citizen, 1968-69; reporter-announcer WCAS Radio, Cambridge, Mass., 1968-69; editor Minute-Man, Bedford, Mass., 1969-74. Journalism instr. night sch. Middlesex Community Coll., 1972, adviser student newspaper, 1973; project coordinator photography class Concord (Mass.) Prison, 1972-73; journalism lectr. Bedford Pub. Schs., 1969—. Mem. Charter Commn., Bedford, 1973-74; mem. Opportunities Industrialization Center, Inc., 1972, Friends of Bedford Library, 1973—; insp. wood, bark, and manure Town of Bedford, 1972-74, mem. publs. com., 1973-74; community cabinet dir. United Way, 1973. Mem. Bedford Democratic Town Com., 1972—; mem. Mass. Ho. of Reps., 1974-77; mem. Mass. Senate, 1977—. Trustee Bedford Pub. Library, 1976-78; chmn. Legis. Water Study Commn., 1977—; mem. Mass. Caucus Women Legislators, 1975—, chmn., 1976-77. Recipient Reporting award New Eng. Press Assn., 1970. Mem. Women in Communications, Nat. Newspaper Assn., New Eng., Mass. Press assns., Alpha Lambda Delta, Sigma Kappa. Mem. Ch. of Christ. Club: Woman's Community (Bedford). Home: 277 The Great Rd Bedford MA 01730 Office: State House Boston MA 02133

AMICK, JAMES ALBERT, electronics researcher; b. Lawrence, Mass., Feb. 18, 1928; s. Chester Albert and Marcella Estella (Hoover) A.; A.B. with honors, Princeton, 1949, M.A., 1951, Ph.D., 1952; m. Nancy Jane Scott, Sept. 9, 1961; 1 dau., D'Maris Ann. Staff mem. electronics research electrophotography, semicondr. processing RCA Labs, Princeton, N.J., 1952-66, Zurich (Switzerland) Labs., 1956-57, group head process research, Princeton, 1966-71, mgr. materials and processes RCA Solid State, Somerville, N.J., 1971-76, spl. assignment solar cell processing RCA Labs, Princeton, 1976; group leader silicon solar cell research Exxon Research & Engring. Center, Linden, N.J., 1976—. Fellow Am. Inst. Chemists; mem. Am. Chem. Soc., Electrochem. Soc., AAAS, Sigma Xi, Alpha Chi Sigma. Presbyterian. Club: Masons. Contbg. author, also contbr. articles to profl. publs.; patentee in field. Home: 76 Leabrook Ln Princeton NJ 08540 Office: Exxon Research and Engring Center Box 8 Linden NJ 07036

AMIDON, RICHARD B., city ofcl.; b. Tully, N.Y., Feb. 16, 1916; s. Frank F. and Bertha (Bush) A.; grad. high sch.; m. Betty Marie Berry, Nov. 29, 1941 (div. 1971); children—Patricia M., Albert Barrett, Gail C. Amidon Brennan, Phyllis M. Amidon Filsinger, Vicki L., Mark C.; m. 2d, Reta J. Leopold, Aug. 31, 1973. Owner, Red Eagle Farms, La Fayette, N.Y., 1937—; supr. Town of La Fayette, 1964—; mem. adv. bd. Marine Midland Bank of Western N.Y., Tully. Dir. Onondago County Extension Service, 1950-54; mem. adv. bd. agr. La Fayette Central Sch., 1951-65; dir. La Fayette Fire Dept., 1961-63; active PTA of Am.; dir. Onondago Soil and Water Dist., 1964—; county legislator 12th Dist., 1968-69; now Onondago County sealer Bur. Weights and Measures. Mem. Empire State Potato Club (exec. sec. 1964), Meaker Hill Game Protective Assn., Onondago Vegetable Growers Assn. (pres. 1962-63), Vegetable Growers Am. (v.p.), Onondago County Farm Bur. (pres. 1955-56), La Fayette C. of C. (pres.), La Fayette Grange, N.Y. Farm Bur., N.Y. State Agrl. Soc., Nat. Potato Council, Hon. Soc. Agfu. Republican. Presbyterian (trustee). Clubs: La Fayette Baseball, Syracuse Anti Sour Puss, La Fayette Athletic. Editor: Potato News. Address: 3234 Eager Rd La Fayette NY 13084

AMMAN, MARGARET CASEY, historian; b. Newport, R.I., Feb. 18, 1932; d. John Raymond and Beatrice Zita (Harrington) Casey; B.A., Salve Regina Coll., 1956, postgrad., 1976. Tchr. U.S. history Thompson Jr. High Sch., Newport, 1956-58, 64—; tchr. U.S. Navy, San Miguel, Zambales, Philippines, 1958-59, Yokosuka, Japan, 1959-60, Newport, R.I., 1960-61; tchr. Creole Petroleum Corp., Judibana, Estado Falcon, Venezuela, 1961-63, Esso Internat. Co., Gach Saran, Iran, 1963-64. Rep. U.S.-Japanese intercultural exchange program Yokohama, 1959-60. Mem. Am., Brit. hist. socs., Nat., R.I. edn. assns., Newport Tchrs. Assn. Roman Catholic. Home: 101 Goat Island Newport RI 02840 Office: Thompson Jr High Sch Broadway St Newport RI 02840

AMODEI, JOSEPH EDWARD, chiropractor; b. N.Y.C.; b. Feb. 12, 1928; John and Rosalie (Barbera) A.; D.C., Chiropractic Inst., 1952; m. Mary Pilieri, June 18, 1949; children—Rosalie Amodei Jordenson, Adrienne, Joseph Jr. Pvt. practice chiropractic, Bklyn.; faculty Columbia Inst. Chiropractic, N.Y., 1970-76. Chmn. chiropractic practice com. Workmens' Compensation Bd., N.Y. Fellow Internat., Am. colls. chiropractic; mem. Am. (council orthopedics), N.Y. State (chiropractor of yr. award 1975, dir., pres. Kings dist. 1976-77), chiropractic assns., Am. Coll. Chiropractice Ortho pedics. Roman Catholic. Clubs: K.C., Moose. Co-author book on Chiropractic Orthopedics and Neurology. Contbr. articles to profl. jours. Home: 145 Buffalo Ave Medford NY 11763 Office: 7522 19th Ave Brooklyn NY 11214

AMORES, ARSENIO JUAN, data processing exec.; b. Camaguey, Cuba, Oct. 18, 1941; s. Tomas Arsenio and Juana F. (Guerra) A.; came to U.S., 1963, naturalized, 1968; B.S. in Electronics, George Washington U., 1967, M.S., 1969; m. Margarita Valdes, Mar. 25, 1965. Chief engr. Qatron Corp., Rockville, Md., 1969-71; design engr. Control Data Corp., Rockville, 1967-69; v.p. Space Age Computer Systems, Inc., Washington, 1971—, bd. dirs., 1975—. Mem. IEEE, Am. Mgmt. Assn., Inst. for Advancement Med. Instrumentation, Sigma Tau. Republican. Roman Catholic. Home: 2 Arlive Ct Potomac MD 20854

AMORNMARN, RUMPA, physician; b. Rangoon, Burma, Oct. 2, 1946; s. C. Peng Moy and Me Cho Che; came to U.S., 1972; M.D., Siriraj Med. Sch., Bangkok, Thailand, 1971. Straight med. intern VA Hosp., Washington, 1972-73; resident and fellow in radiation oncology Johns Hopkins Hosp., Balt., 1973-77; practice medicine specializing in radiology, East Orange, N.J., 1977—; mem. staff VA Hosp., East Orange, 1977—; asst. prof. radiology N.J. Med. Sch., 1978—. Diplomate Am. Bd. Radiology. Mem. Am. Soc. Therapeutic Radiology. Contbr. articles to profl. publs. Home: 360 Park Rd Parsippany NJ 07054 Office: VA Hosp East Orange NJ 07019

AMOROSINO, CHARLES SANTO, JR., med. inst. exec.; b. Boston, Aug. 24, 1943; s. Charles S. and Josephine Theresa (DiGregorio) A.; A.B. in Econs., Stonehill Coll., 1965; M.A., Sch. for Internat. Tng., 1972; m. Dorothy Ruth Roberts, Sept. 8, 1973; children—Sara Roberts, Charles Santo III. Vol., Peace Corps., Philippines, 1965-67; dir. pub. affairs New Eng. area Peace Corps/ACTION, Boston, 1967-71; acting mgr. Mengo Hosp., Kampala, Uganda, 1972; dir. field ops. Commonwealth Inst. Medicine, Boston, 1973-75, asso. exec. dir., 1976-77, exec. dir., 1977—; exec. dir. Mass. Profl. Standards Rev. Council, Boston, 1977—. Trustee Experiment in Internat. Living, Brattleboro, Vt., 1977—; bd. dirs., mem. exec. com. Internat. Inst. Boston, 1970—; Mem. Friends com. Boston Center Arts., 1974-77, treas., 1977—; vol. tchr. Vietnamese Refugee Com. Boston, 1975-76. Mem. Nat. Assn. Med. Care Coordinators, Am. Assn. Med. Soc. Execs., Am. Hosp. Assn. Contbr. articles in field to profl. jours. Home: 17 Ledyard St Wellesley Hills MA 02181 Office: Commonwealth Inst Medicine Mass Professional Standards Review Council 100 Charles River Plaza Boston MA 02114

AMREIN, ROBERT EUGENE, microscopist; b. Akron, Ohio, July 1, 1931; s. Joseph Emery and Florence Marie (Ehrhardt) A.; B.S., Kent State U., 1955; m. Elda Marie Pietrangeli, June 6, 1953; children—Robert S., Lynn M., Joseph E. Microscopist, Goodyear Tire & Rubber Co., Akron, Ohio, 1951-58; project chemist Thiokol Chem. Co., Elkton, Md., 1958-60; microscopist Celanese Fibers Co., Narrows, Va., 1960-63; sr. discipline scientist Cabot Corp., Billerica, Mass., 1963—; cons. in field. County chmn. Giles County ARC, 1961-63; mem. fin. com. Town of Chelmsford (Mass.), 1970-72. Fellow Royal Microscopy Soc.; mem. ASTM (chmn. com. E-23 resinography 1968-69), Electron Microscopy Soc. Am., Am. Crystallography Assn., Soc. Applied Spectroscopy, New Eng. Soc. Electron Microscopy. Episcopalian. Club: Masons. Home: 6 Swart Terr Nashua NH 03060 Office: Concord Rd Billerica MA 01821

AMTMANN, JAMES STEVEN, mktg. exec.; b. Englewood, N.J., Oct. 10, 1947; s. Harry Henry and Emily Victoria (Hjelte) A.; B.S. in Bus. Adminstrn., U. Hartford, 1969; M.B.A., 1974; m. Bonita Therese Kenny, Apr. 25, 1970; children—Eric John, Alisa Marie. Market research analyst Stanley Works, New Britain, Conn., 1969-70; mktg. planner Stanley Hardware div., 1970-71, mktg. mgr., 1971-77, mktg. mgr. consumer products, 1978, v.p. mktg., 1978—; program dir. Stanley Forum, 1974. Named Mktg. Student of Year U. Hartford, 1969. Mem. Am. Mktg. Assn., Packaging Inst. Am. Home: 80 Tamara Circle Avon CT 06001 Office: 195 Lake St New Britain CT 06050

AMY-MORENO, ANGEL ALBERTO, educator; b. San Juan, P.R., Jan. 10, 1945; s. Alberto Sadi Amy and Angeles Moreno; B.A., U. P.R., 1968; M.A. (Title III fellow), State U. N.Y., Fredonia, 1973; postgrad. history Boston U., 1975, in edn. (Title VII Bilingual fellow), 1976—; m. Ana E. Cordero, May 30, 1973; 1 dau., Denise Yaa'hra Amy-Cordero. Tchr. social studies P.R. Pub. Schs., 1969; tchr. history and sociology Madre Cabrini Catholic High Sch., Rio Piedras, P.R., 1969-70; instr. in humanities, art history, history U. P.R., Arecibo, 1970-75; asst. prof. history U. P.R., San Juan, Buchanan campus, 1974-75; asst. prof. social scis. Roxbury Community Coll., 1975—; asst. prof. langs. Boston State Coll. Evening Coll., 1975—; tchr. bilingual edn. Newton (Mass.) Pub. Sch. Systems, 1975. Recipient Eagle with silver palm, 1964, Ad Altare Dei medal 1961, (both P.R. council Boy Scouts Am.). Mem. Mass. Tchrs. Fedn., Ateneo Puerorriqueño, Ateneo de Madrid, Am. Hist. Assn., Archaeol. Inst. Am., Bilingual Tchrs. Assn., Alpha Phi Omega (pres. P.R. chpt. 1964-65, Service award 1965, editor yearbook Omicron Nu chpt. 1968). Democrat. Roman Catholic. Research on Charles V of Spain and Republic of Venice, XVI century, coll. and postsecondary bilingual edn. Home: 12 Holbrook St Jamaica Plain Boston MA 02130 Office: 424 Dudley St Roxbury MA 02119

ANAIN, JOSEPH MARCELO, surgeon; b. Cordoba, Argentina, Dec. 1, 1936; s. Elias Joseph and Maria (Asis) A.; came to U.S., 1969, naturalized, 1972; M.D., U. Cordoba, 1959; m. Anita Masih, Aug. 29, 1959; children—Shirley, Nancy, Joseph Marcelo, Robert, Paul. Intern, Charles Wilson Hosp., Binghamton, N.Y., 1959-60; fellow in surgery Buffalo Gen. Hosp., 1960-61; resident in surgery Sisters Hosp., Buffalo, 1961-65; fellow in angiology Cleve. Clinic, 1965-66; practice medicine specializing in gen. and vascular surgery, Buffalo, 1967—; attending surgeon Emergency and Sisters Hosp., Buffalo; comdr. 365th Army Gen. Hosp., 1974-76. Mem. Am. Coll. Angiology, A.C.S., Buffalo Surg. Soc., Am. Burn Assn., AMA, N.Y. Med. Soc. Republican. Roman Catholic. Club: Transit Valley Country. Home: 393 Dan Troy St Williamsville NY 14221 Office: 2121 Main St Buffalo NY 14214

ANASTASI, JOSEPH ANGELO, advt. exec.; b. Corning, N.Y., Apr. 14, 1947; s. Joseph James and Mary (Dellisante) A.; Asso. Sci., Corning Community Coll. 1967; B.F.A., Alfred U., 1970; postgrad. Elmira Coll., 1970-72; m. Linda Ann Starry, Apr. 29, 1978. Sr. creative designer Thatcher Glass Mfg. Co., Elmira, N.Y., 1970-74; owner, art dir. Design 34, Corning, 1973-76; owner, exec. v.p., creative dir. Jones Anastasi & Mitchell, 1976—. Active United Way of Southeastern Steuben County, 1976, 77. Mem. Erie Advt. Club, Am. Assn. Advt. Agys. Republican. Roman Catholic. Home: 5721 Carriage Hill Dr Apt 8 Erie PA 16509 Office: 3715 Poplar St Erie PA 16508

ANCES, I. G(EORGE), med. educator; b. Balt., July 3, 1935; s. Harry and Fanny A.; B.S., U. Md., 1956, M.D., 1959; m. Marlene Roth, Oct. 23, 1966; 1 son, Beau Mark. Intern Ohio State HU. Hosp., 1959-60, resident in obstetrics and gynecology Univ. Hosp., Balt., 1960-61, 63-65, mem. faculty U. Md. Med. Sch., Balt., 1966—, prof. obstetrics and gynecology, 1975—, dir. labs. obstetrics and gynecol. research and clin. labs., 1967—. Capt. sustaining fund drive Balt. Symphony Orch. Diplomate Am. Bd. Obstetrics and Gynecology. Served with USAF, 1961-63. Fellow Am. Coll. Obstetrics and Gynecology; mem. Endocrine Soc., Soc. Gynecol. Investigation, Soc. Study Reprodn. (charter) Internat. Soc. Research in Biology Reprodn. (charter), Md. Obstetrics and Gynecol. Soc. (sec. 1978-79), Med. and Chirurgical Soc. Md., Soc. Adolescent Medicine, Douglass Obstet. and Gynecol. Soc., English Speaking Union, Md. Conservation Coundil, Sigma Xi. Clubs: Maryland, Towson Golf and Country. Contbr. chpts. to books, articles to profl. jours. Home: 627 E 34th St Baltimore MD 21218 Office: Dept Obstetrics and Gynecology Univ Md Hospital Baltimore MD 21218

ANCONETANI, JOSEPH LOUIS, mfg. co. exec.; b. Ridgefield Park, N.J., Jan. 1, 1925; s. Amilcare and Annunziata A.; B.S. cum laude, Rider Coll., 1949; M.B.A. in Accounting and Taxation magna cum laude, Fairleigh Dickinson U., 1964; LL.B., La Salle Extension U., 1969; m. Jacqueline Faber, Oct. 8, 1960. Contract adminstr. nav. and control Bendix Corp., Teterboro, N.J., 1949-69; sr. contract adminstr. N.J. div. Conrac Corp., Fairfield, 1969-70; mgr. subcontract Kearfott div. Singer Corp., Little Falls, N.J., 1970-74; dir. procurement ITT def. communications div., Nutley, N.J., 1975—. Assessor Hardwick Twp. of Warren County (N.J.), 1967—, Stillwater Twp. of Sussex County (N.J.), 1975—; pres. North Warren Regional High Sch. Bd. Edn., Blairstown, N.J., 1972—. Served with inf. U.S. Army, 1943-46. Certified tax assessor, N.J.; certified profl. contracts mgr. Mem. Nat. Contract Mgmt. Assn. (pres. North Jersey chpt. 1973-74, dir. 1974-75), Internat. Assn. Assessing Officers, Am. Def. Preparedness Assn., U.S. Naval Inst. (asso.), 75th Div. Vets. Assn. Club: Lions. Home: RD 2 Box 401 Blairstown NJ 07825 Office: 100 Kingsland Rd Clifton NJ 07014

ANDELMAN, EDWARD GEORGE, sportscaster; b. Boston, Dec. 3, 1936; s. Maxwell and Bessie (Shriberg) A.; B.S., B.A., Boston U., 1958; M.B.A., Northeastern U., 1961; m. Judith Rosenberg, May 3, 1969; children—David, Michael, Daniel. Pres. Andelman Ins. Agency, Boston, 1958—; co-host Sports Huddle program, Sta. WHOH, Boston, 1977—; v.p. Maxwell Andelman Assoc., Boston, 1969—; sports commentator, Sta. WNAC-TV, Boston, 1972—; Grandstand program, NBC network sports, Boston, 1976. Mem. AFTRA. Author: Sports Fans of the World, Unite, 1972; On Three, 1975; contbr. articles to popular mags. Office: 141 Milk St Boston MA 02109

ANDERBERG, EDWARD, investment co. exec.; b. N.Y.C., Oct. 15, 1918; s. Edward and Winifred (Huntley) A.; B.A., Dartmouth Coll., 1941; M.A., Columbia, 1942; m. Mary Alice Meehan, Jan. 9, 1965; 1 dau., Sarah Elizabeth. Economist, U.S. Tariff Commn., Washington, 1942-45; U.S. fgn. service reserve officer U.S. Embassy, China, 1946-49, Japan, 1950-52; Am. consul, Kingston, Jamaica, 1952-54; with Shields Model Roland Inc. (merged to form Bache Halsey Stuart Shields 1977), White Plains, N.Y., 1956—, v.p., mgr. 1966—. Chmn. Bd. Zoning Appeals, City of White Plains, 1976—; bd. dirs., past pres. Assn. Vis. Nurse Services, White Plains YMCA, Westchester United Way; bd. dirs. Westchester Coalition. Mem. Phi Beta Kappa. Democrat. Episcopalian. Club: Rotary. Home: 9 Pin Oak Ln White Plains NY 10606 Office: 44 Church St White Plains NY 10601

ANDERSEN, ARNOLD MERWIN, paper industry exec.; b. Duluth, Minn., May 1, 1917; s. Samuel and Marie (Rotvik) A.; A.B. cum laude with math. honors, St. Olaf Coll., 1940; M.B.A., Harvard U., 1942; postgrad. Columbia Bus. Sch. Exec. program, 1966; m. Leila Buxton, Mar. 7, 1947; children—Donna, Brent, Laurie, Roger, Tracy, Julie. Supr. mktg. control Marathon Corp. div. Am. Can, Menasha, Wis., 1948-55; with domestic and fgn. sales dept. Potlatch Corp., Atlanta, 1955-62; v.p., bd. mem. Cel-Fibe div. Johnson & Johnson, Milltown, N.J., 1962-67; v.p. mktg. Cellu Products, Inc., Rumson, N.J., 1968—. Served with U.S. Army, 1942-47; PTO; served to lt. col. Res., 1947-67. Named Nat. scholar Harvard U., 1940. Mem. Sales Assn. Paper Industry, Paper Industry Mgmt. Assn., Ret. Officers U.S. Clubs: Shrewsbury Yacht, Harvard of N.Y.C. Home: 11 Bingham Hill Circle Rumson NJ 07760

ANDERSEN, CHRISTOPHER PETER, editor; b. Pensacola, Fla., May 26, 1949; s. Edward Francis and Jeanette (Peterson) A.; B.A. in Polit. Sci., U. Calif., Berkeley, 1971; m. Valerie Jean Hess, Feb. 3, 1972. San Francisco corr. Time mag., 1969-70, contbg. editor, N.Y.C., 1971-72, contbg. editor, Montreal, Que., Can., 1972-74; asso. editor People mag., N.Y.C., 1974—. Author: The Name Game, 1977. Contbr. articles to various publs. including N.Y. Times, Reader's Digest. Home: 200 E 66th St New York City NY 10021 Office: People Mag Time and Life Bldg Rockefeller Center New York City NY 10020

ANDERSEN, DANIEL JOHANNES, lawyer; b. Jamestown, N.Y., Nov. 3, 1909; s. Christian J. and Maria (Hansen) A.; A.B., George Washington U., 1937, J.D., 1940; postgrad. Army War Coll., 1965; m. Alice Klopstad, June 28, 1937; 1 dau., Dianne Marie Andersen Tecklenberg. With U.S. Dept. Labor, Washington, 1933-37; statis. clk., procedures analyst-job analyst Social Security Adminstrn., U.S. Employment Service, Washington, 1937-40; admitted to D.C., U.S. Supreme Ct. bars, 1940; mem. firm Baker, Beedy & Magee, Washington, 1940-42, Magee, Bulow & Andersen, Washington, 1946-58; individual practice law, Washington, 1958—. Mem. men's bd. Florence Crittenton Home and Hosp., 1963—. Bd. dirs. Gettysburg Coll., 1963-73, chmn. devel. com., mem. exec. com., 1965-73; bd. dirs., pres. Dr. O.E. Howe Found. Served with USAAF, 1941-46; ETO, MTO. Mem. Judge Advs. Assn. (pres.), Delta Phi Epsilon, Sigma Chi. Clubs: Newcomers (Washington); Chevy Chase (Md.); Nat. Lawyers, Nat. Press. Author: Job Descriptions and Code Manual, 1937. Home: 4441 Lowell St NW Washington DC 20016 Office: Woodward Bldg Washington DC 20005

ANDERSEN, MARIANNE SINGER, ednl. adminstr., psychotherapist; b. Baden, nr. Vienna, Austria, June 18, 1930; d. Richard and Jolanthe (Garda) Singer; came to U.S., 1940, naturalized, 1946; A.B., Hunter Coll. of City U. N.Y., 1950, M.A., 1974; 1 son, Richard Esten. Book editor specializing in psychology and psychiatry with pub. firms including W.W. Norton, Sterling Pub. Co., E.P.

Dutton, N.Y.C., 1950-71; research asso. Inst. for Research in Hypnosis, N.Y.C., 1971—, dir. workshops Morton Prince Center for Hypnotherapy of Inst. for Research in Hypnosis, 1978—, psychotherapist specializing in hypnotherapy, 1976—; dir. adminstrn. Internat. Grad. U., N.Y.C., 1974-77, dir. continuing profl. edn. workshops, internat. office, 1977—, adminstrv. coordinator, Internat. Grad. Sch. Behavioral Sci. of Fla. Inst. Tech., N.Y.C., 1978; lectr. hypnosis and hypnotherapy to mental and phys. health profls. Fellow in clin. hypnosis Inst. for Research in Hypnosis, 1976. Mem. Soc. for Clin. and Exptl. Hypnosis, Internat. Soc. Clin. and Exptl. Hypnosis (student asso), Am. Psychol. Assn. (asso.), Mensa. Author: (with Louis Savary) Passages: A Guide for Pilgrims of the Mind, 1972; condr. research on treatment of obesity with hypnotherapy. Home: 60 W 57th St New York City NY 10019 Office: 10 W 66th St #24F New York City NY 10023

ANDERSEN, ROBERT ALLAN, govt. ofcl.; b. Denver, Aug. 27, 1936; s. Emmett Christian and Margaret Irene (Maupin) A.; A.B. in Polit. Sci., U. S.C., 1958, M.A., 1961; postgrad. U. Colo. Law Sch., 1958-59; Ph.D. in Internat. Relations, Am. U., 1973; m. Jane Eng, May 13, 1967. Area coordinator for econ. devel. Area Redevel. Adminstrn., Commerce Dept., 1962-64; acting dir. urban projects div., program officer, chief Project Adminstrn., VISTA/OEO, Washington, 1964-66; implementation programming, planning and budgeting system Office Program Planning and Evaluation, Office Edn., 1966-67; staff asst. to dep. postmaster gen. Postal Service, 1967-72, sr. planning officer, 1972-74; now dir. evaluation Immigration and Naturalization Service, 1974—. Bd. dirs. D.C. Assn. Retarded Citizens. Mem. Am. Soc. Pub. Adminstrn., Sigma Phi Epislon. Episcopalian. Home: 5701 Nebraska Ave NW Washington DC 20015 Office: Immigration and Naturalization Service 425 Eye St NW Washington DC 20001

ANDERSEN, THEODORE SELMER, mfg. co. exec.; b. N.Y.C., Dec. 4, 1944; s. Selmer and Irene Frances (McManus) A.; B.Ch.E., Cooper Union, 1965; M.S. Ch.E., U. Pitts., 1967, Ph.D., 1971, M.B.A., 1977; m. Elva Glenna Layden, June 19, 1965; children—Elva Irene, Theodore Christian. With Bettis Atomic Power Lab., Westinghouse Electric Corp., Pitts., 1965—, engring. mgr. naval reactors and civilian power, 1973-77, mgr. personnel compensation, evaluation and tng., 1977-78, mgr. solar project Advanced Energy Systems div., 1978—. Jobs field rep. Nat. Alliance Businessmen, 1973. Bd. dirs. Wesley Inst., Inc., 1974-78; adult tutor St. Clair Village Bethany Ministry, 1968-73; occupational therapy vol. Woodville State Hosp. Registered profl. engr., Pa. Mem. Am. Inst. Chem. Engrs., Am. Chem. Soc., Am. Mgmt. Assn., ABC Flying Club (treas.), Sigma Xi, Beta Gamma Sigma. Republican. Methodist. Office: PO Box 10864 Large PA 15236

ANDERSON, ALFRED JAKOBUS, assn. exec.; b. Tartu, Estonia, Nov. 22, 1901; s. Hans and Auguste (Treufeldt) A.; student U. Tartu, 1922-24, Faculty of Law, 1934; m. Jutta Kurrikoff, Mar. 25, 1940. Came to U.S., 1949, naturalized, 1955. Vice-chmn. Eesti Lihaeksport, Tallinn, Estonia, 1936-40, dir. gen., 1941-44; co-owner Baltic Times, Tallinn, Estonia, 1937-40, co-pub., 1937-40; treas. Estonian Relief Com., Inc., N.Y.C., 1950—. Gov. Estonian Exchange, 1938-40; v.p. Estonian World Council, N.Y.C., 1955-66, pres., 1966—. Mem. Assembly Captive European Nations, 1954-56; mem. II-X Assembly Estonian Am. Nat. Council, 1954—; patron Estonian World Festival, Estonian Salute to Bicentennial, 1976; trustee Found. for Estonia Art and Letters; bd. dirs. Estonian Archives in U.S. Named hon. citizen City of Balt. Mem. Estonian Ednl. Soc., Am. Ordnance Assn. Republican. Lutheran. Office: 243 E 34th St New York City NY 10016

ANDERSON, C(ARL) ALAN, educator; b. Manchester, Conn., July 21, 1930; s. Carl Oscar and Helen Caroline (Anderson) A.; B.A., Am. Internat. Coll., 1952; LL.B., U. Conn., 1955, M.A., 1957, postgrad. 1958-59; Ph.D., Boston U., 1963; m. Luleen Sandefur, Aug. 16, 1963; 1 son, Eric Alan. Instr., Babson Inst. (now Babson Coll.), Babson Park, Mass., 1963-64, asst. prof., 1964-66; asst. prof. Curry Coll., Milton, Mass., 1966-67, asso. prof., 1967-71, prof. philosophy, 1971—, chmn. div. humanities, 1967-77, dir. interdisciplinary studies, 1977—, archivist, 1978—. Mem. Am. Philos. Assn., Metaphys. Soc. Am., Soc. for Study Process Philosophies, Am. Acad. Regigion, Soc. for Sci. Study Religion, Alpha Chi. Mem. Unity Ch. Contbr. articles to religious and philos. jours. Home: 39 Knollwood Rd North Quincy MA 02171 Office: Curry College Milton MA 02186

ANDERSON, CHARLES EDWARD, chemist; b. Alexandria, Tenn., June 6, 1922; s. James Frank and Ida (Evans) A.; B.S., Carson-Newman Coll., 1948; m. Margaret Elizabeth Wiles, Dec. 24, 1942; children—Robert Charles, Charlene Elizabeth. Chemist, E. I. duPont de Nemours & Co., Old Hickory, Tenn., 1948, lab. foreman, 1949-50, lab. shift supr. Savannah River Plant, Aiken, S.C., 1951-52, lab. sr. supr., 1953-65, lab. supr. Seaford Nylon Plant, Seaford, Del., 1966-70, research chemist research and devel., 1971—. Served with USAF, 1942-46. Mem. Am. Chem. Soc. (chmn. Savannah River sect. 1956-57). Baptist. Club: Golf and Country (Seaford, Del.). Home: 742 Woodlawn Ave Seaford DE 19973 Office: PO Box 400 Seaford DE 19973

ANDERSON, CHARLES LEONARD, JR., life ins. co. exec.; b. Bethesda, Md., Nov. 15, 1948; s. Charles Leonard and Mary Alice (Rose) A.; B.C.S. with honors, Benjamin Franklin U., Washington, 1970; m. Agnes Marie Pickett, July 21, 1967; children—Charles Leonard, III, Jeanna Marie. Staff asst. Pargas, Inc., Waldorf, Md., 1966-70; audit sr. Price Waterhouse & Co., C.P.A.'s, Washington, 1970-73; asst. comptroller Acacia Mut. Life Ins. Co., Washington, 1973-75, gen. comptroller, 1975—; v.p., gen. comptroller, dir. Acacia Nat. Life Ins. Co.; dir. Acacia Fin. Corp. C.P.A., Md. Mem. Am., D.C. insts. c.p.a.'s, Met. Washington Bd. Trade, Fin. Execs. Inst. Home: 11 Forest Glenn Ct Waldorf MD 20601 Office: 51 Louisiana Ave NW Washington DC 20001

ANDERSON, CHESTER WASHINGTON, III, data communications engr.; b. Bklyn., Dec. 9, 1942; s. Chester Washington, Jr., and Ruth (Reed) A.; B.A., Wichita U., 1964, M.S., 1966; Ph.D., U. Alta. (Can.), 1970; m. Janet Robinson, Sept. 30, 1971; 1 son, Jay. Mem. Tech. staff Bell Telephone Labs., 1972-75; engring. staff specialist AT & T, Basking Ridge, N.J., 1975-78; mem. tech. staff Bell Labs., Holmdel, N.J., 1978—. Mem. Tinton Falls (N.J.) Bd. Edn., 1976—; bd. dirs. Red Bank (N.J.) Community Center, 1973-75, pres., 1974-75. Served to capt. AUS, 1970-72. Mem. Am. Geophys. Union (com. on minorities and women 1975—), Soc. Exploration Geophysicists, Inst. Nav., AAAS, Kappa Alpha Psi. Author: Handbook on Inductive Interference and Electrical Protection, 1974; Principles of Earth Resistivity and Grounding, 1976. Contbr. articles to tech. jours. Home: 1135 Sycamore Ave Tinton Falls NJ 07724

ANDERSON, CLAUS LUDWIG, physician; b. Phila., Sept. 24, 1934; s. Claus Ludwig and Helen Lachman (Fry) A.; B.A., U. Pa., 1956; M.D., Temple U., 1960; m. Carolyn Harvey, July 26, 1969; children—Catherine Elizabeth, Carl James, Kenneth Claus. Intern, Abington (Pa.) Meml. Hosp., 1960-61; resident in internal medicine Temple U., Phila., 1961-64; fellow pulmonary diseases Western Pa. Hosp., Pitts., 1969; physician Scott-Anderson Ltd., Pitts., 1970—; individual practice medicine specializing in internal medicine and pulmonary diseases, Pitts., 1970—; staff respiratory services Western Pa. Hosp., Pitts., and McKeesport (Pa.) Hosp.; instr. medicine Temple U., 1967; adj. prof. medicine Indiana State U. Pa., 1972—; cons. in field. Served to capt. M.C., USAF, 1964-66. Diplomate Am. Bd. Internal Medicine, Am. Bd. Pulmonary Disease. Fellow A.C.P., Am. Coll. Chest Physicians; mem. Am. Thoracic Soc., Am. Heart Assn., AMA. Home: 114 Woodshire Dr Pittsburgh PA 15215 Office: 4815 Liberty Ave Pittsburgh PA 15224

ANDERSON, DAVID, educator; b. N.Y.C., Nov. 28, 1925; s. Henry Hill and Helen Jennings (James) A.; B.A., Yale, 1949, M.A. with honors, 1970; m. Martha C. Hutchinson, Oct. 6, 1974; children—Tatiana, David H., Edith A., Nicholas J., Helen J., Katherine B., Holley. Mgmt. staff electric boat div. Gen. Dynamics, Groton, Conn., 1949-60, asst. to exec. v.p., N.Y. and Calif., 1960-62; tchr. La Jolla (Calif.) Country Day Sch., 1962-64; librarian, tchr. Norwich (Conn.) Free Acad., 1964—; mem. exec. com. Nat. Program Pre-Coll. Teaching Russian and European Studies. Served with USCG, 1943-46. Named Environ. Tchr. of Yr., Conn., 1974, 78. Mem. Am. Assn. Advancement Slavic Studies, Conn. Council Advancement Slavic Studies, Phi Beta Kappa. Episcopalian. Author (under name Nikolai Kavalenov); Krokodil Tears. Home: RFD 3 Norwich CT 06360 Office: Norton Peck Library Norwich Free Academy Norwich CT 06360

ANDERSON, DAVID GILROY, coll. adminstr.; b. Skaneateles, N.Y., Aug. 3, 1930; s. Edwin C. and Laura L. (Miller) A.; B.S., State U. N.Y., Syracuse, 1953; M.S., U. Utah, 1958; M.P.A., Maxwell Sch., Syracuse U., 1977; divorced; children—Linda C., David A., Timothy S. Instr., then asst. prof. N.Y. State Ranger Sch., Wanakena, N.Y., 1959-65; asso. prof., asst. dean State U. N.Y. Coll. Environ. Sci. and Forestry, Syracuse, 1965-70, v.p. adminstrn. and services, 1970-78, also sec. to bd. trustees, bd. dirs. N.Y. State Coll. Forestry Found.; cons. in field. Elder Onondaga Hill Presbyn. Ch., Syracuse, 1970-78; 1 bd. dirs. Univ. Hill Corp., 1970-78. Served with USNR, 1953-59; Korea, Vietnam. Fellow Am. Council Edn., 1970-71. Mem. Soc. Am. Foresters, AAAS, Am. Soc. Pub. Adminstrn., Sigma Xi. Club: Clayton Yacht. Home: 111 Lafayette Rd Syracuse NY 13205 Office: State Univ NY Coll Environ Sci and Forestry Syracuse NY 13210

ANDERSON, DAVID MARTIN, chem. engr.; b. Boston, July 19, 1930; s. Martin Jens and Dorothy (Finnin) A.; grad. Boston Latin Sch., 1948; B.S., Northeastern U., 1953; S.M., Harvard U., 1955, Ph.D., 1958; m. Marjorie Anne Gilbert, July 19, 1958; children—David Russell, Michael Martin, Anne Marjorie, Stephen Gerald. Research fellow Harvard Sch. Pub. Health, 1953-58; pub. health engr. USPHS, Cin., 1958-60; indsl. health engr. Bethlehem Steel Corp. (Pa.), 1960-67; asst. mgr. environ. quality control, 1967-71, mgr., 1971—. Lectr. air quality standards Pa. State U., 1966-71; vis. lectr. indsl. hygiene engring. Harvard, 1969—; chmn. council tech. advisers Pa. Dept. Environ. Resources, 1964-70, N.Y. Dept. Environ. Conservation, 1974-75; mem. Pa. Gov.'s Task Force on Occupational Health and Safety, 1975-76; mem. com. on biol. effects of atmospheric pollutants Nat. Acad. Scis., 1971-74; mem. nat. air quality criteria adv. com. EPA, 1971-76; mem. Sec. Health, Edn. and Welfare Coal Mine Health Research Adv. Council, 1972-76. Registered profl. engr., Pa. Diplomate Am. Acad. Environ. Engrs. Fellow AAAS, Am. Inst. Chem. Engrs.; mem. Am. Iron and Steel Inst., Am. Chem. Soc., Am. Indsl. Hygiene Assn. (dir. 1968-71), Air Pollution Control Assn. (dir. 1971-74), Am. Acad. Indsl. Hygiene, Sigma Xi, Delta Omega. Mem. bd. asso. editors Atmospheric Environment. Contbr. articles to profl. jours. Research, patentee air cleaning tech. Home: 1037 Westgate Circle Bethlehem PA 18017 Office: Bethlehem Steel Corp Bethlehem PA 18016

ANDERSON, DENNIS RAY, art historian, art dealer; b. Waynesboro, Va., Mar. 8, 1947; s. John L. and Louise F. Anderson; B.A., U. Va., 1972; M.A., U. N.C., 1973. Tech. supr. N.C. Mus. Art, Raleigh, 1974; curator Am. painting Chrysler Mus. at Norfolk, 1974-76; asst. to dir. ACA Galleries, N.Y.C., 1976—. Mem. Art Appraisers Assn. Am. Author books in field including: American Flower Paintings 1850-1950, 1978; Masterpieces in New York Private Collections, 1978; Three Hundred Years of American Art in the Chrysler Collection. Authority on works of Ernest Lawson and Am. impressionists. Address: 9 E 96th St New York NY 10028

ANDERSON, DONALD MORGAN, entomologist; b. Washington, Dec. 27, 1930; s. John Kenneth and Alice Cornelia (Morgan) A.; B.A., Miami U., Oxford, Ohio, 1953; Ph.D., Cornell U., 1958. Grad. teaching asst. Cornell U., 1954-57; asst. prof. sci. State U. N.Y. Coll., Buffalo, 1959-60, research fellow, 1960; research entomologist Dept. Agr., Washington, 1960—. Sigma Xi grantee, 1959. Mem. Entomol. Soc. Washington (corr. sec. 1963-65), Entomol. Soc. Am., Soc. Systematic Zoology, Coleopterists Soc., Am. Inst. Biol. Scis., Sigma Xi, Phi Kappa Phi, St. Andrews Soc. Washington. Contbr. articles to profl. jours. Home: 3701 Connecticut Ave NW Washington DC 20008 Office: Systematic Entomology Lab Dept Agr c/o US Nat Mus Washington DC 20560

ANDERSON, DOUGLAS SCRANTON HESLEY, investment banking exec.; b. Springfield, Mass., Aug. 23, 1929; s. Lloyd Douglas Hesley and Alice Scranton (Eastman) A.; A.B., Harvard Coll., 1951; certificate investment banking Northwestern U., 1959; m. Elizabeth Bartram Radley, Sept. 20, 1969; 1 dau., Katherine Scranton. Gen. partner The Anderson Co., Cambridge, Mass., 1953—; dir. corporate devel. Sterling, Grace & Co. Inc., N.Y.C., 1973—. Pres., Pecksland Rd. Assn., 1977-78. Served to lt. USNR, 1951-53. Mem. Assn. Former Intelligence Officers. Clubs: Round Hill, Fox, West Palm Beach (Fla.) Fishing. Home: 39 Vista Dr Greenwich CT 06830 Office: Sterling Grace & Co Inc 39 Broadway New York City NY 10006

ANDERSON, EDITH HELEN, nursing sch. adminstr.; b. N.J., June 3, 1927; B.S., Manhattanville Coll., 1951; M.A., N.Y. U., 1958, Ph.D., 1963. Staff nurse Halloran VA Hosp., S.I., N.Y., 1948-49; camp nurse Ten Mile River camp Boy Scouts Am., N.Y., 1949; pub. health nurse Vis. Nurse Assn., Elizabeth, N.J., 1950-54, Community Service Soc., N.Y.C., 1954-56; instr. practical nursing program Elizabeth (N.J.) Bd. Edn., 1956-58; teaching fellow grad. program in parent-child nursing N.Y. U., 1958-60, asst. prof., dir. grad. program in parent-child nursing, 1960-64; acting chief nursing sect. Children's Bur., Social and Rehab. Service, HEW, Washington, 1967-68, nursing edn. cons. Nursing Sect. Children's Bur., Welfare Adminstrn., 1964-69; dean Sch. Nursing, Coll. Health Scis. and Social Welfare, U. Hawaii, Honolulu, 1969-76; dean coll. nursing U. Del., Newark, 1976—. Cons. P.R. Dept. Health, U. P.R., 1963, V.I. Dept. Health, 1964, Inst. Tech. Interchange East-West Center, U. Hawaii; tchr./trainer field tng. program Provincial Health Dept., Republic of China, Taiwan, 1969, tchr./trainer Tb control Ryukya Islands, Inst. Tech. Interchange, East-West Center, 1970, Lyndon B. Johnson Tropical Med. Center, Am. Samoa, 1970, 71. Mem. Am., Hawaii (editor mag. 1973-75, chmn. publicity com. 1973-75) nurses assns., Nat. (chmn. maternal child nursing sect. So. region 1965), Hawaii (1st v.p. 1973) leagues for nursing, Am. Acad. Nursing, Pi Lambda Theta, Sigma Theta Tau. Author: Commitment to Child Health, 1967; (with others) Maternity Care in the United States: Gains and Gaps, 1966, Current Concepts in Clinical Nursing, Vol. I, 1967, Vol. II, 1969, Vol. III, 1971, Vol. IV, 1973. Home: 1403 Shallcross Ave Hamilton House Apt 502 Wilmington DE 19806

ANDERSON, HERBERT GODWIN, JR., zoologist, educator; b. Roanoke, Ala., Dec. 29, 1931; s. Herbert Godwin and Ethel Blanche (Taylor) A.; student Jacksonville State U., 1950-51, 55-56; B.S., Auburn U., 1958, M.S. in Zoology, 1960; Ph.D. in Marine Sci., U. Miami, 1964. Fishery biologist U.S. Bur. Sport Fisheries, Highlands, N.J., 1962-64; instr. biol. scis. Central Conn. State Coll., New Britain, 1964-66, asst. prof., 1966-69, asso. prof., 1969-74, prof., 1974—. Served with USN, 1951-55; Korea. Mem. Am. Soc. Parasitologists, Nat., Conn. edn. assns., Sigma Xi, Gamma Sigma Delta. Democrat. Episcopalian (organist 1955-57). Mason. Home: Cheshire Rd Bethany CT 06525 Office: Central Conn State Coll New Britain CT 06050

ANDERSON, HUGOLD BERNDT, JR., mfg. design engr.; b. Providence, Jan. 22, 1915; s. Hugold Berndt and Ernestine (Nelson) A.; student R.I. Sch. Design, 1938-43; m. Barbara Allen Swan, Sept. 4, 1944; children—Barbara Jane (Mrs. Bruce Twickler), Berndt William. Pres., treas. Hugold Anderson, Inc., 1951-63; design engr. Garland Industries (formerly Lew Mfg. Co.), Coventry, R.I., 1963-68, Armbrust Chain Co., Providence, 1968—; treas. Ernick, Inc., until 1963. Mem. Soc. Plastics Engrs. (past sec., dir.), DeMolay Legion of Honor (past pres.). Author: Government Without Taxation, 1965. Inventor Hugold airpress and index tables. Home: 75 Weetamoe Dr Warwick RI 02888

ANDERSON, JACK GARNER, aerospace co. exec.; b. Memphis, Apr. 21, 1922; s. Wilfred John and Ruth (Garner) A.; B.S. in Chem. Engring., U. Louisville, 1943; B.S., USAF Inst. Tech., 1950; m. Patricia Menacher, Dec. 8, 1945; children—Judith, Jack, James, Jerold, Richard, William Donald, Mark. Served as enlisted man U.S. Army Air Force, 1941-42, commd. lt., 1942, advanced through grades to maj., 1951, ret., 1954; v.p. mktg. Hoffman Electronics Corp., Los Angeles, 1954-60, Gen. Dynamics Electronics, Rochester, N.Y., 1960-61, Kollsman Instrument Corp., Elmhurst, N.Y., 1961-68; pres. Kaman Aerospace Corp., Bloomfield, 1969-72, also exec. v.p. Kaman Corp.; pres., chief exec. officer, ILC Industries, Inc., Bohemia, N.Y., 1972—, pres., chief exec. officer, chmn. bd. ILC Data Device Corp., Bohemia, 1976—. Fellow Radio Club Am.; mem. Am. Mgmt. Assn., Am. Rocket Soc., Am. Helicopter Soc., Am. Inst. Aeros., Astronautics. Electronics Industries Assn. (dir. govt. div. 1977—, Nat. Security Indsl. Assn. (v.p. 1972-76, trustee 1976—), Nat. Aero. Assn., Air Force Assn., Assn. U.S. Army, Armed Forces Communications Electronics Assn., Quarter Century Wireless Assn. (dir.), Nat. Aviation Club, Aviation Hall of Fame (bd. nominations 1967—). Club: Avon (Conn.) Country. Home: 64 Hitchcock Ln Avon CT 06001 Office: ILC Industries Inc Airport Internat Plaza Bohemia NY 11716

ANDERSON, JAMES BUELL, lawyer; b. N.Y.C., Feb. 16, 1912; s. Karl James and Helen Edgerton (Buell) A.; B.A., Williams Coll., 1933; J.D., Harvard, 1936; m. Jane Caryl Anderson, Nov. 21, 1952; children—David Buell, Michael James. Admitted to N.Y. bar, 1937, Japan bar, 1952; asso. firm Breed, Abbott & Morgan, N.Y.C., 1936-51; pvt. practice law, Tokyo, 1952-66; partner firm O'Gorman, Nattier & Anderson, N.Y.C. and Tokyo, 1954-60, Anderson, Nattier, Mori & Rabinowitz, N.Y.C. and Tokyo, 1960-63, Anderson, Mori & Rabinowitz, Tokyo, 1963-69; pvt. practice N.Y.C., 1963-68; mem. firm Anderson, Martin & Cable, N.Y.C., 1968-72, Whitman & Ransom, N.Y.C., 1972—; dir. Findlay Millar Timber Co., Manila; mem. nat. panel Am. Arbitration Assn. Served to maj. AUS, 1941-46. Decorated Bronze Star. Mem. Am., N.Y. State, N.Y.C., Tokyo bar assns., Am. Soc. Internat. Law, Am. Fgn. Law Assn., Assn. Ex-Mems. Squadron A (pres. 1978—). Episcopalian. Clubs: Univ., Tokyo Am., Fairfield County Hunt. Home: 3 Stony Point Rd Westport CT 06880 Office: 522 Fifth Ave New York City NY 10036

ANDERSON, JANE VIRGINIA, psychiatrist; b. Boston, Oct. 1, 1931; d. Robert Emery and Virginia (McLean) Anderson; A.B., Smith Coll., 1955; M.D. cum laude, Boston U., 1960; m. Paul Libbey Russell, Oct. 7, 1961 (div. 1973). Med. intern Bellevue Hosp., N.Y.C., 1960-61; resident in psychiatry Mass. Mental Health Center, Boston, 1961-62, 64-65, resident in child psychiatry, 1965-66; resident in adult and child psychiatry Beth Israel Hosp., Boston, 1966-68, asst. in psychiatry, 1968—; teaching fellow in psychiatry Med. Sch., Harvard U., Boston, 1961-62, 64-66, research fellow in psychiatry, 1966-68, asst. in psychiatry, 1968-70, clin. instr. psychiatry, 1970-75, asst. clin. prof. psychiatry, 1975—; courtesy staff McLean Hosp., Belmont, Mass., 1975—. Assn. for Study of Abortion grantee, 1970-71; Pathfinder Fund grantee, 1972. Diplomate Am. Bd. Psychiatry and Neurology. Mem. Am. Psychiat. Assn., Am. Med. Women's Assn., Phi Beta Kappa, Alpha Omega Alpha. Club: Boston Smith Coll. Condr. research psychol. outcome of therapeutic abortion, 1967-74; author profl. papers. Home: 124 Kirkstall Rd Newtonville MA 02160 Office: 1419 Beacon St Brookline MA 02146

ANDERSON, JEAN, author, editor; b. Raleigh, N.C., Oct. 12, 1931; d. Donald Benton and Marian March (Johnson) Anderson; B.S., Cornell U., 1951; M.S. (Pulitzer Traveling scholar), Columbia, 1957. Women's editor N.C. Agrl. Extension Service, 1951-54, Raleigh Times, 1954-56; asst. editor Ladies' Home Jour., N.Y.C., 1957-59, editorial asso., 1959-62, mng. editor, 1963; sr. editor Venture Mag., 1964-71. Recipient So. Women's Achievement award Reed & Barton, 1963, George Hedman Meml. award, 1971. Mem. Am. Home Econs. Assn., Home Economists in Bus., N.Y. Travel Writers, Authors Guild, English Speaking Union, Les Dames D'Escoffier, Gamma Phi Beta, Phi Kappa Phi, Omicron Nu. Author: (with Yeffe Kimball) The Art of American Indian Cooking, 1965; Food Is More Than Cooking, 1968; Henry the Navigator, Prince of Portugal, 1969; The Family Circle 16-Volume Illustrated Library of Cooking, 1972; The Haunting of America, 1973; The Family Circle Cookbook, 1974; (with Elaine Hanna) The Doubleday Cookbook, 1975 (Best Cookbook of Year award, 1975, R.T. French Tastemaker award); Recipes from America's Restored Villages, 1975; The Green Thumb Preserving Guide, 1976; The Grass Roots Cookbook, 1977; Jean Anderson's Processor Cooking, 1979; contbg. editor Family Circle, ASTA Travel News. Office: care McIntosh and Otis 475 Fifth Ave New York City NY 10017

ANDERSON, JERRY ALLEN, investment analyst; b. Ashland, Wis., Feb. 10, 1947; s. Elmer O. and Thelma L. (Fallis) A.; B.B.A., Temple U., 1970, M.B.A., 1976; m. Anne Marie Brown, June 7, 1975; 1 dau., Kristin Marie. With Girard Bank, Phila., 1970—, adminstrv. officer, head consumer products group, 1972-73, investment officer, 1973-77, sr. investment officer, group head, sr. analyst for tng., 1977—; cons. consumer durables field; instr. fin. Temple U. Mem. N.Y. Soc. Security Analysts (sr.), Fin. Analysts Phila., Fin. Analysts Fedn., Beta Gamma Sigma, Theta Chi. Home: 544 Norwyck Dr King of Prussia PA 19406 Office: 4 Girard Plaza Philadelphia PA 19101

ANDERSON, JOHN GASTON, lab. mgr.; b. Dante, Va., Aug. 22, 1922; s. Harvey Ellis and Lenora (Ingram) A.; B.S. in Elec. Engring. with honors, Va. Poly. Inst., 1943; m. Elizabeth Amelia Weller, Sept. 18, 1948; 1 son, David J. Lightning research engr. Gen. Electric Co., 1947-49, high voltage research engr., 1950-64, tech. dir. project extra-high-voltage, 1964-67, mgr., 1967-72, mgr. AC Transmission

Studies, 1972-74; mgr. Gen. Elec. High Voltage Lab., Pittsfield, Mass., 1974—. Asst. dist. commr. Boy Scouts Am., 1970-72, troop committeeman, 1967-72, now mem. Nat. Eagle Scout Assn. Served to Capt. USAAF, 1943-46. Registered profl. engr., Mass. Fellow IEEE (chmn. powers engring. soc. transmission and distbr. com.); mem. AAAS, Internat. Conf. Large High Voltage Systems, Joint Am.-Soviet Com. on Cooperation in Field of Energy (U.S. Working Group on Ulta-High-Voltage Transmission). Congregationalist. Club: Stanley (bd. dirs.). Co-author: Transmission Line Reference Book, 1968; Transmission Line Reference Book, 345 KV and Above, 1975. Editor Gen. Elec. Transmission Mag., 1972-74. Contbr. articles tech. jours. Patentee in field. Home: 31 Stonehenge Rd Pittsfield MA 01201 Office: 100 Woodlawn Ave Pittsfield MA 01201

ANDERSON, JUDITH RAE (MRS. TIMOTHY PARMLEY HORNE), psychologist; b. San Francisco, Feb. 14, 1941; d. Harry Davey and Audrey (Garman) A.; A.B., Vassar Coll., 1962; M.A. in Teaching of English, Stanford, 1965; M.Ed., Boston U., 1972, Ed.D. in Counseling Psychology, 1974; m. Timothy Parmley Horne, Nov. 11, 1965; 1 stepdau., Tara Victoria. Tchr. English, drama, pub. speaking various schs., 1962-64; resident asst. for dean of women Stanford U., 1964-65; tchr. English, Abbot Acad., Andover, Mass., 1966-71, counselor, 1967-71, mem. exec. council, 1969-71; staff psychologist Lawrence Mental Health Center, 1972-73; counselor Salem State Coll., 1973-74, instr. Grad. Sch., 1974-75; pres. Behavioral Devel. Assos., 1974—; practice psychology, N. Andover, 1977—. Benefit chmn. Boston Pops Benefit for Vassar Scholarships, 1967. Episcopalian. Club: Boston Vassar (area chmn. 1966-68, 69-70, mem. spl. gifts com. 1969). Home: Tiralea 94 Porter Rd Andover MA 01810

ANDERSON, KENNETH NORMAN, assn. exec.; b. Omaha, July 10, 1921; s. Duncan McDonald and Letitia Jane (Steed) A.; student U. Omaha, 1939-41, Oreg. State Coll., 1943-44, Stanford, 1944-45, Northwestern U. Coll. Medicine, 1945-46, U. Chgo., 1958-60; m. Lois Elaine Harmon, Jan. 12, 1945; children—Eric Stephen, Randi Laine, Jani Jill, Douglas Duncan. With U.S. Army Finance Office, Nebr. and Mont., 1941-42; engring. aid U.S. Army Engrs., Omaha, 1946; radio news editor sta. KOIL, Omaha, 1946-47; bur. mgr. Internat. News Service, Omaha and Kansas City, Mo., 1947-56; spl. features editor Better Homes and Garden mag., 1956-57; asso. editor Popular Mechanics mag., 1957-59; editor Today's Health mag., pub. by AMA, Chgo., 1959-65; editor Holt, Rinehart & Winston, N.Y.C., 1965-70; exec. dir. Coffee Info. Inst., N.Y.C., 1970—. Lectr. mag. writing New Sch. Social Research, 1959, N.Y.U., 1960, Omaha U., 1961, Rensselaer Poly. Inst., 1964; cons. med. editor Ferguson Pub. Co., 1971—. Sec., Douglas County (Nebr.) Dist. Bd. Edn., 1954-56. Served with AUS, 1942-46. Recipient citation Nat. Poetry Assn., 1946. Mem. Nat. Assn. Sci. Writers, N.Y. Acad. Scis., Am. Pub. Health Assn., AAAS, Soc. Mag. Writers, Am. Inst. Biol. Scis., Am. Med. Writers Assn., Outdoor Writers Assn., Soc. Illustrators, Sigma Delta Chi. Methodist. Clubs: Omaha Press (co-founder); Overseas Press, Deadline (N.Y.C.); Nat. Press (Washington). Co-author: Lawyers' Medical Cyclopedia, 1962; The Family Physician, 1963; Today's Health Guide, 1965; Pictorial Medical Guide, 1967; Field and Stream Guide to Physical Fitness, 1969; New Concise Family Medical and Health Guide, 1971; Complete Illustrated Book of Better Health, 1973; The New Complete Medical and Health Ency., 4 vols., 1977; The Sterno Guide to the Outdoors, 1977; Eagle Claw Fish Cookbook, 1978; Guide to Weight Control and Fitness, 1978; adv. editor Nutrition Today, 1965-75. Home: 23 McQueen St Katonah NY 10536 Office: 60 E 42d St New York City NY 10017

ANDERSON, MILES JEFFERSON, telephone co. exec.; b. N.Y.C., Nov. 13, 1949; s. Thomas D. and Roberta A.; student Va. Union U., 1968-69, Queensborough Community Coll., 1970-73, York Coll., 1975—. Sales clk. Time Square Stores, Inc., 1967-68; with N.Y. Telephone Co., Jamaica, N.Y., 1970—, supr. accounting office, 1976—. Mem. Am. Mgmt. Assn. Democrat. Lutheran. Club: Masons. Home: 163-37 130th Ave Apt 9E Jamaica NY 11434 Office: 88-08 164th St Jamaica NY 11432

ANDERSON, PHILIP WARREN, physicist; b. Indpls., Dec. 13, 1923; s. Harry W. and Elsie (Osborne) A.; B.S., Harvard U., 1943, M.A., 1947, Ph.D., 1949; M.A., Cambridge (Eng.) U., 1967; D.Sc. (hon.), U. Ill., 1978; m. Joyce Gothwaite, July 31, 1947; 1 dau., Susan Osborne. Staff, Naval Research Lab., 1943-45; mem. tech. staff Bell Telephone Labs., Murray Hill, N.J., 1949—, chmn. theoretical physics dept., 1959-60, asst. dir. phys. research lab., 1974-76, cons. dir., 1976—. Fulbright lectr., U. Tokyo, 1953-54, Overseas fellow Chruchill Coll., Cambridge, 1961-62; fellow Jesus Coll., Cambridge, 1969-76, hon. fellow, 1978—. Loeb lectr. Harvard U., 1964; prof. theoretical physics U. Cambridge (Eng.), 1967-75; prof. physics Princeton, 1975—. Recipient Oliver E. Buckley prize, 1964; Dannie Heinemann prize Göttingen Acad. Sci., 1975; Nobel prize in physics, 1977; Guthrie medal Inst. Physics, Eng., 1978. Fellow Am. Phys. Soc., Am. Acad. Arts and Scis.; mem. Nat. Acad. Scis., Phys. Soc. Japan, European Phys. Soc. Author: Concepts in Solids, 1963. Research in quantum theory, especially theoretical physics of solids, spectral line broadening, magnetism, superconductivity. Office: Bell Telephone Lab Murray Hill NJ 07974

ANDERSON, RAYMOND QUINTUS, mfg. co. exec.; b. Jamestown, N.Y., Nov. 27, 1930; s. Paul Nathaniel and Cecille (Ogren) A.; grad. cum laude Phillips Acad., Andover, Mass., 1949; B.S.E., Princeton, 1953; postgrad. Mass. Inst. Tech., 1954; m. Sondra Rumsey, June 5, 1954; children—Heidi, Kristin, Gerrit, Mitchell, Tracy. Brooks. With Dahlstrom Corp., Jamestown, 1957-76, v.p., 1958-66, exec. v.p., 1966-68, pres., chief exec. officer, 1968-76; founder, pres., chief exec. officer Aarque Steel Corp., Jamestown, 1976—; dir. Bankers Trust Co. Western N.Y., Jamestown; pres. Jamestown Furniture Mart, Inc., Jamestown Industries, Inc., Hendrich Bldg. Systems, Inc. Chmn. bd. trustees Jamestown Community Coll.; chmn. United Fund. Served to lt. USNR, 1954-57. Named Outstanding Man of Yr. Mem. Mfrs. Assn. Jamestown (past pres.), Empire State C. of C. (pres.), Tau Beta Pi. Clubs: Moon Brook Country, Sportsmen's, Livingston, Prendergast. Patentee in field. Home: 121 Arlington Ave Jamestown NY 14701 Office: 111 W 2d St Jamestown NY 14701

ANDERSON, RICHARD LOUIS, elec. engr.; b. Mpls., Feb. 4, 1927; s. Ben Walter and Anna Elizabeth (Zitcowicz) A.; B.S., U. Minn., 1950, M.S., 1952; Ph.D., Syracuse U., 1960; D.Sc. (hon.), U. São Paulo (Brazil), 1969; m. Claire Louise Petersen, Sept. 15, 1951; children—Gretchen, Betty Lisa, Karl. Research asst. U. Minn., Mpls., 1950-52; research engr. IBM, Poughkeepsie, N.Y., 1952-60; instr. Syracuse (N.Y.) U., 1954-55, lectr., 1955-60, asso. prof., 1961-66, prof. elec. and computer engring., 1966—; Fulbright-Hays prof. U. Madrid, 1960-61, U. São Paulo, 1967-69; cons. to industry, govtl. agencies, fgn. univs., fgn. govts. NSF grantee, 1974-78; Forge Found. grantee, 1967-69; N.Y. State Sci. and Tech. Found. grantee, 1974-75. Fellow IEEE; mem. Am. Phys. Soc., Electrochem. Soc., AAUP, Brazilian Phys. Soc., Internat. Solar Energy Soc., Sigma Xi. Patentee in field of electronics; contbr. numerous articles on electronic materials and devices, microelectronics, and solar energy conversion to profl. jours. Home: 853 Livingston Ave Syracuse NY 13210

ANDERSON, RICHARD THEODORE, urban planner; b. Bklyn., Oct. 11, 1940; s. Charles Theodore and Lillian Elizabeth (Holmlin) A.; A.B., Rutgers U., 1962; M. Regional Planning, Cornell U., 1964; postgrad. N.Y. U., 1964-67; m. Anasta Frank, Oct. 3, 1970; children—Erik Theodore, Leslie Elisabeth. Vice pres., sec. Regional Plan Assn., N.Y.C., 1964—; instr. dept. city and regional planning Pratt Inst., N.Y.C., 1972—. Bd. dirs. Water Resources Assn. of Delaware River Basin, 1977—, United Way, Pelham, N.Y., 1977—; trustee Big Bros. of N.Y.C. Inc., 1969—; mem. Village Planning Bd., Pelham, 1977—. Mem. Am. Planning Assn. (dir. and treas. 1977—). Lutheran. Home: 69 Young Ave Pelham NY 10803 Office: Regional Plan Assn 235 E 45th St New York City NY 10017

ANDERSON, RICHARD THOMAS, pathologist; b. Bridgeport, Conn., Aug. 16, 1945; s. Charles Henry and Amy Elizabeth (Anderson) A.; B.S. (hons.) in Biology, Tulane U., 1967, M.D. (hons.), 1971; m. Linda Lee Southouse, June 14, 1969; 1 dau., Christina Lee. Intern, Madigan Gen. Hosp. Tacoma, Wash., 1971-72; resident Walter Reed Army Med. Center, Washington, 1972-75, staff pathologist, 1975-77; practice medicine specializing in pathology, Peoria, Ill., 1977—; pathologist Meth. Med. Center, Peoria, 1977—; asso. prof. pathology Uniformed Services Med. Sch., 1977; clin. instr. pathology Peoria Sch. Medicine, 1977. Served with U.S. Army, 1971-77. Fellow Coll. Am. Pathologists; mem. Am. Soc. Clin. Pathologists, Internat. Acad. Pathology, AMA, Central Ill. Pathology Soc., Ill., Peoria County med. socs., Izaak Walton League Am. Clubs: Ill. Valley Yacht and Canoe, Chillicothe Sportsmans. Research and publs. in field. Home: 6933 N Fox Point Dr Peoria IL 61614 Office: 221 N E Glen Oak Ave Peoria IL 61636

ANDERSON, ROBERT JOHN, JR., economist; b. N.Y.C., Sept. 6, 1943; s. Robert John and Ruth Eleanor (Kittleson) A.; B.A., Carleton Coll., 1965; Ph.D., U. Pa., 1969; m. Sonia Maltezou, 1976. Asst. prof. econs. Purdue U., 1969-72; asso. prof. econs. and adminstrn. U. Calif. at Riverside, 1972-73; asso. prof. econs., dir. environ. policy center Pa. State U., 1973-74; v.p., dir. econs. MATHTECH div. Mathematica, Inc., Princeton, N.J., 1974—; cons. EPA, Inst. Def. Analysis, others. Bd. dirs. Lafayette Environ. Action Fedn. Served with USPHS, 1967-69. Mem. Am. Econ. Assn., Am. Inst. Aeros. and Astronautics, Econometric Soc. Home: 148 Conover Rd Robbinsville NJ 08691 Office: Mathematica Inc PO Box 2392 Princeton NJ 08540

ANDERSON, ROBERT RENNER, banker; b. Rochelle, Ill., Dec. 14, 1930; s. Clarence A. and Hazel L. (Renner) A.; A.B., Coll. William and Mary, 1952; postgrad. Harvard, 1953; M.B.A., N.Y. U., 1963; m. Barbara A. Macaulay, May 26, 1956; children—Russell C., Lawrence G. Security analyst Anchor Corp., Elizabeth, N.J., 1957-72; v.p. trust investments Casco Bank & Trust Co., Portland, Maine, 1972—. Served to lt. (j.g.) USNR, 1953-57. Chartered fin. analyst. Mem. N.Y., Boston socs. security analysts. Club: Rotary. Home: Pine Ridge Rd Cape Elizabeth ME 04107 Office: Casco Bank & Trust Co Monument Sq Portland ME 04104

ANDERSON, RONALD JON, mgmt. engr.; b. Weymouth, Mass., June 30, 1948; s. Harold John and Mildred Avis (Chambers) A.; Asso. in Nuclear Engring., Wentworth Inst., 1969; B.S. in Mgmt. Engring., Wentworth Coll., 1972. Design engr. Townsend/Textron Co., Braintree, Mass., 1972-78; staff engr. Foster-Miller Assos., Inc., Waltham, Mass., 1978—. Methodist. Home: 328 Commerical St Braintree MA 02184 Office: 135 2d Ave Waltham MA 02154

ANDERSON, ROY SCOTT, chemist; b. N.Y.C., Jan. 30, 1931; s. David and Pauline (Kollender) A.; B.S., Haverford Coll., 1953; M.S., Tufts U., 1957; Ph.D., Purdue U., 1961; m. Carol Joyce Schneider, June 21, 1958; children—Patricia, Bruce David. Research scientist, mgr. elastic yarns and fibers Uniroyal, Winnsboro, S.C., 1961-65; asst. dir. devel. elastic fabrics div. Deering-Milliken Research Corp., Spartanburg, S.C., 1965-67; mgr. product devel. Tanatex Chem. Corp., Lyndhurst, N.J., 1967-68; mgr. applications research and devel., devel. div. Borg-Warner Corp., Parkersburg, W.Va., 1968-71; mgr. polymer research Acushnet Corp., New Bedford, Mass., 1971-73; mgr. new product devel. dept. PQ Chems., Lafayette Hill, Pa., 1973-77, tech. mgr. internat. div., 1977—. Mem. Marple Long Range Planning Commn., Marple Twp., Pa., 1975—; mem. Gaston County Fluoridation Com., 1962-65. Mem. Am. Chem. Soc., Am. Inst. Chemists, The Chem. Soc. (London), N.Y. Acad. Scis., Sigma Xi, Phi Lambda Upsilon. Contbr. articles in field to profl. jours.; patentee in field. Office: PO Box 840 Valley Forge PA 19482

ANDERSON, STANLEY JAMES, govt. ofcl.; b. Washington, Setp. 24, 1927; s. James Edward and Ethel Anderson; B.S., Howard U., 1948, grad. Sch. Social Work, 1965-67; m. Virginia Alice Ingram, Jan. 12, 1950; children—Stanice Lucretia, Stanley James. With D.C. Recreation Dept., 1946-67, dir. roving leader program, 1961-66, dep. dir. neighborhood centers div., 1966-67; mem. D.C. City Council, 1967-73; mem. Washington Met. Transit Authority, 1970-73, chmn., 1973—; acting dir. Runaway Youth Program, HEW, also acting commr. Office of Youth Devel.; cons. youth, transp. Pres., Hillsdale Civic Assn., 1959-63. Bd. dirs. S.E. Community Hosp., Washington, Eugene and Agnes Meyer Found., Washington Met. Transit Authority Retirement Trust, United Givers Fund. Recipient Melvin C. Hazen award outstanding D.C. govt. service, 1963; Fellowship award Nat. Recreation and Park Assn., 1963. Mem. Am. Recreation Assn. Contbr. articles to profl. jours. Home: 2604 Stanton Rd SE Washington DC 20020 Office: 330 Independence Ave SW Washington DC 20201

ANDERSON, THOMAS WILLIAM, data processing resource mgmt. co. exec.; b. Flushing, N.Y., Jan. 9, 1945; s. Cyril W. and Catherine Elizabeth (Nesbitt) A.; B.A. in Economics, Trinity Coll., 1966; postgrad. U. Hartford, 1974, Stonier Grad. Sch. Banking Rutgers U., 1978—; m. Sara Lynn Jones, July 10, 1970; children—Heather Lynn, Chelsey Brooke. City planner, City of Middletown, Conn. 1967-69; programmer, project mgr. Hartford (Conn.) Nat. Bank and Trust, 1969-73; v.p., mgr. systems planning group Fin. Industry Systems (partnership Hartford Nat. Bank & Trust Co. and Martin Marietta Corp.), Hartford, 1973—. Active Hartford Redevel. Agency, 1972, Hartford area Bd. Edn., Easter Seal Rehab. Data Processing advisory com. Certified data processor; certificate Fed. Civil Def. Tng. Mem. Soc. Mgmt. Info. Systems. Unitarian. Office: 150 Windsor St Hartford CT 06120

ANDERSON, WARREN MATTICE, state senator; b. Bainbridge, N.Y., Oct. 16, 1915; s. Floyd E. and Edna (Mattice) A.; B.A., Colgate U., 1937; J.D., Albany Law Sch., 1940; LL.D., Hartwick Coll., 1976; m. Eleanor C. Sanford, June 28, 1941; children—Warren David, Lawrence, Richard, Thomas. Admitted to N.Y. bar, 1940, since practiced in Binghamton; mem. firm Hinman, Howard and Kattell; individual practice law, 1972; asst. county atty. Broome County (N.Y.), 1940-42; mem. N.Y. State Senate, 1953—, chmn. fin. com., 1966-72, pres. pro tem, maj. leader, 1973—; mem.-at-large Governing Bd. Council State Govt. Trustee Cornell U.; del. Republican State Conv., 1972, 76, mem. platform com. Served with U.S. Army, 1942-45. Mem. Am., N.Y. State bar assns., U.S. Assn. State Govt. Presbyterian. Office: 724 Security Mut Bldg Binghamton NY 13901

ANDERSON, WILLIAM ALPHAUNCE, dermatologist; b. Atlanta, July 21, 1921; s. William A. and Mary Elizabeth A.; B.S., Tuskegee Inst., 1942; M.D., U. Mich., 1953; children—Serena, William A. Intern, U. Mich. Hosp., Ann Arbor, 1953-54; resident VA Hosp., Bronx, N.Y., 1954-57; practice medicine specializing in dermatology, Orange and East Orange, N.J., 1957—; asso. med. dir. Whitehall Labs., N.Y.C., 1965-70; mem. staffs N.Y. Hosp., Meml. Hosp. Cancer and Allied Diseases, Hosp. Center at Orange (N.J.), United Hosps., Newark; clin. asso. prof. dermatology Cornell U. Med. Coll., N.Y.C. Served with U.S. Army, 1942-46. Diplomate Am. Bd. Dermatology. Mem. Am., Nat. med. assns., Am. Acad. Dermatology, Met. Dermatol. Soc. N.Y., N.J. Dermatol. Soc., H.M. Club Am. Contbr. articles in field to med. jours. Home: 594 Seven Oaks Rd Orange NJ 07050 Office: 185 Central Ave East Orange NJ 07018

ANDERSON, WILLIAM CARL, cons. civil engr.; b. Vinton, Iowa, Sept. 24, 1943; s. Ivan Dale and Lois Bernice Anderson; B.S. in Civil Engring., Iowa State U., 1967; m. Elizabeth Ann Dingman, Nov. 12, 1966; children—William Carl III, Erica Dawn. Asst. pub. health engr. N.Y. State Health Dept., Utica, 1967; dir. environ. health Cayuga County Health Dept., Auburn, N.Y., 1968-73; mng. partner Pickard & Anderson, Auburn, 1973—; expert witness U.S. Ho. of Reps., 1975, 76. Mem. health and safety com. Cayuga County council Boy Scouts Am., 1969—. Served with USNR, 1967-68. Recipient Philip F. Morgan medal Water Pollution Control Fedn., 1973, Lewis Van Carpenter award N.Y. Water Pollution Control Assn., 1974. Registered profl. engr., N.Y. State, Iowa; diplomate Am. Acad. Environ. Engrs.; licensed wastewater treatment plant operator, N.Y. State. Mem. ASCE (environ. engring. div., chmn. com. on solid waste mgmt. 1973-75, mem. profl. coordination com. 1977—, awards com. 1977—, publs. com. 1977—, comptroller div. exec. com. 1976—), Am. Cons. Engrs. Council (environ. com. 1976—, chmn. task force on solid waste, 1977—, Chessman, Knights of St. Patrick, Order of Knoll, Chi Epsilon. Republican. Roman Catholic. Clubs: Owasco Country; Iowa State U. Alumni of Syracuse (pres. 1972-75); Rotary. Contbr. articles to profl. jours. Home: 74 Adams Ave Auburn NY 13021 Office: 69 South St Auburn NY 13021

ANDERSON, WILLIAM HENRY, physician; b. Phila., Nov. 10, 1940; s. William Henry Schoen and Elizabeth Winifred (Laverty) A.; B.S., Mass. Inst. Tech., 1962; M.A., U. Pa., 1967; M.D., Thomas Jefferson U., 1967; M.P.H., Harvard U., 1977; m. Catherine Sacchetti, Oct. 7, 1967; 1 dau., Jennifer Ann. Intern, Pa. Hosp., Phila., 1967-68; resident psychiatry Mass. Gen. Hosp., Boston, 1968-71; instr. psychiatry Harvard U., Boston, 1973-75, asst. prof., 1975—; dir. postgrad. edn., dept. psychiatry Mass. Gen. Hosp., 1976—. Served to lt. comdr. M.C., USNR, 1971-73. Diplomate Am. Bd. Psychiatry and Neurology. Mem. AAAS, Mass. Med. Soc., Am. Psychiat. Assn., Am. Coll. Emergency Physicians, Am. Pub. Health Assn., Boston Athenaeum, Sigma Xi. Club: Harvard Boston. Contbg. editor: The New Physician, 1977—. Office: Mass Gen Hosp Boston MA 02114

ANDERSON, WILLIAM JOSEPH, civil engr.; b. Paterson, N.J., July 20, 1922; s. Fredrick William and Julia (Muller) A.; B.S. in Civil Engring., Bucknell U., 1943; m. Eleanor Frances Lennox, Dec. 27, 1946; children—William Thomas. With firm Samworth-Hughes Co., Paramus, N.J., 1946—, v.p. engring., 1961-70, pres., 1971—; pres. W. Anderson Assos., Paramus, 1971—. Mem. bldg. com. Hackensack (N.J.) Hosp., 1967—. Served as ensign C.E.C., USNR, 1943-46. Registered profl. engr., N.Y., N.J., 10 other states. Mem. Passaic County (pres. 1963), N.J. socs. profl. engrs. Clubs: Arcola Country, Ridgewood Country (Paramus). Home: 33 E Allendale Rd Saddle River NJ 07450 Office: PO Box 10 Paramus NJ 07652

ANDERSON, WILLIAM STATON, pediatrician; b. Wilson, N.C., Oct. 7, 1906; s. Wade Hampton and Lalla (Harper) A.; A.B., Duke U., 1927; M.D., Johns Hopkins U., 1931; m. Doris Dunham, June 3, 1933; children—Margaret Anderson Fikioris, Stella Anderson Edmundson. Intern in pediatrics Johns Hopkins Hosp., Balt., 1931-32; asst. resident in pediatrics Cornell U.-N.Y. Hosp., 1932-33, chief resident in pediatrics, 1933-35; practice medicine specializing in pediatrics, Washington, 1935—; mem. staff Children's Hosp. Nat. Med. Center; clin. prof. emeritus George Washington Med. Sch., Washington. Bd. dirs. Children's Hosp. D.C. Diplomate Am. Bd. Pediatrics. Fellow Am. Acad. Pediatrics (pres. 1966-67); mem. Am. Pediatric Soc., Phi Beta Kappa, Omicron Delta Kappa, Alpha Kappa Alpha, Kappa Sigma. Democrat. Methodist. Mem. editorial adv. bd. Pediatric Annals, 1972—. Home: 4502 Tournay Rd Washington DC 20016 Office: 5300 Westbard Ave Washington DC 20016

ANDERSON NOLOSCO, MARYNITA MARGARET, historian; b. Bklyn., Nov. 20, 1947; d. William Thomas and Anita Claire (Wells) Anderson; B.A., St. Joseph's Coll., 1969; M.A. (Ednl. Prof. Devel. Act fellow 1969-71), N.Y. U., 1971, postgrad. (fellow 1976-77), 1974—; m. Anthony L. Nolosco, Oct. 30, 1976; 1 son, Anderson Michael. Instr. history Nassau Community Coll., Garden City, N.Y., 1970-71; travel cons. Salute Travel Agency, N.Y.C., 1971-73; travel planner Bankers Trust Co., N.Y.C., 1973-74; asst. prof. history and polit. sci. St. Francis Coll., Bklyn., 1974—. Mem. Am. Acad. Polit. and Social Scis., AAUP, Am. Hist. Assn., Long Island Hist. Soc., History and Polit. Sci. Soc. of St. Francis Coll. (moderator), Zeta Gamma Alpha (moderator), Phi Alpha Theta. Author tchrs. manual. Office: 180 Remsen St Brooklyn NY 11210

ANDES, LESTER RAY, civil engr., cons. co. exec.; b. Martindale, Pa., Dec. 8, 1931; s. Franklin Ray and Irene (Wenger) A.; B.S. in Civil Engring., Pa. State U., 1955; m. Dorothy Ellen Marsh, Jan. 29, 1955; children—Lucinda Jane, David Bruce. Constrn. engr. Jack and Jim Maser Inc., hwy and heavy contractor, Brownstown, Pa., 1955-58, estimator, 1958-61; constrn. engr. Hempt Bros. Inc., hwy. and heavy contractor, Camp Hill, Pa., 1961-65; project engr. Huth Engrs. Inc., cons. engrs., Lancaster, Pa., 1965-69, chief engr. br., Downingtown, Pa., 1973-75, office mgr., 1975—; city engr. City of Lancaster, 1969-70, dir. pub. works, 1970-73. Mem. Warwick Twp. (Pa.) Planning Commn., 1968, 69. Served with USN, 1951-53; ETO. Registered profl. engr., Pa. Mem. Nat. Soc. Profl. Engrs., Water Pollution Control Fedn., Am. Pub. Works Assn. Clubs: VFW, Elks. Home: 345 E Lexington Rd Lititz PA 17543 Office: 100 E Lancaster Ave Downington PA 19335

ANDORS, LEONARD, educator, oral surgeon; b. Bklyn., Mar. 11, 1924; s. Isidore and Nettie (Gottlieb) A.; student Columbia Coll. Princeton, 1944-46; D.D.S., N.Y.U., 1950; m. Leah Davis, Aug. 17, 1947; children—Sharon Greer, Allison Victor, Louis Jay. Intern in oral surgery Kings County Hosp., Bklyn., 1950-51; resident N.Y. Hosp.-Cornell Med. Center, N.Y.C., 1951-52; practice dentistry specializing in oral surgery, Patchogue, N.Y., 1955-75; dir. dental dept., attending oral surgeon, mem. med. bd. Brookhaven Meml. Hosp., Patchogue, 1967-75; oral surgeon Suffolk County Cleft Palate Rehab. Clinic, 1961—; cons. oral surgery St. Charles Hosp., Central Suffolk Hosp., Greenport Hosp., V.A. Hosp. of Northport, N.Y.; past mem. staffs Meadowbrook Hosp., Brunswick Hosp., Mid-Island Hosp., Lakeside Hosp., Freeport Hosp., Southside Hosp., Good Samaritan Hosp., Mather Meml. Hosp., Southampton Hosp.; full-time asso. prof. bio-dental scis. Suffolk County Community Coll., Selden, N.Y., 1970-75; asst. prof. clin. dental medicine Health Scis. Center of State U. N.Y. at Stony Brook, 1971-76, asst. prof. restorative dentistry

Sch. Dental Medicine, 1976—, clin. dir. Sch. Dental Medicine, 1976—, clin. asso. prof., 1977—. Mem. regional adv. group Nassau-Suffolk Regional med. Program, 1967—, vice chmn., 1972-75; mem. Suffolk County Task Force subcom. on health facilities, 1970; mem. dental adv. group Bd. Coop. Services 2d Supervisory Dist. Suffolk County, 1970-74; mem. dental adv. and utilization com. Suffolk County Med. Adminstrn. Trustee Suffolk County Cancer Soc. Served with USNR, 1942-46, with USAF, 1952-54. Fellow Suffolk County Acad. Medicine (mem. founding bd. trustees 1961—, v.p. 1970-75), Am. Coll. Dentists; mem. N.Y. State (mem. coms.), Suffolk County (pres. 1962-63, exec. bd. 1958—), 10th Dist. (chmn. legis. com. 1968-70, bd. dels 1958-69) dental socs., Am. Dental Assn., N.Y. State Soc. Oral Surgeons, Am. Assn. Dental Schs., Nassau-Suffolk Acad. Dentistry, Am. Assn. Hosp. Dentists, Internat. Assn. Dental Research, Am. Dental Soc. Anesthesiology, Internat. Assn. Study Pain, Am. Cleft Palate Assn., Am. Amateur Radio Relay League, Am. Mus. Natural History, Am. Sch. Health Assn., Nat. Audubon Soc., Alpha Omega. Republican. Jewish religion. Mason. Gen. class licensed radio amateur. Home: 304 Beaver Dam Rd Brookhaven NY 11719 Office: Sch Dental Medicine State U NY Stony Brook NY 11790

ANDOVER, JAMES J., publs. exec.; b. Bronx, N.Y., Nov. 20, 1935; s. Louis and Helen (Szyjarto) A.; B.S. in Mech. Engring., Columbia U., 1960, B.A., Colby Coll., 1957; m. Nilda Zamora, June 17, 1978. Engr., Foster Wheeler Corp., Livingston, N.J., 1960-63, Am. Elec. Power Co., N.Y.C., 1963-65; asso. editor Diesel Equipment Supt. mag., Stamford, Conn., 1965-67; reporter The Herald Statesman, Yonkers, N.Y., 1967-71; news editor Spectrum Mag., IEEE, N.Y.C., 1971-73; editorial dir. Nat. Assn. Credit Mgmt., N.Y.C., 1973-78, dir. publs., 1978—. Mem. Am. Soc. Bus. Press Editors, Am. Mgmt. Assn., N.Y. Bus. Press Editors, N.Y. Press Club. Home: 48-51 43d St Woodside NY 11377 Office: 475 Park Ave S New York City NY 10016

ANDRADE MATTHEWS, ANNE MCILHENNEY (MRS. MICHAEL R. ANDRADE), former newspaperwoman; b. Phila.; d. William and Clara (McCollum) McIlhenney; student U. Buffalo, 1950-54, Ecole des Beaux Arts, Paris, France; D.Litt., Rosary Hill Coll.; m. Burrows Matthews, Oct. 7, 1947 (dec. 1954); m. 2d, Michael R. Andrade, Apr. 1972. Reporter Buffalo Courier Express, 1924-47, aviation editor, 1935-47, also drama critic, motion picture columnist, feature writer, gen. news, reporter, 1935-47, art critic and promotions editor, 1959-63, dir. radio promotions, 1963-64, by-line feature columnist, 1964-75; speech writer, pub. relations Supreme Command, Far East, Tokyo, also NATO, 1952-53; swimming instr. Buffalo Athletic Club, 1927-38, Kensington High Sch., Buffalo, 1938-42. Bd. dirs. Soc. Prevention Cruelty to Animals; trustee Buffalo and County Pub. Library; mem. council Niagara U. Served as maj. WAC, 1942-47. Decorated Purple Heart, Bronze Star. Recipient Someone Cares award Bros. of Mercy, 1972, Liberty Bell award Erie County Bar Assn., 1972, Community Service award 6th dist. VFW, 1972, Americanism award Am. Legion, 1972; also over 30 awards for journalism. Mem. Buffalo Chapitre de la Chaine des Rotisseurs, Eden Citizen's Assn. (dir.). Clubs: Frontier Press (dir.); Saturn; Overseas Press (N.Y.C.) 1st woman named pub. realtions officer in charge U.S. Army; 1st woman dir. Buffalo unit Assn. U.S. Army. Home: 9293 Sission Hwy Eden NY 14057

ANDREWS, CHARLES LAWRENCE, marketing exec.; b. Clinton, Ill., Apr. 23, 1914; s. Lawrence I. and Sarah (Tracey) A.; B.S., U. Ill., 1935; LL.B., LaSalle Extension U., 1949; m. Harriet E. Gilmore, Oct. 3, 1936; children—Beatrice (Mrs. John A. Walker), Lucinda (Mrs. William J. Axtell). Sales Beech-nut Packing Co., 1936-48, legal dept., 1948-52; div. mgr. Frank H. Fleer Corp., 1952-55; asst. sales mgr. F & F Labs., 1955-60; sales mgr. Midwest div., Peter Paul, Inc., 1960-62; sales and marketing, v.p. Beatrice Foods, 1962-70; v.p., dir. marketing M.J. Holloway Co. div. Beatrice Foods 1967-70; pres., sales mgr., dir. marketing Boyer Bros. Inc., Altoona, Pa., 1970—, also dir.; dir. Taconic Farms. Midwest rep. Olympic Swimming Com. Mem. Inst. Food Technologists, Chgo. Exec. Club, Sales Exec. Club, Am. Mgmt. Assn., Am. Marketing Assn., A.I.M. (pres.'s council), Internat. Platform Assn., Chgo. Tobacco Round Table, I Men's Assn., U. of Ill. Alumni Assn., Sigma Chi. Republican. Presbyn. Mason (Shriner). Clubs: Blairmont Country, Heidleberg. Contbr. articles to trade publs. Home: 520 Hickory St Hollidaysburg PA 16648 Office: 821 17th Ave Altoona PA 16601

ANDREWS, DOROTHY MAUD, educator; b. Thornaby-on-Tees, Yorkshire, Eng., Mar. 24, 1922; d. Frederick Lionel and Lena Mary (Hardy) Ellis; came to U.S., 1947, naturalized, 1955; B.Sc., Sheffield (Eng.) U., 1944; Ed.M., Boston U., 1960; m. Robert W. Andrews, Sept. 27, 1947; children—Peter Frederick, Meriel Christine. Biology and chemistry tchr. schs. in Eng. and Mass., 1944-51; gen. sci. tchr. Ridgefield (Conn.) High Sch., 1964-65; tchr. biology, chmn. sci. dept. Bromfield Sch., Harvard, Mass., 1965—; dep. leader Wildlife Conservation Expdn. for Educators to E. Africa, 1973-74. Named Conservation Tchr. of Year, New Eng. Farm and Garden Assn.-Mass. Audubon Soc., 1975; recipient teaching award, recognition star Nat. Sci. Tchrs. Assn., 1978. Mem. Nat. Assn. Biology Tchrs. (named outstanding biology tchr. Mass. 1975), Nat. Sci. Tchrs. Assn., Nat. Assn. Research Sci. Teaching, Essex County Beekeepers Assn. (pres. 1968-72), Bee Research Assn., Boston Mycol. Club, E. African Wildlife Soc., Nat., Mass. Audubon socs., Defenders of Wildlife, Am. Inst. Biol. Scis., Pi Lambda Theta, Phi Delta Kappa. Episcopalian. Contbr. to profl. jours. Home: Old Littleton Rd Harvard MA 01451 Office: Bromfield Sch Harvard MA 01451

ANDREWS, ELLIOTT ELLSWORTH, state ofcl. R.I.; b. Springfield, Mass., Nov. 28, 1921; s. Arthur Albert and Rachal Mae (Thompson) A.; A.B., Brown U., 1947, M.A., 1947; M.L.S., U. R.I., 1967; m. Constance Karen Murlay, June 21, 1949; children—Guy B., Charlotte. Librarian in charge dept. social studies Brown U., 1947-51; librarian, info. dir. Providence (R.I.) Jour. Co., 1951-62; state librarian, dir. State of R.I., Providence, 1962—; cons. in field. Served with U.S. Army, 1942-45, 50-52. Mem. ALA, R.I. Library Assn., Am. Assn. Law Libraries (certified), Spl. Libraries Assn. Roman Catholic. Club: Brown R.I. Contbr. articles in field to profl. jours. Home: Osprey Rd Wakefield RI 02906 Office: State Library State House Providence RI 02908

ANDREWS, GEORGE WARREN, air conditioner mfg. co. exec.; b. New Haven, Aug. 16, 1919; s. Charles Vernon and Doris Evelyn (Dixon) A.; B.S. in Aero. Engring., La. State U., 1942; postgrad. U. Conn., 1944, sales mktg. Yale, 1944-46; m. Helen M. Smith, June 23, 1961; children—Scott W., Deborah J., Barbara Sorensen, Judith Beazley. Flight test engr. United Aircraft Corp., Hartford, Conn., 1941-44; v.p. N.E. Aircraft Corp., New Haven, 1944-50; Atlantic regional mgr. Kresky Mfg. Co., Petaluma, Calif., 1950-56; exec. v.p. Townsend Machine Tool Co., New Haven, 1956-63; br. mgr. York div. Borg-Warner Corp., King of Prussia, Pa., 1964—; mem. Nat. Security Council. Mem. Nat. Soc. Profl. Engrs., Am. Soc. Heating, Refrigeration and Air Conditioning Engrs., Am. Def. Preparedness Assn. (life), Nat. Rifle Assn. (endowment mem.). Republican. Club: Rotary. Author: Mechanized Commercial Farming, 1951. Home: 1615 Stephens Dr Wayne PA 19087 Office: 970 Pulaski Dr King of Prussia PA 19406

ANDREWS, HERBERT DUANE, historian; b. West Paris, Maine, Sept. 19, 1930; s. Alfred Duane and Iona Florence (Littlehale) A.; A.A., Portland Jr. Coll., 1950; A.B., Bowdoin Coll., 1952; M.A., Northwestern U., 1957, Ph.D., 1964; m. Loretta Marie Kreider, Aug. 3, 1957; children—Timothy, Elizabeth, John. Instr., Towson State U., Balt., 1959-62, asst. prof. history, 1962-64, asso. prof., 1964-67, prof., 1967—. Served with USAR, 1952-54. Fulbright fellow, 1961-62; Nat. Endowment for Humanities summer seminar fellow, 1976. Mem. Am., So. hist. assns., Social Sci. History Assn. Home: 343 Rosebank Ave Baltimore MD 21212 Office: Dept History Towson State U Baltimore MD 21204

ANDREWS, JOHN FRASER, physician; b. Norwood, Mass., May 29, 1920; s. Chester Huston and Marjorie Boynton (Fraser) A.; A.B., Amherst Coll., 1947; M.D., Tufts U., 1952; m. Jean Woodruff Shera, Apr. 25, 1947; children—Craig Shera, Marcia Elizabeth, John Fraser, William Seth. Intern, Maine Gen. Hosp., Portland, 1952-53, resident medicine, 1953-54; gen. practice medicine Boothbay Harbor, Maine, 1954—; mem. staff St. Andrews Hosp., med. dir., 1975—; mem. staff Boothbay Harbor, Miles Meml. Hosp., Darmiscotta, Me. Dir. Boothbay Harbor Summer Sch., Inc. Trustee Boothbay Region YMCA, St. Andrews Hosp.; bd. dirs. St. Andrews Hosp., Boothbay Region Scholarship Fund. Served with USCGR, 1941-46. Mem. Am., Maine (mem. council 1968-70), Lincoln-Segadahoc (pres. 1959) med. assns., Pilots Internat. Assn., Aircraft Owners and Pilots Assn. Mason (Shriner). Home: 20 West St Boothbay Harbor ME 04538 Office: St Andrews Ln Boothbay Harbor ME 04538

ANDREWS, LEWIS MARSHALL, JR., map co. exec.; b. N.Y.C., July 10, 1918; s. Lewis Marshall and Mary (Holzmann) A.; B.A., Wesleyan U. Conn., 1939; m. Katherine Englehart, May 5, 1944; children—Lewis Marshall, Mary Katherine, Philip Dawson. Vice pres. Am. Map Co., Inc., N.Y.C., 1945-55, pres., 1955—, chmn. bd., 1966—. Served to lt. comdr. USNR, 1940-45; ETO. Fellow Oceanographic Inst., Am. Geog. Soc.; mem. Map Pubs. Assn, World War Destroyer Escort Comdg. Officers (chmn. 1964-65), Chi Psi. Clubs: Tarrytown (N.Y.) Yacht; Sleepy Hollow Country (skeet and trap com. 1972-73) (Scarborough, N.Y.); Stamford (Conn.) Yacht. Home: 200 E 62d St Apt 5A New York City NY 10022 Office: Am Map Co Inc 1926 Broadway New York City NY 10023

ANDREWS, MARGARET ELIZABETH, rehab. counselor; b. Buffalo, Mar. 19, 1948; d. Arthur Carl and Grace Ellen Metzler; B.A. in Psychology, State U. N.Y., Buffalo, 1970, Ed.M., 1972; m. William Edward Andrews, June 13, 1970; 1 son, Jonathan Luke. Rehab. counselor Niagara Frontier Vocat. Rehab. Center, Buffalo, 1972-73; clin. asso. pvt. psychiat. practice, Williamsville, N.Y., 1973-74; dir. intake DeVeaux Sch., Niagara Falls, N.Y., 1974-76; sr. rehab. counselor dept. child psychiatry and behavioral scis. Children's Hosp. Buffalo, 1976—; co-chmn. Niagara County Rape Task Force, 1973-74. Certified rehab. counselor. Mem. Am. Personnel and Guidance Assn., Nat. Rehab. Assn., Am. Rehab. Counselors Assn. Office: 137 Hodge St Buffalo NY 14222

ANDREWS, RICHARD CECIL, JR., research engr.; b. Tarentum, Pa., May 5, 1927; s. Richard Cecil and Katheryne Merle (Willis) A.; B.S. in Chem. Engring., Grove City Coll., 1951; m. Sarah Ann Lardin, June 11, 1949; 1 dau., Leslie. Research engr. MSA Research Corp., Evans City, Pa., 1951—, mem. cons. team for Comitato Nazionale per l'Energia Nucleare (CNEN-Italian AEC), 1969-70. Served with AAC, 1945-46. Mem. Am. Inst. Chem. Engrs., Am. Nuclear Soc., Kemikos Collegian Hon. Chemistry Soc. Republican. Lutheran. Author tech. papers. Patentee in field. Home: RD 1 Rolling Hills Zelienople PA 16063 Office: MSA Research Corp Evans City PA 16033

ANDREWS, ZELLE WHITMARSH, civic worker; b. Hartford, Conn., Jan. 15, 1938; d. Joseph Church and Bess Evelyn (Whitmarsh) A.; A.B. in Psychology, Wheaton Coll., Norton, Mass., 1960; A.M. (NDEA Title IV fellow), U. Hawaii, Manoa, 1968, Ph.D. in Am. History, 1975; m. Richard L. Larson, Sept. 8, 1962. Course asst. Harvard U. Sch. Bus. Adminstrn., Boston, 1960-61, asso., 1961-62; adj. prof. I div. social and behavioral scis. Westchester Community Coll., Valhalla, N.Y., 1975; pres. NOW-N.Y. State, Albany, 1977-78; mem. NOW Nat. Bd., Washington, 1978—; mem. Hawaii State Comm. on Status Women, 1971-73; N.Y. State commr. Internat. Women's Yr. and ofcl. observer Internat. Women's Yr. Conf., Houston, 1977. Mem. Am. Hist. Assn., Conf. on Peace Research in History, Coordinating Com. on Women in Hist. Profession, Women's Internat. League for Peace and Freedom. Democrat. Congregationalist. Home: 30 Greenridge Ave White Plains NY 10605 Office: One Columbia Pl Albany NY 12207

ANDRIEKUS, LEONARDAS KAZIMIERAS, clergyman; b. Barstyciai, Lithuania, July 15, 1914; s. Kazimieras and Barbora (Jonkute) A.; student Kretinga (Lithuania) Coll., 1937; postgrad. Schwaz Franciscan Sem., Tyrol, Austria, 1937-39, Milan, Italy, 1939-41; D. Canon Law, Pontifical U. Antonianum, Rome, Italy, 1945. Ordained priest Roman Catholic Ch., 1940; editor Cultural Mag. Aidai, 1950-64, 75—; superior Franciscan Monastery, N.Y.C., 1958-64, 70-73, Kennebunkport, Maine, 1973-76; headmaster St. Anthony's High Sch., Kennebunkport, 1964-69; provincial superior Lithuanian Franciscan Fathers, 1964-70. Mem. Lithuanian transmissions Voice Am., 1951-64. Mem. Cath. Acad. Scis., Lithuanian Writers Assn. in Exile (pres. 1970—). Author: (poetry, in Lithuanian) Atviros marios, 1955; Saule Kryziuose, 1960; Naktigone, 1963; Po Dievo antspaudais, 1969; Amens in Amber (selected poems translated by Demie Jonaities), 1968; Uz vasaros vartu, 1976. Address: Franciscan Monastery Kennebunkport ME 04046

ANDRIOLE, RICHARD CHARLES, hosp. exec.; b. Scranton, Pa., Apr. 9, 1941; s. Vincent Anthony and Josephine C. A.; B.S. in Pharmacy, Temple U., 1964, M.B.A., 1971; m. Marion B. Bohlinger, Nov. 4, 1967; children—Richard Charles, Stephanie L. Adminstrv. asst. Wesson Meml. Hosp., Springfield, Mass., 1971-72, div. dir., 1972-73, asst. v.p., 1973-75; asst. dir. med. adminstrn. Baystate Med. Center, Springfield, 1975-78; v.p. Lancaster (Pa.) Gen. Hosp., 1978—; chmn. Regional Emergency Med. Services Com., 1974-75; sec., treas. Hosp. Council Western Mass., 1975-76; mem. Mayor's Med. Adv. Com., 1976-77; active Emergency Health Services Fedn. S. Central Pa., Lancaster chpt. ARC, Hosp. Council Central Pa., 1978—. Mem. Am. Coll. Hosp. Adminstrs., Am. Hosp. Assn., Nat. Ski Patrol Systems (sr.). Office: 555 N Duke St Lancaster PA 17604

ANDRONIC, ALEXE, physician; b. Braila, Romania, Nov. 10, 1922; s. Constantin and Lucia (Stanesco) A.; M.D., U. Bucuresti, 1949; came to U.S., 1965, naturalized, 1970. Extern, intern clin. hosps. Bucuresti, 1945-49; individual practice gen. medicine, Daia-Fratesti, Romania, 1949-51; cons. Oltenitza (Romania) Hosp., 1951-57, internist specialist, 1957-64; house physician Fairlawn Hosp., Worcester, Mass., 1965-66; jr. physician Grafton (Mass.) State Hosp., 1966-67, sr. physician, 1967-73; med. dir. Westborough (Mass.) State Hosp., 1973-74, chief med. physician, 1974—, pres. med. staff, 1973-74; physician gen. R.I. Med. Center, Cranston, 1977—. Vice-pres. Romanian Orthodox Parochial Council, Worcester, 1975—. Mem. AMA (Recognition award 1975, 76, 77, 78), Acad. Psychosomatic Medicine, Nat. Hist. Soc., Smithsonian Assos., Nat. Trust Historic Preservation, Am. Law Enforcement Assn., Early Am. Soc., Audubon Soc., Am. Mus. Natural History, Am. Security Council. Home: 825 Pontiac Ave Apt 15102 Cranston RI 02910

ANDRULIS, RICHARD STANLEY, indsl. psychologist; b. N.Y.C., Nov. 5, 1942; s. Peter Joseph and Irene J. (Richter) A.; B.S., Fordham U., 1964; Ph.D., U. Tex. at Austin, 1968; m. Linda Anne Gould, May 27, 1967; children—Richard Stanley, Jeremy Leonard, Karin Irene. Coordinator research and evaluation Eastern Regional Inst. Edn., U.S. Office Edn., Syracuse, N.Y., 1968-71; lectr. psychology Syracuse U., 1968-71; coordinator Hull Found. for Creative Leadership, 1976-77; Phila., 1977—; indsl. dir. research and evaluation Am. Coll., Bryn Mawr, Pa., 1971-76; indsl. psychologist Haimes Assos., Inc., Phila., 1977—; cons. Midatlantic Research Inst., Washington, 1974-76, Andrulis Research Corp., Washington, 1975—; lectr. Villanova U., Phila., Pa. State U., Phila.; cons. Syracuse Democratic Com., 1971. Bd. dirs. Austin chpt. Big Bros., 1965-67, mem. N.Y.C. chpt., 1963-64. Mem. Am. Psychol. Assn., Nat. Council for Measurement Edn., Assn. Children with Learning Disabilities. Author books; contbr. chpts. to books and articles to profl. jours. Home: 31 Lockwood Rd West Chester PA 19380 Office: 708 S Washington Sq Philadelphia PA 19106

ANDRUS, CECIL D., sec. interior; b. Hood River, Oreg., Aug. 25, 1931; s. Hal S. and Dorothy (Johnson) A.; student Oreg. State U., 1948-49; m. Carol M. May, Aug. 27, 1949; children—Tana Lee, Tracy Sue, Kelly Kay. Asst. mgr. Workmen's Compensation Exchange, 1963-66; agt. Paul Revere Inc. Co., 1967, agy. supr., 1968, field supr., 1969; mem. Idaho Senate; gov. State of Idaho, Boise, until 1977; sec. Dept. of Interior, Washington, 1977—. Served with USNR, 1951-55. Mem. V.F.W. (Man of Year 1959). Democrat. Lutheran. Mason, Elk. Address: RFD Cascade ID 83611 Office: Dept of Interior Office of Secretary Washington DC 20240

ANFINSEN, CHRISTIAN BOEHMER, biochemist; b. Monessen, Pa., Mar. 26, 1916; s. Christian Boehmer and Sophie (Rasmussen) A.; B.A., Swarthmore Coll., 1937, D.Sc., 1965; M.S., U. Pa., 1939; Ph.D., Harvard, 1943; D.Sc., Georgetown U., 1967; m. Florence Bernice Kenenger, Nov. 29, 1941; children—Carol Bernice, Margot Sophie, Christian Boehmer. Am.-Scandinavian Found. fellow Carlsberg Lab., Copenhagen, 1939. Rockefeller fellow, 1954-55; sr. cancer research fellow Nobel Inst., Stockholm, Sweden, 1947, asst. prof. biol. chemistry, Markle scholar Harvard Med. Sch., 1948-50, prof. biochemistry, 1962-63; Guggenheim fellow Weizmann Inst., Rehovot, Israel, 1958; chief lab. cellular physiology and metabolism Nat. Heart Inst., Bethesda, Md., 1950-62; chief lab. chem. biology Nat. Inst. Arthritis and Metabolic Diseases, Bethesda, 1963—. Bd. govs. Weizmann Inst. Sci., Rehovot, Israel. Recipient Nobel prize in chemistry, 1972. Mem. Am. Soc. Biol. Chemists (pres. 1971-72), Am. Acad. Arts and Scis., Nat. Acad. Sci., Fedn. Am. Scientists (treas. 1958-59, vice chmn. 1959-60, 73-74). Author: The Molecular Basis of Evolution, 1959. Contbr. to sci. publs. Office: National Inst Arthritis Metabolic and Digestive Diseases Bethesda MD 20014

ANGELAKOS, EVANGELOS THEDOROU, physician, physiologist, pharmacologist; b. Tripolis, Greece, July 15, 1929; s. Theodore A. and Aglaia (Tsiverioti) A.; student Athens U., 1947-48, Cornell U., 1950-51; M.A., Boston U., 1953, Ph.D., 1956; M.D., Harvard U., 1959; m. Eleanor Pell, Aug. 28, 1954; 1 son, Theodore. Came to U.S., 1948, naturalized, 1966. Faculty, Boston U. Sch. Medicine, 1955-68, prof. physiology, 1963-68; prof., chmn. dept. physiology and biophysics Hahnemann Med. Coll., Phila., 1968—, trustee, sec. bd. hosp. and med. coll., 1977—; dir. biomed. research inst. Center Research and Advanced Studies, U. Maine, Portland, 1971—; research asso. biomath. Mass. Inst. Tech., 1959-60; vis. scientist Karolinska Inst., Stockholm, 1962-63; cons. U.S. Army Labs. Environ. Medicine, Natick, Mass., 1964—, NASA Electronics Research Center, Cambridge, Mass., 1966-68. Med. Found. Research fellow, 1959-60; USPHS Research Career Devel. grantee, 1960-68. Contbr. articles to sci. jours. and textbooks. Home: 602 Washington Sq Philadelphia PA 19106

ANGELERI, LUCY MILNER, counseling psychologist; b. N.Y.C., Apr. 25, 1932; d. Joseph and Lucille B. Milner; student Juilliard Sch. Music, 1955-58, New Sch. Social Research, 1965-68; B.A., Empire State Coll., 1972; M.S., Hunter Coll., 1976; m. Carl J. Angeleri, May 25, 1954; children—Michael, Alvin. Profl. vocalist, tchr., 1959-65; field supr. Am. Research Bur., N.Y.C., 1965-69; community mental health facilitator Catholic Med. Center, Bklyn., 1969; asst. personnel dir. Booth Meml. Med. Center, Flushing, N.Y., 1969-71; counselor Help Line, N.Y.C., 1974-77; pvt. practice psychotherapy, N.Y.C., 1976—; poetry therapist, music therapist. Mem. Poets and Writers, Nat. Rehab. Assn., Am. Personnel and Guidance Assn., Am. Fedn. Musicians, Poet's Coop. Unitarian-Universalist. Author poems: Tidings, 1974. Office: 386 Park Ave S Suite 303 New York City NY 10003

ANGELINI, FRANK SAMUEL, optometrist; b. Trenton, N.J., July 24, 1947; s. Nazarene Frank and Ida (DiBalsi) A.; B.S. in Biology, Delaware Valley Coll., 1968; O.D., Pa. Coll. Optometry, 1972; m. Barbara Corvine, Jan. 1, 1972; children—Frank Todd, Cory, Craig Michael. Gen. practice optometry, Califon, N.J., 1972-73; practice optometry specializing in contact lenses, Moorestown, N.J., 1973—. Certified optometrist, N.J., N.Y., Pa. Mem. N.J. Soc. Optometrists, Better Vision Inst. Roman Catholic. Home: 10 Beth Dr Moorestown NJ 08057 Office: Route 38 and Lenola Rd Morrestown NJ 08057

ANGELL, SAN S., former civic orgn. exec.; b. Buffalo, Oct. 26, 1908; s. S. Joseph and Mary (Baglie) A.; B.S., Canisius Coll., 1929; LL.B., U. Buffalo, 1932, M.S.W., 1939, J.D., 1968; m. Marie Beatrice Caboni, Nov. 28, 1935; 1 dau., M. Faith. Admitted to N.Y. State bar, 1932; practiced in Buffalo, 1933-42; investigator Emergency Relief Bur., Buffalo, 1934-37; case cons., counsel Catholic Charities, Buffalo, 1937-40; counsel, field rep. St. Vincent dePaul Soc., Buffalo, 1937-40; clk. domestic relations, sr. probation officer Buffalo City Ct., 1940-42; field dir., asst. regional dir. ARC, ETO, 1942-46, dir. Home service, exec. dir. Camden County chpt. ARC, Camden, N.J., 1946-55; exec. sec. Community Chest & Council, Camden, 1955-58; exec. v.p., sec. United Fund, Camden County, Camden, 1958-73; vol. Vista, SCORE, 1973—. Council mem. Boy Scouts Am., 1946—; mem. S. Jersey Pub. Relations Assn., 1948-73; bd. dirs. West Collingswood Fire Dept., 1946-66; adv. council United Way Inc., 1962-68, dir., 1968-73. Recipient Silver Beaver award Camden County council Boy Scouts Am., 1953, award Social Workers Assn. Camden County, 1961, Union Orgn. Social Service, 1961, St. George award Camden Diocese, 1970, SCORE award, 1977. Fellow Royal Soc. Health; mem. Am. Overseas Assn. (chpt. pres. 1953, nat. pres. 1973-76), Nat. Assn. Social Workers, Acad. Certified Social Workers, Internat. Platform Assn., Internat. Biographies. Clubs: Kiwanis (pres. Camden 1955); Reciprocity (sec. 1956—) (Camden). Home: 118 Deerfield Dr Cherry Hill NJ 08034

ANGELL, STEPHEN LEROY, JR., lay ch. worker, Friends Gen. Conf.; b. Bronxville, N.Y., Sept. 3, 1919; s. Stephen Leroy and Alice (Angel) A.; B.S., Hamilton Coll., 1941; M.A., U. Chgo., 1947; m. Barbara Elliott Allee, Mar. 6, 1948; children—Marjorie Alice (Mrs. James Alan Van Hoy), Stephen Warder, Thomas Nathaniel, Samuel

John Bowne. Chmn. gen. com. Friends Com. on Nat. Legislation, Religious Soc. Friends, Washington, 1965-74; clk. rep. meeting N.Y. Yearly Meeting Religious Soc. Friends, N.Y.C., 1973-76; clk. Frineds Gen. Conf., Phila., 1975—. Social worker; cons. human services planning; pres. Polytypic Enterprises, Inc. Clinton Corners, N.Y., 1968—. Pres., exec. officer Citizens Community Studies, Inc., White Plains, N.Y., 1976—. Mem. Nat. Assn. Social Workers, Acad. Certified Social Workers, Am. Assn. Planning Ofcls., Nat. Assn. Housing and Redevel. Ofcls., Am. Pub. Health Assn., Am. Pub. Welfare Assn., Nat. Council Crime and Delinquency. Address: Bulls Head Rd Clinton Corners NY 12514*

ANGELO, ANTHONY RICHARD, educator; b. Norwich, Conn., Aug. 4, 1930; s. Thomas Michael and Felicia Rose (Ruffo) A.; B.A., U. Conn., 1954, M.A., 1964; Ed.D., Boston U., 1971. Tchr. primary pub. sch., Ledyard, Conn., 1954-59, East Lyme, Conn., 1959-62; prin. Sayles Sch., Sprague, Conn., 1962-65; asst. prof. reading U. R.I., Kingston, 1965-69; prof. Central Conn. State Coll., New Britain, 1969—; cons. in reading Conn., N.H. In-Service Programs, Xerox Publs., Middletown, Conn., 1973—. NSF fellow DePauw U. Mem. Internat. Reading Assn., Nat., Conn. councils tchrs. English, Phi Delta Kappa, Kappa Delta Pi. Author: Language Problems of the Disadvantaged, 1967; Creativity and the Learning Process, 1970; Syntactic Structures of Children's Oral Language, 1971; Springboards to Creativity, 1974; (with others) Humanizing Reading-Language; (with others) Step by Step, 1978. Home: 18 Inchcliffe Dr Gales Ferry CT 06335 Office: 1615 Stanley St New Britain CT 06050

ANGELOTTI, ROBERT, govt. ofcl.; b. N.Y.C., Oct. 30, 1927; B.A., Transylvania Coll., 1950; M.Sc. (fellow), Ohio State U., 1952, Ph.D. in Microbiology, 1955; m. 1948; 3 children. Research microbiologist Taft San. Engring. Center, USPHS, HEW, 1955-62, chief food microbiology, 1962-65, dep. chief milk and food research program, 1965-67, dir. R&D Nat. Center Urban and Indsl. Health, Cin., 1967-68, dep. asst. commr. for research and devel. Environ. Control Adminstrn., Rockville, Md., 1968-69, dep. dir. div. microbiology Bur. Foods, FDA, 1969-71, dep. dir. Office Food Sanitation, 1971, dir. Office Compliance, 1971—. Served with USNR, 1945-46. Mem. Am. Soc. Microbiology, Am. Pub. Health Assn., Am. Inst. Food Tech. Research in food microbiology, foodborne disease. Office: FDA 200 C St SW Washington DC 20204

ANGUAH-DEI, ANNIE MAY, educator; b. Portsmouth, Va., June 30, 1939; d. John Henry and Pensacola (Bowser) Morgan; B.S., Norfolk State Coll., 1964; M.A., Hampton Inst., 1968; postgrad. U. D.C., 1976-77, George Washington U., 1978—; m. Horace Anguah-Dei, Mar. 20, 1975; 1 dau., Ramona Yvette McCluney. Tchr., Nansemond County, Va., 1964-68; analytical chemist U.S. Naval Hosp., Portsmouth, 1969, Smith-Douglass div. Borden Chem. Co., Norfolk, Va., 1970-71; tchr. Montgomery County pub. schs., Md., 1974-75; tchr. D.C. pub. schs., 1972-73, 76-77, peer asst. tchr., 1977—; coordinator selected sci. programs, co-dir. sci. fair, curriculum and evaluation workshops; cons. in field. Recipient Exemplary Practices award D.C. pub. schs., 1977, named Educator in Spotlight, 1977; EPA grantee, 1977. Fellow Washington Jr. Acad. Sci.; mem. D.C. Sci. Fair Assn. (certificate of service, 1972-78), Am. Fedn. Tchrs., Delta Sigma Theta. Democrat. Baptist. Contbr. to competency based sci. curriculum D.C. Pub. Schs., 1977-78.

ANGULO, MANUEL RAFAEL, lawyer; b. N.Y.C., Sept. 5, 1917; s. Charles and Ysabel (Piedra) A.; B.A., Yale Coll., 1939; LL.B., Harvard U., 1942; grad. exec. mgmt. program Grad. Sch. Bus., Columbia U., 1952; m. Diana Hutchins de Beaulieu, June 12, 1970; children (by previous marriage)—Charles Bonin, M. Ralph. Admitted to N.Y. State bar, 1947; asso. firm Davis Polk Wardwell Sunderland & Kiendl, N.Y.C., 1942-48; attache and econ. analyst Am. embassy, Santo Domingo, 1943-44; with OSS (London), 1944; attache Am. embassy, Lisbon, Portugal, 1944-46; gen. solicitor Creole Petroleum Corp., Caracas, Venezuela, 1948-54; partner Escritorio J. M. Travieso Paul, law firm, Caracas, 1954-61; partner firm Curtis, Mallet-Prevost, Colt & Mosle, N.Y.C., 1961—; lectr. Va. Law Sch., 1963—. Mem. N.Y. State, Internat., Am., Inter Am. bar assns., Société de Legislation Comparée, Pan Am. Soc. U.S., Assn. Bar City N.Y., N.Y. County Lawyers Assn., Am. Fgn. Law Assn., N.Am. Assn. of Venezuela (past pres.), Mexican C. of C. in U.S. (dir.), Peruvian Am. Assn. (dir.), Argentine-Am. C. of C. (dir.), Sigma Xi. Clubs: Yale, Union League, Broad St., Met. Opera (N.Y.C.); Met. (Washington); Merion Criquet (Haverford, Pa.); Farmington Country, Redlands (Charlottesville, Va.). Home: 340 E 64th St New York City NY 10021 Office: 100 Wall St New York City NY 10005

ANGYAN, ANDRÉ JÁNOS, neuropsychiatrist; b. Budapest, Hungary, Oct. 8, 1922; s. Janos B. and Clara Margarete (de Zsedenyi) A.; came to U.S., 1959, naturalized, 1965; B.Sc.B.A., Coll. of Cistercians, Pécs, Hungary, 1940; M.A.M.Sc., U. Med. Faculties, Pécs and Budapest, 1942, M.D., 1944; postgrad. USSR Acad. Med. Sci., Moscow and Leningrad, 1946-47; Ph.D., Hungarian Acad. Sci., 1955; m. Maria de CsecsiNagy, Aug. 2, 1955 (div. 1959); 1 son, John Andre; m. 2d, Barbara Ann Tungly, Dec. 17, 1963; 1 stepdau., Agnes Frimmel Camoro-Angione. Rotating intern Royal Hungarian U., Pecs and Kolozsvar Med. Sch. Clinics, 1943-45; pvt. practice medicine, specializing in endocrinology, neurology, neuropsychiatry and EEG, Pecs. and Budapest, 1946-56; resident psychiatry and neurology U. Budapest Med. Sch., 1956-58; cons., resident, extern, chief of lab., depts. neuropsychiatry and neurosurgery U. Debrecen and Budapest, 1958; guest fellow, cons. electronic div. Tech. U. and Neuropsychiat. Clinic, Vienna, Austria, 1958-59; sr. research scientist Rockland State Hosp., Orangeburg, N.Y., 1959-60; research asst. fellow Jewish Chronic Disease Hosp., Bklyn., 1963-64; asso. research psychiatrist Willowbrook (N.Y.) State Sch., 1964-65; neurophysiol. research physician Westchester Meml. Hosp. and Behavior Biochemistry Research Found., 1965-66; staff psychiatrist, chief EEG and neuropharm. research, resident in neuropsychiatry Essex County Overbrook Hosp. and State Sch., Cedar Grove, N.J., 1967; psychiatrist Big Spring (Tex.) State Hosp., 1969-70; neuropsychiat. cons. VA Hosp., Big Spring, 1970; sr. staff psychiatrist VA Neuropsychiat. Hosp., Pitts., 1970-72; pvt. practice medicine, specializing in family and internal medicine, obstetrics, gynecology, endocrinology, neurology and psychiatry, Bellaire, Tex., 1972-74; physician Internat. Maritime Union Indsl. Clinic at Houston Ship Channel for Kelsey-Seybold Clinic, 1973-74; primary, asst., asso. physician dept. community medicine Baylor Coll. Medicine for Harris County Hosp. Dist., Baytown, 1973-74; chief neuropsychiatrist, cons. in psychosomatic medicine VA Outpatient Clinic, Bklyn., 1974—; faculty U. Pecs Med. Sch., 1943-56, U. Budapest Med. Sch., 1954-58; asst. research prof. physiology U. Calif., Los Angeles, 1959-60; lectr. City of Hope Hosp., Duarte, Calif., 1963; lectr. biology and histology Hunter Coll., N.Y.C., 1966-67; asst. prof. physiology and neurosurgery U. Tex. Med. Br., Galveston, 1967-69; lectr. U. Houston, 1973. Fellow Nat. Acad. Sci., 1958-59; Exchange fellow Hungarian Acad. Scis. and VA NRC, 1976—. Mem. World, Am., Tex. med. assns., Hungarian Med. Soc., Am. and Internat. socs. EEG neurophysiology, N.Y. Acad. Scis., AAAS, IEEE, Am. Soc. Cybernetics, Soc. Neuroscis., Internat. Brain Research Orgn., Bklyn. Neurol. Soc., Am. Fedn. Clin. Research, Am., Tex. psychiat. assns., Internat. Soc. Social Psychiatry, Am. Diabetes Assn., Am. Acad. Family Physicians, N.Y. Soc. Internal Medicine, Nat. Assn. VA Physicians, Eastern Psychiat. Research Assn., Epilepsy Assn., Am. Assn. Advancement Psychotherapy, World Mental Health Assn., Soc. for Biol. Psychiatry, Internat. Platform Assn. Democrat. Mem. Hungarian Reformed Ch. Club: Rotary. Home: 315 E 86th St New York City NY 10028 Office: Dept Neuropsychiatry VA Hosp 35 Ryerson St Brooklyn NY 11205

ANKER, IRVING, edn. ofcl.; b. N.Y.C., Oct. 27, 1911; married, 3 children. B.S. in History, Coll. City N.Y., 1932, M.S.E., in Ednl. Adminstrn., 1939; Ph.D. (hon.) L.I. U., 1975. Dep. chancellor N.Y.C. Bd. Edn., 1970-73, acting chancellor, 1973, chancellor, 1973—; Disting. prof. edn. L.I. U., 1978—; scholar-in-residence Baruch Coll., City U. N.Y., 1978—. Pres. Bklyn. Coop. Soc., 1940-42; trustee Woodward Sch., Bklyn., 1952-54; rep. Episc. and Jewish Communities L.I., 1965; del. Nat. Conf. Ch.-State Relations, 1966. Mem. Am. Assn. Sch. Adminstrs., N.Y. Acad. Pub. Edn., Council Great City Schs., Large City Supts., Large City Bd. Edn. N.Y. State. Editorial bd., contbr.: Know Your World; contbr. articles to profl. jours. Office: 110 Livingston St Brooklyn NY 11201

ANKERMAN, PAUL WILLIAM, research radio engr.; b. Wapakoneta, Ohio, May 21, 1920; s. Roy Edward and Burneta Cleola (Howe) A.; B.S. in Radio Engring., Tri-State Coll., Angola, Ind., 1949; m. Mabel Ann Perdue, Mar. 17, 1950; 1 dau., Peggy Lynn. Electronic, acoustical engr. Stromberg Carlson, Rochester, N.Y., 1950-56; engr. Gen. Dynamics Corp., Rochester, 1956-71; mem. research staff laser fusion feasability project U. Rochester, 1972—. Served with Signal Corps, AUS, 1941-45; ETO. Decorated Bronze Star medal with two oak leaf clusters. Mem. Am. Inst. Physics, Acoustical Soc. Am., Radio Engring. Soc., Sigma Phi Delta. Methodist. Patentee in field. Contbr. articles to profl. jours. Home: 106 Whittington Rd Rochester NY 14609 Office: Univ Rochester 110 Hopeman Engring Bldg Rochester NY 14627

ANKERSTJERNE, WILLIAM DICK, ins. co. exec.; b. N.Y.C., Jan. 11, 1935; s. William and Gwen (Steen) A.; B.S. in Commerce, Rider Coll., 1960; m. Jacquelyn Lyon, Oct. 10, 1964; children—Christine, William. Asst. sales mgr. Comml. Solvents, Inc., N.Y.C., 1960-61; v.p. mfg. Provimi, Inc., Saddle Brook, N.J., 1961-64; group rep. Prudential Ins. Co. of Am., Newark, 1964-65, asso. group mgr., Phila., 1966-68, group mgr., 1968-69, regional group mgr., 1969-75, account exec. Central Atlantic home office, Ft. Washington, Pa., 1975—. Comdt. of cadets CAP, Pa. Wing, 1968-79; active United Way S.E. Pa. Served with U.S. Army Security Agy., 1954-57. Mem. Am. Mgmt. Assn., DAV, VFW, NEA, Zool. Soc. Phila., Tau Kappa Epsilon. Republican. Presbyterian. Club: Spring Haven. Home: 835 Morris Ave Bryn Mawr PA 19010 Office: The Prudential Fort Washington PA 19034

ANNS, ARLENE CLAIR, pub. co. exec.; b. Pearl River, N.Y., d. Frederick Joel and Anna (Behnke) Eiserman; student Bergen Jr. Coll., 1946-48; B.S., Utah State U., 1950; postgrad. Traphagen Sch. Design, 1957, N.Y. U., 1958, Hunter Coll., 1959-60. Research and promotion asst. Archtl. Record, N.Y.C., 1952-56; asst. research dir. Esquire Mag., N.Y.C., 1956-62; research mgr. Am. Machinist, publ. McGraw-Hill, Inc., N.Y.C., 1962-67, mktg. service mgr., 1967-69, 1969-71; v.p. mktg. services Morgan-Grampian, Inc., N.Y.C., 1971-72; dist. sales mgr. Postgrad. Medicine, McGraw-Hill, Inc., 1972-77; sales mgr. contemporary obstetrics and gynecology McGraw-Hill Inc., 1977-78, dir. profl. devel., 1978—. Recipient award as best space rep. of year. Mem. Am. Mktg. Assn. Pharm. Advt. Club, Advt. Women of N.Y., Am. Soc. Tng. Dirs., Pi Sigma Alpha. Home: 1 Brianwood Ct Quinton VA 23141

ANNUNZIATA, FRANK, historian; b. N.Y.C., Oct. 20, 1942; s. Salvatore and Theresa (Martino) A.; B.A., Manhattan Coll., 1964; M.A., City Coll. N.Y., 1965; Ph.D., Ohio State U., 1968; m. Geraldine Gillan, July 3, 1965; 1 son, Paul Gillan. Teaching fellow history Ohio State U., Columbus, 1965-68; Nat. Endowment Humanities postdoctoral fellow Am. history U. Mich., Ann Arbor, 1975-76; asso. prof. history, chmn. Am. studies Eisenhower Coll., Seneca Falls, N.Y., 1968—. Mem. Am. Hist. Assn., Orgn. Am. Historians, Am. Studies Assn. Roman Catholic. Contbr. articles, revs. to hist. publs. Home: Route 1 Box 9 Waterloo NY 13165

ANRIG, GREGORY RICHARD, state ofcl.; b. Englewood, N.J., Nov. 18, 1931; A.B., Western Mich. U., 1953; M.A. in Teaching, Harvard U., 1956, Ed.D., 1963; married; 3 children. Tchr. history, asst. to prin. East View Jr. High Sch., White Plains, N.Y., 1956-60; prin. Battle Hill Elem.-Jr. High Sch., White Plains, 1960-64; supt. Mt. Greylock Regional Sch. Dist., Williamstown, Mass., 1964-67; dir. div. equal ednl. opportunities U.S. Office Edn., 1967-69, exec. asst. to U.S. commr. edn., 1969-70; dir. Inst. Learning and Teaching, U. Mass., Boston, 1970-73; commr. edn. Commonwealth of Mass., Boston, 1973—. Served to 1st lt. U.S. Army, 1953-55; Korea. Recipient Distinguished Service award White Plains C. of C., 1963; Superior Service award HEW, 1970. Office: Mass Dept Edn 182 Tremont St Boston MA 02111*

ANSARY, CYRUS A., lawyer, fin. adviser; b. Shiraz, Iran, Nov. 20, 1933; s. Abdul and Jamali (Mostmand) A.; B.S., Am. U., 1955; LL.B., Columbia U., 1958; m. Janet C. Hodges, Aug. 1, 1970; children—Douglas C., Pary Ann, Jeffrey C., Bradley C. Admitted to Md. bar, 1959, D.C. bar, 1960, Va. bar, 1961; practiced law, Washington, 1959-72; sr. partner firm Ansary, Kirkpatrick and Rosse, 1964-72; chmn. bd. Industry Reports, Inc., Washington, 1960-72; organizer, 1st chmn. bd., pres. Woodland Nat. Bank, Alexandria, Va., 1963-67; dir. Plastic Data Systems, Dallas, 1964-68, Computing and Utilities Services, Inc., Santa Monica, Calif., 1965-68, Resource Mgmt. Corp., Bethesda, Md., 1966-71, Alcorn Combustion Engring. Corp., Yonkers, N.Y., 1967-70; lectr. Sch. Bus. Adminstrn., Am. U., 1967-71; adv. dir. Madison Nat. Bank, Washington, 1967-72; chmn. bd. Fin. Dynamics Corp., Washington, 1967-72, Campbell Music Co., Washington, 1968-72; dir. John L. Lindstrom and Assos., Inc., Washington, 1962—, Fried. Krupp, GmbH, Essen, Ger., 1974—; fin. adviser Govt. Iran, 1974—; pres. Iran-Krupp Investment Co., A.G., Zurich, Switzerland, 1974—; dir. Deutsche Babcock and Wilcox, A.G., Oberhausen, Ger., 1975—. Trustee Am. U., 1968—, Wolftrap Found., Vienna, Va., Inst. Internat. and Fgn. Trade Law, Georgetown U., 1977—. Served with USMCR, 1959-63. Clubs: Nat. Press, Nat. Assn. Execs., Metropolitan (Washington); Congl. Country (Bethesda); Address: 5425 Falmouth Rd Bethesda MD 20016

ANSBACHER, HEINZ LUDWIG, psychologist; b. Frankfurt, W.Ger., Oct. 21, 1904; s. Max and Emilie (Dinkelspiel) A.; Ph.D., Columbia U., 1937; m. Rowena Ripin, June 23, 1934; children—Max G., Benjamin R., Theodore H., Charles A. Mem. faculty Brown U., 1940-43, Bklyn. Coll., 1945-46, Duke U., Durham, N.C., 1946; mem. faculty U. Vt., Burlington, 1946—, prof. psychology emeritus, 1970—. Fulbright fellow, 1954-55; NIMH grantee, 1967-69. Mem. Am., Eastern, Vt. psychol. assns., N.Am. Soc. Adlerian Psychology (past pres.). Editor: (with Rowena R. Ansbacher) The Individual Psychology of Alfred Adler: a systematic presentation in selections from his writings, 1956, rev. edit., 1964; Superiority and Social Interest: a collection of later writings (Alfred Adler), 1964, rev. edit., 1973; Co-operation between the sexes: writings on women, love and marriage, sexuality, and its disorders (Alfred Adler), 1978. Editor Jour. Individual Psychology, 1957-73. Home: 130 East Ave Burlington VT 05401 Office: U Vt Psychology Dept Burlington VT 05401

ANSON, JOYCE NARINS, investment banker; b. N.Y.C., Dec. 30, 1948; d. Charles S. and Frances D. (Kross) Narins; B.A. in Psychology, Wellesley Coll., 1970; M.B.A., Harvard U., 1973; divorced. Asso. corp. fin. Warburg Paribas Becker Inc., Chgo., 1974-75, Goldman, Sachs & Co., N.Y.C., 1973-78; v.p. corp. fin. Paine, Webber, Jackson & Curtis Inc., N.Y.C., 1978—. Mem. Fin. Women's Assn. Club: Harvard (N.Y.C.). Home: 501 E 87th St New York City NY 10028 Office: 140 Broadway New York City NY 10005

ANSPACH, ERNST, bus. economist; b. Glogau, Germany, Feb. 4, 1913; s. Hermann and Margarete (Gurassa) A.; came to U.S., 1936, naturalized, 1943; Js.D., U. Freiburg, Berlin, Munich, Breslau, 1935; M.Sc., New Sch. Social Research, N.Y.C., 1943; m. Ruth Pietsch, Dec. 20, 1950; children—Paul David, Margaret Louise. With German jud. service, 1934-36; fin. analyst Loeb, Rhoades & Co., N.Y.C., 1936-43; reorgn. of adminstrn. Justice in Bavaria and Hesse, 1946-49; gen. counsel and polit. adviser Dept. State, U.S. Land Commr. for Hesse, 1949-52; economist, gen. partner Loeb, Rhoades & Co., investment bankers, N.Y.C., 1952-77; chief economist, 1st v.p. Loeb Rhoades, Hornblower & Co., N.Y.C., 1978—; tchr. adult edn. program Henry St. Settlement, N.Y.C., 1939-43; lectr. U. Munich, Marburg, Frankfurt, 1948-52; lectr. fields econs., polit. sci., theology and primitive art, 1955—. Trustee, Bleuler Psychotherapy Center, 1953—, chmn. bd., 1956-65; trustee Nightingale-Bamford Sch., 1971—; fellow in perpetuity Met. Mus. Art, N.Y.C. Served to capt. AUS, 1943-46. Recipient Army commendation ribbon. Mem. N.Y. Soc. Security Analysts, Nat. Assn. Bus. Economists, Conf. Bus. Economists. Presbyterian (ruling elder 1959—). Club: Wall St. Contbr. articles to sci. jours. Noteworthy collection African Tribal Art exhibited Mus. Primitive Art, N.Y.C., 1967-68. Home: 118 W 79th St New York City NY 10024 Office: 42 Wall St New York City NY 10005

ANTENUCCI, ARTHUR JOSEPH, physician, educator; b. N.Y.C., May 5, 1905; s. Ermindo and Catherine (Mazzeo) A.; B.S., City Coll. N.Y., 1926, M.D., Columbia, 1930; m. Anna Viola Ahlin, June 26, 1933; children—Arthur Joseph, Karin Lila, Nina Ruth, Frances Dale. Intern Roosevelt Hosp., N.Y.C., 1931-33, med. fellow, 1933-35, asst. attending physician, asso. attending physician, 1935-46, attending physician, 1946—, chief 2d med. service, 1953-65, chief medicine, 1965, chief clin. services, 1965-71, exec. officer med. service, 1964-65, cons. physician, 1971—; research vascular pathology, Vienna, Austria, 1933-34; instr., asso. in medicine Columbia, 1935-41, asst. clin. prof. medicine, 1942-54, asso. clin. prof. medicine, 1954-70, asst. prof. clin. medicine Cornell, 1942-43; cons. physician Southampton Hosp., 1948—. Mem. med. adv. bd. Am. Hosp., Paris, France, 1973. Recipient Townsend Harris medal Coll. City N.Y. Alumni Assn., 1974. Diplomate Am. Bd. Internal Medicine. Fellow A.C.P., Acad. Med.; mem. N.Y. State, N.Y. County med. socs., AMA, Roosevelt Hosp. Alumni Assn., Alpha Omega Alpha. Club: Links. Editor-in-chief Am. Jour. Medicine, 1971-74, chmn. adv. bd., 1974-77, editorial dir., 1978—. Contbr. articles to med. jours. Home: 993 Park Ave New York City NY 10028 Office: 112 E 70th St New York City NY 10021

ANTENUCCI, JOSEPH, obstetrician, gynecologist, educator; b. Agnone, Italy, Sept. 28, 1928; s. Luigi and Yolanda (Saulino) A.; came to U.S., 1955, naturalized, 1960; M.D., U. Naples (Italy), 1953; m. Nelda Pasquini, Sept. 22, 1956; children—Eugene, Louise, Sandra. Practice medicine specializing in obstetrics and gynecology, N.Y., 1961—; mem. staff obstetrics and gynecology Booth Meml. Med. Center, Flushing, N.Y., 1961—; clin. asst. prof. obstetrics and gynecology N.Y. U., 1974—. Diplomate Am. Bd. Obstetrics and Gynecology. Mem. Am. Coll. Obstetrics and Gynecology, A.C.S., AMA, Queens Gynecol. Soc. Address: 43-43 Kissena Blvd Flushing NY 11355

ANTHON, CARL GUSTAV, historian, educator; b. Wismar, Germany, May 19, 1911; s. Gustav and Else (Michaelsen) A.; came to U.S., 1924, naturalized, 1931; B.A., U. Chgo., 1938; M.A., Harvard U., 1939, Ph.D. (Holtzer fellow), 1943; m. Margaret Day, Dec. 30, 1949; children—Susan Elizabeth, Gregory. Asst. prof. history Colby Coll., Waterville, Maine, 1945-48, asso. prof., 1948-49; higher edn. adviser U.S. High Commn., Berlin, 1949-52; asso. prof. history Am. U., Beirut, Lebanon, 1955-58; exec. sec. Fulbright Commn., Bonn, W. Ger., 1958-60; prof. history Am. U., Washington, 1961-75, prof. emeritus, 1975—, chmn. dept. history, 1961-67; Fulbright prof. Free U., Berlin, 1967-68. Mem. Am. Hist. Assn., Am. Fgn. Service Assn. Club: Harvard (Washington). Contbr. articles in field of German politics to profl. jours. Home: 4834 Rodman St NW Washington DC 20016 Office: Dept History American Univ Washington DC 20016

ANTHONY, ALBERT JOHN, dentist; b. West Boylston, Mass., June 29, 1931; s. Albert and Mary (Ferrandino) A.; student Worcester Jr. Coll., 1949-51, Boston U., 1951-52; D.M.D., Tufts U., 1956; m. Georgia Maria Kotseas, May 13, 1961 (div. 1978); children—John Albert, Marie Dianne. Pvt. practice dentistry, West Boylston, 1958—; mem. staff Holden Dist. Hosp., 1958—; owner Black Angus Breeding Farm, West Boylston, 1968—. Served to capt. AUS, 1956-58. Mem. Am., Mass. (certificate of merit 1969) dental socs., Central New Eng. Research Study Group, Pierre Fauchard Acad., Worcester Area C. of C., Delta Sigma Delta (grand master 1968). Contbr. articles on tooth transplantation to dental jours. Home: 200 Fairbanks St West Boylston MA 01583 Office: 45 Central St West Boylston MA 01583

ANTHONY, EDWARD LOVELL, II, editor; b. Boston, Sept. 24, 1921; s. DeForest and Dorothy (Dodge) A.; A.B., Harvard U., 1943, M.B.A., 1952; postgrad. Boston U., 1943; m. Constance Foss, Oct. 2, 1954; children—Edward Lovell, Victoria Noble, Richard Geoffrey David. Asst. to pres. Daltry Opera Co., Middletown, Conn., 1938-40; asst. to headmaster Manter Hall Sch., Cambridge and Wianno, Mass., 1941; asso. editor Pub. Affairs Press, Washington, 1945-46; asst. chief photog. intelligence tng. U.S. Navy, 1946-50; dir. publs. Small Bus. Adminstrn., 1952-62; editor Harvard Bus. Sch. Bull., Boston, 1962—, editor Exec. Letter, 1964-70. Vice chmn. Community Fund, Washington, 1960; chmn. adv. com. on devel. Dr. Franklin Perkins Sch.; trustee Vt. Acad. Served with AUS, 1942-45. Mem. Nat. Council Small Bus. Mgmt. Devel., Council Advancement and Support Edn., English Speaking Union, Friends of Boston Symphony Orch., Nat. Assn. Retarded Citizens, Harvard Bus. Sch. Assn. Boston, Navy League U.S. (Boston council), Nat. Free Lance Photog. Assn., Order of Lafayette. Episcopalian (vestryman, warden). Clubs: Country (Brookline, Mass.); Univ. (Washington); Harvard (Boston); Harvard (N.Y.C.); Hundred of Mass. Editor: Management Aids for Small Business Annual, 5 vols., 1955-59; Equity Capital for Small Business, 1960. Home: 68 Woodcliff Rd Wellesley Hills MA 02181

ANTHONY, ROBERT ARMSTRONG, lawyer, govt. ofcl., educator; b. Washington, Dec. 28, 1931; s. Emile Peter and Martha (Armstrong) A.; B.A., Yale U., 1953; B.A., Juris., Oxford (Eng.) U., 1955; J.D., Stanford U., 1957; m. Ruth Barrons, Feb. 7, 1959 (div.); 1 son, Graham B. Admitted to Calif. bar, 1957, N.Y. State bar, 1971, D.C. bar, 1972; asso. firm Pillsbury, Madison & Sutro, San Francisco, 1957-62, Kelso, Cotton & Ernst, San Francisco, 1962-64; asso. prof.

law Cornell U. Law Sch., Ithaca, N.Y., 1964-68, prof., 1968-75, dir. internat. legal studies, 1964-74 (on leave 1972-73); chief counsel, later dir. Office Fgn. Direct Investments, U.S. Dept. Commerce, Washington, 1972-73; chmn. Adminstrv. Conf. U.S., 1974—; lectr. Acad. Am. and Internat. Law, Dallas, 1967-72. Former commr. Sausalito City Planning Commn.; former mem. bd. dirs. Marin Shakespeare Festival; mem. Pres.'s Anti-Inflation Regulatory Council, 1978—. Mem. Am., San Francisco bar assns., State Bar Calif., Assn. Am. Rhodes Scholars, Am. Soc. Internat. Law. Home: 700 New Hampshire Ave NW Washington DC 20037 Office: 2120 L St NW Washington DC 20037

ANTLE, CHARLES EDWARD, educator; b. East View, Ky., Nov. 11, 1930; s. Bayard Pierpoint and Mary Elizabeth (Blaydes) A.; A.A., Lindsey Wilson Coll., 1950; B.S., Eastern Ky. State U., 1954, M.A., 1955; postgrad. U. Ky., 1954-55; Ph.D. (NDEA fellow), Okla. State U., 1962; m. Elna Thomas Hall, Nov. 25, 1953; children—James, Rebecca, Susan Hall, Mark Edward. Sr. aerophysics engr. Gen. Dynamics Corp., Fort Worth, 1955-57; mem. faculty U. Mo., Rolla, 1957-60, 62-68, prof. math., 1966-68; asso. prof. statistics Pa. State U., University Park, 1968-70, prof., 1970—. Served with AUS, 1951-53. Decorated Bronze Star. Mem. Am. Statis. Assn., Royal Statis. Soc., Inst. Math. Statistics. Contbr. articles to profl. jours. Home: 2302 W Branch Rd State College PA 16801 Office: Dept Statistics Pa State U University Park PA 16802

ANTMAN, STUART SHELDON, mathematician; b. Bklyn., June 2, 1939; s. Mitchell and Gertrude (Siegel) A.; B.S., Rensselaer Poly. Inst., 1961; M.S., U. Minn., 1963, Ph.D., 1965; m. Wilma G. Richlin, Mar. 24, 1968; children—Rachel A., Melissa D. Vis. mem. Courant Inst., N.Y. U., 1965-67, asst. prof. N.Y. U., 1967-69, asso. prof., 1969-72; vis. fellow U. Oxford (Eng.), 1969-70, Heriot-Watt U., Edinburgh, Scotland, summer 1972, 77; prof. mathematics U. Md., 1972—; mem. Applied Mathematics Summer Inst., Dartmouth Coll., 1973; prof. Ecole d'Ete d'Analyse Numerique, France, summer 1974; vis. prof. U. Paris, summer 1975, Brown U., 1978-79. NSF grantee, 1972—; Guggenheim fellow, 1978-79. Mem. Am. Mathematics Soc., Soc. Indsl. and Applied Mathematics, Soc. Natural Philosophy (sec. 1974-76). Editor: (with J.B. Keller) Bifurcation Theory and Nonlinear Eigenvalue Problems, 1969; co-editor Springer Tracts in Natural Philosophy, 1972—; editorial bd. Archive for Rational Mechanics and Analysis, 1972—. Home: 10012 Branch View Ct Silver Spring MD 20903 Office: Dept Mathematics U Md College Park MD 20742

ANTOGNOLI, JOHN ANTHONY, psychologist; b. Peckville, Pa., July 26, 1945; s. Anthony Frederick and Lillian Rita A.; B.S., U. Scranton, 1967, M.S., 1969; m. Barbara Mary Yaniga, June 21, 1974. With Lourdesmont Sch., Clarks Summit, Pa., 1970-76, exec. dir., 1976—; adminstr. Diagnostic Center, Phila., 1976; professorial lectr. dept. human resources Grad. Sch., U. Scranton, 1971-76. Mem. human services adv. bd. Keystone Jr. Coll.; mem. leadership assembly Washington province Sisters of Good Shepherd. Mem. Am., Pa. psychol. assns., Nat. Conf. Cath. Charities, Pa., Northeastern personnel and guidance assns., Pa. Assn. on Probation, Parole and Correction Soc., Pa. Alliance for Children. Roman Catholic. Home: 22 Driftwood Dr Clarks Summit PA 18411 Office: 537 Venard Rd Clarks Summit PA 18411

ANTON, ALBERT JOSEPH, JR., investment analyst; b. N.Y.C., Jan. 6, 1936; s. Albert Joseph and Helen (Cichoski) A.; A.B., Columbia, 1957; M.B.A., U. Pa., 1959; m. Sara Jane Lembcke, Sept. 6, 1958; children—Claire Elizabeth, Christopher Paul, Thomas Robert. Vice pres., div. exec. Chase Manhattan Bank, N.Y.C., 1959-69; partner Carl H. Pforzheimer & Co., N.Y.C., 1970—. Mem. investment com. Petroleum and Trading Corp., N.Y.C., 1970—, dir., 1978—. Vice chmn. South Orange-Maplewood YMCA, 1973-77, chmn., 1977-78; bd. dirs. YMCA of Oranges, Maplewood and West Essex, treas., 1977—; trustee Village of South Orange, 1971-73, also chmn. finance com., 1971-73; mem. bd. sch. estimate South Orange-Maplewood, 1971-73; adv. bd. St. Benedict's Prep. Sch., Newark, 1978—. Served with USAF, 1961-62. Chartered financial analyst. Mem. Nat. Assn. Petroleum Investment Analysts (treas. 1976-78, sec. 1978—), Oil Analysts Group N.Y., Inst. Chartered Fin. Analysts, N.Y. Soc. Security Analysts, Ind. Petroleum Assn. of Am., Soc. of Mining Engrs., Delta Upsilon. Roman Catholic. Clubs: Orange Lawn Tennis; City Mid-Day of N.Y. Home: 332 Beech Spring Rd South Orange NJ 07079 Office: 70 Pine St New York City NY 10005

ANTON, ARTHUR CHARLES, cleaning co. exec.; b. Lowell, Mass., July 8, 1925; s. Charles John and Paula (Vacass) A.; B.S. in Bus. Adminstrn., Boston U., 1950; student Nat. Inst. Drycleaning, 1950-51; m. Madeline J. Kanavos, Sept. 2, 1951; children—Diane, Susan, Charles, Arthur Charles, Jr. Trainee Anton's Cleaners, Lowell, 1950, mgr., 1951, gen., 1952-56, pres., 1956—; dir. Union Nat. Bank, Lowell, 1965—. Pres., United Fund Greater Lowell, 1965. Trustee Pierce Coll., Athens, Greece, Hellene Coll., Brookline, Mass., Boston U., Lowell Boys Club; trustee, vice chmn. Lowell Gen. Hosp.; bd. dirs. Merrimack Valley United Fund, 1972—; bd. visitors Boston U. Coll. Bus. Adminstrn., 1972—; nat. chmn. League Greek Orthodox Stewards, 1973—. Served with USAAF, 1943-46. Named Man of Year, Lowell, 1958. Mem. Lowell C. of C. (pres. 1958-60). Order of Ahepa (pres. 1953), Boston U. Alumni Greater Lowell (pres. 1958), Boston U. Coll. Bus. Adminstrn. Alumni Assn. (pres. 1975-77, exec. com.), Cleaning Plant Owners Mass. (v.p. 1955—). Rotarian (pres. 1965-66). Home: 3 Hemlock Dr Chelmsford MA 01824 Office: Anton Bldg 500 Clark Rd Tewksbury MA 01876

ANTON, BARBARA MILLER (MRS. ALBERT ANTON), jewelry designer; b. Pocono Pines, Pa.; d. Walter B. and Emma (Hess) Miller; grad. Gemological Inst. Am., 1964; student various artists; m. Albert Anton, June 23, 1949. Jewelry exhibited in Amsterdam, Holland, Phila. Mus. Art, Boston Mus. Fine Arts; designer jewelry collection Pakiston Pavillion, N.Y. World's Fair, 1964; pres. Barbara Anton, Inc.; contbg. editor Jour. Suisse d'Horlogerie et de Bijouterie, Lausanne, 1966; fashion editor Nat. Jeweler mag., 1966-68; lectr., 1964—. Recipient Diamonds Internat. award, 1963; 3 awards Cultured Pearl Assn. Am. and Japan Ann. Design Competition, 1966, 2 awards, 1967, highest award, 1968, 4 awards, 1969, Spl. award, 1970, 71, 72; 2 awards Retail Jewelers of Am., 1970, Pearl Promotion Soc., Tokyo, 1976; also numerous internat. awards. Compiler: New Anniversary Gemstone List, 1971. Mem. A.S.C.A.P. Contbr. articles on gems and jewelry to publs. Home: Box 533 Alpine NJ 07620 Office: 10 Engle St Englewood NJ 07631

ANTON, HARVEY, textile co. exec.; b. N.Y.C., Nov. 10, 1923; s. Abraham J. and Byrdie (Casin) A.; student Western State Coll. Colo., 1941, Savage Sch. Edn., 1941-42; B.S., N.Y. U., 1949; m. Betty L. Weintraub, Dec. 18, 1949; children—Bruce Norman, Lynne Beth. Pres., Anton Yarn Corp. (merged with Robison Textile Co. to form Robison-Anton Textile Co. 1959), N.Y.C., 1949-50, pres., 1973—. Trustee, Emerson Jewish Center, 1958-59, Erza Charitable Found. Served to 1st lt. AUS, 1943-46. Clubs: Masons, K.P.; N.Y. Univ. Letter (N.Y.C.). Home: 41 Longview Dr Emerson NJ 07630 Office: 175 Bergen Blvd Fairview NJ 07022

ANTONELLI, LUIZ KUSTER, educator; b. Sao Francisco de Assis, Brazil, Feb. 27, 1918; s. Pedro B. and Almerinda (Kuster) A.; student State Tchrs. Coll., Cruz Alta, Brazil, 1935-37; U. Chile, 1947-48; B.A., U. Rio Grande de Sul, 1949; postgrad. U. Denver, 1951-52; M.A., Columbia, 1953, Ed.D., 1961; postgrad. Inst. for Practicing Psychotherapists, N.Y.C., 1962-64, Postgrad. Center for Mental Health, N.Y.C., 1964-68. Came to U.S., 1958. Pres. State Tchrs. Coll., Cachoeira do Sul, Brazil, 1943-50; supt. State of Rio Grande do Sul, Brazil, 1953-54; prof. psychology Inst. Edn., Porto Alegre, Brazil, 1953-54; dean of students Aero. Inst. Tech., San Jose dos Campos, Sao Paulo, Brazil, 1955; dir. Inter-Am. Center, Pan Am. Union, Venezuela, 1956-58; counselor Bklyn. Coll., 1961; dir. div. gen. edn. Voorhees Tech. Inst., N.Y.C., 1961-66; staff mem. Met. Center for Mental Health, N.Y.C., 1963-64; mem. staff Postgrad. Center for Mental Health, 1964-68, staff, 1968-69; asso. prof., dir. counseling and guidance center Queen's Coll., U. City N.Y., 1966—, dir. master tng. program for urban sch. counselors, 1969-72, dir. peer counseling tng. program, 1976—. Hon. chmn. Campaign Against Juvenile Delinquency, Venezuela. Served with Brazilian Army, 1948. Mem. Am. Psychol. Assn., Am. Anthrop. Assn., AAAS, NEA, Am. Ednl. Research Assn., AAUP, Am. Coll. Personnel Assn., Am. Personnel and Guidance Assn., Kappa Delta Pi, Phi Delta Kappa. Address: 25 W 68th St New York City NY 10023

ANTONIADES, HARRY NICHOLAS, biochemist, educator; b. Thessaloniki, Greece, Mar. 12, 1923; s. Nicholas Harry and Eustatia (Manos) A.; B.S., U. Athens (Greece), 1950, Ph.D., 1952; m. Maria Tomaras, Dec. 27, 1953; children—Harry Nicholas, Anna Maria. Came to U.S., 1953, naturalized, 1957. Mem. sci. staff Center Blood Research (name changed from Protein Found. Labs. 1971), Boston, 1954—, asso. investigator, 1957-61, sr. investigator, 1961—. Mem. faculty Harvard U., 1956—, asst. prof. dept. biochemistry Sch. Pub. Health, 1966-70, asso. prof., 1970—, tutor in biol. chemistry Dudley House, 1974—; asso. mem. med. staff Peter Bent Brigham Hosp., Boston, 1961-65; vis. prof. Med. Center, U. Ala., Birmingham, 1963, Inst. Physiology, Med. Sch., U. Buenos Aires (Argentina), 1966, med. schs. Ain Shams U., Cairo, Egypt and Alexandria (Egypt) U., 1971. Recipient Eli Lilly award Am. Diabetes Assn., 1962. Fellow N.Y. Acad. Scis.; mem. AAAS, Am. Soc. Biol. Chemists, Am. Chem. Soc., Endocrine Soc., Am. Diabetes Assn., Am. Heart Assn. (Council on Thrombosis), Internat. Soc. Thrombosis and Haemostasis. Editor: Hormones in Human Plasma, 1960; Hormones in Human Blood, Detection and Assay, 1976. Contbr. to profl. jours. Home: 21 Magnolia Ave Newton MA 02158 Office: 800 Huntington Ave Boston MA 02115

ANTONINI, MARION HUGH, diversified mfg. co. exec.; b. Clinton, Ind., June 7, 1930; s. Valentine and Josephine (Dal Sasso) A.; B.S. in Mech. Engring., U. Toledo, 1952; m. Penelope Sue Fromong, Dec. 20, 1971; children—Caryn Marie, John Marius. Gen. foreman on spl. assignment to works mgr. Willys Motors Inc., Toledo, Ohio, 1952-54; mgr. assembly and mfg. services Willys Overland Export Corp., Toledo, 1955-59; asst. mng. dir. Willys Overseas S.A., Zug, Switzerland, 1959-61; adminstrv. dir. Kaiser Jeep Internat. Corp., Toledo, 1961-64, v.p., mng. dir., Oakland, Calif., 1964-66; group v.p. Eltra Corp., pres. Prestolite Internat. Co., N.Y.C., 1967-75; pres. Eltra Internat. Co., N.Y.C., 1973-75; corp. group v.p. Xerox Corp., 1975—, pres. Canada-Latin Am., Middle East ops., Xerox Corp., 1975—. Mem. U.S. Export Expansion Council, 1960; chmn. bd. Codel Nat. Council, 1974. Bd. dirs. Friends of Philippines Found.; vice chmn. United Way New Canaan, New Canaan YMCA drive. Named Toledo's Outstanding Young Man, 1957, One of Ohio's Five Outstanding Young Men, 1957, One of America's Outstanding Young Men, 1966. Mem. Soc. Automotive Engrs., Woodward Engring. Soc. (pres.), U. Toledo Alumni Assn. (pres.), Blue Key, Kappa Sigma Kappa. Home: 79 Ferris Hill Rd New Canaan CT 06840 Office: Canada-Latin Am Xerox Corp 3 Pickwick Plaza Greenwich CT 06830

ANTONIOU, THEODORE, composer, condr.; b. Athens, Greece, Feb. 10, 1938; s. Vassilios and Maria (Veligradi) A.; came to U.S., 1969, naturalized, 1972; diploma in violin, diploma in theory and harmony Nat. Conservatory of Greece, Athens, 1956, diploma in counterpoint and fugue, 1958; Prof. Music, Ministry Edn. of Greece, 1957; diploma in composition and orchestration Hellenic Conservatory, Athens, 1961; diploma in composition Master Class Hochschule for Musik, Munich, W. Ger., 1964; diploma in electronic music Siemens Studio for Electronic Music, Munich, 1965. Mem. faculty Nat. Conservatory, Athens, 1956-61; composer in residence, vis. prof. composition and orchestration Stanford U., 1968-69, 69-70; composer in residence U. Utah, 1970, 71-72; prof. composition, dir. New Music Group, Phila. Mus. Acad. (now Phila. Coll. Performing Arts), 1970—; founder, dir. Stanford New Music Ensemble, ALEA II, 1969; condr. Phila. Mus. Acad. Symphony Orch., 1970-71, 75-76; numerous compositions, including: Concertino for Piano, 1962 (Hon. 1st prize Athens Tech. Inst. 1962), Violinkonsert, 1965 (1st prize City Stuttgart, Germany 1966), Mikographies for big Orch., 1964 (1st prize in composition Arts Ministry of Greece 1967), Cassandra, ballet, 1969 (Premio Ondas, Barcelona Radi-TV 1970); numerous commns., including Koussevtisky Music Found. Commn., 1972; artistic dir. Athens Centre for Creative Arts, 1973-75; composer, condr., asst. dir. contemporary activities Bergshire Music Center, Tanglewood, 1974—; founder, dir. Hellenic Group Contemporary Music, Athens, 1967—. Recipient 1st prize for composition Hellenic Conservatory, 1961, Richard Strauss prize City of Munich, 1964; Kassimatis Found. fellow, 1961-63; Deutsche Akademische Austauschdienst fellow, 1963-65; State Dept. Program for Leaders and Specialist fellow, 1966; Nat. Endowment for Arts fellow, 1975, 77; John Simon Guggenheim Meml. Found. grantee, 1979. Mem. Internat. Soc. Contemporary Music (co-founder, v.p. Greek chpt. 1965-72), Internat. Soc. Heinrich Schutz (co-founder, v.p. Greek chpt. 1966). Contbr. articles to profl. jours. Office: 250 S Broad St Philadelphia PA 19102

ANTOUN, ANNETTE AGNES, newspaper editor-publisher; b. Franklin, Pa., Mar. 7, 1927; d. Adrien Uriel and Charlotte Mary (McMullen) Adelman; student Allegheny Coll., Meadville, Pa., 1946-47; m. Frederic George Antoun, July 19, 1947; children—Frederic G., Gregory S., Lawrence J., Mark J. (dec.), Laureace A., Scott J., Jonathan M., Lisa A. Founder, 1960, since editor-pub. Paxton Herald, Harrisburg, Pa.; founder, 1972, since owner Graphic Services, advt. and graphics, Harrisburg; co-editor French Creek Patriot, community newspaper, Cochranton, Pa., 1972. Treas., Pa. Lung Assn., 1975-76, sec. bd., 1977—; mem. bd. Am. Lung Assn., 1973-77; sec. bd. Central Pa. Lung Assn., 1969-73; bd. mem. Harris Commn., 1975—; mem. pub. relations com. Tri-County United Way, 1973, com. on children, 1975—; rep. dir. Pa. Lung Assn., 1973, treas., 1975-76; mem. Lower Paxton Coalition Community Assns., 1974—; mem. Lower Paxton Community Planning Com., 1974—; mem. communication com. Catholic Diocese Harrisburg, 1972—, mem. bd. Diocese Cath. Social Service, 1972-76; mem. extension planning com. YMCA, 1975—; mem. pub. relations com. Heart Assn., 1977—; chmn. Dauphin County Juvenile Detention Home bldg. com., 1976—, Dauphin County Citizens Adv. Com., 1977—, Kipona Com., 1977—; chmn. fund raising com. Greater Harrisburg Arts Council, 1977—; bd. mem. Harrisburg Police Athletic League, 1977—. Recipient Advocate award Paxton Area Jaycees, 1968, 73; Golden medallion Pa. State Legion, 1973, 1st pl. pub. relations award, 1974; citation Pa. Ho. of Reps., 1977—; Johnstown Flood Relief award, 1977; also numerous other pub. service awards. Mem. Internat. Platform Assn., Dauphin County Assn. Lawyer Wives, Historic Harrisburg Assn. Club: Pleasant Hills Community. Home: 4910 Earl Dr Harrisburg PA 17112 Office: 101 Lincoln St Harrisburg PA 17112

AOUN, KAMAL HABIB, physician; b. Beirut, Lebanon, Sept. 6, 1929; s. Habib Canaan and Wadad (Dehne) A.; M.D., B.S., St. Joseph's U., Beirut, 1954; m. Raineri, June 29, 1957; 2 sons. Intern, McNeal Meml. Hosp., Berwyn, Ill., 1954-55; resident Good Samaritan Hosp., Cin., 1955-56, Dade County Hosp., Miami, Fla., 1956-57; resident in internal medicine Orange (N.J.) Meml. Hosp., 1957-59; practice medicine, Saudi Arabia, 1959-66; practice family medicine, Franklin, Pa., 1967—; mem. staff Franklin Hosp. Fellow Royal Coll. Health Eng., Internat. Coll. Angiology, Am. Acad. Family Practice; mem. AMA, Pa. Med. Soc., A.C.P., Am. Soc. Internal Medicine. Republican. Roman Catholic. Clubs: Franklin and Wanango Country. Home: 634 Adelaide Ave Franklin PA 16323 Office: 516 Biery Bldg Franklin PA 16323

APFELBAUM, ADEK, civil engr.; b. Lodz, Poland, May 31, 1935; s. Fishel and Bella (Przepiorka) A.; B.S. in Civil Engring., N.Y. U., 1957; m. Doris J. Axman, Oct. 26, 1957; children—Rand, Teri, Scott. Estimator, project mgr. HRH Constrn. Corp., 1957-64; pres., project mgr., chief estimator Dorand Assos., 1964-71; chief ops. Slaydek Constrn. Services, Great Neck, N.Y., 1971-77, pres., 1977—. Bd. dirs. Mid-Hudson Hebrew Day Sch., 1970-71; mem. exec. bd., v.p. North Shore Hebrew Acad., 1972—; trustee Great Neck Synagogue, 1977—. Served with Constrn. Bn., USNR, 1957. Mem. Am. Soc. Profl. Estimators (charter mem., certified profl. estimator), Soc. Am. Mil. Engrs., Am. Assn. Cost Engrs., U.S. Power Squadron. Office: 98 Cuttermill Rd Great Neck NY 11021

APOSTOL, E. ANDRE, ednl. counselor; b. Newark, May 24, 1942; s. Emilio Obispo and Anne Marie (Sherry) A.; B.A., Resurrection Coll., 1964; B.S., Seton Hall U., 1969; M.A., Newark State Coll., 1972; certificate supervision and adminstrn. Kean Coll., 1978; m. Aurea Casas, June 29, 1969; children—Jennifer Frances, David Wesley. Tchr. phys. edn., Fords, N.J., 1965-69; tchr. math, sci., Metuchen, N.J., 1969-72; guidance counselor East Brunswick (N.J.) Pub. Schs., 1972—. Recipient Gov.'s Career Devel. Project grant, 1975, East Brunswick Mini grant, 1977. Mem. Am. (regional coordinator 1974-76), N.J. (membership chmn. 1977-78) sch. counselor assns., NEA, N.J., East Brunswick edn. assns., Am., N.J. personnel and guidance assns., Middlesex County Guidance Assn. Club: East Brunswick Central Photography. Author: A Counselor/Teacher Resource Guide for Sex Fair Counseling and Guidance, 1978. Home: 51 Cori St Parlin NJ 08859 Office: Central Sch Cranbury Rd East Brunswick NJ 08859

APOSTOLOS, MARGARET MORRIS, librarian; d. Berry and Dora Ellen (Gordy) Morris; A.A., Eastern Pilgrim Coll., 1957-59; B.S., Kutztown State Coll., 1961; M.S., Syracuse U., 1966; M.S. in Edn., Temple U., 1978; m. Paul Michael Apostolos, Aug. 17, 1974. Bookkeeper, Salisbury Nat. Bank (Md.), 1948-57; librarian Eastern Shore Book Processing Center, Salisbury, 1961-65; head librarian Owosso (Mich.) Coll., 1966-70; cataloger Kutztown (Pa.) State Coll. Library, 1970-71, chief cataloger, 1972—. Sec. Aux. Penn Wesleyan Coll., Allentown, Pa., 1971-72. Recipient Library Edn. award Kutztown State Coll., 1961. Mem. Am., Pa. library assns., AAUW, Assn. Coll. and Research Libraries, Freedom to Read Found., Kappa Delta Pi, Beta Phi Mu. Mem. Wesleyan Ch. Home: 356 College Blvd Kutztown PA 19530 Office: Kutztown State Coll Library Kutztown PA 19530

APPEL, ABRAHAM BRAM, accountant; b. Montreal, Que., Can., Jan. 13, 1915; s. Israel and Sophie (Hecht) A.; B.Commerce, McGill U., Montreal, 1935; Chartered Accountant, Inst. Chartered Accountants, Que., 1936; m. Bluma Levitt, July 11, 1940; children—David Harry, Mark Gordon. Pres., A. Bram Appel Cons., Inc., Toronto, Ont., 1977—; sec.-treas. Interimco Ltd., Ottawa, 1972—; dir. Pall Corp., Glen Cove, N.Y., RKL Controls, Mt. Holly, N.J., Amalgamated Power Equipment; pres. Canmont Investment Corp., Ottawa, 1966—, Daram Ltd., 1959—, Electroline TV Equipment Inc., 1953— (all Montreal); exec. asst. to minister Energy Mines and Resources, Ottawa, 1966-67; cons. Sec. State and Minister Industry, Trade and Commerce, Ottawa, 1968-72. Recipient Canadian Centennial medal Dominion of Can., 1967. Mem. Order Chartered Accountants (Que.). Club: Cercle Universitaire d'Ottawa. Home: 18A Hazelton Ave E 206 Toronto ON M5R 2E2 Canada Office: 100 Bronson St Suite 1206 Ottawa ON K1R 6G8 Canada

APPEL, VALENTINE, consumer psychologist; b. N.Y.C., Feb. 13, 1926; s. Valentine and Adolphine (Pelzel) A.; B.S.S., Coll. City N.Y., 1949; M.A., N.Y. U., 1951, Ph.D., 1959; m. Patricia Fisher, Apr. 7, 1951; children-Suzanne, Gregory, William, Marguerite. Various research positions, 1950-61; with Ford Motor Co., Dearborn, Mich., 1961; v.p., research dir. Benton & Bowles Advt., N.Y.C., 1961-67; pres. AHF Mktg. Research, N.Y.C., 1967-75, Simmons Market Research Bur., N.Y.C., 1975—. Served with U.S. Army, 1944-46. Decorated Bronze Star with oak leaf cluster, Purple Heart. Fellow Am. Psychol. Assn.; mem. Am. Mktg. Assn., Phi Beta Kappa. Roman Catholic. Contbr. articles to profl. jours. Home: 1501 Strawberry Rd Mohegan Lake NY 10547 Office: 219 E 42 St New York NY 10017

APPELL, WILLIAM THEODORE, psychologist; b. Jamaica, N.Y., Nov. 14, 1926; s. William Theodore and Florence Steele (Logan) A.; Ph.D., Adelphi U., 1953; m. June 21, 1955; 1 dau., Wendy. Pvt. practice psychology, Hudson, N.Y., 1970—; dir. Mental Health, Retardation and Alcoholism Services, Columbia County, N.Y., 1976—. Served with U.S. Army, 1944-46. Mem. Am., N.Y. State psychol. assns., Columbia County Hist. Soc. (pres.). Republican. Episcopalian. Club: Lions. Office: 354 Allen St Hudson NY 12534

APPERSON, POLLY MERRILL, phys. therapist, educator, real estate agt.; b. Norwalk, Conn., Apr. 29, 1910; d. Frank Herbert and Clara (Ryder) Merrill; B.S. in Phys. Edn., Arnold Coll., 1930; B.S. in Phys. Therapy, N.Y.U., 1954; m. Van Doren Apperson, June 25, 1938 (dec.). Tchr. phys. edn. Norwalk Jr. High Schs., 1930-38, Norwalk High Sch., 1938-62, 63-64; phys. therapist N.Y. Hosp.-Cornell Med. Coll., N.Y.C., 1954—, Inst. Phys. Medicine and Rehab., 1962-63, 64-65, Inst. Rehab. Medicine, N.Y.C., 1967-68, 70, Silver Hill Found., New Canaan, Conn., 1971, outpatient dept. U.S. VA, 1972-73; instr. English, An-Lac Orphanage, Saigon, Vietnam, 1967; real estate agt. Montgomery Agy., 1976-78; Yoga instr. Broad River Community Club; staff mem. Sivananda Yoga Vedanta Ashram, Paradise Island, Bahamas, 1969. Asst. troop leader Girl Scouts U.S.A., 1926-27, troop capt., 1944-45; life saving examiner A.R.C., Norwalk, 1930-33, active fund drives, 1941-46, first aid instr., 1941-44, 54-57, tchr. sponsor Jr. Red Cross at Norwalk High Sch., 1961-62, also sponsor exchange visit with St. John, N.B., Can. Jr. Red Cross, 1961-62; active fund dr. Community Chest, Norwalk, 1932; mem. Norwalk Recreation Commn., 1939-41; mem. adv. com. Norwalk Park Commn., 1941-43; air raid warden Silvermine Sector 1, Norwalk, 1941-45; active fund raising drive Silvermine Vol. Fire Co. 1, 1942-43; bd. dirs., 1943-50; mem. common interest group Preservation Mathews Mansion, 1961-62; mem. subcom. edn. Mid-Fairfield County Com. Alcoholism, 1958-59; mem. New Horizons Club; mem. Congregation Temple

Emanu-el, N.Y.C., 1973—. Recipient certificate for 500 hours service Civil Def., 1945. Mem. Nat., Conn. edn. assns., Norwalk Tchrs. Assn. (chmn. social com. 1951-52), Am., Conn. assns. health, phys. edn. and recreation, Am. Registry Phys. Therapists, Am. Phys. Therapist Assn., N.Y.U. Alumni Assn. Divine Life Soc., True World Order; Am. Soc. Dowsers, Nat. Trust for Historic Preservation, Pacifica Found., Spiritual Frontiers Fellowship, Sivananda Yoga Vedanta Center, Silvermine Community Assn., Silvermine River Conservation, Am. Soc. Psychical Research, Nat., Conn. ret. tchrs. assns. Baptist (Sunday Sch. tchr. 1930-33, social chmn. Young Peoples United Ch. League 1931-32). Club: N.Y. U. Alumni (N.Y.C.). Home: PO Box 101 Norwalk CT 06852

APPIGNANI, LOUIS JOSEPH, modeling sch. and cosmetic co. exec.; b. N.Y.C., Mar. 30, 1933; s. Joseph and Susan (Pascale) A.; B.B.A., Coll. City N.Y., 1955; M.S., Columbia U., 1958; postgrad. Ind. U., 1961; 1 son, Andre Louis. Cons. staff Lybrand, Ross Bros. & Montgomery, N.Y.C., 1958-61, Price Waterhouse & Co., N.Y.C., 1962; asst. to fin. v.p. Universal Am. Corp., N.Y.C., 1962-64; cons. Booz, Allen, & Hamilton, Inc., Cleve., 1964-65; pres., chmn. bd. Barbizon Internat., Inc., N.Y.C., 1965—; dir. John Denigris & Co. Bd. dirs. Internat. House Assn., N.Y.C., 1964-65. Served to 1st lt. AUS, 1955-57. Mem. Young Pres.'s Orgn. (exec. com.), Assn. for Better N.Y. (exec. com.). Clubs: Doubles, East Hampton Tennis (N.Y.). Home: Lily Pond Ln East Hampton NY 11937 Office: 689 Fifth Ave New York City NY 10022

APPLETON, DANIEL RANDOLPH, JR., optometrist; b. Boston, June 24, 1942; s. Daniel Randolph and Dorothy (Cheney) A.; B.S., Tufts U., 1965; O.D., Mass. Coll. Optometry, 1969; children—Carole Lee, Deborah Ann, Danielle Marie. Pvt. practice optometry, Newburyport, Mass., 1965—; dir. pediatric clinic Mass. Coll. Optometry, 1969-71, clin. cons., 1971-72; dir. 1st and Ocean Nat. Bank; bd. incorporators Anna Jacques Hosp. Mem. Newburyport Sch. Com., 1975—, sewer commn., 1972—; 2d v.p. ARC. Mem. Am. Optometric Found., Mass. Soc. Optometrists (past dist. chmn., exec. bd. dirs.), Am. Optometric Assn., Jaycees (past pres.). Clubs: Rotary, Shriners. Home: 18 Harris St Newburyport MA 01950 Office: 39 Green St Newburyport MA 01950

APPLETON, HAROLD DONALD, biochemist, educator; b. N.Y.C., July 17, 1918; s. Frank and Jeanette (Goldenberg) A.; B.A., Bklyn. Coll., 1939; M.S., Purdue U., 1943; m. Gladys Frances Tordik, May 25, 1944. Lab. asst. Otisville (N.Y.) Hosp., 1939-42; jr. chemist Bellevue Hosp., N.Y.C., 1946-48; chemist N.Y. U. Research Service and Goldwater Meml. Hosp., 1948-54; sr. chemist Met. Hosp., N.Y.C., 1954-67, dir. dept. clin. chemistry, 1967-73, cons. clin. biochemist, 1972—; asst. prof. biochemistry and pathology N.Y. Med. Coll., 1960-72, asso. prof. clin. biochemistry, 1972-76, prof., 1976—, prof. Grad. Sch. Med. Scis., 1972—; cons. clin. biochemist Flower and Fifth Ave. Hosp., 1972—. Co-chmn. United Jewish Appeal of Greater N.Y., 1959—; bd. dirs., v.p. research Willcox Research Found. Served with inf. U.S. Army, 1942-46; ETO. Diplomate Am. Bd. Clin. Chemistry. Fellow Am. Assn. Clin. Chemistry (Fisher award 1968), Am. Inst. Chemists, N.Y. Acad. Scis.; mem. Am. Chem. Soc., AAAS. Contbr. articles to profl. jours.; chmn. bd. editors Clin. Chemistry, 1957-62, mng. editor, 1962-70; editor Clinica Chimica Acta, 1957-70. Home: Route 39 N Sherman CT 06784 Office: Dept of Biochemistry NY Med Coll Valhalla NY 10595

APPLEYARD, ROBERT BRACEWELL, bishop; b. Jamestown, N.Y., Nov. 17, 1917; s. Albert Edward and Elizabeth (Sharp) A.; A.B., Allegheny Coll., Meadville, Pa., 1940, D.D., 1955; B.D., Union Theol. Sem., 1943; D.D., Trinity Coll., Hartford, Conn., 1962; m. Katharine Louise Gelbach, Sept. 12, 1942; children—Robert Bracewell, Jonathan Briggs, Jane Sharp, Daniel Scott. Ordained priest Episcopal Ch., 1947; asst. dean, dir. program returning service men Union Theol. Sem., 1945-48; asst. minister in N.Y.C., 1945-48; rector Christ Ch., also chaplain Taft Sch., Watertown, Conn., 1948-52; rector Christ Ch., also chaplain Rosemary Hall Sch., Greenwich, Conn., 1952-65; rector in Palm Beach, Fla., 1965-68; bishop Episcopal Diocese Pitts., 1968—; hon. canon Christ Ch. Cathedral, Hartford, St. Luke's Cathedral, Orlando, Fla.; mem. gen. conv. P.E. Ch. Bd. dirs. Action Housing, St. Margaret's Meml. Hosp., Episcopal Ch. Home, A.R.C., YMCA, Planned Parenthood, Religious Leaders, Nat. Safety Council; trustee Book Common Prayer and Hymnal Soc., Am. Ch. Bldg. Fund, Seabury House. Served as chaplain USNR, 1943-46. Mem. Am. Guild Organists, Acad. Religion and Mental Health, Nat. Council Chs. Phi Beta Kappa, Phi Delta Theta. Club: Longue Vue, Duquesne (Pitts.). Home: 715 Amberson Ave Pittsburgh PA 15232 Office: 325 Oliver Ave Pittsburgh PA 15222

APTT, EDWARD BERNARD, penologist; b. Providence, Oct. 24, 1920; s. John F. and Anna (Murphy) A.; B.A., Providence Coll., 1953; B.E., U. R.I., 1955, M. Pub. Adminstrn., 1967; m. Helen M. Kasmicski, May 23, 1942; children—Edward B., Cynthia H., Sharon C., Gregory H., Jeffrey M. Capt., Providence Police Dept., 1949-74, dir. Bur. Prosecution, 1961-72, dir. Acad., 1972-74; asso. prof. criminal justice Bryant Coll., Smithfield, R.I., 1974—, chmn. dept. law enforcement, 1967-72. Mem. Acad. Criminal Justice Sci., Am. Soc. Polit. and Social Scis., Am. Soc. Pub. Adminstrn., Pi Sigma Alpha. Home: 50 Narragansett St North Kingstown RI 02852 Office: Dept Criminal Justice Bryant College Smithfield RI 02852

AQUARO, ANGELO RALPH, architect; b. Rochester, N.Y., Aug. 18, 1921; s. Martino N. and Donata (DiGiorgio) A.; student Drexel Inst. Tech., 1951; m. Catherine Pero. Archtl. designer Equipment Sales Co., 1946-49; Penn Fruit Co., 1949-56, chief architect, 1956-59; partner Aquaro-Gross, architects-engrs., 1959-77, Angelo R. Aquaro, architect-planner assos., 1978—; sec., dir. Aquagro Corp. Served as 1st lt. USAAF, 1943-46; lt. col. Res. 1946—. Decorated Air medal with oak leaf cluster. Mem. AIA, Res. Officers Assn. of U.S., Mil. Order World Wars, Am. Mensa Ltd., Soc. Am. Mil. Engrs., Am. Arbitration Assn. (panel of arbitrators 1972—), Sons of Italy in Am., T Square Club Phila, Res. Officers Assn. Roman Catholic. Home: 1821 S Broad St Philadelphia PA 19148 Office: 1812 Spruce St Philadelphia PA 19103

AQUILINA, JOSEPH PHILIP, engring. co. exec.; b. Queens, N.Y., Apr. 24, 1945; s. Joseph Benjamin and Nicolette (Domato) A.; student Inst. Computer Tech., 1965-66, Hofstra U., 1967-71; m. Wanda Marie Favuzza, Aug. 28, 1971; children-Lisa Ann, Kimberly Renee. Prodn. planner Grumman Aerospace Co., Bethpage, N.Y., 1962-65; prodn. scheduler R.E.F. Dynamics Corp., Mineola, N.Y., 1966-69; buyer Ventil-Aire Corp., Bklyn., 1969-70; buyer I.M.C. Magnetics Corp., Westbury, N.Y., 1971-74; project scheduler/planner Stone & Webster Engring. Corp., N.Y.C., 1974-77; subcontract adminstr. Target Rock Corp., 1978—. Mem. Am. Mgmt. Assn., Computer and Automated Systems Assn., Am. Inst. Indsl. Engrs. (sr.), Soc. Mfg. Engrs. (sr.), Soc. for Advancement Mgmt. Democrat. Home: 659 Nassau Rd Uniondale Long Island NY 11553

ARACENA, AMADO NIORT, lumber co. exec.; b. Antofagasta, Chile, Oct. 3, 1935; s. Amado M. and Carmen (Coltters) A.; came to U.S., 1965; B.B.A., Chilean U., 1960; children—Angelica, Amado J., Daniel A. Mgr. data processing Commonwealth of P.R., N.Y.C., 1965-70, Jarmel Fabrics Inc., N.Y.C., 1970-75; dir. mgmt. info. systems GEM Lumber Inc., N.Y.C., 1975—. Home: 150-49 60th Ave Flushing NY 11355 Office: 97-77 Queens Blvd Rego Park NY 11374

ARAKELIAN, JACK, engring. corp. exec.; b. Alexandria, Egypt, Oct. 2, 1938; s. Garabed and Haigouhi Arakelian; came to U.S., 1960, naturalized, 1970; Asso. Sci., Pasadena City Coll., 1962; B.S., Calif. U. at Los Angeles, 1964; M.S., Brown U., 1966; M.B.A., U. Pa., 1969; m. Marjorie Primeau, July 2, 1966; children—Garabed, Christine. Mgr. market planning and devel. Burroughs Corp., 1971; sr. project engr. Control Data Corp., 1972; founder, pres. Pharos Inc., Broomall, Pa., 1972—; dir. Instrutek Corp.; cons. SBA. Pa. Sci. and Engring. Found. grantee, 1974-75. Mem. Instrument Soc. Am. (sr.), IEEE. Patentee humidity, temperature, pressure sensors. Home: 2305 Oakland Dr Norristown PA 19403 Office: Pharos Inc 1615-17 E Darby Rd Havertown PA 19083

ARAKI, MINORU, pathologist; b. Seattle, June 30, 1920; s. Nisaku and Masa (Araki) Kaneda; student U. Wash., 1942; M.D., Boston U., 1953; m. Pearl Y. Aoyama, June 3, 1944; children—Lynda E., Neil M., Kimberly A. Intern, Meadowbrook Hosp., E. Meadow, N.Y., 1953-54; resident in pathology St. John's Hosp., L.I. City, 1954-58; asst. pathologist Jamaica Hosp., 1958-61; asso. pathologist Syosset (N.Y.) Hosp., 1963-72; dep. med. examiner Nassau County (N.Y.), 1961-74, dep. chief med. examiner, 1974—; dir. pathology Syosset Hosp., 1972—; cons. pathologist Jamaica Hosp. Served with AUS, 1944-46. Diplomate Am. Bd. Pathology. Fellow Coll. Am. Pathologists, Am. Soc. Clin. Pathologists; mem. AMA, N.Y. State Med. Soc., Nat. Assn. Med. Examiners. Home: 8 Southwoods Rd Syosset NY 11791 Office: Med Examiners Office PO Box 160 East Meadow NY 11554

ARAMANY, MOHAMED ABDELAL, prosthodontist; b. Cario, Egypt, Mar. 24, 1935; P.N.S., Cairo U., 1954, D.D.S., 1958; M.S., Sch. Dental Medicine, U. Pitts., 1963, D.M.D., 1973; m. Janet Jacqueline Young, July 31, 1964; children—Jacqueline Elizabeth, Andrew Richard. Intern, Univ. Hosp., Egypt, 1958-59, instr. Sch. Dentistry, 1959-60, asst. prof., 1964-68; resident in prosthodontics U. Pitts. Sch. Dental Medicine and Hosps., 1961-63, teaching fellow Sch. Dental Medicine, 1961-63, asst. prof., 1968-71, asso. prof., 1971-75, prof., 1975—; resident in maxillofacial prosthetics Tex. U. Dental Br., M.D. Anderson Hosp. and Tumor Inst., Houston, 1969-70; dir. Regional Center for Maxillofacial Rehab., Eye and Ear Hosp., Pitts., 1973—; dir. dept. maxillofacial prosthodontics and gen. practice dentistry West Penn. Hosp., Pitts.; cons. maxillofacial prosthodontics VA Hosps., Pitts., Mercy Hosp., Pitts. Diplomate Am. Bd. Prosthodontics; certified N.E. Regional Dental Bd.; licensed dentist, Pa. Fellow Internat. Coll. Dentists; mem. Am. Cleft Palate Assn., Internat. Assn. Dental Research, Am. Prosthodontic Soc., ADA, Pa. Dental Assn., Odontological Soc. Western Pa., Am. Acad. Maxillofacial Prosthetics, Internat. Assn. for Study of Dento Facial Abnormalities, Am. Coll. Prosthodontics, Am. Assn. Dental Schs. Home: 1431 Mayview Rd Pittsburgh PA 15241 Office: Eye and Ear Hosp 230 Lothrop St Pittsburgh PA 15213 also 414 Mellon Pavillion 4815 Liberty Ave Pittsburgh PA 15224

ARAMS, FRANK ROBERT, electronics co. exec.; b. Danzig, Germany, Oct. 18, 1925; s. Richard and Alice (Frank) A.; came to U.S., 1939, naturalized, 1945; B.E.E., U. Mich., 1947; M.S. in Applied Physics, Harvard U., 1948; M.S. in Bus. Mgmt., Stevens Inst. Tech., 1953; Ph.D. in Electrophysics, Poly. Inst. N.Y., 1961; m. Edith Knoll, July 24, 1952; children—Mark, Ronald. Sr. staff mem. RCA Microwave Div., Harrison, N.J., 1948-56; cons. AIL div. Cutler Hammer Corp., Melville, N.Y., 1956-65, head electrophysics and infrared dept., 1965-71; v.p. LNR Communications, Inc., Hauppauge, N.Y., 1971—. Served with AUS, 1942-44. Fellow IEEE; mem. Optical Soc. Am., Am. Inst. Physics. Author: Infrared-to-Millimeter Wave Detectors, 1972; also articles. Home: 37 Schoolhouse Ln Lake Success NY 11020 Office: 180 Marcus Blvd Hauppauge NY 11787

ARAOZ, DANIEL LEON, psychologist; b. Buenos Aires, Argentina, Apr. 23, 1930; came to U.S., 1951, naturalized, 1967; s. Jose Daniel and Maria Lia (Suarez) A.; B.A., Gonzaga U., 1953, M.A., 1954; M.S.T., U. Santa Clara, 1961; M.A., Columbia U., 1964, Ed.D., 1969; m. Dorita Catherine Smyth, July 17, 1964; children—Leon Daniel, Nadine Victoria. Asst. chaplain Coll. Mt. St. Vincent, Bronx, N.Y., 1962-64; psychotherapist Bklyn. Center Psychotherapy, 1966-67; psychotherapist Community Guidance Service, N.Y.C., 1965-72, supr., 1972—; faculty Am. Inst. Psychotherapy and Psychoanalysis, N.Y.C., 1972—; asst. prof. psychology City U. N.Y., 1970-73; asso. prof. counseling L.I. U., 1973—. Registered psychologist, Ill., Pa. Diplomate in counseling psychology Am. Bd. Profl. Psychology. Fellow Am. Inst. Psychotherapy and Psychoanalysis, Am. Soc. Psychosomatic Dentistry and Medicine; mem. Am. Assn. Marriage and Family Counselors (supr. 1973—), Am. Psychol. Assn., Am. Soc. Clin. Hypnosis, Soc. Clin. and Exptl. Hypnosis, Am. Acad. Psychotherapists, Acad. Psychologists in Marital and Family Therapy. Democrat. Roman Catholic. Editor-in-chief Internat. Jour. Family Counseling, 1973-76, founding editor, 1977—; contbr. articles to profl. jours. Address: 5 Surrey Ln New Hyde Park NY 11040

ARBITAL, SAMUEL, optometrist; b. Bklyn., Apr. 11, 1931; s. Abe and Dora (Broftsman) A.; O.D., Chgo. Coll. Optometry, 1952; postgrad. Pacific U. Coll. Optometry, 1952-53; m. Bernice Kirschner, Dec. 29, 1956; children—Lori, Sheri, Scott, Dari. Pvt. practice optometry, Hempstead, N.Y., 1957-72, Plainview, N.Y., 1958—; dep. examiner N.Y. Bd. Regents, 1974-76; owner Thinlite Contact Lens Lab., 1957-65; cons. in field of contact lenses. Served with AUS, 1953-55. Fellow Am. Acad. Optometry mem. Am. Soc. Optometric Clin. Hypnosis, Am. Optometric Assn., Am. Optometric Found., Benjamin Franklin Soc., Omega Epsilon Phi. Address: 54 Country Dr Plainview NY 11803

ARBOGAST, WALTER WILLIAM, JR., chem. engr.; b. Balt., Nov. 16, 1932; s. Walter William and Esther Lee (Heiser) A.; B.S.E. in Chem. Engring., Johns Hopkins U., 1969; M.S. in Engring. Materials, U. Md., 1974; m. Shirley Jean Helmrich, Oct. 29, 1955; children—Deborah Lynn, Tammy Lee. Lab. tester Chevron Asphalt Co., Balt. (Md.) Refinery, 1955-57, lab. leadman, 1957-65, lab. technician, eastern research lab., Balt., 1965-69; project engr. U.S. Army, Aberdeen Proving Ground, Md., 1969—. Mem. Am. Inst. Chem. Engrs. (vice chmn. Md. sect. 1977-78, chmn. 1978-79), Am. Def. Preparedness Assn. Democrat. Methodist. Home: 8220 Arrowhead Rd Baltimore MD 21208 Office: Aberdeen Proving Ground DRDAR-ACW MD 21010

ARCHBOLD, WILLIAM DANA, assn. exec.; b. N.Y.C., Mar. 15, 1923; s. Sherman Dana and Isabel (Hearst) A.; A.B., Princeton U., 1947; postgrad. Harvard U., 1963; m. Harriet Crenshaw White, Sept. 5, 1946; children—Richard Dana, Susan Archbold Macdonald. With Standard Oil Co., N.Y.C., 1947-50; with Imperial Oil Ltd., Toronto, Ont., Can., 1950-73, gen. mgr. mktg. 1970-73, v.p., 1971-73; spl. asst. to pres. U. Toronto, 1973-74; vice chmn. Energy Supplies Allocation Bd., Govt. of Can., 1974-76; pres., exec. dir. Bus. Council on Nat. Issues, 1976—. Bd. dirs., past chmn. bd. Better Bus. Bur. Can.; mem. adv. council, past pres. Can. Save the Children Fund; chmn. bd. govs. Lakefield Coll. Sch. Served to 1st lt. AUS, 1942-46. Mem. Anglican Ch. Clubs: Granite, Donalda (Toronto); Princeton (N.Y.C.). Home: 153 Rochester Ave Toronto ON M4N 1P2 Canada

ARCHER, ALFORD, geographer; b. Garrettsville, Ohio, Apr. 11, 1908; s. John Clark and Cathaline (Alford) A.; student Hiram Coll., 1925-26, Carnegie Inst. Tech., 1927-29; B.S., Columbia, 1935, M.S., 1936; Ph.D., Ohio State U., 1962; m. Barbara Kathleen Dietrich, Oct. 14, 1938; children—John Clark, Joan Elizabeth. Asst. dept. geography Ohio State U., 1936-41; instr. geology and geography Ind. State Tchrs. Coll., 1941-42; asst. prof. commerce and geography, Toledo U., 1942-46, asst. dir. summer session, 1946; with U.S. Bur. Census, 1946-74, geographer geography div., 1946-49, 55-59, 68-71, chief cartographic methods br., 1959-61, Internat. Statis. Programs as census geography adviser loaned to Agy. for Internat. Devel. and assigned to census and statistics offices of Panama, 1949-50, Bolivia, 1950, Honduras, 1951-55, 60, Costa Rica, 1952-54, El Salvador, 1953-55, 61, Thailand, 1961-63, Iran, 1966-68, Argentina, 1969, Paraguay, 1971-72, 74, chief fgn. census research br., 1963-66, staff geographer, 1972-74; geog. adviser to census and statistics office. U. N.C. Population Lab., Kenya, 1975; cartography adviser Central Bur. Statistics, UN Devel. Programme, Indonesia, 1978. Occasional instr. George Washington U., Am. U., U.S. Dept. Agr. Grad. Sch. Mem. adv. com. to Pan-Am. Inst. Geography and History, Nat. Acad. Scis., 1959-62. Pres. Rolling Terrace Civic Assn., Silver Spring, 1958-59, 64-65, Recipient Meritorious Service award from sec. commerce, 1956, Spl. Achievement award Bur. Census, 1972. Mem. Assn. Am. Geographers, Congress on Surveying and Mapping. Home: 711 Forston Dr Takoma Park MD 20012

ARCHER, DAVID HORACE, chem. engr.; b. Pitts., Jan. 20, 1928; s. Horace G. and Inez E. (Eichholtz) A.; B.S., Carnegie Mellon U., 1948; Ph.D., U. Del., 1953; m. Justine Garnic, July 29, 1950 (dec. Sept. 1973); children—Catherine M.I., Miriam A.J., Amy C.A.; m. 2d, Alice Knezovich, July 2, 1976. Instr. chem. engring. U. Del., Newark, 1951-53; asso. prof. Carnegie Mellon U., Pitts., 1953-60; mgr. chem. engring. research Westinghouse Electric, Pitts., 1960—. Mem. Am. Inst. Chem. Engrs. (exec. com. 1971—), Am. Chem. Soc., Combustion Inst., Electrochem. Soc., Am. Guild Organists. Lutheran. Patentee in field. Contbr. to profl. jours. Home: 114 Kentzel Rd Pittsburgh PA 15237 Office: 1310 Beulah Rd Pittsburgh PA 15235

ARCHER, JOHN EMERSON, educator; b. Reading, Pa., Nov. 18, 1934; s. Francis Emerson and Suzanne Agnes (Matlock) A.; B.S. in Secondary Edn., West Chester State Coll., 1956, M.S. in Geography, 1964, postgrad., 1964—; m. Ann Meens, Aug. 17, 1968. Tchr. geography Mt. Pleasant Sch. Dist., Wilmington, Del., 1956—. Served with Del. N.G., 1956-62. Mem. Assn. Am. Geographers, Pa. Council for Geography Edn. (sec. 1976—), Delaware Valley Geog. Assn. (sec.-treas. 1971, 72, 73, exec. bd. 1971—), Fedn. Del. Tchrs. (sec. 1960-63), Nat. Geog. Soc., Nat. Wildlife Fedn., Friends of Brandywine Zoo, Alumni Assn. West Chester State Coll. (life), Am. Fedn. Tchrs. Home: PO Box 2 Claymont DE 19703 Office: Mount Pleasant High School Washington St Extension Marsh Rd Wilmington DE 19810

ARCHER, RONALD DEAN, chemist; b. Rochelle, Ill., July 22, 1932; s. Don Adam and Irma Cecil (Olson) A.; B.S., Ill. State U., 1953, M.S., 1954; Ph.D., U. Ill., 1959; m. Joyce Hilder Carlson, Jan. 31, 1954; children—Paul Dean, Lynn Sue, Sharon Jean, Julie Anne. Tchr., Larson Jr. High Sch., Elgin, Ill., 1954; asst. prof. U. Calif., Riverside, 1959-63; asst. prof. Tulane U., New Orleans, 1963-65, asso. prof., 1965-66; asso. prof. U. Mass., Amherst, 1966-70, prof. chemistry, 1970—, head chemistry dept., 1977—; vis. prof. Tech. U. Denmark, 1972; cons., 1960-63, 64-70, 72—. Served with U.S. Army, 1954-56. Grantee USAF, Research Corp., NSF, Am. Chem. Soc., NIH, Army Research Office. Mem. Am. Chem. Soc. (chmn. Conn. Valley sect. 1979), Am. Crystallographic Assn., Chem. Soc. London, AAAS, Internat. Union Pure and Applied Chemistry, New Eng. Assn. Chemistry Tchrs., Sigma Xi, Phi Lambda Upsilon. Republican. Lutheran. Contbr. chem. articles to research jours. Home: 19 Lantern Lane Amherst MA 01002 Office: Grad Research Tower A U Mass Amherst MA 01003

ARCHIBALD, ARNOLD ADAMS, ret. steel co. exec.; b. Truro, N.S., Can., Sept. 16, 1905; s. Lewis Edgar and Elizabeth May (McCallum) A.; student Truro Pub. Schs., Colchester County Acad., Chauncy Hall Sch., Boston, 1923-24; B.S., Mass. Inst. Tech., 1930; m. Clara West Butler, Dec. 24, 1937; children—Lewis Edgar, II, Roger Williams, John Baird. Came to U.S., 1923, naturalized, 1942. With Jones and Laughlin Steel Corp., Pitts., 1935-70, beginning as metall. asst., successively asst. works metallurgist, metall engr., salesman, asst. to v.p., v.p., 1954-65, adminstrv. v.p. engring., purchasing and research, 1965-70. Served as dollar-a-year man on WPB, 1942-44, 45, Civilian Prodn. Adminstrn., 1946-47. Mem. Am. Iron and Steel Inst., Am. Iron and Steel Engrs., Am. Soc. for Metals. Clubs: Pitts. Athletic Assn., Duquesne (Pitts.); Union (Cleve.); Edgeworth (Sewickley, Pa.). Home: 1327 Coraopolis Heights Rd Coraopolis PA 15108 Office: Union Trust Bldg Pittsburgh PA 15219

ARCOMANO, JOSEPH PETER, radiologist; b. Bklyn., June 7, 1924; s. Frank and Mary G. (Mugavero) A.; B.S., U. Chgo., 1946, M.D., 1949; m. Ellen I. Gustafson, June 4, 1949; children—Peter, Lisa, Paul. Intern, Greenpoint Hosp., 1949; resident in radiology L.I. Coll. Hosp., 1952-55; practice medicine specializing in radiology, Bklyn., 1955-60, Huntington, N.Y., 1960—; mem. staff Northport VA Hosp., Nassau County Med. Center, Mercy Hosp., St. Charles Hosp., Mather Meml. Hosp., Sagamore Children's Hosp.; asso. prof. radiology Sch. Medicine, N.Y. U., 1967-70; prof. radiology Med. Sch., State U. N.Y. Stony Brook, 1977—; dir. radiology North Shore Med. Group, 1970—; dir. sch. radiologic tech. Northport VA Hosp.; mem. X-Ray Technician Bd. of Examiners N.Y. State, 1964-69. Served with U.S. Army, 1942-45, with M.C., 1950-52; Korea. Recipient Dir.'s Outstanding Service award Northport VA Hosp., 1972, 77. Diplomate Am. Bd. Radiology. Fellow Am. Coll. Radiology; mem. AMA (Physicians Recognition award 1969, 72, 77), Radiol. Soc. N.Am., Am. Roetngen Ray Soc., Soc. Nuclear Medicine, Am. Soc. Compensation Medicine, 38th Parallel Med. Soc. Korea. Roman Catholic. Contbr. articles in field to radiol. jours. Home: 1 Richard Ln Huntington NY 11743 Office: 325 Park Ave Huntington NY 11743

ARDEN, GEORGE J., ins. exec.; b. N.Y.C., July 4, 1923; s. James Ezra and Beatrice (Seltzer) A.; B.A., Lafayette Coll., 1944; m. Patricia N. Martin, June 30, 1964; children—Lisa Ann, James, George J., Andrea. Pres., chmn. bd. Physicians Planning Service Corp. of Conn., N.Y.C., 1961—, Gt. Century Life Ins. Co., Phoenix, 1961—, Arden Group of Cos., N.Y.C.; dir. Commodore Ins. Co.; cons. health ins. cos. Mem. pres's. council Brandeis U.; pres. council Lafayette Coll. Served with U.S. Army, 1941-42. Mem. Manhattan League-Indsl. Home for Blind (dir.), Key Biscayne (Fla.) C. of C., Am. Assn. Soc. Execs., Nat. Assn. Residents, Interns (founder, dir., trustee), Am. Profl. Practice Assn. (founder, dir., trustee), Am. Lawyers Assn. (dir., trustee), Am. Bus. Assn. (dir., trustee), Lafayette Coll. Marquis Soc., Throughbred Racing Assn., Murray Hill Assn. Clubs: Jockey (Miami, Fla.); Key Biscayne Beach, Royal Biscayne Bath and Tennis (Key Biscayne); N.Y. Turf and Field, City Athletic, El Morroco (N.Y.C.); Mutiny (Coconut Grove, Fla.); Commodore of Barbados; Westchester County (N.Y.). Contbr. numerous articles on health and accident ins. to profl.

publs.; contbr. numerous articles to profl. jours. including Dental Econs., 1974, Dental Mgmt., 1975, Am. Profl. Practice Assn. Digest, 1970-78, Sethoscope Newsletter, 1970-78. Address: 292 Madison Ave New York City NY 10017

ARENSBERG, FREDERIC SANFORD, psychoanalyst; b. Bklyn., May 22, 1935; s. Sidney and Esther (Caplan) A.; B.S., Queens Coll., 1956; Ph.D., Adelphi U., 1964; postgrad. Center for Mental Health, 1969, 71; m. Leda Glassman, July 1, 1962; children—Sharon, Evan. Mem. faculty Postgrad. Center for Mental Health, N.Y.C., 1970—; supr., dir. group therapy Brookdale Hosp., Bklyn., 1972—; pvt. practice psychoanalysis, N.Y.C., 1964—; group cons. Albert Einstein Coll. Medicine, Bronx, N.Y., 1969-75. NIMH grantee, 1965-67. Mem. Am., N.Y. State psychol. assns., Am. (program com. 1974—, membership com. 1972—, standards and ethics com. 1972—, social action com. 1972—), Eastern (dir. 1973—, sec. 1976) group psychotherapy assns., Tng. Inst. Mental Health Practitioners (chmn. group therapy). Contbr. articles to profl. jours. Home and Office: 255 W 88th St New York City NY 10024

ARENT, RUSSELL ARTHUR, hosp. adminstr., accountant; b. Bklyn., Oct. 19, 1940; s. Arthur A. and Ruth Helen (Griesmer) A.; B.B.A., Adelphi U., 1962; m. Mary Elizabeth Brady, May 12, 1974; children—Gregory Russell, David Brady. Sr. accountant Peat, Marwick Mitchell & Co., N.Y.C., 1962-67, supr., 1967-71; dir. fin. United Hosp., Port Chester, N.Y., 1971—. Treas., mem. council St. Mark's Lutheran Ch., Elmsford, N.Y. Served with USAR, 1962-68. C.P.A. Mem. Am. Inst. C.P.A.'s N.Y. State Soc. C.P.A.'s (award 1962), Hosp. Assn. State N.Y. Hosp. Fin. Mgmt. Assn. (William G. Follmer Merit award 1977). Home: 78 Rivergate Dr Wilton CT 06897 Office: 406 Boston Post Rd Port Chester NY 10573

ARENTH, DONALD CRAIG, interior and indsl. design co. exec.; b. Pitts., Nov. 21, 1933; s. George Paul and Edith Eloise (Craig) A.; B.F.A. in Indsl. Design, Carnegie Mellon U., 1955; m. Linda Magnusson, Oct. 24, 1964; children— Craig Magnus, Sean Lydick. Yacht designer Concorde Yacht div. Brunswick Corp., Balt., 1964-68; partner Arenth & Fish Assos., Towson, Md., 1967-73; dir. mktg. H. Chambers Co., Balt., 1973-74, asso., 1974-76, v.p., 1976—. Served with U.S. Army, 1956-58. Reci Pient Indsl. Design award Indsl. Design Mag., 1970; Arthur Ashe Tennis Racket award, 1970. Mem. Mid Atlantic Designers, Indsl. Designers Soc. Am. Republican. Episcopalian. Home: 1408 Bolton St Baltimore MD 21217 Office: 1010 N Charles St Baltimore MD 21201

AREY, WILLIAM GRIFFIN, JR., govt. ofcl.; b. Shelby, N.C., Feb. 18, 1918; s. William Griffin and Catherine (Roberts) A.; A.B., U. N.C. at Chapel Hill, 1939; m. Louise Turner Craft, Mar. 7, 1942; children—William Griffin III, John G. C. Publisher, editor Cleveland Times Pub. Co., Shelby, 1941-48; pub. affairs officer State Dept., Bogota, Colombia, 1948-51, Panama, Republic Panama, 1951-53; pub. relations officer Panama Canal Co., Balboa Heights, C.Z., 1954-62; with U.S. Travel Service, Commerce Dept., Washington, 1963-76, dir. travel promotion, 1963-67, dep. dir., 1967-70, exec. officer, 1970-73, exec. dir., 1973-76; asst. exec. v.p. Nat. Trust Hist. Preservation, 1976—. Served to 1st lt. USAAC, 1942-45. Recipient Silver medal Commerce Dept., 1973. Mem. Pub. Relations Soc. Am., Internat. Union Ofcl. Travel Orgns. (v.p.), Pacific Area Travel Assn. (dir.), Sigma Nu. Methodist. Club: Rotary. Home: 2700 Virginia Ave NW Washington DC 20037 Office: 740 Jackson Pl NW Washington DC 20006

ARGIRO, LARRY JOSEPH, acoustical engr.; b. Reggio Calabria, Italy, Nov. 23, 1920; s. Joseph and Teresa (Santa Crocci) A.; came to U.S., 1924, naturalized, 1944; B.S. in Elec. Engring., W.Va. U., 1947; postgrad. U.S. Naval Postgrad. Sch., 1955-56, George Washington U., 1970-71; m. Rose Cecelia Demus, Oct. 25, 1947; 1 son, Larry Joseph. Electronics engr. U.S. Naval Engring. Expt. Sta., Annapolis, Md., 1947-53, head, acoustic signal processing br., 1953-67; supervisory engr., head, ship silencing div. U.S. Naval Marine Engr. Lab. (now Naval Ship Research and Devel. Center), Annapolis, 1967—. Served to 1st lt. AUS, 1943-46. Recipient Superior Accomplishment award Navy Dept., 1961, Meritorious Civilian Service award, 1962, 73, George W. Melville award, 1961; commd. adm. Cherry Hill Navy W.Va., 1974. Registered profl. engr., Md.; recipient Navy Superior Civilian Service award, 1977. Fellow Acoustical Soc. Am.; mem. Acoustical Soc. Washington (dir.), Am. Inst. Physics, Severn Tech. Soc. (pres. 1964-66), Md. Soc. Profl. Engrs. (Engr. of Year award 1962, dir. Annapolis chpt. 1963-65). Roman Catholic (bd. dirs. ch. 1963—, pres. Holy Name Soc. 1966-67). Home: 603 Laurel Rd Severna Park MD 21146 Office: Naval Ship Research and Devel Center Annapolis MD 21402

ARGY, DIMITRI, engr., educator; b. Athens, Greece, Mar. 13, 1921; s. Odysseus and Julia (Voga) Argyriades; diploma in chem. engring. Athens Nat. U. Engring. Sci., 1946; student phys. sci. Inst. Tech., Munich, Germany, 1950-51; Doktor-Ingenieur, Inst. Tech., Aachen, Germany, 1955; m. Maria Lycouressi, Aug. 17, 1956; children—Odysseus, Nicolas. With E.I. duPont de Nemours & Co., Inc., 1958-61; sr. research metallurgist Foote Mineral Corp., 1960-61; chief metallurgist, head research and devel. Hoeganes Corp., 1961-63; chief metallurgist Starlite Industries, 1963-65; sect. head metals and controls Tex. Instruments, 1965-67; mem. faculty dept. mech. engring. Southeastern Mass. U., North Dartmouth, 1967—. Cons. materials metallurgist. Mem. Am. Inst. Mining and Metall. Engring., Am. Soc. Engring. Edn., Am. Soc. Metals, Inst. Metals S. Bunsen Gesellschaft, Sigma Xi. Home: Shore Acres Rd South Dartmouth MA 02748 Office: Southeastern Mass U North Dartmouth MA 02747

ARGYIL, MARION H. G., real estate broker; b. New Orleans, Jan. 29, 1912; d. Franklin Johns and Sarah (Henry) Gustine; attended pvt. schs.; widow; 1 son, James E. Med. records librarian Doctors Hosp., Washington, 1944-47; asst. to neurosurgeon VA, Washington, 1948-51; electro-encephalographic tech. service NIH, 1952-55; tchr. real estate Washington Real Estate and Ins. Sch., 1958-60; real estate broker, Washington, 1958—, Va., 1958—, Md., 1959—. Pres. Monetary Mgmt. Inc. Recipient award in recognition of service to Nation, Pres. U.S., 1940; award for vol. work with United China Relief, 1942. Mem. So. Electro-encephalography Soc. Club: Kenwood Golf and Country (Bethesda, Md.). Author: Moonlight Poems; also scenarios under pseudonym Julie de Quistine. Patentee san. disposable baby bottle, payroll safety box, adjustable automobile seat, protective garment. Creator Argyil mortgage plan. Home: 15 E Irving St Chevy Chase Village MD 20015 Office: 810 18th St Washington DC 20015

ARKIN, STANLEY SAMUEL, lawyer; b. Los Angeles, Feb. 28, 1938; s. Jerome Z. and Lillian (Rogo) A.; B.A. magna cum laude, U. So. Calif., 1959; LL.B. cum laude, J.D., Harvard U., 1962; m. Suzanne Salter, Mar. 3, 1963; children—Adam, Alexander, Anthony. Admitted to N.Y. bar, 1963, Calif. bar, 1974, also U.S. Supreme Ct., dist. cts.; asso. firm Harris B. Steinberg, N.Y.C., 1963-69; mem. firm Arkin & Horan, N.Y.C., 1970-73; prin. Stanley S. Arkin, N.Y.C., 1974—; spl. prosecutor 1970 prison riots N.Y. State Dept. Corrections, 1971-72; adj. asst. prof. law N.Y. U., N.Y.C., 1976—; counsel programs on privacy Practicing Law Inst., 1974. Adv. com. criminal procedure law Judicial Conf. State N.Y., 1971-72. Served to capt. JAGC, U.S. Army, 1962-68. Mem. N.Y.C. (chmn. com. criminal cts., law and procedure 1970-72, spl. com. criminal justice 1971-72, com. judiciary 1975—), N.Y. State (chmn. com. standards for judicial competence 1975—), Am. bar assns., Phi Beta Kappa. Home: 11 Governors Rd Bronxville NY 10708 Office: 600 3d Ave New York City NY 10016

ARKLES, BARRY CHARLES, chem. and steel co. exec.; b. Phila., Feb. 1, 1949; s. Sydney J. and Beatrice M. Arkles; B.A., Temple U., 1969, Ph.D., 1975; m. Linda Laffey, Aug. 14, 1967; 1 dau., Elise. Mgr. tech. devel. Liquid Nitrogen Processing Engring. Plastic Co., Malvern, Pa., 1970-76; v.p. Petrarch Systems Inc., Cornwells Heights, Pa., 1975—; pres. M. Arkles & Son Steel Inc., Cornwells Heights, 1976—. Mem. Am. Chem. Soc., Soc. Mfg. Engrs., Soc. Plastic Engrs., Am. Inst. Chem. Engrs., Mensa. Contbr. articles to profl. publs.; patentee polymers, composites, immobilized cell organelles, silanes. Home: 124 Twining Rd Oreland PA 19075 Office: 600 Center Ave Cornwells Heights PA 19020

ARLYCK, RALPH KENNETH, filmmaker; b. Bklyn., Dec. 17, 1940; s. Alexander and Diana (Miller) A.; B.A. in English, Colgate U., 1962; M.S. in Journalism, Columbia U., 1966; postgrad. in film, San Francisco State Coll., 1968-70; m. Elisabeth Cardonne, Dec. 31, 1969; children—Kevin, Matthew. Reporter, The Record, Bergen County, N.J., 1973; Peace Corps vol., Senegal, 1964 66; filmmaker, 1968—; films include Sean, 1969, Natural Habitat, 1970, Enriched Baloney and Homemade Bread, 1972, Centers of Influence, 1974, Undelivered: No Such Country, 1975, Hyde Park, 1977; part-time tchr. film prodn. Recipient 1st prize NSA Film Festival, Lincoln Center, 1969; prize London Film Fest, 1970; grand prize Tours Festival, 1977; Guggenheim fellow, 1978; Am. Film Inst. Prodn. grantee, 1970. Mem. Assn. Ind. Video and Filmmakers. Home: 79 Raymond Ave Poughkeepsie NY 12601

ARMAO, THOMAS ANTHONY, dentist; b. Brooklyn, Aug. 9, 1923; s. Anthony and Maryann (Milazzo) A.; B.S., Manhattan Coll., 1943; D.D.S., Columbia U., 1947. Intern in dentistry Goldwater Meml. Hosp., N.Y.C., 1947-48; practice dentistry and oral surgery, Bklyn., 1948—. Served as lt. (j.g.), Dental Corps, USNR, 1947-48. Mem. ADA, Am. Soc. Contemporary Medicine and Surgery, Soc. Cryobiology, Soc. Cryosurgery, Royal Soc. Health (London), William Jarvie Soc. Dental Research, Am. Coll. Cryosurgery, Internat. Soc. Cryosurgery. Patentee cryosurg. instruments. Home: 1-78th St Brooklyn NY 11209 Office: 1242 56th St Brooklyn NY 11219

ARMISTEAD, HENRY TUCKER, librarian; b. Phila., Sept. 16, 1940; s. George Armistead A. and Elizabeth Russell (Tucker) A.; B.A., U. Pa., 1963; M.S., Drexel U., 1968; m. Mary Elizabeth Mallam, Sept. 3, 1966; children—George Lewis, Mary Douglas, Anne Tucker. Acquisitions librarian Jefferson Med. Coll. Library, Phila., 1968-70, head tech. services Thomas Jefferson Univ. Library, 1970-77, head collection devel., 1977—. Served with AUS, 1963-65. Fellow Delaware Valley Ornithol. Club; Med. Library Assn. (treas. Phila. regional group 1973-75), Brit., Am. ornithologists unions, Wilson, Cooper ornithol. socs., Beta Phi Mu. Democrat. Episcopalian. Book reviewer Library Jour., 1969—, Am. Ref. Books Ann., 1970—, Choice, 1972—; book rev. editor Birding, 1973—. Home: 28 E Springfield Ave Philadelphia PA 19118

ARMOUR, ALLAN A., film co. exec.; b. Bklyn., Apr. 25, 1933; s. Arthur Harris and Gertrude (Kornblue) A.; student New Inst. Film and Television, 1952, N.Y. U. Film Inst., 1956, Sch. Bus., 1956-60; m. Susan Lois Newman, June 25, 1967; children—Steven Douglas, David Newman. Asst. film editor Bray Studios, N.Y.C., 1951-53, asst. to film producer, 1955-57; TV film producer Milton Wynne Advt. Agy., Babylon, N.Y., 1957-59; owner, co-founder Cine Magnetics Inc., N.Y.C., 1961—, also dir.; pres. Projection Systems, Internat., N.Y.C., 1964—. Trustee Lenox Sch., N.Y.C. Served with Signal Corps, AUS, 1953-55. Mem. Nat. Audio Visual Assn. (cons.), Soc. Motion Picture Engrs. Contbr. numerous articles on audio visuals to various publs. Home: 501 E 79th St New York City NY 10021 Office: 730 3d Ave New York City NY 10017

ARMS, KATHARINE HELENA (MRS. JOSEPH EDWARD ARMS), banker; b. Brockton, Mass., July 30, 1922; d. Louis John and Anne Isabel (Murphy) Daniels; student Burdett Coll., 1940-41; m. Robert Sheppard, Mar. 10, 1942 (dec. Nov. 1962); m. 2d, Joseph Edward Arms, Feb. 12, 1967; children—Phillip A. Sheppard, Anne T. Sheppard (Mrs. Bernard M. LaBelle), Stephen D. Sheppard, Edward W. Arms. Payroll clk. Dartmouth Shoe Co., Brockton, 1950-52; with Nat. Bank of Plymouth County (name later changed to First County Nat. Bank, name now Shawmut First County Bank, N.A.), Brockton, 1961—, asst. supr. bookkeeping dept., 1962-63, br. mgr., 1964—. Notary Pub., 1965—. Clubs: Century of Stonehill Coll., Quota (pres.) (Brockton). Home: 38 Hall St Brockton MA 02402 Office: 712 Crescent St Brockton MA 02402

ARMSTRONG, CONRAD ROGER, hosp. adminstr.; b. Woonsocket, R.I., Sept. 29, 1928; s. Wenceslas L. and Laura M. (Capistran) A.; student U. Calif., Los Angeles, 1954-56; B.S. in Bus. U. Rochester (N.Y.), 1959; postgrad. hosp. adminstrn. Brooke Army Med. Center, 1959-60; m. Emily A. Spencer, Aug. 8, 1975; children by previous marriage—Thomas, Patrice, Laurie, Lisa. Adminstrv. asst. U. Rochester Sch. Medicine, 1957-62, asst. adminstr. Strong Meml. Hosp. U. Rochester Med. Center, 1962-67; asso. adminstr. F.F. Thompson Hosp., Canandaigua, N.Y., 1967-68; asst. adminstr. Winchester (Mass.) Hosp., 1968-76, v.p., 1976—; cons. hosp. center USAR Med. Facilities, Bedford, Mass., blood bank ARC, Rochester, 1964-67. Served with USMC, 1945-47, to capt. U.S. Army, 1952-57. Decorated Bronze Star medal. Mem. Am. Coll. Hosp. Adminstrs., Am. Hosp. Assn., New Eng. Hosp. Assembly, Mass. Nursing Home Adminstrs. Office: Winchester Hospital 41 Highland Ave Winchester MA 01890

ARMSTRONG, CRAIG STEPHEN, electric utility exec.; b. Columbus, Ohio, Jan. 18, 1947; s. Albert James and Margaret Ann (Dreschler) A.; B.S. in Edn., Ohio State U., 1972; m. Tamara Taggart, Nov. 26, 1966; children—Amber, Kirsten, Ann-Elise. Engr., announcer, producer WOSU-TV, Columbus, Ohio, 1966-68, 70-72; newscaster WBNS-TV, Columbus, 1968-69; pub. relations counselor Pub. Service Co. of N.H., Manchester, 1969-70, 72—; chmn. Videotape Task Force, Electric Council New Eng.; cons. in field. Active Boy Scouts Am.; bd. dirs. Hancock Found., 1975-77; vice-chmn. Contoocook Valley Regional Sch. Bd., Sharon, N.H., 1975—; pres. Sharon Taxpayers Assn. Served with U.S. Army Res., 1966-77. Mem. Internat. Assn. Bus. Communicators, Indsl. TV Assn., Pub. Relations Soc. Am. (accredited). Home: Rural Route 2 McCoy Rd Peterborough NH 03458 Office: 1000 Elm St PO Box 330 Manchester NH 03105

ARMSTRONG, DEAN ROY, urban and environ. planner; b. Peoria, Ill., July 21, 1945; s. William Martin and Norma June (Campbell) A.; A.B. (Regents Scholar), U. Mich., 1967; M.A., Mich. State U., 1969; m. Mary Ellen Blodgett, Apr. 30, 1967; children—Stephen Blodgett, Jane Mary. Asst. planner City of Hayward, Calif., 1969-70; planning dir., El Cerrito, Calif., 1970-73; project dir. Tri-Cities Seismic Safety and Environ. Resources Study, San Pablo, Calif., 1972-73; planning cons., Berkeley, Calif., spl. cons. to Calif. Gov. Office Emergency Services, 1973-74; county plan coordinator, Md.-Nat. Capital Park and Planning Commn., Upper Marlboro, Md., 1974—; lectr., program cons. U. Calif., Berkeley extension, 1973-74. Mem. Am. Inst. Planners (sec., treas. No. Calif. sect. 1971-72). Episcopalian. Club: Kettering Swim (v.p. 1977—). Dir. major planning studies, author plans and reports, Calif. cities El Cerrito, 1972, Richmond, 1973, San Pablo, 1973, Berkeley, 1974; coordinator proposal of new gen. plan Prince George's County, Md., 1977. Home: 217 Weymouth St Upper Marlboro MD 20870 Office: 14741 Governor Oden Bowie Dr Upper Marlboro MD 20870

ARMSTRONG, EDWARD BRADFORD, JR., oral and maxillofacial surgeon, naval officer; b. Teaneck, N.J., Sept. 24, 1928; s. Edward Bradford and Ruth Elizabeth (Fippinger) A.; A.B., U. Pa., 1950; D.D.S., N.Y.U., 1954; m. Dusanka Vladimirovna Jakovljevic, Nov. 5, 1960; children—Edward Bradford, III, James B., Hugh B. Commd. lt. j.g. U.S. Navy, 1954, advanced through grades to capt. 1971; intern oral surgery Roosevelt Hosp., N.Y.C., 1958, asso. attending oral surgery, 1959—, attending oral surgeon out-patient dept., 1959—, chmn., moderator Oral Surgery Staff Confs., 1963-70; resident Carle Hosp., Urbana, Ill., 1959; asso. attending oral surgeon Flower and Fifth Ave. hosps., N.Y.C., 1960-78; asst. attending oral surgeon Hackensack (N.J.) Hosp., 1963-65; adminstrv. officer Naval Res. Dental Co. 3-2, 1965-68, exec. officer, 1968-71, comdg. officer, 1971-73; comdt.'s rep. 3d Naval Dist., Naval Acad., 1972-78, 3d Naval Dist for Dentistry, 1973-75, group staff officer for dentistry and medicine, 1973-75, Ready Res. Unit 502, 1975-77, VTU 0207, 1977—; asso. clin. prof. oral surgery N.Y. Med. Coll., 1963—; adj. asso. clin. prof. oral surgery Columbia U. Sch. Dentistry, 1973—; chmn. bd. E. & R. Armstrong, Inc., Albany, N.Y., 1966-77; dir. ANS Corp., N.Y.C., Pitts. Graphic Products Corp., 1972-77; dir., mem. exec. com. PGP Internat. Corps, Inc. Bd. dirs., trustee Christian Mission Farms of Paraguay, Inc., 1974-77; v.p., trustee Central Bible Chapel, Palisades Park, N.J.; area rep., ann. giving U. Pa., 1960-68; Blue and Gold officer Naval Acad. Admissions Com.; sec. bd. dirs., trustee Boys' Club of N.Y. Health Services, Inc. Diplomate Am. Bd. Oral Surgery. Fellow N.Y. Acad. Dentistry (sec., dir., pres. 1979—), Am., Internat. colls. dentists, Am. Coll. Oral and Maxillofacial Surgeons (founding); mem. Am. (N.J. rep. Ho. of Dels. 1963-65), N.Y. (chmn. audit and budget com. 1972—) socs. oral surgeons, Am. Dental Assn., First Dist., N.Y., Bklyn., Yokosuka (hon.) dental socs., Assn. Mil. Surgeons U.S., Mil. Order World Wars, Naval Res. Assn. (life), Acaica, Xi Psi Phi, Psi Omega. Plymouth Brethren. Clubs: Union League (chmn. art com. 1973-76, bd. govs. 1974-77, v.p. 1977—), U. Pa. (N.Y.C.). Home: 110 Broad Ave Leonia NJ 07605

ARMSTRONG, GARY RAYMOND, biologist, virologist; b. San Diego, Oct. 26, 1934; s. Harry Raymond and Martha Petrunella (Plo) A.; student in med. tech. Air U., Montgomery, Ala., 1958, San Diego Coll., 1953; student Personnel Mgmt. Sch., Izmir, Turkey, 1961; student in bus. mgmt. U. Md., 1962; student in NIH, virology 1966; m. Ernestine Anne Hester, Sept. 21, 1952; children—Michael J., Gary Raymond, Michele A., Mark L., William H. Joined USAF, 1954, med. technologist, 1954-57, lab. dir., 1957-66, resigned, 1966, biol. lab. technician Nat. Inst. Allergy and Infectious Diseases, NIH, Bethesda, Md., 1966-67, microbiology sect., viral biology br. Nat. Cancer Inst., 1967-70; biologist, primate virus sect., Viral Leukemia and Lymphoma br. NIH Nat. Cancer Inst., Bethesda, 1970-73, biologist viral immunotherapy sect. RNA Tumor Virus Lab. div. Cancer Cause and Prevention, 1973—. Designated hon. aid-de-camp to Gov. of Ala., 1971. Mem. AAAS, Am. Soc. Microbiology, Tissue Culture Assn., Kappa Phi Alpha. Republican. Roman Catholic. Author or co-author papers on viral oncology presented to sci. meetings and contbr. to publs. Home: 329 W Edmonston St Rockville MD 20852 Office: Nat Cancer Inst Bldg 37 Room 1 B 16 Bethesda MD 20014

ARMSTRONG, GEORGE THOMSON, phys. chemist; b. Castor, Alta., Can., Dec. 8, 1916 (parents Am. citizens); s. George Alexander and Margaret (Faris) A.; B.S., U. Fla., 1939, M.S., 1943; Ph.D., Johns Hopkins U., 1948; m. Patricia Eliza Cadigan, June 16, 1945; children—Margaret Lucille Armstrong Chapman, Michael Faris. Grad. asst. U. Fla., Gainesville, 1940-42; scientist Radiation Lab., Mass. Inst. Tech., Cambridge, 1942-45; jr. instr. Johns Hopkins U., 1945-48; instr. chemistry Yale U., 1948-51; lectr. Boston U., 1950-51; phys. chemist U.S. Nat. Bur. Standards, Washington, 1951—, chief thermochemistry sect., 1968-74, chief thermochem. measurements and standards, 1974—, dep. chief chem. thermodynamics div., 1978—; detailed to EPA Office of Toxic Substances, 1979—; cons. in thermochemistry, calorimetry, energy-info. services; mem. Interunion Commn. on Biothermodynamics, 1975—. Mem. Woodside Park Civic Assn., 1960—. Recipient Silver Medal award U.S. Dept. Commerce, 1967. Fellow Am. Phys. Soc., Washington Acad. Scis.; mem. Am. Chem. Soc., Internat. Union Pure and Applied Chemistry (commn. on thermodynamics 1977—), N.Y. Acad. Scis. (life), AAAS (life), U.S. Calorimetry Conf. (dir. 1961-66, chmn. 1963-64, counsellor 1970-74, 77—), Philos. Soc. Washington (council 1973-75, pres. 1978), ASTM (chmn. gaseous fuels com. 1974—), Phi Beta Kappa, Sigma Xi, Phi Kappa Phi, St. Andrews Soc. Mem. United Ch. Christ. Clubs: Cosmos, Potomac Appalachian Trail (Washington). Contbr. articles to profl. jours.; editor Jour. Chem. Thermodynamics, 1977—. Home: 1401 Dale Dr Silver Spring MD 20910 Office: US Nat Bur Standards Washington DC 20234

ARMSTRONG, ROBERT JOHN, ret. chem. engr.; b. Kansas City, Mo., Aug. 3, 1911; s. Robert Elgin and Helen Florence (Valbracht) A.; B.S., U. Mo., Rolla, 1948; M.S., U. Tex., 1949; m. Helen Brady, May 26, 1946; children—Martha Sue, Robert Clyde. With Cook Paint & Varnish Co., Kansas City, 1935-38, Detroit, 1938-41; instr. U. Tex., Austin, 1948-50; heat transfer cons. E.I. duPont de Nemours & Co., Inc., Wilmington, Del., 1950-76. Served to 1st lt., arty. AUS, 1941-45. Decorated Bronze Star, Air medal with 5 oak leaf clusters. Registered profl. engr., Del. Mem. Am. Inst. Chem. Engrs., ASME (chmn. com. on unfired heat-transfer equipment 1960-63), Am. Nat. Standards Inst. (subcom. on heat exchangers 1959-72), Tau Beta Pi, Phi Lambda Upsilon, Omega Chi Epsilon, Alpha Chi Sigma. Presbyterian. Clubs: Masons (32 deg.), K.T. Contbr. articles to profl. jours. Home: 313 Wilson Rd Newark DE 19711

ARMSTRONG, RONALD WILLIAM, educator; b. Balt., May 4, 1934; s. John Paul and Elizabeth (Novotny) A.; B.Engring. Sci., Johns Hopkins U., 1955; Ph.D., Carnegie Mellon U., 1958; M.A. (hon.), Brown U., 1966; m. Mary Ann Manarczyk, Feb. 15, 1958; children—Lisa Joan, Lori Bess. Metallurgist, Westinghouse Electric Corp., Pitts., 1959-64; asso. prof. engring. Brown U., Providence, 1965-68; prof. materials U. Md., College Park, 1968—; cons. Oak Ridge Nat. Lab., 1967-70, Lawrence Livermore (Calif.) Lab., 1968-72, Inst. Def. Analysis, McLean, Va., 1969-75; program mgr. sci. edn. directorate NSF, 1976-77, rotator div. sci. edn. resources improvement, 1976-77. Recipient Robert Lansing Hardy Gold medal Am. Inst. Mining and Metall. Engrs., 1964; research fellow Leeds (Eng.) U., 1958-59, U. Melbourne (Australia), 1964; research grantee Def. Dept., 1963-73, NSF, 1973-75; sr. Fulbright-Hays fellow, Lower Hutt, New Zealand, 1974. Mem. AAAS, Am. Inst. Mining and Metall. Engrs., ASME, Am. Soc. Metals, N.Y. Acad. Scis., Sigma Xi, Phi Kappa Phi, Alpha Sigma Mu, Pi Tau Sigma. Contbr. to profl. jours.

Home: 1514 Rosewick Ave Baltimore MD 21237 Office: Dept Mechanical Engineering Univ Md College Park MD 20740

ARMSTRONG, THOMAS NEWTON, III, museum dir.; b. Portsmouth, Va., July 30, 1932; s. Thomas Newton, Jr. and Mary Saunders (Tabb) A.; student Cornell U., 1950-54, Art Students League, summer 1953, Inst. Fine Arts, N.Y.U., 1965-67; m. Virginia Whitney Brewster, May 18, 1963; children—Thomas Newton IV, Whitney, Eliot, Amory. Personnel coordinator, asst. to chmn. bd. Stone & Webster, Inc., N.Y.C., 1957-65; curator, asso. dir. Colonial Williamsburg-Abby Aldrich Rockefeller Folk Art Collection, Williamsburg, Va., 1967-71; dir. Pa. Acad. Fine Arts, Phila., 1971-73; asso. dir. Whitney Mus. Am. Art, N.Y.C., 1973-74, dir., 1974—. Mem. alumni council Coll. Architecture, Art and Planning, Cornell U., also mem. univ. council com. on alumni trustee nominations; mem. Brandeis creative arts award commn. Brandeis U.; trustee Am. Fedn. Arts, Internat. Exhbns. Found.; mem. U.S. Internat. Council; bd. overseers Hopkins Center of Dartmouth Coll.; mem. bd. Herbert J. Johnson Mus. Art, Cornell U. Served as 1st lt., arty. AUS, 1955-57. Mem. Assn. Art Mus. Dirs. Clubs: Knickerbocker, Century Assn. (N.Y.C.); Fishers Island Country. Home: 765 Park Ave New York City NY 10021 Office: 945 Madison Ave New York City NY 10021

ARMSTRONG, VALERIE, city ofcl.; b. Hamilton, Ont., Can., Sept. 21, 1919; d. Westropp and Winifred (Colquhoun) A.; came to U.S., 1941, naturalized, 1948; student Purdue U., 1937-39, Northwestern U., 1940, U. Chgo., 1942-43, U. Pa., 1956, 57, 61. Campus shopper promotion Mandel Bros., Chgo., 1939; supr. tng. Sears, Roebuck & Co., 1940, methods and time study engr., 1941-44, Phila., 1946-47; asst. mgr. Leave Center for Service Women, Ottawa, Ont., 1944-45; home lighting adviser Phila. Electric Co., 1948; legal recorder Seaboard Fin. Co., 1949-51; statis. analyst RCA Quality Control Lab., 1952-53, Franklin Inst., 1954; records mgmt. analyst City of Phila., 1955-57, adminstrv. analyst, 1957—. Mem. watershed mgmt. com. Water Resources Assn. Del. River Basin. Mem. Am. Soc. Pub. Adminstrn., Pan Am. Assn., Phila. Mus. Art, Univ. Mus., Delaware Valley Protective Assn., Am. Acad. Polit. and Social Sci., World Affairs Council Phila., English Speaking Union, Geneal. Soc. Pa., Hist. Soc. Pa. Episcopalian. Clubs: Plays and Players, Charlotte Cushman, Purdue (sec. 1952-53, dir. 1954, 55, 56, 57, 58), Peale Club Pa. Acad. Fine Arts. Home: The Dorchester 226 W Rittenhouse Sq Apt 1413 Philadelphia PA 19103 Office: Water Dept Philadelphia PA 19107

ARMSTRONG, WILLIAM JAMES, assn. exec.; b. Lynbrook, N.Y., Sept. 7, 1924; s. James Patterson and Gladys Marie (Morris) A.; B.S. in Marine Engring., U.S. Mcht. Marine Acad., 1944; m. Mary Jane Campbell, Aug. 18, 1945; children—Karen Metz, Janet Kempinski, Ann, June. Commd. lt. (j.g.) USN, 1950, advanced through grades to lt. comdr., 1957, ret., 1957; asst. to European passenger mgr. U.S. Lines, 1957-59; exec. officer Internat. Passenger Ship Assn., N.Y.C., 1959-79; N.Am. mgr. Cruise Lines Internat. Assn., N.Y.C., 1976-79. Club: Internat. Skal (past pres. N.Y. chpt.). Home: 12 Fisher Pl Clark NJ 07066 Office: 17 Battery Pl New York City NY 10004

ARMSTRONG, WILLIAM LECKIE, ophthalmologist; b. Croydon, Eng., Feb. 28, 1933; s. Drummond Leckie and Mable (Carmichael) A.; student Aberdeen U., 1952-55; B.A., Oxford U., 1957, B.M., 1960, M.A., 1961; m. Ann Gillian Bardell, Mar. 28, 1959; children—Christopher Leckie, Richard Drummond, Robert William. Intern Radcliffe Inf., Oxford, Eng., 1960-61; resident Westminster and Moorfield hosps., London, Eng., 1962-64, Montreal Gen. Hosp., Montreal, Que., 1964-65; practice medicine specializing in ophthalmology, Victoria, B.C., 1968-76; mem. staff Victoria Gen. Hosp.; asst. prof. U. Conn., Farmington, 1977—. Lectr. U. Aberdeen, 1961-62. Fellow Royal Coll. Surgeons; mem. Canadian Ophthalmol. Assn., Can. Med. Assn. Club: Royal Vancouver Yacht. Office: U Conn Health Center Div Ophthalmology Farmington CT 06032

ARNDT, CYNTHIA, educator; b. N.Y.C., Sept. 27, 1947; d. Charles Joseph and Pura Maria (Rios) A.; B.A., Hunter Coll., 1971, M.A., 1975. Adminstrv. asst. to asst. registrar Hunter Coll., N.Y.C., 1968-69; cataloguer asst. Finch Coll. Library, N.Y.C., 1974; tchr. N.Y. Bd. Edn., N.Y.C., 1974—. Mem. Am. Artist Soc., Assn. Tchrs. Social Studies City N.Y., Center for Inter-Am. Relations, Am., Hispanic Am. hist. socs., Nat. Council for the Social Studies, Nat. Travel Club. Democrat. Roman Catholic. Home: 2 Nantucket Ct Howell NJ 07731

ARNDT, KARL JOHN RICHARD, educator; b. St. Paul, Sept. 17, 1903; s. Edward L. and Marie (Salomon) A.; grad. Concordia Sem., St. Louis, 1927; A.M., Washington U., 1928; postgrad. (Am. Exchange fellow) univs. Marburg and Berlin, 1928-29; Ph.D., Johns Hopkins U., 1933; m. Rosine Anne Linhorst, Dec. 24, 1933 (div. July 1950); 1 son, Karl S. N.; m. 2d, Blanca H. Renner, Oct. 7, 1950; 1 dau., Carola Anne Sylvia. Quartermaster, U.S. Miss. River Survey Service, 1924-25; instr. German and Greek Concordia Coll., Edmonton, Alta., Can., 1925-26; instr. Germanic langs. U. Mo., Columbia, 1929-31; instr. German, Goucher Coll., Balt., 1931-33; jr. instr. German, Johns Hopkins U., Balt., 1931-33; prof. German and Greek, Hartwick Coll., Oneonta, N.Y., 1933-35; asst. prof. Germanics, La. State U., 1935-42, asso. prof., 1942-45; head Edn. and Religious Affairs div. U.S. Mil. Govt. for Germany, Wurttemberg-Baden, Stuttgart and Berlin, 1945-50; prof. German, head dept. Clark U., Worcester, Mass., 1950-69, prof., 1970—; mem. Nat. Adv. Council Am. Ethnic Heritage Studies, 1975—. Guggenheim fellow, 1957-58; Am. Philos. Soc. grantee, 1953, 60, 66, 78; Pabst Found. Wis. grantee, 1965; Nat. Found. on Arts and Humanities grantee, 1967-68; Stiftung Volkswagenwerk grantee, 1967; Lilly Endowment grantee, 1969-71; Deutsche Forschungsgemeinschaft grantee, 1975-76. Mem. Am. Antiquarian Soc., Gesellschaft für deutsche Presseforschung (corr.) (Bremen, Germany), Phi Beta Kappa. Author: (with May E. Olson) German-American Newspapers and Periodicals 1732-1955, Vol. 1, 1965; Vol. 2, 1972; George Rapp's Harmony Society 1785-1847, 1965, rev. edit., 1972; American Pre-Centennial Periodical Literature, 1978; George Rapp's Successors and Material Heirs, 1847-1916, 1971; (with May E. Olson) The German Language Press of the Americas, Vol. I, 1976, Vol. II, 1973; A Documentary History of the Indiana Decade of the Harmony Society 1814-1824, Vol. I, 1975, Vol. II, 1978; The Treaty of Amity and Commerce between Prussia and the United States in 1785, 1977; editor-in-chief Charles Sealsfield: First Complete Edition of his works, Vols. 1-20, 1972-78; contbr. articles to profl. jours. Home: 5 Hazelwood Rd Worcester MA 01609

ARNFELD, LEO, educator, psychologist; b. Warsaw, Poland, Aug. 22, 1939; s. Henry and Sara (Sniadowicz) A.; came to U.S., 1952, naturalized, 1957; B.A., Boston U., 1961, M.Ed., 1964; B.H.L., Hebrew Coll., 1961; Ph.D., U. Sarasota, 1973; m. Lorraine N. Kipnis, July 17, 1964; children—Nina Sara, Aaron Jacob. Staff psychologist Wentworth Inst., Boston, 1965-67; faculty Bristol Community Coll., Fall River, Mass., 1967—, asso. prof. psychology 1971—; pvt. practice clin. psychology, Somerset, Mass., 1974—. Bd. dirs. Mass. Community Coll. Council, 1977—. Fellow Council on Jewish Material Claims Aganist Germany, 1959-61, Garland Jr. Coll. EDPA Inst., 1969. Mem. Am. Personnel and Guidance Assn., AAUP, Am. Coll. Personnel Assn., Mass. Tchrs. Assn., NEA, Am. Psychol. Assn., Zionist Orgn. Am. Club: B'nai B'rith. Office: Bristol Community Coll Fall River MA 02720

ARNOLD, CHARLES BURLE, JR., med. researcher; b. Seattle, Aug. 13, 1934; s. Charles Burle and Ruth Helen (Hadley) A.; B.S. cum laude, U. Puget Sound, 1956; M.D., C.M., McGill U., 1960; M.P.H., U. N.C., 1965; m. Sarah J. Slagle, Dec. 16, 1972; children—Geoffrey, Christopher, Jonathan. Intern U. Wash. Hosp., Seattle, 1960-61, resident, 1961; physician Peace Corps, La Paz, Bolivia and Washington, 1961-64; asst. prof. health adminstrn. U. N.C. at Chapel Hill, 1965-69; asst. prof. Albert Einstein Coll. Medicine, Bronx, 1969-72; prof. pub. adminstrn. and clin. asso. prof. preventive medicine N.Y. U., N.Y.C., 1972—; lectr. community health Mt. Sinai Med. Sch., N.Y.C.; dir. health maintenance inst. Am. Health Found., 1975-78, v.p. research, 1978—. Milbank Faculty fellow, 1967-74; grantee Office Econ. Opportunity, 1968-74, Population Council, 1971-75, Health Research Council N.Y.C., 1972-75, Nat. Cancer Inst., 1975—, Nat. Heart, Lung and Blood Inst., 1977—. Diplomate Am. Bd. Preventive Medicine. Fellow Am. Coll. Preventive Medicine (pres. 1977-78); mem. Pan Am. Community Health Assn. (sec. 1971—). Asso. editor Preventive Medicine Jour., 1975—. Contbr. articles to profl. jours. Research in fertility heart disease and cancer. Home: 25 Forest Ln Scarsdale NY 10583 Office: Am Health Found 320 E 43d St New York City NY 10017

ARNOLD, CHARLES INGERSOLL, forester; b. Woodbridge, Conn., July 14, 1915; s. Harold Sears and Justine (Ingersoll); B.A., Bowdoin Coll., 1939; M.F., Yale U., 1941; m. Dorothy Field Spoor, July 25, 1942; 1 dau., Anne Elizabeth Arnold Biddle. Various temporary forestry jobs U.S. Forest Service, 1941; with forest mgmt. service Union Bag and Paper Co., Savannah, Ga., 1941-42; forest mgmt. teaching Mich. State U., 1947-57; nursery specialist, tree improvement program dir., N.H. State Forest Nursery, 1957—; cons. on forestry and nurseries. Mem. Bowdoin Alumni Council, 1971-73, Yale Alumni Bd., 1966-72. Served with AUS, 1942-46; PTO, ETO. Decorated Purple Heart. Mem. Soc. Am. Foresters (chmn. N.H. 1971-72), Am. Forestry Assn., Assn. Yale Alumni, Yale Forest Sch. Alumni Assn. (pres. 1972-74), Alpha Delta Phi. Republican. Episcopalian. Home: RFD 7 Penacook NH 03301 Office: Dept of Forests and Lands State House Annex PO Box 856 Concord NH 03301

ARNOLD, DAVID RALPH JAQUES, lawyer; b. N.Y.C., Oct. 12, 1896; s. William Campbell and Katharine DeForest (Dashiell) A.; Litt.B., Princeton, 1918; D.J., N.Y. U., 1922; m. Medora Grymes, June 22, 1921; children—William C., Medora A. Vogt. Admitted to N.Y. bar, 1922, since practiced in N.Y.C.; justice Domestic Relations Ct. N.Y., 1936-37. Dir. Netherlands Overseas Corp., Romarco Realty Corp.; past dir. N.Y. & Richmond Gas Co.; trustee S.I. Savs. Bank. Past trustee S.I. Community Chest, S.I. Hosp., S.I. Social Service. Served to ensign USNRF, World War I. Clubs: Richmond County Country (past pres., dir.) (S.I.); Princeton (N.Y.C.); Nassau (Princeton). Home: 231 Benedict Rd Staten Island NY 10304 Office: 152 Stuyvesant Pl Staten Island NY 10301

ARNOLD, EDWARD MILTON, aerostat communications co. exec.; b. Balt., May 5, 1931; s. Milton Anthony and Edna May (Jones) A.; B.Engring., Johns Hopkins U., 1952, B.S. in Bus. Adminstrn., 1960; M.Engring. Adminstrn., George Washington U., 1964; m. Dolores Louise Ruth, Aug. 23, 1952; children—Stephen Edward, Michael Joseph, Richard Gerard, James Christopher. Mgr. ops. systems Westinghouse Electric Co., Balt., 1966-70, mgr. battle survelliance and imaging radar systems, 1970-71, mgr. engring., system devel. div., 1971-72; v.p. TCOM Corp., Columbia, Md., 1972—. Served with C.E., U.S. Army, 1952-54. Decorated Bronze Star medal. Republican. Contbr. articles to profl. jours. Home: 2208 Belleview Rd Baltimore MD 21228 Office: 5575 Sterrett Pl Columbia MD 21044

ARNOLD, FRANK, JR., mfg. co. exec.; b. Balt., July 1, 1934; s. Frank and Anita Elise (Koldewey) A.; B.M.E., Drexel U., 1957; postgrad. Bklyn. Poly. Inst., U. Mo., Purdue U.; m. Elizabeth Nellins Wigton, Jan. 17, 1959; children—Frank Stewart, Elizabeth Nellins, Anne Wigton. Sr. engr. Sperry Gyroscope Co., Lake Success, N.Y., 1957-66; asst. div. mgr. Dynamic Gear Co., Amityville, N.Y., 1966-67; with PMI Motors div. Kollmorgen Corp., Syosset, N.Y., 1967—, v.p. engring., 1972—. Served to 1st lt., C.E., AUS, 1957-58. Mem. ASME, Am. Soc. Metals, Am. Def. Preparedness Assn., Alpha Pi Lambda, Scabbard and Blade. Republican. Office: 5 Aerial Way Syosset NY 11791

ARNOLD, G. DEWEY, JR., accountant; b. Montgomery, Ala., Jan. 30, 1925; s. George D. Dewey and Janie Esther (Terry) A.; B.A. in Econs., U. South, 1949; postgrad. in accounting U. Tenn.; m. Dorothy Louise Wenger, Dec. 4, 1954; children—Susan O., G. Dewey III. With Aladdin Industries, Inc., Nashville, 1949-50; with Price Waterhouse & Co., C.P.A.'s, 1950—, partner, 1961—, partner in charge Washington office, 1966-76, mem. policy com., 1975—, regional mng. partner, 1976—; instr. accounting Robert Morris Sch. Accounting, 1952-53; lectr., course dir. mgmt. accounting Instituto Mexicano de Adminstracion de Negocias, A.C., 1958-64. Bd. dirs. Wolf Trap Found., 1976—, Greater Washington Edn. TV Assn., 1972—, Redskin Found., 1975—; bd. dirs. Landon Sch., 1975—, now chmn. bd. C.P.A., Pa., N.C., D.C., Mich., La., Md. Mem. Am., D.C., Md. insts. C.P.A.'s, Washington Bd. Trade, Am. Arbitration Assn., Beta Alpha Psi. Episcopalian. Clubs: Burning Tree, Congl. Country, Met., Internat. (Washington). Home: 3 Chalfont Ct Bethesda MD 20034 Office: 1801 K St NW Washington DC 20006

ARNOLD, GEORGE, investment co. exec.; b. Phila., May 16, 1930; student pub. schs., Phila.; m. Francoise L. Rengade, Feb. 12, 1969; children—Jay, Julie, Jordon, Gregory. Regional rep. Bache & Co., Phila., 1954-57, Montgomery Scott & Co., Phila., 1958-62; allied mem. N.Y. Stock Exchange, v.p. Gerstley, Sunstein & Co., N.Y.C., 1962-70; pres. Trac Internat., Ltd., Cannes, France, 1971-74; pres. Phila. Pension Securities Corp., Jenkintown, Pa., 1974—, dir., 1974—; sec. Am. Guardian Life Assurance Co.; dir. Phila. Pension Planning Corp., 1975—, PFG Inc., 1975—. Home: 20 Cavendish Dr Ambler PA 19002 Office: Center Bldg York Rd Greenwood Ave Jenkintown PA 19046

ARNOLD, HERBERT MATTHEW, planning ofcl.; b. Endwell, N.Y., Apr. 30, 1922; s. Boyd Everhart and Jennie Ethel (Whispell) A.; A.A.S., State U. N.Y., Delhi, 1971; B.S. in Bus. Adminstrn., Alfred U., 1973; m. Donna Gift Carlson, Mar. 26, 1942; children—Michael, Dawn, Boyd, Pamela, Julie. Supt. ops. Gen. Outdoor Advt. Co., Inc., Binghamton, N.Y., 1950-60; prodn. control supr. Dunn McCarthy Co., Binghamton, 1960's; grants and ops. mgr. So. Tier East Regional Planning Devel. Bd., Binghamton, 1975—. Served with USAAF, 1942-45; PTO. Republican. Methodist. Home: Box 40 Star Route Windsor NY 13865

ARNOLD, JEFFREY, biochemist, business exec.; b. Pitts., Oct. 19, 1937; s. John William and Eleanor Seline (Arnold) Clark; grad. cum laude Choate Sch., 1954; B.A., Yale, 1958; Ph.D. (USPHS fellow), Columbia, 1966; postgrad., N.Y. U., 1968-69, certificate in computer programming, 1974; certificate in taxation Nat. Tax Tng. Sch., 1977, 78; ind. study program in accounting State U. N.Y., 1977—; m. Barbara Wilson Cant, July 21, 1963; children—Jeffrey Cant, Walter Winslow, Elizabeth Weeks. Instr. Rockland Community Coll., Suffern, N.Y., 1966-68; lectr. Lehman Coll., City U. N.Y., Bronx, 1969-73, adj. lectr. Queens Coll., 1973; adj. asst. prof. chemistry Fairleigh Dickinson U., Teaneck, N.J., 1973-74; instr. chemistry Pingry Sch., Hillside, N.J., 1975-77; individual practice as educator and tax cons., 1977-78; retail sales mgr. Channel Home Centers div. W.R. Grace and Co., 1978—. Chmn. adv. com. on pub. opinion Nyack (N.Y.) Bd. Edn., 1971, mem. master plan adv. com., 1976-77; Rockland County Rep. committeeman, Orangetown dist. 5, 1971—; mem. Nyack Zoning Bd. Appeals, 1973—; election inspector, Nyack, 1970-73; mem. citizen's adv. com. Community Devel. Program, City of Nyack, 1974-77, charter mem. recreational adv. com., 1974-78, charter mem. aux. police com., 1975—; chmn. Orangetown Transp. Adv. Com., 1976-78. Trustee, pres., treas., founder Edward Hopper Landmark Preservation Found., Nyack, 1970-73; trustee, sec., publicity officer, founder Tappan Zee Concert Soc., Nyack, 1971-75; chmn. Save the Liberty Sch. Com., 1977-78. Mem. Yale Alumni Assn. (mem. schs. com., past dir.), Cum Laude Soc., Phi Lambda Upsilon, Alpha Chi Sigma. Presbyn. Contbr. articles to profl. publs. Home: 21 Marion St Nyack NY 10960

ARNOLD, JOHN ROLAND, landscape architect; b. Braintree, Mass., June 19, 1919; s. George Allen and Edith (Cain) A.; B.S., Tufts U., 1948; M.Landscape Architecture, Harvard U., 1953; m. Betty Lou Brown, June 12, 1943; children—Dane, Erin, Scott, Lisa. Landscape designer W. Lee Moore, Scarsdale, N.Y., 1953-56; job capt. A. Carl Stelling Co., N.Y.C., 1956-58; chief site design Ferrenz & Taylor, N.Y.C., 1958-62; pvt. practice, Irvington, N.Y., 1962—. Site cons. Croton-Harmon Sch. Dist., 1974—; site planning cons. Mercy Coll., 1975—. Trustee Irvington, 1966-72, mem. Planning Bd., 1960-65, 71-76, acting mayor, 1971-72. Served to 1st lt. AUS, 1941-46 50-52. Mem. Am. Soc. Landscape Architects, Am. Rhododendron Soc., Am. Horticulture Soc., Nat. Audubon Soc. Prin. works include: campus Iona Prep. Sch., New Rochelle, N.Y., 1966, Highland Falls (N.Y.) High Sch., 1971, campus Mercy Coll., Dobbs Ferry, N.Y., 1977, Spencer Meml. Field, Croton-on-Hudson, N.Y., 1976. Address: Lewis Rd Irvington NY 10533

ARNOLD, MERRILL SAWYER, ednl. adminstr.; b. Dallas, June 3, 1944; s. Merrill Sawyer and Jean Loretta (Weidner) A.; B.S., Shippenburg State Coll., 1971, M. Ed., 1973, Ed.D., 1979; 1 dau. by previous marriage, Jennifer Lynn. Tchr. 6th grade Chambersburg (Pa.) Area Sch. Dist., 1971-72; prin. Scotland Elementary Sch., 1972-75, 76-78; elem. supr. Tussey Mountain Sch. Dist., 1978—; research asst. Pa. Sch. Study Council, Pa. State U., 1975-76; lectr., cons. in field. Served with USMCR, 1964-68. Decorated Silver Star, Bronze Star, Purple Heart with 2 clusters. Mem. Assn. Supervision and Curriculum, Am. Assn. Sch. Adminstrs., Pa. Assn. Fed. Program Coordinators, Pa. Assn. Elementary and Secondary Sch. Prins., Internat. Soc. Ednl. Planners, Keystone Personnel and Guidance Assn., C. of C., Phi Delta Kappa. Republican. Lutheran. Clubs: Marine Corps League, V.F.W., Am. Legion, Lions, Masons (32 deg.). Home: PO Box 93 Saxton PA 16678 Office: Saxon-Liberty Elem Sch Saxon PA 16678

ARNOLD, MORRIS FAIRCHILD, bishop; b. Mpls., Jan. 5, 1915; s. LeRoy and Kate (Fairchild) A.; B.A. magna cum laude, Williams Coll., 1936; M.Div., cum laude, Episcopal Theol. Sch., 1940; D.D., Kenyon Coll., 1961, Williams Coll., 1972; children—Jaqueline Fairchild (Mrs. Arnold Crocker), William Morris; m. 2d, Harriet Borda Schmidgall, 1978. Ordained priest Episcopal Ch., 1940; priest-in-charge St. John's Ch., Saugus, Mass., 1940-43; chaplain U.S. Army, 1943-45; rector Grace Ch., Medford, Mass., 1945-50; Episcopal students chaplain, Tufts Coll., Boston, 1945-50; rector Christ Ch., Cin., 1950-72; consecrated suffragan bishop, 1972; suffragan bishop Episcopal Diocese of Mass., 1972—; del. to Anglican Congress from So. Ohio, 1954; dep. to Gen. Convs. of Episcopal Ch., 1958-70; co-founder U.S. Ch. and City Conf., 1959, pres., 1964-66; mem. Joint Commn. on Edn. for Holy Orders, 1961-68, program and budget com. of Episcopal Ch., 1961-70, 77—; pres. Council of Chs. of Greater Cin., 1961-63; treas. Cin. Met. Area Religious Coalition, 1968-72; v.p. Episcopal City Mission, Boston, 1972—. Trustee ARC, 1957-63, Family Service, 1962-71, Better Housing League, 1951-72; mem. Cathedral Deans Assn., 1952-72; mem. steering com. Urban Bishop's Coalition, 1977—. Mem. Soc. for the Relief of Aged or Disabled Clergymen (v.p. 1972—). Alumni Assn. Episcopal Theol. Sch. (pres. 1969-72), Phi Beta Kappa, Delta Phi. Home: 445 Pleasant St Belmont MA 02178 Office: 1 Joy St Boston MA 02108

ARNOLD, PETER WALLACE, banker; b. Bklyn., Jan. 19, 1936; s. Lyndon and Irene Elizabeth (Johnson) A.; B.A., Yale U., 1958; m. Sandra Weeden Marshall, July 12, 1958; children—Deryck Marshall, Peter Hastings. Vice-pres. 1st New Haven Nat. Bank, 1958-72; v.p.-mktg. Washington Trust Co., Westerly, R.I., 1972-75, sr. v.p.-trust, 1975—; pres. Conn. Estate and Tax Planning Council, 1975-76; mem. exec. bd. R.I. Estate Planning Council, 1974—; pres. New Haven Estate Planning Council, 1964-65, Southeastern Conn. Estate Tax Planning Council. Bd. incorporators Westerly Hosp. Served with AUS, 1959-61. Mem. New Eng. Bank Mktg. Assn. (past pres.), Nat. Assn. Estate Planning Councils (regional v.p.), R.I. Life Underwriters Assn., Fin. Planners Assn. Clubs: Quinnipiack, Mory's Assn., Pond View Racquet, Marshneck Gun, S.Shore Wildflowers, Ducks Unltd., YMCA Heritage. Home: 18 Plympton Rd Watch Hill RI 02891 Office: 23 Broad St Westerly RI 02891

ARNOLD, ROSALIND MERCEDA, counselor; b. N.Y.C., July 17, 1947; d. Richard and Mildred Louise (Roderick) Arnold; B.S., State U. of N.Y. at Plattsburgh, 1969; postgrad. L.I. U., 1973. Elementary tchr. Bklyn. Pub. Schs. 307 and 287, 1970-73; program specialist N.Y. State Edn. Dept., N.Y.C., 1973-74; sr. counselor N.Y.C. Tng. Inst. 1974—; cons. Suffolk County Day Care Centers, N.Y.C. Div. Adoption Services. Mem. Am. Personnel and Guidance Assn. Democrat. Methodist. Office: 225 Park Ave S New York City NY 10003

ARNOLD, STEPHEN, physicist; b. Kew Gardens, N.Y., Apr. 16, 1942; s. Albert and Alice (Levine) A.; B.S., U. Toledo, 1964; M.A., Queens Coll., 1967; Ph.D. (Univ. fellow), City U. N.Y., 1970. Asso. engr. Douglas Aircraft Co., Santa Monica Calif., 1963-64; lectr. in physics Queens Coll., 1964-68, instr., 1970-73; research asso. Brookhaven Nat. Lab., Upton, N.Y., 1968-70; sr. scientist N.Y. U., 1973—; cons. Spex Industries, Northrop Municipal Bonds. Mem. Am. Inst. Physics, IEEE, Tau Beta Pi. Research and publs. on electronics, molecular crystals, electro-optics. Home: 1 Washington Sq Village New York City NY 10012 Office: 4 Washington Pl New York City NY 10003

ARNOLD, STEPHEN EDWARD, communications dir.; b. Peoria, Ill., Nov. 17, 1944; s. Willard Burkhardt and Betty Jane A.; B.A., Bradley U., 1966, M.A., 1970; m. Kay Sydney Brewer, Aug. 6, 1968; children—Kelley Sue, Erik Stephen. Coordinator coop. work study program Peoria Pub. Schs., 1967-70; prof. communications Ill. Central Coll.; East Peoria, 1971-73; dir. communication skills program No. Ill. U., DeKalb, 1971-73; mgr. corporate communications NUS Corp., Washington, 1973-77; dir. communications Booz Allen & Hamilton, Washington, 1977—; dir. Nat. Communications Services Inc. Woodrow Wilson fellow, 1965; Duquesne fellow, 1966-67. Mem. Am. Nuclear Soc., Pub. Relations Soc. Am., Soc. Tech. Communications (award 1978). Pub., Communication News, 1977—. Home: 26 Goodport Ct Gaithersburg MD 20760 Office: 4330 East West Hwy Bethesda MD 20014

ARNONE, CAROL FRANCES, counselor; b. S.I., N.Y., Mar. 21, 1950; d. Frank J. and Mary (Carbonaro) A.; A.A. with honors, S.I. Community Coll., 1975; B.A. with honors, Richmond Coll., 1977; 1 son, James P. Sweeney. Tutor, counselor reading center S.I. Probation Dept., 1975-76; counselor S.I. Continuum of Edn., 1977—. Vol. ARC, S.I., 1973—. Mem. Am., N.Y.C. personnel and guidance assns., AAUW. Contbr. article to book, 1978. Home: 81 Lexington Ave Staten Island NY 10302 Office: 130 Stuyvesant Pl Staten Island NY 10301

ARNOW, L(ESLIE) EARLE, scientist; b. Micanopy, Fla., June 22, 1909; s. Joseph Leslie and Mable Annie (Thrasher) A.; Ph.G. and B.S., U. Fla., 1930; Ph.D., U. Minn., 1934, M.B. and M.D., 1940; m. Jennie Martin, July 17, 1933 (dec. Sept. 1976); 1 son, Peter Leslie. Grad. asst. in physiol. chemistry and bio-physics U. Minn., 1931-34, instr. physiol. chemistry, 1934-40, asst. prof., 1940-42; dir. biochem. research, med.-research div. Sharp and Dohme div. Merck & Co., Inc., 1942-44, dir. research, 1944-53, v.p., dir. research, 1953-56; v.p. Merck Sharp & Dohme Research Labs. div. Merck & Co., Inc.; exec. dir. Merck Inst. Therapeutic Research, 1956-58; pres. Warner-Lambert Research Inst., 1958-65; v.p. Warner-Lambert Co., 1958-65, sr. sci. cons., 1965-74. Past pres. bd. trustees Morris County Easter Seal Soc. Recipient Centennial award U. Fla., 1953, Outstanding Achievement award U. Minn., 1955. Fellow AAAS, N.Y. Acad. Scis.; mem. N.J., Morris County med. socs., AMA, Research Dirs. Assn., Am. Chem. Soc., Am. Soc. Biol. Chemists, Soc. Exptl. Biology and Medicine, Am. Soc. Clin. Pharmacology and Therapeutics, Phi Beta Kappa, Sigma Xi, Alpha Omega Alpha, Phi Beta Pi, Gamma Sigma Epsilon, Rho Chi, Phi Sigma, Alpha Epsilon Delta, Gamma Alpha, Sigma Chi. Club: Morris County Golf. Author: Introduction to Physiological and Pathological Chemistry, 1976; Introduction to Laboratory Chemistry, 1976; Health in a Bottle, 1970; Introduction to Organic and Biological Chemistry (with H.C. Reitz), 1949; Food Power, 1972; contbr. articles to tech. publs. Home: 14 Fairfield Dr Convent Station NJ 07961

ARNOWICH, BEATRICE, chemist, educator; b. N.Y.C.; d. Julius and Valia (Patigalla) Arnowich; A.B., Vassar Coll.; M.S., U. Mich.; Ph.D., N.Y. U., 1957; 1 dau., Anne. Chemist, Charles Bruning Co., 1957-59; prin. scientist Interchem. Corp. Clifton, N.J., 1959-68; asst. prof. chemistry Queensborough Community Coll., Bayside, N.Y., 1969-76, asso. prof., 1976—. Fellow AAAS, Am. Inst. Chemists, Chem. Soc. (London); mem. Am. Chem. Soc., N.Y. Acad. Sci. Home: 10 East End Ave New York City NY 10021 Office: Dept Chemistry Queensborough Community Coll Bayside NY 11364

ARONFREED, EVA, educator; b. Phila., July 15, 1911; d. Joseph and Johanna (Scheindling) Aronfreed; B.F.A., U. Pa., 1933, A.M., 1947, Ph.D., 1958. Cons. pub. relations, Phila., 1933-42; asso. editor Pub. Health Nurses, N.Y.C., 1945-46; publs. editor Phila. City Planning Commn., 1947-56; cons. municipal pub. relations, Phila., 1956-61; asst. prof. Monmouth Coll., 1961-62; prof. polit. sci., chairperson polit. sci., econs. dept. Glassboro (N.J.) State Coll., 1962—, now prof., coordinator pub. adminstrn. Served with WAC, 1942-45. Recipient Certificate of Merit, Internat. Union Local Authorities, 1961. Fels Inst. grantee, 1950-57. Mem. Internat. Union Local Authorities, Internat. Polit. Sci. Assn., Internat. Inst. Adminstrn. Studies, Am. Polit. Sci. Assn., Acad. Polit. Scis., Am. Acad. Polit. and Social Scis., Am. Soc. Pub. Adminstrn., League Women Voters, ACLU. Contbr. articles to profl. jours. Home: 403 S Cummings St Glassboro NJ 08028 Office: Glassboro State Coll Glassboro NJ 08028

ARONFY, ANDREW GEORGE, pediatrician; b. Budapest, Hungary, Mar. 1, 1934; s. Anthony and Magdalen (Spiegel) A.; came to U.S., 1949, naturalized, 1955; student Harvard U., 1951-54; M.D., State U. N.Y., Syracuse, 1958; m. Jacqueline Marica Wolfsohn, June 5, 1960; children—Joel David, Amy Dawn. Intern, Washington Hosp. Center, 1958-59; resident in pediatrics Children's Hosp., Washington, 1959-61; practice medicine specializing in pediatrics, Seabrook, Md., 1963—; mem. staff Prince George's Gen. Hosp. and Med. Center; clin. asst. prof. pediatrics Georgetown U. Med. Sch. Served to capt. M.C., AUS, 1961-63. Mem. Am. Acad. Pediatrics, Prince George's County Med. Soc. (chmn. grievance com. 1977—). Democrat. Jewish. Home: 6603 Good Luck Rd New Carrollton MD 20784 Office: 10210 Greenbelt Rd Suite 600 Seabrook MD 20801

ARONIN, JEFFREY ELLIS, architect; b. London, Eng., Aug. 16, 1927; s. Joseph and Bertha (Danziger) A. (father Am. citizen); B.Arch. U. Manitoba, Winnipeg, Can., 1949; M.Arch. magna cum laude, McGill U., 1951. Architect, Frank Grad and Sons, Architects, Newark, 1951-52; architect Shreve Lamb and Harmon, Architects, N.Y.C., 1952-53; architect Voorhees, Walker, Foley and Smith, then Voorhees, Walker, Smith and Smith, Architects, N.Y.C., 1954-56; architect Kahn and Jacobs, N.Y.C., 1956-57; individual practice architecture, N.Y.C., 1957-77; chief architect Kingdom of Lesotho, 1977—; prof. Ecole d'Architecture U. Montreal; lectr. 95 archtl. schs. at univs. in N. Am., Europe, Australia, S. Pacific; moderator WNYC Architecture in the Space Age; mem. N.Y.C. Mayor's Panel of Architects, 1961-76; mem. Mayor's Com. for Better Housing. Treas. Scandinavian-Americans for Rockefeller, 1968. Served with Canadian Army, 1944-47. Certified, licensed architect, numerous states, Canada, U.K., Australia. Fellow Royal Inst. Brit. Architects; mem. AIA, (chmn., mem. many local state, nat. coms., sec., 1968, v.p., 1969,74), N.Y. State Assn. of Architects, Royal Archtl. Inst. Can., La Sociedad de Arquitectos Mexicanos, La Sociedad Venezolana de Arquitectos, Inst. S. African Architects, Lesotho Architects, Engrs. and Surveyors Assn., Nat. Inst. for Archtl. Edn., Brit.-Am. C. of C., Danish-Am. Soc., Rebild Nat. Park Soc., Swedish C. of C. of U.S.A., Am. Arbitration Assn. (mem. nat. panel of arbitrators), St. George's Soc., Internat. Solar Energy Soc., French Engrs. in U.S.A. Clubs: Masons, Canadian University, Hamilton. Author: Climate and Architecture, N.Y., 1953, Climate and Architecture, Moscow, 1959; Climate and Architecture, Boston, 1977. Home: 389 Woodmere Blvd Woodmere NY 11598 Office: PO Box 570 New York City NY 10017

ARONIN, LEWIS RICHARD, materials engr.; b. Norwood, Mass., Aug. 4, 1919; s. Samuel and Celia (Acoff) A.; B.S., Mass. Inst. Tech., 1940; m. Natalie Eleanor Wolfson, June 19, 1947; children—Marlene Aronin Sigel, Terry Susan. Asst. to research dir. Waltham Watch Co. (Mass.), 1940-48; staff mem. Mass. Inst. Tech. Metall. Project, Cambridge, 1949-54; mgr. research and devel. dept. Nuclear Metals, Inc., Concord, Mass., 1954-65; cons. Kennecott Copper Corp., Lexington, Mass., 1966-67; materials engr. Army Materials and Mechanics Research Center, Watertown, Mass., 1967—. Registered profl. engr., Mass. Mem. Am. Inst. Mining, Metall. and Petroleum Engrs., Am. Soc. Metals, Soc. Advancement Materials and Process Engring., Sigma Xi. Clubs: Lions, Masons. Research and publs. on nuclear materials, radiation effects, beryllium and refractory materials; patentee in field. Home: 20 Ingleside Rd Lexington MA 02173 Office: Arsenal St Watertown MA 02172

ARONOVITCH, MICHAEL, physician; b. Montreal, Que., Can., Apr. 15, 1910; s. Isaac and Minnie (Miller) A.; B.Sc., McGill U., 1931, M.D., 1935; m. Katherine Silver, Dec. 30, 1945; children—Jane, Stephen, Carole, Lawrence. Intern, Jewish Gen. Hosp., 1935-36; intern Royal Victoria Hosp., 1936-37, asso. physician, 1948—; resident Grace Dart Hosp., 1937-39; practice medicine specializing in internal medicine, Montreal, 1940—; cons. physician Mt. Sinai Hosp., Prefontaine, Que.; hon. physician Royal Edward Chest Hosp., Montreal; cons. in chest diseases Reddy Meml. Hosp.; asso. prof. medicine and clin. medicine McGill U.; chmn., dir. Fulcrum Investment Co., Ltd., Alphatext Ltd., Ottawa, Ont., Can.; pres., dir. Armika Corp. Ltd. Bd. dirs. Canadian Assn. Mentally Retarded. Served to maj., M.C., Royal Canadian Army, 1942-46. Fellow A.C.P., Am. Coll. Chest Physicians, Royal Coll. Physicians Can.; mem. Am. Trudeau Soc., Canadian Thoracic Soc., Montreal Clin. Soc. (past pres.), Alpha Omega Alpha. Contbr. articles to profl. jours. Home: 1530 Dumfries Rd Town of Mount Royal PQ H3P 2R4 Canada Office: 4119 Sherbrooke St Montreal PQ H3Z 2X8 Canada

ARONS, ANNETTE TRENNER (MRS. LEON ARONS), pub. relations exec.; b. London, Aug. 28, 1912; d. Baron and Leah (Tucker) Trenner; grad. high sch.; m. Leon Arons, May 1, 1942; children—Stephen, Judith Hannah. Came to U.S., 1926, naturalized, 1942. Sec., Robin Hood Dell, symphony orch., Phila., 1930-32; legal sec. Dechert, Bok, Smith & Clark, attys., Phila., 1932-36; account exec. Market Relations Network, N.Y.C., 1956-58; v.p., partner Lem Jones Assos. (merger with J.A. Mansi & Co., name now Corp. Relations Network), pub. relations, N.Y.C., from 1958, partner, sec.-treas. Account exec. Westchester League for Cardiac Children, 1953. Mem. Pub. Relations Soc. Am. Home: 41 Elizabeth Rd New Rochelle NY 10804 Office: 280 Madison Ave New York City NY 10016

ARONS, MARVIN SHIELD, plastic surgeon; b. Derby, Conn., Feb. 13, 1931; s. George and Pauline (Shield) A.; B.S., Yale U., 1952; D.M.D., Harvard U., 1955; M.D., U. Md., 1957; children—Mark David, Jeffrey Alan. Surg. intern Duke Hosp., 1957-58, surg. resident, 1958-59; surg. resident Georgetown U. Hosp., 1961-62; resident in plastic surgery U. Tex. Med. Br., Galveston, 1962-64, chief resident plastic surgery, 1964-65; practice medicine, specializing in plastic and hand surgery, New Haven, 1965—; asso. clin. prof. plastic surgery Yale Med. Sch., 1978—; attending plastic surgeon Yale-New Haven Hosp., West Haven VA Hosp.; chief sect. plastic surgery Hosp. St. Raphael, New Haven; cons. plastic surgery crippled children sect. State Conn., 1965—; cons. hand surgery Workmen's Compensation Commn., New Haven, 1968—; clin. asso. Nat. Cancer Inst., 1959-61. Bd. dirs. New Haven Jewish Community Council, 1971-74, Hosp. St. Raphael Found., 1975—, New Haven Dept. Jewish Edn., 1973-74; trustee Hopkins Day Prospect Hill Sch., New Haven. Am. Cancer Soc. fellow, 1962-65. Diplomate Am. Bd. Plastic Surgery. Fellow A.C.S.; mem. Am. Soc. Plastic and Reconstructive Surgeons, Am. Assn. Hand Surgery, Am. Soc. Maxillofacial Surgeons, Am. Assn. Plastic Surgeons, Plastic Surgery Research Council, New Haven County Med. Soc., Sigma Xi. Club: Woodbridge (Conn.) Country (bd. govs. 1971-74). Home: 66 Hunting Hill Rd Woodbridge CT 06525 Office: 2 Church St S New Haven CT 06519

ARONSON, EDGAR DAVID, brokerage co. exec.; b. N.Y.C., June 17, 1934; s. Aaron Solomon and Ida Claire (Minevitch) A.; A.B., Harvard U., 1956, M.B.A., 1962; m. Nancy Carol Pforzheimer, Dec. 23, 1956; children—Edgar David, Alison C., Edith S., Peter Borrah. Successively trainee, asst. cashier, v.p. First Nat. Bank Chgo., 1962-67; v.p. Republic Nat. Bank N.Y., 1968; trainee Salomon Bros., N.Y.C., 1968-69, ltd. partner, 1970, v.p., 1971-72, gen. partner, 1972—; mng. dir. Salomon Bros. Internat. Ltd., London, 1971-76, dir., 1976—; dir. Salomon Bros. Asia Ltd., Merrie-Go-Round, Inc., Dallas, Burnwood Corp., N.Y.C. Served to 1st lt. USMCR, 1956-60. Mem. Marine Corps Res. Officers Assn., First Marine Div. Assn. Clubs: Harvard (N.Y.C.); The Curzon, Annabel's (London). Co-author: New Old World, 1962; Response to Change, 1963. Home: 115 E 79th St New York City NY 10021 Office: Salomon Bros One New York Plaza New York City NY 10004 also One Moorgate London EC2R 6AB England also 2907 Alexandra House Hong Kong British Crown Colony

ARONSON, PHILIP ROGER, physician; b. Norwich, N.Y., Nov. 26, 1922; s. Sol and Marica S. A.; ed. U. Mich., Ann Arbor, 1940; M.D., L.I. Coll. Medicine, Bklyn., 1948; m. Christine Aronson, Dec. 17, 1953; children—Stuart, Michael, Thomas, Sarah. Intern, Mt. Sinai Hosp., Cleve., 1948-49; resident in internal medicine Boston City Hosp., 1949-51, 54-55; resident in cardiology Sch. Aviation Medicine, Pensacola, 1951; individual practice medicine specializing in internal medicine, Norwich, N.Y., 1955—; asso. prof. medicine State U. Coll. Medicine, Syracuse, N.Y., 1964—; chief coronary care unit Chenango Meml. Hosp., Norwich, 1959—, chief medicine, 1964—. Served with USNR, 1944-46, 51-54. Decorated Purple Heart, Silver Star. Home: Fuller Rd Norwich NY 13815 Office: Med Arts Bldg Norwich NY 13815

ARONSON, SHEPARD GERARD, physician; b. N.Y.C., May 1, 1913; s. Henry and Ida (Kanter) A.; A.B., Cornell U., 1933, M.D., 1937. Intern, Jewish Hosp., Bklyn., 1937-39; extern in surg. pathology N.Y. Hosp., 1940; chief dept. of metabolic diseases and diabetes clinic, Good Samaritan Hosp., N.Y.C., 1955-60; chief diabetes clinic, Stuyvesant Polyclinic, N.Y.C., 1963-64; chief of endocrine clinic, N.Y. U. Hosp., 1964-65; asso. vis. physician Bellevue Hosp., N.Y.C., 1973—; asst. clin. prof. internal medicine N.Y.U. Med. Sch., N.Y.C., 1947—; cons. in internal medicine Inst. Phys. Medicine and Rehab., 1948—, asst. attending physician, 1950—; asso. attending physician N.Y. Infirmary, N.Y.C., 1971—; attending physician Drs. Hosp., N.Y.C., 1973—; mem. Malpractice Mediation Panel apptd. by N.Y. State Supreme Ct.; mem. Interprofl. Com. of Lawyers and Doctors; chmn. criteria com. in internal medicine, N.Y. County Services Review Orgn. Charter mem. NOW, founding chmn. bd. N.Y. Chpt.; med. advisory com. Planned Parenthood N.Y. Served with M.C., U.S. Army, 1942-46. Decorated Bronze Star, Purple Heart. Mem. Soc. Internal Medicine County of N.Y. (pres. 1974-76), Med. Soc. County of N.Y. (Comitia Minora, chmn. pub. relations com., chmn. Medicare peer review com., 1974-78). Contbr. papers to profl. jours. Address: 150 E 56th St New York City NY 10022

ARP, HILDA DORA PAPE (MRS. RUDOLPH ARP), artist; b. Hamburg, Germany; d. Peter Johann and Minna (Warnecke) Pape; student New Sch. Social Research, 1955, Bklyn. Mus., 1956, Art Student League, 1961, Pratt Graphic Center, 1966; m. Rudolph Arp, Oct. 5, 1937; children—Rolf, Rudolf, Peter. Gallery artist Gallery Internat., N.Y.C.; exhibited in group shows throughout U.S., Europe; one-woman shows: A. Artzt Gallery, N.Y., 1962, 65, N.Y. Worlds Fair, 1964, 65; represented in permanent collections: Norfolk (Va.) Mus., Wagner Coll., S.I., N.Y., Union Ch., Bayridge, Bklyn. Dir. adv. bd. John F. Kennedy Library for Minorities, 1972—. Recipient Am. Heritage award, 1972. Mem. Nat. Assn. Women Artists, Am. Fed. Arts, Internat. Platform Assn., Nat. Soc. Arts and Letters, Mus. Modern Art, Bklyn. Mus., Artist Equity Assn. N.Y., Arcanum Artists N.Y. Contemporary Artists Bklyn., Met. Painters and Sculptors, Avant Six. Home: 772 B Hudson Pkwy Crestwood Village Whiting NJ 08759 Office: Gallery Internationale 1095 Madison Ave New York City NY 10028

ARRINGTON, LANCE HARDY, quality control exec.; b. Columbus, Ga., Oct. 16, 1938; s. Clarence Hardy and Virginia Madge (Tucker) A.; B.E.E., Ga. Tech. U., 1961; postgrad. managerial economics N.C. State U., 1968-70; m. Geraldine Carol Burks, Sept. 11, 1960; children—Elaine Camille, Tracy Lynn. Sr. engr. ITT Telecommunications, Raleigh, N.C., 1964-65, mgr. engring. adminstrn., 1965-66, mgr. product engring., 1966-68, quality dir., 1968-70, mgr. quality engring. ITT European Hdqrs., Brussels, Belguim, 1972-77, dir. quality ITT Fed. Electric Corp., Paramus, N.J., 1977-78, dir. quality ITT Telecommunications Tech. Center, Stamford, Conn., 1978—; dir. quality Gen. Datacom Industries, Westport, Conn., 1970-72; internat. lectr. quality mgmt.; tech. and mgmt. cons. in quality control. Recipient Ring of Quality award ITT, 1976. Mem. Am. Soc. Quality Control, Eta Kappa Nu. Home: 54 Butternut Ln Southport CT 06490 Office: ITT Telecommunications Tech Center 1351 Washington Blvd Stamford CT 06902

ARROW, KENNETH JOSEPH, economist; b. N.Y.C., Aug. 23, 1921; s. Harry I. and Lillian (Greenberg) A.; B.S. in Social Sci., City Coll. N.Y., 1940; M.A., Columbia, 1941, Ph.D., 1951, D.Sc., 1973; LL.D., U. Chgo., 1967, City U. N.Y., 1972, Hebrew U. of Jerusalem, 1975, U. Pa., 1976; D.Social and Econ. Scis. (hon.), U. Vienna (Austria), 1971; D.Social Scis. (hon.), Yale, 1974; Doctor (hon.), Universite Rene Descartes, Paris, 1974; D.Polit. Scis. (hon.), U. Helsinki (Finland), 1976; m. Selma Schweitzer, Aug. 31, 1947; children—David Michael, Andrew. Research asso. Cowles Commn. for Research in Econs., 1947-49; asst. prof. econs. U. Chgo., 1948-49; acting asst. prof. econs. and statistics Stanford, 1949-50, asso. prof., 1950-53, prof. econs., statistics and ops. research, 1953-68; prof. econs. Harvard, 1968-74, James Bryant Conant univ. prof., 1974—, exec. head dept. econs., 1954-56, acting exec. head dept., 1962-63; economist Council Econ. Advisers, U.S. Govt., 1962; cons. The RAND Corp. Served as capt. AUS, 1942-46. Recipient John Bates Clark medal Am. Econ. Assn., 1957, Alfred Nobel Meml. prize in econ. scis., 1972. Social Sci. Research fellow, 1952, fellow Center for Advanced Study in the Behaviorial Scis., 1956-57, fellow Churchill Coll., Cambridge, Eng., 1963-64, 70, 73, Guggenheim fellow, 1972-73. Fellow Am. Acad. Arts and Scis. (v.p. 1978), Econometric Soc. (v.p. 1955, pres. 1956), Am. Statis. Assn., Inst. Math. Statistics, Am. Econ. Assn. (exec. com. 1967-69, pres. 1973); mem. Nat. Acad. Scis., Am. Philos. Soc., Inst. Mgmt. Scis. (pres. 1963, chmn. council 1964), Am. Econs. Assn. (v.p. 1978), Finnish Acad. Scis. (hon. fgn.), Brit. Acad. (corr.). Author: Social Choice and Individual Values, 1951; Essays in the Theory of Risk Bearing, 1971; The Limits of Organization, 1974. Co-author Mathematical Studies in Inventory and Production, 1958; Studies in Linear and Nonlinear Programming, 1958; Time Series Analysis of Inter-industry Demands, 1959; Public Investment, The Rate of Return and Optimal Fiscal Policy, 1971; General Competitive Analysis, 1971. Office: 1308 Littauer Center Harvard U Cambridge MA 02138

ARSENAULT, ALFRED JUDE, publishing co. exec.; b. N.Y.C., Sept. 15, 1929; s. George S. and Mary (Roach) A.; B.A., St. John's U., 1960; m. Arlene Jeanne Semon, Aug. 20, 1955; children—James J., Jeanne M., Thomas J., Jane R., Nancy J., Patricia J., Barbara J. Sales rep. Met. Sunday Newspapers, Inc., N.Y.C., 1956-58; sales mgr. Med. Econs., Inc., Oradell, N.J., 1958-64; asst. to pub. Med. World News, N.Y.C., 1965; v.p., dir. advt. Med. World News, N.Y.C. 1966-69; pres. Insight Pub. Co., Inc., 1969—. Served with USN, 1950-54. Club: Cornell of N.Y. Home: 47 Orchard Dr East Williston NY 11596 Office: 501 Madison Ave New York City NY 10022

ARSENEAU, JAMES CHARLES, med. oncologist; b. Syracuse, N.Y., Aug. 29, 1942; s. James Howard and Glenna (Wurth) A.; A.B., Syracuse U., 1964; M.D., Albany Med. Coll., 1968; m. Jane Ellen Macy, July 2, 1966; children—Marc, David. Intern, Strong Meml. Hosp., Rochester, N.Y., 1968-69, resident, 1969-70, fellow med. oncology, 1973-74; clin. asso. med. oncology Nat. Cancer Inst., Bethesda, Md., 1970-73; practice medicine specializing in oncology, Rochester, 1974—; asst. prof. oncology in medicine U. Rochester Cancer Center, 1974—; head med. oncology unit Rochester Gen. Hosp., 1974—; exec. officer New Agents Com., Eastern Cooperative Oncology Group, 1976—; mem. ovarian and chemotherapy coms. Gynecologic Oncology Group, 1977—. Bd. dirs. United Cancer Council, Rochester, 1977—, Am. Cancer Soc., Monroe County unit, Rochester, 1977—; advisory bd. dirs. Make Today Count, Rochester, 1975—. Served with USPHS, 1970-73. Am. Cancer Soc. fellow, 1973; Wilson fellow, 1973-74; Am. Cancer Soc. Jr. Clin. Faculty fellow, 1974-77. Diplomate Am. Bd. Internal Medicine with subsplty. in med. oncology, Nat. Bd. Med. Examiners. Mem. N.Y. State, Monroe County med. socs., AMA, Rochester Acad. Medicine, Am. Soc. Clin. Oncology, Alpha Omega Alpha, Zeta Psi. Republican. Clubs: NIH Alumni, Albany Med. Coll. Alumni. Contbr. articles in field to profl. jours. Home: 24 Vincent Dr Pittsford NY 14534 Office: 1425 Portland Ave Rochester NY 14621

ARSHT, EDWIN DAVID, physician; b. Phila., Oct. 6, 1929; s. Samuel Jacob and Sylvia (Dick) A.; B.A., Swarthmore Coll., 1951; M.D., Jefferson Med. Coll., 1955. Intern Frankford Hosp., Phila., 1955-56; resident gen. practice Mountainside Hosp., Montclair, N.J., 1958-59; pvt. family practice, Springfield, Pa., 1959—; sch. physician, Springfield, 1961—; civil def. physician Springfield Twp., 1960-64; dir. med. edn., dir. employee health service Delaware County Meml. Hosp., Drexel Hill, Pa., 1960-69, chief allergy clinic, 1970; med. dir. Harlee Manor Nursing Home, Springfield, 1975; dir. med. edn. and services Delaware County Meml. Hosp., 1975, dir. dept. family practice, 1976; instr. family medicine Jefferson U. Med. Coll., 1973; clin. instr. dept. family medicine Coll. Medicine and Dentistry N.J.-Rutgers Med. Sch.; med. staff Riddle Meml. Hosp. Pres., Delaware County Jewish Community Center, 1970, chmn. bd. trustees, 1971, man of year, 1971. Served to capt., U.S. Army, 1956-58. Recipient State of Israel award, 1971. Diplomate Am. Bd. Family Practice. Fellow Am. Acad. Family Physicians; mem. Pa. (chmn. com. on edn. 1977), Delaware County (pres. 1962-75) acads. family physicians, Am. Acad. Allergy, Am. Coll. Allergists, Pa. Allergy Soc., Pa. Allergy Assn., Am. Heart Assn., Heart Assn. Southeastern Pa., AMA, Pa., Delaware County med. socs., Assn. Hosp. Med. Edn., Assn. Am. Med. Colls., Soc. Tchrs. Family Medicine, Am. Geriatric Soc., Am. Acad. Med. Dirs., Am. Friends Hebrew U., Delta Upsilon, Phi Delta Epsilon. Republican. Jewish. Clubs: Swarthmore (Phila.); Med. of Delaware County, B'rith Sholom Lodge. Office: 3909 State Rd Drexel Hill PA 19026

ARTASERSE, BONNIE, educator; b. Jersey City; d. Ambrose and Rosina (De Rosa) Artaserse; B.S., Columbia, 1944; pvt. studies with various artists. Tchr. elementary sch., Jersey City, 1919-24; tchr. art Henry Snyder Jr. High Sch., Jersey City, 1924-29, William L. Dickinson High Sch., Jersey City, 1929-40; supr. art, Jersey City, 1940-70; cons. art programs, Jersey City, 1970—; exhibited in group shows at Newark Mus., Montclair Mus., Jersey City Mus. Tchr. design, painting, Jersey City, 1960—. Mem. adv. com. Jersey City Adult Edn. Sch. Mem. exec. com. Jersey City Tercentenary, 1960; active various community fund drives; bd. dirs. Coll. Community Orch. Hudson County; mem. Hudson County Cultural Arts Council.

Recipient First award for oil painting N.J. State Fedn. Women's Clubs, 1960; 1970 Jersey City Pub. Sch. Children's Art Show dedicated in her honor by Jersey City Parents Council; recipient citation Parents Council of Jersey City. Mem. Bus. Profl. Woman's Club (charter), AAUW, Allied Artists N.Y., Jersey City Mus. Assn. (trustee), Hudson Artists, Nat., N.J. art edn. assns., Friends of Music and Art of Hudson County, North Hudson Art League, NEA, N.J., Hudson County edn. assns., Nat. Tchrs. Assn., Friends of N.J. State Mus. Club: Jersey City Woman's. Home: 2016 Kennedy Blvd Jersey City NJ 07305

ARTHER, RICHARD OBERLIN, polygraphist; b. Pitts., May 20, 1928; s. William C. and Florence (Oberlin) A.; B.S., Mich. State U., 1951; M.A., Columbia U., 1960; m. Mary-Esther Wuensch, Sept. 12, 1951; children—Catherine Alice, Linda Diane, William C. Chief asso. John E. Reid & Assos., Chgo., 1951-53; dir. Reid & Assos., N.Y.C., 1953-58; pres. Sci. Lie Detection, Inc., N.Y.C., 1958—; pres. Nat. Tng. Center of Polygraph Sci., 1958—; police sci. staff Bklyn. Coll., 1954-61, Seton Hall U., 1958-61, N.Y. U. Grad. Sch. Pub. Adminstrn., 1959-60, John Jay Coll. Criminal Justice, 1967-68. Mem. N.Y. State Polygraphists (pres. 1964-69, chmn. 1969-72, dir. 1972—), N.J. Polygraphists (sec.-treas. 1965-75), Am. Polygraph Assn. (charter), Am. Assn. Police Polygraphists (charter; dir. 1977-78), Nat. Acad. Lady Polygraphists, Acad. Certified Polygraphists (charter). Author: Interrogation for Investigators, 1959; The Scientific Investigator, 1965; mng. editor Jour. Polygraph Sci., 1966—. Office: 57 W 57th St New York City NY 10019

ARTHUR, JAMES DOUGLAS, dentist; b. Rome, N.Y., May 27, 1921; s. William Morris and Ethel Louise (Warner) A.; student Cornell U., 1939-42; D.D.S., U. Buffalo, 1945; m. Laura Elinor Strobeck, Nov. 13, 1943; children—James Douglas, Joan Arthur Haskins, Janice Arthur Fisher, Jean, Judith, Jonathan. Staff dentist Central N.Y. State Sch. for Deaf, Rome, 1946; pvt. practice dentistry, North Syracuse, N.Y., 1946—. Bd. dirs. Faith Heritage Christian Sch., Syracuse. Served as lt. (j.g.) Dental Corps, USNR, 1945-46, 52-54. Mem. ADA, Fifth Dist., Onondaga County dental socs. Baptist (deacon 1966-73, bldg. fund trustee 1960-73). Clubs: Masons, Rotary (charter mem. N. Syracuse), Gideons. Address: 207 N Main St North Syracuse NY 13212

ARTHUR, PAUL, JR., chemist; b. Detroit, June 20, 1915; s. Paul and Alice Dorothy (Dolan) A.; B.S. cum laude, Loyola at Chgo., 1935; Ph.D., Mass. Inst. Tech., 1938. With duPont Co., Wilmington, Del., 1938—. Harvard U. Corp. fellow, 1958-59; recipient citation Loyola U. Alumni, 1967. Mem. Assn. Computing Machinery (founding), Am. Chem. Soc., Am. Numis. Soc., Am. Mineral. Soc. Patentee chromium dioxide tape, polymer intermediates, x-ray structures. Home: 11 Brandywine Blvd Wilmington DE 19809 Office: duPont Expt Sta Wilmington DE 19898

ARTHUR, WILLIAM CATHCART, JR., mfg. co. exec.; b. Pitts., Dec. 18, 1921; s. William Cathcart and Sara Margaret (Warrick) A.; B.S. in Adminstrv. Engring., Cornell U., 1948; m. Ann Bailey Draper, July 13, 1946; children—Karen Ann, Sara Warrick, Janet Draper, William C. III. Asst. to treas. Norton Co., Worcester, Mass., 1948-54; pres. Anderson Corp., Worcester 1955-76, Anderson div. Dresser Industries, Inc., Worcester, 1977—; dir. Associated Industries of Mass., Boston, 1966—, Esleeck Mfg. Co., Turners Falls, Mass., Mechanics Bank, Worcester, 1963—. Vice chmn. bd. trustees Becker Jr. Coll., Worcester, 1965—; pres. bd. trustees Meml. Hosp. of Worcester, 1973—. Served to capt. U.S. Army 1942-45. Decorated Bronze Star, Order of Leopold, Croix de Guerre (Belgium). Republican. Unitarian. Clubs: Worcester, Tatnuck Country, Beverly Yacht, Five Islands Yacht, U.S. Power Squadron. Home: 71 Berwick St Worcester MA 01602 Office: 1040 Southbridge St Worcester MA 01610

ARTIM, JOHN, artist, designer, advt. agy. exec.; b. Passaic, N.J., Nov. 3, 1903; s. Michael and Maria (Lucacsina) A.; student R.I. Sch. Design, 1931-32, Cooper Inst., 1927-28, Art Students League, 1929-30, Internat. Corr. Schs.; m. Helen Mucha, June 1, 1924; children—John Michael, Florence Helen Artim Pochyla. Designer, Paterson Parchment Co., Bristol, Pa., 1938-41; artist, designer Fleetwings, Bristol, 1941-42; designer Norman Bel Geddes, 1943-44, Warner Corp., N.Y.C., 1945; art dir. Chase Aircraft Co., Trenton, N.J., 1947-55; sales promotion mgr. Curtiss-Wright Corp., East Paterson, 1957-63; established Artim Advt., Yardley, Pa., 1963, dir., owner, 1963—; tchr. Drexel Inst., Phila., 1942, Famous Artists Sch., 1968. Recipient awards including grand prize Art Instrn. Schs., Mpls., 1953, Gold certificate for advt. brochure Phila. Art Dirs. Exhibit, 1967; gold medal real estate sales promotion brochure, silver medal for menus Neographics '76 Showcase, silver medal for indsl. folder Neographics '77 Showcase. Roman Catholic. Clubs: K.C. (past grand knight), Trenton Engrs. Address: 35 Albemarle Rd Hamilton Sq Trenton NJ 08690

ARTURI, FRANK LOUIS, med. instrumentation co. exec.; b. Port Chester, N.Y., Dec. 29, 1921; s. Frank and Mary (Chappa) A.; B.B.A., Pace Coll., 1951; m. Eleanor Wynne, Feb. 4, 1951; children—Lynn, Edythe, Frank Louis. Asso. TV producer/dir. Young & Rubicam, advt., N.Y.C., 1951-54; account exec., mgr. radio-TV dept. Lambert & Feaseley, advt., N.Y.C., 1954-56; account exec. M.B. Scott Co., advt., N.Y.C., 1956-57; asst. advt. and mktg. mgr. Empire Brush Co., Port Chester, 1964-69; corp. advt. mgr. Am. Cystoscope Makers, Inc., Stamford, Conn., 1969—. Served with AUS, 1942-46. Recipient Pub. Service award Stamford Spl. Events Commn., 1976, 77. Mem. Pharm. Advt. Club N.Y.C., Westchester (N.Y.), Fairfield (Conn.) advt. clubs. Club: Stamford Toastmasters Internat. Address: 1394 High Ridge Rd Stamford CT 06903

ARTUSIO, JOSEPH FRANCIS, JR., anesthesiologist; b. Jersey City, Nov. 26, 1917; s. Joseph and Jennie (Cuneo) A.; B.S., St. Peter's Coll., 1939; M.D., Cornell U., 1943; m. Mary Louise Ellis, Oct. 8, 1945; children—Marianne, Suzanne Artusio McIntyre, Evelyn, Joseph Francis, Mark Douglas. Intern, Bellevue Hosp., N.Y.C., 1943-44; resident anesthesiology N.Y. Hosp., 1946-47, asst. attending anesthesiologist, 1947-48, attending anesthesiologist in charge, 1948-57, anesthesiologist-in-chief, 1957—; instr. surgery Cornell U. Med. Coll., 1947-48, asst. prof. surgery, 1948-52, asso. prof., 1952-57, prof. anesthesiology in surgery, 1957-67, prof. anesthesiology in obstetrics and gynecology, 1957-67, prof. anesthesiology, chmn. dept., 1967—. Mem. bd. edn. Pelham (N.Y.) Pub. Schs., 1961-69, pres., 1968-69. Served with M.C., AUS, 1944-46. Diplomate Am. Bd. Anesthesiology. Fellow Am. Coll. Anesthesiologists; mem. AMA, Am. Soc. Anesthesiologists, Am. Soc. Pharmacology and Exptl. Therapeutics, Assn. Univ. Anesthetists, Soc. Exptl. Biology and Medicine (unitarian com. 1956), Med. Soc. State N.Y., N.Y. Acad. Medicine (chmn., sec. anesthesiology and resuscitation 1970), N.Y. State Soc. Anesthesiologists (gen. chmn. postgrad. assembly 1968-70), Soc. Academic Anesthesia Chairmen (chmn. placement com. 1970), Med. Soc. County N.Y. Home: 238 Corlies Ave Pelham NY 10803 Office: 525 E 68th St New York City NY 10021

ARUNASALAM, VICKRAMASINGAM, physicist; b. Jaffna, Ceylon, Aug. 26, 1935; s. Vickramasingam and W. Sithamparam; came to U.S., 1958, naturalized, 1973; B.S., U. Ceylon, 1957; M.S., U. Mass., 1960; Ph.D., Mass. Inst. Tech., 1964; m. S. Saradamani, Mar. 23, 1968; 1 child, Sharmila. Asst. lectr. U. Ceylon, Colombo, 1957-58; instr. U. Mass., Amherst, 1960; research asso. Princeton, 1964-67, mem. research staff, 1967-76, research physicist, 1976—. Mem. Am. Phys. Soc., Sigma Xi. Contbr. articles to profl. jours. Research on plasma physics and quantum theory. Home: 50 Windsor Dr Princeton Junction NJ 08550 Office: Plasma Physics Lab Princeton Univ Princeton NJ 08540

ASADORIAN, WILLIAM RONALD, librarian; b. Jamaica, N.Y., Dec. 27, 1949; s. Harry and Rosanne (Misirian) A.; B.A. in Math., Queens Coll., City U. N.Y., 1971, M.A. in Am. History, 1973, M.L.S., 1976; m. Diana Martirosyan, July 22, 1978. Legal archivist hist. documents collection Queens Coll., 1972-76; asst. curator manuscripts N.Y. Hist. Soc., N.Y.C., 1976—; lectr., cons. in field. Grad. fellow library sci. Queens Coll., 1974-76. Mem. Phi Alpha Theta, Alpha Phi Omega. Presbyterian. Club: Shriners. Contbr. profl. jours. Home: 150-24 Jewel Ave Flushing NY 11367 Office: 170 Central Park W New York NY 10024

ASBURY, MELVIN L., oil co. exec.; b. Concord, N.C., Oct. 21, 1951; s. Beatrice M. Asbury; B.S. in Bus. Adminstrn., N.C. Central U., 1973; M.S. in Indsl. Relations, Purdue U., 1974; m. Brenda L. Pippens, Mar. 2, 1974. Grad. instr. Krannert Grad. Sch., Purdue U., 1973-74; with Exxon Research & Engring. Co., Florham Park, N.J., 1974—, compensation analyst, 1976-78, head of employee relations, 1978—. Mem. N.J. Personnel Assn., Engring. Assos., Omega Psi Phi, Phi Beta Lambda, Gamma Theta Upsilon. Democrat. Lutheran. Address: 126 Pleasantview Ave New Providence NJ 07974

ASCHKINASI, SONJA HENRIETTA, physician; b. Koenigsberg, Germany; d. Joseph and Malvina (Finkelstein) Ashkenazy; Feldscher and midwife Med. Technicum (Yakutsk, U.S.S.R.), 1944; M.D., U. Munich (Germany), 1955. Came to U.S., 1961, naturalized, 1967. Feldscher, Yakutsk Policlinic, U.S.S.R., 1944-45; asst. psychiatrist Univ. Hosp. Psychiatry and Neurology, Munich, 1955-56; asst. dept. dermatology Municipal Hosp., Munich-Schwabing, 1956; asst. gen. pathology Pathology Inst., U. Munich, 1956-57; asst. in neuropathology dept. brain pathology German Research Inst., Max-Plank Inst., 1957-59; resident Montreal (Que.) Childrens Hosp., 1959-60, Allan Meml. Inst., Royal Victoria Hosp., Montreal, Que., 1960-61, dept. psychiatry St. Lukes Hosp., N.Y.C., 1961-62; rotating intern Grand Central Hosp., N.Y.C., 1962, Knickerbocker Hosp., N.Y.C., 1962-63; fellow Mt. Sinai Hosp., N.Y.C., 1963-64, N.Y. Med. Coll., 1964-65; staff psychiatrist child psychiatry clinic and adolescent psychiatry clinic Queens Hosp. Center, N.Y.C., 1965-67; practice medicine, specializing in psychiatry adults, children, N.Y.C., 1964—; Branford, Conn., 1967—; attending clin. asso. child psychiatrist Mt. Sinai Hosp. and Med. Sch., N.Y.C., 1971—; med. dir. adolescent unit Norwich (Conn.) Hosp., 1976-77; Med. dir. Greater Enfield Mental Health Center, 1977-78, exec. dir., 1978—. Diplomate Am. Bd. Psychiatry and Neurology. Home: 33 Totoket Rd Pine Orchard Branford CT 06405 Office: 388 E Main St Branford CT 06405 also 1077 Enfield St Enfield CT 06082

ASH, HOMER LEE, oral surgeon; b. Huntington, W.Va., Sept. 13, 1929; s. Homer Edward and Myrtle (Hayes) A.; B.S., U. Ill., 1951; D.M.D., Harvard U., 1959; children—David Lee, Melinda Lee (dec.), Stephen Edward. Intern, Mass. Gen. Hosp., 1959-60, chief resident, 1961-62; resident Boston U. Sch. Medicine, 1960-61; pvt. practice oral surgery, Framingham, Mass., 1962-66, Keene, N.H., 1966—; examiner Am. Bd. Oral and Maxillo-facial Surgery, 1975—. Chmn. profl. edn. com. Am. Cancer Soc. N.H., 1970-72; Eagle bd. of rev. counselor Algonquin council Boy Scouts Am., 1963-67, Daniel Webster dist. council, 1970-73, commr. Monadnock dist., 1972-74, dist. chmn., 1974-77, recipient award of merit, 1974, Silver Beaver award, 1976. Bd. dirs. Monadnock Health and Welfare Council, Salvation Army, Monadnock United Fund; trustee Cheshire Hosp., 1975—. Served to lt. (j.g.) USNR, 1951-54; ETO. Recipient Student Clinician award Harvard Sch. Dental Medicine, 1959. Diplomate Am. Bd. Oral Surgery. Fellow Am. Dental Soc. Anesthesiology; mem. ADA, New Eng. Dental Soc. (bd. govs. 1972—, pres. elect 1978), N.H. Soc. Oral Surgeons (pres. 1972-73), N.H. Dental Soc. (chmn. council dental health, pres. 1977), Keene C. of C. (dir. 1969-73). Harvard Dental Alumni Assn., Kappa Sigma, Nu Sigma Nu. Mem. Ch. of Christ (mem. Keene planning bd. 1970-74, chmn. 1974). Club: Rotary. Address: 127 Washington St Keene NH 03431

ASH, RENE LEE, trade assn. exec.; b. Brussels, Mar. 14, 1939; s. Curt and Johanna (Kapaun) A.; came to U.S., 1950; naturalized, 1957; student U. Nebr., 1958-60; m. Ethel Botzenmayer, Dec. 22, 1962. Asst. in promotion prodn. Popular Sci. Mag., N.Y.C., 1964-68; publicity dir., editor Internat. Alliance of Theatrical Stage Employees and Moving Picture Machine Operators of U.S. and Can., N.Y.C., 1968—; U.S. rep. Merkur Films, Oslo; research cons. U.S. Dept. Labor. Served with U.S. Army, 1962-64. Mem. Publicists Guild Am. (Eastern v.p. 1973—). Jewish. Author: The Motion Picture Film Editor, 1974; editor IATSE Bull., 1968—; asso. editor Film World, Bombay, India; editor, pub. Show Biz Books; contbr. articles to profl. jours. Home: 33 25 76th St Jackson Heights NY 11372 Office: 1515 Broadway New York City NY 10036

ASH, RONALD MARTIN, civil engr.; b. Worcester, Mass., Feb. 12, 1942; s. Herbert and Mary A.; B.S., U. R.I., 1966, M.S., 1971. With C. E. Maguire, Inc., Providence R.I., 1960—, project mgr., 1965-70, group mgr., 1970-72, asst. v.p., 1973-77, v.p., 1978—; instr. math. Bryant Coll., 1975—; instr. engring. R. W. Coll., 1970—. Chmn., Housing Bd. Review Town of North Providence, 1968-70. Registered profl. engr., R.I., Mass., Fla., N.H., Mem. ASCE (pres. New Eng. council 1972-73), Providence Engring. Soc. (mem. exec. bd. 1970-71), Soc. Mil. Engrs., Municipal Pub. Works Assn. R.I., R.I. Soc. Profl. Engrs., New Eng. Water Works Assn., New Eng. Water Pollution Control Assn., Inc., ASME. Club: Rally Point Tennis. Office: 31 Canal St Providence RI 02903

ASHBAUGH, WILLIAM HATCH, psychologist; b. N.Y.C., July 27, 1929; s. William Leroy and Mary Brownlow (Hatch) A.; B.A., Colby Coll., 1953; M.Ed., U. Maine, 1955; Ph.D., Pa. State U., 1962; m. Carolyn Morton, Aug. 17, 1957; children—Carolyn Ann, William Lee. Sch. psychologist Montgomery County (Md.) Pub. Schs., 1960-62, supr. psychol. services, 1962-64; exec. dir., psychol. services and ednl. research Milw. Pub. Schs., 1964-69; prof. behavioral scis. York Coll. Pa., 1969—, chmn. dept. behavioral scis., 1972-76, 77-78; cons. USOE, Washington, 1965; vis. lectr. U. Wis., 1965-66, Marquette U., 1965. Trustee Upper Midwest Regional Lab., 1966. USPHS fellow, 1962. Diplomate sch. psychology Am. Bd. Profl. Psychology. Mem. Am. (treas., exec. com. 1966-69), Pa. psychol. assns., Am. Ednl. Research Assn. Editorial cons. Profl. Psychology, 1968—; cons. editor Jour. Sch. Psychology, 1967-70. Home: 1906 Ebony Dr York PA 17402

ASHBERY, JOHN LAWRENCE, author; b. Rochester, N.Y., July 28, 1927; s. Chester Frederick and Helen (Lawrence) A.; grad. Deerfield Acad., 1945; B.A. in English Lit., Harvard, 1949; M.A. in English Lit., Columbia, 1951; postgrad. in French lit. N.Y. U., 1957-58. Copywriter, Oxford U. Press, N.Y.C., 1951-54, McGraw Hill Book Co., N.Y.C., 1954-55; art critic European edit. N.Y. Herald Tribune, Paris, France, 1960-65, Art Internat., Lugano, Switzerland, 1961-64; editor Locus Solus, Lans-en-Vercors, France, 1960-62, Art and Lit., Paris, 1963-66; Paris corr. Art News, 1964-65, exec. editor, 1965-72; prof. English, co-dir. MFA program in creative writing Bklyn. Coll., 1974—; poetry editor Partisan Rev., 1976—; art critic New York mag., 1978—. spl. research life and work Raymond Roussel; author: (poems) Turandot and Other Poems, 1953, Some Trees, 1956, 70, The Poems, 1960, The Tennis Court Oath, 1962, Rivers and Mountains, 1966, 77, Selected Poems, 1967, Three Madrigals, 1968, Sunrise in Suburbia, 1968, Fragment, 1969, The Double Dream of Spring, 1970, 76, The New Spirit, 1970, (with Harwood and Raworth) Penguin Modern Poets 19, 1971, Three Poems, 1972, The Vermont Notebook, 1975, Self-Portrait in a Convex Mirror, 1975, Houseboat Days, 1977; (one-act plays) The Heroes, 1952, The Philosopher, 1964; (three-act play) The Compromise, 1956; (novel with James Schuyler) A Nest of Ninnies, 1969, 76; works represented in numerous anthologies; also author numerous articles art criticism, translations. Contbr. verse to lit. periodicals. Recipient Yale Series of Younger Poets prize, 1956; Harriet Monroe Poetry award Poetry Mag., 1963; also Union League Civic and Arts Found. prize, 1966; Nat. Inst. Arts and Letters award, 1969; Shelley award Poetry Soc. Am., 1973; Frank O'Hara prize Modern Poetry Assn., 1974; Harriet Monroe Poetry award U. Chgo., 1975; Nat. Book Critics Circle award for poetry, 1976; Nat. Book award for poetry, 1976; Pulitzer prize for poetry, 1976; Levinson prize for poetry, 1977; Fulbright scholar, Montpellier, France, 1955-56, Paris, France, 1956-57; Poets' Found grantee, 1960, 64; Ingram Merrill Found. grantee, 1962, 72; Guggenheim fellow, 1967, 73. Address: care Georges Borchardt Inc 136 E 57th St New York NY 10022

ASHBEY, WILLIAM NELSON, banker; b. Phila., June 27, 1932; s. William Nightingale and Edmee Kathryn (VanDyke) A.; B.S. in Econs., U. Pa., 1955; m. Julia Elizabeth Stimson Lovett, Mar. 2, 1957; children—Julia Stimson, Katharine VanDyke, Anne Avery. Trainee, Book of the Month Club, N.Y.C., 1958; editor Authenticated News, N.Y.C., 1958-59; investment adminstr. investment adv. div. Bankers Trust Co., N.Y.C., 1959-62, asst. sec., 1962-65, asst. v.p., 1965-69, v.p., 1969—, group head, 1971-76, group head personal investment mgmt. div., 1976-78, mem. product devel. and mktg. group, 1978—. Mem. adv. bd. Mental Retardation Inst., N.Y. Med. Coll., 1975-76; bd. dirs., sec. Hale Matthews Found., Inc., 1972—; bd. dirs. English-Speaking Union Monmouth County (N.J.), 1974—, treas., 1974-77, pres., 1977—; vestryman, chmn. fin. com. All Saints Meml. Ch., Navesink, N.J., 1974-77. Served to lt. (j.g.) USN, 1955-58. Republican. Episcopalian. Club: Seabright Beach. Home: High Point Cottage Chapel Hill Atlantic Highlands NJ 07716 also 350 E 62d St New York City NY 10021 Office: 280 Park Ave New York City NY 10017

ASHBY, CECIL EDWARD, JR., environ. services co. exec.; b. Cumberland, Md., Oct. 16, 1942; s. Cecil Edward and Valeria (Frazee) A.; B.S. in Chem. Engring., W.Va. U., 1965; m. Barbara June Jackson, Dec. 15, 1962; children—Cecil Edward III, Robert Dale. Asst. mgr. polymers ops. Shell Chem. Co., Deer Park, Tex., 1970-73; plant mgr. Logan br., Rollins Environ. Services Inc., Bridgeport, N.J., 1973-74, ops. mgr., 1975-76, v.p. Eastern region, 1977—; cons. engr. Active Boy Scouts Am. Registered profl. engr., N.J. Mem. Am. Inst. Chem. Engrs., Nat., N.J. socs. profl. engrs., Air Pollution Control Assn. Office: Box 221 Bridgeport NJ 08014

ASHDOWN, MARIE MATRANGA (MRS. CECIL SPANTON ASHDOWN, JR.), writer, lectr.; b. Mobile, Ala.; d. Dominick and Ave (Mallon) Matranga; student Maryville Coll. Sacred Heart, Springhill Coll.; m. Cecil Spanton Ashdown, Jr.; children—John Stephen Gartman, Vivian Marie Gartman, Cecil Spanton, Charles Coster. Feature star daily program Sta. WALA, also WALA-TV, Mobile; photographer, model for Louise Sheridan, Mobile; feature columnist Isle Dauphine News, Mobile; lectr. women's clubs, other orgns. Past mem. Am. Women in Radio and TV, Am. Businesswomen's Assn., Mobile. Bd. dirs. Met. Opera Guild. Recipient certificate merit for extraordinary service March of Dimes, 1958. Mem. Nat. Inst. Social Scis. Home: 25 Sutton Pl S New York City NY 10022

ASHE, AMELIA H. (MRS. DAVID I. ASHE), educator; b. Bklyn., Oct. 16, 1916; d. Isadore M. and Sophie (Yancovici) Haimowitz; B.A., Hunter Coll., 1938; M.A. in English, Bklyn. Coll., 1945, M.A. in Guidance and Counseling, 1955; Ph.D. in Guidance and Personnel, N.Y. U., 1966; m. Murray Wexler, June 20, 1937 (dec. 1961); children—Richard Mark, Susan Ellen (Mrs. Stuart Lahn); m. 2d, David I. Ashe, Dec. 26, 1962. Tchr. English, Far Rockaway High Sch., N.Y.C., 1948-59; guidance counselor Plainview (L.I.) High Sch., N.Y., 1959-63; supr. NDEA Inst. Counseling, Bklyn. Coll., summer 1963; instr. guidance and personnel dept. Sch. Edn., N.Y. U., 1963-67, field supr. NDEA Inst. on Guidance for Culturally Disadvantaged, 1963-64; asst. prof., coordinator grad. program in guidance and counseling Richmond Coll., City U. N.Y., 1967-69, asso. prof., 1970-74, prof. emeritus, 1974—; chmn. com. coordinators grad. programs in guidance and counseling City U. N.Y., 1971-74, dir. bilingual counselor edn. grad. program, 1974-75; cons. Center Urban Edn., N.Y. State Dept. Edn.; dir. Consortium for Bilingual Counselor Edn., 1972-75; mem. Bd. Edn. City N.Y., 1974—; mem. N.Y.C. Tchrs. Retirement Bd., 1978—. Mem. Am. Ednl. Research Assn., AAUP, Nat. Council Measurements Used in Edn., N.Y. Acad. Pub. Edn., Kappa Delta Pi, Alpha Epsilon Phi. Home: 1020 Park Ave New York City NY 10028 Office: Board of Education 110 Livingston St Brooklyn NY 11201

ASHE, CARL MALCOLM, engring. service corp. exec.; b. Phila., Nov. 14, 1926; s. Charles Malcolm and Louisa (Burrell) A.; LL.B., Blackstone Sch. Law, 1957; postgrad. Capitol Engring. Inst., 1964, Coll. Textiles and Sci., 1966, U. P.R., 1972, Villanova U., 1978; m. Awilda Batista, Sept. 11, 1971; children—Louis Xavier, Windy Aeleene. Enlisted U.S. Navy, 1943, advanced through grades to sr. chief; served submarine service, 1960-65, ret., 1965; mgr. quality assurance Progress Aerospace Enterprises Inc., Phila., 1968; mgr. measurement equipment labs. Gen. Electric Space Systems, Valley Forge, Pa., 1969-71; mgr. quality assurance Gen. Electric Co. offshore five subs., P.R., 1971-76; v.p. Pa. ops. Unified Industries Inc., Bala Cynwyd, 1976—; mem. ct. appeals Quality Control Center, govt. P.R., 1975-76; bd. dirs. Inst. Quality Control, 1975-76. Recipient Profl. Recognition Program award Gen. Electric Co., Valley Forge Space Center, 1969; NSF alt. fellow, 1965. Mem. IEEE, Am. Soc. Quality Control (sr. chmn. for P.R. 1973-75). Club: DAV. Office: One Bala Plaza Suite 218 Bala Cynwyd PA 19004

ASHLEY, MARIANNE ROSE, pharmacist; b. Flushing, N.Y., Mar. 8, 1948; d. William Michael and Mary Rose (Furey) A.; B.S. in Pharmacy, St. John's U., 1970. Staff pharmacist Plaza Apothecary, N.Y.C., 1971-72, N.Y. Hosp., N.Y.C., 1972-73, Macy's Queens Pharmacy, Elmhurst, N.Y., 1974-75; chief staff pharmacist Buffalo Psychiat. Center, 1976-77, chief pharmacist, 1977—. Health Professions grantee, 1968, 69. Mem. N.Y. Council Hosp. Pharmacists, N.Y. State Dept. Mental Hygiene Pharmacists Assn. Roman Catholic. Office: 400 Forest Ave Buffalo NY 14213

ASHMEN, ROY, educator; b. Camden, N.J., Oct. 15, 1910; s. Alex Jester and Carrie Metzger (Stadtler) A.; B.S. summa cum laude, Drexel U., 1935; M.S., Columbia U., 1936, profl. diploma, 1956; Ph.D., Northwestern U., 1950; m. Frances Rabun Vannerson, Apr. 8, 1944; children—Phyllis Anne (Mrs. Hugh Douglas Marron), Richard Barton. Instr., Okla. State U., 1940, U. Detroit, 1940-41, La. State U., 1941-42; prof., chmn. dept. Am. Grad. Sch. Internat. Mgmt., Phoenix, 1946-47; asso. prof., dept. chmn. U. Kans., 1947-49; prof., dept. chmn. Pace U., N.Y.C., 1950-52; supr., research account contact Young & Rubicam, Inc., N.Y.C., 1952-53; econ. analyst, supr. research and planning NBC, N.Y.C., 1953-58; asso. prof. mgmt. U. Md., College Park, 1958—. Cons. U.S. Dept. Commerce, USIA, FTC (all Washington); spl. tchr. Pentagon, Washington, 1958—. Mem. Am. Mktg. Assn. (v.p. D.C. 1970-71), C. of C. U.S., Nat. Distbn. Council, Am. Acad. Advt. (dean region 2 1964-65), Internat. Radio and Television Soc. (mem. adv. com. 1965-68), Broadcast Pioneers, Am. Econ. Assn., Nat. Assn. Bus. Economists, AAUP, Advt. Club N.Y. (clinic dir. 1952-58), Advt. Sportsman's Club N.Y. (pres., chmn. bd. 1955-57), Kappa Delta Pi (hon.), Alpha Delta Sigma (nat. Outstanding Service Award 1964), Delta Sigma Pi, Phi Delta Kappa, Beta Theta Pi. Contbr. articles to nat. publs. Home: 9010 St Andrews Pl College Park MD 20740 Office: U Md College Park MD 20742

ASHODIAN, MILA JEANETTE (MRS. HOWARD WILLIAM PAYNE), ophthalmologist; b. Providence, Aug. 21, 1925; d. Vahan and Sona (Bahchegulian) A.; A.B., Bryn Mawr Coll., 1945; M.D., Temple U., 1950; m. Howard William Payne; 1 dau., Barbara. Resident, Wills Eye Hosp., Phila., 1952-54, sr. asst. surgeon, 1971—; asso. opthalmologist Lankenau Hosp., Phila., 1954—; clin. instr. U. Pa. Grad. Sch. Medicine, 1956-60; asso. clin. prof. Pa. Med. Coll., 1964-72, Thomas Jefferson Med. U., 1974—. Fellow Am. Acad. Ophthalmology and Otolaryngology, A.C.S.; mem. Am. Med. Women's Assn. (treas. br.), Phila. Club of Med. Women. Club: Phila. Skating. Home: 1014 Centennial Rd Narberth PA 19072 Office: Lankenau Med Bldg Philadelphia PA 19151

ASHTON, DAVID JOHN, educator; b. Somerville, Mass., June 29, 1921; s. Albert Carter and E. Edna (Spry) A.; B.S., Tufts Coll., 1942, M.B.A., Boston U., 1950; M.A., Fletcher Sch. Law and Diplomacy, 1952, Ph.D., 1959; m. Grace Christine Higgins, June 21, 1943; children—Leslie Jean (Mrs. John Koles), Jeffrey Carter, John Mark. Instr., asst. prof. Coll. Bus. Adminstrn., Boston U., 1947-59, asso. prof., 1959-61, prof., 1961—; editor Boston U. Bus. Review, 1958-59; chmn. Internat. Bus. Curriculum, 1958-64, chmn. dept. Internat. Bus., 1964-68, internat. curriculum coordinator, 1968—; mng. dir. Boston U., Brussels, Belgium, 1972-74, 77-78; vis. lectr. U. Libre de Bruxelles, 1972-74; econ. cons. U.S. Naval War Coll., 1963-64, vis. lectr. 1964-65; eocn. and fin. cons. U.S. Dept. Commerce, Fed. Res. Bank of Boston, Ednl. Testing Service, Internat. Exec. Service Corps, New Eng. Econ. Research Found., New Eng. Regional Commn. Mem. Arlington (Mass.) Bd. Pub. Edn., 1955-58, chmn. bd., 1957-58; mem. Planning Bd., Arlington, 1959-62; mem. Tufts Alumni Council, 1959—, mem. exec. com., 1959-62; mem. exec. bd. Fletcher Sch. Alumni Assn., 1958-65; mem. Mass. Gov.'s Adv. Council on Internat. Trade, 1964; mem. Winchester (Mass) Town Meeting, 1964-70, 76—; vice chmn. Town Govt. Study Commn., 1968-70; mem. Town Mgr. Selection Com., 1975. Bd. dirs. Found. for Advancement of Edn. in Internat. Bus., 1962—; Income Fund Boston, Internat. Center New Eng. Served to lt. USNR, 1942-45. Decorated chevalier Order of Leopold II (Belgium); recipient George L. Plimpton Alumni award Tilton Sch., 1976. Mem. Am. Econ. Assn., Nat. Planning Assn., Am. Acad. Polit. and Social Sci., Assn. Edn. Internat. Bus., Am. Arbitration Assn., Delta Tau Delta, Beta Gamma Sigma, Alpha Kappa Psi. Author: New England Manfacturers and European Investments, 1963; The International Component in England's Economic Base, 1968; New England's Exports of Manufactures, 1975; Business Services and New England's Export Base, 1978; also numerous articles in field. Editorial bd. The International Executive. Home: 22 Myrtle St Winchester MA 01890 Office: 685 Commonwealth Ave Boston MA 02215

ASHTON, JOHN K., JR., computer engring. exec.; b. New Paltz, N.Y., Jan. 28, 1927; s. John K. and Elizabeth Ellen (Elliott) A.; B.A., State U. N.Y., New Paltz, 1965; m. Gloria Margaret Seidel, Nov. 20, 1953; children—Laurence, Linda, Robert. Designer, Pratt & Whitney Div., United Aircraft Corp., East Hartford, Conn., 1950-51; with IBM Corp., Poughkeepsie, N.Y., 1951—, project engr., 1972—. Trustee New Paltz Central Schs. Bd. Edn., 1956-62, 72-75. Served with USAAF, 1945-47. Mem. IEEE (internat. tech. com. on fault tolerant computing), Am. Inst. Aeronautics and Astronautics. Home: 542 Albany Post Rd New Paltz NY 12561 Office: Data Systems Div IBM Corp PO Box 390 Poughkeepsie NY 12602

ASKENASY, ALEXANDER ROBERT, social psychologist; b. Frankfurt am Main, Germany; s. Robert Leon Kurt and Dorothea (Wernecke) A.; came to U.S., 1947, naturalized, 1953; B.A., U. Wis., 1950; A.M., Princeton U., 1954; Ph.D., Columbia U., 1962. Research asso. Psychol. Research Assos., Arlington, Va., 1956-58; project co-dir. World Fedn. Mental Health, N.Y.C., 1959-62; asso. prof. in research Am. U., Washington, 1963-69; research scientist N.Y. State Psychiat. Inst., N.Y.C., 1969—; research asso. in psychiatry Columbia U., N.Y.C., 1977-78, asst. prof. psychiatry, 1978—; field research, Peru, Germany, Belgium, Eng., Hawaii. Served with AUS, 1954-56. Walker fellow, 1951-52. Mem. Internat. Assn. Cross-Cultural Psychology, Internat., Am. sociol. assns., Soc. for Psychol. Study of Social Issues, AAUP, World Assn. Pub. Opinion Research, Am., Eastern psychol. assns., World Fedn. Mental Health. Author: Attitudes toward Mental Patients: A Study across Cultures, 1974; Perception of Korean Opinions, 1969; (with B.P. Dohrenwend and B.S. Dohrenwend) Effects of Social Class and Ethnic Group on Judgments of Stressful Life Events, 1977; also monographs on cross-cultural subjects, articles in profl. jours.; presented papers at internat. sci. congresses. Home: 900 W 190th St New York City NY 10040 Office: 722 W 168th St New York City NY 10032

ASKEW, L(OUIE) RUDOLPH, sci. instrument exec.; b. Columbus, Ga., Oct. 12, 1937; s. Louie Elford and Davie Alene (Lawson) A.; B. Chem. Engring., U. Va., 1961; m. Dorothy Patricia Murray, Dec. 5, 1964; children—Eric Fleming, Mary Gillian, Virginia Lawson, Henry Goddard. Quality control engr. U.S. Naval Propellant Plant, Indian Head, Md., 1961-62; mem. tech. sales staff Fisher Sci. Co., Silver Springs, Md., 1962-66; regional mgr. Varian Assos., Houston, 1966-71; product mgr. Instrumentation Lab. Inc., Lexington, Mass., 1971-74; dir. mktg. Environ. Scis. Assos., Bedford, Mass., 1974—. Mem. Am. Chem. Soc., Am. Inst. Chem. Engrs., Profl. Photographers Assn. Home: 1 Indian Hill Rd Winchester MA 01890 Office: 45 Wiggins Ave Bedford MA 01730

ASKINS, ARTHUR JAMES, bus. services co. exec.; b. Phila., Dec. 2, 1944; s. William and Rita (O'Brien) A.; B.S., LaSalle Coll., 1967; M.Ed., Rider Coll., 1971. Tchr. high sch., Phila., 1967-69; sr. staff accountant various pub. accounting firms, Jenkintown, Pa., 1969-74; staff McGinnis Assos., fin. cons., Pitman, N.J. and Phila., 1967—; asst. to controller Hankin Enterprises, Willow Grove, Pa., 1975—. Polit. campaign coordinator various Republican candidates, 1965—, state del. Young Rep. State Conv., 1965, 67, nat. del., 1966. C.P.A. Mem. Nat. Assn. Accountants, Am. Inst. C.P.A.'s, Am. Accounting Assn., Pa. Inst. C.P.A.'s. Roman Catholic. Club: K.C. Home: 43 B Maplewood Dr Mapleshade NJ 08052 Office: 140 S Broadway Pitman NJ 08071

ASLAKSEN, CARROLL, utility exec.; b. Bklyn., Sept. 18, 1926; s. Einar and Anna Caroline (Hansen) A.; B.S. in E.E., Okla. State U., 1950; certificate U. Mich., 1962, Columbia, 1964; m. Anna Marie Smalley, Sept. 3, 1950; children—Carl Edward, Karen Anne. Jr. engr. City Pub. Service Bd., San Antonio, 1950-52; asst. engr. Jersey Central Power & Light Co., Morristown, N.J., 1952-56, engr., 1956-61, asst. transmission engr., 1961-63, transmission engr., 1963-66, transmission and distbn. engr., 1966-70, asst. v.p., 1970-72, v.p., 1972—, also dir. Municipal councilman, Chester, N.J., 1970-72, 75-76, mem. municipal planning bd., 1970-74, mem. municipal bd. adjustment, 1964-70, municipal committeeman, 1962-64. Trustee Upper Raritan Watershed Assn. Served with AUS, 1944-46. Mem. I.E.E.E., Eta Kappa Nu, Sigma Tau, Scabbard & Blade, Tau Kappa Epsilon. Republican. Home: East Fox Chase Rd Chester NJ 07930 Office: Madison at Punch Bowl Rd Morristown NJ 07960

ASSAEL, HENRY, educator; b. Sofia, Bulgaria, Sept. 12, 1935; s. Stanley Isaac and Anna (Behar) A.; B.A. cum laude, Harvard U., 1957; M.B.A., U. Pa., 1959; Ph.D., Columbia, 1965; m. Alyce Friedman, Aug. 19, 1961; children—Shaun Eric, Brenda Erica. Asst. prof. mktg. Sch. Bus., St. John's U., Jamaica, N.Y., 1962-65, Hofstra U., Hempstead, N.Y., 1965-66; prof. mktg. Grad. Sch. Bus. Adminstrn., N.Y. U., 1966—; cons. AT&T, N.Y. Stock Exchange, Nestle Co., Inc., Reuben H. Donnelley Co., Chilton Research Services, Ogilvy-Mather Advt., Am. Can. Co. Mem. Am. Mktg. Assn., Assn. Consumer Research. Author: Educational Preparations for Positions in Advertising Management, 1966; The Politics of Distributive Trade Associations: A Study in Conflict Resolution, 1967; also numerous articles; editor: The History and Development of Marketing Thought, 1978; Early Development and Conceptualization of the Field of Marketing, 1978. Home: 110-45 Queens Blvd Forest Hills NY 11375 Office: 100 Trinity Pl New York City NY 10006

ASSATOURIAN, ALICE HUSISIAN (MRS. HAIG GOURJI KHAN ASSATOURIAN), editing co. exec., cons., critic, lectr.; b. Batoum, Russia, Oct. 15, 1920; d. Leon Nishan and Araxi (Zorian) Husisian; came to U.S., 1923, naturalized, 1944; diploma in gen. edn. and sec. sci. with honors Boston U., 1940; student Clark U., 1943-45; B.S. in English, Columbia U., 1964; M.A., N.Y. U., 1966; m. Haig Gourji Khan Assatourian, Oct. 26, 1946; children—Seta, Sona, Lora. 1st violinist, v.p. Worcester (Mass.) Philharmonic Orch., 1936-43; 1st violinist Phil Spitalny's All-Girl Orch., Springfield, Mass., 1940-41; exec. asst. to pres. Clark U.; research asst. to pres. RKO Film Corp., Worcester, 1943-46; mem. conf. services dept. UN, N.Y.C., 1955-57; co-owner Profl. Editing & Typing Services, N.Y.C., 1957—; cons., lectr. writing and manuscript preparation, 1957—. Instr. swimming YWCA, Worcester, 1942-44; dist. commr. Girl Scouts U.S.A., 1962-64; patron, mem. com. Internat. Debutante Ball, N.Y.C., 1972—. Recipient Spl. award for outstanding services Greater N.Y. council Girl Scouts U.S.A., 1967; 1st place award for mixed doubles Peter Cooper Paddle Tennis Tournament, 1972. Mem. Armenian Gen. Benevolent Union (adviser N.Y. chpt.), Internat. House N.Y. (life), Constantinople Armenian Relief Soc. (cotillian chairwoman N.Y.C. 1970-72), Nat. Assn. for Armenian Studies and Research, Nat. Soc. Lit. and Arts, Armenian Profl. Adv. Council (charter mem., sec.), Modern Lang. Assn. Am. (leader seminar on Non-Slavic peoples of Soviet Union at ann. conv. N.Y.C. 1976), Am. Soc. for Study of Peoples of Eastern Europe and No. and Central Asia (charter mem., sec.-treas.), Daus. Vartan (grand recorder, grand council 1971-73, gen. chairwoman 34th ann. conv. N.Y.C. 1974, matron Ani chpt. 1974-75, grand matron 1975-76, author procedure manuals). Editor: (with Haig Gourji Khan Assatourian) Children and Their Literature, 1969; numerous doctoral dissertations and books on edn. and the humanities. Home: 410 E 20th St New York City NY 10009

ASSATOURIAN, HAIG GOURJI KHAN, research cons., critic, editor; b. Teheran, Iran, Sept. 19, 1911; s. Gourji Khan and Gayaneh (Asdvatzadourian) A.; came to U.S., 1930, naturalized, 1943; A.B., Coll. of Emporia, 1933; M.A., Columbia, 1936; M.B.A., N.Y.U., 1954; m. Alice Husisian, Oct. 26, 1946; children—Seta Assatourian Buchter, Sona Assatourian Davidian, Lora Assatourian. Pres., designer Haig-Howard Corp., N.Y.C., 1947-50; gen. plant mgr. Roman Silversmiths, Inc., 1950-51; pres. Haig Giftware Co., N.Y.C., 1951-56; gen. plant mgr. Laminated Fiberglass Corp. Am., 1956-60; co-owner, operator Profl. Editing & Typing Services, N.Y.C., 1960—; co-leader with Alice Assatoarian, Non-Slavic Peoples of Soviet Union Seminar, Modern Lang. Assn. Am. Ann. Conv., N.Y.C., 1976, 78 Chgo., 1977. Mem. Primate's ways and means com. Diocese Armenian Ch., St. Vartan Cathedral, N.Y.C.; v.p. N.Y. chpt. Armenian Gen. Benevolent Union, 1969, 75—, treas. Eastern dist. com., 1975—, adviser N.Y. chpt., 1978—; publicity dir. Constantinople Armenian Relief Soc., 1971; patron, com. mem. Internat. Debutante Ball, N.Y.C., 1972—. Served with USAAF, World War II; ETO. Mem. Acad. Polit. Sci., Am. Acad. Polit. and Social Scis., Am. Judicature Soc., Modern Lang. Assn. Am., Nat. Assn. Armenian Studies and Research, Armenian Lit. Soc. (hon. dir.), N.Y. Internat. House Alumni (life mem., dir.), UN Assn. N.Y., Armenian Assembly, Armenian Profl. Adv. Council, Am. Soc. for Study of Peoples of Eastern Europe and No. and Central Asia (charter mem., pres.). Clubs: Etchmiadzin Lodge (comdr. 1971-73); Knights of Vartan (gen. chmn. 56th nat. convocation 1974) (N.Y.C.); Mid-Atlantic Interlodge Conf. (chmn. 1975-76). Author articles. Editor, research cons. Children and Their Literature, 1969. Home: 410 E 20th St New York City NY 10009

ASTA, PATRICIA ELLEN, counseling adminstr.; b. Port Chester, N.Y., July 5, 1945; d. David Norbert and Rita Julia (West) A.; B.S. in Psychology magna cum laude (coll. scholar), C. W. Post Coll., 1967; M.S. (scholar), U. Bridgeport, 1969; M.A. in Counseling (scholar), U. So. Calif. 1972; postgrad. bus. mgmt. Pace U., 1973—. Dir., Pirmasens (Ger.) Nursery Sch., 1969; ednl. adminstr. U.S. VA, Kaiserslautern, Germany, 1970-73; asso. dir. counseling Pace U., Pleasantville, N.Y., 1973-75; dir. counseling, tng. and edn. Wildcat Service Corp., N.Y.C., 1975-76; asso. dir. N.J. Job Corps, Edison, 1976-78; mktg. account exec. mgmt. devel. program AT&T Long Lines, Parsippany, N.J., 1978—; instr. psychology, bus., edn. depts. Pace U.; trainer staff devel. ITEL Corp. Cons., group leader YWCA, N. Brunswick, 1977—; mem. town council, Port Chester, N.Y., Pres's. Commn. on Employment of Handicapped; speaker bus. mgmt. classes, civic, ch. groups. Recipient cash award Planned Parenthood, 1967; scholar N.Y. State Regents, 1963-67, Iowa Grad. Sch. Bus. Adminstrn., 1967; certified life skills educator, guidance counselor, therapist, vocat. rehab. counselor. Mem. Am. Personnel and Guidance Assn., Am. Psychol. Assn., Nat. Vocat. Guidance Assn., Assn. Measurement in Edn. and Guidance, Nat. Assn. Student Personnel Adminstrs., Am. Soc. Tng. and Devel., Met. Mental Health Assn. (exec. bd. 1975-78), Sexuality Info. and Ednl. Council, Pub. Offender Counselor Assn., Am. Assn. Higher Edn., AAUW, Nat. Assn. Women Deans and Counselors, Am. Assn. Group Workers, Assn. Humanistic Psychologists, Nat. Assn. Bus. and Profl. Women, N.J. Mental Health Assn., Mid-Hudson Affirmative Action Task Force, Mu Alpha Theta, Psi Chi, Sigma Tau Delta, Pi Gamma Mu. Club: Mensa. Author: Test Your Vocational Aptitude, 1976; How to Score High on the PACE Exam, 1978; contbr. articles to profl. jours. in field; contbr. papers to confs. Address: 5 Byram Ave Dove NJ 07801

ASTARJIAN, NUBAR KRIKOR, surgeon; b. Mosul, Iraq, Dec. 29, 1929; s. Krikor Abraham and Zabel Alexan (Kouyoumdjian) A.; came to U.S., 1960, naturalized, 1970; diploma Baghdad Coll., 1948; M.B., Ch.B., U. Baghdad, 1954; m. Sandra Hintlian Astarjian, Feb. 1, 1975; 1 son, Ara Nubar. Intern, Norwalk (Conn.) Hosp., 1960; resident Columbia U.-Presbyn. and Bellevue hosps., N.Y.C., 1961-65; instr. surgery Columbia U., 1966-68; practice medicine specializing in surgery, Binghamton, N.Y., 1968-76; chief surgery Wilson Hosp., 1975-76; physician, surgeon Gen. Electric Co., Lynn, Mass., 1976—. Diplomate Am. Bd. Surgery. Fellow A.C.S.; mem. AMA, Mass., Essex South med. socs., Armenian Am. Med. Soc. Contbr. articles to profl. jours. Home: 38 Wildewood Dr Lynnfield MA 01940 Office: Bldg 14402 1100 Western Ave Lynn MA 01910

ASTLES, GEOFFREY CLARK, county ofcl.; b. Rochester, N.Y., Oct. 18, 1948; s. Dean Westwood and Mary Elizabeth (Brundage) A.; B.A. in History and Govt., Otterbein Coll., 1970; postgrad. Akron U., 1970-72; m. Janice Marie Ciampa, Feb. 17, 1973. Student intern Civil Service personnel office City of Akron (Ohio), 1971, pub. works dept., 1972; planning technician County of Huntingdon (Pa.), 1972-73; planning dir. Orleans County (N.Y.), 1974—; vis. tchr. Brockport (N.Y.) State U. Bd. dirs. Council on Arts, 1975—, Health Systems Agy. Western N.Y., 1976-77. Home: 163 Clarendon St Albion NY 14411 Office: 151 Platt St Albion NY 14411

ASTON, SHERRELL JERONE, plastic surgeon; b. Nansemond County, Va., July 14, 1942; s. Walter Mathew and Mary Louise (Bracy) A.; B.A., U. Va., 1964, M.D., 1968; m. Michell Sykes, Nov. 24, 1967; children—Walter Mathew III, Sherrell Jerone. Intern, U. Calif. at Los Angeles, 1968-69, resident, chief resident in surgery, 1969-73; Halsted fellow Johns Hopkins Hosp., 1971; resident, chief resident in plastic surgery N.Y.U., 1973-75; chief plastic surgery service Manhattan VA Hosp., 1975—; asso. prof. surgery N.Y. U. Med. Center, 1977—; asso. attending surgeon Inst. Reconstructive Plastic Surgery, N.Y. U. Med. Center, Manhattan Eye, Ear and Throat Hosp., Bellevue Hosp. Diplomate Am. Bd. Surgery, Am. Bd. Plastic Surgery. Fellow ACS, N.Y. Acad. Medicine, Am. Soc. Plastic and Reconstructive Surgery; mem. N.Y. State, N.Y. County med. socs., Soc. Academic Surgeons, Pan Am. Med. Assn. Author numerous surg. publs. Home: 765 Park Ave New York City NY 10021 Office: 176 E 72d St New York City NY 10021

ASUNCION, CELEDONIO MANUEL, pathologist; b. Tarlac, Philippines, Mar. 3, 1928; s. Pedro and Fausta (Manuel) A.; M.D., U. Philippines, 1955; m. Katherine Matthews, Oct. 28, 1961; children—Chris, Keith, Leithia, Stacy. Intern, Mt. Sinai Hosp., Hartford, Conn., 1958-59; resident in pathology St. Mary and Elizabeth Hosp., Louisville, Ky., 1959-61; fellow in pathology Meth. Hosp., Gary, Ind., 1961-63; instr. Chgo. Med. Sch., 1962-63; fellow in pathology Ottawa Civic Hosp., Can., 1963-64; asst. pathologist St. Francis Hosp., Hartford, Conn., 1965-70, asso. pathologist, 1970—, now dir. dept. cytology-cytogenetics; asst. prof. U. Conn. Med. Sch., 1971—. Bd. dirs. Am. Cancer Soc., Hartford, Conn., 1974—; chmn. pub. edn. com. Diplomate Am. Bd. Pathology. Mem. Am. Soc. Clin. Pathologists, Am. Soc. Cytology, Conn. Cytology Assn. (chmn. edn. com.), Conn. State, Hartford County med. assns., Conn. Soc. Pathologists, Assn. Philippines Practicing Physicians Am. Democrat. Roman Catholic. Club: K.C. Office: 114 Woodland St Hartford CT 06105

ASUNCION, JACOBO ROSALES, JR., surgeon, educator; b. Legaspy City, Philippines, June 12, 1932; s. Jacobo Ramirez and Trinidad (Rosales) A.; came to Can., 1961, naturalized, 1971; A.A., U. Philippines, 1949; M.D., C.M., U. Santo Tomas, Philippines, 1956; diploma in anatomy (fellow), Queen's U., Kingston, Ont., Can., 1964; m. Erlinda Yniesta Obellos, Feb. 9, 1963; children—Michael Anthony, Paul Daniel. Intern, Homer G. Phillips Hosp., St. Louis, 1956-57, resident in surgery, 1957-58; resident urology Washington U., St. Louis, 1958-60, chief resident urology, 1960-61; sr. surg. resident Winnipeg Gen. Hosp., Can., 1962-63, chief resident pediatric surgery, 1963; teaching fellow in anatomy Queen's U., 1963-64; lectr. in anatomy Dalhousie U., Halifax, N.S., Can., 1964-66, prof. anatomy Faculty of Medicine, 1966—, Faculty of Dentistry, 1966—, curator Richard L. de C.H. Saunders Med. Mus., 1967—; instr. pub. speaking, human relations and leadership tng. Mgmt. Devel. Center, Warren Adams & Assos., Halifax, 1970—. Founder, pres., bd. dirs., chmn. Filipino Assn. of N.S., 1968-69, 73-74, chmn. standing com. on constn. and by-laws, 1969—, chmn. nominating com., 1976-77; project dir. The Filipino Music Revival, 1975-76; band mgr. Filipino Band of Filipino Assn. N.S., 1975-76. Recipient Distinguished Service award United Council of Filipino Assns. in Can., 1973, Most Outstanding Filipino in Can. award, 1974, Filipino of the Year award Filipino Assn. of N.S., 1975; Canadian govt. grantee, 1975. Diplomate Am. Bd. Urology. Mem. Can. Assn. Anatomists, Dalhousie Research Assn., N.S., St. Thomas Aquinas ednl. assns., Can. Fedn. Biol. Socs., Can. Assn. U. Tchrs., Dalhousie, Santo Tomas U. alumni assns., Filipino Assn. N.S. (chmn. membership com. 1977-78), Fiesta Filipino Exec. Council (social dir., master ceremonies 1978), NW Arm Planning Assn., Filipino Assn. of N.S. Inc. (adviser, dir. 1978—), Phi Xenian Med. Soc., Tau Mu Sigma Phi, Phi Chi. Roman Catholic. Club: K.C. (certificate of recognition 1975). Author course outline series in anatomy, 1967—. Home: 46 Inverness Halifax NS B3P 1X7 Canada Office: Sir Charles Tupper Medical Bldg Faculty of Medicine Dalhousie Univ Halifax NS B3H 4H7 Canada

ATKINS, CHARLES AGEE, investment banker; b. Ashland, Ky., Apr. 25, 1954; s. Orin Ellsworth and Kathryn (Agee) A.; B.A., U. N.C., 1975; M.Sc., London Sch. Econs. and Polit. Sci., 1977, Ph.D., 1978. Internat. economist Ashland Oil, Inc., part-time 1974-75; corp. fin. acco. Lehman Bros., London, part-time 1975-77; fellow Brookings Instn., Washington, 1977-78; gen. partner Securities Group, N.Y.C., 1978—. John Motley Morehead scholar, 1972-75; George C. Marshall scholar, 1975-77; Brookings fellow, 1977-78. Mem. Am. Econs. Assn., Am. Fin. Assn., Royal Inst. Internat. Affairs, Phi Beta Kappa. Republican. Presbyterian. Home: 120 E 75th St New York NY 10021 Office: 375 Park Ave New York City NY 10022

ATKINSON, EUGENE V., Congressman; b. Aliquippa, Pa., Apr. 5, 1927; student U. Pitts. Prin., Atkinson Agy., gen. ins.; dir. customs Port of Pitts., 1962-69; mem. 96th Congress from 25th Pa. dist. Pa. Democratic state committeeman, 1956-72; chmn. Beaver County Dem. party, 1969-77; Beaver County commr., 1972-78. Served with USN. Office: 419 Cannon House Office Bldg Washington DC 20515*

ATKINSON, HAROLD WITHERSPOON, cons. engr., former utility co. exec.; b. Lake City, S.C., June 12, 1914; s. Leland G. and Kathleen (Dunlap) A.; B.E.E., Duke U., 1934; M.S. in Engring., Harvard U., 1935; m. Pickett Rancke, Oct. 6, 1946; children—Henry Leland, Harold Witherspoon. Various positions in sales, engring. Cambridge Electric Light Co. (Mass.), 1935-39, 46-73, asst. mgr. power sales dept., 1946-49, gen. mgr., 1957-68, v.p., 1959-71, exec. v.p., 1971-73, dir., 1959—; mgr. Pee Dee Electric Membership Corp., Wadesboro, N.C., 1939-46; gen. mgr. Cambridge Steam Corp., 1951-59, v.p., 1959-73, dir. 1955—; pvt. cons. engr., 1973—; former mem. corp. Cambridge Savs. Bank; former dir. Electric Inst., Inc., Boston, pres., 1971; former dir. Canal Electric Co., NEGEA. Service Corp. Chmn. Cambridge chpt. ARC, 1969-71; corporate mem., mem. planning and resources com. United Community Services Greater Boston, chmn. allocations com., 1970-71; past corporate mem. Mt. Auburn Hosp., Lesley Coll.; pres. Cambridge Community Services, 1955-56, Cambridge Center Adult Edn. 1962-64; v.p. Cambridge Mental Health Assn.; chmn. Cambridge Traffic Bd., 1961-73; mem. adv. bd. Cambridge council Boy Scouts Am.; mem. corp. Cambridge YMCA, chmn. camp com., 1964-71; bd. dirs. Greater Boston Ednl. Exchange; trustee Trust Funds Town of Harrisville (N.H.); mem. electric council New Eng. Com. on Load Mgmt. Served from pvt. to capt., AUS, 1942-45. Mem. Harvard Engring. Soc., IEEE (sr.), Cambridge C. of C. (pres. 1957-58), Newcomen Soc. N.Am., Nat., Mass. socs. profl. engrs., Phi Beta Kappa, Tau Beta Pi, Pi Mu Epsilon. Clubs: Rotary (pres. Cambridge 1960-61). (Keene); Cambridge Boat, Cambridge (pres. 1971-72); Union (Boston); Civitan (pres. Wadesboro 1940-41); Keene (N.H.) Country. Address: PO Box 125 Harrisville NH 03450

ATKINSON, RICHARD CHATHAM, exptl. psychologist, educator, found. exec.; b. Oak Park, Ill., Mar. 19, 1929; s. Herbert and Margaret (Feuerbach) A.; Ph.B., U. Chgo., 1948; Ph.D., Ind. U., 1955; m. Rita Loyd, Aug. 20, 1952; 1 dau., Lynn Loyd. Lectr. applied math., stats. labs. Stanford (Calif.) U., 1956-57, asso. prof., 1961-64, prof., 1964—, chmn. dept. psychology, 1969-74; asst. prof. psychology U. Calif., Los Angeles, 1957-61; dir. NSF, Washington, 1977—. Served with AUS, 1954-56. Guggenheim fellow, 1967; Center for Advanced Study in Behavioral Scis. fellow, 1963; recipient Distinguished Research award Social Sci. Research Council, 1962. Fellow Am. Acad. Arts and Scis., Am. Psychol. Assn. (pres. exptl. div. 1974, Distinguished Sci. Contbn. award 1977), AAAS (chmn. psychology sect. 1975); mem. Soc. Exptl. Psychologists, Nat. Acad. Scis., Nat. Acad. Edn., Inst. Medicine, Psychonomic Soc. (chmn. 1973), Western Psychol. Assn. (pres. 1975), Psychometric Soc., Sigma Xi. Clubs: Cosmos (Washington); Explorers (N.Y.C.). Author: (with Hilgard and Atkinson) Introduction to Psychology, 7th edit., 1979, Computer Assisted Instruction, 1969; (with Bower and Crothers) An Introduction to Mathematical Learning Theory, 1965; Studies in Mathematical Psychology, 1964; (with Krantz, Luce and Suppes) Contemporary Developments in Mathematical Psychology, 1974; Progress in Psychology, 1975. Home: 2230 California St NW Washington DC 20008 Office: Nat Sci Found 1800 G St NW Washington DC 20550

ATKINSON, RUSSELL WELSH, mfg. co. exec.; b. Somerville, N.J., Sept. 22, 1947; s. Russell Edward and Betty Ramsey (Welsh) A.; B.A. in Mktg., Baldwin-Wallace Coll., Berea, Ohio, 1969; m. Elizabeth Camerden Austin, Oct. 3, 1970; children—Geoffrey Martin, Jamie Lynne. With Affiliated Mfrs., Inc., 1969—, sales mgr., N. Branch., N.J., 1972-77, v.p. mktg., 1977—; v.p., dir. Serigraphico Inc., Wichita Falls, Tex., 1977—, AMI West, Inc., Sun Valley, Calif., 1976—. Mem. Internat. Soc. Hybrid Microelectronics, (chpt. vice chmn.). Author, patentee microelectronic devices. Address: RD 7 Barley Sheaf Rd Flemington NJ 08822

ATKYNS, GLENN CHADWICK, educator; b. Washington, Apr. 26, 1921; s. Willie Lee and Marion Amelia (Van Horn) A.; A.B. cum laude in History, Harvard U., 1948, M.A. in Teaching, 1949; Ph.D., U. Conn., 1958; m. Syme Margaret Vaataja, Dec. 9, 1945; children—Robert Lee, Suzanne. Tchr. social studies W. Hartford Pub. Schs., 1949-59; dir. tchr. edn. U. Conn., Storrs, 1959-64, 65-66; acting dean, 1964-65; chmn. dept. higher tech., adult edn., 1967—; edn. cons. to Rep. of Vietnam AID Nat. Edn. Study Team, 1967; cons. faculty to U.S. Army Command and Gen. Staff Coll., 1969-72; chmn. evaluation teams Nat. Council Accreditation Tchr. Edn., 1966-71. Justice of peace Town of Newington (Conn.), 1955-59, mem. charter revision com., 1959, sec. Democratic Town Com., 1953-59; bd. mgrs. Conn. Baptist Conv., 1966-69. Served to capt. U.S. Army, 1941-46. Decorated Legion of Merit; recipient Distinguished Service award Rep. of Vietnam; named Phi Delta Kappa fellow of year U. Conn., 1974; U.S. Office Edn. grantee, 1969-72. Mem. World Edn. Fellowship (dir. U.S. sect. 1975-78), Am. Assn. Higher Edn., Internat. Edn. Soc., History of Edn. Soc., Orgn. Am. Historians, Assn. Study of Higher Edn., NEA, Phi Delta Kappa. Club: U. Conn. Contbr. articles in field to profl. jours. Home: 83 Brookside Ln Mansfield Center CT 06250 Office: Dept Higher Tech and Adult Edn U Conn Storrs CT 06268

ATKYNS, ROBERT LEE, behavioral scientist; b. Boston, Jan. 20, 1948; s. Glenn C. and Syme M. (Vataja) A.; B.A., Rutgers U., 1971; M.A., U. Conn., 1974; postgrad. Temple U., 1975—. Grad. asst. Communication Div. U. Conn., Storrs, 1971-73; communications researcher drug abuse info. research project, 1971-74; instr. U. Conn., Hartford, 1973-74; health care analyst South Philadelphia Health Action/The Phila. Health Plan, 1974-76, asst. dir. for research and evaluation, 1976-78, dir. research and evaluation, 1978—; cons. to hosps. and industry, 1975—. Mem. Internat. Communication Assn., Am. Assn. Pub. Opinion Research, AAAS, Am. Pub. Health Assn., Am. Acad. Polit. and Social Sci., Group Health Assn. Am., Pa. Evaluation Network. Contbr. to profl. jours. and confs. Home: 120 Webster Ave Wyncote PA 19095 Office: Phila Health Plan 1015 Chestnut St Philadelphia PA 19107

ATLAS, STEVEN ALAN, physician; b. N.Y.C., Sept. 3, 1946; s. Louis and Lillian (Weinberger) A.; student George Washington U., 1964-66; A.B., Johns Hopkins U., 1968, M.D., 1971. Intern and asst. physician, N.Y. Hosp.-Cornell Med. Center, Meml. Sloan Kettering Cancer Center, N.Y.C., 1971-73; research asso. NIH, Bethesda, Md., 1973-75, clin. pharmacologist, 1975-76; instr. in medicine Hypertension Center N.Y. Hosp.-Cornell Med. Center, 1976-77; asst. attending physician, N.Y. Hosp., N.Y.C., 1977—; asst. prof. medicine, Cornell U. Med. Coll., N.Y.C., 1978—; cons. Nat. Heart, Lung and Blood Inst. Served with USPHS, 1973-76. Diplomate Am. Bd. Internal Medicine. Mem. Am. Fedn. Clin. Research, Johns Hopkins Med. and Surg. Assn., A.C.P., The Harvey Soc. Democrat. Jewish. Contbr. research articles in field to profl. pubs. Home: 1161 York Ave New York City NY 10021 Office: 525 E 68th St New York City NY 10021

ATOR, GEORGE JACOB, research co. exec.; b. Hazleton, Pa., Sept. 10, 1935; s. John Daniel and Adelaide (Skoff) A.; B.S., Pa. State U., 1958; postgrad. Duquesne U., 1961—; m. Mary Ann Welkie, June 27, 1959; children—Brian, Mark. Tech. fieldman Equitable Gas Co., Pitts., 1958-60; glass sales forecaster Pitts. Plate Glass Industries, 1960-64; research asso., sales officer Western Pa. Nat. Bank, Pitts., 1964-68; v.p., dir. Feldman & Kahn, Inc., Pitts., 1968-75; pres. Group One Research, Inc., 1976—, Econ. & Market Research Co.; lectr. Grad. Sch. Savs. Banking, Brown U., 1970, 73; instr. mktg. mgmt. U. Mo./SIMSA Mktg. Mgmt. Inst., also U. Mo./Credit Union Execs. Soc. Mktg. Inst.; lectr. U. Mo. confs. and short courses; speaker various fin. instn. trade assns. including Conn., N.Y. savs. bank assns., U.S. Savs. and Loan League, savs. and loan trade assns. in Brazil, others. Ann. mem. United Fund Allegheny County. Chmn. Young Republicans of Baldwin-Whitehall, Pitts., 1961. Bd. dirs. Central Blood Bank of Pitts.; Served with USNR, 1952-60. Licensed pvt. pilot. Mem. Savs. Instns. Mktg. Soc. Am. (chmn. research com. 1971, 74), Am. Mktg. Assn. (past dir. Pitts. chpt.), Pitts. Econ. Club, Pitts. Jr. C. of C., Alpha Kappa Psi. Contbr. articles profl. jours. Home: 3218 Longwood Dr Pittsburgh PA 15227 Office: Granite Bldg 6th and Wood Sts Pittsburgh PA 15222

ATSEFF, TIMOTHY PHILIP, editorial cartoonist; b. Syracuse, N.Y., June 2, 1947; s. Nicholas Peter and Betty (Christoff) A.; B.F.A., So. Ill. U., 1970; m. Susan Gail Stupner, Apr. 18, 1971; 1 dau., Taylor. Editorial cartoonist, art dir., illustrator Syracuse Herald-Jour. and Herald-Am., 1970—; illustrator Am. Psychol. Assn. Monitor, 1975—; free-lance artist: one-man show Paintings Everson Mus. Art, 1975. Mem. Am. Assn. Editorial Cartoonists, Syracuse Press Club. Home: 215 Scottholm Blvd Syracuse NY 13224 Office: Clinton Sq Syracuse NY 13201

ATTAR, AHMAD MANSOUR (ANDY), port ofcl.; b. Damascus, Syria, Nov. 23, 1933; s. Mohamed Kheir and Nazmieh (Subai) A.; came to U.S., 1952, naturalized, 1969; B.S., U. Tex., 1957, M.S. in Archtl. Engring., 1958; postgrad. N.Y. U., 1965-74; m. Ethel Morris, June 4, 1957; children—Yasmin, Laila. Design engr. Wm. A. Moore Cons. Engrs., Houston, 1958-60; chief city planner Municipality of Damascus (Syria), 1960-64; sr. aviation planner Port Authority N.Y. and N.J., N.Y.C., 1965-77, mem. pub. policy task force, mem. com. on the future, 1978—; sr. cons. to several Middle East countries; pres. Orgn. for Devel. Research., 1975-77. Mem. ASCE (chmn. air transport div.), Nat. Soc. Profl. Engrs., Am. Mgmt. Assn. Home: 7 Haven Ct Centerport NY 11721 Office: One World Trade Center Suite 73E New York City NY 10048

ATTRA, HARVEY DAVID, petroleum co. exec.; b. Houston, Feb. 21, 1931; s. John E. and Helen (Faraha) A.; B.S., U. Tex., 1954; m. Aleeta D. Broderick, May 21, 1954; children—John Kevin, Broderick Cory. Prodn. engr. Humble Oil Co., 1954-56, computing coordinator, 1959-62, dist. chief engr., 1965-67, div. chief, reservoir engr., 1967-69; Western Hemisphere adviser gas coordination dept. Standard Oil Co. (N.J.), N.Y.C., 1969—; mgr. marine planning Exxon Corp., 1972-73, prodn. adviser, 1974-75, prodn. mgr. Esso Middle East, 1976—. Bd. govs. Weston Field Club; mem. Republican Town Com. Registered profl. engr., Tex. Mem. Am. Inst. Mining, Metall. and Petroleum Engrs. (Rossiter W. Raymond award 1963), Am. Petroleum Inst., Weston Boosters. Episcopalian (sr. warden, vestryman). Home: Tannery Ln S Weston CT 06880 Office: Rockefeller Plaza New York City NY 10020

ATTWOOD, WILLIAM, publisher; b. Paris, France, July 14, 1919; s. Frederic and Gladys (Hollingsworth) A.; grad. Choate Sch., 1937; A.B., Princeton, 1941; m. Simone Cadgene, June 22, 1950; children—Peter, Janet (Mrs. Richard S. DuPont), Susan Attwood. Corr. New York Herald Tribune in Paris and with UN bur., 1946-49; European corr. Colliers mag., 1949-51; European editor Look mag., 1951-54, nat. editor, 1955-57, fgn. editor, 1957-61; U.S. ambassador to Guinea, 1961-63; spl. adviser U.S. del. to UN, 1963-64; U.S. ambassador to Kenya, 1964-66; editor-in-chief, v.p. Cowles Communications, Inc., N.Y.C., 1966-70; pres., pub. Newsday, Inc., Garden City, N.Y., 1970-78, chmn. bd., 1978—. Mem. John F. Kennedy presdl. campaign staff, 1960; regional alumni trustee Princeton, 1967-71; trustee Kress Found., bd. dirs. Overseas Devel. Council; U.S. del. to UNESCO Gen. Conf., 1978. Served to capt. AUS, 1941-45. Recipient Nat. Headliners award, 1955, 57. George Polk Meml. award, 1956, N.Y. Newspaper Guild Page One award, 1960. Mem. Council Fgn. Relations. Democrat. Club: Century. Author: The Man Who Could Grow Hair, 1949; Still the Most Exciting Country, 1955; (with George B. Leonard, Jr. and J. Robert Moskin) The Decline of The American Male, 1958; The Reds and the Blacks, 1967; The Fairly Scary Adventure Book, 1969. Home: 423 Carter St New Canaan CT 06840 Office: 550 Stewart Ave Garden City NY 11530

ATWOOD, WILLIAM GOODSON, physician; b. Kansas City, Mo., Dec. 14, 1932; s. William Goodson and Jeannette (Morris) A.; A.B., Harvard Coll., 1954; M.D., Columbia U., 1958. Intern, U. Kans. Hosps., Kansas City, 1950-59; resident dermatology Columbia-Presbyn. Med. Center, N.Y.C., 1961-64; pvt. practice medicine, specializing in dermatology, N.Y.C., 1964—; instr. Columbia U. Coll. Phys. and Surgs. Mem. AMA, Am. Acad. Dermatology, Soc. for Investigative Dermatology, Internat. Soc. Tropical Dermatology, Met. Dermatologic Soc. N.Y., N.Y. Dermatologic Soc. Democrat. Club: Harvard (N.Y.C.). Office: 555 Park Ave New York City NY 10021

ATZMON, EZRI, educator, author; b. Radziejow, Poland, June 23, 1915; s. Samuel and Bina (Lajzerowicz) Zajf; came to U.S., 1949, naturalized, 1955; grad. U. London, 1947; M.Ed., Wayne U., 1954; Ph.D., U. Mich., 1958. Tchr. elementary and secondary schs. Palestine, 1937-42; founder, dir. elementary schs. and schs. for rehabilitation of adults, Libya, Africa, 1942-46; lectr. City U. N.Y., 1959-62; Fulbright prof. comparative edn. Philipps U., Marburg, Fed. Republic Germany, 1967-68; asso. prof. ednl. history N.Y. U., 1963-69; prof. edn. Jersey City State Coll., 1969—; vis. lectr. Hacettepe U., Ankara, Turkey, U. Heidelberg, Mannheim, and Marburg, W. Ger., Hebrew U., Jerusalem, Pa. State U.; cons. Ednl. Encyclopedia of Israel, also Hebrew Lang. Acad. Israel, 1972-75; translator and narrator USIA, 1951—. Hon. pres. Educators Council of Fedn. Jewish Philantropies, N.Y., 1960-63; volunteer worker United Jewish Appeal, N.Y., 1973—. Served as volunteer to Brit. Army, 1942-45; cultural officer Israeli Army, 1948-49. Mem. History of Edn. Soc., Comparative Edn. Soc., Comparative Edn. Soc. in Europe, Nat. Edn. Assn., AAUP, Am. Fedn. Tchrs., Democrat. Jewish. Contbg. editor Western European Edn.; author: Hebrew Poetry, 1961; contbr. articles in field to profl. jours. and encys. Home: 165 West End Ave New York City NY 10023 Office: 88 Audubon Ave Jersey City NJ 07305

AUBERT, KENNETH STEPHEN, psychologist, guidance counselor; b. Lowell, Mass., Aug. 19, 1952; s. Harvey A. and Irene (Genest) A.; B.S., U. Mass., 1974; M.Ed., Tufts U., 1976. Psychotherapist in pvt. practice, Reading, Mass., 1977—; guidance counselor Parker Jr. High Sch., Chelmsford, Mass., 1976-78. Mem. Mass. Psychol. Assn., Mass. Sch. Counselors Assn., Am. Personnel and Guidance Assn., Council for Basic Edn., Phi Kappa Phi, Alpha Zeta. Office: 31 Parkerville Rd Chelmsford MA 01824

AUBIN, ALBERT KENNETH, guidance counselor; b. Providence, June 9, 1938; s. Albert Elphege and Doris Irene (Cardin) A.; A.B., Providence Coll., 1961, M.Ed., 1977; Ed.M., R.I. Coll., 1969. Tchr., North Providence (R.I.) Sch. Dept., 1961-70; tchr. various secondary schs., 1970-73; counselor Cranston (R.I.) Manpower and Tng. Dept., 1973-75; counselor Opportunities Industrialization Center of R.I., Providence, 1975-77; pvt. practice counseling, specializing in personal, family and sch. problems, Cranston, 1977—; cons. R.I. Indian Council. Bd. dirs. Cranston Community Action Program, Cranston Mental Health Clinic. Served to 1st lt. U.S. Army, 1962-65. United Comml. Travelers of Am. spl. edn. grantee, 1977. Mem. Nat. Vocat. Guidance Assn., Am., R.I. personnel and guidance assns., Am. Sch. Counselor Assn., Assn. for Counselor Edn. and Supervision. Roman Catholic. Club: K.C. Home: 191 Gladstone St Cranston RI 02910

AUBRECHT, GORDON JAMES, bus. info. co. exec.; b. Maple Heights, Ohio, May 4, 1919; s. James V. and Mary (Sisser) A.; student Fenn Coll., 1937-40; Advanced Mgmt. Program, Harvard, 1969; m. Ernestine Felber, Feb. 14, 1942; children—Gordon II, Mary, Lawrence, John, Robert, Richard, Anita. With Dun & Bradstreet, Inc., N.Y.C., 1946—, v.p. data processing div., 1968, v.p. procurement and facilities, 1968-69, v.p. data processing, 1969—. Served to lt. col. USA, AUS, 1941-63. Home: 21 Manchester Dr Westfield NJ 07090 Office: 99 Church St New York City NY 10007

AUBREY, RACHEL LOWE RUSTOW (MRS. HENRY G. AUBREY), psychotherapist; b. Berlin; d. Adolph and Beatrice (Loewenstein) Lowe; student U. London; A.B., M.S.W., Smith Coll.; certificate in psychotherapy A. Adler Inst., 1972; m. Henry G. Aubrey (dec. Mar. 1970); children—Stephen Lowe, Janet Susan. Came to U.S., 1940, naturalized, 1946. Psychiat. social worker, family agencies, nursery schs., N.Y.C., New Haven, 1946-49; lectr. Sch. Social Work, Stockholm, 1950, Oglethorpe U., 1951-52; ind. field research Family Living and Child Rearing in Modern Turkey, Ankara, 1953-54, 58-60; therapist Jewish Bd. Guardians and Jewish Family Service, N.Y.C., 1960-63; instr., tng. supr. Tchrs. Coll., Columbia U., N.Y.C., 1963—, research asso. Internat. Inst. Study Human Reprodn., 1972-73, staff therapist mental health div. Columbia Health Service, 1973—; pvt. practice psychotherapy, N.Y.C., 1961—; adj. asso. prof. dept. sociology City Coll. N.Y., 1968—. Mem. Nat. Assn. Social Workers, Acad. Certified Social Workers, Am. Orthopsychiat. Assn., Am. Group Psychotherapy Assn. Contbr. articles to profl. publs. Home: 560 Riverside Dr New York City NY 10027 Office: Mental Health Div Columbia U Health Service 519 W 114 St New York City NY 10027

AUDAIN, OWEN ALBERT, urologist; b. Basseterre, St. Kitts, W. Indies, Aug. 13, 1930; s. Henry George and Irene Albertha (Nisbett) A.; came to Can., 1968, naturalized, 1974; M.B. Ch.B., U. Edinburgh (Scotland), 1956; m. Phyllis Imelda Redhead, Aug. 17, 1957; children—Trevor Owen, Anthony Ian. Intern, Rochdale Infirmary, Ryhope Gen. Hosp., 1957-58; resident in urology Victoria Gen. Hosp., Halifax, N.S., Can., 1968-71; gen. practice medicine, St. Kitts, 1957-63, gen. practice surgery, 1966-68; urologist Moncton (N.B. Can.) City Hosp., Dr. Georges Dumont Hosp., Moncton, 1971—. Fellow Royal Coll. Surgeons Edinburgh, Can.; mem. Brit., Canadian med. assns., N.B., Moncton med. socs. Mem. United Ch. Can. Clubs: Golf-Country, Gyro (Moncton). Home: 325 McAllister Ave Riverview NB E1B 1T9 Canada Office: 105 Bon Accord St Moncton NB E1C 1H3 Canada

AUDETTE, LOUIS GIRARD, II, ednl. adminstr., health educator; b. Orange, N.J., Sept. 24, 1939; s. Charles LaPointe and Mary Ford (Haggart) A.; B.A., Yale U., 1962, B.F.A., 1963, M.S. in Anatomy, 1966; m. Anna Brita Held, Aug. 15, 1964; children—Jessie, Alexis. Lectr. anatomy, producer med. TV, Yale U., 1964-69; dir. dept. biomed. communications Health Center, U. Conn., 1970-76, ednl. dir. spl. projects, lectr., researcher health edn., 1977—; project dir. Project Hope, Alexandria, Egypt, 1976-77; ednl. cons. HEW, 1976-77. Conn. Regional Med. Program in Med. Edn. grantee, 1972-73. Mem. Health Sci. Communication Assn. (bd. dirs. 1971-72, 73-77), Assn. Biomed. Communications Dirs. (pres. 1975-76), Nat. Assn. Ednl. Broadcasters, Soc. Motion Picture and TV Engrs. Democrat. Author, editor: Connecticut's Non-Print Resources in the Health Sciences, 1973, mem. editorial rev. bd. Jour. Biocommunications, 1973-75; contbr. articles to profl. jours. Home: 24 Everit St New Haven CT 06511 Office: U Conn Health Center Biomedical Communications Farmington CT 06032

AUDIN, GARY ROBERT, computer cons. co. exec.; b. N.Y.C., July 15, 1941; s. Gabriel and Mildred (Kettner) A.; B.S. in Elec. Engring., N.J. Inst. Tech., 1963; postgrad. Syracuse U., 1966; m. Karen J. Miller, June 15, 1963; children—Robert, Michael, Brian, Jeffrey. Staff systems engr. Western Union Co., Mahwah, N.J., 1967-68; dir. systems projects Informatics Inc., River Edge, N.J., 1969-75; dir. planning research Public Mgmt. Services Inc., McLean, Va., 1975-76; v.p. Logica Inc., N.Y.C., 1977-78; pres. Delphi Inc., Pompton Lakes, N.J., 1978—; lectr. Princeton U., Rutgers U., Am. Mgmt. Assn., Assn. Systems Mgmt. Served to capt. USAF, 1963-67. Decorated Air Force Commendation medal. Mem. IEEE. Home and office: 20 Passaic Ave Pompton Lakes NJ 07442

AUER, EMMA HENRIETTA, educator; b. Ancon, C.Z., July 14, 1913; d. George Harrison and Bertha Evelyn (Weiland) Auer; B.S., U. Ill., 1935, Ph.D., 1968; M.S., Washington U. at St. Louis, 1958. Promotion dir. Boy'd, St. Louis, 1938-51; fashion advt. mgr., fashion dir. Famous-Barr, St. Louis, 1951-58; fashion dir., account liaison MacFarland, Aveyard & Co., Chgo., 1958-59; fashion dir., sales promotion cons. Ind. Retailers Syndicate, N.Y.C., 1959-61; promotion dir. Harper's Bazaar, N.Y., 1962-64; asst. prof. bus. Washington U., St. Louis, 1945-58, No. Ill. U., DeKalb, 1967-68, Kans. U., Lawrence, 1968-69; asso. prof. Fla. State U., Tallahassee, 1969-76; asso. prof. Suffolk U., 1974-75, chmn. dept. mktg., 1976-77; asso. prof. Boston State Coll., 1978—; vis. prof. Purdue U., 1977, Cleve. State U., 1978; congl. intern affairs of the elderly, 1978. Am. Assn. Advt. Agencies grantee, 1969-70, 70-71. Mem. Am. Acad. Advt., Acad. Mktg. Soc., Am. Mktg. Assn., So. Mktg. Assn., Am. Psychol. Assn., European Soc. Opinion Surveys and Market Research, Assn. Consumer Research, The Fashion Group. Contbr. to profl. jours. Home: 101 Fulton St San Marco Apts Boston MA 02113

AUERBACH, ARNOLD ("RED"), profl. basketball exec.; b. N.Y.C., Sept. 20, 1917; s. Hyman and Marie (Thompson) A.; B.S. in Phys. Edn., George Washington U., 1940, M.A. in Edn., 1941; m. Dorothy Lewis, June 6, 1941; children—Nancy, Randy. Pres., gen. mgr. Boston Celtics Basketball Team; coach 11 Consecutive all star games; winner 10 Eastern div. titles, 9 world titles; rep. State Dept. for clinics, demonstrations, exhbns.; dir. basketball sch., Camp Milbrooks, Marshfield, Mass.; sports commentator, lectr.; dir. Seacrest Hotel, North Falmouth, Mass. Chmn. in Mass., Easter Seal Soc. Recipient Boston's Distinguished Achievement medal; Sports Achievement award B'nai B'rith; named to Nat. Basketball Hall of Fame, 1968. Mem. Nat. Coaches Assn., Omicron Delta Kappa, Colonials (George Washington U.). Club: Touchdown (award) (Washington). Author: Basketball for the Player, Fan and Coach; Winning the Hard Way. Home: 4200 Massachusetts Ave NW Washington DC 20016 Office: 150 Causeway St Boston MA 02114*

AUERBACH, BARRY BERNARD, dental surgeon; b. Balt., Aug. 16, 1916; s. Samuel L. and Edith (Handler) A.; B.S., U. Md., 1935, D.D.S., 1939; m. Jean Alma Fretwell, Aug. 10, 1942; 1 dau., Diane Auerbach Meyers. Intern, D.C. Penal Instn., 1939-41, Gallanger Hosp., Washington, 1940-41; practice dentistry specializing in prosthetics and gen. dentistry, Balt.; mem. staff St. Agnes Hosp., Balt., 1946—; pres. Coliseum World Travel, 1976—; dental surgeon under Albert Schweitzer, Lambarane, Gabon, Africa, 1964; researcher cancer of mouth hosps. Cochin and Madras, India, 1972. Bd. dirs. St. Agnes Hosp., Bon Secour Hosp., Balt. Served to lt. comdr. USNR, 1942-46. Mem. ADA, Balt. County Dental Soc. (v.p.), Am. Soc. Clin. and Exptl. Hypnosis, Internat. Soc. Hypnosis, Am. Acad. Oral Roentgenology, Internat. Soc. Clin. and Exptl. Hypnosis, Am. Seminars on Hypnosis Found., Brit. Royal Soc. Health, Am. Soc.

Psychosomatic Dentistry and Medicine, French Fedn. Dentaire Internat., Md. Soc. Med. Research, Assn. Mil. Surgeons U.S., Nat. Acupuncture Research Soc., Am. Acad. Acupuncture Research, Sigma Epsilon Delta. Office: 3322 Frederick Ave Baltimore MD 21229

AUERBACH, LEONARD, pharmacist; b. Newark, Sept. 1, 1920; s. Jacob and Fannie (Rothschild) A.; B.Sc., Rutgers U., 1941; children—Donald, Janice Auerbach Grohs. Owner, pharmacist Maple Pharmacy, Hillside, N.J., 1947-72; pharmacy mgr. Medi Mart Drug Store, Short Hills, N.J., 1973—. Served with AUS, 1942-46. Mem. Nat. Assn. Retail Druggists, Rutgers U. Alumni Assn. Home: 12 Brown Terr Cranford NJ 07016 Office: 800 Morris Turnpike Short Hills NJ 07078

AUGE, BERNARD GIRARD, dentist; b. North Adams, Mass., July 13, 1923; s. Anthony Joseph and Mauda Louise (Boudreau) A.; student U. Notre Dame, 1947; D.M.D., Tufts U., 1952; m. Eleanor Ruth Contois, June 23, 1943; children—Bernard Girard, Christine Ann, Eugene Anthony, Thomas Peter, Timothy John. Gen. practice dentistry, Dalton, Mass., 1952—; instr. dental interns Berkshire Med. Center, Pittsfield Gen. Hosp., 1969—; dental adv. McCann's Regional Sch. for Dental Assts., North Adams, 1969—, Berkshire County Nursing Homes, 1967—; sch. clinic dentist Town of Dalton Pub. Health, 1954-70; dir. cancer research detection pilot program Berkshire County, 1970. Served with US Naval Intelligence, 1943-45. Recipient award for outstanding service in control of cancer Mass. div. Am. Cancer Soc., 1970. Mem. Pierre Fauchard Acad., Acad. Gen. Dentistry, ADA, Mass. (1st dist. trustee 1976-78), Berkshire County (pres. 1972-73) dental socs., U. Notre Dame Nat. Alumni (senate 1970-71), Am. Legion. Clubs: K.C., Rotary, Univ. of Notre Dame of Berkshires (pres. 1970-71, 77-78). Home: 17 Kittredge Rd Pittsfield MA 01201 Office: 498 Main St Dalton MA 01226

AUGUSTINE, JEROME SAMUEL, investment adviser; b. Racine, Wis., May 7, 1928; s. Lester Samuel and Pearl (Hilker) A.; A.B. cum laude, Harvard U., 1950, M.B.A., 1952; m. Camilla Sewell, Feb. 7, 1953; children—Theodore Samuel Purnell, Julia Sewell, Elizabeth Stroebel. Cons., Scudder, Stevens & Clark, Boston, 1952-56; founder, treas., dir. Vencap, Inc., Boston, 1956-58; treas., dir. Consumer Products, Inc., Boston, 1956-58; founder, treas., dir. Microsonics, Inc., Hingham, Mass., 1956-58; treas., dir. Capitol Mgmt. Corp., Boston, 1956-58; cons. Kidder, Peabody & Co., Boston, 1958-64; pres. Cosmos Am. Corp., N.Y.C. 1964-66; founder, pres., dir. Cosmos Securities Corp., 1965-70, Cosmos (Bahamian) Ltd., Nassau, 1964-70, Augustine Fin. Co., Bridgeport, Conn., 1966—; first v.p. Van Alstyne, Noel & Co., N.Y.C., 1973-74; v.p. Wright Investors' Service, Bridgeport, 1974—. Trustee, Low-Heywood Sch. Mem. Boston Fin. Research Assos. (gov. 1960-64, v.p. 1963-64), New Eng. Amateur Rowing Assn. (past pres.). Episcopalian. Clubs: Union Boat (Boston); Harvard (N.Y.C.); Noroton (Conn.) Yacht; Ox Ridge Hunt (Darien, Conn.). Home: 155 Long Neck Point Rd Darien CT 06820 Office: Wright Bldg Bridgeport CT 06604

AUGUSTINE, PATRICK HENRY, personnel exec.; b. Geneva, N.Y., Mar. 27, 1934; s. Henry Joseph and Francis Marie (DiSanto) A.; B.S. in Indsl. Arts, State U. N.Y., Oswego, 1959; m. Suzanne Mary Alfred, July 6, 1957; children—Mark, Pamela, Christopher, Stephen, Amy. High sch. tchr., Canandaigua, N.Y., 1959-61; modelmaker Gen. Elec. Co., Syracuse, N.Y., 1961-63, electronic technician, 1963, foreman, 1964-65, supr. tng. center, 1966-67; tng. and edn. coordinator Link div. Singer Co., 1967-69, mgr. personnel, 1969-71; mgr. personnel Xerox Corp., 1971-73, mgr. home office personnel, 1973-75; pres. H.A. Patrick Assos., Stamford, Conn., 1975—; corp. personnel dir. Databit Corp., Hauppauge, N.Y., 1978—; seminar presenter industry, profl. orgns. Cubmaster Cub Scouts, 1967-69; pres., coach Little League, 1968-70; mem. Jr. C. of C., 1965-67; mem. L.I. Indsl. Wage and Salary Council, 1978—. Served with USMC, 1952-55. Mem. Am. Soc. Personnel Adminstrs, L.I. C. of C., Am. Mgmt. Assn., Eastern Intercollegiate Wrestling Ofcls. Assn. Roman Catholic. Club: Kiwanis (dir. 1977-78). Home: 3 Manor Rd Greenlawn NY 11740 Office: 828 High Ridge Rd Stamford CT 06905

AUGUSTITUS, RICHARD MICHAEL, counselor; b. Hazleton, Pa., Apr. 10, 1932; s. Edward J. and Elizabeth A.; B.A., Hartwick Coll., 1959; M.S., State U. Coll., Oneonta, N.Y., 1962; certificate counseling Cornell U., 1970; m. Shirley Dunn, June 6, 1957; children—Anne, Edward. Tchr., elementary schs., Hancock, N.Y., 1959-62, Corning, N.Y., 1962-70; guidance counselor Home Sch., Corning, N.Y., 1970—. Cub Scout pack leader; bd. dirs. So. Tier Heart Assn. Served with USNR, 1952-56; Korea. Named to Corning Bowling Assn. Hall of Fame, 1976. Mem. N.Y. State Edn. Assn., Corning Tchrs. Assn., N.Y. State Social Workers Assn., Am. Assn. Sex Educators, Counselors, Therapists, Am. Assn. Marriage Family Counselors, NEA, Am. Security Council, N.Y., Am., Genessee Valley personnel and guidance assns., Elementary Guidance Counseling Assn., Assn. Counselor Edn. and Supervision. Republican. Roman Catholic. Clubs: Elmira Country; Corning Country; Elks. Home: 1863 Turner Rd Elmira NY 14905 also Millerton PA 16936 Office: 20 Maple St Corning NY 14830

AUH, YANG JOHN, librarian; b. Mokpo, Korea, Mar. 18, 1934; s. Sam Hyuck and So Yae (Suh) A.; came to U.S., 1962, naturalized, 1971; B.A., Chung-ang U., 1957; M.A. in Library Sci., Western Mich. U., 1964; certificate in library adminstrn. devel. (HEW fellow) U. Md., 1973; certificate in advanced librarianship Columbia U., 1975; m. Karen Kyung-ja Kim, Mar. 11, 1969; 1 dau., Alice Kim. Asst. librarian Korean Nat. Library, Seoul, 1957; tech. services librarian Korean Mil. Acad. Library, Seoul, 1958-61; head union catalog L.I. U. Libraries, Greenvale, N.Y., 1965-68; head catalog dept., tech. services coordinator Wagner Coll. Library, S.I., N.Y., 1968-71, library dir., 1972—. Bd. dirs. Korean Assn. of N.Y., 1967. Mem. ALA, N.Y. State Library Assn. Club: N.Y. Librarians. Office: Horrman Library Wagner College Staten Island NY 10301

AULENBACH, DONALD BRUCE, educator; b. Berwick, Pa., Mar. 7, 1928; s. Henry Israel and Mildred Clara (Schlasman) A.; B.S. (Dist. scholar), Franklin and Marshall Coll., 1950; M.S., Rutgers U., 1952, Ph.D., 1954; m. Marie Pauline Wertz, Aug. 16, 1952; children—Louise Marie, Bruce Donald, Nancy Jean, Brent Thomas. Chemist-bacteriologist State Del. Water Pollution Commn., Dover, 1954-60; asst. prof. Rensselaer Poly. Inst., Troy, N.Y., 1960-65, asso. prof., 1965-73, prof. environ. engring., 1973—; environ. engring. cons. Gen. Electric Co., Hood Milk Co., U.S. Govt., Pownal Tannery, other industries, engring. firms. Pres. West Sand Lake PTA, 1965-66, Sand Lake-Poestenkill Council Chs., 1965-66. USPHS research grantee for grad. edn., 1950-54; registered profl. engr., N.Y. Mem. Am. Chem. Soc., Am. Water Works Assn., N.Y. Water Pollution Control Assn. (sec.-treas. Capital dist. sect. 1965-76, dir. 1977—), Health Physics Soc. (treas. N.E. N.Y. chpt. 1973-75), Assn. Environ. Engring. Profs. (chmn. subcom. on undergrad edn. 1974—), Standard Methods Com. on Ammonia and Nitrate Analyses, Nat. Water Well Assn., Am. Soc. Limnology and Oceanography, Sigma Xi (pres. local chpt. 1969-71). Mem. Ref. Christian Ch. (elder 1973-75). Contbr. chpts. to books, articles to profl. jours. Home: 24 Valencia Ln Clifton Park NY 12065 Office: Rensselaer Poly Inst Troy NY 12181

AULT, JAMES MASE, clergyman; b. Sayre, Pa., Aug. 24, 1918; s. Tracey Everett and Bessie (Mase) A.; A.B. magna cum laude, Colgate U., 1949; B.D. magna cum laude, Union Theol. Sem., 1952, S.T.M., 1964; postgrad. St. Andrews U., Scotland, 1966; D.D., Am. U., 1968; LL.D., Albright Coll., 1973, Ohio Wesleyan U., 1973; m. Dorothy Mae Barnhart, Dec. 22, 1943; children—James Mase, Kathryn Louise, Elizabeth Ann, Christopher John (dec.). Tool engr. Ingersoll-Rand Co., 1936-42; ordained to ministry Meth. Ch., 1950; pastor Meth. Ch., Preston, N.Y., 1946-49; pastor Carlton Hill Meth. Ch., East Rutherford, N.J., 1951-53; pastor Meth. Ch., Leonia, N.J., 1953-58; pastor First Meth. Ch., Pittsfield, Mass., 1958-61; dean students, asso. prof. practical theology Union Theol. Sem., 1961-64, prof. practical theology, dir. field edn., 1964-68; prof. pastoral theology, dean Theol. Sch., Drew U., Madison, N.J., 1968-72; resident bishop Phila. area United Meth. Ch., 1972—. Served to 1st lt. U.S. Army, 1942-46. Faculty fellow Am. Assn. Theol. Schs., 1965-66. Mem. Am. Assn. U. Profs., Acad. Polit. and Social Sci., Phi Beta Kappa. Author: Responsible Adults for Tomorrow's World, 1962. Home: 149 Ridgewood Rd Radnor PA 19087 Office: POB 820 Valley Forge PA 19482

AUMAN, GEORGE EDWARD, exec. cons.; b. Shamokin, Pa., Feb. 2, 1920; s. George Emmett and Millie Senada (Reitz) A.; B.S., Bucknell U., 1941; certificate meteorology U. Chgo., 1945; postgrad. Indsl. Coll. Armed Forces, 1956; m. Martyle Vera Simon, Jan. 20, 1947; children—Sheri Doreen, Sandra Ellen. Meteorologist, U.S. Weather Bur., Washington, 1942-43, 47-52, Pitts., 1943-44, adminstrv. officer, 1952-54; asst. chief mgmt. planning Nat. Bur. Standards, Washington, 1954-61, asst. to dir., 1961-74; owner exec. cons. firm, Gaithersburg, Md., 1974—; exec. sec. com. on fed. labs. Fed. Council for Sci. and Tech., 1960-74; mem. Personnel Officers Research and Devel. Agencies, 1965-72, chmn., 1970-71. Vice pres. Montgomery County (Md.) PTA, 1958-60; mem. Montgomery County Sch. Supts. Com., 1959, County Tax Study Com., 1958. Served to lt. USNR, 1944-46. Decorated Bronze Star medal; recipient Silver medal U.S. Dept. Commerce, 1966, Tao Shu medal Repub. China, 1974. Mem. Fed. Profl. Assn. (nat. pres. 1978—), Internat. Platform Assn., Airline Passengers Assn. Home: 843 Diamond Dr Gaithersburg MD 20760

AUNGST, SHERMAN LESTER, hosp. exec.; b. Lock Haven, Pa., Sept. 14, 1938; s. Sherman Gordon and Lillian Isabell (Maggs) A.; student Lock Haven State Coll., 1956-58; grad. N.H. Coll., 1978; m. Ann Margaret Moffat, Apr. 27, 1963; children—Gordon William, Gayle Lynn, Karyn Leslie. Dir. purchasing Valley Hosp., Ridgewood, N.J., 1968-71; dir. group purchasing N.J. Hosp. Assn., Princeton, 1971-73; dir. purchasing Newark Beth Israel Med. Center, 1973-75, Yale-New Haven Hosp., 1975—. Chmn., advisor Med. Exploring post Valley Hosp., Ridgewood, 1968-71. Served with U.S. Army, 1959-62. Mem. Conn. Hosp. Assn. (regional mgr. 1975—), Nat. Assn. Hosp. Purchasing Mgrs. (dir. 1970-72), N.J. (pres. 1969-70), Am. Hosp. Purchasing Mgrs. Assn., N.J. Purchasing Mgrs. Assn. (pres.), Nat. Orgn. Group Purchasing Dirs. Clubs: Yale Med. Center Bowling, Yale-New Haven Hosp. Softball. Contbr. articles to profl. jours. Home: 40 Hammonassett Meadows Rd Madison CT 06443 Office: 789 Howard Ave New Haven CT 06504

AUSES, JOHN PAUL, analytical chemist; b. Johnstown, Pa., Jan. 28, 1949; s. Frank Frederick and Stephanie Barbara (Pilot) A.; B.S. in Chemistry, St. Francis Coll., Loretto, Pa., 1970; M.S. in Analytical Chemistry, W.Va. U., 1974; m. Christine Wank, Aug. 11, 1973; children—John Anthony, Julia Christine. Asst. dir. Project Upward Bound, St. Francis Coll., Loretto, Pa., 1971; chemist Glyco Chems., Inc., Williamsport, Pa., 1971-72; teaching asst., chemistry dept. W.Va. U., Morgantown, 1972-74; sr. scientist, analytical chemistry div. Aluminum Co. Am., Alcoa Tech. Center, Alcoa, Pa., 1974—; com. mem. Pitts. Conf. on Analytical Chemistry and Applied Spectroscopy, 1976—. Basic life support instr. cardiopulmonary resuscitation, ARC. Recipient Upward Bound award St. Francis Coll., 1970. Mem. Am. Chem. Soc., Soc. Analytical Chemists Pitts., Spectroscopy Soc. Pitts., Tri-City Jaycees (dir. 1975-76, treas. 1976-78, twice named Jaycee of Month). Democrat. Roman Catholic. Office: Alcoa Technical Center Alcoa Center PA 15069

AUSLANDER, DAVID ELY, pharm. scientist; b. N.Y.C., Apr. 27, 1940; s. Samuel and Rose (Remick) A.; B.S., Bklyn. Coll. Pharmacy, 1961; M.S., Columbia U., 1965; Ph.D. (Schering Corp. fellow), Rutgers U., 1972; m. Sheila Kaplan, June 4, 1972; 1 son, Steven Mark. Staff pharmacist N.Y.C. VA Hosp., 1961-62; scientist Schering Corp., Bloomfield, N.J., 1964-70; research investigator E.R. Squibb Inst. Med. Research, New Brunswick, N.J., 1972-77; group head Purdue-Frederick Co., Norwalk, Conn., 1977—; teaching fellow Columbia U., 1962-64. Mem. Am. Pharm. Assn., Sigma Xi, Rho Chi. Contbr. articles to profl. jours. Home: 17 Hemptor Rd New York City NY 10956 Office: Purdue-Frederick Research Center Yonkers NY 10701

AUSTER, DONALD, educator; b. Port Chester, N.Y., Nov. 1, 1922; s. Charles and Sophie (Perkins) A.; A.B., Hofstra U., 1949; M.A., Columbia, 1951; Ph.D., Ind. U., 1959; m. Nancy Eileen Ross, Aug. 18, 1946; children—Carol Jean, Ellen Ruth. Research asso. Ind. U., Bloomington, 1952-56, instr. Southeastern Center, Jeffersonville, Inc., 1956-57; from instr. to prof. sociology, St. Lawrence U., Canton, N.Y., 1959—. Served with U.S. Army, 1942-45. USPHS grantee, 1966-70. Mem. Am. Sociol. Assn., N.Y. State Sociol. Assn., Soc. for Study of Social Problems. Unitarian-Universalist. Author: Men Who Enter Nursing: A Sociological Analysis, 1970; contbr. articles to books and profl. jours. Home: 21 Craig Dr Canton NY 13617

AUSTER, NANCY EILEEN ROSS (MRS. DONALD AUSTER), educator; b. N.Y.C., Aug. 19, 1926; d. Norman Lask and Edith Cornelia (Jacobson) Ross; A.B., Barnard Coll., 1948; M.B.A., Ind. U., 1954; m. Donald Auster, Aug. 18, 1946; children—Carol Jean, Ellen Ruth. Research asso. The Conf. Bd., N.Y.C., 1948-51; research asst. Sch. Bus., Ind. U., Bloomington, 1952-54, editor publs. Bur. Bus. Research, 1954-56; lectr. St. Lawrence U., Canton, N.Y., 1962-66; asst. prof. econs. State U. N.Y. Agrl. and Tech. Coll. at Canton, 1966-70, asso. prof., 1970-73, prof., 1973—, chmn. social sci. dept., 1976—; Canton faculty senator to State U. N.Y. Faculty Senate, 1969-73, mem. exec. com., 1970-71, pres., 1973-75; statistician for USPHS grants, 1966-70. Sec. Thousand Islands Girl Scout council camp com., 1967-69; chmn. adv. planning council St. Lawrence County Comprehensive Employment and Tng. Act, 1977—. Mem. Am. N.Y. State (sec., treas. 1970-71) econ. assns., Am. Statis. Assn., N.Y. State Assn. Jr. Colls., League Women Voters (mem. exec. bd. Canton-Potsdam 1960-62). Unitarian-Universalist. Author: (with Donald Auster) Men Who Enter Nursing: A Sociological Analysis, 1970. Contbr. articles to profl. jours. Home: 21 Craig Dr Canton NY 13617

AUSTIN, ANTHONY, writer, journalist; b. Harbin, China, June 21, 1919; s. Theodore and Lydia (Lebedeff) A.; student pub. and pvt. schs., Shanghai, China; m. Dominique Roncovieri, Dec. 31, 1952; 1 dau., Andrea (Mrs. Walter Williams). Came to U.S., 1949, naturalized, 1955. Reporter, The China Press, The Shanghai Evening Post and Mercury, Shanghai, 1938-41; corr. The United Press, Peking, China, 1945-49, Washington, 1950-58; corr. U.P.I., Moscow and Paris, 1958-61; editor, writer The New York Times, N.Y.C., 1961—. Recipient award best book on fgn. affairs written by Am. journalist Overseas Press Club, 1971, Playboy award best short story in Playboy mag., 1973. Mem. Am. Newspaper Guild. Author: The President's War, 1971. Contbg. author: You and Election '72, 1972. Editor: (with Robert Clurman) The China Watchers, 1969; translator, editor: To Be Preserved Forever (Lev Kopelev), 1977. Home: 315 E 70th St New York City NY 10021 Office: New York Times 229 W 43d St New York City NY 10036

AUSTIN, DAVID WATKINS STUART, educator; b. Tenterden, Kent, Eng., Sept. 5, 1933; s. Llewellyn Thomas and Ivy Myrtle (Stuart) A.; came to U.S., 1965, naturalized, 1978; B.A. in German and French, Cambridge U., 1957, M.A. in Law, 1961; Ph.D. in Social Psychology, Temple U., Phila., 1972; m. Patricia Joanne Moyer, July 22, 1963; children—Candace Lynn, Tara Adrienne. With Lloyds Europe, Paris, 1957-58, Time Inc., N.Y.C., 1959, Case dello Scugnizzo, Naples. Italy, 1960-63, London County Council, 1963-65; mem. faculty Trenton (N.J.) State Coll., 1965-67, Temple U., 1967-71; asst. prof. State U. N.Y., Brockport, 1971-74; dir. resident programs Temple U. Woodhaven Center, also adj. prof. child care, Phila., 1974-78; exec. dir. Community Found. for Human Devel., 1978—; pres. Inter Assn. Child Care Conf., 1975—; cons. OEO, 1974—. Grantee Upward Bound, 1965-67, State U. N.Y., Brockport, 1972, Woodhaven Center, 1973-74, NIMH, 1967-70. Mem. Am. Orthopsychiat. Assn., Child Welfare League Am., Internat. Union Child Welfare, Soc. Psychol. Study Social Issues, Am. Sociol. Assn., Am. Assn. Mental Deficiency. Democrat. Episcopalian. Home: 250 S Chancellor St Newton PA 18940 Office: Ridge Crest PO Box 266 Sellersville PA 18960

AUSTIN, ERNEST AUGUSTUS, physician; b. Bklyn., Nov. 26, 1932; s. Augustin and Mildred Elrica (Davidson) A.; B.S., St. Johns U., 1953; M.D., Howard U., 1957; m. Margaret Patricia Byrd, Aug. 24, 1957; children—Vivian, Jean, Alan. Intern, Kings County Hosp. Center, Bklyn., 1957-58, resident in gen. surgery VA Hosp., Bklyn., 1958-62, practice medicine specializing in surgery, 1962—; chief surgery Fordham Hosp., Bronx, 1966-69; dir. surgery Reynolds Meml. Hosp., Winston-Salem, N.C., 1969-72; chief surgery Provident Hosp., Balt., 1972-73; chief traumatology and surgery U. Md. Inst. Emergency Medicine, Balt., 1974-76, 78—, asst. prof. surgery, 1972—; dir. emergency services U. Md. Hosp., Balt., 1977-78; med. cons. Social Security Adminstrn., Balt., 1976. Bd. dirs. Forsyth unit Am. Cancer Soc., 1970-71, Forsyth-Stokes chpt. Nat. Found., 1971-72. Diplomate Am. Bd. Surgery. Fellow ACS; mem. Am. Trauma Soc. (dir. Md. chpt. 1974-76), Univ. Assn. Emergency Med. Services. Contbr. articles to profl. jours. Office: 22 S Greene St Baltimore MD 21201

AUSTIN, PHILLIP WAYNE, retail exec.; b. Lincoln, Ill., Oct. 21, 1947; s. Charles Clay and Mable Louise (Coats) A.; A.A., Lincoln Coll., 1967; postgrad. Ill. State U., U. Pa.; m. Janis E. Danielson, Aug. 30, 1970; 1 son, Eric Charles. Exec. supr. Spiegel Inc., 1969-70; with J.C. Penney Co., 1970—, personnel mgr., Audubon, N.J., 1972-76, gen. mdse. mgr., Audubon, 1976—; mem. eve. faculty Gloucester County Coll., 1976-77. Retail coordinator United Way Camden County, N.J., 1976. Recipient Baden-Powell award Lincoln Coll., 1967. Mem. Am. Soc. Personnel Adminstrs. Lutheran. Office: JC Penney Co Black Horse Shopping Center Audubon NJ 08094

AUSTIN, STANLEY STUART, musician, educator; b. N.Y.C., Aug. 23, 1914; s. Arthur Thompson and Agnes (Palmer) A.; student Julliard Sch. Music, 1932-35; B.S. in Music Edn., Columbia, 1941, M.A. in Music, 1950; m. Dorothea June Pupke, June 21, 1941; children—David, Peter, Paul, Ruth. Concert debut as violinist, N.Y.C., 1920; mem. N.Y. Symphony, 1929-31; cello soloist CBS Radio, 1930-33; tchr. music pub. schs. N.J., 1932-52; mem. faculty dept. music Trenton (N.J.) State Coll., 1952—, asso. prof., 1958-71, prof., 1971-78, emeritus, 1978—, also supr. grad. music programs, 1957—, condr. Grad. Symphony, 1964-78; condr. Jersey Pops Jazz Symphony; mem. mgmt. Counterpoint Concepts, Inc., N.Y.C.; Chmn. music curriculum task force N.J. Dept. Edn. 1954—, mem. tchr. edn. profl. standards task force, 1968—, improving certification process task force, 1969—. Served with USAAF, 1941—. Recipient 11 teaching merit awards Trenton State Coll., 1960-71, Mem. N.J. (chmn. research com. 1973—), Bergen County (pres.) music edn. assns., N.E.A., N.J. Edn. Assn., Music Educators Nat. Conf., Phi Mu Alpha. Author 34 texts, including Forward March, 1943, Band Development, 1958, String Development, 1970. Composer several works, including Dubut for Trombone and Band, 1954, Suite in G Major for Unaccompanied Cello, 1957, Galaxie for Trombone and Band, 1960, Confrontation for Trumpet Solo and Symphony Orchestra, 1969; The Kancamagus Suite, 1974. Contbr. profl. jours. Home: 4 Hampton Rd Trenton NJ 08638 also Knights Hill Bridgeton ME 04009

AUSTIN, THOMAS SHERWOOD, govt. ofcl.; b. Olean, N.Y., Oct. 10, 1915; s. Claude E. and Ferne (Whipple) A.; B.S. in Biology, Grove City Coll., 1938, Sc.D. (hon.), 1965; M.A. in Zoology, U. Buffalo, 1940; M.A. in Limnology, Yale U., 1942; m. Gretta Jane Martin, June 7, 1941; children—Herbert M., Thomas Sherwood, Claudia Jane Austin Angle. Asst. dir. biol. lab. Bur. Comml. Fisheries, U.S. Dept. Interior, D.C., 1961-64, dir. Tropical Atlantic Biol. Lab., 1964-67; dir. Nat. Oceanographic Data Center, Washington, 1967-70; dir. Environ. Data and Info. Service, NOAA, Dept. Commerce, Washington, 1970—. Recipient citation as outstanding fed. handicapped employee of yr., 1969; Dept. Commerce Gold medal, 1975. Mem. Marine Tech. Soc., Found. for Sci. and Handicapped. Contbr. articles to profl. jours. Home: 9403 Caldran Dr Clinton MD 20753

AUTEN, DAVID CHARLES, lawyer; b. Phila., Apr. 4, 1938; s. Charles Raymond and Emily Lillian (Dickel) A.; B.A., U. Pa., 1960, J.D., 1963; m. Suzanne Crozier Plowman, Feb. 1, 1969; children—Anne Crozier, Meredith Smedley. Admitted to Pa. bar, 1963; partner firm Townsend, Elliott & Munson, Phila., 1963—, chmn., 1977—. Vice pres. N.E. Community Mental Health Center, 1971-72; vice chmn. alumni ann. giving U. Pa., 1971-77, chmn. Benjamin Franklin Assos., 1975-77, pres. Soc. Alumni, 1975—, pres. gen. alumni soc., 1977—; v.p. Assn. Republicans for Educated Action, 1971—. Bd. mgrs. Kearsley Home, 1974—; bd. dirs. St. Peter's Sch., 1975—, pres., 1978—. Mem. Am., Pa., Phila. (vice-chmn. young lawyers sect. 1971-72) bar assns., Juristic Soc. (pres. 1973—), Interfrat. Alumni Council U. Pa. (pres. 1970-74), Phi Beta Kappa, Theta Xi (pres. 1974-76). Episcopalian (vestryman 1974—). Clubs: Rittenhouse (bd. mgrs.), Union League, 4th St. Author articles in field; editor U. Pa. Law Rev., 1962-63. Home: 120 Delancey St Philadelphia PA 19106 Office: 1600 Western Savs Bank Bldg Broad and Chestnut Sts Philadelphia PA 19107

AUTEN, HANFORD LOUIS, JR., ophthalmologist; b. Princeville, Ill., July 17, 1910; s. Hanford Louis and Myra D. (King) A.; A.B., Dartmouth, 1932; M.B., Northwestern U., 1936, M.D., 1937; m. Dawn E. Seavers, May 10, 1939; children—Jon Seavers, Mary Elizabeth, Hanford Louis III. Practice medicine, specializing in ophthalmology, Chgo., 1938-42, Claremont, N.H., 1961—; ophthalmologist-in-charge Dartmouth Eye Inst., Hanover, N.H., 1946-47; ophthalmologist Hitchcock Clinic and Mary Hitchcock

Meml. Hosp., Hanover, 1947-60, Claremont Gen. Hosp., 1961—; cons. U.S. VA Hosp., White River Junction, Vt., 1947-61; instr. abnormal psychology Washburn Coll., Topeka, 1938-39; instr. clin. ophthalmology Dartmouth Med. Sch., 1946-51, asst. prof., 1951-60; dir. Indian Head Nat. Bank of Claremont, 1973—. Moderator, Cornish (N.H.) Sch. Dist., 1970. Served with M.C., USAF, 1942-46; Col. Res. ret. Decorated Air medal, Purple Heart. Fellow A.C.S., AAAS; mem. AMA, N.H. Med. Soc. (pres. 1974), Am. Acad. Ophthalmology and Otolaryngology, Assn. for Research in Vision and Ophthalmology, Aerospace Med. Assn., Pan Am., New Eng. (pres. 1978-79) ophthalmol. socs., N.H. (pres. 1969-71), Am. (dir. 1971-72) heart assns., N.H. Found. for Med. Care (dir., incorporator). Republican. Episcopalian. Home: Homestead Farm South Cornish NH Office: 251 Elm St Claremont NH 03743

AUTERI, ROSE MARY P., sch. adminstr.; b. N.Y.C., June 6, 1928; d. Francesco and Stefana (Patti) A.; B.A., Hunter Coll., 1950; M.A., Columbia U., 1962; Ed.D., Nova U., 1975. Tchr., Dist. 13, Valley Stream, N.Y., 1951-58, asst. prin., 1958-64; prin., Roosevelt, N.Y., 1964-68, Northside Sch., Levittown, N.Y., 1968—; technologist electroencephalography Neurol. Inst., N.Y.C., 1950-58, Mercy Hosp., 1958-78; chmn. parish council Sacred Heart Ch., North Merrick, N.Y., 1976—, pres. religious edn. bd., 1974—. Recipient Arthur A. Hamalainen educator award, 1972. Mem. Nat., N.Y., Nassau County (pres. 1969-70) assns. elementary sch. prins., Nat., N.Y., L.I. assns. (dir. 1971-73) supervision and curriculum devel. Am., Levittown (sec. 1971-72) assns. sch. adminstrs., Nat. Assn. Elementary Sch. Prins., Am. Soc. EEG Technologists, P.T.A. (life), Delta Kappa Gamma, Phi Delta Kappa (historian 1976). Home: 1816 Thomas St Merrick NY 11566 Office: Pelican Rd Levittown NY 11756

AUTH, TONY, editorial cartoonist; b. Akron, Ohio, May 7, 1942; s. William Anthony and Julia Kathleen A.; B.A. in Biol. Illustration, U. Calif., Los Angeles, 1965. Chief med. illustrator Rancho Los Amigos Hosp., Downey, Calif., 1965-71; editorial cartoonist Phila. Inquirer, Phila., 1971—; cartoon anthology: Behind The Lines, 1977. Recipient Pulitzer prize in journalism, 1976. Home: 1137 Rodman St Philadelphia PA 19147 Office: 400 N Broad St Philadelphia PA 19101

AUYANG, KING, chemist; b. Canton, China, Apr. 15, 1928; s. Sing-Kiu and Sook-Ching (Wong) A.; came to U.S., 1959, naturalized, 1974; M.A., Temple U., 1962, Ph.D., 1967; m. Grace Chao, Aug. 4, 1973; children—Ruby, Peter, Edward. NIH postdoctoral fellow U. Pa., Phila., 1966-68; sr. organic chemist W.H. Rorer, Inc., Fort Washington, Pa., 1968-69, group leader, 1969—. Instr. chemistry Temple U., 1966-69. Grantee, Air Force Office Sci. Research, 1966-67. Mem. Am. Chem. Soc., Sigma Xi, Phi Lambda Upsilon, Phila. Organic Chemists Club. Patentee chemicals. Home: 577 Pine Run Rd Doylestown PA 18901 Office: 500 Virginia Dr Fort Washington PA 19034

AVALLONE, MARGARET ANN THORSELL, speech pathologist; b. Chanute, Kans., Jan. 2, 1947; d. Galen Edward and Gertrude Heloise (Walker) Thorsell; B.S., U. Kans., 1969; Ed.M., Pa. State U., 1970; m. Thomas Avallone, Aug. 19, 1972; 1 dau., Jenae Christine. Lab. operator U. Kans. Lang. Lab., Lawrence, 1966-69; recreation aide Parsons (Kans.) State Hosp. and Tng. Center, 1966, counselor, Trail Blazer Camps, Port Jervis, N.Y., 1968-71; intern in speech pathology Children's Hosp., Washington, 1970; tchr. and recreation group leader Children's Center, Hamden, Conn., 1972-73; guest lectr. South Central Community Coll., New Haven, 1974, St. Joseph's Coll., Hartford, Conn., 1978; unit dir. Day Camp, YMCA, Hamden, Conn., 1975-77; lang., speech and hearing clinician New Haven pub. schs., 1970—; private practice speech pathology, 1973—; instr. for lang. devel. workshops, 1977; newspaper adviser After Sch. Program, New Haven, 1977—, vol. instr. of adult sewing class Community Sch. Program Winchester Community Sch., 1978. Recipient Outstanding Young Women of Am. award, 1976; Office of Edn. fellow, 1969. Mem. Am. Fedn. of Tchrs., Am. (certified speech pathologist), Conn. (mem. pub. sch. affairs com. 1975—, conv. panelist 1976, 78), speech and hearing assns., Nat., Conn. (state chmn. for 1978 nat. bus. women's week) fedns. of bus. and profl. women's clubs, State of Conn. Tchrs. Retirement Assn., U. Kans. Alumni Assn. Club: Bus. and Profl. Women's of Milford (pres. 1978). Home: 5 Maplevale Ct East Haven CT 06512 Office: Dept Pupil Personnel Edgewood School Edgewood Ave New Haven CT 06511

AVAMPATO, JOSEPH JAMES, psychologist, hypnotherapist; b. Torrington, Conn., Mar. 27, 1931; s. C. Charles and Anna (Amico) A.; B.A., St. Bernard Coll., 1952; M.A., Seton Hall U., 1965; P.D., Ohio Christian U., 1967; m. Sandra L. Lupinacci, July 13, 1968; children—Joseph, Christa, Maria. Intern in clin. psychology Kings County Hosp., 1966-67; counselor Poly. Inst. Bklyn., 1968; head treatment staff Odyssey House, N.Y.C., 1969; staff psychologist North Shore Child Guidance Center, Manhasset, N.Y., 1970; chief sch. psychologist Beacon (N.Y.) City Sch. System, 1971-72; practice hypnotherapy, Highland, N.Y., practice psychology, Ridgewood, N.J., 1972-76; pres., co-founder, dir. Apple Core, Inc., media occupational lab., Highland, 1976—; chmn. Highland Narcotics Addiction Control Commn., 1974-75. Mem. Am. Psychol. Assn., Nat. Registry Health Service Providers In Psychology, Am. Soc. Clin. Hypnosis, Soc. Priests for Free Ministry, Fellowship Christian Ministries. Home and Office: Apple Core Red Top Rd RD 1 Box 440 Highland NY 12528

AVERSA, ALARICO (RICO), artist; b. Ceccano, Italy, Mar. 18, 1930; s. Francesco and Vincenza (Tomassi) A.; came to U.S., 1961, naturalized, 1965; student Pericle Fazzini, Rome, 1951-52; diploma in scene decorating and modeling Movie Picture Center-Rome, 1956; m. Anna Marchione, Sept. 29, 1964; children—Serena, Frank. Exhibited one-man shows: Italian-Am. Club, Cape Circeo, 1955, Gima's Gallery, Riverside, 1961, Lynn Kottler Gallery, N.Y.C., 1967, Galerie Internationale, N.Y.C., 1973, Duncan Gallery, N.Y.C., 1975, group shows include: 7th Nat. Art Show, Rome, 1954, 16th, 17th, 18th Internat. Art Shows, N.Y.C., 1973, 74, 75, Am. Artists in Paris, 1975; represented in permanent collections: Movie Picture Tng. Center, Rome, Italian-Am. Club, Cape Circeo, Italy; City Hall of Ceccano; Pub. Sch. 34, Bklyn., St. Agatha's Ch. and Convent, Phila. Mem. Nat. Trust Historic Preservation, Association Internationale des Arts Plastigus-UNESCO, Academie Internationale de Lutèce (Paris). Artists Equity Assn., Inter-Am. Soc. Home: 730 Lorimer St Brooklyn NY 11211

AVERSA, JOHN MICHAEL, orthopedic surgeon; b. Bklyn., July 20, 1942; s. Attilio John and Virginia (Adinolfi) A.; A.B., N.Y. U., 1963; M.D., State U. N.Y., 1967; m. Ellen Jane Ferreri, June 17, 1967; children—John Michael, Kristen Rachele, David Mathew. Intern, N.Y. Hosp.-Cornell Med. Center, N.Y.C., 1967-70; resident Yale-New Haven Hosp., 1972-75; practice medicine specializing in orthopedic surgery, New Haven Orthopaedic Group, 1975—; attending surgeon Yale New Haven Hosp., Hosp. of St. Raphael, VA Hosp. West Haven, Yale U. Health Service; clin. instr. surgery Med. Sch., Yale U.; cons. Laurel Heights Hosp., Arden House Convalescent Hosp.; lectr. Quinnipiac Coll. Served to lt. comdr. USN, 1970-72. Charles Ohse grantee, 1974-75. Mem. Am. Acad. Orthopaedics, New Haven County Med. Assn., New Haven Med. Soc., So. N.Eng. Hand Soc., AMA. Roman Catholic. Contbr. articles to profl. publs. Office: 60 Temple St New Haven CT 06510

AVERY, CYRUS STEVENS, II, realtor; b. Tulsa, Oct. 19, 1932; s. Gordon Stevens and Phoebe Jane (Heffner) A.; B.S., U.S. Mil. Acad., West Point, 1954; M.B.A., Harvard U., 1962; m. Ella Jane Wolverton, June 10, 1955; children—Cyrus Stevens, Allyson Anne. Sales rep. Ferris & Co., Washington, 1962-66, br. mgr., 1966-69, partner, 1968-71, sr. v.p., dir., 1971-74; asst. to pres. Internat. Bank, Washington, 1974-77; pres. Fin. Mortgage Realty Corp., Washington, 1974—, also dir.; dir. Fin. Internat. Corp., Intermediate Credit Corp. Chmn. bd. dirs. D.C. Devel. Corp., 1976—. Served with U.S. Army, 1954-60. Mem. D.C. Soc. Investment Analysts, Met. Washington Bd. Trade, Washington Bd. Realtors, West Point Soc. D.C., U.S. Savs. and Loan Assn. (dir. Arlington, Va. chpt. 1979), Harvard Bus. Sch. Club Washington. Republican. Episcopalian. Home: 8016 Georgetown Pike McLean VA 22102 Office: 1701 Pennsylvania Ave NW Washington DC 20006

AVERY, DAVID BURGESS, lawyer; b. Boston, Sept. 2, 1922; s. Herbert Spaulding and Alma (Anderson) A.; student Boston U., 1940; A.A., Suffolk U., 1942, LL.B., 1950; m. Marion E. Fortini, Dec. 26, 1950 (div. Dec. 1972); children—Jonathan Winslow, Faith Anne, Allison Anderson. Admitted to Mass. bar, 1951, since practiced in Boston; sr. mem. firm Avery, Dooley, Post & Avery, 1951—. Pres., treas. New Eng. Greenhouses, Inc., Boston, 1964—; pres., dir. Internat. Protective Products, Inc., Boston; treas., dir. Oliver F. Ames Devel. Corp., Inc., Boston, E.E. Avery Ins. Agy., Inc., Plymouth. Mem. Winthrop (Mass.) Planning Bd., 1946-49; sec. Internat. Christian Leadership Conf., Plymouth, 1960—. Mem. Winthrop Town Meeting, 1946-49; selectman Plymouth, 1951-56; Plymouth Airport Commr., 1951-56; town counsel, Kingston, Mass., 1951-57. Bd. dirs. Mountaintop Fellowship, Inc., 1971—, Life Ministries, Inc., 1971—. Served as lt. USNR, 1942-46. Fellow Mass. Bar Assn.; mem. Internat. Assn. Ins. Counsel, Am., Plymouth, Plymouth County bar assns., Mass. Trial Lawyers Assn., Mass. Def. Counsel Assn., Mass. Ins. Brokers, City Solicitors and Town Council Assn., Mass. Selectmen's Assn., Assn. Ins. Attys., Def. Research Inst., Mass. Police Chief's Assn., State Street Assos., Am. Legion, Am. Judicature Soc., V.F.W., Am. Vets. Assn. (past comdr.), Harlow Family Assn. (v.p. 1949—), EPHATA Internat. Inc. (treas.-dir. 1973—), Mass. Soc. Mayflower Descs., Pa. Claimsmen Assn. Republican. Methodist (trustee). Mason. Home: Shoel Creek NC Office: 141 Tremont St Boston MA 02111

AVERY, HENRY, chem. co. exec.; b. Boston, Oct. 6, 1919; s. Henry P. and Mary Ellen (Mitchell) A.; B.S., Mass. Inst. Tech., 1941; m. Mary Ruth Halverson, June 8, 1947; children—Cynthia Gail, Deborah Lea, Eric Halverson, Sarah Ann. Devel. engr. G.L. Cabot Co., Boston, 1946-51; gen. mgr. Indsl. Chems. div. Pitts. Coke & Chem. Co., 1951-60; exec. v.p., dir. Pitts. Chem. Co., 1960-66; group v.p. devel. USS Chems. div. U.S. Steel Corp., Pitts., 1966-71, v.p. plastics USS Chems. div., 1971-76, v.p. planning and devel. USS Chems. div., 1976—; mem. regional export expansion council Dept. Commerce; civilian aide to sec. army for Western Pa., 1966—. Chmn. Mass. Inst. Tech. Ednl. Counselors, Western Pa., Scholarship Com., Nat. Nominating Com. Served to maj. AUS, World War II. Decorated Legion of Merit; medal of Valor (Italy). Mem. Mfg. Chemists Assn. (chmn. plastics com.), Comml. Chem. Devel. Assn. (pres.), Am. Def. Preparedness Assn. (pres. Pitts. chpt.), Mil. Order World Wars (comdr. Pitts. chpt. 1975-76), Soc. Plastics Industry, Am. Mgmt. Assn., Mass. Inst. Tech. Alumni Assn., Nat. Planning Assn., Greater Pitts. C. of C. (chmn. bd., past pres., chmn. econ. devel. council, dir.) SAR, Soc. Mayflower Descs. Presbyterian (elder). Clubs: Univ.; Duquesne, Press (Pitts.). Author ordnance sect. U.S. Army Mil. Ency., 1945. Home: 2681 Cedarvue Dr Pittsburgh PA 15241 Office: 600 Grant St Pittsburgh PA 15230

AVIADO, DOMINGO MARIANO, pharmacologist; b. Manila, Aug. 28, 1924; s. Domingo and Severina (Mariano) A.; came to U.S., 1945, naturalized, 1952; student U. Philippines, 1940-42, Coll. Medicine, 1942-45; M.D., U. Pa., 1948; m. Asuncion Guevara, Aug. 15, 1953; children—Maria Cristina, Carlos, Domingo, Maria Asuncion. Faculty, U. Pa., 1948-77, prof. pharmacology, 1965-77; sr. dir. biomed. research Allied Chem. Corp., Morristown, N.J., 1977—; mem. staff Phila. Gen. Hosp., 1955-72; vis. lectr. anesthesiology Albert Einstein Med. Center, 1955—, Women's Med. Coll., Phila., 1961-62; adj. prof. pharmacology N.J. Sch. Medicine, Newark, 1978—. Mem. sci. adv. bd. EPA, 1979—. Recipient Rockefeller Found. Travel award, 1961, Linnaeus medal 1st Internat. Pharmacol. Mtg., Stockholm, 1961, Purkinje medal 2d Internat. Pharmacol. Mtg., Prague, 1963, Philippines Presdl. trophy for Most Outstanding Filipino Overseas, 1975; NIH fellow, 1948-50, Guggenheim Found. fellow, 1962-63. Mem. Am. Soc. Pharmacology and Exptl. Therapeutics, Am. Physiol. Soc., AAAS, Am. Heart Assn., Internat. Union Pharmacology, Physiol. Soc. Phila., AMA, Coll. Physicians Phila., Pharmacologic Prins. Med. Practice, Sigma Xi, Alpha Omega Alpha. Author: The Lung Circulation, 2 vols., 1965; Sympathomimetic Drugs, 1970; Propellants and Solvents in the Environment, 1977; sect. editor Chem. Abstracts, 1952-58; asso. editor Circulation Research, 1958-62; editorial cons. Dorland Illustrated Med. Dictionary, 1963-66, Stedman's Med. Dictionary, 1972-75. Research in field of action of drugs on cardiovascular and respiratory systems. Home: 225 Hartshorn Dr Short Hills NJ 07078 Office: PO Box 1021R Morristown NJ 07960

AVITZUR, BETZALEL, mech. engr., educator; b. Haifa, Israel, May 7, 1925; s. Shraga and Nehama (Voronowsky) A.; came to U.S., 1964, naturalized, 1972; B.S., diploma in mech. engring., Technion Israel Inst. Tech., Haifa, 1947; M.S. in Indsl. Engring., U. Mich., 1956, Ph.D. in Mech. Engring., 1960; m. Pnina Stuerman, Aug. 9, 1955; children—Orly, Amir, Tal, Ron. Research engr. Ford Motor Co., Dearborn, Mich., 1959-61; sr. lectr. Technion Israel Inst. Tech., 1961-64; prof. metallurgy and materials sci. Lehigh U., Bethlehem, Pa., 1964—, dir. Inst. Metal Forming, 1970—; cons. engr., pres. Metalforming Inc., Allentown, Pa., 1972—. Mem. ASME, Wire Assn., Metall. Soc. Author: Metal Forming: Processes and Analysis, 1968; contbr. articles on metal forming processes to profl. jours. Patentee in shaping of hollow workpieces, also wire forming processes. Home: 817 N 31st St Allentown PA 18104 Office: Whitaker Lab Dept Metallurgy Lehigh U Bethlehem PA 18015

AVRAMI, LOUIS, physicist; b. Atlantic City, May 7, 1922; s. Thomas and Tali (Leka) A.; B.S., Rutgers U., 1949; M.S., Stevens Inst. Tech., 1952; certificate Internat. Inst. Nuclear Sci. and Engring., 1961; m. Doris Martino, Apr. 23, 1961; children—Louis, Nicole Stephanie, Erica Christine. With Picatinny Arsenal (now ARRADCOM), Dover, N.J., 1950—, successivley asst. chief atomic ammunition br., supervisory physicist reactor requirements office, acting chief physicist, chief physics br. explosives div., chief radiation effects br., 1955-74, research physicist solid state br., 1974—; chmn. Nuclear Survivability Working Group for Propulsion and Ordnance, 1968—. Asst. dir. radiation-chem. div. Morris County (N.J.) Civil Def., Morristown, 1961—. Served with USAAF, 1942-46. Decorated D.F.C. with oak leaf, Air medal with 4 oak leaves; recipient outstanding achievement award Picatinny Arsenal, 1963, research and devel. award, 1973. Mem. Am. Phys. Soc., Am. Nuclear Soc., Combustion Inst., Research Soc. Am., Am. Philatelic Soc., Soc. Philatelic Ams., Morristown Coin Club, Am. Numis. Assn., Sigma Xi. Albanian Orthodox. Contbr. articles to profl. jours.; author govt. publs. Home: 4 Paula Ct Morristown NJ 07690 Office: ARRADCOM Dover NJ 07801

AW, PEGGY, pediatrician; b. Rangoon, Burma, May. 5, 1934; d. Bong Sum and Say Han (Cheah) Khoo; came to U.S., 1971, naturalized, 1977; I.S., U. Rangoon, 1955; M.B., B.S., Inst. Medicine, Rangoon, 1960; m. Robin Aw, May 28, 1960; children—Rocky, Ricky. Rotating intern Rangoon Gen. Hosp., 1960-61; demostrator in physiology Inst. Medicine, Rangoon, 1962-67, asst. lectr. dept. physiology and biochemistry, 1967-69; pvt. practice medicine, Rangoon, 1966-70; rotating intern Morristown (N.J.) Meml. Hosp., 1972-73; resident in pediatrics Staten Island (N.Y.) Hosp., 1974-76; pediatrician N.Y. City Health and Hosp. Corp., East N.Y. Neighborhood Family Care Center, Bklyn., 1976—; pvt. practice medicine specializing in pediatrics, N.Y.C., 1977—. Recipient Physician's Recognition award in continuing med. edn. AMA. 1975-78, 78-81. Mem. intern and resident com., N.Y., 1974-76. Mem. Pub. Health Physician Assn., Kings County Health Care Rev. Orgn. Home: 104 Berry Ave Staten Island NY 10312 Office: 2094 Pitkin Ave Brooklyn NY 11207

AWADA, MICHAEL, lawyer; b. Montreal, Que., Can., Nov. 16, 1930; s. Solomon Moses and Alice (Hanna) A.; B.A., Sir George Williams Coll., 1955; B.C.L., McGill U., 1956; m. Cheryl Sandra Zakaib, Sept. 30, 1962; children—Glenn, Kim. With sales dept. Merck & Co., Ltd., 1949-51; indentured to firm Heward, Holden, Hutchinson, Cliff, McMaster & Meighen, 1956-57; called to Que. bar, 1957, since practiced in Montreal; jr. asso. firm John Jacob Spector, 1957-60; partner firm Awada & Bey, 1960-69, Awada, Gareau & Feifer, 1969-72, Awada & Gareau, 1972-73; partner firm Awada, Gareau & Sumbulian, 1973—; lectr. RCAF Res. Officers Sch., Royal Mil. Coll., Kingston, Ont. Dir. Maisonneuve Distributors, Inc. (Montreal), George Courey & Sons, Ltd. (Montreal), Canadian Granite Industries Assn., Hanna Mfg. Co., Ltd. Hon. legal adviser St. George Orthodox Ch., Montreal. Served with RCAF, 1951-56. Mem. Internat. Platform Assn. Exec. editor McGill Law Jour., 1955-56. Contbr. articles to law jours. Home: 11230 Joseph Casavant Montreal PQ H3M 2B7 Canada Office: 1010 Sherbrooke St W Suite 1011 Montreal PQ H3A 2R7 Canada

AXELROD, HOWARD JAY, elec. engr., economist; b. Albany, N.Y., Sept. 26, 1947; s. Herbert and Frances A.; B.S. in E.E., Northeastern U., 1970, M.S. in E.E., 1971; M.B.A., State U. N.Y., Albany, 1975; postgrad. Rensselaer Poly. Inst., 1976—; m. Nora Perlman, Jan. 8, 1972; children—Jed Ryan, Jill Lauren. Application engr. Gen. Electric Co., Schenectady and Boston, 1968-71; sr. power research analyst N.Y. State Pub. Service Commn., Albany, 1971-76; chief engring. investigations N.Y. State Consumer Protection Bd., Albany, 1976—; mem. econs. dept. faculty Rensselaer Poly. Registered profl. engr., N.Y.; Gen. Electric Co. grantee, 1970-71. Mem. IEEE, Engring. Mgmt. Soc., Power Engring. Soc. Contbr. expert testimony before pub. service commn., also articles to profl. jours. Home: 29 Simon Ln Latham NY 12110 Office: 99 Washington Ave Albany NY 12210

AXELROD, JULIUS, biochemist, pharmacologist; b. N.Y.C., May 30, 1912; s. Isadore and Molly (Leichtling) A.; B.S., Coll. City N.Y., 1933; M.A., N.Y.U., 1941, D.Sc. (hon.), 1971, Ph.D., George Washington U., 1955, LL.D. (hon.), 1971; D.Sc. (hon.), U. Chgo., 1965, Med. Coll. Wis., 1971; LL.D., City Coll. N.Y., 1972; Dr.h.c., U. Panama, 1972; Sc.D., Med. Coll. Phila., 1974; m. Sally Taub, Aug. 30, 1938; children—Paul Mark, Alfred Nathan. Chemist, Lab. Indsl. Hygiene, 1935-46; research asso. 3d N.Y.U. research div. Goldwater Meml. Hosp., 1946-49; asso. chemist sect. chem. pharmacology Nat. Heart Inst., NIH, 1949-50, chemist, 1950-53, sr. chemist, 1953-55, acting chief sect. pharmacology Lab. Clin. Sci., NIMH, 1955, chief sect. pharmacology, 1955—; Otto Loewi meml. lectr. N.Y.U., 1963; Karl E. Paschkis meml. lectr. Phila. Endocrine Soc., 1966; NIH lectr., 1967; Nathanson meml. lectr. U. So. Calif., 1968; James Parkinson lectr. Columbia, 1971; Wartenberg lectr. Am. Acad. Neurology, 1971; Arnold D. Welch lectr. Yale, 1971; Harold Carpenter Dodge distinguished lectr. toxicology U. Rochester, 1971; Bennett lectr. Am. Neurol. Assn., 1971; Harvey lectr., 1971; Mayer lectr. Mass. Inst. Tech., 1971; distinguished prof. sci. George Washington U., 1972; Salmon lectr. N.Y. Acad. Medicine, 1972; Eli Lilly lectr., 1972; Mike Hogg lectr. U. Tex., 1972; Fred Schueler lectr. Tulane U., 1972; vis. scholar Herbert Lehman Coll. City N.Y., 1973. Cons. George Washington U., 1959—; panelist U. S. Bd. Civil Service Examiners, 1958—; mem. research adv. com. United Cerebral Palsy Assn., 1966-69; mem. psychopharmacology study sect. NIMH, 1970-74; mem. Population Crisis Com., Internat. Brain Research Orgn.; mem. research adv. com. Nat. Found., Parkinson Found.; vis. com. Brookhaven Nat. Lab.; bd. overseers Jackson Lab., 1974. Recipient Meritorious Research award Assn. Research Nervous and Mental Diseases, 1965; Gairdner award distinguished research, 1967; Nobel prize med. physiology, 1970; Alumni Distinguished Achievement award George Washington U., 1968; Superior Service award HEW, 1968, Distinguished Service award, 1970; Cluade Bernard professorship and medal U. Montreal, 1969; Distinguished Service award Modern Medicine mag., 1970; Albert Einstein award Yeshiva U., 1971; medal Rudolf Virchow Med. Soc., 1971; Myrtle Wreath award Hadassah, 1972. Fellow Am. Acad. Arts and Scis., Am. Soc. Neuropsychopharmacology; mem. German Pharmacol. Soc. (corr.), Am. Chem. Soc., Am. Soc. Pharmacology and Exptl. Therapeutics (Torald Sollmann award 1973), Am. Soc. Biol. Chemists, AAAS, Nat. Acad. Scis., Am. Neurol. Assn. (hon.), Sigma Xi; hon. mem. Am. Psycholpathol. Assn. Contbr. articles to profl. jours. Editorial bd. Jour Pharmacology and Exptl. Therapeutics, 1956-72, Jour. Medicinal Chemistry, 1962-67, Circulation Research, 1963-71, Currents in Modern Biology, 1966-72; editorial adv. bd. Communication in Behavioral Biology, 1967, Jour Neuroviseral Relation, 1969, Rassegna di Neurologia Vegetativa, 1969—, Internat. Jour. Physchobiology, 1970—; hon. cons. editor Life Scis., 1961-69. Co-author: The Pineal, 1968. Contbr. papers in biochem. actions and metabolism of drugs, hormones, action of pineal gland, enzymes, neurochem. transmission to profl. jours. Home: 10401 Grosvenor Pl Rockville MD 20852 Office: NIH Bethesda MD 20014

AXELROD, NORMAN N(ATHAN), opticist, physicist; b. N.Y.C., Aug. 26, 1934; s. Louis E. and Sadie (Katz) A.; A.B., Cornell U., 1954; Ph.D., U. Rochester, 1959; m. Victoria Ann Grant; 1 dau., Lauren Grant. Aerospace scientist NASA, Goddard Space Flight Center, Washington, 1959-60; research fellow U. London, Eng., 1960-61; asst. prof. U. Del., 1961-65; mem. tech. staff Bell Labs., Murray Hill, N.J., 1965-72; cons. Axelrod Assos., 1972—; dir. World Resources Devel. Co., 1971—. Mem. adv. bd. Del. Dept. Edn., 1963-64; cons. Met. Mus. Art, N.Y.C., 1969-72; participant vis. Scientist program Am. Inst. Physics, 1963-64; adviser to White House, 1969-70; cons. French Ministry Nat. Def. and War, 1971. Fellow AAAS; mem. Am. Phys. Soc., Am. Optical Soc., IEEE, Del., N.Y. acads. sci., Electrochem. Soc., Sigma Xi, Sigma Pi Sigma, Pi Mu Epsilon. Editor: Optical Properties of Dielectric Films, 1968. Book reviewer, cons. John Wiley & Sons, 1965-68, Rheinhold-Van Nostrand, 1968-70, Pergamon Press, 1969-70. Contbr. articles to profl. jours. Patentee in field. Office: 445 E 86th St New York City NY 10028

AXELSON, KENNETH STRONG, corp. exec.; b. Chgo., July 31, 1922; s. Charles F. and Katherine (Strong) A.; A.B., U. Chgo., (John Crerar Scholar 1939-43), 1944; grad. student Va. Poly. Inst., 1943-44; m. Roberta Bearhope, Jan. 23, 1943; children—Kenneth Strong, Jerrold Frederic, Stephen, John. Accountant Arthur Andersen & Co., Seattle, 1946-48; controller Columbia Lumber Co. of Alaska, Juneau, 1948-50; mgmt. cons. McKinsey & Co., Chgo., 1950-52; mgr., mgmt. controls dept. Peat, Marwick, Mitchell & Co. 1952-53, partner, 1953-63; v.p. fin. J.C. Penney Co., Inc. N.Y.C., 1963-67, v.p. fin. and adminstrn., 1967-74, sr. v.p. fin. and adminstrn., 1974-78, dir., 1964—, sr. v.p. fin. and pub affairs, 1978—; dir. Protection Mut. Ins. Co., Discount Corp. N.Y., Grumman Corp. trustee Dry Dock Savs. Bank, 1975—; mem. advisory com. on implementation central market system SEC, 1974-75; dep. mayor fin. N.Y.C., 1975-76; mem. Emergency Fin. Control Bd., N.Y.C., 1976-77. Trustee Fin. Execs. Research Found.; bd. dirs. Lincoln Sq. Neighborhood Center, 1970-77. Served as warrant officer U.S. Army, 1943-46. Recipient 1st ann. lit. award Jour. Accountancy; C.P.A., Ill., Wash., Iowa, N.Mex., N.Y., Va. Mem. Am. Inst. C.P.A.'s (accounting prins. bd. 1968-70), Fin. Execs. Inst. (pres. N.Y.C. chpt. 1975), N.Y. Soc. C.P.A.'s, U. Chgo. Club N.Y. (pres. 1961-62), Nat. Assn. Accountants, Sch. Bus. Assn. U. Chgo. (pres. 1957-58), Assn. for A Better N.Y. (exec. com.), Phi Delta Theta. Baptist. Clubs: India House, Metropolitan (N.Y.C.). Author: Responsibility Reporting, 1961. Editor Mgmt. Controls bus. jour., 1958-63. Home: 115 Central Park W New York City NY 10023 Office: 1301 Ave of Americas New York City NY 10019

AYA, RODERICK HONEYMAN, corp. tax exec.; b. Portland, Oreg., Sept. 17, 1916; s. Alfred Anthony and Grace Myrtle (Honeyman) A.; student U. Oreg., 1935-36, Internat. Accountants Soc., 1937-39, LaSalle Extension U., 1940-42, Walton Sch. Commerce, 1942, U. Calif. Extension, 1945; m. Helen Marjorie Riddle, June 16, 1945; children—Roderick Riddle, Deborah Germaine Aya Reynolds, Ronald Honeyman. Chief statistician Hotel Employers Assn., San Francisco, 1939-42; accountant Pacific Tel. & Tel. Co., San Francisco, 1942-52, spl. accountant, 1952-63; tax accountant 1963-65; spl. accountant AT&T, N.Y.C., 1965-68, mgr. tax studies, 1968-73, mgr. tax research and planning, 1974—; public accountant, San Francisco, 1940—; music tchr., 1959—; v.p., treas., dir. Snell Research Assos., Inc.; guest lectr. on taxes Westchester County Adult Edn. Program. Committeeman, Marin council Boy Scouts Am., 1959-60, com. chmn., 1959-61; mem. Marin County Sheriffs' Res., 1963-65; law enforcement liaison com. on Juvenile Control; sec. Am. Nat. Standards Inst. Com. on Protective Headgear. Vice pres., treas., bd. dirs. Snell Meml. Found.; trustee Snell Meml. Found. (U.K.), Ltd.; dir., past pres. Stuart Highlanders Pipe Band of San Francisco. Recipient Wisdom award Honor, Wisdom Soc., 1970. Mem. ASTM, Nat. Soc. Pub. Accountants, U.S. Yacht Racing Union, U.S. Naval Inst., St. Andrews Soc., Internat. Oceanographic Found., Soc. for Ethnomusicology (contbr. to jour.), Phi Chi, Sigma Nu, Clubs: Corinthian Yacht (Tiburon, Calif.); Sports Car of Am. (regional dir. 1957-59, regional treas. 1957-58). Author: The Legacy of Pete Snell, 1966. Home: Maid of Barra 105 Rowayton Ave Rowayton CT 06853 Office: 195 Broadway New York City NY 10007

AYBAR, ROMEO, architect; b. Buenos Aires, Argentina, Feb. 8, 1930; s. Aristobulo Romeo and Maria Sara (Figoli) A.; B. Arch., U. Buenos Aires, 1954; m. Rose Delia Caceres, Oct. 18, 1954; children—Patricia Monica Aybar Smith, Viviana Sylvia, Cynthia Jenny. Came to U.S., 1960, naturalized, 1965. Pvt. practice architecture, Buenos Aires, 1955-60; sr. draftsman Wiedersum Assos., N.Y.C., 1960-61; job capt. Mahoney Troast, Clifton, N.J., 1961-63; project mgr. R. Cadien Architect, Cliffside Park, N.J., 1963-67; partner Cadien & Aybar, Cliffside Park, 1968-69; prin. Romeo Aybar, architect and planner, Ridgefield, 1969—. Adj. faculty Montclair State Coll., 1971—. Mem. Indsl. Safety Council N.J., 1973-78. Mem. Zoning Bd. Adjustments, Ridgefield, 1969-71, chmn., 1972-73; acting bldg. insp., Ridgefield, 1968. Recipient Directors award, 1971, Vegliante Meml. award, 1973 both from Architect League N.J.; Outstanding Excellence In Design award N.J. Soc. Architects, 1971, 73. Mem. Architect League No. N.J., (pres. 1975), N.J. Soc. Architects (dir. 1973, treas. 1974-75, v.p. 1976, pres.-elect 1978, pres. 1979), AIA (N.J. commr. pub. edn. com. 1971-72), CAP (sr. mem., pilot N.J. wing 1978). Republican. Club: Ridgefield Exchange (pres. 1972, dir. N.J. dist. 1973-74). Home: 550 Oak St Ridgefield NJ 07657 Office: 605 Broad Ave Ridgefield NJ 07657

AYERS, FRANK EDWARD, mcpl. ofcl., civil engr.; b. Saskatoon, Sask., Can., Jan. 14, 1921; s. George William and Otillie (Schwenig) A.; B.S., U. Sask., 1943; m. Doreen Jane Porter, Sept. 13, 1943; children—Carolyn, Paul, David. City engr. City of Ft. William (Ont., Can.), 1947-55; dir. planning and works City of Ottawa (Ont.), 1955-68; works commr. Regional Municipality Ottawa-Carleton (Ont.), 1969—; pres. Can. Inst. Pollution Control, 1964-65; chmn. Rideau Valley Conservation Authority, 1973-74. Served to lt., C.E., Royal Can. Armed Forces, 1943-45. Recipient Can. Centennial medal, 1967; Profl. Engrs. Citizenship award, 1976. Fellow Engring. Inst. Can.; mem. Am. Pub. Works Assn. (Man of Year 1974), Assn. Profl. Engrs. Ont., Mil. Engrs. Assn. Can., Am. Water Works Assn., Pollution Control Assn. Ont. Anglican. Clubs: Ottawa Hunt and Golf, Canadian, Masons. Home: 1049 Castlehill Crescent Ottawa ON K2C 2A7 Canada Office: 222 Queen St Ottawa ON K1P 5Z3 Canada

AYERS, JOSEPH WILLIAMS, chem. co. exec.; b. Easton, Pa., Jan. 6, 1904; s. Charles Pierson and Emma Cottman (Williams) A.; B.Chemistry, Cornell U., 1927, postgrad., 1927-28; m. Caroline Brooke Stone, Oct. 6, 1934; children—Katherine Ayers Hovey, Phyllis Ayers Harmon. Research dir. C.K. Williams & Co., Easton, Pa., 1930-48, v.p., 1945-62; gen. mgr. minerals pigments and metals div. Pfizer, Inc., N.Y.C., 1962-68, pres., 1968-69; pres. Calcium Chem. Corp., Adams, Mass., 1937-48; pres. Agrashell, Inc., Los Angeles, 1939-76, chmn. bd., 1977—; pres. J.W. Ayers, & Co., Easton, 1955-61, The Ayers Co., Easton, 1971—; pres., treas. Joseph Ayers, Inc., Bethlehem, Pa., 1973—; dir. New Eng. Lime Co., Foote Mineral Co.; dir. emeritus Easton Nat. Bank. Chmn., Pa. Hosp. and Health Council, 1971-74, dir., 1975—; v.p. Northampton County Citizens for Regional Progress, 1973—; trustee Greater Valley council Girl Scouts U.S., Bach choir of Bethlehem (Pa.). Mem. Am. Inst. Chem. Engrs., Am. Inst. Chemists, Am. Chem. Soc., AAAS, Soc. Chem. Industries (Eng.), N.Y. Chemist Club, Zeta Psi. Republican. Presbyterian. Clubs: Cornell, Union League (N.Y.C.); Northhampton County Country; Pomfret (Easton); Oyster Harbors, Wianno, Wianno Yacht (Osterville, Mass.); Beach (Craigsville, (Mass.); Los Angeles Athletic. Contbr. articles to profl. jours. Patentee in field. Home: 22 N 14th St Easton PA 18042 Office: RFD 2 Bethlehem PA 18017

AYKAN, KAMRAN, chem. co. exec.; b. Istanbul, Turkey, May 19, 1930; s. Mehmet Emin and Fatma (Hikmet) A.; came to U.S., 1957, naturalized, 1976; student U. Istanbul, 1948-51, M.S. in Chemistry, 1954; postgrad. U. Hamburg (Germany), 1951-53; m. Irmgard Kopp, Jan. 17, 1957. With Bergbau A.G., Koenig Ludwig, Germany, 1956-7; chemist William T. Burnett & Co., Inc., Balt., 1957-58; chemist E.I. DuPont De Nemours & Co., Inc., Wilmington, Del., 1958-71, staff scientist, 1971; mgr. chem. research Engelhard Industries div. Engelhard Minerals & Chem. Corp., Edison, N.J., 1971-72, tech. dir., 1972-74, dir. research and devel., 1974-76, v.p. research and devel., 1976—. Bd. dirs. Research and Devel. Council N.J. Served with Turkish Signal Corps, 1954-56. Mem. Am. Cyrstallographic Assn., Am. Chem. Soc., Research and Devel. Council N.J., Indsl. Research Inst., Am. Ceramic Soc., Catalysis Soc. N.Y. Contbr. articles to profl. jours.; patentee in field. Office: Menlo Park Edison NJ 08817

AYLESWORTH, THOMAS GIBBONS, editor; b. Valparaiso, Ind., Nov. 5, 1927; s. Carrol Wells and Margaret Ruth (Gibbons) A.; A.B., Ind. U., 1950; M.S., 1953; Ph.D., Ohio State U., 1959; m. Virginia Lillian Boelter, Aug. 13, 1949; children—Carol Jean, Thomas Paul. Tchr. Harvard (Ill.) High Sch., 1951-52; New Albany (Ind.) Jr. High Sch., 1952-54; head sci. dept. Battle Creek (Mich.) High Sch., 1955-57; asst. prof. Mich. State U., East Lansing, 1957-61; spl. lectr. Wesleyan U., Middletown, Conn., 1961-64; sr. editor Doubleday & Co., Inc., N.Y.C., 1964—; pres. Update Pub. Corp., 1976—; vis. prof. Ohio State U., Columbus, 1962, Whitewater (Wis.) State U., 1964. Served with AUS, 1946-47. Mem. N.Y. Acad. Scis., Nat. Sci. Tchrs. Assn., Nat. Assn. Biology Tchrs., Nat. Assn. Research Sci. Teaching, Am. Assn. Sci. Writers, Authors Guild, Phi Delta Kappa. Club: Stamford (Conn.) Yacht. Author: Our Polluted World, 1964; Planning for Effective Science Teaching, 1963; This Vital Air, This Vital Water, 1968, rev. edit., 1973; It Works Like This, 1968; Teaching for Thinking, 1969; Into The Mammal's World, 1970; Traveling Into Tomorrow, 1970, Servants Of The Devil, 1970; Mysteries From The Past, 1971; Werewolves And Other Monsters, 1971; Vampires And Other Ghosts, 1972; Monsters from the Movies, 1972; The Alchemists, 1973; Astrology and Fortelling the Future, 1973; Who's Out There?, 1975; The World of Microbes, 1975; Cars, Boats, Trains and Planes of Today and Tomorrow, 1975; ESP, 1975; Movie Monsters, 1975; The Search for Life, 1975; Palmistry, 1976; Graphology, 1976; Science Update, 1977, 78; Science at the Ball Game, 1977; The Story of Vampires, 1977; Earthquakes and Volcanoes, 1978; The Story of Werewolves, 1978. New Eng. editor, American Biology Teacher, 1962-64. Home: 48 Van Rensselaer St Stamford CT 06902 Office: 245 Park Ave New York City NY 10017

AYLSWORTH, JOSEPH LYNN, JR., health care services exec.; b. Phila., June 30, 1916; s. Joseph Lynn and Margaret Eleanor (Wanner) A.; student accounting Peirce Jr. Coll., 1938; m. Marjorie Jane Biedert, June 20, 1942; children—Susan C. Aylsworth Murwin, Joseph Lynn, John Stephen. Registered rep. Butcher Sherrerd, 1946; pres. Mortgage Assos., Inc., 1946-68; exec. v.p. Am. Med. Affiliates, Inc., Jenkintown, Pa., 1968—, also dir. Chmn., Montgomery County chpt. Am. Cancer Soc., 1971; bd. dirs. Erie Osteo. Hosp. (Pa.), Met. Hosp., Phila.; trustee Kirksville Coll. Osteo. Medicine, Keys Community Hosp., Tavernier, Fla. Served to 1st lt. USAAF, 1942-45. Decorated Air medal. Mem. Am. Nursing Home Assn., Health Care Facilities Assn. Pa., Phila. Mortgage Bankers Assn. (pres. 1959). Lutheran (councilman 1972—). Club: Union League (Phila.). Home: 1332 Wright Dr Huntingdon Valley PA 19006 Office: PO Box 608 Foxcroft Sq Apts Jenkintown PA 19046

AYLWARD, LEO JOSEPH ("JAY"), paper co. exec.; b. Montpelier, Vt., Sept. 17, 1939; s. Leo Joseph and Erina (Chiodi) A.; B.S., Norwich U., 1962; m. Bonnie I. Biggs, June 20, 1939; children—Dawn T., Jess W. Customer service rep. Groveton Papers Co. (N.H.), 1967-69, product mgr., 1969-74, v.p., product mgr., 1974-77, v.p., gen. mgr., 1977—, also dir. Served to capt. AUS, 1962-67. Decorated Bronze Star, Air medal. Mem. TAPPI, Paper Industry Mgmt. Assn. Republican. Club: Waumbec Golf. Home: 1 Arlington Ave Groveton NH 03582 Office: Groveton Papers Co Groveton NH 03582

AYOUB, ALFRED, dentist; b. Passaic, N.J., May 25, 1923; s. Anthony and Sadie (Shahadi) A.; A.B. in Chemistry, Drew U., 1948; D.D.S., Temple U., 1952; postgrad. certificate orthodontia N.Y. U., 1961; m. Elaine Orstein, Dec. 24, 1951; children—Richard Anthony, Christopher George, Wendy Drew. Staff dentist Christian Sanitorium, Wychkoff, N.J., 1952-55; mem. staff postgrad. orthodontia div. N.Y. U. Sch. Dentistry, 1957-61; gen. practice dentistry, Pompton Lakes, N.J., 1952—. Served with USNR, 1943-46. Mem. Omicron Kappa Upsilon, Xi Psi Phi. Home: 91 Wilson Ave Wayne NJ 07470 Office: 10 Lenox Ave Pompton Lakes NJ 07442

AYRES, ROBERT CHARLES, ins. co. exec.; b. Erie, Pa., Apr. 18, 1936; s. Horace C. and Edith Ayres; B.S. in Commerce and Finance, Bucknell U., 1958; m. Kathleen Ann Gildea, Oct. 1, 1966; children—Kimberly P., Deborah J. Underwriting trainee Home Ins. Co., N.Y.C., 1958-59; ins. adjuster and supr. Liberty Mutual Ins. Co., Bklyn., 1959-62, N.Y.C., 1962-65; claims supr. Transport Ins. Co., Newark, 1965-66, New Eng. regional claims mgr., 1966-72, New Eng. service and sales mgr., Natick, Mass., 1972—. Mem. Mass. Motor Truck Assn., Maine Motor Transport Assn., New Eng. Motor Carrier Accounting Council, Motor Transport Assn. of Conn. Republican. Episcopalian. Home: 53 Keith Hill Rd Grafton MA 01519 Office: 209 W Central St Natick MA 01760

AZER, MAGDI SELIM, surgeon; b. Cairo, Egypt, Oct. 23, 1933; s. Selim and Fahima (Mahmoudi) A.; P.N.S., Cairo U., 1951; M.B., B.Ch., 1957; m. Karen Wright, May 20, 1967; children—Richard, Michele, Melissa. Came to U.S., 1960, naturalized, 1972. Resident in surgery St. Louis Little Rock Hosp., 1961-65; resident thoracic surgery St. Francis Hosp., Pitts., 1965-67; fellow cardiac surgery Hosp. for Sick Children, Toronto, Ont., Can., 1967-68; practiced medicine specializing in thoracic and cardiovascular surgery, W.Va., 1968-70, Johnstown, Pa., 1970—; thoracic surgeon Lee, Mercy hosps.; chief thoracic and cardiovascular surgery Conemaugh Valley Meml. Hosp., 1971—, chmn. dept. surgery, 1976—; clin. asso. prof. surgery Temple U. Med. Sch., Phila., 1977—. Diplomate Am. Bd. Surgery, Am. Bd. Thoracic Surgery. Fellow A.C.S., Am. Coll. Cardiology, Am. Coll. Chest Physicians; mem. AMA, Soc. Thoracic Surgeons. Club: Sunnehanna Country (Johnstown). Home: 2315 Woodcrest Dr Johnstown PA 15905 Office: 88 Osborne St Johnstown PA 15905

BAAR, JAMES A., pub. relations exec.; b. N.Y.C., Feb. 9, 1929; s. A.W. and Marguerite R. B.; A.B., Union Coll., 1949; m. Beverly Hodge, Sept. 2, 1948; 1 son, Theodore Hall. Washington corr. U.P.I., various other wire services and newspaper assignments, 1949-59; sr. editor Missiles and Rockets mag., 1959-62; mgr. various news bur. operations Gen. Electric Co., 1962-66, mgr. European mktg. communications operation, 1966-70, pres. subsidiary Internat. Mktg. Communications Cons., 1970-72; sr. v.p., dir. pub. relations Lewis & Gilman, Inc., Phila., 1972-74; exec. v.p. Creamer Dickson Basford, Inc., N.Y.C., 1974-78; pres. Creamer Dickson Baseford-New Eng., 1978—. Vestryman, St. Stephen's Ch., Providence. Mem. Nat. Investor Relations Inst., Pub. Relations Soc. Am., Aviation/Space Writers Assn., Internat. Pub. Relations Soc., Chi Psi. Republican. Clubs: Nat. Press, Mohawk (Schenectady); Agawam Hunt (Providence); Dunes (Narragansett, R.I.). Author: Polaris, 1960; Combat Missileman, 1961; Spacecraft and Missiles of the World, 1962; also numerous articles on business, aerospace and polit. subjects. Office: 40 Westminster St Providence RI 02903 also 1301 Ave of Americas New York City NY 10019

BAATZ, CHARLES ALBERT, psychologist, educator; b. Port Chester, N.Y., Apr. 4, 1916; s. Charles Frederick and Anna Marie (Lenherr) B.; B.A., Georgetown U., 1942, licentiate in philosophy, 1943; Ph.D., Fordham U., 1966; m. Olga A. Kozoriz, Jan. 25, 1947; children—Terrence, Barry. Asso. headmaster Oratory Sch., Summit, N.J., 1945-49; prof. edn., philosophy and psychology Seton Hall U., 1949—, chmn. dept. psychology, chmn. gen. profl. edn., co-founder, dir. grad. religious edn.; adj. asso. prof. edn. Fordham U.; lectr. N.Y. U., also Newark Coll. Engring., 1950-62. Pres. Citizens for Responsive Govt., South Orange, N.J., 1969—; v.p. Concerned Parents and Taxpayers, South Orange, 1971—; co-founder, mem. N.J. Council Ednl. Founds.; bd. dirs. Caritas Guild; asso. dir. Upward Bound, 1966-67; dir. Degree Bound, 1967-68; ordained deacon Roman Cath. Ch., 1975. Mem. Internat. Council on Edn. for Teaching, Am. Cath. Philos. Assn., AAUP, World Youth Vocat. Edn. Assn. (co-founder, v.p., dir.), Kappa Delta Pi. K.C. Author: A Critical Analysis of Willmann's Social Philosophy of Education, 1966; The Philosophy of Education: An Introductory Bibliography, 1979. Home: 168 Village Rd South Orange NJ 07079

BABBAGE, JOAN DOROTHY, journalist; b. Montclair, N.J., Jan. 10, 1926; d. Laurence Washburn and Dorothy A. (Davenport) Babbage; B.A. in English, Mt. Holyoke Coll., 1948; postgrad. Art Students League, New Sch. for Social Research; m. Vernon H. Ellsworth, Mar. 6, 1971. Publicist, Paramount Internat. Films, N.Y.C., 1952-58; reporter Newark News, 1960-67, food editor, 1967-72; feature writer, reporter Star-Ledger, Newark, 1972—. Vice pres. jr. group Women's Nat. Republican Club, N.Y.C., 1955. Recipient recommendation award N.J. br. Humane Soc. U.S. Contbr. restaurant revs., bus. articles N.J. Bus. Mag., articles Ofcl. Dog mag. Home: Washington Ave Montclair NJ 07042 Office: Star-Ledger Court St Newark NJ 07101

BABCOCK, BETTY THOMPSON, author, illustrator; b. N.Y.C., Sept. 27, 1900; d. Lewis Steenrod and Geraldine Livingston (Morgan) Thompson; student Art Students League, N.Y.C., 6 yrs.; m. Richard Franklin Babcock, Feb. 7, 1920 (div. Aug. 1942); children—Betsy (Mrs. Robert E. Moulton), Alice Woodward (Mrs. Stacey Lloyd), Anne (Mrs. James D. Bristow). Author, illustrator Polo, Horse and Horseman, The Sportsman, N.Y.C., 1931-40, Horse and Hound, The Field, London, Eng., 1932-39; asso. editor Country Life, N.Y.C., 1940-42; illustrator Grolier Club, N.Y.C., 1938. Active Arts and Skills Corps, A.R.C., 1942-45; dep. sr. warden Civil Def., Woodbury, N.Y.; mem. N.Y. State Citizens Com. for Pub. Schs.; v.p. Central Sch. Dist. No. 2, Syossett; mem. Nat. Com. Support of Pub. Schs. Dir. Brearly Sch., Home Sch., Child Study Assn. Trustee Bd. Edn., Woodbury. Candidate for del.to State Constn. Recipient N.Y. Pub. Library award, 1949, N.Y. State Tchrs. award, 1949, Distinguished Service award N.Y. State Sch. Bds. Assn., 1969. Mem. Nat. Forest Assn., Am. Nus. Natural History, Nat. Audubon Soc. Mem. Soc. of Friends, Nassau-Suffolk Sch. Bds. Assn. (exec. com.). Club: Colony (past gov.). Hon. hunt sec. Meadow Brook Hounds, 1939-42. Author: The Expandable Pig, 1949; Betty Babcock's Illustrated Hunting Diary, 1948. Illustrator: Just Hunting (by H. T. Peters), 1935; Earl American Sport (by Robert Henderson). 1937. Home: Hark Away Woodbury NY 11797 also (summer) Trout Pond Preserve Stoddard NH 03464

BABIGAN, EDWARD C., chemist, educator; b. Lowell, Mass., June 17, 1912; s. Asadoor and Perooz (Jeknavorian) B.; B. Textile Chemistry, Lowell Tech. Inst., 1933; postgrad. Salem (Mass.) State U., 1968, Brown U., 1970, Bowdoin Coll., 1971, 72, Colby Coll., 1973, U. Wis., 1974, U. N.H., 1975; m. Geneva Sooserian, Apr. 30, 1935 (dec.); children—Alan Edward, Lois Ann. Owner, pres. Outlet Fruit Co., Lowell, 1935-67; produce buyer Demoulas Super Markets, Tewksbury, Mass., 1967-68; tchr. physics Lowell High Sch., 1968-69, tchr. chemistry and environ. chemistry, 1969—; cons. in field; ind. researcher U. N.H., 1976, 77. Treas. Armenian Cultural Center drive, 1959-59. NSF grantee, 1970, 71, 72, 73, 74. Mem. Nat. Assn. Environ. Profls. Clubs: Masons, Mt. Pleasant Golf. Home: PO Box 1062 Lowell MA 01853

BABINE, LAWRENCE ROBERT, mfrs. rep.; b. Louisville, Jan. 4, 1919; s. John Rudolph and Josephine (Sullivan) B.; grad. Hebron Acad., 1939; student, Boston Coll., 1940-41; m. Madeline A. Manning, Aug. 30, 1947; children—Lawrence Robert, Nancy M., Sheila A., Patricia E. Clk., McKesson & Robbins Drug Co., Boston, 1945-46; salesman Howley-White Co., mfrs. rep., Boston, 1947-54; pres. Howley-White Assos. Inc., Burlington, Mass., 1954—. Mem. devel. commn., Arlington, Mass., 1958-60, park commn., 1964-70. Chmn. ways and means comm. Arlington Town Democratic Com., 1960-64. Served with AUS, 1941-45. Decorated Croix de Guerre. Mem. Nat. Assn. Drug Mfrs. (pres. 1967), N.E. Cosmetic Assn. (dir.), Small Bus. Assn. New Eng. K. C. Clubs: Wychmere Harbor (Harwich, Mass.); Columbus (Arlington). Home: 91 Stowecroft Rd Arlington MA 02174 Office: 78 Cambridge St Burlington MA 01803

BABITZKE, HERBERT ROLAND, ofcl. U.S. Bur. Mines; b. Eureka, S.D., May 7, 1930; s. Henry and Rosina (Rau) B.; B.S. in Gen. Sci., Oreg. State U., 1959; m. Esther Mae George, Mar. 20, 1954; 1 dau., Tracy Ann. Research chemist Albany (Oreg.) Metallurgy Research Center U.S. Bur. Mines, 1959-70, phys. scientist, Washington, 1970-76, liaison officer for Maine, Augusta, 1976—. Pres. Fir Grove Sch. PTA, Albany, 1961-62. Bd. dirs. Fir Grove Sch., Albany, 1962-66, chmn., 1966-67; bd. dirs. Benton County (Oreg.) Intermediate Edn., 1965-68. Served with USCG, 1949-55. Mem. Am. Soc. Metals, Am. Inst. Mining, Metall. Petroleum Engrs. (vice chmn. chpt. 1974-76), Toastmasters (area gov., dist. lt. gov., Able Toastmaster 1970, Distinguished Toastmaster 1971). Contbr. articles to scientific and engring. jours. Home: 132 Maine Ave Gardiner ME 04345 Office: US Bur Mines Fed Bldg and Post Office 40 Western Ave Augusta ME 04330

BACH, ROBERT BOURREE, ednl. adminstr.; b. Hagerstown, Md., June 11, 1923; s. Carl Christian and Helen Anna (Anderson) B.; student U. Chgo., 1942-43; A.B., Dartmouth Coll., 1947; postgrad. U. Pa., 1948-49, Temple U., 1949; m. Marie Virginia Franke, May 25, 1952 (div. July 1974); children—Del-Bourree Franke, Robin Peel. Tchr., wrestling coach Swarthmore Coll., 1948-52; sales mgr. Q-W Labs., Plainfield, N.J., 1952-60; mfrs. rep., 1960-69; bus. mgr. Wardlaw-Hartridge Sch., Plainfield, 1969—. Exec. bd. ARC, 1978. Served with USNR, 1943-46. Mem. N.J. Assn. Ind. Schs. Bus. Adminstrs. (pres. 1976-77), N.J. Wrestling Ofcls. Assn. (past pres.), Eastern Intercollegiate Wrestling Ofcls. Assn. (past sec.-treas., charter). Club: Kiwanis (pres. 1979—). Author: Wrestling Score Book, 1951. Office: 1295 Inman Ave Edison NJ 08817

BACHARACH, JAMES SIDNEY, market research co. exec.; b. N.Y.C., July 15, 1923; s. Sidney and Blanche Marion (Stroock) B.; B.A., Williams Coll., 1947; m. Dolores Ann Usischon, Nov. 18, 1950; children—Ann, James W., Katherine, Charles, Jean. Advt. copy writer Ruthrauff & Ryan Co., N.Y.C., 1947-51, Warwick & Legler, N.Y.C., 1951-53; advt. account supr. Cecil & Presbrey Co., N.Y.C., 1953-55, Grant Advt. Co., N.Y.C., 1955-58, O.E. McIntyre Co., N.Y.C., 1958-60; mktg. dir. Trendex Inc., Westport, Conn., 1960-63, v.p. sales, 1963-70, chief exec. officer, 1970—. exec. v.p. 1976—. Adv. com. Staples High Sch. work/study, 1969—; chmn. Westport Youth Adult Council, 1970—; v.p. Community Council Westport, 1970-72; chmn. parish council, 1965-68, 70-73; bd. dirs. Westport YMCA, 1966—, A Better Chance, Youth Home Ministry; mem. Westport-Stauffer Com., 1975—. Served to lt. (j.g.) USNR, 1943-46. Fairfield U. fellow. Mem. Am. Mktg. Assn., Am. Assn. Pub. Opinion

Research, Council Am. Survey Research Orgns. Republican. Roman Catholic. Clubs: Williams, Cedar Point Yacht. Home: 4 Stony Brook Rd Westport CT 06880 Office: 15 Riverside Ave Westport CT 06880

BACHER, FREDERICK ADDISON, chemist; b. Northampton, Mass., July 18, 1915; s. Frederick and Minnie Viola (Johnson) B.; S.B., Harvard, 1936; M.Sc., Rutgers U., 1945; m. Margaret T. Hamlin, Aug. 19, 1944 (dec. Mar. 1951); 1 dau., Beatrice; m. Angela Bornn, Jan. 2, 1954; children—Edward, Judith. Asst. chemist E.I. duPont de Nemours & Co., Inc., Leominster, Mass., 1936-38, Merck & Co., Inc., Rahway, N.J., 1939-57; dir. pharm. analysis Merck Sharp & Dohme Research Labs., West Point, Pa., 1957—. Fellow A.A.A.S.; mem. Am. Chem. Soc., Acad. Pharm. Sci., Sigma Xi, Phi Lambda Upsilon. Republican. Episcopalian. Home: Bean & Whitehall Rds RD 3 Norristown PA 19401 Office: Merck Sharp & Dohme Sumneytown Pike West Point PA 19486

BACHL, FREDERICK ANTHONY, architect; b. Bethlehem, Pa., June 24, 1944; s. Ferdinand Joseph and Sophie Bertha (Gonia) B.; B.S., Lawrence Inst. Tech., 1967; m. Carolann Fackenthal, Nov. 8, 1969; children—Todd, Jill, Architect-in-tng. Smith-Hinchman-Grylls, Architects, Detroit, 1967; chief architect/asso. Wallace & Watson Assos., Bethlehem, Pa., 1968—. Active Boy Scouts Am. Mem. AIA (corp.), Nat. Am. Bus. Club (pres. Bethlehem chpt. 1978-79). Lutheran. Coordinating architect Muhlenberg Coll. Center for Arts, 1975. Home: 2652 Boyd St Bethlehem PA 18017 Office: 1 Bethlehem Plaza Suite 900 Bethlehem PA 18018

BACHMAN, CARL OTTO, lawyer; b. Watertown, N.Y., Jan. 4, 1916; s. Otto C. and Marie (Gettings) B.; A.B., Syracuse U., 1937; J.D., Columbia, 1940; m. Ruth Mayer, Sept. 21, 1940; 1 dau., Carla Wynn. Admitted to N.Y. bar, 1941; adjuster Utica Mut. Ins. Co. (N.Y.), 1940-42; with investigations div. CSC, N.Y.C., 1942-43; mem. firm Tripp & Dunk, Watertown, N.Y., 1946-52, Dunk, Conboy, McKay & Bachman, Watertown, 1952-65, Conboy, Bachman & Kendall, 1965—. Mem. Hudson River Black River Regulating Bd., 1964-76. Pres., Watertown Community Chest, 1952-60; mem. character and fitness com. 5th Judicial Dist., N.Y. Supreme Ct., 1966—; chmn. Jefferson County chpt. Nat. Found. March of Dimes, 1966-72, dir. Nat. Found., 1955—, chmn., 1965. Mem. Watertown Bd. Edn., 1955-61, pres., 1958. Trustee Jefferson Community Coll., 1961—, chmn. bd., 1964-67; trustee YWCA, 1965—. Served with AUS, 1943-45; ETO. Decorated Bronze Star medal; Nat. Alumni award Syracuse U., 1977. Fellow Am. Coll. Trial Lawyers; mem. Am., N.Y. State (ho. of dels. 1976—), Jefferson County bar assns., Syracuse U. Alumni Assn. (dir. 1974—), Delta Upsilon, Phi Delta Phi. Presbyn. (elder 1955—). Club: Black River Valley (Watertown) (pres. 1968). Home: 451 Paddock St Watertown NY 13601 Office: 407 Sherman St Watertown NY 13601

BACHMAN, KENNETH LEROY, JR., lawyer; b. Washington, Aug. 24, 1943; s. Kenneth Leroy and Audrey Teresa (Torrence) B.; A.B. summa cum laude, Ohio U., 1965; J.D. cum laude, Harvard U., 1968; m. Sharon Lea Abel, June 18, 1966; children—Laura Ann, Eric Kenneth. Law clk. to Judge Irving Ben Cooper U.S. Dist. Ct., So. Dist. N.Y., 1968-70; admitted to D.C. bar, 1968; asso. firm Cleary, Gottlieb, Steen & Hamilton, Washington, 1970-76, partner, 1976—; faculty Am. Law Inst. seminar, 1976; faculty Practising Law Inst. seminar, 1977. Mem. Am. (vice chmn. emergency econ. controls com. 1978—), D.C. bar assns. Contbg. editor: Oil and Gas Price Regulation Analyst, 1978—. Home: 5412 Duvall Dr Bethesda MD 20016 Office: 1250 Connecticut Ave NW Washington DC 20036

BACHRACH, HENRY MILTON, clin. psychologist; b. N.Y.C., Oct. 4, 1940; s. Joseph Harry and Erika (Oppenheimer) B.; B.S., City Coll. N.Y., 1962, M.A., 1963; Ph.D., U. Chgo., 1967; m. Ilse Klein; 1 son, Michael Keith. Postdoctoral fellow in clin. psychology Menninger Found., Topeka, Kans., 1966-68; instr. psychiatry U. Pa. Med. Sch., Phila., 1968-71, asst. prof., 1971-77, asso. prof., 1977, dir. psychiatry outpatient dept., 1977—. Mem. Psychologists Interested in Study of Psychoanalysis (pres. 1976-77, bd. dirs. 1972—), Am. Psychol. Assn., Am. Psychoanalytic Assn., Soc. Psychotherapy Research, Soc. Personality Assessment. Jewish. Contbr. articles to sci. jours. Office: 3400 Spruce Philadelphia PA 19104

BACHRACH, HOWARD HELMUT, lawyer; b. Kassel, Germany, Nov. 9, 1912; s. Moritz and Anna (Rosenbaum) B.; came to U.S. 1941, naturalized, 1946; B.A., Wilhelmsgymnasium Kassel, 1931; postgrad. U. Munich, 1931-32; Dr. Laws, U. Brussels, 1936; J.D., St. John's U., Bklyn., 1943; m. Ruth Regensburger, Oct. 16, 1941; children—Judith A., Marion J. Legal dept. Sofina Co., Brussels, 1937-40; admitted to N.Y. State bar, 1946; since practiced in N.Y.C.; dir. Glacier Metal Co., Dover Fiduciary Corp., Bawden Enterprises Inc., Orange, Calif., Marcent Internat., Inc., Indussa Corp., N.Y.C.; counsel Belgian Consulate Gen., N.Y.C. Decorated knight Belgian Order Crown. Mem. Am., N.Y.C. bar assns., N.Y. County Lawyers Assn., Fgn. Law Assn., Am. Soc. Internat. Law, Belgian Am. C. of C. (dir.). Jewish (trustee temple). Home: 175 Riverside Dr New York City NY 10024 Office: 1212 Ave of the Americas New York City NY 10036

BACKE, JOHN DAVID, broadcasting exec.; b. Akron, O., July 5, 1932; s. John A. and Ella A. (Enyedy) B.; B.S. in Bus. Adminstrn., Miami U., Oxford, Ohio, 1954; M.B.A., Xavier U., 1961; LL.D. (hon.), Miami U., Xavier U.; m. Katherine A. Elliott, Oct. 22, 1955; children—Kim, John. Various managerial positions in engring., financial and marketing functions Gen. Electric Co., 1957-66; v.p., dir. marketing Silver Burdett Co. div. Gen. Learning Corp., 1966-68, pres., 1968-69; exec. v.p. Gen. Learning Corp., Morristown, N.J., 1969, pres., chief exec. officer, 1969-73; pres. CBS Pub. Group, 1973-76; now pres., dir. CBS, Inc.; dir. Bus. Mktg. Corp., N.Y.C. Trustee Mus. Broadcasting; mem. N.Y. State Alliance to Save Energy, Bus. Com. for Arts; chmn. employee and pub. relations Gen. Electric Park Commn., Cin., 1960; mem. Phoenix City Planning Bd., 1963-64. Trustee United Fund Morris County, 1971-73; bd. dirs. CBS Found. Inc. Served to 1st lt. USAF, 1954-57. Mem. Assn. Am. Pubs. (dirs.). Home: 224 Crest Rd Ridgewood NJ 07450 Office: 51 W 52d St New York NY 10019

BACKENSTOE, GERALD SELER, physician; b. Emmaus, Pa., Aug. 27, 1903; s. Martin John and Agnes (Seler) B.; B.S., Columbia U., 1923; M.D., U. Pa., 1927; m. Harriet Susan Schwartz, Nov. 5, 1929; children—Harriet (Sally) Backenstoe Afflerbach, John E. Intern Allegheny Gen. Hosp., Pitts., 1928, resident in surgery, 1929; practice medicine specializing in family practice, Emmaus, 1929—; mem. staffs Sacred Heart Hosp., Gen. Hosp., Sacred Heart Hosp. and Center (all Allentown, Pa.); med. examiner FAA, 1929—; mem. exec. com., dir. 1st Nat. Bank of Allentown. Served to lt. col. USAAF, 1942-46. Diplomate Am. Bd. Preventative Medicine. Fellow Internat. Coll. Internal Medicine, Am. Acad. Family Physicians (charter), Aero-Space Med. Assn. (v.p. 1929); mem. Am. Geriatrics Soc., Airline Med. Examiners Assn. (pres. 1950), Civil Aviation Med. Assn. (pres. 1952), Pa., Lehigh County (pres. 1964) med. socs., Lehigh Valley Diabetic Assn., World Med. Assn., AMA (Physicians' Recognition award 1972, 76), OX-5 Club Am., Flying Physicians Assn., Lehigh County (Pa.) Hist. Soc. Republican. Mem. Moravian Ch. Clubs: Rotary (past pres.) (Emmaus); United Air Lines Million Mile. Contbr. articles to profl. jours. Ccmpilor records of achievements and histories of mems. class of 1927 of U. Pa. Home and Office: 500 Chestnut St Emmaus PA 18049

BACKUS, DANA CONVERSE, lawyer; b. Bayonne, N.J., Feb. 26, 1907; s. Henry M. and Mary E. (Neilson) B.; A.B., Harvard, 1927, LL.B., 1929; m. Louise B. Laidlaw, Sept. 16, 1933 (dec. July 1973); children—Mary (Mrs. Douglas Rankin), Janet (Mrs. E. Blythe Stason, Jr.), Elizabeth (Mrs. Stephen Stuart Girard, Jr.), Harriet (Mrs. Conrad H. Todd), Anne Converse (dec. 1970). Admitted to N.Y. bar, 1930, since practiced N.Y.C.; partner Kramer, Marx, Greenlee & Backus, 1952-73; now counsel Windels, Marx, Davies & Ives; dir., sec. J.R. Wood & Sons, Inc., 1959-70; dir. Standard & Poors Corp. Bd. dirs. Citizens Union Research Found.; Am. del. Assn. UN to World Fedn. UN Assns., 1946, 47; mem. secretariat UN Conf., San Francisco, 1945; mem. exec. com. Com. for Def. of Constn. by Preserving the Treaty Power, 1952-54. Served from capt. to lt. col. Judge Adv. Gen's. Dept., AUS, 1943-46; col. Res. ret. Mem. Assn. Bar City of New York (mem., chmn. various com.), Harvard Law Sch. Assn. of N.Y.C. (trustee 1937-40, 55-58), Mayflower Soc., Phi Beta Kappa. Democrat. Clubs: Harvard (N.Y.C.); Harvard (dir.) (L.I.); Manhasset Bay Yacht, Appalachian Mountain, Sierra, Pilgrims. Contbr. numerous articles to profl. jours. Home: 180 Middle Neck Rd Sands Point Port Washington NY 11050 Office: care Windels Marx Davies & Ives 51 W 51st St New York City NY 10019

BACON, CHARLOTTE ALZERA MEADE (MRS. EDWARD D. BACON, JR.), educator; b. Alberta, Va.; d. Ollie and Pinkie Ann (Manson) Meade; B.S. with honors, Hampton Inst., 1946; M.Ed., U. Pitts., 1952; m. Edward D. Bacon, Jr., Aug. 11, 1962; children—Judith, Edward, Susan. Tchr. Downingtown (Pa.) Indsl. Sch., 1946-50; tchr. Aliquippa (Pa.) pub. schs., 1950—. Mem. program com. YMCA, Aliquippa, 1955-65; vice chmn. Mayor's Commn. on Human Rights, 1972-75; mem. bd. Beaver-Castle council Girl Scouts U.S.A., Sewickley Community Center; mem. Aliquippa Citizens Adv. Com.; supr. Pa. Fedn. Girl's Clubs, 1974—. Recipient Woman of Year award Aliquippa Negro Bus. and Profl. Women's Club, 1970, Community Involvement award Delta Sigma Theta, 1972. Mem. AAUW (Aliquippa corr. sec. 1971-73, pres. 1977—), Pa. Fedn. Negro Women's Clubs (pres. 1969-73), Nat. Assn. Negro Bus. and Profl. Women's Clubs (life mem.; Sojourner Truth award 1976), Negro Bus. and Profl. Women's Club (pres. 1960-62, 63, 77), Northwestern Dist. Fedn. Women's Clubs (pres. 1974-76), NAACP, World Affairs Council Pitts., NEA, Pa., Aliquippa (rec. sec. 1969-72) edn. assns., Nat. Assn. Colored Women's Clubs (chmn. consumer affairs com. 1977), NE Fedn. Women's Clubs (sec. scholarship com. 1977). Baptist. Club: Sewickley Toastmistress. Home: 311 Chadwick St Sewickley PA 15143 Office: New Sheffield Sch 21st St Aliquippa PA 15001

BACON, DAISY SARAH, editor, writer; b. Pa.; d. Ellsworth and Jessie M. (Holbrook) Bacon; student pvt. tutors. Editor: Love Story mag., 1928—, Ainslee's Mag., 1934-38, Smart Love Stories, 1937-39, Pocket Love mag., 1937, Detective Story and Romantic Range mags., 1940—; pub. paperbound books, 1962—, Gemini Books, 1963—; spl. overseas editor Detective Story mag. for armed forces distbtd. by Spl. Services Div., A.S.F., U.S. Army, 1942-46. Judge Spur awards Western Writers Am., 1967-68. Mem. D.A.R. Republican. Episcopalian. Compiler of four prize-story anthologies annually: Detective Story annual, All Fiction Detective Stories, All Fiction Stories, Love Story Annual. Author: Love Story Writers, 1953, 2d edit., 1959; Love Story Editor, 1964; Playing Magazine, 1974; The Golden Age at Street & Smith, 1975; also author of mag. articles; originator feature People to Learn From. Desc. Gov. William Bradford of Plymouth Colony and Capt. John Holbrook of Weymouth. Home: 7 Hillside Ave Port Washington NY 11050 Office: 520 Fifth Ave New York City NY 10036

BADALAMENTE, MARIE ANN, electron microscopist, educator; b. Bronx, N.Y., July 17, 1949; d. John William and Elizabeth Ann Badalamente; B.A., C.W. Post Coll. L.I. U., 1971, M.S. (Coll. fellow), 1973; Ph.D., Fordham U., 1976. Instr. biology U. City N.Y., Bronx Center, 1973-75; asst. prof., dir. electron microscopy lab. C.W. Post Coll. L.I. U., 1975-78; asst. prof., dir. electron microscopy labs., dept. anatomy and cell biology Downstate Med. Center, Bklyn., 1978—. NIH grantee, 1976-79. Mem. Electron Soc. Am., N.Y. Soc. Electron Microscopists, Am. Soc. Zoologists, AAAS, Sigma Xi. Home: 109 St Marks Pl Roslyn Heights NY 11577 Office: Dept Anatomy and Cell Biology Downstate Med Center Brooklyn NY 11203

BADALAMENTI, ANTHONY FRANCIS, mathematician; b. Bronx, N.Y., Feb. 2, 1943; s. Charles Salvator and Carmella-Maria (D'Ambrosio) B.; B.S. (Italian Charites of Am. Scholar, Bklyn. Poly. Inst. Scholar), Manhattan Coll., 1964; M.S., Stevens Inst. Tech., 1967; Ph.D., Poly. Inst. Bklyn., 1970; m. Karolina V. Kungl. Nov. 30, 1968 (div.); 1 son, Paul Anthony. Mem. tech. staff Bell Telephone Labs., 1964-70; asst. prof. Fairleigh Dickinson U., 1970-72; mem. tech. staff Gen. Research Corp., 1972-74; dir. revenue modelling and reporting Western Union Telegraph Co., 1974; research scientist Rockland Research Inst., Orangeburg, N.Y., 1975—. Mem. Assn. for Computing Machinery, Am. Math. Soc., Soc. for Indsl. and Applied Mathematics, N.Y. Acad. Scis., Bergen County Alumni Soc. Manhattan Coll. (v.p.). Home: 19 Crest St Apt 2A Westwood NJ 07675

BADALAMENTI, FRED LEOPOLDO, artist, educator; b. Long Island City, N.Y., June 25, 1935; s. Leopoldo and Concetta (Vitale) B.; student Pratt Inst., 1953-55; B.A., SUNY, New Paltz, 1961; M.F.A., Bklyn. Coll., 1967; m. Barbara J. Frankenfield, June 14, 1959; children—Katherine, Alexander, Frederick. Tchr. art Newburgh (N.Y.) Secondary Schs., 1961-63, Deer Park (N.Y.) High Sch., 1963-65; mem. art faculty Bklyn. Coll., 1967—, asso. prof. art, 1976—, dep. chmn. for grad. studies in art, 1970—; vis. asso. prof. SUNY, Stony Brook, 1977-78; painting exhbns. in N.Y.C., also in galleries and on campuses in eastern U.S. Bd. dirs. First St. Gallery, 1978-79. Served with USAF, 1955-59. Mem. Coll. Art Assn., Parrish Mus., N.Y. State Tchrs. Assn. Home: 182 Lower Sheep Pasture Rd Setauket NY 11733

BADEN, MICHAEL M., physician; b. N.Y.C., July 27, 1934; s. Harry and Fannie (Linn) B.; B.S., City Coll. N.Y., 1955; M.D., N.Y. U., 1959; m. Judianne Densen Gerber, June 14, 1958; children—Trissa, Judson, Lindsey, Sarah. Intern, first med. div. Bellevue Hosp., N.Y.C., 1959-60, resident, 1960-61, resident in pathology, 1961-63, chief resident in pathology, 1963-64; practice medicine specializing in pathology, N.Y.C.; asst. med. examiner City of N.Y., 1961-65, jr. med. examiner, 1965-66, asso. med. examiner, 1966-70, dep. chief med. examiner, 1970-78, chief med. examiner, 1978—; instr. in pathology N.Y. U., N.Y.C., 1964-65, asst. prof. pathology, 1966-70, asso. prof. forensic medicine, 1970—; adj. prof. law N.Y. Law Sch., N.Y.C.; vis. prof. pathology Albert Einstein Sch. Medicine, 1975; lectr. pathology Coll. Physicians and Surgeons, Columbia U., N.Y.C., 1975; asst. vis. pathologist Bellevue Hosp., N.Y.C., 1965—; lectr. Drug Enforcement Adminstrn., U.S. Dept. Justice, 1973—; vis. lectr. Fairleigh Dickinson Sch. Dentistry, 1968-70; spl. forensic pathology cons. N.Y. State Organized Crime Task Force, 1971-75; mem. med. adv. bd. Andrew Menchell Infant Survival Found., 1969-74; mem. certification bd. Addiction Services Agy., N.Y.C., 1966-69; preceptor health research tng. program N.Y.C. Dept. Health, 1968—; v.p. Council for Interdisciplinary Communication in Medicine, 1967-69. Mem. N.Y. adv. bd. Odyssey House, Inc., 1966—; bd. dirs. N.Y. Council on Alcoholism, sec., 1969—; bd. dirs. Belco Scholarship Found., Inc., 1971—. Diplomate Am. Bd. Pathology, Nat. Bd. Med. Examiners. Fellow Coll. Am. Pathologists (chmn. toxicology subcom. 1972-74), Am. Soc. Clin. Pathologists (mem. drug abuse task force 1973—), Am. Acad. Forensic Scis. (program chmn. 1971-72, sec. sect. pathology and biology 1970-71); mem. Med. Soc. County N.Y. (mem. pub. health com. 1966—), Soc. Med. Jurisprudence (corr. sec. 1971—), Nat. Assn. Med. Examiners, N.Y. Path. Soc., N.Y. State Med. Soc., AMA, Internat. Acad. Law and Medicine, AAAS, Indian Acad. Forensic Medicine, Royal Coll. Health. Author: Alcohol, Other Drugs and Violent Death, 1978; also numerous articles on forensic medicine in profl. jours.; editorial bd. Am. Jour. Drug and Alcohol Abuse, 1973—, Internat. Microfilm Jour. Legal Medicine, 1969—, Contemporary Drug Problems, 1971—. Office: 520 1st Ave New York City NY 10016

BADER, ANNE SHANE, assn. exec.; b. Bklyn., Apr. 2, 1923; d. B. Bevier and Anna E. (Shane) Schoonmaker; m. John Merwin Bader, Jan. 15, 1973; children from previous marriage—Tracy Shane Kramer, Donald L. Shane. Asst. to adj. U.S. Army Base Hosp., New Castle, Del.; exec. dir. Del. Acad. Family Physicians; now exec. dir. Med. Soc. Del., Wilmington, also bus. mgr. Del. Med. Jour. Active A.R.C.; bd. dirs. Blood Bank Del., 1974—. Clubs: Brandywine New Century, Advertising (Wilmington). Home: 1107 Nottingham Rd Wilmington DE 19805 Office: 1925 Lovering Ave Wilmington DE 19806

BADER, FRANZ, gallery dir.; b. Vienna, Austria, Sept. 19, 1903; s. David and Elsa (Steindler) B.; ed. Vienna; m. Antonia Blaustein, Dec. 2, 1928; m. 2d, Virginia Forman, July 31, 1971. Owner, Wallishausser Book Shop, Vienna; v.p., gen. mgr. Whyte Gallery, Washington, 1939-53; pres. Franz Bader Gallery, Washington, 1953—; art appraisals for mus. and pvt. collectors; photographer, exhibited traveling show, Ringling Mus., Sarasota, Fla., 1970, Corcoran Gallery Art, Washington, 1973, Erich Schindler Gallery, Richmond, Va., 1974, Nat. Acad. Scis., Washington, 1975, one-man show Phillips Collection, Washington, 1977; represented in collections Air and Space Mus., Washington, U.S. Ct. Gen. Sessions, Washington, Phillips Collection, Washington, also pvt. collections. Decorated Goldene Ehrenzeichen fuer Verdianste (Austria); Verdienstkreuz Erster Klasse (Germany). Club: George Washington Univ. Home: 2242 48th St NW Washington DC 20007 Office: 2124 Pennsylvania Ave NW Washington DC 20037

BADER, HERBERT IRVING, periodontist; b. N.Y.C., Oct. 18, 1936; s. William and Shirley (Stutman) B.; B.S., Coll. City N.Y., 1957; D.D.S., N.Y. U., 1961; m. Carol Schwartz, June 15, 1957 (div. Nov. 1971); children—William, David, Jeffrey, Todd; m. 2d, Bonnie Epstein, June 25, 1972. Postdoctoral fellow Sch. Dental Medicine, Harvard, 1963-66, asso. in periodontology, 1966-67, lectr. in periodontology, 1967—, mem. staff Dental Service; practice dentistry specializing in periodontics, Concord, Mass., also Acton, Mass., 1967—. Pres., Mass. Parents Assn. for Deaf and Hard of Hearing, 1971—. Served to capt. Dental Corps, AUS, 1961-63. Mem. Am. Acad. Dental Service, ADA, Am. Acad. Periodontists, Harvard Odontological Soc., Northeast Soc. Periodontists, Greater Boston Dental Soc., Mass. Soc. Periodontists. Contbr. articles to dental jours. Home: 26 Newton Rd Sudbury MA 01776 Office: 290 Baker Ave Concord MA 01742 also 418 Massachusetts Ave Acton MA 01720

BADER, I. WALTON, lawyer; b. N.Y.C., June 20, 1922; s. Maximillian and Ida (Sussman) B.; B.A. N.Y.U., 1942, LL.B., 1948; m. Betty Sands, 1972. Admitted to N.Y. State bar, 1948; since practiced in N.Y.C.; asso. firm Duell & Kane, 1948-49; mem. firm Bader & Bader, 1949-70, partner, 1970-78, sr. partner, 1978—; partner firm Richards & Geier, 1970-74; sec. Trade Mark Service Corp., N.Y.C., 1952-70; patent counsel Albert Einstein Coll. Medicine, 1956—, Swingline Inc. and subsidiaries, 1957-72, Yeshiva U., 1965-77; counsel Global Invention Found., 1972—, Ind. Investor Protective League, 1972—. Trustee Heart Disease Research Found., 1960-70, counsel, 1969-77. Mem. Am., N.Y. State, Bklyn., Westchester County bar assns., Am. Arbitration Assn. (nat. panel arbitrators). Mason. Clubs: New York University, Nat. Democratic. Home: 40 Morrow Ave Scarsdale NY 10583 Office: 65 Court St White Plains NY 10601 also 270 Madison Ave New York City NY 10016

BADER, RICHARD E., performing arts exec.; s. Benjamin and Beatrice A. Bader; grad. in econs. Hobart Coll.; M.C.P.A. in City Planning, Yale U. Junior planner Candeub, Fleissig & Assos., Newark, 1960-61; asst. planner Raymond & May Assos. for N.Y.C. Community Renewal Program, 1961-63; dir. sch. planning N.Y.C. Planning Commn., 1963-66; exec. dir. United Parents Assn., N.Y.C., 1966-67; asst. to commr. N.Y.C. Dept. Pub. Works, 1967-68; asst. adminstr. N.Y.C. Parks, Recreation and Cultural Affairs Adminstrn., 1968-72, dep. adminstr., 1972-74; curator met. N.Y.C., N.Y. State Mus., Albany, 1974-76; cons. N.Y. State Mus., N.Y. State Bicentennial Commn., N.Y. City Cultural Affairs Commn., Westchester County Dept. Parks and Recreation, 1976-77; exec. dir. Am. Shakespeare Theatre, Conn. Center for Performing Arts, Stratford, 1977—. Recipient Parks Council award, 1973. Mem. Am. Soc. Planning Ofcls., Am. Assn. Museums, Internat. Council Museums, Friends of Cast Iron Architecture, Conn. Advs. for Arts, Stratford Hist. Soc., Spanish Inst., Yale Engring. Assn. Clubs: Yale; Met. Opera. Home: 47 E 64th St New York City NY 10021 Office: 1850 Elm St Stratford CT 06497

BADER, SAMUEL, exec. recruiter; b. Jersey City, Jan. 13, 1929; s. Harry and Dorothy B.; B.A., Claremont Men's Coll., 1950; M.B.A., N.Y. U., 1955; m. Lila Elson, May 17, 1962; children—Neil, Eric. Asst. editor Super Market Merchandising Pub. Co., N.Y.C., 1954-56; merchandising exec. McCann-Erickson, Inc., Chgo., 1956-58, N.Y.C., 1959; account exec. Kenyon & Eckhardt Inc., N.Y.C., 1959-65; account supr. William Esty Co., N.Y.C., 1965-68; pres. Mgmt. Recruiters Inc., N.Y.C., 1968—. Served with U.S. Army, 1951-53. Mem. Assn. Personnel Consultants N.Y. State (treas. 1973-75), Nat. Assn. Personnel Consultants (dir.), Claremont Men's Coll. Alumni Assn. (pres. E. Coast chpt. 1959-76). Home: 1070 Park Ave New York City NY 10028 Office: 535 Fifth Ave New York City NY 10017

BADERTSCHER, DAVID GLEN, librarian; b. Morrow, Ohio, Jan. 31, 1935; s. Glen C. and Blanche (Cluff) B.; B.S., Ind. State U., 1957, M.S., 1962; M.A., Rosary Coll., 1967; m. Betty Jo Shafer, June 25, 1965. Tchr., Rockville (Ind.) High Sch., 1957-59, Medinah Elementary Sch., 1961-63; librarian Elgin (Ill.) Acad., 1963-64; tchr. Beachwood (Ohio) High Sch., 1964-65; librarian Chgo. Pub. Library, 1965-66; circulation, asst. reference librarian U. Chgo. Law Sch., 1966-70; librarian Schiff Hardin Waite Dorschel & Britton, Chgo., 1970-73; exec. librarian Georgetown U. Law Center, Washington, 1973-78; dir. library Milbank, Tweed, Hadley & McCloy, N.Y.C., 1978—; cons. Urban Research Corp., Chgo., 1970-73, Herner & Co.,

1977—; adviser Computer Law Service, 1972—, EIS, 1978—. Served with AUS, 1959-61. Conv. grantee Am. Assn. Law Libraries, 1970. Mem. Medinah Tchrs. Assn. (pres. 1962-63), Am. (chmn. com. automation, sci. devel. 1970-72), Chgo. (pres., conf. chmn. 1970-72) assns. law librarians, Nat. Micrographics Assn., Am. Soc. Info. Sci. (editor SIG/Law Newsletter 1975—), Am. Bar Assn. (asso.). Home: 46 Colony Ct New Providence NJ 07974 Office: 1 Chase Manhattan Plaza New York City NY 10005

BADILLO, HERMAN, congressman; b. Caguas, P.R., Aug. 21, 1929; s. Francisco and Carmen (Rivera) B.; B.B.A. magna cum laude, Coll. City N.Y., 1951; LL.B. cum laude, Bklyn. Law Sch., 1954, J.D., 1967; LL.D., U. City N.Y., 1972; m. Irma Deutsch, May 7, 1961; 3 children. Admitted to N.Y. State bar, 1955; asso. Ferro, Berdon & Co., C.P.A.'s N.Y.C., 1951-55; mem. firm Permut & Badillo, N.Y.C., 1955-61; dep. commr. N.Y.C. Dept. Real Estate, 1962; commr. N.Y.C. Dept. Relocation, 1962-65; pres. Borough of Bronx, 1966-69; mem. firm Stroock & Stroock & Lavan, 1970, of counsel, 1971-73; mem. 92d-95th Congresses from 21st N.Y. Dist., resigned, 1978; dep. mayor for mgmt. N.Y.C., 1978—; adj. prof. Fordham U. Grad. Sch. Urban Edn., 1970—. C.P.A., N.Y. Author: A Bill of No Rights: Attica and the American Prison System, 1972. Home: 405 W 259th St Riverdale Bronx NY 10471 Office: City Hall New York City NY 10007

BADMAJEW, PETER, physician; b. Warsaw, Poland, Feb. 19, 1929; s. Wlodzimierz and Tamara (Brzozowski) B.; came to U.S., 1967, naturalized, 1973; M.D., Med. Acad. Lodz (Poland), 1952. Asst. in surgery County Hosp., Garwolin, Poland, 1952-57; sr. asst. First Surg. Clinic, Postgrad. Sch. Medicine, Warsaw, 1957-62; surg. fellow Surg. Med. Inst., U. Alta. (Can.), Edmonton, 1962-63; rotating intern St. Mary's Hosp., Passaic, N.J., 1964; dep. chief dept. thoracic surgery Sanatorium Otwock (Poland), 1965; asst. cardiosurg. dept. Univ. Hosp., Zurich, Switzerland, 1966-67; resident in surgery Wilson Meml. Hosp., Johnson City, N.Y., 1967-68; sr. resident thoracic dept. New Eng. Deaconess Hosp., Boston, 1968-69; practice medicine specializing in family practice, Jamesport, N.Y., 1969—; mem. staff Central Suffolk Hosp., Riverhead, N.Y. Served with Polish Home Army, 1943-44, in German prison camp, 1944-45. Certified specialist in gen. surgery, Poland; diplomate Am. Bd. Family Practice. Mem. AMA. Roman Catholic. Home and office: Main Rd Jamesport NY 11947

BAECHEL, CHARLES WILLIAM, ins. co. exec.; b. Akron, Ohio, Feb. 17, 1921; s. Arthur Albert and Mildred (LaCave) B.; m. Bessie B. Bovey, Feb. 24, 1939; children—Kenneth Earl, Constance Susan, Charles William. Draftsman, McConnell Heating Co., Akron, 1945-49; salesman Gerber Baby Foods, Akron, 1949-50; field underwriter Mut. N.Y., Akron, 1950-55, asst. mgr., 1955-57, tng. asst., N.Y.C., 1957-58; mgr., Des Moines, 1958-64, mgr. Albany, N.Y., 1964-73; prin. Baechel Assos., Albany, 1973—; dir. Epoch Resources, Inc. Served with USAAF, 1943-45. Decorated Air medal with six oak leaf clusters. Mem. Gen. Agts. and Mgrs. Iowa (1st v.p., 1962-63, pres. 1963-64), Des Moines Life Underwriters Assn. (1st v.p. 1962-63, pres. 1963-64), Des Moines Gen. Agts. and Mgrs., Central Iowa Health Assn. (pres., 1961-62), N.Y. State (pres. 1978—), Albany (pres. 1972-73) assns. life underwriters, Capital Dist. Sales and Marketing Execs., Albany C. of C., Catholic War Vets. (pres. 1947-48). Kiwanian (pres. Akron 1955). Club: Woolferts Roost Country. Home: 24 Park Ln E Albany NY 12204 Office: 6 Automation Ln Albany NY 12205

BAEHREL, PETER WILLIAM, mfg. co. exec.; b. Jamaica, N.Y., July 15, 1940; s. William Julius and Frances Elizabeth (Gingell) B.; student U. Fla., 1958-60; m. Judith Geuder, June 20, 1970; children—Michael Christian, Suzanne Michelle. Office mgr. Mehron Inc., N.Y.C., 1960-64; supr. facilities AMF Inc., White Plains, N.Y., 1965-73, mgr. facilities and equipment, purchasing agt., 1974-78, mgr. adminstrv. services and purchasing agt., 1978—. Served with Army N.G., 1961-68. Mem. Nat. Assn. Food Service Mgmt., Nat. Fire Protection Assn. Home: 8 Van Dyke Ave Suffern NY 10901 Office: 777 Westchester Ave White Plains NY 10604

BAER, HAROLD, JR., lawyer; b. N.Y.C., Feb. 16, 1933; s. Harold and Edna (Jacobus) B.; grad. magna cum laude, Hobart Coll., 1954; LL.B., Yale, 1957; m. Suzanne Harris, Aug. 18, 1957; children—Elizabeth Jane, Linda Gail. Admitted to N.Y. bar, 1959, U.S. Supreme Ct., 1964; asst. U.S. atty. So. Dist. N.Y., 1961-66; exec. dir. civilian complaint rev. bd., N.Y.C. Police Dept., 1966-67; mem. firm Guggenheimer & Untermyer, N.Y.C., 1968—. 1st dep. asst. U.S. Atty., chief criminal div. U.S. Atty.'s Office, So. Dist. N.Y., 1970-71; mem. faculty New Sch. Social Research, 1972—; dir. Supreme Ins. Co., Ltd., Hamilton, Bermuda, Omnia Properties Inc., Casio Inc. Trustee Community Service Soc., chmn. commn. criminal and juvenile justice, 1976—. Bd. dirs. Retarded Infants Services, Brotherhood-in-Action; trustee Dr. I Fund Found.; mem. N.Y. Gov.'s Task Force on Crime. Mem. N.Y. County Lawyers Assn. (v.p.), N.Y. State Bar Assn. (grievance com. 1978—), Assn. Bar City N.Y. Contbr. articles to profl. jours. Home: 302 W 12th St New York City NY 10014 Office: 80 Pine St New York City NY 10005

BAER, MAX, mfg. co. exec.; b. Karlsruhe, Germany, Feb. 23, 1910; s. Berthold and Frieda B.; m. Hilde. Pres., Ferum Co., Inc., Bronx, N.Y. Served with U.S. Army, 1943-45. Office: 815 E 136th St Bronx NY 10454

BAER, SANFORD, chem. co. exec.; b. Newark, Sept. 29, 1932; s. Benjamin and Yetta (Liss) B.; B.S., N.Y. U. 1958; m. Lenore M. Yavner, Nov. 16, 1958; children—Jill, Jonathan. Gen. agent Am. Nat. Life Ins. Co., Galveston, Tex., 1965-68; pres. ECO-TROL Labs, Inc., West Orange, N.J., 1968-72; sales mgr. DuBois Chemical Corp., East Rutherford, N.J., 1972—. Dist. leader West Orange Democratic Party, 1975-77; vice chmn. Englishtown Civic Assn., West Orange, 1974—. Served with USN, 1951-55. Democrat. Jewish. Clubs: West Orange Dems., B'nai B'rith. Home: 7 Nottingham Rd West Orange NJ 07052 Office: DuBois St East Rutherford NJ 07073

BAER, THOMAS JAMES, lawyer; b. N.Y.C., May 11, 1927; s. Edward J. and Catherine A. (Long) B.; B.S., Columbia, 1955, LL.B., 1957; m. Margaret C. Hill, Aug. 28, 1951; children—Thomas James, Stephen Michael, Margaret Jane, Julie Ellen, Maura Beth. Admitted to N.Y. bar, 1958; since practiced in N.Y.C., partner firm Hawkins, Delafield & Wood, 1967—. Mem. Am., N.Y. State bar assns., N.Y. Municipal Forum, Internat. Bridge, Tunnel and Trunpike Assn. Roman Catholic. Home: 22 Westcott St Old Tappan NJ 07675 Office: Hawkins Delafield & Wood 67 Wall St New York City NY 10005

BAERGER, PAUL JOSEPH, dentist; b. N.Y.C.; s. William Paul and Ducie (Schildknecht) B.; B.S., City Coll. N.Y., 1954; D.D.S., N.Y. U., 1958, M.S. in Dentistry (USPHS fellow), 1964; children—Richard Freed, Dana Royce. Practice dentistry N.Y.C., 1960—; chief dept. dentistry and oral surgery Park East Hosp., N.Y.C., 1970-77; prof. dept. health Kean Coll. N.J.; faculty dept. preventative dentistry, mem. postgrad. faculty Inst. for Grad. Dentists, N.Y.C., 1971—; mem. staff, postgrad. lectr. preventive dentistry and implantology Deepdale (N.Y.) Hosp.; lectr. dept. preventive dentistry, oral medicine and community health N.Y. U. Dental Center; postgrad. lectr. Albert Einstein Coll. Medicine, 1973—; postgrad. lectr. 1st, 2d, 8th, and 11th Dist. dental socs., N.Y. Bd. dirs. Birch Wathen Sch., N.Y., 1969-71. Served to capt., Dental Corps, AUS, 1958-60. Fellow Acad. Preventive Medicine, Royal Soc. Health (Eng.); mem. Am. Dental Assn., Fedn. Dentaire Internationale, Am. Acad. Implant Dentistry, Soc. for Dental Research (past pres.), Midtown Dental Soc. (dir. 1962-70), Am. Acad. Psychodentistry (a founder, pres. 1970-75), Inst. for Endo-osseous Implantology, 1st Dist. Dental Soc., Internat. Acad. Preventive Medicine (trustee 1971-74), Am. Soc. for Preventive Dentistry (founding, program chmn. N.Y. State br. 1971), Council on Dental Health, Omicron Kappa Upsilon. Discoverer Kreb's acid cycle in mouth. Office: 57 W 57th St New York City NY 10019

BAFFA, FRANK PATRICK, union ofcl.; b. N.Y.C., May 14, 1923; s. Pasquale and Maria Sophie (Buglari) B.; ed. high sch.; m. Catherine Di Biaso, Jan. 27, 1945; one dau., Lorraine. Laborer, tractor and crane operator Penn Stevedoring Piers Piers 27-30, North River, N.Y., 1939-42, foreman, 1942-46, gen. supt. labor, 1946-53; sec.-treas. Local 976 Internat. Longshoremen's Assn., Jersey City, 1953—, dir. welfare fund, 1967—, adminstr. pension fund, 1971—; organizer, bus. agt. Local 518 Internat. Brotherhood Teamsters, N.J., 1962-63. Adv. bd. Nat. Security Council, 1976; active fundraising Muscular Dystrophy Assn., 1967-68. Mem. Nat. Assn. Jointly Adminstered Trusts, Nat. Rifle Assn. Roman Catholic. K.C. (3 deg.). Club: Callicoon Gun (co-founder 1974, exec. v.p. 1974—). Home: 4 Gramercy Ln Hillsdale NJ 07642 Office: Internat Longshoremen's Assn 215 14th St Jersey City NJ 07302

BAGATTINE, JOHN PETER, chemist; b. N.Y.C., Nov. 22, 1945; s. Carl and Rose (Paparella) B.; B.S., L.I.U., 1968, M.S., 1971; m. Judith Ann Hans, Sept. 16, 1972; children—Christian John, Andrea Marie. With Kingsbrook Jewish Med. Center, Bklyn., 1967—, phys. chemist, 1971—; adj. asst. prof. in organic chemistry Nassau Community Coll., 1972—; adj. instr. biochemistry L.I. U., 1977—; adj. instr. chemistry Queensborough Community Coll., 1978—, Suffolk Community Coll., 1978—; research cons. dept. hematology L.I. Jewish Med. Center, New Hyde Park, N.Y. Licensed clin. technologist, N.Y.C. Mem. AAAS, Am. Chem. Soc., Am. Inst. Chemists. Contbr. articles to profl. jours. Home: 16 Peacock Ln Levittown NY 11756

BAGBY, JAMES WILLIS, JR., psychologist; b. Waynesville, N.C., Feb. 27, 1912; s. James Willis and Lucile (Shuford) B.; B.S., Tenn. State Coll., 1934; M.A., Duke, 1937; postgrad. Washington Sch. Psychiatry, 1948-52; Ph.D., Columbia, 1955; m. Betty J. Adair, July 7, 1943 (div.). Tchr. pub. schs., Johnson City, Tenn., 1932-36, Montgomery County, Md., 1937-41; dir. personnel research and tng. Glenn L. Martin Co., Balt. and Omaha, Nev., 1941-43; psychologist N.Y. Postgrad. Hosp., N.Y.C., 1946-48; research cons. Princeton, 1954-56; asso. psychologist Roosevelt Hosp., N.Y.C., 1956, sr. psychologist, 1966—; sr. psychol. cons. Ednl. Services Bur., 1967—; pvt. practice, 1956—. Served from lt. (j.g.) to lt., USNR, 1943-46; from lt. to lt. comdr., psychologist in med. dept., 1948-54. Fellow A.A.A.S.; mem. Am. Orthopsychiat. Assn., Am. Psychol. Assn., Soc. for Research in Child Development, Pi Gamma Mu. Kappa Delta Pi. Presbyn. Home: Signal Hill Hardscrabble Rd North Salem NY 10560 Office: 151 E 80th St New York City NY 10021

BAGDAN, GLORIA, milk co. exec.; b. Bronx, N.Y., May 24, 1929; d. Max and Molly (Trufelman) Green; student Coll. City N.Y., 1947-49, Inst. Interior Design, 1964, Wharton Sch., 1977; m. Kenneth Bagdan, Nov. 25, 1948 (dec. 1974); children—Meryl Bagdan Mitchel, Scott, Stacy. Founder, 1st pres. Bronx Municipal Hosp. Aux., 1955-60; interior designer, Scarsdale, N.Y., 1964—; v.p., treas. Gold Medal Farms, Bronx, 1974—. Active in fundraising Grasslands Hosp. Heart Assn.; cons. Mental Health Assn., 1967—. Democrat. Jewish. Club: Atrium (N.Y.C.). Home: 31 Sheridan Rd Scarsdale NY 10583 Office: 1157 E 156th St Bronx NY 10474

BAGGISH, MICHAEL SIMEON, obstetrician, gynecologist; b. Hartford, Conn., July 22, 1936; s. William Radford and Sylvai Raff (Zachariah) B.; B.S., U. Louisville, 1957, M.D., 1961; m. Caryl Jane Flumbaum, Sept. 11, 1960; children—Jeffrey Steven, Mindy Ann, Cindy Beth, Stuart Harrison. Intern in gen. surgery Johns Hopkins Hosp., Balt., 1961-62, asst. resident in obstetrics and gynecology, 1962-67, chief resident in gynecology and obstetrics, 1967-68, fellow in gynecologic pathology, 1970-72, Am. Cancer Soc. clin. fellow, 1965-67, asst. prof. gynecology and obstetrics, 1970-72; USPHS fellow Kandang Kerbau Hosp., U. Singapore, 1967-68; fellow dept. gynecology and obstetrics Johns Hopkins U. Sch. Medicine, 1962-68; asso. prof. gynecology and obstetrics Sch. Medicine, U. Conn., Farmington, 1972-77, prof. gynecology and obstetrics, 1978—, asso. prof. pathology, 1976—; mem. staff Mt. Sinai Hosp., Hartford, Conn., 1972—, chief dept. obstetrics and gynecology, 1972—; pres. Gender Identity Clinic New Eng., 1973—; state med. dir. Planned Parenthood League Conn., 1975—. Bd. dirs. Am. Cancer Soc., chmn. pub. issues com., 1977—. Served as comdr. USNR, 1968-70. Diplomate Am. Bd. Obstetrics and Gynecology. Fellow Am. Coll. Obstetricians and Gynecologists; mem. Am. Assn. Gynecologic Laparoscopists, AMA, Am. Soc. for Colposcopy and Colpomicroscopy, Assn. Planned Parenthood Physicians, Pan Am., Conn., Hartford County med. assns., New Eng. Obstet. and Gynecol. Soc., Med. and Chirurg. Faculty Md., Balt. City Med. Soc., Conn. Assn. Bd. Certified Obstetricians and Gynecologists, Johns Hopkins Med. Soc. Contbr. articles to med. jours. Home: 37 Fox Chase St West Hartford CT 06107

BAGGOT-GUISE, JACK A., data processor, cons.; b. Bklyn., June 18, 1934; s. John A. and Helen C. (Paden) B.-G.; B.S., M.S. in Physics, N.Y. U., 1952, M.S., 1957, D.Sc., 1957; B.A. in Sociology, City U. N.Y., M.A., 1971; m. Jeanette A. Guyse, June 3, 1972; children—James, Joyce, Sean. Mem. advanced planning staff, instr. tng. and devel. Dept. Def., N.Y.C., 1964-68; dir. tech. services and electronic data processing Hanksley Enterprises, 1968-71; mgr. spl. projects and applications City U. N.Y., 1971-73; dir. econ. and ednl. devel. N.Y.C. Poverty Programs, 1973-75; pres. King Assos., Inc., Bklyn., 1963—; asso. Rand Inst.; bd. mem. Commn. on Sci. Advancement for Humanity; exec. dir. automated data processing Communications Media, Inc.; adj. prof. automated data processing City U. N.Y.; cons. IBM, Honeywell, Inc., RCA, NCR, Saks Fifth Ave. Staff mem. Pres.' Adv. Council, 1960-64; chmn. N.Y. State Pub. Adv. Com. on Automated Data Processing, 1969-70; mem. Nat. Democratic Com. on Privacy and Security, 1964-67. Served to lt. comdr. USNR, 1950-59. Decorated Silver Star, Bronze Star, Purple Heart, Naval Commendation medal; recipient awards Dept. State, Dept. Def.; certified data processor. Mem. Humanists, Sci. Writers Assn., Am. Soc. Physicists, Systems and Procedures Assn. Roman Catholic. Clubs: Toastmasters Internat., Friendly Sons of St. Patrick. Editor: Advancements in ADP Sciences. Contbr. articles to sci. publs. Patentee communications and computer systems designs. Home: 215 Ave F Brooklyn NY 11218 also 534 Spruce Ave Keismutter Pinehurst NJ*

BAGLEY, BRIAN G., physicist; b. Racine, Wis., Nov. 20, 1934; s. Wesley John and Ethel (Rasmussen) B.; B.S., U. Wis., 1958, M.S., 1959; A.M., Harvard U., 1964, Ph.D., 1968; m. Dorothy Elizabeth Olson, Nov. 20, 1959; children—Brian John, James David, Kristin Marie. Metall. engr. U. Wis., Madison, 1959-60; tech. staff Bell Telephone Labs., Inc., Murray Hill, N.J., 1967—. Served to 1st lt. AUS, 1960-61. Mem. Am. Phys. Soc. Home: 467 Ridge Rd Watchung NJ 07060 Office: Bell Telephone Labs Inc Murray Hill NJ 07974

BAGLEY, EDYTHE SCOTT, educator; b. Marion, Ala.; d. Obie and Bernice (McMurry) Scott; B.S. in Edn., Ohio State U., 1949; M.A., Columbia U., 1954; M.F.A., Boston U., 1965; m. Arthur M. Bagley, June 5, 1954; 1 son, Arturo Scott. Instr. English, Westside High Sch., Talladega, Ala., 1949-52; asst. prof. English, Elizabeth City (N.C.) State Coll., 1953-55, Albany (Ga.) State Coll., 1955-56, A & T Coll. N.C., Greensboro, 1956-57, Norfolk (Va.) State Coll., 1963-65; asso. prof. drama Cheyney (Pa.) State Coll., 1971—, now chmn. dept. spl. asst. to Mrs. Martin Luther King, Jr., 1968-71. Bd. dirs. Martin Luther King Jr. Center for Social Change, Atlanta, 1968—. Mem. Am. Theatre Assn., Am. Nat. Theatre and Acad., Theater Assn. Pa., Womens Internat. League Peace and Freedom, NAACP, NEA, Pa. Edn. Assn., The Links Inc., Alpha Psi Omega. Methodist. Home: 124 W Lafayette St West Chester PA 19380 Office: Dept Drama Cheyney State Coll Cheyney PA 19319

BAGLEY, FENTON LLOYD, JR., project engr.; b. Van Wert, Ohio, Sept. 29, 1934; s. Fenton Lloyd and Mildred Ida (Ries) B.; B.S., Purdue U., 1956; M.S., Mass. Inst. Tech., 1960; postgrad. Carnegie Inst. Tech., 1964-68; m. Jessie Marie Barnett, June 2, 1956; children—Fenton Dean, Enora Marie, Joan Lea. With Bendix Aviation Corp., Mishawaka, Ind., 1956-57; metal cutting research Watertown (Mass.) Arsenal, 1958-60; indsl. research PPG Industries, Harmar, Pa., 1960-65; mem. faculty Steel Valley Area Tech. Sch., West Mifflin, Pa., 1965-66, Allegheny Campus, Pitts., 1966-73, also cons. engr., Pitts., 1965-73; project engr. Snap-Tite, Inc., Union City, Pa., 1973-78; product engr. Reed Mfg., Erie, Pa., 1978—. Pack sec. Cub Scouts Am., 1966. Served with Ordnance Corps, AUS, 1957. Recipient award Fisher Body craftsman's guild competition, 1951. Mem. ASME, Pershing Rifles, Pi Tau Sigma. Contbr. articles to profl. jours. Home: RD 4 Concord Rd Union City PA 16438 Office: Reed Mfg Erie PA

BAHAM, GARY JOSEPH, cons. engr.; b. New Orleans, Mar. 14, 1941; s. Harold and June Margaret (Pavageau) B.; B.S., U. Calif., Los Angeles, 1964; M.S., George Washington U., 1974; m. Alexis Juanita DeClouette, Feb. 24, 1968; children—Michelle, Jocelyn, Nicole, Brian. Research asst. McDonnell-Douglas Aircraft, Long Beach, Calif., 1962-65; mech. engr. So. Calif. Edison Co., Los Angeles, 1965-68; gas turbine engr. United Technologies Corp., Hartford, Conn., 1968-69; sect. mgr. Litton Industries, Culver City, Calif., 1969-72; mgr. dept. George G. Sharp, Inc., Hyattsville, Md., 1972-76; prin. research scientist Hydronautics Inc., Laurel, Md., 1974-76; pres. Baham Corp., Columbia, Md., 1976—. Mem. ASME, Soc. Naval Architects and Marine Engrs., Am. Soc. Naval Engrs. Club: Howard County Bus. (sec. 1977-78) (Columbia). Home and Office: 5538 Coltsfoot Ct Columbia MD 21045

BAHAT, ARI, architect, designer; b. Jerusalem, May 4, 1941; s. Asher and Miriam (Kamin) B.; came to U.S., 1967, naturalized, 1975; B.A. cum laude, Technion, Israel Inst. Tech., 1967; m. Shulamith Hochberg, July 20, 1967; 1 son, Roy Eadon. Designer, Rouse, Dubin & Ventura, Architects-Engrs., N.Y.C., 1967-68; architect Paul Rudolph, Architect, N.Y.C., 1968-69; pres. Ari Bahat Inc., Architects-Designers, N.Y.C., 1970—; cons. in field. Leader, Boy Scouts Israel, 1960-61; asst. to dir. Grand Music Hall Israel, 1967. Served with Paratroops, Israeli Army, 1959-62. Technion awardee, Ratner scholar, 1963-65. Mem. AIA. Designer, developer concept glass blocks in interiors, furniture. Office: Plaza Hotel 768 Fifth Ave New York City NY 10019

BAILES, STEPHEN MARTIN, data processing exec.; b. N.Y.C., Nov. 30, 1932; s. George and Sara (Cheifitz) B.; A.B., Columbia Coll., 1954; M.B.A., N.Y. U., 1961; m. Leah E. Cohen, Sept. 2, 1956; children—Craig D., Ian K. Mgr. systems procedures IBM Corp., Yorktown Heights, N.Y., 1958-66; dir. bus. operational systems Western Union, Mahwah, N.J., 1966-69; mgr. hdqrs. info. systems Xerox Corp., Stamford, Conn., 1969-73; v.p. systems services Irving Trust Co., N.Y.C., 1973—; author, lectr. in field. Mem. Occoneechee Council exec. com., Boy Scouts Am., 1956-57, membership chmn., 1961-62; Eagle scout. Served with U.S. Army, 1955-57. Mem. Columbia Alumni Assn., Tau Epsilon Phi. Republican. Home: 104 Hoyt St Darien CT 06820 Office: One Wall St New York City NY 10015

BAILEY, ANNE MARIE, dietitian; b. West Reading, Pa., May 25, 1945; d. George Dundore and Mae (Zeller) Oxenreider; B.S. with honors, U. Del., 1967; m. Kenneth D. Bailey, Jan. 28, 1967. Tchr., Fort Monmouth Nursery Sch., Eatontown, N.J., 1967-68; asst. dietitian Wernersville (Pa.) State Hosp., 1968-69, food service dir., 1969—; mem. adv. com. Reading Area Community Coll. Mem. Am., Pa. dietetic assns., Berks County Nutrition Edn. Com. (chairperson 1977-78), Reading Dial-a-Dietitian, AAUW, Tulpehocken Hist. Soc., Historic Schaefferstown, Inc. Lutheran. Home: RD 2 Box 423B Myerstown PA 17067 Office: Wernersville State Hosp Wernersville PA 19565

BAILEY, CHRIS HARVEY, mus. dir., genealogist; b. Robinson, Ill., Aug. 4, 1946; s. Ray Kenneth and Imogene Ilene (Roberts) B.; Asso. Sci., B.S., Brigham Young U., 1970. Geneal. research analyst, tchr. seminars Brigham Young U. Geneal. Research Center, Provo, Utah, 1971-72; curator Am. Clock and Watch Mus., Inc., Bristol, Conn., 1972-73, mng. dir., 1973—. Missionary, Ch. of Jesus Christ of Latter Day Saints, So. Australia, 1966-68. Mem. Utah Geneal. Assn. (contbg. editor jour. 1972-76), Conn. Hist. Soc., Brigham Young Univ. Soc. for Local History and Genealogy (pres. 1968), Nat. Assn. Watch and Clock Collectors (nat. dir. 1975—), Am. Assn. for State and Local History, Antiquarian Horological Soc. (Eng.), Am. Assn. Museums, Rolls Royce Owner's Club, Ill. Geneal. Assn. Author: 200 Years of American Clocks and Watches, 1975. Editor: Highsmiths in America, 1971. Contbr. articles on horological research and genealogy to profl. publs. Home: Castle Largo 230 Center St Bristol CT 06010 Office: 100 Maple St Bristol CT 06010

BAILEY, DAVID ROLLINS, health care adminstr.; b. New Haven, Aug. 19, 1943; s. Carl Williams, Jr., and Edna May (Bailey) B.; B.S. in Accounting, Syracuse U., 1965; M.P.H. in Hosp. Adminstrn., Yale U., 1967; m. Patricia Lois Jordan, Feb. 12, 1966; children—Michael Rollins, Stephen Walsh. Asst. adminstr. Sewickley (Pa.) Valley Hosp., 1969-71; asst. exec. dir. Hosp. Planning Assn. Allegheny County, Pitts., 1971-73; exec. dir. D.T. Watson Home for Crippled Children, Pitts., 1973-76; exec. dir. McLean Home, Simsbury, Conn., 1976—; adj. instr. U. Pitts.; guest lectr. U. Conn; cons. Mr. Rogers TV show. Bd. mgrs. Farmington Valley YMCA; bd. dirs. Simsbury Youth Hockey Assn.; mem. End-stage Renal Disease Network Exec. Com., Hartford County Profl. Standards Rev. Orgn. Served with USPHS, 1967-69. Mem. Am. Coll. Hosp. Adminstrs., Am. Coll. Nursing Home Adminstrs., Yale U. Hosp. Adminstrn. Alumni (treas.). Republican. Club: Rotary. Contbr. articles in field to hosp. jours. Home: 9 Fox Den Rd W Simsbury CT 06092 Office: McLean Home 75 Great Pond Rd Simsbury CT 06070

BAILEY, DON, Congressman; b. July 21, 1945; B.A. in Polit. Sci., U. Mich., 1967; LL.B., Duquesne U., 1976. Past staff asst. Pa. Democratic Com.; mem. 96th Congress from 21st Pa. dist. Served in armed forces in Vietnam. Office: 116 Cannon House Office Bldg Washington DC 20515*

BAILEY, GEORGE WILLIAM, optometrist; b. Ogdensburg, N.Y., 1896; s. Charles Owen and Bell Bradley (Pickup) B.; O.D., Rochester Sch. Optometry, 1921; m. Grace Olive Putman, Feb. 14, 1923; children—Donald William, Charles Putman. Pvt. practice optometry, Cortland, N.Y., 1923-37, Ogdensburg, N.Y., 1938-72; dir. N.Y. adv. bd. ophthalmic dispensing, 1955-63. Served with M.C., USN, 1917, USMCR, 1918-19. Decorated D.S.C., Verdun Medal (French). Mem. N.Y., Am.(life), No. N.Y. (pres. 1941-44) optometric assns., Am. Legion, VFW. Republican. Universalist. Clubs: Rotary (pres. Ogdensburg 1941), Masons, Army and Navy Legion of Valor. Inventor in field. Home: 417 Elizabeth St Ogdensburg NY 13669

BAILEY, HAROLD WHITNEY, JR., publisher; b. Detroit, Aug. 7, 1937; s. Harold Whitney and Virginia (Rose) B.; B.A., Tufts U., 1959; M.B.A., M.A., U. Chgo., 1966; m. Allison Floy Heaney, Oct. 24, 1964; children—Wendelin Floy, Harold Whitney. Staff cons. Touche Ross & Co., Detroit, 1967-68; asst. to pres., dir. corp. strategy Pneumo Corp., Boston, 1968-70; pres. Suncraft Internat. Corp., N.Y.C., 1970—; publisher, editor Filmmakers Monthly, N.Y.C., 1970—. Served to lt. USN, 1959-62. Mem. Omicron Delta Epsilon. Club: Detroit Athletic. Home: 30 Gray Rd Andover MA 01810 Office: 41 Union Sq West New York City NY 10003

BAILEY, JAKE SCHULTZ, elec. engr.; b. Middlesboro, Ky., Dec. 29, 1927; s. Charles Wise and Mary Elizabeth (Nice) B.; B.S., U. Ala., 1949; postgrad. U. Minn., 1956, Westminster Theol. Sem., 1977—; m. Barbara Jean McClelland, Sept. 11, 1947; children—Linda Elaine, Mary Marjorie, Alan Curtis. Design engr. Memphis Light, Gas and Water Div., 1949-52; electronics design engr. Boeing Airplane Co., Wichita, Kans., 1952-54; design engr. Honeywell, Inc., Mpls., 1954-58; sr. electronics engr. Link div. Gen. Precision, Inc., Binghamton, N.Y., 1958-60; mgr. exptl. methods and tech., computer cons. Gen. Electric Co., King of Prussia, Pa., 1960-69; pres., co-owner B & G Corp., Valley Forge, Pa., 1969-74; chief elec. engr. Zenith Engrs., Inc., Ardmore, Pa., 1974-75; prin. Jake S. Bailey, Elec. Engring. Cons., Phoenixville, Pa., 1975—; pub. speaker; former instr. Dale Carnegie Sch. Mem. Illuminating Engring. Soc., Aircraft Owners and Pilots Assn. Nat. Rifle Assn., Nat. Small Bus. Assn. Home and Office: 28 N Forge Manor Dr Phoenixville PA 19460

BAILEY, KENNETH ALAN, sports exec.; b. Bklyn., Feb. 28, 1944; s. Stanley and Ruth (Vizbara) B.; B.S., L.I. U., 1965, M.B.A., 1974; m. Margaret A. Korb, May 4, 1968; children—Joseph Peter, Patricia Margaret, Michael Kenneth. Sr. accountant Price Waterhouse & Co., 1965-71; asst. controller Donovan Lesiure-Newton & Irvine, 1971-72; adminstr., controller, Townsley, Updike, Carter & Rodgers, N.Y.C., 1972-75; staff auditor Equitable Life, N.Y.C., 1975-76; controller Nat. Basketball Assn., 1976—. Sec.-treas. Phi Kappa Theta Nat. Properties, 1973—. C.P.A., N.Y. Mem. Am. Inst. C.P.A.'s, N.Y. Soc. C.P.A.'s. Home: 28 Pitman Pl Wayne NJ 07470 Office: 645 Fifth Ave New York City NY 10022

BAILEY, LAWRENCE RANDOLPH, lawyer; b. Panama, C.Z., Mar. 31, 1918; s. Charles Wesley and Alma (Small) B.; A.B., Howard U., 1939, J.D., 1942; m. Norma Thomas, May 20, 1961; children—Lawrence Randolph, Bruce, Lamont, Susan. Admitted to N.Y. State bar, 1943, U.S. Supreme Ct. bar; practiced in N.Y.C. Former counsel Jamaica Community Corp., Queens County Youth Athletic Centre, Queens County-Merrick Community Centre; former asst. counsel to pres. N.Y.C. Council, 1951-53. Mem. Met. Transp. Authority. Bd. dirs. Legal Aid Soc., Queens Urban League, N.Y. Urban League, Greater Jamaica Devel. Corp.; bd. dirs. Jamaica br. N.A.A.C.P., former chmn. legal redress com., former chief counsel N.Y. State Conf. brs., now hon. v.p. Mem., counsel Community Planning Bd. 10. Served with AUS, Judge Advocate div. Decorated Bronze Star medal. Mem. Harlem Lawyers Assn. (dir., past pres.), Nat. Bar Assn. (regional dir., dir., chmn. constl. revision com.), Am. Arbitration Assn. (arbitrator accident cases), Howard U. Alumni N.Y. (pres., counsel), Kappa Alpha Psi. Elk. Home: 112-05 175th St Jamaica NY 11433 Office: 360 W 125th St New York City NY 10027

BAILEY, MILTON, govt. ofcl.; b. N.Y.C., May 20, 1917; s. Abraham and Lillian (Ruderman) Bialek; B.B.A., Coll. City N.Y., 1940, M.S., 1949; certificate Pratt Inst., 1951; postgrad. Bklyn. Coll., 1958-61; m. Lucille Rubin, Jan. 9, 1954; 1 son, Joseph Adam. Editor newspaper and ednl. materials Adj. gen.'s office Dept. Army, 1941-43; feature editor S. Pacific Daily News, 1945-46; chem. supt. Ruderman Inc., N.Y.C., 1946-52; leather chemist U.S. Naval Supply Research and Devel. Facility, 1952-67; phys. sci. adminstr. USN Clothing and Textile Research Unit, Natick, Mass., 1967—. Lectr. Coll. City N.Y., 1951-52, N.Y.C. Community Coll., 1953-61. Arbitrator, Am. Arbitration Assn., 1973; sec. Am. Leather Chemists Assn.-ASTM, 1960-64; chmn. subcom. safety shoe com. Am. Nat. Standards Inst., 1973. Served with AUS, 1943-46. Recipient commendation Undersec. Navy, 1964. Mem. Soc. Fed. Labor Relations Profls., Am. Leather Chemists Assn., ASTM, N.Y. Acad. Sci. Club: Toastmasters (area gov. Bklyn. 1963). Patentee in field. Home: 18 Bayfield Rd Wayland MA 01778 Office: 21 Strathmore Rd Natick MA 01760

BAILEY, RALPH E., oil co. exec.; b. Pike County, Ind., Mar. 23, 1924; s. Enos M. and Gertie L. (Taylor) B.; B.S. in Mech. Engring., Purdue U., 1949; m. Bettye J. Holder, Sept. 2, 1945; children—Douglas G., Cinda C., Rhonda Y., Lisa A. With No. Ill. Coal Corp., 1949-50, Sinclair Coal Co., 1950-53; with Peabody Coal Co., 1955-65, v.p. charge mining operations, 1963-64, exec. v.p. operations, 1964-65; v.p. Consolidation Coal Co., Pitts., 1965-68, sr. v.p., 1968-70, exec. v.p. 1970-74, pres., 1974-77; pres. Continental Oil Co., 1977—. Address: Continental Oil Co Ridge Park Stamford CT 06904*

BAILEY, ROBERT WILLIAM, policy analyst; b. Bklyn., Jan. 27, 1951; s. Vincent Joseph and Theresa (Mulhearn) B.; B.A., Fordham U., 1974; diploma U. Vienna (Austria), 1973; postgrad. City U. N.Y. Grad. Center, 1974—. Research asso. Temporary Commn. on City Fin., N.Y.C., 1975, 76; policy analyst N.Y. State Emergency Fin. Control Bd., 1976-77; cons. Office of Chancellor of Schs., City of N.Y., 1978—. Mem. trustees' subcom. on coll. relations and devel. Manhattan Coll., 1970-71. Austrian Ministry of Edn. grantee, 1973. Mem. Am. Polit. Sci. Assn., Am. Hist. Assn., Soc. Historians, of Am. Fgn. Relations. Home: 19 Laura Ln Park Ridge NJ 07656

BAILEY, SAMUEL ALBERT, personnel cons.; b. Charlestown, W.Va., June 13, 1944; s. Milton Albert and Edith Corena (Davis) B.; A.S., Ricker Coll., Houlton, Maine, 1969; m. Madone Dumas, July 6, 1968; 1 dau., Monique Debbie. With Union Mut. Ins. Co., 1970-72, Maine Employment Service, 1972-74; pres. Careers Inc., personnel cons./placement, Lewiston, Maine, 1974—. Served with USAF, 1965-68. Roman Catholic. Address: 1105 Washington Ave Portland ME 04012

BAILEY, WILLIAM O., ins. co. exec.; b. Syracuse, N.Y., July 1, 1926; s. William E. and Kate (Olliver) B.; A.B. in Econs., Darmouth Coll., 1947; M.B.A. in Ins., Wharton Sch., U. Pa., 1949; m. Emily Wood, Oct. 7, 1950; children—George, Janet, Thomas, Carolyn. Asst. sect. Nat. Bur. Casualty Underwriters, 1952-54; with Aetna Life & Casualty Co., Hartford, Conn., 1954—, sr. v.p. casualty and surity div., 1968-72, exec. v.p., dir., 1972—. Corporator, mem. ins. com. Hartford Hosp.; trustee Hartford Rehab. Center; bd. corporators Hartford Sem. Found.; bd. dirs. St. Francis Hosp. Served with USNR, World War II. Mem. Oil Ins. Assn. (past pres.), Soc. C.P.C.U.'s. Home: 29 Harvest Ln West Hartford CT 06117 Office: 151 Farmington Ave Hartford CT 06115*

BAILIS, LAWRENCE ALAN, educator; b. Cleve., Sept. 1, 1946; s. Wilbur and Edith (Michaelovitz) B.; B.S., L.I. U., 1968; M.A., U. Mo., Kansas City, 1970; Ph.D., Case Western Res. U., 1974. Intern, Tchr. Corps, Kansas City, Mo., 1968-70; instr. John Carroll U., Cleve., 1974-75, Union County Community Coll., N.J., 1975-76; post-doctoral fellow U. Pa., 1976-77; asst. prof. Community Coll. Phila., 1977—; mem. Columbia U. Seminars on Death. Mem. Am. Ednl. Research Assn., Am. Ednl. Studies Assn., Found. Thanatology. Contbr. numerous articles in field of thanatology to profl. jours. Home: 610 S 10th St Philadelphia PA 19147 Office: 34 S 11th St Philadelphia PA 19107

BAILLIE, DAVID, ednl. counselor; b. N.Y.C., Nov. 30, 1938; A.A., Holyoke Community Coll., 1974; B.A., U. Mass., 1976; M.Ed., Antioch Coll., 1978; postgrad. Southeastern U.; m. Rose Mary; children—David II, Daniel, Patrick, Donald, Dawn, Douglas, Devin. Ins. agt., Western Mass. area, 1966-70; owner, mgr. Springfield franchise Westfield Newspapers, 1968-71, circulation dept. mgr., 1971; asst. mgr. Merit Oil Corp., Westfield, Mass., 1971, mgr., 1971-72; counselor, deptl. asst., program coordinator, dir. counseling assistance for older students U. Mass., Amherst, 1976-78; exec. dir. Older Wiser Learens, 1978—. Advisor, Nat. Eagle Scout Assn., 1971—; active Boy Scouts Am., 1946—. Served with AUS, 1956-62. Mem. Am. Personnel and Guidance Assn., Am. Assn. Higher Edn., Adult Edn. Assn. U.S.A. Alpha Phi Omega. Home: Box 596 Amherst MA 01002

BAILOWITZ, STANLEY ALLAN, accountant; b. Bklyn., Nov. 22, 1938; s. Meyer and Jeanne B.; B.S. in Accounting, Bklyn. Coll., 1962; m. Sandra T. Knecht, June 10, 1961; children—Jordan, Andrea. Staff accountant Fred Landau & Co., C.P.A.'s, N.Y.C., 1960-65; field controller Lawrence A. Wien and affiliated cos., N.Y.C., 1965-72; pres. Property Group, Inc. affiliate Donaldson, Lufkin & Jennette, N.Y.C., 1972—; guest lectr. Paul Smith Hotel Coll.; exec. trainee IBM; Legis. co-ordinator PTA. C.P.A., N.Y. State. Mem. N.Y. State Soc. C.P.A.'s, Am. Inst. C.P.A.'s. Office: 140 Broadway New York City NY 10005

BAILY, ALFRED EWING, environ. engr.; b. Carmichaels, Pa., Jan. 20, 1925; s. Richard L. and Alta (Hebel) B.; student Waynesburg (Pa.) Coll., 1943, Bethany (W.Va.) Coll., 1943-44; B.S. in Physics, Duke U., 1945, B.S. cum laude in Civil Engring., 1949; m. Hannah Jane Drake, Sept. 1, 1946; children—Judith Ann, Frank Henry, Louise Jane, Nancy Lee. With Chester Engrs., Coraopolis, Pa., 1949—, partner, 1969, dir. municipal services, 1974, pres., dir., 1977—. Mem. Scott Twp. Planning Commn., 1963-64. Served from ensign to lt., USNR, 1943-46, 52-53. Registered profl. engr., D.C., Del., Pa., W.Va., Ky., N.Y., Md., Va.; diplomate Am. Acad. Environ. Engrs.; certified Nat. Council Engring. Examiners. Fellow ASCE; mem. Water Pollution Control Assn. W.Va., Nat. Soc. Profl. Engrs., Pollution Control Fedn., Am. Water Works Assn., Pa. Soc. Profl. Engrs., Tau Beta Pi. Presbyterian (elder). Office: 845 4th Ave Coraopolis PA 15108

BAIN, DONALD EUGENE, JR., historian; b. Nyack, N.Y., May 29, 1943; s. Donald Eugene and Virginia Geraldine (Boire) B.; B.A., State U. N.Y. at Buffalo, 1969, M.A., 1972, Ph.D., 1974; m. Margaret Anne Stevens, Jan. 15, 1968; children—Donald Eugene III, Genevieve Elizabeth. Dir. field electronics Columbia U./NASA Geophys. Expdn. to Campo del Ciello, Argentina, 1966; asst. prof. history and urban studies Coll. Charleston (S.C.), 1974-75; asst. prof. history St. John Fisher Coll., Rochester, N.Y., 1975—; adj. faculty Rochester Inst. Tech., 1976—; chmn. Rochester Area Colls. Historians Com. Mem. Charleston Bicentennial Com., 1974-75; mem. Town of Brighton (N.Y.) Conservation Bd., 1978—. Served with U.S. Naval Air Force, 1961-65. Nat. Endowment for Humanities fellow, Yale, 1978. Mem. Am. Hist. Assn., Internat. History Honors Soc., Smithsonian Instn. Contbr. articles to profl. jours. Home: 166 Warrington Dr Rochester NY 14618 Office: Dept History St John Fisher Coll Rochester NY 14618

BAIN, GEORGE KEITH, province ofcl.; b. Brampton, Ont., Can., Apr. 5, 1928; s. George J. and Jean (Keith) B.; B.A., McMaster U., 1953; M.A., Syracuse U., 1958; m. Helen Jean Peart, Sept. 12, 1953. Asst. head, subdivision sect., community planning br. Dept. Planning and Devel., Govt. of Ont. (Can.), 1956-60, head, ofcl. plans sect. community planning br. Dept. Municipal Affairs, 1962-72, dir. planning policy br. econs. and intergovtl. affairs Ministry Treasury, 1972-75; dir. local planning policy br. Ministry Housing, 1975—. Instr. ann. town planning course to students qualifying as Ont. land surveyors, 1965-74. Mem. Can. Inst. Planners, Assn. Am. Geographers, Canadian Assn. Geographers, Assn. Ont. Land Economists, Soc. Mayflower Descs. Home: 45 Blyth Hill Rd Toronto ON M4N 3L6 Canada Office: 56 Wellesley St E Queen's Park Toronto 5 ON Canada

BAINES, JAMES DALTON, ednl. inst. adminstr.; b. Pampa, Tex., July 27, 1932; s. William Marcus and Willia Agnes (Peitzcker) B.; B.A., Southwestern U., Georgetown, Tex., 1943; M.A., Baylor U., 1957; Ph.D. (Univ. grad. fellow), Tulane U., 1967; m. Marjorie Alice Drumm, Sept. 9, 1955; children—Joel David, Stephen Brett, Catherine Kay. Teaching fellow in speech and drama Southwestern U., 1957, asst. prof., 1957-60; dir. theater McMurry Coll., Abilene, Tex., 1961-65, Lambuth Coll., Jackson, Tenn., 1965-66; asso. prof. of theater, also play-wright-in-residence Ark. Arts Center, Little Rock, 1966-68; prof. Okla. State U., Tulsa, 1968-69, also vis. prof. of urban studies Northeast Iowa Consortium of Colls., Waverly; prof. urban edn., also dir. Community Affairs Inst. William Paterson Coll., Wayne, N.J., 1969—; cons. to Interfuture Co., N.Y.C., 1975—; cons. in peace studies Paterson Diocese Office of Edn., Wayne, 1975—; tng. cons. to community workers. Chmn., Mayor's Youth Opporunity Council, Paterson, N.J., 1970-71; bd. dirs. Bergan-Passaic County (N.J.) Lung Assn., 1973-75, Greater Paterson Planning Assn., 1975-76; co-chmn. Criminal Justice Coordinating Com. of Passaic County, 1974-76. Served with M.C., AUS, 1953-55. Mem. World Future Soc., Consortium on Peace Research, Edn. and Devel., Assn. for World Edn., Common Cause. Democrat. Episcopalian. Developer curriculum programs in peace studies, urban studies and community corrections. Home: 530 E 27th St Paterson NJ 07154 Office: R-16 William Paterson Coll Wayne NJ 07470

BAINUM, PETER MONTGOMERY, aerospace engr.; b. St. Peterburg, Fla., Feb. 4, 1938; s. Charles Joseph and Mildred Trincher (Salyer) B.; B.S. in Aero. Engring., Tex. A. and M. U., 1959; S.M. in Aeros. and Astronautics, Mass. Inst. Tech., 1960; Ph.D. in Aerospace Engring., Cath. U. Am., 1967; m. Carmen Cecilia Perez, Sept. Bainum and Mildred (Trincher) Salyer; Peter. Sr. engr. Martin Co., Orlando, Fla., 1960-62; staff engr. IBM Fed. Systems Div., Bethesda, Md., 1962-65; sr. staff engr., cons. Johns Hopkins U. Applied Physics Lab., 1965-69, 69-72; mem. faculty Howard U., 1969—, prof. aerospace engring., dir. grad. studies, 1973—; v.p. research, cons. WHF & Assos. Inc., Upper Marlboro, Md., 1977—. Summer faculty fellow NASA/Am. Soc. Engring. Edn., 1970-71; recipient Teetor award Soc. Automotive Engrs. Fellow Brit. Interplanetary Soc.; asso. fellow Am. Inst. Aeros. and Astronautics; mem. Am. Astronautical Soc. (v.p. tech.). Contbr. articles to profl. jours. Home: 2400 Queens Chapel Rd Hyattsville MD 20782 Office: Dept Mech Engring Howard Univ Washington DC 20059

BAIR, MEDILL, ednl. cons.; b. Aberdeen, S.D., Aug. 6, 1914; s. Carl M. and Hazel (Collins) B.; A.B., Trenton State Coll., 1935; M.A., Columbia, 1939; postgrad. Harvard; H.H.D., Nova U., 1970; m. Sophia Slutzky, Oct. 12, 1936; children—Bonnie B., Penny (Mrs. Kurt Aguer), Nicki. Tchr.-prin. Inlaystown, N.J., 1935-39, Needham, Mass., 1939-42; supt. schs. East Greenwich, R.I., 1942-46, Cape Elizabeth, Me., 1946-48, Pennsbury Schs., Fallsington, Pa., 1948-59, Lexington, Mass., 1959-63, Carmel, Cal., 1963-66, Hartford, Conn., 1966-72; pres. Edn. Collaborative for Greater Boston, Cambridge, 1972-75, EDIC, Inc., 1975—; cons. Office of Edn., Washington; mem. bd. Ed.D. program Nova U., 1970; mem. Ednl. Software Devel. Commn., 1972; adviser Nat. Center for Ednl. Research and Devel., 1972; chmn. bd. Ednl. Dynamics, Inc. of Conn., 1971-75. Trustee, bd. mem. Ednl. Devel. Corp., Newton, Mass. Mem. Mass. Advocacy Center, Mass. State Occupational Task Force. Mem. Am. Assn. Sch. Adminstrs. (mem. jury exhbn. sch. architecture; mem. 1973 conv. planning com., mem. com. on state assns.). Co-author: Team Teaching in Action, 1964. Contbr. articles to profl. jours. Home and Office: Morningside Ln RD 2 Lincoln MA 01773

BAIRD, CHARLES FITZ, bus. exec.; b. Southampton, N.Y., Sept. 4, 1922; s. George White and Julia (Fitz) B.; A.B., Middlebury Coll., 1944; grad. Advanced Mgmt. Program, Harvard U., 1960; m. Norma Adele White, Sept. 13, 1947; children—Susan Fitz, Stephen White, CHarles Fitz, Nancy Williams. With Standard Oil Co. N.J. (now Exxon), 1948-65, dep. European fin. rep., London, 1955-58, asst. treas., 1958-62, dir. Esso Standard SA Francaise, Paris, 1962-65; asst. sec. fin. mgmt. U.S. Navy, 1965-67, undersec. of navy, 1967-69; v.p. fin. Inco Ltd. (formerly Internat. Nickel Co. Can. Ltd., 1969-72, sr. v.p., 1972-76, vice chmn., 1976-77, pres., 1977—, also dir.; dir. Bank of Montreal (Que., Can.); trustee Union Dime Savs. Bank; mem. Pres.'s Commn. Marine Sci., Engring. and Resources, 1967-69, Nat. Adv. Commn. on Ocean and Atmosphere, 1972-74; mem. bd. advisers Naval War Coll., 1970-74. Trustee Bucknell U., 1969—, chmn. bd., 1976—. Served as capt. USMC, 1943-46, 51-52. Mem. Council Fgn. Relations (Can.-Am. com.), Can. Inst. Mining and Metallurgy, Chi Psi. Clubs: Chevy Chase (Md.); Met. (Washington), India House, Econ. (N.Y.C.); Short Hills (N.J.), Links, Union, Wequetonsing (Mich.) Golf; Lawn Tennis of U.S.A. Home: 109 Forest Dr Short Hills NJ 07078 Office: 1 New York Plaza New York City NY 10004

BAIRD, HENRY WELLES, III, pediatric neurologist; b. Fort Leavenworth, Kans., Oct. 10, 1922; s. Henry Welles and Elizabeth (Tower) B.; B.S., Yale, 1945, M.D., 1949; m. Eleanora C. Gordon, Apr. 21, 1950; children—Henry Welles IV, Douglas G., Bruce C., Matthew C. Fellow, resident neurology and pediatrics Temple U. Sch. Medicine, Phila., 1950-53, faculty pediatrics, 1953—, asso. prof., 1963-68, prof. pediatrics, 1968—; practice medicine specializing in pediatric neurology, Phila., 1953—; attending pediatrician St. Christopher's Hosp. for Children, Phila., 1966—. Served to capt. M.C., AUS, 1950-56. Mem. Soc. Pediatric Research, Am. Acad. Pediatrics, Am. Acad. Cerebral Palsy. Author: The Child with Convulsions, 1972. Mem. editorial bd. Devel. Medicine and Child Neurology, 1971—. Contbr. articles to profl. jours. Home: 263 Kent Rd Wynnewood PA 19096 Office: 2600 N Lawrence St Philadelphia PA 19133

BAIRD, JAMES DAVID, materials handling equipment mfg. co. exec.; b. Rochester, N.Y., Oct. 5, 1939; s. James and Margaret (MacFadyen) B.; B.B.A., Bryant Coll., 1961; m. Carol A. Pascale; children—Douglas James, Jeanne Elizabeth. With Castle div. Sybron Corp., Rochester, 1961-65, contract sales, 1962-64, credit mgr., 1964-65; credit mgr. Am. Sterilizer Co., Erie, Pa., 1966-67, mgr. contract financing, 1967-68; treas. Lamson div. Diebold Inc., Syracuse, N.Y., 1968-72, v.p. gen. mgmt., 1972—. Chmn. mfg. div. Onondaga County chpt. United Way, 1970-73; bd. dirs. Huntington Family Center. Mem. Mfrs. Assn. Syracuse, Syracuse C. of C., Material Handling Inst. Mason. Clubs: University Lakeshore Yacht and Country (Syracuse); Meadows Racquet. Home: 4177 Lucan Rd Liverpool NY 13088 Office: Lamson St Syracuse NY 13201

BAIRD, JOHN ABSALOM, JR., coll. ofcl.; b. Honolulu, Sept. 13, 1918; s. John Absalom and Helen (Bates) B.; grad. Lawrenceville Sch., 1936; A.B., Princeton, 1940; postgrad. Johns Hopkins, 1941; m. Virginia Walton, Mar 8, 1941; children—Suzanne W. Baird Perot, Linda W. Baird Livingston, Barbara Baird Rogers. Asst. supt. Charles S. Walton Co., 1942-47, asst. sec. and dir., 1947-52, v.p. 1952-72; asst. pres. Eastern Baptist Theol. Sem., Phila., Eastern Coll., St. Davids, Pa., 1952-61, v.p., 1961—. Bd. corporators, bd. dirs. Presbyn. Ministers Fund Ins. Co., Phila. Main Line dist. chmn. Valley Forge council Boy Scouts Am., 1952-54, dist. commr., 1954-56; vice chmn. Main Line br. YMCA Greater Phila., 1947-63; trustee, v.p. Pa. Lupus Found.; v.p. Pa. chpt. Lupus Found. Am.; trustee Vol. Services for Blind, Phila.; mem. adv. bd. Phila. Home for Incurables; trustee 4th Bapt. Mission Found.; chmn. trustees Shipley School, Bryn Mawr, Pa.; v.p., dir. Am. Sunday Sch. Union (Phila.) 1957-69; dir. Watchman Examiner Corp. (N.Y.C.), 1958-70; dir. Pa. United Theol. Sem. Found. (Pitts.), Am. Ednl. and Hist. Film Center (St. Davids). Recipient Freedom Founds. Honor medal, 1973. Mem. Am. Bapt. Pub. Relations Assn., Am. Alumni Council, Am. Coll. Pub. Relations Assn., U.S. Naval Inst., U.S. Naval Found., Loyal Legion, Soc. of Cincinnati (pres. Del. 1972-75, sec. gen. 1977—), Soc. Colonial Wars, Order Fgn. Wars, S.R., Am. Assn. Sem. Staff Officers (pres. 1966-68), Pa. Acad. Fine Arts, Am. Rose Soc., Am. Philatelic Soc., English-Speaking Union, Hist. Soc. Pa., Nat. Hist. Soc., Newcomen Soc. N.Am., Geneal. Soc. Pa. Republican. Baptist. Clubs: Princeton (Phila.); Merion Cricket (Haverford, Pa.). Author: A Leap of Faith; the Whole Gospel for the Whole World; All Things Are Thine; Profile of a Hero. Contbr. articles to profl. jours. Home: 226 Broughton Ln Villanova PA 19085 Office: Eastern Baptist Theol Sem City Line and Lancaster Ave Philadelphia PA 19151

BAIRD, LINDSAY LAIRE, JR., mgmt. cons.; b. Jamaica, N.Y., Apr. 16, 1932; s. Lindsay Laire and Louise (Hummel) B.; B.S., U. Md., 1959; M.B.A., Hofstra U., 1967; ml. Elizabeth Catherine Jay, Mar. 19, 1955; children—Lisbeth Louise, Bruce Jeffery. Commd. 2d lt. U.S. Army, 1953, advanced through grades to lt. col., Mil. Police Corps, 1968, ret., 1973; gen. mgr. Advanced Computer Techniques Corp., N.Y.C., 1973-76; pres. Baird Stevens Waugh White, Inc., Denville, N.J., 1976—, Indsl. Listing Network, Inc., Denville, 1976—; lectr. U. Md., College Park, 1961-64. Camping and activities chmn. Boy Scouts Am., 1969. Decorated Bronze Star. Mem. Am. Soc. Indsl. Security (chmn. 1975-78), Data Processing Mgmt. Assn. (legis. com. 1978),

Internat. Assn. Chiefs of Police, Computer Security Inst. (adv. bd.). Republican. Roman Catholic. Clubs: Picatinny Arsenal Officers, Mountain Lakes. Contbr. articles to profl. jours.; editorial bd. Computer Fraud and Security Bull. (U.K.). Home: 98 Crestview Rd Mountain Lakes NJ 07046

BAIRD, MARTHA JOANNA, editor, author; b. Dodge City, Kans., June 10, 1921; d. Harry Charles and Mary Lou (Jones) B.; B.A., State U. Iowa, 1943; m. Eli Siegel, Oct. 7, 1944. Radio writer Sta. WGN, Chgo., 1943; sec. Am. Guild Variety Artists, N.Y.C., 1944-45, Soc. Aesthetic Realism, 1946—; editor Definition Press, 1961—; tchr. music criticism, 1973—; author; (poems) Nice Deity; also articles; co-author: Personal and Impersonal, 1959; Two Aesthetic Realism Papers, 1971. Editor: Definition: A Journal of Events and Aesthetic Realism, 1961-67; The Press Boycott of Aesthetic Realism: Documentation, 1978; co-editor: James and the Children, 1968; Goodbye Profit System, 1970; The Williams-Siegel Documentary, 1970. Home: 67 Jane St New York City NY 10014 Office: 141 Greene St New York City NY 10012

BAIRD, RONALD JAMES, surgeon, educator; b. Toronto, Ont., Can., May 3, 1930; s. Robert Whitney and Mary Agnes (Williamson) B.; M.D., U. Toronto, 1954, B.S., 1956, M.S., 1960; m. Fern Elaine Sarles, July 23, 1955; children—Ronald, Fraser, Catherine. Intern, Toronto Gen. Hosp., 1954-55, resident, 1958-59, mem. staff cardiovascular surgery, 1960-64, chief cardiovascular surgery, 1977—; resident Hosp. for Sick Children, Toronto, 1959-60, mem. staff cardiovascular surgery, Toronto Western Hosp., 1964-72, chief, 1972—, dir. surg. research, 1968—, chmn. animal care com., 1970—, asso. surgery U. Toronto, 1960-64, asst. prof., 1964-68, asso. prof., 1968-73, prof., 1973—, dir. surg. research, 1972—, head cardiovascular surgery, 1977—. Bd. govs. Canadian Heart Found., 1970—, Ont. Heart Found., 1970—. Served as surgeon lt. Royal Candian Navy, 1955-60. Recipient Roscoe Graham award, 1960; Lister award in surgery, 1964; Royal Coll. medal in surgery, 1969. Fellow Internat. Surg. Soc., Royal Coll. Physicians and Surgeons of Can., Am. Coll. Surgeons (gov. 1970-76); mem. Ont. Canadian med. assns., Acad. Medicine Toronto, Canadian Cardiovascular Soc. (councillor 1969-72, sec. treas. 1970-74, pres. 1976-77), Am. Heart Assn., Canadian Coll. Surgeons, Canadian Soc. Clin. Investigation, Internat. Cardiovascular Soc. (v.p. N.Am. chpt. 1973, v.p., 1974-75), Soc. Vascular Surgery (recorder 1977—), Soc. Univ. Surgeons (councillor 1966-70), Am. Assn. for Thoracic Surgery, Soc. Thoracic Surgeons, Am. Surg. Assn., Internat. Soc. Surgery, Alpha Omega Alpha. Conservative. Clubs: University (Toronto), Caledon Mountain Trout. Mem. editorial bd. Canadian Jour. Surgery, 1965—, Med. Post, 1966-75, Jour. Thoracic and Cardiovascular Surgery, 1977—, Surgery, 1977—, Current Surgery, 1977—. Contbr. numerous articles to profl. jours. Home: 72 Clarendon Ave Toronto ON M4V 1J3 Canada Office: Suite 8-100 Univ Wing Toronto Gen Hosp 101 College St Toronto ON M5G 7L7 Canada

BAIS, DALJIT SINGH, structural engr.; b. Nabha, India, Aug. 17, 1939; s. Thakur Kanwar Singh and Daropadi (Devi) B.; came to U.S., 1965, naturalized, 1976; B.S. in Civil Engring., Punjab U., 1962; M.B.A., Pace U., 1974; M.S. in Structural Engring., U. Ill., 1966; m. Pammi Thakur, Aug. 2, 1967; children—Rajney Monica, Rajeev Kumar. Asst. engr. Heavy Engring. Corp., Ranchi, India, 1962-64; design engr. Parsons, B.Q. & D. Inc., N.Y.C., 1966-67; structural engr. Port Authority of N.Y. and N.J., N.Y.C., 1967—. Chairperson planning and design com. United Hindu Temple N.J., 1977—; co-chairperson com. Indian Ams. for Pub. Affairs, 1978-79. Registered profl. engr., N.Y., N.J. Mem. ASCE, Nat. Soc. Profl. Engrs. AIA, Soc. Ednl., Cultural and Tech. Assistance, Inc. (pres. 1977-78). Home: 987 New Dover Rd Edison NJ 08817 Office: 57 West 1 WTC New York City NY 10048

BAISLEY, ROBERT WILLIAM, educator; b. New Haven, Apr. 5, 1923; s. Joseph V. and Mary (Bergin) B.; Mus.B., Yale, 1949; M.A., Columbia, 1950; m. Jean Shanley, July 30, 1955; children—Joan Ann, Susan Jean, Elizabeth Veronica. Tchr., Cherry Lawn Sch., Darien, Conn., 1950-51; dir. Neighborhood Music Sch., New Haven, 1951-56; asst. prof. piano Sch. Music, Yale U., New Haven, 1956-65; chmn. dept. music Pa. State U., University Park, 1965—, prof. music, 1965—. Concert pianist in various concerts, recitals, radio and TV. Vol. United Fund, New Haven, 1951-65; rep. to Council of Social Agencies, New Haven, 1951-60; mem. adv. council Salvation Army, New Haven, 1963-65. Bd. dirs. Central Pa. Festival of Arts (pres. 1969-71). Served with AUS, 1941-45. Mem. Coll. Music Soc., Lechetizsky Assn., Music Educators Nat. Council, Am. Assn. for Composers and Conductors, Internat. Soc. for Contemporary Music, Yale U. Sch. Music Alumni Assn. (exec. com. 1977—) Rotarian. Home: 454 Park Ln State College PA 16801 Office: Music Dept Pa State U University Park PA 16802

BAKAL, ABRAHAM ITSHAK, food scientist; b. Baghdad, Iraq, July 5, 1936; s. Joseph and Naomi (Hacham) B.; came to U.S., 1968, naturalized, 1977; B.S. in Chem. Engring., Technion-Israel Inst. Tech., Haifa, 1962, M.S. in Food and Biotechnology, 1965; Ph.D. in Food Sci., Rutgers U., 1970; m. Frida Shomer, Nov. 15, 1966; children—Gil, Amir. Tech. head Food Advisory Sta., Haifa, Israel, 1964-66; asst. prof. food sci., U. Sask., Saskatoon, Can., 1966-67; research asst. Rutgers U., New Brunswick, N.J., 1967-70; research dir. Foster D. Snell div. Booz, Allen & Hamilton Inc., Florham Park, N.J., 1970—, on leave as 1st tech. dir. Centro Indsl. Exptl. Para La Exportacion, San Felipe, Venezuela, 1973-75; product devel., mktg. strategies cons. French Nat. Research Council grantee, 1965. Mem. Inst. Food Technologists, N.Y. Acad. Scis. Jewish. Contbr. articles in field to tech. jours. Home: 10 Stafford Rd Parsippany NJ 07054 Office: 66 Hanover Rd Florham Park NJ 07932

BAKELMAN, JACK SAM, corp. exec.; b. Bronx, N.Y., June 10, 1929; s. Isadore and Bertha Bakelman; B.B.A., City Coll. N.Y., 1950; m.Harriette Finkenthal, Dec. 20, 1953; children—Eve, Ned. Jr. accountant firm Haas, Schlesinger & Mayer, N.Y.C., 1950-52; sr. accountant firm Ben Miller, N.Y.C., 1952-57; tax accountants, tax. mgr. Book-of-the-Month club., Inc., N.Y.C., 1957-70; tax mgr. firm Touche, Ross & Co., N.Y.C., 1970-71; tax mgr. Neptune Meter Co., N.Y.C., 1971-72; asst. dir. taxes Gen. Signal Corp., Stamford, Conn., 1972—. Served with N.G., 1948-63. C.P.A., N.Y. State. Mem. Am. Inst. C.P.A.'s, N.Y. Soc. C.P.A.'s (spl. tax award 1971), Tax Execs. Inst. Club: Masons. Home: 200-04 15th Rd Bayside NY 11360 Office: High Ridge Park Stamford CT 06904

BAKER, BENJAMIN BEALE, transp. adminstr.; b. Boston, July 1, 1939; s. Talbot and Polly N. (Beale) B.; A.B., Harvard, 1961; M.Regional Planning, U. N.C., 1967. Planning cons., Boston, 1967; asst. dir. Model Cities, New Bedford, Mass., 1968; city planner City of New Bedford, 1969-75; adminstr. Southeastern Regional Transit Authority, 1975—. Mem. exec. com. Nat. Assn. City Planning and Mgmt. Agys., 1972-75. Mem. Planning Bd., Millis, Mass., 1967-69; mem. Millis Conservation Commn., 1967-69; mem. New Bedford Planning Bd., 1969—. Served with USCGR, 1958—. Mem. Am. Inst. City Planners, Am. Soc. Planning Ofcls., Nat. Assn. Housing and Redevel. Ofcls., New Bedford Preservation Soc., Urban and Ft. Taber Assn., New Eng. Transit Club (dir.), Am. Pub. Transit Assn., Res. Officers Assn. (life), Port Support of New Bedford. Clubs: Harvard of Boston; Buzzards Yacht. Home: 132 School St New Bedford MA 02740 Office: 1213 Purchase St New Bedford MA 02740

BAKER, ELSWORTH FREDRICK, psychiatrist, med. orgonomist; b. Summit, S.D., Feb. 5, 1903; s. Niles Albert and Effie Anna (Cartwright) B.; student Regina Coll., 1920-21, U. Man., 1922-23; M.D. cum laude, Man. Med. Coll., 1928; certificate in psychiatry and neurology U. Vienna, 1929; m. Marguerite Martha Mayberry, Sept. 28, 1941; children—Courtney Fredrick, Allan Elsworth, Michael Bruce. Intern Vancouver (B.C.) Gen. Hosp., 1927-28; resident State Hosp., Greystone Park, N.J., 1928-31; chief women's service State Hosp., Marlboro, N.J., 1931-48; pvt. practice psychiatry, med. orgonomy, N.Y.C., 1948—, Fair Haven, N.J., 1948—; asst. psychiatrist Monmouth Med. Center, Long Branch, N.J., 1940-62. Pres. Orgonomic Publs., N.Y.C., 1967—. Trustee Orgonomic Research Found., N.Y.C., 1967—. Decorated knight comdr. Justice Sovereign Order St. John of Jerusalem, Knight of Malta. Diplomate Am. Bd. Psychiatry and Neurology. Fellow Am. Psychiat. Assn., Am. Coll. Orgonomy (pres. 1968—), Royal Soc. Health, A.A.A.S.; mem. Monmouth County Med. Soc., A.M.A., N.J. Neuropsychiat. Assn., Internat. Platform Assn. Author: Man In The Trap, 1967 (N.J. Tchrs. English award). Editor Jour. Orgonomy, 1967—. Contbr. profl. jours. Home: 51 Hance Rd Fair Haven NJ 07701 Office: 200 East End Ave New York City NY 10028

BAKER, HAROLD JAY, JR., mgmt. cons.; b. Wellston, Okla., Sept. 2, 1908; s. Harold Jay and Helen Josephine (Woods) B.; B.S., Purdue U., 1931; M.Sc., Mass. Inst. Tech., 1933; m. Jean Harmon, June 5, 1948; 1 dau., Amy Woods. Chem. engr. Sinclair Refining Co., East Chicago, 1933-39, E.I. duPont de Nemours & Co., Inc., Wilmington, Del., 1939-44, Standard Oil Co./Exxon, N.Y.C., 1944-71; mgmt. cons., Dobbs Ferry, N.Y., 1971—. Registered profl. engr., N.Y. Mem. Nat. Soc. Profl. Engrs., Am. Inst. Chem. Engrs., Chem. Mktg. Research Assn., AAAS, SAR, Beta Theta Pi. Episcopalian. Mason. Patentee in petroleum refining. Address: 300 Broadway Dobbs Ferry NY 10522

BAKER, HAROLD KENT, educator; b. Portsmouth, Va., Nov. 13, 1944; s. David Harold and Ruby Lee (Peek) B.; B.S. in Bus. Adminstrn., Georgetown U., 1967; M.B.A., U. Md., 1969, D.Bus. Adminstrn., 1972, M.Ed., 1974; m. Patricia Marie Stachura, July 31, 1972; 1 dau., Stacey Marie. Asst. to dean U. Md. Coll. Bus. and Pub. Adminstrn., 1969-72; asst. dean Georgetown U. Sch. Bus. Adminstrn., 1972-74; asso. prof. Am. U. Sch. Bus. Adminstrn., 1975—; adv. dir. D.C. Nat. Bank, 1966-70. Mem. Am., Eastern, So., finance assns., Fin. Mgmt. Assn., Am. Inst. Decision Scis., Alpha Sigma Nu, Beta Gamma Sigma, Phi Kappa Phi, Delta Sigma Pi. Contbr. to profl. jours. Home: 12618 English Orchard Ct Wheaton MD 20906 Office: Sch Bus Adminstrn American Univ Washington DC 20016

BAKER, HOUSTON ALFRED, JR., educator; b. Louisville, Mar. 22, 1943; s. Houston A. and Viola Elizabeth (Smith) B.; B.A., Howard U., 1965; M.A. (John Hay Whitney fellow), U. Calif., Los Angeles, 1966, Ph.D., 1968; m. Charlotte Marie Pierce, Sept. 10, 1966; 1 son, Mark Frederick. Instr., Howard U., summer 1966; instr. English, Yale, 1968-69, asst. prof., 1969-70; asso. prof., mem. Center Advanced Studies, U. Va., 1970-73, prof., 1973-74; prof., dir. Afro-Am. studies U. Pa., 1974—; Phi Beta Kappa vis. scholar, 1975-76. Recipient Alfred Longueil Poetry award U. Calif., Los Angeles, 1966. Mem. Modern Lang. Assn., Nat. Assn. Black Profs., Phi Beta Kappa. Author: Long Black Song, 1972; Singers of Daybreak, 1974; A Many-Colored Coat of Dreams, 1974; editor: Black Literature in America, 1971; 20th-Century Interpretations of Native Son, 1972; Reading Black: Essays in the Criticism of African, Caribbean and Black American Literature, 1976; contbr. articles and revs. to profl. jours. Home: 613 E Phil-Ellena St Philadelphia PA 19119 Office: Dept English U Pa Philadelphia PA 19174

BAKER, JACK THOMAS, design engr.; b. Linton, Ind., Nov. 7, 1924; s. George J. and Oneta L. Baker; B.S., U.S. Maritime Acad., 1945; m. Sylvia E. Tofte, July 1, 1971; children—Frances, Robert, Catherine, Cynthia, Christine, Jason, Justin. With Henry Heide Co., 1948-50, Senator Frozen Products Co., 1950-60, Gordon Baking Co., 1960-65, Interstate Brands Corp., 1965-74; design engr. Sebco Mfg. Co., Greenwich, N.Y., 1974—; cons. in field. Author articles. Office: PO Box 36 Greenwich NY 12834

BAKER, JAMES BARNES, architect; b. N.Y.C., Feb. 18, 1933; s. William Edgar and Violet (Twachtman) B.; A.B., Princeton, 1954; M.Arch., Yale, 1960; children—Mary Morgan, James Edgar, Catriona Griswold, Frederick Alden. With firms Blake & Neski, N.Y.C., 1960-62, George Lewis, N.Y.C., 1962-63, Kahn & Jacobs, N.Y.C., 1963-64; partner firm Baker & Blake, N.Y.C., 1964-72, Baker/Grinnell, N.Y.C., 1972-74; cons., 1974-78; pres. Park/Tower Devel. Group, Cleve. and N.Y.C., 1978—; vis. prof. Sch. Architecture, City U. N.Y., 1967—. Trustee Darrow Sch. Recipient Design awards HUD, AIA. Fellow AIA (dir.); mem. Am. Arbitration Assn. Clubs: Coffee House, Holland Soc., St. Nicholas Soc. Home: 105 E 63d St New York City NY 10021

BAKER, JAMES EARL, plant physiologist; b. Cowen, W.Va., Dec. 1, 1931; s. Henry Floyd and Dora (Justus) B.; B.S., U. Md., 1953, M.S., 1955; Ph.D., N.C. State U., 1958; m. Dorothy Ann Vinansky, May 6, 1961. Research in plant physiology U.S. Dept. Agr., Ithaca, N.Y., 1958-60, Beltsville, Md., 1960—. Vis. scientist U. Calif. at Los Angeles, 1965-66, Nat. Research Inst. of Tea, Kanaya, Japan, 1971; vice chmn. 1st Gordon Research Conf. on Plant Senescence, 1976. Recipient research award for fgn. specialists Japanese Govt., 1971. Mem. Am. Soc. Plant Physiologists, Am. Inst. Biol. Sci., Am. Chem. Soc., Japanese Soc. Plant Physiologists, AAAS, Sigma Xi, Phi Kappa Phi. Contbr. articles to profl. jours., chpts. to books. Home: 7004 Chansory Ln College Heights Estates MD 20782 Office: US Dept Agriculture SEA Fed Research Post Harvest Physiology Lab Beltsville MD 20705

BAKER, JOSEPHINE L. REDENIUS (MRS. MILTON G. BAKER), pub. relations dir.; b. Oceanville, N.J., Aug. 31, 1920; d. Jacob and Josephone (Palmer) Redenius; student Columbia, 1948-49, L.I. U., 1957-58, George Washington U., 1947-48; M.A. in Journalism, Am. U., 1963; L.H.D., Temple U., 1964. Enlisted as pvt. WAAC, 1943, advanced through grades to lt. col. U.S. Army, 1963; intelligence officer atomic installations throughout U.S. and Can., 1943-53; asst. in Office Chief of Staff, Army Forces Far East, Japan, 1954-56; pub. info. officer Office Chief of Information, Washington, 1958-61; chief Women's Army Corps Recruiting, U.S. Army, 1962-66; info. liaison officer U.S. Army, 1966-67, ret., 1967; dir. pub. relations and devel. Valley Forge Mil. Acad. and Jr. Coll., Wayne, Pa., 1967-71, dir., 1970—; pres. Intercounty Trading Co., Inc., Surfside, Fla., 1976—; pres. bd. dirs. Surf Club Apts., Surfside. Bd. dirs. Valley Forge Freedom Valley dist. Girl Scouts Am., Republican Women of Pa., Opera Guild of Miami; pres. bd. dirs. St. Cornelius the Centurian Found. Decorated Legion of Merit, Pa. Meritorious Service medal; U.S. Army Commendation medal with oak leaf cluster; named Distinguished Alumnus Am. U., 1969. Mem. Pub. Relations Soc. Am., Am. Personnel and Guidance Assn., Am. Coll. Personnel Assn., Nat. Vocat. Guidance Assn., Am. Sch. Counselors Assn., Am. Legion Aux., Ret. Officers Assn., Assn. U.S. Army (Anthony J. Drexel Biddle medal 1968), Army-Navy Union, Soroptomist Club, Assn. Measurement and Evaluation in Guidance, Am. Legion, La Boutique Des Hult Chapeaux et Quarante Femmes, Emergency Aid of Pa., Women in Communications, Mil. Order World Wars. Presbyterian. Clubs: Surf, La Gorce Country, Bald Peak Colony (N.H.), St. David's Golf. Address: Tower House Eagle and Radnor St Rds Wayne PA 19087 also Surf Club Apts 9133 Collins Ave Surfside FL 33154

BAKER, LOIS MEADOWCROFT, educator; b. Phila., Dec. 30, 1918; d. Earle Lewis and Estella Firth (Dove) Meadowcroft; B.S. in Home Econs., Drexel Inst. Tech., 1941; M.A., Columbia, 1945; postgrad. U. St. Andrews (Scotland), 1968, Radbrook Coll., Shrewsbury, Eng., 1968, Pa. State U., 1971; m. George W. Baker, IV, Mar. 31, 1945; 1 son, Bruce Meadowcroft. Tchr. pub. schs., Colwyn, Pa., 1941-45, Phila., 1945-50; with Drexel U. (formerly Drexel Inst. Tech.), Phila., 1950—, dir. Drexel Early Childhood Center (formerly nursery sch.), asso. prof., 1970—, acting head dept. human behavior and devel., 1973-76; mem. Pa. Bd. Pvt. Academic Schs., Harrisburg, 1971—. Grantee U.S. Office Child Devel., 1972-75, Pa. Dept. Welfare, 1975-76. Mem. Delaware Valley Assn. for Edn. Young Children (past pres.), AAUP, AAUW, Am. (life), Pa. home econs. assns., Home Econs. Assn. Phila., Internat. Fedn. for Home Econs., Assn. for Supervision and Curriculum Devel., U.S. com. l'Organisation Mondiale pour l'Education Prescholaire, Nat. Assn. for Edn. of Young Children, NEA, Am. Assn. for Childhood Edn. Internat., Brit. Assn. for Early Childhood Edn., Alpha Sigma Alpha. Home: 1507 Woodland Ave Folcroft PA 19032 Office: Drexel U Philadelphia PA 19104

BAKER, MALCOLM C., geologist, geophysicist; b. Gilboa, N.Y., July 6, 1909; s. Elmer andl Blanche C. (Clapper) B.; A.B., Colgate U., 1929; postgrad. Cornell U., 1933; m. Lucille Wallin, Sept. 23, 1933; children—Wayne A., Neal W. With Seismic Computer dept. Humble Oil, Houston, 1934-45; Seismic interpreter Tropical Oil, Bogota, Columbia, 1946-48; geophysicist Creole Petroleum, Caracas, Venezuela, 1948-56, Standard-Vacuum, White Plains, N.Y., 1957-59, Philippines, 1959; pres. Am. Magnetic Reduction Inc., Georgetown, Conn., 1961-65; cons. Broken Hill Pty. Ltd., Melbourne, Australia, 1962-63; cons. Nat. Iranian Oil Co., Teharan, 1963-64; cons. Weeks Natural Resources, Westport, Conn., 1971-78; ret., 1978. Mem. Am. Assn. Petroleum Geologist. Club: Explorers. Home: 155 Umpawaug Rd West Redding CT 06896 Office: Westport CT

BAKER, NANCY ANN, librarian; b. Charleston, W.Va., Oct. 6, 1921; d. Donald James and Genevieve P. (Gaskill) Baker; B.S. in Edn., U. Pa., 1943; M.L.S., U. Pitts., 1965. Classroom tchr., Spring City, Pa., 1943-44, Upper Darby, Pa., 1944-48; tchr. Mt. Lebanon Sch. Dist., Pitts., 1948-65, librarian, 1965—. Mem. Am., Pa., Pitts., Suburban library assns., Friends of Library, Nat., Pa., Mt. Lebanon (sec.-treas. 1962-63) edn. assns., Zeta Tau Alpha. Home: 19 Ralston Pl Pittsburgh PA 15216 Office: Markham Sch Crescent Dr Pittsburgh PA 15228

BAKER, RICHARD BROWN, art collector; b. Providence, Nov. 5, 1912; s. Harvey Almy and Marion North (Brown) B.; B.A., Yale, 1935; B.A. (Rhodes scholar), Christ Ch. Oxford U., 1943, M.A., 1943; student Students Internat. Union, Geneva, 1932; D.F.A. (hon.), R.I. Sch. Design, 1978. Reporter, edit. librarian Providence Jour., 1938-40; attache, Am. embassy, Madrid, Spain, 1940; editorial asst. FCC, Washington, 1941; asso. social sci. analyst Western European sect. div. spl. information Library Congress, 1941-43; research analyst Western European sect. research and analysis br. OSS, Washington, London, Paris, 1943-45; research analyst Office Intelligence Research, Dept. State, 1945-47; fgn. affairs officer CIA, 1947-48; nongovt. observer Internat. League Rights of Man UN, 1954-56; mem. museum com. R.I. Sch. Design, 1966-75, mem. fine arts com. of mus. council, 1976—; mem. com. on art gallery Univ. Council, Yale, 1962-66, 71-76; mem. governing bd. Yale U. Art Gallery, 1974—, mem. acquisitions com., 1978—; collection of contemporary art has been basis for exhibits at R.I. Sch. Design Mus., Providence, 1959, 64, 73, Drew U., Madison, N.J., 1960, 62, Walker Art Center, Mpls., 1961, Wellesley (Mass.) Coll. exhibit, 1963, Yale, New Haven, 1963, 75, Larry Aldrich Museum, Ridgefield, Conn., 1965, Oakland U., Rochester, Mich., 1967, 74, U. South Fla., Tampa, 1967, 69, Selected Works World Art, Mexico City, 1968, U. Notre Dame, South Bend, Ind., 1969, San Francisco Mus. Art, 1973, U. Pa., Phila., 1973, Stamford (Conn.) Mus., 1978; mem. N.Y.C. Art Commn., 1977—. Fellow Morgan Library; mem. Met. Mus. (life), Art Students League (life), Am. Fedn. Arts, Archives of Am. Art, Friends Am. Arts at Yale, Mus. Modern Art, Mus. Art R.I. Sch. Design, Guggenheim Mus. (asso.), Yale Library Assos., Friend of Columbia Libraries, Phi Beta Kappa. Clubs: Hope (Providence); University (Washington); Grolier, Yale (N.Y.C.). Author: THe Year of the Buzz Bomb: A Journal of London, 1944, 1952; Stairways to Another Stage: Verse, 1952. Home: 1185 Park Ave New York City NY 10028

BAKER, ROGER DAVID, pediatrician; b. Winsted, Conn., Feb. 11, 1936; s. Louis Herman and Agatha Pauline (Knight) B.; B.A., U. Vt., 1959, M.D., 1962; m. Carolyn Grace Spencer, July 11, 1959; children—David, Bruce, Stephen. Intern, Meth. Hosp., Indpls., 1962-63; resident in pediatrics Coll. Medicine, U. Vt., 1963-65; practice medicine specializing in pediatrics, Rutland, Vt., 1967—; mem. staff Rutland Hosp., 1967—, chmn. dept. pediatrics, 1976-78; vol. clin. instr. pediatrics U. Vt. Past bd. dirs. Vt. Heart Assn., Rutland area Vis. Nurse Assn.; pediatric cons., mem. profl. advisory com. Vt. Achievement Center. Served with U.S. Army, 1965-67. Diplomate Nat. Bd. Med. Examiners, Am. Bd. Pediatrics; Mem. Am. Acad. Pediatrics, Vt., Rutland County med. socs., Rutland Region C. of C., Phi Beta Kappa, Sigma Xi (asso.). Methodist. Home: 57 Hillside Rd Rutland VT 05701 Office: 98 Allen St Rutland VT 05701

BAKER, SETH NOEL, textile co. exec.; b. Freeport, N.Y., Jan. 3, 1915; s. C. Dwight and Emma Louise (Parshall) B.; B.A., Washington and Lee U., 1938; m. Geraldine T. Sullivan, Dec. 25, 1941; children—Geraldine Diane, Kathryn Louise, Susan Noel. Copyboy, N.Y. Daily News, 1938; feature writer Telegraph Desk, Newsday, 1938-41; personnel mgr. Sharp & Dohme, Inc., Phila., 1946-50, pub. relations dir., 1950-56; personnel dir. Plax Corp., Hartford, Conn., 1956-64; asst. labor relations mgr. Monsanto Co., St. Louis, 1964-65; personnel dir. Celanese Plastics Co., Newark, 1965-72; v.p. employee relations Celanese Fibers Internat. Co., N.Y.C., 1972—. Chmn. Sch. Authority Commn. Springhouse (Pa.), 1949-51; chmn. Econ. Devel. Com. Twp. of Chatham, N.J., 1970; mem. Planning Bd. Chatham Twp. Served to maj. AUS, 1941-46. Mem. Pub. Relations Soc. Am. (pres. Phila. chpt. 1955-56), Internat. Personnel Assn., Sigma Delta Chi, Omicron Delta Kappa. Episcopalian. Home: 50 Nicholson Dr Chatham NJ 07928 Office: 1211 Ave of Americas New York NY 10036

BAKER, THOMAS, pharmacologist; b. Mineola, N.Y., Sept. 19, 1933; s. Raymond Ira and Agatha (Carroll) B.; A.B., Hunter Coll., City U. N.Y., 1968; M.S., Grad. Sch. Med. Scis., Cornell U., 1971; m. Marion Whitaker, Nov. 11, 1951; children—Patricia Anne, Susan, Thomas, Peter, David, Marian. Research asst., Med. Coll., Cornell U., N.Y.C., 1962-68, research asso., 1968-76, asst. prof. pharmacology, 1976—. Mem. Ramapo Valley Ambulance Corps. Mem. AAAS, N.Y. Acad. Scis., Am. Soc. Pharmacology, Soc. Neurosci. Contbr. articles to profl. jours. Office: Cornell University Medical College Dept Pharmacology 1300 York Ave New York City NY 10021

BAKER, VERNA TOMLINSON (MRS. EARL M. BAKER), librarian; b. Phila., Apr. 14, 1915; d. Joseph Ullman and Mabel (Dolton) Tomlinson; student (scholar) Temple U., 1937-39, Phila. Coll. Bible, 1959-62; B.S., Bryan Coll., 1963; M.A., George Peabody Coll., 1964; M.A., Chgo. Grad. Sch. Theology, 1970; m. Earl M. Baker, Dec. 31, 1938 (dec. Nov. 1958); children—Earl M. III, B. Kimball. Asst. to expediter Brit. Admiralty Delegation, Naval Aviation Supply Depot, Phila., 1944-45; sec., manuscript reader Westminster Press, Phila., 1947-53; librarian Ben Lippen Sch., Asheville, N.C., 1953-58; gen. library work Nashville Pub. Library, 1963-64; with King's Coll., Briarcliff Manor, N.Y., 1964—, reader services librarian, 1967—. Mem. N.Y., Westchester library assns. Christian Librarians fellow, 1965—. Author: Here in the Spring, 1968. Editor: Poems Revisited, 1976. Contbr. poems to anthologies, various mags. Office: King's Coll Briarcliff Manor NY 10510

BAKER, WALTER LOUIS, elec. engr., educator; b. Earlton, N.Y., Aug. 7, 1924; s. Alberti and Louise (Schmidt) B.; B.E.E., Clarkson Coll. Tech., 1944; M.S., Pa. State U., 1954; m. Janet Katherine Sprague, Sept. 7, 1944 (dec.); children—Walter Kent (dec.), Lawrence Albert, Linda Louise, Louis Milton; m. 2d, Marion M. King, July 1, 1976. Tech. asst. Tenn. Eastman Corp., Oak Ridge, 1944-45; sr. engr. Philco Corp., Phila., 1945-49; research asso., prof. Pa. State U., University Park, 1949—, lectr. engring. acoustics, 1965—. Cons. Jitco, 1952-68, HRB-Singer, 1958-67, Spartan Electric Corp., 1960-61, USMC, 1965, Environmental Sci. Services Adminstrn., 1966—. Recipient Navy Meritorious Pub. Service citation, 1975. Registered profl. engr., Pa. Mem. IEEE (sr., past chmn., sec., treas. Central Pa. sect.), Acoustical Soc. Am., N.Y. Acad. Scis., Sigma Xi. Methodist. Contbr. articles to profl. jours. Home: 117 Wildot Dr State College PA 16801 Office: Pa State U University Park PA 16802

BAKER, WILLIAM HERBERT, hosp. assn. exec.; b. Buffalo, Oct. 23, 1932; s. Guy Andrew and Ella Mae (Beeler) B.; B.S. in Econs., Purdue U., 1954; postgrad. Ball State U., 1956-58; m. Nancy Ann Brown, Nov. 5, 1955; children—Scott Andrew, Karen Lynn. Prodn. supr., safety dir., labor relations supr. Gen. Motors Corp., Muncie, Ind., New Brunswick, N.J., Anderson, Ind., 1956-69; dir. personnel mgmt. N.J. Hosp. Assn., Princeton, 1969-75, v.p., 1975—; mem. faculty hosp. seminars. Mem., v.p. Montgomery Twp. Bd. Edn.; bd. dirs. Am. Heart Assn. N.J. affiliate; officer, bd. dirs. Princeton Area United Fund. Served with CIC, AUS, 1954-56. Mem. Am. Mgmt. Assn., Soc. Advancement Mgmt. Lutheran. Home: RD 1 Cleveland Circle Skillman NJ 08558 Office: 760 Alexander Rd CN 1 Princeton NJ 08540

BAKER, WILLIAM JESSE, diagnostic pharm. co. exec.; b. East Florenceville, N.B., Can., Dec. 25, 1932; s. Frank Jesse and Ellen Jane (Pryor) B.; student U. N.B., 1949-50, B.S., 1957; M.S., Wayne State U., 1960, Ph.D., 1967; m. Joyce Elizabeth Bevans, Aug. 8, 1953; children—Susan Jane, Nancy Joyce, Timothy William. Med. lab. technologist N.B. Dept. Health, St. John, Moncton, Fredericton, N.B., 1951-53; research asso. Wayne State U., Detroit, 1959-60; scientist, Ortho Pharm. Corp., Raritan, N.J., 1960-67; dir. diagnostic services internat. Johnson & Johnson Internat., Raritan, 1967-74; dir. mfg., Ortho Diagnostics Inc., Raritan, 1974—; guest lectr., Rutgers U. Sch. Med., 1963-66. Com. mem. Boy Scouts Am., 1972-75; bd. dirs. Hunterdon Occupational Tng. Center, 1975—, pres. bd. trustees, 1978—. Recipient Gov. Gen's. Medal, Can., 1957. Mem. N.Y. Acad. Scis., AAAS, Am. Assn. Blood Banks, Am. Assn. Clin. Chemists, Am. Inst. Chemists, Inst. Med. Lab. Technologists, Canadian Soc. Lab. Tech., Sigma Xi. Contbr. papers, text sections to sci. publs. Office: Ortho Diagnostics Inc Route 202 Raritan NJ 08869

BAKEWELL, CHARLES ADAMS, energy econs. cons.; b. Hartford, Conn., Apr. 12, 1940; s. Henry Palmer and Hester Livingstone (Adams) B.; B.A., Yale, 1963; M.B.A., Columbia, 1966; m. Lucia Ruth Urban, June 22, 1963; children—Geoffrey Ward, Andrea Whitney, Christine Ashley. Various fin. positions Gen. Foods Corp., White Plains, N.Y., 1966-74, category fin. mgr., 1974-75; mgr. budgets, profit analysis and gen. acctg. Sperry Remington Consumer Products Div., Bridgeport, Conn., 1975-78; sr. fin. analyst Gruy Fed., Inc., Arlington, Va., 1978—. Treas., Westport (Conn.) chpt. Am. Field Service, 1970-71, Westport Republican Town Com., 1978-79; del. Conn. Rep. Conv., 1978; participant Campaign Mgmt. Inst., 1977; vestryman Christ Holy Trinity Ch., Westport, Conn., 1974-77, canvass chmn., 1974, 75. Episcopalian. Home: 7900 Old Falls Rd McLean VA 22101 Office: Suite 701 2001 Jefferson Davis Hwy Arlington VA 22202

BAKHRU, HASSARAM CHOITHRAM, physicist, educator; b. Rohri, Sindh, India, June 2, 1937; s. Choithram and Heer (Ahuja) B.; came to U.S., 1965; M.S., Banaras Hindu U., India, 1960; Ph.D., Saha Inst. Nuclear Physics, Calcutta, 1964. Asso. dir. Heavy Ion Accelerator, Yale U., 1966-69; asst. prof. physics State U. N.Y. at Albany, 1970-73, asso. prof., 1973—, dir. nuclear accelerator lab., 1972—. Grantee Research Found. State N.Y., 1971; Frederick Gardner Cottrell grantee Research Corp., 1971; AEC grantee, 1971—; NSF grantee 1973. Mem. Am. Phys. Soc., Health Physics Soc., Soc. Nuclear Medicine, Sigma Xi. Contbr. articles on nuclear and atomic physics to profl. publs.; lectr. in field. Home: 500 Pittsfield Rd Lenox MA 01240 Office: Physics Dept State U NY Albany NY 12222

BAKSH, MUSTAPHA KEMAL, economist; b. San Fernando, Trinidad, Nov. 17, 1940; s. Rassul A. and Salima H. Baksh; came to U.S., 1961; B.S. in Biology, U. N.Mex., 1965, M.A. in Econs., 1966; m. Janet Ruth Hall, Mar. 17, 1967; 1 son, Peter Rassul. Asst. prof. econs. Belknap Coll., Center Harbor, N.H., 1966-70; dir. Intersate Investments, Cranston, R.I., 1969—, Russul Baksh Enterprises, San Fernando, 1958—, Bancar Internat., East Providence, 1970—; prof. econs., chmn. dept. bus. and econs. Roger Williams Coll., Bristol, R.I., 1970—. Fellow World Acad. Scholars; mem. Am., Western econ. assns., AAUP, Am. Fin. Assn., NEA, U.S. Com. for Caribbean, Greater Providence C. of C. Home: 2 Seabrook Dr East Providence RI 02914 Office: Roger Williams Coll Bristol RI 02809

BALABAN, EDWARD ELLIOT, educator; b. Bklyn., Mar. 21, 1952; s. Milton and Roslyn (Dubrow) B.; student (N.Y. Regents Coll. scholar) City U. N.Y., 1969-70; B.S., State U. N.Y., Oswego, 1973; M.S., Syracuse U., 1974; Cert. Advanced Study, Hofstra U., 1978; m. Diane Lee Axelrod, July 4, 1976. Pub. relations asst. State U. N.Y., Oswego, 1971-74; sales promotion dir. Syracuse (N.Y.) Stingers Box Lacrosse Club, 1974; tchr., info. officer Uniondale (N.Y.) pub. Schs., 1974—. Mem. exec. bd. Turtle Hook Jr. High Sch. PTA, Uniondale, 1974—. Permanent teaching and adminstrs. certs., N.Y. Mem. Pub. Relations Soc. Am., Nat. Sch. Pub. Relations Assn., L.I. Sch.-Community Relations Assn., Stuyvesant Alumni Assn., U.S. CB Radio Assn., Epsilon Pi Tau. Club: Blue Line (Oswego). Home: 5 Crab Ave Lynbrook NY 11563 Office: Turtle Hook Jr High Sch Jerusalem Ave Uniondale NY 11553

BALABAN, MAXINE I., sch. adminstr.; b. Providence, July 28, 1929; d. Bert Eli and Anne Miriam (Gorman) Israel; B.A., Brown U., 1951; M.A., U. Conn., 1969; m. Leonard J. Balaban, Jan. 6, 1951; children—Michael David, Steven I., Rachel Ida Beth. Tchr. English, Holmes County (Fla.) Schs., 1960-67; guidance counselor Naugatuck (Conn.) High Sch., 1969—. Mem. Am. Personnel and Guidance Assn., Nat. Vocat. Edn. Assn., Assn. Humanistic Edn. and Devel., NEA, Am. Fedn. Tchrs. Home: 111 Lake Ave West Haven CT 06516 Office: 543 Rubber Ave Naugatuck CT 06770

BALANCHINE, GEORGE, choreographer; b. Petrograd, Russia, Jan. 9, 1904; s. Meliton and Marie Balinchinvadze; grad. Imperial Sch. Ballet, 1921, student Conservatory of Music, Petrograd; L.H.D., Brandeis U., 1965; m. Tanaguil LeClerq, Dec. 31, 1952 (div. 1969). Came to the U.S., 1933. Danced in state theatres of opera and ballet, Russia, 1915-24; toured Europe, then joined Ballets Russes de Serge Diaghilev; became dir. Royal Theater Copenhagen, 1929; helped organize Ballets Russes de Monte Carlo, 1932; with Met. Opera House, N.Y. City, 1934-37; helped organize Sch. Am. Ballet, 1934, now dir.; founded (with Lincoln Kirstein) Ballet Soc., 1946, now N.Y. City Ballet (toured U.S. and abroad, 1950—); Artistic dir., N.Y. City Ballet, 1948, choreography for motion pictures, plays, On Your Toes, Goldwyn Follies, Boys from Syracuse, Cabin in the Sky, I Married an Angel, ballets: The Nightingale, 1925; Barabau, 1925; Pastorale, 1927; Triumph of Neptune, 1927; Jack-in-the-Box, 1927; Apollon, 1928; Le Bal, 1929; Prodigal Son, 1929; Cotillion, 1932; Mozartiana, Errante, Seven Deadly Sins, 1933; The Nutcracker, 1954; Liebeslieder Waltzer, Ivesiana, Agon, Bugaku; Don Quixote, 1965, Sonatine, 1974, numerous others; collaborated on many ballets with Igor Stravinsky. Decorated Order Legion Honor (France). Mem. Greek Orthdox Ch. Author: Balanchine's Book of Ballet. Office: 144 W 66th St New York City NY 10023*

BALAZS, DENES VILMOS, physician; b. Budapest, Hungary, Nov. 5, 1941; s. Denes Vilmos and Katalin (Seidl) B.; came to U.S., 1960, naturalized, 1966; B.S., Columbia U., 1968; M.D., Albert Einstein Coll. Medicine, 1972; m. Janie Sacks, Mar. 28, 1970; children—Andre, Nicole, Damien. Intern, New Britain (Conn.) Gen. Hosp., 1972-73; resident Beth Israel Med. Center, N.Y.C., 1973-74, Hartford (Conn.) Hosp., 1974-75; pvt. practice internal medicine, West Hartford, Conn., 1975—; asst. prof. clin. medicine U. Conn. Med. Center, 1976—; attending in medicine Hartford Hosp., 1975—. Diplomate Am. Bd. Internal Medicine. Mem. Am. Soc. Internal Medicine, Hartford County Med. Assn. Home and Office: 1043 Farmington Ave West Hartford CT 06107

BALBIN, JULIUS YUL, educator; b. Cracow, Poland, Jan. 12, 1917; s. Fryderyk and Balbina (Meisler) Löwy; came to U.S., 1951, naturalized, 1957; M.A., Jagiellonian U. (Poland), 1939; Ph.D., U. Vienna, 1950. Translator, Marks and Clerk, Patent Attys., N.Y.C., 1953-57; researcher, writer U.S. Joint Publs. Research Service, N.Y.C., 1957-59; asst. prof. French and Russian, U.S. Mcht. Marine Acad., Kings Point, N.Y., 1959-63; instr. French, German, Russian, Italian and Spanish, Internat. Sch. of Langs., N.Y.C., 1965-67; asso. prof. German, French, Spanish and English, Essex County Coll., Newark, 1969—. Recipient numerous awards for original and translated poetry in Esperanto. Mem. Modern Lang. Assn., Am. Council Teaching of Fgn. Langs., AAUP, Am. Soc. Geolinguistics, Linguistic Soc. Am., Am. Inst. Writing Research, Universal Esperanto Assn. Author and translator; contbr. articles and poetry to scholarly and lit. publs. Home: 340 Riverside Dr New York City NY 10025 Office: Essex County Coll Newark NJ 07102

BALCAR, GERALD P., glass mfg. co. exec.; b. Elizabeth, N.J., July 2, 1932; s. Frederick Rhinehart and Genevieve (Pierce) B.; A.B., Cornell U., 1954; m. Carol Mintern Edlund, June 17, 1955 (div. 1977); children—Sherry Elizabeth, Peter Rhinehart, Joanne Wendell. Mem. staff Tradeways, Inc., mktg. consultants, 1954-58; supr. mktg. research Collins Radio Co., Richardson, Tex., 1958-60; asst. to pres. Acoustica Assos., Inc., Los Angeles, 1960-62; asst. to pres. Atco Chem. Indsl. Products, Inc., Franklin, N.J., 1962-65; nat. sales mgr. Potters Bros., Inc., Carlstadt, N.J., 1965-71; v.p., dir. mktg. Potters Industries, Inc., 1971—. Chmn. Pub. Affairs Com.; chmn. West Milford Bd. Edn., 1971-73. Mem. Am. Ordnance Assn. Club: Chemists (N.Y.). Home: 1111 River Rd Edgewater NJ 07020 Office: 377 Route 17 Hasbrouck Heights NJ 07604

BALDING, BRUCE EDWARD, financial co. exec.; b. Chgo., Oct. 15, 1931; s. John Barnard and Dorothy (Davis) B.; grad. St. Mark's Sch., 1950; A.B., Harvard, 1953, M.A., 1954; m. Barbara Whitney, Feb. 25, 1955; 1 dau., Elizabeth; m. 2d, Elizabeth T. Whitman, June 21, 1975. Portfolio mgr. Wellington & Co., N.Y.C., 1962-67; partner firm Emannel, Deetjen & Co., N.Y.C., 1967-69; pres. Controlled Equities Inc., N.Y.C., 1970—, also dir.; dir. Fairmont Advisers Ltd., Grand Cayman, B.W.I., Frequency Electronics Co., New Hyde Park, N.Y., Combined Metals Reduction, Salt Lake City. Bd. dirs. Nat. Soc. Prevention Blindness, N.Y.C., Young Adult Inst. and Workshop, N.Y.C. Served with 8th Army, AUS, 1955-56; Korea. Mem. N.Y. Soc. Security Analysts. Clubs: Piping Rock, Locust Valley (N.Y.); Harvard of New York City; Leash, Links, River (N.Y.C.). Home: Wheatley Rd Glen Head NY 15545 Office: Rockefeller Center 1270 Ave of Americas New York City NY 10020

BALDINGER, STANLEY, govt. ofcl.; b. St. Paul, Jan. 11, 1932; s. Samuel Charles and Ethel Sylvia (Yaffe) B.; B.A., U. Minn., 1953, M.A., 1956; M.S., Columbia, 1969; m. Judith Gittl Altman, Dec. 20, 1970. Fgn. service officer State Dept., Washington, Rome, 1957-64; program organizer for fgn. govt. ofcls. Social Security Adminstrn., Washington, 1964-66; adminstrv. asst. to dept. dir. Nat. Capital Planning Commn., Washington, 1966-67; chief overall program design D.C. Office Planning and Mgmt., Washington, 1970-75; sr. planning coordinator D.C. Municipal Planning Office, Washington, 1975—. Recipient Merit award D.C. Office Planning and Mgmt., 1972; Mayor's Outstanding Performance award, 1976, 78; Towser Found. fellow, 1956, William Kinne Fellows fellow, 1968. Mem. Am. Acad. Polit. and Social Sci., World Future Soc., Nat. Trust for Historic Preservation, Smithsonian Instn. Author: Planning and Governing the Metropolis: The Twin Cities Experience, 1971. Home: 5533 Warwick Pl Chevy Chase MD 20015 Office: 1329 E St NW Washington DC 20004

BALDWIN, CHARLES DICKINSON, editor; b. Orange, N.J., Dec. 19, 1928; s. Charles G. and Kathrina C. (Condict) B.; B.S., Rider Coll., 1955; m. Jane McCrea, Apr. 17, 1953; children—Diane, Brenda. Editor, Gen. Electric Co., Toronto, Ont., Can., 1955-57, McLean Pub. Co., Toronto, 1957-59, Rosenthal Smythe, Inc., Summit, N.J., 1959-64, Haire Pub. Co., N.Y.C., 1964-68, Baldwin-Dickinson, Inc., pub., Madison, N.J., 1968-77; ret., 1977; free-lance writer, 1978—. Served with AUS, 1951-53. Recipient Jesse H. Neal Am. Bus. Press award of merit for outstanding journalism, Summit, 1961. Home: Crest Dr Bernardsville NJ 07924

BALDWIN, ESTHER EBERSTADT (MRS. ROBERT HOWE BALDWIN), personnel and ins. co. exec.; b. East Orange, N.J.; d. Edward Frederick and Elenita Contreras (Lembcke) Eberstadt; B.A., Notre Dame Coll. Md., 1919, M.A. (hon.), 1941, LL.D., 1958; Mus.B., Am. Inst. Applied Music, 1921; m. Robert Howe Baldwin, June 7, 1933. Pres., Mrs. E.E. Brooke, Inc., personnel consultants, 1923—, Robert H. Baldwin, Inc., Ins. Brokers, 1955—; v.p. Davis, Dorland & Co., 1955— (all N.Y.C.). Lectr. to colls., bus. and profl. groups. Mem. nat. council U.S. Com. for Refugees, 1963-64; mem. White House Conf. For World Refugee, 1963; mem. nat. council Am. Friends of Middle East, 1956-63, Pakistan-Am. Students Assn., 1957-62; mem. Greater N.Y. council Boy Scouts Am., 1956-58; Greater N.Y. chpt. ANTA. Life mem., former dir., mem. exec. com. Women's Nat. Republican Club. Pres. Robert H. Baldwin Found., 1956—; bd. dirs., chmn., pres. Am. Com. to Befriend Arab Refugees, 1958—; bd. dirs. Council on Islamic Affairs, 1957-65, vice-chmn., 1958-63; bd. dirs. Near East Found., Notre Dame Coll. Md., Reziob Coll., Iran, Baldwin Clinic, Iran, Boys Clubs of Jordan, Robert H. Baldwin Fund for Arab Students, Camp Fire Girls, Inc., Internat. Ednl. Devel.; trustee Robert H. Baldwin Library, Iraq; council Met. Opera, 1967—; mem. Pres.'s Council Columbia. Decorated by Shah of Iran. Fellow Archeol. Inst. Am., Am. Geog. Soc.; founding mem. Jr. League of Oranges (Orange, N.J.); life mem. Acad. Polit. Sci., Am. Mus. Natural History, Assistance League So. Calif., Met. Mus. Art, N.Y. Zool. Soc.; mem. Nat. Inst. Social Scis., Pakistan-Am. C. of C., Soc. Women Geographers, AAUW, English Speaking Union, Assos. of Columbia U., Arab and Am. Women's Friendship Assn. (founder, life mem.), Soc. of Jesus (hon.), Delta Epsilon Sigma. Author: The Girl and Her Job, 1933; Career Clinic, 1940; The Right Job For You and How To Get It, 1944; Career Guide, 1943; Guide to Career Success, 1947; You and Your Personality, 1949. Contbr. articles to Cosmopolitan, Good Housekeeping, Mademoiselle, others. Home: 4 Pleasant St Woodstock VT 05091 Office: Near East Found 54 E 64th St New York City NY 10021 also Davis Dorland & Co 99 Church St New York City NY 10007

BALDWIN, RICHARD ANTHONY, chemist; b. Phila., Oct. 17, 1946; s. Richard Kaelker and Violet Marie (Iacaruso) B.; B.S., Chemistry, St. Joseph's Coll., 1968, M.S. in Chemistry, 1970; m. Barbara Lee Potter, Sept. 6, 1969; children—Mark Richard, Ruth Anne. Lab. aide St. Joseph's Coll., Phila., 1965-68; jr. chem. tech. IRC div. TRW Corp., Phila., 1968; teaching asst. St. Joseph's Coll., 1968-70; sci. instr. Sch. of the Holy Child, Rosemont, Pa., 1969-70; chemist U.S. FDA, Phila., 1970-75, Rockville, Md., 1975-77, dir. edn. and tng. staff, 1977—. Recipient certificate of appreciation FDA, 1973, 75, awards, 1973, 75, 78. Mem. Twinbrook Civic Assn., Am. Chem. Soc., AAAS, Assn. Ofcl. Analytical Chemists, Central Atlantic State Assn. Food and Drug Ofcls. Home: 313 Farragut Ave Rockville MD 20851 Office: 5600 Fishers Ln (HFO-11) Rockville MD 20857

BALDWIN, RICHARD SARGENT, accountant, tax cons.; b. Peterborough, N.H., Oct. 22, 1940; s. Harrison Copp and Elizabeth Brockway (Sargent) B.; student New Eng. Coll., 1960-63; Profl. Accounting Certificate, Pierce Coll., 1965; B.S., LaSalle Extension U., 1976. Staff auditor Nat. Grange Mut. Ins. Co., Keene, N.H., 1966-69; audit supr. SCM Crop., N.Y.C., 1969-75; resident auditor Pechiney Ugine Kuhlmann, Greenwich, Conn., 1975-77; owner Richard S. Baldwin, Bookkeeping and Tax Service, Hillsborough, N.H., 1977—. Treas., Town of Hillsborough, 1978—. Served with Army N.G., 1959-65. Certified internal auditor. Mem. Inst. Internal Auditors, Nat. Assn. Accountants, Hillsborough Area Jaycees, Am. Mgmt. Assn. Club: Admirals. Home: Lower Village Hillsborough NH 03244 Office: School St Hillsboro NH 03244

BALDWIN, THOMAS FRERRICHS, interior designer, space planning cons.; b. Iowa City, Nov. 4, 1914; s. Harry and Hattie Johanna (Frerrichs) B.; student schs. Clinton, Iowa; m. Catherine Keane, July 8, 1944; children—Linda, Thomas, Barbara, Kevin, James, Catherine, William. Set designer, 1932-36; dir. design P. J. Nee Co., Washington, 1948-53, M.S. Ginn, Washington, 1953-58, N. Frank and Son, Rockville, Md., 1958-70; pres. Baldwin Design Assos., Bethesda, Md., 1970—; tutor design renderings to coll. grads.; space planning cons. Served with USNAF, 1940-48. Democrat. Roman Catholic. Asso. designer habipod home. Home: 5911 Ryland Dr Bethesda MD 20034

BALDWIN, VELMA NEVILLE, ofcl. Exec. Office Pres.; b. Meade, Kans., Aug. 31, 1918; d. Charles Chester and Anna Velma (Neville) Wilson; A.B., U. Kans., 1940; m. Claude David Baldwin, Jan. 31, 1942 (dec. Nov. 1976). Student placement U. Kans., 1940-42; personnel adminstrn. War Dept., Washington, 1942-45; asst. to Dr. A.C. Kinsey, Ind. U., 1946-47; legal sec. Carter Oil Co., Denver, 1948-50; personnel, budget and security officer Bur. of Budget, Washington, 1951-55; asst. to dir. personnel Treasury Dept., 1955-59; personnel officer, asst. to dir. for adminstrn. Office Mgmt. and Budget, 1959—. Mem. Soc. Personnel Adminstrn. (exec. bd. 1966-69), Am. Soc. Pub. Adminstrn. (adviser 1961), Mortar Bd., Phi Beta Kappa. Presbyterian. Home: 2234 49th St NW Washington DC 20007 Office: Office Mgmt and Budget Washington DC 20503

BALFE, HARRY, II, educator; b. Bklyn., Apr. 27, 1922; s. Raymond Adams and Dorothy (MacDonald) B.; B.A., Trinity Coll., 1947; J.D., Cath. U., 1952; M.A., Am. U. Sch. Internat. Service, 1964; m. Judith Lee Huggins, May 8, 1965; children—Thomas James, Jennifer Linda. Advt. asst. to v.p. Macy's Dept. Store, 1946-47; intelligence research analyst Georgetown U. Research Project, Washington, 1953-57; tchr. history, econs. Montclair (N.J.) Acad., 1957-66, asst. prof. history Montclair State Coll., Upper Montclair, N.J., 1966-69, asst. prof. polit. sci., 1969—; asso. Danforth Found., 1970—. Chmn., Mayor's Com. UN Week, Montclair, 1966; mem. Charter Commn. Study Group, Montclair, 1963; N.J. election supr. NBC, 1970-73; Democratic party candidate N.Y. State Assembly, N.Y.C., 1946; mem. Essex County Dem. Com., 1962-65, 68-78; mem. nat. bd. dirs. Am. Vets. Com., 1970-73; mem. bd. Nat. Consumers League, 1977—; bd. dirs. Consumers League N.J., 1967—, Montclair Adult Sch., 1974-78. Served with USAAF, 1943-46. Mem. Amnesty Internat. U.S.A., ACLU, UN Assn., Am. Polit. Sci. Assn., Am. Soc. Internat. Law, Supreme Ct. Hist. Soc., Pi Gamma Mu. Unitarian-Universalist. Home: 94 Mount Hebron Rd Montclair NJ 07043

BALISTOCKY, MARVIN HAROLD, physician; b. Phila., May 18, 1923; s. Meyer and Tillie (Wright) B.; B.A., U. Pa., 1946; postgrad., 1946-47, Sch. Medicine, 1953-54; M.D., Hahnemann Med. Coll., 1951; m. Loretta Rabinowitz, Nov. 3, 1957; children—Anne Rose, Paul Howard. Intern, Phila. Gen. Hosp., 1951-53, resident surgeon in ophthalmology, 1954-56, asst. chief, 1958-61; ship's surgeon S.S. Santa Barbara, Grace Line, 1954; pvt. practice medicine specializing in ophthalmology, Norristown, Pa., 1958—; chief opthalmology Sacred Heart Hosp., 1976—, Norristown State Hosp., 1968—; staff Wills Eye Hosp., Jefferson U., Montgomery Hosp., Suburban Gen. Hosp.; cons. staff Phoenixville Hosp., Valley Forge Hosp. and Med. Center, Med. Diagnostic Center Norristown; mem. glaucoma screening bd. Sr. Adult Activities Center, 1975—, Montgomery County Assn. for Blind, 1970-75. Served with inf. AUS, 1943-45, USCGR, 1954, to lt. M.C., USNR, 1956-58. Diplomate Am. Bd. Ophthalmology. Fellow Internat. Coll. Surgeons; mem. AMA (Physician's Achievement awards 1972, 75), Pa., Montgomery County, Hahnemann Alumni, Blockley med. socs., Am., Pa. acads. ophthalmology and otolaryngology, Contact Lens Assn. Ophthalmologists, Intercounty Ophthal. Soc. Pa. Contbr. articles to profl. jours. Home: 1601 Northview Blvd Norristown PA 19401

Office: 1320 Dekalb St Norristown PA 19401 also 491 Allendale Rd King of Prussia PA 19406

BALISTRERI, WILLIAM FRANCIS, pediatrician, gastroenterologist; b. Geneva, N.Y., June 24, 1944; s. Francis William and Mary (Yannotti) B.; student St. Bonaventure U., 1962; B.A., U. Buffalo, 1966, M.D., 1970; m. Rebecca Ann McLeod, May 31, 1969; children—Anthony Michael, Jennifer Rebecca, William Philip. Intern, Children's Hosp. Med. Center, Cin., 1970-71, resident in pediatrics, 1971-72; fellow in gastroenterology Children's Hosp. Research Found. and Mayo Clinic, Rochester, Minn., 1972-74; asst. prof. pediatrics U. Pa., Phila., 1976—. Served with M.C., USN, 1974-76. Mem. Am. Assn. Study of Liver Disease, Am. Fedn. Clin. Research, AAAS, N.Am. Soc. Pediatric Gastroenterology, Phila. Pediatric Soc. Office: 34th St and Civic Center Blvd Philadelphia PA 19104

BALL, BURTON MARSH, health physicist; b. Rutland, Vt., Dec. 16, 1919; s. Clarence Franklin and Mary Olive (Marsh) B.; B.S., Union Coll., 1943, postgrad., 1947-49; m. Ruth Mary Elliott, Dec. 27, 1945; children—Mary Ann, Nancy Louise, Richard Marsh. Asst. radiol. engr. Knolls Atomic Power Lab., Schenectady, N.Y., 1948-55; health physicist Alco Products, Inc., Schenectady, 1955-57; radiol. safety engr. U.S. AEC, Schenectady, 1957-62; v.p. Taylor & Ball, Inc., Rutland, Vt., 1962-66; tech. asst. radio. and environ. Vt. Yankee Nuclear Power Corp., Vernon, 1966-78; cons. in health physics, 1962-66. Served with AC, U.S. Navy, 1942-46; PTO. Decorated Air medals (two); certified Am. Bd. Health Physics. Mem. Am. Nuclear Soc., Am. Pub. Health Assn., Internat. Radiation Protection Assn., Health Physics Soc. Republican. Clubs: Masons, Shriners. Home: 99 Chesterfield Rd Hinsdale NH 03451 Office: PO Box 157 Vernon VT 05354

BALL, EDWARD CHARLES, educator; b. Hoosick Falls, N.Y., July 15, 1922; s. Charles Edward and Margaret Mary (Canfield) B.; B.A., Syracuse U., 1948, M.A., 1949; m. Wilma Wayne Boyette, Aug. 20, 1946; children—Barbara Susan, Pamela Ann, William Minton. Tchr., Rome (N.Y.) Free Acad., 1949—, chmn. dept. social studies, 1963—. Supr. Colgate U. High Ability Seminars for Secondary Students, 1958—; lectr. Mohawk Valley Community Coll., 1968-70; cons. Colgate U., 1958—, N.Y. State Am. Revolution Bicentennial Commn., 1973—; pres. Lake Delta P.T.A., 1961-62; mem. hist., archtl. landmarks com. Oneida-Herkimer Counties, 1966-67; pres. chmn. bd. trustees Rome Hist. Soc., 1968—; gen. chmn. Rome Pub. Schs. Council of Bicentennial of Am. Revolution, 1975—; mem. Rome Bicentennial Commn., 1975—; mem. Contract Com. To Erect Tomb of Unknown Revolutionary Soldiers at Rome, 1976. Served with USAAF, 1943-46. Mem. Acad. Am. Educators, Kappa Phi Kappa, Alpha Chi Rho. Republican. Club: Lake Delta Yacht (Rome). Author: The American Strategy and French Role in the Fort Stanwix Treaty of 1784, 1972; The First Stars and Stripes to Defy Foe Flown at Fort Stanwix, 1972. Editor, contbg. author: Survey and Evaluation of Fifty Historic Buildings and Sites at Rome, N.Y., 1966. Home: Grand View Ave RD 3 Rome NY 13440 Office: Bd Edn Bldg 108 E Garden St Rome NY 13440

BALL, EDWIN LAWRENCE, biologist; b. Collins, Iowa, Jan. 31, 1913; s. Benjamin Alfred and Crescy Ellen (Downing) B.; A.B., U. No. Iowa, 1938; Ph.M., U. Wis., 1939, Ph.D., 1947; m. Harriet Josephine Barnes, Oct. 30, 1948; children—Carl Benjamin, Jane Elizabeth. Lab. asst. Iowa State Tchrs. Coll., Cedar Falls, 1936-38; successively research asst., teaching asst., univ. fellow U. Wis., Madison, 1938-43; research mycologist Lederle Labs. div. Am. Cyanamid Co., Pearl River, N.Y., 1943-56, devel. chemist, 1956-78; ret., 1978. Mem. supervisory com. Lederle Employees Fed. Credit Union. Mem. troop com. local Boy Scouts Am., 1962-73; mem. parents adv. com. Hamilton Coll., 1969-72; mem. Beaver Coll. Circle Parents, 1973-77. Mem. Soc. Indsl. Microbiology, A.A.A.S., Soc. Am. Microbiologists, Soc. Am. Plant Physiologists, N.Y. Acad. Sci., Sigma Xi. Republican. Lutheran (ch. council, treas.). Patentee in field. Home: 33 Convent Rd Nanuet NY 10954 Office: Bldg 120 Lederle Labs N Middletown Rd Pearl River NY 10965

BALL, LAWRENCE, govt. ofcl.; b. Albion, N.Y., Aug. 10, 1933; s. Harold W. and Gladys (Gibbs) B.; B.S., Antioch Coll., 1957; M.S., Ohio State U., 1962; postgrad. U. Colo., 1963-66; grad. Inst. Applied Sci., 1973; m. Caroline Nicoll Moran, June 20, 1957; children—Daniel Lawrence, Logan Edward, Stacey Laura, Ryan Laird. Sr. engr. Deco Electronics Corp., Boulder, Colo., 1962-66, Westinghouse Georesearch Lab., Boulder, 1966-74, Westinghouse Ocean Research Lab., Annapolis, Md., 1974-75; program mgr. for geothermal energy ERDA, Washington, 1975-77, U.S. Dept. Energy, Washington, 1977—; emergency med. technician Anne Arundel County, Md., 1977—. Mem. Boulder Res. Police, 1968-74; scoutmaster Long's Peak council Boy Scouts Am., 1971-74. Mem. IEEE, AAAS, Soc. Exploration Geophysicists, Nat. Rifle Assn. Methodist. Clubs: Toastmasters Internat., Cape St. Claire Yacht. Contbr. numerous articles on geophysics to sci. jours. Office: Dept Energy 20 Massachusetts Ave NW Washington DC 20545

BALL, PETER PAUL, JR., chemist; b. Springfield, Mass., Dec. 6, 1931; s. Peter P. and Jennie W. (Wasko) B.; B.A., Am. Internat. Coll., Springfield, 1953, M.A., 1961; M.S., Simmons Coll., Boston, 1971; Ph.D., U. Mass., Amherst, 1979; m. Joyce E. McDowell, Mar. 1, 1958; 1 son, Wayne A. Tchr. chemistry, physics, biology and gen. sci. high schs. in Mass., 1954-67; mem. faculty Westfield (Mass.) State Coll., 1967—, asst. prof. chemistry, 1971—; cons. in field. Mem. AAAS, New Eng. Assn. Chemistry Tchrs., Am. Chem. Soc., Mass. Assn. Sci. Tchrs. Author: A Mechanistic Approach to Organic Chemistry, 1970. Home: 109 Winona Dr West Springfield MA 01089 Office: Westfield State Coll Westfield MA 01085

BALLARD, CLAUDE MARK, JR., ins. co. exec.; b. Memphis, Sept. 27, 1929; s. Claude Mark and Elsie May (Miner) B.; m. Mary Theresa Birnbach, July 11, 1953; children—Karen Sue, Mary Melinda, Robin Lisa. With Prudential Ins. Co. Am., 1948-69, v.p., regional treas. SW ops., Houston, 1967-73, v.p. real estate investment dept., Newark, 1973—; dir. PIC Realty Co., Newark; guest lectr. Cornell U., 1974-78, Mich. State U., 1975-78, N.Y. U., 1975, Harvard U., 1976; mem. fin. com. Am. Hotel and Motel Assn. Chmn. Econ. Devel. Com., Houston, 1972-73; trustee Urban Land Inst., 1975—, mem. exec. com., 1977—; pres., trustee Urban Land Research Found., Washington, 1977—. Mem. Am. Inst. Real Estate Appraisers. Contbr. articles in field to profl. jours. Home: 37 Knob Hill Dr Summit NJ 07901 Office: 20 Prudential Plaza Newark NJ 07101

BALLARD, LOWELL DOUGLAS, mech. engr.; b. Seiling, Okla., June 27, 1933; s. Auty Wayne and Mabel (Henderson) B.; B.S., U. Md., 1962. Mech. engr. Rabinow Inc., Rockville, Md., 1962; mech. engr. Nat. Bur. Standards, 1962—; panel mem. Nat. Elec. Code, 1975 edit. Vice-pres. South Townhouse Assn., 1974-77, pres., 1978. Served with USAF, 1954-58. Fellow Wash. Acad. Sci.; sr. mem. IEEE; mem. Am. Def. Preparedness Assn., Philos. Soc. Washington, Optical Soc. Am. Presbyterian. Home: 722 S Colonial St Sterling Park VA 22170 Office: National Bureau of Standards Washington DC 20234

BALLARD, PATRICIA JOAN, paralegal; b. Houston, Jan. 21, 1954; d. Walter W., Jr. and Joanne (Brown) Ballard; B.A., Bowling Green State U., 1976. Intern, Nat. Women's Polit. Caucus, 1976, Women's Equity Action League Fund, 1976-77; paralegal, antitrust litigation with firm Howrey & Simon, Washington, 1977—. Gov., Colo. Columbine Girls State, 1971; law rep. from Pueblo (Colo.) to Pres.'s Nat. Congress Explorer Scouts, 1971; mem. D.C. Women's Polit. Caucus; affirmative action chairperson Women's Equity Action League; observer Internat. Women's Year Conf.; mem. Nat. Women's Polit. Caucus, ERA Commn.; mem. steering com. Democratic Nat. Convs., 1972, 76. Mem. Nat. Nations Capitol Area, Pitts. paralegal assns., NAACP, Urban League, Nat. Hook-up Black Women. Methodist. Home: 1343 Childress St NE Washington DC 20002 Office: 1730 Pennsylvania Ave NW Washington DC 20006

BALLARD, ROBERT WILSON, physician; b. Trenton, Mar. 4, 1922; s. Arthur Crosley and Mary Eliza (Wilson) B.; student Cornell, 1940-43; M.D., N.Y. Med. Coll., 1947; m. Renata Margaret Crisi, June 20, 1970; children—Christina Marie, Marshall Wilson. Intern, Moses Taylor Hosp., Scranton, Pa., 1947-48; resident W. Side Hosp., Scranton, 1948-49; gen. practice medicine, Nelsonville, Ohio, 1949-50, 53-55, Baldwinsville, N.Y., 1955-59; asst. med. dir. White Labs., Kenilworth, N.J., 1959-60; asst. dir. clin. research, Warner-Lambert Research Inst., Morris Plains, N.J., 1960-61; med. dir. Pitman-Moore Co., Indpls., 1961-63; dir. med. research, v.p. Winthrop Labs., N.Y.C., 1963-66; exec. and med. dir. McNeil Labs., Ft. Washington, Pa., 1966-68; gen. practice medicine, Wappingers Falls, N.Y., 1968-69, 71—; med. dir. Vassar Bros. Hosp., Poughkeepsie, N.Y., 1969-70; partner Hopewell Med. Group, Hopewell Junction, N.J., 1971—; chmn. utilization rev. com. Central Dutchess Nursing Home, 1971—; chmn. utilization rev. com. Hyde Park Nursing Home, Staatsburg, N.Y., 1974-76, med. dir., 1976—; mem. Dutchess County Mental Health Bd., 1975—. Trustee Hudson Valley Health Services Found., Inc., Poughkeepsie, 1974—. Served with U.S. Army, 1943-46; served to capt. USAF, 1950-53. AEC fellow, 1951-52. Mem. Dutchess County, (pres. 1975-76), N.Y. State med. socs., Am. Soc. Clin. Pharmacology and Therapeutics. Home: 21 Hilltop Dr Wappingers Falls NY 12590 Office: Hopewell Medical Group Hopewell Junction NY 12533

BALLESTEROS, RUBEN FRANCISCO, surgeon; b. Sorsogon, Philippines, Apr. 5, 1940; s. Roque B. and Esther M. (Francisco) B.; M.D., U. Philippines, 1964; m. Adelaida De Guzman, Sept. 2, 1967; children—Ruben, Maria, Michael. Came to U.S., 1965, naturalized, 1978. Intern, Washington Hosp. Center, 1965-66; resident gen. surgery Wayne State U., Detroit, 1966-69; resident in plastic surgery La. State U., New Orleans, 1969-72; asst. prof. surgery U. Md., Balt., 1977—; chief div. plastic surgery Mercy Hosp. Balt., 1977—; individual practice medicine, specializing in plastic surgery Balt., 1973—. Diplomate Am. Bd. Plastic Surgery. Fellow A.C.S.; mem. AMA, Am. Soc. Plastic and Reconstructive Surgeons. Roman Catholic. Address: 7401 Osler Dr Baltimore MD 21204

BALLO, FRANK RUSSELL, brewing co. ofcl.; b. Ashtabula, Ohio, May 19, 1934; s. Frank Edmund and Ellen Irene (Niemi) B.; B.S. in Bus. Adminstrn., Kent State U., 1956; M.Ed. in Guidance, Framingham State Coll., 1965; postgrad. N.Eng. Sch. Law, 1970-72; m. Jean Forbes, May 10, 1970; children—Lee Russell, Brett Matthew. Production foreman Dayton Tire and Rubber Co. (Ohio), 1958-60; gen. foreman SW Industries, Inc., Newton, Mass., 1960-63, dir. employee relations, 1963-68; personnel dir. Revere Sugar Refinery subs. United Brands, Boston, 1968-71, v.p. ops., 1971-73; mgr. employee relations F. & M. Schaefer Brewing Co., Lehigh Valley Brewery, Allentown, Pa., 1973—. Mem. Am. Coll. Personnel Assn., Nat., Pa. vocat. guidance assns., Am. Rehab. Counseling Assn., Am. Soc. Personnel Adminstrn. Club: Elks (Bethlehem, Pa.). Home: 1014 Lawrence Dr Emmaus PA 18049 Office: PO Box 2568 Allentown PA 18001

BALLOU, ELLEN BARTLETT (MRS. NORMAN V. BALLOU), author; b. Pitts., Sept. 24, 1905; d. Dwight Kellogg and Maud (Orr) Bartlett; A.B., Wellesley Coll., 1927; M.A., Northwestern U., 1929; m. Norman V. Ballou, June 29, 1932. Actress, New Playwrights Theatre, 1927; dir. of drama Wheaton Coll., 1929-41; with outpost desk OSS, 1945-46; dean Katharine Gibbs Sch., 1948-55; asst. English dept. Brown U., 1955-62. Mem. N.H., R.I. hist. socs., Peterborough Hist. Soc., Friends of Houghton Library (Harvard), Boston Athenaeum, Soc. for Protection N.H. Forests. Clubs: Boston Authors; Dublin Lake, Garden of Dublin; Garden of America; Chilton (Boston). Author: The Centennial (plays), 1935; The Building of the House, Houghton Mifflin's Formative Years, 1970. Address: Blueberry Hill Box 271 Dublin NH 03444

BALLOU, KENNETH WALTER, univ. adminstr.; b. Boston, June 6, 1930; s. Thomas Walter and Anne M. (Blanck) B.; A.B., Tufts U., 1953, Ed.M., 1954; postgrad. Rutgers U., 1955-56, U. Calif. at Los Angeles, 1978; m. Ann Dysart, Aug 14, 1954; children—Stephen K., Jeffrey S., Laura A., Ellen S. Tchr. pub. schs., Verona, N.J., 1954-56; asst. dir. admissions Northeastern U., Boston, 1954-59, dir. admissions, 1959-65, dean univ. relations, 1965-69, dean Univ. Coll., 1969-74, dean adult edn., 1974—; cons. U.S. Office of Edn., various colls. Chmn., Framingham (Mass.) Sch. Com., 1962-68; corporator Framingham Union Hosp., 1969—; bd. dirs. Mass. Osteo. Hosp., 1970-72; mem. nat. council Northeastern U., 1969—. Mem. AAUP, Assn. for Higher Edn., Adult Edn. Assn., Am. Assn. for Continuing Higher Edn., Council for Advancement of Edn., Am. Personnel and Guidance Assn. Democrat. Roman Catholic. Author monographs in field of adult edn. Home: 527 Grove St Framingham MA 01701 Office: 360 Huntington Ave Boston MA 02115

BALLOU, RAYMOND JAMES, elec. engr.; b. Rochester, N.Y., July 21, 1945; s. Ivan Oliver and Elizabeth Alida (Barrett) B.; B.S. in Elec. Engring., Gen. Motors Inst., 1968; m. Nora Ann Roupe, Nov. 12, 1966; children—Raymond, Kevin, Deanna, Nathan. Sr. research engr. Rochester Products div. Gen. Motors Corp., Rochester, N.Y., 1971-72, supr. mfg. research, 1972-73, gen. supr. mfg. devel., 1973-74, gen. supr. prodn. engring., 1974-77, supt. prodn. engring., 1978—. Adult leader Otetiana council Boy Scouts Am., 1976—. Mem. Rochester Area C. of C. (dir. Greece council 1977—), Rochester Engring. Soc. Republican. Roman Catholic. Patentee digital logic test probe, numerical base translator. Home: 172 Chimney Hill Rd Rochester NY 14612 Office: 1000 Lexington Ave Rochester NY 14603

BALSAM, MURRAY, dentist; b. Newark, June 20, 1917; s. Abraham A. and Ruth A. (Sumka) B.; B.S., U. Va., 1938; D.D.S., U. Pitts., 1942; m. Mildred Lande, June 20, 1942; children—William L., Stefanie B. (Mrs. David Hertzog). Pvt. practice dentistry, East Orange, N.J., 1942-58, West Orange, N.J., 1958—; chief anesthesia dept. Beth Israel Med. Center, Newark, 1969-74, asst. chief oral surg. service, 1965-74, lectr., 1960-74; pres. Hidden Spring Walking Horses, Inc., 1974—. Pres. Orange Mt. council Boy Scouts Am., 1957-58; trustee, West Orange (N.J.) Community House, 1970-74. Served to capt. Dental Corps, AUS, 1942-44. Recipient Silver Beaver award Boy Scouts Am., 1957. Fellow Acad. Gen. Dentistry, Am. Coll. Dentists; mem. ADA, N.J. Dental Soc., N.J. Soc. Anesthesia, Am. Dental Soc. Anesthesia, Am., N.J. (steward 1970-74) horse show assns., Am. Walking Horse Assn. (dir. 1972-74), Tenn. Walking Horse Breeders Assn., Tenn. Squires. Club: Lions (1st v.p. 1971-72). Home: 39 Lenox Terr West Orange NJ 07052 Office: 391 Northfield Ave West Orange NJ 07052

BALTER, LESLIE MARVIN, educator; b. N.Y.C., Feb. 27, 1920; s. Harry and Rose Balter; B.S. in Elec. Engring., Columbia U., 1941; postgrad. Rutgers U.; M.A., N.Y. U., 1969; children—Kenneth Robert, Sheila Beth. Civilian radio engr. Signal Corps Development Lab., Ft. Monmouth, N.J., 1941-45, in ETO, 1942; chief engr. Masters Crystal Co., quartz crystal prodn., 1945-46; founder Jersey City Tech. Inst., dir., 1947—, founded br. operation as Paterson (N.J.) Inst., 1956—; founder Sch. Bus. Machines, teaching IBM machines, 1958—; cons. test engr. Consumers Research, Washington, N.J. Mem. N.J. Vocat. Edn. Master Plan Com. Communications chmn. Jersey City Civil Def. Council, 1950-53. Mem. IEEE, N.J. Assn. Pvt. Career Schs. (pres. 1971), N.J. Bus. Edn. Assn., Delta Pi Epsilon. Mason. Contbr. articles to Electronic Design Mag., Bus. Edn. World. Clubs: Stuyvesant Yacht, Adventurers (N.Y.C.). Home: Montague NJ also PO Box 305 RD 4 Port Jervis NY 12771 Office: Plaza School Garden State Plaza Paramus NJ 07652

BALTIMORE, DAVID, microbiologist, educator; b. N.Y.C., Mar. 7, 1938; s. Richard I. and Gertrude (Lipschitz) B.; B.A. with high honors in Chemistry, Swarthmore Coll., 1960; postgrad. Mass. Inst. Tech., 1960-61; Ph.D., Rockefeller U., 1964; m. Alice S. Huang, Oct. 5, 1968; 1 dau., Teak. Research asso. Salk Inst. Biol. Studies, LaJolla, Calif., 1965-68; asso. prof. microbiology Mass. Inst. Tech., Cambridge, 1968-71, prof. biology, 1972, Am. Cancer Soc. prof. microbiology, 1973. Recipient Gustav Stern award in virology, 1971; Warren Triennial prize Mass. Gen. Hosp., 1971; Eli Lilly and Co. award in microbiology and immunology, 1971; U.S. Steel Found. award in molecular biology, 1974; Gairdner Found. ann. award, 1974; Nobel prize in medicine, 1975. Mem. Nat., Pontifical acads. scis. Mem. editorial bd. Jour. Virology. Home: 28 Donnell St Cambridge MA 02138 Office: Mass Inst Tech Cambridge MA 02139

BALTIMORE, IDA WRIGHT, nurse; b. S.C., Sept. 11, 1914; d. Joseph and Louise (Clyburn) Wright; R.N. diploma Fordham Hosp. Sch. Nursing, 1946; B.S., N.Y. U., 1958, M.A., 1960; m. Herman Lee Baltimore, Jr., Oct. 10, 1934; 1 dau., Bessie Louise. With N.Y.C. Municipal Hosp. System, 1947—, supr., 1955-62, asst. dir. nursing, 1962-74, dep. asso. exec. dir. nursing, 1974—; mem. nurse's adv. com. N.Y.C. div. Am. Cancer Soc. Mem. Am., N.Y. State, Dist. 13 nurses assns., Am. Soc. Hosp. Nursing Service Adminstrs., Am. Pub. Health Assn., N.Y. U. Nurses Alumni, Chi Eta Phi. Congregationalist. Office: 1901 1st Ave New York City NY 10029

BAMBERGER, FRITZ, coll. adminstr.; b. Frankfurt-am-Main, Germany, Jan. 7, 1902; s. Max and Amalie (Wolf) B.; Ph.D., U. Berlin, 1923; m. Kate Schwabe, Mar. 21, 1933 (dec.); children—Michael Albert, Gay; m. 2d, Maria E. Nussbaum, Sept. 29, 1963. Came to U.S., 1939, naturalized, 1944. Research prof. Acad. for Jewish Research, Berlin, 1926-33; prof. philosophy Coll. Jewish Studies, Berlin, 1933-34; dir. Bd. Edn. for Jews, Berlin, 1934-38; also pres. Jewish Tchrs. Coll. of Prussia; mem. Bd. Jewish Edn. of Chgo., faculty mem. Coll. Jewish Studies 1939-44; dir. research Coronet and Esquire mags., 1942-48; editorial dir. Coronet, 1948-52, editor, 1952-56; exec. dir. Esquire and Coronet, 1956-61; prof. intellectual history, also asst. to pres. Hebrew Union Coll., 1962—; mem. exec. com. scholars Inst. Advanced Studies in Religion and the Humanities; v.p. Leo Baeck Inst.; vice chmn. N.Am. bd. World Union Progressive Judaism; mem. bd., exec. bd. Selfhelp Community Services; mem. bd. United Help. Mem. Am. Acad. Polit. and Social Sci., Overseas Press Club. Author: Entstehung des Wertproblems, 1924; Moses Mendelssohn, 1929; Das System des Maimonides, 1935; Des neunte Schuljahr, 1937 (all pub. in Germany); Zunz's Conception of History, 1941; Leo Baeck-The Man and the Idea, 1958; The Philosophy of Julius Guttmann, 1960; Books Are the Best Things, 1962. Editor or compiler: Lehren des Judentums, 1928-30; Moses Mendelssohn's Gesammelte Schriften, 1929-32, rev. edit., 1971-77; Denkmal der Freundschaft, 1929; Das Buch Zunz, 1932; Herder's Blaetter der Vorzeit, 1936 (all pub. in Germany). Contbr. to various publs. Home: 415 E 52d St New York City NY 10022 Office: 40 W 68th St New York City NY 10023

BAMBERGER, JEFFREY LEE, textile co. exec.; b. York, Pa., Jan. 5, 1952; s. A. J. and Betty Mae (Trimmer) B.; B.S. in Accounting, York Coll., 1973; m. Brenda Elaine Zellers, Apr. 1, 1972; children—Marisa Renee, Lauren Rebekah. Staff accountant Dentsply Internat. Inc., York, Pa., 1973-76, asst. accounting mgr., 1977-78; asst. accounting mgr. Duling Optical Corp. subs. of Dentsply Internat. Inc., 1976-77; plant controller Travis Mills Inc., Lititz, Pa., 1978—. Mem. Nat. Assn. Accountants (Named Most Valuable Member York chpt. 1975-76). Republican. Mem. United Ch. of Christ. Club: Shiloh Rod and Gun. Home: 345 Ashford Dr Lancaster PA 17601 Office: 201 W Lincoln Ave Lititz PA 17543

BAMDAD, JALIL, psychiatrist; b. Neiriz, Iran, Mar. 27, 1929; s. Ali A. and Jahan S. (Farahmandi) B.; came to U.S., 1957, naturalized, 1965; M.D., Tehran (Iran) Med. Sch., 1954; m. Harriet A. Thomet, Apr. 6, 1974; children—Christina Marie, Shareen Jahan, Michale Jon. Intern, Bayonne (N.J.) Hosp., 1957; resident Utica Psychiat. Center Upstate N.Y. Med. Center, Syracuse; individual practice psychiatry, Utica 1963—, sr. in psychiatry Utica-Marcy Psychiat. Center, 1963—, supervising psychiatrist, 1964-68, chief edn. and tng. 1968-69, dep. dir. clin., 1968—, pres. med. staff, 1977-79; mem. staff St. Elizabeth Hosp., St. Luke's Hosp., Faxton Hosp. Bd. dirs. Utica chpt. Epilespy Found. Mem. N.Y. State, Oneida County (trustee) med. socs., Am. Psychiat. Assn. (pres. no. N.Y. dist. br. 1976—). Home: 6 Deerpath Ct New Hartford NY 13413 Office: 1705 Genesee St Utica NY 13501

BAMFORD, JOSEPH CHARLES, JR., physician, educator; b. Paterson, N.J., Oct. 23, 1930; s. Joseph Charles and Luise (Whitehead) B.; B.S., Rutgers U., 1952; M.D., N.Y. Med. Coll., 1956; m. Susan Jane Hall, Apr. 13, 1951; children—Joseph Charles III, Elizabeth Ann. Intern, U. Vt., 1956-57; resident obstetrics and gynecology N.Y. Med. Coll., N.Y.C., 1957-60, asst. clin. instr. dept. obstetrics and gynecology, 1960-64, clin. instr., 1964-65, asst. prof., 1965-70, asso. prof., 1970-72, asst. dean, 1966-68, asso. dean, 1968-72, acting v.p. hosp. affairs, 1971-72; sect. chief psychosomatic obstetrics and gynecology Met. Hosp. Center, N.Y.C., 1963-72, chief service, 1971-72; practice medicine specializing in obstetrics and gynecology, Paterson, N.J., 1962-66, St. Johnsbury, Vt., 1972-76; asst. obstetrician and gynecologist Flower and Fifth Ave Hosps., N.Y.C., 1960-66, asst. attending, 1966-70, attending, 1970-72; asst. vis. obstetrician and gynecologist Met. Hosp. Center, N.Y.C., 1960-66, asso., 1968-70, vis., 1970-72; clin. asst. obstetrics and gynecology Paterson Gen. Hosp., 1962-64, asso. attending, 1964-66, attending, 1966-67, cons., 1967—; attending obstetrician and gynecologist Northeastern Vt. Regional Hosp., St. Johnsburg, 1972-76, cons., 1976—; cons. Beatrice D. Weeks Meml. Hosp., Lancaster, N.H., 1972—; chmn. subcom. for fact finding Mayor's Com. for Hosp. Facilities Planning, Paterson, 1964-66; chmn. med. adv. com. Passaic County (N.J.) Com. for Planned Parenthood, 1965-67; mem. N.J. Com. on Med. Edn., 1965-66; trustee Greater Paterson Gen. Hosp., 1966—. Served to lt. comdr. USNR, 1960-62. Diplomate Am. Bd. Obstetrics and Gynecology. Fellow Am. Coll. Obstetricians and

Gynecologists (mem. com. on course coordination 1977—); mem. No. New Eng. Acad. Medicine, Obstet. and Gynecol. Soc. N.Y. Med. Coll. (mem. exec. com. 1968-75), Vt. (mem. judicial com. 1975-77), Caledonia County (v.p. 1974-75) med. socs. Contbr. articles to profl. jours. Home: Spaulding Rd St Johnsbury VT 05819 Office: Box 369 St Johnsbury VT 05819

BAMPTON, ROSE ELIZABETH, dramatic soprano; b. Cleve.; d. Samuel and Henrietta (Hunt) B.; Mus.B., Curtis Inst. Music, Phila., 1932; L.H.D. (hon.), Drake U., 1950, Hobart and William Smith Colls., 1978; m. Wilfrid Pelletier, May 24, 1937. With Met. Opera, 1932-50, Teatro Colon, Buenos Aires, 1945-50, Covent Garden, 1937; performed in opera houses throughout world; mem. voice faculty Manhattan Sch. Music, 1963-78, Juilliard Sch. Music, 1974—; rec. artist RCA Victor Records; mem. profl. com. Met. Opera Auditions; tchr. master classes Temple U., 1972-73, Snowbird-U. Utah, 1976, Banff (Man., Can.), Music Sch., 1977, Duquesne U., 1977, Cin. U., 1978, Shawnigan, B.C., Can., 1978; pres. Bagby Found. Mem. Nat. Assn. Tchrs. Singing, N.Y. Singing Tchrs. Assn. Home: 322 E 57th St New York City NY 10022 Office: Julliard Sch Music Lincoln Center New York City NY 10023

BANAY-SCHWARTZ, MIRIAM, chemist, educator; b. Sibiu, Rumania, Oct. 9, 1929; M.Sc., Hebrew U., Jerusalem, 1954, Ph.D. in Biochemistry, 1961; m. 1951; 2 children. Came to U.S., naturalized. Instr. biochemistry Albert Einstein Coll. Medicine, Bronx, N.Y., 1962-68, asst. prof., 1968—; sr. research scientist N.Y. State Research Inst. Neurochemistry and Drug Addiction, N.Y.C., 1968—. Mem. Am. Inst. Chemists, Am. Soc. Neurochemistry, N.Y. Acad. Scis. Research on intermediate metabolism, electron transport. Office: NY State Research Inst Neurochemistry & Drug Addiction Ward's Island New York City NY 10035

BANCHERI, LOUIS PETER, JR., educator; b. Flushing, N.Y., July 17, 1928; s. Frances Nella (Mascali) B.; B.S., Georgetown U., 1949; M.A., Hofstra U., 1950, M.S., 1957; m. Patricia Marie Hynes, July 9, 1955; children—Susan E., James L., Robert W., Kathryn J. Tchr. biology Sewanhaka High Sch., Floral Park, N.Y., 1954-57; chmn. sci. dept. H. Frank Carey Jr.-Sr. High Sch., Franklin Square, N.Y., 1957-75, Sewanhaka High Sch., Floral Park, N.Y., 1975—; adj. prof. Molloy Coll., Rockville Centre, N.Y., 1967-68; cons. Diocese of Rockville Centre, 1965-67, Rand McNally Pub. Co., 1971, Seaford Pub. Schs., 1968. Mem. citizens adv. com. South Huntington Pub. Schs., 1960-61. Bd. dirs. Netherwood Civic Assn., 1957-60. Recipient William Gaston Educator of Year award Georgetown U., 1974. NSF fellow, 1966-71, NSF/Leadership Devel. Inst., U. Md., 1973-74. Fellow Sci. Tchrs. Assn. N.Y. State; mem. AAAS (life), Nat. Sci. Tchrs. Assn. (life), Nat., N.Y. State, Nassau County (pres. 1968) sci. suprs. assns., Phi Delta Kappa (pres. L.I. chpt. 1974-75). Author: (with M. Stock) Investigations in Modern Biology, 1971, 77; Reading Embracing All Disciplines-Science, 1970; contbg. author Laboratory Exercises in Marine Sciences, 1969; Energy, Its Alternate Forms, 1977; contbg. editor Concepts in Modern Biology (D. Kraus), 1970, 75. Home: 18 Glendale Dr Huntington Station NY 11746 Office: 500 Tulip Ave Floral Park NY 11001

BANCROFT, PAUL, III, investment co. exec.; b. N.Y.C., Feb. 27, 1930; s. Paul and Rita (Manning) B.; B.A., Yale, 1951; postgrad. Georgetown Fgn. Service Inst., 1952; children—Bradford, Kimberly, Stephen, Gregory. Account exec. Merrill Lynch Pierce Fenner & Smith, N.Y.C., 1956-57; asso. corporate finance dept. F. Eberstadt & Co., N.Y.C., 1957-62; partner Draper, Gaither & Anderson, Palo Alto, Calif., 1962-67; v.p. Bessemer Securities Corp., 1967-73, sr. v.p., 1974-76, pres., chief exec. officer, dir., 1976—; chmn., dir. Nat. Venture Capital Assos.; dir. Measurex Corp., Fotomat Corp., Intersil, Inc., Scudder Devel. Fund, Scudder Spl. Fund. Served from 2d lt. to 1st lt. USAF, 1952-56. Clubs: The Brook, Yale (N.Y.C.); Pacific Union, Bohemian (San Francisco); Burlingame (Calif.). Home: 238 Newtown Turnpike Redding CT 06896 Office: 245 Park Ave New York City NY 10017

BANDEEN, ROBERT ANGUS, ry. exec.; b. Rodney, Ont., Can., Oct. 29, 1930; s. John Robert and Jessie Marie (Thomson) B.; B.A., U. Western Ont., 1952, LL.D. (hon.), 1975; Ph.D., Duke, 1959; m. Mona Helen Blair, May 31, 1958; children—Ian Blair, Mark Everett, Robert Derek, Adam Drummond. Asst. economist Can. Nat. Rys., Montreal, Que., 1955-56, research statistician, 1956-58, staff officer planning, 1958-60. chief costs and statistics. 1960, chief devel. planning, 1960-66, dir. corp. planning, 1966-68, v.p. corp. planning and finance, 1968-71, v.p. Great Lakes region, 1971-72, exec. v.p. finance and adminstrn., 1972-74; pres., chief exec. officer Canadian Nat. Rys., 1974—; chmn. bd., dir. Grand Trunk Corp., Grand Trunk Western R.R., Central Vt. Ry., Duluth Winnipeg & Pacific Ry., CN (France), CN Tower Ltd., CN Marine, Canaven; dir. Via Rail Can. Inc., MICE Investments Ltd., Participaction. Mem. Conf. Bd., Can. Econ. Policy Com., Can. Transp. Research Forum. Mem. Stratford Shakespeare Festival Found. Can.; mem. corp. Bishop's U.; hon. v.p. Que. Provincial council Boy Scouts. Decorated comdr. Order of St. John. Mem. Arctic Inst. N. Am., Nat. Freight Traffic Assn., Can., Toronto ry. clubs, Que. Gen. Council Industry Clubs: Montreal Amateur Athletic Assn., Mount Royal, Saint James's (Montreal). Home: 3120 Daulac Rd Montreal PQ H3Y 2A2 Canada Office: 935 Lagauchetiere St W Box 8100 Montreal PQ H3C 3N4 Canada

BANDEIAN, JOHN JACOB, physician; b. Garen, Armenia, Mar. 15, 1912; s. John and Flora (Gureghian) B.; B.S., Harvard, 1935; M.D., Tufts U., 1941; m. Alice M. Kechijian, Apr. 4, 1952; children—Natalie, John Jacob, Stephen H. Intern, Med. Center Jersey City, 1941-42, Mass. Meml. Hosp., 1942; resident in diseases of chest Trudeau San., Saranac Lake, N.Y., 1943, in surgery, Pondville State Hosp., Walpole, Mass., 1943-45; fellow gynecology Mass. Gen. Hosp., Boston, 1945-46; surg. resident Beverly (Mass.) Hosp., 1946-48; practice surgery, Holyoke, Mass., 1948—; pres. John J. Bandeian M.D. Assos., Inc., Vestryman, St. Paul's Ch. Diplomate Am. Bd. Surgery. Fellow A.C.S., AMA, Mass. Med. Soc. (councilor), Hampden Dist. Med. Soc. (pres. 1971-72); mem. C. of C. Republican. Home: 1265 Northampton St Holyoke MA 01040 Office: 210 Pine St Holyoke MA 01040

BANDI, WILLIAM RICHARD, chemist; b. Tarentum, Pa., July 26, 1924; s. William Grover and Hazel Manilla (Sharrar) B.; B.S. in Chemistry, U. Pitts., 1949, postgrad., 1950-57; m. Lucie Camille Petit, Sept. 3, 1948; children—Richard W., Faye C. Research chemist Allengheny Ludlum Steel, Brackenridge, Pa., 1950-54; asso. technologist U.S. Steel Corp., Monroeville, Pa., 1954-56, scientist, 1956-58, sr. scientist, 1958-60, supervising chemist, 1960-66, asso. research cons., 1966—; abstractor Thermal Abstracts. Councilman Borough of Monroeville (Pa.), 1957-61; active Monroeville Human Relations Commn. Served to tech. sgt. USMC, 1943-46. Recipient Lundell-Bright award in analytical chemistry, 1978. Mem. ASTM, Am. Chem. Soc., Pitts. Conf. on Analytical Chemistry and Applied Spectroscopy, Internat. Confederation Thermal Analysis, N.Am. Thermal Analysis Soc. Democrat. Episcopalian. Contbr. articles on chemistry, metallurgy to tech. jours., books. Home: 338 Skyview Dr Monroeville PA 15146 Office: 125 Jamison Ln Monroeville PA 15146

BANDLER, BERNARD, physician; b. N.Y.C., Aug. 9, 1904; s. Leon and Miriam (Haas) B.; B.S., Harvard U., 1926, M.A., 1928; M.D., Columbia U., 1938; m. Louise Silbert, July 13, 1942; children—Susan, Jane, Judith, Deborah, Kate, Barry. Intern Cin. Gen. Hosp., 1938-39; grad. asst. psychiatry Mass. Gen. Hosp., 1942-43, asst. phychiatry, 1943-46, asst. psychiatrist, 1946-47; asst. psychiatry Harvard Med. Sch., 1940-42, 43-46, instr. 1946-47; staff psychiat. clinic Boston Psychoanalytic Soc. and Inst., Inc., 1942-47, tng. analyst, 1948-66; dir. psychiatry clinic University Hosp., 1947-57, asso. vis. physician, 1949-54, vis. physician, 1954—, psychiatrist-in-chief, 1958-70, trustee, 1960-70; asst. prof. psychiatry Boston U. Sch. Medicine, 1947-49, asso. prof., 1949-53, prof., chmn., 1953-70, emeritus, 1970—, chmn. div. psychiatry, 1958-70; acting area dir. Boston U.-Commonwealth Mass. Community Mental Health and Retardation Center, 1963-70; sr. cons. Boston U. Med. Sch., 1976—, Solomun Fuller Carter Community Mental Health Center, 1976—. Dir. Research Project on Relations of Epilepsy to Sexual Life of Women, 1950; mem. spl. adv. com. to Dept. Mental Health, Commonwealth Mass., 1960-64, gov.'s recess commn. mental health Commonwealth Mass., 1961-70; chmn. exec. com. med. staff Univ. Hosp., 1960-63; mem. adv. council, co-chmn. task force on tng. Mass. Mental Health Planning Project, 1963-65; mem. city relocations com. Boston Redevel. Authority, 1967-70; cons. com. on tng. NIMH, 1960-63, chmn. tng. com., 1963-64, acting dir. psychiatry tng. br. div. manpower tng., 1970-71, acting dir. div. manpower and tng., 1971-72, spl. cons. on tng. to dir., 1972—. Mem. test com. Nat. Bd. Med. Examiners, 1965-69. Mem. Group Advancement Psychiatry (chmn. com. on therapy 1953-56, com. on therapeutic care 1971—), Boston Psychoanalytic Soc. and Inst. (chmn. ednl. com. 1950-52, 54-55), Am. Psychoanalytic Assn. (pres. 1959-60, chmn. bd. profl. standards 1955-58), Am. Psychiat. Assn. (chmn. ad hoc com. on edn. in pub. hosps. 1953-61, mem. program com. 1960-63, mem. com. on community psychiatry 1967—, chmn. com. on psychiatry and psychology 1969-70, council med. edn. and career devel. 1971), Am. Coll. Psychoanalysts (pres. 1978—), Mass. Med. Soc. (sec. sect. on psychiatry and neurology 1965, chmn. 1966), AMA, Am. Assn. for Research in Psychosomatic Medicine, Suffolk Dist. Med. Soc., Mass. Psychiat. Soc., Boston Soc. Neurology and Psychiatry. Editor: Psychiatry in a General Hospital, 1966; mem. editorial bd. Am. Survey of Psychoanalysis, Vol. 1, 1950, Jour. Nervous and Mental Diseases; asso. editor Am. Jour. Psychiatry, 1965-72. Contbr. articles to profl. jours. Home: 157 Brattle St Cambridge MA 02138 Office: 350 Beacon St Boston MA 02116

BANDYOPADHYAY, ALOK KUMAR, microbiologist; b. Rangpur, India (now Bangladesh), Apr. 20, 1944; s. Satyadas and Sati (Mukhopadhyay) B.; Ph.D., Calcutta U. and Ind. U., 1970. Postdoctoral fellow U. Conn. Health Center, Farmington, 1969-71; research asso. Baylor Coll. Medicine, Houston, 1971-72; sr. scientist Frederick (Md.) Cancer Research Center, 1972-76; sr. investigator Balt. Cancer Research Center, 1976—; adj. asso. prof. U. Md. Sch. Medicine, 1978—; lectr. in field. Fulbright travel grantee, 1969; Am. Cancer Soc. grantee, 1971-72, fellow, 1969-71. Mem. Am. Assn. Cancer Research, Am. Soc. Biol. Chemists (travel awardee Internat. Bio Congress for Biochemists), Soc. Gen. Microbiology (U.K.), Am. Soc. Microbiology. Contbr. articles to profl. jours. Home: 6129 Sinbad Pl Columbia MD 21045 Office: Baltimore Cancer Research Center 655 W Baltimore St Howard Hall Baltimore MD 21201

BANE, MARILYN ANNETTE, advt. co. exec.; b. Ft. Worth, Aug. 26, 1943; d. Forest Nelson and Wilma Grace (Orr) Bane; A.B., U. Tex., Austin, 1967. Copywriter, Ted Bates and Co., Inc., N.Y.C., 1967-69, Grey Advt., Inc., N.Y.C., 1969-70; v.p., copy supr. Gary F. Halby Assos., Inc., N.Y.C., 1970-73; v.p., account supr. Chester Gore Co., Inc., N.Y.C., 1973-78; v.p., account supr. Wells, Rich, Greene, Inc., N.Y.C., 1978—; mktg. and advt. prof. Marymount Weekend Coll., Tarrytown, N.Y.; mem. mktg. adv. com. to bd. trustees Marymount Coll.; mktg. cons. to bd. dirs. Consumer Credit Counseling Service, N.Y.C. Mem. pub. relations com. Al-anon Family Group Hdqrs., N.Y.C., 1973-76. Republican. Episcopalian. Office: 767 Fifth Ave New York NY 10022

BANERJEE, UMESH CHANDRA, biologist, educator; b. Aligarh, Uttar Pradesh, India, July 15, 1937; s. Suresh Chandra and Mrinalini Devi (Bhattacharya) B.; came to U.S., 1963, naturalized, 1976; B.Sc., Muslim U., Aligarh, India, 1958, M.Sc., 1961; M.S., U. Mass., 1967; Ph.D., Harvard, 1973; m. Sumana Ganguly, Aug. 14, 1966; 1 dau., Sonali. Govt. India fellow Council Sci. and Indsl. Research at Muslim U., Aligarh, 1961-63; teaching fellow in botany U. Mass., Amherst, 1963-66; electron microscopist dept. biology Yale, 1966-68; electron microscopist Harvard, 1968-69, 72-73, teaching fellow, 1969-72, postdoctoral fellow, 1973-74, hon. research fellow in palynology bot. museum, 1975—; asst. prof. Boston U., 1974-75; lectr. U. Mass., 1975—. Recipient Gold medal Muslim U., 1961. Mem. New Eng. Bot. Soc., Electron Microscopic Soc. Am., Bot. Soc. Am., Am. Assn. Stratigraphic Palynologists, Internat. Assn. Wood Anatomists, Palynological Soc. India (life), Sigma Xi. Hindu. Contbr. numerous articles to profl. publs. Home: 21 Redwood Rd Newton Centre MA 02159 Office: 22 Divinity Ave Harvard U Cambridge MA 02138

BANEY, JOHN EDWARD, ins. co. exec.; b. Pitts., May 27, 1934; s. James V. and Mathilde M. (McGary) B.; B.A., U. Pa., 1957; m. Joan A. McGrath, June 14, 1958; children—Jay E., Diane L., Timothy J. With trust dept. First Pa. Bank & Trust, Phila., 1957-58, Remington Rand, Phila., 1958-62; brokerage cons. Conn. Gen. Life Ins. Co., Phila., 1962-68, brokerage mgr., Detroit, 1968-72, dir. agys., Hartford, 1972-73, v.p. brokerage div., 1973-77, v.p. branch div., 1977—; pres. bd. dirs. CG Equity Sales Co., Bloomfield, Conn., 1973—; exec.-in-residence Baylor U., 1976. Mem. port affairs com. Delaware Valley Council, Phila., 1960-68; pres. Simsbury (Conn.) Little League, 1976—; bd. dirs. Birmingham (Mich.) YMCA, 1970-71, N. Central Conn. Jr. Achievement. Served with U.S. Army Res., 1958-64. C.L.U. Mem. Am. Council Life Ins., C.L.U. Assn. Republican. Roman Catholic. Club: Hopmeadow Country. Home: 4 Musket Trail Simsbury CT 06070 Office: 900 Cottage Grove Rd Bloomfield CT 06152

BANIK, SAMBHU NATH, state hosp. adminstr.; b. Joypara, India, Nov. 7, 1935; s. Padma L. and Kadambini (Datta) B.; B.Sc., Vedyasagar Coll., 1956; M.Sc., Calcutta U., 1958; Ph.D., Bristol (Eng.) U., 1964; m. Promila Roy, Nov. 16, 1968; children—Sharmila, Kakali. Came to U.S., 1971. Staff psychologist Des Moines Child Guidance Center, 1965-66; sr. psychologist Univ. Hosp., Saskatoon, Sask, Canada, 1966-68, dir. psychol. services, 1969-71; dir. tng. and research, chief psychologist Glenndale Hosp. (Md.), 1971—; chief psychologist D.C. Geriatric Center, Washington, 1974—. Lectr., U. Sask., 1966-68, asst. prof., 1968-71; vis. prof. Bowie (Md.) State Coll., 1972—. Patron, Saskatoon Art Center and Orchestral Soc., 1969-71; edn. chmn. Canadian Council Christians and Jews, 1968-70; pres. Prabashi, Bowie, Md. Mem. Am. Psychol. Assn., Am. Group Psychotherapy Assn., World Fedn. for Mental Health, Internat. Assn. Social Psychiatry, Pan Am. Med. Assn. Lectr. yoga TV, 1970. Contbr. articles to profl. jours. Home: 8606 Bradmoor Dr Bethesda MD 20034 Office: Glenndale Hospital Glenn Dale MD 20709

BANK, ARNOLD HARVEY, obstetrician-gynecologist; b. N.Y.C., May 16, 1941; s. Paul and Helen (Panzer) B.; A.B. cum laude, Columbia U., 1962, M.D., 1966; m. Sharon Gwen Fishbein, July 10, 1965; children—Pamela, Matthew. Intern, Montefiore Hosp., N.Y.C., 1966-67; resident in obstetrics-gynecology Mt. Sinai Hosp., N.Y.C., 1967-71; practice medicine specializing in obstetrics, gynecology, Port Jefferson, N.Y., 1973-74, Cedarhurst, N.Y., 1974—; med. dir. Planned Parenthood Assn., Nassau County, N.Y., 1975—. Served to maj. M.C., U.S. Army, 1971-73. Diplomate Am. Bd. Obstetrics and Gynecology. Fellow Am. Fertility Soc.; mem. N.Y. State, Nassau County med. socs., Phi Beta Kappa. Office: 650 Central Ave Cedarhurst NY 11516

BANK, WALTER JOSEPH, bus. services co. exec.; b. Marlborough, Mass., Jan. 15, 1926; s. Curt Paul and Margaret Mary (Lally) B.; B.S., Worcester Poly. Inst., 1946, M.S., 1950; m. Janet W. Smith, Oct. 28, 1950; children—Gretchen Gilbert, Holden Joseph. Communications engr. Raytheon Co., Waltham, Mass., 1947-48; radio tube engr. Sylvania Electric Products Inc., Kew Gardens, N.Y., 1950-51; tech. coordinator govt. relations Sylvania Electric Co., Washington, 1953-62, mgr. Navy relations, 1962-64; marketing mgr. Trident Labs., Washington, 1964-67; Navy marketing mgr. Control Data Corp., Washington, 1967-72; marketing mgr. Systems Cons.'s, Inc., Washington, 1972—. Pres. Stone Ridge Fathers Club, 1969-71; swimming ofcl. AAU, 1969—; v.p. Solotar swim team, 1975-76; term trustee Worcester Poly. Inst., 1976—. Served with USNR, 1943-47, 51-53; PTO. Mem. Nat. Energy Resources Orgn., Armed Forces Communications and Electronics Assn., Navy League, Am. Soc. Naval Engrs., Assn. Old Crows, Am. Def. Preparedness Assn., Nat. Security Indsl. Assn., Worcester Poly. Inst. Alumni Assn. (nat. pres. 1973-75). Roman Catholic. Clubs: Bethesda Country; Worcester Poly. Inst. Alumni (Washington). Home: 7704 Massena Rd Bethesda MD 20034 Office: Systems Cons 1054 31st St NW Washington DC 20007

BANKER, HARRY JOHN, arborist; b. Poughkeepsie, N.Y., Oct. 20, 1913; s. Harry H. and Veronica (Tworek) B.; student Rutgers U., 1941, 47-49, Bartlett Sch. Tree Surgery, 1939-41; m. Patricia Vadnais, June 19, 1937; children—Harry Paul, Joan Marie (Mrs. Robert Trivane), Patricia Ann (Mrs. Russell DeSantis), Thomas Andrew. Salesman, F.A. Bartlett Tree Expert Co., 1938-42; pres. Trees, Inc., West Orange, N.J., 1945—; owner-operator Banker & Co., West Orange, 1957—. Nat. exec. sec. Nat. Arbor Day Com., 1957-76, nat. chmn., 1976—; pres. N.J. Tree Expert Bur., 1960-63; chmn. West Orange Shade Tree Adv. Com., 1955—, West Orange Environ. Commn., 1970-74. Mem. N.J. Soc. Certified Tree Experts (pres., recipient citation 1967), Internat. Soc. Arboriculture, N.J. Fedn. Shade Tree Commns. (achievement award 1968, pres.), Internat. Shade Tree Conf. (award of merit 1972), West Orange Environ. Commn., Arborists Assn. N.J., Soc. Municipal Arborists, Joyce Kilmer Birthplace Assn., N.J. Hort. Adv. Com., Essex County Bd. Agr. Contbr. articles to periodicals. Home: 63 Fitzrandolph Rd West Orange NJ 07052 Office: 640 Eagle Rock Ave West Orange NJ 07052

BANKERT, BURNELL HAROLD, postal union ofcl.; b. Hanover, Pa., Mar. 30, 1924; s. Harry Franklin and Carrie Viola (Sterner) B.; diploma Thompson Bus. Coll., 1951-53; m. Anna Mae Mowrer, Aug. 29, 1943; children—Barry Burnell, Barbara Bea. Last puller, bottom finisher Beaudin Shoe Factory, Hanover, Pa., 1941-43; stock clk., scout dept. mgr. J.C. Penny Co., Hanover, 1943-44; clk., asst. mgr. Maudra Shoppe, Hanover, 1944-49; substitute rwy. mail clk. U.S. Post Office, Hanover, 1949-53, clk., 1953-58, clk., pring Grove, Pa., 1958-61, rural letter carrier, 1961—; treas. Letter Carriers Rural Nat. Assn., 1963—. Active Boy Scouts Am. Pres., Bethel Ch., Spring Grove, 1968-71. Served with U.S. Army, 1943. Named Carrier of Year, Nat. Rural Letter Carrier Assn. Pa., 1968. Mem. Pa. Rural Letter Carriers Assn. (dep. dir. labor relations 1978, area steward 1974-78), Am. Legion, VFW. Democrat. Home: RFD 3 Hanover PA 17331

BANKS, ARTHUR SPARROW, research center exec.; b. Quincy, Mass., May 30, 1926; s. Gordon Thaxter and Miriam (Goodspeed) B.; B.A., Cornell U., 1951; M.A., George Washington U., 1954, Ph.D., 1967. Lectr. govt. dept. U. N.H., 1959-61; research asso. Internat. Devel. Research Center, Ind. U., 1963-65; asst. prof., research asso. George Washington U., 1966-68; asso. prof. dept. polit. sci., dir. Center for Comparative Polit. Research, State U. N.Y. at Binghamton, 1968-76, prof. dept. polit. sci., sr. fellow Center for Social Analysis, 1976—. Served with USMC, 1943-45. Wenner-Gren Found. grantee, 1961, NSF grantee, 1969-71. Mem. Am., N.Y. polit. sci. assns., Peace Research Soc., Internat. Studies Assn., Pi Gamma Mu, Pi Sigma Alpha. Author: A Cross-Polity Survey, 1963; Cross-Polity Time-Series Data, 1971; Political Handbook of the World, 1975, 76, 77, 78. Contbr. articles to profl. jours. Home: Center Rd Shirley MA 01464 Office: Center for Social Analysis State University of New York Binghamton NY 13901

BANKS, DAVID OWEN, pub. relations exec.; b. Huntington Park, Calif., Dec. 9, 1940; s. Willard Louis and Winifred Paula (Regan) B.; B.S., U. Dayton (Ohio), 1964; m. Lyneth Diane Soinski, Aug. 10, 1963; children—Matthew David, Michael Joseph, Joseph Stephen. Sports editor Fostoria (Ohio) Rev.-Times, 1960-62; sports writer Dayton Jour.-Herald, 1962-64; legis. asst. U.S. Senator Stephen M. Young, Washington, 1965; nat. exec. sec. Young Democratic Clubs Am., Washington, 1966-67; asst. dir. pub. affairs Dem. Nat. Com., Washington, 1968-69; sr. v.p. pub. relations Daniel J. Edelman Inc., Washington, 1969—. Press asst. presidential campaign v.p. Hubert H. Humphrey, 1968. Mem. Pub. Relations Soc. Am., Nat. Registry Emergency Med. Technicians, Va. State Fireman's Assn. Roman Catholic. K.C. Home: 2421 Silver Fox Ln Reston VA 22091 Office: 1730 Pennsylvania Ave NW Washington DC 20006

BANKS, KARL DEON, program analyst; b. Paulsboro, N.J., Mar. 20, 1938; s. Silius Walter and Susie Ellen (Corbin) B.; B.A., Rutgers U., 1959; M.A., U. Conn., 1960; postgrad. U. Pa., 1962-65. Probation officer County Ct., Phila., 1962-65; clin. psychologist Dept. Human Resources, Washington, 1965-74; various adminstv. positions, Washington, 1974-77; program analyst on inter-agency loan to HEW, Washington, 1977—; prof. Combs Coll., Phila., 1962-65. Jesse Smith-Noyes Found. fellow, 1955-59; N.J. State scholar, 1955-59. Mem. D.C. Psychol. Assn., Am. Psychol. Assn., Nat. Council of Health Care Providers. Home: 700 7th St SW Washington DC 20024

BANKS, SAMUEL LEE, educator; b. Norfolk, Va., Apr. 21, 1931; B.A. in History and Polit. Sci., Howard U., Washington, 1956, M.A. in Edn., and History, 1970; Ed.D. in Edn. Adminstrn., George Washington U., Washington, 1976; married; 2 children. Tchr. social studies Balt. City Pub. Schs., 1959-69, dir. social studies, 1972—, curriculum specialist, 1969-70; tchr. Johns Hopkins U., Balt., summers 1970, 75, 76. Pres. Urban Advisory Communications Council, Balt., 1971—; bd. dirs. Urban League, Balt., 1974—, Balt. council Boy Scouts Am. Nat. Humanities fellow Harvard U., summer 1978. Mem. Nat. Council Social Studies, Assn. Study Afro. Am. Life and History, History Tchrs. Md., Phi Delta Kappa, Kappa Delta Pi, Tau Kappa Alpha, Alpha Phi Alpha. Author: Stony the Road: The Black American in the American Experience, 1972. Home: 9006 Walkerton Dr Lanham MD 20801 Office: 1401 E Oliver St Baltimore MD 21213

BANKS, TALCOTT MINER, lawyer; b. Englewood, N.J., June 23, 1905; s. Talcott Miner and Olive H.S. (Dawes) B.; student Hotchkiss Sch., 1921-24; B.A., Williams Coll., 1928; LL.B., Harvard, 1931; LL.D., Northeastern U., 1971, Williams Coll., 1975; m. Kathleen Macy Hall, July 23, 1935 (dec. May 1966); children—Ridgway Macy, Oliver Talcott, Helen; m. 2d, Ann Monks, June 23, 1967 (dec. 1970); m. 3d, Elisa Brooks, Aug. 8, 1973. Pres. Nat. Intercollegiate Lawn Tennis Assn., 1927-28; mem. editorial staff Time mag., N.Y.C., 1930; admitted to Mass. bar, 1931; practice in Boston; asso. firm Palmer & Dodge and predecessor firms, Boston, 1931-41, mem. firm, 1944—; gen. counsel Bd. of Investigation and Research, Washington, 1941-44. Dir. Comstock & Wescott, Inc. Pres. Boston Opera Assn., 1956-69, hon. pres., 1969—; pres. Boston Symphony Orch., 1968-77, chmn. bd., 1977—; pres. Sterling & Francine Clark Art Inst., 1966-77, hon. trustee, 1977—; trustee New Eng. Conservatory Music; trustee emeritus Williams Coll. Mem. Am., Mass., Boston bar assns., Am. Law Inst., Am. Judicature Soc., Cruising Club. Am. Alpine Club, Phi Beta Kappa, Kappa Alpha. Unitarian. Clubs: University (N.Y.C.); Agawam Hunt (Providence, R.I.); Dunes (Narragansett); St. Botolph (pres. 1949-53), Somerset (Boston). Contbr. articles to profl. jours. Home: Bedford Rd Lincoln MA 01773 Office: 1 Beacon St Boston MA 02108

BANNING, JOHN PECK, JR., art dealer and appraiser; b. Mt. Vernon, N.Y., June 12, 1939; s. John Peck and Irene Emma (Finer) B.; A.B., Brown U., 1962; 1 son by previous marriage, John Peck, III. Fgn. service officer Dept. State, Washington, 1962-63; 3d sec. Am. embassy Buenos Aires, Argentina, 1963-65; vice consul Am. embassy Manila, Philippines, 1965-67; moderator broadcasting, owner Campus Radio Voice, N.Y.C., 1968-70; v.p. real estate N.Y.C. Off-Track Betting Corp., 1970-71, v.p. mktg., 1971-72; exec. v.p. Manhattan Cable TV subs. Time, Inc., N.Y.C., 1972-74; pres. Banning & Elm, Ltd., N.Y.C., 1974—; lectr. Cooper-Hewitt. Mgr. campaign Norman Mailer for Mayor, N.Y.C., 1969; dep. campaign mgr. Howard Samuels for Gov. N.Y., 1970, 74. Served with USAR, 1962-68. Recipient Emmy award, 1974. Mem. Appraisers Assn. Am., Internat. Poster Dealers' Assn. (founder), Phi Delta Theta. Democrat. Episcopalian. Contbr. articles on the poster to mags.; poster collector. Home: 50 Riverside Dr New York NY 10024 Office: 174 Ninth Ave New York NY 10011

BANOV, ABEL, editor, writer; b. Charleston, S.C., Aug. 10, 1915; s. Samuel Lazara and Rachel (Karesh) B.; B.S., Coll. of Charleston, 1937; postgrad. Northwestern U., 1937, New Sch. for Social Research, 1951-52; m. Joan Heineman, Apr. 3, 1941; 1 dau., Beverly Heineman Banov Brown. Reporter, Columbia (S.C.) Record, 1937-38; English editor La Correspondencia de P.R., San Juan, 1938-39; asst. supr. English, P.R., 1939; corr. N.Am. Newspaper Allia, Caribbean and Spain, 1939-40; founder, editor P.R. World Jour., 1940-41; editor Nat. County Agent, Phila., 1947-48, Food Trade News, Phila., 1949-50; mktg. dir. Am. Inst. Food Distbn., N.Y.C., 1951-52; pres. Abel Banov Assos., N.Y.C., 1952-60; editor Am. Paint Jour., N.Y.C., 1960—; lectr. engring. dept. U. Wis.; dir. Chem. Coordinators, Inc., Chem. Research Assos. Del. Democratic Nat. Conv., P.R., 1940. Served with USAAF, 1942-45. Mem. Am. Chem. Soc., ASTM, Assn. Bridge Constrn. and Design. Jewish. Author: Paints and Coatings Handbook, 1972; The Book of Successful Painting, 1975; Wallcovering and Decoration, 1976. Home: 110 Overlook Terr East Hills Roslyn Heights NY 11577 Office: 370 Lexington Ave New York City NY 10017

BANOV, JOAN HEINEMANN (MRS. ABEL BANOV), artist; b. Mainz, Germany, May 17, 1921; d. Richard and Aenne (Berney) Heinemann; student Bazirkschule, Mainz, 1936-37; pvt. art instrn. with Herman Lissman of Bauhaus, 1937-38; student Ringling Art Sch., Sarasota, Fla., 1944-45, Pa. Acad. Fine Arts, 1946; m. Abel Banov, Apr. 3, 1941; 1 dau., Beverly. One-man shows Bryant Library Gallery, Roslyn, N.Y., 1963, 68, 69, 73, Contemporary Arts, Inc., N.Y.C., 1963, Shelter Rock Library, 1974; exhibited in group shows Ringling Art Assn., Phila. Art Alliance, Nat. Arts Club, N.Y.C., Heckscher, Suffolk museums, Argent Gallery, Nat. Acad. Fine Arts, N.Y.C., Lever House, N.Y.C., Carolina Art Assn., Charleston, S.C., Contemporary Arts, Inc., N.Y.C., Artium Gallery, Port Washington Gallery, Village Gallery, Sea Cliff, L.I., N.Y., Donnell Art Library, N.Y.C., North Shore Portfolio, others; represented in permanent collections Honolulu, Phila., N.Y.C., Swarthmore, Pa., U.S. Embassy, Tokyo, Japan, others; traveling exhbns. Nat. Assn. Women Artists, S. Am., 1963-65, France, 1965, also univs. and museums U.S.; traveling show of graphics maj. colls. L.I. Tchr. art adult edn., Roslyn, N.Y. Recipient 1st prize watercolors Ringling Art Assn., 1945; prizes Carolina Art Assn., Manhasset Art Assn.; 2d prize in oil, Manhasset Art Assn., 1965, 1st prize for watercolor, 1974, for graphics, 1976. Mem. Profl. Artists Guild, Nat. Assn. Women Artists (recipient Elizabeth Morse Genius Meml. prize 1966, Elizabeth Erlanger Meml. prize for oil 1976), Manhasset Art Assn., Collectors Am. Art. Home: 110 Overlook Terr Roslyn Heights NY 11577 Office: 156 Fifth Ave New York City NY 10010

BANTA, JOHN JOSEPH, law librarian; b. Astoria, N.Y., May 24, 1932; s. William John and Frances T. (Vlacancich) B.; student Pace U., 1956-58; m. Joan Walker, Dec. 31, 1955; children—Linda, William, Edward. Dep. law librarian Assn. Bar City N.Y., 1959-65; law librarian Fried, Frank, Harris, Shriver & Jacobson, 1965-67, Hughes, Hubbard & Reed, 1967-69, Cadwalader, Wickersham & Taft, N.Y.C., 1969-75; chief law librarian White & Case, N.Y.C., 1975—. Mem. legislative adv. com. to Assemblyman John G. LoPresto, 1973-76. Served with AUS, 1952-54. Mem. Am. Assn. Law Libraries, Law Library Assn. Greater N.Y., Assn. Law Librarians Upstate N.Y. Home: 22 46 75th St Jackson Heights NY 11370 Office: 14 Wall St New York City NY 10005

BANTEY, BILL, pub. relations co. exec.; b. Québec City, Que., Can., Dec. 16, 1928; s. Louis and Maria (deLuce) B.; grad. high sch.; m. Judith Doonan, July 9, 1948; children—Daniel, Mark, Paul. Reporter, Que. Chronicle Telegraph, Québec City, 1944; police reporter Montreal Star, 1945-52; polit. writer, columnist Montreal Herald, 1952-56; feature writer, columnist Montreal Gazette, 1956-69; pres. Bill Bantey & Assos. Ltd., Montreal, 1968—, Gagné, Bantey et Cie., Montreal, 1972—. Guest lectr. McGill U., Montreal, 1973-74, Carleton U., Ottawa, 1967. Mem. Canadian Pub. Relations Soc. (dir. 1975, financial adminstrn. bd. 1975-76, awards of excellence 1975, 76), Pub. Relations Soc. Am. Club: Mt. Royal Tennis. Founding English editor City Montreal ofcl. mag. Montréal, 1964-69; editor M quar. rev. Montreal Mus. Fine Arts, 1970—. Author guidebooks to Expo 67, Man and His World, Old Montreal. Home: 3440 Beausejour St St Laurent PQ H4K 1W6 Canada Office: 2015 Peel St Suite 255 Montreal PQ H3A 1T8 Canada

BANYARD, RICHARD DAVID, ophthalmologist; b. Trenton, Jan. 18, 1941; s. Alfred Lothian and Sarah Alice (Hammer) B.; A.B., Princeton U., 1963; M.D., Columbia U., 1967; m. Sandra Marie Geissler, Jan. 20, 1973; children—Victoria Lynn, Richard David, Elizabeth Allison. Intern, Greenwich (Conn.) Hosp., 1967-68; resident in ophthalmology Edward Harkness Ins. Ophthalmology, N.Y.C., 1968-71; staff ophthalmologist Portsmouth (Va.) Naval Hosp., 1971-73; practice medicine, specializing in ophthalmology, Greenwich, 1973—; asso. attending Greenwich Hosp., 1973—; asst. in clin. ophthalmology Columbia U., 1973—; asst. ophthalmologist Edward Harkness Inst. Ophthalmology, 1973—. Served with USNR, 1971-73. Diplomate Am. Bd. Ophthalmology. Fellow A.C.S.; mem. Am. Acad. Ophthalmology, AMA, Greenwich, Fairfield County, Conn. med. socs., Am. Assn. Ophthalmology, Soc. Mil. Surgeons, Soc. Mil. Ophthalmologists. Research on opthalmol. aspects lasers, 1969-70. Home: 100 Oneida Dr Greenwich CT 06830 Office: 4 Deerfield Dr Greenwich CT 06830

BAR, KANAI LAL, elec. engr.; b. Calcutta, India, Oct. 22, 1939; s. Abhoy Charan and Chandramani B.; came to U.S., 1966, naturalized, 1977; B.Sc. with honors, U. Calcutta, 1961, B.Tech., 1963, M.Tech., 1964; M.S. in Elec. Engring. (Univ. fellow), Columbia U., 1967; M.S. in Mgmt., Rensselaer Poly. Inst., 1970; m. Iti Basak, May 11, 1965; children—Jay, Eva, Neil and Paul (twins). Lead engr. Northeast Utilities Service Co., Hartford, Conn., 1967-73; asst. supervising engr. United Engrs. & Constructors, Phila., 1973-75, supervising engr., 1975-76; group supervising engr. Burns & Roe, Inc., Oradell, N.J., 1976, asst. chief elec. engr., 1977—; cons. engr. to power projects. Registered profl. engr., Mass., Pa., N.J. Mem. IEEE (sr.), Nat., N.J. socs. profl. engrs. Home: 4 Pawtucket Dr Cherry Hill NJ 08003 Office: 30 S 17th St Philadelphia PA 19101

BARAF, CHARLES SELIG, physician; b. Bklyn., Jan. 19, 1935; s. Samuel Lewis and Onnie Miriam (Salem) B.; B.S., U. Mich., 1957; M.D., State U. N.Y., 1961; children—Andrew, Susan. Intern, L.I. (N.Y.) Jewish Hosp., 1961-62; resident in dermatology Kings County Hosp. Center, Bklyn., 1962-65; practice medicine specializing in dermatology, Manhasset, N.Y., 1967—; mem. staff N. Shore Univ. Hosp., Manhasset; mem. staff L.I. Jewish Hosp., New Hyde Park, N.Y., 1967—, physician in charge div. dermatology, 1977—; physician in charge Hillside Med. Center, New Hyde Park, 1978—; cons. chief dermatologist Jewish Inst. Geriatric Care, 1972—. Served to capt. M.C., U.S. Army, 1965-67. Diplomate Am. Bd. Dermatology. Fellow A.C.P., mem. L.I. Dermatological Soc. (treas. 1974—), N.Y. Acad. Medicine, Am. Acad. Dermatology, AMA, N.Y. State, Nassau County med. socs., Dermatology Found., N.Y. State Dermatologic Soc., Internat. Soc. Tropical Dermatology. Club: Old Westbury Golf and Country. Contbr. articles in field to med. jours. Address: 535 Plandome Rd Manhasset NY 11030

BARAHENI, REZA, poet, humanist, educator; b. Tabriz, Iran, Apr. 7, 1935; s. Mohammad-Taghi and Zahra-Soltan (Shokoohtazeh) B.; came to U.S., 1974, permanent resident, 1977; B.A., U. Tabriz, 1957; Ph.D., U. Istanbul (Turkey), 1960; m. Sanaz Sehhati, Sept. 24, 1971; 1 dau. by previous marriage, Aleca; 1 son, Oktay-Mohammad. Faculty of Letters, Teheran U., Iran, 1963-74, asst. prof. English, 1963-67, asso. prof., 1967-74; asso. prof. English, U. Tex., Austin, 1972, U. Utah, Salt Lake City, 1973; poet in residence U. Iowa, Iowa City, 1974; prof. creative writing Ind. U., Bloomington, 1975; prof. English, U. Md. Baltimore County, 1977—. Served with Iranian Army. 1960-61. Hon. fellow writing U. Iowa, 1977—; hon. chairperson Com. Artistic and Intellectual Freedom in Iran, N.Y.C., 1975—. Recipient award Overseas Press Club Am., 1977. Mem. AAUP, PEN, Writers Assn. Iran. Author: Oil Revolution and Identity, 1979; Khayyam and FitzGerald Within the Framework of the Victorian Era, 1960; God's Shadow, prison poems, 1976; The Crowned Cannibals, essays and poetry, 1977, other books in Persian. Contbr. articles to profl. publs., translator books. Editor-in-chief Jahane No, Iran, 1966; lit. editor Ferdowsi mag., Iran, 1964-68; lectr., reader poetry, TV, radio Appearances. Office: U Md Baltimore County 5401 Wilkens Ave Baltimore MD 21228

BARAHURA, WOLODYMYR BOHDAN DMYTRO, mag. editor; b. Nemyriw, Ukraine, Nov. 8, 1910; s. Ivan and Eustachia (Mushynsky) B.; came to U.S., 1949, naturalized, 1956; M.Philos., U. Lwiw (Ukraine), 1929-34; student U. Vienna, 1945; m. Maria Kushnir, Oct. 7, 1939; 2 children. Tchr., Ukraine, 1935-39; editor Veselka (The Rainbow), Jersey City, 1954—; contbg. editor daily Svoboda, Jersey City, 1949—. Active Plast, Ukrainian youth orgn. Mem. Assn. Ukrainian Writers for Children, Ukrainian Journalists Assn. U.S.A. Author: Sword and Book (Mech i Knyha) for children, 1954. Editor, contbr. Ukrainian ednl. mags. Home: 91-19 87th Woodhaven NY 11421 Office: 30 Montgomery St Jersey City NJ 07303

BARAMKI, THEODORE ATALLAH, gynecologist; b. Jerusalem, Palestine, May 6, 1931; s. Atallah Theodore and Cecile (Madbak) B.; M.D., Cairo U., 1957; m. Ingrid Ringe, Dec. 27, 1969. Intern, Cairo U. Hosp., Egypt, 1957-58; resident in gynecology and obstetrics Johns Hopkins U. Hosp., Balt., 1960-64; postdoctoral fellow in gynecologic endocrinology Johns Hopkins U. Sch. Medicine, 1964-66, instr. gynecology and obstetrics, 1966-68, asst. prof. gynecology and obstetrics, 1968—; cons. John F. Kennedy Inst. Handicapped Children, 1972. Recipient medal Independence 1st class (Jordan). Diplomate Am. Bd. Obstetrics and Gynecology with subsplty. in reproductive endocrinology. Fellow Am. Coll. Obstetricians and Gynecologists; mem. Md. Obstetrical and Gynecologic Soc. (pres. 1976-77). Republican. Author: Medical Cytogenetics, 1967. Home: 605 Coventry Rd Baltimore MD 21204 Office: 550 N Broadway Baltimore MD 21205

BARAN, BRADLEY RONALD, vocat. sch. dir.; b. Hartford, Conn., Aug. 2, 1945; s. Phyllis (Siegel) B.; B.A., U. Conn., 1967; M.B.A., Am. U., 1968; M.A., Central Conn. Coll., 1971; m. Barbara Dale Levin, Dec. 21, 1973; 2 children. Instr. Hartford Bd. Edn., 1968-72; dir., pres. Tech. Careers Inst., Milford, Conn., 1972—; pres. Coastal Welding & Tech. Inst., Tex., 1976—. Mem. Milford C. of C., Better Bus. Bur., Conn. Assn. Proprietary Sch., Higher Ed. Assn. Home: 360 Amity Rd Bethany CT Office: 11 Kimberly Ave Milford CT 06460

BARANASKAS, ROBERT CHARLES, distilling co. exec.; b. Jersey City, May 30, 1947; s. Charles George and Dorothy Jean (Hohenstein) B.; B.S., Fairleigh Dickinson U., 1970. Auditor Arthur Andersen & Co., Newark, 1970-73; auditor, sr. fin. analyst Standard Brands Inc., N.Y.C., 1973-74, v.p. fin., planning and adminstrn. wine and spirits group, 1977-78, sr. v.p. beverage group, 1978—. Served with U.S. Army Res., 1970-76. C.P.A., N.J. Mem. N.J. Soc. C.P.A.'s, Am. Inst. C.P.A.'s. Roman Catholic. Office: Wine and Spirits Group Standard Brands Inc 3003 New Hyde Park Rd New Hyde Park NY 11040

BARANSKI, CARL THOMAS, computer specialist; b. Detroit, Oct. 8, 1945; s. Carl William and Stella Ann (Witkos) B.; B.A., Oakland U., 1966; M.B.A., Shippensburg State Coll., 1976. Computer programmer U.S. Army Tank Automotive Command, Warren, Mich., 1966-68, Mobility Equipment Command, St. Louis, 1968-69, 71, Logistics Data Center, Long Binh, Vietnam, 1969-71, computer specialist Logistics Systems Support Activity, Chambersburg, Pa., 1971—. Certified computer programmer. Mem. Assn. Computing Machinery, Data Processing Mgmt. Assn., Am. Hist. Assn., Orgn. Am. Historians. Home: RD 1 PO Box 693 Shippensburg PA 17257

BARATTA, EDMOND JOHN, chemist; b. Somerville, Mass., June 22, 1928; s. Joseph and Rose (Giorgi) B.; student Washington and Jefferson Coll., 1948-49, Boston U., 1949; B.S., Northeastern U., 1953; m. Rose Marie Doucette, July 25, 1953; 1 dau., Susan. Chemist, Shell Oil Co., Houston, 1953-55, USN, Newport, R.I., 1956-59; sr. profl. Nat. Lead Co., Inc., Winchester, Mass., 1959-61; chief analytical service Bur. Radiol. Health, USPHS, Winchester, 1961-67, chief analytical quality control services, 1967-70; chief analytical quality control services Office Radiation Programs, Environmental Protection Agy., Winchester, 1970-72; chief radiol. analytical lab. FDA, Winchester, 1972—. Pres., Marycliff Acad. Fathers Club, Winchester, 1966-67. Served with USNR, 1946-48. Recipient Superior Performance award Dept. Health, Edn. and Welfare, 1963. Mem. Am. Chem. Soc., Health Physics Soc., Assn. Ofcl. Analytical Chemists, Assn. Lab. Employees (pres., 1964). Contbr. articles to profl. jours. Home: 5 Fairlane Terr Winchester MA 01890 Office: 109 Holton St Winchester MA 01890

BARBA, J. WILLIAM, lawyer; b. Arlington, N.J., May 22, 1923; s. John and Rose (Lettiere) B.; A.B., Princeton, 1947; LL.B., U. Pa., 1950; m. Susan Vartanian; 1 dau., Susan Elizabeth. Admitted to N.J. bar, 1950, D.C. bar, 1969; practiced in Newark, 1950-53; asst. spl. counsel to Pres. U.S., 1954-57; partner firm Shanley & Fisher, Newark, 1957—. Chmn. N.J. Republican Finance Com. Served as lt. (j.g.) USNR, 1943-46. Mem. Am., D.C., Essex County bar assns. Republican. Roman Catholic. Clubs: Metropolitan (Washington, D.C.); Essex (Newark). Asso. editor U. Pa. Law Rev. Home: Long Hill Rd New Vernon NJ 07976 Office: 550 Broad St Newark NJ 07102

BARBANEL, SIDNEY WILLIAM, cons. engring. firm exec.; b. N.Y.C., July 2, 1921; s. Morris A. and Sadie (Rosenbloom) B.; m. Hilda Helen Hirsch, Oct. 10, 1942; children—Marsha Barbanel Elser, Stephanie Barbanel Simon, Geraldine, Samara Barbanel Rosenberg, Karen Sue. Owner, exec. Sidney W. Barbanel, Long Island City, N.Y., cons. engr. internat. practice, designer shopping centers, housing complexes, comml., indsl. facilities, energy systems. Trustee Hebrew Acad. Nassau County, 1962, pres., 1974-76. Registered profl. engr. 16 states including Md., Pa., Mass., Conn., D.C., N.J., N.Y. Mem. N.Y. Assn. Profl. Engrs., Internat. Council Shopping Centers. Club: Nassau Yacht (commodors 1975). Home: 59 Overlea S Massapequa Park NY 11762 Office: 29-28 41st Ave Long Island City NY 11101

BARBARO, ANTHONY JOSEPH, chemist, educator; b. N.Y.C., July 26, 1926; s. Salvatore and Dina B.; B.S., Wagner Coll., 1950; M.S., Western Conn. State Coll., 1972; diploma So. Conn. State Coll., 1978; m. Rose Borrelli, Sept. 9, 1951; children—Valerie Jean, Pamela Gail. Research chemist chemotherapy Am. Cyanamid Co., Stamford, Conn., 1950-51; chemist Amsco, Carteret, N.J., 1952-53; petroleum engr. Swan-Finch Oil Co., Hackensack, N.J., 1953; dye chemist Pfister Chem. Co., Ridgefield, N.J., 1954-55; explosives chemist Naval Propellant Factory, Indian Head, Md., 1955; patent examiner U.S. Patent Office, Washington, 1955-59; patent agt. Nopco Chem. Co., 1959-60; title examiner Home Title Co., White Plains, N.Y., 1960-65; investigator Dept. Treasury, N.Y.C., 1965-66; chemist City of N.Y., 1966; tchr. biology Dover Plains (N.Y.) High Sch., 1967-75, coordinator phys. sci., 1975—; item writer chemistry N.Y. State Regents. Translator, Am. Chem. Soc. Patentee amides preparation. Home: Box 149 Cross River NY 10518

BARBARO, RONALD DELANO, environ. quality mgmt. firm exec.; b. Bklyn., Aug. 5, 1933; s. Michael and Louisa (De'feo) B.; B.A., Providence Coll., 1956; M.S., U. R.I., 1961; Ph.D. (fellow), Rutgers U., 1966; m. Ellen C. Lydon, July 3, 1956; children—Michele, Andrea, Ronald, Mark. Chief recreational water quality studies, tech. assistance br. Fed. Water Pollution Control Adminstrn., Athens, Ga., 1966-68; acting chief extramural program br. Office Manpower Devel., Nat. Air Pollution Control Adminstrn. (EPA), Research Triangle, N.C., 1968-70; v.p. Princeton Aqua Sci., New Brunswick, 1970-72; mgr. air and water quality programs Glass Containers, Mfrs. Inst., Washington, 1972-73; pres. GBC Assos., Falls Church, Va., 1971—. Cons., World Bank Group, 1971—; asst. prof. No. Va. Community Coll., Woodbridge, 1973. Mem. Am. Chem. Soc., Water Pollution Control Fedn., Air Pollution Control Assn., Sigma Xi. Author: (with F. Cross) Primer on Environmental Impact Assessment, 1973. Patentee device for determination of waste water treatability. Home: 996 Ocean Ave West Haven CT 06516 Office: 7036 Lee Park Ct Falls Church VA 22042

BARBE, DAVID FRANKLIN, supervisory research elec. engr.; b. Webster Springs, W.Va., May 26, 1939; s. Damon and Mary K. (Cooper) B.; B.S. with high honors in Elec. Engring., W.Va. U., 1962, M.S. in Elec. Engring., 1964; Ph.D. in Solid State Materials and Electronics, Johns Hopkins U., 1969; m. Elizabeth K. Munyon, June 26, 1965; children—John David, Jane Suzanne. Instr. elec. engring. W.Va. U., Morgantown, 1962-65; fellow engr. Westinghouse Advanced Tech. Lab., Balt., 1964-71; head functional devices sect. Electronics Div., Naval Research Lab., Washington, 1971-74, head microelectronics br. Electronics Tech. Div., 1974—; Navy mem. adv. group on electron devices Dept. Def., 1971—; mem. Navy Strategy Com. for Electron Devices, 1977—. Mem. steering coms. Internat. Conf. on Charge Coupled Devices, Edinburgh, Scotland, 1974, 76, San Diego, 1975; lectr. 1st Internat. NATO Congress on Charge Coupled Devices, U. Louvain-La-Neuve, Belgium, 1975. Westinghouse fellow, 1965-69. Fellow IEEE (asso. editor Electron Devices Newsletter 1972—, mem. standards com. on charge coupled devices 1974, mem. steering com. Internat. Solid State Circuits Conf. 1977); mem. Am. Phys. Soc., Sigma Xi, Tau Beta Pi, Eta Kappa Nu. Democrat. Roman Catholic. Contbr. numerous articles on electronics to profl. publs.; patentee in field. Home: 6905 Bradford Ct Laurel MD 20810 Office: Code 5260 Naval Research Lab Washington DC 20375

BARBEE, WILLIAM HENRY, JR., mgmt. cons.; b. Washington, Nov. 8, 1937; s. William Henry and Margaret Catherine (Coffman) B.; B.A., U. Md., 1970; M.P.A., U. So. Calif., 1976; m. Elizabeth Ann Baumgardner, June 27, 1959; children—William Henry III, Marta Elizabeth, Erica Gardner, Christian Michael. Reservations sales agt. Pan Am. World Airways, Inc., Washington, 1960; sales Rep. Varig Airlines, Inc., Washington, 1961-63; sr. sales rep. Trans World Airlines, Inc., Louisville, 1963-64; U.S. sales mgr. Civil Air Transport Co. Ltd., Washington and Taipei, Taiwan, 1964-70; chief transp. br., spl. asst., cons. ACTION, Washington, 1970-72; mgmt. analysis officer VA, Washington, 1972—; bd. dirs. VA Central Fed. Credit Union; instr. Prince George's Community Coll., Largo, Md.; mng. dir. Barbee Assos. Served with USN, 1955-58. Mem. Am. Soc. Pub. Adminstrn., Met. Area Credit Union Mgmt. Assn., Advt. Club Met. Washington, VFW, THETA Assn., Am. Soc. Psychical Research, Assn. Research and Enlightenment, Parapsychol. Assn., Sigma Chi. Democrat. Methodist. Author: (with Richard Pell, Jr.) A Program Evaluation - VA Chaplain Service, 1977. Home: 6610 Adrian St Oakwood Knolls New Carrollton MD 20784 Office: VA 810 Vermont Ave NW Washington DC 20420

BARBEITO, MANUEL SERAFINO, microbiologist; b. Freeland, Pa., Jan. 23, 1930; s. Jobino and Almirinda Mary (DiPronio) B.; X-Ray Technician, Franklin Sch. Sci. and Arts, 1948; B.S., Pa. State U., 1956; postgrad. U. Md., 1956-61, N.Y. U., 1958; m. Eva Rebecca Rhoderick, Apr. 26, 1958; children—David K., Diane M., Ronald M. Microbiologist, biol. labs. Army Dept., Ft. Detrick, Md., 1956-60, supervisory microbiologist, 1960-72; supervisory microbiologist Nat. Cancer Inst., Bethesda, Md., 1972-75, asst. safety mgr., 1975—; cons. U.S. Govt. agys., univs., hospitals, pharm. labs., other related comml.

cos. Exec. com. PTA, Frederick, Md., 1967, 68, 69; com. chmn. Cub Scouts Am., Frederick, 1968-71; asst. scoutmaster Boy Scouts Am., Frederick, 1971-76, scoutmaster, 1976—. Served with USN, 1948-52. Recipient Outstanding Performance award U.S. Govt., 1970, Bronze Medal adult scouter award Boy Scouts Am., 1973, Superior Service award USPHS, 1978. Mem. Am. Soc. Microbiology, Am. Acad. Microbiology, Sci. Research Soc. N.Am., Am. Legion, Sigma Xi. Roman Catholic (com. chmn. parish council 1968-70). Home: 2105 Runny Meade Ct Frederick MD 21701 Office: Office of Research Safety Nat Cancer Inst Bethesda MD 20014

BARBER, EDMUND AMARAL, JR., ret. engr.; b. East Providence, R.I., Oct. 20, 1916; s. Edmund Amaral and Clara Veronica (Amaral) B.; Sc.B., Brown U., 1938; postgrad. Mass. Inst. Tech., 1951, Syracuse U., 1955-57; m. Marion McKelvy Yost, Mar. 15, 1941; children—Marion Elizabeth (Mrs. Robert Barry Goodrich), Jean Claire (Mrs. Peter Raymond Concklin). Designer, New Eng. Butt Co., Providence, 1936-38; with IBM, 1938-71, mgr. research, Endicott, N.Y., 1952-55, engring. mgr., Owego, N.Y., 1955-59, lab. adminstrn. mgr., Owego, 1959-64, spl. asst., Owego, 1964-66, avionics systems adminstrn. mgr., 1966-67, staff adminstrn. mgr., 1967-68, facility plans mgr., 1968-69, tech. staff mem., 1969-70, data mgr., 1970-71; ret., 1971; mem. Ithaca (N.Y.) chpt. Service Corps Ret. Execs., 1976—. Mem. Town of Owego Planning Bd., 1956-72. Pres. Tioga County Indsl. Devel. Corp., 1970-72, sec.-exec. dir., 1972, dir., 1967-72; adminstrv. dir. Tioga County Indsl. Devel. Agy., 1972; v.p. N.Y.-Penn Health Planning Council, 1969-72, dir., 1968-72; mem. exec. com., dir. N.Y.-Penn Health Mgmt. Corp., 1972; mem. exec. com. Tioga Gen. Hosp., Waverly, N.Y., 1962-72, dir., 1961-72, chmn. planning com., 1964-72; v.p. Owego Boys' Club, 1963-66, dir., 1962-66; pres. Christmas League, Owego, 1963-64, dir., 1961-70; bd. mgrs. Tompkins County Hosp., Ithaca, N.Y., 1976, sec., 1976, chmn. planning com., 1976. Mem. Am. Soc. M.E., Nat., N.Y. socs. profl. engrs., Sigma Xi, Tau Beta Pi. Republican. Roman Catholic. Clubs: Elks, Rotary (pres. Owego 1962-63, sec. 1965-66). Patentee in field of data processing machine and med. research equipment. Home: 42 Fairview Sq Ithaca NY 14850 also 2650 Pearce Dr Apt 311 Clearwater FL 33520

BARBER, GLENN VERNON, hosp. adminstr.; b. Duluth, Minn., Dec. 29, 1925; s. Albert Edward and Florence Dora (Gathercole) B.; M.B.A., Rensselaer Inst., 1975; m. Florence Elvira Brainard, Nov. 9, 1947; children—Lynn Elizabeth, Bruce Paul. Foreman, standards lab. Sonotone Corp., Elmsford, N.Y., 1951-56; quality control mgr. Otarion Electronics, Ossining, N.Y., 1956-62; mgr. ops. space battery lab., Sonotone Corp., Elmsford, 1962-64; production mgr. Chronteics, Mt. Vernon, N.Y., 1964-65; quality control engr. Eaton, Yale & Towne, Rye, N.Y., 1966-72; sr. mgmt. engr. St. Luke's Hosp. Center, N.Y.C., 1972-75, asst. controller, 1975—; adj. asst. prof. mgmt. Rensselaer Poly. Inst., Troy, N.Y., 1976—. Bd. dirs. Friends of Yorktown (N.Y.) Mus., 1978—. Mem. Hosp. Fin. Mgmt. Assn., Hosp. Mgmt. Soc., Am. Inst. Indsl. Engrs., Am. Soc. for Quality Control. Republican. Home: 2038 Midland Dr Yorktown Heights NY 10598 Office: Amsterdam Ave at 114th St New York City NY 10025

BARBER, RICHARD DAVIS, naval officer; b. Point Pleasant, N.J., Mar. 19, 1939; s. Albert Stanley and Marie Margaret (Stockton) B.; B.S. summa cum laude, So. Ill. U., 1976; m. Georgia Faith Kessler, Sept. 26, 1959; children—David Allan, Mark Steven, Anne-Marie, Michael Anthony. Enlisted man, warrant officer U.S. Navy, 1957, advanced through grades to lt., 1976; career retention specialist Repair Ship Cadmus, Newport, R.I., 1968-70, USS Wasp, Quonset Point, R.I., 1970-72; adminstrv. officer Navy Mine Warfare Command Hdqrs., Charleston, S.C., 1972-75; Navy word processing program mgr. Office of the Chief of Naval Ops., Washington, 1975—; instr. Trident Tech. Coll., Charleston, 1973-75; lectr. in field. Pres., PTA, Woodbridge, Va., 1977-78; cubmaster Boy Scouts Am., Charleston, 1973-74, scoutmaster, 1968-70, scout troop committeeman, 1972-75, spl. edn. adv. bd. chmn., 1970-72. Decorated Navy Commendation Medal. Mem. Am. Mgmt. Assn., Vocat. Tchrs. Assn., Fed. Govt. Word Processing Council. Presbyterian. Club: Masons. Editor, Keystrokes newsletter, 1975—. Home: 4208 Glendale Rd Dale City VA 22193 Office: Navy OPNAV-OP-09B11 Pentagon Rm 4D471 Washington DC 20350

BARBER, STEPHEN GUY, journalist; b. Tanta, Egypt, Dec. 24, 1921; s. Clement Richard and Margaret (Mole) B.; ed. Bristol (Eng.) U.; m. Deirdre Christine Knewstub, Mar. 21, 1953; 1 son, Simon Guy Bernard. Reporter, sub-editor Egyptian Gazette, 1940; war corr. AP, 1942-45; fgn. corr. Mideast, Korea, Africa, Indochina, then asst. editor News Chronicle, London, 1945-60; with London Daily Telegraph, 1961—, bur. chief, Washington, 1968—. Mem. Inst. Journalists, Overseas Writers Assn., White House, State Dept. corr. assns., Senate and House Press Gallery. Mem. Ch. of Eng. Clubs: London Press; Nat. Press (Washington). Author: America in Retreat, 1969; collaborator: A Grand Original, 1971, The Six Day War, 1967. Home: 2700 35th Pl NW Washington DC 20007 Office: 1366 Nat Press Bldg Washington DC 20045

BARBER, WAYNE SIDMAN, psychiatrist; b. N.Y.C., Feb. 16, 1938; s. Sidman Ira and Bernardine Katherine (Herring) B.; B.A., Amherst Coll., 1960; M.D., Duke U., 1964; m. Patricia Ann Wood, June 24, 1961; children—Christopher Edward, Molly Elizabeth, Margaret Eileen. Intern, U. Rochester (N.Y.), 1964-65, resident in child psychiatry, 1965-69; practice child and adult psychiatry, Summit, N.J., 1971—; clin. coordinator Glen Kirk Sch., Morristown, N.J., 1973—; cons. Hanover Ave. Sch., Morris Plains, N.J., 1975—, Matheny Sch., Peapack, N.J., 1977—, also various N.J. sch. dists.; instr. sex edn. Pingry Sch., 1977—; founding mem. Clin. Assos. Psychiat., Psychol. and Ednl. Services, Summit and Basking Ridge, N.J., 1974—. Served to maj. USAF, 1969-71. Bd. dirs. Millburn Short Hills Scholastic Boosters. Mem. Am. Acad. Child Psychiatry, N.J. Council Child and Adolescent Psychiatry. Republican. Episcopalian. Clubs: Canoe Brook Country; Univ. Glee (N.Y.C.). Home: 10 Sheridan Dr Short Hills NJ 07078 Office: 22 Bank St Summit NJ 07901

BARBIERI, CHRISTOPHER GEORGE, assn. exec.; b. Bklyn., Jan. 9, 1941; s. Nicholas Joseph and Marie Anne (Bacigalupo) B.; B.S., Cornell U., 1962; M.S., U. Vt., 1964; m. Joanne Lee Barnett, Jan. 30, 1965; children—Matthew, Deborah, Lisa. Adminstrv. asst., asst. new products mgr., new products mgr., retail sales mgr. H.P. Hood & Sons, Boston, 1964-69; exec. v.p. Vt. C. of C., Montpelier, 1969—. Bd. dirs. Vt. Charitable Found., 1974-75. Served with Vt. Air N.G., 1964-70. Mem. Vt. Soc. Assn. Execs. (pres. 1972), Vt. Assn. Chamber Execs. (pres. 1971), Small Bus. Advisory Council, U.S. C. of C. (pub. affairs com.). Republican. Roman Catholic. Clubs: Kiwanis of Burlington (pres. 1972-73); Worcester Rangers; Snowmobile; Vt. Assn. Snow Travellers. Home: Box 344 Worcester VT 05682 Office: Box 37 Montpelier VT 05602

BARBIERI, DAVID JAMES, systems analyst; b. Gt. Barrington, Mass., Apr. 2, 1945; s. Emil John and Evelyn Louise (Hart) B.; A.S., Tunxis Community Coll., 1975; student Central Conn. State Coll., 1974—; certificate in data processing Inst. for Certification of Computer Profls., 1978; m. Mary Ellen Welch, Aug. 5, 1967; children—Karin Lee, Pamela Ann. Systems analyst NCR, Hartford, Conn., 1969-70; programmer analyst Loctite Corp., Newington, Conn., 1970-72, ops. supr., 1973-76, asst. mgr. EDP, 1976, systems analyst, 1977—, founding dir. employees credit union, 1976—, treas./mgr., 1976—. Served with USAF, 1963-67. Mem. Conn. Credit Union League (v.p. L.R. Nixon chpt. 1978—). Roman Catholic. Office: 705 N Mountain Rd Newington CT 06111

BARBOUR, JOSEPH PIUS, JR., psychiatrist; b. Spartanburg, S.C., Aug. 16, 1923; s. Joseph Pius and Olee (Littlejohn) B.; student Lincoln U., 1940-43; M.D., Meharry Med. Coll., 1946; m. Marie T. Drake, Nov., 1947, (div. Dec. 1960); children—Joseph Pius III, Russell, Warren; m. 2d, Elizabeth Louise, Feb. 1963; children—Robert, Charlene, Benjamin. Intern Mercy Douglas Hosp., Phila., 1946-47; pvt. practice medicine, Phila., 1946-50; sch. physician, Phila., 1947-48; pub. health physician City Phila., 1955-56; sr. psychiatrist Commonwealth of Pa., 1956—; clin. dir. Phila. State Hosp., 1955—; mem. tng. and research com. psychiatry and neurology, 1959—, dir. forensic psychiatry, psychiat. cons. Eastern Correctional Inst., Phila.; exec. dir. Phila. Psychiat. Community Mental Health Center; asst. clin. prof. psychiatry Temple U. Med. Sch.; clin. dir. North Central Phila. Community Mental Health Center Phila. State Hosp. Bd. mgrs. Phila. Youth Study Center, 1977—. Served to capt. USAF, 1950-52. Mem. Pa. Psychiat. Soc., Am. Psychiat. Assn. Episcopalian. Contbr. articles to profl. jours. Home: 730 W Mt Airy Ave Philadelphia PA 19119 Office: 7100 Germantown Ave Philadelphia PA 19119

BARCHET, STEPHEN, naval med. officer; b. Annapolis, Md., Oct. 25, 1932; s. Stephen George and Louise (Lankford) B.; student Brown U., 1949-52; M.D., U. Md., 1956; m. Marguerite Joan Racek, Aug. 9, 1965. Commd. ensign U.S. Navy, 1955, advanced through grades to rear adm. M.C., 1978; intern Naval Hosp., Chelsea, Mass., 1956-57, resident in obstetrics and gynecology, 1958-61; resident in gen. surgery Naval Hosp., Portsmouth, Va., 1957-58; fellow in obstetric-gynecologic pathology Med. Sch., Harvard U., Boston, 1959-60; obstetrician-gynecologist, Naval Hosp., Naval Support Activity, Naples, Italy, 1961-63; obstetrician-gynecologist, Naval Hosp., Portmouth, N.H., 1963-64, Beaufort, S.C., 1964-66, Bremerton, Wash., 1967-70; comdr. mil. provincial hosp. assistance program, Hoi An, Quang Nam Province, Rep. S. Vietnam, 1966-67; chief obstetric-gynecology service Naval Hosp., Boston, 1970-73; asst. head tng. br. Bur. Medicine and Surgery, Washington, 1973, head, 1973-75, dept. spl. asst. to Surgeon Gen. of Navy, 1975; physician mem. Chief of Naval Ops. Select Com. to Review Navy Health Care, Washington, 1975-76; asso. dean Sch. Medicine, Uniformed Services U. Health Scis., Bethesda, Md., 1976-77, exec. sec. bd. regents, 1976-77; dir. Navy Med. Dept. Edn. and Tng., spl. asst. to Navy Surgeon Gen. for edn. and tng., Bur. Medicine and Surgery, Washington, 1977—; comdg. officer Naval Health Scis. Edn. and Tng. Command, Nat. Naval Med. Center, Bethesda, 1977—; clin. asst. prof. obstetrics and gynecology Sch. Medicine, Boston U., 1971—; adj. prof. allied health George Washington U. Sch. Medicine; dir. residency obstetrics-gynecology, Naval Hosp., Boston/Newport, 1971-73; chmn. Med.-Dental Com., Interservice Tng. Review Orgn., Washington, 1977—; alt. regent Nat. Library Medicine, Bethesda, 1977—; panelist on evaluation of allied health personnel Nat. Bd. Med. Examiners, Phila., 1978; chmn. com. on admissions Uniformed Services U. Health Scis., Sch. Medicine, Bethesda, 1976-77; Surgeon Gen's. rep. to Sec. of Navy adv. bd. on edn. and tng., 1974. Decorated Bronze Star, Meritorious Service medal; recipient certificates of merit Rep. Vietnam, 1966, 67. Diplomate Am. Bd. Obstetrics and Gynecology. Fellow Am. Coll. Obstetricians and Gynecologists; mem. Baker-Channing Soc., Md. State Med. Soc., Med. Alumni Assn. U. Md., Internat. Soc. Study of Vulvar Diseases, Assn. Mil. Surgeons U.S., Soc. Med. Cons.'s to Armed Forces. Prin. contbr. four volumne edit. Rev. of Navy Health Care System, 1976; contbr. articles to sci. publs., exhibits to sci. confs. Home: 8220 Windsor View Terr Potomac MD 20854 Office: Naval Health Sciences Education and Training Command Bethesda MD 20014

BARCLAY, GORDON LANIER, psychologist; b. Chgo., Jan. 24, 1907; s. Wade Crawford and May (Hartley) B.; B.S., Northwestern U., 1928; postgrad. U. Ill., U. Nebr., Syracuse U.; Ed.D., Columbia U., 1940; m. Mary Abigail Johnson, Dec. 21, 1934 (dec. Oct. 1949); 1 son, John Gordon Lanier; m. 2d, Katherine Taylor Campbell Johnson, May 22, 1953 (dec. Nov. 1974); 1 stepson, Roderick Carter Johnson (dec.). Asst. in psychology U. Ill., 1928-29; asst. instr., clin. psychologist U. Nebr., 1929-30; instr. psychology, chmn. grad. resident counseling program, asst. prof. Syracuse U., 1930-36; asst. prof., asso. prof., head psychology dept., dir. freshmen, dir. Sch. Edn. Russell Sage Coll., 1937-40; asso. research sci. Rockland State Hosp., Orangeburg, N.Y., 1961-66; asst. commr. N.Y. State Dept. Mental Hygiene, Albany, 1966-74, cons., 1977—; cons. Internat. Com. Against Mental Illness, 1961—; mng. dir. Research Found. Mental Hygiene, Inc., 1970-77, treas., 1975-77. Vice pres., dir. N.J. Research Found. Mental Hygiene; dir. Psychiat. Research Found. Dir. Albany Boys Clubs. Served to col. U.S. Army, 1940-62. Mem. AAAS (life), Am. Acad. Polit. and Soc. Sci., Am. Judicature Soc., Council for Exceptional Children, Nat. Conf. on Social Welfare, N.Y. State Assn. for Mental Health, Am. (life), Eastern Psychol. Assn. (life), Met. Assn. for Applied Psychology, N.Y. Acad. Scis., World Fedn. for Mental Health, Am. Pub. Health Assn., Am. Assn. Suicidology, Royal Soc. Health (life, London), Soc. Research Adminstrs., Nat. Assn. Sci. Writers, N.Y. Geneal. and Biog. Assn., Scottish Geneal. Soc. (Edinburgh), S.A.R. (past dir. Empire State), Mil. Order World Wars (past dir.), St. Andrews Soc. (life, pres., past chmn. bd. N.Y. State), Sigma Xi, Phi Kappa Sigma. Presbyterian. Clubs: University, Overseas Press, Army and Navy (N.Y.C.); University (Albany); Schuyler Meadows (Loudonville); Army-Navy (Washington). Contbr. articles to profl. jours. Home: 302 Loudonville Rd Loudonville NY 12211 Office: 44 Holland Ave Albany NY 12229

BARCLAY, ROBERT, JR., chemist; b. Mt. Vernon, N.Y., Apr. 1, 1928; s. Robert and Emma Josephina (Neher) B.; B.A., Cornell U., 1948; postgrad. Poly. Inst. Bklyn., 1949-51; Ph.D. (pre-doctoral fellow U. Md. Office Naval Research, 1954-55, also Celanese Corp.), U. Md., 1957. Chemist, Allied Chem. Corp., Edgewater, N.J., 1948-51, Am. Cyanamid Co., Linden, N.J., 1951-52; project scientist Union Carbide Corp., Bound Brook, N.J., 1956-69; sr. research scientist Thiokol Chem. Div., Trenton, N.J., 1969—. Mem. Am. Chem. Soc., Am. Inst. Chemists, N.Y. Acad. Scis., Phi Beta Kappa, Sigma Xi. Roman Catholic. Home: 6 Berrywood Dr Trenton NJ 08619 Office: PO Box 8296 Trenton NJ 08650

BARCUS, GILBERT MARTIN, med. products co. exec.; b. N.Y.C., Sept. 20, 1937; s. Leon A. and Dorothy (Brownstein) B.; B.S., N.Y. U., 1959; M.B.A., L.I. U., 1969; m. Sondra Ettin, May 6, 1961; children—David A., Ruth A. Stock broker Ernst & Co., N.Y.C., 1962-65; sales mgr. McNeil Labs., Ft. Washington, Pa., 1965-75, mktg. mgr. U.S.A. Devices Ltd., New Brunswick, N.J., 1976-77; dir. product mgmt. Stimtech. Inc., Mpls., 1978—; asso. adj. prof. bus. dept. City U. N.Y.; lectr. dept. bus. Brookdale Coll. Chmn. Bd. Fire Commrs. Marlboro (N.J.). Home: 23 Millay Rd Morganville NJ 07751 Office: 9440 Science Center Dr Minneapolis MN 55428

BARDES, JUDITH LEOPOLD (MRS. CHARLES ROBERT BARDES), fin. exec., community worker; b. Phila., Aug. 17, 1931; d. Charles Stein and Marian Rose (Bettman) Leopold; B.A. cum laude, Bryn Mawr Coll., 1953; m. Charles Robert Bardes, June 20, 1953; children—Charles Leopold, Peggy Anne, Diane Lisa. Librarian, William Jeanes Meml. Library, Plymouth Meeting, Pa., 1961-68; exec. sec. Alfred and Mary Douty Found., Plymouth Meeting, 1969—; agt. Sun Life Assurance Co. Can., Phila., 1970-76; security salesman Suncan Equity Services Co., Boston, 1971-76; dir. Families and Friends Program Bryn Mawr Coll., 1975-78; life income trust officer U. Pa., 1978—. Co-chmn. Com. for A New Library, Lafayette Hill, 1968; adv. com. William Jeanes Meml. Library Bldg. Fund, Plymouth Meeting, 1970-71; mem. Citizens' Council Whitemarsh Twp.; trustee Alfred and Mary Douty Found., 1969—; trustee William Jeanes Meml. Library, Lafayette Hill, 1968—, v.p., 1969-73, pres., 1973-78; bd. dirs. Friends of William Jeanes Meml. Library, Plymouth Meeting, 1963—, pres., 1964-68; mem. adv. bd. Grad. Sch. Social Work and Social Research Bryn Mawr Coll., 1974—; mem. resource devel. com. YWCA, Phila., 1976-78; chmn., 1977—, bd. dirs., 1977—; mem. fin. devel. com. Greater Phila. council Girl Scouts U.S.A., 1977—. Mem. Pa. Library Assn., Women and Founds./Corp. Philanthropy, Phila., Plymouth Meeting Hist. Soc. Clubs: Bryn Mawr (v.p. 1973-76), U. Pa. Faculty (Phila.). Home: 5070 Militia Hill Rd Plymouth Meeting PA 19462 Office: U Pa 3451 Walnut St I/6 Philadelphia

BAREFOOT, GARY SAYLOR, pollution control devices exec.; b. Greensburg, Pa., July 4, 1948; s. Bernard Blackburn and Lois (Saylor) B.; B.S. in Mech. Engring., Lehigh U., 1970; m. Diane Lou Cotton, Aug. 3, 1968; children—Dena Kathleen, Emily Grace, Carrie Anne. Project engr., mgr. firm B.B. Barefoot & Assos., Inc., Monroeville, Pa., 1970-72, v.p., dir. engring., 1973—; application engr. Wheelabrator & Frye, Inc., Pitts., 1972-73. Mem. Air Pollution Control Assn., Nat. Assn. Power Engrs., Engrs. Soc. Western Pa. Club: Monroeville Photography. Home: 5129 Mamont Rd Murrysville PA 15668 Office: 3821 Wm Penn Hwy Murrysville PA 15668

BARER, SEYMOUR, chem., mech. and environ. engr.; b. Bklyn., Apr. 10, 1923; s. Morris and lMollie (Altman) B.; B.S. in Chem. Engring., U. Minn., 1944, M.S., 1950; grad. U.S. Naval War Coll., 1965; m. Goldie Halbrecht, Oct. 26, 1957; children—David, Ronald, Shari, Andrew. Engring. research asst. U. Minn., St. Paul, 1947-50; mfg. chemist Doughnut Corp. Am., N.Y.C., 1951; sr. process design engr. Blaw-Knox Co., Pitts., 1951-53; cons. engr. Am. Machine & Foundry Co., N.Y.C., 1955, Foster D. Snell, Inc., N.Y.C., 1954-55, Allen Porter Lee, Inc., Bolivia, 1954; project mgr., mgr. design and standards, mgr. cost engring. Toms River Chem. Corp. (N.J.), 1955-66; pres. Barer Engring. Co., cons. engrs., Lakewood, N.J., 1966—; acting dir. inspections Lakewood Twp., 1973. Chmn., Lakewood Indsl. Commn., 1960-64; trustee Lakewood Hebrew Day Sch., 1964—, pres., 1976—. Served to comdr., expert air intelligence officer USNR, 1943-46; PTO. Decorated Bronze Star, Silver Star; registered profl. engr., N.J.; fallout shelter analyst Dept. Def. Mem. Nat., N.J. socs. profl. engrs., Cons. Engrs. Council, Water Pollution Control Fedn. Patentee in field; designed and developed indsl. wastewater treatment plants; specialist in indsl. process and pollution control engring., product liabilities and accidents investigation. Office: 145 Ocean Ave Lakewood NJ 08701

BARET, ALEXANDER CHARLES, surgeon; b. Mt. Carmel, Pa., Feb. 26, 1921; s. Charles Stanley and Mary Ann (Gozel) B.; B.S. summa cum laude, Rutgers U., 1949; M.D., U. Pa., 1953, postgrad. 1958; children by former marriage—Nicole Andrea, Alexander Scott. Intern, Hosp. U. Pa., Phila., 1953-54, resident in surgery, 1954-59; asso. in surgery, 1959-70; asst. clin. prof. surgery Hahnemann Med. Coll., Phila., 1970-74, asso. clin. prof., 1975—; chief surgery Freehold Area Hosp. (N.J.), 1971-72; attending surgeon Monmouth Med. Center, Long Branch, N.J., 1969-76, chief vascular and out-patient surg. clinic, 1970—; practice surgery, specializing in vascular surgery, Long Branch, 1960—. Pres. Monmouth County Heart Assn., N.J., 1971-72; bd. govs. Monmouth County chpt. Am. Cancer Soc. Served with Signal Corps, U.S. Army, 1943-45. Recipient Rose Meadow Levinson prize cancer research, 1952; Nat. Found. clin. fellow, 1955, Am. Cancer Soc. clin. fellow, 1957-58. Diplomate Am. Bd. Surgery. Fellow A.C.S., Am. Coll. Angiology, Soc. Clin. Vascular Surgery, Am. Soc. Abdominal Surgeons, Internat. Cardiovascular Soc.; mem. Am. Soc. for Parenteral and Enteral Nutrition, Phi Beta Kappa, Sigma Xi. Roman Catholic. Contbr. articles to profl. publs. Home: 480 Ocean Ave West End NJ 07740 Office: 279 3d Ave Long Branch NJ 07740

BARETSKI, CHARLES ALLAN, polit. scientist, librarian, educator, historian; b. Mt. Carmel, Pa., Nov. 21, 1918; s. Charles Stanley and Mary Ann (Gorzelnik) B.; B.A. cum laude (scholar), Rutgers U., 1945; B.S. in L.S. (Edna Sanderson fellow), Columbia, 1946, M.S. in L.S. (Newark Pub. library scholar), 1951; diplomas in archival adminstrn. Am. U., 1951, 55; M.A. in Polit. Sci. (research fellow), U. Notre Dame, 1957, Ph.D., 1958; M.A. in Govt. and Internat. Relations, N.Y. U., 1965, Ph.D. in Politics, 1969; m. Gladys Edith von Nyitrai Yartin, Aug. 19, 1950. Research intern Am. State Dept. Archives, Nat. Archives, 1951; from reference librarian to sr. librarian Newark Pub. Library, 1938-54, librarian Van Buren br., 1954-56, br. dir., 1957—, dir. fgn. lang. book collection, 1954—; coordinator Slavic-Am. hist. studies Sr. Citizens' Inst., Essex County Coll., Newark, 1978—; dir. Baretski Tutorial Service, 1935-68; founder, dir. Ethnic Research Archives, 1971—; pres. Asso. Community Councils Newark, 1969—; pres. Ironbound (Newark) Community Council, 1961—; lectr., cons. Am. Ethnic Polit. History, 1968—; mem. adv. council North Essex Ednl. Center, Essex County Coll., Belleville, N.J., 1973—; treas., chmn. N.J. Coalition for Safe Communities, Anti-Crime N.J. State-wide Fedn., 1978—; Republican Clean Govt. candidate for U.S. Congress, 10th Dist. N.J., 1962; N.J. chmn. Polish-Am. Citizens Goldwater, 1964; N.J. liaison dir. Polish Am. Rep. Nat. Council, 1971—; research dir., pub. relations dir. Polish-Am. Rep. Club N.J. Founder, dir. Inst. Polish Culture, Seton Hall U., South Orange, N.J., 1953-54; state del. Polish Hungarian World Fedn., 1977—; founder, pres. Newark Pub. Library Employees Union Local 2298, Am. Fedn. State, County and Municipal Employees, AFL-CIO, 1971-77, del. internat. convs., 1974, 76, 78, trustee N.J. Pub. Employees Council 52, No. N.J. Pub. Employee Unions, 1978—; mem. exec. bd. Newark Labor Coalition, 1972—; bd. dirs. N.J. chpt. Confedn. Am. Ethnic Groups; active numerous other civic orgns. Recipient Presdl. Leadership and Distinguished Service award Am. Fedn. State, County and Municipal Employees, 1972, Service awards Newark Pub. Library, 1972, 74, Nat. Am. Heritage award J.F. Kennedy Library for Minorities, 1972, Outstanding State Labor Leader award N.J. Pub. Employees, AFL-CIO, 1978; New Internat. award Polish Govt. in exile, London, also various others; decorated Knight's cross Polonia Restituta. Mem. Polish-Am. Unity League, Polish-Am. Hist. Assn., Writers Soc. N.J. (exec. dir. 1947-56), Am. Polit. Sci. Assn., Am. Soc. Internat. Law, Am. Sociol. Assn., Soc. Historians Am. Fgn. Relations, Am. Hist. Assn., N.Y. Library Club, Polish-Hungarian World Fedn., Immigration History Soc., N.J., Middle States councils social studies, Am. Council Polish Cultural Clubs, Newark Pub. Library Guild (founder, pres. 1970), Library Pub. Relations Council, ALA, N.J. Library Assn., Essex County Librarians Assn. Roman Catholic. Clubs: Polish U. (Newark). Author: Our Quarter Century: History of the American Council of Polish Cultural Clubs 1948-1973, 1973; editor: Higher Horizons Ednl. Program N.Y.C., 1961; editor and pub. Ironbound (N.J.) Counselor, Newark, 1965. Contbr. articles to numerous profl. jours., also chpts.

to books. Research on contbns. Polish and other immigrants to Am. culture and history. Home: 229 Montclair Ave Newark NJ 07104 Office: 140 Van Buren St Newark NJ 07105

BARKAN, STANLEY HOWARD, jour. pub.; b. Bklyn., Nov. 20, 1936; s. Joseph and Rose (Schwartz) B.; B.Ed., U. Miami (Fla.), 1962; M.A., N.Y. U., 1967, postgrad., 1967—; m. Beverly (Bebe) Adrian Rosenfeld, June 21, 1964; children—Jacqueline Mia, Joseph Scott. Tchr. Boys High Sch., N.Y.C., 1964-73, Beach Channel High Sch., N.Y.C., 1973—; pub. Cross-Cultural Communications 1972—; chmn. Cross-Cultural Communications Inst., L.I. U., 1971-72, lectr. in Swahili and English as 2d lang., 1969-71; dir. English as 2d lang. Greek Center, N.Y.C., 1969-70. Editor El Verano newspaper, San Miguel de Allende, Mexico, 1967; asso. editor Bitterroot poetry quar., N.Y.C., 1972-74; dir. cultural activities Internat. Center, N.Y.C., 1973-75; U.S. rep. Struga Poetry Evenings, Macedonia, Yugoslavia, 1976, 77, 78; dir. Internat. Poetry Serries, Merrick, N.Y., 1977—. Coordinator Internat. Festival Poetry and Art, N.Y.C., 1972, 73. Served with Signal Corps, AUS, 1956-59. N.Y. State Council Arts poetry grantee, 1972, 73. Mem. Am. Soc. Geolinguistics (dir. 1970), Modern Lang. Assn., ASCAP, Internat. Linguistics Assn., N.Y. Poetry Forum, Shakespeare Assn. Am., Am. Name Soc., Am. Dialectic Soc., Internat. Soc. Gen. Semantics, Alliance N.Y. Writers and Pubs., Internat. Platform Assn., Kappa Delta Pi, Phi Delta Kappa. Author: The Blacklines Scrawl, 1976. Editor: Cross-Cultural Rev., 1978—; contbg. editor Poets, 1978—; compiling editor To Struga With Love, 1978; poetry editor Sunstorm, 1978—. Contbr. poetry to jours. Home: 239 Wynsum Ave Merrick NY 11566 Office: PO Box 383 Merrick NY 11566

BARKAT, SAMUEL, coll. adminstr.; b. Sialkot, Pakistan, Aug. 1, 1932; s. Barkat Rehmat and Sardar G. (Masih) Khan; came to U.S., 1958, naturalized, 1975; B.A., Murray Coll., Pakistan, 1955; B.A., Tenn. Temple Coll., 1960; M.S., U. Tenn., 1961, Ed.D., 1963; m. Shelia J. Din, Dec. 29, 1955; children—Johnston, James. Instr. langs. Murree (Pakistan) Lang. Sch., 1952-55; asst. prof. psychology Tenn. Temple Coll., Chattanooga, 1963-64; vis. lectr. psychology Nyack (N.Y.) Coll., 1965-70; prof., chmn. dept. psychology King's Coll., Briarcliff Manor, N.Y., 1964—, v.p. for academic affairs, 1971—. Trustee, elder Community Bible Ch., Ossining, N.Y., 1974—; trustee Am. Inst. Pakistan Studies. Mem. Am., Eastern psychol. assns., Am. Sci. Affiliation, Christian Assn. Psychol. Studies, Am. Assn. Higher Edn., Am. Conf. Academic Deans. Home: 149 Central Dr Briarcliff Manor NY 10510 Office: King's Coll Briarcliff Manor NY 10510

BARKER, ELIZABETH ANNE, nurse, naval officer; b. Roanoke, Ala., Nov. 14, 1933; d. Frank Hendricks and Lena Inez (Cooper) B.; diploma Charity Hosp. Sch. Nursing, New Orleans, 1954; B.S.N. cum laude, Boston U., 1965; M.S.N., U. Pa., 1972. Commd. lt. (j.g.) U.S. Navy, 1958, advanced through grades to capt., 1977; supr. U.S. Naval Hosp., Phila., 1972-74; chief nurse U.S. Naval Hosp., Subic Bay, Philippines, 1975-76; dir. nursing service Naval Submarine Med. Center, Groton, Conn., 1976—. Decorated Bronze Star with combat V; Republic of Vietnam Gallantry Cross unit citation. Mem. Am. Nurses Assn., Council Nursing Facilitators, Nat. League Nursing, Nat. Forum Nursing Service Adminstrs., Assn. Mil. Surgeons. Home: 75 Inchcliffe Dr Gales Ferry CT 06335 Office: Naval Submarine Med Center Groton CT 06340

BARKER, HAROLD GRANT, surgeon; b. Salt Lake City, June 10, 1917; s. Frederick George and Jennetta (Stephens) B.; A.B., U. Utah, 1939, postgrad., 1939-41; M.D., U. Pa., 1943; m. Kathleen Butler, July 29, 1949; children—Janet Stephens, Douglas Reid. Intern Hosp. U. Pa., 1943-44, asst. resident in surgery, 1947-51, sr. resident in surgery, 1951-52, asst. attending surgeon, 1952-53, also asst. instr., research fellow U. Pa., 1946-51, instr., research fellow, 1951-52, asso. in surgery, 1952-53; asst. prof. clin. surgery Columbia U., 1953-57, asso. prof., 1957-68, prof., 1968—; asst. attending surgeon Presbyn. Hosp., 1953-57, asso. attending surgeon, 1957-69, attending surgeon, 1969—, dir. med. affairs, 1974—; pvt. practice, Phila., 1952-53, N.Y.C., 1953—. Served from 1st lt. to capt., M.C., AUS, 1944-46, ETO. Diplomate Am. Bd. Surgery. Fellow A.C.S.; mem. Soc. U. Surgeons, N.Y. Surg. Soc., Am. Physiol. Soc., Soc. Exptl. Biology and Medicine, Am. Fedn. Clin. Research, AMA, Halsted Soc., N.Y. State (chmn. surg. sect. 1961-62), N.Y. County med. socs., N.Y. Acad. Scis., Am. Surg. Assn., N.Y. Gastroent. Assn., Societe Internationale de Chirurgie, Soc. Surgery Alimentary Tract, Am. Assn. History of Medicine, Whipple Surg. Soc., Collegium Internationale Chirurgiae Digestivae, Sigma Xi. Clubs: Century Assn. (N.Y.); Am. Yacht; Manursing Island; Charaka. Contbr. articles to med. jours. Home: 1 Forest Ave Rye NY 10580 Office: 161 Ft Washington Ave New York City NY 10032

BARKER, KENNETH RAY, educator; b. Memphis, Oct. 30, 1939; s. Ray Whitman and Etta Mae (Sexton) B.; B.S. Southwestern U., Memphis, 1961; M.S., U. Miss., 1963; Ph.D., U. Tex., 1966; m. Marilyn Ann Koteras, May 22, 1971; children—Ray Clinton, Dara Lorraine. Instr. cell biology U. Tex., Austin, 1966, NIH fellow 1967; research fellow U. Witwatersrand, Johannesburg, S. Africa, 1968; asso. prof. biology Canisius Coll. Buffalo, 1969—; vis. prof. U. Tex. at Austin, 1976-77. Served with M.C. U.S. Army, 1958. Sigma Xi grantee, 1963-64; Am. Philos. Soc. grantee, 1967-68, Am. Heart Assn. grantee, 1967-68. Mem. AAAS, Am. Cell Biology, Can. Soc. Genetics. Contbr. articles in field to profl. jours. Home: 171 Woodward Ave Buffalo NY 14214 Office: Dept Biology Canisius College Main St Buffalo NY 14208

BARKER, ROBERT RANKIN, bus. exec.; b. Brookline, Mass., July 12, 1915; s. James Madison and Margaret (Rankin) B.; A.B. magna cum laude, Harvard U., 1936; m. Elizabeth VanDyke Shelly, Mar. 7, 1942; children—James Robertson, Ann Shelly, William Benjamin, Margaret Welch. With investment and credit analysis, investment adv. depts. J. P. Morgan & Co., 1936-49; with Wm. A.M. Burden & Co., N.Y.C., 1949-78, gen. partner, 1954-78; gen. partner Robert R. Barker & Co., 1973—. Spl. asst. to asst. sec. commerce for air U.S. Dept. Commerce, 1942-43. Past chmn. adv. com. endowment mgmt. Ford Found. Past trustee Am. Geog. Soc., New Canaan Country Sch., Silvermine Guild Artists, New Canaan Library; trustee Mus. Modern Art, Am. Mus. Natural History, Am. Farm Sch. Thessaloniki, Greece, Hudson Inst., Florence V. Burden Found., Perkin Fund; mem. vis. com. univ. resources Harvard U. Served as officer USNR, 1943-46. Mem. Council Fgn. Relations, N.Y. Soc. Security Analysts, Phi Beta Kappa. Clubs: University, Harvard, Brook, Hemisphere, (N.Y.C.). Home: 809 Oenoke Ridge New Canaan CT 06840 Office: 630 Fifth Ave New York City NY 10020

BARKER, VERLYN LLOYD, clergyman; b. Auburn, Nebr., July 25, 1931; s. Jack Lloyd and Olive Clara (Bollman) B.; A.B., Doane Coll., 1952, D.D., 1977; B.D., Yale U., 1956, S.T.M., 1960; Ph.D., St. Louis U., 1970. Ordained to ministry United Ch. of Christ, 1956; sec. for ministries in higher edn. Bd. for Homeland Ministries, N.Y.C., 1961—; pres. United Ministries in Higher Edn., N.Y.C., 1970-78. Mem. Am. Assn. Higher Edn., Am. Hist. Assn., Am. Studies Assn., UN Assn., ACLU, Doane Coll. Alumni Assn. (pres. 1957-58), Assn. Yale Alumni. Democrat. Club: Yale of N.Y.C. Mem. adv. com. Jour. Current Social Issues, 1972—, contbr. articles, 1972-75. Home: 392 Central Park W New York City NY 10025 Office: 287 Park Ave S New York City NY 10010

BARLOW, EDWARD VERNON, librarian; b. North Providence, R.I., Jan. 8, 1924; s. Peter Henry and Emma Cora (Baron) B.; student Bryant Coll., Providence, 1947; m. Florence E. Johnson, June 17, 1944; children—David E., Stephen P., Robert A. Second asst. law librarian State R.I., Providence, 1950-69, 1st asst., 1969-72, law librarian, 1972—. Served with USCGR, 1942-45, USNR, 1951; Korea. Mem. Am. Assn. Law Librarians, New Eng. (v.p. R.I. 1971-72), North Providence (pres. 1969-72) amateur hockey assns. Home: 78 Cottage Ave North Providence RI 02911 Office: 250 Benefit St Providence RI 02903

BARLOW, GEORGE BARTON, physician; b. Ossining, N.Y., Apr. 11, 1906; s. John C. and Josephine (Bassett) B.; B.A., Williams Coll., 1928; M.D., Columbia U., 1932; m. Alice Denison Fisher, June 27, 1931; children—John Denison, Peter Bassett. Intern, Bklyn. Hosp., N.Y., 1932-33, med. resident, 1933-34; practice medicine specializing in cardiology, Englewood, N.J., 1934—; asst. in medicine Vanderbilt Clinic, N.Y.C., 1934-39; asst. attending physician in pediatric cardiology, out-patient dept. Babies Hosp., N.Y.C., 1937-41; asso. attending physician, also tchr. Post-Grad. Hosp., N.Y.C., 1936-50; asst. chief medicine Keesler Field Sta. Hosp., Biloxi, Miss., 1942-43; asst. physician Englewood Hosp., 1935-38, attending physician, 1938-70, pres. med. staff, 1950-51, chief of medicine, 1953-70, cons. in medicine and cardiology, 1970—; dir. internal medicine Bergen Pines County (N.J.) Hosp., 1952-57, cons. in medicine, 1957—, pres. med. staff, 1954-55; mem. council's subcom. on therapeutic procedures in heart disease N.J. Regional Med. Program, 1970-72. Jr. vestryman St. Paul's Episcopal Ch., Englewood, 1936-42. Served to maj. M.C., USAAF, 1942-46. Recipient (with wife) Du Pont Trophy award Del. Mus. Natural History, 1974; named to Wisdom Hall Fame, 1973; diplomate Am. Bd. Internal Medicine, subsplty. cardiovascular diseases. Fellow A.C.P., Am. Coll. Chest Physicians, Am. Coll. Cardiology, Am. Coll. Angiology, Acad. Medicine N.J., Am. Heart Assn. Council Clin. Cardiology; mem. Am. (Silver Distinguished Achievement medallion 1972), Bergen County (pres. 1965-67), N.J. (mem. exec. com. 1967-73, 1st. v.p. 1970-72) heart assns., Med. Soc. N.J. (chmn. various coms. 1947-63), Pan Am. Med. Assn., Am. Soc. Peripheral Vascular Disease (v.p. 1956-59), Englewood Hosp. Assn. (Distinguished Service award 1970), Bergen County Med. Soc. (pres. 1952-53). Republican. Episcopalian. Clubs: Englewood; Knickerbocker Country. Home: 76 Westervelt Ave Tenafly NJ 07670 Office: 155 N Dean St Englewood NJ 07631

BARLOW, WALTER GREENWOOD, pub. opinion analyst, mgmt. cons.; b. Liverpool, Eng., Sept. 10, 1917; s. Walter and Sarah Ellen (Greenwood) B.; came to U.S., 1920, naturalized, 1928; B.A., Cornell U., 1939; widower; children—Eric, Francine, Deborah, Alison. Reporter, Washington Daily News, 1940-41; mem. editorial staff Time mag., 1941; with Opinion Research Corp., N.Y.C., 1946-65, pres., 1960-65; pres. Howard Chase Assos. Inc., N.Y.C., 1965-68, Research Strategies Corp., N.Y.C., 1966—; sr. partner Partners for Growth, Inc., 1968-71; dir. A.D. Publs., N.Y.C., 1970—, pres., 1976-78. Mem. N.J. Bd. Pub. Welfare, 1966—, vice chmn., 1973—; trustee Cornell U., 1968-76, mem. univ. council, 1968—; bd. dirs. support agy. United Presbyn. Ch. U.S.A., 1973—; bd. dirs. Family Service Assn., 1958-69, pres., 1967-69. Served to maj. U.S. Army, 1941-46. Mem. Pub. Relations Soc. Am., Am. Statis. Assn., Am. Mgmt. Assn., Am. Assn. Pub. Opinion Research, Am. Mktg. Assn., Electric Power Research Inst. (adv. council 1977—), Phi Beta Kappa, Sigma Delta Chi, Phi Kappa Phi. Club: Cornell (N.Y.C.); Presbyn. Home: RD 1 Poor Farm Rd Pennington NJ 08534 Office: 1270 Ave of Americas New York City NY 10020

BARNA, GARY STANLEY, mfg. co. exec.; b. Newark, Dec. 1, 1940; s. Benjamin and Clara (Berenfeld) B.; student Union Coll. at Cranford, N.J., 1965-66; B.S., Rutgers U., 1972; m. Roberta Babat, Mar. 24, 1962; children—Jeffrey, Scott, Claire. Mem. trust accounting dept. Fidelity Union Trust Co., Newark, 1964-65; mem. staff accounting dept. Enjay Chem. Co., Cranford, 1965-67; controller Weldon Roberts Rubber Co., Newark, 1967-70, v.p., gen. mgr., 1970—, also. dir.; chmn. bd., pres., treas., dir. Brightboy Abrasives Inc., Newark, 1974—. Served with USAF, 1958-60. Mem. Nat. Assn. Accountants, Grinding Wheel Inst., Abrasive Engring. Soc., Am. Inst. Corp. Controllers, Am. Soc. Notaries, AIM, N.J. Bus. and Industry Assn., Rutgers U. Alumni Assn., N.J., Newark chambers commerce. Odd Fellow, Lion. Club: Rutgers U. Alumni-Faculty. Office: 351-365 6th Ave Newark NJ 07107

BARNARD, WALTHER M., educator; b. Hartford, Conn., May 30, 1937; s. Walter Monroe and Florence Elzada (Wheeler) B.; B.S., Trinity Coll., 1959; M.A., Dartmouth, 1961; Ph.D., Pa. State U., 1965. Asst. prof. dept. geology State U. N.Y., Fredonia, 1964-70, asso. prof., 1970-77, prof., 1977—, dir. NSF undergrad. research programs, summers 1975-78. Recipient grant-in-aid Research Found. of State U. N.Y., 1964, 66, 69, 72, faculty research fellowship, summers 1966, 70, 73; research grant Research Corp., 1965; Lake Erie Environmental Studies Research fellowship State U. N.Y., Fredonia, summers, 1972-76, 78. Mem. AAAS, AAUP, Am. Geophys. Union, Am. Inst. Chemists, ASTM, Geochem. Soc., Geochem. Soc. Japan, Geol. Assn. Can., Geol. Soc. Am., Internat. Assn. Geochemistry and Cosmochemistry, Internat. Assn. Theoretical and Applied Limnology, Mineral. Assn. Can., mineral. socs. Gt. Britain, Am., Nat. Assn. Geology Tchrs., N.Y. Acad. Scis., Soc. for Applied Spectroscopy, Soc. for Environmental Geochemistry and Health, Am. Chem. Soc., Am. Soc. Agronomy, Crop Sci. Soc. Am., Internat., Can. socs. soil sci., Fedn. Am. Scientists, Soil Sci. Soc. Am., Sigma Xi. Contbr. articles to profl. jours. Home: 2950 Straight Rd Fredonia NY 14063

BARNERT, ALAN H., physician; b. N.Y.C., June 23, 1914; s. Cyril and Rose (Stone) B.; A.B., Columbia, 1940, M.D., 1937; m. Libby Tillman, Feb. 14, 1954; children—David, William, Ruth. Intern, Morrisania Hosp., N.Y.C., 1937-39; resident in ophthalmology Mt. Sinai Hosp., N.Y.C., 1940-42; practice medicine, specializing in ophthalmology, N.Y.C., 1946—; attending ophthalmologist Manhattan Eye, Ear and Throat Hosp., 1960—, Beth Israel Hosp., 1970—; asso. ophthalmologist Mt. Sinai Hosp., 1948—; cons. ophthalmologist Beekman-Downtown Hosp., 1970—, Manhattan State Hosp., 1970—, Harlem Hosp., 1960—; clinician The Lighthouse, 1964—; asso. clin. prof. ophthalmology Mt. Sinai Sch. Medicine, 1972—. Served to capt. M.C., AUS, 1942-46. Recipient Jacobi medallion Asso. Alumni Mt. Sinai Hosp., 1971. Mem. AMA. N.Y. County Med. Soc., ACS, N.Y. Acad. Medicine, N.Y. Soc. for Clin. Ophthalmology (past pres.), Manhattan Ophthal. Soc. (past pres.), Am. Acad. Ophthalmology and Otolaryngology (life). Jewish religion. Home: 62 Stony Run New Rochelle NY 10804 Office: 1047 Park Ave New York City NY 10028

BARNES, CHAPLIN BRADFORD, assn. exec.; b. New Haven, Apr. 7, 1941; s. Irston Roberts and Lidorra Holt (Putney) B.; grad. Choate Sch., 1958; B.A. magna cum laude, Yale, 1962, LL.B., 1965; postgrad. Univ. Coll., Oxford (Eng.) U., 1965-67; m. Lila Cummings, May 13, 1972; children—Sarah Southworth, Diana Brewster. With firm Breed, Abbott & Morgan, N.Y.C., 1968-69; with Nat. Audubon Soc., N.Y.C., 1969—, asst. to pres., 1969-73, dir. Office of Internat. Activities, 1973-75, dir. internat. activities, 1975—. Mem. adv. bd. Center for Internat. Environ. Info. Bd.; trustee Rare Animal Relief Effort, 1974—, Watch Hill Chapel Soc., 1977—; mem. exec. bd. Am. Com. for Internat. Conservation, 1974—. Episcopalian. Clubs: Union (N.Y.C.); Misquamicut (Watch Hill, R.I.). Home: 190 Hurlbutt St Wilton CT 06897 Office: 950 3d Ave New York City NY 10022

BARNES, DAVID KENNEDY, chem. co. exec.; b. Concordia, Kans., Apr. 23, 1923; s. Richard A. and Leiella (Hudson) B.; B.S., Olivet Coll., 1943; A.M., Ind. U., 1944, Ph.D., 1947; m. Martha Ann Snapp, Dec. 24, 1942; children—David Kennedy, John A., Katharine Barnes Wesolowski, Jeffrey C. Sr. chemist Stanolind Oil & Gas Co., Tulsa, 1947-53; sr. chemist E. I. duPont de Nemours & Co., textile fibers dept., Kinston, N.C., 1953-57, tech. supr., Seaford, Del., 1957-63, mgr. prodn., Wilmington, Del., 1963-66, dir. mfg., 1966-67, dir. mfg. indsl. and biochems. dept., 1967-69, asst. gen. mgr. electrochems. dept., 1969-72, asst. gen. mgr. indsl. chems. dept., 1972-74, v.p., gen. mgr. energy and materials dept., 1974-77, v.p. textile fibers, 1977—. Trustee Olivet (Mich.) Coll. Served with C.E., U.S. Army, 1944-46. Ind. U. grad. fellow, 1946-47. Mem. Am. Chem. Soc., Soc. Chem. Industry, Sigma Xi. Republican. Unitarian. Clubs: Torch, Wilmington Country, DuPont Country (Wilmington, Del.). Patentee in field. Home: 3704 Centerville Rd Wilmington DE 19807 Office: 1007 Market St Wilmington DE 19898

BARNES, ELIZABETH CHESNUT (MRS. WILSON KING BARNES), club woman; b. Balt., Oct. 28, 1905; d. William Calvin and Florence E. (Carroll) Chesnut; A.B. cum laude, Bryn Mawr Coll., 1928; J.D., cum laude, U. Md., 1936; student Johns Hopkins, 1929-32, Peabody Inst., 1928-32; m. Wilson King Barnes, Apr. 30, 1938; children—William Calvin Chesnut, Wilson King. Mem. Schenley Rd. Community Center, 1944-71; dep. coordinator Civil Def., Balt., 1956-59. Mem. D.A.R. (nat. chmn. nat. def. com. 1959-62, state chmn. 1958-61, chpt. regent 1958-61, vice chmn. nat. resolutions com. 1960-63, state vice regent 1961-64, Md. state regent 1964-67, organizing sec. gen. nat. soc. 1968-71, state chmn. D.A.R. schs. 1971-73, speakers bur. 1971—), Colonial Dames Am., Daus. of 1812 (3d v.p. 1956-58, state chmn. 1958-60, rec. sec. 1959-60, historian 1959-62, chmn. nat. def. com., by-law com. 1961-65, state parliamentarian 1964-67), Daus. Colonial Wars (state chmn. nat. def. com.; state pres. 1968-71), Magna Charta Dames, Colonial Dames of 17th Century (state historian 1969-70, rec. sec. Terra Marine chpt. 1972-73, nat. chmn. nat. def. 1971-73), Colonial Order of Crown, Hist. Annapolis Soc. for Preservation Md. Antiquities, Descs. Knights of Garter, Minute Women U.S. (chmn. Md. 1962-64), Descs. Lords of Md. Manors Magothy River Assn., Cylburn Wildflower Preserve and Garden Center (chmn. hort. com. 1959-60). Clubs: Green Thumb Garden (past pres.), Woman's (Roland Park, Md.); Three Arts (vice chmn. publicity com. 1958-60) (Homeland, Md.). Author: Sharing Trade Secrets (brochure), 1938; What Do the Daughters Do, 1957; United Nations Unmasked; The Peace Corps—A Pig in a Poke; Two Faced NATO; DAR Calendar for Chapter Regents; Promoting and Conserving Our Chapters, also brochures. Home: 111 Ridgewood Rd Baltimore MD 21210

BARNES, EMMETT GEORGE, physicist; b. Paterson, N.J., Mar. 26, 1940; s. Emmett Eugene and Sophie Doris (Mosiewicz) B.; B.S., Stevens Inst. Tech., 1962; postgrad. W. Tex. State U., 1965; m. Audrey Mae Matthews, Sept. 15, 1962; children—Joyce, Lorraine. Physicist, U.S. Naval Weapons Sta., Dahlgren, Va., 1962; physicist U.S. Army Armament Research and Devel. Command, Dover, N.J., 1965—; mem. steering com. Dept. Def. Ann. Conf. on Nondestructive Testing, 1967-69. Served with USAF, 1962-65. Recipient Picatinny Arsenal Research and Engring. awards, 1971, 1976; registered profl. engr., Calif. Mem. Am. Soc. Nondestructive Testing. Episcopalian. Contbr. articles in field to profl. jours. Home: 41 Mountain Ave Mendham NJ 07945 Office: DRDAR-QAS US Army ARRADCOM Dover NJ 07801

BARNES, FRANK CLYDE, glass co. exec.; b. Phila., Jan. 25, 1935; s. Clyde and Theresa M. (Brabazon) B.; A.B., Ursinus Coll., 1961; m. Vera Johanna Cole, Mar. 24, 1956; children—Margaret Ann. Distbn. mgr. Alan Wood Steel Co., Conshohoken, Pa., 1956-67; cons. Alexander Proudfoot, N.Y.C., 1967-68; quality control and assurance mgr. Wheaton Industries, Millville, N.J., 1968—; lectr. in field. Served with USMC, 1953-56. Mem. Am. Mgmt. Assn., Am. Soc. for Quality Control (chmn. So. Jersey sect. 1978-79). Contbr. articles in field to profl. jours. Home: 2916 Garwood Ln Vineland NJ 08360 Office: 3d and G Sts Millville NJ 08332

BARNES, GEORGE HENRY, electronic engr.; b. Portland, Oreg., Feb. 27, 1923; s. Brown Emerson and Cordelia (Hill) B.; B.S. magna cum laude, Harvard Coll., 1944, M.A., 1948; m. Vera Glora Lewis, May 4, 1972; children—George Henry III, Margaret Morris. Med. technician Trudeau Found., N.Y., 1948-50; research scientist Franklin Inst. Labs. Research and Devel., Phila., 1950-55; engr. Burroughs Corp., Paoli, Pa., 1955—, supr. sect., 1961-63, sr. staff engr., 1964—. Served with U.S. Army, 1944-46. Mem. IEEE (sr.), Acoustic Soc. Am., Sigma Xi. Contbr. articles to profl. publs. computer design. Patentee in field. Home: 767 Mancill Rd Wayne PA 19087 Office: Burroughs Corp Box 517 Paoli PA 19018

BARNES, MICHAEL DARR, congressman; b. Washington, Sept. 3, 1943; s. John P. and Vernon (Smith) B.; B.A., U. N.C., 1965; postgrad. Inst. Higher Internat. Studies, Geneva, 1965-66; J.D. with honors, George Washington U., 1970-72; m. Claudia Fangboner, June 13, 1970; 1 dau., Sarah Dillon. Spl. asst. to Sen. Edmund S. Muskie, Muskie for Pres. Com., 1970-72; admitted to D.C. bar, 1973; asso. firm Covington & Burling, Washington, 1972-75; exec. dir. Nat. Democratic Platform Com., Dem. Nat. Conv., 1975-76; mem. Public Service Commn. Md., 1975-78; mem. 96th Congress from 8th Congl. Dist., Md.; vice chmn. Washington Met. Area Transit Commn., 1976-78. Served with USMC, 1967-69. Recipient Magnum medal U. N.C., 1965; named Disting. State Ofcl. of 1977, Young Dems. Md. Mem. Am. Bar Assn., D.C. Bar Assn., Nat. Assn. Regulatory Utility Commrs., Am. Legion, Marine Corps Res. Officers Assn. Asst. editor Dem. Rev. Mag., 1974-78. Office: 1607 Longworth House Office Bldg Washington DC 20515

BARNES, ROBERT MORSON, investment exec.; b. Poughkeepsie, N.Y., May 30, 1940; s. Willand Ogden and Marie (Bell) B.; B.S. in Math., Rensselaer Poly. Inst., 1962; M.S. in Math., Lehigh U., 1964; m. Elizabeth L. Bell, June 29, 1963; children—Bryan, Jeffery. Sr. engr. Raytheon Co., Portsmouth, R.I., 1967-70; v.p. Investment Scis., Meadowbrook, Pa., 1970-71; pub. mgr. Research Found., State U. N.Y., Albany, 1971-73; pres. Barnes Tech. Corp., investment mgmt., Albany, 1973—. Mem. Am. Assn. Commodity Traders. Author: The Dow Theory Can Make You Rich, 1973; also articles in field. Home: 3 Ashley Dr Ballston Lake NY 12019 Office: 105 Wolf Rd Albany NY 12205

BARNETT, DAVID, pianist, educator; b. N.Y.C., Dec. 1, 1907; s. Samuel and Bertha (Margolis) B.; diploma, Juilliard Sch., 1925, Ecole Normale de Musique, 1928; B.A., Columbia U., 1927; Mus.D., Elon Coll., 1953; m. Josephine Wolff, Dec. 31, 1929; 1 son, Jonathan. Mem. faculty Wellesley Coll., 1935-65, Harvard U., 1955-59, New Eng.

Conservatory Music, 1946-65, Columbia U., summers 1946-62; prof. music U. Bridgeport (Conn.), 1967—; vis. lectr. Assn. Am. Colls.; lectr. WGBH, Boston; pianist concert tours east and mid-west; recitals in Carnegie Hall, Town Hall, Jordon Hall, Gardner Mus., Salle Pleyel; soloist with Boston Symphony, St. Louis Symphony, Cin. Symphony, Orchestre Symphonique de Paris; dir. Wellesley Concert Series, Westport Friends of Music. Bd. dirs. Boston Old South Meeting House. Mem. Nat. Assn. Am. Composers, Coll. Music Soc., Am. Soc. for Aesthetics, Conn. State Music Tchrs. Assn. (v.p. 1977—), AAUP, Pi Kappa Lambda, Kappa Gamma Psi (hon.), Tau Zeta Epsilon (hon.). Composer: Seven Interludes and Pieces in Dance Tempi for Piano; Fantasie for Clarinet and Piano; Rhapsody and Scherzo for Violin and Piano; Ballade for Viola and Piano; Tonight (song). Author: Living With Music; They Shall Have Music; Manual for Grade Teachers; The Performance of Music; recs. include Three Cycles of Robert Schumann with Josephine Barnett. Contbr. articles to profl. jours., popular mags. Home: 3 Ledgebrook Ct Weston CT 06880 Office: Music Dept U Bridgeport Bridgeport CT 06602

BARNETT, JOSEPHINE (MRS. DAVID BARNETT), actress; b. N.Y.C., July 20, 1909; d. Marks A. and Jennie (Weise) Wolfe; B.S., Tchrs. Coll. of N.Y., 1928; postgrad. Cornell U., 1929-30; Columbia 1930-31, 35-36; m. David Barnett, Dec. 31, 1929; 1 son, Jonathan. Tchr. N.Y.C. Pub. Schs., 1929-35; tchr. drama Master Inst., 1931-32; profl. staff Westport Country Playhouse, 1946-50; dir. drama N.E. Conservatory of Music, 1950-59; spl. lectr. Emerson Coll., Boston, 1957-58; active actress Westport Country Playhouse, 1946-49. Exec. bd. Friends of Wellesley Library, Alliance Unitarian Soc. of Westport; mem. Darien Community Assn.; sec., mem. exec. bd. Westport Friends of Music; mem. drama com., exec. bd. Weston-Westport Arts Council. Mem. Boston Mus. Fine Arts, Nat. League Am. Pen Women (past pres.), League Women Voters (past pres.), Sigma Alpha Iota. Unitarian. Address: 3 Ledgebrook Ct Box 1304 Weston CT 06880

BARNETT, LESTER ALFRED, surgeon; b. N.Y.C., Mar. 11, 1915; s. Benjamin and Rae Viola (Marcus) B.; student Ohio State U., 1932-35; B.A. (spl. hon.), George Washington U., 1936, M.D., 1939; m. Jean Wolfe, Apr. 16, 1939; children—Barbara Jane Barnett Grossman, James A. Intern, Gallinger Municipal Hosp., Washington, 1939-40; resident St. Peter's Gen. Hosp., New Brunswick, N.J., 1940-41, Walter Reed Gen. Hosp., Washington, 1942-43, Grasslands Hosp., Valhalla, N.Y., 1944-46; practice medicine specializing in surgery, Long Branch, N.J., 1945—; mem. staff Monmouth Med. Center, 1946—, dir. dept. surgery, 1961-71, pres. med. staff, 1970-73, trustee 1975—, bd. mgrs. Sch. Nursing, 1953-65; clin. prof. surgery Hahnemann Med. Coll., 1970—; asso. in surgery U. Pa. Sch. Medicine; cons. surgery Jersey Shore Med. Center, Neptune. Trustee Monmouth Coll., 1971-78. Served to 1st lt. M.C., AUS, 1942-43. Diplomate Am. Bd. Surgery. Fellow Am. Coll., Gastroenterology, A.C.S.; mem. AMA, N.J., Monmouth County (pres. 1959-60) med. socs. Jewish. Clubs: Hollywood Golf (Deal, N.J.); Ocean Beach (Elberon, N.J.); Masons, B'nai B'rith (past lodge pres.). Author sci. articles. Home: 675 Ocean Ave West End NJ 07740 Office: 255 3d Ave Long Branch NJ 07740

BARNETT, PROCTOR HAWTHORNE, former ins. co. exec.; b. Birmingham, Ala., Dec. 11, 1906; s. Frank Willis and Maude (Proctor) B.; student Samford U., 1924-26, U.S. Mil. Acad., 1927-28, Columbia, 1953; m. Mary Reeder, Dec. 11, 1929; 1 dau., Mary Frances. Sec., dir. Jackson Securities & Investment Co., Birmingham, 1929-33; with Prudential Ins. Co. Am., 1933-72, successively mortgage loan insp., mortgage loan appraiser, Birmingham, asst. mgr. prodn., Dallas, asst. gen. mgr., gen. mgr., exec. dir., Newark, 1933-56, exec. gen. mgr. western region, 1956-63, v.p., Newark, 1963-65, sr. v.p., 1965-72; pres. Pic Realty Corp., 1968-71. Dir. council for better cities ACTION, mem. governing com. Urban Renewal div.; mem. governing com. Urban Redevel. div. mem. governing com. urban redevel. div. Urban Am., Inc. Served to col. USAAF, 1941-46. Mem. Exec. Assn. (chmn. exec. com.), Regional Plan Assn. N.Y. (dir. class of 1971), Nat. Assn. Home Builders (redevelopers and spl. programs council), Navy League, Am. Legion, U.S. C. of C. (ins. com.), Urban Land Inst., Pi Kappa Alpha. Club: Essex County Country (West Orange, N.J.). Home: 19 Kings Hill Ct Summit NJ 07901

BARNETT, WILLIAM ARNOLD, econometrician; b. Boston, Oct. 30, 1941; s. Marcus Jack and Elizabeth Leah (Forman) B.; B.S., Mass. Inst. Tech., 1963; M.B.A., U. Calif., Berkeley, 1965; Ph.D., Carnegie-Mellon U., 1974; m. Maxine Harriet Goldstein, July 10, 1969. Engr., Rocketdyne div. Rockwell Internat. Corp., Canoga Park, Calif., 1963-65, system devel. engr. Apollo project, 1965-69; research econometrician Bd. Govs. Fed. Res. System, Washington, 1973—; research asso. U. Chgo., summer 1977. NSF research grantee, 1977—; Richard King Mellon fellow, 1969-70, NDEA fellow 1970-71, NSF fellow, 1971-73. Mem. Am. Econ. Assn., Econometric Soc., Am. Statis. Assn., Fedn. Am. Scientists, Sigma Xi, Omicron Delta Epsilon. Club: M.I.T. (Washington). Contbr. articles to Econometrica, Jour. Am. Statis. Assn., Jour. Polit. Economy. Editor spl. edit. Jour. Econometrics. Home: 613 N Armistead St Alexandria VA 22312 Office: Federal Reserve Board Washington DC 20551

BARNHARD, IVAN HAROLD, educator, investment co. exec.; b. Bklyn., Jan. 2, 1934; s. Daniel S. and Sydelle (Lowenthal) B.; B.A., L.I.U., 1956; M.A., Auburn U., 1962; Ph.D., 1969; m. Vivian Blancato, June 20, 1957; children—David William, Linda Carol, Lisa Ann. Tchr., adminstr. pub. schs., Yonkers, N.Y., 1962—; pres. Profl. Investment Group, 1967—, Hudson Holding Assos., 1969—, Marine Investor Assos., 1969—; chmn. bd. Pine Investment Assos., 1969—; exec. v.p. Ednl. Analysis Assos., 1971—; vice chmn. bd. People's Nat. Bank Rockland County; dir. P.I.A. Inc., Packease-Servease Corp., Electro Motion Corp.; adminstr. Yonkers (N.Y.) High Sch. S., 1972—. Recipient Jenkins Meml. award Yonkers PTA, 1970. Mem. Am. Ednl. Research Assn., Nat., Assn. Secondary Sch. Prins., N.Y. State Assn. Secondary Sch. Adminstrs., Ga. Acad. Sci., Mensa, Phi Delta Kappa, Tau Delta Phi, Phi Beta Mu. Author numerous articles on edn. and investments. Home: 29 Culver Dr New City NY 10956

BARNHARD, SHERWOOD ARTHUR, printing co. exec.; b. Newark, Mar. 14, 1921; s. Charles L. and Blanche (Tarnow) B.; B.S., Franklin and Marshall Coll., 1942; m. Esther Lasky, Feb. 21, 1946; children—Ronald Harris, Paul Ira. With Lasky Co., Millburn, N.J., 1946—, exec. v.p., 1956-61, pres., 1961—, v.p., trustee Jewish News. Trustee, Temple Israel, South Orange, N.J.; bd. govs. Pleasant Valley Home For Aged, West Orange, N.J. Mem. Printing Industries N.J. (past pres.), Printing Industries Met. N.Y. (mem. bd.), Met. Lithographers (dir., labor com.), Mktg. Communications Execs. Internat., Zeta Beta Tau. Clubs: Village (South Orange); Crestmont Golf and Country (West Orange). Home: 408 Long Hill Dr Short Hills NJ 07079 Office: 67 E Willow St Millburn NJ 07041

BARNHART, CHARLOTTE KENNEDY (MRS. HOWARD KENNETH BARNHART), research co. exec.; b. Chambersburg, Pa., Jan. 29, 1919; d. John Harry and Marguerite (Hafer) Kennedy; grad. high sch., Chambersburg; m. Howard Kenneth Barnhart, June 22, 1939; children—Joy Ann (Mrs. James K. Knox), Virginia Kay, Pamela Ellen. Propr. Park Ave. Style Shop, Chambersburg, 1950-53; sec., dir. Facts, Inc., Chambersburg, 1960—. Mem. Kittochtinny Hist. Soc., Internat. Platform Assn., Sr. Hosp. Aux. Republican. Methodist. Clubs: Order Eastern Star, Chambersburg Women's (pres. 1967-68). Artist and art collector. Home: 280 Park Ave Chambersburg PA 17201 Office: Trust Co Bldg Chambersburg PA 17201

BARNHART, JEFFERSON CLIFFORD, lawyer; b. Cleona, Pa., July 30, 1918; s. Thomas Jefferson and Reba (Wentling) B.; A.B., Lebanon Valley Coll., 1938; LL.B., Columbia, 1948; m. Mary Elizabeth Zartman, Dec. 26, 1949; children—Jeffrey Clifford, Stephen Harry. Tchr. Hershey (Pa.) High Sch., 1938-41; admitted to Pa. bar, 1948; since practiced in Harrisburg, Pa.; mem. firm McNees, Wallace and Nurick, 1948—. Pres. REC, Inc., 1969—. Lectr. Practicing Law Inst., 1965—; solicitor, dir. Hershey (Pa.) Nat. Bank; solicitor Dauphin County Register of Wills., 1967—. Mem., sec., pres. Hershey Sch. Bd., 1960-66; solicitor Derry Twp. Suprs., Hershey, 1958-67. Trustee, Lebanon Valley Coll., Hershey Jr. Coll.; sec., dir. Alpine Nursing and Convalescent Home, Inc. Served to capt., AUS, 1941-46, 51-53. Decorated Bronze Star medal, Purple Heart; recipient distinguished alumnus award Lebanon Valley Coll., 1969. Mem. Pa., Dauphin County bar assns., Pa. Soc. Republican. Mem. Evang. U.B. Ch. (trustee). Mason (32 deg.). Author: Principles of the In-Finite Philosophy, 1955; The Alephs, 1977; Aleph-Nought, 1978. Home: 306 Bahia Ave Hershey PA 17033 Office: 100 Pine St Harrisburg PA 17033 also Ruhehaus Ln Hershey PA 17033

BARNHILL, GREGORY HURD, investment banker; b. Balt., Feb. 20, 1953; s. Robert Bell and Margaret Katherine (Hurd) B.; student Institut d'Etudes Européenes, Banque Nat. de Paris, 1974; B.A. in Econs., Brown U., 1975; postgrad. Inst. Fin., N.Y.C., 1975. Registered rep. Alex. Brown & Sons, Investment Bankers, Balt., 1975—; v.p., dir. BOACO, Inc.; partner Barnhill/Phillips; dir. CPU, Inc. Chmn., Ridgely Archtl. Com., 1978; adv. bd. Institut d'Etudes Européenes. Lic. N.Y. Stock Exchange/Nat. Assn. Securities Dealers. Mem. Bond Club Md., Nat., Md. assns. realtors, Greater Balt. Bd. Realtors, Md. Hist. Soc., Brown U. Club—Md. (pres. 1976—), McDonogh Sch. Alumni Assn. (dir. 1976—), Sigma Chi. Republican. Home: Bond Ct 628 Washington Blvd Baltimore MD 21230 Office: Alex Brown & Sons 135 E Baltimore St Baltimore MD 21202

BARNHOUSE, RUTH TIFFANY, physician; b. La Mur, Isere, France, Oct. 23, 1923 (parents American citizens); d. Donald Grey and Ruth (Tiffany) Barnhouse; came to U.S., 1925; student Vassar Coll., 1940-41; B.A., Barnard Coll., 1945; M.D., Columbia, 1950; Th.M., Weston Coll. Sch. Theology, Cambridge, 1974; m. Francis C. Edmonds, Jr., Aug. 11, 1941 (div. July 1947); children—Francis C. III, Ruth T.; m. 2d, William F. Beuscher, Apr. 6, 1950 (div. June 1968); children—Robert Conrad, William David, Christopher Grey, Thomas Frederick, John Franklin. Intern, Monmouth Meml. Hosp., Long Branch, N.J., 1950-51; resident McLean Hosp., Waverly, Mass., 1953-55; USPHS fellow in psychiatry Mass. Gen. Hosp., Boston, 1955-56; practice medicine, specializing in psychiatry, 1955—; mem. staff McLean Hosp., 1958-79; courtesy staff Sibley Meml. Hosp., Washington, 1978—; asst. in psychiatry Harvard, 1959-79; dir. clin. psychiatry Children's Unit Met. State Hosp., Waltham, Mass., 1956-58; staff psychiatrist Mass. Mental Health Center, Boston, 1958-59. Lectr., supr. Weston Coll. Sch. Theology, Cambridge, Mass., 1971-78, vis. lectr. pastoral theology, 1975-76; adj. prof. pastoral theology Va. Theol. Sem., Alexandria, 1978—; lectr., workshops, radio and TV appearances on psychiatry and religion, sexuality, prayer and spirituality, occult movement, 1969—; participant Conf. on Catholics and divorce Paulist Center, Boston, 1972; mem. planning com., speaker Symposium for Laity and Clery on women and priesthood, 1973; del. Anglican-Roman Catholic Commn., spl. cons. on women and priesthood, 1975; mem. joint commn. in health and human affairs Gen. Conv., Episcopal Ch., 1977—; mem. Commn. on Women and ministry Episcopal Diocese of Mass., 1977-78; bd. dirs. Anchor Soc., 1975-78, Found. for Edn. in Human Relations. Nat. Exec. Council of the Episcopal Ch. grantee. Diplomate Am. Bd. Psychiatry and Neurology. Fellow Am. Psychiat. Assn.; mem. AAAS, Washington Psychiat. Soc., Med. Soc. of D.C., Mass. Psychiat. Soc., Am. Med. Women's Assn., Episcopalian. Bd. dirs. Anglican Theol. Rev., 1975—. Author: Homosexuality: A Symbolic Confusion, 1977. Editor: (with Urban T. Holmes) Male and Female: Christian Approaches to Sexuality, 1976. Contbr. articles to profl. publs. Home: 2311 Connecticut Ave NW Apt 402 Washington DC 20008

BARNUM, WILLIAM MILO, architect; b. N.Y.C., June 17, 1927; s. Phelps and Catharine (Davis) B.; student Phillips Andover Acad., 1942-45; B.A., Yale, 1950; M.Arch., U. Pa., 1952; m. Katharine Miller, Aug. 10, 1971; children—Anne Lyttleton, Catharine Hollerith, William Milo, Nathaniel Phelps, Caleb Townsend. Archtl. asst. job capt. Eggers & Higgins, 1952-54; job capt. W. Stuart Thompson & Phelps Barnum, architects, 1954-58, jr. partner, 1958-60; sr. partner Phelps Barnum & Son, N.Y.C., 1960-68; prin. William Milo Barnum Assos., N.Y.C., 1968—. Chmn. Archtl. Rev. Bd., Greenwich. Mem. selectmen's com. High Sch. Property, Greenwich, Conn., 1964—; bd. dirs. Community Chest, Greenwich, 1964—. Mem. alumni council Phillips Acad., Andover, Mass., 1965—; v.p. bd. trustees Putnam Indian Field Sch. Served with USNR, 1945-46. Mem. Concrete Industry Bd. (dir.), A.I.A. (N.Y. chpt. office practices com.), Met. Builders Assn., (liaison com.), Andover Alumni Assn. N.Y.C. (pres. 1964-65). Clubs: Yale (council 1958—, pres. 1970—) (N.Y.C.); Field (gov. 1965—) (Greenwich, Conn.). Prin. works include Westminster Sch. Chapel, 1961, Westminster Sch. Acad. Center, 1964, Howmet Office Bldg., Greenwich, Conn., Mfrs. Hanover Bank, Bklyn., Pickwick Plaza, Greenwich, R.T. Vanderbilt Corp. Hdqrs., Norwalk, Conn., Union Trust Sq., Greenwich, Gen. Host Corp. Hdqrs., Stamford, Conn., Gateway Center, Greenwich. Office: 255 Glenville Rd Greenwich CT 06830

BARON, CHARLES JESSE, govt. ofcl.; b. Winston Salem, May 20, 1936; s. Walter Theodore and Vinnie (Eggleton) B.; B.S., N.C. Central U., 1958, M.S., 1965; J.D., Howard U., 1968; m. Martha Louise Carter, Nov. 25, 1967; children—Adrian Renee, Cristal Jacque, Charles Jesse. Tchr., D.C. Govt., Washington, 1961-70; exec. dir. Greater Omaha Community Action Agy., 1970-71; dep. regional dir. of Action for Region IV, Atlanta, 1972-73; dep. asst. dir. for adminstrn. Dept. Human Resources, Washington, 1973-74; spl. asst. to the dir. and chief, Office Jud. Affairs, Washington, 1975—; admitted to D.C. bar, 1971; lectr. Elizabeth City State U., 1969. Active Met. Dems. Assn., Washington, 1975-76, Citizens United for Progress, Washington, 1976—. Served with U.S. Army, 1958-61. Named Outstanding Sr. of Month, N.C. Central U., 1958; Named Outstanding Alumnus, Howard U., 1972; Outstanding Leadership award, 1971, Omaha C. of C. Hon. Citizen of Omaha award, 1971. Mem. Am., Nat., D.C., Nebr. bar assns., So. Poverty Law Center, Am. Pub. Welfare Assn., Am. Assn. Pub. Welfare Attys. (regional chmn. 1976—), Screen Actors Guild, AFTRA, Phi Alpha Delta. Home: 1328 Juniper St NW Washington DC 20012 Office: Dept Human Resources 1350 E St NW Washington DC 20004

BARON, COLIN SAMUEL, counselor, ednl. adminstr.; b. Hamburg, Germany, May 16, 1918; s. Karl Friedrich and Gertrud Bertha (Cohen) Kunreuther; came to U.S., 1947, naturalized, 1952; B.Sc., N.Y. U., 1951, M.A., 1952; tchr. certificate Hebrew Union Coll., 1955, prin. certificate, 1967; m. Mila Freudman, June 30, 1950; children—Freda Baron Friedman, David, Jeffrey. With Shell-Mex and B.P. Ltd., London, 1936-47; elementary sch. tchr. various pub., pvt. schs., N.Y., 1952-59; guidance counselor pub. schs., Yonkers, N.Y., 1959-65; dean students Scarsdale (N.Y.) High Sch., 1965—. Prin. Sinai Temple Religious Sch., Mt. Vernon, N.Y., 1967-69. Served with Brit. Army, 1940-46. Mem. Am., N.Y. State, Westchester, Rockland, Putnam personnel and guidance assns., Scarsdale Tchrs. Assn. (exec. bd.). Democrat. Home: 77 Darling Ave New Rochelle NY 10804 Office: Scarsdale High Sch Post Rd Scarsdale NY 10583

BARON, HAROLD, educator, poet; b. Bklyn., Aug. 25, 1932; s. David and Jean (Berner) B.; B.A., Bklyn. Coll., 1954; M.A., N.Y.U., 1955; M.S., Hofstra Coll., 1961; Ph.D., N.Y.U., 1970; m. Sondra Joy Winthrop, Sept. 26, 1954; children—Pamela Jean, Ellen Cecile. Tchr. dept. English, Sr. High Sch., East Islip (N.Y.) Sch. Dist., 1959—; adj. asst. prof. English, Suffolk Community Coll., 1965-71; adj. asso. prof. English, Dowling Coll., Oakdale, N.Y., 1967—; lectr. East Islip Pub. Library; lectr. Celtic witchcraft, Tarot, Kabbalistic magic; cons. drug program Suffolk Med. Assn. Served with AUS, 1955-58. Recipient certificate of merit East Islip Sch. Dist., 1963; Founders Day award N.Y.U., 1971. Mem. AAUP, Dowling Coll. Adj. Faculty Assn. (pres. 1972—), N.Y. State United Tchrs., Nat. Council Tchrs. English. Home: 91 Fawn Dr East Islip NY 11730 Office: Dowling Coll Oakdale NY 11769

BARON, ROBERT ALEX, theatrical mgr., noise abatement advocate, writer; b. Chgo., Sept. 2, 1920; s. Morris and Emma (Bagus) B.; B.S. cum laude, U. Ill., 1943; M.A., Smith Coll., 1949; m. Joan DeKeyser, Dec. 19, 1956 (div. 1976); 1 dau., Stacey. Pub. health officer State of Ill., 1942-43; bus. mgr. theatre dept. Smith Coll., 1947-49; press agt. Off-Broadway play Right You Are, 1950; asst. Broadway press agt. Arena Theatre, 1950; mem. staff Anta play series, 1950; pub. relations staff Locust Valley Music Festival, 1950; asst. stage mgr., actor Arms & The Man, Arena Theatre, 1950-51; production asst. Razzle Dazzle, Arena Theatre, 1951; unit stage mgr. Anta album, 1951; dir. TV script dept. Frieda Fishbein, 1952; treas. Westport (Conn.) Country Playhouse, 1955; statis. research and presentation staff Report to the Legitimate Theatre Industry, 1952-55; asst. stage mgr., understudy Broadway play Hook N Ladder, 1952; dir. Equity summer stock Pine Bush, N.Y., 1952; advance dir. Evelyn Keyes package I Am a Camera, 1953; resident dir., production stage mgr. Norwich (Conn.) Summer Theatre, 1973; gen. mgr. Theater Tours, 1956-75, Broadway play Love Me Little, 1958, A Mighty Man is He, 1958, At the Drop of a Hat, 1959, Actor's Studio production Strange Interlude, 1963; v.p., sec. Interscope, Inc., 1957; co. mgr. Broadway plays The First Gentleman, 1957, The Man in the Dog Suit, 1958, pre-Broadway tryout Listen to the Mocking Bird, 1958-59, Broadway and nat. tour An Evening With Yves Montand, 1961-62, Laurence Olivier's Becket, 1960-61; Broadway plays Seidman and Son, 1962, Bicycle Ride to Nevada, 1963, The Deputy, 1964, Summer of the 17th Doll, 1958; theatre mgr. Shubert Theatre, Cin., 1965, George Abbott Theatre, N.Y.C., 1966, Blackstone Theatre, Chgo., 1974. Mem. theatre adv. com. Smith Coll., 1946—; mem. tech. adv. bd., noise abatement panel U.S. Dept. Commerce; founder, Citizens for a Quieter City, Inc., 1966, exec. v.p., 1966—. Served with AUS, 1944-46. Recipient Eleanor Roosevelt Humanitarian award N.Y. League for Hard of Hearing, 1970; Ford Found. grantee, 1970-72. Mem. AFTRA, Acoustical Soc. Am. Club: Smith Coll. (N.Y.C.). Author: The Tyranny of Noise, 1970; speaker confs. and symposia on noise. Address: 110 West End Ave 17D New York City NY 10023

BARON, SYDNEY STUART, pub. relations and mgmt. cons. co. exec.; b. N.Y.C., May 30, 1920; s. Hyman C. and Anne (Stuart) B.; B.S., St. John's U., 1942; m. Sylvia Schreibman, Oct. 23, 1938; children—Barbara Joyce Baron Balsam, Eric, Richard, Daniel Henry. Practice as publicist, 1940-50; chmn. bd. Sydney S. Baron and Co., N.Y.C., 1952—; dir. Shopwell, Inc.; pub. relations, mgmt. cons. to Aluminum Co. Am., Am. Can Co., Am. Ship Bldg. Co., Atlantic Cement Co., Inc., Panax Corp., Japan Bearing Indsl. Assn., Columbia U., Commodity Exchange, Inc., Electronic Industries Assn. Japan, Reliance Ins. Group, Republic of China (Taiwan), Republic of South Africa, others; instr. polit. sci. N.Y. U., 1954-58; dep. commr. N.Y.C. Dept. Marine and Aviation, 1950; dep. commr., dir. promotion N.Y.C. Dept. Commerce, 1951. Bd. dirs. Nat. Assn. Retarded Children, N.Y.C. Big Bros. Movement; chmn. bd. dirs. Beth Jacob Schs., N.Y.C., 1956—; trustee Maimonides Hosp., N.Y.C. Recipient Civic Merit award N.Y.C., 1951; certificate commendation Jewish War Vets. U.S.A., 1960. Mem. AIM (pres.'s council), Pub. Relations Soc. Am., U.S. C. of C., Am. Mgmt. Assn., Soc. of Silurians. Democrat. Clubs: Atrium, Masons, Board Room, Lone Star Boat Friars (N.Y.C.); Fenway Golf (White Plains, N.Y.). Author: One Whirl, 1942; Men Without Humor, 1944; The Bells Ring Loudly, 1946. Contbr. numerous articles to popular mags. Producer Broadway stage shows including Tambourines to Glory. Home: Scarsdale NY 10583 Office: 540 Madison Ave New York City NY 10022

BARONE, ROSE MARIE PACE (MRS. JOHN A. BARONE), educator, clubwoman; b. Buffalo, Apr. 26, 1920; d. Dominic and Jennie (Zagara) Pace; B.A., U. Buffalo, 1943; M.S., U. So. Cal., 1950; certificate of advanced study Fairfield U., 1963; m. John A. Barone, Aug. 23, 1947. Mem. faculty Angola High Sch., 1943-46, Puente High, 1946-47, Jefferson High, 1947-50; dir. Warren Inst., 1951-53; instr. U. Bridgeport (Conn.), 1953-54; tchr., counselor Bassick High Sch., Bridgeport, 1954-74, Harding High Sch., Bridgeport, 1974—. Instr. certified profl. secs. course Fairfield U., 1969, 70. Pres. Conn. UN Assn. of U.S.A., 1970—, chmn. area UN day 1960—, pres. UN Assn. Bridgeport, 1968-70; state chmn. UNICEF, 1970—; historian Pen Woman of Bridgeport Area, 1966—, recipient nat. historian award, 1976. Recipient Playwriting prize Conn. Fedn. Women's Clubs, 1955; Auerbach Found. Scholarship, 1956. Mem. NEA, Conn., Bridgeport (rec. sec. 1966) edn. assns., AAUW, United Bus. Edn. Assn., Eastern, Conn. (area research chmn.) bus. educators assns., League Women Voters, Fairfield Philatelic Soc. (sec.), Fairfield Philatelic Jrs. (founder), Internat. Platform Assn., Pi Omega Pi. Clubs: Southport Woman's, Fairfield University Women (founder, 1st pres. and v.p. 1973-74, pres. 1974—). Author play, articles. Co-editor handbook, 1966. Home: 1283 Round Hill Rd Fairfield CT 06430

BAROODY, WILLIAM JOSEPH, research orgn. exec.; b. Manchester, N.H., Jan. 29, 1916; s. Joseph A. and Helen (Hasney) B.; B.A., St. Anselm's Coll., Manchester, 1936, LL.D. (hon.), 1965; postgrad. U. N.H., 1937-38, Am. U., 1938; m. Nabeeha Marion Ashooh, Oct. 15, 1935; children—Anne Mary Baroody Gallagher, William Joseph, Joseph D., Helene Baroody Payne, Michael E., Maryfran Baroody Cummiskey, Katherine Jane. Asst. statistician N.H. Unemployment Compensation Div., 1937-40, supr. fiscal, research and legis. planning sects., 1941-44; dir. statis. div. N.H. War Fin. Com., 1943-44; research asso. N.H. Legis. Commn. on Disability Benefits, 1940-44; chief research and statis. div., readjustment allowance service VA, Washington, 1946-49; exec. sec. Com. on Econ. Security, U.S. C. of C., asso. editor Am. Econ. Security, 1950-53; exec. v.p. Am. Enterprise Assn. (now Am. Enterprise Inst. for Pub. Policy Research), Washington, 1954-62, pres., 1962-78, counsellor, chmn. devel. com., 1978—. Former mem. Am. Revolution Bicentennial Adv. Council; chmn. bd. Woodrow Wilson Internat. Center for Scholars; mem. adv. com. for social devel. and world peace U.S. Cath. Conf.; mem. adv. council Va. Poly. Inst. and State U., Blacksburg; mem. bd. advisors DeSales Grad. Sch. Theology; mem.

bd. consultants Nat. War Coll., 1973-75; mem. exec. com. Georgetown Center for Strategic and Internat. Studies; mem. bd. overseers Hoover Instn., Stanford; trustee St. Mary's Sem. and U., Balt., 1973—; bd. dirs. Herbert Hoover Birthplace Found., Near East Found., Georgetown U.; trustee Lehrman Inst., St. Anselm's Coll.; treas., trustee Inst. for Social Sci. Research. Served to lt. (j.g.) USNR, 1944-45. Mem. Acad. Polit. Sci., John Carroll Soc., Newcomen Soc. Clubs: Belle Haven Country (Alexandria); Carlton, F Street, Army-Navy (Washington); K.C. Home: 1111 Francis Hammond Pkwy Alexandria VA 22302 Office: 1150 17th St NW Washington DC 20036

BAROWSKY, HARRY, physician; b. Kiev, Russia, Apr. 15, 1906; came to U.S., 1911, naturalized, 1917; s. Samuel and Rachel (Schleffar) B.; B.S., Coll. City N.Y., 1927; M.D., N.Y. Med. Coll., 1931; m. Dorothy Riesenberg, Jan. 17, 1935. Intern, Beth David Hosp., N.Y.C., 1931-32; resident Flower Hosp., N.Y.C., 1932-33; pvt. practice medicine specializing in gastroenterology, N.Y.C., 1933—; mem. staff Flower and Fifth Av., Met., Bird S. Coler hosps., N.Y.C.; dir. Sarah C. Upham Gastrointestinal Clinic, N.Y.C., 1968-74; instr. dept. medicine N.Y. Med. Coll., 1933-40, asst. prof., 1940-52, asso. prof., 1952—. Pres. 83d St. Tenants Inc. Fellow Am. Coll. Gastroenterology (Outstanding Service plaque 1972, trustee 1957-72, sec. 1963-67, v.p. 1968-69), N.Y. Acad. Gastroenterology (pres. 1954-56), Am. Soc. Gastrointestinal Endoscopy; mem. A.M.A., N.Y. County, N.Y. State med. socs., N.Y. Med. Coll. Alumni Assn. (bd. govs.). Contbr. numerous articles to profl. jours. Address: 8 E 83d St New York City NY 10028

BARQUIST, WALTER ERIC, physician; b. Newton, Iowa, Mar. 23, 1943; s. Richard Fenn and Rose Fay (Scott) B.; B.S., George Washington U., 1964; M.D. N.Y. U., 1969. Intern, St. Elizabeth's Hosp., Washington, 1969-70, resident, 1972-74, staff psychiatrist, 1974—, dir. Nichols-Haydon Outpatient dept., 1977—; pvt. practice medicine specializing in psychiatry, Washington, 1973—. Served with USPHS, 1970-72. Mem. Am. Psychiat. Assn., Washington Psychiat. Soc., AMA, D.C., St. Elizabeth's med. Socs., St. Elizabeth's Assn. Psychiatrists (pres. 1977-78). Home: 11457 Waterview Cluster Reston VA 22090 Office: 3000 Connecticut Ave NW Washington DC 20008

BARR, CHARLES B., assn. exec.; b. Bryn Mawr, Pa., Aug. 10, 1908; s. Charles Hagan and Sarah (Ricketson) B.; grad. pub. high sch.; m. Myrtle Kennedy, Feb. 5, 1941; children—William Kennedy, Dorothy (Mrs. David J. Peckham), Nicholas Easton. Prin. firm Charles Barr & Assos., West Haven, Conn., 1932—; sec. Conn. Bakers Assn., Inc., Milford, Conn., 1937-65; exec. v.p. Conn. Florists Assn., Inc., West Haven, 1938—; sec. treas. Allied Florists Assn. Central Conn., Inc., 1950—. Owner West Haven Letter Shop, 1945—. Exec. sec. Conn. Tree Protective Assn., Inc., 1970—, Conn. Recreation and Park Assn., 1972-74; pres. Conn. Agrl. Info. Council, 1969-71; mem. Conn. Vo-Ag Adv. Com.; sec. Conn. food adv. com. to U.S. Dept. Agr., 1942-43; treas. Conn. Nutrition Council, 1950-54. Served with AUS, 1943-45. Recipient Man Year award Conn. Bakers Assn., 1956; Service award Conn. Florists Assn., 1966; Merit award Conn. Nurserymen's Assn. Inc., 1971; named Hon. State Farmer, Conn. chpt. Future Farmers Am., 1966. Mem. Am. Soc. Assn. Execs., Am., New Eng. socs. assn. execs., Nursery Assn. Execs. U.S. (sec.-treas. 1960-74), Floral Assn. Council (nat. chmn. 1956-58), Soc. Am. Florists, Am. Acad. Florists, Conn. (exec. sec. 1960-77), New Eng. (exec. sec. 1965-77) nurserymen's assns., Conn. Bus. and Industry Assn., West Haven C. of C. (pres. 1965), West Haven Hist. Soc. (pres. 1963-65). Mason, Rotarian (pres. West Haven club 1947-48). Home: 135 Center St West Haven CT 06516 Office: 421 Campbell Ave West Haven CT 06516

BARR, HUGH THOMPSON, telephone co. exec.; b. Pitts., Oct. 20, 1939; s. Russell Alexander and Finis (Durkee) B.; B.A., Am. U., 1961. Mem. staff Congressman William G. Bray, Washington, 1959-61, Senator John Tower, Washington, 1961-62; sr. underwriter Aetna Life & Casualty Co., Hartford, Conn., 1965-68; with So. New Eng. Telephone, W. Hartford, Conn., 1968—, staff mgr. Revenue Requirements Dept., 1978—. Mem. Conn. Gov.'s Vacation-Travel Council, 1977-78; co-chmn. Sammy Davis Jr. Greater Hartford Open, 1970-71; pres. Greater Hartford Jaycees, 1974-75; trustee Hartford Easter Seal Rehab. Center, 1975-77. Served with USN, 1962-64. Republican. Methodist. Home: 964 N Main St West Hartford CT 06117 Office: 227 Church St Room 410 New Haven CT 06506

BARR, JOHN WILMER BROWNING, med. council exec.; b. Lanark, Ont., Can., Dec. 7, 1916; s. James and Mary Allan (Browning) B.; M.D., C.M., Queen's U., Ont., 1940; Diploma in Hosp. Adminstrn., U. Toronto (Ont.), 1959; m. Marion Sarah Crawford, May 10, 1945. Enlisted Canadian Army, 1940, commd. lt., 1940, advanced through grades to maj.-gen., 1970; stationed overseas, 1941-46, dep. command med. officer, Winnipeg, Man., 1947-50, comdg. officer Royal Canadian Army Med. Sch., Borden, Ont., 1950-52; sr. Canadian med. officer, Europe, 1953-54; asst. dir. med. services, Ottawa, Ont., 1954-57; comdg. officer Canadian Forces Hosp., Kingston, Ont., 1958-61; dir. med. personnel Canadian Forces Med. Services, Ottawa, 1961-64; dep. surgeon gen., Ottawa, 1966-70, surgeon gen., 1970-73; ret., 1973; registrar Med. Council Can., Ottawa, Ont., 1973—; chief med officer Priory of St. John in Can., Ottawa, 1977—; col. comdt. med. br. Canadian Forces, 1976. Dir. Ottawa br. Canadian Cancer Soc., 1973-76. Decorated comdr. Order of Mil. Merit, 1973; knight of grace Order St. John Jerusalem, 1978; named Queen's hon. physician, 1966-73, 77—; recipient Robert Wood Johnson award, Johnson & Johnson Ltd. Can., 1959. Mem. Canadian, Ont. med. assns., Defence Med. Assn. Can., Canadian Coll. Health Service Execs., Inst. Assn. Execs., United Services Inst. Mem. United Ch. Can. Club: Mason. Home: 429 Huron Ave Ottawa ON K1Y 0X3 Canada Office: 1867 Alta Vista Dr Ottawa ON K1G 3H7 Canada

BARR, JOSEPH DANIEL, JR., metall. engr.; b. Phila., Feb. 26, 1944; s. Joseph Daniel and Gertrude Angela (Quaid) B.; B.S., Drexel U., 1972; M.S., U. Conn., 1974; m. Ann Elizabeth Amon, Sept. 4, 1971; 1 son, Joseph Daniel III. With Ampco Metal Inc. (formerly Phila. Bronze & Brass Corp.), 1962-68; mgr. quality control, metallurgist Phila. Bronze Corp., 1968-72; engr. test devel. United Technologies Corp., East Hartford, Conn., 1972-74; chief metallurgist Jenkins Bros., Inc., Bridgeport, Conn., 1974—. Mem. Am. Foundrymen's Soc., Am. Soc. Metals, ASTM, Am. Soc. Quality Control, Corrosion Soc., Metall. Soc. Republican. Roman Catholic. Office: 510 Main St Bridgeport CT 06609

BARR, SOLOMON EFREM, allergist; b. Washington, Mar. 24, 1929; s. Barney and Jennie Florence (Brickman) B.; B.A. (Emma K. Carr scholar 1948-49; Maria M. Carter scholar), George Washington U., 1951, M.D., 1954; m. Rita Zeasla Cohan, June 20, 1954; children—Linda, Steven, Carol, Sharon. Intern, Phila. Gen. Hosp., 1954-55; resident D.C. Gen. Hosp., 1957-58, George Washington U., 1959-60; practice medicine specializing in allergies, Silver Spring, Md., 1960-78, Rockville, Md., 1978—; mem. staff Holy Cross Hosp., George Washington U., Suburban Hosp., Bethesda, Md., Washington Adventist Hosp., Takoma Park, Md.; asso. clin. prof. medicine George Washington U. Sch. Medicine. Served as capt. M.C., U.S. Army, 1955-57. Recipient Freshman award in chemistry Alpha Chi Sigma, 1948, award in Chemistry, Sigma Kappa, 1948, John Ordronaux award in medicine George Washington U., 1954; diplomate Am. Bd. Internal Medicine, Am. Bd. Allery and Immunology. Fellow Am. Acad. Allergy, A.C.P., Am. Coll. Allergists, Am. Assn. Certified Allergists; mem. Washington Allery Soc., Montgomery County, Md. State med. socs., AMA (Physician's Recognition award 1974-77, 77-80), Smith-Reed-Russell, William Beaumont, Jacobi Med. Soc. Washington, Phi Beta Kappa, Alpha Omega Alpha. Jewish. Club: Phi Delta Epsilon Grad. of Washington (pres. 1971-72). Contbr. articles to med. publs., the most recent being mainly on insect sting allery. Home: 6613 Kenhill Rd Bethesda MD 20034 Office: 4701 Randolph Rd Rockville MD 20852

BARRACK, WILLIAM SAMPLE, JR., fuel co. exec.; b. Pitts., July 26, 1929; s. William Sample and Edna Mae (Henderson) B.; B.S. in Engring., U. Pitts., 1950; m. Evelyn Irene Ball, Sept. 12, 1953; children—William Peter, Elizabeth Irene. With Texaco, Inc., 1953—, mgr. distbn. devel. Texaco Services Ltd., Brussels, Belgium, 1967, area dir., 1968-70, v.p., 1969—, gen. mgr., 1970-71, v.p. internat. sales Europe Texaco, Inc., N.Y.C., 1971—, v.p. producing Eastern Hemisphere Texaco, Inc., 1976—, v.p personnel and corporate services, 1977—; dir. Texaco Can. Ltd., Toronto, Deusche Texaco A.G., W.Ger. Served with USNR, 1950-53; now comdr., Res. Club: Cloud (N.Y.C.); Woodway Country, Ox Ridge Hunt (Darien, Conn.); Ida Lewis Yacht (Newport, R.I.). Office: 2000 Westchester Ave White Plains NY 10604

BARRESI, CHARLES ANTHONY, architect; b. N.Y.C., July 3, 1940; s. Philip Charles and Grace (Buchetta) B.; Asso. in Applied Scis., Pratt Inst., 1963; m. Jean Daddino, Nov. 11, 1961; children—Philip, Charles. Draftsman, Abraham Grossman, Architect, N.Y.C., 1958-63, Harrison & Abramovitz, Architects, N.Y.C., 1963-65; project capt. Max O. Urbahn & Assos., Architects, N.Y.C., 1965-67; project mgr. John Carl Warnecke & Assos., Architects, N.Y.C., 1967-70; asso. Kennerly, Slomanson & Smith, Architects, N.Y.C., 1970—; archtl. cons. various interior design groups. Active Clarke St. Civic Assn., S.I., S.I. Hist. Soc. Mem. AIA, N.Y. State Soc. Architects. Home: 207 Park St Staten Island NY 10306

BARRETO, ERNESTO, physicist; b. Bogota, Colombia, Nov. 9, 1934; s. Ernesto and Evangelina (Gomez) B.; came to U.S., 1952, naturalized, 1965; B.A., N.Y.U., 1958, M.S., 1960; m. Lucia Paramo, June 11, 1960; children—Gilberto, Ernest. Research asso. N.Y.U.-Bellevue Med. Center, N.Y.C., 1959-60; sci. dir. Marks Polarized Corp., Whitestone, N.Y., 1960-64; project engr. Curtiss-Wright Corp., Woodridge, N.J., 1964-69; sr. research asso. Atomspheric Scis. Research Center, State U.N.Y. at Albany, 1969—. Cons. Am. Petroleum Inst., Mobil Research Corp., Nat. Acad. Scis., USCG. Office of Naval Research grantee, 1965——; Am. Petroleum Isnt. grantee, 1971-74. Mem. Am. Phys. Soc., Am. Geophys. Union, Am. Inst. Aeros. and Astronautics. Contbr. articles to profl. jours. Home: 1123 Rosehill Blvd Scotia NY 12309 Office: 1400 Washington Ave Albany NY 12222

BARRETT, HERBERT, artists mgmt. assn. exec.; b. N.Y.C., May 31, 1910; s. John and Mollie (Pike) B.; B.A., Cornell U., 1930; m. Betty Palash, May 29, 1937; children—Nancy, Katherine. Pub. relations council Cadillac Car Co., N.Y.C., 1934—, Gen. Motors, N.Y.C., 1935—; mgr., pres. Herbert Barrett Mgmt., artists mgmt. assn., N.Y.C., 1940—. Mem. adv. com. Town Hall, N.Y.C., 1970—; mem. recommendation bd. Avery Fisher Artist Program, Lincoln Center Performing Arts, presenter Great Performers series, 1965-66; mem. adv. bd. Van Cliburn Internat. Piano Competition. Mem. Little Orch. Soc. (treas. 1970—, mgr. 1967—), Internat. Assn. Festival and Concert Mgrs. (exec. bd. 1969—), Phi Beta Kappa. Home: 15 W 72nd St New York City NY 10023 Office: 1860 Broadway New York City NY 10023

BARRETT, MONTGOMERY BRINTON, librarian; b. Phila., Aug. 16, 1913; s. Charles Smith and Mae Cecillia (Barry) B.; grad. William Penn Charter Sch., 1931; A.B., U. Pa., 1935, M.S., 1940; Diplôme, Ecole Universitaire de Hautes Etudes Internationales, Geneva, Switzerland, 1935-37; B.S. in L.S., Drexel Inst. Tech., 1940. Asst. librarian Cooper Union for Advancement Sci. and Art, 1940-43, Lawrenceville (N.J.) Sch., 1943-48; librarian Bloomfield (N.J.) Coll. and Sem., 1948-51; chief reference librarian USIS, Paris, France, 1951-54; mgr. New Yorker Bookshop, 1955-57; library asst., dep. dir. Smithtown (N.Y.) Library, 1957-75, dir., 1975—. Mem. Civil Service Employees Assn. (pres. Smithtown unit 1969-70, mem. scholarship com.), N.Y. Suffolk County library assns. Mem. Soc. of Friends. Editor Sch. Library Jour., 1946-49. Home: 7 Fordham Dr Smithtown NY 11787 Office: 1 N Country Rd Smithtown NY 11787

BARRETT, TONI, interior designer; b. Paterson, N.J.; s. Joseph and Bertha (Berger) B.; student N.Y. Sch. Interior Design, 1950, Pratt Inst.; 1 son, William G. Fashion designer, N.Y.C., 1933-43; instr. painting, N.Y.C., 1947-50; interior designer, partner design firm, N.Y.C., 1950-52; pvt. practice residential and indsl. design, N.Y.C., 1952-78, E. Hampton, N.Y., 1978—; painter; lectr. on design. Mem. Am. Soc. Interior Designers (profl.). Designer, supr. residential, indsl. constrn., N.Y., Conn., N.J., Mass., Fla., R.I.; designer lighting and space plans, furniture. Office: 24 Lilla Ln East Hampton NY 11937

BARRETT, WALTER HARMON, mfg. co. exec.; b. Providence, May 17, 1933; s. Walter Harold and Annie Ellen Barrett; grad. USAF Aircraft Technician Sch., 1953, USAF Sr. Aircraft Technician Sch., 1955, USAF T-29 Engring. Sch., 1956; m. Nancy Murphy, Jan. 24, 1953; children—Walter Alan, David Lawrence, Steven Daniel, Nancy Louise, John Scott. Process engr. Mackenzie Walton Corp., Pawtucket, R.I., 1950-53, 57-60; owner Hi-View Farms Corp., Johnston, R.I., 1960-67; owner Barrett Automotive Engring. and Research Inc., Woonsocket, R.I., 1967-76; pres. Solar-Tech, Inc., Woonsocket, 1974-76; ops. mgr. Columbia Chase Solar Energy Div., Holbrook, Mass., 1976—; instr. Hall Inst. Bd. govs. Hall Inst.; capt. CAP, 1974-78. Served with USAF, 1953-57. Mem. Solar Energy Industries Assn., New Eng. Solar Energy Industries Assn., New Eng., R.I. solar energy assns., Solar Energy Inst. Am., N.E. Council Task Force for Solar Energy. Episcopalian. Inventor patented flat plate solar collector with fiberglass molded box; contbr. articles to profl. jours. Home: RD 1 Douglas Pike North Smithfield RI 02895 Office: 55 High St Holbrook MA 02343

BARRICK, ANN HENDERSON, ednl. adminstr.; b. Durham, N.C., Dec. 4, 1938; d. James J. and Julia (Hicks) H.; B.S., Hampton Inst., 1960; M.A., Temple U., 1966, postgrad., 1977—. Itinerant speech and lang. pathologist Sch. Dist. 4, Phila., 1960-72, program developer and mgr. program for pre-sch. communicatively impaired, 1972-75, supr. itinerant speech and lang., 1975-78, dir. fed. project presch. spl. edn., 1978—; clin. communication cons. St. Francis of Assisi Sch., 1965; lang. arts cons. Phila. Dept. Engring. Edn., 1969; Pa. Dept. Edn. fellow, 1971; speech and language pathologist; lang. arts cons.; guest lectr. Chestnut Hill Coll., West Chester Coll. Bd. dirs. Singing City. Mem. Am. (nat. com. on supervision, nat. com. urban and ethnic minorities, nat. task force), Pa. (com. on profl. standards and practices) speech and hearing assns., Nat. Assn. Edn. young Children, AAUW, Council on Exceptional Children, Urban League, NAACP, Delta Sigma Theta. Home: Mayfair House Lincoln Dr and Johnson St Philadelphia PA 19144 Office: Div Spl Edn Sch Dist Phila Philadelphia PA 19103

BARRIE, JOSEPH ROLLIN, surgeon; b. Bklyn., Aug. 22, 1935; s. David Joseph and Bertha (Rollin) B.; B.S., Yale, 1956; M.D., Harvard, 1960; m. Sylvia Jean Smith, Oct. 6, 1962; children—John Rollin, Susan Smith. Surg. intern Mass. Gen. Hosp., Boston, 1960-61, asst. resident in surgery, 1961-65; sr. surg. resident Meml. Sloan-Kettering Cancer Center, 1967-69; fellow in surgery Cornell U. Med. Coll., 1968-69; practice medicine specializing in surgery, Concord, Mass., 1969—; active staff Emerson Hosp., Concord, clin. asso. in surgery Mass. Gen. Hosp., 1969—; clin. instr. surgery Tufts U. Sch. Medicine, 1973—. Bd. dirs. Health Planning Council for Greater Boston, 1971-75. Served with USNR, 1965-67, Nat. Cancer Inst. and Am. Cancer Soc. fellow, 1967-69. Diplomate Am. Bd. Surgery. Mem. ACS, AMA, Mass. Med. Soc., Boston Surg. Soc., Soc. Surg. Oncology. Republican. Clubs: Harvard, Yale (Boston). Author publs. on cancer. Home: 116 Acton St Carlisle MA 01741 Office: John Cuming Bldg Concord MA 01742

BARRINGTON, THOMAS MARTIN, educator, former coll. pres.; b. N.Y., July 8, 1916; B.A., State U. N.Y., Albany, 1937, M.A., 1942; Ed.D., Columbia U., 1951; L.H.D., Clarkson Coll., Potsdam, N.Y., 1974; LL.D., St. Lawrence Coll., Canton, N.Y., 1977. Tchr., coach, prin. schs. in N.Y. State, 1937-47; dean students, then v.p. student affairs State Univ. Coll., Potsdam, 1947-69, pres., 1969-78, prof., 1950—; mem. Bd. Coop. Ednl. Services St. Lawrence County; trustee Asso. Colls. St. Lawrence Valley; vice chmn. trustees Wadhams Hall Coll.; cons. Mater Dei Coll., Ogdensburg, N.Y.; dir. St. Lawrence Nat. Bank; adv. bd. St. Lawrence County Nat. Bank. Adv. com. Catholic Charities Ogdensburg. Served to lt. USNR, 1942-46. Mem. Am., N.Y. State personnel and guidance assns., Am. Coll. Personnel Assn., Nat. Assn. Student Personnel Adminstrs., Nat. Orgn. Legal Problems in Edn., N.Y. State Sch. Bds. Assn., Am. Assn. U. Adminstrs. Contbr. profl. jours. Address: 3 Garden Dr Clifton Park NY 12065

BARRON, GLORIA JOAN, historian, educator; b. Bklyn., May 19, 1933; d. Maurice Lee and Irene Barron; A.B., Wellesley Coll., 1954; M.A., Columbia U., 1956, postgrad., 1958-59; postgrad. U. Chgo., 1964-65; Ph.D. (AAUW fellow), Tufts U., 1971. Registrar, tchr. history Newton Jr. Coll., Newtonville, Mass., 1956-58; tchr. history upper sch. Brimmer & May Sch., Chestnut Hill, Mass., 1959-63; chmn. history dept. Winthrop (Mass.) High Sch., 1963-64; edn. specialist HEW, Washington, 1965-66; asst. prof. history Framingham (Mass.) State Coll., 1970—. Mem. Am. Hist. Assn., Orgn. Am. Historians. Author: Leadership in Crisis: FDR and the Path to Intervention, 1973. Home: 50 Park St Brookline MA 02146 Office: Framingham State Coll May Hall Framingham MA 01701

BARRON, MABEL AMMONS, ret. hosp. adminstr.; b. Somerset, Pa., Dec. 28, 1906; d. Edward C. and Carrie M. (Berkey) Barron; R.N., Western Pa. Hosp. Sch. Nursing, Pitts., 1928; student Tchrs. Coll., Columbia U., Summers, 1931-35; B.S. with high honor, U. Pitts., 1943, M.A. in Sociology, 1944; D.H.L., Geneva Coll., 1962. Head nurse West Penn Hosp., Pitts., 1928-29, med. supr., 1930-31, instr., 1931-36, asst. prin., 1936-39; asst. adminstr., Elizabeth Steel Magee Hosp., Pitts., 1939-52, dir. nursing, 1940-52; asst. instr. U. Pitts. Sch. Nursing, 1940-43, instr., 1943-44, asst. prof., 1944-53, spl. lectr., 1954-63; adminstr. Ellwood City (Pa.) Hosps., 1952-73. Bd. dirs. Ellwood City council Girl Scouts U.S.A., 1953-68, Lawrence County Mental Health Clinic, 1960-73; v.p. Lawrence County Mental Health Assn., 1963-64; bd. dirs. Lawrence County Vis. Nurse Assn., 1967-73; mem. Lawrence County Mental Health-Mental Retardation Bd., 1968-69, Lawrence County Cancer Bd., 1969-73. Recipient Distinguished Service award, sr. citizen Jr. C. of C., Ellwood City, Pa., 1961; named Distinguished Dau. of Pa. Fellow Am. Coll. Hosp. Adminstrs., 1961; mem. Hosp. Assn. Pa. (past pres.; chmn. council hosp. auxs. 1962-63), Middle Atlantic Hosp. Assembly (1st v.p. 1961-62, pres. 1962-63, bd. govs.), Am., Pa. (past dist. pres.), Lawrence County nurses assns., Nat., Pa. (past pres.) leagues nursing edn., Am. (del. 1961-66), Northwest Regional hosp. assns., Pa. Assn. Hosp. Auxs. (counsellor 1967-74), Sigma Theta Tau. Presbyn. (trustee). Clubs: Zonta, Bus. and Profl. Women's. Home: 110 2d St Ellwood City PA 16117

BARRON, ROBERT PAUL, chemist; b. Dickson City, Pa., June 5, 1940; s. Walter and Mary (Bandurick) B.; A.A., Keystone Jr. Coll., 1960; B.S., U. Scranton, 1964; grad. certificate Am. U., 1974; m. Marilyn Elizabeth Connors, Nov. 28, 1970. Chemist, Berkeley chemistry dept. Millmaster Onyx Corp., Berkeley Heights, N.J., 1964-66; research chemist Bur. Foods, FDA, Washington, 1966-70, Bur. Drugs, Div. Drug Chemistry, 1973—; chemist Spl. Testing and Research Lab., Drug Enforcement Adminstrn., McLean, Va., 1970-73. Mem. Chem. Soc. Washington (treas. 1975, 76), Downtown Jaycees (Distinguished Service award 1972, sec. 1973), Am. Soc. Mass Spectrometry, Am. Chem. Soc. (mem. council, governing body 1977—), AAAS, Assn. Analytical Chemists, Sigma Xi. Roman Catholic. Clubs: Toastmasters, K.C. Contbr. articles to profl. jours. Home: 7358 Shenandoah Ave Annandale VA 22003 Office: 200 C St SW Washington DC 20204

BARROWS, TIMOTHY MANNING, aero. engr.; b. Rochester, N.Y., June 27, 1944; s. Walter Loring and Mary Rose (Reichard) B.; B.S. (scholar), Princeton U., 1966; Ph.D., Mass. Inst. Tech., 1970; m. Ruth Louise Helfrich, Apr. 20, 1972; 1 dau., Miranda. With U.S. Dept. Transp., Washington, 1970; engr. Transp. Systems Center, Dept. Transp., Cambridge, Mass., 1970—. Recipient (with others) Wake Vortex Hazard Evaluation Team Group Achievement award, 1975; NSF traineeship, 1966-68. Mem. Am. Inst. Aeros. and Astronautics, Phi Beta Kappa. Contbr. articles on subject wings in ground effect to profl. jours. Home: 51 Otis St Newton MA 02160 Office: Transp Systems Center Dept Transp Kendall Sq Cambridge MA 02142

BARRY, ALLEN IVES, pollution control mfg. co. exec.; b. Bklyn., July 18, 1915; s. George Stone and Florence Peck (Allen) B.; B.Ch.E., Rensselaer Poly. Inst., 1938; m. Nancy Collins, Feb. 22, 1940 (div. Oct. 1966); children—Barbara (Mrs. Harry Brawley III), David (dec.); m. 2d, Alison King, Apr. 14, 1967; children—Bruce, Kristin. Plant supr. Monsanto Chem. Co., Springfield, Mass., and Marshall, Tex., 1938-44, Charles Pfizer Co., Bklyn., 1944-48; plant mgr. Argenta Products Co., Eastport, Maine, 1948-50; project engr. F.S. Gibbs Co., Newton Lower Falls, Mass., 1950-54; sales engr. Badger Co., Cambridge, Mass., 1954-58; pres., mfrs. rep. Barry & Assos., Milton, Mass., 1958-73; pres. Barry & Assos., Inc., 1973—. Registered profl. engr., Mass. Mem. Am. Inst. Chem. Engrs. (chmn. N.E. sect., 1966), Water Pollution Control Fedn. Republican. Unitarian. Club: Appalachian Mountain. Contbr. to prof. jours. Home: 337 Adams St Milton MA 02186 Office: PO Box 117 Milton MA 02186

BARRY, DAVID MICHAEL, lawyer, state senator; b. Manchester, Conn., Nov. 7, 1930; s. John Francis and May (D'Arcy) B.; B.A., Trinity Coll., 1952, LL.B., Boston U., 1955; m. Judith Ann Leclerc, Sept. 12, 1959; children—Joan, David, Michael, Mark, Ryan, Bridget. Admitted to Conn. bar, 1955, Mass. bar, 1959; practiced in Manchester, 1958—; corp. counsel Town of Manchester, 1971-73,

77—; state rep. Conn. Gen. Assembly, Manchester, 1959-61; mem. Conn. Senate from 4th Senatorial Dist., 1966-71, 75—, counsel to Democratic majority, 1971. Vice chmn. Conn. Adv. Council on Aging, 1969-71. Chmn. Manchester Charter Revision Commn., 1960, mem. town bd. dirs., 1962-66, dep. mayor, 1964-66; mem. Manchester Democratic Town Com., 1960-78; pres. Young Dem. Club of Manchester, 1960. Served as spl. agt. CIC, AUS, 1955-57. Recipient Distinguished Service award Manchester Jr. C. of C., 1964. Mem. Am., Conn., Hartford County. Manchester bar assns., Manchester Area Mental Health Assn. (treas. 1961-62). Democrat. Roman Catholic. Home: 473 East Center St Manchester CT 06040 Office: 178 E Center St Manchester CT 06040

BARRY, FRANCIS EDWARD, gynecologist; b. Lynn, Mass., Aug. 5, 1922; s. Francis E. and Mary J. (O'Connor) B.; B.A., Holy Cross Coll., 1944; M.D., Tufts U., 1946; m. Ruth Helene Pineault, Feb. 15, 1947; children—Sheila Marie, John Francis, Kathleen Ann. Intern, Carney Hosp., Boston, 1946-47; resident in obstetrics and gynecology St. Francis Hosp., Wichita, Kans., 1949-52; individual practice medicine specializing in obstetrics and gynecology Lynn, Mass., 1955—; mem. staff Union Hosp., chief obstetrics, gynecology 1970-76; mem. staff Lynn Hosp. Trustee Union Hosp. Served with M.C., USAF, 1947-49, 52-55. Diplomate Am. Bd. Obstetrics and Gynecology. Mem. AMA, Mass. Med. Soc., Am. Coll. Obstetricians and Gynecologists, A.C.S., Am. Assn. Gynecologic Laparoscopists. Roman Catholic. Office: 480 Lynnfield St Lynn MA 01904

BARRY, JOHN PATRICK, occupational health engr.; b. Bangor, Maine, July 12, 1947; s. John Thomas and Patricia Josephine (Byrnes) B.; B.A. in Zoology, U. Maine, 1969; M.Sc. in Pub. Health, U. Mass., 1971; Sc.D. in Acoustics (Rotary Found. fellow 1972-73, USPHS fellow 1973-76), U. Pitts., 1976. USPHS trainee U. Mass., 1969-71; health engr. Southeastern region Mass. Dept. Pub. Health, 1971-72; research fellow in occupational hygiene U. Manchester (Eng.), 1972-73; research asst. dept. otolaryngology Eye and Ear Hosp., Pitts., 1974-76; specialist in noise control and hearing conservation Phila. regional office Dept. Labor Occupational Safety and Health Adminstrn., 1976—. Registered sanitarian, Mass.; certified occupational hygienist, U.K. Mem. Acoustical Soc. Am. (mem. faculty Delaware Valley chpt. noise control seminars), Am. Inst. Physics, Audio Engring. Soc., Am. Conf. Govtl. Indsl. Hygienists, Brit. Inst. Occupational Hygiene, Phila. Museum Art, Sigma Xi. Roman Catholic. Home: 2400 Chestnut St Apt 2108 Philadelphia PA 19103 Office: Dept Labor Occupational Safety and Health Adminstrn 3535 Market St Philadelphia PA 19104

BARRY, KEVIN GERARD, physician; b. Newton Center, Mass., May 12, 1923; s. Michael L. and Catherine (Coleman) B.; student The Citadel, 1943-44; grad. Johns Hopkins U., 1945; M.D., Georgetown U., 1949; m. Gisela Radek, Sept. 13, 1973. Joined U.S. Army, 1943, advanced through grades to lt. col., 1962; intern Walter Reed Army Hosp., 1949-50, resident internal medicine, 1953-56; fellow in hematology, 1956; bn. surgeon 418th Combat Engrs., Germany, 1950-51; med. officer 98th Gen. Hosp., Munich, Germany, 1951-52; bn. surgeon 43d Combat Engrs., Germany, 1952-53; chief of medicine U.S. Army Hosp., Ft. Jay, N.Y., 1956-58; research internist dept. metabolism Walter Reed Army Inst. Research, 1958-61; dir. div. medicine, chief dept. metabolism Walter Reed Army Inst. Metabolism, Walter Reed Army Inst. Research, chief enlisted male gen. medicine and metabolism sect. Walter Reed Gen. Hosp., 1965-66; dir. med. edn., chief renal and metabolic diseases Washington Hosp. Center, 1966-69; chief div. medicine Georgetown Service, D.C. Gen. Hosp., 1969-70; med. dir. Cafritz Hosp., Washington, 1970-76; pvt. practice nephrology, Gambrills, Md., 1976—. Mem. sci. adv. com. D.C. chpt. Nat. Kidney Found. Decorated Army Commendation medal, Legion of Merit. Fellow A.C.P., Am. Coll. Clin. Pharmacology and Chemotherapy; mem. AMA, Internat. Assn. Internal Medicine, Am. Fedn. Clin. Research, Am. Soc. Artificial Internal Organs, Am. Heart Assn. (council on circulation, program com. 3d Internat. Congress Nephrology 1966). Contbr. articles to profl. jours. Patentee on Barry Peritoneal Cannula. 1st physician to use mennitol for prevention renal failure. Home: 1295 Lavall Dr Gambrills MD 21054

BARRY, RONALD MAKEPEACE, child psychiatrist, educator; b. Melbourne, Australia, Apr. 26, 1926; s. Norman Makepeace and Mavis Pauline (Haliday) B.; came to U.S., 1967; M.B.B.S., Melbourne U., 1963; m. Gaye Rosemary Scott Rogers, Jan. 29, 1966; children—Teana Louise, Astra Maria, Dana Louis. Intern, Prince Henry's Hosp., Melbourne, 1964; resident in psychiatry Heidelberg Gen. Hosp., Victoria, Australia, 1965-66, resident in gen. psychiatry Rockingham Hosp., Victoria, 1966-67, resident in gen. psychiatry Inst. Psychiatry & Human Behaviour, U. Md., Balt., 1967-69, resident in child psychiatry, 1969-71; dir. psychiatric edn., tng. Regional Inst. Children & Adolescents, Balt., 1971-74; dir. inpatient service, med. dir. psychiat. day care service SW Balt. County Community Mental Health Program, 1974-76; dir. youth services Southeastern Balt. County Community Mental Health Centre, 1976-77, dir. centre, 1978—; clin. asst. prof. dept. child psychiatry U. Md., 1971—; instr. in pediatrics Johns Hopkins Hosp., Balt., 1973—; cons. OEO Day Care Program, 1968-72, Boys Home Soc., 1968—, adv. bd. Woodbourne Center, Inc., 1975—, bd. appeals for excess cost dept. edn. State of Md., 1974—. Licensed physician, Australia, Gt. Brit., Md.; diplomate Am. Bd. Psychiatry and Neurology (child psychiatry). Fellow Royal Soc. Health London; mem. Am. Acad. Child Psychiatry, Md. Regional Council Child Psychiatry (sec. 1978—). Home: 2552 Ridge Rd Baltimore MD 21207

BARSAM, PAUL CHARLES, ophthalmologist; b. Worcester, Mass., July 8, 1926; s. Charles and Novart (Keljikian) B.; B.S., Tufts U., 1948, M.A., 1949; M.D., U. Geneva, 1959; m. Joyce Lorna Shushan, Sept. 25, 1966; children—Julie R., Charles A., Ara P. Intern, Newton-Wellesley Hosp., 1960; resident in ophthalmology Univ. Hosp., Boston, 1961-62, Bronx (N.Y.) Eye and Ear Infirmary, 1962-64; asst. dir. div. chronic diseases Mass. Dept. Pub. Health, Boston, 1964-66; practice medicine, specializing in ophthalmology Arlington, Mass., 1967—; clin. instr. Boston U. Sch. Medicine, 1968—; cons. ophthalmology WHO, Geneva; cons. in field. Com. rep. Nat. Assn. Armenian Studies and Research, Harvard U., 1965—, rep. Armenian Assembly, Washington, 1973-75, chmn. bd. trustees Armenian Library and Mus. Am., 1975—; asso. dir. Friends Armenian Culture Soc.; trustee Holy Trinity Armenian Apostolic Ch. Served with USNR, 1944-46. Recipient Silver medal Am. Acad. Ophthalmology and Otolaryngology, 1971. Fellow A.C.S.; mem. Mass., Armenian-Am. (founding pres. 1972-75) med. assns., Mass. Soc. Eye Physicians and Surgeons, New Eng. Ophthal. Soc., Contact Lens Assn. of Ophthalmologists, Am. Intraocular Implant Soc., Council Armenian Execs., Sylvanus Packard Soc. Tufts U. Author: (with Frank Reynolds) Adult Health, 1967. Contbr. articles to med. jours. Home: 170 Rutledge Rd Belmont MA 02178 Office: 279 Massachusetts Ave Arlington MA 02174

BARSON, NORMAN, chem. engr.; b. Omaha, Jan. 17, 1926; s. Harry Leon and Rae (Shabashov) B.; student U. Omaha, 1946-48; B.A. in Chem. Engring., Iowa State U., 1950, M.S. in Chem. Engring., 1952, Ph.D., in Chem. Engring., 1954; m. Celia Ann Keller, Aug. 1, 1954. Engr., Esso Research & Engring. Co., Linden, N.J., Florham Park, N.J., 1954-65; sr. research engr., supr. Tech. Info. Center, Celanese Research Co., Summit, N.J., 1965—. Served with U.S. Army, 1944-46. Registered profl. engr., Iowa. Mem. Mfg. Chemists Assn. (Celanese rep. com. on info. retrieval). Home: 7 Ridge Ct East Brunswick NJ 08816 Office: 86 Morris Ave Summit NJ 07901

BART, LEONARD EUGENE, educator, psychologist; b. Bklyn., May 24, 1926; s. Irving and Pauline (Greenberg) B.; A.B., Washington U., St. Louis, 1949; M.S., St. John's U., 1968, Ph.D., 1971; m. Muriel Singer, Feb. 15, 1953; children—Andrew, Jonathan. Instr., Rockland Community Coll., Suffern, N.Y., 1968; counselor, Instr. Pace U., N.Y.C., 1969-71, asst. prof. psychology, 1971-77, asso. prof., 1977—, supr. interns Sch. Psychology, 1972—; pvt. practice, Bklyn., 1972—; sales mgr. Bart Novelty Co., Bklyn., 1949-64; pres. L.I. Discount Center, 1959-69, Queens Discount City, 1961-66. Served with AAF, 1944-46; PTO. Certified psychologist, N.Y. Mem. Am., N.Y. State psychol. assns., Nat. Assn. Sch. Psychologists, A.A.A.S., N.Y. Acad. Scis., Sigma Xi, Psi Chi. Home: 21-20 77th St Jackson Heights NY 11370 Office: 100 8th Ave Brooklyn NY 11215

BARTALOS, MIHALY, physician; b. Pozsony, Czechoslovakia, May 27, 1935; s. Mihaly and Roza (Knyazoviczky) B.; came to U.S., 1960, naturalized, 1965; student U. Budapest, 1953-56; M.D. cum laude, U. Heidleberg, 1960; m. Eva Paula Starhoczki, Oct. 19, 1957; children—Michael A., Gabriel Z., Gregory B. Intern Czerny Hosp., U. Heidelberg, 1960; resident in Internal medicine USPHS Hosp., Balt. 1968-70; fellow in pathology and medicine Johns Hopkins, 1961-64; practice medicine, specializing in med. genetics, Washington, 1965-68, N.Y.C., 1971—; chief med. genetics unit, research scholar, asst. clin. prof. pediatrics, dir. heredity clinic Howard U., Washington, 1965-68; asst. chief internal medicine in charge of primary care clinic USPHS Hosp., Balt., 1970; asst. prof. human genetics and devel., asst. prof. clin. pediatrics, cons. psychiatry Columbia, 1971—; co-dir. Birth Defects and Genetic Disease Center, St. Mary's Hosp., 1976—; cons. Harlem Hosp. Center, N.Y.C., 1976—. Bd. dirs. Am.-Hungarian Found., 1975-76. Served with USPHS, 1968-70. Mem. Am. Soc. Human Genetics, Semmelweis Sci. Soc. (pres. 1974-75), Internat. Platform Assn. Westchester County Med. Soc., Sigma Xi. Author: (with T.A. Baramki) Medical Cytogenetics, 1967; Genetics in Medical Practice, 1968. Office: 630 W 168th St New York City NY 10032

BARTBERGER, CHARLES LOUIS, underwater acoustics researcher; b. Pitts., Feb. 5, 1914; s. Edward William and Elsie Emma (Smith) B.; B.S., Allegheny Coll., 1935; A.M., Harvard, 1936; postgrad. Carnegie Inst. Tech., 1936-40; m. Helen Marie Tritinger, Sept. 4, 1940; children—Charles Edward, Carol Ann Bartberger Veil. Physicist Naval Aircraft Factory, Phila., 1941-52; physicist Naval Air Devel. Center, Warminster, Pa., 1952-66, research in underwater acoustics, 1967—. Mem. U.S. Navy Underwater Sound Adv. Group, 1962-63. Mem. Acoustical Soc. Am. Author: Lecture Notes on Underwater Acoustics, 1965. Home: 31 Bright Rd Hatboro PA 19040 Office: Naval Air Development Center Warminster PA 18974

BARTH, ERNEST, chem. co. exec.; b. Vienna, Austria, Feb. 17, 1926; s. Jacob and Regina (Hecht) B.; m. Rita Spiegel, Dec. 30, 1951; 1 dau., Karen Nina. Pres., Continental Fertilizer Corp. N.Y.C., also v.p. Continental Ore Corp., 1953-72; pres. Agrico Internat., Inc., Tulsa, also N.Y.C., 1972-73; pres. Beker Internat. Corp., Greenwich, Conn., also sr. v.p. Beker Industries, 1973-75, 77-78; v.p. Philipp Bros./Engelhard Minerals & Chem. Corp., N.Y.C., 1975-77; pres. Minex Corp., Greenwich, Conn., 1978—; dir. affiliated cos. Mem. Food for Peace Council, 1962; co-chmn. U.S. Indsl. Mission to Korea, 1962. Clubs: Burning Tree Country (Greenwich); Board Room (N.Y.C.); Landmark (Stamford, Conn.). Home: 25 Lindsay Dr Greenwich CT 06830 Office: 35 Mason St Greenwich CT 06830

BARTHOLD, JAMES CARL, newspaper editor; b. Phila., Apr. 17, 1950; s. Elmer Albert and Doris (Tilney) B.; B.S. in Journalism, Temple U., 1972; m. Rita A. Minard, Mar. 24, 1973. Reporter, photographer Wildwood (N.J.) Leader, 1972-74, editor, 1974-77; editor Cape May County Gazette, 1976-77, Gazette-Leader, N. Wildwood, N.J., 1977—. Recipient Spl. Humanitarian award Asso. Humane Socs., 1976; first prize N.J. Press Assn., 1976; various prizes for newspaper writing. Mem. N.J. Press Assn., Jaycees (sec. Greater Wildwood-So. Cape sect.). Lutheran. Clubs: Stone Harbor Golf. Home: Breakwater Rd RD 2 Cape May NJ 08204 Office: 1212 Atlantic Ave North Wildwood NJ 08260

BARTHOLOMEW, GEORGE ANDERSON, chem. engr.; b. Pitts., June 21, 1924; s. Tracy and Sarah Jane (Anderson) B.; A.B., Haverford Coll., 1946; B.S. in Chem. Engring., U. Pitts., 1947, M.S., 1948; m. Nancy Davis Large, July 26, 1947; children—Susan, Tracy II. Pilot plant coordinator Consolidation Coal Co., Library, Pa., 1948-50; research fellow Mellon Inst., Pitts., 1950-55; research sect. leader U.S. Steel Corp., Monroeville, Pa., 1955-57; tech. rep. raw materials. Pitts., 1957-68; v.p. research and devel. Burrell Constrn. Co., New Kensington, Pa., 1968—. Bd. dirs. Blackridge Civic Assn.; mem. Republican Exec. Com. 14th Ward Pitts.; elder Presbyteran Ch. Served with AUS, 1943-46. Decorated Purple Heart. Mem. Nat. Slag Assn. (past chmn. research), AAAS, Am. Inst. Chem. Engrs., Am. Ceramic Soc., N.Y. Acad. Scis., Pa. Asphalt Pavement Assn. (environ. com.), Pa. Ready Mixed Concrete Assn. (bd. dirs.), Air Pollution Control Assn. (tech. council), Sigma Xi, Phi Lambda Upsilon, Beta Sigma Sigma, Sigma Tau, Beta Rho Sigma. Clubs: Longue Vue, Masons. Contbr. articles to profl. jours. Patentee in slag processing and mech. separations. Home: Riding Trail Ln Pittsburgh PA 15215 Office: 1 5th St New Kensington PA 15068

BARTHOLOMEW, GEORGE EDWARD, railroad exec.; b. Boston, Oct. 23, 1942; s. Edward Langdon and Sarah (LeBlanc) B.; student U. Ariz., 1960-66; m. Mary Handy, July 29, 1967; children—Kathy, Michael. Owner, Fairhaven Robo Car Wash (Mass.), 1968-73, Willimantic Robo Car Wash (Conn.), 1971-74; pres., chmn. bd. Edaville R.R. steam powered tourist railroad, South Carver, Mass., 1970—; partner Leisure Pool Co., Wareham, Mass., 1971-73; pres. Bay Colony R.R. Corp., Wareham. Mem. Bicentennial Com. Southeastern Regional Planning and Econ. Devel. Dist., 1973—; mem. Nantucket Conservation Found.; bd. dirs., v.p. Plymouth County Devel. Council; bd. dirs. Moby Dick council Boy Scouts Am. Mem. Cranberry Area (v.p., dir., 1972—), Cape Cod, Plymouth Area chambers commerce, Nat. Carwash Council, New Eng. Travel Council (exec. bd.). Home: 60 Water St Marion MA 02738 Office: Rochester Rd South Carver MA 02566

BARTHOLOMEW, PHILLIP RAYMOND, lawyer; b. New Castle, Pa., Oct. 12, 1942; s. Francis O. and Rena L. (Clepper) B.; B.A., Westminster Coll., 1964; J.D., Vanderbilt U., 1967; m. Jane K. Barkley, June 21, 1969. Admitted to Pa. bar, 1968; law clk. Ct. of Common Pleas, Mercer County, Pa., 1967; partner firm Cusick, Madden, Joyce & McKay, Sharon, Pa., 1968—; atty. Shenango Valley Osteo. Hosp., Farrell, Pa., 1969—; solicitor West Middlesex (Pa.) Area Sch. Dist., 1971—. Trustee, Shenango Valley Osteo. Hosp., 1969—; pres. Pa. Christian Endeavor Union, 1972-76; v.p. Internat. Christian Endeavor, 1975-77; sec. Mercer County Young Republicans, 1964-74; elder Unity United Presbyterian Ch., Mercer, Pa., 1976-78. Mem. Am., Pa., Mercer County bas assns., Order of Coif, Omicron Delta Kappa. Home: 90 Wick Ave Sharon PA 16146 Office: First Federal Bldg Sharon PA 16146

BARTH-WEHRENALP, GERHARD, chem. co. exec.; b. Teplitz-Schoenau, Czechoslovakia, Oct. 19, 1920; s. Burghard and Kaethe (Bechert) von B.-W.; student U. Hamburg, Germany, 1942-43; Ph.D. maxima cum laude, U. Innsbruck, Austria, 1949; m. Waltraut von Weber, Apr. 8, 1952; children—Christian, Gerald, Markus. Came to U.S., 1951, naturalized, 1957. Chemist, Inst. Beverage Tech., Bad Homburg, Germany, 1943-44, Breganzia Food Corp., Bregenz, Austria, 1945-46; lectr., asst. U. Innsbruck, 1949-51; research asso. Temple U., 1951-52; asst. prof. LaSalle Coll., Phila., 1952-54; research chemist Pennwalt Corp., Phila., 1953-55, group leader, 1955-57, dir. inorganic research, 1957-63, mgr. research, 1963-70, asst. to chmn., 1971, corporate v.p., tech. dir., 1971-74, sr. v.p., tech. dir., 1974—. Austrian rep. to Younger Chemists Internat. Project, Tech. Assistance Program, 1951; chmn. phosphorus-nitrogen chemistry symposium Gordon Research Conf., 1960; dir. U.S. Commn. for WHO; mem. pres.'s council LaSalle Coll., Phila. Mem. Am. Chem. Soc., Am. Rocket Soc. (pres. Phila. sect. 1958), Soc. Chem. Industry, Am. Com. for Economic Edn. Contbr. articles to profl. jours. Holder U.S., Canadian, British, German, French, Italian patents. Home: Johns Ln Ambler PA 19002 Office: Pennwalt Bldg 3 Parkway Philadelphia PA 19102

BARTKY, MURRAY S., psychologist; b. N.Y.C., May 22, 1929; s. Samuel and Lena (Jacobs) B.; B.A., Bklyn. Coll., 1958; M.S., Yeshiva U., 1961; Ph.D. (scholar), Ariz. State U., 1970; m. Cynthia Huss, Dec. 25, 1955; children—Richard, Elliott, Eric, Jonathan, David. Research psychologist Center for Urban Edn., N.Y.C., 1965-68; supervising clin. psychologist Essex County Guidance Center, East Orange, N.J., 1970—, chmn. ednl. com., 1972—. Staff psychotherapist Bleuler Psychotherapy Center, Jamaica, N.Y., 1970-75; adj. prof. Montclair (N.J.) State Coll., 1971-72; cons. psychologist, 1973—. Served with M.C., AUS, 1951-53. Mem. Am., N.J., N.Y. State psychol. assns. Home: 375 Walnut St Livingston NJ 07039 Office: 160 S Livingston Ave Livingston NJ 07039

BARTLESON, MICHAEL MYERS, physician; b. Amarillo, Tex., Aug. 9, 1944; s. Horace Blair and Halcyon (Myers) B.; B.A., Northwestern U., 1966; M.D., U. Ill., 1970. Intern, Boston VA Hosp., 1970-71; teaching fellow in medicine Boston U. Sch. Medicine, 1970-71; resident Boston VA Hosp., 1971-73; fellow in nephrology, med. dir. kidney transplant unit Loyola U., Hines VA Hosp., Maywood, Ill., 1973-75; practice medicine specializing in internal medicine-nephrology, Westford, Mass., 1975—; mem. staff Nashoba Community Hosp. Diplomate Am. Bd. Internal Medicine. Mem. Mass. Med. Soc., Beta Beta Beta, Phi Gamma Delta. Home: 19 Maple Rd South Chelmsford MA 01824 Office: 190 Littleton Rd Westford MA 01886

BARTLETT, CHRISTOPHER ERIC, museum dir., artist, educator; b. Stratford-upon-Avon, Eng., Dec. 11, 1944; s. Eric Henry and Doreen Amy (Yeats) B.; came to U.S., 1971; Cert Ed. (Distinction), St. Paul's Coll., Eng., 1970; B.Ed. with 1st class honors, Bristol (Eng.) U., 1971; M.F.A., Syracuse U., 1978. Tchr. art Gloucestershire (Eng.) High Schs., 1967-70; chmn. design div. Md. Coll. Art and Design, 1971-72, asso. prof., 1972-74, dean, 1972-73, pres., 1973-74; adj. instr. Howard Community Coll, Md., 1972; instr. Center for Visual Arts, Antioch U., Columbia, Md., 1974; dir. gallery Towson (Md.) State U., 1974—; vice-chmn. bd., ednl. cons. Chesapeake Sch. Marine Ecology; exhbns. of drawings and sculpture include: Balt. Arts Festival (purchase prize Rouse Co.), 1972, Antioch U., 1974, Hannah Moore Art Center, 1976, Nat. Audubon Soc., Washington, 1976, Nat. Paper and Clay Juried Show, Memphis State U., 1978. Mem. Nat. Assn. Schs. Art, Artists Equity Assn., Am. Craft Council, Md. Craft Council. Office: Towson State U Towson MD 21204

BARTLETT, MABEL, librarian, educator; b. Bklyn.; d. William Cushing and Mabel (Worman) Bartlett; B.A., Conn. Coll. for Women, 1930; B.S., Columbia, 1938. Cataloger, reference librarian L.I. Hist. Soc., Bklyn., 1940-43; reference and circulation asst. Pub. Library, New London, Conn., 1943-44; cataloger State U. Iowa Library, Iowa City, 1944-46; head catalog dept. Osterhout Free Library, Wilkes-Barre, Pa., 1946-48; head tech. processes dept. L.I.U., Library, Bklyn., 1948-77, asst. prof., 1948-54, asso. prof., 1954-70, prof., 1970-77. Mem. ALA Am. Bible Soc., N.Y. Tech. Services Librarians, AAUP, (chpt. treas. 1966-77). Republican. Episcopalian. Home: 143 Linden Blvd Brooklyn NY 11226

BARTLETT, MARSHALL KINNE, surgeon; b. New Haven, Jan. 18, 1904; s. Charles J. and Genevieve (Kinne) B.; B.A., Yale U., 1924; M.D., Harvard U., 1928; m. Barbara Frazier Hume, Dec. 21, 1935; children—Charles Joseph, Barbara Hume, Susan Bartlett Demb. Intern, Mass. Gen. Hosp., Boston, 1928-31; resident Free Hosp. for Women, Brookline, Mass; practice medicine specializing in surgery, Boston, 1932-73; adminstrv. dir. operating rooms Mass. Gen. Hosp., Boston, 1973—; clin. prof. surgery emeritus Harvard Med. Sch., Boston; sr. surgeon, Mass. Gen. Hosp., Boston, 1970—. Served to lt. col., M.C., AUS, 1942-46. Decorated Bronze Star Medal. Diplomate Am. Bd. Surgery. Mem. Boston, New Eng. surg. socs., Mass. Med. Soc., Am. Med. Assn., ACS, Am. Surg. Assn. Contbr. articles in field to med. jours. Home: 43 Chestnut St Dedham MA 02026 Office: Mass Gen Hosp Fruit St Boston MA 02114

BARTLETT, RALPH THEODORE, accountant; b. Lyndhurst, N.J., Sept. 5, 1924; s. Ralph and Elinor (Chambers) B.; B.S., Lehigh U., 1947; postgrad. N.Y. U., 1948-49; m. Natalie G. Khun, Apr. 19, 1947; children—Deborah, Jeffrey, Thomas. Staff, Deloitte, Haskins & Sells, C.P.A.'s, Newark, 1947—, partner, 1961—, in charge New Haven and Hartford, Conn., offices, 1970-73, Newark, 1973-78, Exec. Office, N.Y.C., 1978—. Trustee St. Timothy's House, home for boys, Newark, 1965-68; chmn. profl. div. United Appeals Newark, 1967-68; mem. diocesan loans com., funding commn. Episcopal Diocese Newark, 1973—. Served with A.C., USNR, 1943-45. C.P.A. Mem. N.J. Soc. C.P.A.'s (pres. 1963-64), Am. Inst. C.P.A.'s (council 1962-70, nat. rev. bd. 1977—), Conn. Soc. C.P.A.'s (chmn. com. accounting and auditing 1971-72). Republican. Clubs: Essex (treas. 1976—) (Newark); Lehigh No. N.J. (pres. 1975-77), Fairmount Country, Madison Golf, Milford (Conn.) Yacht, US Power Squadron, Minisink Tennis and Swim (pres. Chatham, N.J. 1962-63), Kiwanis (chmn. audit com. Newark 1961-62). Editor: N.J. C.P.A. Jour., 1955-56. Home: 164 Green Ave Madison NJ 07940 Office: Deloitte Haskins & Sells 1114 Ave of Americas New York City NY 10036

BARTO, WALTER WEAVER, JR., health care exec.; b. Phila., Oct. 25, 1937; s. Walter Weaver and Mary Kraybill (Strickler) B.; B.S. in Econs., Temple U., Phila., 1962; m. Diana Magee, Aug. 20, 1960; children—Stacy, Stephanie, Susan, Jennifer. Salesperson, Nat. Dairy Corp., 1961-63; with Smith Kline Corp., Phila., 1963-79, dir. govt. and industry affairs, 1973, v.p. corp. affairs, 1974-78, v.p. mktg., 1978-79; exec. President's Commn. Personnel Interchange, 1972; acting dep. dir. Office Pub. Affairs, EPA, 1973-73; commnr. Interchange Commn., 1976-79. Elder, Abington (Pa.) Presbyn. Ch.; trustee Adington Free Library Soc.; bd. dirs. S.E. Pa. chpt. ARC. Served with Chaplains Corps, AUS, 1956-58. Mem. NAM, Pharm. Mfrs. Assn., Pub. Relations Soc. Am., Internat. Mgmt. ad Devel. Inst. Clubs: Nat.

Press, Univ. (Washington). Home: 1441 Stocton Rd Meadowbrook PA 19046 Office: 1500 Spring Garden St Philadelphia PA 19101 Died Jan. 27, 1979.

BARTOK, FREDERICK FRANCIS, ednl. adminstr.; b. Johnstown, Pa., May 22, 1943; s. Francis Andrew and Margaret Veronica (Ritko) B.; B.A., U. Pitts., 1965; M.Ed., Duquesne U., 1969; children—Rory Elizabeth, Keri Helene. Asst. mgr. br. office div. Mellon Nat. Bank, Pitts., 1966-69; asso. prof. banking and finance Community Coll. Allegheny County, Monroeville, Pa., 1969-74, asst. to exec. dean, 1974-76, asst. acad. dean, 1976—. Named Outstanding Educator of Am., 1974-75. Mem. AAUP, Am. Fedn. Tchrs., Financial Mgmt. Assn., Banking and Bus. Assn. (dir. 1970-74) Monroeville C. of C. (ednl. task force), Nat. Staff Devel. Orgn. Democrat. Roman Catholic. Author: Personal Economics, 1976. Home: 801 Mac Arthur Dr North Huntingdon PA 15642 Office: 595 Beatty Rd Monroeville PA 15146

BARTOL, CARL RICHARD, clin. pathologist; b. Hazle Brook, Pa., Aug. 3, 1932; s. Wante and Charlotte (Feissner) B.; student Mining Mech. Inst., 1946-50; B.A., Lehigh U., 1954; M.D., U. Innsbruck, 1960; postgrad. cum laude U. Heidelberg; m. Karin Springmeier, June 9, 1960; children—Susan Ann, Brenda Lee, Carl Albert, David. Intern, St. Francis Hosp., Poughkeepsie, N.Y., 1960-61; resident St. Luke's Hosp., Newburgh, N.Y., 1961-62, White Plains (N.Y.) Hosp., 1962, No. Westchester Hosp., 1967-69; practice medicine specializing in pathology, 1969—; asst. pathologist St. Clare's Hosp., N.Y.C., 1969-71, asso. pathologist, 1971—; chief pathologist St. Elizabeth's Hosp., N.Y.C., 1971—. Served to maj. U.S. Army, 1962-67. Diplomate Am. Bd. Pathology in anatomic and clin. pathology. Fellow Am. Soc. Clin. Pathologists, Coll. Am. Pathologists; mem. Am. Med. Soc. Vienna (life), N.Y. State Soc. Pathologists, N.Y. State Med. Soc., Pathologists Club, Westchester County Med. Soc., Westchester Acad. Medicine, Internat. Acad. Pathology, Nat. Guard Assn. Republican. Roman Catholic. Clubs: Elks., K.C. Contbr. articles in field to med. jours. Home: 19 Woodland Pl Scarsdale NY 10583 Office: 689 Ft Washington Ave New York City NY 10040

BARTOLOMEO, ROBERT SALVATORE, physician; b. Bklyn., Jan. 25, 1946; s. Angelo and Josephine Concetta (Muscarella) B.; B.S., U. Notre Dame, 1967; M.D., N.Y. Med. Coll., 1971; m. Joyce Mitgang, Oct. 23, 1976. Intern, Met. Hosp. Center, N.Y.C., 1971-72, resident, 1972-73; resident in internal medicine Beth Israel Med. Center, N.Y.C., 1973-74; fellow gastroenterology program Yale U., New Haven, 1974-76; practice medicine specializing in gastroenterology, Mineola, N.Y., 1976—; attending physician Nassau Hosp., Mineola, 1976—; asso. attending physician Nassau County Med. Center, Stony Brook U. Med. Sch., 1976—. Diplomate Am. Bd. Internal Medicine. Mem. L.I. Gastroenterologic Assn. Home: 167 Brookville Ln Glen Head NY 11545 Office: 222 Station Plaza N Nassau Profl Bldg Mineola NY 11501

BARTOLOTTA, PETER LOUIS, telephone co. exec.; b. Bklyn., Apr. 11, 1947; s. Louis Peter and Ida Rita (Melito) B.; A.A., Nassau Coll., 1968; m. Deirdre Elizabeth Giglio, Feb. 13, 1971; children—Heather Louise, Derek Peter, Adam George. Sales rep. SCM, L.I., 1970-71; mfg. systems specialist Xerox Corp., L.I., 1971-74; nat. mktg. mgr. corr., electronic mail systems Bowne Time Sharing Co., N.Y.C., 1974-78; mktg. mgr. Am. Tel & Tel. Co., Morristown, N.J., 1978—. Scout master Nassau County council Boy Scouts Am. Mem. Soc. Consumer Affairs Profls. in Bus., Electronic Mail Users Assn. (charter mem.), Sales Exec. Club (N.Y.). Episcopalian. Home: 25 Williamson Ln Chester NJ 07930 Office: 1776 On-the-Green Morristown NJ 07960

BARTOLOTTI, VIRGINIA LAURA, educator/counselor; b. Bklyn., Oct. 10, 1942; d. Emanuel Anthony and Rose (Campagna) B.; B.S., Bklyn. Coll., 1964; M.A., N.Y. U., 1967; M.S., Bklyn. Coll., 1975, profl. degree, 1976; doctoral candidate N.Y. U., 1976—. Secondary sch. tchr., curriculum devel. math./career-edn. specialist, office pupil personnel services, adviser student support systems, coordinator career edn./guidance jr. high sch., Bklyn., 1964-78, dir. funded program. skills devel. making rational choices, coordinator/dir. career edn. and curriculum devel., profl. staff tng., 1978—; profl. staff devel. instr. human relations and career edn., coordinator career edn., div. edn. planning and support N.Y.C. Bd. Edn., 1975—; guest lectr. Bklyn. Coll., 1976-77; presenter profl. devel. workshops; cons. crisis intervention. Vol. counselor Bklyn. Coll. Project Chance, 1977—. Recipient certificate in drug and alcohol prevention Adelphi U. Nat. Tng. Labs., 1977. Mem. Am. Psychol. Assn., Nat. Council Tchrs. Math., Am., N.Y. State personnel and guidance assns., Columbia Assn. N.Y.C. Bd. Edn. Office: 360 Smith St Brooklyn NY 11231

BARTON, CHARLES ANDREWS, JR., clergyman; b. Memphis, Apr. 25, 1916; s. Charles Andrews and Martha Lee (Stewart) B.; B.S., Southwestern U. Memphis, 1937, D.D., 1964; M.S., N.Y. U., 1939; M.Div., Union Theol. Sem., 1950; m. Jane Irby Teague, Aug. 19, 1950; children—Martha, Carol, Stewart, Susan. Chief sales engr., wire and cable Dept. U.S. Rubber Co., N.Y.C., 1939-47; ordained to ministery United Methodist Ch., 1952; pastor City Island Ch., N.Y.C., 1952-54, Crawford Meml. Ch., N.Y.C., 1954-56, 1st Ch. Jamaica, N.Y.C., 1956-67, Mt. Kisco Ch., N.Y.C., 1967-73; asso. exec. dir. United Meth. City Soc., N.Y.C., 1973—; pres. bd. missions N.Y. Conf. United Meth. Ch., 1968-72, pres. bd. evangelism, 1962-68; v.p. Bklyn. Deaconess Fund, 1973—, Five Points Mission, 1973—; pres. Chinese Meth. Community Center, 1977—; bd. dirs. Harlem Interfaith counseling Service; sec. ethics com. Mt. Kisco, 1971-74; chmn. Mt. Kisco Narcotics Guidance Council, 1970-73; mem. Mt. Kisco, Park Commn., 1970-73; v.p. bd. Anchor House, 1974. Served as 1st lt. Signal Corps, U.S. Army, 1942-46. Named Distinguished Citizen Mt. Kisco, 1972. Mem. Am. Camping Assn. (dir. N.Y. sect. 1975—), Internat. Platform Assn., Pi Kappa Alpha. Democrat. Home: 42 Otsego Ave New Rochelle NY 10804 Office: Room 1922 475 Riverside Dr New York City NY 10027

BARTON, GEORGIE READ (MRS. GEORGE THOMAS BARTON), artist; b. Summerside, P.E.I., Can., Apr. 7, 1902; d. John Lefurgey and Nellie (Hillson) Read; grad. Mt. Allison Sch. Fine Arts, 1927, Art Students League, 1934; came to U.S., 1940, naturalized, 1956; m. George Thomas Barton, May 17, 1942; 1 son, George Thomas II. One-man shows Hudson River Mus., Yonkers, N.Y., 1953, Awards Gallery, Eastchester, N.Y., 1963, Confedn. Art Gallery, P.E.I., 1965, Epworth Hall, Summerside, P.E.I., 1969, Marine Sch., Summerside, 1973, 77, Owens Art Gallery, Mt. Allison U., Sackville, N.B., 1978; exhibited in group shows at Royal Canadian Acad., 1927-28, Hudson Valley Art Assn., 1956—, Acad. Artists of Springfield, 1958—, Nat. Arts Club, 1968, 71-72, Allied Artists Am., 1963-64, 70—, Am. Artists Profl. League, 1963—, Catherine Lorrilard Wolfe Art Club, 1963—, Council Am. Artists Socs., 1964-66, also Royal Palace, Monaco; represented in permanent collections Confedn. Art Gallery, P.E.I., IBM, Art of Western Hemisphere, Bruckner Mus., also numerous pub. and pvt. collections; tchr., Ottawa Ladies Coll., 1934-40, St. Agnes Sch., Albany, N.Y., 1940-44; pvt. tchr. art, 1950—. Bd. dirs. P.E.I. Council of the Arts, 1974—; mem. P.E.I. Heritage Found. Recipient bronze medal IBM, 1941, Distinguished Service award Am. Artists Profl. League, 1978, also numerous other awards. Treas. P.E.I. Council of the Arts, 1974—. Fellow Royal Soc. Arts, Am. Artists Profl. League (dir. nat. bd. 1964—); mem. Council of Am. Artists Socs. (dir. 1966—), Hudson Valley Art Assn. (sec. 1958-65, pres. 1966-69, 1st v.p. 1970—, gold medal 1963, citation of honor 1972, Gold medal of honor 1972, top award for landscape 1973), Salmagundi Club. Address: 3 Hillside Ave Summerside PE C1N 4H3 Canada

BARTON, LUCIAN ANTHONY, chemist; b. Wilno, Poland, Mar. 27, 1921; s. Waclaw and Jadwiga (Wirpszo) Bartoszewicz; came to U.S., 1951, naturalized, 1957; B.A., Rutgers U., 1957, postgrad., 1957-61; m. Carolina Salerano, Aug. 8, 1949; 1 dau., Elena. Sr. technician Thiokol Chem. Corp., 1952-55; mem. tech. staff RCA Labs., David Sarnoff Research Center, Princeton, N.J., 1955—. Served with Polish Corps, Brit. Army, 1942-48. Decorated Bronze Star medal; recipient Achievement awards in sci. RCA, 1966, 70, 72, Gold medal David Sarnoff Research Center, 1969. Fellow Am. Inst. Chemists; mem. Am. Chem. Soc. Contbr. articles to profl. jours. Patentee in field. Office: RCA Labs Princeton NJ 08540

BARTON, SIDNEY MEDEL, real estate investor; b. N.Y.C., Apr. 16, 1912; s. William and Ester (Von Grover) B.; A.B., N.Y. U., 1935, LL.B., 1936; (div.); 1 dau., Shari; m. 2d, Lady Dorothea McCarthy May, Aug. 31, 1964. Real estate and oil bus., N.Y.C., 1945—; owner Sidney M. Barton Co., N.Y.C., 1951—. Clubs: Turf and Field, Lotos. Home: 3 E 69th St New York City NY 10021 also 2 Palm Bay Ct Miami FL 33138 Office: 400 Madison Ave New York City NY 10017

BARTON, STANLEY, business exec.; b. Halesowen, Worcestershire, Eng., Dec. 30, 1927; s. Lazarus and Alice (Faulkner) B.; B.S. with honors, U. Birmingham (Eng.), 1949, Ph.D., 1952; m. Marion Brittain, Dec. 20, 1952; children—Carolyn Francesca, Andrea Elizabeth. Came to U.S., 1957, naturalized, 1963. Group leader Naval Research Establishment, Halifax, N.S., Can., 1953-56; project coordinator Def. Research Chem. Labs., Ottawa, Ont., Can., 1956-57; devel. engr. Procter & Gamble, Cin., 1957-58, research and devel. group leader, 1958-59, research and devel. sect. head, 1959-69; tech. dir. food products/natural resources ITT Corp., N.Y.C., 1969-76; sr. v.p.-tech. and quality ITT Rayonier, Inc., N.Y.C., 1977—. Dist. chmn. United Appeal campaigns, Cin., 1964-65. Sec., Planning and Zoning Commn., Greenhills, Ohio, 1966-68. Mem. Am. Inst. Chem. Engrs., Am. Theater Organ Soc., Cinema Organ Soc. Home: 10 White Woods Ln Westport CT 06880 Office: 605 3d Ave New York City NY 10016

BARTON, WILLIAM DAVID, computer co. exec.; b. N.Y.C., June 22, 1933; s. William David and Martha (McCurdy) B.; B.B.A., So. Meth. U., 1960. Sales rep. Penn Metal Co., Inc., Houston, 1960-65, Honeywell, Inc., Houston and N.Y.C., 1965-69; mgr. Digitronics Corp., N.Y.C., 1969-73; pres. Teldata Systems Corp., N.Y.C., 1973-76, also dir.; pres., dir. Datel Systems Corp., 1976—; dir. Telecommunications Systems. Served with USNR, 1955-59. Mem. Am. Mgmt. Assn. Episcopalian. Home: 201 E 83d St New York City NY 10028 Office: 1211 Ave of Americas New York City NY 10036

BARTON, WILLIAM RENALD, govt. ofcl.; b. Boston, May 13, 1928; s. William Renald and Katherine Veronica (Byrd) B.; B.A. in Geology, Boston U., 1951, M.A. in Geology, 1955; Certificate in Econs. of Nat. Security, Indsl. Coll. Armed Forces, 1960; m. Mercedes Lambert, Oct. 25, 1948; children—William, Marilyn, Barbara. Geologist, U.S. Geol. Survey, Grand Junction, Colo., 1951-57; phys. scientist U.S. Bur. Mines, Washington, 1957-61, Rumford, Maine, 1961-64, Arlington, Va., 1964-68, supervisory phys. scientist, Knoxville, Tenn., 1968-70, liaison officer, Newmarket, N.H., 1970—. Mem. N.H. Gov.'s Council on Mineral and Energy Resources, 1971—, New Eng. Council Natural Resources Com., Boston, 1973-77; dep. regional dir. Emergency Minerals Adminstrn., 1975—. Served with Signal Corps, AUS, 1946-48. Mem. Am. Inst. Mining, Metall. and Petroleum Engrs., Maine Mineral Resources Assn., Soc. Econ. Geologists, Am. Inst. Profl. Geologists. Contbr. articles to profl. jours. and govt. publs. Office: Federal Bldg Newmarket NH 03857

BARTOW, JEROME E., corp. exec.; b. Orange, N.J., June 15, 1930; s. William D. and Florence Lillian (Jones) B.; B.A., Va. State Coll., 1951; M.A., Columbia U., 1955, Ph.D., 1967; m. Louise D. Tolson, Apr. 1, 1949; children—Sharon Lillian Bartow Veasey Mitchell, Jerome E. Dean of students State U. N.Y. at Buffalo 1961-65; dist. mgr. N.Y. Telephone Co., Buffalo, 1965-69; mgr. exec. placement ITT Hdqrs., N.Y.C., 1969-74, dir. employee relations ops., 1974-77, dir. personnel/indsl. relations, 1977—. Vice pres., bd. dirs. Nat. Fedn. Settlements and Neighborhood Centers, N.Y.C., 1974—; co-chmn. nat. adv. com. Black Exec. Exchange Program, Nat. Urban League, 1970—; mem. Diocesan council Episcopal Council Newark, 1977—. Served to lt. U.S. Army 1951-53. Recipient Man of Year award, Buffalo, 1967. Mem. Am. Personnel and Guidance Assn., Am. Coll. Personnel Assn., Nat. Urban League. Episcopalian. Office: ITT 320 Park Ave New York City NY 10022

BARTZ, ALICE PUGH, librarian; b. Burnswick County, Va., June 19, 1915; d. John Warner and Camelia (Brooks) Pugh; B.A., Westhampton Coll., U. Richmond, 1936; B.S. in Library Sci., U. N.C., 1938; m. Warren Frederick Bartz, Sept. 6, 1940; children—Warren Frederick, John Davis. Children's librarian, Richmond, Va., 1936-38, N.Y.C., 1938-40, Free Library Phila., 1940-43; sch. librarian Germantown Acad., 1955-60, Abington (Pa.) Sch. Dist., 1961-68; dir. Eastern Area Br., Div. Sch. Library Media Programs, Pa. Dept. Edn.-Sch. Dist. Phila., 1968—; mem. Newbery/Caldecott Award Com., 1978. Mem. ALA, Pa. Library Assn., Pa. Sch. Librarians Assn. (Outstanding Contbr. award 1978), Nat. Council Tchrs. English, Assn. Edn. Communication and Tech., Internat. Reading Assn., AAUW, Noble Improvement Assn., Phi Delta Kappa. Democrat. Presbyterian. Contbr. articles to profl. jours. Home: 646 Pine Tree Rd Jenkintown PA 19046 Office: Horn Sch Frankford and Castor Aves Philadelphia PA 19124

BARUCH, JOHN ALFRED, pharmaceutical co. exec.; b. Herford, Germany, Sept. 22, 1926; s. Bernard and Marie Adrienne (Theblee) B.; student Northampton Town and Country, England, 1940-43; A.B., Harvard, 1950; m. Doris Kartun, July 1, 1951; children—Marianne, Peter Bernard. Rep. med. service Ortho Pharm., 1950-55, mgr. advt. 1959-62; asst. mgr. advt. Warner-Chilcott Labs., 1955-57; mgr. pub. relations Warner-Lambert, 1957-59; dir. mktg. Winthrop Labs., N.Y.C., 1962-67; exec. v.p. Reed & Carnrick, Kenilworth, N.J., 1967-70, pres., 1970—; guest lectr. Coll. of Pharmacy, U. Miss. Pres. Assn. Queens (N.Y.) Independents, 1954-56; pres. bd. trustees Morristown/Morris Twp. (N.J.) Library, 1976-77. Served with AUS, 1944-46. Mem. Pharm. Advt. Club (pres. 1964), Pharm. Mfrs. Assn. (program chmn. 1965), Am. Med. Writers Assn. Democrat. Clubs: Harvard (N.Y.C.); Harvard (N.J. pres. 1974-75), Kellogg (dir.). Home: 19 Hilltop Circle Morristown NJ 07960 Office: 30 Boright Ave Kenilworth NJ 07033

BARWIN, BERNARD NORMAN, obstetrician, gynecologist; b. Transvall, South Africa, Mar. 8, 1938; s. Aron and Rita (Miller) B.; Ch.B., M.B., B.Obstetrics, Queen's U., M.D., 1972; m. Myrna Zelkow, Jan. 7, 1962. Lectr. dept. physiology and midwifery and gynecology Queen's U., 1969; intern Belfast City Hosp., 1965-66; resident Royal Maternity and Royal Victoria hosps., Belfast, 1967-69; asso. prof. dept. obstetrics and gynecology U. Ottawa (Ont., Can.), 1973—, co-dir. infertility clinic, 1974—; dir. high risk pregnancy, cons. Ottawa Gen. Hosp., 1973—; cons. Eastern Ont. Children's Hosp.; adv. bd. Canadian Fertility Council, WHO. Fellow Am. Coll. Obstetricians and Gynecologists, Irish Acad. Sci., Ottawa Acad. Medicine, Am. Soc. Andrology (founding), mem. Canadian Fertility Soc. (v.p. 1976-77). Jewish religion. Clubs: Nepean Sports, B'nai B'rith. Author: (with others) Outlines of Obstetrics and Gynecology, 1972. Home: 26 O'Kanangan St Ottawa ON K2H 7G1 Canada Office: 43 Bruyere St Ottawa ON K1N 5C8 Canada

BARYSH, NOAH, physician; b. Edinburgh, Scotland, Oct. 17, 1906; s. Aaron and Bertha (Wasserman) B.; B.S., City Coll. N.Y., 1928; M.D., U. Chgo., 1932; m. Gertrude Genviève Katsh, Jan. 19, 1939; children—Alan, Ann. Resident in cardiology Sunset Cardiac Camp, Antioch, Ill., 1932, Edward Sanitarium, 1932, Michael Reese Hosp., Chgo., 1932-34; practice medicine, Jamestown, N.Y., 1935-37, Bklyn., 1937-40, N.Y.C., 1946-52, New Milford, Danbury, Conn., 1953—; emeritus mem. staff Lenox Hill Hosp., N.Y.C.; emeritus mem. staff New Milford Hosp., pres. med. staff, 1963; mem. staff Danbury Hosp., 1953—. Mem. New Milford Bd. Edn., 1968-77, chmn. sch. health com., 1970-77; pres., co-founder Temple Sholom, New Milford, 1959. Served with M.C., U.S. Army, 1940-45. Decorated Bronze Star, Silver Star; diplomate Am. Bd. Pediatrics, Am. Bd. Allergy and Immunology. Fellow Am. Acad. Pediatrics, Am. Coll. Allergy, Am. Acad. Allergy. Clubs: Lake Waramaug Country, Errol Estates Country, Masons, Lions. Home: 82 Chestnutland Rd New Milford CT 06776 Office: 93 West St Danbury CT 06810

BARZANTI, SERGIO, educator; b. Rome, Oct. 4, 1925; s. Domenico and Pierina (Casadei) B.; Baccalaureat, Liceo, Rome, 1943; Dr. J., U. Rome, 1947; M.A., N.Y. U., 1958, Ph.D., 1962; postgrad. U. Paris, 1959; m. Gabriele A. Stormer, Oct. 24, 1968 (div. 1973); children—Simonetta, Paul, Mark, Lorenzo. Came to U.S., 1955, naturalized, 1961. Mem. faculty Fairleigh Dickinson U., Rutherford, N.J., 1963—, asst. prof., 1964-67, asso. prof., 1967-75, prof. history and internat. studies, 1975—. Fulbright grantee, 1965. Mem. AAUP, Am. Polit. Sci. Assn. Author: The Underdeveloped Areas Within the Common Market, 1965. Home: 540 80th St Brooklyn NY 11209 Office: Dept Social Sciences Fairleigh Dickinson U Rutherford NJ 07070

BASAR, RONALD JOHN, electrophotographic engr.; b. Kingston, Pa., Mar. 28, 1950; s. John and Sophie Barbara (Turowski) B.; B.S. in Chem. Engring. (Mich., Regents scholar, Monsanto fellow), Wayne State U., 1972; M.B.A. in Fin., Rochester Inst. Tech., 1978; m. Karen Marie Jarvis, June 1, 1974; 1 dau., Amber Lynn. Photog. engr. Eastman Kodak Co., Rochester, N.Y., 1972-74, electrophotog. engr., 1974—. Mem. Am. Inst. Chem. Engrs., Assn. M.B.A. Execs., Soc. Photog. Engrs., Eastman Kodak Mgmt. Club, Tau Beta Pi, Phi Lambda Upsilon. Democra Roman Catholic. Club: Am. Health Spa. Research on dual sequestrant formula, electrophotog. low temperature toner Home: 145 Andiron Ln Rochester NY 14612 Offic Eastman Kodak Co Kodak Park Rochester NY 14650

BASCOM, ROBERT HOLDEN, accountant; b. Pittsfield, Mass., Feb. 11, 1940; s. Ralph Benjamin and Ethel Charlotte (MacRoberts) B.; student Berkshire Bus. Coll., 1957-58. Staff accountant George P. Hunt, Accountant, Pittsfield, Mass., 1958-65; accountant Hunt, Bascom & Co., Pittsfield, 1965-74; prin. Robert H. Bascom, 1974—. Treas., St. Stephens Ch. Served with USCGR, 1961-69. Mem. Nat., Mass. assns. pub. accountants. Episcopalian. Club: Kiwanis (treas. Pittsfield 1965-74, pres. 1977, sec. 1978). Home: 153 South St Pittsfield MA 01201 Office: 74 North St Pittsfield MA 01201

BASES, ALBERT LOUIS, lawyer; b. Bklyn., July 14, 1929; s. Rudolph and Frances (Ponzo) B.; student Long Island, U., 1949-51; LL.B., Bklyn. Law Sch., 1954; m. Eileen McClarnon, Sept. 4, 1954; children—Patricia Mary, John Albert, Joseph Jude, Matthew Luke. Admitted to N.Y. bar; adjuster, All-State Ins. Co., N.Y.C., 1954-55; atty. Republic Ins. Co., N.Y.C., 1955-56; mem. com. grievances Assn. Bar N.Y.C., 1956-59; mem. firm Dominic J. Cornella, N.Y.C., 1959-60; atty. Exchange Mut. Ins. Co., N.Y.C., 1960-63; mem. firm Mendes & Mount, Esqs., N.Y.C., 1963-72; atty., partner firm Doran, Colleran, O'Hara, Pollio & Dunne, P.C., Garden City, N.Y., 1972-76, Bases Russo Lawrence & Ciovacco, Garden City, 1977—. Mem. N.Y. Bar Assn., Fedn. Ins. Counsel, Def. Research Inst., Trial Lawyers Am., Aircraft Owners and Pilots Assn. Republican. Roman Catholic. Author: (with Irwin Grey) Product Liability: A Management Response, 1975; Lawyers' Professional Liability: The Experience in New York and Elsewhere, 1977. Home: 579 Babbling Brook Ln Valley Cottage NY 10989 Office: 1415 Kellum Pl Garden City NY 11530

BASHORE, DONALD RAY, educator; b. Newark, Aug. 4, 1921; s. Willard Emmons and Della Blanche (Burris) B.; B.A., Susquehanna U., 1947; M.Ed., Pa. State U., 1948; postgrad. (Coe Found. scholar), Bucknell U., 1961-62, Eastern Psychiat. Inst., St. Christopher's Hosp. for Children, Temple U., 1977-78; m. Blossom E. Farnum, Apr. 2, 1943; children—James Willard, Donna (Mrs. Robert Shuman), Barbara (Mrs. John Roeder). Tchr., football coach, Yeagertown, Pa., 1947-49; prin., elementary sch. Mifflintown, Pa., 1950-53; psychologist Selinsgrove (Pa.) Epileptic Colony, 1955; tchr., coach Juniata Joint High Sch., Mifflintown, 1953-60; asso. prof., counselor Bloomsburg (Pa.) State Coll., 1960—. Cons., Pa. Dept. Health, 1963-72; tchr., counselor Pottsville (Pa.) Gen. Hosp., Ashland (Pa.) Gen. Hosp., Hazelton (Pa.) Gen. Hosp., 1964—; tchr. continuing edn. psychology Pa. State U., 1963-74; pastor Emanuel's Ref. Ch., Mainville, Pa., 1969—. Served with USMCR, 1942-46, 50-53; Korea. Decorated Bronze Star. Fellow Nat. Found. Research in Clin. Hypnosis; mem. Am., Pa. psychol. assns., Assn. Ethical Hypnosis, Nat. Assn. Sch. Counselors, AAUP, Am. Acad. Human Scis., Inst. Noetic Sci. Mason (K.T.). Home: RD 3 Bloomsburg PA 17815 Office: Dept Psychology Bloomsburg State College Bloomsburg PA 17815

BASILI, VICTOR ROBERT, educator; b. N.Y.C., Apr. 13, 1940; s. Basil and Marie (Tesoriero) B.; B.S., Fordham Coll., 1961; M.S., Syracuse U., 1963; Ph.D., U. Tex., 1970; m. Patricia Ann D'Amato, Dec. 27, 1967; children—Alexander John, Brian Joseph, Theodore James. Asst. prof. math. and computer sci. Providence Coll., 1965-67; curriculum coordinator S.W. Region Edn. Computer Network, U. Tex. at Austin, 1969-70; asst. prof. computer sci. U. Md., College Park, 1970-75, asso. prof. computer sci., 1975—; cons. at Naval Research Lab., 1975—, Naval Surface Weapons Center, Dahlgren, 1975—, Inst. Computer Applications in Sci. and Engring., NASA, Langley Field, 1974—, NASA, Goddard Center, 1976—. Office Naval Research grantee, 1972-76; NASA grantee, 1975—. Mem. Assn. Computer Machinery (chpt. pres. 1964-65), AAUP, IEEE. Editor: (with T. Baker) Structured Programming: A Tutorial, 1975. Contbr. articles in field to profl. jours. Home: 7102 Good Luck Rd Lanham MD 20801 Office: Computer Sci Dept Univ Md College Park MD 20742

BASINSKI, ZBIGNIEW STANISLAW, metal physicist; b. Wolkowysk, Poland, Apr. 28, 1928; s. Antoni and Maria Zofia Anna (Hilferding) B.; B.A., Oxford (Eng.) U., 1951, B.Sc., 1952, D.Phil., 1954, D.Sc., 1965; m. Sylvia Joy Pugh, Apr. 1, 1952; children—Stefan Leon Hilferding, Antoni Stanislaw Hilferding. Immigrated to Can.,

1956, naturalized, 1961. With div. indsl. cooperation Mass. Inst. Tech., 1954-55; mem. staff Nat. Research Council Can., 1956—, prin. research officer, 1965—; Ford distinguished vis. prof. Carnegie Inst. Tech., 1963-64; Commonwealth vis. prof. Oxford U., 1969-70, fellow Wolfson Coll., 1969-70. Recipient 1st Canadian Metal Physics medal, 1977. Fellow Royal Soc. Can. Contbr. articles to sci. jours. Home: 108 Delong Dr Ottawa ON K1J 7E1 Canada Office: NRC Ottawa ON K1A 0R6 Canada

BASKERVILLE, CHARLES ALEXANDER, coll. dean; b. Queens, N.Y., Aug. 19, 1928; s. Charles H. and Annie M. (Allen) B.; B.S., Coll. City N.Y., 1953; M.S., N.Y. U., 1958, Ph.D., 1965; m. Ruth Corrine Cuestas, Apr. 5, 1953; children—Mark Dana, Shawn Allison. Asst. civil engr. N.Y. State Dept. Transp., N.Y.C. and L.I., 1953-66; soils engr. McFarland-Johnson Cons. Engrs., Binghamton, N.Y., 1967; sr. engr. soils and geology Madigan-Hyland Engrs., Long Island City, N.Y., 1968; prof. engring. geology City Coll. N.Y., 1966-69, dean Sch. Gen. Studies, 1970—; cons. to industry; engring. geol. cons. N.Y.C. corp. counsel-bd. water supply City of N.Y. Mem. nat. adv. com. on minority participation Dept. of Interior, 1972-75. Recipient award for excellence in engring. geology Nat. Consortium Black Profl. Devel., 1978. Fellow Geol. Soc. Am.; mem. N.Y. Acad. Scis., Assn. Engring. Geologists (chmn. N.Y.-Phila. sect., nat. bd. dirs. 1973), Assn. Profl. Geol. Scientists, Sigma Xi. Office: 138th St at Convent Ave New York City NY 10031

BASKOUS, ATHAN ALEXANDER, state ofcl.; b. Schenectady, June 12, 1921; s. Alexander and Beatrice (Aliferis) B.; B.C.E., Cornell U., Ithaca, 1943; M.P.H., U. Mich., 1956; m. Dena Xanthos, Feb. 7, 1945 (dec. Dec. 1968); children—Alexander, Patricia (Mrs. David Lambert); m. 2d, Bertha Caranikas, Aug. 26, 1973. Engr., Havens and Emerson, cons. engrs., Cleve., 1946-49; asst. san. engr. N.Y. State Dept. Health, Albany, 1949-51, sr. san. engr., 1951-56, asso. san. engr., 1956-63, regional engr., 1963-71; regional dir. N.Y. State Dept. Environ. Conservation, Albany, 1971-77, regional dir. environ. quality, 1977—. Dist. commr. Boy Scouts Am., 1950-55, troop com., 1957-59, merit badge counselor, 1959-74. Served to 1st. lt. Med. Service Corps, USAAF, 1945-46. Registered profl. engr., N.Y. Mem. Water Pollution Control Fedn., Air Pollution Control Fedn. Catskill Center, Am., Adirondock water works assns., Hudson River Environ. Soc., Am. Hellenic Ednl. Prog. Assn., Chi Epsilon. Greek Orthodox (ch. bd. dirs. 1963-67). Club: Niskayuna Field Archers (Schenectady). Contbr. articles in field to profl. jours. Home: 825 Jamaica Rd Schenectady NY 12309 Office: NY State Dept Environmental Conservation Region 4 Office 50 Wolf Rd Albany NY 12101

BASS, HOWARD LARRY, lawyer; b. Bklyn., Feb. 6, 1942; s. Samuel and Esther (Gold) B.; B.A., Adelphi Coll., Garden City, N.Y., 1963; J.D., Bklyn. Law Sch., 1966. Admitted to N.Y. State bar, 1967; law clk., N.Y.C., 1966-67; tchr. N.Y.C. pub. schs., 1967-68; spl. counsel firm Rudnick & Sheps, N.Y.C., 1978—; composer-lyricist; lectr. New Sch. for Social Research, 1976. Mem. Am. Bar Assn. Author: Divorce Law, 1976; also articles, poems; collected poems pub. in Hindi as Lava Poetry, 1978. Address: 330 E 49th St New York City NY 10017

BASS, HYMAN B., orgn. exec., author; b. Vilno, Poland, Nov. 27, 1904; s. Rubin and Ida (Gilden) B.; came to U.S. 1922, naturalized, 1937; student Jewish Tchrs. Sem., Vilno, 1920-22, N.Y.C., 1922-24; D.Jewish Lit. (hon.), Jewish Tchrs. Sem. and Horace M. Kallen Center for Jewish Studies, N.Y.C., 1978; m. Rebecca R. Rosemblum, July 10, 1935 (dec. July 1951); 1 dau., Vivian M.; m. 2d, Sulamitis Kreplak, Aug. 22, 1952. Lectr. tchr's. courses Arbeiter Ring, 1935-48, nat. v.p., 1958-60, 70-72, chmn. ednl. com., 1962-66, 68-70, treas., 1974-76; overseas staff Joint Distbn. Com., 1945-48; mem. profl. staff United Services For New Ams., 1948; lectr. Jewish Tchrs. Sem., N.Y.C., 1948-72, bd. dirs., 1950—; ednl. dir. Congress for Jewish Culture, 1948-53, exec. dir., 1953—, lectr. Inst. Jewish Affairs, 1957-58. Treas. Jewish Book Council, 1959-63, v.p., 1963-66, pres., 1966-68, citation, 1969; adminstrv. com. Jewish Labor Com., 1969—; council Nat. Found. Jewish Culture, 1960—; mem. planning com. World Conf. Jewish Edn. in Jerusalem, 1961-62; mem. exec. bd. Nat. Council Jewish Edn., 1965; bd. dirs. Foward Pub. Assn., 1971—; mem. commn. cultural affairs Jewish Welfare Bd., 1971-72; trustee, mem. exec. bd. Meml. Found. for Jewish Culture, Inc.; trustee Am. Assn. for Jewish Edn. Recipient Shaban Lit. award Congress Jewish Culture, 1950; N. Chanin Lit. award, 1973. Mem. P.E.N. Author: Der Ursprung fun Pesach, 1926; Arbets Buch Fun Yiddisher Geschichte, 1931; Undzer Vort, 1932; Yidn Amol, 1933; Yidn Amol un Haint, 1937; Mein Shprach Buch (2 vols.), 1938, 42; Dos Yiddishe Vort, 1947; Shprach un Dertsiung, 1950; Program fun Yiddisher Geshichte, 1952; Undser Dor Muz Antsheiden, 1963; Shreiber un Verk, 1971. Editor: Bleter Far Yiddisher Dertsiung, 1949-62; Dertsiungs Entsiklopedie, 3 vols., 1957-59; Pinkos far der Forshung fun der Yiddisher Literatur, 1972; Literary Diary of S. Niger-Charney (1907-1955) (with introductory study by editor), 1973; Antologie fun der Yiddisher Literatur far Yugnt., vol. 2, 1976; Di Yiddishe Drame Fun 20th Yorhundert, 2 vols. (with introductory study by editor), 1977; mem. editorial bd. Jewish Audio-Visual Aid Materials Rev., 1950-69; co-editor Zukunft, 1965—; mem. editorial adv. bd. Jewish Book Ann., 1954—, asso. editor, 1971—. Weekly radio commentator. Home: 164 E 78th St New York City NY 10021 Office: 25 E 78th St New York City NY 10021

BASS, WARNER S., condr., Composer, educator; b. Brandenburg, Germany, Oct. 6, 1915; s. Eugene Seeley and Helene B.; M.A. Equivalency, Berlin U.; M.Music Equivalency with honors, State Acad. Music, Berlin; Music B., N.Y. Coll. Music, M.A., N.Y.U.; m. Marion Corda, Apr. 27, 1941; Condr. opera, composer stage music State Opera, Kassel, Germany; condr. Kulturbund Theater, Berlin; asso. condr. Am. Symphony Orch., 1962-64; condr., arranger, orchestrator RCA Victor Rec. Co.; vis. prof. music Southampton Coll. L.I. U., 1965; adj. asso. prof. music N.Y.U., 1967-69; asst. prof. music City U.N.Y. Kingsborough, 1969-71, asso. prof., 1971-75, prof., 1975—; guest condr. with major orchs. Served with U.S. Army, World War II. Mem. ASCAP, Coll. Music Soc., Am. Musicol. Soc., Nat. Hist. Soc. Composer Overture and Fugue Song of Hope; Adagio (Taps) for String Orch., Trumpet and Percussion; Suite for String Orch.; Serenata Concertante for Viola and Strings; 96th Psalm for Tenor Solo, Chorus and Organ; Sonatas for Viola and for Trumpet and Piano.

BASSECHES, ROBERT TREINIS, lawyer; b. N.Y.C., Jan. 24, 1934; s. J.T. and Paula (Treinis) B.; B.A., Amherst Coll., 1955; LL.B., Yale, 1958; m. Harriet Itkin, July 6, 1958; children—Karen, Joshua, Jessica. Admitted to N.Y. State bar, 1959, D.C. bar, 1962; law. clk. Judge David L. Bazelon, U.S. Ct. of Appeals for D.C., 1958-59, Justice Hugo L. Black U.S. Supreme Ct., Washington, 1959; asso. firm Shea & Gardner, Washington, 1960-63 partner firm, 1963—. Pres. Chevy Chase (Md.) Village Citizens Assn., 1976, mem. exec. com., 1976—; pres., 1976—, trustee, bd. trustees Green Acres Sch., 1973-75. Mem. Maritime Adminstrv. (pres. 1969-71), Am. (chmn. maritime transp. com. 1969-71), D.C. bar assns., Order of Coif, Phi Beta Kappa, Phi Alpha Delta. Office: 734 15th St NW Washington DC 20005

BASSETT, GLENN ARTHUR, mfg. co. exec.; b. Fort Collins, Colo., Dec. 19, 1930; s. Glenn Willard and Rosalie Alberta (Morrish) B.; B.A. cum laude, U. Calif. at Berkeley, 1954; M.A., Calif. State Coll. at Long Beach, 1958; Ph.D., Yale U., 1978; m. Olivette Irene Potts, Aug. 20, 1977; children—Glenna Lynn, Glenn Arthur, John, Olivette. Underwriter, field rep., various ins. cos. 1954-60; employment mgr. Climax Molybdenum Co., Leadville, Colo., 1960-62; personnel mgr., specialist social sci. research applications Gen. Electric Co., N.Y.C., 1962—. Cons., Mgmt. Assos., Chgo., Boston, N.Y.C., 1964—, London, Eng., 1973—. Bd. dirs. 23d Assembly Dist. Democratic Club, 1972-74. Served with USAF, 1950-53. Mem. Am. Psychol. Assn., Am. Soc. Personnel Adminstrn., Am. Assn. Pub. Opinion Research. Author: Practical Interviewing, 1965; Management Styles, 1966; New Face of Communication, 1968; Personnel Systems, 1971; Advanced Communication Techniques, 1976. Contbr. to profl. jours. Home: 135 Blueberry Rd Trumbull CT 06611 Office: Easton Turnpike Fairfield CT 06431

BASSETT, MARION PRESTON, writer; b. Bklyn., June 24, 1894; d. Edward Murray and Annie Rebecca (Preston) Bassett; B.A., Wellesley Coll., 1916; postgrad. Columbia, 1920-21, 42-44, New Sch. For Social Research, 1946; m. James C. Luitweiler, Oct. 8, 1917 (div. 1941); children—Preston B., James C. Research analyst in investments Baker Kellogg & Co., N.Y.C., 1921-34; chmn. finance Planned Parenthood Fedn. State of N.J., 1939-42; mem. exec. com. League for Indsl. Democracy, N.Y.C., 1944-48; mem. Tri-State Council on Family Relations, 1947-76, pres., 1947-48; co-founder Am. Assn. Marriage Counselors, 1942; mem. governing bd. Wellesley Summer Inst. for Social Progress, 1933-52; co-founder Farmington Hist. Soc., 1954, exec. sec., 1955-60; active Women's Universal Movement, 1964-76; co-founder Central Conn. chpt. NOW, 1967, mem. exec. bd., 1974. Recipient plaque for distinguished service Am. Assn. Marriage Counselors, 1967. Mem. League Women Voters, Conn. Civil Liberties Union, Planned Parenthood League Conn., Women Strike for Peace. Author: New Sex Ethics and Marriage Structure, 1961; (with Joseph K. Folsom) The Family and Democratic Society, 1948; contbr. articles to popular mags., also internat. quar. Women Speaking. Home and office: 24 Hatters Ln Farmington CT 06032

BASSETT, MARY GRACE, journalist, govt. ofcl.; b. Spokane, Aug. 17, 1927; d. Joseph Elliott and Jane Olive (Jones) Bassett; B.A., Whitman Coll., 1947; M.S. in Journalism, Columbia U., 1948; postgrad. U. Paris, U. Frankfurt, 1950-51, U. Mich. Law Sch., 1977. Freelance writer, Europe, 1949-52; staff writer urban affairs Washington Post, 1952-57; Congl. corr. Washington Star, 1957-67; radio interview program, 1964-67; writer on politics, domestic and urban affairs King Features, Washington, 1969-76; asst. sec. HUD, 1976-77. Asst. campaign mgr. Eugene McCarthy Presdl. campaign, 1968. Russell Sage Found. fellow, 1967; recipient Outstanding Polit. Writing citation Am. Polit. Sci. Assn.; Newspaper Guild prizes. Home: 2704 N St NW Washington DC 20007 Office: South River Farm Loch Haven Rd Edgewater MD 21037

BASSETT, PRESTON CROSBY, actuary; b. Portland, Oreg., Nov, 4, 1917; s. William Waters and Olive Rafina (Crosby) B.; B.A., Reed Coll., 1940; m. Helen Margaret Edmonds, May, 25, 1941; children—Katherine Morris, Preston C. With Prudential Ins. Co., Newark, 1940-50; actuary Towers, Perrin, Forster & Crosby, N.Y.C., 1950-59, v.p., actuary, 1959-60, dir., 1960-77. Mem. adv. council to U.S. Dept. Labor, 1972—. Served with USN, 1943-46; PTO. Fellow Soc. Actuaries (v.p.), Conf. Actuaries in Pub. Practice (past pres.); mem. Am. Acad. Actuaries (v.p.), Internat. Assn. Cons. Actuaries (past pres.), Br. Inst. Actuaries, Council on Employee Benefits, Assn. Pvt. Pension and Welfare Plans, Pension Research Council. Clubs: Union League (Phila.), Springhaven Country. Contbr. articles to profl. jours. Home and office: Tanglewood Circle Wallingford PA 19086

BASSETT, RAYMOND FRANCIS, realtor; b. Buckmanville, Pa., Jan. 13, 1924; s. Frank Faulkner and Jennie (Atkinson) B.; B.B.A., Lansdale Sch. Bus., 1948; m. Georgeann Birdsong Longsdorf, May 22, 1965. Clk. U.S. Post Office, Wrightstown, Pa., 1948-52, U.S. Steel Corp., Fairless Hills, Pa., 1952-60; treas. Bucks County (Pa.), 1960-64, assessor, 1964-72; realtor Newtown, Pa., 1968—. Auditor Wrightstown Twp. (Pa.), 1954-60; sec. Lingohocken Vol. Fire Co., 1948-54, v.p., 1955-64; mem. Newtown Bicentennial Com., 1976. Served with USNR, 1943-46. Mem. Bucks County Bd. Realtors, Pa. Realtors Assn., Nat. Assn. Real Estate Bds., Nat. Assn. Real Estate Appraisers, Bucks County Firemen's Assn. Republican. Clubs: Newtown Reliance (v.p. 1974—), Newtown Hist. Soc. Club: Masons. Home: 281 N Lincoln Ave Newtown PA 18940 Office: 255 S State St Newtown PA 18940

BASSINOR, PAUL, antiquarian bookseller; b. Boston, Dec. 6, 1912; s. Harry and Sarah Bertha (Spitt) B.; A.B., Clark U., 1934; M.A., McGill U., 1935, Harvard, 1939; m. Sarah Ester, Apr. 2, 1938; 1 son, Alan. Owner, Book Den, N.Y.C., 1941-46, Univ. Book Res., Boston, 1946-51, Hull, Mass., 1951—. Mem. Antiquarian Booksellers Assn. Am. (v.p. New Eng. chpt. 1950-52, emeritus), Shaw Soc. U.S., Shaw Soc. Gt. Britain, Delta Phi Alpha. Author: An outline of Chaucer, 1945; A Critical outline of Don Quixote, 1954; outline Confessions of St. Augustine, 1956; Plays of Ibsen, 1959. Home: 75 Main St Hull MA 02045 Office: 815 Nantasket Ave Hull MA 02045

BASSIS, MICHAEL STEVEN, sociologist, educator; b. N.Y.C., Sept. 8, 1944; s. Lewis and Barbara (Fay) B.; A.B., Brown U., 1967; Ph.D., U. Chgo., 1974; m. Mary Wilson, Dec. 27, 1977; children—Anne Elizabeth, Christina Lyons. Faculty U. R.I., Kingston, 1971—, asso. prof. sociology, 1977—, asst. dean Coll. Arts and Scis., 1977—. NIMH fellow, 1967-71. Mem. AAUP, Am., Eastern sociol. assns. Author: The Social Organization of Nautical Education: The U.S., Britain and Spain, 1976. Home: 274 Church St Apt 3E Guilford CT 06437

BASTARACHE, EDOUARD GERALD, physician; b. Arvida, Que., Can., Jan. 30, 1942; s. Joseph Augustin and Marie Clara (Savard) B.; B.A., Laval U., 1962, M.D., 1966; m. Francine Ginette Pellerin, May 31, 1975. Intern Hotel-Dieu, Chicoutimi, Que., 1966-67; resident in surgery and internal medicine Laval U. Hosp., 1967-70; med. researcher Laval Hosp. and Endocrine Lab., Québec City, Que., 1967-71; founding dir. Centre Recherches Appliques Richelieu Yamaska, Sorel, Que., 1971—; individual practice medicine, specializing in environ. health, Sorel, 1971—; cons. environ. health. Served with M.C., Royal Can. Army, 1962-70. Grantee Laval U., Med. Research Council Can., Nat. Sci. Research Inst., Royal Can. Army Med. Corps. Mem. Can. Pub. Health Assn., Internat. Med. Assistance Assn. Liberal Party. Roman Catholic. Contbr. articles to profl. publs. on hyperlipemias, endocrine physiology, environ. lung diseases. Home: 2340 des Erables Sorel PQ J3R 2W3 Canada Office: 30 Ferland St Sorel PQ J3P 3C7 Canada

BASTARDI, ANTHONY VINCENT, smoking cessation co. exec.; b. Newark, Aug. 30, 1944; s. Anthony Vincent and Josephine (Gerardo) B.; B. Engring. with honors, Stevens Inst. Tech., 1966; M.S. in Indsl. and Mgmt. Engring. (Grad. scholar 1966-67), Columbia, 1967; m. Marilyn P. Petrozzino, June 24, 1967; children—Noelle, Anthony Vincent III, Matthew, Christian. Dist. sales mgr. Gen. Precision Systems, Inc., Wayne, N.J., 1967-68; chmn. bd., pres. Mgmt. Computer Systems Corp., Florham Park, N.J., 1968-73, Infotel Corp., Florham Park, N.J., 1971-73, Am. Recycling Corp., Cedar Knolls, N.J., 1973-77; adminstrv. v.p. Smok Enders, Inc., Phillipsburg, N.J., 1977—. Recipient Arthur J. Grymes Jr. award Stevens Inst. Tech., 1966. Mem. Tau Beta Pi, Phi Sigma Kappa (chpt. pres. 1965-66). Home: 40 Polhemus Terr Whippany NJ 07981 Office: 525 Memorial Pkwy Phillipsburg NJ 08865

BASTIAN, GLENN PICKERING, realtor; b. Chemung, N.Y., June 28, 1927; s. Lloyd Franklin and Mary Ellen (Pickering) B.; student Mansfield Coll., 1948-49; m. Martha Ann Bogaczyk, Nov. 17, 1950; children—Glenn Pickering, Scott C., Barbara Bastian MacNamara. Broker, West's Farm Agy., Pitts., 1953-55, pres., Mansfield, Pa., 1955-64; v.p. Safe Buy Real Estate Agy., Inc., Little Rock, 1964-73; sales mgr. Capital Industries Avis, Pa., 1966-71; owner The Real Estaters, Mansfield, 1973—; instr. Pa. State U. Served with U.S. Mcht. Marines, 1944-45, U.S. Navy, 1946, AUS, 1946-48, 50-53. Mem. N. Central Bd. Realtors (past pres., Realtor of Year, 1973), Pa. Real Estate Exchangers (founder), Pa. Farm and Land Brokers (past pres.), Met. Washington, Va., Fla., real estate exchangors, Creative Real Estate Workshop, Pa. Assn. Realtors, Pa., Nat. farm and land insts., VFW, Am. Legion. Republican. Methodist. Author: How to Buy and Sell Real Estate, 1958; Ten Lesson Real Estate Course, 1959. Home: 241 N Main St Mansfield PA 16933 Office: RFD 1 Box 41 Mansfield PA 16933

BASTOMSKY, CHARLES HENRY, endocrinologist; b. Johannesburg, S. Africa, Feb. 28, 1935; s. Boris and Millie B.; came to Can., 1965, naturalized, 1970; M.B., B.Ch., U. Witwatersrand, Johannesburg, 1957; M.R.C.P., Royal Coll. Physicians Edinburgh (Scotland), 1960. Intern, Coronation Hosp., Johannesburg, 1957-58, resident in medicine 1958-59; research fellow Seton Hall Coll. Medicine, Jersey City, 1961-63, Boston U. Sch. Medicine, 1963-65; Med. Research Council Can. research fellow McGill U. Sch. Medicine, Montreal Que., Can., 1965-68, Med. Research Council Can. scholar, 1968-74, asst. prof. exptl. medicine, 1968-76, asso. prof., 1976—, chief clin. thyroid lab. service Royal Victoria Hosp., Montreal, 1974—. Mem. Canadian Soc. Clin. Investigation, Can. Soc. Cell Biology, Am. Fedn. Clin. Research, Am. Thyroid Assn., Endocrine Soc. Jewish religion. Contbr. articles on thyroid physiopathology to profl jours. Home: Apt 1722 3450 Drummond St Montreal PQ H3G 1Y2 Canada Office: 687 Pine Ave W Montreal PQ H3A 1A1 Canada

BASU, SAMARENDRA, biophysicist, electron microscopist; b. Calcutta, India, July 21, 1942; s. Sachindra Krishna and Nihar Bala (Ghosh) B.; came to U.S., 1969, naturalized; Ph.D., Calcutta U., 1968; m. Helen Jean Sabat, Nov. 28, 1975. Research fellow Saha Inst. Nuclear Physics, Calcutta, 1965-68; research asso. and scientist, biophysics dept. U. Chgo., 1969-72; sr. research fellow, cytology dept. Sloan-Kettering Inst. Cancer Research, N.Y.C., 1972-73; sr. cancer research scientist, biophys. dept. Roswell Park Meml. Inst., Bufflao, 1973-76, sr. research scientist, dept. electron optics, div. lab. and research N.Y. State Dept. Health, Albany, 1976—. Recipient DPI merit stipend Govt. of West Bengal (India), 1958-64. Mem. Biophys. Soc. Am., Am. Soc. Cell Biology, Electron Microscopy Soc. Am., Am. Microscopy Soc. Hindu. Research and publs. on cancer cell activity, chromosome structure and function, optical and spectroscopic methods for elucidating detailed orgns. of chromosomes, chromatins and cell surfaces in their near native state. Home: Menands Garden Apts Bldg 7 Apt 3 Menands NY 12204 Office: NY State Dept Health Div Lab and Research Albany NY 12201

BATA, ANDREW, transp. engr., planner; b. Budapest, Hungary, Sept. 13, 1948; s. Rudolf and Elizabeth (Simor) B.; came to U.S., 1963, naturalized, 1972; B.A. in Urban Geography, Hunter Coll., 1971; M.S. in Transp., Northwestern U., 1973; certificate in Energy Engring., Poly. Inst. of N.Y. 1977. Research asso. The Transp. Center, Northwestern U., Evanston, Ill., 1973; transp. engr. Gibbs and Hill, Inc., N.Y.C., 1973—. Transport steering com. mem. local planning bd., N.Y.C. U.S. Dept. Transp. Urban Mass Transp. fellow, 1971-73; Rotary Internat. group study exchange fellow, Japan, 1978. Mem. Am. Inst. Planners, Transp. Research Bd., Nat. Acad. of Scis., Transp. Research Forum. Contbr. to research projects and reports on railways and advanced transport systems. Office: 393 Seventh Ave New York City NY 10001

BATA, EVELYN JOAN, mgmt. cons., educator; b. Buffalo, Mar. 22, 1931; d. James John Heigl; B.A., U. Md., 1967, M.Ed., 1969, Ph.D., 1972; m. John Bata, Jr., Feb. 21, 1959; children—Constance Jean, Lawrence Lee, Cynthia Sue. Partner, Quality Inns, Silver Spring, Md., 1960—; program dir. Urban Service Corps, Washington, 1967-69; curriculum cons. Gen. Conf. Seventh Day Adventists, Washington, 1970-73; instr. English, Prince George's Community Coll., Largo, Md., 1970—; partner Bata Assos. Gen. chairperson Commn. for Women of Prince George's County, 1973-74, chairperson legal status of women com. docent Nat. Gallery Art, 1973-74; vol. probation officer Md. Div. Parole and Probation, 1973—; chairperson Task Force on Abused Women, 1975—; chmn. Hyattsville Citizens Adv. Bd., Urban Renewal Program, 1974—; chmn. New Quality Implementation Com. Prince George's County, 1975—; active Citizens Com. on Modernization Md. Cts. and Justice, 1973—, Prince George's County Manpower Planning Adv. Council, 1973-75, rules and regulations com. Sheriffs Dept. Prince George's County, 1975—, U. Md. Human Resources Adv. Council, 1975—, Personnel Bd. Prince George's County, 1975—, Hyattsville Bicentennial Com., 1975—; chmn. criminal justice com. Hyattsville LWV, 1973-75; chmn. employment com. Womens Polit. Caucus, 1974-75. Recipient Citizenship award Md. Div. Corrections Vol. Programs, 1974, citation for service Dept. Parole and Probation Prince George's County, 1975, certificate of recognition Internat. Women's Year Task Force, Prince George's County, 1975, Disting. Leadership award City of College Park, 1975. Mem. Nat. Council Tchrs. English, AAUP, Nat. Women's Polit. Caucus, AAUW (sec. Md. 1974—, pres. Silver Spring 1975—, Internat. Women's Year award Silver Spring 1975), Prince George's C. of C. (Outstanding Service award 1974, dir. 1974—), Bus. and Profl. Women's Club College Park (pres. 1974-75), So. Md. Dental Soc. Women's Assn. (pres. 1965-66), Md. Fedn. Bus. and Profl. Women (sec. 1975—). Md. Fedn. Women's Clubs (chmn. Prince George's County pub. affairs dept. 1973-75), Nat. Assn. Dental Assts. Clubs: Hyattsville Women's (pres. 1975—). Address: 5403 Queens Chapel Rd Hyattsville MD 20782 Office: care Quality Inn 7200 Baltimore Ave College Park MD 20740

BATCHELOR, BARRINGTON DEVERE, educator; b. Lucea, Jamaica, W.I., July 2, 1928; s. Reginald Augustus and Vera Louise (O'Connor) B.; B.Sc. with honors (Elias Issa Scholar), U. Edinburgh, 1956; Ph.D. (Commonwealth scholar), U. London, 1963; m. Alison Yvonnie Johnston, Sept. 14, 1960; children—Roger, Nicola, Wayne. Asst. engr. Sir William Halcrow & Partners, London, Eng., 1956-58; exec. engr. Ministry Edn., Jamaica, 1958-63, sr. exec. engr., 1963-64; partner Franks & Batchelor, cons. engrs., Kingston, Jamaica, 1964-66; asst. prof. civil engring. Queen's U., Kingston, Ont., Can., 1966-68, asso. prof., 1968-72, prof., 1972—. Mem. task force for devel. of Ont. hwy. bridge design code Ministry of Transp. and Communications. Mem. Am., Canadian socs. civil engrs., Am. Concrete Inst., Instn. Civil Engrs. (U.K.), Instn. Engrs. (Jamaica). Home: 784 Ashley Crescent Kingston ON Canada Office: Dept Civil Engring Queen's Univ Kingston ON Canada

BATCHELOR, SHIRLEY STAGG, concert pianist, educator; b. Paterson, N.J.; d. Theodore and Janet (De-Witt) Stagg; student Oberlin Conservatory of Music, 1943-44; B.S., Juilliard Sch. Music, 1948; M.A., Columbia U., 1949; postgrad. N.Y. U.; student of Carl Friedberg, Edward Steuermann, Karl Ulrich Schnabel; 1 dau., Martha Suzanne. Asst. prof., lectr. humanities Lebanon Valley Coll., Annville, Pa., 1950-54, Young Artists Series, Sta. WNYC, 1950-54; concert appearances throughout Eastern sect. of U.S., 1943; asst. prof. Trenton State Coll., 1962—; head music dept. and concert appearances summers at Les Chalets Francais, Deer Isle, Maine, 1963—; reviewer books on keyboard harmony, piano pedagogy; chamber music and solo concerts, 1970—; adjudicator, mem. Am. Music Scholarship Assn.; adjudicator state contests, 1975—. Mem. Nat., N.J. edn. assns., AAUP, Music Educators Nat. Conf. (adjudicator state contests 1974, 75), N.J. Music Tchrs. Assn. (1st v.p. 1972—). Home: 261 State Rd Princeton NJ 08540 Office: Trenton State Coll Trenton NJ 08625

BATE, WALTER JACKSON, educator; b. Mankato, Minn., May 23, 1918; s. William G. and Isabel (Melick) B.; A.B., Harvard U., 1939, M.A., 1940, Ph.D., 1942; L.H.D., Ind. U., 1969, U. Chgo., 1973; Litt.D., Merrimack Coll., 1970, Boston Coll., 1971; Rutgers U., 1979. Mem. faculty English, Harvard U., Cambridge, Mass., 1946—, prof., 1956—, chmn. dept. history and lit., 1955-56, chmn. dept. English, 1956-63, 66-68, Abbott Lawrence Lowell prof. humanities, 1962—. Guggenheim fellow, 1956, 65. Mem. Am. Philos. Soc., Am. Acad. Arts and Scis., Phi Beta Kappa (Christian Gauss award lit., history and criticism 1956, 64, 70). Author: Negative Capability, 1939; The Stylistic Development of Keats, 1945; From Classic to Romantic, 1946; Criticism: the Major Texts, 1952; The Achievement of Samuel Johnson, 1955; Prefaces to Criticism, 1959; Writings of Edmund Burke, 1960; John Keats, 1963 (Pulitzer Prize 1964); Coleridge, 1968; The Burden of the Past and the English Poet, 1970; Samuel Johnson, 1977 (Pulitzer Prize 1978, Nat. Book award 1978, Nat. Book Critics award 1978). Contbr. editor Yale edit. of Works of Samuel Johnson. Home: Warren House Harvard U Cambridge MA 02138*

BATEN, EUGENE CARL, mgmt. cons.; b. Braddock, Pa., Aug. 10, 1941; s. Robert Eugene and Hazel Irene (Madison) B.; B.A., Juniata Coll., 1963; M.Ed., Temple U., 1966; M.B.A., U. Pa., 1974; m. Anita Louise Washington, Sept. 3, 1966; children-Christopher Gene, Phillip Kerry. Tchr., Phila. Sch. Dist., 1963-69; dir. Entrepreneurial Devel. Tng. Center, Phila., 1969-72; sr. cons. Peat, Marwick, Mitchell & Co., Phila., 1974—; adviser religious and fraternal orgns. Mem. advisory bd. McKinley Sr. Citizens Center, 1976—. Council Opportunity Grad. Mgmt. Edn. fellow, 1972-74. Mem. Nat. Black M.B.A. Assn., Nat. Rifle Assn. (life). Democrat. Baptist. Home: 703 Brook St Willow Grove PA 19090 Office: 1500 Walnut St Philadelphia PA 19102

BATES, BARBARA J. NEUNER (MRS. HERMAN MARTIN BATES, JR.), municipal ofcl.; b. Mt. Vernon, N.Y., Apr. 8, 1927; d. John Joseph William and Elsie May (Flint) Neuner; B.A., Barnard Coll., 1947; m. Herman Martin Bates, Jr., Mar. 25, 1950; children—Roberta Jean, Herman Martin III, Jon Nicholas. Confidential clk. to supr. town Ossining (N.Y.), 1960-63; pres. BNB Assos., Briarcliff Manor, N.Y., 1963—, Upper Nyack Realty Co., Inc., Briarcliff Manor, 1966-71; receiver taxes Town of Ossining (N.Y.), 1971—. Pres., Hackley Sch. Mother's Assn., 1966-68; v.p. Ossining Young Republican Club, 1958; pres. Young Womens Rep. Club Westchester County (N.Y.), 1959-60; regional committeewoman Assn. N.Y. State Young Rep. Clubs, 1960-62; mem. Westchester County Rep. Com., 1963—. Mem. Jr. League Westchester-on-Hudson, Ossining Bus. and Profl. Women's Club, D.A.R., R.I., Briarcliff/Scarborough, Westchester County hist. socs., N.Y. State Assn. Tax Receivers and Collectors, Am. Soc. Notaries. Conglist. Home: 78 Holbrook Ln Briarcliff Manor NY 10510 also RFD 2 Chepachet RI 02814 Office: Municipal Bldg Ossining NY 10562

BATES, CHARLES WILLIAM, county ofcl.; b. Mpls., Feb. 19, 1928; s. Leon Scoville and Isabelle (Ranum) B.; B.A., St. Olaf Coll., 1952; M.S.W., La. State U., 1956; m. Ruth Kuhlman, Oct. 4, 1952; children—Michael Paul, Timothy John, Joseph William. Caseworker, Lake of the Woods City Welfare Dept., Baudette, Minn., 1952-54; child welfare cons. and dist. welfare rep. Minn. Dept. Pub. Welfare, St. Paul, 1956-60; dir. casework Children's Home of Cin. and Ohio Humane Soc., Cin., 1960-64; exec. dir. Child Care Centers, Inc., Milw., 1964-68, Boston Children's Service Assn., 1968-72; dir. Ohio Dept. Pub. Welfare, Columbus, 1972-75; commr. social services County of Westchester (N.Y.), White Plains, 1975—; lectr., cons. Served with AUS, 1946-47. Mem. Acad. Certified Social Workers, Nat. Assn. Social Workers, Lutheran. Home: 103 Midland Ave Rye NY 10580 Office: DSS 150 Grand St White Plains NY 10601

BATES, DON, assn. exec.; b. Boston, May 16, 1939; s. Clifford H. and Helen G. (MacCormick) B.; B.A. cum laude Northeastern U., 1965; m. Helen Minkoff, Nov. 3, 1973; 1 dau., Kelly. Communications specialist Western Electric Co., Inc., N.Y.C., 1965-68; dir. pub. affairs Community Relations Conf. So. Calif., Los Angeles, 1968-70; dir. pub. relations Nat. Assn. Social Workers, Washington, 1970-73; dir. field ops. UN Assn., N.Y.C., 1973-74; exec. dir. Nat. Communication Council Human Services Inc., N.Y.C., 1974-77; mem. pub. affairs com. Nat. Health Council, 1975-77; mem., co-chmn. pub. service com. Pub. Relations Soc. Am., 1975-78, dir. spl. projects, 1977—; adj. prof. Columbia U. Sch. Social Work, 1977—. Bd. dirs. Nat. Conf. Social Welfare, 1973—, Quality of Life Found., 1975-77, Karen Horney Psychoanalytic Inst., 1976—. Recipient newspaper fund award, 1963. Mem. Nat. Acad. TV Arts and Scis., Am. Soc. Assn. Execs., Pub. Relations Soc. Am. (accredited), UN Assn., Greenpeace Found., Sierra Club, ACLU, Common Cause. Author: (with Anne L. New) Using Standards To Strenghten Public Relations, 1977. Home: 150 E 18th St New York City NY 10003 Office: 845 3d Ave New York City NY 10022

BATES, FRANK JOSEPH, athletic coach; b. Paterson, N.J., July 22, 1912; s. Andrew and Michalina (Jablonski) B.; student pub. schs., Paterson; m. Helen Raclawski, Dec. 25, 1937; children—Bonnie Dewitt, Valerie Polumbo, Andrew Fantusi. Coach, referee, weight lifting, 1976—; referee Olympic Games, 1975; coach Pan Am. Games, Mexico City, 1975; coach, mgr., New Zealand, 1975; coach Friendship Cup Contest, USSR, 1974; referee world championships; tchr. Olympic style weight lifting, mem. U.S. Olympic Weight Lifting Com. Elected to Helem's Hall Fame, Paterson, 1968; Old Timer's Hall Fame, Paterson, 1969. Mem. Nat. AAU (pres. N.J. assn.), Internat. Weightlifting Fedn. Club: Tri County Pistol. Contbr. articles on weight tng. to mags. Home: 6 Greenwood St Haskell NJ 07420 Office: 752 Belmont Ave North Haledon NJ 07504

BATES, MARTHA COPENHAVER, guidance counselor; b. Abilene, Tex., Dec. 22, 1933; d. Robert Madison and Mildred (Manton) Copenhaver; B.S. in Psychology, Coll. of William and Mary, 1956; M.Ed. in Guidance and Counseling, Loyola Coll. of Balt., 1974; m. Charles Benjamin Bates, Apr. 9, 1960; children—Benjamin Madison, Lelia Ann, William Andrew. Tchr. 1st grade Montgomery County Pub. Schs., Md., 1956-57; mem. staff subscriber service and enrollment depts. Group Hospitalization, Inc., Washington, 1957-59; tchr. 1st grade Bd. of Edn., Balt. County, Md. 1959-61, tchr. 2nd, 3rd grades 1962-64, elementary sch. guidance counselor 1973—. Recipient advanced profl. certificate elementary guidance and counseling, Md. Mem. Balt. County Counselors Assn., Am., Md. sch. counselors assns., Am., Md. personnel and guidance assns., Tchr. Assn. of Balt. County, Md. State Tchrs. Assn., NEA, Democrat. Methodist. Developer ann. parents' communication group, staff devel. series, contbr. catalog of guidance media, Balt. County Schs. Home: 202 Frazier Ct Joppa MD 21085 Office: 5101 Hazelwood Ave Baltimore MD 21206

BATES, RAYMOND NELSON, real estate and ins. broker; b. Medina, N.Y., May 24, 1928; s. Clarence Nelson and Lillian (Rook) B.; student Rochester Bus. Inst., 1949-50; m. Frances Yevonne Capurro, Jan. 28, 1952; children—Robert Nelson, Betty (Mrs. James A. Moule). Rural mail carrier U.S. Post Office, Lyndonville, N.Y., 1955—; ins. broker, Lyndonville, 1958—; real estate broker, owner, operator Benson Realty, Medina, N.Y., 1974, Lyndonville Realty, 1960—; treas. Bates Modular Homes Sales Inc., Lyndonville, 1972—. Mem., past pres. Orleans County Real Estate Bd., Lyndonville Area Found. Served with AUS, 1946-47. Mem. N.Y. State Firemen's Assn. (life), Nat., N.Y. State real estate bds., Nat. Rural Letter Carriers Assn. Republican. Presbyterian. Clubs: Sportsmen (pres. Yates 1968), Lions (pres. 1967). Home: 15 Lake Ave Lyndonville NY 14098

BATES, WILLIAM EATON, ins. agt.; b. Pitts., June 30, 1942; s. William Palmer and Emma Ruth (Eaton) B.; grad. Shady Side Acad.; 1960; A.B., Franklin & Marshall Coll., 1964; M.B.A., Washington U., 1972; m. LaDonna Joyce Green, Nov. 27, 1971; 1 son, Douglas Green Eaton, Sept. 9, 1978. Asst. buyer Strawbridge and Clothier, Phila., 1964-66; sales rep., mktg. rep. PPG Industries, N.Y.C., St. Louis, Pitts., 1966-74; asso. Edward F. Halderman & Assoc., Pitts., 1974—. Dep. del. ann. conv. Episcopal Diocese of Pitts.; mem. Shady Side Acad. Alumni Council. Recipient Nat. Quality award, State Mut. Circle of Honor, Nat. Sales Achievement award Nat. Assn. Life Underwriters. Mem. State Mut. Inner Circle, Washington U. Alumni Assn., Pitts. Life Underwriters Assn., Nat. Assn. Life Underwriters, Phi Kappa Psi. Republican. Episcopalian. Clubs: Chartiers Country, Franklin and Marshall Coll. (pres.), Pitts. Alumni. Home: 1500 Spreading Oak Dr Pittsburgh PA 15220 Office: 2000 Gateway Center 3 Pittsburgh PA 15222

BATKY, GYULA, electron microscopist; b. Bratislava, Chechoslovakia, Nov. 21, 1935; s. Ferenc and Amalia (Szabo) B.; came to Can., 1960, naturalized, 1966; B.Sc., Royal Danish Agr. and Vet. Coll., Copenhagen, 1959; m. Eva Sylvia Puskas, Dec. 2, 1961; 1 son, John Denis. With Leo Pharm. Products, Copehagen, 1960, Connaught Med. Research Lab., U. Toronto, 1960-61, electron microscopy lab. dept. physics Ont. Research Found., 1961-66, electron microscopy lab. dept. biology Carleton U., 1966-68; electron microscopist electron microscopy lab. dept. anatomy McGill U., 1968—; pres. J.B. EM Services Inc., Montreal, Que. Danish Red Cross scholar, 1957-59. Mem. Electron Microscopy Soc. Am., Micros. Soc. Can., Japanese Soc. Electron Microscopy. Roman Catholic. Office: 128 Ronald Dr Montreal PQ H4X 1M8 Canada

BATT, RONALD ELMER, obstetrician, gynecologist; b. Buffalo, Sept. 24, 1933; s. Elmer Lawrence and Mary Catherine (Roll) B.; student Niagara U., 1951-54; M.D., U. Buffalo, 1958; m. Carol Mary Schaab, Dec. 28, 1957; children—Paula, Douglas, Thomas, Neil, Jennifer, John. Intern, Millard Fillmore Hosp., Buffalo, 1958-59; resident in obstetrics-gynecology State U. N.Y., Buffalo, 1959-60, 62-66; research fellow Harvard U. Med. Sch., 1963-64; asst. in surgery Peter Bent Brigham Hosp., Boston, 1963-64; spl. fellow in gynecologic surgery Mayo Clinic, 1965; practice medicine specializing in gynecology, infertility, obstetrics, Buffalo, 1966—; clin. asst. prof. gynecology, obstetrics State U. N.Y. Served with M.C., USN, 1960-62. Fellow Royal Coll. Surgeons Can.; Am. Coll. Obstetricians and Gynecologists, A.C.S.; mem. Royal Soc. Health, Am. Fertility Soc., Soc. Study Reproduction, Am. Assn. History Medicine, Internat. Soc. History Medicine, Western N.Y. Geneal. Soc. (dir. 1974-76), Med. Hist. Soc. Western N.Y. (pres. 1976), Buffalo and Erie County Hist. Soc. Office: 2900 Main St Buffalo NY 14214

BATTAGLIA, JOHN D., banker; b. Bklyn., May 6, 1940; s. Joseph and Esther (Thapani) B.; B.S., Seton Hall U., 1962; m. Patricia Peters, Nov. 14, 1965; children—Valerie, Joseph, Tracy, Anthony. Sr. auditor Ryan, Harrington & Mortenson, C.P.A.'s, Newark, 1962-66; v.p. James Talcott Inc., Newark, 1966-74, Nat. Bank N. Am., Somerset, N.J., 1974-76; pres. Franklin Comml. Corp., Somerset, 1979—; sr. v.p. Franklin State Bank, Somerset, 1979—; dir. Franklin Comml. Corp. Coach, Pop Warner Football, Little League, Marlboro Basketball. Mem. Bankers Comml. Fin. Assn. (pres. 1977), Nat. Comml. Fin Conf. (dir.), Matawan Italian Am. Assn. Democrat. Roman Catholic. Home: 12 Markham Dr Morganville NJ 07751

BATTERMAN, STEVEN CHARLES, mech. engr.; b. Bklyn., Aug. 15, 1937; s. Jacob and Anna (Abramowitz) B.; B.C.E., Cooper Union, 1959; Sc.M. (NSF fellow), Brown U., 1961, Ph.D., 1964; M.A. (hon.), U. Pa., 1971; m. Judith Wilpon, Mar. 29, 1959; children—Scott David, Risa Karen, Daniel Adam. Mem. faculty U. Pa., 1964—, asst. prof. mech. engrng. and applied mechs., 1964-68, asso. prof., 1968-74, prof., 1974—, asso. prof. orthopaedic surgery research Sch. Medicine, 1972-75, prof. bioengrng., 1974—, profl. biomechs. in vet. medicine, 1975—; cons. Dept. Def., USN, Franklin Inst.; cons. to industry, ins. cos., lawyers. NSF grantee, 1964-70, postdoctoral fellow, 1970-71; Nat. Inst. Dental Research grantee, 1973-77. Mem. ASCE, ASME, Am. Acad. Mechs., Am. Soc. Engrng. Edn., Biomed. Engrng. Soc., Soc. Exptl. Stress Analysis, Soc. Automotive Engrs., Am. Soc. Safety Engrs., Am. Acad. Forensic Scis., Sigma Xi, Tau Beta Pi, Chi Epsilon. Jewish. Contbr. articles to profl. jours.; patentee periodontal diagnostic apparatus. Home: 109 Charlann Circle Cherry Hill NJ 08003 Office: 111A Towne Bldg U Pa Philadelphia PA 19104

BATTERSBY, MARK EDWIN, writer, cons.; b. Phila., Dec. 17, 1941; s. Mark and Carolyn Troupe (Bradley) B.; B.S., U. Kyushu (Japan), 1967; B.A., Temple U., Phila., 1971. Writer, cons. taxation, finance Ardmore, Pa., 1967—. Served with M.I., AUS, 1963-67. Recipient vol. service award Salvation Army, Phila., 1975. Mem. Asso. Bus. Writers Am., Internat. Platform Assn., Pa., Nat. socs. pub. accountants. Episcopalian. Club: Optimists (optimist of year Ardmore 1970-71, pres. 1974-75). Contbr. articles to trade, consumer-oriented publs. Home: 20 Rittenhouse Pl Ardmore PA 19003 Office: 63 W Lancaster Ave Ardmore PA 19003

BATTLE, RONALD OWEN, architect; b. Washington, July 13, 1947; s. Bennett Owen and Mary A. (Sears) B.; B.Arch., Howard U., 1971; M.City Planning and Urban Design, Harvard U., 1974; m. Cynthia Ingrid Goins, May 6, 1972; 1 son, Karif Owen. Planner/architect Skidmore, Owings & Merrill, Washington, 1969-72; asst. instr. dept. city and regional planning Harvard U. Grad. Sch. Design, Cambridge, Mass., 1973-74; project architect/planner Mass. Inst. Tech., Cambridge, 1973-74; sr. asso., project mgr. Perkins & Will, Washington, 1974-78. Recipient design award Progressive Architecture mag. 1978; Howard U./Skidmore, Owings & Merrill fellow, 1969, Skidmore, Owings & Merrill scholar/grantee, 1972-73, Harvard U. scholar, 1972-73. Mem. AIA, Am. Inst. Planners. Democrat. Presbyterian. Club: Harvard (Washington). Address: 2348 14th St NE Washington DC 20018

BATTLE, TURNER CHARLES, III, artist, educator, business exec.; b. Oberlin, Ohio, Mar 13, 1926; s. Turner and Annie (McClellan) B.; student Andrews U., 1944-45; B.A., Oakwood Coll., 1950; postgrad. Wagner Inst. Sci., 1953-54, Cheyney State Coll., 1957-58, Sch. Edn., Temple U., 1959-60, Tchrs. Coll., Columbia, 1960, N.Y. U., 1970—; M.F.A., Tyler Sch. Art, Temple U., 1958; children—Anne Elizabeth, Turner Charles IV. Exhibited in group shows Eastern U.S., including Bucknell U., Phila. Art Alliance, Newport (R.I.) Art Assn., Phila. Mus. Art, Sesquehanna U., Atlantic City Boardwalk Show, shows Greenwich Village, N.Y.C., and many others; represented in permanent collections throughout U.S., India, Eng., Africa, Japan; instr. art Oakwood Coll., Huntsville, Ala., 1946-50; instr. art, Phila., 1956-66; head, Sch. Gifted Children, Phila., 1959-66; asst. prof. art Elmira (N.Y.) Coll., 1966-68; asso. prof. art Moore Coll. Art, Phila., 1968-70; vis. asso. prof. N.Y.U., 1970, teaching fellow, 1971-72; vis. asso. prof., also dir. program Westminster Choir Coll., 1971-74; art cons., lectr. pvt. and pub. orgns., 1958—. Exec. dir. Higher Edn. Coalition Southeastern Pa., 1969-71; dir. Open Door Program, LaSalle Coll., 1969-70; edn. cons. community planners group U.S. Office Edn., 1969-70; asst. exec. dir. United Negro Coll. Fund, N.Y.C., 1974—. Mem. Am. Assn. Higher Edn., Nat. Soc. Lit. and Arts, Tyler Sch. Temple U. Alumni Assn. (pres. 1965-66), Univ. Council for Art Edn., Phi Delta Kappa. Office: 500 E 62d St New York City NY 10021

BATTLE, WILLIAM CLEMENT, psychiatrist; b. Asheville, N.C., Aug. 31, 1925; s. George Cullen and Sarah Jenkins B.; M.D., Duke U., 1949; m. Carolyn Marlowe Calhoun, Jan. 27, 1961; children—Susan Marlowe, Cynthia Lynn. Intern, Duke Hosp., Durham, N.C., 1949-50; resident in pediatrics L.I. Hosp. and U. Rochester (N.Y.) Hosp., 1950-52; practice medicine specializing in pediatrics, Huntington, N.Y., 1954-59; resident in psychiatry Johns Hopkins Hosp., 1960-63; practice medicine specializing in psychiatry, Towson, Md., 1963—; asst. prof. psychiatry Johns Hopkins Hosp., 1971—; asst. prof. child psychiatry U. Md., 1965-66; dir. Dundalk Mental Health Clinic, Balt., 1964-66. Bd. dirs. NE Balt. Symphony Soc.; mem. steering com. North Balt. YMCA. Served with M.C., USAF, 1952-54. Diplomate Am. Bd. Pediatrics. Mem. AMA, Am., Md. psychiat. assns., Md. Assn. Pvt. Practicing Psychiatrists. Home: 309 Lochview Terr Timonium MD 21093 Office: 7710 York Rd Towson MD 21204

BATTLES, MICHAELE SNYDER, lawyer; b. Pitts., July 3, 1942; d. Irvin and Janet Rene (Birken) Snyder; B.A. Ohio State U. 1964; J.D. Boston U. 1967; m. Philip Morton Battles, III, Aug. 31, 1969; 1 son, Alexander. Admitted to U.S. Supreme Ct. bar, 1971, Pa. bar, 1967, D.C. bar, 1972; lawyer sch. desegration cases HEW, Washington, 1967-69; specialist in race race, sex, handicapped and vets. discrimination cases U.S. Dept. Labor, Washington, 1969—, asst. counsel for Equal Opportunity Programs, 1976—; adjunct faculty mem. on employment of handicapped and vets. Cornell Sch. of Indsl. and Labor Relations, N.Y.C., 1974—; lctr. Exec. Enterprises, N.Y.C. 1975—, various others. Commnr. Arlington (Va.) Commn. on Status of Women 1976—; nat. bd. dirs. ACLU, Washington, 1973-76, nat. capitol area bd. dirs. 1970-76; mem. Fiscal Affairs Advisory Com., Arlington, Va. 1974-76, Com. of 100, Arlington 1975—; bd. dirs. Dept. of Labor Day Care Center, Washington, 1977—. Mem. Am., D.C. bar assns., Arlingtonians for a Better County, N.Va. Jewish Community Center, Smithsonian Assos., Wolf Trap Assts. Clubs: Reston Country, Overlee Swim, Soc. for Celebration of Barthmonia, various others. Author untitled book on employment of handicapped, 1978; contbr. articles to profl. jours. Home: 1560 Forest Villa Ln McLean VA 22101 Office: Room 2414 N 200 Constitution Ave Washington DC 20210

BATTOCCHIO, JOHN FRANK, tool mfg. co. exec.; b. Bronx, N.Y., June 6, 1917; s. Frank and Frances (De Valeria) B.; student pub. schs., Mt. Vernon, N.Y.; m. Grace Rella, Dec. 13, 1942; 1 dau., Dolores. Diemaker, Arma Corp., Bklyn., 1942-43, Ward Leonard Co., Mt. Vernon, 1943-46; toolroom and fabricator mgr. Airequipt Co., New Rochelle, N.Y., 1946-53; pres. Batco Inc., Pelham Manor, N.Y., 1953-69; owner, operator Battocchio Co., Ossining, N.Y., 1970—. Mem. Am. Def. Preparedness Assn. Clubs: Pine Island Beach, New Rochelle Rowing. Developer hosp. equipment, including vein and kidney connectors, oxygenators, machinery in med. field. Home: 730 Pelham Rd New Rochelle NY 10805 Office: 59 Central Ave Ossining NY 10562 also PO Box 187 Scarsborough NY 10510

BATTON, DELMA-JANE HECK (MRS. JAMES HAROLD BATTON), librarian; b. Tampa, Fla., Dec. 10, 1915; d. William Claude and Myfanwy (James) Heck; student N.J. State Tchrs. Coll., 1935-36, Coll. of William and Mary, 1937-38, U. Pa., summer 1946; B.S. in L.S., U. Ill., 1950, postgrad., 1951; m. James Harold Batton, July 21, 1951; children—David Jeffrey, Nancy Janine (Mrs. William D. Goodwin, Jr.), Thomas William. Asst., Princeton (N.J.) Pub. Library, 1930-32; librarian State Home for Girls, Trenton, N.J., 1934-35; asst. acquisitions and circulation Princeton U. Library, 1935-37; asst. children's and adult Free Library of Phila., 1938-43; asst. Naval Hosp. Library, Phila., 1943-46; order librarian Principia (Ill.) Coll., 1946-48; catalog asst. U. Ill. Library, 1948-51; field cons. State Library Commn., Dover, Del., 1961-69, acting state librarian, 1964-65, 67-68; dir. Dover Pub. Library, 1969—. Ednl. rep. Del. Assn. for Retarded Children, Dover, 1963-64; mem. Del. Adv. Council on Right to Read, 1973—. Mem. Am. (adv. com. to J.C. Good Reading), Del. (editor bull., sec., pres., pres. pub. library div. 1978—) library assns., NEA, Dover Storytellers League (pres. 1975—), Daus. of Union, D.A.R., AAUW, Soroptimists (corr. sec. Dover 1973-74). Home: 1081 S Bradford St Dover DE 19901 Office: Dover Pub Library Dover DE 19901

BAUDER, FREDERICK WILLIAM, educator; b. Newark, July 25, 1897; s. John F. and Anna M. (Boehm) B.; B.S., Worcester Poly. Inst., 1920; M.S., Stevens Inst. Tech., 1945; postgrad. Columbia U., N.Y. U.; m. Florence A. Mehne, June 24, 1922; 1 dau., Stephanie Ann. Plant chemist Cooper Chem. Co., 1920-26; prod. chemist Congoleum-Nairn Co., 1926-27; mgr. Holdt Paint Co., 1928-29; instr. chemistry N.J. Inst. Tech., 1929-41, asst. prof., 1941-48, asso. prof., 1948-56, prof., 1956—; owner Bauder Products, 1930—; cons. in field.; indsl. waste treatment and sewage treatment cons. Dir. Mullaly Meml. Coatings Lab., Newark Coll. Engrng. Served with USN, 1918. Registered profl. engr.; certified profl. chemist. Fellow Am. Inst. Chemists; mem. Am. Chem. Soc., Am. Soc. Engrng. Edn., Fedn. Socs. for Paint Tech., Phi Sigma Kappa, Omicron Delta Kappa. Mason. Contbr. articles to profl. jours. Home: 19 Great Hills Terr Short Hills NJ 07078 Office: 323 High St Newark NJ 07102

BAUER, CHARLES HENRY, pediatrician; b. Vienna, Austria, Oct. 6, 1927; came to U.S., 1939, naturalized, 1945; s. Ernest and Annie (Farchy) B.; A.B. with honors (Eisenhower scholar), Columbia, 1949; M.D., Harvard, 1953; m. Arlene Malvin, May 29, 1957; children—Russell B., David J. Intern, San Francisco Gen. Hosp., U. Calif., 1953-54; resident and fellow in pediatrics N.Y. Hosp.-Cornell U. Med. Center, 1954-58, dir. Inst. Care Premature Infants, 1958-68; practice medicine specializing in pediatrics, N.Y.C., 1958—;

attending pediatrician, Roosevelt Hosp., N.Y.C., 1958—, chief neonatology and pediatric gastro-enterology, 1965-75; asso. attending pediatrician, chief pediactric gastro-enterology N.Y. Hosp., N.Y.C.; clin. asso. prof. pediatrics Cornell U. Med. Coll.; med. specialist N.Y.C. Dept. Health. Bd. dirs. Found. Internat. Child Health, 1965-75; bd. mgrs. West Side YMCA, chmn. br. council, 1971-74, pres. Leaders Club, 1969-71. Served to maj., M.C. AUS, 1954-63. Diplomate Am. Bd. Pediatrics. Mem. Am. Acad. Pediatrics (pres. sect. perinatology 1975—), Met. Perinatal Soc. N.Y. (exec. com. 1974—), N.Y. County Med. Soc. (com. on infant mortality 1966—), N.Y. Pediatric Soc. (pres. 1973-74), N.Y. Acad. Gastroenterology, N.Y. Gastroenterol. Assn., Phi Beta Kappa. Author: Dr. Bauer's Baby Book. Editor pediatric series Marcel Decker Pub.; editorial cons. Pediatric Annals, 1972—. Contbr. articles to med. jours. Home: 345 E 69th St New York City NY 10021 Office: 1111 Park Ave New York City NY 10028

BAUER, GREGG DAVID, marketing exec., elec. engr.; b. Lodi, Ohio, Aug. 30, 1953; s. Wayne Lichty and J.Ilene (Cleveland) B.; B.S. in Elec. Engring., Ohio U., 1975. Grounds supr. Village of Columbiana, Ohio, 1967-71; asst. engr. Ohio Edison Co. Akron, 1971-75; sr. sales engr. Reliance Electric Co., Syracuse, N.Y., 1975—, marketing exec., 1976—; dir. Todd-Bauer Ins. Inc., 1976—. Registered profl. engr., Ohio. Mem. IEEE, Am. Mgmt. Assn., Aircraft Owners and Pilots Assn., Tau Beta Pi, Omicron Delta Kappa, Eta Kappa Nu, Phi Gamma Delta. Republican. Presbyterian. Home: 7300 Cedar Post Rd Liverpool NY 13088 Office: 6836 E Genesee St Fayetteville NY 13066

BAUER, JOHN PETER, food co. exec.; b. Fuerth, Bavaria, Germany, Nov. 14, 1925; s. August and Agnes (Rosenfeld) B.; came to U.S., 1940, naturalized, 1943; M.B.A., Lycee Janson de Sailly, Paris, 1930; postgrad. N.Y.U., 1941-42, 44-46; m. Marion Rosenstein, June 19, 1949; children—Steven, David. Vice pres. BNS Internat. Sales Corp., N.Y.C., 1946-65; pres., owner Bauer Industries, Inc., N.Y.C., 1965—; pres., owner Poultry and Dairy Corp Am., N.Y.C., AG fuer Agrar handel and Finanzierung, Zurich, Am. European Agrl. Commodities Co. Inc., Transcontinental Packing Corp.; pres. Packers Products Marketing Co., Inc.; owner Bauer Internat. (Europe) GmbH, Frankfurt/Main. Pres., John P. Bauer Found., Inc. Served with AUS, 1942-44. Mem. Inst. Am. Poultry Industries, Am. Meat Inst., Dairy Soc. Internat. Home: 1085 Park Ave New York City NY 10028 Office: PO Box W New York City NY 10028

BAUER, RAYMOND GALE, mfrs. rep.; b. Merchantville, N.J., June 19, 1934; s. Robert Irwin and Florence Winifred (Guyer) B.; A.A., Monmouth Coll., West Long Branch, N.J., 1955; B.B.A., U. Miami, 1958; m. Jayne Whitehead, Feb. 15, 1955; 1 dau., Linda Joan. Div. mgr. R.J. Reynolds Tobacco Co., Winston-Salem, N.C., 1959-68; Middle Atlantic mgr. U.S. Envelope Co., Springfield, Mass., 1968-74; div. sales mgr. Eastern Tablet Corp., Albany, N.Y., 1974-75; owner Ray Bauer Assos., mfrs. reps., Haddonfield, N.J., 1975—. Served with USAF, 1959-64. Mem. Friends of Haddonfield Library, Haddonfield Civic Assn., Smithsonian Assos., Monmouth Coll., U. Miami alumni assns., USAF Aux. (officer), Air Force Assn., Am. Security Council, Am. Mgmt. Assn., Nat. Philatelic Soc., Lambda Sigma Tau, Lambda Chi Alpha. Clubs: Republican, U.S. Senatorial, Arrowhead Racquet, Iron Rock Swim and Country. Home and Office: 132 Maple Ave Haddonfield NJ 08033

BAUER, RICHARD CARLTON, nuclear engr.; b. Batavia, N.Y., July 15, 1944; s. Willard Ronald and Ethel Ann (Roth) B.; B.S. in Chem. Engring. (Clarkson Trustee scholar), Clarkson Coll. Tech., 1966; M.Engring., Cornell U., 1968; Ph.D. in Nuclear Sci., Engring. (Bettis Doctoral Program fellow), Carnegie-Mellon U., 1974; m. Madeline Joy Amreich, June 28, 1969; children—Jason Todd, Cheryl Robyn. Technician, Graham Mfg. Co., Batavia, N.Y., summer 1965; engr. Linde div. Union Carbide Corp., Tonawanda, N.Y., summer 1966; hot cell operator asst. Cornell U., Ithaca, N.Y., 1967; sr. engr. Bettis Atomic Power Lab. div. Westinghouse Corp., West Mifflin, Pa., 1968—; employee tng. lectr. reactor safety, sec. lab. reactor ops. safety com. Chmn. Cornell Secondary Schs., Pitts.; chmn. P.E.I. Pitts. Regents fellow, 1962; AEC spl. fellow, 1967; registered profl. engr., Pa.; certified fallout shelter analyst, multiprotection designer. Mem. Nat., Pa. soc. profl. engrs.; Cornell Soc. Engrs. (regional v.p.), Am. Nuclear Soc., Am. Inst. Chem. Engrs., Tau Beta Pi, Sigma Xi, Omega Chi Epsilon, Triangle Frat. Contbr. articles to sci. jours.

BAUERNFEIND, JACK (JACOB) C(HRISTOPHER), nutritionist, food technologist; b. N. Branch, N.Y., Apr. 30, 1914; s. Edward and Nellie (Metzger) B.; B.S., Cornell U., 1936, M.S., 1939, Ph.D., 1940; m. Lillian Rose Nurmi, July 23, 1939; children—Kathleen, Michael, Edmund. Nutritionist, research chemist Hiram Walker & Son, Inc., Peoria, Ill., 1940-44; chief applied nutrition Hoffmann-La Roche, Inc., Nutley, N.J., 1944-55, dir. food and agrl. product devel., 1955-61, dir. agrl. research, 1961-68, dir. agrochemistry and asst. to v.p. for chem. research, 1968-71, nutrition research coordinator, 1972—. Trustee Grace Presbyterian Ch., Montclair, N.J., 1973-76, v.p., 1975; mem. adv. com. to pres. Montclair State Coll., 1969-72; mem. Nutley Bd. Edn., 1948-50; bd. dirs. Bergen County (N.J.) Community Chest, 1965-66; supt. Glen Rock (N.J.) Community Ch., 1962-64. Life fellow Inst. Food Technologists (indsl. achievement award 1968); mem. Am. Chem. Soc., N.Y. Acad. Sci., Poultry Sci. Assn. (research award 1940), World Poultry Sci. Assn., Am. Soc. Animal Sci., Animal Nutrition Research Council, Agrl. Research Inst., Am. Inst. Nutrition, Am. Soc. Clin. Nutrition, Soc. Nutrition Edn., Nutrition Today Soc., Sigma Xi. Contbr. numerous articles to profl. jours. Research in nutrition, biochemistry, food tech., agrochemistry, vitamins, food colors, animal health, drugs, food additives. Home: 3664 NW 12th Ave Gainesville FL 32605 Office: Hoffmann-La Roche Inc 340 Kingsland St Nutley NJ 07110

BAUGHMAN, URBANUS EDMUND, ret. chief U.S. Secret Service; b. Camden, N.J., May 21, 1905; s. Urbanus Edmund and Alberta (Faunce) B.; student U. Pa., 1931-33; m. Ruth Louise Yessel, Aug. 5, 1936; 1 son, William E. With U.S. Secret Service, Washington, 1927-61, chief of secret service, 1948-61. Mem. law enforcement adv. com. Ocean County Coll., Toms River, N.J., 1976—. Recipient Albert Gallatin award U.S. Treasury Dept., 1961, Exceptional Service award, 1961. Mem. Internat. Assn. Chiefs of Police (life), Chiefs of Police of Southeastern Pa., Md. Law Enforcement Assn., Assn. Former Agts. of U.S. Secret Service, Ocean County Hist. Soc., Sons of Union Vets. of Civil War. Clubs: Ocean Acres Golf, Beachwood Yacht. Author: Secret Service Chief, 1961. Home: 306 Wayne Ave Pine Beach NJ 08741

BAULKNIGHT, CHARLES WESLEY, research scientist, environ. and energy problems cons.; b. Concord, N.C., Nov. 15, 1911; s. Charles Henry and Martha (Freeman) B.; B.S. in Chemistry, Johnson C. Smith U., 1935, D.Sc. (hon.), 1959; postgrad. U. Pa., 1938-40, 52-55; postdoctoral study St. John's U., 1965; m. Helen Madelon Pryor, Dec. 21, 1946; 1 son, Charles Jeffery. Research asso. Thermodynamics Lab., U. Pa., Phila., 1944-45, Mellon Inst., Pitts., 1945-46; phys. chemist Frankford Arsenal, Phila., 1946-56; research scientist Gen. Electric Co., Valley Forge, Pa., 1956-63, Grumman Aerospace Corp., Bethpage, N.Y., 1963-76; congressional sci. counselor to U.S. Rep. Jerome A. Ambro, 1974—; founder, chmn. bd., pres. Inst. for Sci. Inquiry, Inc., 1977—. Trustee Johnson C. Smith U., 1965—, Dowling Coll., Oakdale, N.Y., 1973; trustee Friends of Nassau County Mus., 1975—, also mem. air space com.; v.p. J.F.K. Democratic Club, 1976, pres., 1977; ruling elder Presbyterian Ch. Recipient Congressional Record citation, 1976; named Young Man of Year Christian St. YMCA, 1960. Fellow Am. Inst. Chemists, Am. Inst. Aeros. and Astronautics (asso.); mem. Am. Chem. Soc. (sec.-treas. L.I. sect. 1976-77), Am. Phys. Soc., AAAS, Sigma Xi, Beta Kappa Chi, Alpha Phi Alpha. Contbr. articles to profl. jours. Home: 19 Romscho St Bethpage NY 11714 Office: S Oyster Bay Rd Bethpage NY 11714

BAUM, ALAN EDMUND, physician; b. Fairfield, Conn., July 26, 1921; s. Seymour J. and Anne Margaret (Lynch) B.; A.B., Columbia U., 1942, M.D., 1945; m. Cecelia Jane Connolly, Aug. 17, 1946; children—Gregory, Douglas, Alan Edmund Jr., William, Reyne. Resident in radiology L.I. Coll. Hosp., 1948-51; practice medicine specializing in radiology, Hicksville, also Huntington, N.Y., 1951—; chief radiology VA Hosp., Northport, N.Y., 1968—; asso. prof. radiology State U. N.Y. at Stony Brook, 1974—, acting chmn. radiology, 1977-78; sec.-treas. BAB Rad., P.C., Huntington, N.Y., 1974-78, pres., 1978—; pres. Hicksville Profl. Bldg. Inc., 1954—. Past pres. Laurel Cove Property Owners Assn. Served with USNR, 1942-47, 53. Fellow Am. Coll. Radiology, Nassau Acad. Medicine; mem. AMA, Med. Soc. State N.Y., L.I. Radiol. Soc. (past pres.), Radiol. Soc. N.Am. Republican. Roman Catholic. Club: Meadowbrook (Jericho). Home: 230 Laurel Cove Rd Oyster Bay Cove NY 11771 Office: 7 Lawrence Hill Rd Huntington NY 11743

BAUM, EMANUEL LESTER, cons. co. exec.; b. N.Y.C., July 15, 1922; s. B. and E. (Cogan) B.; B.S., Cornell U., 1942; M.S., Iowa State U., 1947, Ph.D., 1949; m. Norma G. Goldsmith, July 3, 1946; children—Kenneth H., Steven R., Bryan A. Asst. prof. Wash. State U., 1949-54; chief agrl. econs. br. TVA, 1954-61; sr. economist, dir. regional devel. U.S. Dept. Agr., Washington, 1961-67; v.p. Acres Am. Inc., also Acres Cons. Services Ltd., Washington and Buffalo, 1967—. Served with Inf. AUS, 1942-46. Decorated Purple Heart, Bronze Star. Mem. Am. Agrl. Econs. Assn., Regional Sci. Assn., Am. Econs. Assn. Author: Capital and Credit Problems in a Changing Agriculture, 1961; Economic and Technical Analyses of Fertilizer Innovations and Resource Use, 1957. Home: 5707 English Ct Bethesda MD 20034 Office: 1750 Pennsylvania Ave NW Suite 1105 Washington DC 20006 also Suite 900 Liberty Bank Bldg Buffalo NY 14202

BAUM, GILBERT, ophthalmologist; b. Apr. 29, 1922, N.Y.C.; s. Louis and Minnie (Wang) B.; B.A., U. Wis., 1942; M.D., L.I. Coll. Medicine, 1945; m. Barbra Nusbaum, 1951; children—David, Robert, Margo. Intern, Bklyn. Jewish Hosp., 1945-46; resident Bronx (N.Y.) VA Hosp.; practice medicine specializing in opthalmology, Port Chester, N.Y., 1951—, prof. ophthalmology AlbertEinstein Coll. Medicine, Bronx, 1952—, dir. ultrasound lab., 1955—; mem. staffs Montefiore Hosp., Bronx Municipal Hosp. Served with AUS, 1946-48. Diplomate Am. Bd. Ophthalmology. Fellow Internat. Soc. for Diagnostic Ultrasound in Ophthalmology (hon.); mem. Am. Inst. Ultrasound in Medicine (past pres., Recognition award 1977), World Fedn. for Ultrasound in Medicine and Biology (pres.), Am. Acad. Ophthalmology and Otolaryngology, N.Y. State, Westchester County med. socs., IEEE, Am. Internat. Symposium on Ultrasonic Diagnostics in Ophthalmology. Author: Fundamentals of Medical Ultrasonography, 1975; also articles, chpts. in books. Mem. adv. editorial bd. Ultrasound in Medicine and Biology; cons. editorial bd. Jour. Clin. Ultrasound. Office: 333 King St Port Chester NY 10573

BAUM, INGEBORG RUTH, librarian; b. Berlin, Germany, Sept. 20, 1916; d. Ella Koch; Oberlyceum (scholar), Kassel, Germany, 1926-33; postgrad. Georgetown U., 1963-70; m. Albert Otto Baum, Feb. 16, 1938 (div. 1960); children—Harro Siegward, Helma Sigrun (Mrs. George Meadows). Came to U.S., 1951, naturalized, 1957. Export corr. Bitter-Polar, Germany, 1933-35, Henschel Locs, Germany, 1936; exec. sec. Fieseler Airplane Mfrs., Germany, 1936-38; interpreter, sec. UNRRA, Germany, 1946-48; payroll supr., civilian dept. U.S. Army, Wetzler PX, Germany, 1948-51; asst. librarian Supreme Council, Ancient and Accepted Scottish Rite, Washington, 1951-70, acting librarian and museums curator, 1970—. Vice pres. Merical Elec. Contractors, Inc., Upper Marlboro, Md. Free-lance contbr. to Pabelverlag, Rastatt, Germany, Harie, Ofcl. Publs., Inc., others. Mem. Am. Soc. Appraisers. Mem. Ch. of Jesus Christ of Latter-day Saints. Home: 2480 16th St NW Apt 416 Washington DC 20009 Office: 1733 16th St NW Washington DC 20009

BAUM, JOHN LEACH, museum curator; b. N.Y.C., Mar. 25, 1916; s. Dwight James and Lucia Katharine (Crouse) B.; grad. Berkshire Sch., 1935; B.A., cum laude, Harvard, 1939; m. Augusta Theodora Gallagher, June 24, 1940; children—Dwight Gallagher, Peter Nicholas. Mineral exploration geologist N.J. Zinc Co., Franklin, N.J., 1939-71; curator Franklin Mineral Mus., 1965—. cons. geologist municipal water supplies, 1971—. Mem. Sussex County Municipal Utilities Authority, Newton, N.J., Franklin Pub. Works Dept., 1956-60, Hamburg (N.J.) City Council, 1965-66. Fellow Geol. Soc. Am.; mem. Sussex County Hist. Soc. (trustee), Franklin-Ogdensburg Mineral. Soc. (past pres.), Mineral. Soc. Am. Contbr. articles to profl. jours. New mineral species baumite named for contbns. to mineralogy, 1973. Home: 70 Route 23 N Hamburg NJ 07419 Office: 76 Evans St Franklin NJ 07416

BAUM, RICHARD THEODORE, engring. co. exec.; b. N.Y.C., Oct. 3, 1919; B.A., Columbia U., 1940, B.S., 1941, M.S., 1948. Engr., Electric Boat Co., Groton, Conn., 1941-43; with Jaros, Baum & Bolles, N.Y.C., 1946—, partner, 1958—. Mem. adv. council, faculty of engring. and applied sci. Columbia U., 1972—. Served to 1st lt. USAAF, 1943-46. Registered profl. engr., N.Y., Mass., Conn., N.J., others. Fellow Am. Cons. Engrs. Council, ASME, Am. Soc. Heating, Refrigerating and Air-Conditioning Engrs.; mem. Nat. Soc. Profl. Engrs., Am. Arbitration Assn. (panel of arbitrators 1973—). Club: Univ. (N.Y.C.). Office: 345 Park Ave New York City NY 10022

BAUM, SHARON ENLOE, banker; b. Kansas City, Mo., Jan. 3, 1940; d. Herbert I. and Emma Bonnadell (Clibourn) Enloe; student U. Stockholm, 1960-61; B.A., Randolph-Macon Women's Coll., 1962; M.B.A., Harvard U., 1965; m. Stephen H. Baum, Mar. 16, 1969; children—Benjamin Clibourn, Samuel David. Mgr. mktg. planning Eastern Airlines Co., N.Y.C., 1965-66; mgr. women's promotion Pan Am Airways Co., N.Y.C., 1966-69; v.p., dir. advt. Chem. Bank, N.Y.C., 1970—. Mem. AAUW, DAR, Zeta Tau Alpha. Republican. Baptist. Clubs: Harvard, Princeton, Harvard Bus. Sch. (N.Y.C.). Home: 850 Park Ave New York City NY 10021 Office: Chem Bank 20 Pine St New York City NY 10015

BAUM, SHELDON, physician; b. Monticello, N.Y., Oct. 31, 1927; s. Abraham and Ida (Rosenbaum) B.; B.S. cum laude, Georgetown U., 1951; M.D., U. Pa., 1955; m. Maureen Gardiner, Apr. 26, 1966; children—David, Robert, Stephanie. Intern U. Chgo. Hosps., 1955-56; resident Francis Delafield Hosp., N.Y.C., 1956-57, Hartford (Conn.) Hosp., 1957-60; practice medicine, specializing in nuclear medicine, 1964—; dir. nuclear medicine Pa. State U. Coll. Medicine, 1976—, asso. prof. radiology, 1976—. Served with U.S. Army, 1946-47. Diplomate Am. Bd. Nuclear Medicine Imaging, 1979; editor-in-chief: Clin. Nuclear Medicine, 1976. Home: 10 Dogwood Dr Hershey PA 17033 Office: 500 University De Hershey PA 17033

BAUM, SIEGMUND JACOB, physiologist; b. Vienna, Austria, Nov. 14, 1920; s. Joseph L. and Marie (Leiser) B.; came to U.S., 1939, naturalized, 1943; B.A., U. Calif. at Los Angeles, 1949, M.A., 1950; Ph.D., at Berkeley, 1959; m. Arline Renee Weber, Apr. 1, 1947; children—Jonathan W., Andrew M., Vicki M., Joseph L., Anthony P. Sr. project leader radiobiology U.S. Naval Radiol. Def. Lab., San Francisco, 1950-60; group leader physiology and radiobiology Douglass Missile & Space Div., Santa Monica, Cal., 1960-62; div. head Armed Forces Radiobiology Research Inst., Bethesda, Md., 1962-64, chmn. exptl. pathology dept., 1964-76, chmn. exptl. hematology dept., 1976—; lectr. physiology Georgetown U., Washington, 1970-71; prof. dept. physiology Sch. Medicine, Uniformed Services U. of Health Scis., Bethesda, 1978—. Served with AUS, 1942-45. Recipient 1st ann. award for sci. achievement Naval Radiol. Def. Lab., 1960, Exceptional Civilian Service award Def. Nuclear Agy., 1973. Mem. Am. Physiol. Soc., Internat. Soc. Exptl. Hematology, Transplantation Soc., Radiation Research Soc., Sigma Xi. Toastmaster (pres., 1963-64). Contbr. articles to profl. jours. Home: 6600 Greyswood Rd Bethesda MD 20034 Office: Armed Forces Radiobiology Research Inst Nuclear Defense Agy Bethesda MD 20014

BAUM, STANLEY ALLEN, advt. agy. exec.; b. N.Y.C., Mar. 6, 1928; s. Louis and Olga (Pasternack) B.; B.A., N.Y.U., 1949. Advt. writer Dancer-Fitzgerald-Sample, N.Y.C., 1950-56, copy supr., 1956-69, v.p., creative dir., 1969—; prin. Stanley Baum Assos., N.Y.C., 1970-72; pres. Robert L. Smock Staff, Princeton, N.J., 1972—, Creative Corps., N.Y.C., 1974—. Mem. Dramatist's Guild, ASCAP. Clubs: N.Y. University, Players. Home: 235 Lincoln Pl Brooklyn NY 11217 Office: 330 E 49th St New York City NY 10017

BAUM, WILLIAM, Cardinal; b. Dallas, Nov. 21, 1926; s. Harold E. and Mary Leona (Hayes) W.; student Kenrick Sem., St. Louis, 1947-51, U. St. Thomas Aquinas, Rome, 1956-58; S.T.L., Muhlenberg Coll., Allentown, Pa., 1957, S.T.D., 1968, D.D., 1967; LL.D. (hon.), Georgetown U., 1973, St. John's U., Bklyn., 1973. Ordained priest Roman Cath. Ch., 1951; elevated to cardinal, 1976; asso. pastor St. Aloysius Parish, St. Therese's Parish and St. Peter's Parish, Kansas City, Mo., 1951-56, 61-64, 67-68; adminstr. St. Cyril's Parish, Sugar Creek, Mo., 1960-61; pastor St. James Parish, Kansas City, Mo., 1968-70; chancellor Diocese Kansas City-St. Joseph, 1967-70; bishop of Springfield-Cape Giradeau, Mo., 1970-73; archbishop of Washington, 1973—; instr., then prof. Avila Coll., Kansas City, Mo., 1954-56, 58-63. Hon. chaplain of the Pope, 1961; peritus 2d Vatican Council, 1962-65; hon. prelate of the Pope 1968; 1st exec. dir. Bishops' Commn. Ecumenical and Inter-religious Affairs 1964-67; mem. Joint Working Group, reps. Cath. Ch. and World Council Chs., 1965-69; mem. Mixed Commn., reps. Cath. Ch. and Lutheran World Fedn., 1965-66; mem. Vatican Congregation Cath. Edn., also mem. secretariat for Non-Christians; observer Vatican Secretariat Promoting Christian Unity; chmn. doctrine com., com. pastoral research and practices U.S. Cath. Conf.-Nat. Conf. Cath. Bishops; mem. Nat. Catechetical Directory Com., Commn. Contemplative Nuns, Bishop's Welfare Relief Com., adminstrv. com. Nat. Conf. Cath. Bishops. Trustee Cath. U. Am. Author: The Teaching of Cardinal Cajetan on the Sacrifice of the Mass, 1958; Considerations Toward the Theology on the Presbyterate, 1961. Office: 1721 Rhode Island Ave NW Washington DC 20036*

BAUMAN, CAROL DAWSON, writer; b. Indpls., Sept. 8, 1937; d. Ernest Eugene and Hilda Lou (Carroll) Dawson; B.A., Dunbarton Coll., Washington, 1959; m. Robert Bauman Nov. 19, 1960; children—Edward Carroll, Eugenie Marie, Victoria Anne, James Shields. Exec. sec. Youth for Nixon-Lodge, 1959-60; legis. aide U.S. Congressman Donald C. Bruce of Ind., 1961-63; dep. dir. info. Goldwater-Miller campaign, 1963-64; editor New Guard mag., Washington, 1965-66; dir. info. Am. Conservative Union, 1967-68; news analyst Exec. Office President 1969; staff reporter Easton (Md.) Star-Democrat, 1971; writer Md., Horse and Horse Play mag., 1972-73, editor horse sports page, 1976-77; free-lance writer, 1969—; realtor asso. Latham Realtors, Easton, Md., 1977—. Chmn. Talbot County (Md.) Right to Life Com., 1973-74. Pres. Dunbarton Coll. Young Republicans, 1958-59; co-chmn. Nat. Coll. Young Reps., 1959-60; bd. dirs. Young Americans for Freedom, 1960-64; vice chmn. Talbot County Rep. Central Com., 1970-74. Mem. 93d Congl., Rep. Congl. wives clubs, Talbot County Rep. Women's Club, Talbot County Kennel Club, Talbot County Horse Show Assn. Roman Catholic. Clubs: Talbot County Women's; Capitol Hill. Home: Glebe House Route 5 Easton MD 21601 Office: 29 Dover St Easton MD 21601 also 118 Cannon Bldg Washington DC 20515

BAUMAN, MARY KINSEY, psychologist, agency exec.; b. Phila., Nov. 10, 1910; d. Abram D. and Mary Jane (Huber) Kinsey; B.S., U. Pa., 1930, M.S., 1945; postgrad. Pa. State U., Temple U.; m. Nathan P. Bauman, Sept. 1, 1933. Mem. staff Psychol. Clinic, U. Pa., Phila., 1930-42; asst. dir. Trainee Acceptance Center Phila., 1942-45; co-dir., dir. Personnel Research and Guidance, Phila., 1945-73; dir. Nevil Interagency Referral Service, Phila., 1973—; exec. sec. Assn. for Edn. Visually Handicapped, 1969-77; condr. research, cons., psychol. evaluation and rehab. of visually and physically handicapped, N.J., Pa., Md., Del., Va., S.C.; pres. Am. Assn. Workers for the Blind, 1977—, Pa. Consumer-Provider Council, 1976-78; v.p., bd. dirs. Radio Info. Center for the Blind, Gov. appointee State Bd. Vocat. Rehab., 1963-72, chmn. policy and planning bd. Comprehensive Statewide Planning for Vocat. Rehab., 1966. Mary E. Switzer fellow, 1977-78; lic. psychologist, Pa.; certified pub. sch. psychologist, Pa. Diplomate Am. Bd. Profl. Psychologists. Fellow Am. Psychol. Assn.; mem. Eastern, Pa. psychol. assns., Nat. (life), Pa. (pres. 1964-65) rehab. assns., Assn. Edn. Visually Handicapped (life; sec.-treas. 1965-69), Council for Exceptional Children, AAUW, Council of and for Blind of Delaware Valley, Women's Personnel Group Phila. Contbr. articles to profl. publs. in field; author books. Home: 400 Orchard Ln Fort Washington PA 19034 Office: 919 Walnut St Philadelphia PA 19107

BAUMAN, ROBERT E., congressman; b. Apr. 4, 1937; s. John Carl and Florence (House) B.; B.S. in Internat. Affairs, Georgetown U., 1959, J.D., 1964; m. Carol Gene Dawson, 1960; children—Edward Carroll, Eugenie Marie, Victoria Anne, James Shields. Various staff positions U.S. Ho. of Reps., including House page, staff Judiciary com., minority floor staff, 1953-68; admitted to Md. bar, 1964, practice, 1968—; mem. 93d-96th Congresses from 1st Md. Dist. Founder, nat. chmn. Young Ams. Freedom, 1962-65; founder, dir. Am. Conservative Union, 1964—, now nat. chmn.; del. Republican nat. conv., 1964, alt. del., 1972; mem. Md. State Senate, 1970-73. Mem. Am., Md. bar assns., Md. Farm Bur., Isaac Walton League, YMCA. Club: Elks. Address: 2443 Rayburn House Office Bldg Washington DC 20515

BAUMAN, WILLIAM ALLEN, pediatrician; b. N.Y.C., Nov. 23, 1923; s. Louis and Stella (Kraus) B.; student Harvard U., 1942-43, 46; M.D., Columbia U., 1947, postgrad. in Biostatistics, Sch. Pub. Health, 1960-63; m. Joan Carlsen, June 28, 1952; children—William Carlsen,

Phillip Allen, Pamela Joan. Intern, L.I. Div. Kings County Hosp., Bklyn., 1947-48; resident Babies Hosp., N.Y.C., 1948-50; dir. pediatric clinic Vanderbilt Clinic, N.Y.C., 1954-65; practice medicine specializing in pediatrics, N.Y.C., 1953—; dir. med. data processing Presbyn. Hosp., N.Y.C., 1966-74, asso. attending pediatrician, 1973—; v.p. med. adminstrv. services Group Health Inc., N.Y.C., 1974-77; chmn. bd. govs. Hillcrest Gen. Hosp.-Group Health Inc., 1975—, attending pediatrician 1975—; sr. v.p. Health Services Group Health Inc., 1977—; asso. clin. prof. pediatrics Columbia U., 1973—, mem. com. for study of sci. in human affairs, 1967—; mem. med. bd. Maternity Center Assn., 1969—; chmn. faculty-student advisory bd. P&S Club Coll. Physicians and Surgeons, Columbia U., 1970—; chmn. com. on data processing New York County Health Rev. Orgn., 1976—. Served with M.C. USAF, 1951-52. Fellow N.Y. Acad. Medicine; mem. Am. Acad. Pediatrics, New York County Med. Soc., Med. Soc. State N.Y. (chmn. com. on data processing in medicine 1967—), Assn. Ambulatory Pediatrics, Assn. Computing Machinery, Soc. Computer Medicine (trustee), Bioengring. Inst., Am. Soc. Info. Scis., N.Y. Acad. Scis., N.Y. State Assn. professions. Contbr. articles to med. jours. Home: 20 Country Club Dr Larchmont NY 10538 Office: 326 W 42d St New York City NY 10036

BAUMBACH, RICHARD CARTER, oral surgeon; b. Scranton, Pa., Mar. 7, 1929; s. Clifford Weber and Irene Matilda (Carter) B.; B.A. magna cum laude, Syracuse U., 1950; D.D.S. cum laude, U. Pa., 1954, certificate in oral surgery, 1957; m. Mary Ellen Grove, Sept. 18, 1954; children—Peter G., Philip F., S. Andrew. Intern, then resident in oral surgery Henry Ford Hosp., Detroit, 1958-60; practice dentistry specializing in oral surgery, Shillington, Pa., 1960—; mem. ambulatory care com. Reading (Pa.) Hosp.; mem. adv. com. Am. Bd. Oral Surgery, 1974-78. Exploring chmn. Apalachian Dist. Haw Mountain council Boy Scouts Am., 1969—. Served to lt. (s.g.) USNR, 1954-56. Recipient Sight Conservation award Sinking Spring Lions Club, 1966. Diplomate Am. Bd. Oral Surgery. Mem. Am., Pa., Middle Atlantic, Central Pa. (chmn. ethics com.) socs. oral surgeons, Am. Dental Assn., A.M.A. (spl. affiliate), Phi Beta Kappa, Psi Chi, Alpha Epsilon Delta, Alpha Chi Rho, Xi Psi Phi. Republican. Lutheran (mem. ch. council 1964-67, v.p. 1966). Lion (pres. Sinking Spring 1967-68). Club: Heidelberg Country (Bernville, Pa.). Home: 401 S Tulpehocken Rd Reading PA 19601 Office: 517 E Lancaster Ave Shillington PA 19607

BAUMEISTER, VICTOR FLOYD, architect; b. Georgetown, Del., Nov. 12, 1919; s. Victor Leroy and Mary Estelle (Taylor) B.; student Logan Coll., 1937-40, Wilmington Acad. Fine Arts, 1941, Internat. Corr. Schs., 1947-51; m. Virginia Lee Williamson, Apr. 18, 1942; children—Richard Mark, Marcia Lee (Mrs. Dennis Grant Sutton), Robert Victor. Draftsman, designer, job capt. Weston H. Blake, Architect, Wilmington, 1947-51, Walter Carlson, Architect, 1951-60; with Whiteside, Moeckel & Carbonell architects, Wilmington, 1960—, chief specification writer, mgr. specification dept., 1964—. Mem. USCG Aux., 1959—, commodore, 1971, 72; active Boy Scouts Am. Served with AUS, 1942-46; ETO. Mem. AIA, Constrn. Specifications Inst. Republican. Episcopalian. Clubs: Masons, K.T. Home: RD 4 West Chester PA 19380 Office: 29 Hill Rd Wilmington DE 19899

BAUMGAERTNER, IMRE V., oceanographer-geologist, educator; b. Szentendre, Hungary, Nov. 19, 1937; s. Bela v. and Ilona (Tilkowszky) B.; came to U.S., 1961, naturalized, 1969; Rockefeller Found. scholar U. Innsbruck (Austria), 1957; U. Graz (Austria), 1957-61; m. Erika Mandy, Oct. 19, 1962. Research asst. Lamont Doherty Geol. Observatory, Columbia U., Palisades, N.Y., 1968-72; research asst. Goddard Space Flight Center NASA, N.Y.C., 1971; cons., French Nickel Co., France, 1971, U.S. Nat. Parks Service, 1974-75; pvt. cons., dept. geology Fairleigh Dickinson U., Rutherford, N.J., 1972—; dir. M&C Environ. Cons., Freeport, N.Y., 1974—; adj. prof. N.J. Marine Scis. Conservatory, Sandy Hook, 1974, 76; asst. prof. dept. geology and geography C.W. Post Center, L.I. U., Greenvale, N.Y., 1977—; contbr. to N.C. ednl. TV series, 1975. Roman Catholic. Contbr. articles to encys. and profl. jours. Address: 48 E 2nd St Freeport NY 11520

BAUMHOFER, WALTER MARTIN, painter, illustrator; b. Bklyn., Nov. 1, 1904; s. Henry and Marie (Wolters) B.; grad. (Sch. scholar), Pratt Inst., 1925; m. Alureda Moore Leach, June 28, 1930. One man shows Soc. Illustrators, N.Y.C., 1941, Le Nid Galerie, Northport, N.Y., 1976; exhibited in group shows in Soc. Illustrators, 1943-54, Bklyn. Mus. Art, 1942, Stony Brook (N.Y.) Mus., 1951; Cashi, Orlando, Fla., Capricorn Galleries, Bethesda, Md.; represented in permanent collections in Custer Mus., Monroe, Mich., Riveredge Found., Calgary, Alta., Can., Guardian Fed. Savs. & Loan Assn., Northport, N.Y., Irving Trust Co., Taipei, Taiwan. Republican. Illustrator: Argosy, 1951-61, Outdoor Life, 1960-74, True Mag., 1953, Esquire, 1951-66, McCall's, 1940-49, Ladies Home Jour., 1944-50, Woman's Home Companion, 1940-51, Redbook, 1940-49, Cosmopolitan, 1940-50, American, 1937-56, This Week, 1936-50, Liberty, 1935-40, Reader's Digest, 1964-73, Steelways, 1955-60, Womans Day, 1949-65. Home and office: 56 School St Northport NY 11768

BAUNACH, LYNNE GUERKE, educator; b. Orange, N.J., Oct. 11, 1943; d. Ralph Martis and Rosa (Mitchell) Guerke; B.A. in Chemistry, Goucher Coll., 1965; m. Aug. 14, 1965; children—Dawn Michelle, Mark Warren. Tchr. chemistry Hanover Park High Sch., East Hanover, N.J., 1965-66; tchr. chemistry and honors physics Morris Catholic High Sch., Denville, N.J., 1974—; mem. Hanover Park Regional Bd. Advisory Council. Bd. dirs. Theatre Arts Guild Hanover Twp., 1976—. Certified high sch. sci. tchr., N.J. Mem. Am. Chem. Soc. Roman Catholic. Home: 17 Valley Forge Dr Whippany NJ 07981 Office: Morris Cath High Sch Morris and Kitchell Aves Denville NJ 07834

BAVAR, DAVID IAN, real estate co. exec.; b. Jamestown, N.Y., Sept. 30, 1935; s. Gus and Sylvia (Tissenbaum) B.; B.S., Pa. State U., 1957; M.B.A., U. Pa., 1959; m. Betty Jean Axel, July 26, 1969; children—Robert Axel, Adrienne Fay. Accountant, Burke, Landsberg & Gerber, Balt., 1960-62; real estate broker Manekin Corp., Balt., 1962-71; partner Kayne, Levin, Neilson, Bavar Realtors, Balt., 1971—; dir. Greater Balt. Bd. Realtors, 1975-76; pres. Mt. Vernon Belvedere Improvement Assn., 1970-71; 1st v.p. Comprehensive Housing for the Aged, 1971—; chmn. real estate div. Asso. Jewish Charities, 1974-75; mem. campaign cabinet, 1975—; mem. econ. task force Regional Planning, 1975—. Served with U.S. Army, 1959-60. Soc. Indsl. Realtors (pres. Md.-Wash. chpt. 1975-76; nat. bd. dirs. 1976—), Nat. Assn. Realtors, Balt. Jr. Assn. Commerce (distinguished grad. 1972, treas., 1969). Clubs: The Center, The Towson. Home: 4 Windsong Ct Baltimore MD 21208 Office: Suite 1204 Fidelity Bldg Baltimore MD 21201

BAVASI, PETER JOSEPH, baseball exec.; b. Bronxville, N.Y., Oct. 31, 1942; s. Emil Joseph and Evit E. (Rice) B.; B.A. in Philosophy, St. Mary's Coll., 1964; m. Judith Marzonie, June 13, 1964; children—Patrick, Christina. Minor league gen. mgr. Los Angeles Dodgers, 1964-68; dir. minor league ops. San Diego Padres, 1968-73, v.p., gen. mgr., 1973-76; pres., chief exec. officer Toronto (Ont.) Blue Jays, 1976—. Mem. sports adminstrs. council Laurentian U.; mem. Friends bd. Seneca Coll. Club: Variety (Toronto). Office: care Toronto Blue Jays Exhibition Stadium Exhibition Pl Toronto ON Canada*

BAX, RONALD FRANK, med. electronic engr.; b. Niagara Falls, N.Y., Oct. 30, 1941; s. Frank Lou and Margaret Violet (Hallenbeck) B.; student (Alumni Assn. scholar) Syracuse U., 1959-60; B.A. in Physics, George Mason U., Fairfax, Va., 1977; m. Gail Ann Barber, Aug. 26, 1961; children—Keith Robert, Bronwyn Lee. Electronic engr. Scope Electronics Co., Reston, Va., 1966-67, sr. engr., 1967-69; sr. electronic engr. Recognition Equipment Co., Rockville, Md., 1969-72, Acuity Systems Co., Reston, 1972-75; prin. engr. Pfizer Med. Systems Co., Columbia, Md., 1975—; cons. in field. Commr. Boy Scouts Am., 1975-77. Served with USAF, 1960-64. Roman Catholic. Patentee in field. Home: 5592 Eaglebeak Row Columbia MD 21045 Office: 9052 Old Annapolis Rd Columbia MD 21045

BAXLEY, MARVIN OWEN (MAX), newspaper editor; b. Toledo, Oct. 2, 1934; s. David Ermal and Mollie Ethel (Howard) B.; B.E., U. Toledo, 1956. Promotion dir. Libbey Glass div. Owens-Ill., Inc., Toledo, 1956-62; prodn. editor, then copy-editing supr. trade books div. Prentice-Hall, Inc., Englewood Cliffs, N.J., 1962-64; asst. editor, then asso. editor Food and Drug Packaging mag., Mags. for Industry, Inc., N.Y.C., 1965-66, mng. editor, then editor Hard Goods and Soft Goods Packaging mag., 1966-69; asso. editor, then exec. editor Civil Service Leader, N.Y.C., 1970-73, editor, 1973—. Mem. Common Cause, Skye Terrier Club Am., Tau Kappa Epsilon. Democrat. Unitarian-Universalist. Home: 48-10 45th St Woodside NY 11377 Office: 233 Broadway New York NY 10007

BAXTER, RUTH HOWELL, ednl. adminstr.; b. Washington; d. Robert R. and Georgie (Murray) Lassiter; B.S., D.C. Tchrs. Coll., 1958; M.A., George Washington U., 1961, certificate in Edn., 1965; certificate (N. Am. Com. of Oslo scholar) Oslo U., Norway, 1970; m. Dudley H.G. Baxter; children—Robert, Astrid, Mova, Mava. Tchr., D.C. Pub. Schs., 1958—; dir., propr. Jewels of Ann Pvt. Day Sch., Washington, 1970—; tchr. Newlands Infant, Southampton, Eng., 1965-67; instr. math. demonstration lessons dept. edn. Howard U.; dir. early childhood edn. workshop Brent Elementary Sch., Washington, 1974; tchr. adult edn. Bel Air Sch., Woodbridge, Va., 1977; mem. Ednl. Instn. Licensure Commn. Task Forces, 1978; mem. Mayor's Pre-White House Conf. on Libraries and Info. Services, 1978; exec. high sch. internship program D.C. Pub. Schs., 1978. Fulbright scholar, 1965; named Outstanding Tchr. of Year, Future Tchrs. Am.; Outstanding Contbn. award Nat. Assn. Negro Women, 1976. Mem. Jack and Jill Club, Bus. and Profl. Women, Columbia Women, Zeta Phi Beta. Presbyterian. Author: A Norwegian Birthday Party, 1979; contbr. children's stories to various publs. Home: 13349 Delaney Rd Dale City Woodbridge VA 22193 Office: 2011 Bunker Hill Rd NE Washington DC 20018

BAYARD, ALEXIS IRENEE DU PONT, lawyer; b. Wilmington, Del., Feb. 11, 1918; s. Thomas F. and Elizabeth (duPont) B.; B.A., Princeton, 1940; LL.B., U. Va., 1947; m. Jane Brady Hildreth, Apr. 24, 1944 (dec. July 1960); children—Alexis Irenee du Pont, Eugene H., Richard H., Jane H., John F., William B. Admitted to Del. bar, 1948; practiced in Wilmington, 1948—; sr. partner firm Bayard, Brill & Handelman, 1965—; dir. Farmers Bank State Del. Mem. Nat. Commn. on Uniform Laws, 1962-71; chmn. Del. River and Bay Authority, 1967-69; bd. dirs. Del. Project Hope, 1962-70, Blood Bank of Del., 1955-70, Del. region NCCJ, 1964—; state chmn. Nat. Found. March Dimes, 1966—. Lt. gov. Del., 1949-53; campaign chmn. Del. Democratic Com., 1954; chmn., 1967-69; chmn. Del. Citizens for Kennedy and Johnson, 1960, Del. citizens for Johnson-Humphrey, 1964; mem. finance com. Nat. Dem. Com., 1970—; adv. bd. Del. Law Sch. Served from pvt. to lst lt., USMCR, 1942-45. Decorated Purple Heart. Fellow Harry S. Truman Library Inst. Nat. and Internat. Affairs (hon.); mem. Am., Del. bar assns., Assn. Bar City of N.Y., Am. Judicature Soc., Soc. Mayflower Descs., S.A.R., Mil. Order World Wars, Del. Swedish Colonial Soc., Hist Soc. Del., Marine Res. Officers Assn., Am. Road Bldg. Assn., Am. Acad. Polit. and Social Sci. Episcopalian. Clubs: Wilmington, Wilmington Country, Greenville, University. Home: 9 Red Oak Rd Wilmington DE 19806 Office: 901 Market St Wilmington DE 19801

BAYER, CHRISTOPHER ALAN, clin. psychologist; b. N.Y.C., Dec. 26, 1945; s. Sanford Alan and Valerie B.; A.B., Clark U., 1968; M.A., U. Man., (Can.), 1971, Ph.D., 1975; m. Nancy Ray Bueller, June 22, 1969; children—Robert, Jonathan. Research asso. Center for Settlement Studies U. Man., 1970-72, clin. extern Psychol. Service Center, 1972; psychology extern Marshfield (Wis.) Clinic, 1971; psychology intern Norristown (Pa.) Hosp., unit co-adminstr., 1972-75; staff psychologist Hillside Hosp., Glen Oaks, N.Y., 1975—; coordinator psychol. services, psychiat. liaison and cons. service L.I. Jewish-Hillside Med. Center, New Hyde Park, N.Y.; cons. psychologist Office Vocat. Rehab., State of N.Y.; cons. Community Guidance Service, N.Y.C.; pvt. practice clin. psychology, Forest Hills, N.Y. Recipient Vineberg research prize in psychology, U. Man., 1970. Mem. Am., Eastern, Nassau County psychol. assns., N.Y. Soc. Clin. Psychologists. Author: (with J.B. Nickels and L. Sexton) Life Satisfaction in a Resource Frontier Community, 1976; contbr. research articles to symposium, publs. U.S. and Can. Home: 69 Parkway Dr Syosset NY 11791 Office: 109-23 71st Rd Forest Hills NY 11375

BAYER, ROBERT ADOLPH, JR., asphalt mfg. and constrn. co. exec.; b. Wilkes-Barre, Pa., Feb. 1, 1949; s. Robert Adolph and Brunhilde Marian (Lanterman) B.; Asso. Civil Engring., Pa. State U., 1969; m. Debra Gail Tanner, May 4, 1974. Chief survey crew Gannett, Fleming, Corddry & Carpenter Co., Harrisburg, Pa., 1969-72; cost estimator Am. Asphalt Paving Co., Inc., Shavertown, Pa., 1973—. External v.p. Back Mountain chpt. U.S. Jaycees, 1977-78; bd. dirs., treas. Dallas Area Fall Fair, 1976—; mem. Back Mountain Drug and Alcohol Abuse Council. Mem. Nat. Wildlife Fedn., Pa. State U. Alumni Assn. Republican. Lutheran. Home: 120 N Main St Shavertown PA 18708 Office: RD 7 Box 95 Shavertown PA 18708

BAYUK, JOHN FRANK, cons. engr.; b. Chisholm, Minn., Jan. 18, 1911; s. John and Mary (Vaida) B.; Asso. in Mech. Engring., U. Minn., 1933; m. Ruth Marie Larson, Feb. 14, 1953; children—John Carl, Leonard. Draftsman Burke Mining Co., Gilbert, Minn., 1934-36; plant engr. Jenkins Bros., Bridgeport, Conn., 1940-53; dir. plant engring. AVCO Lycoming, Stratford, Conn., 1953-76; cons. engr., 1976— cons. Solar Engring. Sales, Stratford, 1978—. Asst. city assessor Eveleth (Minn.), 1937-39; chmn. bd. bldg. appeals Easton (Conn.), 1973-76, bd. fin., 1973-77, chmn. bd. tax rev., 1978—. Registered profl. engr., Conn. Mem. Nat. Soc. Profl. Engrs., Nat. Inst. Plant Engrs. Republican. Roman Catholic. Clubs: Rotary, Bridgeport Architects, KSKJ, K.C. Home: 160 Far Horizon Dr Easton CT 06612 Office: 160 Far Horizon Dr Easton CT 06612

BAZELON, DAVID LIONEL, judge; b. Superior, Wis., Sept. 3, 1909; B.S. in Law, Northwestern U., 1931, LL.D., 1974; LL.D. (hon.), Colby Coll., 1966; LL.D., Boston U., 1969, Albert Einstein Coll. Medicine of Yeshiva U., 1972, U. So. Calif., 1977; m. Miriam M. Kellner, June 7, 1936; children—James A., Richard Lee. Admitted to practice in Ill., 1932, asst. atty. gen. U.S., 1946-49; judge U.S. Ct. of Appeals for D.C. Circuit, 1949—, chief judge, 1962-78; lectr. psychiatry Johns Hopkins U. Sch. Medicine, 1964—; clin. prof. socio-legal aspects of psychiatry George Washington U., 1966—; Robert S. Marx lectr. U. Cin. Coll. Law, 1972; 12th Ann. James Madison lectr. N.Y.U. Law Sch., 1971; cons. Judge Baker Guidance Center of Children's Hosp. and Med. Center-Harvard Med. Sch., 1974—. Chmn. task force on law Pres.'s Panel on Mental Ratardation, 1961-62; chmn. steering com. Model Sch. Subsytem, Washington, 1964-66; mem. adv. com. program on tech. and soc. Harvard, 1966-71; mem. nat. adv. mental health council USPHS, 1967-71; mem. U.S. mission on mental health USSR, 1967; mem. adv. com. child devel. NRC, Nat. Acad. Scis., 1971—; chmn. adv. bd. Boston U. Center for Law ahd Health Scis., 1970; nat. adv. com. J.F. Kennedy Center for Research on Edn. and Human Devel., 1968-77; adv. com. Behavioral Law Center, Inst. Behavioral Research, 1973-74; bd. dirs. Washington Sch. Psychiatry, Coop. Health Info. Center Vt., Nat. Council Crime and Delinquency; bd. vistors City Coll. of City U. N.Y. trustee Salk Inst. for Biol. Studies, William Alanson White Found., Washington; mem. panel on human rights and U.S. fgn. policy UN Assn., 1978—; mem. recombinant DNA guidelines group NIH, 1976. Recipient Isaac Ray award Am. Psychiat. Assn., 1960. Hon. fellow Am. Psychiat. Assn. (Distinguished Service award 1975), Am. Coll. Legal Medicine; fellow Am. Acad. Arts and Scis.; mem. Am. (commn. mentally retarded 1973-74), Fed., D.C. bar assns., Inst. Medicine of Nat. Acad. Scis. (sr.), Am. Orthopsychiat. Assn. (pres. 1969-70, dir.). Jewish. Democrat. Club: Cosmos. Cons. Children Today, 1973—. Home: 2700 Virginia Ave NW Washington DC 20037 Office: Court of Appeals Washington DC 20001

BAZEWICZ, ROBERT JOSEPH, architect, city planner; b. Paterson, N.J., Mar. 19, 1947; s. John Vincent and Mary B.; B.Arch., U. Okla., 1970, M. City and Regional Planning, 1973; children—Amanda, Kimberly. Planner, Passaic County Planning Bd., Paterson, 1971-72; architect Reynolds & Morrison, Oklahoma City, 1972; asst. planning dir. Midwest City (Okla.) Planning Dept., 1972-73; planner, architect Oklahoma State Dept. Tourism and Parks, 1973; dir. planning and devel. Richard Browne Assos., Wayne, N.J., 1974—; cons. planner Morristown, West Paterson, Green Brook, N.J., 1975—. Commr. Paterson Parking Authority, 1976-77, sec.-treas., 1977. Served with USAR, 1969-76; Lic. profl. planner, N.J. Mem. Am. Inst. Planners, Am. Soc. Planning Ofcls., AIA. Home: 6 Prospect Pl Morristown NJ 07960 Office: 50 Galesi Dr Wayne NJ 07470

BAZIN, ALBERT JEIL, corp. exec.; b. Caracas, Venezuela, Sept. 20, 1904; s. Miguel Uzcategui and Rosa (Sarria) B.; B.C.S. cum laude, N.Y.U., 1929; m. Mildred Davidson, July 18, 1931 (dec. 1971); 1 son, James D.; m. 2d, Frances Sichel, Apr. 7, 1973. Came to U.S., 1910, naturalized, 1935. Asst. treas. Jaeger Watch Co., N.Y.C., 1929-35; sec.-treas. Albert B. Ashforth, Inc., N.Y.C., 1935-59, v.p., treas., 1959-72, sr. v.p., treas., 1972-75, sr. v.p., 1975, also dir.; sec.-treas., dir. Duff & Conger, Inc., Comml. Mgmt. Corp., 1946—; dir. Western Hemisphere Export Co., Inc., N.Y.C. Trustee Employees Profit Sharing Retirement Trust. Licensed real estate broker, N.Y. State, Conn. Mem. Real Estate Bd. of N.Y., Greenwich Bd. Realtors, Beta Gamma Sigma, Alpha Kappa Psi. Club: Wykagyl Country (past gov.). Home: 25 Old Orchard Rd Port Chester NY 10573 Office: 2 Greenwich Plaza Greenwich CT 06830

BEACH, CARTER LEROY, constrn. co. exec.; b. Coloma, Mich., June 10, 1926; s. LeRoy Howard and Belle (Carter) B.; student U. Wis., 1944, Va. Poly. Inst., 1945; B.S. in Civil Engring., U. Mich., 1948; m. Mary Ann Lawton, Aug. 20, 1949; children—Margaret Lynn, Eric Lawton, Christine Lou. Constrn. supr. Blaw Knox Co., Pitts., 1948-61; v.p. constrn. Crawford and Russell, Inc., Stamford, Conn., 1961—, also dir. Served with U.S. Army, 1944-46. Registered profl. engr., La. Mem. Nat. Constructors Assn. (dir. 1969—, exec. com. 1974-75). Club: Masons. Home: 103 Old Easton Turnpike Weston CT 06883 Office: 14 Amelia Pl Stamford CT 06904

BEACH, DAVID NELSON, III, mgmt. cons.; b. Pawtucket, R.I., July 22, 1926; s. David Nelson and Marguerite (Mills) B.; A.B., Yale, 1949; M.A. (scholar), U. Cin., 1951, Ph.D., 1963; m. Janet Rae Simpson, Jan. 26, 1952; children—Claudia G., David Nelson, Victoria S. Cons., United Indsl. Services, 1950-53, also Children's Home Cin.; dir. indsl. relations Dulany Foods, Inc., Fruitland, Md., 1953-57; v.p. Mahler Assos., Inc., cons., Midland Park, N.J., 1957-70; pres., dir. Learning Inc., edn. and tng. cons., Wyckoff, N.J., 1968—; prin. David N. Beach Assos., Inc., mgmt. consultants, Wyckoff, 1971—. Asso. prof. psychology U. Md., 1953-57. Served with AUS, 1946-47; Japan. Mem. Am. Psychol. Assn., Inst. Mgmt. Cons. (founding), Am. Arbitration Assn., Met. (N.Y.) Assn. Indsl. Psychologists. Author: Management by Commitment, 1968; Management by Goals, 1969; Counseling and Coaching, 1970. Home and office: 753 Janice Ct Wyckoff NJ 07481

BEACH, LOUIS ANDREW, physicist; b. Greenville, Ind., June 2, 1925; s. George Covert and Clara (Kiesler) B.; B.S., Ind. U., 1944, M.S., 1947, Ph.D., 1949; m. Virginia Ann McHugh, Oct. 20, 1956; children—Andrew, Ann Marie, Ruth Christine, Covert John. Research asso. Lab. Nuclear Studies, Cornell U., 1949-51; physicist Naval Research Lab., Washington, 1951—, head shielding sect., 1953-55, head nuclear reactions br., 1955-66, head physics I sect., cyclotron br., 1966-71, head nuclear physics sect., 1971-76, head radiation damage simulation sect., 1976—. Lectr. grad. program nuclear engring. Catholic U. Am., 1960-66. Served with AUS, 1944-46. Fellow Washington Acad. Sci.; mem. Am. Phys. Soc., A.A.A.S., Philos. Soc. Wash. Democrat, Roman Catholic. Home: 1200 Waynewood Blvd Alexandria VA 22308 Office: Code 6674 Naval Research Lab Washington DC 20375

BEACH, PAUL MAYNARD, JR., surgeon; b. East Orange, N.J., Sept. 20, 1931; s. Paul M. and Dorothy Henrietta (Hughson) B.; A.B., Lehigh U., 1954; M.D., Temple U., 1958; m. Deborah Lyons, Aug. 11, 1956; children—Elizabeth, Rebecca, Paul M. Intern, Beverly (Mass.) Hosp., 1958-59; resident Peter Bent Brigham Hosp., Boston, 1961-66, Children's Hosp. Med. Center, Boston, 1963-64; research fellow in surgery Harvard Med. Sch., Boston, 1964-65; chief resident Mary Hitchcock-Dartmouth Med. Center, Hanover, N.H., 1966-67; resident in thoracic and cardiac surgery Columbia Presbyn. Med. Center, N.Y.C., 1968-69; practice medicine specializing in thoracic surgery, Pa., 1959, Mass., 1963, N.Y., 1968, Calif., 1973, Maine, 1974; asst. attending surgeon Columbia Presbyn. Med. Center, 1970-73, Harlem Hosp. Center, 1970-73, Francis Delafield Hosp., 1970-73, Kaiser Found. Hosp., Los Angeles, 1973-74; chief surg. services Eastern Maine Med. Center, Bangor, 1974—; asst. attending surgeon St. Joseph Hosp., Bangor, 1974—; asst. prof. surgery Columbia U., Coll. of Physicians and Surgeons, N.Y.C., 1970-73. Served to lt. comdr. USN, 1959-61. Diplomate Am. Bd. Surgery, Am. Bd. Thoracic Surgery. Mem. A.C.S., Soc. Thoracic Surgeons, Am. Thoracic Soc., N.Y. Soc. Thoracic Surgery, N.Y. County, Penobscot County med. socs., Maine Vascular Soc., Maine Med. Assn., AMA, Am. Heart Assn., Maine Lung Assn., Assn. Acad. Surgery, Bangor Med. Club. Contbr. articles on cardiovascular surgery to med. jours. Home: 900 State St Bangor ME 04401 Office: 431 State St Bangor ME 04401

BEACH, ROSE MARY RANDALL, librarian; b. Waterloo, Iowa, Dec. 11, 1921; d. Charles Warren Milton and Rose Ellen (MacDonald) Randall; B.A., State U. Iowa, 1943; M.S., Drexel U., 1971; children—Charles Randall, Thomas Christopher Coffing, Murray MacDonald. Opinion researcher Audience Research, Inc., Princeton, N.J., 1944; radio news and feature writer A.P. Radio, Rockefeller Center, N.Y.C., 1944-47; instr. Green Mountain Jr. Coll., Poultney, Vt., 1951-54; instr. Goldey Beacom Coll., Wilmington, Del., 1956-69, library dir., 1970—. Mem. Nat. Bus. Tchrs. Assn., Am., Del. library assns., Phi Beta Kappa, Beta Phi Mu, Kappa Tau Alpha, Sigma Delta Chi. Episcopalian. Home: RD 1 Box 335 Landenberg PA 19350 Office: 4701 Limestone Rd Wilmington DE 19808

BEACHER, LAWRENCE LESTER, optometrist, educator; b. Cherne, Czechoslovakia, Aug. 18, 1905; s. Frank A. and Jennie (Berger) B.; O.D., Pa. State Coll. Optometry, 1927; D.O.Sc., (hon.), No. Ill. Coll. Optometry, 1937; Ph.D., Phila. Coll. and Infirmary Osteopathy, 1945; L.H.D., Philathea Coll., London, Ont., 1961, M.A., 1959, Ph.D., 1962; Sc.D., Dearborn Coll. Phys. and Surg., 1946, Studiorum Collegium Academicum, 1967, London Coll. Applied Sci. (Eng.), 1968, Ind. No. U., 1972; Litt.D., Sem. St. Francis of Assisi, 1947; Ed.D., Ohio Coll. Podiatric Medicine; LL.D., Nat. Police Acad., 1970, London Coll. Applied Sci., 1970; Dr. Optometric Sci., sci. sect. Beta Sigma Kappa; M.D., McCormick Med. Coll., 1948, Homeopathic Med. Coll. South Africa, 1975; m. Sylvia Budoff, Jan. 12, 1930; 1 son, Melvin M. Instr. geometrical optics. Pa. State Coll. Optometry, 1927-29, asst. prof., 1929-31; chief staff, head ednl. div. Bronx Co. Optometrical Clin. Service, 1929-31; lectr. contact lens impression methods Optometric Found., 1944-50; prof. psychology Philathea Coll., 1957-72, chancellor, 1967-72, emeritus, 1972—; vis. lectr. Pa. State Coll. Optometry, 1962-71, emeritus, 1971—, also vis. clin. staff; prof. contact ophthalmology and lens therapy McCormick Med. Coll., 1946-52; vis. lectr. So. Coll. Optometry, 1962-64; Ill. Coll. Optometry, intermittently, 1944—; vis. prof. Ind. No. U., 1972-73. Mem. N.Y. Guard 9th Regt., 1943-45; maj. CAP (Aux. USAF), chief eye cons. N.J. Wing, 1945-62; ret., 1962. Decorated Grand Cross Eloy Alfano Internat. Found. of Panama: Maltese Cross. Order St. John Jerusalem; recipient Martin Buber award Midway Counseling Center; award Mass. Gov.'s Council, 1971; Hall of Fame, Nat. Police Acad., Venice, Fla.; Wisdom Hall of Fame award Wisdom Soc., 1971; Good Citizenship medal Nat. Soc. S.A.R., 1971; Archbishop Benjamin C. Eckardt award, 1971; J.F.K. Humanitarian award J.F.K. Library for Minorities, 1978. Diplomate Am. Bd. Examiners in Psychotherapy. Fellow Am. Psychotherapy Assn. (pres. 1971-72), Am. Assn. Clinic Physicians and Surgeons, Assn. Social Psychology, Distinguished Service Found. Optometry, Am. Acad. Optometry (diplomate contact lens bd.), A.A.A.S., Philos. Soc. Eng., Royal Soc. Arts, Royal Soc. Health, Am. Coll. Clinic Adminstrs., Internat. Coll. Physicians and Surgeons (homeopathic), Internat. Soc. Psychologists (Eng.); mem. Internat. Coll. Ocular Sci. (dir. edn.), Am. Acad. Med. Adminstrn., N.J., N.Y. acads. scis., Essex County Optometric Soc., N.J. (past chmn. contact-lens sect., Sci. achievement award 1975, 50 Yr. Appreciation award 1977), Am. optometric assns., Md. Homeopathic Med. Soc., World Med. Assn. (asso.), La. Psychol. Assn. (life), Mark Twain Lit. Soc. (hon.), Circolo Italiano U. Conn. and U.S. Fla., Beta Sigma Kappa (chmn., ret. board regents sci. sect., gold medal 1976), Phi Delta Alpha. Jewish. Mason. Forester. Author: Ocular Refraction and Diagnosis, 1931; Practical Optometry, 1934; Contact Lens Technique, 1941, 5th ed., 1974; Your Precious Eyesight, 1952; Corneal Contact Lenses, 1956; A Study of Practical Psychology, 1962; How Can I Improve Myself, 1962; Psychological Manifestations in Ocular Science, 1968; also 100 articles. Home and office: 63 Whittingham Pl West Orange NJ 07052

BEAGLE, CHARLES WELLINGTON, cons. civil engr.; b. Media, Pa., Oct. 25, 1910; s. John Andrew and Ella Mae (Hartman) B.; B.S., Pa. State U., 1933, C.E., 1939; m. Alice Rosa Rigg, July 6, 1946; children—Joann (Mrs. Morris Bricks), Rosana (Mrs. Duncan B. McGill), Charles Andrew, Ruth Ella (Mrs. Peter Jackson Allen). Jr. civil engr. U.S. Forest Service, Pa., 1933-39; chief constrn. engr. Bendix Aviation Corp., Teterboro, N.J., 1940-44; project engr. George M. Brewster, Inc., Bogota, N.J., 1945-49; pres. R & B Constrn. Co., South Plainfield, N.J., 1950-55; municipal engr., dir. pub. works, South Plainfield, 1955-60, New Providence, N.J., 1960-62, Woodbridge, N.J., 1962-76; cons., lectr., 1976—. Vice chmn. South Plainfield Redevel. Agy., 1967-70. Served with U.S. Army, 1939-40, USNR, 1944-45. Recipient Industry Recognition award Nat. Asphalt Pavement Assn., 1965, Asphalt Leadership award Poly. Inst. Bklyn., 1972, Pioneer award N.J. Asphalt Pavement Assn., 1974, award for outstanding contbn. Rutgers Asphalt Paving Conf., 1976; named to honor roll Asphalt Inst., 1976. Mem. Hwy. Research Bd., Am. Rd. Builders Assn., Assn. Asphalt Paving Technologists (dir., pres. 1974), Am. Pub. Works Assn. (Pub. Works Man of Year 1966), Nat., N.J. (Engr. of Year 1971, govt. profl. devel. award 1974, state trustee) socs. profl. engrs., N.J. Soc. Municipal Engrs. (merit award 1961), Am. Arbitration Assn. (nat. panel arbitrators), Am. Legion, VFW, Alpha Sigma Phi. Elk. Home: 102 W Nassau Ave South Plainfield NJ 07080 Office: 1 Main St Woodbridge NJ 07095

BEAHM, RALPH EUGENE, mus. adminstr.; b. Aaronsburg, Pa., May 8, 1905; s. Henry Oscar and Emma Susan (Zerby) B.; student Susquehanna U., 1924-30; B.A., Bucknell U., 1948; M.A., State U. Ia., 1949; m. Bernice Evelyn Shook, Apr. 20, 1950. Tchr., Haines Twp. pub. schs., Pa., 1925-42; supt. prin. Miles Twp. Schs., Pa., 1945-52; tchr. Pa. Valley Schs., 1952-70; tchr. ednl. and hist., dir. Aaronsburg Hist. Mus., 1968—. Pres. Civic Club, Aaronsburg, 1967-72. Twp. auditor Aaronsburg, 1970—; chmn. planning bd., Aaronsburg; chmn. Haines Twp. Bicentennial Commn. Served with AUS, 1942-45. Mem. Pa. State (dir.), Centre County (pres. 1970—) Sabbath sch. assns., Pa. State Edn. Assn. (treas. local chpt. 1948-51), Sch. Master's Assn. (pres. 1950-51), Susquehanna U. Alumni Club (pres. 1930-35), Centre County Hist. Soc. (pres. 1972-74), Jr. Order United Am. Mechanics, VFW, Am. Legion. Odd Fellow. Contbr. articles to hist. jours. Home: Aaron Sq Aaronsburg PA 16820 Office: Aaronsburg Hist Mus Aaron Sq Aaronsburg PA 16820

BEAKES, KENDALL DOUGLAS, govt. ofcl.; b. Washington, Pa., Nov. 17, 1923; s. Edwin August and Elsie (Hauck) B.; B.A., Western Md. Coll., 1948; student U. Paris, 1948-49, U. Aix Marseille, 1949, U. Strasbourg, 1949-50; Docteur es Lettres, U. Besancon (France), 1964; LL.D. (hon.), Ball State U., 1972; m. Maria M. Haas, Aug. 16, 1954; children—Douglas Edwin, Christine Maria. Edn. adviser U.S. Army, Austria, 1950-54, edn. cons., Morocco, 1954-56; liaison officer for edn. USAF, Germany, 1956-58; dep. dir. U.S. Armed Forces Inst., Germany, 1958-61; dir. edn. USAF, Europe, 1961—. Active Boy Scouts Am. Served with AUS, 1943-45. Recipient Meritorious Civilian Service award, Exceptional Service medal, Air Force Outstanding award (3), Air Force Sustained Superior award. Mem. European Programmed Instrn. Assn. (v.p. 1962, 65), Beta Beta Beta, Gamma Beta Chi. Author: Moroccan Arabic Simplified, 1955; Skiing in Austria, 1953; East and West at Stalingrad, 1969. Home: 2 Heilengenbornstrasse Wiesbaden 62 Federal Republic of Germany Office: Hdqrs USAFE (DPXE) APO NY 09633

BEAL, ALEXANDER SIMPSON, real estate co. exec.; b. Boston, July 22, 1908; s. Julius and Adelaide (Simpson) B.; B.S., Harvard, 1931; m. Leona Madeleine Rothstein, Mar. 29, 1930 (dec. July 1977); children—Bruce Anthony, Robert Lawrence. With Henderson & Ross Boston, 1931-34, James D. Henderson & Son, Boston, 1934-40; asso. Henderson & Beal Co., Boston, 1940-53; asso. Beal & Co. Inc., Boston, 1953-75, chmn. bd., 1975—; dir. Grove Hall Savs. Bank. Mem. Mass. Airport Mgmt. Bd., 1954-59; bd. dirs. Boston Municipal Research Bur.; chmn. bd. Grahm Jr. Coll., 1973-75. Mem. Spl. Commn. on Revision of Eminent Domain Laws, 1966-70; exec. adv. com. Mass. Transp. Commn., 1957; pres. Temple Ohabei Shalom, Brookline, Mass., 1977—; trustee Beth Israel Hosp. Served with USNR, 1943-45. Mem. Bldg. Owners and Mgrs. Assn. (pres. 1961-63), Mass. Bd. Real Estate Appraisers (pres. 1961-63), Urban Land Inst., Nat., Mass. assns. real estate bds., Inst. Real Estate Mgmt. (certified property mgr.). Club: Harvard. Home: 180 Beacon St Boston MA 02116 Office: 15 Broad St Boston MA 02109

BEAL, BRUCE A., real estate cons., developer; b. Boston June 28, 1936; s. Alexander S. and Leona R. (Rothstein) B.; B.A., Rollins Coll., 1958; postgrad. Boston U. Law. Sch.; m. Enid L. Levine, Mar. 22, 1964; children—Christopher L., Alexandra S., Bruce A. Vice pres. Beal & Co., Inc., real estate, Boston, 1960-69, v.p., treas., 1973-75, pres., 1976—; corporate officer H. N. Gorin & Leeder Co., Inc., Boston, 1969-70; v.p. devel., financing Wasserman Devel. Corp., Boston, 1970-73; lectr. Harvard U., Northeastern U.; cons. Stop & Shop, Inc., Walco Nat. Corp., Cities Service Oil Co., U.S. Ry. Assn. in reorgn. Penn Central. Trustee Mass. Eye and Ear Infirmary; mem. examining com., chmn. assos. Boston Pub. Library bd. dirs. Children's Mus. Center House Found.; mem. Mayor's Com. on Cultural Affairs; mem. vis. com. contemporary arts Boston Mus. Fine Arts; mem. Land Conservation Commn., Town of Lincoln (Mass.); trustee Washington Center for Addictions; trustee combined Jewish Philanthropies, Jewish Family and Children's Services. Mem. Am. Soc. Real Estate Counselors, Mass., Greater Boston real estate bds., Nat. Inst. Real Estate Brokers, Realtors Nat. Mktg. Inst., Bldg. Owners and Mgmt. Assn. Clubs: Belmont Country. Contbr. articles to profl. jours. Home: Old Winter St Lincoln MA 01773 Office: 15 Broad St Boston MA 02109

BEAL, CARL LEWIS, tech. cons.; b. Phillips, Maine, Nov. 21, 1901; s. Benjamin Frank and Cynthia (Prescott) B.; B.S., U. Maine, 1924; m. Grace Ellen Bearce, Sept. 18, 1926; children—Blaine Lewis, Calvin Howard. Research chemist Eastman Kodak Co., Rochester, N.Y., 1924-27; devel. chem. engr. B.F. Goodrich Co., Akron, Ohio, 1927-29, chem. engr. synthetic rubber, 1942-44; devel. engr., mgr. devel. and engring. Am. Anode, Inc., Akron, 1929-42; v.p., gen. mgr. Ideal Latex Corp., Hollis, N.Y., 1944-50; mgr. tech. and research tape div. Behr-Manning Corp., Troy, N.Y., 1950-52; tech. adviser, tech. cons. various orgns. in rubber and plastics field, 1952—. Recipient Modern Pioneer award N.A.M., 1940. Mem. Am. Chem. Soc., Am. Inst. Chem. Engrs., Soc. Plastic Engrs., AAAS, Chemists' Club N.Y., Soc. Mayflower Descs., Phi Eta Kappa, Alpha Chi Sigma, Phi Kappa Phi, Tau Beta Pi. Patentee in field. Home: 477 Grace Trail Orange CT 06477

BEAL, RICHARD BARRATT, business exec.; b. Williamsport, Pa., June 20, 1929; s. Walter Hubert and Dorothy (Barratt) B.; grad. Haverford Sch., 1947; A.B., Colby Coll., 1951; m. Margaret Knight Voorhees, June 9, 1951; children—Walter Barratt, Todd Voorhees, Douglas Welch, Dayna Middlekauff. Asst. exec. dir. Found. for Full Service Banks, Phila., 1961-65, exec. v.p., sec. 1965-73; pres. Bankstream, Inc., pub. Outside In, 1973-75; dir., mng. partner The Mktg. Dept., Villanova, Pa. Past pres. Gladwyne Civic Assn.; trustee, pres. Holt-Elwell Meml. Found. (N.H.); bd. dirs. Lower Merion-Narberth Watershed Assn., Riverbend Environ. Center; committeeman Montgomery County Republican Com. Served to 2d lt. AUS, 1951-53. Mem. Phila. Adv. Tennis Assn. (past pres.), Delta Kappa Epsilon (past pres. Phila.). Presbyn. (elder, trustee). Clubs: Merion Golf, Colby (past pres.) (Phila.). Home: 936 Merion Square Rd Gladwyne PA 19035

BEALE, EVERETT MINOT, percussionist, educator; b. Rockland, Mass., July 7, 1939; s. Minot Alfred and June (Thornton) B.; B.Mus. in Applied Percussion, New Eng. Conservatory of Music, 1962; children—Dawn, Tania. Percussionist, Boston Symphony Orch., Boston Pops Orch., 1961—; asst. timpanist, prin. percussionist Boston Ballet and Boston Opera Orchs., 1964—; head percussion dept. U. Lowell (Mass.), 1968—; TV concerts and recs. on Polydor, Deutsche Grammophon, R.C.A. with Boston Symphony, Boston Pops. Apptd. mem. World Symphony Orch. by Arthur Fiedler, 1971. Mem. Percussive Arts Soc., Phi Mu Alpha Sinfonia. Author: The Playing and Teaching of Percussion Instruments, 1975. Contbr. articles to profl. jours. Home: 104 Red Gate Rd Tyngsboro MA 01879 Office: Music Dept Univ of Lowell 1 University Ave Lowell MA 01854

BEALE, GEORGIA ROBISON (MRS. HOWARD KENNEDY), historian; b. Chgo., Mar. 14, 1905; d. Henry Barton and Dora (Sledd) Robison; A.B., U. Chgo., 1926, A.M., 1928; Ph.D., Columbia, 1938; student Culver-Stockton Coll., 1921-24. Sorbonne, Coll. de France, 1930-34; m. Howard Kennedy Beale, Jan. 2, 1942; children—Howard Kennedy, Henry Barton Robison, Thomas Wight. Reader history U. Chgo., 1927-29; lectr. Barnard Coll., 1937-38; instr. Bklyn. Coll., 1937-39; asst. prof. history Hollins Coll., 1939-41, Wellesley College 1941-42, Castleton (Vt.), State Coll., 1968-70; vis. asso. prof. history U. Ky., 1970-72. Mem. women's com. Madison Civic Music Assn.; hon. trustee Culver-Stockton Coll. Mem. Am. Hist. Assn., So. Hist. Assn., Am., Brit. socs. for eighteenth century studies, Soc. for French Hist. Studies, Western Soc. French History, AAUW, Phi Beta Kappa, Pi Kappa Delta, Pi Lambda Theta, Phi Alpha Theta. Author: Revelliere-lépeaux, Citizen Director, 1938, reprinted, 1972; contbg. author Consortium on Revolutionary Europe, 1973. Home: The Ridge Orford NH 03777 also 2816 Columbia Rd Madison WI 53705 also 1020 19th St NW Washington DC 20036

BEALL, HARRY SPURGEON, JR., impresario; b. Olney, Md., Mar. 4, 1927; s. Harry Spurgeon and Hazel Maria (Long) B.; student Western Md. Coll., 1944-45, George Washington U., 1947-49; m. Mary Lester, Nov. 10, 1956; children—Martin Long, Andrew Lester. Div. asso., tour mgr. Lily Pons and Van Cliburn, Columbia Artists Mgmt., N.Y.C., 1949-59; dir. press and pub. relations Boston Symphony Orch., 1959-63; v.p. Judson O'Neill Beall and Steinway, N.Y.C., 1963-70; pres. Arthur Judson Mgmt., 1970-72, Harry Beall Mgmt., N.Y.C., 1972—; mem. Avery Fisher Artist Award Recommendation Bd., 1974—. Vestryman, Ch. of the Atonement, Tenafly, N.J., 1973-76. Served with AUSAF, 1945-46. Recipient Harriett Lane Johnson award, 1940, Superior award Nat. Fedn. Music Clubs, 1942. Mem. Assn. Coll., U. and Community Arts Adminstrs., Internat. Soc. Performing Arts Adminstrs., Assn. Am. Dance Cos., Met. Opera Guild. Republican. Episcopalian. Club: Englewood Field. Home: 23 Park St Tenafly NJ 07670 Office: Beall Mgmt 119 W 57th St New York City NY 10019

BEAM, MARGARET ALEXINE, educator; b. Pitts., Feb. 20, 1907; d. George Samuel and Katherine Veronica (Collins) Beam; B.A., Seton Hill Coll., 1940; M.S., U. Pitts., 1943; M.A., St. Mary Coll., 1955; NSF fellow U. Notre Dame, 1960-63. Entered Sisters of Charity, Roman Catholic Ch., 1923; elementary tchr., Pitts. and Greensburg, Pa., 1925-36; tchr. sci. St. James High Sch., Pitts., 1941-50, St. Luke High Sch., Pitts., 1950-56, Sacred Heart High Sch., Pitts., 1956-70; tchr. Central Cath. High Sch., Greensburg, 1970—, chmn. sci. dept., 1970—; tutor underprivileged children. Cardio-pulmonary resusitation trainee ARC, 1977. Named Outstanding Sci. Tchr. in Pa., Pa. Tchr. Accrediting Assn., 1964; Outstanding Biology Tchr. in Pa., Biology Tchr. Assn., 1971; recipient Spectroscopy Soc. award, 1965; Jones-Laughlin Steel Co. award, 1973; VFW award, 1963; Allegheny County Med. Soc. award, 1973; Master Brewers Assn. Am. award, 1971, 75; E. Liberty C. of C. award, 1964; others. Mem. Am. Mus. Natural History, Nat. Sci. Tchrs. Assn., Pitts. Math and Sci. Tchrs. Assn. Roman Catholic. Contbr. articles to profl. jours. Address: 925 Armory Dr Greensburg PA 15601

BEAN, CALVIN, clothing mcht.; b. Chicora, Pa., July 7, 1906; s. Joseph M. and Mary (Decker) B.; student pub. schs.; m. Kathryn Larsen, Apr. 7, 1932; 1 son, John W. Traveling salesman, 1922-35; owner Ideal Shirt Co., mfrs. hunting and fishing clothes, Sykesville, Pa., 1935-56; pres. Ideal Products, Inc., 1957—; v.p., dir. Keystone Nat. Bank (Pa.); dir. Symmco, Inc. Active Boy Scouts Am. Trustee Ideal Retirement Trust. Democrat. Methodist. Mason. Club: Sportsman of Am. (life). Home: 124 N Park St Sykesville PA 15865 Office: Ideal Products Inc Du Bois PA 15801

BEAN, CARL BENNETT, physician; b. Cochranton, Pa., Apr. 3, 1917; s. John S. and Maude (McCracken) B.; student Clarion State Coll., 1934-36, Duke, 1938, Pa. State U., 1940; B.S., Northwestern U., 1942, M.B., 1943, M.D., 1944; m. Ida Jane Fordyce, Apr. 18, 1942; children—Mary Jane, John David. Intern, U. Pitts. Med. Center, Pitts., 1943-44; resident in radiology Yale, 1947-48, W. Penn Hosp., Pitts., 1948-50; practice medicine specializing in radiology, Altoona, Pa., 1952-63; dir. dept. radiology Mercy Hosp., Altoona, 1952-63, cons. 1963-66; cons. Tyrone (Pa.) Hosp., 1955-66, Nason Hosp., Roaring Spring, Pa., 1963-66; mem. radiology service VA Hosp., Lebanon, 1967-76, Butler, Pa., 1976—; clin. asst. prof. radiology Pa. State U. Coll. Medicine, Hershey, 1971-75; lectr. in field. Served from 1st lt. to capt., M.C., USAAF, 1944-46. Diplomate Am. Bd. Radiology. Mem. Am. Coll. Radiology, Radiol. Soc. N.A., Pitts. Roentgen Soc., Soc. Nuclear Medicine. Presbyterian. Rotarian (pres. 1962-63). Author: Manual of Diagnostic X-Ray Technique, 1958. Home: 164 W Orchard Dr Butler PA 16001

BEARD, EDWARD P., congressman. Mem. 94th-96th congresses from 2d R.I. Dist. Office: Room 131 Cannon House Office Bldg Washington DC 20515

BEARD, LILLIAN MCLEAN, physician; b. N.Y.C., Nov. 15, 1943; d. John Wilson and Woodie M. (Durden) McLean; B.S., Howard U., 1965, M.D., 1970; m. De Lawrence Beard, Aug. 20, 1967. Intern Children's Hosp. Nat. Med. Center, Washington, 1970-71, resident in pediatrics 1971-73, dir. Child Devel. Services, 1973-74; practice medicine specializing in pediatrics, Washington, 1973—; dir. pediatric services Nat. Children's Center, Inc., Washington, 1974—; clin. asst. prof. child health and devel. George Washington U. Sch. Medicine, Washington, 1973—; cons. in field; bd. dirs. Washington Home for Foundlings, 1972—, Community Psychiat. Clinic, Bethesda, Md., 1973—. Bd. dirs. Family and Med. Counselling Service; mem. Head Start Advisory Bd. Met. Washington. Diplomate Am. Bd. Pediatrics, Nat. Bd. Med. Examiners. Mem. Nat., Am. med. assns., Am. Med. Women's Assn., D.C. Pub. Health Assn., Nat. Capital Med. Found., Medico-Chirurgical Soc. D.C., Med. Soc. D.C. Home: 11917 Hunting Ridge Ct Potomac MD 20854 Office: 5505 5th St NW Washington DC 20011

BEARD, TIMOTHY DONAHUE, III, food technologist; b. Hart, Mich., July 6, 1936; s. Elmer Augusta and Bernice Silvia (Tupes) B.; B.S. in Horticulture, Mich. State U., 1958, M.S. in Food Sci., 1960; m. Mary Louise Stonecliffe, Dec. 10, 1960; children—Michelle Louise, Timothy Donahue IV. Chemist, Campbell Soup Co., Napoleon, Ohio, 1960-61, asst. mgr. quality control, 1961-62, mgr. juices quality control, Saratoga, Ind., 1962, mgr. poultry frozen foods quality control, Chestertown, Md., 1962-64, research technologist subs. Campbell Inst. Food Research, Camden, N.J., 1964-68, sr. research technologist, 1968-69, tech. dir. subs. Champion Valley Farms, Inc., Camden, 1969-75; dir. resources devel. Technol. Resources Inc., Camden, 1975—. Youth officer Burlington County YMCA, 1975-76, v.p., 1976-77, sec., 1977. Served with USN, 1978. Fellow Am. Inst. Chemists; mem. Inst. Food Tchnologists, AAAS, Assn. Pacific Fisheries Technologists, Pa., Mass. hort. socs., Mich. State U. Alumni Assn. (pres. Phila. 1970, dir. 1975—). Republican. Methodist. Home: 2157 Whitman Ct Cinnaminson NJ 08077 Office: PO Box 391 Camden NJ 08101

BEARDS, ASHLEY HARRIS, dentist; b. Bklyn., Mar. 27, 1948; s. William L. and Ila C. (Bartell) B.; B.A., Hunter Coll., 1969; D.M.D., Fairleigh Dickinson U., 1973; certificate in periodontics N.Y.U., 1975. Gen. practice dentistry, N.Y.C., 1974; practice limited to periodontics, Scarsdale, N.Y., 1975—; asst. prof. periodontics N.Y. U., 1975-77, Fairleigh Dickinson U., 1975—. Mem. ADA, N.Y. State Dental Assn., Northeastern Soc. Periodontics, Am. Acad. Periodontics, Am. Acad. Oral Medicine, Alpha Omega. Home: 77 Livingston Rd Scarsdale NY 10583 Office: 50 Walworth Ave Scarsdale NY 10583

BEARDSLEE, WILLIAM EARL, civil engr.; b. N.Y.C., June 7, 1947; s. Lester Frisbee and Rose (Lieberman) B.; B.S. in Civil Engring., N.J. Inst. Tech., 1972; m. Francine Andriach, Mar. 24, 1968; children—William Earl, Marc David. Draftsman, Boswell Engring Co., Ridgefield Park, N.J., 1966-67, party chief, 1967-68, project engr., 1968-70; sr. engr. Twp. of Teaneck (N.J.), 1970-72; hwy. project engr., right of way and utility engr. A.G. Lichtenstein & Assos., Teaneck, 1972-76; chief engr. Urban Planning and Engring., Franklin Lakes, N.J., 1976—; pres. Beardslee Engring. Asso., Franklin, N.J., 1974—. Registered profl. engr., N.J., Pa., Conn.; lic. land surveyor, Pa., N.J.; lic. profl. planner, N.J. Mem. Nat., N.J. socs. profl. engrs., Engrs. and Surveyors Assn., Am. Rd. and Transp. Builders Assn., Builders Assn. No. N.J., N.J. Inst. Tech. Alumni Assn., Alpha Tau Omega Alumni Assn. Roman Catholic. Home and Office: RD 1 46 Deerfield Dr Franklin NJ 07416

BEARDSLEY, THEODORE S(TERLING), JR., hispanist; b. East St. Louis, Ill., Aug. 26, 1930; s. Theodore S. and Margaret (Kienzle) B.; B.S., So. Ill. U., 1952; M.A. (Max Bryant fellow), Washington U., St. Louis, 1954; postgrad. U. Heidelberg (Germany), 1955-56; Ph.D., U. Pa., 1961; m. Lenora J. Fierke, May 26, 1955; children—Theodore Sterling III, Mark A., Mary Elizabeth. Asst. d'anglais Lycee Wilson, Chaumont, France, 1952-53; from instr. to asst. prof., also chmn. modern lang. Rider Coll., 1957-61; asst. prof. Spanish So. Ill. U., 1961-62, U. Wis., 1962-65; dir. The Hispanic Soc. Am., N.Y.C., 1965—; adj. prof. Spanish, N.Y.U., 1967—, Adelphi U., 1966—, Columbia U., 1969—. Spl. cons. Hispanic bibliography Library of Congress, 1973; linguistic research Instituto Caro y Cuervo, Bogota, Colombia, 1973. Chmn., Museums Council N.Y., 1972-73. Bd. dirs. Spanish Inst., N.Y.C., 1967—. Served with AUS, 1954-56; Germany. Decorated Orden de Mérito Civil (Spain); recipient Premio Bibliofilia, Barcelona, 1973. Fulbright grant, 1952-53; Jusserand traveling fellowship, 1963; Am. Council Learned Socs. research grantee, 1964; Fulbright lectr., Ecuador, 1974. Mem. Renaissance Soc. Am. (exec. council 1974—), Real Academia de Bellas Artes de San Carlos, Royal

Spanish Acad. (corr.), Hispanic Soc., Academia Guatemalteca, Sigma Delta Pi, Sigma Tau Gamma. Club: Grolier. Author: Hispano-Classical Translations 1482-1699, 1970; Tomas Navarro Tomas, A Tentative Bibliography (1908-1970), 1971; (text) Ponce de Leon, 1973; (TV series) Hispanic Immigration in the United States, 1973. Editor: El hispanismo universitario en los Estados Unidos, 1971-72; mem. adv. bd. Hispanic Rev. Contbr. articles to profl. jours. Recordings: Charla con Camilo Jose Cela. Archive of Recorded Voice, 1966; Visita a The Hispanic Society, 1969; also Spanish lang. recorded tours Mus. Natural History, Nat. Gallery Art, Boston Mus. Sci., Smithsonian Instn. Office: 613 W 155th St New York City NY 10032

BEARSCH, LEE PALMER, architect, city planner; b. Binghamton, N.Y., July 5, 1942; s. Frederick James and Mildred Jane (Palmer) B.; B.Arch., Clemson U., 1965; M.Planning, Leverhulme Sch. Archtl. Assn., London, 1970; m. Christine Cromer, Dec. 31, 1972; children—Frederick Cromer, Benjamin Palmer. Project dir. Llewelyn-Davies Assos., London, N.Y. and Racine, Wis., 1970-75; partner firm Bearsch-Compeau & Assos. and predecessor firms, 1976—; dir. Northside Redevel., Inc., Racine, 1973-74. Mem. South Harbor Commn., Racine, 1972-73; chmn. Bicycle Commn., Racine, 1974; mem. Broome County Planning Adv. Bd., Binghamton, 1978—. Registered profl. architect, N.Y., Pa., Wis. Mem. AIA (area dir. 1978—), Am. Inst. Planners, N.Y. Assn. Architects, Archtl. Assn. (Eng.). Democrat. Club: Broome Breakfast (pres.). Office: 122 State St Binghamton NY 13901

BEARSS, WILLIAM STANLEY, X-ray co. exec.; b. Buffalo, Feb. 19, 1930; s. Stanley Leroy and Ruth Magdalene (Busch) B.; B.S., U. Buffalo, 1952; m. May 28, 1955. Founder, pres. Buffalo X-Ray Corp., 1952—; part owner Elicott Sq. Office Bldg. Mem. adv. com. of material sci. tech. dept. Erie Community Coll., 1969—. Fellow Am. Soc. for Non-Destructive Testing (chmn. Western N.Y. sect. 1965-66); mem. Am. Soc. for Metals, Radiologic Technologists Soc. N.Y. State (asso.). Republican. Clubs: Masons, Shriners. Office: 81-83 E Market St Buffalo NY 14204

BEASLEY, WAYNE MACHON, materials scientist, educator; b. Everett, Mass., May 23, 1922; s. William Francis and Elsie May (Machon) B.; B.S. cum laude in Astronomy, Harvard, 1946; M.S. in Phys. Ceramics, Mass. Inst. Tech., 1965; m. Evelyn Harriet Eddy, Feb. 28, 1945; 1 dau., Dawn Linda. Physicist, Clarostat Mfg. Co., Dover, N.H., 1951-55; physicist nuclear products div. Metals & Controls Corp., Attleboro, Mass., 1955-57; research prof. Engring. Expt. Sta., U. N.H., Durham, 1957-71, prof. materials sci., mech. engring. dept., 1971—, dir. X-ray Diffraction Lab., 1963-71; cons. in materials tech. to electronics industry, 1957—; mem. Inst. on Energy Options for Future, Oak Ridge Asso. Univs., 1977—. Active Barrington (N.H.) Waste Disposal Study Commn., 1975—. Served to lt. USNR, 1942-46. Invited by Royal Soc. to Bragg Symposium, 1970. Mem. Brit. Inst. Metals, N.H., N.Y., acads. Scis., Am. Crystallographic Assn., Am. Soc. Metals (pres. N.H. chpt. 1959), Am. Phys. Soc. (chmn. nominating com., mem. program com. 1977) N.E. sect. 1976), N.E. Soc. Electron Microscopy, Sigma Xi. Club: Harvard of N.H. Contbr. articles to profl. jours.; patentee in field. Home: 22 Weeks Ln Rochester NH 03867 Office: Mech Engring Dept U NH Durham NH 03824

BEATON, ROBERTA ANN JENSEN, civic and polit. worker; b. Modesto, Calif., Mar. 27, 1925; d. James Robert and Ann Marie Elizabeth (Bladt) Jensen; B.A., Pomona Coll., 1945; M.A. in Internat. Relations, Columbia, 1948; m. Donald Grant Beaton, Sept. 13, 1952; children—Heather Anne, Rodney Towers. With Offices Nelson A. Rockefeller, 1949-50; sec., adminstrv. asst. to head planning and head info. Radio Free Europe, N.Y.C., 1950-53; tchr. music St. Joseph Acad., N.Y.C., 1969-71. Co-chmn. polit. com. Womens Nat. Republican Club, 1971, mem. luncheon com., 1975, treas., 1975; co-chmn. Parent's Assn., Jack and Jill Nursery Sch., St. George's Ch., N.Y.C., 1964-78; mem. solicitation com. ARC, N.Y.C. Mem. Acad. Polit. Sci., Am. Acad. Polit. and Social Sci., Nat. Catholic Music Educators Assn., Leschetizky Assn., Nat. Vols. in Action, English Speaking Union, Nat. Trust for Historic Preservation. Episcopalian. Home: 531 E 20th St New York NY 10010

BEATTIE, DIANA SCOTT (MRS. ROBERT NATHAN STUCHELL), biochemist, educator; b. Cranston, R.I., Aug. 11, 1934; d. Kenneth Allen and Lillian Francis (Barton) Scott; B.A., Swarthmore Coll., 1956; M.S., U. Pitts., 1958, Ph.D., 1961; m. Benjamin Howard Beattie, June 30, 1956 (div. 1975); children—Elizabeth, Sara, Rachel, Ruth; m. 2d, Robert Nathan Stuchell, Feb. 6, 1976. Research asso. U. Pitts., 1961-67, VA Hosp., Pitts., 1967-68; asst. prof. Mount Sinai Sch. Medicine, N.Y.C., 1968-70, asso. prof., 1970-76, prof., 1976—; mem. grad. faculty biomed. scis. City U. N.Y., 1968—, biochemistry, 1971—, biology, 1974—. NIH grantee, 1966—, NSF grantee, 1970—. Mem. Am. Soc. Biol. Chemists, Am. Soc. Cell Biology, Biophysics Soc. Contbr. articles to profl. jours. Research on subcellular biochemistry, mitochondrial metabolism and biogenesis. Home: 141-21 33d Ave Flushing NY 11354 Office: Dept Biochemistry Mount Sinai Sch Medicine Fifth Ave and 100th St New York City NY 10029

BEATTIE, EDWARD JAMES, JR., physician; b. Phila., June 30, 1918; B.A., Princeton U., 1939; M.D., Harvard U., 1943; m. Nicole Mary; 1 son, Bruce Stewart. Intern, resident in surgery Peter Bent Brigham Hosp., Boston, 1942-46; Mosely traveling fellow (Harvard) to U. London (Eng.), 1946-47; surg. fellow, Markle scholar George Washington U., 1947-52; chief thoracic surgery Presbyn. Hosp. and chmn. dept. surgery Presbyn.-St. Luke's Hosp., Chgo., 1952-65; chief thoracic surgery Meml. Hosp., N.Y., 1965-75, chmn. dept. surgery, 1966-78, chief med. officer, 1966—, gen. dir., chief exec. officer, 1974—; prof. surgery U. Ill., 1954-65; prof. surgery Cornell U., 1965—; mem. Sloan-Kettering Inst., 1966—. Mem. Am. Bd. Med. Specialties, Inc. Diplomate Am. Bd. Thoracic Surgery (bd. 1960-69). Fellow A.C.S.; mem. Am. Assn. Thoracic Surgery. Am. Cancer Soc., Am. Broncho-Esophageal Assn., Am. Assn. Med. Colls., Am. Coll. Chest Physicians, Am. Fedn. Clin. Research, Am. Thoracic Soc., James Ewing Soc., Soc. Vascular Surgery, Soc. Thoracic Surgeons, AMA, Chgo. Surg. Soc., Am., Central, Pan Pacific, Western surg. assns., Pan Am. Med. Assn., Harvard Med. Soc., Soc. Clin. Surgery, Physician's Sci. Soc., AAAS, Transplantation Soc., Am. Radium Soc. Republican. Mem. editorial bd. Jour. Thoracic and Cardiovascular Surgery, 1962—, Pediatric Digest, 1962—, Jour. Surg. Oncology, 1972—. Home: 430 E 67th St New York City NY 10021 Office: Meml Hosp 1275 York Ave New York City NY 10021

BEAUCHEMIN, PAUL THOMAS, cons. engr.; b. Montreal, Que., Can., Mar. 26, 1931; s. Jules Armand and Marie Anne (Gervais) B.; B. Letters, Coll. Montreal, 1949; B.A., Coll. Ste Marie, 1951; B.Applied Sci., U. Montreal, 1956; C.E., Ecole Polytechnique, 1956; m. Lise E. Roy, Oct. 8, 1955; children—Louis, Sophie, Patrick. Jr. partner Beauchemin-Beaton-Lapointe, 1956-64, sr. partner, 1964-72; pres. Beauchemin-Beaton-Lapointe, Inc., Montreal, 1972-77, chmn. bd., 1977—; dir. Via Rail Can. Ltd., Les Consultants en Aeroports Internationaux de Montreal Ltée. Trustee Research Inst. on Pub. Opinions. Recipient award Engring. Inst. Can., 1955, Orders of Merit, U. Montreal, 1955, Ecole Polytechnique, 1954. Mem. Assn. Cons. Engrs. Can. (pres. 1976), Assn. Cons. Engrs. Que. (pres. 1975), Corp. Engrs. Que. (pres. cons. engrs. sect. 1969), Assn. des Diplomes de Polytechnique (dir. 1968), Assn. Quebecoise des Techniques de l'Eau, Assn. Quebecoise des Techniques Routieres, Community Planning Assn. Can., Engring. Inst. Can., Inst. Transp. Engrs., Order Engrs. Que., Profl. Corp. Urbanists Que., Societe Francaise d'Urbanisme, Canadian Inst. Planners, Montreal C. of C. Roman Catholic. Club: Cercle Universitaire. Home: 3781 The Boulevard Westmount PQ H3Y 1T3 Canada Office: 1134 W Ste Catherine Montreal PQ H3B 1H4 Canada

BEAUCHEMIN, ROGER OLIVIER, cons. engr.; b. Donnacona, Que., Can., May 20, 1923; s. Jules Armand and Marie Anne (Gervais) B.; Bach. Applied Scis., Ecole Polytechnique, U. Montreal (Que.), 1950; m. Andree Decarie, June 29, 1950; children—Francois, Denys, Anne-Marie, Roger. Engr., tech. sales dept. Canada Cement Co. Ltd., Montreal, 1950-55; partner Beauchemin-Beaton-Lapointe Cons. Engrs., Montreal, 1956—; dir. Mont Tremblant Lodge Inc., Martin Black Wire Ropes Can. Ltd., BG Checo Inc., The United Provinces Ins. Co., Cansilo Ltd., Atometics Ltd. Councillor, Municipality of Mont-Tremblant, Que., 1965-74; pres. Chambre de Commerce du Dist. de Montreal, 1969-70; vice-chair and mem. exec. com. Montreal Port Authority, 1971-76; chmn. Montral Heart Inst., 1976—; chmn., chief exec. officer Montreal Port Authority, 1977—. Recipient Canadian Design of Merit citations, 1966; award Grad. Soc. of Ecole Polytechnique, 1978. Mem. Order Engrs. Quebec, Assn. Cons. Engrs. Can., Inst. Transp. Engrs. (pres. Canadian sect. 1971), Canadian Transp. Research Forum. Roman Catholic. Clubs: St. Denis, Mount Royal. Chmn. project exec. com. for writing and publishing Manual of Geometric Design for Canadian Roads and Sts. Home: 4345 Westmount Ave Westmount PQ H3Y 1W4 Canada Office: 1134 Ste Catherine West Montreal PQ H3B 1H4 Canada

BEAULIEN, MARCEL LAURENT, cuisine adminstr., educator; b. Montreal, Que., Can., July 26, 1926; s. Rodrigue and Blanche (Talbot) B.; ed. pub. schs.; m. Rita Gallienne, Dec. 26, 1946; children—Liliane, Louise, Johanne, Caroline, Pierre. Staff Murray's Restaurant, Montreal; chef Can. Nat. Bank, Montreal, Old Ford Hotel, Montreal, Molson Brewery, Montreal; chef instr. Que. Restaurant Assn.; cons. in field. Served with Can. Service Corp, 1944-45. Named Chef of Year Que., 1974, recipient Ordre du Merite de la Restauration; named mem. of honor Conseilles de la Gastronomie Française. Mem. Chaine des Rotisseurs (culinary cons. for Can.), Fedn. Chefs Can., Food Assn. London (master craftsman), Assn. Cuisinier Paris, Chef Soc. (pres. 1971-72). Roman Catholic. Clubs: United Comml. Travelers Am., K.C., Gourmet (pres. chpt. 1974-75). Author cooking books, recipes. Home: 220 Lucerne St Rosemere PQ J7B 1A4 Canada Office: 1555 Notre Dame St E Montreal PQ J7B 1A4 Canada

BEAVER, HOWARD OSCAR, JR., steel co. exec.; b. Lebanon, Pa., May 18, 1925; s. Howard Oscar and Lessie Katherine (Yocum) B.; student U.S. Naval Acad., 1944; B.S. in Metallurgy, Pa. State U., 1948; student Mgmt. Program for Execs., U. Pitts., 1967; m. Jean Lillian Shollenberger, June 14, 1945; children—Bonne Jean (Mrs. James Riefenstahl), Thomas. With Carpenter Tech. Corp., Reading, Pa., 1948—, successively, metallurgist, 1948-57, mgr. mill metallurgy, 1957-60, asst. gen. supt., 1960-66, asst. v.p. steel mfg., 1966-68, v.p. prodn., 1968-69, group v.p. steel, 1969-71, pres., chief exec. officer, 1971—, also dir.; dir. Girard Bank, Phila., Girard Co. Mem. troop com. Boy Scouts Am., 1960-69, dist. activities chmn. Daniel Boone council, 1967, bd. dirs. Hawk Mountain council, 1969—, pres., 1973-76; active YMCA; v.p. Muhlenberg area Ambulance Assn., 1963-68. Adv. bd. Berks Campus Pa. State U., chmn., 1972; trustee Pa. State U., 1978—; bd. dirs. United Way, Chit-Chat Found. Served with USNR, 1943-44. Fellow Am. Soc. for Metals (Bradley Stoughton award, Lehigh Valley chpt. 1967, David Ford McFarland award Pa. chpt. 1972); mem. Mfrs. Assn. Berks County (bd. dirs., pres. 1978), Am. Assn. Iron and Steel Engrs., Am. Inst. Mining, Metall. and Petroleum Engrs., Am. Iron and Steel Inst. (dir. 1971—), Nat. Assn. Mfrs., Newcomen Soc. N.Am., C. of C. Reading and Berks County. Lion (pres. 1962-63). Lutheran (lay pres. ch. council). Clubs: Wyomissing, Berkshire Country, Moselem Springs Golf (Reading); Skytop (Pa.). Patentee in field. Home: 320 Hain Ave Muhlenberg Park Reading PA 19605 Office: 101 W Bern St Reading PA 19603

BEAVERS, ALLEN LOUIS, JR., assn. exec.; b. Scranton, Pa., May 26, 1930; s. Allen Louis and Angeline (Evans) B.; B.S. in Edn., Boston U., 1958, Ed.M., 1962; m. Cynthia Norma VanNote, Aug. 20, 1960; children—Cynthia Lynne, Scott Allen. Asst. to dean of men Boston U., 1958-62; asso. gen. dir., camping dir. YMCA, Quincy, Mass., 1962-66; exec. dir. camping services Hartford (Conn.) YMCA, 1966-77, asso. exec. dir., 1977—; pres. Allen Beavers Enterprises, Inc., Hartford. Bd. dirs. Hartford council Am. Youth Hostels; mem. Mass. DeMolay Assn., ednl. youth found. Pres., Hartford council Campfire Girls U.S.A., 1977-79; v.p. Webster Hill Sch., PTA, West Hartford, Conn., 1970-71, pres., 1976-77; chmn. building com. West Hartford Methodist Church, 1970-71. Served as sgt. U.S. Army, 1950-54. Recipient Legion of Honor award, 1972. Mem. Assn. Profl. Dirs. YMCA, Am. (dir. nat. bd. 1970-74, 77—, arrangements chmn. nat. conv. 1968, life mem.), New Eng. (pres. 1972-74) camping assns., Nat. Rifle Assn., Alpha Phi Omega, Sigma Phi Epsilon. Certified profl. camp dir., Conn. Clubs: Adirondack Mountain, Appalachian Mountain, Masons. Contbr. articles to camping mags. Home: 14 Rumford St West Hartford CT 06107 Office: 160 Jewell St Hartford CT 06103

BECHIS, KENNETH PAUL, astrophysicist; b. Boston, July 22, 1949; s. Zenon Krispin and Helen (Usevich) B.; grad. Boston Latin Sch., 1966; B.A. with honors (Coll. scholar), Harvard, 1970; S.M., Mass. Inst. Tech., 1973, postgrad., 1974; Ph.D., U. Mass., 1976; m. Donna Sharon Friedman, June 5, 1976. Lab. technician Harvard Coll. Obs., Cambridge, Mass., 1966-68, research asst. radio astronomy project, 1968-71; research asst. research lab. electronics dept. physics Mass. Inst. Tech., Cambridge, 1971-74; physicist Radiotech. Inc., Wakefield, Mass., 1974-75; research asst. physics/astronomy dept. U. Mass., Amherst, 1975, sr. research asso., lectr., 1977—, sta. mgr. Five Coll. Radio Astronomy Obs., 1976—; pres., chmn. exec. bd. Harvard Radio Broadcasting Co., Cambridge, 1969-70; sta. mgr. WHRB-FM, Cambridge, 1969; cons. TASC, Reading, Mass., 1978—, TRG div. Alpha Industries, Woburn, Mass., 1978—. Pres. jr. service league Mus. Sci., Boston, 1965-66. Served with USNR, 1970. Decorated Nat. Def. Service medal, 1970. Mem. Am. Astron. Soc., IEEE, Sigma Xi. Clubs: Community Boating (Boston). Contbr. articles to profl. jours. Office: Physics-Astronomy Dept 619I-GRC U Massachusetts Amherst MA 01003

BECHTLE, JON MICHAEL, coast guard officer; b. Riverhead, L.I., N.Y., Aug. 17, 1956; s. Walter Eugene and Rose Elaine (Reidy) B.; B.S. in Ocean Engring., U.S. Coast Guard Acad., 1978. Enlisted U.S. Coast Guard, 1974, commd. ensign, 1978; service as deck watch officer, engr.-in-tng. USCGC Ironwood, 1978—. Engr.-in-tng., Conn. Mem. U.S. Coast Guard Acad. Alumni Assn. Methodist. Home: 662 N Arnistead St Alexandria VA 22312 Office: USCGC Ironwood (WLB-297) FPO Seattle WA 98799

BECHTOLD, CHARLES LOUIS, chem. engr.; b. North Bergen, N.J., Feb. 29, 1928; s. Charles Frederick Andrew and Marion Elizabeth (Norris) B.; B.Chem. Engring., Poly. Inst. Bklyn., 1952, M.Chem. Engring., 1956; m. Helen Pauline Lang, June 24, 1956; children—Charles Frederick, Linda Helen. With Colgate Palmolive Co., 1952—, now sect. head process devel. household specialities, Jersey City. Served with U.S. Army, 1946-48. Mem. Am. Inst. Chem. Engrs., Phi Lambda Upsilon, Tau Beta Pi. Presbyterian. Clubs: Perth Amboy (N.J.) Rifle, Masons. Patentee in field. Home: 116 Hazelwood Ave Edison NJ 08817 Office: 105 Hudson St Jersey City NJ 07302

BECK, ADRIAN ROBERT, pediatric surgeon; b. N.Y.C., June 8, 1932; s. Alexander George and Frances (Price) B.; B.S., Union Coll., 1954; M.D., Albany Med. Coll., 1958; m. Marcia Perlmutter, Aug. 18, 1963; children—Adrienne, David. Intern, Beth Israel Hosp., N.Y.C., 1958-59; asst. resident surgery Mt. Sinai Hosp., N.Y.C., 1959-63, Dazian fellow in surg. research 1960-61, chief resident, 1963-64; chief resident pediatric surgery Buffalo Children's Hsop., 1964-66; practice medicine specializing in pediatric surgery, N.Y.C., 1968—; asso. clin. prof. surgery Mt. Sinai Sch. of Medicine, N.Y.C., 1966-78, clin. prof., 1978—; asso. attending surgeon, asso. dir. div. pediatric surgery Mt. Sinai Hosp., asso. attending surgeon City Hosp. at Elmhurst; attending surgeon, dir. div. pediatric surgery, Beth Israel Med. Center. Diplomate Am. Bd. Surgery. Fellow Am. Bd. Surgery, Am. Acad. Pediatrics, Am. Coll. Surgeons; mem. Am. Pediatric Surg. Assn., N.Y. Acad. of Sci., N.Y. Pediatric Soc., N.Y. State Med. Soc., N.Y. Soc. of Pediatric Surgery, N.Y. Surg. Soc., Soc. for Surgery of Alimentary Tract. Democrat. Jewish. Contbr. articles in field to profl. jours. and chpt. to book. Home: 4919 Goodridge Ave Riverdale NY 10471 Office: 45 E 85th St New York NY 10028

BECK, ALBERT, fire protection co. exec.; b. N.Y.C., Jan. 14, 1928; s. Albert Christian and Mabel Agnes (Dunn) B.; B.S., Fairleigh Dickinson U., 1950; M.S., Rutgers U., 1956; m. Jean Norma Russ, June 16, 1951; children—Nancy, Richard, Douglas. Product line mgr. Tung-Sol Electric, Inc. div. Wagner Electric Co., Bloomfield, N.J., 1951-66; dir. quality control IT&T, Brussels, 1966-69, asst. dir.-product ops. staff, 1969-72, dir. N.Am. staff, N.Y.C., 1972-73; sr. v.p.-Eastern ops. Grinnell Fire Protection Systems Co., Inc., Providence, 1973—; instr. evening div. Rutgers U., 1957-61. Mem. curriculum com. Wayne (N.J.) Bd. Edn., 1964. Served with A.C., USNR, 1945-47. Mem. Am. Soc. Quality Control (sr.). Republican. Baptist. Club: Quidnessett Country (N.Kingston, R.I.). Home: 216 Hemlock Dr East Greenwich RI 02818 Office: 10 Dorrance St Providence RI 02903

BECK, AUDREY PHILLIPS, state senator; b. Bklyn., Aug. 6, 1931; d. Gilbert Wesley and Mary (Reilly) Phillips; B.A. with high honors and distinction in econs., U. Conn., 1953, M.A., 1955; m. Curt Frederick Beck, Aug. 4, 1951; children—Ronald Pierson, Meredith Wayne. Instr. econs. U. Conn., Storrs, 1960-68; planning economist Windham Regional Planning Agy., 1968; mem. Conn. Ho. of Reps., 1969-75, asst. minority leader, 1973-75; mem. Conn. Senate, 1975—, chmn. joint fin. com., asst. majority leader, 1975—. Vis. prof. practical politics Center Am. Women and Politics, Eagleton Inst. Politics Rutgers U., 1973; vis. prof. politics Central Conn. State Coll. Mem. liaison com. Mansfield (Conn.) U., 1967-68, mem. community devel. action program, 1968-71; mem. Mansfield Bd. Fin., 1965-71, mem. town govt. study com., 1967-68; pres. Tolland County Democratic Assn.; del. UN Conf. on Habitat, Vancouver, 1976; del. Dem. nat. conv., 1972; mem. com. legislative ethics and campaign financing Nat. Legislative Conf., 1973; mem. regional tax com. Council of State Govts.; del. Internat. Women's Year, Houston; del. White House Conf. on Balanced Growth, 1978. Recipient outstanding state ofcl. award, 1973. Mem. League Women Voters, NOW, Am. Soc. Planning Ofcls. (pres. 1976-77), Women's Polit. Caucus. Alert, Women's Legislative Rev., AAUW, Conn. Fedn. Dem. Women's Clubs, Artus, Phi Beta Kappa, Phi Kappa Phi, Gamma Chi Epsilon, Delta Sigma Rho. Home: Dunham Pond Rd Storrs CT 06268 Office: Room 409-A State Capitol Hartford CT 06115

BECK, DOROTHY FAHS, social work research dir.; b. N.Y.C.; d. Charles Harvey and Sophia (Lyon) Fahs; student Randolph-Macon Women's Coll., 1924-26; A.B., U. N.C., 1928; M.A., U. Chgo., 1932; Ph.D., Columbia U., 1944; postdoctoral student, 1955-56; m. Hubert Park Beck, Aug. 20, 1930; 1 dau., Brenda E.F. Dir. econ. research Am. Dental Assn., 1929-32; social worker Emergency Relief Adminstrn., Linden, N.J., 1933, Morristown, N.J., 1933; statistician N.J. Emergency Relief Adminstrn., 1934; statis. analyst U.S. Office Edn., 1935-36; asso. social economist U.S. Central Statis. Bd., 1936-38; research supr., author Am. Coll. Dentists, 1940-42; statistician Am. Heart Assn., 1947-53; asst. prof. biostatistics Am. U., Beirut, Lebanon, 1954; dir. research Family Service Assn. Am., N.Y.C., 1956—; cons. Gilder fellow, 1934-35; Am.-German student exchange fellow, 1928-29. Fellow Am. Sociol. Assn.; affiliate Am. Assn. Marriage and Family Counselors; mem. Nat. Conf. Family Relations (vice chmn. counseling sect.), Groves Conf., Am. Statis. Assn., Nat. Assn. Social Workers, Am. Pub. Health Assn., Soc. Study of Social Problems, Acad. Certified Social Workers, Phi Beta Kappa. Mem. Liberal Party. Unitarian-Universalist. Author: Costs of Dental Care Under Specific Clinical Conditions, 1943; (with I.S. Wright and C.D. Marple) Myocardial Infarction, 1954; Patterns in Use of Family Agency Service, 1962; (with J.C. Sacks and P.M. Bradley) Clients' Progress within Five Interviews, 1970; (with M.E. Jones) Progress on Family Problems, 1973, How to Conduct a Client Follow-Up Study, 1974; (with E. Bradshaw) Marriage and the Family Under Challenge, 1976; New Treatment Modalities, 1978. Contbr. to Treating Relationships (David Olson, editor), 1976. Home: 523 W 121st St New York City NY 10027 Office: Family Service Association of America 44 E 23d St New York City NY 10010

BECK, EARL HENRY, JR., packaging cons.; b. Chester, Pa., Apr. 29, 1935; s. Earl Henry and Amelia S. (Connelly) B.; B.S. in Mech. Engring., U. Del., 1957; m. Ruth M. Scherer, Aug. 22, 1959; children—Karen, Scott, Tracey. Sr. engr. Scott Paper Co., Chester, Pa., 1957-61; supr. product devel. Container Corp. Am., Chgo., 1961-69; mgr. new products Continental Group, N.Y.C., 1969-74; sr. v.p. Raymond Eisenhardt Inc., Oakland, N.J., 1974—. Served with USNR, 1958. Registered profl. engr., Del. Mem. World Packaging Orgn., TAPPI, ASTM, Packaging Inst., Soc. Packaging and Handling Engrs. (certified). Republican. Presbyterian. Club: Redding Country. Patentee. Home: 74 Old Driftway Wilton CT 06897 Office: 95 Bauer Dr Oakland NJ 07436

BECK, FELIX M., mortgage banker; b. N.Y.C., Mar. 12, 1926; s. Louis and Jane (Cohen) B.; B.S., Rutgers U., 1949, M.B.A. (hon.), 1953; m. Doris Lew, June 18, 1950; children—Jeffrey, Bruce, Steven. Sec., Carteret Savs. & Loan Assn., Newark, 1950-57; exec. v.p. J.I. Kislak Mortgage Corp., Newark, 1957-69; chmn. bd. Margarette & Co. Inc., Perth Amboy, N.J., 1969—; instr. mortgage bankers schs.; cons. in field; dir. Berg Enterprises Inc.; trustee, pres. Berg Realty Trust; chmn. N.J. Mortgage Study Commn., 1972. Asst. sec. Newark CD Council, 1955; chmn. Essex County Mental Health Assn. fund-raising campaign, 1972, Multiple Sclerosis campaign, 1965, Newark March of Dimes campaign, 1967; mem. Indsl. Commn. Livingston (N.J.), 1970; trustee Rutgers U. Served to 1st lt. AUS, 1944-46. Mem. Mortgage Bankers Assn. N.J. (pres. 1974—),

Mortgage Bankers Assn. Am. (Washington com.). Democrat. Jewish. Clubs: 200 of Essex County, Scarlet R. Home: 70 Springbrook Rd Livingston NJ 07039 Office: 280 Maple St Perth Amboy NJ 08861

BECK, FRANCES PATRICIA, playwright, producer, dir.; b. Phila.; d. Lido and Agnes (DiAnnuntis) Speca; B.A. in Psychology, Columbia, 1957; grad. Am. Acad. Dramatic Arts, 1958; student Herbert Berghof, Tom West, Fred Steele; m. John Beck, Apr. 18, 1956; children—Alisa, John. Tchr., Am. Acad. Dramatic Art, N.Y.C., Phila. Dramatic Sch., N.Y. Acad. Dramatic Arts; founder, tchr. Creative Acad. Dramatic Arts, N.Y.C.; prin. Fran Beck Enterprises, N.Y.C., 1974—; dir. Betty Hughes Show, Philadelphia Presents; dir. numerous commls., documentaries, travelogs; writer, dir., producer Will the Real Zooperman Please Stand Up, Sex is . . .?; dir., actress numerous plays for community theatre, summer stock; dir., producer TV talk shows including Merv Griffin, Joe Franklin, Johnny Carson, Midday Show; appeared in TV prodns. Days of Our Lives, Bewitched, Edge of Night, TV Sound Stage, Omnibus, Naked City, others; appeared in movies North by Northwest, Splendor in the Grass, La Bonanza, also numerous commls., travelogs and indsl. films; cons. in field; tchr., cons. Lincoln Sq. Community Center, 1973-75. Recipient Vol. Tchr. award, 1959, 63; Phila. Drama award, 1971; George Foster Peabody award, 1976. Mem. Soc. Stage Dirs. and Choreographers, AFTRA, Actor's Liberation (pres.), Am. Guild Variety Artists, Screen Actors Guild, Actors Equity, NOW. Author: Gene of Jean, 1972; (poetry) Fannie, Fannie, 1970, Your Side, 1977; (plays) Choose It, 1966, Lara Peters, 1970, Answers Switch Me On, 1971, Zooperman, Sex Is ...?, 1972, Dutch Bride, 1978, others. Home: 319 E 24th St New York City NY 10010 Office: 110 E 23d St New York City NY 10010

BECK, GASPER PAUL, city ofcl.; b. New Brunswick, N.J., May 6, 1915; s. Andrew and Rose (Kovacs) B.; student Rutgers U., 1945-46, Am. Sch. Chgo., 1943-48; m. Ethel Nagy, June 27, 1936; children—Ilene (Mrs. Joseph Iassagna), Paul A., Patricia (Mrs. James Ladota), Christine (Mrs. John Puk), Rosemary (Mrs. Frank Murphy). With Johnson & Johnson, North Brunswick, 1933—, staff engr., 1963—; mayor, Highland Park, N.J., 1972-76; sec.-treas. Middlesex County Conf. Mayors, 1973; pres., 1974-75; bd. dirs. N.J. Conf. Mayors, 1975, asso., 1976—. Democratic County committeeman, 1960-71; mem. Dem. Council, 1963-71; v.p. Hungarian Am. Dem. Assn. Middlesex County, 1974, pres., 1976-77; chmn. March of Dimes, 1964, Mental Health Fund drive, 1966, United Fund drive, 1967-68; vice chmn. carousel ball Hungarian Studies Found., 1974, chmn., 1975; mem. Profl. Devel. Com., 1970—; bd. dirs. Villanova U. Devel. Council, 1978; bd. dirs. Am. Hungarian Found., 1975, treas., 1976—; mem. parish council St. Pauls Ch., 1972-76, St. Ladislaus Ch., 1977—. Merit badge counselor Girls Scouts U.S.A., 1947—, bd. dirs., 1955-60. Registered profl. engr., N.J. Mem. N.J. Vocat. Advisory Council, Assn. Energy Engrs. (charter mem.). Roman Catholic. Clubs: Johnson and Johnson Mgmt., Lions, K.C. Patentee in field. Home: 118 S 5th Ave Highland Park NJ 08904 Office: US Hwy 1 North Brunswick NJ 08902

BECK, JOHN HARRY, musician, educator; b. Lewisburg, Pa., Feb. 16, 1933; s. Harry T. and Mary Anna Virginia (Osman) B.; B.Mus., Eastman Sch. Music, 1955, M.Mus., 1962; m. Audrey J. Schulz, June 20, 1959; children—John R., Laurie Jean. Mem. U.S. Marine Band, Washington, 1955-59; percussionist Rochester Philharmonic Orch., 1959-62; timpanist, 1962—; instr. percussion Eastman Sch. Music, 1960-67, asst. prof. percussion, 1967-76, asso. prof., 1976—. Organizer rudimental drum contest Monroe County (N.Y.) Bicentennial Commn. Mem. Nat. Assn. Coll. Wind and Percussion Instrs. (past columnist jour.), N.Y. State Sch. Music Assn. (past chmn. percussion), Percussive Arts Soc. (pres. N.Y. State chpt., host internat. conv. 1976), AAUP, Music Educators Nat. Conf., Phi Mu Alpha Sinfonia, Mu Phi Epsilon (Musician of Year 1976). Club: Faculty. Author: Practical Approach to the Drum Set, 1967; record reviewer Woodwind World, Brass and Percussion mags. Composer: Rhapsody for Percussion and Band, 1970; Sonata for Timpani, Jazz Variants for Ensemble, 1972; Colonial Drummer, 1975; Colonial Capers, 1976; Overture for Percussion Ensemble, 1976; Episode for Solo Percussion, 1978; Episode for Percussion Trio, 1979; numerous recs. Vox Home: 23 Chelsea Way Fairport NY 14450 Office: Eastman Sch Music 26 Gibbs St Rochester NY 14604

BECK, MICHAEL JOHN, psychologist; b. Jamaica, N.Y., Sept. 3, 1942; s. Ernest and Helen May (Wallace) B.; B.A., St. John's U., 1964, Ph.D., 1972; m. Stanis A. Marusak, Dec. 17, 1967; children—Seanna Michele. Psychol. trainee Bronx (N.Y.) VA Hosp., 1965; psychotherapist Jamaica Center for Psychotherapy, 1965-73; asso. psychologist Kings Park State Hosp., 1967-73; treatment team leader Central Islip (N.Y.) State Hosp., 1973-76; adminstrv. supr. Manhattan Center for Modern Psychoanalytic Studies, 1973—; mem. faculty Advanced Inst. for Analytic Psychotherapy, 1972-73; pvt. practice, Babylon, N.Y., 1973—. Mem. Am., Suffolk County psychol. assns., Western Suffolk Personnel and Guidance Assn., Am. Assn. Marriage and Family Counselors. Contbr. articles to profl. jours. Home and office: 534 Deer Park Ave Babylon NY 11702

BECK, ROBERT ARTHUR, ins., co. exec.; b. N.Y.C., Oct. 6, 1925; s. Arthur C. and Alma B.; B.S. summa cum laude, Syracuse U., 1950; m. Frances Kenny, Aug. 7, 1948; children—Robert II, Stephen, Kathleen, Theresa. Financial analyst Ford Motor Co., Detroit, 1950-51; with Prudential Ins. Co. of Am., 1951—, salesman, 1951, mgr., Cin., 1956, dir. agy., Jacksonville, Fla., 1957-63, exec. gen. mgr., Newark, 1963-65, v.p., 1965-66, sr. v.p., Chgo., 1966-67, Newark, 1967-70, exec. v.p., 1970-73, pres., 1974-78, chmn. bd., chief exec. officer, 1978—, also dir.; dir. Xerox Corp., Campbell Soup Co. Bd. dirs., past chmn. Health Ins. Assn. Am.; mem. adv. council Grad. Sch. Bus., Columbia U.; bd. dirs., vice chmn. long range planning com. United Way; trustee Syracuse U.; chmn. silver anniversary N.J. Coll. Fund, Garden State Bowl Com. Served as 1st lt. parachute inf., AUS, World War II. Mem. Life Ins. Mktg. and Research Assn. (past chmn. bd.), Greater Newark C. of C. (chmn.), N.J. Hist. Soc. (dir., past pres.), Am. Council Life Ins. (dir.), Bus. Arts Found., Bus. Com. for Arts, Bus. Council, Bus. Roundtable, Conf. Bd. Clubs: Navesink, Essex, Knights of Malta, Seabright, Ocean Reef. Home: 8 Somerset Dr Rumson NJ 07760 Office: Prudential Plaza Newark NJ 07101

BECK, ROBERT EDWARD, ednl. adminstr.; b. Bklyn., June 23, 1946; s. Fred and Roslyn (Dodge) B.; B.A. with distinction in Psychology, State U. N.Y., Buffalo, 1968, M.S. in Edn., 1970; M.Ed., Columbia U., 1972, Ed.D., 1975; m. Anna Margret Edwards, June 11, 1977. Tchr., Bd. Edn., Buffalo, 1968-70; dir. Red Balloon Child Care Center, N.Y.C., 1971-72; sr. clin. sch. psychologist Manhattan Children's Psychiat. Center, Wards Island, N.Y., 1973-77; asst. adj. prof. psychology and human services City U. N.Y., Laguardia Coll., 1974-77; dir. pupil services/sch. psychologist Am. Embassy Sch., New Delhi, India, 1977—; lectr. in field; instr. adult edn. course in child psychology Am. Embassy Sch., New Delhi, 1977-78. Community police liaison worker Youth Bur., Buffalo, 1968-69. Named Employee of Yr., Intermediate Unit, Manhattan Children's Psychiat. Center, 1976; Heft scholar Columbia U., 1972. Mem. Am. Psychol. Assn., Am. Mental Health Counselors Assn., Am. Personnel and Guidance Assn., Day Care and Child Devel. Council Am., Assn. for Childhood Edn. Internat. Contbr. articles in field to profl. jours. Address: Am Embassy Sch New Delhi care Dept of State Washington DC 20520

BECK, ROBERT RANDALL, investment mgmt. co. exec.; b. San Francisco, July 2, 1940; s. Lester L. and Eunice (Hague) B.; A.B. with certificate in pub. affairs, Woodrow Wilson Sch., Princeton, 1962; M.B.A., Harvard, 1967. Producer, dir., Les Films Numero Uno, Paris, France, 1963-65; with State St. Research & Mgmt. Co., Boston, 1967—, partner, 1973—; dir. Edn. for Mgmt., Inc., United Artists Theatres, Inc., Graphics Mktg. Group, Inc. Mem. corp. New Eng. Deaconess Hosp.; bd. dirs. Modern Theatre. Served with USN, 1962-64. Mem. Boston Soc. Security Analysts. Home: Forest Rd East Alstead NH 03602 Office: 225 Franklin St Boston MA 02110

BECK, WILLIAM, physician; b. N.Y.C., Apr. 28, 1935; s. Allen and Belle Blanche (Barr) B.; A.B. summa cum laude, Boston U., 1956; M.D. cum laude, Downstate Med. Sch. N.Y., 1960; m. Paula Gertzman, Mar. 27, 1959; children—Bonnie, Wendy. Intern, Maimonides Hosp., Bklyn., 1960-61; resident ophthalmology Montefiore Hosp., Bronx, N.Y., 1961-64; dir. ophthalmology, Kew Gardens, N.Y., 1964—; asst. clin. prof. ophthalmology Albert Einstein Coll. Medicine, 1964—; attending ophthalmologist Montefiore and Jacob hosps., 1964—. Diplomate Am. Bd. Ophthalmology. Mem. Am. Acad. Ophthalmology and Otolaryngology, A.C.S., Phi Beta Kappa, Sigma Xi. Office: 125-10 Queens Blvd Kew Gardens NY 11415

BECKER, ARTHUR BERNARD, ins. co. exec.; b. Norwich, Conn., Mar. 25, 1928; s. Frank Edward and Rose (Goldstein) B.; student U. Conn., 1945-48; LL.B., Boston U., 1951; m. Gloria Ethel Oxman, Sept. 4, 1950; children—William B., Ross J. Admitted to Conn. bar, 1951, Pa. bar, 1976; practiced in Norwich, 1951-57, Farmington, 1957-60; group counselor, Aetna Life, Hartford, 1957-60; atty., asst. counsel Continental Casualty, Chgo., 1960-65; counsel, sec. Nat. Ben Franklin Companies, Chgo., 1965-69; sec., gen. counsel Colonial Penn Life, Phila., 1970-75, v.p., 1970—; v.p. Colonial Penn Franklin, 1971—, Colonial Penn Ins. Co., 1975—; sr. counsel Colonial Penn Group, Inc., 1975—, dep. corp. counsel, 1975-77, dir. govt. relations, 1978—. Sec., exec. com. Industry Adv. Com. Conf. Ins. Legislators, 1975-76, vice chmn., 1976-77, chmn., 1978—; mem. advisory com. on Medicare supplement ins., mem. industry adv. coms. Nat. Assn. Ins. Commr.'s Task Forces, Pa. Ins. Dept. Served with USN, 1945-46. Mem. Pa., Conn., Am. bar assns., Ins. Fedn. Pa. (dir., chmn. life and health legis. com. 1975—), Am. Council Life Ins. (group subcom. regulatory matters 1973-77), Am. Ins. Assn. (com. on fed.-state relations 1977—), Phila. Assn. Ins. Counsel, Am. Soc. Life Ins. Counsel. Club: Masons. Home: 337 Echo Valley Ln Newtown Square PA 19073 Office: 5 Penn Center Plaza Philadelphia PA 19103

BECKER, EDWARD PAUL, steel co. exec.; b. Bethlehem, Pa., Oct. 20, 1929; s. Joseph Horace and Anna Catherine (Kimenhour) B.; B.S. in Civil Engring., Lehigh U., 1951, M.S., 1954; m. Helen Elinor Becker, Oct. 9, 1954; children—Stacey Jane, Jill Anne. Structural engr. Cons. Engrs., Harrisburg, Pa., 1954-61; structural engr. Lehigh Structural Steel Co., Allentown, Pa., 1961-68, chief engr., 1968—. Served with C.E., AUS, 1951-53. Registered profl. engr., Pa., S.C., Tex. Fellow ASCE; mem. Nat. Soc. Profl. Engrs. (dir. 1974-79), Pa. Soc. Profl. Engrs. (pres. 1977-78), Am. Welding Soc. Democrat. Catholic. Office: Lehigh Structural Steel Co Box 626 Allentown PA 18105

BECKER, JAY JOSEPH, educator; b. N.Y.C., Nov. 23, 1943; s. William and Rose (Kalman) B.; B.A., Queens Coll., N.Y.C., 1968, M.A., 1970, adminstrn. and supervision certificate, 1973; m. Florence Laura Feinstein, June 14, 1964; children—Corey, Heidi. Tchr. law, dir. legal studies program Adrien Block Jr. High Sch., Flushing, N.Y., 1968—; dir. Sports Center, Sch. Athletic League, 1968-74; cons. legal studies N.Y.C. Bd. Edn., 1974; prof. Am. govt. N.Y. Inst. Tech., 1976; dir. Bay Terr. Corp., 1970-73; claims investigator Seaborad Adjustment Bur., 1972-76, Probus Investigations, 1978. Mem. Aux. Police, N.Y.C. Police Dept., 1975—. Tchr. Leadership Program fellow U. Houston, 1972, Taft Found. fellow, 1972; Am. Bar Assn. grantee, 1974. Mem. Law Studies Assn. New York, Nat. Bus. and Profl. Council. Democrat. Club: K.P. Author: Trade in the British Colonies: The Administration of the Customs Service, 1970; Curriculum Guide to Teaching Law, 1973; Auxiliary Commander's Training Course, 1976. Office: 34-65 192d St Flushing NY 11358*

BECKER, JERRY ELLSWORTH, cons. engring. co. exec.; b. Harrisburg, Pa., Oct. 9, 1936; s. Clarence William and Anna Mae (Lego) B.; ed. high sch.; m. Georgia Ann Baker, July 4, 1958; children—Kaye Ellen, Timothy John, Joseph Edward. Surveyor, Glace & Glace Inc., Harrisburg, Pa., 1954-57, draftsman, designer, constrn. insp., 1957-64; chief designer Tracy Engrs. Inc., Lemoyne, Pa., 1964-65, sr. project engr., LeMoyne/Camp Hill, Pa., 1965-73, v.p., Camp Hill, 1973—, also dir. Bd. dirs. Harrisburg Natural History Soc., 1967—; active Boy Scouts Am., 1970-74. Mem. Pa. Water Pollution Control Assn., Water Pollution Control Fedn. Republican. Methodist. Clubs: Masons, Shriners. Home: Route 1 Box 429-P Palmyra PA 17078 Office: Box 702 702 Lisburn Rd Camp Hill PA 17011

BECKER, KIP, ednl. adminstr., prof.; b. Phila., Apr. 3, 1946; s. Paul. E. and Claire B.; B.A. in Psychology, U. Del., 1972, M.Ed. in Counseling, 1973; Ph.D. in Profl. and Clin. Services, Fla. State U., 1978. Research asst., residence hall dir. U. Del., 1970-73, instr. dept. nursing, 1977-78; program evaluation specialist Gov.'s Commn. on Criminal Justice, State of Del., 1976-77; human relations expert Apalachee Community Mental Health Services, Tallahassee, 1974-75; cons. to City of Wilmington (Del.) Citizen Dispute Settlement, 1978; dir. criminal justice dept. Wilmington Coll., 1977—, dir. of security, 1977—. Served to CW-2, U.S. Army, 1966-70. Helicopter pilot, decorated D.F.C., 30 Air medals; Vietnamese Cross of Gallantry. Mem. Am. Acad. of Criminal Justice Scis., Am. Personnel and Guidance Assn. Home: 1502 Delaware Ave Wilmington DE 19806 Office: Criminal Justice Dept Wilmington College 320 Dupont Hwy New Castle DE 19720

BECKER, LAFOLLETTE, communications, urban affairs, community relations cons.; b. N.Y.C., July 4, 1924; d. Frank and Friedy (Wegeli) Becker; ed. N.Y. U., Columbia. Advt. exec. consumer and indsl. accounts Ben Sackheim, Inc., 1951-53; indsl. pub. relations editor-writer, translator in German and French, George Fischer Ltd., Schaffhausen, Switzerland, 1953-56; advt. exec. indsl. accounts Hazard Advt. Co., Inc., 1957; non-profit pub. relations editor-writer Nat. Council Chs. in U.S.A., 1958-61; ednl. pub. relations-alumni devel. editor-writer Pratt Inst., N.Y.C., 1961-62; dir. corp. pub. relations and consumer-trade advt. Incabloc Corp., N.Y.C., 1963; dir. fin. pub. relations Franklin Soc. Fed. Savs. & Loan Assn., N.Y.C., 1965-68; communications cons. mktg., advt., pub. relations programs for banks, bus., govt., 1969-72; state housing ofcl., pub. affairs and community relations adminstr. Empire Housing Found., N.Y. State Div. Housing and Community Renewal, 1972-75; communications cons. urban affairs and community relations, 1975—; founder, co-chmn. Community Action Council, 1970; lectr. women in bus. seminar New Sch., 1977; mem. regional adv. council U.S. SBA, 1976-78, lectr. mgmt. workshops, 1977; host community relations features Cable TV, 1977; adj. lectr. continuing edn. program Columbia U., 1978—. Republican candidate for N.Y. State Assembly, 1964; mem. Manhattan Community Bd. 8, 1975-77. Recipient Editorial awards Am. Alumni Council, 1962; Mktg. awards Savs. Inst. Mktg. Soc. Am., 1968; Freedoms Found. award, 1968; Silver Good Citizenship medal Nat. Soc. S.A.R., 1977. Mem. Pub. Relations Soc. Am., Fin. Advt. and Mktg. Assn. Met. N.Y., N.Y. U. Alumni Fedn., Citizens Union, Washington Hdqrs. Assn., East Mid-Manhattan C. of C. (dir. 1972, v.p. 1973, pres. 1976, permanent mem. exec. com. 1977—, community relations achievement awards 1973-75, 77). Contbr. articles to fin. and other publs. Home: 305 E 88th St New York City NY 10028

BECKER, LEON ROBERT, mfg. co. exec., occupational safety specialist; b. Carmel, N.Y., June 12, 1915; s. Joseph and Yette (Levitt) B.; B.S. with honors, Rutgers U., 1954; M.S., N.Y. U., 1954; m. Pearl Leah Kopelov, Aug. 10, 1943; children—Richard S., Harold A. Supr., Swift & Co., Newark, 1936-41; safety officer Huntsville Chem. Warfare Arsenal, 1943-45; mgr. safety, indsl. hygiene and security areas Mut. Chem. Co. Am., Jersey City, 1945-50; safety and fire protection mgr. indsl. chemistry div. Am. Cyanamid Co., Wayne, N.J., 1950-57, corp. sr. safety engr., 1957-65; corp. dir. safety and med. services Crane Co., Chgo., 1965-69; corp. dir. safety and loss prevention Becton, Dickinson and Co., Rutherford, N.J., 1969—; mem. N.J. Indsl. Safety Com., 1946—, Pres.'s Conf. on Occupational Safety and Health, 1948-72; chmn. legal sect. N.J. Gov.'s Conf. Occupational Safety, 1960-62; participant world-wide safety congress WHO and ILO, 1974—; lectr., adv. to profl. socs., univs., fed. and local govts. on occupational safety. Served with Chem. Corps, U.S. Army, 1941-46; lt. col. Res. Decorated Army Commendation medal; recipient spl. commendation for outstanding service in indsl. security, safety and related tng. Pres. U.S.; letters of commendation for contbn. to occupational safety legis., mems. U.S. Congress; spl. commendations from various profl. socs.; cert. safety profl.; cert. hazard control mgr.; accredited profl. diplomate. Mem. Am. Soc. Safety Engrs. (asst. v.p. and chmn. editorial adminstrn. bd. 1965-70, mem. tech. paper evaluation com. 1976—), Am. Indsl. Hygiene Assn., NAM, N.J. C. of C., Vets of Safety. Clubs: B'nai B'rith, Masons. Office: Beckton Dickinson and Co Mack Centre Dr Paramus NJ 07652

BECKER, MARY LOUISE, polit. scientist; b. St. Louis; d. W. R. and Evelyn (Thompson) Becker; B.S., Washington U., St. Louis, 1949, M.A. (Blewett fellow), 1951; Ph.D. (resident fellow 1952-56), Radcliffe Coll., 1957; postgrad. (Fulbright scholar) U. Karachi, Pakistan, 1953-54; married (div.); children—James, John. Intelligence research analyst Dept. State, Washington, 1957-59; internat. relations officer AID, Washington, 1959-64, community relations officer, 1964-66, sci. research officer, 1966-71, UN relations officer, 1971—; adviser U.S. dels. 19th, and 21st and 23d Governing Council sessions UN Devel. Program. Lectr. internat. relations civic orgns., student groups, 1954—. Mem. adv. bd., chmn. student placement Washington Citizenship Seminar, Nat. YMCA-YWCA, Washington, 1961-71. Mem. Am. Polit. Sci. Assn., Soc. for Internat. Devel., Assn. Asian Studies, Asia Soc., Am. Soc. Pub. Adminstrn., Am. Assn. U. Women, Mo. Soc. Washington (sec. 1959-60), Mortar Bd., Chimes, Alpha Lambda Delta, Beta Gamma Sigma, Eta Mu Phi, Pi Sigma Alpha. Presbyn. Club: International (Washington). Author: Muhammed Iqbal, 1965. Contbg. editor: Concise Ency. of Middle East, 1973. Contbr. articles to govt. publs. Office: Agy for Internat Devel Washington DC 20523

BECKER, NATALIE ROSE HARRITON (MRS. STANLEY M. BECKER), artist; b. Phila., Dec. 13, 1933; d. Frank and Zelda (Saltzman) Harriton; Asso. in Sci., Temple U., 1951; student Acad. Fine Arts, 1957-58, Art Students League, 1970-72; m. Stanley M. Becker, Oct. 27, 1957; children—Pamela Sue, Mitchell Douglas, Andrew David. One-man shows at Gallery 9, Chatham, N.J., 1969, Bloomfield Coll., 1971, Pen and Brush Club, N.Y.C., 1975; exhibited in group shows at Fine Arts Mus., Carnegie Inst., Jersey City Mus., N.A.D., Nat. Arts Club, Bergen County Mus., Capricorn Gallery, Bklyn. Mus.; represented in permanent collection at Bloomfield Coll.; tchr. art Union Coll., Cranford, N.J. Recipient Leon Lehrer Meml. prize for landscape, 1972, Grumbacher award of merit, 1972, many others. Fellow Am. Artists Profl. League (N.J. dir. 1971-76); mem. Audubon Artists, Pen and Brush Club, Burr Artists N.Y., Catharine Lorillard Wolfe Art Club. Club: Salmagundi (N.Y.C.). Home: 97 Barchester Way Westfield NJ 07090

BECKER, PAUL W., hosp. adminstr.; b. Madison, Wis., May 9, 1940; s. Paul F. and Margaret E. (Fisher) B.; B.S., U. Wis., 1962; M.S., Ohio U., 1964, Ph.D., 1967; m. Marianne Ritchie, Aug. 30, 1971; children—Eric Courtland, Todd James Paul. Pub. health services officer Fed. Reformatory, Chillicothe, Ohio, 1963; psychol. intern Norristown (Pa.) State Hosp., 1967, co-dir. intensive rehab. unit, 1968-70, adminstr. active patient treatment unit, 1971-72, sr. staff psychologist, 1970—, adminstr. departure unit, 1973—; pvt. practice as psychologist, 1970—. Registered Nat. Register of Health Service Providers in Psychology. Fellow Pa. Psychol. Assn.; mem. Am. Psychol. Assn., Psychologists in Pvt. Practice, Sigma Xi, Psi Chi (service award 1966, certificate of merit 1967). Contbr. articles to profl. jours. Office: Dept Psychology Norristown State Hospital Norristown PA 19401

BECKER, ROBERT LOUIS, JR., lawyer; b. Milw., July 28, 1925; s. Robert Louis and Marion Merrill (Jaynes) B.; student Franklin and Marshall Coll., 1943-44, U. Pa., 1944-45; J.D., Cornell U., 1949; m. Patricia Mansfield Osborne, Aug. 2, 1950; children—Anne Baldwin Becker Hulley, Emily Merrill, Robert Louis III. Admitted to Pa. Supreme Ct. bar, 1950; partner firm Kirkpatrick, Lockhart, Johnson & Hutchison, Pitts., 1949—; dir. Anderson Equipment Co. Trustee Children's Hosp., Pitts., Sarah Scaife Found. Served as ensign USNR, 1943-46. Mem. Am., Pa., Allegheny County bar assns., Cornell Law Assn., Am. Law Inst., Phi Gamma Delta, Phi Delta Phi. Republican. Presbyterian. Clubs: Duquesne, Pitts. Golf. Home: 5029 Amberson Pl Pittsburgh PA 15232 Office: 1500 Oliver Bldg Pittsburgh PA 15222

BECKER, SARAH RUSKIN, stockbroker, ret. psychologist; b. N.Y.C., May 4, 1914; d. Max and Bessie (Sirotkin) Ruskin; student Hunter Coll., 1931-34; B.A., Adelphi Coll., 1957; M.A. Hofstra Coll., 1961; m. Irving Becker, Dec. 11, 1938; children—Barbara Joan (Dr. Martin Edward Kantor), Carol Doree (Mrs. Manny Goldberg). Tchr. math Nassau County, N.Y., 1957-59; grad. asst. Hofstra Coll., Hempstead, N.Y., 1958-60, lectr., freshman counsellor, 1964-65; sch. psychologist Union Free Sch. Dist. 2, East Williston, N.Y., 1959-68, Locust Valley (N.Y.) Sch. Dist., 1963-64, Central Sch. Dist. 4, Plainview, N.Y., 1967-71; stockbroker Liberty Securities Co., New Hyde Park, N.Y., 1971-74. Active Girl Scouts U.S.A., 1952-56. Mem. Am., N.Y. State, Nassau County (treas. 1963-69) psychol. assns., Psi Chi, Pi Gamma Mu. Mem. B'nai B'rith (fin. sec. 1952-54). Home: 1 Horseshoe Ln Roslyn Heights NY 11577

BECKER, STEPHEN PHILIP, electronics co. exec.; b. Newton, Mass., Apr. 4, 1943; s. Frederick Leon and Julia Jean (Rattet) B.; B.S., Boston U., 1966, M.Ed., 1968, certificate advanced grad. study adult edn., 1971; m. Brenda Phyllis Marmer, May 28, 1967; children—Adam Jay, Marc Austin, Sheri Jill. Mgmt. tng. specialist

Polaroid Corp., Cambridge, Mass., 1968-70; dir. tng. St. Johnsbury Trucking Co., Cambridge, 1970-77; v.p. orgn. and mgmt. devel. M/A-COM Inc., 1978—. Mem. Adult Edn. Assn. Mass. (dir.), Am. Soc. Tng. and Devel., Nat. Soc. Performance and Instrn. (Outstanding Communication award 1978), Adult Edn. Assn. U.S.A., Nat. Orgn. Devel. Network, Mgmt. Devel. Forum, N.Y.C., Phi Delta Kappa. Contbr. articles Tng. mag. Home: 23 Swanson Rd Framingham MA 01701 Office: South Ave Burlington MA 01803

BECKER, WILLIAM ADOLPH, ins. co. exec.; b. Kenosha, Wis., July 2, 1933; s. Adolph Gustav and Helen Marie (Rasmussen) B.; B.A., Coll. William and Mary, 1957; diploma Cornell U., 1958; C.L.U., Am. Coll. Life Underwriters, 1971; m. Mildred Lois Behr, Dec. 13, 1952; children—Verne W., Bradford S., Gregory T. Mgr., Commodore Maury Hotel, Norfolk, Va., 1957-59; field underwriter Home Life Ins. Co. of N.Y., Norfolk, 1959-61; asst. to gen. agt. Union Mut. Life Ins. Co., Richmond, Va., 1961-65; supr. Aetna Life & Casualty, Richmond, Va., 1965-70, mktg. dept. field dir., 1970-71, gen. agt., Utica, N.Y., 1971-74, Syracuse, N.Y., 1974—; moderator Life Underwriter Tng. Council, 1964, 66; instr. C.L.U. diploma program, 1973-74. Served with USN, 1950-54. C.L.U., N.Y.; recipient Louis I. Dublin award for pub. service, 1976, 77. Mem. Am. Soc. C.L.U.'s (pres. Mohawk Valley chpt. 1973-74), Central N.Y. Mgrs. Assn., Utica Assn. Life Underwriters (pres. 1972-73), N.Y. Assn. Life Underwriters (regional v.p. 1977-78), Nat. Assn. Life Underwriters, Syracuse Assn. Life Underwriters, Soc. for Advancement Mgmt., Am. Soc. Personnel Adminstrs., Am. Mgmt. Assn., Gen. Agts. and Mgrs. Assn. Republican. Club: Univ. Home: 507 Churchill Ct Fayetteville NY 13066 Office: 258 Genesee St Power Bldg Suite 510 Utica NY 13502

BECKETT, WILLIAM WADE, lawyer; b. Charleston, S.C., Feb. 2, 1928; s. Theodore Ashe and Mary (Scroggs) B.; B.S., The Citadel, 1948; J.D., George Washington U., 1956; m. Kathryn Rae Sims, June 4, 1955; children—Kathryn Elizabeth, Nancy Ellen, Mary Sims. Engr. Am. Bridge Co., Ambridge, Pa., 1948; with Burns, Doane, Benedict & Irons, 1953-60; mem. firm Irons, Birch, Swindler & McKie, Washington, 1960-69, Schuyler, Birch, Swindler, McKie & Beckett, 1969—. Trustee Internat. Students, Inc., 1962-65. Served to 1st lt. AUS, 1948-53. Mem. Am., D.C. bar assns., Am. Patent Law Assn., Washinton Patent Lawyers Club (sec. 1965-66, pres. 1966-67, area com. Young Life campaign 1965—), Delta Theta Phi. Presbyn. (elder). Clubs: Univ.; Bethesda (Md.) Country. Home: 9300 Renshaw Dr Bethesda MD 20034 Office: 1000 Connecticut Ave Washington DC 20036

BECKSTED, WILLIAM FREDRICK, engring. mfg. co. exec.; b. Oswego, N.Y., Jan. 24, 1948; s. William Fredrick and Dorothy (Skinner) B.; Asso. Applied Sci., State U. N.Y. at Delhi, 1969; m. Gail JoAnn Cline, June 28, 1969; children—William Fredrick, Genevieve Ann, Jason David. Mgr. quality control No. Steel Corp., Oswego, N.Y., 1971-75; mgr. quality assurance Lyons Iron Works Inc., Manchester, N.H., 1975-77, Bergen-Paterson Pipesupport Corp., Laconia, N.H., 1977—. N.Y. State Regents Acad. scholar, 1966. Mem. Am. Soc. Quality Control, Am. Welding Soc., ASTM. Club: Masons. Home: 33 Pine Notch Circle Laconia NH 03246 Office: 48 Winnisquam Ave Laconia NH 03246

BEDDOW, JOHN HEBERT, hosp. adminstr.; b. Elizabeth, N.J., July 11, 1919; s. George and Bessie (Hartenstein) B.; student Rider Coll., 1939-40, Rutgers U., 1946; m. Louise Audrey Applebaum, May 12, 1946; children—Gail, Erica, Alison. Adminstrv. v.p., gen. mgr. Middlesex Gen. Hosp., New Brunswick, N.J., 1954-60; exec. dir. Chronic Disease Hosp., Bklyn., 1960-61; asst. to pres. N.Y. Med. Coll., adminstr. Flower and Fifth Avenue Hosp., N.Y.C., 1961-65; mng. dir. The Valley Hosp., Ridgewood, N.J., 1965-68; adminstr. Raritan Valley Hosp., Greenbrook, N.J., 1968-69; pres. Tuxedo Meml. Hosp., Tuxedo Park, N.Y., 1969—; preceptor Columbia, 1957-59, Xavier U., Cin., 1964-65. Mem. Pres.'s White House Conf. on Health, 1965. Served with USAAF, 1942-45, ETO. Recipient Urban League Human Relations award, 1958. Mem. Am. Coll. Hosp. Adminstrs., Am. N.J. hosp. assns. Home: Tuxedo Park NY 10987 Office: Myers Rd Tuxedo Park NY 10987

BEDELL, FOREST KEITH, pension cons.; b. Olympia, Wash., Feb. 25, 1929; s. Issac Foster and Alda Rose (Mosher) B.; A.A., Clark U., 1950; B.A., N.Y. U., 1956; m. Gaynell Pack, Nov. 21, 1966. Corporate trust officer Central Hanover Bank, N.Y.C., 1953-56; sales Pa. Mut. Life Ins. Co., N.Y.C., 1957-60; exec. dir. Pension & Estate Inc., N.Y.C., 1960-66; pres., dir. Quality Pension Consultants Inc., N.Y.C., 1967—, Forest K. Bedell Assos. Inc., N.Y.C., 1966—, Garna Planning Corp., N.Y.C., 1969-75; pres., dir. Integrated Investors Service Inc., Scarsdale, N.Y., 1975—; dir. Lowenberg Bakery, Inc., Meyco Products Inc. Served with AUS, 1945-48. Mem. Am. Soc. Pension Actuaries, Nat. Assn. Life Underwriters. Home: 25 Sutton Pl S New York City NY 10022 Office: 342 Madison Ave New York City NY 10017

BEDELL, JOHN ROBERT, metall. engr.; b. Bklyn., Nov. 16, 1928; s. Chester Styles and Anita Paulina (Geise) B.; B.S., Mass. Inst. Tech., 1950; M.S., Bklyn. Poly. Inst., 1955; m. June Larson, Feb. 2, 1951; children—J. Chris, Curtis Styles. Metallurgist, Sperry Gyroscope, Great Neck, N.Y., 1950-52; sr. engr. Sylvania Atomic Energy Div., Bayside, N.Y., 1952-56; group leader Glenn Martin Aircraft, Middle River, Md., 1956-57; product mgr. Photocircuits Corp., Glen Cove, N.Y., 1957-64; techniques mgr. Consol. Controls Corp., Bethel, Conn., 1964-71; project mgr. Allied Chem. Corp., Materials Research Center, Morristown, N.J., 1971—; v.p., sec. Thermotek Corp., Madison, N.J., 1978—. Mem. Am. Soc. Metals, Am. Inst. Mining, Metall. and Petroluem Engrs., IEEE, Nat. Soc. Profl. Engrs. Presbyterian. Home: 15 Wyndehurst Dr Madison NJ 07940 Office: Box 1021-R Morristown NJ 07960

BEDELL, SUSANNA E., lawyer; b. Budapest, Hungary; d. Jozsef and Rosemarie (Kenyeres) Eszenyi; came to U.S., 1938, naturalized, 1948; A.B., Vassar Coll., 1940; J.D., Columbia U., 1944; m. Wallace Canaday Bedell, Aug. 30, 1947 (div. 1967); children—Susanna Elizabeth, Wallace Canaday. Admitted to N.Y. bar, 1948, D.C. bar, 1953, U.S. Supreme Ct. bar, 1952; asso. Shearman & Sterling & Wright, N.Y.C., 1944-51; pvt. practice law, Poughkeepsie, N.Y., 1951-52, 54—; asso. firm Wilmer & Broun, Washington, 1953-54; of counsel Van De Water & Van De Water, Poughkeepsie, 1970—. Mem. Hoover Commn., 1948; panelist World Affairs Conf., U. Colo., 1968. Pres. W.W. Smith Center, 1956-58; trustee Poughkeepsie Day Sch., 1958-65; area chmn. Columbia U. Campaign, 1968-69; legis. chmn. Region III, N.Y. State Mental Health Soc., 1966-67; pres. Dutchess County Women's Republican Club, 1960-64; mem. Rep. County Com., 1962-73; v.p., bd. dirs. Astor Child Guidance Clinic, 1966—; bd. dirs. Dutchess County Mental Health Soc., 1962—, Mid-Hudson Legal Services Project, 1974-77; chmn. bd. trustees Dutchess County Supreme Ct. Library, 1968—; mem. women's aux. Dutchess County Med. Soc., 1951-67; treas., bd. dirs. Mid-Hudson Meml. Soc., 1971-77; pres., dir. Mid-Hudson Legal Services, Inc., 1977-78. Mem. Am., N.Y. State, Dutchess County (chmn. continuing legal edn. com. 1975—) bar assns., Bar Assn. City N.Y., LWV, Jr. League, Asso. Alumnae Vassar Coll. (1st v.p., dir. 1954-57). Club: Poughkeepsie Tennis. Contbr. articles to periodicals. Home: 20 Sunrise Ln Poughkeepsie NY 12603 Office: 40 Garden St Poughkeepsie NY 12602

BEDFORD, RUTH ALICE HAEDIKE (MRS. EDWIN GARRARD BEDFORD), librarian; b. Chgo.; d. William Henry and Alice (Lohr) Haedike; student Beloit Coll., 1932-33; B.S., U. Ill., 1936, M.S., 1954, postgrad.; m. Edwin Garrard Bedford, June 6, 1942; children—David Edwin, Ellen Louise. Instr. U. Ill. Library, Urbana, 1954-64; asst. prof. library sci. U. Utah Libraries, Salt Lake City; 1964-68; asso. librarian Butler Library, State U. Coll., Buffalo, 1968—, mem. personnel com. tech. services div., 1972-75, chmn., 1974-75, mem. faculty adv. council instructional resources, 1971-73. Mem. tech. services com. Western N.Y. Library Resources Council, 1968-73. Mem. State U. N.Y. Librarians' Assn., AAUP, ALA, Kenan Center (charter mem.), Delta Phi Alpha. Club: Order Eastern Star. Home: 905 Charlesgate Circle East Amherst NY 14051 Office: 1300 Elmwood Ave Buffalo NY 14222

BEDROSIAN, SAMUEL DER, systems engr., educator; b. Marash, Turkey, Mar. 24, 1921; s. Sahag Der and Zabel (Chorbajian) B.; came to U.S., 1922, naturalized, 1942; A.B., State U. N.Y., 1942; M.E.E., Poly. Inst. Bklyn., 1951; Ph.D., U. Pa., 1961; m. Agnes Morjigian, Nov. 24, 1951; children—Camille, Gregory. Project engr., sect. chief Signal Corps Engring. Labs., Ft. Monmouth, N.J., 1946-55; systems engr. Burrough Research Center, Paoli, Pa., 1955-60; mem. faculty U. Pa., Phila., 1960—, prof. systems engring., 1973—, chmn. dept. systems engring., 1975—; cons. to RCA Corp., 1968—, Aydin Monitor Systems, 1976, Norden Systems, 1977—. Served to 1st lt. Signal Corps, U.S. Army, 1943-46; PTO. Recipient Kabakjian award Armenian Students Assn., 1976. Fellow IEEE; mem. Franklin Inst. (asso. editor Jour. 1966—), Sigma Xi, Eta Kappa Nu. Home: 35 Bryan Ave Malvern PA 19355 Office: 371 Moore School Univ of Pa 200 S 33rd St Philadelphia PA 19104

BEEBE, WILLIAM DOW, utility ofcl.; b. Bridgeport, Conn., Dec. 7, 1917; s. Ira Dow and Mary Margaret (Bell) B.; student George Washington U.; m. Hazel Emma Fowler, Apr. 2, 1954; children—William Dow, Donald James, Barbara Ann, Margaret Frances. With Potomac Elec. Power Co., Washington, 1937—, relay tester high voltage power apparatus, 1949-53, supr. tech. tng., foreman of substa. test dept., 1953—; instr. continuing edn. George Washington U. First aid instr. A.R.C.; mem. adv. com. United Fund, 1960-75; past pres. Friends of Woodrow Wilson Library; v.p., trustee Barcroft Terrace Citizens Assn., 1968-70; mem. exec. com. P.T.A., 1957-58, 72-73; active Boy Scouts Am.; mem. Fairfax County (Va.) Planned Land Use Study Com., 1974-75, Fairfax Legacy Action Group, 1975; mem. Fairfax County Republican Com.; del. Va. Rep. Convs., 1976-77. Served with Signal Corps, AUS, 1943-46; PTO. Recipient Silver Beaver award Boy Scouts Am., 1958. Mem. I.E.E.E., PEPCO Engrs. Assn. (past sec.), UN Assn. Methodist. Mason (32 deg.). Home: 6227 Parkhill Dr Alexandria VA 22312 Office: 1900 Pennsylvania Ave NW Washington DC 20006

BEECHHOLD, HENRY FRANK, educator; b. Miami, Fla., July 25, 1928; s. Irvin Frank and Dorothy Berenice (Stone) Mitchell; student Western Res. U., 1947-48; B.S., Okla. State U., 1951, M.A., 1952; Ph.D., Pa. State U., 1956; m. Irene S. Pollack, Jan. 31, 1954; children—Adrienne, Matthew S. Tech. writer Cushing & Nevell, N.Y.C., 1951, 52; instr. English, Okla. Mil. Acad., Claremore, Okla., 1952-53; teaching asst. Pa. State U., 1953-56; from instr. to asso. prof. U. Maine, Orono, 1956-63; asso. prof. English and linguistics Trenton (N.J.) State Coll., 1963-67, prof., 1967—, chmn. interdisciplinary program in linguistics, 1972—, tchr. Hunter Coll. City U. N.Y., 1970-73; cons. in curriculum; ednl. program cons. ABC, N.J. Writers Conf.; exec. v.p. Power Techs., Inc.; participant TV series Grammar Rock. Mem. nat. council Irish Am. Cultural Inst., 1972—; U.S. resident dir. Tagore Inst. Creative Writing, Madras, India, 1974-76. Served with AUS, 1945-47. Named N.J. Edn. Writer of Year, N.J. Assn. Tchrs. English, 1972; Lit. Luminary of N.J., N.J. Writers Conf., 1977. Licensed pvt. pilot. Mem. Linguistic Soc. Am., Internat., N.J. (founder, pres.) linguistic assns., Linguistics Assn. Gt. Britain, Coll. English Assn., N.J. Assn. Tchrs. English, Phi Kappa Phi. Democrat. Author: The Creative Classroom, 1971; The Science of Language and The Art of Teaching, 1972; (plays) Tohu Bohu, 1969, The Waiting Room, 1970, Third Act, 1971; (opera) Between the Shadow and the Dream, 1972. Asso. editor Eire-Ireland, 1973—; exec. editor Bitterroot, 1974—. Contbr. poetry to publs. Home: 13 Perry Dr West Trenton NJ 08628 Office: Dept English Trenton State Coll Trenton NJ 08625

BEEDE, BENJAMIN RIPLEY, librarian; b. Portland, Maine, Jan. 12, 1939; s. Kenneth Allen and Virginia Carolyn (Maddocks) B.; A.B., Rutgers U., 1961, M.L.S., 1963. Supervising reference librarian Linden (N.J.) Free Pub. Library, 1968-69; tech. services librarian Sch. Law Library, Rutgers U., Camden, N.J., 1969-71, asst. law librarian for pub. services, 1971—; cons. N.J. Dept. CS. Served with U.S. Army, 1964-67. Decorated Army Commendation medal. Mem. ALA, Am., N.J. (sec.-treas. 1975—) polit. sci. assns., Am. Hist. Assn., Spl. Libraries Assn., AAUP (pres. N.J. conf. 1977—), N.J. Library Assn., Phi Beta Kappa, Phi Sigma Alpha. Congregationalist. Author: The Legal Sources of Public Policy, 1977; Independence Documents of the World, 1977; contbr. articles to profl. jours. Home: 7 Thrush Mews North Brunswick NJ 08902 Office: 5th and Penn Sts Camden NJ 08102

BEEMAN, WILLIAM ORMAN, linguistic anthropologist, educator; b. Manhattan, Kans., Apr. 1, 1947; s. William Orman and Florence Lucille (O'Kieffe), B.; student Grinnell Coll., 1964-65; B.A., Wesleyan U., 1968; M.A., U. Chgo., 1971, Ph.D., 1976. Vis. lectr. Wesleyan U., Middletown, Conn., 1972-73; asst. prof. anthropology Brown U., Providence, 1973—. Asso., Maqam Middle East Consultants, 1975—. Mem. Am. Anthrop. Assn., Middle East Studies Assn., Soc. Applied Anthropology, Soc. for Iranian Studies, Afghan Studies Assn., Linguistic Soc. Am. Contbr. articles to profl. jours. Home: 108 Webster Ave Providence RI 02912 Office: Box 1921 Brown U Providence RI 02912

BEER, DAVID WELLS, architect; b. N.Y.C., June 29, 1934; s. Walter Eugene and Florence Louise (Fay) B.; B.A., Harvard, 1956; M.Arch., 1959; m. Laura DeKay Houghton, Apr. 28, 1962; children—Elizabeth Amory, Andrew David. With Pedersen & Tilney-Architects, N.Y.C., 1959-62, Hoberman & Wasserman-Architects, N.Y.C., 1962-65; with Welton Becket Assos.-Architects, N.Y.C., 1965—, sr. v.p., 1970—, dir. design, 1970—. Bd. dirs. Travel Program for Fgn. Diplomate, N.Y. council United Negro Coll. Fund. Co-recipient 1st prize Franklin Delano Roosevelt Competition, 1960. Mem. AIA, Alpha Chi Rho. Clubs: River, Met. Opera (N.Y.C.); Delphic (Cambridge, Mass.). Home: 131 E 66th St New York City NY 10021 Office: Care Welton Becket Assos 110 E 59th St New York City NY 10022

BEER, JEANETTE MARY AYRES, educator; b. Wellington, N.Z.; d. Alexander Samuel and Una Doreen (Castle) Scott; B.A. 1st class, Victoria U., N.Z., 1954, M.A. 1st class, 1955; B.A. 1st class Oxford U., Eng., 1958, M.A., 1962; Ph.D. (fellow), Columbia, 1967; m. Colin Gordon Beer, June 27, 1959; children—Stephen James Colin, Jeremy Michael Alexander. Asst. lectr. French, Victoria U., Wellington, 1956; lectrice French and English, Universite de Montpellier, France, 1958-59; instr. French, Otago U., Dunedin, N.Z., 1963-64, Barnard Coll., Columbia, N.Y.C., 1966-68; asst. prof. French, Fordham U., Bronx, N.Y., 1968-69, asso. prof., 1969-77, prof., 1977—, acting asso. dean Thomas More Coll., 1972-73, dir. medieval studies, 1972—. Mem. nat. bd. consultants Nat. Endowment for Humanities, 1978—. Grantee Nat. Endowment for Humanities, 1975. Mem. Modern Lang. Assn., Medieval Acad., Internat. Arthurian Soc., Soc. Rencesvals, Comparative Lit. Assn., Am. Assn. Tchrs. French, Anglican. Author: Villehardouin—Epic Historian, 1968; A Medieval Caesar, 1976. Gen. editor Teaching Language through Literature, 1971—. Contbr. articles to profl. jours. Home: 256 W Hudson Ave Englewood NJ 07631 Office: Dept Medieval Studies Fordham U Bronx NY 10458

BEER, ROBERT AUGUR, Realtor; b. Balt., Oct. 14, 1924; s. Robert Augur and Marie (McLaughlin) B.; grad. George Washington U., 1946; m. Kathleen Costello, Feb. 18, 1950; children—Robert Carey, Tracy Augur, Elizabeth West. Asst. v.p. James W. Rouse Co., mortgage bankers, Washington, 1944-55; exec. v.p., mortgage specialist Ivor B. Clark Co., Inc., Washington, 1957—; dir. Am. Nat. Bank, Silver Spring, Md. Served with USNR, World War II, Home: 10621 S Glen Rd Potomac MD 20854 Office: 1511 K St NW Washington DC

BEERS, DAVID MONROE, hosp. exec.; b. Pelham, N.Y., July 12, 1934; s. Ernest Monroe and Jean (Thoman) B.; B.A., Wesleyan U., 1955; M.P.A., Syracuse U., 1956, postgrad.; postgrad. Yale U. Div. Sch.; m. Jean Tubbs, Dec. 28, 1965; children—Terri Mi Sook, Mia Linn. Exec. dir. Univ. Hill Corp., Syracuse, N.Y.; dir. joint legis. com. on housing and urban devel. N.Y. State Legislature; pres. Crouse-Irving Meml. Hosp., Syracuse, 1969—; chmn. bd. Va. & Md. R.R., Md. & Del. R.R.; chmn. Central N.Y. Emergency Med. Services Adv. Council. Served with USAR, 1956-58. Mem. Hosp. Assn. N.Y. State (trustee), Hosp. Assn. Central N.Y. (vice chmn.). Home: 219 Goodrich Ave Syracuse NY 13210 Office: 736 Irving Ave Syracuse NY 13210*

BEERS, ROBERT GEORGE, water co. exec.; b. Shenandoah, Pa., Oct. 27, 1919; s. Elmer R. and Margaret (Bees) B.; E.E., Lehigh U., 1937-41; m. Nancy Jane Black; 1 son, Robert George, III. With E.R. Beers Electric Co., Bloomsburg, Pa., 1941—, pres., 1955—, dir., 1955—; with Bloomsburg Water Co., 1946—, pres., 1958—, dir., 1941—; sec. Bloomsburg Sand & Gravel Co., Inc., 1967—, dir., 1967—. Served with USAAF, 1942-46. Lutheran. Mason. Home: RD 4 Bloomsburg PA 17815 Office: 143 W Main St Bloomsburg PA 17815

BEERY, EDWIN NEWMAN, ophthalmalogist; b. Bklyn., Apr. 14, 1910; s. Edwin Milton and Minnie L. (Newman) B.; A.B., Colgate U., 1931; M.D., Columbia U., 1934; m. Evelyn V. Onken, Oct. 11, 1941 (div. July 1977); children—Lillian Beery Willis, Edwin Newman, William Stocktill; m. 2d, Caroline T. Marabello, Jan. 24, 1978. Intern, St. John's Episc. Hosp., 1934-36, asst. to cons. ophthalmologist, 1938—; resident in ophthalmology Bklyn. Eye and Ear Hosp., 1936-38, attending ophthalmic surgeon, 1938-76; practice medicine specializing in ophthalmology, Bklyn., 1938-77; med. officer U.S. Postal Service, Bklyn., 1977—; asso. attending Kings County Hosp., 1938-47; cons. Carson C. Peck and Meth. Hosp., 1946—, Bklyn. Thoracic Hosp., 1946-55, Hosp. of St. Giles, 1946-78, Bklyn. Hosp., 1978—; mem. physician's rev. com. Blue Shield of N.Y., 1965—; malpractice rev. panel Bklyn. Supreme Ct., 1975—. Trustee Adelphi Acad., Bklyn., 1941—, pres., 1965—; treas. Brooklyn Hts. Montessori Sch., 1969-71; pres. First Presbyn. Ch. of Bklyn., 1965-71, elder, 1941—. Served to col. U.S. Army, 1940-46. Decorated Legion of Merit; recipient various awards Brooklyn Eye & Ear Hosp.; gymnasium at Adelphi Acad. named in his honor, 1978. Diplomate Am. Bd. Ophthalmology. Fellow A.C.S., Am. Acad. Ophthalmology and Otolaryngology, Internat. Soc. Eye Surgeons, Am. Acad. Compensation Medicine, AMA; fellow N.Y. State, Kings County med. socs., Assn. Research in Ophthalmology, Bklyn. (past pres.), N.Y. State (dir.) ophthalmol. socs., Bklyn. Eye & Ear Hosp. Alumni (founder, past pres.). Conservative. Clubs: Bklyn.; Rembrandt; Ihpetonga (past pres.); Rotary of Bklyn. Home: 260 65th St Apt 2F Brooklyn NY 11220 Office: Room 369 271 Cadman Plaza E Brooklyn NY 11201

BEETON, DIANA LAFAY, casting dir.; b. Washington, Oct. 17, 1934; d. John Ewing and LaFay (Gentry) Beeton; B.A., Coll. William and Mary, 1956. Asst. traffic mgr. Dancer, Fitzgerald & Sample, Inc., N.Y.C., 1956-57; with Batten, Barton, Durstine & Osborne, Inc., N.Y.C., 1957-62, Talent Assos., Ltd., N.Y.C., 1962-65; casting dir. Papert, Koenig & Lois, Inc., N.Y.C., 1965-67; sr. casting dir. Foote, Cone & Belding, Inc., N.Y.C., 1967-69; casting dir., prodn. asst. Alton/Melsky Prodns., Inc., N.Y.C., 1969-70; casting dir. Howard Zieff, Inc., N.Y.C., 1970-72; dir. casting Ogilvy & Mather, Inc., N.Y.C., 1972-74; free-lance casting The Casting Couch, N.Y.C., 1972—. Mem. Nat. Acad. TV Arts and Scis. Home: 315 E 68th St New York City NY 10021

BEGASSE, BRUCE KENNETH, equipment sales co. exec.; b. Binghamton, N.Y., Jan. 21, 1925; s. Otto A. and Miriam B.; B. Bldg. Constrn., Rensselaer Poly. Inst., 1950; M. Mil. Sci., Command and Gen. Staff Coll., 1968; M.B.A., State U. N.Y., 1964; m. Patricia A. Hamlin, June 17, 1950; children—Thomas, Susan, Margaret, Gail, John. Engr. supt. The Ferber Co., Hackensack, N.J., 1950-54; pres. Otto A. BeGasse & Son., Inc., Binghamton, 1955-75, Mobile Spray, Inc., Endwell, N.Y., 1965—; owner So. Tier Hotsy Co., Johnson City, N.Y., 1977—; partner BFG Co., Johnson City, 1975—; dir. PDCA. Mem. Planning Commn. Binghamton, 1964-76; bd. dirs. Roberson Center Arts and Scis. Served to col. U.S. Army, 1943-45, 51-53. Decorated Silver Star (2), Bronze Star (2), Purple Heart, N.Y. Legion of Merit. Mem. Painting and Decorating Contractors Assn., Associated Bldg. Contractors (v.p.), Res. Officers Assn., Assn. U.S. Army, Nat. Pilots Assn., Aircraft Owners and Pilots Assn., Mil. Order of World Wars, Am. Def. Preparedness Assn., VFW, Rensselaer, 10th Mountain Div. alumni assns. Republican. Roman Catholic. Clubs: Oasis (Binghamton); Sertoma, Elks. Contbr. articles in field to profl. jours. Home: Box 152 RD 1 Brackney PA 18812 Office: 236 Corliss Ave Johnson City NY 13780

BEGELL, WILLIAM, publisher; b. Wilno, Poland, May 18, 1928; s. Ferdinand and Liza (Kowarski) Beigel; came to U.S., 1947, naturalized, 1953; B. Chem. Engring., Coll. City N.Y., 1953; M. Chem. Engring., Poly. Inst. Bklyn., 1958; postgrad. Columbia U., N.Y.C., 1958-59; m. Esther Kessler, May 27, 1948; children—Frederick Paul, Alissa Maya. Engring. mgr., heat transfer research facility, dept. chem. engring. Columbia U., N.Y.C., 1953-59; co-founder, exec. v.p. Scripta Technica, Inc., Washington, 1959-74; founder, pres. Hemisphere Pub. Corp., Washington, 1974—; lectr. in pub. U. Pa., 1974, State U. N.Y., Stony Brook, 1974, George Washington U., Washington, 1977-78; pub. cons. McGraw-Hill Book Co. Mem. nat. adv. bd. Center for the Book, Library of Congress. Mem. Am. Inst. Chem. Engrs., ASME, Assn. Am. Pubs., Internat. Centre for Heat and Mass Transfer, Washington Book Pubs. (founder). Jewish. Editor books including: Theory of Energy and Mass Transfer (V. Luikov), 1963; Heat Transfer-Soviet Research, 1968-74; Heat Transfer-Japanese Research, 1971-74. Contbr. articles to profl. jours. Patentee electromagnetic measurements. Home: 46 E 91st St New York NY 10028 Office: 1025 Vermont Ave NW Washington DC 20005 also 19 W 44th St New York NY 10036

BEGLEY, THOMAS DEVLIN, JR., lawyer; b. Phila., May 2, 1938; s. Thomas Devlin and Margaret (Moore) B.; B.S., Georgetown Coll., 1959, J.D., 1962; m. Anne Glass, June 24, 1962 (dec. Feb. 1977); children—Thomas Devlin, Sharon A., Mark L. Partner firm Begley & Begley, Burlington, N.J. and Moorestown, N.J., 1962—; dir. Farmers & Mechanics Savs. & Loan Assn.; municipal atty. Twp. Shamong, 1976—; municipal ct. judge Twp. Hainesport, Woodland, 1973—. Mem. Am., N.J., Burlington County bar assns. Roman Catholic. Club: Swim (pres. 1973-75) (Moorestown). Home: 753 Stonehouse Rd Moorestown NJ 08057 Office: Suite 204 214 W Main St Moorestown NJ 08057

BEGNER, EDITH, author; b. N.Y.C., Mar. 6, 1918; d. Herrman and Anna Elita (Dorfman) Friedman; student Wellesley Coll., 1936-37, Columbia U., 1937-42; m. Jacob Anthony Begner, Dec. 22, 1937; 1 son, Thomas Lewis. Sculptor, 1937-42, exhibited Artists for Victory Exhbn., Met. Mus. Art, 1942; author, 1943—; works include: Just Off Fifth, 1960; Son and Heir, 1961; Red in The Morning, 1963; A Dark and Lonely Hiding Place 1968; Accident of Birth, 1977; Dressing to the Left, 1980. Nurse's aide ARC, 1941-44. Mem. P.E.N.

BEGUIN, FRED PAUL, environ. acoustics engr.; b. Brussels, Belgium, Oct. 13, 1909; s. Florent Ch. and Maria (Tuerlinckx) B.; B.S. in Electronics Engring., Tech. State Coll. Brussels, 1931; M.S. in Physics, Nat. Inst. Radioelectricity, Brussels, 1944; postgrad. Syracuse U., 1951; grad. profl. bus. mgmt. inst. Gen. Electric Co., 1957-58; certificate in noise control engring. and audiometry Colby Coll., 1971; m. Sophie Koubekova, Nov. 6, 1934; 1 dau., Natalie. Came to U.S., 1948, naturalized Dec. 4, 1956. Project and patent engr. Compagnie Francaise Thomson-Houston, Paris, 1931-34; tonmeister engr. Philips Rec. Studios, Eindhoven, Holland. 1934-37; research engr. Philips Physical Labs., also tech. dir. Philips Internat. TV Operations, 1937-44; prof. electroacoustics Nat. Radioelectronics Inst., Belgium, 1944-46; tech. dir. Decca Records of Belgium, 1944-46; tech. dir. in Benelux countries for Motorola, Acme Electric, Internat. Harvester, 1946-50; project engr. electronics div. Gen. Electric, Syracuse, N.Y., 1950-54, audio-cons. with Gen. Electric, audio products devel. for internat. original equipment mfrs., 1954-59; dir. electroacoustics research and devel. Am. Optical Corp., Southbridge, Mass., 1959-72; dir. Hearing Conservation and Noise Control Center, Harrington Meml. Hosp., Southbridge, 1972-77; environ. engr., sr. scientist, Sturbridge, Mass., 1977—; govt. expert in U.S.-European trade, from 1946-54; cons. to Mutual Security Adminstrn. productivity teams, 1952; voting mem., industry rep. bioacoustics and noise com. Am. Nat. Standards Inst., 1968-75. Fellow Audio Engring. Soc. (Nat. Sci. Achievement award 1970); mem. N.Y. Acad. Scis., IEEE (sr. mem.; vice chmn. electroacoustics com.), Am. Inst. Physics, Acoustical Soc. Am., Nat. Soc. Profl. Engrs. (sr.), Indsl. Safety Equipment Assn. (hon.). Patentee in field. Home: Southbridge Rd RFD 1 Sturbridge MA 01566 Office: PO Box 122 Southbridge MA 01550

BEHAN, RICHARD LOWELL, oral and maxillofacial surgeon; b. Long Island City, N.Y., June 13, 1942; s. John Howard and Lillian Mary (Zemek) H.; student Lycoming Coll., 1960-63; D.D.S., U. Md., 1967, postgrad. oral surgery, 1967-70; children—Bradley J., Brendon O., Henry A., Angela C. Intern, U. Md., 1967-68, resident, 1968-70; pvt. practice oral surgery, Hagerstown, Md., 1970—; mem. staff Waynesboro Hosp.; mem. staff Washington County Hosp., chief oral surgery, 1978; chief dental sect. Chambersburg Hosp., 1977; cons., Md. Correctional Inst., 1970-74. Mem. Big Bros. Balt., 1964-67. Served to maj. USAF. Recipient Service certificate Big Brothers, 1967, 68, 69. Diplomate Am. Bd. Oral Surgery. Fellow Am. Dental Soc. Anesthesiology; mem. Washington County Dental Soc. (v.p. 1971-72, pres. 1974), Md., Am. dental assns., Am., Middle Atlantic, Pa., Md. (pres. 1978) socs. oral and maxillofacial surgeons, Pierre Fauchard Acad., Assn. Mil. Surgeons, Kappa Delta Rho, Xi Psi Phi. Clubs: Chambersburg Golf, Fountain Head Country, North Country Rod and Gun (pres. 1973-79), Exchange (Hagerstown); Rotary. Home: 980 Northern Ave Hagerstown MD 21740 Office: 1707 Potomac Ave Hagerstown MD 21740 also 1101 Sheller Ave Chambersburg PA 17201

BEHL, WISHVENDER KUMAR, research chemist; b. Dhariwal, Punjab, India, Dec. 26, 1935; s. Amar Nath and Vidya Wati (Trehan) B.; came to U.S., 1962, naturalized, 1973. B.S., U. Delhi, 1955, M.S., 1957, Ph.D., 1962; m. Ravi Sharma, Feb. 15, 1977. Jr. chem. asst. Govt. Test House, Calcutta, India, 1957-58; jr. research fellow chemistry U. Delhi (India), 1958-62; postdoctoral research scientist chemistry N.Y. U., 1962-64; postdoctoral research asso. Brookhaven Nat. Lab., Upton, N.Y., 1964-67; research chemist Power Sources div. Electronics Tech. and Devices Lab., U.S. Army Electronics Research and Devel. Command, Ft. Monmouth, N.J., 1967—. Univ. merit scholar, 1955-57. Fellow Am. Inst. Chemists, mem. Am. Chem. Soc. (exec. com. Monmouth County sect. 1971-74), Electrochem. Soc. Club: Schussboomer Ski (pres. 1974-75). Contbr. articles to profl. publs. Patentee in field. Home: 210A Paul Ave Eatontown NJ 07724 Office: Power Sources Div Electronics Tech and Devices Lab US Army Electronics Research and Devel Command Ft Monmouth NJ 07703

BEHNKE, JOHN ALDEN, sci. editor; b. Appleton, Wis., June 4, 1905; s. Henry John and Mabel (Wolcott) B.; student Lawrence Coll., Appleton, 1923-25; B.A. in Humanities, U. Wis., 1928; M.A., Harvard, 1929; m. Frances Lucille Berry, Dec. 30, 1957; children—Roger W., Barbara (Mrs. Michael deLaszlo). Dean of freshmen U. Wis., 1927-28; with Macmillan Co., 1929-39; head coll. dept. W.B. Saunders Co., 1939-47; co-founder, v.p. W.H. Freeman & Co., 1947-52; asso. adminstv. sec. AAAS, 1952-56; v.p. Ronald Press Co., 1956-70; editor of jour. BioSci., Am. Inst. Biol. Scis., 1971—. Trustee Gordon Research Confs. in Chemistry; mem. ednl. policies com. Nat. Acad. Scis. Nat. Research Council. Mem. Adult Edn. Assn. (pres. council nat. orgns.), AAAS, Bot. Soc. Am., N.Y. Zool. Soc., Am. Assn. Ret. Persons, Sigma Xi. Clubs: Univ. (N.Y.C.); Harvard Faculty; Torrey Bot. Author: Challenging Biol. Problems, 1972; The Dilemmas of Euthanasia, 1975; The Biology of Aging, 1978. Home: Box 32 Pine Plains NY 12567 Office: Dept Natural Scis Marist College Poughkeepsie NY 12601

BEHREND, WILLIAM LOUIS, elec. engr.; b. Wisconsin Rapids, Wis., Jan. 11, 1923; s. Albert and Eva Mae (Barney) B.; B.S. in Elec. Engring., U. Wis., Madison, 1946, M.S., 1947; m. Manet Louise Whitrock, July 7, 1945; children—Jane Louise, Ann Elizabeth. Research engr. RCA Corp., David Sarnoff Research Center, 1947—, advanced devel. engr. comml. systems div. Meadow Lands, Pa., 1964-66, prelimary design and systems analyst, 1966—. Served with USNR, 1944-46. Recipient RCA David Sarnoff Research Center award, 1956, 59, 63. Fellow IEEE (Scott Helt award 1971); mem. AAAS, Sigma Xi. Author, patentee in field. Address: 479 Carnegie Dr Pittsburgh PA 15243

BEHRENS, JOHN CHARLES, journalist, author, educator; b. Lancaster, Ohio, Feb. 7, 1933; s. Charles H. and Dorothy P. Behrens; B.S.J., Bowling Green State U., 1955; M.A., Pa. State U., 1956; m. Patricia A. Behrens, June 17, 1956; children—Cynthia Sue, Mark Andrew. Gen. assignment reporter Pacific Stars & Stripes, Seoul (Korea) Bur., 1957-58; sports editor Lancaster (Ohio) Eagle-Gazette, 1958-62; corr. Columbus (Ohio) Citizen, AP, 1958-62; acting chmn. journalism dept. Ohio Wesleyan U., Delaware, 1962-63; asst. prof. journalism dept. Marshall U., Huntington, W.Va., 1963-65; asst. prof. journalism, pub. relations Utica Coll. of Syracuse (N.Y.) U., 1965-68, prof. journalism, pub. relations, 1975—, dir. pub. relations, 1968-70, cons. publs., 1970—; author: Magazine Writers Workbook, 1972; Reporting Worktext, 1974; The Typewriter Guerrillas: Closeups of 20 Top Investigative Reporters, 1977. editor: Wood and Stone: Landmarks of the Upper Mohawk Region, 1972; contbr. numerous articles to periodicals including Financial Weekly, U.S. Oil Week, Mankind, Writer's Digest, Radio & TV Weekly, True, Nieman Reports, Vocat. Biographies, Nat. Enquirer, N. Am. Newspaper Alliance, Quill; bus. columnist Elks Mag., 1976—; columnist Inland Printer, 1978—; dept. editor Coll. Press Rev., 1969—; contbg. editor Quartet, 1969-70; curator Student Press in Am. Archives, 1968—; cons., publs., colls., small bus. Adminstrv. asst. former congressman Walter Moeller from Ohio, 1966; mem. A Better Chance Bd., Clinton, N.Y.; treas. Mohawk Valley Council Chs. Served with AUS, 1956-58. Recipient Research award Utica Coll., 1973. Mem. Nat. Council Coll. Publs. Advisers (Hall Fame 1972, Presdl. citation 1973, Distinguished Service Plaque 1975), Am. Soc. Journalists and Authors, Authors Guild, AAUP, Sigma Delta Chi. Lutheran. Home: 57 Stebbins Dr Clinton NY 13323 Office: Utica Coll Burrstone Rd Utica NY 13502

BEHRMAN, HAROLD RICHARD, research inst. adminstr.; b. Vidora, Sask., Can., Nov. 26, 1939; s. Henry Fred and Minnie Alice (Waslenko) B.; B.S., U. Man., Winnipeg, 1959-64; Ph.D., N.C. State U., 1967; m. Josephine Lynne Messenger, Sept. 11, 1959; children—Tracy Lea, Terri Lynne, Russell Norman. Research fellow Harvard Med. Sch., Boston, 1967-71; asst. prof. Harvard Med. Sch., Boston, 1971-72; dir. reproductive biology Merck Inst., Rahway, N.J., 1972-75; asso. prof. gynecology and pharmacology, dir. reproductive biol. sect. Yale, 1975—. Recipient fellowship Med. Research Council Can., 1967-70, research award Lalor Found., 1971-72. Mem. Soc. Exptl. Biology and Medicine, Am. Physiol. Soc., Endocrine Soc., Soc. for Study Reproduction, Soc. Endocrinology, Canadian Physiol. Soc., AAAS. Editor: (with others) Methods of Radioimmunoassay, 1974. Home: 99 Summer Hill Rd Madison CT 06443 Office: Medical School Yale New Haven CT 06510

BEIER, LEONARD SAMUEL, physician; b. N.Y.C., Aug. 14, 1932; s. Louis and Anna (Resnik) B.; A.B., N.Y. U., 1953, M.D., 1957; m. Helen Sylvia Freed, Mar. 26, 1961; children—Michele Beth, Gail Joyce. Intern and resident in medicine Bellevue Hosp., N.Y.C., 1957-60; resident in medicine Wadsworth VA Hosp., Los Angeles, 1960-61; clin. asst. in medicine Sch. Medicine, U. Calif., Los Angeles, 1960-61; sr. attending physician Nyack (N.Y.) Hosp., 1964—, sec. to cardiology sect., 1974—; active staff Community Hosp., Spring Valley, N.Y., 1964—; sch. physician East Ramapo Sch. Dist., 1965—; practice medicine specializing in internal medicine, Spring Valley, 1964—. Served to capt. M.C., U.S. Army, chief medicine Army Hosp., Ft. Monroe, Va., 1961-64. Diplomate Am. Bd. Internal Medicine. Mem. AMA, A.C.P., N.Y. State, Rockland County med. socs. Contbr. articles to profl. jours. Home: 11 Wesel Rd Nanuet NY 10954 Office: 254 N Main St Spring Valley NY 10977

BEILSTEIN, HENRY RICHARD, microbiologist; b. Phila., Dec. 2, 1920; s. Henry Nicholas and Elizabeth Anna (Binder) B.; B.S., Phila. Coll. Pharmacy and Sci., 1943, M.S., 1961, Ph.D., 1970; grad. Phila. Coll. Bible, 1949; m. Grace Alta Marple, June 8, 1946; children—Janet (Mrs. Jack Bittner), Richard Alan (dec.), David Richard. Chemist, Merck Sharp & Dohme, Glenolden, Pa., 1943-45; biol. processor Phila. Dept. Pub. Health Lab., 1945-53, sr. microbiologist, 1953-61, asst. dir., 1961-70, acting dir., 1970, dir., 1970—. Vis. asso. prof. dept. microbiology Hahnemann Med. Coll., Phila., 1970—; adj. asst. prof. dept. microbiology and immunology Temple U. Sch. Med., Phila., 1969—; prof. microbiology and med. tech., dir. evening sch. Franklin Sch. Sci. and Arts, Phila., 1956-71; asso. prof. dept. microbiology Pa. Coll. Podiatric Medicine, 1975—; cons. Smith Kline Diagnostics, Phila., 1971—. Recipient Chapel of 4 Chaplains award, 1978. Fellow Am. Pub. Health Assn., Am. Soc. Microbiology, Am. Acad. Microbiology (registered microbiologist and specialist microbiologist); mem. Christian Med. Soc., Conf. Pub. Health Lab. Dirs., Am. Sci. Affiliation, Greater Phila. Alliance for Eradication Veneral Disease. Presbyterian (elder 1945-72, Sunday Sch. supt. 1950-72). Club: Delaware Valley Torch (dir. 1976—). Contbr. articles to profl. jours. Home: 1032 E Mt Pleasant Ave Philadelphia PA 19150 Office: Pub Health Lab 500 S Broad St Philadelphia PA 19146

BEINFIELD, MALCOLM SYDNEY, surgeon; b. Bklyn., Mar. 24, 1921; s. Henry Harold and Jennie (Joseloff) B.; B.A., Yale, 1942; M.D., State U. N.Y. at Bklyn., 1945; m. Marjorie May Koster, Dec. 16, 1945; children—Harriet Lynn, Bruce, Elizabeth. Intern, King's County Hosp., Bklyn., 1945-46, resident Cleve. City Hosp., 1946-48, Harlem Hosp., N.Y.C., 1948-51; practice medicine specializing in surgery, Westport, Conn., 1951—; mem. staff Norwalk Hosp., 1951—, dir. dept. surgery, 1966-69, asst. chief staff, 1976—, trustee, 1976—; mem. faculty dept. anatomy Yale Sch. Medicine, 1950-53. Diplomate Am. Bd. Surgery. Fellow ACS. Democrat. Contbr. to med. lit. Home: 17 Hockanum Rd Westport CT 06880 Office: The Willows Westport CT 06880

BEINHOCKER, GILBERT DAVID, computer co. exec.; b. Phila., July 7, 1932; s. Joseph A. and Florence (Shlifer) B.; B.A., Pa. State U., 1954; M.S., U. Pa., 1958; D.Eng., U. Detroit, 1968; m. Barbara Broadley, Dec. 17, 1960; children—Eric David, Elizabeth Broadley, Robert Marc. Engring. dir. Epsco, Inc., 1958-61; pres. Syber Corp., Natick, Mass., 1961-64; div. mgr. Tech. Measurement Corp., 1964-65; dir. advanced planning Am. Optical Co., 1965-66; chmn. bd. Microdyne Instruments, Inc., Waltham, Mass., 1967-69; pres., chief exec. officer, dir. Nat. Information Services, Inc., Cambridge, Mass., 1970-74, pres., chief exec. officer, dir. Eurocom Inc., Cambridge, 1974—; v.p. Moors & Cabot, Boston, 1977—; dir. Stanway Corp., Elmendorf Bd. Corp., New Boston Bank & Trust Co., Nat. Remote Computer Devices, Inc. Sr. lectr. U. Detroit, 1967-68. Recipient Nat. Fight for Sight citation Nat. Council to Combat Blindness, 1963. Mem. AAAS, IEEE, Assn. Computing Machinery, Internat. Fedn. Med. Electronics and Biol. Engring., Internat. Soc. Clin. Electroretinography, Assn. Research Ophthalmology, Am. Ordnance Assn., Am. Mgmt. Assn., Instrument Soc. Am., Am. Assn. Med. Instrumentation, Pi Lambda Phi. Democrat. Author: Theory and Operation of Stardac Computers, 1960, also articles. Patentee in field. Home: 36 Beatrice Circle Belmont MA 02178 Office: 675 Massachusetts Ave Cambridge MA 02139

BEISER, LEO, image and data tech. cons. and research co. exec.; b. N.Y.C., Sept. 18, 1924; s. Sigmund N. and Sarah (Weiner) B.; B.S., Hofstra U., 1964, M.A., 1964; m. Edith Vegotsky, Aug. 31, 1946; children—Helene Ronnie, Steven Scott. Asst. chief engr. CBS, N.Y.C., 1951-56; project mgr. Polarad Electronics Corp., N.Y.C., 1956-60; staff cons. Gen. Instrument Corp., L.I., N.Y., 1960-61; research mgr. Telechrome Corp., 1961-62; staff research specialist Autometric-Raytheon Corp., 1962-63; sr. staff physicist and dir. Dennis Gabor Labs., CBS Labs., Stamford, Conn., 1963-76; pres., dir. research Leo Beiser Inc., Flushing, N.Y., 1976—. Mem. council judges N.Y.C. Sch. Sci. Fairs, 1960-66. Served with USAAF, 1943-46; CBI. Recipient 1st prize for oil painting N. Queens Art Fair, 1965. Fellow Soc. Info. Display (regional dir. 1975—, recipient spl. recognition award for laser scanning and rec. 1978); mem. Optical Soc. Am., Soc. Photog. Instrumentation Engrs., Soc. Motion Picture and TV Engrs. Contbr. articles to profl. jours.; inventor in field. Home: 151-77 28th Ave Flushing NY 11354

BEISHLAG, GEORGE ALBERT, educator; b. Syracuse, N.Y., Mar. 4, 1907; s. Everett Webster and Anne (Sturgeon) B.; A.B., Wayne U., 1930; M.A., Clark U., 1937; Ph.D., U. Md., 1953; student Universidad Nacional de Mexico, 1941, Fgn. Service Inst., U.S. Dept. State, 1948; m. Bernice Ethel Townsend, May 23, 1936. Pub. sch. tchr., Detroit, 1931-42; intelligence specialist U.S. Govt., 1942-49; lectr. Postgrad. Naval Intelligence Sch., 1946, Am. U., 1949-53; research geographer Rural Land Classification Survey, Govt. P.R., 1951; prof. geography Towson State U., Balt., 1954-77, prof. emeritus, 1977—, chmn. dept. geography, 1965. Vis. prof. U. Man., summer 1964; cons. to librarian Secretariat UN, 1946, OSS, 1942-45, Baltimore County Office of Planning, 1958. Fellow Am. Geog. Soc.; mem. Assn. Am. Geographers, Nat. Council for Geog. Edn., Phi Delta Kappa, Phi Kappa Phi. Contbr. to World Book Ency., Book of Knowledge Ency. Home: 1530 Taylor Ave Baltimore MD 21234

BEISWINGER, GEORGE LAWRENCE, retail co. exec.; b. Salem, Mo., Mar. 15, 1924; s. Lawrence and Bessie (Pines) B.; B.S., Washington U., St. Louis, 1949, postgrad., 1953; postgrad. Harvard, 1949; m. Virginia Marie Graves, Dec. 24, 1950; children—Gail Anne, George William. Personnel mgr. Continental Baking Co. (name now changed to ITT Continental Baking Co.), St. Louis, 1953-58; supr. tng. and communication Monsanto Co., Columbia, Tenn., 1958-63; communication coordinator Dodge Truck Plant, Chrysler Corp., Detroit, 1963-64; communication supr. research and styling Chrysler Engring., Detroit, 1964-66, group mgr. communication, car assembly group, 1966-67; corporate dir. communication Acme Markets, Inc., Phila., 1967-77, v.p. communication, 1977—. Served with USAAF, 1942-46. Recipient award Freedoms Found., 1963. Mem. Pub. Relations Soc. Am. (pres. Phila. chpt. 1976—, mem. nat. eligibility com. 1973). Republican. Episcopalian. Home: 708 Conestoga Rd Berwyn PA 19312 Office: 124 N 15th St Philadelphia PA 19101

BEITEL, HERBERT MANSON, food service co. exec.; b. Kokomo, Ind., Apr. 1, 1925; s. Orville Charles and Vesta Ann (Oliver) B.; student Emory U., 1943-44; B.S. cum laude, U. S.C., 1946; J.D., U. Chgo., 1949. Admitted to Ind. bar, 1950, Ill. bar, 1950; asst. chief title examiner Calumet Title Co., Crown Point, Ind., 1950-52; asst. to pres., atty. First Fed. Savs. & Loan Assn., Chgo., 1952-55; legislative counsel, eastern mgr., counsel Nat. Automatic Merchandising Assn., Chgo., 1955-60, 66-68, sec., dir. Cantop Machinery Corp., Bala Cynwyd, Pa., 1960-65; exec. dir. Pa. Automatic Merchandising Council, Phila., 1963-68; pub. editor Vend mag. Billboard Publs., Inc., N.Y.C., 1968-72; dir. mktg. services and communications Servomation Corp., N.Y.C., 1972—. Nat. treas. Young Republicans, 1951-53, asst. gen. counsel, 1953-55. Served to lt. (j.g.) USNR, 1943-46. Recipient Jesse H. Neal award journalism. Mem. Am., Ill., Ind. bar assns., Newcomen Soc., Blue Key, Phi Beta Kappa. Mason. Contbr. articles in field profl. jours. Home: 300 Winston Dr Cliffside Park NJ 07010 Office: 777 3d Ave New York City NY 10017

BEJ, EMIL, educator; b. Stryy, Ukraine, Apr. 26, 1925; s. Joseph and Klementyna (Kozieja) B.; LL.B., Ukrainian Free U., Munich, 1949, Ph.D., 1970; B.C.S., Detroit Bus. Inst., 1957; M.A., U. Detroit, 1966; postgrad. Temple U., 1967-70, fellow, 1968-69; m. Vera A. Szwabiuk, Oct. 7, 1961; children—Mark Daniel, Andrew Emil. Came to U.S., 1949, naturalized, 1954. Tchr. St. Mary High Sch., Mt. Clemens, Mich., 1965-67; instr. Detroit Coll. of Bus., Detroit, 1966-67; grad. asst. Temple U., 1967-69; asst. prof. econs. Shippensburg (Pa.) State Coll., 1969-78, asso. prof., 1978—. Chmn. ways and means com. Rep. Nationalities Council, Hamtramck, Mich., 1962-65; v.p. Eastern European Research Inst., Phila., 1962-67. Mem. Am., Atlantic, Eastern econ. assns., Can. Assn. Slavists, NEA. Contbr. articles to profl. jours. Home: RD 4 Forest Ridge Acres Shippenburg PA 17257

BEJARANO, JOSE RAFAEL, internat. bus. cons.; b. Mexico; M.S. in Elec. Engring., Columbia U., 1938. Formerly sr. v.p. Xerox Corp., Stamford, Conn., sr. v.p. Xerox Consultants Inc., Stamford, and pres. Xerox Latin Am. div.; mem. internat. adv. bd. State Nat. Bank of Conn.; dir. Parsons Brinckerhoff Inc. (Engrs.), N.Y.C. Home and Office: 138 Pecksland Rd Greenwich CT 06830

BEJARANO, LUIS ENRIQUE, univ. ofcl.; b. Bklyn., Aug. 9, 1917; s. Jose Miguel and Trinela (Lillo) B.; A.B., Columbia U., 1938, M.S., 1940; m. Valerie Garrett, Jan. 1, 1944; children—Valerie (Mrs. Gary Carter), Luis Enrique Jr., Joel, Carlos, Andrea, Deena. Asso. prof., head library dept., pub. relations dir. U.S. Mcht. Marine Acad., 1946-59; pub. relations, devel. dir. Hillside Hosp., Glen Oaks, N.Y., 1959-61; coordinator devel. Hofstra U., Hempstead, N.Y., 1961-68, v.p. devel., 1968-75, spl. adviser to pres., 1975—; pres. Luis E. Bejarano Assos., Inc., 1975—; devel. cons. Alliance Minority Group Leaders, Inc., U.S. Mcht. Marine Acad. Alumni Assn., Arthur Research Found., Lutheran High Sch., Belnap Coll., Purdue U., Niagara U., Huntington Arts Council, L.I. Symphony Orch. Pres., trustee Bd. Edn., Malverne, 1961-66, Egelersky Ballet, 1978—; former Pro Arte Symphony Orch.; former mem. bd. dirs. L.I. Adv. Council State Commn. Human Rights; founding trustee, chmn. Nassau County Research Library; mem. legis. adv. bd. N.Y. State Assembly. Served to lt. comdr. USNR, 1942-46; ETO; capt. Res. (ret.). Mem. AAUP, Council for Support and Advancement Edn., Hofstra Council, Hofstra Library Assos., Archons of Colophon, Friends of Fine Arts, Navy League U.S., Am. Legion, Alpha Sigma Lambda, Alpha Sigma Phi, Pi Delta Epsilon, Sigma Pi, Sigma Delta Pi. Republican. Lutheran. Clubs: University (L.I.). Asso. editor L.I. Jewish Exec. quar. Contbr. articles to profl. jours. Home and Office: 87 Grove St Lynbrook NY 11563

BEKKER, PETER OTTO ERIK, JR., broadcasting exec.; b. Boise, Ida., Apr. 3, 1952; s. Peter Otto Erik and Gloria Eileen (Stroebel) B.; B.A. in Communications, Lindenwood Colls., St. Charles, Mo., 1974. Reporter, writer, editor Sta. KMOX, St. Louis, 1974-75; exec. news producer, writer Sta. WCBS, N.Y.C., 1975—, also syndicated music commentator CBS Radio; instr. radio prodn. and theory, Lindenwood Coll. Recipient Spl. Mention award, Peabody nominee for KMOX radio documentary, 1975. Mem. Writers Guild Am., AFTRA, N.Y. Press Club. Office: 51 W 52d St New York City NY 10019

BELAFSKY, MARK LEWIS, otolaryngologist; b. Perth Amboy, N.J., June 8, 1939; s. Henry Abraham and Rose (Buckner) B.; A.B., U. Pa., 1960; M.D., Chgo. Med. Sch., 1964; m. Betty Forman, Dec. 25, 1962; children—Caryn, Peter. Intern, Thomas Jefferson U. Hosp., Phila., 1964-65, resident, 1967-71; practice medicine specializing in otorhinolaryngology and facial plastic surgery, Cherry Hill, N.J., 1971—; clin. asst. prof. otorhinolaryngology Thomas Jefferson U. Sch.

Medicine, 1971—. Bd. dirs. Jewish Fedn. So. N.J. Served with U.S. Army, 1965-67. Decorated Army Commendation medal. Diplomate Am. Bd. Otolaryngology. Fellow Phila. Coll. Physicians, A.C.S., Am. Acad. Ophthalmology and Otolaryngology; mem. Acad. Facial Plastic and Reconstructive Surgery, Pediatric Otolaryngologic Soc., Am. Assn. Cosmetic Surgeons, Pa. Laryngological Soc., Am. Soc. Head and Neck Surgeons. Home: 921 Francine Dr Cherry Hill NJ 08003 Office: 905 Kings Hwy N Cherry Hill NJ 08003

BELCHIKOFF, KARIN JO, ednl. adminstr.; b. Detroit, Oct. 8, 1950; d. James Peter and Johann Audrey (Banwell) Headlee; B.A., Western Mich. U., 1972; M.B.A., U. Conn., 1978. Tchr. math Eastern High Jr. Sch., Greenwich, Conn., 1972-76; adminstr. Pub. Schs., Greenwich, 1976—. Mem. Greenwich, Conn. edn. assns., Nat. Math Tchrs. Assn., Phi Kappa Sigma, Beta Gamma Sigma. Episcopalian. Home: 8 Glen Rd New Fairfield CT 06810 Office: 51 Hendrie Ave Riverside CT 06878

BELDEN, FREDERICK HESLEY, bishop; b. Watertown, N.Y., Sept. 25, 1909; s. Stacy Beardsley Denn and Emma May (Hesley) B.; B.A., Hartwick Coll., 1932; S.T.B., Gen. Theol. Sem., 1936, S.T.D., 1972; m. Dorothy Elizabeth Reumann, Nov. 26, 1936; children—David Allan, Jeffrey Owen, Patricia (Mrs. Paul Conrad Carlson), Bruce Edward. Ordained to ministry Episcopal Ch., 1935; rector Christ Ch., Duanesburg, N.Y., 1936-37, Christ Ch., Walton, N.Y., 1937-42, St. Johns Ch., Johnstown, N.Y., 1942-49, St. Pauls Ch., North Kingstown, R.I., 1949-71; bishop coadjutor Diocese of R.I., 1971-72; bishop of R.I., Providence, 1972—. Pres. R.I. State Council Chs., 1964-65. Trustee Gloversville (N.Y.) Library, 1943-49. Mem. Guild of Ascension (warden 1961-69). Club: University (Providence). Home: 10 Brown St Providence RI 02906 Office: 275 N Main St Providence RI 02903

BELDEN, REED HOLMAN, chem. co. exec.; b. Brainerd, Minn., Feb. 18, 1932; s. Wyman Reed and Alice Mildred (Holman) B.; B.S., U. Nebr., 1953; m. Suzanne Adams, June 7, 1954; children—Lynda Sue (Mrs. Gregory R. Paulsen), John Reed, Dane Adams. Internal mgmt. cons. Allied Chem. Corp., Morristown, N.J., 1971-73; gen. mgr. Thermosets-Plastics div., Toledo, 1973-74, v.p., gen. mgr. plastics dept., Splty. Chems. div., Morristown, N.J., 1974—; dir. Nypel Inc., West Conshohocken, Pa., Synres-Almoco B.V., Hoek of Holland; asso. dir. Corp. Engring. Tech. Center, 1977—. Fellow Am. Inst. Chemistry; mem. Soc. Plastics Industry, Soc. Plastic Engrs., Am. Chem. Soc., AAAS, Morris County (pres. 1977-78), Morristown (treas.) 1975-76) hist. socs. Presbyn. Patentee in field. Home: Clark Rd Bernardsville NJ 07924 Office: PO Box 1087R Morristown NJ 07960

BELDEN, WILLIAM MERRILL, devel. found. exec.; b. Cumberland, Md., Jan. 14, 1934; s. Harris J. and Orma (Merrill) B.; B.S. in Landscape Architecture, Syracuse U., 1956; M.S. in Land Use and Regional Planning, 1970; postgrad. Corcoran Sch. Art, 1960-61; m. Margaret Anna Norris, May 20, 1960; children—Lorraine, Kathryn, Patricia, Timothy. Landscape architect Nat. Park Service, Washington, 1956-63; sr. planner Fred W. Tuemmler & Assos., 1963-67; lectr., research asso. Sch. Landscape Architecture, N.Y. State Coll. Forestry, Syracuse U., 1967-69; exec. dir. Three Rivers Devel. Found., Corning, N.Y., 1969—; pres. Three Rivers Realty Corp., Corning, 1969—; cons. in planning, landscape architecture and devel., 1960-69; vis. lectr. various univs. Mem. Com. for Nation's Capital, 1960-65; sec. S.E. Steuben County (N.Y.) Area Planning Bd., 1971—; chmn. street festival Corning Philharmonic Soc., 1971; mem. Corning Area Bicentennial Com., Corning Area Recreation Found., So. Finger Lakes Devel., Inc. Served with U.S. Army, 1956-58. Recipient Spl. Service act award Nat. Park Service, 1962, honor award for design excellence HUD, 1976. Mem. Am. Soc. Landscape Architects (sec.-treas. N.Y. Upstate chpt. 1975-77), Am. Inst. Planners, Am. Soc. Planning Ofcls., Nat., N.Y. State assns. housing and redevel. ofcls., Internat. City Mgrs. Assn., Greater Corning C. of C. (dir. 1974-77). Episcopalian. Contbr. articles to profl. publs.; redesigner rose garden, White House, 1962; designer Bryce Park, Washington, 1961. Home: 70 E 4th St Corning NY 14830 Office: 34-36 W Market St Corning NY 14830

BELDOCK, DONALD TRAVIS, financial exec.; b. N.Y.C., May 29, 1934; s. George and Rosa (Tribus) B.; B.A., Yale, 1955; m. Lucy Geringer, Apr. 23, 1971; children—John Anthony, Gwen Ann, James Geringer Christopher. Mdse., fin. exec. R. H. Macy & Co., N.Y.C., 1955-60; financial cons. D. T. Beldock & Co., N.Y.C., 1961-66; chmn. finance com. Basic Resources Corp. (formerly White Shield Corp.), N.Y.C., 1966-69, chmn. bd., pres., chief exec. officer, 1970—; pres., dir. Beaver St. Research Corp., N.Y.C., 1966—; dir. Automatic Toll Systems, Inc., N.Y.C., Phila. Printing Properties, Inc., Original Print Collectors Group Ltd., N.Y.C., Dynaflair, Ltd., Toronto, Ont., Can., Trustee, treas. Strang Clinic-Preventive Medicine Inst.; bd. advisers Colo. Timberline Acad. Clubs: Yale, Westchester Country. Home: 784 Park Ave New York City NY 10021 Office: 595 Madison Ave New York City NY 10022

BELEFONTE, CARMEN PAUL, lawyer; b. Wilmington, Del., Nov. 27, 1940 s. Charles Carl and Mary Rita (DiSabatino) B.; B.B.A., U. Notre Dame, 1962; LL.B., Dickinson Sch. Law, 1965; postgrad Grad. Sch. Law George Washington U., 1968; m. Elke Elisabeth Kreutz, Apr. 10, 1965; children—Stephanie Lynne, Andrea, Dina Anne. Admitted to Pa. bar, Pa. Supreme Ct. bar, 1965, U.S. Ct Mil. Appeals, 1966, U.S. Supreme Ct. bar, 1969, asso. firm Kassab, Cherry, Curran & Archbold, Media, Pa., 1969-73, partner, 1973—; solicitor Dist. Justices Assn. Delaware County, Sheriffs Office Delaware County, Coroners Office Delaware County. Vice pres. bd. Commrs. Marple Twp., 1974. Served with JAG, U.S. Army, 1966-69. Mem. Pa., Phila., Delaware County bar assns., Pa., Am. trial lawyers assns., Nat. Assn. Criminal Def. Lawyers. Club: Optimists. Home: 100 N Morgan Ave Havertown PA 19083 Office: 214 N Jackson St PO Box 626 Media PA 19063

BELETZ, ELAINE ETHEL, nurse, assn. exec.; b. N.Y.C., Jan. 5, 1944; d. Harry and Rose Beletz; diploma in nursing Mt. Sinai Hosp. Sch. Nursing, N.Y.C., 1968; B.S. in Nursing, Fairleigh Dickinson U., 1970; M.A., N.Y. U., 1974; M.Ed., Columbia U., 1978, Ed.D., 1978. Staff nurse Mt. Sinai Med. Center, N.Y.C., 1968-70, asst. head nurse, 1970, adminstrv. supervisory relief nurse, 1973-74; clin. instr. Roosevelt Hosp. Sch. of Nursing, 1970-73; nurse gerontologist St. Luke' Hosp. Center, N.Y.C., 1974; asst. dir. nursing Bklyn. Hosp., 1975-77. Registered nurse, N.Y. Mem. Am., N.Y. State (treas. 1977-78, pres. elect 1978—), N.Y. Counties (dir.) nurses assns., Am. Hosp. Assn., Indsl. Relations Research Assn., Sigma Theta Tau. Home: 95 W 95th St Apt 18B New York City NY 10025

BELFIORE LOCONTE, GIOVANNI, metall. engr.; b. Ceglie del Campo, Bari, Italy, Sept. 1, 1950; s. Francesco and Laura (Accettura) B.L.; came to U.S., 1961; B.S., Poly. Inst. Bklyn., 1974; postgrad. Poly. Inst. N.Y., 1975—; m. Larraine Sarnelle, Dec. 4, 1977. Metallurgist, Sandvik Inc., Fairlawn, N.J., 1974-76, prodn. supr., 1976-77, project engr., 1977-78, quality control mgr., 1978—; lectr. in field. Mem. Am. Soc. Metals, Cemented Carbide Producers Assn. Roman Catholic. Home: 1602 Pollitt Dr Fairlawn NJ 07410 Office: 1702 Nevins Rd Fairlawn NJ 07410

BELKIN, GARY STUART, educator; b. Bklyn., Mar. 7, 1945; s. Robert M. and Doris (Isaacs) B.; B.A., L.I.U., 1966, M.S., 1967; Ed.D. (NDEA Title IV fellow 1967-69), Columbia, 1974; m. Melanie R. Ciletti, July 16, 1975; 1 son, Jordan Robert. Asso. prof. counseling L.I.U., 1970—; pvt. practice counseling and psychotherapy, Bklyn., 1974—. Mem. Am. Psychol. Assn., Am. Personnel and Guidance Assn. Author: Practical Counseling in the Schools, 1975; Educational Psychology: An Introduction, 1977; also articles Editor: Foundations of Counseling, 1974; Counseling: Directions in Theory and Practice, 1976. Home: 140 Berkeley Pl Brooklyn NY 11217 Office: Dept Counseling Long Island Univ Room M616 Brooklyn NY 11201

BELKIN, MARVIN, distillery co. exec.; b. N.Y.C., Apr. 6, 1931; s. Max and Rose (Gold) B.; B.S., Coll. City N.Y., 1953; M.A., Columbia, 1960; m. Amy Elizabeth Stone, Aug. 10, 1969; 1 son, Jeffrey Alan. Research asst. Internat. Research Assos. Inc., N.Y.C., 1956-59; research asso. Med. and Health Research Assn. Inc., N.Y.C., 1959-63; research project supr. Kenyon & Eckhardt Inc., N.Y.C., 1963-65; asso. dir. market research Pepsi Cola Co., N.Y.C., 1965-70, Am. Cyanamid Co., N.J., 1970-72; mgr. consumer research Joseph E. Seagram & Sons Inc., N.Y.C., 1972—. Mem. Am. Mktg. Assn., AAAS, Am. Sociol. Assn., Am. Assn. for Pub. Opinion Research. Contbr. articles to profl. publs. Home: 205 West End Ave New York City NY 10023 Office: 800 3d Ave New York City NY 10022

BELKNAP, MICHAEL H. P., real estate service co. exec.; b. South Bend, Ind., Oct. 27, 1940; s. Paul E. and Mary Elizabeth (Gibb) B.; B.A., Harvard U., 1963, J.D., 1967; LL.B., Cambridge (Eng.) U., 1965; m. Dorothy Callaway, Aug. 12, 1967; children—Michael, Jenny Warner, Matthew Gibb. Admitted to N.Y. bar, 1969; asso. Sullivan & Cromwell, N.Y.C., 1967-70; dir. Council on Environment, Office of Mayor City of N.Y., 1970-72; v.p., gen. counsel Corporate Property Investors, N.Y.C., 1972-75; v.p. Levitt & Sons Inc., Greenwich, Conn., 1975-78; pres. Belknap Co. Ltd., Greenwich, 1978—. Adv. bd. Wave Hill. English Speaking Union fellow, 1963-64. Mem. Builders Inst. Westchester, Urban Land Inst. Democrat. Episcopalian. Home: 108 Greenwich Hills Dr Greenwich CT 06830 Office: 270 Greenwich Ave Greenwich CT 06830

BELL, CALVIN MILES, supermarket chain exec.; b. Newark, Jan. 17, 1927; s. Samuel and Gussie (Pinkos) B.; student pub. schs., Matawan, N.J.; m. Pearl Keller, Nov. 25, 1951; children—Nina Ruth, Scot K. Sec.-treas. Foodtown of Matawan (Bell Beef Co. Inc.), 1946—; pres. Foodtown Supermarkets; sec. Twin Co. Grocers, Edison, N.J.; chmn. N.J. Food Council, Com. Good Govt., Trenton. Pres. Bayshore Community Hosp., Holmdel, N.J. Served with USN, 1945-46. Home: 13 Galloping Hill Rd Holmdel NJ 07793 Office: 124 Main St Matawan NJ 07747

BELL, CHARLES ROBERT, broadcasting exec.; b. Phila., Jan. 7, 1917; s. Harry P. and Jeanne K. (Klein) B.; B.A., Swarthmore Coll., 1939; m. Elise Stone, Sept. 13, 1941; children—Jean (Mrs. Albert Rodriquez), Wendy (Mrs. Fredrik Bjorkan), Robert Mead. Asst. nat. pub. relations dir. Am. Legion, N.Y.C., 1948-50; producer, dir. Voice of Am., N.Y., 1951-53; film dir. WOR-TV, N.Y.C., 1954-59; dir. WABC-TV, N.Y.C., 1959, ABC-TV, 1960-66; dir. Project Reach, North Bellmore, N.Y., 1967-69; gen. mgr. WLIW-TV, Garden City, N.Y., 1970—; free-lance writer. Producer documentary film Children's Aid Soc., N.Y.C., 1953. Trustee, Village Roslyn (N.Y.), 1956-58, mayor, 1958-60. Served from ensign to lt. comdr., USNR, 1941-45, 46-47. Mem. Dirs. Guild Am., Sigma Delta Chi. Author: (with wife) Television and Teamwork, 1962; producer, dir. Enrichment Materials, 1951-70. Home: 100 E Broadway Roslyn NY 11576 Office: Ellington Ave W Garden City NY 11530

BELL, CHARLES SPENCE, artist; b. Tulsa, Feb. 2, 1935; s. Ivan Wallace and Edith Mildred B.; B.B.A., U. Okla., 1957. One-man shows include: Meisel Gallery, N.Y.C., 1972, 74, 77, Morgan Gallery, Shawnee Mission, Kans., 1976; group shows include: Setay Gallery, Beverly Hills, Calif., 1968, DeYoung Mus., San Francisco, 1968, Meisel Gallery, N.Y.C., 1969, 73, 75, 77, Allentown (Pa.) Mus., 1974, Brooks Meml. Art Gallery, Memphis, Wadsworth Atheneum, Hartford, Conn., 1974, Tokyo Met. Art Mus., 1974, Krannert Art Mus., Champaign, Ill., 1975, Butler Inst. Am. Art, Youngstown, Ohio, 1975, Barrington Gallery, Auckland, N.Z., 1975, Waikato Art Mus., Hamilton, N.Z., 1975, Internat. Art Fair, Paris, Vancouver (B.C., Can.) Centennial Mus., 1976, Winnipeg Art Gallery, 1977, Musée d'Art Contemporain, Montreal, P.Q., Can., 1977, Windsor (Can.) Art Gallery, Jacksonville (Fla.) Mus., 1977, Art Gallery of Hamilton (Can.); represented in permanent collection Solomon Guggenheim Mus. Home: 267 6th Ave Brooklyn NY 11215

BELL, CYNTHIA MARIE, ednl. adminstr.; b. Lexington, N.C., May 24, 1942; d. Marshall and Lula Mae (Hogan) B.; B.S., N.C. Central U., 1964; M.Ed., Johns Hopkins U., 1971; Ph.D., U. Md., 1977. Tchr. jr. high schs., Centreville, Md., 1964-66, Balt., 1966-69; counselor jr. high sch., Balt., 1969-72, sr. high sch., Balt., 1972-74; project mgr. Balt. City Pub. Schs., 1974—; cons., tchr. in field. Mem. Am., Md. (certificate of recognition 1976) personnel and guidance assns., Assn. Nonwhite Concerns in Personnel and Guidance, Balt. City Guidance Assn., N.C. Central U. Alumni Assn., Pub. Sch. Adminstrs. and Suprs. Assn. Balt. City, Kappa Delta Pi, Phi Delta Kappa, Delta Sigma Theta. Home: 5128 Chalgrove Ave Baltimore MD 21215 Office: 2702 Keyworth Ave Baltimore MD 21215

BELL, ERNEST LORNE, III, lawyer; b. Boston, June 12, 1926; s. Ernest L. and Ellamay (Currier) B.; B.A. cum laude; Harvard Coll., 1949; J.D., U. Mich., 1952; m. Margaret Van Nostrand Depue, Apr. 14, 1951; children—David E., Robin E., Roseanne Margaret. Admitted to N.H. bar, 1952; individual practice law Keene, N.H., 1952-78; partner firm Bell and Falk, Keene, N.H., 1972-78. Mem. exec. bd. Daniel Webster council, Boy Scouts Am., 1970—. Recipient Silver Beaver award Boy Scouts Am. Mem. N.H. (pres. 1978-79), Lawyer Pilots (founding, dir. 1972-78), Am., Cheshire County bar assns., Def. Research Inst. (v.p. 1969-73). Episcopalian. Clubs: Keene County, Harvard of Boston. Home: 54 School St Keene NH 03431 Office: 29 Center St Keene NH 03431

BELL, GEORGE BROWN, accountant; b. Phila., Nov. 5, 1915; s. George Dickes and Bessie I. (Brown) B.; B.S. in Commerce, Temple U., 1938; m. Grace M. Freed, Feb. 8, 1940; children—Janice Bell Lamphere, G. Bruce, Gary Douglas, Curtis Dwight. Staff accountant George D. Bell & Co., C.P.A.'s, Phila., 1934-41, partner, 1948-60; contractor, Balt., 1941-46; partner Stockton Bates & Co. (merged with George D. Bell & Co.), Phila., 1960—; lectr. Ursinus Coll. Evening Sch., 1957—. C.P.A., Pa. Mem. Pa., Am. insts. C.P.A.'s. Clubs: Union League of Phila., Temple U. Downtown. Home: 1841 Howe Ln Maple Glen PA 19002 Office: Robinson Bldg Philadelphia PA 19102

BELL, GRIFFIN B., atty. gen.; b. Americus, Ga., Oct. 31, 1918; s. A.C. and Thelma (Pilcher) B.; student Ga. Southwestern Coll.; LL.B. cum laude, Mercer U., 1948, LL.D., 1967; m. Mary Foy Powell, Feb. 20, 1943; 1 son, Griffin B. Admitted to Ga. bar, 1947; practiced in Savannah and Rome, 1947-53; partner firm King & Spalding, Atlanta, 1953-59, mng. partner, 1959-61; U.S. judge 5th Circuit, 1961-76; sr. partner firm King & Spalding, 1976; atty. gen. U.S., 1977—. Chief of staff Gov. Vandiver of Ga., 1959-61; chmn. Atlanta Commn. on Crime and Delinquency, 1965-66; mem. vis. com. Law Sch., Vanderbilt U.; trustee Inst. Continuing Legal Edn. in Ga.; bd. dirs. Fed. Jud. Center, 1974-76. Served to maj. AUS, 1941-46. Mem. Am. Law Inst., Am. Bar Assn. (chmn. div. jud. adminstrn. 1975-76), Order of Coif. Baptist. Office: Dept Justice Constitution Ave between 9th and 10th Sts Washington DC 20530

BELL, HASKELL HARMAN, railroad salesman; b. Keyser, W. Va., Aug. 23, 1922; s. Guy Harman and Myrtle (Paugh) B.; student Catherman's Bus. Sch., Cumberland, Md., 1940-41; m. Katye Sheffield, Feb. 1, 1946; children—Larry Alton, Brian Kent, Thane Craig, Mark Brook. Apprentice clk. B & O R.R., Cumberland, 1941; stenographer Western Md. Ry., Cumberland, 1941-42, 46-49, sr. clk., stenographer, Hagerstown, Md., 1949-52, chief clk., Hagerstown, 1952-55, traffic rep., Elkins, W. Va., 1955-66, sales rep., Elkins, 1967-72, legis. committeeman, 1970-72; salesman Home (Amana) Food Plan, Hagerstown, 1954-55; dist. chmn. ASTRO, 1970-71. Pres. YMCA, 1969-70; bd. dirs. Randolph County unit Am. Cancer Soc.; asst. dir.-gen. Mountain State Forest Festival, 1960-61; pres. Elkins Sch. Band Aux., 1963; v.p. P.T.A., 1960. Served with inf. AUS, 1942-46; ETO. Decorated Bronze Star; named Ky. Col., 1968. Mem. Kanawha Valley Transp. Club, Western Md. Ry Fellowship Club (pres. 1959), Western Md. Ry. Social Club, Hagerstown Traffic Club (dir.), Brotherhood Ry., Airline and S.S. Clks., Elkins C. of C. (exec. sec. 1956-58), Internat. Platform Assn., 99th Inf. Div. Assn. Methodist. Clubs: Masons (Master 1966), Elks, Rotary (pres. 1960-61). Home: 941 Noland Dr Hagerstown MD 21740 Office: Western Md Ry Elgin Blvd Hagerstown MD 21740

BELL, HOWARD HUGHES, assn. exec., lawyer; b. N.Y.C., June 27, 1926; s. George H. and Mary Elizabeth (Hughes) B.; B.J., U. Mo., 1948; postgrad. George Washington U., 1954-55; J.D., Catholic U. Am., 1960; m. Corinne Chandler, Aug. 30, 1947; children—Mary Elizabeth, Jeffery Chandler, Laurinda Louise. Sales promotion mgr. Evening Star Broadcasting Co., Washington, 1948-51; v.p., asst. to pres., dir. code authority Nat. Assn. Broadcasters, 1951-68; admitted to Md. bar, 1961; pres. Am. Advt. Fedn., Washington, 1968—; exec. sec. Assn. for Profl. Broadcast Edn.; instr. sales promotion Am. U. Mem. Nat. Yellow Pages Adv. Council; mem. parents council Marietta Coll.; bd. dirs. U. Mo. Freedom of Info. Center, Ednl. Found. Served with USNR, 1944-46. Mem. Am. Bar Assn., Advt. Council (bd. dirs.), Nat. Advt. Rev. Council, Soc. Assn. Execs., Broadcast Pioneers, Delta Theta Phi (Alumni award), Pi Kappa Alpha, Alpha Delta Sigma. Episcopalian. Clubs: Washington Advertising, Internat.; Congressional Country, Sky (N.Y.C.); World Trade (San Francisco). Home: 14510 Faraday Dr Rockville MD 20853 Office: 1225 Connecticut Ave Washington DC 20036

BELL, JAMES FREDERICK, lawyer; b. New Orleans, Aug. 5, 1922; s. George Bryan and Sarah Barr (Perry) B.; A.B. cum laude, Princeton, 1943; LL.B., Harvard, 1948; m. Jill Cooper Arden, Apr. 14, 1951; children—Bradley Cushing, Sarah Perry, Ashley Arden. Admitted to D.C. bar, 1949, asso. firm Pogue & Neal (name changed to Jones, Day, Reavis & Pogue 1967), Washington, 1948-53, partner, 1953—; gen. counsel Conf. State Bank Suprs., 1951—. Dir., Inst. for Internat. Devel., Inc., Washington, 1975-77; chmn. com. on canons and other bus. Episcopal Diocese of Washington, 1960-78; pres. Episc. Center for Children, Washington, 1966-67. Served to lt., USNR, 1943-46. Mem. Am., Fed., D.C. bar assns. Clubs: Metropolitan, George Town (Washington). Home: 5307 Elliott Rd NW Washington DC 20016 Office: 1100 Connecticut Ave NW Washington DC 20036

BELL, JAMES MILTON, physician; b. Portsmouth, Va., Nov. 5, 1921; s. Charles Edward and Lucy (Barnes) B.; student Va. State Coll., 1939-40; B.S., N.C. Central U. (formerly N.C. Coll.), 1943; M.D., Meharry Med. Coll., 1947. Rotating intern, Harlem Hosp., N.Y.C., 1947-48; asst. physician to clin. dir. Lakin (W.Va.) State Hosp., 1948-51; fellow gen. psychiatry Menninger Sch. Psychiatry-Menninger Found., Topeka, Kans., 1953-56, tng. child psychiatry, 1957-58; resident Winter VA Hosp., Topeka, 1953-56; asst. sect. chief childrens unit Topeka State Hosp., 1956-58; clin. teaching staff Menninger Sch. Psychiatry, 1956-58; med. cons. psychiatry Irwin Army Hosp., Ft. Riley, Kans., 1957-58; clin. dir., psychiatrist Berkshire Farm Center and Services for Youth, Canaan, N.Y., 1959—; clin. asst. to clin. asso. prof. psychiatry Albany Med. Coll., Union U., 1959—, mem. admission com., 1972—; psychiatrist-in-charge Albany Home for Children, N.Y., 1959-77; staff psychiatrist Parsons Child and Family Center, 1977—; asst. dispensary to dispensary psychiatrist Albany Med. Center Clinic, 1960; trainee cons. Albany Child Guidance Center Psychiat. Service, Inc., 1961; cons. Astor Home for Children, Rhinebeck, N.Y., 1965; instrnl. staff Frederick Amman Meml. Inst. Delinquency and Crime, St. Lawrence U., 1965-70; cons. adolescence N.Y. State Div. Youth, 1966-76, mem. med. rev. bd., 1974-76; mem. Child Abuse Adv. Council, Albany; bd. dirs., mem. com. on proposed policy N.Y. Spaulding for Children; lectr. in field. Bd. dirs., exec. com. Gould Farm, Barrington, Mass. Served to capt. M.C., AUS, 1951-53; now col. Res.; comdg. officer 364th Gen. Hosp., USAR, Albany, 1967-76, assigned 344th Gen. Hosp., USAR, Ft. Totten, N.Y., 1976, 815th Sta. Hosp., Stewart Army Subport, Newburgh, N.Y., 1977; cons. Keller U.S. Army Hosp., U.S. Mil. Acad., West Point, N.Y. Diplomate in psychiatry and child psychiatry Am. Bd. Psychiatry and Neurology, Pan. Am. Med. Assn. (mem. council psychiatry sect.); certified N.Y. State Dept. Mental Hygiene. Fellow Am. Psychiat. Assn. (chmn. council nat. affairs 1973-75, past vice-chm.), Am. Acad. Child Psychiatry (chmn. com. facilities for children and adolescence 1973-75), AAAS, Am. Orthopsychiat. Assn. (past dir.), N.Y. Acad. Scis., Am. Coll. Psychiatrists (past mem. Stanley Dean award com.); mem. Group for Advancement of Psychiatry (com. on child psychiatry), Inst. Religion and Health (charter), Council for Exceptional Children, Nat. Assn. Tng. Schs. and Juvenile Agys., Assn. of N.Y. Educators of Emotionally Disturbed, AMA, Nat., N.Y. State, Columbia Country med. assns., Am. Psychopath. Assn., Assn. Child Care Workers (dir. 1978), Soc. Adolescent Psychiatry, Assn. Psychiat. Treatment of Offenders, N.Y. Acad. Scis., Am. Acad. Polit. and Social Sci., N.Y. State Soc. Med. Research, N.Y. Capitol Dist. Council Child Psychiatry (pres. 1974), Internat. Platform Assn., Alpha Omega Alpha. Rotarian. Contbr. numerous articles to profl. jours. Home: Hudsonview Old Post Rd N Croton-on-Hudson NY 10520 Office: Berkshire Farm Center and Services for Youth Canaan NY 12029

BELL, JOSEPH EMEAL, ednl. specialist; b. Mobile, Ala., June 9, 1945; s. Hubert Thomas, Sr., and Theresa (Thomas) B.; B.S., Ala. State U., 1967; postgrad. Hampton Inst., 1970-71; M.A., Howard U., 1974; 1 dau., Tonya Renee. Tchr., bd. edn., Phenix City, Ala., 1967-68, St. Paul, 1968-70; instr. Hampton (Va.) Inst., 1970-71; coordinator, dir. spl. service for disadvantaged students Howard U., Washington, 1971—; cons., teaching and career cons. to high sch. and coll. students. Recipient outstanding service award Howard U., 1974, Office of Edn. HEW, 1975, citation Inst. for Urban Affairs and Research, Howard U., 1978, numerous others. Mem. Am. Personnel and Guidance Assn., D.C. Consolidation Edn. Services (pres. 1978—), Mid-Eastern Assn. Ednl. Opportunity Program Personnel (exec. bd. 1978—), Am. Assn. Higher Edn., Nat. Coordinating Council Ednl. Opportunities, Nat. Assn. Black Social Workers, Assn.

Non White Concerns, Kappa Alpha Psi. Roman Cahtolic. Home: 3932 7th St NE Washington DC 20017

BELL, JULIUS ARTHUR, lawyer; b. N.Y.C., Jan. 14, 1916; s. Harry and Anita (Atran) B.; LL.B., N.Y. U., 1940; m. Rita M. Taylor, Apr. 8, 1945; children—Tina Sharon Bell Gilford, Stephen Elliot. Admitted to N.Y. bar, 1942, U.S. Supreme Ct. bar, 1961; practiced in N.Y.C., 1949—, partner firm Resnick Barr & Resnick, 1963-66; with U.S. Office Housing Expediter, Bklyn., 1949-50; with Am. Home Products Corp., N.Y.C., 1966-72, sr. atty., 1972—; house counsel Hunter Douglas Aluminum Corp., N.Y.C., 1961-63. Bd. dirs., sec., treas. Atran Found., Inc.; pres. Westbury (N.Y.) Hebrew Congregation, 1964-65, chmn. bd. trustees, 1965-66. Served to capt. AUS, 1942-46; ETO. Recipient award for Outstanding Service, Fedn. Jewish Philanthropies of N.Y., 1966, award of Merit, United Jewish Appeal, 1962. Mem. Pharm. Mfrs. Assn. (chmn. trademark and copyright com. on Far and Middle East), Am. Bar Assn., Assn. Bar City N.Y., U.S. Trademark Assn., N.Y. Patent Law Assn. Democrat. Jewish. Home: 109 Aspen Dr E Woodbury NY 11797 Office: Atran Found Inc 60 E 42d St New York City NY 10017

BELL, MARTIN HAROLD, equipment engr.; b. Provo, Utah, Jan. 26, 1940; s. Harold Cyril and Ruth (Dunn) B.; Asso. Sci., Brigham Young U., 1967, B.S., 1969; m. Debra Joan Davis, June 26, 1975; children—Robert, Jay, Crystal, Jeffrey, Katharine. Sr. equipment engr. Corning Glass Works (N.Y.) 1970-72, supr. equipment engr., 1972-74, supr. mfg. engring., 1974-75; mgr. fiber optics Am. Cystoscope Makers, Stamford, Conn., 1975-77; mgr. engring. Innotech Corp., Trumbull, Conn., 1977—; tchr. Utah Tech. Coll., 1965-67. Served with USN, 1958-65. Mem. IEEE, Instrument Soc. Am. (sr. mem.). Republican. Mem. Ch. of Jesus Christ of Latter-day Saints. Home: 6 Cayer Circle Huntington CT 06484 Office: 2285 Reservoir Ave Trumbull CT 06611

BELL, MORLEY BRUCE, astronomer; b. Orillia, Ont., Can., Oct. 7, 1937; s. Melville Lorne and Irene (Wyley) B.; B.Sc., U. Western Ont., 1960, M.S., 1962. Research asst., dept. elec. engring. U. Toronto (Ont.), 1962-65; asst. research officer NRC, Ottawa, Ont., 1965-75, asso. research officer, 1975—. Mem. Am., Canadian (charter) astron. socs., Profl. Inst. Pub. Service Can. Contbr. tech. papers to profl. jours. Research in high resolution observations of active regions on the sun. Home: 20 Eastpark Dr Ottawa ON K1B 3Z8 Canada Office: Herzberg Inst Astrophysics Nat Research Council Ottawa ON K1A 0R8 Canada

BELL, PAUL ALBERT, patent examiner; b. New London, Conn., July 27, 1945; s. Richard G. and Martha L. (Casselman) B.; B.S. in Aerospace Engring., U. Okla., 1968; postgrad. U. N.Mex., 1971-72; m. Lynda L. Storm, Mar. 2, 1973; children—Crystal, Tamera, Daniel, Melody, Robert. Research asst. nuclear and chem. engring. dept. U. N.Mex., 1972-73; patent examiner U.S. Patent & Trademark Office, Washington, 1973—. Bd. dirs. Good Shepherd United Methodist Ch., Woodbridge, Va., 1977-78; active Dalewood Musical Theatre, 1977—; founder Albuquerque Melodrama Theatre, 1972; mem. Albuquerque Civic Light Opera, 1969-72. Served with U.S. Army, 1968-71. Mem. Am. Inst. Aeros. and Astronautics, Am. Nuclear Soc., Patent Office Soc. (dir. 1974—, sec. 1976-78). Republican. Lutheran. Author: Plowshare: A Look at Problems with Tritium, 1972; (with G.A. Whan) Material Resources Analysis, 1973, The Nuclear Device, 1973; (with P.G. Johnson and G.A. Whan) Radioactive Contamination, 1973. Office: US Patent and Trademark Office Washington DC 20231

BELL, RANDALL WILLIAM, ophthalmic surgeon; b. N.Y.C., Jan. 20, 1938; s. William Randall and Frances Veronica (Dwyer) B.; B.S., U.S. Mil. Acad., 1959; M.D. (Chubb Found. fellow), Cornell U., 1966; m. Carole Ann Gilligan, June 6, 1959; children—Randall, Deborah, Kevin, Thomas, James. Commd. 2d lt. U.S. Army, 1959, advanced through grades to col., 1975; intern Walter Reed Gen. Hosp., Washington, 1966-67, resident, 1967-70; chief ophthalmology Valley Forge (Pa.) Gen. Hosp., 1970-72; practice medicine specializing in ophthalmology, USAR 338th Med. Group, Wayne, Pa., 1972—; mem. staffs Scheie Inst., Presbyn. U. Pa. Med. Center, Wills Eye Hosp., Phila., Jefferson Hosp., Phila., Bryn Mawr (Pa.) Hosp., Paoli (Pa.) Hosp., Sacred Heart Hosp., Norristown, Montgomery Hosp., Norristown; asst. prof. Thomas Jefferson U., Phila., 1972-76, U. Pa., 1978. Diplomate Am. Bd. Ophthalmology, Nat. Bd. Med. Examiners. Fellow ACS, Pa. Acad. Ophthalmology and Otolaryngology, Am. Acad. Ophthalmology, Phila. Coll. Physicians; mem. AMA, Pa., Delaware County med. socs., Assn Research in Vision and Ophthalmology, Soc. Contemporary Ophthalmology, Soc. Mil. Ophthalmologists, West Point Soc. Phila. (bd. govs. 1975—). Republican. Roman Catholic. Clubs: Merion Cricket, Aronimink Golf, Union League of Phila., Cornell. Contbr. articles to profl. jours. Home: 1102 DeKalb St Norristown PA 19401 Office: 200 Eagle Rd Strafford Bldg 2 Wayne PA 19087

BELL, ROBERT EDWARD, univ. prin.; b. New Malden, Eng., Nov. 29, 1918; s. Edward R. and Edith (Rich) B.; B.A., U. B.C., 1939, M.A., 1941; Ph.D., McGill U., 1948; m. Jeanne Atkinson, July 5, 1947; 1 dau., Alison Ann. Radar devel. Nat. Research Council, Ottawa, Can., 1941-45; nuclear research Chalk River Nuclear Labs., 1946-52; prof. physics McGill U., Montreal, Que., 1956—, Rutherford prof., 1960—, dir. Foster Radiation Lab., 1960-69, vice dean arts and sci., 1964-67, dean Faculty Grad. Studies and Research, 1969-70, prin., vice chancellor, 1970—. Fellow Am. Phys. Soc., Royal Soc. (London), Royal Soc. (Can.) (pres. 1978—); mem. Can. Assn. Physicists (pres. 1965-66). Home: 363 Olivier Ave Montreal PQ H3Z 2C8 Canada

BELL, ROBERT LAWRENCE, pub. co. exec.; b. Everett, Mass., Feb. 21, 1919; s. Joseph and Mary (Kiernan) B.; B.S. in History with honors, Bowdoin Coll., 1942; m. Rose Edith Hogan, June 2, 1942; children—Marlene Bell Andre, Robert Lawrence, Stephen, Christine. Prop. Bell's Card Shops, Boston, 1950-67; pres. Advance Corp., Boston, 1960—; pres., pub. Crescendo Pub. Co., Boston, 1968-76; pres. Cuarta Corp., 1971—; v.p., sales mgr. Allied Pub. Co., Portland, Oreg., 1956-60; pres. Reliance Corp., Boston, 1960-68; sales rep., trainer Rust Craft Greeting Cards, Boston, 1951-56. Trustee Bridgton Acad., Robse Realty Trust. Served to lt. (s.g.), USNR, 1942-45. Mem. ASCAP. Clubs: Union Boat, Bowdoin (past pres.) (Boston); Bellevue Country. Office: 48-50 Melrose St Boston MA 02116

BELL, STEPHEN (STEVE) SCOTT, TV news corr.; b. Oskaloosa, Iowa, Dec. 9, 1935; s. Howard Arthur and Florance Louise (Scott) B.; B.A., Central Coll. Iowa, 1959; M.S.J., Northwestern U., 1963; Ph.D. in Journalism (hon.), Central Coll., 1969; m. Joyce Dillavou, June 16, 1957; children—Allison Kay, Hilary Ann. Announcer KBOE radio, Oskaloosa, 1955-59; reporter WOI Radio-TV, Ames, Iowa, 1959-60; news writer WGN Radio-TV, Chgo., 1960-61; chief newscaster WOW-TV, Omaha, 1962-65; newscaster WNEW Radio, NYC, 1965-67; corr. ABC News, N.Y. Radio, 1967-70, Combat corr., Vietnam, 1970-71, So. Bur. chief, Atlanta, 1971, chief Asia corr., Hong Kong, 1971-75, anchorman ABC Morning News, Good Morning America program, 1975—. Recipient Emmy nomination, 1964, 1974; overseas press club award ABC News, 1969; Headliner's award, 1976. Mem. White House, Radio-TV corrs., assns., Radio-TV News Dirs. Assn., Headliners Club, Hong Kong Fgn. Corrs. Club. Presbyterian. Office: ABC News 1124 Connecticut Ave NW Washington DC 20036

BELL, THOMAS ROBERT, III, chem. engr., tech. co. exec.; b. Phila., Jan. 8, 1920; s. Thomas Robert and Ada Byram (Wells) B.; B.S., Lehigh U., 1941; m. Mabel Doris Missimer, June 26, 1943; children—Janis Nancy, Thomas Robert IV, Richard Missimer. Coll. apprentice Gen. Chem. div. Allied Chem. Corp., Marcus Hook, Pa., 1941-42, shift supr. TNT Gen. Chem. Def. Corp., Point Pleasant, W.Va., 1942-45, chem. engr. research and devel., Gen. Chem. div., Marcus Hook, 1945-51; with Pennwalt Corp. (formerly Pa. Salt Mfg. Co.), King of Prussia, Pa., 1951—, gen. mgr. tech. center, 1974—. Mem. Research Mgmt. Group Phila., Pa. Economy League, Lambda Chi Alpha. Republican. Episcopalian. Club: Aronimink Golf. Patentee in field. Office: 900 1st Ave King of Prussia PA 19406

BELLAMY, JOE DAVID, educator; b. Cin., Dec. 29, 1941; s. Orin Ross and Beulah Pearl (Zutavern) B.; student Duke, 1959-61; B.A., Antioch Coll., 1964; M.F.A., U. Iowa, 1969; m. Connie Sue Arendsee, Sept. 16, 1964; children—Lael Elizabeth, Samuel Ross Carlos. Editor, Antiochian, Antioch Coll., Yellow Springs, Ohio, 1965-67; instr. English, Pa. State Coll., Mansfield, 1969-70, asst. prof. English, 1970-72; asst. prof. English, St. Lawrence U., Canton, N.Y., 1972-74, asso. prof., 1974—; editor, pub. Fiction Internat., 1972—; cons. editor U. Ill. Press, 1974—; book reviewer Chgo. Daily News, 1975-76, Saturday Rev., 1976—; dir. ann. St. Lawrence U. Writers' Conf., 1974—; bd. dirs. Coordinating Council Lit. Mags., 1976—. Bread Loaf scholar Middlebury Coll., 1973; Nat. Endowment for Humanities grantee, 1974. Mem. Modern Lang. Assn., AAUP, Coordinating Council Lit. Mags. Author: Apocalypse: Dominant Contemporary Forms, 1972; The New Fiction, 1974; Superfiction, or The American Story Transformed, 1975; (poems) Olympic Gold Medalist, 1978; contbr. fiction, poetry, criticism to popular, profl. publs. Home: 14 Jay St Canton NY 13617 Office: Dept English St Lawrence U Canton NY 13617

BELLANTE, E. LAWRENCE, cons. engr.; b. Easton, Pa., Apr. 16, 1925; s. Santo and Carmelia (Italiano) B.; B.S. in Indsl. Engring., Lehigh U., 1949; m. Ann Helstrom, May 28, 1949; John, Carl (twins), Susan, David. Engring. rep. Gilboy and O'Malley, Cons. Engrs., and predecessor firms, Scranton, Pa., 1949-50, project engr., 1950-53, pres., gen. mgr., 1953-54; pres. Bellante, Clauss, Miller & Partners, Inc. and predecessor firms, Scranton, 1954—; pres. Cycon, Inc., Scranton, 1959—; dir. N.Am. Music Industries, Inc., Nickey-Bellante Internat., Northeastern Bank of Pa. (Chmn. drive Lackawanna (Pa.) United Fund, 1966-67, pres., 1968, 69; chmn. South Abington (Pa.) Planning Commn., 1961-66; sec. South Abington Bd. Adjustment, 1962-66; chmn. bd. trustees U. Scranton, 1973-78; bd. dirs. Geisinger Hosp., Danville, Pa., 1977—, Myer Davidow Meml. Found., 1970—; bd. govs. Scranton Area Found., 1970—. Served with USAAF, World War II. Recipient Engr. of Year award NE chpt. Pa. Soc. Profl. Engrs. Mem. Nat., Pa. socs. profl. engrs., C. of C. Scranton (dir. 1965—, pres. 1972-73). Contbr. articles to profl jours. Home: 24 Oakford Glen RD # 4 Clark's Summit PA 18411 Office: 130 N Washington Ave Scranton PA 18503

BELLARD, AMERICO (MAX), engring. co. exec.; b. Phillipsburg, N.J., Nov. 2, 1919; s. Espartero and Esterina (Goretti) Belardinelli; A.S. in M.E., U. New Haven, 1953; m. Lydia Manocchi, Feb. 2, 1946; children—Robert Louis, Gary Steven, David Alan. With Sikorsky Aircraft, 1947-77, chief elec. design devel. and test br., 1965-77; mfr.'s rep. application engring. aircraft elec. systems A.M. Bellard, Orange, Conn., 1977—; cons. elec. and electronic instrument design and installation FAA, 1965—. Served with USAAC, 1942-45. Mem. Am. Helicopter Soc. (sec.-treas. N.E. region 1970-77, certificate of appreciation 1976), Am. Def. Preparedness Assn., Soc. Automotive Engrs. (chmn. A-2c subcom., mem. A-2 subcom.), Engring. Club Bridgeport (pres. 1961-62), Army Aviation Assn. Am., Air Force Assn. Roman Catholic. Contbr. articles to profl. jours. Home and office: 64 Andrew Ln Orange CT 06477

BELLAS, HUGH WALLACE, church exec., ret. chem. co. exec.; b. Phila., Oct. 19, 1912; s. Hugh Edwin and Emily Louise (Roescher) B.; B.Chem. Engring., U. Pa., 1933; m. Mary G. Wickes, June 14, 1947; 1 dau., Betty Joan (Mrs. William J. Bain). With E.I. duPont de Nemours & Co., Wilmington, Del., 1933-77, plants tech. engr. and supt., 1940-50, process supt., 1950-77. Bd. dirs. Nether Providence Community Classes, 1965—, finance chmn., 1973—, vice chmn., 1978—. Mem. Am. Inst. Chem. Engrs. Episcopalian (mem. pres. bishop's nat. advisory com. on evangelism and renewal 1978—, mem. exec. com. Del. Deanery 1978—). Mem. Brotherhood of St. Andrew (nat. pres. 1971-76, exec. asst. to pres. 1977-78), Pewsaction (nat. chmn. 1978—). Author: Filtration, 1954, 2d edit., 1966. Home: Rose Valley Rd Box 153 Moylan PA 19065 Office: 373 W Market St York PA 17405

BELLE, JOSEPH VINCENT, environ. engr.; b. Medford, Mass., Apr. 14, 1920; s. John Dennis and Elena Frances (Lo Sciuto) B.; B.S. in Civil Engring. cum laude, Tufts U., 1943; m. Grace Marie Rando, Oct. 23, 1949; children—Joseph Michael, Margaret Elaine, Christine Ann. Engr., Bur. Aeronautics, Bur. Naval Weapons, Navy Dept., Washington, 1946-63, civil engr. Bur. Yards and Docks, Naval Facilities Engring. Command, 1963-73; environmental engr. ManTech of N.J. Corp., Washington, 1973-78, PA Engring., Corte Madera, Calif, 1978—; officer, dir. King Charles Apts., Ltd. Vice pres. Annandale Terrace Civic Assn., 1966. Served to lt. USNR, 1943-46. Registered profl. engr., Mass. Mem. Soc. Am. Mil. Engrs., Nat. Assn. Ret. Fed. Employees, Am. Concrete Inst. (hon.), Tau Beta Pi. Democrat. Roman Catholic. Club: K.C. Author govtl. publs. Home: 7452 Madeira Pl Annandale VA 22003 Office: 7452 Madeira Pl Annandale VA 22003

BELLER, MARTIN LEONARD, orthopaedic surgeon; b. N.Y.C., Apr. 30, 1924; s. Abraham Jacob and Ida (Fishkin) B.; A.B. with honors, Columbia U., 1944, M.D., 1946; m. Wilma Gertrude Kjelgaard, June 29, 1947; children—Alan Lewis, Beatrice Ann, Peter James. Intern Mt. Sinai Hosp., N.Y.C., 1946-47; resident orthopaedic surgery Hosp. Joint Diseases, N.Y.C., 1949-52; practice medicine specializing in orthopaedic surgery, Phila., 1952—; asst. prof. orthopaedic surgery U. Pa. Sch. Medicine, Phila., 1967-72, asso. prof., 1972—; attending orthopaedic surgery Hosp. U. Pa., 1963—; asso. attending orthopaedic surgeon Albert Einstein Med. Center, 1960-70, chmn. dept. orthopaedic surgery Daroff div., 1970—; Served from 1st lt. to capt., M.C., AUS, 1947-49. Am. Orthopaedic Assn. exchange fellow Gt. Britain, 1963. Diplomate Am. Bd. Orthopaedic Surgery. Fellow A.C.S., Am. Acad. Orthopaedic Surgeons (bd. councilors 1978—), Internat. Soc. Orthopaedic Surgery and Traumatology; mem. Eastern Orthopedic Assn., Pa. Orthopedic Soc. (pres. 1975-77), Pa. Com. on Trauma (chmn. 1978—), Orthopaedic Research Soc., Am. Rheumatism Soc., N.Y. Acad. Sci., Phila. Coll. Physicians, Phi Beta Kappa, Alpha Omega Alpha, Phi Delta Epsilon (nat. pres. 1975-76). Republican. Episcopalian (vestryman 1966-70, 71—). Club: Union League of Phila. Author: (with I. Stein and R. O. Stein) Living Bone in Health and Disease, 1955, (with I. Stein) Clinical Densitometry of Bone, 1970. Home: 1813 Blackberry Ln Gladwyne PA 19035 Office: 1936 Spruce St Philadelphia PA 19103

BELLER, STEPHEN MARK, coll. adminstr.; b. Chgo., Aug. 14, 1948; s. Irving Elliott and DeVera (Jameson) B.; B.S., U. Ill., 1970; M.S., Western Ill. U., 1972; Ph.D., Oreg. State U., 1977; m. Luanne Evelyn Heyl, June 28, 1970; 1 dau., Clancy Dee. Asst. head ednl. awards div. Rotary Found., Evanston, Ill., 1972-73; teaching asst. Office of Student Services, Oreg. State U., 1973-77; asst. dean students State U. Coll. Arts and Sci. at Geneseo, N.Y., 1977—. Mem. Am. Personnel and Guidance Assn., Am. Coll. Personnel Assn., Nat. Assn. Student Personnel Adminstrs., Am. Assn. U. Adminstrs., United U. Professions, Phi Delta Kappa, Delta Sigma Pi, Alpha Epsilon Pi, Phi Kappa Phi. Club: Rotary Internat. Home: 19 Ward Pl Geneseo NY 14454 Office: 109 Erwin Bldg State U Coll Geneseo NY 14454

BELLIN, MARTIN R., psychologist; b. Bklyn., July 17, 1935; s. James Jacob and Shirley (Farber) B.; B.A., Bklyn. Coll., 1958; M.S. (Danziger fellow), Yeshiva U., 1962; m. Barbara Sue Langdon, Aug. 20, 1967; children—Devra Lee. Psychologist, pub. schs., Mineola, N.Y., 1962-69, West Islip, N.Y., 1969—. Psychotherapist, Jamaica Center for Psychotherapy, Hempstead, N.Y., 1971-76; dir. Head Start, 1967-69; columnist, writer Setter Mag., 1976-78; free-lance writer Dog World Mag., 1976—, Setter Mag., 1976—. Trustee, Comsewogue Pub. Schs., Port Jefferson Station, N.Y., 1965-68. Bd. dirs. Family Service, Inc., North Suffolk County. Recipient Community Leader of Am. award News Pub. Co., 1969; grantee Project Able, 1958-60. Recipient award Assn. for Children with Downs Syndrome, 1973. Mem. Am. Psychol. Assn. Home: 178 Lower Sheep Pasture Setauket NY 11733 Office: West Islip Public Schools West Islip NY 11795

BELLINGER, JACK WAITSTILL, govt. ofcl.; b. Mt. Vernon, N.Y., Nov. 17, 1910; s. James Waitstill and Mary (Dwight) B.; student Pace Coll., 1934-35; B.S., N.Y.U., 1940; B.C.S., Southeastern U., 1954, M.C.S., 1955; m. Adelande H. Irving, Aug. 2, 1941; children—Dorthy Ann, Dwight Allen. Auditor, N.Y. Telephone Co.; instr. Ft. Myer Sch. Adminstrn.; auditor Navy S.C.I. 3rd dist., War Assets Adminstrn., FHA; with Nat. Park Service, Dept. Interior, Washington, 1950-67, chief financial control br., asst. chief auditor, acting chief auditor, dep. chief auditor, 1955-66, regional audit mgr., Washington region, 1966-67; regional audit mgr. N.Y. region CAB, N.Y.C., 1967-73. C.P.A., N.J. Mem. Am. Mgmt. Assn., Fed. Govt. Accountants Assn., Wilderness Soc. Am., N.Y.U. Alumni Assn., Eastern Nat. Parks and Monuments Assn., Research Assn. Am. Inst. C.P.A.'s, Southeastern U. Honor Soc., N.J. Soc. C.P.A.'s. Episcopalian. Home: 82 Tierney Dr Cedar Grove NJ 07009

BELLMORE, MANDELL, business exec.; b. Washington, May 22, 1935; s. Bernard and Dorothy (Kraft) B.; B.S., U. Md., 1957; M.E.E., Catholic U. Am., 1961; Ph.D., Johns Hopkins, 1965; m. Carol Ann Block, June 23, 1957; children—Robyn Eileen, Stacy Joy. Engr. electronics div. ACF, Riverdale, Md., 1960-61; sr. engr. Martin Marietta Corp., Balt., 1961-63; tech. staff Mitre Corp., Arlington, Va., 1963-65; asst. prof. Johns Hopkins U., Balt., 1965-70, asso. prof., 1970-72; dir. research and devel. Block, McGibony and Assos., Silver Spring, Md., 1972-73, pres., 1973—. Operations research cons. Sci. and Tech. Task Force, Pres. Commn. on Law Enforcement and Criminal Justice, 1967; adviser Project Acorn, Office Law Enforcement Assistance, U.S. Dept. Def., 1969; mem. adv. com. for sec. of health and mental hygiene State of Md., 1970-71; trustee Southeastern U., Washington, 1975—. Served to 1st lt. USAF, 1957-60. Mem. Operations Research Soc. Am., Inst. Mgmt. Scis., Assn. Computing Machinery, Tau Epsilon Phi (chpt. pres. 1957). Contbr. articles to profl. jours. Home: 3609 Woodvalley Baltimore MD 21208

BELLO, MICHAEL JOSEPH, JR., accountant; b. Elmira, N.Y., May 23, 1944; s. Michael Joseph and Betty (Surgeoner) B.; student Syracuse U., 1962-66; m. Paulette Marie Denero, Sept. 25, 1971; children—James Daniel, Brian Michael. Retail accountant Nettleton Shoes, Inc., Syracuse, 1969-72; comptroller Syracuse Symphony Orch., 1972—; cons. in field. Trustee, treas. Syracuse Area Landmark Theatre, 1978—. Mem. Am. Symphony Orch. League, Nat. Assn. Accountants, Beer Can Collectors Am. Roman Catholic. Club: Riverside Country. Home: 2924 Court St Syracuse NY 13208 Office: 411 Montgomery St Syracuse NY 13202

BELLOMO, CHARLES MICHAEL, city ofcl.; b. Needham, Mass., May 19, 1924; s. Jerry and Mary (Morreale) B.; diploma E.W. Wiggins Airway's Aviation Technician Sch., 1943; m. Antoinette Marie Ferrera, June 8, 1947; children—Gerald Philip, Frank Charles. Fed. aviation insp. E.W. Wiggins Airway's, Norwood, Mass., 1943-45, aircraft inspector, 1945-48; with Needham Fire Dept., 1948—, dep. fire chief, 1969—; cons. in fire safety to various hosps., nursing homes and instns. in New Eng., 1960—; mem. staff Mass. Firefighting Acad., 1978—; guest speaker to various civic groups and schs., 1959—. Served to sgt. USAAF, 1943-45. Mem. Nat. Fire Protection Assn., Mass. Fire Prevention Assn., Internat. Soc. of Fire Service Instrs., Mass. Inst. of Fire Dept. Instrs., Norfolk County Firefighters Assn. Roman Catholic. Contbr. articles on fire prevention and rescue procedures to various newspapers. Home: 43 Norfolk St Needham MA 02192 Office: Needham Fire Dept 88 Chestnut St Needham MA 02192

BELLOTTI, FRANCIS XAVIER, state ofcl.; b. Dorchester, Mass., May 3, 1923; A.B., Tufts Coll., 1947; LL.B., Boston Coll., 1952; J.D. (hon.), New Eng. Sch. Law, 1977. Admitted to Mass. bar, 1952, U.S. Supreme Ct. bar, 1965; individual practice law, Quincy, 1952-74; lt. gov. Mass., 1963-64; atty. gen. Mass., 1975—; chmn. Criminal History System Bd., Com. on Criminal Justice, Organized Crime Control Council, Com. on Privacy and Consumer Rights. Fellow Am. Coll. Trial Lawyers, Internat. Acad. Trial Lawyers; mem. Nat. Assn. Def. Lawyers in Criminal Cases, Am. Trial Lawyers Assn. (dir. Mass. chpt.), New Eng. Law Inst., Am. Judicature Soc., Justinian Law Soc. Office: One Ashburton Pl Boston MA 02108

BELLOWS, HOWARD ARTHUR, business exec.; b. Chgo., May 13, 1902; s. John and Dora (May) B.; student Va. pub. schs.; m. Rita Maffitt, Jan. 30, 1934; children—Howard Arthur, Judith Anne (Mrs. Clifford G. Allen, Jr.). Salesman, Gen. Tire & Rubber Co., 1924-27, asst. div. mgr., 1927-30, div. mgr., 1930-51, nat. mgr. retail merchandising, 1951-52, v.p. replacement tire sales, 1952-57, mgmt. cons. and adviser, 1958-67, 69—; v.p., mgmt. adviser R.K.O., 1957-58; mgmt. cons. Clubs: Philadelphia Country, Union League (Phila.); Akron City. Home: 221A Old Nassau Rd Jamesburg NJ 08831

BELLOWS, HOWARD ARTHUR, JR., hardware products mfg. co. exec.; b. N.Y.C., Mar. 10, 1938; s. Howard Arthur and Rita Jennie (Maffitt) B.; B.A., Princeton, 1960; M.B.A., Harvard, 1964; m. Mary Josephine Boyd, Sept. 7, 1968; children—Maffitt Vodrey, Alexander Scott, Hillary Newland. Dir. mktg. Olga Co., Van Nuys, Calif., 1964-66; chmn. bd., co-chief exec. officer Triangle Corp., Stamford, Conn., 1967-71, chmn. bd., pres., chief exec. officer, 1971—; dir. United Media, Inc., Seattle, Hovermarine Corp., Pitts. Served to lt. (j.g.) USNR, 1960-62. Mem. Young Presidents Orgn. Clubs: River, Racquet and Tennis (N.Y.C.); Stanwich (Greenwich, Conn.). Home:

15 Upper Cross Rd Greenwich CT 06830 also Pond Ln Southampton NY 11968 Office: 72 Cummings Point Rd Stamford CT 06902

BELLUCCI, RICHARD JOHN, physician; b. N.Y.C., Apr. 22, 1914; s. Frank and Letezia (Marrella) B.; B.S., N.Y. U., 1936; M.S., 1938; M.D., Creighton U., 1942; m. Eleanor DePaoli, Aug. 13, 1949; 1 dau., Eleanor. Intern, Grasslands Hosp., Valhalla, N.Y., 1942-43, resident, 1943-44; resident Manhattan Eye Ear & Throat Hosp., N.Y.C., 1944-46, now chmn. dept. otolaryngology, practice medicine specializing in otology, N.Y.C., 1947—; chmn. dept. otolaryngology Manhattan Eye, Ear and Throat Hosp.; chmn. dept. otolaryngology Met. Hosp.; chmn. dept. otolaryngology, attending staff Flower and Fifth Ave. Hosp.; prof., chmn. dept. otolaryngology N.Y. Med. Coll., 1966—. Mem. Columbus Citizens Com. Mem. Am. Otological Soc., Am. Laryngological and Rhinological and Otolgical Soc. Author: (with D. Wolf) Microscopic Anatomy of Temporal Bone, 1957, rev. edit., 1971. Contbr. articles to profl. jours. Home and office: 162 E 71st St New York City NY 10021

BELLWIN, ALEXANDER, physician; b. Russia, Oct. 17, 1922; s. Alexander and Bessie (Fine) B.; A.B., Columbia U., 1943; M.D., N.Y. U., 1945; m. Barbara Ann Rosenbloom, Nov. 1, 1964; children—Robert, Richard, Peter, Jane, Nancy, John. Intern, Kings County Hosp., N.Y.C., 1945; resident in pathology R.I. Hosp., Providence, 1948-49; resident in obstetrics Brookdale Med. Center, N.Y.C., 1949-51; resident in surgery, gynecology Mt. Sinai Hosp., N.Y.C., 1951-54; practice medicine specializing in obstetrics and gynecology, Stamford, Conn.; attending obstetrician Stamford Hosp., obstetrician in chief, 1971-77; asst. prof. obstetrics and gynecology N.Y. Med. Coll. Served to capt. M.C., USAAF. Diplomate Am. Bd. Obstetrics and Gynecology. Mem. AMA, Fairfield County, Stamford med. socs., Am. Coll. Obstetricians and Gynecologists, A.C.S. Democrat. Jewish. Office: 144 Morgan St Stamford CT 06905

BELOTE, WILLIAM MILTON, author, educator; b. Bellevue, Wash., Oct. 4, 1922; s. William Milton and Adelaide (Hine) B.; A.B., U. Wash., 1948, M.A., 1949; Ph.D., U. Calif., at Berkeley, 1953; m. Marilyn Pape, Feb. 8, 1952; 1 son, Alan Richard. Asst. prof. history Miss. State U., 1953-56; asst. prof. U.S. Naval Acad., Annapolis, Md., 1956-62, asso. prof., 1962-68, prof., 1968—. Served with USAAF, 1943-46. Mem. Am. Hist. Assn., Am. Mil. Inst., U.S. Naval Inst., AAUP, Com. History Second World War, Soc. French Hist. Studies. Christian Scientist. Contbg. author: Essays in European History in Honor of F.C. Palm, 1956; Sea Power and Naval History, 1960; co-author; Corregidor The Saga of a Fortress, 1967; Typhoon of Steel, 1970; Titans of the Seas, 1975. Home: 324 Beach Dr Annapolis MD 21403 Office: Dept History US Naval Acad Annapolis MD 21403

BELSKY-STETSENKO, IVAN, artist; b. Ukraine, Oct. 8, 1923; s. Chariton and Stepanida (Zelena) Stetsenko; student Coll. Arts, Dniepropetrovsk, Ukraine, 1941; m. Nadia Szymkiw, May 19, 1962; children—Gregory, Igor. One man shows: Belsky's Gallery, Caracas, Venezuela, pvt. galleries Can.; group shows include: Museo de Bellas Artes, Caracas and Valencia, Venezuela; represented in permanent collections including Hist. Mus. of Trujillo, Sanctuary of Isnotu, Hist. Mus. of Merida, Cathedral of Merida, State Palace of St. Cristobal, Air Force Acad. of Maracay (all Venezuela), Gallery of Am. Fathers' Sta. Maria (both Colombia), St. Joseaphat's Cathedral, St. Mary Ch. (both Toronto, Ont., Can.), St. Wladimir Ch., Windsor, Ont. Mem. Inst. Painters (dir.), Art Gallery Ont. Home and office: 22 Brule Gardens Toronto ON M6S 4J2 Canada

BELT, DAVID LEVIN, lawyer; b. Wheeling, W.Va., Jan. 13, 1944; s. David Homer and Mae Jean (Duffy) B.; B.A. magna cum laude, Yale, 1965, LL.B., 1970; m. Carolyn Emery Copeland, July 22, 1967; children—David Clifford, Amy Elizabeth. Mem. firm Jacobs, Jacobs & Grudberg, P.C., New Haven, 1970—. Trustee First United Meth. Ch. of New Haven. 1972-74; chmn. Madison (Conn.) Democratic Town Com., 1974-76. Served with Mil. Intelligence Br., U.S. Army, 1965-67. Decorated Bronze Star. Mem. Am., Conn. (exec. com. antitrust sect.), New Haven County bar assns., Conn. Trial Lawyers Assn., Assn. Trial Lawyers Am., Nat. Assn. Criminal Def. Lawyers, Phi Beta Kappa, Omicron Delta Epsilon. Congregationalist. Club: Yale of N.Y.C. Home: Chestnut Hill Rd Killingworth CT 06417 Office: 350 Orange St New Haven CT 06503

BEMIS, HAL LAWALL, engring. and bus. exec.; b. Palm Beach, Fla., Jan. 30, 1912; s. Henry E. and Elise (Lawall) B.; grad. Haverford Sch., 1931; B.S., Mass. Inst. Tech., 1935; m. Isabel Mead, June 27, 1942; children—Elise, Carolyn, Claudia. With Campbell Soup Co., 1935-53, mgr., asst. to pres., v.p., dir. Campbell Soup Co., Ltd., 1946-53; organizer, pres. Mariner Corp., 1954—; v.p. Hosp. Food Mgmt., Inc., 1954-57; sec., treas. Belle Key Corp., 1955—; pres. Jennings Machine Corp., 1957—; v.p. Coral Motel Corp., 1963—; cons. Coopers & Lybrand, 1973—; dir. Publicker Industries, Phila. Reins. Corp. Past pres. Commn. Twp. of Lower Merion; dir. Phila. Port Corp., West Phila. Corp., Phila. Indsl. Devel. Corp. Bd. dirs., vice chmn. Spring Garden Coll.; past trustee Haverford Sch.; chmn. bd. dirs. Am. Cancer Soc.; bd. dirs. Del. Valley area Nat. Council on Alcoholism, Am. Diabetes Assn., Mass. Inst. Tech. Devel. Fund; mem. advisory bd. Salvation Army; exec. bd. Com. of 70; trustee United Fund, Young Men's Inst.; pres., trustee Greater Phila. Found.; corp. bd. Garrett-Williamson Found., Goodwill Industries. Served from 1st lt. to lt. col., U.S. Army, 1942-45. Decorated Legion of Merit with oak leaf cluster, Bronze Star Medal (U.S.); Croix de Guerre (France). Mem. C. of C. Greater Phila. (past chmn., pres.), S.R., S.A.R., Pa. Soc., Newcomen Soc., Am. Legion (post comdr.), Tau Beta Pi, Delta Psi. Clubs: Union League (pres.), Racquet, St. Anthony Phila.); St. Anthony (N.Y.C.); Merion Cricket (dir.) Merion Golf, Pine Valley Golf, Bachelor's Barge, IV Street, Rittenhouse, Sunday Breakfast, Right Angle, Penn, Toronto Golf, Royal Canadian Yacht, Mil. Order World Wars, Mil. Order Fgn. Wars of U.S., Brit. Officers. Home: 256 W Montgomery Ave Haverford PA 19041 Office: 355 W Lancaster Ave Haverford PA 19041

BENANDER, LAURENCE EDWIN, civil engr.; b. Richland, Kans., Sept. 7, 1941; s. Edwin Francis and Inez Ethel (Coultis) B.; B.S. in Bus. Adminstrn., U. Kan., 1965, B.S. in Civil Engring., 1965, M.S. in Water Resources Engring., 1966; postgrad. Va. Poly. Inst., 1970-72; m. Elizabeth Jean Cook, June 28, 1969; children—Julia Cook, Mark Cook. Sr. asst. san. engr. USPHS Radiol. Health Lab., Winchester, Mass., 1966-68; planning hydrologist Va. Div. Water Resources, Richmond, 1968-73; water resources engr. Gannett, Fleming, Corddry & Carpenter, Engrs., Harrisburg, Pa., 1973—. Mem. Nat. Soc. Profl. Engrs., ASCE, Am. Geophys. Union. Club: Harrisburg Bicycle. Home: 1 Columbia Dr Camp Hill PA 17011 Office: PO Box 1963 Harrisburg PA 17105

BENARESH, EHSANOLLAH, anesthesiologist; b. Kashan, Iran, Apr. 22, 1934; s. Leon and Cecile B.; came to U.S., 1958, naturalized, 1969; B.S., Alborz Coll., Teheran, Iran, 1951; M.D., U. Teheran, 1957; m. Marcelle A. Gold, July 9, 1964; children—Lamont, Jennifer. Intern, Beth David Hosp., N.Y.C., 1958-59; resident in anesthesia Bellevue Hosp., N.Y.C., 1959-61; chief resident in anesthesia Jewish Hosp., Bklyn., 1961-62; practice medicine specializing in anesthesiology, N.Y.C., 1961-73; mem. staff Flower Fifth Ave. Hosp. N.Y. Med. Coll., Bronx Lebanon Hosp. Center, Nyack (N.Y.) Hosp.; asst. prof. anesthesia Albert Einstein Coll. Medicine, Bronx, N.Y., 1973—. Diplomate Am. Bd. Anesthesiology. Recipient AMA Continuing Med. Edn. award, 1970, 73, 76. Fellow Am. Coll. Anesthesiologists; mem. N.Y. Soc. Anesthesiologists, Am. Soc. Anesthesiology, N.Y., Rockland County (N.Y.) med. socs., Internat. Anesthesia Research Soc. Home: 11 Ethan Allen Ct Orangeburg NY 10962 Office: Nyack Hospital Nyack NY 10960

BENDA, HAROLD WILLIAM, former coll. dean; b. Brule County, S.D., Aug. 19, 1914; s. John William and Amy Linnea (Mortenson) B.; B.A., No. Iowa U., 1934; M.A., State U. Iowa, 1941; Ed.D., N.Y. U., 1956; m. Adele Guthormson, Apr. 8, 1944; 1 dau., Karen Dae (Mrs. Dennis J. Barkow). Tchr., Liberty Consol. Sch., Clemons, Iowa, 1935-38; tchr., Decorah, Iowa, 1938-39, Ft. Dodge, Iowa, 1939-42, 45-49; prof. edn. West Chester (Pa.) State Coll., 1949-53, prof., dean Sch. Edn., 1956-75; asst. dir. curriculum and instrn. N.J. Dept. Edn., Trenton, 1953-56. Served with USCG, 1942-45. Mem. Pa. State Edn. Assn. (citation), Pa. Future Tchrs. Am. (hon. life). Club: Masons. Author: (with Cressman) Public Education in America, 1966; also articles. Home: 1154 Lake Dr West Chester PA 19380

BENDER, ADAM NORMAN, physician, educator; b. N.Y.C., June 29, 1942; s. Morris B. and Sara (Spirtes) B.; A.B., Columbia, 1964, M.D., 1968; m. Estelle Darlene Pisetsky, Dec. 26, 1965; 1 dau., Melissa Amy. Intern Columbia U.-Harlem Hosp., N.Y.C., 1968-69, resident, 1969-70; resident, Columbia U.-Neurol. Inst. N.Y., 1970-73; clin. asso. med. neurology br. NIH, USPHS, Bethesda, Md., 1973-75; asst. prof. neurology Mt. Sinai Sch. Medicine, N.Y.C., 1975—, also dir. Muscular Dystrophy Assn. Neuromuscular Clinic. Mem. med. adv. bd. Myasthenia Gravis Found. N.Y. Recipient NIH career tchr.-investigator award, 1976. Diplomate Am. Bd. Psychiatry and Neurology. Mem. Am. Acad. Neurology, AMA, N.Y. Soc. Electron Microscopists, Assn. for Research in Nervous and Mental Disease, N.Y. State, New York County med. socs., Histochem. Soc., Soc. for Neuroscis., Am. Assn. Neuropathologists, N.Y. Acad. Medicine. Home: 1212 Fifth Ave New York City NY 10029 Office: Dept Neurology Mt Sinai Sch Medicine New York City NY 10029

BENDER, COLEMAN COALPORT, educator; b. Coalport, Pa., Mar. 30, 1921; s. Harry and Annie Bender; B.A., Pa. State U., 1946, M.A., 1947; Ph.D. (Univ. fellow in speech), 1955; m. Pauline Bender, Apr. 5, 1947; children—Sue Ann, David. Instr., Pa. State U., 1946-48, U. Ill., 1948-51; asst. prof. speech communication Emerson Coll., 1951-52, asso. prof., 1952-54, prof., 1955—; cons. Harvard U. Sch. Pub. Health, New Eng. Inst. Law Enforcement. Mem. Watertown (Mass.) TV Cable Commn., 1974-76. Served with USAAF, 1941-46. Named Mass. Speaker of Yr., Mass. Speech Assn., 1970. Mem. Internat. Communication Assn., Speech Assn. Am. Author: (with McCabe) Speaking Is A Practical Matter, 1968, 3d edit., 1976; (with Zachris) Speech Communication, 1976. Home: 81 Bromfield St Watertown MA 02172 Office: 148 Beacon St Boston MA 02116

BENDER, FILMORE EDMUND, educator; b. Bakersfield, Calif., Aug. 9, 1940; s. Marvin Edmund and Edna (Spitzer) B.; B.S., U. Calif. at Davis, 1961; M.S. (NDEA fellow), N.C. State U., 1965, Ph.D., 1966; m. Christine Norton, Jan. 31, 1958; children—Karl Alten, Frederick Jacob, Kurt Edmund, Tonja Alysse. Asst. prof. agrl. econs. U. Md., College Park, 1964-68, asso. prof. agrl. econs. and bus. adminstrn., 1968-73, prof. agrl. and resource econs., 1973—; mem. grad. faculty Food Sci. program Central U. Venezuela, 1974—; dir. RPL, Inc., Annapolis, Md. Research adviser Nat. Broiler Council, 1969-72; mem. faculty Center Profl. Advancement, 1975—; spl. cons. Exotech Systems, Inc., Washington. Mem. Am. Econs. Assn., Am. Agrl. Econs. Assn., Greenbelt Jaycees (pres. 1971-72, chmn. bd. 1972-73), Alpha Zeta, Phi Kappa Phi. Republican. Mem. Ref. Ch. in U.S. Author: Systems Analysis for the Food Industry, 1976. Home: 129 Rosewood Dr Greenbelt MD 20770 Office: Dept Agrl and Resource Econs Symons Hall U Md College Park MD 20742

BENDER, JOSEPH, physician; b. Phila., Dec. 28, 1927; s. Rudolph C. and Mary (Zeitchick) B.; B.A., U. Pa., 1949; M.D., McGill U., 1953; m. Maejean Swartzman, June 27, 1954; children—Alison Ann, Laura Ellen, Robin Leigh, Rodd William. Rotating intern Pa. Hosp., Phila., 1953-54; resident internal medicine Bryn Mawr (Pa.) Hosp., 1954-55, chief med. resident, 1955-57; Nat. Cancer Inst. fellow Hosp. U. Pa., Phila., 1957-58; practice medicine, specializing in internal medicine, Norristown, Pa., 1959—; physician Pa. R.R. Co., Phila., 1958-62; dir. med. and diabetic clinics Norristown State Hosp., 1962—; chief medicine Sacred Heart Hosp., Norristown, 1977—. Bd. govs. SE Pa. chpt. Am. Heart Assn., 1974—. Served with Ordnance dept. U.S. Army, 1946-48. Fellow Am. Coll. Gastroenterology; mem. Montgomery County Med. Soc. (dir. 1975—), AMA, Pa. Med. Assn., A.C.P., Am. Soc. Internal Medicine, Phi Beta Kappa, Alpha Omega Alpha. Republican. Jewish. Club: Phila. Aviation Country. Home: 1993 Virginia Ln Norristown PA 19401 Office: 1544 DeKalb St Norristown PA 19401

BENDERLY, ROSE H., counselor; b. N.Y.C., Aug. 8, 1912; d. Nathan and Dora (Steinberg) Hochman; B.A. cum laude, Hunter Coll., 1933; M.A., Tchrs. Coll. Columbia U., 1960, Ed.D., 1977; m. Nadav A. Benderly, July 29, 1936 (dec. Sept. 1977); 1 son, Jordan. Asst. to exec. sec. N.Y.C. cancer com. Am. Cancer Soc., 1933-40; developer parent edn. program, leader discussion groups PTA, Mt. Vernon, N.Y., 1948-53; elementary sch. tchr. Port Chester (N.Y.) Pub. Schs., 1953-61, jr. high sch. counselor, coordinator guidance, 1961-68, counselor, cons. in early childhood, 1968-77; cons. day care centers, 1978—; pvt. practice counseling, cons. early childhood devel., learning and emotional problems, family relationships, Hartsdale and New Rochelle, N.Y., 1977—; guest lectr. at various colls., 1948—, including Tchrs. Coll. Columbia U., Bank St. Coll.; leader parent discussion groups, 1948—. Mem. PTA N.Y. State (life), Am., N.Y. State, Westchester, Putnam, Rockland personnel and guidance assns., N.Y. Assn. Learning Disabled, Assn. Mentally Ill Children Westchester, Am. Sch. Counselor Assn., Assn. Counselor Edn. and Supervision, N.Y. State Assn. Humanistic Edn. and Devel., Phi Beta Kappa. Editor: (with M. Huberman, others) Guidance in the Elementary Schools: A Collection of Readings, 1970; author pamphlets in field. Home and Office: 177 E Hartsdale Ave Hartsdale NY 10530

BENDETSEN, KARL ROBIN, lawyer, forest products mfr.; b. Aberdeen, Wash., Oct. 11, 1907; s. Albert M. and Anna (Bentson) B.; A.B., Stanford, 1929, J.S.D., 1932; m. Billie McIntosh, Sept. 8, 1938; 1 son, Brookes McIntosh; m. 2d, Maxine Bosworth, Sept. 19, 1947; 1 dau., Anna Martha; m. 3d, Gladys Ponton de Arce Johnston, Aug. 19, 1972. Admitted to Calif., Oreg., Wash., Ohio, N.Y., D.C. bars; in law practice, Aberdeen, 1932-40; mgmt. counsel, 1946-47; spl. cons. to Sec. Def., 1948; asst. sec. Army, 1948-52, undersec. Army, 1952; chmn. bd. Panama Canal Co., 1950-54; dir. gen. U.S. Railroads, 1950-52; with Champion Internat., Inc. (formerly U.S. Plywood-Champion Papers Inc.), Stamford Conn., 1952-54, Tex. div. mgr., 1954-55, v.p., gen. mgr. Tex. div. Pasadena, Tex., 1955-57, v.p., gen. mgr. pulp and paper mfg., 1958-59, exec. v.p. ops. group, 1959-60, pres., 1960-72, chmn. bd., 1965—, also chief exec. officer, 1967-73, also chmn. exec. com., 1973-75, dir.; dir. Westinghouse Electric Corp. Mem. Nat. Indsl. Conf. Bd.; mem. governing bd. N.Y. Stock Exchange. Spl. asst. to Sec. Def. for German Affairs, also for Philippines, 1956; spl. U.S. rep. to W. Ger. and Philippines with rank ambassador, 1956; chmn. adv. com. on gen. mil. instrn. Office Sec. Def., 1962; vice chmn. Def. Manpower Commn., 1974-76; mem. council U. Chgo. Grad. Sch. Bus.; bd. visitors Stanford U. Law Sch.; overseer Hoover Instn., Stanford U. Served in active mil. service, 1940-46; as col. Gen. Staff Corps. U.S. Army, 1940-46. Decorated D.S.M. with oak leaf cluster, Silver Star, Legion of Merit with 2 oak leaf clusters, Bronze Star with 2 oak leaf clustgrs and V device, Medal of Freedom, Disting. Civilian Service award (U.S.), Croix de Guerre with palm, officer Legion of Honor (France), Order Brit. Empire (Eng.); knight comdr. Order St. John Jerusalem, Knights Malta. Mem. Theta Delta Chi. Episcopalian (vestryman 1968-74). Clubs: Pacific Union, San Francisco, Bohemian (San Francisco); Wash. Athletic (Seattle); Tejas, Bayou, Houston Country, Petroleum, (Houston); Commonwealth (Cin.), Metropolitan (N.Y.C.); Chicago; Brook, Links (N.Y.C.); Washington F St., Georgetown (Washington); Everglades, Bath and Tennis (Palm Beach). Home: 2918 Garfield Terr NW Washington DC 20008 Office: Suite 990 N 1800 M St NW Washington DC 20036

BENDZ, DIANA JEAN, chemist, devel. engr.; b. Newark, Jan. 21, 1946; d. Arthur Peterson and Martha Clarisa (Vroom) Knight; B.S. in Forestry, State U. of N.Y., 1968; B.S. in Chemistry, Syracuse U., 1978; m. Gerald Andrei Bendz, Oct. 10, 1970; children—Daniel Andrei, Christopher Paul. Jr. engr. IBM, Endicott, N.Y., 1968-70, asso. engr., E. Fishkill, N.Y., 1970-72, sr. asso. engr., 1972-75, project engr., Endicott, 1975-78, devel. engr., 1978—. Recipient various invention awards, IBM. Mem. Am. Chem. Soc., IEEE. Roman Catholic. Patentee in field. Home: RD 2 Box 79A Vestal NY 13850 Office: U90 032-3 IBM North St Endicott NY 13760

BENEDICK, DALE RAYMOND, electronic engr.; b. York County, Pa., Oct. 11, 1941; s. Raymond Albert and Mae Leader (Gingerich) B.; A.Sci., York Coll. Pa., 1961; B.S., Pa. State U., 1963; postgrad. U. Conn., 1967-69, U. Md., 1970-72; m. Sandra Mae Henry, July 15, 1962; 1 dau., Carol Ann. Elec. engr. U.S. Navy, Mechanicsburg, Pa., 1963-65; sr. elec. engr. Pratt & Whitney Aircraft, E. Hartford, Conn., 1965-69; sr. engr. Fairchild Hiller Corp., Germantown, Md., 1969-70; sr. mem. tech. staff Computer Sci. Corp., Falls Church, Va., 1970-73; staff engr. Ensco Inc., Springfield, Va., 1973-74; sr. project engr. Indsl. Solid State Controls, Inc., York, Pa., 1974—; cons. in field. Mem. IEEE, Nat. Soc. Profl. Engrs., Instrument Soc. Am. Republican. Contbr. articles in field to profl. jours. Home: 559 Norman Rd York PA 17402 Office: 435 W Philadelphia St York PA 17405

BENEDICT, DEAN EDWIN, clergyman; b. Batavia, N.Y., Nov. 21, 1937; s. Donald Charles and Gertrude Valentine (Hutton) B.; B.S. in Edn., Salem State Coll., 1964; S.T.B., S.T.M., Boston U., 1967; m. Jean Mabel Learned, June 21, 1958; children—Rebecca Lynn, David Charles. Ordained to ministry, Methodist Ch., 1967; asst. minister Maple St. Meth. Ch., Lynn, Mass., 1959-61; pastor South St Meth. Ch., Lynn, 1961-64; asso. pastor Centre Ch., Malden, Mass., 1964-67; pastor Quincy Centre Meth. Ch., Quincy, Mass., 1967-70; sr. pastor Crawford Meml. United Meth. Ch., Winchester, Mass., 1970-74, 1st United Meth. Ch., Hudson, Mass., 1974—. Chaplain, Quincy Hosp., 1968-70; staff cons. for religious activities New Eng. Rehab. Center, Woburn, Mass., 1972—. Mem. Malden (Mass.) Model Cities Planning Com., 1965-67; comptroller So. New Eng., United Meth. Conf. Bd. Evangelism, 1969—. Mason (32 deg., K.T., Shriner). Clubs: Friars, Itinerants (Boston). Home: 16 Richardson Rd Hudson MA 01749 Office: Felton and Pleasant Sts Hudson MA 01749

BENEDICT, JOSEPH HAROLD, JR., univ. adminstr.; b. Albany, N.Y., Aug. 13, 1941; s. Joseph Harold and Frances Ellen (Long) B.; B.S., State U. N.Y. Brockport, 1965; M.S., State U. N.Y., Albany, 1966; m. Elizabeth Ann Roberts, July 8, 1967; children—Brian Arthur, Timothy Joseph. Asst. dir. student activities State U. N.Y. at Farmingdale, 1967-72; coordinator student activities Rockland Community Coll., Suffern, N.Y., 1966-67; dir. student activities C.W. Post Center L.I. U., Greenvale, N.Y., 1972—. Mgmt. coordinator Region III, Assn. Coll. Unions, 1977—. Served with U.S. Army, 1959-60. Mem. Assn. Coll. Unions-Internat., L.I. Personnel and Guidance Assn. Roman Catholic. Home, office: C W Post Center Greenville NY 11548

BENEDICT, LINDA SHERK, ins. co. exec.; b. Hartford, Conn., Jan 25, 1945; d. Robert William and Marjorie Joan (Drysdale) S.; A.B. magna cum laude, Harvard, 1967; m. Geoffrey C. Benedict, Sept. 13, 1969. Sr. mktg. research analyst Polaroid Corp., Cambridge, Mass., 1967-70; mgr. mktg. research Transaction Tech., Cambridge, 1970-72; mgr. mktg. research and new products Ocean Spray Cranberries, Hanson, Mass., 1972-76; dir. corporate mktg. Conn. Gen. Life Ins. Co., Hartford, 1976—; cons. in field. Cons., Bloomfield Community Awareness Task Force, 1977. NSF grantee, 1966-67. Mem. Am. Mktg. Assn., Soc. Advancement Mgmt., Bloomfield (pres. 1977-79), Greater Hartford (dir. 1977-79) chambers commerce. Office: Cottage Grove Rd Hartford CT 06152

BENEDICT, LLOYD HARVEY, ins. broker; b. Centralia, Wash., Jan. 7, 1919; s. John Merrill and May (Sloan) B.; A.B., Whitman Coll., 1941; m. Murrell Van Zandt, Mar. 20, 1956; children—Francis, Lloyd, William, Melisa. Mgr., Am. Fgn. Ins. Assn., Sao Paulo, Brazil, 1947-53, country mgr., Bogota, Colombia, 1953-58; with Johnson & Higgins, N.Y.C. and Milan, Italy, 1959—, partner, v.p., N.Y.C., 1972—. Served with USNR, 1941-46; PTO. Mem. Phi Delta Theta, Delta Sigma Rho. Club: India House (N.Y.C.). Home: 126 Lowell Rd Glen Rock NJ 07452 Office: 95 Wall St New York City NY 10005

BENEDICT, ROBERT CLYDE, govt. ofcl.; b. Bethel, Vt., Nov. 29, 1940; s. Leslie Roy and Marjory (Haseltine) B.; B.S., Eastern Mich. U., Ypsilanti, 1965; M.P.A., U. Mich., 1969; certificate U. Mich.-Wayne State U. Inst. Gerontology, Ann Arbor, 1969; m. Joanne Marie Cleland, Jan. 22, 1966; children—Amy Marie, David Matthew. Intern, Mich. State Legislature, 1960, Peace Corps, Washington, 1963, Pa. Dept. Pub. Welfare, 1970; organizer, dir. Campus Service Corps, Eastern Mich. U., 1963-65; staff asso. for human services Mich. Human Resources Council, Exec. Office of Gov., Lansing, 1965-67; dir. Low Income Family Planning Program, Ann Arbor, 1968-69; staff asso. faculty mem., dir. short term tng., dir. Residential Inst. on Aging Program, U. Mich.-Wayne State U. Inst. Gerontology, 1969-72, also cons.; dir. Bur. for Aging, commr. Office for Aging, Pa. Dept. Pub. Welfare, Harrisburg, 1972-78; commr. on aging Office Human Devel. Services, HEW, Washington, 1978—; cons. Center on Aging, Duke U., Internat. Center on Social Gerontology, Nat. Center on the Black Aging, Macy Found., Nat. Council on Aging. Mem. certification bd. Homes for Aged, United Ministries of Methodist Ch., 1971-73. Mem. Am. Soc. for Pub. Adminstrn., Am. Acad. Polit. and Social Sci., Gerontology Soc. (co-chmn. elect pub. info. com.), Nat. Assn. State Units on Aging. Office: 330 Independence Ave SW Room 4760 HEW Washington DC 20201*

BENEDIKT, LUCIE, social worker, health planner; b. Vienna, Austria; d. Benjamin and Stephanie (Politzer) Benedikt; B.A., Hunter Coll., 1948; M.S. in Social Work, Columbia, 1950, M.S. in Adminstrv. Medicine, 1969; postgrad. N.Y. U., 1969—. Caseworker social service dept. Columbia-Presbyn. Med. Center, N.Y.C., 1949-52, Beth Israel

Hosp., Boston, 1952-55; sr. social worker social service dept. Maimonides Hosp., Bklyn., 1955-59; sr. social worker dept. home care, faculty Home Care Tng. Inst. Montefiore Hosp. and Med. Center, Bronx, 1959-63; asst. supr. social service dept. Maimonides Med. Center, Bklyn., 1963-67; program rep. N.Y. Met. Regional Med. Program, N.Y.C., 1969-70; social service exec. Barnert Meml. Hosp. Center, Paterson, N.J., 1971-76; pub. health social worker N.Y. State Dept. Health, 1977—. Vol., Internat. Center in N.Y. Fellow Am. Pub. Health Assn.; mem. Nat. Assn. Social Workers, Acad. Certified Social Workers, Pub. Health Assn. N.Y.C., Soc. Hosp. Social Work Dirs., Royal Soc. Health, N.Y. Alumni Internat. House, Sierra Club. Club: Appalachian Mountain. Contbr. articles to profl. jours. Home: 58 W 8th St New York City NY 10011

BENENSON, EDWARD HARTLEY, realty co. exec.; b. N.Y.C., Mar. 27, 1914; s. Robert C. and Nettie (Rachstein) B.; B.A., Duke U.; m. 2d, Gladys Steinberg, Apr. 5, 1962; 1 dau., Lisa; children by previous marriage—Thomas Hartley, James Stuart, Amy Roberta. Pres., Benenson Mgmt. Co., Inc., Benenson & Co., Benenson Funding Corp., Yale Motor Inn. Conn., Conn. Equities Corp., Benenson Investment Corp., Greenwich Devel. Corp., Sedgefield Realty N.C., Thomas James Corp., Arbee Properties of Fla., Edward Stephen of Tampa, Inc. Chmn. Urban Redevel. Commn., 1957-58; mem. Mayor's Youth Adv. Group, N.Y.C., 1956-58; trustee Albert Einstein Coll. Medicine, Bronx Lebanon Hosp., Duke Med. Center, Hampton Med. Center; trustee Fedn. Jewish Philanthropics N.Y., mem. exec. com., 1960-66; trustee Synagogue Council; pres. YM-YWHA of Bronx, 1958-63, now dir.; chmn. Friends Duke Museum Art. Served to 2d lt., 77th Inf. Div., AUS, 1939-43. Decorated officier Ordre du Merite Agricole (France); recipient gold medal Renaissance Francaise, Bronze medal City of Paris. Mem. Real Estate Bd. N.Y., Confrerie des Chevaliers du Tastevin (chmn. N.Y. commanderie, Grand Camerlingue), Culinary Inst. Am. (dir.), Les Amis d'Escoffier Soc., Grand Jury Assn., Commerce and Industry Assn. N.Y., Nat. Bd. Realtors, Internat. Real Estate Fedn. (charter), Order of Lafayette, Croix de Guerre Assn., Profl. Engrs., Soc. France, Fedn. War Vets (France), Chaine des Rotisseurs-Bailli Delegue des U.S.A. (council of honor), Am. Soc. Italian Legions Merit (Cavalier), Les Chevaliers de la Croix de Lorraine (Resistance), Commanderie de Bordeaux, du Bailliage N. Am., Res. Officers Assn. Conseil de la Croix du Combattant de l'Europe. Jewish religion. Clubs: Century Country, Harmonie (bd. govs.), Presidents, Paris Am., Wine and Food; Raffles; Noyac Country. Home: 510 Park Ave New York City NY 10022 also Georgica Rd East Hampton NY 11937 Office: 445 Park Ave New York City NY 10022

BENENSON, ESTHER SIEV (MRS. WILLIAM BENENSON), nursing home adminstr.; b. Jerusalem, Aug. 16, 1925 (parents Am. citizens); d. Joshua and Anna (Sanders) Siev; A.A.S., Queens Coll., 1957; B.S., Hunter Coll., 1972, M.S., 1974; Ed.M., Tchrs. Coll., Columbia, 1976; m. William Benenson, Sept. 15, 1957; children—Michael J., Sharon G., Amy L., Blanche S. Exec. dir. Flushing (N.Y.) Manor Nursing Home, 1959—, Flushing Manor Care Center, 1974—. Registered nurse; licensed X-ray technician; adj. asso. prof. C.W. Post Coll., also mem. advisory bd., dept. health care and pub. adminstrn.; mem. Bd. Examiners Licensing Nursing Home Adminstrs. N.Y. State, 1970-74; adv. council N.Y. State Health Planning Commn. Fellow Am. Coll. Nursing Home Adminstrs., Am. Acad. Med. Adminstrs., Royal Soc. Health; mem. Soc. Pub. Health Educators, Gerontol. Soc., Bus. and Profl. Women's Club Greater Flushing, Med. Soc. County Queens Women's Aux., Med. Soc. State N.Y. Women's Aux., Am. Pub. Health Assn., Am. Geriatrics Soc. Home: 36-21 Parsons Blvd Flushing NY 11354 Office: 35-15 Parsons Blvd Flushing NY 11354

BENEVENTANO, THOMAS CARMINE, radiologist; b. Maspeth, N.Y., Mar. 20, 1932; s. Joseph Anthony and Mildred Carmela (Citera) B.; A.B., N.Y. U., 1953; M.D., State U. N.Y., 1957; m. Marilyn Louise Rarrick, June 15, 1957; 1 son, Thomas Martin. Intern, Kings County Hosp., Bklyn., 1957-58, resident in radiology, 1960-63; radiologist Montefiore Hosp. and Med. Center, Bronx, 1963—; prof. radiology Albert Einstein Coll. Medicine, Bronx, 1978—. Served to capt. M.C., U.S. Army, 1958-60. Diplomate Am. Bd. Radiology. Fellow Am. Coll. Radiology, N.Y. Acad. Gastroenterology, N.Y. Acad. Medicine; mem. Radiol. Soc. N.Am., N.Y. Roentgen Soc., AMA, N.Y., Bronx County med. socs., Soc. Gastrointestinal Radiologists, Assn. Univ. Radiologists. Co-author: Radiologic Examination of the Orohypopharynx and Esophagus, 1977. Address: 6 Eastwind Rd Yonkers NY 10710

BENEVENTI, FRANCIS ANTHONY, urol. surgeon; b. Chgo., Oct. 13, 1906; s. Dr. Vito and Lucia (Mangieri) B.; student U. Ill., 1923-26, Marquette U., 1926-28; M.D., L.I. Coll. Hosp., 1930; m. Mary Elizabeth Lockwood, Apr. 30, 1938; children—Lucinda Beneventi Findley, Arthur. Intern St. Francis Hosp., Evanston, Ill., 1930-31, Fifth Ave. Hosp., N.Y.C., 1931-32, Passavant Hosp., Chgo., 1932-33; pvt. practice, N.Y.C., 1934—; asst. attending urology S.B. Brady Found., N.Y. Hosp., 1936-72; dept. chmn., chief of urology French-Polyclinic Med. Sch. and Health Center, 1958-77; clin. affiliate N.Y. Hosp. Cornell Med. Center, 1977; cons. urologist St. Clares Hosp., Mercy Hosp., USPHS, S.I. Served as lt. USNR, 1942-46. Recipient grants Squibb Co., Pfizer Co. Diplomate Am. Bd. Urology. Fellow A.C.S., Internat. Coll. Surgeons (past pres. sect. urology), N.Y. Acad. Sci., N.Y. Acad. Medicine, Am. Urol. Assn. (pres. N.Y. sect. 1965-66; chmn. prize essay com. 1964-70); mem. Internat. Coll. Surgeons (pres. GU sect. 1954), Internat. Soc. Urologie, AMA, Am. Med. Art Assn., Soc. Am. Med. Writers, Soc. N.Y. Hosp., Am. Geriatric Soc. Clubs: Garden City Golf, University. Author: Retropublic Prostatecomy, 1954; also sci. articles in surg. jours. Deviser several surg. operations and instruments. Home: 126 Stratford Ave Garden City NY 11530 Office: 65 E 76th St New York City NY 10021

BENI, GERARDO, physicist; b. Florence, Italy, Feb. 21, 1946; s. Edoardo and Assunta (Bazzanti) B.; came to U.S., 1970, naturalized, 1976; Laurea, U. Florence, 1965-70; Ph.D., U. Calif., Los Angeles, 1974; m. Ruth Ellen Cook, Jan. 4, 1971. Research asso. Bell Telephone Labs., Murrary Hill, N.J., 1974-76, mem. tech. staff, 1976—. IBM fellow, 1973-74. Mem. Am. Phys. Soc. Home: 306 Harrison Ave Westfield NJ 07090 Office: 600 Mountain Ave Murrary Hill NJ 07974 also Holmdel NJ 07733

BENJAMIN, CHESTER RAY, govt. research adminstr.; b. Alliance, Ohio, Jan. 23, 1923; s. Isaac Marshall and Eva Verlin (Skaggs) B.; B.S., Mt. Union Coll., 1948; M.S., State U. Iowa, 1954, Ph.D., 1955; m. Margaret Elliott Hart, June 8, 1947; 1 dau., Karen. Research mycologist U.S. Dept. Agr., Peoria, Ill., 1955-60, leader mycology investigations, Beltsville, Md., 1960-71, asst. dir. internat. programs div. Agrl. Research Service, Hyattsville, Md., 1975-78, asst. dir. internat. programs staff Sci. and Edn. Adminstrn., 1978—; dep. dir. agrl. directorate Bur. Internat. Orgn. Affairs U.S. Dept. State, Washington, 1971-74. Chmn. U.S. toxic microorganisms panel U.S.-Japan Cooperation in Natural Resources, 1964-69; sec. U.S. nat. com. Internat. Union Biol. Scis., 1969-71; mem. numerous U.S. dels. to meetings FAO. Mem. adult edn. com. YMCA, Peoria, 1958-59; sec.-treas. bd. trustees Am. Type Culture Collection, Rockville, Md., 1968-71, vice chmn. bd., 1972, exec. com., 1968-74. Served with USNR, 1943-45. Recipient Citation, Plaque Japanese Govt. Toxic Microorganisms Panel, 1969. Fellow AAAS, (mem. Council) mem. Smithsonian Inst. (hon. curator, hon. research asso. 1961-68), NRC, Mycol. Soc. Am. (pres. 1966-67), Internat. Nomenciature Com. for Fungi, Lichens, Botan. Soc. Am., Sigma Xi. Contbg. author: Ency. Americana, 1973. Editorial adv. bd. Abstracts of Mycology, 1966—. Contbr. articles on fungi to profl. jours. Inventor in field. Home: 315 Timberwood Ave Silver Spring MD 20901 Office: Internat Programs Staff Sci and Edn Adminstrn US Dept Agr Fed Bldg Hyattsville MD 20782

BENJAMIN, GILBERT LEON, counselor; b. Bklyn., Dec. 28, 1936; s. Carl and Esther B.; B.A., Bklyn. Coll., 1958; M.S., Grad. Sch. Bus. Columbia U., 1960, postgrad. Tchrs. Coll., 1960-62; 6th year certificate advanced study N.Y. U. Grad. Sch. Edn., 1969; m. Joan Warshaw, Apr. 15, 1962; children—Marc, Daniel. Employment interviewer, vocat. counselor Hotel Placement Office and Youth Placement Service, N.Y. State Dept. Labor, N.Y.C., 1960-63; sr. counselor B'nai B'rith Career Counseling Service, N.Y.C., 1963-68; asst. prof., counselor, office student services, coordinator evening session counseling services Coll. S.I., 1968—. Vice pres. Tiny Tots Transit Corp., Englishtown, N.J., Pied Piper Playhouse Nursery Sch., Englishtown; exec. sec. bd. trustees N.J. Jewish Marriage Experience, 1978—. Certified in student personnel services, N.J. Mem. Am., N.Y., N.J., N.Y.C. personnel and guidance assns., Adult Student Personnel Assn., Nat. Vocat. Guidance Assn. (profl.), Am. Coll. Personnel Assn., N.J. Psychol. Assn., N.J. Vocat. Guidance Assn., Nat. Council Student Devel., Student Personnel Assn. N.Y. State, N.J. Assn. Profl. Psychologists (asso.), Middle Atlantic Career Counseling Assn., Kappa Delta Pi. Jewish. Club: B'nai B'rith. Home: 7 McCue Rd Morganville NJ 07751 Office: 715 Ocean Terr Staten Island NY 10301

BENJAMIN, JEFFREY LLOYD, plastic surgeon; b. Bklyn., June 28, 1941; s. Shepherd M. and Rose S. Benjamjn; A.B. cum laude, Princeton U., 1963; M.D., N.Y. U., 1967; children—Scott Adam, Lisa Joelle. Intern, N.Y. U. Med. Center and Bellevue Hosp., N.Y.C., 1967-68, resident in surgery, 1968-69, 71-74; resident in plastic surgery Inst. Reconstructive Plastic Surgery, N.Y.C., 1974-76; head transplantation surgery br. Naval Med. Research Inst., Bethesda, Md., 1969-71; practice medicine specializing in plastic surgery, Stamford, Conn., 1976—. Served as lt. comdr. M.C., USNR, 1969-71. Diplomate Am. Bd. Surgery. Mem. Transplantation Soc., Assn. Academic Surgery, A.C.S., Am., N.Y. Regional, New Eng. socs. plastic and reconstructive surgery, Conn. Soc. Am. Bd. Surgeons, Conn., Fairfield County, Stamford med. socs. Club: Princeton of New Canaan. Contbr. articles in field to profl. jours. Office: 47 Oak St Stamford CT 06905

BENJAMIN, SIDNEY HERBERT, ret. newspaper editor; b. Hazleton, Pa., Nov. 12, 1911; s. Jacob Louis and Mayme (Singer) B.; B.A. (Sigma Delta Chi scholar), Pa. State U., 1933; m. Eva Maude Fleshman, Oct. 7, 1944; children—Ronald Lee, Barbara Belle Benjamin Burger. Sports editor Hazleton Plain Speaker, 1934-54; with Scranton (Pa.) Times, 1954—, fed. ct. reporter, 1958-71, columnist, show bus., 1955—, editor Sunday mag., Sunday Times, Scranton, 1971-77; lectr. journalism U. Scranton, 1974—. Served with AUS, 1942-45. Mem. Newspaper Guild, Pa. State U. Alumni Assn. (pres. Lackawanna County). Democrat. Jewish. Clubs: Masons, Lions (pres., Distinguished Service award 1970, 72). Home: 341 W Main St Dalton PA 18414

BENJAMIN, THEODORE SIMON, pub. and mktg. exec.; b. Jacksonville, Fla., Feb. 3, 1926; s. Roy A. and Phyllis M. (Meyer) B.; B.A. with high honors, U. Fla., 1948; m. Edith Lipner, Sept. 7, 1949; children—Phyllis A., Jill; m. 2d, Barbara Joyce Bloch, Sept. 20, 1964; adopted children—Elizabeth J. Sanders, Ellen J. Benjamin. Mgr. Leitman Assos., Geneva, Switzerland, 1948-49; head western office Tire Mart, N.Y.C., Los Angeles, 1949-53; exec. v.p. Benjamin Co., Inc., N.Y.C., 1953—. Freelance cons. promotional, marketing and pub. activities. Mem. White Plains (N.Y.) Dem. Com., 1958-70, Westchester County Dem. Com., 1964-68. Served with inf. AUS, 1944-46; ETO. Decorated Bronze Star. Mem. Nat. Premium Sales Execs., Assn. Am. Publishers, Direct Mail Mktg. Assn., Hundred Million Club, Premium Mktg. Assn. Am., Phi Beta Kappa, Pi Lambda Phi, Phi Kappa Phi, Phi Eta Sigma. Home: 21 Dupont Ave White Plains NY 10605 Office: 485 Madison Ave New York City NY 10022

BENJAMINSON, MORRIS AARON, microbiologist; b. N.Y.C., Aug. 6, 1930; s. Abraham Jacob and Anna (Schwartz) B.; B.S., L.I. U., 1951; M.S., N.Y. U., 1961, Ph.D., 1967; m. Barbara Jane Brodmerkel, July 4, 1958; children—Brina Michal, Ari Jonathan. Sr. biol. technician Sloan Kettering Inst., N.Y.C., 1954-55; med. technician VA Hosp., N.Y.C., 1956-59; research asst. Margaret M. Caspary Inst. for Vet. Research, N.Y.C., 1959-61; research asso. Bronx-Lebanon Hosp. Center, Bronx, 1961-64; sr. task leader, microbiologist Naval Applied Sci. Lab., Bklyn., 1964-69; asst. prof. microbiology N.Y. U., 1969-75; asso. prof., coordinator med. tech. City U. N.Y., 1964-75; supervisory bacteriologist Bendiner & Schlessinger, N.Y.C., 1976-77; exec. v.p., dir. research and devel. BioDor Chem. Products, Inc., Bridgeport, Conn., 1978—; dir. North Star Research, N.Y.C., 1975—; research asso. in microbiology N.Y. Ocean Sci. Lab., Montauk, N.Y., 1979; vis. research scientist Inst. for Dental Research, N.Y. U. Dental Center, 1978; asso. prof. public health Coll. Pharmacy, L.I. U., Bklyn., 1979; adviser in aerobiology Dept. Air Resources of City of N.Y. Mem. York Coll. Senate, 1975-76. Served with U.S. Army, 1952-54; Korea. Certified in pathogenic bacteriology and virology Nat. Registry of Microbiologists, Am. Acad. Microbiology; licensed clin. lab. supr. Health Services Adminstrn. of City of N.Y. Dept. Health. Mem. AAAS, Am. Soc. for Microbiology, Am. Inst. Biol. Scis., Am. Assn. Textile Chemists and Colorists, N.Y. Acad. Scis., Sigma Xi. Jewish. Contbr. articles in field to profl. jours. Home: 342 E 55th St New York NY 10022 Office: NSR 170 Broadway Suite 201 New York NY 10038 also BioDor Chem Products Ltd. Bridgeport CT 06605

BENKENDORF, MARY BELL, rehab. counselor; b. Phila., Apr. 7, 1953; d. Clarence Deshong and Mary (James) Bell; B.A. in Psychology, Washington Coll., Chestertown, Md., 1974; M.Ed. in Rehab. Counseling, Pa. State U., 1975; m. Donald W. Benkendorf, May 1, 1976. Vocat. counselor adminstrv. service Community Mental Health Center, Crozer-Chester Med. Center, Upland, Pa., 1976-77, vocat. counselor transitional living service, 1977—. Certified rehab. counselor. Mem. Am. Personnel and Guidance Assn., Am. Rehab. Counseling Assn., Nat. Vocat Guidance Assn., Am. Mental Health Counselors Assn., Aston (Pa.) Town Watch. Republican. Roman Catholic. Address: 2206 Lee Ln Aston PA 19014

BENN, MICHAEL ANDREW, urban planner; b. New Amsterdam, Guyana, Sept. 28, 1943; s. Andrew Adolphus and Aileen DeTracy (Alleyne) B.; B.S., Ohio State U., 1966; M.A., M.C.P., U. Cin., 1970; m. Cynthia Insolio, Aug. 13, 1977. Came to U.S., 1962, naturalized, 1971. Project dir. Lucas & Edwards, N.Y.C., 1970-72; planning officer Harvard, 1972-76; with facilities planning and engring. dept. Digital Equipment Corp., Maynard, Mass., 1976—; guest lectr. dept. architecture Mass. Inst. Tech., Cambridge, 1976. Post leader Explorer program Cambridge council Boy Scouts Am. Recipient citation Progressive Architecture, 1972. Mem. Assn. Am. Geographers, Am. Soc. Planning Ofcls. Works include Manhattanville Health Park (N.Y.C.). Home: 80 Strathmore Rd Apt 6 Boston MA 02146 Office: Digital Equipment Corp Maynard MA 01754

BENNER, B. K. BUCK, govt. ofcl.; b. Muscatine, Iowa, Aug. 2, 1922; s. Lauren Franklin and Ocean Lela (LaGrille) B.; student Southeastern Community Coll., 1940-41, 1946-47; grad. Nat. Law Enforcement Acad., 1949, U.S. Army CID Sch., 1951, 1955, Japanese Acad. for Sci. Study, Control and Prevention Crime, 1959, U.S. Treas. Law Enforcement Sch., 1973; m. Patricia R. Knowles, July 10, 1976. Enlisted USMC, 1942, ret., 1965; chief law enforcement and security Employment and Tng. Adminstrn., Dept. Labor, Washington, 1965—; cons. lectr. in field. Pres., Beverly Forest Citizens Assn., Springfield, Va., 1962-74. Decorated Bronze Star. Fellow Acad. Police Sci.; mem. Fed. Law Enforcement Assn., Am. Fedn. Police, N.Mex. Sheriff's Assn., Internat. Acad. Criminology, Internat. Chiefs Police Assn. Presbyterian. Clubs: Mason. Home: 7032 Beverly Ln Springfield VA 22150 Office: 601 D St NW Room 6122 Washington DC 20213

BENNER, RICHARD EDWARD, JR., cosmetic co. exec.; b. Jersey City, Dec. 7, 1932; s. Richard E. and Dorothy (Linstead) B.; B.S., Lehigh U., 1954; postgrad. N.Y. U., 1959-63; m. Virginia E. Hart, Aug. 3, 1963; children—Linda Elaine, Richard Edward III, Christopher Daniel. Data processing salesman, IBM, 1954-58; product counselor Avon Products, N.Y.C., 1959, sales planner, 1960-63, mgr. sales planning, 1963-68, v.p. mktg. research, 1968, v.p. merchandising, 1969-71, group v.p. mktg., 1971—, group v.p. mktg. Europe, 1973-75, group v.p. mktg. internat., 1975—. Vice chmn. Lehigh Centennial Fund, 1964-65; fund-raiser Boy Scouts Am., 1966; exec. committeeman United Fund Drive; dir. Tenafly Youth Services Com., 1978—. Served with inf., U.S. Army, 1955-56. Clubs: N.Y. Athletic (N.Y.C.); Beaverkill Trout (dir. 1976) (Livingston-on-Manor, N.Y.); Englewood Field. Home: 21 Edgewood St Tenafly NJ 07670 Office: 9 W 57th St New York City NY 10019

BENNET, DAVID HUGHES, physicist, former navy officer; b. Dallas, July 14, 1934; s. David H. and Francis Bennet; B.S. with highest honors in Physics, U. Tex., 1962, B.S. with highest honors in Mathematics, 1962, M.A. in Physics, 1963; M.L.A. in Physics, Johns Hopkins U., 1970; m. Betty Louise Moore, Feb. 14, 1954; children—David, Stephan, Richard, Melanie, Christopher, Cynthia. Served as enlisted man U.S. Navy, 1952-64; commd. officer, 1964, advanced through grades to lt. comdr., 1972; instr., dept. head Navy Nuclear Power Sch., Bainbridge, Md., 1968; acoustics project officer Office of Naval Research, Arlington, Va., 1969; sonar engring. div. dir. Naval Ship Systems Command, Arlington, 1972-73; ret., 1973; asst. dir. engring. NAVSHIPS, Arlington, 1974-76; dep. project mgr. MK 48 Torpedo, NAVSEA, Arlington, 1976; tech. dir. ALWT Project, 1976; pres. Dynamic Systems, Inc., Gaithersburg, Md., 1977—; cons. mgmt., corporate planning and devel. and orgn., underwater acoustics and undersea warfare. Mem. Gen. Systems Research Soc., Am. Soc. Naval Engrs., Phi Beta Kappa, Sigma Pi Sigma. Contbr. articles in area of undersea warfare, also organizational devel. Home: 12313 Pueblo Rd Gaithersburg MD 20760 Office: 1517 West Branch Dr McLean VA 22101

BENNETT, CLINTON WENDELL, accountant, mgmt. engr.; b. Bennett, Que., Can., July 29, 1894; s. Lambert L. and Emma H. (Beattie) B.; m. Ethel G. Taylor, Sept. 25, 1917. Partner firm Touche, Ross & Co., accountants and mgmt. cons., Boston, now ret.; trustee Winchester Savs. Bank. Mem. corp. Bentley Coll. C.P.A., Mass., N.H., S.C. Registered profl. engr., Mass. Mem. Mass. Soc. C.P.A.'s (past pres.), Nat. Assn. Accountants (past pres., dir.), Am. Inst. C.P.A.'s, ASME, Nat. Soc. Profl. Engrs. Democrat. Episcopalian. Author: Standard Costs—How They Serve Modern Management; also articles for bus. and tech. press; speaker bus. gatherings. Home: 10 Everell Rd Winchester MA 01890 Office: Touche Ross & Co Wellesley Office Park 20 Williams St Wellesley MA 02181

BENNETT, EDWARD HENRY, reins. exec.; b. Glens Falls, N.Y., July 22, 1917; s. Harry and Elizabeth Chandler (Clark) B.; A.B., Princeton U., 1940;m. Louise Faris, Aug. 3, 1946; children—Faris Elizabeth, Anne Louise. With Guy Carpenter & Co., Inc., N.Y.C., 1940—, v.p., 1954-76, dir., 1963-76, vice chmn., chief adminstrv. officer, 1976—; pres., dir. Am. Overseas Reins. Co., Phila.; dir. Balis & Co., Inc., Phila. Ins. Data Processing, Inc., Jenkintown, Pa., George F. Rutledge & Co., Inc., Des Moines, Reaseguradora Delta C.A., Venezuela. Served to maj. USAAF, 1942-46; lt. col. Res. Decorated Legion of Merit. Mem. Res. Officers Assn., Am. Def. Preparedness Assn., S.A.R. Republican. Episcopalian. Clubs: Wall St., Drug and Chem., Princeton (N.Y.C.), Nassau (Princeton), Hartford, Adirondack Mountain. Home: RFD 1 West Circle Bedford NY 10506 Office: 110 William St New York City NY 10038

BENNETT, EUDORA SMITH, hosp. adminstr.; b. W. Franklin, Pa., July 16, 1924; d. Merton Henry and Ruby-Estelle Grace (Allen) Smith; R.N., Robert Packer Hosp. Tng. Sch. Nurses, Sayre, Pa., 1945; m. Raymond Leslie Bennett, Dec. 21, 1946; children—Ann Marie, Donald Hasbrouck, Stanley Douglas. Gen. duty nurse Robert Packer Hosp., 1945-46, supr. pediatrics, 1947-48; pvt. duty nurse Carbondale (Pa.) Gen. Hosp., 1948-49; supr. Monmouth Meml. Hosp., Long Branch, N.J., 1950-51; adminstr. Montrose (Pa.) Med. Center, 1951—, also dir.; adminstr. Montrose Gen. Hosp.; dir. Med. Arts Nursing Center, Montrose; a founder Med. Arts Clinic, Montrose, 1952. Mem. bd. N.Y.-Pa. Health Planning Council, 1969—, chmn. Susquehanna County chpt., 1971-72; bd. dirs., mem. exec. com., mem. planning com. Statewide Health Coordinating Council of Pa., 1976—; mem. bd. Northeastern Human Parts Assn., 1971—; mem. Susquehanna County Ambulance and Emergency Services Assn., 1971—; bd. dirs., mem. exec. com. N.Y.-Pa. Health Systems Agy. Named Spirit of Nursing, Robert Packer Hosp., 1945. Mem. Am., Pa. (planning com. 1977—) hosp. assns., Health Care Facilities Assn. Pa. Republican. Presbyn. Club: Y-Gradale (Montrose). Home: 42 Maple St Montrose PA 18801 Office: 3 Grow St Montrose PA 18801

BENNETT, GORDON LOCKHART, lt. gov. P.E.I.; b. Charlottetown, P.E.I., Can., Oct. 10, 1912; s. J. Garfield and Annie (Lockhart) B.; B.Sc., Acadia U., 1937, M.Sc. in Chemistry, 1947, D.C.L., 1976; m. Doris L. Bernard, Aug. 10, 1937; 1 dau., F. Diane Bennett Campbell. Elementary, secondary and univ. tchr., 1939-66; mem. Provincial Legislature of P.E.I., 1966-74, pres. exec. council, 1966-74; minister of edn. P.E.I., 1966-72, minister of justice and atty. gen., 1970-74, provincial sec., 1970-74, lt. gov., 1974—; Can. del. UNESCO, Paris, 1972, Commonwealth Parliamentary Assn., Sri Lanka, 1974. Mem. Liberal Party. Mem. United Ch. Can. Club: Masons. Address: Government House Charlottetown PE C1A 7L9 Canada

BENNETT, HARRIET, painter; b. N.Y.C.; d. John and Henrietta (Jantzen) Bultman; student Art Students League N.Y., Bklyn. Mus., New Sch. for Social Research, Pratt Graphic Art Center. One-woman shows at Marino Gallery, N.Y.C., 1958, Condon Riley Gallery, N.Y.C., 1959, Cichi Gallery, Rome, Italy, 1962. Galerie de l'Université, Paris, France, 1962, Woodstock Gallery, London, Eng., 1965. Recipient Falmouth Artists Guild award, 1962, Internat. Women's Slide Exhbn. award, 1975-76. Mem. Long Beach Art Assn.,

Mus. Modern Art, Women's Interart Center, Artists Equity Assn. N.Y. Address: PO Box 3738 Grand Central Station New York City NY 10017

BENNETT, HENRY GARLAND, philosopher, educator; b. Stillwater, Okla., May 25, 1940; s. Phil Connell and Frances Elizabeth (Corbin) B.; student Mass. Inst. Tech., 1958-60; B.A., Okla. State U., 1962, M.A., 1964; postgrad. U. Wash., 1964-66; m. Jane Martha Allen, Oct. 19, 1974; children—Phil Connell II, Gina Michelle, Paul Corbin, Suzanne Lynn, Richard Craig. Instr. philosophy Wichita (Kans.) State U., 1966-68. Capital U., Columbus, Ohio, 1968-69; assoc. prof. philosophy Corning (N.Y.) Community Coll., 1969—; cons. manpower devel. Nat. Endowment for Humanities fellow, 1975-76. Mem. Am. Philos. Assn., Nat. Trust for Hist. Preservation, Friends of Old Sturbridge Village. Republican. Episcopalian. Home: 15 Morningside Dr Painted Post NY 14870 Office: Humanities Div Corning Community Coll Corning NY 14830

BENNETT, IVAN LOVERIDGE, JR., physician, univ. adminstr.; b. Washington, Mar. 4, 1922; s. Ivan Loveridge and Ruby (Jenrette) B.; A.B., Emory U., 1943, M.D., 1946; m. Martha Rhodes, June 24, 1944; children—Susan, Paul, Katherine, Jeffrey L. Intern, Grady Meml. Hosp., Atlanta, 1946-47, resident, 1951-52; fellow, asst. in pathology Johns Hopkins Hosp., Balt., 1949-50; asst. resident Duke Hosp., Durham, N.C., 1950-51; asst. in medicine Emory U., 1951-52; asst. prof. internal medicine Yale U., 1952-54; asso. physician Grace New Haven Hosp., 1952-54; asso. prof. medicine Johns Hopkins U., 1954-57, prof., 1957-58, Baxley prof. pathology, dir. dept., 1958-66; dep. dir., acting dir. Office Sci. and Tech., Exec. Office Pres., Washington, 1966-69, cons., 1976—; v.p. for health affairs N.Y. U., 1969-76, exec. v.p., 1976, prof. medicine, 1970—, dir. Med. Center, 1969-73, provost, 1973—, dean Sch. Medicine, 1970—; mem. energy research adv. bd. U.S. Dept. Energy, 1978—; mem. bd. human resources Nat. Acad. Scis., 1970—; trustee Med. Library Center of N.Y., 1970—; mem. health Research Council City N.Y., 1972—; mem. adv. com. on health manpower Health Planning Council N.Y., 1977—. Served to lt. USNR, 1947-49. Recipient Emory U. Med. Alumni Assn. award, 1972; Abraham Flexner award for disting. service to med. edn., 1978. Fellow A.C.P., N.Y. Acad. Scis., Am. Soc. Clin. Pathologists, Am. Acad. Arts and Scis.; mem. Am. Fedn. Clin. Research (pres. 1957-58), Assn. Am. Med. Colls. (chmn. 1976, chmn. council deans, 1974), Med. Soc. County N.Y. (pres. 1975-76, bd. censors 1971—), AMA, Am. Soc. Exptl. Pathology, Am. Soc. Clin. Investigation, Harvey Soc., Phi Beta Kappa, Alpha Omega Alpha, other assns. Clubs: Cosmos, Century. Contbr. chpts. to books, articles to profl. jours. Home: 5 The By-Way Bronxville NY 10708 Office: 550 1st Ave New York NY 10016*

BENNETT, JAMES DAVISON, lawyer, town ofcl.; b. Mineola, N.Y., Dec. 2, 1938; s. John Davison and Mildred (Schwindt) B.; B.A., Cornell U., 1960, J.S.D., 1963; m. Aug. 11, 1962; children—Fernanda, Anne, Jill. Admitted to N.Y. State bar, 1965; individual practice law, Rockville Centre, N.Y., 1963-65; partner firm Bennett, Kaye & Scholly, Rockville Centre, 1965—; councilman Town of Hempstead (N.Y.), 1966-77, supr., 1978—; lectr. in field. Exec. com. Cornell Law Sch., 1978—; v.p. L.I. Loves Bus., Inc., 1978—, also bd. dirs. Served to 1st lt. U.S. Army, 1963-65. Mem. Am., N.Y. State bar assns. Republican. Methodist. Clubs: Cherry Valley, Gardiners Bay Country. Home: 34 Hilton Ave Garden City NY 11530 Office: Bennett Kaye & Scholly 255 Merrick Rd Rockville Centre NY 11570

BENNETT, JAMES GORDON, JR., educator, business exec.; b. Scranton, Pa., Oct. 9, 1935; s. James Gordon and Mary Theresa (Collins) B.; A.A., Keystone Jr. Coll., 1959; B.S., Syracuse U., 1961, M.B.A., 1964; Ph.D., Ohio State U., 1969; m. Patricia Daly, June 30, 1961; children—James Gordon III, Rob, Susan. Prof. bus. and distributive edn. Polk Jr. Coll., Winter Haven, Fla., 1964-66; dir. coop. edn. Pan Am. Airlines, Cocoa Beach, Fla., 1966-67; research asso. Ohio State U., 1967-69; asst. prof. Rutgers U., New Brunswick, N.J., 1969-74; sr. research asso. Cornell U., 1974-76; dir. mktg. Citizens Savs. Bank, 1976-78; account exec. E.F. Hutton, 1978—; vis. prof. U. N.C., Greensboro, 1973-74, Winthrop Coll., Rock Hill, S.C., 1974-75. Mem. troop exec. com. Boy Scouts Am., Ithaca, N.Y.; mgr. Kiwanis Baseball, Ithaca. Served with USNR, 1954-56. Found. for Econ. Edn. fellow, 1964; Ohio State U. Center for Vocat.-Tech. Edn. grantee, 1967-69; Law Enforcement Adminstrn. Act grantee, 1975. Mem. Am. Vocat. Assn. (life), Phi Delta Kappa, Iota Lambda Sigma, Delta Pi Epsilon. Republican. Episcopalian. Clubs: Masons, Rotary. Author: Model Curricula for Vocational Teacher Education, 1971; The Evaluation of Instructional Materials in Occupational Education, 1975; Careers in Marketing, 1976; Individualized Vocational Education Programs for the Incarcerated, 1977. Home: 420 Hanshaw Rd Ithaca NY 14850 Office: One Marine Midland Tower Warren St Syracuse NY 13204

BENNETT, JOHN EUGENE, physician; b. El Centro, Calif., Mar. 6, 1933; s. Ray Crawford and Helene (Thomas) B.; B.S., Stanford, 1955; M.D., Johns Hopkins, 1959; m. Shirley Fern Kendrick, Aug. 30, 1958; children—Byard, Colin. Intern, Johns Hopkins, Balt., 1959-60, lectr. dept. microbiology Sch. Medicine, 1974; U. Wash., Seattle, 1960-61, Washington U., St. Louis, 1964-65; now research physician NIH, Bethesda, Md. Cons. anti-infective agents div. Food and Drugs Adminstrn., 1969—; mem. ad hoc study group on bacterial and mycotic diseases Army Dept., 1973—; cons. on mycoses Am. Pub. Health Assn., 1970, 75; prof. medicine Uniformed Services U. of Health Scis., Bethesda, 1977—. Served with USPHS, 1961-64. Diplomate Am. Bd. Internal Medicine. Fellow A.C.P.; mem. Am. Assn. Immunologists, Am. Soc. Clin. Investigation, Am. Fedn. Clin. Research, Internat. Soc. Human and Animal Mycology, Soc. Exptl. Biology of Medicine, Infectious Disease Soc. Am. (council 1978—), Am. Soc. Microbiology. Editorial bd. Antimicrobial Agents and Chemotherapy, 1972-76, Jour. Clin. Microbiology, 1976—. Contbr. to publs. in field. Home: 10913 Candlelight Ln Potomac MD 20854 Office: Room 11N210 Bldg 10 Clinical Center NIH Bethesda MD 20014

BENNETT, MARION TINSLEY, fed. judge; b. Buffalo, Mo., June 6, 1914; s. Philip Allen and Mary Bertha (Tinsley) B.; A.B., S.W. Mo. State U., 1935; J.D., Washington U., St. Louis, 1938; m. June Young, Apr. 27, 1941; children—Ann Bennett Guptill, William Philip. Admitted to Mo. bar, 1938, D.C. bar, 1956; individual practice law, Springfield, Mo., 1938-43; mem. 78th to 80th Congresses from 6th Mo. Dist.; trial judge U.S. Ct. of Claims, Washington, 1949-72, chief trial judge, 1964-72, appellate judge, 1972—. Served to col. USAF Res., 1950-74. Decorated Legion of Merit; recipient Patriotic Service medal Am. Coalition Patriotic Socs., 1963, Outstanding Alumnus award S.W. Mo. State U., 1964. Mem. Am., Fed., D.C. bar assns., Res. Officers Assn., Nat. Lawyers Club, Delta Theta Phi. Methodist. Club: Nat. Exchange. Author: American Immigration Policies, A History, 1963; Annals, Am. Acad. Polit. and Social Sci., 1966; History, U.S. Court of Claims, 1855-1976, 1977. Home: 3715 Cardiff Rd Chevy Chase MD 20015 Office: 717 Madison Pl NW Washington DC 20005

BENNETT, MELVIN, engring. librarian; b. Mangum, Okla., Nov. 23, 1919; s. Lewis Irving and Kate Edna (Martin) B.; student Okla. State U., 1937-41; B.A. in L.S., U. Okla., 1947, B.A. in Econs., 1948; M.Librarianship, Emory U., 1950. Reference librarian S.E. Mo. State Coll., 1947-49, Tex. A. and M. U., 1950-51; head tech. library Air Force Missile Test Center, Cocoa Beach, Fla., 1951-56; research librarian Radiation, Inc., Melbourne, Fla., 1957; asst. head sci. tech. dept. Carnegie Library, Pitts., 1958-65; head engring. library Pa. State U., University Park, 1965—. Cons. Melbourne Friends of Library, 1954-55. Prodn. mgr. Melbourne Little Theatre Group, 1952-57. Served with AUS, 1942-45. Mem. Am. Philatelic Soc., Pa. (chmn. spl. libraries div. 1975-76), Spl. library assns., Am. Soc. Engring. Edn. (guidelines com. for engring. libraries). Republican. Episcopalian (vestryman), lay reader, resolutions com. Mason. Author: Science and Technology, 1963; Compiler Index Guide for U.S. Patents Issued Prior to 1860, 1965; Pennsylvania State University Serial Holdings, 4 vols., 1967—; Science and Technology: A Purchase Guide for Branch and Public Libraries, 1963—. Home: 2006 N Highland Dr State College PA 16801 Office: Hammond Bldg University Park PA 16802

BENNETT, RICHARD KISTLER, found. exec.; b. N.Y.C., Dec. 25, 1916; s. John Mills and Emily Barbara (Keller) B.; student Am. Inst. Banking, 1935-39, Inst. Arts and Scis., Columbia U., 1940, Boston U., 1944-45, Northeastern U., Boston, 1945-46, Harvard, 1945; m. Louisa Anna Mueller, Apr. 17, 1943; 1 dau., Barbara Louise Shadden. With N.Y. Sun, 1934-35, Chem. Bank and Trust Co., N.Y.C., 1935-41; with Am. Friends Service Com., 1946-56, nat. sec. community relations div., 1948-56; spl. asst. dept. social affairs UN, 1949; cons. Phoebe Waterman Found., 1955-56, dir. welfare projects, 1956-62, exec. dir., 1963-68; exec. dir. Phila. Found., 1958-61; v.p. Haas Community Fund, Phila., 1968-72; exec. v.p. William Penn Found., Phila., 1972—, also mem. bd., corporation mem., exec. com.; cons. in field. Charter mem. bd. Nat. Com. Against Discrimination in Housing, 1952-54; nat. panel arbitrators Am. Arbitration Assn., 1952-63; mem. Phila. Manpower Commn., 1960-62, Phila. Mayor's Anti-Poverty Task Force, 1962-63; mem. automation com. Pa. Dept. Pub. Edn., 1961; advisory bd., chmn. fin. com. Phila. Youth Conservation Com., 1961-63; chmn., pres., mem. bd. Phila. Council Community Advancement 1965-68; pres., bd. dirs. Maple Corp., 1968-76; chmn. Pa. com. U.S. Commn. Civil Rights, 1968-72; bd. dirs. Phila. chpt. ACLU, 1969-70, Phila. Housing Devel. Corp., 1969-73, Walnut St. Theatre, 1970-76; mem. corp. Med. Service Assn. Pa., 1970—; trustee pretrial services agy. U.S. Dist. Ct. for Eastern Pa., 1975—; trustee, fin. chmn. Phila. Award, 1976—; bd. dirs. council on founds., 1977—. Recipient Key award Opportunity Industrialization Centers; Nat. award Carver Assos., 1961, Humanitarian award Our Neighbors Civic Assn.; award Phila. YWCA, 1972; also citations. Mem. NAACP (life), mem. Fellowship Reconciliation, Nat. Com. U.S.-China Relations. Quaker. Clubs: Sunday Breakfast, Peale (Phila.). Contbr. articles, to jours. Home: 1237 Lois Rd Ambler PA 19002 Office: 1617 John F Kennedy Blvd Philadelphia PA 19103

BENNETT, ROBERT CLEMENT, health care co. exec.; b. Hackensack, N.J., Dec. 27, 1925; s. John Caldwell and Josephine Elizabeth (Trul) B.; B.S., Seton Hall U., 1954; M.B.A., Rutgers U., 1955; m. Verna Lois Stevens, Nov. 11, 1956; children-Karen, Kevin, Kenneth. Asst. to pres. Schering-Plough Inc., Kenilworth, N.J., 1954-58; dir. mktg. and econ. research Hoffman LaRoche, Inc., Nutley, N.J., 1958-66, gen. mgr. ROCOM div., Nutley, 1967-75; pres. Healthcom, Inc., Towaco, N.J., 1976—; pres., dir. Profl. Market Research, Inc., Phila., 1978—; dir. Nelson Barry, Inc.; chmn. bd. dirs. Healthcom, Inc., 1976—; guest lectr. Fairleigh Dickinson U., 1970-72, Rutgers U., 1973-74. Bd. dirs. Jr. Achievement, 1965-73, Myesthenia Gravis Found., 1973-76, Hosp. Audiences, 1972-74; trustee Milton Sch., 1973-78; mem. nat. adv. council Nat. Inst. Drug Abuse, 1974-75, FDA, 1975-76; mgmt. advisor Sm. Bus. Adminstrn., 1970-78. Served with USAAF, 1944-46. Named Man of the Year, Cath. Parents Assn., 1975; recipient Golden Eagle awards Council Non-Theatrical Events, 1972, 73, 75; recipient Silver Medal, Internat. Film and TV Festival, 19—. Fellow Acad. Health Care Adminstrn., Menninger Found.; mem. Am. Econ. Assn., Internat. Platform Soc., Am. Film Acad., Am. Mktg. Assn., Union League, Delta Sigma Phi. Episcopalian. Clubs: Friars, Pharm. Advt. Home: 20 Mary Dr Towaco NJ 07082 Office: 2 Penn Center Philadelphia PA 19102

BENNETT, ROWLAND FRANCIS, librarian; b. Rochester, N.Y., Oct. 17, 1940; s. Harold Francis and Xantha Blanche (Gallaher) B.; B.A., Wheaton (Ill.) Coll., 1962; M.L.S., Case Western Res. U., Cleve., 1966; M.A., Princeton Theol. Sem., 1973; m. Margaret Johnson, Sept. 4, 1965; children—Chad Hamilton, Kyle Francis. Vol., U.S. Peace Corps, Malawi, Africa, 1963-64; reference librarian Princeton Pub. Library, 1967-71, asst. dir., 1971-73; dir. Maplewood (N.J.) Meml. Library, 1974—. Mem. ALA, N.J. Library Assn. Presbyterian. Home: 61 Burnet St Maplewood NJ 07040 Office: 51 Baker St Maplewood NJ 07040

BENNETT, WALKER GARDNER, II, hosp. adminstr.; b. Washington, June 1, 1922; s. Floyd Wesley and Mary Taylor (Hungate) B.; M.E., U. Pa., 1939; B.S. in Elec. Engring., U.S. Naval Acad., 1944; m. Rosline Weisman, Oct. 7, 1972; children—Walker G. III, Stanley T., Kristine McAnelly, Jay Barnett. Chief, proposal devel. Gen. Dynamics/Astronautics, San Diego, 1953-62; tech. dir. Data Mgmt., Inc., San Diego, 1962-63; configuration mgr. Litton Systems, Inc., Woodland Hills, Calif., 1963; dep. mgr. program control, dir. tech. adminstrn. Northrop Ventura, Newberry Park, Calif., 1963-66, dir. ops., project mgr. NIKE-X, dir. bus. adminstrn. Northrop Corp., 1966-70; pres., chief exec. officer Augustana Hosp. and Health Care Center, Chgo., 1970-74; exec. v.p., chief exec. officer Ellis Hosp., Schenectady, 1974—. Mem. Pres.'s Com. on Equal Employment; sec. bd. social ministry Pacific SW synod Lutheran Ch. in Am., 1960-66, chmn. bd. social ministry S.E. Synod, 1966-70; vice chmn. Luth. Services San Diego; chmn. Citizen's Council for Edn.; bd. dirs. City Rescue Mission. Served to 2d lt. USMC, 1944-45, as chief mate U.S. Maritime Service, 1946. Fellow Am. Acad. Med. Adminstrs.; mem. Am. Astronautical Soc. (sr.), Electronic Industries Assn., Am. Mgmt. Assn., Am., Protestant, Luth. hosp. assns., Am. Coll. Hosp. Adminstrs., Assn. N.Y. State, Naval Acad. Alumni Assn. Republican. Club: Mohawk (Schenectady). Home: 1799 Randolph Rd Schenectady NY 12308 Office: 1101 Nott St Schenectady NY 12308

BENNING, CALVIN JAMES, chemist; b. Chgo., Aug. 6, 1925; s. Earl Edmund and Caroline Marie (Schmitt) B.; B.S., U. Notre Dame, 1950; Ph.D., Ohio State U., 1953; m. Genevieve H. Hunstiger, June 21, 1952; children—Christopher, Kathleen, Matthew, Therese, Richard. Chief chemist Hudson Foam Plastics Co., Yonkers, N.Y., 1954-55; sr. research chemist M.W. Kellogg Co., Jersey City, 1955-57; dir. rigid containers, mgr. plastic application research W.R. Grace Co., Clarksville, Md., 1957-68; mgr. new tech., dir. indsl. packaging Internat. Paper Co., Tuxedo Park, N.Y., 1968-77; tech. dir. Spl. Chem. div. Essex Chem. Co., Clifton, N.J., 1977—; founder, 1st chmn. Gordon Research Conf., 1964. Served with USNR, 1943-46. Recipient Internat. Plastic Foam award German Plastic Soc., 1973. Fellow Am. Inst. Chemists; mem. Soc. Plastics Engrs. (dir. polyolefin div.), Am. Chem. Soc., TAPPI, Plastic Inst. Am. (trustee), Forest Products Research Soc. Roman Catholic. Author: Plastic Foams, Vols. I and II, 1969; contbr. sci. articles to profl. jours. Patentee in field. Home: 103 Malcolm Rd Mahwah NJ 07430 Office: Essex Chem Co Crossman Rd Sayerville NJ 07882

BENNION, SCOTT DESMOND, physician; b. Casper, Wyo., July 26, 1948; s. Desmond J. and Wanda (Tolman) B.; B.A. cum laude, U. Wyo., 1971, M.S., 1972; M.D., U. Utah, 1975; m. Mary Marie Blanton, June 9, 1972; children—Scott B., Beau B. Intern, Rutgers U. Med. Sch., 1975-76, resident in internal medicine, 1976-77; commd. capt., M.C., U.S. Army, 1978—. Diplomate Am. Bd. Internal Medicine. Mem. AMA, A.C.P. (asso.), Phi Kappa Phi. Republican. Mem. Ch. Jesus Christ Latter-day Saints. Home: Box 47 USA MEDDAC Würzburg APO NY 09801

BENNUN, ALFRED, educator; b. Buenos Aires, Argentina, July 9, 1934; s. Leon and Ana (Odesser) B.; Pharmacist, U. Cordoba (Argentina), 1954, Biochemist, 1957, Ph.D., 1963; m. Nelida Prilutzky, Jan. 31, 1961; 1 dau., Irene Ruth. Came to U.S., 1964, naturalized, 1972. Instr., research fellow U. Buenos Aires, 1958-63, fellow Argentine Research Council, 1961-63; postdoctoral fellow Weizmann Inst. Sci., 1963-64; research asso. Duke Med. Center, 1964-65; postdoctoral fellow Pub. Health Research Inst., NIH, N.Y.C., 1965-66; spl. NIH fellow Cornell U., 1966-67; lectr., asst. prof. U. P.R., 1967-69; asso. prof. biochemistry Rutgers U., Newark, 1969—, mem. sci. council, 1970-73; vis. scientist Centre National de la Recherche Scientifique, France, 1974. Bd. dirs. Cancer Research Council, Rutgers-Newark. Recipient prin. investigator research grant NIH, 1968-71, Research Corp., 1968—; grantee Rutgers Research Council, 1969-72, Charles and Johanna Busch Meml. Fund, 1974—. Mem. Am. Chem. Soc., Am. Nuclear Soc., Internat. Union Pure and Applied Biophysics (com. bioenergetics), Am. Soc. Biol. Chemists, Biophys. Soc., N.Y. Acad. Scis., Genetics Soc. Am., Am. Soc. Plant Physiologists, Biochem. Soc., Am. Soc. Photobiology, Fedn. Am. Scientists. Mem. editorial bd. Jour. Bioenergetics and Biomembranes. Contbr. to books and jours. Home: 22 Passaic Ave Nutley NJ 07110

BENOIT, RICHARD CHARLES, JR., electronic engr.; b. East Orange, N.J., May 16, 1917; s. Richard Charles and Mary F. (Tierney) B.; student RCA Insts., 1936-37; certificate Air U. Command and Staff Coll., 1958; grad. Modern Engring. Program Syracuse U., 1969; D. Engring., Am. Internat. Open U., 1976; m. Josephine M. Rasulo, June 5, 1943 (dec. June 1971); children—Richard Joseph, Joseph Edward; m. Marilyn Heit Chazan, Apr. 28, 1973. Pvt. practice radio and theatre sound servicing, Highlands, N.J., 1934-40; electronic technician U.S. Army Signal Corps Labs., Ft. Monmouth, N.J., 1940-42; from project engr. to unit chief USAF Watson Labs., Red Bank, N.J., 1945-50; from unit chief to sect. chief in areas of radio nav. and Telecommunications USAF Rome Air Devel. Center, Griffiss AFB, N.Y., 1950-68, chief communications processing and distbn. sect., 1968—; mem. U.S. del. to NATO Telecommunications Conf., 1959-67; USAF tech. adviser on telecommunications to Spanish Air Force; spl. communications cons. Albany (N.Y.) Med. Coll., Union U., 1959-64; U.S. project officer for telecommunications, mut. tech. data exchange program between U.S. and NATO nations and Republic Korea. Chmn. Non-Partison Tech. Adv. Com. to Congressman Mitchell of N.Y.; mem. citizens adv. council Marcy (N.Y.) Psychiat. Center. Served with USCGR, 1942-43; to ensign U.S. Maritime Service, 1944-45; mem. USNR, 1947-78. Recipient Key to City of Utica for pub. service contbns. (N.Y.) Utica C. of C., 1959, Mayor of Utica, 1960; 4 awards and recognition certificates for invention contbns. Dept. Air Force, 1959-60, Air Force Superior Performance award, 1963; certificate of merit Air Force Systems Command, 1973. Fellow IEEE (internat. bd. dirs. 1974-75, del. to USSR Popov Soc. Congress 1974, mem. U.S. activities bd. 1974-75, 77-78, various awards for contbns. to engring. profession 1957-77), AAAS; mem. Société Francaise des Electriciens des Electroniciens et des Radioélectriciens. Roman Catholic. Club: K.C. (4 deg.). Author numerous tech. papers on telecommunications. Home: 10 Windsor Terr Utica NY 13501 Office: USAF Rome Air Devel Center DCLT Griffiss AFB NY 13441

BENSEL, ARLINGTON, dermatologist; b. Newark, Aug. 14, 1915; s. Arlington and Edith Mary (Driver) B.; A.B., Dartmouth Coll., 1938; M.D., Temple U., 1942; m. Mildred V. Herdman, July 12, 1941; children—Arlington III, Marianne Bensel McClure. Intern, St. Vincents Hosp., N.Y.C., 1942-43, U.S. Naval Hosp., St. Albans, N.Y., 1943; resident in dermatology Mass. Gen. Hosp., Boston, 1948-51; fellow in dermatology Harvard U. Med. Sch., 1948-51; practice medicine specializing in dermatology, Point Pleasant, N.J., 1951—; staff Columbia Presbyn Hosp., N.Y.C., 1951-58. Served to 2d lt. USMC, 1934-38, with M.C. USN, 1943-46. Diplomate Am. Bd. Dermatology. Mem. Am. Acad. Dermatology (award), AMA, Med. Soc. N.J., Ocean County Med. Soc., Soc. Investigative Dermatology, N.Am. Clin. Dermatology Soc., Internat. Soc. Tropical Dermatology. Republican. Clubs: Masons, Eagle, Globe and Anchor (v.p.). Contbr. articles in dermatology to med. publs. Home: 401 Laurel Ave Brielle NJ 08730 Office: River Rd Point Pleasant NJ 08742

BENSKINA, MARGARITA O. (PRINCESS ORELIA), dancer, singer, musician; b. Colon, Panama; d. Jose and Amelia Benskina; ed. Catholic schs., Havana, Cuba, and Colon, Panama; Harren High Sch., N.Y.C.; diploma N.Y. Acad. Theatrical Arts, 1962; grad. N.Y. Sch. Floral Designing, 1971; student Queen's Coll.; 1 dau., Pearl Astrona Quintyne. Naturalized U.S. citizen, 1956. Has appeared in theatres, night clubs, etc., in various cities of U.S.; in Dance with Your Gods, Calling All Stars, Broadway Parade, N.Y.C., 1935—; toured with Osadata Dafara Dance Opera, Kykunkoi, 1947; mem. Afro-Cuban dance team, Orelia and Pedro, 1942; now doing solo appearances; toured Canada with own dance company, Bacanal, 1950; starred in UN program Stars of W.I., also TV program Tropical Holiday, C.B.S.; toured with Sam Manning Calpso Concert Co., 1954; vocalist Caribbean Folk Lores; personal mgr. Rouse-Watkins Les Modes Quintet, 1956—; owner, mgr. Orelia's Tropical Garden, retail religious articles, N.Y.C., 1957—; dir., producer Afra-Ghan concert, N.Y.C., 1960; producer, dir., choreographer, star Pot Purri at Judson Concert Hall, N.Y.C., 1965; mem. B.M.I. Corp., toured East and West Africa for dances and rhythmns. Ordained minister spiritual sci. Internat. Spiritual Healers Fellowship, 1956. Recipient Am. Honorarium citation, 1966; Heritage award John F. Kennedy Library for Minorities, 1972. Mem. Nat. Council Negro Women (life), N.Y. Bus. Civics and Cultural Assn. Negro Women Council of Am., Broadcasting Music, Inc. for composers and writers, Synanon, Writers Sch. Conn. Author: No Longer Defeated and Other Poems, 1972; The Inflammable Desire to Rebel and Other Poems, 1974; I Have Loved You Already, 1975; I Thank You, Father, 1976; To Whom It May Concern, 1978. Composer: Princess; One-Two-Three-Four-O in Syncopation; (with Charles Rouse and Herbert G. Brown) One Day; (with Charlie Rouse) Un Dia (One Day), 1965. Home: 192-22 100th Ave Hollis NY 11423

BENSON, DOUGLAS BRUCE, systems analyst; b. Atlanta, Sept. 29, 1948; s. Edwin Bruce and Elizabeth (Boogher) B.; B.S. in Econs., Rider Coll., Trenton, N.J., 1970; M.S. in Indsl. Adminstrn., Union Coll., Schenectady, N.Y., 1972; m. Jean Marie McThomas, Aug. 29, 1970; children—Christen, Timothy. Mgmt. systems analyst Burroughs Corp., Plainfield, N.J., 1973-75; lead systems analyst Pitney Bowes, Stamford, Conn., 1975—; owner, mgr. MB Innovations, Inc., Somerville, N.J. Served to capt., AUS, 1972. Certified data processor. Mem. Assn. Systems Mgmt., Ridgefield Jaycees (exec. bd.), Omicron Delta Epsilon. Home: 32 Virginia Ct Ridgefield CT 06877 Office: 69 Walnut St Stamford CT 06904

BENSON, RICHARD LEWIS, sci. equipment mfg. co. exec.; b. Flushing, N.Y.; s. Philip and Blanche (Silver) B.; A.A., RCA Inst. Electronic Engring., 1968; m. Patricia Haase, Feb. 14, 1970; children—Scott Aaron, Danielle Suzanne. Sales engr. Tracerlab Nuclear Co., 1963-65, Whatman Corp., 1965-68; sales and mktg. engr. Fisher Sci. Co., 1968-72; sales mgr. Abbott Labs., 1972-75; pres. Benson Biomed. Products Co., Ridgefield, N.J., 1975-76; v.p. mktg. and sales Centaur Sciences Inc., Stamford, Conn., 1976—; cons. in field. Served with USAFR, 1963-69. Mem. Biomed. Mktg. Assn., ASTM. Home: 375 Elm St Monroe CT 06468 Office: 180 Harvard Ave Stamford CT 06902

BENSON, ROBERT DALE, fin. mgmt. cons.; b. Little River, Kans., June 4, 1912; s. Leslie Robert and Vernena (Sherer) B.; grad. Hutchinson Jr. Coll., 1932; student Northwestern U., 1939-40; grad. Army Indsl. Coll., 1944; m. Nelle Malick Payne, Dec. 23, 1933 (dec.); children—Robert Payne, Robin Sherwood; m. 2d, Gertrude Marie Trudeau, June 21, 1975. Chief accountant, Asso. Dairies Wichita, Kans., 1933-34; with Spurrier, Wood, C.P.A.'s, Wichita, 1935; chief accountant, comptroller Steffen Ice and Ice Cream Corp., Wichita, 1936; partner Spurrier, Wood & Benson, accountants and auditors, Hutchinson, Kans., 1941-43; with firm P.H. Willems, accountants and auditors, McPherson, Kans., 1937; partner Willems & Benson, accountants and auditors, McPherson, 1937-43; chief fixed price audits, spl. audit and termination audits brs. Hdqrs., U.S. Army Air Force, 1943-47; chief spl. audits br., asst. chief indsl. audits div. Hdqrs., U.S. Army Audit Agy., 1947-48; dep. auditor gen. U.S. Air Force, 1948-53, dep. for accounting and fin. mgmt. to asst. sec. air force, 1953-58, dep. asst. sec. air force for fin. mgmt., 1958-69, prin. dep. asst. sec. air force for fin. mgmt., 1969-71; chmn. bd. Internat. Finance and Mgmt. Corp., Washington, 1971-72; pres. Robert D. Benson & Assos., mgmt. cons., Washington, 1972—; guest lectr. George Washington U., 1953-56. Mem. bd. U.S. Civil Service Examiners, 1955-71. Recipient Air Force Decoration for Exceptional Civilian Service, 1953, 55, 69-71; named Outstanding Young Man Kans., 1942. Mem. U.S. Jr. (v.p. 1943-44, treas. 1944-45, dir. 1941-45), Kans. (dir. 1942-43), Kans. Jr. (pres. 1942-43) chambers commerce, Assn. Govt. Accountants, Kans. State Soc. Licensed Municipal Pub. Accountants, Am. Accounting Assn., Air Force Assn., Ordre Des Compagnons Du Bontemps-Medoc et Graves Bordeaux France (hon. comdr.), Internat. Wine and Food Soc., Les Amis du Vin. Clubs: Kenwood Golf and Country (Bethesda, Md.); Nat. Aviation (Washington); Century XXI (Germantown, Md.); Town and Country; Rotary. Asso. editor Future Magazine, 1944. Home: 3506 Manor Rd Chevy Chase MD 20015

BENSON, WILBUR MAXWELL, physician; b. Honeyford, N.D., May 9, 1915; s. August and Betsy (Swanson) B.; B.S., N.D. State U., 1939; M.S., U. Fla., 1941; M.D., U. Wis., 1948, Ph.D., 1949; m. Esther Pauline Weller, Feb. 22, 1946; children—Elizabeth Ann Benson Peterson, Ellen Christine Benson Brehm. Intern Calif. Hosp., Los Angeles, 1949-50; sr. pharmacologist Hoffman-LaRoche, Inc., Nutley, N.J., 1950-57; Hill prof. pharmacology U. Minn. Med. Sch., 1957-60; dir. neuropharmacology and psychopharmacology Mead Johnson Research Center, 1960-62; sr. pharmacologist, chmn. dept. pharmacology Stanford Research Inst., 1962-69; asst. med. dir. Bristol Myers Co., N.Y.C., 1969-70; asso. med. dir. USV Pharm. Corp., Tuckahoe, N.Y., 1971-75; asso. dir. clin. research Boehringer Ingelheim Ltd., Ridgefield, Conn., 1975—. Mem. Nat. Sci. Adv. Com. Recipient Borden Med. Student award, 1948; Alumni Achievement award N.D. State U., 1963. Mem. AAAS, AMA, Am. Soc. Clin. Pharmacology and Therapeutics, Am. Soc. Pharmacology and Exptl. Therapeutics, N.Y. Acad. Scis., Am. Pharm. Assn., Sigma Xi, Phi Kappa Phi, Rho Chi, Phi Sigma, Phi Beta Pi. Lutheran. Co-author: Tranquilizing and Antidepressive Drugs, 1962. Contbr. to profl. jours. Home: 24 Sherry Ln Danbury CT 06810 Office: Box 368 Ridgefield CT 06877

BENT, HENRY EVERETT, agrl. engr.; b. Annapolis Royal, N.S., Can., Dec. 27, 1947; s. Trueman P. and Esther E. (Orde) B.; diploma Agrl. Engring., N.S. Agrl. Coll., 1970; B. Agrl. Engring. N.S. Tech. Coll., 1972; m. Margo E. Staples, May 30, 1970; children—Kimberly, Jennifer. Chem. sales Allied Chem. Can. Ltd., Moncton, N.B., 1972-74; chem. sales, service Apollo Chem. Corp., Moncton, 1974; project engr., mgr. MacLaren Atlantic Ltd., Moncton, 1974-76, office mgr./project mgr., Fredericton, N.B., 1976-78; pres. ABP Cons. Ltd., Fredericton, 1978—. Mem. Am., Can. socs. agrl. engrs., N.B., P.E.I. assns. profl. engrs. Home: 158 Burpee St Fredericton NB E3A 1M5 Canada Office: PO Box 321 Fredericton NB E38 4Y9 Canada also 91 Regent St Fredericton NB E3B 3W3 Canada

BENTIVEGNA, PETER IGNATIUS, architect; b. N.Y.C., Dec. 2, 1941; s. Peter and Catherine (Cardillo) B.; B.Arch., Pratt Inst., 1963; m. Antoinette Janis, Aug. 26, 1961; children—Pierrette, Scott, Peter. Sr. cons. Bolt, Beranck & Newman, Inc., N.Y.C., 1966-69, Mauchly Constrn. Mgmt. Inc., N.Y.C., 1969-71; dir. design Am. Medicorp, Inc., Bala Cynwyd, Pa., 1971-74, v.p., 1975-78; exec. v.p. Medifac Inc., Elkins Park, Pa., 1978—. Chmn., Doylestown Zoning Bd., 1973-78; pres. Doylestown Twp. Civic Assn., 1971-74. Served with U.S. Army, 1964-66. Registered architect, W. Va., Tex., Pa. Mem. AIA, Pa. Soc. Architects, Constrn. Specifications Inst. Co-author: Capital Projects for Health Care Facilities. Home: 2162 Turk Rd Doylestown PA 18901 Office: Med Arts Bldg 60 E Township Line Elkins Park PA 19117

BENTLEY, JAMES FRANCIS, fluid power distbg. co. exec.; b. Buffalo, Sept. 16, 1927; s. John Sinclair and Florence (Sullivan) B.; B.B.A., U. Buffalo, 1956; m. Shirley Evelyn Service, June 11, 1949; children—Mary, James Francis. Salesman, H.D. Taylor Co., Rochester, N.Y., 1946-50; sales engr. Buffalo Rubber & Supply Co., 1950-51, 52-54; supr. B.R. DeWitt Co., Rochester, 1954-56; sales engr. R.C. Neal Co., Buffalo, 1956-59; v.p., prin. Goll Corp., Buffalo, 1959-68; pres. Bentley & Callahan, Inc., Buffalo, 1968-71, J.F. Bentley Co., Inc., Williamsville, N.Y., 1971—; exec. v.p., prin. Colloid-A-Tron of the Virginias, Inc., Williamsville, 1974—, dir., 1973—; dir. Superior Mgmt. Corp., Superior Security Systems, Western N.Y. Restaurants, Inc. Served with USNR, 1944-46, 51-52. Mem. Fluid Power Soc. (founder, past pres. Niagara Frontier chpt.), Delta Sigma Pi. Republican. Roman Catholic. Clubs: Clarence Shooting; Buffalo Curling. Contbr. articles to profl. jours. Home: 326 Getzville Rd Snyder NY 14226 Office: 35 California Dr Williamsville NY 14221

BENTLEY, ROBERT ASA LINCOLN, mgmt. cons.; b. Buffalo, Feb. 12, 1908; s. Ora Willis and Myrtle (Crawford) B.; B.S., N.Y. U., 1938, M.B.A., 1963; m. Charlotte Marie Fowler, Feb. 26, 1943. Commd. 2d lt. U.S. Army, advanced through grades to col.; stationed at N.Y. Port of Embarkation, 1941, Office of Q.M. Gen., Washington, 1941-43, Hdqrs. USAAF-CBI, India, 1943-46, 3d Army Hdqrs., 1950-51, G.H.Q., Tokyo, 1952-54, N.Y. Mil. Dist. Hdqrs., 1954-57; with res., 1957-68; ret., 1968; sr. cons. Robert Bentley Assos., N.Y.C., 1957—. Decorated grand cross Order Souverain et Militarie du Temple de Jerusalem; knight comdr. Ordre Souverain de Saint Jean de Jerusalem; grand cross Eloy Alfaro Internat. Found. Panama; grand cross Order St. Constantine and St. George. Mem. Am. Mgmt. Assn., Am. McAll Assn. (treas.), Mil. Order World Wars, Mil. Order Fgn. Wars (comdr.), Order Lafayette, St. Andrew's Soc., St. Nicholas Soc., Pilgrims, Am. Legion (past post comdr.), Vet. Corp. Arty., Ret. Officers Assn., S.R., New Eng. Soc. Presbyterian. Mason (32 deg., K.T.). Home: 390 1st Ave New York City NY 10010 Office: 71 W 23d St New York City NY 10010

BENTON, ALLEN HAYDEN, educator; b. Ira, N.Y., Sept. 4, 1921; s. Haydon Willey and Pearl Amelia (Diddy) B.; B.S., Cornell U., 1948, M.S., 1949, Ph.D., 1952; m. Marjorie Lois Hall, Aug. 16, 1947; children—Thomas Hall, Christopher Allen, Holly Anne. Jr. wildlife biologist U.S. Fish and Wildlife Service, 1949; asst. prof. biology State U. N.Y. at Albany, 1949-57, asso. prof., 1957-62; prof. biology State U. N.Y. at Fredonia, 1962—, distinguished teaching prof., 1973—, faculty exchange scholar, 1975—; vis. prof. Stephen F. Austin Coll., 1957, Concord Coll., Athens, W.Va., 1969-70, U. Minn. Biol. Sta., 1970; cons. Nuclear Fuel Services, Inc., Calspan, Inc., Environ. Analysts Inc. Life mem. P.T.A.; cons. Environmental Def. Fund, Nature Conservancy. Bd. dirs. Fredonia Coll. Found. Served with cav. AUS, 1942-46. Decorated Bronze Star. Grantee Research Found., State U. N.Y., 1963, NSF, 1972, E.N. Huyck Found., 1976-78. Mem. Am. Ornithologists Union, Am. Inst. Biol. Sci., AAAS, Am. Soc. Mammalogists, Ecol. Soc., Wilson Ornithol. Soc., N.Y. Entomol. Soc., Intecol, Fedn. N.Y. State Bird Clubs (pres.), Sigma Xi, Phi Kappa Phi. Author: (with W.E. Werner, Jr.) Field Biology and Ecology, 3d edit., 1974, Manual for Field Biology and Ecology, 5th edit., 1972; (with Margaret M. Stewart) Keys to Northeastern Vertebrates, Excluding Birds, 3d edit., 1971. Contbr. articles to profl. jours. Home: 292 Water St Fredonia NY 14063

BENTON, DONALD STEWART, publishing co. exec.; b. Marlboro, N.Y., Jan. 2, 1924; s. Fred Stanton and Agnes (Townsend) B.; B.A., Columbia U., 1947, J.D., 1949; LL.M., N.Y.U., 1953; student U. Leeds (Eng.), 1945. Admitted to N.Y. State bar, 1953; practiced in N.Y.C., 1953-56; atty. N.Y. State Banking Dept., 1954-55; v.p. Found. Press, Inc., Bklyn., 1957-60; exec. asst. to exec. v.p. N.Y. Stock Exchange, 1960-61; dir. reference book dept. and spl. projects editor Appleton Century Crofts, N.Y.C., 1962-71; sr. editor Matthew Bender & Co., Inc., N.Y.C., 1974-77; editor Warren, Gorham & Lamont, Inc., N.Y.C., 1977—. Mem. Cresskill (N.J.) Zoning Bd. Adjustment, 1969-71; mem. Cresskill Planning Bd., 1971-74; councilman City of Cresskill, 1972-74. Served with AUS, 1943-46, 50-52. Decorated Bronze Star. Mem. N.Y. Bar Assn., Phi Delta Phi. Mem. Reformed Ch. in Am. Home: 117 Heatherhill Rd Cresskill NJ 07626

BENTON, JOSEPH EDWARD, JR., city and county ofcl.; b. Camden, N.J., Mar. 17, 1944; s. Joseph Edward and Margaret Marie (Zeisweiss) B.; B.S., Rutgers U., 1972; M.A., Rider Coll., 1978; student Camden Police Acad., 1968; m. Kathleen T. Viggiano, Aug. 19, 1972; 1 son, Joseph E. III. Patrolman, Camden Police Dept., 1968-69, planning and research officer, 1969-70, crime analysis officer, 1970, adminstrv. aid, grant coordinator Officer Dir. of Pub. Safety, 1970-72, criminal justice planner, 1972—; criminal justice instr. Camden County Coll., 1972—. Mem. Navy League (pres. 1976—), U.S. Coast Guard Aux., Internat. Assn. Chiefs of Police, Kappa Upsilon. Home: RD 30 Fernwood Ave Atco NJ 08004 Office: 2276 N 43d St Pennasuken NJ 08110

BENTON, PETER, banker; b. Boston, July 4, 1925; s. Jay Rogers and Frances (Hill) B.; grad. Browne and Nichols Sch., 1944; Asso. degree, Boston U., 1950, B.S., 1956; m. Marilyn M. Moore, Sept. 11, 1948; children—Jeffrey Willard, Douglas Chamberlin, Andrew Jay, Sarah Warren. With John Hancock Mut. Life Ins. Co., Boston, 1950-73, dir. pub. relations Midwest region, Chgo., 1963-73; v.p., dir. mktg. First Vt. Bank, Brattleboro, 1973—; mem. evening faculty Northeastern U. Coll. Bus. Adminstrn., 1958-63. Asst. Chmn. Greater Boston United Fund Health and Fitness Fair, 1961; mem. Chgo.-Cook County Com. on Criminal Justice, 1970-73; bd. dirs. Greater North Mich. Ave. Assn., Chgo. Conv. and Tourist Bur., 1972-73; pres., dir. Brattleboro Mus. and Art Center; governing mem. Chgo. Symphony Orch., 1967-71; trustee Browne and Nichols Sch., 1960-68, Vt. State Symphony; bd. dirs. Vt. Symphony Orch., Vt. Pub. Radio; mem. nat. alumni council Boston U. Served with USMCR, 1943-46. Recipient Francis W. Hatch award for advt. excellence, Gamma award for photog. excellence. Mem. Pub. Relations Soc. Am. (dir. New Eng. chpt. 1958-63, pres. 1961, chmn. 15th nat. conf. 1962, award for profl. excellence). Clubs: Chgo. Athletic Assn., Marine Memorial (San Francisco). Home: Dummerston Center VT Office: 215 Main St Brattleboro VT 05301

BENTZEN, OLE HANS, civil engr.; b. Frederikssund, Denmark, Mar. 23, 1906; s. Niels Peter and Helga (Hendriksen) B.; Cand. Philosophy, U. Copenhagen (Denmark), 1925; M.Sc., Polyteknisk Laereanstalt, Copenhagen, 1929; m. Gertrude Marie Moses, Jan. 10, 1936 (dec.). Design and constrn. engr. Bjorn Petersen, Copenhagen, 1929-38; constrn. engr., br. mgr. Christiani & Nielsen (S. Africa), Cape Town, also Durban, S. Africa, Mombasa, Kenya, 1938-46, asst. mgr., Durban, 1946-49; joint mgr. Owen Falls Constrn. Co., Jinja, Uganda, 1949-53; chief engr. Christiani & Nielsen A/S, Copenhagen, 1953-56; project mgr. Fenco, Christiani & Nielsen Can. Ltd., Vancouver, B.C., Can., 1956-59; exec. v.p. Christiani & Nielsen Can. Ltd., Vancouver, 1959-75, also dir.; pres. Christiani & Nielsen Corp., N.Y.C., 1963—, also dir. Served with intelligence sect. 19th Coastal Bn. S. Africa, 1942. Registered profl. engr., Wash., B.C. Mem. ASCE, Assn. Profl. Engrs. B.C., Am. Soc. Danish Engrs. (past pres.), Arbitrators Inst. Can. Clubs: Vancouver, Canadian of New York. Home: 3 Ploughmans Bush Riverdale NY 10471 Office: 350 Fifth Ave New York City NY 10001

BENZ, EDWARD JOHN, clin. pathologist; b. Pitts., June 11, 1923; s. Henry John and Gertrude Nora (Heffernan) B.; B.S., U. Pitts., 1943, M.D., 1946; M.S., U. Minn., 1952; m. Verna Marie Cuddyre, June 20, 1945; children—Edward John, Thomas James, Gregory Paul, Mary Louise. Intern, St. Joseph's Hosp., Pitts., 1946-47; resident, fellow Mayo Found., Mayo Clinic, 1949-53; pathologist, dir. labs. St. Luke's Hosp., Bethlehem, Pa., 1953—; adj. prof. microbiology Lehigh U., Bethlehem, 1956—; pres. Lab. Clin. Pathology, Bethlehem, 1956—; cons. Palmerton (Pa.) Hosp., Allentown (Pa.) State Hosp.; past dir. Miller Meml. Blood Bank, Bethlehem. Mem. adv. com. Pa. Sec. Health on Clin. Labs., 1973—; mem. health sci. adv. com. Lehigh U., 1973—. Trustee St. Luke's Hosp., 1968-71. Served as capt. M.C., AUS, 1947-49. Fellow Coll. Am. Pathologists (past chmn. anat. path. commn., past del. from Pa.), Am. Soc. Clin. Pathologists; mem. AMA, Internat. Acad. Pathology, Am. Assn. Pathologists and Bacteriologists, Am. Assn. Blood Banks, Sigma Xi, Alpha Omega Alpha. Club: Saucon Valley Country (Bethlehem). Contbr. articles to profl. publs. Home: 288 E Macada Rd Bethlehem PA 18017 Office: St Luke's Hosp Bethlehem PA 18015

BERADUCCI, JOHN ANGELO, ednl. inst. exec.; b. Bklyn., July 24, 1927; s. Joseph and Michelina (Pace) B.; student Internat. Corr. Schs., 1953-54, State U. Agrl. and Tech. Inst., Farmingdale, N.Y., 1956-57; m. Joyce Marie Joneson, Sept. 7, 1947; children—Vicki, Joseph, Anne. Maintenance engr. Continental Can Co., Maspeth, N.Y., 1958-68; maintenance supr. Avco, Lycoming, Conn., 1968-69; dir. bldgs. and grounds Culinary Inst. Am., Hyde Park, N.Y., 1969—. Mem. Dutchess County Sheriff's Dept. Served with USN, 1945-49. Certified plant engr. Mem. Am. Inst. Plant Engrs., Phys. Plant Dirs. Assn., Am. Inst. Maintenance, Assn. Phys. Plant Adminstrs. of Univs. and Colls. Republican. Roman Catholic. Club: Dutchess County Pistol. Home: 43 Ninham Ave Wappingers Falls NY 12590 Office: Route 9 Hyde Park NY 12538

BERANEK, LEO LEROY, communications co. exec.; b. Solon, Iowa, Sept. 15, 1914; s. Edward Fred and Beatrice (Stahle) B.; A.B., Cornell Coll., 1936, D.Sc. (hon.), 1946; M.S., Harvard, 1937, D.Sc., 1940; D.Eng. (hon.), Worcester Poly. Inst., 1971; m. Phyllis Knight, Sept. 6, 1941; children—James Knight, Thomas Haynes. Instr. physics Harvard, 1940-41, asst. prof. applied physics, 1941-43, dir. electro-acoustics and systems research labs., 1941-46, asso. prof. communications engring. Mass. Inst. Tech,, 1947-58, lectr., 1958—, tech. dir. acoustics lab., 1947-53, mem. council arts, 1972—; pres., dir. Bolt, Beranek & Newman, Inc., Cambridge, 1953-69, cons., dir., 1969—; pres., dir. Boston Broadcasters, Inc., 1963—; chmn. bd. Mueller-BBM GmbH, Munich, Germany, 1962—. Thomas Hawksley lectures Inst. Mech. Engrs., London, 1958; chmn. panel on acoustics Research and Devel. Bd., Dept. Def., 1949-52; mem. Mass. Commn. Ocean Mgmt., 1967-71, Spl. Commn. Marine Boundaries and Resources, Mass., 1969-71; mem. Gov.'s Task Force Coastal Resources, 1974—, Gov.'s Com. Fgn. Bus., 1977—; bd. dirs. World Affairs Council Boston, 1973—, pres., 1975-78; bd. dirs. Boston Opera Co., pres. 1961-63; pres., dir. Cambridge Soc. for Early Music, 1964-71, chmn., 1971—; bd. overseers Boston Symphony Orch., 1968—, chmn., 1977—, trustee, 1977—; trustee Cornell Coll., 1955-71, Longy Sch. Music, 1971-75, Emerson Coll., 1974—; bd. overseers Harvard Coll., com. to visit Center Behavioral Scis., 1964-71, com. to visit dept. biology, 1971-77, adv. com. on mgmt. devel. programs Grad. Sch. Bus. Adminstrn., Harvard, 1966-71; bd. dirs. Boston 200 Corp., 1975-77, United Way Mass. Bay, 1975—, Flaschner Jud. Inst., Boston, 1978—; mem. Positive Program for Boston NAACP, 1973—; chmn. bd. Greater Boston Fund Internat. Affairs, 1978—. Recipient Presdl. certificate of merit, 1948, Cornell Coll. Alumni citation, 1953, NAACP media award, 1975, Abe Lincoln award TV Commn. So. Bapt. Conv., 1976. John Guggenheim fellow, 1946-47. Registered profl. engr., Mass. Fellow Nat. Acad. Engring. (dir., com. pub. engring. policy, marine bd., aeros. and space engring. bd.), Acoustical Soc. Am. (exec. council 1944-47, pres. 1954-55, asso. editor 1946-60, biennial award 1944, Sabine award 1961, Gold medal 1975), Am. Phys. Soc., AAAS, I.E.E.E. (chmn. profl. group on audio 1950-51), Audio Engring. Soc. (exec. v.p. 1966-67, pres. 1967-68, gov. 1966-71, gold medal award 71), Am. Acad. Arts and Scis.; mem. Am. Nat. Standards Inst. Inc. (chmn. acoustical standards bd. 1955-68, dir. 1963-66), Inst. Noise Control Engring. (charter pres. 1971-73), Mass. Broadcasters Assn. (dir. 1973—, v.p. 1977-78, pres. 1978-79), Groupement des Acousticiens de Langue Francaise (1st silver commemorative medal 1966), Boston Community Media Council (treas. 1973-76, v.p. 1976-77), Greater Boston C. of C. (dir. 1973—, v.p. 1976—), Execs. Club Greater Boston (dir. 1970-72), Phi Beta Kappa, Sigma Xi, Eta Kappa Nu. Clubs: St. Botolph (Boston); Winchester Country; Mass. Institute Technology Faculty. Author: Principles of Sound Control in Airplanes, 1944; Acoustic Measurements, 1949; Acoustics, 1954; Noise Reduction, 1960; Music, Acoustics and Architecture, 1962; Noise and Vibration Control, 1971. Editor: Noise Control Mag., 1954-55; asso. editor Sound, 1961-63; editorial bd. Noise Control Engring., 1971-77. Contbr. articles on acoustics, audio, TV communications systems and effects of noise on people to tech. publs. Home: 7 Ledgewood Rd Winchester MA 01890 Office: 5 TV Pl Needham MA 02192

BERANEK, PHYLLIS KNIGHT (MRS. LEO L. BERANEK), club woman; b. Boston, Oct. 18, 1917; d. Hardy Jay and Ethel (Beal) Knight; B. Dental Hygiene, Tufts U., 1937; m. Leo L. Beranek, Sept. 6, 1941; children—James Knight, Thomas Haynes. Fgn. students worker Mass. Inst. Tech., Cambridge, 1948-58, entertainment supr. spl. summer programs, 1953, 55, 57, 60, 64, 67, 72, 75; chmn. ladies com. Internat. Congress Acoustics, Cambridge, 1958, meeting Acoustics Soc., Am., Boston, 1966, meeting Audio Engring. Soc., N.Y., 1968, Inter-Noise 72, Washington, 1972, Inter-Noise 77, Zurich, Switzerland, 1977; sustaining sponsor Opera Co. of Boston, Inc., 1960—; mem. Silver Ball com. World Affairs Council of Boston, 1976. Episcopalian. Clubs: Winton, Winchester Country, Mass. Institute of Technology Faculty; Great Britain Ski; Murren (Switzerland) Ski. Home: 7 Ledgewood Rd Winchester MA 01890

BERARDUCCI, ARTHUR ANGELO, health services adminstr.; b. Ithaca, N.Y., Aug. 8, 1946; s. Romeo and Ida (Miccoli) B.; B.S., State U. N.Y., 1968; M.P.H. (USPHS fellow), Yale U., 1970; m. Marie T. Keefe, Apr. 3, 1971; 1 dau., Lisa Marie. Adminstrv. resident Harvard Community Health Plan, Boston, 1970; asst. dir. Beth Israel Hosp., Boston, 1970-74; asso. dir. health policy and mgmt. program Harvard U., 1974-76; dir. ambulatory services planning Peter Bent Brigham Hosp., Boston, 1976—; cons. Harvard Community Health Plan, Assn. Am. Med. Colls., Am. Hosp. Assn.; sr. program cons. Robert Wood Johnson Found., 1976-77; lectr. health services adminstrn., 1976—. Served with USAR, 1968-74. Mem. Am. Hosp. Assn. Center for Ambulatory and Home Care Services (mem. governing council 1976—), Am. Hosp. Assn., Am. Pub. Health Assn., Yale Univ. Alumni in Hosp. Adminstrn., Beta Gamma Sigma. Roman Catholic. Editor: Jour. Ambulatory Care Mgmt., 1977—. Contbr. articles to profl. jours. Office: Harvard Sch Pub Health 677 Huntington Ave Boston MA 02115

BERC, KENNETH MYLES, psychiatrist; b. N.Y.C., May 7, 1942; s. Ira Lee and Viola Helene (Lebowitz) B.; B.A. cum laude, Colgate U., 1963; M.D., Harvard U., 1967. Intern, St. Luke's Hosp. Center, N.Y.C., 1967-68, resident in psychiatry, 1968-71, chief resident, 1972; cons. rapid intervention project Family Ct. N.Y. State, 1972-74; emergency room psychiatrist St. Luke's Hosp. Center, N.Y.C., 1972-74; acting dir. psychiat. in-patient services St. Luke's Hosp., 1974-76, asso. attending psychiatrist, 1972—; asso. clin. instr. Columbia Coll. Phys. and Surgs., N.Y.C., 1972—; med. dir. N.Y.C. Service Program for Older People, 1975—; faculty Brookdale Center on Aging, Hunter Coll., N.Y.C., 1977—; practice psychiatry, N.Y.C., 1972—; lectr. in field. Served in U.S. Army, 1969-70. NIMH grantee, 1974; recipient Audi Math. prize Colgate U., 1963, Physics prize, 1963. Diplomate Am. Bd. Psychiatry and Neurology. Mem. AMA (Physicians Recognition award 1972), Am. Psychiat. Assn., N.Y. Acad. Sci. (life), N.Y. Acad. Medicine, Am. Geriatrics Soc., Boyleston Soc. Club: Harvard of N.Y. Home: Montauk Hwy Box 525 East Hampton NY 11937 Office: 155 E 76th St New York City NY 10021 also Montauk Hwy East Hampton NY 11937

BERCK, MARTIN G., journalist; b. N.Y.C., Feb. 5, 1928; s. Samuel M. and Florence (Gans) B.; A.B., N.Y. U., 1947; M.S. in Journalism, Columbia U., 1953, Russell Sage fellow, 1967-68; m. Lenore Fierstein, July 12, 1953; children—Jonathan, Judith, David. Newsman, AP, 1953-56; successively reporter, UN corr., nat. editor N.Y. Herald Tribune, 1956-66; writer, editor, producer NBC News, 1966-72; editorial writer, corr., fgn. editor Newsday, 1972—; adj. asso. prof. journalism N.Y. U., 1973—. Served with AUS, 1950-52. Mem. UN Corrs. Assn., Overseas Press Club, Nat. Press Club. Clubs: N.Y. U. Faculty, Columbia Journalism Alumni (N.Y.C.). Home: 604 Ramapo Rd Teaneck NJ 07666 Office: Newsday 550 Stewart Ave Garden City NY 11530

BERDICK, MURRAY, research exec.; b. New Rochelle, N.Y., June 27, 1920; s. Joseph and Sarah (Simmons) B.; B.S. in Engring. (Carter scholar), George Washington U., 1942; postgrad. Union Coll., Schenectady, 1944-46; M.S. in Chemistry, Poly. Inst. Bklyn., 1949, Ph.D. (Lilly Research fellow, NSF fellow), 1954; m. Joan Jacobstein, Dec. 6, 1947; 1 dau., Dena Anne. Research asst. Nat. Bur. Standards, 1940-42; test engr. Gen. Electric Co., 1942-43, chemist, 1943-46; research project leader Evans Research & Devel. Corp., 1946-51, coordinator research, 1953-60, v.p., dir. research, 1960-61; mgr. research Chesebrough-Pond's Inc., 1962-65, dir. Clinton (Conn.) labs., 1965-68, dir. Research Labs., 1969-70, dir. applied research, 1971-75, dir. regulatory affairs, 1975—. Recipient CIBS award Cosmetic, Toiletry and Fragrance Assn., 1971. Fellow N.Y. Acad. Scis., Am. Inst. Chemists (past chmn. N.Y. chpt.), Soc. Cosmetic Chemists (medal award 1975); mem. Am. Chem. Soc., Soc. Chem. Industry, Assn. Research Dirs., Cosmetic, Toiletry and Fragrance Assn. (chmn. sci. sect. 1969-70), Inter-industry Color Com. (chmn. 1971-76), Soc. for Investigative Dermatology, Chemists Club. Contbr. chpts. to books. Home: 16 Oak Gate Dr Branford CT 06405 Office: care Chesebrough-Ponds Inc Trumbull CT 06611

BERDON, ROBERT IRWIN, judge; b. New Haven, Dec. 24, 1929; s. Louis J. and Jean C. (Cohen) B.; B.S. in Accounting, U. Conn., 1951, J.D., 1957; m. Nancy Tarr, Aug. 30, 1964; 1 son, Peter Adlai. Admitted to Conn. bar, 1957, Supreme Ct. Conn. bar, 1957, U.S. Dist. Ct. Conn. bar, 1958, U.S. Ct. Appeals bar, 1962, U.S. Tax Ct. bar, 1958; partner firm Berdon, Berdon and Young, 1960-73; treas. State of Conn., Hartford, 1971-73; judge Conn. Superior Ct., 1973—. Arbitrator, Am. Arbitration Assn., 1968-73; dir. Conn. Attys. Title Guaranty Fund, Inc. Sec., bd. dirs. Arts Council Greater New Haven, 1965-70; mem. Humane Soc. U.S., New Haven Assn. Retarded Children, 1965—. Mem. Branford (Conn.) Republican Town Com., 1967-72, counsel, 1967-70. Served with AUS, 1951-53. Recipient Distinguished Service award Nat. Jewish Fund, 1961, New Haven Rep. Town Com., 1968; Distinguished Alumni award U. Conn., 1977; award for judiciary Conn. Trial Lawyers Assn., 1976. Mem. Am., Conn., New Haven law assns., Jr. C. of C. Internat. (life), New Haven Jewish Community Center, U. Conn. Alumni Assn. Jewish. Mem. B'nai B'rith (past sec.), Mason (Shriner). Contbr. articles to profl. jours. Home: Flax Mill Rd Branford CT 06405 Office: 235 Church St New Haven CT 06510

BEREDAY, GEORGE ZYGMUNT FIJALKOWSKI, lawyer, sociologist of edn.; b. Warsaw, Poland, July 15, 1920; s. Zygmunt B. and Halina (Piwko-Barylska) B.; B.Sc., U. London, 1944; B.A., U. Oxford, 1950, M.A., 1953; Ph.D., Harvard, 1953; J.D., Columbia, 1976; m. Mary Hale Gillam, Dec. 21, 1954; children—Cornelia Krystyna, Mariko, Thaddeus Matthew Sigmund. Came to U.S., 1950, naturalized, 1955. Mem. faculty Columbia, 1955-59, prof. comparative edn., 1959-78, prof. juvenile law, sociology and edn., 1978—; exchange prof. U. Moscow, 1961; Fulbright prof. U. Tokyo, 1962; vis. prof. U. Hawaii, 1969-70; Carnegie fellow in law and polit. sci. Harvard, 1963-65, Burton lectr., 1972; dir. Japanese-Am. tchr. program Ford Found., 1964-68; Convocation lectr. U. Wis., 1958; Phi Delta Kappa lectr. U. Ohio, 1964; Wolfson lectr. U. Oxford, 1971; Rosner lectr. City U. N.Y., 1975. Mem. U.S. cultural mission to USSR, 1958, U.S. mission to Finland, 1966; U.S. del. 4th U.S.-Japan Cultural Conf., 1969; cons. U.S. Office Edn., 1966-70, OECD, 1970-71, UNESCO, 1971, Edn. Law Center, Rutgers Law Sch., 1974-75, Child Welfare League, 1974-75. Served with Polish Cavalry, 1938-42, Brit. Parachute Regiment, 1942-45. Decorated Virtuti Militari of Poland, 1944. Mem. AAUP, Am. Hist. Assn., Am. Sociol. Soc., Am., N.Y., Hawaii bar assns., Comparative Edn. Soc., Harvard, Columbia law sch. assns. Clubs: Royal Automobile (London); Harvard (N.Y.C.). Author, editor; Public Education in America, 1958; Liberal Traditions in Education, 1958; Politics of Soviet Education, 1960; Changing Soviet School, 1960; Comparative Method in Education, 1964; Essays on World Education, 1969; Modernization and Diversity in Soviet Education, 1971; American Education through Japanese Eyes, 1973; Universities for All, 1973. Founder, editor Comparative Edn. Rev., 1957-67; joint editor World Year Book Edn., 1957-67; gen. editor Columbia Comparative Edn. Studies, 1964—. Home: 106 Morningside Dr New York City NY 10027 also 4818 Kahala Ave Honolulu HI 96815

BERENBAUM, ARTHUR ABRAHAM, physician; b. Phila., Jan. 6, 1907; s. Harry and Sophie (Zimring) B.; B.S., U. Pa., 1927, M.D., 1930; postgrad. internal medicine and cardiology Columbia U., 1939-40; m. Grace B. Novak. Intern, Albert Einstein Med. Center, 1930-31, clin. asst., 1932-37, asso. in medicine, 1936-46; asso. in cardiology U. Pa. Sch. Medicine, 1946; chief outpatient dept. St. Luke's Med. Center, 1937-46; med. cons. SSS, 1940-42; cons. physician in medicine St. Luke's and Children's Med. Center Phila., 1940-62, cons. physician in internal medicine and cardiology, 1962—; cons. in internal medicine and cardiology Rolling Hill Hosp. and Diagnostic Center, Elkins Park, Pa., Oxford Hosp., Phila.; attending cardiologist Grad. Hosp. U. Pa.; faculty U. Pa. Sch. Medicine. Vice chmn. Phila. physicians div. Allied Jewish Appeal-Israel Emergency Fund. Served from capt. to maj. M.C., AUS, 1942-46. Fellow Internat. Soc. Cardiology, Am. Coll. Cardiology, Pa. Acad. Cardiology, Jerusalem Acad. Medicine, Am. Coll. Angiology, Am. Geriatric Soc., A.C.P. Internat. Coll. Angiology, Internat. Cardiology Found., Royal Soc. Health, Intercontinental Biog. Assn.; mem. Am., Internat. socs. internal medicine, AMA, AAAS, FAS, Pa., Phila. County med. socs., Am. Heart Assn. (council clin. cardiology, council basic sci., rheumatic fever, congenital heart disease, hypertension, arteriosclerosis), N.Y. Acad. Scis., Israel Med. Assn., Am., Pa, thoracic socs., AAUP, Diabetes Assn., Maimonides Soc. (charter), Royal Soc. Medicine, African Flying Drs. Soc., African Med. and Research Soc., Physicians Fellowship Com., Fellowship Commn., Internat. Platform Assn., Smithsonian Instn., Am. Friends Hebrew U. (exec. com.). Jewish (pres. congregation). Manuscript reviewer Am. Heart Jour., 1966—. Contbr. to med. jours. Home: 7414 Richards Rd Melrose Park PA 19126 Office: 1930 Chestnut St Philadelphia PA 19103

BEREND, ROBERT WILLIAM, lawyer; b. Miami Beach, Fla., Dec. 31, 1931; s. George Harry and Miriam (Wagner) B.; A.B., N.Y.U., 1952; LL.B., Yale, 1955. Admitted to N.Y. bar, 1955; practiced in N.Y.C., 1955—; asst. gen. atty. to trustee Hudson & Manhattan R.R. Co., N.Y.C., 1958-61; asso. firm Delson, Levin & Gordon, N.Y.C., 1961-65; partner firm Delson & Gordon, 1965-76; sr. v.p., gen. counsel Mgmt. Assistance Inc., 1976—, sec., dir., 1970—. Served with AUS, 1956-58. Mem. Am., N.Y. State, N.Y.C. bar assns., Phi Beta Kappa. Jewish. Club: Yale (N.Y.C.). Home: 132 E 35th St New York City NY 10016 Office: 300 E 44th St New York City NY 10017

BERENS, NORMAN, pharm. co. exec.; b. Bklyn., Jan. 25, 1934; s. Isaac Philip and Pearl Ida (Bor) B.; A.A.S., State U. N.Y., 1953; B.Chem. Engring., City Coll. N.Y., 1958; postgrad. N.Y. U., 1961-62; m. Eileen Kadish, June 12, 1954; children—Lance Philip, Scott Martin, Clark Spencer. Devel. chem. engr. Lederle Labs. div. Am. Cyanamid, 1958-61; supr. planning and projects, plant mgr. Sun Chem. Co., 1962-67; mgr. ops. planning E.R. Squibb & Sons, Inc., New Brunswick, N.J., 1968-75, mgr. project devel., Princeton, N.J., 1975—. Mem. Twp. Bldg. Adv. Com., 1970—; chmn. Proper Regional Inter Devel. Effort, 1970, sec., 1969; committeeman George Washington council Boy Scouts Am., 1968-75, sec., 1968-70, Cub Scout committeeman, 1969-75; chief radiac monitor Civil Def., 1952; mem., leader Ednl. Goals Conf., 1972; mem. religious affairs com. Princeton Jewish Center, 1973-76, chmn., 1975-76, v.p., 1976-77; budget dir. PTA, 1971; mgr., coach Little League Baseball, 1969-73. Recipient Otto Klitgord award State U. N.Y., 1953, Charles A. Marlies award Coll. City N.Y., 1958. Certified cardio-pulmonary resuscitation instr. trainer Am. Heart Assn. Mem. A.A.A.S., Am. Inst. Chem. Engrs. (pres. student chpt. 1957-58). Home: 24 Taylor Rd RFD 4 Princeton NJ 08540 Office: PO Box 4000 Princeton NJ 08540

BERENSON, JOSEPH S., lawyer, accountant; b. N.Y.C., May 23, 1898; s. Wolfe and Rose (Sukenik) B.; B.C.S. cum laude, N.Y.U., 1920; LL.B., N.Y. Law Sch., 1926; m. Birdie Bergman, June 17, 1928; children—Robert Kenneth, David Alan. Auditor, Bur. Investigation and Statistics, City N.Y., 1918-19; sr. partner Berenson & Berenson, C.P.A.'s, N.Y.C., 1920—; prof. accounting St. John's U., Bklyn., 1930-68, City Coll. N.Y., 1930-71. Mem. UN Assn. U.S.A., Internat. Platform Assn., Am. Soc. U. Profs., Am, Accounting Assn., N.Y. State Soc. C.P.A.'s, Beta Gamma Sigma, Alpha Beta Psi. Jewish religion. Mason; mem. B'nai B'rith. Home: 93 Baraud Rd Scarsdale NY 10583 Office: 100 Park Ave New York City NY 10017

BERENT, DAVID, clergyman; b. N.Y.C., Feb. 28, 1907; s. Louis and Esther R. (Botschko) B.; Rabbi, Ez Chayim Sem., Montreux, Switzerland, 1933; postgrad. Coll. City N.Y., 1925-28, Dropsie Coll., 1930-32, Tchrs. Coll. Columbia U., 1940-41; D.D., Colonial Acad., 1955; H.H.D., Nasson Coll., Springvale, Maine, 1957; m. Gertrude Weiner, Aug. 5, 1934; 1 son, Jonathan Alan. Rabbi, Congregation Beth Judah, Wildwood, N.J., 1937-40, Congregation Beth Jacob, Lewiston, Maine, 1940-75, rabbi emeritus, 1975—; chaplain VA Center and Hosp., Togus, Maine, 1941—; aux. chaplain U.S. Naval Air Sta., Brunswick, Maine, 1945—; adj. prof. dept. theology St. Joseph's College, North Windham, Maine; instr. dept. philosophy U. Maine; Jewish Chautauqua Soc. lectr. Bates, Bowdoin, Colby colls., U. Maine Del. Mid-Century White House Conf. on Youth; mem. Govs. Com. Vets Affairs and Child Health Welfare, Little Hoover Commn., 1952; mem. commn. character building and Bible accredition State Bd. Edn.; mem. State Bd. Mediators, 1958—, chmn., 1960—. Civilian chaplain Camp Keyes, Maine, 1943-45; chaplain, capt. Maine State Guard, 1954; aux. chaplain USAF, Topsham, Maine. Recipient citation Outstanding Citizen of Lewiston, Elks, 1949; Silver Beaver, Boy Scouts Am., 1952; medal and 2d prize Freedoms Found., 1959, medal, 1961; Humanitarian award State of Maine B'nai B'rith, 1962; Distinguished Service award State of Maine, 1963, NCCJ, 1969. Mem. Am. Assn. Higher Jewish Studies, Religious Zionists Am. (v.p. New Eng. region), Mental Hosp. Chaplains Assn. (New Eng. regional chmn.), Am. Acad. Polit. and Social Sci., Rabbinical Assn. Am., Zionist Orgn. Am., Mizrachi, Rabbinical Council New Eng., Rabbinical Assn. Maine (pres. 1959—), Mental Health Chaplains Assn., Mil. Chaplains Assn., Internat. Platform Assn., Am. Acad. Religion, Nat. Council Family Relations, Soc. for Sci. Study of Sex, Soc. for Advancement Higher Jewish Learning, Soc. for Advancement Edn., Va'ad Harabanim Greater Mass. (trustee), Am. Assn. for Higher Edn., Acad. Religion and Mental Health, Coll. Theology Soc., Am. Jewish Commn., Polit. Affairs Club Columbia (pres. 1941—). Clubs: Masons (grand chaplain Maine 1954—), Shriners, Odd Fellows, K.P., B'nai B'rith. Contbr. to Universal Jewish Ency., Anglo-Jewish Press. Home: 12 Bardwell St Lewiston ME 04240 Office: 2 Shawnut St Lewiston ME 04240

BERESTON, EUGENE SYDNEY, dermatologist; b. Balt., Feb. 21, 1914; s. Arthur and Sarah Bertha (Hillman) B.; A.B., Johns Hopkins, 1933; M.D., U. Md., 1937; M.Sc., U. Pa., 1945, D.Sc., 1955; m. Marion Ableman, Jan. 15, 1942 (dec. May 1975); children—Linda (Mrs. Richard Katz), David, Michael; m. 2d, Carol Ephraim, May 30, 1976; 1 dau., Patricia (Mrs. Robert Schulman). Intern, Meml. Hosp., Johnstown, Pa., 1937-38, Mercy Hosp., Balt., 1938-39; resident U. Pa., Phila., 1939-40, Montefiore Hosp., N.Y.C., 1940-41; practice medicine, specializing in dermatology, Balt., 1946—; faculty U. Md., 1946—, prof. medicine in dermatology, 1972—; instr. dermatology Johns Hopkins, 1946-60; chief dermatology Mercy Hosp., 1968—; cons. dermatology VA Hosp., 1951-76, Spring Grove State Hosp., 1952—; part-time chief dermatology VA Hosp., Washington, 1977—. Bd. dirs., chmn. Religious Sch. Temple Oheb Shalom, 1967-72, trustee, 1977—. Served to maj. M.C., AUS, 1941-46; PTO. Recipient research grant U.S. Army, 1951-57, award Ner Israel Rabbinical Coll., 1970. Diplomate Am. Bd. Dermatology. Fellow A.C.P., Am. Acad. Dermatology, Royal Soc. Health (Eng.); mem. Am. Legion (comdr. 1971-73), A.M.A., Soc. Investigative Dermatology, Dermatology Found., Md. Dermatologic Soc., Md. State, Balt. City med. socs. Clubs: Civitan (dir. 1964-78), Johns Hopkins (Balt.). Contbr. numerous articles to dermatol. jours. Home: 7707 Park Heights Ave Baltimore MD 21208 Office: 22 E Eager St Baltimore MD 21202

BERG, ALAN SULZBERGER, oil co. exec.; b. Phila., June 7, 1930; s. Abram Sulzberger and Elsie (Freidman) B.; student Bergen Jr. Coll., 1948-49, Gen. Motors Inst. Tech., 1950-51; children—Alan S., Andrew G., Eileen H. With Neatsfoot Oil Refiners Corp., Phila., 1952—, pres., 1968—; pres. Calber Chem., Inc., 1971-77, Glue Specialty Co., Inc., Phila., 1954—. Mem. Phila. Oil Trade Assn. (dir., golf chmn.), Am. Oils and Fats Assn. Club: Philmont Country. Home: 7911 Ronaele Dr Elkins Park PA 19117 Office: Neatsfoot Oil Refiners Corp E Ontario and Bath Sts Philadelphia PA 19134

BERG, GERALD ROBERT, physician; b. N.Y.C., May 31, 1942; s. Alban Aaron and Sylvia B.; B.S. magna cum laude, Coll. City N.Y., 1963; M.D. (Jonas Salk scholar 1963-67), U. Rochester, 1967; m. Barbara Less, June 15, 1963; children—Adam Seth, Jason David, Melissa Anne. Intern, resident in internal medicine Bronx Municipal Hosp., Albert Einstein Coll. Medicine, 1967-69; research asso. NIH, Bethesda Md., 1969-71; resident in radiology Mass. Gen. Hosp., Boston, 1971-74; attending radiologist Waterbury (Conn.) Hosp. Health Center, 1974—; instr. radiology Harvard Med. Sch., 1971-74; asst. prof. diagnostic radiology Yale U. Med. Sch., 1974—. Bd. dirs. Marrakech Inc., 1974-78. Served as lt. cmdr. USPHS, 1969-71. George Hoyt Whipple scholar, 1967-68; diplomate Am. Bd. Internat Medicine, Am. Bd. Diagnostic Radiology, Am. Bd. Nuclear Medicine. Mem. Conn. Soc. Ultrasound in Medicine (pres. 1976-78), Am. Coll. Radiology, Soc. Nuclear Medicine, Am. Inst. Ultrasound in Medicine, Conn., New Haven County, Waterbury med. socs., Phi Beta Kappa, Alpha Omega Alpha. Contbr. articles to profl. jours. Office: 134 Robbins St Waterbury CT 06720

BERG, LOIS ANNE, dietitian; b. Akron, Ohio, Feb. 14, 1934; d. Donald Valentine and Anna Johanna (Moewe) Berg; B.S. in Dietetics, Coll. St. Mary of Springs, Columbus, Ohio, 1956. Intern dietetics, then dietitian Miami Valley Hosp., Dayton, 1956-58; adminstrv. dietitian Riverside Methodist Hosp., Columbus, 1958-77, Weirton (W.Va.) Gen. Hosp., 1977—. Mem. Am., Columbus dietetic assns., Am. Soc. Hosp. Food Service Adminstrs. Democrat. Roman Catholic. Home: 553 Oaklynn Ct Apt TH Pittsburgh PA 15220 Office: Weirton Med Center Colliers Way Weirton WV 26062

BERG, LOUIS LESLIE, investment exec.; b. Vienna, Austria, Dec. 27, 1919; s. Gustav and Hedwig (Kohn) B.; came to U.S., 1938, naturalized, 1943; student U. Vienna, 1937-38, Coll. City N.Y., 1941-43; m. Minnette Whitman, Aug. 28, 1959; children—Sharon, Randee, Michel. Pres., Gt. Empire Corp., N.Y.C., 1946—, Bendalou Real Estate Corp., N.Y.C., 1950-60, Netherlands Securities Co., Inc., N.Y.C., 1959-62, Imported Automotive Parts, Ltd., L.I. City, N.Y.; dir. Internat. Aviation Corp., Cosmos Industries, Kane-Miller Corp., Knickerbocker Toy Co., Inc., Wernitron Corp., Jet Aero Corp., Fidelity Am. Finance Corp., S.W. Fla. Enterprises, Sulray Inc., U.S. Airlines, Commuter Airlines, Aviation Equipment, I.A.P. Inc., Lyndhurst, N.J. Mem. Am. Mgmt. Assn. Club: Wings. Home: 945 Fifth Ave New York City NY 10021 also 50 Hagivah Savyon Israel Office: 220 Clay Ave Lyndhurst NJ 07071

BERGAU, FRANK CONRAD, educator; b. N.Y.C., Sept. 17, 1926; s. Frank Conrad and Mary Elizabeth (Davie) B.; B.A. in English, St. Francis Coll., Loretto, Pa., 1950; M.S. in Edn. and English, Potsdam (N.Y.) State U., 1969; m. Rita I. Korotkin; children—Mary, Rita, Francis, Theresa, Veronica. Tchr. English Gouverneur (N.Y.) Schs., 1962—, dir. continuing edn., 1968—, summer prin., 1974—; project dir. St. Lawrence County (N.Y.) Bd. Co-op. Ednl. Services, Canton, 1974. Bd. dirs. St. Lawrence County Assn. Retarded Children, 1965—, Gouverneur Library. Mem. Gouverneur C of C (dir. 1963-66), NEA, N.Y. Assn. Continuing Edn. (dir.). Certified as tchr., supr., adminstr., N.Y. Club: Gouverneur Luncheon. Home: 52 Wall St Gouverneur NY 13642 Office: 133 Barney St Gouverneur NY 13642

BERGEN, CATHARINE MARY, ret. educator; b. Garden City, N.Y., Jan. 16, 1912; d. John Oldfield and Alice (Terry) Bergen; A.B., Wellesley Coll., 1933; M.A., Columbia, 1935, Ph.D., 1942. Elementary sci. cons. Garden City pub. schs., 1934-37; asst. in physics Hofstra Coll., 1939-40; elementary sci. Tchrs. Coll., Columbia, 1940-43; sci. workshop, extra-mural U. Chgo., Hastings, Mich., summer 1941; asso. prof. sci. Jersey City State Coll., 1941-54, prof. sci., 1954-69, prof. physics, 1969-72, prof. emeritus, 1974—, chmn. sci. dept., 1954-58. Mem. Am. Phys. Soc., AAAS, AAUP, AAUW (past pres. Jersey City br., past dir. N.J.), NEA, Nat., N.J. (past pres.) sci. tchrs. assns., Am. Inst. City of N.Y., Pi Lambda Theta, Kappa Delta Pi. Author: Childrens Science Information, 1943. Home: 39 Duncan Ave Jersey City NJ 07304

BERGEN, DANIEL PATRICK, librarian, educator; b. Albert Lea, Minn., May 25, 1935; s. Francis Joseph and Grace Frances (Donovan) B.; A.B. in History-Philosophy, U. Notre Dame, 1957, M.A. in Polit. Sci., 1962; M.A. in Librarianship, U.Chgo., 1961, postgrad. (Univ. fellow), 1963, certificate of advanced study in librarianship, 1969; M.A. in Am. Studies, U. Minn., 1968, Ph.D. in Am. Studies (Univ. fellow), 1970; postgrad. in philosophy, summer 1973-75; postgrad. U.Conn. Law Sch., fall 1977; m. Carol Lee Janson, Apr. 11, 1958; children—Mary Clare, Paula Maureen, Brent Daniel, Gregory Joseph. Grad. asst. dept. polit. sci. U. Notre Dame, 1957-58, 61-62; asst. librarian, instr. polit. sci. St. Benedict's Coll., 1962-63; asst. dean, lectr. Sch. Library Sci. Syracuse U., 1964-65; asst. prof. Sch. Library, Info. Services U. Md., 1965-66; asso. prof. library sci. U. Miss., 1966-70, chmn. dept. library sci., 1966-68; asso. prof. U. R.I., 1970-75, prof., 1975—. Served with USAF, 1958-60. U. R.I., 1970-75, prof., 1975—. Served with USAF, 1958-60. U. R.I. teaching effectiveness grantee, 1975. Mem. AAAS, AAUP, ALA, Am. Studies Assn., Assn. Am. Library Schs., New Eng., R.I. (exec. bd. 1974-78, pres., 1976-77) library assns., Soc. Gen. Systems Research, Beta Phi Mu. Contbr. articles to profl. publs. Home: 41 Highland Ave Wakefield RI 02879 Office: Grad Library Sch U RI Kingston RI 02881

BERGER, BERTRAM, civil engr.; b. Boston, Feb. 3, 1931; s. Benjamin and Anna Bella (Ullian) B.; B.S., Northeastern U., 1954; postgrad. Mass. Inst. Tech., 1956-57; m. S. Frances Forman, Oct. 31, 1954; children—Beth Lee, Robin Carole, Gwenne Cheryl, Lynne Ann. With E.W. Branch, Quincy, Mass., 1950-52; with Fay, Spofford & Thorndike, Boston, 1952—, v.p., dir., head transp. dept.; mem. energy conservation com. Mass. Dept. Community Affairs. Mem. Bd. Appeals Sharon (Mass.), 1969-72; chmn. United Fund, 1972-73; v.p., dir. Temple Israel. Served with U.S. Army, 1954-56. Registered profl. engr., Mass. Mem. ASCE, Boston Soc. Civil Engrs. (past pres.), Inst. Transp. Engrs., Met. Assn. Urban Designers and Environ. Planners, Soc. Am. Mil. Engrs., Nat., Mass. socs. profl. engrs. Jewish. Home: 126 Billings St Sharon MA 02067 Office: One Beacon St Boston MA 02108

BERGER, EUGENE Y., physician; b. Phila., Dec. 11, 1919; s. Charles and Pearl Fan (Wagner) B.; B.A. (Ario Pardee scholar 1936), Lafayette Coll., 1940; M.D., N.Y. U., 1944; m. Betty Bratter Levy, May 27, 1951; children—Arthur Wagner, Ann Rothschild. Intern Newark Beth Israel Hosp., 1944-45; resident Goldwater Meml. Hosp., N.Y. U. Research Service, 1946-48, research fellow, 1948-50, research asst., 1951-53, research asso., 1953-56, asso. dir., 1956—; asst. in medicine N.Y. U. Sch. Medicine, N.Y.C., 1948-51, instr., 1951-53, asst. prof., 1953-61, asso. prof. medicine, 1961—; med. dir. Morningside House, N.Y.C., 1973—; mem. staff Goldwater Meml. Hosp. Served to lt. (j.g.) M.C., USNR, 1945-46, 53-54. Recipient N.Y. Heart Assn. fellowship, 1949. Diplomate Am. Bd. Internal Medicine. Fellow N.Y. Acad. Scis.; mem. Am. Chem. Soc., Am. Fedn. Clin. Research, Am. Physiol. Soc., Am. Soc. Clin. Investigation, Harvey Soc., N.Y. Acad. Medicine, N.Y. Acad. Scis., Soc. Exptl. Biology and Medicine, Alpha Omega Alpha. Contbr. articles to profl. jours. Home: 126 Ritchie Dr Yonkers NY 10705 Office: 1000 Pelham Pkwy New York City NY 10461

BERGER, HARVEY ROBERT, psychologist; b. Quincy, Mass., Nov. 3, 1927; s. Joel Joseph and Helen Esther (Stone) B.; B.A., Tufts U., 1949, M.A., 1950; Ph.D., U. Mo., 1953; m. Thelma Lee Cohen, July 11, 1954. Psychologist, Marblehead (Mass.) Pub. Schs., 1953—; dir. psychol. services Federally Assisted Programs, Salem (Mass.) Pub. Schs., 1967-76; asso. prof. Salem State Coll., 1963; clin. dir. North Shore Psychol. Counselling and Testing Center, 1963-75; pres. Paul Revere Savs. & Loan Assn., 1971-76, William Dawes Realty Corp. Mem. Nat. Commn. on Safety Edn., 1952-54; capt., Mass. comdt. U.S. Naval Cadet Program, 1966—; pres. Area Bd. on Mental Health and Retardation, 1975-78; vice chmn. Greater Lynn Council for Children, Mass. Office for Children, 1977-78. Auditor Republican City Com., Lynn, Mass., 1970—. Pres. Mass. Am. Legion Coll., 1964-66; pres. NEA Mut. Fund; chmn. bd. NEA Income Fund; trustee Ida C. Romanow Fund. Served with AUS, 1945-47. Fellow Sch. Alcohol Studies, Yale, 1957. Diplomate Am. Bd. Examiners Profl. Psychology. Fellow Am. Assn. Mental Deficiency, Royal Soc. Health; mem. Am. Psychol. Assn., Soc. for Personality and Social Psychology, Nat. Assn. Sch. Psychologists, Am. Psychology-Law Soc., Soc. for Advancement Social Psychology, Soc. Behaviorists, Religious Zionists Am. (life), Mass. Bar Assn., NEA (life), Am. Legion (life), VFW, Navy League (life), U.S. Naval Inst. (life), Nat. Soc. Profs. (life), Am. Assn. Higher Edn. (life), D.A.V. (life), Phi Beta Kappa, Phi Delta Kappa. Jewish. Mason (32 deg, Shriner); mem. Order Eastern Star. Home: 31 Tudor St Lynn MA 01902 Office: Sch Dept Marblehead MA 01945

BERGER, HENRY, psychiatrist; b. Marburg, Germany, Jan. 17, 1947; s. Oscar and Rose (Engelstein) B.; came to U.S., 1948, naturalized, 1953; B.A., Columbia U., 1968, M.S., 1971, Ph.D., 1973; M.D., Dartmouth Med. Sch., 1978; m. Elizabeth Ann Blum, Oct. 27,

1974. Practice clin. psychology specializing in psychotherapy, Scarsdale and N.Y.C., 1973-75; practice medicine specializing in psychiatry, Hanover, N.H., 1978—; instr. Columbia U., 1972-73; asso. psychologist Lenox Hill Hosp., N.Y.C., 1973-74; psychiatrist Dartmouth-Hitchcock Med. Center, 1978—. NIMH fellow, 1968-72; Nat. Council Alcoholism fellow, 1977-78. Mem. Am., Vt. psychol. assns., Harry Stack Sullivan Soc., Sigma Xi. Office: Dept Psychiatry Dartmouth-Hitchcock Med Center Hanover NH 03755

BERGER, HERBERT, physician; b. Bklyn., Dec. 14, 1909; s. Louis and Augusta (Feldman) B.; B.Sc., N.Y. U., 1929; M.D., U. Md., 1932; m. Sylvia Berger, Oct., 1930; children—Leland S., Shelby L. (Mrs. William Jakoby). Intern, Morrisania City Hosp., Bronx, N.Y., 1932-34; resident U.S. Naval Hosps., 1941-45; practice medicine, 1934—; cardiologist Sea View Hosp., S.I., 1934—; attending physician Flower-Fifth Ave. Hosp., Met. Hosp.; cons. USPHS Hosp.; prof. medicine N.Y. Med. Coll., 1962—; pres. med. staff, dir. medicine emeritus Richmond Meml. Hosp., 1975—. Dir., Group Health Ins. Inc. Served to comdr. USNR, 1942-45. Recipient Gold medal U. Md., 1978. Diplomate Am. Bd. Internal Medicine Fellow Am. Coll. Physicians, Am. Coll. Chest Physicians; mem. Internat. Coll. Angiology, N.Y. Acad. Medicine (chmn. sect. on medicine, vice chmn. com. med. edn.), Brit. Soc. Health Edn., Richmond County (past pres.), N.Y.C. (past pres.) med. socs., Med. Soc. State N.Y. (past v.p.), Blood Banks Assn. (past pres.), N.Y. State Soc. Internal Medicine (past pres.), Internat. Soc. for Study Addictions (past pres.). Republican. Jewish. Clubs: Richmond County Country, Richmond County Yacht. Contbr. over 150 articles to med. jours., chpts. med. text books. Cons. editor: Medical Times; Internat. Jour. of the Addictions. Home: 25 Bloomingdale Rd Staten Island NY 10309 Office: 7440 Amboy Rd Staten Island NY 10307

BERGER, OSCAR, artist; b. Presov (Eperjes), Czechoslovakia, May 12, 1901; s. Henry and Regina (Berger) B.; art study in Europe; m. Ann Arany I. Varga, Feb. 9, 1937. First visit to U.S., 1928, naturalized, 1955. Sketched 1945 UN Conf. in San Francisco for N.Y. Times, London (Eng.) Daily Telegraph; caricaturist of world celebrities drawn from life, including: Winston Churchill, Eleanor Roosevelt, Queen Elizabeth II, Pres. Pompidou, Molotov, Edison, Prince Philip of Eng., Queen Wilhelmina, Premier Alexei Kosygin, King Paul I of Greece, Pres. Tito, Pope Pius XII, Pope Paul VI, Franklin D. Roosevelt, Herbert Hoover, Harry S. Truman, Dwight D. Eisenhower, Anna Pavlova, Carl Sandburg, Emperor Haile Selassie, Albert Einstein, John F. Kennedy, Chancellor Willy Brandt, Jacqueline Kennedy-Onassis, Golda Meir, Anwar Sadat, Robert Frost, Bernard Shaw, Toscanini, Charles De Gaulle, King Baudouin, King Faisal, Premier Khrushchev, Leonid Brezhnev, Lyndon Baines Johnson, Pres. Richard Nixon, Gerald Ford, Jimmy Carter, numerous others; sketched meetings of League of Nations, Geneva, 1925, House of Commons, London, 1935-45, UN confs., 1945-78, UN gen. assemblies, 1946—; works represented in permanent collections Library of Congress, Nat. Portrait Gallery, Met. Mus., also pvt. collections and museums. Author: Tip & Top, 1933; Aesop's Foibles, 1947; A La Carte, 1948; Famous Faces, 1950; My Victims, 1952; I Love You, 1960; The Presidents, 1969; contbr. articles, illustrations, caricatures, cartoons to Am. and European newspapers and mags., Nat. Register Indsl. Art Designers, London, 1944. Club: Nat. Press (Washington). Address: Berkeley House 120 Central Park S New York City NY 10019

BERGER, RICHARD A., ednl. adminstr.; b. Sayville, N.Y., Mar. 1, 1917; married, 2 children. B.S. in Edn., N.Y. U., N.Y.C., 1951, M.A. in Guidance, 1953. With Sachem Central Sch. Dist., Holbrook, N.Y., 1955—, asst. supt. instruction and facilities, 1966-75, supt., 1975—. Mem. Am. Assn. Sch. Adminstrs., Suffolk County Sch. Execs. Assn., Islip Town Chief Sch. Adminstrs., Bd. of Coop. Ednl. Services, Chief Sch. Adminstrs. Contbr. articles in field to profl jour. Office: 245 Union Ave Holbrook NY 11779

BERGER, ROBERT IRVING, computer specialist; b. Bklyn., July 25, 1943; s. Ralph Oscar and Ida B.; A.A.S., RCA Inst., 1965; degree in Computer Tech., Bklyn. Poly. Inst., 1969; m. Susan Diane Davis, June 13, 1965; children—Rochelle Joy, David Edward. Asst. mem. tech. staff Bell Telephone Labs., Holmdel, N.J., 1965-69; mgr. programming and ops. Transnet Corp., Union, N.J., 1969-71; mgr. minicomputers ITT World Hdqrs., N.Y.C., 1971-75; asst. v.p. Bankers Trust, N.Y.C., 1975—, in-house trainer for programmers; cons. small bus. N.Y. State scholar, 1961-65. Mem. IEEE, Assn. Small Computer Users, Decus. Home: 5 Buck Rd East Brunswick NJ 08816 Office: 1 Bankers Trust Plaza New York NY 10006

BERGER, ROBERT NORMAN, metals co. exec.; b. New Brunswick, N.J., July 27, 1935; s. George and Helen (Beck) B.; B.S.C., Rider Coll., 1958; postgrad. Acad. Advanced Traffic, 1961; m. Helene Kassoff, June 3, 1956; children—Michael Steven, Sharon Ilean. Traffic rep. Westinghouse Corp., Trenton, N.J., 1966-69; traffic mgr. Circle F Industries, Trenton, 1969-71; traffic mgr. N.J. Aluminum Co., North Brunswick, N.J., 1959-65, mgr. distbn. and purchasing, 1971—; mem. safety com. Pvt. Truck Council. Election dist. judge, Levittown, Pa., 1973-76; active Boy Scouts Am.; mem. Newportville 1 Fire Co. Served with AUS, 1958-59. Elk, Odd Fellow. Home: 70 Mill Dr Levittown PA 19056 Office: POB 73 North Brunswick NJ 08902

BERGER, SANFORD EARL, exec. search co. exec.; b. Chgo., Aug. 11, 1928; s. Joseph Abraham and Anna (Goodman) B.; B.S.S., CCNY, 1950; LL.B., Tulane U., 1957; m. Barbara Scheckter, Feb. 22, 1959; children—Dana, Glen, Laura. Admitted to La. bar, 1957; account exec. Merrill Lynch, Paramus, N.J., 1958-65; br. mgr. Hayden Stone, N.Y.C., 1965-68; regional mgr. Blair & Co., Stamford, Conn., 1968-69; br. mgr. Thomson & McKinnon, N.Y.C., 1969-72, Bache & Co., N.Y.C., 1972-74; pres. Dunhill of Paramus, Inc. (N.J.), 1975—. Served with USCG, 1952-54. Presdl. scholar Tulane U., 1955-57. Mem. N.J. Assn. Personnel Cons. (pres. 1978), Assn. Investment Brokers (dir.), Nat. Assn. Security Dealers. Club: Rotary (pres. River Vale 1973). Home: 606 Sargent Rd River Vale NJ 07675 Office: 27 Madison Ave Paramus NJ 07652

BERGGREN, JOHN PHILIP, ins. co. exec.; b. Middletown, Conn., July 11, 1918; s. John Philip and Hannah Josephine (Anderson) B.; B.S., Worcester Poly. Inst., 1942; postgrad. Mass. Inst. Tech.; m. Lorraine Ann Grubelich, Apr. 9, 1955; children—Jill Alane, Wendy Sue, Bradley Scott. Safety engr. Aetna Life & Casualty Co., Hartford, 1946-57, mgr. engring., Buffalo, 1957-65, Syracuse, N.Y., 1965-67, supt. tech. services, Hartford, 1967-69, asst. sec. engring. dept., Hartford, 1969-77, dir., 1977—. Trustee Village of East Aurora, N.Y., 1965; mem. Glastonbury (Conn.) Sewer Commn., 1969-78, chmn., 1975-78. Served to lt. comdr. USNR, 1942-46, 51-52. Registered profl. engr., Conn. Mem. Am. Ins. Assn., Am. Nat. Standards Inst., Nat. Fire Protection Assn., Am. Indsl. Hygiene Assn. (pres. Conn. River Valley sect. 1972-73), Phi Sigma Kappa. Republican. Episcopalian. Home: 285 Buttonball Ln Glastonbury CT 06033 Office: 151 Farmington Ave Hartford CT 06115

BERGIN, CHARLES KYRAN, JR., lawyer; b. Lexington, Mass., Dec. 12, 1940; s. Charles Kyran and Eleanor Elizabeth (Cove) B.; B.A. in Econs., St. Francis Coll., 1962; LL.B., Boston Coll., 1965; m. Judith Emma Wentzel, Sept. 5, 1964; children—Charles Kyran, III, Daniel Raymond, Kristin Mary. Admitted to Mass. bar, 1965; trial atty., criminal div. U.S. Dept. Justice, Washington, 1965-67; mem. firm Robinson, Donovan, Madden & Barry, Springfield, Mass.; U.S. magistrate Dist. of Mass., Springfield, 1971—. First asst. city solicitor, Springfield, 1967-70. Mem. Am., Mass., Hampden County bar assns., (v.p. young lawyers 1969-70), Assn. Trial Lawyers Am. (state committeeman 1974—), Mass. Acad. Trial Attys. (bd. govs. 1973—), Order of Coif Democrat. Roman Cahtolic. Mem. editorial staff Boston Coll. Indsl. and Comml. Law Rev., 1964, 65. Home: 93 Northfield Rd Longmeadow MA 01106 Office: 127 State St Springfield MA 01103

BERGLAND, BOB SELMER, govt. ofcl.; b. Roseau, Minn., July 22, 1928; grad. U. Minn. Sch. Agr., 1948; m. Helen Elaine Grohn, 1950; children—Dianne, Linda, Stevan, Jon, Allan, Billy, Franklyn. Mem. 92d to 94th Congresses from 7th Minn. dist.; mem. Agr. Com., mem. Conservation and Credit Subcom., Livestock and Grains Subcom.; mem. Sci. and Astronautics Com.; mem. Select Com. on Small Bus.; sec. Dept. Agr., Washington, 1977—. Mem. Farmers Union, Nat. Farmers Orgn. Mem. Democratic Farm Labor party. Lutheran. Mason, Lion, Eagle. Office: Dept Agr The Mall between 12th & 14th St NW Washington DC 20250

BERGLAND, GLENN DAVID, computer systems research exec.; b. Forest City, Iowa, Aug. 12, 1940; s. Glenn Woodrow and Delia (Twenge) B.; B.S. in E.E., Iowa State U., 1962, M.S. in E.E., 1964, Ph.D. in E.E., 1966; m. Marilyn Ardis Stevens, Dec. 27, 1961; children—Kara, Eric, Matthew. Computer engr. Dept. Def., Ft. Meade, Md., 1963; tchr., research asst. Iowa State U., 1963-66; mem. tech. staff, tech. group supr. Computer Systems Studies Group, Bell Telephone Labs., Whippany, N.J., 1966-72, head software systems and advanced computer arch. depts., Naperville, Ill., 1972-77, head digital systems research dept., Murray Hill, N.J., 1977—; lectr. short course Nat. Engring. Consortium. Recipient hon. mention as outstanding young elec. engr. Eta Kappa Nu, 1969; named Outstanding Young Alumnus, Iowa State U., 1970. Mem. IEEE, Assn. Computing Machinery, AAAS, Sigma Xi, Eta Kappa Nu, Tau Beta Pi, Phi Kappa Phi, Phi Mu Alpha Sinfonia. Republican. Lutheran. Patentee digital signal processing algorithms, spl. purpose arch. Home: 106 Wentworth Dr Berkeley Heights NJ 07922 Office: 600 Mountain Ave Murray Hill NJ 07974

BERGLUND, ALICE MAE, tech. translator; b. Medford, Mass., Jan. 19, 1943; d. Allan D. and Mary E. (Turner) Russell; B.A. in Russian, U. Mass., 1964; postgrad. in doctoral program U. Calif. at Berkeley, 1964-66; postgrad, Harvard U., 1968-77. U. Lowell, 1977—; m. Arthur E. Berglund, Mar. 25, 1975; children—Joan, Elise. With CIA, Washington, 1966-67; tech. librarian and translator Norton Research Co., Cambridge, Mass., 1967-70; asst. dir. Etymon Research, Medford, Mass., 1970-73; dir. Internat. Translation Co., Peabody, Mass., 1973—. NDEA fellow, 1964-66. Mem. Am. Translation Assn., New Eng. Translators Assn. (v.p. 1976-78), AAAS. Contbr. articles in field to profl. jours.; editor New Eng. Translators Assn. News, 1976—; translator: Y. A. Solonskii's Solar Rotation, 1977. Address: 35 Catherine Dr Peabody MA 01960

BERGMAN, BARRY EDWARD, ins. exec.; b. Bronx, Aug. 13, 1945; s. Mortimer Aaron and Mary (Axelrod) B.; A.A., Queensborough Coll., 1965; B.A., Queens Coll., 1967; m. Iris Libow, Aug. 26, 1967; children—Jill Renee, Lauren Rae, Jeremy Scott, Jonathan Reid. Adminstrv. asst. to ops. partner Eastman Dillon & DuPont Glove Forgan Inc., N.Y.C., 1967-70; with Prudential Ins. Am., Bohemia, N.Y., 1970—, div. mgr., 1971-73, agy. mgr., 1973—. CLU. Mem. Nat. Assn. Life Underwriters, Gen. Agents and Mgrs. Conf., Am. Soc. CLU, Suffolk County Life Underwriters Assn. (dir.). Liberal. Club: Kiwanis. Home: 3 Tarleton Ct Fort Salonga NY 11768 Office: 40 Orville Dr Bohemia NY 11716

BERGMAN, CHARLES CABE, orgn. exec.; b. Boston, May 1, 1933; s. Sidney Meyer and Esther Rachel (Cabe) B.; A.B., Harvard U., 1954. Account asst. Ketchum, MacLeod & Grove, Inc., Pitts., 1955-57; asso. dir. devel. and alumni affairs Browne & Nichols Sch., Cambridge, Mass., 1957-59; asso. v.p. Lavin Co., Inc., Boston and N.Y.C., 1959-61; v.p. People to People Health Fedn., Washington, 1962-63; v.p. Inter-Am. Found. for the Arts, N.Y.C., 1963-65; exec. v.p., treas., trustee Acad. Religion and Mental Health, N.Y.C., 1965-72; exec. v.p., chief operating officer, dir., mem. exec. com. Insts. Religion and Health, 1972-78. Dir. George Nelson & Co., N.Y.C. Cons. Adminstrv. Psychiatry Program, Yale Med. Sch., New Haven, 1971, Nat. Inst. Mental Health, Argentina, 1969, Center for studies Child and Family Mental Health, NIMH, Washington, 1971; spl. adviser Pres.'s Com. on Mental Retardation, Washington, 1971—, White House Conf. on Children and Youth, Washington, 1970, Maurice Falk Med. Fund, 1971—; vis. lectr. U. Colo. Mem. council New Directions; chmn. internat. council Am. Field Service Internat. Intercultural Programs; mem. exec. com., bd. mgrs. Silver Hill Found.; spl. cons. President's Commn. on Mental Health; pres., chief exec. officer, bd. dirs., exec. com. Program for New World Anthropology; trustee Lenox Sch.; bd. dirs. Pro Musicis Found.; chmn. internat. council Bklyn. Mus. Clubs: Century Assn.; Harvard (Boston); Harvard-Yale-Princeton (Pitts.); Cosmos (Washington). Home: 25 E 37th St New York City NY 10016 Office: 200 E 42d St 27th Floor New York City NY 10017

BERGMAN, JAMES ABERT, assn. exec.; b. Watertown, Wis., Jan. 6, 1945; s. Abert Virgil and Alice Lucille Marie (Trachte) B.; B.S., U. Wis., 1967; m. Terry Jane Trowbridge, June 28, 1969; 1 son, Samuel Trowbridge. Dir. Legal project of Council of Elders, Inc., Roxbury, Mass., 1969-72; dir. program devel. Mass. Dept. Elder Affairs, Boston, 1972-73; asst. sec. dept. 1973-75; New Eng. regional dir. Legal Research and Services for the Elderly (project Nat. Council Sr. Citizens), Boston, 1975—; pres. Workers With Elderly; chmn. Elderly Legal Coalition; mem. profl. adv. com. Dept. Elder Affairs. Del., Wis. Republican Conv., 1967, 68, 69. Mem. Gerontol. Soc., Mass. Gerontology Assn., Mass. Assn. Older Ams., Common Cause, Mass. Hort. Soc. Democrat. Home: 47 Carville Ave Lexington MA 02173 Office: 2 Park Square Boston MA 02116

BERGMANN, ARTHUR, county ofcl.; b. Bklyn., Nov. 24, 1927; s. Augustus H. and Johanna Bergmann; B.S. in Polit. Sci. and Pub. Adminstrn., Empire State Coll., Old Westbury, N.Y., 1974; postgrad. in pub. adminstrn. C.W. Post Coll.; m. Shirley H. Lipsman, Dec. 24, 1948; children—Susan M., Joel M., Kathy G., Jonathan M. With N.Y. Herald Tribune, 1945-63; asst. news editor Riverhead News, 1949-50; Suffolk County (N.Y.) corr. for N.Y.C. newspapers, 1949-63; news editor Moriches (N.Y.) Tribune, 1950-51; mem. staff Newsday, 1951-71, Suffolk County polit. editor, columnist, 1965-71; chief dep. Suffolk County Exec., Hauppauge, N.Y., 1972—. Chmn., Suffolk Criminal Justice Coordinating Council, 1975, Arson Action Com.-Suffolk Arson Task Force, 1978, County/State Released Mental Patient Liaison Com., 1973, N.Y. State/Suffolk County Mental Health Demonstration Project Bd., 1978; mem. Juvenile Justice Task Force, 1975-77, MTA Permanent Citizens Adv. Com., 1978, Nassau/Suffolk Emergency Med. Services Council, 1976; adv. council N.Y. State Crime Victims Compensation Bd., 1978; chmn. Nassau. Suffolk Govt./Bus. Econ. Devel. Com., 1976-77; interim adminstr. Suffolk County Dept. Econ. Devel. 1977-78; adv. bd. Suffolk County Dept. Transp., 1977; trustee Suffolk Acad. Medicine, 1976; chmn. med./govt. liaison com. Suffolk Acad. Medicine-Suffolk County Med. Soc., 1977; adv. council Empire State Coll., 1977, W. Averell Harriman Coll. Urban and Policy Scis., 1977; trustee, bd. dirs. planning com. United Way Nassau-Suffolk. Served with USAAF, 1946-47. Recipient Distinguished Service award United Jewish Appeal, 1976; Pub. Adminstrn. award C.W. Post Coll., 1977; Distinguished Service plaque L.I. Assn. Commerce and Industry, 1977. Mem. Acad. Polit. Sci., Soc. Silurians, Am. Soc. Pub. Adminstrs., Nat. Assn. County Adminstrs., Pi Delta Delta. Address: 10 Estate Rd Center Moriches NY 11934

BERGMANN, WARREN CLARENCE, mech. engr.; b. Lyndhurst, N.J., May 21, 1921; s. Frank A. and Matoria C. (Tribout) B.; B.M.E., Newark Coll. Engring., 1950; m. Phyllis E. Rule, Sept. 10, 1949; 1 son, Brian P. Devel. engr. Walter Kidd & Co., Belleville, N.J., 1951-56; chief engr. Pneu-Hydro Valve Corp., Cedar Knolls, N.J., 1956-69; sr. design engr. Curtiss-Wright Corp., Caldwell, N.J., 1970; sr. project engr. Valcor Engring. Corp., Kenilworth, N.J., 1970-73; chief engr. Angar Sci. Controls, a Brunswick Co., East Hanover, N.J., 1973—. Served with AUS, 1943-46; ETO. Registered profl. engr., N.J. Mem. Nat. Soc. Profl. Engrs., Am. Soc. Metals, N.J. Inst. Tech. Alumni Assn. (past pres., trustee), Am., Garden State theatre organ socs., Am. Legion. Patentee cable-cutting shut-off valve. Home: 35 Spruce Run Rd Clinton NJ 08809 Office: B 8-9 Merry Ln East Hanover NJ 07936

BERGQUIST, PHILIP EUGENE, accountant; b. Danbury, Conn., Aug. 23, 1924; s. Gustav Victor and Vena Frances (Anderson) B.; B.B.A., Pace Coll., 1949; m. Kathryn Elizabeth Hill, Oct. 16, 1954. Bookkeeper, Am. Hatters & Furriers Co., Inc., Danbury, 1951-61; staff accountant Seward and Monde, C.P.A.'s, Danbury, 1961—, mgr. br. office, 1971—. Chmn. supervisory com. Conn. State Grange Fed. Credit Union, 1972—. Served with AUS, 1943-45. C.P.A., D.C., Conn. Mem. Am. Inst. C.P.A.'s, Conn. Soc. C.P.A.'s, Nat. Assn. Accountants. Republican. Methodist. Clubs: Kiwanis (treas. 1971—), Grange. Home: 348 N Salem Rd Ridgefield CT 06877 Office: 234 Main St Danbury CT 06810

BERGSTROM, GARY LEONARD, fin. mgmt. co. exec.; b. Chgo., Mar. 4, 1941; s. Nils E. and Anna (Granberg) B.; B.S., Purdue U., 1962, M.S., 1963; postgrad. Indian Inst. Mgmt., Calcutta, 1966-67; Ph.D., Mass. Inst. Tech., 1968; m. Joan Lois Margosian, Sept. 4, 1966; 1 son, Craig. Instr. Sloan Sch. Mgmt., Mass. Inst. Tech., Cambridge, 1967-68; with Putnam Mgmt. Co., Boston, 1968-77, asst. v.p., 1969-71, v.p., 1971-77; v.p. Putnam Internat. Adv. S.A. (Luxembourg), 1976—; pres. Acadian Fin. Research Inc.; lectr. fin., investments Babson Coll., 1972-73. Treas. Fayerweather St. Sch., Cambridge, 1971-73. Ford Found. fellow, 1964-66. Mem. Sylvanus Packard Soc. of Tufts U., Boston Soc. Security Analysts, Inst. Mgmt. Scis. Author: Resource Utilization in Indian Manufacturing, 1972. Contbr. articles on investment mgmt. to profl. publs. Office: 265 Franklin St Boston MA 02110 also 320 E 43d St New York City NY 10017

BERGSTROM, JOHN, actor, dir.; b. Kewanee, Ill., July 23, 1941; s. Leland Warren and Edith (Rusk) B.; B.A., Ill. Wesleyan U., 1963; student Stovring, Denmark, 1961-62; M.A., Ind. U., 1966; certificate in acting Acad. of Dramatic Art, Rochester, Mich., 1971; m. Brenda Curtis, June 9, 1967. Instr. drama Ill. Wesleyan U., Bloomington, 1966-69; prin. mem. acting co. Cleve. Play House, 1971-75; appeared in Gt. Lakes Shakespeare Festival, 1971, 73, And So to Bed, N.Y.C., 1975; appeared on Broadway in Ceasar and Cleopatra, 1977; actor in commercials and TV soap operas. Mem. Actors Equity, Screen Actors Guild, AFTRA. Home: 25 W 68 St New York City NY 10023

BERING, EDGAR ANDREW, JR., neurosurgeon; b. Salt Lake City, Feb. 18, 1917; s. Edgar Andrew and Ilse (Billing) B.; B.A., U. Utah, 1937; M.D., Harvard U., 1941; postgrad. Columbia U., 1947; m. Harriet Crocker Aldrich, Nov. 3, 1944; children—Edgar Andrew, Charles C., Harriet A. Surg. house officer Boston City Hosp., 1941-42; spl. research asso. Dept. Phys. Chemistry, Harvard Med. Sch., Boston, 1942-44; asst. in neurosurgery, spl. research asso., demonstrator in anatomy N.Y. Med. Coll. and Flower Fifth Ave. Hosp., N.Y.C., 1946-48; Moseley travelling fellow of Harvard Med. Sch., Nat. Hosp., Queens Sq., London, and clin. clk., 1948-49; resident in neurosurgery Childrens Hosp. and Peter Bent Brigham Hosp., Boston 1949-50; practice medicine, specializing in neurosurgery, Easton, Md., 1952—; teaching fellow in surgery Harvard Med. Sch., Boston, 1949-50, asst. in surgery, 1952, clin. asso. in surgery, 1956-59, asst. clin. prof. surgery, 1959-65; research fellow in neurosurgery Children's Hosp., Boston, 1950-51, asst. neurosurgeon, 1950-55, dir. neurosurg. research lab., 1952-63, asso. neurosurgeon, 1955-64; Harvey Cushing fellow Peter Bent Brigham Hosp., Boston, 1950-51, jr. asso. in neurol. surgery, 1950-63; sr. fellow in polimoyelitis, NRC, 1951-52; cons. in surgery of nervous system Lemuel Shattuck Hosp., Jamaica Plain, Mass., 1953-55; attending neurosurgeon West Roxbury VA Hosp., 1954-63; vis. lectr. neurosurgery U. Calif. at Los Angeles Med. Sch., 1958; vis. scientist Nat. Inst. Neurol. Diseases and Blindness, NIH, Bethesda, Md., 1963-65; spl. asst. to dir. for program analysis Nat. Inst. Neurol. Diseases and Stroke, NIH, 1965-71; cons. to advisory com. on coagulation components Commn. on Plasma Fractionation and Related Products, 1954—; chief spl. programs br. Collaborative and Field Research, Nat. Inst. Neurol. Diseases and Stroke, NIH, Bethesda, 1971-74; asso. clin. prof. neurol. surgery Georgetown U., Washington, 1968—; cons. neurol. and electroencephalographic dept. Eastern Shore Hosp., Cambridge, Md., 1975—; cons. Neurosurg. Dept., Johns Hopkins Hosp., Balt., 1975—; active staff neurosurg. and electroencephalographic dept. Meml. Hosp., Easton, 1974—. Served with M.C., USN, 1942-46. Rockefeller fellow, 1940; diplomate Am. Bd. Neurol. Surgery. Mem. Am. Acad. Neurology, AAAS, Am. Assn. Neurol. Surgeons, Soc. for Neurosci. (founding mem.), Internat. Soc. for Pediatric Neurosurgery (founding mem.), Soc. Neurology, Psychiatry and Neurosurgery (Argentina), Chilean Soc. Neurosurgery and Neurology, D.C. Med. Soc., Neurosurg. Soc. D.C., Neurosurg. Soc. Am., Scandinavian, New Eng. neurosurg. socs., N.Y. Acad. Sci., Royal Soc. Medicine (London), Am. Assn. Neurol. Surgeons (founding mem.), Research Soc. Neurosurg. Surgeons (founding mem.), Sigma Xi. Patentee fibrin foam used in surgery; contbr. numerous articles in field to profl. jours. Home: Creek House Oxford MD 21654 Office: 4 Talbottown Ln Easton MD 21601

BERK, HAROLD LEE, dentist; b. Bklyn., May 10, 1931; s. Ben and Anne (Richstein) Berkowitz; B.A. summa cum laude, N.Y. U., 1952, D.D.S., 1955; m. Rosalind Fortunoff, Sept. 6, 1953; children—Emily Judith, Jeffrey David, Shari Elizabeth. Pvt. practice gen. dentistry, Bklyn., 1957—. Served to capt., U.S. Army, 1955-57. Recipient Dr. Leon Ringer award N.Y. U., 1955. Certified flight instr., FAA. Mem. N.Y. Acad. Dental Practice Adminstrn., Med. Amateur Radio Council (founder), N.J. Pilots Assn., Mensa, Omicron Kappa Upsilon. Mem. B'nai B'rith (past pres.). Clubs: Metropolitan Rod and Gun (Bklyn.); Hawk Flying (pres.). Home: 40 Independence Dr East Brunswick NJ 08816 Office: 297 Ave X Brooklyn NY 11223

BERK, NATHANIEL GABRIEL, physician; b. Baranowicz, Poland, Mar. 10, 1910; s. Boris and Zlata Berkowitz; came to U.S., 1920, naturalized, 1927; B.A., U. Pa., 1931, M.D., 1935; m. Sylvia Shwartz, Aug. 18, 1940; children—Robert Henry, Richard Seth. Intern, Phila.

Gen. Hosp., 1935-37; resident internal medicine Eagleville (Pa.) Sanatorium (chest diseases), 1937-38; practice medicine specializing in internal medicine and cardiology, Wyncote, Pa., 1956—; cons. internal medicine and cardiology VA Hosp., Phila., 1954-64; asso. prof. medicine Hahnemann Med. Coll., Phila., 1956-64, clin. prof. clin. cardiology, 1964-67; chmn. div. medicine Albert Einstein Med. Center, Phila., 1964-66, sr. attending medicine, 1956-73, emeritus, 1973—; dir. S. Hillman Med. Center, Phila., 1973—, Willow Crest Skilled Nursing Facility, Phila., 1973-75; cons. in field. Diplomate Am. Bd. Internal Medicine. Fellow A.C.P., Am. Coll. Cardiology; mem. Am. Heart Assn., Phila Acad. Cardiology, Phila. Coll. Physicians, Alpha Omega Alpha. Researcher coronary disease. Home: 1405 Juniper Ave Elkins Park PA 19117 Office: Cedarbrook Hill 3 Wyncote PA 19095

BERK, PETER DAVID, veterinarian; b. N.Y.C., Oct. 22, 1930; s. Harry and Frances (Giarry); B.S., Iowa State U., 1952; D.V.M., U. Mo., 1956; m. Marjorie Lee Stinson, Sept. 17, 1954; children—Jeffrey Thomas, Andrew Charles, Kathryn Ann. Gen. practice veterinary medicine, Canton, Conn., 1956—; prin. United Aircraft Crop. Bioscis. Labs., 1962-66; research surgeon Hartford Hosp., 1962-64; cons. vocat. agr. State of Conn. Dept. Edn., 1970—. Adv. bd. Future Farmers Am., 1970—. NIH grantee, 1963. Mem. Am., Hartford County (pres. 1970-71) vet. med. assns., Am. Animal Hosp. Assn. Republican. Clubs: University. Home: 97 Mallard Dr Farmington CT 06085 Office: Lovely St Canton CT 06019

BERKELEY, IRVING HERMAN, dentist; b. N.Y.C., Aug. 20, 1914; s. Herman and Beatrice (Wagner) B.; student Alfred U., 1932-34; D.D.S., Ohio State Coll., 1939; certificate in oral rehab. N.Y.U. Coll. Dentistry; D.D., Universal Life Ch.; m. Paulette G. Bezin, July 31, 1946; 1 dau., Colette F. Practice dentistry, Bklyn., 1939—; faculty mem. on staff N.Y.U. Coll. Dentistry. Cons. to dentists. Director of Herman & Appley, Inc. Served from 1st lt. to maj., AUS, 1943-46. Fellow Acad. Gen. Dentistry, Royal Soc. Health; mem. AAUP, N.Y.U. Oral Rehab. Soc., Internat. Narcotic Enforcement Officers Assn., Am. Acad. Electrosurgery, Acad. Oral Medicine, Flatbush Med. Soc., Am. Legion, ADA, Am. Dental Soc. Anesthesiology, 2d Dist. Dental Soc., Internat. Soc. Anesthesiologists, Internat. Acad. Orthodontists, Fedn. Dentaire Internat., Am. Cancer Soc., U.S. Power Squadron. Invented Berkeley Post for use in broken teeth, 1941; pioneer methods of mouth rehab. Address: 261 Ocean Pkwy Brooklyn NY 11218 also 16B E Tiana Rd Hampton Bays Southampton NY 11946

BERKELEY, NORBORNE, JR., banker; b. Bethlehem, Pa., June 5, 1922; s. Norborne and Dorothea (Randolph) B.; B.A., Yale, 1947; LL.B., U. Va., 1949; grad. Advanced Mgmt. Program, Harvard, 1966; m. Rowena B. Dewey, July 28, 1972; children by previous marriage—Sally, Anne, Norborne III. Admitted to N.Y. bar, 1950; asso. firm Root, Ballatine, Harlan, Bushby & Palmer, N.Y.C., 1949-50; with Chem. Bank N.Y.C., 1950—, exec. v.p. 1968-73, pres. 1973—, also dir.; chmn. bd. Wildcat Service Corp., 1973—; pres., dir. Chem. N.Y. Corp.; dir. Freeport Minerals Co. (N.Y.), The Hartz Mountain Corp., Harrison. N.J., Uniroyal Inc., Middlebury, Conn. Trustee Nat. Recreation Found., Arlington Va., treas., 1965—; bd. dirs. Beekman Downtown Hosp., N.Y.C., Vera Inst. Justice; trustee Whitney Mus. Am. Art; mem. Pres.'s Adv. Com. Trade Negotiations. Served with AUS, 1943-45; ETO. Mem. Assn. Res. City Bankers. Republican. Episcopalian. Clubs: Links, Yale (N.Y.C.); Bedens Brook (Princeton); Nat. Golf Links Am. (Southampton, N.Y.); Maidstone (East Hampton, N.Y.). Home: 41 Westcott Rd Princeton NJ 08540 Office: 20 Pine St New York City NY 10005

BERKELEY, NORMA LIFSON (MRS. ARNOLD D. BERKELEY), educator; b. N.Y.C.; d. Michael Alexander and Clara (Kaufmann) Lifson; B.A., Hunter Coll., 1947; M.A., Columbia, 1948; m. Arnold D. Berkeley, June 25, 1950; children—Amy, Jeb, Barbara. Mem. speech and drama faculty N.Y.C. high schs., 1947-51; lang. devel. specialist United Cerebral Palsy Devel. Center, 1953-59; v.p. Md. Modernizers, 1961-62; lang. devel. specialist Montgomery County Head Start, 1965-69; asso. prof. dept. speech and drama Montgomery Coll., Rockville, Md., from 1969, now prof., chmn. dept.; voice cons. Washington Theatre Club. Mem. Speech Communication Assn., Am. Theater Assn., Eastern Communication Assn., Met. Washington Speech Communication Assn., League Women Voters (v.p. 1959). Home: 8818 Tallyho Trail Potomac MD 20854 Office: Montgomery Coll Rockville MD 20850

BERKMAN, JACK NEVILLE, lawyer, corp. exec.; b. London, Eng., Feb. 12, 1905; s. H. L. and Sarah (Hellman) B.; came to U.S., 1908, naturalized, 1922; A.B., U. of Mich., 1926; J.D., Harvard, 1929; m. Sybiel B. Altman, Aug. 27, 1933 (dec. May 1964); children—Myles P., Stephen L., Monroe B.; m. 2d, Lillian Rojtman, Jan. 26, 1970. Formerly Sr. mem. firm Berkman, Anglin & McCann, Steubenville, Ohio; chmn. exec. com., vice chmn. bd., also dir. Rust Craft Greeting Cards, Inc., N.Y., Boston; vice chmn., dir. Rust Craft Broadcasting Co.; pres., dir. Rust Craft Broadcasting of N.Y., Inc., N.Y.C., Rust Craft Broadcasting of Pa., Inc., Phila., Rust Craft Broadcasting of Tenn., Inc., Radio Buffalo Inc.; dir. Rust Craft, Ltd., Toronto, Volland Ltd., Asso. Am. Artists, Inc., Rust Craft Greeting Cards (U.K.), Ltd. Trustee the Sybiel B. Berkman Found., Steubenville; mem. Am. bd. govs. Technion; Haifa, Israel; mem. Am., Internat., Ohio, Jefferson County bar assns., Fed. Communications Commn. Bar Assn., Am. Judicature Soc., Radio and TV Exec. Soc., Steubenville C. of C. Clubs: Variety Harvard-Yale-Princeton (Pitts.); Broadcasters (Washington); Harmonie, Friars, Harvard (N.Y.C.), Steubenville Country. Author: Playing God, a play, 1931; also short stories. Home: 22 E 64th St New York City NY 10021 Office: Rust Craft Broadcasting Co 680 Fifth Ave New York City NY 10019

BERKO, FRANCES GIDEN, health service adminstr.; b. N.Y.C., Mar. 20, 1922; d. Archie and Rosa (Goldstein) Giden; A.B., Hunter Coll., 1941; J.D., Fordham Law Sch., 1944; M.A. in Vocat. Rehab., N.Y. U., 1946; M.A. in Speech Therapy, Wichita State U., 1956; L.H.D. (hon.), Ithaca Coll., 1975. Admitted to N.Y. State bar, 1944, asso. firm Giden & Giden, N.Y.C., 1944-45; dir. research Fedn. of Handicapped, N.Y.C., 1945-47; research asst. to dir. Inst. Logopedics, Wichita, Kans., 1947-50, tchr. of spl. edn., also supr. of curriculum and tchr. tng. in spl. edn., 1959-62; exec. dir. Spl. Children's Center, Ithaca, N.Y., 1963-74; chief treatment services Suffolk Developmental Center, Melville, N.Y., 1974—; clin. adviser Chemung County (N.Y.) Parent Group for Cerebral Palsied, 1964-74; mem. exec. com. Tompkins County (N.Y.) Comprehensive Health Planning Com., 1967-74; mem. spl. edn. adv. com. Tompkins-Seneca-Tioga Bd. of Co-op Ednl. Services, 1967-72, adv. com. on adaptive phys. edn. for the handicapped, 1969; mem. advocacy com. United Cerebral Palsy of N.Y. State, 1972-74; del. White House Conf. on Children, 1970; mem. N.Y. State Gov.'s Com. on Children and Youth, 1970; bd. visitors Broome State Sch., Binghampton, N.Y., 1974. Recipient Pioneer Service award United Cerebral Palsy of N.Y. State, 1968, 71, Al Felmet Achievement award, 1974. Fellow Am. Acad. Cerebral Palsy, Am. Assn. Mental Deficiencies; mem. Assn. Med. Rehab. Dirs. and Coordinators (clin. mem.), Nat. Rehab. Assn., Council for Exceptional Children, Assn. Med. Rehab. Dirs. and Coordinators (certified), Profl. Workers in Cerebral Palsy Assn., United Cerebral Palsy Assn. (pres. spl. task force 1975-76), Assn. on Mental Health Adminstrn. Jewish. Author: (with M. Meachem and M. J. Berko) Speech Therapy in Cerebral Palsy, 1960; Communication Training in Childhood Brain Damage, 1966; (with M. J. Berko and S. Thompson) Management of the Brain Damaged Child, 1970. Editor-in-chief Cerebral Palsy Rev., 1952-56. Home: 216 Old South Path Melville NY 11746 Office: Suffolk Development Center Box 788 Melville NY 11746

BERKOFF, CHARLES EDWARD, pharm. co. exec.; b. London, Eng., Sept. 29, 1932; s. Maurice and Dora (Landy) B.; B.Sc. with 1st class honors, U. London, 1956, Ph.D., 1959; postdoctoral Johns Hopkins (Fulbright scholar), 1959-60, U. Southampton (Eng.), 1960-61; m. F. Elaine Price, Aug. 18, 1961; children—Timothy Alexander, David Charles, Kevin Richard. Came to U.S., 1963, naturalized, 1975. Asst. to v.p. research and devel. Nicholas Research Inst., Eng., 1961-62; asst. dir. research and devel. BioRex Labs., Eng., 1962; group leader Wyeth Labs., Pa., 1963-65; successively group leader, asst. dir., mgr. tech. assessment Smith, Kline & French Corp., Phila., after 1964, now dir. organic chemistry. Recipient awards London County, 1954-56, Monsanto Bursary, 1956-59. Chartered chemist. Fellow Royal Inst. Chemistry, Am. Inst. Chemistry; mem. Am., Italian, French chem. socs., Chem. Soc. London, Phila. Organic Chemists Club, N.Y. Acad. Scis., AAAS, Entomol. Soc. Am. Unitarian (trustee). Contbr. articles to profl. jours. Patentee in field. Home: 1850 Terwood Rd Huntingdon Valley PA 19006 Office: 1500 Spring Garden St Philadelphia PA 19101

BERKON, MARTIN, artist; b. Bklyn., Jan. 30, 1932; s. Samuel F. and Sara (Hodes) B.; student Pratt Inst., 1952; B.A., Bklyn. Coll., 1954; M.A., N.Y. U., 1959; m. Eileen Phyllis Eichel, July 10, 1960. One man shows Smolin Gallery, N.Y.C., 1962, 20th Century West Gallery, N.Y.C., 1967, Soho Center for Visual Artists, N.Y.C., 1974, Genesis Galleries, N.Y.C., 1978; exhibited in group shows Bklyn. Mus., 1958, Silvermine (Conn.) Guild Artists, 1963, Ohio U. Gallery, 1964, Ball State U., 1965, Wesleyan Coll. at Ga., 1965, Butler Inst. Am. Art, 1965, 67, 69, Aldrich Mus. Contemporary Art, Ridgefield, Conn., 1974, 75, New Britain (Conn.) Mus., 1974, Am. Fedn. Arts traveling show, 1975-77, Meadowbrook Art Gallery Oakland U., Rochester, Mich., and Flint (Mich.) Inst. Art, 1975-76; represented in permanent collection Aldrich Mus. Contemporary Art; mem. adj. faculty Fairleigh Dickinson U., 1966, Nassau Community Coll., 1966-67; lectr. City Coll., City U. N.Y., 1968-69; guest lectr. Middlebury Coll., 1977. Recipient Patrons' prize Nat. Soc. Painters in Casein, 1965. Mem. Coll. Art Assn. Am. Home: 51-25 Van Kleek St Elmhurst NY 11373

BERKOWITZ, BERNARD SOLOMON, lawyer; b. Trenton, N.J., June 13, 1930; s. Samuel and Sarah (Jansil) B.; B.A., Cornell U., 1952; LL.B., 1956; LL.M., N.Y.U., 1958; m. Edith Anne Collins, June 11, 1960 (dec. Nov. 1975); children—Laura J., Philip T., Amy Lee; m. 2d, Rita Nancy Sobel, Dec. 5, 1976; children—Robert L., Alexa and Richard D. Sobel. Admitted to N.Y. State bar, 1956, N.J. bar, 1957; asso. atty. Hannoch, Weisman, Stern & Besser, and predecessor, Newark, 1956-61, partner, 1961—; prin. organizer, sec., dir. N.J. Life Ins. Co., Newark, 1964—; organizer State St. Life Ins. Co., Boston. Bd. dirs. Community Service Council of Oranges and Maplewood; trustee Berkowitz Found., Orange Orphan Soc.; trustee, gen. campaign chmn. United Way of Essex and West Hudson. Served to 2d lt. AUS, 1952-54. Decorated Bronze Star. Mem. Am., N.J., Essex County, N.Y. County bar assns., Order of Coif, Phi Epsilon Pi. Unitarian. Clubs: Mountain Ridge Country, Woodstock Country. Home: 249 N Ridgewood Rd South Orange NJ 07079 Office: 744 Broad St Newark NJ 07102

BERKOWITZ, CARL MITCHELL, city planning exec.; b. N.Y.C., Dec. 5, 1940; s. Abraham and Miriam (Rappaport) B.; B.C.E., City Coll. N.Y., 1963; M.B.A., Baruch Coll., 1967; M.S.T.P., Bklyn. Poly. Inst., 1971, postgrad., 1971—; m. Michelle Spiegel, Jan. 30, 1965; children—Keith Wayne, Eric Scott. Jr. engr. N.Y.C. Transit Authority, 1962-63; transp. planning engr. N.Y. State Dept. Transp., Hauppauge, 1963-67; asso. planner N.Y. State Office Planning Services, N.Y.C., 1967-70; dir. spl. projects and applied research N.Y.C. Transp. Aminstrn., 1970-76, exec. dir., Bur. Ferries, N.Y.C. Dept. Transp., 1976—; asst. prof. City U. N.Y., 1972-73; asst. prof. transp. St. John's U., S.I., N.Y., 1974—; prof. mgmt. N.Y. Inst. Tech., 1976—. Pres. Arden Heights Jewish Center, 1974; pres. Council of Jewish Orgns., 1977-78; bd. dirs. Jewish Community Center, 1976-78; del. Jewish Community Relations Council of N.Y., 1976-78; mem. Community Planning Bd., 1974-76; bd. guardians Jewish Family Service, 1976—; del. N.Y. Council Jewish Poverty, 1976—; exec. sec. S.I. Democratic County Com., 1977—; adv. bd. Nat. Bicycle Fedn., 1975—. Registered profl. engr., N.Y., N.J., Fla. Mem. Am. Inst. Planners, Met. Assn. Urban Designers and Environ. Planners (pres. 1969-78), Marine Transit Assn. (pres., founder 1977-78), ASCE (chmn. waterborne transp. com. 1975-76), Transp. Research Bd. (chmn. waterborne passenger com. 1978—), Profl. Engrs. Soc. (dir. chpt. 1973-76), Staten Island Zool. Soc. Village Green Homeowners Assn. Clubs: Victory Dem., Masons. Contbr. articles on transportation to profl. jours. Home: 170 Forest Green St Staten Island NY 10312 Office: Dept Transp Bur of Ferries Battery Maritime Bldg New York City NY 10004

BERKOWITZ, EDWARD, supt. schs.; b. Bklyn., July 10, 1929; s. Abraham S. and Lillian (Landesberg) B.; B.A., Bklyn. Coll., 1951, M.A., 1952; Ed.D., Tchrs. Coll. Columbia, 1962; m. Barbara May Kestenbaum, Apr. 1, 1951; children—Ruth Carol, Susan Mira, Marc Jay. Tchr. elementary schs., N.Y.C., 1951-59; asst. prin. Pub. Sch. 289K, N.Y.C., 1959-62; project supr. Audio Visual Devel. and Appraisal Center, N.Y.C., 1962-64; prin. Willets Rd. Sch., East Williston, N.Y., 1964-71; adj. asst. prof. edn. Bklyn. Coll., City U. N.Y., 1965-70; supt. schs., Northvale, N.J., 1970-72; asst. supt. schs. Carroll County (Md.), 1972-77; asst. supt. schs., Port Washington, N.Y., 1977—. Vice pres. Carroll County Arts Council; bd. dirs. Carroll Players Community Theatre, Carroll County council Boy Scouts Am.; bd. dirs. Carroll Players; mem. ednl. advisory com. Nassau County Mental Health Assn. Served with USNR, 1952-56. Mem. NEA, Am. Assn. Sch. Adminstrs., Am. Ednl. Research Assn., Nat. Soc. for Study Edn., Nat. Assn. Elementary Sch. Prins., Assn. for Supervision and Curriculum Devel., Phi Delta Kappa, Kappa Delta Pi. Home: 66 Flower Ln Jericho NY 11753

BERKOWITZ, WESLEY IAN, psychotherapist, family counselor; b. Queens, N.Y., Dec. 9, 1950; s. Edward and Evelyn (Miller) B.; B.A., Hofstra U., 1973, M.S., 1974, profl. diploma, 1977, family therapy certificate, 1978; postgrad. Duke U., 1975-76. Guidance counseling intern Wheatley Sch., Old Westbury, N.Y., 1974; counselor Manhasset Jr. Sr. High Sch. (N.Y.), 1974-75; counselor, tchr. project friend, Ridgewood Jr. Sr. High Sch., Ridgewood, N.Y., 1975; guidance counselor Willets Rd Sch., East Williston, N.Y., 1976-77, Dix Hills, N.Y., 1978, Sachem, N.Y., 1978-79; pvt. practice psychotherapy, Port Washington, N.Y., 1978—. Mem. Am., N.Y. State, Western Suffolk, L.I. personnel and guidance assns. Democrat. Jewish. Club: Bridge Great Neck. Home and Office: 33 Longview Rd Port Washington NY 11050

BERKSON, JAMES HAROLD, research analysis and mgmt. cons. exec.; b. Kansas City, Mo., Nov. 5, 1920; s. Harry and Mary (Applebaum) B.; B.M.E., U. Kans., 1942; J.D., Pacific Coast U., 1955; postgrad. U. Calif. at Los Angeles, 1958. Admitted to Calif. bar, 1965, D.C. bar, 1973, U.S. Supreme Ct. bar, 1973; with U.S. Govt., 1946-56; adminstrv. contracting officer Hughes Aircraft Co., 1955-56; contract and fiscal adminstr., SDD, The Rand Corp., Santa Monica, Calif., 1956-57; treas. System Devel. Corp., Santa Monica, 1957-64; mgmt. cons., practice of law, Los Angeles, 1964—, Washington, 1973—; head corporate projects Aerospace Corp., El Segundo, Calif., 1965-66; sr. v.p. dir., CACI, Inc., 1966—; sec.-treas., dir. Advanced Software Resources, Inc., Arlington, Va., 1971-74; asst. sec., dir. CACI Ltd., Hamilton, Bermuda, 1974—; sr. v.p., dir. CACI Inc.-Benelux, Arlington, Va., 1975—; sr. v.p., dir. CACI, Inc.-Comml., Arlington, 1975—; dir. CACI-Ireland, Ltd., Dublin; sr. v.p., dir. CACI, Inc.-Del., 1977—; CACI Inc.-France, 1977—; treas., dir. Watergate South, Inc., Washington, 1976-78, pres., dir., 1978—. Served with U.S. Army, 1942-46. Mem. Nat. Contract Mgmt. Assn. (dir. 1962—, nat. treas. 1963-65, nat. v.p. 1965-66), Am. Calif., D.C. bar assns., Am. Judicature Soc., U. Calif. at Los Angeles Exec. Assn. Home: Watergate South Apts 700 New Hampshire Ave NW Washington DC 20037 Office: 1815 N Fort Myer Dr Arlington VA 22209 also 12011 San Vicente Blvd Los Angeles CA 90049

BERL, ETHEL GARFUNKEL, psychologist; b. Jersey City, May 1, 1906; d. Samson and Rose Garfunkel; B.A. cum laude, Hunter Coll., 1927, M.A., Columbia U., 1928; Ph.D., N.Y. U., 1940; m. Alexander Berl, July 31, 1932. Mem. faculty Hunter Coll., City U. N.Y., 1927-74, prof. psychol. founds. and mental health, 1928-74, prof. emeritus, 1974—; cons. Brookdale Center on Aging, 1976-78; pvt. practice counseling and cons. psychology, N.Y.C., 1958—. Mem. edn. com. Greater N.Y. council Girl Scouts U.S.A., 1945-51. Named to Hunter Hall of Fame, 1972. Certified psychologist, N.Y. Mem. Am., N.Y. State psychol. assns., Alumni Assn. Hunter Coll. (past 1st, 2d, 3d v.p., past dir.; dir. scholarship and welfare fund 1951—), Phi Beta Kappa, Pi Mu Epsilon, Kappa Delta Pi.

BERLER, LAWRENCE SHELDON, gallery exec.; b. Bklyn., Aug. 11, 1939; s. Gustave L. and Laura (Engel) B.; student N.Y. U., 1957-60; B.A., Queen's Coll., 1968; postgrad. Faculte de medecine, Academie de Paris, 1968-69. Narcotics rehab. officer Bayview Rehab. Center, N.Y.C., 1967; lab. asst. cancer research Francis Delafield Hosp., N.Y.C., 1968; owner, auctioneer, dir. Victoria Galleries, N.Y.C., 1971—. Mem. Internat. Platform Assn., Tau Epsilon Phi. Office: 106 Greenwich Ave New York City NY 10011

BERLIN, CLEM, plant engr.; b. Knox, Pa., July 15, 1922; s. Howard A. and Anna M. (Jackson) B.; student pub. schs., Knox, Pa.; m. Esther Weaver, July 15, 1946; 1 dau., Karen L. Berlin Demyanovich. With Glass Container Corp., Knox, Pa., 1939—, plant engr., 1978—. Served with U.S. Army, 1942-46. Lutheran. Clubs: Servicemens, Masons. Expert Mental quick Math., particularly sq. root computation. Office: Knox PA 16232

BERLIN, DONALD ROBERT, rabbi; b. Montreal, Que., Can., June 30, 1936; s. Saul Schnair and Isabel (Riven) B.; B.A. in Philosophy, U. Toronto (Can.), U. Cin., 1961; B. Hebrew Letters, Hebrew Union Coll., Jewish Inst. Religion, 1963, M.A. in Hebrew Lit., 1969; m. Norma Brass, Nov. 26, 1959; children—Seth Daniel, Sharon Leah. Ordained rabbi, 1965; rabbi, Temple Emanuel, Roanoke, Va., 1965-71, Congregation Keneseth Israel, Allentown, Pa., 1971-76; sr. rabbi Temple Oheb Shalom, Balt., 1976—; chaplain VA Hosp., Salem, Va., 1965-71; instr. philosophy Va. Western Community Coll., 1969-70; lectr. Jewish Chautauqua Soc.; instr. Judaism, Mary Immaculate Conception Sem., Northampton, Pa., 1974-75; instr. dept. religion Goucher Coll., 1977—; chmn. rabbinic edn. com. Camp Harlam. Mem. admissions and allocations panel United Way Central Md., 1977-78. Recipient Brotherhood citation award NCCJ, 1970, Legion of Honor, Chapel of Four Chaplains, 1976; Shofar award Boy Scouts Am., 1978. Home: 28 Millstone Rd Randallstown MD 21133 Office: 7310 Park Heights Ave Baltimore MD 21208

BERLINER, WILLIAM MICHAEL, educator; b. N.Y.C., Aug. 24, 1923; s. Samuel L. and Anna (Josephine) B.; B.S., N.Y. U., 1949, M.B.A., 1953, Ph.D., 1956; m. Bertha A. Hagedorn, Apr. 27, 1946. With Continental Casualty Co., 1941-42, 45-46; retail div. mgr. B.F. Goodrich Co., 1949-50; asst. purchasing agt. Cutler-Hammer Inc., 1950-51; mem. faculty N.Y.U., N.Y.C., 1951—, prof. mgmt., chmn. dept. mgmt. and indsl. relations, 1965-74; dir., cons. OTI Services, Inc., 1958—; cons. Mfrs. Hanover Trust Co., 1956—; edn. adviser Am. Inst. Banking sect. Am. Bankers Assn., 1962—; Ford Found. cons. exec. program N.Y.C. and Met. Area 1961-65; mem. policy com. external degree program Regents of U. State N.Y. Kellog Found. cons. exec. program Boys Clubs Am., 1962-67; faculty Stonier Grad. Sch. Banking, 1970—. Served to 1st lt, USAAF, 1942-45. Decorated D.F.C., Air medal with 6 oak leaf clusters, Purple Heart. Ford Found. grantee, 1960. Mem. Acad. Mgmt., Am. Mgmt. Assn., Am. Mktg. Assn., Beta Gamma Sigma, Alpha Kappa Psi. Author: (with F.A. DePhillips and J.J. Cribbin) Management of Training Programs, 1960; (with W.J. McLarney (dec.) Management Practice and Training, Cases and Principles, 1974. Home: 27 Perkins Rd Greenwich CT 06830 Office: N Y U Grad School Business Adminstrn 100 Trinity Pl New York City NY 10006

BERMACK, CHARLES K(ALMON), pub. accountant, lawyer; b. Lutck, Russia, Mar. 17, 1902; s. Koss and Bessie (Wallach) B.; brought to U.S., 1913, naturalized, 1926; B.C.S., N.Y.U., 1924, J.D., 1928, LL.M., 1934; m. Lillian Freeman, Nov. 23, 1926; children—Eugene, Ruth (Mrs. Robert Rosenberg). Pvt. practice accounting, N.Y.C., 1927-39; sr. partner Charles K. Bermack & Co., 1939—; admitted to N.Y. State bar, 1934; now asso. firm Bermack & Bermack. Active Flatbush Jewish Community Council, past chmn., co-chmn. United Jewish Appeal, Roslyn area, L.I. Mem. orgn. com. Albert Einstein Med. Sch. C.P.A., N.Y. Mem. Am. Inst. C.P.A.'s, N.Y. State Soc. C.P.A.'s N.Y. Credit and Financial Mgmt. Assn., Jewish Chautauqua Soc., Zionist Orgn. Am., Delta Mu Delta. Mason. Home: 45 Strawberry Ln Roslyn Heights NY 11577 Office: 175 Great Neck Rd Great Neck NY 11021

BERMACK, EUGENE, lawyer; b. N.Y.C., June 16, 1929; s. Charles K. and Lillian (Freeman) B.; B.A., N.Y.U., 1951; J.D., Rutgers U., 1954; m. Elaine Dalberg, Mar. 18, 1951; children—Alison, Kiri, Marla. Admitted to N.Y. bar, 1956; partner firm Bermack & Bermack, Great Neck, 1957—; partner Charles K. Bermack & Co., C.P.A.'s, 1959—. C.P.A., N.Y. Mem. N.Y. County Lawyers Assn., Am. Inst. C.P.A.'s, N.Y. Soc. C.P.A.'s, Great Neck Lawyers Assn. (dir. 1978), Common Cause (steering com.). Clubs: Temple Judea of Manhasset (trustee 1969-73), Masons. Home: 70 Knolls Dr North Manhasset Hills NY 11040 Office: 175 Great Neck Rd Great Neck NY 11021

BERMAN, ALLAN, psychologist, educator; b. Boston, Sept. 27, 1940; s. Edward Isadore and Irene (Milesky) B.; B.A., U. Mass., 1962; M.Ed., Boston U., 1964; Ph.D., La. State U., 1968; m. Jerianne Louise Hoddes, June 21, 1964; children—Jennifer Ann, Andrew I., Michael Ross. Chief psychologist R.I. Dept. Corrections, Cranston, 1968-70; prof. psychology U. R.I., Kingston, 1970—; cons. to Governor Med. Center, Providence, 1969-77; clin. dir. Delta Consultants, 1977—; dir.

neuropsychology lab. R.I. Tng. Sch., Howard, 1970-74; mem. Gov.'s Adv. Council on Correctional Services, 1971-75, R.I. Council of Community Services. Mem. Am., Eastern, New Eng., R.I. (exec. bd. 1971—, pres. 1973-75) psychol. assns., Nat. (exec. bd. 1975—), R.I. (profl. adviser, pres. 1977—) assns. for children with learning disabilities. Contbr. articles to profl. jours. Home: 15 Candle Hill Ct Warwick RI 02886 Office: Psychology Dept 407 Chafee Center University of RI Kingston RI 02881

BERMAN, ALLAN BERTRAND, media specialist; b. Bayonne, N.J., May 13, 1931; s. Benjamin Maurice and Celia (Katz) B.; diploma Bayonne Jr. Coll., 1951; A.B., Montclair State Coll., 1954; M.A., Columbia, 1961; postgrad. Montclair State Coll., Kean Coll., 1961-69; m. Harriet Sondra Werner, Mar. 30, 1958; children—Robert Lee, Beth Lisa, Faith Marcia. Tchr., Bayonne Pub. Schs., 1957-58, Central Sch., Orange, N.J., 1958-59; tchr. social studies South Orange (N.J.) Jr. High Sch., 1959-67, media specialist, 1967—. Camping specialist; mem. reference dept. South Orange Pub. Library. Served with USNR, 1954-56. Mem. NEA, N.J., Essex County, South Orange-Maplewood edn. assns., Am., N.J. assns. ednl. communications and tech., N.J. Sch. Media Assn., Essex County Sch. Library Assn., Bayonne Hebrew Benevolent Assn., Rohwec, Phi Delta Kappa. Jewish. Home: 18 Highland Pl Maplewood NJ 07040 Office: 70 N Ridgewood Rd South Orange NJ 07079

BERMAN, BARRY, educator; b. Bklyn., Dec. 2, 1944; s. Abraham Louis and Goldie (Boyarsky) B.; B.B.A. cum laude, Coll. City N.Y., 1966, M.B.A., 1968; Ph.D., City U. N.Y., 1973; m. Linda Grossman, June 9, 1968; children—Glenna Laurie, Lisa Naomi. Asso. dean Sch. Bus., Hofstra U., Hempstead, N.Y., 1973—, asso. prof. mktg., 1974—; cons. N.Y. State Edn. Dept., external degree program, com. on non-collegiate sponsored instruction; cons. Suffolk County Fed. Savs. & Loan Assn., Centereach, N.Y., N.Y. Telephone. NDEA fellow. Mem. Am. Mktg. Assn., Baruch Coll. Alumni Assn. (dir.), Beta Gamma Sigma, Mu Gamma Tau. Author: Study Guide to Modern Marketing, 1975; (with others) Study Guide to Marketing Strategy and Structure, 1975; (with others) Retail Management: A Strategic Approach, 1978, Applying Retail Management: A Strategic Approach, 1978; Applying Retail Management: A Strategic Approach, 1978. Asso. editor Mktg. Rev. 1970—. Home: 2037 Oliver Way Merrick NY 11566 Office: 1000 Fulton Ave Hempstead NY 11550

BERMAN, BERNARD ALVIN, physician; b. Boston, Mar. 12, 1924; s. Hyman Irving and Elise Marion (Davb) B.; M.D., Tufts U., 1948; m. Lois Deborah Landau, Aug. 27, 1957; children—Susan, Steven, Laura. Intern, resident pediatrics Jewish Hosp., Bklyn., 1948-51; intern, resident Children's Hosp., Boston, 1953-55, fellow in pediatric allergy Strong Meml. Hosp., Rochester, N.Y., 1955-57; pvt. practice specializing in allergy, Brookline, Mass., 1957—; chief pediatric allergy St. Elizabeth Hosp., Boston, 1965—; asso. clin. prof. Tufts U., 1959—. Nat. trustee Nat. Jewish Hosp., Denver, 1975—; trustee Krebs Sch., 1971-75. Served with USNR, 1944-48, 51-53. Diplomate Am. Bd. Pediatrics, Am. Bd. Allergy and Immunology (dir.). Fellow Am. Coll. Allergists (past pres.), Am. Acad. Allergy, Am. Coll. Chest Physicians, Am. Acad. Pediatrics, Assn. Asthmatic and Convalescent Homes (past pres.), Greater Boston Med. Soc. (past pres.), Phi Delta Epsilon (past pres.). Contbr. articles to profl. jours. Home: 31 Hyslop Rd Extension Brookline MA 02146 Office: 1714 Beacon St Brookline MA 02146

BERMAN, DANIEL ELIHU, dentist; b. Balt., July 13, 1919; s. Benjamin and Dorah (Yavner) B.; student Balt. City Coll., 1935, U. Md., 1935-37; D.D.S., U. Md., 1941; m. Sally Esther Boyette, Jan. 16, 1943; children—Joel Lee, Deborah, Linda Rae, Thomas Alan. Intern, resident Sinai Hosp., Balt., 1941-43; practice dentistry, Balt., 1943—; established 1st active civilian blood bank at Sinai Hosp., Balt. 1942, chief oral diagnosis and prosthetic dentistry, 1950-62; dental cons. Md. State Criminal Injuries Commn. Pres., PTA, Balt., 1959-60; pres. Balt. Council Temple Brotherhoods, 1962-64; charter mem. Mt. Washington Improvement Assn., 1948-62; mem. sch. facilities com. Citizens Sch. Adv. Commn., 1964-65; pres. Council Jewish Temple Brotherhoods, 1964-66; temple trustee, 1967-70. Recipient certificate of honor Gorgas Odontological Soc., 1964; citation Nat. Fedn. Temple Bro., Temple O.S., Temple Beth Shalom, 1966. Mem. Balt. City Dental Soc. (v.p. 1971-72, pres. 1974), Am., Md. (bd. govs.) dental assns., Am. Dental Soc. Anesthesiology (charter), Pierre Fauchard Acad., Sigma Epsilon Delta (pres. 1950). Club: Masons (32 deg.). Home: 28 Farmhouse Ct Pikesville MD 21208 Office: Med Arts Bldg Baltimore MD 21201

BERMAN, HERBERT LAWRENCE, furnace engring. specialist; b. Bklyn., Jan. 8, 1931; s. Moses and Bertha (Silberman) B.; B.Chem. Engring., Poly. Inst. Bklyn., 1952; postgrad. N.Y. U., 1955-56; m. Pearl M. Lieberman, Mar. 30, 1957; children—Stacey P., Marcy E. Refinery engr. Shell Oil Co., Houston, 1952-53; engr. Petro-Chem. Devel. Co., furnace equipment, N.Y.C., 1955-60; sr. engr. Foster Wheeler Corp., furnace equipment, N.Y.C., 1960-62; mgr. proposal engring. Alcorn Combustion Co., furnace equipment, N.Y.C., 1962-72; furnace engring. specialist, cost engr. Caltex Petroleum Corp., N.Y.C., 1972—. Adviser, Chem. Engring. mag., 1974, mem. product research panel, 1975-78. Served with AUS, 1953-55. Recipient Order of Arrow, Boy Scouts Am., 1945. Registered profl. engr., N.Y. Mem. Am. Petroleum Inst. (task force on fired heater mech. standard, task force on fired heater performance test procedure, subcom. heat transfer equipment), Am. Inst. Chem. Engrs. (lectr.), ASME, Am. Assn. Cost Engrs., Nat. Geog. Soc. Mem. editorial quality audit Plant Engring. Mag., 1975-78. Patentee in field. Home: 23-20 Bell Blvd Bayside NY 11360 Office: Caltex Petroleum Corp 380 Madison Ave New York City NY 10017

BERMAN, IRWIN, machinery mfg. co. exec.; b. Bronx, N.Y., Oct. 16, 1925; s. Morris and Fannie (Rosen) B.; B.S., Coll. City N.Y., 1948; M.S., Stevens Inst. Tech., 1953; Ph.D., Poly. Inst. N.Y., 1959; m. Diana Leonora Styler, Nov. 17, 1956; children—Kenneth Howard, Benjamin Seth. Head analysis sect. Wright Aero. Div., Woodridge, N.J., 1948-54; research asso. Poly. Inst. N.Y., 1954-56; head solid mechanics dept. Foster Wheeler Corp., Livingston, N.J., 1956-76, tech. dir. engring. sci. and tech. research, 1976—; adj. prof. mech. engring. N.Y. U., 1960-71. Served with inf. AUS, 1944-46; ETO. Decorated Purple Heart. Fellow ASME (v.p.); mem. Soc. Exptl. Stress Analysis, Montclair Soc. Engrs., Tau Beta Pi, Pi Tau Sigma, Sigma Gamma Tau. Editor: Computer Software in Structural Analysis, 1970; Computer Software-Verification, Qualification, Certification, 1972. Editor: Jour. Pressure Vessel Tech., 1973-78. Contbr. articles to profl. jours. Patentee in field. Home: 530 Valley Rd Montclair NJ 07043 Office: 12 Peach Tree Hill Rd Livingston NJ 07039

BERMAN, JANE WEINSTEIN, historian; b. Stamford, Conn., Apr. 5, 1951; d. Morris M. and Rosalyn (Rothman) Weinstein; B.A., Johns Hopkins U., 1973; M.A., State U. N.Y., Buffalo, 1976, postgrad., 1976—; m. Donald E. Berman, June 16, 1974. Grad. asst. history State U. N.Y., Buffalo, 1973-74, 74-75, teaching asst., 1975-76, grad. resource access devel. grantee, 1976; lectr. in history Endicott Coll., 1978-79. Mem. Am. Hist. Assn., Coordinating Com. on Women in Hist. Profession, AAUW. Home: 207 Pepper Ridge Rd Stamford CT 06905

BERMAN, JUDITH ROBBINS, ednl. adminstr.; b. Hartford, Conn., May 10, 1940; d. Irving George and Anne Gertrude (Zaiman) B.; A.A., Hartford Coll. Women, 1961; B.A., Brandeis U., 1963; Ed.M., Harvard U., 1965; Ed.D. (fellow 1972-73, Jane Addams fellow 1974-75), Boston U., 1975; m. William Howard Berman, Sept. 3, 1966; children—James Irving, Mayer Berman, Benton Alan, Robbins Berman. Staff psychologist Wrentham (Mass.) State Sch., 1964-66; spl. edn. tchr. Watertown (Mass.) Schs., 1971-72, dir. music/reading, 1972-74, cons., 1975-76; coordinator spl. edn. pub. schs., Lexington, Mass., 1975-76; ednl. dir. Manville Sch.-Judge Baker Guidance Center, Boston, 1976—. Mem. Mass. Assn. Children with Learning Disabilities, Internat., Mass. reading assns., Internat. Neuropsychiat. Soc., Nat. Council Tchrs. English, AAUW, N.E. Ednl. Research Assn., Am. Psychol. Assn. Home: 175 Pine Ridge Rd Waban MA 02168 Office: 295 Longwood Ave Boston MA

BERMAN, LEONARD DAVID, exptl. pathologist; b. Bklyn., July 7, 1933; s. Harry and Mabel (Kasnetz) B.; B.A. cum laude, Hobart Coll., Geneva, N.Y., 1953; M.D., N.Y. U., 1957; D.C.P., Postgrad. Med. Sch., London, Eng., 1961; m. Audrey Buchman, June 3, 1962. Intern Charity Hosp., New Orleans, 1957-58; resident Mallory Inst. Pathology, Boston, 1958-60, Children's Hosp. Med. Center, Boston, 1961-62; surgeon USPHS, NIH, Bethesda, Md., 1962-64; Eleanor Roosevelt fellow, vis. scientist Nat. Inst. for Med. Research, Mill Hill, Eng., 1964-66; NIH fellow Institut de Recherche sur le Cancer, Villejuif, France, 1966-67; vis. scientist Karolinska Inst., Stockholm, Sweden, 1967-68; pathologist Mallory Inst. Pathology, Boston City Hosp., 1968—; chief lab. service Boston VA Hosp., 1973—; acting chief lab service West Roxbury VA Hosp., 1975-76; pathologist Jewish Meml. Hosp., Roxbury, Mass., 1971—; asst. prof. pathology Harvard Med. Sch., 1968-73, lectr. pathology, 1973—; asso. prof. pathology Boston U. Sch. Medicine, 1973-78, prof., 1978—. Mem. Am. Assn. for Cancer Research, Am. Soc. for Microbiology, Am. Assn. Immunologists, New Eng. Soc. Pathologists (sec. 1972-74, treas. 1974-76, v.p. 1976-77, pres. 1977-78), Mass. Med. Soc., Assn. VA Chiefs Lab. Service (pres. 1977-78), Am. Assn. Pathologists and Bacteriologists, Boston Cancer Research Assn., Harvard Musical Assn., Boston Philat. Soc., Amateur Chamber Music Players, Phi Beta Kappa, others. Contbr. articles to profl. jours. Home: 53 Bothfeld Rd Newton Centre MA 02159 Office: 150 S Huntington Ave Boston MA 02130

BERMAN, MALCOLM FRANK, hosp. adminstr.; b. Boston, Oct. 30, 1941; s. Marcus Wolfe and Evelyn Bernice (Sachs) B.; B.A. in Biology, U. Pa., 1963; M.S. in Hygiene, U. Pitts., 1966; m. Natalie Sue Peikin, June 27, 1965; children—Lisa E., Jeremy R. (dec.), Wendy B., Bradley D. Adminstrv. asst. St. Francis Gen. Hosp., Pitts., 1966; adminstr. Meml. Hosp., Monogahela, Pa., 1966-67; staff asst. Western Pa. Regional Med. Program, Pitts., 1967; asst. to exec. dir. St. Francis Gen. Hosp., 1967—, also mem. hosp. adv. coms. home health and community mental health; adminstr. St. Francis Community Mental Health/Mental Retardation Center, 1972—. Pres. Rodef Shalom Jr. Congregation, 1972-73; treas. Group Against Smog and Pollution, Pitts., 1972-75. Served with AUS, 1963-64. Decorated Army Commendation medal. Fellow Am. Coll. Hosp. Adminstrs.; mem. Am. Hosp. Assn., Assn. Mental Health Adminstrs., Hosp. Assn. Pa. (chmn. council psychiat. service providers), Pitts. Mineral and Lapidary Soc. (past pres.), U. Pitts. Grad. Sch. Pub. Health Alumni Assn., Theta Rho (past chpt. sec., v.p.). Republican. Address: 104 Emily Dr Pittsburgh PA 15215

BERMAN, MARSHALL FOX, lawyer; b. Portsmouth, Va., Aug. 27, 1939; s. Israel and Etta (Fox) B.; B.A., U. Va., 1961, postgrad. in Rhetoric, 1961-62; J.D., Am. U., 1967; LL.M. in Labor Law, George Washington U., 1970; m. Barbara Pressner, Aug. 29, 1965; children—Richard Joseph, Deborah Lynn. Admitted to Va. bar, 1967, D.C. bar, 1971, U.S. Supreme Ct. bar, 1971; tchr. reading pub. schs., Washington, 1965-66; mem. staff D.C. Minimum Wage, Indsl. Safety Bd., 1966-67; atty. NLRB, Washington, 1968-71; asso. firm Gall, Lane & Powell, Washington, 1971-75; partner firm Dow, Lohnes & Albertson, Washington, 1975—. Mem. Am., Fed., D.C., Va. bar assns, Phi Alpha Delta. Editorial staff Am. U. Law Rev., 1965-67. Home: 3735 N Vernon St Arlington VA 22207 Office: Dow Lohnes & Albertson 1225 Connecticut Ave NW Washington DC 20036

BERMAN, MARTIN, physicist, govt. adminstr.; b. N.Y.C., Jan. 24, 1938; s. Albert Stanley and Betty (Samuels) B.; student in elec. engring. Cooper Union, 1955-58; B.S. in Engring. Physics, N.Y. U., 1960; M.S. in Physics, Brown U., 1964; m. Roslyn Marie Liebman, Aug. 28, 1960; 1 son, Stanley Arthur. Research physicist solid state physics group Pitts. Energy Research Center, U.S. Bur. Mines, 1964-72; asst. dir. Pitts. Energy Tech. Center, U.S. Dept. Energy, 1972—; pres. POLYH Corp., Pitts., 1972—. Fellow AAAS; mem. Am. Phys. Soc. Research Adminstrs., Am. Math. Soc., Assn. Computing Machinery, Sierra Club, Tau Beta Pi, Sigma Pi Sigma. Clubs: Explorers, Appalachian Mountain, South Hills Swim (pres. 1974-75). Contbr. articles to profl. jours. Patentee in field. Home: 373 Macassar Dr Pittsburgh PA 15236 Office: US Dept Energy 4800 Forbes Ave Pittsburgh PA 15213

BERMAN, RICHARD ANGEL, health care adminstr.; b. Cin., Jan. 23, 1945; s. Isidore Alexander and Cecelia (Angel) B.; B.B.A. with distinction, U. Mich., 1966, M.B.A. with distinction, M.H.A., 1968; m. Sara Hoberman, July 30, 1966; 1 son, Joshua. Spl. asst., asst. sec. health, dir. health policy Economic Stabilization Program, HEW, Washington, 1974; sr. program cons. Robert Wood Johnson Found., Princeton, N.J., 1974-77; asst. dean, asso. hosp. dir. N.Y. Hosp., Cornell Med. Center, N.Y.C., 1974-77; dir. N.Y. Office Health Systems Mgmt., Albany, 1977—; cons. in field. Served with USPHS, 1968-70. Fellow Am. Coll. Hosp. Adminstrs., N.Y. Acad. Medicine (asso.); mem. Am. Hosp. Assn., Am. Pub. Health Assn., Pub. Health Assn. N.Y.C. Jewish. Contbr. articles in field to profl. jours. Home: 43 Willow Ave Larchmont NY 10538 Office: Tower Bldg Empire State Plaza Albany NY 12237

BERMAN, ROBERT DONALD, dentist, contract bridge player; b. N.Y.C., Aug. 2, 1921; s. Emil and Cecelia (Jack) B.; B.A., Bklyn. Coll., 1942; D.D.S., N.Y. U., 1946; m. Marilynn Himmelstein, Mar. 28, 1944; 1 dau., Ellen Beth. Dental intern Grasslands Hosp., Valhalla, N.Y., 1946-47, dental resident, 1947-51; pvt. practice dentistry, White Plains, N.Y., 1947-51, Levittown, N.Y., 1953—; writer, tchr., adminstr., tournament player contract bridge. Trustee Levittown Pub. Library, 1964—, pres. bd., 1967-68, 70-71, 74-75, Nassau Library System, 1976. Mem. Am. Dental Assn., Am. Contract Bridge League (life master), Nassau-Suffolk (pres. 1962-64, dir.), Nassau-Suffolk Library Trustees Assn., Greater N.Y. (v.p. 1969-70, dir.) bridge assns. Home: 3626 Regent Ln Wantagh NY 11793 Office: 133 Gardiners Ave Levittown NY 11756

BERMAN, SIDNEY, physician; b. Washington, July 31, 1908; s. Saul and Gertrude (Berman) B.; B.S., Georgetown U., 1928, M.D., 1932; m. Claire Richardson, Nov. 23, 1935; 1 dau., Sarah Miriam Berman Schlein. Intern, D.C. Gen. Hosp., 1932-33; jr. med. officer, resident in psychiatry St. Elizabeth's Hosp., Washington, 1933-35; sr. med. officer VA Hosp., Northport, N.Y., 1935-41; Commonwealth Fund fellow in child psychiatry U. Md. Med. Sch. and Hosp., 1941-42, dir. Mental Hygiene Clinic, 1942-43; dir. Washington Inst. Mental Hygiene, 1946-48; clin. prof. psychiatry George Washington U. Sch. Medicine, Washington, 1948—; sr. adv. staff Children's Hosp. Nat. Med. Center, Washington, 1948—; tng. and supervising analyst Washington Psychoanalytic Inst., 1957—; practice medicine, specializing in child and adult psychiatry and psychoanalysis, Washington, 1948—; cons. Walter Reed Gen. Hosp., 1960-71, NIH, 1953—. Founder, Nat. Consortium Child Mental Health Services, 1971; Mental Health Manpower rep. to Congress, 1971-74. Served to maj. M.C., USAAF, 1943-46. Diplomate Am. Bd. Psychiatry and Neurology with subsplty. child psychiatry. Mem. Am. Acad. Child Psychiatry (pres. 1969-71), Washington Psychoanalytic Soc. (pres. 1963-65), Washington Psychiat. Soc. (pres. 1962), Med. Soc. D.C., AMA, Am. Psyciat. Assn., Group for Advancement of Psychiatry, Am. Orthopsychiat. Assn., Am. Psychoanalytic Assn., Internat. Psychoanalytic Assn., Pan-Am. Med. Assn. Jewish. Club: George Washington U. Contbr. articles to profl. jours. Home: 5534 Warwick Pl Chevy Chase MD 20015 Office: 4301 Massachusetts Ave NW Washington DC 20016

BERMAN, SIMEON MOSES, educator; b. Rochester, N.Y., Mar. 28, 1935; s. Jeremiah Joseph and Rose (Rappaport) B.; B.A., Coll. City N.Y., 1956; M.A., Columbia, 1958, Ph.D., 1961; m. Iona Toby, Dec. 28, 1955; children—Jeremy, Jessica, Daniel, Zachary, Migdana, Tehilah. Lectr., Coll. City N.Y., 1957-60; asst. prof. Columbia, 1961-65; asso. prof. math. N.Y. U., N.Y.C., 1965-77, prof., 1977—, prin. investigator NSF grant in math., 1966—. Jewish (pres. congregation 1973). Author: The Elements of Probability, 1969; Mathematical Statistics, 1971; Calculus for the Nonphysical Sciences, 1974. Home: 334 Marlboro Rd Brooklyn NY 11226 Office: 251 Mercer St New York City NY 10012

BERNALD, EUGENE, internat. corp. exec.; b. Rostov, Russia, Jan. 23, 1908; s. Edouard K. and Vera (Sviatoslav-Gurekoff) B.; came to U.S. 1913, naturalized, 1942; grad. Columbia, 1929; m. Mary Blanche Dual, Dec. 15, 1940; children—Mary Ann, Eugene Robert, Edward Arthur, Barbara Elaine. Asso. with Mfrs. Trust Co., N.Y.C., 1929-30; jr. exec. trust dept. J. Schanzenbach & Co., N.Y.C., 1931-36; asst. to pres. PABCO, Inc., N.Y.C., 1936-47, v.p., 1947-65, pres., 1965—; dir. Pan Am. Broadcasting Co., Internat. Media Co., Radio Am. West Indies, Inc., St. Croix, V.I., Radio Anchorage, Inc., Alaska, South Eastern Alaska Broadcasters, Inc., Juneau, Drum Trading Corp., Ltd., Lagos, Nigeria, Intercontinental Ltd., Salisbury, Rhodesia. Adv. com. Operation Crossroads Africa, Inc., N.Y.C., 1960—; chmn. radio industry com. Am. Korean Found., 1957—. Adviser minority groups presdl. elections Republican Nat. Com., Washington, 1956-64. Bd. dirs. Asia Found. Mem. Internat. Broadcasting Soc. (dir.), Internat. Advt. Assn., Lutheran Laymen's League. Author: Primer of International Broadcasting, 1938; Economics of Broadcasting, 1940; Broadcasting Overseas, 1948; Reaching Minority Groups, 1952; Communications for Underdeveloped Countries, 1960. Club: Overseas Press (N.Y.C.). Home: 83 Somerstown Rd Ossining NY 10562 also Long Pond Rd Willsboro NY 12996 Office: 275 Madison Ave New York City NY 10017 also 4320 Stevens Creek Blvd San Jose CA 95157

BERNARD, LAWRENCE, editor; b. N.Y.C., Mar. 18, 1927; s. Jacob and Rose (Kroll) B.; A.B. in Journalism and English, Syracuse U., 1950; postgrad, N.Y. U., 1952-54, New Sch., N.Y., 1955-56, Columbia U., 1956-57; m. Anne G. Kroll, Sept. 5, 1954; children—Russel Samuel, Donald Alan. With editorial dept. Newsweek Mag., N.Y.C., 1947; asso. editor, sr. editor, internat. editor Advt. Age, N.Y.C., 1950-64; dir. publs. div., founder Interpub. Press, Interpub. Group of Cos., N.Y.C., 1965-67; editor Bus. Mgmt. mag. Crowell, Collier & MacMillan, Inc., Greenwich, Conn., 1968-71; pres. Gamblers World, Inc., editor, pub. Gamblers World mag., N.Y.C., 1972-75; cons. pub. relations, mktg., 1955—; asso. staff mem. Columbia Ency., 1964—; lectr. pub. relations and publicity N.Y. Inst. Tech., 1976-77; adj. prof. communication art & skills St. John's U., N.Y., 1978—. Mem. communications council Great Neck (N.Y.) Bd. Edn., 1970—, vice chmn., 1971-72; mem. Syracuse U. Alumni Counseling Com., 1963—, bd. advisors, 1977—. Served with USAAF, 1945-47. Mem. Overseas Press Club Am., Am. Soc. Mag. Editors, Am. Soc. Bus. Press Editors, Authors League, Sigma Delta Chi. Club: Deadline. Home: 22 Ascot Ridge Great Neck NY 11021 Office: 141 Moonachie Rd Moonachie NJ 07074

BERNARD, MARCELLE THOMASINE, physician; b. N.Y.C., Aug. 11, 1920; d. Rene Jules and Antoinette (Byrnes) B.; A.B. magna cum laude, Coll. of St. Elizabeth, 1941; M.D., N.Y. Med. Coll., 1944; m. Ebmund D. Marinucci, Mar. 30, 1967. Intern, Flower and Fifth Av. Hosps., 1944-45; gen. practice medicine and geriatrics, N.Y.C., 1947—, Norwalk, Conn., 1974—; attending physician St. Francis Hosp., Bronx, N.Y., 1950-65, Union Hosp., N.Y.C., 1957—; attending staff Frances Schervier Home and Hosp., N.Y.C., 1952-76, pres. med. bd., 1959-60, sec., 1962; attending staff St. Patrick's Home, N.Y.C., 1954—, pres. med. bd., 1962; med. dir. St. Joseph's Heritage House, Danbury, Conn., 1972-75; mem. med. bd. Notre Dame Convalescent Home, Norwalk, Conn., 1974—; asst. attending physician, sec. dept. family practice Norwalk Hosp. Mem. bd. examiners nursing home adminstrs., N.Y., 1973-77; mem. exec. com. Bronx Tb and Health Assn., 1956-60; hon. surgeon Life Sav. Service N.Y.C., 1959—; v.p. Bronxboro Commn. on Aging, 1961-63; adv. bd. Bronx Mental Health Assn., 1964-69, Bronx div. Salvation Army, 1964—, Norwalk div., 1977—; mem. exec. com. Bronx chpt. Am. Cancer Soc., 1965-75, chmn. profl. edn., 1966-68, co-chmn. adv. bd., 1970-75, bd. dirs. So. Fairfield County (Conn.) Unit, 1974—, med. affairs Com., 1974—; mem. adv. bd. Boy Scouts Am., 1962-66; mem. Conn. Region IV Area Agy. on Aging, 1976—; mem. long-term health care com. Norwalk Commn. on Aging, 1976—; bd. dirs. Blue Cross/Blue Shield (N.Y.), 1975—; mem. Ladies of Charity. Served as lt., M.C., Womens Res., USN, 1945-47. Decorated Lady Equestrian Order Holy Sepulchre of Jerusalem. Diplomate Nat. Bd. Med. Examiners. Fellow Am. Acad. Family Physicians (charter; pres. Bronx chpt. 1969-72), Am. Geriatrics Soc.; mem. N.Y. State Acad. Family Physicians (legislative com., pub. relations com.), N.Y. State (chmn. pub. med. care com. 1963-65, chmn. aging and nursing homes com. 1973-77), Bronx County (pres. 1965-66, bd. censors 1966-68), Norwalk (sec. 1974—), Fairfield County med. socs., Bronx Catholic Physicians Guild (exec. com.), Mil. Surgeons U.S. Asst. editor Jour. Am. Med. Womens Assn., 1949-55. Contbr. articles on geriatrics to med. jours. Home: Pine Hill Rd East Norwalk CT 06855 Office: 635 E 211th St New York City NY 10467 also 156 East Ave Norwalk CT 06851

BERNARDI, RALPH EUGENE, educator; b. Scranton, Pa., May 4, 1927; s. Narciso and Emma (Franchi) B.; B.S., cum laude, U. Scranton, 1949; M.A., N.Y. U., 1955, Ph.D., 1967. Instr., Georgetown Prep. Sch., Washington, 1950-51, Scranton Pub. Schs., 1951-63; asso. prof. Marywood Coll., Scranton, 1963—, chmn. dept. edn. Grad. Sch. Arts and Scis., 1968—. Prof., Kilroe Sem., 1968. Mem. Humane Soc. Lackawanna County, 1969—; mem. alumni bd. admissions N.Y. U., 1965—. Recipient Founder's Day award N.Y. U., 1967. Mem. NEA (life), Internat. Reading Assn. (pres. Scranton chpt.

1967), AAUP (pres. Marywood chpt. 1971), Phi Delta Kappa (pres. 1977). Home: 304 Prescott Ave Scranton PA 18510

BERNARDO, PETER, pharm. chemist; b. Sagamore, Pa., Aug. 21, 1937; s. John and Helen (Lecorchick) B.; B.S., Duquesne U., 1959; M.S., U. Mich., 1963, Ph.D., 1966; m. Loretta Stapor, Aug. 26, 1961; children—Carol Sue, John Peter, Alice Ann. Asst. mgr. Gray Drug Co., 1959-60; asst. research pharmacist Parke Davis & Co., 1960-61; sr. investigator Smith Kline Corp., Phila., 1966-76; head dept. formulation devel., research and devel. sect. Lederle Labs., Pearl River, N.Y., 1976—. Mem. Am. Pharm. Soc. (Eastern regional sect. program com. 1969-73, program chmn. 1972, gen. chmn. 1973), Acad. Pharm. Scis. (chmn. membership com., resolution com. Bask sect. 1971-72), Am. Chem. Soc., Sigma Xi, Rho Chi, Phi Lambda Upsilon. Republican. Roman Catholic. Office: RFD 3 Mount Holly Rd Katonah NY 10536

BERNAY, ELAYN KATZ, market research cons., educator; b. Paterson, N.J., July 29, 1928; d. Max and Leah (Rosen) Katz; M.B.A., City Coll. N.Y., 1965; Ph.D. City U. N.Y., 1973; m. Paul Bernay, Feb. 1, 1948; 1 dau., Laura. With Harper's/Atlantic/Natural History, N.Y.C., 1958-76; dir. research Ms. Mag., N.Y.C., 1976—; faculty Baruch Coll., City U. N.Y., 1970—, asso. prof. mktg., 1977—; asso. prof. Grad. Sch. Bus., Pace U., 1978—. Mem. com. to establish consumer product safety standard for power lawn equipment U.S. Product Safety Commn., 1974-76. Mem. AAAS, Am. Assn. Pub. Opinion Research, Am. Mktg. Assn. (pres. N.Y. chpt. 1976—, nat. dir. 1975—), Am. Psychol. Assn., Am. Council on Consumer Interests, Am. Statis. Assn., Media Research Dirs. Assn., Advt. Research Found., Travel Research Assn. (chpt. pres. 1976), Assn. Consumer Research, Advt. Women N.Y. (dir. 1978—), Beta Gamma Sigma. Mem. editorial bd. Jour. Bus. Research, Jour. Travel Research. Home: 201 E 17th St New York City NY 10003 Office: 370 Lexington Ave New York City NY 10003

BERNAYS, EDWARD L., pub. relations cons.; b. Vienna, Austria, Nov. 22, 1891; s. Ely and Anna (Freud) B.; came to U.S., 1892, naturalized; B.S., Cornell U., 1912; L.H.D. (hon.), Boston U., 1966; LL.D. (hon.), Babson Coll., 1977; m. Doris Elsa Fleischman, Sept. 16, 1922; children—Doris Fleischman Bernays Held, Anne Fleischman Bernays Kaplan. Co-producer Damaged Goods, N.Y.C., 1913; editor Dietetic & Hygienic Gazette, N.Y.C., 1913; asso. editor Med. Rev. of Revs., N.Y.C., 1913; free-lance writer, newspapers in N.Y.C., 1913-15; partner Met. Musical Bur., N.Y.C., 1916-18; publicity mgr. Caruso, Diaghileff Russian Ballet, 1916-18; mem. U.S. Com. on Pub. Info., N.Y.C. and Paris, 1918-19; counsel on pub. relations, N.Y.C., 1919-62, Cambridge, Mass., 1962—, partner Edward L. Bernays, Counsel on Pub. Relations, 1922—; prof. pub. relations N.Y. U., 1949-50, U. Hawaii, 1950, Boston U., 1968; cons. State Dept., 1970-75, HEW, 1976, Dept. Commerce, 1977-78. Trustee New Eng. Conservatory Music; mem. advisory com. Ford Hall Forum, Boston, 1972-79; pres. Edward L. Bernays Found., N.Y.C.; mem. advisory com. Edward R. Murrow Center Fletcher Sch. Law and Diplomacy. Decorated King Christian 10th medal (Denmark); named Officer Pub. Instruction, French Govt., 1926; recipient medallion of Honor, City N.Y., 1961, Honor award Ohio U., 1970, Distinguished Service award Pub. Relations Council Health and Welfare Services, 1975. Mem. Pub. Relations Soc. Am. (Gold Anvil award 1976, Lincoln award N.E. chpt. 1976), Soc. Psychol. Study Social Issues, Nat. Multiple Sclerosis Soc. (hon. trustee), Columbia U. Pub. Communication Seminar, Women in Communications. Clubs: Harvard Faculty (Cambridge); Cornell U. (N.Y.C., Boston); Columbia U. Faculty, Overseas Press (N.Y.C.). Author books, including: Crystallizing Public Opinion, 1923; Propaganda, 1928; Public Relations, 1952; Biography of an Idea, 1965; editor, contbg. author: An Outline of Careers, 1927, Engineering of Consent, 1955; co-editor: The Case for Reappraisal of U.S. Overseas Information Policies and Programs, 1970. Contbr. articles to profl. jours. Home and office: 7 Lowell St Cambridge MA 02138

BERNBACH, WILLIAM, advt. exec.; b. N.Y.C., Aug. 13, 1911; s. Jacob and Rebecca (Reiter) B.; B.C.S., N.Y. U., 1933; m. Evelyn Carbone, June 5, 1938; children—John Lincoln, Paul. Dir. research N.Y. World's Fair, 1939-40; dir. postwar planning Coty, Inc., 1943-44; v.p. Grey Advt. Agy., 1945-49; pres. Doyle Dane Bernbach Inc., 1949-67, chmn., chief exec. officer, 1968-74, chmn. exec. com., chief exec. officer, 1974—; distinguished adj. prof. N.Y.U. Vice chmn. Lincoln Center Film Com., bd. dirs., mem. exec. com. Salk Inst. Biol. Studies; bd. dirs. Legal Aid Soc., Mary Manning Walsh Home, Internat. Eye Found., Municipal Arts Soc.; bd. dirs., vice chmn. Citizens Com. for N.Y.C.; bd. dirs., v.p. AAAA Ednl. Found., Inc. Named Man of Year, Pulse, Inc. 1966; mem. Copywriters Hall of Fame, Advt. Hall of Fame; recipient Madden Meml. award, 1968; Am. Acad. Achievement award, 1976. named Top Advt. Agy. Exec., 1969; named One Person Who Did Most for the Progress of Advt. Industry, 1963, 65, 66. Mem. Urban Design Council City of N.Y. Club: N.Y. University Alumni; City Athletic Home: 870 UN Plaza New York City NY 10017 Office: 437 Madison Ave New York City NY 10022

BERNER, ROBERT KENNETH, mktg., advt. and pub. relations exec.; b. Weehawken, N.J., Aug. 28, 1928; s. Samuel and Minerva (Rosenthal) B.; student Ohio State U., 1945-46, L.I. U., 1946-48; m. Evelyn Gurewitz, June 29, 1961. News film coordinator NBC, N.Y.C., 1953-58; reporter Ridgewood (N.J.) News, 1959; reporter Paterson (N.J.) News, 1960-61; publicist Madison Square Garden, 1961-62; editor Dell Pub. Co., N.Y.C., 1962; freelance pub. relations cons., Passaic, N.J., 1963; pres. Robert K. Berner Assos., Clifton, N.J., 1964—. Served with U.S. Army, 1950-52. Mem. Pub. Relations Soc. Am., Bus./Profl. Advt. Assn., Am. Jewish Com. Club: B'nai B'rith. Home: 140 Hepburn Rd Clifton NJ 07012 Office: 50 Mt Prospect Ave Clifton NJ 07013

BERNEY, THOMAS EDWARD, microfilm co. exec.; b. Chgo., Oct. 5, 1928; s. James T. and Mary E. Berney; grad. DePaul U., 1949; m. Catherine E. O'Connor, Aug. 14, 1954; children—James, Jean, Ellen, Sandra, Dorothy, William, Barbara, Laura. Salesman, Charles Bruning Co., Chgo., 1953-61; with Bell & Howell Co., Chgo., Washington, 1961—, mgr. sales devel., 1961-65, mgr. fed. govt. sales, 1966-71, Mid-Atlantic area mgr., 1971-72, regional mgr., 1972-77, mgr. advance planning, 1978—; mem. 16mm microfilm container standards task group Am. Nat. Standards Assn., 1969-75. Served with U.S. Army, 1950-52. Mem. Nat. Micrographics Assn. (pres. Nat. Capitol chpt. 1973-74, mem. exec. bd.). Republican. Roman Catholic. Home: 7214 Ridgewood Ave Chevy Chase MD 20015 Office: 4820 Fairmont Ave Bethesda MD 20014

BERNFELD, GERALD EDWARD, pharm. co. exec.; b. New Britain, Conn., Nov. 2, 1939; s. Edward Emil and Helena Betty (Jenosky) B.; student Pa. State U., 1957-59; diploma in Russian, Ind. U., 1960; A.B., Edison Coll., 1973; m. Elizabeth L. Jack, July 11, 1964; children—Edward, Michael, Maria. Translator, editor Library of Congress, Washington, 1963-65; intelligence officer, fgn. tech. div. Wright-Patterson AFB, Ohio, 1965-67; translation mgr. Frank C. Farnham Co., Phila., 1967-72; sr. clin. info. scientist Squibb Inst., Princeton, N.J., 1972-76, dir. clin. data sect., 1976—. Served with USAF, 1959-63; mem. U.S. Army Res. Mem. Am. Translators Assn. (past dir.), Del. Valley Translators Assn. (past v.p.), Guild Profl. Translators (adv. bd. 1972—), Am. Med. Writers Assn. (chpt. v.p. 1978), Drug Info. Assn., Soc. Tech. Communication (sr.). Democrat. Roman Catholic. Translator: Introduction to Medical Cybernetics (Parin and Bayevskiy), 1968. Contbr. numerous articles on clin. research to profl. jours. Home: 1503 Cliff Rd Philadelphia PA 19151 Office: Squibb Inst Med Research POB 4000 Princeton NJ 08540

BERNFELD, HERBERT, real estate cons.; b. Jersey City, June 17, 1919; s. Max and Florence (Kislak) B.; student Union Coll., 1938; M.B.A., Columbia Grad. Sch. Bus., 1940; m. Marilyn Solomon, Sept. 15, 1946; children—Thomas Jay, Ellen Marie. Pres., Cumberland Estates Inc., Teaneck, N.J., 1948, Cottage Shops Inc., Englewood, N.J., 1949-53; sr. v.p. C. B. Snyder Realty Inc., Jersey City, 1953-71; prin. Herbert Bernfeld Assos., Tenafly, N.J., 1971—; chmn. bd. E.M.B. Prodns. Inc., N.Y.C. Mem. Grad. Realtors Inst., Nat. Assn. Realtors, Nat. Inst. Real Estate Brokers (past regional v.p.), Central Bergen County Bd. Realtors (dir.), N.J., Assn. Realtors Bds. (past dir., exec. com.), Hoboken Bd. Realtors (past pres.), Nat. Assn. Real Estate Bds. (recipient Nat. Trade of the Year award, 1958, 61, 63, sr. instr.), Realtors Nat. Mktg. Inst. (v.p.), Internat. Traders Club. Omega Tau Rho. Clubs: Bergen, Mason. Contbr. articles to profl. jours. Home: 21 S Park Dr Tenafly NJ 07670 Office: Herbert Bernfeld Assos Tenafly NJ 07670

BERNFELD, PETER HARRY WILLIAM, biochemist; b. Leipzig, Germany, June 1, 1912; s. Isidor and Elsa (Gutfreund) B.; M.S., U. Leipzig, 1935; Ph.D., U. Geneva (Switzerland), 1937; m. Helen Cecily Kroch, Nov. 21, 1940; children—Michele Marion, Mark Raymond. Came to U.S., 1949, naturalized, 1955. Research fellow U. Geneva, 1937-39, chief chemist dept. chemistry, 1939-49, privat docent enzymology, faculty sci., 1947-49; asst. prof. dept. biochemistry and nutrition Sch. Medicine Tufts U., 1949-51, asso. prof., 1951-57, biochemist, cancer research unit, 1949-57; sr. v.p., dir. research Bio-Research Inst. and Bio-Research Cons., Cambridge, Mass., 1957—. Recipient Werner medal Swiss Chem. Soc., 1948. Mem. Am. Soc. Biol. Chemists, Soc. Exptl. Biology and Medicine, Am. Chem. Soc., Am. Inst. Chemists, Am. Assn. Cancer Research, AAAS, N.Y. Acad. Sci., Sigma Xi. Editor, contbg. author Biogenesis of Natural Compounds, 1963, 2d edit., 1967. Contbr. articles to profl. jours. Home: 247 Farm Ln Westwood MA 02090 Office: 9 Commercial Ave Cambridge MA 02141

BERNHANG, ARTHUR MAURICE, orthopaedic surgeon; b. N.Y.C., June 21, 1934; s. Emanuel Abraham and Claire (Kessler) B.; A.B., U. Rochester, 1955; M.D., Chgo. Med. Sch., 1959; m. Judith Lynne Pertz, Dec. 3, 1961. Intern, Hosp. for Joint Diseases, N.Y.C., 1959-60, resident in surgery, 1960-61, resident in orthopaedics, 1961-64; attending orthopaedist Huntington (N.Y.) Hosp., 1968—; asst. prof. orthopaedic surgery State U. N.Y., Stony Brook, 1975—. Served to lt. comdr. USNR, 1966-68. Fellow Am. Acad. Orthopaedic Surgeons, A.C.S.; mem. Am. Orthopaedic Soc. Sports Medicine, Eastern Orthopaedic Assn., Soc. Advanced Med. Systems, Internat. Orthopaedic Club Bermuda, N.Y. State Orthopaedic Soc., Med. Soc. State N.Y. (mem. com. on med. aspects of sports). Contbr. articles to profl. jours. Office: 124 Main St Huntington NY 11743

BERNHARDT, LEWIS JULES, securities rep., lectr., educator; b. N.Y.C., Sept. 22, 1937; s. Henry and Jean (Dickov) B.; B.A., U. Md., 1964, M.A., 1965; M.A. (NDEA fellow), Princeton U., 1967, Ph.D. (Ford Found. regional studies grantee, Harold W. Dodds fellow), 1970; m. Rochelle Solomon, Aug. 7, 1960; children—Marc Stuart, Jay Michael. Asst. in instrn. and comparative lit., Princeton U., 1969-70; asst. prof. Slavic Langs. and Lit., Rutgers U., New Brunswick, N.J., 1970-76; municipal securities rep. Halpert, Oberst and Co., Millburn, N.J., 1976—; Internat. Research and Exchange Bd. research grantee, Bulgaria, 1971, USSR, 1973; mem. acad. adv. bd. Citizens Exchange Corps, 1970-74. Served with U.S. Army, 1960-63. Mem. AAUP, Modern Lang. Assn., Bulgarian Studies Group, Assn. Devel. Computer-Based Instructional Systems, Soc. Israel Philatelists (sec. Central Jersey chpt. 1976—), Am. Bridge Tchrs. Assn., Am. Crytogram Assn., Judaica Hist. Philatelic Soc., Internat. Platform Assn. Jewish. Club: Princeton of N.Y. Editor: The Poems and Idylls of Saul Chernikhovsky, (in Russian), 1974; contbr. articles and revs. to scholarly jours.; developer Rusjaz (computer drills in Russian). Home: 5 Norton Rd East Brunswick NJ 08816 Office: Halpert Oberst and Co 284 Millburn Ave Millburn NJ 07041

BERNHOLZ, WILLIAM FRANCIS, chem. co. exec.; b. N.Y.C., Jan. 26, 1924; s. Edward Louis and Lillian Ruth (Polhemus) B.; B.S. in Chemistry, Manhattan Coll., 1945; M.S. in Organic Chemistry, Fordham U., 1948; m. Rosalie Cecile Eckel, Feb. 19, 1949; children—Elinor Ruth, Catherine Cecile, Frances Marie. Asso. chemist Gen. Foods Corp., Hoboken, N.J., 1948-57; research chemist Avon Products, Inc., Suffern, N.Y., 1957-62; research chemist Colgate Palmolive Co., Inc., Piscataway Twp., N.J., 1962; indsl. research mgr. PVO Internat. Inc. (formerly Drew Chem. Corp.), Boonton, N.J., 1963—, dir. research, 1976—; cons. in field. Chmn. promotional com. Wayne Library referendum, 1962; mem. Friends of Wayne Pub. Library, 1959-66. Served with USNR, 1944-46; PTO. Mem. Am. Chem. Soc. Republican. Roman Catholic. Contbr. articles to profl. jours. Patentee man-made fiber processing, modifications of flexible packaging film. Home: 11 Ledge Rd Wayne NJ 07470 Office: 416 Division St Boonton NJ 07005

BERNIER, RAYMOND JOSEPH, educator, designer; b. Fall River, Mass., May 26, 1930; s. Joseph and Rose Anna (Chouinard) B.; B.S., Southeastern Mass. U., 1958; M.Ed., Bridgewater (Mass.) State Coll., 1960; M.A., Smith Coll., 1967; m. Natalie Jane Moquin, June 18, 1966; children—Kristian Charles, Erika Jane. Asst. prof. theater, tech. dir., designer U. N.H., Durham, 1967—; instr./designer, dir. theater Phillips Exeter (N.H.) Acad., summers 1972-76; art instr., Fall River, 1958-65; cons. tech. theater, schs./community theaters. Served with U.S. Army, 1949-50. Mem. Am. Theatre Assn. Roman Catholic. Home: Route 4 Durham Rd Dover NH 03820 Office: Paul Arts Center U NH Durham NH 03824

BERNOSKY, HERMAN GEORGE, retail gasoline dealer; b. Minersville, Pa., Aug. 16, 1921; s. Peter and Mary Bernosky; student Rider Coll., Trenton, N.J., 1947-48. With Bernosky's Exxon Sta., Llewellyn, Pa., 1940-42, 46—, owner, operator, 1949—. Treas. Minersville Area Bicentennial, 1976. Served with AUS, 1942-46; ETO. Decorated Bronze Star (3). Mem. Am. Legion. Democrat. Roman Catholic. Club: Minersville Lions (past pres., dir. 1957—). Home: 622 Lytle St Minersville PA 17954 Office: PO Box 170 Llewellyn PA 17944

BERNS, H(ERMAN) JEROME, restaurateur; b. N.Y.C., Feb. 19, 1907; s. Abraham and Sophia (Bazin) B.; student Columbia, 1925; B.A., U. Cin., 1929, D.C.S. (hon.), 1962; m. Suzanne Pogany, Mar. 3, 1977. children—Cecily (Mrs. Michael Fuhrmann), Diane (Mrs. Gerald Stein). Drama critic, editor Cin. Enquirer, 1929-38; v.p., sec., 21 Club, Inc., N.Y.C., 1945—; sec. Iron Gate Products, Inc., N.Y.C., 1951—. Pres., Kriendler-Berns Found.; co-chmn. restaurant div. United Fund N.Y., 1960—; chmn. restaurant div. N.Y. Heart Assn., 1962-63. Trustee Local No. 1 Waiters Union Pension Fund; vice chmn. U. Cin. Found. Recipient William Howard Taft medal U. Cin., 1972, Outstanding Alumni award, 1973. Diplomate Nat. Inst. Food Industry, 1976. Mem. Restaurant League N.Y. (chmn. bd. 1958), Nat. (dir., Nat. Restaurateur of Yr. 1978), N.Y. State (exec. com. 1960, v.p. 1962, sec.-treas. 1963) restaurant assns., Culinary Inst. Am. (vice chmn. exec. com. 1971—), Wine and Food Soc. N.Y. (treas., dir. 1955-73), Internat. Wine and Food Soc. (Andre Simon medal 1977), N.Y. Conv. and Visitors Bur. (exec. com. 1960, v.p., treas. 1963-74), U. Cin. Alumni Assn. (regional v.p. 1963), U. Cin. Alumni Club N.Y. (treas. 1950). Home: 14 E 75th St New York City NY 10021 Office: 21 W 52d St New York City NY 10019

BERNSTEIN, ARTHUR GEORGE, mech. engr.; b. N.Y.C., Sept. 1, 1922; s. Irving and Stella (Roth) B.; student City Coll. N.Y., 1938-43; B.S., Pa. State U., 1948; m. Marilyn J. Treppel, June 19, 1950; children—Ellen, Janet, Andrew, Joan. Engr., mgr. EDP, United Engrs. & Constructors Inc., Phila., 1948-68, mgr. cost evaluation and analysis, 1977—; mgr. cost control Allied Chem. Corp., Morristown, N.J., 1968-70; supr. cost Control Gibbs & Hill Inc., N.Y.C., 1970-72; cons. in field. Trustee, treas. Pennsauken Library Assn., 1955-60. Served with C.E., U.S. Army, 1943-46. Mem. ASME, Jenkintown Improvement Assn., Jenkintown Library Assn. Democrat. Home: 605 Runnymede Ave Jenkintown PA 19046 Office: United Engrs & Constructors Inc 30 S 17th St Box 8223 Philadelphia PA 19101

BERNSTEIN, DAVID, surgeon; b. Minsk, Russia, Oct. 20, 1910; s. George and Anna (Rossoff) B.; came to U.S. 1912, naturalized, 1932; B.S., N.Y.U., 1930, M.D., 1935; m. Dorothy Ashery, Sept. 2, 1937; children—Helen Miriam (Mrs. Peter Young), Herbert Jacob. Intern Bellevue Hosp.-N.Y.U., N.Y.C., 1935-37, resident in ear, nose, throat and facial plastic surgery, 1937-39; clin. prof. otorhinolaryngology, chief of plastic surgery N.Y.U. Med. Center, 1966—; chief otolaryngology service Maimonides Med. Center, 1966—; cons. otorhinolaryngol. plastic surgery VA Hosp., N.Y.C.; attending otolaryngologist plastic surgery Bellevue, N.Y.U. Hosp.; pres. exec. com. of med. staff Met. Geriatric Center, 1974-75, mem. joint com. bd. trustees, 1975—; cons. otorhinolaryngology and maxillofacial plastic surgery Coney Island Hosp., Bklyn. Served to maj. M.C., AUS, 1944-46. Fellow Am. Acad. Ophthalmology and Otolaryngology, Am. Acad. Facial Plastic and Reconstructive Surgery, Am. Assn. Cosmetic Surgeons, Internat. Coll. Surgeons; mem. N.Y., Vienna acads. medicine, N.Y.U. Med. Sch. Alumni Assn. (pres. 1974-75), N.Y.U. Alumni Fedn. (dir.), Phi Beta Kappa. Jewish (adv. com. to bd. trustees temple). Club: N.Y.U. Contbr. articles to profl. jours. Pioneer surg. techniques in rhinoplastic, otoplastic and maxillofacial surgery. Home and office: 1342 51st St Brooklyn NY 11219

BERNSTEIN, EMMANUEL MOSES, psychologist; b. Balt., Apr. 23, 1930; s. Emmanuel Moses and Hortense Elinor (Gans) B.; student New Sch. for Social Research, 1952-53, Colo. State Coll., 1955; B.S.E., U. Pa., 1952; M.A., Columbia, 1960; postgrad. State U. N.Y., 1954-55, Boston U., 1961-63, U. Hawaii, 1966; Ph.D., U. Oreg., 1971; m. Pearl Marie Gross, Nov. 30, 1968; children—Roberta Marie, Vauna Kathleen, Arthur Frank Alexander. Interviewer, Psychol. Corp., N.Y.C., 1952-54; recreation worker, preadolescent psychiat. ward Bellevue Hosp., N.Y.C., 1952-53; tchr. Manhattanville Nursery, N.Y.C., 1952-53; tchr. elementary and jr. high, Plattsburgh, N.Y., 1955-56, elementary sch., Warwick, N.Y., 1956-57; instr. Paul Smith's (N.Y.) Coll., 1958-60; counselor, jr.-sr. high sch., Atco, N.Y., 1960-61; caseworker Family and Children's Service, Boston, 1961-63; tchr. emotionally disturbed Kingsley Sch., Boston, 1963-65; elementary counselor, pub. schs. Johnston, R.I., 1965-67; sr. psychologist United Counseling Orgn., Eugene, Oreg., 1967-68; cons., learning coordinator Met. Learning Center, Portland, Oreg., 1969-71; psychologist Permanent Mental Health Clinic, Portland, 1971-72; psychologist Adirondack Counseling, Glenwood Estates, Saranac Lake, N.Y., 1972—. Cons., St. Agnes Sch., Lake Placid, 1972—, Med. Center Hosp. Vt., Burlington, 1973; pvt. practice psychology, Portland, 1969-72, Saranac Lake, N.Y., 1972—; prin. psychologist Ray Brook State Rehab. Center (N.Y.), 1973-75; cons. St. Lawrence State Hosp., Saranac Lake Gen. Hosp., 1973—, Center for Advancement Developmentally Disabled, 1974—, Camelot Boys Home, 1976—, Sunmount Developmental Center, 1977—. Pres., Tri-Lakes Humane Soc., 1972-75, v.p., 1975—; mem. Am. Humane Assn., 1974-76, Humane Soc. U.S., 1974—. Bd. dirs. Center for Advancement of the Developmentally Disabled, 1973-74, Day Care Center, 1975—, Franklin County Mental Health Bd., 1977—. Recipient William Stillman Meritorious Service award Am. Humane Assn., 1948, Nat. Def. Edn. Act grant, Hawaii, 1966. Mem. Am. Psychol. Assn., Am. Assn. Marriage and Family Counselors. Contbr. articles to profl. jours. Home: Glenwood Estates Saranac Lake NY 12983 Office: Adirondack Counseling Glenwood Estates Saranac Lake NY 12983

BERNSTEIN, EUGENE HAROLD, lab. exec.; b. N.Y.C., Sept. 26, 1926; s. Max and Anna (Cohen) B.; B.S., U.S. Mcht. Marine Acad., 1947; B.S. in Biology, Rutgers U., 1951, M.S. (Instnl. fellow), 1952, Ph.D. in Biochemistry and Physiology (Nutrition Found. fellow, Am. Cancer Soc. fellow), 1955; m. Bernice Alberta Frant, Dec. 21, 1952; children—Andrew Mark, Robert Stuart, Jill Terri. Asst. dir. New Brunswick Clin. Lab., 1953-55; biochemist Sloan-Kettering Inst. Cancer Research, N.Y.C., 1955-56; biochemist, enzymologist Colgate-Palmolive Co., 1956-58; head biochemistry and enzymology sect. Colgate-Palmolive Biol. Research Labs., Rutgers U., 1958-60; vis. investigator Inst. Microbiology of Rutgers U., 1959-68; dir. research Univ. Labs., Inc., Highland Park, N.J., 1960—, pres., dir., 1964—; dir. In Vivo, Inc., Somerville, N.J. Served to ensign USNR, 1944-47; PTO. Fellow Am. Inst. Chemists; mem. N.Y. Acad. Scis., AAAS, Am. Chem. Soc., Am. Soc. Microbiology, Am. Med. Technologists, Internat. Leukemia Assn., N.J. Acad. Scis., Phi Beta Kappa, Sigma Xi. Patentee skin packaging process to prolong shelf life of biol. materials. Home: 901 S Park Ave Highland Park NJ 08904 Office: 810 N 2d Ave Highland Park NJ 08904

BERNSTEIN, IRVING, fund raising exec.; b. N.Y.C., Aug. 9, 1921; s. Jacob and Ethel (Potasewitch) B.; B.A., City Coll. N.Y., 1942; M.A., Columbia, 1946; m. Judith Muniz, Jan. 2, 1952; children—Robert, Joseph. Secondary sch. tchr. N.Y.C. Pub. Sch. System, 1946; social worker N.Y.C. Dept. Welfare, 1947; field rep. United Jewish Appeal, 1948-50, West Coast regional dir., 1950-62, nat. asst. exec. vice chmn., 1962-68, nat. exec. vice chmn., N.Y.C., 1969—; asso. mem. bd. govs. Jewish Agency (Israel); mem. Jewish Agency Internat. Fund-raising Com.; founder Jewish Agency Inst. for Fund-Raising; mem. Am. Friends Internat. Edn. Seminar for Middle Eastern Educators, Harvard. Bd. dirs. Brandeis U. Hornstein Program, grad. studies in Jewish communal services; mem. exec. com. Hebrew Union Coll., Los Angeles; mem. exec. com. Nat. Jewish Conf. Served with USAF, 1942-45. Clubs: Stuyvesant, Lambs. Contbr. articles to profl. jours. Home: 1 Stoneleigh Rd Scarsdale NY 10583 Office: United Jewish Appeal 1290 Ave of Americas New York City NY 10019

BERNSTEIN, LEONARD, conductor, pianist, composer; b. Lawrence, Mass., Aug. 25, 1918; s. Samuel Joseph and Jennie (Resnick) B.; A.B., Harvard U., 1939; grad. Curtis Inst. Music, 1941; studied conducting with Fritz Reiner and Serge Koussevitzky; studied piano with Helen Coates, Heinrich Gebhard and Isabella Vengerova; numerous hon. degrees from various colls. and univs.; m. Felicia

Montealegre Cohn, Sept. 5, 1951; children—Jamie, Alexander, Nina. Asst. to Serge Koussevitsky at Berkshire Music Center, 1942; asst. condr. N.Y. Philharmonic Symphony, 1943-44; condr. N.Y.C. Symphony, 1945-48; frequent condr. Israel Philharmonic Orch., 1947—, mus. adviser, 1948-49; faculty Berkshire Music Center, 1948-55, head conducting dept., 1951-55; prof. music Brandeis U., 1951-56; co-condr. with Dimitri Mitropoulas of N.Y. Philharmonic, 1957-58, music dir., 1958-69, apptd. laureate condr. Philharmonic for life; condr. major orchs. of U.S. and Europe in tours, 1946—; condr. opera at La Scala, Milan, also Met. Opera, N.Y.C. and Vienna State Opera; shared transcontinental tour in U.S. with Koussevitzky and Israel Philharmonic, 1951; toured Europe with Vienna Philharmonic Orch., 1970; gala Bicentennial tour Am. and Europe with N.Y. Philharmonic, 1976; Charles Eliot Norton prof. poetry Harvard U., 1972-73; Works include: Clarinet Sonata, 1942; Seven Anniversaries for Piano, 1942; Song Cycle, I Hate Music, 1943; Four Anniversaries for Piano, 1948; Song Cycle, La Bonne Cuisine, 1949; Symphony No.2-The Age of Anixety, 1949; Trouble in Tahiti (1 act opera; also wrote libretto), 1952; Symphony No. 3, Kaddish, 1963; Chichester Psalms (for mixed chours, boys' choir, orch.), 1965; score for musical show On The Town; ballets Fancy Free, 1944, Facsmile, 1946; incidental score for prodn. Peter Pan, 1950, The Lark, 1957; mus. score for Broadway prodn. Wonderful Town, 1953, Broadway mus. Candide, 1956, West Side Story, 1957, film On the Waterfront, 1954; songs Afterthought, 1945, Silhouette, 1951, Two Love Songs, 1949; Serenade (for violin and string orch. with percussion), 1954; Five Anniversaries for Piano, 1964; Mass (theatre piece for singers, players and dancers), 1971; ballet score Dybbuk, N.Y.C. Ballet Co., 1974, Dybbuk Variations, Suites No 1 and 2 (from ballet by Jerome Robbins), 1974. Recipient Emmy award for Young People's Concerts, 1960, for Outstanding Classical Music Program, Leonard Bernstein and the N.Y. Philharmonic, 1976; The Handel Medallion, 1977. Author: The Joy of Music, 1959 (Christopher award); Leonard Bernstein's Young People's Concerts for Reading and Listening, 1962, rev. edit., 1970; The Infinite Variety of Music, 1966; The Unanswered Question: Six Talks at Harvard, 1976. Office: 205 W 57th St New York NY 10019*

BERNSTEIN, MARIANNE E. (MRS. ROBERT S. WIENER), scientist; b. Goettingen, Germany; d. Felix and Edith (Magnus) Bernstein; came to U.S., 1934, naturalized, 1943; B.A., Barnard Coll., 1938; M.S., N.Y.U., 1940; Ph.D., U. Rome, 1951; m. Robert S. Wiener, July 11, 1952; 1 son, Ronald Albert. Statistician U.S. Govt., 1943-46; instr. Syracuse and Purdue univs., 1947-49; human geneticist Radcliffe Coll., 1951-52; cons. and lectr. human genetics Boston Hosp. and Schs., 1957—; lectr. C. Gini Inst., Rome, 1966; hon. research fellow dept. biology Harvard, 1973—. Fulbright fellow, Norway, 1949-50; postdoctoral fellow Radcliffe Coll., 1952. Mem. League Women Voters, Am. Soc. Human Genetics, Genetics Soc. Am. Author articles in field. Office: 112 Water St Room 405 Boston MA 02109

BERNSTEIN, MARVER HILLEL, univ. pres.; b. Mankato, Minn., Feb. 7, 1919; s. Meyer M. and Esther (Alpert) B.; B.A., U. Wis., 1940, M.A., 1940; Ph.D. in Politics, Princeton, 1948; Litt.D., Jewish Theol. Sem. Am., 1975; D.H.L., Northeastern U., 1978, Duquesne U., 1978; m. Sheva Rosenthal, Sept. 19, 1943. Budget examiner U.S. Bur. Budget, 1942-46; research asso. Princeton, 1946-47, instr. politics, 1947-48, asst. prof., 1948-54, asso. prof., 1954-58, prof., 1958-72, dean Woodrow Wilson Sch. Pub. and Internat. Affairs, 1964-69; pres. Brandeis U., Waltham, Mass., 1972—; cons. State Controller of Israel, 1953-57; dir. New Eng. Mchts. Nat. Bank, 1973—, New Eng. Mchts. Co., 1976—. Mem. Mass. Ethics Commn., 1978—; bd. dirs. WGBH Ednl. Found., 1972—; trustee Joint Distbn. Com., 1978—. Recipient Ann. citation of merit NCCJ, 1975. Mem. Am. Soc. Pub. Adminstrn., Am. Polit. Sci. Assn., Nat. Acad. Pub. Adminstrn., Am. Acad. Arts and Scis. Jewish religion. Clubs: Cosmos (Washington); Princeton (N.Y.C.). Author: Regulating Business by Independent Commission, 1955; The Politics of Israel, 1957; The Job of the Federal Executive, 1958; (with others) American Democracy, various edits., 1951—. Home: 32 Orchard Ave Weston MA 02193 Office: 415 South St Waltham MA 02154

BERNSTEIN, PHILIP, charitable assn. exec.; b. Cleve., June 6, 1911; s. Jacob and Anna (Golufchin) B.; B.A., U. Mich., 1932; M.S., Western Res. U., 1934, LL.D., 1966; m. Florence Michaelson, June 12, 1938; children—Joel, Paul, Judith. Asst. dir. Cleve. Jewish Welfare Fedn., 1934-43; sec. Cleve. Jewish Community Council, 1935-43; instr. community orgn. Western Res. U. Grad. Sch. Applied Social Scis., 1936-40; dir. field service Council Jewish Fedns. and Welfare Funds, N.Y.C., 1943-47, asso. dir., 1947-55, exec. v.p., 1955—. Mem. bd. overseers Sch. Advanced Social Studies, mem. adv. com. Inst. Contemporary Jewish Affairs, Brandeis U., 1965-73; Jewish co-chmn. steering com. Nat. Interfaith Consultation on Social Welfare, 1965-74; mem. exec. com. Citizens Crusade Against Poverty, 1965-70; pres., Nat. Conf. Jewish Communal Service, 1953. Bd. dirs., mem. exec. com. Nat. Conf. Social Welfare, 1965-68; bd. dirs., chmn. social issues and policies forum Nat. Assembly Social Policy and Devel., Inc., 1964-74; asso. mem. exec. com. Jewish Agy. for Israel, 1971—. Mem. Nat. Assn. Social Workers, Nat. Conf. Social Welfare, Nat. Conf. Jewish Communal Service, Phi Beta Kappa, Phi Eta Sigma, Alpha Kappa Delta, Phi Kappa Phi. Home: 320 Central Park W New York City NY 10025 Office: 575 Lexington Ave New York City NY 10022

BERNSTEIN, ROBERT LOUIS, dentist; b. N.Y.C., Mar. 23, 1924; s. Herman and Lillian (Kaplan) B.; student N.Y. U., 1940-43; D.D.S., St. Louis U., 1946; grad. in field dentistry U.S. Army Med. Field Service Sch., Ft. Sam Houston, Tex., 1951, in mgmt. Am. Mgmt. Assn., 1978. Practice dentistry, N.Y.C., 1947—; head dental div. Manhattan Med. and Dental Assts. Sch., 1954-67; dir. dental therapeutics Pharm. Food and Drug Assos., Inc., Roslyn Heights, N.Y., 1964-76; dental dir. United Wire Metal and Machine Health Center, N.Y.C., 1976-77; house dentist Regency Hotel, N.Y.C., 1966-71; dental advisor Blue Cross, Blue Shield of Greater N.Y., N.Y.C., 1976—; lectr. continuing edn. program Dental Assts. Soc. N.Y. Mem. N.Y.C. Mayors Community Council, 19th precinct, 1976—; state community mayor of Madison Ave., State Community Mayors Assn., N.Y.C., 1977—. Served with USNR, 1943-47, U.S. Army, 1951-53; Korea. Decorated Army Commendation medal. Fellow Royal Soc. Health (London); mem. ADA, N.Y. State, First Dist. N.Y. dental socs., N.Y. Soc. Dentistry for Children, Met. Research Inst., Acad. Oral Medicine, N.Y. Acad. Scis., Internat. Dental Fedn., Acad. Gen. Dentistry, Eastern Dental Soc. (exec. bd. 1977—, chmn. publ. com. and editor bull. 1978), N.Y. U. Coll. Dentistry Century Club, Pierre Fauchard Acad., Am. Pub. Health Assn., Am. Assn. Dental Editors, AAAS, Am. Mgmt. Assn., N.Y. Vet. Police Assn., Alpha Phi Omega, Alpha Omega, N.Y. Power Squadron. Home: 155 E 73d St New York City NY 10021 Office: 30 E 60th St New York City NY 10022

BERRIE, ROBERT HARRIS, oral surgeon; b. Bronx, N.Y., June 16, 1935; s. Julius and Martha (Loventhal) B.; B.S., Coll. City N.Y., 1956; D.D.S., N.Y. U., 1960, M.S. in Dentistry, 1966; m. Barbara Rita Lincoln, Apr. 7, 1963; children—Andrea, Jaclyn. Intern oral surgery Elmhurst Gen. Hosp., Queens, N.Y., 1962-63, resident, 1963-65; research fellow oral surgery Mt. Sinai Hosp., N.Y.C., 1965-66; practice oral surgery, Lindenhurst, N.Y., 1966—; mem. attending staff Southside, Good Samaritan, Brunswick hosps. Served to capt. Dental Corps, AUS, 1960-62. Diplomate Am. Bd. Oral surgery. Fellow Am. Dental Soc. Anesthesiology; mem. Am. Soc. Oral and Maxillo-Facial Surgeons, Am. Dental Assn., 10th Dist. Dental Soc. Home: 4 Talisman Dr Dix Hills NY 11746 Office: 150 E Sunrise Hwy Lindenhurst NY 11757

BERRONE, LOUIS, educator; b. Hartford, Conn., Feb. 25, 1932; s. Louis and Antoinette (Pastormerlo) B.; B.A., Trinity Coll., 1954, M.A. (fellow), 1958; postgrad. Drama Sch., Yale, 1960-61; Ph.D., Fordham U., 1973; m. Nina Perez, Aug. 30, 1952; children—Carla, Teresa, Lisa, Annette, Julia. Tchr. West Hartford (Conn.) Pub. Schs., 1955-59, Amity Regional Pub. Schs., Woodbridge, Conn., 1961-65; prof. English, Fairfield (Conn.) U., 1965—; tchr. Conn. Center for Continuing Edn., Fairfield, 1976. Mem. Woodbridge Democratic Com., 1973—. Recipient Superior Tchr. award West Hartford Pub. Schs., 1957; Fairfield U. grantee, 1967, 75; Caesare Barbieri Center for Italian Studies grantee, 1977. Mem. Modern Lang. Assn. Am., Nat. Council Tchrs. English, James Joyce Founds., Ltd., Dickens Soc. Am., Dramatists Guild, Authors League Am. Democrat. Roman Catholic. Playwright: Tenebrae for Holy Children; Hornets. Author: James Joyce in Padua, 1977. Home: 110 Peck Hill Rd Woodbridge CT 06525 Office: Fairfield U North Benson Rd Fairfield CT 06430

BERRY, CARLTON FREDERICK, JR., actor, educator; b. Tarrytown, N.Y., Nov. 30, 1926; s. Carlton F. and Mildred (Morrow) B.; B.S., Springfield Coll., 1951; M.A., U. Mich., 1963. Tchr., prin. pub. schs., Deerfields, Mass., 1951-55; tchr. pub. schs., Jackson, Mich., 1955-60, Tarrytown, 1960-66; prof., drama dir., dir. student activities Norwich, U., Northfield, Vt., 1966—; profl. actor area theatres. Dir., Northfield Meml. Park, summers 1967, 74, steering com. mem., 1977—. Served with Signal Corps, U.S. Army, 1945-46. Norwich grantee, Oxford and Cambridge, summer 1975. Mem. Am. Theatre Assn., Speech Communication Assn. Republican. Home: 12 Byam St Northfield VT 05663 Office: Norwich Univ Northfield VT 05663

BERRY, DAVID CHRISTOPHER, ednl. adminstr., cons.; b. Lamar, Okla., Sept. 23, 1918; s. Andrew Earl and Hattie Luella (Reynolds) B.; student Okla. Bapt. U., 1937-39, U. Dijon (France), 1945, B.A., Southwestern Inst. Tech., Okla., 1941; M.A., U. Md., 1952, Ed.D., 1974; m. Eugenia Mae Lowe, June 10, 1966; children—Geraldine Lynn, David Wesley; stepchildren—Elizabeth Frances, Eugenia Elaine. Tchr. social scis. Canton (Okla.) Pub. Schs., 1941-42; instr. tng. officer 7th U.S. Army, Heidelberg, Germany, 1945-46; edn. officer, Frankfurt, Germany, 1946-49, Heidelberg, 1949-50, Ft. George G. Meade, Md., 1950-59; dir. edn. 2d U.S. Army, Ft. George G. Meade, 1959-65, 1st U.S. Army, 1965-72; edn. cons. Hdqrs. U.S. Army Europe and 7th Army, 1972-74; ednl. cons. ARC, Lancaster, Pa., 1975—; pub. relations officer Ret. Officer Assn., Lancaster; cons. armed forces edn. Nat. U. Extension Assn. Ann. Conf., 1971; mem. panel on career devel. for educators Dept Army, chmn. Md. Edn. Conf., 1961; chmn. Exec. Devel. Conf., 1st U.S. Army, 1965; chmn. judges com. Scholarship Program, Ft. George G. Meade, 1965-66; chmn. employee profl. devel. and tng. com. 1st U.S. Army, 1970-71. Deacon, United Ch. of Christ, 1976; pres. University Park PTA, 1955-56; del. Md. Congress PTA, 1957; del. Gov.'s Conf. on Edn., Balt., 1960. Served with AUS, 1942-45. Decorated Army Commendation medal; recipient Meritorious Service award Dept. Army, 1950, Outstanding Performance of Duty award, 1956. Mem. Am. Assn. Sch. Adminstrs., NEA, Phi Delta Kappa (del. Biennial Council 1961, pres. U. Md. chpt. 1961). Clubs: Mason, Lions, Slumbering Groundhog Lodge of Quarryville, Pa. Author: Higher Education in the United States Army, 1977. Contbr. articles to profl. jours. Home and Office: 215-I Oakridge Dr Tanglewood PO Box 32 Quarryville PA 17566

BERRY, ROBERT GIFFORD, b. Fall River, Mass., Aug. 3, 1921; s. Ralph Doe and Lida (Gifford) B.; A.B., Brown U., 1947; m. Christiane Laus. Adminstrv. asst. W. R. Grace & Co., 1947-48; service research supr. Booz, Allen & Hamilton, 1948-50, mgmt. cons. 1950-55; coordinator mktg. research and product devel. Union Bag-Camp Paper Corp., 1955-56; exec. asst. to pres. J. Walter Thompson Co., 1956-59, account supr., account rep., 1959-64; product mgr. Bayer Aspirin, Glenbrook Labs. div. Sterling Drug, Inc., 1964-66, group product mgr., 1966-67, v.p., mem. mgmt. com., 1967-76; mgmt. cons., 1976-77; nat. dir. fund raising U.S. Olympic Com., 1977—; lectr. Internat. Council Museums, 1965. Mem. exec. com. Project HOPE, 1961-64; mem. membership com. Mus. of Modern Art, 1968-70, mem. print council, 1976—; mem. Internat. Study Center Com., 1968—; trustee, chmn. fin. com. Mus. Am. Indian, 1977—; trustee Brown U., 1974—. Served from pvt. to 1st lt., AUS, 1942-46; PTO. Mem. Am. Assn. Museums, Internat. Council Museums, Asso. Alumni Brown U. (pres. 1971-73), Grand Jury Assn. N.Y. County. Club: Brown U. N.Y. (bd. govs. 1958-75, v.p. 1961-63). Home: 185 E 85th St New York City NY 10028 Office: 57 Park Ave New York City NY 10016

BERRY, ROBERT WORTH, lawyer; b. Ryderwood, Wash., Mar. 2, 1926; s. John Franklin and Anita Louise (Worth) B.; B.A. in Polit. Sci., Wash. State U., 1950; J.D., Harvard U., 1955. Admitted to D.C. bar, 1956, Pa. bar, 1961, Calif. bar, 1967; research asso. Harvard U., 1955-56; atty. Office of Gen. Counsel, U.S. Dept. Def., Washington, 1956-60; staff counsel Philco Ford Co., Phila., 1960-63; asst. gen. Counsel Litton Industries, Beverly Hills, Calif., 1963-67, dir. Washington office, 1967-71; gen. counsel U.S. Dept. Army, Washington, 1971-74, civilian aide to sec. to army, 1975-77; col. U.S. Army, prof., head dept. law U.S. Mil. Acad., 1978—; resident partner Quaries and Brady, Washington, 1974-78. Served with U.S. Army, 1944-46, 1951-53; Korea. Decorated Bronze Star; recipient Distinguished Civilian Service medal U.S. Dept. Army, 1973, 1974. Mem. Am., Fed. bar assns., Nat. Lawyers Club, Phi Beta Kappa, Phi Kappa Phi. Methodist. Clubs: Army Navy, Army Navy Country. Home: 120 A Washington Rd West Point NY 10996 Office: Dept Law US Mil Acad West Point NY 10996

BERRY, WALTHALL MADDEN, counselor, coll. adminstr., artist; b. Balt., Nov. 14, 1922; s. Joseph Bernard and Beulah L. (Madden) B.; B.F.A., Phila., Coll. Art, 1951; M. Ed., U. Md.; postgrad. State U. N.Y. at Buffalo, 1966, Portland (Oreg.) State Coll., 1967, Boston U., 1968; m. Louise Pyles, Dec. 30, 1951. Tchr., Balt. Pub. Schs., 1951-65, counselor, 1965-69; counselor Community Coll. Balt., 1969-75, dir. counseling, 1975—. Organizer Rosemount Neighborhood Orgn., 1951-58; exec. bd. Windsor Hills Neighbors, 1959-62; lay leader Douglas Meml. Community Ch., 1955—, ch. choir, 1957—. Served with U.S. Army, 1942-46, 50-51. Gen. Electric Corp. fellow, 1968; NDEA fellow, 1966-67. Mem. Am. Personnel and Guidance Assn., Am. Sch. Counselor Assn., Nat. Vocat. Guidance Assn., Am. Coll. Personnel Assn., NEA, NAACP, Phi Delta Kappa, Kappa Alpha Psi. Democrat. Researcher counseling, peer relationships, career planning high-sch. youth, role models and inner-city youth. Home: 3919 Duvall Ave Baltimore MD 21216 Office: Community Coll Balt 2901 Liberty Heights Ave Baltimore MD 21215

BERSON, ROBERT MORDECAI, investment banking co. exec.; b. N.Y.C., Mar. 10, 1939; s. Leo Einhorn and Tillie (Altman) B.; B.S., Pa. State U., 1960; J.D., Fordham U., 1963; m. Natalie Ann Cofsky, June 25, 1961; 1 son, Scott Daniel. Admitted to N.Y. bar, 1964; staff atty., trial counsel N.Y. regional office SEC, 1964-66, chief atty., 1966-68; with Blyth & Co., Inc., N.Y.C., 1968—, v.p., gen. counsel, 1972—; 1st v.p. Blyth Eastman Dillon & Co., Inc., 1973-77; asst. gen. counsel Norton Simon, Inc., 1977—; v.p., sec., gen. counsel, dir. Shields Model Roland Inc.; gen. partner Moore & Schley, Cameron & Co., 1978—; allied mem. N.Y. Stock Exchange. Adviser to youth activities Temple Israel Center, White Plains, N.Y., 1962-70. Served as 1st lt. Signal Corps AUS, 1963. Mem. Am. Bar Assn., N.Y. County Lawyers Assn. Home: 4 Stone Dr West Orange NJ 07052 Office: 44 Wall St New York City NY 10005

BERSON, SIDNEY HARRY, energy co. exec.; b. Hartford, Conn., Oct. 7, 1924; s. George and Fannye Rebecca (Brook) Berson; student U. Pa., 1952; m. Willie Perlysky, Apr. 29, 1956; children—Steven, Lori, Linda. Ops. mgr. Berson Bros., Inc., New Britain, Conn., 1940-43, sec., mgr., 1946-47 (name changed to Oilpower, 1950), sec., chief exec. officer, 1950-69; pres., chief exec. officer Energy Unltd., Inc., New Britain, Conn., 1969—; pres., chief exec. officer Lawrence Park (Conn.) Heat Light and Power Co., 1973—; dir. Royal Par Industries, Inc. Mem. Conn. Gov.'s Emergency Energy Commn., 1974-75; mem. fuel oil mktg. adv. com. U.S. Dept. Energy, 1978—. Served with U.S. Army, 1943-45. Mem. Home Builders Assn., Ind. Conn. Petroleum Assn., New Eng. Fuel Inst., Nat. Oil Jobbers Council. Republican. Hebrew. Office: 50 Harvard St New Britain CT 06051

BERSTEIN, IRVING AARON, research and devel. exec.; b. Providence, Oct. 11, 1926; s. Robert Louis and Laura (Sperber) B.; Sc.B., Brown U., 1946; Ph.D. (teaching fellow), Cornell U., 1951; m. Suzanne D'Amico, Apr. 16, 1972; children—Jonathan, Robert Laurance. Pres., tech. dir. Controls for Radiation, Inc., Cambridge, Mass., 1957-68; dir. med. div., v.p. AGA Corp., Secaucus, N.J., 1969-71; program officer research program devel. div. health scis. and tech. Harvard-Mass. Inst. Tech., Cambridge, 1972-74, asst. dir., research program devel., 1974—; cons. for mgmt. research and devel. new med. instrumentation, 1971—; Mem. Sigma Xi. Francis Wayland scholar. Home: 42 Buckman Dr Lexington MA 02173 Office: Mass Inst Tech Room 26-167 Massachusetts Ave Cambridge MA 02139

BERTISCH, ABRAHAM MAURICE, economist; b. N.Y.C., July 23, 1942; s. Sacher and Anna Clara (Eckstein) B.; B.A., Bklyn. Coll., 1965, M.A., 1967; postgrad. N.Y. U., 1978; m. Sara Laufer, June 21, 1973; children—Rochelle, Jason. Tchr. social studies Seward Park High Sch., N.Y.C., 1965-69; adj. lectr. Queensboro Community Coll., 1968-76; stringer corr. Israel Economist, Jerusalem, 1976-78; dir. Nassau Coll. Summer Inst. in Israel, 1972-78; producer radio program Popular Econs., WHPC-FM, L.I., N.Y.; asso. prof. econs. Nassau Community Coll., Garden City, N.Y., 1978—, also chmn.; mem. Nassau Coll. Speakers Bur.; participant Fed. Res. Bank's 16th Central Banking Seminar, 1976, Consumer Law Tng. Center, N.Y. Law Soc., 1976; guest on Radio Sta. WEVD-AM/FM program Issues and Events, 1976. Meml. Found. for Jewish Culture grantee, 1977. Mem. Joint Council on Econ. Edn., Am. Econ. Assn., Am. Profs. for Peace in Middle East. Asst. editor, Introductory Economics, 1976. Contbr. articles to profl. jours.

BERTOLET, WILLIAM BOWDEN, indsl. devel. exec.; b. Glendon, Pa., July 25, 1911; s. Howard Benjamin and Margaret Bessie (Bowden) B.; B.S.E.E. summa cum laude, Lafayette Coll., Easton, Pa., 1932, M.S. in Physics, 1934; grad. utility exec. course, U. Mich., 1954; m. Kathryn Elizabeth Brong, July 16, 1938; children—William Bowden, Suzanne. Instr. physics Lafayette Coll., 1932-34; with Met. Edison Co., 1934-76, mgr. corp. relations, Reading, Pa., 1975-76; acting exec. dir. Northampton County Indsl. Devel. Authority, Easton, 1977—; chmn. Indsl. Devel. Commn. Easton Area, 1970-74, Northampton County Indsl. Devel. Commn., 1974-77; adminstr. Pa. State U. Extension Sch., Easton, 1938-41. Sec., Glendon Boro Sch. Dist., 1934-41; campaign chmn. Easton United Way, 1970; bd. dirs. Easton chpt. ARC, 1967—; past trustee Calvary United Methodist Ch.; past bd. dirs. Downtown Improvement Group. Served to maj. AUS, 1940-46. Kiwanis scholar, 1928-32; recipient various service awards, certificates appreciation; registered profl. engr., Pa. Mem. Nat., Pa. socs. profl. engrs., IEEE (sr., life), Illuminating Engring. Soc. (asso.), Nat. Rifle Assn. (life), Phi Beta Kappa, Tau Beta Pi. Republican. Methodist. Clubs: Leigh Valley (Allentown); Pomfret (Easton); Masons, Shriners. Home: 120 Ridgewood Rd Easton PA 18042 Office: 157 S 4th St Easton PA 18042

BERTOLINO, EMIL M., drug co. exec.; b. Rochester, N.Y., June 3, 1928; s. Sebastian and Anna B.; student City U. N.Y., 1947-49; m. Ruth Carleo, Aug. 5, 1950; children—Dianne, Daniel, Dean. Market analyst Sherman & Marquette Advt. Agency, N.Y.C., 1947-53; media buyer Lennen & Newell Advt. Agency, N.Y.C., 1953-58, asso. media dir., 1958-62, v.p., account supr., 1962-68; v.p., account supr. C.C.I. Advt. Agency, N.Y.C., 1968-71; mktg. dir. Brioschi, Inc., Fairlawn N.J., 1971—; cons. in field. Active Boy Scouts Am., 1977—; treas., pres. Liberty St. PTA, West Nyack, N.Y., 1958-59; pres. Rockland County (N.Y.) Full Gospel Bus. Men's Fellowship Internat., 1974-75. Mem. 742d Ord. Officers Assn., Res. Officers Assn. Home: 7 Pheasant Dr West Nyack NY 10994 Office: 1901 Pollitt Dr Fairlawn NJ 07410

BERTRAM, JOHN GEORGE, travel orgn. exec.; b. Rotterdam, Netherlands, July 4, 1935; s. Dirk Johannes and Dirkje (Visser) B.; came to U.S., 1970; grad. Internat. Bus. Sch. of Nijenrode, Utrecht, Netherlands, 1959; m. Elizabeth Bellew Doyle, Nov. 6, 1972. Dep. sec. Found. for Representation Dutch Industry for Internat. Relations, 1959-62; mgr. Fairbanks Internat. Bus. Devel., Ltd., London, Eng., 1962-66; European rep. Party Time, Inc., Stockholm, 1966-68; mgr. Anthony Veder Internat. Co., Rotterdam, 1968-70; dir. N.Am. br. Netherlands Nat. Tourist Office, N.Y.C., 1970—; chmn. European Travel Commn., N.Y.C., 1974—; adv. bd. World Meeting Planners Congress, 1972—. Recipient Students of Am. award Student Travel Mag., 1973; named Travel Man of Year, 1976. Mem. Assn. Group Travel Execs. (v.p.), Am. Soc. Travel Agts. Clubs: Rotary, Netherlands of N.Y. Home: 50 Sutton Pl S New York City NY 10022 Office: Netherlands Nat Tourist Office 576 5th Ave New York City NY 10036

BERTRAM, LUCY VIRGINIA, med. masseuse; b. S. Norfolk, Va., Dec. 1, 1929; d. Aaron Browning and Cleo Beatrice (White) Keen; B.S., Coll. William and Mary, 1951; m. John Elwood Bertram, June 22, 1952; 1 son, John David. With David Taylor Model Basin Aero. div. U.S. Dept. Navy, 1951-52; with DuPont Lavoisieur Library, Wilmington, Del., 1952; with Fisher Sci. Co., N.Y.C., 1953-57; med. masseuse, Pleasantville, N.Y., 1978—. Mem. Phelps Meml. Hosp. Aux., N. Tarrytown, N.Y., 1973—, gen. fair chmn., 1975, aux. treas., 1976. Democrat. Methodist. Home: 123 River Rd Scarborough NY 10510 Office: Andersens Inst Inc 8 Hays Hill Rd Pleasantville NY 10570

BERTRAND, JOHN PETER, elec. engr.; b. Athens, Greece, Feb. 2, 1943; s. Peter John and Vasso (Tsoli) B.; came to U.S., 1962, naturalized, 1977; B.S., Columbia U., 1966, Ph.D., 1970; M.E.E., U.

Calif. at Berkeley, 1967; m. Daphne Apostoleri, June 30, 1972; 1 dau., Cleo Vasso. Mem. tech. staff Research Center for Nat. Def., Athens, 1971-72; sr. mem. tech. staff Rockland Systems Corp., Rockleigh, N.J., 1972—; adj. asst. prof. elec. engring. Columbia U., 1973-77, adj. asso. prof., 1979—. Served in Tech. Corps, Greek Army, 1970-71. Eugene and Mona Gee fellow, 1967. Mem. IEEE, Acoustical Soc. Am. (asso.), Sigma Xi, Tau Beta Pi, Eta Kappa Nu. Patentee in field. Home: 211 Hilltop Ln Upper Nyack NY 10960 Office: Rockland Systems Corp Rockleigh Indsl Park Rockleigh NJ 07647

BERTSCH, JACK HERMAN, educator; b. Columbus, Ohio, Jan. 7, 1928; s. John H. and Margaret (Dunn) B.; A.B., Denison U., 1949; LL.B., Columbia U., 1952; Ph.D., Ohio State U., 1968. Admitted to U.S. Supreme Ct. bar, 1958; asst. atty. gen., Columbus, 1952-55; gen. practice Carlton S. Dargusch, Columbus, 1955-60; faculty philosophy dept. Ohio State U., 1960-64; asst. prof. philosophy U. Tampa, 1965-69; asso. prof. philosophy Clarion (Pa.) State Coll., 1969—. Mem. Am. Philos. Assn., Philosophy of Sci. Assn., Blue Key, Phi Beta Kappa, Tau Epsilon Phi, Tau Kappa Epsilon, Omicron Delta Kappa, Pi Sigma Alpha, Tau Kappa Alpha. Mem. Disciples of Christ Ch. Mason. Contbr. articles to profl. jours. Home: 700 Liberty St Clarion PA 16214

BERUBE, BERNICE GERMAINE, credit corp. exec.; b. Stamford, Conn., Dec. 25, 1937; d. Leo O. and Anna T. B.; student Norwalk (Conn.) State Tech. Coll., 1965-68, Akron U., 1971-72. Personnel asst. AMF, Inc., Stamford, 1961-64; personnel and security mgr. Bosley Assos., Stamford, 1964-68; employment specialist Gen. Electric Credit Corp., Stamford, 1968-70, supr. employment and tng., 1970-71, adminstr. employee and community relations, Canton, Ohio, 1971-72, mgr. personnel services, Stamford, 1972-74, mgr. compensation, benefits and practices, 1974—. Mem. Human Resources Commn., Community Beautification Com., Canton, Ohio, 1971-72; co-chmn. commerce and industry div. United Way, Stamford, 1974-76, chmn. loaned exec. program, 1976-78; bd. dirs. YWCA, Stamford, 1976. Recipient Good Egg award United Way, 1977, Gold award, 1978. Mem. Am. Mgmt. Assn., Adminstrv. Mgmt. Soc. (dir., v.p. chpt. 1978-79), Am. Soc. Personnel Adminstrn., Am. Compensation Assn., Internat. Assn. Personnel Women, Mental Health Assn. Clubs: Midday, Gen. Electric Co.'s Elfun Soc. Office: 260 Long Ridge Rd Stamford CT 06904

BERY, RAJENDRA NATH, engring. co. exec.; b. Cuttack, India, Dec. 4, 1930; s. Kashi R. and Bhagwati (Bhandari) B.; sr. sch. certificate U. Cambridge (Eng.), 1945; B.S. in Chem. Engring., U. Mo., 1951; M.S. in Chem. Engring., N.J. Inst. Tech., 1954, M.S. in Mgmt. Engring., 1956; m. Marjorie Adele Bauernfeind, Apr. 14, 1956; children—Renuka, Rajan. Research engr. Agrico Chem. Co., Carteret, N.J., 1951-57; sr. tech. officer Imperial Chem. Industries Ltd., Calcutta, India, 1957-60; process mgr., proposal mgr., sales mgr. Foster Wheeler Corp., Livingston, N.J., 1960—; v.p. FW Mgmt. Ops. Ltd., Milan, Italy. Cons. and tech. witness on synthetic gas energy, hydrogen mfg. Trustee Far Brook Sch., Short Hills, N.J. Mem. Am. Inst. Chem. Engrs., Am. Chem. Soc., Asia Soc. Contbr. articles to profl. jours. Research and devel. design on synthetic gas, hydrogen, fertilizers and metall. plants. Home: 42 Whittingham Terr Millburn NJ 07041 Office: 110 South Orange Ave Livingston NJ 07039

BESHAR, CHRISTINE, lawyer; b. Paetzig, Germany, Nov. 6, 1929; d. Hans and Ruth (von Kleist-Retzow) von Wedemeyer; student U. Hamburg (Germany), 1950-52, U. Tuebingen (Germany), 1952; B.A., Smith Coll., 1953; m. Robert P. Beshar, Dec. 20, 1953; children—Cornelia, Jacqueline, Frederica, Peter. Admitted to N.Y. bar, 1960, U.S. Supreme Ct. bar, 1971; asso. firm Cravath, Swaine & Moore, N.Y.C., 1964-70, partner, 1971—; dir. Bus. Mktg. Corp., N.Y.C.; mem. nat. adv. council Practising Law Inst., N.Y.C. Trustee Colgate U. Recipient Distinguished Alumnae medal Smith Coll., 1974; Studienstiftung fellow, Germany. Fellow Am. Coll. Probate Counsel; mem. Catalyst (dir.), UN Assn., Fgn. Policy Assn., Assn. Bar City N.Y., N.Y. State (exec. com.), Am., Internat., N.Y. County bar assns. Republican. Presbyterian. Clubs: Wall St., Gipsy Trail, Cosmopolitan. Home: 120 East End Ave New York City NY 10028 Office: Cravath Swaine & Moore 1 Chase Manhattan Plaza New York City NY 10005

BESHAR, ROBERT PETER, lawyer; b. N.Y.C., Mar. 3, 1928; A.B. (scholar of the House), Yale U., 1950, LL.B., 1953; m. Christine von Wedemeyer, Dec. 20, 1953; children—Cornelia, Jacqueline, Frederica, Peter. Vol. law clk. Hon. Jerome N. Frank, 2d Circuit Ct. Appeals, 1952-53; admitted to N.Y. bar, 1954; asst. gen. counsel Waterfront Commn. N.Y. Harbor, 1954-55; law sec. Hon. Charles D. Breitel, Appellate Div. 1st dept. N.Y. Supreme Ct., N.Y.C., 1956-58; dep. asst. sec. Commerce, dir. Bur. Internat. Commerce, nat. export expansion coordinator Commerce Dept., Washington, 1971-72; practice law, N.Y.C., 1972—; bus. adv. panel Nat. Commn. Rev. of Antitrust Laws, 1978; spl. hearing officer Dept. Justice, 1967-68; dir. Nat. Semicondr. Corp. Bd. dirs. Community Action for Legal Services, Inc.; bd. dirs. Manhattan Legal Services Corp, chmn. legal services com. Mem. Internat., Am., N.Y. State bar assns., Assn. Bar City N.Y., N.Y. County Lawyers Assn., Am. Judicature Soc., Fed. Bar Council, Phi Beta Kappa. Presbyterian. Clubs: Gipsy Trail (Carmel, N.Y.); Elizabethan (New Haven). Author: Current Legal Aspects of Doing Business with Sino-Soviet Nations, 1973; editor: Manhattan Auto Study, 1973; contbg. editor Boardroom Reports, 1974—. Home: 120 East End Ave New York NY 10028 Office: 25 Broad St New York NY 10004

BESLEY, RICHARD NORTON, psychiatrist; b. New Brunswick, N.J., Aug. 30, 1937; s. Harry Elmer and Elizabeth (Norton) B.; B.S., Tufts U., 1959; M.D., Jefferson Med. Coll., 1963; m. Jeanne Alva Taylor, June 11, 1966; children—Lisa Jeanne, Nicole Suzanne. Intern, Middlesex Gen. Hosp., New Brunswick, 1965-66; resident in psychiatry N.Y. Hosp.-Cornell Med. Coll., 1967-69; practice medicine specializing in psychiatry, Hartsdale, N.Y., 1969—; mem. staff St. Agnes Hosp., White Plains, N.Y., Westchester County Med. Center; clin. instr. psychiatry N.Y. Med. Coll., 1977—. Mem. AMA, Am. Psychiat. Assn., Am. Soc. for Adolescent Psychiatry, Westchester County Med. Soc., Psychiat. Soc. Westchester. Office: 80 E Hartsdale Ave Hartsdale NY 10530

BESNER, CLAUDE EDOUARD, physician; b. Maniwaki, Que., Can., May 27, 1937; s. Arthur Michel and Rita Jocelyne (Therrien) B.; B.A., Ottawa U., 1958, M.D., 1964; m. Ghislaine Asselin, Aug. 13, 1961; children—Manon, Julie, Marc. Intern, Ottawa Gen. Hosp., 1965-66; pvt. tng. in anesthesiology U. Ottawa, 1965; gen. practice medicine, Maniwaki, 1965—; mem. staff St. Joseph Hosp., Maniwaki, 1970—; dist. coroner, 1967—. Served with Canadian Army, 1953-57. Mem. Canadian Coll. Family Physicians, Am. Geriatric Soc., Internat. Anesthesia Research Soc. Roman Catholic. Home: 367 Des Oblats St Maniwaki PQ J9E 1H1 Canada Office: 218 Commerciale St Maniwaki PQ J9E 1P4 Canada

BESS, HAROLD LEON, osteo. physician; b. Atlantic City, Oct. 25, 1924; s. Edward and Lillian (Rubenstien) B.; A.B. cum laude, Rutgers U., 1950; D.O., Coll. Osteo. Physicians and Surgeons, 1954; m. Elaine Sabott, Aug. 22, 1948; children—Alan, Ronald, Barbara. Intern Mass. Osteo. Hosp. Boston, 1954-55; resident Bristol Gen. Hosp. Bristol, Pa., 1955-57; chmn. dept. gen. practice Del. Valley Hosp., Bristol, Pa., also chmn. utilization com., chief of staff, dir. med. edn., 1968—, pres. of bd. dirs., 1976-77; pvt. practice Levittown, Pa., 1957—; pres. bd. dirs. Exit Drug Treatment Center, Del. Valley Hosp., 1976-78. Served with USNR, 1943-46. Decorated three bronze stars. Certified in gen. practice, 1976. Fellow Acad. Psychosomatic Medicine; mem. AAAS, Internat. Soc. Gen. Semantics, Inst. Gen. Semantics, Acad. Psychosomatic Medicine, Internat. Soc. Comprehensive Medicine, Am. Osteo. Assn., Internat. Soc. Transactional Psychiatry, Bucks County Osteo. Soc. (sec. treas. 1959-62), Pa. Osteo. Assn., Am. Coll. Neuropsychiatry, Am. Coll. Gen. Practitioners, Phi Sigma Gamma. Club: Masons. Contbr. to profl. jours. Address: 2 Red Rose Dr Levittown PA 19056

BESSETTE, RUSSELL WILLIAM, physician; b. Albany, N.Y., July 22, 1942; s. Emery William and Alice Zulma (LeBoeuf) B.; B.S., Manhattan Coll., 1964; postgrad. SUNY at Albany, 1964-65; D.D.S., SUNY at Buffalo, 1969, postgrad. (fellow), 1969-71, M.D., 1975; m. Beth Sharon Ostrofsky, Oct. 21, 1966; children—Carolyn, Matthew. Instr. dept. oral medicine SUNY at Buffalo, 1971-73, asst. prof., 1973-74; pvt. practice ltd. to periodontics, 1972—; resident in surgery Buffalo Gen. Hosp., 1976-79, resident in plastic surgery, 1979—, also diagnostic cons.; cons. Strong Meml. Hosp., Rochester, N.Y.; asso. prof. oral pathology SUNY at Buffalo. Mem. ADA, AAAS, Am. Acad. Periodontology, Internat. Assn. Dental Researchers, Internat. Soc. Electromyographic Kinesiology. Contbr. articles to profl. jours. Home: 55 Wynngate Lane Williamsville NY 14221 Office: 50 High St Buffalo NY

BESSOM, MALCOLM EUGENE, writer, editor; b. Boston, Sept. 27, 1940; s. Harold Eugene and Mina (Townley) B.; B.Mus., Boston U., 1962, postgrad., 1962-63. Grad. asst. Boston U., 1962-63; dir. vocal music pub. schs., Chelmsford, Mass., 1963-67; asst. editor Allyn & Bacon Inc., Boston, 1967-68, assoc. editor, 1968-70; asst. editor Music Educators jour., Washington, 1970-71, editor, 1971-77, Reston, Va., 1975-77; dir. publs. Music Educators Nat. Conf., Reston, Va., 1976-77; freelance writer, 1977—; pres. David Allen Press, 1978; participant White House Conf. on Arts Edn., Washington, 1976. Recipient Distinguished Achievement award in journalism Ednl. Press Assn. Am., 1973, 74, 75, 76, 78. Mem. Music Educators Nat. Conf. (exec. staff 1970-77), Mass. Music Educators Assn., Washington Edpress, Internat. Platform Assn., Pi Kappa Lambda, Phi Mu Alpha Sinfonia. Author: Supervising the Successful School Music Program, 1969; Teaching Music in Today's Secondary Schools, 1974; How to Sell Your Songs Like Professionals Do, 1978; contbg. author: This Is Music For Today Books 6, 7, 8, 1970-71. Editor: Music in Special Education, 1972; Careers and Music, 1977. Contbr. numerous articles, columns, musical arrangements to profl. publs. Home: Apt 315 4114 Davis Pl NW Washington DC 20007

BESSOR, WILLIAM DINSMORE, aluminum foundry co. exec.; b. Washington, Pa., Jan. 7, 1927; s. George Blymer and Florence (Dinsmore) S.; B.S., Thiel Coll., 1950, U. Pitts., 1952; m. Joyce Ann Miller, Apr. 8, 1953; children—Bryan William, Carrie Ann. Co-founder, Besco Mfg. Co., Zelienople, Pa., 1952, v.p., treas., 1965-73, pres., chmn. bd., 1973—. First aid instr. A.R.C., 1952—; asst. chief, Zelienople Vol. Fire Co. Councilman, Borough Zelienople, 1958—, v.p., 1970-74, pres., 1974—; corp. mem. North Hills Passavant Hosp., 1974—; Republican nominee for Congress 25th Pa. dist., 1958; trustee, Butler County Community Coll., Butler, Pa., chmn. bd., 1974—. Served with AUS, 1944-46; PTO. Named Distinguished Citizen Zelienople area Jr. C. of C., 1969. Mem. Zelienople C. of C. (dir. 1973), Sigma Phi Epsilon (charter mem. Penn Nu chpt.). Clubs: Lions, Masons, Shriners, Jesters. Home: 401 S Green Ln Zelienople PA 16063 Office: Ziegler St Zelienople PA 16063

BEST, EDGAR EVERETT, rehab. services cons.; b. Elrama, Pa., Mar. 21, 1904; s. Edward Everett and Ella Jane (Wray) B.; B.S., California (Pa.) State Coll., 1940; m. Pauline Phillips, Sept. 4, 1943; 1 dau., Ellen Rae Best Krall. With Carnegie Illinois Steel Corp., Clairton, Pa., 1925-40, insp. steel quality, 1934-40; tchr. vocat. machine shop and indsl. arts Prince George's County (Md.) Bd. Edn., Upper Marlboro, 1940-42; with VA, 1945-69; chief manual arts therapy and ednl. therapy, acting chief corrective therapy, spl. asst. to dir. central office, Washington, 1951-69; cons., exec. dir. Rehab. Cons. Service, Beltsville, Md., 1970—. Served to maj. USAAF, 1942-45. Recipient Meritorious Service award Tri-Organizational Rehab. Conf., 1970. Mem. Registry Med. Rehab. Therapists, Specialists. Am. Assn. Rehab. Therapy (life, Wise Owl award 1969), Epsilon Pi Tau (Hon. citation 1964, Corrective Therapy award Mid-Atlantic chpt. 1968). Methodist. Clubs: Masons, Shriners, Craftsmen of U.S. (life mem.). Contbr. articles to profl. publs. Home and Office: 4112 Kenny St Beltsville MD 20705

BETE, JOHN MORRIS, cardiologist; b. Brockton, Mass., Aug. 28, 1938; s. John Upham and Mary Inez (Morris) B.; B.S. in Biology, Tufts U., 1960; M.D., Boston U., 1965; m. Annette Carolyn Lareau, Apr. 22, 1967; children—John, Laura, Kimberly. Intern in medicine D.C. Gen. Hosp., Washington, 1965-66, asst. resident, 1966-67; sr. asst. resident in medicine Hosp. of U. Pa., Phila., 1969-70; clin. trainee in cardiology Tufts-New Eng. Med. Center Hosps., 1970-71, teaching fellow in cardiology, 1971-72; research fellow in medicine Harvard Med. Sch., 1971; clin. and research fellow in medicine Mass. Gen. Hosp., 1972-73; practice medicine specializing in cardiology, Hyannis, Mass., 1973—; mem. staff Cape Cod Hosp. Served to lt. comdr. USNR, 1967-69. Diplomate Am. Bd. Internal Medicine, Nat. Bd. Med. Examiners; lic. physician, Mass. Fellow Am. Coll. Cardiology; mem. AMA, Mass. Med. Soc. Club: Hyannis Yacht. Home: 141 Scudder Bay Circle Centerville MA 02632 Office: 34 Park St Hyannis MA 02601

BETER, PETER DAVID, legal and fin. cons., commentator; b. Huntington, W.Va., June 21, 1921; s. David Sowan and Sophia Moron (Morone) B.; student U. Detroit, 1943-46; B.A., W.Va. U., 1947; J.D., George Washington U., 1951, LL.M., 1958; m. Lillian Olga Fink, July 23, 1965; children—Alexander Mathias, Joseé-Marie Elizabeth, Petra Christina. to D.C. bar, 1951, W.Va. bar, 1959; practiced in Washington, 1951-61; gen. counsel Am. Gold Assn., Washington, 1958-61; legal counsel Export-Import Bank U.S., Washington, 1961-67; dir., treas., gen. counsel Sodesmir, S.P.R.L., Kinshasa Republic du Zaire (Congo), 1968-73; commentator Dr. Beter Monthly Audio Letter (tape cassettes) Audio Books, Inc., Ft. Worth, 1974—; at Georgetown U. Fgn. Service Sch., Washington, 1952-53. Pres. S.W. Citizens Assn., Washington, 1952-54; dir. Citizens Crime Commn. Met. Washington, 1952-61; Republican candidate for gov. W.Va., 1967-68. Mem. Fed. Bar Assn., U.S. Naval Inst., Royal Commonwealth Soc. (London). Roman Catholic. Club: Bankers of America (N.Y.C.). Author: Gold Positions of U.S.A., 1958; Gold and Gold, 1959; The Conspiracy Against The Dollar, 1973. Editor: Spiritual Practices, 1972. Producer (record) Chorale Congo, 1968. Office: 1629 K St NW Washington DC 20006

BETHE, HANS ALBRECHT, physicist, educator; b. Strassburg, Alsace-Lorraine, July 2, 1906; s. Albrecht Theodore and Anna (Kuhn) B.; ed. Goethe Gymnasium, Frankfurt on Main, U. Frankfort; Ph.D., U. Munich, 1928; D.Sc., Bklyn. Poly. Inst., 1950, U. Denver, 1952, U. Chgo., 1953, U. Birmingham, 1956, Harvard U., 1958; m. Rose Ewald, 1939; children—Henry, Monica. Came to U.S., 1935. Instr. in theoretical physics, univs. of Frankfort, Stuttgart, Munich and Tubingen, 1928-33; lectr. univs. of Manchester and Bristol, Eng., 1933-35; asst. prof. Cornell U., 1935, prof., 1937-75, prof. emeritus, 1975—; dir. theoretical physics div. Los Alamos Sci. Lab., 1943-46. Mem. Presdl. Study Disarmament, 1958; mem. President's Sci. Adv. Com., 1956-60. Recipient A. Cressy Morrison prize N.Y. Acad. Sci., 1938-40; Presdl. Medal of Merit, 1946; Max Planck medal, 1953; Enrico Fermi award 1961; Nobel Prize in physics, 1967, Nat. Medal of Sci., 1976. Fgn. mem. Royal Soc. London; mem. Am. Philos. Soc., Nat. Acad. Scis. (Henry Draper medal 1968), Am. Phys. Soc. (pres. 1954), Am. Astron. Soc. Author: Mesons and Fields, 1953; Elementary Nuclear Theory, 1957; Quantum Mechanics of One-and Two-Electron Atoms, 1957; Intermediate Quantum Mechanics, 1964. Contbr. to (books) Handbuch der Physik, 1933; Reviews of Modern Physics, 1936-37; Phys. Rev., 1935—. Office: Lab Nuclear Studies Cornell U Ithaca NY 14853

BETHEA, SAMMIE, real estate broker; b. Marion, S.C., Oct. 9, 1924; s. Daniel and Agnes (Crawford) B.; B.S. in Chemistry, U. Md., 1966; m. Beulah Williams, June 26, 1948; 1 dau., Val Jeane Bethea Creighton. Analytical chemist FDA, Washington, D.C., 1960-68; subs. chemistry tchr. pub. schs., Washington, 1969-74; owner, real estate broker Ocean Realty, North Myrtle Beach, S.C., 1975—; owner, mgr. Bethea Family Inn, Atlantic Beach, S.C. Licensed real estate broker, S.C. Mem. Grand Strand Bd. of Realtors, Assn. Ofcl. Analytical Chemists, Am. Chem. Soc., Inst. Food Technologists. Research in analytical chemistry and determination of food toxicity for human consumption. Contbr. scientific articles to profl. jours. Home: 1413 34th St Washington DC 20020 Office: 611 31st Ave S North Myrtle Beach SC 29582

BETTENHAUSEN, LEE HERMAN, govt. ofcl.; b. Hazleton, Pa., Dec. 14, 1934; s. William H. and Gertrude (Bradney) B.; B.S., Pa. State U., 1956; Ph.D., U. Va., 1974; m. Mary Ann Cavalovitch, Sept. 29, 1962; children—Maia Ann, Tod William, Lia Marie. Research scientist Battelle Meml. Inst., Columbus, Ohio, 1959-66; mem. faculty U. Va., Charlottesville, 1971-74; rep. for radiation programs EPA, Phila., 1974—; dir. A.J. Assos., Inc., Charlottesville. Served with USAF, 1956-59. Registered profl. engr., Ohio, Va. Mem. IEEE, Am. Nuclear Soc., Va. Acad. Sci., Delaware Valley Soc. Radiation Safety, Sigma Xi, Sigma Tau, Phi Eta Sigma. Patentee in field. Home: 7 Long Ln Malvern PA 19355 Office: US Environmental Protection Agency 6th and Walnut Sts Philadelphia PA 19106

BETTER, MICHAEL ISAAC, pharmacist; b. Leeds, Eng., Aug. 29, 1945; s. Eddie and Sonia (Marder) B.; came to U.S., 1947, naturalized, 1963; B.S. in Pharmacy, Columbia U., 1968; M.S. in Hosp. Pharmacy Adminstrn., Bklyn. Coll. Pharmacy, 1976; m. Jane Wolheim, Feb. 10, 1973. Staff pharmacist Booth Meml. Med. Center, Flushing, N.Y., 1972-74; dir. pharmacy Interboro Gen. Hosp., Bklyn., 1974—; clin. instr. St. Joseph's Coll., 1978—. Served with U.S. Army Res., 1969. Mem. N.Y.C. Soc. Hosp. Pharmacists (exec. com. 1977-79, rec. sec. 1978), Am. Soc. Hosp. Pharmacists, Am. Pharm. Assn., N.Y. State Council Hosp. Pharmacists, Am. Hist. Inst. of Pharmacy, Rho Chi. Office: 2749 Linden Blvd Brooklyn NY 11208

BETTS, FRANCIS MARION, III, ednl. cons.; b. Buffalo, May 5, 1935; s. Frank M., Jr. and Helen (Kennedy) B.; B.S. in Econs., U. Pa., 1957, Ed.D., 1977; m. Renée Josephine Allard, Jan., 1976; 1 son, Ian McNair; children by previous marriage—Lori Hill, Melinda Adelaide, Jennifer Kennedy. Staff positions U. Pa., 1960-73, successively in admissions and fin. aid, dir. Student Union, instl. research, long range planning, archtl. programming and design, asst. to v.p. coordinated planning, 1960-69, asst. to pres. for external affairs, 1969-73, also instr. statistics and operations research Wharton Sch. Fin., 1960-66; partner Ednl. Mgmt. Assos., Phila., 1973-77; founder, pres. Betts/Allard Assos., Phila., 1977—; instr. psychology Widener Coll., 1974; instr. urban studies and community devel., Rutgers U., 1974-75; coordinator curriculum and research Gt. Lakes Colls. Assn., Phila. Urban Semester, 1975—. Bd. dirs. University City Arts League, Dist. 1 Community Edn. Center, West Phila. Community Free Sch., University City New Sch., Peoples' Health Services W. Phila., Unit 3 Housing Corp.; city committeeman, Phila., 1971. Served as lt. (j.g.) USN, 1957-60. Recipient award Inst. Ednl. Mgmt., Harvard, 1970; selected for Rowing Hall of Fame Nat. Assn. Amateur Oarsmen, 1977; Ford Found. fellow, 1971-73. Mem. Sphinx (past pres.), Phi Delta Kappa. Contbr. articles to profl. jours. Home: 2524 Naudain St Philadelphia PA 19146 Office: 37 S 13th St Philadelphia PA 19107

BETZ, ALFRED ANTHONY, court reporter; b. Fountain Hill, Pa., Jan. 28, 1949; s. Alfred A. and Theresa M. (Bendekovitz) B.; student Balt. Inst., 1967, 68; m. Kay L. Frantz, July 25, 1969; 1 son, Matthew Scott. Hearing reporter, Workmen's Compensation Commn., Balt., 1969-70; court reporter, Salomon Reporting Service, Balt., 1970-71; ofcl. court reporter, U.S. Dist. Ct., Dist. Md., Balt., 1971—; mem. advisory council for court and conf. reporting course Essex (Md.) Community Coll.; faculty seminars, Dallas, 1973, Ocean City, Md., 1975, Washington, 1976, New Orleans, 1977, Albuquerque, 1977, Kansas City, Mo., 1977; mem. adv. council Baron Data Systems, Oakland, Calif., 1977—. Recipient certificates proficiency and merit, Nat. Shorthand Reporters Assn., award of excellence, certificate of distinguished service, Md. Shorthand Reporters Assn.; certified shorthand reporter, Md., registered profl. reporter Nat. Shorthand Reporters Assn. Mem. Nat. (com. computer-aided transcription, chmn. nat. com. state assns. 1978—), Md. (pres. 1976-78, chmn. pub. relations com.) shorthand reporters assns., U.S. Ct. Reporters Assn. Roman Catholic. Editor: In Session, 1975-78. Home: 502 Sunbrook Rd Reisterstown MD 21136 Office: Room 528 101 W Lombard St Baltimore MD 21201

BETZ, GREGOR WILLIAM, cons. and mfg. rep.; b. Springdale, Pa., Sept. 17, 1924; s. Gregor and Anna (Paterson) B.; B.S. in Mech. Engring., U. Pitts., 1945; m. Mary Margaret Tunney, Oct. 29, 1955; children—Mary Kathleen, Marcella Ann, Susan Louise. Jr. engr. Wyckoff Steel Co. (became div. Ampco Pitts. Corp. 1969), Ambridge, Pa., 1945-50, plant engr., 1950-53, asst. chief engr., 1953-57, chief engr., 1957-67; exec. v.p., dir. Cumberland Steel Co. (Md.), 1967-73; v.p. mfg. Ramco Steel Inc., Buffalo, 1973-75, exec. v.p. 1975-77; pres. G.W. Betz Assos., Inc., cons. and mfg. reps., East Amherst, N.Y., 1977—; cons. mech. engr., 1960—; instr. engring. extension sch. Pa. State U., 1952-57. Registered profl. engr., Pa. Mem. Assn. Iron and Steel Engrs., Steel Service Center Inst., ASME, Nat. Soc. Profl. Engrs., Aircraft Owners and Pilots Assn., Phi Delta Theta, Sigma Tau. Republican Roman Catholic. Elk, K.C. Clubs: Park Country (Buffalo); Youngstown (Ohio) Country; Tuscarora (Lockport, N.Y.). Home: 35 Brandywine Chapel Woods Williamsville NY 14221 Office: 9350 Transit Rd Box 67 Amherst NY 14051

BETZ, JEAN, investment securities co. exec.; b. Utica, N.Y., Mar. 1, 1927; d. Walter John and Anna (Pomichowska) Hapanowicz; student Utica Free Acad., 1941-45; B.S., Rider Coll., 1949; postgrad. Beaver Coll., 1964-65; m. Frank Theodore Betz, Apr. 18, 1949; children—Frank, Eleanor Jean, Richard Walter. Editorial writer Book Publishers Projects, Inc., N.Y.C., 1967-68; sec., dir. Frank T. Betz & Co., Inc., investment securities, Phila., 1966—. Editor: The First Book of Magic, 1968. Home: 1554 Hower Rd Abington PA 19001 Office: Philadelphia National Bank Bldg Philadelphia PA 19107

BEUBE, FRANK EDWARD, periodontist, educator; b. Kingston, Ont., Can., July 1, 1904; s. Gabriel and Fannie Bessie (Florence) B.; L.D.S., D.D.S., U. Toronto, 1930; m. Edith Schweitzer, Oct. 5, 1930; children—Eric, Stephen. Came to U.S., 1930, naturalized, 1937. Clin. asst. div. periodontology Sch. Dental and Oral Surgery, Columbia, 1930-37, instr., 1937-41, asst. prof., 1941-46, asso. prof., 1946-53, head div., 1948—, clin. prof. dentistry, 1953—; head dept. periodontology Presbyn. Hosp., N.Y.C., 1941-70; lectr. dept. periodontology, Dental Sch. N.Y. U., 1973—; found. mem. Hebrew U. Diplomate Am. Bd. Periodontology (dir., v.p. 1963-64). Fellow AAAS, Am. Coll. Dentists, Am. Acad. Periodontology (councilman 1962, chmn. edn. com. 1963, chmn. com. on coms. 1964, pres. 1964-65, chmn. exec. council 1965-66); mem. ADA (chmn. periodontia sect. 1964-65), Western Soc. Periodontology (hon.), Academy Oral Pathology, So. Acad. Periodontology (hon.), Internat. Assn. Dental Research, First Dist. Dental Soc. (past pres. pathodontia sect.), Sigma Xi. Author: Periodontology: Diagnosis and Treatment, 1953; Prevention of Periodontal Diseases, 1956; Gingivectomy in the treatment of Periodontal Diseases, 1957; Disadvantages of Surgical Techniques, 1960. Contbr. articles to dental jours. Research in study of healing of cementum and bone, periodontal diseases and their treatment. Home: 10 London Terr New Rochelle NY 10804 Office: 9 W 57th St New York City NY 10019

BEUTEL, WILLIAM STEEL, elec. mfg. co. exec.; b. Spring Valley, N.Y., Mar. 7, 1924; s. George and Susie (Jones) B.; B.A., Bergen Jr. Coll., 1951; B.S., Rutgers U., 1955; m. Martha Kammermayer, June 6, 1945; children—William Michael, Bonnie Marthel. With Lederle Labs. div. Am. Cynanamid Co., Pearl River, N.Y., 1948-55, Electrol, Inc., Kingston, N.Y., 1955-63, Carbic Hoechst Corp., Mountainside, N.J., 1963-65, Lamborn & Co., N.Y.C., 1965-68, Tyton Corp. Am., Metuchen, N.J., 1968-69; controller Oborne Machine Co., Warren, N.J., 1969-72, S.S. White Indsl. Products, Piscataway, N.J., 1972-74; pub. accountant, 1974—. Cubmaster Boy Scouts Am., 1956-61, neighborhood commr., 1960-61; life mem. Vol. Fire Dept. Served with AUS, 1943-46; ETO. Mem. Indsl. Mgmt. Club, Nat. Assn. Accountants, Rutgers Alumni Assn., Nat. Parks Assn. Clubs: Humble Travel, Jackson Perkins Experimental Rose (Somerville, N.J.). Home: 607 Foxcroft Rd Bridgewater NJ 08807

BEUZEVILLE, CARLOS ADALBERTO, physician; b. Lima, Peru, Aug. 17, 1926; s. Arturo and Yolanda (Ferro) B.; Médico-cirujano, U. San Marcos, Lima, 1956; m. Graciela Alvarez, May 26, 1950. Fellow Bryn Mawr Coll., 1956-58; asso. prof. San Agustín Med. Sch., Arequippa, Peru, 1958-60; asst. prof. physiology Albert Einstein Coll. Medicine, N.Y.C., 1961-69; trainee pediatrics Montafiore and L.I. Jewish Hosps., N.Y.C., 1969-72; pvt. practice pediatrics, Mamaroneck, N.Y., 1972—. Mem. N.Y. State, Westchester med. socs. Home: 313 Heathcote Ave Mamaroneck NY 10543 Office: 640 W Boston Post Rd Mamaroneck NY 10543

BEVACQUA, RONALD ANTHONY, bus. exec.; b. Jersey City, N.J., Dec. 14, 1945; s. Guido Ferrar and Anna (Lostumbo) B.; B.S., N.Y. U., 1967; m. Joan Marie Stanley, May 25, 1968; children—Dawn, Stefanie. Sr. accountant Price Waterhouse & Co., N.Y.C., 1967-71; dir. corporate fin. reporting Cooper Labs., Inc., Wayne, N.J., 1971-73; mgr. budgeting and accounting IU Internat. Corp., Phila., 1973-77; controller Nat. Bottle Corp., Bala Cynwyd, Pa., 1977; dir. fin. planning Pepperidge Farm, Inc., Norwalk, Conn., 1977—. Mem. Am. Inst. C.P.A.'s, N.J. Soc. C.P.A.'s, Nat. Assn. Accountants. Roman Catholic. Home: 26 Bonnie Brook Dr Huntington CT 06484

BEVACQUA, SAVERIO FRANCIS, tech. specialist; b. Fulton, N.Y., July 16, 1929; s. Samuel and Mary B.; N.Y. State Regents diploma with honors, 1946; m. Teresa A. Lumbrazo, Nov. 14, 1953; children—Samuel, Marie, Robert. Mgr. wholesale and retail bus. Farmer's Dog Food Co., Syracuse, N.Y., 1951-52; with Gen. Electric Co., Syracuse, 1952—, tech. specialist, advanced tech. lab., semicondr. products dept., mem. group solid state applications, 1959—; cons. wafer diffusion. Served in U.S. Army, 1948-51. Mem. VFW. Republican. Roman Catholic. Club: K.C. Contbr. articles to tech. jours. Co-developer world's first solid state visible light laser. Home: 464 W 1st St Fulton NY 13069 Office: Gen Electric Co Electronics Park Bldg 7 Syracuse NY 13201

BEVARD, RALPH EDWARD, eraser mfg. co. exec.; b. Newark, O., Mar. 20, 1915; s. Leroy Herman and Elizabeth Sarah (Strear) BeV.; B.S. in Bus. Adminstrn., Syracuse U., 1962; m. Renate Monika Odorff, Sept. 15, 1967; children—Virginia (Mrs. Donald Stone), Ralph Edward, Peter, Marilyn (Mrs. James Keggeries), Karen (Mrs. Bruce Steenberg), Jon, James, Marcus. Prodn. mgr. Reliance Electric and Engring. Co., Cleve., 1935-47; pres. Am. Prodn. Co., Syracuse, N.Y., 1948—; pres. Eraser Co., Inc., Syracuse, 1960—, also dir.; pres. Eraser Internat. Co., Syracuse, 1972—; dir. Eraser Internat., Ltd., Am. Prodn. and Grinding Co.; adviser SBA, 1952-64. Bd. dirs. Eraser Co. Pension Fund, Eraser Co. Profit Sharing Fund, Community Council on Careers; chmn. adminstrv. bd., capital funds drive Methodist Ch. Mem. Syracuse Jr. C. of C. (pres. 1949-50). Clubs: Syracuse U., Syracuse Press. Patentee. Bevard Community Room in Onondaga County Civic Center named in his honor. Home: 108 Woodmancy Ln Fayetteville NY 13066 Office: 1342 Oliva Dr Syracuse NY 13201

BEVER, CHRISTOPHER THEODORE, psychiatrist; b. Munich, Germany, Mar. 12, 1919; s. Rudolf Paul and Maria (Bever) Berliner; came to U.S., 1936, naturalized, 1943; A.B. cum laude, Harvard U., 1940, M.D., 1943; postgrad. Washington Psychoanalytic Inst., 1947-53; diploma Washington Sch. Psychiatry, 1952; m. Josephine Jordan Morton, Mar. 12, 1944; children—Christopher Theodore, Caroline Stackpole, Edward Watts M., Sarah Sayward. Intern, Hartford (Conn.) Hosp., 1944; resident in psychiatry St. Elizabeths Hosp., Washington, 1947-48, psychiatrist, 1948-50; psychiatrist Washington Inst. Mental Hygiene, 1950-51; dir. Montgomery County (Md.) Mental Hygiene Clinic, 1951-54; asso. prof. psychiatry U. N.C., 1954-56; practice medicine specializing in psychiatry and psychoanalysis, Washington, 1956—; mem. staff George Washington U. Hosp., 1956—; mem. faculty Washington Psychoanalytic Inst., 1954—, Washington Sch. Psychiatry, 1956—; faculty George Washington U., 1957—, clin. prof., 1974—; cons. Walter Reed Hosp., 1972-75; bd. dirs. Community Psychiat. Clinic, Bethesda, Md., 1958—, pres., 1973-75; bd. dirs. D.C. Inst. Mental Hygiene, 1966-73, pres., 1966-68, trustee, 1973—. Trustee William Alanson White Found., Washington, 1974—. Served with U.S. Army, 1944-47. Diplomate Am. Bd. Psychiatry and Neurology. Fellow Am. Psychiat. Assn., Am. Orthopsychiat. Assn. (life), Am. Acad. Psychoanalysis; mem. Am. Psychoanalytic Assn., AMA. Home and Office: 6812 Connecticut Ave Chevy Chase MD 20015

BEVERLY, LAURA ELIZABETH, educator; b. Glen Jean, W.Va., Nov. 26, 1935; d. Sidney and Alma Lee (Davis) Logan; B.A. in Elementary Edn., W.Va. State Coll., 1960; postgrad. Hofstra U., 1961-63, N.Y. U., 1967-70, Oxford (Eng.) U., 1974; M.S. in Edn. Retarded Children, Bklyn. Coll., 1969; m. Albert Beverly, 1962 (dec. 1970). Tchr. spl. children Nassau County Bd. Coop. Ednl. Services, Jericho, N.Y., 1963—; cooperating tchr. Hofstra U., 1973. Mem. Royal Soc. Health (London), Smithsonian Instn., Council Exceptional Children, Internat. Platform Assn., Nat. Hist. Soc., Nat. Audubon Soc., Phi Delta Kappa, Delta Sigma Theta. Home: 150 Washington St Apt 6-B Hempstead NY 11550

BEVILACQUA, JOSEPH A., judge; b. Providence, Dec. 1, 1918; s. John and Angelica (Inonnoti) B.; B.A., Providence Coll., 1940; J.D., Georgetown, U., 1948; m. Josephine Amato, 1946; children—John J., Angelica H., Joseph A., Mary Ann. Admitted to R.I. bar; asst. adminstr. charitable trusts dept. State of R.I. Atty. Gen., 1950-54; mem. R.I. Ho. of Reps., 1955, dep. majority leader, 1965-66, majority leader, 1966-68, speaker, 1969; chief justice R.I. Supreme Ct. Mem. Democratic State Com. R.I., 1950-54; del. Dem. Nat. Conv., 1968. Served as 1st lt. U.S. Army, 1941-46. Office: RI Supreme Ct Providence RI 02903

BEYER, FRANCIS DAVID, JR., physician; b. Altoona, Pa., Nov. 19, 1926; s. Francis David and Frances (Murdock) B.; B.A., Pa. State U., 1947; M.D., U. Pa., 1951; m. Pat Krehlik, Aug. 30, 1968; children—David, Robert. Intern, Presbyn. Hosp., Phila., 1951-52; resident in pathology VA Hosp., Pitts., 1955-59, pathologist Magee-Woman's Hosp., Pitts., 1959-64, Washington (Pa.) Hosp., 1964-67, Latrobe (Pa.) Area Hosp., 1967—, Frick Hosp., Mt. Pleasant, Pa., 1967—. Served with USNR, 1944-46. Fellow Am. Coll. Pathologists; mem. Soc. Clin. Pathologists, AMA. Club: Elks. Home: 3021 Williamsburg Dr Latrobe PA 15650

BEYRER, NANCY ELIZABETH, newspaper editor; b. Oceanside, N.Y., Feb. 10, 1933; d. Kenneth Ely and Irene Florence (Hall) Nagle; B.A., Keuka Coll., 1955; Deutsche Fur Auslander, U. Bern (Switzerland), 1961; m. Charles R. Beyrer, Dec. 22, 1956; children—Anne, Christopher, Kate, Jacqueline, Judith. Editor, Beacon Newspaper, Babylon, N.Y., 1977—. Trustee Hewlett Sch. of East Islip; editor Unitarian Soc. of S. Suffolk Newsletter, 1975-78, N.Y. State Council on the Arts and Islip Town Writer's Workshop Jour., 1974-76; moderator-co-producer AAUW TV show Female Focus, 1974-75. Mem. Press Club L.I., AAUW. Home: 11 Dana Ln East Islip NY 11730 Office: 45 Deer Park Ave Babylon NY 11702

BHAGAT, PHIROZ MANECK, educator; b. Poona, India, Oct. 28, 1948; s. Maneck Phirozshaw and Khorshed Eduljee (Batliwala) B.; came to U.S., 1970; B.Tech., Indian Inst. Tech., 1970; M.S.E., U. Mich., 1971, Ph.D., 1975. Research fellow in applied mechanics Harvard U., Cambridge, Mass., 1975-77; asst. prof. mech. engring. Columbia U., N.Y.C., 1977—. Horace H. Rackham fellow, 1973-75; J. N. Tata scholar, 1970; K.C. Mahindra scholar, 1970. Mem. ASME, Sigma Xi, Tau Beta Pi. Club: Harvard. Contbr. articles in field to profl. jours. Office: Dept Mech Engring Columbia Univ New York City NY 10027

BHAMRE, SURESH TUSHIRAM, SR., psychiat. social worker; b. Vadjai, India, Mar. 21, 1935; s. Tulshiram Bhagwan and Muktabai T.; B.A., U. Poona, 1956; M.A., Tata Inst. Social Scis., 1958; Ph.D., Bernadean U., 1979; m. 1960; children—Shrikant, Ravindra. Publicity officer Coal Mines Labor Welfare Orgn., India, 1959-64; asst. prof. abnormal psychology C.W. Post Coll., 1969-71, New Sch. Social Research, 1970-74; Yoga Philosophy and social work supervision Central Islip Psychiat. Center. Pres., founder World Yoga Soc. Mem. Acad. Cert. Social Workers, India Assn. L.I. Hindu. Contbr. articles to yoga jours. Address: 135 Calvert Ave Ronkonkoma NY 11779

BHANDARI, NARENDRA CHAND, educator; b. Jodhphur, India, Oct. 5, 1938; B.Commerce, SMK Coll., Jodhpur, 1960, M.Commerce, 1962; M.A. with distinction, U. Ga., 1966, M.B.A., 1968, Ph.D., 1972; came to U.S., 1963; married; 2 children. Grad. asst. U. Ga., 1967-68; asst. prof. mgmt. Va. Commonwealth U., Richmond, 1968-73; prof. Nat. Inst. Tng. in Indsl. Engring., Vilhar Lake, Bombay, India, 1973-74; asso. prof. mgmt. U. Balt., 1974-78; prof. mgmt. Pace U., 1978—; mgmt. cons. and trainer; UNIDO expert on small bus. Fellow Govt. Rajasthan, Ga. Rotary Student Fund, U. Ga., Pfizer Internat. Corp., Ashland Oil Found. Mem. Acad. Mgmt., So. Mgmt. Assn., Am. Soc. Tng. and Devel., Internat. Council for Small Bus. Author: Cases in Small Business Management; editor Am. Jour. Small Business; author numerous articles, papers. Address: 4803 Ebenezer Rd Baltimore MD 21236

BHAR, TARAK NATH, elec. engr., educator; b. Calcutta, India, July 31, 1941; s. Panchu Gopal and Bhagabati (Das) B.; came to U.S., 1969; B.S., Calcutta U., 1964, M.S., 1965; M.S., Baylor U., 1970; Ph.D., Tex. A. and M. U., 1973; m. Sikha Das, July 26, 1974. Design elec. engr. W.B.S.E.B., Calcutta, 1965-69; asst. prof. dept. elec. engring. Howard U., Washington, 1973—. Mem. IEEE, Electron Device Soc., Sigma Pi Sigma, Eta Kappa Nu. Club: Sankriti (sec.). Contbr. articles to profl. jours. Research growth and characterization GaAs liquid phase epitaxial layers, fabrication microwave solid-state devices, solar cells. Home: 6980 Maple St #12 Washington DC 20012 Office: Dept Elec Engring Howard U Washington DC 20059

BHATT, JAGDISH JEYSHANKER, scientist, educator; b. Umreth, India, Feb. 17, 1939; B.Sc. with honors, U. Baroda (India), 1961; M.S., U. Wis., Madison, 1963; postgrad. U. N.Mex., 1966-67, U. Calif. at Santa Barbara, 1968-69; Ph.D., U. Wales, 1972; postdoctoral work Stanford U., 1971-72; m. Maena Jagdish, Jan. 22, 1970; 1 child, Amar. Instr. phys. scis. and chemistry Jackson (Mich.) Jr. Coll., 1964-65, Panhandle State U., Goodwill, Okla., 1965-66; asst. prof. State U. N.Y., Buffalo, 1972-74; asst. prof. geol. sci. and oceanography R.I. Jr. Coll., Warwick, 1974-78, asso. prof., 1979—, chmn. ocean tng. program com., 1977-78, advisor Geol. Club, 1974—; mem. R.I. Ocean Task Force, 1975-76; environ. cons. Warwick City Hall, 1976-77; judge R.I. Sci. Expo, 1975-77. Mem. Geol. Soc. Am., Internat. Oceanographic Found., Oceanic Soc. Author: Cretaceous History of Himalayan Geosyncline, 1966; Environmentology: Earth's Environment and Energy Resources, 1975; Geochemistry and Petrology of South Wales Main Limestones, 1976; Oceanography: Exploring the Planet Ocean, 1978; Laboratory Manual on Physical Geology, 1966; Laboratory Manual on Physical Sciences, 1966; Geologic Exploration of Earth, 1976; Instructor's Manual on Oceanography, 1978; also articles. Home: 11 Midlands Dr East Greenwich RI 02818 Office: RI Jr Coll 400 East Ave Warwick RI 02886

BHATTACHARJI, PARES CHANDRA, city planner; b. Calcutta, India, Dec. 25, 1923; s. Probodh Chandra and Surabala (Chakravarty) B.; came to U.S., 1958, naturalized, 1973; B.S., Scottish Ch. Coll., Calcutta, 1944; B.Engring., Bengal Engring. Coll., 1947; M.S. in Civil Engring. (Univ. scholar), Mich. State U., 1949; M.City Planning, Mass. Inst. Tech., 1952; m. Arati Mookerjee, Oct. 8, 1957; 1 son, Sandip C. Bridge Design engr. Steinman, Boynton, Gronquist & London, cons. engrs., N.Y.C., 1949-50, 52-54, 58-61; dep. dir. Nat. Bldgs. Orgn., Govt. of India, New Delhi, 1955-58; asso. prof. planning Sch. Planning and Architecture, Govt. of India, New Delhi, 1958; zoning and urban renewal cons. N.Y.C. Housing and Devel. Adminstrn., 1961-66, 68-69; chief of residential study Smith, Haines, Lundberg & Waehler, cons., Santurce, P.R., 1966-68; prin. planning cons. N.Y.C. Planning Commn., 1969-76, adminstrv. mgr., 1977—. Recipient Progressive Architecture award Rockefeller Family Fund, 1977. Mem. Am. Inst. Planners, Am. Soc. Planning Ofcls., Indian Inst. Town Planners, Mass. Inst. Tech. Alumni Assn., Mich. State U. Alumni Assn., Bengal Engring. Coll. Alumni Assn. East Coast (pres. 1973—). Editor Nat. Bldgs Orgn. Jour., 1955-58. Home: 98-40 64th Ave Forest Hills NY 11374

BHATTACHARYA, ARUN KUMAR, chemist; b. Allahabad, India, Apr. 9, 1938; s. A. K. and Madhabi Mukherjee B.; came to U.S., 1966, naturalized, 1977; B.Sc., U. Saugar (India), 1956, M.Sc., 1958, Ph.D., 1960; m. Purobi Banerjee, Dec. 3, 1962; children—Ashish, Sujit. Asst. prof. chemistry U. Saugar (India), 1958-65; vis. research asso. chemistry Antioch Coll., Yellow Springs, Ohio, 1966; research asso. chemistry Aerospace Research Lab., Wright-Patterson AFB, Ohio, 1967-68, sr. scientist Air Force Materials Lab., 1969-74; sect. leader Hooker Chem. Research Center, Grand Island, N.Y., 1974-78; supr. analytical chemistry Mobil Chem. Co., Edison, N.J., 1978—. Mem. bd. edn., Dayton, Ohio, 1972-74, chmn. nomination com., 1973; active Little League Baseball, Cub Scouts Am. Recipient Bedi Gold medal U. Saugar, 1957. Mem. Am. Chem. Soc., Soc. Applied Spectroscopy, Royal Soc. Chemistry, Am. Soc. Mass Spectroscopy, Indian Sci. Congress Assn. Home: 8 Edward St East Brunswick NJ 08816 Office: Mobil Chem Co PO Box 240 Edison NJ 08817

BHATTAD, SITRAM MANIKALAL, food technologist, microbiologist; b. Ambada, India, June 23, 1941; s. Manikalal J. and Kashi M. (Bharadia) B.; came to U.S., 1970, naturalized, 1977; B.S. (D. Tech.), Nat. Dairy Research Inst., Punjab (India) U., 1967; M.S. in Food Sci., U. Sask. (Can.), 1970; postgrad. Ohio State U., 1970-72; m. Chanda A. Dammani, May 1, 1968; children—Vijay Kumar, Jay Kumar. Research asso. Ohio State U., 1970-72; quality control supr. Shasta Beverages div. Consol. Foods Corp., 1972-73; food technologist, project coordinator Kitchens Sara Lee div. Consol. Foods Corp., Deerfield, Ill., 1973-74; microbiologist, mgr. lab. and tech. services Libby McNeill & Libby div. Nestle Enterprises, Chgo., 1974-78; gen. mgr. tech. services Foodways Nat. Inc. div. H. J. Heinz, Wethersfield, Conn., 1978—; dir. food and agr. U.S. Tech., Livonia, Mich., 1976—. Named to Merit Roll, Punjab U., 1967; named Outstanding Citizen of Year, Citizenship Council Met. Chgo., 1977. Mem. Am. Soc. Quality Control (sr.), Inst. Food Technologists (profl.). Democrat. Hindu. Club: Toastmasters (Outstanding Toastmaster of Year 1975, 76, pres. local club 1977, area gov. area 12 1978). Research, publs. on lactic bioanhancers; founder, editor Dairy Sci. Coll. mag., 1967. Home: 950 Maple St Rocky Hill CT 06067 Office: 1000 Silas Deane Hwy Wethersfield CT 06109

BHIRUD, SURESH L., fin. co. exec.; b. Rozode, India, Sept. 14, 1948; s. Laxamn L. and Sarojini L. (Mahajan) B.; B. in Engring., Regional Engring. Coll., Durgapur, India, 1970; M.B.A., Columbia, 1972. With First Boston Corp., N.Y.C., 1972—, v.p., 1976—. Mem. N.Y. Soc. Security Analysts. Home: 1601-29 3d Ave New York City NY 10028 Office: The First Boston Corp 20 Exchange Pl New York City NY 10005

BHOI, PARAMJIT SINGH, physician; b. Nakuru, Kenya, Dec. 22, 1941; s. Bhajan Singh and Jajgjit (Kaur) B.; came to U.S., 1965; licentiate Royal Coll. Physicians and Surgeons, Dublin, Ireland, and London, Eng., 1965; m. Gwennyth R. Swerdfeger, Mar. 2, 1965; children—Daniel, Paul, Peter. Intern St. Mary's Hosp., Saginaw, Mich., 1965-66; resident Hurley Hosp., Flint, Mich., 1966-68, U. Hosp., U. Sask. (Can.), 1968-69, Ottawa (Ont. Can.), Gen. Hosp., 1969-70; practice medicine specializing in internal medicine, Ottawa, 1970—; mem. staff Riverside Hosp., Ottawa, cons. St. Louis de Montfort Hosp., Children's Hosp., Eastern Ont. Diplomate Am. Bd. Internal Medicine. Fellow Coll. Physicians of Can., Am. Coll. Chest Physicians, Acad. of Medicine of Ottawa; mem. Canadian, British Med. Assns., Royal Coll. Surgeons, Canadian Def. Med. Assn., A.C.P. Home: 2010 Hollybrook Crescent Ottawa ON K1J 7Y6 Canada Office: 194 Main St Room 202 Ottawa ON K1S 1C2 Canada

BHUSHAN, BHARAT, mech. engr.; b. Jhinjhana, India, Sept. 30, 1949; s. Narain Dass and Devi (Vati) Agarwal; came to U.S., 1970, naturalized, 1977; B.Engring. with honors in Mech. Engring. (Govt. of India Merit Scholar), Birla Inst. Tech. and Sci., 1970; M.S. in Mech. Engring. (Ford Found. fellow), Mass. Inst. Tech., 1971; M.S. in Mechanics, U. Colo., 1973, Ph.D. in Mech. Engring. (U. Colo. fellow), 1976; m. Manju Agarwal, June 14, 1975; 1 child, Ankur Agarwal. Mem. research staff dept. mech. engring. Mass. Inst. Tech., Cambridge, 1970-72; research asst., instr., dept. mech. engring. U. Colo., Boulder, 1972-76; expert investigator Automotive Specialists, Denver, 1973-76; sr. engring. scientist Mech. Tech. Inc., Latham, N.Y., 1976—; propr., mgr. computer operation, India. Grantee U.S. Navy, NASA, Dept. of Energy, DuPont Co., USAF, Chrysler Corp. Mem. ASME (certificate of recognition Design Engring. Conf.), Am. Soc. Lubrication Engrs., Am. Acad. Mechanics, Soc. Automotive Engrs., Soc. for Exptl. Stress Analysis, Internat. Humanists Soc., Tri-City India Assn., Sigma Xi, Tau Beta Pi. Hindu. Club: Rotary. Contbr. numerous articles to profl. jours. Patentee in field. Home: 15 Lake Shore Dr Apt 1D Watervliet NY 12189 Office: Mech Tech Inc Latham NY 12110

BHUYAN, KAILASH CHANDRA, ophthalmologist, biochemist; b. Assam, India, Jan. 1, 1937; s. Bipin Chandra and Giribala (Talukdar) Khataniar; student Cotton Coll., Gauhati U., 1955-57; M.B., B.S., Assam Med. Coll., India, 1962; diploma Ophthalmology, Assam Med. Coll., 1965; M. Surgery in Ophthalmology, All India Inst. Med. Scis., New Delhi, 1967; m. Durga S. Ghanekar, Aug. 12, 1967; children—Parthapratim K., Parkashpratim K. Resident house surgeon dept. ophthalmology and gen. surgery Assam Med. Coll. Hosp., India, 1963-65; clin. resident in ophthalmology All India Inst. of Med. Scis., New Delhi, 1965-67; research asso. in corneal center Inst. of Ophthalmology, Coll. of Physicians and Surgeons, Columbia U., N.Y.C., 1968-69; research asso. biochemistry lab. The Eye-Bank/Sight Restoration, N.Y., 1969-71, dir. biochemistry research, 1971—; asst. prof. dept. ophthalmology Mt. Sinai Sch. Medicine, U. City N.Y., 1978—. Recipient scholarship, Dir. Gen. of Health Services, India, 1965-67; NIH grantee, 1975, 78; Fight for Sight, Inc., grantee, 1969-71, Sea Train Lines, Inc. grantee, 1971-73. Mem. Assn. for Research in Vision and Ophthalmology, Inc., All India Ophthalmol. Soc., N.Y. Acad. Sci. Contbr. articles in field to profl. jours. Home: 362 Lantana Ave Englewood NJ 07631 Office: Fifth Ave and 100th St New York City NY 10029

BIAGGI, MARIO, congressman; b. N.Y.C., Oct. 26, 1917; s. Salvatore and Mary (Campari) B.; LL.B., N.Y. Law Sch., 1963; LL.D., New Eng. Sch. Law; m. Marie Wassil, Apr. 20, 1941; children—Jacqueline, Barbara, Richard, Mario. Detective lt. N.Y.C. Police Dept., 1942-65; community relations specialist, N.Y.C., 1961-63; admitted to N.Y. bar, 1963; asst. sec. state N.Y. State, 1963-65; sr. partner firm Biaggi, Ehrlich and Lang, N.Y.C., 1966—; mem. 91st-93d congresses from 24th Dist. N.Y., 94th and 96th congresses from 10th Dist. N.Y. Past 1st v.p., acting pres. Patrolmen's Benevolent Assn.; past bd. dirs. Police Widows Relief Fund, Police Recreation Center, Police Pension Fund, Municipal Credit Union; del. Law of Sea Conf. Decorated Star of Solidarity, 1961, cavaliere, knight comdr. Order of Merit (Italy); Order of Cyprus; Nat. Front gold medal (Bulgaria); recipient medal of honor N.Y.C. Police Dept., 1960; Public Service award Greek Orthodox Archdiocese; named to

Italian Am. Hall of Fame, 1976, Nat. Police Officers Hall of Fame. Mem. Nat. Police Officers Assn. Am. (medal of honor for valor 1961; mem. Hall of Fame 1961; pres. 1967), Am., Bronx County bar assns., Trial Lawyers Assn., Navy League, Columbia Assns. in Civil Service (pres. nat. council 1958—). Democrat. Club: K.C. Home: 100 Mosholu Pkwy New York City NY 10458 Office: Rayburn House Office Bldg Washington DC 20515

BIALAS, PAUL ANTHONY, internist; b. Portage, Pa., Jan. 15, 1949; s. Frank A. and Florence (Solarczyk) B.; B.S. magna cum laude, Pa. State U., 1970; M.D., Jefferson Med. Coll., 1973; m. Deborah L. Cann, June 6, 1970; children—Nichole Marie, Bridget Lynn, Corinn Louise. Intern, Presbyn. U. Hosp., U. Pitts., 1973-74, resident, 1974-76, chief med. resident, instr. medicine, 1976-77; clin. instr. U. Pitts., 1977—; attending physician Warren (Pa.) Gen. Hosp., 1977—; practice medicine specializing in internal medicine, Warren, 1977—, teaching physician St. Vincent's Health Center, Erie, Pa., 1978—. Diplomate Am. Bd. Internal Medicine. Mem. Pa. Med. Soc., Am. Heart Assn., ACP, AMA, Phi Kappa Phi, Phi Alpha Sigma. Roman Catholic. Contbg. editor Med. Challenge, 1977-78; contbr. articles to profl. jours. Home: 14 Jackson Ave Warren PA 16365 Office: 514 W 3d Ave Warren PA 16365

BIALER, IRVING, psychologist; b. Bklyn., Dec. 8, 1919; s. Charles and Dora (Librader) B.; B.A., Bklyn. Coll., 1943; M.A., George Peabody Coll., 1957, Ph.D. (NIMH fellow), 1960; m. Judith R. Levine, Aug. 3, 1947; children—Cheryl Anne, Robin Sue, Jeffrey Stuart. Engaged in various comml. enterprises, 1946-54; with div. grad. studies Bklyn. Coll., 1954-56; chief clin. psychologist Clover Bottom Hosp. and Sch., Nashville, 1960-64; dir. research Kennedy Child Study Center, N.Y.C., 1964-70; prin. research scientist N.Y. State Dept. Mental Hygiene, child psychiat. evaluation research unit, Bklyn., 1970-77; prin. research scientist div. child mental health L.I. Research Inst., Stony Brook, N.Y., 1977—; adj. asst. prof. to adj. asso. prof. ednl. psychology N.Y. U., 1965—, Bklyn. Coll., 1970—; clin. asso. prof. psychiatry Downstate Med. Center, Bklyn., 1971—; cons. Summit Sch., Forest Hills, N.Y., 1968—, Kennedy Clinic, Bklyn., 1973—. Served with C.E., AUS, 1942-46. Fellow Am. Psychol. Assn., Am. Assn. Mental Deficiency; mem. N.Y. Acad. Sci. Research on motivational and personality devel. in retarded children, pediatric psychopharmacology. Home: 124 Regent Dr Lido Beach NY 11561 Office: LI Research Inst Div Child Mental Health Health Services Center T-10 Stony Brook NY 11794

BIANCO, CELSO, immunologist, cell biologist; b. Sao Paulo, Brazil, May 23, 1941; s. Jose Antonio and Paulina (Schor) B.; came to U.S., 1969; M.D., Med. Sch. of Sao Paulo, 1966; m. Barbara Mei. Resident in internal medicine Hosp. Sao Paulo, 1967-68; postdoctoral fellow to instr. N.Y. U., 1969-72; asst. prof. pathology N.Y. U., 1972-73; asst. prof. cellular physiology and immunology Rockefeller U., N.Y.C., 1973-77; asso. prof. pathology State U. N.Y., Downstate Med. Center, Bklyn., 1977—; advisor in immunology WHO. Recipient career devel. research award NIH, 1976; Leukemia Soc. Am. scholar, 1975-76. Mem. Am. Assn. Immunologists, Am. Soc. Cell Biology, N.Y. Acad. Scis., Am. Fedn. Clin. Research, Harvey Soc., Sigma Xi. Contbr. articles to sci. jours. Home: 140 West End Ave New York City NY 10023 Office: Box 25 Downstate Med Center Brooklyn NY 11203

BIASSEY, EARLE LAMBERT, psychiatrist; b. New Brunswick, N.J., Jan. 20, 1920; s. Earle Henry and Lillian (Craig) B.; B.S. in Chemistry, Upsala U., 1943; M.D., Howard U., 1947; M.S., in Psychiatry, U. Mich., 1953; m. Marie Davis, Sept. 22, 1946; children—Sharon Marie, Earle Lambert, Eric Wayne, Sandra Jane. Intern, Jersey City Med. Center, 1947-48, resident internal medicine medicine, 1948-50; resident psychiatry VA Hosp., Fort Custer, Mich., 1950-51, U. Mich. Hosp., Ann Arbor, 1951-52; psychoanalytic tng. N.Y. Med. Coll., Flower and Fifth Ave. Hosp., 1959-62; practice medicine specializing in psychiatry, Stratford, Conn., 1957—; mem. staffs Bridgeport (Conn.) Hosp.; cons. Bridgeport Ednl. Systems, 1969-76, Whiting Forensic Inst., Middletown, Conn., Mental Health Services and Afro-Am. Inst., Wesleyan U., Middletown. Chmn. profl. adv. com. Bridgeport Mental Health Assn., 1969-75; mem. mental health council com. Community Mental Health Center, 1969-75; mem. bd. assos. U. Bridgeport, 1968-73; mem. exec. bd. Planned Parenthood League, 1969-71; bd. dirs. Mental Hygiene Assn. Greater Bridgeport. Served with AUS, 1944-46, capt. M.C., 1953-55. Diplomate Am. Bd. Psychiatry and Neurology. Fellow Am. Psychiat. Assn., Am. Acad. Psychoanalysis; mem. Conn. Psychiat. Soc. (chpt. pres. 1971), Conn., Bridgeport, Christian, Fairfield County med. socs., Soc. Med. Psychoanalysts, Omega Psi Phi. Republican. Congregationalist. Club: Rotary. Home: 163 Inwood Rd Fairfield CT 06432 Office: 39 Stonybrook Rd Stratford CT 06497

BIBAUD, RICHARD EDGAR, computer services co. exec.; b. Amesbury, Mass., Nov. 21, 1937; s. Raoul Ulric and Marguerite Adrienne (Brochu) B.; B.S. cum laude (Navy Dept. engring. scholar), Northeastern U., 1962; m. Joan Gail McGrath, June 21, 1958; children—Maryanne, Richard, Scott, Suzanne, Marc. Indsl. engr. Portsmouth (N.H.) Naval Shipyard, 1962-65, head methods engr., 1965-66; mgr. mgmt. systems Avco Systems Div. Avco Corp., Wilmington, Mass., 1966-72, dir. Avco Computer Services, 1972—; seminar leader New Eng. Purchasing Mgmt. Assn., 1968; lectr. Advanced Mgmt. Research, Inc., 1970-71. Mem. adv. bd. Whittier Regional Vocat. Tech. High Sch., Haverhill, Mass., 1972—. Recipient Coop. Edn. award Northeastern U., 1962. Mem. Am. Inst. Indsl. Engrs. (exec. bd. computer info. systems div.), Am. Mgmt. Assn., AAAS, Am. Def. Preparedness Assn., Data Processing Mgmt. Assn., Alpha Pi Mu. Roman Catholic. Newsletter editor Am. Inst. Indsl. Engrs., 1971-73; contbr. articles in field to profl. jours. Home: 80 High St Amesbury MA 01913

BIBB, D. PORTER, III, magazine publisher; b. Louisville, Apr. 2, 1937; s. D. Porter, Jr. and Margot (Clark) B.; B.A., Yale U., 1959; postgrad. London Sch. Econs., 1961; children—Hilary Walker, Addison Porter. Writer, editor, White House corr. Newsweek mag., 1959-60; founder, mng. dir. Interbro Ltd., econ. research and investment, London, 1962; pub. Rolling Stone mag., 1970-72; ind. film producer, screen writer, author, 1972-76; pub. US mag., 1977-; Lectr. film, communications and the media. Served with USMCR, 1959-60. Mem. Inst. Dirs., Screen Writers Guild, Motion Picture Producers Assn. Democrat. Club: University (N.Y.C.). Author: screen play) Bessie, 1974—; (non-fiction) CB Bible, 1976. Producer: (film) Gimme Shelter, 1970. Home: 45 E 89th St New York City NY 10028 Office: 488 Madison Ave New York City NY 10022

BIBBO, MICHAEL PAUL, psychologist; b. Milford, Mass., June 18, 1946; s. Michael Arthur and Mary Lucy (Savino) B.; A.B., Clark U., 1968; M.A., Assumption Coll., 1971; Ed.D., Boston U., 1974. Tchr. sci. Milford High Sch., 1968-70; dir. psychol. services Univ. Center, Boston, 1970-73; intern psychol. service Devereux Found., Devon, Pa., 1973-74, postdoctoral fellow in clin. psychology, 1974-75, sr. clin. psychologist Glen Lock West, 1975—; pvt. practice psychology, 1978—; instr. Pa. State U. Recipient certificate of commendation Mass. Assn. Mental Health, 1970. Certified rehab. counselor; licensed psychologist, Pa.; certified sch. psychologist, Pa. Mem. Am. Psychol. Assn., Am. Personnel and Guidance Assn., Assn. for Counselor Edn. and Supervision, Am. Rehab. Counselor Assn. Home: 612 Meadow Dr West Chester PA 19380 Office: 891 E Boot Rd West Chester PA 19380

BIBLE, CHARLES JAMES, author, illustrator; b. Waco, Tex., Apr. 22, 1937; s. Julius Vernon and Willie Mae (Chatman) B.; student San Francisco State Coll., 1968, Pratt Inst., 1969-70; B.A., Queens Coll., 1976; m. Evelyn Nebeling, July 13, 1969; 1 son, Jax. One man shows Blackmans Art Gallery, San Francisco, 1967, Queens Coll., N.Y., 1974, Dorseys Gallery, Bklyn., 1976; exhibited in group shows Lowell Colbus Gallery, Sausalito, Calif., 1967, San Francisco State Coll., 1968, Coll. Pacific, Hayward, Calif., 1968, Queens Coll., 1976, Sunday Gallery, White Plains, N.Y., 1975, Stoneybrook (N.Y.) Coll., 1977, A & S Hempstead (N.Y.) Gallery, 1977, Gallery 52, Bklyn., 1977, Bedford Stuyvesant Resoration Corp., Bklyn., 1977; represented in permanent collection Fillmore and Fell Corp., San Francisco, Harlem State Office Bldg., N.Y.C.; illustrator: Brooklyn Story (Sharon B. Mathis), 1970; Black Means. . ., 1970; Spin a Soft Black Song 1971; author, illusttrator: Hamdaani, A Tradiational Tale from Zanzivar, Zanzibar, 1977; Jennifer's New Chair, 1978; also posters of Malcolm X, Frederick Douglass, Niki Giovanni, Sonia Sanchez, Gwendolyn Brooks, Phyllis Wheatley, Langston Hughes, Paul Dunbar, and others. Served with USN 1954-56. Recipient Virginia Kiah award Nat. Conf. Artists, 1975-76. Mem. Authors' League, Nat. Conf. Artists, Am. Inst. Graphic Arts, Council on Interracial Books for Children (corr., columnist Illustrators Showcase, 1973—), L.I. Black Artists Assn. Democrat. Roman Catholic.

BICK, MALCOLM WAGNER, ophthalmologist; b. Bklyn., June 20, 1915; s. Harry J. and Mildred (Wagner) B.; A.B., Yale U., 1936; M.D., Harvard U., 1940; m. Esther Sagalyn, Sept. 6, 1938; children—Michael S., Elizabeth Bick Lonsdorf, Katherine Bick Weitberg. Intern, Bklyn. Hosp., 1940-42; resident and house officer in ophthalmology Johns Hopkins Hosp., Balt., 1945-48, asst. ophthalmologist, 1948-49, Andrew W. Mellon fellow in ophthalmology, 1948-49; practice medicine specializing in ophthalmology, Northampton, Mass., 1950-77, Springfield, Mass., 1949—; spl. cons. NIH, Washington, 1949-50; ophthalmologist Cooley Dickinson Hosp., 1950-73, chief of ophthalmology, 1951-73; attending ophthalmologist Wesson Meml. Hosp., 1950—, ophthalmologist in chief, 1975-77; cons. ophthalmologist Soldier's Home, Holyoke, Mass., 1951-62, Northhampton State Hosp., 1973-75; attending ophthalmologist Baystate Med. Center, Springfield, 1975-78; pres. Eye Assos., Springfield, 1975—; dir. Visual Aids, Inc., Springfield, 1965—; lectr. in ophthalmology Cooley Dickinson Hosp. Sch. Nursing, 1952-65; guest lectr. Worcester Art Mus., 1977. Mem. art adv. com. Mt. Holyoke Coll., 1976-78; fellow Morgan Library, N.Y.C., 1974—; bd. corporators Springfield Orch. Assn., 1955—. Served to capt., M.C., U.S. Army, 1942-45. Decorated Purple Heart. Diplomate Am. Bd. Opthalmology and Otolaryngology. Fellow Am. Acad. Ophthalmology, Royal Soc. Health; mem. Nat. Soc. Prevention of Blindness, Springfield Acad. Medicine, Royal Soc. Medicine, Greater Springfield (pres. 1970-72), New Eng. ophthal. socs., AMA, NAACP, Sigma Xi. Club: Yale N.Y.C. Contbr. articles on ophthalmology to med. jours. Office: 33 Mulberry St Springfield MA 01105

BICKEL, WILLIAM CROFT, performing arts exec.; b. Pitts., Feb. 20, 1918; s. William Forman and Florence Graham (Croft) B.; A.B., Princeton U., 1939; m. Minnette Chapman Duffy, Jan. 3, 1947; children—Minnette Chapman, Susan B. Scioli. With Gulf Oil Corp., various locations, 1946-78, v.p. mktg., Tulsa, 1965-71, Atlanta, 1971-74, v.p. govtl. relations, Washington, 1974-75, mgr. community relations, Pitts., 1976-78; chmn., mng. dir. Heinz Hall for the Performing Arts. Served as pilot USMC, 1941-46. Decorated D.F.C. with stars, Air medal with stars. Mem. Pa. (dir. 1975—), Pitts. chambers commerce. Presbyterian. Clubs: Harvard Yale Princeton, Pitts. Golf, Fox Chapel Golf (Pitts.), Boston (New Orleans); Hyannisport (Mass.); Beach (Centreville, Mass.); Capitol Hill (Washington). Home: 816 St James St Pittsburgh PA 15232 Office: Heinz Hall for the Performing Arts 600 Penn Ave Pittsburgh PA 15222

BICKFORD, ELWOOD DALE, indsl. corp. ofcl.; b. Conventry, Vt., Aug. 7, 1927; s. Robert Lee and Evangeline B. (Tyler) B.; B.S., U. Vt., 1957, M.S., 1959; m. Gladys M. Doyle, Dec. 27, 1953; children—Dale Robert, Mary Jane. Teaching asst. U. Vt., Burlington, 1957-59; sci. tchr. Freeport (N.Y.) High Sch., 1959-60; research scientist, Olin Corp., New Brunswick, N.J., 1960-62; photobiologist, GTE Sylvania, Danvers, Mass., 1962-76; mgr. environ. lighting, Duro-Test Corp., North Bergan, N.J., 1976—; tchr. continuing edn. N.Y. Bot. Garden. Mem. Mosquito Control Bd., Environ. Adv. Com., Conservation Comm., Town of Topsfield (Mass.), 1965-72. Served with Signal Corps, U.S. Army, 1951-53. Recipient outstanding service award Nat. Mgmt. Assn., 1968. Mem. Illuminating Engring. Soc., Am. Inst. Biol. Scis., Am. Soc. Photobiology, Am. Soc. Hort. Sci., Am. Soc. Agrl. Engrs. Sr. author: Lighting for Plant Growth, 1972; contbr. IES Lighting Handbook, also articles to publs. in field. Home 760 Park Rd Morris Plains NJ 07950 Office: 2321 Kennedy Blvd North Bergan NJ 07047

BICKFORD, JOHN HOWE, psychologist; b. Plainfield, N.J., July 13, 1940; s. John H. and Lydia Gray (Shaw) B.; B.A., Swarthmore Coll. (Pa.), 1962; M.A., Columbia U., 1966, Ed.D., 1972; m. Anya Helin, Jan. 5, 1968; children—Tatyana Lydia, Catherine Virginia. Intern counseling psychology Queens Coll., N.Y.C., 1969-70, counseling psychologist, 1970-72; staff psychologist Franklin D. Roosevelt VA Hosp., Montrose, N.Y., 1972—; asst. prof. psychology Pace U., Pleasantville, N.Y., 1976—; coordinator halfway house, cons. in field. Vice chairperson EEO com. Montrose VA Hosp., 1977—. Mem. Am. Psychol. Assn. Home: 81 Tuttle Rd Briarcliff Manor NY 10510 Office: Franklin D Roosevelt VA Hosp Montrose NY 10548

BICKING, CHARLES ALBERT, research exec.; b. Wilmington, Del., Nov. 22, 1908; s. William Laurence and Clara (Albert) B.; B.S. in Mech. Engring., U. Del., 1930; M.S. in Bus. and Engring. Adminstrn., Mass. Inst. Tech., 1931; m. Blanche Malcom, Feb. 21, 1935; children—Martha (Mrs. Paul J. Nagy), Marjorie, William Laurence II, Charles Malcom. Power sales and rate study engr. Del. Power & Light Co., 1931-41; quality control engr. Hercules Power Co., 1941-51; chief design expt. unit, research and devel. U.S. Army Ordnance, 1951-56; mgr. math. br., research and devel. div. Carborundum Co., 1956-71; lectr. State U. N.Y. at Buffalo, 1971; cons. exptl. design and quality assurance White Sands Missile Range, 1956-69; mem. rev. bd. quality standards NASA, 1962; U.S. rep. com. statistics in industry Internat. Statis. Inst., 1958-61, ofcl. U.S. del., Rome, 1953, NSF, Japan Soc. Promotion Sci. Seminar, Tokyo, 1965, Honolulu, 1970; expert in indsl. mgmt./quality control UNIDO, 1971-74; vis. scientist Israel Inst. Tech., Haifa, 1972; cons. indsl. mgmt. and quality control, 1974; mgr. mgmt. scis. dept. Tracor Jitco, Inc., Rockville, Md., 1975-76, dep. dir. scis. div., 1977—. Travel grantee NSF, Rio de Janeiro, 1955. Registered profl. engr., N.Y. Fellow AAAS, Am. Statis. Assn., Am. Soc. Quality Control (exec. sec. 1965-66, Shewhart medalist 1967, vice chmn. environ. tech. com. 1978), N.Y. Acad. Scis., Internat. Acad. for Quality (dir. info. services 1969—), ASTM (award of merit 1962, chmn. com. statis. methods 1962-68, chmn. liaison com. 1976); mem. Biometric Soc., Internat. Assn. for Statistics in Phys. Scis., Soc. de Statistique Paris, Tau Beta Pi, Phi Kappa Phi. Editor: Index of Internat. Periodical Lit. on Quality Control and Reliability, 1973; Procedure for the Evaluation of Environmental Monitoring Labs., 1975; Guidelines for Quality Assurance in Biol. Research and Environmental Monitoring, 1977. Mem. editorial bd. Internat. Jour. Abstracts on Statistics, 1953-59; editorial bd. Indsl. Quality Control, 1954-59, book rev. editor, 1967. Home: 5936 Muncaster Mill Rd Rockville MD 20855

BICKLEY, GEORGE, JR., corp. exec.; b. Abington, Pa., Jan. 31, 1940; s. George and Phyllis (Keevill) B.; B.A., Cornell U., 1961. With Clarke Can Co., Inc., Phila., asst. sales mgr., 1964-65, operations mgr., 1965-66, asst. to pres., 1966-68, v.p. corporate finance, 1968-69; with Clarke Corp., Phila., v.p. corporate planning and devel., 1969-71, sr. v.p., 1971—; sec., dir. Capitol Corp. Resources; dir. Eastern Bancorp.; guest lectr. Am. Mgmt. Assn., 1972—. Mem. pres. council Am. Inst. Mgmt. Served to 1st lt. Intelligence Corps AUS 1961-63. Mem. Am. Mgmt. Assn., Sigma Alpha Epsilon (v.p. 1961). Republican. Lutheran. Clubs: Pine Valley Golf, Squires Golf (Ambler, Pa.); Pa. Soc.; Curzon House (London). Home: 408 Welsh Rd Ambler PA 19002 Office: PO Box 179 S Pennsylvania Ave Morrisville PA 19067

BICOFSKY, DAVID MARC, telephone co. exec.; b. N.Y.C., Mar. 11, 1947; s. Samuel and Dorothy (Krinsky) B.; B.A. in Polit. Sci., Hunter Coll., 1969; m. Jennifer Lynn Wyzan, Sept. 3, 1967; 1 dau., Robyn Joy. Sportswriter Yonkers (N.Y.) Herald Statesman, 1966-68; layout editor The Record, Hackensack, N.J., 1968-70; editor N.Y. Telephone, N.Y.C., 1970-73; pub. relations supr. A.T. & T., N.Y.C., 1973-76; dist. pub. relations mgr. N.Y. Telephone Co., N.Y.C., 1976—; lectr. in field. Vol. Ambulance Corps, Ridgefield Park, N.J., 1969-75; bd. dirs. Solomon Schechter Day Sch. of Bergen County. Recipient 1st. prize Employee Publs. Internat. Assn. Bus. Communicators, 1975. Mem. Pub. Relations Soc. Am. (accredited), Soc. Profl. Journalists, Sigma Delta Chi, Tau Epsilon Phi (life). Republican. Jewish. Office: NY Telephone Room 2506 1095 Ave of the Americas New York NY 10036

BIDA, MICHAEL CHARLES, systems engr.; b. Sharon, Conn., Aug. 5, 1946; s. Michael Charles and Elizabeth Marie (McDonald) B.; A.A.S. in Data Processing, Dutchess Community Coll., 1970; B.A. in Computer Sci., Potsdam State U. N.Y., 1972. Programmer analyst Eastman Kodak Co., Rochester, N.Y., 1973-75, systems engr., N.Y.C., 1975—. Served with U.S. Army, 1966-69; Vietnam. Mem. Nat. Micrographics Assn., Data Processing Mgmt. Assn. Democrat. Roman Catholic. Home: 1675 York Ave New York City NY 10028

BIDDLE, NICHOLAS, JR., securities exec.; b. Boston, Nov. 15, 1940; s. Nicholas and Virginia (Morris) B.; A.B., Harvard Coll., 1963; postgrad. U. Va. Law Sch., 1963-64; m. Joan Alanson Moore, Dec. 10, 1966; children—Virginia M., Barbara M., Katharine M. Salesman, team leader Kidder, Peabody & Co., Inc., N.Y.C., 1964-70; salesman, v.p. Kuhn, Loeb & Co., N.Y.C., 1970-76; instl. salesman Paine, Webber, Jackson & Curtis, Inc., N.Y.C., 1976-77; v.p., stockholder Keefe, Bruyette & Woods, Inc., N.Y.C., 1977—. Bd. dirs. treas. Lloyd Harbor Hills Assn., Huntington, N.Y., 1973-75; victory fund sponsor Nat. Republican Congl. Com., 1972—; mem. Nat. Right to Work Com., 1976—; class agt. St. Paul's Sch., Concord, N.H., 1974—. Served with USMCR, 1964-65. Mem. Investment Assn. of N.Y. Republican. Episcopalian. Clubs: C.S.H. Beach, Huntington Country. Home: 14 Harbor Hill Dr Lloyd Harbor Huntington NY 11743 Office: 1 Liberty Pl New York City NY 10006

BIDEN, JOSEPH ROBINETTE, JR., U.S. senator; b. Scranton, Pa., Nov. 20, 1942; A.B., U. Del.; J.D., Syracuse U.; m. Jill Jacobs; children—Joseph R. III, Robert Hunter, Naomi Christina (dec.). Admitted to Del. bar, 1968, practiced in Wilmington 1968-72; U.S. senator from Del., 1972—, mem. fgn. relations, budget, intelligence oversight, judiciary com. Mem. New Castle (Del.) County Council. 1970-72. Democrat. Office: 347 Russell Bldg Washington DC 20510

BIDWELL, DONALD, mfg. co. exec.; b. Southington, Conn., Feb. 2, 1930; s. Charles H. and Alma (Hull) B.; B.S. in Accounting, U. Hartford, 1962; m. Helen Anne Synic, Oct. 13, 1954; children—Michael, Anne, Donald. Cost accountant Internat. Silver Co., Meriden, Conn., 1950-63; asst. controller Times Wire & Cable, Inc., Wallingford, Conn., 1963-68; controller, Stewart Stamping Corp., Yonkers, N.Y., 1968-71; div. controller Burndy Corp., Norwalk, Conn., 1971-72; controller Raymond Engring. Inc., Middletown, Conn., 1962-78; corporate controller Raymond Industries, Middletown, 1978—. Republican candidate for town council, Meriden, 1975; treas. Rep. Town Comm., Meriden, 1976-77. Served with U.S. Army, 1947-48. Mem. Nat. Assn. Accountants, Nat. Contract Mgmt. Assn., Fed. Govt. Accountants Assn., Planning Execs. Inst., Am. Def. Preparedness Assn. Home: 28 Kim Ln Meriden CT 06450 Office: 217 Smith St Middletown CT 06457

BIDWELL, ROBERT ERNEST, research co. exec.; b. Bklyn., Jan. 15, 1926; s. Ernest Martin and Helen (Hamilton) B.; degree in Archtl. Design, Pratt Inst., 1953; m. Patricia Murphy, July 1, 1950; children—Robert Bruce, Kerry Martin, Jane James Patrick. Designer, Harrison & Abramovitz, Rockefeller Center, N.Y.C., 1955-58; pres. Robert Bidwell Assos., Farmingdale, N.Y., 1958-68; gen. mgr., dir. design Bioresearch, Inc., Farmingdale, 1968—. Served with AUS, 1944-46. Mem. Soc. Plastic Engrs. (sr.), Am. Soc. Metals, Assn. Advancement Med. Instrumentation, Def. Preparedness Assn. Democrat. Christian Ch. Inventor in field; patentee in field. Home: 27 Montrose Pl Melville NY 11747 Office: 315 Smith St Farmingdale NY 11735

BIELENBERG, URSULA, electronmicroscopist; b. Germany, Aug. 25, 1934; d. Alfred and Magdalene (Roeder) Setz; came to U.S., 1959, naturalized, 1965; B.S. in Chemistry, Mass. Inst. Tech., 1970; postgrad. Lehigh U., Bethelem, Pa., 1974; m. James G. Bielenberg, Nov. 29, 1974; 1 adopted son, James T.D. Chemist in Ger., 1956-58; electronmicroscopist Internat. Nickel Co., 1959-70, Airco Co., Murray Hill, N.J., 1970-74, St. Barnabas Med. Center, Livingston, N.J., 1974-76, Lyons (N.J.) VA Hosp., 1976—. Mem. Am. Soc. Metals (edn. com. 1974-75, program com. N.J. chpt. 1975—), Micro beam Analysis Soc. (chmn. 1972-73, exec. council 1973-74), Electron Microscopy Soc. Am., N.Y. Soc. Electron Microscopy, AAAS, Nat. Geog. Soc., YWCA. Recipient awards for tech. photography ASTM. Home: 51 Ormont Rd Chatham NJ 07928 Office: VA Hosp Lyons NJ 07939

BIEMILLER, RUTH COBBETT (MRS. REYNARD BIEMILLER), writer; b. Morristown, N.J., June 5, 1914; d. Fredrick Burford and Margaret (Dickinson) Cobbett; B.A., Coll. William and Mary, 1935; postgrad. N.Y. U., 1947-48, 52-53, New Sch. for Social Research, 1963, 66, 75; m. Reynard Biemiller, Nov. 5, 1938; 1 son, Christopher Cobbett. Mem. editorial staff Mut. Benefit Life Ins. Co., Newark, 1937-41; crossword puzzle editor N.Y. Herald Tribune, 1952-66; freelance writer and editor books, mags., corporate newsletters, 1966—; mem. pub. relations staff N.Y. Hosp.-Cornell Med. Center, N.Y.C., 1975-76; writer articles for mags. including N.Y. Mag., N.Y. Times Sunday Book Rev., Chem. Week, Sat Rev., Retirement Living, 1966—; contbg. editor Family Bible Ency.; puzzle editor Nat. Star, 1973. Served to lt. (j.g.) USNR, 1942-44. Mem.

Newswomen's Club of N.Y. (dir. 1960-66), Overseas Press Club Am. (bd. govs. 1972—, chmn. bull. com. 1972-73, house com. 1975-76, hospitality com. 1975—), Mortar Board, Chi Delta Phi. Author: (with others) Nat. Fein's Animals, 1955; Dance: The Story of Katherine Dunham, 1969; Next Stop . . . Paris, 1974; also series of 4 crossword puzzle paperbooks. Home: Water Mill Towd Rd Southampton NY 11968

BIENSTOCK, HERBERT, govt. ofcl.; b. N.Y.C., Dec. 25, 1922; s. Nathan and Anna (Flaum) B.; B.B.A., City Coll. N.Y.; student N.Y. U., 1945-47; LL.D., CUNY, 1976; m. June M. Klein, June 28, 1947; children—Ruth, Josh. Economist; U.S. Dept. Labor, N.Y.C., 1945—; commr. labor statistics Middle Atlantic Region, Bur. Labor Statistics, N.Y.C., 1962—; adj. prof. Hunter Coll., 1963—, Cornell U., 1969—, Baruch Coll. of U. City N.Y., 1969—, Yeshiva U., 1966—; prof. labor mgmt. relations Pace U., 1973—, chmn. indsl. relations dept. Grad. Sch. Bus.; mem. exec. council City U. N.Y. Inst. Occupational Research, 1972—. Co-chmn., NCCJ Labor-Mgmt. Dialogue, 1967—; mem. Mayor's Com. on Youth and Work, 1962-65; mem. Chancellor's Adv. Com. to Promote Equal Opportunity, 1974—. Served with AUS, 1944. Fellow Am. Statis. Assn., Am. Econ. Assn.; mem. Indsl. Relations Research Assn. (v.p. N.Y. chpt. 1973-74, pres. 1974—). Home: 53-12 Oceania St Bayside NJ 11364 Office: 1515 Broadway New York City NY 10036

BIERLY, MAHLON ZWINGLI, JR., physician, pharm. co. exec.; b. Phila., Apr. 24, 1922; s. Mahlon Zwingli and Edna Charlotte (Wentzel) B.; B.S., Franklin & Marshall Coll., 1943; M.D., Jefferson Med. Coll., 1946; m. Lois Rutledge Brinkman, Nov. 10, 1944; children—Mahlon Zwingli III, Steven Talmadge. Intern, Bryn Mawr (Pa.) Hosp., 1946-47; resident in pediatrics Phila. Hosp. for Contagious Diseases, 1949-50, Children's Hosp., Phila., 1951-52; practice medicine specializing in pediatrics, Wayne, Pa., 1952-53; with Wyeth Labs., Phila., 1953—, med. exec. asst. to v.p. adminstrn., 1970—; adj. asso. prof. biology Millersville State Coll., 1972—. Served with M.C., USN, 1947-49. Diplomate Am. Bd. Pediatrics. Mem. Am. Acad. Pediatrics, Am. Pub. Health Assn., Am. Coll. Preventive Medicine. Republican. Methodist. Clubs: Martin's Dam, Aronimink Golf, Masons. Home: 1707 Thomas Rd Wayne PA 19087 Office: PO Box 8299 Philadelphia PA 19101

BIERMAN, ARNOLD, optometrist; b. N.Y.C., May 6, 1943; s. William Leonard and Dora (Paiken) B.; student City Coll. N.Y., 1961-64; B.S., Pa. Coll. Optometry, 1966, O.D., 1968; m. Carol Ann Feigin, Dec. 26, 1965; 1 dau., Julie Elise. Pvt. practice optometry, Lansdale, Pa., 1968—; clin. instr. Pa. Coll. Optometry, 1968-72, asst. prof., 1972—; visual cons. Montgomery County Intermediate Unit. Chmn. optometric div. N. Pa. United Fund. Recipient Keyman award Lansdale Jaycees, 1970. Fellow Am. Acad. Optometry; mem. Am., Pa., Bucks Montgomery optometric socs., Beta Sigma Kappa. Club: Kiwanis (bd. dirs.) Contbg. editor Jour. Pa. Optometric Assn. Office: 762 E Main St Lansdale PA 19446

BIERNAT, LILLIAN M. NAHUMENUK, interior designer; b. Phila., Apr. 27, 1931; d. Peter and Anna (Wolonick) Nahumenuk; student pub. schs.; m. Joseph Anthony Biernat, July 22, 1951; children—Joseph A., Daria Ann, Karen Marie, Mark Allen, Brent Hilary. Receptionist, sec. Mayer, Magaziner & Brunswick, lawyers, Phila., 1950-53; owner Town House Interiors, Columbia, Conn., Newton Square, Pa., 1956—. Mem. fund raising com. Girl Scouts U.S.A., 1968; exec. bd. Conn. Opera Guild, Friends of Hartford Ballet. Clubs: Womens, Garden (Newtown Square); Villagers Womens (Columbia). Address: 30 Hurdle Fence Dr Avon CT 06001

BIGELOW, JOHN BRITTAIN, headmaster; b. Stamford, Conn., July 8, 1909; s. Frank Hoffnagel and Mabel Augusta (Brittain) B.; grad. Kent Sch., 1929; A.B., Harvard, 1933; m. Margarete Koenig, Mar. 15, 1969; children by previous marriage—John Brittain, Blair F. Tchr., dormitory master, admissions officer Rectory Sch., Pomfret, Conn., 1933-35, asst. headmaster, 1935-37, headmaster, 1937-74, now emeritus; mem. Pomfret Bd. Edn., 1937-39. Corporator Day Kimball Hosp.; trustee Becket Acad.; mem. adv. bd. Carroll, Kildonan schs. Mem. Orton Soc. (adv. bd.). Episcopalian (lay reader). Clubs: Harvard (Boston and N.Y.C.). Home: Thompson CT 06277 Office: Rectory School Pomfret CT 06258

BIGGE, ROBERT JAMES, health care adminstr.; b. Pitts., Sept. 12, 1943; s. William B. and Louise M. (Loxterman) B.; B.A., Indiana U. Pa., 1965; M.P.H., U. Pitts., 1971; m. Dianne Arlette Teetsell, Jan. 23, 1965; children—Robert, Matthew, Christine. With McKeesport (Pa.) Hosp., 1970—, asso. exec. dir., 1973, exec. dir., 1974—; mem. acad. planning bd. Walden U., Naples, Fla.; preceptor U. Pitts. Grad. Sch. Public Health. Chmn. Mon Yough Justice Commn. Mem. Am. Coll. Hosp. Adminstrs., Assn. Hosp. Med. Edn., Am. Acad. Health Adminstrn., Am. Public Health Assn., Hosp. Assn. Pa., Pa. Cancer Coordinating Com. Clubs: Youghiogheny Country, Rotary. Office: 1500 5th Ave McKeesport PA 15132*

BIGGS, JEREMY HUNT, investment co. exec.; b. N.Y.C., Aug. 16, 1935; s. William R. and Geogene N. (William) B.; B.A., Yale, 1958; postgrad. London Sch. Econs. and Polit. Sci., 1958-59; m. Brenda Ann Bolton, Oct. 1, 1960; children—Fiona, Allegra, Melissa, Robin. Investment officer Kleinwort, Benson Ltd., London, 1959-60; investment mgr. U.S. Steel and Carnegie Pension Fund, N.Y.C., 1960-69; mng. partner, sr. v.p., sec., dir. Davis, Palmer & Biggs, Inc., N.Y.C., 1969—; gen. partner Fifth Ave. Capital Assos., N.Y.C., 1971—. Bd. dirs., v.p. N.Y. Venture Fund; bd. dirs., vice chmn. Union Settlement Assn.; trustee, treas. St. James Sch.; bd. visitors Boston U. Mem. Chartered Fin. Analysts Assn., N.Y. Soc. Security Analysts. Clubs: Pilgrims, Univ. Home: 150 E 73d St New York City NY 10021 Office: 330 Madison Ave New York City NY 10017

BIGGS, SHERIDAN CHAPMAN, JR., accountant; b. Schenectady, Apr. 9, 1934; s. Sheridan Chapman and Dorothy (Miller) B.; B.S. with Honors, Lehigh U., 1956; m. Sheila McKivergan, June 27, 1959; children—Sarah E., James S., Andrew G. Accountant, Price Waterhouse & Co., N.Y.C., 1963—, partner, 1972—. Sr. warden Zion Episcopal Ch., 1972-76. Served as lt. USN, 1956-63. C.P.A., N.Y. Mem. Am. Inst. C.P.A.'s, N.Y. State Soc. of C.P.A.'s, Am. Soc. Mining Engrs. Clubs: Mining, Whitehall (N.Y.C.); Ardsley (N.Y.) Country. Home: Hudson Rd E Ardsley-on-Hudson NY 10503 Office: 153 E 53d St New York City NY 10022

BIGLEY, WILLIAM JOSEPH, JR., control engr.; b. Union City, N.J., May 8, 1924; s. William Joseph and Mary May (Quigley) B.; B.M.E., Rensselaer Polytech. Inst., 1950; M.S. in Elec. Engring., N.J. Inst. Tech., 1962; M.S. in C.S., N.J. Inst. Tech., 1973; Sc.D. (hon.), Colo. State Christian Coll., 1973; m. Hannelore Hicks, June 24, 1950; children—Laura C., William Joseph IV, Susan J. Project engr. Tube Reducing Corp., Wallington, N.J., 1953-58, Flight Support, Inc., Metuchen, N.J., 1958-59, Airborne Accessories, Inc., Hillside, N.J., 1959-61; supr. control engring. Lockheed Electronics Co., Lockheed Aircraft, Plainfield, N.J., 1961-70, sr. staff engr., 1970—; prof. engring. electronics N.J. Inst. Tech., 1961-62; prof. cons. engr. Automatic Control Systems, 1958—. Mem. council Boy Scouts Am., Scotch Plains, N.J., 1960-63. Served with AUS, 1943-44; served with USNR, 1944-46. Registered profl. engr., N.J., N.Y. Mem. Nat. Soc. Profl. Engrs., IEEE, ASME, AAAS, Nat. Mgmt. Assn., Nat. Rifle Assn., Instrument Soc. Am. Contbr. articles in field to profl. jours. Home: 1641 Terrill Rd Scotch Plains NJ 07076 Office: Lockheed Hiway 22 Plainfield NJ 07060

BIHN, JOHN PHILIP, educator; b. Queens, N.Y., Aug. 19, 1947; s. Philip and Madeline Bridget (King) B.; B.S., St. John's U., 1968, M.S., 1970, Ph.D., 1975; m. Kathleen Lee Lewis, Oct. 16, 1971. Nat. Sci. Found. research fellow St. John's Univ., Jamaica, N.Y., 1968-72; instr. cell biology LaGuardia Community Coll., L.I., N.Y., 1973-75, asst. prof., 1975-78, asso. prof., 1978—. Mem. Am. Inst. Biol. Scis., Am. Soc. Microbiology, Am. Soc. Zoologists, Soc. Protozoologists, N.Y. Acad. Scis. Roman Catholic. Home: 82-18 267th St Floral Park NY 11004 Office: 31-10 Thomson Ave Long Island City NY 11101

BIJLFELD, WILLEM ABRAHAM, educator; b. Tobelo, Halmahera, Indonesia, May 8, 1925; s. Jan and Johanna (van Dijk) B.; came to U.S., 1966; B.D., U. Groningen (Netherlands), 1946, D. Theol., 1950; Dr. Theol. cum laude, U. Utrecht, 1959; m. Catherine S. Vriezen, Oct. 7, 1950; children—Evelyn Astoeti, Wilhelmina T., Joke C., Marjolijn. Univ. chaplain to overseas students, Leiden, Netherlands, 1950-55; adviser Islam in Africa project, Nigeria, 1959-64; asst. prof. religious studies and Arabic-Islamic studies U. Ibadan (Nigeria), 1964-66; asso. prof. Islamic studies Hartford Sem. Found., Hartford, Conn., 1966-68, prof., 1968—, acad. dean, 1969-74, dir. Duncan Black Macdonald Center for Study of Islam and Christian-Muslim Relations, 1974—; prof. Qur'anic studies McGill U., Montreal, P.Q., Can., 1975-78. Fellow Middle East Studies Assn.; mem. Am. Soc. for Study of Religions, Am. Acad. Religions, Deutsche Gesellschaft fur Religions und Missionswissenschaft. Mem. United Ch. of Christ. Author: Islam as a Post-Christian Religion, 1959. Editor: The Muslim World, 1967—; mem. editorial bd. Jour. of Religion in Africa, 1967—, Islamic Culture, 1977—. Contbr. articles in field to profl. jours. Home: 94 Sherman St Hartford CT 06105 Office: 111 Sherman St Hartford CT 06105

BIL, FEYZI NECAT, mech. engr.; b. Gaziantep, Turkey, Mar. 27, 1925; s. Mehmet Ali and Tacurrical Leyla Bil; came to U.S., 1958, naturalized, 1972; M.Engring., Swiss Fed. Inst. Tech., 1950; m. Helsie Morton, Sept. 10, 1952. With r.r. and refrigeration plants, Turkey, 1950-58; asso. cons. engr. Fred S. Dubin Assos., Hartford, Conn., and N.Y.C., 1958-66; partner Kallen and Lemelson, cons. engrs., N.Y.C., 1966—. Mem. Nat. Soc. Profl. Engrs. Democrat. Club: Southampton North Colony Yacht. Designer archtl. works related to energy conservation. Home: 37 Shorthill Rd Forest Hills NY 11375 Office: 1271 Ave of Americas New York City NY 10020

BILBOW, JAMES ROBERT, police officer; b. Phila., Feb. 2, 1923; s. James Michael and Jane Marie (Barrett) B.; Asso. Aero. Engring., Pa. Inst. Tech., 1954-56; m. Blanche Colley, Sept. 1, 1951. Technologist survival equipment U.S. Naval Air Engring. Center, Phila., 1951-75, program mgr. life support equipment, 1975—; lt. staff Delaware County Park Police Dept., Media, Pa., 1977—, now officer in charge tactical unit. Pres., Delaware County Police Officers Legal Rights Fund, 1975—; nat. adv. bd. Am. Police Hall of Fame, 1975—. Mem. bd. Hero Scholarship Fund Delaware County, chmn. Hero Scholarship Day. Served with USMRC, 1942-51; ETO, PTO, Korea. Recipient Freedoms Found. awards, 1977-78; certified sr. engring. technician instr. police firearms and profl. law enforcement skills. Mem. Am. Law Enforcement Officers Assn. (Good Samaritan award 1975, Commendation awards 1974, 76, Honor award 1976, nat. v.p. publs. 1977), Fraternal Order Police (dir. Delaware County Lodge 27, 1977—), Internat. Acad. Criminology, Nat. Police Officers Assn. (certificates of commendation 1975, 76), Police Marksman Assn., Nat. Assn. Chiefs of Police, U.S. Assn. Firearms Instrs. and Coaches, other orgns. Home: 2724 Prescott Rd Havertown PA 19083 Office: Delaware County Park Police Court House Media PA 19063

BILELLO, FRANK LEONARD, pension cons.; b. Bklyn., May 19, 1937; s. Barney and Maria (Corsentino) B.; B.S., Queens Coll. City U. N.Y., 1959; m. Concetta Ingoglia, Sept. 8, 1962; children—Barney F., Jack M. Actuarial asst. U.S. Life Ins. Co., N.Y.C., 1960-65; pension actuarial asst. Marsh & McLennan, N.Y.C., 1965-66; actuarial mgr. Am. Life Ins. Co. N.Y., N.Y.C., 1966-70; actuarial supr. Coopers & Lybrand, N.Y.C., 1970-76; sr. pension cons. Met. Life Ins. Co., N.Y.C., 1976—. Served with U.S. Army Res., 1959. Enrolled actuary. Mem. Am. Acad. Actuaries, Conf. Actuaries in Pub. Practice, Am. Pension Conf. Home: 99 Slabey Ave Malverne NY 11565 Office: Met Life Ins Co 1 Madison Ave New York City NY 10010

BILELLO, MICHAEL ANTHONY, meteorologist; b. N.Y.C., Oct. 24, 1924; s. James and Anna (LaSala) B.; student Mohawk Coll., 1948; B.Sc., U. Wash., 1950; M.Sc., McGill U., 1972; m. Thelma Marie Hvammen, June 23, 1951; children—Catherine, Vincent, Christine, Elisabeth, Daniel. Meteorologist, U.S. Weather Bur., Washington, 1950-54, Nat. Weather Analysis Center, 1954-56; research meteorologist U.S. Army Snow Ice Permafrost Research Establishment, Evanston, Ill., 1956-61, Cold Regions Research and Engring. Lab., Hanover, N.H., 1961—; instr., lectr. Dartmouth Coll., 1964, 68. Served with USNR, 1943-46; PTO. Grad. tng. grantee U.S. Dept. Army, 1970; recipient Outstanding Performance Rating and Quality Increase awards U.S. C.E., 1973, Ann. Grad. award Canadian Assn. Geographers, 1973. Mem. Glaciological Soc., Canadian Geog. Soc., Am. Meteorol. Soc. Club: Dartmouth Handel Society (Hanover). Home: 12 Spencer Rd Hanover NH 03755 Office: Box 282 Hanover NH 03755

BILES, GEORGE EMERY, educator; b. Charlotte, N.C., Nov. 5, 1934; s. George Walter Frank and Ethyl (Emery) B.; B.S., U.S. Naval Acad., 1956; M.A., George Washington U., 1963; Ph.D., Ohio State U., 1969; m. Lillian Sloane Yates, Mar. 24, 1958; children—George Emery II, Spencer Yates. Commd. ensign U.S. Navy, 1956, advanced through grades to comdr., 1969; comdg. officer U.S.S. Nimble, 1964-66, Mine Div. 81, 1970-71, Mine Div. 21, 1971-72; head Manpower Programming Office, Dept. Navy, 1973-76, ret., 1976; pres. Comdrs. Four, Inc., Bethany Beach, Del., 1970—; owner, mgr. George Biles & Assos., mgmt. consultants, Washington, 1973—; prof. personnel adminstrn. Am. U., Washington, 1972—, dir. personnel and indsl. relations program, 1976—. Decorated Bronze Star medal with V, Meritorious Service medal, Navy Commendation medal, Air Force Commendation medal, Navy Achievement medal, Vietnamese Medal of Honor. Mem. Am. Soc. Personnel Adminstrn., Am. Soc. for Tng. and Devel., Indsl. Relations Research Assn., Acad. Mgmt., Washington Personnel Assn., So. Mgmt. Assn., Washington Tech. Personnel Forum, SAR. Episcopalian. Clubs: Army-Navy Country, Masons. Contbr. articles to profl. jours. Home: 5302 Ravensworth Rd North Springfield VA 22151 Office: Sch Bus Adminstrn Am U Washington DC 20016

BILINSKY, YAROSLAV, polit. scientist; b. Lutsk, Ukraine, USSR, Feb. 26, 1932; s. Peter Bilinsky and Natalia (Balabaj) Bilinska; A.B. magna cum laude, Harvard U., 1954, postgrad. in Soviet affairs, 1956-57; Ph.D., Princeton, 1958; m. Wira Rusaniwskyj, Feb. 18, 1962; children—Peter Yaroslav, Sophia Vera Yaroslava, Nadia Yaroslava, Mark Paul Yaroslav. Asso., Harvard Russian Research Center, 1956-58; instr. polit. sci. Douglass Coll., Rutgers U., New Brunswick, N.J., 1958-61; asst. prof. U. Del., Newark, 1961-65, asso. prof., 1965-69, prof., 1969—; visiting instr. U. Pa., 1961; vis. prof. Columbia U., N.Y.C., 1976. Corr. sec. Peter and Paul Ukrainian Orthodox Ch., Wilmington, Del., 1965-66, trustee, 1967-71. Mem. Am. Polit. Sci. Assn., Am. Assn. Advancement Slavic Studies, Ukrainian Acad. Arts Scis. in U.S. Author: The Second Soviet Republic: The Ukraine after World War II, 1964. Home: 2 Mimosa Dr Newark DE 19711 Office: Political Science Department University Delaware Newark DE 19711

BILLARD, ALBERT CALVIN, physician; b. Nfld., Can., Aug. 6, 1925; s. Samuel and Harriet (Edwards) B.; B.S., Acadia U., 1946; M.D., C.M., Dalhousie U., 1951; m. Margaret Hope MacMichael, Oct. 31, 1952; 1 son, Samuel. Gen. practice medicine, Inverness, N.S., 1951-53; gen. practice surgery, Sheet Harbour, N.S., 1957-59, Bathhurst, N.B., 1960—; chief staff Chaleur Gen. Hosp., 1971-76, chief dept. surgery, 1970—. Served with Royal Navy, 1944-45. Fellow Royal Coll. Surgeons Can.; mem. N.B. Med. Soc. (pres. 1973-74). Anglican. Club: Gowan Brae Gold and Country. Home: 540 Murray Ave Bathurst NB E2A 1T6 Canada Office: 1745 Vallee Lourdes Dr Bathurst NB Canada

BILLECI, ANDRE GEORGE, sculptor, educator; b. N.Y.C., Dec. 2, 1933; s. Salvatore Daniel and Rosaria Grace (Turco) B.; B.F.A. cum laude, SUNY, Alfred, 1960, M.F.A., 1961; m. Carol Loretta Farinola, Sept. 1, 1956; children—Andrew, John. One man shows: Pilkington Glass Mus., Lancashire, Eng., 1973, Corning Mus. Glass, 1970, 72, Mus. Contemporary Crafts, 1970; instr. art Coll. Ceramics SUNY, Alfred, 1961-69, asst. prof., 1969-71, asso. prof., 1971—. Trustee, N.Y. State Craftsmen Bd. Dirs., 1968-72, Naples Mill Sch. Arts & Crafts, 1972-74. Served with USAF, 1952-56. Corning Glass Works Found. research grantee, 1974. Mem. AAUP, Am. Crafts Council. Home: Thurston Studio RFD 1 Campbell NY 14821 Office: Dept Art Coll Ceramics SUNY Alfred NY 14802

BILLER, HENRY BURT, educator, psychologist; b. Providence, Oct. 30, 1940; s. David and Thelma (Rodin) B.; A.B. magna cum laude, Brown U., 1962; Ph.D. (USPHS fellow), Duke U., 1967; m. Lana Golderg, June 11, 1961; children—Jonathan, Kenneth, Cameron, Michael. Asst. prof. psychology U. Mass., Amherst, 1967-69, George Peabody Coll., Nashville, 1969-70; prof. U. R.I., Kingston, 1970—; cons., Northampton (Mass.) Welfare Dept., 1968-69, Protestant Youth Center, Baldwinville, Mass., 1969, Cape Cod (Mass.) Mental Health Center, 1970, Newport (R.I.) County Mental Health Center, 1970-71, VA Hosp., Providence, 1972-76, Emma Pendleton Bradley Hosp., Riverside, R.I., 1970—; pvt. practice, Warwick, R.I., 1970—. Fellow Am. Psychol. Assn.; mem. Soc. Research in Child Devel., AAAS, AAUP, R.I. Psychol. Assn., Phi Beta Kappa, Sigma Xi. Author: Father, Child and Sex Role, 1971; Paternal Deprivation, 1974; Father Power, 1974; The Other Helpers, 1977. Contbr. profl. jours. Home: 244 Love Ln Warwick RI 02886 Office: Dept Psychology Univ RI Kingston RI 02881

BILLERA, FRANKLIN A., men's clothing mfg. co. exec.; b. Northampton, Pa., Feb. 21, 1936; s. Anthony and Anna (Licata) B.; grad. Pa. State U., 1956; m. Ann M. Eby, Jan. 26, 1957; children—Anthony, Charles. Asst. treas., asst. sec., labor relations Cross Country Clothes, Northampton, 1956-65, v.p. mktg. and sales, N.Y.C., 1965-73, exec. v.p., 1973-75, pres., 1975—; partner B & C Motel Corp., 1965-70; exec. v.p. Holiday Bristol Motel Corp., 1967-72. Dir., co-founder Lake Wallenpanpack Watershed Ecol. Assn., 1971—, sec., 1971-72; trustee Cross Country Clothes Retirement Plan Fund; exec. v.p. Reuben Bloch Health Fund. Mem. Sigma Chi (life). Clubs: N.Y. Athletic; Englewood Field. Home: Box 23 Alpine NJ 07620 Office: 1290 6th Ave New York City NY 10019 also 39 W 21st St Northampton PA 18067

BILLHARZ, ROGER WILLIAM, cons. engr.; b. France, Sept. 16, 1911; s. William John and Anna Marie (Minvielle) B.; came to U.S., 1912, naturalized, 1921; B.S. in Mech. Engring., U. Mich., 1935; m. Constance Clark, Jan. 12, 1946; children—David, Judy Billharz Lott, Roger Clark. Engr., Gen. Motors Corp. Works Engring., 1935-41, Albert Kahn, architects and engrs., Detroit, 1941-42, Smith, Hinchman & Grylls, architects and engrs., Detroit, 1942-44; dir. Sunnyside Savs. & Loan Assn., Queens, N.Y. Registered profl. engr., N.Y. Mem. Cons. Engrs. Council (past pres. Mid-Hudson chpt.), Nat., N.Y. State (pres. Westchester chpt. 1970, Outstanding Engr. in Pvt. Practice award Westchester 1973) socs. profl. engrs., Am. Soc. Heating, Refrigeration and Air Conditioning Engrs., IEEE, Am. Arbirration Assn. (panel). Club: Univ. of Mich. (N.Y.C.). Home: 467 Munroe Ave Tarrytown NY 10591 Office: 65 S Broadway Tarrytown NY 10591

BILLIG, DONAL MICHAEL, surgeon; b. N.Y.C., Feb. 19, 1931; s. Richard L. and Sylvia Irma (Nydorf) B.; A.B., U. Louisville, 1952, M.D., 1956; children—Pamela Susan, Andrea Lynn. Intern, First (Columbia) Med. Div., Bellevue Hosp., N.Y.C., 1956-57, resident, 1958-59; fellow cardio-pulmonary lab. Columbia Coll. Physicians and Surgeons, N.Y.C., 1958-59; resident in gen. and thoracic surgery Baylor Coll. Medicine, instr. surgery Baylor Coll. Medicine and chief cardiovascular surgery Houston VA Hosp., 1966-68; asst. prof. surgery Tufts U. Sch. Medicine, Boston, chief pediatric thoracic surgery New Eng. Med. Center Hosps. and chief thoracic surgery Boston VA Hosp., 1968-72; asso. prof. surgery Hahnemann Med. Coll. Phila., 1972, prof., 1973—, dir. div. cardio-thoracic surgery, 1972-76; attending thoracic and cardiovascular surgeon Monmouth Med. Center, Long Branch, N.J., 1976—. Trustee Monmouth County Heart Assn. Served to lt., M.C., USN, 1958-60. Recipient Baylor Coll. Medicine Teaching award, 1968, Phi Chi award for Excellence in Teaching, 1968. Diplomate Am. Bd. Surgery, Am. Bd. Thoracic Surgery. Fellow A.C.S., Am. Coll. Cardiology, Am. Coll. Chest Physicians, Am. Acad. Pediatrics, Royal Soc. Health, Phila. Acad. Surgeons; mem. Soc. Thoracic Surgeons, Soc. Vascular Surgery, Phila., New Eng. pediatric socs., Mass., Pa., Monmouth County (exec. com. 1977), Camden County med. socs., Am., N.J. thoracic socs., Royal Soc. of Health, Med. Soc. N.J., Am., Monmouth County heart assns., Pa. Assn. Thoracic Surgery, AMA, Internat. Cardiovascular Soc., Michael E. DeBakey Internat. Cardiovascular Soc., Alpha Epsilon Delta. Contbr. numerous articles on cardiovascular surgery to med. jours.; sr. editor Chest, 1974; author: Management of Neonates and Infants with Congenital Heart Disease, 1973. Home: 4 Spier Ave Allenhurst NJ 07711 Office: 279 Third Ave Long Branch NJ 07740

BILLINGS, GERARD, health assn. exec.; b. Jamaica, N.Y., Nov. 11, 1923; s. Herbert Bennett and Edna (Meeks) B.; B.S., Cortland State Coll., 1948; M.S.P.H., Columbia U., 1949; m. Valma Bigg, Mar. 4, 1944; children—Patrick, Evelyn Billings Weidenhammer, Theresa Billings Thomas, Michael, Timothy, Daniel. Health educator Greater Hartford (Conn.) Tb and Health Soc., 1949-50; exec. dir., Adams, Arapahoe and Jefferson County TB and Health Assn., Denver, 1950-58; exec. dir. Am. Lung Assn. of Berks County, Reading Pa., 1958—; chmn. Conf. of Agency Execs., 1972-73; prof. adv. com. Vis. Nurses Assn., 1973—. Chmn. Berks County Interagy. Health Council; mem. planning div. and coms. United Way, 1971-77. Served with USN, 1941-45; PTO. Mem. Am., Pa. pub. health assns., Conf. of Lung Assn. Pa., Congress of Lung Assn. Staff. Roman Catholic. Home: 106 Center Ln Reading PA 19606 Office: Box 137 611 Walnut St Reading PA 19603

BILSKI, PETER, music publishing co. exec., bowling exec.; b. Archbald, Pa., Jan. 9, 1918; s. Michael and Mary (Shereda) B.; student Villanova Coll., 1939-40, Akron U., 1943-44, Coll. City N.Y., 1960; m. Oct. 10, 1942; children—Peter, Andrew, Christopher, Victoria. Owner, Re-Nu Bowling Pin Co., Ozone Park, N.Y., 1947-60, B & M Wood Co., Ozone Park, 1949-51; prop. Anton Hotel, Salisbury Mills, N.Y., 1951-52; partner Festive Music Pub. Co., N.Y.C., 1975—. Co-chmn. Rockland Pub. Edn. and Religious Liberty, dir. exec. com. N.Y. State chpt. Served with USAAF, WW II. Decorated Air medal with oak leaf cluster. Home: 126 Cara Dr Pearl River NY 10965

BINDER, FREDERICK MOORE, coll. pres.; b. Atlantic City, N.J., Nov. 18, 1920; s. Paul R. and Kathryn (Moore) B.; A.B., Ursinus Coll., 1942, LL.D., 1960; M.A., U. Pa., 1948, Ph.D., 1955; L.H.D., Wagner Coll., 1965, Rider Coll., 1967; Pd.D., Susquehanna U., 1969; m. Grace Irene Brandt, May 27, 1943; children—Janet Binder Houts, Roberta Lynn. Instr. in history Temple U., Phila., 1946-55; v.p. acad. affairs, Thiel Coll., Greenville, Pa., 1955-59; pres. Hartwick Coll., Oneonta, N.Y., 1959-69; asso. commr. Higher II Edn., N.Y. State Edn., Albany, 1969-70; pres. Whittier (Calif.) Coll., 1970-75; pres. Juniata Coll., Huntingdon, Pa., 1976—. Cons. to Ford Found., 1966, 74, 78. Trustee Russell Sage Coll., 1967-69, Fox Meml. Hosp., Oneonta, N.Y., 1962-69, J. C. Blair Hosp., Huntingdon, 1975—. Served to lt. comdr. USNR, 1942-45. Fulbright grantee, 1967-68. Mem. Am. Hist. Assn., Orgn. Am. Historians, Alpha Chi Rho. Republican. Episcopalian. Rotarian. Club: Union League (Phila.). Author: The Serbian Assignement, 1972; Coal Age Empire, 1974. Home: Taylor Highlands Huntingdon PA 16652 Office: Juniata Coll Huntingdon PA 16652

BINGHAM, ANDREW WILLIAM, publishing co. exec.; b. London, Apr. 20, 1935; s. David and Gezina Bingham; B.A. cum laude, Harvard U., 1957; M.B.A., N.Y. U., 1967; m. Caelia Ruth Bell, Nov. 8, 1958; children—Sarah, Catherine, George. Reporter, edn. editor Washington Star, 1957-60; reporter Valley Times Today, North Hollywood, Calif., 1960-61; asst. mgr. budget and fin. analysis Time Inc., N.Y.C., 1961-64; v.p., gen. mgr. Dictionary, Am. Heritage, N.Y.C., 1965-71; v.p., dir. prodn. Ency. Brit. Ednl. Corp., Chgo., 1971-73; v.p., publisher text div. Scholastic Mag., Inc., N.Y.C., 1974; mem. sch. div. exec. com. Assn. Am. Pubs., N.Y.C., 1976—. Home: 68 Douglas Rd Glen Ridge NJ 07028 Office: 50 W 44th St New York City NY 10036

BINGHAM, ELIZABETH CLAUGHTON (MRS. HAROLD J. BINGHAM), historian, librarian; b. Auburn, Ala., Apr. 11, 1918; d. William Posey and Anna Eustacia (Dawson) Claughton; student U. Montevallo (Ala.), 1932-34; A.B., Hollins Coll., 1936; M.A., Vanderbilt U., 1937; M.S. in L.S., Columbia U., 1964; postgrad. U. So. Calif., 1950-51, 55-56, 64-66; m. Harold Jaynes Bingham, Sept. 2, 1937 (dec. 1973); children—Harold Jaynes, Annette de Vane. Asst. historian Army Service Forces, War Dept., Washington, 1942-45; adj. lectr. European history Central Conn. State Coll., New Britain, intermittently 1946-58; reference librarian U. So. Calif., 1964-66; humanities bibliographer Sterling Meml. Library, Yale U., 1966-72; v.p., sec. Found. for Internat. Cultural Integration, Arawana, Middletown, Conn., 1975—; Chmn. study and orgn. com. Cromwell United Fund, 1960-61, pres., 1961-63; bd. dirs. Conn. Valley Mental Health Assn., 1957-64, pres., 1961-63; bd. dirs. Conn. Mental Health Assn., 1958-64, sec., 1960-64. Mem. AAUW, (v.p. Middletown br. 1962-63, chmn. state com. on legislation 1963-64), Cromwell Hist. Assn. (charter, pres. 1978-79). Club: Cromwell Home (pres. 1963-64, 78-79). Home: 93 Shunpike Rd Cromwell CT 06416 Office: Arawana Middletown CT 06457

BINGHAM, FRANK GEORGE, JR., bus. services co. exec.; b. Providence, Oct. 26, 1940; s. Frank George and Mary Elizabeth (Compton) B.; B.B.A., Bryant Coll., 1961, M.B.A., 1972; certificates Brown U., 1965, U. R.I., 1966, N.Y. U., 1973; m. Caryl Ann Whitcher, Oct. 27, 1962; children—Deborah Ann, Pamela Francis. Asst. dir. purchasing Speidel div. Textron Inc., Providence, 1965-73; corporate dir. material flow Uniroyal, Inc., Providence, 1973-74; corporate dir. materials mgmt. So. Cross Industries, Atlanta, 1974-75; freelance cons. purchasing, material flow, East Greenwich, 1976—; owner, operator Country Card & Gift Shop, East Greenwich, 1975—; owner, pres. Country Sales, East Greenwich, 1976—; lectr. in field. Mem. Nat. Assn. Pruchasing Mgmt. (certified profl. purchaser; dir. Dist. 9 1974-75), Am. Soc. Quality Control. Clubs: K.C., Lions. Home: 99 Blueberry Dr East Greenwich RI 02818

BINGHAM, JONATHAN B(REWSTER), congressman; b. New Haven, Apr. 24, 1914; s. Hiram and Alfreda (Mitchell) B.; student Groton Sch.; B.A., Yale, 1936, J.D., 1939; m. June Rossbach, Sept. 20, 1939; children—Sherrell (Mrs. Richard Downes), June Mitchell (Mrs. Erik C. Esselstyn), Timothy Woodbridge, Claudia R. Admitted to N.Y. State bar, 1940, practiced in N.Y.C., 1939-41, 46-51, 53-54, 59-61; with OPA 1941-42; chief Alien Enemy Control Sect., Dept. of State, 1945-46, asst. dir. Office Internat. Security Affairs, 1951, dep. adminstr. Tech. Cooperation (Point Four) Oct., 1951-53; mem. law firm Goldwater & Flynn, 1959-61; sec. to gov. N.Y. State, 1955-58; U.S. rep. in UN Trusteeship Council, 1961-63, pres., 1962, alternate rep. 15-18th Gen. Assemblies, prin. adviser to U.S. rep. to UN on colonial and trusteeship questions, 1961-63; U.S. rep. (ambassador) UN Econ. and Social Council, 1963-64; mem. 89th-92d Congresses from 23d N.Y. Dist., 93d-95th congresses from 22d dist., mem. internat. relations and interior coms. Pres. Bronx County Soc. Mental Health, 1960-62; pres. bd. mgrs. Bronx Boys Club, 1959-64. Served to capt. AUS, 1943-45. Fellow Yale Corp., 1949-51. Recipient War Dept. Staff citation, 1945. Mem. Am., Bronx County bar assns., Assn. Bar City N.Y., Council Fgn. Relations, N.Y.C. Club: Century Assn. (N.Y.C.). Author: Shirt Sleeve Diplomacy-Point 4 in Action, 1954; (with Alfred M. Bingham) Violence and Democracy, 1970, also articles. Home: 5000 Independence Ave Bronx NY 10471

BINKLEY, HOWARD LEE, assn. exec.; b. Knoxville, Tenn., Nov. 21, 1924; s. Lee Andrew and Mabel Lee (Fisher) B.; B.S., U. Del., 1950; M.B.A., U. Pa., 1952; postgrad. U. London, 1955, Case Western Res. U., 1957, U. So. Calif., 1959; D. Polit. Economics Japan U., 1958; m. Iluminda Segarra, Dec. 12, 1975; children by previous marriage—Lynn, Andrea, Shanna, Michele, Ronald. Asst. mgr. fabrics and finishes E.I. duPont de Nemours, Europe and Asia, 1945-48; dir. AFSC/UNESCO Latin Am. devel. projects, 1952; pres. Ameurex Co., Madison, Ind., 1955-60; with Pharm. Mfrs. Assn., Washington, 1960—, v.p., econ. research and mgmt. planning, 1971—; dir. Top-a-Telix Inc., Color Code Inc., Lisle Internat. Fellowship Inc.; adj. prof. Hanover Coll., 1954-60; adj. prof. bus. and pub. adminstrn. U. Md., 1961-71. Served with inf. AUS, 1943-45. Decorated Bronze Star with oak leaf cluster, Purple Heart. Lilly Endowment grantee, 1950-52; Danforth fellow 1956; Lisle fellow Jr. Chamber Internat. Asian Devel. Progr, 1959. Fellow Royal Economic Soc.; mem. Am. Economic Assn., Am. Statis. Assn., Am. Acad. Polit. and Social Sci., AAAS, Am. Pub. Health Assn., Am. Mktg. Assn. (pres. chpt. 1968-69), Nat. Economists Soc. (founder 1968, pres. 1971, chmn. bd. govs. 1972, founder found. 1973), Pi Gamma Mu. Quaker. Clubs: Rotary, Tantallon Country, Army-Navy Country, Potomac Yacht, Shannondale, Univ. Author: Public Finance; Business Law; Mathematics of Finance; Health Economics; Marketing Principles, others. Office: Suite 900 1155 15th St NW Washington DC 20005

BINSTOCK, ARNOLD IRWIN, accountant; b. N.Y.C., Sept. 21, 1933; s. Benjamin and Dotty Binstock; m. Elieen Ruth Niewood, Sept. 8, 1963; children—Debra, David. B.B.A., City Coll. N.Y. Jr. accountant firm Philip Trager, C.P.A., N.Y.C., 1955-56, firm Milton Bogen, N.Y.C., 1956; sr. accountant S. George Greenspan & Co., N.Y.C., 1958-65; controller Ruder & Finn, Inc., N.Y.C., 1965-68; partner Elmer Fox, Westheimer & Co., N.Y.C., 1968—. C.P.A., N.Y. State. Mem. Am. Inst. C.P.A.'s, N.J., N.Y. State socs. C.P.A.'s, Am. Orchid Soc., Indoor Light Gardening Soc. Am., African Violet Soc. Am., Saint Paulia Internat., Am. Gloxinia and Gesneriad Soc. Contbr. articles to profl. jour. Home: 3 Ardmore Rd Marlboro NJ 07746 Office: 1211 Ave of Americas New York City NY 10036

BINTZER, WILLIAM WINFIELD, civil engr.; b. Perkasie, Pa., Apr. 29, 1921; s. William O. and Florence C. (Barndt) B.; B.S. in Civil Engring., Drexel U., 1947; m. Anna Lou Wilson, May 8, 1948; children—William Roy, Jeanne Ann. Civil engr., Kuljian Corp., Phila., 1947-49, Am. Viscose Corp., Phila., 1950, Engring. Cons., Phila., 1950-53; with Wallace & Warner architects and engrs., 1953-57; with Lukens Steel Co., Coatesville, Pa., 1957—, project engr., 1966, supr. engring. design, 1966-77, spl. projects engrs., 1977—. Served with AUS, 1943-46. Registered profl. engr., Pa., N.J., Del., Md. Mem. Soc. Am. Mil. Engrs., Am. Inst. Mining Metall. and Petroleum Engrs., Assn. Iron and Steel Engrs., Pi Kappa Phi. Lutheran. Patentee in field. Home: 28 Wood Ln Malvern PA 19355 Office: Lukens Steel Co Coatesville PA 19320

BIONDI, ANGELO MARIO, editor, found. exec.; b. Buffalo, Sept. 27, 1933; s. Carmelo and Angela (Pisano) B.; B.A., U. Buffalo, 1957; M.S., State U. N.Y., Buffalo, 1976; m. Sharon D. English, Sept. 26, 1959; children—Mark C., Renée M., Matthew M. Adminstrv. asst. Creative Edn. Found., Buffalo, 1958-59, exec. dir., 1973—, mng. editor Jour. Creative Behavior, 1967—; asst. dir. devel. U. Buffalo, 1959-62; asso. dir. devel. U. Pitts., 1962-66; mng. editor Paideia, 1977—; adj. prof. State U. Coll. at Buffalo. Served with U.S. Army, 1953-55. Mem. Creative Leadership Council, Galielo Soc. Author: The Creative Process, 1972: Have an Affair with your Mind, 1974; Assessing Creative Growth, 1976; (with S.J. Parnes, R.B. Noller) Guide to Creative Action, 1976; (with Noller, Parnes) Creative Actionbook, 1976. Office: 1300 Elmwood Ave Buffalo NY 14222

BIRCH, ROBERT LOUIS, librarian; b. Mobile, Ala., Aug. 9, 1925; s. William Ekin and Anita Elizabeth (Bowles) B.; B.A., U. Miami (Fla.), 1948; M.L.S., Cath. U. Am., 1958; m. Daisy Grace Kay, Oct. 24, 1951; children—John, David, Paul, Mary, Joseph, Rose, Eve, Daisy. Acquisitions librarian Georgetown U., 1955-57; librarian U.S. Patent Office Library, Washington, 1957-59, 60-68; bilingual sci. info. specialist OAS, Washington, 1959-60; librarian Nat. Agrl. Library, Washington, 1968—; bibliographer Pres.'s Commn. on Patent System, 1964-65; founder-coordinator Sci. Index Group, 1957-64; tchr. grad. sch. U. S. Dept. Agr., 1958—; lectr. on memory systems. Pres., Lincoln Group of D.C., 1968. Served with U.S. Army, 1951-53. Recipient medal Vets. of the Polish Resistance in France, 1956. Mem. Mil. Order of World Wars (past program dir. Arlington chpt.), Spl. Libraries Assn., Memory Research Group, Mensa, D.C. Library Assn. Roman Catholic. Research in history of phonetic pattern of the alphabet; application of memory systems to math. and rhetoric. Home: 3108 Dashiell Rd Falls Church VA 22042 Office: Nat Agrl Library Room 1052-S US Dept Agr Washington DC 20250

BIRD, BARNARD TAYLOR, bldg. material distbg. co. exec.; b. Clear Lake, S.D., June 18, 1914; s. George Washington and Mary Ludeema (Mohler) B.; B.S., Linfield Coll., 1936; m. Dorothy Ilean Calvin, Feb. 23, 1943; children—Danielle Kathryn, Donyn Karel; stepdau., Deidre Kathleen. Order filler, stockman Montgomery Ward, Portland, Oreg., 1936-38; stock controller, Pacific Coast buyer Montgomery Ward, Oakland, Calif., 1938-42, 46-51, 53-59, nat. retail sales mgr. bldg. materials, Chgo., 1960-61, nat. buyer, 1961-65; purchasing coordinator Lumberman Merchandising Corp., Wayne, Pa., 1966-71, v.p., 1972—. Republican committeeman, 1957; elder Presbyterian Ch. Served with USN, 1942-46, 51-53; comdr. Res. ret. Mem. V.F.W. Republican. Home: Creek Dr Apt 306 St Davids PA 19087 Office: 107 N Aberdeen Ave Wayne PA 19087

BIRD, JOHN MALCOLM, geologist, educator; b. Newark, Dec. 27, 1931; s. John Robert and Beryl Elizabeth (Wright) B.; B.S., Union Coll., 1955; M.S., Rensselaer Poly. Inst., 1959, Ph.D., 1962; m. Marjorie Ann Kelleher, Apr. 18, 1957; children—Anne Elizabeth, Marsha Jean. Grad. asst. Rensselaer Poly. Inst., Troy, N.Y., 1958-61; instr. State U. N.Y., Albany, 1961-62, asst. prof., 1962-63, asso. prof., 1963-70, prof., 1970-72, chmn. dept. geol. scis., 1969-72, vis. research prof., 1972-76; research asso. Dudley Obs., 1964-72; sr. research asso. Lamont-Doherty Geol. Obs., Columbia, 1970-73; prof. geology Cornell U., Ithaca, N.Y., 1972—; distinguished vis. scientist Am. Geol. Inst., 1971; chmn. Appalachian working group U.S. Geodynamics Com., 1971-73; Nat. Acad. Scis. exchange vis. scientist to Polish Acad. Scis., 1967; Am. Assn. Petroleum Geologists distinguished lectr., 1977-78; cons. in geotech. engring. and mineral exploration. Served with AUS, 1955-57. Research grantee NSF, 1964, 68, 72, 73, 74, 75, 77, 78, Nat. Acad. Scis., 1969, Petroleum Research Fund, 1975-77, Nat. Geog. Soc., 1977, Office Naval Research, 1978. Fellow Geol. Soc. Am. (vice chmn. N.E. sect. 1974-75, chmn. 1975-76), Canadian Geol. Soc.; mem. Am. Geophys. Union, Geochem. Soc., Sigma Xi, Chi Psi. Club: Explorers. Asso. editor Jour. Geophys. Research, 1971-74. Contbr. articles to profl. jours. Home: 681 Snyder Hill Rd Ithaca NY 14850

BIRD, L. RAYMOND, investor; b. Plainfield, N.J., Jan. 22, 1914; s. Lewis Raymond and Bessie (MacCallum) B.; student N.Y. U., 1946-47; m. May Ethel Siercks, June 5, 1949. With shipping dept. Horn & Hardart Co., 1936-46, control auditor, 1946-49, gen. supt. in commissary, 1949-51; asst. to treas. Lockheed Electronics Co. (formerly Stavid Engring., Inc.), 1951-55, treas., 1955-60; pres., dir. State Bank of Plainfield (N.J.), 1960-62; investor, 1962—. Plainfield area committeeman Young Life Campaign, Inc.; pres. Plainfield Camp of Gideons, 1956—; mem. exec. com., treas. Christian Bus. Men's Com. of Central Jersey, 1956—. Bd. dirs. Sudan Interior Mission; chmn. trustees Barrington Coll.; trustee Evangelistic Com. Newark and Vicinity. Served from pvt. to 1st lt. 6th Armored Div., AUS, 1941-45. Mem. Am. Mgmt. Assn., Plainfield Area C. of C. Baptist (deacon). Home: 18 Maplewood Dr Whiting NJ 08759

BIRD, THOMAS EDWARD, educator; b. Rome, N.Y., Mar. 28, 1935; s. Harry J. and Paula W. (Boyce) B.; A.B. magna cum laude, Syracuse U., 1956; postgrad. Harvard, 1958-59; M.A., Middlebury Coll., 1960; Ph.D. candidate, Princeton, 1965; m. Mary Lynne Miller, Aug. 23, 1958; children—Matthew David, Lisa Bronwen. Lectr., Slavic langs. and lit. Queens Coll., City U. N.Y., 1965—, asst. chmn. dept., 1973—, dir. Scholars program, 1970-72. Bd. dirs. Pax Romana Grad. and Profl. Commn., Benyumin Shekhter Found., Cymdeithas Madoc, Center for Study Ethics and Pub. Policy. Fellow Soc. for Values in Higher Edn.; mem. Columbia U. Faculty Seminars, Byelorussian Inst. Arts and Scis., Polish Inst. Arts and Scis., Ukrainian Acad. Arts and Scis., Hon. Soc. of Cymmrodorion, Modern Lang. Assn., AAUP, Dobro Slovo, Phi Beta Kappa, Phi Kappa Alpha. Club: Princeton. Author: Patriarch Maximos IV, 1964. Founding editor Diakonia, 1966-75. Editor: Modern Theologians: Christians and Jews, 1967; Aspects of Religion in the Soviet Union, 1971; The Ecumenical World of Orthodox Civilization, 1974; The Third Hour, 1976; At the Border, 1977; mem. editorial bd. Polish Rev., Zapiski, Zapisy. Office: Academic II Queens Coll 65-30 Kissena Blvd Flushing NY 11367

BIRD, WILLIAM FREDERICK JAMES, mfg. co. exec.; b. London, Sept. 13, 1941; s. William Frederick and Lucy Elizabeth (Paulyn) B.; came to U.S., 1969; B.B.A., U. London, 1969, M.B.A., 1969; Diploma Inst. Purchasing Supply, London, 1970; m. Melodee Marie Kelly, Sept. 8, 1967; children—Cindy Lee, William Frederick Joseph. Metals buyer Gen. Motors Ltd., London, 1971; Corp. buyer Western Electric Co., N.Y.C., 1969-74; corp. purchasing mgr. Alpha Metals Co., Jersey City, 1974—. Served with Royal Navy, 1958-60. Mem. Nat. Assn. Purchasing Mgmt., Internat. Fedn. Purchasing Materials Inst., Inst. Purchasing Supply, Brit. Inst. Mgmt., Purchasing Mgmt. Assn. N.J. Clubs: Airborne Arms Flying, Elco Yacht, Alhambra. Contbr. articles to profl. jours. Office: 600 Route 440 Jersey City NJ 07304

BIRDSALL, NATALIE AUDIBERT, writer; b. Washington, Jan. 31, 1919; d. Xavier Marie and Natalie (Whiting) Audibert; student Rockland Community Coll., 1967-68, New Sch. for Social Research, 1968-71, m. Gregg C. Birdsall, Oct. 24, 1945; children—Marie, Isabelle. Research worker Newsweek, 1944-45, Film Counselors, Inc., 1945-46. Treas., Warner House Assn. (nat. hist. landmark), 1973-77, gov., 1972—. Mem. Seacoast, Dover writers. Club: Wentworth Fairways. Ballad author: New Hampshire Profiles, 1975; articles in various mags. Home: Portsmouth Ave New Castle NH 03854

BIRGER, JORDAN, bus. exec.; b. Winthrop, Mass., Nov. 10, 1922; s. Louis John and Ruth (Berman) B.; B.S., Tufts U., 1943; m. Barbara Ann Featherman, Aug. 7, 1955; children—S. Chet Bradley, Jon Sanford. Founder, treas. Orkney Assos., Waltham, Mass., 1950-70; founder Bee Plastics, Inc., Waltham, 1960, pres., 1960-68; treas. 214 Assos., Inc., Waltham, 1966-68; partner Ridge Assos., Cambridge, Mass., 1968-69; mgr. consumer products div. Amoco Chem. Corp., Waltham, 1968-71; founder, pres. Family Products, Inc., Tyngsborough, Mass., 1972—. Mem. alumni council Tufts U.; mem. exec. com. Yale Parents Fedn. Served with AUS, 1944-46. Recipient Distinguished Service award Tufts U. Coll. Engring., 1973. Mem. Am. Chem. Soc., Soc. Plastic Engrs., Phi Epsilon Pi. Jewish. Republican. Club: Masons. Home: 145 Sargent Rd Brookline Center MA 02146 Office: Family Products Inc Tyngsborough MA 01879

BIRINGER, PAUL PETER, elec. engr., educator; b. Marosvásárhely, Hungary, Oct. 1, 1924; s. Arpad and Eszter (Izsak) B.; Diploma Engring., U. Budapest; M.Applied Sci., U. Stockholm (Swedeen), 1951; Ph.D., U. Toronto, 1956; m. Barbro E.G. Rengman, Apr. 15, 1952; children—Anne Barbro, Monica Eva. Came to Can., 1952, naturalized, 1957. Research asso. Royal Inst. Tech., Stockholm, 1947-52; research asso. U. Toronto (Ont., Can.), 1952-57, asst. prof., 1957-61, asso. prof., 1961-65, prof. elec. engring., 1965—; pres. Elec. Engring. Consociates Ltd., 1968-71; cons. in field. Vice chmn. bd. govs. George Brown Coll. Applied Arts and Tech., 1976. Recipient Pleyel award for Research, 1950, Son's of Martha medal, 1968; sr. research fellow NRC, 1967. Fellow IEEE: mem. Engring. Inst. Can., Assn. Profl. Engrs., Am. Soc. Engring. Edn., Congress Internat. Grands Reseaux, Internat. Electric Commn., other orgns. Clubs: Kiwanis, Toronto Lawn Tennis, Empire. Contbr. articles to profl. publs. Patentee in field; inventor magnetic frequency changer. Home: 6 Lumley Ave Toronto ON M4G 2X4 Canada Office: U Toronto Toronto ON M5S 1A4 Canada

BIRKE, ARNOLD A., educator; b. N.Y.C., May 20, 1932; s. Samuel Sidney and Frances (Limmer) B.; B.S., Coll. City N.Y., 1954, M.A., 1963; M.S., Clarkson Coll., 1970; m. Malvine Suss, July 1, 1962; children—Sheryl, Barbara. Chemist, Nopco Chem. Co., Harrison, N.J., 1954-57, Reichbold Chems. Inc., Elizabeth, N.J., 1957-58, Hungerford Plastics Inc., Morristown, N.J., 1958; tchr. chemistry N.Y.C. Sch. Dist., 1958-67, 1968—, Clarkstown Central Sch. Dist., 1967-68. Mem. Am. Chem. Soc., Nat. Sci. Tchrs. Assn., Chemistry Tchrs. Club N.Y. (pres. 1969-70). Home: 850 Mulberry Rd Valley Cottage NY 10989

BIRKEN, STEVEN, protein biochemist; b. Bklyn., Dec. 17, 1945; s. William and Mollie (Finkelstein) B.; B.A. magna cum laude, N.Y. U., 1967; M.A., Hofstra U., 1969; Ph.D. in Biology (univ. fellow, NSF fellow), St. John's U., 1972; m. Fae Myrna Weiss, June 25, 1972. Teaching asst. Hofstra U., Hempstead, N.Y., 1968-69; NIH postdoctoral fellow in protein biochemistry Columbia Coll. Phys. and Surg., 1972-75; research asso. Columbia Coll. Physicians and Surgeons, 1976—. Recipient Biology prize, Founder's Day award N.Y. U., 1967. Mem. Am. Soc. for Microbiology, Fedn. Am. Scientists, AAAS, Phi Beta Kappa. Contbr. articles to profl. jours. Home: 120 Oneida Ave Dumont NJ 07628 Office: Dept Medicine 630 W 168th St New York City NY 10032

BIRKETT, EASTMAN, lawyer; b. Pann Yan, N.Y., Dec. 14, 1919; s. Claude Henry and Pauline (Eastman) B.; B.A. magna cum laude, Dartmouth Coll., 1942; J.D., magna cum laude, Harvard, 1949; m. Kathaleen Wood, Aug. 8, 1944; children—Peter W., Sally Lorraine, Joel E. Admitted to N.Y. State bar, 1949, D.C. bar, 1972; asso. firm Simpson Thacher & Bartlett, N.Y.C., 1949-60, partner, 1961-69; 1st dep. county exec. Nassau County, 1969-70; partner firm Hale Russell Gray Seaman & Birkett, N.Y.C., 1971—; dir. Airfleets, Inc., 1950-53, No. Metropolis Corp., 1950-51. Pres. Manhasset Democratic Club, 1975; trustee Meadowbrook Hosp., Nassau County, 1963-69; dir. Community Service Center, Manhasset, N.Y., 1973—. Served with AUS, 1942-46. Mem. ACLU, Am. Soc. Internat. Law, Am., N.Y. State (chmn. civil rights com. 1968-72), Nassau County bar assns., Assn. Bar of City N.Y. (chmn. fed. legis. com. 1965-68, chmn. com. children's rights 1974—), Phi Beta Kappa, Theta Delta Chi. Unitarian. Clubs: Plandome Country, Players, Yale, Marco Polo, Dartmouth N.Y.C. Editor Harvard Law Rev., 1947-48. Home: 15 Middle Dr Plandome NY 11030 Office: 122 E 42d St New York City NY 10017

BIRKHOLZ, GERTRUD MARIA, lawyer, educator; b. Annaberg, Germany, 1922; d. Johannes and Gertrud Theresia (Sandmann) Birkholz; came to U.S., 1951, naturalized, 1957; R.N., Md., 1955; B.S., Johns Hopkins, 1962; J.D., Balt. U., 1970. Supr. nursing services Johns Hopkins Hosp., Balt., 1958-62; tchr. health occupation Balt. Pub. Schs., 1965-68; tchr. practical nursing program Balt. County Pub. Schs., 1968—; admitted to Md. bar, 1970, since practiced in Balt. Mem. Am., Md. bar assns., Tchrs. Assn. Balt. County (faculty rep. 1971—), N.E.A., Iota Tau Tau. Address: 6205 The Alameda Baltimore MD 21239

BIRKIMER, DONALD LEO, civil engr.; b. New Lexington, Ohio, Sept. 6, 1941; s. Edgar Earl and Virginia Eileen (Johnson) B.; B.S. in Civil Engring., Ohio U., 1963; M.S., U. Cin., 1965, Ph.D., 1968; grad. Program Mgmt. Devel., Harvard U., 1973; m. Edith Marie Lowe, Aug. 25, 1962; children—Mark Austin, Thomas Edgar, Julie Lee. Research structural engr. Battelle Meml. Inst., Columbus, Ohio, 1968-69; acting chief constrn. materials br. U.S. Army Construction Engring. Research Lab., Champaign, Ill., 1969-71; asst. head tech. applications Advanced Systems dept. Naval Surface Weapons Center, Dahlgren, Va., 1971-75; tech. dir. Coast Guard Research and Devel.

Center, Avery Point, Groton, Conn., 1975—. Registered profl. engr., Ohio. Mem. Fed. Lab. Consortium, Mass. Inst. Tech. Marine Industry Collegium, Naval Undersea Warfare Research and Devel. Council, Nat. Soc. Profl. Engrs., Chi Epsilon. Roman Catholic. Clubs: Harvard, Elks. Contbr. articles in field to profl. jours. Home: 16 Bob White Trail Gales Ferry CT 06335 Office: US Coast Guard Research and Development Center Avery Point Groton CT 06340

BIRNBACH, SEYMOUR, prosthodontist; b. N.Y.C., Oct. 4, 1920; s. George and Rose (Bornstein) B.; B.S., L.I. U., 1941; D.D.S., U. Buffalo, 1944; certificate N.Y. U., 1960, 63; m. Ruth Saal, June 22, 1947; children—Ritsue Birnbach Charlestein, Steven Jay, David Joel. Pvt. practice gen. dentistry, Queens Village, N.Y., 1946-60, ltd. to prosthodontics, Queens Village, 1961—; clin. prof. prosthodontics N.Y. U., dir. maxillofacial prosthodontics Coll. Dentistry; adj. prof. speech pathology C.W. Post Coll.; attending prosthodontist, chief service L.I. Jewish Hosp.-Queens Hosp. Center Affiliation, 1948-69, Booth Meml. Hosp., 1969-74, North Shore Univ. Hosp., N.Y. U. Hosp.; vis. prof. Tel Aviv U. Sch. Medicine, 1973; vis. scholar prosthodontics Hebrew U.-Hadassah Sch. Dental Medicine, 1972; dir. dental residency programs, attending prosthododontist, chief service Peninsula Hosp. Center; dir. maxillofacial prosthodontics Jamaica Hosp.; cons. in prosthodontics Cath. Med. Center of Bklyn. and Queens. Instr. ARC; active Hollis Hill Jewish Center, Fedn. Jewish Philanthropies, Queens-Nassau Physicians and Dentists. Served to capt. Dental Corps, AUS, 1943-46. NIH trainee rehab., 1964; Cancer Div. NIH fellow, 1967-68. Mem. Am. Dental Assn., Dental Soc. State N.Y., Am. Prosthodontic Assn., Am. Acad. Maxillofacial Prosthetics, Am. Cleft Palate Assn., Am. Equilibration Soc., Am. Coll. Dentists, Internat. Coll. Dentists, N.Y. Acad. Dentistry, L.I. Acad. Odontology, Greater N.Y. Acad. Prosthodontics, Am. Coll. Prosthodontics, Alpha Omega. Club: Masons. Home: 80-67 222d St Queens Village NY 11427 Office: 206 Hillside Ave Queens Village NY 11427

BIRNBAUM, JACOB, community service exec.; b. Vienna, Dec. 10, 1926; s. Solomon Asher and Irene Rikl (Grunwald) B.; came to U.S., 1963; B.A. with honors, U. London, 1951; m. Freda Bluestone, Nov. 21, 1971. Tchr., Avigdor Secondary Sch., London, 1951-52; dean students Sunderland Theol. Coll., County Durham, U.K., 1952-55; dir. Hackney Jewish Community Center, London, 1955-57; dir. Jewish Community Council Manchester and Salford, U.K., 1957-59; founder, nat. dir. Student Struggle for Soviet Jewry, 1964—, Center for Russian and East European Jewry, N.Y.C., 1966—; co-founder N.Y. Coordinating Com. for Soviet Jewry, 1966; founder, hon. pres. Bklyn. Coalition for Soviet Jewry, 1969—; founding mem. Greater N.Y. Conf. on Soviet Jewry, 1971, hon. chmn., 1977—; founding mem., bd. govs. Nat. Conf. on Soviet Jewry, 1971—. Home: 656 W 162d St New York City NY 10032 Office: Center for Russian and East European Jewry 200 W 72d St New York City NY 10023

BIRNBAUM, MELVYN, customs ofcl.; b. N.Y.C., Jan. 18, 1934; s. Harry and Mollie (Kugelmas) B.; B.S., Columbia U., 1959, postgrad., 1960; postgrad. N.Y. U., 1976. Import specialist U.S. Customs Service, Jamaica, N.Y., 1961-71, ops. officer, 1971-74, br. chief classification and value, 1974—. Mem. Community Bd., 1977; mem. exec. com. Jewish Labor Com.; 3d v.p. Council of Jewish Orgns. in Civil Service; del. Jewish Community Relations Council. Served with Security Agy., U.S. Army, 1953-56. Office: US Customs Service Cargo Bldg JFK Airport Jamaica NY 11430

BIRNBAUM, ROBERT BENJAMIN, pub. co. exec.; b. Wilkes-Barre, Pa., June 10, 1922; s. Louis and Elvira (Peters) B.; B.S., U. N.H., 1946; student U. Grenoble (France), 1945; postgrad. N.Y. U., 1946-47; m. Florence Harriet Green, Sept. 6, 1948; children—Marie Ann, William David. With various consumer and trade publs., 1947-52; sr. v.p. Breskin Publs., Inc., N.Y.C., 1952-65; exec. v.p. Franklin Sq. Agy., Teaneck, N.J., 1965-66; v.p. mktg. Billboard Publs., Inc., N.Y.C., 1966-70; v.p. pub. services Lebhar-Friedman, Inc., N.Y.C., 1970-76; pres. Bob Birnbaum Co., Mountainside, N.J.; dir. Breskin Publs., 1960-64; guest lectr. Fairleigh Dickinson U., 1976; chmn. Audit Bur. Circulations Businesspaper Industry Com., 1974-76. Served with U.S. Army, 1943-46; ETO. Decorated Bronze Star. Mem. Mag. Pubs. Assn. (chmn. pub. mgmt. com. 1975-76), Am. Mktg. Assn., Advt. Club N.Y. Jewish. Contbr. articles in field to profl. jours. Home and Office: 1173 Blazo Terr Mountainside NJ 07092

BIRNBAUM, ROGER WILLIAM, health adminstr.; b. N.Y.C., Aug. 6, 1936; s. David and Betty (Risk) B.; B.S., U. Rochester, 1958; M.B.A., Harvard U., 1960; m. June Cannell, Dec. 20, 1970; children—Cara, Amy. Med. economist, asst. to v.p. Kaiser-Permanente Med. Care Program, Oakland, Calif., 1962-67; asso. dir. Harvard Community Health Plan, Boston, 1967-72; exec. dir. Rutgers Community Health Plan, New Brunswick, N.J., 1972—; bd. dirs. Central Jersey Health Planning Council; mem. adv. council Nat. Health Care Mgmt. Center, U. Pa.; adj. asst. prof. Rutgers Med. Sch., 1972—; vis. lectr. public health Yale U. Sch. Medicine, 1976—; cons. HEW; mem. alternative health systems adv. com. N.J. State Health Dept. Served with U.S. Army, 1960-61. Guggenheim fellow, 1972. Mem. Group Health Assn. Am. (dir.), Am. Public Health Assn. Author: Health Maintenance Organizations: A Guide to Planning and Development, 1976. Home: 204 Harrison Ave Highland Park NJ 08904 Office: 57 US 1 New Brunswick NJ 08901

BIRNBAUM, SHEILA L., lawyer, educator; b. N.Y.C., Mar. 5, 1940; d. Louis and Belle (Trotter) Lubetsky; B.A., Hunter Coll., 1960, M.A., 1962; LL.B., N.Y. U., 1965. Admitted to N.Y. bar, 1965; with Emile Z. Berman & A. Harold Frost, Attys., N.Y.C., 1965-72, partner, 1970-72; legal research asst. Supreme Ct., New York County, 1965; asso. prof. law Fordham U., 1972-76, prof., 1976—; lectr. Practicing Law Inst., 1972—; vis. prof. law N.Y. U., 1975-76, prof. law, 1978. Co-chmn. lawyers gen. practice for practicing attys. course N.Y. County. Mem. Assn. Bar City of N.Y. (mem. ins. com. 1970-72, civil ct. com. 1973-76, consumer law com. 1976-77, judiciary com. 1977—, exec. com. 1978), Am. Bar Assn. (vice chmn. faculty liaison com., product liability com., ins., negligence and compensation sect.), N.Y. Women's Bar Assn. (2d v.p. 1971-72, 1st v.p. 1972, pres. 1974, dir. 1975—, chmn. judiciary com.), N.Y. State Bar Assn., Phi Beta Kappa. Co-editor Product Liability, Law Practice, Science, 1975. Contbr. articles to profl. jours. Home: 220 Central Park South New York City NY 10019

BIRNBAUM, SOLOMON ASHER, philologist, palaeographer; b. Vienna, Dec. 24, 1891; s. Nathan and Rosa (Korngut) B.; naturalized Brit. citizen, 1939; student U. Vienna, 1910-12, 18, U. Zurich, 1919, U. Berlin, 1919-21; Dr.phil., U. Wurzburg, 1921; m. Irene Grunwald, Aug. 5, 1925; children—Jacob, Eva, Eleazar, David Joseph. Dozent, Hamburg U., 1922-33; prof. London U., 1936-57; ret., 1957; with Brit. Nat. Service, 1939-45. Recipient Brit. Def. medal, 1945. Jewish. Author 33 books, booklets and pamphlets, including: The Bar Menasheh Marriage Deed, 1962, The Hebrew Scripts, 1955-72, Yddish-A Survey and a Grammar, 1979; contbr. articles to learned jours. and encys. Home: 114 Invermay Ave Downsview ON M3H 1Z8 Canada

BIRNBERG, JACK, corporate exec.; b. June 15, 1937; s. Max and Yetta (Halpern) B.; B.S., Fairleigh Dickinson U., 1959; m. Louise Rothstein, June 7, 1959; children—Michael, Steven, John, Jeffrey. Accountant firm Scholtz, Simon & Miller, 1960-61; controller, officer Scott, Harvey Co., Inc., 1962-63; pres. M. A. Allan & Co., Inc., Clifton, N.J., 1963-71, dir., 1963-71; exec. v.p., dir. Tappan-Zee Small Bus. Investment Corp., 1973—; dir. Tolchin Instruments, N.Y.C., 1970-71, Kraftware Corp., N.Y.C., 1969-71, San Sebastian Gold Mines, 1969-71, Color Canvas, Inc., N.Y.C., 1969-72, Cytoarchectronics, N.Y.C., 1970-72, Tech.-Am. Resources Corp., Paterson, N.J., 1970-71, Joy Footwear Corp., 1974—; chmn. bd. Computerized Security Automation, Clifton, 1970—, Internat. Equities, Ltd., Clifton, 1970-71, Edios, Inc., 1969-77; asso. dir. Home State Bank; dir. Authenticolor, Inc. Mem. Midwest Stock Exchange, 1968-76. Phila.-Balt.-Washington Stock Exchange, 1966-72. Pres. Passaic County Childrens Shelter, 1967-68; dir. Boys Club, Paterson, N.J., 1970—; chmn. met. div. United Jewish Appeal, 1970; dir. greater Paterson (N.J.) YW-YMHA, 1970-75. Bd. dirs. Birnberg Found., 1969—, Barnert Hosp., 1971—, Daus. Miriam, 1971—, Employee Retirement Benefit Assn., 1975—, Barnert Temple, 1976—; chmn. Expo 200 Barnert Temple, 1976—. Jewish religion (dir. temple). Clubs: B'nai B'rith (trustee Greater Clifton chpt. 1962-64); Preakness Hills (N.J.) Country; Inverarry Country (Fla.). Home: 409 Carriage Ln Wyckoff NJ 07481 Office: 120 N Main St New York City NY

BIRO, KENNETH LOUIS, pharm. co. exec.; b. N.Y.C., Nov. 5, 1921; s. John Eugene and Elizabeth (Marcus) B.; B.S. in Bus. Adminstrn., Rutgers U., 1947, M.A. in Econs., 1950; postgrad. Syracuse (N.Y.) U., 1951; m. Gilda Jane Ratner, June 16, 1946; children—Douglas, David, John. With RCA, 1952-58; salary adminstr. Miles Labs., Elkhart, Ind., 1958-62; mgr. salary and benefits Schering div. Schering-Plough Co., Kenilworth, N.J., 1962—; past mem. adj. faculty Syracuse, Rutgers univs. Pres. Union County Urban League, 1970-72; bd. dirs. Elkhart Symphony, 1956-58, Union County Anti Poverty Council, 1968-69. Served to 1st lt. USAAF, 1942-45. Decorated D.F.C., Air medal with 4 oak leaf clusters, Purple Heart; named N.J. Vol. of Year, Vols. in Cts. and Corrections Assn., 1977. Mem. Am., N.J. compensation assns. Address: 2000 Galloping Hill Rd Kenilworth NJ 07040

BIRO, LASZLO, dermatologist; b. Czeckoslovakia, May 31, 1929; s. Sandor and Margaret (Klein) B.; came to U.S., 1956, naturalized, 1963; M.D., Kossuth U., Debrecen, Hungary, 1947; m. Dolores Macchiaroli, July 9, 1961; children—David, Lisa, Deborah, Michele. Intern, Kings County Hosp., Bklyn., 1957-58; resident Bellevue Hosp., N.Y.C., 1958-60; practice medicine specializing in dermatology, N.Y.C., 1960-61, Bklyn., 1960—; chief dept. dermatology Bklyn. Hosp., Luth. Med. Center; clin. asso. prof. dermatology State U. N.Y., Downstate Med. Center, 1971—. Diplomate Am. Bd. Dermatology. Fellow A.C.P., Am. Acad. Dermatology, N.C. Acad. Medicine; mem. AMA, N.Y., Kings County, Bay Ridge med. socs. N.Y., Bklyn. dermatol. socs., Internat. Soc. Tropical Dermatology, N.Y. Acad. Scis., Am. Coll. Cryosurgery. Contbr. articles in field to profl. jours. Office: 7502 Ridge Blvd Brooklyn NY 11209

BIRON, JACQUES, lawyer; b. Drummondville, Que., Can., Sept. 29, 1935; s. Antoine and Therese (Gendron) B.; B.A., Brebeuf Coll., 1956; L.L.L., U. Montreal, 1960; m. Louise Thibodeau, Aug. 15, 1959; children—Yves, Marie-Claude. Called to Que. bar, 1960; mem. firm Biron & Biron, Drummondville, 1960-75; firm Biron, Jutres & Hinse, 1975—. Mem. Que., Can., Rural, Arthabaska bar assns. Progressive Conservative. Roman Catholic. Home: 117 rue Biron Drummondville PQ J2C 2Y8 Canada Office: 147 rue Lindsey Drummondville PQ J2B 6W3 Canada

BIRRELL, DONALD GEORGE, physician; b. Lancaster, Pa., June 3, 1924; s. George William and Margaret Caroline (Kunzler) B.: B.S., Franklin and Marshall Coll., 1946; M.D., Jefferson Med. Coll., 1948; m. Patricia Lou Clarke, Sept. 26, 1953; children—Andrew Stuart, Jeffrey Clarke, Janice Kay. Intern, Gen. Hosp., Lancaster, 1948-49; resident Magee Hosp. U. Pitts., 1949-51, 53-55; individual practice medicine specializing in obstetrics, gynecology Pitts., 1955—; staff Magee Women's Hosp., Pitts., 1955—, pres. med. staff, 1969-71; v.p. asso. Thomas E. Allen and Assos. Inc., Pitts., 1955—; clin. asso. prof. obstetrics-gynecology U. Pitts., 1978—. Served with M.C., U.S. Army, 1951-53. Diplomate Am. Bd. Obstetrics and Gynecology; mem. A.C.S., Am. Coll. Obstetrics and Gynecology, AMA, Pa., Allegheny County med. socs., Pitts. Obstetrics-Gynecology Soc., Pitts. Acad. Medicine. Presbyterian. Republican. Club: Oakmont Country (gov. 1977—). Home: 828 12th St Oakmont PA 15139 Office: 204 Craft Ave Pittsburgh PA 15213

BIRREN, FABER, author, color cons.; b. Chgo., Sept. 21, 1900; s. Joseph P. and Crescentia (Lang) B.; student U. Chgo., 1919-20; M.G. (hon.) Arnold Coll., 1941; m. Wanda Martin, Apr. 25, 1934; children—Zoe Birren Kirby, Fay Birren Koedel. Ind. color cons., 1936—; developer manuals of color practice U.S. Navy, 1948, 53, 69, U.S. Coast Guard, 1952, 65, U.S. Army, 1968, 72. U.S. rep. World Conf. on Indsl. Productivity and Safety, Rome, 1955. Recipient Silver Seal, Nat. Council State Garden Clubs, 1969; citation for contributions to safety Japanese Govt., 1974. Mem. Am. Soc. Photobiology, Optical Soc. Am., AIA, Inter-Soc. Color Council, Color Mktg. Group. Democrat. Unitarian. Responsible for establishment of Faber Birren Collection Books on Color, Yale Art and Architecture Library. Author: Color in Vision, 1928; Color Dimensions, 1934; Printer's Art of Color, 1934; Color in Modern Packaging, 1935; Functional Color, 1937, Wonderful Wonders of Red-Yellow-Blue, 1937; Monument to Color, 1938; American Colorist, 1939, rev. edits., 1948, 66; The Story of Color, 1941; Selling with Color, 1945; Color Psychology and Color Therapy, 1950, rev. edit., 1961; Your Color and Your Self, 1952; New Horizons in Color, 1955; Selling Color to People, 1956; Creative Color, 1961, (German transl. 1971); Color, Form and Space, 1961; Color in Your World, 1966; Color for Interiors, 1963; Color-A Survey in Words and Pictures, 1963; History of Color in Paintings, 1965; Principles of Color, 1969; Light, Color and Environment, 1969; Color Perception in Art, 1976; Color and Human Response, 1978. Editor numerous books including A Grammar of Color (Albert H. Munsell), 1969; The Color Primer (Wilhelm Ostwald), 1969; The Elements of Color (Johannes Itten), 1970; Modern Chromatics (Ogden N. Rood), 1973. Contbr. numerous articles on color to tech., profl., trade mags. Home: 77 Prospect St Stamford CT 06902 Office: 184 Bedford St Stamford CT 06901

BIRUTIS, GEORGE, elec. engr.; b. Kaunas, Lithuania, May 13, 1938; s. Stasys and Aldona (Carneckis) B.; brought to U.S., 1949, naturalized, 1956; B.E.E., Coll. City N.Y., 1960; M.S. in Elec. Engring., Poly. Inst. Bklyn., 1966; m. Donna Grajauskas, July 20, 1963; children—Tadas, Paul, Adria. Microwave engr. Polarad Electronics, Long Island City, N.Y., 1959-60; with Dorne & Margolin Inc., Bohemia, N.Y., 1960—, microwave engr., 1960-68, engring. section mgr., 1968-70, chief engr., 1970-71, v.p. ops., 1971-76, v.p. engring., 1976-78, v.p. mktg., 1978—. Mem. IEEE. Home: 29 Autumn Dr East Northport NY 11731 Office: 2950 Veterans Memorial Hwy Bohemia NY 11716

BISHOFF, LEE EDWARD, plastics co. exec.; b. Lowell, Mass., Jan. 7, 1951; s. Maurice Allen and Shirlie Elaine (Gordon) B.; B.S. in Psychology magna cum laude, U. Mass., 1972; M.Ed. in Counseling, Northeastern U., 1976. Dir., Lowell Hebrew Community Center, 1972-76; counseling intern Youth Devel. Program, Newton, Mass., 1975-76; sch. psychologist intern Claflin Elementary Sch., Newton, 1976-77; product mgr. Form-Fit Plastics, Inc., Dracut, Mass., 1977—. Commonwealth scholar, 1969-72. Mem. Phi Eta Sigma, Phi Kappa Phi, Kappa Delta Pi. Home: 16 Nottinghill Rd Brighton MA 02135 Office: 100 Pleasant St Dracut MA 01826

BISHOP, EVERETT GEORGE, ins. co. exec.; b. Providence, Oct. 14, 1950; s. Everett Gurney and Emma Charlotte (Berger) B.; B.A., Northeastern U., Boston, 1973; m. Donna Jean Park, May 19, 1979. Actuarial asst. Am. Mut. Ins. Cos., Wakefield, Mass., 1976-77, asst. v.p., 1977—. Asso. Casualty Actuarial Soc.; mem. Internat. Actuarial Assn., Phi Kappa Phi. Home: 244 Kennedy Dr Apt 810 Malden MA 02148 Office: Am Mut Ins Cos Quannapowitt Pkwy Wakefield MA 01880

BISHOP, FRANK EUGENE, JR., filter mfg. co. exec.; b. North Bergen, N.J., Nov. 8, 1929; s. Frank Eugene and Elizabeth (Koch) B.; B.E., U. Detroit, 1952; M.M.E., N.Y. U., 1957; M.B.A., L.I. U., 1974; m. Dolores M. Vendette, Aug. 29, 1953; children—Jeanne M., Lois E., Jacqueline C. Research engr. Grumman Aircraft Co., L. I., N.Y., 1952-54; project engr. Lummus Co., N.Y.C., 1956-58; with Aircraft Porous Media, Inc., Glen Cove, N.Y., 1958—, v.p., 1972—. Served with U.S. Army, 1954-56. Mem. ASME, Soc. Automotive Engr., Am. Soc. Naval Engrs., Internat. Standards Orgn. Club: Huntington Bay. Contbr. articles in field to profl. jours. Home: 3 Harmony Rd Huntington NY 11743 Office: 30 Seacliff Ave Glen Cove NY 11542

BISHOP, FREDERICK THOMAS, ceramics co. exec.; b. Toronto, Ont., Can., Jan. 2, 1933; s. Frederick Thomas and Florence Elizabeth (McBride) B.; student Scarborough Coll., 1945-50, Ryerson Inst. Tech., 1950-53, McMaster U. Extension, 1962-65; m. Marilyn Joan Johnson, Sept. 10, 1955; children—Evelyn Dianne, Carolyn Elizabeth, Roslyn Elaine. Engring. research-transformers Canadian Gen. Electric Co., Guelph, Ont., 1953-55; asst. plant mgr. Toronto Brick Co., 1955-65; gen. mgr. NATCO Bldg. Products, Ltd., Burlington, Ont., 1965-77; pres. Halton Ceramics Ltd., 1977—. Mem. Canadian Ceramic Soc. (pres. 1972-73), Ont. Assn. Certified Engring. Technologists, Am. Ceramic Soc. Mason. Home: 1771 Waterdown Rd Burlington ON L7R 3X5 Canada Office: 1200 Unsworth Ave Burlington ON L7R 3X5 Canada

BISHOP, GORDON BRUCE, journalist; b. Paterson, N.J., Jan. 1, 1938; s. Charles Edward and Freda Mary (Romyns) B.; B.A., Rutgers U., 1967; postgrad. (scholar) Inst. Internat. Edn., U. Manchester (Eng.), 1972; m. Jeanne Reed, June 30, 1962; children—Jennifer, Elizabeth. Writer, Herald-News, Passaic, N.J., 1959-67, columnist, 1962-67; columnist Star-Ledger, Newark, 1969—, environmental editor, 1971—. Lectr., Rutgers U., 1970—, Princeton U., 1978—. Recipient Edward J. Meeman Nat. Environ. award Scripps-Howard Found., 1971, 72, 73, 74, 75, Thomas Stokes Nat. Conservation award Washington Journalism Center, 1971, 72, Conservation award N.J. Audubon Soc., 1973, Distinguished Pub. Service award Sigma Delta Chi, 1972, 73, 76, Nat. Recycling award Nat. Recycling Assn., 1973; Good Govt. award N.J. Conf. Mayors, 1974; Media award U.S. EPA, 1975; Pub. Service award N.J. Soc. Profl. Engrs., 1976; named Man of Yr., Congregation AABC, 1973; also Congl. commendations from U.S. senators Harrison A. Williams and Clifford P. Case; also 9 awards N.J. Press Assn. Author: (with Frank Papps) The Purple Canary, 1963. Home: 18 Ruth Pl Eatontown NJ 07724 Office: Star Ledger Plaza Newark NJ 07101

BISHOP, JOHN BYRON, psychologist, univ. adminstr.; b. Pitts., Nov. 5, 1942; s. J. Byron and Gladys L. (Brown) B.; B.A., Albright Coll., 1964; M.S., Ohio U., 1966, Ph.D., 1969. Asst. dir. residence Ohio U., Athens, 1966-68; intern counseling center Duke U., Durham, N.C., 1969-70; counseling psychologist U. Del., Newark, 1969-72, asso. dir. counseling, student devel., 1972-76, dir. counseling, career services, 1976—, asst. prof. edn.; mem. steering com. Univ. and Coll. Counseling Center Dirs.; cons. drug info. action line, Opportunities Industrialization Center. Trustee Newark Pastoral Counseling and Consultation Center; faculty bd. Ferris Sch. for Boys, State Del. Corrections Dept. Mem. Am., Del. psychol. assns., Am. Personnel and Guidance Assn., Am. Coll. Personnel Assn., Assn. Counselor Edn. and Supervision. Methodist. Contbr. articles in field to Jour. Counseling Psychology, Jour. Coll. Student Personnel, Personnel and Guidance Jour., Assn. Counselor Edn. and Supervision Jour., Nat. Assn. Student Personnel Adminstrs. Jour. Home: PO Box 68 Kemblesville PA 19347 Office: 210 Hullihen Hall U Del Newark DE 19711

BISHOP, MILO ELLIS, spl. educator; b. Buhl, Idaho, Oct. 2, 1939; s. Henry Milo and Gertha Irene B.; B.S., U. Utah, 1966; M.A., U. N.Mex., 1969; Ph.D., Purdue U., 1972; m. Marcia A. Morgan, Nov. 25, 1961; children—Bradley James, Laura Ann, Lynnette Carol, Paul Steven. Trainee, Utah Sch.for the Deaf, Ogden, 1965-66, instr. and researcher, 196668; asst. prof./research asso. Nat. Tech. Inst. for the Deaf, Rochester, N.Y., 1972-74, asst. dean, 1974-77, asso. prof., 1976, asso. dean, 1977—; tchr. communications Rochester Inst. Tech., 1973-78; cons. to schs. Active Boy Scouts Am.; mem. Greece Central Bd. Edn., 1977—. Served with U.S. Army, 1958-61. Office of Edn. fellow, 1967; USPHS fellow, 1968-69; Nat. Inst. Neurol. Diseases and Stroke fellow, 1969-71; PTA spl. edn. scholar, 1964-65. Mem. Acoustical Soc. Am., Alexander Graham Bell Assn., Am. Ednl. Research Assn., Am. Instrs. of the Deaf, Conf. Execs. Am. Schs. Deaf, Am. Mgmt. Assn., Am. Speech and Hearing Assn., Acad. Rehabilitative Audiologists, Nat. Sch.Bds. Assn., Soc. Research Adinstrs. Mormon. Co-author: Mainstreaming Bibliography, Vol. I, Vol. II; asso. editor Jour. Speech and Hearing Research, 1973-75, Mainstreaming, Practical Ideas for Educating Hearing Impaired Students; contbr. articles to profl. jours. Home: 350 Ridgemont Dr Rochester NY 14626 Office: One Lomb Memorial Dr Rochester NY 14623

BISSELL, PELHAM ST. GEORGE, III, jurist; b. N.Y.C., Oct. 20, 1912; s. Pelham St. George and Mary V. Y. (Bissell) B.; student Columbia U., 1931-34; A.B., Rutgers U., 1936; LL.B., N.Y.U., 1939; m. Mary Alascia, Dec. 24, 1934. Admitted to N.Y. State bar, 1941; asso. firm Barnes, Richardson & Colburn, N.Y.C., 1939-41, 45-51; law sec. to Judge Jacob Gould Schurman, Ct. of Gen. Sessions, 1945-51; justice Municipal Ct., N.Y.C., 1952-62; judge Civil Court, N.Y.C., 1962—. Served from 2d lt. to lt. col., 1st Inf. Div., AUS, 1941-45; Judge Adv. V Corps, 1945; N. African, European campaigns; col. Res. ret. Decorated Bronze Star medal with cluster, French Croix de Guerre, Belgian Croix de Guerre. Mem. Am. Bar Assn., Assn. Bar City N.Y., N.Y. County Lawyers Assn., S.R. (past nat. pres.), Soc. Am. Wars (past comdr.), Mil. Order Fgn. Wars (past N.Y. State comdr.), Soc. Mayflower Descs. (past nat. asst. gov.), N.Y. State Bar Assn., Order Founders and Patriots, Order Lafayette, New Eng. Soc., St. Nicholas Soc., Soc. Colonial Wars, St. David's Soc., St. George's Soc., Soc. Colonial Order Acorn, Soc. 1st Div. (past nat. bd. dirs.), Grand St. Boys Assn., Am. Legion (past post comdr.), 40 and 8, Vets. Corps. Arty., Mil. Order World Wars, N.Y. Soc. Mil. and Naval

Officers World Wars, VFW, Res. Officers Assn., Judge Advs. Assn., Sojourners, Delta Psi, Phi Delta Phi. Republican. Episcopalian. Clubs: Union League, Church, N.Y. Athletic (N.Y.C.); Army and Navy (Washington); St. Anthony; Masons (33 deg.), Elks. Home: 22 E 36th St New York City NY 10016 Office: 111 Centre St New York City NY 10013

BISSINGER, ELEANOR LEBENTHAL (MRS. H. GERARD BISSINGER II), investment banker; b. N.Y.C., Mar. 5, 1927; d. Louis S. and Sayra (Fischer) Lebenthal; B.A., Smith Coll., 1948; m. H. Gerard Bissinger II, May 11, 1950; children—Ann Louise, H. Gerard III. Editorial asst. UNIFRUITCO mag., 1948-50; letters corr. Life Mag., 1950-52; with market research dept. Norman Craig & Kummel, 1957-58; asst. to producer-dir. plays, motion picture Laurette, There Must Be A Pony, To Kill a Mockingbird, N.Y.C., 1960-63; v.p. Lebenthal & Co., Inc., N.Y.C., 1963-68, adminstrv. v.p., 1970-78, exec. v.p., 1976—, also dir.; exec. asst. Ladenburg Thalmann & Co., 1968-70. Decade chmn. fund raising drive Smith Coll. 1965-66 master of ceremonies Smith Coll. reunions, 1949, 53, 58, 63, 73. Bd. dirs. Bronx River Neighborhood Centers, Consumers Action Now, Inc., American Place Theatre; bd. advisers Sun Day, N.Y., 1978. Club: Smith College of N.Y. Office: 1 State St Plaza New York City NY 10004

BISSON, ROBERT ANTHONY, environ. services co. exec.; b. Laconia, N.H., Feb. 20, 1946; s. Reginald Anthony and Frances Adrienne (Shastany) B.; student U. N.H., Fla. Altantic U., Faculte des Sciences, Marseilles, France; m. Linda Gale Gaillardetz, Mar. 10, 1965; 1 dau., Theresa Adrienne. Technician, research diver Office Francais de Recherche Sous-Marine, Marseilles, France, and Musee D'Oceanographique, Monaco, 1966-67; master diver, conshelf exploration Divcon Internat., London, Eng., 1967-68; project dir. conshelf exploration Ocean Sci. & Engring., Inc., Riviera Beach, Fla., 1968-69; project dir. ecol. studies Normandeau Asso. Inc., Manchester, N.H., 1969-72; pres. Biospheric Cons. Internat., Inc. (now BCI-Geonetics, Inc.), Meredith, N.H., 1972—; v.p., dir. Biospherics Group Ltd., Halifax, N.S., Can., 1973—; pres., dir. BCI Map Corp., Laconia, N.H., 1976-77; Program leader N.H. Hydrospace Explorers, Boy Scouts Am., 1975—; trustee Center for Environmental Studies, 1976—; bd. dirs. Lake Winnipesaukee Assn., 1977—, pres., 1978-79. Certified master deep-sea diver Divcon Advanced Mixed-Gas Diving Unit, Gt. Yarmouth, Eng., 1967. Mem. AAAS, Marine Tech. Soc. Home: 21 Parker Pl Laconia NH 03246 Office: Homestead Bldg US Route 3 Meredith NH 03253

BISSONNETTE, GEORGES LOUIS, clergyman; b. Central Falls, R.I., July 22, 1921; s. George Joseph and Alida (Provost) B.; B.A., Assumption Coll., 1943; S.T.B., Laval U., 1947, S.T.L., 1949; M.A., Fordham U., 1953; M.H., Columbia, 1957, Ph.D., 1962; fellow Russian Inst. Columbia, 1957. Instr. Assumption Coll., 1943-45, 49-51, dir. Sch. Fgn. Affairs, dean faculty, prof. polit. sci., 1962-68, pres., 1968-71, asst. dir. devel., 1971—, prof. polit. sci., 1971—; ordained priest Roman Catholic Ch., 1949; chaplain of Americans in USSR, and apostolic adminstr. of USSR, 1953-55; lectr.-cons. U.S. Army Command and Gen. Staff Coll., Leavenworth. Recipient 175th Anniversary Medal of Honor, Georgetown U., 1964. Author: Moscow Was My Parish, 1956. Address: Assumption Coll Worcester MA 01609

BISSOONDOYAL, DAN, neurologist; b. Mauritius, Mar. 7, 1938; s. Sookdeo and Annie (Pandou) B.; M.B.B.S., Univ. Coll. Hosp., London, Eng., 1964; postgrad. McGill U. (Can.), 1965-70; m. Georgine Gauthier, Jan. 17, 1970; children—François, Alain. Came to Can., 1965, naturalized, 1970. Intern Univ. Coll. Hosp., London, 1964-65; resident McGill Univ. Hosps., Montreal, Que., Can., 1965-70; practice medicine specializing in neurology, Montreal, 1971—; cons. neurologist St. Luc Hosp., 1972—, Hotel Dieu, 1971—; asst. prof. neurology U. Montreal, 1973—. Mem. Am. Acad. Neurology, Canadian Neurol. Soc. Home: 5201 Brillon St Montreal PQ H4A 1H6 Canada Office: 315 Dorchester Blvd E Montreal PQ Canada

BISTRIAN, BRUCE RYAN, physician; b. Southampton, N.Y., Oct. 22, 1939; s. Peter and Mary Laura (Ryan) B.; student Clarkson Coll., 1956-58; B.A., N.Y. U., 1961; M.D., Cornell U., 1965; M.P.H., Johns Hopkins U., 1971; Ph.D., Mass. Inst. Tech., 1976; m. Eleanor Alice Dix, Sept. 3, 1964; children—Tennille Ryan, Jordan Brooke, Britton Perry. Intern, Bellevue Hosp., N.Y.C., 1965-66; fellow in metabolism U. Vt. Med. Sch., Burlington, 1968-69; resident internal medicine, 1969-70; practice medicine specializing in clin. nutrition, Boston, 1975—; mem. staffs Boston City Hosp., New Eng. Deaconess Hosp.; research asso. Mass. Inst. Tech., Cambridge, 1975—; clin. asst. prof. medicine Harvard U., 1976—. Served to capt. M.C., AUS, 1966-68. Decorated Army Commendation medal. Diplomate Am. Bd. Internal Medicine. Mem. Am. Inst. Nutrition, Am. Soc. Clin. Nutrition, Fedn. Am. Soc. Exptl. Biologists, Am. Soc. Clin. Research, Mass. Med. Soc., Mass. Soc. Mayflower Descs., Sigma Xi, Phi Beta Kappa. Presbyterian. Contbr. articles in field to profl. jours. Home: Argilla Rd Ipswich MA 01938 Office: 194 Pilgrim Rd Boston MA 02215

BITTICK, ROBERT LUCIAN, hosp. adminstr.; b. Eagle Pass, Tex., Jan. 28, 1948; s. Robert Luther and Sara (Cheatham) B.; B.S., Johns Hopkins U., 1966; M.A., Harvard U., 1969, Ph.D., E.E., 1970; M.D., Med. Coll. Ga., 1973. Med. research asst. Johns Hopkins U., 1965-66; med. research asso. Harvard U., 1968-70; pres. Syntron Corp., Atlanta, Los Angeles, Key West, Fla., 1973-75; chief dir. tech. and devel. Johns Hopkins Balt. City Hosp., 1975—; pres. Bugs (Balt. Small Computers Users Group); cons. patent devel. Chmn. Scientists Com. to Elect Carter, 1975-76; cons. Presdl. Sci. Advisory Council, 1976—. Asso. mem. NSF; mem. IEEE. Episcopalian. Co-author (with John H. Freeman) Steamboat Springs, Colorado, 1969; Surge of All Seas, 1978. Patentee microcomputer/human nervous system: direct interface, periscope imprinting code resolution, DNA Activation Enzyme Synthesis. Home: Beethoven South #202 1518 Park Ave Baltimore MD 21217 Office: Tech and Devel Bldg D-5 West 4940 East Ave Baltimore MD 21224

BITTMAN, LORAN RICE, state ofcl.; b. N.Y.C., Dec. 24, 1916; s. Loran Rice and Winifred (Hall) B.; student Stevens Inst., 1943-44; B.A., N.Y. U., 1942, M.S., 1952, Ph.D., 1953; postgrad. Adelphi U., 1955-56, Bklyn. Poly. Inst., 1956-59; m. Beryl Maureen Boult, July 23, 1955; children—Lorna Maureen Rose, Mace Percy. Physicist, Westinghouse Electric Corp., Bloomfield, N.J., 1942-49; project engr. Sperry Gyroscope Co., Great Neck, N.Y., 1952-59; prin. staff scientist Martin Co., Balt., 1959-64; resident dir., prof. elec. engring. U. Fla., Gainesville, 1964-67; sect. head lasers Raytheon Co., Waltham, Mass., 1967-69, prin. engr., 1969-70; cons. systems analyst, dept. pub. welfare Commonwealth Mass., Boston, 1970-73, dir. statistics, 1973—. Named Engr. of Yr., Fla. Engring. Soc., 1967. Mem. Am. Phys. Soc., IEEE. Rotarian. Home: 39 Blake Rd Lexington MA 02173 Office: 600 Washington St Boston MA 02111

BITTNER, NORMAN DOUGLAS, dentist; b. Glen Ridge, N.J., July 8, 1930; s. Norman Meuser and Marion (Reilly) B.; B.A., Upsala Coll., 1953; D.D.S., U. Pa., 1957; certificate in prosthodontics N.Y. U., 1969; m. Dorothy Platte, Nov. 25, 1958; children—Elisabeth Anne, Christine Carol, Douglas Meuser. Practice dentistry, specializing in prosthodontics, Upper Montclair, 1959—; instr., lectr. Fairleigh Dickenson U. Sch. Dentistry, 1959-65; now asso. prof. N.J. Coll. Medicine and Dentistry; cons. to Warner Lambert Corp., also Armed Forces. Served as lt. Dental Corps, USNR, 1957-59. Diplomate Am. Bd. Prosthodontics. Charter fellow Am. Coll. Prosthodontics; mem. Am. Prosthodontic Soc., N.Y. Acad. Dentistry, U.S. Combined Tng. Assn., Eastern States Dressage Assn. (treas.). Conglist. Club: Spring Valley (N.J.) Hounds. Home: RD 1 Box 76 North Maple Ave Basking Ridge NJ 07920 Office: 286 Park St Upper Montclair NJ 07043

BIXBY, R. BURDELL, lawyer; b. Schenectady, Oct. 11, 1914; s. Raymond O. and Mabel A. (Rumsey) B.; A.B., Colgate U., 1936; J.D., Albany Law Sch., 1940; m. Anne M. Hardwick, Oct. 25, 1941; 1 son, Robert Hardwick. Admitted to N.Y. bar, 1940; asst. sec. to Gov. of N.Y. State, 1948-50, exec. asst., 1950-52, sec., 1952-54; sec.-treas. N.Y. State Thruway Authority, 1950-60, chmn., 1960-74; partner law firm Dewey, Ballantine, Bushby, Palmer & Wood, N.Y.C., 1955—; trustee Hudson City Savs. Inst. Treas. New York Rep. Com., 1959-61. Trustee Albany (N.Y.) Law Sch. Served with USAAF, 1942-46. Mem. Am., N.Y. State, Columbia County bar assns., N.Y. County Lawyers Assn., Assn. Bar City N.Y., Am. Legion. Clubs: City Midday (N.Y.C.); Masons. Home: 7 Joslen Pl Hudson NY 12534 Office: 140 Broadway New York City NY 10005

BIXLER, HERBERT EDWARDS, transp. cons.; b. New London, Conn., June 10, 1911; s. James Wilson and Mabel (Seelye) B.; grad. Phillips Exeter Acad., 1928; A.B., Amherst Coll., 1932; M.S., Yale, 1933; m. Agnes MacAulay Rodgers, June 26, 1937; children—Sidney Rodgers, Agnes Seelye (Mrs. Thomas E. Kurtz), Elizabeth James (Mrs. Arnold W. Yanof). With N.Y., N.H. & H. R.R., 1936-50, gen. supt. transp., 1947-48, gen. mdse, mgr., 1948-49; gen. supt. transp. Boston & Maine R.R. and Maine Central R.R., 1950-54; asst. to pres. Boston and Maine R.R., 1954-55; asst. to pres. Northeast Airlines, Boston, 1956-62; asso. Systems Analysis and Research Corp., Boston, 1962-64, v.p., 1964-70; transp. cons., Jaffrey Center, N.H., 1971—. Mem. Mass. Legislative Commn. To Investigate Massachusetts Bay Transit Authority, 1967-70, Greater Boston Econ. Study Com., 1958-60, Mass. Tomorrow, 1973; bd. dirs. New Eng. Council for Econ. Devel., 1951-54. Mem. Transp. Research Forum (pres. 1972), Assn. ICC Practitioners (pres., chpt. 1, 1972-73), Am. Assn. R.R. Supts. (pres., 1952-53), Ry. Systems and Mgmt. Assn., New Eng. R.R. Club, Aero Club New Eng. Clubs: Yale (N.Y.C.); Harvard (Boston). Contbr. articles to profl. jours. Address: South Hill Rd Jaffrey Center NH 03454 also 30 Boylston St Cambridge MA 02138

BIZER, LAWRENCE STANLEY, surgeon; b. Detroit, July 11, 1935; s. Abraham Victor and Frieda Lillian (Auslander) B.; B.S., U. Mich., Ann Arbor, 1956, M.D., 1960; m. Linda Susan Nussdorf, Aug. 21, 1958; children—Mark, David, Karen. Intern, U. Mich. Hosp., Ann Arbor, 1960-61, resident in surgery 1961-66, instr. in surgery, 1966; asst. prof. of surgery Wayne State U., Detroit, 1968-69; chief of surgery Western Mass. Hosp., Westfield, 1969-71; chief of surgery Wing Meml. Hosp., Palmer, Mass., 1971-78; cons. surgeon Western Mass. Hosp., Westfield, 1971-78; asst. prof. surgery Albert Einstein Coll. Medicine, Bronx, N.Y., 1978—; asso. attending in surgery Montefiore Hosp., Bronx, 1978—, North Central Bronx Hosp., 1978—. Served to chief of surgery 2nd M.A.S.H., AUS, 1966-68; Vietnam. Decorated Bronze Star. Diplomate Am. Bd. Surgery. Fellow ACS, Victor Vaughn Soc.; mem. Alpha Omega Alpha, Phi Delta Epsilon, Sigma Alpha Mu. Jewish. Contbr. articles to profl. jours. Home: 43 Morgan Circle Amherst MA 01002 Office: North Central Bronx Hosp Bronx NY 10467

BLACHARSH, CARL, periodontist; b. Bklyn., June 12, 1918; s. Alex and Minnie (Goodnow) B.; B.S. cum laude, Coll. City N.Y., 1938; D.D.S., N.Y.U., 1942, certificate periodontia, 1958; m. Anne Bernstein, Mar. 18, 1945; children—Phyllis Susan, Jill June. Intern Harlem Hosp., N.Y.C., 1942-43; pvt. dental practice, N.Y.C., 1944-56, ltd. to periodontics, West Hempstead, N.Y., 1957—; staff periodontist L.I. Jewish Med. Center; asso. prof. clin. periodontics Sch. Dental Medicine, State U. N.Y. at Stony Brook. Diplomate Am. Bd. Periodontology. Fellow Am. Coll. Dentists; mem. Am. Acad. Periodontology, Northeastern Soc. Periodontists, ADA, N.Y. State, 10th Dist. dental socs., Phi Beta Kappa. Contbr. articles profl. jours. Home and Office: 680 Howard Ave West Hempstead NY 11552

BLACHER, STANLEY PAUL, city ofcl.; b. Providence, June 5, 1926; s. Harry and Bertha (Adler) B.; A.B., Brown U., 1947; postgrad. Bryant Coll., 1947-48; m. Marcia Miriam Cohan, May 29, 1949; children—Richard Evan, John Michael. Mem. Providence Redevel. Agy., 1967—, chmn., 1972—; pres., treas., dir. Blacher Bros., Inc., Providence, 1972—, Harben Realty Co., Providence, 1962—; v.p., treas., dir. Donstan Corp., Providence, 1962—, Valley Metal Stampings, Inc., Providence, 1963—; dir. Woonasquatucket Reservoir Co., Indsl. Nat. Bank. Mem. corp. Jewish Family and Children's Service, 1968—; mem. nat. campaign cabinet Israel Bond Orgn., R.I. chmn., 1972-74; mem. nat. council Am. Jewish Joint Distbn. Com. Inc., 1975—; mem. R.I. council Nat. Jewish Hosp. and Research Center, Denver, 1974-75, trustee, 1975—. Bd. dirs. Camp Jori; bd. dirs. Jewish Fedn. R.I., mem. exec. com., 1970—, v.p., 1975—; trustee Miriam Hosp., 1971—, mem. exec. com., 1975—, chmn. med. matters com.; mem. corp. Women and Infants Hosp., 1976—; trustee Jewish Home for the Aged, 1972—, The Blacher Found.; mem. corp. Butler Hosp., 1975—; trustee Temple Emanuel, 1971—, mem. exec. com., 1976—. Served with USNR, World War II. Jewish. Clubs: Turks Head, Univ. Home: 20 Old Tannery Rd Providence RI 02906 Office: PO Box 1417 299 Carpenter St Providence RI 02901

BLACK, CAROLYN LAPP, coll. adminstr.; b. Indpls., Jan. 25, 1924; d. Harry R. and Carol H. (Crouch) Lapp; student Ohio State U., 1942-43; B.S., Skidmore Coll., 1948; M.S., Kearney State Coll., 1968; m. Roe Coddington Black, Jan. 19, 1947; children—Donna Carolyn, Avis Elizabeth, Thomas Roe, Phillip Coddington. Asst. mgr. Black Ranches, San Antonio, Tex., Aurora, Nebr., 1949-51; tchr. English, Social Studies Bradshaw (Nebr.) Sch. Dist., 1960-64, dir. guidance and counseling, 1964-69; asst. dean student affairs Pa. State U., 1969—; cons. and lectrs. in field. Chmn. swimming program Hamilton County (Nebr.) Red Cross. Served with U.S. Navy, 1944-46. Gen. Electric fellow, 1964. Mem. Pa. Coll. Personnel Assn. (pres. 1977-78), Pa. (councilman 1974-78), Montgomery County, Greater Phila. (pres. 1974-75), Am. personnel and guidance assns., Am. Coll. Personnel Assn., Nat. Assn. Women Deans and Counselors, Delta Kappa Gamma, Alpha Xi Delta. Home: 233 Kent Rd Warminster PA 18974 Office: 1600 Woodland Rd Abington PA 19001

BLACK, EDWARD BARNWELL, radiologist; b. Greenville, S.C., Jan. 8, 1944; s. Hugh Clifton and Harriet (Barnwell) B.; B.A., U. of the South, 1966; M.D., Duke U., 1970. Intern in medicine Duke U. Hosp., Durham, N.C., 1970-71; resident in diagnostic radiology Mass. Gen. Hosp., Boston, 1973-76; clin. fellow in radiology Harvard Med. Sch., Boston, 1973-76; instr. radiology, 1976—; dir. abdominal and pelvic ultrasound lab. Mass. Gen. Hosp., Boston, 1976—, asst. radiologist, 1976—. Served with USPHS, 1971-73. Diplomate Am. Bd. Radiology. Episcopalian. Home: 84 Prescott St Apt 46 Cambridge MA 02138 Office: Dept of Radiology Massachusetts General Hospital Boston MA 02114

BLACK, EUGENE CHARLTON, educator, historian; b. Boston, Dec. 15, 1927; s. Knox Charlton and Margaret Kirkley (Henely) B.; A.B., Coll. William and Mary, 1948; M.A., Harvard U., 1954, Ph.D., 1958; m. Anne Galt Kirby, Nov. 10, 1948; children—Alexander Charlton, Rebecca Galt, Andrew Gavin. Teaching fellow history and lit. Harvard U., Cambridge, Mass., 1956-58; instr. history Brandeis U., Waltham, Mass., 1958-60, asst. prof., 1960-63, asso. prof., 1963-69, prof. history, 1969-70, Leff prof. history, 1970-72, Springer prof. history, 1972—, asso. dean of faculty, 1964-65, dean Grad. Sch. Arts and Sci., 1971-72, acting dean of faculty, 1971-72, chmn. dept. history, 1970-72, 1973—; vis. prof. history Boston U., 1969; chmn. panelist, speaker profl. meetings. Mem. Wellesley (Mass.) Town Democratic Com., 1964—. Served to capt. with USAFR, 1948-53. Fellow Royal Hist. Soc.; mem. Am. Hist. Assn., Conf. on Brit. Studies, Hist. Assn. U.K., Econ. History Soc. U.K., New Eng. Hist. Assn., Bus. History Soc., Victorian Studies Group, Acad. Polit. Sci. Democrat. Episcopalian. Club: Internat. Golf. Author 5 books, and contbr. numerous articles in field to profl. jours. Home: 22 Lathrop Rd Wellesley MA 02181 Office: Dept History Brandeis U Waltham MA 02154

BLACK, IRA BARRIE, neurologist, educator; b. N.Y.C., Mar. 18, 1941; s. Samuel and Frances B.; A.B., Columbia U., 1961; M.D., Harvard, 1965; m. Janet Marie Lindquist, Sept. 26, 1969. Intern, Boston City Hosp., 1965-66; resident, 1966-67; research asso. Lab. Clin. Sci., NIMH, Bethesda, Md., 1966-70; William O. Moseley Traveling fellow Cambridge (Eng.) U., 1970-71; tchr.-investigator spl. awardee NIH, 1971-76; asst. prof. neurology Cornell U. Med. Coll., 1973-75, faculty, grad. sch. med. sci., 1973, asso. prof. neurology, dir. div. developmental neurology and lab. developmental neurology, 1975; invited mem. Hypertension Task Force, NIH, 1976; mem. med. adv. bd. Dysautonomia Found., 1977—; mem. neurology B study sect. NIH, 1977—; adv. com. on developmental neurobiology Med. Coll. Pa., 1977—; adv. com. Dysautonomia Treatment and Evaluation Center, N.Y. U. Med. Center, 1977—. Served with USPHS, 1967-70; Irma T. Hirschl Career Scientist award, 1976—. Mem. Am. Acad. Neurology (chmn. spl. course on autonomic nervous system 1977), Am. Soc. Pharmacology and Exptl. Therapeutics, Soc. Neurosci., AAAS, N.Y. Acad. Sci., N.Y. State Med. Soc., Harvey Soc. Contbr. articles, mem. editorial bd. profl. jours. Office: 515 E 71st St Cornell U Sch Medicine New York City NY 10021

BLACK, LEWIS STANLEY, lawyer; b. Wilmington, Del., June 29, 1938; s. Lewis Stanley and Pauline May (Priestley) B.; A.B., Princeton U., 1960; LL.B., Yale U., 1963; m. Kathryn Marie Robbins, July 29, 1972. Admitted to Del. bar, 1964, D.C. bar, 1965, N.Y. bar, 1966; law clk. U.S. Dist. Ct. Del., 1963-65; asso. firm Milbank, Tweed, Hadley & McCloy, N.Y.C., 1965-68; asso. firm Morris, Nichols, Arsht & Tunnell, Wilmington, Del., 1968-70, partner, 1970—; dir. Home Fed. Savs. and Loan Assn. Treas. Del. Ave. Community Assn. Mem. Am., Del., Dist. of Columbia, N.Y. bar assns. Republican. Presbyterian. Club: U. & Whist. Author numerous articles in field. Home: 2601 W 17th St Wilmington DE 19806 Office: 12th and Market Sts Wilmington DE 19899

BLACK, MARTIN MAX, physician; b. Syracuse, N.Y., July 15, 1924; s. Meyer Leon and Rose (Cohen) B.; B.A., Syracuse U., 1947; M.D., State U. N.Y., Syracuse, 1951; m. Ethel May Freeman, Dec. 19, 1948; children—Gerald, Deborah, Michael, Robert. Intern, Upstate Med. Center State U. N.Y., Syracuse, resident, 1952-55, now staff, clin. prof. medicine, 1977—; practice medicine specializing in internal medicine, Syracuse, 1955—; mem. staff Community Gen. Hosp., Syracuse, 1963—, dir. medicine, 1970—; mem. staff VA Hosp., St. Joseph's Hosp., Syracuse; Bd. dirs. Heart Assn. Upstate N.Y., Health Services Assn. Served with USAAF, 1943-46. Diplomate Am. Bd. Internal Medicine. Fellow Am. Coll. Cardiology, A.C.P., mem. Am. Soc. Internal Medicine, Am. Heart Assn., AMA, Med. Soc. State N.Y., Onondaga County (N.Y.) Med. Soc. Jewish. Home: 5191 Winterton Dr Fayetteville NY 13066 Office: Physicians Office Bldg Broad Rd Syracuse NY 13215

BLACK, PERRY, neurosurgeon; b. Montreal, Que., Can., Oct. 2, 1930; s. Ovido and Rose (Vasilevsky) B.; B.Sc., McGill U., 1951, M.D., C.M., 1956; m. Phyllis Naomi Rubin, June 2, 1963; children—Daniel Ovid, Julie Miriam, Amy Rose. Came to U.S., 1959. Intern, asst. resident medicine and gen. surgery Jewish Gen. Hosp., Montreal, 1956-58; asst. resident neurology Montreal Neurol. Inst., 1958-59; resident neurosurgery Johns Hopkins Hosp., 1959-63, neurosurgeon, 1964—, dir. child head injury project, dept. neurol. surgery, 1963-70; NIH fellow physiology Johns Hopkins Sch. Medicine, 1961-62, mem. faculty, 1964—, asso. prof. neurol. surgery, 1969—, asso. prof. psychiatry, 1970—; dir. lab. neurol. scis. Friends Med. Sci. Research Center, Balt., 1964—, chmn. central research authority, 1972—; vis. neurosurgeon Balt. City Hosps., 1965—; neurosurg. cons. Good Samaritan Hosp., Balt., 1970—, North Charles Gen. Hosp., Balt., 1975—. Mem. neurology A study sect. NIH, 1973-77; mem. com. fifty Epilepsy Found. Am., 1970-75; bd. dirs. Epilepsy Assn. Central Md., 1966-77, chmn. profl. advisory bd., 1973-75. Recipient resident's paper award So. Neurosurg. Soc., 1963. Diplomate Am. Bd. Neurol. Surgery. Mem. Congress Neurol. Surgeons (exec. com. 1972-75, editor newsletter 1972-75, chmn. sci. program com. 1971-72, chmn. internat. com. 1975-79, mem. nominating com. 1975-77, Distinguished Service award 1977), Am. Assn. Neurol. Surgeons (chmn. ad hoc com. Rev. Joint Commn. Accreditation Manual for Hosps. 1973), Internat. Assn. Study Pain, AAUP, Internat. Soc. Research Stereoencephalatomy, Soc. Neurosci., Pavlovian Soc. N.Am., Research Soc. Neurol. Surgeons, Am. Epilepsy Soc., Am. Neurol. Assn., Internat. Neurosurg. Forum. Editor: Drugs and The Brain, 1969; Physiological Correlates of Emotion, 1970; asso. editor Neurosurgery, 1976—, internat. editor, 1976—. Contbr. to profl. jours. Home: 5600 Greenspring Ave Baltimore MD 21209 Office: Dept Neurosurgery Johns Hopkins Hosp Baltimore MD 21205

BLACK, RICHARD THOMAS, constrn. co. exec.; b. Passaic, N.J., Oct. 25, 1937; s. Raymond and Alice (Brandreth) B.; B.S., Fairleigh Dickinson U., 1961; M.B.A., Seton Hall U., 1964; postgrad. N.Y. U., 1975-78; m. Patricia Ann Kelly, Jan. 22, 1961; children—Kathleen Marie, Sheila Ann. Systems analyst, asst. to chief accountant Chubb & Son, Inc., Short Hills, N.J., 1961-67; mgr. gen. accounting RCA Records, Rockaway, N.J., 1967-72; chief fin. officer Halecrest Co., Edison, N.J., 1972-74; mgr. project and field accounting Chemico Air Pollution Control Co. div. Envirotech Corp., 1974-75, dir. accounting ops., 1975—. Asso. dir., bus. mgr. 10th Ann. North Jersey Bus. Show, 1969-70. Treas. Hackettstown (N.J.) Recreation Commn., 1971-72; dist. chmn. Hackettstown Community Hosp. Fund Drive, 1968; trustee Colonial Musketeers Fife and Drum Corps, 1977—. Recipient Jaycee of Year and Key Man awards Hackettstown Jaycees, 1968-69. Mem. Nat. Assn. Accountants, Hackettstown Area Jaycees (chmn. bd. 1970-71, pres. 1969-70, dir. 1965-71). Home: 123 College View Dr Hackettstown NJ 07840 Office: 1 Penn Plaza New York City NY 10001

BLACK, ROBERT ATTICKS, JR., policy analyst, polit. scientist; b. Charleston, S.C., Feb. 20, 1942; s. Robert Attick and Margarette MacRae Whitaker (de Saussure) B.; B.S., U.S. Naval Acad., 1963; certificate with honors, Def. Lang. Inst., 1967; postgrad. George

Washington U., 1969, Am. U., 1969; M.A., Columbia, 1974, certificate, 1975, M.Phil., 1976, Ph.D., 1977. Apptd. midshipman U.S. Navy, 1959, advanced through ranks to capt., USMC, 1966; mem. Belgian Navy Exchange Program, 1962; exec. officer Mar Det U.S.S. Randolph, 1964-65; platoon and co. comdr. 2d Marines, 1965-66; logistics officer, logistics support unit comdr. Caribbean Ready Force, 1966-67; hdqrs. commdt., intelligence officer, co. comdr. 1st Marines, Vietnam, 1967-68; spl. projects officer manpower div. Hdqrs. USMC, Washington, 1968-69; ret., 1969; instr. Columbia, 1970-71, asst. to dir. and asso. dean, cons. Internat. Fellows Program, 1971-74; asst. to dir., research asso., cons. Inst. Western Europe, N.Y.C., 1974—; instr. U. Montreal, 1975; project asso., cons. Conf. Bd., 1976-78; dir. programs Council on Learning, 1978—; cons. spl. acad. programs and mil. programs and studies; interpreter, translator; research analyst energy and environ. affairs. Pres. N.Y. region Concerned Acad. Grads, 1970-72, Op Sail, 1964, 76. Decorated Silver Star, Cross of Gallantry; Internat. fellow, 1970-71; Herbert Lehman fellow, 1970-74; recipient Inst. Western Europe research grant, 1974, 75, Am. Legion edn. award, 1959. Mem. Internat., Am. polit. sci. assns., Policy Studies Orgn., Internat. Studies Assn., Viet Studies Group, Am. Soc. Internat. Law, Am. Acad. Polit. and Social Scis., UN Assn. U.S.A., UN Assn. of N.Y. (dir.), Scientists Inst. Pub. Info., U.S. Naval Inst., U.S. MarCor Assn., Nat. Geog. Soc., Nat. Wildlife Fedn., Nat. Trust Hist. Preservation, Friends of the Hermitage, Preservation Soc. Charleston, U.S. Naval Acad. Alumni Assn., Naval Acad. Athletic Assn., Soc. Internat. Fellows, Soc. Colonial Wars, Huguenot Soc. Episcopalian. Author: (with others) Multinationals in Contention: Responses at Governmental and International Levels. Contbr. articles to profl. jours., chpts. to books. Md. 3-weapon fencing champion, 1963, foil champion, 1963. Office: 1305 IAB 420 W 118th St New York City NY 10027 also Council on Learning NBW Tower New Rochelle NY 10801

BLACK, WILLIAM, philanthropist, restaurant exec.; b. Bklyn.; grad. Columbia, 1926, L.H.D. (hon.), 1967; m. Jean Martin, 1951 (div. 1962); 1 dau. Melinda; m. 2d, Page Morton, Mar. 27, 1962. Checker, Washington Market; retail mcht. shelled nuts, N.Y.C.; organizer chain of stores Chock Full O' Nuts, N.Y.C., converted to restaurants, past pres., chmn. bd., chief exec. officer; also owner coffee producing firm. Founder Parkinson's Disease Found., 1957; bd. dirs. New Rochelle Hosp; founder Page & William Black Postgrad. Sch. Medicine at Mount Sinai Hosp., William Black Hall of Nursing at Lenox Hill Hosp., William Black Med. Research Bldg. at Columbia-Presbyn. Med. Center. Home: Premium Point New Rochelle NY 10802 Office: 425 Lexington Ave New York City NY 10017

BLACK, WILLIAM FISHER, govt. ofcl.; b. Mt. Vernon, N.Y., Mar. 15, 1937; s. William Richard and Emma Florence (Fisher) B.; B.M.E., Cornell U., 1957; B.S.B.A., N.Y. U., 1960, M.B.A., 1962; grad. Fed. Exec. Inst., Charlottesville, Va., 1974; m. Jacquelyn G. Furman, June 19, 1976. Mem. lab. staff Bell Telephone Labs., N.Y.C., 1960-61; asst. chief packaging engr. Chesebrough-Ponds Co., N.Y.C., 1961-63; tech. asst. to dir. and chief insp. Bur. Explosives, Assn. Am. R.R.'s, N.Y.C., 1963-68; transp. safety cons. Dept. Transp., Washington, 1968-69, chief div. hazardous materials, 1969—; cons. fire sci. tng. Mem. Cornell Soc. Engrs., Fed. Exec. Inst. Alumni Assn., Nat. Fire Protection Assn., Cousteau Assn., Va. Jaycees (v.p. 1971-72). Episcopalian. Clubs: Masons (Mamaroneck, N.Y.): K.T. (White Plains, N.Y.). Home: 4012 N 35th St Arlington VA 22207 Office: 2100 Second St SW Washington DC 20590

BLACK, YUILL, allergist; b. Falkirk, Scotland, Aug. 15, 1928; s. Samuel and Mary (Martin) B.: came to U.S., 1951, naturalized, 1954; M.B., Ch.B., U. Glasgow (Scotland), 1960; m. Michele Black; children—Jeffrey, Stephen, Laura, John. Resident Bismarck Hosp., 1961-62, United Mineworkers Hosp., 1962-63; practice medicine, specializing in allergy, Washington, 1965—; staff Doctors Hosp., Washington, Arlington (Va.) Hosp.; instr. Georgetown U. Med. Sch., Washington, 1967-69. Served with U.S. Army, 1954-56. Recipient Burns prize in internal medicine U. Glasgow Med. Sch., 1957; Henry Ford Hosp. fellow, 1964-65; Am. Acad. Allergy grantee, 1965. Fellow Am. Acad. Allergy, Am. Assn. Clin. Immunology and Allergy; mem. AMA, D.C. Med. Soc. Office: 916 19th St NW Washington DC 20006

BLACKBURN, BENJAMIN COLEMAN, botanist; b. Ridgeway, N.Y., May 2, 1908; s. Jay Earl and Maud Scott (Coleman) B.; B.S., Cornell, 1929; Ph.D., Rutgers U., 1949. Landscape plantsman, Locust Valley and Sterlington, N.Y., 1930-35; instr., specialist, landscape gardening Rutgers U., New Brunswick, N.J., 1936-42, adminstr. Willowwood Arboretum, Gladstone, N.J., 1972—; adj. prof. botany Drew U., Madison, N.J., 1949-72, prof. emeritus, 1972—. Bd. dirs. Willowwood Found., 1960—. Served with AUS, 1942-46. Mem. Internat. Dendrology Soc., Internat. Assn. Plant Taxonomy, Royal Hort. Soc. (London), Hort. Soc. N.Y., N.J. Acad. Sci., Sigma Xi. Author: Your Garden This Week, 1939, Trees and Shrubs of New Jersey, 1949, Trees and Shrubs in Eastern North America, 1952. Home: Box 125 Gladstone NJ 07934 Office: Willowwood Arboretum of Rutgers U Hacklebarney Rd Gladstone NJ 07934

BLACKBURN, GEORGE L., surgeon; b. McPherson, Kans., Feb. 12, 1936; s. George Ralph and Betty (Warrick) B.; B.A., U. Kans., 1958, M.D., 1965; Ph.D. (NIH fellow), Mass. Inst. Tech., 1973, m. Kathleen Mary Hunt, Jan. 14, 1973; children by previous marriage—David George, Amy Lee, Mathew Russell. Intern, Boston City Hosp., 1965-66, resident in surgery, 1966-70; fellow in surgery Harvard Med. Sch., Boston, 1966-70, instr. surgery, 1971-72; practice medicine, specializing in surgery, Boston, 1971—; asst. vis. surgeon Boston City Hosp., 1971-73, dir. Office of Alimentation, 1972-75, staff surgeon, 1973-75; investigator Gen. Clin. Research Center, Mass. Inst. Tech., Cambridge, 1971-73, research asso., dept. nutrition, 1973-77, lectr., 1977—; asso. surgeon New Eng. Deaconess Hosp., Boston, 1972-75, staff surgeon, 1975—, dir. hyperalimentation service, 1973—, mem. Cancer Research Inst., 1973-75, mem. Cancer Research Inst., 1976—; dir. liver div. Sears Surg. Research Lab., Boston, 1972—; cons. surgeon Falmouth (Mass.) Hosp., 1973—; asst. prof. surgery Harvard Med. Sch., Boston, 1973-75, asso. prof., 1975—. Served to lt. USN, 1958-61. Mem. Mass. Cancer Soc., N.Y. Acad. Scis., Mass. Med. Soc., Am. Fedn. Clin. Research, A.C.S., Am. Soc. Parenteral and Enteral Nutrition (pres.), Assn. Acad. Surgeons, Soc. Alimentary Tract Surgeons, Soc. Trauma Surgeons, Am. Inst. Nutrition, Alpha Omega Alpha. Contbr. articles to profl. jours. Home: 100 Memorial Dr Cambridge MA 02142 Office: 110 Francis St Boston MA 02215

BLACKBURN, MARGARET IRWIN, violist, ret. educator; b. McKeesport, Pa., July 18, 1908; d. James Power and Emma Claire (Menk) B.; A.B., Wellesley Coll., 1930; M.A., Carnegie Mellon U., 1935; postgrad. Dalcroze Inst., 1935-37, Juilliard Sch., 1936-38, Columbia U., 1937-39, U. Geneva (Switzerland), 1959, Mozarteum, Salzburg, Austria, 1967. Tchr. music dept. Pitts. Pub. Schs., 1947-71, ret., 1971; violist McKeesport Symphony Orch., 1959—; mem. chamber music groups, Pitts. Area; composer Sigma Alpha Iota Nat. Hymn, 1939. Mem. Pitts. Tuesday Mus. Club, Sigma Alpha Iota. Republican. Presbyterian. Home: 1905 Jenny Lind Ave McKeesport PA 15132

BLACKEY, EDWIN ARTHUR, JR., geologist; b. Tamworth, N.H., Oct. 19, 1927; s. Edwin Arthur and Flora (Whipple) B.; B.S., U. N.H., 1951; postgrad. Worcester (Mass.) Poly. Inst., 1955-56; m. Patricia Ann Matthews, Jan. 22, 1955; children—Mark Edwin, Janet Angove. Geologist, NE Div Corps Engrs., Waltham, Mass., 1951-72, div. geologist, 1972—. Chmn. Hist. Dists Commn. Sudbury (Mass.); trustee Sudbury Hist. Soc.; mem. Earth Removal Bd. Sudbury; past pres. Sudbury Jr. Ski Program. Served with U.S. Army, 1946-47. Certified geologist, Maine. Mem. Assn. Engring. Geologists (nat. chmn. bldg. codes com., dir. New Eng. sect.), Am. Geologic Inst. Episcopalian. Club: U.S. Eastern Ski. Contbr. articles in field to profl. jours. Home: 62 King Philip Rd Sudbury MA 01776 Office: US Army Corps Engrs Trapelo Rd Waltham MA 02154

BLACKHAM, ANN ROSEMARY (MRS. JAMES W. BLACKHAM, JR.), realtor; b. N.Y.C., June 16, 1927; d. Frederick Alfred and Letitia L. (Stolfe) DeCain; A.B., Ohio Dominican Coll., 1949; M.A., Ohio State U., 1950; m. James W. Blackham, Jr., Aug. 18, 1951; children—Ann C., James W. III. Mgr. br. store Filene & Sons, Winchester, 1950-52; broker Porter Co., real estate, Winchester, 1961-66; sales mgr. James T. Trefrey, Inc., Winchester, 1966-68; pres., founder Ann Blackham & Co., Inc., realtors, Winchester, Mass., 1969—; corporator, trustee Charlestown Savs. Bank; mem. bd. econ. advisers to gov., 1969-74; participant White House Conf. on Internat. Cooperation, 1965; mem. Presdl. Task Force on Women's Rights and Responsibilities, 1969; mem. exec. council Mass. Civil Def., 1965-69; chmn. Gov.'s Commn. on Status of Women, 1971-75; mem. adv. commn. Dept. Def., 1977—; pres. Scholarship Found., 1977—; regional dir. Interstate Assn. Commn. on Status of Women, 1971-74; mem. Gov. Task Force on Mass. Economy, 1972; mem. regional selection panel White House fellow; mem. Ad Hoc. Judicial Selection Com. Pres. Mass. Fedn. Republican Women, 1964-69; sec. Nat. Fedn. Rep. Women, 1967-71, 2d v.p., 1972-78; New Eng. regional dir., 1967-78; pres. Women's Rep. Club Winchester, 1960-62; dep. chmn. Mass. Rep. State Com., 1965-66; sec. Mass. Rep. State Conv., 1970, del., 1960, 62, 64, 66, 68, 70, 74; state vice chmn. Mass. Rep. Finance Com., 1970; alt. del. at large Rep. Nat. Conv., 1968, 72. Recipient Pub. Service award Commonwealth Mass., 1969, 78, Merit award Rep. Party, 1969, Pub. Affairs award Mass. Fedn. Women's Clubs, 1975; named Civic Leader of Yr. Mass. Broadcasters, 1962. Mem. Greater Boston Real Estate Bd. (dir.), Mass. Assn. Real Estate Bds., Nat. Assn. Realtors (women's council), Mass. Assn. Realtors (dir., Million Dollar Club), Brokers Inst., Doric Dames (2d v.p. 1971-74). Clubs: Capitol Hill (Washington); Winchester Boat, Winchester Country. Home: 40 Wedgemere Ave Winchester MA 01890 Office: 11 Thompson St Winchester MA 01890

BLACKMUN, HARRY ANDREW, asso. justice U.S. Supreme Ct.; b. Nashville, Ill., Nov. 12, 1908; s. Corwin Manning and Theo H. (Reuter) B.; B.A. summa cum laude, Harvard U., 1929, LL.B., 1932; numerous hon. degrees; m. Dorothy E. Clark, June 21, 1941; children—Nancy Clark, Sally Ann, Susan Manning. Admitted to Minn. bar, 1932; law clk. for John B. Sanborn, judge 8th circuit, U.S. Ct. of Appeals, St. Paul, 1932-33; asso. Dorsey, Colman, Barker, Scott & Barber, Mpls., 1934-38, jr. partner, 1939-42, gen. partner, 1943-50; instr. St. Paul Coll. Law, 1935-41, U. Minn. Law Sch., 1945-47; resident counsel Mayo Clinic, Mayo Assn., Rochester, 1950-59, mem. sect. adminstrn., 1950-59; judge 8th Circuit, U.S. Ct. of Appeals, 1959-70; asso. justice U.S. Supreme Ct., 1970—. Rep. jud. br. Nat. Hist. Publs. and Records Commn.; adv. com. on jud. activities Jud. Conf.; mem. faculty Salzburg Seminar in Am. Studies (Law), 1977. Mem. bd. members Mayo Assn. Rochester, 1953-60; bd. dirs. mem. exec. com. Rochester Meth. Hosp., 1954-70; trustee Hamline Univ., St. Paul, 1964-70, William Mitchell Coll. Law, St. Paul, 1959-74. Mem. Am., Minn., Olmsted County, 3d Jud. Dist. bar assns., Phi Beta Kappa. Contbr. profl. articles legal, med. jours. Office: Supreme Ct US Washington DC 20543

BLAI, BORIS, educator; b. Rovno, Russia, July 24, 1897; s. Michael and Esther (Anatopole) B.; grad. Imperial Acad. Fine Arts, Kieve, Russia, 1911, Imperial Acad. Fine Arts, Leningrad, Russia, 1913; student Ecole des Beaux Arts, Paris, 1913-15; studied under Rodin; LL.D., Glassboro State Coll., 1975; m. Manya Gorenko. Mar. 29, 1921 (dec. 1961); 1 son, Boris; m. 2d, Bertha Rosenberg, Apr. 14, 1965; children—Ruth Leventhal, Anita Simon. Came to U.S., 1917, naturalized, 1931. One man show Grand Central Galleries, N.Y.C., 1934; exhibited in group shows, including 1st Open air show Rittenhouse S., Phila., 1928, 30, Ann. Show Acad. Fine Arts, Pa., 1924, Chgo., Art Inst., 1934; exhibited in Europe; asso. with R. Tait McKenzie in work Canadian Meml., Edinburgh, Scotland, Statue of Gen. Wolfe, London; represented in permanent collections Phila. Art Mus., Temple U., Fla. So. Coll., Lakeland, Rosenwald Collection, also many pvt. collections. Dir. art Oak Lane County Day Sch., 1927-34; founder, also dean Stella Elkins Tyler Sch. Fine Arts, Temple U., 1934-60, dean emeritus, 1960—; founder, hon. pres. Found. Arts and Scis., Long Beach Island, N.J., 1947—; founder, dir. Boris Blai Coll. Contemporary Art, Forked River, N.J., 1966-72; dean duCret Sch. Art, Plainfield, N.J., 1969—; founder Blai Sch. Fine Arts, Melrose Park, Pa., 1972—; artist-in-residence Glassboro (N.J.) State Coll., 1973-76. Trustee Harcum Jr. Coll., Bryn Mawr, Pa., Delaware Valley Coll., Doylestown, Pa. D.F.A., Fla. So. Coll., 1950. Recipient Page One award Newspaper Guild Greater Phila., 1960, Phila. Art Alliance medal, 1960, Samuel S. Fels medal Fels Found., 1962. Mem. Phila. Art Alliance, Acad. Fine Arts, Phila., Grand Central Galleries, N.Y. Home: 4th and High Ave Melrose Park PA 19126 Office: Tyler Sch Fine Arts Temple U Beech and Penrose Ave Elkins Park PA 19126

BLAIR, BENJAMIN FRANKLIN, JR., engr. and constrn. cons.; b. Bryn Mawr, Pa., Dec. 22, 1942; s. Benjamin Franklin and Ann Redman (Willits) B.; B.Civil Engring., Union Coll., 1966; M.S. in Civil Engring., Northwestern U., 1972; m. Gail Wheaton Starr, Sept. 12, 1964; children—Megan Starr, Benjamin Webster. Project engr. John G. Reutter Assoc., Camden, N.J., 1966-73; mgr. environmental engring. dept. John G. Reutter Assoc., Camden, 1973-75; dir. project mgmt. div., 1975-77; dir. engring. Hill Internat., Inc., Willingboro, N.J., 1977—; dir. John G. Reutter Assos., Camden, 1977; coadj. instr. Rutgers U., New Brunswick, N.J., 1973—; lectr. Center for Profl. Advancement, E. Brunswick, N.J., 1978—. Mem., Haddonfield (N.J.) Citizens Adv. Task Force on Sewer Regionalization, 1975, mem. site plan review com. Haddonfield Planning Bd., 1977—; treas. bd. trustees Haddonfield Friends Sch., 1975—. Fed. Water Quality Adminstrn. research grantee, 1970-72; diplomate Am. Acad. Environ. Engrs. Mem. ASCE (pres. S.J. br. 1977-78), Water Pollution Control Fedn., Nat. Soc. Profl. Engrs., Sigma Xi. Office: Garden Plaza Bldg Willingboro NJ 08046

BLAIR, DAVID WILLIAM, mech. engr.; b. Santa Barbara, Calif., Oct. 5, 1929; s. David Sutherland and Norah Irene (Higgins) B.; B.S., Oreg. State Coll., 1952; M.S., Columbia, 1954, Ph.D., 1961; m. Rosemary Constance Miles, Jan. 30, 1954; children—Karen E., Barbara A., M. Maria, Amanda M., David B., Rachel P. Instr. mech. engring. Columbia, 1954-58, 59; research asso. aero. engring. Princeton, 1958-61; research engr. AeroChem. Research Labs., Princeton, N.J., 1961-62; asso. prof. mech. engring. Poly. Inst. Bklyn., 1963-69; sr. research engr. Exxon Research and Engring. Co., Linden, N.J., 1969-74, engring. asso., 1974—; instr. mech. engring. Stevens Inst. Tech., 1961-63, 69-70; adj. asso. prof. mech. engring. Columbia, 1975—. Committeeman, Princeton Twp., 1976—. Royal Norwegian Inst. Indsl. and Sci. Research postdoctoral fellow, 1962-63. Mem. Am. Phys. Soc., ASME, Combustion Inst., Sigma Xi, Pi Mu Epsilon, Tau Beta Pi, Sigma Tau, Pi Tau Sigma, Phi Kappa Phi. Author chpt. in book. Home: 1108 Princeton-Kingston Rd Princeton NJ 08540 Office: PO Box 45 Linden NJ 07036

BLAIR, EDWARD JOSEPH, clothing mfg. co. exec.; b. Balt., Aug. 25, 1944; s. Charles Ignasius and Gladys Virginia (Pitcher) B.; student Loyola Coll., Balt., 1963-65; B.A., U. Balt., 1968; A.A., Essex Community Coll., 1975; m. Jeanne Marie Kilroy, Nov. 28, 1964; children—Karen Janine, Janine Marie, Melissa Denise. Asst. mgr. warehouse L. Grief Co., Balt., 1963-64, mgr., 1964-66, indsl. engr., 1966-68, prodn. mgr. Verona plant, 1968-71; asst. plant mgr. Webster Clothes, Balt., 1972-74; mgr. central distbn. and warehouse Joseph A. Bank Clothiers Inc., Balt., 1974-75, plant and mfg. mgr., 1976-79, v.p. mfg., 1979—; cons. indsl. engring. Mem. Towson (Md.) Recreation Council, 1977—; bd. dirs. Stone Oaks Condominium Assn. Mem. Am. Inst. Indsl. Engrs. Clubs: Green Spring Racquet, U. Balt. Bee, Loyola Alumni, Downtown Racquet. Office: Joseph A Bank Clothiers Inc 123 Market Pl Baltimore MD 21202

BLAIR, JAMES WALTER, JR., specialty metals co. exec.; b. Douglas, Ariz., Mar. 26, 1936; s. James Walter and Edithe Ann (Watson) B.; M.E., U. Ariz., 1959; m. Jeanne Daily, Aug. 30, 1958; 1 son, James Walter III. With Gen. Electric Co., San Jose, Calif. and Schenectady, 1959-73; pres. Handy & Harman Tube Co., Norristown, Pa., 1973-76, group v.p. Handy & Harman, N.Y.C., 1976—. Mem. Am. Mgmt. Assn. Republican. Presbyterian. Clubs: Mason (Lynn, Mass.); Shriners (San Francisco). Home: 77 Greenhaven Rd Rye NY 10580 Office: 850 3d Ave New York City NY 10022

BLAIR, JOHN AITKEN, plastics co. exec.; b. Birmingham, Ala., Nov. 21, 1927; s. Robert Swan and May (Aitken) B.; B.S. in Chem. Engring., U. Auburn, 1951; postgrad. U. Del., 1960-61; m. Irene Hagood, Dec. 15, 1948; children—John Aitken, Judith Ann, Steven Swan, Robert Swan. With E.I. duPont de Nemours & Co., Wilmington, Del., 1951—, area supr., film dept., 1966-67, quality control supr., film, 1967-68, cons. plastics, 1968-72, sr. cons. plastics, 1972-76, mgr. standards programs, 1976—; tchr. extension courses U. Del. Mem. adv. bd. Underwriters Lab.; chmn. furniture com. Nat. Fire Protection Assn., 1973—. Active Boy Scouts Am., 1950-68. Served with USNR, 1946-47. Mem. Am. Inst. Chem. Engrs., ASTM, Nat. Fire Protection Assn., Internat. Standards Orgn., Soc. Plastics Industry (chmn. coordinating com. on consumer safety), Soc. Plastics Engrs. Club: DuPont Country. Contbr. articles to profl. jours. Office: 1007 Market St Wilmington DE 19898

BLAIR, MCCLELLAN GORDON, new bus. ventures co. exec.; b. Pitts., Oct. 20, 1938; s. David Hall and Elinor (Gordon) B.; B.S., Yale U., 1960; M.A., U. Rochester, 1962, Ph.D., 1967; m. Britta Louise Nesbitt, Aug. 26, 1960; children—Elizabeth Hall, Christina Reinhardt, Janet Nesbitt, James Gordon. Scientist, Nuclear Materials and Equipment Corp., Apollo, Pa., 1967-69, sr. scientist, 1970-71; artificial heart project mgr. Arco Nuclear Co., Leechburg, Pa., 1971-75, chmn. radiation com., nuclear pacemaker product mgr. Arco Med. Products Co., 1976, asst. to v.p. new products, ventures, Pitts., 1977—. Pres., White Twp. Community Assn., 1970-72; del. tech. trade seminar U.S. Dept. Commerce to Poland, Czechoslovakia, Hungary, 1977; scoutmaster Boy Scouts Am., 1968-73, recipient Scouter's Key award, 1972. Nat. Heart and Lung Inst. devel. grantee, 1970-73. Mem. Am. Phys. Soc., Assn. Advancement Med. Instrumentation, Am. Soc. Artificial Organs, Am. Philatelic Soc., Bur. Issues Assn., Antique Automobile Club Am., Buick Club Am. Patentee in fields med. devices, solar energy. Home: 3000 Warren Rd Indiana PA 15701 Office: Suite 101 1000 RIDC Plaza Pittsburgh PA 15238

BLAKE, ALFRED GREENE, mining co. exec.; b. Pitts., June 22, 1902; s. William F. and Blanche (Johnson) B.; C.E., Lehigh U., 1925; spl. student U. Pa., 1933-34; m. Mildred I. Cordeaux, July 27, 1929; children—Johnson C., Phyllis I. Spl. rep. Standard Sanitary Mfg. Co., Pitts., 1925-32; mgr. dealer div. Phila. Gas Works Co., 1932-37; mgr. Eastern operations Ruud Mfg. Co., Pitts., 1937-45; partner Rogers & Slade, mgmt. cons., N.Y.C., 1945-50; v.p. Edgar Bros. Co., Metuchen, N.J., 1950-54, merged with 4 other cos. to form Minerals & Chems. Corp. of Am., exec. v.p., dir., mem. exec. com., 1954-60; exec. v.p., dir., mem. exec. com. Minerals & Chems. Philipp Corp., 1960-64, pres., chief exec. officer Minerals & Chems. div., 1964-67, co. merged with Engelhard Industries to form Engelhard Minerals & Chems. Corp. 1967; exec. v.p., dir., mem. exec. com. Engelhard Minerals & Chems. Corp., 1967-71, chmn. bd., mem. exec. com., 1971-75, mem. exec. com., dir., 1967-76, dir. emeritus, 1976—; pres. minerals and chems. div., 1967-69, chmn. div., 1969-71; v.p. Porocel Corp., 1954-67, pres., 1967-70, chmn. 1970-75, dir., 1954-76; v.p. Chemstone Corp., 1955-67, pres., 1967-70, chmn., 1970-75, dir., 1955-76; v.p. Cuyahoga Lime Co., 1955-67, pres., 1967-70, chmn., 1970-75, dir., 1955-76; pres. Eastern Magnesia Talc Co., 1967-70, chmn., 1970-75, dir., 1967-76; dir. Commonwealth Bank of Metuchen. Dir. operations U.S. Govt. Tng. Within Industry div. War Manpower Commn., 1942-45; trustee Lehigh U., N.J. Coll. Fund Assn.; bd. dirs. Syracuse Pulp and Paper Found., pres., 1970-71. Mem. Lehigh U. Alumni Assn. (pres., dir., exec. com. 1969-70), TAPPI. Clubs: Masons, Union League (N.Y.C.); Baltusrol (N.J.) Golf; Saucon Valley (Pa.) Country; Lauderdale Yacht (Fla.). Home: 970 Glenway Ave Plainfield NJ 07060 Office: Engelhard Minerals & Chems Corp Menlo Park Edison NJ 08817

BLAKE, RICHARD DOUGLAS, biochemist; b. Greenfield, Mass., Sept. 24, 1932; s. Charles Samuel and Vena Beatrice Blake; B.S., Tufts Coll., 1958; postgrad. Harvard U., 1958-60; M.S., Rutgers U., 1963; Ph.D., Princeton U., 1967; m. Jeanne Marie Mango, Aug. 16, 1958; children—Hannah Elizabeth, Jonathan Dresser. Research asst. Harvard U., Cambridge, Mass., 1958-60; research asso. Princeton (N.J.) U., 1967-68, mem. research staff, 1968-73; asst. prof. biochemistry U. Maine, Orono, 1973-77, asso. prof., 1977—; dir. Worthington Biochem. Corp., Freehold, N.J., 1968-77. Served with USAF, 1950-54. HIH research grantee, 1975-79. Mem. Biophys. Soc., Am. Soc. Biol. Chemists, Sigma Xi. Contbr. articles in field to profl. jours. Home: 540 College Ave Orono ME 04473 Office: Dept Biochemistry U Maine Orono ME 04473

BLAKELY, ALLISON, historian; b. Clinton, Ala., Mar. 31, 1940; s. Ed Walton and Alice B.; student Oreg. State U., 1958-60; A.B. with honors in History, U. Oreg., 1962; M.A. (Woodrow Wilson fellow), U. Calif., Berkeley, 1964, Ph.D. in Russian History, 1971; m. Shirley Ann Reynolds, July 5, 1968; children—Shantel Lynn, Andrei. Research asst., teaching asst. U. Calif., Berkeley, 1965, 68, 69; instr. European history Stanford (Calif.) U., 1970-71; asso. prof. modern European history, dir. grad. program dept. history Howard U., Washington, 1971—; reader advanced placement exams. Ednl. Testing Service, Princeton, N.J. Mem. Sligo Park Hills Civic Assn., N.Chevy Chase PTA. Served to capt. U.S. Army, 1966-68. Decorated Bronze Star, Purple Heart; Andrew Mellon fellow in Humanities, Aspen Inst., 1976-77. Mem. Am. Hist. Assn., Am. Assn. Advancement of Slavic Studies, Assn. Study of Afro-Am. Life and History, Phi Beta Kappa. Democrat. Unitarian. Contbr. articles on

Russian history to Jour. Negro History and 2 vols. on Russian history. Home: 8 Belmont Ct Silver Spring MD 20910 Office: Dept History Howard U Washington DC 20059

BLAKELY, JAMES RUSSELL, pub. co. exec., fin. editor; b. Princeton, Ind., Mar. 21, 1935; s. Russell Harold and Mildred Mae (Newman) B.; B.A., U. Ill., 1957, postgrad. in law, 1957-58; m. Martha Marelen Mitchell, Aug. 31, 1968; children—Karen Holmes, Thomas Howard. Reporter, Champaign (Ill.) News-Gazette, 1964-65; feature writer Sunday mag. Chgo. American, 1965-67; consumer affairs editor Rochester (N.Y.) Democrat and Chronicle, 1967-72; asst. editor Consumer Reports Mag., Mt. Vernon, N.Y., 1972-74; mng. editor Gold & Silver Newsletter, New Rochelle, N.Y., 1974-76; editor/pub. Silver & Gold Report, Newtown, Conn., 1976—; pres., treas. Precious Metals Report, Inc., Newtown, 1976—. Served with AUS, 1958-59. Mem. Soc. Profl. Journalists, Phi Alpha Theta, Theta Delta Chi. Club: Nat. Press. Home: Old Green Rd Sandy Hook CT 06482 Office: PO Box 325 Newtown CT 06470

BLAKEMAN, THOMAS LEDYARD, ret. regional planner; b. Melville, Mont., Dec. 24, 1909; s. Thomas Greenleaf and Charlotte Phillips (VanCleve) B.; B.Arch. in City Planning, Mass. Inst. Tech., 1936; m. Virginia Downie Davidson, Sept. 15, 1934; children—Virginia Leal, Beatrice Bruce, Phillip VanCleve, Hannah Hall. Planner, City of Richmond (Va.), 1937-40; planner State of N.J., 1941-48; dir. Detroit Regional Planning Commn., 1948-56; planning advisor State of Conn., N.J. Dept. Econ. Devel. and Dept. Agr., also Office Gov. N.Y. State, 1956-72; lectr. state and regional planning Sch. Pub. Adminstrn. N.Y. U., 1959-69. Mem. Am. Inst. Planners, Am. Soc. Planning Ofcls. Democrat. Episcopalian. Home: Box 264 Cataumet MA 02534

BLANCHARD, BERTIE JOSEPH, bldg. contractor; b. N.S., Can., Aug. 5, 1914; s. John J. and Mary (Burns) B.; student Wentworth Coll., 1935-36, Boston U., 1938; m. Dorothy M. McAuliffe, June 17, 1946; children—John G., Susan M. Came to U.S., 1924, naturalized, 1932. With J.J. Blanchard Sons, East Weymouth, Mass., 1936—, owner, 1945—; pres. Blan Fitz Corp. Boston, 1965; treas. M & B Realty, Weymouth, 1967—; chmn. Weymouth Housing Authority, 1968—, treas., 1964; treas. Bamby Realty Trust, 1972. Served with USNR, 1942-45. Kiwanian. Home: 100 Mt Vernon St W East Weymouth MA 02189

BLANCHARD, BRUCE, govt. ofcl.; b. Ft. Stotsenburg, Philippines, Dec. 26, 1932; s. Wendell and Marcelia (Palmer) B.; S.B. in Civil Engring., Mass. Inst. Tech., 1957, S.M. in Civil Engring., 1964; children—Wendell, Laura, Renee. Teaching and research asst. Mass. Inst. Tech., 1957-59; hydraulic engr. Bur. Reclamation, Dept. Interior, Denver, 1959-60, 60-61, water resources planning engr., Phoenix, 1961-66; sr. staff specialist Water Resources Council, Washington, 1966-69; environ. specialist Office of Sec. Dept. Interior, Washington, 1970-71, dir. Office Environ. Project Rev., 1971—. Served with U.S. Army, 1951-53, 60; lt. Ariz. N.G., 1961-66; maj. Md. N.G., 1967—. Recipient Commendation medal State of Md., 1976. Mem. ASCE, AAAS, Am. Geophys. Union, Am. Water Resources Assn., N.G. Assn. U.S., Soc. Am. Mil. Engrs., U.S. Armor Assn., Phi Gamma Delta. Club: Explorers. Editor of The Nation's Water Resources, 1968. Home: 1264 Palmer Rd Oxon Hill MD 20022 Office: Interior Bldg Washington DC 20240

BLANCHARD, HELEN M., counselor, ednl. adminstr.; b. Boonton, N.J., Oct. 19, 1918; d. Schuyler Colfax and Bertha (Brundage) Blanchard; B.A., Wellesley Coll., 1940; M.A., Montclair State Coll., 1951; postgrad. Rutgers U., 1961-68. Tchr., counselor Mountain Lakes (N.J.) Bd. Edn., 1940-62; counselor Fair Lawn (N.J.) Bd. Edn., 1962-65; counselor, dir. guidance No. Highlands Regional High Sch. Bd. Edn., Allendale, N.J., 1965—; resident fellow Mt. Holyoke Coll. Advisory com. Bergen Community Coll. Lab. Tech. program, 1976—; bd. dirs. East Bergen Fed. Tchrs. Credit Union; vice-chmn. Boonton County Com. Republican party, 1950-54. Wellesley scholar, Mem. No. Highlands, Bergen County, N.J. (life), Nat. (life) edn. assns., Bergen County Guidance Assn.(exec. com. 1968—), N.J. (exec. com.), Am. personnel and guidance assns., N.J., Am. sch. counselors assns., Nat. Assn. Coll. Admission Counselors, Delta Kappa Gamma. Presbyterian. Address: 1306 Ferry Heights Fairlawn NJ 07410

BLANCHET, BERTRAND, bishop; b. Montmagny, Que., Can., Sept. 19, 1932; s. Louis and Alberta (Nicole) B.; B.A., Ste. Anne de la Pocatiere, 1952; L.Th., U. Laval, 1956, M.Sc., 1965, D.Sc., 1975. Ordained priest Roman Catholic Ch., 1956, bishop, 1973; tchr. Coll. de Ste. Anne de la Pocatiere, 1956-69, Collége Enseignement Général et Professionnel la Pocatiere, 1969-73; bishop of Gaspe, Que., 1973—; mem. Comite Catholique (Ministere de l'Edn. du Que.); mem. Fonds de Recherches Forestieres, U. Laval. Mem. Conseil Quebecois de L'Environ nement. Club: Chevaliers de Colomb. Home and Office: 172 rue Jacques Cartier Gaspe PQ G0C 1R0 Canada

BLANCK, ROBERT FRANKLIN, lawyer; b. Phila., Jan. 19, 1926; s. Oscar F. and Anna (Tippett) B.; A.B., Muhlenberg Coll., 1949; LL.D., 1976; LL.B., U. Pa., 1952; m. Barbara Jefford Steel, June 10, 1949; 1 dau., Meredith S. Admitted to Pa. bar, 1952, since practiced in Phila.; mem. firm McWilliams, Wagoner & Troutman, 1952-66, partner, 1957-66; partner firm La Brum and Doak, 1973—. Mem. bd. mgrs. Germantown Settlement, Phila., 1960-69, pres., 1964-69; mem. del. assembly Delaware Valley Settlement Alliance, Phila., 1963-70, pres., 1967-70; mem. exec. bd. Eastern Pa. Synod. Luth. Ch. Am., Phila., 1966-68, Southeastern Pa. Synod, 1968-73, 74—, chmn. planning com., 1968; mem. cons. com. on theol. edn. Luth. Ch. Am., 1974-76; trustee Luth. Theol. Sem., Phila., 1970—, vice chmn., 1973-76, chmn., 1976—, chmn. fin. com., 1970-76; bd. dirs. Council for Luth. Theol. Edn. in NE; sec., bd. dirs. Inst. for Cancer Research, 1969-72; bd. dirs. Met. Christian Council Phila., 1969—74, also treas. and chmn. fin. com. Served with USAAF, 1944-46. Mem. Am., Pa., Phila. bar. assns., Am. Judicature Soc., Socialegal Club. Lutheran (trustee 1956—, pres. bd. 1966—). Clubs: Masons (trustee 1961—); Union League (Phila.); Ocean City (N.J.) Yacht. Home: 122 W Springfield Ave Philadelphia PA 19118 Office: Suite 700 1700 Market St Philadelphia PA 19103

BLANK, ROBERT GERHARD, engring. cons.; b. Boston, Feb. 20, 1942; s. Gerhard August and Winifred Anne (Karalczyk) B.; B.S.M.E., Northeastern U., 1964; m. Irene Marie Fantini, Feb. 16, 1969; children—Rachelle, David, Vanessa. Mech. design engr. Metcalf & Eddy, Inc., Boston, 1964, sr. mech. engr., 1968-73; mech. design engr. Fay, Spofford & Thorndike, Boston, 1976; asst. mgr. Anderson-Nichols & Co., Inc., Boston, 1973—. Served with U.S. Army, 1964-66. Registered profl. engr., Mass., Maine, N.H., N.Y., R.I., Conn. Mem. Nat. Soc. Profl. Engrs., Mass. Soc. Profl. Engrs., ASME. Office: 150 Causeway St Boston MA 02114

BLANKENSHIP, EDWARD GARY, architect; b. Martin, Tenn., June 22, 1943; s. Edward Gary and Martha Lucille (Baldridge) B.; B.Arch., Columbia, 1966, M.Sc. in Arch., 1967; M.Litt. Arch., U. Cambridge (Eng.), 1971; m. Lynda Maria Meredith, Dec. 5, 1970. Architect, Warner Burns Toan Lunde, Architects, N.Y.C., 1967-68; facilities planner Am. Airlines, N.Y.C., 1968, 71-73; dir. systems facilities and planning design TWA, N.Y.C., 1973—. William Kinne fellow, 1966; Fulbright fellow alt. to Eng., 1967. Registered architect, N.Y. Mem. AIA. Episcopalian. Clubs: United Oxford and Cambridge Univ., Tenn. Soc. in N.Y., Auburn, Cord and Duesenberg Club of Am. Author: The Airport—Architecture, Urban Integration, Ecological Problems, 1974. Home: 44 East End Ave New York City NY 10028 Office: 605 3d Ave New York City NY 10016

BLANKFEIN, ROBERT JEROME, neurologist; b. N.Y.C., Nov. 5, 1931; s. Jules and Freda (Slavin) B.; B.A., Yale U., 1954; M.D., N.Y. Med. Coll., 1958. Intern, San Francisco Gen. Hosp., 1958-59; resident in internal medicine and neurology Bronx (N.Y.) VA Hosp., 1960-63, vis. fellow neurology Columbia Presbyn. Hosp., N.Y.C., 1962-63; research fellow neurology U. Pa., Phila., also asst. instr. neurology and electroencephalagraphy Hosp., 1963-65; dir. neurology Bird S. Coler Hosp., N.Y.C., 1965-67; practice medicine specializing in neurology, Jackson Heights, N.Y., 1967—; mem. staff Flower Fifth Ave., Met. hosps., N.Y.C.; dir. medicine and neurology Physicians Hosp., N.Y.C., 1971—; clin. asst. prof. N.Y. Med. Coll., 1971-75, clin. asso. prof., 1975—; cons. Cath. Med. Center Queens, 1973—. Chmn. emergency fund, physicians div. United Jewish Appeal, Queens County, 1973, 76. Diplomate Am. Bd. Psychiatry and Neurology. Fellow Am. Acad. Neurology, N.Y. Acad. Medicine, ACP; mem. N.Y. Neurol. Soc., Am. Epilepsy Soc., N.Y. Acad. Scis., AAUP, AMA, Am. Med. EEG Assn., Am. EEG Soc., Royal Soc. Medicine, N.Y. Med. Soc. Queens County, N.Y. Soc. Med. Research, Assn. for Research in Nervous and Mental Disease, Pan Am. Med. Assn., Yale Sci. and Engring. Assn. Club: Yale (N.Y.C.). Cons. editor: Hospital Physician, Health Practitioner. Contbr. articles to profl. jours. Participant sci. exhbns. Home: 501 E 87th St New York City NY 10028 Office: 34-01 73d St Jackson Heights NY 11372

BLANKMAN, RUTH COSTA, mayor Canton (N.Y.); b. Woodhaven, N.Y., June 17, 1921; d. Pedro and Ethel (Ellis) Costa; student St. Lawrence U., 1939-41: m. Edward James Blankman, June 10, 1942; children—Peter, Gail, James, Edward. Sec., Union Free Sch. Dist., Tuckahoe, N.Y., 1942-44; sec.-buyer Barbour's, Canton, N.Y., 1953—; village trustee Village of Canton, 1974-75, mayor 1975—; 2d v.p. St. Lawrence County Mayors Assn., 1978—. Pres. Guild of Noble Hosp., Canton, 1950-52, 52-53; dir. Black River-St. Lawrence Econ. Devel. Commn., 1976—. Mem. St. Lawrence Figure Skating Club (pres. 1952-54). Democrat. Unitarian. Home: 67 State St Canton NY 13617 Office: Municipal Bldg Canton NY 13617

BLANTON, EDWARD LEE, JR., lawyer; b. nr. Hope Mills, N.C., Oct. 31, 1931; s. Edward Lee and Margaret M. (Bullard) B.; B.S., Davidson Coll., 1953; M.A., Vanderbilt U., 1954; LL.B., U. Md., 1960; m. Cathleen Estelle Edwards, Aug. 13, 1960; children—Edward Lee III, Cathleen Estelle, Margaret Ellyn. Tchr. math. Balt. City Schs., 1956-59; admitted to Md. bar, 1960; law clk. to judge, Washington, 1960-62; practiced in Balt., 1962-65, 69—; mem. firm Adelberg, Rudow & Blanton, Balt., 1969—; asst. atty. gen. State of Md., Balt., 1965-68. Dir. Aiken Fund, Inc., Balt., United Credit Bur. Am.; chmn. subcom. drafting revision Md. election laws Md. Legislative Council, 1966-67; chmn. subcom. drafting revision Md. income tax laws Hughes Commn., 1966-67. Bd. dirs. United Christian Citizens, 1971—; bd. dirs. Central Balt. Ecumenical Sch. Christian Edn., 1971—, sec., 1972-73, pres., 1974-75. Served as 1st lt. AUS, 1954-56; capt. Md. N.G., 1957-62. Mem. Am., Fed., Md. bar assns., Bar Assn. City Balt., Newcomen Soc. N. Am., Delta Theta Phi. Republican. Presbyn. (elder). Clubs: Merchants, Center, Masons, K.T., Shriners. Home: Avondell Glen Arm MD 21057 Office: Suite 210 Bosley Bldg 210 Allegheny Ave Baltimore MD 21204

BLANTON, LAWTON WALTER, coll. dean; b. Perry, Fla., Oct. 25, 1914; s. Lawton Walter and Minnie Florelle (Truesdale) B.; B.S., U. Fla., 1936, M.S., 1941; postgrad. U. Chgo., 1949, Columbia, 1951-53. Research asso. U. Fla., Gainesville, 1941-42, asst. prof. math., 1942-53; asst. dean students Coll. City N.Y., 1955-57; dir. admissions Montclair Coll., Upper Montclair, N.J., 1957-61, dean students, 1961—. Mem. Am. Assn. Higher Edn., Nat. Assn. Student Personnel Adminstrs., Am., N.J. personnel and guidance assns., N.Y. Schoolmasters, Eastern Assn. Coll. Deans and Advisers of Students, N.J. State Coll. Chief Student Affairs Officers (pres. 1977-78), Nat. Collegiate Honors Council, Am. Hort. Soc., Men's Garden Clubs Am., Am. Hemerocallis Soc., Am. Plant Life Soc., Am. Rhododendron Soc., Am. Magnolia Soc., Am. Boxwood Soc. Home: 1 Oak Crescent Little Falls NJ 07424 Office: Montclair State Coll Normal Ave Upper Montclair NJ 07043

BLANZACO, ANDRE CHARLES, obstetrician, gynecologist; b. Phila., July 28, 1934; s. Laurent and Simone C. (Vurpillot) B.; B.S., Ursinus Coll., 1955; M.D., U. Pa., 1959; m. Janet Ruth Keller, June 7, 1974; children—David Paul, Suzanne Louise, Stephen Mark, Lauren Elizabeth. Intern, Chestnut Hill Hosp., Phila., 1959-60, mem. staff, 1965—, dir. dept. obstetrics and gynecology, 1975—; resident in obstetrics and gynecology Germantown Hosp., Phila., 1960-63, mem. staff, 1965—; practice medicine specializing in obstetrics and gynecology, Phila., 1965—; mem. staff Rosborough Meml. Hosp. Served with U.S. Army, 1963-65. Decorated Army Commendation medal. Diplomate Am. Bd. Obstetrics and Gynecology. Fellow Am. Coll. Obstetricians and Gynecologists; mem. AMA, Pa., Phila. County med. socs., Phila. Obstet. Soc., Am. Fertility Soc., Am. Assn. Gynecologic Laparoscopists, Greater Phila. Alliance for Eradication of Venereal Disease. Republican. Lutheran. Author: V.D. Facts You Should Know, 1970. Home: 409 Washington Ln Fort Washington PA 19034 Office: 717 Bethlehem Pike Philadelphia PA 19118

BLASCO, ANDREW PATRICK, nuclear chemist, army officer; b. Harrisburg, Pa., Apr. 15, 1937; s. Andrew George and Patricia Vera (May) B.; B.S. in Chemistry, Loyola Coll., 1959; M.S. in Nuclear Chemistry, Ohio State U., 1963; student Army Command and Gen. Staff Coll. 1971; m. Catherine Yvonne Shauck, June 13, 1959; children—Michael, Tracy, Lisa, Kelly. Commd. 2d lt. U.S. Army, 1959, advanced through ranks to lt. col., 1975; assigned to Ft. Carson, Colo., 1959-61, Vint Hill Farms Station, Warrenton, Va., 1963-65, Ft. McClellan, Anniston, Ala., 1965, Korean Mil. Advisory Group, Seoul, Korea, 1966-68, Saigon, Vietnam, 1971-72, Rocky Mountain Arsenal, Denver, 1972-74; asst. prof. mathematics U.S. Mil. Acad., West Point, N.Y., 1968-71; chmn. bio-chem. dept. Armed Forces Radiobiology Research Inst., Bethesda, Md., 1974-77; nuclear, biol., chem. advisor to Supreme Allied Comdr., Europe, SHAPE, Beigium, 1977—; biochem. cons. Nat. Cancer Inst., NIH, Bethesda, 1974-77. Mem. Denver C. of C., 1972-74, Adams County (Colo.) C. of C. 1972-74. Decorated Bronze Star, Meritorious Service medal; named Boss of Yr., Bethesda chpt. Nat. Sec. Assn., 1976. Mem. Def. Preparedness Assn., Toastmasters Internat. Democrat. Roman Catholic. Author research papers in field. Home: 4 Clover Ln Elizabethtown PA 17022 Office: SHAPE PANDP APO New York 09055

BLASI, ROBERT VINCENT, transp. engr.; b. Providence, Oct. 16, 1946; s. Rocco Vincent and Pasqualina Louise (Cascella) B.; B.S.C.E., U. R.I., 1969; m. Susan Marie Aldworth, Aug. 16, 1969; children—Kevin Vincent, Ryan Robert. Cons. engr. C. E. Maguire, Providence, 1967-70, sr. liaison engr., sr. traffic engr., Wethersfield, Conn., 1970-74, project mgr., dept. chief, New Britain, Conn., 1974-77; sales engr. Traffic Engring. and Sales, Providence, 1977—. Registered profl. engr., N.Y., Conn. Mem. Inst. Transp. Engrs., Internat. Municipal Signal Assn. (traffic rep. Empire sect.). Home: RFD 1 Victoria Dr Colchester CT 06415 Office: PO Box 2267 Providence RI 02905

BLASLAND, WARREN VINCENT, JR., cons. engr.; b. N.Y.C., Jan. 16, 1945; s. Warren Vincent and Mary Clare (McCarthy) B.; B.C.E., Manhattan Coll., 1966; M.S., Syracuse U., 1971; children—Warren, David Alan, Brian Joseph. Project engr. Havens & Emerson, Cons. Engrs., N.Y.C., 1966; project engr. O'Brien & Gere Engrs., Inc., Syracuse, N.Y., 1966-71, mng. engr., 1971-77, v.p., 1977—; lectr. Syracuse U. Engring. Grad. Sch., 1976. Mem. N.Y. State Soc. Profl. Engrs. (pres. 1975-76, dir. 1976—), Am. Pub. Works Assn. (dir. 1978—), Am. Water Works Assn., N.Y. Water Pollution Control Fedn., Internat. City Mgrs. Assn. Home: 8408A Shallowcreek Rd Liverpool NY 13088 Office: 1304 Buckley Rd Syracuse NY 13221

BLASS, JOHN PAUL, physician; b. Vienna, Austria, Feb. 21, 1937; s. Gustaf and Jolan (Wirth) B.; A.B. summa cum laude, Harvard U., 1958; Ph.D., U. London, 1960; M.D., Columbia U., 1965; m. Birgit Annelise Knudsen, Dec. 20, 1960; children—Charles, Lisa. Postdoctoral fellow Am. Cancer Soc., Columbia U., 1962-63; intern Mass. Gen. Hosp., Boston, 1965-66, resident in medicine, 1966-67; research asso. Nat. Heart and Lung Inst., Bethesda, Md., 1967-70; asst. prof. psychiatry and biol. chemistry UCLA Med. Sch., 1970-76, asso. prof., 1976-78; mem. staff UCLA Hosps. Clinics, 1970-78; Winifred Masterson Burke prof. neurology, prof. medicine Cornell U. Med. Center, 1978—; attending neurologist N.Y. Hosp. Served as asst. surgeon USPHS, 1967-70. Mem. Soc. Neurosci., Biochem. Soc., Am. Soc. Biol. Chemists, Soc. Neurochemists, Am. Soc. Clin. Investigation, Am. Geriatrics Soc., Am. Chem. Soc., Phi Beta Kappa, Sigma Xi, Alpha Omega Alpha. Jewish. Contbr. articles to profl. jours. Home: 1 Orchard Pl Bronxville NY 10708 Office: 785 Mamaroneck Ave White Plains NY 10605

BLASZCZAK, JOSEPH WLADYSLAW, oncologist; b. Sanok, Poland, July 8, 1914; s. Anthony and Maria (Niemiec) B.; A.B., Acad. Veterinary Medicine, Lwow, Poland, 1939; D.V.M., U. Bologna (Italy), 1948; m. Isolde M.T. Staedele, May 20, 1961; 1 son, Stefan J. Asst. Exptl. Inst. Sicily, Palermo, Italy, 1948-49; experimentor Instituto Superiore di Sanita, Rome, Italy, 1950-54; pvt. practice veterinary medicine, Rome, 1950-54; researcher, Pasteur Inst., Paris, France, 1954, London (Eng.) Sch. Hygiene and Tropical Diseases, London U., 1955-58, Gustave Roussy Inst. de Recherches sur le Cancer, Paris U., 1958-60; founder, owner Polonine Devel. Lab., Woodside, N.Y., 1966—. Served with Polish Army under Brit. Commd., 1941-46. Mem. N.Y. Acad. Scis., AAAS. Patentee two synthetic antimetabolites: antimetabolite Polonine which is aribonucleoside, active against cancer; antimetabolite P-2 which is active on RNA viruses of man, animals and plants. Home: 19 Dosoris Way Glen Cove NY 11542 Office: PO Box 7 5702 Woodside Ave Woodside NY 11377

BLATCHLEY, DAVID BOYD, communications exec.; b. Montour Falls, N.Y., June 4, 1942; s. Robert Purdy and Alice (Pitcher) B.; B.S., State U., N.Y., 1966; M.S.W., Syracuse, U., 1972; m. Sharon Lee Hines, Sept. 10, 1966; 1 dau., Caitlin Sharon. Probation officer Cortland County Probation Dept., 1966-68; psychiat. social worker Marcy State Hosp., Uitca N.Y., 1968-73; psychiat. social worker Syracuse (N.Y.) Developmental Center, 1973, intake and services coordinator, 1974, dir. communications, 1974—; adj. prof. Syracuse U., 1977—. Mem. Cortland County Comprehensive Health Service Planning Bd., 1973-75; chmn. Cortland County Social Services Adv. Bd., 1973-75. Mem. Pub. Relations Soc. Am., Profl. Photographers Am., Cortland County Jaycees (pres.). Republican. Methodist. Home: 170 Groton Ave Cortland NY 13045

BLATE, SAMUEL ROBERT, educator; b. Bklyn., July 20, 1944; s. Bernard Joseph and Sonya Frances (Sroelov) B.; student (Emma Carr scholar), George Washington U., 1961-63; A.B. in English and Polit. Sci., U. N.C., Chapel Hill, 1966; postgrad. U. N.C., Greensboro, 1966-67; m. Toni Lee Bress, 1976. Asso. prof. English, Montgomery Coll., Rockville, Md., 1967—, chmn. faculty senate, 1971-73, parliamentarian, 1973—, advisor lit. mag., 1970-71, 76, mem. Speakers Bur., 1970—; cons. in tech. writing COMSAT, 1970, Fairchild Industries, 1976, IBM, 1977; exhibited photographs Holton-Arms Sch., 1977, Framers Gallery and Workshop, 1978; founder Free U., U. N.C., Greensboro, 1966. Mem. Modern Lang. Assn. Am., S. Atlantic Modern Lang. Assn., Coll. English Assn., AAUP, Izzak Walton League Am., Smithsonian Resident Assos., Potomac Appalachian Trail Club, Asso. Photographers Internat. Humanistic Existentialist. Editorial staff Carolina Quar., 1963-66; editorial staff Potomac Appalachian Mag., 1973-77, editor in chief, 1975; contbr. fiction, articles, photographs, and book revs. to lit. jours., mags. and newspapers. Home: 10331 Watkins Mill Dr Gaithersburg MD 20760 Office: Dept English Philosophy Montgomery Coll Rockville MD 20850

BLATZ, LINDA JEANNE, sales exec.; b. N.Y.C., Dec. 8, 1950; d. William Edmund and Jeanne Grace (Hyman) B.; B.S., U. Md., 1972. Mgmt. trainee Milliken & Co., N.Y.C., 1972, sales rep., 1972-74, regional sales mgr., 1974—. Recipient Milliken Service award, 1977. Mem. U. Md. Alumni Group, Alpha Gamma Delta. Congregationalist. Clubs: St. Bartholomew's, N.Y.C. Panhellenic. Home: Two Tudor City Pl Apt 2I-NO New York NY 10017 Office: 1045 6th Ave New York NY 10018

BLATZ, WILLIAM EDMUND, indsl. security co. exec.; b. Bklyn., Mar. 31, 1919; s. William John and Jane Veronica (Jones) B.; B.B.A., N.Y. U., 1950; m. Jeanne Grace Hyman, Sept. 27, 1947; children—Linda J., Susan L., Edward W. With Babaco Alarm Systems, Inc., Hackensack, N.J., 1946—, v.p., 1967—; v.p. Babaco, Chgo., Inc. Deacon, United Ch. of Christ, Manhasset, N.Y., 1975—. Served with AUS, 1942-46; ETO. Decorated Army Commendation medal. Mem. Internat. Assn. Chiefs of Police, Nat. Assn. Transp. Security Officers, Marine Multi Peril Soc. Chgo. Clubs: Nassau Country (Glen Cove, N.Y.); Plandome (N.Y.) Country; Roslyn (N.Y.) Racquet. Contbr. articles to profl. jours. Home: Meadowridge Ln Old Brookville NY 11545 Office: 508 Hudson St Hackensack NJ 07601

BLAUFOX, MORTON DONALD, physician, educator; b. N.Y.C., July 19, 1934; s. Emanuel and Elizabeth (Rosenblum) B.; student Harvard, 1952-55; M.D., State U. N.Y., 1959; Ph.D., U. Minn., 1964; m. Paulette Goldberg, Dec. 20, 1958; children—Laurie Beth, Ellen Ruth, Andrew David. Intern, Jewish Hosp. of Bklyn., N.Y.C., 1959-60; fellow in medicine Mayo Found. Med. Edn. and Research, Rochester, Minn., 1960-64; advanced research fellow Am. Heart Assn., 1964-66; research fellow in medicine, Harvard Med. Sch., Boston, 1964-66; asst. in medicine and radiology, Peter Bent Brigham Hosp., Boston, 1964-66; asst. prof. in radiology, also asso. in medicine Albert Einstein Coll. Medicine, Bronx, N.Y., 1966-71, dir. sect. nuclear medicine, 1966—, chmn. sect., 1975, asso. dir. clin. research center, 1966-70, co-dir. div. hypertension, 1974-76, asst. prof. medicine, 1968-72, asso. prof. radiology, 1971-76, prof. radiology, 1976—, asso. prof. medicine, 1972-78, prof. medicine, 1978—; asst.

attending physician Bronx Municipal Hosp. Center, 1966-71, asso. attending, 1972, attending physician, 1972—; dir. div. nuclear medicine Montefiore Hosp. and Med. Center, 1976—; Mem. adminstrv. council nuclear medicine VA, 1970-73; mem. panel on radiopharmaceuticals U.S. Pharmacopeia, 1970—. Fellow ACP; mem. Am. Heart Assn., AMA, Am. Physiol. Soc. Recipient Edward Nobel Found. award. Diplomate Am. Bd. Internal Medicine, Am. Bd. Nuclear Medicine. Mem. Am. Fedn. Clin. Research, Soc. Nuclear Medicine (pres. Greater N.Y. chpt. 1976-77, chmn. acad. council 1976-77), Internat. Soc. Nephrology, Internat. Hypertension Soc., Council on High Blood Pressure Research (med. adv. bd.), Am. Heart Assn., N.Y. Med. Soc., N.Y. Nephrology Soc., Sigma Xi. Editor: Seminars in Nuclear Medicine; Evaluation of Renal Function and Disease with Radionuclides, 1972; Radionuclides in Nephrology, Procs. Internat. Symposium, 1971, 75. Contbr. articles to profl. jours. Editorial bd. Jour. Nuclear Medicine, Uroradiology, Am. Jour. Radiology, Nephron; asso. editor Barnet's Pediatrics. Research of renal function and evaluation of renal function with radioisotopes, renal blood flow and renin secretion. Home: 101 Drake-Smith Ln Rye NY 10580 Office: Eastchester Rd and Morris Park Ave Bronx NY 10461

BLAUGRUND, STANLEY MARVIN, surgeon; b. El Paso, Tex., Sept. 20, 1930; s. David and Birdie (Stark) B.; B.A., Tex. Western Coll. (now U. Tex.), El Paso, 1951; M.D., U. Tex. Southwestern, Dallas 1955; m. Annette Weintraub, Feb. 12, 1961; children—Andrea, James, Jonathan. Intern, D.C. Gen. Hosp., 1955-56; asst. resident surgery Mt. Sinai, N.Y.C., 1958-59, asst. resident dept. otolaryngology, 1959-61, resident, 1961-62; USPHS trainee, 1959-62; spl. fellow head, neck and facial plastic surgery Pack Med. Group and St. Vincent's Hosp., N.Y.C., 1963-65; practice medicine specializing in head, neck and facial plastic surgery, N.Y.C.; attending otolaryngologist Mt. Sinai, N.Y.C.; surgeon dir. N.Y. Eye and Ear Infirmary, N.Y.C.; asso. clin. prof. otolaryncology, Mt. Sinai Sch. Medicine, City U. N.Y., N.Y.C. Served to capt. USAF, 1956-58. Diplomate Am. Bd. Otolaryngology. Fellow ACS; mem. Am. Laryncological Assn., Am. Triological Soc., Am. Bronchoesophagological Assn., Am. Acad. Facial Plastic and Reconstructive Surgery, Am. Acad. Otolaryngology, N.Y. Acad. Medicine (past chmn. sect.). Club: Gardiners Bay Country. Research laryngeal surgery. Home: 44 W 77th St New York City NY 10024 Office: 115 E 61st St New York City NY 10021

BLAUVELT, HOWARD W., oil co. exec.; b. N.Y.C., Feb. 11, 1917; s. Harry and Lilian (Woelfert) B.; B.A., Yale, 1939; postgrad. Columbia Grad. Sch. Bus. Adminstrn., nights 1939-42; m. Margaret D. Hahn, Sept. 2, 1939 (dec. Feb. 1970); children—Harry, Margaret; m. 2d, Mary E. Cassity, July 25, 1970. Controller Continental Oil Co., Houston, v.p., charge coordinating and planning now chmn., chief exec. officer, also dir. Served with USNR, 1944-46. C.P.A., N.Y. Mem. Financial Execs Inst., Am. Petroleum Inst., Phi Beta Kappa, Beta Gamma Sigma. Presbyterian. Home: 59 Londonderry Dr Greenwich CT 06830 Office: Continental Oil Co High Ridge Park Stamford CT 06904

BLAUVELT, JAMES ANDREW, clergyman, camp adminstr.; b. Paterson, N.J., Dec. 1, 1939; s. Andrew Myers and Lela May (South) B.; B.S. in Animal Husbandry, Iowa State U., 1961; M.Div., Asbury Theol. Sem., 1972; m. Joyce Evelyn Cooley, Aug. 26, 1967; children—Andrew James, Susannah Maria, Sarah Elizabeth, Christena Alethea, Jeremy David. Licensed to ministry Methodist Ch., 1959; ordained to elder's ministry Apostolic Cath. Ch., 1972; pastor Buck Creek-Marne-Monroe Circuit of Iowa, Methodist Ch., 1965-68; asst. pastor, edn. dir. 1st United Meth. Ch., Lexington, Ky., 1969-71; pastor Agape House Fellowship, Lexington, 1971-75; dir. Living Waters and Green Pastures, camp and retreat, Pittstown, N.J., 1975—. Served from 2d lt. to 1st lt. Field Artillery, U.S. Army, 1962-63. Mem. Holland Soc. N.Y., Assn. Blauvelt Descs., David Ackerman Descs. 1662, N.Y. Aberdeen-Angus Breeders Assn., N.J. Farm Bur., N.J. Agrl. Soc. Home and Office: RD 1 Box 44 Race St Pittstown NJ 08867

BLAUVELT, ROBERT WARD, internat. trade and finance co. exec.; b. Paterson, N.J., Dec. 25, 1918; s. Ernest Elvin and Elizabeth Marion (Addy) B.; A.B., Williams Coll., 1941; postgrad. Universidad Obrero, Mexico City, Mexico, 1942, N.Y. U., 1947-49; m. Elizabeth Sheila Anderson, Apr. 1, 1952; children—Ardath Noni, Gillian Elizabeth, David Anderson. With U.S. Dept. State, Mexico, 1942; investigator AEC, Santa Fe, 1946-47; mgr. fgn. operations Alcoa Steamship Co., Alcoa Internat., N.Y.C., 1947-64, asst. treas., 1961-64; v.p., dir. Porcella, Vicini & Co., Inc., N.Y.C., 1965-75, pres., 1975—; v.p., dir. Empreses Dominicanas, Compañia por Acciones, Santo Domingo, Dominican Republic, 1965—; Mercantile Santo Domingo, 1965—; trustee A.N.B. Trust, U.S. Trust Co. Mem. exec. bd. Bergen council Boy Scouts Am., 1972—; mem. City of Santo Domingo Sch. Bd., 1953-56, City of Santo Domingo Ch. Council, 1953-56; mem. Town of Franklin Lakes (N.J.) Bd. Adjustment, 1960-63. Served with M.I., AUS, 1942-46. Mem. Holland Soc. N.Y., Assn. Blauvelt Descs. (v.p. 1973—), Theta Delta Chi. Club: Masons. Home: 735 Franklin Lakes Rd Franklin Lakes NJ 07417 Office: Porcella Vicini & Co Inc 1 World Trade Center New York City NY 10048

BLEICHER, SHELDON JOSEPH, endocrinologist; b. N.Y.C., Apr. 9, 1931; s. Max and Fannie (Klieger) B.; A.B., N.Y.U., 1951; M.S., Western Ill. U., 1952; M.D., Downstate Med. Center, 1956; m. Anne C.M. Ames, July 28, 1967; children—Erick Max, Phillip Thaddeus Samuel. Intern, L.I. Jewish Hosp. Center, New Hyde Park, N.Y., 1956-57; resident Boston City Hosp., 1959-60; research fellow medicine Harvard-Thorndike Meml. Lab., Boston, 1960-63; chief metabolic research unit Jewish Hosp. Med. Center, Bklyn., 1963-67, chief div. endocrinology and metabolism, 1967-77; practice medicine, specializing in endocrinology and diabetes, Bklyn. and Upper Brookville, N.Y., 1963—; prof. medicine Downstate Med. Center, State U. N.Y., 1975—; chmn. dept. internal medicine Bklyn.-Cumberland Med. Center, 1978—; cons. IAEA, Vienna, 1966—. Served to capt. M.C., USNR., 1957-59. NIH fellow, 1960-63; NIH research career devel. award, 1970. Mem. Am., N.Y. (pres. 1975—) diabetes assns., Endocrine Soc., AAAS, Harvey Soc. Jewish. Club: Sag Harbor, Sagamore Yacht (L.I.). Contbr. articles to profl. jours. Office: 121 DeKalb Ave Brooklyn NY 11201

BLEILER, FREDERICK FAY, educator; b. Montour Falls, N.Y., Nov. 17, 1935; s. Delmar F. and Charlotte R. (Lewis) B.; B.S., Ithaca Coll., 1957, M.S., 1959, dir. certificate, 1962; m. Alice Marion Decker, Aug. 23, 1958; children—Timothy, Sharlene, Steven, Kathy. Tchr., Trumansburg (N.Y.) Central Sch., 1957-59; dir. athletics Ovid (N.Y.) High Sch., 1959-68; div. phys. edn., asst. prof. Eisenhower Coll., Seneca Falls, N.Y., 1968—. Bd. dirs. Seneca County chpt. ARC, 1974—, chmn., 1976—; sec.-treas. Pvt. Coll. Athletic Conf., 1972—; area rep. Nat. Assn. Intercollegiate Athletics, 1975-76. Named Ithaca Coll. Sr. Athlete of Yr., 1957. Mem. AAUP, Internat. Assn. Approved Basketball Ofcls. (dir. 1958), Upstate N.Y. Track and Field Assn. (vice chmn. 1974—). Episcopalian. Home: 3354 Garden St Seneca Falls NY 13148 Office: Eisenhower Coll Seneca Falls NY 13148

BLEIWEISS, EUGENE, mfg. co. exec.; b. N.Y.C., Apr. 24, 1925; s. Mortimer and Sadie (Rosensweig) B.; B.S. in Mech. Engring. cum laude, Coll. City N.Y., 1950; postgrad. Stevens Inst., 1958-59, Fairleigh Dickinson U., 1965-67; m. Lorraine Adler, Sept. 11, 1949; children—John, Robert, Nancy. Asst. plant supt. Premier Textile Machinery Co., Bklyn., 1950-52; gen. mgr. Apco div. Wilnes Corp., Bronx, N.Y., 1953-60; pres. Magnus Mfg. Corp. div. Wilnes Corp., 1960-62, Nepperhan Plastics Corp. div. Yonkers, N.Y., 1960-63, v.p. mfg., engring., dir. Metaframe Corp. div., Maywood, N.J., 1961-68, sr. v.p. operations, 1969-70; sr. v.p. operations, dir. Metaframe Corp. div. Mattel, Inc., 1970-74; pres. Ebcon Co., 1975—. Democratic committeeman 27th election dist. N.Y., 1961-62. Served with AUS, 1943-45; ETO. Recipient Am. Legion N.J. State award Aid to Handicapped, 1969. Mem. Am. Soc. Prodn. and Inventory Control, Am. Inst. Indsl. Engrs., ACLU, Audubon Soc., Tau Beta Pi, Pi Tau Sigma. Patentee artificial slate, heater element, all-glass aquarium. Home and office: RD Box 259 Belvidere NJ 07823

BLENKO, ARDIS JONES (MRS. WALTER J. BLENKO), civic worker; b. Iron Mountain, Mich., Mar. 29, 1899; d. John Tyler and Rachel Ann (Milligan) Jones; B.Sc., U. Pitts., 1920; m. Walter John Blenko, Sept. 15, 1921; children—Walter John, Don Balman. Copywriter, Joseph Horne Co., Pitts., 1920-23; writer weekly program Sta. KDKA, 1923-24; fashion writer, spl. women's advt. Frank & Seder, 1924-26. Lectr. specializing in blown glass and garden topics, 1946—. Mem. women's adv. bd. Duquesne U., 1959; mem. Passavant Hosp. Suburban Aides, 1968-70. Bd. dirs. Curtis Home for Girls, 1945-60. Mem. Nat. League Am. Penwomen, D.A.R., Allegheny (bd. mem. 1941-48), Pa. (sec. 1947-48) leagues women voters, Delta Delta Delta. Clubs: Twentieth Century, College, Fortnightly and Linden Garden (Pitts.). Home: 4073 Middle Rd Allison Park PA 15101

BLICK, JOSEPH GREELEY, govt. ofcl.; b. Chgo., June 15, 1926; s. Joseph John and Ella (Gillespie) B.; B.S. in Mech. Engring., U. Ill., 1950, M.S., in Mech. Engring., 1952; m. Florence Elizabeth Kaluzny, May 15, 1955; children—Jeffrey, Jennifer, Julia. Research asst. in mech. engring. U. Ill., 1950-52; mech. engr. U.S. Army Ordnance Ammunition Command, Joliet, Ill., 1952-59; chief prodn. div. U.S. Army Munitions Command, Dover, N.J., 1959-73; dir., logistics engr. U.S. Army Armament Readiness Command, Rock Island, Ill., 1973-77; asso. tech. dir. U.S. Army Armament Research and Devel. Command, Dover, N.J., 1977—. Council commr., mem. exec. bd. Morris-Sussex Area council Boy Scouts Am. Served with USAAF, 1944-46; ETO. Recipient Silver Beaver award Boy Scouts Am.; Meritorious Civilian Service award U.S. Army, 1970, 1973. Mem. Nat. Soc. Profl. Engrs., Am. Def. Preparedness Assn., VFW, U. Ill. Alumni Assn., Sigma Xi, Pi Tau Sigma, Chi Gamma Iota. Clubs: Masons, Shriners, Kiwanis. Home: 18 Cambridge Dr Sparta NJ 07871 Office: U.S. Army Armament Research and Devel Command care Picatinny Arsenal Dover NJ 07801

BLIGH, VERONICA MARIE, counselor; b. N.Y.C., Dec. 21, 1908; d. Dominic Francis and Mary Elizabeth (Egan) Bligh; B.A., St. John's U., Jamaica, N.Y., 1945, M.S., 1963, profl. diploma, 1970; postgrad. Fordham U., 1964-66, (Wall St. Jour. fellow in journalism) Marquette U., 1967, (Gen. Electric fellow) Boston U., 1968, (Univ. fellow in guidance) U. Wis., 1969. Joined Dominican Sisters of Amityville (N.Y.), Roman Catholic Ch., 1927; prin., Our Lady of Perpetual Help, Lindenhurst, N.Y., 1945-55, Good Shepherd Sch., Bklyn., 1955-61; tchr. English, journalism St. Agnes High Sch., Rockville, Centre, N.Y., 1961-64; guidance counselor St. Agnes High Sch., College Point, N.Y., 1964-68, St. Michael's Sch., East, N.Y., 1968-70, Maria Regina, Uniondale, N.Y., 1968—; drug counselor; lectr. in adolescent psychology; intern State Hosp., Independent, Iowa, 1970; asst. chaplain Nassau County Med. Center Psychiat. Div. Mem. exec. bd. Regina Residence for Unwed Mothers, Rockville Centre Diocese. Mem. Am., L.I. (exec. bd.) personnel, guidance assns., Nat. Cath. Guidance Assn., Nat. Cath. Guidance Conf. (chmn. state divs. and councils, exec. bd.), Rockville Centre Diocesan Guidance Assn. (pres. 1972—). Author: My English Book, series, 1955-60. Home and Office: 1333 Admiral Ln Uniondale NY 11553

BLIND, WILLIAM CHARLES, lawyer; b. Chgo., May 18, 1911; s. William Alfred and Josephine Margaret (Koenig) B.; A.B. cum laude, U. Notre Dame, 1932; J.D., Harvard, 1935; m. Peggy Anne Kauffman, Oct. 20, 1937; children—William Charles, Anne Cochran (Mrs. Peter T. Cook). Admitted to N.Y. bar, 1936; since practiced in N.Y.C.; asso. firm Patterson, Eagle, Greenough & Day, 1935-37, Kauffman, Tuttle & McCarthy, 1937-42, Hines, Rearick, Dorr & Hammond, 1942-59; mem. firm Clark, Carr & Ellis (now Kelley Drye & Warren), N.Y.C., 1959—; dir. Dodge Cork Co., Inc., Giant Portland Cement Co., George W. Rogers Constrn. Corp. Sec. Englewood Hosp. Assn., 1947-51, treas., 1951-52, trustee, 1947—. Mem. N.Y. County Republican Com., 1939-41. Served with USNR, 1943-46. Mem. Am., N.Y. State, bar assns., Bar Assn. City N.Y., Am. Judicature Soc., Am. Arbitration Assn., Nat. Panel Arbitrators, Newcomen Soc. N.Am. Roman Catholic. Clubs: Knickerbocker (N.J.); Lancaster (Pa.) Country; Webhannet (Maine) Golf; Englewood Field, University, Knickerbocker (N.Y.C.); Hamilton (Pa.); Englewood Men's. Home: 224 Cedar St Englewood NJ 07631 Office: 350 Park Ave New York City NY 10022

BLISKO, LAWRENCE BERNARD, advt./pub. relations co. exec.; b. Bronx, N.Y., Dec. 21, 1944; s. William and Pauline (Schmugler) B.; student Fairleigh Dickinson U., 1963-68, Montclair State Coll., 1974-77; m. Paula Sharon Lakind, Dec. 22, 1968; children—Marni Chandra, David Solomon. Tchr. Paterson (N.J.) Bd. Edn., 1968-70; chief reporter Spectator News Syndicate, Englewood, N.J., 1970-72; investigative reporter Union City (N.J.) Dispatch, 1972-74; v.p., Shena Pearl & Assos. Inc., Paterson, 1974—; vice-chmn. bd. Community Mgmt. Cons.'s, Paterson, 1976—; dir. SPA Research Inc., W.G. DeWolfe, Inc. Press sec. to Peter M. Mocco, mayor City of North Bergen (N.J.), 1974-75; campaign mgr. Ft. Lee (N.J.) Democratic Assn., 1978—. Recipient Traffic Safety Writing award Am. Automobile Assn., 1972, 2d pl. spot news N.J. Press Assn., 3d pl. features, 1974; Pub. Relations award N.J. Sch. Bds. Assn., 1975. Mem. N.J. Press Assn., Am. Soc. Pub. Adminstrs., Am. Inst. Social and Polit. Scis., Acad. Polit. Scis., Pub. Relations Soc. Am., Am. Mgmt. Assn. Office: Shena Pearl Assos Inc 801 11th Ave Paterson NJ 07514

BLISS, ANTHONY ADDISON, lawyer, opera exec.; b. N.Y.C., Apr. 19, 1913; s. Cornelius Newton and Zaidee (Cobb) B.; B.A., Harvard, 1936; LL.B., U. Va., 1940; m. Barbara Field, Dec. 22, 1937 (div. Dec. 1941); 1 dau., Barbara Mestre; m. 2d, Jo Ann Sayers, June 9, 1942 (div. July 1967); children—Eileen Bliss Andahazy, Anthony Addison, John Wheeler; m. 3d, Sally Brayley, July 24, 1967; children—Mark Brayley, Timothy Newton. Admitted to N.Y. State bar, 1943; mem. firm Milbank, Tweed, Hadley & McCloy, N.Y.C.; exec. dir., bd. dirs., mem. exec. com. Met. Opera Assn., pres., 1956-67. Trustee U.S. Trust Co. N.Y.; chmn. bd. Found. for Am. Dance, Inc.-City Center Joffrey Ballet; bd. dirs. N.Y. Found. for Arts, Inc.; mem. Nat. Council on Arts, 1965-68; trustee Portledge Sch.; co-chmn. Nat. Corp. Fund for Dance, Inc. Served in USNR, 1942-45. Decorated Air medal. Mem. Am., Internat., N.Y. State, Nassau County bar assns., Assn. Bar City N.Y. Clubs: Century, Creek, Beaver Dam Winter Sports, Cove Neck Tennis. Home: Centre Island Oyster Bay NY 11771 Office: Met Opera Assn Lincoln Center Plaza New York NY 10023

BLISS, DENNIS LESLIE, state ofcl.; b. Trenton, N.J., July 22, 1941; s. Gerald B. and Helen M. (Molnar) B.; B.A., Rutgers U., 1964; J.D., Ind. U., 1967; m. Carolyn E. Moss, Nov. 30, 1968. Admitted to N.J. bar, 1969, D.C. bar, 1968; dep. atty. gen., chief Internal Affairs Bur., N.J. Div. Criminal Justice, Trenton, 1970-75, spl. asst. to atty. gen., 1975-76, dir. adminstrn., dept. law and pub. safety, 1977—; chief legal counsel to N.J. State Police, Police Tng. Commn., Office State Med. Examiner, State Racing Commn., 1975-77, State Law Enforcement Planning Agy., 1972—; legal adviser to chief of staff Dept. Def., 1977—; instr. N.J. State Police in-service tng. programs; mem. N.J. Adv. Council, Project STAR; mem. N.J. Adv. Councils on Drug Abuse and Alcohol Problems, 1972-75; nat. bd. cons. Police Services Study, Ind. U., 1974-78; rep. Gov.'s Adv. Council for Emergency Services, 1975—, Gov.'s Cabinet Subcom. on Urban Affairs, 1975—, County Counsel's Assn. N.J., 1975-77; mem. Statewide Police Emergency Radio Network Task Force, 1977—, chmn., 1977; mem. Gov.'s Adv. Com. for Implementation N.J. Penel Code, 1978—; chmn. Motor Vehicles Div. Service Delivery Task Force, 1978—. Trustee Monmouth County Mental Health Assn., 1967-70. Mem. Am., D.C., N.J. (mem. com. on tng. programs for law enforcement personnel 1976—), Monmouth County bar assns., Am. Judicature Soc., Nat. Dist. Attys. Assn., Internat. Assn. Chiefs of Police, Phi Delta Phi, Delta Sigma Phi. Home: 19 Statesir Pl Red Bank NJ 07701 Office: Room 104 State House Annex Trenton NJ 08625

BLISS, PHILIP JAMISON, med. services ofcl.; b. N.Y.C., Jan. 24, 1921; s. Julius and Inez (Mueller) B.; student Columbia, 1939-41; B.S. in Pub. Adminstrn., U. Mo., 1945; m. Janell Leon Davis, June 22, 1945 (div. Mar. 1971); children—Donald Philip, Ellen Inez; m. 2d, Jeanne King Lockrow, May 15, 1971. Ramp agt. Mid-Continent Airlines, Kansas City, Mo., 1945-46; personnel technician City Kansas City, Mo., 1946; Westchester County, N.Y., 1947; research asst. Bur. Municipal Research, Inc., Newark, 1948; field sec. N.J. Laundryowners' Assn., Newark, 1948-49; prin. personnel technician State N.J., Dept. Civil Service, Trenton, 1949-51; personnel dir. N.J. Turnpike Authority, New Brunswick, 1951-55; office mgr. Batten, Barton, Durstine and Osborn, N.Y.C., 1956-69, v.p., office mgr., 1969-74; regional emergency med. services coordinator SW Conn. region, 1975—. Life mem. Chatham Emergency Squad, Inc., Inc., pres., 1961, capt., 1964-65; organized New Canaan (Conn.) Vol Ambulance Corps., 1975, capt., 1975-76; 1st aid instr. Madison-Chatham and Somerset Hills chpts. ARC., 1956-73 New Canaan chpt., 1974—; mem., former 1st asst. chief Chatham Vol. Fire Dept. Vice chmn. Boro Republican Com., Chatham, N.J., 1964, chmn., 1965. Served 2d lt. inf., AUS, 1941-43. Mem. Advt. Agy. Office Mgrs. Assn. N.Y. (charter; pres. 1962-63), Phi Gamma Delta, Delta Sigma Pi. Home: 270 Smith Ridge Rd New Canaan CT 06840

BLISS, ROBERT PORTER, JR., ins. agy. exec.; b. St. Albans, Vt., Sept. 8, 1923; s. Robert Porter and Edith (Tuscany) B.; student Vt. pub. schs.; m. Dorothy J. Kidder, Feb. 15, 1947; children—Robert G., John A. Estate planner Conn. Gen. Life Ins. Co., St. Albans, 1947-52; ins. agt. A.N. Deringer, Inc., St. Albans, 1952-57; v.p. S.S. Watson Co., Inc., St. Albans, 1957-64, pres., chief exec. officer, 1964—; pres. Porter Orgn., Ltd., St. Albans, 1971—; dir. Franklin Lamoille Bank, Central Vt. Pub. Service Corp., Rutland. Mem. St. Alban's Sch. Commn., 1970-73; justice of peace, 1971—; mem. St. Albans Planning Commn., 1965-70; mem. Vt. Whey Authority, 1968-71. Served with USMCR, 1943-47, 50-51. Named Vt. Ins. Man of Yr., 1967, Outstanding Citizen, Jaycees, 1971; recipient Legion of Honor, Order of Demolay, 1972. Mem. Nat. Assn. Ins. Agts. (presdl. citation 1972), Nat. Assn. Real Estate Appraisers, Ind. Ins. Agts. Am., Nat. Assn. Rev. Appraisers, Ind. Mut. Agts. New Eng., Nat. Assn. Realtors. Republican. Methodist. Clubs: Rotary, Owls, Elks, Masons (Mason of year 1976). Contbr. monthly column to Green Mountain Agt. Mag., 1965—; contbr. articles to mags. Home: 177 N Main St Saint Albans VT 05478 Office: 81 N Main St Saint Albans VT 05478

BLITZ, DANIEL, electronics engr.; b. N.Y.C., Feb. 8, 1920; s. Samuel and Amelia (Hirsch) B.; B.S., Mass. Inst. Tech., 1940; m. Peggy Schulder, Aug. 5, 1963. Research engr. RCA, Camden, N.J., 1940-43, Princeton, N.J., 1943-47; research engr. Raytheon Mfg. Corp., Waltham, Mass., 1947-51; research engr., co-founder Sanders Assos., Inc., Waltham, 1951-52, Nashua, N.H., 1952—, corp. engr., 1974—. Mem. IEEE, Soc. Photog. Scientists and Engrs., AAAS, Soc. Motion Picture and TV Engrs. Patentee in field (50). Home: 242 Beacon St Boston MA 02116 Office: Daniel Webster Hwy S Nashua NH 03061

BLOCH, HENRY SIMON, economist; b. County Kehl (Baden), Germany, Apr. 6, 1915; s. Edward and Claire (Bloch) B.; M.B.A., U. Nancy (France), 1935, Dr. of Laws-Econs., 1937; fellow Acad. Internat. Law, The Hague, summer 1937; Dr. Econ., Polit. and Social Scis. (honoris causa), Univ. Libre de Bruxelles, Belgium, 1969; 1 dau., Miriam (Mrs. H. Feuerstein). Came to U.S., 1937, naturalized, 1943. Research asst., instr. econs., instr. Army and Navy officers program U. Chgo., 1938-45; cons. Fgn. Econ. Adminstrn., 1945; economist Treasury Dept., 1945-46, mem. Treasury del. for tax treaty negotiations with Western Europe, 1946; sect. chief to dir. fiscal and fin. br. UN, dir. Bur. Tech. Assistance Ops., dep. commr. for tech. assistance, 1946-62; pres. Zinder Internat. Ltd., 1962-66; v.p., dir. E.M. Warburg Co., Inc., 1967-70; sr. v.p., dir. E.M. Warburg, Pincus & Co., Inc., 1970-75, exec. v.p., dir., 1976—; dir. affiliated cos.; adviser banks, corps., govtl. agys.; vis. prof. econs. Yale, 1955; lectr. law Columbia U., 1955-63, adj. prof. law and internat. relations, 1963—; dir., chmn. UNITAR Seminar on Internat. Monetary Systems for 37 govts., 1972; spl. adviser UN Panel on Fgn. Investment, Amsterdam, 1969; adviser UN Consultative Com. for Asian Devel. Bank, Bangkok, Thailand, 1965. Mem. Am. Econ. Assn., Council Fgn. Relations, Soc. Royale d'Economie Politique de Belgique (hon.). Clubs: Cosmos (Washington). Author: The Challenge of the World Trade Conference, 1965; Financial Strategy for Developing Nations, 1969; Export Financing Emerging as a Major Policy Issue, 1976; Foreign Risk Judgment for Commercial Banks, 1977; (with others) Legal-Economic Problems of International Trade, 1961; The Global Partnership, 1968; Financial Integration in Western Europe, 1969. Office: 277 Park Ave New York City NY 10017

BLOCH, JACQUES W., hosp. food services adminstr.; b. Baden-Baden, Germany, June 19, 1920; s. Maurice and Betty (Kahn) B.; came to U.S., 1941, naturalized, 1943; Brevet Hôtelier, Collège Technique Hôtelier, Strasbourg, France, 1935-38; student City Coll. N.Y., 1945-48; m. Jean H. Dreyfuss, Aug. 7, 1949; children—Norman Arthur, Elaine Regina. Asst. prodn. supt. Maxson Food System, Queens Village, N.Y., 1945-46; asst. to purchasing and catering dir. Commodore Hotel, N.Y.C., 1947-48; food prodn. mgr. Johns Hopkins Hosp., Balt., 1949-53; dir. food services Montefiore Hosp. and Med. Center, Bronx, N.Y., 1954—; lectr. univs. N.Y.; cons. on food service Am. Hosp. Assn., 1961-74, also to govt. and pvt. agencies. Mem. adv. bd. Dietetic Service, N.Y.C. Health & Hosps. Corp., N.Y.C., 1970-72; mem. food trades ednl. adv. commn. N.Y.C. Bd. Edn., 1970—; food adv. com. Joint Purchasing Corp., Fedn. Jewish Philanthropies, 1954—, chmn.-elect, 1978. Served with U.S. Army, 1943-45. Decorated Purple Heart medal. Mem. Am. Soc. Hosp. Food

Adminstrs. (pres. 1967-68), Am. Hosp. Assn., Hosp. Food Adminstrs. Assn. Greater N.Y. Inc. (pres. 1960-62), Council on Hotel, Restaurant and Instl. Edn., Internat. Food Service Execs. Assn. Jewish. Office: 111 E 210th St Bronx NY 10467

BLOCH, JOSEPH LORING, hosp. adminstr.; b. N.Y.C., Sept. 11, 1935; s. Melvin Harold and Eva Gertrude (Seiden) B.; B.A. cum laude, Alfred U., 1956; M.A. in Pub. Adminstrn., Am. U., 1959; m. Carla Zinn, June 25, 1959; children—David Peter, Nancy Jill. Asst. to dean personnel Washington, 1958-59; employment devel. asst. U.S. Civil Service Commn., Washington, 1959-60, employment devel. officer, 1960-61; fed. coll. recruitment rep., N.Y. region, 1961-62; asst. personnel officer N.Y. VA Hosp., 1962-64; asst. adminstr. Peninsula Hosp. Center, Far Rockaway, L.I., N.Y., 1964-66, adminstr., 1966-68, exec. dir., 1968-74, adminstr., v.p., 1974—; mem. bd. examiners N.Y. State Nursing Home Adminstrs., 1971—; mem. advisory council Sch. of Bus. Adminstrn. Alfred U., 1976. Dir., Far Rockaway/5 Towns Rotary, 1967-72; budget advisory com. Hewlett Woodmere Sch. Dist., 1968-69, mem. sch. bd., 1972-73; dir. C. of C. Rockaways, 1967; mem. Greater N.Y. council Boy Scouts Am., 1967. Served with USAF, 1958-59, USAFR, 1958-64. Named guest of honor Rockaway Coll., 1974, United Jewish Appeal, 1975, State of Israel Bonds, 1978. Fellow Royal Soc. Health; mem. Am. Coll. Hosp. Adminstrs., Am. Coll. of Nursing Home Adminstrs., Am. Hosp. Assn., Am. Pub. Health Assn., Adminstrs. Conf. Group, N.Y. State Pub. Health Assn., Greater N.Y. Hosp. Adminstrs. (bd. govs.), Pi Sigma Alpha, Pi Gamma Mu, Pi Delta Epsilon, Blue Key. Jewish religion. Clubs: Woodmere. Home: 53 Bergman Dr Hewlett NY 11557 Office: 51-15 Beach Channel Dr Far Rockaway NY 11691

BLOCH, KONRAD, biochemist; b. Neisse, Germany, Jan. 12, 1912; s. Frederick D. and Hedwig (Steimer) B.; Chem. Eng., Technische Hochschule, Munich, Germany, 1934; Ph.D., Columbia U., 1938; m. Lore Teutsch, Feb. 15, 1941; children—Peter, Susan. Came to U.S., 1936, naturalized, 1944. Asst. prof. biochemistry U. Chgo., 1946-50, prof., 1950-54; Higgins prof. biochemistry Harvard U., 1954—. Recipient Nobel Prize in physiology and medicine, 1964. Fellow Am. Acad. Scis.; mem. Nat. Acad. Scis., Am. Philos. Soc. Home: 16 Moon Hill Rd Lexington MA 02173 Office: 38 Oxford St Cambridge MA 02138

BLOCH, RAPHAEL S., ophthalmologist; b. N.Y.C., Feb. 16, 1942; s. Abraham P. and Belle B.; B.A., Yeshiva U., 1963; B.H.L., 1963, M.D., 1967; m. Dorothy Richard, June 16, 1964; children—David, Joel. Intern, Montefiore Hosp., N.Y.C., 1967-68, resident in ophthalmology, 1968-71; practice medicine specializing in ophthalmology, Mt. Kisco, N.Y., 1973—; asso. attending physician No. Westchester Hosp., Mt. Kisco, 1974—; asst. clin. prof. Albert Einstein Coll. Medicine, 1974—. Served to maj., M.C., U.S. Army, 1971-73. Diplomate Am. Bd. Ophthalmology and Otolaryngology. Fellow A.C.S.; mem. Am. Acad. Ophthalmology and Otolaryngology, N.Y. State, Westchester County med. socs. Club: B'nai B'rith. Office: 332 Main St Mt Kisco NY 10549

BLOCHER, MAURICE HENRY, purchasing agt., writer; b. Hampstead, Md., Oct. 13, 1920; s. John Henry and Annie (Shamer) B.; student U. Balt., 1937-38; B.A., Western Md. Coll., 1948; m. Nancy Meade, Apr. 14, 1945; children—Susan, Thomas Henry. Ins. insp. Retail Credit Co., Chambersburg, Pa., 1948-49; purchasing asst. to mgr. Anteitam Paper Co., Hagerstown, Md., 1949-54, asst. purchasing agt., 1954-55, purchasing agt., 1955—. Served with USAAF, 1942-45. Decorated D.F.C., Air medal with 2 oak leaf clusters. Republican. Author: New Hope, 1939; Blocher, 1969; Blocher Families in America, 1972. Contbr. articles to various newspapers. Home: 501 Dunn Irvin Dr Hagerstown MD 21740 Office: 37 W Antietam St Hagerstown MD 21740

BLOCK, CY, life ins. co. exec., former athlete; b. Bklyn., May 4, 1919; s. Abraham and Jennie (Levinsky) B.; grad. high sch.; m. Harriet Spektor, Apr. 8, 1943; children—Bette Block Simonson, Margy (Mrs. Lawrence Bauman), Nancy (Mrs. Les Perlson). Profl. baseball player, Paragould, Ark., Class D., 1938, Chgo. Cubs, 1942-48, Buffalo Internat. League, 1948-51; with Mut. Benefit Life Ins. Co., N.Y.C., 1948-77, mem. Hall of Fame, 1951—. Pres., Oakland Little League, Bayside, N.Y., 1951-53; commr. Lake Success Little League, 1954-59, Lake Success Girls Soccor Baseball, 1960-70. Served with USCG, 1942-45. Mem. Mut. Benefit Nat. Assos. (pres. 1957), Million Dollar Roundtable (life), Top of Table, Five Million Dollar Forum. Author: So You Want to be a Major Leaguer, 1965. Home: 4 Old Field Ln Lake Success NY 11020 Office: 3 E 54th St New York City NY 10022

BLOCK, FREDERICK HENRY, lawyer; b. N.Y.C., Feb. 6, 1909; s. Frederick and Selma (Rosenbluth) B.; B.A., Columbia, 1930; LL.B., Fordham U., 1935; m. Bernice Rocker, Aug. 31, 1965; children—Elizabeth, Frederick L. Admitted to N.Y. State bar, 1935, U.S. Supreme Ct. bar, 1950; asso. various firms in N.Y.C., 1935-42; asst. U.S. atty. criminal and criminal appeals divs. for So. Dist. N.Y.C., 1942-43, 46-51; individual practice law, partner various firms, N.Y.C., 1951-65; partner firm Bernstein, Seawell, Kaplan & Block, N.Y.C., 1965-75; counsel Zimmer, Fishbach & Hertan, N.Y.C., 1975—. Pres. Community Synagogue, Rye, 1955-57, Temple Shaaray Tefila, N.Y.C., 1973. Served with AUS, 1943-45; capt. JAG Res., 1945-48. Mem. Am., N.Y. State bar assns., Assn. Bar City of N.Y. (trial counsel to com. on grievances 1951-61), N.Y. County Lawyers Assn. (dir. 1976—), Fed. Bar Council, N.Y. State Dist. Attys. Assn. Clubs: Lawyers Sq. (trustee), City, Masons. Home: 10 E 76th St New York City NY 10021 Office: 919 3d Ave New York City NY 10022

BLOCK, MARCUS THEODORE, physician; b. N.Y.C., Aug. 13, 1903; s. Arthur and Lena (Halperin) B.; A.B., Cornell U., 1925; B.S. in Medicine, U. Kans., 1928; M.D., U. Chgo., 1931; part-time student Cook County Grad. Sch. Medicine and Surgery, 1947-51, N.Y. Skin and Cancer Sch., 1953; m. Frances Eleanor McBride, Nov. 7, 1932 (div.); children—Jane Audrey, Arthur, Marcus Theodore; m. 2d, Dorothy Dean Greb, Aug. 4, 1962 (dec. Aug. 1969). Intern, Newark City Hosp., 1930-32; in pvt. practice, Newark, 1932—; attending dermatologist Am. Legion Tri County Meml, Columbus, Newark City hosps.; asst. dermatologist Babies Hosp.; courtesy staff Presbyn., Beth hosps., clin. asst. prof. medicine (dermatology) N.J. Coll. Medicine and Dentistry. Fellow Internat. Soc. Tropical Dermatology; mem. Internat. Congress Dermatology, AMA, N.J., Essex County med. socs., Soc. Investigative Dermatology, N.J. Dermotol. Soc. (pres.), Am. Heart Assn., Am. Acad. Dermatology (life), N.J. Hosp. Assn., U. Chgo., U. Kans. alumni assns., Am. Mus. Natural History, Acad. Medicine N.J., Friends Presbyn. Hosp., Benjamin Rush Med. Soc., Phi Sigma, Phi Delta Epsilon. Clubs: Masons, Odd Fellows, Elks, Cornell of Essex County, Cornell of N.Y.C., U. of Chgo. Contbr. articles med. jours. Home: 402 Mt Prospect Ave Newark NJ 07104 Office: 515 Mt Prospect Ave Newark NJ 07104

BLOCK, WILLIAM, newspaper publisher; b. N.Y.C., Sept. 20, 1915; s. Paul and Diana (Wallach) B.; A.B., Yale, 1936; m. Maxine Horton, May 23, 1944; children—William, Karen Block Ayars, Barbara L., Donald. With circulation, other depts. Toledo Blade, 1937-39, asst. to gen. mgr., 1939-41; co-pub. Pitts. Post-Gazette and Toledo Blade, 1941—; pres. Post-Gazette; v.p. Toledo Blade. Bd. dirs. Pitts. Regional Planning Assn., Pitts. Communications Found., Pitts. World Affairs Council; trustee Am. Assembly; sponsor Allegheny Conf. on Community Devel. Served as pvt., inf., A.U.S., 1941-42; officer C.A.C. (Anti-Aircraft), 1942-46; disch. capt.; served in mil. govt. in Korea, 1945-46. Mem. Internat. Press Inst. (dir.), Am. Soc. Newspapers Editors. Pitts. Symphony Soc. (dir.) Home: 215 Hillcrest Rd Pittsburgh PA 15238 Office: 50 Blvd of Allies Pittsburgh PA 15222

BLODGETT, ANNE WASHINGTON, artist; b. N.Y.C., Apr. 17, 1940; d. Thomas Peabody and Martha (Allen) Blagden; B.A., Smith Coll., 1961; student Sch. Mus. Fine Arts, Boston, 1961-62; m. Thomas Noyes Blodgett, Sept. 15, 1962; children—Joanne Washington, Laura Landon, Thomas Noyes. One-woman shows: Caravan House Gallery, N.Y.C., 1971, 74, Berkshire Mus., Pittsfield, Mass., 1971, Medici Gallery, London, 1973, N.E. Harbor (Maine) Library, 1973, 75, TV Channel 24, Hartford, Conn., 1976, Bodley Gallery, N.Y.C., 1976, 79, Scott-Carspechen Gallery, Wilmington, Del., 1979; group shows: New Crafton Gallery, London, 1972, Grist Mill, Farmington, Conn., 1973, 75, Buck Hill Falls (Pa.) Art Assn., 1974, Red Bar, Fishers Island, N.Y., 1974, 76, Pioneer Gallery, Coopertown, N.Y., 1974, 76; represented in permanent collections: Fitzwilliam Coll., Cambridge, Eng., Berkshire Mus., Charles River Assos., Inc., Boston, Energy Absorption Systems, Inc., Chgo., Research Media, Inc., Cambridge, Mass., Crane Paper Co., Dalton, Mass., also pvt. collections. Home: 830 Park Ave New York NY 10021

BLOEDE, VICTOR GUSTAV, advt. exec.; b. Balt., Jan. 31, 1920; s. Victor Gustav, Jr. and Helen (Yoe) B.; student St. John's Coll., Annapolis, Md., 1937-39, U. Md., 1941; m. Merle Huie, Mar. 11, 1945; children—Victor Gustav, Susan Lohn. Vice pres., copy chief French & Preston, N.Y.C., 1947-50; with Benton & Bowles, Inc., N.Y.C., 1950—, v.p., creative dir., 1957-61, sr. v.p., 1961-62, sr. v.p. charge creative services, 1962-63, exec. v.p., 1963-68, chmn. plans bd., 1963-67, pres., chief exec. officer, 1968-71, chmn. bd., chief exec. officer, 1971-74, chmn., 1974—; dir. at large Am. Assn. Advt. Agys., vice chmn., 1972-73, chmn., 1973-74, chmn. adv. com., 1974—; dir. Am. Advt. Fedn.; mem. Nat. Advt. Rev. Bd. dirs. Travelers Aid Soc. N.Y., Am. Cancer Soc., 1976—; mem. bd. visitors and govs. St. John's Coll., 1972—. Served to capt. USAAF, 1942-45. Decorated Air medal with 6 oak leaf clusters. Mem. Phi Sigma Kappa. Clubs: Sands Point (L.I.) Golf (gov.), Sandspoint Bath and Tennis (v.p., gov. 1962); Coral Beach (Bermuda); Manhasset Bay Yacht, Economic (N.Y.C.). Contbg. author: The Copy Writer's Guide, 1958. Home: 160 Bayview Rd Plandome Manor Long Island NY 11030 Office: 909 3d Ave New York City NY 10022

BLOGOSLAWSKI, WALTER JOSEPH, physician; b. New Britain, Conn., Mar. 18, 1900; s. Casimir and Catherine Estelle; student Fordham U., 1922-24; M.D., Georgetown U., 1927; m. Ann Petuskis, July 17, 1932; children—Walter, Ona Blogoslawski Barta. Intern, Georgetown U. Hosp., Washington, 1928; practice medicine specializing in internal medicine, New Britain, Conn., 1976—. Mem. AMA, Conn., New Britain med. socs. Home and Office: 199 W Main St New Britain CT 06052

BLOMBERG, RICHARD DAVID, mgmt. cons.; b. N.Y.C., July 29, 1945; s. Philip Dean and Hylde Theodora (Vogel) B.; m. Susan Evelyn Konigsbacher, Aug. 10, 1969; children—Jeffrey Adam, Pamela Faith. Vice pres. Arden Radio Stores, Inc., N.Y.C., 1964-68; v.p. Dunlap and Assos., Inc., contract research; mgmt. cons., Darien, Conn., 1968—. Guest instr. Columbia Grad. Sch. Engring. Chmn. bd. dirs. Hampshire House, Inc., Stamford, Conn., 1971-73; NSF trainee, 1967-68. Recipient Illig medal Columbia, 1967. Mem. Ops. Research Soc. Am., Assn. Consumer Research, Sigma Alpha Mu, Tau Beta Pi, Alpha Pi Mu. Home: 27 Fawn Dr Stamford CT 06905 Office: 1 Parkland Dr Darien CT 06820

BLOMFIELD, RICHARD BEST, brokerage co. exec.; b. Kamuela, Hawaii, Mar. 24, 1919; s. John Harold Stewart and Eirene Alice (Best) B.; A.B. cum laude, U. Hawaii, 1945; postgrad. Harvard U., 1945-46; M.A., Columbia U., 1947; m. Laurel Currey, May 18, 1957; children—John Roe, Christiane Jane, Mary Rachel. Analyst, Amfac, Inc., Honolulu, 1947-50; mgr. salary adminstrn. Union Carbide Corp., N.Y.C., 1950-59; dir. personnel adminstrn. Mack Trucks, Inc., Plainfield, N.J., 1959-61; dir. personnel Am. Standard Inc., N.Y.C., 1961-63; v.p. Am. Mut. Ins. Cos., Wakefield, Mass., 1964-69; sr. v.p., sec., dir., mem. exec. com. Hornblower, Weeks Noyes & Trask, Inc., N.Y.C., 1969—; 1st v.p. Loeb Rhoades, Hornblower & Co., N.Y.C., 1978—; gen. partner Hornblower & Weeks-Hemphill, Noyes, Inc., N.Y.C., 1969-72, sr. v.p., sec., dir., 1972—; sec., treas., dir. Lincoln Industries Corp., H&W-H,N Ill., Hornblower & Weeks, Inc., 8 Hanover St. Corp.; sec. Stuyvesant Asset Mgmt. Corp.; sec., dir. 1st N.Y. Options Inc., Hornblower Growth Fund, Inc.; dir. Henry Hornblower Fund, Inc. allied mem. N.Y. Stock Exchange. Adviser Nat. Exec. Inst., Boy Scouts Am.; bd. dirs. Morris County Mental Health Assn.; mem. adv. bd. Am. Cleft Palate Edn. Found., Ins. Inst. Boston U., 1967-69; chmn. Hornblower Pension and Profit Sharing Trust; mem. Lexington (Mass.) Town Meeting, also mem. appropriations com. Served to lt. USNR, 1941-45. Mem. Am. Soc. Tng. and Devel., Wall St. Corporate Secs. Assn., Am. Soc. Personnel Adminstrn., Securities Industry Assn., Morris Mus. Mineral Soc., Nat. Audubon Soc., Am. Mus. Natural History, Smithsonian Inst., Am. Heritage Soc., N.J., Morris County hist. assns., Friends of Mineralogy, Am. Hemercallis Soc., Frelinghuysen Arboretum, Internat. Oceanographic Soc. Episcopalian (vestryman). Clubs: Downtown Athletic, Broad St. (N.Y.C.); Spring Brook Country (Morristown). Contbr.: How to Prepare for Management Responsibilities, 1962; Leadership in the Office, 1963; contbr. articles to profl. jours. Home: 44 Rolling Hill Dr Morristown NJ 07960 Office: 14 Wall St New York City NY 10005

BLOMQUIST, JANE MARGARET, advt. and art cons.; b. Phila., Aug. 20, 1943; s. Frank Ernest and Willamay Jane (Moore) Blomquist; ed. Phila. Coll. Art, Charles Morris Price Sch. Advt. and Journalism, Samuel Fleisher Sch. Art, Sch. Visual Arts. Formerly various positions advt. and pub. relations firms, Phila.; advt. sales mgr. Thursday's Drummer, 1971-72; operator art and advt. cons. firm, N.Y.C., 1973—, art cons. Manhattan Life Ins. Corp. Ward leader congl. campaign, Phila., 1971-72; art dir. McGovern presdl. campaign Pa., 1972. Mem. Mus. Modern Art, N.Y. Art Dirs. Club. Address: 42 W 13th St New York City NY 10011

BLONDELL, ALLAN ST. JOHN, ednl. adminstr.; b. Nassau, Bahamas, Mar. 6, 1947; s. Charles Andre (stepfather) and Yvonne Lucille Rouboneau; A.A., Miami-Dade Community Coll., 1967; B.A., Howard U., 1971; M.A., Va. Poly. Inst. and State U., 1977; m. Helena Sheryl Duhart, May 31, 1969; 1 son, Allan St. John. Program coordinator, counselor Arlington County (Va.) Adult Edn., 1971—; counselor Catonsville Community Coll., 1977; off-campus adminstr. No. Va. Community Coll., 1978—; tutor Right-to-Read Programs; tutor Arlington County Recreation Dept., 1971-73. Vice pres. Cinnamon Tree Community Assn., Columbia, Md., 1976, pres., 1977—; del. Columbia (Md.) Townhouse and Condominium Assns. Mem. Am. Personnel and Guidance Assn., Am. Coll. Personnel Assn., Nat. Md. assns. measurement and evaluation in guidance, Assn. Non-White Concerns in Guidance, Adult Edn. Assn. U.S.A., Adult Edn. Assn. Va. Roman Catholic. Counselor career edn. workshop. Home: 6287 Centre Stone Ring Columbia MD 21044 Office: 3011 N 7th St Arlington VA 22204

BLOOD, ROBERT JUSTUS, architect, designer; b. Phila., Feb. 26, 1931; s. William Christy and Marie Giesse (Holme) B.; B.A., Pratt Inst., 1958; m. Nancy Jane Anson, Dec. 26, 1952; children—Margaret Ann, Nancy Jane, Nina Elizabeth. Designer, job capt., project dir. Walter Dorwin Teague Asso., N.Y.C., 1955-67; pres., architect/designer Q5 Inc., East Orange, N.J., 1967—, also dir. Served with AUS, 1950-52. Presbyterian. Home: 12 Cedric Rd Summit NJ 07901 Office: 141 S Harrison St East Orange NJ 07018

BLOOM, EDWIN JOHN, JR., mgmt. cons.; b. Yonkers, N.Y., Nov. 12, 1931; s. Edwin John and Marion Reata (Baude) B.; B.S., Cornell U., 1957; student Columbia U., 1951, 54; m. Mary Caciola, June 9, 1956; children—Mary Catherine, Edward Joseph, Theresa Ann, Donna Marie. Supr. employment and employee services Ansco div. GAF Corp., Binghamton, N.Y., 1957-65; mgr. indsl. relations Philco Ford Corp., Phila., 1965-70; dir. employee relations Rauland div. Zenith Radio Corp., Chgo., 1970-72; v.p. personnel Lechmere Sales div. Dayton Hudson Corp., Cambridge, Mass., 1973-77; pres. Employee Relations Assocs., Inc., Concord, Mass., 1977—; lectr. Lasell Jr. Coll., Newton, Mass., 1977—, Bunker Hill Community Coll., Charlestown, Mass., 1978—. Pres., Minute Man Assn. for Retarded Citizens, 1977, bd. dirs., 1974—; bd. dirs. Concord Area Bd. Mass. Dept. Mental Health, 1975—. Served with U.S. Army, 1951-54. Recipient Certificate of Merit, Mass. Dept. Mental Health, 1978; Award of Merit, United Way, 1974. Mem. Indsl. Relations Research Assn., Smaller Bus. Assn. New Eng., Mass. Businessmen's Assn., Concord C. of C. Roman Catholic. Home: 265 Oak Hill Circle Concord MA 01742 Office: PO Box 1036 Concord MA 01742

BLOOM, FLORENCE TEICHER, historian; b. N.Y.C., Dec. 12, 1920; d. Max and Etta (Platzman) Teicher; A.B., Hunter Coll., 1943, M.A. (N.Y. State Tchr. Edn. Program scholar), 1960; Ph.D., (City Univ. Grad. Center grantee), U. City N.Y., 1970; m. Nathan Bloom, Dec. 25, 1941 (dec. Feb. 1976); children—Beth Susan, Kenneth Lawrence, Carrie Ellen. Clk. U.S. Air Force, Newark, 1943, registrar, Madison, Wis., 1944-45; tchr., chmn. dept. social studies Tappan Zee High Sch., South Orangetown (N.Y.) Sch. Dist., 1958-66; prof. history, chairperson social sci. dept. Ladycliff Coll., 1966—; rep. of pres. Ladycliff Coll. at Associated Colls. Mid-Hudson Region. N.Y. Edn. Dept. grantee Columbia U., summer 1962. Mem. Orgn. Am. Historians, AAUP, Am. Hist. Assn., AAUW. Quaker. Research on family life styles of lower strata working women in early 20th century Am., on Leonora O'Reilley. Home: PO Box 23 Valley Cottage NY 10989

BLOOM, MELVYN HAROLD, assn. exec.; b. Chgo., Oct. 20, 1938; s. William and Lillian (Antkes) B.; student Roosevelt U., 1955-56; B.S. in Journalism with honors in Polit. Sci., Northwestern U., 1958, M.S.J., 1959; postgrad. Coll. Jewish Studies, Chgo., 1958-60, U. Calif. at Los Angeles, 1964; M.A. in Polit. Sci., New Sch. for Social Research, 1971, postgrad., 1971—; m. Priscilla Newman, June 15, 1958; children—Jeffrey, Alan, Steven, Bradley. Dir. pub. relations Cooley & Borre, Park Ridge, Ill., 1958-59; news editor, reporter, producer CBS News, Chgo., 1959-62; pub. relations dir., program exec. Johnson Found., Racine, Wis., 1962-66; asso. Murden & Co., N.Y.C., 1966-70; dir. pub. relations, nat. office United Jewish Appeal, N.Y.C., 1970-74, asst. exec. vice chmn., 1974—, nat. campaign dir., 1975—; vis. prof. Inst. for Leadership Devel., Jerusalem, 1978; cons. Ford Found., 1967—. Civil rights officer Chgo. Commn. on Human Relations, 1960-61; mem. adv. bd. Nat. Reading Is Fundamental Program, 1970—; mem. program and publs. com. Anti-Defamation League, 1967—; mem. communications com. Nat. Urban League, 1969—; mem. bd. edn. Beth El Synagogue, New Rochelle, 1973—; pub. affairs dir. White House Conf. on Internat. Cooperation, 1965; press sec. Campaign Congressman Lynn Stalbaum, 1964; campaign mgr. Wis. state senator Henry Dorman, 1965. Served with U.S. Air N.G., 1956-62. Recipient Citation, Sec. State, 1965; Gold Key award Pub. Relations News, 1977. Mem. Am. Polit. Sci. Assn., UN Assn. (dir. N.Y. chpt. 1971-73), Pub. Relations Soc. Am. (dir., program chmn. Wis. chpt. 1964-66), N.Y. Deadline Club, Northwestern U., Roosevelt U., New Sch. alumni assns., Sigma Delta Chi. Democrat. Jewish. Mem. B'nai B'rith. Author: Public Relations and Presidential Campaigns: A Crisis in Democracy, 1973; also scripts, articles. Contbr. articles to profl. jours. Home: 445 Wolf's Ln Pelham Manor NY 10803 Office: United Jewish Appeal 1290 Ave Americas New York City NY 10019

BLOOM, SAMUEL MICHAEL, physician; b. Portland, Me., Dec. 27, 1908; s. Max Laib and Bessie Deborah (Baum) B.; B.S. cum laude, N.Y. U., 1932, M.D., 1935; m. Zita S. Greene, June 17, 1945; children—Lloyd Jay, Betty Ann Bloom Berson. Intern Mt. Sinai Hosp., N.Y.C., 1935-36; resident Chesapeake and Ohio Hosp., Clifton Forge, Va., 1936-37; resident Mt. Sinai Hosp., N.Y.C., 1937-39, clin. asst., 1939-40, 46-48, adj., 1948-60, asso. attending, 1960-70, cons. otolaryngologist, 1970—; pvt. practice otolaryngology and plastic surgery, N.Y.C., 1947—; asso. clin. prof. emeritus otolaryngology Mt. Sinai Sch. Medicine, N.Y.C., 1966—. Served to maj. M.C., AUS, 1941-46. Decorated Bronze Star medal. Diplomate Am. Bd. Otolaryngology. Mem. Am. Defenders Bataan and Corregidor (nat. comdr. 1958-59), Am. Friends Hebrew U., Am. Physicians Fellowship, Israel Med. Assn., Jewish War Vets., Zionist Orgn. Am., Am. Acad. Facial Plastic and Reconstructive Surgery (treas. 1969-74), Am. Acad. Otolaryngology, ACS, Am. Laryngol., Rhinol. and Otol. Soc., Med. Soc. County N.Y., N.Y. Acad. Medicine, N.Y. State Med. Soc., Virchow Pirquet Med. Soc., Alpha Omega Alpha. Jewish. Contbr. to books and med. jours. Home: 150 E 77th St New York City NY 10021 Office: 55 E 86th St New York City NY 10028

BLOOM, STEPHEN ROGER, fin. exec.; b. N.Y.C., Dec. 30, 1942; s. Hyman and Frances Roslyn (Hart) B.; B.S., Tulane U., 1964; M.A. in Accounting, N.Y. U., 1965; m. Dale Isacson, May 30, 1966; children—Jodie, Joshua. Staff accountant Mach, Rosenston & Co., N.Y.C., 1965-68, Anchin, Block & Anchin, N.Y.C., 1968-72; controller Papers Sales Corp., Darien, Conn., 1972—, chief fin. officer, fin. v.p., 1974—. C.P.A., N.Y. State. Mem. N.Y. State Soc. of C.P.A.'s. Jewish. Club: Hampshire Country. Home: 13 Old Orchard Rd Port Chester NY 10573

BLOOMENTHAL, ABRAHAM PHILIP, physician; b. Vilna, Russia, Jan. 15, 1908; s. Joseph J. and Ida (Kapansky) B. came to U.S., 1909, naturalized, 1910; certificate, Syracuse U., 1929, M.D., U. Middlesex, 1933; m. Sara Novick, Nov. 26, 1938; children—Leslie, Nowell, Robert. Intern, Beth El Gen. Hosp., Colorado Springs, Colo., 1930, Jefferson Park Hosp., Chgo., 1933; resident Onondaga Gen. Hosp., Syracuse, N.Y., 1934; former mem. staff Onondaga Sanatorium; gen. practice medicine, Waltham, Mass., 1935—; mem. staffs Allerton, Brookline, Mass., Waltham hosps.; physician Mass. Dept. Pub. Safety, Maccabee Athletic Team; surgeon AAU Boxing Team. Mem. Profl. Standards Rev. Orgn. Sec., Boston Investment Assos. Active Combined Jewish Appeal, 1960—. Exec. dir. Waltham Boys' Club; bd. dirs. United Synagogue Council, Middlesex Healing Arts Found. Brandeis U. Served to capt. M.C., AUS, 1943-45. Decorated Bronze Star (three); recipient adv. award, 1968; Man of Year award Jewish War Vets., 1969. Fellow Am. Acad. Family

Practice; mem. AMA, Assn. Mil. Surgeons. Am. Acad. Gen. Practice (mem. credential and membership com.), New Eng. Obstetrics and Gynecology Soc., World, Israel, Ausscalapius, Greater Boston, Charles River, Mass. med. socs., Blue Shield Soc. Physicians, Nat. Assn. Ringside Physicians, Jewish War Vets. U.S. (surgeon gen. Mass. 1967-73), Nat. Sojourners New Eng., VFW, Am. Legion (past post surgeon Waltham), Lexicon, Phi Lambda Upsilon. Jewish (pres. temple). Clubs: Masons (32 deg.), Shriners (surgeon), Moose, Odd Fellows, Eagles, Lions, GranDad's. Home: 55 Woodchester Rd Waltham MA 02154 Office: 5 Banks St Waltham MA 02154

BLOOMER, WILLIAM DAVID, radiation therapist; b. Washington, Aug. 19, 1944; s. Ward LaVern and Vera Catherine (Rochefort) B.; A.B., U. Pa., 1966; M.D., Jefferson Med. Coll., Phila., 1970. Intern Univ. Hosps., Cleve., 1970-71; clin. fellow in radiation therapy Harvard U. Med. Sch., 1971-74, instr., 1974-76, asst. prof., 1976—, mem. sr. common room Lowell House, 1973—. Diplomate Am. Bd. Radiology, Am. Bd. Nuclear Medicine. Mem. Am. Coll. Radiology, Am. Soc. Therapeutic Radiologist, Soc. Nuclear Medicine, Am. Radium Soc., AAAS, Radiation Research Soc., Am. Assn. Cancer Research. Club: Harvard (Boston). Contbr. profl. pubis. Home: 116 Hampshire Rd Wellesley Hills MA 02181 Office: 50 Binney St Boston MA 02115

BLOOMFIELD, NERICE SIEGEL, guidance counselor; b. Hartford, Conn., Apr. 5, 1936; d. Samuel and Mollie (Backer) Siegel; B.S., Simmons Coll., 1958; M.Ed., U. Hartford, 1973; m. Donald Peter Bloomfield, Aug. 18, 1958; children—Maryanne, Paul. Teacher, Wintonbury Sch., Bloomfield, Conn., 1958-60; counselor-intern Sage Park Jr. High Sch., Windsor, Conn., 1973; grad. asst. U. Hartford, 1973-74; counselor Windsor High Sch., 1974—, career specialist, 1978—, fin. aid chairperson, 1977-78. Certified counselor, Conn. Mem. Am., Conn. personnel and guidance assns. Home: 21 Proctor Dr West Hartford CT 06117 Office: 50 Sage Park Rd Windsor CT 04095

BLOOMFIELD, PHILIP EARL, physicist; b. Erie, Pa., Aug. 28, 1934; s. Simon Richard and Ruth Rose (Strauss) B.; B.A., U. Chgo. 1956, B.S. in Physics and Math., 1957, M.S. in Physics, 1959, Ph.D. (Gen. Electric Co. fellow, Woodrow Wilson fellow), 1965; m. Rachael Melhado, Aug. 28, 1958; children—Sharon Rose, Alexa Lynne. Research asso. John Crerar Library, Chgo., 1957; instr., Coll. of U. Chgo., 1958-59, physicist in lab. for applied scis., 1958-60, research physicist lab. of molecular structure, 1959-60, research asst. Inst. for Study of Metals, 1960-64; asst. prof. U. Pa., Phila., 1964-70; asso. prof. Drexel U., Phila., 1969-70, Coll. City N.Y., 1970-73; cons. Pittman Dunn Labs., Frankford Arsenal, Phila., 1967-74; physicist Bur. of Standards, Gaithersburg. Md., 1974-77; sr. research physicist Pennwalt Technol. Center, King of Prussia, Pa., 1977—; guest lectr. magnetic resonance and elec. properties of metals, magnetic alloys and dielectrics in various research insts., colls. and univs, 1964—. Recipient Research and Devel. award for devel. piezopolymer materials U.S. Army, 1976; Advanced Research Project Agy. grantee, 1964-70. Mem. Am. Phys. Soc., AAAS, Sigma Xi. Contbr. numerous articles on solid state physics to sci. jours. and articles on thermodynamics to McGraw-Hill Ency.; research in surface impedance, magnetoresistance and optical properties of metals, magnetic materials, non-linear dielectrics, piezoelectricity, ferroelectricity, superconductivity, and polymer physics. Home: 21 W Dartmouth Rd Bala Cynwyd PA 19004 Office: Pennwalt Corp 900 1st Ave King of Prussia PA 19406

BLOOMFIELD, WILLIAM MENDEL, human services and communication cons.; b. Akron, Ohio, Mar. 10, 1948; s. Jerome and Ruth Bloomfield; B.A. in Edn., U. Akron, 1970; postgrad. Bank St. Coll., N.Y.C., 1976; m. Lynne M. Hirsch, May 28, 1972. Adminstr., Green Art/Graphic House, Farmingdale, N.J., 1970-72; cons., dir. edn. Venture Theatre Inc., Metuchen, N.J., 1972-76; mgr. Newark Boys Chorus, 1976; ind. cons. human services and communication, 1976—; field staff/cons. Urban Reinvestment Task Force, Washington, 1977—; communication therapist Carrier Clinic Found., Belle Mead, N.J., 1976—; trainer, designer in-service tng. programs. Mem. steering com. Mayor Plainfield (N.J.) Task Force Youth, 1976-78; mem. Supt. Edn. Plainfield Ednl. Support Team, 1976-78; neighborhood commnr. Boy Scouts Am., 1973-78. Recipient Outstanding Achievement award theatre dept. Akron U., 1968, 70. Mem. Am. Personnel and Guidance Assn., Assn. Humanistic Edn. and Devel., Nat. Vocat. Guidance Assn., Assn. Specialists in Group Work. Author 15 plays for young people; drama critic N.J. Music and Arts mag., 1974-75. Address: 132 E 9th St Plainfield NJ 07060

BLOOMQUIST, HOWARD RICHARD, bus. exec.; b. Mpls., Sept. 16, 1918; s. Richard P. and Ruth M. (Holmgren) B.; student U. Minn., 1937-40; grad. Advanced Mgmt. Program, Harvard, 1958; m. Ingrid M. Brostrom, Feb. 14, 1941; children—Dennis, Diane (Mrs. W. Mowry Connelly), Laurel (Mrs. Paul Shields). Asst. advt. mgr. Pillsbury Mills, Inc., 1941-46; advt. mgr. Toni div. Gillette Co., 1946-49; gen. mgr. Lever Bros. Co., 1949-53; with Gen. Foods Corp., 1953-68, gen. mgr., 1962-63, v.p., 1963-67, group v.p., 1967-68; dir., sr. partner McKinsey & Co., 1969-71; pres. Grocery Products group, v.p. W.R. Grace, Inc., 1971-73; sr. v.p., pres. consumer products group, dir. Warner Lambert Corp., Morris Plains, N.J., 1973-77, sr. v.p. corp. mktg., 1977—. Trustee Greenwich Acad. Mem. Am. Mgmt. Assn., Assn. Nat. Advertisers. Mem. Community Ch. (chmn. ofcl. bd.). Clubs: Field (Greenwich, Conn.); Harvard Business School (N.Y.C.). Home: Round Hill Rd Greenwich CT 06830 Office: 201 Tabor Rd Morris Plains NJ 07950

BLOOMSTEIN, MICHAEL IRA, microbiologist; b. Bklyn., Nov. 8, 1944; s. Herman A. and Bertha M. (Monisoff) B.; B.S. (N.Y. State Regents scholar), Cornell U., 1966; Ph.D. (NIH fellow), Northwestern U. Med. Sch., 1971; m. Cheryle S. Greenston, June 15, 1968; 1 son, Daniel Seth. Research fellow Hoffman-LaRoche Inst. Molecular Biology, Nutley, N.J., 1971-73; mgr. biol. quality control Pall Corp., filter mfg., Glen Cove, N.Y., 1973-76; sr. microbiologist Hoechst Roussel Pharmaceuticals Inc., Somerville, N.J., 1976-77, group leader, 1978—. Mem. Am. Soc. Microbiology, Soc. Indsl. Microbiology, Parenteral Drug Assn. Home: 50 Prospect Ave Bridgewater NJ 08807 Office: Hoechst Roussel Pharmaceuticals Inc Route 202-206 North Somerville NJ 08876

BLOORE, ERNEST WILLIAM, metallurgist; b. Bklyn., July 31, 1931; s. John William and Cynthia Louise (Burrowes) B.; A.A.S., N.Y. State A. and T. Inst., 1951; B.S., Johns Hopkins U., 1960; Ph.D., U. Utah, 1971; m. Dorothy Frances Spear, July 25, 1953; children—Deborah Ann, Barbara Ann, Pamela Ann. Technician, Brookhaven Nat. Lab., 1951-54; chemist. U.S. Army Nuclear Def. Lab., Md., 1956-69; chemist U.S. Army Ballistic Research Lab., Aberdeen Proving Ground, Md., 1969-71, metallurgist, 1971-78; chief materials tech. br., fire control and small caliber weapons systems lab. U.S. Army Armament Research and Devel. Command, Dover, N.J., 1978—. Served with AUS, 1954-56. Mem. Am. Soc. Metals, Md. Inst. Metals, Chespeake Wine Soc. Research in radioactive waste disposal, radioactive fallout, ballistic materials. Home: 70 Warren Rd Sparta NJ 07871 Office: US Army Research and Devel Command Dover NJ 07801

BLOUGH, WILLIAM MILTON, musician, ret. educator; b. Meyersdale, Pa., Mar. 9, 1914; s. John A. and Orpha E. (Barndt) B.; B.S. in Music Edu., Juniata Coll., 1936; M.F.A. in Music Edn., Carnegie-Mellon U., 1948; student Peabody Conservatory, Eastman Sch. Music, Syracuse U., Acad. Music, Vienna, Austria; m. Olive Elizabeth Harley, Sep. 1, 1938; children—William Milton, Donald Harley. Tchr., Meyersdale (Pa.) Pub. Schs., 1936-37, Bellevue (Pa.) Pub. Schs., 1937-39; choral dir. William Penn High Schl., Harrisburg, Pa., 1939-45; choral dir., supr. Farrell (Pa.) Pub. Schs., 1945-48; dir. music. edn. Sharon (Pa.) sch. dist., 1948-75; music lectr. Pa. State U., 1971-72, 75, 76-77; condr. Sharon Steel Male Chrous, 1947-64; music dir. Shenango Valley Chorale, 1972—; bd. dirs. Community Concerts Assn., 1946-75; voice tchr., guest condr. music festivals, clinician, lectr., adjudicator, ch. music dir. Mem. Mayor's Bicentennial Com., Mayor's Arts Com. Mem. Am. Fedn. Musicians (hon.), NEA, Pa. Music Educators Assn., Music Educators Nat. Conf., Am. Choral Dir. Assn., Nat. Assn. Tchrs. Singing, Nat. Ret. Tchrs. Assn., Phi Mu Alpha Sinfonia. Republican. Methodist. Clubs: Rotary, Music (Sharon). Home: 1635 Highland Rd Sharon PA 16146

BLOUNT, KENNETH MORGAN, JR., service co. ofcl.; b. Akron, Ohio, July 31, 1946; s. Kenneth Morgan and Louisa Marie (Geul) B.; A.B. in History, Middlebury, Coll., 1968; m. Cheri J. D. Zwieg, May 25, 1974; children—Raechel Ann, Kameron Marie. Staff asst. personnel, SCM Corp., N.Y.C., 1968-71; dir. Diners Club Inc., Denver, 1971-74; dir. indls. relations IPCO Hosp. Supply Corp., White Plains, N.Y., 1974-76; dir. personnel Avis Rent A Car, Garden City, N.Y., 1976—; guest lectr. Middlebury Coll. Served with U.S. Army, 1969-71. Decorated Bronze Star. Mem. Am. Soc. Personnel Adminstrn., Adminstrv. Mgmt. Soc. Republican. Episcopalian. Clubs: Stamford Yacht (com. chmn.), Denver Athletic. Home: 29 Ralsey Rd Stamford CT 06902 Office: 900 Old Country Rd Garden City NY 11530

BLOUSTEIN, EDWARD J., ednl. adminstr.; b. N.Y.C., Jan. 20, 1925; s. Samuel and Cecilia (Einwohner) B.; B.A., N.Y. U., 1948; B.Phil. (Fulbright scholar), Wadham Coll., Oxford (Eng.) U., 1950; Ph.D., Cornell U., 1954, J.D., 1959; LL.D. (hon.), Coll. Charleston, 1976, U. Pa., 1975, N.Y. U., 1972, Cedar Crest Coll., 1970; m. Ruth Ellen Steinman, Oct. 6, 1951; children—Elise, Lori. Polit. analyst Dept. State, 1951-52; instr. logic and philosophy Cornell U., Ithaca, N.Y., 1954-55; admitted to N.Y. bar, 1959; prof. law N.Y. U., 1961-65; pres. Bennington (Vt.) Coll., 1965-71, Rutgers U., New Brunswick, N.J., 1971—; mem. spl. com. to study copyright laws Am. Assn. Law Schs.-Am. Assn. Colls., 1972—; chmn. commn. on financing higher edn. Nat. Assn. State Univs. and Land-Grant Colls., 1974—, chmn. legal affairs com., 1975—; chmn. acad. adv. com. Jewish Acad. Without Walls, 1973—; mem. spl. com. to study tort liability of acad. instns. Am. Assn. Colls., 1973—; mem. adv. council Cornell U. Law Sch., 1974—; adv. council dept. philosophy Princeton U., 1973—; bd. visitors Sch. Internat. Tng., Expt. for Internat. Living, 1968—. Mem. exec. com. Cancer Inst. N.J., 1975—. Mem. Bar Assn. City of N.Y. (mem. spl. com. on 2d Century 1975—), Phi Beta Kappa. Contbr. articles to legal jours. Editor-in-chief Cornell Law Quar., 1959. Clubs: Century, University (N.Y.C.). Address: 1245 River Rd Piscataway NJ 08854

BLUE, ROSE, author, educator; b. N.Y.C., Dec. 3, 1931; d. Irving and Frieda (Rosenberg) Bluestone; B.A., Bklyn. Coll., 1953; postgrad. Bank St. Coll. Edn., 1967. Tchr., N.Y.C. pub. schs., 1955—. Mem. Authors' Guild Am., Authors' League Am., MENSA, Profl. Women's Caucus, Broadcast Music, Inc. Author: A Quiet Place, 1969, Black, Black Beautiful Black, 1969, How Many Blocks Is The World, 1970, Bed-Stuy Beat, 1970, I Am Here (Yo Estoy Aqui), 1971; A Month of Sundays, 1972; Grandma Didn't Wave Back, 1972; Nikki 108, 1973; We are Chicano, 1973; The Preacher's Kid, 1975; Seven Years from Home, 1976; The Yo Yo Kid, 1976; The Thirteenth Year, 1977; lyricist: Drama of Love, 1964, Let's Face It, 1961, Give Me a Break, 1962, My Heartstrings Keep Me Tied To You, 1963, Homecoming Party, 1966. Contbg. editor: Teacher mag. Home and office: 1320 51st St Brooklyn NY 11219

BLUE SPRUCE, GEORGE, JR., health ofcl.; b. Santa Fe, N.Mex., 1931; D.D.S. (Elks fellow), Creighton U.; M.P.H., U. Calif. Sch. Pub. Health, 1967; married. Formerly practiced dentistry; liaison officer for Am. Indian Affairs, Washington; now dir. Office Native Am. Programs Dept. HEW, Washington. Office: Dept Health Edn and Welfare Washington DC 20201

BLUESTEIN, BERNARD RICHARD, chem. co. exec.; b. Phila., Oct. 7, 1925; s. Joseph and Minnie (Ravkin) B.; B.S., U. Pa., 1946; M.S., U. Ill., 1947, Ph.D. in Organic Chemistry, 1949; M.B.A., Fairleigh Dickinson U., 1967; m. Claire Kraiman, June 22, 1947; children—Rhona, Sherrie, Hazel, Carol. Research asso. in chemistry Rutgers U., New Brunswick, N.J., 1949-51; research fellow Purdue U., West Lafayette, Ind., 1951-52; asst. prof. Coe Coll., Cedar Rapids, Iowa, 1952-55; sr. research chemist Sonneborn Chem. & Refining Co., Petrolia, Pa., 1955-59, asst. supt., 1959-62, dir. research, 1960-62; mgr. corporate research labs., asst. dir. corporate research and devel. Witco Chem. Corp., Oakland, N.J., 1962-75, dir. central research, 1976—; prof. continuing edn. Pa. State U. Extension, 1957-61. Pres. Petrolia Vol. Fire Dept., 1960-61; active Boy Scouts Am., 1956-62. Bd. dirs. Glen Rock (N.J.) Jewish Center, 1963—. Mem. Am., Brit. chem. socs., Am. Inst. Chemists, Iowa Acad. Sci., Sigma Xi. Editor: Amphoteric Surfactants, 1974. Contbr. articles to profl. jours. Patentee in field. Home 358 Dunham Pl Glen Rock NJ 07452 Office: 100 Bauer Dr Oakland NJ 07436

BLUH, GEORGE KENNETH, historian; b. Astoria, N.Y., Mar. 28, 1932; s. Arthur and Frieda (Reich) B.; B.S., U. Colo., 1958, M.A., 1964; student Yale U. Summer Lang. Inst., 1962; postgrad. U. Wash., 1966-69; m. Cynthia Hubbard, Feb. 25, 1961; children—Geoffrey, Alexandra, Joshua, Rebecca. Chmn. dept. social studies Frontier Regional Sch., Deerfield, Mass., 1969-70; tchr. emotionally distrubed teenage boys Conn. Jr. Republic, Litchfield, 1964-66; free-lance writer, tutor in Chinese lang., 1971-74; asst. to pres. Greenfield (Mass.) Community Coll., 1974-75, instr. history and philosophy, 1975—; project cons. Mass. Found. for Humanities and Pub. Policy. Pres. Franklin County Big Brother/Big Sister Assn., 1977-78; mem. Com. Concerned Asian Scholars, 1967-71; active Asian Studies Outreach. Served with USAF, 1951-55. NDEA Lang. fellow, 1966. Mem. Am. Hist. Assn., Assn. for Asian Studies, Mass. Audubon Soc., Psi Chi, Phi Alpha Theta. Democrat. Unitarian. Clubs: Norman Bird, Appalachian Mountain. Author: The Kuldja Crisis: An Historical Survey, 1964. Home: Mathews Rd Conway MA 01341 Office: Greenfield Community Coll Greenfield MA 01301

BLUM, JAMES DAVID, SR., realtor; b. Pitts., May 23, 1906; s. Harry Morton and Celia B.; student U. Balt., Am. U. Sch. Law, Washington; m. Fiola Shapiro, Sept. 14, 1930; children—James D., Harry M. Owner, operator Harry M. Blum & Son, Balt., 1928-38; mdse. mgr. Hecht Bros., Balt., 1941-49; broker Fiola Blum, Inc., Realtors, Balt. 1948-66, pres., 1966—. Mem. Nat. Assn. Realtors, Greater Balt. Bd. Realtors (dir. 1973-74), Md. Assn. Realtors (dir. 1974-75), Md. Realtors Polit. Action Com. (treas. 1973—, life), Citizens Planning and Housing Assn. Jewish. Club: Suburban of Balt. County. Home: 11 Slade Ave Pikesville MD 21208 Office: 110 Slade Ave Pikesville MD 21208

BLUM, JOHN JAY, hosp. adminstr.; b. N.Y.C., Oct. 26, 1945; s. John and Sybil (Levy) B.; student Marquette U., 1973; B.S. in Biology, St. John's U., 1967; postgrad. Howard U., 1967-68, N.Y. U. Sch. Medicine, 1968-71; M.S., State U. N.Y., 1976; m. Sharon Dukette, Feb. 25, 1970. Pub. relations exec. Pinkerton Nat. Detective Agy., N.Y. World's Fair div., 1963-65; field supr. Neighborhood Youth Corps, N.Y.C., 1965-68; program adminstr. Astoria Youth in Action, N.Y.C., 1968; health researcher in infant mortality study Cornell U. Med. Sch., N.Y.C., 1969; therapeutic activities group leader Bellevue Hosp., dept. psychiatry, N.Y.C., 1969-70; founder, pres. Am. Med. and Dental Assn. Students, 1969-70; v.p. Student Nat. Med. Assn., 1970-71; psychol. researcher High Scope Ednl. Found., 1972-73; adminstrv. resident Sydenham Hosp. Neighborhood Family Care Center, N.Y.C., 1973—, exec. dir., 1976—, asso. dir., 1975-76; preceptor health care adminstrn. program Coll. City N.Y., 1976—; cons. health services and systems, 1978. Mem. N.Y.C. mayor's task force; pres. N.Y. Com. to Save Arts and Culture, 1977. Martin Luther King fellow, 1968-71; named Outstanding Young Man Am., U.S. Jaycees, 1977; lic. nursing home adminstr. Mem. Am. Hosp. Assn., Am. Pub. Health Assn., Internat. Acad. Preventive Medicine, Acad. Polit. Sci., Assn. Fin. Mgmt. Home: 5800 Arlington Ave Riverdale NY 10471

BLUM, LUDWIG LEONHARD, physician; b. Pfungstadt, Germany, July 15, 1911; s. Julius J. and Agathe (Jeidel) B.; came to U.S., 1938, naturalized, 1943; student Goethe U., Frankfurt, Germany, 1930-33; M.D., U. Geneva, 1938; m. Mary Joanne Hoyt; children—Claire, Jonathan; 1 dau. by previous marriage, Arlene. Intern, Jackson Park Hosp., Chgo., 1941-42; resident Research Hosp., U. Ill., Chgo., 1942-44; practice medicine specializing in anesthesiology, Chgo., 1948-51, N.Y.C., 1951-65, Franklin Delanoe Roosevelt Hosp., Montrose, N.Y., 1965—; instr. anesthesiology Albert Einstein Coll. Medicine, N.Y.C., 1960-73, asst. prof., 1973—; rep. surg. service VA at com. of Nat. Standards Inst. and Internat. Standard Orgn., 1974—. Served to capt. USPHS, 1945-47. Mem. Am. Coll. Anesthesiology, Am., N.Y. State socs. anesthesiology, Am. Soc. Clin. and Exptl. Hypnosis, Am. Soc. Clin. Hypnosis, Internat. Soc. Hypnosis, N.Y. State, New York County med. socs., N.Y. Acad. Sci. Office: Franklin Delanoe Roosevelt Hosp Montrose NY 10548

BLUM, MAURICE DAULTON, bus. exec., interior designer; b. San Francisco, July 27, 1925; s. Julian Jack and Juliette Vivian (Cohen) B.; B.S., U. Calif. at Los Angeles, 1945; postgrad. Rudolph Schaeffer Sch. Design, 1950. Vice-pres. John J. Greer-Maurice D. Blum Assos., Inc., Washington, 1957-77; pres. Interior Design Cons., 1967—. Founder mem. Friends of Kennedy Center; mem. visual arts com. D.C. Commn. for Endowment Arts and Humanities, 1974-75. Served with USNR, 1942-45, 47-49. Mem. Am. Inst. Interior Designers, Zeta Beta Tau. Club: Black Tie (Washington). Address: 2248 49th St NW Washington DC 20007

BLUMBERG, ARNOLD GEORGE, physician; b. Bklyn., Apr. 25, 1920; s. Max and Edith (Miller) B.; B.S., Coll. City N.Y., 1941; M.S., U. Pa., 1942; M.D., N.Y.U., 1945; m. Barbara Salmanson, June 19, 1949; children—Florence Ellen Schwartz, Martin Jay, Emily Anne. Tng. internal medicine and neuropsychiatry Goldwater Meml. Hosp., N.Y.U. Div., 1948-51; fellow in medicine N.Y.U. Coll. Medicine, 1950-52; pvt. practice specializing in internal medicine, Manhasset, N.Y., 1950—; dir. med. services Hillside Hosp., Glen Oaks, N.Y.; dir. medicine Manhasset (N.Y.) Hosp., also pres. exec. com. of med. staff; attending staff L.I. Jewish, North Shore hosps.; asso. prof. medicine State U., Stoney Brook. Chmn. Lake Success Citizens Party, 1962; mem. Nassau County Democratic Com. Served to capt. AUS, 1946-48. Diplomate Am. Bd. Internal Medicine. Fellow A.C.P., Am. Coll. Clin. Pharmacology, Am. Acad. Clin. Toxicology; mem. A.M.A., N.Y. State, Nassau County med. socs., Am. Psychosomatic Soc., Am. Heart Assn., Gerontol. Soc. Club: Glen Oaks. Contbr. articles to profl. jours. Home: 12 Birch Hill Rd Lake Success NY 11020 Office: 1554 Northern Blvd Manhasset NY 11030

BLUMBERG, BARBARA SALMANSON (MRS. ARNOLD G. BLUMBERG), civic worker; b. Bklyn., Oct. 2, 1927; d. Sam and Mollie (Greenberg) Salmanson; B.A., De Pauw U., 1948; postgrad. New Sch. for Social Research, N.Y.C.; m. Arnold G. Blumberg, June 19, 1949; children—Florence Ellen Schwartz, Martin Jay, Emily Anne. Pub. relations Nate Fein & Co., N.Y.C., 1948-51; free lance, 1960—; councilwoman, North Hempstead, 1975—. Pres., UN Assn. Great Neck, N.Y., 1967-69, chmn. China Study Workshop, 1966-67; pres. Shalom chpt. Hadassah, 1955-57; exec. v.p. Lakeville P.T.A., Great Neck, 1963-65; exec. v.p. Great Neck S. Jr. High Sch., 1965-66; co-chmn. Great Neck UNICEF, 1968-70, mem. speakers bur., 1971—; v.p. Herricks Community Life Center, 1976-77, B'nai B'rith, Lake Success, N.Y.; coordinator, 6th Congl. Dist., N.Y. McGovern for Pres.; bd. dirs. New Democratic Coalition of Nassau; v.p. Reform Dem. Assn. Great Neck; bd. dirs. Citizen's Sch. Com., Great Neck; mem. platform com. Nassau Dem. Com.; mem. adv. com. to speaker N.Y. State Assembly. Recipient award Anti-Defamation League, New Hyde Park, N.Y., 1975, Alumni award DePauw U., 1977. Mem. N.Y. Alumni Club DePauw U. (trustee), North Shore Archeol. Assn. (chmn. study group), Women in Communication, Internat. Platform Assn., Alpha Lambda Delta. Club: Glen Oaks. Home: 12 Birch Hill Rd Great Neck NY 11020 Office: 220 Plandome Rd Manhasset NY 11030

BLUMBERG, BARUCH SAMUEL, research physician; b. N.Y.C., July 28, 1925; s. Meyer and Ida (Simonoff) B.; B.S., Union Coll., Schenectady, 1946; M.D., Columbia, 1951; Ph.D., Balliol Coll., Oxford (Eng.) U., 1957; m. Jean Liebesman, Apr. 4, 1954; children—Anne, George, Jane, Noah. Intern, resident Columbia div. Bellevue Hosp., N.Y.C.; fellow in medicine Columbia-Presbyn. Med. Center, N.Y.C.; chief geog. medicine and genetics sect. NIH, Bethesda, Md., 1957-64; asso. dir. clin. research Inst. Cancer Research, Phila., 1964—; univ. prof. medicine, also prof. anthropology U. Pa. Med. Sch. Served to ensign USNR, 1943-46. Recipient Albion O. Bernstein M.D. award Med. Soc. State of N.Y., 1969; Grand Sci. award Phi Lambda Kappa, 1972, Ann. award Eastern Pa. br. Am. Soc. Microbiology, 1972; Eppinger prize U. Freiburg (Germany), 1973; Passano award Williams and Wilkens Co., 1974; Modern Medicine Distinguished Achievement award, 1975; Internat. award Gairdner Found., 1975; Karl Landsteiner Meml. award Am. Assn. Blood Banks, 1975; Nobel prize, 1976. Fellow ACP; mem. Nat. Acad. Scis., Assn. Am. Physicians, Am. Soc. Clin. Investigation, Am. Soc. Human Genetics, Am. Soc. Phys. Anthropologists, John Morgan Soc., Chesapeake and Ohio Canal Soc. Clubs: Provincetown Yacht, Explorers. Contbr. articles to profl. jours. Discoverer causative agt. hepatitis B. Office: Inst Cancer Research 7701 Burholme Ave Philadelphia PA 19111

BLUMBERG, GERALD, lawyer; b. N.Y.C., July 25, 1911; s. Saul and Amelia (Abramowitz) B.; A.B. cum laude (scholar), Cornell U., 1931; J.D. cum laude (scholar), Harvard U., 1934; m. Rhoda Shapiro, Jan. 6, 1945; children—Lawrence, Rena, Alice, Leda. Instr. econs. Cornell U., Ithaca, N.Y., 1931; admitted to N.Y. State bar, 1934, Mass. bar, 1934; practiced in N.Y.C., 1934—. Bd. dirs. nat. urban affairs com. Anti-Defamation League; mem. nat. estate affairs com. Cornell U. Council; bd. dirs. of Am. com. Weizmann Inst. Sci. Mem. Am., Internat., Fed., N.Y. State, Westchester, Yorktown bar assns., N.Y. County Lawyers Assn., Phi Beta Kappa, Phi Kappa Phi. Home: Baptist Church Rd Yorktown Heights NY 10598 Office: 1 Rockefeller Plaza New York City NY 10020

BLUMBERG, HAROLD, surgeon; b. Cin., Mar. 3, 1930; s. Oscar and Rae (Bernstein) B.; B.S., U. Cin., 1952, M.D., 1956; m. Amy Burnshaw, June 12, 1959; children—Kathryn, John, Jennifer. Intern, Jewish Hosp., Cin., 1956-57; resident in gen. surgery Bronx Mcpl. Hosp., N.Y.C., 1957-59, 61-64; practice medicine specializing in surgery Poughkeepsie, N.Y., 1965—; mem. staff Vassar Brothers Hosp., St. Francis Hosp. (Poughkeepsie); dir. intensive care unit Vassar Brothers Hosp., 1971—. Served with USAF, 1959-61. Diplomate Am. Bd. Surgery. Fellow ACS.; mem. AMA, Dutchess County Med. Soc., Mid Hudson Surg. Soc., Phi Beta Kappa. Home: 160 Kingwood Park Poughkeepsie NY 12601 Office: 7 Fox St Poughkeepsie NY 12601

BLUMBERG, JOEL MYRON, cardiologist; b. N.Y.C., Oct. 17, 1940; s. Howard Godfrey and Lily Ruth (Goldberg) B.; B.A., DePauw U., 1962; M.D., N.Y.U., 1966; m. Judith Ellen Green, Aug. 23, 1964; children—Amy, Hillary, Michelle. Intern, N.Y.U.-Bellevue Med. Center, N.Y.C., 1966-67, resident in internal medicine, 1969-71; fellow in cardiology Cornell U.-N.Y. Hosp., 1971-73; pvt. practice internal medicine and cardiology, Old Greenwich, Conn., 1973—; asso. attending staff Greenwich Hosp., 1973—, coronary care cons., 1973—; physician to out-patients N.Y. Hosp., 1973—; med. dir. Electrolux Corp., Old Greenwich, 1975—; clin. instr. Cornell U. Med. Coll., 1971—, Yale Sch. Medicine, 1975—; lectr. in preventive cardiology to civic groups. Trustee, Temple Sholom, Greenwich, Conn. Diplomate Am. Bd. Internal Medicine. Fellow A.C.P., Am. Coll. Cardiology; mem. Am. Soc. Internal Medicine, N.Y. Heart Assn., Greenwich, Fairfield County, Conn. State med. socs. Club: B'nai B'rith (Stamford, Conn.). Contbr. articles to profl. jours. Home: 59 Old Stone Bridge Rd Cos Cob CT 06807 Office: 8 West End Ave Old Greenwich CT 06870

BLUMBERG, LAWRENCE, orthopaedic surgeon; b. Westchester, Pa., May 26, 1947; s. Howard and Sylvia Ruth (Richards) B.; B.A., Western Md. Coll., 1967; M.D., U. Md., 1971; m. Joan S. Laytin, June 15, 1971; children—Eric, Michael. Intern, U. Md. Hosp., 1971-72, resident, 1972-75; practice medicine specializing in orthopaedic surgery, Balt., 1975—; instr. dept. surgery U. Md. Med. Sch., Balt., 1975. Served with U.S. Army, 1971-77. Diplomate Am. Bd. Orthopaedic Surgery. Mem. Md. Orthopaedic Soc., Med.-Chi Faculty Md., U. Md. Surg. Soc., Baltimore County Med. Soc. Republican. Jewish. Office: 1900 E Northern Pkwy Baltimore MD 21239

BLUME, JAMES BERYL, real estate developer; b. N.Y.C., Apr. 9, 1941; s. Philip F. and Mary R. (Kirschman) B.; B.A., Williams Coll., 1963; M.A., Harvard, 1966. With Faulkner, Dawkins & Sullivan, N.Y.C., 1966-73, sr. v.p., 1971-73; partner Omega Properties, N.Y.C., 1973-75; v.p. Arthur M. Fischer, Inc., 1975-76, exec. v.p., 1976-77, cons., 1978—; dir. Koger Properties, Inc., Jacksonville, Fla., 1969-74; mem. faculty, L.I. U., 1972, Bklyn. Coll., 1974-75. Mem. Lexington Democratic Club, 1968—; campaign mgr. southern Vt., Philip Hoff, 1970; mem. Dem. County Com., N.Y.C., 1972—; bd. dirs. Sydney Found., N.Y.C. Mem. Williams Coll. Soc. Alumni (exec. com. 1970-75). Clubs: Williams, Harvard (N.Y.C.); Tennis Center. Home: 108 E 91st St New York City NY 10028 Office: Sharpstown Shopping Center PO Box 36201 Houston TX 77019

BLUME, ROBERT MURRAY, ret. army officer, psychologist, county ofcl.; b. Detroit, Jan. 13, 1929; s. Arthur and Rose (Glass) B.; B.A., Providence Coll., 1951; M.S.W., Boston U., 1953; M.A., New Sch. for Social Research, 1962; M.Ed., Columbia, 1970, Ed.D., 1971; m. Suzanne Achison, May 24, 1952; children—Howard, Richard, Barbara, Carol. Commd. 1st lt. U.S. Army, 1955, advanced through grades to lt. col., 1968; psychiat. social worker Mental Health Clinic, Fort Ord, Calif., 1955-57; chief psychiat. social worker Mental Health Clinic, Ft. Monmouth, N.J., 1957-60; mental health cons. Mental Health Clinic, Ft. Dix, N.J., 1960-63; chief social worker and mental health cons. U.S. Army Hosp., Wurzburg, Germany, 1963-65; instr. psychology and sociology European Extension program U. Md., Wurzburg, 1963-65; asst. chief social work service Fitzsimmons Gen. Hosp., Denver, 1965-66; chief mental retardation sect. Office of Surgeon Gen., Dept. Army, Washington, 1966-68; chief psychiat. br. Biomed. Stress Research Div., Office of Surgeon Gen., 1971-72, chief Biomed. Stress Research Div., U.S. Army Research and Devel. Command, Office of Surgeon Gen., 1972-73; chief social work service Walter Reed Army Med. Center, Washington, 1973-74; ret., 1974; dep. commr. Nassau County Dept. Mental Health, Mineola, N.Y., 1974—; adj. prof. C.W. Post Coll., L.I. U., 1976; mem. Comprehensive Health Planning Council of Nassau-Suffolk Counties, 1974—. Bd. dirs. Econ. Opportunity Commn. of Nassau City, Inc., 1974—, Mobilization Community Resources, 1974—; chmn. Nassau County legis. com. Nassau/Suffolk Health Systems Agy.; mem. Nassau County Title XX Adv. Council Nassau County Dept. Social Services. Mem. Am. Psychol. Assn., Nat. Assn. Social Workers, Ret. Officers Assn., Am. Assn. Marriage and Family Counselors. Contbr. articles to profl. jours. Home: 39 Edgewood Pl Great Neck NY 11024 Office: Nassau County Dept Mental Health 240 Old Country Rd Mineola NY 11501

BLUMENBERG, ROBERT MURRAY, surgeon; b. Rochester, N.Y., Jan. 5, 1934; b. Rochester, N.Y., Jan. 5, 1934; s. Theodore P. and Esther S. Blumenberg; A.B. cum laude, Amherst Coll., 1955; M.D., Albany Med. Coll., 1959; m. Linda B. Dibble, Dec. 13, 1962; children—Andrew, Dara, Laura. Intern, Strong Meml. Hosp., Rochester, 1959-60; asst. resident in surgery Albany (N.Y.) Med. Center Hosps., 1960-64, chief resident, 1964-65; pvt. practice gen. and vascular surgery, Schenectady, 1968—; attending surgeon Ellis Hosp., St. Clare's Hosp.; cons. surgeon Glenridge, Sunnyview Bellevue hosps., Schenectady, also VA Hosp., Albany; clin. instr. surgery Albany Med. Coll., 1968—. Servde with U.S. Army, 1965-67. Recipient various fellowships; diplomate Am. Bd. Surgery. Fellow A.C.S.; mem. Viet Nam Vascular Registry, Internat. Cardiovascular Soc., Soc. Clin. Vascular Surgery, Upstate N.Y. Vascular Surg. Soc., Am. Trauma Soc. Republican. Jewish. Club: Schuyler Meadows (Loudonville). Contbr. articles to profl. jours. Home: 2259 Algonquin Rd Schenectady NY 12309 Office: 1412 Union St Schenectady NY 12308

BLUMENGARTEN, GAIL RACHEL, tchr.; b. Springfield, Mass., Oct. 27, 1945; d. Irving and Ada (Cohen) Weiner; B.S. in Elem. Edn., Am. Internat. Coll., 1968; M.Ed. in Counseling, Boston State Coll. 1974; m. Jerome A. Blumengarten, Aug. 7, 1977. Tchr. grades 2, 3, 4, Lincoln Sch., Melrose, Mass. 1967-77; admnstrv. asst. Internat. Mktg. Inst., Cambridge, Mass. 1969-(76; coordinator lawyers in classroom program Open Doors, N.Y.C. 1977—. Certified tchr., counselor, admnstr. of WISC tests, Mass. Mem. NEA, Mass. Tchrs. Assn., Melrose Tchrs. Assn., Nat. Council for Social Studies, Am. Personnel and Guidance Assn. Jewish. Home: 3215 Ave H Apt 4-L Brooklyn NY 11210

BLUMENTHAL, ELLIOTT DAVIS, JR., obstetrician, gynecologist; b. Savannah, Ga., Mar. 30, 1920; s. Elliott and Ruby (Jankower) B.; B.S., U. Ga., 1939; M.D., Columbia U., 1943; m. Julia Hutzler Schaefer, May 7, 1944; children—Elliott J., David M., Mary S. Intern Beth Israel Hosp., N.Y.C., 1943, resident, 1947-50, now attending obstetrics and gynecology; resident Hosp. Joint Diseases, N.Y.C., 1951-52; practice medicine specializing in obstetrics and gynecology, N.Y.C., 1952—; asso. obstetrics and gynecology Univ. Hosp., 1968—; attending obstetrics and gynecology Bellevue Hosp., N.Y.C., 1968—; dir. cytology labs. Univ. Hosp., Beth Israel Med. Center, N.Y.C., 1957—; clin. prof. obstetrics and gynecology N.Y. U. Med Sch., N.Y.C., 1977—; asso. dir. obstetrics and gynecology Beth Israel Med. Center, 1974—. Lectr. obstetrics and gynecology Mt. Sinai Sch. Medicine, N.Y.C., 1970—. Served to capt. M.C., AUS, 1944-46. Am. Cancer Soc. fellow, 1952. Diplomate Am. Bd. Obstetrics and Gynecology. Fellow Am. Coll. Obstetrics and Gynecology; mem. Am. Soc. Cytology, N.Y. Acad. Medicine, Pan Am. Med. Assn., N.Y. Gynecol. Soc., N.Y. Acad. Scis. Contbr. articles to med. jours. Home: 4731 Grosvenor Ave Riverdale NY 10471 Office: 200 E 78th St New York City NY 10021

BLUMENTHAL, JOSEPH, designer-printer, printing historian; b. N.Y.C., Oct. 4, 1897; s. Solomon and Rose (Hart) B.; student Cornell U., 1915-17; m. Apr. 25, 1929. Founder, owner, operator Spiral Press, N.Y.C., 1926-71; exhibited books and ephemera at Cornell U., 1961, Pierpont Morgan Library, N.Y.C., 1966, also nat. libraries of Belgium, Holland, Scotland and Israel; designer Emerson typeface; now printing historian. Mem. Am. Inst. Graphic Arts (medal 1952), Grolier Club N.Y. (hon.), Boston Soc. Printers (hon.). Author: The Spiral Press Through Four Decades, 1966; Art of the Printed Book 1455-1955, 1973; The Printed Book in America, 1977. Home and Office: Box 86 West Cornwall CT 06796

BLUMENTHAL, W. MICHAEL, govt. ofcl.; b. Berlin, Germany, Jan. 3, 1926; s. Edward and Rose Valerie (Markt) B.; came to U.S., 1947, naturalized, 1952; B.S., U. Calif. at Berkeley, 1951; M.A., Princeton U., 1953, M.P.A., 1953, Ph.D., 1956; m. Margaret Eileen Polley, Sept. 8, 1951; children—Ann Margaret, Gillian, Jane Eileen. Research asso. Princeton U., 1954-57; labor arbitrator State of N.J., Trenton, 1955-57; v.p., dir. Crown Cork Internat. Corp., Jersey City, 1957-61; dep. asst. sec. state, Washington, 1961-63; ambassador, Pres.'s dep. spl. rep. for trade negotiations, Geneva, Switzerland 1963-67; pres., chief operating officer Bendix Internat. (operating group of Bendix Corp.), N.Y.C., 1967-70; vice chmn. Bendix Corp., 1970, pres., chief operating officer, dir., 1971-72, chmn., pres., chief exec. officer, 1972-77, also dir. numerous fgn. affiliated cos.; sec. Dept. of the Treasury, Washington, 1977—. Trustee Princeton Found. Mem. Am. Econ. Assn., Council Fgn. Relations, Phi Beta Kappa. Author profl. articles. Office: Dept of Treasury 15th St & Pennsylvania Ave Washington DC 20220

BLUMSTOCK, ROBERT EDWARD, sociologist, educator; b. N.Y.C., Oct. 5, 1934; s. Ernest and Sari (Berger) B.; B.A., Coll. City N.Y., 1956; Ph.D., U. Oreg., 1964; m. Ruth Babara Singer, Jan. 19, 1958; children—Judith Evelyn, Miriam Rita. Instr. dept. sociology U. Conn., Storrs, 1962-64; asst. prof. to asso. prof. sociology McMaster U., Hamilton, Ont., Can., 1964—; chmn. dept. sociology, 1968-71; vis. lectr. Karl Marx U., Budapest, Hungary, 1972; researcher Canadian Center for Folk Culture Studies, Nat. Mus. of Man, Ottawa, Ont. Social Sci. Research Council Can. grantee, 1966; Can. Council grantee, 1968. Served with U.S. Army, 1957-59. Mem. Canadian Sociology and Anthropology Assn., Am. Sociol. Assn. Jewish. Author: Public Opinion in Hungary. Contbr. articles to profl. jours. Home: 8 Daleview Ct Hamilton ON L8S 3L8 Canada Office: Dept Sociology McMaster U Hamilton ON L8S 4M4 Canada

BOAL, BERNARD HARVEY, cardiologist; b. Winnipeg, Man., Can., May 14, 1937; s. Charles and Bessie (Carr) B.; came to U.S., 1964; B.S. in Medicine, U. Man., 1962, M.D., 1962; m. Pamela Sharon Brownstone, Oct. 28, 1962; children—Steven, Jeremy, Hilary. Intern, Winnipeg Gen. Hosp., 1962-63, resident in medicine, 1963-64; resident in medicine U. Utah Hosps., Salt Lake City, 1964-66; USPHS trainee in Cardiology N.Y. U. Med. Center, N.Y.C., 1966-68; practice medicine specializing in cardiology, Flushing, N.Y., 1969—; mem. Booth Meml. Med. Center, Flushing, 1969—, chief sect. cardiology, 1969—; mem. staff Univ. Hosp., Hosp., Bellevue Hosp.; instr. clin. medicine Sch. Medicine, N.Y.U. Chmn. Booth Meml. div. United Jewish Appeal Greater N.Y., 1976-77, chmn. physicians div. Queens County Cabinet, 1978—. Served as capt. M.C., USAR, 1970-73. Licenciate Med. Council Can.; diplomate Nat. Bd. Med. Examiners, Am. Bd. Internal Medicine in medicine and cardiology. Fellow Am. Coll. Cardiology (chmn. med. devices com. Heart House campaign 1976-78), A.C.P. (treas. Queens chpt. 1976-78, sec. 1978—); mem. Assn. for Advancement of Med. Instrumentation (pacemaker standards com.), Am., N.Y. heart assns., Contbr. articles to med. jours. Co-inventor Kolker-Boal Cardiac Pacemaker Electrode. Office: Booth Meml Med Center Flushing NY 11355

BOARD, FRED CARL, orgn. exec.; b. Chgo., Mar. 10, 1924; s. Hyman L. and Elsa (Eppsteiner) B.; B.S. Cornell U., 1949; m. Anne P. Tepper, Aug. 31, 1946; children—Michael Joseph, Gail Lynne. Spl. service mgr. Sunset Appliance Stores, N.Y.C., 1949-51; tech. writer Sperry Gyroscope Co., L.I., N.Y., 1951-54; asst. dir. Just One Break, Inc., N.Y.C., 1954-56, exec. dir., 1956—. Cons. various univs., Human Resources Center, Nat. Rehab. Assn. Mem. Pres.'s Com. on Employment of Handicapped, 1959—, Gov.'s Com., 1961—, Gov.'s Adv. Council on Disabled, 1977-78; past pres. Job Placement div. Nat. Rehab. Assn.; mem. N.Y. State Council on Handicapped, 1978—. Bd. dirs. Met. chpt. Nat. Rehab. Assn.; mem. adv. bd. L.I. U. Served with AUS, 1942-45. Decorated Purple Heart, Silver Star medal. Mem. D.A.V., Am. Pub. Health Assn., N.Y. Personnel Mgmt. Assn., Adminstrv. Mgmt. Soc., N.Y. Assn. Workers for Blind (dir.). Contbr. articles to profl. jours. Home: 15 Boulevard Dr Hicksville NY 11801 Office: 373 Park Ave S New York City NY 10016

BOARDMAN, JOSEPH THOMAS, civil engr.; b. Fall River, Mass., Sept. 17, 1928; s. Joseph T. and Mary Etta (Dougherty) B.; B.C.E., Ind. Inst. Tech., 1956; m. Norma Jean Michael, June 28, 1956; children—Joseph, Edward, William. Project engr., sr. engr. C.E. Maguire, Inc., Providence, 1957—. Instr. first aid and water safety, also instr. cardio-pulmonary resuscitation ARC, 1975—, chmn. safety programs, Pawtucket, R.I., 1975—; instr. cardio-pulmonary resuscitation R.I. Heart Assn. Served with AUS, 1950-53. Recipient Service award Boys Clubs Am., 1975, awards ARC, 1974, 75, 76; registered profl. engr., R.I., Mass., Maine, N.H., Vt. Mem. ASCE, Nat. Soc. Profl. Engrs. Roman Catholic. Office: 31 Canal St Providence RI 02903

BOATES, TILBURY THOMAS, JR., clergyman; b. Newton, Mass., Oct. 18, 1933; s. Tilbury Thomas and Mildred (Parlee) B.; A.B., Eastern Nazarene Coll., 1954; B.D., Nazarene Theol. Sem., 1957; S.T.M., Boston U., 1968; m. Barbara Ellen Pope; children—Ellen (Mrs. Donald C. Clark, Jr.), T. Thomas III, John H. Ordained to ministry, 1959; minister East Baltimore Ch. of Nazarene, 1957-59, North Congregational Ch., New Bedford, Mass., 1960-64, 1st Federated Ch., Beverly, Mass., 1964-68; asso. minister Old South Church, Boston, 1968-75; area conf. minister Met. Suffolk Area, N.Y. Conf. United Ch. of Christ, N.Y.C., 1975—. Bd. dirs. L.I. Council Chs. and Council Churches N.Y.C.; chmn. Com. Denom. Execs., N.Y.C.; mem. Citizens Adv. Com., New Bedford, 1963-64; chmn. Beverly (Mass) Redevel. Authority, 1966-68. Mem. Acad. Parish Clergy, Soc. for Sci. Study Religion. Home: 47 Fern St Floral Park NY 11001 Office: NY Conference 297 Park Ave S New York City NY 10010

BOATNER, MRS. EDMUND BURKE (MAXINE TULL BOATNER), writer, lectr.; b. Kentwood, La., Feb. 23, 1903; d. James Porter and Emma Mai (Bailey) Tull; B.A., Millsaps Coll., 1924; M.A., Gallaudet Coll., 1926, L.H.D., 1960; M.A., Yale U., 1951, Ph.D., 1952; m. Edmund Burke Boatner, July 19, 1928; 1 dau., Emma Barbara. Tchr., Belzoni (Miss.) Pub. Schs., 1925-26, Miss. Sch. for Deaf, Jackson, 1926-28; writer Cleve. Plain Dealer, Cleve. News, 1928-31; tchr. Kendall Sch. for Deaf, Washington, 1932-33, N.Y. Sch. for Deaf, N.Y.C., 1933-35, Am. Sch. for Deaf, Hartford, Conn., 1935-49; writer, lectr., Hartford, 1935—. Active bd. mem. Hartford Symphony Soc.; bd. dirs. Conn. Opera Guild, The Hartt Opera-Theatre Guild of U. Hartford, Conn. Citizens for Pub. Schs.; mem. bd., women's com. U. Hartford; dir. hist. research, hon. mem. Conf. Execs. Am. Schs. for Deaf; mem., dir. Hartley-Salmon Child Guidance Clinic, Inc.; sec. bd. Mark Twain Library and Meml. Commn.; pres. women's aux. Cerebral Palsy; bd. dirs. Newington Children's Hosp., Newington Children's Hosp. Aux., Hartford Conservatory. Recipient Edward Allen Fay award Conf. Execs. Am. Schs. for Deaf; Woman of Year award Woman's Recreation Com. of Gallaudet Coll., Washington, 1970. Mem. Library Assos. Council Trinity Coll. and Yale U., AAUW, Nat. Soc. Arts and Letters, Nat. League Am. Pen Women, Inc. (4th nat. v.p.), Kappa Delta, Chi Delta Phi. Clubs: Town and County (Hartford); Women's Press (N.Y.C.). Author: Voice of the Deaf: A Biography of Edward Miner Gallandet, 1959; contbr. poetry, articles on deafness to profl. and popular jours. Compiled Dictionary of Idioms for the Deaf, 1966. Spl. work with deaf related to work of pioneer Thomas Hopkins Gallaudet. Home: 2 Linbrook Rd West Hartford CT 06107

BOBBY, ANNETTE M., spl. services counselor; b. Pitts., Oct. 31, 1951; d. Margaret (Sisak) Bobby; B.S.B.A. cum laude, U. Dayton, 1973; M.Ed. in Guidance and Counseling cum laude, Slippery Rock State Coll 1975. Grad. employee counselor, grad. asst. in student devel. Slippery Rock State Coll., 1974-75; counselor Pitts. Job Corps Center, 1975-77; spl. services counselor Burling County Coll., 1977; Act 101 counselor Phila. Coll. Art, 1977—; cons. YWCA; vol. counselor, program tng. cons. Contact Pitts., 1975-77. Mem. Am. Personnel and Guidance Assn. (conv. panelist 1978), Nat. Vocat. Guidance Assn., Smithsonian Instn., YWCA, Internat. House Phila. Office: Act 101 Program Phila Coll Art Broad and Spruce Sts Philadelphia PA 19102

BOCCHINO, ROBERT LOUIS, mktg. communications cons.; b. Phila., May 28, 1936; s. Daniel and Gertrude Rita (LaBattaglia) B.; B.A., Temple U., 1964, M.B.A., 1973; m. Nancy Lee Keeler, Dec. 20, 1969; children—Robert Louis, Steven Robert. Gen. assignment reporter, news writer Westinghouse Broadcasting Co., Phila., 1964-70; prin. Robert L. Bocchino, exec. communications cons., Bryn Mawr, Pa., 1973—; freelance TV, movie actor bicentennial prodns. Independence, 1975, Adams Chronicles, 1976. Mem. energy adv. com., econ. adv. com. PENJERDEL. Mem. Greater Phila. C. of C. (dir., life mem., awards 1978), Am. Mktg. Assn., TV and Radio Advt. Club Phila., Am. Mgmt. Assn., Phila. Orch. Assn., Franklin Inst., Bishop's Mill Hist. Inst., Independence Nat. Hist. Park. Clubs: Yesper, Poor Richard. Office: PO Box 1128 Bryn Mawr PA 19010

BOCK, ARTHUR EMIL, educator; b. Dubuque, Iowa, Sept. 30, 1916; s. Emil Martin and Alvina (Kupferschmidt) B.; student U. Dubuque, 1934-36; B.S. in Mech. Engring., Kans. State U., 1939; M.S. (Grad. fellow), Va. Poly. Inst. and State U., 1940; m. Betty Louis O'Shaughnessy, Dec. 27, 1943. Instr. mech. engring. Va. Poly. Inst. and State U., Blacksburg, 1940-42, asst. prof., 1942-44; civilian mem. faculty of engring. U.S. Naval Acad., Annapolis, Md., 1946—; vis. prof. Va. Poly. Inst. and State U., summer 1960, 62, U.S. Naval Marine Engr. Lab., Annapolis, 1963. Served with USNR, 1944-46. Registered profl. engr., Md. Mem. ASME, Am. Soc. for Engring. Edn., Am. Soc. Naval Engrs., Nat. Soc. Profl. Engrs., Sigma Tau, Pi Tau Sigma. Author: (with others) Elements of Applied Thermodynamics, 1950, rev. 4th edit., 1978. Home: 9 Cove of Cork Ln Annapolis MD 21401

BOCK, HARRY H., banker; b. N.Y.C., July 15, 1914; s. Harry C. and Frieda M. (Honold) B.; B.S. in Econs., Wharton Sch. U. Pa., 1936; postgrad. N.Y. U., 1946-51, Am. Inst. Real Estate Appraisers, 1963-64; m. Virginia D. Porter, Oct. 14, 1950; children—Gordon, Gary, Geoffrey. Investment analyst Dominick & Dominick, 1936-41; with N.Y. Trust Co., 1946-52, asst. treas., 1949-52; asst. v.p. Franklin Savs. Bank, N.Y.C., 1953-55, v.p., 1955-69, trustee, 1959, v.p., sec., 1965-69, pres., 1969—, chmn. bd., 1973—; dir. Savs. Banks Trust Co. Vice pres., treas., bd. dirs. West Side Assn. Youth Found. Served to lt. col. U.S. Army, World War II, Korea. Mem. Investment Officers Assn. Savs. Banks N.Y. State (pres. 1963), Nat. Assn. Mut. Savs. Bank (dir.), West Side Assn. Commerce, Phi Gamma Delta. Clubs: Union League (N.Y.C.); Shenorock Shore (Rye, N.Y.); St. Andrews Golf (Hastings-on-Hudson, N.Y.). Home: 161 Brewster Rd Scarsdale NY 10583 Office: 380 Madison Ave New York City NY 10017

BOCKIAN, JAMES BERNARD, computer systems exec.; b. Jersey City, Sept. 16, 1934; s. Abraham and Evelyn (Skner) B.; B.A., Columbia U., 1953; M.B.A., U. Mich., 1955; M.A., Yale U., 1957. Vice consul, 3d. sec. embassy U.S. Dept. State, Washington and abroad, 1957-61; sr. systems analyst J.C. Penney Co., N.Y.C., 1961-64; bus. systems cons. Western Union-Mgmt. Info. Systems div., N.Y.C., 1964-66; dir. applications devel. Megasystems Inc., N.Y.C., 1966-67; mgr. systems services, prin. cons. McDonnell Douglas Automation Co., East Orange, N.J., 1967-76; prin. James B. Bockian and Assos., publs. computer systems, Fort Lee, N.J., 1966—; v.p. AG Systems Assos., Inc., Rowayton, Conn., 1977—; lectr. in field. Univ. fellow 1954-55; grad. scholar Yale U., 1956. Mem. Assn. Computing Machinery, Data Processing Mgmt. Assn., Systems and Procedures Assn., Am. Mgmt. Assn., Assn. Internat. Cybernetics. Democrat. Jewish. Clubs: Yale (N.Y.C.); Royal Danish Yacht (Copenhagen). Author: Project Management: Planning and Control, 1975; Management Manual for Systems Development Projects. Address: 26 Farmhouse Ln Morristown NJ 07960 also AG Systems Assos Inc 119 Rowayton Ave Rowayton CT 06853

BODDEN, HUGH EDWARD, utility exec.; b. Bklyn., Jan. 16, 1923; s. Hugh A. and Kathleen Beryl (Walters) B.; B.S., N.Y. State Maritime Coll., 1944; m. Bernice Shirley Rose, Jan. 5, 1946; children—David E., James A., Douglas R., Barbara L. Service engr. O'Brien Industries, Jersey City, 1948-50; engr. Burroughs Corp., Park Ridge, N.J., 1950-52, Travelers Ins. Co., Newark and Reading, Pa., 1952-56; mgr. generation maintenance Met. Edison Co., Reading, 1976—, tech. engr. 1956-58, asst. supt. Crawford sta., 1958-59, supt., 1959-66, supt. Titus Sta., 1966-69, supt. Portland Sta., 1969-72, mgr. gen. maintenance, 1972-75, mgr. generation operation, 1975-76. Deacon, 1st. Baptist Ch., E. Stroudsburg, Pa., 1970-72; bd. dirs. Hope Rescue Mission, 1976—; trustee Limerick Chapel, 1978—. Served with USNR, 1944-46. Registered profl. engr., Pa. Mem. ASME, Pa. Soc.

Profl. Engrs. Republican. Baptist. Home: Boone Rd Birdsboro PA 19508 Office: 2800 Pottsville Pike Reading PA 19640

BODLEY, HARLEY RYAN, JR., editor; b. Dover, Del., Nov. 24, 1936; s. Harley Ryan and Mildred (Carver) B.; B.A., U. Del., 1959; m. Lois May Deputy, July 1, 1961. Sports editor Del. State News, Dover, 1959-60; with News Journal Co., Wilmington, Del., 1960—, asst. sports editor, 1967-71, sports editor, 1971—. Moderator, Diamond State Profile, Del. Football Report, Sta. WHYY-TV, Wilmington, 1967-74; safety counselor, FAA, 1970—. Dir. publicity Del. Found. for Retarded Children, All-Star football games, 1965-71. Bd. dirs. Nat. Football Found. and Hall of Fame, 1970. Named Del. Sportswriter of Year, Nat. Sportscasters and Sportswriters Assn., 1961, 63, 65, 67, 68, 69, 70, 73, 74, 75. Mem. Wilmington Sportswriters and Broadcasters Assn. (pres. 1963, exec. sec.-treas. 1964—), Aircraft Owners and Pilots Assn., U.S. Power Squadrons, Baseball Writers Assn. Am. (chmn. Phila. chpt. 1977-78, nat. bd. dirs. 1978), AP Sports Editors Assn. (nat. sec.-treas. 1977—), U. Del. Alumni Assn., Am. Press Inst., Sigma Delta Chi. Clubs: N.E. Md. River Yacht (North East, Md.); Wilmington Country. Home: Route 1 Box 59 Middletown DE 19709 Office: 831 Orange St Wilmington DE 19899

BODNAR, JOHN PAUL, educator; b. Pitts., Oct. 5, 1927; s. John P. and Helen D. (Benzer) B.; B.E. in English, Duquesne U., 1962; M.Ed. in English, Shippensburg State Coll., 1965; postgrad. Western Md. Coll., 1965-67, Pa. State U., 1967-68, U. Md., 1968-74. Advt. and pub. relations writer Kaufmann's, Pitts., 1953-59; tchr. high sch. English, Pitts. Pub. Schs., 1962-65; prof. English, Shippensburg (Pa.) State Coll., 1965-68; prof. English, Prince George's Community Coll., Largo, Md., 1968—, asso. dean for English studies, 1971-74; free-lance writer, 1968—; writing cons. Prince George's County Exec. Writing Program. Frick scholar, 1962-65. Mem. Nat. Council Tchrs. of English, AAUP, Conf. Coll. Composition and Communication, N.E. Regional Conf. English in the Two-Year Coll., Nat. Writers Club, Nat. Jr. Coll. Council. Republican. Roman Catholic. Editor The Pyramid, 1977. Home: 306 G St SE Washington DC 20003 Office: Prince George's Community Coll 301 Largo Rd Largo MD 20870

BODNER, RICHARD MARTIN, environ. engr.; b. Poughkeepsie, N.Y., Apr. 28, 1945; s. Gadlin and Dorothy Ida (Handler) B.; B.S. in Civil Engring., Clarkson Coll. Tech., 1967, M.S., 1969; m. Brenda Agnes Norton, June 11, 1967; children—Kevin, Steven. Engr., Barton, Brown, Clyde & Loguidice, Syracuse, N.Y., 1967-68; pub. works engr., City of Balt., 1969-70; prin. engr. Nassaux-Hemsley Inc., Chambersburg, Pa., 1971-72; pres. Martin & Martin Inc., Chambersburg, 1973—; partner CDR Assos., Chambersburg, 1974—; lectr., cons. in field. Pres. Coldbrook Meadows Homeowners Com., 1972-73. Registered profl. engr., N.Y., Pa., W.Va., Md., Fla., N.J. Mem. Nat. Soc. Profl. Engrs., ASCE, Am. Pub. Works Assn., Chi Epsilon. Club: Chambersburg Country. Pioneer design Purox pyrolysis plants. Home: 14 Downing Ct Chambersburg PA 17201 Office: 149 E Queen St Chambersburg PA 17201

BOE, NILS ANDREAS, fed. judge; b. Baltic, S.D., Sept. 10, 1913; s. Nils and Sissel Catherine (Finseth) B.; B.A., U. Wis., 1935, LL.B., 1937; LL.D. (hon.), Huron (S.D.) Coll., 1972. Admitted to Wis. bar, 1937, S.D. bar, 1938, D.C. bar, 1970, U.S. Supreme Ct. bar; dep. states atty., Minnehaha County, S.D., 1938-42; partner firm May, Boe & Johnson, Sioux Falls, S.D., 1946-65; chief judge U.S. Customs Ct., N.Y.C., 1971-77, judge, 1977—. Mem. S.D. Legislature, 1951-59; speaker S.D. Ho. of Reps., 1955-59; lt. gov. S.D., 1963-65, gov., 1965-67, 67-69; dir. Office Intergovernmental Relations, Exec. Office of Pres., 1969-71. Served to lt. USN, 1942-46. Mem. Am., Wis., S.D., D.C. bar assns., Am. Legion, VFW, Phi Alpha Delta. Clubs: Elks; Odd Fellows; New York Athletic. Home: 71 Island Dr Rye NY 10580 Office: One Federal Plaza New York NY 10007

BOE, ROY LARS MAGNUS, basketball team exec.; b. Bklyn., Sept. 14, 1929; s. Magnus and Marta Elizabeth (Mortensen) B.; B.A., Yale U., 1951; m. Deon Woolfolk, Nov. 12, 1953; children—Susan Lys, Roy Lars Magnus, Amanda Harding, Jeremy Clarke, Todd Erling. Food broker Henry Kilian, Inc., N.Y.C., 1954-61; pres. Boe Jests, Inc., wearing apparel, Stamford, Conn., 1954-61; chmn. bd., pres. L.I. Sports Enterprises, Inc., owners N.Y. Nets of Am. Basketball Assn., Carle Place, N.Y., 1969—, R.L.M. Sports, Inc., gen. partner Nassau Sports N.Y., Islanders of Nat. Hockey League, Carle Place, 1972—. Served to 1st lt. U.S. Army, 1953. Episcopalian. Clubs: Wee Burn Country (Darien); Yale, Canadian (N.Y.C.); Nassau Country (Glen Cove, N.Y.). Office: 1 Landmark Sq Stamford CT 06901*

BOE, SUE LOHMEYER, pub. relations exec.; b. St. Louis, May 8, 1920; d. Emil H. and Claire Marie (Roy) Lohmeyer; B.S. cum laude, Kans. State U., 1939; M.A., U. Iowa, 1940; m. John R. Boe, July 19, 1941 (div. 1966); children—Christine, Susan. Free-lance radio and TV program personality, Kansas City, Mo., 1936-57; staff field rep. AMA, Chgo., 1965-67; asst. v.p. consumer affairs Pharm. Mfrs. Assn., Washington, 1968—; adj. prof. dept. allied health scis. Kent (Ohio) State U.; vice chmn. womens conf. Nat. Safety Council, 1973-75, 76-77. Fellow Am. Sch. Health Assn.; mem. Pub. Relations Soc. Am. (accredited). Contbr. articles to profl. jours. Home: 13907 Piscataway Dr Ft Washington MD 20022 Office: 1155 15th St NW Washington DC 20005

BOEHM, ALICE E(VELYN), research psychologist; b. Prague, Czechoslovakia; d. Leopold and Bertha (Bohm) Bohm; came to U.S., 1941, naturalized 1946; Ph.D., German U. Prague, 1938. Research asst. N.J. State Hosp., Trenton, 1941-42; ind. research, N.Y.C., 1947—; asso. World Fedn. Mental Health. Fellow Internat. Council Psychologists, AAAS; mem. Am., Eastern, N.Y. State psychol. assns., N.Y. Acad. Scis. Contbr. articles in field to profl. jours. Address: 30 E 81st St New York City NY 10028

BOEHM, EDWARD GORDON, JR., univ. adminstr.; b. Washington, Jan. 30, 1942; s. Edward Gordon and Catherine A. (Murray) B.; B.S., Frostburg State Coll., 1964; M.Ed., Am. U., 1970, Ph.D., 1977; m. Regina Ellen Evans, June 25, 1966; children—Evan Arnold, Andrew Edward. Tchr., Montgomery County (Md.) Pub. Schs., 1964-68; instr., soccer coach Am. U., Washington, 1968-70, asst. dir. admissions, 1970-73, asso. dean freshman admissions, fin. aid, vet. affairs, programs and services, 1973-75, interim dean, 1978, dean students, 1975-77, dir. univ. devel., 1977—; mem. Coll. Entrance Exam Bd., 1976—; exec. bd. Am. Coll. Test Program to Md./D.C., 1976-78. First nat. chmn. Washington Coll. Fair, 1974; bd. dirs. Project Open, Washington, 1971-75, Friends of Nat. Zoo, Washington, 1975—. Mem. Nat. Assn. Coll. Admissions Counselors (exec. bd. 1975-76), Am. Assn. Higher Edn., Am. Coll. Testing Program, Am. Personnel and Guidance Assn., Council Advancement and Support of Edn., Nat. Assn. Coll. Admissions Officers, Phi Gamma Mu. Democrat. Roman Catholic. Contbr. articles in field to profl. jours. Home: 4829 Powder House Dr Rockville MD 20853 Office: 5010 Wisconsin Ave Am Univ Washington DC 20016

BOEKER, GILBERT FERBER, ret. physicist, educator; b. N.Y.C., Apr. 29, 1905; s. Alfred and Louise (Schloendorff) B.; A.B., Columbia, 1925, B.S., Engring. Sch., 1926, M.E., 1927, Ph.D. in Physics (fellow), 1933; m. Mary I. Draper, Sept. 4, 1937. Engr., Power Splty. Co. (now Foster Wheeler Co.), Dansville, N.Y., 1927-29; asst., instr. physics dept. Columbia, 1929-31, research asso. dept. mech. engring., 1945-58; instr., asst. prof. City Coll. N.Y., 1933-41, asst. prof., asso. prof. math. dept., 1945-50, prof., 1950-70, prof. emeritus, 1970—; purchasing mgr., mem. sci. staff Underwater Sound Labs., U.S. Navy, 1941-42; sect. leader mech. engring. sect. S.A.M. Labs., 1942-45. Mem. Am. Phys. Soc., Am. Assn. Physics Tchrs., Sigma Xi, Tau Beta Pi, Phi Gamma Delta. Republican. Episcopalian. Clubs: Norfolk (Conn.) Country, Norfolk Trout. Contbr. articles on physics, math., engring. to profl. publs. Inventor in field. Home: Greenwoods Rd E Norfolk CT 06058

BOGART, GRACE ELIZABETH, librarian; b. Bolton, Mass., June 10, 1923; d. Francis Gould and Grace Effie (Smith) Mentzer; B.S., U. Mass., 1945; M.S., Simmons Coll., 1975; m. Lindsay Boyd, Aug. 6, 1944 (dec.); children—David Gordon, Bethanne, Sandra Lindsay; m. 2d, Victor Brociner, Nov. 13, 1971 (dec.); m. 3. Stanley C. Bogart, Aug. 7, 1977. Librarian, Lincoln Lab. Library, Mass. Inst. Tech., Lexington, 1959-77; dir. info. services Roberts Info. Services, Inc., Fairfax, Va., 1977-78, Bogart-Brociner Assos., Annapolis, Md., 1978—. Mem. Spl. Libraries Assn. (chmn. spl. com. translation problems 1973-76; rep. Nat. Transl. Center John Crerar Library, Chgo. 1973-77), Am. Soc. Info. Sci. (local arrangements chmn. nat. conf. Boston, 1975, rep. Nat. Transl. Center John Crerar Library, Chgo., 1978—), Soc. Fed. Linguists. Compiler: A Guide to Scientific and Technical Journals in Translation, 1972; How to Obtain a Translation, 1976. Home: 47 Williams Dr Annapolis MD 21401 Office: Bogart-Brociner Assos 47 Williams Dr Annapolis MD 21401

BOGART, WILLIAM HARRY, lawyer; b. Sayre, Pa., Mar. 5, 1931; s. Harry M. and Luella C. Bogart; A.B., Duke U., 1953; A.A.A., The Hague Acad. Internat. Law, 1962; J.D., Syracuse U., 1963; m. Karin Rudolph, Dec. 12, 1962; children—Barbara, Silke. Admitted to N.Y. bar, 1964; mem. firm Ali, Gerber, Parr & Bogart, Syracuse, N.Y., 1966-67, Bogart & Andrews, Syracuse, 1967-77; mem. firm Bogart, Andrews & Huffman, Syracuse, 1977—; cons. in field to various govts, fin. instns., ednl. instns.; lectr. in field. Mem. missionary com. Presbyterian Ch., 1974-77. Served with USMC, 1950-51. Mem. Am. Arbitration Assn., Am., N.Y. State, Onondaga County bar assns., Assn. of Attenders and Alumni, Lawyers Intergroups, World Ct., Assn. Atty. and Advocates. Democrat. Clubs: Univ., Witte Soc. Dem Hague, Masons (32 deg). Contbr. articles in field to profl. jours. Home: 110 E Lake Rd Skaneateles NY 13152 Office: 1000 Carrier Tower Syracuse NY 13202

BOGDAN, JOSEPH CARL, pediatrician; b. Jersey City, Apr. 21, 1938; s. Stanley Peter and Virginia (Rozwadowski) B.; B.S., St. Peters Coll., 1960; M.D., N.J. Coll. Medicine, 1964; m. Daphne Ellen Menchin, June 13, 1964; children—Joseph, Doreen, Gregory, Robert. Intern, Jersey Shore Med. Center, Fitkin Hosp., Neptune, N.J., 1964-65, resident in pediatrics, 1965-67; practice medicine, specializing pediatrics, partner Pediatric Assoc., Neptune and Marlboro, N.J., 1967—; dir. dept. pediatrics Jersey Shore Med. Center, 1978—; clin. instr. dept. pediatrics N.J. Coll. Medicine, Martland Med. Center, 1968—; mem. Children Cancer Leukemia Group A, 1972. Served with N.J. N.G., 1964-72. Recipient Certificate of Appreciation, N.J. Mil. Coll., 1972; Physician's Recognition award AMA, 1969-77. Diplomate Am. Bd. Pediatrics. Fellow Am. Acad. Pediatrics (exec. council N.J. chpt. 1973-78); mem. Am. Med. Assn. Contbr. articles in field to med. jours. Home: 20 Ludlow Ave Springlake NJ 07762 Office: 2100 Corlies Ave Neptune City NJ 07753

BOGEN, STANLEY MAURICE, stockbroker; b. N.Y.C., May 11, 1937; s. Max and Marcy (Drucker) B.; B.S., U. Pa., 1958; M.B.A., N.Y. U., 1959; children—Lauren, Edmund. Vice pres. First Hanover, (name now changed to First Devonshire), N.Y.C., 1959-69; v.p. S.C. Bernstein Co., N.Y.C., 1969—. Treas. Am.-Israel Cultural Found., 1973-76; treas. Am. Friends Hebrew U., 1972-77, pres., 1977—. Mem. Am. Technion Soc. (dir. 1973), Zeta Beta Tau. Club: Friars (N.Y.C.). Home: 50 E 79th St New York City NY 10021 Office: 717 Fifth Ave New York City NY 10022

BOGGIO, GEORGE JOHN, investment banker; b. Passaic, N.J., June 27, 1940; s. Ercole and Ida (Boggio) B.; B.S., Fairleigh Dickinson U., 1961; m. Mary Louise Sachau, Aug. 24, 1963; children—George John III, Michael Christopher, James Hamilton and Richard Winston (twins). Accountant, Seidman & Seidman, N.Y.C., 1961-64; C.P.A., LaFrance, Walker, Jackley & Saville, N.Y.C., 1964-66; v.p., treas., sec. Fred Alger & Co., Inc., N.Y.C., 1967—, also dir.; sec.-treas. Castle Convertible Fund, Inc., Spectra Fund, Inc. Township committeeman Holmdel, N.J., 1972-75; mayor of Holmdel, 1974-75; mem. Holmdel Planning Bd., 1974-75. Served with AUS, 1962. C.P.A., N.Y., N.J. Mem. Am. Inst. C.P.A.'s, N.Y. State Soc. C.P.A.'s. Roman Catholic. K.C. Office: 26 Broadway New York City NY 10004

BOGIN, ALVIN, civil engr.; b. Hartford, Conn., Dec. 20, 1916; s. Bernard and Esther (Bloom) B.; B.S., U. Conn., 1948; m. Alberta Baron, Dec. 22, 1946; children—Carol, Betsy. Surveyor, John Henderson, Hartford, 1937-40; hwy. engr. Conn. Dept. Transp., Wethersfield, 1947-72; cons. engr., West Hartford, Conn., 1972-78; instr. hwy. design Hartford State Tech. Coll., 1955; planning and zoning engr. Town of Oxford (Conn.), 1972-73. Served with C.E., U.S. Army, 1941-45. Recipient certificate of meritorious service USAAF, 1946, certificate of merit award Gov. Conn., 1957; registered profl. engr., land surveyor, Conn. Mem. ASCE, Nat. Soc. Profl. Engrs. Expert witness Superior Cts., Conn. Home and Office: 25 Carlyle Rd West Hartford CT 06117

BOGLEY, SAMUEL W., state ofcl. Lt. gov. Md., 1979—. Office: Office: of Lt Gov State House Annapolis MD 21404*

BOGNAR, CHARLES RALPH, mgmt. and mktg. exec.; b. Phila., Feb. 2, 1926; s. Charles S. and Anna Bognar; student Pa. State U., 1957-67; m. Bernadine L. Schantz, Oct. 2, 1948. Tool and model maker in machine shop Franklin Inst. Research Labs., Phila., 1949-55, sr. tech. asso. friction lubrication div., 1955-70, sr. test engr. utilities services group, 1970-73; mgr. test ops. and co-founder of Turbo Experimental div. of Turbo Research, West Chester, Pa., 1973-75; co-founder Energy Tech., Inc., West Chester, 1975, v.p., dir. mktg. 1975-79; new bus. devel. Mktg. Spl. Services div. Ebasco Services, Inc., N.Y.C., 1979—. Mem. ASME, Research Engrs. Soc. Am., Sigma Xi. Mem. Christian Ch. Home: Blair House 1-M Two Hamilton Rd Morristown NJ 07960 Office: Two Rector St New York NY 10006

BOGOSIAN, JOHN SARKIS, photog. equipment co. exec.; b. Phila., July 17, 1927; s. Sarkis and Sirarpi (Savoulian) B.; student George Washington U., 1951; certificate of accounts and finances U. Pa., 1955; m. Marjorie Berberian, Nov. 6, 1955; children—John Paul, Joanne, Karen. With Camera Shop, Inc., Broomall, Pa., 1946—, v.p., 1955-60, pres., 1960—; pres. Visual Sound Co., 1967—; mem. retail adv. bd. Bell & Howell Co., Delaware County Community Coll.; mem. adv. bd. Argus and Graflex. Pres., Armenian Students Assn. Am., 1954-56, trustee, 1956-71, chmn. bd. trustees, 1967-71; mem. Nat. Small Bus. Council; vice-chmn. Am. Bicentennial Commemoration Com., 1976. Served with USNR, 1945-47, 50-52. Recipient B'nai B'rith award Delaware County, 1963; named Photog. Retailer of Yr., 1975, Bell & Howell Photo Specialist Dealer of Yr., 1976. Mem. Photog. Research Orgn. (sec., dir.), Photog. Marketing Assn. (trustee-at-large), Lawrence Park Mchts. Assn. (pres.), Delaware County C. of C. (v.p., dir.), Nat. Audio Visual Assn., Delaware Valley Photo Dealers Assn., Knights of Vartan. Conglist. Rotarian (pres. Broomall 1973, dist. gov.'s rep.). Home: 131 Charles Dr Havertown PA 19083 Office: 485 Parkway S Broomall PA 19008

BOGOSIAN, PAUL JOHN, real estate co. exec.; b. Providence, Mar. 1, 1924; s. John J. and Mary (Melkonian) B.; diploma in real estate U. R.I., 1964; grad. Realtors Inst., 1974; m. Ethel May Bailey, Oct. 6, 1951; 1 son, Paul John. Partner, Parick Jewelry Co., Providence, 1952-59, Richard Alan, Realtors, Warwick, R.I., 1959—; pres. Kent County Bd. Realtors, 1972, 73. Pres. Kent County XPTR Nat. Found., March of Dimes, 1962, mem. exec. com. R.I. XPTR Nat. Found., 1963—. Served with U.S. Army, 1943-46. Named Realtor of Year, Kent County Bd. Realtors, 1974. Mem. R.I. Assn. Realtors (v.p. 1974-75, pres. 1977, pres. state-wide multiple listing service 1976), Nat. Assn. Realtors (nat. dir. 1976—), R.I. Builders Assn. Methodist. Clubs: Greenwich (past v.p.), Greenwich Bay Power Squadron, Masons. Dir., producer Miss R.I. Pageant, 1962-72. Home: 120 Sunnybrook Dr North Kingstown RI 02852 Office: 3604 Post Rd Warwick RI 02886

BOHLMANN, HANS HEINRICH, rubber co. exec.; b. Itzehoe, Holstein, Germany, May 7, 1906; s. Johannes Heinrich and Marie Henriette (Jensen) B.; came to U.S., 1926, naturalized, 1937; grad. Am. Inst. Banking, 1929; m. Margaret Goodenow Williams, Feb. 7, 1935. With fgn. dept. Chase Nat. Bank, N.Y.C., 1926-29; asst. cashier Am. Express Co., Inc., Berlin, Munich, Germany, 1929-31, asst. accountant, Hong Kong, 1931, cashier, accountant Shanghai, China, 1931-37; export sales exec. Firestone Tire & Rubber Export Co., Akron, Ohio, 1937-40; asst. export mgr. Seamless Rubber Co., New Haven, 1940-42, export mgr., 1942-64; pres. Conintrade Co., North Haven, Conn., 1964—; internat. trade cons., mem. U.S. Trade Mission to S.E. Asia, 1957; mem. World Trade Adv. Com. U.S. Dept. Commerce, Washington, 1957-61, mem. Task Force, 1958; mem. Conf. on Nat. Planning for Export Expansion, Washington, 1960, Export Trade Promotion Conf., 1960, White House Conf. Export Expansion, 1963, Washington Conf. on Magnuson-Adams Export Expansion Bill, 1965, New Eng. Regional Export Expansion Com., 1960-63, Conn. Gov.'s Conf. on Exporting, 1972; mem. Conn. Regional Export Expansion Council, 1963-74, chmn., 1963-65. Recipient certificate of appreciation for service as mem. regional export expansion council, Sec. Commerce, 1974. Mem. New Haven C. of C. (past chmn. fgn. trade com.). Mfrs. Assn. Conn. (past chmn. fgn. trade com.), Internat. Execs. Assn. (dir. 1963-66), Internat. Platform Assn., Yale-China Assn., Combination Export Mgrs. Assn. Conn. (pres. 1967-72). Republican. Lutheran. Club: Shanghai Tiffin (N.Y.C.). Contbr. articles to leading publs. Home: Bubbling Well Farm North Haven CT 06473 Office: 222 Rimmon Rd North Haven CT 06473

BÖHM, EMANUEL THEODORE, chemist, cons.; b. Vrutky, Slovakia, Feb. 1, 1909; s. Emanuel and Amalia (Srnka) B.; came to U.S., 1952, naturalized, 1957; B.S., Charles U., Prague, 1931, M.S., 1931, Ph.D., 1934; m. Maria Dziakova, Sept. 27, 1941. Prof. chemistry and natural scis. Michalovce, Kosice, 1936-41; editor daily newspaper Slovenska Jednota, Budapest, 1941-45; freedom fighter during World War II writing History of Years 1938-45 in Central Europe; congressman Prague Parliament, 1946-48, dep. speaker, commr. for health; dir. research Newlands Bros., London, 1948-52; dir. research Hoffman Beverage Co., Newark, 1952-65, 66-71; dir. beverage research Refined Syrups & Sugars div. CPC Internat., Inc., Yonkers, N.Y., 1971-74, mgr. tech. sales service-beverages Indsl. div., 1974—. Served to capt., arty., Czechoslovakian Army, 1934-36. Recipient replica of Statue of Liberty for contbn. to well being of Am. people and Democracy, Hoffman Beverage Co., 1962. Mem. Inst. Food Technologists, Soc. Soft Drink Technologists, Chem. Soc. Roman Catholic. Club: Slovak-Am. (N.Y.C.). Contbr. articles to profl. jours. Patented Q Plus Research Tool, 1971.

BOHMAN, RAYNARD FREDERICK, JR., trade assn. exec.; b. Boston, July 31, 1933; s. Raynard F. and Theresa (Conlon) B.; B.S. in Econs., U. Pa., 1955; m. Douglas Ann Watson Boutin, Sept. 24, 1955; children—David John, Jack Duncan, Andrew MacKenzie. With Nat. Furniture Traffic Conf., Inc., Gardner, Mass., 1955—, pres., 1968—; pres. Bohman Indsl. Traffic Consultants, Inc., Gardner, 1955—; cons. to various nat. trade assns. Served to 1st lt. AUS, 1956. Mem. Am. Soc. Assn. Execs., Phi Gamma Delta. Episcopalian. Club: Eastward Ho Country (Chathamport). Author: Guide to Maximizing Recovery of Loss and Damage Claims, 1976; editor: Furniture Packaging, 1960—, Furniture Transporter, 1966—, Bohman Traffic News Summary, 1976—; contbg. editor Furniture Production mag., 1968—, Gift and Accessories mag., 1976—. Home: 27 Bay Ln Chatham MA 02633 Office: 335 E Broadway St Gardner MA 01440

BOHN, NELSON RANSON, accountant; b. Frederick, Md., Oct. 27, 1920; s. Harry Howard and Mamie (May) B.; B.S., U. Md., 1951; m. Bettie Mae Stultz, Sept. 14, 1943; children—Phil D., William H., Robert T. Adminstrv. officer, comptroller U.S. Army, Fort Terry, Plum Island, N.Y., 1951-54; pvt. practice C.P.A., Frederick, 1955-69; partner Stoy, Malone & Co., Bethesda, Md., 1969—; pres. Catoctin Properties, Inc., Frederick, 1967—, B & N Enterprises, Inc., Frederick, 1968-78; dir. Moreland Farms, Inc. Pres., Frederick County Heart Assn., 1959-60. Served to 2d lt. USAAF, 1940-44. Mem. Am. Inst. C.P.A.'s, Md. Assn. C.P.A.'s (chpt. pres. 1969-70). Lion (past pres.). Clubs: Kenwood Golf and Country, Green Hill Yacht and Country. Home: 10201 Grosvenor Pl Rockville MD 20852 also 134 E Rustic Dr Salisbury MD 21801 Office: 7315 Wisconsin Ave Bethesda MD 20014

BOHN, WILLIAM CHANLER, audio-acoustic cons.; b. Ithaca, N.Y., June 29, 1921; s. William Christian and Alida (Chanler) B.; student YMCA Trade Sch., N.Y.C., 1941-42, Harvard U., 1946-48; m. Helen Louise Reary, Dec. 17, 1953; children—Cynthia Nancy, Peter Willoughby. Audio engr. ABC, N.Y.C., 1951-52; owner, engring. designer Bohn Music Systems Co., 1952-58; dir. tech. info. Indsl. Acoustics Co., Inc., Bronx, N.Y., 1958-59; audio-acoustic cons., N.Y.C., 1959—; owner, mgr. Hi-Fi Doctor Service. Served to lt. U.S. Mcht. Marine, 1942-46, 48-50. Decorated Meritorious Service medal. Mem. Acoustical Soc. Am., Audio Engring. Soc., AAAS, Am. Inst. Physics, Fedn. Am. Scientists, IEEE, Soc. Motion Picture and TV Engrs., Am. Inst. Aeros. and Astronautics, Vet. Wireless Operators Assn., Soc. Wireless Pioneers, Am. Radio Relay League. Club: Camden (Maine) Yacht. Contbr. articles to mags.; host, writer radio program The Art of High Fidelity, 1958-59. Office: 45 W 45th St New York City NY 10036

BOHON, MARLANE GELDART, wine co. exec.; b. Haverhill, Mass., June 20, 1933; d. Clarence B. and Jean O. (Kyle) Geldart; student Drexel U., 1951-52, Lebanon Valley Coll., 1952, Bucks County Community Coll., Villanova U.; children—Jeannie K., Kevin V. With personnel dept. Yale & Towne, Phila., 1954; sec., purchasing agt. Richardson Mints, Phila., 1955-56; sec. to v.p. John Wagner Wines & Spirits Co., Frazer, Pa., 1970-71, sec. to pres., 1972, asst. to pres., 1974-75, v.p. adminstrn., 1976—, also sec.; v.p., sec. Ratnor

Wines & Spirits Co. Sec., Jr. Women's Club of Southampton, 1966-68, pres., 1968-70; bd. dirs. Southampton Free Library, 1968-70, Western Assn. of Ladies for Relief & Employment of Poor, 1960—, exec. sec., 1968—; active Friends of Southampton Free Library. Mem. Am. Bus. Women's Assn. Presbyterian. Home: 35 Chetwynd Rd Paoli PA 19301 Office: Wagner Wines & Spirits Co 53 Great Valley Pkwy Frazer PA 19355

BOHY, DAVID WELDON, hosp. adminstr., personnel exec.; b. Sumas, Wash., June 22, 1938; s. Leon Alfred and Sarah Virginia (Snyder) B.; B.A. in Religion and Philosophy, Aurora (Ill.) Coll., 1960; M.D.P.H., Harvard U, 1977; m. Cynthia Cross, July 2, 1960; children—Jonathan M., Joel R. Asst. pastor Capitol Hill Advent Christian Ch., Seattle, 1959-61; asst. mgr. Gilchrist's Co., Stoneham, Mass., 1961-65; personnel mgr. Addison-Wesley Pub. Co., Reading, Mass., 1965; personnel officer N.R.C. divs. Norton Co., Worcester, Mass., 1965-68; dir. personnel McLean Hosp., Belmont, Mass., 1968—; instr. Radcliffe Coll.; lectr. Clark U.; condr. seminars on human resource mgmt.; cons. in field. Mem. town personnel bd., Burlington, Mass., 1965-68; pres. bd. trustees Lexington (Mass.) Christian Acad., 1969-76; adv. bd. Middlesex Community Coll., Bedford, Mass., 1972-77; mem. tech. adv. group Manpower Linkage Project, Commonwealth of Mass., 1974-77. Mem. Mass. Hosp. Personnel Dirs. Assn. (pres. 1975-76), Am. Soc. Personnel Adminstrn. (accredited exec.), Am. Mgmt. Assn. Contbr. articles to profl. jours.; editorial adv. bd. Nursing Pulse of New Eng., 1976—. Office: McLean Hosp 115 Mill St Belmont MA 02178

BOIKESS, OLGA SHNIPER, lawyer; b. Jamaica, N.Y., Dec. 25, 1938; d. Robert and Bella (Jarus) Shniper; B.A., Barnard Coll., 1960; J.D., U. Calif., Los Angeles, 1964. Admitted to Calif. bar, 1964, D.C. bar, 1969; law clk. U.S. Dist. Ct. for So. Dist. Calif., 1964-65; atty. gen. counsel's office, Office Econ. Opportunity, Exec. Office President, Washington, 1965-68; asso. firm Galland, Kharasch, Calkins & Brown, Washington, 1968-74; mem. firm Galland, Kharasch, Calkins & Short, Washington, 1975—; cons. in health services and econ. devel. for fed. agencies and govt. contractors, 1968—. Contbr. articles to profl. jours. Office: 1054 31st St NW Washington DC 20007

BOJARSKYJ, ISYDORA, chartist; b. Palczynci, Ukraine, July 8, 1917; d. Ivan and Olena (Chemeryavskvj) Maluca; came to U.S., 1949, naturalized, 1955; student Sch. Comml. Art, Lviv, Ukraine, 1941-44; M.A. in Folklore, Munich, Ger., 1950; m. Bohdan Bojarskyj, Feb. 14, 1966. Tchr. art vocat. high schs. Lviv, also Karlsfeld, Ger., 1942-47; factory worker Flexnit Co., Newark, 1950-62; chartist, A.C. Nielsen Co., N.Y.C., 1962-70, Hackensack, N.J., 1970—. Mem. Ukrainian Shevchenko Sci. Soc. Ukrainian Catholic. Author: (Ukrainian lang.) Ukrainian Christmas Customs, 1950; contbr. essays from Folks Calendar to Ukrainian mags., newspapers in Germany, 1946-49. Lecture traditional Ukrainian Easter eggs. Home: 65 Clinton Pl Hackensack NJ 07601 Office: 401 Hackensack Ave Hackensack NJ 07601

BOK, DEREK CURTIS, univ. pres.; b. Ardmore, Pa., Mar. 22, 1930; s. Curtis and Margaret (Plummer) B.; B.A., Stanford U., 1951; LL.B., Harvard U., 1954; M.A., George Washington U., 1958; m. Sissela Ann Myrdal, May 7, 1955; children—Hilary Margaret, Victoria, Thomas Jeremy. Fulbright scholar, Paris, France, 1954-55; faculty Harvard U. Law Sch., Cambridge, Mass., 1958-71, prof., 1961-71, dean Law Sch., 1968-71; pres. Harvard U., Cambridge, 1971—. Served to 1st lt. AUS, 1956-58. Mem. Am. Bar Found., Am. Law Inst., Phi Beta Kappa, Phi Kappa Sigma. Author: (with Archibald Cox) Labor Law, 1962; (with John T. Dunlop) Labor and the American Community, 1970. Home: 33 Elmwood Ave Cambridge PA 02138 Office: University Hall Cambridge MA 02138

BOKSER, LEWIS, newspaper publisher; b. Phila., Mar. 23, 1904; s. David and Yetta B.; student U. Pa., 1930-31, Temple U., 1972, Villanova U., 1972-73; m. Sara A. Lipschutz, Feb. 11, 1931. Mgr., announcer Sta. WNAT, Phila., 1924-27; paving contractor, Phila., 1924-54; pub. Phila. Beacon, 1943-50, Phila. Civil Service Sentinel, 1945-50; sec.-treas. Lewis Bokser Inc., Phila., 1957—. Alt. del. Republican Nat. Conv., 1952; nat. bd. dirs. Yeshiva U., N.Y.C., 1950-60; co-founder Einstein Coll. Medicine, N.Y.C., 1950. Jewish. Clubs: Fourth Estate Sq., Centurions (cofounder 1946), Mason (master lodge 1945). Editor Am. sect. Jewish Travel Guide. contbr. hist., humanitarian articles to newspapers. Home: 5108 N 10th St Philadelphia PA 19141 Office: 2829 N Broad St Philadelphia PA 19132

BOLAND, EDWARD P., congressman; b. Springfield, Mass., Oct. 1, 1911; ed. Classical High Sch., Bay Path Inst., Boston Coll. Law Sch. Mem. Mass. legislature, 1935-40; register of deeds Hampden County, 1941-52; mem. 83d-96th Congresses, 2d Mass. Dist. Served from pvt. to capt. AUS, 1942-46, PTO. Democrat. Home: Springfield MA 01101 Office: Rayburn House Office Bldg Washington DC 20515

BOLAND, GERALD LEE, financial exec.; b. Harrisburg, Pa., Apr. 2, 1946; s. Vincent Harry and Alice Jane (Geiste) B.; B.S., Lebanon Valley Coll., 1968; m. Mary Hannalora Shultz, June 17, 1972. Accounting trainee Armstrong Cork Co., Millville, N.J., 1968; payroll supr., plant ops. accountant, 1969-70; sr. fin. accountant Lancaster (Pa.) Gen. Hosp., 1970-71, mgr. gen. accounting, 1972; corporate accounting mgr. HMW Industries, Inc., Lancaster, 1972; corporate controller Fleck-Marshall Co. subs. Gable Industries, Lancaster, 1973-74, sec.-treas., 1974-75; controller Dominion Psychiat. Treatment Center, Falls Church, Va., 1975-76; controller, dir. fin. Miller & Byrne, Inc., Rockville, Md., 1976—. 1976—. Mem. Am. Accounting Assn., Nat. Assn. Accountants, Hosp. Fin. Mgmt. Assn., Eastern Fin. Assn., Am. Hosp. Assn., Am. Mgmt. Assn., Fin. Mgmt. Assn. Methodist. Home: 6032 Westchester Park Dr College Park MD 20740

BOLANDE, ROBERT PAUL, pathologist, educator; b. Chgo., Apr. 16, 1926; s. Herman Asher and Florence (Levy) B.; B.S., Northwestern U., 1948, M.S., 1952, M.D., 1952; m. A. Suzanne Hiss, Apr. 1, 1954; children—Deborah, Jennifer, Miriame, Hyam Asher. Intern, Chgo.-Wesley Meml. Hosp., 1952-53; resident Children's Meml. Hosp., Chgo., 1953-54; resident, instr. pathology Case Western Res. U., Cleve., 1954-56, chief pediatric pathology, 1956-66, asso. prof. pathology, 1960-72; dir. labs. Akron (Ohio), Childrens Hosp., 1966-72; dir. pathology Montreal (Que., Can.) Children's Hosp., prof. pathology McGill U., Montreal, 1972—, also prof. pediatrics, 1975—. Served with USNR, 1944-46. Mem. Am. Assn. Pathologists and Bacteriologists, Pediatric Pathology Club, Inc. (councillor 1965—). Author: Cellular Aspects of Development Pathology, 1967; editor Perspectives in Pediatric Pathology, 1973; contbr. articles in field to profl. jours. Home: 23 Barat Rd Montreal PQ 217 Canada Office: 2300 Tupper St Montreal PQ Canada

BOLDUC, REGINALD JOSEPH, agrl. scientist; b. Lac Drolet, Que., Can., July 28, 1939; s. Wilfrid and Lucienne (Deslongchamps) B.; B.E.S.A., Laval U., Que., 1960, B.Sc.Agr., 1964; Ph.D., Purdue U., West Lafayette, Ind., 1968; m. Dorothy Roy, June 6, 1964; 1 son, Yann J. Kevin. Research asst. in plant physiology and biochemistry Purdue U., 1964-68; asso. prof. agr. Laval U., 1968-72, asst. prof., 1972—; research scientist Can. Agr., Quebec, 1972—; postdoctoral research fellow Centre National de la Recherche Scientifique, Gifyvette, France, 1969, Que. Ministry Edn., 1964-68. Mem. Corp. Agr. Province Que., Agrl. Inst. Can., Agrl. Soc. Can., Conseil des Prodns. Vegetales du Que., Canadian Soc. Plant Physiology, Fedn. Biol. Soc. Can., Assn. Sci., Engring. and Technol. Community Can., Assn. Canadienne Française pour l'Avancement des Scis., Sigma Xi. Contbr. articles to profl. jours. Home: 31 Robitaille St Breakeyville PQ G0S 1E0 Canada Office: Research Sta Can Dept Agr 2560 Blvd Hochelaga PQ G1V 2J3 Canada

BOLEY, ROBERT EUGENE, assn. exec.; b. Washington, Nov. 25, 1925; s. Charles Taylor and Viva (Weightman) B.; A.B., George Washington U., 1953, M.A., 1958; m. Janet Elizabeth McCarty, May 26, 1950; 1 stepson, Stephen C. Sole. Geographer Fed. Govt., 1953-54; research asso. George Washington U., 1954-56; dir. Indsl. Devel. Com. of Prince George County (Md.), 1956-57; with Urban Land Inst., Washington, 1957-73, exec. dir., 1968-73; cons. Soc. Indsl. Realtors, 1973, exec. v.p., 1974—. Served with AUS, 1943-46. Decorated Air medal. Mem. Assn. Am. Geographers, Am. Indsl. Devel. Council, League Econ. Devel. Orgns., Nat. Assn. Corporate Real Estate Execs., Lambda Alpha, Pi Gamma Mu. Club: National Press. Contbr. Industrial Development Handbook, 1975, Guide to Industrial Site Selection, 1979, Industrial Real Estate, 3d edit., 1979. Home: 2900 Chesapeake St NW Washington DC 20008 Office: 925 15th St NW Washington DC 20005

BOLEY BOLAFFIO, RITA, artist; b. Trieste, Italy; d. Angelo and Olga Senigaglia; came to U.S., 1939, naturalized, 1944; ed. Kunstgewerbe Schule, Vienna, Austria; student of Josef. Hoffmann; diploma violin Music Conservatory, Vienna; m. Orville F. Boley; children—Lucius R., Bruno A. Fashion and textile designer, Vienna, Milan, Italy; murals and displays throughout U.S., maj. exhbns. collage and assemblage include Mus. of Art, Columbia, S.C., Am. House, N.Y.C., J.L. Hudson Gallery, Detroit, Pen and Brush Club, N.Y.C., Richard Kollmar's Gallery, N.Y.C., Guild Hall Mus., East Hampton, N.Y., James Pendleton Gallery, N.Y.C. Mem. arts group ARC, 1942-44. lMem. Composer, Author and Artists Am. Home and Studio: 310 W 106th St New York City NY 10025

BOLGER, JACK, advt. co. exec.; b. Montclair, N.J., Dec. 12, 1934; s. Lewis Theodore and Edythe (Haynes) B.; B.S., Moravian Coll., 1958; m. Dorothea Pool, Aug. 16, 1958; children—Aric Daniel, Glen David, Rod Andrew. Vice pres. Indsl. Mktg. Services, Inc., Sparta, N.J., 1958-62; v.p., creative dir. Newman-Marwel, Inc., Bloomfield, N.J., 1962-68; pres. Advt. Mktg. Asso., Inc., Bloomfield, 1968—; creative cons. various advt. agys. Mem. Sparta Twp. Zoning Bd. of Adjustment, 1976-77; bd. dirs. Sch. of Arts, Stillwater, N.J., 1960-64, chmn., 1960-63; bd. dirs. Madison (N.J.) Area YMCA, 1966-67; trustee Kittatinny Recreation and Tourist Assn., 1970-72; councilman Twp. of Sparta, 1977—. Contbr. articles to profl. jours. Home: 55 Fox Ridge Rd Sparta NJ 07871 Office: 46 Main St Sparta NJ 07871

BOLT, EDWIN RALPH, logistics mgr.; b. Sugar Grove, Va., July 10, 1927; s. Joseph Marion and Ava Mabel (Schuler) B.; student Pa. State U., Mont Alto, 1969-70, Shippensburg State Coll., 1972-73, Mt. St. Mary's Coll., 1972-73; m. Leah Ruth Greenstreet, Dec. 30, 1950; children—James Edwin, David Joseph. With U.S. Govt., 1948—; staff mgr. hdqrs. U.S. Army Munitions Command, Dover, N.J., 1964-68; staff officer maintenance engring. field office Army Material Command, Chambersburg, Pa., 1968-73; systems analyst Logistics Systems Support Agy., Chambersburg, Pa., 1973-77; staff liaison Officer U.S. Army Depot System Command Liaison office, Alexandria, Va., 1977—. Pres., Aberdeen Elementary Sch. PTA, 1962-63; sect. chmn. United Fund campaign, 1976. Served with Fin. Corps, U.S. Army, 1945-46, M.C., 1950-51. Recipient Outstanding Performance awards U.S. Govt., 1970, 73. Mem. Am. Def. Preparedness Assn., Am. Security Council (adv. bd.), Profl. Photographers Am. Home: RD 3 Box 212 Fayetteville PA 17222 Office: Eisenhower Ave Alexandria VA 22333

BOLT, RICHARD EUGENE, family practitioner; b. Boston, Jan. 27, 1943; s. Richard Henry and Katherine (Smith) B.; A.B., Antioch Coll., 1966; M.D., U. Rochester, 1970; m. Ann Marie Brayfield, Oct. 9, 1965; children—Elaine, Joyce, Richard. Intern, U. Rochester (N.Y.), 1970-71, resident and chief resident in family medicine, 1973-76, fellow in family medicine, 1976; family physician, med. dir. Fight Sq. Health Center, Westside Health Services, Rochester, 1976—, supr. nurse practitioner, 1976—; clin. instr. family medicine Sch. Medicine and Dentistry, U. Rochester; asst. physician, asst. pediatrician Strong Meml. Hosp. Mem. community bd. mgmt. Arnett Br. YMCA, 1976—; chairperson bank investment subcom. Housing Task Force 19th Ward Community Assn., 1977—; mem. Council of Adoptive Parents, 1976—. Served with USPHS, 1971-73. Recipient letters of commendation Dir. Office Research and Devel., Indian Health Services, 1973. Mem. Am. Acad. Family Physicians, Cheyenne-Arapaho Tribe of Okla., Gourd Dancing Clan, Golden Link Folk Singing Soc., Country Dance and Song Soc. Am., Country Dancers of Rochester, Irish Musician's Group. Democrat. Profl. folk music performer as violinist, vocalist and guitarist. Home: 203 Elmdorf Ave Rochester NY 14619 Office: 288 Troup St Rochester NY 14608

BOLTON, BARBARA WEEKS (MRS. JOHN DICKSON BOLTON, JR.), communications cons.; b. Oil City, Pa., Jan. 16, 1930; d. Charles Raymond and Edna Alice (Baumbach) Weeks; B.A., Muskingum Coll., 1951; postgrad. U. Pitts., 1951-52, N.Y. U., 1954, Columbia U., 1963; m. John Dickson Bolton, Jr., Nov. 29, 1952. Columnist, feature writer, corr. Zanesville News, New Concord Enterprise, 1948; dir. radio, TV, films Community Chest of Allegheny County, 1951-54; fund raising and pub. relations dir. Western Pa. Heart Assn., 1954-67; exec. dir. Western Pa. Nat. Cystic Fibrosis Research Found., 1967-69; free lance pub. relations and devel. cons., 1969-72; account supr. Vic Maitland & Assos., 1972-74; asso. dir. Inst. for Ednl. Research, Pitts., 1972-74; pub. relations cons. Nat. Poison Center Network, Children's Hosp. of Pitts., 1974-76; free lance writer, communications cons., 1976—. Mem. community relations com. Goodwill Industries Pitts., 1974-77; mem. communications com. Pitts. Presbytery, 1975-77; feature writer Pitts. Presbyterian, 1977—. Recipient Golden Reel award Pitts. Radio and TV Club, 1976. Mem. Christian Assos. S.W. Pa. (communications com., chmn. edn. cons. com. 1975-77), Sigma Tau Delta. Office: 832 Graham Blvd Pittsburgh PA 15221

BOMBARD, DONALD KEITH, JR., broadcast exec.; b. Syracuse, N.Y., Dec. 16, 1948; s. Donald Keith and Betty (Stuhlman) B.; student Syracuse U., 1965-69; m. Martina M. Harrison, Oct. 31, 1975. Announcer, Sta. WNDR, Syracuse, 1967-68, announcer, music dir., asst. program dir., 1970-74; music dir., announcer Sta. WOLF, Syracuse, 1968-70, announcer, program dir., 1976-77; production dir. Sta. WKTQ, Pitts., 1977—; pres. Don Bombard Disco, Inc., 1975-76. Audio co-ordinator Muscular Dystrophy Assn. dance marathons Syracuse U., 1972-76, Cystic Fibrosis marathon, Syracuse, 1975, Easter Seal marathon, Pitts., 1978. Producer (with Ron Wray) History of Syracuse Music Albums, 9 vols., 1969-76. Home: 907 Tropical Ave Pittsburgh PA 15216 Office: Broadcast Plaza Crane Ave Pittsburgh PA 15220

BONA, FREDERICK EMIL, chem. co. exec.; b. Union City, N.J., Mar. 3, 1939; s. Henry C. and Clementina A. (Buzzi) B.; B.S. in Mktg., Fairleigh Dickinson U., 1962; m. Doris Hurlbert, May 27, 1961; children—Lauri, Dawn, Christine, Rick. Pub. relations rep. W.R. Grace & Co., N.Y.C., 1962-70, corp. mgr. press relations, 1970—. Mem. Planning Bd., Boonton (N.J.) Twp., 1977—. Served with U.S. Army, 1959-66. Mem. Pub. Relations Soc. Am., Nat. Fgn. Trade Council, Am. Petroleum Writers Assn., Chem. Industry Assn., Chem. Communications Assn., N.Y. Bus. Press Editors. Club: Overseas Press. Home: Boonton NJ 07005 Office: 1114 Ave of the Americas New York City NY 10036

BONAGUIDI, LAWRENCE PAUL JOHN, lawyer; b. Albuquerque, Mar. 17, 1936; s. Dino L. and Olga Pauline (Dinelli) B.; B.A. cum laude, Harvard U., 1957; J.D., Yale U., 1961. Admitted to N.Y. State bar, 1962; dep. asst. atty. gen. State of N.Y., Albany, 1962-63; asso. firm Davies, Hardy & Schenck, N.Y.C., 1963-68; partner firm Davies, Hardy, Loeb Austin & Ives, N.Y.C., 1968-72; sr. partner firm Burns, Van Kirk, Greene & Kafer, N.Y.C., since 1973—. Chmn. Higher Edn. Devel. Fund N.Y.C., 1971—; pres. E. 63d. St. Assn., 1972—; mem. Local Planning Bd. 8 N.Y.C., 1975—; trustee Metro I.L.A. Pension Fund. Mem. Am. Bar Assn., Assn. Bar City N.Y. Home: 975 Park Ave New York City NY 10028 Office: Burns Van Kirk Greene & Kafer 521 Fifth Ave New York City NY 10017

BONAMICI, DANIEL ROBERT, accountant; b. N.Y.C., Aug. 4, 1931; s. Daniel Victor and Rose Marie (Slepesky) B.; B.S. cum laude, Rider Coll., 1955, postgrad., 1959-60; postgrad. Rutgers U., 1958-59; m. Gloria Anne Smith, July 4, 1959; children—Kendall, Kirk, Kimball. Self employed pub. accountant, 1959-63; partner Furey & Bonamici, 1963-67; owner Bonamici Co., Spotswood, N.J., 1967—; dir. Multi-Investment Group, Central Jersey Savs. & Loan Assn. Sec. Jamesburg Bd. Edn., 1963-77, Helmetta Bd. Edn., 1969—; adviser, hon. mem. Monroe First Aid Squad, Jamesburg First Aid Squad; chmn. East Brunswick Indsl. and Comml. Advisory Council, So. County Hosp. Com., Brain-Injured Children's Assn.; past pres. Democratic Club East Brunswick; chmn. Raritan Valley Workshop; budget dir. East Brunswick Bicentennial Commn.; mem. Indsl. Commn., Spotswood; past chmn. Middlesex County Indsl. Devel. Com.; bd. dirs., former treas. Easter Seal Soc. N.J. Served with U.S. Army, 1950-52. Mem. Nat. Soc. Pub. Accountants, N.J. Assn. Pub. Accountants, N.J. Sch. Bd. Ofcls., East Brunswick (dir.) C. of C., Am. Legion, VFW, Phi Sigma Epsilon (past nat. v.p.). Democrat. Presbyterian. Clubs: Elks, Lions; Battleground (Englishtown, N.J.). Home: 23 Carter Rd East Brunswick NJ 08816 Office: 406 Main St Spotswood NJ 08884

BONANNO, ANTHONY KENNETH, mfg. co. exec.; b. Lawrence, Mass., Apr. 17, 1949; s. Anthony Francis and Lucille Adella (Mignanelli) B.; B.S. in Accounting, Northeastern U., Boston, 1971; M.B.A. in Mgmt., N.H. Coll., Manchester, 1977; m. Julia Ann Chaykowsky, Apr. 29, 1972; 1 son, Anthony Kenneth, II. Supr. gen. accounting Shepard & Morse Co., Brookline, Mass., 1971-72; forecast accountant, supr. budgets and planning Sanders Assos., Nashua, N.H., 1972-74, sr. fin. analyst, 1974-76; adminstr. procurement planning Raytheon Co., W. Andover, Mass., 1976-78, sr. subcontract adminstr., 1978—; mem. part-time faculty econs. and accounting Fitchburg (Mass.) State Coll, N.H. Coll. Adviser Greater Lawrence Jr. Achievement, named advisor of yr., 1978. Clara and Joseph Ford scholar, 1971. Mem. Nat. Assn. Accountants (chpt. pres. 1978), Assn. M.B.A. Execs., Raytheon-Andover Mgmt. Club, Delta Chi (alumni trustee). Democrat. Roman Catholic. Home: 314 Lowell St Methuen MA 01844 Office: 350 Lowell St West Andover MA 01810

BONANNO, PHILIP CARL, plastic and reconstructive surgeon; b. Bklyn., Mar. 5, 1938; s. Peter Victor and Rose (Castoro) B.; B.A., Hofstra Coll., 1959; M.D., Albany Med. Coll., 1963; m. Diane Cassetta, Oct. 19, 1963; children—Dominique, Peter, Philip. Intern in surgery Kings County Hosp., N.Y.C., 1964; resident in gen. surgery State U. N.Y. Downstate Med. Center, 1964-68, resident in plastic surgery Inst. Reconstructive Plastic Surgery, N.Y.C., 1968-70; practice medicine specializing in plastic and reconstructive surgery, White Plains, N.Y., 1970—; mem. staff United Hosp., Portchester, N.Y., St. Agnes Hosp., White Plains, No. Westchester Hosp., Mt. Kisco, N.Y., White Plains Hosp.; asso. clin. prof. plastic surgery N.Y. U-Bellevue Med. Center. Mem. Am. Soc. Plastic and Reconstructive Surgery, Am. Soc. Maxillo-facial Surgeons, Am. Assn. Surgery of Trauma. Republican. Roman Catholic. Clubs: Dutchess Valley Rod and Gun, Hilltop Gun, Westchester Country. Office: 7 Lake St White Plains NY 10603

BONAVENTURA, MARIA MIGLIORINI, chemist, educator; b. Somerville, Mass., June 29, 1938; d. Andrew and Maria Civita (Gallinaro) Migliorini; B.A. cum laude, Regis Coll., 1960; Ph.D., Tufts U., 1965; m. Andrew Salvatore Bonaventura, June 9, 1963. Research asst. Tufts U., Medford, Mass., 1960-64, research asso., 1965-66; asst. prof. Suffolk U., Boston, 1965-68, asso. prof., 1968-71, prof., 1971—, chmn. dept. chemistry, 1972—; research asso. Bio-Research Inst., Cambridge, Mass., 1968. Faculty rep. to trustees Joint Council on Univ. Affairs, Suffolk U., 1973-77; convenor President's Commn. on Status of Women, 1974-78, speaker ednl. policy com., 1972-73. Mem. Am. Chem. Soc. (alt. councillor, 1976-79, councillor, 1979—, dir. Northeastern sect. 1976—, chmn. pub. relations sect. 1977-79), The Chem. Soc. (London), New Eng. Assn. Chemistry Tchrs., AAUP (pres. chpt. 1970), Sigma Xi (pres. chpt. 1972-73), Sigma Zeta (sec. chpt. 1970—), Alpha Lambda Delta, Delta Epsilon Sigma. Contbr. articles to profl. jours. Home: 28 Lawndale Rd Stoneham MA 02180 Office: Suffolk University Beacon Hill Boston MA 02114

BOND, DAVID JAY, architect, city planner; b. Cedar Falls, Ia., Apr. 1, 1930; s. Leland T. and Florence (McKee) B.; B.Arch., Carnegie-Mellon U., 1957; M City Design, Miami U., Oxford, Ohio, 1958; m. Patricia Joan Dotterway, Oct. 25, 1952; children—Cecelia Elizabeth, Leland David. Sr. planner Pitts. Regional Planning Assn., 1958-62; planning dir. Urban Redevel. Authority, Pitts., 1962-67, asst. exec. dir., 1968-71; asso. prof. site planning grad. sch. pub. and internat. affairs U. Pitts., 1964—; pres. Environmental Resources Assos.; dir. planning and research div. Port Authority of Allegheny County, 1972-76; mem. Pa. Transp. Adv. Com., 1974—. Chmn., Bethel Park (Pa.) Planning Commn., 1958-71; mem. Ch. Planning Bd. Southwestern Pa., 1967-69. Served with USCG, 1951-53; now comdr. Res. Mem. AIA, Pa. Soc. Architects, Am. Inst. Planners, Phi Kappa Phi, Tau Sigma Delta. Home: 644 Rolling Green Dr Bethel Park PA 15102 Office: PO Box 24 Bethel Park PA 15102

BOND, ELIZABETH DUX, chemist; b. Altoona, Pa., June 17, 1923; d. Herbert Elmer and Irene (Moore) Dux; B.S., Pa. State U., 1944, M.S., 1951; Ph.D., Rutgers U., 1973; m. Arthur C. Bond, Apr. 19, 1973. Asst. prof. Rutgers U., New Brunswick, N.J., 1973-74; research chemist Cities Service Co., Cranbury, N.J., 1974-76; sr. scientist Hoffman-LaRoche Inc., Nutley, N.J., 1976—. Lever Bros. fellow, 1970-71. Mem. Am. Chem. Soc., Sigma Xi, Iota Sigma Pi, Sigma Pi Sigma, Sigma Delta Epsilon. Home: 27 Meadowbrook Ln Piscataway NJ 08854 Office: Hoffmann-La Roche Inc 340 Kingsland St Nutley NJ 07110

BOND, HAROLD HERANT, poet, editor; b. Boston, Dec. 2, 1939; s. Khorin and Ovsanna (Avakian) B.; A.B. in English - Journalism, Northeastern U., Boston, 1962; M.F.A. in Creative Writing, U. Iowa, 1967. Instr. poetry writing Cambridge (Mass.) Center Adult Edn., 1968—, Model Cities Higher Edn. Program, Boston, 1972, Poets-in-the-Schools program,Mass., 1971-74, 78—, N.H., 1973-76; author: The Northern Wall, 1969; Dancing on Water, 1970; The Way It Happens to You, 1979; co-author: 3X3, 1969; editor Ararat mag., 1969-70, editorial bd., 1968—; work included in anthologies, poems pub. in mags. and revs. including The New Yorker, Saturday Rev., Harper's, The New Republic; reader poetry in colls. and univs., also on radio. Recipient 1st prize poetry Armenian Allied Arts Assn. Am., 1963, 64, 65, Kansas City Star, 1967, 68; grantee in creative writing Nat. Endowment Arts, 1976. Mem. Poets Who Teach. Address: 11 Chestnut St Melrose MA 02176

BOND, JAMES PHILLIPS, physician; b. Bethlehem, Pa., July 24, 1931; s. John Henry and Eileen (Phillips) B.; B.S., Lehigh U., 1953; M.D., U. Pa., 1963; m. Nancy Hall Bond, June 13, 1959; children—Jeffrey Hall, Lynn Kathleen, John William. Geophysicist, Gulf Oil Corp., Ft. Worth, 1953-58; intern U. Pa., Phila., 1963-64, resident, 1964-66, fellow in hematology, 1966-67; chief med. resident U. Pa. Med. Div., VA Hosp., Phila., 1967-68; staff hematologist U. Pa. Med. Sch., Phila., 1967-71, asst. prof. medicine, 1971—; attending physician Service of Hematology and Oncology, Bryn Mawr (Pa.) Hosp., 1974—; dir. internal medicine Bryn Mawr Rehab. Center, 1971—. Served with Chem. Corps, U.S. Army, 1956-57. Diplomate Am. Bd. Internal Medicine, Am. Bd. Hematology. Mem. County Hematology Soc. Club: Bryn Mawr Med. Jour. (pres. 1977-78). Democrat. Presbyterian. Contbr. articles in field to profl. jours. Home: 825 Hunt Rd Newtown Square PA 19073 Office: 933 Haverford Rd Bryn Mawr PA 19010

BONDY, HEINZ ERIC, ednl. adminstr.; b. Gandersheim, Germany, June 2, 1924; s. Max and Gertrud (Wiener) B.; came to U.S., 1938, naturalized, 1943; B.A., Swarthmore Coll., 1948; M.A., Bryn Mawr Coll., 1949; m. Carolyn Ann Louks, Jan. 20, 1966; children—Peter, Eric. Asst. headmaster Windsor Mountain Sch., Lenox, Mass., 1949-50, headmaster, 1950-75; spl. asst. to chancellor U. Mass., Boston, 1975-77, asso. v.p. for univ. relations, 1978—. Served with AUS, 1943-45; ETO. Decorated Purple Heart. Contbr. articles to profl. publs. Address: 55 Park Ave Wellesley MA 02181

BONE, JOHN HENRY, psychologist; b. Nanticoke, Pa., Apr. 21, 1914; s. Charles Alfred and Margaret (Knarr) B.; B.S., Bucknell U., 1938, M.S., 1943; D.Ed., Pa. State U., 1957; m. Jessie Slayton Green, Dec. 18, 1943; children—Barbara Joyce, Constance Gheen. Tchr., Nanticoke High Sch., 1939-42; tng. officer VA, Williamsport, Pa., 1945-52; dir. guidance Bellefonte (Pa.) Area Sch. Dist., 1952-57; dean of students and admissions Lock Haven (Pa.) State Coll., 1957-73, emeritus, 1973—; pvt. practice psychology, Lock Haven, 1957—. Mem. Jersey Shore (Pa.) Sch. Bd., 1969-73; mem. Lycoming-Clinton Counties Mental Health and Mental Retardation Bd., 1967-70. Served with AUS, 1942-45. Diplomate Am. Bd. Profl. Psychology (clin.). Fellow Am., Pa. psychol. assns.; mem. Am. Personnel and Guidance Assn. Home and office: 328 S Main St Jersey Shore PA 17740

BONE, LARRY EARL, library exec.; b. Memphis, Oct. 31, 1932; s. Blondell Foster and Thelma Catherine (Crouch) B.; B.A., Southwestern at Memphis, 1954; M.S. in L.S., Case Western Res. U., 1955. Asst. reference librarian San Francisco State Coll., summer 1955; br. librarian Memphis Pub. Library, 1955-57; asst. head gift sect. Library of Congress, 1958; librarian George Mason Coll., U. Va., 1958-59; head librarian Avon Lake (Ohio) Pub. Library, 1959-62; dir. Mentor (Ohio) Pub. Library, 1962-63; county librarian Shelby County Libraries, Memphis, 1963-66; vis. asst. prof. Sch. Librarianship, U. Wash., summer 1968; vis. dep. librarian Am. Library in Paris, France, 1968-69; asst. dir., asst. prof. Grad. Sch. Library Sci., U. Ill., 1966-70; asst. dir. libraries for pub. services Memphis Pub. Library and Info. Center, 1970-75; vis. asst. prof. George Peabody Coll. for Tchrs., summer 1970, 76, 78; vis. prof. Columbia U., Sch. Library Service, summer 1972; vis. lectr. dept. library service Memphis State U., 1973-75; dir. Burrow Library, asso. prof. bibliography Southwestern at Memphis, 1975-77; dir. libraries Mercy Coll., Dobbs Ferry, N.Y., 1977—; cons. various libraries; staff ALA Library/U.S.A., New York Worlds Fair, 1965. Ford Found. Council on Library Resources fellow, 1974. Mem. ALA (council 1972-76, chmn. outstanding reference books com. 1971-73, chmn. com. for third edit. Reference Books for Small and Medium-Sized Libraries 1977-78, pres. reference and adult services div. 1978—), Tenn. (chmn. intellectual freedom com. 1963-65), Ohio (chmn. reference sect. 1959-60), Lake County (Ohio) (chmn. 1962-63) library assns., Memphis Librarians Council (chmn. 1964-65), Phi Beta Kappa, Beta Phi Mu. Democrat. Author: Library Education: An International Survey, 1968; Library School Teaching Methods, Courses in the Selection of Adult Materials, 1969; Reference Books for Small and Medium-sized Libraries, 1979. Issue editor Library Trends, 1972, 76. Home: 513 3d Ave New York NY 10016 Office: 555 Broadway Dobbs Ferry NY 10052

BONFIELD, EDWARD HARVEY, educator, mktg. specialist; b. Birmingham, Ala., Apr. 28, 1938; s. Louis and Gertrude (Kessler) B.; B.S., U. Ala., 1962, M.S., 1963; Ph.D., U. Ill. at Urbana-Champaign, 1972; m. Phyllis Ann Kline, May 16, 1965; children—Brett, Jeffrey, Robin. Research analyst, asso. study dir. Market Facts, Inc., Chgo., 1963-66; research asst. U. Ill. Survey Research Lab, Urbana, 1966-68, staff research asst Bur. Bus. Mgmt., 1968-70; lectr. mktg. U. Ala., Tuscaloosa, 1970-72, asst. prof., 1972-76; asso. prof. Temple U., Phila., 1976—. Bd. dirs., treas. Temple Emanu-el, Tuscaloosa, 1973-76; bd. dirs. Consumer Credit Counseling Service, Tuscaloosa, 1970-72; pres., chmn. bd. U. Community Cooperative U. Ala., 1972-75. Ford Found. grantee U. Ala., 1973; recipient outstanding prof. award Morris L. Mayer award U. Ala., 1975. Mem. Am. Mktg. Assn., Am. Psychol. Assn., Am. Statis. Assn., Assn. Consumer Research, S. Mktg. Assn., Acad. Mktg. Sci.; asso. mem. Smithsonian Inst. Democrat. Mem. Old York Rd. Temple-Beth Am., Abington, Pa. Contbr. articles in field to profl. jours. Home: 2028 Fortune Rd Glenside PA 19038 Office: Mktg Dept Sch of Business Temple U Philadelphia PA 19122

BONFORTE, RICHARD JAMES, physician, hosp. adminstr.; b. Newark, Feb. 27, 1940; s. James Sebastian and Lillian Viola (Reiss) B.; A.B. cum laude, Seton Hall U., 1961; M.D. cum laude, Georgetown U., 1965. Intern, Mt. Sinai Hosp., N.Y.C., 1965-66, resident, 1966-68, fellow in infectious disease and immunology, 1970-72, dir. pediatric out-patient dept., 1972—, dir. pediatric ambulatory care, 1977—, asso. prof., 1972—, dir. Cystic Fibrosis Care and Teaching Center, 1971—, dir. Pediatric Pulmonary Center, 1977—. Served with AUS, 1968-70. Fellow Am. Acad. Pediatrics; mem. AAAS, Am. Soc. Microbiology, Am. Thoracic Soc., N.Y., Bela Schick (sec. 1970—) pediatric socs., Alpha Omega Alpha. Home: 140 Hepburn Rd Clifton NJ 07012 Office: Mount Sinai Sch Medicine 1 Gustave L Levy Pl 100th St and Fifth Av New York City NY 10029

BONGIOVANNI, CARL, social services planner; b. Niagara Falls, N.Y., Jan. 15, 1944; s. Carmen Joseph and Rose Theresa (Spatorico) B.; student U. Buffalo, 1963-64; B.S. in Edn., Fredonia Coll., 1966; postgrad. Fredonia Coll., 1971-73; m. Judith Arlene McKie, Mar. 29, 1971. Tchr., Union-Endicott (N.Y.) Pub. Schs., 1966-67; social caseworker City of Binghamton (N.Y.), 1967-68; with Niagara County, Dept. Social Services Niagara Falls, 1969—, now title XX planner. Active United Way, 1978—. Mem. Nat. Assn. Social Workers, Am. Planning Assn., N.Y. State Assn. for Human Services, Gerontol. Soc., Sertoma. Lutheran. Home: 1321 Ashland Niagara Falls NY 14301 Office: 301 10th Niagara Falls NY 14302

BONK, JUDITH ANN, interior designer; b. Pitts., Feb. 26, 1946; d. Walter Louis and Sophia Joan (Leja) B.; asso. degree in interior design Art Inst. Pitts., 1973; B.S. in Interior Design, LaRoche Coll., 1974. Custom software mfr., 1965-75; owner, operator Montage, interior design studio, custom softwares, Pitts., 1975—; lectr. interior design dept. LaRoche Coll., 1977—, lectr. interior design Project Phoenix, 1976—, project placement supr., 1976—. Home: 399 Sunderland Dr Pittsburgh PA 15237 Office: 3333 Babcock Blvd Pittsburgh PA 15237

BONNER, CHARLES DOUGLASS, physician; b. New Haven, May 1, 1917; s. Fred D. and Charlotte (Stokes) B.; A.B., Lincoln U., Pa., 1939, D.Sc. (hon.), 1966; M.D., Boston U., 1944; m. Frances E. Jones, Dec. 18, 1943; children—Carol, Dale. Intern, Boston City Hosp., 1944-45, asst. resident, 1947-48, resident, 1948-49, asst. in medicine, 1949—; Damon Runyan fellow in cancer research Tufts U., 1949-52, trainee Nat. Cancer Inst., 1952-55, instr. medicine, 1949-56, asst. clin. prof., 1956-58; asst. in medicine Boston U., 1949-54, instr., 1954-56, lectr., 1956-58, asst. prof., 1958—; asst. in medicine Faulkner Hosp., 1955-59, asso. staff, 1960-76; asst. in medicine St. Elizabeth's Hosp., 1956-62, asst. vis. physician in medicine, 1962—, cons. phys. med. and rehab., 1962—; courtesy staff Carney Hosp., 1954-76; physician-in-charge Cardinal Cushing Rehab. Center of Youville Hosp., 1958—, v.p. staff, 1960-61, pres. staff, 1961-62; cons. VA Hosp., Northampton, Mass., 1963-66; cons. medicine Cambridge City Hosp., 1967—; cons. phys. medicine and rehab. Brockton VA Hosp., 1974-77; med. dir. Youville Hosp., 1968—, pres. med. staff, 1971-72; chief phys. med. div. Cambridge Hosp., 1968—; adv. bd. Sch. Practical Nursing, 1960-66; lectr. phys. medicine and rehab. Tufts U., 1961. Mem. Pres.'s Commn. Employment of Handicapped, 1968—, Mass. Med. Assistance Adv. Council, 1966; mem. Cambridge Rehab. Com., 1956-62; mem. United Community Services Rehab. Council, 1957-62, mem. adv. bd., 1958-60; Mass. del. White House Conf. Aging, 1961; chmn. health and social services com. Mass. Council Aging, 1961-65; v.p. Cambridge Tb and Health Assn., 1961-65, pres., 1965-67; chmn. stroke com. Mass. Heart Assn., 1965-67, bd. dirs., 1964—, chmn. com. programming in low income and minority areas, 1972-77; adv. bd. Region I Pub. Health Service, 1968; bd. dirs. Mass. div. Am. Cancer Soc., 1970-74; trustee Lesley Coll., 1971-77; mem. corp. Mt. Auburn Hosp., 1971—. Served from 1st lt. to capt., AUS, 1945-47. Recipient Region I, Nat. Rehab. Assn. award for meritorious service, 1967; Better Life award Fedn. Nursing Homes, 1970; Distinguished Alumnus award Boston U. Sch. Medicine, 1971; Distinguished Pub. Service award Alumni Assn. Boston U., 1973; Meritorious Service award Mass. Rehab. Assn., 1977. Fellow A.C.P.; mem. AMA, Mass. Med. Soc., N.Y. Acad. Scis., Am. Assn. Cancer Research, Am. Congress Rehab. Medicine, Am. Heart Assn. (dir. 1970-75, v.p. 1972-73, exec. com. 1973-75, nominating and awards com. 1973-75; v.p. Mass. affiliate 1974-76, pres. 1978—; award of merit 1975, Louis B. Russell award 1978), New Eng. Rheumatism Soc., New Eng. Soc. Phys. Medicine and Rehab. (councilor, 1960-63, sec. 1963-64, treas. 1964-65, 2d v.p. 1965-66, 1st v.p. 1966-67, pres. 1967-68), Mass. Assn. Occupational Therapy (adv. bd. 1964-65), Am. Phys. Therapy Assn. (adv. bd. dirs. Mass. chpt. 1961-63), Cambridge Tb Health Assn. (chmn. rehab. com., mem. bd. mgrs., 1958-68), Mass. Soc. Internal Medicine, Am. Hosp. Assn. (governing council chronic disease and rehab. sect.), Cambridge Med. Improvement Soc., Boston U. Med. Sch. Alumni Assn. (pres. 1968-69). Contbr. numerous articles to profl. jours. Home: 160 Lake Ave Newton Centre MA 02159 Office: 1575 Cambridge St Cambridge MA 02138

BONNER, MARIE A., educator; b. Pottstown, Pa., Apr. 24, 1924; d. Fred W. and Annette M. (Tosh) B.; B.S., Albright Coll., 1946; M.A., Columbia U., 1954; M.Ed., U. Del., 1971; postgrad. Phila. Coll. Pharmacy and Sci., summer 1965, Villanova U., summer, 1966, Beaver Coll., summer 1967, U. Del., 1970-71. Tchr., Kutztown (Pa.) High Sch., 1946-53; tchr. biology Scott Sr. High Sch., Coatesville, Pa., 1953-59; traveling sci. tchr. Oak Ridge Inst. Nuclear Studies, 1959-60; tchr. chemistry, chmn. sci. dept. Alexis I. duPont High Sch., Greenville, Del., 1960—, on leave, 1977-78; mem. Del. Sci. Curriculum Com., Dover; cons., lectr. in field. Delta Kappa Gamma scholar, 1970-71; NSF summer grantee, 1962-70; recipient award as Outstanding Sci. Tchr. in Del., Am. Chem. Soc., 1969; Am. Psychiat. Assn. commendation, 1969; award of excellence, Nat. Sci. Fair Internat., Am. Inst. Mining, Metall. and Petroleum Engrs., 1968. Mem. NEA, Del. Tchrs. Sci., Nat. Sci. Tchrs. Assn., Nat. Sci. Suprs. Assn., Delta Kappa Gamma. Address: 1614 W Lynn Dr West Chester PA 19380

BONNEY, JEAN COZZA (MRS. RUSSELL NORWOOD BONNEY, JR.), ednl. adminstr.; b. Orange, N.J., Sept. 9, 1940; d. Stanley and Margaretta (Meyer) Cozza; B.A. in Math., U. Del., 1962; M.S. in Math., Stevens Inst. Tech., 1967; m. Russell Norwood Bonney, Jr., Sept. 14, 1963; children—Lesley Suzanne, Andrea Kay. Mem. tech. staff Bell Labs., Whippany, N.J., 1962-71; asst. dir. computer center Rutger's U., New Brunswick, N.J., 1971-77; dir. academic and research computing services Mass. Inst. Tech., Cambridge, 1977—; session chmn. 7th ann. conf. computers in undergrad. curricula, 1976. Sunday sch. tchr. Congregational Ch.; mem. citizens' goals com. Madison (N.J.) Pub. Schs., 1975. Mem. Assn. Computing Machinery (spl. interest groups-computers in edn., programming langs., univ. computer centers, gen. chmn. user services conf. 1975, reviewer Computing Revs. 1974—, dir. spl. interest group on computing centers 1976-79), Mortar Bd., Kappa Delta Pi. Home: 146 Ministerial Dr Concord MA 01742 Office: Mass Inst Tech Cambridge MA 02139

BONOYER, JOHN JOSEPH, mech. engr.; b. Providence, June 30, 1949; s. Louis Francis and Elizabeth Angela (Smith) B.; student R.I. Jr. Coll., 1968-70, Bryant Coll., 1970-71, Roger Willia Coll., 1974-76; m. Constance Mary Seaver, July 12, 1967; children—John Joseph, Cristine Mary. Machine operator Brown & Sharp Co., 1967-68; asso. engr. Foxboro Co. (Mass.), 1970-72, tech. technician, 1972-74, test engr., 1974-76, quality control engr., 1976-78, supr. systems test and quality control engring., 1978—. Home: 48 East Ave Harrisville RI 02830 Office: Foxboro Co Mechanics St Foxboro MA 02830

BONSALL, EDWARD HORNE, III, real estate exec.; b. Phila., Aug. 14, 1930; s. Rodney Tunnelle and Emilie Bartholomew (Harned) B.; student U. Pa., 1949-51; B.S. in Bus., Benedictine Coll., 1967; M.B.A., U. Pa., 1973; m. Patricia Ziegler, Jan. 4, 1958; children—Gwen Fontaine, Katherine Harned, Suzanne Tunnelle, Richard Spencer. Enlisted U.S. Army, 1951, commd. lt., 1952, advanced through ranks to lt. col., 1967; served in Korea, 1952-53, in Germany, 1958-62; served as comdr. with 3d Squadron, 6th Armed Cavalry, 1969-70, with 3d Squadron, 3d Armored Cavalry, 1970-71; sr. v.p., mgr. property mgmt. div. Jackson-Cross Co. Realtors, Phila., 1975—. Bd. dirs. Chestnut Hill Acad., Phila., 1977—; gen. staff Mil. Order of World Wars, Phila., 1976—. Served with U.S. Army, 1951-74. Decorated Legion of Merit, Meritorious Service medal, Bronze Star with V and 3 clusters, Air Medal, Purple Heart, others. Mem. Bldg. Owners and Mgrs. Assn., Phila. Bd. Realtors, Assn. M.B.A. Execs., Assn. U.S. Army, Soc. Real Property Adminstrs. Republican. Episcopalian. Clubs: Union League, Rittenhouse, Phila. Cricket. Home: 7711 Saint Martins Ln Philadelphia PA 19118 Office: 2000 Market St Philadelphia PA 19103

BONVILLIAN, JOHN DOUGHTY, psychologist; b. Caldwell, Idaho, Sept. 4, 1948; s. William Doughty and Florence Elizabeth (Boone) B.; B.A., Johns Hopkins U., 1970; Ph.D., Stanford U., 1974. Asst. prof. dept. psychology Vassar Coll., Poughkeepsie, N.Y., 1974—; vis. asso. prof. U. Va., Charlottesville, 1978-79. NSF fellow, 1970-73. Mem. AAUP, Am. Psychol. Assn., N.Y. Acad. Scis., Soc. Research in Child Devel. Democrat. Episcopalian. Mem. bd. adv. editors Sign Lang. Studies, 1977—. Office: Vassar Coll Poughkeepsie NY 12601

BOODEY, CECIL WEBSTER, JR., educator; b. Yonkers, N.Y., June 10, 1931; s. Cecil Webster and Dorothy (Mitchell) B.; B.A., U. N.H., 1949-53; postgrad. Princeton U., 1953-54; M.A. (Penfield scholar), N.Y. U., 1960; m. Phyllis Ann Stensland, July 9, 1955; children—William Mitchell, John Barton, Pamela D. Ellen. Tng. program Arabian-Am. Oil Co., Dhahran, Saudi Arabia, 1954; with N.Y. Telephone Co., Westchester, 1957-62; instr. polit. sci. Fashion Inst. Tech., N.Y.C., 1964-68, asst. prof., 1968-72, asso. prof., 1972—, chmn. social sci. dept., 1971-73. Treas. Richards Boys Club, Yonkers, 1962-63; v.p. Manasquan-Brielle (N.J.) Little League, 1969; sec. Manasquan Babe Ruth League, 1972—; Democratic municipal chmn., Manasquan, 1970-78; pres. 11th Ward Democratic Club, 1962; bd. dirs. Manasquan Area Human Relations Council, 1973—. Served with U.S. Army, 1954-56. Ford Found. fellow, 1953-54. Mem. Am. Polit. Sci. Assn., Assn. Asian Studies, Internat. Studies Assn., Asia Soc., Phi Beta Kappa, Phi Kappa Phi, Pi Mu Epsilon, Pi Gamma Mu. Methodist. Home: 80 Allen Ave Manasquan NJ 08736 Office: 227 W 27th St New York City NY 10001

BOOKER, ALVIN EUGENE, pub. exec.; b. Phila., Jan. 17, 1928; s. Samuel Bear and Yetta (Stein) B.; B.A., Temple U.; m. Janice Leah Lekoff, Dec. 16, 1951; children—Ellis Carl, Susan Barbara. Social worker YMHA, 1950-51; pres. Shopper Publns., Inc., 1952—; cons. to hosps. on office procedures. Trustee, pres. Oak Lane Day Sch. Home: 530 Elkins Ave Elkins Park PA 19117 Office: 202 York Rd South Jenkintown PA 19046

BOOKHOUT, LELAND TRAVIS, real estate cons., appraiser; b. Bath, N.Y., Apr. 22, 1939; s. Lynn Milton and Iola Maude (Grover) B.; B.S., Cornell U., 1961; m. Martha Elizabeth Swan, Aug. 17, 1963; children—Thomas Nathan, Jodi Lynne. Asst. agrl. agt. N.Y. State Coop. Ext. Service, Jamestown, 1961; real estate appraiser C.L. Orbaker and Assos., Poughkeepsie, N.Y., 1963-67; real estate appraiser, market analyst, v.p. H.R. Fountain and Co., Inc., Pleasant Valley, N.Y., 1967-70; pres., real estate cons., appraiser L.T. Bookhout, Inc., Hyde Park, N.Y., 1971-77, 78—; sr. comml. appraiser Poughkeepsie Savs. Bank, 1977-78; instr. Dutchess County Community Coll., 1968-73, 76-77; mem. nat. teaching staff Soc. Real Estate Appraisers; instr. Tri-State Real Estate Inst., Concord, N.H. Treas., deacon Hyde Park Baptist Ch. Served with U.S. Army, 1961-63. Mem. Urban Land Inst., Am. Right of Way assn., Am. Soc. Farm Mgrs. and Rural Appraisers (nat. legis. com. 1969-70, dir. N.E. Soc. chpt. 1970-73), N.Y. State Soc. Real Estate Appraisers (gov. 1978-80), Nat. Assn. Realtors, Dutchess County Bd. Realtors, Am. Inst. Real Estate Appraisers, Soc. Real Estate Appraisers (pres. 1973, dir. 1974, 78 Mid Hudson chpt.). Republican. Club: Mid-Hudson Valley Cornell (treas., dir.). Home: 3 Long Meadow Dr Staatsburg NY 12580 Office: 42 Albany Post Rd Hyde Park NY 12538

BOOKHOUT, ROBERT MARSHALL, ins., real estate exec.; b. Oneonta, N.Y., Oct. 15, 1921; s. I. Jay and Lila B. (Bell) B.; B.A., Amherst Coll., 1943; m. Wahneta Crawford, Mar. 2, 1947; children—David Alan, Robert Dale, Bruce Frederick, Allison Jay. Lighting engr. N.Y. State Electric & Gas Co., Oneonta, 1945-47; v.p. Otsego Wholesale Electric Co., Oneonta, 1947-49; pres. Bookhout Agency, Inc., Oneonta, 1949—; chmn. divisional bd. Mechanics Exchange Savs. Bank, Oneonta, 1972—. Bd. dirs. Fox Meml. Hosp., Oneonta. Mem. Oneonta C. of C. (pres. 1970-71), Ind. Ins. Agts. Am., Ind. Mut. Agts., Nat. Assn. Realtors. Republican. Methodist. Clubs: Rotary (pres. Oneonta 1959-60), Elks, Eagles, Masons. Home: 170 East St Oneonta NY 13820 Office: 41 Dietz St Oneonta NY 13820

BOOKOUT, ARTHUR ROSCOE, JR., former chem. co. exec.; b. Grover, N.C., Jan. 5, 1918; s. Arthur Roscoe and Carrie (Beam) B.; B.S. in Chem. Engring., 1939; postgrad. Va. Poly. Inst., 1943-45, U. Del., 1947-49; m. Mary Pelham Whitley, June 21, 1941; children—Jean Pelham, Susan Frances, Anne Elizabeth, Arthur William. Chief chemist Kerr Bleaching & Finishing Works, Concord, N.C., 1939-41; chemist War Dept., U.S. Army, Radford, Va., 1941-43; with Hercules Inc., 1943-78, chem. engr., Radford, Va., 1943-45, Wilmington, Del., 1945-50, chem. engr., research supr., Brunswick, Ga., 1950-54, sr. project engr. engring. dept., 1954-67, project mgr., 1967-72, mgr. design, 1972-75, mgr. design and constrn., 1975-78, ret., 1978. Registered profl. engr., Ga., Del., Ore., La., S.C. Mem. Nat. Soc. Profl. Engrs., Am. Inst. Chem. Engrs., Am. Chem. Soc., AAAS. Republican. Lutheran. Home: 2623 Longwood Dr Wilmington DE 19810 Office: Hercules Inc Wilmington DE 19899

BOOKS, KENNETH WILSON, newspaper editor; b. Pa., Apr. 20, 1949; s. Robert Merl and Pearl Anna B.; A.A., Harrisburg (Pa.) Area Community Coll., 1969; certificate Nikon Sch. Photography, 1976. Dir. pub. re Moore Assos., Harrisburg, 1973-74, Leedpak, Inc., Pa., 1974-75; editor, gen. mgr. The Citizen-Standard, Valley View, Pa., 1975—; active local schs. Newspaper in Edn. program. Pub. relations dir. Wambach for Congress campaign, 1974. Served with USN, 1969-73; Vietnam. Recipient Am. Cancer Soc. award, 1977; Am. Legion award for outstanding journalism, 1978. Mem. Nat. Newspaper Assn., Pa. Newspaper Pubs. Assn., Americans for a Free Press. Libertarian Party of Pa. Home: 16 E Main St Elizabethville PA 17023 Office: 121 W Main St Valley View PA 17983

BOOKSTAVER, JULIAN BARNET, dentist; b. N.Y.C., Mar. 22, 1914; s. Barnet Seymour and Anna (Bockar) B.; B.S., N.Y. U., 1936; D.D.S., U. Md., 1940; m. 2d, Lillian Rose, Oct. 1969. Practice denistry specializing in oral surgery, Teaneck, N.J., 1940-56, practice ltd. to oral surgery, Ramsey, also Ft. Lee, N.J., 1956—; dental surgeon Teaneck Police Dept., 1940-56; mem. oral surgery staff Holy Name Hosp., Teaneck; engaged in real estate mgmt., N.Y.C., Ft. Lee, 1958—. Mem. Gorgas Odontological Honor Soc. of U. Md. Dental Sch. Club: Lions (pres. Teaneck 1949-50). Originator dental method of personal identification; procedure for multiple extractions and immediate dentures (demonstrated U. Paris 1962); contbr. articles to profl. jours. Address: 371 Audubon Rd Englewood NJ 07631

BOOKWALTER, JOHN ROBERT, surgeon; b. Youngstown, Ohio, May 23, 1938; s. Lee Bookwalter; B.A., Amherst Coll., 1960; M.D., Harvard U., 1964; m. Judy Newberg, July 20, 1963; children—William, Thomas. Intern, then resident in surgery Boston City Hosp., 1964-70; resident in thoracic surgery New Eng.

Deaconess Hosp., Boston, 1972-73; practice medicine specializing in surgery, Brattleboro, Vt., 1973—; mem. staff Brattleboro Meml. Hosp., Rockingham Meml. Hosp.; med. adviser Rescue, Inc. Chmn. trustees Putney (Vt.) Grammar Sch. Served to maj. M.C., U.S. Army, 1970-72. Diplomate Am. Bd. Surgery, Am. Bd. Thoracic Surgery. Fellow A.C.S. Home: Dusty Ridge Rd Putney VT 05346 Office: 9 Belmont Ave Brattleboro VT 05301

BOONE, CHARLES WALTER, pathologist; b. Berkeley, Calif., Dec. 21, 1925; s. Harmon Dunscomb and Florence Celia (Chandler) B.; student U. Tex., 1943-45; B.A., Harvard U., 1947; M.D., U. Calif. at Berkeley, 1951; Ph.D., U. Calif. at Los Angele 1964; m. Doris Watson, Nov. 17, 1951; 1 dau., Catherine; m. 2d, JoAnn Brinkman, May 22, 1965; stepchildren—Joyce, Arthur. Intern, Los Angeles City and County Hosp., 1951-52; gen. practice medicine, Los Angeles, 1952-56; resident in pathology U. Calif. at Los Angeles Center for Health Scis., 1956-60, grad. fellow Dept. Biol. Chemistry, 1960-64; research fellow Dept. Cell Biology Albert Einstein Coll. Medicine, N.Y.C., 1964-65; head cell biology sect. Lab. Viral Carcinogenesis, Nat. Cancer Inst., NIH, Bethesda, Md., 1965—; clin. prof. pathology Georgetown U., Washington, 1976—. Served with USN, 1943-45. Mem. Am. Assn. Cancer Research, Am. Soc. Exptl. Pathology, Am. Soc. Biol. Chemists, Am. Soc. Cell Biology. Democrat. Methodist. Contbr. articles in field to med. jours.; asso. editor Jour. Nat. Cancer Inst., 1969—. Home: 9414 Balfour Dr Bethesda MD 20014 Office: Room 1C09 Bldg 37 Nat Cancer Inst NIH Bethesda MD 20014

BOORSTEIN, BEVERLY WEINGER, lawyer; b. Chgo., Apr. 25, 1941; d. Morris Aaron and Bess (Meisel) Weinger; B.A., Brandeis U., 1961; J.D., Boston U., 1964; m. Sidney Lester Boorstein, July 3, 1962; children—Robin Anne, Michelle Loren. Admitted to Mass. bar, 1964; with firm Siskind & Siskind, Boston, 1965-68; pvt. practice, Boston, 1969—. Mem. women's council Solomon Schechter Day Sch.; women's aux. West Edn House Boys Club. Bd. dirs. young women's div. Combined Jewish Philanthropies, 1968-70, bd. dirs. lawyers div., 1971—; contbg. asso. Weizmann Inst. Sch.; president's councillor Brandeis U. Mem. Am., Mass., Boston bar assns., Mass. Assn. Women Lawyers (rec. sec. 1969-70), Brandeis U. (nat. reunion chmn. 1971, v.p., bd. dirs. Greater Boston chpt. 1970, nat. exec. bd. 1978-79), Boston U. Law Sch. alumni assns., Mass. Audubon Soc., Nat. Council Jewish Women, Am. Jewish Com., Boston Zool. Soc., Hadassah. Home: 41 Exeter St West Newton MA 02165 Office: 185 Devonshire St Boston MA 02110

BOOSER, EARL RICHARD, engr.; b. Harrisburg, Pa., Jan. 7, 1922; s. Charles Edgar and Etta (Paul) B.; B.S., Pa. State U., 1942, M.S., 1944, Ph.D., 1949; m. Katherine Swavely, Sept. 9, 1944; children—Judith Booser Eimicke, Joan Booser Ropel. Research asst. in petroleum refining, instr. chem. engring. Pa. State U., State College, 1943-48; engr., unit mgr. in bearing, lubrication and mech. equipment devel. Gen. Electric Co., Lynn, Mass., 1948-55, Schenectady, 1955—. Registered profl. engr., N.Y. Fellow Am. Soc. Lubrication Engrs. (nat. pres. 1957), Am. Chem. Soc., ASME, Sigma Xi. Mem. Community Ch. (governing bd. 1970—). Author: (with D.F. Wilcock) Bearing Design and Application, 1957; contbr. articles to profl. jours. Home: 65 St Stephens Ln Scotia NY 12302 Office: Gen Electric Co Schenectady NY 12345

BOOTH, GEORGE WARREN, artist, advt. co. exec.; b. Omaha, July 6, 1917; s. George H. and Rae (McGrady) B.; A.B., summa cum laude, Ohio U., 1940, M.A., 1942; postgrad. John Huntington Poly. Inst., 1941, Chouinard Sch. Art, 1945-46; m. Nancy Jane Schuele, Dec. 6, 1968; children—George Geoffrey, Katherine Ellen, Robert Alan. Art dir. J.Walter Thompson Co., N.Y.C., 1947-58, Gardner Advt. Co., N.Y.C., 1958-60, Ted Bates Co., N.Y.C., 1960-64; exhibited numerous 1-man shows in N.Y.C., Calif., Washington, Md., 1972—, group shows: NAD, N.Y.C., Am. Water Color Soc., N.Y.C., Allied Artists Am., Calif. Watercolor Soc., Los Angeles, Los Angeles Mus. Art, San Francisco Mus. Art, Butler Art Inst., others; represented in permanent collections; teaching fellow photography Ohio U., Athens, 1941-42; cons. in field. Served with Signal Corps, U.S. Army, 1942-44. Recipient Art Dirs. Club N.Y.'s gold medal, 1954, Kerwin H.Fulton medal, 1954. Mem. Soc. Illustrators N.Y.C., Art Dirs. Club N.Y., Fla. Thoroughbred Breeders Assn. Clubs: Rowfant (Cleve.); Golden Hills Golf and Turf (Ocala, Fla.). Home: 314 E 41st St New York City NY 10017

BOOTH, JAMES EDWARD, chem. co. exec.; b. North Hornell, N.Y., Feb. 5, 1942; s. Claude William and Ruth L. (Lockwood) B.; student Park Coll., 1960-61, Alfred U., 1961-62, Broome Community Coll., 1970-71; m. Cynthia Louise Allen, Sept. 3, 1960; children—Pamela Ruth, Marcella Jane, James Allen. Credit mgr. Sherwin-Williams Co., Olean, N.Y., 1962-63, asst. br. mgr., Ashland, Ky., 1963-64, br. mgr., Dunkirk, N.Y., Binghamton, N.Y., 1964-72; dist. mgr. Glidden-Durkee Div., SCM Corp., Pittston, Pa., 1972-76; div. sales mgr. Grow Chem. Corp., Pennsauken, N.J., 1976-78; regional mgr. The Valspar Corp., Bound Brook, N.J., 1978—; chmn. mktg. group Grow Chem. Coatings Corp. Deacon, 1st Presbyn. Ch., 1962-63, 65-68, elder, 1968-70, 73-76; committeeman Republican party, Dunkirk, Pa., 1968-70, Pittston, 1974-76; pres. Pa. United Services Agy., 1974-76; v.p. YMCA, Pittston, 1975-76. Recipient Community Sharing Success award, Scranton, Pa., 1974; Ky. col. Mem. Constrn. Specifications Inst. (dir., Scranton, Pa. 1973-76), Painting and Decorating Contractors (asso.), U.S. Jr. C. of C. (dist. pres. 1969-70, Appreciation award N.Y. State chpt., 1970). Club: Lions. Home: 118 Westbury Ct Marlton NJ 08053 Office: Chimney Rock Rd Bound Brook NJ 08805

BOOTH, ROBERT GRAY, ins. co. exec.; b. N.Y.C., Feb. 28, 1913; s. Robert McNeilly and Violet Chambers (Gray) B.; A.B., Colgate U., 1936; m. Eleanor C. Wood, Oct. 18, 1940. Asst. dir. publs. Boy Scouts Am., N.Y.C., 1938-45; account exec. J. Walter Thompson Co., N.Y.C., 1945-61; v.p. advt. Met. Life Ins. Co., N.Y.C., 1961—. Mem. Assn. Nat. Advertisers (dir.), Life Ins. Advertisers Assn., Advt. Rev. Bd. N.Y., Sigma Nu. Republican. Presbyterian. Home: 4 Hillside Ct E Morris Plains NJ 07950 Office: 1 Madison Ave New York City NY 10010

BOPP, RAYMOND KARL, thoracic surgeon; b. Kirkwood, Mo., Dec. 17, 1930; s. Ferdinand G. and Marie (Christofferson) B.; B.A., Valparaiso U., 1952; M.D., Vanderbilt U., 1956; m. Jacqueline Bergmann, Sept. 11, 1954; children—Sandra Lynne, Jeffrey Ray, Ellen Ruth. Intern in surgery Yale New Haven Med. Center, 1956-57, cardiovascular research fellow, 1957-58, asst. resident in surgery, 1960-62, resident in gen. and thoracic surgery, 1962-63, resident in cardiovascular surgery, 1963-64; instr. surgery Yale U., New Haven, 1962-64; practice medicine specializing in gen., thoracic, and vascular surgery Willimantic, Conn., 1969—; surgeon Windham Community Meml. Hosp., Willimantic, 1969—; pres. Windham Surg. Group, Willimantic, 1974-75. Served to maj. M.C., USAF, 1958-60, 65-69. Decorated Air Force Commendation Medal with 3 oak leaf clusters; Aid Assn. for Lutherans scholar, 1951; licensed physician, Conn., Tenn.; diplomate Am. Bd. Surgery, Am. Bd. Thoracic Surgery. Mem. A.C.S., Soc. Thoracic Surgeons, Soc. Air Force Clin. Surgeons, Am. Heart Assn., AMA, Sigma Xi. Republican. Lutheran. Home: 533 Wormwood Hill Rd Mansfield CT 06250 Office: 150 Mansfield Ave Willimantic CT 06226

BORABY, MIGUEL ANGEL, psychiat. social worker, social service adminstr.; b. Camaguey, Cuba, Apr. 19, 1935; s. Agmed and Santa Ana (Pinero) B.; came to U.S., 1963, naturalized, 1969; student N.Y. U., 1965-66; certificate Columbia U., 1967; M.S.W., Fordham U., 1970; postgrad. in family therapy N.Y. Med. Coll., 1973; m. Margarita Santander, May 24, 1969. Counselor, Catholic Charities, Family Services, N.Y.C., 1966-67; asst. caseworker Shield's Inst. for Retarded Children, Bronx, N.Y., 1967-68; family counselor Catholic Charities Guidance Inst., N.Y.C., 1969-70; psychiat. social worker Upper Manhattan Aftercare Clinic, N.Y.C., 1970-71, Williamsburg Residential and Tng. Center, Bklyn., 1971-72; psychiat. social work supr. Manhattan Developmental Center, N.Y.C., 1972—; pvt. practice psychotherapy, N.Y.C., 1971—. Mem. Am. Assn. Marriage and Family Counselors, Nat. Assn. Social Workers, N.Y. State Soc. Clin. Social Workers. Democrat. Roman Catholic. Home: 31-56 31st St Astoria NY 11106 Office: 60 Gramercy Park N New York City NY 10010

BORDELEAU, NANCY VIVIAN MCINTOSH (MRS. ROLAND J. BORDELEAU), pub. welfare exec.; b. Boston, Aug. 30, 1934; d. Edmund and Dorothy (Goldstein) McIntosh; B.Ed., R.I. Coll. Edn., 1955; m. Roland J. Bordeleau, June 18, 1955; children—John Michael, Lisa Marie, Michele Denise. Tchr., Hugh B. Bain Jr. High Sch., Cranston, R.I., 1955-57; social caseworker R.I. Div. Pub. Assistance, Dept. Social Welfare, 1957-60; substitute tchr. secondary schs., Cranston, 1965; dir. Pub. Welfare, Cranston, 1966—; cons. Legislative Commn. to Study Day Care in R.I., 1968-73, chmn. Community Action Program Com. Cranston, 1969-70; mem. adv. bd. Cranston Ret. Sr. Vol. Program, 1976—; legis. chmn. Mental Health Assn. R.I., 1977, R.I. Assn. Mental Health Bds., 1977; past pres. Cranston Community Mental Health Bd., Cranston Council PTA's, D.D. Waterman PTA; moderator local Baptist Ch., 1977-78, chmn. diaconate, 1975, mem. ABCORI social concerns com., 1975-78; bd. dirs. Cranston Dist. Nursing Assn., Cranston Day Care Com., Inc.; trustee Butler Hosp.; mem. Area IV Comprehensive Mental Health Bd. Named Woman of Year, Cranston Bus. and Profl. Women's Club, 1966, Outstanding Young Woman of R.I., 1967; recipient Charles B. Willard Achievement award R.I. Coll. Alumni Assn., 1978. Mem. R.I. Dirs. Pub. Welfare Assn. (past pres.), R.I. Conf. Social Work (v.p. 1975-78), Nat. Conf. Social Welfare, Am. Pub. Welfare Assn., Kappa Delta Pi. Home: 70 Poppy Dr Cranston RI 02920 Office: 1090 Cranston St Cranston RI 02920

BORDEN, ENID ALANA, journalist; b. Bklyn., Feb. 15, 1950; B.A., Alfred U., 1972; M.A. in Speech and Theatre Arts, Adelphi U., 1973. Editor, Sta. KKFM, Colorado Springs, Colo., 1977; pub., editor Wings of the Springs, Colorado Springs, 1976-77; polit. reporter The Beacon Newspapers, Babylon, N.Y., 1977-78; free-lance writer, 1978—; congl. press sec. for 5th Dist. Conn., Waterbury, 1978; tchr. community schs., Colorado Springs, 1977. Founder, dir. Rainbow Repertory Co., Lawrence, N.Y., summer 1976. Mem. Am. Theatre Assn. Composer musical score for children's theatre prodn., 1974. Home and Office: 38 Dubonnet Rd Valley Stream NY 11581

BORDEN, GEORGE ASA, educator; b. Elmira Heights, N.Y., June 16, 1932; s. Arthur Leroy and Matilda Catherine (Hartman) B.; student Bible Inst. Los Angeles, 1950-52, N.Mex. State U., 1955-57; B.A. in Mathematics, U. Denver, 1958, M.A. in Mathematics, 1959, M.A. in Communication Methodology, 1962; Ph.D. in Speech Behavior, Cornell U., 1964; children—Sherrie, Cynthia, Curtis. Mathematician, Marathon Oil Co., Littleton, Colo., 1959-62; from asst. prof. to prof. Pa. State U., University Park, 1964-75; prof. dept. communication U. Del., Newark, 1975—, chmn. dept., 1975-78; cons. Augmented Human Intellect Project of Rome Air Devel. Center; mem. nat. advisory bd. Eric Clearinghouse on Reading and Communication Skills. Served with U.S. Army, 1952-54. Mem. Am. Psychol. Assn., Internat. Communication Assn., Speech Communication Assn., Assn. Lit. and Linguistic Computing. Author: (with Gregg and Grove) Speech Behavior and Human Interaction, 1969; Introduction to Human Communication Theory, 1971; (with Stone) Human Communication: The Process of Relating, 1976; contbr. articles to profl. jours. Home: 11 Myers Rd Newark DE 19713 Office: U Delaware Newark DE 19711

BORDERS, WILLIAM DONALD, archbishop; b. Washington, Ind., Oct. 9, 1913; s. Thomas M. and Zelpha Ann (Queen) B.; student St. Meinrad (Ind.) Sem.; M.S. in Edn., U. Notre Dame, 1947; D.D., LL.D., Notre Dame Sem., New Orleans, 1969. Ordained priest Roman Cath. Ch., 1940; consecrated bishop, 1968; apptd. archbishop, 1974; asso. pastor several parishes in New Orleans, 1940-47; chaplain AUS, World War II; instr. U. Notre Dame, 1946-47; chaplain Cath. Student Community, La. State U., 1947-62; pastor Holy Family Parish, Port Allen, La.; rector St. Joseph Cathedral and St. Joseph Prep. Sch., Baton Rouge, 1962-68; bishop Diocese of Orlando (Fla.), 1968-74; archbishop of Balt., 1974—; mem. boundaries of dioceses and provinces com., cons. moral values com., mem. nomination of bishops com. Region 4, Nat. Conf. Cath. Bishops, mem. adminstrv. com., 1977—, mem. com. on adminstrn. and personnel, 1977—; past chmn. edn. com. U.S. Cath. Conf., mem. adminstrv. bd., 1977—. Trustee Cath. U. Am.; bd. dirs. Commn. for Cath. Missions Among the Colored People and Indians. Address: 320 Cathedral St Baltimore MD 21201

BORECKY, ISIDORE, bishop Ukrainian Cath. Ch. in Can.; b. Ostrovec, Ukraine, Oct. 1, 1911. Ordained priest, 1938; titular bishop of Amathus and exarch of Toronto (Ont. Can.), 1948-56; bishop of Toronto (Ukrainian), 1956—. Address; 61 Glen Edyth Dr Toronto ON M4V 2V8 Canada

BORER, EDWARD TURNER, investment banker; b. Phila., Nov. 30, 1938; s. Robert Chamberlin and Helen Elizabeth (Clawges) B.; B.S., U. Pa., 1960; m. Amy Hamilton Ryerson, Aug. 8, 1959; children—Edward Turner, Catherine Hamilton, Elizabeth Taft. Rep., Hopper Soliday & Co., Inc., Phila., 1960-67, v.p. research, 1967-73, sec., 1971—, sr. v.p., 1973—, also dir., dir. Manchester Gas Co. (N.H.), 1965—, pres., 1970, chmn. bd., chmn. exec. com., 1970—; founder, treas., sec., dir. Creative Info. Systems, Inc., Chadds Ford, Pa., 1967-77; chmn. West Met. Area-Wide Com., Regional Med. Program, 1969-70. Pres. Swarthmore Home and Sch. Assn., 1973-74; treas., trustee George W. South Meml. Ch. of the Advocate, 1978—. Served to 1st lt. Q.M.C., AUS, 1961-62. Chartered fin. analyst. Mem. Fin. Analysts Fedn., Fin. Analysts Phila., N.Y. Soc. Security Analysts, Bond Club Phila., Phila. Securities Assn., Delta Upsilon. Episcopalian. Club: Union League (Phila.). Home: 125 Guernsey Rd Swarthmore PA 19081 also St John VI 00830 Office: 1401 Walnut St Philadelphia PA 19102

BORG, MALCOLM AUSTIN, newspaper pub. co. exec.; b. N.Y.C., Jan. 28, 1938; s. Donald Gowen and Flora (Austin) B.; grad. The Hill Sch., 1956; B.S. in English Lit., Columbia, 1965; postgrad. Harvard Sch. Bus., 1970; m. Sandra Jean Agemian, Sept. 9, 1961; children—John Austin, Jennifer Ann, Stephen Agemian. With The Bergen Evening Record, Hackensack, N.J., 1959—, v.p., 1967-68, exec. v.p., 1968-70, chmn. bd., pres., 1971—; chmn. bd. Toms River Pub. Co., Inc., Monmouth News, Inc., Freehold Transcript, Inc.; chmn. bd., pres. Gremac, Inc.; chmn. bd. Gateway Communications, Inc. Exec. bd. Bergen council Boy Scouts Am., 1967-74; mem. exec. bd. N.J. Dept. Health Comprehensive Health Planning Council, 1971-72; mem. nursing adv. com. Bergen Community Coll., 1968-70; mem. health care adminstrn. bd. N.J. Dept. Health, 1972-76; bd. dirs. Palisades Interstate Park Commn., 1974—, Boys' Club of Paterson, 1966-69, Wolfeboro Camp, 1970—, The Newspaper Comics Council, Inc., 1970-73; trustee Hackensack Area Community Chest, 1968-71, Three Sch. Devel. Found., 1973-76, N.J. Health Facilities Planning Council, 1965-69, N.E. Ice Hockey Ofcls. Assn., 1976—; bd. mgrs. Bergen Pines County Hosp., 1974—. Served with AUS, 1956-58. Recipient Torch of Liberty award Soc. Fellows Anti-Defamation League, B'nai B'rith N.J., 1973; William H. Spurgeon III council award Bergen council Boy Scouts Am., 1972; Service to Others award N.J. div. Salvation Army, 1977; named Man of Year, Holy Name Hosp., Teaneck, N.J., 1977; Community Leadership award No. N.J. Interprofl. Council, 1977. Mem. Am. Soc. Newspaper Editors, AP Mng. Editors Assn., N.J. Press Assn., Am. Newspaper Pubs. Assn., Columbia U. Club Bergen County, Harvard Bus. Sch. Clubs Greater N.Y. (dir. 1973—), Harvard Bus. Sch. Assn. (pres. 1976-78), Alumni Assn. Hill Sch. (pres. 1973-76), Bergen County C. of C. (dir. 1967-74), Sigma Delta Chi. Clubs: Arcola Country (Paramus, N.J.); Bath and Tennis of Spring Lake (N.J.); Englewood Field (N.J.); Harvard of N.Y.; Mid-Ocean, Tuckers Town (Bermuda). Home: 8 Forest Rd Tenafly NJ 07670 Office: 150 River St Hackensack NJ 07602

BORGE, CARLOS, civil engr.; b. Esparta, Costa Rica, Oct. 26, 1919; s. Agamenon and Maria Luisa (Calvo) B.; came to U.S., 1953, naturalized, 1956; B.S. in Civil Engring., U. Costa Rica, 1947; M.S., U. Minn., 1953; m. Margaret Irene Campbell, Aug. 3, 1949. Chief engr. hydraulics dept. Govt. of Costa Rica, San Jose, 1948-53; design engr. Thomas Worcester, Inc., Boston, 1953-54, Edwards, Kelcey & Beck, Inc., Boston, 1954-55, Metcalf & Eddy, Boston, 1955-58, Diamato Engrs., Boston, 1958-60; adviser water supply programs in Honduras, 1960-63; city engr. East Chicago, Ind., 1963-64; engring. analyst Inter-Am. Devel. Bank, Washington, 1965—. U.S. State Dept. fellow, 1948-49. Registered profl. engr., Ind., Mass. Fellow ASCE; mem. Nat. Soc. Profl. Engrs., Am. Acad. Environ. Engrs. (diplomate 1968), Inter-Am. Assn. San. Engrs., Internat. Platform Assn. Republican. Episcopalian. Home: 815 Hayward Ave Takoma Park MD 20012 Office: 808 17th St NW Washington DC 20577

BORGOS, STEPHEN JOHN, mktg. and mgmt. cons., educator; b. Yonkers, N.Y., June 2, 1941; s. William and Stephanie J. (Samoyedny) B.; student Clarkson Coll., 1958-59; B.S. in Mktg., State U. N.Y., Albany, 1963, M.S. in Mktg., 1965; m. JoAnn Leone, July 16, 1966; children—Patricia, William, Michael, Kelli, Sharon. Vice pres. Robinson Laundry, Inc., South Glens Falls, N.Y., 1963-64, sales mgr., 1964-65; real estate salesman Maple Realty, Glens Falls, N.Y., 1963—; dir. mktg. Thruway Travel Service, Inc., Lake George, N.Y., 1965-66; asso. prof. bus. Adirondack Community Coll., Glens Falls, 1966—; chmn. bd. dirs., pres. Traveltown, Inc., Glens Falls, 1967—; mktg. and mgmt. cons., Glens Falls, N.Y., 1969—. Mem. Queensbury (N.Y.) Central Vol. Fire Co., 1972—, pres., 1977—; fire warden N.Y. State, 1974—; co-chmn. fund drive Moreau (N.Y.) chpt. ARC, 1963; chmn. fund drive Muscular Dystrophy, Moreau, 1963; mem. bd. assessment rev. Town of Queensbury, 1975-77. Mem. Am. Mktg. Assn., Am. Forestry Assn., Epsilon Delta Epsilon. Republican. Roman Catholic. Club: Rotary (v.p. Glen Falls club 1977-78). Home and Office: Butler Pond Rd RD 2 Glens Falls NY 12801

BORGSTEDT, HAROLD HEINRICH, pharmacologist, physician, educator; b. Hamburg, Germany, Apr. 21, 1929; s. Gustav Johannes and Anni (Wulf) B.; came to U.S., 1956, naturalized, 1962; M.D., U. Hamburg, 1956; m. Agneta D. von Rehren, Apr. 3, 1957; children—Eric von R., Astrid Ann. Intern, Rochester (N.Y.) Gen. Hosp., 1956-57; fellow pharmacology and anatomy U. Rochester, 1957-59, instr. pharmacology, 1959-63, sr. instr., 1963-65, research sr. instr. anesthesia, 1963-65, asst. prof. pharmacology, research asst. prof. anesthesiology, 1965—. Mem. AAAS, Rochester Acad. Medicine, N.Y. Acad. Scis., Am. Soc. Pharmacology and Exptl. Therapeutics, Soc. Toxicology, Internat. Narcotic Enforcement Officers' Assn., Leica, Photog. hist. socs., Internat. Platform Assn., Sigma Xi. Unitarian. Contbr. to sci. jours., books. Home: PO Box 7 Henrietta NY 14467 Office: 601 Elmwood Ave Rochester NY 14642

BORITZ, MYRA ARLENE FREILICH, physician, editor, writer; b. N.Y.C., Dec. 27, 1942; d. Louis and Gertrude (Staff) Freilich; B.S. cum laude, Coll. City N.Y., 1963; M.D., State U. N.Y. Upstate Med. Center, 1963-67; m. Pepi Isaac Boritz, Dec. 25, 1967. Research asst. anatomy Columbia Coll. Physicians and Surgeons, 1961-63; summer fellow Syracuse (N.Y.) Psychiat. Hosp., 1965; profl. asso. Media Medica, Inc, N.Y.C., 1968-69; asst. to pubs. Medcom, Inc., N.Y.C., 1969-73; exec. producer, writer 8 filmstrip library on care of newborn; med. cons. slide series Famous Teachings in Modern Medicine; dir. med. copy Synapse Communication Services, Inc., 1973-74; freelance, 1974—. Mem. Am. Med. Women's Assn., Am. Med. Writers Assn., Met. Mus. Art, Mus. Modern Art, Phi Beta Kappa. Contbg. editor tech. monographs; chief contbg. writer to teaching manuals on med. gynecology, gastro-enterology and infant nutrition for pharm. salesmen. Address: 945 Fifth Ave Apt 10 E New York City NY 10021

BORKE, ROBERT FRANCIS, rehab. counselor; b. Syracuse, N.Y., Aug. 21, 1947; s. Robert Paul and Theresa Dolores (Pacini) B.; B.S., State U. N.Y., Cortland, 1971; M.S., Syracuse U., 1973; m. Carol Francis Suskin, Apr. 17, 1971; 1 son, Brandon Robert. Sr. rehab. counselor, out patient team leader St. Mary's Hosp., Syracuse, N.Y., 1973-75; rehab. counselor Sequin Community Services, Syracuse, 1975-78; treatment team tchr. Syracuse Developmental Center, 1978—; cons. to ARC, Madison and Cortland. Certified rehab. counselor. Mem. Am. Personnel and Guidance Assn., Nat. Rehab. Counseling Assn., Kappa Delta Phi. Home: 140 Grant Blvd Syracuse NY 13206

BORKIN, ANDREW, EDP co. exec.; b. N.Y.C., Mar. 14, 1947; s. Daniel Wolkind and Ruth Vivian B.; B.A., State U. N.Y. at Fredonia, 1968; M.S., State U. N.Y. at Albany, 1972; m. Dana Sue Nelson, Jan. 24, 1970; children—Scott, Mary Beth, Carol Ann. Personnel counselor Rockland Community Coll., Suffern, N.Y., 1972-74; divisional personnel coordinator L'Oreal of Paris, N.Y.C., 1974-76; personnel adminstr. Itel Corp., Data Services Group, White Plains, N.Y., 1976-78; supr. compensation and benefits, mktg. and refining div. Amerada Hess, Woodbridge, N.J., 1978—; cons. in field. Served to 1st. lt., USAF, 1969-72. Mem. Am. Soc. Personnel Adminstrs., Am. Compensation Assn. Office: Amerada Hess 1 Hess Plaza Woodbridge NJ 07095

BORKOWSKY, ROMAN, librarian; b. Hlubichok Velykyi, Ukraine, Dec. 24, 1915; s. Taras and Kateryna (Popovych) B.; came to U.S., 1949, naturalized, 1955; student Lviv U., 1934-37; LL.D., Ukrainian Free U., 1949; M.S., Columbia, 1959; m. Maria Struminsky, June 17, 1951; 1 son, Taras. Clk. trainee N.Y. Pub. Library, N.Y.C., 1957-59, librarian, 1959-61, sr. librarian, lang. specialist Ukrainian, Polish and Russian, 1961—. Mem. Ukrainian Librarian Assn., Assn. for Free Ukraine (chmn. 1956—). Republican. Ukrainian Catholic. Editor: American Idea, 1976. Home: 184 Hillside Ave Yonkers NY 10703 Office: 20 W 53d St New York City NY 10019

BORLAND, BARBARA DODGE (MRS. HAL BORLAND), author; b. Waterbury, Conn.; d. Harry G. and Grace (Cross) Dodge; student Oberlin U., 1922-23, Columbia U. Sch. Journalism, 1923; m. 2d, Hal Borland, Aug. 10, 1945; 1 dau., Diana (Mrs. James C. Thomson, Jr.). Editorial cons. various pubs., 1923-35; condr. Writers Workshop, N.Y.C. 1934-38; writer, also collaborator with husband, fiction for Colliers, McCalls, Good Housekeeping, Cosmopolitan, Redbook, others, 1946-56; garden columnist Berkshire Eagle, Pittsfield, Mass., 1960. Recipient distinguished alumna award St. Margaret's Sch., 1972. Congregationalist. Mem. Authors League Am. Author: The Greater Hunger, 1962 (chosen Ambassador Book, English Speaking Union 1963). Address: Weatogue Rd Salisbury CT 06068

BORLAND, JOHN NELSON, III, publishing co. exec.; b. N.Y.C., Feb. 21, 1929; s. J. Nelson and Leslie (Fuller) B.; grad. high sch.; m. Isabelle Clarke, Mar. 15, 1953 (div. 1968); children—Susan Madeleine, Tory Lloyd, Leslie Fuller; m. 2d, Virginia Stockfish, Nov. 17, 1969. Reporter, U.P.I., N.Y.C., 1948-50; export sales promotion mgr. Fairbanks Morse & Co., N.Y.C., 1950-53; publicity writer Hazard Advt. Co., N.Y.C., 1953-54, copywriter, 1954-55, account exec., 1955-60, account supr., 1960-63, v.p., 1963-65, exec. v.p., 1966-71, treas., dir., 1967-71; pres. J. Nelson Borland & Co., Inc., 1971-74; pres., pub. Muse Pub. Co., N.Y.C., 1974—. Clubs: N.Y. Yacht, Raquet and Tennis, Met. Opera (N.Y.C.). Home: 110 East End Ave New York City NY 10028 Office: 663 Fifth Ave New York City NY 10019

BORLAND, VIRGINIA ANN, fashion specialist, fiber co. exec.; b. N.Y.C., Mar. 8, 1929; d. Charles Peter and Margaret Elise (Swane) Stockfish; B.A., Wells Coll., 1951; m. J. Nelson Borland, Nov. 13, 1969. Fashion publicist Grey Advt., N.Y.C., 1956-60; fashion dir. Cunningham & Walsh, advt., N.Y.C., 1960-61, FMC Fibers (formerly Am. Viscose Co.), N.Y.C., after 1961; now with Avtex Fibers Inc. (formerly FMC Fibers and Am. Viscose Corp.). Vol. pediatric ward Meml. Hosp., 1953—. Mem. Fashion Group (gov. 1975-77), Inner Circle Am. Printed Fabrics Council, Color Assn. U.S.A. (dir. 1978—), Nat. Home Fashions League, N.Y. Jr. League Episcopalian. Contbg. editor Intermezzo Mag. Home: 110 East End Ave New York City NY 10028 Office: 1185 Ave of Americas New York City NY 10036

BORLE, ANDRE BERNARD, physiologist; b. La Chaux-de-Fonds, Switzerland, May 27, 1930; s. Andre Leon and Fernande Alice (Rubeli-Courvoisier) B.; came to U.S., 1956, naturalized, 1969; M.D., U. Geneva, 1955; m. Beverly Ann George, Dec. 17, 1966; children—Michael, Caroline, Christian Dominique. Ship surgeon Johnson Line, Stockholm, 1956; intern Mt. Auburn Hosp., Cambridge, Mass., 1956-57; research fellow in biochemistry Harvard U. Med. Sch., Boston, 1957-59; asst. in medicine Peter Bent Brigham Hosp., Boston, 1957-59; resident in medicine Clinique Therapeutique Universitaire, Hosp. Cantonal, Geneva, 1959-61; instr. dept. radiation biology and biophysics U. Rochester (N.Y.) Sch. Medicine, 1961-63; asst. prof. physiology U. Pitts. Sch. Medicine, 1963-70, asso. prof., 1970-75, prof., 1975—; cons. research program Atomic Energy Project, U. Rochester, 1969, 72, program-project com. Div. Research Grants, Arthritis and Metabolic Diseases, NIH, 1971, 72, mem. Arthritis and Metabolic Diseases Program Project Com., 1973-77. Bd. dirs. Association Pour La Création D'une Foundation Pour Recherches Médicales, Geneva, 1967-72. Recipient Lederle Med. Faculty award, 1964-67; Prix Andre Lichtwitz, Republique Francaise, 1970. Mem. Endocrine Soc., Am. Physiol. Soc., Biophys. Soc., Assn. Des Medecins Assts. (pres. Geneve sect. 1960-61). Contbr. articles to profl. jours. Home: 900 Delafield Rd Pittsburgh PA 15215

BORMEL, JOSEPH, realtor; b. Balt., Nov. 8, 1927; s. Harry and Anna (Weinblatt) B.; student McCoy Coll., 1956-71. Appraiser real estate, Balt., 1966—, realtor, 1956—. Chmn. Comptroller S. Harbor Com., 1956—; pres. Hart-Miller Island Environ. Group, 1974—; mem. Md. Boat Act advisory com., 1972-77. Served with USNR, 1944-46. Named Md. conservationist of year 1973, 75. Mem. Md. Boating Assn. (pres. 1968-72), Nat. Assn. Real Estate Appraisers, Nat., Md. assns. realtors, Greater Balt. Bd. Realtors, Md. Wildlife Fedn. Club: U.S. Power Squadrons. Author: Around the World on Fifty Dollars, 1956. Office: 36 N Linwood Ave Baltimore MD 21224

BORNEMAN, HERMAN FRANCIS, investment banker; b. Newark, Aug. 3, 1930; s. Herman Francis and Marie (Ryan) B.; B.S., Lehigh U., 1952; M.B.A., Cornell U., 1956; m. Nancy Winifred Mooney, Feb. 1, 1956; children—Peter Copeland, Lisa Wolters, Brooke Ann. Treas.'s asst. Socony Mobile Oil Co., N.Y.C., 1956-59; sr. security analyst Schroder Rockefeller & Co., N.Y.C., 1959-60, asst. treas., 1960-61, treas., 1961-63, v.p., 1963-67; v.p., dir. Schroder Securities Corp. 1962-65, Woodrock Bus. Capital Corp., N.Y.C., 1961-67; dir. Teaching Systems Corp., 1962-67, Trans-Video (N.Y.C.); 1963-67, Computer Systems Labs, 1968-69; mng. partner Exchequer Assos., N.Y.C.; pres., chmn. bd. B.M.S. Service Corp., N.Y.C., 1968-71; v.p. W.H. Reaves & Co. Inc., 1972-74; sr. v.p. Jesup & Lamont Inc., 1974—. Mem. adv. council Grad. Sch. Bus. and Pub. Adminstrn., Cornell U. Served to 1st lt. USAF, 1952-54. Mem. Thelta Delta Chi. Clubs: Lunch, Cornell (N.Y.C.); Monmouth Beach Bath and Tennis; Ponte Verdra; Rumson Country. Home: Rumson Rd and Bellevue Ave Rumson NJ 07760 Office: 25 Broadway New York City NY 10004

BORNEMANN, ALFRED HENRY, economist, educator; b. Queens, N.Y., Nov. 30, 1908; s. Ernest and Carrie (Wolters) B.; B.A. cum laude, N.Y. U., 1933, M.A., 1937, Ph.D., 1941; student U. Goettingen, summer 1929; m. Bertha Kohl, Aug. 20, 1938; 1 son, Alfred Richard. Accountant, Cities Service Co., 1923-33, Am. Water Works & Electric Co., Inc., 1934-40; instr. Rutgers U., 1941-44; vis. lectr. N.Y. U., 1944-45. Bklyn. Coll., summer 1945; asst. prof. Boston U., 1945-46, L.I. U., 1946-48; asso. prof. Muhlenberg Coll., 1948-50, Fla. State U., 1950-51; prof., head econs. and bus. adminstrn. dept. Norwich U., 1951-58; chmn. econs. dept. St. Francis Coll., 1958-60; prof. econs., bus. adminstrn. C.W. Post Coll. of L.I. U., 1960-66, with City U. N.Y.-Hunter, Kingsborough, 1967-74; lectr. econs. Fairleigh Dickinson U., 1966, 75; prof. Bklyn. Coll., 1977-78, St. Francis Coll., 1978—. Mem. Bus. History Conf., Am. Mktg. Assn., Am. Accounting Assn., Acad. Mgmt., Am. Econ. Assn., Am. Fin. Assn., Vt. Hist. Soc., Alpha Kappa Psi (dep. councilor 1953-54; dist. dir. 1954-67, regional dir., 1962, chmn. expansion com., 1956-62, chmn. history com. 1965-68), Omicron Delta Epsilon, Pi Gamma Mu. Author: J. Laurence Laughlin: Chapters in The Career of an Economist, 1940; Fundamentals of Industrial Management, 1963; Essentials of Purchasing, 1974; contbr. articles to profl. jours. Home: 151 Engle St Englewood NJ 07631

BORNSCHEUER, GEORGE CHARLES, civil engr.; b. N.Y.C., Feb. 24, 1922; s. Charles F. and Susane B.; B.C.E. cum laude, Poly. Inst. N.Y., 1955; m. Doris A. Woods, Feb. 3, 1945; children—Doris J., Susan A. Designer, M. W. Kellogg Co., N.Y.C., 1946-48; asst. chief engr. Fellheimer & Wagner, N.Y.C., 1948-57; chief engr. Maiman Assos., N.Y.C., 1957-58; v.p., dir. Washington ops. Burns & Roe Internat., Washington, 1965—; cons. structural engr. Served with USNR, 1942-45. Mem. Am. Nuclear Soc., Nat. Soc. Profl. Engrs., Mgmt. Assn., Soc. Am. Mil. Engrs., Washington Soc. Engrs., Xi, Tau Beta Pi, Chi Epsilon. Clubs: Bethesda Country, Internat. Club of Washington, Capital Hill. Home: 6828 Old Stage Rd Bethesda MD 20852 Office: 1850 K St NW Washington DC 20006

BORNSTEIN, ABRAHAM BENJAMIN, cardiologist; b. Bilerfeld, Germany, May 7, 1947; s. Israel and Lila B.; came to U.S., 1950, naturalized, 1952; B.A., Boston U., 1969; M.D., Tufts U., 1973. Intern, Tufts-New Eng. Med. Center, 1973-74, resident, 1974-75, fellow in cardiology, 1975-78, sr. cardial catheterization fellow, 1977-78; instr. in medicine and cardiology Tufts U., 1973-78; asst. clin. prof. cardiology N.Y. Med. Coll., 1978—; with Cardiology Assos. of Darien (Conn.), 1978—. Diplomate Am. Bd. Internal Medicine and subsplty. in cardiology. Fellow A.C.P. (asso.), Clin. Council Cardiology, Am. Coll. Cardiology (asso.); mem. AMA, Am., Mass. heart assns., Mass., Am. socs. internal medicine. Democrat. Jewish. Office: 17 Old King's Hwy S Darien CT 06820

BORNSTEIN, MYER SIDNEY, obstetrician and gynecologist; b. Boston, Sept. 7, 1938; s. Abram and Celia (Stein) B.; B.S., Northeastern U., 1961; M.D., U. Vt., 1965; m. Janet L. Difonzo, July 15, 1977; 2 children; 3 children by previous marriage. Intern, Rochester (N.Y.) Gen. Hosp., 1965-66, resident, 1966-69; practice medicine specializing in obstetrics and gynecology, 1970—; chief obstetrics and gynecology Kinchloe AFB, Mich., 1969-71; asst. chief Weibaden (Germany) Regional Hosp., 1971-74; attending physician Truesdale Hosp., Fall River Mass., 1974—; cons. in obstetrics and gynecology Fall River Community Devel. Center. Bd. dirs. chpt. Am. Cancer Soc., Greater Fall River Children's Protective Services; asst. coach Fall River Youth Hockey Assn. Served to lt. col. USAF, 1969-74. Diplomate Am. Bd. Obstetrics and Gynecology. Mem. AMA, Fall River Med. Soc., Am. Soc. for Gynecological Laparascopy, Am. Soc. for Colposcopy, Mass. Med. Soc., Bristol South Med. Assn., Am. Coll. Obstetricians and Gynecologists, Am. Legion.

BOROSON, HAROLD ROBERT, nuclear engr.; b. Schenectady, Dec. 24, 1923; s. Morris and Rebecca Beatrice (Lobel) B.; B.S., Union Coll., 1944; M.S., U. Ill., 1946; Ph.D., U. Md., 1972; m. Adele Rosenbluth, Aug. 2, 1953; children—Ronald, Kenneth, David, Michael. Grad. asst. in physics U. Ill., 1947; physicist Naval Research Lab., Washington, 1948-50; electronic scientist Naval Ordnance Lab., White Oak, Md., 1950-61; lectr. elec. engring. U. Md., 1961, 77—; aerospace technologist, Goddard Space Flight Center, NASA, Greenbelt, Md., 1961-63; head systems intergration div. David W. Taylor Naval Ship Research and Devel. Center, Annapolis, Md., 1963—. Active Boy Scouts Am., Wheaton Boy's Club, PTA, Temple Emanuel Youth Com. Served to lt. (j.g.) USNR, 1943-46. Recipient Meritorious Civilian Service award Navy Dept., 1953, Outstanding Performance award, 1971, Sustained Superior Performance award, 1971. Mem. IEEE, Am. Phys. Soc., Am. Geol. Inst., Am. Geophysics Union, Am. Soc. Naval Engrs., Am. Nuclear Soc., AAAS, Phi Kappa Phi, Sigma Xi, Tau Beta Pi. Jewish. Patentee linear wide range magnetometer. Author: Experiments on POGO Satelite, 1963; Project SEA BED Propulsion/Machinery Report, 1965; Review of Naval Uses of Electric Power, 1968. Home: 11201 Bucknell Dr Silver Spring MD 20902 Office: David W Taylor Naval Ship Research and Devel Center Annapolis MD 21402

BOROW, LAWRENCE STEPHEN, obstetrician, gynecologist; b. Phila., Apr. 19, 1944; s. Willard and Florence May (Pincus) B.; B.A., Franklin and Marshall Coll., 1966; M.D., Temple U., 1970; m. Susan Radbill, May 28, 1970; 1 son, Todd. Intern, Pa. Hosp., Phila., 1970-71, resident in obstetrics and gynecology, 1971-74; practice medicine specializing in obstetrics and gynecology, Phila., 1974—. Diplomate Am. Bd. Obstetrics and Gynecology. Fellow Am. Coll. Obstetricians; mem. Am. Soc. Colposcopy and Cervical Pathology, Am. Fertility Soc., Phila. Colposcopy Soc. (dir. pres.), Pa. State, Philadelphia County med. socs. Jewish. Editor: Atlas of Gynecologic Laparoscopy and Hysteroscopy (Kurt Semm), 1977. Home: 516 Craig Ln Villanova PA 19085 Office: 7348 Drexel Rd Philadelphia PA 19151

BOROWICH, ABBA EMANUEL, psychiatrist; b. N.Y.C., July 17, 1942; s. Samuel Z. and Janet Z. (Rotczyld) B.; B.A., Yeshiva U., 1963; M.D., State U. N.Y., 1967; m. Sandra Pearl Horowitz, Aug. 25, 1968; children—David Eric, Jillian Sheryl. Intern, Roosevelt Hosp., N.Y.C., 1967-68; chief resident dept. of psychiatry Mt. Sinai Hosp., N.Y.C., 1971-72, sr. chief resident, 1972-73; practice medicine specializing in psychiatry, N.Y.C. and New Rochelle, N.Y., 1973—; instr. psychiatry Mt. Sinai Sch. Medicine, City U. N.Y., N.Y.C., 1972-73, asso. in psychiatry, 1973-76, sr. clin. instr., 1976-77, asst. clin. prof., 1977—, liaison psychiatrist Neoplastic Disease Research Center; sr. clin. asst. psychiatrist Mount Sinai Hosp., N.Y.C., 1973-77, asst. attending psychiatrist, 1977—, asso. dir. of ambulatory services, 1973-75, in-patient unit chief, 1975—; cons. to Rabbinical Coll. of Am., Morristown, N.J., Ohel Children's Home, Bklyn.; mem. Doctor's Advisory Com., Shaare Zedek Hosp., Jerusalem, 1973—. Active United Jewish Appeal. Served with NIMH, USPHS, 1968-70. Recipient M. Ralph Kaufman award Mount Sinai Sch. of Medicine, 1973; named Outstanding Young Man in Am., U.S. Jaycees, 1975; diplomate Am. Bd. Psychiatry and Neurology. Fellow Soc. for Values in Higher Edn., Inst. on Human Values in Medicine, Israel Med. Assn. (Am. physician); mem. Am. Psychiat. Assn., N.Y. Soc. for Clin. Psychiatry, Am. Acad. of Psychiatry and the Law, Assn. for the Advancement of Psychotherapy, N.Y. State, N.Y. County med. socs., Inst. of Soc., Ethics and the Life Scis., Soc. for Health and Human Values, Fedn. of Jewish Philanthropies (mem. task force on mental health 1974—), Young Physicians Leadership Cabinet, Syracuse Med. Alumni Assn., Yeshiva U. Alumni Assn., Assn. Orthodox Jewish Scientists, Young Israel of Westchester. Guest editor Jour. Psychiatry and Law, 1975. Office: 40 E 89th St New York City NY 10028

BORRA, EMIL JOSEPH, advt. exec.; b. Beadling, Pa., Nov. 21, 1932; s. John and Emilia (Angelo) B.; B.A. in Journalism, Pa. State U., 1954; m. Sarah Jane Hodgkin, Feb. 13, 1965; children—John Emil, Jill Alexandra. Merchandising exec. Young & Rubicam Inc., N.Y.C., 1958-61, account exec., supr., 1962-67; v.p., dir. account services, Grey Advt. Ltd., Toronto, Ont., Can., 1967, exec. v.p., gen. mgr., 1968-75, also, dir.; pres., chief exec. officer, Doyle Dane Bernbach Advt. Ltd., Toronto, 1975—; dir., instr. Inst. Canadian Advt. Bd. dirs. Canadian Opera Co. Served with USAF, 1954-57. Mem. Am. Mktg. Assn. (pres.). Roman Catholic. Home: 1438 Birchwood Dr Mississauga ON L5J 1T2 Canada Office: 2 Bloor St W Toronto ON M4W 8O4 Canada

BORSCH, ROMAN NICKOLAS, psychiatrist, psychoanalyst; b. Brooklin, Ont., Can., Apr. 23, 1932; s. Nickolas and Anna (Sych) B.; M.D., U. Toronto, 1957; m. Dolores Marie Brunelle, June 13, 1959; children—Anne Marie, Barbara Lynn, Linda Susan, Michael Roman. Intern, St. Michael's Hosp., Toronto, 1957-58; mem. staff St. Thomas Psychiat. Hosp. (Ont.), 1958; resident in psychiatry Topeka State Hosp., 1959-62; clin. dir. Osawatomie (Kans.) State Hosp., 1962-64; staff psychiatrist C.F. Menninger Meml. Hosp., Topeka, 1964-66; individual practice medicine, specializing in psychiatry and psychoanalysis, Toronto, 1966—; cons. in field. Diplomate Am. Bd. Psychiatry and Neurology. Fellow Royal Coll. Physicians and Surgeons; mem. Am., Ont. psychiat. assns., Can. Med. Assn., Canadian, Toronto psychoanalytic socs., Acad. Medicine Toronto, Canadian, Am. owners and pilots assns. Greek Catholic. Clubs: Toronto Bd. Trade, Golfers. Contbr. articles on religion and psychiatry, food in psychiatry, psychotherapy problems to profl. publs. Home: 299 Forest Hill Rd Toronto ON M5P 2N7 Canada Office: 400 Walmer Rd Toronto ON M5P 2X7 Canada

BORSCHING, ROBERT RICHARD, SR., photog. mfg. co. exec.; b. Little Falls, N.Y., Oct. 7, 1923; s. Richard Joseph and Cornelia (Roulette) B.; student pub. schs., Rochester, N.Y.; m. Elizabeth Amelia Ray, Nov. 29, 1949; children—Robert Richard, Betty Jean, Bruce Alton, Bonnie Lea, Bryan Lee, Bilene Joni. Supr., O-At-Ka Burial Vault Co., 1948-49; owner, mgr. Aero Printing Co., 1949-51; adminstrv. asst. Eastman Kodak Co., Rochester, N.Y., 1951-70, supr. stock control, 1970—; pres. Artisan Flying, Inc., 1969. piper Damascus Pipe Band; notary public; pvt. pilot. Served with U.S. Army, 1946-49; ETO. Decorated Purple Heart. Mem. Air Force Assn. (life), Am. Def. Prepardness Assn. (life), Internat. Platform Assn., Am. Numis. Assn., N.Y. State Flying Farmers (pres. 1974-75). Mem. Ch. Jesus Christ Latter-day Saints. Clubs: Toastmasters (dist. gov. 1972-73), Masons, Shriners. Contbr. articles to profl. jours. Home: 50 East St Honeoye Falls NY 14472 Office: 20 Ave E Rochester NY 14650

BORSHER, HARRY NATHAN, lawyer; b. N.Y.C., Mar. 29, 1911; s. Nathan and Tillie (Tendler) B.; LL.B., N.Y. Law Sch., 1934; m. Ruth Rosenthal, Feb. 9, 1939; children—Cathy Ellen Borsher Gold, Elissa Ann Borsher Terris. Admitted to N.Y. bar, 1935; practiced in N.Y.C., 1935—; mem. firm Paley, Levy & Borsher Esqs., N.Y.C., 1962—. Served with AUS, 1942-46; PTO. Recipient service award, B'nai B'rith, 1963. Mem. Naussau County, N.Y. County lawyers assns., Customs Bar Assn., Am. Vets. (comdr. N.Y. state 1947-48). Mem. B'nai B'rith. Home: 270-03A Grand Central Pkwy Floral Park NY 11005 Office: 80 Broad St New York City NY 10004

BORSODY, ROBERT PETER, lawyer; b. N.Y.C., Oct. 6, 1937; s. Benjamin F. and Edith Nora (Corcoran) B.; B.E.E., U. Va., 1961, LL.B., 1964; diploma, U. Teheran (Iran), 1959; m. Paula Jane Bercutt, Oct. 14, 1973; children—Lisa M., Daniel B. Admitted to N.Y. State bar, 1965, D.C. bar, 1978; asso. firm Sullivan & Cromwell, N.Y.C., 1964-69; dir. Legal Services for Elderly Poor, 1969-71; dir. Community Health Law Project, 1971-73; individual practice law, N.Y.C., 1973-78; partner firm Epstein Becker Borsody & Green, N.Y.C., 1978—; bd. dirs. Health Law Project, Phila., 1971-73; adj. prof. Manhattan Coll., 1977—. Sec., N.Y. Statewide Health Coordinating Council, 1978—; mem. N.Y. State Council Health Care Financing, 1978—. Mem. N.Y. State Bar Assn. (chmn. public health com.), Assn. Bar N.Y.C., Am. Bar Assn., Am. Assn. Hosp. Attys., Nat. Assn. Health Lawyers. Club: Univ. Home: 4 Acorn Ln Larchmont NY 10538 Office: 380 Madison Ave New York NY 10017

BORTZ, BERNARD JACK, cons. engr.; b. N.Y.C., July 16, 1921; s. Samuel and Fannie (Cooper) B.; B.Chem.Engring., Coll. City N.Y., 1943; M.Chem. Engring., Poly. Inst. Bklyn., 1947; m. Phyllis Elkin, July 3, 1947; children—Joyce Gail, John Gordon, Jean Grace. Chem. engr. Kellex Corp., Jersey City, 1943-44; engr. M.W. Kellogg Co., Jersey City, 1944-49; process engr. Wigton-Abbott Corp., Newark, 1949-51; chem. engr., sr. engr., chief chem. engr., cons. engr., project mgr. Ford, Bacon & Davis, Inc., N.Y.C., 1951—. Chmn. citizens advisory com. 1954, Plainedge Sch. Dist., trustee Plainedge Sch. Bd., 1951-54. Registered profl. engr., Del., Calif., Fla., La., Md., Maine, Mich., N.J., N.Y., Pa., Okla., Tenn., Tex. Mem. Nat., N.Y. State socs. profl. engrs., Am. Inst. Chem. Engrs., Sigma Xi, Phi Lambda Upsilon. Home: 307 Albany Ave Massapequa NY 11758 Office: 2 Broadway Ave New York City NY 10004

BORUM, RODNEY LEE, trade assn. exec.; b. nr. High Point, N.C., Sept. 30, 1929; s. Carl Macy and Etta (Sullivan) B.; student U. N.C., 1947-49; B.S., U.S. Naval Acad., 1953; m. Helen Marie Rigby, June 27, 1953; children—Richard Harlan, Sarah Elizabeth. Design-devel. engr. Gen. Electric Co., Syracuse, N.Y., Cape Kennedy, Fla., 1956-58, missile test condr., Cape Kennedy, 1958-60, mgr., ground equipment engr., 1960-61, mgr. Eastern Test Range Engring., 1961-65; adminstr. Bus. and Def. Services Adminstrn. U.S. Dept. Commerce, 1966-69; pres. Printing Industries of Am., Inc., 1969—, also mem. exec. com., dir.; gov. Comprint Internat.; dir. Inter-Comprint Ltd., Strangers Cay, Ltd.; founding trustee Graphic Arts Edn. and Research Trust Fund; bd. dirs. Graphic Arts Council N.Am.; mem. edn. council bd. dirs. Graphic Arts Tech. Found. Bd. dirs. United Fund, Brevard County, Fla., 1963—, v.p., 1964-65; exec. council Cub Scouts Am., 1965; bd. dirs. Brevard Beaches Concert Assn., 1964. Republican candidate Fla. Ho. of Reps., 1960. Served to 1st lt. USAF, 1953-56. Named Boss of Yr., Jr. C. of C., 1965; recipient Bausch and Lomb sci. award; award Am. Legion. Mem. U.S. Naval Inst., U.S. Naval Acad. Alumni Assn., Phi Eta Sigma. Methodist. Clubs: Columbia Country, City Tavern. Home: 4008 Glenrose St Kensington MD 20795 Office: 1730 N Lynn St Arlington VA 22209

BOSCH, ALBERT CASPER, educator; b. N.Y.C., Jan. 15, 1934; s. Emanuel and Augusta (Babel) B.; B.S., Coll. City N.Y., 1955, M.A., 1958; Ph.D., N.Y. U., 1972; m. Marie Adele Pepenella, July 10, 1957; children—William Michael, Vivienne Louise. Tchr. biology Forest Hills (N.Y.) High Sch., 1957-73; adj. asst. prof. biology Bronx Community Coll., 1962-65, Coll. City N.Y., 1965—; asst. prof. biology Hostos Community Coll., N.Y.C., 1973—. Recipient Honor Scholar award N.Y. U., 1972, study grants NSF, 1960-62. Mem. AAAS, Am. Inst. Biol. Scis., Nat. Assn. Biology Tchrs., Nat. Sci. Tchrs. Assn., Nat. Assn. for Research in Sci. Teaching, Nat. Soc. for Study Edn., N.Y. Biology Tchrs. Assn., N.Y. U., City Coll. N.Y. alumni assns., Phi Delta Kappa. Home: Greenwich Rd Bedford Village NY 10506 Office: 475 Grand Concourse New York City NY 10451

BOSE, GURU P., city ofcl.; b. Calcutta, India, June 21, 1945; s. Ranajit L. and Jyotsnamoyee (Guha) B.; came to U.S., 1970, naturalized, 1976; B.C.E., Jadavpur U., 1968; M.B.A., Drexel U., 1974; m. Kamala Bagchi, Jan. 31, 1971. Jr. engr. Architects and Engrs., Calcutta, 1968-70; civil engr. Yule, Jordan & Assos. Inc., Phila., 1970-73; san. engr. Catalytic Inc., Phila., 1973-75; supr. water dept. City of Phila., 1975—; instr. structural analysis Jadavpur U. Archtl. Engring. dept., 1968-70. Founder, past treas. Indian Cultural Assn. of Greater Phila.; active Society Hill Civic Assn. Mem. Am. Water Works Assn., ASCE, Water Pollution Control Fedn., Engrs. Club, Instrument Soc. Am., Internat. Water Supply Assn. Research create new treatment processes in water industry. Home: 200 Locust St Apt 23F Philadelphia PA 19106 Office: 3545 Fox St Philadelphia PA 19129

BOSIN, MAXINE BETH, guidance counselor; b. Passaic, N.J., June 26, 1941; d. Arnold Joseph and Ruth (Grossman) Barta; B.S., Fairleigh Dickinson U., 1963; M.A., Montclair (N.J.) State Coll., 1970; m. Seth Bosin, May 4, 1961; children—Corey, Andrew. With Passaic (N.J.) Bd. Edn., 1964—, tchr. English as 2d lang., 1972-74, elementary guidance counselor, 1974—; cons. Wyckoff Drug Abuse Council. Mem. Am. Personnel and Guidance Assn., Am. Sch. Counselor Assn., NEA, N.J., Passaic edn. assns., League Women Voters (past dir. Passaic), Nat. Council Jewish Women (dir. 1966-70), Sports for Israel, Hadassah. Address: 537 Carlton Rd Wyckoff NJ 07481

BOSS, BERDELL GLADSTONE, elec. motors mfg. co. exec.; b. Lake Geneva, Wis., Apr. 22, 1938; s. Robert Albert and Edna Victoria (Henderson) B.; A.A.S., Mohawk Valley Community Coll., 1959; B.S., Rochester Inst. Tech., 1962; m. Carolyn Chase, Aug. 8, 1959; children—Joel, Thad. Mfg. mgmt. program Gen. Electric Co., Schenectady, 1962-65, mfg. engr., 1965-67, mgr. prodn. control, 1967-69, mgr. quality control, product service, Scotia, N.Y., 1969-74; mgr. mfg. Rotron Inc., Woodstock, N.Y., 1974-78, Stow Mfg. Co., Binghamton, N.Y., 1978—. Commr. Rip Van Winkle council Boy Scouts Am., 1978—. Mem. Soc. Mfg. Engrs., Am. Product Inventory Control Soc., Soc. Die Casting Engrs. Republican. Unitarian-Universalist. Home: Box 640B Route 8 Old State Rd Binghamton NY 13904 Office: PO Box 490 Binghamton NY 13902

BOSSE, MALCOLM JOSEPH, writer, educator; b. Detroit; s. Malcolm Clifford and Thelma (Malone) B.; B.A., Yale U., 1950; M.A., U. Mich., 1956; Ph.D. (Univ. scholar), N.Y. U., 1969; m. Marie-Claude Aullas, July 4, 1969; 1 son, Malcolm-Scott. Editorial writer Barron's Fin. Weekly, N.Y.C., 1950-52; freelance writer, N.Y.C., 1957-66; prof. English, City Coll. N.Y., 1969—. Served with USN, 1950-54. Decorated 2 Bronze Stars. Recipient Masefield award Yale U., 1949, 2 Hopwood awards Univ. Mich., 1956; Nat. Endowment for Arts fellow, 1977-78; Fulbright lectr., India, 1978—. Mem. Modern Lang. Assn., Soc. Eighteenth Century Studies, Authors' Guild, Phi Beta Kappa. Clubs: Yale of N.Y.C., Andiron. Author: The Journey of Tao Kim Nam, 1960; The Incident at Naha, 1972 (nominated for Edgar Allen Poe award 1974), in England, 1973, in Germany, 1974; The Man Who Loved Zoos, 1974 (nominated for Edgar Allen Poe award 1975), in England, Italy and France, 1975, in Germany, 1976, in Holland, 1978; Introductory Essay to Charles Johnstone's Chrysal 1760-65, 1978; co-editor: Foundations of the Novel, 1973; sr. editor: Flowering of the Novel, 1975; contbr. short stories to Voyages, Calif. Quar., Artesian, Mich. Quar., Remington Rev., N. Am. Rev., Mass. Rev. Home: 40 E 10th St New York City NY 10003 Office: Dept English City College City University New York City NY 10031

BOSTELLE, THEODORE THOMAS, artist; b. West Chester, Pa., Nov. 16, 1921; s. Rudolph William and Viola (McLaughlin) B.; student pub. schs.; m. Mary Heed Price, July 6, 1943; children—Jessie, Jonathan, James, Mary. Welder, Empire Lukens Steel, Coatesville, Pa.; aesthetic adviser animated films Phillip Ragan Assos., Phila., 1948-50; exhibited in one-man shows at Chester County Art Assn., Suburban Sta. Gallery, Phila., Dubin Gallery, Phila., Phila. Art Alliance, Ferargil Gallery, N.Y.C., Hewitt Gallery, N.Y.C., Bianchini Gallery, N.Y.C., Selected Artists Galleries, N.Y.C., Franz Bader Gallery, Washington, Warehouse Gallery, Wilmington, Del., Aeolian Palace, Pocopson, Pa.; exhibited in group shows at Corcoran Loan Library, Washington, Balt. Mus. Loan Library, Del. Art Mus., Pa. Acad. Fine Arts, Walker Art Center, Mpls., Graham Gallery, N.Y.C., Grippi Gallery, N.Y.C., Calif. Palace of Legion of Honor, Mus. Modern Art, Paris, Spoleto (Italy) Art Festival of Two Worlds; retrospective exhbns. at Chester County Art Assn., 1955, 1966, George Washington U., Washington, 1969, Del. Art Mus., 1973, Woodmere Gallery, Phila., 1977; represented in permanent collections at Del. Art Mus., Chester County Art Assn., West Chester Coll., Butler Art Inst., Youngstown, Ohio, Chadds Ford Sch., Tower Hill Sch., Wilmington, others, also pvt. collections; adviser Art for Embassies Com., Washington, 1964-65. Served with U.S. Army Engrs., 1943-46. Recipient Christian Brinton Meml. award Chester County Art Assn., 1946, 48, 60; N.C. Wyeth award, 1963; 1st prize Fidelity Trust Regional Show, Phila., 1963, Breck's Mill Cronies, Wilmington, Del., 1964; ofcl. agt. Aeolian Palace. Featured in articles in art mags. Home: 408 1/2 E Lancaster Ave Downingtown PA 19335 Office: Aeolian Palace Box 8 Pocopson PA 19366

BOSTELMAN, WILLIAM TOWNSEND, pub. relations exec.; b. Jersey City, Aug. 10, 1920; s. William K. and Harriet (McGimpsey) B.; B.S. cum laude, N.Y. U., 1943; m. Leta Buchanan, Apr. 25, 1947; children—John Townsend, Patricia Shaw. With treas.'s dept. Gen. Motors Corp., 1940-43, pub. relations dept., 1946-47; news editor Automotive Industries mag., 1947-51; gen. mgr. Bernard Relin Assos., 1951-57, exec. v.p., 1957, pres., 1957-67; pres. Bostelman Assos., Inc., N.Y.C., 1967—. Served as lt. (j.g.) USNR, 1943-46. Decorated theatre ribbon with 7 battle stars; Philippine Liberation medal with 2 battle stars. Mem. Pub. Relations Soc. Am., Beta Gamma Sigma. Clubs: Nat. Press (Washington); Madison Square Garden, N.Y. Univ., N.Y. Athletic (N.Y.C.); Knickerbocker Country (Tenafly, N.J.). Author articles on pub. relations. Home: 7 Forest Rd Tenafly NJ 07670 Office: 663 Fifth Ave New York City NY 10022

BOSTIAN, DAVID BOONE, JR., fin. co. Exec.; b. Charlotte, N.C., Feb. 12, 1943; s. David Boone and Clara Edna (Kanoy) B.; A.B. (Distinguished Mil. grad.), Davidson Coll., 1964; M.B.A. (Bus. Found. scholar), U. N.C., 1965; m. Mary Rodgers Hunter, Sept. 11, 1965; 1 son, Robert Boone, Dir. market services Hayden, Stone Inc., N.Y.C., 1967-72; v.p. and dir. market research Loeb, Rhoades & Co., N.Y.C., 1972-76; pres. Bostian Research Assos., 1977—; lectr. N.Y. Inst. Fin. Served to lt. U.S. Army, 1965-67. Mem. Am. Fin. Assn., N.Y. Soc. Security Analysts, Inst. Chartered Fin. Analysts, Fin. Analysts Research Found., Nat., N.Y. assns. bus. economists, Market Technicians Assn. N.Y., Alenda Soc., Alpha Phi Omega. Republican. Methodist. Author: (with others) Methods and Techniques of Business Forecasting, Encyclopedia of Stock Market Techniques; A Question of National Economic Security; Market Analysis and Portfolio Strategy. Home: Suffolk Ln Tenafly NJ 07670 Office: 25 Broadway New York City NY 10004

BOSTIN, MARVIN JAY, health services cons.; b. Toronto, Ont., Can., July 3, 1933; s. Samuel and Rose (Mandel) B.; came to U.S., 1956; B.S., U. Toronto, 1955; M.S. in Hosp. Adminstrn., Columbia U., 1958; Ph.D. in Pub. Adminstrn. (Gottlieb Meml. scholar), N.Y. U., 1972; 1 son, Shepard Craig. Pharmacist, New Mount Sinai Hosp., Toronto, 1953-56; asst. adminstr. L.I. Jewish Hosp., New Hyde Park, N.Y., 1958-62; asso. dir. Mt. Sinai Med. Center, Miami Beach, Fla., 1962-65; exec. v.p. E.D. Rosenfeld Assos. Inc., hosp. and health services cons. White Plains, N.Y., 1965—; guest scholar Brookings Instn., Washington, 1965; lectr. Sch. of Pub. Health and Adminstrv. Medicine, Columbia U., N.Y.C., 1965—, Grad. Sch. of Pub. Adminstrn., N.Y. U., N.Y.C., 1967; lectr. Grad Sch. of Architecture and Planning, Columbia U., N.Y.C., 1975—; cons. to Bur. of Hearings and Appeals, Social Security Adminstrn., HEW, 1967-68; spl. cons. to Office of Equal Health Opportunity, Office of Surgeon Gen., USPHS, 1966-67. Mem. Dade County (Fla.) Welfare Planning Council, Miami, 1962-65; bd. dirs. South Fla. Hosp. Council, Miami, 1963-65. Fellow Royal Soc. Health (London), Am. Pub. Health Assn., Am. Assn. Hosp. Cons. (chmn. monograph series com. 1970-71, exec. com. 1972-75, profl. standards com. 1974-76), mem. Am. Hosp. Assn., Am. Acad. Health Adminstrn., Am. Assn. Hosp. Planning, Am. Acad. Med. Adminstrs., Am. Soc. Pub. Adminstrn., Am. Coll. Hosp. Adminstrs., AIA (mem. com. on architecture for health 1974—), Canadian Coll. Health Service Execs. (fgn. affiliate), Internat. Hosp. Fedn., Canadian Pharm. Assn. Address: 235 Main St White Plains NY 10601

BOSTON, ROBERT MCCAULEY, hosp. adminstr.; b. Ballymacarratt, Ireland, Jan. 14, 1911; s. Robert and Sara (McCauley) B.; came to U.S., 1928, naturalized, 1939; student Carnegie Inst. Tech., 1930-33; m. Olive May Miller, June 8, 1940; children—Judith Findley Boston Skillman, Olive Lawrence Boston Davidson. Prevention of blindness dir. Center for Blind, Phila., 1953-72; dir. devel. and community relations Wills Eye Hosp., Phila., 1973-75. Cons. Pa. Acad. Ophthalmology and Otolaryngology, 1958—; pres. Rudolphy Residence for Blind, 1977—; mem. Pa. Gov.'s Com. for Blind, 1964-72, vice chmn., 1968, chmn., 1969-70; exec. com. Comprehensive Rehab. Study, 1967-74; bd. dirs. Southeastern Pa. chpt. Nat. Kidney Found., 1973-76, Pa. Indsl. Home for Blind, 1973-76, pres., chmn. bd., 1977—; cons. Sci. for the Blind, 1973-75; cons., TV producer Telegroup, Inc., 1973-77. Served with USNR, 1943-46. Mem. Nat. Aid to Visually Handicapped (chmn. tech. adv. com. 1961-70, vice chmn. 1970-71), Nat. Soc. Prevention of Blindness (state rep. 1957-72), Am. Assn. Workers for Blind (dir. Pa.-Del. chpt. 1970-72), Pa. Fedn. Blind, Phila. County Med. Soc. (rep. of eye sect. 1956—), Pa. Soc., Scotch-Irish Soc. Presbyterian. Home: 120 Birch Ave Bala Cynwyd PA 19004

BOSWELL, ALFRED CHESTER, JR., advt. co. exec.; b. Washington, May 7, 1947; s. Alfred Chester and Gladys (Amos) B.; B.F.A., Md. Inst., 1969; m. Cecilia Diane Baker, June 3, 1967; children—Cameron David, Amy Dulane. Publs. rev. editor U. Md., College Park, 1969; pres., chmn. bd. Boswell Prodns., Columbia, Md., 1964—; pres., chmn. bd., founder Graphica Internat., Washington, 1974—; pres., chmn. Par Excellence, Ltd., Washington, 1978—; chmn. Image Processing Media, Inc., 1978—, Edits., Ltd., 1977—, Creative Environs., 1979—; pres. Boswell Puppets, 1964—; dir. Eastport Litho, Inc., Point of View Photography. Served with USAF, 1969-73. Mem. Printing Industries Met. Washington, Printing Industries Am., Am., Hampton Rds. hort. socs. Methodist. Author: Don't Steal a Meal (musical comedy), 1969. Home: 5608 Thunder Hill Rd Columbia MD 21045 Office: Graphica Internat Inc 1302 18th St NW Washington DC 20036

BOSWORTH, PHYLLIS RUTH, broadcasting exec.; b. Long Beach, N.Y., June 5, 1934; d. Louis and Natalie Rose (Jacobs) Bosworth; B.S., Cornell U., 1956. Researcher, CBS News, N.Y.C., 1961-72, asso. producer documentary films, 1972-75, producer documentary films, 1975—. Mem. Writers Guild Am. East. Office: 524 W 57th St New York City NY 10019

BOSWORTH, ROSWELL SEWELL, JR., publisher; b. Bristol, R.I., Sept. 2, 1926; s. Roswell S. and Edith H. (Howard) B.; student U. Mass., 1944; A.B., U. R.I., 1949; m. Sarah Hodgman, May 26, 1951; children—Barbara, Peter; m. Marcia Walls, Feb. 15, 1975. Founder Barrington Times, Warren Times-Gazette and Sakonnet Times; pres., pub. Phoenix-Times Pub. Co., Bristol, R.I., 1969—; pres., dir. Suburban Newspapers Am. Chmn., Bristol Charter Commn., 1969-70; chmn. Harbor Devel. Commn., Bristol, 1955-70. Served with USAAF, 1944-45. Recipient U. R.I. award, 1969. Mem. New Eng. Press Assn. (pres. 1958-59, dir., recipient Distinguished Service award). Episcopalian. Mason. Clubs: University (Providence); Bristol Yacht. Home: 8 Woodmont Ct Barrington RI 02806 Office: 1 Bradford St Bristol RI 02809

BOTH, ROBERT L., trading co. exec.; b. Vienna, Austria, Apr. 19, 1917; s. Louis and Sally (Syrop) B.; came to U.S., 1954, naturalized, 1959; student in chemistry and pharmacology U. Vienna, 1935-38; m. Edith Knoll, July 25, 1950; 1 son, Stewart L. Liaison officer new constrn. to traffic dept. Anglo-Iranian Oil Co., Abadan, Iran, 1942-46; advisory asst. Consol. Refineries Ltd., Haifa, Israel, 1946-50, traffic mgr., 1951-53; v.p. in charge steel dept. Pan Am. Trade Devel. Corp., N.Y.C., 1954—. Home: 67-07 180 St Fresh Meadows NY 11365 Office: 2 Park Ave New York City NY 10016

BOTHNE, RALPH EDWARD, control mfg. co. exec.; b. Portland, Oreg., Aug. 22, 1929; s. Elmer Justinus and Ethel Louise (Lewis) B.; B.S. in Elec. Engring., Oreg. State U., 1964; m. Patricia Anne Cole, Aug. 28, 1949; children—Marjorie M., Rebecca E., Melissa C. Painter, electrician So. Pacific Co., 1948-51; control engr. Mobil Oil Co., 1964-68; mgr. system engring. Foxboro Co., 1968-71; self-employed cons., 1971-74; founder, 1974, since pres. EMC Controls, Inc., Cockeysville, Md.; founder Internat. User Distributed Control Systems Soc., 1976; instr. Skagit (Wash.) Valley Jr. Coll., 1965, U. Wash., Seattle, 1966. Grantee So. Pacific Co., 1962, NAM, 1962. Sr. mem. Instrument Soc. Am. (Service award 1965; past sect. pres.); mem. Distributed Control Soc. (past pres.). Author, patentee pneumatic multiplexing system. Office: PO Box 242 Cockeysville MD 21030

BOTTO, RICHARD ALFRED, artist; b. Union City, N.J., May 5, 1931; s. Alfred and Cesarina (Bagnoli) B.; certificate Pratt Inst., 1956, A.S. in Applied Sci., 1958; student Art Students League, 1955-60; m. Marguerite A. Downing, Apr. 28, 1962; children—Richard Alfred, Lisa Christine. One-man shows: La Salle Coll., Phila., 1972, George Washington Carver Mus., Ala., 1973, Union County Library, Monroe, N.C., 1973, Brandeis U., Waltham, Mass., 1973, La Fonda Hotel, Santa Fe, 1973; exhibited in group shows: Corcoran Gallery, Washington, 1968, Hammond Mus., N.Y.C., 1968, NAD, N.Y.C., 1971, Allied Artists Am., N.Y.C., 1972, 74, Trenton (N.J.) Mus., 1970, Am. Artists Profl. League, N.Y.C., 1972, 74, Hudson Valley Art Assn., White Plains, N.Y., 1972, State Exhbn., N.J. State Mus., Trenton, 1972, Dallas Pub. Library, 1972, U. Mo. at Kansas City, DeLand (Fla.) Mus., 1973; represented in permanent collection Jersey City Mus.; mural executed at St. Paul Convent Chapel, Clifton, N.J.; instr. fine art Frank Reilly Sch. Art, N.Y.C., 1964-68, pres., 1967-68; chmn. dept. fine arts Jersey City Mus., 1968-69; founder, dir. Renaissance Sch. Art, Ridgefield Park, N.J., 1974—. Active Bergen council Boy Scouts Am., 1973-75. Served with USNR, 1952-53. Recipient Best-in-show medal Jersey City Mus., 1967. Mem. Allied Artists Am. (rec. sec. 1973-74, award 1971, 73), Hudson Valley Art Assn., Hudson Artists (pres. 1966-68, chmn. bd. 1969-77), Am. Artists Profl. League (gold medal award 1972), Painters and Sculptors Soc. N.J. Address: 138 Union Pl Ridgefield Park NJ 07660

BOTTONE, EDWARD JOSEPH, microbiologist; b. N.Y.C., Feb. 18, 1934; s. Salvatore and Lillian (Squillante) B.; B.S., Coll. City N.Y., 1965; M.S., Wagner Coll., 1968; Ph.D., St. John's U., 1973; m. Ida Marie Spano, June 2, 1962; children—Laura Marie, Rina. Bacteriologist, Green Point Hosp., Bklyn., 1962-64; sr. bacteriologist Elmhurst City Hosp., Queens, N.Y., 1964-68; asso. dir. microbiology Mt. Sinai Hosp., N.Y.C., 1969-73, acting dir. dept. microbiology, 1974-75, dir. dept. microbiology, 1975—; asst. prof. microbiology Mt. Sinai Med. Sch., 1973-76, asso. prof., 1976—. Served with AUS, 1957-59. Mem. Am. Soc. for Microbiology (councilor N.Y.C. br. 1973—, membership chmn. N.Y.C. br. 1974, program chmn. clin. sect. N.Y.C. br. 1976), Mycology Soc. N.Y. Contbr. articles to profl. jours.; mem. editorial bd. Jour. Clin. Microbiology, 1978-80. Home: 91 Dogwood Ln Irvington NY 10533 Office: Mt Sinai Hosp 100th St and Fifth Ave New York City NY 10029

BOTWINICK, JOSEPH WILLIAM, transp. engr.; b. N.Y.C., June 2, 1929; s. Jacob Herman and Martha (Rachlin) B.; Aero. Engr., N.Y. U., 1956; m. Ruth Betty Bamberger, Nov. 20, 1960; children—Mark Robert, Lynn Marie. Asst. to chief design engring. Insuline Corp. Am., L.I., N.Y., 1952-53; project engr. Abel Mfg. Co., L.I. City, N.Y., 1953-54; microwave test engr. Polarad Electronics Corp., Long Island City, 1954-57; asst. staff div. engr. N.Y.C. Transit Authority, Bklyn., 1958—; cons. in field. Mem. Community Planning Bd. 13, Queens County, N. 1973—; bd. dirs. Laurelton (N.Y.) Civic Assn., Laurelton Safety Patrol; active Boy Scouts Am. Served with USAF, 1947-50, 68. Mem. IEEE, Soc. Am. Mil. Engrs., Jewish War Vets. (comdr. post 1973-78, vice-comdr. county 1978-79). Jewish. Pioneer design underground radiating and above-ground communications system, transp. control center for City of Boston, 1969-73. Home: 2566 Howard Rd North Bellmore NY 11710 Office: 370 Jay St NYC Transit Authority Brooklyn NY 11201

BOTWINICK, LEO, dentist; b. Bklyn., Oct. 4, 1919; s. Sam and Bessie (Jacobson) B.; B.A., Bklyn. Coll., 1939; D.D.S., N.Y. U., 1943; m. Libbie Brown, June 25, 1950; children—Lisa, Howard Michael. Intern, Beth Moses Hosp., Bklyn., 1943; pvt. practice dentistry, 1944-54, specializing in endodontics, N.Y.C., 1954—; clin. prof. endodontia N.Y. U.; cons. USPHS; endodontist Sydenham Hosp.; lectr. 1st Dist. Dental Soc., other dental socs. Served to comdr. USNR, 1954-56. Recipient Meritorious Service award N.Y. U., 1966; diplomate Am. Bd. Endodontics. Fellow Am. Assn. Endodontists, Am. Acad. Oral Medicine (hon., pres. 1975-76), Am. Coll. Dentists; mem. ADA, N.Y. 1st Dist. Dental Soc., Alumni Assn. N.Y. U. Coll. Dentistry (pres. 1963-64), Am. Soc. Anesthetists, Sigma Xi. Author: Must You Lose That Tooth?, 1947; contbr. articles to profl. jours. Home: 131 Shoreward Dr Great Neck NY 11021 Office: 57 W 57th St New York City NY 10019

BOTWINICK, MICHAEL, museum dir.; b. N.Y.C., Nov. 14, 1943; s. Joseph and Helen (Shlisky) B.; B.A., Rutgers U., 1964; M.A., Columbia U., 1967; m. Harriet Maltzer, Aug. 14, 1965; children—Jonathan Seth, Daniel Judah. Instr., Columbia U., N.Y.C., 1968-69, City Coll., N.Y., CUNY, 1969; asst. curator medieval art Cloisters, Met. Mus. Art, N.Y.C., 1969, asso. curator medieval art Cloisters, 1970, asst. curator in chief, 1971-73; asst. dir. art Phila. Mus. Art, 1973-74; dir. Bklyn. Mus., 1974—; pres. Cultural Instns. Group, 1975-76; mem. N.Y.C. Adv. Commn. Cultural Affairs, 1975-76, N.Y.C. Urban Design Council, 1975—. Mem. Assn. Art Mus. Dirs. (mem. profl. practices, legis. coms.), Am. Assn. Museums (mem. ethics com.), Coll. Art Assn., Soc. Archtl. Historians, Internat. Center Medieval Art. Office: Bklyn Mus 188 Eastern Pkwy Brooklyn NY 11238*

BOU, MARY ELLEN, psychologist; b. San Jose, Costa Rica, Nov. 30, 1931; d. Alfredo and Maria (Jimenez) Mata; came to U.S., 1937, naturalized, 2954; B.A., Barnard Coll., 1953; M.S., Pa. State U., 1955; m. Edward C. Bou, July 19, 1956; children—Christopher, Stephen, Wendy, Lawrence. Sch. psychologist Beauvoir Sch., Washington, 1969—; pvt. practice psychology, Washington, 1972—. Mem. Am., Va., D.C. psychol. assns. Club: Dollology of D.C. Home: 5607 Ontario Circle Washington DC 20016 Office: 5428 MacArthur Blvd NW Washington DC 20016

BOUCHARD, CARL EDWARD, agrl. engr.; b. Ft. Kent, Maine, Mar. 19, 1941; s. Gilman Leonide and Isabel (Caron) B.; student East Carolina Coll., 1962-63; B.S. in Agrl. Engring., U. Maine, 1966; m. Janet Louise Gilchrist, Nov. 26, 1966; children—Stephen Edward, Janice Leigh. Asst. to engr. Walter Carpenter Assos., Orono, Maine, 1964-66; agrl. engr. N.B. (Can.) Dept. Agr., Fredericton, 1966-67; civil engr., hydrologist Soil Conservation Service, U.S. Dept. Agr., Orono, 1967-74, planning engr., 1974-76; asst. water resource planning specialist N.E. Tech. Service Center, Soil Conservation Service, U.S. Dept. Agr., Broomall, Pa., 1976—. Served with USAF, 1959-63. Named Young Engr. of Yr. in Maine, 1975. Registered profl. engr., Maine. Mem. Am. Soc. Agrl. Engrs., Soil Conservation Soc. Am., Nat. Soc. Profl. Engrs. Episcopalian (accounting warden 1978-79). Home: 1548 Wickerton Dr Westchester PA 19380 Office: 1974 Sproul Rd Broomall PA 19008

BOUCHARD, GILMAN DONALD, optometrist; b. Madawaska, Maine, Dec. 29, 1927; s. Levite and Emelda (Beland) B.; O.D., Pa. State Coll. Optometry, 1953; m. Jean M. Mavor, July 27, 1948; children—Michael, Mary, Ann. Pvt. practice optometry, Old Town, Maine, 1953-60, Lewiston, Maine, 1960—. Police commr. Town of Lewiston, 1967-70. Served with 1st cavalry div., U.S. Army, 1946-48. Mem. New Eng. Council Optometrists (pres. 1975-76), Maine (pres. 1970), Am., New Eng. optometric assns., Nat. Eye Research Assn. Democrat. Roman Catholic. Club: K.C. Home: 32 Delcliff Ln Lewiston ME 04240 Office: 25 Ash St Lewiston ME 04240

BOUCHARD, PATRICIA JEAN, health care orgn. ofcl.; b. Ogdensburg, N.Y., Mar. 21, 1931; d. Joseph Francis and Sena (Denny) LaRue; student St. Louis U. Catholic Hosp. Assn., m. Robert Stanley Bouchard, Oct. 2, 1965; children—Deborah Anne, Karen Lynn. Cashier, trainer cashiers A & P Tea Co., 1953-63; teller, trainer tellers, receptionist Marine Midland Bank, Watertown and Potsdam, N.Y., 1964-73; purchasing agt. Central St. Lawrence Health Services, Potsdam, 1974—. Mem. No. Group Purchasing (organizer), Potsdam Bus. and Profl. Women's Club (pres. 1973-74), Potsdam Hosp. Guild. Home: Route 1 Box 164 Norwood NY 13668 Office: 50 Leroy St Potsdam NY 13676

BOUCHER, JACK EDWARD, archtl. photographer, writer; b. Buffalo, Sept. 4, 1931; s. John L. and Alma L. (Hookey) B.; student Winona Sch. Profl. Photography, Nat. Trust of Eng. Summer Sch.; m. Mary M. Sullivan, Sept. 25, 1965; children—Jack J., Paul E. Photographer, writer Atlantic City Tribune, 1949-52; chief photographer, exhibits specialist N.J. Hwy. Authority, 1952-58; sr. photographer U.S. Nat. Park Service, 1958-66; chief historic sites State of N.J., 1966-69; free-lance archtl. photographer, writer, lectr., 1969-70; supr. photography and pictorial records U.S. Nat. Park Service, Office of Archaeology and Hist. Preservation, 1971—; photog. works exhibited at Library of Congress. Fellow Royal Photog. Soc. Great Britain; mem. Archtl. Photographers Assn., Profl. Photographers Am., Nat. Trust for Historic Preservation, Am. Assn. State and Local History, Nat. Trust of Eng., Atlantic County Hist. Soc. (trustee, past pres.). Author: Absegami Yesteryear, 1963; Of Batsto and Bog Iron, 1964; History of the Atlantic City Lighthouse, 1965; History of Margate Elephant, 1970. Address: 37 Laurel Ave Linwood NJ 08221

BOUCHER, MARY BETH, hosp. adminstr.; b. Ossining, N.Y., July 15, 1946; d. Arthur G. and Helen V. (Heron) Floodquist; student U. Hartford, 1966-67, Northeastern U., 1976-77; m. Neal M. Boucher, Dec. 17, 1977. Personnel sec., asst. Colt Industries, Hartford, 1968-69, employment specialist, 1969; placement counselor Ed Devoe Personnel Systems, Hartford, 1969; employment mgr. St. Francis Hosp., Hartford, 1970-72; dir. personnel Anna Jaques Hosp., Newburyport, Mass., 1972—. Bd. dirs. John Ashford Link House, Inc., 1974—, v.p., 1977-78; mem. personnel com. Merrimack Valley Health Planning Council, 1976—. Mem. Mass. Hosp. Personnel Dirs. Assn., Am. Soc. Hosp. Personnel Adminstrn. Democrat. Roman Catholic. Office: 25 Highland Ave Newburyport MA 01950

BOUCHER, RAYMOND MARCEL GUT, physicist; b. Toul, France, Apr. 28, 1921; s. Gustave and Marie Madelaine B.; E.N.S.I.C., U. Nancy (France), M.S. in Physics and Chemistry; Ph.D., U. Paris, Sorbonne; m. Michelle Le Landias, Aug. 23, 1945; children—Sylviane, Veronique. Physicist, Physico Chem. Lab. French Coal Bd., 1946-48, head, microparticles research lab., 1948-50; chief physicist Brit. CECA Co., London, 1950-52; project dir., sr. research scientist, head, ultrasonic lab. N.Y. U. Research Div., 1959-62; founder, pres. Macrosonics Corp., Rahway, N.J., 1962-69; pres. Wave Energy Systems, Inc., N.Y.C., 1969—. Served with French Navy. Decorated Cross of War, Cross of Resistance; recipient Order of Merit French Govt. Mem. French Nat. Order Research and Invention, ASME, AAAS, Am. Assn. Med. Instrumentation, N.Y. Acad. Scis., Marine Tech. Soc., Internat. Microwave Power Inst. Contbr. physics articles to profl. jours.; 55 patents, 10 trademarks in field. Home: 200 E 64th St Apt 12D New York City NY 10021 Office: 655 Madison Ave New York City NY 10022

BOUCHER, RITA JEANNETTE, educator; b. Woonsocket, R.I., Nov. 1, 1934; d. Donat A. and Juliette A. (Levesque) Boucher; B.S. in Nursing, Salve Regina Coll., 1956; M.S., Boston U., 1962, certificate advanced study in Rehab. Nursing, 1963, Ed.D. in Ednl. Adminstrn. and Andragosy (Am. Jour. of Nursing fellow), 1970. Mem. staff Our Lady of Fatima Hosp., N. Providence, R.I., 1956-57, also head nursing, 1956-77, also instr. obstetrics and pediatric nursing, 1958-60; lectr. medical and surg. nursing Simmons Coll., Boston, 1961; instr. fundamentals of nusing and med.-surg. nursing New Eng. Baptist Hosp., Boston, 1962; asst. clin. instr. rehab. nursing workshop for pub. health nurses, Boston U., 1963, instr. rehab. nursing, 1963-65, asst. prof. rehab. nursing, 1965-67, dir. field experience in rehab. nursing, 1965-67, adj. asso. prof. rehab. nursing, 1967-70; asso. prof. nursing State U. of N.Y., Buffalo, 1970—, adviser grad. students, 1971—; asst. dean, asso. prof. Coll. Nursing U. R.I., 1977—; cons. dept. adult health and continuing edn., 1970; cons. E.J. Meyer Meml. Hosp., Buffalo, 1971, New Eng. Deaconess Hosp., Boston, 1969, Bristol Nursing Home, New Bedford, Mass. HEW grantee, 1962. Mem. Am., R.I., N.Y. State nurses assns., Nat., N.Y. State leagues for nursing, Assn. of Nurse Clinicians, AAUP, Senate Profl. Assn., Am. Congress of Rehab. Medicine, Sigma Theta Tau. Roman Catholic. Co-author book Guidelines in Primary Care. Contbr. articles to profl. publs. Home: 2 Top Hill Dr PO Box 38 Kingston RI 02881

BOUDREAU, ALLAN, librarian; b. Albany, N.Y., Aug. 1, 1936; s. Alexander and Lillian (Allan) B.; B.S., Russell Sage Coll., 1958; M.B.A., N.Y. U., 1964, Ph.D., 1973; M.S., Columbia, 1972; children—Kirstin Rosamund, Andrew Allan. Jr. adminstrv. asst. N.Y. State Dept. Edn., 1958-59; adminstrv. officer N.Y. State Library, 1959-62; asst. dir. N.Y. U. Libraries, 1962-73; sr. research asso. N.Y. U., 1973-74; sec. Library Trustees Found., 1973—; librarian Grand Lodge Masons N.Y., 1974—. Pub. accountant, 1961—; cons. libraries, museums, research orgns., mfrs., architects, state and local govtl. units; lectr. colls. and profl. groups. N.Y. State Exempt vol. fireman; pres. Ind. Royal Found., 1968-78, trustee, 1978—. Served with AUS, 1953-55. Recipient Founders Day award N.Y. U., 1973. Mem. ALA (life), N.Y. Library Assn., N.Y. State Assn. Library Bds. (dir. 1973—), Am. Legion. Clubs: N.Y. Athletic; Masons (32 deg.). Author: The Library and Scholarly Research, 1964; The Research Resources at Washington Square, 1831-1970, 1972. Mem. editorial bd. Library Scene, 1970. Contbr. articles to profl. jours. Home: 1 Washington Sq Village New York City NY 10012 Office: 71 W 23d St New York City NY 10010

BOUDREAU, FRANCIS HELIER, obstetrician, gynecologist; b. Cambridge, Mass., Aug. 29, 1934; s. Odina and Fabiola (Delaney) B.; A.B., Harvard U., 1956; M.D., Boston U., 1962; m. Laura O'Brien, Feb. 23, 1963; children—Francis, Laura, Renee, Nicole, Jacques, Jean-Paul, Micheline, Andre, Danielle. Intern, St. Vincent's Hosp., N.Y.C., 1962-63, resident, 1963-68; practice medicine specializing in obstetrics, gynecology, Brookline, Mass., 1968—; mem. staff Boston Hosp. for Women, St. Elizabeth's Hosp., Mass. Gen. Hosp.; clin. asst. Harvard Med. Sch., Tufts U. Med. Sch. Served with USNR, 1956-58. Mem. Boston Obstet. Soc., Am. Coll. Obstetrics and Gynecology, Am. Fertility Soc. Roman Catholic. Club: Harvard. Home: 4 Pleasant St Dover MA 02030 Office: 1180 Beacon St Brookline MA 02146

BOUFFORD, RONALD P., real estate developer; b. Keene, N.H., Jan. 3, 1945; s. Edward L. and Mary E. (Cantlin) B.; m. Joan M. Shea, Jan. 20, 1968; children—Ronald P., Colleen M., Kenneth A., Jeffrey A., Nathan M. Mgr., OK Fairbanks Co., Keene, 1963-70; pricing specialist, buyer Assoc. Grocers New Eng., Manchester, N.H., 1970-73; div. mgr. Westwood Realty, Inc., Manchester, 1973—; owner Enfield Properties, Manchester, 1977—; mem. Homebuilders and Suppliers Legal Action Com., 1977—. Justice of the peace, Manchester, 1974—; mem. St. Francis of Assissi Sch. Bd., 1978—. Mem. Nat. Assn. Homebuilders, N.H., Manchester homebuilders assns., Manchester Hist. Assn., Hillsborough County Law Enforcement Assn., Conservative Caucus. Republican. Roman Catholic. Home: 1023 S Beech St Manchester NH 03103 Office: 50 Queen City Ave Manchester NH 03103

BOUGAS, JAMES ANDREW, cardio-thoracic surgeon; b. Bismarck, N.D., Jan. 25, 1925; s. Andrew James and Mary (Psaltiras) B.; student Mass. Inst. Tech., 1940-44; M.D., Harvard U., 1948; m. Tiina Parlin, June 27, 1953; children—Karen Louise, Tiina Maria. Intern, Columbia div. Bellevue Hosp., 1948-49; resident, 1949-50; resident Presbyterian Med. Center, N.Y.C., 1950-54; practice medicine specializing in cardio-thoracic surgery, Boston, 1954—; asso. Overholt Thoracic Clinic, Boston, 1954-65; asso. prof. surgery Boston U. Sch. Medicine, 1965—; mem. vis. staff Boston City Hosp., active staff Goddard Meml. Hosp., Stoughton, Mass., Carney, N.E. Deaconess, Univ. hosps., Boston, sr. active staff N.E. Baptist Hosp., Boston; asso. staff N.E. Med. Center Hosps.; cons. Athol (Mass.) Meml. Hosp., Barnstable County Hosp., Pocasset, Mass., Boston Hosp. for Women, Boston City Hosp., Tobey Hosp., Marion, Mass., Lemuel Shattuck Hosp., Boston, Quincy (Mass.) City Hosp., Symmes Arlington (Mass.) Hosp., USPHS Hosp., Brighton, Mass., VA hosps., Boston, Providence, West Roxbury, Mass.; lectr., Tufts U. Sch. Medicine, 1955—; chmn. Gordon Research Confs., 1967-68; dir. cardiopulmonary lab. N.E. Deaconess Hosp., 1956-65. Pres., Greater Boston chpt. Mass. Heart Assn., 1967-69; trustee Boston Tb Assn.; bd. dirs. Mass. Heart Assn. Served with AUS, 1943-44. Mem. AAAS, Am. Assn. Thoracic Surgery, Am. Coll. Cardiology, Am. Coll. Chest Physicians (mem. gov.'s com. 1965—), A.C.S., Am. Fedn. Clin. Research, Am. Heart Assn. (mem. council on cardiovascular surgery 1965—), AMA, Am., Mass. thoracic socs., Soc. Thoracic Surgeons, N.Y. Acad. Scis., N.E. Cardiovascular Soc., Mass. Med. Soc., Mass. Tb and Health League, Boston Surg. Soc. Club: Longwood Cricket (Chestnut Hill, Mass.); Beverly Yacht, Sippican Tennis (Marion, Mass.); Badminton and Tennis (Boston). Home: 25 Valley Rd Chestnut Hill MA 02167 Office: 110 Francis St Boston MA 02215

BOUISSAC, PAUL ANTOINE, educator; b. Perigueux, France, Jan. 7, 1934; s. Antoine Louis and Marguerite Marie (Frêne) B.; came to ., 1962; Licence-es-Lettres, U. Paris, 1956, D.Linguistics, 1970. in French, Victoria Coll., U. Toronto, 1962-65, asst. prof., 9, asso. prof., 1969-74, prof., 1974—; vis. prof. State U. N.Y., 1975, U. South Fla., 1975. Served with French Air Force, 1959-61. Can. Council grantee, 1968, 70, 77-78; Wenner-Gren Found. grantee, 1970; Netherlands Inst. for Advance Studies fellow, 1972-73; Guggenheim Found. fellow, 1973-74. Mem. Modern Lang. Assn., Am. Anthrop. Assn., Am. Folklore Soc., Linguistics Soc. Am., Semiotic Soc. Am., N.Y. Acad. Scis. Author: Les Demoiselles, 1970; La Mesure des Gestes, 1973; Circus and Culture, 1976. Office: 73 Queen's Park Toronto ON M5S 1K7 Canada

BOULWARE, ELIZABETH FAYE, counselor; b. Harrisburg, Pa., Sept. 17, 1952; d. Henry W. and Barbara A. (Hill) B.; B.A., Cheyney State Coll., 1973; M.S., Shippensburg State Coll., 1977. Mgr., Torch Products, Harrisburg, 1974; student intern Dept. Pub. Welfare, Office of Children and Youth, Harrisburg, 1973; caseworker, homemaker supr. County of Dauphin Child Care Service, Harrisburg, 1978—; pvt. family and group counseling, 1978—. Mem. Am. Personnel and Guidance Assn., NAACP, YWCA. Mem. A.M.E. Zion Ch. Home: 617 N 16th St Harrisburg PA 17103

BOURDON, DAVID (JOSEPH, JR.), art critic, editor; b. Glendale, Calif., Oct. 15, 1934; s. David Joseph and Marilyn Edythe (Casale) B.; B.S., Columbia U., 1961. Asst. editor Life Mag., N.Y.C., 1966-71; asso. editor Saturday Rev. of the Arts, N.Y.C., 1972, Smithsonian mag., Washington, 1972-74, Arts Mag., N.Y.C., 1973—; art critic The Village Voice, N.Y.C., 1964-66, 74-77; N.Y. corr. Du, Zurich, 1976—; columnist Vogue, N.Y.C., 1978—; contbr. articles to profl. jours.; organizer exhbns.; lectr. Mem. Internat. Assn. Art Critics. Author: Christo, 1972; Carl Andre Sculpture 1959-1977, 1978; cons. editor: Christo: Running Fence, 1979. Home and Office: 30 Fifth Ave New York City NY 10011

BOURKE, ROBERT SAMUEL, neurosurgeon; b. Malden, Mass., Feb. 20, 1935; s. Robert William and Beatrice (Hoberman) B.; A.B. cum laude, Harvard U., 1956; M.D. cum laude (Mosby scholar 1959), Tufts U., 1960; m. Marlene Cohen, Feb. 6, 1965; children—Jaron Robert, Andrew Benjamin, Intern, Barnes Hosp., St. Louis, 1960, gen. surg. asst. resident, 1961, asst. resident neurosurgery, 1964-65, resident neurosurgery, 1966, fellow neurosurgery, 1967; research asso. Lab. Neurochemistry, Nat. Inst. Neurol. Diseases and Blindness, NIH, Bethesda, Md., 1960-64, chief sect. on devel. neurochemistry, 1967-69; isotope physics Oak Ridge Nuclear Inst., 1963; acting chief neurosurg. service Georgetown U., D.C. Gen. Hosp., 1967-69, instr. neurosurgery Georgetown U., 1967-69; asso. prof. neurosurgery State U. N.Y., Buffalo, 1969-74; chief dept. neurosurgery Roswell Park Meml. Inst., Buffalo, 1969-74; prof., chmn. div. neurosurgery Albany (N.Y.) Med. Coll., 1974—. Served with USPHS, 1961-64. Diplomate Am. Bd. Neurol. Surgeons. Mem. AMA, AAAS, Congress Neurol. Surgeons, D.C. Med. Soc., Assn. Research Neurosurgeons, Am. Assn. Neurol. Surgeons, Soc. Neurosci., Soc. Neurol. Surgeons, Soc. Univ. Neurosurgeons, Alpha Omega Alpha, Phi Delta Epislon. Contbr. articles in field to profl. publs. Office: Div Neurosurgery Albany Med Coll Albany NY 12208

BOURNE, AVIS COTTRELL (MRS. C. FRED BOURNE), educator; b. Boston, Sept. 1, 1905; d. Charles T. and Carolyn (Frink) Cottrell; A.B., Boston U., 1927, A.M., 1931; certificate U. Grenoble, 1927; m. Charles Fred Bourne, Aug. 14, 1932; 1 son, Richard Cottrell. Tchr., Sterling, Mass., 1927-28, 34—, asst. prin., 1948-62, dir. guidance, 1962-71; tchr., Walpole, Mass., 1928-31, Norwood, Mass., 1931-32; mem. adv. council women's div. Mass. Dept. Commerce. Mem. Wachusett Regional Sch. Dist. Com., 1955-67, chmn., 1958-59; mem. Sterling Historical Commn., 1968—. Named Woman of Achievement, Bus. and Profl. Women's Club, 1963. Mem. AAUW (pres. No. Mass. br. 1957-61; organizer, charter pres. Sterling br.), Mass. (various com. chairmanships and offices; state pres. 1957-59, dist. chmn.; state parliamentarian 1969-71), Nat. (nat. legis. com.) fedns. bus. and profl. women's clubs, Am. Personnel and Guidance Assn., Mass. Sch. Guidance Assn. (chpt. sec., state membership com., v.p. jr. high sch. div.), N. Central Mass. Guidance Assn. (pres.), Daus. Colonial Wars, Nat. Soc. New Eng. Women (v.p. Augusta, Maine colony 1978—), Daus. Am. Colonists (state regent Mass. 1973-76, nat. historian 1976—), Piscataqua Pioneers, Mass. Daus. of 1812 (v.p. 1977-78), DAR, Mass. Ret. Tchrs. Assn. (legis. chmn. North Worcester County br.), NEA, Sterling Hist. Soc. (founder, trustee, charter pres.), Lancaster League Hist. Socs. (treas. 1972-74), Daus. Am. Colonists (nat. historian 1976—, hon. state regent Mass., mem. nat. officers club, asso. mem. Maine), Belgrade Lakes C. of C., Pi Lambda Theta, Phi Sigma Pi, Theta Upsilon, Delta Kappa Gamma (state com. on personal growth and services). Club: Waterville (Maine) Community Garden (asst. treas. 1978—), Oakland (Maine) Garden (sec.). Home: Clinton Rd Sterling MA 01564 also Long Lake Belgrade Lakes ME 04918

BOURNE, MARY BONNIE MURRAY (MRS. SAUL HAMILTON BOURNE), music publishing co. exec.; b. Salix, Iowa, Sept. 13, 1903; d. Thomas William and Kathryn (McDermott) Murray; student Morningside Normal Coll., 1922-23; student Am. Banking Inst., N.Y.C.; m. Saul Hamilton Bourne, Apr. 12, 1928; 1 dau., Mary Elizabeth. Appeared with George White Scandals, Ramblers, Cocoanuts, Ziegfeld Follies, 1925-28; owner, mgr. Bourne Co., N.Y.C., 1960—. Mem. social work recruiting com. United Hosp. Fund. Trustee S.H. Bourne Found., Coll. New Rochelle; trustee N.Y. Infirmary, 1945—, chmn. social service youth bd., 1947—, bd. visitors Sch. Music, Catholic U. Am., Washington. Mem. A.S.C.A.P. (dir., pubs. adv. com.). Home: 14 E 75th St New York City NY 10021 Office: 1212 Ave of Americas New York City NY 10036

BOURQUE, JEAN JACQUES, psychiatrist, clin. dir.; b. Windsor, Que., Can., Sept. 22, 1937; s. Herve and Jeanne (Fredette) B.; B.A., Laval U., Que., 1959, M.D., 1964; diploma in psychiatry McGill U., Montreal, Que., 1972; m. Marguerite Daniele Houle, Jan. 2, 1961; children—Dominique, Pierre. Intern, Hôtel Dieu, Quebec City, 1963-64; resident in psychiatry Royal Victoria Hosp., Montreal, 1968, Douglas Hosp., Montreal, 1969, Albert Prevost Inst., Montreal, 1970, Ste. Justine's Hosp., Montreal, 1971; practice medicine specializing in psychiatry, Montreal, 1972-76; dir. outpatient team for adolescence, Charles LeMoyne Hosp., Montreal, 1974—; dir. adolescent service Allan Meml. Inst. Royal Victoria Hosp., 1975—; demonstrator McGill U., 1975; clin. demonstrator U. Montreal, 1977. Served officer M.C., Canadian Army, 1964-68. Fellow Royal Coll. Physicians (Can.); mem. Société Québécoise des Psychiatres de L'Adolescence (pres. 1978), Assn. Psychiatrists Que., Canadian Psychiat. Assn., Am. Soc. Adolescent Psychiatry, Canadian Med. Assn., Assn. French Physicians Que. Parti Quebecois. Roman Catholic. Office: 116 Guilbault St Longueuil PQ Canada

BOUSAADA, TONY FARID, indsl. engr.; b. Beirut, Lebanon, Dec. 28, 1946; s. Farid M. and Zahia J. B. came to U.S., 1969, naturalized, 1979; Asso. Sci. in Mfg. Engring., Waterbury State Tech. Coll., 1974; B.S. in Indsl. Tech., Central Conn. State Coll., 1979. Jr. indsl. engr. Seal Inc., Naugatuck, Conn., 1970-75, machine shop dept. mgr., 1975-76, indsl. engr., 1976—. Mem. Soc. Mfg. Engrs., Am. Inst. Indsl. Engrs. Club: Am.-Lebanese (Waterbury). Home: 174-1 Maybury Circle Waterbury CT 06705 Office: Emhart Industries Hard Div Berlin CT 06037

BOUT, JAN, ret. ins. co. exec.; b. Rotterdam, The Netherlands, Apr. 7, 1915; s. Cornelius and Hendrika (Bosch) B.; ed. Rotterdam, Leiden and pub. schs. Pasadena, Calif.; m. Katherine D. Bassett, May 12, 1936; children—Jan II, Jacqueline. With C. Bout and Sons, 1934-36; tour mgr. Tanner Tours, Ltd., Grey Line, also ind. tours, 1936-40; passenger traffic dept. A.T. & S.F. Ry., 1941-47; traffic and conv. mgr. Prudential Ins. Co. Am. 1947-56, mgr. travel and conf. div., 1956-66, dir. conf. arrangements, Newark, 1966-75. Mem. No. N.J., Am. orchid socs. Clubs: 1,000,000 Milers; American Airlines Admirals; Clipper; Beaver. Contbr. articles on transp. and tourism to profl. publs. Home: 21 Country Club Dr Chatham NJ 07928

BOUTIETTE, RICHARD CLIFFORD, municipal ofcl.; b. Worcester, Mass., Mar. 19, 1930; s. Clifford L. and Regina Marie (Vigeant) B.; B.S., Worcester Poly. Inst., 1952; m. Helen Carol Rembiszewski, Oct. 1, 1955; children—Judith Ann, John Richard. Civil engr. Mass. Dept. Pub. Works, 1955-56; sr. civil engr. Edwards & Kelcey, Boston, 1956-58; town engr. Town of Reading (Mass.), 1958-61; dir. pub. works Town of Wakefield (Mass.), 1961—. Chmn. tech. adv. com. Met. Area Planning Council. Served as lt. USMCR, 1952-54. Mem. Am. Soc. C.E., Am. Rd. Builders Assn., Am. Pub. Works Assn. (past pres., dir. New Eng. chpt., chpt. Man of Yr. award 1977), Norfolk-Bristol-Middlesex Hwy. Assn. (past pres., dir.). K.C., Lion (pres. 1964-65). Home: 40 Morrison Rd W Wakefield MA 01880 Office: 1 Lafayette St Wakefield MA 01880

BOUTILLIER, ROBERT JOHN, accountant; b. Newark, Jan. 1, 1924; s. William and Millicent (Davies) B.; B.S., Rutgers U., 1948; m. Marie C. Humphries, June 24, 1945; children—Robert Allan, Suzanne Marie. With Peat, Marwick, Mitchell & Co., 1943—, partner, 1955—, partner charge Newark office, 1960—, mem. advisory com. and Eastern Area, partner, 1965—, partner-in-charge U.S. ops., 1970—, vice chmn., 1977; lectr., Rutgers U. Bd. dirs. Newark YM-YWCA. C.P.A., N.J. Mem. Am. Inst. C.P.A.'s, N.J. Soc. C.P.A.'s, Newark Jr. C. of C. (pres. 1956-57, outstanding young man of yr. award 1957), Newark Assn. Commerce and Industry, Delta Sigma Pi, Beta Gamma Sigma. Republican. Presbyterian. Clubs: Rotary of N.Y., Baltusrol Golf (v.p., gov.). Home: 920 Minisink Way Westfield NJ 07090 Office: 345 Park Ave New York City NY 10022

BOUTWELL, HARVEY BUNKER, traffic engr.; b. Concord, N.H., May 16, 1924; s. Harley and Helen Louise (Bunker) B.; B.S., Yale U., 1946; m. Margaret Ann Hindinger, July 6, 1946; children—Margaret Helen, William Bruce. Traffic research engr. N.H. Dept. Pub. Works and Hwys., Concord, 1954-64; research asso. Yale U., 1964-68; mem. Kaehrle Traffic Assoc., W. Hartford, Conn., 1968-71; owner, traffic engr. Hwy. Traffic Cons., Cheshire, Conn., 1971—; cons. in field; asso. lectr. So. Conn. State Coll., 1968—; chmn. Cheshire Safety Commn., 1974-76. Served with USNR, 1943-46. Recipient Distinguished Service award New Eng. sect. Inst. Transp. Engrs., 1975; registered profl. engr., N.H., Mass., Conn., Calif. Fellow Inst. Transp. Engrs. (internat. dir. 1974-76, dist. chmn. 1977, pres. New Eng. sect. 1970, sec. cons. council 1974-77); mem. Nat. Soc. Profl. Engrs., Transp. Research Bd., Order of Engr. Republican. Episcopalian. Clubs: Exchange, Masons (master Eureka Lodge 1957-58), Shriners, IOOF chief patriarch Penacook Encampment 1949). Address: 30 Bates Dr Cheshire CT 06410

BOUVIER, EDMOND EDWARD, chem. process co. exec.; b. Wilmington, Mass., Jan. 21, 1924; s. Damase and Helene (Filiatrault) B.; student Marist Coll., 1943-45; B.S. Edn., Fordham U., 1950, M.S. in Chemistry, 1954; m. Jodie Marie DiStadio, Apr. 8, 1956; children—Lisette, Marc, Luke, Margaret. Research chemist Allied Chem. Co., N.Y.C., 1952-54; research chemist Sci. Design Co., Port Washington, N.Y., 1954-59, asst. dir. research, 1959-61; safety dir. Halcon Internat., Inc., Little Ferry, N.J., 1961—, dir. analytical research, 1970—; cons. N.Y.C. Air Resources Bur., 1967-70. Mem. bd. trustees Westwood (N.J.) Regional Bd. Edn., 1971-77, pres., 1974-76; chmn. Troop 47 com. Bergen council Boy Scouts Am., 1971-74. Mem. Am. Chem. Soc., Nat. Safety Mgmt. Soc., Internat. Hazard Control Bd. (certified hazard control mgr., master level). Author numerous corp. manss.; inventor continuous analyzer for peroxides in chem. process streams, 1973. Home: 48 Lowell St Westwood NJ 07675 Office: Philips Pkwy Montvale NJ 07645

BOUVIER, LEON FRANCIS, demographer, sociologist, educator; b. Moosup, Conn., Feb. 24, 1922; s. Stanislas A. and Rose A. (Donais) B.; B.S. cum laude in Sociology, Spring Hill Coll., 1961; M.A. in Sociology, Brown U., 1964, Ph.D. in Sociology (fellow), 1971; m. Theresa Olive Fallon, Feb. 19, 1944; children—Thomas, Lynne, Linda, Kenneth. Instr. Siena Coll., Loudonville, N.Y., 1963-65; asst. prof. sociology U. Scranton (Pa.), 1965-66; from instr. to asso. prof. sociology U. R.I., Kingston, 1966-75; profl. lectr. Center for Population Research, Georgetown U., Washington, 1972—; v.p. Population Reference Bur., Washington, 1975-76; mem. bd. of tech. cons. to U.S. Com. on Vital and Health Statistics, 1974-75; sr. social sci. cons. Smithsonian Instn., 1976; demographic adviser Internat. Statis. Programs Center U.S. Bur. Census, 1976-78; spl. cons. Select Com. on Population, U.S. Ho. of Reps., 1978-79. Named Distinguished Tchr. of the Year, U. R.I., 1970-71. Mem. Population Assn. of Am. (editor PAA Affairs 1978-79), Internat. Union for Sci. Study of Population, World Population Soc., AAUP, So. Regional Demographic Group (pres. 1978). Contbr. numerous articles and monographs on demographic studies and urban ecology to profl. jours. Home: 217 S Virginia Ave Falls Church VA 22046

BOVA, ROBERT JOSEPH, elec. mfg. co. exec.; b. Boston, Jan. 19, 1936; s. Frank Joseph and Mildred Louise (Falino) B.; B.S., Boston U., 1963. Pub. relations rep. Boston U., 1963-65; asst. dir. pub. relations Children's Hosp. Med. Center, Boston, 1965-68; mgr. communication support Gen. Electric Co., Lynn, Mass., 1968—. Served with USN, 1955-59. Mem. Internat. Assn. Bus. Communicators, New Eng. Bus. Communicators. Club: Publicity (Boston). Home: 38 Carlson Ave Revere MA 02151 Office: 1100 Western Ave Lynn MA 01910

BOVARNICK, BENNETT, engring. co. exec.; b. Lawrence, Mass., June 22, 1924; s. Jacob and Rose Cecille (Fineman) B.; B.S., Calif. Inst. Tech., 1946; A.M., Boston U., 1949, Ph.D., 1958; J.D., New Eng. Sch. Law, 1978; m. Evelyn Singer, Dec. 28, 1948; children—Deborah, Ellen, Daniel. Materials scientist, chief powder metals and ceramics br. U.S. Army Watertown Arsenal (Mass.), 1951-59; materials scientist Raytheon Co., Waltham, Mass., 1959-61; sr. metall. engr., Arthur D. Little, Inc., Cambridge, Mass., 1961-74; pres. Bennett Bovarnick, Inc., Newton, Mass., 1974—. Served with U.S. Army, 1943-45. Decorated Purple Heart. Mem. Am. Inst. Mining and Metall. Engrs., Am. Powder Metals Inst. Office: 41 Brentwood Ave Newton MA 02159

BOVE, HENRY JOSEPH, chem. engr.; b. New London, Conn., Jan. 24, 1925; s. Loreto and Rose (Tolo) B.; B.S., Worcester Poly. Inst., 1947, M.S., 1948; m. Yolanda H. Ferrigno, Sept. 10, 1950; 1 son, Lawrence J. Cons. and design engr. Day & Zimmermann, Inc., Phila., 1948-68, v.p. engring. research, 1966-67, v.p. planning and research, 1967-68; project mgr. chem. div. United Engrs. & Constructors, Inc., Phila., 1968—. Served with AUS, 1944-46. Registered profl. engr. Pa., N.Y., La., Ala., Ga., Ind., Del., Md. Mem. Am. Inst. Chem. Engrs., Am. Assn. Cost Engrs., Franklin Inst., Phila. Engrs. Club, Licensing

Exec. Soc., Internat. Platform Assn., Pa. Soc., Italian Execs. Am. Inc., Sigma Xi, Tau Beta Pi, Phi Kappa Theta. Republican. Roman Catholic. Home: 125 N Ormond Ave Havertown PA 19083 Office: 30 S 17th St Philadelphia PA 19101

BOVIS, HENRY EUGENE, govt. ofcl.; b. Kenansville, Fla., Mar. 31, 1928; s. Henry P. and Vassie Curtis (Wright) B.; B.A. cum laude, U. Fla., 1948, M.A., 1950; certificats d' etudes francaises, ler et 2e degres, U. Grenoble, France, 1951; Ph.D., Am. U., 1968; m. Beatrice Louise Wilfong, June 24, 1958; 1 son, Henry Eugene. Arabic lang. and area trainee U.S. Fgn. Service, Beirut, 1953-54; research analyst Dept. State, 1954-57, Hebrew lang. trainee U. Pa., 1957-58, 2d sec. Am. embassy Tel Aviv, 1958-60, consul, Haifa, 1960-63, polit./econ. officer Dept. State, 1963-69, 2d sec. U.S. interests sect. Spanish embassy, Cairo, 1969-71; vis. lectr., asst. prof. polit. sci. USAF Acad., 1971-73; coordinator polit. studies Dept. State Fgn. Service Inst., Washington, 1973-77; counselor for polit. affairs Am. embassy, Jidda, Saudi Arabia, 1977—. Sec. sch. bd. Cairo (Egypt) Am. Coll., 1970-71; mem. sch. bd. Schutz Sch., Alexandria, Egypt, 1969-71. Rotary Found. fellow, 1950-51. Mem. Internat. Studies Assn., Am. Fgn. Service Assn., Am. Polit. Sci. Assn., Middle East Studies Assn., Middle East Inst., Soc. Mayflower Descs., Phi Beta Kappa. Author: The Jerusalem Question, 1971. Office: Am Embassy APO New York City NY 09697

BOWDITCH, JAMES LOWELL, educator; b. Boston, Jan. 30, 1939; s. Richard Lyon and Mabel (Rantoul) B.; B.A., Yale U., 1961; M.A., Western Mich. U., 1965; Ph.D. in Indsl. Psychology (Richardson Found. fellow 1966-67), Purdue U., 1969; m. Felicity Joan Sexton, Apr. 4, 1964; children—Matthew Sexton, Andrew Rantoul, Sarah Lowell. Asst. prof. Sch. Mgmt., Boston Coll., Chestnut Hill, Mass., 1969-72, asso. prof., 1972—, dir. honors program, 1972-77. Served to 1st lt. AUS, 1961-64. NSF grantee, 1961; Carnegie Corp.-Gilman fellow, 1974—. Mem. Am. Psychol. Assn., Acad. Mgmt., AAAS, Sigma Xi, Beta Gamma Sigma. Democrat. Episcopalian (chmn. strategy com. 1972-73, sec. long-range planning com. 1973—, both Diocese Mass.). Clubs: Camden (Maine) Yacht; Megunticook Golf (Rockport, Maine). Author: (with E.F. Huse) Behavior in Organizations: A Systems Approach to Managing, 1973, 2d edit., 1977, Spanish edit., 1976. Home: 103 Loring Rd Weston MA 02193 Office: Boston Coll Chestnut Hill MA 02167

BOWE, EDWARD THOMAS, obstetrician, gynecologist; b. N.Y.C., May 12, 1930; s. Edward and Letitia (Tate) B.; B.S., Columbia U., 1957, M.D., 1961; m. Hope Mullen, 1957; children—Deirdre, Daphne, Ashton, Christopher, Cordelia. Intern, Upstate Med. Center Hosp., Syracuse, N.Y., 1961-62; resident in obstetrics, gynecology Columbia Presbyn. Med. Center, 1962-67; instr. in obstetrics, gynecology Columbia U., 1967-69, asst. prof. obstetrics, gynecology, 1970-75, asso. prof. clin. obstetrics, gynecology, 1975—; pvt. practice medicine specializing in obstetrics, gynecology, N.Y.C., 1968—; dir. obstet. service Presbyterian Hosp., N.Y.C., 1976—. Served with U.S. Army, 1951-53. Diplomate Am. Bd. Obstetrics and Gynecology. Mem. Am. Coll. Obstetrics and Gynecology, N.Y. Obstetrical Soc., Phi Beta Kappa. Contbr. articles on monitoring fetus, RH disease and fetal physiology to med. publs., 1967-77. Home: 1295 Pennington Rd Teaneck NJ 07666 Office: 161 Fort Washington Ave New York City NY 10032

BOWEN, JOHN SHEETS, advt. exec.; b. Chelsea, Mass., Feb. 4, 1927; s. Charles Parnell and Helen (Sheets) B.; B.A., Yale, 1949; m. Catherine Leigh Stander, June 28, 1952; children—Mark Stander, Charles Parnell III, Holly Leigh. Salesman, Procter & Gamble Co., 1949-51, unit mgr., 1952; account exec. McCann-Erickson, Inc., 1952-58, with Benton & Bowles, Inc., 1959—, mgmt. supr., 1964—, sr. v.p., 1965-68, exec. v.p., 1968-71, pres., 1971—, also chief exec. officer. Served with AUS, 1945-46; ETO. Mem. Am. Assn. Advt. Agys. (dir.-at-large). Episcopalian. Home: 44 Grace Church St Rye NY 10580 Office: 909 3d Ave New York City NY 10022

BOWEN, WILLIAM GORDON, univ. pres., economist; b. Cin., Oct. 6, 1933; s. Albert A. and Bernice (Pomert) B.; B.A., Denison U., 1955; Ph.D., Princeton, 1958; m. Mary Ellen Maxwell, Aug. 25, 1956; children—David Alan, Karen Lee. Mem. faculty Princeton, 1958—, prof. econs., 1965—, dir. grad. studies Woodrow Wilson Sch. Pub. and Internat. Affairs, 1964-66, provost, 1967-72, pres., 1972—; dir. NCR Corp., 1975—. Trustee Center for Advanced Study in the Behavioral Scis.; bd. dirs. Am. Council on Edn. Mem. Am. Econ. Assn., Am. Acad. Arts and Scis., Indsl. Relations Research Assn., Phi Beta Kappa. Author: The Wage-Price Issue: A Theoretical Analysis, 1960; Wage Behavior in the Postwar Period; An Empirical Analysis, 1960; Economic Aspects of Education; Three Essays, 1964; (with W. J. Baumol) Performing Arts; The Economic Dilemma, 1966; (with T.A. Finegan) The Economics of Labor Force Participation 1969. Office: 1 Nassau Hall Princeton U Princeton NJ 08540

BOWERING, JOHN RENVILLE, psychologist, clergyman; b. Bklyn., Dec. 29, 1933; s. William Gilbert and Rita (Snow) B.; student Union Jr. Coll., 1951-53; A.B., Upsala Coll., 1953-56; postgrad Drew U., 1956-58, Temple U., 1958-59, Princeton U., 1965-66; B.D., Crozer Sem., 1960; D.D., Am. Div. Sch., 1959; S.T.D., 1970; Ph.D., Thomas Edison Coll., 1972; M.Div., Colgate Rochester U., 1974; m. Bernice Lee Souchek, Aug. 20, 1960; children—John W.G. Bowering, Tami Lee, Jani Rae. Chaplain, Rahway (N.J.) State Prison, 1955-59; ordained to ministry United Methodist Ch., 1958; pastor chs. Perth Amboy, N.J., 1954-55, East Millstone, N.J., 1956-58, Linden, N.J., 1958-59, West Creek-Warren Grove, 1960-63, 1st United Meth. Ch., Island Heights, 1963-70, Cedar Grove United Methodist Ch., 1965-70, Manasquaq United Meth. Ch., 1970-73, Hightstown United Meth. Ch., 1973—; marriage counselor, 1963—; capt. (chaplain) N.J. State Police, 1976—; chaplain Boy Scouts Am., 1958—. Mem. Island Heights Planning Bd. and Bd. Edn., 1963-70; juvenile judge, Hightstown, 1974-78. Served with USNR, 1951-58. Decorated Order St. John Jerusalem Mem. Internat., N.J. chiefs of police, N.J. Narcotic Enforcement Officers Assn., Am. Scizophrenia Found., Am. Correctional Assn., N.J. Counselors Alcohol Problems, Am. Personnel and Guidance Assn., Am. Rehab. Counselling Assn., Assn. Counselor Edn. and Supervision. Clubs: Lions, Masons, Shriners. Home: 100 Academy St Hightstown NJ 08520

BOWERS, CHARLES EDWARD, resource recovery exec.; b. Crestview, Fla., Feb. 15, 1933; s. Michael Alexander and Lillian Lobelia (Searcy) B.; B.S., Morehead State U., 1956; M.S. in Nuclear Engring., U. Wash., 1965; m. Joan Austin, June 25, 1969; children—Charles, Andrea, Randy, Michele. Reactor physicist Gen. Electric Corp., Richland, Wash., 1956-65; mfg. mgr. United Nuclear, Richland, 1965-71; quality control mgr. Gen. Electric Corp., Wilmington, N.C., 1971-73; engring. mgr. United Nuclear, Montville, Conn., 1973-74, gen. mgr. fuel recovery operation, Wood River Junction, R.I., 1974—; cons. AEC, Oak Ridge, 1967-68; dir. U.S. Nuclear Corp., Oak Ridge. Chmn., Silent Majority, Richland, 1971; pres. Pasco (Wash.) PTA, 1963; chmn. trustees Columbia Basin Coll., 1970-71. Mem. Am. Nuclear Soc., Am. Mgmt. Assn. Republican. Methodist. Clubs: Oak Ridge Country, Masons Elks. Office: Fuel Recovery Operation Wood River Junction RI 02894

BOWERS, ETHEL MAY, educator; b. Clifton Heights, Pa., Sept. 29, 1900; d. Frank and Jennie (Pyle) Bowers; A.B., Brenau Coll., 1924; student N.Y. U., 1927-29; m. Ben Solomon, Sept. 8, 1929. Chmn. dept. phys. edn. Brenau Coll., 1922-27; specialist Recreation for Girls and Women, Nat. Recreation Assn., 1928-45; mng. editor Youth Leaders Digest, 1945-68; mng. editor Leadership Library, Putnam Valley, N.Y., 1968-74, pres., 1974—; lectr., cons. recreation for girls and women. Mem. Nat. Recreation and Parks Assn., World Leisure and Recreation Assn., Am. Youth Hostel Assn. Author: Recreation for Girls and Women.

BOWERS, EUGENE VINCENT, educator; b. Buffalo, Nov. 14, 1921; s. Roy Thomas and Margaret Cecelia (Ryan) B.; B.S. magna cum laude, State U. N.Y., 1949, M.S., 1952; Ed.D., U. Rochester, 1972; m. Gloria Myrtle McLaughlin, Apr. 20, 1946; children—Leslie Gene, Deborah Lynn. Tchr. of deaf, 1949-57; health coordinator Greece Central Sch., Rochester, N.Y., 1953-55, vice prin., 1955-56, prin. jr. high sch., 1956-61, coordinator pupil personnel services, 1961-63; prof. health sci. State U. N.Y. at Brockport, after 1963, now prof. emeritus; cons., writer in field. Bd. dirs. Learning Disabilities Assn., Am. Cancer Soc. Served with USAAF, 1942-45. Mem. Royal Soc. Health. Episcopalian (warden, lay leader, vestryman). Home: PO Box 2 Woodgate NY 13494 Office: State U NY Brockport NY 14420

BOWERS, GRAYSON HUNTER, bldg. parts mfg. co. exec.; b. Frederick, Md., Nov. 18, 1897; s. Grayson Eichelberger and Chrisse Byrd Dell (Firestone) B.; ed. Gettysburg Coll., 1919; m. Isabel Houck, June 6, 1921 (dec. Dec. 1961); children—Grayson Hunter, Charles R., Alice Josephine Bowers Butler; m. 2d, Frances L. Crilly, June 20, 1964. Vice pres. William D. Bowers Lumber Co. and pres. allied corps., Frederick, 1919—; pres. Fidelity Bldg. & Loan Assn., Mt. Olivet Cemetery Co.; sr. v.p., dir. Fredericktown Bank & Trust Co.; dir., officer Lumbermens Merchandising Corp., Wayne, Pa., 1945-70. Alderman City of Frederick, 1928-34; pres. Bd. Election Suprs., 1934-38, Frederick City Planning Commn., 1943-70; trustee Hood Coll., 1950-74; mem. adv. council Md. Hosp. Constrn., 1968-71. Served to 1st lt. U.S. Army, 1919. Club: Masons. Mem. Frederick County Hist. Soc. (pres.). Home: Route 10 Box 38 Frederick MD 21701 Office: 6th and East Sts Frederick MD 21701

BOWERS, JACK FREDERIC, ophthalmologist; b. Easton, Pa., Apr. 1, 1934; s. Charles Franklin and Helen Shell (Kantner) B.; B.A. cum laude, Lafayette Coll., 1955; M.D., Yale U., 1959; m. Edith Anna Hollmann, Oct. 8, 1960; children—Allegra Ann, Charles Allston. Intern, Lankenau Hosp., Phila., 1959-60; resident in ophthalmology Washington Hosp. Center, 1960-63; chief of ophthalmology U.S. Naval Hosp., Portsmouth, N.H., 1963-65; practice medicine specializing in ophthalmology, Haverhill, Mass., 1965—; pres. med. staff Hale Hosp., Haverhill; mem. active staff Mass. Eye & Ear Infirmary, Boston; clin. asst. in ophthalmology Harvard U. Sch. Medicine. Treas. West Boxford (Mass.) Library, 1970. Guild Opticians fellow, 1960-63; diplomate Am. Bd. Ophthalmology. Mem. Mass. Med. Soc. (pres. ophthalmology sect. 1975), New Eng. (chmn. program com. 1978—), Mass. ophthal. socs. (pres. 1975), Am. Assn. Ophthalmology, Am. Acad. Ophthalmology. Clubs: N. Andover Country (treas.), Cederdate Tennis. Author: (under pseudonym Allegra Charles) How to Win at Ladies Doubles, 1975; contbr. articles in ophthalmology to med. jours. Home: 691 Great Pond Rd North Andover MA 01845 Office: 215 Summer St Haverhill MA 01830

BOWERS, JAMES SUTPHEN, bus. cons.; b. Morristown, N.J., Dec. 22, 1928; s. Frank Nicolas and Marguerite (Sutphen) B.; B.A., Cornell U., 1951; M.B.A., Rutgers U., 1960; m. Nancy Ferber Berntsen, June 28, 1969; children by previous marriage—Carl B., Pamela Joan, David Paul. Plant-customer corr. Gen. Motors Corp., N.Y.C., 1953-56, mktg. analyst, 1956-59, asst. to product mgr., 1959-61; sr. investment analyst Prudential Ins. Co. Am., Newark, 1961-63; supervising mktg. specialist Mack Trucks, Inc., Allentown, Pa., 1963-65; gen. mgmt. cons. Price Waterhouse & Co., Phila., 1965-67; asst. v.p. Phila. Nat. Bank, 1967-71; v.p. Anchor Savs. Bank, N.Y.C., 1971-74; pres., propr. Princeton Cons. Assos. (N.J.), 1974—, Real Estate Investment Co. (N.J.), 1964—; instr. Univ. Coll., Rutgers U., 1975—; instr. bus. Centenary Coll., Hackensack, N.J. Treas. Princeton Area United Fund; past pres. bd. trustees, trustee scholarship fund Cornell Delta Phi Assn.; past deacon Nassau Presbyterian Ch.; former troop committeeman Boy Scouts Am. Served to 1st lt. USAF, 1951-53. Mem. Am. Mktg. Assn., Princeton C. of C. (dir.). Clubs: Rotary (Princeton); Skytop (Pa.); Vesper (Phila.). Contbr. articles to periodicals. Home and Office: 209 Shady Brook Ln Princeton NJ 08540

BOWERS, PATRICIA ELEANOR FRITZ, economist; b. N.Y.C., Mar. 21, 1928; d. Edward and Eleanor (Ring) Fritz; student (scholar) Goucher Coll., 1946-48; B.A., Cornell U., 1950; M.A., N.Y. U., 1953, Ph.D., 1965. Statis. asst. Fed. Res. Bank N.Y., N.Y.C., 1950-53; lectr. Upsala Coll., East Orange, N.J., 1953-59; research Fortune Mag., N.Y.C., 1959-60; instr. N.Y. U., 1960-64, teaching fellow, 1960-62; economist Bklyn. Coll., City U. N.Y., 1964—. Mem. Econometric Soc., Met. (sec. 1963-68, pres. 1974-75), Am. econ. assns., Am. Statis. Assn. (univs. chmn. annual forecasting confs. 1970-71, 71-72). Club: Talbot Country (Easton, Md.). Author: Private Choice and Public Welfare, 1974. Home: 145 E 16th St New York City NY 10003 Office: Dept Econs Brooklyn Coll City U NY Brooklyn NY 11210

BOWERS, PAUL EUGENE, telephone co. exec.; b. Stoystown, Pa., July 21, 1925; s. John Thomas and Mary (Zimmerman) B.; student I.C.S., 1950-51; m. Rosemary Gardner, Sept. 25, 1948; children—Cathy, Robert, Paul Jr., Calvin. Gen. supt. Carstensen Inc., Johnstown, Pa., 1946-64; co-propr. Vanguard of Erie Co. (Pa.), 1964-65; land, bldg. planning mgr. Gen. Telephone Co. of Pa., Erie, 1965—. Chmn. Harborcreek Twp. Bldg. Authority, 1966-73; vice-chmn. Harborcreek Twp. Sewer Authority, 1969-73, mem., 1975—; mem. bldg. com. Erie E. YMCA, 1976—, bd. mgrs., 1977—; bd. dirs. Greater Erie YMCA, 1976—; bd. dirs. Met. Erie Housing Devel. Corp. Served with USMCR, 1942. Mem. Constrn. Specifications Inst. (sec. 1971-72, 75-76, 1st v.p. 1977-78). Home: 425 Fair Ave Erie PA 16511 Office: 150 W 10th St Erie PA 16512

BOWERS, RICHARD PHILIP, mfg. co. exec.; b. Reading, Pa., July 27, 1931; s. Clarence Philip and Lottie Rose (Linkowski) B.; student St. Bonaventure U., 1949-51; m. Dolores Rita Dombrowski, June 21, 1952; children—Richard Philip, Karen Marie, Lisa Ann, Julie Louise. Sales trainee Bowers Battery & Spark Plug Co., Reading, 1954-55, sales mgr., 1955-58, v.p. sales, Gen. Battery Corp. (merger Bowers Battery & Spark Plug Co.), Reading, 1958-64; exec. v.p., dir., East Pa. Mfg. Co., Lyons Station, Pa., 1964—; pres. Pioneer Auto Parts, Phila.; dir. Miller Export, Hillsdale, N.J. Served with AUS, 1952-54. Mem. Ind. Battery Mfg. Assn. (dir.; chmn. marketing com. 1967-70), Battery Council Internat. (mem. merchandising com.), Am. Legion. Democrat. Roman Catholic. Clubs: Moselem Springs (Pa.) Golf, Second Generation. Home: 537 N Brobst St Shillington PA 19607 Office: East Pa Mfg Co Lyons Station PA 19536

BOWES, DENNIS MICHAEL, accountant; b. Framingham, Mass., Feb. 6, 1944; s. Francis Henry and Mary Gertrude (Craven) B.; B.S. in Acctg., Coll. of Holy Cross, 1965; m. Eileen R. Hodge, Oct. 21, 1973; 1 dau., Amanda Jean. Staff comptroller dept. Prudential Ins. Co., Boston, 1965-66; sr. accountant Spark Mann & Co., Boston, 1966-72; audit mgr. Sullivan Bille & Co., Tewksbury, Mass., 1972—, partner, 1979—. C.P.A., Mass. Mem. Mass. Soc. C.P.A.'s, Am. Inst. C.P.A.'s. Clubs: United Citizens Band Assn., Inc., (v.p. 1977, treas. 1978), Knights of Columbus. Home: 36 Fernwood Ave Lynn MA 01904 Office: 500 Clark Rd Tewksbury MA 01876 also 1 Boston Pl Boston MA

BOWIE, JACK EDWARD, med. info. systems scientist; b. Lakewood, Ohio, Jan. 31, 1946; s. William Edward and Frances (Fullam) B.; B.S., Mass. Inst. Tech., 1970, M.S., 1970, Sc.D., 1973; m. Sharon Diane Smoot, June 22, 1968; children—Lisa Diane, Jennifer Diane. Research engr. NASA Electronics Research Center, Cambridge, Mass., 1968, 69; staff programmer Digilab, Inc., Cambridge, 1971-72; computer systems analyst Lab. Computer Sci., Mass. Gen. Hosp., Boston, 1972—; research asso. in medicine Harvard U. Mem. Assn. Computing Machinery, Sigma Xi, Eta Kappa Nu, Tau Beta Pi. Office: Massachusetts General Hospital Boston MA 02114

BOWKER, LAWRENCE WAYNE, dental products co. exec.; b. Wrightstown, N.J., July 7, 1944; s. Russell Lewis and Marie Alice (Cliver) Baker; B.S., Rider Coll., Lawrenceville, N.J., 1978; M.B.A., Fairleigh Dickinson U. Software specialist IBM Corp., Trenton, N.J., 1966-69; systems cons. Office Treas. N.J., Trenton, 1969-71, Petroleum Data Corp., Princeton, N.J., 1971-76; project mgr. J & J Dental Products Co., E. Windsor, N.J., 1976—. Served with USN, 1962-66. Mem. Data Processing Mgmt. Assn., Am. Prodn. and Inventory Control Soc. (edn. chmn.). Address: J & J Dental Products Co 20 Lake Dr East Windsor NJ 08520

BOWLING, JAMES CHANDLER, tobacco co. exec.; b. Covington, Ky., Mar. 29, 1928; s. Van Dorn and Belinda (Johnson) B.; B.S., U. Louisville, 1951; m. Ann Jones, Oct. 20, 1951; children—Belinda, Nancy, James, Stephanie. From campus rep. to pub. relations dir. Philip Morris, Inc., N.Y.C., 1951-62, asst. to pres., 1962-64, v.p., dir. sales, corporate relations, 1964-67, v.p. parent co., group v.p. Philip Morris U.S.A., 1967-69, v.p., asst. to chmn. bd., dir. corporate affairs, dir., 1969—, sr. v.p., 1976—; chmn. pub. relations Tobacco Inst., Washington, 1958-64, 75-78. Mem. Nat. council Boy Scouts Am., 1961—; Justice of Peace, Rowayton, Conn., 1960-68; mem. admissions adv. bd. U. Louisville; trustee Midway Coll., Berea Coll., Low Haywood Sch.; bd. dirs., chmn. bd. Keep Am. Beautiful; bd. dirs. U. Ky. Devel. Council; vice chmn. Clean World Internat., 1978. Served with AUS, World War II; PTO. Recipient Kolondy award as outstanding young exec. in industry, 1963; named Outstanding Young Businessman of Year, St. John's U., 1967, Man of Year, Tobacco and Allied Trades div. Anti-Defamation League, 1969, Outstanding Grad., U. Louisville Coll. Bus., 1970, Kentuckian of Yr., 1977; named to Tobacco Industry Hall of Fame, 1976. Mem. Nat. Assn. Tobacco Distbg. (v.p. exec. mgmt. div.), Nat. Automatic Merchandising Assn. (dir.), Sales Execs. Club N.Y. (dir.), Pub. Relations Soc. Am., Kentuckians, Lambda Chi Alpha. Episcopalian (vestryman). Club: Wee Burn Country. Author: How To Improve Your Personal Relations, 1959. Home: Tokeneke Trail Darien CT 06820 Office: 100 Park Ave New York City NY 10017

BOWLING, JOHN KNOX, JR., aviation co. exec.; b. Duncan, Okla., Feb. 26, 1940; s. John Knox and Lula (Hatley) B.; B.A., U. Tex. at Austin, 1963, B.J., 1963; m. Diantha Lee King, July 13, 1967; 1 dau., Tanisha Lee. Advt. trainee Ted Bates & Co., Inc., N.Y.C., 1963-64, comml. broadcast producer, 1964-66, broadcast supr., 1966-67; Western pub. relations mgr. Air France, Los Angeles, 1968-73, advt., merchandising and creatvie service mgr. for U.S.A., N.Y.C., 1973—. Recipient Grand Chevalier de lvOrdre de Vieux Moulin, France, 1963. Republican. Presbyterian. Clubs: Univ. N.Y., Blue Hill Troupe (N.Y.C.); Ardsley Country (Ardsley-on-Hudson, N.Y.). Home: Clifton Pl Irvington NY 10533 Office: 1350 Ave of the Americas New York City NY 10019

BOWLSBEY, LEONARD STANLEY, JR., educator; b. Balt., Sept. 9, 1930; s. Leonard Stanley and Blanche Carolyn (Ford) B.; B.A., Western Md. Coll., 1952, M.Ed., 1959; Ph.D., U. Iowa, 1969; m. Jo Ann Harris. Tchr. English, Balt. Jr. Coll., 1955-64, dean of faculty, 1966-69; prof. edn., chmn. dept. edn., dir. grad. program Western Md. Coll., Westminster, 1969—; mem. Md. Tchr. Edn. Advisory Council, 1969-74, chmn., 1973-74; mem. Md. Profl. Standards Bd., 1974—, chmn., 1977-78. Served with AUS, 1952-54. Mem. Assn. Supervision and Curriculum Devel., AAUP, Nat. Soc. Study Edn. Home: 1600 Green Mill Rd Finksburg MD 21048 Office: Western Md Coll Westminster MD 21157

BOWMAN, CLAUDE CHARLTON, sociologist; b. Harrisburg, Pa., Sept. 13, 1908; s. Claude C. and Jane Given (Sprout) B.; A.B., Dickinson Coll., 1928; Ph.D., U. Pa., 1937; m. Mary S. Carson, June 29, 1929. Instr. chemistry Dickinson Coll., Carlisle, Pa., 1928-29; fellow in sociology U. Kans., Lawrence, 1929-30; instr. sociology Temple U., Phila., 1930-37, asst. prof., 1937-45, prof., 1945—, acting dean men, 1942-44, dean students, 1944-45; lectr. in field. Bd. dirs. Horizon House, Planned Parenthood Assn. S.E. Pa., Phila. ACLU, Phila. Ams. Democratic Action. Mem. Am. Sociol. Assn., AAUP (chpt. pres. 1953-54), Internat. Assn. Applied Psychology, Phi Beta Kappa. Clubs: Franklin Inn, Art Alliance (Phila.). Author: The College Professor in America, 1938; Humanistic Sociology, 1973; contbr. articles to sociol., psychiat. jours. Home: 331 Hamilton Rd Merion Station PA 19066 Office: Temple U Philadelphia PA 19122

BOWMAN, JAMES FLOYD, II, geologist; b. Orange, N.J., Feb. 22, 1932; s. Floyd Smith and Margaret Nagel (Gramm) B.; A.B., Rutgers U., 1956, Ph.D., 1966; m. Mary Michael McKenna, Aug. 10, 1968; children—Steven McMath, John Peter, Patricia Anne, Jennifer Cooper. Lectr. geology Hunter Coll., City U. N.Y., 1965-66, instr. Herbert H. Lehman Coll., Bronx, N.Y., 1966-69, asst. prof. geology, 1970—, expert to media in geology, 1972—; sedimentologist Hudson Estuary Survey Program, N.Y.C. Inst. Oceanography, 1973—; participant 10th Internat. Field Inst., Spain, 1971; contest judge Project Skylab, NASA, N.Y.C. High Schs., 1972. Served with AUS, 1952-54. Mem. Geol. Soc. Am., AAUP, Internat. Assn. Mathematics in Geology, Soc. Econ. Paleontologists and Mineralogists, Nat. Assn. Geology Tchrs., Am. Geophys. Union, VFW, N.Y. Acad. Scis. Office: Geology Dept Lehman Coll City U NY Bronx NY 10468

BOX, THEODOR MAX, plastic injection molding co. exec.; b. Berlin; Aug. 23, 1906; s. Sam Max and Johanna Maria (Markwald) B.; came to U.S., 1957, naturalized, 1962; Dr. merc., Koelnisches Gymnasium, Berlin; m. Ruth Pardo, Apr. 11, 1935; children—Thomas, David. Agt., Bata Kotva Zlin, Czechoslovakia, 1933-40; self-employed in pub. relations and advt., Haifa, Palestine, 1945-47; hon. German consul, Cyprus, 1950-56; agt. Wacker Chemie K.C., Munich, Germany, 1956-57; founder, pres. Tedruth Plastics Corp., Farmingdale, N.J., 1961—. Mem. Com. for UN Day, 1975; bd. dirs. Jersey Shore Med. Center, Neptune, N.J. Served as capt., Brit. forces, 1940-45. Recipient German Sports decoration; Achievement award United Inventors and Scientists Am., 1977. Clubs: Rotary, Masons, Shriners. Patentee in field. Home: 1108 Aileen Rd Brielle NJ 08730 Office: Tedruth Plaza Farmingdale NJ 07727

BOXER, THEODORE, govt. ofcl.; b. Bklyn., May 17, 1918; s. Louis and Sarah (Lillian) B.; B.A. cum laude, Bklyn. Coll., 1940; postgrad. U. Md. and Johns Hopkins, 1947-51; M.S., Stevens Inst. Tech., Hoboken, N.J., 1953; m. Terry R. Rubinfeld, Sept. 24, 1944; children—Loretta Boxer Kerstein, Susan (dec.). Various positions in govt. in teaching and engring. field, 1940-59; dir. Ordnance Lab., W.L. Maxson Co., N.Y.C., 1959-61; mgr. ordnance dept. Kollsman Instrument Corp., Elmhurst, N.Y., 1961-64; chief Pyrotechnic Br., Explosives Div., Feltman Research Lab., Picatinny Arsenal, Dover, N.J., 1964-77; chief tech. br., energetic materials div., large caliber weapons systems lab. Army Research and Devel. Command, 1977—; U.S. nat. rep. Internat. Tech. Com. for Pyrotechnic Research; tchr. thermodynamics and math. Newark Coll. Engring., Fairleigh Dickinson U., Madison, N.J. Served with AUS, 1944-46. Mem. Am. Ordnance Assn., Sigma Xi. Club: Masons. Author, contbr. govt. publs. Patentee in field. Office: Army Research and Devel Command Bldg 407 Dover NJ 07801

BOXER, TIM, journalist, photographer; b. Winnipeg, Man., Can., May 12, 1934; s. Gabriel and Annie (Gampel) B.; student United Coll., Can., 1951-52, Herzl Jr. Coll., 1952-54, Northwestern U., 1954-55, Hebrew Theol. Coll., 1952-56; m. Nina Naham, June 12, 1977. News editor Nat. Jewish Post, Chgo., 1956-57; reporter City News Bur., Chgo., 1957-59; city editor Sentinel of Chgo., 1958-60; asst. pub. relations dir. Israel Bonds of Chgo., 1960; publicist for Dick Gregory, Chgo., 1960-61; Eastern publicity mgr. Playboy mag. and Playboy Club of N.Y., 1961-62; freelance pub. relations specialist, 1963-67; asst. to Earl Wilson, N.Y.C., 1967—; freelance photographer, 1967—; columnist Jewish Week of N.Y., 1978—; producer Manhattan Cable TV, 1974—. Served with AUS, 1957. Mem. Am. Soc. Mag. Photographers, Nat. Press Photographers Assn., Royal Photog. Soc. Gt. Britain, Profl. Photographers Am., Photog. Soc. Am., Internat. Platform Assn., Young Israel, Am. Israel Numis. Assn., United Zionists Revisionists Am. Home: 102-10 66th Rd Forest Hills NY 11375

BOXILL, GALE CLARK, toxicologist; b. Indpls., Jan. 28, 1919; s. Harold Augustus and Lillian Alcoke (Gale) B.; B.A., Washington and Lee U., 1947; M.S., U. Tenn., 1951, Ph.D., 1954; m. Irene Victoria Byk, July 20, 1946; children—William, Judith Anne. Asst. pharmacologist William S. Merrell Co., 1947-49; sr. scientist Mead Johnson & Co., Evansville, Ind., 1953-59; sr. pharmacologist Warner Lambert Research Inst., 1959-62, dir. toxicology, Morris Plains, N.J., 1962-70; mgr. toxicology Wyeth Lab., Malvern, Pa., 1970-78, asso. dir. biol. research, 1978—; asst. prof. pharmacology U. Ga., Athens, 1951-52. Mem. bd. edn., Morris Plains, 1961-65. Served to 1st lt. AUS, 1943-46. Mem. Soc. Toxicology (sec. 1975—), Am. Soc. Pharmacology and Exptl. Therapeutics, AAAS, N.Y. Acad. Sci., Sigma Xi. Home: 708 Timberlake Dr Exton PA 19341 Office: PO Box 861 Paoli PA 19301

BOXWILL, FRANK E., sch. psychologist; b. Georgetown, Guyana, June 25, 1926; s. Isaac and Stella (Bunbury) B.; came to U.S., 1946, naturalized, 1960; student Howard U., 1947-48; B.S., Wagner Coll., 1953; postgrad. New Sch. Social Research, 1954, L.I. U., 1956-58, U. Oreg., 1958-59, Ph.D., East Coast U., 1971; children—Frank E., Eric, Yvette, Hope, Francyne, Dave, André. Fellow in psychology Bklyn. Psychiat. Center, 1959-61; clin. psychologist Kings County Hosp., Bklyn., 1961-65; psychotherapist Bklyn. Center Psychotherapy, 1964-66; psychotherapist Bleuler Center Psychotherapy, Jamaica, N.Y., 1967—; sch. psychologist Brentwood (N.Y.) Pub. Schs., 1965-66, Amityville (N.Y.) Pub. Schs., 1967—; sr. research asso. Tng. Resources for Youth, Bklyn., 1965-66; coordinator research Harlem Psychat. Rehab. Center, Columbia U., N.Y.C., 1966-67; dir. Center Advancement and Mgmt. of Edn., N.Y.C., 1970, Family Inst. for More Effective Living, Westbury, 1973. Cons. in child devel., learning, marital and family relations. Fellow Royal Soc. Health (Eng.); mem. Am., N.Y. State, County psychol. assns. Republican. Author: The Troubled Youngster in the Classroom, 1971; Understanding Ego Development of the Troubled Youngster; Learning Disabilities, a Multi-disciplinary Approach. Office: 496 Jefferson St Westbury NY 11590

BOYCE, THOMAS KENNETH, psychiatrist; b. Middletown, N.Y., Apr. 26, 1923; s. Thomas A. and Lillian F. (Hackett) B.; R.N., Middletown State Hosp. (N.Y.), 1947; postgrad. Marietta (Ohio) Coll., 1951, Columbia, 1953; M.D., Cath. U. Louvain (Belgium), 1961. Staff nurse Middletown (N.Y.) State Hosp., 1947, intern, 1962, resident in psychiatry, 1963-66, sr. psychiatrist, 1965-66, supervising psychiatrist, 1966-67, psychiatrist II, 1969-70, psychiatrist III, chief of service Orange County unit, 1970-76; cons. in field; individual practice medicine, specializing in psychiatry Middletown, 1966—. Served with USNR, 1943-46; ETO. USPHS scholar, 1952. Mem. Am. Psychiat. Assn., A.C.P., AMA, N.Y. State, Orange County med. socs., Am. Legion, Middletown Psychiat. Center Sch. Nursing Alumni Assn. Roman Catholic. Home and office: 150 N Beacon St Middletown NY 10940

BOYD, DONALD WILLIAM, JR., editor, publisher, assn. exec.; b. Buffalo, Feb. 7, 1923; s. Donald William and Nan (Smith) B.; A.B., Colgate U., 1943; m. Winifred G. Boyd, Sept. 10, 1955; children—Donald William III, Nancy J., Geoffrey G. Asst. dir. pub. relations Champlain Coll., Plattsburgh, N.Y., 1946; dir. pub. relations Clarkson Coll., Potsdam, N.Y., 1947-52; dir. univ. press div. Wm. J. Keller, Inc., Buffalo, 1952-53; dir. pub. relations Canisius Coll., Buffalo, 1953-62; pres. Profl. Program Mgmt. Inc., and predecessor co., Buffalo, 1963—; exec. sec. Am. Assn. Indsl. Editors, 1965-70, Purchasing Mgmt. Assn., Buffalo, 1963—, Greater Buffalo Advt. Club, 1974—, Profl. Skaters Guild Am., 1978—; editor, pub. Niagara Frontier Purchaser mag., 1960—. Assn. chmn. Buffalo and Erie County council Girl Scouts U.S.A., 1969-72, 75-77, bd. dirs., 1972-77; scoutmaster Boy Scouts Am., 1968-76, dist. commr., 1970-73; bd. dirs. Jr. Achievement Niagara Frontier, 1966—. Served to lt. (j.g.) USNR, 1944-46. Mem. Alpha Tau Omega. Home: 541 Crescent Ave Buffalo NY 14214 Office: 802 Kenmore Ave Buffalo NY 14216

BOYD, JOHN, mech. engr.; b. Pitts., Nov. 21, 1906; s. Vinton W. and Priscilla (Patterson) B.; B.S. in Mech. Engring., Carnegie Inst. Tech., 1929, M.S., 1934; m. Wanda Nielsen, Jan. 10, 1933; 1 day., Joanne. Sect. mgr. research lab. Westinghouse Co., Pitts., 1933-67, cons. engr., 1967-71, cons. engr. Westinghouse Atomic div., Cheswick; Pa., 1967-71, ret., 1971; mem. mech. engring. faculty U. Pitts., 1934-45; instr. Carnegie Inst. Tech., 1933-45. Instr., Internat. Exec. Service Corps, Korea, 1973. Fellow Am. Soc. Lubrication Engrs. (pres. 1954, editor jour. 1957-71, Alfred E. Hunt award 1976), ASME (Mayo D. Hersey award 1970). Republican. Author: Standard Handbook Lubrication, 1958. Home: 219 Bevington Rd Pittsburgh PA 15221

BOYD, RACHEL ELIZABETH, educator; b. Hanger, Va., Jan. 30, 1905; d. Burton Marvin and Charlotte (Van Dyke) Boyd; B.S., U. Del., 1929; M.S., Cornell U., 1946; summer study U. Md., Purdue U., W.Va. U. Tchr. home econs. Schs. of Cecil County, Md., 1929-48, supr. home econs. edn. and sch. lunch program, 1947-70. Adviser, region E. Md. Future Homemakers Am., 1957-70; mem. leadership tng. com. Newcastle Presbyterial Assn., 1974-78. Mem. Am., Md. (chmn. scholarship com. 1958-60, sec.) home econs. assns., Md. Sch. Food Service Assn. (pres. 1953-54), Am. Vocat. Assn. (treas. home econs. sect. 1951-53), Cecil County Hist. Soc., Delta Kappa Gamma. Democrat. Presbyterian. (coordinator women's assn.). Club: Women's College (treas. 1970-78), Woman's (dir. 1975-77) (Elkton). Home: 4 Walter Boulden St Elkton MD 21921

BOYD, ROBERT, journalist; b. Chgo., Jan. 11, 1928; grad. Harvard, 1949; married, 4 children. With Dept. State, 1949-52; reporter Lafayette (La.) Daily Advertiser, 1953; state editor Benton Harbor (Mich.) News-Palladium, 1954-57; reporter Detroit Free Press, 1957-60; mem. Knight Newspapers' Bur., Washington, 1960—, chief, 1967—. Recipient Pulitzer prize for nat. reporting, 1973. Office: care Knight-Ridder Newspapers Nat Press Bldg Washington DC 20045

BOYD, ROBERT JAMES, orthopedic surgeon; b. Detroit, July 1, 1930; s. DeVere Robert and Frances (Richardson) B.; A.B., Harvard U., 1952; M.D.C.M., McGill U., 1956; m. Sanda L. Hibbard, June 25, 1955; children—Elizabeth Ann, Sarah Catherine. Intern, San Francisco Gen. Hosp., 1956-57; resident in surgery, research fellow surgery Stanford U., 1959-61; resident in orthopedics Harvard U. Med. Sch., Boston, 1962-65; practice medicine specializing in orthopedic surgery, Boston, 1965—; asst. orthopedic surgeon Mass. Gen. Hosp., 1965—; clin. instr. orthopedics Harvard U. Med. Sch., 1965-77, asst. clin. prof. orthopedic surgery, 1977—. Served with M.C., AUS, 1957-59. Fellow Am. Acad. Orthopedic Surgeons, Am. Assn. Surgery of Trauma, A.C.S.; mem. AMA, Mass. Med. Soc., Orthopedic Research Soc. Home: 87 Sylvan Ln Weston MA 02193 Office: Zero Emerson Pl Boston MA 02114

BOYD, WILLIAM JAMES DAVID, assn. exec.; b. Coffeyville, Kans., Dec. 7, 1930; s. Joseph David and Zona Carol (Vernon) B.; B.A., U. Calif., Santa Barbara, 1957; postgrad. Stanford U., 1957-58, Princeton U., 1958-60; M. Pub. Adminstrn., N.Y. U., 1978. Mem. staff Nat. Municipal League, N.Y.C., 1960-78, asst. dir., 1969-78; dir. dept. for the city Community Service Soc. N.Y., 1978—; mem. citizens adminstrv. advisory com. N.Y. State Tax Commn., 1976—; advisory com. reapportionment to N.Y. State Legislature, 1965-66; dir. dist. ct. N.Y.C. Community Sch. Bd. Elections, 1970, 73, 75; bd. dirs. Com. for Modern Courts; bd. dirs., exec. com. Citizens Union, 1967—; co-chmn. N.Y. State Com. Fair Representation, 1967; exec. com. Com. for Effective Constitution, 1967. Served with USN, 1951-54. Ford Found. Behavior Sci. scholar, 1957-58; Danforth Found. fellow, 1958-60. Mem. Am. Polit. Sci. Assn., Am. Soc. Pub. Adminstrn., Govtl. Research Assn., LWV, Regional Plan Assn. Mem. Disciples Christ. Author: Changing Patterns of Apportionment, 1965; After the Electoral College, 1968; editor: Court Decisions on Legislative Apportionment, 33 vols., 1962-71; contbr. articles to profl. publs. Home: PO Box 21 243 Mine Rd Fort Montgomery NY 10922

BOYD-MONK, HEATHER GWENDOLINE, nurse, hosp. ofcl.; b. Luanshya, No. Rhodesia, May 24, 1936; d. Robert Danby and Edith Francis (Torr) Boyd-M.; came to U.S., 1964, naturalized, 1977. S.R.N., Addenbrooke's Hosp., Cambridge, Eng., 1962; B.S. in Nursing, U. Pa., 1981. Staff nurse Addenbrooke's Hosp., 1962-63, Doctors Hosp., Toronto, Ont., Can., 1963-64; head nurse pediatric dept. Wills Eye Hosp., Phila., 1965-67, relief supr., 1968-74, relief head nurse, 1968-74, supr., 1974-76, edn. coordinator, dir. staff devel., 1976—. Mem. Soc. Opthalmic Nurses. Presbyterian. Contbr. articles to nursing jours. and books. Home: 702 S Park Towne Pl 2200 Benjamin Franklin Pkwy Philadelphia PA 19130 Office: 1601 Spring Garden St Philadelphia PA 19130

BOYER, GEORGE KENNETH, investment co. exec.; b. Wallington, N.J., Jan. 18, 1931; s. George Gabriel and Theresa Catherine (Derzsak) B.; grad. Realtors Inst., 1970, Revac Investment Inst., 1971, Nat. Inst. Real Estate Brokers, 1972; m. Priscilla A. Fryer, Nov. 18, 1952; children—Sandra Lee, Kim Anne, Kathryn Marie, Kenneth George. Owner, dir. Boyer Agy., New London, Conn., 1963—; sr. investment analyst Boyer Realty Investments, New London, 1971—, pres. Conn. Comml. Investment div., 1976—; pres. Conn. Real Estate Securities and Syndication Inst., 1974—; v.p. New Eng. Real Estate Securities Syndication Inst.; bd. dirs. New London Bd. Realtors, Conn. Devel. Council. Served with USCG, 1948-61. Mem. Home Builders Assn. Southeastern Conn. (dir.), Home Builders Assn. Conn. (dir., pres. Eastern Conn. comml. investment div. 1971-73), New Eng. Appraisal Soc., Nat., Conn. assns. real estate bds., Nat. Inst. Real Estate Brokers, Nat. Assn. Home Builders, U.S. Navy League. Home: 85 Prospect Hill Rd Noank CT 06340 Office: 261 Williams St New London CT 06320

BOYER, JERE MICHAEL, educator; b. Lebanon, Pa., Feb. 24, 1946; s. Carl William and June (Arnold) B.; B.S., U. Scranton, 1968; M.A., Millersville State Coll., 1971; Ph.D., St. John's U., 1975; m. Charlotte Bailey, Sept. 29, 1971. Teaching fellow St. John's U., N.Y.C., 1971-74; instr. Phila. Coll. Osteo. Medicine, 1974-75, asst. prof. microbiology, 1975—; cons. Nat. Bd. Examiners for Osteo. Physicians. NSF grantee, 1974, NDEA grantee, 1964-68. Fellow Am. Coll. Osteo. Allergists and Immunologists (asso.); mem. Am. Soc. Microbiology, Soc. Indsl. Microbiology, Pa. Acad. Sci., Med. Mycol. Soc. N.Am. Republican. Roman Catholic. Club: K.C. Contbr. articles in field to profl. jours. Home: 6 Kathleen Ct Havertown PA 19083 Office: Phila Coll Osteo Medicine 4150 City Ave Philadelphia PA 19131

BOYES, FRED HOWARD, mktg. research co. exec.; b. Pulaski, Va., Apr. 16, 1933; s. Fred and Justine (Boyes) Vaden; B.A. cum laude in Mathematics, Ohio State U., 1957; M.S. in Psychology (Wis. Alumni Research Found. fellow), U. Wis., 1960; m. Sandra Elizabeth Papay, Sept. 6, 1958; children—Alexandra, Gregory. Research psychologist Gen. Motors Corp., Warren, Mich., 1960-62; research account exec. firm Campbell-Ewald, Detroit, 1962-64, mgr. advt. evaluation, 1964-66; staff cons. Mktg. Strategy Inc., Detroit, 1966-67, v.p., 1967-68; consumer research mgr. May Dept. Stores Co., St. Louis, 1968-70; v.p., asso. dir. research Kenyon & Eckhardt Advt., N.Y.C., 1970-72; v.p. Data Devel. Corp., N.Y.C., 1973-75; exec. v.p. R.H. Bruskin Assos., New Brunswick, N.J., 1975—. Mem. Am. Psychol. Assn., Am. Mktg. Assn., Retail Research Soc., Market Research Soc. (Gt. Britain), Am. Assn. Pub. Opinion Research, Phi Beta Kappa. Club: Huntington Yacht (N.Y.). Home: 88 Preston Ct Huntington NY 11743 Office: 303 George St New Brunswick NJ 08901

BOYLAN, WILLIAM ALVIN, lawyer; b. Marshalltown, Iowa, Sept. 18, 1924; s. Glen D. and Dorothy I. (Gibson) B.; student U. Iowa, 1943-44; B.A., Drake U., 1947; LL.B., Harvard U., 1950; m. Nancy Dickson, Aug. 5, 1950; children—Ross, Laura. Admitted to Ill. bar, 1950, N.Y. bar, 1952, since practiced in N.Y.C.; mem. firm Windels, Marx, Davies & Ives, and predecessor firms, 1963—; dir. Tribune Oil Corp., N.Y.C. Served with USAAF, 1943-46. Mem. Am., N.Y. State bar assns., Assn. Bar City N.Y., Phi Beta Kappa, Sigma Alpha Epsilon. Episcopalian. Club: Harvard. Contbr. articles to profl. jours. Home: 108 E 82d St New York City NY 10028 Office: Windels Marx Davies & Ives 51 W 51st St New York City NY 10019

BOYLE, CAROL ANN, editor; b. Elizabeth, N.J., Mar. 11, 1945; d. Frank Joseph and Domicella M. (Sakotski) Brescher; B.A., Moravian Coll., 1967; M.L.S., Rutgers U., 1968; m. Edward T. Boyle, Oct. 5, 1968. Librarian, cataloger Baker & Taylor, Somerville, N.J., 1968; asst. librarian Marist Coll., Poughkeepsie, N.Y., 1969, Rondout Valley High Sch., Stone Ridge, N.Y., 1969-75; editor Discar, Canine Abstracts, Hurley, N.Y., 1975—, The High Fallonian, 1979—; v.p., dir. Profl. Breeding Services, Hurley, 1972—. Mem. Dog Writers Assn. Am. (Best Article award 1978), Am. Dog Owners Assn., Pyrenean Fanciers N.E., Mid-Hudson Kennel Club, Great Pyrenees Club Am. Editor: Dogs; A Hobby or Profession, Vol. I, 1978. Home: RD 3 Box 142D Kingston NY 12401 Office: Route 209 PO Box 176 Hurley NY 12443

BOYLE, EDWARD LEO, JR., ophthalmologist; b. Saratoga Springs, N.Y., Nov. 19, 1943; s. Edward Leo and Margaret (Lautrup) B.; A.B., Dartmouth Coll., 1965; M.D., Albany Med. Coll., 1970; m. Mary Elizabeth Knight, June 29, 1968; children—Ryan Fitzgerald, Lauren Alexandra. Research asst. Baker Research Labs., Med. Sch. Harvard U., Boston, 1965-66; med. intern Dartmouth Affiliated Hosps., Hanover, N.H., 1970-71; fellow in ophthalmic pathology Albany (N.Y.) Med. Coll., 1971-72, resident in opgthalmology, 1972-75; practice medicine specializing in ophthalmology, Saratoga Springs, N.Y., 1977—; mem. staff Saratoga, Glens Falls, Albany Med. Center hosps. Served to lt. comdr., M.C., USN, 1975-77. USPHS grantee, 1971-72 Diplomate Am. Bd. Ophthalmology, Mem. N.Y. State Ophthalmologic Soc. (legis. com.), Saratoga County Med. Soc., Northeastern N.Y. Eye, Ear, Nose and Throat Soc., Am. Assn. Ophthalmology. Home: 41 Fieldstone Dr Route 2 Gansevoort NY 12831 Office: 31 Myrtle St Saratoga Springs NY 12866

BOYLE, RICHARD JOHN, museum ofcl.; b. N.Y.C., June 3, 1932; s. James and Gertrude (Eichhorn) B.; B.A. in English Lit., Adelphi U., 1954; certificate fine arts Oxford U., 1959; postgrad. Art Students League, N.Y.C., 1959-61; m. Patricia, June 19, 1971; children—Patrick, Cheryl, Barbara, Eric. Tchr., 1962-63; curator Internat. Art Found., R.I., 1962; dir. Middletown (Ohio) Fine Arts Center, 1963-65; curator Cin. Art Mus., 1965-73; dir. Pa. Acad. Fine Arts, Phila., 1973—. Chmn. Fine Arts Commn., Phila. Redevel. Authority; bd. dirs. Center City Found. Served with M.C., U.S. Army, 1954-56. Benjamin Franklin fellow Royal Soc. Art, London. Mem. Assn. Am. Art Mus. Dirs., Nat. Trust Historic Preservation, Nat. Assn. Art and Lit. Clubs: Franklin Inn, Sunday Breakfast (Phila.). Author: American Impressionism, 1974. Collaborator: Genius of American Painting, 1973. Contbr. articles to profl. jours. Home: 2121 Delancey St Philadelphia PA 19103 Office: Pa Acad Fine Arts Broad and Cherry Sts Philadelphia PA 19102

BOYLE, ROBERT JOSEPH, editor; b. Lansford, Pa., Mar. 25, 1927; s. Samuel John and Olive Margaret (Bonner) B.; grad. high sch.; m. Mildred Clark, Apr. 6, 1953; children—Colleen, Robert Joseph. Reporter, photographer Lansford Record, 1948-54; reporter Pottstown (Pa.) Mercury, 1954-55, county editor, 1955-56, wire editor, 1956-57, city editor, 1958-68, mng. editor, 1968-69, editor, 1969-75; founder, pub. Pottstown Guardian, 1975—. Served with USNR, 1944-45. Mem. Soc. Newspaper Editors, Am. Soc. Newspaper Editors. Home: 527 Clearview St Pottstown PA 19464 Office: 40 High St Pottstown PA 19464

BOYLE, WILLIAM LEO, JR., coll. pres.; b. Utica, N.Y., July 23, 1933; s. William Leo and Gladys (Kuney) B.; A.B., Colgate U., 1955; postgrad. Cornell U. Law Sch., 1960-61; M.A., Columbia U., 1964, Profl. Diploma in Ednl. Adminstrn., 1967, Ed.D., 1969; postgrad. Harvard U., 1979. Participant advanced mgmt. program, ednl. adviser Procter & Gamble Co., Cin., 1958-60; legis. aide N.Y. State Senate, Albany, 1961-62; account exec., ednl. cons. Batten, Barton, Durstine & Osborn, N.Y.C., 1962-64; asst. dir. devel., presdl. asst. Wesleyan U., Middletown, Conn., 1964-65; program cons. Council for Fin. Aid to Edn., N.Y.C., 1965-70, asst. v.p., 1970-72, v.p., 1972-75; pres. Keuka Coll., Keuka Park, N.Y., 1975-78; pres. Curry Coll., Milton, Mass., 1978—, also trustee. Vice chmn. nat. bus. and industry com. Colgate U., Hamilton, N.Y., 1974—, mem. Nat. Council, 1975—, mem. annual fund exec. com., 1975—; ednl. cons. Pres. Ford Com., Washington, 1976. Served to 1st lt. USAF, 1955-58. Mem. various ednl. and profl. orgns. Clubs: Eire Soc., Gridiron (Boston); Harvard U. Educators Round Table (Cambridge); Columbia U. (N.Y.C.). Author: The National Corporate Educational Support Movement, 1954-66, 1969; contbr. articles to ednl. and profl. jours. Home: 956 Brush Hill Rd Milton MA 02186 Office: Curry College Milton MA 02186

BOYLEN, DANIEL BERKLEY, architect; b. Pitts., Dec. 12, 1941; s. Sidney Daniel Thomas and Virginia Mae (Walker) Boylen; m. Mary Virginia Bond, May 1, 1965; children—Nina Danielle, Daniel Berkley. Project architect Harvey L. Gordon & Assos., Alexandria, Va., 1969-72; project architect McDonald & Williams, Washington, 1972-73; staff architect D.C. Govt. Office of Housing and Community Devel., 1973-75; quality control rep. Spradlin Constrn. Co., Wheaton, Md., 1975; prin. Daniel B. Boylen, Washington, 1975-78; partner Architects Consortium, Washington, 1978—; prin. Daniel B. Boylen, Richmond, Va., 1978—. Mem. AIA. Club: Ski-Mates. Home: 60 Underwood Pl NW Washington DC 20012 Office: 700 E Main St Richmond VA 23219

BOYLES, CHARLES WILLIAM, aerospace co. exec.; b. Flemington, W.Va., June 2, 1928; s. Charles Arthur and Gertrude May (Hoffmann) B.; B.E.E., Internat. Schs., 1954; B.S. summa cum laude, Rutgers U., 1964; M.B.A. magna cum laude, Fairleigh Dickinson U., 1968; m. Ann M. Galla, May 31, 1950; children—Patricia Ann, William Charles. Supr., TV Labs., Cleve., 1949-51; supervising service engr. Westinghouse Electric Corp., Balt., 1951-60; dir. ops. adminstrn. Lockheed Electronics Corp., Plainfield, N.J., 1960-71; dir. mktg. ITT, Paramus, N.J., 1971-73; pres. Decision Studies Group div. Sci. Mgmt. Corp., Washington, 1973-77; v.p., program dir. Lockheed Aircraft Internat., Jeddah, Saudi Arabia, 1977—. Served with USN, 1945-48. Mem. IEEE, Armed Forces Communications and Electronics Assn., Am. Def. Preparedness Assn., U.S. Space Pioneers, Am. Businessmen of Jeddah (exec. com.), Nat. Indsl. Security Assn. Home: 48 Queen Ann Ct Marlton NJ 08053 Office: PO Box 6308 Jeddah Saudi Arabia

BOYNTON, EDWIN FRANK, actuary; b. Mansfield, Mass., May 20, 1929; s. Charles Thomas and Mary Gertrude (Tucker) B.; A.B. magna cum laude, Brown U., 1952; m. Mary Cecelia Gadrow, Sept. 17, 1955; children—Nancy, David, Thomas, Carol, Robert. Actuarial asst. Conn. Gen. Life Ins. Co., Hartford, Conn., 1952; cons. actuary The Wyatt Co., Washington, 1956—; dir. The Wyatt Co. Chmn. bd. actuaries U.S. Civil Service Retirement System; actuarial cons. Commn. on R.R. retirement, 1972-74; mem. pension research council Wharton Sch. Com. chmn. Boy Scouts Am., 1969-75. Served to lt. Finance Corps, AUS, 1953-56. Fellow Soc. Actuaries, Conf. Actuaries in Pub. Practice; mem. Am. Acad. Actuaries (dir. 1972-74, v.p. 1975-76, pres. elect 1977, pres. 1978), U.S. C. of C. (com. on employee benefits 1967—). Clubs: Manor Country, Internat. (Washington). Home: 4135 Great Oak Rd Rockville MD 20853 Office: The Wyatt Co 1990 K St NW Washington DC 20006

BOZORTH, SQUIRE NEWLAND, lawyer; b. Portland, Oreg., Oct. 25, 1935; s. Squire Smith and Ethel Elizabeth (Newland) B.; B.S., U. Oreg., 1958; LL.B., N.Y. U., 1961; m. Louise Crosby Mathews, Aug. 9, 1967; children—Squire Mathews, Caroline Rutgers. Admitted to N.Y. bar, 1961; asso. firm Milbank, Tweed, Hadley & McCloy, N.Y.C., 1961-70, partner, 1970—; asso. counsel Rockefeller U.,

1973—. Bd. dirs., mem. exec. com., sec. Fedn. Protestant Welfare Agencies. Mem. Am., N.Y. State bar assns., Assn. Bar City N.Y. Episcopalian. Club: Down Town Assn. (N.Y.C.). Home: 38 Olmsted Rd Scarsdale NY 10583 Office: 1 Chase Manhattan Plaza New York City NY 10015

BOZZA, DOROTHEA MARIAN, lawyer; b. Newark; d. Frank B. and Adele (Bianco) Bozza; student Rutgers U., Newark Colls., 1940-44; LL.B., Rutgers U., 1947, J.D., 1965. Admitted to D.C. bar, 1948; stenographer, claim examiner, law research asst. Prudential Ins. Co. of Am., Newark, 1940-48, atty., 1949-59, asst. counsel, 1959-65, asst. gen. counsel, 1965—. Mem. AAUW, League Women Voters. Club: Zonta Internat. (pres. chpt. 1977-79). Office: Prudential Plaza Newark NJ 07101

BOZZA, RICHARD GEORGE, educator; b. N.Y.C., Nov. 17, 1949; s. Richard J. and Marian (Reed) B.; B.S. in Secondary Edn., Monmouth Coll., West Long Branch, N.J., 1971, M.S. in Edn., 1975; postgrad. in Sch. Adminstrn., Rutgers U.; 1 dau., Erika. Tchr. Spanish, Long Branch (N.J.) pub. schs., 1970-74, job placement coordinator, 1974—, also dir. ESEA Title VII and ESAA Title VII. Mem. Long Branch, Monmouth County, N.J. edn. assns., Assn. for Supervision and Curriculum Devel., Am. Assn. Sch. Adminstrs., Phi Delta Kappa. Club: Exchange. Office: 364 Indiana Ave Long Branch NJ 07740

BRACHFELD, JONAS, physician; b. Antwerp, Belgium, Dec. 1, 1924; s. Chaskiel and Rosa (Spira) B.; came to U.S., 1944, naturalized, 1953; B.S., Calif. Inst. Tech., 1947; M.D., U. Pa., 1952; m. Rosalind Roth, Apr. 5, 1956; children—Claude, Renee, Eric. Intern, fellow, resident various hosps., Phila.; co-founder Rancocas Valley Hosp., Willingboro, N.J., chmn. dept. internal medicine, chmn. bd. dirs., 1967-68; founder, pres. Brachfeld Med. Assos.; asso. clin. prof. medicine Temple U., 1975—. Mem. Moorestown (N.J.) Bd. Edn., 1968-69. Fellow A.C.P., Am. Coll. Cardiology, Am. Heart Assn. Jewish. Author articles on mgmt. of emergency room coronary patients. Home: 227 Nicholson Dr Moorestown NJ 08057 Office: Rancocas Valley Hosp Willingboro NJ 08046

BRACK, HAROLD ARTHUR, educator; b. East Moline, Ill., Oct. 8, 1923; s. Willis and Mary Christina (Petrie) B.; B.A., Augustana Coll., 1948; B.D., Garrett Bibl. Inst., 1951; M.A., Northwestern U., 1951, Ph.D., 1953; Th.D., Immaculate Conception Sem., 1976; m. Mary Lou Lundahl, Aug. 9, 1952; children—Barbara Anne, Susan Elizabeth, Janet Lee. Ordained to ministry United Methodist Ch., 1952; pastor Meth. Ch., Preemption, Ill., 1950-51; instr. Northwestern U., Chgo., 1951-52; mem. faculty Drew U., Madison, N.J., 1953—, prof. speech and homiletics, 1968—; vis. prof. homiletics Immaculate Conception Sem., Darlington, N.J., 1971—; adj. prof. San Francisco Sem., 1973-77; chmn. TV, radio and film com. No. N.J. ann. conf. United Meth. Ch., 1967-76. Served with AUS, 1943-46; PTO. Mem. Speech Communications Assn. Author: (with Kenneth G. Hance) Public Speaking and Discussion for Religious Leaders, 1961, Effective Oral Interpretation For Religious Leaders, 1964. Home: 57 Madison Ave Madison NJ 07940

BRACKBILL CLETUS, RALPH, elec. engr.; b. Lancaster, Pa., Apr. 8, 1919; s. Ralph McQuate and Sally Bertha (Mease) B.; B.S. in Elec. Engring., Pa. State U., 1941; m. Helen Dorothy Hart, Oct. 17, 1941; children—Carolyn Lee, Connie Elaine. With RCA Corp., 1945-71, standards engr., 1961-71; nuclear startup and test engr. GAI, Reading, Pa., 1971—. Served to 1st lt. C.E., U.S. Army, 1941-45. Mem. IEEE (sr.), Am. Legion. Republican. Lutheran. Home: 19 Sunrise Ave Lancaster PA 17601 Office: GAI PO Box 1498 Reading PA 19603

BRACKETT, ERNEST WALKER, lawyer; b. Mohawk, N.Y., Dec. 8, 1902; s. Jay and Jennie (Walker) B.; A.B., Cornell U., 1925; postgrad. govt. exec. course U. Chgo., 1958; m. Beatrice L. Paul, Apr. 24, 1926; 1 dau., Jaclin (Mrs. Richard Farrell). Admitted to N.Y. bar, 1928; mem. firm Griffith & Brackett, Utica, N.Y., 1928-42; with procurement div. Air Force Dept., Washington and Dayton, Ohio; 1946-59; dir. procurement and supply NASA, Washington, 1959-65, chmn. bd. contract appeals, 1965-74; pres. Nat. Conf. Bds. Contract Appeals, 1971-73; gen. counsel Don Sowle Assos., Inc., mgmt. cons., 1978—. Served with AAC, 1942-46. Mem. Am., Fed. bar assns., Acacia, Phi Alpha Delta. Clubs: Masons, Rotary, Nat. Aviation. Home: 2820 Northampton St NW Washington DC 20015

BRADBURY, BIANCA RYLEY, author; b. Mystic, Conn., Dec. 4, 1908; d. Thomas Wheeler and Blanche (Keigwin) R.; B.A., Conn. Coll. for Women, 1930; m. Harry Burdette, Aug. 14, 1930; children—William Wyatt, Michael Ryley. Mem. New Milford (Conn.) Bd. Edn., 1956-65; bd. trustees New Milford Pub. Library, 1966—. Mem. Authors League. Democrat. Author numerous books including The Three Keys, 1966; The Blue Year, 1966; To a Different Tune, 1967; Lucinda, 1968; Nancy and Her Johnnie-O, 1969; Red Sky at Night, 1969; The Loner, 1970; The New Penny, 1971; Those Traver Kids, 1973; Boy on the Run, 1974; In Her Father's Footsteps, 1976. Address: Mount Tom Rd New Milford CT 06776

BRADDOCK, PETER SAMUEL, elec. engr.; b. Paterson, N.J., Aug. 26, 1931; s. John C.T. and Henrietta T. (Stapert) B.; B.S.E.E., Newark Coll. Engring., 1970; m. Josephine Tiritilli, Nov. 12, 1955; children—Peter John, Paul Carmine. Test technician Bogue Electric Co., Paterson, 1953-57; lab. technician Nat. TV Tube Inc., Saddlebrook, N.J., 1957-58; sr. project engr. Regulators, Inc., Allendale, N.J., 1958-70; elec. engr. Fermont div. Dynamics Corp. Am., Bridgeport, Conn., 1970; chief engr. White Metal Mfg. Co., Hawthorne, N.J., 1970—. Served with U.S. Army, 1949-52. Mem. IEEE, Am. Soc. for Metals, Nat. Soc. Profl. Engrs. Home: 24 New Read St Pequannock NJ 07440 Office: 220 Goffle Rd Hawthorne NJ 07506

BRADFIELD, WALTER SAMUEL, mech., aero. engr.; b. Sheridan, Ind., Sept. 23, 1918; s. Walter Samuel and Margaret (Mitchell) B.; B.S. in Mech. Engring., Purdue U., 1941; M.S., Calif. Inst. Tech., 1945; Aero. Engr., U. Mich., 1953; Ph.D., U. Minn., 1957; m. Mimi Kirilova, Sept. 2, 1940; 1 son, Timothy Alan. Flight test engr. Allison div. GMC, Indpls., 1941-44; supr. aero. design, applied physics lab. Johns Hopkins U., 1945-47; co-supr. supersonic wind tunnel labs. U. Mich., Ann Arbor, 1947-49; lectr., project scientist U. Minn., Mpls., 1949-57; sr. staff scientist research lab. Convair, San Diego, 1957-61; prof. engring. State U. N.Y., Stony Brook, 1961—; pres. Hydrosail, Inc., 1972—. Mem. Inst. Aeros. and Astronautics, Am. Inst. Chem. Engrs. Contbr. articles to profl. jours. Home: Anchorage Rd Port Jefferson NY 11777 Office: Dept Mech Engring State U NY Stony Brook NY 11790

BRADFORD, CHARLES ALLEN, securities analyst; b. Flushing, N.Y., July 10, 1941; B.S., U. N.C., 1963; M.B.A., U. Pa., 1965; m. Eileen Carol Gottlieb, Dec. 27, 1964; children—Karen Denise, Stacey Lynn. Sr. security analyst Mut. Benefit Life Ins. Co., Newark, 1965-68, Goodbody & Co., N.Y.C., 1968-70; supervising analyst. R.W. Pressprich & Co., N.Y.C., 1971-72; v.p., Jas. H. Oliphant & Co. Inc., N.Y.C., 1974-75; v.p. Merrill Lynch, Pierce Fenner & Smith Inc., N.Y.C., 1975—; mem. steel experts panel Office of Tech. Assessment, U.S. Congress. Vice pres. Florham Park (N.J.) Republican Club, 1971-72. Mem. N.Y. Metals Mining Analysts Assn. (pres. 1975-76), N.Y. Soc. Security Analysts, Am. Inst. Mining Engrs., Non-ferrous Metals Analysts Assn., Steel Analysts Group (sec. 1976-77). Mem. all Am. research team Instnl. Investor mag., 1974-78. Office: 165 Broadway New York City NY 10000

BRADFORD, LELAND POWERS, orgn. devel. cons.; b. Chgo., July 12, 1905; s. Theron Draper and Ivy Blanche (Powers) B.; A.B., U. Ill., 1930, A.M., 1935, Ph.D., 1939; L.H.D. (hon.). Boston U., 1968, Lesley Coll., 1973; LL.D., U. Cin., 1976; m. Martha Irene DeMaeyer, Oct. 12, 1933; 1 son, David Lee. Dir. bur. visual aids U. Ill., 1935-36, instr., 1938-41; state dir. adult edn. WPA, Ill., 1941-43; chief tng. U.S. Immigration and Naturalization Services, 1943-44, FSA, 1944-45; dir. div. adult edn. service NEA, Washington 1945-62, exec. sec., dept. adult edn., 1945-50, dir. Nat. Tng. Labs., NEA, 1947-67; exec. dir. Nat. Inst. Applied Behavioral Sci., 1967-70; cons. orgn. devel., 1971—; mem. nat. com. on study grants in adult edn. Ford Found. Fund for Adult Edn., 1952-54; Fulbright adv. selection com., 1952-56; mem. Am. Mission Human Relations Tng. Team to Austria, 1954-55, Am. delegation Internat. Conf. on Human Relations in Industry, Rome, Italy, 1956; cons. European Productivity Agy., Paris, 1955; del. UN Conf. on Elimination of Prejudice, 1955; sec. Internat. Com. Adult Edn., World Confedn. Orgns. Teaching Profession: del. UNESCO World Conf. Adult Edn., Montreal, Can., 1960. Trustee Lesley Coll., First Distinguished fellow Nat. Tng. Labs. Fellow Am. Psychol. Assn.; mem. Soc. Psychol. Study Social Issues, NEA, Am. Sociol. Assn., Nat. Soc. Study Communication, Adult Edn. Assn. (exec. com. 1951-54, coordinator research and tng. 1953-56), N.Y. Acad. Sci., AAAS, Phi Delta Kappa. Clubs: Pinehurst, Country of N.C. Author: The History of the National Training Laboratories; Making Meetings Work; Group Development; editor: Adult Edn. Bull., 1942-50; co-editor: T Group Theory and Laboratory Method; Laboratory Method of Learning and Changing; contbr. articles to ednl. publs. Address: Box 247 Center Lovell ME 04016

BRADFORD, ROBERT ALLEN, stationary engr.; b. Orange, Tex., Aug. 2, 1947; s. Brady H. and Doris Gene (Thomas) B.; student pub. schs., Cambridge, Md.; m. Nina Susan Garrett, July 6, 1972; children—Robert Allen, Carol Ann. Div. mgr. Sears, Roebuck & Co., Cambridge, Md., 1965-68, 70-73; quality control engr. Rotork Inc., Cambridge, Md., 1973-74; chief engr. Graf-comm., Easton, Md., 1974-75; town engr. Town of Trappe (Md.), 1975-76; supt. wastewater treatment facility, Trappe, 1976—; stationary engr. Dorchester Gen. Hosp., Cambridge, Md., 1976—. Served with USN, 1968-70. Mem. Am. Soc. Hosp. Engring. Republican. Methodist. Home: 311 Maryland Ave Cambridge MD 21613 Office: 300 Byrn St Cambridge MD 21613

BRADFORD, ROBERT ERNEST, motion picture exec.; b. Berlin, May 25, 1927; s. Siegfried and Doris (Herzberg) B.; came to U.S., 1946, naturalized, 1953; student Marie Curie Coll., Paris, 1937; A.B., U. Geneva, 1945; m. Barbara Taylor, Dec. 24, 1963. Prodn. cons. Distbn. Corp. Am., N.Y.C., 1946-53; exec. v.p. Jesse L. Lasky Prodns., Beverly Hills, Calif., 1953—; exec. v.p., dir. Samuel Bronston Prodns., N.Y.C., 1955—; exec. v.p. Franco London Films Internat., Ltd., Montreal, Que., Can.; pres. Franco London Film, S.A., Paris, Franco London Music Ltd., London; head feature prodn., exec. producer Hal Roach Studios, Hollywood, Calif., 1959—; dir. Hy-Ford Prodns., Inc., Hy-Ford Europea, Rome, Jack London Prodns.; producer John Paul Jones, Warner Bros., 1958, The Scavengers, Hal Roach Studios, 1959, If You Remember Me, 1959-60, The Golden Touch, 1959-60, Simon Bolivar, 1965, To Die of Love, 1971, Sweet Deception, 1972, Impossible Object, 1973; fgn. corr. Overseas News Agy., 1951—; lectr. internat. affairs, interracial problems, 1950—; press relations cons. Senator Herbert H. Lehman, 1952-53; cons. dir. Nat. Found. for Good Govt., 1952; cons. Internat. Study Tour Alliance, 1951—. Pub. relations dir. one world award com. Am. Nobel Anniversary Com. Served with French Intelligence, 1940-45. Recipient citation for outstanding work and civic achievements Greater N.Y. Citizens Forum, 1952. Mem. Internat. Inst. Arts and Letters (dir.), Internat. Platform Assn. Home: 135 E 83d St New York City NY 10028 Office: 9200 Sunset Blvd PH3 Beverly Hills CA 90024

BRADISH, SANDRA MARIE, counselor; b. Charleroi, Pa., Oct. 27, 1950; d. Andrew and Elizabeth Bradish; B.S., U. Pitts., 1972, M.Ed., 1973. Rehab. counselor St. Francis Gen. Hosp., Pitts., 1974-77, Crawford Rehab. Services, Inc., Pitts., 1977—. Bd. dirs. Magic Carpet, orgn. for handicapped, Pitts., Info. and Vol. Services Allegheny County. Mem. Am. Personnel and Guidance Assn., Am., Nat. rehab. counseling assns., Nat. Rehab. Assn., Pitts. Claims Assn., Pitts. Jaycees (program mgr. 1978-79), Phi Delta Gamma. Club: Pitts. Ski. Home: 2311 Sherbrook St Pittsburgh PA 15217 Office: Room 255 2020 Ardmore Blvd Pittsburgh PA 15221

BRADISH, THOMAS JAMES, JR., mech. engr.; b. Greensburg, Pa., June 26, 1947; s. Thomas H. and Mary B.; B.A. in Math., St. Vincent Coll., 1968; B.M.E., Pa. State U., 1970; m. Linda L. Smith, Aug. 22, 1975. Systems engr. tests Penelec, Johnstown, Pa., 1971-73, div. engr. maintenance, 1973-76, supr. mobile maintenance, 1976-77, supt. maintenance planning, 1977—. Mem. ASME, Am. Welding Soc. Home: RD 2 Box 218 Ligonier PA 15658 Office: 1001 Broad St Johnstown PA 15907

BRADLEE, THOMAS FRANCIS, publisher; b. Buffalo, Nov. 18, 1946; s. Russell Lamont and Helen Barbara (Ruf) B.; grad. pub. schs.; m. Carol Elizabeth Ireland, Oct. 1, 1975; children—Christina, Russell Thomas. Asst. gen. mgr. Tri-State Pub. Co., Elkton, Md., 1970-74; gen. mgr. Bi-State Pub. Co., Seaford, Del., 1974-77, pub., 1977—. Bd. dirs. Nanticoke Meml. Hosp., Seaford. Served with USMCR, 1966-68. Mem. Greater Seaford C. of C. (dir. 1972-75, v.p. 1975-78), Md.-Del.-D.C. (dir. 1975—), Nat. (vice-chmn. futures com. 1977—, Del. chmn. 1976—) newspapers assns. Republican. Roman Catholic. Home: 121 S Conwell St Seaford DE 19973 Office: 616 Water St Seaford DE 19973

BRADLEY, ELEANOR REHILL, assn. exec.; b. White Plains, N.Y., June 25, 1919; d. Charles P. and Grace M. (Purdy) Rehill; B.A., U. Rochester, 1942; postgrad. N.Y. U., 1945-46, U. Buffalo, 19—; m. James F. Bradley, Feb. 11, 1950; children—Anna E., Kevin P. Sales engr. Johns Manville Corp., N.Y.C., 1943-47; personnel supr. women Niagara Falls (N.Y.) br. E. I. DuPont De Nemours & Co., Inc., 1947-50; with YWCA, various locations, 1958—, exec. dir., Lockport, N.Y., 1972—. Republican committeewoman in Dist. 26, Town of Cheektowaga (N.Y.), 1974-75. Roman Catholic. Home: 250 S Huxley Dr Cheektowaga NY 14225 Office: 32 Cottage St Lockport NY 14094

BRADLEY, MARK EDMUND, physician, naval officer; b. Balt., Nov. 29, 1936; s. John Edmund and Kathryn (Davis) S.; B.S., U. Notre Dame, 1958; M.D., U. Md., 1962; M.S., U. Pa., 1968; M.P.H. (fellow), Harvard U., 1971; 1 dau., Meghan. Intern, U. Va. Hosp., Charlottesville, 1962-63; commd. capt. U.S. Navy, 1976; med. officer U.S.S. Robert E. Lee and U.S.S. Stonewall Jackson, 1964-65; med. officer Submarine Escape Tng. Tank and Submarine Base, Pearl Harbor, Hawaii, 1965-66; med. officer Aquanaut U.S. Navy Sealab program, 1967-70; chmn. hyperbaric medicine and physiology dept. Naval Med. Research Inst., Bethesda, 1973—; v.p. Undersea Life Scis., Inc. Diplomate Am. Bd. Preventive Medicine. Fellow A.C.P., Am. Coll. Preventive Medicine, Aerospace Med. Assn.; mem. Am. Physiol. Soc., Undersea Med. Soc. Roman Catholic. Home: 32 Orchard Way S Rockville MD 20854 Office: Hyperbaric Medicine and Physiology Dept Naval Med Research Inst Bethesda MD 20014

BRADLEY, MURRAY LEE, librarian; b. Balt., July 20, 1941; s. Howard Lee and Isabel (Biggs) B.; B.S. in Social Sci., Loyola Coll., Balt., 1963; M.S. in L.S., Catholic U. Am., 1969. Reference and circulation librarian U.S. Naval Acad., Annapolis, Md., 1964-68, asst. acquisitions librarian, 1968-70, sci. and tech. librarian, 1970-72, acquisitions librarian, 1972-77; head readers service div. U.S. Naval War Coll. Library, Newport, R.I., 1977—. Mem. ALA, Spl. Libraries Assn., Am. Soc. Info. Sci. (sec. Chesapeake Bay chpt. 1973-74, program chmn. 1974-75, chmn. 1975-76), Beta Phi Mu. Republican. Roman Catholic. Clubs: Mountain Club Md., Catholic Alumni Club Am. (treas. Balt. chpt. 1975). Home: 6 Halidon Terr Newport RI 02840 Office: Hewitt Library US Naval War Coll Newport RI 02840

BRADLEY, NORMAN ROBERT, lawyer; b. Phila., May 24, 1917; s. William A. and Eliza (Gwinnutt) B.; A.B., U. Ala., 1939; J.D. (with honors), Dickinson S Law, 1942; m. Sharlee Merner Elsworth, June 24, 1978; children—Christine, Evelyn, Joan, Suzanne D. Elsworth. Admitted to Pa. bar, 1942; practiced in Phila., 1946—; partner firm Saul, Ewing, Remick & Saul, Phila., 1963—, head litigation dept., 1964—; lectr. trial practice Temple U., 1974—; mem. Commn. Jud. Selection, Retention and Evaluation; chmn. Com. Evaluation Fed. Judges; adv. bd. Acad. Advocacy. Mem. budget rev. com. United Fund Phila. and vicinity, 1965-70, central allocations com., 1968-70. Trustee Unitarian Soc. Germantown, 1965-68; dir. World Affairs Council, Phila., 1975—; mem. adv. bd. Phila. area council World Federalists U.S.A. Served to lt. USNR, 1942-46. Mem. Am., Pa., Phila. bar assns., Phila. Assn. Def. Counsel (v.p. 1978, pres. 1979), ACLU, Internat. House Phila., Phila. Art Alliance, Pa. Acad. Fine Arts, Phi Beta Kappa, Theta Chi. Clubs: Wissahickon Skating, Germantown Cricket, Main Line Ski, Delaware Valley Sail (Phila.). Democrat. Unitarian. Editorial bd. Dickinson Law Rev., 1941-42. Home: 752 St George's Rd Philadelphia PA 19119 Office: 3800 Centre Sq W Philadelphia PA 19102

BRADLEY, RAYMOND EDGAR, JR., anesthesiologist; b. New Vineyard, Maine, Aug. 10, 1932; s. Raymond Edgar and Josephine Anastasia (Jellison) B.; B.A., U. Mass., 1953; M.D., N.Y. Med. Coll., 1958; m. June Arlene Cronen, Oct. 4, 1958; children—June Ellen, Paul Joseph. Intern St. Vincent Hosp., Worcester, Mass., 1953-59, resident in anesthesiology, 1959-61; attending physician Griffin Hosp., Derby, Conn., 1961—, chief anesthesiologist, 1965—, asst. chief of staff, 1969-73, chief of staff, 1973—. Served with M.C. U.S. Army Res., 1968. Diplomate Am. Bd. Anesthesiology. Fellow Am. Coll. Anesthesiologists; mem. Conn., New Haven, med. socs., Am., Conn. socs. anesthesiology. Clubs: Woodbridge (dir. 1973), New Haven Racquet, Cross Court Tennis. Home: 20 Center View Rd Woodbridge CT 06525 Office: 130 Division St Derby CT 06418

BRADLEY, WILLIAM WARREN (BILL), U.S. Senator; b. Crystal City, Mo.; b. July 28, 1943; s. Warren and Susan Crowe (Rasom) B.; B.A., Princeton U., 1965; postgrad. (Rhodes scholar) Oxford (Eng.) U., 1965-67. Player, N.Y. Knickerbockers, NBA 1967-77; U.S. senator from N.J., 1979—. Recipient Sullivan award for outstanding U.S. amateur athlete, 1965; named Coll. Player of Year, AP, Basketball Writers, Helms, Nat. Assn. Basketball Coaches, UPI, 1965; named to Helms Hall of Fame, 1965; named to Eastern Conf. All-star team NBA, 1973. Mem. U.S. Olympic team, Tokyo, 1964 (gold medal), U.S. team World Univ. Games, Hungary, 1965. Democrat. Office: 315 Russell Senate Office Bldg Washington DC 20510*

BRADSHAW, JOSEPH GEORGE, assn. exec.; b. Trenton, N.J., Oct. 12, 1918; s. Thomas Rupert and Elizabeth Batchelder (White) B.; B.S.E.E., Princeton, 1940; m. Dorothy Carey, Mar. 28, 1942; children—Jane Bradshaw Jost, Laura Bradshaw Tyler. With Koppers Co., Inc., Pitts., 1940-58, dir. electronics computing, 1955-58; alumni sec., bus. mgr. Princeton (N.J.) U., 1958-68; v.p., treas. J.P. Cleaver Co. orgn. devel., Princeton, 1968-74, also dir.; pres. Internat. Marine Inst., Clinton, N.J., 1974—; lectr. Princeton U., 1964-68. Trustee, treas. Peddie Sch., Hightstown, N.J., 1964—. Mem. Am. Inst. Chem. Engrs., Assn. Computing Machinery, Internat. Oceanographic Found. Clubs: Nassau (Princeton); HPY (Pitts.). Home: RD 1 Box 129 Pittstown NJ 08867 Office: 181 Center St Clinton NJ 08809

BRADSHAW, LAWRENCE ALLEN, educator; b. Phila., Sept. 23, 1932; B.S. in Edn., Shippensburg (Pa.) State Coll., 1960, M.Ed., 1966; Coe Found. scholar Bucknell U., 1962-63; U.S. Office Edn. scholar U. Vt., 1968; Rockefeller fellow Ball State U., Muncie, Ind., 1973-74; postgrad. Am. U., Washington, 1976-78; m. Mary Ellen Osgood, Dec. 28, 1974. Adminstrv. positions U.S. Fed. Civil Service, 1951-57; tchr. social studies and geography Shippensburg Area Jr. High Sch., 1961-62; tchr. English and humanities Shippensburg Area Sr. High Sch., 1962-69; asst. prof. English, Shippensburg State Coll., 1969—, asst. dir. admissions, 1969-70, asst. dean admissions, 1970-72, dir. PREP Program for Disadvantaged Students, 1970-74, asst. to v.p. acad. affairs, 1972-73, acting asst. to pres., 1974-75, spl. asst. to pres., 1975—. Vestryman, St. Andrews Episcopal Ch., 1967-69, organist, 1962—; bd. dirs., radio tchr. Franklin County Sunday Sch. Assn., 1966—; first pres. Shippensburg chpt. Am. Field Service; bd. dirs. United Way of Chambersburg (Pa.), Served with U.S. Army, 1953-55. Named Outstanding Educator Am., 1974-75. Mem. Am. Guild Organists, Nat., Pa. edn. assns., Nat. Council Tchrs. English, Coll. English Assn., Am. Assn. Univ. Adminstrs., Am. Assn. Higher Edn., Phi Sigma Pi, Pi Nu Epsilon, Phi Delta Kappa. Clubs: Kiwanis (dir.), Cumberland Valley Torch (sec.). Home: Beth-Adoram Route 3 Box 446 Fayetteville PA 17222 Office: Office of Pres Shippensburg State Coll Shippensburg PA 17257

BRADSHAW, WILLIAM DANIEL, real estate co. exec.; b. Balt., May 24, 1933; s. William D. and Emily M. Bradshaw; B.A., Yale U., 1955; postgrad. Boston U.; divorced; children—Priscilla DeRosset, William Daniel. With R.M. Bradley & Co., Inc., comml. and indsl. real estate, Boston, 1955—, sr. v.p., 1970—. Chmn. real estate com. Mass. United Fund, 1971; treas. Wellesley chpt. Mass. Assn. Children with Learning Disabilities, 1969; mem. Wellesley Town Meeting, 1965-68.

Mem. Nat. Assn. Indsl. and Office Parks (pres. New Eng. chpt. 1977-79), Greater Boston Real Estate Bd. (asso.), Greater Boston C. of C. Clubs: Harvard, Yale (Boston). Home: 770 Boylston St Apt 17H Boston MA 02199 Office: 250 Bolyston St Boston MA 02116

BRADY, GENE PAUL, security analyst; b. nr. Wexford, Pa., July 8, 1927; s. John Arthur and Frances Augusta (Aven) B.; B.S., U.S. Naval Acad., 1950; M.B.A., U. Pa., 1958; m. Helena Marie Real, Feb. 1, 1958. Commd. ensign U.S. Navy, 1950, advanced through grades to lt., 1956; aviator, 1952-55, exec. officer mine sweeper U.S.S. Loyalty, 1956; security analyst Laird, Bissell and Meeds, N.Y.C., 1958-61, Orvis Brothers, N.Y.C., 1961-66, W.E. Hutton, N.Y.C., 1966-74, Reynolds Securities, 1975-77, Dean Witter Reynolds, 1978—. Mem. N.Y. Soc. Security Analysts. Republican. Roman Catholic. Author: Tripling Your Money in the Stock Market with Techno-Fundamental Strategies; A Master Plan for Winning in Wall Street. Home: 432 Scarborough Road Scarborough NY 10510 Office: 1 Battery Park Plaza New York City NY 10004

BRADY, H(ERBERT) WAYNE, polit. scientist; b. McConnellsburg, Pa., May 21, 1944; s. Oakley Herbert and Marie Ardella B.; B.A. in Social Sci. (Jesse S. Heiges scholar, Elks scholar), Shippensburg State Coll., 1966; M.A. (Univ. scholar), Lehigh U., 1969; M.A., Montclair State Coll., 1977; m. Jane Diehl Zepp, Feb. 27, 1966; children—Peter Wayne, Ethan Wayne. Sales service rep. Am. Can. Co., Chambersburg, Pa., 1966-68; instr. social scis. Middlesex County Coll., 1969-74, asst. prof. social scis., 1974-76, asso. prof. govt. and history, 1976—, fellow Robert A. Taft Inst. Govt., summer 1973; legis. aide to Assemblyman John Froude N.J. Gen. Assembly, 1974—. Auditor Waynesboro (Pa.) Borough, 1966-68; mem. Edison (N.J.) Cable-TV Adv. Com.; mem. Middlesex County Coll. Found.; trustee Upsala Coll.; coll. rep. to Woodbridge (N.J.) and Edison chambers commerce. Mem. Acad. Polit. Sci., Am. Acad. Polit. and Social Sci., Am., Northeastern, N.J. polit. sci. assns. Democrat. Lutheran. Author: (with Charles Foley) Citizens Opinions in Middlesex County: Choices for '76, 1974. Home: 7 Fayette St Edison NJ 08817 Office: Middlesex County Coll Edison NJ 08817

BRADY, JOHN JOSEPH, food products co. exec.; chem. engr.; b. Weymouth, Mass., Dec. 9, 1927; s. George Francis and Mary Agnes (Gallivan) B.; B.S. cum laude in Chem. Engring., Tufts U., 1952; m. Ann C. Dalesandro, Sept. 3, 1950; children—Christine Ann, Mary Ann, John Joseph. Research engr. Socony Mobile Oil Co., Paulsboro, N.J., 1952-53; process devel. engr. Raytheon Mfg. Co., Quincy, Mass., 1953-56; research mgr. Walter Baker div. Gen. Foods Corp., Boston, 1956-63, H.P. Hood & Sons, Inc., Boston, 1963-65; exec. v.p. Brady Enterprises, Inc., East Weymouth, Mass., 1965—; dir. South Shore Nat. Bank, Quincy, Mass. Trustee, South Shore Hosp., Weymouth, Mass. Served with AUS, 1946-48. Registered profl. engr., Mass. Mem. Am. Inst. Chem. Engrs., Inst. Food Technologists. Democrat. Roman Catholic. Clubs: South Shore Country, Cohasset Country. Home: 10 Heritage Ln E Weymouth MA 02189 Office: 167 Moore Rd E Weymouth MA 02189

BRADY, JOSEPH JOHN, assn. exec.; b. Ossining, N.Y., Sept. 23, 1926; s. William and Kathryn Mary (Bell) B.; B.S., N.Y. U., 1949; postgrad. John Jay Center, Coll. City N.Y., 1968-69; m. Barbara Jane Kenney, Mar. 31, 1951; 1 son, Joseph John. Asst. v.p. sales and pub. relations Nat. Indsl. Conf. Bd., N.Y.C., 1952-63; v.p., gen. mgr. Benziger Bros., Inc., N.Y.C., 1963-67; pres. Hosp. Bur., Inc., Pleasantville, N.Y., 1967-77; exec. v.p. Assn. Cons. Mgmt. Engrs., Inc., N.Y.C., 1977—; mem. Westchester bd. Chem. Bank, 1971-77; speaker Am. Hosp. Assn. Insts., 1970-77. Chmn. (commr.) Police Bd., Westchester County Pkwy. Police, 1967-74; mem. Westchester Crime Control Planning Bd., 1970-74; mem. exec. bd. Washington Irving council Boy Scouts Am., 1969-74; mem. devel. bd. Westchester Med. Center, 1973-74; mem. FBLA adv. bd. N.Y. Dept. Edn., 1970-77. Served with USAAF, 1944-45; as lt. USAF, 1951-52. Mem. Alpha Delta Sigma. Republican. Roman Catholic (pres. parish council 1971-73). Clubs: Seaview Country (Absecon, N.J.); N.Y. Yacht. Home: 32 Browning Dr Ossining NY 10562 Office: 230 Park Ave New York City NY 10017

BRADY BURKS, ADELAIDE, pub. relations agy. exec.; b. N.Y.C., June 27, 1926; d. Earl Victor and Audrey (Calvert) Burks; B.S., Boston U., 1946; m. James Francis Brady, Jr., June 22, 1946 (div. 1953); 1 son, James Francis. Exec. v.p. Media Enterprises, 1952-55; dir. group relations Save the Children Fedn., N.Y.C., 1955-59; dir. pub. affairs div. Girl Scouts U.S.A., N.Y.C., 1959-69; pres. Communication Internat., Inc., Washington, 1969-73, Burks Brady Communications, N.Y.C., 1972—, Angel Shopper Catalog Inc., Pleasant Valley, N.Y., 1976—; exec. v.p. Arts in the Parks Inc., Washington, 1971—. Mem. Nat. Women's Republican Club, 1968—; bd. dirs. Lenox Hill Hosp., N.Y.C.; past bd. dirs. Achievement Rewards for Coll. Scientists Found. Recipient Silver Reel award for film The Children of Now, Save the Children Fedn.; decorated Order St. John of Jerusalem (Eng.), 1974. Mem. Nat. Assn. Women Bus. Owners, Pub. Relations Soc. Am., AAUW, NEA, Am. Women in Radio and TV, Nat. Ednl. Broadcasters Assn., Women Execs. in Pub. Relations, N.Y. Press Women (v.p.), Nat. Fedn. Press Women (state pres.). Episcopalian. Club: Capitol Hill (Washington). Home: 785 Park Ave New York City NY 10021 Office: 575 Madison Ave New York City NY 10022 also Main St Pleasant Valley NY 12569

BRAGAGNOLO, JULIO ALFREDO, physicist; b. Buenos Aires, Argentina, Oct. 6, 1941; s. Efrain Domingo and Maria Elvira (Bustillo) B.; came to U.S., 1976; Licenciado en Fisica, Universidad Nacional de Buenos Aires, 1965; Ph.D., U. Del., 1973; m. Elsa Beatriz Iturbe, Dec. 15, 1965; 1 dau., Celina Maria. Instr., U. Buenos Aires, 1965-66; post-doctoral fellow Inst. of Energy Conversion, U. Del., 1973; research asso. Microelectronics Lab., Inst. for Sci. and Technol. Research of the Armed Forces, Buenos Aires, 1974-76; research asso. Inst. Energy Conversion, U. Del., Newark, 1976—. Mem. Consejo Nacional de Investigaciones Cientificas Y Tecnicas, Am. Vacuum Soc. Roman Catholic. Contbr. articles in field of solid state physics and tech., solar energy to profl. jours. Home: 490 Stamford Dr Newark DE 19711 Office: 1 Pike Creek Center Wilmington DE 19808

BRAGDON, DAVID HUGH, ednl. adminstr.; b. Durham, N.C., Oct. 18, 1939; s. Ralph Mayne and Janet Elisabeth (Seville) B.; student (W.C. Teagle scholar), Mass. Inst. Tech., 1958-61; B.A., U. Del., 1962; M.Ed., Tufts U., 1968; m. Jill Virginia Morgan, Aug. 24, 1967; children—Gwyneth Moss, Jeremy Seville. Coordinator Well High Sch., Peterborough, N.H., 1970-72; dir. Van Sch., Hancock, N.H., 1972-77; chmn. dept. math. and dir. computation center Brunswick Sch., 1977—; mem. Nonpub. Sch. Study Com., 1972—. Chmn. Brunswick Sch. Bicentennial Com., 1975-76; Address: 100 Maher Ave Greenwich CT 06830

BRAGG, JOHN KENDAL, chemist; b. Washington, Nov. 12, 1919; s. Kendal Benjamin and Kathleen (Bowes) B.; B.S., Harvard, 1941, Ph.D., 1948; m. Mary Fulton Roberts, Sept. 25, 1943; children—Janet Bragg Campbell, John Kendal, Kathleen Bragg Lindquist, Arthur Hampton. Asst. prof. chemistry Cornell U., Ithaca, N.Y., 1948-50; research asso. Gen. Electric Research and Devel. Center, Schenectady, 1950-53, project analyst, 1957-63, mgr. research and devel. cons., 1964-70; pres. Ops. Research Inc., Silver Spring, Md., 1953-57; asst. v.p., dir. research and devel. Singer Co., N.Y.C., 1970-77; cons. scientist, 1978—; adj. prof. Siena Coll., 1950-51; rep. Indsl. Research Inst., 1970—; trustee Textile Research Inst., 1972—; mem. indsl. panel sci. and tech. NSF, 1974—; mem. industry com. Am. Inst. Physics, 1976; mem. at large evaluation panel NRC-Nat. Bur. Standards, 1976—; cons. Nat. Bur. Standards, 1977—. Served to lt. comdr. Submarine Corps USNR, 1941-46. Home: 100 W 57th St New York City NY 10019

BRAGG, JOSEPH LEE, journalist; b. Jackson, N.C., July 6, 1937; s. John and Addie B.; B.A., City U. N.Y., 1976; student Georgetown U. Sch. Fgn. Service; m. Barbara Brandom, July 6, 1968; 1 dau., Barbara Jonetta. News reporter Sta. WHN, Storer Radio, Inc., N.Y.C., 1968—, city hall bur. chief, 1975—; newscaster Mut. Black Network, 1971. Bd. dirs. Nat. Arts Consortium, N.Y.C. Served in U.S. Army. Recipient 1st pl. Spot News award Uniform Firefighters Assn. Mem. Inner Circle (pres.), N.Y. Press Club (past pres.), Black Citizens for Fair Media. Club: Masons (32 deg.). Home: 95 W 95 St New York City NY 10025 Office: 400 Park Ave New York City NY 10022*

BRAGINSKY, BENJAMIN MARTIN, psychologist; b. Bklyn., June 27, 1934; s. Herman and Anna (Flaumenbaum) B.; B.B.A., Coll. City N.Y., 1958; M.A., New Sch. Social Research, 1960; Ph.D., Columbia U., 1965; children—Claudia Lynn, Craig Hal. Research social psychologist Conn. Valley Hosp., Middletown, 1966-67; research asso. Yale U., New Haven, 1967-68; asst. prof. psychology Wesleyan U., Middletown, 1968-70, asso. prof., 1970—; cons. in field; with Shield Inst. of N.Y. Served with USNR, 1953-55. Mem. Am. Psychol. Assn., Sigma Xi. Contbr. to profl. jours. Home: 640 Mix Ave Hamden CT 06514 Office: Dept Psychology Wesleyan Univ Middletown CT 06457

BRAHA, THOMAS I., bus. exec.; b. Austin, Tex., Sept. 3, 1947; s. Jacob and Valentine (Capone) B.; B.S.M.E., U. Tex., 1969; M.B.A., Temple U., 1971; postgrad. N.Y. U., 1971-73; m. Nancy Elizabeth Rowe, Mar. 31, 1973; children—Nancy Elizabeth, Jeanne Valentine. Engr., Davis Electronics, Inc., Austin, 1967, Whirlpool Corp., Evansville, Ind., 1968; project engr. ITE Imperial Corp., Phila., 1969-71; sr. supply analyst Mobil Oil Corp., N.Y.C., 1971-74; pres. Western Hemisphere Bulk Oil (U.S.A.), Inc., N.Y.C., 1974-75; pres., chief exec. officer Braha Co., N.Y.C., 1975—; dir. Braha Oil, Inc., Braha Oil, Ltd., Braha Oil B.V., Braha Estates, Inc., Braha Farms, Western Paper, Inc., Braha Profit and Pension Trusts. Mem. Am. Mgmt. Assn., ASME, Am. Petroleum Inst. Office: 336 E 50th St New York City NY 10022

BRAIDWOOD, CLINTON ALEXANDER, chem. co. exec.; b. Snover, Mich., Nov. 14, 1914; s. Irving Alexander and Blanche (Tyrrell) B.; B.S., Mich. State U., 1940, postgrad., 1941-42; postgrad. Rensselaer Poly. Inst., 1964; m. Helene Guillaume, Jan. 23, 1942; children—John, Anne, Susan. Mech. goods devel. U.S. Rubber Co., Detroit, 1940-42; asst. dir. research Reichhold Chems. Inc., Detroit, 1942-49; v.p. research and mfg. Schenectady Chems. Inc. (N.Y.), 1949-71, exec. v.p., 1971-73, pres., 1973—. Pres., Schenectady County Community Coll. Found., 1977—; trustee Schenectady Savs. Bank, Blue Shield Schenectady; bd. dirs. Sunnyview Hosp. Mem. AAAS, Am. Chem. Soc., Am. Inst. Chem. Engrs., Am. Mgmt. Assn. Fellow Am. Inst. Chemists. Mem. Niskayuna Reformed Ch. Clubs: Mohawk Golf, Mohawk. Patentee in field. Home: 2319 Algonquin Rd Schenectady NY 12309 Office: PO Box 1046 Schenectady NY 12301

BRAIOTTA, LOUIS, JR., accounting educator; b. Tucson, Oct. 2, 1943; s. Louis and Frances (Aloia) B.; B.B.A., Pace U., 1969; M.B.A., Iona Grad. Sch. Bus., 1975; C.P.A., State U. N.Y., 1972; m. Virginia A. Hogan, Apr. 10, 1976; 1 son, Timmy. Asst. chief accountant Empire Brushes, Inc., Port Chester, N.Y., 1963-66; in-charge accountant Ernst & Ernst, White Plains, N.Y., 1969-70; sr. internal auditor GAF Corp., N.Y.C., 1970-72; instr. accounting Westchester Bus. Inst., White Plains, 1972-73, Orange County Community Coll., Middletown, N.Y., 1973-76; asst. prof. adj. Pace U. Grad. Sch. Bus., Pleasantville, N.Y., spring 1976; asst. prof. accounting N. Adams (Mass.) State Coll., 1976-78; asso. prof. accounting Alfred (N.Y.) U. Sch. Bus., 1978—; cons. pub. accounting firms. C.P.A., N.Y.; Dyson Found. scholar, 1966-67. Mem. No. Berkshire C. of C. (treas. 1977-78, mem. exec. com. 1977-78), No. Berkshire Indsl. Mgmt. Club (seminar coordinator 1977-78). Contbr. articles to profl. jours. Home: 18 Meadowbrook Ct Wellsville NY 14895 Office: Alfred U Alfred NY 14802

BRAKE, EDWARD THOMAS, ednl. adminstr.; b. Springfield, Mo., June 16, 1942; s. Elbridge Thomas and Geraldine Frances (Gallagher) B.; B.S. in Edn., diploma in voice S.W. Mo. State U., 1964; M.S. in Edn., So. Ill. U., 1966. Dean students, instr. psychology, dir. fin. aid Bethany Coll., Lindsborg, Kans., 1966-70; dir. fin. aid Trenton (N.J.) State Coll., 1970-76; dir. admissions Phila. Coll. Performing Arts, 1976—. Mem. Singing City Chorale, Phila., 1972-77; mem., dir. pub. relations All-Phila. Boy Choir and Men's Chorale, 1973—; judge Miss Phila. Pageant, 1977. Named Outstanding Young Man of Yr., U.S. Jaycees, 1977; recipient Service award Trenton State Coll., 1977. Mem. Nat. Assn. Student Personnel Adminstrs., Am. Personnel and Guidance Assn., Soc. of Notaries, Nat., N.J. (sec.) assns. student fin. aid adminstrs., Sigma Phi Epsilon, Kappa Delta Pi, Phi Mu Alpha Sinfonia. Home: 1406 Spruce St Philadelphia PA 19102 Office: Phila Coll Performing Arts 250 S Broad St Philadelphia PA 19102

BRAKELEY, GEORGE ARCHIBALD, JR., fundraising counsel; b. Washington, Apr. 18, 1916; s. George Archibald and Lillian (Fay) B.; B.A., U. Pa., 1938; m. Roxana Byerly, Sept. 7, 1946; children—George Archibald, Deborah Fay Brakeley Buri, Joan Keller, Linda Smith Brakeley Terry. Vice pres., dir. John Price Jones Co., Inc., N.Y.C., fund-raising counsel, 1938-50; v.p. Jones & Brakeley, Inc., advt. and indsl. publicity, 1948-53; pres., treas. John Price Jones Co. (Can.) Ltd., Montreal, 1950-53, became G. A. Brakeley & Co., Ltd., 1954, chmn., 1954-61; chmn. G. A. Brakeley & Co., Inc., San Francisco, 1956-76, chmn., treas., 1958, dir., 1976—, became Brakeley, John Price Jones Inc., 1975. Served to capt. C.E., AUS, World War II. Mem. Am. Assn. Fund-Raising Counsel, Atlantic Salmon Assn., Zeta Psi. Episcopalian. Clubs: Univ. (N.Y.C., Chgo., Washington); Montreal Racket, Wee Burn Country (Darien, Conn.); Sky, Anglers (N.Y.C.); Racquet (Phila.); Mill Reef (Antigua); Flyfishers (London). Home: 1 Pilgrim Rd Darien CT 06820 Office: 6 E 43d St New York City NY 10017

BRAKL, HEINZ JOSEPH, research co. exec.; b. Vienna, Austria, July 9, 1932; s. Leopold and Gisela (Krall) B.; came to U.S., 1952, naturalized, 1954; B.S., Columbia, 1958; M.S. in Geophysics, N.Y. U., 1960; m. Mary Jane Hill, Jan. 27, 1968; 1 dau., Vicki Lee. Marine geologist Hudson Labs., Columbia U., Dobbs Ferry, N.Y., 1959-69; dir., sec. treas., geologist, geophysicist Ocean & Atmospheric Sci. Inc., Dobbs Ferry, 1970—; geophysicist Geotechnics & Resources Co., White Plains, N.Y., 1961-62; sec.-treas. 56 Locust Hill Corp., Yonkers, N.Y., 1966-71; pres. Wylan Corp., Dobbs Ferry, 1968-72; sec. treas., dir. Information Flow Inc., Dobbs Ferry, 1971-74. Served with AUS, 1953-55. Mem. Soc. Exploration Geophysicists, European Assn. Exploration Geophysicists. Office: 145 Palisades St Dobbs Ferry NY 10522

BRALY, EARL BURK, pub. relations counselor; b. Eastland, Tex., Feb. 5, 1919; s. Robert Burk and Maud (Gray) B.; B.A., Tex. Tech. Coll., 1939, M.A., 1946; Ph.D., U. Tex., Austin, 1955. Mem. staff pub. relations dept. Southwestern Bell Telephone Co., Dallas and St. Louis, 1948-51; account exec. Weldon-Hart, John Van Cronkhite Assos., Austin, 1952-53; pres. sec., exec. asst. to gov. Tex., 1953-54; dir. student publs., lectr. journalism, U. Tex., Austin, 1954-56; asst. dir. Tex. Legis. Council, 1956-60; research info. coordinator Human Resources Research Office, George Washington U., Washington, also lectr. English, 1960-62; mgr. info. services Systems Tech. Center, Philco-Ford Corp., Arlington, Va., 1962-66; prof. English, asst. to pres. Tex. Tech. Coll., Lubbock, 1966-68; ind. pub. relations cons, Washington, 1971—. Served with AUS, 1941-46, 51-52, 68-71. Decorated Army Commendation medal. Mem. Pub. Relations Soc. Am., Tex. Pub. Relations Assn., English Speaking Union, Sigma Delta Chi. Clubs: Arts, Nat. Press (Washington). Home: 53 Lake Shore Dr Hampton VA 23666 Office: Nat Press Bldg 14th and F Sts NW Washington DC 20045

BRAM, LEONARD, pediatrician; b. Bklyn., Dec. 11, 1935; s. Irving and Ruth (Gluckson) B.; A.B., Columbia U., 1956; M.D., State U. N.Y., 1960; m. Carolyn Helene Honig, Nov. 19, 1961; children—Benjamin, Jonathan, Elizabeth. Intern, Jewish Hosp., Bklyn., 1960-61, resident, 1961-63; practice medicine, specializing in pediatrics, pres. Merrimack Valley Pediatric Assocs., Inc., Billerica, Mass., 1965—; active staff Children's Hosp. Med. Center, Boston, New Eng. Med. Center, Boston, St. John's and St. Joseph's Hosp., Lowell, Mass. Served with USPHS, 1963-65. Diplomate Am. Bd. Pediatrics. Fellow Am. Acad. Pediatrics; mem. Mass. Med. Soc., New Eng., Merrimack Valley pediatric socs. Office: 221 Boston Rd Billerica MA 01862

BRAM, STEPHEN BENNETT, elec. engr.; b. Bklyn., Dec. 9, 1942; s. Vincent and Helen (Shattls) B.; B.S.E.E., Mass. Inst. Tech., 1963; M.B.A., N.Y. U., 1966, postgrad., 1966—; m. Constance Lieberman, Mar. 21, 1964; children—Jeffrey, Neal. With Consol. Edison Co. N.Y., Inc., N.Y.C., 1963—, chief generation planning engr., 1973—, mgr. system ops., 1977—, asst. v.p., 1978—; adj. asst. prof. Pace U. Grad. Sch. Bus. Adminstrn., N.Y.C., 1967—; chmn. N.Y. Power Pool Generation Planning Adv. Subcom., 1973-77, chmn. task force, 1977—. Mem. IEEE. Home: 9 Irene Ct Edison NJ 08817 Office: 128 West End Ave New York City NY 10023

BRAME, EDWARD GRANT, JR., spectroscopist; b. Shiloh, N.J., Mar. 20, 1927; s. Edward Grant and Susan Lilian (Musser) B.; B.S., Dickinson Coll., 1948; M.A., Columbia, 1950; Ph.D., U. Wis., 1957; m. Grace Adolphsen, Aug. 10, 1957. Chemist, Corn Products Refining Co., Argo, Ill., 1950-53; research chemist plastics dept. E.I. duPont de Nemours & Co., Inc., Wilmington, Del., 1957-64, spectroscopist, elastomer chems. dept., 1964—. Pres. Wycliffe Civic Assn., 1969-70. Served with USNR, 1945-46. Mem. Am. Chem. Soc., Soc. for Applied Spectroscopy (eastern analytical symposium 1964-72), Fedn. Analytical Chemistry and Spectroscopy Socs., N.Y. Acad. Scis., Sigma Xi, Phi Lambda Upsilon. Republican. Lutheran. Editor Applied Spectroscopy Revs., 1967—; editor-in-chief Practical Spectroscopy, 1976—. Home: 13 North Cliffe Dr Wilmington DE 19809 Office: Du Pont Co Experimental Station Wilmington DE 19898

BRAMFITT, BRUCE LIVINGSTON, research metallurgist; b. Troy, N.Y., Feb. 4, 1938; s. Thomas and Ruth (Livingston) B.; B.S., U. Mo.-Rolla, 1960, M.S., 1962, Ph.D., 1966; m. Joan Flora Sunukjian, June 30, 1963; children—Christopher Livingston, David Livingston. Metall. trainee Allegheny Ludlum Steel Corp., Watervliet, N.Y., 1957; metallurgist Watervliet Arsenal, summers 1959-64; research engr. Bethlehem Steel Corp. (Pa.), 1966—; lectr. metallurgy U. Mo.-Rolla, 1960-66; chmn. iron and steel com. Edn.-Engring.-Industry 1975-76. Wheelabrator fellow, 1963-64, Texaco fellow, 1964-65; Foundry Ednl. Found. scholar, 1959-60; recipient Vilella award ASTM, 1974; C.D. Moore award Iron and Steel Soc., 1977. Mem. Am. Soc. Metals (exec. com. Lehigh Valley chpt. 1975-78), Assn. Iron and Steel Engrs., Am. Inst. Mining, Metall. and Petroleum Engrs., Instn. Metallurgists (London), Sigma Xi, Alpha Sigma Mu, Sigma Gamma Epsilon, Kappa Sigma. Contbg. author, contbr. articles to profl. publs.; patentee in field. Home: 16 Pleasant Dr RD 7 Bethlehem PA 18015 Office: Homer Research Labs Bethlehem Steel Corp Bethlehem PA 18016

BRAMOWITZ, ALAN DAVID, cardiologist; b. Chgo., June 29, 1942; s. Harry and Sonya (Tureck) B.; B.S., U. Ill., 1964, M.D., 1968; m. Marsha Weiss, Nov. 4, 1972; 1 dau., Emily Alison. Intern, Michael Reese Hosp., Chgo., 1968-69, resident internal medicine, 1969-71, chief resident, 1971-72; fellow in cardiology U. Calif. at Los Angeles Med. Center, 1972-74; individual practice medicine, specializing in cardiology, Pitts., 1976—; clin. instr. medicine U. Pitts., 1976—. Served as lt. comdr., M.C., USNR, 1974-76. Diplomate Am. Bd. Internal Medicine, Am. Bd. Cardiovascular Diseases. Fellow Am. Coll. Cardiology; mem. AMA, Am. Heart Assn., Council Clin. Cardiology, Pitts. Press Club. Jewish. Home: 708 Pinetree Rd Pittsburgh PA 15243 Office: South Hills Med Bldg Jefferson Center Coal Valley Rd PO Box 18137 Pittsburgh PA 15236 also Aiken Profl Bldg 532 S Aiken Ave Pittsburgh PA 15232

BRAMWELL, FITZGERALD BURTON, chemist, educator; b. Bklyn., May 16, 1945; s. Fitzgerald and Lula (Burton) B.; B.A. in Chemistry, Columbia U., 1966; M.S. in Chemistry, U. Mich., 1967, Ph.D. in Chemistry (Phillips Petroleum fellow), 1970; m. Charlott Burns, Aug. 12, 1973; 1 son, Fitzgerald Timothy. Research chemist ESSO Research & Engring. Co., Linden, N.J., 1970-71; asst. prof. dept. chemistry Bklyn. Coll., 1971-75, asso. prof., 1975—; cons. Bell Labs., Murray Hill, N.J., 1974—; guest speaker in seminars at various univs., 1974—; judge 35th Sci. Fair, Am. Inst. of N.Y.C., 1973. Recipient NSF summer award, 1968-69, faculty devel. award, 1977-78. Mem. Am. Chem. Soc., Am. Phys. Soc., N.Y. Acad. Scis., Sigma Xi, Phi Lambda Upsilon (pres. Delta chpt. 1969-70). Author: (with others) General Chemistry 1 Laboratory Manual, 1975, General Chemistry 2 Laboratory Manual, 1975; Investigations in General Chemistry, 1977; contbr. articles and book revs. to profl. publs. Office: Dept of Chemistry Brooklyn College Brooklyn NY

BRANCH, EDNA RAPHAEL BERNADETTE, economist; b. Washington, Sept. 19, 1946; d. Wadsworth Schuyler and Raphael Christine (Taylor) B.; A.B., Howard U., 1969; postgrad. Dept. Agr. Grad. Sch., 1973, 75, 76; U. So. Calif., fall 1977, summer 1978. Research asst. Inst. Def. Analysis, Arlington, Va., 1969-72; survey statistician Bur. Census, Suitland, Md., 1972-73; economist Bur. Labor Statistics, Washington, 1973—. Asst. coordinator for N.C., liaison Presdl. Campaign for Congresswoman Shirley Chisholm, 1972; active Penn Naylor Civic Assn., 1976—; dep. chief trustee Naylor Dupont Community Assembly, 1976. Mem. Am. Statis. Assn., Am. Econ. Assn., Am. Soc. Pub. Adminstrs. Democrat. Roman Catholic.

BRANCH, LAURENCE GEORGE, psychologist; b. Cleve., Oct. 31, 1944; s. John Howard and Mercedes (Brachle) B.; B.A., Marquette U., 1967; M.A. Loyola U., Chgo., 1969, Ph.D., 1971; m. Patricia Mary Skalski, June 24, 1967; children—Kathryn Helen, Carolyn Mercedes, Daniel Laurence. Research psychologist Army Labs., Natick, Mass., 1970-73; program dir. Center for Survey Research U. Mass. at Boston,

Hassel Lansdale Lloyd, May 18, 1974; children—Jenny, Arnold; 1 stepson, Timothy Mayhew. Intern, Lenox Hill Hosp., N.Y.C., 1961-62; resident in psychiatry Bellevue Hosp., N.Y.C., 1962-63, St. Luke's Hosp., N.Y.C., 1963-65; practice medicine specializing in psychiatry, Pleasant Valley, N.Y., 1967—; asst. dir. Dutchess County (N.Y.) Mental Health Clinic, 1967-68; courtesy staff Sharon (Conn.), Hosp., 1967—; attending staff Craig House Hosp., Beacon, N.Y., 1977—; cons. psychiatrist Bennett Coll., Millbrook, N.Y., 1967-77, Greer Children's Services, Millbrook, 1968-77. Mem. vestry Grace Episcopal Ch. Millbrook, 1974-77. Served to capt. USAF, 1965-67. Diplomate Am. Bd. Psychiatry and Neurology. Fellow Am. Psychiat. Assn. (sec. Mid-Hudson Dist. br. 1974-76, del. to regional council 1976-77, pres. 1977—); mem. Dutchess County, N.Y. State med. socs. Republican. Clubs: Millbrook Hunt, Millbrook Golf & Tennis. Contbr. articles to profl. jours. Home: Deep Hollow Farm Millbrook NY 12545 Office: Main St Pleasant Valley NY 12569

BUDD, HARRIET, therapist, educator, adminstr; b. Brookline, Mass., June 9, 1953; d. Louis and Muriel (Goff) Budd; A.A., U. Hartford, 1974; B.A. in Psychology and sociology magna cum laude, U. Mass., 1976; M.S. in Counselor Edn., M.Ed. magna cum laude (fellow), Suffolk U., 1977. Dir. orientation U. Mass., Boston, 1974-76; supr. Schneider Coll. Center, Wellesley (Mass.) Coll., 1977—; instr. psychology, mental health counselor Quincy (Mass.) Jr. Coll., 1977—; instr. behavioral scis. N. Shore Community Coll., Beverly, Mass., 1978—; cons. career counseling and psychol. testing Beacon Counseling Inc., Brookline, Mass., 1977—. Mem. Am. Coll. Personnel Assn., Am. Personnel and Guidance Assn., Am. Mental Health Counselors Assn., Am. Counselors and Suprs. Assn., Alpha Kappa Delta. Home: 45 Salisbury Rd Newton MA 02158

BUDD, HERBERT FRANKLIN, physicist; b. N.Y.C., Mar. 17, 1937; s. Morris and Lillian (Epstein) B.; B.S., Mass. Inst. Tech., 1959, M.S., 1959; D.Sc., Ecole Normale Superieure, Paris, 1963; m. Guislaine Matte, June 19, 1971; children—Jeffrey, Laurent, Valerie. Research asst. Ecole Normale Superieure, Paris, 1959-63, research master, 1967-73; group leader Xerox Corp. Research Lab, Webster, N.Y., 1963-67; dir. Centre National de la Recherche Scientifique-USA, N.Y.C., 1973—; tchr. U. Rochester, U. Paris, Internat. Centre Theoretical Physics, Trieste; cons. UN Sci. and Tech. Office, Xerox Corp., Compagnie Generale d'Electricité, France, IBM Corp. Mem. Am. Phys. Soc., Société Française de Physique, Assn. Internationale des Docteurs es-Sciences, Ingenieurs Civils de France, Sigma Xi, Eta Kappa Nu. Contbr. articles to profl. jours. Home: 500 E 77th St New York City NY 10021 Office: 972 Fifth Ave New York City NY 10021

BUDD, REGINALD (REX) MASTEN, advt. cons.; b. Bklyn., June 20, 1902; s. William Henry and Jane O. (Witbeck) B.; B.S., U. Pa., 1924; m. E. Elizabeth Charlton, Oct. 17, 1931; children—Richard M., John S., Peter C., Thomas W. With Campbell Soup Co., Camden, N.J., 1924-67, beginning as asst. advt. mgr., successively advt. mgr., 1946-50, gen. advt. mgr. U.S. and Can., 1950-53, v.p. advt. Campbell Soup Co. Ltd. (Can.), 1953, dir. advt. for U.S., 1954-67, v.p. Campbell Soup Co., Ltd., 1962-67, also dir., v.p. advt. U.S., 1966-67, ret.; self employed advt. and mktg. cons., 1967—; cons. Lewis and Gilman, Phila. dir. Beck Engraving Co. Former coordinator U.S. Treasury Savs. Bonds Campaign. Recipient Hess-Daubman Merchandising award U. Pa., 1950; U.S. Treasury award, 1956. Mem. Alpha Sigma Phi. Clubs: Huntington Valley (Pa.) Country; Seaview Country; Buck Hill Country; Union League (Phila.). Home: Buck Hill Falls PA 19436 Office: Lewis and Gilman 1700 Market St Philadelphia PA 19103

BUDD, RICHARD WADE, communications scientist, educator; b. Henderson, Md., Aug. 24, 1934; s. Bryan William and Dorothea Marie (Fouvy) B.; B.A., Bowling Green U., 1956; M.A., U. Iowa, 1962, Ph.D., 1964; m. Beverly Ann Knight, Aug. 28, 1955; children—Kimberly, Richard Wade, Janna. Reporter, staff writer Dayton (Ohio) Daily News, 1956-57; research asso., instr., asst. prof., dir. inst. communication studies U. Iowa, Iowa City, 1960-71; prof., distinguished prof., chmn. dept. human communication Rutgers U., New Brunswick, N.J., 1971—; chmn. bd. Newstatements Communication Cons.'s, New Brunswick, 1973—; cons. in field. Mem. Community Arts Council East Brunswick (N.J.), 1973—; exec. council East Brunswick Youth Baseball Program, 1974; active Boy Scouts Am. Served to lt., USNR, 1957-60. Mem. Internat. Communication Assn. (pres. 1976-77), AAAS, Speech Communication Assn., Am. Assn. Pub. Opinion Research, Assn. Edn. in Journalism. Episcopalian. Author: Introduction to Content Analysis, 1964; Content Analysis of Communication, 1967; Approaches to Human Communication, 1972; Human Communication Handbook Simulations and Games, 1975; Mass Communication: Dialogue and Alternatives, 1976. Asso. editor Human Communication Research, 1974—, Communication Quar., 1975—; editorial bd. Jour. Communication, 1976—. Home: 3 Pilgrim Run East Brunswick NJ 08816 Office: Dept Human Communication Van Dyck Hall Rutgers U New Brunswick NJ 08903

BUDESHEIM, NORMAN ELLSWORTH, ret. govt. ofcl., pub. utilities cons.; b. Washington, July 22, 1908; s. Harry and Minnie Amelia (Rothauge) B.; B.C.S., Strayer Coll., 1938, M.C.S., 1939; m. Annie Laurie Miller, Sept. 30, 1933; children—Norma Ann, Mildred Linda Budesheim Gilliam, Harry Paul. Head accountant, adminstrv. asst. to dir. and chief engr. Pub. Works Adminstrn., Washington, 1938-41; prin. fiscal accountant clk. Office of Chief Engrs., C.E., Washington, 1941; accountant, auditor Pub. Utilities Commn., Washington, 1941-48, accountant, sr. auditor, 1948-51; pub. utilities specialist Transp. and Pub. Utilities div. GSA, Washington, 1951-59; pub. utilities accountant FPC, Washington, 1959-64, systems accountant, 1964-70; pub. utilities cons., Silver Spring, Md., 1954-57, 70—. Mem. Republican Nat. Com., 1976. Mem. Assn. Govt. Accountants, Am. Accounting Assn., Nat. Assn. Accountants. Presbyterian. Address: 8408 11th Ave Silver Spring MD 20903

BUDLONG, BARRY IVES, ednl. adminstr.; b. Binghamton, N.Y., Sept. 6, 1937; s. Benjamin Harrison and Myrtle Edith (Ives) B.; B.S., St. Lawrence U., 1960; M.P.A., U. Hartford, 1972; m. Ruth Carling, June 25, 1960; children—Scott, Kristen. Group tng. supr. Travelers Ins. Co., Hartford, Conn., 1963-68; reins. rep. Phoenix Mut. Life Ins., Hartford, 1968-69; asso. dir. devel. U. Hartford, 1969-72; adminstr. Conn. Office of Intergovtl. Programs, Hartford, 1972-77; dir. devel. Am. Sch. for the Deaf, West Hartford, 1977—. Served with U.S. Army, 1960-62. Mem. Am. Inst. Planners, Am. Soc. Pub. Ofcls. Home: 14 Remington Rd Windsor CT 06095 Office: 139 N Main St West Hartford CT 06107

BUDNE, THOMAS ALLEN, mgmt. cons.; b. Jersey City, Nov. 2, 1918; s. Philip and Sarah B.; B.A., Montclair State Coll., 1940, M.A., 1941, M.Ph., Columbia U., 1977; m. Betty Levine, Sept. 6, 1953; children—Daniel, Leah, Philip. Instr., Montclair State Coll., 1943-47; dir. quality control Hughes Aircraft Co., Culver City, Calif., 1947-52; mem. internat. team UN Mission to India, 1952-53; dir. quality control Philip Morris Inc., 1953-56; mgmt. cons., pres. T.A. Budne & Assos. Inc., Great Neck, N.Y., 1957—; mem. teaching faculty Montclair State Coll., Rutgers U., Hofstra U., N.Y. U., Calif. at Los Angeles, U. Conn., Air Force Inst. Tech.; instr. teaching programs IEEE and Am. Soc. Quality Control. Served with Signal Corps, U.S. Army, 1942-43. Certified reliability engr., quality engr.; qualified statis. expert fed. cts. Fellow AAAS, Am. Soc. Quality Control; mem. Am. Mgmt. Assn., Am. Mktg. Assn., IEEE, Biometrics Soc., Am. Statis. Assn., Ops. Research Soc. Am. Contbr. articles to profl. jours.; holder patents on bldg. joint connector, standard deviation determining apparatus. Office: 3 Dunster Rd Great Neck NY 11021

BUDNER, STANLEY GORDON, news agency exec.; b. Norfolk, Va., Dec. 9, 1927; s. Erwin M. and Ruth (Glickman) B.; B.S., U. Del., 1950; m. Doris Hollett, Mar. 26, 1948; children—Hope Ann, Faith Rose, Alisa Joy. Pres., Delmar News Agency Inc., Wilmington, Del., 1950—; v.p., Delmar Photo Service, Inc., Wilmington, 1951—; pres., Key News Agency, Inc., Marathon, Fla., 1964—; partner, Del. Candy & Tobacco, Wilmington, 1969—; newsstand sales mgr. Games Mag., 1977—. Democratic committeeman, 1966-69; active Boys' Club, Red Feather; solicitor United Jewish Appeal, 1965; Del. Outward Bound rep., 1977; mem. Am. Jewish Com., 1976; active Jewish Nat. Fund, 1978. Served in U.S. Army, 1946-47. Recipient award Anti-Defamation League, 1975; named Man of Yr., Jewish Nat. Fund, 1978. Mem. Mag. Pubs. Mktg. Inst. (treas.), Atlantic Coast Ind. Distbrs. Assn. (v.p., past dir.), Council for Periodical Distbrs. Assn. (v.p. 1970-74), Bur. Ind. Pubs. & Distbrs., Phi Kappa Phi. Jewish. Clubs: Brandywine Country, New Castle Sailing. Home: 17 Gumwood Dr Wilmington DE 19803 Office: 848 Church St Wilmington DE 19801

BUDZEIKA, GEORGE, economist; b. Vilnius, Lithuania, May 19, 1921; M.A., U. Innsbruck (Austria), 1946, Ph.D., 1947, N.Y. U., 1970. Came to U.S., 1949, naturalized, 1955. Economist, Am. Inst. Econ. Research, Great Barrington, Mass., 1950-54; instr. econs. Manhattan Coll., N.Y.C., 1954-57; economist Fed. Res. Bank N.Y., N.Y.C., 1957—; faculty Baruch Coll. of City U. N.Y., N.Y.C., 1958—, adj. asso. prof. econs., 1970—. Mem. Am. Econ. Assn., Am. Fin. Assn. Contbr. articles to profl. jours. Home: 34 1/2 Van Corlear Pl New York City NY 10463 Office: 33 Liberty St New York City NY 10045

BUECHLER, PETER ROBERT, chemist; b. N.Y.C., Oct. 7, 1919; s. Peter N.A. and Anna (Regan) B.; B.S., Fordham U., 1941; M.S., U. Denver, 1946; Ph.D., U. Cin., 1949; m. Mary Frances Hartman, June 12, 1946; children—Ruth Anne, Mary Frances, Sarah Ellen, Elizabeth Jean, Peter Charles. Asst. prof. U. Cin., 1946-51; sr. scientist Olin-Mathieson Chem. Co., New Haven, 1951-54; gen. mgr. Tanners Research Corp. of N.J., Newark, 1954-56; research group leader Rohm & Haas Co., Phila., 1956-66; head, applications research sect. Central Coatings lab., Mobil Chem. Co., Edison, N.J., 1966-69; dir. research and devel. K.J. Quinn & Co., Malden, Mass., 1969-73; sr. devel. asso. coatings and resins research and devel. PPG Industries, Inc., Allison Park, Pa., 1973—. Cons. VA, 1949-51, Johnson & Johnson, Inc., 1949-51; lectr. LaSalle Coll., 1961-69; invited lectr. U. Detroit polymer symposia, 1970, 72, 73. Dir. Seacoast Boys Club, N.H., 1970-73. Mem. Adv. Commn. for Neshaminy Sch. Bd., 1959-69, chmn., 1962; chmn. curriculum study com. Neshaminy Sch. Dist., 1960-61. Fellow Am. Inst. Chemists (Pa. dir. at large 1978-79); mem. Am. Chem. Soc., Soc. for Paint Tech., Am. Leather Chemists Assn., Soc. for Leather Trades Chemists (Brit.), Sigma Xi, Phi Lambda Upsilon. Republican. Roman Catholic. Lion (pres. Langhorne, Pa., 1965-66, dir. 1968-69; dir. Hampton 1970-72). Patentee in field. Home: 5300 Richland Rd Gibsonia PA 15044 Office: PO Box 9 Allison Park PA 15101

BUELL, ELTON HOLLISTER, nuclear and mech. engr.; b. Avon, Conn., Nov. 12, 1928; s. Clarence G. and Florence H. (Hollister) B.; A.A., Phoenix Coll., 1948; B.S. with honors in Mech. Engring., U. Ariz., 1950, postgrad., 1953-54; postgrad. U. Idaho, 1957-58, Inst. Gas Tech., 1955, U. Mich., 1967, U. Calif. at Los Angeles, 1958-60; m. Norma F. Neal, May 18, 1951; children—Cynthia Kay, Sherry Elaine. Engr., Ariz. Pub. Service Co., Phoenix, 1950-56, assigned Rocky Mountain-Pacific Nuclear Research Group, Nat. Reactor Testing Sta., Idaho Falls, Idaho and San Diego, 1956-61, mgr. sci. research, Phoenix, 1963-75; v.p. Resources Co., Phoenix, 1966-75, also dir.; adminstr. Kaiparowits Coal Project, 1964-75; v.p. Bixco, 1972-73; energy cons., Phoenix, 1975—76; mgr. advanced energy conversion systems dept. Gilbert/Commonwealth Cos., 1976-78, program mgr., 1978—; mem. Ariz. AEC Technol. Devel. Subcom., 1966-71, Western Energy Supply and Transmission Assos. Energy Conversion Task Force, 1973-75, Electric Power Research Inst. Advanced Systems Task Force, 1974-75, Gas-Cooled Fast Reactor Program Rev. Com., 1972-75, Utah Kaiparowits Planning and Devel. Adv. Council, 1974-75. Served in C.E., AUS, 1951-52. Registered profl. engr., Calif., Ariz. Mem. Am. Nuclear Soc. (chmn. Ariz. chpt. 1974-75), ASME, Internat. Solar Energy Soc., Nat., Ariz. (achievement award 1975) socs. profl. engrs., Soc. Advancement Mgmt., Intertel Inc., Am. Mensa Ltd., S.A.R., Sigma Xi (asso.). Co-author: SELECTOR (nuclear core optimization code); contbr. articles to various publs. Home: 2112 Rosewood Ct Wyomissing PA 19610

BUELL, EUGENE F(RANKLIN), lawyer; b. Elrama, Pa., Dec. 3, 1916; s. Frank Currey and Altina (Ecklund) B.; B.S., St. Vincent's Coll., 1938; grad. student Carnegie Inst. Tech., 1938-40, U. Pitts., 1941, Johns Hopkins U., 1942; J.D., Duquesne U., 1944; m. Elizabeth Ellen Foster, Dec. 28, 1940; children—Ellen E. (dec.), Erik Foster. Admitted to D.C. bar, 1949, Canadian Patent Office, 1949; chemist U.S. Steel Corp., 1938-42, chief chemist Homestead works, 1942-45; with Stebbins, Blenko & Webb, 1945-48; partner firm Blenko, Hoopes, Leonard & Glenn, 1949-52, Blenko, Hoopes, Leonard & Buell, Pitts., 1953-66, Blenko, Leonard & Buell, 1966-72, Blenko, Buell, Ziesenheim & Beck, 1973—; pres., dir. Tartan Industries, Inc.; sec. Porta-Drill, Inc.; dir. Metaltronics, Inc.; instr. Law Sch. U. Pitts., 1954-59, adj. prof. law, 1959—. Past pres. Richland Com. for Better Govt.; sch. dir. Richland Twp. Mem. Am. Bar Assn., Am. Patent Law Assn., Engrs. Soc. Western Pa., Pa. Soc., Assn. Bar City N.Y., Licensing Exec. Soc., Order of Coif. Clubs: Masons, Kiwanis (pres. Richland), Elks, Duquesne, Press, Allegheny. Home: RD 2 Box 418 Gibsonia PA 15044 Office: 301 5th Ave Pittsburgh PA 15222

BUERGER, ANNE FORTUNE (MRS. DAVID BERNARD BUERGER), civic worker; b. Pitts., Oct. 28, 1909; d. Joseph and Katharina (Ritter) Fortune; student U. Pitts., 1940, Duquesne U., 1968; m. David Bernard Buerger, June 30, 1946; 1 son, David Charles. Organizer, mem. Hampton Civic Assn., Allison Park, Pa., 1948—, pres., 1960-61, editor handbook, 1960, 64, 68, 72, 76; mem. Route 8 Civic Improvement Assn., Allegheny County, Pa., 1965—; mem. Pitts. Symphony Soc., 1948—; chmn. North Hills, 1962, chmn. Hampton Community Center Allison Park, 1962-1963; pres. Allegheny Acad., 1971-72, v.p., 1973-76; bd. dirs. Divine Providence Aux., Pitts., Allegheny Gen. Hosp. Flower Cart Service, Pitts.; aux. worker Parkwood chpt. Meals on Wheels; chmn. Easter com. St. Ursula's Roman Cath. Ch., 1962—, chmn. fashion show and luncheon 1963. Mem. Woman's Nat. Farm and Garden Assn. (nat. pres. 1968-70, internat. del. to Ireland 1965, Norway, 1971, Africa, 1977, chmn. various coms. 1954-72, nat. Bicentennial chmn. 1975-76), Asso. Country Women of World (internat. council 1968-70). Clubs: Hoe and Harvest Garden (organizer), Country Lane Garden (organizer, pres. 1955, 78—), Pittsburgh Garden Center, Federated Garden Clubs, Wildwood Golf (chmn. several ladies' coms. 1960-65). Home: 3000 McCully Rd Allison Park PA 15101 also George St Conneaut Lake Park PA 16316

BUERGER, DAVID BERNARD, lawyer; b. Phila., Dec. 1, 1909; s. Charles B. and Ada (Fischel) B.; A.B. with honors, U. Pitts., 1928, A.M., 1929; J.D., Columbia, 1932; m. Anne M. Fortun, June 30, 1946; 1 son, David C. Admitted to Pa. bar, 1932, since practiced in Pitts.; partner firm Buchanan, Ingersoll, Rodewald, Kyle & Buerger, and predecessors, 1947—. Lectr. taxation and corp. law Com. Continuing Legal Edn., Am. Law Inst., 1951—; engaged in litigation trials and arguments in 47 states; pres. Jersey City Investment Co., Fourteen Bell Corp.; v.p. dir. Tapatco Industries Ltd., R. Munroe & Sons Mfg. Co.; sec., dir. Vantage Broadcasting Co., Carriage Trade Realty Inc., Pitts. Stage, Inc.; gen. counsel Magee Womens Hosp., Hunt Found., Roy A. Hunt Found., Allegheny Acad. Pres. Hampton Civic Assn., 1956-57. Trustee Davis and Elkins Coll., Helen Clay Frick Found. Fellow Am. Bar Found.; mem. Am. Law Inst., Am. Arbitration Assn. (nat. panel), Am. Judicature Soc., Am. Bar Assn., Sigma Alpha Mu, Omicron Delta Kappa. Club: Wildwood Golf. Editor: Columbia Law Rev., 1930-32. Home: 3000 McCully Rd Allison Park PA 15101 Office: 600 Grant St Pittsburgh PA 15219

BUESCHER, ADOLPH ERNST, JR., aerospace exec.; b. St. Louis, Oct. 6, 1922; s. Adolph E. and Eugnie K. (Stroh) B.; B.S., U. Mo., 1946; M.S., Stanford U., 1950; postgrad. U. Calif. at Los Angeles, 1951-52; m. Ruth L. Flemming, Aug. 21, 1948; children—Timothy, Philip. Engr., Eastman Kodak, Rochester, N.Y., 1946-49; flight test supr. Northrop Aircraft, Inc., 1950-53; cons. engr., mgr. controls and instrument sect. Sverdrup & Parcel, Inc., St. Louis, 1953-56; with Gen. Electric Co., Valley Forge, Pa., 1956—, mgr. devel. plans, missile and space div., 1963-69, mgr. strategic planning Aerospace group, 1969—; instr. refresher course for N.Y. profl. engring. licensing exam, 1948-49; lectr. tech. mktg. Engring. Club Phila., 1967. Vice pres. Whitemarsh Citizens Council, 1961-66; chmn. Whitemarsh Twp. Planning Commn., 1975—. Served with USAAF and AUS, 1942-46. Registered profl. engr., N.Y., Calif., Mo. Asso. fellow Am. Inst. Aeros. and Astronautics; mem. Am. Security Council, Greater Phila. C. of C., Pi Tau Sigma, Tau Beta Pi. Club: Explorers (N.Y.C.). Patentee automatic celestial nav. systems. Home: 6044 Cannon Hill Rd Ft Washington PA 19034 Office: PO Box 8555 Philadelphia PA 19101

BUGG, CAROL DONAYRE, interior designer; b. N.Y.C., June 8, 1937; d. Carlos G. and Frances (Burkhart) Donayre; A.A., Georgetown Visitation Jr. Coll., 1957; postgrad. Georgetown U., 1959-60; Internat. Inst. Interior Design, 1963-67; m. James Simon Bugg, Dec. 24, 1968. Interior design draftsman W. & J. Sloane, Washington, 1967-68; interior designer H. Chambers Co., Washington, 1968-69; dir. design, Internat. Cosmetic Co., Washington, 1969-71; residential comml. interior designer Stix, Baer & Fuller, St. Louis, 1971-72; interior designer Burklew Design Assos., Rockville, Md., 1973-76; pres. Carol Donayre Bugg & Assocs., Chevy Chase, Md., 1976—; owner Model Home Interior Design Co., Chevy Chase, 1976—; lectr. Smithsonian Inst., Washington, 1976; cons. in field. Mem. Am. Soc. Interior Designers (chmn. chpt. ways & means com., dir. 1979), Surburban Md. Home Builders Assn., Nat. Assn. Women Bus. Owners. Contbr. article to profl. jours. Home and office: 3717 Bradley Ln Chevy Chase MD 20015

BUGNOLO, DIMITRI S., cons.; b. Atlantic City, Feb. 3, 1929; s. Carlo and Mafalda (Trovero) B.; B.S. in Elec. Engring., U. Pa., 1952; M.Engring., Yale, 1955; Sc.D., Columbia, 1960; children—John, Dimitri, Alexis. Instr., Columbia, 1956-60, asst. prof., 1961-63, sr. research scientist, 1966-68; mem. tech. staff, cons. Bell Telephone Labs., 1963-66; pvt. cons., Portsmouth, R.I., 1968—; faculty marine engring. sci. Mass. Maritime Acad.; cons. Institut Nat. de la Recherche Scientifique U. Que. (Can.), 1971-73. Served with USN, World War II. Mem. Am. Phys. Soc., Sigma Xi. Contbr. numerous articles to profl. jours. Home 71 Canonchet Dr Portsmouth RI 02871 Office: Dept Marine Engring Mass Maritime Acad Buzzards Bay MA 02532

BUIST, JEAN MACKERLEY, veterinarian; b. Newton, N.J., Dec. 24, 1919; d. Ackerson Jacob and Mary Morris (Morford) Mackerley; D.V.M., Cornell U., 1942; m. Richardson Buist, Oct. 2, 1948; children—Peter Richardson, Jean Morford, Mary Elizabeth (Mrs. Morrissey). Veterinarian, Summit (N.J.) Dog and Cat Hosp., 1942-48; pvt. practice vet. medicine, Sparta, N.J., 1948—. Mem. Sparta Twp. Bd. Health, 1962—, chmn., 1972—. Mem., sec. N.J. State Bd. Vet. Med. Examiners. Bd. dirs. N.J. Acad. Vet. Medicine and Surgery, 1972—, sec., 1975—. Recipient Gaines award Newton Kennel Club, 1970. Mem. Sussex County 4-H Horse Club Leaders Assn. (pres. 1970-76). Home: 143 Old Stanhope Rd Sparta NJ 07871

BUIST, RICHARDSON, trust banker; b. Bklyn., Aug. 8, 1921; s. George Lamb and Adelaide (Richardson) B.; student Yale; m. Jean Mackerley, Oct. 2, 1948; children—Peter Richardson, Jean Morford, Mary Elizabeth Buist Morrissey. Advt. copy writer Ecloss Co., Sparta, N.J., 1946-48; advt. mgr. Sussex County Ind., 1948-50, Dover Advance, 1950-53; bus. mgr. N.J. Herald, Newton, 1953-70, pub., 1969-70; dir., v.p. N.J. Herald, Inc., 1958-70; asst. sec.-treas. Morford Co., 1968-72; trust officer Midlantic Nat. Bank/Sussex & Mchts., 1971—, Midlantic Nat. Bank, 1972—. Pres. Sussex County chpt. Am. Cancer Soc., 1956-58, Sussex County Music Found., 1959-61; mem. Morris-Sussex Area Health Facilities Planning Council, 1965-68; v.p. Sussex County Council of Arts, 1971-73; trustee Sussex County Music Found., 1955—; v.p., chmn. fin. devel. com. Newton Meml. Hosp., 1966-68, pres. bd. govs., 1968-70, chmn. bd. govs., 1971-73; v.p., mem. exec. com. Regional Health Planning Council, 1976—. Mem. N.J. Press Assn. (dir. 1968-70), Am. Peony Soc. Club: Rotary (pres. 1967-68). Home: RR 1 Box 668A Hamburg NJ 07419 Office: 161 Madison Ave Morristown NJ 07960

BULDRINI, GEORGE JAMES, lawyer; b. N.Y.C., May 14, 1947; s. Frederick Paul and Emily Geraldine (Bewick) B.; B.A., St. John's U., 1969, J.D., 1972; LL.M., N.Y. U., 1976. Admitted to N.Y. bar, 1973; sr. atty. Counsel's Office, N.Y. Dept. Health, Albany, 1974—. Mem. Am., N.Y., Fed. bar assns., Am. Hist. Assn. Office: NY State Dept Health Counsel's Office Tower Bldg 12th Floor Empire State Plaza Albany NY 12237

BULIAN, MAX JOSEPH, obstetrician, gynecologist; b. Boston, Sept. 8, 1922; s. Joseph and Esther (Lipofsky) B.; B.S., Tufts U., 1943, M.D., 1946; M.P.H., Harvard U., 1966; m. Adele Landau, June 28, 1947; children—John, Joseph, Emily. Intern, Albert Einstein Med. Center, Phila., 1946-47; resident in obstetrics and gynecology Sinai Hosp., Balt., 1949-53, Johns Hopkins Hosp., Balt., 1951-52; research fellow in gynecology, Free Hosp. for Women (Harvard U.), Brookline, Mass., 1953-54; practice medicine specializing in obstetrics and gynecology, Brookline, 1954—; asst. prof. obstetrics and gynecology Harvard U., 1962, Tufts U., 1956—; cons. maternal and child health Mass. Dept. Pub. Health, 1966; wrote City of Boston Maternity and Infant Care Project, 1966; mem. adv. com. to dept. obstetrics and gynecology Harvard Med. Sch. Served to capt. M.C., U.S.Army, 1947-49. Diplomate Am. Bd. Obstetrics and Gynecology. Mem. Am. Coll. Obstetrics and Gynecology, Boston Obstet. Soc., Am., Mass. pub. health assns., Mass., Norfolk Dist. med. socs. Home: 44 Valley

Rd Chestnut Hill MA 02167 Office: 1180 Beacon St Brookline MA 02146

BULKLEY, BERNADINE HEALY, physician; b. N.Y.C., Aug. 2, 1944; d. Michael J. and Violet (McGrath) Healy; A.B. summa cum laude, Vassar Coll., 1965; M.D. cum laude, Harvard U., 1970; m. Gregory Bartlett Bulkley, Aug. 13, 1967. Intern in medicine Johns Hopkins Hosp., Balt., 1970-71, asst. resident in medicine, 1971-72; staff fellow Nat. Heart and Lung Inst., NIH, Bethesda, Md., 1972-74; fellow cardiovascular div. Johns Hopkins U. Sch. Medicine, Balt., 1974-75, dept. pathology and medicine, 1975-76; practice medicine specializing in cardiology, Balt.; asst. prof. medicine Johns Hopkins U. Sch. Medicine, 1976-77, asst. prof. of pathology, 1976—, asso. prof. medicine, 1977—; dir. coronary care unit Johns Hopkins Hosp., 1977—, mem. staff, 1976—; cons. Nat. Heart, Lung and Blood Inst., NIH, 1976—; mem. cardiology adv. com. HEW; editorial cons. Annals of Internal Medicine, Am. Jour. Cardiology, Johns Hopkins Med. Jour. Bd. dirs. Bethesda-Chevy Chase (Md.) YMCA, 1974-75. Stetler Research fellow, 1976-77. Diplomate Am. Bd. Internal Medicine, Am. Bd. Cardiology. Fellow Am. Coll. Cardiology (state gov.), Am. Heart Assn. Council on Clin. Cardiology; mem. Am. Fedn. Clin. Research (councilor Eastern sect. 1977—, sec.-treas. Eastern sect. 1978-79), Alpha Omega Alpha, Phi Beta Kappa, A.C.P. Contbr. numerous articles on cardiovascular disease to med. jours. Home: 4002 St Paul St Baltimore MD 21218 Office: 600 N Wolfe St Baltimore MD 21205

BULLARD, GREGORY NELSON, librarian; b. Mt. Vernon, N.Y., Dec. 27, 1927; s. John Nelson and Victoria Marie (Chibouk) B.; B.A., Champlain Coll., Plattsburgh, N.Y., 1953; M.S. in L.S., Syracuse U., 1954; children—Deborah, Victoria, John, Patricia, Howard. Acquisitions librarian Harpur Coll., State U. N.Y., Binghamton, 1954-60; asst. dir. tech. services State U. N.Y., Binghamton, 1960-74, acting dir. libraries, 1970, 71-72; asst. dir. tech. and automated services Syracuse (N.Y.) U., 1974—; bd. dirs. Five Asso. Univ. Libraries, 1971-72, vice chmn., 1972; mem. com. on compilation of SCRLC Union List of Serials, S.Central Research Library Council, 1973-74; chmn. tech. services com. CENTRO Fin. Com., 1976—; v.p., trustee Central N.Y. Library Resources Council, 1977—; mem. network dirs. OCLC, Inc., 1978—. Served with USMC, 1945-46. Mem. Am., N.Y. library assns., Library Info. Tech. Assn. Home: 685 E Seneca Turnpike Syracuse NY 13205 Office: Syracuse U Libraries 222 Waverly Ave Syracuse NY 13210

BULLARD, JOHN KILBURN, urban planner; b. New Bedford, Mass., Aug. 21, 1947; s. John Crapo and Katharine (Kilburn) B.; B.A. magna cum laude, Harvard U., 1969; M.Arch., Mass. Inst. Tech., 1974, M.City Planning, 1974; 1 son, Matthew Havens. Agt., Waterfront Hist. Area League, New Bedford, Mass., 1974—. Trustee Archtl. Conservation Trust Mass.; chmn. New Bedford Bicentennial Commn., 1974-77; mem. New Bedford Fairhaven Harbor Master Planning Commn., 1977—, Greater New Bedford Forum, 1977—. Mem. Nat. Trust Historic Preservation, Soc. Preservation New Eng. Antiquities, Assn. Preservation Technology. Unitarian. Home: 19 Irving St New Bedford MA 02740 Office: 13 Centre St New Bedford MA 02740

BULLEN, ALLAN GRAHAM ROBERT, civil engr., educator; b. Wellington, N.Z., Dec. 8, 1936; s. Allan Richard and Lorna (Sharpe) B.; came to U.S., 1967; B.Sc., U. N.Z., 1960, M.Sc. with honors, 1962; M.S., Northwestern U., 1964, Ph.D., 1969; m. Mary Victoria Wesney, Apr. 14, 1972; children—Andrew James, Johanna Jane. Traffic engr. N.Z. Govt. Dept. Transport, 1955-66; research engr. Northwestern U., Evanston, Ill., 1967-69; asst. prof. civil engr. U. Ill., Urbana, 1969-70; asso. prof. civil engring. U. Pitts., 1970—, dir. environ. systems engring., 1973-76; cons. Westmoreland Engring., Monessen, Pa., Peat, Marwick, Mitchell & Co., Washington. Internat. Road Fedn. fellow, 1963-64; recipient O'Farrill Hwy. award as Outstanding Student of Year, 1964. Mem. ASCE, Inst. Traffic Engrs., Transp. Research Bd., Transp. Research Forum, Sigma Xi. Presbyterian. Home: 711 Rockwood Dr Gibsonia PA 15044 Office: 1140 Benedum Hall U Pitts Pittsburgh PA 15261

BULLOUGH, JOHN FRANK, educator; b. Washington, Oct. 15, 1928; s. John and Mabel Jean (McCalip) B.; A.B., George Washington U., 1954; S.M.M., Union Theol. Sem., 1958; m. Dorothy Baines, Apr. 10, 1950; children—John Frank, Lynn Diane, Patricia Ann. Organist, asst. prof. music Hartford (Conn.) Theol. Sem. Found., 1958-64; asst. prof. music Fairleigh Dickinson U., 1964-70, asso. prof., 1970-74, prof., 1974—, chmn. dept. fine arts, 1974—; music dir. Hartford Center Ch., 1960-64; organist, choirmaster St. Paul's Episcopal Ch., Englewood, N.J., 1973—. Vice-pres. bd. trustees Bergen (N.J.) Philharmonic Orch., 1973—. Mem. AAUP, Am. Guild Organists (dean Hartford chpt. 1963-64, dean No. Valley chpt. 1975-78), Coll. Music Soc. Episcopalian. Contbr. articles to profl. jours. Home: 488 Fairidge Terr Teaneck NJ 07666 Office: Fairleigh Dickinson U Teaneck NJ 07666

BULLUCK, LINWOOD VONRAE, social worker; b. Rocky Mount, N.C., Jan. 28, 1932; s. Ponce and Mary Etta (Dickens) B.; B.A., N.C. Central U., Durham, 1954; M.S.W., N.Y. U., 1966; D.S.W., Adelphi U., 1978; div.; 1 dau., Rhonda M. Caseworker, unit supr., case supr., spl. asst. to commr. in family planning N.Y.C. Dept. Social Services, 1957-68, 69-75; instr. SUNY, Farmingdale, 1969-75; asst. prof. Grad. Sch. Social Work, Adelphi U., Garden City, N.Y., 1972—; pvt. practice psychotherapy, Westbury, N.Y., 1972—; exec. dir. Youth and Family Counseling Agy. of Oyster Bay-East Norwich, Inc., 1969—. Served with U.S. Army, 1954-56. Recipient various grants and scholarships. Mem. Nat. Assn. Social Workers, Acad. Certified Social Workers, Assn. Black Social Workers, Nat. Orgn., NAACP. Republican. Home: 280 Grand Blvd Westbury NY 11590 Office: 193 South St Oyster Bay NY 11771

BULMASH, GARY FRANKLIN, accounting, educator; b. Balt., Apr. 13, 1945; s. Gilbert and Dorothy (Goldstein) B.; B.S., U. Md., with high honors, 1966, M.B.A., 1968, D. Bus. Adminstrn., 1974. Instr. accounting U. Md., College Park, 1968-73; mgr. exams. div. Am. Inst. C.P.A.'s, N.Y.C., 1973-75; asst. prof. accounting Am. U., Washington, 1975—; cons. in field. Bd. dirs. Washington chpt. Accountants for Pub. Interest. C.P.A., Md. Mem. Nat. Assn. Accountants (bd. dirs. Washington chpt.), Acad. Accounting Historians, Am. Taxation Assn., Am. Inst. C.P.A.'s, Md. Assn. C.P.A.'s, Am. Accounting Assn., Phi Kappa Phi, Beta Gamma Sigma. Democrat. Jewish religion. Home: 12000 Old Georgetown Rd Apt C1002 Rockville MD 20852 Office: Sch Bus Adminstrn Am U Washington DC 20016

BULMASH, GILBERT, accountant; b. Balt., Oct. 22, 1914; s. Samuel and Rose (Kitt) B.; certificate in accounting and bus. adminstrn. U. Balt., 1937; m. Dorothy Goldstein, June 28, 1942; children—Gary Franklin, Patsy Beth Bulmash Milner. Partner, Kushner, Bulmash & Co., C.P.A.'s, Balt., 1946-73, Donald E. Webster & Co., C.P.A.'s, Balt., 1973-76; officer Naron, Wagner & Vosrow, Chartered, C.P.A.'s, 1976—; dir. Universal Bldg. & Loan Assn., Inc., Balt., 1951-73, Harley's Restaurants, Inc., H. & A. Commissary Corp. Exec. bd., scholarship com. PTA, Balt., 1959-62. C.P.A., Md. Mem. Am. Inst. C.P.A.'s, Am. Accounting Assn., Md. Assn. C.P.A.'s (sec. profl. ethics com.), U. Balt. Alumni Assn. (bd. govs.), Gamma Eta Sigma (past grand high priest). Home: 2800 Steele Rd Baltimore MD 21209 Office: Suite 1200 Sun Life Bldg 20 S Charles St Baltimore MD 21201

BULOVA, ERNST, psychologist; b. Vienna, Austria, June 24, 1902; s. Richard and Valerie B.; came to U.S., 1940, naturalized, 1946; Ph.D., U. Vienna, 1936; m. Ilse Simachowitz, Sept. 1933; children—Stephen, Joanne. Dir. Exptl. Sch., Berlin, 1927-33; prin. Radio Berlin, 1930-33; asso. Beltane Sch., London, 1934-40; dir. Buck's Rock, New Milford, Conn., 1943—; psychologist, N.Y.C., 1944—. Recipient Pearl Merrill award, 1962. Mem. Am., N.Y. State psychol. assns., N.Y. Soc. Clin. Psychologists, Am. Camping Assn., Assn. Pvt. Camps. Author films: Their Voices Rise, 1946, Thus We Learn, 1932, also 2 books, numerous radio plays, articles in profl. jours. Home: PO Box 87 New Milford CT 06776

BULSON, WALTER THEODORE, chem. engr., research scientist; b. Tompkins Cove, N.Y., June 6, 1926; s. Theodore and Grace Elizabeth (Baisley) B.; B. Chem. Engring., Clarkson Coll. Tech., 1947; M.S. in Chemistry, Franklin and Marshall Coll., 1969; m. Carolyn Jean Longfritz, June 25, 1949; children—Linda Ruth, Nancy Grace. Project engr. Kay Fries Chems., West Haverstraw, N.Y., 1947-52, research engr., 1952-55; research engr. Armstrong Cork Co., Lancaster, Pa., 1955-62, supr. chem. pilot plant, 1962-64, sr. research scientist, 1964—. Chmn. constrn. com. Civic Assn., 1952-54. Registered profl. engr., Pa. Mem. Am. Inst. Chem. Engrs., Am. Assn. Cost Engrs. (v.p. Del. Valley sect. 1970-71, pres. 1971-72, dir. 1972-73), Am. Chem. Soc. (chmn. publs. and edn. sect. 1956-58), Soc. Advancement Mgmt. (chmn. 1968), Lancaster Toastmasters (pres. 1975), Lancaster Table Tennis Assn. (pres. 1959-64), Lancaster Speaker's Bur. Republican. Presbyn. (elder). Patentee in field. Home: 903 Forest Rd Lancaster PA 17601 Office: Research and Devel Center Armstrong Cork Co Lancaster PA 17604

BUMSTEAD, JOHN CHAMBERS, cons. engr.; b. Saratoga Springs, N.Y., Apr. 16, 1913; s. Arthur Irving and Gertrude Ursula (Boller) B.; C.E., Rensselaer Poly. Inst., 1935; m. Lenore Fox, Feb. 27, 1971; children—Elsa, Ann. Asst. city engr. Saratoga Springs (N.Y.), 1935-41; asst. engr. TVA, 1941-42; constrn. engr. Havens & Emerson, Walnut Ridge, Ark., 1942; design engr. Gannett, Eastman & Fleming, Andrews Field, Washington, 1942-43; asst. editor Engring. News Record, McGraw-Hill Pub. Co., N.Y.C., 1946-48, asso. editor, 1948-51; asso. engr. Alfred LeFeber & Assos., Cin., 1952-55; asst. water pollution control engr. City of Cin., 1956-57; asso. Alden E. Stilson & Assos., Cleve., 1957-64; cons. Ohio Dept. Health, Cleve., 1964-65; asso. engr. comprehensive planning N.Y. State Dept. Health, Albany, 1965-68, dir. utilities mgmt., 1968-70, dir. bur. pub. water supplies, 1970-78, ret., 1978; cons. engr., 1978—. Served from 1st lt. to lt. col. AUS, 1943-46. Decorated medal of War, Brazil, 1946; diplomate Am. Acad. Environ. Engrs. Fellow Am. Water Works Assn., ASCE (div. sec. 1951-55); mem. Water Pollution Control Assn. (sec. san. engring. div.). Contbr. articles to profl. jours.; author numerous studies and tech. reports. Home: 39 Beach Ave Albany NY 12203

BUNDY, RICHARD FRANKLIN, marriage counselor; b. Syracuse, N.Y., June 4, 1941; s. Stanley Anderson and Myrta Carolyn (Doyle) B.; A.B., Syracuse U., 1962; B.Div., Princeton Theol. Sem., 1965, Th.M., 1966; postgrad. Med. Sch., U. Pa., 1971-72; m. Marjorie Robinson, Dec. 22, 1962; one dau., Heather Lynn. Ordained minister Presbyn. Ch., 1966; asst. pastor New Brunswick, N.J., 1966-68, asso. pastor, 1968-71; Protestant chaplain Middlesex County Jail, New Brunswick, 1968—; marriage counselor Rutgers U., New Brunswick, 1971-73; pvt. practice marriage counseling, Highland Park, N.J., 1972—; cons. in field; adj. faculty Rutgers U. chmn. fund raising com., mem. exec. com. of bd. dirs. Del.-Raritan Lung Assn.; bd. dirs. Am. Lung Assn. of N.J. NIMH grantee, 1971-72. Certified marriage counselor N.J. Bd. Marriage Counselor Examiners. Mem. Am. Assn. Marriage and Family Counselors (clin.), N.J. Assn. Marriage and Family Counselors, Am. Assn. Sex Educators, Counselors and Therapists. Kiwanian (v.p. New Brunswick 1972-73). Home: 208 S 2d Ave Highland Park NJ 08904 Office: 24 N 3d Ave Highland Park NJ 08904

BUNDY, ROBERT FLEMING, engring. physicist; b. Phila., Jan. 7, 1912; s. Robert Fleming and Sarah Frances Bundy; A.B., U. Pa., 1935, postgrad., 1936, 67; postgrad. Bklyn. Poly. Inst., 1943, Northeastern U., 1964; m. Ora L. Mitchell, Dec. 15, 1972; children by previous marriage—Robert Fleming, Karen, Robin, Rhoda. Group leader U.S. Signal Corps Radar Labs., 1942-45; mem. research staff Allen B. DuMont Labs., 1956-60; gen. engr. U.S. Dept. Transp., 1972—; evaluation engr. microwave landing systems FAA, Atlantic City, 1976—. Recipient citation from chief signal officer U.S. Signal Corps, 1944; Citizen of Year award Masons, 1977; honored by Phila. Electric Co., 1977. Mem. Franklin Inst. Phila., IEEE, Soc. for Non-Destructive Testing, Nat. Tech. Assn., Nat. Patent Lawyers Assn., Alpha Phi Alpha (hon.). Club: Frontiers Internat. Patentee waveguide commutator for x-y matrix. Designer airport baggage x-ray inspection system. Office: FAA Nat Aviation Facilities Exptl Center Atlantic City NJ 08405

BUNKE, EDWARD WILLIAM DIEDRICH, mech. engr.; b. Milford, Conn., Sept. 16, 1915; s. John Henry August and Elsa Louise Sophie (Weber) B.; M.E., Stevens Inst. Tech., 1936; m. Marjorie Alice Clifton, June 12, 1943; 1 dau., Margaret E. With Gen. Electric Co., 1936—, with Knolls Atomic Power Lab., 1954-62, with Apollo Support Dept., 1962-65, advance systems engr. Armaments Systems Dept., Burlington, Vt., 1965—; dir. Weber-Bunke-Lange, Inc. Registered profl. engr., N.Y. Mem. ASME, Am. Def. Preparedness Assn., U.S. Naval Inst., Tau Beta Pi, Theta Xi. Republican. Lutheran. Office: General Electric Co Lakeside Ave Burlington VT 05402

BUNTING, NINA LOU, educator; b. Md., Oct. 7, 1942; d. William R. and Olive (McCabe) Ringler; B.S. in Early Childhood, U. Del., Newark, 1973; M.A., 1979; m. Franklin O. Bunting; children—Lucinda Kay, Sandra Deanne, Franklin O. Tchr. pvt. Kindergarten, Millsboro, Del., 1963-70; tchr. Indian River Sch. Dist., Frankford, Del., 1971—. Active Am. Field Service, Indian River, Del., SMS Band Boosters. Named Del. Tchr. of Year, 1979. Certified in Nursery and Kindergarten, Del. Mem. Delta Kappa Gamma. Methodist. Home: Route 1 Box 15 A Dagsboro DE 19939 Office: Lord Baltimore Elementary Sch Ocean View DE 19970

BUNZEL, KENNETH WILLIAM, securities co. exec.; b. Chester, Pa., July 14, 1943; s. John W. and Elizabeth B.; B.S., Pa. State U., 1964; postgrad. in mgmt. Rutgers U., 1968-71; m. Dawn E. Camillo, Mar. 18, 1962; children—Tracy Lyn, Melissa Kay. With Hess Oil Co., Port Reading, 1965-68; with Lever Bros., N.Y.C., 1968-69; asst. dir. Am. Stock Exchange, N.Y.C., 1969-73; v.p. ops. dept. Goldman, Sachs & Co., N.Y.C., 1973—. Mem. econ. council N.Y. Com. to Aid N.Y.C., 1972. Mem. computer user groups. Clubs: Plainfield Kennel; Hawk Flying; N.Y.C. Bridge; Masons. Home: 74 Yorktown Rd East Brunswick NJ 08816 Office: 55 Broad St New York NY 10004

BUONOCORE, FREDRIC J., educator; b. Rahway, N.J., Mar. 11, 1933; B.A. in Philosophy, St. Bonaventure U., Olean, N.Y., 1956; M.A. in Adminstrn., Supervision, Seton Hall U., South Orange, N.J., 1960; Ph.D. in Adminstrn., Supervision, Methods of Elementary and Secondary Edn., Fordham U., N.Y.C., 1966; married; 2 children. Tchr., Woodbridge (N.J.) Twp. Sch. Dist., 1956-63, prin., 1963-69, asst. supt., 1969-72, supt. schs., 1972—. Bd. trustees Woodbridge Library, 1972—; mem. Middlesex County Career Coordinating Council, N.J. Sch. Devel. Council. Mem. Am., N.J., Middlesex County assns. sch. adminstrs., N.J. Adv. Council Vocat. Edn. Phi Delta Kappa. Office: PO Box 428 School St Woodbridge NJ 07095

BURBA, JOHN VYTAUTAS, radiopharmacologist; b. Jurbarkas, Lithuania, Oct. 1, 1926; s. Joseph and Marcella (Paznok) B.; B.Sc. with honors, U. Montreal, 1951; Ph.D., U. Ottawa, 1962; postgrad. Yale, 1967-68; m. Charlotte Boisclair, Apr. 21, 1955; children—Johanne, Tanya. Asst. prof. pharmacology U. Ottawa (Ont., Can.), 1962-65; sci. advisor, research scientist Health Protection Br., Ottawa, Ont., Can., 1965-73; head radiopharmacology sect. Radiation Protection Bur., Ottawa, Ont., Can., 1973—. Cons. proprietary and patent medicine unit Health Protection Br., 1968-73. Ont. Research Found. scholar, 1959-62; Med. Research Council grantee, 1963-65. Mem. Pharmacological Soc. Can., Soc. Nuclear Medicine, Chem. Inst. Can., Ottawa Humane Soc. Home: 1357 Fontenay Crescent Ottawa ON K1V7K5 Canada Office: Brookfield Rd Ottawa ON K1A1C1 Canada

BURBACH, RODNEY VAN, psychiatrist, educator; b. Wichita, Kans., Apr. 19, 1942; s. Marvin Imo and Lila (Bitzer) B.; B.A. (NSF fellow), Union Coll., Lincoln, Nebr., 1964; M.D., Loma Linda U., 1968; postgrad. in Psychoanalysis, U. N.C.-Duke Psychoanalytic Tng. Program, 1970—; m. Ivy Joy Wiesher, June 12, 1966; 1 dau., Anne Cristina. Intern in medicine Loma Linda U. Hosp., 1968-69; resident in psychiatry Duke U., 1969-71, Letterman Army Hosp., San Francisco, 1971-72; research psychiatrist Walter Reed Army Inst. Research, Washington, 1972-75; instr. psychiatry Georgetown U. Sch. Medicine, 1975—; staff psychiatrist Washington VA Hosp., 1975-76; practice medicine specializing in treatment of alcoholism, Washington, 1975—; cons. Eastern Shore Hosp. Center, 1972—. Served to maj. M.C., U.S. Army, 1971-75. Recipient Physics Achievement award Chem. Rubber Co., 1961-62. Diplomate Am. Bd. Psychiatry and Neurology. Mem. Am. Psychiat. Assn., Washington Psychiat. Soc., D.C. Med. Soc. Clubs: Carderock Springs Swimming and Tennis, Washington Blue Book. Home: 8608 Fenway Rd Bethesda MD 20034 Office: 2029 Q St Washington DC 20009

BURBANK, ROBINSON DERRY, crystallographer; b. Berlin, N.H., Oct. 3, 1921; s. Paul William and Hazel Louise (Robinson) B.; A.B. cum laude, Colby Coll., 1942; Ph.D., Mass. Inst. Tech., 1950; children—Paul Robinson, Claudia Olive. Research asst. Manhattan Project, Mass. Inst. Tech., 1942-45, research asst. Lab. Insulation Research, 1945-50; sr. physicist Gaseous Diffusion Plant, Oak Ridge, Tenn., 1950-53; group leader in crystallography Olin Industries, New Haven, 1953-55; mem. tech. staff Bell Telephone Labs., Murray Hill, N.J., 1955—, research materials specialist, 1977—. Mem. U.S.A. Nat. Com. Crystallography, 1968-70, 71-73, ex-officio mem., 1974-76; mem. U.S. del. to gen. assembly Internat. Union Crystallography, Stony Brook, N.Y., 1969, Amsterdam, Netherlands, 1975; mem. Com. of Sci. Soc. Presidents, 1975-76. Mem. AAAS, Am. Phys. Soc., Am. Crystallographic Assn. (treas. 1965-68, v.p. 1974, pres. 1975), Chester Twp. Taxpayers Assn. (dir. 1962-65, 70-74, pres. 1973), Sigma Xi, Phi Beta Kappa. Club: Appalachian Mountain (Boston). Home: 45 Woodland Ave Summit NJ 07901 Office: Bell Labs 600 Mountain Ave Murray Hill NJ 07974

BURBIDGE, FREDERICK STEWART, transp. co. exec.; b. Winnipeg, Man., Can., Sept. 30, 1918; s. Frederick Maxwell and Susan Mary (Stewart) B.; B.A., U. Man., 1939, LL.B., 1946; m. Cynthia Adams Bennest, Apr. 27, 1942; children—John Bennest, George Frederick. With law dept. Canadian Pacific Ltd., Winnipeg, 1947-50, Montreal, 1950-62, asst. v.p. traffic, 1962-66, v.p. rail adminstrn., 1966-67, v.p., exec. asst., 1967-69, v.p. marketing and sales CP Rail, 1969-71, sr. exec. officer CP Rail, also v.p. parent co., 1971-72, pres., dir., mem. exec. com. parent co., Montreal, Que., Can., 1972—; dir. Canadian Pacific Investments Ltd., Canadian Pacific Steamships Ltd., Canadian Pacific Transport Co., Canadian Pacific (Bermuda) Ltd., Canadian Industries Ltd., Cominco Ltd., Marathon Realty Co., Ltd., Soo Line R.R. Co., Toronto, Hamilton & Buffalo Ry. Co.; dir., mem. exec. com. Bank of Montreal; mem. adv. council to Minister of Industry, Trade and Commerce. Hon. v.p. Que. Provincial council Boy Scouts Am. Bd. dirs. Royal Victoria Hosp. Found.; mem. citizens adv. bd. Salvation Army. Mem. Gen. Council Industry, Montreal Bd. Trade, La Chambre de Commerce, Canadian Ry. Club, Traffic Club Montreal, Law Soc. Manitoba. Clubs: St. James's, Mt. Royal. Office: Canadian Pacific Ltd Windsor Sta Montreal PQ H3C 3E4 Canada

BURCH, FRANCIS BOUCHER, lawyer, state ofcl.; b. Balt., Nov. 26, 1918; s. Louise Claude and Constance (Boucher) B.; Ph.B. summa cum laude (scholar 1937-41), Loyola Coll., Balt., 1941; LL.B. (scholar 1941-43), Yale U., 1943; m. Mary Patricia Howe, Apr. 12, 1947; children—Francis Boucher, Catherine Howe Jenkins, Richard Claude, Constance Boucher, Edwin Howe, Robert Stuart, Mary Patricia. Admitted to Md. bar, 1943, also U.S. Supreme Ct.; pres. Balt. CSC, 1960-61; mem. Balt. Bd. Estimates, 1961-63; city solicitor, Balt., 1961-63; ins. commr. Md., 1965-66; atty. gen. Md., 1966-78; with firm Weinberg and Green, Balt.; instr. bus. law Loyola Coll., Evening Sch., 1945-57. Chmn. bd. Lauderdale '70, Inc., Ft. Lauderdale, Fla., 1964-68; partner Sheraton Fontainebleau Hotel, Ocean City, Md.; bd. dirs. Balt. Credit Union, 1961-63; mem. Pension Study Com. Balt., 1962; chmn. Mayor Balt. Com. Scholarship Program, 1961, Mayor Balt. Com. Mass. Transit, 1961; mem. Standard Salary Bd. Md., 1960-61, Mayor Balt. Com. Conflict of Interest, 1960; chmn. Md. Cancer Crusade, 1967-68, Constl. Prayer Found., 1963-66; pres. Balt. Safety Council, 1963-65, chmn. exec. com., 1965-67, v.p., 1958-62; lay chmn. Papal Vols. Com. Latin Am., Archdiocese Balt., 1962-65; vice chmn. Alumni div. Loyola Coll. Devel. Program, 1957, chmn. spl. gifts div., 1971; chmn. Md. Catholic Lawyers Retreat, 1957-59; pres. Reciprocity Club Balt., 1956-57, bd. dirs., 1954-59; bd. dirs. Legal Aid Bur. Balt., 1954, Goodwill Industries Balt., 1959-65; trustee Loyola Coll., Balt., 1974—, Camp Fire Girls Balt., 1960-65; chmn. maj. gifts div. Loyola and Notre Dame Coll. (Balt.) Library Devel. Dr., 1972. Served with USCGR, 1944-45. Recipient Spiritum award Cardinal Gibbons High Sch., Balt., 1966; Man of Year award Hibernian Soc. Md., 1967; Pub. Servant award Md. Cath. War Vets., 1967; Humanitarian award Nu Beta Epsilon, 1967; Nat. Jewish Hosp. award, 1969; Alumnus of Year award Loyola Coll., 1970; Andrew White medal for distinguished citizenship Loyola Coll., 1973. Mem. Am., Md., Balt. bar assns., Am. Arbitration Assn. (panel 1954—), Nat. Assn. Attys. Gen. (pres. 1970-71, exec. com. 1969—, Wyman award 1975), Council State Govts. (exec. com. 1971—), So. Md. Soc., Hibernian Soc. Md., St. Thomas More Soc. (pres. Md. 1962-63), St. Georges Soc. Md., Friendly Sons of St. Patrick. Clubs: Paint and Powder (bd. govs. 1957-63), Balt. Country; Tri-State Anglers (Md.-Del.-Va.). Author: On Calling of a Constitutional Convention, 1950. Home: 207 Chancery Rd Baltimore MD 21218 Office: 10 Light St Baltimore MD 21202

BURCH, FRANCIS FLOYD, clergyman, educator; b. Balt., May 15, 1932; s. Thaddeus Joseph and Frances Fidelis (Greenwell) B.; B.A., Fordham U., 1956, M.A., 1958; Ph.L., Woodstock Coll., 1957, S.T.L., 1964; Docteur d'universite de Paris, Sorbonne, 1967. Joined Soc. of Jesus, 1950, ordained priest Roman Catholic Ch., 1963; tchr. Gonzaga High Sch., Washington, 1957-60; asst. prof. St. Joseph's Coll., Phila., 1967-71, asso. prof., 1971-76, prof. English, 1976—, asst. acad. dean, 1972-74, bd. dirs., 1971-76, sec. bd. dirs. 1971-75; artist-scholar-in-residence Millersville (Pa.) State Coll., 1978. Mem. AAUP, Eastern Assn. Coll. Deans and Advisors of Students, Modern Lang. Assn. Am., Renaissance English Text Soc., Alpha Epsilon Delta. Author: Tristan Corbiere: l'originalite des "Amours jaunes" et leur influence sur T.S. Eliot, 1970. Editor: (with P.O. Walzer) Tristan Corbiere: Oeuvres completes, 1970; Sur Tristan Corbiere: lettres inedites adressees au poete et premieres critiques le concernant, 1975. Contbr. articles to profl. jours. Home: 5841 Overbrook Ave Philadelphia PA 19131

BURCH, JOHN THOMAS, JR., lawyer; b. Balt., Feb. 22; s. John T. and Katheryn Estella (Peregoy) B.; B.A., U. Richmond, 1964, J.D., 1966; LL.M., George Washington U., 1971; student JAG Sch., 1969, 72; m. Linda Anne Shearer, Nov. 1, 1970; children—John Thomas, Richard James. Admitted to Va. bar, 1966, D.C. bar, 1974, U.S. Supreme Ct. bar, 1969; asso. firm Lane, Paul and Rudd, Richmond, Va., 1966, Sadur, Pelland, Braude and Caplan, Washington, 1974-75; partner firm Pompan and Burch, Washington, 1976-77; pres. firm Burch, Kerns and Klimek, Washington, 1977—; pres. Internat. Procurement Cons.'s, Ltd., Washington, 1977—. Committeeman City of Alexandira (Va.) Republican Com., 1975—; aide-de-camp Gov. of Va., 1976—. Served to maj., JAGC, U.S. Army, 1966-74; Vietman. Decorated Bronze Star. Mem. Am. (sec. pub. contract law sect. 1976-77), Fed. bar assns., Am. Arbitration Assn., Alexandria Contractors Assn., Va. Soc. SAR (state pres. 1975-76, Patriots medal 1978, Good Citizenship medal 1970), SCV, Scabbard and Blade, Phi Sigma Alpha. Republican. Episcopalian. Home: 1015 N Pelham St Alexandria VA 22304 Office: 1320 19th St NW Washington DC 20036

BURCHESS, EDWIN WALTER, briquetting co. exec.; b. Shenandoah, Pa., May 16, 1919; s. Walter Benjamin and Julia Rose (Roman) B.; student U. Scranton, 1946, 47, Internat. Corr. Schs., 1959, Alexander Hamilton Inst., 1970; m. Helen Joan Mack, May 17, 1941; children—Mary D. (Mrs. Roger D. Harris), Damian E. Miner, Phila. & Reading Coal & Iron Co., Reading, Pa., 1938-43; lab. technician Reading Briquet Co., St. Nicholas, Pa., 1945-47; chemist Am. Briquet Co., Lykens, Pa., 1947-58; exec. v.p. Internat. Briquetting Corp., Balt., 1958—; briquetting cons. So. Cross Steel Co., South Africa, 1973—. Chmn. troop com. Boy Scouts Am., 1963-72. Served with USNR, 1943-45. Mem. Inst. Briquetting and Agglomeration (exec. com. 1972—), DAV, VFW. Republican. Roman Catholic. Elk. Home: 105 Furnlea Dr Glen Burnie MD 21061 Office: 2805 Light St Baltimore MD 21061

BURD, ROBERT MEYER, physician; b. N.Y.C., Aug. 25, 1937; s. David and Anne (Popkin) B.; A.B., Columbia U., 1959, M.D., 1963; m. Alice Stoller, May 30, 1964; children—Russell J., Stephen J. Intern, Albert Einstein Med. Sch., N.Y.C., 1963-64, resident in internal medicine, 1964-66; hematology fellow Montefiore Hosp., N.Y.C., 1966-67; practice medicine, specializing in hematology and oncology, Fairfield, Conn., 1969—; asst. prof. medicine Yale U., New Haven, 1975; mem. staff Park City, St. Vincent's, Yale-New Haven hosps. Active Leukemia Soc. Am., Hemophilia Found. Served to lt. comdr. USN, 1967-69. Diplomate Am. Bd. Internal Medicine. Fellow A.C.P.; mem. Am. Soc. Hematology, Am. Soc. Internal Medicine, AMA. Editorial bd. Conn. Medicine, 1974-78. Office: 1305 Post Rd Fairfield CT 06430

BURDETT, LESLIE ROBERT, publishing exec.; b. Corvallis, Oreg., Aug. 11, 1945; s. Leslie Robert and Hannah Genevieve (Stroh) Burdette; B.A., Portland State U., 1967; postgrad. U. Wis., 1967-68, U. Toronto, 1969-72. Editor social scis. Holt, Rinehart & Winston Can. Ltd., Toronto, 1972; exec. coordinator The Roundstone Council Arts, Toronto, 1973-76; head pub. relations Sch. Continuing Studies, U. Toronto, 1976-78; head pub. div. Canadian Broadcasting Corp., 1978—; tutor U. Toronto, 1969-70, 70-71. Bd. dirs. Roundstone Council Arts, 1972-73. Recipient Travel award Can. Council, 1973; Ont. grad. fellow, 1969-70, 70-71, Central Mortgage and Housing Corp. fellow, 1971-72. Editor: Canadian Artists in Exhibition, 1972-73, 73-74. Home: 206 St George St Toronto ON M5R 2N6 Canada Office: PO Box 6471 Sta A Toronto ON M5W 1X3 Canada

BURGE, FURMAN HORACE, JR., geologist; b. Doland, S.D., Feb. 26, 1924; s. Furman Horace and Olga A. (Sannes) B.; B.S. in Geol. Engring., S.D. Sch. Mines and Tech., 1950; M.S. in Geology, U. Mich., 1955; m. Dorothy Louise Anderson, May 17, 1952; children—Catherine Alice, Charles Furman, Carolyn Louise. Geologist, Oliver Iron Mining Co., Duluth, Minn., 1951-52, Mich. Limestone Co., Detroit, 1952-58; project engr., internat. engring. and raw materials dept. U.S. Steel Corp., Pitts., 1958-61, geologist internat. dept., 1962-65, chief geologist for devel., 1965-76, chief geologist coal and stone investigations, also resource devel., 1976—; pres. Mina Matilde Corp., 1967-71; resident mgr. P.T. Pacific Nikkel, Jakarta, Indonesia, 1975. Served with USNR, 1942-46. Mem. Soc. Econ. Geology, Soc. Mining Engrs., Geol. Soc. Am., Canadian Inst. Mining and Metallurgy, Sigma Xi, Sigma Tau. Office: 600 Grant St Pittsburgh PA 15230

BURGER, PAUL FREDERICK, ins. co. exec.; b. Bridgeport, Conn., May 22, 1939; s. Zoltan and Ida M. (Miller) B.; student St. Lawrence U., 1957-59, U. Bridgeport, 1960-61; m. Frances Fulton Ashby; 1 son, Douglas. Salesman, Burger & Burger, Inc., Bridgeport, 1960-68; founder, pres. Realestate Ins. Mgmt. (RIM) div. Burger & Burger, Inc., N.Y.C., 1968-73; exec. v.p., sec., dir. Burger & Burger, Inc., Stratford, Conn., 1962—; v.p. Nordstrom-Larpenteur Agy., Inc., Mpls., 1973-74; founder, pres. Air Plan, 1978—. Trustee, Zoltan Burger Found., 1967—; bd. dirs. Westport and Bridgeport (Conn.) YMCA's. Recipient President's Club award Gt. Am. Life Ins. Co., 1968; named Gen. Agt. of Year, 1967, 68, 69; named Leading Life Ins. Broker U.S., Conn. Gen. Life Ins. Co., 1968; named to All-Star Honor Roll, Ins. Salesman Mag., 1968, 69. Licensed pvt., multiengine, instrument and comml. pilot. Mem. Million Dollar Round Table (life), Crown Life Club (v.p. U.S., regional v.p. Eastern U.S. 1969), Phi Sigma Kappa. Club: Windham (N.Y.) Mountain. Contbr. articles to profl. jours.; host of weekly radio program. Home: 18 Godfrey Rd Weston CT 06883 Office: 4021 Main St Stratford CT 06497

BURGER, PHILIP CLINTON, educator; b. Elgin, Ill., Sept. 22, 1940; s. Lloyd Philip and Marion (Morgan) B.; B.S. (Ill. State scholar), Ill. Inst. Tech., 1962; M.S., Purdue U., 1963, Ph.D., 1968; m. Virginia M. Craig, June 19, 1965; children—Jennifer, Craig. Asst. prof. Northwestern, U., Evanston, Ill., 1967-73; asso. prof. State U. N.Y., Binghamton, 1973—; research asso. Advanced Research Orgn., 1976—; cons. Elrick and Lavidge, Chgo., 1970—, NSF, 1973-74, Inland Steel Corp., Chgo., 1972-73, Chgo. Conv. and Tourism Bur., Mgmt. Research and Planning, Inc., Evanston. Mem. Am. Mktg. Assn., Ops. Research Soc. Am., Am. Inst. Decision Sci., ACLU. Methodist. Author: Marketing Research: Fundamentals and Dynamics, 1975; Cases in Marketing Research, 1975; The Management of New Products and Services, 1977; Managerial Career Advancement: A Comparative Analysis, 1978; Inventions-The COMP System for Analyzing New Products Success, 1972; also FCC report. Home: 1204 Wildwood Ln Binghamton NY 13093 Office: Sch Mgmt State U Binghamton NY 13901

BURGER, WARREN EARL, chief justice U.S.; b. St. Paul, Sept. 17, 1907; s. Charles Joseph and Katharine (Schnittger) B.; student U. Minn., 1925-27; LL.B. magna cum laude, St. Paul Coll. Law (now Mitchell Coll. Law), 1931; m. Elvera Stromberg, Nov. 8, 1933; children—Wade Allan, Margaret Elizabeth. Admitted to Minn. bar, 1931; partner firm Faricy, Burger, Moore & Costello and predecessor firms, 1935-53; faculty Mitchell Coll. Law, 1931-48; asst. atty. gen. U.S., 1953-56; judge U.S. Ct. Appeals, Washington, 1956-69; chief justice U.S., 1969—. Hon. master bench Middle Temple, 1969; pres. Bentham Club, U. Coll. London, 1972-73; hon. chmn. Inst. Jud. Adminstrn., criminal justice project Am. Bar Assn. Chancellor, bd. regents Smithsonian Instn.; chmn. bd. trustees Nat. Gallery Art, Washington; trustee emeritus Mitchell Coll. Law, Macalester Coll., St. Paul, Mayo Found., Rochester, Minn.; trustee Nat. Geog. Soc. Office: Supreme Ct Bldg Washington DC 20543

BURGESS, CARL(TON) MICHAEL, plastics engr.; b. Detroit, Dec. 2, 1919; s. Carlton M. and Clara B. (Smith) B.; student Mich. State Coll., 1939-42, U. Mich., 1947; m. Mary Louise Wilcox, Feb. 2, 1946; children—Craig, Kathryn (Mrs. Alvin Gentzler), Gretchen (Mrs. Gary G. Wyman), Randall (dec.), Todd, Andrea. Chief chemist, metallurgist Kelvinator div. Am. Motors Corp., Grand Rapids, Mich., 1948-56; chief chemist Barnum Bros. Fiber Co., Detroit, 1956-58; dir. research, fiber forming div. Arvey Corp., Olean, N.Y., 1958-60; sr. project engr. Harrison Radiator div. Gen. Motors Corp., Lockport, N.Y., 1960—. Neighborhood commr. Boy Scouts Am., 1962-64; adult adviser Order of DeMolay, 1968-75. Served with AUS, 1942-45. Mem. ASTM, Soc. Plastics Engrs. (pres., dir. Buffalo chpt., nat. dir. 1976—), Smithsonian Assos., DAV (life). Republican. Conglist. Mason. Patentee in field. Home: 631 Locust St PO Box 704 Lockport NY 14094 Office: A & E Bldg Lockport NY 14094

BURGESS, MARY LOUISE DODSON, ednl. adminstr.; b. Washington, May 4, 1946; d. Clifton H. and Hazel I. (Price) Dodson; B.S., Towson State U., 1968; Ed.M., U. Md., 1975; m. Michael Allen Burgess, Sept. 13, 1968; children—Scott Allen, Lance Michael. Tchr. English, Prince Georges County (Md.) Bd. Edn., 1968-72; research asst. dept. agr. U. Md., College Park, 1972; tchr. vocat. English, Charles County (Md.) Bd. Edn., 1973-74, guidance counselor, 1974-77, vocat. evaluator, 1977—. Mem. Task Force for Writing Goals, Charles County, Md., 1973-75; active in orgn. and adminstrn. community food coop., 1974—. Named Tchr. of Year, Crossland High Sch., 1969. Mem. NEA, Am., Md. personnel and guidance assns., Nat. Vocat. Guidance Assn., Educators Assn. Charles County (mem. profl. devel. com. 1977-78), Measurement and Evaluation Assn., Profl. Women's Assn., Prince Georges (Md.) Tchrs. Assn. (fed. credit union rep. 1977—, bd. dirs. nominating com.), Md. Vocat. Evaluators Concerns Com. (sec. 1978-79), Am. Coll. Women, NOW. Republican. Home: Route 2 Box 9A La Plata MD 20646 Office: Vocational Evaluation Unit Charles County Vo-Tech Center Route 2 Box 75 Pomfret MD 20675

BURGESS, ROBERT BLUNDON, JR., mfg. co. exec.; b. Washington, June 3, 1934; s. Robert Blundon and Kathryn (Roberts) B.; A.B. in Bus. and Indsl. Mgmt., Johns Hopkins, 1956; postgrad. McCoy Coll., 1959; m. Alice Lee Tomlin, Mar. 5, 1960; children—Sarah Watt, Robert Blundon III. Indsl. engr. Armco Steel Co., Balt., 1956-61; project mgr. Brunswick Corp., Marion, Va., 1962-63; internat. cons. Wofac Co., U.K., South Africa, Germany, Moorestown, N.J., 1963-71; group v.p. internat. Joy Mfg. Co., N.Y.C., 1971-75; sr. v.p. United Techs. Internat., Hartford, 1975-77, pres., 1977—. Commr. Blue Ridge dist. Boy Scouts Am., 1962-63. Chmn. Smythe County Republican Com., 1963. Served to lt. inf. AUS, 1957-58; Korea. Mem. Work Factor Assos. East Coast (dir. 1971—), Nat. Fgn. Trade Council (dir. 1977—), Phi Gamma Delta. Clubs: University, Wings (N.Y.C.); Johns Hopkins Faculty (Balt.), Hartford, Hartford Gun, University (Hartford); Farmington (Conn.) Country, Farmington Field. Contbr. articles to German bus. publs. Home: 44 Dorset Ln Farmington CT 06032 Office: United Techs Bldg Hartford CT 06101

BURGET, DEAN EDWIN, JR., plastic surgeon; b. Toledo, June 29, 1936; s. Dean Edwin and Marie (Alwine) B.; student Denison U., 1954-57; B.S., U. Toledo, 1958; M.D., Yale, 1962; m. Anna Undine Ehrman, Mar. 16, 1957; children—Anna Undine, Mark Andrew, Kevin Phillips. Intern surgery U. Hosp., Cleve., 1962-63, resident anaesthesia, 1963-64; resident surgery Hannemann Hosp., Phila., 1966-68; resident plastic surgery Temple U. Hosp., Phila., 1968-70, asst. prof. plastic surgery, dir. div. plastic and reconstructive surgery Hahnemann Med. Coll. and Hosp., Phila., 1971-74. Served as capt. M.C., USAF, 1964-66. Diplomate Am. Bd. Plastic Surgery. Fellow A.C.S.; mem. AMA, Am. Burn Assn., Pa. Med. Soc., Am. Cleft Palate Assn., Am. Soc. Plastic and Reconstructive Surgeons, Soc. Colonial Wars Pa., Soc. War of 1812 of Pa., Valley Forge Hist. Soc. (dir.), Pa. Soc. S.R., Colonial Soc. Pa. Clubs: Yale, Rittenhouse, Penn, Racquet, Pickering Hunt (Phila.). Address: West Meadow Farm Chester Springs PA 19425

BURGGRAF, FRANK BERNARD, JR., state ofcl.; b. L.I., N.Y., Nov. 13, 1932; s. Frank Bernard and Johanna (Verbaan) B.; B.S. in Landscape Engring. and Recreation Mgmt., State U. N.Y., Syracuse, 1954; M.Landscape Architecture, U. Pa., 1958; m. Jane Rannenberg, June 25, 1955; children—Helen Marguerite, Frank Bernard III, John Christian. Asst. prof. U. Ga., Athens, 1958-63; asst. prof. Pa. State U., University Park, 1963-66, asso. prof., 1966-70; chief transmission facilities certification Office Environmental Planning, N.Y. State Dept. Pub. Service, 1970—. Cons. landscape architect Clarence C. Combs Co., N.Y.C., 1954; landscape architect Nat. Park Service, Phila., 1958, Bye & Harrmann Co., Rye, N.Y., 1959; cons. architect, Ga. and Pa., 1958-66; cons. landscape architect, partner Burggraf & King Co., State College, Pa., 1966-70; instr. nat. ednl. television, University Park, 1966; mem. N.Y. State Bd. Landscape Architecture, State U. N.Y., 1977—. Served to 1st lt. USAF, 1954-57, 62, lt. col. Res. Registered landscape architect, Ga., Ohio, Md., Mass., Pa., N.Y. Mem. Am. Soc. Landscape Architects (pres. North Central sect. 1968-69), Am. Soc. Planning Ofcls., Illuminating Engrs. Soc., Regional Plan Assn., Wilderness Soc., Western Pa. Conservancy, Am. Inst. Urban and Regional Affairs, Am. Judicature Soc., Nat. Trust for Historic Preservation. Author: (with C.S. Oliver and J.R. Nuss) Landscaping the Home Grounds, 1970; contbr. chpt. to the Handbook of Landscape Architectural Construction, 1975. Contbr. articles to profl. jours. Home: 56 Fernbank Ave Delmar NY 12054 Office: NY State Dept Public Service Office Environmental Planning Empire State Plaza Albany NY 12223

BURGI GHIGLIONE, WALTER EMILIO LUIS, statis. co. exec.; b. Rosario, Argentina, July 9, 1938; s. Emilio and Maria (Luisa) (Ghiglione) Burgi; came to U.S., 1960, naturalized, 1971; D.Math. and Statistics, U. Litoral (Argentina) 1960; m. Mafalda Rita Romano; children—Andrianne, Sabrina. Dir. statis. services Benton & Bowles, N.Y.C., 1963-70; owner Burgi Internat., Inc., N.Y.C., 1970—; chmn. Norsearch Internat. Inc., 1975—; prof. U. Buenos Aires (Argentina), 1959-60, U. Litroal, 1959-60. Mem. Am. Mktg. Assn. (chpt. dir. 1976-77, chpt. v.p. 1978—). Roman Catholic. Contbr. articles in field to profl. jours. Home: 47 Beechknoll Rd Forest Hills Garden NY 11375 Office: 1350 Ave of the Americas New York City NY 10019

BURGIN, WALTER HOTCHKISS, JR., educator; b. Harrisburg, Pa., Apr. 14, 1935; s. Walter H. and Wilhelmina (Buntin) B.; grad. Mercersburg Acad., 1953; A.B., Dartmouth, 1957; postgrad. (NSF fellow), Princeton, 1957-59; M.Ed., Harvard, 1964; postgrad. (Shell Merit fellow), Cornell U., 1964; m. Barbara I. Waddell, June 15, 1957; children—Christine, Jennifer. Tchr., Mercersburg (Pa.) Acad., 1959-64, Phillips Exeter Acad., 1964-72; headmaster Mercersburg Acad., 1972—. Vice chmn. Pa. State Bd. for Pvt. Acad. Schs., 1973—; mem. exec. com. Assn. Ind. Schs. Greater Washington, 1975-77. Mem. exec. com. council higher edn. United Ch. of Christ, 1974—. Named Outstanding Young Educator in N.H., Jr. C. of C., 1968. Mem. Math. Assn. Am., Nat. Council Tchrs. Math. (com. on supplementary publs. 1966-68), Nat., Pa. assns. ind. schs., English-Speaking Union (chmn. com. on sch. exchange programs), Headmasters Assn., Phi Beta Kappa, Phi Delta Theta. Democrat. Mem. United Ch. of Christ. Address: Mercersburg Acad Mercersburg PA 17236

BURK, RICHARD JAMAR, JR., assn. exec.; b. Balt., Jan. 17, 1940; s. Richard Jamar and Mary (Via) B.; B.A., Coll. William and Mary, 1963; postgrad. Am. U., 1968-70; m. Sue Carol Patterson, Aug. 21, 1964; children—Brett Jamar, Jill Leigh. Asst. to gen. mgr. Am. Inst. Biol. Scis., Washington, 1964-65, adminstr. for spl. projects, 1965-66, dep. dir. office biol. edn., 1966-68; exec. dir. Radiation Research Soc., Washington, 1968—, Am. Soc. Photobiology, 1973—, Environmental Mutagen Soc., 1973—, Health Physics Soc., 1974—. Cons. non-profit and sci. assns.; adv. bd. Archival Center for Chem. Mutagenesis. Pres., State Homeowners Assn., Gaithersburg, 1972, bd. dirs., 1971-72. Served with USCGR, 1963-64. Mem. Soc. Assn. Mgrs. (pres. 1969), Am. Inst. Biol. Scis., Am. Soc. Assn. Execs. Home: 17800 Vinyard Ln Derwood MD 20855 Office: 4720 Montgomery Ln Bethesda MD 20014

BURKAVAGE, WILLIAM JOSEPH, civil engr.; b. Scranton, Pa., Nov. 20, 1919; s. Joseph and Matilda (Gudinas) B.; Asso. in Sci., Keystone Jr. Coll., 1939; B.C.E., Lehigh U., 1941; m. Frances Elizabeth Streit, July 5, 1947; children—William Joseph, Marilyn Beth, John David. Partner, Von Storch and Burkavage, Clarks Summit, Pa., 1950-78, sr. partner successor firm Burkavage-Evans Assos., 1978—; mem. Nat. Engrs. Examining Council; mem., sec. Pa. State Registration Bd. Profl. Engrs. Served to comdr., C.E., USN, 1942-46, 51-53. Mem. ASCE, Nat., Pa. socs. profl. engrs., Am. Def. Preparedness Assn., Soc. Am. Mil. Engrs. Roman Catholic. Clubs: Springhaven Country (Wallingford, Pa.); Seaview Country (Absecon, N.J.); Lions (Springfield, Pa.); K.C. Author textbook: Cements and Aggregates, 1971. Home: 468 Conard Dr Springfield PA 19064 Office: Colonial Bldg Media PA 19063 also 709 N State St Clarks Summit PA 18411

BURKE, AUSTIN EMILE, bishop; b. Sluice Point, N.S., Can., Jan. 22, 1922. Ordained priest Roman Catholic Ch., 1950; bishop of Yarmouth (N.S.), 1968—. Address: PO Box 278 53 Park St Yarmouth NS B5A 2A9 Canada*

BURKE, CHARLES BRIAN, anesthesiologist; b. Worksop, Eng., Oct. 9, 1931; s. William Beaufort and Dorothy Mabel (Johnson) B.; student Bradfield Coll., 1945-48; B.A., U. Dublin, 1953, M.B., B.Chir., 1956, M.A., 1958; m. Elizabeth Stewart Andison, Aug. 30, 1955; children—Nicholas, Timothy, Louise. Came to U.S., 1962, naturalized, 1968. Intern, Welsh Regional Hosp., 1956-57, resident anesthesiology, 1957-60; practice medicine, specializing in anesthesiology, Sydney, N.S., Can., 1960-62; staff anesthesiology, dir. inhalation dept. Dartmouth/Hitchcock Med. Center, Hanover, N.H., 1962—. Clin. asst. prof. anesthesiology Dartmouth Med. Sch., 1970—; cons. anesthesiology VA, 1966—; fellow Faculty Anaesthetists, Royal Coll. Surgeons in Ireland, 1972. Diplomate Am. Bd. Anesthesiology. Fellow Am. Coll. Chest Physicians, Am. Coll. Anesthesiologists; mem. N.H. Med. Soc. (mem. ho. of dels. 1964—, sec. 1975—). Club: East India Sports and Public Schools (St. James, London). Home: Juniper Ln Blueberry Hill Etna NH 03750 Office: Hitchock Clinic Hanover NH 03755

BURKE, D(ANIEL) BARLOW, lawyer, govt. ofcl.; b. Phila., Oct. 12, 1902; s. John Julius and Phoebe J. (Barlow) B.; B.S., U. Pa., 1925; J.D., N.Y. U., 1930; M.B.A., U. Pa., 1928; m. Virginia May Friedrich, Nov. 25, 1936; children—D. Barlow, Brian Charles. Admitted to Pa. bar, 1930; asst. dist. atty. Phila., 1938-45; dep. prothonotary, Phila., 1945-55, prothonotary, 1955-70; referee State Workmen's Compensation, 1970-72; asst. prof. law and govt. Drexel Inst. Tech., 1930-40; asst. prof. polit. sci. U. Pa., 1931-38, 41-42; lectr. civil procedure class Temple Sch. Law, 1947-60. Mem. law com. Phila. Republican City Com., 1947-50; bd. dirs. Internat. House, Phila., Central Phila. chpt. ARC, Internat. Inst., Phila.; chmn. bd. council Home for Aged, Phila. Served as lt. comdr. USNR, 1942-45. Mem. Am., Pa., Phila. (dir. profl. placement 1968—) bar assns., Conf. Adminstrv. Law Judges (asso.), SAR (chancellor Pa. Soc. 1957-59, pres. Continental chpt.), Am. Polit. Sci. Assn., N.Y. U. Law Alumni Assn. (pres. Phila. chpt.), Presbyn. Social Union Phila. (pres. 1969-70), Phi Kappa Tau. Presbyterian (trustee, elder 1966-71). Clubs: Lawyers (dir. 1962), Union League (Phila.); Overbrook Farms (dir. 1965-66, v.p. 1967—), Univ. Author articles in field. Home: 200 N Wynnewood Ave Wynnewood PA 19096 Office: City Hall Annex Philadelphia PA 19107

BURKE, DANIEL J., lawyer; b. Medford, Mass., Jan. 22, 1939; s. Myles T. and Gertrude (McCarthy) B.; A.A., U. Notre Dame; B.A., Boston U.; LL.B.; J.D., New Eng. Coll. Law, 1970. Commr., Essex County, Mass., 1960-76, chmn., 1963-64, 1967-76; adminstrv. asst. to lt. gov. State of Mass., 1962-64. Cons. motivational research W.G. Haughey & Co., Boston, 1962-69. Chmn., Essex County March of Dimes, 1967, Essex County United Fund Drive, 1968; area dir. Boston U. drive. Trustee Essex County Hosp., Essex Tech. Inst.; mem. exec. bd. St. John's Prep. Sch., Danvers, Mass. Recipient awards United Fund, Lions, March of Dimes. Mem. Am., Mass., Essex County bar assns., Trial Lawyers Assn., Mass. Assn. County Ofcls., Cardinal Cushing Charities Guild, Jr. C. of C. Democrat. Home: 11 Horton St Gloucester MA 01930 also 8 Sylvan Circle Lynnfield MA 01940 Office: 550 Walnut St Lynn MA also 11-13 Horton St Gloucester MA 01930

BURKE, EDWARD NEWELL, radiologist; b. Wakefield, Apr. 28, 1916; s. Charles Edward and Laura Cecilia (Doherty) B.; B.S., Holy Cross Coll., 1938; M.D., C.M., McGill U., 1942; postgrad. Brit. Postgrad. Med. Sch., 1946, John Hopkins Sch. Pub. Health, 1943; m. Mary A. Bryon, Nov. 26, 1949; children—Laureen, Martha, Newell, Laurence. Resident in pathology Mallory Inst., Boston City Hosp., 1942-43; intern Salem (Mass.) Hosp., 1946-47, resident in radiology, 1947-50; asso. radiologist Mass. Meml. Hosp., Boston, 1951-56; radiologist Lawrence Meml. Hosp., also Charles Choate Hosp., Medford, Mass., 1956—; individual practice medicine specializing in radiology Medford, 1956—; radiologist St. Joseph's Hosp., Lowell, Mass., 1956-64, Hooper Inf., Tufts Coll., Medford, 1970—; chmn., chief depts. radiology Lawrence Meml. Hosp., 1961—, Charles Choate Meml. Hosp., 1963—; asso. prof. radiology Boston U., 1951-56; asst. clin. prof. radiology Tufts U., 1971—; pres. Charles Choate Hosp. med. staff, 1974-76, incorporator, trustee, 1974—; incorporator Lawrence Meml. Hosp., 1972—; lectr. in field. Served with U.S. Army, 1943-46. Diplomate Am. Coll. Radiology. Fellow Am. Coll. Radiologists; mem. AMA, New Eng. Roentgen Ray Soc., Radiol. Soc. N.Am., Mass. Radiol. Soc., Soc. Nuclear Medicine, Mass. Med. Soc. Roman Catholic. Clubs: Clover Boston, Winchester Country. Contbr. articles to med. publs. Home: 40 Pine Ridge Rd West Medford MA 02155 Office: 170 Governors Ave Medford MA 02155

BURKE, FRED GEORGE, state ofcl. N.J.; b. Collins, N.Y., Jan. 1, 1926; s. Fred and Sophie (Blesy) B.; B.A. magna cum laude, Williams Coll., 1953; M.A. in Polit. Sci., Princeton U., 1955, Ph.D., 1958; postgrad. Nuffield Coll., Oxford (Eng.) U., 1955-56; LL.D. (hon.), Bryant Coll., 1971; m. Virginia Mount, Oct. 5, 1975; children by previous marriage—Rebecca, Frederick, Daniel, Adam. Asst. prof. polit. sci. Ohio Wesleyan U., Delaware, Ohio, 1957-60; prof. polit. sci. Syracuse (N.Y.) U., 1961-68; dean internat. studies, prof. social scis. and adminstrn., State U. N.Y., Buffalo, 1968-70; commr. edn. State of R.I., 1971-74; commr. edn. State of N.J., 1974—; cons. Kenya govt., 1956, UN Econ. Commn. for Africa, 1968; mem. govt./acad. interface com. on internat. edn., Am. Council on Edn.; mem. Council of Chief State Sch. Officers task force on ednl. dissemination and rep. to adv. com. on ednl. finance for Am. Commn. on Intergovtl. Relations; chmn. N.J. State Bd. Examiners. Served with USAF, 1943-46, 50-51. Nat. Woodrow Wilson fellow, 1953-55; Sanaxy fellow, 1954-55; Social Sci. Research Council fellow, 1955; Ford Found. fellow, 1955-57; Eagleton and Citizenship Clearing House Democratic Conv. fellow, 1960; recipient Kimburough Owens award, 1958. Mem. Council for Internat. Exchange of Scholars, Am. Polit. Sci. Assn. (life), Am. Assn. Sch. Adminstrs., African Studies Assn., World Future Soc., Am. Edn. Fin. Assn., N.J. Police Tng. Commn., Gov's. Commn. on Drug Abuse. Author: Africa's Quest for Order, 1964; Local Government and Politics in Uganda, 1965; Tanganyika-Preplanning, 1965; Transformation of East Africa-Studies in Political Anthropology, 1966; Sub-Saharan Africa, 1966; Africa, Selected Readings, 1969; Africa, 1970; contbr. articles to publs. Office: 225 W State St Trenton NJ 08625

BURKE, HAROLD P., fed. judge; b. Fairport, N.Y., June 6, 1895; s. Peter and Jennie B.; LL.B., U. Notre Dame, 1916; m. June 30, 1927. Admitted to N.Y. bar, 1920; judge U.S. Dist. Ct., Rochester, 1937—. Served with U.S. Army, 1918-19. Democrat. Roman Catholic. Home: 30 Lakeview Park Rochester NY 14613 Office: 272 US Courthouse Rochester NY 14614

BURKE, HAROLD REYNOLDS, educator; b. Sterling, Conn., May 17, 1915; s. Harold and Louise Grace (Gallup) B.; B.S., Springfield Coll., 1940, M.Ed., 1942; D.Ed., Boston U., 1955; m. Mary J. Bathchelder, Nov. 3, 1956; children—Richard, Patricia, Sally, Harold, Lawrence, Alysa. With YMCA, Boston, 1941-43, Springfield, Mass., 1943-46; asst. prof. Springfield Coll., 1953-54; counselor Boston U.; with U. Conn. at Storrs, 1954-65; dean student affairs Western Conn. State Coll., Danbury, 1965-76, prof. psychology, 1976—; cons. psychologist, cons. orgn. devel. and human relations Nat. Tng. Labs.; adult edn. specialist. Mem. Democratic Town Com., 1963-65; justice of the peace, 1963-65. Bd. dirs. Human Resources Center of Conn., 1969-71. YMCA, 1970-73. Named Educator of the Year Student N.E.A., 1972. Mem. Am. Personnel and Guidance Assn., Am. Coll. Personnel Assn., Phi Delta Kappa, Psi Chi. Lion (dist. gov., 1964-65). Home: 21 Homestead Ave Danbury CT 06810 Office: 181 White St Danbury CT 06810

BURKE, HERBERT THOMAS, educator; b. Fort Washington, Pa., Feb. 15, 1923; married, 3 children. B.B.A. in Econs., Upsala Coll., East Orange, N.J., 1952; M.A. in Bus. Edn., Seton Hall U., South Orange, N.J., 1967; Mus.D. in Piano, Inst. Music, London, 1975. Prodn. mgr. Curtis-Wright Corp., Wood-Ridge, N.J., 1952-55, ops. mgr., 1962-63; engr. Westinghouse Electric Corp., Bloomfield, N.J., 1955-62; tchr., coordinator Perth Amboy (N.J.) High Sch., 1969—. Founder, dir. Central Jersey Sch. of Music. Mem. Perth Amboy Edn. Assn., Inc. (pres. 1970-75), N.J. Am. Fedn. Tchrs. Author tchrs. guides. Home: 749 Stephen Ave Perth Amboy NJ 08861 Office: Edn Center Perth Amboy High Sch Perth Amboy NJ 08861

BURKE, JACKSON FREDERICK, author; b. Alameda, Calif., Aug. 6, 1915; s. Francis Frederick and Elisabeth May (Wood) B.; B.A. in English, U. Calif., Berkeley, 1944; m. Rosa de Sa Aleixo, Dec. 25, 1958. Tchr., Kamehameha Sch., Honolulu, 1944-45; mem. faculty U. Calif., Berkeley, 1945-47; novels include: Noah, 1969, Location Shots, 1974, Death Trick, 1975, The Kama Sutra Tango, 1977, Crazy Woman Blues, 1978. Mem. Authors Guild, Authors League Am. J.F. Burke Collection established at Mugar Meml. Library, Boston U. Office: James Seligmann Agy 280 Madison Ave New York City NY 10016

BURKE, JOHN FRANCIS, surgeon, educator; b. Chgo., July 22, 1922; s. Frank A. and Mary B.; B.S., U. Ill., 1947; M.D., Harvard U., 1951; m. Agnes Redfearn Goldman, June 24, 1950; children—John Selden, Peter Ashley, Ann Campbell, Andrew Thomas. Intern, Mass. Gen. Hosp., Boston, 1951-52, resident, 1952-57; practice medicine specializing in surg. infection, burn trauma treatment, Boston, 1958—; asso. prof. surgery Harvard Med. Sch., Cambridge, Mass., 1969-75, prof., 1975-76, Helen Andrus Benedict prof., 1976—; mem. staff Mass. Gen. Hosp., Shriners Burns Inst. - Boston Unit, chief of staff, 1969—; vis. prof. dept. nutrition and food sci. Mass. Inst. Tech.; program dir. New Eng. Burn Demonstration Program, 1977—. Served with USAAF, 1942-45. Moseley Traveling fellow Harvard Med. Sch. - Lister Inst. Preventive Medicine, London, 1955. Mem. N.Y. Acad. Scis., AMA, Am. Thoracic Soc., Mass. Med. Soc., A.C.S., Boston, New Eng. surg. socs., Am. Surg. Assn., Soc. Univ. Surgeons, Infectious Disease Soc. Am., Am. Assn. Surgery of Trauma, Am. Soc. Contamination Control, Am. Assn. Thoracic Surgery, Internat. Soc. Burn Injuries, Am. Burn Assn., Am. Trauma Soc., Am. Assn. Med. Instrumentation. Contbr. articles in field to med. jours. Home: 216 Prospect St Belmont MA 02178 Office: Mass Gen Hosp Boston MA 02114

BURKE, JOSEPHINE MARY, educator; b. N.Y.C., July 21, 1914; d. Joseph T. and Maggie (Kloeti) Burke; B.A., Hunter Coll., 1936; M.A., Columbia, 1937. Temporary instr. Hunter Coll. of City U. N.Y., 1936-38, tutor, 1938-42, instr., 1943-48, asst. prof., 1949-60, asso. prof. phys. edn., 1960-66, prof., 1967-75, prof. emeritus, 1975—, chmn. dept., 1968-71, chmn. womens' div. dept. phys. edn., 1961-71. Mem. U.S. Olympic Volley Ball Sports Com. for XVIII Olympiad, 1961-72; mem. U.S. Pan-Am. Sports Com., 1962-63; organizer, operator, adminstr., supr. children's camp, 1951-62; staff mem. Nat. Red Cross Aquatic Sch., 1947-49, dean of women, staff mem., 1949. Recipient gold medal Finnish League for Phys. Edn. of Women, 1962; Golden Eagle award Girl Scouts U.S.A., 1934; named to Volley Ball Hall of Fame, Los Angeles, 1956, Hunter Coll. Hall of Fame, 1975. Fellow AAHPER; mem. U.S. Volley Ball Assn. (mem. at large exec. bd. 1952—). Home: 5 Howard Rd Bayville NY 11709

BURKE, MARVIN MURRAY, govt. ofcl.; b. Toronto, Ont., Can., Jan. 24, 1930; s. Jacob and Fanny B.; student U. Toronto, 1951-52; diploma Maritime Sch. Social Work, Dalhousie, 1970. Music specialist Toronto YM & YWHA, 1948-49; dept. head Univ. Settlement House, Toronto, 1950-52; supr. dept. gerontology and creative arts YM & YWHA, Montreal, Que., Can., 1952-54; program dir. Jewish Community Center, Ottawa, Ont., 1954-55; entertainer, musician, broadcaster, theatrical agt., producer, mem. Raftsmen, RCA Victor Rec. Artists, 1955-66; writer, researcher, broadcaster Canadian Broadcasting Co., Halifax, N.S., 1965—; coordinator neighborhood services Halifax Neighborhood Centre Project, 1966-68; acting exec. dir. Halifax-Dartmouth Welfare Council, 1970; dir., therapist Assos. for human Relations and Counselling Ltd., Halifax, 1970-71; exec. dir. N.S. Commn. on Drug Dependency, 1971—; cons. Study on Youth Programmes, Halifax Jewish Community, 1966; cons. social animation and human relations tng. Youth Agy., Province N.S., 1968-70; cons. seminar sex and the family, Dalhousie, 1970; mem. panel Symposium on Drug Abuse, Dalhousie, 1969; profl. resources person to com. on gerontology Montreal Council Social Agys., 1952-54. Mem. Halifax Bd. Trade, 1966—; vice-chmn. Halifax-Dartmouth Welfare Council, 1971; producer Jolly Tar Hornpipe, Folk Festival, Halifax, Natal Day, 1966-68; pres. N.S. Folk Arts Council, 1967; exec. com. Canadian Addictions Found., 1976-78, pres., 1977-78; exec. com., bd. dirs. Halifax Sr. Citizens Housing Corp., 1969-71; chmn. bd. dirs. Help Line, Halifax, 1971-72; bd. dirs. Interim Social Planning Council, Halifax, Dartmouth and County, 1971—. Fellow Royal Soc. Health; mem. Internat. Council Alcohol and Addictions (exec. com. 1972—), Am. Assn. Automotive Medicine, Canadian Pub. Health Assn., Canadian Assn. Social Workers, N.S. Assn. Social Workers, N.S. Press Gallery Assn., Assn. Canadian TV and Radio Artists, Am. Fedn. Musicians. Home: PH6/211 Willett St Halifax NS B3M 3C7 Canada Office: 5871 Spring Garden Rd Halifax NS B3H 1Y2 Canada

BURKE, MARY LOU, med. technician; b. Holyoke, Mass., May 15, 1936; d. Edmund A. and Mary L. (McCabe) B.; B.A., Coll. of Our Lady of Elms, 1957; grad. Mercy Hosp. Sch. Med. Tech., 1957. Hematologist, Mercy Hosp., Springfield, Mass., 1957, teaching supr., 1966; tech. rep. in New Eng., Hycel Inc., Houston, 1966-69, dir. edn., 1966-71, dir. profl. consultation, 1971-73; product coordinator Instrumentation Lab. Inc., Lexington, Mass., 1973-74, mgr. tech. services, biomed, div., 1974—. Mem. Am. Assn. Clin. Chemistry, Am. Soc. Med. Tech. (Clay Adams research grant 1963, certified AUC med. technologist), Mass. Assn. Med. Tech. Roman Catholic. Home: 378 Park Ave Arlington Heights MA 02175 Office: 113 Hartwell St Lexington MA 02173

BURKE, MICHAEL, sports exec.; b. Enfield, Conn., June 8, 1918; s. Patrick and Mary (Fleming) B.; B.S., U. Pa., 1939; m. Faith Long, June 10, 1939 (div. Dec. 1945); 1 dau., Patricia; m. 2d, Timothy Campbell, Nov. 17, 1946; children—Michele, Doreen, Peter. Spl. adviser to U.S. high commr. for Germany, 1951-54; v.p., gen. mgr. Ringling Bros. Barnum & Bailey Circus, 1954-56; program exec. CBS TV Network, 1956-57; program dir. CBS TV Network, Europe, 1957-58; mng. dir., pres. CBS Europe, Zurich, Switzerland, 1958-62, CBS Ltd., London, 1958-62; mng. dir. CBS Prodns. Ltd., London, 1958-62; v.p. CBS, Inc., N.Y.C., 1962-73; chmn., pres. N.Y. Yankees, Inc., 1966-73; partner, cons. N.Y. Yankees, 1973—; pres. Madison Square Garden, 1973—. Vice pres., bd. dirs. Repertory Theatre of Lincoln Center, N.Y.C. Served to lt. (j.g.) USNR, 1942-45. Decorated Navy Cross, Silver Star, Medaille de la Resistance (France). Clubs: Garrick, Special Forces (London); Players (N.Y.C.). Home: 52 Gramercy Park New York City NY 10010 Office: Madison Square Garden 2 Pennsylvania Plaza New York City NY 10001

BURKE, ROYDON, photographer; b. Quincy, Mass., Dec. 21, 1901; s. Walter Edward and Zayma (King) B.; A.B., Harvard U., 1923; m. Jean Attwood, Oct. 24, 1931 (div.); 1 dau., Janet. Ins. broker, Quincy, 1924-34; pictorial and portrait photographer, Quincy, 1939—; one-man shows include: Mass. Inst. Tech., 1966, N.Y. Photog. Soc., N.Y.C., 1976; photographs exhibited in numerous internat. salons, including: Boston Internat. Salon, Los Angeles Internat. Exhbn., Photog. Soc. Hong Kong Internat. Salon, 1957-77; represented in permanent collections, including Photog. Soc. Am.; photog. judge, commentator; lectr., tchr. in field. Recipient numerous medals, cups and other awards for photography, including gold statuette S.E. Asia Photog. Soc., 1964, Seiko Cup Chinese Photog. Assn., 1968, goldmedal Photog. Soc. Am., 1971, gold medal Sarawak Internat. Salon, 1977. Fellow S.E. Asia Photog. Soc. (hon.), Photog. Salon Exhibitors Assn. (Hong Kong); mem. Royal Photog. Soc. Gt. Brit. (asso.), Federation Internationale de L'arte Photographique (artiste), Rochester Salon (hon.), Photog. Soc. Am. (asso., master of salon workshop), South Shore, Hong Kong YMCA (hon.), Del. (asso.), Boston camera clubs, Quincy Hist. Soc. Republican. Episcopalian. Clubs: Neighborhood of Quincy, Harvard of Quincy. Author: Fantasy, 1925; Night Song, 1931; Reverie, 1937; asso. editor Poetry world, 1929-30; contbr. photograph to rep. U.S. in 1975 World Cup Competition. Home: 284 Adams St Quincy MA 02169

BURKE, THOMAS EDWARD, hotel co. exec.; b. Akron, Ohio, July 29, 1930; s. Paul Mark and Mary Leocadia (Ley) B.; B.Communications, Am. U.; m. Elizabeth Maxine Wells, Apr. 18, 1953; children—Nancy Elizabeth Burke Harmon, Thomas Edward, Timothy Paul, Daniel Patrick, David Gerard. Reporter, Painesville (Ohio) Telegraph, 1954-57; mgr. pub. relations Seiberling Rubber Co., Akron, Ohio, 1961-63; pub. relations staff rep. Carrier Corp., Syracuse, N.Y., 1963-66; pub. relations dir. Wyandotte (Mich.) Chem. Corp., 1966-69; dir. corporate relations Merriott Corp., Washington, 1969-72, v.p. corporate affairs, 1972-78, sr. v.p. corporate affairs, asst. to pres., 1978—; guest lectr. Am. U., Washington, Georgetown U., Washington. Past dir. Washington Bd. Trade; trustee Fed. City Council. Served with U.S. Army, 1951-53. Mem. Pub. Relations Soc. Am., Bethesda-Chevy Chase C. of C. (past dir.), Nat. Press Club. Republican. Roman Catholic. Club: Congressional Country. Home: 521 Haven Ln Great Falls VA 22066 Office: Marriott Dr Washington DC 20058

BURKE, THOMAS GEORGE, educator; b. Bklyn., Mar. 16, 1947; s. George Joseph and Dorothy (Hohl) B.; B.A. in Psychology (State Regents scholar), St. John's U., 1968, M.A. in Clin. Psychology, 1971; postgrad. New Sch. Social Research, 1973—. Tchr., student drug counselor St. John's Prep. High Sch., Bklyn., 1969-72; psychologist New High Sch., Bklyn., 1972-73; adj. instr. dept. psychology St. John's U., Jamaica, N.Y., 1973—, S.I. Community Coll. (N.Y.), 1973—; acad. coordinator psychology N.Y. Inst. Tech., Old Westbury, 1974—; psychotherapist Personal Awareness Center, 1977—. Vol. psychologist Creedmoor State Mental Hosp., Queen's Village, N.Y., 1972—. Mem. Am. (asso.), N.Y. State (asso.) psychol. assns., N.Y. State Doctoral Assn. (v.p.), Delta Sigma Phi. Roman Catholic. Author: Contemporary Issues in Abnormal Psychology and Mental Illness, 1976. Composer (with Charles Frazer) Jack in the Box, 1969. Home: 79-57 Juniper Valley Rd Middle Village NY 11379 Office: NY Inst Tech CAPP Office Old Westbury Campus Wheatley Rd PO Box 170 Old Westbury NY 11568

BURKERT, JOHN WALLACE, SR., cons. engring. firm exec.; b. Phila., June 29, 1926; s. John Alphonses and Violet Sidonia (Stark) B.; B.S. in E.E., Pa. State U., 1949; m. Phyllis Marion Blasdale, Sept. 18, 1948; children—John Wallace, Mary I., Andrew M. Power specialist engr. E.I. du Pont deNemours Co., Inc., Newark, Del., 1950-66; pres. Del. Engring. and Design Corp., Newark, 1966—. Guest lectr. Pratt Inst. Life Support Systems, 1973-74; gen. chmn. Engrs. Week Banquet for State Del., 1972; pack chmn. Cub Scouts Am., Newark, 1958-60; pres. Jennie Smith PTA, Newark, 1958-59; mem. Newark Council PTA, 1960. Served with USAF, 1944-45. Mem. Am. Soc. Heating, Refrigeration and Air Conditioning Engrs. (pres., organizer Del. chpt. 1969-70, sec. nat. com. 1972—, dir., chmn. region III), Sanford Soc. (dir.). Episcopalian (jr. warden 1969-71). Rotarian (pres. 1969). Home: 58 W Park Pl Newark DE 19711 Office: 153 Chestnut Hill Rd Newark DE 19711

BURKHARDT, CHARLES HENRY, author, assn. exec., lectr.; b. Bklyn., June 17, 1915; s. Adolph Michael and Mildred (Herman) B.; B.S., St. Johns U., 1938; postgrad Pratt Inst., 1947-48; m. Lillian Sanders, Jan. 31, 1942; children—Gregory Charles, Christopher Michael. Service mgr., asst. sales mgr. Concord Oil Corp., N.Y.C., 1939-43; instr. heat engring. Walter Hervey Jr. Coll., N.Y.C., 1947-49; dir. edn. Perfex Corp., Milw., 1949-51; gen. mgr. Paragon Maintenance Co., Mineola, N.Y., 1951-55; mng. dir., sec.-treas. Oil Heat Inst. Am., N.Y.C., 1955-60; v.p. Nat. Oil Fuel Inst., N.Y.C., 1960-62; exec. v.p. New Eng. Fuel Inst. Boston, 1962—. Cons., Standard Oil Co. N.J., 1957-58, Bacharach Instrument Co., 1947, Richfield Mfg. Co., 1948; mem. Mktg. Viability Task Force, U.S. Dept. Energy, 1977, also mem. fuel oil adv. com.; del. New Eng. Energy Congress, 1978, White House Conf. on Small Bus. Served to capt. AUS, 1943-46. Recipient Distinguished Achievement award New Eng. Oil Heat Industry, 1972; Certificate of Commendation, Conn. Petroleum Assn., 1974; Oil Man of New Eng. award Better Home Heat Council N.H., 1975; Certificate of Appreciation, Soc. Mfg. Engrs., 1976; 15th Anniversary commendation New Eng. Fuel Inst., 1977. Mem. Am. Soc. Heating, Refrigeration and Air Conditioning Engrs., Am. Soc. Assn. Execs., Paulist League. Republican. Roman Catholic. Author: Residential and Commercial Air Conditioning, 1959, Baseboard Heating, 1952, Domestic and Commercial Oil Burners, 1969. The Oil Heating Technician, 1957. Home: 770 Boylston St Boston MA 02199 Office: 20 Summer St Watertown MA 02172

BURKHARDT, DOLORES ANN, library cons.; b. Meriden, Conn., July 28, 1932; d. Frederick Christian and Emily (Detels) Burkhardt; B.A., U. Conn., 1955; M.S., So. Conn. State Coll., 1960; postgrad. Central Wash. State Coll., 1962, Columbia, 1964—; 6th yr. diploma U. Conn., 1972. Asst. librarian So. Conn. State Coll. Library, summers 1960, 62; sch. library tchr. Farmington High Sch., Unionville, Conn., 1955-65; library cons.; media specialist East Farms Sch., Farmington, Conn., 1967-70; sch. library coordinator K-12, Durham-Middlefield, Conn., 1970-72; media specialist regional dist. 10, Burlington-Harwinton, Conn., 1972-78; ednl. media cons., 1978—. Instr. Boston U. Media Inst. Spl. cons. Conn. Dept. Edn., 1965—. Mem. AAUW (sec. 1956-58), NEA, Conn. Edn. Assn., New Eng. (pres. 1969-70), Conn. (2d v.p. 1965—, chmn. sch. library devel.; chmn. standards com. 1970-72, chmn. instructional materials selection policy com. Region 10) sch. library assns., Am. Assn. Sch. Librarians, New Eng. Sch. Devel. Council, Phi Delta Kappa. Lutheran. Home and office: 812 Savage St Southington CT 06489

BURKS, JUANITA HARRIETTE, trade co. exec.; b. N.Y.C., May 2, 1947; d. Alvin Lee and Harriette Juanita (Hope) B., B.A., City Coll. N.Y., 1970; M.Pub. Adminstrn., N.Y. U., 1974. Tng. dir. N.Y.C. Housing and Devel. Adminstrn., 1970-74; asst. dir. pub. relations Black Arts Found., San Francisco, 1974-77; systems sales mgr. Acme Visible Systems, N.Y.C., 1977—. Pres. Concerned Democrats Washington Heights, N.Y., 1974-75; adv. bd. N.Y. State Assembly, 1975-76. Martin Luther King Jr. scholar, 1972-73. Mem. Am. Inst. Planners, Nat. Housing Conf., Am. Soc. Pub. Adminstrn., Nat. Assn. Housing and Redevel. Democrat. Lutheran. Clubs: Sales Exec. N.Y., City Coll. Alumni. Home: 17 Ft George Hill New York City NY 10040

BURLAGA, LEONARD FRANCIS, physicist; b. Superior, Wis., Oct. 1, 1938; s. Edward Walter and Helen Katherine (Plachta) B.; B.S., U. Chgo., 1960; M.S., U. Minn., 1962, Ph.D. in Physics, 1966; m. Catherine M. McDonough, Mar. 18, 1972; 1 dau., Anna Marie. From teaching asst. to research asso. physics U. Minn., 1960-66; astrophysicist Goddard Space Flight Center, NASA, Greenbelt, Md., 1966—. Mem. Am. Phys. Soc., Am. Geophys. Union. Author research papers. Home: 3108 Shield Ln Bowie MD 20715 Office: Code 692 NASA/GSFC Greenbelt MD 20771

BURLESON, HAL EUGENE, AID ofcl. State Dept.; b. Ala., Dec. 26, 1932; s. Emmit Howard and Vertie (Green) B.; ed. U. Md.; m. Joung Hee Lee, Aug. 13, 1952; 1 dau., Charlene. Procurement officer, gen. service officer UNC/OEC State Dept., Korea, 1956-61; gen. ser. officer, area exec. officer ICA, State Dept. Afghanistan, 1961-63; gen. service officer, supply and procurement adviser AID, State Dept., Yemen, 1963-64, field support and asst. exec. officer, Panama, 1964-66, dep. exec. officer, then exec. officer, Vietnam, 1966-69, adminstrv. officer, New Delhi, 1969-73, Washington, 1973-74; dep. exec. officer, Panama, 1974-77; exec. officer, Swaziland, 1977—. Served with AUS, 1949-55. Home: Route 1 Brilliant AL 35548 Office: Dept State AID Washington DC 20523

BURLINGHAM, MARY S., ins. exec.; b. Dayton, Ohio, Sept. 14, 1938; d. John J. and Mary (McCarthy) Sullivan; student Freeman Sch. Bus., Geneva, N.Y., 1957; m. Gene Burlingham, Sept. 16, 1961; children—Wanda B. Edgcomb, Janne B. Harrison. Exec. sec., Brown-Hoyt, Inc., Canandaigua, N.Y., 1960-61; partner Burlingham Agy. Inc. ins., Fairport, N.Y., 1963—, v.p., sec., 1963—. Pres., Ontario County Hist. Soc., 1978-79; pres. Hist. Soc. East Bloomfield, 1973-75; sec. Zoning Bd. Village East Bloomfield, 1972-76. Mem. Bloomfield Holcomb C. of C. (sec. 1962), Bloomfield Dramatics Club, Nat. Secs. Assn. (past chpt. pres.), Regional Conf. Hist. Agencies. Club: Hunt Hollow Ski. Home: 1 Howard Ave Holcomb NY 14469 Office: 6780 Pittsford Palmyra Rd Fairport NY 14450

BURLIUK, NICHOLAS, artist; b. Moscow, Apr. 11, 1915; s. David Davidovich and Maria Nikiforovna (Yelenevskaya) B.; came to U.S., 1922, naturalized, 1940; Certificate in Journalism, N.Y.U., 1938; B.S., U. Idaho, 1940; M.A., Columbia, 1950; m. Freda Jeannette Boyd, Apr. 22, 1944; children—Mary Burliuk Holt. One man shows at Harry Salpeter Gallery, N.Y.C., 1947; Burliuk Gallery, N.Y.C., 1950, 51, 52; Wellons Gallery, N.Y.C., 1953; State Assembly, State Capitol, Albany, N.Y., 1962; Artiques Gallery, Hicksville, N.Y., 1970; Baiter Gallery, Huntington, N.Y., 1971; Burliuk Gallery, Hampton Bays, N.Y., 1974; exhibited in group shows at Butler Art Inst., 1954; Board Coll., 1959; Pietrantonio Gallery, N.Y.C., 1963; World's Fair, N.Y.C., 1964; C.W. Post Coll., 1964; Adelphi U., 1968; Silvermine Gallery, Conn., 1969, numerous others; represented in permanent collections in U.S. and Can.; owner, dir. Burliuk Gallery, N.Y.C., 1950-53, Hampton Bays, L.I., 1967—; judge Westhampton Beach (L.I.) Outdoors Art Shows, 1972. Served with M.C., U.S. Army, 1942-46. Recipient 1st prize Royal St. Art Sch., New Orleans, 1943, Parrish

Mus., Southampton, L.I., 1947, Guild Hall, L.I., 1949, 50, Heckscher Mus., Huntington, L.I., 1958; 2d prize, Guild Hall, Easthampton, L.I., 1953. Mem. L.I. Art Tchrs. Assn., N.Y. State Tchrs. Assn., N.Y. State Parents and Tchrs. (hon. life). Republican. Methodist. Editor: (with Katherine S. Dreier) Burliuk, 1944. Editor Color and Rhyme Art mag., 1948-67. Home: 184 Twin Ln N Wantagh NY 11793 also Hampton Bays NY 11946

BURLTON, ROGERS CHRISTOPHER, psychiatrist; b. Beaumont, Tex., Sept. 28, 1935; s. Carl Christopher and Catherine Rose (Rinkel) B.; B.A., DeMazenod Scholasticate, 1958, U. St. Thomas, 1960; B.S., Lamar State Coll. Tech., 1963; M.D., U. Tex., 1967; m. Camille Ellis, Oct. 10, 1964. Intern, Bryan Meml. Hosp., Lincoln, Nebr., 1967-68; resident in psychiatry Walter Reed Gen. Hosp., Washington, 1968-71, child psychiatry fellow, 1971-73; asst. chief dept. psychiatry, chief out-patient psychiatry clinic, chief child guidance clinic Dwight D. Eisenhower Army Med. Center, Augusta, Ga., 1973-75; pvt. practice child, adolescent and adult psychiatry Psychiat. Assos., Gaithersburg, Md., 1975—; cons. in field. Served to maj., U.S. Army, 1968-75. Mem. Am. Psychiat. assn., Am. Acad. Child Psychiatry, Am. Soc. Adolescent Psychiatry. Home: 13800 Loree Ln Rockville MD 20853 Office: 19221 Montgomery Village Ave Suite C-14 Gaithersburg MD 20760

BURMAN, DAVID JAY, educator; b. N.Y.C., June 11, 1938; s. Louis Robert and Frances Beatrice (Cohen) B.; B.S., N.Y. U., 1961, M.S., 1962; M.P.A., Nova U., 1976; m. Luise L. Alterman, Aug. 23, 1964; children—Rona Susan, Michael Jonathan. Mgr., Ohrbach's, 1961-62; asst. gen. mdse. mgr. Gimbel's, 1962; owner B. Casual, Inc., 1963-66; dir. coop. edn., asst. prof. bus. adminstrn. Central Conn. State Coll., 1967—; cons. retail field; pres. Merch-a-Matic; pres., dir. Vestamatic, Inc. Mem. Coop. Edn. Assn. (charter), Am. Vocat. Assn. (life), West Hartford, Hartford chambers commerce, Nat. Assn. Mgmt. Edn., Am. Acad. Consultants, Am. Collegiate Retailing Assn. (dir.), Am. Mktg. Assn., Am. Soc. Pub. Adminstrn., Newcomen Soc. N.Am., U.S. C. of C. Execs., Eta Mu Pi (nat. dir.), Pi Sigma Epsilon. Home: 100 Mohawk Dr West Hartford CT 06117 Office: 1615 Stanley St New Britain CT 06050

BURNES, ALAN JEFFREY, diversified co. exec.; b. Boston, Nov. 21, 1935; s. Justin Irwin and Jeanette (Olins) B.; B.A. (Rufus Choate scholar), Dartmouth Coll., 1957; student Amos Tuck Sch. Bus. Adminstrn., 1961; Ed.D. (Lehman scholar), Harvard, 1966; m. Karen Lois Hirschmann, Sept. 11, 1971; children—Alan Jeffrey, Jonathan Nels, Kristopher Olins. Asst. prof. grad. psychology and edn. Boston Coll., 1966-67; exec. dir. Behavioral Scis. Center, Cambridge, Mass., 1966-69; sr. asso. Behavioral Scis. Tech., Inc., N.Y.C., 1969-70; exec. dir. Bristol Acres, residential treatment center, Taunton, Mass., 1970-71; sr. asso. Human Scis., Inc., N.Y.C., 1971; mgr. profl. and service devel. Corning Glass (N.Y.), 1972-75; dir. human resources Textron, Inc. (R.I.), Providence, 1975-76; chmn. The Compass Group, Westport, Mass., 1978—; dir. Nav., Inc., Internat. Homes Group, Internat. Seafoods Group, Constrn. Tech. Group, Internat. Protection Group, Med. Tech. Group, Personal Products Group; dir. Teknos, Inc., N.Y.C., W. African Investments Corp.; mem. council Conf. Bd., 1976—. Mem. Venereal Disease Control Commn., 1967. Served to capt. USMC, 1957-61. Fellow Am. Psychol. Assn.; Am. Soc. Tng. and Devel., Kappa Phi Kappa, Delta Upsilon, Phi Delta Kappa. Clubs: Harvard; Dartmouth (Boston). Author: (with Sheldon R. Roen) Community Adaptation Schedule, 1966. Editor: Urban Problems Series, 1970. Contbr. articles profl. publs. Home: 1286 Drift Rd Westport MA 02790 Office: PO Box 295 Westport Point MA 02791

BURNETTE, MAHLON ADMIRE, III, nutritionist; b. Leesville, Va., May 18, 1936; s. Mahlon Admire and Alda (Mergler) B.; B.S., Va. Poly. Inst., 1968; M.Phil., Rutgers U., 1973, Ph.D., 1974; m. Sheryl Patricia Rutledge, July 31, 1976. Research asst. Rutgers U., 1971-74; dir. sci. affairs Grocery Mfrs. Am., Washington, 1974—. Served with inf. U.S. Army, 1969-70; Vietnam. Decorated Bronze star. Mem. Inst. Food Technologists, Am. Inst. Nutrition, Soc. for Nutrition Edn., Am. Chem. Soc., AAAS, Mensa, Sigma Xi, Alpha Zeta. Club: Washington Golf and Country. Home: 2940 Harvest Glen Ct Herndon VA 22070 Office: 1010 Wisconsin Ave NW Suite 800 Washington DC 20007

BURNEY, GLORIA GREGORY, personnel cons.; b. Winthrop, Mass., July 21, 1926; d. Gregory John and Lucy Elizabeth (Yeganian) Gregory; B.A. in Psychology, U. N.H., 1948; m. Spencer Worthington Burney, Sept. 8, 1956; children—Meredith Leigh, Priscilla Elizabeth. Vice pres. personnel Sigma Instruments, Inc., 1951-70; personnel cons., Wellesley, Mass., 1970—. Bd. dirs. Bur. Vocat. Counsel, Inc., 1960-76. Mem. AAUW, Am. Soc. Personnel Adminstrn. Republican. Mem. Ch. of Christ. Club: Armenian Women's Ednl. Home and Office: 27 Thackeray Rd Wellesley MA 02181

BURNHAM, ANITA LOUISE, ednl. adminstr.; b. Troy, N.Y., July 18, 1949; d. Henry Paul and Eleanor Mary (Bocchi) Stockwicz; B.A. in French, Goucher Coll., 1971; M.S., State U. N.Y., Albany, 1977. Dance tchr. YWCA Gloversville, N.Y., 1966-67; tchr. French and Spanish, Vincentian Inst., Albany, 1971-73, Ichabod Crane Middle Sch., Valatie, N.Y., 1973-75; asst. dean student affairs Skidmore Coll., Saratoga Springs, N.Y., 1975—. Vol. usher Saratoga Performing Arts Center, summers, 1968, 69, 77. Mem. Am. Personnel and Guidance Assn., Student Personnel Assn. N.Y. State. Republican. Roman Catholic. Home: Sleepy Hollow Manor Rowland St Ballston Spa NY 12020 Office: Skidmore Coll Saratoga Springs NY 12866

BURNHAM, HAROLD ARTHUR, physician, pharm. co. exec.; b. Boston, Nov. 6, 1929; s. Howard Rowland and Edna Adelaide (Teachout) B.; B.S., Union Coll., 1951; M.A., Middlebury Coll., 1952; postgrad. Albany State Tchrs. Coll., 1953-54, Adelphi U., 1958-59, Nassau Community Coll., 1961-62; M.D., U. Md., 1966; m. Lucienne Jeanne Seas, June 28, 1952; children—Philippe Henri, Isabelle Jeanne. Tchr. sci., French and track team coach S. Glens Falls (N.Y.) Central High Sch., 1952-54; med. rep., hosp. salesman Upjohn Co., Bklyn., 1956-62; intern S. Balt. Gen. Hosp., 1966-67; resident Glen Cove (N.Y.) Community Hosp., 1967-69; practice family medicine, Glen Cove, 1969-75; asso. med. dir. Winthrop Labs. div. Sterling Drug Inc., N.Y.C., 1975-76, med. dir. Glenbrook Labs. div., N.Y.C., 1977; v.p. for med. affairs, sr. v.p. Winthrop Products Inc., N.Y.C. and N.J., The Sydney Ross Co. and Sterling Products Internat., N.Y.C., 1977—; instr. Sch. Practical Nursing, Glen Cove, Community Hosp., 1970-75; cons., clinician in medicine Nassau County Pub. Health Dept., 1975—. Scoutmaster, Boy Scouts Am., Glens Falls, N.Y., 1953-54, com. mem., 1968—, merit badge counsellor for first aid, pub. health, emergency care, chemistry and mammals for Sagamore Dist., 1968—. Served in U.S. Army, 1954-56. Recipient Continuing Edn. awards AMA, 1969, 72, 75. Diplomate Am. Bd. Med. Examiners, Am. Bd. Family Practice. Mem. AMA, Pan Am., N.Y. State, Nassau County med. socs., Am. Acad. Family Physicians, Am. Fertility Soc., Nu Sigma Nu. Episcopalian. Office: 90 Park Ave New York City NY 10016

BURNS, ALEX ANDREW, life sciences co. exec.; b. Monroe, La., Sept. 15, 1940; s. Alex A. and Ollie M. (Hamilton) B.; B.S., So. U., 1962; postgrad. (NIH Predoctoral fellow) State U. of N.Y., 1966-67. Asst. cancer research scientist Roswell Park Meml. Inst., Buffalo, 1964-69; mgr. cell production Asso. Biomedic Systems, Inc., Buffalo, 1969-71, asst. to pres., 1971-73, v.p. corp. devel., 1973-74; exec. v.p., 1974-75, pres., 1975—, also dir.; chmn. of bd., pres. HTI Corp., Buffalo, 1975—, also dir.; cons. Inst. for Sci. and Social Accountability, Washington; mem. Human Subjects Com., State U. of N.Y. at Buffalo. Active Buffalo Urban League. Served with U.S. Army, 1962-64. Mem. Am. Soc. for Microbiology, Tissue Culture Assn., Internat. Assn. for Plant Tissue Culture, Alpha Phi Alpha. Home: 525 Humboldt Pkwy Buffalo NY 14208 Office: 872 Main St Buffalo NY 14202

BURNS, ANNE, coll. dean; b. Phila., Mar. 28, 1927; d. Michael and Mary (McFadden) B.; A.B. in English and History, Immaculata (Pa.) Coll., 1957; M.Ed. in Latin and Edn., U. Va., 1964, Ed.D. in Counseling Psychology, 1970. Tchr. Latin, guidance counselor Norfolk (Va.) Catholic High Sch., 1958-67; prefect Notre Dame Acad., Miami, Fla., 1967-69; grad. asst. U. Va., Charlottesville, 1969-70; tchr. edn. Immaculate Coll., 1970-73, tchr. psychology, 1973—, dean of coll. devel., 1978—; dir. self-esteem workshops and managerial seminars. Mem. Am. Psychol. Assn., Am. Coll. Tchrs. Assn., Am., Pa. personnel and guidance assns., Classical Assn. (Rome), Nat. Cath. Guidance Counsel, Kappa Delta Pi, Delta Tau Kappa. Fulbright scholar Am. Acad., Rome; contbr. articles to profl. jours. Home: Immaculata Coll Immaculata PA 19345

BURNS, ARNOLD IRWIN, lawyer; b. N.Y.C., Apr. 14, 1930; s. Herman Leon and Rose (Lauterstein) B.; A.B., Union Coll., Schenectady, 1950; LL.B., Cornell U., 1953; postgrad. Parker Sch. Internat. Law, 1960; m. Felice Bernstein, June 17, 1951; children—Linda Susan, Douglas Todd. Admitted to N.Y. State bar, 1953; partner firm Burns Jackson Jacoby Miller, Summit & Jacoby, and predecessors, N.Y.C., 1960—; dir. Space & Leisure Time Ltd., Felsway Co. Counsel, N.Y. State Joint Legis. Com. on Ethics, 1964; trustee Union Coll., Schenectady; bd. govs. Union U. Served from pvt. to capt. AUS, 1953-57. Mem. Am., Fed., N.Y. State bar assns., Fed. Bar Council, Am. Arbitration Assn. (panel arbitrators), N.Y. County Lawyers Assn., Assn. Bar City N.Y., Cornell Law Assn. (exec. com.), Order of Coif, Phi Kappa Phi, Kappa Nu, Alpha Phi Omega. Republican. Jewish. Clubs: Cornell, Atrium, Merchants, Friars (N.Y.C.); Army and Navy (Washington). Note editor Cornell Law Quar., 1952-53. Home: 25 Sutton Pl S New York City NY 10022 also 425 Lopez Dr West Hempstead NY 11552 Office: 445 Park Ave New York City NY 10022

BURNS, DENNIS RAYMOND, hosp. adminstr.; b. Erie, Pa., June 29, 1943; s. Raymond and Virginia Marie (Hoffman) B.; B.S., Alderson-Broaddus U., 1966; postgrad. Edinboro State U., 1969-71, Pa. State U., 1972-74, Gannon U., 1975—; m. Joan Virginia Thomas, June 11, 1966; children—Jeffrey, Christopher. Head orderly, operating room Hamot Med. Center, Erie, Pa., 1971-72, adminstrv. asst. dept. nursing, 1972-75, dir. distbn. service, 1975-76, dir. material mgmt., 1976—. Vice pres. Hamot United Charities, 1974—. Served with AUS, 1966-69. Decorated Bronze Star. Mem. Internat. Material Mgmt. Soc. Republican. Clubs: Mason, Shriner. Home: 4628 Budd Dr Erie PA 16506 Office: 201 State St Erie PA 16512

BURNS, FRANCIS LOVIS, JR., restaurant co. exec.; b. Cambridge, Mass., Oct. 9, 1948; s. Francis Louis and Bella (Morin) B.; B.S. in Bus. Adminstrn., Babson Coll., Wellesley, Mass., 1969, certificate fin. mgmt., 1976. Div. sales mgr. Sears, Roebuck & Co., Natick, Mass., 1975-77; food service mgr. Brandeis U., Waltham, Mass., 1977-78; mgr. Red Lobster Inns Am., Burlington, Mass., 1978—. Recipient Charles Davis award Charles Davis Found., 1966; Student Activity Key, Babson Coll., 1969. Mem. Am. Mgmt. Assn., Babson Coll. Alumni Assn. Home: 408 Winsor Ridge Dr Westboro MA 01581 Office: Red Lobster Inn Middlesex Turnpike and Bedford Rd Burlington MA 01803

BURNS, JOHN FRANCIS, dentist; b. Gardiner, Maine, July 2, 1934; s. Earl Francis and Jeannette (Ross) B.; student Bowdoin Coll., 1952-55; D.D.S., N.Y. U., 1959; m. Eileen Marie Donohue, Dec. 29, 1956; children—Jane Elizabeth, Sean Michael, Michael Gerard. Practice dentistry, Brunswick, Maine, 1959-63; intern, resident in oral surgery N.Y.U. Bellevue Med. Center, N.Y.C., 1963-66; practice dentistry specializing in oral and maxillofacial surgery, N.Y.C., 1966—; asso. clin. prof. oral surgery N.Y. U. Coll. Dentistry, 1966—; dir. dentistry Beekman-Downtown Hosp., N.Y.C., 1972—; dir. dentistry, chief oral and maxillofacial surgery World Health Med.-Dental Center, World Trade Center. Diplomate Am. Bd. Oral Surgery. Mem. Am., N.Y. State, 1st Dist. dental assns., Am., N.Y. State socs. oral surgeons, Bellevue Oral Surgery Alumni Assn. Roman Catholic. Home: 85 E 10th St New York City NY 10003 Office: 69 Gold St New York City NY 10038

BURNS, JOHN SPINNEY, bus. exec.; b. Evanston, Ill., June 30, 1943; s. John Lawrence and Beryl Mignon (Spinney) B.; A.B., Princeton, 1966; postgrad. Harvard, 1968; m. Dana Brown, July 15, 1972; 1 son, Geoffrey. Treas., Min-a-matic Inc., Absecon, N.J., 1968-69; exec. v.p. fin. Culligan Communications, Inc., N.Y.C., 1969-70; v.p. fin. Seaboard Am. Corp., N.Y.C., 1970-73; asst. v.p. Citibank, N.Y.C., 1973-75; pres., prin. Burns Aviation Inc., Newburgh, N.Y., 1975-77; pres. Interair, Inc., Greenwich, Conn., 1977—. Club: Round Hill (Greenwich). Home: Chateau Ridge Dr Greenwich CT 06830 Office: 32 Porchuck Rd Greenwich CT 06830

BURNS, MARY MEHLMAN, educator; b. Gloucester, Mass., Sept. 5, 1927; d. David Eddy and Sara Isabelle (Kennedy) Mehlman; A.B., Mt. St. Mary Coll., 1949; M.A., Boston Coll., 1950; M.S., Simmons Coll., 1966; m. Richard James Burns, July 17, 1954; 1 son, Christopher. Tchr. Mount St. Mary Sem., Nashua, N.H., 1950-52; children's librarian Boston Pub. Library, 1952-58; instr. dept. history Framingham (Mass.) State Coll., 1962-69, coordinator curriculum library, 1969—, asst. prof. children's lit., 1969—, mem. grad. faculty, 1974—. Hewins-Melcher lectr., 1971. Bd. dirs. New Eng. Round Table of Children's Librarians, 1973-77; judge Boston Globe Horn Book award, 1976; dir. Internat. Seminar on Children's Lit., Loughborough, 1978. Sec. adv. bd. Mt. St. Mary Coll., 1959-61; corporator Framingham Union Hosp. Mem. Am. (chairperson children's services div. award jury 1975), New Eng., Mass. library assns., Mass. Assn. Coll. and Univ. Reading Educators, Nat., Mass. councils tchrs. English, Mass. Reading Assn., Catholic Library Assn. (bd. dirs. New Eng. Unit 1972-74), Mount Saint Mary Coll. Alumnae Assn. (pres. 1960-61), Framingham Hist. Soc., Village Improvement Soc., Internat. Seminar Children's Lit., Delta Kappa Gamma, Kappa Delta Pi. Club: Framingham Catholic Women's. Contbr. articles to profl. jours., reference book. Home: 11 Joanne Dr Framingham MA 01701 Office: Framingham State Coll State St Framingham MA 01701

BURNS, PADRAIC, psychiatrist; b. Des Moines, Aug. 31, 1929; s. Charles and Ethel (Bentz) B.; B.A., U. Chgo., 1948; postgrad. N.Y. U., 1949-51; M.D., Yale, 1955; grad. Boston Psychoanalytic Inst., 1976; m. Ikuko Kawai, Oct. 18, 1959; children—Kenneth Charles, Amelia Patricia, Margaret Asa. Rotating intern Pa. Hosp., Phila., 1955-56; resident in psychiatry Yale, 1956-57, 59-61; fellow in child psychiatry James Jackson Putnam Children's Center, Mass. Gen. Hosp., Harvard, 1961-62; fellow child psychiatry Boston U. Med. Center, 1962-63, NIMH spl. fellow, research tng. child psychiatry, Boston U. Med. Center, 1963-65, research psychiatrist, child devel. unit, 1965-69; asst. to dir., dept. child psychiatry, Sch. Medicine Boston U., 1969-70, coordinator med. student edn., dept. child psychiatry, also staff psychiatrist Center Exceptional Children, 1970-77, asso. prof. psychiatry, div. psychiatry, 1972—; asso. dir. Psychiatry Out-patient Clinic, Univ. Hosp., 1978—; practice medicine specializing in adult and child psychiatry and adult psychoanalysis. Served to capt., M.C., AUS, 1957-59. Diplomate Nat. Bd. Med. Examiners, Am. Bd. Psychiatry and Neurology. Fellow Am. Acad. Child Psychiatry; mem. Am. Psychiat. Assn., Mass. Med. Soc., AMA, New Eng. Council Child Psychiatry, Soc. Research Child Devel., Boston Psychoanalytic Soc. Contbr. articles in field to psychiat. jours. Home: 9 Downing Rd Brookline MA 02146 Office: Boston Univ Medical Center 80 E Concord St Boston MA 02118 also 7 Orchard Rd Brookline MA 02146

BURNS, ROBERT F., state ofcl.; m. Peg Burns; 1 son, Robert. Former mem. and pres. Pawtucket City Council; past mayor Pawtucket, 4 terms; sec. of state State of R.I., Providence, 1972—; past pres. R.I. Municipal Chief Execs. Assn. Past chmn. Pawtucket Democratic Party. Office: Office of Sec of State 220 State House Providence RI 02903*

BURNS, ROBERT MILTON, indsl. engr.; b. Muncy, Pa., Sept. 12, 1925; s. Robert Bernard and Nina Gertrude (Snyder) B.; Pa. State U., 1953-65; m. Ruth E. Thomas, Dec. 17, 1949; children—Roberta Ann, Robert Louis. Comml. pilot, instr. Baker Aeroservice, Muncy, 1947-52; with Sylvania Electric Products, Inc., Montoursville, Pa., 1946-49, quality control technician, 1949-53, indsl. engr., 1953-56, sr. engr., 1956-69; plant mgr. Shop-Vac Corp., Williamsport, Pa., 1969-70; with GTE Sylvania, Inc., Montoursville, 1970—, sr. engr. for spl. projects, 1977—. Mgmt. cons. comdr. of cadets CAP, 1950-52, squadron comdr., 1952-55; pres. Com. for Traffic Safety Muncy, 1953-58; chmn. Muncy Shade Tree Commn., 1964-68; vestryman St. James Episcopal Ch., Muncy, 1954-56; Republican Ward Committeeman, 1957-70. Served with USAAF, 1943-45. Decorated Air medal with 5 oak leaf clusters, D.F.C.; Certificate of Service, Shade Tree Commn., 1968, CAP, 1955. Mem. Am. Inst. Indsl. Engrs. (pres. 1966-67), Trout Unltd., Am. Legion, U.S. Coast Guard Aux. Clubs: Susquehanna Boat, Sylvania Mgmt. Inventor trout flies. Home: 1 Feigles Rd Muncy PA 17756 Office: 1050 Broad St Montoursville PA 17754

BURNS, RONALD GREGORY, pub. relations exec.; b. Phila., Dec. 12, 1932; s. Herbert Norman and Caroline Rose (Glatt) B.; B.S., St. Joseph's Coll., 1957; postgrad. Fordham U., 1957-59; m. Marie B. Wood, Nov. 21, 1959; children—Ronald Joseph, Suzanne Marie, Gregory John. Editor, McGraw-Hill Pub. Co., N.Y.C., 1960-63; mgr. employee publs. Abex Corp., N.Y.C., 1963-67; asst. sec. pub. relations Mfrs. Hanover Trust Co., N.Y.C., 1967-69; v.p. investor relations div. U.S. Industries, Inc., N.Y.C., 1969-71; pub. relations cons., Phila., 1972-75; pub. relations, advt. account exec. Gray & Rogers, Inc., Phila., 1975-78; dir. communication Selas Corp. Am., 1979—. Publicity dir. 41st Internat. Eucharistic Congress, Phila., 1976; active Boy Scouts Am. Served with U.S. Army, 1950-53. Mem. Pub. Relations Soc. Am. Roman Catholic. Home: Media PA Office: Selas Corp Am Dresher PA 19025

BURNS, STANLEY BENJAMIN, ophthalmic surgeon; b. Bklyn., Dec. 3, 1938; s. Harry and Estelle (Saltzman) B.; A.B. cum laude, Bklyn. Coll., 1960; M.D., State U. N.Y., Syracuse, 1964; children—Elizabeth Amiel, Jason Lawrence. Intern, USPHS Hosp., San Francisco, 1964-65, resident in gen. surgery, 1965-66; resident in ophthalmology USPHS Hosp., S.I., N.Y., 1967-70; clin. asst. ophthalmologist Manhattan Eye, Ear and Throat Hosp., 1970; asst. attending surgeon, 1972—; asst. adj. ophthalmologist Lenox Hill Hosp., N.Y.C., 1970; clin. asst. ophthalmologist Mt. Sinai Hosp. and Mt. Sinai Med. Sch., 1970; ophthalmologist to outpatients N.Y. Hosp., 1970; adj. ophthalmologist Lenox Hill Hosp., 1972—; dir. New China Med. Corp., Med. Archivists of N.Y. State; vis. mem. dept. history of medicine Albert Einstein Coll. Medicine; malpractice mediation panelist in ophthalmology Appellate Div. of N.Y. State Supreme Ct.; adv. bd., dir., curator photog. archives Israeli Inst. Med. History. Served with USPHS, 1964-70. Diplomate Am. Bd. Ophthalmology. Fellow A.C.S.; mem. Am. Acad. Ophthalmology and Otolaryngology, N.Y. State, N.Y. County med. socs., AMA, Soc. Med. Jurisprudence, N.Y. Soc. Clin. Ophthalmology, Am. Intra Ocular Lens Soc., Am. Assn. History of Medicine, Photog. Hist. Soc. Am. Exhibitor: A Thousand Words, a History of Photography 1839-1890, Adelphi U., 1978. Office: 30 E 60th St New York City NY 10022

BURNS, STEPHEN HAMILTON, educator; b. Damariscotta, Maine, July 22, 1939; s. Byron Ludwig and Wilma Catherine (Cushman) B.; A.B., Bowdoin Coll., 1960; A.M., Harvard, 1961, Ph.D. (NSF fellow), 1966; m. Joanne Watt Radue, Sept. 14, 1963; children—Catherine, Josephine. Research asst. Harvard, 1963-65, research fellow, 1965-66; asst. prof. elec. engring. U.S. Naval Acad., Annapolis, Md., 1966-72, asso. prof., 1972—. Mem. Acoustical Soc. Am., AAAS, Am. Assn. Physics Tchrs., Phi Beta Kappa. Republican. Methodist. Contbr. articles to profl. jours. Home: 1821 Old Annapolis Blvd Annapolis MD 21401

BUROS, OSCAR KRISEN, editor, publisher; b. Lake Nebagamon, Wis., June 14, 1905; s. Herman R. and Tona (Ferguson) B.; B.S., U. Minn., 1925; postgrad. Tchrs. Coll., Columbia U., 1928; D.Sc. (hon.), Upsala Coll., 1973; m. Luella Gubrud, Dec. 21, 1925. Instr., Central High Sch., Superior, Wis., 1926-27, Tchrs. Coll., Columbia U., 1929-30; prin. Washington Sch., Millburn, N.J., 1930-32; from asst. prof. to prof. Rutgers U., 1932-65, prof. edn. emeritus, 1965—; founder, dir. Inst. Mental Measurements, Highland Park, N.J., 1967—; asso. dir. evaluation staff study Progressive Edn. Assn., 1934-35; chmn. Invitational Conf. on Testing Problems, 1949; Fulbright lectr. Makerere U., Kampala, Uganda, 1956-57; Ford Found. prof. Nat. U., Nairobi, Kenya, 1965-66. Bd. dirs. Buros Found. Served to maj. AUS, 1942-45. Recipient Disting. Service award Ednl. Testing Service, 1973. Fellow Am. Statis. Assn.; mem. Am. Ednl. Research Assn., Nat. Council Measurements in Edn. (v.p. 1964-65), Am. Psychol. Assn., Assn. Measurements and Evaluation in Guidance. Editor, founder Mental Measurements Yearbooks, 1938—, also related publs. Home: Playwicky Box 64 Star Route New Hope PA 18938 Office: 220 Montgomery St Highland Park NJ 08904. *Died Mar. 19, 1978*

BURRELL, MORTON IRWIN, radiologist; b. Phila., May 20, 1941; s. Louis and Susan Burrell; B.S. cum laude, Bklyn. Coll., 1962; M.D., State U. N.Y., 1966; m. Barbara Marie McCann, June 7, 1970; children—Lynn Meredith, Mark Francis. Intern, Kings County Hosp., N.Y.C., 1966-67; resident in internal medicine Kings County Hosp., 1967-68; resident in diagnostic radiology Yale-New Haven Hosp., 1970-73 attending radiologist, 1973—; asst. prof. diagnostic radiology Yale U., New Haven, and chief gastrointestinal radiology, 1973-76, asso. prof. diagnostic radiology, chief gastrointestinal radiology, 1976—; cons. in radiology West Haven VA Hosp., 1973—. Served with USNR, 1968-70. Fellow A.C.P.; mem. Coll. Med.

Imaging (dir.), Radiologic Soc. N. Am., Am., New Eng. Roentgen ray socs., Am. Coll. Radiology, Soc. Gastrointestinal Radiologists, Am. Gastroent. Assn., ACP, Conn. Radiology Soc. Asso. editor Gastrointestinal Radiology. Contbr. articles in field to profl. jours. Home: 374 Augusta Dr Orange CT 06477 Office: 789 Howard Ave New Haven CT 06504

BURRIDGE, ROBERT, educator; b. Essex, Eng., Dec. 6, 1937; s. Sydney Stanmore and Phebe Mercy (Raven) B.; came to U.S., 1971; B.A. (Major scholar King's Coll.), U. Cambridge (Eng.), 1959, M.A., 1962, Ph.D., 1963; m. Elizabeth Nelson Bingham, Sept. 22, 1962; children—Rosalind, Lucinda, Robert. Research fellow Calif. Inst. Tech., Pasadena, 1963-64; research geophysicist U. Calif., Los Angeles, 1964-65; asst. lectr. U. Cambridge, 1965-67; research fellow U.K. Atomic Energy Authority, 1967-71; fellow King's Coll., Cambridge, 1965-71; asso. prof. math. N.Y. U., N.Y.C., 1971-75, prof., 1975—; cons. seismic studies and fracture phenomena. Recipient Adams prize in math. U. Cambridge, 1971; NSF research contract in earthquake mechanism studies, 1971—. Fellow Cambridge Philos. Soc., Explorers Club; mem. Am. Geophys. Union, Seismol. Soc. Am. Editorial bd. Soc. Indsl. and Applied Math., Wave Propagation (Internat.); contbr. papers on applied math. and theoretical seismology to tech. jours. Home: 110 Bleecker St New York City NY 10012 Office: NY Univ Courant Inst Math Sci 251 Mercer St New York City NY 10012

BURROUGHS, FREDERICK SIDNEY, cons., mfg. co. exec.; b. Olympia, Wash., Apr. 3, 1914; s. Frederick Sidney and Margueriete (Annis) B.; grad. Phillips Exeter Acad., 1932; A.B., Princeton, 1936; postgrad. Columbia, also N.Y. U., 1937; m. Virginia Claire Sackett, Nov. 25, 1938; children—Frederick Sidney, Cynthia (Mrs. Dwight Nadeau). Asst. mgr. pub. relations Shell Oil Co., N.Y.C., 1940-46; owner Vita-Frost Foods Co., Newton, N.J., 1946-50; v.p. Nat. Oil Fuel Inst., N.Y.C., 1951-63; v.p. firm West, Weir & Bartel Inc., N.Y.C., 1963-66; mng. dir. Wallcovering Mfrs. Assn., N.Y.C., 1966-74; pres. Intera Wallfashions, Inc., 1975-77; pres. Fred S. Burroughs & Assos., wallcovering consultants and mktg. reps., Little Falls, N.J., 1977—. Mem. Am. Soc. Assn. Execs., U.S. C. of C., Trout Unltd. (chmn. N.J. council 1971-73, nat. dir.), Color Marketing Group. Home: 1 Rustic Ridge Little Falls NJ 07424 Office: E-22 Great Notch Village Little Falls NJ 07424

BURROUGHS, RICHARD H., III, geologist, oceanographer; b. New Haven, July 5, 1946; s. Richard Hansford and Mary Drummond (Page) B.; A.B., Princeton U., 1969; Ph.D., MIT-Woods Hole Oceanographic Inst., 1975. Intern Council on Environ. Quality Washington, 1972; staff officer Nat. Acad. Scis.-NRC, 1974-77; sr. fellow Ecosystems Center, Marine Biol. Lab., Woods Hole, Mass., 1977—; lectr. Sch. Forestry and Environ. Studies, Yale U., 1979—; grad. research fellow Woods Hole Oceanographic Instn., 1969-74. Mem. AAAS, Am. Geophys. Union, Geol. Soc. Am., Marine Tech. Soc., Sigma Xi. Contbr. profl. jours. Home: Box 273 Woods Hole MA 02543 Office: Marine Biol Lab Woods Hole MA 02543

BURROWES, JOSEPH J., mfrs. rep.; b. Phila., Jan. 7, 1919; s. Joseph Thomas and Katie Lewis (McBlain) B.; B.A., Temple U., 1940, postgrad. Law Sch., 1940-42; m. Helen Leola Berkelbach, Nov. 10, 1942; children—Leola (Mrs. Robert Trainor Zintl, Jr.), Lisa Jo (Mrs. David A. Lough). Tech. sales rep. R.M. Hollingshead Corp., Camden, N.J., 1947-52; owner, Pakoil Co., Havertown, Pa., 1952—. Served as pilot, maj. AUS, 1942-46. Mem. Soc. Packaging and Handling Engrs. (nat. v.p. 1970-71, exec. v.p. 1972-73, pres. 1974-75, chmn. bd. 1976-77), Am. Def. Preparedness Assn., Am. Ordnance Assn., Nat. Inst. Packaging and Handling and Logistics Engrs. Mason. Clubs: Lianerch Country, Seaview Country. Home and office: 7 N Drexel Ave Havertown PA 19083

BURROWS, RAY IRVING, city ofcl.; b. Durham, N.H., Mar. 17, 1928; s. William Henry and Ethel Ora (Stevens) B.; student pub. schs., Dover, N.H.; m. Beverly Ruth Record, Aug. 12, 1950; children—Robert William, Janice Rae. Heating plant fireman U. N.H., Durham, 1947-54, Simplex Wire & Cable Co., Newington, N.H., 1954-55; oil burner technician Robinson-Rudd Oil Service, Durham, 1955-60; police officer, Durham, 1957-61, chief police, 1961—; mem. Police Standards and Tng. Council, 1971-75; mem. Nat. Exec. Law Enforcement Adv. Council, Montrose, Calif., 1973-74; mem. Police Profl. Standards and Goals Com., 1972. Past dep. dir. Durham Civil Def.; baseball coach Durham Youth Assn., 1961-67; chief instr. N.H. chpt. Nat. Rifle Assn. hunter safety program. Served with USN, 1945-47. Recipient certificate of Achievement, Am. Legion, 1967; New Eng. Coll., 1972. Mem. Internat., New Eng., N.H., (past pres.) assns. chiefs police, N.H. Police Assn., N.H. Criminal Investigations Assn., Strafford County Law Enforcement Assn., Am. Legion (past comdr., sgt. at arms). Republican. Baptist. Clubs: Masons, Shriners. Home: 27 Schoolhouse Ln Durham NH 03824 Office: Police Dept Dover Rd Durham NH 03824

BURROWS, WILLIAM E., author, educator; b. Phila., Mar. 27, 1937; s. Eli William and Helen (Marino) B.; B.A., Columbia U., 1960, M.A., 1962; m. Joelle Bentley Hodgson, Nov. 19, 1966; 1 dau., Lara Julie. News asst. N.Y. Times 1962-65; reporter Richmond (Va.) Times-Dispatch, 1965-66, Washington Post, 1966-67, N.Y. Times, 1967-68; asso. prof. journalism, dir. undergrad. studies N.Y. U., 1974-79; author: On Reporting the News, 1977; Richthofen, 1969; Vigilante., 1976; also articles. Danforth asso., 1978. Mem. AAAS, Am. Acad. Polit. and Social Sci., Kappa Tau Alpha, Pi Sigma Alpha, Sigma Delta Chi (award 1977). Home: 154 Burns St Forest Hills NY 11375 Office: 1021 Main Bldg 100 Washington Sq E New York City NY 10003

BURRY, ANTHONY, clin. psychologist; b. N.Y.C., Jan. 29, 1939; s. Solen and Mathilde (Rothgans) B.; B.A., City U. N.Y., 1961; M.A., New Sch. Social Research, 1966; Ph.D. (VA trainee), U. Ky., 1971; m. Veena Steen, Oct. 25, 1963; children—Alexander Solen, Theodore Victor. Psychologist, Counseling and Testing Center, U. Ky., Lexington, 1968-71, asst. clin. psychologist, outpatient psychiat. clinic Med. Center, 1970-71; dir. testing services, asst. dir. clin. psychology internship, supr., faculty Postgrad. Center Mental Health, N.Y.C., 1971—; staff psychologist St. Vincent's Guidance Inst., N.Y.C., 1971-74; pvt. practice psychotherapy, psychodiagnostic testing, N.Y.C., 1970—. Fellow Am. Orthopsychiat. Assn.; mem. Am., N.Y. State psychol. assns., N.Y. Soc. Clin. Psychologists. Address: 386 Park Ave S New York NY 10016

BURSILL, CLAUDE, instn. adminstr.; b. London, Eng., July 26, 1920; s. Bernard and Thekla (Weber) B.; M.A., Cambridge (Eng.) U., 1950, Ph.D., 1953; m. Vera Morgan, Oct. 24, 1943; children—Charmian, Mark Eliot. Sr. geologist Bur. Mineral Resources, Australia, 1951-53; asst. consulting geologist Anglo Am. Corp. S.A. Ltd., S. Africa, 1953-60; exec. asst. research to mng. dir. Rank Orgn., London, 1960-63; exec. dir. N.B. (Can.) Research and Productivity Council, 1963—. Hon. research asso. U. New Brunswick, 1966; mem. Standards Council Can., Nat. Adv. Bd. Sci. and Technol. Info. Bd. dirs. Atlantic Research Bd., Atlantic Forestry Inst., N.B. Devel. Corp., Canadian Research Mgmt. Assn., Non-Profit Indsl. Research Assn. Can. Served with RAF, 1940-45. Mem. geol. socs. S. Africa, Australia, London. Home: 549 Woodstock Rd Fredericton NB E3B 2J2 Canada Office: POB 6000 Fredericton NB E3B 5H1 Canada

BURSTEIN, DONALD ALAN, psychologist, med. adminstr.; b. Springfield, Mass., Apr. 17, 1941; s. Rubin M. and Sylvia (Burke) B.; B.A. in Psychology, Am. Internat. Coll., 1962; M.Ed., Springfield Coll., 1963, Advanced Study Clin. Psychology certificate, 1964; Ph.D., Walden U., 1977; m. Linda N. Karol, May 30, 1965; children—Mark, Fran. Staff psychologist Northampton State Hosp., 1964; psychology supr. Phila. State Hosp., 1965-69; dir. partial hospitalization service N.W. Center Community MH/MR Programs, Phila., 1969—. Instr., Bucks County Community Coll., Newtown, Pa., 1974—; mem. adult com. Phila. Forum of Community Mental Health Centers. Bd. dirs. Bucks County Psychiat. Center, Pendel and Chalfont, Pa., Lenape Valley Found., Chalfont. Licensed clin. psychologist, Pa. Mem. Assn. Mental Health Adminstrs., Nat. Register Health Service Providers in Psychology, Am., Pa., Eastern psychol. assns., Delaware Valley Partial Hospitalization Assn., Psi Chi. Home: 55 Sunshine Rd Southampton PA 18966 Office: 35 E Mount Airy Ave Philadelphia PA 19119

BURSTEIN, STEPHEN DAVID, neurosurgeon; b. Bklyn., Apr. 10, 1934; s. Moe and Anna (Bloch) B.; B.A., U. Mich., 1954; M.D., State U. N.Y., 1958; M.S. in Neurosurgery, U. Minn., 1965; m. Ronnie Sue Deutsch, Oct. 8, 1972; 1 dau., Alissa Aimee. Intern, Johns Hopkins Hosp., 1958-59; resident Mayo Clinic, Rochester, Minn., 1961-65; asso. chief dept. neurosurgery S. Nassau Communities Hosp., Oceanside, N.Y., 1976—; chief dept. neurosurgery Franklin Gen. Hosp., Valley Stream, N.Y., 1977—; practice medicine specializing in neurosurgery, Freeport, N.Y., 1965—. Served to lt. U.S. Navy, 1959-61. Diplomate Am. Bd. Neurol. Surgery. Fellow A.C.S.; mem. L.I. Hearing and Speech Soc. (1st v.p., dir. 1969—), Congress Neurol. Surgeons, Am. Assn. Neurol. Surgeons, AMA, Med. Soc. State N.Y., Nassau Physicians Guild, N.Y. Soc. Neurosurgery, N.Y. State Neurosurg. Soc., Nassau Surg. Soc., Nassau County Med. Soc., Sigma Xi, Alpha Omega Alpha. Office: 88 S Bergen Pl Freeport NY 11520

BURSUK, LAURA ZELMAN, educator; b. N.Y.C., Mar. 1, 1926; d. Aaron and Jennie (Warshaw) Zelman; B.A. cum laude, Hunter Coll., 1946; M.A., Coll. City N.Y., 1950; Ph.D. (Doctoral proposal scholar), N.Y. U., 1969; m. Samuel Bursuk, Aug. 13, 1955; children—Barbara, Lois. Early childhood edn. tchr. N.Y.C. Bd. Edn., 1947-56; reading cons. South Huntington (N.Y.) Schs., 1963-64; reading specialist Lawrence (N.Y.) High Sch., 1964-69; adj. asst. prof. ednl. psychology N.Y. U., 1967-73; asso. prof. tchr. preparation York Coll., City U. N.Y., 1969—; research cons. N.Y. U. Office Field Services, 1968-69; field cons. to schs., 1969—. Mem. Internat. Reading Assn., Nassau Reading Council (bd. dirs.), Nat. Congress Parents and Tchrs., Phi Beta Kappa, Kappa Delta Pi, Pi Lambda Theta. Author instructional modules for teaching reading; contbr. articles to Resources in Edn., 1975—, Acad. Therapy, The Principal. Office: York Coll City U NY Jamaica NY 11451

BURT, MARVIN ROGER, research firm exec.; b. Los Angeles, Mar. 5, 1937; s. Henry Howard and Iris Faith (Green) B.; student Los Angeles City Coll., 1955-56; B.A., U. Calif. at Los Angeles, 1958; M.P.A., George Washington U., 1965, D.Pub. Adminstrn., 1969; m. Joy Lee Rougk, July 20, 1958; children—Sandra Marie, Scott Marvin. Mgmt. intern, program analyst Dept. Army, Washington, 1962-64; program analyst Def. Supply Agy., Alexandria, Va., 1964-65, Office Econ. Opportunity, Washington, 1965-66; mem. tech. staff Research Analysis Corp., McLean, Va., 1966; sr. research analyst, dir. program analysis Resource Mgmt. Corp., Bethesda, Md., 1966-67; sr. cons. Peat, Marwick, Livington and Co., Washington, 1967-68; sr. staff mem. Urban Inst., Washington, 1969-72; pres. Burt Assos., Inc., pub. policy research and cons., Bethesda, 1972—; pres. Inst. Human Resources Research, Bethesda, 1973—. Asso. professorial lectr. George Washington U., 1969-72; lectr. U.S. Civil Service Commn., 1969-72, U.S. Gen. Accounting Office, 1969-72; cons. fed., state and municipal govt. agys. Served with USMCR, 1958-61. Fellow AAAS; mem. Operations Research Soc. Am. (editor C-E Newsletter 1969-70, mem. council 1970-73), Am. Soc. Pub. Adminstrn., Inst. Mgmt. Sci. Methodist (adminstrv. bd. 1971-73, chmn. council on ministries 1972-73). Author 6 books. Contbr. articles, papers to publs. Home: 8809 Harness Trail Potomac MD 20854 Office: 7315 Wisconsin Ave Bethesda MD 20014

BURT, WARREN BROOKER, lawyer; b. N.Y.C., May 16, 1934; s. ConAmore V. and Mazie Gladys (Brooker) B.; student Princeton, 1951-54; B.S., U. Nebr., 1956; LL.B., U. Va., 1959; m. Cynthia Jane Henderson, June 8, 1956; children—David Henderson, John Warren. Admitted to Del. bar, 1960; clk. U.S. Dist. Ct., Dist. of Del., Wilmington, 1959-60; asso. firm Prickett & Prickett, Wilmington, 1960-65; partner firm Prickett Ward Burt & Sanders, Wilmington, 1965—; dept. atty. gen. State of Del., 1962-63. Mem. Del. State Ho. of Reps., 1968-70. Mem. Am., Del. State bar assns. Republican. Presbyterian. Home: 4810 Lancaster Pike Wilmington DE 19807 Office: 1310 King St Wilmington DE 19899

BURTT, ELIZABETH ALLENE, nurse; b. Exeter, N.H., July 31, 1926; d. William Abbot and Elizabeth Pride (Cole) Burtt; diploma in Nursing, Hillborough County Gen. Hosp., 1947; B.S., Johns Hopkins U., 1961, M.P.H., 1977; M.S. in Pub. Health Nursing, Boston U., 1965. Staff nurse Mass. Gen. Hosp., Boston, 1948-49; head nurse, supr. emergency dept. Johns Hopkins Hosp., Balt., 1950-55; resident sch. nurse Oldfields Sch., Glencoe, Md., 1955-60; sr. pub. health nurse Balt. City Health Dept., 1961-63; instr. pub. health nursing U. R.I., Kingston, 1965-68; asst. prof. pub. health nursing U. N.H., Durham, 1968-72; pub. health nurse epidemiologist N.H. Div. Pub. Health Services, Concord, 1972-73, ednl. cons., 1973-75, dir. Bur. Pub. Health Nursing, 1975—; summer camp nurse Vt., 1955-59, N.Y., 1965, Mass., 1966, R.I., 1968; pub. health nurse cons. Exeter Vis. Nurse Assn., 1967. Chmn. Epping (N.H.) Health Com., 1969-70; bd. dirs. N.H. League Nursing; chmn. N.H. Immunization Task Force, 1977—. Fellow Royal Soc. of Health; mem. Am. Nurses Assn., Am. Pub. Health Assn., Assn. State and Ter. Dirs. Nursing, Nat. League for Nursing, Am. Sch. Health Assn., Sigma Theta Tau. Home: Route 1 Exeter NH 03833 Office: 61 S Spring St Concord NH 03301

BURTT, J(OSEPH) FREDERIC, educator; b. Lowell, Mass., Apr. 4, 1908; s. Walter N. and Edith (Flint) B.; student Hebron Acad., 1925-27; B.S., Lowell Tech. Inst., 1931; M.S., Mass. Inst. Tech., 1958; Asso. Bus. Adminstrn., Boston U., 1942; m. Marguerite T. Richards, July 16, 1938; children—Joseph Frederic, John Robert, Richard F. Trainee, Horner Bros. Woolen Mills, Eaton Rapids, Mich., 1931; prodn. mgr. Newmarket Mfg. Co., Lowell, 1931-33; supr. time study Abbot Worsted Co., Westford, Mass., 1933-35, asst. supt., 1936-41, supt., personnel mgr., prodn. mgr., 1942-49; asst. prof. Lowell Tech. Inst., 1950-59, asso. prof. physics and engring. sci., 1959—; sr. textile technologist Q.M.C. Research and Engring. Command, Natick, Mass., 1957-59; research fellow Lowell Tech. Inst. Research Found., 1950—; Fulbright lectr. Alexandria U., Egypt, 1965-67; mem. Workshop Indsl. and Tech. Research, Djarkarta, 1971, Indian Inst., U.S. Dept. Edn., 1971-73. Vice pres. Piscataqua Pioneers, 1968-71; mem. Lowell Conservation Commn., 1971—; mem. Lowell Centennial Commn., 1960-64; pres. Lowell Hist. Commn., 1960-62; bd. dirs. N.E. Found. Am. Indian Culture, Inc., 1962-66, Lowell Tech. Inst., WBZ-TV Sci. Countdown, 1958-66, Mental Health Assn. Greater Lowell, 1969—. Recipient medallion merit Alexandria U., 1967, C.B. Price Meml. award N.H. Archeol. Soc., 1965, DeMolay Cross of Honor and Legion of Honor, 1936; hon. mem. St. Francis-Abenaki Tribe, 1977. Fellow Pa. Inst. Anthropology; mem. Am. Assn. Textile Tech., Interstate Textile Assn., Nat. Assn. Woolen and Worsted Mgrs. Assn., AAAS, Am. Assn. Engring. Edn., Mass. (v.p. 1954), N.H. (editor, pres. 1962-66) archael. socs., Nat., Indonesian acads. sci., Sigma Xi, Omicron Pi. Congregationalist. (deacon 1960—). Club: Masons (32 deg.), Shriners (master 1948-50). Co-author: History of the City of Lowell, 1976; co-editor, pub.: Colby's Indian History, 1975; contbr. articles to profl. jours. Home: 97 Hoyt Ave Lowell MA 01852

BUSBY, JAMES MERWIN, bus. machines co. exec.; b. Williamsburg, W.Va., May 18, 1931; s. Calvin and Rose (Ray) B.; B.S., Empire State Coll., 1978; m. Emilie Saundra DeBernardis, Dec. 28, 1968; children—Nancy Ann Marler, Karl Ray, Gary Wayne, Christopher Lud, Allison Brooke. Enlisted U.S. Army, 1952, advanced through grades to maj., 1973; ret., 1973; mgr. spl. projects Xerox Corp., Rochester, N.Y., 1973—. Committeeman, Monroe County Republican Com., 1975—; pres. Roundtree Homeowners Assn., 1975—. Decorated Bronze Star medal. Mem. Xerox Mgmt. Assn., IEEE, Ret. Officers Assn. (pres. 1975-76), U.S. Golf Assn. Republican. Roman Catholic. Home: 14 Shagbark Way Fairport NY 14450 Office: Xerox Corp Xerox Square Rochester NY 14644

BUSCH, ALLEN CYRIL, govt. ofcl.; b. Cin., Aug. 21, 1931; s. Walter Albert and Lillian (Voegtle) B.; B.A., Miami U., Oxford, Ohio, 1955, M.A., 1958; m. Patricia L. Burr, Mar. 23, 1957; children—Michael A., Melany M., Eric C., Craig A. Sect. chief, research and advanced devel. div. Avco Corp., Wilmington, Mass., 1959-62; staff psychologist HRB Singer Inc., State College, Pa., 1962-64; research psychologist L.G. Hanscom Field, USAF, Bedford, Mass., 1964-67; with FAA/NAFEC, Atlantic City, 1967—, br. chief analysis br., 1973—. Served with USMC, 1951-52. Mem. Am. Psychol. Assn., IEEE (sr.), Human Factors Soc., AAAS, Aviation Psychologists Assn. Contbr. articles in field to profl. jours. Home: 1014 Richard Dr Linwood NJ 08221 Office: FAA/NAFEC AMA 220 Atlantic City NJ 08405

BUSCH, BENJAMIN, lawyer; b. N.Y.C., June 12, 1912; s. S. Henry and Dorothy (Busch) B.; student Coll. City N.Y., 1928-30; LL.B., St. Lawrence U., 1933; m. Phyllis Toby Schnell, Nov. 8, 1935; children—Frederick Matthew, Eric Edwin. Admitted to N.Y. State bar, 1934; partner firm Katz & Sommerich, 1946-76; counsel firm Hamburger, Weinschenk, Molnar & Busch, 1976—. Adj. prof. internat. and comparative law N.Y. Law Sch., 1973—. Explorer, adv. Boy Scouts Am. Served from pvt. to sgt. Mountain Troops, 1944-45. Decorated Bronze Star Medal, Purple Heart. Mem. Am. Bar Assn. (div. vice chmn. sect. internat. and comparative law 1967-71, chmn. 1972-73, observer to UN 1974-79), Am. Fgn. Law Assn. (v.p. 1966-69, pres. 1969-71, dir. 1971—), consular Law Soc. (dir.), Am. Soc. Internat. Law, Assn. Bar City N.Y. (com. internat. law 1973-76, com. fgn. law 1978—), N.Y. State Bar Assn., Fed. Bar Council (co-chmn. program com. 1974-75, co-chmn. internat. law com. 1974-75). Author (with Otto C. Sommerich) Foreign Law—A Guide to Pleading and Proof, 1959. Contbr. articles to profl. jours. Office: 630 Fifth Ave New York City NY 10020

BUSH, ALVIN GLENN, JR., elec. engr.; b. Weston, W.Va., Feb. 4, 1928; s. Alvin Glenn and Jessie Emma B.; student Glenville State Coll., 1946-48; B.E.E., Washington U., St. Louis, 1955; postgrad. Johns Hopkins, 1955-74; m. Shirley Mae Forcade, May 24, 1951; children—Richard A., Rodney B., Rhonda C. With Union Electric Co., St. Louis, 1954; research asst. Washington U., St. Louis, 1953-55; with applied physics lab. Johns Hopkins U., Laurel, Md., 1955—, asst. group supr. reliability engring., space dept., 1978—. Deacon Presbyterian Ch., Belleville, Ill., 1951, Columbia, Md., 1968-70; den father Cub Scouts, 1967-71. Served with USAF, 1948-52. Mem. Armed Forces Communications Assn. (charter mem. Belleville), IEEE, Internat. Soc. Hybrid Microelectronics. Office: Applied Physics Lab Johns Hopkins U Johns Hopkins Rd Laurel MD 20810

BUSH, DAVID FREDERIC, psychologist, educator; b. Watertown, N.Y., July 12, 1942; s. Frederic Ralph and Charlotte Mary (Ellingworth) B.; B.A., U. South Fla., 1965; M.A., U. Wyo., 1968; Ph.D., Purdue U., 1972. Instr. psychology Hiram Scott Coll., Scottsbluff, Nebr., 1967-69, Purdue U., West Lafayette, Ind., 1971-72; asso. prof. psychology West Chester (Pa.) State Coll., 1972-73; asst. prof., chmn. grad. program psychology Villanova (Pa.) U., 1972-77, asso. prof., 1978—; instr. seminar Am. Coll. Life Underwriters, Bryn Mawr, Pa., 1976—; cons. in field. Mem. council Unitarian fellowship Lafayette, Ind., 1970-72; bd. dirs. Ars Moriendi, Dennis Burton Day Care Center, 1971-72, Life Guidance Services, Inc., 1977-82. NDEA fellow 1969-71, David Ross summer fellow, 1972, Am. Inst. Pakistan Studies fellow, 1978; Unitarian Universalist grantee, 1973, Villanova U. grantee, 1974, 77. Mem. Am., Eastern, Midwestern, Pa. psychol. assns., Soc. Psychol. Study Social Issues, Am. Ednl. Research Assn., Soc. Research Child Devel., Soc. Advancement Social Psychology, Sigma Xi, Psi Chi. Author: Human Development: The Psychology of the Life-Span, 1974. Editor: Social Sci. Forum: An Interdisciplinary Jour. Researcher moral devel., Piagetian logical devel. in children, cognitive styles and adult learning, group processes and communication. Home: 290 Iven Ave Apt 2D St Davids PA 19087 Office: Dept Psychology Villanova U Villanova PA 19085

BUSH, DEREK VERNON, hosp. adminstr.; b. King's Lynn, Eng., Aug. 4, 1929; s. Robert Leslie and Edna Maud (Jary) B.; came to U.S., 1962; certificate Cambridge (Eng.) U., 1945; student U. Man. (Can.), 1961-62; m. Marguerite Hartlen, Sept. 3, 1963. Adminstr., WKM Hosp., Berwick, N.S., Can., 1958-62; asso. adminstr. Hyack (N.Y.) Hosp., 1962-65; adminstr. Mt. Desert Island Hosp., Bar Harbor, Maine, 1966-69; pres. Maine Cost Meml. Hosp., Ellsworth, 1969—; chmn. Maine Hosp. License Bd., 1975-77, Vol. Budget Rev. Orgn. Maine, 1978—. Chmn. County Health Planning Agy., 1973-75; pres. Project Hancock, 1973—; bd. dirs. Genetic Counseling, Inc., 1974—, Maine Blue Cross, 1969-71, 78—, Hancock Auditorium, Inc., 1975—. Served with Royal Navy, 1947-54, Royal Canadian Navy, 1954-58. Recipient Blue Ribbon award New Eng. Hosp. Assembly, 1969, 72, 76. Fellow Am. Coll. Hosp. Adminstrs. (Maine rep. Council of Regents 1977—); mem. Internat. Platform Assn., Arthritis Assn., Multiple Sclerosis Soc., Am. Assn. Hosp. Planning, Am. (dir. center for small or rural hosps. 1978—), New Eng., Maine (pres. 1969-71, 1st Distinguished Service award 1977) hosp. assns., Am. Rose Soc., Nat. Hist. Soc. Congregationalist. Home: 102 Eden St Bar Harbor ME 04609 Office: 50 Union St Ellsworth ME 04605

BUSH, HENRY LEON, hosp. fin. adminstr.; b. Reading, Pa., Apr. 4, 1916; s. Lewis Leon and Bertha (Ringler) B.; certificate of proficiency U. Pa. Wharton Extension Sch., 1936; m. Mallory Florence Texter, Jan. 27, 1940. Asst. to dir. indsl. relations Textile Machine Works, Reading, 1933-40; chief accountant Vanity Fair Mills, Inc., Reading, 1940-49; controller Riverside Metal Co. (N.J.), 1949-50; staff accountant Ernst & Ernst, Phila., 1950-56; asst. to pres. Spring City Knitting Co. (Pa.), 1956-61; treas. L.W. Foster Sportswear Co., Phila., 1961-62; treas. L'Aiglon Apparel, Inc., Phila., 1962-66;

v.p. fin. St. Luke's Hosp. of Bethlehem (Pa.), 1966—; dir. Pentamation Enterprises, Inc. Mem. Pa., Am. insts. C.P.A.'s, Hosp. Fin. Mgmt. Assn. Republican. Episcopalian. Clubs: Masons, Lehigh Valley, Pike Twp. Sportsmens Assn. Home: 1600 Lehigh Pkwy E Regency Towers Apt 10H Allentown PA 18103 Office: 801 Ostrum St Bethlehem PA 18015

BUSH, JOHN, psychotherapist; b. Madison, Wis., Sept. 11, 1930; s. Chilton Rowlette and Myrtle Holmes (Stocking) B.; B.A., Stanford U., 1950; postgrad., U. Florence (Italy), 1951-52; M.A., New School for Social Research, 1973, postgrad., 1973—; m. Judith Coyle, Apr., 1952 (div. 1978); children—Alexandra (dec.), Elizabeth, Jonathan, Iain. Pres., John Bush and Assos., N.Y.C., 1967-71; inst., student advisor, grad. faculty New School for Social Research, N.Y.C., 1973-77; mng. dir. Center for Humanistic Psychoanalysis, N.Y.C., 1978—. Mem. Mayor's Council for the Environment, N.Y.C., 1968-73; pres. Berkeley Pl Assn., 1969-72; trustee Park Slope Civic Council, 1970. Mem. Am. Psychol. Assn. (asso.), Assn. Humanistic Psychology. Democrat. Episcopalian. Home and Office: 207 Berkeley Pl Brooklyn NY 11217

BUSHEY, ARTHUR MERRICK, dentist; b. Balt., Mar. 9, 1924; s. Arthur Clifton and Marjorie (Merrick) B.; student Coll. William and Mary, 1941-42, U. N.C., 1942-43; D.D.S., U. Md., 1950. Intern, resident in oral surgery and anesthesiology U. Md. Hosp., 1950-52; instr. oral surgery U. Md. Dental Sch., 1952-57, instr. pathology, 1956; practice dentistry, Towson, Md., 1952—; dir. oral surgery clinic, children's dental health program Balt. City Health Dept., 1952—; dir. Dental Treatment Center for Handicapped, dept. chief James Lawrence Kernan Hosp. for Crippled Children, Balt. vis. staff Md. Gen. Hosp., Greater Balt. Med. Center; sr. cons. dentist Montebello State Hosp. for Chronically Ill; cons. staff Balt. City Hosps.; attending dentist William S. Baer Sch. Crippled Children. Mem. camping adv. com. Balt. League Crippled Children, 1961—; bd. dirs., chmn. camp com. Balt. council Camp Fire Girls, 1958—, sec. bd., 1961; cubmaster Boy Scouts Am., 1960—; Served with Hosp. Corps, USNR, 1943-46. Fellow Royal Soc. Health; mem. ADA, Am. Soc. Dentistry for Children, Md., Balt. dental socs., Photog. Soc. Am., Am. Camping Assn., Soc. Cincinnati, Soc. Ark and Dove, Psi Omega. Episcopalian. Clubs: Gibson Island Country, Yacht Squadron. Home: Hampton House Apt 909 204 E Joppa Rd Towson MD 21204 Office: 8019 York Rd Towson MD 21204

BUSHEY, BRANSBY WALTER, mech. engr.; b. Harrisburg, Pa., Mar. 31, 1931; s. Walter Glenn and Elsie A. (Boesch) B.; student Gettysburg Coll., 1948-50; B.S. with honors, Va. Poly. Inst., 1953; M.S., U. Pa., 1963; m. Alice Plank, June 20, 1953; children—Glenn W., Ann Elizabeth, Bransby Walter Jr. Archtl. engr. Deere & Co., Moline, Ill., 1953-54; project engr. Frankford Arsenal, Phila., 1956-64; chief projectile devel. and engring. br., 1964-69, chief arty. ammunition lab., 1969-71, chief mfg. tech. directorate, 1971-77; chief munitions metal parts engring. br. munitions systems div. Army Ammunition Research and Devel. Command, Dover, N.J., 1977—. Active Boy Scouts Am., 1968-72; mem. ch. council Immanuel Lutheran Ch., Phila., 1971-76, v.p., 1973, 75-76, pres., 1974. Served with Ordnance, U.S. Army, 1954-56. Recipient Research and Devel. Achievement award U.S. Army, 1970, Sustained Quality Performance award Dept. of Army, 1977. Registered profl. engr., Pa. Mem. Am. Def. Preparedness Assn., Sigma Xi, Phi Kappa Phi. Republican. Patentee in field. Home: 348 Shelmore St Philadelphia PA 19111 Office: Munitions Systems Div Ammunition Research and Devel Command U S Army Dover NJ 07801

BUSHMAN, THERESA, nurse; b. Totowa Boro, N.J., June 11, 1920; d. Harry and Julia (Offringa) Bushman; R.N., Paterson (N.J.) Gen. Hosp., 1941; B.S. in Nursing Edn., N.Y.U., 1954, M.A. in Nursing Adminstrn., 1951. Staff nurse Paterson (N.J.) Gen. Hosp., 1941-42, obstet. supr., instr., 1942-60; dir. nursing Christian Health Care Center, Wyckoff, N.J., 1960—; mem. Wyckoff Bd. Health. Bd. dirs., pres. women's aux. Eastern Christian Children's Retreat; v.p., bd. dirs. Florence Christian Home, Greater Paterson Gen. Hosp.; founder Eastern Christian Children's Retreat. Recipient Distinguished Alumnus award Eastern Christian High Sch., 1975. Mem. Am. Nurses Assn., Paterson Gen. Hosp. Alumni, N.J. Hosp. Nursing Adminstrs., N.J. Licensed Nursing Home Adminstrs., Am. Coll. Nursing Home Adminstrs. Home: 307 Calvin Ct Wyckoff NJ 07481 Office: 301 Sicomac Ave Wyckoff NJ 04781

BUSHNELL, CLARENCE WILLIAM, hosp. adminstr.; b. Lowville, N.Y., Nov. 25, 1916; s. Robert Emmett and Isabelle (Webster) B.; R.N., Hudson River State Hosp., 1937; A.B., N.Y. U., 1947; M.P.H., Yale U., 1951; m. Ethel Victoria Loving, Apr. 26, 1943; children—Sandra Lynn, Paul George, Susan Lisa. Various adminstrv. and indsl. nursing positions, 1937-51; asst. adminstr. Mass. Meml. Hosp., Boston, 1951-62; adminstr. Bridgeport (Conn.) Hosp., 1962—; lectr. pub. health and hosp. adminstrn. Yale U., 1963—. Active United Community Services. Trustee, New Eng. Hosp. Assembly. Served with USCG, 1942-45. Mem. Conn. Hosp. Assn. (past pres., past trustee). Conglist. (trustee, deacon). Rotarian. Home: 300 Hill Ave Bridgeport CT 06610 Office: Bridgeport Hosp 267 Grant St Bridgeport CT 06602*

BUSLER, MICHAEL RONALD, economist, writer; b. Phila., Sept. 18, 1949; s. Harry Arthur and Sally (Levin) B.; B.S., Drexel U., 1972, M.B.A., 1973. Sr. fin. analyst Philco-Ford Corp., 1973-74; fin. mgr. FMC Corp., Phila., 1974-76; pres. Michael Busler Group, King of Prussia, Pa., 1976—; asst. prof. Montgomery County Community Coll.; lectr. Phila. Coll. Textiles and Scis. Republican. Jewish. Home: 22 Cypress Ln Berwyn PA 19312

BUTCHER, (CHARLES) PHILIP, educator, author; b. Washington, Sept. 28, 1918; s. James William and Jennie Lawrence (Jones) B.; B.A., Howard U., 1942, M.A., 1947; Ph.D., Columbia, 1956; m. Ruth Ann Batch, Dec. 27, 1948; children—Wendy Ann (Mrs. Smith W. Davis), Laurel Ruth (Mrs. Peter J. Miles). Instr. English, Morgan State U., Balt., 1947-49, asst. prof., 1949-56, asso. prof., 1956-59, prof. English, 1959—, chmn. div. humanities, 1960-66, dean Grad. Sch., 1972-75. Occasional lectr. U. Pa., U. Ia., U. N.C., Va. State Coll., N.C. Central U. Served with AUS, 1943-46. Gen. Edn. Bd. fellow, 1948-49, John Hay Whitney Found. Opportunity fellow, 1951-52; recipient Creative scholarship award Coll. Lang. Assn., 1964, research grants Am. Philos. Soc., 1968-69, 73. Mem. Modern Lang. Assn., Coll. Lang. Assn., Soc. for Study of So. Lit. Democrat. Author: George W. Cable: The Northampton Years, 1959; George W. Cable, 1962; The William Stanley Braithwaite Reader, 1972; The Minority Presence in American Literature, 1600-1900, 2 vols., 1977. Asso. editor Coll. Lang. Assn. Jour., 1969-77. Contbr. articles to profl. jours. Home: 9326 Mellenbrook Rd Columbia MD 21045 Office: Dept English Morgan State Univ Baltimore MD 21239

BUTCHER, RUSSELL DEVEREUX, author, photographer; b. Bryn Mawr, Pa., Feb. 8, 1938; s. Devereux and Mary Frances (Taft) B.; student Colo. State U., 1957-58; B.A., U. Colo., 1960; postgrad. U. Mich. Law Sch., 1960-61; m. Pamela Richards, Apr. 12, 1967; 1 dau., Wendy Nan; children by previous marriage—Pamela Marie, Neill Devereux. Research editor Sierra Club, San Francisco, 1961-65; publicity writer Save-the-Redwoods League, San Francisco, 1963-65; conservation specialist Nat. Audubon Soc., N.Y.C., 1965-66, also mem. editorial bd. Audubon mag.; chief of pub. relations and publs. Mus. of N.Mex., Santa Fe, 1967-69; free lance writer, photographer and author, 1969—; editorial writer N.Y. Times, 1963—. Mem. Save-the-Redwoods League (life), Nat. Parks and Conservation Assn., Nat. Wildlife Fedn., Maine Audubon Soc. (pres. Down East chpt. 1978—), Sierra Club (life). Episcopalian. Author: Maine Paradise, 1973; New Mexico: Gift of the Earth, 1975; The Desert, 1976; Field Guide to Acadia National Park, Maine, 1977; contbr. articles to environ. jours. Home and Office: Box 155 Seal Harbor ME 04675

BUTCHER, WILLARD CARLISLE, banker; b. Bronxville, N.Y., Oct. 25, 1926; s. Willard F. and Helen (Calhoun) B.; student Middlebury Coll., 1945; B.A., Brown U., 1947; m. Sarah Catherine Payne, Oct. 8, 1949 (dec. Jan. 1955); children—Sarah Carlisle, Helen Catherine; m. 2d, Elizabeth Allen, Jan. 28, 1956; children—Barbara Downs, John Carlisle. With Chase Nat. Bank (now Chase Manhattan Bank), N.Y.C., 1947—, asst. treas. Grand Central br., 1953-56, asst. v.p., 1956-58, v.p., 1958-61, sr. v.p., 1961-69, exec. v.p., 1969-72, vice chmn., 1972, pres., 1972—, also chmn.; dir. ASARCO, Inc., Firestone Tire & Rubber Co., Akron, Ohio. Served with USNR, 1944-45. Mem. Phi Beta Kappa, Sigma Nu. Congregationalist. Clubs: Union League, Economic, Wall Street, Knickerbocker, Links (N.Y.C.); Silver Spring Country (Ridgefield, Conn.); Blind Brook (Port Chester, N.Y.); Norwalk (Conn.) Yacht. Home: 39 Trail's End Rd Wilton CT 06897 Office: 1 Chase Manhattan Plaza New York City NY 10015

BUTLER, ANNA MABEL LAND (MRS. FLOYD BUTLER), author; b. Phila.; d. John Weaver and Edith Frances (Jones) Land; student Trenton State Tchrs. Coll., 1920-22, 36, Temple U., 1953, U. Md., 1942-45; m. Maurice Alexander Hayes, June 1925 (div.); 1 son, Maurice Alexander (dec. 1943); m. 2d, Floyd Butler, Mar. 10, 1934. Tchr. pub. schs., Atlantic City, 1922-64; newspaper corr. Pitts. Courier, 1936-65; Atlantic City reporter Phila. Tribune, 1965—; now dir., head tchr. Morris Child Care Center. Mem. edn. council Human Resources Atlantic County-Anti-Poverty Program, 1965—; founder Black History-News Scrapbook Contest, 1969; pres. Seaboard Council Heritage House, 1954—, Atlantic City Study Center, 1959—; rec. sec. Episcopal Women, Diocese of N.J., now v.p.; pres. Episc. Churchwomen, St. Augustine's Ch., Atlantic City; mem. interracial planning com. Bal Masque, Atlantic City. Mem. Nat. (trustee), Northside (pres. 1961-65, v.p. 1960-61) bus. and profl. women's clubs, N.J. Orgn. Tchrs. (v.p. 1960—), Nat. Assn. Negro Bus. and Profl. Women, Heritage House and Cotillion Soc. (dir. 1956—), Catholic Poetry Soc., Am. Poets Fellowship Soc., Nat. Soc. Poets, Nat. Soc. Lit. and Arts, Atlantic City Tchrs. Assn. (life, exec. bd. 1962-64), Atlantic City C. of C. (chmn. judges boardwalk div., planning com. ann. children's parade), Nat. Links (pres. Atlantic City chpt., nat. chmn. creative writing), Wednesday Lit. Club (pres.), Phi Delta Kappa (charter). Author: Album of Love Letters—Unsent, 1952; Touchstone, 1962; High Noon, 1970; poems pub. in various anthologies; editor Responsibility, 1955-59, asso. editor, 1953—; Eastern area editor Nat. Links Jour., 1968—. Home: 410 N Kentucky Ave Atlantic City NJ 08401

BUTLER, BENJAMIN, ret. judge; b. Farmington, Maine, Aug. 7, 1905; s. Frank W. and Alice (Smith) B.; ed. Phillips Exeter Acad., 1924; A.B., Bowdoin Coll., 1928; LL.B., Boston U., 1932; m. Natalie C. Sturges, May 23, 1932; children—Diane Clare Butler Brinkman, Benjamin Sturges. Admitted to bar, 1932; pres., gen. mgr. Forster Mfg. Co., 1934-43; dir. Livermore Falls Trust Co., 1934; county atty., 1941-46; state senator from Franklin County, 1953-58; judge Franklin Municipal Court, 1961-65; atty., dir., registrar Sugarloaf Mountain Corp., 1955-74, clk., 1966-74. Assessor Farmington Village Corp., 1940-56, 60—; selectman Village of Farmington, 1948-51; mem. Farmington Sch. Com., 1948, chmn., 1949-53; mem. Farmington Budget Com., 1954-59; pres. Farmington Pub. Library, 1954-77; clk. Maine Citizens for Historic Preservation, 1972—, trustee, 1976—; trustee Franklin County. Recipient certificate of commendation Am. Assn. State and Local History, 1970; award Maine Historic Preservation Commn., 1972. Mem. Am., Maine, Franklin County bar assns., Newcomen Soc., New Eng. Historic Geneal. Soc., Maine, Farmington (treas. 1975—) hist. socs., Mayflower Soc. (gov. 1946-48, dep. gov.-gen. 1949-75), Chi Psi. Republican. Mason (Shriner, K.T., Scottish Rite, 32 deg.). Author: (with wife) History Old South Church of Farmington from 1814 to 1965, 1966; also Pilgrimage booklets for hist. soc. Home: 93 Main St Farmington ME 04938 Office: 7 Broadway Farmington ME 04938

BUTLER, CHARLES HENRY, hosp. adminstr.; b. N.Y.C., Oct. 12, 1932; s. Charles Henry and Theresa Edith (Simmons) B.; A.A., N.Y. City Community Coll., 1960; B.S., L.I. U., 1962; M.P.A., N.Y. U., 1970; m. Lois Evelyn Belle, Jan. 14, 1956; children—Charles Henry, Craig Aron. Advt. claims adjuster N.Y. Times, N.Y.C., 1950-65; br. office mgr. Bklyn. Union Gas Co., 1965-67; corp. personnel specialist Endicott Johnson Corp., Endicott, N.Y., 1967-69; sr. indsl. relations rep. Kennecott Copper Corp., N.Y.C., 1969-70; dir. personnel N.Y.C. Health & Hosps. Corp., 1970—, Greenpoint Hosp., 1970-75, Queens Hosp. Center, 1975-78, Cumberland Hosp., 1978—; faculty Marymount Coll., Tarrytown, N.Y., 1975-76. Pres. PTA, N.Y.C., 1966-67; chmn. adv. com. Citizens Affirmative Action, N.Y.C., 1974-76. Served with USNR, 1953-55; maj. USAF Res. Recipient Certificate of Appreciation, N.Y.C. Bd. Edn., 1967; award N.Y. State Dept. Mental Hygiene, 1975. Mem. Am. Mgmt. Assn., Res. Officers Assn., NAACP, Am. Soc. Personnel Adminstrn., N.Y. U. Alumni Assn., 100 Black Men, Council Concerned Black Execs. Presbyterian. Contbr. articles in field to profl. jours. Home: 6 Foxcroft Dr Nanuet NY 10954 Office: 39 Auburn Pl Brooklyn NY 11205

BUTLER, HENRY GEORGE, JR., textile products co. exec.; b. Providence, Jan. 5, 1918; s. Henry George and Deborah Rose (Conley) B.; student Brown U., 1935-38, Northeastern U., 1938-39; m. Norma Avis Anderton, Oct. 12, 1942; children—Judith Butler Hilburger, Jill Butler Vitko, Janet Butler Blair. Warehouse mgr. Lans Warehouse Co., Providence, 1946-47; traffic mgr., prodn. mgr. Textron, Inc., East Greenwich, R.I., 1947-54; material mgr. William Heller div. Uniroyal, Inc., Coventry, R.I., 1954-75; mgr. Spring-Green Corp., Warwick, R.I., 1975—; mgr., mem. bd. dirs. Quidnessett Meml. Cemetery, 1977—. Mem. Sch. Planning Commn., North Kingstown, R.I., 1957-59; chmn. bldg. com. Town of North Kingstown, 1965-68, chmn. sch. com., 1969-72. Served to 1st lt. AUS, 1941-45. Methodist (bd. trustees 1968-71, mem. adminstrv. bd. 1953—). Home: 235 Forge Rd North Kingstown RI 02852 Office: 6365 Post Rd North Kingstown RI 02852

BUTLER, JAMES EDWARD, realty co. exec.; b. Montreal, Que., Can., July 22, 1932; s. Ambrose Clifford and Winefred (Farrell) B.; B.S., Sir George Williams U., 1962; m. Elspeth Jewett, Feb. 1, 1954; 1 dau., Susan Elspeth. Constrn. auditor Place Ville Marie Corp., Montreal, 1959-63; mgr. Montreal Trust Co., 1963-74; gen. mgr. ops. Marathon Realty Co. Ltd., Montreal, 1974—; dir. Found.-Scottish Properties Ltd., New Brunswick Cold Storage Co. Mem. Real Estate Inst. Can. (dir.), Bldg. Owners and Mgrs. Assn. Montreal (dir.), Inst. Real Estate Mgmt. (past pres.), Montreal Real Estate Bd., Adminstrv. Mgmt. Soc., Montreal Bd. Trade. Mem. Anglican Ch. Clubs: LeCardinal Golf, St. Hyacinthe Golf. Home: 2121 Belvedere Circle Deux Montagnes PQ J7R 1G5 Canada Office: Suite 1800 Place du Canada Montreal PQ H3B 2N2 Canada

BUTLER, JONATHAN PUTNAM, architect; b. Portchester, N.Y., June 6, 1940; s. Jonathan Fairchild and Mary Elizabeth (Putnam) B.; B.A., Princeton U., 1962, M.F.A., 1965; M.Arch., Columbia U., 1966; m. Deborah Day Rogers, Mar. 18, 1967; children—Jonathan Rogers, Pauline Washburn, Benjamin Putnam. Constrn. adminstr. Landis Gores, New Canaan, Conn., 1965; designer, programmer, planner Skidmore Owings & Merrill, Architects, N.Y.C., 1966-68; asso. Rogers, Butler & Burgun, N.Y.C., 1968-71; partner Rogers, Butler, Burgun & Shahine, 1971—. Mem. Mystic (Conn.) Seaport Planning Com. Mem. AIA, Am. Hosp. Assn., N.Y. Soc. Architects, N.Y. State Assn. Architects, Columbia Archtl. Alumni Assn., Nat. Council Archtl. Registration Bds. (certified). Presbyterian. Clubs: Union, Princeton. Home: 108 E 82d St New York City NY 10028 Office: 521 Fifth Ave New York City NY 10017

BUTLER, LORETTA MARIE, research psychologist, univ. dean; b. St. Louis, Jan. 23, 1932; d. Raymond John and Loretta Mary (Cronin) B.; B.A., Fontbonne Coll., 1955; student U. Geneva, 1974; M.A., Columbia U., N.Y. U., 1968; B.A., M.A., Pius XII Inst., Italy, 1960; Ph.D., Fordham U., 1973; postgrad. U. Mich., 1975, Harvard U., 1978. Research asst. Mineola Arts Project, Rockefeller Found., Mineola, N.Y., 1969-72; mem. staff tchr. corps Fordham U., N.Y.C., 1972-74, asst. dean Fordham U., 1975—; dir. instl. research St. Thomas Aquinas Coll., N.Y., 1974-75; conf. participant Nat. Tchr. Corps. and others; trustee Washington Workshops, 1974-78. Recipient Myron Taylor study award, Florence, Italy, 1959; NDEA grantee in French, 1962, 64, 66, 68. Democrat. Roman Catholic. Exhibitor in art show, N.Y.C., 1963; contbr. articles to Piagetian ann. conv. reports, 1976-77. Home: 605 1st Ave New York City NY 10016 Office: Fordham Univ 113 W 60th St New York City NY 10023

BUTLER, NATALIE STURGES (MRS. BENJAMIN BUTLER), writer; b. Melrose, Mass., July 13, 1908; d. Dwight Case and Clare (Vaughan) Sturges; student Vesper George Art Sch., 1926-28; M.A. (hon.), U. Maine, Farmington, 1972; m. Benjamin Butler, May 23, 1932; children—Diane-Clare Butler Brinkman, Benjamin Sturges. Librarian, decorator Irving & Casson-A. H. Davenport Co., Boston, 1928-31; pres. Sturdia Corp., Farmington, Maine, 1955—. Franklin County chmn. Maine Sesquicentennial, 1970; mem. Maine Citizens for Hist. Preservation 1971—, sec., 1971, trustee, 1976—; mem. Maine Mus. Commn., 1974-76; trustee Farmington Pub. Library Assn., 1950—, treas., 1958-74, sec., 1958-77; trustee Franklin County Meml. Hosp., 1963-70; mem. Maine League Hist. Socs. and Museums, 1964—, trustee, 1973-76; co-chmn. Union Baptist Ch. Restoration Project, 1975-78. Recipient certificate of commendation Am. Assn. State and Local History, 1970; Hist. Preservation award Maine Hist. Preservation Commn., 1972. Mem. Maine Soc. Mayflower Descs., Maine Hist. Soc., John Howland Soc., New Eng. Hist. Geneal. Soc., Delta Kappa Gamma (hon.). Republican. Congregationalist (deaconess 1963-68). Author: (with Ben Butler) History of Old South Church, Farmington, Maine, 1966, Little Red Schoolhouse, 1971, Farmington's Musical Heritage, 1975, The Falls: Where Farmington, Maine, Began in 1776, 1976; Dwight C. Sturges: Etcher of an Era, 1974; (with Ben Butler and Don McKeen) Zephaniah Builds a Schoolhouse—Among Other Things!, 1975; also Pilgrimage booklets for hist. soc., and articles. Home: 93 Main St Farmington ME 04938

BUTLER, PAUL RICHARD, mgmt. cons.; b. East Orange, N.J., Dec. 12, 1946; s. Thomas Edgar and Dorathea Clarice (May) B.; U. Fla., 1972, B. Indsl. Engring., 1973, M.Ed., 1977, specialist in edn., 1977. Asst. mgr. J. Wayne Reitz Union, U. Fla., Gainesville, 1972-75; arcade mgr. Pint Pleasant Pavilion, Point Pleasant Beach, N.J., 1975-76; mgr., counselor, 1977—; counselor Drug Project, Gainsville, 1973-77. Served with AUS, 1966-68. Mem. Am. Inst. Indsl. Engr., Am. Personnel and Guidance Assn., IEEE, Nat. Assn. Student Personnel Adminstrs., Ocean County, U. Fla. alumni assns. Home: 110 St Louis Ave Point Pleasant Beach NJ 08742

BUTLER, ROBERT NEIL, physician, psychiatrist; b. N.Y.C., Jan. 21, 1927; s. Fred and Easter (Dikeman) B.; B.A., Columbia U., 1949, M.D., 1953; m. Myrna Lewis, May 17, 1975; children by previous marriage—Ann Christine, Carole Melissa, Cynthia Lee. Intern St. Lukes Hosp., N.Y.C., 1953-54; resident U. Calif. Langley Porter Clinic, 1954-55, NIMH, 1955-56; research psychiatrist NIMH, USPHS, 1955-62; founder geriatric unit Chestnut Lodge, 1958, adminstr., 1958-59; research psychiatrist Washington (D.C.) Sch. Psychiatry, 1962-76; dir. Nat. Inst. Aging, NIH, 1976—. Mem. faculty George Washington U. Med. Sch., Washington, 1962—, Howard U. Sch. Medicine; cons. NIMH, 1967-76, U.S. Senate Spl. Com. on Aging. Chmn. D.C. Adv. Commn. on Aging, 1969-76; bd. dirs. Nat. Council on Aging, Nat. Caucus on Black Aged; mem. Inst. Medicine, Nat. Acad. Scis., 1978—. Served with U.S. Martime Service, 1945-47. Recipient Pulitzer prize for non-fiction, 1976. Fellow Am. Psychiat. Assn., Am. Geriatrics Soc.; mem. Group for Advancement Psychiatry (trustee). Gerontol. Soc. Club: Cosmos (Washington). Author: (with others) Human Aging, 1963; (with Myrna I. Lewis) Aging and Mental Health, 1973; Why Survive? Being Old in America, 1975; (with M.I. Lewis) Sex After Sixty, 1975. Mem. editorial bd. Jour. Geriatric Psychiatry. Aging and Human Devel., Geriatrics. Contbr. articles to publs. Address: 3815 Huntington St NW Washington DC 20015

BUTLER, WALTER JOHN, union ofcl.; b. N.Y.C., Aug. 6, 1927; s. Walter James and Marion (Wynn) B.; student Russell Sage Coll., 1947-48; B.S., Cornell U., 1951; m. Linda Marie Hoke, Apr. 14, 1976; children from previous marriage—Jo-Ann, Walter James, Suzanne, Constance, Scott. Internat. rep. Service Employees Internat. Union, AFL-CIO, 1951—, mem. exec. bd., 1968—, trustee Local 200, 1951—, pres., 1953—, pres. Local 234, 1951—, also sec.-treas. Fla. State Council, sec.-treas. N.Y. State Service Employees Council, 1970—, Eastern Conf. Service Employee Unions, 1975—; 1st v.p. Greater Syracuse Labor AFL-CIO, 1960—; vice-chmn. N.Y. State Service Employees Legis. Council, 1962—. Mem. Appeal Bd. Upstate Selective Service System, 1969-73; bd. dirs. Group Health Inc., 1969—; mem. Temporary State Com. Living Costs and the Economy, 1973-75. Served with USN, 1943-46. Mem. Cornell U. Alumni Assn. Club: Cavalry Country. Office: 3060 Erie Blvd E PO Box 1200 Syracuse NY 13201

BUTORAC, FRANK GEORGE, adminstrv. librarian; b. Crosby, Minn., Feb. 12, 1927; s. Frank and Mary (Paun) B.; A.B., U. Mich., 1950, A.M., 1956, A.M.L.S., 1958; postgrad. Cornell Law Sch., 1950-51, Harvard U., 1953, U. Notre Dame, 1959, 60-62, Holy Cross Coll., 1962-66, Cath. U., 1963, Georgetown U., 1965, Cambridge U., 1975; Ph.D. candidate, N.Y. U., 1970; m. Mary Regis McGowan Ratigan, Apr. 8, 1972; stepchildren—Helen Elizabeth, Nicholas. Sales corr., trainee U.S. Rubber, Mishawaka, Ind., 1952-53; tchr. 6th grade Jefferson Sch., Wayne, Mich., 1953-54; tchr. social studies Slauson Jr. High Sch., Ann Arbor, Mich., 1954-55; supervising tchr. social studies Lincoln Consol. High Sch. Eastern Mich. U., Ypsilanti, 1955-57; circulation librarian, engring. librarian U. Mich., Ann Arbor, 1958-59; joined Congregation of Holy Cross, 1959; seminarian and temporary profession, 1959-66; novice Sacred Heart Novitiate, Jordan, Minn.,

1959-60; order librarian Holy Cross Coll., Washington, 1962-66; registrar Trenton (N.J.) Jr. Coll., 1966-67; registrar Mercer County Community Coll., Trenton, N.J., 1967-68, asst. dir. community and extension services, 1968-70, dir. evening and extension ops., 1970-71, dir. spl. programs, 1971-74, chmn. library services dept., 1974—; cons. library tech. programs. Chmn. Anna B. Stokes Found., Trenton, 1974-75. Served with USN, 1944-47. Recipient Tall Cedars of Lebanon award for Community Service, Trenton, 1974. Mem. ALA, N.J. Library Assn. (exec. bd. 1977-78), Am. Assn. U. Adminstrs., Cornell Law Assn., Purnell, George sch. parents assns., Hun Sch. Fathers Assn., St. Mary's Hall-Doane Acad. Parent-Faculty Assn., Theta Delta Chi, Phi Delta Phi, Phi Delta Kappa, Alpha Phi Omega. Democrat. Roman Catholic. Clubs: Nassau (Princeton, N.J.); Princeton (N.Y.C.); Trenton Lions (pres. 1972), Trenton Torch (pres. 1972), Cornell of Central N.J. (pres. 1977-78). Home: 44 E Union St Bordentown NJ 08505 Office: 1200 Old Trenton Rd Trenton NJ 08690

BUTT, GENE WILLARD, writer, hist. researcher, cons.; b. Toronto, Ont., Can., June 15, 1918; s. George Willard and Lillian May (Everett) B.; B.A. in Polit. Sci., York U., 1974, B.A. in Sociology with honors 1972; m. Margaret L. Baker, Nov. 25, 1950. Lectr. Ont. Coll. Art, 1957; chmn. dept. extension and evening classes Ont. Coll. Art, 1965, dep. prin., 1966, acting prin., 1969-71; co-ordinator edn. services Art Gallery Ont., Toronto, 1974-76; head of exhbns. Fine Art Dept., Robert Simpson, Ltd., Toronto, 1940-45. Fellow Royal Horticulture Soc. (Eng.); mem. Canadian Polit. Sci. Assn., Canadian Hist. Assn., Canadian Sociology and Anthropology Assn., Am. Sociol. Assn., Teihard Centre for Future of Man (Eng.). Conservative. Anglican. Clubs: University Club (Toronto), Arts and Letters. Editor Colour Comments, 1962-65. Home: Glendyer Rural Route 4 Mabou Cape Breton NS B0E 1X0 Canada

BUTTACI, SALVATORE ST. JOHN, editor, educator; b. Corona, N.Y., June 12, 1941; s. Michael Salvatore and Josephine (Amico) B.; B.A. in Communication Arts, Seton Hall U., South Orange, N.J., 1965; m. Susan Linda Gerstle, Mar. 9, 1974. Tchr. elementary English, St. Anne Sch., Fair Lawn, N.J., 1967-68, vice prin., then prin., 1968-71; instr. English, Saddle Brook (N.J.) schs., 1972—; co-editor New Worlds Unltd., 1974—. Mem. N.J. Edn. Assn., Nat. Amateur Press Assn., Com. Small Mag. Editors and Pubs., N.J. Poetry Soc., Poetry Club Terre Haute (Ind.), Internat. Platform Assn. Roman Catholic. Poetry pub. in anthologies, mags. and revs. Home: 100 Maple St Apt 53 Garfield NJ 07026 Office: New Worlds Unltd PO Box 556 Saddle Brook NJ 07662

BUTTERLY, MARGARET PARDEE, violinist, violist, educator; b. Valdosta, Ga., May 10, 1920; d. William Augustus and Frances Ross (Burton) Pardee; diplomas Inst. Mus. Art, Juilliard Sch. Music, 1940, postgrad. diploma, 1942; diploma Juilliard Grad. Sch., 1945; m. Daniel Rogers Butterly, July 5, 1944. Mem. Faculty Manhattanville Coll. of Scared Heart, 1942-54; tchr. violin and viola Juilliard Sch. Music, N.Y.C., 1942—; mem. faculty Meadowmount Sch. Music, Westport, N.Y., 1956—; debut recital N.Y. Town Hall, 1952; toured as soloist and with chamber music groups; concertmaster Gt. Neck Symphony, 1954—. Mem. Internat. Viola Research Soc., Music Tchrs. Nat. Assn., Am. Fedn. Musicians, N.Y. State Music Tchrs. Assn., Asso. Music Tchrs. League N.Y., Soc. for Strings (dir. 1969—). Office: care Juilliard Sch Lincoln Center Plaza New York City NY 10023

BUTTINGER, JOSEPH ANTHONY, author; b. Reichersbeuern, Germany, Apr. 30, 1906; s. Anton and Maria (Birkenauer) B.; student pub. schs.; hon. doctorate U. Klagenfurt (Austria, 1977; m. Muriel Morris, Aug. 1, 1939; 1 step dau., Constance Mary (Mrs. Harold Harvey.) Came to U.S., 1939, naturalized, 1943. Sec., Social Democratic party Carinthia, Austria, 1928-34, chmn. central com., 1934-38; vice chmn. bd. dirs. Internat. Rescue Com., N.Y. N.Y.C., 1945-56, European dir., Geneva, Switzerland, 1945-47; chmn. exec. com. Am. Friends of Vietnam, N.Y.C., 1955-64. Decorated Golden Order of Merit (Austria), 1971. Author: In The Twilight of Socialism, 1952; The Smaller Dragon-A Political History of Vietnam, 1958; Vietnam: A Dragon Embattled, 1967; Vietnam: A Political History, 1968; A Dragon Defiant: A Short History of Vietnam, 1972; Vietnam: The Unforgettable Tragedy, 1977; Manko of Mankoland, 3 vols., 1977; also history of Vietnam, Ency. Brit. Home: Brookdale Farm Rural Route 1 Box 264 Pennington NJ 08534

BUTTON, BLAND BALLARD, investment banker; b. Louisville, June 25, 1915; s. Bland Ballard and Alleene Harwood (Wilson) B.; B.S., U. Chgo., 1938; m. Patricia Spooner, Sept. 20, 1969; children—Justine, Louise, Marcy, Kenneth. With Diversey Corp., Chgo., 1939-62, exec. v.p., 1959-62; v.p. Internat. Minerals & Chem. Corp., Libertyville, Ill., 1962-68; dir. spl. services Olin Corp., Stamford, Conn., 1969-72; investment banker F. Eberstadt & Co., N.Y.C., 1972-76; pres. Bland B. Button & Assos., Bronxville, N.Y., 1976—; chmn. bd., dir. Chemvet Labs., Inc., Kansas City, Kans.; dir. Bonewitz Chems. Inc., Burlington, Iowa. Mem. citizens bd. U. Chgo., 1958—. Republican. Episcopalian. Clubs: St. Andrews Golf, N.Y. Caledonian Curling, Indian Hill, University (Chgo.). Home and office: 65 Durham Rd Bronxville NY 10708

BUTTON, DANIEL EVAN, writer; b. Dunkirk, N.Y., Nov. 1, 1917; A.B., U. Del., 1938; M.S., Columbia, 1939; m. Rebecca B. Pool; children—Nancy, Sarah, Daniel, Jefferson, Mary; m. 2d, Rena P. Posner, 1969. Reporter, editor News-Journal Papers, Wilmington, Del., and Asso. Press, N.Y.C., 1939-46; dir. pub. relations U. Del., 1947-51; asst. to pres. State U. of N.Y., 1952-58; staff Rensselaer Polytech. Inst., 1959; editorial page editor Times-Union, Albany, N.Y., 1959-60, exec. editor, 1960-66; mem. 90th to 91st Congresses from 29th Dist. of N.Y.; exec. dir., pres. The Arthritis Found., 1971-75; editor Sci. Digest, 1976—. Home: South Egremont MA 01258

BUTTON, FORD LINCOLN, cartoonist; b. Wellsboro, Pa., June 22, 1924; s. Howard Henry and Beatrice Charlotte (Larson) B.; B.S. Edn., Mansfield State Coll., 1952; postgrad Buffalo State U., N.Y. U., Rochester Inst. Tech.; m. Joyce Marie Fullagar, Aug. 5, 1956; children—Lisa, Sally, Connie, Jeffrey, Christopher. Tchr. art, Ramapo Central Sch. #2, Spring Valley, N.Y., 1952-56, Churchville (N.Y.) Chili Central Sch., 1956-62; art cons. Gates Chili Central Sch., 1962-69, tchr. art, 1962—; freelance cartoonist Good Housekeeping, Nation's Bus., Christian Sci. Monitor, Phi Delta Kappan, and others, 1956—; exhibited Internat. Salon Cartoons, Montreal. Served with AUS, 1943-45; ETO. Mem. N.Y. United Tchrs. Presbyterian. Home: 3398 Chili Ave Rochester NY 14624 Office: 3227 Lyell Rd Rochester NY 14606

BUTTRICK, CARLTON ELWIN, humane soc. exec.; b. Hampstead, N.H., Oct. 29, 1910; s. Charles C. and Mabel (Mills) B.; B.A., U. N.H., 1932, LL.D. 1962; postgrad. Yale U., 1938; m. Florence E. Middlebrook, Oct. 14, 1936; 1 son, Richard O. Boys dir. Gilbert Home, Winsted, Conn., 1935-38; boys supr. Mitchell House, Hartford, Conn., 1938; dir. edn. Conn. Humane Soc., Hartford, 1938-45; dir. field services Am. Humane Assn., Denver, 1945-49, pres., 1954-55, treas., 1973-74, also dir.; pres. Animal Rescue League of Boston, 1949-77, also dir.; treas. Internat. Soc. for Protection of Animals, Boston, 1959-61, pres., 1961-65, regional chmn. Western Hemisphere, 1965-67, 1st v.p., 1967-69, asst. treas., 1969-71, treas., 1971—, also dir., 1967—; bd. dirs. Eastern Slopes Animal Welfare League, 1972—; dir. N.H. Soc. Prevention Cruelty to Animals, 1972-76; chmn. Boston Animal Control Commn., 1972-76; dir. Am. Fondouk, Fez, Morocco; corporator Hibernia Savs. Bank, Boston. Recipient Gold medal award Danish Soc. Protection Animals, 1962; Gold medal award West German Fedn. Animal Protective Socs.; Royal Soc. Prevention Cruelty to Animals Queen Victoria medal in Silver, 1965; certificate of merit Am. Humane Assn., 1965; Gold medal Swedish Soc. Protection Animals, 1976. Wisdom award of honor, 1970. Mem. Dedham Hist. Soc., New Eng. Fedn. Humane Socs. (pres. 1966-67), Boston Zool. Soc. (trustee), Phi Kappa Phi. Episcopalian (vestryman). Club: Rotary (pres. chpt. 1963-64, dist. gov. 1967-68). Editor: Our Fourfooted Friends, 1949-77. Home: PO Box 532 Cataumet MA 02534

BUTTS, JOHN WILLIAM, real estate broker; b. Lancaster, Pa., Feb. 10, 1912; s. Harry Walter and Sarah Ann (Kunkel) B.; student U. Pa., 1934-35, Lancaster Bus. Coll., 1937-38, Franklin and Marshall Coll., 1936-38, Pa. State U., 1946-47; m. Esther Christiana Kauffman, June 28, 1933; children—Laurence A., David M., Kathleen D. Butts Seely. Indsl. engr. Armstrong Cork Co., Lancaster, 1942-43, safety engr., 1943-46; real estate broker; pres. John W. Butts, Inc., Manor Shopping Center, Lancaster; instr. Pa. State U., 1964-76; cons. City Renewal Authority, 1961-62; owner, pub. E.S.P. Orbit, 1974-77. Mem. Lancaster City and County Sub Housing Com., Mayor's Housing Conf. Rev. Com.; bd. dirs. Lancaster Health and Welfare Found; past pres. Child Devel. Center; past pres. council Lutheran Ch. Mem. Greater Lancaster Bd. Realtors (pres. 1955-56, Realtor of Year 1967, Distinguished Service award 1976) Club: Kiwanis (past lt. gov., past dist. sec.). Home: 2250 Fruitville Pike Lancaster PA 17601 Office: Manor Shopping Center PO Box 135 Lancaster PA 17604

BUTTZ, CHARLES WILLIAM, mgmt. cons.; b. Aberdeen, S.D., Aug. 8, 1932; s. Ward Leland and Mary (Eddy) B.; student No. State Coll., Aberdeen, 1949-50, U.S. Mil. Acad., 1950-54; B.C.E., Rensselaer Poly. Inst., 1956; M.B.A., U. Conn.; m. Teresa Margarita Castro, July 28, 1956; children—Jean, Teresa, Charles Leland, William, James. Planning engr., project mgr. Tippetts-Abbett-McCarthy-Stratton, Engrs., N.Y.C., 1956-65; chief traffic engr. Kuala Lumpur Transp. Study, Malaysia, 1963-64; mgmt. cons. Booz, Allen & Hamilton, Inc., N.Y.C., 1965-67; sr. asso., prin., dir. Knight, Gladieux & Smith, Inc., Mgmt. Cons., N.Y.C., 1967-74; group mgr. Boeing Computer Services Cons. Div., N.Y.C., 1974-76; v.p. Middlesex Research Center, 1976-77; pres. Eastern Shelter-All, Inc., 1977—. Chmn. troop com. Boy Scouts Am., 1967—; v.p. Darien United Fund and Community Council, 1970; v.p., sec. Darien YMCA. Served to maj. C.E., U.S. Army Res., 1956-70. Registered profl. engr., N.Y., N.J. Mem. ASCE, Inst. Transp. Engrs. (asso.), Transp. Research Bd., Regional Plan Assn. Episcopalian (vestryman, layreader 1968—). Home: PO Box 222 Buck Hill Falls PA 18323 Office: PO Box 152 Mountainhome PA 18342

BUTZNER, JAMES IRVIN, engr.; b. Scranton, Pa., Nov. 10, 1920; s. John Decker and Bess (Robison) B.; B.Chem. Engring., U. Va., 1942; m. Mary Catharine Schoen, Sept. 5, 1942; children—Jane, Ann, William. Engr. and adminstr. Mobil Research & Devel. Corp., Paulsboro, N.J., 1942—, mgr. bldgs. and adminstrv. services, 1969—. Founding chmn. bd. trustees Gloucester County Coll., 1966-74; pres. N.J. Council County Colls., 1973-74; mem. N.J. State Bd. Higher Edn., 1973-74; mem. Woodbury City Council, 1958-64; founder Gloucester County Coll. Found., pres., 1975-78. Named Outstanding Citizen Woodbury, 1970; recipient award Gloucester County, 1972, achievement award Woodbury Exchange Club, 1973, Service to Community award Gloucester County Coll., 1976. Mem. Am. Chem. Soc., S. Jersey Purchasing Agts. Assn. (past pres.), Gloucester County Hist. Soc. (past trustee), Greater Woodbury C. of C. (dir.), SAR. Republican. Presbyterian. Club: Exchange of Woodbury. Home: 556 Myrtle Ave Woodbury NJ 08096 Office: Billingsport Rd Paulsboro NJ 08066

BUXBAUM, COLMAN LAZAR, biomedical engr.; b. N.Y.C., Nov. 16, 1930; s. Joseph H. and Gertrude (Abbe) B.; B.Elec. Engring., City Coll. N.Y., 1953; M.S., Adelphi U., 1961; m. Rita T. Bachman, Jan. 26, 1957; 1 dau., Cheryl Rose. Radar design engr. Sperry Gyroscope Co., Great Neck, N.Y., 1955-59; project mgr. mil. systems programs Airborne Instrument Lab., Deer Park, N.Y., 1959-67; med. electronics systems mgr. Hoffmann La Roche Inc., Cranbury, N.J., 1967-76; mgr. engring. med. ultrasound div. Picker Corp., Northford, Conn., 1976—. Served with AUS, 1953-55. Fellow Soc. Advanced Med. Systems; mem. Nat. Elec. Mfrs. Assn. (nat. chmn. tech. com. ultrasound sect.), Assn. Advancement Med. Instrumentation, IEEE (sr.) Patentee in field. Home: 100 State St North Haven CT 06473 Office: 12 Clintonville Rd Northford CT 06472

BUXBAUM, MARTIN DAVID, writer, ret. editor, poet; b. Richmond, Va., June 27, 1912; s. David Martin and Sadie St. Clair (McGuffin) Noll.; student Columbia Tech. Coll., 1934-38, Newman Sudduth Sch. Art, 1936-38; m. Alice Lee Lyons, Sept. 4, 1938; children—Joan Buxbaum Galope, Alice Buxbaum Dick, Rosemary Buxbaum Redding, Martha Buxbaum Newpher, Roberta Buxbaum Walker, Kathleen Buxbaum Stubbs, Martin L., William. Editor, Hechinger Co., Washington, 1933-38; timekeeper Diamond Constrn. Co., Washington, 1938-39; free lance writer, photographer, 1939-41; editor Engring. & Research Corp., Riverdale, Md., 1941-45; editor So. Dairies, Inc., Washington, 1945-53; dir. communications Marriott Corp., Bethesda, Md., 1953-76, editor Table Talk, 1953—; now freelance writer. Recipient George Washington medal of honor, 1964, 70, 71, 72, 73, 75; named Poet of Year, Md. Poetry Soc., 1967; named Ky. Col., 1970. Mem. Md. Poetry Soc. Kiwanian. Author: Rivers of Thought, 1958; The Underside of Heaven, 1963; The Unsung, 2 vols., 1964, 65; Whispers in the Wind, 1966; Around Our House, 1968; Once Upon a Dream, 1970; Table Talk, 1972; The Warm World, 1974. Counselor Sunshine Mag., 1968—; asso. editor Playtime Mag., 1970—; advisor Praying Hands mag., 1975—; columnist Jour. Papers, 1978. Home and office: 7819 Custer Rd Bethesda MD 20014

BUXTON, EDWARD FULTON, publisher, writer; b. Boston, May 8, 1917; s. Edward William and Grace (Hurlburt) B.; B.A., U. Wis., 1941; postgrad. Northwestern U., 1942; m. Susan Elizabeth Abrams, Jan. 14, 1962; children from former marrage—Gail, Leslie. Reporter/rewriteman Wis. Press Bur., 1940-42; creative supr. Ellington Co., 1946-50, Compton Co., 1950-55, J. Walter Thompson Co., 1955-62, D'Arcy Advt. Co., 1962-65; pres. Exec. Communications Inc., diversified pub. co., N.Y.C., 1965—; author: Promise Them Anything, 1973, Creative People at Work, 1976; writer articles trade press, lectr. in field. Served to lt. (j.g.), USNR, 1942-46. Democrat. Home: 185 E 85th St New York City NY 10028 Office: 400 E 54th St New York City NY 10022

BUZZELL, SCOTT PRESCOTT, shopping center adminstr.; b. Springfield, Mass., Feb. 23, 1943; s. Francis Prescott and Irene (Peaulieu) B.; B.A., U. Hartford, 1969; m. Carol T. Speer, Nov. 19, 1966. Flight instr. Burnside-Ott Tng. Center, Miami, 1969-70; supr. property mgmt. div. Allstate Ins. Co., Farmington, Conn., 1970-75; asst. mgr. Westfarms Mall, West Hartford, Conn., 1975; center mgr. Mall at Short Hills (N.J.), 1976-78; dir. property mgmt. La Percq Realty Corp., N.Y.C., 1978—. Mem. bus. adv. council Town of Bloomfield (Conn.), 1974-75. Office: La Percq Realty Corp 345 Park Ave New York NY 10022

BYCER, ROBERT ELLIOTT, health care exec.; b. Darby, Pa., Dec. 16, 1952; s. Manuel Max and Mildred (Charlestein) B.; B.S., Drexel U., 1975; M.B.A., Adelphi U. Sales rep. J & T Snack Food Corp., Pennsauken, N.J., 1975-76; bus. mgr., dept. medicine Temple U. Sch. Medicine, Phila., 1976-77; asst. controller Jewish Inst. for Geriatric Care, New Hyde Park, N.Y., 1977—. Mem. Hosp. Fin. Mgmt. Assn., Am. Hosp. Assn., Assn. M.B.A. Execs., Am. Mgmt. Assn. Home: 15 Schenck Ave Apt 3C Great Neck NY 11021 Office: 271-11 76th Ave New Hyde Park NY 11040

BYE, ARTHUR EDWIN, JR., landscape architect; b. Arnhem, Holland, Aug. 25, 1919; (parents Am. citizens) s. Arthur Edwin and Mary (Heldring) B.; B.S. in Landscape Architecture, Pa. State U., 1942. Partner firm Bye & Herrmann, Rye, N.Y., 1951-63; sole practice, Ridgefield, Conn., 1963—. Prof., Cooper Union, N.Y.C., 1951—, Columbia, N.Y.C., 1952-74. Recipient merit award U.S. Housing and Urban Devel. Dept., 1968, 3 nat. awards Am. Assn. Nurserymen, 1971—. Fellow Am. Soc. Landscape Architects (recipient honor award 1970, bd. dirs. Found.); mem. Archtl. League N.Y. Contbr. to profl. jours. Home: 803 N Salem Rd Ridgefield CT 06877 Office: 186 Sound Beach Ave Old Greenwich CT 06870

BYERS, ARTHUR MAHLON, JR., clergyman, sem. adminstr.; b. Phila., Jan. 21, 1915; s. Arthur Mahlon and Edna (Shallcross) B.; A.B., Wesleyan U., Middletown, Conn., 1936; M.S., U. Pa., 1941; B.D., Princeton Theol. Sem., 1950; D.D. (honoris causa), Westminster Choir Coll., 1974; m. Margaret Heilman McDaniel, Oct. 22, 1942; children—Elizabeth Jean, Ruth Anne, David Arthur, John William. Head sci. dept. Chestnut Hill Acad., 1939-41; instr. chemistry Drexel Inst. Tech., 1946-47; ordained to ministry Presbyn. Ch., 1950; pastor Wissinoming Presbyn. Ch., Phila., 1950-53; sec. audiovisual prodns. Dept. Stewardship and Promotion, United Presbyn. Ch., N.Y.C., 1953-64; sec. Princeton Theol. Sem., 1964—. Chmn. Assistance Bd. Princeton Twp., 1964-71; mem. Princeton Community Action Council, 1965-68. Trustee Westminster Choir Coll., Princeton, 1961-73, vice chmn., 1966-68, chmn., 1968-73; trustee N.J. State Prisons, Trenton, 1971-72. Served to capt. AUS, 1941-45; ETO. Mem. Am. Chem. Soc., Sigma Chi. Club: Nassau. Home: 45 Audubon Way Princeton NJ 08540

BYERS, FRANCES REES, ednl. research asso.; b. Phila., Oct. 14, 1940; d. Joseph Arthur and Frances Rees (Hollihan) Byers; B.A., Rosemont Coll., 1962; Ph.D. (U.S. Office Edn. fellow, U. Pa. Dissertation Year fellow), U. Pa., 1976. Computer programmer Bell Telephone Co. Pa., Phila., 1962-64; statis. asst. U. Pa. Office Admissions, Phila., 1964-66, teaching asst. Grad. Sch. Edn., 1970; research asst. Office Research and Evaluation Sch. Dist. Phila., 1970-71, research asso., 1971—. Bd. dirs. Spruce Hill Community Assn., 1975-79, Friends of Clark Park, 1976-79. Mem. Nat. Council on Measurement in Edn., Am. Ednl. Research Assn. (rep. on student com. 1971-73, research tng. com. 1971-73), Psychometric Soc., Phila. Assn. Sch. Adminstrs., Nat. Hist. Soc., Nat. Trust for Historic Preservation, AAAS, Acad. Natural Scis. Phila., Phila. Art Mus., Franklin Inst., Pi Lambda Theta, Phi Delta Kappa. Democrat. Roman Catholic. Home: 4409 Baltimore Ave Philadelphia PA 19104 Office: Sch Dist Philadelphia Office Research and Evaluation 21st St and Ben Franklin Pkwy Philadelphia PA 19103

BYINGTON, FREDERICK DOLLIVER, educator; b. Oakland, Calif., May 2, 1930; s. Horace D. and Zoe (Burdick) B.; A.B., B.A., Pomona Coll., 1952; postgrad. Calif., Los Angeles, 1952-53; M.S., U. So. Calif., 1956, M.Ed., 1956; postgrad. Columbia, 1959-60, N.Y.U., 1956—, U. Pa., 1976—; m. Jennifer S. Grant, Aug. 1, 1955 (dec. 1961). Teaching asst. U. So. Calif., 1953-55; tchr. Chadwick Sch., Rolling Hills, Calif., 1955-57; tchr., supr. Mt. Vernon (N.Y.) Pub. schs., 1958-59; founding dir. Yokaya Prep. Sch., Redlands, Calif., 1956-58; chmn. dept. secondary edn. Farleigh Dickinson U., 1959-62; instr. secondary edn. Hofstra U., 1962-63; founding dir. Byton Schs., Southbury, Conn., Adams, Mass., 1963-74, Phila., 1978—; dir. secondary academically talented program Phila. Pub. Schs., 1973-78. Mem. Ad Hoc Com. on Edn. for Gifted and Talented, Pa. Dept. Edn. Chmn. bd. govs., exec. dir. Ednl. Service Found. Mem. Nat. Assn. Biology Tchrs., Am. Inst. Biol. Scis., AAAS, NEA, Nat. Sci. Tchrs. Assn., Nat. Assn. for Gifted, Phi Delta Kappa, Alpha Phi Omega, Alpha Tau Omega, others. Republican. Christian Scientist. Lion. Home: 1500 Locust St Philadelphia PA 19102

BYINGTON, JOHN WILLIAM, bus. exec.; b. Lansing, Mich., May 14, 1947; s. Walter Montgomery and Jeanette Julia (Celentino) B.; B.A. cum laude, Mich. State U., 1969; M.B.A., U. Cin., 1972; postgrad. N.Y. U., 1975—. With market research dept. Chesebrough-Pond's, Inc., Greenwich, Conn., 1972-76; supr. test mktg. dept. Gen. Foods Corp., White Plains, N.Y., 1976-77; dir. syndicated industry services NPD Research, Inc., Floral Park, N.Y., 1977—; dir. Byington Family Fund, Lansing, Mich., 1973—. Mem. adv. bd. U. Cin. Coll. Bus. Mem. Am. Mktg. Assn., N.Y. U. Bus. Forum, Beta Gamma Sigma, Phi Kappa Psi, SAR. Democrat. Home: 14 Horatio St New York City NY 10014 Office: 15 Verbena Ave Floral Park NY 11001

BYINGTON, S. JOHN, lawyer; b. Grand Rapids, Mich.; Pha m.B., Ferris State Coll.; Pharm.D. (hon.), Albany (N.Y.) Sch Pharmacy; student U. Mich. Law Sch.; J.D., Georgetown U., 1963; m. Sally Ruth Meyer; children—Nancy, Barbara. Dir. pub lic relations Am. Pharm. Assn., Washington, 1961-64; asst. prosecuting atty. Kent County, Mich., 1964-65; mem. staff Mich. Gov. George Romney, 1965-68; practiced law, held vari corp. posts in communication and internat. trade firms, 1968-72; dir. Detroit office, then dep. dir. and nat. expo mktg. dir. Office Field Ops., Dept. Commerce, 1972-74; dep dir. Office of Consumer Affairs, HEW, dep. spl. asst. to pres. for consumer affairs, 1974-76; chmn. Consumer Product Safety Commn., 1976-78; mng. partner firm Bushnell, Gage, Reizen & Byington, P.C., Washington, 1978—. Bd. dirs. Hamilton Found., 1972—; mem. adv. council Center for Study of Presidency, nat. adv. bd. Citizen's Choice, Inc.; hon. bd. dirs. Am. Coll. Toxicology; mem. task force on product liability Nat. Chamber Found. Mem. Am. Pharmacists Assn., Mich. Pharmacists Assn., Am. Bar Assn., Fed. Bar Assn., D.C. Bar Assn., Mich. Bar Assn., Acad. Polit. Sci. Office: Bushnell Gage Reizen & Byington PC 1899 L St NW Washington DC 20036

BYRAM, THOMAS LESLIE, hosp. adminstr.; b. Madison, Ind., Sept. 30, 1931; s. Leslie A. and Hazel A. (Pangburn) B.; B.S., Ind. U., 1953; M.S. in Hosp. Adminstrn., Northwestern U., 1957. Adminstr., Bloomsburg (Pa.) Hosp., 1960-65; cons. hosp. adminstrn. N.Y.C. Regional Office, N.Y. State Health Dept., 1969-72; exec. dir. Bapt. Hosp., Bklyn., 1972—; dir. Am. Baptist Homes and Hosps., 1974—. Mem. Am. Coll. Hosp. Adminstrs., Am. Hosp. Assn., Am. Pub. Health Assn., Ind. U. Northwestern U. alumni assns., Alpha Delta Mu, Theta Chi. Episcopalian. Office: Baptist Hospital 759 President St Brooklyn NY 11215

BYRD, ALICIA DELORIS, ednl. counselor; b. Tachakawa AFB, Japan, May 16, 1953; d. William Lee and Myrtice Ernestine (Mickens) Byrd; A.B. in Psychology, Wheaton Coll., 1975; M.A. in Human Devel. Counseling, Sangamon State U., 1977. Student asst. psychology dept. Wheaton (Ill.) Coll., 1975; Outreach coordinator YWCA, Springfield, Ill., 1975-76; Outreach counselor Youth Service Bur., Springfield, 1976-77; asso. dean students Gordon Coll., Wenham, Mass., 1977—; Woman-to-Woman Workshop leader Sangamon State U., 1976, 77. Campaign worker Carter Presdl. campaign, 1976. Mem. Am. Personnel and Guidance Assn., Assn. for Non-White Concerns in Counseling, Am. Coll. Personnel Assn., Nat. Black Christian Student Conf. Democrat. Home: PO Box 94 Beverly Farms Station Beverly MA 01915

BYRD, EDWIN (EDDIE) LEONARD, JR., graphic arts co. exec.; b. Paso Robles, Calif., Nov. 19, 1943; s. Edwin Leonard and Helen Catherine (Konat) B.; student Corcoran Gallery Sch. Art, 1962-63; m. Mary Lee Wittig, May 14, 1960; children—Catherine Lee, Diana Lynn. Graphic designer IBM Corp., Washington, 1962-66; art dir. Beveridge & Asso., Inc., Washington, 1966-70; sr. adv. graphic designer Westinghouse Electric Co., Pitts., 1970-74; pres., owner Byrd Graphic Design Inc., Pitts., 1974—. Cited as one of most important U.S. graphic designers Idea Mag., Tokyo, 1978. Mem. Am. Inst. Graphic Arts, Pitts. Assn. Indsl. Advertisers. Club: Highland Country. Home and Office: 728 Harden Dr Pittsburgh PA 15229

BYRD, WILLIAM TED, educator; b. Clover, Va., Dec. 13, 1941; s. Ralph and Virginia Saunders (Jones) B.; B.A., Greensboro Coll., 1964; postgrad. Towson State Coll., 1968-76. Tchr. Perry Hall Sr. Sch., Balt., 1964-65, Patapsco Sr. Sch., Balt., 1967—. Served with AUS, 1965-67. Mem. Tchrs. Assn. Baltimore County, NEA, Md. Tchrs. Assn., Pi Gamma Mu. Home: 8236 Gray Haven Rd Baltimore MD 21222 Office: 8100 Wise Ave Baltimore MD 21222

BYRD, WILLIAM THOMAS, JR., theatrical and interior designer; b. Lancaster, Pa., Feb. 14, 1942; s. William Thomas and Mary Catherine (Parker) B.; B.Arch., Cath. U. Am., 1965, M.F.A., 1968. Archtl. designer Richard Malesardi, Washington, Robert Schwinn, Silver Spring, Md., 1966-68; instr. theatre arts U. Notre Dame (Ind.), 1968-70; owner Bill Byrd Jr., N.Y.C., 1970—; designer Little Theatre on the Square, Sullivan, Ill., 1970-72; designer Showboat Dinner Theatre, Pinellas Park, Fla., 1972, Homestead Theatre, Hot Springs, Va., 1973; Guest instr. communication arts dept. Marymount Manhattan Coll., N.Y.C., 1972; asst. prof. theatre arts Stockton State Coll., Pomona, N.J., 1972-74; asst. to Eldon Elder, 1974-76; asso. Asso. Theatrical Designers, N.Y.C., 1974-76; guest instr. Marymount Coll., Tarrytown, N.Y., also Bklyn. Coll., 1975; archtl. cons. Sarac Theatre Devel. Project, S.E. Alaska Regional Arts Council, 1976; theatre devel. cons. Entertainment Center, Fair Lane Conf. Center, U. Mich., Dearborn, 1977; asso. Interspace, Inc., 1978. Mem. U.S. Inst. Theatre Tech., Am. Theatre Assn., Actor's Equity Assn., Sigma Beta Kappa. Office: 145 W 71st St New York City NY 10023 also 1940 Biltmore St NW Washington DC 20009

BYRDSONG, CHARLES ELLIOTT, chemist; b. Atlanta, Jan. 10, 1945; s. Earl and Jannie B.; B.S., Clark Coll., 1968; grad. George Washington U., 1975; m. Brenda Elizabeth Walker, Nov. 19, 1977. Analytical chemist, aerospace and electronic systems div. Westinghouse Electric Co., Balt., 1968—, sr. process engr., 1974—. Mem. Am. Electroplaters Soc. Home: PO Box 57 Linthicum MD 21090 Office: Box 746 Westinghouse Electric Co Baltimore MD 21203

BYRNE, BRENDAN THOMAS, gov. N.J.; b. West Orange, N.J., Apr. 1, 1924; grad. Princeton, 1949; LL.B., Harvard, 1951; m. Jean Featherly; 7 children. Admitted to N.J. bar; asst. counsel to N.J. Gov. Robert B. Meyner, 1955-56, exec. sec., 1956-59; prosecutor, Essex County, N.J., 1959-68; pres. N.J. Pub. Utilities Commn., 1968-70; judge N.J. Superior Ct., 1970-73; gov. N.J., Trenton, 1974—. Served with USAAF, World War II. Roman Catholic. Home: Morven Gov's Mansion Princeton NJ 08540 Office: State Capitol Bldg Trenton NJ 08625

BYRNE, GEORGE PETER, JR., trade assn. exec.; b. Decatur, Ill., Mar. 23, 1916; s. George Peter and Eula (Mason) B.; A.B. cum laude, Harvard, 1938; LL.B., Boston U., 1941; m. Eleanor Rose Westervelt, Jan. 1, 1943; children—Barbara Anne, Karen Louise, Richard Chase. Spl. agt. FBI, U.S. Dept. of Justice, Washington, Little Rock, San Francisco, San Jose, Calif., Chgo., 1941-46; trade assn. exec., N.Y.C., 1946—; mng. dir., sec. Nat. Trade Assn., Tubular Exchanger Mfrs. Assn., Steatite Mfrs. Assn., Expansion Joint Mfrs. Assn., Powder Actuated Tool Mfrs. Inst., Hand Tools Inst., Tapping Screw Service Bur., U.S. Machine Screw Service Bur.; pres., dir. Assn. Orgn., Inc.; pres., sec. Industry Service Bureaus, Inc. Mem. Am. Nat. Standards Inst. Presbyn. Clubs: Harvard, Larchmont Yacht. Home: 2 Pryer Ln Larchmont NY 10538 Office: 331 Madison Ave New York City NY 10017

BYRNE, JOHN JAMES, corp. exec.; b. Anaconda, Mont., June 14, 1920; s. Peter J. and Emma (Eakin) B.; B.S., Poly. Coll. Engring., 1942; m. Florence Rinker, Feb. 11, 1950; children—Katharine Anne, Lael Meredith, Marilyn Rosamond. Jr. engr. Richmond (Calif.) Shipbuilding Corp., 1942; mech. engr., sales engr. Adherite Corp., Oakland, Calif., 1946-51; head field service engring., E. W. Bliss Co., Canton, Ohio, 1953-55, mgr. launching and recovery equipment div., 1955-61, dir. research and engring., 1961-69, v.p. research and engring., 1964-69, group v.p. press divs. 1969-70; v.p. engring., research and devel. G & W Indsl. Products Co., 1970-72; v.p. Advanced Devel. and Engring. Center G & W Industries, 1972—. Served with USNR, 1942-46, to lt. comdr., 1951-53. Mem. Am. Def. Preparedness Assns., Am. Mgmt. Assn., N.A.M., Soc. Mfg. Engrs. Patentee in field. Home: 321 Ellis Rd Havertown PA 19083 Office: 101 Chester Rd Swarthmore PA 19081

BYRNES, BERNARD CHRISTOPHER, oceanographer; b. Barnesboro, Pa., Mar. 6, 1923; s. William Henry and Effie Matilda (Ladenberger) B.; B.S., St. Francis Coll., 1948; m. Helen Jane McGregor, June 4, 1952; children—William, James, Nancy, Patricia. Geophysicist, Coast and Geodetic Survey, Washington, 1948-51; supervisory geophysicist to head geomagnetics br. Hydrographic Office USN, Washington, 1951-61, dep. dir., marine surveys div. Oceanographic Office, 1961-62, dir. devel. surveys div., 1962-74, dir. nearshore surveys div., 1974—. Trustee Heart Assn. So. Md., 1972—. Served to lt. USNR, 1943-45. Recipient Superior Achievement awards USN, 1955, 60, 64, Navy Meritorious Civilian Service award, 1977. Home: 2503 Lorring Dr District Heights MD 20028 Office: US Naval Oceanographic Office Washington DC 20373

BYRNES, JAMES DONOVAN LEICESTER, educator; b. Rye, N.Y., Nov. 9, 1929; s. John Francis and Gertrude Claire (Donovan) B.; B.A., St. Ambrose Coll., 1953; M.A., City Coll. N.Y., 1955, Columbia, 1962; Ph.D. (Erwin fellow), U. Md.. 1967; postgrad. John Jay Coll. Criminal Justice, 1972. Lectr., instr. govt. and politics U. Md., College Park, 1965-67; asst. prof. macro polit. systems Emory U., Atlanta, 1967-68; asst. prof. polit. sci. Fairleigh Dickinson U., Madison, N.J., 1968-72, chmn. dept. social scis.; vis. scholar Hoover Inst. on War, Revolution and Peace, Stanford (Calif.) U., summer 1972; prof. polit. sci. Edinboro (Pa.) State Coll., 1972—; prof. grad faculty Inst. Community Service. Bd. dirs. Erie (Pa.) Philharmonic Orch., 1973-75; virgir Cathedral of St. Philip, Atlanta. Mem. Nat. Collegiate Conf. Assn. (dir. 1970-72), Am. Polit. Sci. Assn., Am. Soc. Pub. Adminstrn., Pa. Soc. Polit. Sci. and Pub. Adminstrn., Inst. Middle Eastern and N. African Affairs, Delta Epsilon Sigma, Phi Sigma Alpha. Author: Bourguibism: A Study in Decision Making, 1968; (with Jean D. Andrew) Blue Book for Bureaucrates, 1973; editor: On the Twenty-Fifth Anniversary of the United Nations, 1970; contbr. articles in field to profl. jours. Home: RD 2 Eureka Rd Girard PA 16417 Office: Dept Polit Sci Edinboro State Coll Edinboro PA 16444

BYRNES, JANE LOUISE, sch. prin.; b. Syracuse, N.Y.; d. James Joseph and Catherine Agnes (O'Neill) Byrnes; B.S. magna cum laude, Syracuse U., 1945, M.S., 1949, Ed.D., 1966; postgrad. Stanford, 1956. Prin., Cleveland Sch., Syracuse, 1946-49, U.S. Grant and Garfield schs., 1949-50, Clinton Sch., 1950-53, Salem Hyde Sch., 1953—; mem. faculty State U. N.Y., Plattsburgh, summers 1957, 58, 59. Trustee, Onondaga Community Coll., Maria Regina Coll.; bd. dirs. Met. Comml. Council Careers, v.p. 1975; bd. govs. Citizens Found., 1976-78. Named Woman of Achievement of Edn., Syracuse Post-Standard, 1974; recipient Am. educators medal Freedoms Found., 1976. Mem. Met. Council (v.p. 1975), Citizens Found., N.Y. State Assn. Elementary Sch. Prins. (pres. 1957), N.Y. State Council Adminstrv. Leadership (v.p. 1959), Syracuse Assn. Adminstrs. (pres. 1962), Bus. and Profl. Women's Club Syracuse (Pres. (pres. 1971-72), Nat. Fedn. Bus. and Profl. Womens Club, Zonta. Roman Catholic. Office: 450 Durston Ave Syracuse NY 13203

BYROM, DAVID GENE, psychologist; b. Honolulu, Apr. 19, 1940; s. Harold and Cornelia (Butters) B.; A.A., Trenton Jr. Coll., 1960; B.A., Adelphi Coll., 1962; Ph.D. (USPHS trainee), Adelphi U., 1969; m. Ann Elaine Hedderick, June 16, 1962; children—David Gene, Eric Michael, Lisa Ann. Dir. psychol. services, cons. for tng. and program evaluation Head Start Program Suffolk County, L.I., N.Y., 1967-71; pvt. practice clin. psychology specializing in psychotherapy and psychoanalysis, Huntington, N.Y., 1970—. Clin. psychologist Huntington and Babylon community mental health centers, 1965-73; adj. prof. Union Grad. Sch., Antioch Coll., Yellow Springs, Ohio, 1971-76; asso. with Postdoctoral Psychotherapy Center, Adelphi U., Garden City, N.Y.; dir. Middle Country Center for Psychotherapy, Nesconset, N.Y.; cons. in field, 1967—. Mem. Am., N.Y. State, Nassau and Suffolk Counties (exec. bd.) psychol. assns., Am. Acad. Psychotherapists, N.Y. Soc. Clin. Psychologists, Acad. Psychologists in Marital and Family Therapy, N.Y. Inst. Gestalt Therapy. Home: 27 Fairview St Huntington NY 11743 Office: 27 Fairview St Huntington NY 11743

BYRON, BEVERLY BUTCHER, congresswoman; b. Balt., July 27, 1932; d. Harry C. and Ruth B. Butcher; student Hood Coll., 1963-64; m. Goodloe Edgar Byron, 1952 (dec. 1978); children—Goodloe Edgar, Barton Kimball, Mary McComas. Mem. 96th Congress from 6th Dist. Md. Campaign mgr. Goodloe E. Byron campaign for Md. Ho. of Dels., 1962, Md. Senate, 1966, U.S. Ho. of Reps., 1970, 72, 74, 76, 78; treas. Md. Young Democrats, 1962, 65; bd. dirs. Am. Hiking Soc., Frederick County (Md.) chpt. ARC; bd. assos. Hood Coll.; sec. Frederick Heart Assn.; mem. Frederick Phys. Fitness Commn., Md. Phys. Fitness Commn. Mem. Frederick County Hist. Soc., Frederick County Landmarks Found., John F. Kennedy 50-Mile Meml. Hike. Episcopalian. Club: Frederick Garden. Home: 306 Grove Blvd Frederick MD 21701 Office: US Ho of Reps Office of Clk of House H-105 The Capitol Washington DC 20515*

BYRON, GLORIA BLUM (MRS. STUART DAVID BYRON), writer, pub. relations cons.; b. N.Y.C., June 10, 1937; d. Joseph and Theresa (Philip) Blum; student Bernard M. Baruch Sch. Bus. and Pub. Adminstrn., 1955-57, Fashion Inst. Tech., 1957-58; m. Stuart David Byron, Nov. 20, 1971; children—Linda Beth, Lisa Joan. Asst. fashion dir. Leather Industries Am., N.Y.C., 1958-62; account exec. Robert S. Taplinger Assos., Inc., N.Y.C., 1962-64; account exec. Daniel J. Edelman, Inc., N.Y.C., 1964-68, v.p., 1968-71; v.p. Rowland Co., Inc., N.Y.C., 1972-73; pub. relations counselor, free-lance writer, 1973—; lectr. on career opportunities in pub. relations for various groups. Vol. spl. pub. relations project Adlai E. Stevenson Inst. Fgn. Affairs, 1971; worker John V. Lindsay mayoralty campaign, 1965; mem. membership, pub. relations coms. Knickerbocker League for Children's Asthma Research Inst. and Hosp., Denver, 1963-64. Mem. Pub. Relations Soc. Am., Fashion Group, Inc., Nat. Writers Club. Contbr. articles to popular mags. Home: 324 E 41st St New York City NY 10017

BYSTRYN, SARA WOLSKI (MRS. ISER BYSTRYN), importer; b. Brest Litovsk, Russia; d. Charles and Louba (Prilouk) Wolski; student Sorbonne, Paris, 1930-33; m. Iser Bystryn, Dec. 23, 1930; children—Denise Bystryn Kandel, Jean-Claude. Came to U.S., 1949, naturalized, 1954. Owner, pres. Ibis Export Import Co., N.Y.C., 1951—. Active mem. French Resistance, 1942-44. Home: 800 West End Ave New York City NY 10025 Office: 250 W 57th St New York City NY 10019

BYUN, YOUNG HO, trading co. exec.; b. Kyungbuk Province, Korea, Feb. 11, 1937; s. Hee Yong and Soon Chun (Park) B.; B.A., Korea U., 1959; M.A., Kent State U., 1964; M.A. (AID fellow 1965), U. Pa., 1969; m. Hwa Young Rhee, Dec. 28, 1964; children—Sonya, Sharon, Harold. Pres., Byun Trading Co., Inc., 1969—, Crystal of Penn., Inc., Phila., 1977—; partner Eurasia Joy Travel Agency, Phila., 1975—. Trustee Korea Credit Union, 1976—; sec.-gen. Korean Assn. Greater Phila., 1971-72, trustee, 1972—, chmn., 1975-76. Served with Korean Army, 1959-60, 74-75. Recipient citation Ministry Fgn. Affairs Korea, 1976. Mem. Korean Businessmen's Assn. (pres. 1974-75). Presbyterian. Home: 260 Clearview Ave Huntingdon Valley PA 19006 Office: 613 W Cheltenham Ave Philadelphia PA 19126

CABAUP, JOSEPH JOHN, educator; b. Bronx, N.Y., Nov. 5, 1940; s. Joseph Christopher and Angelina (DeVenuta) C.; B.A. in Physics, Hunter Coll., 1962; M.S. in Geology, U. N.C., 1969; m. Barbara Louise Mellor, June 26, 1965; children—Joseph Ernest, Jean Marie. Asst. prof. chemistry and physics Winthrop Coll., Rock Hill, S.C., 1967-70, Franconia (N.H.) Coll., 1970-71; tchr. Dartmouth (Mass.) High Sch., 1971-72; asst. prof. physics R.I. Jr. Coll. at Warwick, 1972-74; asso. prof. natural resources mgmt. N.H. Vocat. Tech. Coll., Berlin, 1974—; environmental cons. Environ. Survey & Analysis, Bethlehem, N.H., 1971—; dir. North Country Streams Environments Symposium, 1973, Environ. Conf. Narragansett Bay, 1974. Pres. White Mountain Nature Mus., Franconia, 1970-74, also trustee. Mem. AAAS, Nat. Assn. Geology Tchrs., Geol. Soc. Am., AAUP. Home: Bethlehem Junction RFD 2 Whitefield NH 03598

CABEBE, FERNANDO SALVA, physician, air force officer; b. Narcavan, Philippines, Jan. 29, 1932; s. Benito and Rufina (Salva) C.; came to U.S., 1959, naturalized, 1970; M.D., Santo Tomas U., Manila, Philippines, 1959; m. Romana C. Moises, June 17, 1961; children—Anthony, Belinda, Christina. Intern, Prospect Heights div. L.I. Coll. Hosp. Bklyn., 1959-60, resident in family practice Community Gen. Hosp., Reading, Pa., 1960-62; practice medicine specializing in emergency medicine, Riverhead, N.Y., 1964—; chief, emergency dept. and house staff physicians Brookhaven Meml. Hosp., Patchogue, N.Y., 1962-64; chief emergency physician. house staff physician Southampton Hosp., Central Suffolk Hosp., Riverhead, 1964-76; dir. family practice team USAF Hosp., Chanute AFB, Ill. lt. col. M.C., USAF, 1976—. Named Outstanding Profl. in Human Services, Am. Acad. Human Services, 1975. Mem. Am. Assn. Fgn. Med. Grads., Am. Profl. Practice Assn., Am. Acad. Family Physicians, Am. Coll. Emergency Physicians, Setaukets (N.Y.) Civic Assn. Club: Filipino Social (N.Y.C.). Home: 28 Lynx Ln East Setauket NY 11733

CABLE, CHARLES ALLEN, educator; b. Akeley, Pa., Jan. 15, 1932; s. Elton Thomas and Margaret Fredora (Fox) C.; B.S., Edinboro State Coll., 1954; M.Ed. (NSF fellow) U. N.C., 1959; Ph.D. (NSF faculty fellow, NDEA fellow), Pa. State U., 1969; m. Mabel Elizabeth Yeck, Dec. 19, 1955; children—Christopher A., Carolyn E. Tchr. math. Interlaken (N.Y.) High Sch., 1954-55, Tidioute (Pa.) High Sch., 1957-59; instr. math. Juniata Coll., Huntingdon, Pa., 1959-62, asst. prof., 1962-67; asso. prof. math. Allegheny Coll., Meadville, Pa., 1969-75, prof., 1975—, chmn. dept. math., 1970—, chmn. sci. div., 1974-76. Served with AUS, 1955-57. Gen. Electric fellow, summer 1958, NSF Summer Inst. fellow, 1961, 73. Mem. Math. Assn. Am. (chmn. Allegheny Mountain sect. 1973-75), Am. Math. Soc., AAUP (pres. Allegheny Coll. chpt.), Pi Mu Epsilon. Republican. Presbyn. Kiwanian. Home: 199 Jefferson St Meadville PA 16335 Office: N Main St Meadville PA 16335

CABLE, DANA GERARD, educator, b. Sewickly Valley, Pa., Aug 27, 1943; s. Boyd and Jean (Clover) C.; A.B., W.Va. Wesleyan Coll., 1965; M.A. (NDEA fellow, 1968-71), W.Va. U., 1971, Ph.D., 1972; m. Sylvia Kaufman, Mar. 19, 1977; children—David, Jennifer. Research asst., dept. psychology, W.Va. Wesleyan Coll., Buckhannon, 1965-68; instr. W.Va. U., Morgantown, 1970-72, vis. asst. prof. psychology, 1972; asst. prof. psychology, Hood Coll., Frederick, Md., 1972-75, asso. prof., 1975—, co-chmn. dept., 1976-78; treas. Md. Consortium for Gerontology in Higher Edn.; lectr. on death and dying. Trustee Citizens Nursing Home; bd. dirs. Home Care Inc. Mem. Am., Eastern, Md. psychol. assns., Gerontol. Soc., Psychometric Soc., Forum for Death Edn. and Counseling, W.Va. Acad. Scis., AAUP, Internat. Platform Assn., Psi Chi. Methodist. Club: Kiwanis. Contbr. and reviewer articles in profl. jours. Home: Pinecliffe Route 6 Box 178 Frederick MD 21701 Office: Dept Psychology Hood Coll Frederick MD 21701

CABOT, THOMAS TARVIN GRAY, educator; b. Boston, June 25, 1939; s. Oliver Hazard Perry and Anne Randolph (Gray) C.; B.A. in Spanish Lang. and Lit., Williams Coll., Williamstown, Mass., 1961; M.A. in Spanish Lit., N.Y. U. and U. Madrid, 1964; M.Ed. in Ednl. Media, Worcester (Mass.) State Coll., 1973; m. Maria Dolores Rosa Montserrat Buldú-Prim y Galián-Camerero de Cabot; children—Celeste-Ann Buldú, Corinne-Aissa Buldú, Michéle-Elena Buldú. Tchr. langs. Pingry Sch., Elizabeth, N.J., 1961-65; head learning lab. Eaglebrook Sch., Deerfield, Mass., 1965-67; dir. dept. langs., dir. audio visual Quabbin Regional High Sch. Dist., Barre, Mass., 1967-70, dir. media services, fed./state programs coordinator, 1970—; instr. Spanish, Assumption Coll.; instr. media adminstrn. Worcester (Mass.) State Coll. Mem. adv. council Mass. Bd. Library Commrs., 1974—; interpreter, cons., translator Spanish Govt. Ministry of Tourism, Madrid, 1972-74; bd. dirs. Sociedad Cultural Hispana. Mem. New Eng. Ednl. Media Assn. (exec. bd., pub. relations chmn.). Certified secondary sch. prin., audio visual specialist, sch. librarian, unified media specialist, Spanish tchr., Mass. Author study aids in Spanish and French; cons. ednl. media design and use. Home: 20 Ridgewood RD Holden MA 01520 Office: Quabbin Regional Sch Dist Barre MA 01005

CABRERA-ROSETE, JORGE ARMANDO, mfg. co. exec.; b. Mexico, Mar. 1, 1942; s. Pedro and Concepcion (Rosete) C.; B.A., U. Kans., 1964; M.A., Stanford U., 1965; m. Karin Inge Fiedler, June 15, 1978. Asst. sales mgr. Chrysler Corp., Mexico, 1969-72; regional sales rep. Xerox Corp., Stamford, Conn., 1972; market mgr. Latin Am. ITT Rayonier, Inc., N.Y.C., 1973-76, asst. gen. mgr. internat., N.Y.C., 1976—. Served with Peace Corps, Colombia, 1966-68. Mem. Am. Mgmt. Assn. Club: Reform athletic. Home: 43 Middlesex Rd Darien CT 06820 Office: 605 3d Ave New York City NY 10016

CACCAMISE, DANIEL A., dentist; b. Rochester, N.Y., Mar. 18, 1933; s. Dominic H. and Mary A. (LaDuca) C.; B.A., U. Buffalo, 1954, D.D.S. (N.Y. Profl. Regents scholar), 1960; dental research student fellow U. Rochester, summers 1957, 58, 59; m. Susan Pak, Aug. 2, 1962; children—Glenn, Kimberly Ann. Practice gen. dentistry, Rochester, 1964—. Bd. dirs. Sigl Center Charity Golf Tournament; founder, bd. dirs. Doover Golf Classic. Served with AUS, 1960-63. Mem. Am., 7th Dist. dental assns., Monroe County Dental Soc., Am. Soc. Writers, Phi Kappa Psi. Clubs: Green Hills Country; Tennis (Rochester). Home: 7 Spier Ave Rochester NY 14620 Office: 1500 Clinton Ave S Rochester NY 14620

CACCAMISE, JAMES WILLIAM, bus service exec.; b. Leroy, N.Y., July 23, 1931; s. Anthony Charles and Bernice (Abelt) C.; grad. Leroy pub. schs., 1950; 1 dau., Christine A. Mechanics helper Buick Dealer, Leroy, 1952-55, mechanic, 1955-64, sales mgr., 1964-68; founder, operator Batavia (N.Y.) Bus Service, 1968-71; designer, operator dial-a-bus system Rochester (N.Y.) Genesee Regional Transp. Authority, 1971-73; founder, operator Genesee Bus Co., Inc., Batavia, 1973—. Served with U.S. Army, 1950-52. Mem. Sch. Bus Operators Assn., Am. Legion. Roman Catholic. Club: Elks. Address: 5577 E Main Rd Batavia NY 14020

CACCIA, ALEXANDER LOUIS, lawyer; b. N.Y.C., Feb. 26, 1911; s. Alexander Joseph and Adeline Anna (Brizzi) C.; B.S., Coll. City N.Y., 1932; J.D., St. John's U., 1935; m. Gertrude Elaine Yoell, Nov. 7, 1936; children—Regina (Mrs. Walter Pedersen), Paul. Admitted to N.Y. bar, 1936, U.S. Supreme Ct. bar, 1964, Conn. bar, 1968; practiced in N.Y.C., 1936—; atty. Mut. Life Ins. Co. N.Y., N.Y.C., 1936-44; asso. firm Turk, Marsh, Kelly & Hoare, N.Y.C., 1944-60, mem. firm, 1961—. Pres. Forest Hills Civic Assn., 1944-49, counsel, 1959-62; pres. Forest Hills Youth Activities Assn., 1961-64. Trustee Marymount Manhattan Coll., 1965—, counsel, 1970—. Mem. Am. Bar Assn., N.Y. County Lawyers Assn., Columbian Lawyers Assn., Nat. Assn. Coll. and Univ. Attys., Phi Kappa Theta. Clubs: Olquom of Forest Hills (pres. 1955-60), West Side Tennis, Hemisphere. Office: Turk Marsh Kelly & Hoare 575 Lexington Ave New York City NY 10022

CACELLA, ARTHUR FERREIRA, textile co. exec.; b. New Bedford, Mass., Nov. 26, 1920; s. Antonio Ferreira and Francelina Medeiros (Albino) C.; B. Chem. Engring., N.C. State Coll., 1947; M.S. in Physics and Chemistry, Inst. Textile Tech., 1949; M.A. in Phys. Chemistry, Princeton, 1952; m. Evelyn Ruth Bishop, June 10, 1950; children—Rose Zane, Arthur, Alicia, Linda, Barry. Research fellow Textile Research Inst., Princeton, 1949-54; research chemist E.I. duPont, Waynesboro, Va., 1954-59; synthetic fibers research asso. Inst. Textile Tech., 1959-60; dir. research Globe Mfg. Co., Fall River, Mass., 1960-62; v.p. research and devel. Ameliotex, Inc., Rocky Hill, N.J., 1962—. Served with AUS, 1942-45; ETO. Decorated Bronze

Star. Fellow Am. Inst. Chemists; mem. N.Y. Acad. Scis., Am. Chem. Soc., Am. Assn. Textile Chemists and Colorists, Amateur Astronomers, Inc. (past pres.), Sigma Xi, Phi Kappa Phi. Republican. Roman Catholic. Patentee in field. Home: 16 Hillwood Rd East Brunswick NJ 08816 Office: POB 238 Rocky Hill NJ 08553

CADAVERO, DAVID ANTHONY, ednl. adminstr.; b. Yonkers, N.Y., June 18, 1947; s. Alfred F. and Justine A. (Ferraro) C.; M.A., New Sch. Social Research, 1971; m. Nadia Bekersky, Nov. 22, 1970. Guidance counselor Greater N.Y. Acad., Woodside, 1968-70, asst. prin., 1971-75, prin., 1976—. Recipient Disting. Alumni award Greater N.Y. Acad., 1973; citation Jr. Achievement, 1976. Mem. Am. Assn. Sch. Adminstrs., Am. Psychol. Assn., Assn. Seventh Day Adventist Educators, Am. Personnel and Guidance Assn. Seventh Day Adventist. Home: Rural Route 1 Box 129C Tuxedo NY 10987 Office: Greater NY Acad 4132 58th St Woodside NY 11377

CADDELL, FOSTER, artist; b. Pawtucket, R.I., Aug. 2, 1921; s. Foster and Clara (Bamford) C.; student R.I. Sch. Design, 1940-43; pvt. study with Peter Helck, Robert Brackman, Guy Wiggins; m. June A. Kaufmann, Apr. 10, 1943. Artist, Providence Lithograph Co. (R.I.), 1939-52; free-lance illustrator, 1951-65; owner, instr. Foster Caddell's Art Sch., Voluntown, Conn., 1958—; one-man shows: Providence Art Club, 1948, 63, South County (R.I.) Art Assn., 1967, Slater Mus., Norwich Acad., 1976; group shows include: Springfield Mus. Fine Arts, 1962-77, Am. Watercolor Soc., 1973, NAD, 1973, Am. Artists Profl. League (awards 1953, 71, 72), Acad. Artists Am. (awards 1968, 73, 75), Providence Art Club (award 1978), Nat. Arts Club, 1978, Internat. Soc. Artists (award 1978), others; specialist in portraiture, 1965—. Served as artist USAAC, World War II. Recipient awards Norwich Acad., 1947, Ogunquit Art Center, 1949, Conservative Painters R.I., 1962, Salmagundi Club, 1973. Mem. Providence Art Club, Am. Artists Profl. League, Acad. Artists Am., Salmagundi Club, Portraits Inc., Pastel Soc. Am., Internat. Soc. Artists. Author: Keys to Successful Landscape Painting, 1976; Keys to Successful Color in Landscape Painting, 1979. Address: Northlight RFD 1 Route 49 Voluntown CT 06384

CADEMARTORI, GARY MARTIN, accountant; b. Jersey City, Sept. 16, 1941; s. Joseph John and Patricia Lillian (Harrigan) C.; B.S., St. Peter's Coll., 1963; M.B.A., Seton Hall U., 1971; m. Patricia Maryann Feehan, Oct. 16, 1965; children—Jill Ann, Glenn Martin, Gregg Martin. Accounting supr. Merck & Co., Inc., Rahway, N.J., 1965; accountant Haskins & Sells C.P.A.'s, Newark, 1965-69; treas. B.S.A. Inc., Nutley, N.J., 1969; partner Touche Ross & Co. C.P.A.'s, Newark, 1969; lectr. in field. Exec. com. Tamarack council Boy Scouts Am., 1974—, Columbian Found., 1976-77. Served to 1st lt. U.S. Army, 1963-65. C.P.A. Mem. Am. Inst. C.P.A.'s, N.J. Soc. C.P.A.'s, Nat. Assn. Accountants, Am. Accounting Assn., Ironbound Mfg. Assn., Glen Ridge (N.J.) Civic Assn. Roman Catholic. Clubs: Glen Ridge Country, Rotary (asso.). Home: 224 Forest Ave Glen Ridge NJ 07028 Office: Touche Ross & Co Gateway 1 Newark NJ 07102

CADMAN, CHARLES ROBERT, educator; b. McKeesport, Pa., Apr. 24, 1945; s. Harry Elmer and Elizabeth (Smart) C.; B.S., Calif. State Coll., 1966, M.Ed., 1972. Chemistry and physics thcr. Monessen (Pa.) High Sch., 1966-70; chemistry tchr. McKeesport (Pa.) Area High Sch., 1970-76; phys. sci. tchr. McClure Jr. High Sch., White Oak, Pa., 1976-77; chemistry tchr. McKeesport (Pa.) Area High Sch., 1977—; chmn. sch. judging Mon-Yough C. of C. Sch. Sci. Fair, 1971—. Sec. bd. trustees Victory Meth. Ch., 1970-78, organist, 1961-78. Recipient Sci. Tchr. award Buhl Planetarium, 1974, Sci. Tchr. award Master Brewers Assn. Am., Pitts. sect., 1976, Tchr. award Westinghouse Air Brake Co. switch and signal div., 1975. Mem. NEA, Pa. State, McKeesport edn. assns., Chi Beta Psi. Home: 2651 Douglas Run Rd Elizabeth PA 15037 Office: 1960 Eden Park Blvd McKeesport PA 15132

CAFARO, PAUL JAMES, nuclear physicist; b. N.Y.C., Nov. 10, 1942; s. Paul Henry and Mary Petrina (Alascia) C. Nuclear physicist Atomic Ammunition Devel. Lab., Nuclear Engring. Directorate, Picatinny Arsenal, Dover, N.J., 1967-69, concepts and effectiveness div., 1969-77; phys. sci. analyst U.S. Army Research and Devel. Command, Large Caliber Weapon Systems Lab., nuclear applications div., 1977—; lectr., cons. in field. Chmn. Nat. and World Movement Toward Human Understanding, 1967-74. Served in civilian service U.S. Army, 1967—. Recipient hon. doctorate in pub. service, law certificate, sci. award. Mem. Am. Inst. Physics, Astron. Soc. N.J., Mensa Soc. N.Y. Clubs: Chess, Tennis, Ski, Art, Photography N.Y. Contbr. articles to profl. jours. Home: 214 Daniel Rd N North Massapequa NY 11758 Office: ARRADCOM/DRDAR-F Bldg 65 N Dover NJ 07801

CAFFREY, ANDREW AUGUSTINE, U.S. judge; b. Lawrence, Mass., Oct. 2, 1920; s. Augustine J. and Monica A. (Regan) C.; A.B. cum laude, Holy Cross Coll., 1941; LL.B. cum laude, Boston Coll., 1948; LL.M., Harvard U., 1948; m. Evelyn F. White, June 26, 1946; children—Augustine J., Andrew A., James E., Mary L., Francis J., Joseph H. Admitted to Mass. bar, 1948, U.S. Supreme Ct. bar, 1958; asso. prof. law Boston Coll. Law Sch., 1948-55; asst. U.S. atty., chief civil div., Dist. Mass., 1955-59, 1st asst. U.S. atty. Dist. Mass., 1959-60, U.S. dist. judge, 1960—, chief judge, 1972—. Served with U.S. Army, World War II; ETO. Mem. Jud. Conf. U.S. (exec. com., jud. panel on multidist. legislation), Am., Fed., Boston bar assns., Am. Law Inst., Harvard Law Sch. Assn. Mass., Order of Coif, Alpha Sigma Nu, Delta Epsilon Sigma. Club: Merrimack Valley, Holy Cross Alumni (past pres., dir.). Address: 1629 Post Office Bldg Boston MA 02109

CAGGIANO, ANTHONY PATRICK, obstetrician/gynecologist; b. Passaic, N.J., May 11, 1939; s. Anthony P. and Ellen Elizabeth (Donlon) C.; B.A., Seton Hall U., 1960; M.D., Georgetown U., 1964; m. Faith Messina, May 16, 1964; children—Anthony, Tracy Lynn, Dawn, Danielle, Marcus, Erik. Intern, Newark City Hosp., 1965-68, resident in obstetrics/gynecology, 1970-72; practice medicine specializing in obstetrics/gynecology, Glen Ridge, N.J., 1972—; attending physician Mountainside Hosp., Montclair, N.Y., 1976—, dir. obstetrics/gynecology div. family practice residency, 1976—; clin. asst. prof. obstetrics/gynecology N.J. Coll. Medicine and Dentistry, Newark, 1976—. Served to capt. USAF, 1968-70. Fellow A.C.S., Am. Coll. Obstetricians and Gynecologists. Roman Catholic. Clubs: Glen Ridge Country, K.C. Home: 437 Ridgewood Ave Glen Ridge NJ 07028 Office: 123 Highland Ave Glen Ridge NJ 07028

CAGUIN, FEODOR CAGANDAHAN, surgeon; b. Philippines, Oct. 27, 1932; s. Felix A. and Rafaela C.; came to U.S., 1956, naturalized, 1965; A.A., U. Santo Tomas, 1954, M.D., 1956; m. Mary Ann Casiello, Mar. 5, 1962; children—Carla, Thomas, Robert, Michael. Chief resident gen. surgery Kate Bitting Meml. Hosp., Winston—Salem, N.C., 1959-60, Hosp. St. Raphael, New Haven, 1960-62; fellow cardiology Hosp. St. Raphael, New Haven, 1963; practice medicine specializing in thoracic surgery, Balt., 1965—; mem. staffs N. Charles, Provident Luth., Bon Secours, Good Samaritan hosps. Mem. AMA, Med. and Chir. Faculty, Soc. Philippine Surgeons, Balt. City Med. Soc., Md. Thoracic Soc. Office: 230 E 25th St Baltimore MD 21218

CAHILL, JOHN CARROLL, services co. exec.; b. Ossining, N.Y., Apr. 2, 1937; s. Patrick Joseph and Mary Agnes (Carroll) C.; B.S., Manhattan Coll., 1959; M.B.A., CCNY, 1965; m. Barbara Ann Beaudouin, Sept. 2, 1961; children—Barbara, John Jr., Maureen, Steven. Sr. interviewer N.Y. Central R.R., N.Y.C., 1960-63; personnel mgr. AMF, 1963-66; indsl. relations Am. Bank Note Co., N.Y.C., 1966-70; v.p. Eastern States Bankcard Assn. Inc., Lake Sucess, N.Y., 1970—, Eastern States Monetary Services, Inc., Lake Sucess, 1977—; instr. Manhattan Coll., 1966-70; adj. asst. prof. St. John's U., N.Y., 1970—. Bd. advisers Queensborough Community Coll., 1977—; mem. community relations com. N.Y.C. Police Dept., 1968-70, Mayor Lindsay's com. tng. hard core unemployed, 1968. Served with N.Y. Army N.G., 1960-66. Mem. Am. Soc. Personnel Adminstrn. (accredited), Am. Soc. Tng. and Devel., Am. Mgmt. Assn., Conf. Bd., Planning Execs. Inst., World Future Soc. (newsletter editor 1978), N.Am. Soc. Corp. Planning, L.I. Planners Assn., Nat. Indsl. Recreation Assn. Republican. Roman Catholic. Home: 4 Keel Ct Oyster Bay NY 11771 Office: 4 Ohio Dr Lake Success NY 11040

CAHILL, MARY-CAROL, psychologist; b. N.Y.C.; d. Harold Daniel and Mildred Eva (Gessler) Cahill; A.B. (N.Y. State Regents scholar), Coll. New Rochelle; A.M. (NSF fellow), Fordham U., Ph.D., (N.Y. State Regents fellow), 1967. Human factors engr. Life Scis. div. Grumman Aerospace Corp., Bethpage, N.Y., 1967-70; asst. prof. dept. psychology Rensselaer Polytech. Inst., Troy, N.Y., 1970-74; asst. prof. dept. psychology Fordham U., Bronx, N.Y., 1974-76, asso. prof., 1976—; cons. in human factors engring. and environ. design. Mem. Am., Eastern psychol. assns., AAAS, Assn. Women in Sci., AAUP, Human Factors Soc. (pres. Met. chpt. 1979), Soc. Info. Display (vice chmn. Mid-Atlantic chpt. 1976-77), N.Y. Zool. Soc., Am. Mus. Nat. History, N.Y. Acad. Scis., Sigma Xi. Contbr. articles to sci. and profl. jours. Home: 60 Stratford Rd Scarsdale NY 10583 Office: Dept Psychology Grad Sch Arts and Scis Fordham Univ Bronx NY 10458 Scis Fordham Univ Bronx NY 10458

CAHILL, VINCENT J., JR., communications exec.; b. N.Y.C., Jan. 5, 1944; s. Vincent J. and Marian T. (Corcoran) C.; B.E.E., Manhattan Coll., 1965; children—Jennifer, Jeremy. With N.Y. Telco, N.Y.C., 1965-70; sr. sales engr. ITT Communications Systems, N.Y.C., 1970-72, br. sales mgr., 1972-73, area mgr., 1973-78, dist. Sales mgr., 1978—. Served with USAR, 1967-73. Certified nuclear shelter analyst, Dept. of Def. Mem. Am. Mgmt. Assn., Little Falls Jaycees (treas. 1976-77).

CAIN, MICHAEL GENT, lawyer, restaurant exec.; b. Evanston, Ill., Mar. 20, 1946; s. George R. and Mary Jane (Gent) C.; B.A., U. Vt., 1969; J.D., Syracuse U., 1972; m. Beverly I. Hall, Sept. 24, 1968; children—Alexandra S.G., Lindsey M. Admitted to Vt. bar, 1973; with firm Burditt & Calkins, Chgo., 1972-73; individual practice law, Grand Isle, 1973—; state's atty. Grand Isle County, 1974—; mem. firm Bing, Bauer & Cam, Burlington, Vt., 1975—; owner Pierce Restaurant, Inc., Colchester, Vt., Burrito and Friends, Ltd., B.T. McGuires, Burlington, Burgher Baron, Internat., Ltd., Barre, Vt.; partner Peg Realty, Burlington. Mem. Am., Vt. bar assns., Nat. Dist. Attys. Assn. Address: 350 Main St Burlington VT 05401

CAIN, MICHAEL HANEY, lawyer; b. Chicoutimi, Que., Can., Mar. 26, 1929; s. Murray Vincent and Anna Marie (Feeney) C.; B.A., McGill U., 1950, B.C.L., 1953; m. Huguette Potvin, Sept. 20, 1954; children—Murray, Evelyn. Called to bar Que., 1954; partner firm Fradette, Bergeron, Cain & Assos., and predecessors, Chicoutimi, 1954-71, 72—; justice Superior Ct. Que., Chicoutimi and Quebec City, 1971-72; mem. Canadian Inst. for Adminstrn. of Justice. Founding pres. Found. U. Quebec at Chicoutimi Inc.; mem. Que. Human Rights Commn.; pres. com. on discipline Order of Nurses of P.Q. Mem. Que. (v.p. 1970-71), Can. (v.p. Que. 1973-74, pres. 1974-75) bar assns., Bar of Saguenay (batonnier 1970-71). Home: 315 Chabanel St Chicoutimi PQ G7H 3S1 Canada Office: 110 Racine St Chicoutimi PQ G7H 1R2 Canada

CAIOLA, JAMES CLIFFORD, mfg. co. exec.; b. Bronx, N.Y., Nov. 2, 1933; s. Vincent James and Lola (DeFelice) C.; B.B.A., Iona Coll., 1955; m. Josephine Orlando, July 12, 1953; children—Valerie, Vincent. With Arthur Young & Co., N.Y.C., 1955-59; asst. gen. mgr. Renault, Inc., N.Y.C., 1959-64; fin. officer Baxter, Kelly & Faust, Inc., N.Y.C., 1964-69; with Murdock Webbing Co., Inc., Central Falls, R.I., 1969—, pres., dir., 1971—, pres., dir. subsidiaries Electroweave, Inc., Eezee Life Sling Co., Inc., 1971—. Sec. planning bd., East Brunswick, N.J., 1966-67, chmn., 1968-69. Recipient Key Man award East Brunswick Jr. C. of C., 1965. C.P.A., N.J. Mem. Nat. Assn. Accountants, Am. Assn. Seat Belt Mfrs., Am. Inst. C.P.A.'s, R.I. Inst. C.P.A.'s, Textile Narrow Fabric Inst. Home: 37 Elizabeth Circle Framingham MA 01701 Office: 27 Foundry St Central Falls RI 02863

CAIRNES, WALTER JOSEPH, fin. cons., philanthropic organizer; b. Newark, Mar. 18, 1946; s. John Matthew and Virginia Alice C.; A.B., U. Miami (Fla.), 1967; M.P.A., U. So. Calif., 1977; M.Ed., Harvard U., 1977; D.Phil. candidate in econs. Magdalen Coll. Oxford U. Centre for Mgmt. Studies. Pvt. practice fin. cons., 1969-71; founder, coordinator Sea Ventures, Highlands, N.J., 1971-76, chmn. bd. trustees; developer Sea Ventures program with U.S. Dept. Interior, Nat. Park Service, ACTION, airline industry; creator Bicentennial Sail, 1976; lectr., participant in numerous confs. in field. Served as officer USMC, 1967-68. Recipient Distinguished Service award Jaycees of N.J., 1975. Roman Catholic. Address: 1105 Massachusetts Ave Cambridge MA 02138 also 3 Murray Ct 80 Banbury Rd Oxford OX2 6JT England

CAIRO, ARMON ANTHONY, psychiatrist, educator; b. Steelton, Pa., Jan. 5, 1925; s. Salvatore and Josephine (Priete) C.; B.S., Franklin Marshall Coll., 1945; M.D., Georgetown U., 1948; m. Laura Irene Jones, May 28, 1955; children—Michael, Richard, Susan, Catherine, James. Intern, Georgetown U., Washington, 1948-49; resident in internal medicine, also psychiatry and neurology Mt. Alto VA Hosp., Georgetown U., George Washington U., 1950-55, 61-64; practice medicine specializing in psychiatry, Chevy Chase, Md., 1964—; instr. medicine Georgetown U., Washington, 1954-56, asst. prof. medicine, exec. officer dept. medicine, dir. diagnostic services, med. center, cons. medicine, hosp., 1956-61, clin. asso. prof. medicine, 1964-71, clin. asso. prof. psychiatry, 1971—; cons. medicine D.C. Gen. Hosp.; cons. medicine and psychiatry Bur. Hearing Appeals Social Security Agency, 1969—. Served with USNR, 1943-46, 48-50, 52-54. Diplomate Am. Bd. Internal Medicine, Am. Bd. Psychiatry and Neurology. Mem. Am. Psychiat. Assn., Am. Soc. Physician Analysts, Washington Psychiat. Soc., D.C. Med. Soc., Montgomery County Med. Assn., John Carroll Soc. Republican. Roman Catholic. Editor Grand Rounds Diary, Georgetown Bull., 1954-61. Home: 6002 Corewood Ln Bethesda MD 20016 Office: 35 Wisconsin Circle Chevy Chase MD 20015

CALABRESE, ALPHONSE FRANCIS XAVIER, psychoanalyst; b. Bklyn., Apr. 27, 1923; s. Charles Angelo and Josephine (Ambrosino) C.; B.A., St. John's U., 1950; M.S.W, Cath. U. Am., 1952; student Postgrad. Inst. Mental Health, 1953-58; Ph.D., Fla. Christian Coll., 1965; postgrad. N.Y. U., 1973—; m. Florence Elizabeth Shumacher, Aug. 4, 1950; children—Charles A., Therese S., Thomas M., Catherine A., Eileen M., John A., Bernadette M., James A. Psychotherapist, Cath. Charities, Bklyn., 1952-53; staff, group psychoanalyst Postgrad. Inst. Mental Health, N.Y.C., 1955-66; practice psychoanalysis, N.Y.C., 1956-68, L.I., 1960-68; faculty L.I. Consultation Center, Queens, N.Y., 1968-70; exec. dir. Christian Inst. Psychotherapeutic Studies, Hicksville, N.Y., 1972—; practice psychoanalysis, Hicksville. Bd. advisers Christian Counseling Center, Narbeth, Pa. St. Vincent de Paul grad. scholar, 1950; Postgrad. Inst. Mental Health grantee, 1956, 59. Mem. Nat. Assn. Social Workers, Am. Group Psychotherapy Assn., Nat. Accreditation Inst. Psychoanalysis, Christian Assn. Psychol. Studies, Am. Acad. Psychotherapy, Council Basic Edn., Religious Edn. Assn., N.Y. Soc. Psychoanalytic Psychotherapists. Republican. Roman Catholic. Author: (with William Proctor) Rx The Christian Love Treatment, 1976. Home: 120 Hunters Dr Syosset NY 11791 Office: Christian Inst Psychotherapeutic Studies 183 S Broadway Hicksville NY 11801

CALABRO, JOSEPH FRANCIS, utility exec.; b. Carbondale, Pa., Sept. 25, 1942; s. Dominick Joseph and Mary Louise (Delfino) C.; B.S., U. Scranton, 1964; M.S., Seton Hall U., 1966, U. Conn., 1969, Ph.D., 1971; m. Diane Bendersky, June 11, 1966; children—Joseph Christopher, Jeffrey Michael. Water quality mgr. Pa. Gas and Water Co., Wilkes-Barre, 1970—; instr. Pa. State U., Worthington Scranton campus, Dunmore, 1971—, U. Scranton, 1974-77; instr. Municipal Tng. div. Pa. Bur. Local Govt. Services, 1972—. NSF fellow, 1969. Certified water works Class A Type 1, Pa. Dept. Environ. Resources. Mem. Am. Water Works Assn. (chmn. Dist. II Pa. 1974), Am. Soc. Microbiology, Water Works Operators Assn. Pa., Eastern Pa. Water Pollution Control Operators Assn., Am. Fedn. Musicians. Roman Catholic. Club: Lions. Home: 604 Fern St Clarks Summit PA 18411 Office: 135 Jefferson Ave Scranton PA 18503

CALABRO, NATALIE, educator; b. Providence; d. Anthony and Josephine (Caliri) Calabro; A.B., Hunter Coll.; M.B.A., N.Y. U., 1957, Ph.D., 1966. Market analyst-statistician Charles Pfizer & Co., 1946-52; market analyst-statistician Allied Chem. & Dye, 1952-58; research exec. statistician Chesebrough-Pond's, 1958-63, Look Mag., N.Y.C., 1963-68; asso. prof. quantitative methods St. John's U. Grad. Sch.-Coll. Bus. Adminstrn., 1968—. Cons., statistician-tchr. Mem. Am. Statis. Assn. (chpt. pres. 1973-75, dir. 1975-78), Ops. Research Soc. Am., Am. Mktg. Assn. Contbr. articles to profl. jours. Home: 102-30 66th Rd Forest Hills NY 11375

CALANTONE, ROGER JAMES, educator; b. Passaic, N.J., Mar. 12, 1949; s. Carl and Rosalie (Fili) C.; B.A., Canisius Coll. 1970, M.B.A., 1972; Ph.D., (Am. Mktg. Assn. Doctoral Consortium fellow), U. Mass., 1976. Dir. computational lab. Canisius Coll., Buffalo, 1970-72; teaching asso. U. Mass., Amherst, 1972-75; prof. mktg., 1975—; cons. fin. instns., U.S. and abroad. Mem. Am. Mktg. Assn., Assn. Consumer Research. Roman Catholic. Home: 85 Lafayette Ave Passaic NJ 07055 Office: McGill U Dept Mgmt Montreal PQ Canada

CALATAYUD, JUAN BAUTISTA, physician; b. Valencia, Spain, May 17, 1928; s. Agustin and Carmen (Llobat) C.; M.D., U. Valencia (Spain), 1952; m. Helen T. Lupton, July 2, 1960; children—Mary Carmen, Juan Cesar. Intern, Alexian Bros. Hosp., Elizabeth, N.J., 1955; resident St. Pauls Hosp., Dallas, 1956-57; fellow in medicine George Washington U. Hosp., 1957-60, asst. prof. medicine, 1962-69, asso. rpof., 1969-70, asso. clin. prof., 1977—; asso. dir. med. edn. Doctors Hosp., Washington, 1970—, dir. heart sta. and exercise EKG Lab., 1974—, sec. profl. staff, 1973, also dir.; research asst. U. Montreal (Que., Can.), Sch., 1960, Guggenheim fellow medicine Montreal Gen. Physician Debroah Hosp., Browns Mills, N.J., 1961-62; practice medicine specializing in cardiology, Washington, 1962—; cons. VA Center, Martinsburg, W.Va., 1965—. Fellow Am. Coll. Angiology; mem. A.M.A., Am., Washington heart assns., Am. Fedn. Clin. Research (v.p. 1966-67, pres. 1967-68), D.C. Med. Soc., AAAS, Pan Am. Med. Assn., Peruvian Cardiac Soc. (hon.), Peruvian Angiology Soc. (hon.). Contbr. articles in field to profl. jours. Home: 6217 Cheryl Dr Falls Church VA 22044 Office: 1712 I St NW Washington DC 20006

CALDERONE, RONALD JOHN, govt. ofcl.; b. Scranton, Pa., July 5, 1951; s. Joseph John and Virginia Lucille (Mattson) C.; B.S. in Computer Sci. and Math., King's Coll., Wilkes-Barre, Pa., 1973; M.S.A. in Ops. Research and Systems Analysis, George Washington U., 1977; m. Paulette Mary Hoban, June 16, 1973. Asst. psychology dept. King's Coll., 1972-73; ops. research analyst GAO, Washington, 1973—. Active local Boy Scouts Am. Mem. Assn. Pub. Program Analysis, GAO Employees Assn. (v.p. 1977-78). Lutheran. Home: 1624 S Stafford St Arlington VA 22204 Office: Room 4001 GAO Bldg 441 G St Washington DC 20548

CALDERWOOD, JAMES ALBERT, lawyer; b. Washington, Dec. 4, 1941; s. Charles Howard and Hilda Pauline C.; B.S., U. Md., 1964; J.D. with honors (Univ. scholar), George Washington U., 1970; postgrad. Oxford (Eng.) U., 1977. Admitted to Md. bar, 1970, D.C. bar, 1973, U.S. Supreme Ct. bar, 1974; trial atty. antitrust div. Dept. Justice, Washington, 1970-73, 74-78; atty. Gabeler & Gastley, McLean, Va., 1978—; asst. U.S. atty. D.C., 1973. Mem. alumni council U. Md., 1974—, pres. Young Alumni Club, 1976-77. Served to capt. USAF, 1964-68. Mem. Am. (award of achievement 1973), Fed. (nat. co-chmn. council on younger lawyers 1972-73, Outstanding Com. Chmn. 1973, chmn. com. regulated industries 1976—), Md. bar assns., D.C. Bar, Soc. Govt. Economists (gen. counsel 1972-75), U. Md., George Washington U. alumni assns., Prince George's Jaycees, Delta Sigma Pi Alumni Club, Pi Sigma Alpha. Lutheran. Editorial bd. Fed. Bar Jour., 1975—. Home: 3120 Parkway St Cheverly MD 20785 Office: 6623A Old Dominion Dr McLean VA 22101

CALDWELL, JIMMY MICHAEL, engr., govt. ofcl.; b. Manning, S.C., Apr. 23, 1952; s. Jesse and Tinnie (Bell) C.; B.S. in Civil Engring Tech., 1974; m. Alice Rovena Carter, July 8, 1978. Contract adminstr. Naval Facilities Engring. Command, Dept. of Navy, 1974-78; gen. engr. GSA, Crystal City, Va., 1978—. Mem. S.C. State Coll. Alumni Assn. (D.C. chpt.). Baptist. Office: Gen Services Adminstrn Crystal Mall 4 Crystal City VA 24506

CALDWELL, RONALD FRANCIS, physicist; b. Columbus, Ohio, Mar. 1, 1938; s. Francis Everett and Lillian Faye (Casto) C.; B.S., Capital U., 1960; M.S., U. Ill., 1962, Ph.D., 1966; m. Martha Anne Michael, Sept. 18, 1966; children—Andrea Lenore, Douglas Allen. With Eastman Kodak Co., Rochester, N.Y., 1966—, project physicist, 1966-76, sr. research physicist, 1976—. Mem. Am. Phys. Soc., Sigma Xi. Home: 60 Drumlin View Dr Mendon NY 14506 Office: 901 Elmgrove Rd Rochester NY 14650

CALHOUN, GEORGE DONALD, mfg. co. exec.; b. Utica, N.Y., Feb. 3, 1950; s. Grant Dye and M. Helen (Welch) C.; B.S. in Agrl. Engring., Cornell U., 1972, M.Engring., 1974; m. Darlene Linda Spytko, May 27, 1978. Nat. product mgr., waste mgmt. DeLaval Separator Co., Poughkeepsie, N.Y., 1973-75, nat. product mgr., manure and feeding product lines, 1975—. Mem. Northeast Dairy Practices Council, Water Pollution Control Fedn., N.Y. Assn. Milk, Food and Environ. Sanitarians, Alpha Gamma Rho. Republican. Baptist. Office: 350 Dutchess Turnpike Poughkeepsie NY 12602

CALHOUN, JOHN COZART, fin. and mktg. co. exec.; b. Ft. Oglethorpe, Ga., Aug. 6, 1937; s. James Paul and Geneva F. (Fortson) C.; LL.B., Blackstone Sch. Law, 1970; B.A., Eastern Nebr. Coll., 1972; LL.D. (hon.), Edward Waters Coll., 1975, Morris Brown Coll., 1976, Daniel Payne Coll., 1976; Ph.D. (hon.), Va. Coll., 1976, Am. Internat. U., 1977. Intelligence analyst NATO, Izmir, Turkey, 1959; corr. Stars and Stripes, Dept. Def., 1959-60; newspaper editor, Ft. Myer, Va., 1961-63; news editor Radio VUNC, Okinawa, 1963-64; pub. affairs rep. Dept. Def., Maine-N.H.-Vt., 1964-67; Tokyo pub. affairs rep. UN, 1967-68; chief community relations Mil. Dist. Washington, 1969-70; dir. pub. affairs Nat. Farmers Union, 1970-71; dir. minority communications Peace Corps, 1971-73; staff asst., dep. spl. asst. to Pres. for minority affairs, 1973-74; spl. asst. to Pres., also dir. for media relations The White House, Washington, 1975-76; v.p. Bamieh Assos., Washington, 1977—; dir. Am.-Asian Trading Co., Am. Bionics Enterprises. Bd. dirs. Bel-Pre Civic Assn., 1973-76; mem. Nat. Adv. Council on Edn. for Disadvantaged Children. Served with U.S. Army, 1955-59. Decorated Army Commendation ribbon; recipient award Middle Atlantic Assn. Indsl. Editors, 1961; Clio award Am. TV and Radio Comml. Festival Group, 1971; Andy award Advt. Club N.Y., 1971; Nat. Man of Year award Nat. Inst. Rural Agrarian Life, 1976; Distinguished Pub. Service award Prairie View A. and M. U., 1976. Mem. Internat. Communication Assn., Am. Mgmt. Assn., Acad. Polit. Sci., DAV (life), Nat. Press Club, Capital Press Club (dir. 1969—), Rep. Nat. Com. Assos. Republican. Club: Capital Office: Box 8015 SW Station Washington DC 20024

CALHOUN, WILLIAM DICE, cons. engr.; b. Petersburg, W.Va., Dec. 30, 1941; s. Richard Frailey and Annah Renick (Harper) C.; B.S. in Civil Engring., W.Va. U., 1963, M.S. in Civil Engring., 1965; m. Gloria Jean Robertson, Dec. 29, 1962; children—Lori Lyn, Gina Kaye, William Dice II. With State Rd. Commn. W.Va., Morgantown, 1959-65; project engr. Delta Engrs., Cumberland, Md., 1965-68; prin. engr. Nassaux-Hemsley, Inc., Chambersburg, Pa., 1968-74; dir. engring. Delta Internat., Ltd., Chambersburg, 1974-76; cons. civil/structural engr., Chambersburg, 1976—. Supt. Sunday sch. Calvary United Methodist Ch., 1970-72; Webelo den leader Boy Scouts Am., 1974-77. Registered profl. engr., W.Va., Md., Pa., N.J., N.Y., Ind.; profl. land surveying certificate, Md., Pa., Mem. Nat., Pa. (pres. Franklin chpt.) socs. profl. engrs., ASCE, Am. Concrete Inst., Prestressed Concrete Inst., Chi Epsilon. Democrat. Club: Chambersburg Rod and Gun. Home: Route 8 Box 434 Chambersburg PA 17201 Office: PO Box 532 Chambersburg PA 17201

CALIFANO, JOSEPH ANTHONY, JR., govt. ofcl.; b. Bklyn., May 15, 1931; s. Joseph Anthony and Katherine (Gill) C.; A.B., Holy Cross Coll., 1952; LL.B., Harvard U., 1955; m. Gertrude Zawacki, July 4, 1955; children—Mark Gerard, Joseph Anthony, Claudia Frances. Admitted to N.Y. State bar, 1955, D.C. bar; with firm Dewey, Ballantine, Bushby, Palmer & Wood, N.Y.C., 1958-61; spl. asst. to gen. counsel Dept. Def., 1961-62; spl. asst. to sec. army, 1962-63; gen. counsel Dept. Army, 1963-64; spl. asst. to sec. and dep. sec. def., 1964-65; spl. asst. to Pres. U.S., 1965-69; partner Arnold & Porter, Washington, 1969-71; mem. firm Williams, Connolly & Califano, Washington, 1971-76; sec. HEW, Washington, 1977—. Served to lt. USNR, 1955-58. Recipient Distinguished Civilian Service award Dept. Army, 1964, Dept. Def., 1968; Man of Year award Justinian Soc. Lawyers, 1966; One of Ten Young Outstanding Men Am., U.S. Jr. C. of C., 1966. Mem. Am., Fed. bar assns., Am. Judicature Soc. Democrat. Author: The Student Revolution: A Global Confrontation, 1969; A Presidential Nation, 1975; (with Howard Simons) The Media and the Law, 1976, The Media and Business, 1979. Home: 3551 Springland Ln Washington DC 20008 Office: HEW 200 Independence Ave SW Washington DC 20201

CALIGIURI, ANGELO MICHAEL, clergyman; b. Buffalo, Sept. 26, 1933; s. Rosario and Sebastiana (Glanpaolo) C.; B.A., Niagara U., 1955; S.T.L., Pontifical Gregorian U., Rome, Italy, 1959, Ph.L., 1964, Ph.D., 1966. Ordained priest Roman Catholic Ch., 1958; prof. Diocesan Prep. Sem., Buffalo, 1961-63; prof. theology St. Clare Coll., Williams, N.Y., 1962-63, Loyola U. of Chgo., Rome Center, 1966; prof. philosophy and Christian ethics St. John Vianney Sem., East Aurora, N.Y., 1966-74; vicar for religious Diocese of Buffalo, 1975—. Carnegie Found. grantee for Summer Inst. in Philosophy, 1967. Mem. Cath. Theol. Soc. Am., Metaphys. Soc. Am., Am. Cath. Philos. Assn. Author: The Concept of Freedom in the Writings of Erich Fromm, 1966. Contbr. to Rev. for Religious, Spiritual Life, The Priest, Sisters Today. Home: 10330 Main St Clarence NY 14031 Office: 100 S Elmwood Ave Buffalo NY 14202

CALIGUIRI, RICHARD S., mayor Pitts.; b. Pitts., Oct. 20, 1931; grad. Pitts. Tech. Inst.; m. Jeanne Conte; children—Greg, David. Mem. City Council Pitts., 1970-77, pres., 1977; mayor of Pitts., 1977—. Served with USAF, 1950-54. Office: Office of Mayor City Hall 414 Grant St Pittsburgh PA 15219

CALKINS, EVAN, physician, educator; b. Newton, Mass., July 15, 1920; s. Grosvenor and Patty (Phillips) C.; grad. Milton Acad., 1939; A.B., Harvard, 1942, M.D., 1945; m. Virginia McC. Brady, Sept. 9, 1946; children—Sarah Whiton, Stephen, Lucy McCormick, Joan Grosvenor, Benjamin, Hugh, Ellen Rowntree, Geoffrey, Timothy. Intern, asst. resident medicine Johns Hopkins, 1945-46, 48-50; practice medicine, specializing in internal medicine, Boston, 1951-61, Buffalo, 1961—; NRC fellow dept. biochemistry Harvard, 1950-52, instr., asst. prof. medicine, 1952-61; staff mem. Mass. Gen. Hosp., 1952-61; prof. medicine State U. N.Y., Buffalo, 1961—, chmn. dept., 1965-77, head div. geriatrics and gerontology, 1978—; head dept. medicine Buffalo Gen. Hosp., 1961-68; dir. medicine E.J. Meyer Meml. Hosp., 1968-78; cons. Buffalo VA Hosp., Roswell Park Meml. Inst., Millard Fillmore Hosp., Sisters of Charity Hosp.; cons. Nat. Inst. Arthritis and Metabolic Diseases Tng. Grants Com., 1958-62, Program Project Com., 1964-68; mem. Nat. Insts. Spl. Study Sect. for Health Manpower, 1969-71. Served to capt., M.C., AUS, 1943-45, 46-48. Mem. Am. Soc. Internal Medicine, Am. Soc. for Exptl. Pathology, Gerontol. Assn., Am. Rheumatism Assn. (pres., past chmn. Med. Council), A.C.P., Am. Clin. and Climatological Assn., Am. Soc. Clin. Investigation, Assn. Am. Physicians, Assn. Profs. Medicine (sec.-treas. 1970-73), Assn. Behavioral Scis. and Med. Edn., Central Soc. Clin. Research, Asociacion Medica Argentina (hon.). Contbr. articles to profl. publs. Home: 3799 Windover Hamburg NY 14075 Office: 462 Grider St Buffalo NY 14215

CALKINS, GARY NATHAN, lawyer; b. N.Y.C., Mar. 1, 1911; s. Gary Nathan and Helen R. (Williston) C.; student Ecole Internationale, Geneva, Switzerland, 1926-27, Storm King Sch., 1927-29; A.B., Columbia U., 1933; LL.B., Harvard U., 1936; m. Constantia Hommann, June 22, 1940 (div. Dec. 1948); m. 2d, Susannah Eby, Nov. 19, 1949; children—Helen, Margaret, Sarah, Abigail. Admitted to N.Y. bar, 1936, D.C. bar, 1955; asso. firm Beekman & Bogue, N.Y.C., 1936-41; staff Civil Aeros. Bd., 1941-56, chief internat. and rules div., 1947-56; partner firm Galland, Kharasch, Calkins & Short and predecessor firms, Washington, 1956—. Dir. Dune House Condominium, Ocean City, Md., 1969—, pres., 1973-75. Mem. U.S. del. legal com. Internat. Civil Aviation Orgn., 1947-55, delegation chmn. 1st, 3d, 5th, 9th and 10th meetings; chmn. U.S. delegation Internat. Diplomatic Conf. for Revision of Warsaw Conv., The Hague, 1955; chmn. legal div. U.S. Air Coordinating Com., 1955-56. Served as lt. USNR, 1943-45. Mem. Am., D.C. bar assns., Soc. Quiet Birdmen, Psi Upsilon. Clubs: Nat. Aviation, Internat. Aviation, George Town (Washington). Asso. editor United States and Canadian Aviation Reports, 1956; asso. editor Jour. Air Law and Commerce, 1956-58, editor-in-chief, 1958-63. Author profl. papers. Home: 6504 Dearborn Dr Falls Church VA 22044 Office: Canal Sq 1054 31st St Washington DC 20007

CALLAHAN, JOHN WILLIAM, biochemist, educator; b. Welland, Ont., Can., July 9, 1942; s. Cyril James and Elizabeth Sarah (Burden) C.; B.S. with honors in Biology and Chemistry, U. Windsor (Ont.), 1965, M.S., Biochemistry, 1966; Ph.D. in Biochemistry, McGill U., Montreal Que., Can., 1970; m. Marilyn MacDonald, Dec. 9, 1969; children—Andrew S., Matthew J. Investigator, Research Inst., Hosp. for Sick Children, Toronto, Ont., 1972—; asst. prof. dept. pediatrics U. Toronto, 1973—, asst. prof. dept. biochemistry, 1975—. Med. Research Council of Can. fellow, 1970-72, scholar, 1973-78. Mem. Am. Soc. for Neurochemistry, Can. Biochem. Soc., Can. Soc. Clin. Investigation, AAAS, N.Y. Acad. Scis. Roman Catholic. Contbr. articles on biochemistry to profl. jours. Home: 479 Karen Park Crescent Mississauga ON L5A 3E1 Canada Office: 555 University Ave Toronto ON M5G 1X8 Canada

CALLAHAN, MICHAEL EDSON, instrument co. exec.; b. Tacoma, Wash., June 26, 1940; s. Edson Jess and Marjorie Mabel (Lee) C.; student Tacoma Vocat. Inst., U. Puget Sound; m. Lenita Marjean Hickok, Feb. 8, 1964; children—Kevin, Kelly. Instrumentation engr., research asst. Boeing Co., Seattle, 1960-68; sales rep. computer products Digital Equipment Corp., Seattle, 1968-70, mgr. Seattle office, 1970-75, mktg. mgr., Maynard, Mass., 1975—. Bd. dirs. Eastside Amateur Hockey Assn., 1975-76; chmn. program com. local Cub Scouts. Mem. Am. Mgmt. Assn. Club: Elks. Author various articles in field. Home: 65 Angelica Dr Framingham MA 01701 Office: 146 Main St Maynard MA 01701

CALLAHAN, MONITA (MRS. ROY H. CALLAHAN), bus. exec.; b. Grand Saline, Tex., Dec. 15, 1927; d. Cecil Stone and La Rue (Smith), Chaney; student So. Meth. U., 1945-48; m. Roy Haney Callahan, Dec. 27, 1952; children—Roy Haney, Michael Chaney, Monita. Vice pres., sec., dir. Round Hill Limousine Service, Inc., Greenwich, Conn., 1960-61; asst. sec., dir. Round Hill, Inc., 1960-61; asst. sec., dir. Wilder Transp. Co., 1960-61, pub. relations rep., 1962; sec., dir. Airport Service Corp., 1961, Mid-City Taxi Co., 1961—; exec. adminstr. N.Y. met. region Duracell Products. Co-chmn. Westport com. Mid-Fairfield County Child Guidance Council. Bd. dirs. Women's League of Mid-Fairfield County Youth Mus.; trustee Greenwich Country Day Sch., Whitley Sch. Mem. Greenwich C. of C. (edn. com. 1959-61), Round Hill Community Guild (chmn. children's fair 1959-60). Republican. Office: 1 Old Easton Turnpike Westport CT 06883

CALLAHAN, ROY HANEY, lawyer, transp. facilities cons., naval officer, business exec.; b. Marceline, Mo., July 7, 1904; s. William Paxton and Malvina (Haney) P.; A.B., U. Mich., 1926; J.D., 1929; LL.M., So. Meth. U.; children—Roy Haney, Michael C., Monita. Librarian, 1924-29; naval aviator, 1929-31, 40-46 as aircraft carrier exec. officer, task group ops. officer, task group chief of staff, asst. to dept. chief, Bur. Aeros, asst. to asst. sec. navy for air, also asst. to sec. navy; exec. dir. N.Y.C. Airport Authority, also asst. commr. Marine and Aviation for N.Y.C., 1946; admitted to N.Y. state bar, 1931, Mich. bar, 1931, Tex. bar, 1949; asso. firm White & Case, N.Y.C., 1931-40; mem. Callahan & Durant, Ft. Worth, 1949-55, Kilgore & Kilgore, Dallas, 1955-56; v.p., gen. mgr. Airlines Terminal Corp., also Airlines Nat. Terminal Service Co., 1946-48; exec. dir. Greater Fort Worth Internat. Air Terminal Corp., 1950-51; lectr. U. Mich. Law Inst., 1940; pres. Simpson Grain Co., Inc., 1956—; pres. Swan Finch Oil Corp., pres., dir. Keta Oil & Gas Co., Olean Industries, Inc., Doeskin Products, Inc. 1956-57; v.p. Epsco, Inc., 1959; pres., gen mgr. Round Hill Limousine Service, Inc., 1960; exec. asst. to v.p. Eastern Air Lines, 1961-69; exec. v.p. Airlines Facilities Corp. Am., 1969—, AFCOA Inc., 1969—; dir. Bradley Facilities, Inc., Airlines Terminal Corp., Airlines Nat. Terminal Service Co. Trustee Southwestern Inst. for Alcohol Research. Res. officer with U.S. Army, 1926-29, reserve enlisted man or officer, 1929—, capt. USNR, 1945-55, rear adm., 1955—. Mem. Navy Roper Bd., 1948; occasional spl. asst. to sec. of navy, 1948. Mem. Bur. Aeros. Naval Res. Advisory Council, 1946—. Decorated Bronze Star medal, Air medal, Reserve medal Pacific. Life mem. Southwestern Legal Found.; mem. Com. of 100 on behalf of U. Mich. Phoenix Project for Atomic Research; mem. Am., City of N.Y., Tex., Fort Worth, Dallas bar assns. Mason. Clubs: University, New York Athletic; Cipango (Dallas). Author: The Corporate Mortgage under Texas Law; Rescue and Slavage in the Everglades; A Neglected Air Market; The Robinson Patman Act; Impact of the Next Two Aircraft Generations on Airport Design; Airport Role in the Community; co-author: National Policy for Aviation, 1946; Airports for Future Aircraft-A Planning Guide. Home and Office: 1 Old Easton Turnpike Weston CT 06883

CALLAM, JAMES MONROE, ednl. adminstr.; b. E. Orange, N.J., Jan. 1, 1927; s. Alexander James and Catherine Ruth (Monroe) C.; B.A. cum laude, Montclair State Coll., 1950; A.M., Columbia U., 1953; Ed.D., Rutgers U., 1968; m. Ella Ruth Torgerson, June 23, 1951; 1 dau., Pamela Ruth. Tchr. English, Passaic Valley High Sch., Little Falls, N.J., 1950-52, Roosevelt Jr. High Sch., Westfield, N.J., 1952-56; adminstrv. prin. Brielle (N.J.) Sch., 1956-57; dir. personnel Westfield (N.J.) Pub. Schs., 1964-71; prin. McKinley Sch., Jefferson Sch., Westfield, 1957-64; supt. schs. Pt. Pleasant Beach (N.J.) Schs., 1971—; pres. Ocean County Supts. Round Table; pres. N.J. Sch. Devel. Council, Rutgers U. Chmn., Central Jersey Christian Businessmen's Com., 1957-67; fund raiser Westfield YMCA, Am. Cancer Soc. Served with U.S. Army, 1945-46. Mem. Am., N.J. assns. sch. adminstrs., N.J. Schoolmasters, N.J. Council Edn., N.J. Sch. Bds. Assn., Kappa Delta Pi, Phi Delta Kappa. Republican. Club: Rotary (dir. 1972-78). Home: 2 Blair Ct Wayside NJ 07712 Office: Cook's Ln Point Pleasant Beach NJ 08742

CALLENDER, CARL OSWALD, legal adminstr.; b. N.Y.C., Nov. 16, 1936; s. Joseph and Ida (Burke) C.; A.B., Hunter Coll., 1964; J.D., Howard U., 1967; m. Leola Rhames, Aug. 1, 1970. Editor, Prentice-Hall Tax Reports, Englewood Cliffs, N.J., 1967-68; admitted to N.Y. bar, 1968; staff atty. Community Action for Legal Services, N.Y.C., 1968-71; dir. Community Law Offices, N.Y.C., 1971—; dir. Housing Litigation Bur., N.Y.C. Dept. Housing Devel. Adminstrn., 1975-77, dep. commr. adminstrn., 1977—; chmn. NYPCA Enterprises, Inc., 1972—; exec. editor Nat. Drum, 1970—; ordained minister of Gospel, 1972. Chmn. bd. Nat. Young People's Christian Assn., Inc.; asst. gen. supt. Christian Mission U.S.A., 1977—; pres. Christian Leaders United, Inc., 1969—. Served with USAF, 1955-58. Reginald Heber Smith fellow, 1969-70. Home: 415 Louis Ave South Floral Park NY 11011 Office: 125 Church St New York City NY 10007

CALLENDER, CLIVE ORVILLE, surgeon; b. N.Y.C., Nov. 16, 1936; s. Joseph and Ida (Burke) C.; A.B., Hunter Coll., 1959; M.D. (Nat. Med. Assn. aux. scholar 1961, 63, Joseph Collins scholar 1961-63), Meharry Med. Coll., 1963; m. Fern Irene Marshal, May 25, 1968; children—Joseph, Ealena, Arianne. Intern, U. Cin., 1963-64; asst. resident Harlem Hosp., N.Y.C., 1964-65; asst. resident Howard U. and Freedmans Hosp., Washington, 1965-66, 67-68, chief resident, 1968-69, instr. dept. surgery, 1969-71; asst. resident Meml. Hosp. for Cancer and Allied Diseases, N.Y.C., 1966-67; cons. surgery Port Harcourt Gen. Hosp., Nigeria, 1970, 71; med. officer D.C. Gen. Hosp., 1970-71; postdoctoral research and clin. transplant fellow U. Minn., 1971-73; asst. prof. surgery Howard U. Med. Coll., Washington, 1973-76, asso. prof., 1976—, dir. transplant center, 1973—; transplantation cons., Bermuda, 1977, V.I., 1978; G.P.A. Ford Meml. lectr., 1978. Recipient Hoffman LaRoche award, 1961, Charles Nelson Gold medal, 1963, Hudson Meadows award, 1963, Charles R. Drew research award, 1968, Daniel Hale Williams award, 1969; William Alonzo Warfield award, 1977. Diplomate Am. Bd. Surgery. Fellow Am. Cancer Soc., A.C.S.; mem. D.C. Med. Soc., Soc. Acad. Surgeons, Transplantation Soc., Am. Soc. Transplant Surgeons, Kidney Found. (dir. Nat. Capital area), Alpha Omega Alpha, Alpha Phi Omega, Alpha Phi Alpha. Mem. editorial adv. bd. New Directions, 1974. Contbr. articles to med. jours. Home: 509 Kimblewick Dr Silver Spring MD 20904 Office: 2041 Georgia Ave Washington DC 20060

CALO, TINA CAROL, guidance counselor; b. East Cleveland, June 3, 1939; d. Vincent James and Maria Angelina (Caruso) C.; B.S. in Edn., Ohio U., 1961, M.Ed., 1969. Tchr., Stafford Elementary Sch., Maple Heights, Ohio, 1961-67; counselor Tyler Elementary Sch., Naha Air Base, Okinawa, 1967-70, Am. Elementary Sch., Berlin, 1970-71, Mc Gogney Elementary Sch., Washington, 1971-72, Hahn Elementary Sch., Hahn Air Base, Germany, 1972—. Mem. NEA, Ohio Edn. Assn. (v.p.), Hahn Edn. Assn., Am. Personnel and Guidance Assn., Am. Sch. Counselor Assn. Office: PSC Box 1149 APO New York 09109

CALOBRISI, DOMINICK, psychiatrist; b. Binghamton, N.Y., June 18, 1929; s. Anthony Mico and Vicenzina (Trabucco) C.; B.A., Syracuse U., 1951; M.D., U. Rome (Italy), 1959; m. Franca de Palma, Aug. 2, 1959; children—Antonio Rosario, Stella DiVina. Intern, Binghamton Gen. Hosp., 1960-61, resident in psychiatry and child psychiatry, 1961-62; resident N.J. Neuropsychiat. Inst., 1962-65; pvt. practice psychiatry, Manhasset, N.Y., 1965—; unit chief psychiatry L.I. Jewish Hosp., New Hyde Park, N.Y., 1970-72; med. dir. Mental Health Center North East Nassau (N.Y.), 1972-75; dir. dept. psychiatry St. Francis Hosp., Roslyn, N.Y., 1975—; asst. prof. clin. psychiatry State U. N.Y., Stony Brook, 1972—. Diplomate Am. Bd. Psychiatry and Neurology. Mem. Am. Psychiat. Assn., AAAS, N.Y. Acad. Scis. Roman Catholic. Club: Sands Point Skeet. Home: 237 Sussex St Manhasset NY 11030 Office: 100 Port Washington Blvd Roslyn NY 11576

CALOMIRIS, WILLIE DONALD, realtor, builder; b. Washington, Mar. 8, 1925; A.B.A. (Joseph Jolles Meml. award 1965), Am. U., 1963; m. Helen G. Dennis; children—Janice, George Donald. Engaged in real estate bus., 1940—, in constrn. bus., 1952—; treas., dir. William Calomiris Investment Corp., Washington, Calomiris Constrn. Corp.; dir., chmn. exec. com. Central Nat. Bank Md.; professorial lectr. property mgmt. Am. U., 1962—; trustee, chmn. bus. and fin. com. Am. U., 1974—. Served with AUS, World War II. Recipient Distinguished Alumni award Sch. Bus. Adminstrn., Am. U., 1975; Alumni Recognition award Am. U. Alumni Assn., 1978. Mem. Washington Bd. Realtors (dir. 1966-67, 69-70, past chmn. coms.; Property Mgmt. Transaction of Year award 1962, Realtor of Year award 1968), Nat. Assn. Realtors (Mgr. of Year 1967), Inst. Real Estate Mgmt. (pres. 1967; Omega Tau Rho medallion 1967), Washington Bd. Trade, Am. Legion (past post comdr.; Outstanding Comdr. award 1965), Rho Epsilon (past pres.; Honoris Causis award 1967, Rho Epsilon award 1967, 71), Lambda Alpha, AHEPA. Greek Orthodox. Address: 910 17th St NW Washington DC 20006

CALTER, PAUL, mech. engr., educator, author, artist; b. N.Y.C., June 18, 1934; s. Arthur and Frances (Bankowitz) C.; B.S., Cooper Union, 1962; M.S., Columbia, 1965; m. Margaret Jolind Carey, May 13, 1959; children—Amy, Michael. Sr. research asst. Columbia, 1952-60; engr. Kollsman Instrument Co., N.Y.C., 1960-65; sr. project engr. Intertype Co., N.Y.C. 1965-68; pres. Med. Computation Service, Randolph, Vt., 1973-76; asso. prof. math. Vt. Tech. Coll., Randolph Center, 1968—; cons. optical design; dir. UMS Inc., Reading, Pa., 1973-76. Served with AUS, 1957-59. Recipient Ralph Horton Meml. award in Sci., 1952. Mem. ASME, Am. Soc. Engring. Edn., Optical Soc. Am., Vols. in Tech. Assistance. Democrat. Club: University. Author: Problem Solving with Computers, 1973; Solution of Differential Equations, 1975; Magic Squares, 1976; Outline of Technical Mathematics, 1978. Sculptor Focus, steel sculpture Vt. Tech. Coll. campus, 1971. Home: 33 S Pleasant St Randolph VT 05060 Office: Vt Tech Coll Randolph Center VT 05061

CALVIELLO, JOSEPH ANTHONY, scientist; b. Genzano, Italy, Nov. 29, 1933; s. Nicola and Grazia (Lomuto) C.; came to U.S., 1952, naturalized, 1955; B.E.E., Poly. Inst. Bklyn., 1962, M.S. in Electrophysics, 1966; m. Carmela M. Ciaramella, Dec. 26, 1959; 1 son, Joseph John. Engring. asst. Poly. Microwave Research Inst., Bklyn., 1956-61; with AIL Central Research Lab., Melville, N.Y., 1961—, sr. research scientist, 1973—. Mem. IEEE (sr.), Am. Mgmt. Assn., Sigma Xi. Roman Catholic. Club: Smithtown Landing Country. Contbr. articles in field to profl. jours. Home: 30 Ashland Dr Kings Park NY 11754

CAM, MARCIALITO FELIPE, social welfare and adminstrv. programs cons., author; b. Phila., Feb. 15, 1934; s. Toribio and Lucille (Gregory) C.; B.A., Franklin and Marshall Coll., 1955; M.S.W., Adelphi U., 1957; postgrad. Temple U., Bryn Mawr Coll.; m. Bettye Owens, Apr. 27, 1957; 1 dau., Lise Tinnele. Various adminstrv. and field positions in social work, N.Y., Washington and Phila., 1957-72; faculty Grad. Sch. Edn., Antioch Coll., 1972-73; social welfare, adminstrv. and program cons., Phila., 1972—; mem. bd. Vol. Services for Blind. Recipient plaque Am. Acad. Human Services, 1974, Outstanding Community Service award Chapel of Four Chaplins, 1964. Mem. Dramatist Guild, AAUP, ACLU, Am. Sociol. Assn., Nat. Assn. Social Workers, Acad. Certified Social Workers. Dramatist, novelist, poet. Address: 706 W Carpenter Ln Philadelphia PA 19119

CAMERON, ARTHUR STUART, educator; b. Winchester, Mass., Nov. 15, 1936; s. Arthur Stewart and Jessie Martha (Cole) C.; A.A., Boston U., 1961, B.S., 1963, Ed.M., 1964; postgrad. Lamar U., 1966-67, State Coll., Bridgewater, Mass., 1967-68, Boston Coll., 1970-71, Princeton, 1969-70. Tchr. earth sci. Belmont (Mass.) High Sch., 1965-77, chmn. sci. dept., 1977-78, sci. edn. coordinator, 1978—. Bd. dirs. Mass. Sci. Fair Com., 1966-70. Served with Army Security Agy., 1957-60. NSF grantee, 1966, 67, 68, 70. Mem. Mass., Middlesex County, Belmont (pres. 1972-73, chmn. legis. action com. 1966-68) tchrs. assns., NEA, Nat. Sci. Tchrs. Assn., Nat. Assn. Geology Tchrs., Mass. Assn. Sci. Tchrs., Phi Delta Kappa (chpt. historian 1972-73, treas. 1973-74, editor newsletter 1972-73). Home: 66 Richardson Rd Belmont MA 02178 Office: 221 Concord Ave Belmont MA 02178

CAMERON, DOUGLAS GEORGE, physician; b. Folkestone, Eng., Mar. 11, 1917; s. George L. and Rowena (Shaver) C.; B.S., U. Sask., 1937; M.D., McGill U., 1940; B.S., U. Oxford, 1948; m. Jeanne

Sutherland Thompson, Feb. 23, 1946; children—George, Jane, Heather, Bruce, Nancy, Marian. Physician-in-chief Montreal Gen. Hosp., 1957—, dir. McGill U. Med. Clinic, 1957—; prof. medicine McGill U., 1957—, chmn. dept. medicine, 1964-69, 74—. Served to lt. col. M.C., Royal Canadian Army, 1940-46. Fellow A.C.P., Royal Coll. Physicians (London), Royal Coll. Physicians and Surgeons (Can.) (v.p. 1970-78, pres. 1978); mem. Am. Clin. and Climatol. Assn., Am., Canadian socs. clin. investigation, Med. Research Soc. London, Internat., Am. socs. hematology, Assn. Am. Physicians, Canadian, Que. (past pres.) med. assns. Contbr. articles to profl. jours. Home: 227 Portland Ave Town of Mount Royal Montreal PQ H3R 1V3 Canada Office: 1650 Cedar Ave Montreal PQ H3G 1A4 Canada

CAMERON, RANDOLPH WHITNEY, cosmetic co. exec.; b. Jersey City, Apr. 6, 1936; s. Hugh J. and Anneatta R. (Alleyne) C.; B.S., Del. State Coll., 1958; m. Martha R. Billingsley, Apr. 10, 1965; children—Randolph Whitney, Michele Renee. Mgr., D. Parke Gibson Assos., N.Y.C., 1962-64, v.p., 1966-71, dir., 1964-66; div. sales mgr. Avon Products, Inc., N.Y.C., 1972-73, mktg. dir., 1973-78, dir. gen. communications, 1978—. Served with U.S. Army, 1959-61. Mem. Nat. Assn. Market Developers, Am. Mktg. Assn., Del. State Coll. Alumni Assn. Home: 100 W 94th St New York City NY 10025 Office: Avon Products 9 W 57th St New York City NY 10019

CAMERON, SCOTT CHARLES, tech. service rep.; b. Highland Park, Mich., June 8, 1951; s. Walter Alexander and Phyllis Cameron (Klein) Leikett; certificate in computer tech. Control Data Inst., 1973; certified in laser-photo Asso. Press Service Sch., 1975; m. Mariwyn Glowe, Jan. 21, 1976. Technician Sycor, Inc., Ann. Arbor, Mich., 1973-74; technician AP, Detroit, 1974-75, field technician, Harrisburg, Pa., 1976, technician, N.Y.C., 1977—, chmn. N.Y. local union, 1977—. Served with U.S. Army, 1971-72. Mem. Am. Def. Preparedness Assn., Smithsonian Assos., N.Y. Zool. Soc., Nat. ABATE. Home: 264-49 Langston Ave Glen Oaks NY 11004 Office: 50 Rockefeller Plaza New York City NY 10020

CAMILLERY, GEORGE LEWIS, pediatrician, pediatric and adult allergist; b. N.Y.C., Apr. 23, 1945; s. Joseph and Sylvia (Tayara) C.; B.S. cum laude, Fordham U., 1968; M.D., N.Y. Med. Coll., 1972; m. Rosemary Ann Holland, Feb. 14, 1975. With data processing and med dept. IBM, N.Y.C., 1965-74; fellow in forensic pathology Med. Examiner's Office, N.Y.C., 1969; med. technologist N.Y. Med. Coll., Flower Fifth Ave. Hosp., N.Y.C., 1970-72; intern in pediatrics Bellevue Hosp., N.Y. U. Med. Center, N.Y.C., 1972-73; resident in pediatrics Beth Israel Hosp., N.Y.C., 1973-75; elective fellow in immunology, allergy Hammersmith Hosp., London, 1975; elective studies Cooke Allergy Inst., Roosevelt Hosp., N.Y.C., 1975; v.p. house staff Bellevue Hosp., 1972, pres., 1973, bd. dirs. Bellevue Hosp. Center, 1973; attending physician in pediatrics Newark Wayne Community Hosp. (N.Y.), 1975—; lectr. health care, travel, N.Y. State, 1978. Recipient Physician's Recognition award AMA, 1975-78; diplomate Nat. Bd. Med. Examiners. Mem. Student AMA, N.Y. State, Wayne County med. socs. Home: 205 Grace Ave Newark NY 14513 Office: 106 Washington St Newark NY 14513

CAMLIN, JAMES ALEXANDER, artist; b. Hopkinton, Mass., Jan. 16, 1918; s. Alexander and Elizabeth Patterson (Gray) C.; student Sch. Practical Art, Boston, 1938-40, 45-46, with Aldro T. Hibbard, 1946; m. Ruth Helen James, Aug. 29, 1942; 1 dau., Cheryl Ruth. Exhbns.: Nat. Acad. Gallery, N.Y.C., 1970, Nat. Arts Gallery, N.Y.C., 1971, Lever House Gallery, N.Y.C., 1971-76, Springfield (Mass.) Mus. Fine Arts, 1969, Mcpl. Casino, Cannes, France, 1974, l'Oeuvres Contemporaine, Geneva, 1974, Colchester (Eng.) Castle, 1944; dot etch artist Artographic Corp. div. Rust Craft Printers & Pubs., Dedham, Mass., 1951—. Served with USAAF, 1942-45; ETO. Recipient diplome d'honneur, Cannes, 1974. Mem. Am. Artists Profl. League, North Shore Art Assn., Ogunquit Art Assn., Internat. Platform Assn. Home: 234 W Emerson St Melrose MA 02176

CAMMARATA, ANGELO, physician; b. Cerami, Italy, Aug. 27, 1936; s. Joseph and Josephine (Ruggiero) C.; came to U.S., 1951, naturalized, 1974; A.B., Upsala Coll., 1958; M.D., N.Y. Med. Coll., 1962; m. Diane M. Donner, Apr. 25, 1965; children—Joseph, Marisa, A. Michael, Christina. Intern, N.Y. Polyclinic, 1962-63; resident in surgery N.Y. Med. Coll.-Met. Hosp. Center, N.Y.C., 1963-67, chief surg. resident, 1967; resident surg. oncology Meml. Hosp. Cancer and Allied Diseases, N.Y.C., 1967-68; asst. attending surgeon Cabrini Med. Center, N.Y.C., Flower-Fifth Ave Hosp., N.Y.C., asso. vis. surgeon Met. Hosp., 1972; clin. asst. prof. surgery N.Y. Med. Coll., N.Y.C., 1974—; practice medicine specializing in gen. surgery, N.Y.C., 1969—. Diplomate Nat. Bd. Med. Examiners, Am. Bd. Surgery. Mem. A.C.S., Internat. Coll. Surgeons, N.Y. Cancer Soc., N.Y. County Med. Soc., Surg. Soc. N.Y. Med. Coll., Pan Am. Med. Assn., N.Y. Met. Breast Cancer Group. Roman Catholic. Club: Alpha. Office: 700 Park Ave New York City NY 10021

CAMMAROTA, CHARLES CARMINE, clin. psychologist; b. Phila., May 11, 1940; s. Carmine Charles and Dorothy Cecelia (Pahler) C.; A.B., LaSalle Coll., 1962; M.Ed., West Chester State Coll., 1969; M.A., Glassboro State Coll., 1969; Ed.D., Rutgers U., 1975; postgrad. U. Pa., 1975; m. Marie Elizabeth Cardile, Aug. 14, 1965; 1 dau., Sharon Marie. Clin. psychologist Pa. Bur. Corrections, 1964-66; asst. chief clin. psychologist Diagnostic and Relocation Service Corp., Phila., 1966-67; sch. psychologist Washington Twp. (N.J.) Bd. Edn., 1967-69, 78—; psychologist, later dir. counseling center Glassboro State Coll., 1969-71; clin. psychologist Salem County (N.J.) Child Guidance Center, 1969-71; coordinator psychol. services Alfred I. duPont Sch. Dist., Wilmington, Del., 1971-74; clin. psychologist Inst. Pa. Hosp., Phila., 1974-78; pvt. practice, N.J., 1978—; intern Yale, summer 1972. Licensed clin. psychologist, Pa., N.J., marriage counselor, N.J. Mem. Am., N.J., Camden County, Pa. psychol. assns., Am. Assn. Mental Deficiency, Soc. Clin. and Exptl. Hypnosis, Franklin Inst. Sci., Kappa Delta Pi, Psi Chi. Mason (32 deg., Shriner). Address: 44 Bryant Rd Blackwood NJ 08012

CAMOUGIS, GEORGE, physiologist, cons. co. exec.; b. Concord, Mass., May 10, 1930; s. Charles George and Angeliki (Georgekopoulou) C.; B.S. (Olmstead fellow), Tufts Coll., 1952; M.A., Harvard U., 1957, Ph.D., 1958; m. Irene Andreson, Nov. 18, 1961; children—Caroline A., Elizabeth M., Sarah A. Asst. prof. physiology Clark U., 1958-62, asso. prof., 1962-64, affiliate prof., 1964—; sr. neurophysiologist Astra Pharm. Products, Inc., Worcester, Mass., 1964-66, head sect. neuropharmacology, 1966-68; pres., research dir., dir. New Eng. Research, Inc., Worcester, 1968—; affiliate prof. Worcester Poly. Inst., 1970—; panelist NSF; mem. corp. Bermuda Biol. Sta. for Research, 1968—; lectr. in field, U.S., Can.; mem. Worcester Sci. Center Planning Com., 1963. Bd. dirs. Worcester Children's Friend Soc., 1968—, v.p., 1978. Served with USNR, 1952-54; Korea. Virginia B. Gibbs scholar, 1954-55; E.L. Mark fellow 1956; USPHS fellow, 1957-58; NIH grantee, 1962-64; Office Naval Research grantee, 1963-64. Mem. AAAS, Biophys. Soc., Am. Soc. Zoologists, Am. Physiol. Soc., N.Y. Acad. Scis., ASTM, Phi Beta Kappa, Sigma Xi. Republican. Greek Orthodox. Club: Tatnuck Country (Worcester). Author: Nerves, Muscles and Electricity, 1970; contbr. numerous articles to profl. jours., 1959—; patentee drug; cons. editor Acad. Press, Inc., 1978. Home: 10 Wheeler Ave Worcester MA 01609 Office: 15 Sagamore Rd Worcester MA 01605

CAMP, HAZEL LEE BURT, artist; b. Gainesville, Ga., Nov. 28, 1922; d. William Ernest and Annie Mae (Ramsey) Burt; student Md. Inst. Art, 1957-58, 62-63; m. William Oliver Camp, Jan. 24, 1942; children—William Oliver, David Byron. One man shows at Ga. Mus. Art, Rockville Art Mus., Coll. Notre Dame (Balt.), U. Md., Balt. Vertical Gallery, Cleveland Meml. Gallery (Balt.), others; exhibited in juried shows at Peale Mus., Balt., Wilmington (Del.) Fine Arts Center, Smithsonian Instn., Turner Gallery, Balt., others; represented in permanent collections Ga. Mus. Art, Peabody Inst. (Balt.), numerous pvt. collections. Recipient 1st prize Md. Chpt. Artists' Equity, 1967; St. Marys County Art Assn., 1964, 67, 1st prize still life Cape May, N.J., 1969, Catonsville (Md.) Community Coll., 1969, St. John's Coll., 1969, Best in Show York (Pa.) Art Assn. Gallery, 1972, 2d award Md. Inst. Alumni Founding Chpt., Balt., 1976, Best in Show Three Arts Club, 1978, others. Mem. Nat. League Am. Pen Women (pres. Carroll br. 1968-70, editor The Quill 1975-76), Artist's Equity, Rehoboth Art League, Md. Fedn. Art, Md. Inst. Alumni Assn., Balt. Watercolor Soc. Democrat. Methodist. Contbr. illustrations to mags., booklets. Home: 921 Breezewick Circle Baltimore MD 21204

CAMP, MARGARET WHITTLESEY PERKINS (MRS. MORTIMER HART CAMP), ret. lawyer; b. New Britain, Conn., Nov. 27, 1897; d. John Russell and Mary Whittlesey (Brown) Perkins; A.B., Radcliffe Coll., 1919; J.D., U. Chgo., 1924; m. Mortimer Hart Camp, June 2, 1928. Tchr., La Veta (Colo.) High Sch., 1919-21; admitted to Conn. bar, 1925; practiced in New Britain, 1925-30; partner firm Camp, Williams & Richardson, 1930-66. Mem. cello sect. New Britain Symphony Orch., 1930-62. Dir. New Britain C. of C., 1949-51; trustee New Britain Inst., 1949—; corporator New Britain Gen. Hosp., 1942—. Mem. Am., Hartford County, New Britain bar assns., D.A.R., Order of Coif, Phi Beta Kappa. Republican. Methodist. Clubs: New Britain Musical, Woman's (pres. 1943-45), Shuttlemeadow Country. Home 37 Russell St New Britain CT 06052 Office: 130 W Main St New Britain CT 06050

CAMPBELL, ALEXANDER BRADSHAW, judge; b. Summerside, P.E.I., Can., Dec. 1, 1933; s. Thane A. and Cecilia B. Campbell; B.A., Dalhouse U., LL.B., 1959; LL.D., McGill U., 1967; m. Marilyn Ruth Gilmour; children—Blair Alexander, Heather Kathryn, Graham Melville. Practiced law in Summerside, 1959-66, partner firm; mem. legislature P.E.I., from 1965; leader of Liberal party P.E.I., 1965-78; premier, P.E.I., 1966-78, atty. gen., 1966-69, minister of devel., 1969-72, agriculture and forestry, 1972-74, minister justice, atty. gen., from 1974; judge Supreme Ct, P.E.I., 1978—; mem. Privy Council for Can., 1967—. Past sec. Summerside Bd. Trade. Mem. United Ch. Can. (elder). Club: Y's Men's (past pres.). Home: 330 Beaver St Summerside PE C1N 2A3 Canada Office: Supreme Ct Charlottetown PE Canada

CAMPBELL, CATHERINE F. GRAY (MRS. WALLACE ARNOLD CAMPBELL), writer, civic worker; b. Balt.; d. Ernest Guy and Catherine (Daly) Gray; B.S., Md. Coll.; M.S., Johns Hopkins; postgrad. Columbia, C.W. Post U.; m. Wallace Arnold Campbell, July 22, 1945; 1 dau., Catherine Frances. Tchr. pub. schs., Balt., N.Y.C.; writer various newspapers, L.I., N.Y., 1955-65, Los Angeles, 1966-69; writer for travel mags., 1960—; writer for Balt. City ednl. system, vol. groups, guides; lectr. world travel, various travel clubs, women's clubs, tchr. groups, 1958—. Chmn. vol. groups Glen Cove (N.Y.) Community Hosp., 1958-65; group chmn. Salvation Army, 1960-62; vice chmn. YMCA, Glen Cove, 1958-65; bd. dirs. Meals-on-Wheels, 1974—, v.p., 1976—; publicity dir. Greenwich Garden Center, 1975—, conservation chmn., also bd. dirs.; mem. Round Hill Guild. Mem. AAUW, Nat. Writers Club, Kappa Delta Pi, Pi Delta Gamma, Pi Lambda Theta. Clubs: Garden (pres. 1965) (Sea Cliff, N.Y.); Am. Women's (London, Eng.); Greenwich Country (chmn. 9-hole golf 1977-78). Editor, pub. Newsletter monthly Woman's Club of Greenwich, Inc., 1970-74. Home: Rockwood Ln Greenwich CT 06830

CAMPBELL, COLIN GOETZE, univ. pres.; b. N.Y.C., Nov. 3, 1935; s. Joseph and Marjorie (Goetze) C.; A.B., Cornell U., 1957; J.D., Columbia U., 1960; M.A. (hon.), Wesleyan U., 1970; LL.D., Amherst Coll., 1972, Williams Coll., 1973; m. Nancy Nash, June 20, 1959; children—Elizabeth, Jennifer, Colin, Blair. Admitted to Conn. bar, 1961; atty. Cummings & Lockwood, Stamford, Conn., 1960-62; asst. to pres. Am. Stock Exchange, N.Y.C., 1962-63; sec., 1963-64, v.p., 1964-67; adminstrv. v.p. Wesleyan U., Middletown, Conn., 1967-69, exec. v.p., 1969-70, pres., 1970—; dir. Pitney Bowes, Middlesex Mut. Assurance Co., Middletown; trustee No. Energy Corp.; corporator Liberty Bank for Savs. Bd. dirs. Middlesex Meml. Hosp., 1972—; Charles E. Culpeper Found., Inc.; trustee Inst. Architecture and Urban Studies. Mem. New Eng. Assn. Schs. and Colls. (chmn. commn. instns. higher edn.), Psi Upsilon, Phi Delta Phi. Episcopalian. Club: Century Assn. Home: 269 High St Middletown CT 06457

CAMPBELL, DIX MCDILL, architect; b. Boston, Apr. 14, 1938; s. Walter E. and Loraine L. (Leeson) C.; A.B., Harvard, 1960; M. Arch., U. Pa., 1963; m. Elizabeth H. Miller, June 24, 1960; children—Benjamin Dix, Jessica, Elizabeth. Designer, Hugh Stubbins and Assos., Cambridge, Mass., 1965-69; asso. Sasaki Assos., Watertown, Mass., 1969-74; partner, Campbell and Searson Architects, Cambridge, 1974—. Mem. com. town govt. Watertown; mem. exec. com. Belmont (Mass.) Day Sch. Recipient Parker medal, 1963, Arthur Spayde Brooke medal, 1963 (both U. Pa.). Registered architect, Mass., N.H. Mem. AIA, Boston Soc. Architects. Clubs: St. Botolph, Belmont Hill. Home: 150 Prospect St Belmont MA 02178 Office: 625 Mt Auburn St Cambridge MA 02138

CAMPBELL, DOUGLAS EATON, trade assn. exec.; b. Lewiston, Idaho, Mar. 28, 1922; s. Wilbur Lee and Elizabeth (Eaton) C.; student U. Idaho, 1940-42; B.S., U. Mich., 1944; J.D., N.Y. U., 1949. Research asst. Merck & Co., Inc., Rahway, N.J., 1944-50; asst. sec. Mfg. Chemists Assn., Washington, 1950-53; research asso., asst. to v.p. Nat. Aniline div. Allied Chem. Co., N.Y.C., 1953-58; research asso. Denver Chem. Co., 1958-59; sec.-treas. Pulp Chems. Assn., N.Y.C., 1959—. Mem. TAPPI, Am. Chem. Soc., Am. Oil Chemists Soc., Am., N.Y. socs. assn. execs. Clubs: University (Washington). Home: 10 Afterglow Ave Verona NJ 07044 Office: 60 E 42d St New York City NY 10017

CAMPBELL, EUGENE PAUL, physician, ret. pub. health adminstr., ret. govt. ofcl.; b. St. Paul, July 22, 1907; s. Eugene Paul and Fan (Berry) C.; B.A. in Zoology, U. Calif. at Los Angeles, 1929; M.D., Johns Hopkins, 1933; M.P.H., Pa. Sch. Pub. Health, 1942; m. Reba Lowe, Oct. 3, 1936; 1 dau., Marilyn Joyce. Intern Balt. City Hosp., 1933-34, asst. resident in medicine, 1935; practice medicine specializing in preventive medicine, 1939—; ward officer Communicable Disease sect. Walter Reed Hosp., Washington, 1935-39; asst. prof. epidemiology U. Pa. Sch. Pub. Health, Phila., 1939-42; chief of Co-op Health Program, Guatemala, 1942; field dir. Central Am. Co-op Health Programs, 1943-45; chief Co-op Health Program, Brazil, 1945-55; dep. chief pub. health div. ICA, Washington, 1955-57; dir. Office of Pub. Health, Washington, 1959-62; chief pub. health div. AID, New Delhi, India, 1962-65; attache health Am. Embassy, India, 1962-65; chief pub. health div. AID, Brazil, 1966-70, ret., 1970, now cons.; mem. U.S. Delegation WHO Gen. Assembly, 1957, 58, 60. Bd. dirs. Am. Sch., Rio de Janeiro, Brazil, Strangers Hosp., Rio de Janeiro. Decorated grand ofcl. Order Med. Merit, Brazil, 1955; recipient Meritorious Service citation U.S. Govt., 1956, Merit citation Nat. Civil Service League, 1958. Fellow Am. Pub. Health Assn., A.C.P.; mem. Royal Acad. Tropical Medicine and Hygiene, Am. Soc. Tropical Health and Hygiene, Indian Assn. Advancement Med. Edn., Royal Soc. Health, Brazilian Soc. Hygiene. Home: 4701 Willard Ave Chevy Chase MD 20015

CAMPBELL, HELEN ZOTT, apparel mfrs. assn. exec.; b. Des Moines, Feb. 7, 1919; d. John Henry and Perna A. (Jones) Zott; student Fairmont Jr. Coll., 1938, Strayer Bus. Coll., 1939-40, George Washington U., 1943-45, Orgn. Mgmt. Inst., U. Del., 1973—; m. Robert A. Campbell, Jr., Sept. 4, 1948; children—Karen Leigh, Debra Arlene. Accounting clk. George Washington U., Washington, 1940-46; sec., bookkeeper NEA, Washington, 1946-47; sec., accountant W.E. Cumberland Washington 1947-52; accountant Am. Apparel Mfrs. Assn., Inc., Arlington, Va., 1967-72, asst. treas., 1972—, dir. fin. services, 1973—. Jr. bd. George Washington U. Hosp., Washington, 1948-50, pres., 1950-52; bd. govs. English Speaking Union, Sydney, Australia, 1963-65. Recipient citation Philippine Govt., 1958, citation Children of Libya, 1963. Mem. Nat., Am., Washington socs. assn. execs., Nat. Assn. Exec.'s Clubs, Soc. for Preservation Va. Antiquities, Assn. Fgn. Service Women, Arlington C. of C., Zonta Internat., Kappa Delta. Republican. Presbyterian. Clubs: Capital Hill, Nat. Press, Capital Speakers, Washington. Home: 4701 Willard Ave Washington DC 20015 Office: 1611 N Kent Arlington VA 22209

CAMPBELL, ISOBEL AGNES BRYDON (MRS. WENDELL CHESLEY CAMPBELL), nursing cons.; b. Fergus, Ont., Can., Dec. 15, 1912; d. Donald Harvey and Margaret May (McIntosh) Brydon; grad. Guelph (Ont.) Coll. Vocational Inst., 1925-30; R.N., Hamilton (Ont.) Civic Hosp. Sch. Nursing, 1931-34; m. Wendell Chesley Campbell, Aug. 30, 1952. Pvt. duty nurse, Hamilton, 1934-39; gen. staff nurse Hamilton Civic Hosps., 1939-41, asst. nurse, 1941-44, head nurse, 1944-58, supr., 1958-77, v.p. Vol. Assn. Exec. sec. Central Service Assn., Province Ont., 1968-77; now cons. Mem. Alumni Assn. (pres. 1969-72). Home: 347 Arlington Rd Hamilton ON L8K 3K6 Canada Office: 237 Barton St E Hamilton ON Canada

CAMPBELL, JACK DUNCAN, mayor Northport (N.Y.); b. Los Angeles, Nov. 13, 1926; s. Jack Duncan and Pauline Howard (Lockwood) C.; B.F.A., Art Center Sch., Los Angeles, 1951; m. Marilyn Tostenrud, Dec. 1952; children—Douglas, Halla, Duncan. Designer, Raymond Lowe Assos., 1951-53, 56, Donald Deskey & Assos., 1953-56, Koodin-Lapow, 1956-57, Lee Vitale Assos., 1957-62, Frank Gianninoto & Assos., 1962-67, E. C. Kozlowski, 1967-73; art dir. Sterling Products Internat., 1973—; mem. Village of Northport Planning Bd., 1965-70, mayor, 1974—. Co-founder, 1st pres. Northport Homeowners Assn., 1960, Unity Polit. Party, 1963. Served with USNR, 1944-45. Mem. Northport Hist. Soc., Northfort/Commack/Smithtown Concert Assn. (dir.). Democrat. Unitarian. Home: 52 Norwood Ave Northport NY 11768 Office: 90 Park Ave New York City NY 10016

CAMPBELL, JAMES FRANKLIN, bank exec.; b. Valley Stream, N.Y., June 20, 1938; s. Edward C. and Anna (Becker) C.; A.A.S., State U. N.Y., Farmingdale, 1958; postgrad. Harvard U., 1972; m. Arlene Walther, Sept. 17, 1966; children—Lorraine, Arlene, James. Vice pres. Nat. Bank of N. Am., N.Y.C., 1958-72; adviser to security mortgage investors, exec. v.p., chief lending officer Semorco, Inc., N.Y.C., 1973-74; sr. v.p., mortgage officer Manhattan Savs. Bank, N.Y.C., 1974—. Asso. bd. dirs. S. Nassau Comminity Hosp., Oceanside, N.Y. Mem. Real Estate Bd. N.Y., Rho Epsilon. Clubs: E. Rockaway Yacht (sec.-dir), Kiwanis. Contbr. articles in field to profl. jours. Office: The Manhattan Savs Bank 385 Madison Ave New York City NY 10017

CAMPBELL, JAMES RAY, mfg. co. exec.; b. July 16, 1941; s. Ray E. and Anne Louise (Wooten) C.; B.S., U. Houston, 1965; postgrad. in behavioral sci. Case Western Res. U., 1967-68. Personnel asst. Standard Oil Co. (Ohio), Cleve., 1966-68; dir. equal opportunity programs Turner Constrn. Co., Cleve., 1968-73; employment project dir. Nat. Assn. on Drug Abuse Problems, N.Y.C., 1973-74; exec. dir. Cuyahoga Plan Ohio, Inc., Cleve., 1974-77; equal opportunity compliance mgr. Continental Group, Inc., N.Y.C., 1978—; expert witness HUD, 1970, U.S. Ho. of Reps. subcom., 1972. Task force chmn., mem. steering com. Cleve. Fedn. for Community Planning's Manpower Planning and Devel. Commn., 1971-73; mem. Cleve. Press Community Adv. Bd., 1972; co-chmn. speakers' bur. Arnold Pinkney's campaign for mayor Cleve., 1972. Served with USAF, 1958-62. Named 1 of 10 Outstanding Young Men of Yr., Cleve. Jr. C. of C., 1970, Outstanding Community Service award Urban League Cleve., 1972. Mem. Am. Soc. Personnel Adminstrn. (accredited personnel diplomate), World Future Soc., Omicron Delta Kappa (circle v.p. 1965, Gold Key 1965). Author profl. publs. Home: 130 W 67th St New York NY 10023 Office: 633 Third Ave New York NY 10017

CAMPBELL, MARSHALL DENDY, bus. exec.; b. Greenville, S.C., Mar. 19, 1936; s. Perry Boyce and Jetty Daisy (Hughes) C.; B.A. in Math., Berea (Ky.) Coll., 1957; postgrad. Ohio U., Rutgers U.; m. Connie Radford, Sept. 1, 1957; children—Cheryl, Bryan, Denise, Tonya. Mgmt. trainee Goodyear Atomic Corp., Wavely, Ohio, 1957-60; with System Devel. Corp., 1960-64, 3d level mgr., Omaha, 1963-64; with Western Union Corp., 1964-71, dept. mgr., Mahwah, N.J., 1966-71; pres. Distronics Corp., Cherry Hill, N.J., 1971—. Deacon Baptist Ch., Santa Monica, Calif., 1964-66, Presbyn. Ch., Ramsey, N.J., 1969-72. Home: 400 Chester Ave Moorestown NJ 07960 Office: 1060 Kings Hwy N Cherry Hill NJ 08034

CAMPBELL, MICHAEL ROBERT, interior designer; b. Lockport, N.Y., July 10, 1947; s. Robert D. and Audrey (Shallow) C.; grad N.Y. Sch. Interior Design, 1965. Interior designer William Fleming Interiors, Kingston, N.Y., 1967-69; spl. rep. N.Y. State Senate Fin. Com., Albany, 1969-71; interior designer John B. Hauf, Inc., Albany, 1971-73, Campbell-Moreau Assos., Inc., Boston, 1973—; interior design editor Mass. Apt. and Condominium Living mag., 1974-77. Served with U.S. Army, 1966-67. Mem. Am. Soc. Interior Designers (asso.), Designers Lighting Forum (bd. dirs., ednl. chmn. 1977—), Mass. Hort. Soc. Roman Catholic. Office: 174A Newbury St Boston MA 02116

CAMPBELL, NANCY HACKETT, hosp. adminstr.; b. Arlington, Iowa, June 10, 1935; d. Ferdinand Morgan and Esther Ellene (Thomas) Hackett; certificate in Personnel and Communications, Electronic Radio-TV Inst., Omaha, 1955; student Univ. Coll., U. Md., 1971—, U.S. Army Acad. Health Scis., 1976—; m. George Andrew Campbell, July 26, 1957; children—Teresa Ann, Ferrell Sue. Various clerical positions, Iowa, Nebr., D.C., 1949-58; sec. to surgeon, Hdqrs., Mil. Dist., Washington, 1958-62; clk.-typist, Kimbrough Army Hosp., Ft. Meade, Md., 1963-64; supervisory clk. dept. pathology, U.S. Army Med. Lab., Ft. Meade, 1964-75; mgmt. asst. dept. pathology and area lab. services, Walter Reed Army Med. Center, Washington, 1975—; lectr. on adminstrn. and mgmt. in Army. Asst. treas., bus. adminstr., advisory council mem. Beulah Retreat and Conf. Center, Inc., 1976—;

publicity com. Nat. Cystic Fibrosis Research Found., Washington, 1960-62, fund raising community chmn., 1963. Served with USN, 1954. Recipient performance awards, commendations, employee service certificates, U.S. Army. Mem. Am. Mgmt. Assn., Met. Washington Assn. Cytology (founding), Am. Mus. Natural History, Resident Assos. Smithsonian Inst. (sustaining). Democrat. Home: 238 Old Line Ave Laurel MD 20810 Office: Dept Pathology and Area Lab Services Walter Reed Army Med Center Washington DC 20012

CAMPBELL, NORMAN AMBROSE, pharm. educator; b. Pawtucket, R.I., Jan. 21, 1936; s. Norman Harper and Victoria Helen (Moussally) C.; B.S., R.I. Coll. Pharmacy, 1957; M.B.A., U. Wis., 1961, Ph.D., 1972; J.D., New Eng. Sch. Law, 1968; m. Mary Hodde, Sept. 7, 1957; children—Debra Mary, Linda Ann, Michael Joseph. From instr. to asso. prof. Mass. Coll. Pharmacy, 1961-69; vis. asso. prof. pharmacy adminstrn., asst. to provost for health sci. affairs U. R.I., 1970-71, asso. prof. pharmacy adminstrn., 1971-76, prof., 1976—, chmn. dept., 1971—; admitted to Mass. bar, 1969. Mem. town meeting, Needham, Mass., 1966-69. Bd. dirs. South County div. Am. Cancer Soc., 1971—. Recipient Squibb Pres.'s award, 1976, A.H. Robins Bowl of Hygeia award, 1977. Fellow Am. Found. Pharm. Edn., 1969-70; recipient award Pharm. Mfrs. Assn., 1969-70. Registered pharmacist, R.I., Wis., Mass. Mem. Am., R.I. (pres. 1975-76) pharm. assns., Am. Mktg. Assn., Am. Bar Assn., Am. Assn. Colls. Pharmacy (dir. 1976-78), AAUP, Am. Soc. Pharmacy Law (nat. steering com. 1974-76), Kappa Psi (historian 1965-67, grand regent 1972-74). Clubs: Narragansett Lions (dir. R.I. Lions Sight Found. 1976—), K.C. (3 deg.). Home: 15 Avice St Narragansett RI 02882 Office: Coll Pharmacy Univ RI Kingston RI 02881

CAMPBELL, OLIVER ALOYSIUS, dentist; b. Jersey City, June 21, 1927; s. Oliver Aloysius and Kay (Deevy) C.; B.S., Fordham U., 1950; D.D.S., Georgetown U., 1956; m. Monika Conrad, Aug. 21, 1965; children—Christopher, Jennifer, Julienne. Intern, Guggenheim Dental Clinic, N.Y.C., 1957; practice dentistry specializing in pedodontics, Plainfield, N.J., 1959—; attending dentist Matheny Sch. for Cerebral Palsy, Peapack, N.J., Children's Specialized Hosp., Westfield, N.J.; cons. children's dentistry All Soul's Hosp., Morristown, N.J., Muhlenberg Hosp., Plainfield; clin. instr. in pedodontics Seton Hall Dental Sch., 1958-64; instr. in pedodontics Fairleigh-Dickinson Dental Sch., 1969-77, clin. asst. prof., 1977—. Pres., Martinsville (N.J.) Rescue Squad, 1975-77. Served to cpl. M.C., AUS, 1950-52. Fellow N.Y. Acad. Dentistry, Am. Coll. Dentists; mem. Am. Acad. for Cerebral Palsy, Acad. Dentistry for Handicapped, Am. Acad. Pedodontists, Am., N.J. dental assns., Plainfield Dental Soc., Nat. Registry Emergency Med. Technicians, Psi Omega. Contbr. articles to profl. jours. Home: 2221 Brookside Dr Martinsville NJ 08836

CAMPBELL, RAYMOND ELLSWORTH, med. adminstr.; b. Boston, Jan. 15, 1934; s. Arthur Hulock and Ruby Maude (LaRaque) C.; degree in Radiology Adminstrn., Northeastern l)., 1963; m. Patience Webster, Aug. 14, 1965; 1 dau., Susan Lee. Emergency technician Harvard U. Health Service, Cambridge, 1960-65; coordinator tech. sch., asst. chief technologist Mass. Gen. Hosp., Boston, 1962-65; asst. dir. sch., chief technologist radiology Monmouth Med. Center, Long Branch, N.J., 1965-70, adminstrv. asst. radiology, 1970—. Advisor Bd. Health City of Long Branch, 1972-77; mem. juvenile conf., Long Branch, 1972—; trustee Long Branch Pub. Library Bd., 1978. Served with U.S. Army, 1954-56. Mem. Internat. Phantom Soc., Am. Hosp. Radiology Adminstrs. (charter mem., pres. N. Atlantic region 1976-77, chmn. fin. com. nat. 1977-78), N.J. (chmn. pub. relations 1968-69), Am., Mid-Eastern socs. radiologic technologists (chmn. edn. 1967-68). License examiner N.J. Dept. Environ. Health, 1968-70; sch. insp. radiology schs. N.J. Bd. Environ. Health, 1970—. Home: 8 Chelton Way Long Branch NJ 07740 Office: 300 Second Ave Long Branch NJ 07740

CAMPBELL, ROBERT DUFF, pub. co. exec.; b. Billings, Mont., Dec. 19, 1917; s. Robert James and Mary Truman (Duff) C.; ed. Northwestern U., 1939; grad. Advanced Mgmt. Program, Harvard U., 1969; m. Julia Briggs, Dec. 8, 1951; children—Julia Clay, William Duff. Vice pres. Champion Textile Co., Chgo., 1945-47; advt. salesman Macfadden Publs., Los Angeles, 1947-48; with Newsweek mag., 1949—, mng. dir. internat. edits., 1967-69, exec. v.p., 1969-72, pub., 1972—, pres., chmn. bd., 1976—; dir. Washington Post Co., Sawyer Ferguson, Walker Co. Served to brig. gen. USAF, 1941-45, 51-52, 61-62. Decorated D.F.C., Air medal with clusters, Air Force medal. Mem. Com. on Econ. Devel., Conf. Bd., Fgn. Policy Assn., NAM, N.Y. Bd. Trade, Mag. Pubs Assn., Pacific Basin Econ. Council, Council Fgn. Relations. Presbyterian. Clubs: Chicago; Economic of N.Y., Marco Polo (N.Y.C.); Fairfield (Conn.) Country; Internat. (Washington); Bob O'Link Golf. Office: Newsweek Mag Newsweek Bldg 444 Madison Ave New York NY 10022*

CAMPBELL, ROY KENNEDY, planning exec.; b. Chester, Pa., Aug. 31, 1929; s. John and Mary (Yuile) C.; student Columbia, 1954-64; m. Ana Rivero, Sept. 29, 1956; children—Lisa Anne, Patricia Alice. Account exec. Dun & Bradstreet, N.Y.C., 1957-66, v.p. planning and devel., 1975—; asst. dir. mktg. Am. Bankers Assn., N.Y.C., 1966-68; v.p. mktg. research Mfrs. Hanover Trust Co., N.Y.C., 1968-75. Served with USN, 1950-54. Mem. Bank Mktg. Assn. (dir. 1972-75), Info. Industry Assn. (sec. and dir. 1978—), Am. Mktg. Assn., Nat. Rifle Assn. (life), Assn. for Computing Machinery. Home: 31 Sagamore Rd Bronxville NY 10708 Office: 99 Church St New York City NY 10007

CAMPBELL, THOMAS CURTIS, physician; b. Boston, Feb. 23, 1947; s. Curtis and Eunice Gould (Murray) C.; A.B., Harvard Coll., 1969, M.D., 1973; m. Rosemary Loring, Sept. 26, 1970; children—William Caleb, Suzanne Bailey. Intern, New Eng. Deaconess Hosp., Boston, 1973-74, resident, 1974-76, pulmonary fellow NEDH, 1976-77; practice medicine specializing in internal and pulmonary medicine, Boston, 1977—; mem. staff New Eng. Deaconess Hosp. Diplomate Am. Bd. Internal Medicine. Mem. A.C.P. Episcopalian. Home: 100 Edgewater Dr Needham MA 02192 Office: 110 Franics St Suite 9D Boston MA 02215

CAMPEL, ROBERT J., hosp. adminstr.; b. Perth Amboy, N.J., Mar. 22, 1938; s. John and Josephine C.; A.B. in Econs., Rutgers U., 1961; M.P.A. in Health, N.Y. U., 1979; m. Joan Notaro, July 6, 1963. Claims rep. Liberty Mut. Ins. Co., Boston, 1964-66; exec. dir. Middlesex County (N.J.) chpt. Am. Cancer Soc., 1966-68; mgmt. engr. Brooks Internat., Westwood, N.J., 1968-69, United Research Co., Woodcliff Lake, N.J., 1969-71; asso. project dir. Kings County Hosp. Center, Bklyn., 1971—; preceptor, guest lectr., curriculum adv. com. Downstate Med. Center, State U. N.Y. Served with U.S. Army, 1961-63. Mem. Am. Hosp. Assn., Hosp. Mgmt. Systems Soc., Am. Acad. Health Adminstrn., Am. Pub. Health Assn. Club: Jaycees Internat. (senator). Office: 451 Clarkson Ave Brooklyn NY 11203

CAMPO, IVON NORBERTO, physician; b. Rafaela, Argentina, Oct. 10, 1939; s. Francisco Luis and Elida (Martini) C.; came to U.S., 1964, naturalized, 1973; B.S., Nat. Coll. Rafaela (Argentina), 1956; M.D., Nat. U., Cordoba, Argentina, 1963, Doctor in Medicine and Surgery, 1972; m. Lidia M. Cassina, Nov. 13, 1965; children—Peggy Ann, Carla Patricia, Adrian Norberto. Intern, Meml. Hosp., Pawtucket, R.I., 1964; jr. asst. resident in internal medicine Boston U., 1965; sr. asst. resident Boston City Hosp., 1967-68; resident in internal medicine, Bronx VA Hosp., 1968-69; resident cardiology Montefiore Hosp. and Med. Center, Bronx, 1969-70, chief resident, 1970-71, adj. attending in medicine and cardiology, 1971—; active cons. attending Prospect Hosp., Bronx, 1971—; practice medicine specializing in internal medicine and cardiology, Bronx, 1971—; clin. instr. medicine Albert Einstein Coll. Medicine, 1973—; mem. med. bd. Prospect Hosp., Bronx, 1978—. Served to capt. USAR, 1965-67. Diplomate Am. Bd. Internal Medicine, Am. Bd. Cardiology, Am. Bd. Utilization Rev. and Quality Assurance. Fellow Am. Coll. Cardiology; mem. Am. Med. Assn., N.Y. State, Bronx County med. socs., Am. Coll. Utilization Rev. Physicians, Alpha Beta Chi. Roman Catholic. Club: YM-YWHA. Contbr. articles to med. jours.

CAMPSEN, HERMAN (MARTIN), JR., ret. educator; b. N.Y.C., Sept. 6, 1900; s. Herman Martin and Mary (Meyer) C.; A.B., Columbia, 1922, A.M., 1923; postgrad. Tchrs. Coll., Columbia, City Coll., N.Y. U., U. London; m. Anna Hoppe, 1930; 1 dau., Anne-Marie (Mrs. Tietjen); tchr. gen. sci. Jefferson Jr. High Sch., Meriden, Conn., 1924-26; tchr. chemistry Bklyn. Tech. High Sch., N.Y.C., 1926-30; tchr. chemistry and physics DeWitt Clinton High Sch., N.Y.C., 1930-38; founder, chmn. dept. phys. sci. Bronx High Sch. Sci., N.Y.C., 1938-67; ret. sci. edn. cons. Dir. war courses N.Y.C. High Schs., World War II; cons. NASA Service Series; cons. to War Dept., U.S. Office Edn. on secondary Sch. Pre-Induction Courses, Am. Soc. for Metals, Am. Petroleum Inst., Ford Found., Conant Commn.; past chmn. Sci. Textbook Appraisal com. for N.Y.C. Bd. Edn.; organizer, cons. N.Y.C. Sci. Fairs; historian, North Congl. Ch., Woodbury, Conn.; past pres. Heritage Village Condominium Bd. Dirs., 1977; alt. mem. Heritage Village Bd. Trustees, 1978. Served with AUS, 1918. Mem. Am. Chem. Soc. (cited for outstanding contbns. to chemistry N.Y. Sect. 1958), AAAS, Frat. Emile, Chemistry Tchrs. Club N.Y. (past pres., Foster award 1963), Phys. Sci. Chmns. Assn. (past pres.), N.Y.C. Physics Club. Club: Masons. Co-Author: Fundamentals of Automotive Mechanics, 1942; Physics in the High School; contbr. ednl. articles. Home: 122B Heritage Village Southbury CT 06488

CAMUTI, LOUIS J., veterinarian; b. Italy, Aug. 30, 1893; s. Gaspare and Corinne (Pomarelli) C.; B.S., Cornell U., 1916; D.V.S., N.Y. U., 1920; m. Alessandra V. Landi, 1920; children—Nina Camuti Danielson, Louis J. (dec.). Practice veterinary medicine, N.Y.C., 1921—, specializing in feline medicine, 1932—; insp.-in-charge poultry N.Y.C. Dept. Health, 1923-24; founder, supr. live poultry inspection N.Y. Poultry Commn. Mchts. Assn., 1924-26, exec. sec., 1926-27; pres., sec.-treas. Dexter Poultry Co., 1927-32; mem. Senator R. Copeland's staff for preparation Fed. Food and Drug Act, 1932-38; pres. Research Consultants, Inc., 1939-67; Served 2d lt., lt. U.S. Army, World War I, capt. Vet. Corps. N.Y. N.G., 1921-1940. Mem. AVMA, N.Y. Soc. Mil. and Naval Officers of World Wars. Author: Park Avenue Vet, 1962 (transl. into German); contbr. numerous articles to various publs., also column to Feline Practice mag., 1971—. Address: 249 E Devonia Ave Mount Vernon NY 10552

CANCRO, RALPH, clin. psychologist, educator; b. N.Y.C., June 28, 1928; s. Joseph and Marie Elena (Cicchetti) C.; B.S., Columbia, 1951, M.A., 1953, Ph.D., 1963; m. Marcella Rosignoli, Aug. 9, 1952; children—Lawrence, Barbara, Susan, Lorraine. Clin. psychologist Burke Rehab. Center, White Plains, N.Y., 1953-56, dir. psychol. and vocational services, 1956—, asso. dir., mental hygiene services, 1958—; asso. prof. psychology, Marymount Coll., Tarrytown, N.Y., 1967-73, prof., 1973—, dir. counselling center, 1968—; instr., dept. phys. medicine and rehab., State U. N.Y. Sch. Medicine at Bklyn., 1963-67. Served with USAAF, 1946-47. N.Y. State Vets. scholarship N.Y. State Regents, 1952-55. Mem. Am., Westchester psychol. assns., Nat. Honor Soc. in Psychology, State Assn. Rehab. Facilities (sec.-treas. 1962-64, pres. 1965-66), Psi Chi. Home: 64 Archer Dr Bronxville NY 10708 Office: 5 Old Mamaroneck Rd White Plains NY 10605

CANDEE, EDWARD DEFOREST, pub. relations co. exec.; b. N.Y.C., May 14, 1915; s. Hamilton and Gertrude (Sayler) C.; B.A., Princeton U., 1937; m. Anita Simms Jones, Feb. 12, 1941; children—Barbara Candee McCarthy, Joan Candee Collins, Virginia, Catherine, Hamilton, Paul. Securities salesman Smith, Barney & Co., N.Y.C., 1937-41; spl. asst. to chmn. War Prodn. Bd., Washington, 1941-45; asst. dir. pub. relations Gen. Outdoor Advt. Co., Washington, 1946-50; dep. exec. sec. Office Def. Moblzn., Washington, 1951-52; v.p. Fred Smith Pub. Relations, N.Y.C., 1953-54, Walker & Crenshaw, N.Y.C., 1954-57; dir. advt. and pub. relations Cyanamid Internat. div. Am. Cyanamid Co., Wayne, N.J., 1957-68, mgr. communications and pub. affairs Am. Cyanamid Co., 1968-75, dir. internat. pub. affairs, 1975—; lectr. in field. Mem. Internat. Pub. Relations Assn., Internat. Advt. Assn. (dir. 1962-66). Home: 150 Heights Rd Ridgewood NJ 07450 Office: 859 Berdan Ave Wayne NJ 07470

CANDER, LEON, physician, med. sch. adminstr.; b. Phila., Oct. 7, 1926; s. Joseph Harry and Anna (Glick) C.; M.D., Temple U., 1951; m. Geraldine Piontkowski, Dec. 11, 1954; children—Alan Drew, Harris Scott. Research fellow in physiology Grad. Sch. Medicine U. Pa., 1952-56; resident in medicine Beth Israel Hosp., Boston, 1956-58; asst. in medicine Harvard U. Med. Sch., 1957-58; practice medicine specializing in internal medicine, Boston, Phila. and San Antonio, 1958—; sr. instr. medicine Tufts U. Med. Sch., Boston, 1958-60; asst. prof. medicine Hahnemann Med. Coll., Phila., 1960-63, asso. prof., 1963-66; prof. and chmn. dept. physiology and medicine U. Tex. Med. Sch., San Antonio, 1966-72; chmn. dept. medicine, dir. med. edn. Daroff Div. Albert Einstein Med. Center, Phila., 1972—; prof. medicine Jefferson Med. Coll., Phila., 1972—; mem. nat. adv. council on black lung. Research fellow Nat. Acad. Scis., 1954-55. Fellow Am. Coll. Physicians; mem. Am. Thoracic Soc., Am. Physiol. Soc. Editor: (with J.H. Moyer) Aging of the Lung, 1963. Home: 317 Cherry Ln Wynnewood PA 19096 Office: 1429 S 5th St Philadelphia PA 19147

CANESTRARI, CHARLES JOSEPH, govt. ofcl.; b. Cohoes, N.Y., Oct. 26, 1916; s. Emmanuel and Raffaella (Massi) C.; student pub. schs.; m. Anne Pusatere, Apr. 16, 1939; children—Charles, Carol (Mrs. George Durant). With Montgomery Ward & Co., 1939-40; with Watervliet (N.Y.) Arsenal, 1940—. Served with USNR, 1935-39, 44-46; PTO, ETO. Mem. Cohoes Hist. Soc. (trustee). Address: Van Schaick Mansion Cohoes NY 12047

CANFIELD, JACK, ednl. adminstr.; b. Fort Worth, Aug. 19, 1944; s. Elmer Elwyn Canfield and Ellen (Taylor) Canfield Angelis; B.A., Harvard U., 1966; M.Ed., U. Mass., 1973; m. Judy Sue Ohlbaum, July 1, 1973 (div. Nov. 1977); children—Oran David, Kyle Danla; m. 2d, Georgia Lee Noble, Sept. 9, 1978. Dir. Tchr. Tng. Program, Job Corps Center, Clinton, Iowa, 1968-69; asso. dir. achievement motivation programs W. Clement and J.V. Stone Found., Chgo., 1969-70, edn. programs Combined Motivation Edn. Systems, Chgo., 1970; founder, dir. New Eng. Center, Amherst, Mass., 1971-77; dir. Inst. Wholistic Edn., Amherst, 1976—; co-dir. Center for Whole Being, Amherst, 1977—; bd. advisers Nat. Humanistic Edn. Center, Ky. Center for Psychosynthesis, Kopp Center Continuing Edn.; Cons. numerous sch. systems; instr. U. Mass., 1977—; pvt. practice gestalt therapy; field faculty Humanistic Psychology Inst.; program adviser Campus Free Coll. Recipient Certificate of Appreciation, U.S. Job Corps, 1969. Mem. Planetary Citizens, Assn. Humanistic Edn. (pres. 1978-79), Assn. Humanistic Psychology, Assn. Transpersonal Psychology, Transpersonal Edn. Network, Am. Assn. Study Mental Imagery, Internat. Transactional Analysis Assn., Transpersonal Edn. Network, Mich. Assn. Affective Edn., Confluent Edn. Devel. and Research Center, Nat. Assn. Humanistic Gerontology. Author: About Me, 1970; (with Harold Wells) 100 Ways to Enhance Self-Concept in the Classroom, 1976. Editor: Wholistic Education: Jour. Humanistic and Transpersonal Edn., 1976—; (with others) Yearbook in Humanistic and Transpersonal Edn., 1977; edn. editor New Age Jour., 1977—. Home and office: Box 575 Amherst MA 01002

CANN, WILLIAM FRANCIS, judge; b. Somerville, Mass., Oct. 10, 1922; s. William Arthur and Frances (Hardy) C.; student Tufts U., 1940-42; LL.B., Boston U., 1948; grad. Nat. Coll. State Judiciary, Reno, 1972; m. Ellen Catherine Hughes Watts, Sept. 6, 1958; stepchildren—Ellen (Mrs. Dale H. Lockhart), Allan Craig Watts. Admitted to Mass. bar, 1948, N.H. bar, 1959; sr. claim examiner Am. Mut. Liability Ins. Co., Wakefield, Mass., 1948-60; law asst. Office of Atty. Gen., State of N.H., Concord, 1960-61, asst. atty. gen., 1961-67, dep. atty. gen., 1967-71; asso. justice N.H. Superior Ct., 1971—. Mem. adv. bd. Community Corrections Center of N.H. State Prison, Franklin Pierce Law Center, Civic Intern Program. Served with USAAF, 1942-45. Mem. Am., N.H., Merrimac County bar assns., Am. Judicature Soc. Home and Office: 36 Roger Ave Concord NH 03301

CANNAVO, JOSEPH JACK, indsl. nurse; b. Buffalo, Dec. 26, 1921; s. Jack and Rose (Aveni) C.; R.N., Westchester Sch. Nursing at Valhalla, N.Y., 1943; R.T., E.J. Meyer Meml. Hosp. Sch. X-Ray Technology, Buffalo, 1949; certificate Rutgers U. Sch. Alcohol Studies, 1963; certificate in supervisory tng. Nat. Safety Council, 1964; m. Ida S. Catalino, Sept. 6, 1952; children—Thomas Jack, Joanne Marie. Psychiat. head nurse Grasslands Hosp., Valhalla, N.Y., 1943-44; indsl. nurse Bell Aircraft Corp., Buffalo and Niagara Falls, N.Y., 1944-45; pvt. duty nurse Emergency Hosp., Buffalo, 1945-46; nurse operating room VA Hosp., Buffalo, 1950-53; supr. med. services Bond plant Hydronics div. Am.-Standard, Inc., Buffalo, 1946-49, 53-63, supr. safety and med. services, 1963-75; safety engr. J.H. Williams div. TRW, Buffalo, 1975, supr. safety and health, 1976—; mem. profl. nurses resource com. D'Youville Coll., Buffalo, 1974—. Bd. dirs., pres. Western N.Y. Safety Conf.; bd. dirs. Western N.Y. Com. for Edn. on Alcoholism; exec. com. Buffalo and Erie County Community Welfare Alcoholism Council. Certified safety profl. Bd. Certified Safety Profls. Ams.; certified occupational health nurse Am. Bd. Certified Occupational Health Nurses. Mem. Buffalo Area C. of C. (chmn. safety com.), N.Y., Western N.Y. assns. indsl. nurses, Am. Soc. Safety Engrs. (pres. Niagara Frontier chpt.). Author profl. articles. Home: 154 Washington Ave Kenmore NY 14217

CANNELLA, JOHN MATTHEW, fed. judge; b. N.Y.C., Feb. 8, 1908; s. Joseph and Laura (Gullo) C.; B.S., Fordham U., 1930, LL.B., 1933; m. Ida Rutnik, Dec. 26, 1938; children—Lauretta Cannella Kushay, Christine Cannella Phelan, John Matthew. Admitted to N.Y. State bar, 1934, practice in N.Y.C., 1934-40; asso. U.S. atty., 1940-42; commnr. Water Supply Gas and Electricity, N.Y.C., 1946-48, Dept. Licenses, 1948-49; mem. N.Y.C. Ct. Spl. Sessions, 1949-59, N.Y.C. Co. Gen. Sessions, 1957-58, N.Y.C. City Ct., 1959-61, N.Y.C. Criminal Ct., 1963; U.S. judge So. Dist. N.Y., N.Y.C., 1963—. Mem. Cath. Lawyers Guild, Fed. Bar Assn., Columbian Lawyers Assn. Served with USCGR, 1942-45. Office: US Dist Courthouse Foley Sq New York City NY 10007

CANNON, DANIEL PAUL, nuclear engr., air force officer; b. Allentown, Pa., Dec. 21, 1934; s. James Peter and Helen Katherine (Briody) C.; B.S. in Chem. Engring. with honors, Lehigh U., 1956; M.S. in Nuclear Engring. with distinction, Air Force Inst. Tech., 1967; m. Anna Marie Appleby, Aug. 25, 1962; children—Michael J., Mark, Dawn Michelle. Commd. 2d lt. USAF, 1956, advanced through grades to col., 1978; duty in Greenland, Philippines, Vietnam and Thailand; chief spl. programs and air def. br., Thailand, 1969-70; nuclear research officer, then chief threat br., intelligence Hdqrs. SAC, 1970-74; chief strategic and nuclear research br., directorate of threat applications, asst. chief of staff Intelligence USAF, Pentagon, Washington, 1974-78; dep. asst. dir. planning Office Mil. Applications Dept. Energy, 1978—. Decorated Bronze Star, Air medal, Meritorious Service medal. Mem. Am. Nuclear Soc. (Outstanding Student Paper award 1966, 67), Tau Beta Pi. Republican. Roman Catholic. Home: 13801 Wisteria Dr Germantown MD 20767 Office: Dept Energy Mail Stop A-362 Washington DC 20545

CANNON, DAVID EVANS, program mgmt. specialist; b. Salt Lake City, June 25, 1930; s. Abrahm H. and Leone (Evans) C.; B.S. in Engring., U.S. Naval Acad., 1953; m. Jacqueline Murtha, June 14, 1953; children—John, Thomas, Deborah. Commd. ensign U.S. Navy, 1953, advanced through grades to lt. comdr., 1973; with Submarine Service, 1954-59, 61-66, dir. basic enlisted submarine sch., 1959-61, with strategic system project office, 1966-69; chief engr., tech. dir. naval plant rep. Gen. Electric Co., Pittsfield, Mass., 1969-73, ret., 1973; program mgmt. specialist Singer Co., Wayne, N.J., 1973—. Home: 42 Park Rd Sparta NJ 07871 Office: 150 Totowa Rd Wayne NJ 07470

CANNON, JOHN, investment adviser; b. Phila., Jan. 17, 1930; s. John F. and Anne (Carlin) C.; B.S., U. Pa., 1954; M.B.A., Drexel Inst. Tech., 1956; m. Edythe Marple Grebe, Aug. 16, 1952; children—John III, Lynne, Anne. Financial analyst Bishop & Hedberg, Inc., Phila., 1956-58; rep. Stone & Webster Securities Corp., Phila., 1958-62; nat. sales mgr. municipal bond dept. Hallowell & Sulzberger, Phila., 1962-64; pres., dir. Cannon & Co., Inc., Flourtown, Pa., 1964—, PRO Fund, Inc., Flourtown, 1967-71, 75—, Pro Income Fund Inc., 1975—; v.p. Janney, Montgomery, Scott, Inc., 1972-73. Served with USMCR, 1950-51. Mem. Financial Analysts Am., Nat. Found. Health, Welfare and Pension Plans, Phila. Securities Assn. Republican. Episcopalian. Mason. Club: Manufacturer's Golf and Country (Oreland, Pa.). Home: 531 Willow Ave Ambler PA 19002 Office: 1107 Bethlehem Pike Flourtown PA 19031

CANNY, J. FRANCIS, psychologist, exec.; b. Norwich, N.Y., Feb. 20, 1913; s. Anthony Joseph and Bridgit (Redden) C.; B.A. in Psychology, U. Rochester, 1935; M.A. in Personnel Adminstrn., Columbia, 1946; student Wharton Sch. Finance and Commerce, 1935-36; m. Helen Jane Stofer, Apr. 20, 1940; 1 son, Christopher Richard. Sect. mgr. R. H. Macy & Co., Inc., 1936-38; salesman Eastman Kodak Stores, Inc., 1938-41; instr., vocat. counselor Bklyn. Poly. Inst., 1946-48; asst. to v.p. for personnel R. H. Macy and Co., 1948-52; dir. personnel adminstrn. McKinsey and Co., 1952-54; chmn. bd. Canny, Bowen, Inc., 1954-77; v.p., dir. Golightly & Co. Internat., N.Y.C., 1978—. Bd. dirs. Westchester United Fund, 1963-64, Community Fund, Bronxville, 1957-59, Westchester Co. Council Social Agys., 1969-64, Graham-Windham Child Care, 1968—, Parish Counseling Centers, Inc., 1971-73. Served to lt. comdr. USNR, 1941-45. Mem. Am., N.Y. State psychol. assns., Assn. Exec. Recruiting Cons. (pres. 1959-61). Episcopalian (vestryman 1965-73). Clubs: Wharton (dir.); Columbia University (gov. 1956-60); Cloud (gov. 1964-71). Home: 45 Sutton Pl S New York City NY 10022 Office: 1 Rockefeller Plaza New York City NY 10020

CANTILLI, EDMUND JOSEPH, engr., planner, educator; b. Yonkers, N.Y., Feb. 12, 1927; s. Ettore and Maria (deRubeis) C.; A.B., Columbia, 1954, B.S., 1955; certificate Yale Bur. Hwy. Traffic, 1957; Ph.D. in Transp. Planning, Poly. Inst. Bklyn., 1972; m. Nella Franco, May 15, 1948; children—Robert, John, Teresa. Traffic engr. Port of N.Y. Authority, N.Y.C., 1955-69, project planner, 1958-60, terminals analyst, 1960-62, engr. traffic safety research and studies, 1962-67, supervising traffic engr., 1967-69; research asso. div. transp. planning Poly. Inst. Bklyn., 1969-72, asso. prof. transp. planning, 1972-74; asso. prof. transp. planning Poly. Inst. N.Y., 1974-77, prof., 1977—; tchr. Italian, algebra, traffic engring., urban planning, urban and transp. geography, land use planning, aesthetics, environment, safety, 1965—; pres. Urbitran Assos., 1973—; cons. community planning, traffic engring., transp. planning, transp. safety, environ. impacts, 1969—; pres., chmn. bd. Inst. for Safety in Transp., Inc., 1977—. Served with AUS, 1945-49, 50-51. Fellow ASCE, Inst. Traffic Engrs.; mem. Am. Soc. Planning Ofcls., Am. Inst. Planners, Am. Soc. Safety Engrs., Mensa, Sigma Xi. Author: Programming Environmental Improvements in Public Transportation, 1974; Transportation and the Disadvantaged, 1974. Editor: Transportation and Aging, 1971; Pedestrian Planning and Design, 1971; Traffic Engineering Theory and Control, 1973; editor and calligrapher There Is No Death That Is Not Enobled By So Great a Cause, 1976. Contbr. articles to profl. jours. Home: 134 Euston Rd S West Hempstead LI NY 11552 Office: Poly Inst NY 333 Jay St Brooklyn NY 11201 also Urbitran Assos 101 Park Ave New York City NY 10017

CANTON, STEVE, govt. ofcl.; b. N.Y.C., Jan. 30, 1915; s. Ciro and Rose (Di Vita) C.; student pub. schs.; m. Ruth Pearl, Sept. 28, 1939; children—R. Marcia, Steven J., Amy B., Maryann F. and Christopher C. (twins). Free-lance writer, N.Y.C., 1936-42; pub. relations rep. Air and Rail Express divs. Ry. Express Agy., N.Y.C., 1942-52, dir. publs., N.Y.C., 1952-59; editor Babcock & Wilcox, N.Y.C., 1959-62; editor Air Force Civil Engineer, U.S. Air Force, Dayton, Ohio, 1962-66, editor Air Force Comptroller, and spl. asst. to comptroller of Air Force, The Pentagon, Washington, 1966—; cons. Armed Forces mag. Am. Soc. Mil. Comptrollers, 1976—. Served with AUS, 1944-45. Mem. House Mag. Inst., Internat. Council Indsl. Editors, Am. Ry. Mag. Editors Assn. (treas. 1958-59), Fed. Editors Assn. Republican. Roman Catholic. Club: Pinecrest Golf. Patentee device to draw precision stars, pentagons, circles, etc. Home: 5503 Flag Run Dr North Springfield VA 22151 Office: The Pentagon Washington DC 20330

CANTOR, ALFRED J(OSEPH), physician; b. Syracuse, N.Y., Mar. 14, 1913; s. Abraham B. and Fannie (Sirlin) C.; B.A. magna cum laude, Syracuse U., 1933, M.D. magna cum laude, 1936; m. Eleanor Weschler, June 9, 1938; children—Pamela C., Alfred J. Intern, Lenox Hill Hosp., 1937-38; pvt. practice, 1939—; cons. surgeon proctology Jersey City Med. Center; dir. research in proctology Intestinal Research Inst. Dir. UNITROL Teaching Inst. Pres. governing regents Internat. Bd. Proctology. Diplomate Internat. Bd. Applied Nutrition. Hon. fellow Internat. Coll. Applied Nutrition; fellow Am. Med. Writers' Assn., Internat. Acad. Proctology (founding pres., sec.); mem. Acad. Psychosomatic Medicine (founder, treas., pres. emeritus), Phi Beta Kappa, Phi Kappa Phi, Alpha Omega Alpha. Author: Ambulatory Proctology, 1942; Cancer Can Be Cured, 1949; A Handbook of Psychosomatic Medicine, 1951; Painless Rectal Surgery, 1951; Immortality, 1958; How to Lose Weight The Doctor's Way, 1959; Control of Constipation, 1962; Dr. Cantor's Longevity Diet, 1964; Unitrol, 1964; Ridding Yourself of Psychosomatic Health Wreckers, 1965; Doctor Cantor's Longevity Program, 1966; How To Turn On The Power of Your Mind, 1973-74; Dr. Cantor's Revitalization Diet, 1978; also articles on proctology. Editor in chief: Am. Jour. Proctology, 1950—. Home: 96 Wildwood Rd PO Box L Kings Point Great Neck NY 11023

CANTOR, ELI, writer, typographic co. exec., mgmt. cons.; b. N.Y.C., Sept. 9, 1913; s. Sol M. and Bertha (Seidler) C.; B.S., N.Y. U., 1934, M.A. (Ogden Butler fellow in Philosophy), 1935; J.D., Harvard, 1938; m. Beatrice Mink, Oct. 4, 1942; children—Ann, Fred. Of counsel CBS, N.Y.C., 1939; mem. editorial staff Esquire, Coronet mags., Chgo., 1940-41; editor-in-chief Research Inst. Report, Research Inst. Am., Inc., N.Y.C., 1951-61; pres. The Photo-Composing Room, Inc., N.Y.C., 1961-65; chmn. bd. The Composing Room, Inc., 1965-71, chmn. emeritus, 1971—; chmn. bd. Printing Industries Met. N.Y., 1971-73; chmn. Printing Industries Am., 1973-74; mem. printing and journalism advisory commns. Bd. Edn., N.Y.C., 1972—; chmn. exec. com. Advt. Typography Assn., N.Y., 1967-70; chmn. research-tech. com. Graphic Arts Tech. Found., 1971-76; cons. fed. graphics Nat. Endowment Arts, 1975—; industry rep. before Congress. Pres. Columbian Hook and Ladder Co., Croton Fire Dept., 1951; trustee Croton Free Library. Named to O'Brien Roll of Honor, Yaddo; Menninger Found. fellow, 1978—. Club: Harvard of N.Y. (trustee). Author numerous short stories, articles, poems for popular publs., TV plays NBC. Author: (plays) Candy Store, 1948, The Golden Goblet, 1959; (novels) Baron of Darkness, Enemy in the Mirror, Love Letters. Lectr. and educator in fields of econs., bus., graphic arts. Home: 15 W 81st St New York City NY 10024 Office: 15 W 81st St New York City NY 10024

CANTU, ROBERT CLARK, surgeon; b. Santa Rosa, Calif., Aug. 31, 1938; s. Robert L. and Frances (Clark) C.; A.B., U. Calif., 1960, M.A., 1962; M.D., U. Calif., San Francisco, 1963; m. Jane Quale, Aug. 6, 1964; children—Robbie, Kelley. Intern in surgery Presbyn. Hosp., N.Y.C., 1963-64; asst. resident in neurosurgery Mass. Gen. Hosp., Boston, 1964; research fellow in physiology Harvard Med. Sch., Cambridge, 1964-67, teaching fellow in surgery, 1967-68; chief resident in neurosurgery Boston City Hosp., 1967; practice medicine specializing in neurosurgery, Boston and Concord, Mass., 1968—; clin. asst. in neurosurgery Mass. Gen. Hosp., 1967-68, clin. and research fellow in neurosurgery, 1968, clin. asso. in neurosurgery, 1968—; asst. in surgery Harvard Med. Sch., 1968-69, instr. surgery, 1969; acting asst. dir. neurosurgery Boston City Hosp., 1968-70, dir. pediatric neurosurgery, 1968-70; chief neurosurg. service Emerson Hosp., Concord, Mass., 1969—; neurosurg. cons. to Nashoba Community Hosp., Ayer, Mass., 1970—. Recipient Borden Research award, 1963; diplomate Am. Bd. Neurology and Surgery. Mem. A.C.S., Am. Fedn. Clin. Research, Am. Assn. of Neurol. Surgeons, AMA, Am. Soc. for Pharmacology and Exptl. Biology, Soc. of Neurosci., Internat. Soc. for Pediatric Neurosurgery, Mass. Med. Soc., Am. Physiology Soc., Microcirculatory Soc., Soc. of Mil. Surgeons, Am. Coll. of Angiology, Am. Heart Assn., New Eng. Neurosurg. Soc., AAAS, Presbyn. Hosp. Alumni Assn., Calif. Med. Alumni Soc., Congress of Neurol. Surgeons, Am. Assn. for the History of Medicine. Author: Ventriculocisternostomy, 1970; contbr. numerous articles to profl. jours. Home: Great Meadows Farm Concord MA 01742 Office: John Cuming Bldg Concord MA 01742

CAPALBO, ROBERT FRANK, univ. adminstr.; b. Greenwich, Conn., May 21, 1940; s. Frank Alfonso and Mary Grace (Avantino) C.; A.B., Boston Coll., 1962, M.A., 1974. Instr. polit. sci. Regis Coll., Weston, Mass., 1964-65; instr. history Framingham (Mass.) State Coll., 1965-66; asst. prof. polit. and hist. studies Curry Coll., Milton, Mass., 1966-77, asst. dean students, 1967-70, dean men, 1970-73, dean student life, 1973-77; asst. dir. univ. housing Boston Coll., Chestnut Hill, Mass., 1977—. Named man of year Curry Coll., 1973. Mem. Boston Coll., St. Mary High Sch. (pres. 1958-62) alumni assns., Boston Assn. Coll. Housing Adminstrs., Nat. Assn. Student Personnel Adminstrs., Am. Coll. personnel and guidance assns., Am. Coll. and Univ. Housing Officers, Mass. Coll. Personnel Assn., Boston Assn. Coll. Housing Adminstrs. Address: Housing Office Boston Coll Chestnut Hill MA 02167

CAPASSO, EDWARD JOSEPH, environ. scientist; b. Newark, Sept. 18, 1945; s. Edward and Lillian (Jacheo) C.; B.A., Rutgers U., 1967; M.A. with honors, Montclair State Coll., 1978; m. Francine Vitale, Sept. 20, 1969. Bacteriologist, N.J. Dept. Health, Trenton, 1967; chemist Suburban Air Pollution Commn., West Orange, N.J., 1967-69; prin. envrion. specialist N.J. Dept. Environ. Protection, Trenton, 1969—; environ. cons. Mem. Hillside (N.J.) Bd. Edn., 1976—, fin. chmn., 1976, v.p., 1977, pres., 1978; bd. dirs. Union County (N.J.) Ednl. Services Commn., 1976—. Recipient certificate of award State N.J., 1977, Service award Rotary Club, 1978. Mem. Air Pollution Control Assn., N.J. Assn. Environ. Educators, N.J. Sch. Bds. Assn., ASTM, N.J. Edn. Assn., Rutgers Alumni Assn., Italian-Am. Assn., Phi Kappa Phi. Club: Republican. Home: 120 Woodruff Pl Hillside NJ 07205 Office: John Fitch Plaza PO Box 2807 Room 1108 Trenton NJ 08625

CAPELL, FRANK ALPHONSE, editor, publisher; b. N.Y.C., May 1, 1907; s. Anthony and Caroline (Brautigam) C.; student pub. schs., Army mil. intelligence courses; m. Adele Neighbour, July 9, 1948; children—Harold Joseph, James W., Francis J., William J., Ralph A., George L. Confidential investigator to police commrs. and dist. attys., 1930-38; chief investigator Westchester County (N.Y.) Sheriffs office, 1938-42; personnel and intelligence Douglas Aircraft Co., U.S. and Africa, 1942-43; personnel officer Sperry Gyroscope Co., Bklyn., 1943-44; personnel cons. Personnel Service Bur., Inc., N.Y.C., 1944-52; personnel counsellor Capell Employment Agy., S.I., N.Y., 1952-63; editor, pub. Herald of Freedom, Manville, N.J., 1963—. Cons. Cath. War Vets. State of N.J., 1966. Chmn. Richmond County Com. Juvenile Decency, 1955-63; pres. bd. dirs. S.I. chpt. Vols. Am., 1960-64; dir. S.I. Aid to Retarded Children, 1960-62; v.p. Citizens for Decent Lit., 1960-64; dir. Am. Edn. Council, 1962—. Kiwanian (past pres. and lt. gov.), Knight of Malta. Author: Freedom Is Up To You, 1963; The Threat From Within, 1963; The Strange Death of Marilyn Monroe, 1964; Treason Is The Reason, 1965; The Strange Case of Jacob Javits, 1966; Robert F. Kennedy: A Political Biography, 1968; The Untouchables, 1968; The Untouchables, Book II, 1969, Henry Kissinger—Soviet Agent, 1974. Contbg. editor Rev. of the News. Home: Box 16A School House Rd Somerset NJ 08873 Office: Box 3000 Manville NJ 08835

CAPELL, ROBERT GOODE, cons. chem. engr.; b. Defuniak Springs, Fla., Oct. 13, 1911; s. Robert Spratley and Ida (Stallworth) C.; B.S., Ga. Inst. Tech., 1935; M.S., Columbia, 1946; m. Margaret Elizabeth Yerg, Oct. 5, 1940; children—Margaret Capell Sadler, John, Peter. Vice pres., tech. dir., dir., Floridin Co., Warren, Pa., 1941-46; sr. fellow Mellon Inst. Indsl. Research, Pitts., 1946-61; dir. comml. devel. chem. dept. Gulf Oil Corp., Pitts., 1961-66, research asso., mem. research adv. com. Gulf Research & Devel. Co., Pitts., 1966-73; research analyst Internat. Research Tech., Arlington, Va., 1973-75; cons. chem. engr., Pitts., 1975—. Mem. bd. mgmt. local YMCA; active Boy Scouts Am. Registered profl. engr., Pa. Mem. Am. Chem. Soc., Am. Inst. Chem. Engrs., AAAS, Comml. Devel. Assn., Pitts. Chemists Club. Democrat. Methodist. Contbr. articles in field to profl. jours.; patentee in field. Home and office: 630 Olympia Rd Pittsburgh PA 15211

CAPELLA, RAFAEL F., physician; b. Colombia, Aug. 2, 1933; s. Pablo and Soledad (Fernandez) C.; M.D., Universidad Javeriana, Bogota, Colombia, 1958; m. Cecilia Lozano, May 3, 1958; children—Pablo, Gina, Joseph. Intern, Maryview Hosp., Portsmouth, Va., 1959-60; resident in surgery Jewish Hosp., Cin., 1960-64; practice medicine specializing in surgery, Tuxedo Park, N.Y., 1967; mem. staff Good Samaritan Hosp., Suffern, N.Y., 1968—; chief surgery Tuxedo Meml. Hosp., 1968—. Fellow A.C.S.; mem. AMA. Roman Catholic. Club: Tuxedo. Home: Laurel Rd Tuxedo Park NY 10987

CAPELLI, JOHN PLACIDO, nephrologist; b. Hammonton, N.J., May 23, 1936; s. John L. and Marie C.; B.S. in Biology, Villanova U., 1958; M.D., Jefferson Med. Coll., 1962; m. Patricia Ann Verna, Nov. 4, 1961; children—John L., Elizabeth Ann, David S. Intern, Michael Reese Hosp., Chgo., 1962-63; resident Thomas Jefferson U. Hosp., 1963-65, postdoctoral fellow in nephrology NIH, 1965-67, Martin E. Rehfuss chief resident internal medicine, 1967-68; practice medicine specializing in nephrology, 1968—; dir. div. clin. pharmacology Jefferson Med. Coll., Phila., 1968-69; dir. hemodialysis unit Our Lady of Lourdes Hosp., Camden, N.J., 1969—, dir. div. nephrology and transplantation, 1974—; asso. prof. medicine Thomas Jefferson U., Phila., 1974—; mem. chronic renal disease advisory com. N.J. State Dept. Health, 1969—, chmn., 1971-73, 74-75. Diplomate Am. Bd. Internal Medicine. Mem. Am. Soc. Nephrology, Internat Soc. Nephrology, Renal Physicians Assn. (pres. 1977—), AMA, Med. Soc. N.J., Am. Fedn. for Clin. Research, Am. Soc. Artificial Internal Organs, Southeastern Organ Procurement Found., Nat. Kindey Found. Roman Catholic. Discoverer hormone Renin also located in human uterus, 1968; contbr. articles in field to med. jours. Office: 35 Kings Hwy E Haddonfield NJ 08033

CAPER, SAMUEL PHILIP, physician, health adminstr.; b. Los Angeles, July 22, 1938; s. Gene Harold and Anabelle (Cohn) C.; A.B., UCLA, 1960, M.S., 1963, M.D., 1965; m. Jane Ann Carpenter, Aug. 19, 1973; children—Dana Victoria, Adam, Sara. Intern, Harvard Med. Unit, Boston City Hosp., 1965-66, asst. resident, 1966-67, chief resident, 1969-70; research asso. Nat. Cancer Inst., NIH, 1967-69; fellow Harvard Center for Community Health and Med. Care, Harvard U. Med. Sch. and Sch. Public Health, 1969-71; mem. prof. staff U.S. Senate Subcom. on Health, 1971-76; dep. chancellor U. Mass. Med. Sch., 1976—; mem. Nat. Council on Health Planning and Devel., HEW, 1977—; mem. Mass. Statewide Health Coordinating Council, 1977—. Served with USPHS, 1967-69. Recipient Richard H. Schlesinger award Am. Public Health Assn., 1975. Mem. Mass. Med. Soc., Worcester (Mass.) Dist. Med. Soc., Am. Health Planning Assn. (dir., chmn. subcom. on tech. and productivity), Alpha Omega Alpha. Club: U.S. Power Squadron. Author Senate report. Home: Laurel Dr Lincoln MA 01773 Office: U Mass Med Center 55 Lake Ave N Worcester MA 01605

CAPLAN, LESTER, optometrist; b. Balt., Mar. 27, 1924; s. Hyman and Jeannette (Frank) C.; student Wheaton (Ill.) Coll., 1943-44, U. Md., 1946-47; B.S. in Visual Optics, No. Ill. Coll. Optometry, Chgo., 1948, summa cum laude, O.D., 1949; M.Ed., Loyola Coll. Balt., 1967; m. Florence Shenker, Sept. 8, 1946; children—Bruce E., Eric Scott. Practice optometry, Balt., 1950—; chief of staff Contact Lens Clinic, Optometric Center Md., 1975-77; optometric cons., clinician Sinai-Druid Comprehensive Child Care Clinic, 1967-68; cons. to dir. Indian Health Service, USPHS, 1969—; adviser dir. profl. services Fed. Health Programs Services, 1972-73—, NIH Bur. Health Manpower, 1972, Nat. Health Service Corps, 1973-76; adv. council Md. Comprehensive Health Planning Agy., 1971-77, Md. Statewide Profl. Standard Rev. Council Advisory Group, 1978—; mem. profl. adv. com. Optometric Center Md., 1973-75, v.p. bd. dirs., 1975; mem. Md. Bd. Examiners in Optometry, 1975—; instr. adult edn. Balt. County Pub. Schs., 1968-69; vision cons. Prince Georges County Pub. Schs., 1968-70; instr., cons. Howard Community Coll., Columbia, Md., 1976—. Pres., Beth Israel Congregation, Randallstown, Md., 1966-67. Served with AUS, 1943-46; PTO. Mem. Am. (named Nat. Optometrist of Year 1975), Md. (Optometrist of Year 1974) optometric assns., Am. Pub. Health Assn., Am. Optometric Found., Nat. Eye Research Found., Am. Assn. Comprehensive Health Planning, Optometric Extension Program, Md. Optometric Assn., Md. Pub. Health Assn., Optometric Hist. Soc. Home: 1 Stonehenge Circle Baltimore MD 21208 Office: 6660 Security Blvd Baltimore MD 21207

CAPLAN, RONALD MERVYN, gynecologist, obstetrician; b. Montreal, Que., Can., Dec. 12, 1937; s. Philip and Betty (Gamer) C.; came to U.S., 1971; B.Sc., McGill U., Montreal, 1958, M.D., C.M., 1962; m. Marilyn Gail Amdur, Dec. 23, 1962; children—Randy Sue, Gordon. Resident, Royal Victoria Hosp., Montreal, 1963-67; instr. in obstetrics and gynecology McGill U., 1968-71; practice medicine specializing in obstetrics and gynecology, Montreal, 1968-71, N.Y.C., 1971—; mem. attending staff Royal Victoria Hosp., Montreal, 1968-71; asst. attending physician in obstetrics and gynecology N.Y. Hosp., N.Y.C., 1971—; clin. asst. prof. obstetrics and gynecology Cornell U. Med. Coll.; mem. med. advisory bd. Nat. Cancer Cytology Center, N.Y.C. Fellow A.C.S., Am. Coll. Obstetricians, Gynecologists, Royal Coll. Surgeons (Can.); mem. AMA, N.Y. Med. Soc., Que. Med. Assn., N.Y. Gynecol. Soc. Clubs: Fairview Country (Greenwich, Conn.); Griffis Faculty of Cornell U. Editor: (with William J. Sweeney, III) Advances in Obstetrics and Gynecology (Williams, Wilkins). 1978. Office: 460 E 63d St New York City NY 10021

CAPLIN, JERROLD LEON, health physicist; b. Phila., Jan. 25, 1930; s. Samuel Harry and Katherine C.; A.B., Temple U., 1951, postgrad., 1952-53; postgrad. (AEC fellow) Vanderbilt U., 1951-52. Supervisory health physicist U.S. Army C.E., Fort Belvoir, Va., 1959-61; health physicist AEC, U.S. Nuclear Regulatory Commn., Washington, 1961—. Served to lt. USNR, 1953-58. Mem. Am. Nat. Standards Inst., Health Physics Soc., Am. Conf. Gov. Indsl. Hygienists, (chmn. com. 1977—), Internat. Radiation Protection Assn., Am. Assn. Physics Tchrs., AAAS, U.S. Naval Inst., Am. Film Inst., Nat. Wildlife Fedn., Nat. Geog. Soc. Resident asso. Smithsonian Instn., 1970—. Home: 9 Goodport Ln Gaithersburg MD 20760 Office: Hdqrs US Nuclear Regulatory Commn Washington DC 20555

CAPO, LARRY GENE, educator; b. Pontiac, Mich., Oct. 30, 1948; s. Joseph Peter and Marion Louise (Gately) C.; B.A. (Univ. scholar), Central Mich. U., 1970, M.A. (Univ. scholar), 1971; postgrad. U. Mo., Columbia, 1971—. Art coordinator Mt. Pleasant (Mich.) Elementary Schs., 1969-71; instr. fine arts and theatre Rider Coll., 1974—, chmn. dept. fine arts, 1975—; vis. profl. lectr. Hun Sch., Princeton, N.J., 1975; ednl. cons. for external degrees Edison Coll., 1975—. Named Outstanding Theatre Student, Central Mich. U., 1968, Outstanding Grad. Teaching Asst. U. Mo., Columbia, 1973. Mem. Speech Communication Assn., Am. Theatre Assn., Central States, So. States speech assns., Alpha Psi Omega, Pi Kappa Delta. Democrat. Club: Order DeMolay. Prodns. directed include: Company, Cabaret, Ralph Roister Doister, Exit the King. Home: 44 Park Pl Princeton NJ 08540 Office: 2083 Lawrenceville Rd Lawrenceville NJ 08648

CAPOBRES, RUDOLFO M., JR., anesthesologist; b. Manila, Philippines, Jan. 9, 1938; s. Rudolfo S. and Alfreda M. (Mary) C.; M.D., Manila Central U., 1963. Resident in anesthesiology Albert Einstein Med. Center, Phila., 1965-67; fellow in pediatric anesthesiology Children's Hosp., Detroit, 1971-72; research asso., teaching fellow Wayne State U., Detroit, 1973; chief anesthesiologist Canonsburg (Pa.), 1974—; asso. anesthesiologist Pitts. Anesthesia Assos.; mem. staff Mercy Hosp., St. Clair Hosp., Central Med. Pavilion, St. Margaret's Hosp. Diplomate Am. Bd. Anesthesiology. Mem. AMA, Pa. State, Washington County med. socs., Pa., Western Pa. socs. anesthesiologists. Office: 1400 Locust St Pittsburgh PA 15219

CAPONE, DOM ANTHONY, guidance counselor; b. N.Y.C., Feb. 10, 1942; s. John Louis and Antoinette Margaret (Charchietta) C.; B.A. in History, Hunter Coll., 1963, M.A. in Social Studies, 1966; postgrad. degree Manhattan Coll., 1975; postgrad. in counseling psychology Fordham U.; m. Rosalie Maria Reda, June 11, 1967; 1 son, Don-Anthony. Tchr. French, Spanish and Italian, bilingual counselor Jr. High Sch. 55, Bronx, N.Y., 1963-64; tchr. French, Spanish and social studies DeWitt Clinton High Sch. Bronx, N.Y., 1964-74; tchr. fgn. langs., coll. adviser Harry S. Turman High Sch., Bronx, 1974-77; tchr. fgn. langs., bilingual counselor Evander Childs High Sch., Bronx, 1977—, also bilingual cons. to the prin.; mem. fng. lang. task force for preparation student tchr. curriculum Lehman Coll. of City U. N.Y., 1975-76. Mem. Columbia Assn. of Bd. of Edn., N.Y.C. Mem. Am. Personnel and Guidance Assn., N.Y. State Tchrs. Fgn. Lang., Kappa Delta Pi. Office: 800 E Gun Hill Rd Bronx NY 10467

CAPONE, THOMAS ALBERT, psychologist; b. Bronx, N.Y., Mar. 30, 1940; s. Carmine Thomas and Margaret Violanda (Paliotta) C.; B.A., N.Y. U., 1962; M.A. (State scholar), Syracuse U., 1965; Ph.D., Fordham U., 1969; m. Juliane Robba, July 29, 1967; children—Thomas, Daniel. Research asst. N.Y. State Mental Health Research Unit, Syracuse, 1963-64; clin. psychology intern VA Hosps., Syracuse, Montrose, N.Y., 1963-65; psychol. asst. Upstate Med. Center, N.Y., 1965; research asst. Albert Einstein Coll. Medicine and Psychiatry, Bronx, N.Y., 1965-66; ednl. researcher N.Y.C. Bd. Edn., 1967-72; dir. psychol. services Nassau County Dept. Drugs and Alcohol Addiction, Carle Place, N.Y., 1972—; research cons. Mt. Vernon (N.Y.) Bd. Edn., 1968-73; adj. asst. prof. Fordham U., 1969-70; adj. asso. prof. L.I. U., 1970—; psychologist Jamaica Center Psychotherapy, Hempstead, N.Y., 1970-71; cons. psychologist Nassau Psychol. Services, Nassau County, N.Y., 1970—; individual practice psychology and psychotherapy, 1970—; psychol. cons. N.Y. State Office Vocat. Rehab., 1973—; faculty asso. Hofstra U., 1974—; clin. cons. Oceanside Counseling Center. Asst. in Senator James Buckley's investigation N.Y. State drug treatment program, 1973. Diplomate in clin. psychology Am. Bd. Profl. Psychology. USPHS fellow, 1962. Mem. Am., Nassau County (exec. bd.) psychol. assns. Roman Catholic. Contbr. articles to profl. lit. Home: 150 Parkway Dr Plainview NY 11803 Office: Nassau County Med Center Bldg 0 East Meadow NY

CAPORALI, RONALD VAN, glass tech. cons.; b. Arnold, Pa., June 22, 1936; s. Gustave John and Letitia Emily (Succo) C.; B.S. in Ceramic Tech., Pa. State U., 1958, M.S., 1964, Ph.D., 1969; m. Carol June Wagner, Sept. 10, 1956; children—Leslie Ann, Carolyn Sue, Ronald Van, Amy Lou. Ceramic engr. Am. Glass Research Inc., Butler, Pa., 1958-62, chief glass technologist, 1969-76; asso. ceramic tech. dept. Pa. State U., 1962-69; cons. glass tech., West Sunbury, Pa., 1976—. PPG Co. scholar, 1955-58; G.C.I.R.C. fellow, 1963-64; NSF grantee, 1964-69. Mem. Am. Ceramic Soc., Soc. Glass Tech., ASTM,

Soc. Soft Drink Technologists, Keramos, Sigma Xi. Democrat. Address: RD 1 Box 19 West Sunbury PA 16061

CAPOZZI, MARIAN RITA, librarian; b. Balt.; d. Daniel Michael and Frances Jane (Ziolkowski) Capozzi; B.S., U. Md., 1949; M.S. in L.S., Catholic U. Am., 1967. Tchr. Baltimore County Schs., 1950-55; librarian, tchr., adviser U.S. Dependent Schs., Stuttgart, Germany, also Rochefort, France, 1955-57; librarian Baltimore County Schs., 1957-61; librarian Westchester (N.Y.) County Schs., 1962-65; supr. library services Bd. Edn. of Baltimore County, Towson, 1966—. Mem. ALA, Md. Library Assn., Am. Assn. Sch. Librarians, Assn. for Library Service to Children (2d v.p. 1975), Md. Ednl. Media Orgn., Md. Assn. for Supervision and Curriculum Devel., Internat. Platform Assn., Beta Phi Mu, Delta Delta Delta. Club: Soroptimist. Author: Elementary School Media Programs: An Approach to Individualizing Instruction; Drumming up Children's Interest in Literature. Home: 6802 Dunhill Rd Baltimore MD 21222 Office: 6901 N Charles St Towson MD 21204

CAPPIELLO, WILLIAM ANTONIO, surgeon; b. Newark, Dec. 27, 1914; s. Frank and Theresa (DiGiacomo) C.; B.S., Seton Hall U., 1936; M.D., Jefferson Med. Coll., 1940; m. Elizabeth A. Calabro, June 19, 1949; children—William F., John A., Robert A., Richard A. Intern, Newark City Hosp., 1940-42; resident Presbyn. Hosp., Newark, 1946-48, N.Y.U.-Bellevue Hosp., N.Y.C., 1948-49, Newark City Hosp., 1949-50; practice medicine specializing in surgery, 1953—; attending surgeon Lower Bucks Hosp., Bristol, Pa., 1954—; dir. surgery St. Mary's Hosp., Langhorne, Pa., 1972—. Served with U.S. Army, 1942-46. Decorated Bronze Star; diplomate Am. Bd. Surgery. Fellow Am., Internat. colls. surgeons; mem. Pa., Bucks County med. socs. Republican. Roman Catholic. Club: K.C. Home: 57 Rust Hill Rd Levittown PA 19056 Office: 5 Lakeside Dr Levittown PA 19054

CAPRARO, RICHARD THOMAS, personnel indsl. relations exec.; b. Plainfield, N.J., Sept. 24, 1943; s. Leonard Charles and Mary (Kostura) C.; B.S. in Commerce, W.Va. U., 1965. Mgr. compensation AMF, Inc., White Plains, N.Y., 1966—. Served with USAR, 1966-72. Mem. Compensation Assn. (chmn.), Am. Mgmt. Assn., Am. Compensation Assn. Office: AMF Inc 777 Westchester Ave White Plains NY 10604

CAPRETTA, UMBERTO, chemist; b. Nereto, Italy, Mar. 5, 1922; s. Pasquale and Vincenza (Buschi) C.; came to U.S., 1955, naturalized, 1960; D. Indsl. Chemistry, U. Naples (Italy), 1952; m. Leda Durpetti, Sept. 7, 1950; children—Mara, Capretta Dinolfo, Richard. Tchr. sci. high sch., Teramo, Italy, 1952-55; lab. technician Eastman Kodak Co., Rochester, N.Y., 1955-60, analytical chemist, 1960-68, sr. engr., 1968—. Served with Italian Air Force, 1943. Mem. Am. Chem. Soc., ASTM, Am. Inst. Chemists, Soc. Applied Spectroscopy, N.Y. Acad. Sci., AAAS, Rochester Soc. Quality Control. Research methods of analysis, X-ray spectrometry, atomic absorption and polarography. Home: 187 River St Rochester NY 14612 Office: 1669 Lake Ave Rochester NY 14650

CAPRIO, RAPHAEL JOHN, educator; b. Newark, May 26, 1945; s. Michael Frank and Mary Mildred (DiSisto) C.; A.B., Rutgers U., 1967, Ph.D. in Urban Geography, 1973; A.M. (Nat. Def. Edn. Act fellow), U. Cin., 1969; m. Joan Kelly, Dec. 20, 1969. Teaching asst. Livingston Coll., Rutgers U., New Brunswick, N.J., 1969-70; instr. geography Barnard Coll., N.Y.C., 1970; instr. geography Rutgers U., Newark, 1970-73, acting chmn. dept. geography, 1973, asst. prof., chmn. dept. urban studies, 1973-75, asso. prof., chmn. dept. urban studies, 1975-76, asso. prof., asso. dean Coll. Arts Scis., 1976—; cons. to municipal and state agencies. Bd. dirs. North Ward Cultural and Ednl. Center, Newark. Mem. Assn. Am. Geographers. Contbr. articles to profl. jours. Home: 9 Yarmouth Rd Chatham NJ 07928 Office: Rutgers U Coll Arts Sciences Deans Office Newark NJ 07102

CAPUTO, ANTHONY ROBERT, ophthalmologist; b. Newark, May 24, 1941; s. Anthony R. and Pauline A. (Cascella) C.; B.S. in Biology, St. Bonaventure U., 1963; postgrad. Seton Hall U. Grad. Sch., 1963-64; M.D., U. Bologna, Italy, 1969; m. Catherine Smith, Aug. 13, 1966; children—Karen, Kathryn, Kerry. Intern, Martland Hosp., Newark, 1970-71; resident Associated Eye Residencies of N.J., Newark, 1971-74; fellow in pediatric ophthalmology Wills Eye Hosp., Phila., 1974-75; practice medicine specializing in ophthalmology, Newark, 1975—; attending ophthalmologist Jersey City Med. Center, Martland Med. Center, Columbus Hosp., United Hosps. of Newark; dir. Fight for Sight Children's Eye Clinic, Eye Inst. of N.J., 1975—; dir. pediatric ophythalmology and adult motility Newark Eye and Ear Infirmary, 1975—; asst. med. dir. Eye Inst. of N.J., Newark, 1975—; asst. prof. ophthalmology Coll. of Medicine and Dentistry, Newark, 1975—; cons. Riverside Hosp., Secaucus, N.J., 1977—, St. Barnabus Hosp., Livingston, N.J., 1976—, Clara Maas Hosp., Belleville, N.J., 1975—; guest lectr. various hosps., schs. and profl. orgns. Chmn. Screening Program, State Instns. of N.J., 1977. Diplomate Am. Bd. Ophthalmology. Mem. Am. (First Prize award 1975, examiner 1975—), N.J. acads. of ophthalmology and otolaryngology, Am. Acad. Pediatric Ophthalmology. Contbr. articles on pediatric ophthalmology to med. jours. Home: 223 Edgewood Terr South Orange NJ 07079 Office: 15 S 9th St Newark NJ 07107

CAPUTO, BRUCE F., former congressman; b. Yonkers, N.Y., Aug. 7, 1943; s. Anthony and Doris (Burke) C.; B.A. cum laude, Harvard, 1965, M.B.A., 1967; J.D., Georgetown U., 1971. Founder, dir. I.C.F., Inc., N.Y.C., 1969—; mem. 95th Congress from 23d N.Y. dist.; cons. HEW, HUD, U.S. Cost of Living Council. Mem. N.Y. State Assembly from 87th Dist., 1973-77. Bd. dirs. Westchester Assn. Retarded Children. Home: 250 Pondfield Rd W Yonkers NY 10708*

CARABITSES, NICHOLAS LAMPROS, cons. elec. engr., electrochemist; b. Boston, Aug. 29, 1914; s. Lampros N. and Diamond (Govostes) C.; B.S. in Elec. Engring., McKinley Roosevelt U., 1936; Ph.D. in Elec. Engring., U. Mich., 1938; D.Sc. in Electrochemistry, Thomas Edison Coll.; D.Sc. in Electro-biology, Royal Coll. of Sci.; hon. degree Inter-Am. U., Mexico; m. Pauline Anna Papas, Nov. 13, 1938; children—Thelma, Anna. Elec. engr. United Engring. Co., Boston, 1938-40; chief engr. New Eng. Engring. Co., Manchester, N.H.; now cons. elec. engr. Hudson and Carabitses, cons. engrs., Providence; prin. Nicholas L. Carabitses, electrochemist, Providence; owner research lab.; pres. St. John's Ch., Boston. Recipient award Greek Gov. of Athens. Registered profl. engr. Mem. Electrochem. Soc., Am. Astronautical Soc., Am. Helicopter Soc., Am. Soc. of Naval Engrs., Am. Inst. of Sci. (v.p.), Aerospace Med. Assn., Am. Soc. of Mil. Engrs., Greek Am. Progressive Assn., Hellenic Profl. Assn. Am. Internat. (founder, pres. exec. bd., exec. trustee), Am. Hellenic Ednl. Progressive Assn., Internat. Platform Assn. Mem. Greek Orthodox Ch. Contbr. articles on electro-biology to sci. pubis.; writer sci. column for Greek Sunday News. Home: 44 Asheville Rd Hyde Park MD 02136 Office: 419 Industrial Bank Bldg Providence RI 02903

CARALEY, DEMETRIOS, educator, author; b. N.Y.C., June 22, 1932; s. Chris and Stella (Psaras) C.; B.A. summa cum laude, Columbia U., 1954, Ph.D., 1962; m. Jeanne Louise Benner, Sept. 7, 1957; children—James Christopher, David Andrew, Anne Leslie. Mem. faculty Barnard Coll. and Columbia, N.Y.C., 1959—, prof. polit. sci., 1968—, dir. Columbia Grad. Program in Pub. Affairs and Adminstrn., 1978—. Mem. North Tarrytown Zoning Bd. Appeals, 1970-71; mem. North Tarrytown Bd. Trustees, 1971-73, dept. mayor and acting mayor, 1972-73; chmn. North Tarrytown Planning Bd., 1977—. Served with USNR, 1954-56. Mem. Am. Polit. Sci. Assn., Acad. Polit. Sci., Phi Beta Kappa. Democrat. Author: Politics of Military Unification, 1966; New York City's Deputy Mayor—City Adminstrator, 1966; Party Politics and National Elections, 1966; (with R. H. Connery) Governing the City, 1969; City Governments and Urban Problems, 1977; American Political Institutions in the 1970's, 1976; (with M.A. Epstein) The Making of American Foreign and Domestic Policy, 1978. Contbr. American Politics and Public Policy, 1978. Editor: Polit. Sci. Quar., 1973—. Home: 24 Hemlock Dr North Tarrytown NY 10591 Office: Dept Political Science Barnard College Columbia Univ New York City NY 10027

CARBONE, JOSEPH ENRICO, mech. engr.; b. Messina, Italy, May 3, 1919; s. Stellario and Natala (DePasquale) C.; came to U.S., 1921, naturalized, 1943; B.S. in Mech. Engring., Coll. City N.Y., 1944; postgrad. Blkyn. Poly. Inst., 1944-45; m. Julia Anita Alessio, June 29, 1947; children—Natalie Grace, Joseph Enrico. Research engr. Republic Aviation Co., Farmingdale, L.I., N.Y., 1944-47; asst. mech. engr. N.Y.C. Bd. Transp., 1947-50; sr. design engr. Vitro Corp. Am., N.Y.C., 1951-53; asso. partner Syska & Hennessy, Inc., N.Y.C., 1953—; mem. mech. tech. adv. com. bd. N.Y.C. Community Coll., Bklyn., 1968—. Registered profl. engr., N.Y. State, N.J., Fla., S.C. Mem. ASME, Am. Soc. Heating, Refigerating and Air Conditioning Engrs. Contbr. articles to profl. jours. Home: 83-12 168th Pl Jamaica NY 11432 Office: 110 W 50th St New York City NY 10020

CARDACI, MICHAEL MARIO, JR., communications exec.; b. Boston, Mar. 5, 1951; s. Michael Mario and Anne M. (Moreno) C.; student Harvard U., 1968-71, Reed Coll., 1971-72; m. Susan Leslie Dost, Feb. 22, 1974. Founder Panvidicon Video Assurance Program, Norwood, Mass., 1974, pres., gen. mgr., 1975-76, chief exec. officer, vice chmn. bd., 1976—; chmn. bd. Forbes Consol. Bus. Services Corp., 1975—; cons. in field. Founder, Fastracs/U.S.A. Mem. Internat. TV and Program Producers Assn., Asso. Audio Visual Communicators Am., Soc. Internat. TV Arts, New Eng. Smaller Businessmens Assn., New Eng. Mfrs. Assn., New Eng. Advt. Assn., Mass. C. of C., Nat. Assn. Franchises, New Eng. Home Inventory Assn., Nat. Home Security Assn., Mass. Arts Assn. (mem. fund-raising com.), Ind. Ins. Agts. and Brokers Assn. Roman Catholic. Clubs: Harvard, Masons. Home: 200 Fruit St Mansfield MA 02048

CARDARELLI, ALBERT PETER, educator, sociologist; b. Boston, June 30, 1936; s. Albert and Kathleen Frances (Broderick) C.; B.A. in Psychology, Boston U., 1961; M.A. in Labor and Indsl. Relations, U. Ill., 1963; M.A. in Criminology, U. Pa., 1965, Ph.D. in Sociology, 1973. Research cons., correction div. Am. Found., Phila., 1963; field research asst. U.S. Fed. Probation Office, Phila., 1965-66; instr. Coll. Edn., Temple U., 1966-68; research analyst, planning coordinator Mass. Com. on Law Enforcement and Adminstrn. of Criminal Justice, Boston, 1968-70; cons. law enforcement Central Mass. Regional Planning Commn., Worcester, 1970-71, Center for Criminal Justice, Boston U., 1971; staff criminologist Office of Justice Adminstrn., City of Boston, 1970-71; asso. profl. New Eng. Bur. for Criminal Justice Services, Dedham, Mass., 1972-74; asst. prof., co-dir. community sociology program, dept. sociology Boston U., 1974-78; co-dir. Nat. Evaluation of Delinquency Prevention in U.S., 1975-76; cons. Gov.'s Com. on Criminal Justice, Boston, 1973-74; mem. Nat. Humanities Faculty, Concord, Mass. Mem. Boston Democratic Ward Com., 1976—. Served with AUS, 1956-58. Am. Fedn. Tchrs. grantee, 1968-69; NIH research fellow, 1965-66. Mem. Am. Soc. Criminology, Am. Sociol. Assn., Soc. Study of Social Problems, Nat. Council Crime and Delinquency. Contbr. articles to profl. jours. Home: 271 Corey Rd Brighton MA 02146 Office: Boston U 100 Cummington St Boston MA 02215

CARDENAS, RAUL RUDOLPH, JR., civil engr., educator; b. Galveston, Tex., Feb. 5, 1929; s. Raul R. and Clementina (Munoz) C.; B.A., U. Tex., 1951, postgrad. in bacteriology, 1955-57; M.S. in Environ. Health Sci., N.Y. U., 1963, Ph.D., 1970; m. Mary R. Gaglio, Nov. 23, 1961; children—Dianne, Patricia, Randy. Research asso. Manhattan Coll., Bronx, N.Y., 1964-66, adj. asst. prof. civil engring., 1963-66; sr. microbiologist Republic Aviation Farmingdale, N.Y., 1963; instr. dept. civil engring. N.Y. U., N.Y.C., 1966-70, asst. prof. sanitary engring., 1970-72; asso. prof. dept. civil engring., Poly. Inst. of N.Y., Bklyn., 1973—; cons. in environ. health sci. to various agys. and mfg. cos., 1968—; sr. sci. adviser Natural Resources Def. Council, 1970—; sci. reviewer EPA, 1973-75; guest speaker Adelphi U., 1971, Northeastern U., 1972, Worcester Poly. Inst., 1973, U. R.I., 1973; cons. to U.S. Atty.'s Office, N.Y. and N.J., 1971-72; organizer Environ. Forum Workshops, Marymount Coll., Tarrytown, N.Y., 1974. Served with inf. AUS, 1952-54. Recipient Founders Day award N.Y. U., 1970. HEW grantee, 1974-75. Mem. Water Pollution Control Fedn. (standard methods com. 1971-72), Am. Soc. for Microbiology, InterAm. Assn. of Sanitary Engrs., Hudson River Environ. Socs., AAAS, Sigma Xi. Contbr. numerous articles on environ. pollution control to profl. publs. Home: 66 Pine Tree Ln Tappan NY 10983 Office: Polytechnic Institute of New York Dept of Civil Engineering 333 Jay St Brooklyn NY 11201

CARDI, PAUL, inventor; b. Pitts., Sept. 16, 1916; s. Domenico and Rosa (Corpolongo) C.; student pub. schs.; m. Clara Pannone, Aug. 29, 1938; children—Domenico, Paula. Stock and shipping clk. Carlan Instrument, Inc., Cranston, R.I., 1933-40, foreman heavy constrn. equipment, 1940-50, owner, operator, 1950-65; researcher automotive field, 1965—; various inventions including bead stringing machine for jewelry. Address: 1375 Park Ave Cranston RI 02920

CARDILLO, THOMAS EDWARD, assn. exec., physician; b. Rochester, N.Y., Oct. 19, 1924; s. Joseph and Josephine (Battaglia) C.; student U. Minn., 1943-44; A.B., U. Rochester, 1947, M.D., 1951; m. Valerie A. Post, July 3, 1948; children—Thomas S., Linda C., David P., Joseph J., Michael G. Intern in medicine Strong Meml. Hosp., Sch. Medicine and Dentistry, U. Rochester (N.Y.), 1951-52; asst. resident in medicine U. Hosp. of Good Shepherd, Upstate Med. Center, Syracuse, N.Y., 1952-53, resident, 1953-54; USPHS cardiac trainee Nat. Heart Inst., 1953-55; asst. in medicine cardio-pulmonary lab. Sch. Medicine and Dentistry, U. Rochester, 1954-55; pvt. practice medicine specializing in internal medicine and cardiology, Rochester, 1955-61; asso. chief examiner New Eng. Life Ins. Co., 1955-61; internist, sr. cardiology examiner Met. Life Ins. Co., 1955-61; cardiology cons., staff physician Eastman Kodak Co., Rochester, 1955-65; mgr. clin. services, med. dir. Aerojet-Gen. Corp., NASA Marshall Space Flight Center, Huntsville, Ala., 1965-68; dir. heart disease program Rochester Regional Med. Program, 1968-73; pvt. practice medicine Eastside Med. Group, Webster, N.Y., 1973-75; exec. dir. Monroe County (N.Y.) Med. Soc., 1975—; sr. asso. physician Strong Meml. Hosp., Rochester, 1968—; dir. cardiology unit Monroe Community Hosp., Rochester, 1968—; instr. in medicine U. Rochester, 1955-60, clin. sr. instr., 1960-64, clin. asst. prof. medicine, 1964-65, asso. prof. 1968-75, clin. asso. prof., 1975—; clin. asst. prof. U. Ala., 1965-68. Bd. dirs. Genesee region Profl. Standards Rev. Orgn., 1974—; Genesee Valley Med. Found., 1976—; bd. dirs. Monroe Plan for Med. Care, Inc., 1969-76, v.p. 1971-72. Served with USAF, 1943-45. Mem. AMA, Med. Soc. State N.Y., Monroe County Med. Soc. (v.p. 1970-71, dir. 1970-76, pres. 1974-75, exec. dir. 1975—), Genesee Valley Heart Assn. (dir. 1954-65, 68-74), N.Y. State Heart Assembly, Am. Heart Assn. (Distinguished Service award 1965), Rochester Acad. Medicine, Rochester Soc. Internal Medicine (sec.-treas. 1962-63, pres. 1964). Independent Republican. Roman Catholic. Contbr. articles to profl. jours. Office: 1441 East Ave Rochester NY 14610

CARDINALE, KATHLEEN CARMEL O'BOYLE, nurse; b. County Donegal, Ireland, July 13, 1933; d. Denis and Mary (Cannon) O'Boyle; came to U.S., 1958, naturalized, 1966; B.A. magna cum laude in Health Edn., Jersey City State Coll., 1972, M.A. in Health Sci. and Health Adminstrn., 1973; m. Anthony Cardinale, Aug. 28, 1965. Head nurse, relief supr. Manhattan Gen. Hosp., 1959-63; staffing coordinator, asst. dir. nursing Bernsteins Inst., Beth Israel Med. Center, N.Y.C., 1963-70; clin. specialist surg., intensive care unit Beth Israel Med. Center, N.Y.C., 1970-73; asst. dir. nursing Cabrini Health Care Center, N.Y.C., 1974-77, asso. dir. nursing, 1977, asst. adminstr. nursing services, 1977-78, sr. v.p. nursing services, 1978—. Mem. Am. Nurses Assn. Democrat. Roman Catholic. Home: 545 E 14th St Apt 1E New York City NY 10009

CARDINALI, ALBERT JOHN, lawyer; b. N.Y.C., Apr. 24, 1934; s. John and Ines (Clara) C.; B.A., Coll. City N.Y., 1955; LL.B., Columbia, 1958; LL.M., N.Y. U., 1965; m. June DuRose Seaman, Apr. 21, 1977; children—Kathleen, John, Raymond. Admitted to N.Y. bar, 1961; law asso. firm Thacher, Proffitt, Prizer, Crawley & Wood, N.Y.C., 1960-68; partner firm Thacher, Proffitt & Wood, N.Y.C., 1969—. Served with AUS, 1958-60. Mem. Am. (chmn. com. on partnerships, sect. on corporate banking and bus. law 1973—), N.Y. State (exec. com. tax sect. 1972-74) bar assns., Assn. Bar City N.Y. Clubs: Shenorock Shore (Rye, N.Y.), City-Miday, Univ. (N.Y.C.). Home: 9 Franklin Ave Rye NY 10580 Office: 40 Wall St New York City NY 10005

CARDONI, JOHN JOSEPH, elec. engr.; b. Worcester, Mass., Jan. 14, 1952; s. Frank Joseph and Verna Rose (Rindos) C.; B.S. in Elec. Engring. magna cum laude, Lowell Tech. Inst., 1974; M.S. in Elec. Engring., U. Lowell, 1976. Teaching asst. Lowell (Mass.) Tech. Inst., 1974-75, U. Lowell, 1975-76; systems test engr. Data Gen. Corp., Southboro, Mass., 1976, new products mfg. engr., 1976-77, sr. prodn. test supr. Micronova computer systems, 1977—. Mem. Lowell Tech. Inst., U. Lowell alumni assns., Tau Epsilon Sigma, Eta Kappa Nu. Home: 3 Vendora Rd Worcester MA 01606 Office: Route 9 Southboro MA 01772

CARDOZO, BENJAMIN MORDECAI, lawyer; b. N.Y.C., May 15, 1915; s. Sidney Benjamin and Eva Cecile (Mordecai) C.; B.A., Dartmouth, 1937; J.D., N.Y. U., 1941; m. Barbara Schaffer, Sept. 21, 1941; children—Enid (Mrs. Edward Lamon), Ellen (Mrs. Isaac Sonsino). Admitted to N.Y. State bar, 1942, U.S. Supreme Ct. bar, 1947, U.S. Dist. Ct. So. Dist. N.Y., 1949, 2nd Ct. Appeals, 1954, Conn. bar, 1954; atty. Office Alien Property, Dept. Justice, N.Y.C., 1946-49; asso. firm Cardozo & Nathan, N.Y.C., 1949-51, Cardozo & Cardozo, N.Y.C., 1952—. Served with AUS, 1941-43. Mem. N.Y. State, Fed., Am. bar assns., State Bar Assn. Conn., N.Y. County Lawyers Assn. (surrogate ct. com. 1961-66, legal aid com. 1966-72), N.Y. Trial Lawyers Assn., Assn. Bar City N.Y. Home: 325 E 79th St New York City NY 10021 Office: 11 E 44th St New York City NY 10017

CARDOZO, JACK GEORGE, bus. machines co. exec.; b. Westfield, N.J., Nov. 16, 1931; s. Jack George and Marion Dorothy C.; B.A., Rutgers U., 1953; m. Virginia Ann Knill, Feb. 6, 1954; children—Richard, Karen, Craig. Systems analyst Prudential Ins. Co., Newark, 1956-60; mgr. Am. Cyanamid Co., Wayne, N.J., 1960-65; mgr. corp. staff IBM Corp., Armonk, N.Y., 1965—. Mem. Hosp. Study Com., Wayne, 1961-62; cons. chmn. Cub Scouts, 1967-73. Served with USMC, 1954-56. Mem. Assn. Computing Machinery. Home: 5 Highwood Rd Westport CT 06880 Office: Old Orchard Rd Armonk NY 10504

CARERE, ROMULUS PETER, physician; b. Guelph, Ont., Can., Jan. 19, 1926; s. Giacomo and Vincenza C.; student U. Toronto, 1946-47; M.D., U. Ottawa, 1954; m. Madeleine Lapointe, July 30, 1954; children—Paula, Ronald, Claudia, Marc, Monica, Cosmo. Intern, U. Ottawa, 1954, fellow in pathology, 1954-55, fellow in medicine, 1955-56; asso. medicine Dr. R.B. Cronk, Belleville, Ont., 1956-57; fellow in medicine Johns Hopkins, 1957-58; asst. resident internal medicine U. Ottawa, 1958-59; pvt. practice medicine, specializing in internal medicine, Guelph, 1959—; chief of staff St. Joseph's Hosp., Guelph, 1971-75, past chief of medicine; med. rep. Wellington County Dist. Health Council; cons. in field. Coroner Province of Ont. for Waterloo and Wellington. Fellow Royal Coll. Physicians and Surgeons Can.; mem. Wellington County Med. Soc. (pres. 1960), Royal Soc. Medicine (London), Nutrition Today Soc., Am. Coll. Cardiology, A.C.P. (asso.), Acad. Medicine Toronto, N.Y. Acad. Sci. Roman Catholic. Office: 77 Westmount St Guelph ON N1H 8J1 Canada

CAREWE, SYLVIA, painter, tapestry artist; b. N.Y.C.; d. Louis and Esther (Oghstal) Carewe; student Columbia, Atelier 17; pupil Hans Hoffman, Kunyoshi; 1 son, John. One-man shows (paintings) A.C.A. Gallery, N.Y.C., 1948, 51, 53, 54, 56, 58, Three Arts, Poughkeepsie, N.Y., 1947, 52, 54, 58, 61, Barnett Aden Gallery, Washington, 1950, Art. Assn. Richmond, Ind., 1955, U. Ind., 1955, Ball State Tchrs. Coll., 1955, Terza Karlis Gallery, 1955, N.C. U., 1958, Decatur Art Center, 1955, Butler Art Inst., 1955, W.Va. U., 1956, Butler Inst. Am. Art (tapestry), 1960, Galerie Katia Granoff, Paris, 1957, Exhbn. '22 X 28" etchings Witterborn Gallery, N.Y.C.; received sponsorship of French cultural ambassador, 1959; 1st Am. artist creating tapestries executed by Ambusson; one-man shows of tapestry at Butler Inst. Am. Art, 1960, ACA Gallery, N.Y.C., 1961, French & Co., N.Y.C., 1960, 62, show of tapestries and banners Fordham U., 1970; exhbn. Paintings for Tapestry Donnell Art Library, N.Y.C., 1968; N.C. Mus. Show, 1972; created headdresses for Aristophanes; play The Birds; exhibited group shows Whitney Mus. Am. Art, Mus. of Modern Art N.Y., Boston Museum of Fine Arts, Audubon Soc., Bklyn. Museum Phila. Print Club, Vassar Coll., Smith Mus. Apringfield, Mass., Bruge Mus., Belgium, Staadliche Mus., Holland, many others, represented in permanent collections Met. Mus. Art, Whitney Mus. Am. Art, Muse de l'Art Modern, Paris, Musee Nationale de Jakarta, Indonesia, Brandeis U., Butler Art Inst., Howard U., Art. Assn. Richmond, Tel Aviv Mus., Norfolk Mus., many pvt. collections, including Joseph H. Hirshboen, Julius Fleischman, others; lectr. on tapestry Columbia; poetry readings Sta. WNEW, 1969; 100 signed posters distributed by State Dept., 1972. Recipient 1947 ann. A.C.A. Gallery competition for 1st one-man show. Contbr. works and articles to numerous jours. and mags. Address: 500 E 83d St New York NY 10028

CAREY, DONALD EDMUND, civil engr.; b. Bronx, N.Y., Oct. 28, 1925; s. Donald Edmund and Naomi Gillis (Fitzpatrick) C.; B.S.C.E., Pa. Mil. Coll., 1951; m. Loretta Marty, Feb. 20, 1965; 1 dau., Joyce Ann. Jr. engr. N.Y. Water Service Co., 1951-53; distbn. engr. Hackensack Water Co., 1953-55; supt. transmission and distbn. Elizabethtown (N.J.) Water Co., 1960-65, supt. planning and engring.,

1965-70; exec. dir. South Brunswick (N.J.) Utility Authority, 1970-71; bus. adminstr. City of South Brunswick, 1971-72; mgr. water and sewer tech., Lakewood, N.J., 1972-74; exec. dir. Fla. Keys Aqueduct Authority, 1974-75; water supt. City of New Brunswick, N.J., 1975—; Served with USNR, 1944-46. Mem. N.J. Operators Assn. (pres.), Am. Water Works Assn. (chmn. N.J. sect.), Water Pollution Control Assn., Am. Water Resources Assn. Democrat. Roman Catholic. Clubs: Lions, Exchange. Home: 507 St Clair Ave Spring Lake NJ 07762

CAREY, GRANT ELDON, chemist; b. Campbell's Bay, Que., Can., July 6, 1935; s. Allen B. and Erma D. (Smith) C.; came to U.S., 1957, naturalized, 1977; student Carleton U., Ottawa, Ont., Can., 1954-56; B.S., Roberts Wesleyan Coll., 1963; M.S., State U. of N.Y. at Brockport, 1969; postgrad. U. So. Calif., 1970, U. Mont., 1972, Hope Coll., 1974; m. June Georgina Potter, Mar. 2, 1957; children—Allen Grant, Brian Edward, Peter Michael. Tchr., Churchville (N.Y.)-Chili Central Sch., 1963-65, Greece (N.Y.) Olympia High Sch., 1966-67; adj. instr. chemistry Roberts Wesleyan Coll., N. Chili, N.Y., 1969-70; chemistry tchr. Churchville-Chili Central Sch., 1967—. Recipient internship for devel. of career edn., Rochester Area Indsl. Mgmt. Council, 1978. Mem. Nat., N.Y. edn. assns., Churchville-Chili Tchrs. Assn., Nat. Sci. Tchrs. Assn. Democrat. Methodist. Clubs: Gideon's Internat. (treas.), Riga Conservation Group, Audubon, Nat. Wildlife. Home: 31 Chili-Riga Townline Rd Churchville NY 14428

CAREY, HUGH LEO, gov. N.Y. State; b. Bklyn., Apr. 11, 1919; s. Dennis J. and Margaret (Collins) C.; LL.B., St. John's Coll., 1951, LL.D., 1967; m. Helen Owen, Feb. 27, 1947 (dec. Mar. 1974); children—Alexandria, Christopher, Susan, Peter (dec.), Hugh L. (dec.), Michael, Donald, Marianne, Nancy, Helen, Bryan, Paul, Kevin, Thomas. Sales mgr., then v.p. Peerless Oil and Chem. Corp. L.I. City; as dir. affiliate Peerless Chems., P.R.; admitted to N.Y. bar, 1951; mem. 87th Congress from 12th Dist. N.Y., mem. Interior and Insular Affairs com.; mem. 88th-93d congresses from 15th N.Y. Dist.; gov. N.Y. State, Albany, 1975—. Active local Boy Scouts Am.; bd. visitors Mcht. Marine Acad.; bd. dirs. Gallaudet Nat. Inst. Deaf, St. Vincent's Home for Boys. Served to Maj., infantry, AUS, World War II; lt. col. Res. Decorated Bronze Star medal, Combat Inf. award; Croix de Guerre with silver star (France); named knight Holy Sepulcher of Jerusalem (Pope Pius XII). Mem. Salesmen's Assn. of Am. Chem. Industry, Sales Execs. Club N.Y.C., V.F.W., Am. Legion, Cath. War Vets., Emerald Assn., Galway Men's Assn. (hon.). Democrat. Roman Catholic. K.C. Clubs: Montauk, Cathedral (Bklyn.). Office: Office of Governor State Capitol Albany NY 12224*

CAREY, JAMES EDWARD, plastics cons.; b. Baker, Mont., Feb. 22, 1920; s. Edward Sylvester and Cecil Jean (Markin) C.; B.S. in Chem. Engring., Mont. State U., 1942; postgrad. U. Wis., 1945, M.I.T., 1959-60; m. Elizabeth Jane Bryant, May 12, 1945; 1 dau., Lisa Messinger. With Shell Cos., U.S. and Europe, 1942-75; cons. in plastics industry, Mullica Hill, N.J., 1975—; mem. nat. materials adv. bd. com. organic matrix composites, 1978—. Served with USAAF, 1943-45. Mem. Am. Chem. Soc., Soc. Plastics Engrs., Sigma Xi, Tau Beta Pi. Club: Royal Ocean Racing. Patentee in field; contbr. articles to profl. jours. Address: PO Box 201D Route 538 Mullica Hill NJ 08062

CAREY, WILLIAM JOSEPH, banking exec.; b. N.Y.C., May 15, 1922; s. Cornelius M. and Ellen (Gannon) C.; m. Barbara L. Garrison, Aug. 24, 1946; children—Kathleen, Eileen, Christine, Robert. Mgr., Ernst & Ernst, N.Y.C., 1949-59; controller Reynolds & Co., N.Y.C., 1959-61; exec. v.p. Bache & Co., Inc., N.Y.C., 1961-69; exec. partner Goodbody & Co., N.Y.C., 1970-71; v.p. Paine, Webber, Jackson & Curtis, N.Y.C., 1971-73; controller, treas. J. Henry Schroder Banking Corp., N.Y.C., 1973—, v.p. Schroders Inc. Served with U.S. Navy, 1941-45. Decorated Purple Heart. Mem. N.Y. State Soc. C.P.A.'s, Am. Inst. C.P.A.'s, Fin. Execs. Inst., Nat. Assn. Security Dealers. Home: 861 Huron Rd Franklin Lakes NJ 07417 Office: 1 State St New York City NY 10015

CARICKHOFF, JOHN EDWARD, JR., trade co. exec.; b. Phila., June 16, 1938; s. John Edward and Eleanor Harriet (Cunningham) C.; B.S., Villanova U., 1961. Staff accountant Haskins and Sells, Phila., 1962-65; asst. controller Harry F. Ortlip Co., Phila., 1965-66, controller, corporate sec., 1966-75, v.p., controller, sec., 1975—. Served with USMCR, 1962. C.P.A. Mem. Am., Pa. insts. C.P.A.'s, Fin. Execs. Inst. Roman Catholic. Clubs: Peale, Alpha. Office: Harry F Ortlip Co 50 N 18th St Philadelphia PA 19103

CARIOTO, SALVATORE, veterinary surgeon; b. Ottawa, Ont., Can., Apr. 26, 1925; s. Salvatore and Maria C.; B.A., B.S., U. Ottawa, 1947; D.V.M., U. Toronto, 1957; m. Elisabeth Ruig, Dec. 9, 1969; children—Salvatore, Jennifer, Susanne. Veterinary surgeon Care Animal Hosp., Ottawa Acadian Vet. Clinic, Rockland 1966—. Mem. Am., Can. Ont. vet. med. assns., Am. Assn. Hosp. Adminstrs., Italian Bus. and Profl. Med. Assn., Sicula Soc. (pres., coordinating com. Italian socs.), Dante Aligheri Soc. (v.p. 1975), Mardi Gras Soc. Home: 30 Rothwell Dr Ottawa ON K1J 7G4 Canada Office: 631 Montreal Rd Ottawa ON K1K 0T4 Canada

CARISSIMO, PETER WALTER, realtor; b. Rome, N.Y., Jan. 6, 1949; s. Dominick Michael and Pauline Margaret (Burth) C.; B.S., Empire State Coll., 1978; m. Sharon Joy Conboy, Oct. 13, 1973; 1 dau., Brooke DiMichael. Listing specialist William F. Lennon Real Estate, Rome, N.Y., 1971-74; partner, broker Stropp Real Estate, Rome, 1974-75; owner, pres. Peter W. Carissimo Real Estate, Rome, 1975—; staff housing legislation N.Y. State Lt. Gov. Adminstr. Urban Homesteading expt. Community Services Adminstrn., Utica, N.Y. Mem. Soc. Real Estate Appraisers (asso.), Nat., N.Y., Rome real estate bds., Am., N.Y., Rome heart funds, Rome Area C. of C. Contbr. articles to local newspapers. Home and Office: 8138 Turin Rd Rome NY 13440

CARLE, ERIC, artist, author; b. Syracuse, N.Y., June 25, 1929; s. Erich Wilhelm and Johanna (Oelschlager) C.; student Akadamie der Bildenden Kunste, Stuttgart, Germany, 1946-50; m. Dorothea Wohlenberg, June 5, 1954 (div. Mar. 1967); children—Cirsten, Rolf; m. 2d, Barbara A. Morrison, June, 1973. Poster designer U.S. Information Center Germany, Stuttgart, 1950-52; designer promotion dept. N.Y. Times, N.Y.C., 1952-55; art dir. pharm. advt. L.W. Fromlich Co., N.Y.C., 1952-63; guest instr. Pratt Inst., N.Y.C., 1963; exhibited in group shows including Soc. Illustrators, Am. Inst. Graphic Arts, 1970; author, illustrator: 1, 2, 3 to the Zoo, 1968; The Very Hungry Caterpillar, 1970; Pancakes, 1970; The Tiny Seed, 1970; Do You Want To Be My Friend?, 1971; The Secret Birthday Message, 1972; Walter The Baker, 1972; The Rooster Who Set Out To See The World, 1972; Have You Seen My Cat?, 1973; I See A Song, 1973; All About Arthur, 1974; The Mixed Up Chameleon, 1975; Eric Carle's Storybook, 1976; The Grouchy Ladybug, 1977; Hans Christian Andersen by Eric Carle, 1978; Watch Out! A Giant!, 1978. Served with AUS, 1952-54. Recipient 10 Best Book of Year N.Y. Times, 1969; 10 Best poster of year 1952; 1st prize for children's books Internat. Childrens Book Fair, 1970, 72; Deutscher Jugendbuch preis, 1970, 72, selection du Grand Prix des Treize, 1972, 73, Readers prize, Japan, 1975; one of best children's books, Eng., 1971. Home and studio: W Hill Rd West Hawley MA 01339

CARLEONE, JOSEPH, adminstrv. mech. engr.; b. Phila., Jan. 30, 1946; s. Frank Anthony and Amelia (Ciaccia) C.; B.S., Drexel U., 1968, M.S., 1970, Ph.D., 1972; m. Shirley Elizabeth Atwell, June 29, 1968; children—Gia Maria, Joan Marie. Civilian engring. trainee, mech. engr. Phila. Naval Shipyard, 1963-68; grad. asst. applied mechanics Drexel U., Phila., 1968-72, postdoctoral research asso., 1972-73, NDEA fellow, 1968-71, adj. prof. grad. mechanics, 1974-75, 77—; chief research engr. Dyna East Corp., 1973—. Mem. Health Systems Agency, S.E. Pa., 1977—. Mem. ASME, Sigma Xi, Tau Beta Pi, Pi Tau Sigma, Phi Kappa Phi. Contbr. articles in field to profl. jours.; researcher explosive and metal interaction, ballistics, projectile penetration, impact of plates. Home: 3333 Shelmire St Philadelphia PA 19136 Office: 3132 Market St Philadelphia PA 19104

CARLETON, BUKK GRIFFITH, investment counsel; b. N.Y.C., May 30, 1909; s. Bukk G. and Clarice (Griffith) C.; A.B. magna cum laude, Harvard, 1931, LL.B., 1934; m. Mary Elizabeth Tucker, June 16, 1934; children—Elizabeth Holland, Bukk Griffith III. Admitted to N.Y. bar, 1935; asso. Larkin, Rathbone & Perry, N.Y.C., 1934-36; asst. counsel, asst. sec. Gen. Chem. Co., 1936-41; v.p., sec., dir. Parma-Bilt Homes, Inc., 1941-42; counsel RFC, 1942-44; head N.Y. law office Montgomery Ward & Co., 1944-46; mem. legal dept. Sinclair Refining Co., 1946-56; owner, investment counsel Griffith Carleton, 1946—. Trustee Hicks-Stearns Mus. Mem. Am., N.Y. bar assns., New Eng. Soc., Phi Beta Kappa. Mem. Soc. Friends (mem. com. on nat. legislation 1957-58). Clubs: Metropolitan, Sleepy Hollow, Harvard (N.Y.C.); Woodway Country, Quinnatisset Country (Conn.); R.I. Country; New Canaan Country, Harvard (New Canaan). Address: Parade Hill Ln New Canaan CT 06840 also Bukkskin East Killingly CT 06243

CARLETON, BUKK GRIFFITH, III, real estate exec.; b. N.Y.C., May 27, 1940; s. Bukk Griffith and Mary Elizabeth (Tucker) C.; grad. cum laude St. Paul's Sch., Concord, N.H., 1957; A.B. cum laude, Harvard, 1961; M.B.A. with honors, Stanford, 1964; m. Mary Oliver Lee, July 8, 1967; children—Samantha, Heather. Trust trainee First Nat. City Bank, N.Y.C., 1961-62; fin. analyst Am. Friends Service Com., 1964-66, cons., 1966-69, mem. finance com., 1973—; partner Investment Assos., Washington, 1965-72; v.p., treas. Landtest Corp., Phila., 1966-73, pres., 1974—; pres. L.T. Developers, Phila., 1969—, Landtest New Eng., 1976—, Burlington Tennis Co., Inc., 1977—; dir. Landplan Corp., Phila., Beckett Devel. Corp., Phila., Pier 30 Corp., Phila., fin. cons. Stanford Research Inst., Menlo Park, Calif., 1969-70. Mem. Soc. Friends. Clubs: Harvard (N.Y.C.); Gulph Mills, Harvard, Racquet, Merion Cricket (Phila.); Norwich (Vt.) Racquet; D.U., Hasty Pudding Inst. (Cambridge, Mass.). Home: New Boston Rd Norwich VT 05050 Office: 3 Lebanon St Hanover NH 03755

CARLETON, JAMES WILLIAM, investment counselor; b. Weymouth, Mass., Mar. 16, 1929; s. Henry Alfred and Ruth Marion Burrill C.; diploma Rutgers U., 1966; m. Lorraine E. Smith, July 2, 1949; children—James, Elizabeth, Mary Kate. Trust investment officer 2d Nat. Bank of New Haven, 1952-68; account exec. and asst. v.p. Wood Struthers & Winthrop, Inc., New Haven, 1968-77; instl. sales mgr. Fahnestock & Co., New Haven, 1978—; tchr. Am. Inst. Banking, 1969—. Pres., United Civic Assn. of W.Haven, 1969—; asst. treas. New Haven Heart Assn., 1965-68; dist. dir. Quinnipiac council Boy Scouts Am., 1970-71; pres. parish council, chmn. fin. com., trustee Our Lady of Victory Ch. Served with U.S. Army, 1950-52. Recipient Outstanding Community Service award W.Haven Jaycees, 1970. Mem. Conn. Assn. Fin. Execs. (pres.), Hartford Soc. Fin. Analysts (charter). Roman Catholic. Club: Quinnipiac (bd. govs.) (New Haven); Landmark (Stamford, Conn.). Home: 29 Mullen Rd West Haven CT 06516 Office: 129 Church St New Haven CT 06510

CARLIN, GABRIEL S., corp. exec.; b. N.Y.C., Mar. 19, 1921; s. Samuel and Lena (Franco) C.; B.S., N.Y. U., 1951, M.B.A., 1954; m. Rosalind Goldberg, Apr. 17, 1943; children—Donald B., Beverly J. Army-Navy purchasing coordinator Dept. Def., 1947-49; gen. sales mgr. Old Town Corp., Bklyn., 1950-60; div. gen. mgr., mem. world planning group Xerox Corp., Rochester, N.Y., 1960-64; exec. v.p. Savin Bus. Machines Corp., Valhalla, N.Y., 1964—, dir., 1965—; dir. Rapifax Corp., Fairfield, N.J. Served to 1st lt. AUS, 1942-46. Author: The Power of Enthusiastic Selling, 1962; How to Persuade and Motivate People, 1964. Home: 1807 Long Ridge Rd Stamford CT 06903 Office: Savin Business Machines Corp Valhalla NY 10595

CARLINO, ROSE THERESE, nursing adminstr.; b. Bklyn., Oct. 3, 1928; d. Anthony and Clara (Bella) Carlino; R.N., St. Catherine's Hosp. Sch. Nursing, 1949; B.S. in Nursing, St. John's U., 1955, M.S. in Nursing Edn., 1960, M.A. in Sociology, 1976. Staff nurse St. Catherine's Hosp., 1949-51, asst. head nurse, 1951-52, head nurse, 1952-55, asst. clin. instr., supr. surgery, 1955-59, asst. dir. nursing service, 1959, asso. dir., 1959-64, dir., 1964-65; dir. nursing service Evangelical Deaconess Hosp., Bklyn., 1966-67; dir. nursing Deepdale Gen. Hosp., Little Neck, N.Y., 1967-69; asso. prof. Queensborough Community Coll., Bayside, N.Y., 1969-70, adj. profl. instl. research, 1971-73, adj. prof., cons. nursing and allied health curriculum devel., 1973—; asst. v.p. nursing Luth. Med. Center, Bklyn., 1970-75; v.p. and sec. bd. dirs. Queens Med. and Health Program, 1974-75. Mem. N.Y. State Nurse's Assn., Nat. League for Nursing, Cath. Nurses' Assn., Am. Hosp. Assn. Soc. for Nursing Service Adminstrs., St. Catherine's Hosp. Sch. of Nursing Alumni Assn., St. John's U. Alumni Fedn., Nat. Council for Women, Bklyn. Lung Assn. (nursing adv. com.). Co-author: A Survey of Health Needs in Queens, 1971; Community Nursing, Clinical Associate, 1972. Home: 83-52 264th St Floral Park NY 11004

CARLISLE, HOWARD, ednl. adminstr.; b. Phila., July 7, 1918; s. Raphael and Yetta (Brody) C.; B.S., Temple U., 1938, Ed.D., 1971; A.M., U. Pa., 1948. Tchr. English pub. schs., Phila., 1946-51, 53-57, head English dept., 1957-62, vice prin., 1962-69; pres. Central High Sch., 1969—; tchr. English, Pa. area colls., 1946-48; trustee Coll. Entrance Examination Bd., 1974—. Served to lt. col., AUS, 1941-45. Decorated Bronze Star medal. Mem. Temple U. Ednl. Adminstrn. Alumni Assn. (pres.), Nat. Assn. Secondary Sch. Prins., Am. Assn. Sch. Adminstrs., Phi Delta Kappa. Home: 1739 Lombard St Philadelphia PA 19146 Office: Central High Sch Ogontz and Olney Aves Philadelphia PA 19141

CARLISLE, LILIAN MATAROSE BAKER (MRS. E. GRAFTON CARLISLE, JR.), author, lectr.; b. Meridian, Miss., Jan. 1, 1912; d. Joseph and Lilian (Flournoy) Baker; student Dickinson Coll., 1929-30, Peirce Coll. Bus. Adminstrn., 1930-31; m. E. Grafton Carlisle, Jr., Jan. 9, 1933; children—Mrs. E. S. Schwerdtle, Mrs. Leroy G. Meshel. Legal sec. A. W. Sanson, Phila., 1931-35; adminstrv. sec. Royal Air Force Ferry Command, Montreal, Que., Can., 1942-43; vol. stenographer ARC Missing Persons Enquiring Bur., Montreal, 1944-45; vol. sec. McGill U. Sch. Social Work, Montreal, 1945-46; legal sec. Frederick P. Smith, Burlington, Vt., 1948-50; exec. staff mem. in charge collections, research Shelburne (Vt.) Mus., 1951-61; exec. sec. Burlington Area Community Health Study, 1963-64; lectr. Am. culture seminars N.Y. State Hist. Assn., 1970, Henry Ford Mus., 1977; faculty Elder Hostel program U. Vt., 1976-77. Council registrar Girls Scouts U.S.A., 1951-52, chmn. cookie sale, 1952; sec. Burlington PTA, 1948, v.p., 1947-49, pres., 1949-51, dist. radio chmn., 1948-51, state corr. sec., 1951-53, chmn. summer workshop, 1951; treas. Burlington Community Council for Social Welfare, 1951, v.p., 1956-58, pres., 1959-61, 72-75; lay mem. Gov.'s Conf. on Problems of Aging for White House Conf., 1960; project dir. Medicare ALERT, 1966; asst. coordinator Vt. Mental Retardation Planning Project, 1965; mem., chmn. publs. com. Vt. Bicentennial Commn.; v.p., mem. exec. com. Interfaith Sr. Citizens, 1975—, pres., 1977-79; mem. Vt. House of Reps., 1968-70; pres. adv. com. Chittenden County Extension Service, 1977; mem. adv. com. Vt. State Extension Service, 1978-80; dir. pub. relations Champlain Valley Exposition, 1968-77. Mem. Vt. Hist. Soc. (past trustee), Vt. Old Cemetery Assn., Vt. Folklore Soc., Zonta (pres. 1964-65), League of Vt. Writers (pres. 1967-69), Chittenden County Hist. Soc. (pres. 1969-72), Nat. League Am. Pen Women, Order Women Legislators (pres. Vt. br. 1972-74), Chi Omega. Co-author: The Story of the Shelburne Museum, 1955; Profile of the Community, 1964; Vermont Clock and Watchmakers, Silversmiths and Jewellers, 1778-1878, 1970; also numerous pamphlets on Shelburne Mus. Editorial cons. Burlington Social Survey, 1967; editor heritage book series Chittenden County Hist. Soc., 1972-77; contbr. numerous articles to profl. jours. Home: 117 Lakeview Terr Burlington VT 05401

CARLSEN, LLOYD NIELS, surgeon; b. Wauchope, Sask., Can., Feb. 29, 1932; s. Martin and Dora (Sorensen) C.; A.A., Luther Coll., Sask., 1951; M.D., C.M., Queens U., Kingston, Ont., Can.; m. Elizabeth Ruth Craig, Apr. 26, 1958; children—Ian, Thor, Lisa. Intern, Vancouver (B.C.) Gen. Hosp., 1957-58; resident Queens U., 1958, Glasgow U., (Scotland) 1959-60, resident in plastic surgery, 1960-61, Mt. Vernon Plastic Surgery Centre, London, 1961-62, Toronto (Ont.) East Gen. Hosp., 1962-63, Roosevelt Hosp., N.Y.C., 1961-64; practice medicine specializing in plastic surgery, Toronto, 1964—; mem. staff Scarborough (Ont.) Gen. Hosp., 1964—, chief of plastic surgery, 1966—, chief of surgery, 1975—; dir. Cosmetic Surgery Hosp., Woodbridge, Ont., Can., 1972—. Served with Royal Canadian Navy Res., 1949-62. Named Man of Year, Jr. C. of C., 1971; recipient citation Minister of Health, Vietnam, 1971. Fellow Royal Coll. of Surgeons (Can.), A.C.S.; mem. Ont., Canadian med. assns., Canadian, Brit. socs. of plastic surgeons, Am. Soc. for Plastic and Reconstructive Surgeons, Am. Soc. of Hand Surgery, Internat. Soc. of Aesthetic Surgeons, Toronto Acad. of Medicine, Am. Burn Assn. Progressive Conservation Party. Lutheran. Clubs: Alpine Ski, Bayview Golf. Home: 60 Fairway Heights Dr Thornhill ON Canada Office: 2901 Lawrence Ave East Scarborough ON Canada

CARLSON, ALBERT WILLIAM DAVID, JR., pub. co. exec.; b. Balt., June 10, 1937; s. Albert William David and Clio (Mansfield) C.; B.A. in English, U. Va., 1959; m. Barbara Sosman Eames, Apr. 29, 1977; children—Daniel, Hannah. Asst. advt. mgr. McGraw-Hill Book Co., N.Y.C., 1960-62; writer/illustrator children's books and films, 1962-67; dir. marketing Ednl. Supplements Corp., N.Y.C., 1969-72; pres. U.S. Learning Corp., N.Y.C., 1972-75; pres. Rivercross Learning Corp., N.Y.C., 1975—. Served with AUS, 1959-60. Recipient award of excellence Soc. of Illustrators, 1970; first prize Internat. Center for Typographic Arts, Germany, 1971. Mem. Authors Guild, Am. Inst. for Graphic Arts, Authors League Am. Illustrator: Perkins and the Brain, 1964; The House of Perkins, 1965; Miss Maloo, 1967; The Human Apes, 1972. Author, illustrator: Goodmorning Danny, 1972; Goodmorning Hannah, 1971; Awful Marshall, 1972; The Last Show, 1974. Home: 555 Main St Roosevelt Island NY 10044 Office: 172 E 75th St New York City NY 10021

CARLSON, ALMA JANE, educator; b. Dobbs Ferry, N.Y., July 12, 1937; d. Gustav Leonard and Christine Mildred (Cushman) Carlson; B.A. cum laude, Marymount Coll., 1959; M.S., Hunter Coll., 1962; postgrad. William Paterson Coll. N.J., 1969-73. Tchr. elementary schs., Ossining, N.Y., 1959-65; tchr. elementary schs., Oakland, N.J., 1965—, math. coordinator Heights Sch., 1977—. Mem. Ossining Schs. In-Service Steering Com., 1962-65, Com. Reading Curriculum Revision, Oakland, 1970—; mem. Instructional Council Oakland, 1970-71, 75-77. Mem. Nat., N.J. edn. assns., Oakland Tchrs. Assn. (rep. council 1971-75), Curian Honor Soc., Nat. Soc. Study Edn., Alpha Delta Kappa (charter mem. chpt., pres. Tau chpt. 1976-78). Home: 81 Manito Ave Oakland NJ 07436 Office: Heights Sch Seminole Ave Oakland NJ 07436

CARLSON, GLENN HERBERT, lawyer; b. Summit, N.J., June 10, 1940; s. Ben Herbert and Billie Benium (Finnegan) C.; B.A., Am. U., 1962, J.D., 1964, M.A., 1968; m. Dianne Patricia Behme, Dec. 30, 1966; children—Glenn Herbert, Jr., Sara Lent. Admitted To D.C. bar, 1965; since practiced in Washington, 1965—; research asso., project dir. Am. U. Research Center, Washington, 1966-68, sr. research asso. Devel. Edn. and Tng. Research Inst., 1968-70; of counsel Perito, Rose and Duerk, 1975; prin. atty. Perito, Duerk and Carlson, 1976—; adj. prof. dept. anthropology and sociology, 1970-76, Montgomery Community Coll., adj. prof. dept. mgmt. tech., 1975—; dir. Georgetown U. Inst. Manpower Resources Legal Asst. Program, Washington, 1974-75. Bd. dirs. Health and Welfare Council Nat. Capital Area, Voluntary Action Center, 1971-74, chmn. pub. relations task force, 1972, chmn. search com. for dir., 1973. Bd. dirs., gen. counsel Washington-Waldorf Sch., Inc., 1975—. Mem. Am. Bar Assn., Am. Sociol. Assn., Am. Univ. Alumni Assn. (nat. bd. govs., exec. com. 1972-73, pres. 1973-74), Am. Arbitration Assn. (panel of arbitrators), Phi Alpha Delta, Sigma Delta Chi. Contbr. articles to profl. jours. Home: 5343 32d St NW Washington DC 20015 Office: 1001 Connecticut Ave Suite 1200 Washington DC 20036

CARLSON, J(OHN) PHILIP, lawyer; b. Shickley, Nebr., Apr. 16, 1915; s. Christopher Theodore and Klara (Blomquist) C.; student Luther Coll., Wahoo, Nebr., 1931-33; A.B., Wayne State Coll. (Nebr.), 1935; M.A., Columbia, 1967; J.D., Georgetown U., 1951; m. Maryjo Suverkrup, Oct. 14, 1950. Tchr., coach high sch., Bristow, Nebr., Carroll, Nebr., Ashland, Nebr., 1935-42; vets. relations adviser OPA, Washington, 1946-47; tng. specialist Dept. Navy, Washington, 1947-56; minority counsel Com. on Govt. Operations, Ho. of Reps., Washington, 1956—; admitted to D.C. bar, 1952, U.S. Supreme Ct. bar, 1957, U.S. Ct. Mil. Appeals bar, 1970; Am. Polit. Sci. Assn. congl. staff fellow Columbia, 1964-65, 66-67. Served from aviation cadet to capt. USAAF, 1942-45; lt. col. USAF Res. ret. Decorated D.F.C., Air Medal with oak leaf cluster. Mem. Am. Econ. Assn., Am., Fed. bar assns., Am. Judicature Soc. Republican. Lutheran. Clubs: Nat. Lawyers, Capitol Hill, Nat. Economists (Washington); Belle Haven Country (Alexandria, Va.). Home: 2206 Belle Haven Rd Alexandria VA 22307 Office: 2153 Rayburn Bldg Washington DC 20515

CARLSON, JANE, pianist; b. Hartford, Conn.; d. John Berger and Lena (Stoneholm) Carlson; B.Mus., Shenandoah Conservatory Music, 1940; diploma, Juilliard Sch. Music, 1946. Concert pianist U.S. and abroad, 1945—; soloist Gordon String Quartet, 1945-46; Town Hall debut, N.Y.C., 1947; soloist Telephone Hour, 1947; recital Carnegie Hall, N.Y.C., 1951, Lincoln Center, 1970, Tully Hall, Lincoln Center, 1972, Lincoln Center-Juilliard Theater, 1976; European concert tour, 1952, 54, 63, 65, 66, 67, 70, 76; appearances with numerous Am. symphony orchs. recordings include Ludus Tonalis (Hindemith), 1965, re-released 1972; tchr. L'Ecole Hindemith, Blonay, Switzerland, summer 1974; asst. in Carl Friedberg, Juilliard Sch. Music Summer Sch., 1947-52; tchr. piano Juilliard Sch. Music, 1946—, Berkley Summer Sch. Music, Springvale, Maine, 1958-60, Congregation of Arts, Dartmouth, Coll., summers 1963-65. Recipient award Nat. Music League, 1946, Naumburg Found award, 1947. Contbr. articles to Piano Quar. Home: 257 W 86th St New York NY 10024 Office: Juilliard Sch lincoln Center Plaza New York NY 10023

CARLSON, JOHN PAUL, advt. and sales promotion exec.; b. Worcester, Mass., May 31, 1940; s. Hilding Verner and Hanna Marie (Doherty) C.; A.A., Worcester Jr. Coll., 1962, 77; B.S., Suffolk U., 1964; postgrad. Quinsigamond Community Coll., 1968, Clark U., 1969; m. Nancy Ellen Maylott, Aug. 24, 1964; children—Mark Christopher, Michael John. Staff tech. writer David Clark Co., Worcester, 1964-65; advt. mgr. Waters Assos. Inc., Framingham, Mass., 1965-68; product promotion mgr. Fenwal Inc., Ashland, Mass., 1968-69; mgr. advt. and sales promotion Alden Electronic & Impulse Recording Equipment Co., Inc., Westborough, Mass., 1969—; cons. in field. Served with USNR, 1958-60. Recipient Martin J. Flaherty Meml. prize, 1964; William M. Cavanaugh Meml. scholar, 1963. Contbr. articles to profl. publs. Office: 1 Washington St Westborough MA 01581

CARLSON, JOHN SWINK, lawyer, petroleum co. exec.; b. Ft. Collins. Colo., June 16, 1911; s. George A. and Rosa (Alps) C.; A.B., U. Colo., 1932; LL.B., Harvard, 1936; m. Sara A. Mott, June 22, 1940; children—John Swink, Lucie Pamela, Ann Brockenbrough, Virginia Charles, Thomas George (dec.); m. 2d, Barbara C. Spencer, Oct. 5, 1973. Admitted to Okla. bar, 1937; legal staff Shell Oil Co., 1936-37, Turman Oil Co., 1937-38; legal asso. Yancey & Spillers, Tulsa, 1938-39; legal counselor Chapman, Barnard & McFarlin, oil, cattle and investments, Tulsa, 1939-42; gen. counsel Selsmograph Service Corp., Tulsa, 1942-49; pra cticed in Tulsa, 1949-51; sr. partner firm Carlson, Lupardus, Matthews, Holliman & Huffman, Tulsa, 1951-61; head legal firm John S. Carlson, 1961—; gen. counsel, exec. com., dir. Century Geophys. Corp., 1951-71, sr. v.p., 1957-71; sec., dir., gen. counsel Hayward-Wolff Research Corp., 1951-61; v.p., sec., dir., gen. counsel Exploration Cons., Inc., 1951-63, Canadian Geophys. Measurements, Ltd., 1954-66, Venezuela Geophys. Measurements, S.A., 1957-66, Enterprises & Businesses, Inc., 1960-65, The Jameson Corp., 1961; pres., dir., gen. counsel Petroleum Research Corp., 1957-66, Western Petroleum Co., Inc., 1960-65; chmn. bd. dirs., gen. counsel Community Merchandisers, Inc., 1959—; sec., dir. Western Hemisphere Trade & Credit Corp., 1960; dir. Hemisphere Constrn. Co., 1960, v.p., 1961; pres., gen. counsel, dir. Oil Enterprises, Inc., 1965—; v.p., gen. counsel, sec., dir. Digital Resources Corp., 1972—; dir., counsel Applied Devices Corp. Mem. Am., Okla., Okla. Jr. (pres. 1943, 44) bar assns., Am. Judicature Soc., Am. Soc. Internat. Law, Phi Beta Kappa, Delta Sigma Rho. Clubs: Tulsa, Harvard (pres. 1949, 50). Editor: Compendium of Laws Relating to the Problems of Men in the Armed Forces, 1943. Home: 912 B Woodside Circle Kissimmee FL 32741 Office: 1604 Fourth Nat Bank Bldg 15 W 6th St Tulsa OK 74119 also 60 Plant Ave Hauppauge NY 11787 also 2931 N Poinsiana Blvd Kissimmee FL 32741

CARLSON, ROBERT EUGENE, surgeon; b. Bloomfield, N.J., Nov. 15, 1928; s. Carl O. and Ingeborg Anna (Frisell) C.; B.S., Tufts U., 1948; M.D., Columbia U., 1952 m. Eva-Maria C. Wuerker, Jan. 8, 1955; children—Gilbert, Christine, Lorin. Intern, Bellevue Hosp., N.Y.C., 1953; resident in surgery Columbia Presbyn. Med. Center, N.Y.C., 1955-59; chief resident surgery Bellevue Hosp. Center, N.Y.C., 1959; chief surgery, dir. emergency services Montgomery Hosp., Norristown, Pa., 1975—, pres. med. staff, 1976-78; asso. surgery Sacred Heart Hosp., Norristown, 1960—. Health officer Whitpain Twp. (Pa.), 1968-76. Served to capt., M.C., U.S. Army, 1953-55; ETO. Diplomate Am. Bd. Surgery. Mem. Am., Pa. med. socs., A.C.S. (treas. Pa. com. on trauma 1978—), Am. Cancer Soc., Internat., Am. burn socs. Episcopalian. Home: 3 John's Ln Ambler PA 19002 Office: 21 W Fornance St Norristown PA 19401

CARLSON, ROGER DAVID, psychologist, educator; b. Berkeley, Calif., Nov. 19, 1946; s. George Clarence and Elizabeth (Norris) C.; A.B., Sacramento State Coll., 1968, M.A., 1969; Ph.D., U. Oreg., 1972; m. Ema T. Paviolo, June 11, 1977. Grad. asst. Sacramento State Coll., 1969-70; research asst. Psychol. Survey and Testing Service, Sacramento, 1970; grad. teaching fellow U. Oreg., Eugene, 1971-72; asst. prof. psychology Lebanon Valley Coll., Annville, Pa., 1972—. Mem. Friends of Radio Sta. KPFA, v.p. 1969, pres. 1970. Recipient Presdl. Sports award. Mem. Am., Eastern psychol. assns., Soc. for Philosophy and Psychology (exec. com. 1975-76), AAUP, Aerobics Internat. Research Soc., Psi Chi. Club: Appalachian Athletic. Contbr. research papers at convs. on genetic epistemology, child devel., cognition and psycholinguistics. Home: RD 2 Box 208 Annville PA 17003

CARLSON, RUTH HARTWELL, realtor; b. Brockton, Mass., Apr. 29, 1915; d. Edwin S. and Mary S. (Hoyt) Hartwell; student Pawtucket (R.I.) Sch. Bus., 1934; m. J. Frederick Carlson, Apr. 19, 1938; children—Judith Ann, Burce Frederick, Priscilla Ruth, Jonathan Edwin. Operator New Eng. Tel. & Tel., 1935-50; co-owner, operator The Old Village Store, West Barnstable, Mass., 1955-71; prin. J.F. Carlston, Realty, West Barnstable 1971—. Mem. West Parish Meml. Found., Women's Guild (charter), Dig and Delve Garden Club, West Barnstable Civic Assn. Barnstable Hist. Zoning Com. (sec.). Contbr. chpt. Seven Villages of Barnstable, 1976. Home: Willow St West Barnstable MA 02668 Office: Route 149 West Barnstable MA 02668

CARLSON, THEODORE JOSHUA, lawyer, utility exec.; b. Hartford, Conn., Jan. 4, 1919; s. John and Hulda (Larson) C.; A.B., Montclair State Coll., 1940; J.D., Columbia U., 1948, A.M., 1951; postgrad. U. Chgo., 1942; m. Jacqueline L. Coburn, Apr. 25, 1953; children—Stephanie, Christopher J., Victoria, Antoinette. Admitted to N.Y. State bar, 1948, since practice in N.Y.C.; asso. firm Gould & Wilkie, 1948-54, partner, 1954—, sr. partner, 1970—; dir. Central Hudson Gas & Electric Corp., Poughkeepsie, N.Y., 1968—, chmn. bd., 1975—, prin. officer, 1975—; dir. Empire State Electric Energy Research Corp., Empire State Power Resources, Inc. Chmn. bd. of exec. com. N.Y. Power Pool, 1977-78; pres. United Fund Rockville Centre, 1966; chmn. Westchester County adv. bd. Salvation Army, 1977—, chmn. N.Y. State adv. bd., 1977—; bd. dirs., mem. exec. com. Mid-Hudson Pattern for Progress, Inc., 1975—; trustee, chmn. finance com. King's Coll. Served to capt. USAAF, 1942-46. Mem. Fed. Power Bar Assn., Edison Electric Inst. (dir., mem. legal com. 1958-75), Energy Assn. N.Y. State (chmn. exec. com. 1976-77), Am., N.Y. bar assns., Bar Assn. City N.Y. (mem. spl. com. on energy and environment 1972-73, chmn. pub. utility sect. post admissions-legal edn. com. 1970-73). Club: Rotary (hon.). Home: 52 Dalmeny Rd Briarcliff Manor NY 10510 Office: 284 South Ave Poughkeepsie NY 12602 also 1 Wall St New York City NY 10005

CARLSON-GUMBINER, DALE, author; b. N.Y.C., May 24, 1935; d. Edgar M. and Estelle (Cohen) Bick; student Riverdale Country Sch., 1947-53; B.A., Wellesley Coll., 1957; m. Albert W. D. Carlson, Jr., Nov. 24, 1962; children—Daniel Bick, Hannah Bick. Vice pres. Parents League N.Y., 1967-72. Mem. Authors Guild, Author's League Am. Author: Perkins the Brain, 1964; The House of Perkins, 1965; Miss Maloo, 1966; The Brainstormers, 1966; Frankenstein, 1968; Counting Is Easy, 1969; Your Country, 1969; Arithmetic I, II, III, 1969; The Electronic Teabowl, 1969, Warlord of the Genji, 1970; Awful Marshall, 1971; The Beggar King of China, 1971; The Mountain of Truth, 1972; The Human Apes, 1972; Goodmorning Danny, 1972; Goodmorning Hannah, 1972; Girls Are Equal Too, 1973; Baby Needs Shoes, 1974; Triple Boy, 1977; The Plant People, 1977; Where's Your Head?, 1977; The Wild Heart, 1977; The Shining Pool, 1979; Lovingsex for Both Sexes, 1979; The Story of Practically Everybody, 1979. Address: 116 E 63d St New York NY 10021

CARLTON, CYRUS MORRIS, mktg. exec.; b. N.Y.C., Apr. 10, 1931; s. Paul and Rae (Cohen) C.; A.B., U. Mich., 1952; postgrad. N.Y. U., 1956-62; m. Doris H. Cohen, June 10, 1965; children—Paula, Thomas, Peter. With Grey Advt., N.Y.C., 1954-56, Compton Advt., N.Y.C., 1956-58; dir. advt. Carlton Record Corp., N.Y.C., 1958-61; asst. dir. tape club Columbia Record Club, N.Y.C., 1962; asst. sales mgr. Goodren Products Corp., Englewood, N.J., 1963-67; founder, pres. Carlton Display Corp., Rowayton, Conn., 1967—; founding partner, exec. v.p. 3-D Marketing Corp., Phila., 1969—; dir. Copeland & Laird, Phila., 1974. Pres. Davenport Ridge Sch. PTA, Stamford, Conn., 1976-77; mem. Democratic City Com., Stamford, Conn., 1975-78; pres. Caucus of Stamford Dems., 1970-71; bd. dirs. Caucus of Conn. Dems., 1970-76, vice chmn., 1976-77; bd. dirs. N. Stamford Dem. Club, 1971—. Served with U.S. Army, 1952-54. Mem. Am. Mktg. Assn., U. Mich. Alumni Assn., Point of Purchase Advt. Inst. (mem. pub. relations com. 1974-75), United Jewish Fedn. (adminstrv. vice chmn. 1978), Sigma Delta Chi. Jewish Religion. Clubs: City of N.Y.; N. Stamford Dem.; B'nai B'rith; U. Mich. of Lower Fairfield County (Ct.). Home: 52 Eden Rd Stamford CT 06907 Office: PO Box 162 Rowayton CT 06853

CARLTON, SARA BOEHLKE (MRS. MASON GANT CARLTON), occupational therapist; b. Black River Falls, Wis., July 1, 1937; d. Ralph William and Hazel Olive (Drecktrah) Boehlke; B.S., U. Wis., 1959; m. Mason Gant Carlton, Sept. 9, 1961; children—Holly Gant, John Frederick. Occupational therapist VA Hosp., Lyons, N.J., 1960-65; occupational therapist Hunterdon Med. Center, Flemington, N.J., 1968-71, dir. occupational therapy, 1971-73, dir. child devel. program, 1973—; mem. adv. bd. Inst. for Study Exceptional Children, Ednl. Testing Service, Princeton, N.J., 1977—; v.p. Hunterdon Council for Children, Flemington, 1977—. Mem. Hilland Twp. Bd. Edn., Hunterdon County, N.J., 1972-77, v.p., 1974-76; trustee Hunterdon Occupational Tng. Center, Flemington, 1972—, v.p., 1974-75, pres., 1975-78; trustee Hunterdon County Bd. Mental Health, 1975-77; mem. bd. Christian edn. Presbyterian Ch. Mem. Am., N.J. occupational therapy assns. Club: Woman's (exec. bd. 1971-72) (Milford, N.J.). Home: RTE 1 Box 130 Milford NJ 08848 Office: Hunterdon Med Center Flemington NJ 08822

CARMAN, FLOYD SHETLER, accountant; b. Cambridge, Mass., Aug. 2, 1945; s. Russell Elmer and Margurite Elizabeth (Dingee) C.; B.S.A. in Accounting, Bentley Coll., 1968; m. Ann Lillian Dailey, Oct. 10, 1971; children—Bradford Floyd, Dean Edward. Heade cash dept. Stop & Shop, Cambridge, 1963-68; accountant John Hancock Mut. Life Ins. Co., Belmont, Mass., 1971-74; advanced accountant, 1974-77, sr. accountant securities accounting div., 1977—. Mem. Budget Com. Belmont, 1977-78. Served as capt., inf., U.S. Army, 1968-71. Mem. Res. Army Assn. Republican. Address: 184 Brighton St Belmont MA 02178

CARMAN, JAMES RUSSELL, maritime service exec., govt. ofcl.; b. Springfield, Mass., Nov. 24, 1920; s. Ernest W. and Jessie Bailey (Caton) C.; grad. Mass. Maritime Acad., 1941; A.B., Harvard U., 1950; postgrad. U. Wis., 1952-53; M.A. in Econs., Cleve. State U., 1976; m. Pauline Isabel Ecklund, Sept. 25, 1953 (div. 1971); children—Jean Audrey, Jessie Caton. Chief officer Grace Line, Inc., N.Y.C., 1941-46; planner Chainbelt Co., Milw., 1950-54; traffic mgr. MacFarlane Steamship Agy., Detroit, 1954-59; region mgr. U.S. Nav. Co., Cleve., 1959-64; exec. dir. Lorain Port Authority (Ohio), 1964-68; v.p. Terminal Import Export Co., Lorain, 1968-71; transp. editor Indsl. Pub. Co., Cleve., 1972-76; program mgr. Maritime Adminstrn. Office of Port and Intermodal Devel., Washington, 1976—; part-time instr. internat. trade and transp. Wayne State U., Detroit, 1956-59, Western Res. U., Cleve., 1960-62, Fenn Coll., Cleve., 1963-64; transp. program mgr. Cuyahoga Community Coll., Cleve., 1973-76. Mem. Mayor's Com. on Port Devel., Cleve., 1962; v.p., trustee Westshore Unitarian Ch., 1967-70, chmn. funds com., 1965-67. Served with U.S. Mcht. Marine, 1941-46. Holder Master's License. Mem. Am. Soc. Traffic and Transp. (asso. examiner 1976—; certified), Transp. Logistics Inst. (founder 1972, pres. 1972-76, trustee 1972—), Am. Econ. Assn., Traffic Club Washington, Transp. Research Forum (dir. D.C. chpt. 1977—), Nat. Ski Patrol System, Nat. Geog. Soc., Traffic Clubs Internat., Interlake Sailing Class Assn., Omicron Delta Epsilon. Unitarian-Universalist. Clubs: Harvard of Washington; Circumnavigators, Podickory Yacht. Contbr. articles on shipping to tech. jours. Home: 1830 N Forest Court D Crofton MD 21114 Office: 14th and E Sts NW Washington DC 20230

CARMEL, ALAN STUART, lawyer, diversified co. exec.; b. Balt., July 24, 1944; s. Isaac and Sylvia (Sirulnik) C.; A.A. magna cum laude, U. Balt., 1963, J.D., 1966; m. Ellen Freda Hobman, June 29, 1969; children—Shana Miriam, Jason Mark, Jarre Paige. Admitted to Md. bar, 1966; sec., asst. counsel 1st Federated Life Ins. Co., Balt., 1966-69; dir. equity mktg. U.S. counsel Mfrs. Life Ins. Co., Toronto, Ont., Can., 1970-75; v.p., dir. ManEquity, Inc., Denver, 1970-75; pres., dir. ManuLife Holding Corp., 1970-75; v.p., gen. counsel, sec., dir. Atlantic Internat. Corp., Balt., 1975—, Atlantic Internat. Mktg. Corp., Balt., 1975—, Atlantic Mfg. Corp., Balt., 1975—; mng. dir. Atlantic Mobile GmbH, Frankfurt, W. Ger., 1976—; dir. Atlantic Industries, Inc.; gen. counsel AI Services, A.G., Zug, Switzerland, 1976—; exec. mgr. Atliran, P.J.S.C., Tehran, Iran. Fellow Life Mgmt. Inst.; mem. Internat., Am., Md. bar assns., Am. Judicature Soc., Am. Soc. Internat. Law, Mensa. Home: 2425 Diana Rd Baltimore MD 21209 Office: 111 Chesapeake Park Plaza Baltimore MD 21220

CARMEL, SIMON JACOB, phys. chemist, govt. ofcl., deaf community leader; b. Balt., Apr. 30, 1938; s. Joseph and Ann (Miller) C.; student Georgetown U., 1959, Am. U., 1960-61, Catholic U., 1960-61; B.S. with honors in Physics and Math. Gallaudet Coll., 1961; postgrad. Nat. Bur. of Standards Grad. Sch., 1965. Physicist, Nat. Bur. of Standards, Gaithersburg, Md., 1961-63, phys. chemist, 1963—; mem. U.S. Swimming Team, 9th Internat. Summer Games for the Deaf, Helsinki, Finland, 1961; ofcl. Russian interpreter 10th World Summer Games for the Deaf, Washington, 1965; coach, team mgr. of U.S. Deaf Ski Team, W. Germany, 1967; actor Frederick Hughes Meml. Theatre, Washington, 1964-69, mem. steering com., 1968-69, mem. publicity com., 1970-71; organizer Eastern Deaf Skiers Race Championships, Wilmington, Vt., 1970-71; organizer Nat. Tournament for Deaf Magicians, Nat. Assn. Deaf, 1970; ski tech. del. Internat. Com. Silent Sports, 1971—, dir. U.S. Deaf Ski Team, 7th World Winter Games, Switzerland, 1971; gen. chmn. Lake Placid Organizing Com., World Winter Games for the Deaf, 1975. Founder, co. chmn. Nat. Congress of Jewish Deaf Conv.'s teenagers activities program, Washington, 1962, chmn. teenagers activities program, 27th Conv., Washington, 1964; rep. of Nat. Congress of Jewish Deaf at Council of Orgns., Washington, 1968. Recipient Silver Trophy award Italian Sports Fedn. of the Deaf, 1973, Nat. Vol. award Nat. Center for Voluntary Action, 1974, Medallion award Alpine Deaf Skiers Assn., 1968, Robey Burns Sportsman of Yr. award Block "G" Club Gallaudet Coll., 1975-76. Mem. U.S. Deaf Skiers Assn. (Leadership award 1972, editor Newsletter 1968-76, v.p. 1968-72, pres. 1972-76), Nat., Md. assns. of the deaf, Am. Athletic Assn. of the Deaf, U.S., Eastern (award for outstanding service to eastern deaf skiers 1975) ski assns., Nat. Fraternal Soc. of the Deaf, Deaf Telecommunicators of Greater Washington. Author: International Hand Alphabet Charts, 1975; contbr. articles in skiing to various local and nat. mags. for the deaf. Home: 10500 Rockville Pike Apt 1028 Rockville MD 20852

CARMEN, ESTHER CORA MAYO, coll. counselor; b. Bolton, Ga., Apr. 8, 1921; d. Walter Augusta and Lillie May (Lord) Mayo; student Miami U., 1939-41; B.S. with honors in Elementary Edn., U. Del., 1968, M.Ed. in Coll. Counseling and Student Personnel Services, 1971; m. John William Carman, June 13, 1942; children—David, Melinda, Michele, John Jared, Richard. Undergrad. teaching asst. U. Del., 1967-68, grad. adminstrv. asst., 1968-69, acad. counselor, 1969-70, asst. to dean Coll. of Edn., 1970-77, dir. student services for tchr. edn., 1977—. Active Windy Hills Civic Assn. Mem. Am. Personnel and Guidance Assn., Am., Del. coll. personnel assns., Kappa Delta Pi, Phi Kappa Phi. Mem. Reorganized Ch. of Jesus Christ of Latter-day Saints. Club: Eastern Star. Home: 80 Welsh Tract Rd Apt 309 Newark DE 19713 Office: 120 Willard Hall W Main Newark DE 19711

CARMICHAEL, CAROL ELIZABETH ROGERS, realtor; b. Boston, June 15, 1934; d. Lemuel James and Dorothy Hawthorne (Sewell) Rogers; student Fisher Jr. Coll., 1952-54; student U. Mass., 1964-68. Asso., D.H. Jones Real Estate Agy., Amherst, Mass., 1968-75; pres. Landmark Properties, Inc., Northampton, Mass., 1976—; mem. faculty adv. com. for real estate certificate program U. Mass., 1977-78. Co-chmn. drive UNICEF, 1967; mem. Amherst Task Force on Growth and Housing. Mem. Realtors Nat. Mktg. Inst., Nat., Mass. assns. real estate bds., Mass. Assn. Realtors (comml. and investment div.), Acad. Creative Real Estate, UN Assn., Hampshire County Bd. Realtors (treas. 1977-78), Hampshire County Mental Health Assn. (treas. 1967-68), Leverett Artists and Craftsmen Assn. (co-chmn. spring show and sale 1968). Home: Wendell Rd Shutesbury MA 01072 Office: 47 Gothic St Northampton MA 01060

CARMICHAEL, DONALD WOODS, stockbroker; b. St. Catherines, Ont., Can., Jan. 29, 1923; s. Harry John and Marie (Moren) C.; student Assumption Coll., Windsor, Ont., 1942-45; student commerce McGill U., Montreal, Que., 1945-46; m. Maryon Misner, June 26, 1948 (dec.); children—Harry John, Lee Anne. Founder, owner, mgr. Carmichael Heat and Power Co. Ltd., Toronto, Ont., 1947-57; trainee Baker Weeks, N.Y.C., 1957-58, securities salesman, Toronto, Ont., 1958-71; stockbroker Donald R. Watt Securities (name changed to Watt Carmichael Securities Ltd. 1972), Toronto, 1971—, partner, 1972—, v.p., 1972-76, pres., 1976—, also dir. Bd. govs. Lady of Mercy Hosp., Toronto, 1955-69, Scarborough Gen. Hosp., Seven Years, Ont., 1958-60. Mem. Toronto Stock Exchange, Metro Bd. Trade, Delta Kappa Epsilon. Roman Catholic. Clubs: Toronto Hunt, Rosedale Golf, Granite, Metropolitan (N.Y.C.); Canadian of N.Y. Home: 15 Lauderdale Dr Willowdale ON M2L 2A8 Canada Office: PO Box 276 Toronto-Dominion Centre Toronto ON M5K 1J5 Canada

CARMICHAEL, HERBERT WARREN, motel exec.; b. Portland, Maine, Jan. 1, 1936; s. Herbert Warren and Helen Julia (Malloy) C.; student U. Maine, 1954-57; B.S., Boston U., 1963; postgrad. Mont. State U., 1971; m. Rebecca Mitchell, Nov. 2, 1968; children—Herbert W., Joshua Brooks. Indsl. relations specialist AVCO Corp., Glasgow, Mont., 1968-71; personnel asst. Mont. State U., Bozeman, 1971-72; personnel mgr. W.H. Nichols Co., Portland, Maine, 1972-76; personnel dir. Wright, Pierce, Barnes & Wyman, cons. engrs., Topsham, Maine, 1976-78; owner Buoy Motel, Falmouth, Maine, 1978—. Mem. ann. fund com. Maine Med. Center; past pres. awards com. Maine Community Betterment Assn. Mem. So. Maine Personnel Execs. Council, Greater Portland Personnel Mgmt. Assn. (past pres.), Associated Industries Maine (v.p.), Am. Soc. Personnel Adminstrn. Clubs: Personnel Mgmt., Rotary (Portland). Home and Office: 374 US Hwy #1 Falmouth ME 04105

CARMIEN, DONALD CHARLES, lawyer; b. Peoria, Ill., July 20, 1932; s. Ernest Donald and Helen (Tench) C.; A.B., Albion Coll., 1954; LL.B., Syracuse U., 1958; m. Janice F. Redhead, Sept. 4, 1954; children—Nancy Ann, Carol Jean, Michael Charles, Mark Ernest. Admitted to N.Y. bar, 1958; practiced in Binghamton, N.Y., 1958—; partner firm Chernin and Gold, 1961-70, Drazen, Carmien & Young, 1970-72, Carmien & Young, 1972—. Chmn. bd. Broome County Heart Assn., 1971-72, pres., 1970-71; bd. visitors Syracuse U. Coll. Law, 1968—. Served with USN, 1954-56. Mem. Motor Carrier Lawyers Assn., Am. (chmn. N.Y. state membership com. 1972—), N.Y. State (sect. chmn. 1967, exec. com. 1968, chmn. young lawyers sect. 1968, chmn. profl. econs. sect. 1969-71, mem. com. of appraisal 1972—) bar assns., Broome County C. of C. (chmn. transp. com. 1969-71), Delta Nu Alpha, Delta Tau Delta. Presbyn. (deacon). Home: 416 W Benita Blvd Vestal NY 13850 Office: 22 Riverside Dr Binghamton NY 13901

CARNAHAN, PETER MALOTT, state ofcl.; b. Buffalo, Mar. 31, 1931; s. Edmund Haynes and Margaret (Malott) C.; B.A. magna cum laude, Amherst Coll., 1952; student Stratford Shakespearean Festival Can., 1954; postgrad. Inst. in Arts Adminstrn., Harvard U., 1973; m. Mary Frances Morris, Feb. 13, 1960; children—Brian Morris, Edmund Malott. Dir. Orpheus Prodns., Royal Playhouse, N.Y.C., 1954-56; bus. mgr. Poets' Theatre, Cambridge, Mass., 1956-57; mng. dir. Joe Jefferson Players, Mobile, Ala., 1957-61, Harrisburg (Pa.) Community Theatre, 1961-72; mem. theatre adv. panel, asst. dir. Commonwealth of Pa., Council on Arts, 1972-74, dir. performing arts, 1974-78, acting dir., 1978—. Served with AUS, 1952-54. Mem. Theatre Assn. Pa. (dir. 1969-72), Harrisburg Arts Council (exec. com. 1970-71), Ala. Theatre Conf. (mem. exec. council 1959-61). Stage adaptation Tolstoy's Anna Karenina, Harrisburg Community Theatre, 1971; TV adaptations and documentaries WITF-TV, Hershey, Pa., 1965-67. Author: Early American Society Guide to Central Pennsylvania, 1975. Contbr. People of the Revolution series to Early Am. Life Mag., 1976; (poetry) Paris Rev., 1978. Home: 1524 Greening Ln Harrisburg PA 17110 Office: 2001 N Front St Harrisburg PA 17102

CARNE, EDWARD BRYAN, elec. engr.; b. Hendon, Middlesex, Eng., Aug. 20, 1928; s. Sydney and Dorothy (Hall) C.; B.S. in Engring. with 1st class honours, U. London, 1949, Ph.D., 1952; postgrad. advanced mgmt. program Harvard, 1968-69; m. Joan Marie Ferry, Sept. 18, 1954; children—John Joseph, Margaret Mary, Michael Joseph, Brian Joseph, Kevin Joseph. Came to U.S., 1952, naturalized, 1959. Engr., Remington Rand Corp., South Norwalk, Conn. 1952-56, chief devel. engr., Utica, N.Y., 1957-59; group leader Nat. Carbon Co., Cleve., 1956-57; mgr. advanced computer lab. Melpar, Inc., Falls Church, Va., 1960-62, mgr. intelligence dept., 1962-65; dir. engring. LTV Electrosystems, Inc., Greenville, Tex., 1965-67, v.p., 1967-69; asso. dir. research, dir. Electronic Systems Lab., Gen Telephone and Electronics Labs., Inc., Waltham, Mass., 1969—. Chmn., Hunt County March of Dimes, 1966. Nominated for Nat. Capital award Washington, 1962. Mem. I.E.E.E. (sr. mem.). Author: Artificial Intelligence Techniques. Contbr. articles on fuse phenomena, computing techniques, artificial intelligence, telecommunications to tech. publs. Home: 38 Juniper Circle Concord MA 01742 Office: 40 Sylvan Rd Waltham MA 02154

CARNES, JAMES MCCABE, nuclear engr.; b. Canton, Ohio, Dec. 24, 1914; s. William Stuart and Nellie Ethel (McCabe) C.; B.S., U.S. Naval Acad., 1937; m. Edna Ramona Adams, Feb. 1, 1943; children—Diana May, Linda Louise, William Stuart. With United Engring. & Fdy. Co., Pitts., 1937-59; gen. supt. Arthur G. McKee & Co., Cleve., 1959-70; constrn. mgr. Westinghouse Nuclear Concepts div., Pitts., 1970-72, Ebasco Services, N.Y.C., 1972—. Served to lt. comdr. U.S. Navy, 1941-45. Mem. Am. Nuclear Soc., Assn. Iron and Steel Engrs., Mil. Order World Wars, U.S. Naval Inst. Republican. Club: Masons. Home: 2 Nappa Ln Westport CT 06880 Office: 2 Rector St New York City NY 10006

CARNEY, WILLIAM, congressman; b. Bklyn., July 1, 1942; s. Joseph James and Sarah Gertrude (Regan) C.; student Fla. State U., 1960-61; m. Barbara Ann Haverlin, May 14, 1966; children—Jackie, Julie. Sales rep. heavy equipment firm, 1972-76; mem. Suffolk County (N.Y.) Legislature, 1976-79, chmn. transp. and commerce com.; mem. 96th Congress from 1st Dist. N.Y. Vice pres. Suffolk County council Boy Scouts Am., L.I. Loves Bus., Inc.; active Suffolk County chpt. Am. Heart Assn. Served with M.C., U.S. Army, 1961-64. Conservative. Roman Catholic. Club: Kiwanis. Home: 7 Garvey Dr Hauppauge NY 11787 Office: Room 1113 Longworth House Office Bldg Washington DC 20515

CARNOCHAN, JOHN LOW, JR., aluminum co. exec.; b. Hagerstown, Md., Oct. 19, 1918; s. John Low and Susan (Long) C.; A.B., Western Md. Coll., 1940, M.Ed., 1947; Ed.D., Columbia, 1963; m. Emily Kent Linton, July 3, 1943; children—John, David, Susan, Jean, Carol, Robert. Tchr. pub. schs., Washington County, Md., 1941-53; vice-prin. schs., Hagerstown, Md., 1953-55; prin., Maugansville, Md., 1955-56, Williamsport, Md., 1956-61; ednl. TV project coordinator, Harrison, N.Y., 1961-62; asst. to state supt. schs. Md. Dept. Edn., Balt., 1962-63; asst. supt. county schs., Frederick, Md., 1963-64, supt. county schs., 1964-76; mgr. community relations Eastalco Aluminum Co., Frederick, 1976—; chmn. bd. Home Care Research, Inc. Mem. Md. adv. council Vocat. Tech. Edn. Served from pvt. to capt., AUS, 1941-46; now lt. col. Res. (ret.). Danforth fellow, 1974. Mem. Am. Assn. Sch. Adminstrs., Md. Assn. Sch. Supts. (past pres. and legis. chmn.), Pub. Relations Soc. Am., Md. C. of C. (dir.), Phi Delta Kappa, Delta Kappa Pi. Club: Kiwanis. Home: Round Hill Rd Frederick MD 21701 Office: Route 9 Box 128 Frederick MD 21701

CARONIA, VICTOR STEPHEN, dentist; b. Bklyn., July 1, 1927; s. Stephen and Mary (Lamanna) C.; student Kerpel Sch. Dental Tech., 1947-49, Hofstra Coll., 1951-53; D.D.S., Columbia, 1957; m. Marian J. Vento, Apr. 22, 1950; children—Susan Mary, Stephen Michael. Pvt. practice dentistry, N.Y.C., 1957—. Asso. prof. dentistry Sch. Dental and Oral Surgery, Columbia U., 1957—; cons. in prosthodontics USPHS Hosp., S.I., N.Y., 1967—. Pres. Montvale (N.J.) Republican Club, 1966-67; v.p. Montvale Bd. Edn., 1968-69, pres., 1969-70; mem. Montvale Sewer Commn., 1967-72; mem. Youth Guidance Council, Montvale, 1971-72; councilman Borough of Montvale, 1972-78. Served with USNR, 1945-46. Recipient Rowe-Wiberg medal, Ella Maria Ewell medal, award in pedodontics, Columbia U., 1957; Psi Omega award, 1957; Omicron Kappa Upsilon key, 1957. Fellow Am. Coll. Dentists, N.Y. Acad. Dentistry; mem. William Jarvie Soc. for Dental Research, Am. Assn. Dental Schs., Am. Prosthodontic Soc. Aide to cons. editor Stedman's Med. Dictionary, 21st edn., 1966. Home: 9 Donnybrook Rd Montvale NJ 07645 Office: 16 E 79 St New York City NY 10021

CAROSSO, VINCENT PHILLIP, historian; b. San Francisco, Mar. 19, 1922; s. Vincent G. and Lucia M. (Barale) C.; A.B., U. Calif., Berkeley, 1943, M.A., 1944, Ph.D. (Panama-Pacific Fellow in History, 1945-46, LeConte Meml. Fellow, 1946-47), 1948; m. Rose Celeste Berti, Aug. 23, 1952; 1 son, Steven Berti. Instr. history San Jose (Calif.) State Coll., 1949-50; asst. prof. Carnegie Inst. Tech., Pitts., 1950-53; asst. prof. N.Y. U., N.Y.C., 1953-56, asso. prof., 1956-62, prof. history, 1962-76, William R. Kenan Prof. History, 1976—; vis. asso. research prof. Harvard U., 1961-62, vis. lectr., 1963-64; Fulbright-Hays sr. lectr., Italy, 1973, 76. Harvard postdoctoral fellow, 1948-49; Nat. Endowment for Humanities fellow, 1976-77. Mem. Am. Hist. Assn., Orgn. Am. Historians, Econ. History Assn., Bus. and Econ. History Conf. (trustee 1973-76). Author: California Wine Industry, 1830-95, 1951; (with George Soule) American Economic History, 1957; (with Henry Parkes) Recent America, 2 vols., 1963; Investment Baking in America, 1970; editor: Wall Street and Security Markets, 1975; co-editor: Companies & Men: Business Enterprise in America, 1976; asso. editor Jour. Econ. History, 1955-61; editorial bds. Business Hist. Rev., 1957-61, Jour. Am. History, 1968-71; contbr. articles to profl. jours. Home: 375 Riverside Dr New York City NY 10025

CAROUSSO, DOROTHEE HUGHES, author, pub. relations exec.; b. Winthrop, Mass., Oct. 4, 1909; d. Patrick Lawrence and Luella (Nowell) Hughes; student pub. schs., St. Agnes Acad., N.Y.C., Kurt's Bus. Sch., Los Angeles; L.H.D., Combs Coll., 1968; m. Georges Carousso, Dec. 31, 1930 1 dau., Dorothee Nowell (Mrs. George Neil McKinnon). Author: (fiction) Open Then the Door, 1942; Sports Afield, 1960; (TV plays) Climax, Studio One; also fiction, verse in Collier's, Household, All-Story, Gothic Stories, mags., Woman's Home Companion, Canadian Home Jour.; geneal. works have appeared in Geneal. Mag. N.J., Pa. Geneal. Mag., Nat. Geneal. Soc. Quarterly, Md. and Del. Genealogist, New Eng. Hist. and Geneal. Register; pres. Georges Carousso & Assos., Inc.; trustee Nat. Bd. Certification in Geologists, 1976—. Book critic Bklyn. Eagle. Fellow Geneal. Soc. Pa. (v.p.); mem. Hist. Soc. Pa., Nat. Geneal. Soc., Montgomery County (Pa.), Chester County (Pa.), Berks Co., (Pa.), Buck County (Pa.), hist socs., Nat. Soc. Colonial Dames Am., D.A.R., Descs. Colonial Clergy, Colonial Daus. 17th Century, Bucks County Writers Guild, New Eng. Historic Geneal. Soc., N.Y. Geneal. and Biog. Soc., Daus. Utah Pioneers, Pa. Soc. New Eng. Women, Library Co. Phila. Address: 234M Blair Mill Village East Horsham PA 19044

CARP, GEORGE, electronics co. exec.; b. N.Y.C., May 28, 1921; s. Emil Z. and Florence (Singer) C.; B.S., Coll. City N.Y., 1949, B.A., 1942; m. Bernice Jeanne Levy, Oct. 1, 1944; children—Joy Nina, Michael Harrison. Lab. design engr. Ward Leonard Electric Co., Mt. Vernon, N.Y., 1948-50; exec. mgr. elec. controls G. Carp & Co., South Norwalk, 1950-54; evening instr. Bridgeport Engring. Inst., 1950-57; dir. engring. York Research Corp., Stamford, Conn., 1954-57, tech. dir., 1959-60; dir. electronic design Sperry Semicondr. div. Sperry Rand Co., 1957-59; dir. engring. Conn. Tel. & Electric Corp., Meriden, 1960-61, exec. v.p., 1961-62, pres., 1962—; pres. Holtzer Cabot Corp., North Attleboro, Mass., 1971-73; evening instr. Bridgeport Engring. Inst., 1950-57. Served with AUS, 1943-46. Fellow AIM (pres.'s council); mem. IEEE, AAAS, Inst. Environ. Sci., Nat., Conn. socs. profl. engrs. Patentee in field. Home: Hyland Rd Wilton CT 06897 Office: 38 Elm St Meriden CT 06450

CARPENTER, ASORA ESTHER TOATLEY (MRS. DARIOUS CARPENTER), social worker; b. Ashburn, Ga., July 11, 1919; d. Walker Alexander and Lucille (Walker) Toatley; student Wilberforce U., 1936-40; B.S., Temple U., 1963; M.S.W., U. Pa., 1965, postgrad. 1966-67; m. William Cochran, Apr. 17, 1945 (dec. Sept. 1957); 1 dau., Cheryl Ann; m. 2d, Darious Carpenter, Oct. 23, 1965. Caseworker Philadelphia County Bd. Assistance, Phila., 1946-57; caseworker Delaware County Bd. Assistance, Chester, Pa., 1957-59, supr. social work, 1959-65, social work tng. specialist, 1965-68; social worker III, marriage counsellor Family Services, Camden, N.J., 1968; dir. community and social services Comprehensive Group Health Services, Phila., 1968-70; dir. Phila. Community Coordinated Child Care Council, Franklin Inst. Research Labs., Phila., 1970-72; social work student supr. U. Pa., Phila, 1966-67; asst. prof. Temple U., Phila., 1969—, social work student supr., 1971-74; dir. social services, community services, mental health services Neighborhood Health Center, Trenton, 1973—; social work student supr. Trenton State Coll., 1973-74, Rider Coll., Trenton, 1973-74; adj. prof. social work Camden County Coll., Blackwood, N.J. Mem. Nat. Assn. Social Workers, Am. Pub. Welfare Assn., Acad. Certified Social Workers, Child Welfare League Am., Bus. and Profl. Women's Club, Advocates for School-Age Parents, South Jersey Continentals, Nat. Community Coordinated Child Care Council (dir. 1973—), Coalition for Children, Day Care and Child Devel. Council Am., Nat. Council Negro Women, Alpha Kappa Alpha. Home: 313 Farmdale Rd Moorstown NJ 08057 Office: 321 N Warren St Trenton NJ 08618

CARPENTER, CHARLES BERNARD, immunologist, educator; b. Melrose, Mass., Sept. 11, 1933; s. Seymour Charles and Pauline Annette (Freeman) C.; A.B., Dartmouth, 1955, D.M.S., 1956; M.D., Harvard, 1958; m. Sandra Davis, Aug. 4, 1956; children—Bradford Dana, Scott Charles. Intern, resident medicine II (Cornell) med. div. Bellevue Hosp., N.Y.C., 1958-60; research fellow Harvard Med. Sch., 1962-65; investigator Howard Hughes Med. Inst., 1973—; instr., asst. prof., asso. prof. Harvard Med. Sch., 1966—; sr. asso. in medicine Peter Bent Brigham Hosp., Boston; mem. transplantation and immunology com. NIH, 1974-78. Served with USN, 1960-62. Recipient NIH Research Career Devel. award, 1968-72; named Outstanding Young Man of Greater Boston, 1968. Diplomate Am. Bd. Internal Medicine. Mem. Am. Assn. Immunologists, Am. Soc. Clin. Investigation, Transplantation Soc., Am. Assn. Clin. Histocompatibility Testing (pres. 1977-78). Baptist. Contbr. articles to profl. jours.; editorial bd. Transplantation, Jour. Immunology, Immunopharmacology. Home: 242 Glen Rd Weston MA 02193 Office: 721 Huntington Ave Boston MA 02115

CARPENTER, CHARLES WHITNEY, II, educator; b. N.Y.C., Jan. 2, 1918; s. George W. and Dorothy (Millen) C.; A.B., Cornell U., 1943; M.A., U. So. Calif., 1952; grad. Indsl. Coll. Armed Forces, 1961; Ph.D., N.Y.U., 1968; M.S. Ed., Bucknell U., 1973; m. Dorothy Anne Byford, June 5, 1958; children—Anne Whitney (by previous marriage), Suzanne Whitney. Lectr., Wagner Coll., S.I., N.Y., 1954-55; teaching asst. Princeton, 1955-56; instr. N.Y. U., Bronx, 1956-59; asst. prof. Bronx Community Coll., 1959-62; instr. Adelphi Coll., Garden City, L.I., N.Y., evenings 1961-62, U. Vt., Burlington, 1962-63; instr. German, U. Hawaii, Honolulu, 1963-65; asst. prof. German, Buena Vista Coll., Storm Lake, Iowa, 1965-66; asso. prof. dept. fgn. langs. Bloomsburg (Pa.) State Coll., 1966-69, prof., 1969—; gen. partner Jesup & Lamont Stock Brokers, N.Y.C., 1946-48, ltd. partner, 1948-61. Served with Armed Services as 2d lt., 1939-42. Decorated Silver Order of Merit, Golden medal Spl. Membership, Japanese Red Cross, 1964, Golden Order of Merit, 1977; recipient Bronx Community Coll. award Student Council, Spl. Faculty award, 1962. N.Y. U. honors scholar, 1969. Fellow Intercontinental Biog. Assn. (life); mem. German Soc. City N.Y., Inst. Germanic Studies (London), Busch-Reisinger Mus. Friends Princeton Library, S.I. Inst. Arts and Scis., Bishop Mus. Assn., Cornell Alumni Athletic Assn., Mod. Lang. Assn., Am. Assn. Tchrs. German, AAUP, Order of Lafayette (life), Soc. Colonial Wars (life), St. Nicholas Soc. (life), Holland Soc., Am. Inst. Mgmt. (pres's council), NEA (life), Am. Ordnance Assn. (life), S.I. Hist. Soc. (life), Princeton Grad. Alumni Assn. (life), SAR (life), Linguistic Soc. Am., 1st Armored Div. Assn., Hawaii Assn. Lang. Tchrs., Linguistic Circle N.Y., Mil. Order World Wars, Nat. Rifle Assn. (endowment life), N.Y. U. Assn. for Libraries, Friends of Princeton Library, Orders and Medals Soc. Am., Pilgrim Soc. U.S., Schlaraffia-Nova Yorkin, United Hunts Racing Assn., Verein der New Yorker Deutschlehrer, Gen. Alumni Assn. U. So. Calif. (life), Bishop Mus., Imperial German Mil. Collectors Assn., Am. Assn. Higher Edn., Nat. Police Res. Officers Assn., Delta Phi Alpha, Phi Delta Kappa (life), Phi Kappa Phi, Delta Psi. Clubs: Racquet and Tennis, Princeton, St. Anthony, Regency-Whist (N.Y.C.); Nassau (Princeton, N.J.). Home: 144 W 4th St Bloomsburg PA 17815

CARPENTER, EARLE FRANKLYN, cons. civil engr.; b. Woodstock, N.B., Can., Nov. 16, 1936; s. Raymond S. and Katherine L. (Van Derbeck) C.; B.S., U. N.B., 1959; M.S., U. Del., 1967; m. E. L. Joey MacDonald, Apr. 1, 1961; children—Jennifer, Jamie, Arthur. Research engr. Nat. Bur. Standards, Washington, 1967-69; tech. staff Mitre Corp., MacLean, Va., 1969-74; pres. E.F. Carpenter Assos. Ltd., Fredericton, N.B., 1974—; pres. Misty Mirror Gift Shops Ltd., Fredericton, 1975—; dir. Field & Stream Machinery Ltd. Research fellow U. Del. 1964-66. Registered profl. engr. Md., Maine, N.B. Mem. ASCE, Assn. Profl. Engrs. N.B. Contbr. articles to profl. publs. Home: 22 Grey St Fredericton NB Canada Office: 469 Waterloo Row Fredericton NB E3B 1V7 Canada

CARPENTER, GEORGE BENTON, marine geophysicist; b. Beacon, N.Y., June 23, 1941; s. Ellsworth Ray and Frances (Bartenstein) C.; B.S. in Geology, State U. N.Y. at Oneonta, 1969. Cons. geophysicist Seismograph Service Corp., Tulsa, 1969-70; research asso., Lamont-Doherty Geol. Obs., Palisades, N.Y., 1970-77; geophysicist U.S. Geol. Survey, Washington, 1978—; cons. Danish govt., 1977, Naval Underwater Systems Command, New London, Conn., 1972-74. Served with USNR, 1960-63. Mem. Soc. Exploration Geophysicists. Contbr. articles in field to profl. jours. Home: 7811 Enola St McLean VA 22102 Office: US Geological Survey 1725 K St NW Washington DC 20006

CARPENTER, HARRY GLENN, JR., oil co. exec.; b. Greensburg, Pa., Mar. 16, 1939; s. Harry Glenn and Mary Louise (Rose) C.; B.A. in English, U. Pitts., 1961; m. Mary Jane Scheidhauer, Aug. 27, 1966; children—Robert Glenn, William Calvin. Instr. English, Pa. State U., also U. Pitts., 1965-66; personnel mgr. Gulf Oil Corp., Pitts., 1967-73, gen. mgr. internat. marine sales, 1977—; v.p. human resources Gulf Trading and Transp. Co., Pitts., 1974-77. Mem. bd. advisers Pitts. Jr. Achievement, 1967-69; bd. dirs. Pitts. YMCA, 1975-76; loaned exec. Pitts. United Way, 1972. Served as officer USMC, 1961-64; lt. col. Res. Teaching fellow U. Pitts., 1965-66. Mem. Am. Mgmt. Assn., Am. Compensation Assn., Marine Corps Res. Officer Assn. Republican. Methodist. Clubs: Pittsburgh, Pitts. Athletic. Home: 430 Morrison Dr Pittsburgh PA 15216 Office: Gulf Bldg 439 7th Ave Pittsburgh PA 15230

CARPENTER, HOYLE DAMERON, educator; b. Stockton, Calif., Aug. 8, 1909; s. William Horace and Mabel (Hanna) C.; Mus.B., U. Pacific, 1930; Mus.M., U. Rochester, 1932; Ph.D., U. Chgo., 1951-57; postgrad. U. Calif. at Berkeley, 1949-50; m. Rose Mick, Feb. 24, 1968. Instr. Ft. Hays (Kans.) State Coll., 1942-44; asst. prof. Grinnell Coll., 1944-57; faculty Glassboro (N.J.) State Coll., 1957—, asst. prof., 1957-60, asso. prof., 1960-61, prof., 1961—. Treas. Gloucester County Mental Health Assn., 1963-68. Committeeman Glassboro Democratic Com., 1964; v.p. Glassboro Dem. Club, 1964-66. Mem. Am., Internat. musicological socs., Music Tchrs. Nat. Assn. (sec. Eastern div. 1962-64), Music Educators Nat. Conf., Renaissance Soc. Am., Am. Guild Organists, AAUP, N.J. Music Tchrs. Assn. (pres. 1961-63), Pi Kappa Lambda. Author: Teaching Elementary Music without a Supervisor, 1959; also edits. Holyoke's Instrumental Assistant, 1959, Crequillon Pisne me peult venir, 1962; also several poster sets on music, 1970, also articles. Home: 512 S Woodbury Rd Pitman NJ 08071

CARPENTER, ROBERT R.M., baseball club exec.; b. Chgo., Dec. 12, 1917; grad. high sch., Chgo.; married; children—Robert R. M. III, Mary Kaye. Played football Tower Sch., also Duke; staff pub. relations dept. E.I. DuPont de Nemours & Co.; pres. Phila. Baseball Club, 1943—, also chmn. bd.; owner Wilmington Bombers, Am. Baseball League. Served with U.S. Army, 1944-46. Club: Wilmington Sportsmen's (pres.). Office: Phila Baseball Club Broad St and Pattison Ave Philadelphia PA 19148*

CARPENTER, STANLEY WATERMAN, paper co. exec.; b. Lowell, Mass., June 25, 1921; s. Daniel Albert and Edith May (Redfern) C.; student Lowell Textile Inst., 1939-42; m. Marie Kurth, May 12, 1957; children—Cheryl J., Mark S. With Thorp & Martin Co., Boston, 1947-49; self employed distbr. Ditto, Inc., 1949-51; marketing mgr. U.S. Envelope Co., Springfield, Mass., 1951-65; with N.Y. Envelope Corp., L.I., N.Y., 1965—, v.p. sales, 1969—. Asst. dir. CD, Bedford, Mass., 1946-49. Served with AUS, 1942-46. Decorated Army Commendation medal. Mem. Am. Mktg. Assn. Clubs: Saugatuck Harbor Yacht (Westport, Conn.); Connecticut Gun Guild (Hartford). Home: 14 Owenoke Park Westport CT 06880 Office: 29-10 Hunters Point Ave Long Island City NY 11101

CARPER, ANNA MARY, librarian; b. Palmyra, Pa.; d. Frank S. and Ella (Ebersole) Carper; A.B. cum laude, Elizabethtown Coll., 1941; M.S., Columbia, 1951. Tchr., librarian Fredericksburg (Pa.) High Sch., 1941-47; tchr. South Lebanon Schs., Lebanon, Pa., 1947-50; head cataloger U. Md., College Park, 1951-60; head librarian Elizabethtown (Pa.) Coll., 1960—, also dir. Mem. Am., Pa. (2d v.p. 1978-79), Lancaster County library assns., Delta Kappa Gamma (Beta Theta chpt.). Mem. Ch. of Brethren. Home: 316 E Plum St Apt A Elizabethtown PA 17022 Office: Zug Meml Library Elizabethtown PA 17022

CARR, ARTHUR CHARLES, psychologist, educator; b. Buffalo, Nov. 27, 1918; s. John E. and Katherine (Haas) C.; B.S., Buffalo State Tchrs. Coll., 1941; M.A Tchrs. Coll., Columbia U., 1946; Ph.D., U. Chgo., 1952; postgrad. William Alanson White Inst., 1953-54, Inst. Group Therapy, 1957-58, N.Y. Soc. Clin. Psychologists, 1954, 60. Trainee clin. psychology VA 1947-52; sr. clin. psychologist Creedmoor State Hosp., Queens Village, N.Y., 1952-56; prin. clin. psychologist N.Y. State Psychiat. Inst., N.Y.C., 1956—. Asst. prof. psychology Adelphi Coll., Garden City, L.I., N.Y., 1952-56; asso. prof. med. psychology, dept. psychiatry Coll. Phys. and Surg., Columbia U., 1956-71, prof., 1971-78; clin. prof. psychology in psychiatry Cornell Med. Coll., N.Y.C., 1978—. Served to maj. AUS, 1941-46. Diplomate Am. Bd. Examiners in Profl. Psychology, N.Y. State Edn. Dept. Fellow Am. Psychol. Assn., Soc. Projective Techniques (bd. mem. 1961-64, pres. 1971-72); mem. Eastern, N.Y. State psychol. assns., N.Y. Soc. Clin. Psychologists. Author: (with Shervert Frazier) Introduction to Psychopathology, 1964; (with Herbert Hendin, Willard Gaylin) Psychoanalysis and Social Research, 1965. Editor: (with Bernard Schoenberg and Helen Pettit) Teaching Psychosocial Aspects of Patient Care, 1968; author, editor: (with B. Schoenberg, D. Peretz, A. Kutscher) Loss and Grief, 1970; Psychosocial Aspects of Terminal Care, 1972; The Terminal Patient, 1973; Anticipatory Grief, 1974; Bereavement, 1975. Editorial bd., cons. editor Jour. Projective Techniques, 1967-73; asso. editor Jour. Abnormal Psychology, 1966-70, Jour. Thanatology, 1971—; editor-in-chief Man and Medicine, 1975—. Contbr. articles to profl. publs. Home: 560 Riverside Dr New York City NY 10027 Office: Westchester Div NY Hosp 21 Bloomingdale Rd White Plains NY 10605

CARR, ELLIOTT GRABILL, assn. exec.; b. Hanover, N.H., Sept. 24, 1938; s. Robert K. and Olive (Grabill) C.; A.B cum laude, Dartmouth, 1960; M.B.A., Harvard, 1964; postgrad. Princeton, 1961; m. Susan Wheatley, July 6, 1968; children—Priscilla, Sarah. With Central Nat. Bank Cleve., 1961-64; with Mass. Indemnity Life Ins. Co., Boston, 1965-69, treas., chief investment officer, 1969; research dir. Savs. Bank Assn. Mass., Boston, 1969-73, exec. v.p., 1973—; dir. Cape Cod Clam Co., Marion, Mass., Abington Mut. Ins. Co. Vice chmn. Silver Lake Regional Sch. Com.; trustee So. Mass. Shellfish Trust; chmn. bd. assessors, Pembroke, Mass. Mem. Pembroke Hist. Soc. Club: East Pembroke Community. Author: Better Management of Business Giving, 1966; Observation on the Competitive Position of Massachusetts Mutual Savings Banks, 1973. Contbr. articles to profl. jours. Home: Country Rd Pembroke MA 02359 Office: 50 Congress St Boston MA 02115

CARR, JOHN JEFFREY, social worker; b. N.Y.C., Jan. 5, 1943; s. John Croston and Rita Maria (Quinn) C.; A.B., Providence Coll., 1964; M.S., Simmons Coll., 1968; m. Mary L. Mellor, Feb. 20, 1965; children—Jayson, Kathy. Social worker R.I. Dept. Social Welfare, 1964-68, casework supr., 1968-71; casework supr. Childrens' Friend and Service, Providence, 1971-72; exec. dir. Family Service Soc., Pawtucket, R.I., 1972-78; mem. faculty Boston Coll., Boston U., Simmons Coll., Salva Regina Coll. Mem. supervisory bd. R.I. Gov.'s Justice Commn. Recipient M.E. Kelley award Simmons Coll., 1976. Mem. Acad. Cert. Social Workers, Am. Assn. Marriage and Family Counselors, Am. Orthopsychiat. Assn. Project team dir. police crisis teams Pawtucket. Office: 33 Summer St Pawtucket RI 02860

CARR, LAWRENCE EDWARD, JR., lawyer; b. Colorado Springs, Colo., Aug. 10, 1923; s. Lawrence Edward and Lelah R. (Rubert) C.; B.S., U. Notre Dame, 1948, LL.B., 1949; LL.M., George Washington U., 1954; m. Agnes Isabel Dyer, Dec. 26, 1946; children—Mary Lee, James Patrick, Lawrence Edward III, Eileen Louise, Thomas Vincent. Admitted to Colo. bar, 1949, D.C. bar, 1952, Md. bar, 1961; with Travelers Ins. Co., 1949-51; practiced in Washington, 1952—; sr. partner firm Carr, Jordan, Coyne & Savits, and predecessor firms, 1960—. Pres., Capital Investment Co. of Washington, 1962—. Served with USMCR, 1943-46, 51-52; col. Res. Mem. Am. Bar Assn. (ho. dels. 1974), Bar Assn. D.C. (dir. 1969-71, pres. 1974-75), Internat. Assn. Ins. Counsel. Home: 12001 Piney Glen Ln Potomac MD 20854 Office: 900 17th St NW Washington DC 20036

CARR, MARTIN DOUGLAS, TV dir., producer; b. Flushing, N.Y., Jan. 20, 1932; s. Irving Conovitz and Isabel (Hochdorf) C.; B.A. summa cum laude, Williams Coll., 1953; postgrad. Neighborhood Playhouse Sch. Theatre, 1956. Producer, CBS News, N.Y.C., 1957-69, NBC News, N.Y.C., 1969-71, ABC News, N.Y.C., 1973—; producer The Saturday Night Kid, N.Y.C., 1959. Served to lt. (j.g.), USNR, 1953-55. Recipient Emmy award, Nat. Acad. TV Arts and Scis., 1966, 67, 68, 71, Peabody award U. Ga. Sch. Journalism, 1968, 70, 71, Robert F. Kennedy Journalism award Robert F. Kennedy Found., 1970, Sidney Hillman Found. Found. award, 1971,

DuPont/Columbia Journalism award, 1971, Gavel award Am. Bar Assn., 1972. Mem. Phi Beta Kappa. Club: Williams (N.Y.C.). Major TV prodns.: CBS Reports, Hunger in America; NBC White Paper, Migrant, This Child Is Rated X, The Search For Ulysses, ABC Close-up: The Culture Thieves. Home: 305 W 86th St New York City NY 10024

CARR, PATRICK WILLIAM, pub. relations exec.; b. Denver, Dec. 17, 1920; s. John Spencer and Mary Irene (Freeman) C.; grad. high sch.; m. Judith Ann Starr, Oct. 7, 1960; children—Shanon Kathleen, Douglas Spencer, Jennifer Ann. Reporter, writer Middletown (Ohio) Jour., Kansas City (Mo.) Star, 1946-49; writer, editor UPI, Kansas City, Topeka, N.Y.C., 1949-56; pub. relations exec. Firestone, Akron, Ohio, 1956-58, Young & Rubicam, N.Y.C., 1959-66, P.R. Assos., N.Y.C., 1966-67; pres. Patrick Carr Assos., pub. relations, N.Y.C., 1967—; lectr. St. John's U.; creative writer. Mem. Pub. Relations Soc. Am. (counselors sect.), Soc. Silurians. Democrat. Roman Catholic. Clubs: Princeton of N.Y., Overseas Press Am. Home: Skyline Ridge Bridgewater CT 06752 Office: 147 E 50th St New York City NY 10022

CARR, RALPH LIONEL, JR., indsl. chemist; b. Charlestown, Mass., Nov. 2, 1917; s. Ralph Lionel and Helen Elizabeth (Swift) C.; Asso. Chemistry, Lincoln Tech. Inst., Boston, 1949; B.B.A. in Engring. and Mgmt., Northeastern U., 1956; m. Violet Cornell, July 2, 1949. Chief chemist BIF unit Gen. Signal Corp., W. Warwick, R.I., 1951—; judge sci. fairs, R.I.; tchr. mineralogy; cons. chemistry; lectr.-demonstrator crystals and mineralogy. Chief observer Ground Observer Corps, Cranston, R.I., 1953-56; counselor in sci. Cranston dist. Boys Scouts Am. Served with inf. AUS, 1942-45; ETO. Decorated Bronze Star. Mem. Am. Chem. Soc., Am. Inst. Chemists, Am. Water Works Assn., Narragansett Water Pollution Control Assn., Fine Particle Soc., AAAS, R.I. Mineral Hunters (pres. 1969-70, 75-76), Am. Topical Assn. Co-editor Bowen-Lite, 1973—; contbr. articles in field to profl. jours. and books. Home: 25 Farnum Rd Warwick RI 02888 Office: 1600 Division Rd West Warwick RI 02893

CARR, WILLIAM HENRY ALEXANDER, pub. relations exec., author; b. Albany, N.Y., Nov. 25, 1924; s. John Joseph and Ruby (Sokol) C.; student U. Chgo., 1944-46; m. Margaret McCormick, Dec. 19, 1976. Reporter City News Bur., Chgo., 1943-44, Chgo. Sun, 1944-45, 47-48, Chgo. Times, 1945-46; news editor ABC, 1946-47; pub. relations client counsel John Price Jones Co, N.Y.C., 1949-52; asso. dir. pub. relations United Community Def. Services, N.Y.C., 1952-55; reporter, columnist, editor N.Y. Post, N.Y.C, 1955-64; pub. relations cons. INA Corp., Phila., 1967-71, 71-72; dir. pub. info. State of Pa., Harrisburg, 1971; sr. speechwriter N.Y. Life Ins. Co., N.Y.C., 1975-76; account exec. Jack Raymond & Co., N.Y.C., 1977—; books include: JFK: A Complete Biography, 1962, rev. edit., 1963, The Emergence of Red China, 1966, The Du Ponts of Delaware (award Friends of Am. Writers), 1964, The Basic Book of the Cat, 1963, rev. edit., 1978; others. Mem. Md. Gov.'s Task Force on Crime Prevention and Community Involvement, 1968-69; mem. exec. com. Pa. Pub. Com. for Humanities, 1971-76. Served with USAAF, World War II. Recipient Albert Schweitzer medal for Humanitarianism Animal Welfare Inst. 1961. Mem. Phila. Writers Conf. (dir.), Authors Guild Am., Aircraft Owners and Pilots Assn., Nat. Pilots Assn. Clubs: Overseas Press, N.Y. Press. Contbr. articles to numerous mags.; columnist Dog World Mag, 1958-65. Home: 71 Letchworth Ave Yardley PA 19067 Office: 488 Madison Ave New York City NY 10022

CARR, WILSON MURRAY, III, govt. ofcl.; b. Charlottesville, Va., Oct. 29, 1934; s. Wilson M. and Catherine (Stoneham) C.; B.A., U. Va., 1960; postgrad. Pa. State U.; m. Mary Frances Beck, Mar. 4, 1960; children—Mary Catherine, Elizabeth Stoneham. Investigator, U.S. Civil Service, Washington, 1961-68; budget analyst Dept. of Justice, Washington, 1968-69; sr. mgmt. analyst Interstate Commerce Commn., Washington, 1969-75; mgmt. officer Bur. of Reclamation, Dept. of Interior, Washington, 1975—. Active U. Va. Student Aid Found. Served with U.S. Army, 1954-56. Mem. Assn. of Fed. Investigators, Airborne Assn., Fairfax Hosp. Assn., Smithsonian Assos. Episcopalian. Home: 10930 Fairchester Dr Fairfax VA 22030 Office: Bur of Reclamation Dept of Interior 18th & C St NW 7550 Washington DC 20240

CARRATELLO, DOMENICO, chem. engr.; b. Santa Croce Camerina, Sicily, Italy, May 9, 1949; s. Giovanni and Carmela (Mandara) C.; came to U.S., 1966, naturalized, 1974; B.S. in Chem. Engring., Newark Coll. Engring., 1972, postgrad. in chem. engring., 1974—. Process engr. E.I. du Pont de Nemours & Co., Newark, 1972-73, Inmont Corp., Hawthorne, N.J., 1973-74; plant environ. control specialist Ford Motor Co., Mahwah, N.J., 1974—. Mem. Am. Inst. Chem. Engrs., No. N.J. Amateur Soccer Assns., Omega Chi Epsilon. Home: 160 Woodside Ave Ridgewood NJ 07450 Office: Ford Motor Co NJ State Hwy 17 N Mahwah NJ 07430

CARREL, JEFFREY MACK, podiatrist; b. Buffalo, Mar. 7, 1942; s. Ralph and Gertrude (Rosen) C.; student U. Buffalo, 1959-61; Dr. Podiatric Medicine cum laude, N.Y. Coll. Podiatric Medicine, 1965; m. Sheila Rose, June 21, 1964; children—Aaron, Mitchell, David. Resident Woodward Gen. Hosp., Highland Park, Mich., 1965-66, Kern Hosp., Detroit, 1965-66; practice podiatric medicine, Buffalo, 1966—; mem. staff, Rosa Coplan Jewish Home and Infirmary, Buffalo, 1967—, also Sheridan Park Hosp., Tonawanda, N.Y.; Staff Deaconess Hosp., Buffalo, podiatry cons. Family Practice Center, 1977—. Bd. dirs. Erie County unit Am. Cancer Soc., Buffalo. Recipient, sr. research award N.Y. Podiatry Soc., 1965, William J. Stickel Research award Am. Podiatry Assn., 1968; diplomate Am. Bd. Podiatric Orthopedics, Am. Bd. Podiatric Surgery. Fellow Am. Coll. Foot Orthopedists (nat. sec. 1972-74, pres. 1975-76, trustee 1977-78), Am. Coll. Foot Surgeons; mem. N.Y. Acad. Scis., Acad. Podiatry. Mason. Contbg. author Modern Therapy, Basic Foot Problems. Asso. editor neurology sect. Yearbook of Podiatry; editorial bd. Archives of Podiatric Medicine and Surgery, Jour. Am. Podiatry Assn. Contbr. articles to profl. jours. Home: 152 President's Walk Williamsville NY 14221 Office: 409 Brisbane Bldg Buffalo NY 14203 also 388 Evans St Williamsville NY 14221 also 1220 Main St Niagara Falls NY

CARRETTA, ROBERT WILLIAM, med. center adminstr.; b. Queens, N.Y., Mar. 10, 1946; s. Alphonso and Agnes Mary (Daw) C.; student Suffolk County Community Coll., 1963-64, U.S. Armed Forces Inst., 1966-68, C.W. Post Coll., 1970-71; m. Claire Mary Grayson, Oct. 5, 1968; children—Jon, Lisa. Engring. plant adminstr. Grumman Aircraft Engring. Corp., N.Y.C., 1964-66; corp. adminstr., 1968-71; adminstrv. asst. methadone maintenance treatment, 1971-72, communications asst., 1972, communications coordinator, 1972-73, asst. dir. purchasing, 1973-74, asso. dir. purchasing, 1974-76, dir. materials mgmt., 1976—. Mem. adv. com. Joint Purchasing Corp. of Fedn. Jewish Philanthropies N.Y., 1973—. Served with USNR, 1966-68. Mem. Am. Soc. Hosp. Purchasing and Materials Mgmt., Nat. Assn. Ednl. Buyers, Am. Hosp. Assn., Hosp. Communication Assn. N.Y. Republican. Roman Catholic. Home: 102 Grandview St Huntington NY 11743 Office: 10 Nathan D Perlman Pl New York City NY 10003

CARRIERA, ANTHONY JOHN, JR., banker; b. Stamford, Conn., Oct. 23, 1941; s. Anthony and Anna (Vieta) C.; B.S., U. Bridgeport, 1974; m. Diane Scognamiglio, July 6, 1968; children—Danielle R., Tracey L. With State Nat. Bank of Conn., Bridgeport, 1962—, v.p., loan officer, retail accounts group, 1975—; dir. Project Own, Inc., Bridgeport, 1976—; adviser fin. com. Mini Store, Inc., Bridgeport, 1976—; adj. prof. accounting U. Bridgeport, 1977—. Bd. dirs. Monks of Brotherhood of St. Francis, Cambridge, N.Y., 1972—; fin. adviser Sisters of St. Claire, Cambridge, 1973—. Served with U.S. Army, 1959-62. Mem. Nat. Assn. Accountants. Home: 26 Barberry Rd Southport CT 06490 Office: 10 Middle St Bridgeport CT 06604

CARRINO, FRANK GAETANO, educator; b. Lima, Ohio, Feb. 15, 1922; s. Ralph and Concetta (Fortuna) C.; A.B., Baldwin-Wallace Coll., 1946; M.A., U. Wis., 1945; Ph.D., U. Mich., 1956; m. Elnora M. Drafahl, Feb. 4, 1950; 1 dau., Constance Anne. Instr. Spanish, Muhlenberg Coll., Allentown, Pa., 1947-48; from instr. to asso. prof. Romance langs. State U. N.Y. at Albany, 1948-59, prof., 1959—, chmn. dept. Hispanic langs. and lit., Italian and Portuguese, 1976—, asst. to pres., 1961-62, fgn. student adviser 1961-65, dir. Center for Inter-Am. Studies, 1961—. Dir. Binat. Center, USIS, Asuncion, Paraguay, 1959-61; dir. fgn. study program U. Guadalajara; cons. Internat. U., Fla., 1971. Mem. World Affairs Council, Albany, N.Y., 1953-54; bd. dirs. Albany Internat. Center, 1963-65. Served with USAAF, 1942-45. Dept. State grantee, 1962, 64, 65; Am. Specialist grantee, Dominican Republic, 1964-66; Fulbright-Hayes scholar U. Ams., Mexico, 1965; State U. N.Y. Research Found. grantee, 1974. Mem. Am. Assn. Tchrs. Spanish and Portuguese, Latin Am. Studies Assn., State U. Latin Americanists, Schenectady Hispanic Soc., Phi Sigma Iota, Mu Lambda Alpha. Author: (with Ana Manarimi) Let's Talk English, Vols. II and III, 1960, 61. Co-editor bilingual edit. Martin Fierro, 1967; co-translator UNESCO edit. the Gaucho Martin Fierro, 1974. Contbr. articles to profl. jours. Home: 34 Loudon Pkwy Loudonville NY 12211 Office: 1400 Washington Ave Albany NY 12222

CARROL, WILFRED, physician; b. Russia, Mar. 18, 1909; s. Israel and Jennie C.; came to U.S., 1910, naturalized, 1932; A.B., Columbia U., 1929, M.D., 1933; postgrad. Mt. Sinai Med. Sch., 1944, N.Y. U., 1948, Seton Hall Med. Coll. (now N.J. Coll. Medicine), 1947-49; m. Ruth Gluck, Feb. 11, 1938; children—Laura Carrol Guthart, Edward N. Intern, Clara Maass Meml. Hosp., Newark, 1933-34; practice internal medicine, Newark and Maplewood, N.J., 1935—; asso. attending physician Newark-Beth Israel Med. Center, 1954-75, emeritus, 1975—; clin. asso. prof. medicine Coll. Medicine and Dentistry N.J., 1969—; draft bd. physician, Newark, 1941-45. Recipient certificate of appreciation, Pres. F.D. Roosevelt, 1944; diplomate Am. Bd. Internal Medicine. Fellow A.C.P., N.J. Acad. Medicine; mem. AMA. Home: 74 Parker Ave Maplewood NJ 07040

CARROLL, CHARLES MICHAEL, data processing co. exec.; b. Elizabeth, N.J., July 23, 1948; s. William and Marie Agatha (Washington) C.; B.A., Rutgers U., 1970; M.B.A., Seton Hall U., 1972; m. Virginia Marilyn Maneri, Oct. 24, 1970; children—Christine, Charissa. Chief accountant Monarch Corp. div. Bristol-Myers Corp., Hillside, N.J., 1970-71; sr. accountant consolidations Research-Cottrell Inc., Bound Brook, N.J., 1971-73; dir. corporate accounting Automatic Data Processing Inc., Clifton, N.J., 1973—; cons. fed., local income taxes. N.J. State scholar, 1966-70; licensed pub. accountant, N.J. Mem. Nat., Am. assns. accountants. Home: also 30 Lord Stirling Dr Morris Township NJ 07960 Office: 405 Route 3 Clifton NJ 07015

CARROLL, CYRIL JAMES, educator; b. Phila., Sept. 28, 1933; s. Michael James and Sara Marie (Timony) C.; B.A., Pa. State U., 1959; M.A., U. Md., 1970; m. Ann Cary Sanson, Dec. 18, 1965; children—Deborah Ann. Tchr., Prince George's County, Md., 1959-69; teaching fellow U. Md., College Park, 1969-70; lectr. Prince George's Community Coll., Largo, Md., 1968-70, asso. prof. speech communication and theatre, 1970—; cons. to various schs. and theatres. Served with AUS, 1956-58. Recipient certificate Region II, Am. Theatre Coll. Festival, 1974; named Outstanding Play Dir., Md. Drama Assn., 1966, 67, 68. Mem. Am. Theatre Assn. (certificate of appreciation Mid-Atlantic chpt. 1977), Univ. and Coll. Theatre Assn., Md. (pres. 1977-78), Eastern, Met. Washington speech communication assns., Smithsonian Resident Asso., Soc. Literature and Arts, Pa. State U. Alumni Assn., Assn. for Children With Learning Disabilities (pres. Prince George's chpt. 1977-78). Democrat. Roman Catholic. Home: 13403 Queen's Ln Fort Washington MD 20022 Office: Prince George's Community College 301 Largo Rd Largo MD 20870

CARROLL, EDWARD GONZALEZ, bishop; b. Wheeling, W.Va., Jan. 7, 1910; s. Julius Sylvester and Florence (Dungee) C.; B.A., Morgan State Coll., 1930, LL.D. (hon.), 1967; B.D., Yale U., 1933; M.A., Columbia U. Union Theol. Sem., N.Y., 1941; Ed.D., Columbia U.; m. Phenola Valentine, July 3, 1934; children—Edward Gonzalez, Nansi Ethelene. Ordained to ministry United Methodist Ch., 1935; served congregations Md., N.Y., Va., W.Va., 1935-68; pastor Marvin Meml. Ch., Silver Spring, Md., 1968-72; consecrated bishop Northeastern Jurisdictional Conf., 1972; resident bishop Maine, N.H., So. New Eng. confs., Boston, 1972—; past instr. ethics and philosophy, dir. vol. religious activities Morgan State U.; ministerial del. Gen. Conf. United Meth. Ch., 1972. Past asso. sec. Nat. Student YMCA; bd. dirs. Sibley Hosp., Washington, Wesley Theol. Sem., Washington, Urban League, NAACP. Served to maj. AUS, 1941-45. Contbr. articles to religious jours. Home: 53 Worthington Rd Brookline MA 02146 Office: 581 Boylston St Room 81 Boston MA 02116

CARROLL, MARGUERITE RUTH, educator; b. Medford, Mass., June 25, 1926; d. Harry Anthony and Rose (Melanson) Carroll; B.S., Boston U., 1947; M.Ed., Boston Coll., 1954; Ed.D., St. John's U., 1974. Tchr. Great Mills (Md.) High Sch., 1947-51; dir. guidance Ware (Mass.) High Sch., 1953-54; sch. counselor North Jr. High Sch., Waltham, Mass., 1954-58, Darien (Conn.) High Sch., 1958-64; dir. guidance Weston (Conn.) Pub. Schs., 1964-68; asst. prof. Fairfield (Conn.) U. Grad. Sch. Edn., 1969-75, asso. prof., 1975—, dept. chmn. div. counseling and sch. psychology, 1972-75, coordinator Tomorrow's Woman Today program div. counseling and community services, 1975—. Bd. dirs. Woman Place, Darien, Conn., 1974-77. Mem. Am. (treas. 1969-70, nat. cons. task force group procedures 1969-71), Conn. (pres. 1967-68) sch. counselor assns., Am. Psychol. Assn., Am. (chmn. bd. jour. editors, mem. research awards com. 1971-72), Conn., Fairfield County (pres. 1962-63) personnel and guidance assns., New Eng. Guidance Conf. (exec. com. 1968-70), Assn. Counselor Edn. and Supervision (chmn. licensure research com. 1975-76), Conn. Assn. Counselor Edn. and Supervision (pres. 1978—), Assn. Specialists in Group Work (sec. 1976-77, senator 1977—, publs. chmn. 1977—), New Eng. Assn. Specialists in Group Work (pres.-elect 1977—). Asso. editor The School Counselor, 1971-72, editor, 1972—. Home: 9 Longview Dr Ridgefield CT 06877 Office: Fairfield U Fairfield CT 06430

CARROLL, STEPHEN JOHN, JR., educator; b. Boston, Aug. 23, 1930; s. Stephen John and Helene Ann (Roach) C.; B.S., U. Calif., Los Angeles, 1957; M.A., U. Minn., 1959, Ph.D., 1963; m. Donna June Freeman, June 24, 1961; children—Christopher Wayne, Alisa Helene. Research fellow, instr. U. Minn., 1957-61; asst. prof. Villanova U., 1961-64; asst. prof. U. Md., College Park, 1964-67, asso. prof., 1967-70, prof., 1970—, chmn. faculty organizational behavior and indsl. relations, 1972-77, also chmn. div. personnel/human resources Acad. Mgmt., 1973-74, editorial bd. jour., 1974—. Served with USNR, 1947-53. Mem. Am. Psychol. Assn., Acad. Mgmt., Alpha Kappa Psi, Beta Gamma Sigma, Iota Rho Chi. Author: (with Henry L. Tosi) Management by Objectives: Applications and Research, 1973, Management: Contingencies, Structure, and Process, 1976; (with Frank T. Paine and John B. Miner) The Management Process: Cases and Readings, 2d edit., 1977; (with Allan N. Nash) The Management of Compensation, 1974; (with Henry L. Tosi) Organizational Behavior, 1977. Contbr. articles to profl. jours. Home: 3901 Foreston St Beltsville MD 20705

CARRUTH, DAVID BARROW, landscape architect; b. Woodbury, Conn., June 28, 1926; s. Gorton Veeder and Margery Barrow (Dibb) C.; student N.Y. U., 1946-47; B.S. in Land Planning, Cornell U., 1951, M. Landscape Architecture, 1952; Landscape architect, asso. Clarke & Rapuano, Inc., cons. engrs., landscape architects, N.Y.C., 1952-70; pres. Kane and Carruth, landscape architects, Pleasantville, N.Y., 1970—; mem. N.Y. State Bd. Landscape Architecture, 1970—; pres. Council Landscape Archtl. Registration Bds., 1975, Interprofl. Council on Registration, 1975, Landscape Archtl. Registration Bds. Found., 1975. Trustee Bayard Cutting Arboretum; mem. Katonah-Lewisboro Sch. Bd., 1963-73. Served with USNR, 1944-46. Licensed landscape architect, N.Y., Conn., Pa., Fla., Mass.; nat. certification as landscape architect. Mem. Am. Soc. Landscape Architects. Office: 70 Memorial Plaza Pleasantville NY 10570

CARSON, ELLAREETHA, dietitian; b. Marianna, Fla., July 25, 1934; d. Edward David and Rosa (Williams) Trueblood; B.S., Fla. A. and M. U., 1955; m. Sydney W. Marshall, Jr., Jan. 17, 1959; 1 son, Sydney W.; m. 2d, A. Lincoln Carson, Jan. 8, 1977. Staff dietitian Fla. A. and M. U., Tallahassee, 1955-56; dietetic intern Freedmen's Hosp., Washington, 1956-57; therapeutic dietitian Mt. Sinai Hosp., Hartford, Conn., 1957-64, Lankenau Hosp., Phila., 1967-69; dietitian Odgen Foods, Phila., 1969; asst. dir. dietetics Mt. Sinai Hosp., Hartford, 1969-72, dir. dietetics, 1972—, supr. clin. dietetic students, sponsor dietetic traineeship programs, 1971-73, 74-75. Recipient certificate of merit Fla. A. and M. U. Alumni Assn., 1976. Mem. Am., Conn., No. Conn. dietetic assns., Conn. Soc. Hosp. Food Adminstrs., Fla. A. and M. U. Alumni Assn. (chpt. v.p. 1976-77). Methodist. Home: 33 Split Rock Dr Waterbury CT 06706 Office: 500 Bluehills Ave Hartford CT 06112

CARSON, GEORGE WILLIAM, clergyman; b. Island Falls, Me., Jan. 27, 1918; s. William Alonzo and Laura Blanche (Green) C.; B.A., Gordon Coll. Theology and Missions, 1943; M.A., Boston U., 1944; B.D. (fellow), Princeton Theol. Sem., 1947, Th.M., 1949; postgrad. U. Edinburgh (Scotland), 1947-48; D.D., Ricker Coll., 1964; m. Irene Maud Haugh, Sept. 16, 1947; children—Philip Green, Lois Elaine, Stephen George. Ordained to ministry Presbyn. Ch., 1947; supply minister Blackwood (N.J.) Presbyn. Ch., 1945-47, St. Michael's Ch. Scotland, Cupar-Fife, 1947-48; minister Chestnut Level Presbyn. Ch., Quarryville, Pa., 1948-52, First Presbyn. Ch., Williamsport, Pa., 1952-58, Trinity Presbyn. Ch., Beaver Falls, Pa., 1958—; moderator Presbytery of Donegal, 1951; commr. Gen. Assembly U.P. Ch., 1953, 55, 62, 75; moderator Beaver Butler Presbytery, 1961, chmn. com. overtures and records, 1972—; vice moderator Synod Pa., 1956, 71; bd. dirs. Beaver County Council Chs., 1962-64, 73-76, v.p., 1976-78, pres., 1978-80; news reporter World Council Chs., Evanston, Ill., 1954. Mem. Upper Beaver Valley Human Relations Com., 1963-69, Speakers' Bur., Beaver County United Fund, 1965-69, Beaver County Salvation Army Adv. Bd., 1965-70; mem. Beaver Falls Area Centennial Corp., 1966-68, chmn. spl. events div., 1968; mem. exec. bd. Allegheny Trails council Boy Scouts Am., 1966—, chmn. Alum Rock Dist., 1968-70; chmn. Friends Scouting, 1967, 74; bd. dirs. Beaver County unit Am. Cancer Soc., crusade chmn., 1972, v.p., 1976-79; bd. dirs. Community Concert Assn.; mem. advisory com. Womens Center of Beaver County, 1976-78. Recipient George Washington Bronze medal (8), Valley Forge, Pa., intermittently 1950-67; Tri-State Zionist Orgn. fellow study tour of Israel, 1967; Tri-State Zionist award, 1969; Tour host, Holy Lands, 1970; named Beaver Valley Man of Year, 1968. Mem. Internat. Platform Assn. Clubs: Masons, K.T. (grand prelate 1967), Rotary (dist. gov. 1965-66, dist. rep. to internat. conv. Mexico City 1970). Home: 144 Rama Rd Gravenhurst Beaver Falls PA 15010 Office: 8th Ave and 11th St Beaver Falls PA 15010

CARTER, ALEXANDER, bishop; b. Montreal, Que., Can., Apr. 16, 1909; s. Thomas and Mary (Kerr) C.; M.Th., M.C.L., LL.D., Montreal Coll. 1930; ed. Sem. Philosophy and Grand Sem. Montreal, 1936; M.Th., M.C.L., Canadian Coll., Rome, 1939; LL.D. (hon.), Laurentian U., Sudbury, Ont., 1962. Ordained priest Roman Cath. Ch., 1936; bishop of Sault Ste. Marie, 1957—; chancellor U. Sudbury, 1962—. Pres. Canadian Cath. Conf., 1967-69. Mem. Vanier Inst. Address: 480 McIntyre St W North Bay ON Canada

CARTER, JAMES EARL, JR. (JIMMY), Pres. of U.S.; b. Plains, Ga., Oct. 1, 1924; s. James Earl and Lillian (Gordy) C.; student Ga. Southwestern U., 1941-42, Ga. Inst. Tech., 1942-43; B.S., U.S. Naval Acad., 1947; postgrad. Union Coll., 1952; J.D. (hon.), U. Notre Dame, 1977; m. Rosalynn Smith, July 7, 1946; children—John William, James Earl III, Donnel Jeffrey, Amy Lynn. Commd. ensign USN, 1947, advanced through grades to lt., 1950, ret., 1953; farmer, warehouseman, 1953-77; mem. Ga. Senate, 1962-66; gov. Ga., 1971-74; Pres. of U.S., 1977—. Chmn. Sumter County (Ga.) Sch. Bd., 1955-62; pres. Plains Devel. Corp., 1963, Sumter County Devel. Corp., 1963; chmn. West Central Ga. Area Planning and Devel. Commn., 1964; deacon, Sunday sch. tchr. Plains Bapt. Ch., to 1977; candidate Gov. Ga., 1966. Democrat. Club: Lions (dist. gov. 1968-69). Author: Why Not the Best?, 1975. Home: 1 Woodland Dr Plains GA 31780 Office: White House 1600 Pennsylvania Ave Washington DC 20500

CARTER, MARC EDGAR, artist; b. North Tarrytown, N.Y.; s. Marcellus Edgar and Mary Louise (Shannon) C.; student Columbia, 1945, Art Students League N.Y., 1946-51, Sch. Visual Arts, 1965. Animator Terrytoons, New Rochelle, N.Y., 1950-54; artist Bunker Ramo Corp., Trumbull, Conn., 1955—; one-man shows at Wellons, New Age, Scarborough galleries, Greenburgh Town Hall, 1976; exhibited in group shows at Wellons Gallery, N.Y.C., Ann Ross Gallery, White Plains, N.Y., Scarborough Gallery, Altoona Mus.; represented in permanent collection at Altoona Mus. Tchr. art Westchester Art Soc., White Plains, 1966-74. Mem. arts and culture com. Town of Greenburgh (N.Y.), 1970—. Mem. Westchester Arts and Crafts Guild (pres. 1960-62), Westchester Art Soc. (dir. 1964-74; v.p. 1970-71, 74).

CARTER, RICHARD JOHN, chem. specialties co. exec., chemist; b. Bklyn., Aug. 31, 1941; s. James Vincent and Rose (Sanseviera) C.; B.S., St. Francis Coll., 1962; M.S. in Chemistry, State U. N.Y., 1971; postgrad. in bus. adminstrn. Fairleigh Dickinson U.; m. Elaine Bucalo, Sept. 1, 1963; children—John Michael, Thomas James. Chemist, Nat. Can Corp., Mespeth, N.Y., 1962-67; staff chemist FMC Co., Carteret,

N.J., 1967-68, chem. supr., 1969-73; mgr. quality control Airwick Industries, Carstadt, N.J., 1973-75, asst. dir. quality control, 1975-76; coordinator regulatory affairs Boyle-Midway Inc., Cranford, N.J., 1976-77, dir. regulatory affairs, 1977-78, dir. advt. and regulatory affairs, 1978—. Pres. Parish Confrat. Christian Doctrine, Bklyn., 1966-68, mem. Parish Council, 1973-74. Recipient Franciscan Spirit award St. Francis Coll., 1962. Mem. Am. Chem. Soc., Chem. Specialties Mfrs. Assn., Am. Soc. Quality Control. Home: 76 Cypress Ln Aberdeen NJ 07747 Office: Boyle-Midway Inc South Ave and Hale St Cranford NJ 07016

CARTER, ROBERT AYRES, advt. agy. exec., writer; b. Omaha, Sept. 16, 1923; s. George Whitfield and Zeta Aylene (Hart) C.; student U. Chgo., 1942-44; A.B., New Sch. for Social Research, 1949; Certificats avec Mentions Honorables (Fulbright scholar), U. Paris, 1949-50; m. Marjorie Anne Marker, Dec. 29, 1954; children—Jonathan Barlow, Randall Ayres; m. 2d Winifred Allen Scott, Apr. 23, 1973. Instr. French, Stephens Coll., Columbia, Mo., 1951-53; copywriter Denhard & Stewart Advt. Agy., N.Y.C., 1953-56; advt., pub. mgr. Funk & Wagnalls, N.Y.C., 1956-58; adv. mgr. Trade Dept., McGraw-Hill Book Co., N.Y.C., 1958-60, Doubleday & Co., N.Y.C., 1960-68; dir. advt. and pub. Mus. Modern Art, N.Y.C., 1960-66, dir. books for young readers, 1966-68, dir. publs., 1968-70; v.p. Franklin Spier Inc., N.Y.C., 1971—; lectr. in field; Star adj. prof. Hofstra U., 1976; lectr. N.Y. U., 1979. Served with USAF, 1943-46; PTO. Recipient Russell L. Reynolds award Nat. Assn. Coll. Stores, 1965. Mem. Authors Guild, The Players. Christian. Club: Pub. Ad. Author: Manhattan Primitive, 1971. Home: 142 E 16 St Apt 9E New York City NY 10003 Office: 270 Madison Ave New York City NY 10003

CARTER, ROSALYNN SMITH, wife of Pres. of U.S.; b. Plains, Ga., 1927; student Ga. Southwestern Coll., 1945-47; m. James Earl Carter, Jr., July 7, 1946; children—James Earl III, John William, Donnel Jeffrey, Amy Lynn. Chmn., Ga. Commn. on Mental Health Services, 1971; bd. dirs. Nat. Assn. Mental Health. Baptist. Home: White House 1600 Pennsylvania Ave Washington DC 20500 also 1 Woodland Dr Plains GA 31780

CARTER, RUTH B. (MRS. JOSEPH C. CARTER), assn. exec.; b. Charlotte, Vt.; d. Ira E. and Sadie M. (Congdon) Burroughs; Ph.B., U. Vt., 1931; m. Joseph C. Carter, June 28, 1935. Prin., Newton Acad., Shoreham, Vt., 1931-35; substitute tchr. Spaulding High Sch., Barre, Vt., also Woodbury (Vt.) High Sch., 1935-36; tchr. Craftsbury Acad., Craftsbury Common, Vt., 1936-38; sales mgr., buyer Vt. Music Co., Barre, 1939-44; statistician Syracuse U., 1944-46; instr. English, Temple U., Phila., 1946-47; records clk. sec., 1947-56; tchr. English, Central High Sch., Phila., 1957, Springfield Twp. Sr. High Sch., Montgomery County, Pa., 1964-65; sec. Women's Univ. Club, Phila., 1961-64, treas., 1965-67. Exec. sec. White-Williams Found., 1966-73, exec. dir., 1973—. Mem. AAUW (admissions chmn.; treas.; rec. sec. Phila. br.), D.A.R. (treas., historian, com. chmn., budget dir. Germantown chpt.), New Eng. Historic Geneal. Soc., Geneal. Soc. Vt., Soc. Mayflower Descs. Republican, Methodist. Clubs: Temple University Faculty Women's (pres. Center City Group), Temple University Women's. Author: (with Joseph C. Carter) Anchors Aweigh Around the World with Ernest Vail Burroughs, 1960. Home: D-4 Glenside House Glenside PA 19038 Office: The Pkwy at 21st St Philadelphia PA 19103

CARTNICK, EDWARD NATHANIEL, gynecologist; b. Garfield, N.J., Oct. 18, 1914; s. Louis Charles and Mary (Schwartz) C.; B.A., Harvard U., 1936; M.D., Tufts U., 1940; m. Marie Cody Mitten, Apr. 11, 1942; children—Christine Merritt, Lois Germano, Edward Cody. Intern, Kings County Hosp., Bklyn., 1940-42, resident in obstetrics and gynecology, 1946-49; practice medicine specializing in gynecology, Garden City, N.Y., 1949—; mem. staff, mem. exec. com. Mercy Hosp., Rockville Center, N.Y., 1962-76, dir. obstetrics and gynecology, 1967-76; dir. gynecol. oncology Nassau County Med. Center, East Meadows, N.Y., 1960—; asso. prof. obstetrics and gynecology State U. N.Y., Stony Brook, 1972—. Served as maj. M.C., U.S. Army, 1942-46. Fellow ACS (v.p. Long Island chpt.), Am. Coll. Obstetrics and Gynecology; mem. Am. Cancer Soc. (past dir., certificate merit), Nassau Surg. Soc. (pres.), Nassau Obstetrical, Gynecology Soc. Inc. (pres.), N.Y. State Med. Soc. (chmn. maternal mortality, obstetrics and gynecology div., chmn. obstetrics and gynecology div. 1972-74), AMA, Med. Soc. State N.Y., Long Island Cancer Council. Home: 113 Whitehall Blvd Garden City NY 11530 Office: 520 Franklin Ave Garden City NY 11530

CARTON, EDWIN BECK, chemist, plastics mfg. co. exec.; b. Balt., Apr. 27, 1927; s. Jacob G. and Gertrude (Beck) C.; B.A. in Chemistry, Johns Hopkins U., 1949; M.S. in Organic Chemistry, U. Md., 1952; Ph.D. in Organic Chemistry, Pa. State U., 1955; m. Lonnie Frances Caming, June 19, 1949; children—Evan Bruce, Deborah Ann, Paula Bette. Research chemist Scott Paper Co., Chester, Pa., 1955-57, project leader, 1957-60; dispersions research and devel. mgr. Cabot Corp., Phila. office, 1960-64, head corp. applications research and devel., Billerica, Mass., 1964-66, mgr. mktg. oxides div., 1966-68; mgr. applications engring. dept. Chomerics Inc., Woburn, Mass., 1968-69; asst. dir. research and devel. U.S. M. Chem. Co., Middleton, Mass., 1969-76; pres., dir. Sharpe Plastic Products Inc., Concord, Mass., 1976—, dir. RIM Plastics, Inc., Concord, 1978—; instr. Pa. State U., 1952-55. Founder, dir. Suburban Jewish Sch., Phila., 1957-64; chmn. United Fund, Chestnut Hill, Mass., 1966. Served with USAAF, 1945-46. Fellow Am. Inst. Chemists, AAAS; mem. Am. Chem. Soc. (chmn. Phila. sect. budget and audit com. 1961-63, mem. investment bd. trustees 1963-64), ASTM, Soc. Plastics Industry, N.Y. Acad. Scis., Am. Optical Soc., Soc. Plastics Engrs. (chmn. thermoplastic and foams div. 1968-69, dir. 1969—), Phi Lambda Upsilon. Contbr. articles on plastics and organic chemistry to sci. jours. and encys. Patentee in field. Home: 25 Sheffield Rd Newtonville MA 02160 Office: 152 Commonwealth Ave Concord MA 01742

CARUBA, ALAN, writer, editor; b. Newark, Oct. 9, 1937; s. Robert and Rebecca Margaret (Friedlander) C.; B.A., U. Miami (Fla.), 1959. City editor N.J. weeklies, 1962-64; columnist Morris County (N.J.) Daily Record, 1964-65; pub. relations positions for agys. in N.J., N.Y.C. area, 1971-74; editorial cons. N.Y. State Housing Fin. Agy., N.Y.C., 1968-76; freelance writer, 1971—; dir. publs. N.J. Inst. Tech., Newark, 1974-76; author: People Touch, 1972; 1776 Relived, 1972; Angelface, 1976; contbg. author: Travel Guide to Scenic America, 1972; contbr. articles to N.Y. Times, popular mags.; syndicated columnist Bookviews, The Jewish Future. Served with AUS, 1960-62. Recipient Met. Printing Industries awards 1969, 70, 71, N.J. Tchrs. English Authors award, 1972, Newark Coll. Engring. Authors award, 1973, N.J. Inst. Tech. Authors award, 1974, 76, Lit. Luminary of N.J. award 10th ann. N.J. Writers' Conf., 1977, Notable Achievement award Dist. 1, Internat. Assn. Bus. Communicators, 1977, Nat. Sch. Pub. Relations Assn. award, 1977. Mem. Authors League Am., Am. Soc. Journalists and Authors (sec., exec. council), Nat. Book Critics Circle, N.J. Assn. Communicators, Nat. Press Photographers Assn. Democrat. Jewish. Home: PO Box 40 9 Brookside Rd Maplewood NJ 07040

CARUCCI, VICTOR JOHN, computer co. exec.; b. Utica, N.Y., July 31, 1928; s. John and Lena (Donvito) C.; B.S., Syracuse U., 1950; m. Mary Anne Tringo, Sept. 2, 1950; children—John B., Victor L. Surveyor, N.Y. State Thruway, 1950-51; indsl. engr. Internat. Heater Co., 1951-58; indsl. engr. Sperry Univac, Utica, N.Y., 1958-60, Naples, Italy, 1960-61, cost reduction specialist, 1961-62, supr. indsl. engring., 1962-67, chief indsl. engr., 1967-71, mgr. indsl. engring. and planning, 1971—. Recipient Achievement award Mohawk Valley Engrs. Exec. Council, 1968. Mem. Nat., N.Y. State socs. profl. engrs., Am. Inst. Indsl. Engrs. (pres. Mohawk Valley chpt. 1963-64, regional community services project chmn. 1973-75), Indsl. Mgmt. Club Utica (pres. 1964-65), Sperry Univac Mgmt. Assn., Greater Utica C. of C. (chmn. rds. subcom., transp. com. 1973—), Alumni Assn. Syracuse U. Home: 38 Whitford Ave Whitesboro NY 13492 Office: 311 Turner St Utica NY 13501

CARULLO, MARIA ELENA GARCIA (MRS. DOMINIC JOSEPH CARULLO), educator; b. N.Y.C., Oct. 13, 1934; d. Laureano Benigno and Maria Elena (Alvarez) Garcia; B.A., Coll. New Rochelle, 1956; M.A., Columbia, 1962, M.Ed., 1975, M.Philosophy, 1977; m. Dominic Joseph Carullo, June 9, 1956. Tchr. St. Rose of Lima Sch., Murfressboro, Tenn., 1957-58, Haverstraw (N.Y.) Elementary Sch., 1958-59, New Rochelle (N.Y.) High Sch., 1959-65; head fgn. lang. dept. Ardsley (N.Y.) High Sch., 1965—. Cons. N.Y. State Edn. Dept., 1964-75. Mem. Am. Assn. Tchrs. of Spanish and Portuguese (chpt. pres. 1963-68), N.Y. State Assn. Fgn. Lang. Tchrs. (dir. 1967-70), Modern Lang. Assn., Spanish Inst., Am. Assn. Tchrs. of French, Am. Assn. Tchrs. Italian, Am. Classical League, Classical Assn. of Empire State, Am. Council on Teaching of Fgn. Langs., Council of Fgn. Lang. Suprs. of Westchester, Ardsley Tchrs. Assn. (pres. 1971-72), Alpha Delta Kappa (chpt. pres. 1970-72), League Women Voters. Contbr. articles in field to profl. jours. Home: 77 Elk Ave New Rochelle NY 10804 Office: 300 Farm Rd Ardsley NY 10502

CARUSO, PATRICK FRANCIS, supt. schs.; b. Jersey City, Jan. 16, 1921; s. Carmine and Josephine (Gatto) C.; B.A., Western Md. Coll., 1946; M.A., Seton Hall U., 1949; m. Mary Iannuzzelli, Sept. 1, 1946; children—Richard, Gerald, Thomas, Margaret. Tng. specialist VA, Northern N.J., 1946-50; wage adjustment examiner Dept. Labor, N.J., 1950-51, wage-salary cons., N.Y. met. area, 1951-53; tchr., asst. prin., dir. adult edn., asst. supt. Morris Hills Regional Dist., 1953-68; supt. schs. Morris Hills (N.J.) Regional Bd. Edn., 1968—. Chmn., Morris County Career Coordinating Council, 1970-71; trustee Morris County LPN Assn., 1967; chmn. manpower and edn. com. Greater Dover Area Econ. Action Com., 1975-76; mem. Adv. Com. to Establish Free Pub. Library, Fairfield, N.J., 1968, 69. Served to capt. USMCR, 1943-46. Decorated Purple Heart. Mem. N.J. Assn. Sch. Adminstrs. (exec. com. 1977, 78-79), Morris County Assn. Sch. Adminstrs. (pres. 1974-75), Assn. Supervision and Curriculum Devel., Am. Assn. Sch. Adminstrs., N.J. Sch. Masters, DAV (comdr. West Essex chpt. 1951-53). Roman Catholic. Contbr. articles to profl. jours. and newspapers. Home: 14 Ward Pl Caldwell NJ 07006 Office: Knoll Dr Denville NJ 07834

CARUSO, PAUL JOHN, real estate exec.; b. Long Branch, N.J., July 21, 1948; s. Joseph John and Lucy (Straniero) C.; B.S. in Bus. Adminstrn., Monmouth Coll., 1970; m. Laurie Lee Gersh, Nov. 17, 1972; children—Kristina Lea, Justin Tate. Treas., W. Hills Day Camp Inc., Huntington, N.Y., 1972—; v.p. Sweet Hollow Bus Corp., Huntington, 1976—; mgr. dir. Univ. Gardens Apts., Port Jefferson Sta., N.Y., 1977—. Mem. L.I. Builders Inst., Apt. House Council. Home: 7 Sweet Hollow Rd Huntington NY 11743 Office: 460 Old Town Rd Port Jefferson NY 11776

CARVALHO, JULIE ANN, psychologist; b. Washington, Apr. 11, 1940; d. Daniel Henry and Elizabeth Cecilia (Gardiner) Schmidt; B.A. with high honors, U. Md., 1962; M.A., George Washington U., 1966; postgrad. U. Md., 1973; m. Joao M.P. de Carvalho, June 7, 1977; 1 son, Joshua Emmanuele; children from previous marriage—Alan Richard, Dennis Michael, Melanie Dawn, Celeste Angelene. Social sci. research analyst Mental Health Study Center, NIMH, 1963-67; edn. and tng. analyst Computer Applications Inc, 1967-68; edn. program specialist U.S. Office Edn., 1969-70, program analyst/specialist, 1970-73; 1970-73; equal opportunity specialist Office of Sec. HEW, 1973-77; legis. analyst Office for Civil Rights, HEW, Washington, 1977—. Mem. steering com. Alliance for Child Care. Mem. Am. Psychol. Assn., Soc. Psychol. Study Social Issues, Federally Employed Women (editor News and Views 1974-75, 78), Am. Soc. Pub. Adminstrn., HEW Employees Assn. (bd. dirs.). Home: 11668 Mediterranean Ct Reston VA 22090 Office: 330 Independence Ave SW Washington DC 20201

CARVER, KENDALL LYNN, ins. co. exec.; b. Spencer, Iowa, Nov. 4, 1936; s. Marion and Letha G.; B.S., U. Iowa, 1958; m. Carol Lee Spiers, July 1, 1961; children—Merrian, Kendra, Lee, Christine. Rep. field sales Washington Nat. Ins. Co., Evanston, Ill., 1958-73, regional dir., 1974-77, pres., N.Y.C., 1977—, chief exec. officer, 1978—. C.L.U. Fellow Life Mgmt. Inst.; mem. Nat. Assn. Life Underwriters, Am. Coll. Life Underwriters, Life Ins. Council N.Y. Republican. Home: 5 Tanglewood Trail Darien CT 06820 Office: Washington Nat Life Ins Co 500 Fifth Ave New York City NY 10036

CARY, FRANK TAYLOR, bus. machines co. exec.; b. Gooding, Idaho, Dec. 14, 1920; s. Frank Taylor and Ida C.; B.S., U. Calif. at Los Angeles, 1943; M.B.A., Stanford U., 1948; m. Anne Curtis, 1943; children—Marshall, Bryan, Steven, Laura. With IBM, 1948—, dist. mgr., San Francisco, 1957-61, pres. Service Bur. Corp., N.Y.C., 1959-61, asst. dir. corp. staff 1961-62, v.p. data processing div., White Plains, N.Y., 1962-64, pres., from 1964, v.p., group exec., from 1966, now chmn. bd., chief exec. officer, Armonk, N.Y. Served with AUS, 1944-46. Home: 6 Haskell Ln Darien CT 06820 Office: IBM Corp Armonk NY 10504

CASAPULLA, ROBERT TERRANCE, customer service rep.; b. Paterson, N.J., Apr. 20, 1944; s. Edward J. and Edmea O. (Colongo) C., Sr.; A.A. in Bus. with honors, Edward Williams Coll., 1975; m. Frances A. Tiseo, Sept. 20, 1969; 1 dau., Rebecca Ann. Technician, N.J. Micro-Film Corp., Haledon, 1962-64; security specialist U.S. Army Security Agency, Homestead, Fla., 1965-67; letter carrier U.S. Postal Service, Paterson, N.J., 1964-71, customer service rep., 1971—, instr., 1975-76, ad hoc hearing officer non-bargaining unit employees No. N.J. Dist., 1978—. Rec. sec. Fidelians of Am., N. Haledon, 1978. Served with U.S. Army, 1965-67. Mem. Nat. Assn. Postal Suprs. (br. pres. 1976-77, state bd. rep. 1978—). Roman Catholic. Club: P.O. War Vets. Home: 90 N 13th St Hawthorne NJ 07506 Office: 194 Ward St Paterson NJ 07510

CASARINO, JOHN PHILIP, psychiatrist; b. Bklyn., Oct. 19, 1940; s. John Joseph and Grace (Esposito) C.; B.S., U. Notre Dame, 1961; M.D., Med. Coll. Ala., 1965. Intern, Meadowbrook Hosp., East Meadow, N.Y., 1965-66, resident pediatrics, 1966-67; resident psychiatry St. Vincent's Hosp. and Med. Center N.Y., N.Y.C., 1967-69, 71-72; asst. attending, 1972—, chief partial hospitalization service, 1973—; staff psychiatrist Luth. Med. Center, Bklyn., 1972-73; cons. in field. Bd. dirs. Fedn. Partial Hospitalization Study Groups, 1977—. Served to maj. USAF, 1969-71; Vietnam. Decorated Meritorious Service medal. Diplomate Am. Bd. Psychiatry and Neurology (examiner 1974). Mem. N.Y. State Soc. Clin. Psychiatry, Am. Psychiat. Assn., AMA, Med. Soc. County N.Y. Home: 115 Central Park W New York City NY 10023 Office: 144 W 12th St New York City NY 10011

CASAZZA, JOHN ANDREW, mgmt. cons.; b. Bklyn., Jan. 3, 1924; student Cooper Union, 1941-43; B.E.E., Cornell U., 1945; m. Madeline Russo, Apr. 24, 1949; children—John Anthony, Joan Bernadette. Engr. trainee Pub. Service Electric and Gas Co., Newark, 1946-48, asst. engr., 1948-53, sr. engr., 1953-57, transmission planning engr., 1957-63, asst. system planning and devel. engr., 1964-67, system planning and devel. engr., 1968-70, mgr. system planning, 1970-71, gen. mgr. planning and research, 1971-74, v.p. planning and research, 1974-77; v.p. Stone & Webster, mgmt. cons., N.Y.C., 1977—. Chmn. seminar on hydrogen, 9th World Energy Conf. 1974; trustee N.J. Marine Scis. Consortium, 1974—, N.J. Energy Research Inst., 1976-77; v.p. U.S. nat. com. Internat. Conf. Large High Tension Electric Systems, 1974—. Served with USNR, 1943-45. Registered profl. engr. Fellow IEEE, Edison Electric Inst. (chmn. system planning com. 1971-73), Regional Plan Assn. Roman Catholic. Club: Essex (Newark). Contbr. numerous articles to publs. Home: 302 Passaic Ave Hasbrouck Heights NJ 07604 Office: 90 Broad St New York City NY 10004

CASCIEGNA, JILL PATON, food co. exec.; b. N.Y.C., Aug. 25, 1936; d. John Hezekiah and Millicent Alice Ora (Ford) Paton; student Bradford Jr. Coll., 1956; Asso. B.A., Tobe Coburn Sch. Fashion Merchandising, 1959; m. Salvatore Casiegna, Jan. 9, 1977. Vice pres. Golden Blossom Honey, N.Y.C., 1970-71; chmn. bd., pres. John Paton, Inc., N.Y.C., 1971—. Home: PO Box 93 Point Pleasant PA 18950 Office: 73 E State St Doylestown PA 18901

CASCIERI, TITO, JR., toxicologist; b. Winthrop, Mass., Feb. 1, 1948; s. Tito and Helena (Pascucci) C.; B.A., Northeastern U., 1970; Ph.D. (Grad. asst. 1970-75), Pa. State U., 1975; m. Margaret A. Schmalhofer, June 24, 1972. Group leader, toxicology and environ. group. FMC Corp., Princeton, N.J., 1975—. Served as lt. U.S. Army, 1975. Recipient Analytical Chemistry Award Northeastern U. chpt. Am. Chem. Soc., 1969; Sci. Research award Pa. State U. chpt. Sigma Xi, 1974. Mem. Nat. Environ. Health Assn., Am. Pub. Health Assn., Am. Chem. Soc., AAAS, Am. Soc. Microbiology, ASTM, N.Y. Acad. Sci., Regulatory Affairs Profl. Soc., Am. Coll. Toxicology, Genetic Toxicology Assn., Environ. Mutagen Soc., Sigma Xi, Phi Kappa Phi, Phi Sigma, Phi Lambda Upsilon. Office: FMC Corp PO Box 8 Princeton NJ 08540

CASCIO, THOMAS MICHAEL, mgmt. cons., govt. ofcl.; b. Bklyn., July 25, 1937; s. Thomas Romano and Inez Clair (LaBelle) Cacioppi; B.S. in Mgmt. Engring., Rensselaer Poly. Inst., 1960, M.S., 1961; m. Carol Ann Michalski, July 6, 1963; children—Marc, Michael, Cynthia. Mgr. mgmt. sci. Gen. Electric Co., Schenectady, 1970-71; mgmt. cons. Stochos, Inc., Schenectady, 1972; mgmt. cons. ops. analysis N.Y. State Dept. Transp., Albany, 1973—; adj. asso. prof. adminstrn. and mgmt. Union Coll., Schenectady. Mem. com. mgmt. YMCA. Mem. Ops. Research Soc. Am. (asso.), Phi Kappa Theta, Psi Chi. Author: Facilities Modeling, 1969; Manufacturing Simulation, 1970; Fleet Replacement Analysis in the Public Sector, 1977. Home: 2065 Lexington Pkwy Schenectady NY 12309 Office: Bldg 4 NY State Campus Albany NY 12226

CASE, CLIFFORD PHILIP, lawyer, former U.S. senator; b. Franklin Park, N.J., Apr. 16, 1904; s. Clifford P. and Jeannette (Benedict) C.; A.B., Rutgers U., 1925, LL.D., 1955; LL.B., Columbia, 1928; LL.D., Middlebury Coll., 1956, Rollins Coll., 1957, Rider Coll., 1959, Bloomfield Coll., 1962, Columbia, 1967, Princeton, 1967, Upsala Coll., 1969, Yeshiva U., 1976; Dr. Pub. Service, Seton Hall U., 1971; m. Ruth M. Smith, July 13, 1928; children—Mary Jane (Mrs. William M. Weaver), Ann (Mrs. John C. Holt), Clifford Philip III. Asso. law firm Simpson, Thacher & Bartlett, N.Y.C., 1928-39, mem. firm, 1939-53. Mem. Rahway (N.J.) Common Council, 1938-42; mem. House of Assembly of N.J., 1943, 44; mem. 79th to 83d Congresses, 6th N.J. Dist.; resigned Aug. 1953; pres. Fund for the Republic 1953-54. U.S. senator from N.J., 1955-79. Hon. trustee Roper Pub. Opinion Research Center at Williams Coll., Williamstown, Mass., bd. dirs. Columbia Jour. Law and Social Problems. Mem. N.J. Hist. Soc. (hon. trustee), Assn. Bar City N.Y., N.Y. County, N.Y. State, Am. bar assns., Council Fgn. Relations, Phi Delta Phi, Delta Upsilon, Phi Beta Kappa. Republican. Presbyn. Clubs: Century Assn. (N.Y.C.); Essex (Newark); Federal City, (Washington). Home: 191 W Milton Ave Rahway NJ 07065 Office: 2728 Dumbarton Ave NW Washington DC 20007

CASEY, MURRAY JOSEPH, physician; b. Armour, S.D., May 1, 1936; s. Meryl Joseph and Gladice (Murray) C.; student Chanute Jr. Coll., 1954-55, Rockhurst Coll., 1955-56; A.B., U. Kans., 1958; M.D., Georgetown U., 1962; postgrad. Suffolk U. Law Sch., 1963-64, Howard U., 1965; m. Virginia Anne Fletcher; children—Murray Joseph, Theresa Marie, Anne Franklin, Francis X. Intern, USPHS Hosp.-Univ. Hosp., Balt., 1962-63; staff physician USPHS Hosp., Boston, 1963-64; staff asso. Lab Infectious Diseases, Nat. Inst. Allergy and Infectious Diseases, NIH, Bethesda, Md., 1964-66; virologist, resident physician Columbia-Presbyn. Med Center, also Francis Delafield Hosp., N.Y.C., 1966-69; USPHS sr. clin. trainee, 1969-70; fellow gynecol. oncology, resident dept. surgery Meml. Hosp. for Cancer and Allied Diseases, Meml. Sloan-Kettering Cancer Center, N.Y.C., 1969-71, Am. Cancer Soc. fellow, 1969-71; ofcl. observer in radiotherapy U. Tex. M.D. Anderson Hosp. and Tumor Inst., Houston, 1971; vis. scientist Radiumhemmet Karolinska Sjukhuset and Inst., Stockholm, Sweden, 1971; asst. prof. obstetrics and gynecology U. Conn. Sch. Medicine, 1971-75, asso. prof., 1975—, dir. gynecologic oncology, 1971—, also mem. med. bd.; chmn. research adv. com., mem. council Conn. Cancer Epidemiology Unit. Bd. dirs., mem. exec. com., chmn. profl. edn. com. Hartford unit Am. Cancer Soc. Diplomate Am. Bd. Med. Examiners, Am. Bd. Obstetrics and Gynecology. Fellow Am. Coll. Obstetricians and Gynecologists, A.C.S.; mem. AAAS, N.Y. Acad. Scis., Am. Soc. Colposcopy, Am. Fertility Soc., Soc. Gynecologic Oncologists, St. George Soc. Contbr. articles to profl. jours., chpts. to books. Research in oncogenesis and tumor immunology. Home: Farmington CT 06032 Office: New Britain Gen Hosp New Britain CT 06050 also Dept Obstetrics and Gynecology U Conn Health Center Farmington CT 06032

CASEY, SISTER NATALIE, coll. pres.; b. Cleve., Oct. 12, 1916; d. Bernard T. and Phoebe (Cornell) Casey; B.A., Manhattan Coll., 1951; M.S. in Edn., Fordham U., 1955; M.S. in Chemistry, Syracuse U., 1963; postgrad. Columbia, 1964-70. Tchr. Holy Cross Sch., N.Y.C., 1938-42, St. Paul's High Sch., Daytona Beach, Fla., 1942-49, St. Pius Sch., Bronx, N.Y., 1949-55; asst. prin. Acad. Our Lady of the Blessed Sacrament, Goshen, N.Y., 1955-65; instr. Dominican Coll., Blauvelt, N.Y., 1965-66, pres., 1966—. Mem. com. evaluating secondary schs. Archdiocese of N.Y., 1963-65. Trustee Dominican Coll. NSF grantee in physics, 1958, in biology, 1959. Mem. AAUP, Council for Advancement Small Colls. (dir.), Kappa Gamma Pi, Pi Lambda Theta. Home: 722 Bradley Pkwy Blauvelt NY 10913

CASGRAIN, ARDOIN EDMOND, cons., ret. govt. ofcl.; b. Winchester, Mass., Feb. 23, 1897; s. Louis Amedee and Zelia (Goddu) C.; student U.S. Mil. Acad., 1918, Brown U., 1928-30, Northwestern U., summer 1934, in Edn., Harvard U., 1938, in Pub. Adminstrn., Am. U., 1941; m. Mildred Chaloner Davis, Feb. 21, 1934; children—Norman Williams, Charlotte Ardoin, Louise Amedee Casgrain Noyes. Asst. sec. Providence (R.I.) C. of C., 1928-30; sec. Watertown (Mass.) C. of C., 1931-35; adult edn. dir. fed. works program Community Service, Boston, 1935-36; regional adviser So. states U.S. Office Edn., 1937-39; regional info. rep. U.S. Housing Authority, Washington, 1939-41; regional rent dir. OPA, N.Y.C., 1941-42, regional homes use dir., 1943; civilian moblzn. adviser Office Civil Def., Washington, 1944; chief UN Relief and Rehab., Washington, 1945-46; exec. dir. Nat. Com. Atomic Information, Washington, 1947; chief community relations Dept. Army, Washington, 1948-49, dep. dir. community services adj. gen. office, 1950-53, adminstrv. officer, mgmt. analyst, 1954-65; program adviser adminstrn. aging HEW, 1966-67; asst. dir., cons. community services Sr. Aides Program Dept. Labor, Washington, 1968—; mem. cons. panel Volt Service Corp., Washington, 1969—; lectr. Simmons Sch. Social Work, Boston, 1934, N.Y. Sch. Social Work, 1943. Mem. bd. Nat. Council Sr. Citizens, Washington, 1969; spl. adviser govt. employee groups, 1967-69; cons. older Am. problems various nat. orgns.; program asst. Inst. Lifetime Learning, 1970-76. Served with U.S. Army, World War I. Recipient Meritorious Civilian Employee award Dept. Army, 1966, HEW Adminstrn. on Aging, 1970. Mem. Am. Legion, Assos. U.S. Mil. Acad., Am. Assn. Retried Persons (pres. Nat. Capital chpt. 1971-72, 75-76). Address: 4000 Cathedral Ave NW Washington DC 20016 Died Aug. 25, 1978.

CASHDOLLAR, ROBERT MURREL, psychologist; b. Pitts., Sept. 6, 1924; s. Walter M. and Florence B. (Gardner) C.; B.S., Calif. State Coll., 1949; postgrad. Westminster Coll., 1952; M.A., U. Pitts., 1961; m. Frances A. Wagner, June 21, 1945; children—Richard L., Linda. Tchr. pub. schs., Mercer, Pa., 1949-54, Grove City, Pa., 1954-56; counselor Butler (Pa.) Area Schs., 1956-64, psychologist, 1964—; practice psychology, Butler, 1964—. Scoutmaster Boy Scouts Am.; vice chmn. Mental Health/Mental Retardation Bd. Served with USAAF, 1942-46. Mem. Am., Pa. psychol. assns., Nat. Assn. Sch. Psychologists, NEA, Pa. Edn. Assn., U.S. Coast Guard Aux. (vice comdr.). Home: 874 Mercer Rd Butler PA 16001 Office: 167 Newcastle Rd Butler PA 16001

CASHMAN, GEORGE WASHINGTON, lawyer, judge; b. Boston, Feb. 22, 1911; s. Frank and Annie (Cummings) C.; LL.B., Boston U., 1934; m. Jacqueline Harris, Oct. 8, 1941; children—Robert H., Daniel F., Deborah L. Admitted to Mass. bar, 1934; pvt. practice law, Newton, 1934-42; commr. Mass. Commn. Investigating Communism and Subversive Activities, 1953—, Mass. Commn. Against Discrimination, 1954-56; judge Boston Juvenile Ct., 1956—; clk., gen. counsel Stedfast Rubber Co., Inc., 1950—; former partner firm Goldman, Goldman, Curtis & Cashman. Trustee Agassiz Village, 1959—, hon. dir. Kiddie Kamp Corp.; bd. overseers governmental relations Brandeis U. Served from pvt. to capt., AUS, 1942-46. Mem. Nat. Council Juvenile Ct. Judges, Mass. Trial Lawyers' Assn., Anti-Defamation League, World Affairs Council (dir.), N. Am., Judges Assn., Am. Arbitration Assn., Zeta Beta Tau. Mem. B'nai B'rith. Editor: Desk Guide to Italy, 1945. Home: 20 Damien Rd Wellesley Hills MA 02181 Office: Boston Juvenile Ct Pemberton Sq Boston MA 02108

CASHMAN, THOMAS JOSEPH, state ofcl.; b. Newburyport, Mass., July 2, 1920; s. Thomas Joseph and Mary C. (Carens) C.; B.S. in Chem. Engring., U. R.I., 1947; m. Margaret Stedman, June 16, 1947; children—Margaret, Anne Cashman Miller, Thomas, Joan, Mary Ellen. Chem. engr. J.T. Baker Chem. Co., Phillipsburg, N.J., 1947-49; various managerial positions Gen. Electric Co., Schenectady, 1949-67; dir. Bur. Radiol. Health, N.Y. State Heatlh Dept., Albany, 1968-70; dir. Bur. Radiation, N.Y. State Dept. Environ. Conservation, Albany, 1970—. Registered profl. engr., N.Y. State. Mem. Am. Inst. Chem. Engrs., Am. Nuclear Soc., Conf. Radiation Control Program Dirs. Club: Helderberg Ski. Home: 35 Saint Stephens Ln Scotia NY 12302 Office: 50 Wolf Rd Albany NY 12233

CASO, ADOLPH, educator, author; b. Mirabella, Italy, Jan. 7, 1934; s. Ralph and Prisca (DeLuca) C.; B.A., Northeastern U., 1957; M.A. (fellow), Harvard, 1964; m. Amelia E. Maruffa, June 6, 1959; children—Richard, Robert, Liana. Pres., Dante Univ. Cultural Center, Boston, 1975—; tchr., dir. bilingual dept. Waltham (Mass.) Pub. Schs., 1964—. Pres. Davis Sch. P.T.A., Newton, Mass., 1970-71; bd. dirs. Beaverbrook Guidance Center, Belmont, Mass., Dante Alighieri Soc.; founder, pres. Dante U. Am. Found., Inc., 1978. Served to lt. col. Signal Corps, U.S. Army, 1957-62. Fulbright scholar, 1966. Mem. Modern Lang. Assn., Res. Officer Assn., Am. Assn. Tchrs. Italian, Culture Commn., Sons of Italy, Lit. Guild of Cambridge. Author: The Straw Obelisk (novel), 1971; America's Italian Founding Fathers, 1975; Alfieri's Ode to America's Independence, 1976; Water and Life (poetry), 1976; They Too Made America Great (non-fiction), 1978; Issues in Foreign Language and Bilingual Education, 1978. Home: 158 Hickory Rd Weston MA 02193 Office: 55 School St Waltham MA 02154

CASON, JUNE MACNABB, musician, educator; b. Phila., June 21, 1930; d. Vernon C. and Eleanor (Scarlet) Macnabb; student Eastman Sch. Music, Rochester, N.Y., 1948-52, U. Houston, 1965-69; m. Roger Lee Cason, June 12, 1952; children—David Alan, Diane Louise, Nancy Lynn. Soloist ch. and music groups, Charleston, W.Va., 1957-63; dir. youth chorus St. John's Episcopal Ch., Charleston, 1956-63; founder, dir. summer music camp for Episcopal Diocese W.Va., 1961-62; pvt. voice tchr., Houston, 1965-71; tchr. voice San Jacinto Coll., Pasadena, Tex., 1969-71; soloist Christ Ch. Cathedral, Houston, 1963-71, Gilbert and Sullivan Soc., Houston, 1970; pvt. voice tchr., Wilmington, Del., 1971—; mem. faculty Wilmington Music Sch., 1973-77; founder, gen. mgr., soloist Minikin Opera Co., Wilmington, 1972—; mem. Del. Pro Musica, Wilmington, 1973—, chmn., 1975—; instr. music Albert Einstein Acad., Wilmington, 1975-76; dir. music Immanuel Episcopal Ch., Wilmington, 1973-75. Recipient Theta Eta award U. Rochester, 1952. Mem. Nat. Assn. Tchrs. Singing, Del. Music Tchrs. Assn., Met. Opera Guild, Nat. Opera Service. Sigma Alpha Iota (Sword of Honor 1971). Republican. Contbr. articles to profl. jours. Address: 1125 Grinnell Rd Wilmington DE 19803

CASON, ROGER LEE, chem. co. exec., mech. engr.; b. Madison, Wis., Aug. 13, 1930; s. Hulsey and Eloise (Boeker) C.; B.S. in Mech. Engring. with high distinction, U. Rochester, 1951, M.S., 1952; M.B.A., U. Del., 1977; m. June Ely MacNabb, June 12, 1952; children—David Allan, Diane Louise, Nancy Lynn. With E.I. DuPont de Nemours & Co., various locations, 1955—, sr. mech. engr., prodn. supr., mech. supr. Houston, 1963-70, staff bus. analyst, Wilmington, Del., 1971-75, bus. analysis mgr., 1975—. Served with C.E., USNR, 1952-55. Registered profl. engr., Del., W. Va. Mem. ASME, FMA Honor Soc., Wilmington Power Squadron (officer 1978—, instr. boating course 1977-78), Green Acres Recreation Assn. (officer 1971-73), Beta Gamma Sigma, Phi Beta Kappa, Sigma Xi (asso. mem.), Tau Beta Pi. Republican. Episcopalian. Contbr. articles to profl. publs. Home: 1125 Grinnell Rd Green Acres Wilmington DE 19803 Office: DuPont Co Chems Dyes and Pigments Dept Wilmington DE 19898

CASPERSEN, BARBARA MORRIS, food co. exec.; b. Phila., Feb. 27, 1945; d. Samuel Wheeler and Eleanor May (Jones) Morris; B.A., Wellesley Coll., 1967; m. Finn M.W. Caspersen, June 17, 1967; children—Finn M.W., Erik M.W., Samuel M.W., Andrew W.W. Treas., dir. Westby Corp., Wilmington, Del., 1971—, Westby Mgmt. Inc., Andover, N.J., 1967—, Tri-Farms, Inc., Andover, 1967—; pres., dir. Clark Hill Sugary Inc., Canaan, N.H., 1971—. Bd. dirs. v.p. O.W. Caspersen Found., 1967—; trustee Hoosac Sch., 1968-76; trustee Hilltop Sch., 1974—, pres., 1976—. Mem. English-Speaking Union U.S. (dir. 1972-73, dir. N.Y. chpt. 1970-75). Presbyterian. Club: Colony (N.Y.C.). Office: Westby Corp PO Drawer W Andover NJ 07821

CASPERSEN, FINN MICHAEL WESTBY, fin. co. exec.; b. N.Y.C., Oct. 27, 1941; s. Olaus Westby and Freda C.; A.B. with honors in Econs., Brown U., 1963; LL.B. cum laude, Harvard, 1966; m. Barbara Morris, June 17, 1967; children—Finn Michael Westby, Erik M.W., Samuel M.W., Andrew W.W. Admitted to Fla. bar, 1966, N.Y. State bar, 1967; asst. firm Dewey, Ballantine, Bushby, Palmer & Wood, N.Y.C., 1969-72; asso. counsel Beneficial Mgmt. Corp., Morristown, N.J., 1972-75; gen. counsel, dir. Central Nat. Life Ins. Co. of Omaha, Morristown, 1973-75; v.p., dir. Beneficial Corp. 1975, vice chmn., mem. exec., fin. coms., 1976, chmn., chief exec. officer, 1976—; dir., mem. exec. com. Peoples Bank & Trust Co., Wilmington, Del.; dir. Spiegel Inc., Chgo., Midatlantic Nat. Bank/Sussex & Mchts., Beneficial Ins. Group Cos. Western Auto Supply Co., Kansas City, Mo.; pres. Westby Corp., TriFarms Inc.; chmn. bd. Clark Hill Sugary. Trustee, mem. exec. com., chmn. Peddie Sch., Hightstown, N.J.; trustee Camp Nejeda; trustee O.W. Cusperson Found., Brown U.; mem. State Bd. N.J. Higher Edn.; bd. dirs. Com. Econ. Devel. Served to lt. USCG, 1966-69. Mem. Am., N.Y. State, Fla. bar assns., Nat. Consumer Fin. Assn. (dir., mem. exec. com.). Clubs: Harvard, (N.Y.), Knickerbocker; University (Sarasota, Fla.); Panther Valley Country (N.J.); Carlton. Home: PO Drawer W Andover NJ 07821 Office: 200 South St Morristown NJ 07960

CASS, PAUL TAYLOR, physician; b. Chester, Pa., Oct. 1, 1945; s. Charles Albert and Mary (Cohen) C.; B.S., Juniata Coll., 1967; M.D., Hahnemann Med. Coll. and Hosp., 1971; m. Deetra Leeds, Aug. 26, 1967; 1 dau., Kelly Nicole. Resident in internal medicine Hahnemann Hosp., Phila., 1971-74; attending physician Crozer Chester Med. Center, Chester, Sacred Heart Gen. Hosp., Chester; asst. prof. medicine Hahnemann Hosp., 1974—. Methodist. Home: 804 General Sterling St West Chester PA 19080 Office: Check House 15th and Upland Sts Upland PA 19015

CASSAK ALBERT LOEB, pub. co. exec.; b. N.Y.C., Sept. 12, 1917; s. Michael and Lena (Pincus) C.; B.S., N.Y.U., 1940, M.B.A., 1953; m. Dorothy Mildred Reinke, Feb. 28, 1943; children—Laurie Nan, David James, Lance Douglas. Account exec. Ernest W. Greenfield Advt., Phila., 1946-47; salesman Surg. Bus. Mag., N.Y.C., 1947-53, v.p., 1953-68; pres. Cassak Publs., Inc., Union, N.J., 1968—; industry tech. rep. U.S. Med. Equipment Catalog Exhbn., Johannesburg, Capetown, S. Africa, 1976; ITR U.S. Med. Equipment Catalog Exhbn., India, 1979. Served to maj. U.S. Army, 1941-46. Health Industry Mfrs. assn., Pharm. Advt. Club, Overseas Press Club, Union C. of C., Smithsonian Asso., Nat. Hist. Soc. Jewish. Club: Masons. Home: 16 Notch Hill Dr Livingston NJ 07039 Office: 2009 Morris Ave Union NJ 07083

CASSARA, NUNZIO GIUSEPPE, systems mgr., communications co. exec.; b. Bklyn., Mar. 19, 1929; s. Emanule and Rose (Farce) C.; grad. Walter Hervey Coll., 1952; certificate N.Y. U., 1966; m. Dolores Ann Heath, Oct. 12, 1952; children—Ann, Chris, Lisa. Programmer, Associated Food Stores, Inc., N.Y.C., 1962-63; sr. programmer N.Y. Hilton Hotel, Inc., N.Y.C., 1963-65, ops. supr., 1963-64; instr. (part-time) computer programming ADR Programming Inst., N.Y.C., 1966-68, RCA Inst., 1968-72, CPU Inst., N.Y.C., 1972-74; lead programmer analyst Datamor, Inc., N.Y.C., 1965-67; project leader NBC-TV Network, N.Y.C., 1969-73, mgr., 1973—, system analyst, 1967-69; mem. Center Island Columbian Assos., Inc.; lectr. N.Y. U., 1978—. Served with U.S. Army, 1947-50. Mem. Am. Mgmt. Assn. Republican. Author: Instructor's Manual for BAL Programming course, 1967. Home: 209 Aster St Massapequa Park NY 11762 Office: 30 Rockefeller Pla New York NY 10020

CASSCELLS, SAMUEL WARD, physician; b. N.Y.C., Nov. 15, 1915; s. Samuel Ward and Marguerite (Hafslund) C.; M.D., U. Va., 1939; m. Sarah Ohseda Dyson, June 10, 1949; children—Samuel Ward III, Christopher D., Elizabeth Anne, Margaret. Intern, St. Lukes Hosp.-Met. Hosp., Cleve., 1939-40, resident, 1940-42; resident orthopaedic service Alfred I. duPont Inst., 1947-48, now cons.; resident orthopaedic service U. Va., 1948-49; practice medicine specializing in orthopedic, Wilmington, Del., 1949—; acting chief orthopedics Wilmington Med. Center, 1959, St. Francis Hosp., 1959. Served to capt., M.C., AUS, World War II. Mem. Am., Eastern orthopedic assns., Am. Acad. Orthopedic Surgeons, Internat. Arthroscopy Assn., Internat. Soc. Knee. Republican. Episcopalian. Clubs: Wilmington Country, Vicmead Hunt. Contbr. articles to med. jours. Home: Guyencourt Montchanin DE 19710 Office: 1205 Gilpin Ave Wilmington DE 19806

CASSEL, DAVID EDWARD, chemist; b. Phila., Jan. 7, 1933; s. Samuel Ernest and Edna (Schnoke) C.; student St. Joseph's Coll., Phila., 1963-66; m. Lois M., Aug. 29, 1959; children—Carolann, Kathleen, David Edward. Asst. salesmann, tour condr. Thomas Cook & Son, Phila., 1954-57; jr. chemist Allied Chem., Barrett div., Phila., 1957-58; technician E. J. Lavino & Co., Sheridan, Pa., 1959-62, Alco Standard Corp., Alco Chem., Phila., 1962-69; chemist Monroe Chem., Aico Standard Corp., Eddystone, Pa., 1969-73; sr. technician Phila. Quartz Research and Devel. Center, Lafayette Hill, Pa., 1973—. Served with USN, 1952-53. Republican. Patentee in field. Office: PO Box 258 Lafayette Hill PA 19444

CASSIDY, CARL EUGENE, physician; b. Salineville, Ohio, Dec. 4, 1924; s. Clifford J. and Dortha (Lance) C.; A.B., Kenyon Coll., 1946; M.D., Western Res. U., 1948; m. Helen Ruth Skinner Collord, Dec. 21, 1961; children—George L. Collord III, Frederick Perkins Collord. Intern, Youngstown (Ohio) Hosp. Assn., 1948-49; fellow in medicine Cleve. Clinic Found., 1951-54; research fellow in endocrinology Pratt Clinic, New Eng. Med. Center Hosps., Boston, 1954-56, asst. physician, 1956-67, sr. physician, 1968-72; physician-in-chief Med. Center Western Mass., 1972-76; program dir. Postgrad. Med. Inst., Boston, 1978—; asst. in medicine Tufts U. Sch. Medicine, Boston, 1954-56, clin. instr. medicine, 1956-58, instr., 1958-59, sr. instr., 1959-62, asst. prof., 1962-68, asso. prof., 1968-73, clin. prof., 1973—. Served with USNR, 1943-45, to lt., M.C., 1949-51. Mem. AMA, Mass. Med. Soc., Am. Thyroid Assn., Endocrine Soc. Clubs: Longwood Cricket (Chestnut Hill, Mass.); Badminton and Tennis (Boston). Co-editor: Clinical Endocrinology II, pub. 1968. Contbr. articles to med. jours. Office: 2 Boylston Plaza Prudential Center Boston MA 02199

CASSIDY, JACK, educator; b. Phila., Mar. 12, 1941; B.A. in English, Gettysburg Coll., Phila., 1962; M.Ed. in Secondary Edn., Temple U., Phila., 1965, Ph.D. in Ednl. Psychology, 1975, married; 2 children. Tchr., Hawaii Dept. Pub. Instruction Island Kauai, Lihue, Hawaii, 1965-69; instr. Temple U., 1970-71; reading supr. Newark (Del.) Sch. Dist., 1972-78; asso. prof. reading and gifted edn. Millersville (Pa.) State Coll., 1978—. Coach Community Swim Teams, Kapaa, Hawaii, 1967-68. Mem. Internat. Reading Assn. (mem. legis. com. 1975-76, dir. 1976-79), Diamond State Reading Assn. (pres. 1974-75) Nat. Council Tchrs. English, Council Exceptional Children, Del. Assn. Sch. Adminstrs., Assn. Gifted, Nat. Assn. Gifted. Phi Delta Kappa. Contbr. articles in field to profl. jours. Home: Robins Nest Kemblesville PA 19347 Office: Millersville State College Millersville PA 17551

CASSIDY, JAMES J(OSEPH), pub. relations counsel; b. Norwood, Ohio, Dec. 31, 1916; s. Martin D. and Helen (Johnston) C.; student U. Cin., 1934-38; m. Rita Hackett, Oct. 18, 1941; children—Claudia, James. Dir. spl. events, internat. broadcasts Crosley Broadcasting Corp., 1939-44, war corr., 1944-45, dir. pub. relations, 1946-50; also war corr. NBC, 1944-45; account exec. Hill & Knowlton, Inc., N.Y.C., 1950-53, v.p., 1953-61, sr. v.p., 1961-66, exec. v.p., 1966-71, pres., 1971-74, vice chmn., 1974-75; vice chmn. Burson-Marsteller, Washington, 1975—. Recipient Variety award, 1944; citation for reporting in combat areas from Sec. War, 1945. Mem. Air Force Assn., Public Relations Assn. Am. (past pres. N.Y. chpt.), Profit Sharing Council Am. (past chmn.), Internat. Soc. Aviation Writers, Aviation-Space Writers Assn. Clubs: Sky, Nat. Press, Overseas Press Am., Georgetown. Home: 2801 New Mexico Ave NW Washington DC 20007 Office: 1800 M St NW Washington DC 20036

CASSIDY, ROBERT STERLING, state ofcl.; b. Attleboro, Mass., June 13, 1933; s. Edward M. and Margaret H. (Nihan) C.; A.A., Boston U., 1953, B.S., 1955; m. Dora M. Weir, Aug. 24, 1957; children—Robert E., Jan. M., Lee S. Employment counselor, interviewer Div. Employment Security, Attleboro, 1957-60; dir. pub. assistance Dept. Pub. Welfare, Attleboro, 1960-66; former pres. Plymouth County Relief Office; regional coordinator Mass. Dept. Pub. Welfare. Chmn. govtl. div. United Fund, Attleboro, 1961-62; mem. Attleboro Housing Authority, 1962-74; mem. Regional Comprehensive Health Planning Bd., 1971—, Region VII Mental Health Bd., 1971—. City Councilman Attleboro, 1972—. Served with AUS, 1955-57. Mem. Plymouth County Relief Officers Assn. Democrat. Roman Catholic. Elk. Editor: Pub. Relations Com. News, 1962-64. Home: 20 Foley St Attleboro MA 02703 Office: 39 Boylston St Boston MA 02116

CASSIE, WILLIAM BREMNER MACGREGOR, mgmt. cons., educator; b. Lowville, N.Y., June 3, 1937; s. Charles MacGregor and Anna (Ferrara) C.; A.B., Hamilton Coll., 1960; postgrad. (Am. Chem. Soc. grantee 1961), U. Calif., Berkeley, 1961-62; M.S. (Nat. Research Council Can. fellow 1964-65), U. Alta., 1965; M.B.A., Harvard, 1967; Ph.D., U. Minn., 1971; D.H.A., U. Montreal, 1976; m. Josephine Lena Meyer, June 12, 1965; children—JoAnna, William Andrew, Charles. Engring. asst. Westinghouse Corp., Washington, 1958-59; supr. polymer products devel. Shell Oil Co., San Francisco, 1961-63; supr. plastics mktg. research Dow Chem. Co., Midland, Mich., 1966; dir. comml. products devel. Radiation Chems. Corp., Palo Alto, Calif., 1967-68; mgmt. cons. MacGregor-Cassie Assos., Halifax, N.S., 1968-70; prof. Concordia U., Montreal, Que., Can., 1970-72; asso. dean of faculty Bus. Ryerson Inst., Toronto, Ont., 1972-73; prof. Coll. de Maisonneuve, Montreal, 1973-75; pvt. practice cons., Montreal, 1975—; founder, mem. bd. dirs. Canadian Inst. Entrepreneurial Studies, Toronto; instr. bus. devel. programs Can. Ministry Manpower, Inst. Canadian Bankers; cons. Pillsbury Co., Green Giant Co., Amicon Corp., Med. Testing, Inc., Can. ministries of Indian Affairs, Agr., Trade and Industry, Health and Welfare; del. France-Que. Mgmt. Cons. Mission, 1978. Founder, dir. Nat. Save the Orchards Assn.; Quebec chmn. research com. Harvard Bus. Sch. Assn.; campaign mgr. Parti Quebecois Vercheres Riding Assn. Recipient Beta Gamma Sigma Internat. award, 1970, Concordia Student Assn. outstanding prof. award, 1971, Internat. Assn. Commerce and Econs. Students award, 1972. Mem. Am. Mktg. Assn., Canadian Coll. Health Service Execs., Canadian Pub. Health Assn., Quebec Hosps. Assn., Canadian Town Planning Assn. Republican. Mormon. Clubs: Tennis, Sailing, Curling, Mensa Internat. (maritime coordinator), Swiss Am. Author: Consumer Behavior in a Bicultural Milieu, 1978; (with G.L. Cassie) The Cassie Family in the United States and Canada, 1976; Consumer Behavior in the Health Care Services Setting, 1971; (with R.N. Cardozo) Robertson Electronics Company: A Case in Product Strategy Planning, 1970; contbr. articles, reports, speeches to publs. and meetings. Home: Les Bouleaux Stone Ridge Estates Mont Saint Hilaire PQ J3H 1S5 Canada Office: 3800 Sherbrooke est Montreal PQ H1X 1Z7 Canada

CASSO, LEONARD ANTHONY, comml. arbitrator; b. Sanford, Fla., Oct. 18, 1931; s. Emmanuel Leonard and Edna (Allen) C.; spl. studies in retailing U. Uppsala, 1969-71; B.A., York Coll. of City U. N.Y., 1978; children—Emmanuel, Angela, Lenora. Journalist, UPI, Europe and Africa, 1954-56; job developer Mayor's Office, City of Boston, 1956-66; book negotiator Albert Bonniers Forlag, Stockholm, Sweden, 1969-71; comml. arbitrator, bus. cons. Libra Assos., Jamaica, N.Y., 1965—. Advisor in community relations, Mayor's Office, N.Y.C., 1972-76; advisor Borough Pres. of N.Y., 1972-76; mem. Commn. for Profl. Devel., Nat. Assn. for Fgn. Student Affairs, 1973-75. Served with U.S. Army, 1950-53; Korea. Mem. Am. Arbitration Assn. (mem. comml. panel), Am. Soc. for Psychical Research, Internat. Assn. for Parapsychology, Friends of Earth, Am. Cryptography Assn., Am. Translators Assn., Am. Polit. Sci. Assn., P.E.N. (guest 34th Congress 1966), Am. Chess Assn., Am. Econ. Assn., Am. Mgmt. Assn., Aquarian Found. of Seattle, Solar Quest, Internat. Healing Fellowship. Unitarian. Office: PO Box 2257 Astoria NY 11102

CASTAGNA, EUGENE GENNARO, chem. engr.; b. Newark, Mar. 30, 1928; s. Nicholas A. and Angelina (DeJianne) C.; B.S. in Chem. Engring., Newark Coll. Engring., 1949; M.S., Stevens Inst. Tech., 1953; Ed.D., N.Y. U., 1977; m. Mary Louise Craven, June 21, 1958; children—Gina Marie, Marie Angela, Lisa Ann, Nicholas Arthur, Eugene Andrew. Asso. chemist Allied Chem. Corp., Morristown, N.J., 1948-51; materials engr. Picatinny Arsenal, U.S. Govt., N.J., 1951-54; materials and processes engr. Westinghouse Elec. Co., Balt., 1957-61; plastics engr. Esso Research & Engring. Co., Linden, N.J., 1961-63; sales service engr. Chevron Chem. Co., San Francisco, 1963-68; product devel. mgr. Dart Industries, Paramus, N.J., 1968—. Adj. faculty mem., supr. plastics program Newark Coll. Engring., 1964—. Served with AUS, 1954-56. Mem. Soc. Plastics Engrs. (dir.), Pi Kappa Phi. Roman Catholic. Patentee magnetic dielec. jointure. Home: 29 Hillside Ave Clark NJ 07066 Office: W115 Century Rd Paramus NJ 07083

CASTELLI, HELEN SIMS, publicist; b. Lilly, Ga., Dec. 7, 1920; d. Ulysses Grant and Emma (Sims) Johnson; B.A., Tift Coll., 1942; student Columbia U., 1944-45; M.A., U. Okla., 1960; Ph.D., U. Colo., 1975; m. Joseph R. Castelli, Jan. 14, 1950; children—Marc, Joseph, Jeffrey. Newspaper writer, photographer, 1943-76; tchr. Dalton Sch., N.Y.C., 1944-46, Edgewood Sch., Greenwich, Conn., 1946-47,

Low-Heywood Sch., Stamford, Conn., 1947-48, Colorado Springs (Colo.) Sch., 1964-67, Cheyenne Mountain Sch., Colorado Springs, 1967-68; French instr. U. Okla., 1959-60, U. Colo., 1966-69; family editor Pocono Record, Stroudsburg, Pa., 1975-76; mem. bd., publicity dir. Quiet Valley Hist. Farm, Stroudsburg, 1976—, Am. Cancer Soc., 1976—, Arthritis Found., 1977—. Mem. bd. Monroe County Hosp. Aux., Stroudsburg, 1977-78. Grantee, Sorbonne, Paris, summer 1966. Mem. Am. Hist. Assn., Assn. Asian Studies, AAUW, Soc. French Hist. Studies, Modern Lang. Assn., Pa. Women's Press Assn., Société des Professeurs Français en Amérique. Republican. Clubs: Shawnee Country, Water Gap Country. Contbr. to Anglo-American Contributions to Basque Studies: Essays in Honor of Jon Bilbao. Home: PO Box 631 East Stroudsburg PA 18301

CASTELLS, SALVADOR, pediatrician, endocrinologist, educator; b. Barcelona, Spain, Dec. 4, 1935; s. Domingo and Rosa (Cuch) C.; came to U.S., 1962, naturalized, 1967; M.D., U. Barcelona, 1960; postgrad. Cambridge (Eng.) U., 1962; m. Jean Proudfit, Feb. 24, 1962; children—David, Brewster. Clin. asst. dept. pediatrics Barcelona Med. Sch., 1960-62; rotating intern Women's Hosp., Balt., 1963; pediat. intern Sinai Hosp., Balt., 1963-64; resident in pediatrics Jefferson Med. Sch., Phila., 1964-66; NIH fellow in metabolic and endocrine diseases Lab. Devel. Genetics, Dept. Pediatrics, Yale Med. Sch., New Haven, 1966-67, dept. nutrition and food sci. Mass. Inst. Tech., Cambridge, 1967-68, research asso., 1968; asst. prof. pediatrics N.Y. State U. Downstate Med. Center, Bklyn., 1968-71, asso. prof., 1971-77, prof., 1977—; mem. med. staff Yale-New Haven Hosp., 1966-68; asst. attending physician Kings County (N.Y.) Hosp., 1968-71, asso. attending physician, 1971—; asso. attending physician Downstate Med. Center, 1968—, dir. unit of growth and metabolism, 1972—, dir. pediatric research. Diplomate Am. Bd. Pediatrics. Mem. Soc. for Pediat. Research, The Endocrine Soc., The Lawson Wilkins Soc. for Pediat. Endocrinology, N.Y. Diabetes Assn. (mem. diabetes detection com. 1972—), N.Y. Acad. Sci., AAAS, Bklyn. Acad. Pediatrics, Bklyn. Endocrine and Metabolic Pediat. Assn., Sigma Xi. Contbr. articles to profl. jours. Home: 3333 Henry Hudson Pkwy Riverdale NY 10463 Office: 450 Clarkson Ave Bklyn NY 11203

CASTER, BERNARD HARRY, artist; b. Wolcott, N.Y., May 27, 1921; s. Edward Everett and Effie Armenia (Reed) C.; A.A., Syracuse U., 1956, B.A., 1960; m. Katherine Jane Capron, Nov. 29, 1941; children—Carol Sue (Mrs. Karl Schantz III), Cyril Everett, Allan David. One-man shows at Galerie Paula Insel, N.Y.C., Univ. Coll. Syracuse (N.Y.) U., Edinborough (Pa.) State Tchrs. Coll.; exhibited in group shows at Syracuse Mus. Fine Arts, Rochester (N.Y.) Meml. Art Gallery, Albright Art Gallery, Buffalo; represented in permanent collections at Sainte Croix at Neuilly, Paris, France, Galerie Paula Insel, Muggleton Gallery Fine Arts, Auburn, N.Y., St. Lawrence U., Canton, N.Y., Newark Pub. Library. Served with USAAF, 1942-45; PTO. Recipient Wilner award Cayuga Mus. History and Art, Auburn, 1962, Ceramic award, 1966, Crafts prize, 1972; Mem. Am. Crafts Council, N.Y. State Craftsmen. Home: Box 154 South Butler NY 13154

CASTERGINE, JOHN, hosp adminstr.; b. Cranston, R.I., Apr. 15, 1917; s. Joseph and Victoria Diana C.; student Cornell U., 1940; degree in Hosp. Mgmt. (hon.), Rider Coll., 1965; m. Janene Johnson, Oct. 22, 1962; children—Irene, Margie Rae, Stuart. Gen. mgr. Gow Mgmt. Trust, restaurant chain, Boston, 1940-57; dir. dietary hosp. Mercer Med. Center, Trenton, N.J., 1957-67; hosp. food cons., Morrisville, Pa., 1967-70; dir. hosp. food mgmt. ARA Services, Phila., 1970-75; dir. dietary Monmouth Med. Center, Long Branch, N.J., 1975—; cons. Pennsbury Sch. System. Served with inf. U.S. Army, 1942-45. Recipient Culinary Art award Hosp. Food Dirs. Assn., 1962; Dietetic grantee Howard Johnson's, 1940-45. Mem. Am. Soc. Hosp. Food Service Adminstrs., Am. Hosp. Assn., Hosp. Dirs. Assn., Nat. Soc. Hosp. Food Cons. Republican. Presbyterian. Clubs: Rotary, Boosters, Morrisville Men's. Home: 47 Girard St Marlboro NJ 07746 Office: 3d and Pavillion Ave Long Branch NJ 07740

CASTLETON, VIRGINIA, editor, writer; b. Fairbanks, La.; d. Pierre Ariel and Vada Al Berta (Nolan) Castleton; student Temple U., 1951-52, New Sch. Social Research, 1962, U. Paris, 1964; 1 son, Ronald Michail. Corr., MacNen's News Agy., Paris, France, 1966-67; feature writer Phila. Bull., 1968-71; beauty editor Prevention mag., Emmaus, Pa., 1970—. Mem. Overseas Press Club, Bucks County Writers Guild. Author: The Calendar Book of Natural Beauty, 1973; Look Younger, Look Prettier, 1972; My Secrets of Natural Beauty, 1972; The Handbook of Natural Beauty, 1975. Home: 236 Century House W Doylestown PA 18901

CASTOR, RICHARD GILBERT, corp. exec.; b. Woodbury, N.J., Dec. 26, 1927; s. George F. and E. Dorothy (Supplee) C.; B.A., Adelphi Coll., 1956; m. Constance R. Flink, Sept. 2, 1957; children—Kimberly Susan, Lisa Beth, Holly Jennifer, Jill Catherine. Pres., Interstate Risk Mgmt. Corp. and Interstate Coverage Corp., Bedford, N.Y., 1951—. Chmn. bd. Scripture Union-U.S.A., Phila.; corp. mem. Inter-Varsity Christian Fellowship, Madison, Wis.; vice chmn. Union Biblica en Las Americas Consejo Regional, Lima, Peru; bd. mgrs. Am. Bible Soc. Served with USMC, 1945-46. C.L.U., C.P.C.U. Mem. Soc. C.P.C.U.'s, Profl. Ins. Agts. N.Y. (state bd. 1967-73, v.p. 1971-73), Nat. Safety Assn., Campus Safety Assn. Home: RFD 2 Box 72 Bedford Village NY 10506 Office: Hunting Ridge Mall Bedford NY 10504

CASTRO, ANTONIO OSCAR, counselor; b. Santruce, P.R., Feb. 16, 1943; s. Jose Antonio Luis and Cristina (Pagan Hahn Villa-Lobos) Castro Ossorio; profl. counseling diploma U. P.R., 1970, M. Rehab. Counseling, 1972; Tchr. elementary sch., Santruce, 1969-70; vocat. rehab. counselor Dept. Social Services P.R., Bayamon, 1970-72; psychiat. rehab. counselor Health and Hospitals Corp., N.Y.C., 1972—; pvt. practice counseling and therapy, 1975—. Mem. Nat. Rehab. Assn., Nat., Am. rehab. counseling assns., Am. Personnel and Guidance Assn. Home: 33-20 70th St Jackson Heights NY 11372 Office: 37-60 92d St Jackson Heights NY 11372

CASTRUCCI, PAUL PHILIP, engring. exec.; b. St. Johnsville, N.Y., July 10, 1934; s. Filiberto and Josephine (Granati) C.; B.S. in Physics, Union Coll., 1952-56; m. Margaret Davis, Apr. 1, 1956; children—Janice Ellen, Lynda Ann, David Paul, Ellen Lyn. Jr. engr. IBM, Poughkeepsie, N.Y., 1956-66, devel. engr. components div., Fishkill, N.Y., 1966—, mgr. devel. semicondr. device pilot line, 1964—, sr. engr. components div., 1968, mono memory component program mgr., 1969, developed 1st bipolar monolithic memory used in computers, developed first FET monolithic memory, 1970, mgr. FET Memory Mfg. group, 1971, Future Mfg. Systems, 1972, 73, SPD HQ mfg. staff, 1975, dir. mfg. planning, 1977—. Served to capt. USAAF, 1956-59. Recipient IBM Invention Achievement awards, 1966-71, IBM Outstanding Contbn. awards, 1967, 69, IBM Outstanding Invention awards, 1970, 75. Mem. Am. Phys. Soc., IEEE, Research and Engring. Soc. Am. (asso.). Patentee in field. Home: 41 Pheasant Way South Burlington VT 05401 Office: IBM Gen Technology Div Essex Junction VT 05452

CASTURO, DON JAMES, banker; b. McKeesport, Pa., Nov. 9, 1942; s. Charles and Elizabeth B. (Barno) C.; B.A., Mich. State U., 1964; M.B.A., U. So. Calif., 1965; m. Judith K. Erkman, Aug. 22, 1964; children—Don J.E., Christian D.E. Participant mgmt. devel. program Mellon Bank, Pitts., 1966-67, investment researcher, 1967-73, asst. investment officer, 1969-71, investment officer, 1971-73, asst. v.p., 1973—; pres. Equity Asset Mgr., 1973—. Pitts. co-chmn. enrichment program Mich. State U. Mem. Pitts. Soc. Fin. Analysts (past pres., chmn. exec. com., dir.), Fin. Analysts Fedn. (chartered fin. analyst). Am. Bankers Assn., Sigma Nu. Republican. Orthodox Catholic. Home: 2339 Morton Rd Pittsburgh PA 15241 Office: Mellon Bank NA Mellon Sq Pittsburgh PA 15230

CATACOSINOS, WILLIAM JAMES, electronics co. exec.; b. N.Y.C., Apr. 12, 1930; s. James and Penelope (Paleologos) C.; B.S., N.Y. U., 1951, M.B.A., 1952, Ph.D., 1962; m. Florence Maken, Oct. 16, 1955; children—William, James. Asst. editor 20th Century Fox, N.Y.C., 1951-52; asst. dir. bus. mgmt. and adminstrn. Brookhaven Nat. Lab., 1956-69; pres. Applied Digital Data Systems Inc., Hauppauge, N.Y., 1969—. Adj. asst. prof. N.Y. U., 1962-64; mgmt. counselor, 1962-69; chmn. bd. dirs. Corometrics Med., 1968-74; dir. The Alpha Group Inc., RDC Industries Inc. Mem. Brookhaven Town Indsl. Commn., 1956-77; mem. Brookhaven Indsl. Devel. Com. Inc., 1970—. Bd. dirs. Suffolk County Am. Cancer Soc., 1969-77. Home: Cleft Rd Mill Neck NY 11765 Office: 100 Marcus Blvd Hauppauge NY 11787

CATALDO, LOUIS, city ofcl.; b. East Boston, Mass., June 11, 1920; s. Lawrence and Angela (Ciampa) C.; grad. FBI Nat. Acad., 1955; m. Lora Ruth Gardner, June 15, 1947; children—Steven, Michael, Louis G. Dep. sheriff Bur. Criminal Investigation, Barnstable County Sheriff's Dept., Barnstable, Mass., 1948-74, dir., also chief dep. sheriff, 1970-74; dir. Barnstable County Police Acad., 1960-74; chief police, Dennis, Mass., 1974—. Intelligence officer Barnstable County CD, 1960—; bd. dirs. Cape Cod United Fund, 1962-76, pres., 1971-73; chmn. Barnstable Hist. Commn., 1969—; founder, pres. Tales of Cape Cod, Inc., 1949—; co-chmn. Barnstable Civil War Centennial Com., 1961-66; coordinator Nat. Bicentennial Commn., Barnstable, 1973-76. Mem. Barnstable Republican Town Com., 1963-74; bd. dirs. Cape Cod Com. on Alcoholism, 1964—; founding dir. Cape Cod YMCA, 1966; founder, mem. bd. dirs. Donald G. Trayser Mus., 1960—; bd. dirs. Old Indian Church Meeting House Authority, Mashpee, 1959-76, sec., 1968-74. Named B'nai B'rith Citizen of Year, 1974, hon. dep. sec. state Mass., 1974; recipient hon. citation Mass. Senate and Ho. of Reps., 1974. Mem. Internat. Assn. for Identification (regional v.p. 1972-74), Mass. Police Tng. Officers Assn., (pres. 1972—), Nat. Sheriffs Assn., Mass. Dep. Sheriffs Assn., Cape Cod Investigators Assn. (coordinator 1970-73), V.F.W. Elk. Home: 47 Cherry St Hyannis MA 02601 Office: Cataldo Detective Agency 58 Falmouth Rd Hyannis MA 02601

CATALDO, LUCILLE ANN, microbiologist; b. N.Y.C.; d. Vincent Francis and Pauline Rosemary (Diesa) Cataldo; B.S. in Biology, Fordham U., 1968; M.A., Columbia, 1969. Med. technologist, mycologist, teaching supr. microbiology clin. lab. St. Vincent's Hosp. and Med. Center N.Y., N.Y.C., 1969—, teaching supr., lectr. hosp. sch. med. tech., 1971—. Recipient Supr.'s license N.Y.C. Dept. Health. Mem. Nat. Registry of Microbiologists, Am. Soc. Clin. Pathologist, N.Y. Mycology Soc., Am. Soc. Microbiology, Phi Beta Kappa.

CATANELLO, IGNATIUS ANTHONY, clergyman; b. Bklyn., July 23, 1938; s. Nicholas Anthony and Mary Grace (DeFalco) C.; B.A. in Philosophy, St. Francis Coll., 1962; S.T.B., Cath. U., 1966; M.S. in Counselling, St. John's U., 1971, M.A. in Theology, 1974. Ordained priest Roman Catholic Ch., 1966; asso. pastor St. Rita's Ch., Long Island City, N.Y., 1966-76, St. Helen's Ch., Howard Beach, N.Y., 1976-78; chmn. Bklyn. Diocesan Ecumenical Commn., 1975—; pres. priests senate Diocese of Bklyn., 1973-75; asst. prof. theology St. John's U., Jamaica, N.Y., 1971—; chmn. Com. of Religious Leaders City of N.Y., 1978—. Recipient Pres.'s medal St. John's U., 1975; Brotherhood award NCCJ, 1975; N.Y. State Disting. Service award, 1975. Mem. Am. Acad. Religion, Coll. Theology Soc., Cath. Bibl. Assn., Soc. Sci. Study of Religion, Ecumenical Clergy Assn., N.Y. State Personnel and Guidance Assn. Home: 157-04 82d St Howard Beach NY 11414 Office: 75 Greene Ave Brooklyn NY 11202

CATANIA, JOSEPH VINCENT, govt. auditor; b. N.Y.C., Sept. 2, 1917; s. Philip Joseph and Anne (Gianni) C.; B.S., St. Johns U., 1941; M.B.A, N.Y. U., 1950; m. Catherine Rosary Munna, Oct. 15, 1950; 1 dau., Anne Elizabeth (Mrs. William Armstrong Dixon). Cost accountant Bendix Aviation Corp., N.Y.C., 1942-43; accountant H.S. Pollack & Co., C.P.A.'s, N.Y.C., 1946-56; staff asst. for audits AEC (now Nuclear Regulatory Commn.), Washington, 1956—. Served with USAAF, 1943-46. Decorated Bronze Star. Mem. Assn. Govt. Accountants, Am. Accounting Assn., Inst. Nuclear Materials Mgmt., Am. Mgmt. Assn., Fin. Mgmt. Assn. Roman Catholic. K.C. Home: 3613 Tarkington Ln Silver Spring MD 20906 Office: US Nuclear Regulatory Commn Washington DC 20555

CATCHI, (CATHERINE CHILDS), artist; b. Phila., Aug. 27, 1920; d. William Henry Harrison and Catherine Stuart (Oeland) Childs; student Briarcliff Jr. Coll. 1937, Comml. Illustration Studios, 1938-39; studied with Leon Kroll, Harry Sternberg, Hans Hoffman and Angelo Savelli, Positano, Italy; children—Diane Childs Willis (Mrs. Neuse), Heather Childs Willis (Mrs. Sargent), Charles Everett Willis III, Jeffrey Childs Willis (dec.). Exhibited in shows at A.C.A. Gallery, Allied Artists, Lever House, Royal Acad. Galleries, Edinburgh, Scotland, Denver Art Mus., Pepsi Cola Show, Contemporary Arts, Springfield (Mass.) Mus., Hofstra U., L.I., Knickerbocker Artists, Queens Coll., Royal Soc. Artists Galleries, Eng., others; exhibited one-man shows at Queens Coll., Art Gallery North Shore, Heckscher Mus., Port Washington Pub. Library, Hofstra U., Alfredo Valente Gallery, N.Y.C., Southwestern U., Galeria Mediteranio, Rosenberg Library, Galveston, Tex., 1977, Monika Beck Gallery, Homburg, Germany, 1978; group exhbns. include U.S. Congress Rayburn Hall, Washington, 1968, 76; Universalist Art Gallery, Atlanta, Country Art Gallery, Locust Valley, N.Y.; represented in Rosenberg Found., Hofstra U. collections, also individual collections. Art adv. council Port Washington Pub. Library. Recipient 1st prize L.I. Regional Show, 1953; 2d prize Knickerbocker Artists, Riverside Mus., 1955; 3 time winner 1st prize Guild Hall, East Hampton; Lillian Cotton award and medal of honor Nat. Assn. Women Artists, 1966, 1st prize, 1973, Goldie Paley award, 1977; Grumbacher award, 1963; Irene Sickle Feist Meml. prize, 1971; 1st prize Internat. Platform Assn., 1973; 1st prize Ligoa Duncan Gallery, 1963, others. Mem. Nat. Assn. Women Artists (v.p., dir.), Audubon Artists (dir.), Manhasset Art Assn. (pres. 1962-64), Internat. Platform Assn., N.Y. Soc. Women Artists (v.p.), Internat. Platform Assn. (art com.), Exec. and Profl. Hall of Fame. Home and studio: 2 Grist Mill Ln Manhasset NY 11030

CATE, CURTIS WILSON, author; b. Paris, May 22, 1924 (parents Am. citizens); s. Karl Springer and Josephine (Wilson) C.; B.A. in History magna cum laude, Harvard U., 1947; degree in Russian, Ecole des Langues Orientales, Paris, 1949, Magdalen Coll., Oxford U., 1952; m. Elena Bajanova, Oct. 16, 1965. European editor Atlantic Monthly, 1958-66; author: Antoine de Saint-Exupéry (translated into French, recipient Grand Prix Lit. l'Aéro-Club de France 1973), 1970; George Sand, 1975; The Ides of August, 1978. Served with AUS, 1943-46. Address: care Harold Matson Co 22 E 40th St New York City NY 10016

CATENA, ANNA LORRAINE FIORITO, pharmacist; b. Newark, Aug. 28, 1912; d. Giovanni and Filomena (Greci) Fiorito; Registered Pharmacist, Coll. Pharmacy, Rutgers U., 1934; m. Louis R. Catena, June 26, 1938; children—Robert L., Diana M. Staff pharmacist Christ Hosp., Jersey City, 1936-41; staff pharmacist St. Barnabas Med. Center, Livingston, N.J., 1941-49, chief pharmacist, 1950-64, dir. pharmacy, 1965—; lectr. in pharmacy. Active Girl Scouts U.S.A. Mem. Am., N.J. socs. hosp. pharmacists, Am. Pharm. Assn. Home: 268 Brooklake Rd Florham Park NJ 07932

CATHCART, ALAN, statistician; b. N.Y.C., Mar. 29, 1925; s. Ernest William and Alice Elizabeth (Bergmann) C.; B.A., Columbia, 1944, M.A., 1945, postgrad., 1945-48. Mathematician, Weiss & Klau, Bronx, N.Y., 1948-60; time analyst N.Y.C. Dept. Real Estate, 1960-66; statistician Ins. Data Processing Center, N.Y.C., 1966-68; mathematician Pub. Service Mut. Ins. Co., N.Y.C., 1968-69; analyst Ch. Life Ins. Corp., N.Y.C., 1969-75; remedial asst. in math. Manhattan Community Coll., N.Y.C., 1975—. Mem. Am. Math Soc., Fedn. Greater N.Y. Rifle and Pistol Clubs, Nat. Rifle Assn. Am., Conn. Rifle and Revolver Assn., U.S. Revolver Assn. Republican. Home: 730 Ft Washington Ave New York City NY 10040 Office: 135 W 70th St Room 807 New York City NY 10023

CATTANEO, DONALD JEROME, pharm. co. exec.; b. Floral Park, N.Y., Jan. 25, 1932; s. Dante A. and Mildred S. (Weitemeyer) C.; B.S., Fordham U., 1954; M.B.A., N.Y. U., 1958; postgrad. Hofstra Coll., 1959-60, Adelphi Coll., 1960-61; m. Barbara H. Sanchez, Jan. 8, 1955; children—Elizabeth, Christopher, Matthew, Dante. Asst. to v.p. mfg. Am. Chicle Co., L.I., N.Y., 1956-57; asst. head tablet dept. E.R. Squibb & Sons, Bklyn., 1958-63; asst. mgr. tech. liaison dept. Internat. Div., Schering Corp., Bloomfield, N.J., 1963-66; gen. prodn. mgr. Endo Labs., Garden City, N.Y., 1966-69; pres., dir. Pharmacia Inc., Piscataway, N.J., 1969-76; v.p. ops. Astra Pharm. Products Inc., Worcester, Mass., 1977—. Trustee, Community Leukemia Fund. Served to 1st lt. AUS, 1954-56. Mem. Am. Pharm. Assn., Parental Drug Assn., Swedish-Am. C. of C. Republican. Roman Catholic. Clubs: Worcester Rotary, K.C. Office: 7 Neponset St Worcester MA 01606

CATTANI, DEBRA ANN, mfg. co. exec.; b. N.Y.C., Feb. 20, 1953; d. Frank and Anita (Acciani) C.; A.A., Nassau Community Coll., 1973; B.S., N.Y. Inst. Tech., 1975, postgrad., 1976—. Sec., Rosenfeld, Steinman & Blau, Great Neck, N.Y., 1974-75; tchr. Katharine Gibbs Secretarial Sch., N.Y.C., 1975-76; adminstrv. asst. to br. mgr. and br. control mgr. Xerox Corp., Woodbury, N.Y., 1976-78, market support rep., N.Y.C., 1978—; pvt. tutor. Mem. Bus. Tchrs. Assn. N.Y., Bus. Edn. Assn. Metro N.Y., Delta Mu Delta, Phi Theta Kappa. Republican. Roman Catholic. Home: 135 South St New Hyde Park NY 11040 Office: 40 W 57th St New York City NY

CAUDLE, GARY CRAIG, educator; b. Rochester, N.Y., Dec. 24, 1947; s. Jack Craig and Joan R. (Woods) C.; B.S., State U. N.Y. at Geneseo, 1970, M.S. in Edn., 1973; postgrad. State U. N.Y. Buffalo, Amherst, 1975—, Inst. Spl. Edn. State U. N.Y., Geneseo, 1976-77; postgrad. indoctoral program (doctoral fellow) State U. N.Y., Albany, 1977-78; Elementary sch. tchr., Scottsville, N.Y., 1970-72; sociotherapist Convalescent Hosp. for Children, 1972-74; reading specialist Rochester Mental Health Center, 1974-75; instr. spl. edn. dept. State U. N.Y. at Geneseo, 1975-76, dir. reading tutoring lab., 1975-77, diving coach, 1975—; ednl. therapist Convalescent Hosp. for Children, 1978—. Mem. NEA, New Eng. Ednl. Research Orgn., Council Exceptional Children, N.Y. State Univ. Tchrs., Nat. Reading Conf., Internat. Reading Assn., Eastern Ednl. Research Orgn. Address: 6459 Upper Railroad Ave Conesus NY 14435

CAUTELA, JOSEPH RICHARD, educator; b. Boston, Feb. 21, 1927; s. Salvatore and Domenica (D'Amico) C.; A.B., Boston Coll., 1949; M.A. Boston U., 1950, Ph.D., 1954; m. Joan Therese Gleason, May 6, 1972. Research asst. Harvard, 1952; dir. guidance evening sch. Boston Coll., 1954-59, asst. prof., 1954-59, asso. prof., 1959-66, prof. psychology, 1966—, dir. doctoral program in behavior modification, 1973—; teaching fellow psychiatry med. sch. U. Va., 1965; cons. Mass. Mental Health, 1965-70, Cushing Hosp., 1965-68, div. vocat. rehab. State R.I., U.C., 1966-70, div. legal medicine, Commonwealth of Mass., Shirley Indsl. Sch., 1965-69, Conn. Valley Hosp., Middletown, 1967-70, VA, 1969—; pvt. practice with Behavior Therapy Inst., Sudbury, Mass.; dir. behavior modification unit Boston State Hosp., 1970-72. Served with USNR, 1945-46. Fellow Mass. Psychol. Assn.; mem. Am., Eastern, New Eng. psychol. assns., AAAS, Assn. Advancement of Behavior Therapy (bd. profl. affairs 1967-74, pres. 1972-73), Sigma Xi. Author: (with June Groden) Relaxation; Behavior Analysis Forms for Clin. Intervention, 1977. Contbr. numerous articles to profl. jours. Home: 10 Phillips Rd Sudbury MA 01776

CAVALET, JAMES ROGER, civil engr.; b. Dean, Pa., Jan. 5, 1942; s. Irvin Gordon and Elizabeth Ann (Nevling) C.; Asso. Mech. Engring. Tech., Pa. State U., 1963; postgrad. U. Pitts., 1973—; m. Margaret Joan Burkey, June 17, 1961; children—Peggy Ann, James Roger, Beth Ann, Deborah. Sturctural engr. Peter F. Loftus Corp., Pitts., 1965-66; chief civil engr. Acme Design Co., Pitts., 1966-67; asst. mgr. civil engring. Auburn Engring. Inc., Pitts., 1967-69; asst. chief civil engr. Dravo Corp., Pitts., 1969—, cons. engr./chief engr. Brazilian subs., 1976-77. Mem. tech. adv. com. Pa. State U., McKeesport campus, 1977—. Registered profl. engr. Pa., Ohio, N.J., W.Va., Minn. Mem. ASCE. Roman Catholic. Home: 1438 Swede Hill Rd Greensburg PA 15601 Office: One Oliver Plaza Pittsburgh PA 15222

CAVALIERI, ANTHONY SIMONE, accountant; b. N.Y., Aug. 27, 1946; s. Charles Joseph and Angela Maria (Yezzo) C.; B.S., St. John's U., 1968; M.B.A., Fordham U., 1974. Pub. accountant Price Waterhouse, N.Y.C., 1968-71; sr. fin. analyst Gulf & Western, N.Y.C., 1971-74; with The Mennon Co., Morristown, N.J., 1974—, dir. corporate accounting, 19—; faculty Fairleigh Dickinson U., 1976—. Served with USAR, 1969-75. C.P.A., N.Y., N.J. Mem. Am. Inst. C.P.A.'s, N.Y., N.J. socs. C.P.A.'s, Alpha Kappa Psi. Office: E Hanover Ave Morristown NJ 07960

CAVALLARO, JAMES ANTHONY, sch. adminstr.; b. Phila., July 7, 1941; s. Anthony C.and Rita E. (Baldino) C.; B.B.A., U. Pa., 1976; m. Mary E. Doonan, May 21, 1965; children—Cheryl, Gina, James. Accountant, U. Pa., Phila., 1962-65, bus. adminstr., 1965-69, bus. mgr., 1969—; tchr. basic tax class H & R Block, Inc. Mem. environ. com. Springfield Twp.; election judge Springfield Twp.; bd. dirs. YMCA Indian Guide program. Served with USAR, 1961. Recipient Dean's award, Wharton Sch. U. Pa., 1969. Mem. Soc. Research Adminstrs., Assn. Bus. Adminstrs., Night Watch Honor Soc. Republican. Roman Catholic. Clubs: Italian Ams. Del. County, K.C. Home: 317 Rambling Way Springfield PA 19064 Office: Cardiovascular-Pulmonary Div 874 Maloney Bldg Hosp U Pa 3600 Spruce St Philadelphia PA 19104

CAVALLO, ROBERT MICHAEL, lawyer; b. N.Y.C., Dec. 8, 1932; s. Dominick and Mary (DiStefano) C.; B.S., Manhattan Coll., 1954; LL.B., St. John's U., 1957; m. Ellen Beach, Nov. 6, 1963; 1 son, Robert Beach. Admitted to N.Y. bar, 1958; asso. firm Thomas J. Flood, N.Y.C., 1958-61, James I. Lysaght, N.Y.C., 1961-62; individual practice law, N.Y.C., 1962—; instr. photography and the law N.Y. U., 1974—. Mem. N.Y. State Bar Assn., Fed. Bar Council, Colombian Lawyers Assn., Dramatists Guild. Author: (with Stuart Kahan) Photography: What's the Law?, 1976; Do I Really Need A Lawyer?, 1979; contbr. numerous articles on photography law to mags. Home and office: 1065 Park Ave New York City NY 10028

CAVANAUGH, PAUL EDWARD, wholesale co. exec.; b. Fall River, Mass., July 20, 1942; s. Frank and Avis (Grey) C.; B.S., Southeastern Mass. U., 1964; m. Karin Bergquist, July 9, 1966; children—Kelly Ann, Pamela Lynn. Br. mgr. First Nat. Bank of Md., Balt., 1970-72; credit mgr. Texaco, Inc., Balt., 1972-73, Cherry Hill, N.J., 1973-75, Boston, 1975-77; credit mgr. A.E. Borden Co., Inc., Boston, 1977-78, sales mgr. indsl. div., 1978—. Served to lt. USN, 1964-68. Mem. New Eng. Assn. of Credit Mgmt. Home: 945 Riverside Dr Apt 25A Methuen MA 01844 Office: A E Borden Co Inc 184 Everett St Boston MA 02134

CAVANAUGH, WILLIAM JOSEPH, acoustical engring. cons.; b. Boston, June 27, 1929; s. Francis Xavier and Catherine Marie (Hennessey) C.; B.Arch., Mass. Inst. Tech., 1951; m. Louise V. Huff, May 3, 1953; children—Joan M., Lauren C., William J., Mark A. John W. Asso. engr. Polaroid Corp., Cambridge, Mass., 1953; cons., mgmt. exec. Bolt Beranek & Newman, Inc., Cambridge, 1954-70, div. v.p., 1966-70, div. dir., 1969-70; pvt. practice as acoustical engring. cons., Natick, Mass., 1970—; partner Cavanaugh & Copley Assos., Newton, Mass., 1970-75, Cavanaugh & Tocci Assos., Natick, Mass., 1975—. Vis. lectr. Mass. Inst. Tech., 1959, div. archtl. studies R.I. Sch. Design, Providence, 1961-66, 72—, others. State coordinator admissons program U.S. Mil. Acad. Served as 1st lt. C.E., AUS, 1951-53; col. Res. Fellow Acoustical Soc. Am. (chmn. tech. com. archtl. acoustics, com. on regional chpts., pub. policy com., membership com.); mem. Inst. Noise Control Engring. (bd. examiners), Nat. Council Acoustical Consultants (v.p. 1975-76, pres. 1977—), Audio Engring. Soc., Soc. Am. Mil. Engrs., AAAS, Boston Archl. Center (vice chmn. com. on continuing profl. edn. 1967—). Contbr. sect. on acoustics Time Saver Standards, 4th edit., 1966; also articles to profl. jours. Address: 3 Merifield Ln Natick MA 01760

CAVANNA, ALICE MAY, nurse; b. South Glastonbury, Conn., Aug. 10, 1923; d. Anthony and Jennie (Gilmetti) C.; B.S. in Nursing, Tchrs. Coll., Columbia U., 1960, M.A. in Nursing Service Adminstrn., 1962; R.N., Kings County Hosp. Sch. Nursing, 1944. Gen. duty nurse Hartford (Conn.) Hosp., night supr., staff nurse, urol. unit, asst. head nurse urol. unit, head nurse med.-surg. unit; asst. dir. nursing, Mt. Sinai Hosp., Hartford, 1962-74, asso. dir. nursing, 1974—. Served with Nurse Corps, U.S. Army, 1945-46; ETO. Conn. Bd. Nursing Examiners grantee. Mem. AAHPER, Conn. Nurses Assn., St. Augustine's Altar Guild. Roman Catholic. Home: 2008 New London Turnpike Glastonbury CT 06033

CAVEN, ROBERT EMERSON, physician; b. Atlantic City, June 6, 1938; s. Waldo Emerson and Malissa Jane (Bryant) C.; B.A., U. Va., 1960; M.D., U. Pitts., 1964; m. Judith May Edmond, July 6, 1963; children—Timothy, Dean, Tobias, Leilani, Rebecca, Jeremiah. Intern, Providence Hosp., Portland, Oreg., 1964-65; resident in internal medicine Maine Med. Center, Portland, 1968-71; commd. capt. M.C., U.S. Air Force, 1965, advanced through grades to maj., 1977; family physician Air Force hosps., Hawaii, 1965-68, Eng., 1977—; family physician Kauai Med. Group, Lihue, Hawaii, 1971-73; asso. dir. family practice residency tng. program Maine Med. Center, Portland, 1973-77; asst. prof. community medicine Tufts U., Boston, 1974—. Diplomate Am. Bd. Family Practice. Fellow Am. Acad. Family Physicians; mem. A.C.P., Soc. Tchrs. Family Physicians, Anglo-Am. Med. Soc. Home: The Old Rectory Stoke Doyle Peterborough United Kingdom Office: Box 2371 APO New York City NY 09238

CAVENY, LEONARD HUGH, mech. engr.; b. Atlanta, Oct. 30, 1934; s. Elmer Leonard and Dorothy (Franklin) C.; B.M.E., Ga. Inst. Tech., 1956, M.S., 1960; Ph.D. in Mech. Engring., U. Ala., 1969; m. Joyce Ellen Rodal, Apr. 10, 1957; children—Polly J., Rebecca R., Teresa L., Leslie Y., Susan C. With Thiokol Chem. Corp., Huntsville, Ala., 1960-67, sr. engr., supr. Thermodynamics group, 1963-65, prin. engr., 1965-67, supr. tech. staff, 1967; sr. mem. profl. tech. staff Princeton, 1969—. Cons., U.S. Army Research Office, 1969—, pvt. industry, 1970—; rep. Interagy. Chem. Rocket Propulsion Group. Served to lt. (j.g.) USN, 1956-59. Recipient M.A. Ferst award Sigma Xi, 1961, A.T. Colwell merit award Soc. Automotive Engrs., 1972. Registered profl. engr., Ala. Asso. fellow Am. Inst. Aeros. and Astronautics (chmn. Princeton sect.); mem. A.A.A.S., Combustion Inst., ASME, Sigma Xi, Pi Tau Sigma, Pi Mu Epsilon. Contbr. articles to profl. jours. Patentee in field. Home: 23 Galston Dr Rural Route 4 Robbinsville NJ 08691 Office: Mech and Aerospace Engring Dept Princeton U Princeton NJ 08540

CAZAN, MATTHEW JOHN, educator; b. Beclean, Romania, Mar. 10, 1912; s. John and Marie (Sipos) C; student U. Bucharest Law Sch., Youngstown Coll., Georgetown U. Sch. Fgn. Service; m. Sylvia Marie Buday, July 14, 1935; 1 son, Matthew John George. Lectr. Georgetown U., 1942-44; spl. lectr. Indsl. Coll. of the Armed Forces, 1947; asso. in Romanian Georgetown U. Inst. Langs. and Linguistics, 1949—, lectr. polit. sci. and econs. Sch. Fgn. Service, 1943-57; lectr. The Inst. Fgn. Service Officer Preparation, 1953—; lectr. polit. sci. George Washington U., 1963—; spl. employee U.S. Dept. of Justice, 1947-60, 63—; internat. claims analyst fgn. claims settlement commn., 1960-63. Chmn. Lobarca youth guidance com. Va. Gov.'s Conf. Youth. Mem. Am. Assn. U. Profs., Am. Polit. Sci. Assn., Am. Soc. Internat. Law, Conf. Democratic Theory, Pi Gamma Mu. Home: 6369 Lakeview Dr Lake Barcroft Estates Falls Church VA 22041 Office: George Washington U Washington DC 20052 also Dept Justice Washington DC 20530

CAZEAU, CHARLES JAY, geologist, educator; b. Rochester, N.Y., June 25, 1931; s. Floyd Alfred and Nan Marie (Barbehenn) C.; B.S., U. Notre Dame, 1954; M.S., Fla. State U., 1955; postgrad. Va. Poly. Inst., 1958; Ph.D., U. N.C., 1962; children—Sharon Lee, Suzanne Carroll. Geologist, Humble Oil and Refining Co., Houston, 1955-58; asst. prof. geology Clemson (S.C.) U., 1960-63; asst. prof. geology State U. N.Y., Buffalo, 1963-67, asso. prof., 1967—; cons. Tenn. Gas and Pipeline Co., 1967-68, Dillingham Corp., LaJolla, Calif., 1966-67, McLain Industries, 1967-68; pres. CPF Assos., environ. consultants. NIH grantee, 1965-66, Sigma Xi grantee, 1965. Mem. N.Y. Acad. Scis., Am. Assn. Petroleum Geologists, Soc. Econ. Paleontologists and Mineralogists, Carolina Geol. Soc., Nat. Assn. Geology Tchrs., AAAS, Sigma Xi. Author: Physical Geology Laboratory Manual, 1971; Earthquakes, 1974; Physical Geology, 1976; Great Mysteries of the Earth, 1978. Home: 300 Paradise Rd East Amherst NY 14051

CEBRIK, MICHAEL MELVIN, physician; b. Newark, Jan. 15, 1943; s. Michael and Melvina (Nemo) C.; A.B., Dartmouth Coll., 1964, M.B.S., 1966; M.D., Harvard U., 1968; m. Priscilla Hopkins, June 12, 1965; children—Michael Bryant, David Michael, Jeffrey Roger, Deborah Susan. Intern, Jewish Hosp., St. Louis, 1968-69, resident, 1969-70; resident Maine Med. Center, Portland, 1972-74; practice medicine specializing in internal medicine and cardiology, Bath, Maine, 1974—; staff Bath Meml. Hosp., 1974—, Regional Meml. Hosp., Brunswick, Maine, 1974—, Maine Med. Center, Portland, 1974—, Parkview Hosp., Brunswick, 1974—. Mem. Brunswick Planning Bd., 1977-80; mem. music com. First Parish Ch., Brunswick, 1976-79; trustee Bath Meml. Hosp., 1977—. Served with M.C., U.S. Army, 1970-72. Diplomate Am. Bd. Internal Medicine. Mem. A.C.P., Am. Soc. Internal Medicine. Congregationalist. Home: Board Rd RFD 5 Brunswick ME 04011 Office: 14 Oak Grove Ave Bath ME 04530

CECCARELLI, JOHN F., aircraft hydraulic equipment co. exec.; b. N.Y.C., Jan. 16, 1921; s. Angelo and Josephine (Medici) C.; B.S., Ind. Inst. Tech., 1942; m. Violet M. Pepe, Apr. 30, 1949; children—John, Joanne Ceccarelli-Egan, Jeanne, Gerard, Stephen. Stress engr. Glenn L. Martin Co., Balt., 1942-44, Republic Aviation Corp., Farmingdale, N.Y., 1946-47; mgr. engring. and devel. Electrol, Inc., Kingston, N.Y., 1948-55; v.p. engring. and mktg. Ozone Industries, Ozone Park, N.Y., 1955—. Served with USAF, 1944-46. Mem. Inst. Aeros. and Astronautics, Am. Helicopter Soc., Soc. Automotive Engrs., Holy Name Soc. Republican. Roman Catholic. Clubs: Sagamore Yacht, (Oyster Bay, N.Y.); K.C. Home: 253 Peach Tree Dr East Norwich NY 11732 Office: Ozone Industries Inc 101-32 101st St Ozone Park NY 11416

CELENTANO, DOMENICK, food co. exec.; b. Newark, Jan. 22, 1923; s. John and Lucy C.; student pub. schs.; m. Doris Bastardi, Jan. 11, 1953; children—Domenick A., Anthony, Tina. Founder, pres. Celentano Brothers Inc., frozen Italian foods, Verona, N.J. Served with AUS, 1942-45. Republican. Office: 120 Bloomfield Ave Verona NJ 07044

CELLA, ELISA, mgmt. cons. firm exec.; b. Paterson, N.J., May 23, 1938; d. Alexander and Frances (Biggio) Cella; B.S., Fairleigh Dickinson U., 1960, postgrad., 1960-62; postgrad. N.Y. U., 1965-67. Controller Rogers, Slade & Hill, Inc., cons. to mgmt., N.Y.C., 1962-72; corporate sec. Pipeco Steel Corp., 1970-72; sec.-treas. Golightly & Co. Internat., Inc., N.Y.C., 1972—. Home: 412 Pompton Ave Cedar Grove NJ 07009 Office: 1 Rockefeller Plaza New York City NY 10020

CELLA, EUGENE ANTHONY, accountant; b. St. Albans, N.Y., Mar. 7, 1940; s. Anthony Joseph and Regina Ann (Ohm) C.; B.B.A., St. Francis Coll., 1961; m. Noeleen M. McEvoy, Apr. 27, 1963 (separated); children—Eugene Anthony, Robert J. Staff accountant Patterson & Ridgway, C.P.A.'s, Hempstead, N.Y., 1961-62, 65-68; treas., dir. Colgate Mgmt. Corp., N.Y.C., 1968-69; operational dir. Upstairs at Wantagh (N.Y.), 1976—; corporate v.p. TOC Security Corp., Patchague, N.Y., 1976-77; pvt. practice accountant Wantagh, 1970—. Mem. Nassau County Com. Conservative Party, 1972—; active Boy Scouts Am. Served with U.S. Army Air Def. Command, 1962-65, C.P.A.; certified supervisory mgr. Am. Mgmt. Assn. Mem. N.Y. State Sheriff Assn. (hon.), Am. Inst. C.P.A.'s, N.Y. State Soc. C.P.A., Nat. Assn. Accountants, St. Francis Alumni Assn. Club: Elks. Home: 1601 George Rd Wantagh NY 11793 Office: 78 Rockaway Ave Valley Stream NY 11580☆

CELLIERS, PETER JOUBERT, internat. pub. relations specialist; b. Vogelfontein, South Africa, May 21, 1920; s. Bartilimy and Elsie Blanche (Goldberg) C.; ed. Eng. and Europe; m. Helen Rassaby, Sept. 10, 1949; children—Gordon A.J., Jennefer A.J. Bur. chief Reuters, Washington, 1942-43; polit. intelligence officer British Fgn. Office, San Francisco, 1944-45; mng. editor N.Am. Newspaper Alliance, N.Y.C., 1946-50; departmental editor Farm Jour. group, Washington, 1951-56; sr. editor Redbook, N.Y.C., 1957-59; cons. to fgn. govts., internat. corps. Peter J. Celliers Co., N.Y.C., 1960-68; dir. for N.Am., Mexican Nat. Tourist Council, 1962-72; chief fgn. press services XIX Olympic Games, Mexico City, 1968; owner Ellis Assos., N.Y.C., 1969—; tech. adviser on tourism devel. to UN, hotels, carriers, govts. Mem. Pub. Relations Soc. Am. (counsellors sect.), Soc. Am. Travel Writers (past pres.), N.Y. Assn. Travel Writers, Internat. Assn. Exchange Students Tech. Experience (nat. com.), Am. Soc. Journalists and Authors. Clubs: Nat. Press (Washington); Overseas Press, Dutch Treat (N.Y.C.). Home: 131 Fenimore Rd New Rochelle NY 10804 Office: 304 E 42d St New York City NY 10017

CELNIK, MAX, librarian, editor, cons.; b. Berlin, Germany, June 15, 1933; s. Leib and Gussie (Schnall) C.; came to U.S., 1939; B.A., Bklyn. Coll., 1955; B. Hebrew Lit., Sem. Coll. Jewish Studies, Jewish Theol. Sem., 1957; M.L.S., Rutgers U., 1956; m. Faith Caplan, Mar. 25, 1958; children—Eli, Gerald. Library researcher N.Y. Pub. Library, 1956-57; librarian, instr. in research methodology Stern Coll. for Women, Yeshiva U., N.Y.C., 1957-67, asst. prof. library sci., 1967-69, chief librarian, 1957-69, lectr. Grad. Sch. Edn., 1958-60 dir. High Sch. Libraries, 1961-69; librarian Congregation Shearith Israel, N.Y.C., 1956-76, cons., 1976—; mng. editor, library cons. Nat. Cash Register Co., PCMI Library Information System, 1969-72; v.p., editor in chief Microlections Pub. Corp., 1973-74; dir. libraries Touro Coll., 1971—, asst. to pres., 1976—. Library cons. United Synagogue Am., 1959—, Crowell Collier MacMillan Corp., 1966—. Library cons. Fedn. Jewish Philanthropies N.Y., 1965-78, mem. child guidance com., mem. Judaica Libraries Com. 1962—, library cons. mental retardation library program Maimonides Sch. Exceptional Children, 1966-67; cons. med. library Mid-Island Hosp., N.Y.C., 92d St. YMHA Library and Archives, 1978—. Recipient Distinguished Service award Fedn. Jewish Philanthropies of N.Y., 1965. Mem. AAUP (v.p. Yeshiva U. chpt. 1961-63), Jewish Librarians Assn. (sec. 1958-64), Am. Coll. and Research Librarians, ALA Spl. Libraries Assn. Author: The Synagogue Library; Organization and Administration, 1960; 2d edit., 1968; A Basic Book List for Synagogue and Religious School libraries, 1960; A Bibliography on Judaism and Jewish Christian Relations, 1965; How to Organize and Administer the Y Camp Library, 1975. Editor: Physicians Book Compendium, 1969-70. Bibliographer: Jews in American Life, 1967, 68. Contbr. articles to profl. jours. Designed Judaica library classification system. Home: 1739 E 3d St Brooklyn NY 11223 Office: Touro College 30 W 44th St New York City NY 10036

CENTURIONI, MARY KATHLEEN, ednl. adminstr.; b. Pitts., July 15, 1941; d. Gilbert Anthony and Catherine Margaret (Sprung) Carney; B.S. in Edn. cum laude, Duquesne U., 1964; M.Ed. (HEW fellow), Wayne State U., 1965, Ph.D., 1972; postgrad. Villanova U., 1977; 1 dau., Kierstin. Coordinator aural rehab. services Wayne State U. Hearing/Speech Clinic, Detroit, 1965-68; supr. auditory tng. programs Detroit Pub. Schs. Speech/Hearing Clinic, 1968-71; pediatric audiologist, supr. lang. devel. program St. Christopher's Hosp. for Children, Phila., 1972-73; coordinator speech and hearing services Child Devel. Center, Norristown, Pa., 1972-76, asso. dir. profl. services, 1976-77, dir. profl. services, 1977—; cons. to speech therapists Detroit Bd. Edn., 1968-71; field supr. student affiliate programs in speech pathology/audiology Temple U., 1976-78. Mem. advisory bd. Main Line Day Care, Ardmore, Pa., 1972-74; program chmn. advisory bd. Main Line Care Assn., 1974-75. Mem. Am., Pa. speech and hearing assns., Alexander Graham Bell Assn. for Deaf, Council for Exceptional Children, Wayne Home/Sch. Assn., Main Line Night Sch. Assn. Contbr. edn. and med. articles to profl. jours. Home: 219 Sugartown Rd J-101 Wayne PA 19087 Office: 1605 W Main St Norristown PA 19403

CERBULIS, JANIS, biochemist; b. Latvia, Dec. 5, 1913; s. Karlis and Karline (Abolins) C.; Ph.D., U. Latvia, 1944; M.S., U. Pa., 1956; Ph.D., Rutgers U., 1966; m. Anna Dombrovskis, June 14, 1952; children—Ilze, Dace, Karlis Andrejs. Came to U.S., 1949, naturalized, 1955. Asso. prof. Baltic U., Germany, 1947-49; research chemist Stephen F. Whitman & Sons, Phila. 1951-55; research chemist Agrl. Research Service, U.S. Dept. Agr., Phila., 1956—. Farmer/rancher, Pa. Served with Latvian Army, 1934-35. USPHS maintenance grantee, 1961-63; Am. Cancer Soc. research grantee-in-aid, 1963. Mem. Am. Latvian Assn. Agronomists (v.p. 1946-68), Am. Latvian Assn. U. Profs., Am. Chem. Soc., Am. Latvian Assn., Sigma Xi. Lutheran. Contbr. articles to profl. jours. Home: RD 2 Boyertown PA 19512 Office: US Dept Agr Philadelphia PA 19118

CERIO, JAMES VINCENT, interior designer, restaurant owner, musician; b. Elmira, N.Y., Oct. 16, 1939; s. James Joseph and Matilda Alice (Crusade) C.; A.A.S. in Bus. and Fine Arts, Elmira Coll., 1959; postgrad. State U. N.Y., Delhi, 1959-61; m. Rebecca Kimber, Sept. 23, 1974; children—Julie Beth, Charles Andrew, James Vincent; stepchildren—Laura Fox, Linda Fox. Interior designer Crusade and Smith, Elmira, N.Y., 1957-64; interior designer, partner Crusade and Cerio, Elmira, 1964—; owner, mgr. Fast Food Service,1976—; profl. musician, leader own group, 1956—; design cons. archtl. and contracting cos., lectr., instr. interior design and music. Citizen for Encampment scholar, 1961. Mem. Interior Design Adv. Panel, Am. Fedn. Musicians, Nat. Assn. Home Furnishings. Clubs: Rotary (Elmira Heights, bd. dirs., 1974-77, bulletin editor, Best of Dist. Award, 1977), Interested Musicians' Scholarship Fund (pres.). Home: 928 Grand Central Ave Horseheads NY 14845 Office: 2024 Lake Rd Elmira NY 14903

CERJANEC, RUTH LILIAN WADE, educator; b. Central Falls, R.I., 1913; d. John Thomas and Susanna (McDowell) Wade; A.B. magna cum laude (Overton scholar 1929-30), Pembroke Coll., 1933; postgrad. Brown U. Grad. Sch., 1934-35, R.I. Coll., 1932-55, Providence Coll., 1941, U. R.I., 1964, U. Wash., 1965, U. Colo., 1968, Western Mich. State U., 1969, Kent State U., 1970-72; M.S., Simmons Grad. Sch. Library Sci., 1960, postgrad., 1963; m. Earl Franklin Cerjanec, July 7, 1945 (dec. Mar. 1967); children—Nicholas Wade, Derek McDowell. Tchr., librarian high sch., Central Falls, R.I., 1933-43; head librarian U.S. Naval Air Facilities, R.I., 1943-47; part time tchr., R.I., Mass., 1947-52; dir. nursery sch., Central Falls, 1952-57; tchr. high sch., Barrington, R.I., 1957-59; librarian Dighton-Rehoboth Regional High Sch., Mass., 1960-66; cons. sch. media centers, coordinator Title II R.I. Dept. Edn., Providence, 1966-72; dir. library media services Cranston (R.I.) Sch. Dept., 1972-73; cons. continuing edn. for women U. R.I., 1973—. Adv. bd. U. R.I. Grad. Sch. Library Sci.; sec. Pembroke Coll. Class of 1933, 1957—, chmn. class secs., 1962-63, chmn. nomination com., 1965-66. Sec. women's com. R.I. Bicentennial Commn., 1973—; mem. Central Falls Bicentennial Commn. R.I. Sch. Design scholar, 1924-26. Mem. ALA (chmn. young adults services dir. nomination com. 1972-73), Am. Assn. Sch. Librarians, R.I. (chmn. library edn. 1970-71), New Eng. library assns. (chmn. pub. relations 1969-70) New Eng. Sch. Library Assn., R.I. Women Educators (sec. 1972—), R.I. Assn. Supervision and Curriculum Devel., Mass., Central Falls (v.p. 1938-43), Bristol County (coordinator library sect. 1961, 63), tchrs. assns., Am. Fedn. Tchrs., Asso. Alumni Brown U. (dir.), Phi Beta Kappa. Editor Media News, 1966—, Newsline for Women Educators, 1972—. Contbr. articles to profl. jours. Home: 22 Binford St Central Falls RI 02863 Office: U RI Promenade St Providence RI 02908

CERMAK, JOSEF RUDOLF CENEK, lawyer; b. Skury, Czechoslovakia, Nov. 15, 1924; s. Rudolf and Rosalie (Zahalkova) C.; student Charles U., Prague, Czechoslovakia, 1945-48; LL.B., U. Toronto (Ont., Can.), 1958. Called to Ont. bar, 1960, created Queen's counsel, 1975; mem. firm Borden, Elliot, Kelley & Palmer, Toronto, 1960-61; mem. firm Wahn, Mayer, Smith, Creber, Loyons, Torrance & Stevenson (name now Smith, Lyons, Torrance, Stevenson & Mayer), Toronto, 1962—, partner, 1967—; dir. Wright Line Can. Ltd., Carleton Homes Ltd., Galahad Investments Ltd., Abksteel Ltd., D.W. Naylor Ltd., Muskoka Properties Ltd. Actor, New Theatre, Toronto, Snizek Theatre, N.Y.C. Mem. Exec. Pro Arte Orch. Assn., 1963-66. Mem. Canadian, Ont. bar assns., Czechoslovak Soc. Arts and Scis. Am. (pres. Toronto chpt. 1970—), Czechoslovak Nat. Assn. Can. (mem. exec. 1958-70). Club: Sokol Symnastic Assn. (Toronto). Author: Pokorne Navraty, 1955; Going Home, 1963. Editor: Zpravy News, 1965-67; chmn. editorial bd. Nase Hlasy, Toronto Czech Weekly, 1960-68. Office: Suite 3800 Toronto-Dominion Centre Toronto ON M5K 1C7 Canada

CERNIUS, VYTAUTAS (VYTAS), psychologist; b. Mazeikiai, Lithuania, Apr. 26, 1926; s. Juozas and Julia (Nevardauskas) C.; came to U.S., 1951, naturalized, 1957; student U. Münster (Germany), 1948-51; B.A., Boston U., 1953; M.A., U. Chgo., 1957, Ph.D., 1966; children—Linas, Sigita. Instr., U. Chgo. Sch., 1957-62; sch. psychologist Thornton Twp. Spl. Edn. Assn. (Ill.), 1962-66; research project U. Chgo., 1965-66; dir. guidance and sch. psychologist Ind. State U. Lab. Sch., Terre Haute, 1966-67; prof. psychoednl. processes Grad. Sch. Temple U., Phila., 1967—; cons. U.S. and Europe. Certified psychologist, Pa. Mem. AAUP, Am. Psychol. Assn. Author: (with others) Chancen und Probleme der Lebensmitte, 1978. Co-founder, co-convenor Nat. Confs. Teaching of Group Psychology. Home: 116 Glenview Ave Wyncote PA 19095 Office: Temple U Grad Sch Philadelphia PA 19122

CERRUTO, JOSEPH ANGELO, corp. devel. exec.; b. Amityville, N.Y., June 28, 1936; s. Joseph Peter and Angela (LaMarca) C.; B.B.A., Clarkson Coll. Tech., 1958; M.B.A., Adelphi U., 1966; m. Patricia Mary Carroll, Oct. 4, 1959; children—Joseph Thomas, Richard Guy, Wendy Ann, Michele Lynn, Patricia Mary. Subcontract adminstr. Grumman Aerospace Corp., Bethpage, N.Y., 1960-64, subcontract supr., 1965, asst. support program mgr., 1966-67, career and profl. devel., 1967-69, adminstr. corporate devel., 1970-72, mgr. market planning Grumman Health Systems Co., Melville, N.Y., 1972-73, product mgr., 1973, asst. to v.p. corporate devel., Grumman Corp., Bethpage, N.Y., 1973—. Mem. Suffolk County Conservative party com., 1968—, exec. com., 1969-72, founder, chmn. John Paul Jones club, 1968-69, co-founder, vice-chmn. Islip Town Council party clubs, 1968, chmn., 1969-70, chmn. Islip Town party, 1970-72, mem. state party com., 1970-74; del. 10th Judicial Dist. convs., 1973-74; mem. Montauk Broadway Civic Assn., 1973—, sec. 1974-75, dir., 1974—, 1st v.p., 1975-77, chmn., 1977—; active Boy Scouts Am.; mem. Suffolk County Conservation Council, 1974-75. Served to 1st. lt. U.S. Army Res., 1959-60. Mem. N.Am. Soc. Corp. Planning, Assn. Corporate Growth, Alpha Kappa Psi, Delta Upsilon. Roman Catholic. Clubs: Clarkson Coll. L.I. Contbr. articles to civic, polit. jours. Home: 44 Amy Dr Sayville NY 11782 Office: 1111 Stewart Ave Bethpage NY 11714

CERTO, NATALIE MARY, pharmacist, coll. educator; b. Pitts.; d. Louis and Anna Mary (Antonnuccio) C.; B.S. magna cum laude, U. Pitts., 1945, M.S. in Pharmacy Adminstrn., 1961, Ph.D. in Pharmacy

Adminstrn., 1975. Intern, Carrolls' Pharmacy, Pitts., 1942-45, pharmacist, 1945-50: pharmacist Hites' Drug Store, Pitts., 1950-54; asst. dir. pharmacy St. Francis Gen. Hosp., Pitts., 1952-61; dir. pharmacy service Children's Hosp., Pitts., 1961—; clin. prof. pharmacy U. Pitts., 1977—; dir. pharmacy service Children's Hosp., Pitts. Researcher, Thornburg for Gov., Penn. Recipient awards dispensing pharmacy, pharm. econs. Mem. Am. (jud. bd. 1977—), Allegheny County pharm. assns., Am., Western Pa., Pa. socs. hosp. pharmacists, Am. Assn. Colls. Pharmacy, Rho Chi. Republican. Roman Catholic. Clubs: Churchill Valley Country, Italian Philanthropic Orgn. Contbr. articles to profl. jours. Office: Childrens' Hosp Pitts 125 De Soto St Pittsburgh PA 15213

CERULLI, MAURICE ANTHONY, gastroenterologist; b. San Antonio, Dec. 7, 1944; s. Frank and Anne (Anastasio) C.; B.A. in Chemistry, Cornell U., 1966; M.D., State U. N.Y., 1972; m. Sandra Laghi, Dec. 28, 1968. Intern, State U. Kings County Med. Center, Bklyn., 1972-73, resident, 1973-75; fellowship in gastroenterology Johns Hopkins U., 1975-77; practice medicine specializing in gastroenterology, Bklyn., 1977—; chief sect. gastroenterology Bklyn. Cumberland Med. Center, 1977—; asst. prof. medicine Downstate Med. Center, 1977—. Diplomate Am. Bd. Internal Medicine. Mem. A.C.P., AMA, Am. Gastroenterol. Assn., Eastern Gut Club. Roman Catholic. Contbr. articles to profl. jours. Home: 24 Andover Rd Rockville Centre NY 11570 Office: 121 De Kalb Ave Brooklyn NY 11201

CERVENKA, ARTHUR FRANK, cons. engr.; b. Bohemia, L.I., N.Y., July 8, 1917; s. Frank and Mary (Bernard) C.; B.S. in Mech. Engring., Columbia, 1941; m. Gladys E. Hunt, July 9, 1944. With Grumman Aerospace Engring. Corp., Bethpage, N.Y., 1941—, mgr. equipment and process engring., 1959-63, dir. facilities, 1963-65, staff engr. mfg. mgmt., 1965-68, corporate operation staff, 1968-69, pres.'s staff, 1969-71, exec. staff, 1971-77; cons. engr., 1977—; chief engr. N.Am. Hovercraft Corp., N.Y.C., 1978—. Recipient certificate Am. Soc. M.E., 1964; named hon. citizen State of Okla., 1967, hon. mem. Kiowa Indian Tribe, Okla., 1967. Registered profl. engr., N.Y. Life fellow Instn. Prodn. Engrs. London; mem. Soc. Mfg. Engrs. (life; chmn. chpt. 88, 1953-54, chmn. nat. constrn. and bylaws com., 1957-60, field editor monthly pub., 1957-68, nat. sec., 1961-62, nat. dir., 1961—, treas., 1962-63, 4th v.p., 1963-64, 2d v.p., 1965-66, v.p., 1963-67, internat. pres., 1967-68, chmn. intgrnat. honor awards com. 1976—, award merit, 1959), Am. Standards Assn. (chmn. com. 25 1956-63), Aerospace Industries Assn. (past chmn. mfg. equipment com.), N.Y. State, Nat. socs. profl. engrs., Am. Soc. for Quality Control (regional councilor automotive div. 1970-74), Am. Soc. Appraisers (asso. mem.), Columbia Coll., Columbia Engring. School (life) alumni assns., Dowling College Library (hon. charter mem.), Theta Tau. Republican. Home: 435 Vanderbilt Blvd Oakdale NY 11769 Office: N Am Hovercraft Co One World Trade Center Suite 5255 New York City NY 10048

CERVIK, JOSEPH, geophysicist; b. Boswell, Pa., Feb. 6, 1928; s. George J. and Mary (Kolok) C.; B.S., Pa. State U., 1953, M.S., 1955; m. Audrey J. Rylke, Aug. 31, 1957; children—Darlene Jo, Linda Leigh. Geophysicist Gulf Research and Devel. Co., Pitts., 1955-57; physicist Crucible Steel Research and Devel. Co., Pitts., 1957-60; research physicist Research and Devel. Lab., Pitts. Plate Glass Co., 1960-64; project leader U.S. Bur. Mines, Pitts., 1964-70, supervisory geophysicist, 1970—. Served with USN, 1946-49. Mem. Soc. Exploration Geophysicists, Sigma Gamma Epsilon, Pi Mu Epsilon. Contbr. articles to profl. jours. Research in degasification of coalbeds. Home: 195 Main Entrance Dr Mount Lebanon PA 15228 Office: 4800 Forbes Ave Pittsburgh PA 15213

CERVINO, GRACE, restaurant and real estate co. exec.; b. Haledon, N.J., Dec. 16, 1933; d. Dominick and Grace (Puccio) Scordato; m. Jan. 31, 1954; children—Michelle, Daniele, Thomas, Sec.-treas. Bradmal Bldg., Tenafly, N.J., 1972—, Cervino Plaza, Tenafly, 1973—; corporate treas. Cervino's Brick House Inn, Danshelmas Inc., Wyckoff, N.J., 1968—. Tchr., St. Elizabeth Catholic Ch., Wyckoff. Mem. Ridgewood (N.J.) C. of C. (past pres.), N.J. Restaurant Assn., Police Benevolent Assn. Wyckoff (recipient Silver badge). Office: 179 Godwin Ave Wyckoff NJ 07481

CERVONE, DOMENIC DONALD, composer, conductor, educator; b. Meadville, Pa., July 27, 1932; s. Samuel Domenick and Rose Elnora (Martignetti) C.; student Allegheny Coll., 1950-52; Mus.B., Eastman Sch. Music, U. Rochester, 1955, Ph.D., 1970; Mus.M., U. Ill., 1960; m. Bernice Mary Clare Kuenzig, Sept. 26, 1959; children—Gian Carlo, Davide Piero, Maria Anina, Cristina Maria. Composer-in-residence, Ford Found., Nat. Music Council fellow, State of Mont. Pub. Schs., 1960-61, Milw. Pub. Schs., 1961-62; tchr. David Hochstein Meml. Music Sch., Rochester, N.Y., 1962-66; dir. instrumental music, Bishop Kearney High Sch., Irondequoit, N.Y., 1964-65; prof., dir. music, St. Bernard's Sem., Rochester, 1967-68; asst. prof. music, State U. N.Y. Coll. at Brockport, 1966-71, asso. prof., 1971—; lectr. Nazareth Coll. of Rochester, 1964, 66; condr., music dir., The Brockport Singers, Pro Musica Consort, Sinfonia Pro Musica, The Ragazzi Consort; guest condr. (own works), Buffalo Philharmonic, Milw. Civic, Northwest Pa. Symphony, Brockport Symphony orchs., Brockport Chorus. Served with U.S. Army, 1956-58. State U. N.Y. research council faculty fellow, 1968, 69; recipient Edward B. Benjamin Award, 1965, Lincoln (Nebr.) Pub. Schs. Festival finale composition contest, 1966; Jewish Community Center - Yale Gordon Found. Composers Award, 1970. Commns.: Community Savs. Bank, Rochester, children's opera, 1965; Allegheny Coll. work for dedication of Fine Arts Center, 1971; State U. N.Y. at Brockport, music for the Crucible, 1968, What Is a College?, 1968, Rosencrantz and Guildenstern, 1974, An Evening of Renaissance plays, 1974; composer music for orch., piano, solo instruments, chorus, operas, song cycles. Home: 3318 Brockport-Spencerport Rd Spencerport NY 14559 Office: Music Dept State Univ Coll at Brockport Brockport NY 14420

CESS, ROBERT DONALD, educator; b. Portland, Oreg., Mar. 3, 1933; s. Harold Francis and Louise Elizabeth (Teasdale) C.; B.S., Oreg. State U., 1955; M.S. (Westinghouse fellow), Purdue U., 1956; Ph.D. (Westinghouse fellow), U. Pitts., 1960; m. Patricia Ann Peirano, Dec. 23, 1953; children—Barbara Ann, Curtis Maxwell. Research engr. Westinghouse Research Labs., 1956-60; asso. prof. engring. N.C. State U., 1960-61; asso. prof. engring. State U. N.Y., Stony Brook, 1961-65, prof. engring., 1965—; adj. prof. U. Pitts., 1959-60; cons. Westinghouse Electric Corp., 1960-64. Mem. Brookhaven Town Adv. Com., 1969—. NSF research grantee, 1960—. Mem. Am. Phys. Soc., AAAS, Sigma Xi. Republican. Presbyterian. Author: (with E.M. Sparrow) Radiation Heat Transfer, 1966. Contbr. articles to profl. jours. Home: 42 Puritan Path Port Jefferson NY 11777 Office: State U NY Stony Brook NY 11790

CHABALLA, PAUL VINCENT, nurse; b. Lansford, Pa., June 30, 1924; s. Michael J. and Mary (Koltiska) C.; R.N., Jersey City Med. Center, 1950; certificate hosp. mgmt. Rutgers U., 1970; certified registered nurse anesthetist Sacred Heart Hosp., 1951; m. Kathleen T. Huelsenbeck, Oct. 20, 1949; children—Paul Vincent, John, Susan, James, Eileen. Nurse anesthetist St. Elizabeth Hosp. (N.J.), 1951-60, dir. spl. services, 1960-67; coordinator spl. services St. Marys Hosp., Orange, N.J., 1967—. Mem. Essex County Disaster Council; scoutmaster Boy Scouts Am., 1955—, roundtable commr. Unami dist. 1975-77, promotion chmn. dist., 1977—. Served with USNR, 1943-47. Recipient Silver Beaver award, 1976. Mem. Am. Assn. Nurse Anesthetists, Am. Assn. Respiratory Therapy, Am. Soc. Hosp. Engrs., Am. Hosp. Assn. Democrat. Roman Catholic. Home: 621 Marshall St Elizabeth NJ 07206 Office: 135 Center St S Orange NJ 07050

CHABINSKY, IRVING JOHN, indsl. co. exec.; b. N.Y.C., Oct. 4, 1921; s. Samuel and Sylvia (Britten) C.; student Clarkson Coll. Tech., 1945-49; B.S. in Bus. Mgmt., Syracuse U., 1950; m. Elizabeth Jane Oley, June 11, 1946; children—David Britten, Douglas John, Diane Elizabeth. Engring. supr. dept. mil. equipment Gen. Electric Co., Syracuse, N.Y., 1951-60; program mgr. Bendix Corp., Ann Arbor, Mich., 1960-63; market mgr. systems and research center Honeywell Inc., Mpls., 1963-69, radiation center, Lexington, Mass., 1969-74; dir. bus. devel. Comstock & Wescott, Cambridge, Mass., 1974-76; microwave indsl. processing equipment Raytheon Co., Waltham, Mass., 1976—; cons. in new ventures and acquisitions, 1973-76. Bd. dirs. Young Republican Club of Clay (N.Y.), 1955-60; active Boy Scounts Am., 1955-63; Republican Committeeman, 1956-60. Served with AC, U.S. Army, 1942-44; PTO. Mem. ASCE, Am. Inst. Aeros., Astronautics, TAPPI, Am. Chem. Soc., Sigma Delta. Republican. Episcopalian. Clubs: Lions, Masons. Designer crib dam for recreational purposes, St. Regis Falls, N.Y., 1948. Home: 8 Paul Revere Rd Acton MA 01720 Office: Foundry Rd Waltham MA 02154

CHACKO, GEORGE KUTTICKAL, operations researcher; b. Trivandrum, India, July 1, 1930; s. Geevarghese Kuttickal and Thankamma (Mathew) C.; certificate advanced tng. Indian Statis. Inst., Calcutta, India, 1951; B. Commerce, Calcutta U., 1952; M.A., Madras U., Tambaram, India, 1950; Ph.D., New Sch. Social Research, 1959; m. Yo Yee, Aug. 10, 1957; children—Rajah Yee, Ashia Yo. Came to U.S., 1953. Asst. editor Indian Finance, Calcutta, 1951-53; comml. corr. Times of India, Calcutta, 1953; asso. test devel. math. Ednl. Testing Service, Princeton, N.J., 1955-57; dir. mktg. mgmt. research Royal Metal Mfg. Co., N.Y.C., 1958-60; ops. research cons. RAND Corp., Santa Monica, Calif., 1961-62; mgr. ops. research dept. Hughes Semicondr. div., Newport Beach, Calif., 1960-61; ops. research cons. Union Carbide Corp., N.Y.C., 1962-63; staff mem. Research Analysis Corp., McLean, Va., 1963-65; staff mem. MITRE Corp., Arlington, 1965-67; sr. staff scientist TRW Systems Group, Washington, 1967-70; asst. in research Princeton, 1953-54; asst. prof. U. Calif., Los Angeles, 1961-62, research fellow Western Mgmt. Sci. Center, 1961; lectr. U.S. Dept. Agr. Grad. Sch., 1965-67, asst. professorial lectr. George Washington U., Washington, 1965-68, Ph.D. thesis dir., 1965-67, professorial lectr. Am. U., Washington, 1967-70, Ph.D. examiner, 1969-70, adj. prof., 1970; vis. prof. systems mgmt. U. So. Calif., 1970-71, prof., 1971—; cons. to numerous cos., govt. agys.; tech. proposal reviewer, chmn. tech. evaluation panel NSF, Washington. Sec.-treas. Am. Com. Friends of Serampore, N.Y.C., 1963-65; youth cons. World Council Chs. Fellow AAAS (nat. council 1968-73), Am. Astron. Soc. (nat. v.p. publs. 1969-71, dir. 1972-74, rep. to AAAS 1968-71); mem. Ops. Research Soc. Am.) rep. to AAAS, 1972—, rep. to Internat. Inst. Applied Systems Analysis 1974—), Inst. Mgmt. Sci. (rep. to Internat. Inst. Applied Systems Analysis 1976—), World Future Soc., Washington Ops. Research Council (trustee 1968-70), Policy Scis. Assn., AAUP, Societe des Consultants Independants et neutres de la Communauté Européenne (corr.). Presbyn. (nat. council 1969-71, co-dean ch. reunion 1977). Mem. Mar Thoma Syrian Ch. of India (youth leader, congl. nurture dir., rep. to World Council Chs.). Kiwanian (charter pres. Friendship Heights chpt. 1972-73). Author: India-Toward an Understanding, 1959; International Trade Aspects of Indian Burlap-An Econometric Study, 1961; Today's Information for Tomorrow's Products, an Operations Research Approach, 1966; Studies for Public Men, 1969; Applied Statistics in in Decision-Making, 1971; Computer-Aided Decision-Making, 1972; Technological Forecontrol-Prospects, Problems, Policy, 1975; Systems Approach to Public and Private Sector Problems, 1976; Operations Research Approach to Problem Formulation and Solution, 1976; Management Information Systems, 1979. Translator: Mar Thoma Syrian Liturgy, 1956; Mar Thoma Syrian Church-Order of Holy Matrimony, 1957; acting mng. editor Jour. Astronaut. Scis., 1969-70, mng. editor, 1971-74; editor Am. Astron. Soc. Newsletter, 1968-70; also editor or co-editor numerous other books and publs.; contbr. articles to profl. jours. Home: 6809 Barr Rd Washington DC 20016 Office: U So Cal Systems Mgmt Center 5510 Columbia Pike Arlington VA 22204

CHACKO, MATHEW CHETHIPURCKAL, psychotherapist, clergyman; b. Thalavady, Kerala, India, Dec. 19, 1932; s. Varkey C. and Sosamma Koprapurayil (Mathew) C.; came to U.S., 1968; B.Sc., U. Travancore, 1954; B.D., Bishop's Coll. (Calcutta), 1957; Ph.D., Hartford Sem. Found., 1973; S.T.M., Uhion Theol. Sem., 1969; M.A., Kerala U., 1964; m. Ruthamma Thomas, May 25, 1969; children—Jacob, Susan. Ordained priest Orthodox Ch. of India, 1957; pastor parishes Trivandrum, India, 1960-64, Kerala, 1966-68, Madras, India, 1966-67, Calcutta, India, 1967-68; tchr. Mar Geevarghese Dionysius High Sch., 1958-59; asst. minister various chs. U.S.A., including Armenian Ch., Bayside, N.Y., 1968-69, Meml. Bapt. Ch., Hartford, Conn., 1969-70, United Meth. Ch., Westfield, Mass., 1970-71, United Ch. of Christ, Terryville, Conn., 1971-72; psychotherapist Flushing (N.Y.) Consultation Center, 1975; chaplain Sea View Hosp. and Home, Health & Hosps. Corp., N.Y.C., 1977—; chaplain, psychotherapist Luth. Med. Center, Bklyn., 1975-77; asso. minister St. Baselios Orthodox Ch. of India, Bklyn., 1977-78, St. George Orthodox Ch. of India, S.I., 1978—. Chmn., Bharat Aid Assn., 1974; mem. working com. Am. Zone of the Orthodox Ch. of India, 1975—. Kerala U. research fellow, 1964-66; Fulbright scholar, 1968-72; Luddington fellow, Union Theol. Sem., 1968-69. Mem. Am. Psychol. Assn., Assn. for Clin. Pastoral Edn. Chief editor, Basellos Beacon, 1976-78. Home: 29 Bache St Staten Island NY 10302 Office: 460 Brielle Ave Staten Island NY 10314

CHADBOURN, ERIKA MARIANNE (MRS. JAMES HARMON CHADBOURN), curator of archives; b. Nuremberg, Germany, Jan. 21, 1915; d. Georg and Luise (Rabus) Sammeth; came to U.S., 1934, naturalized, 1943; B.A., U. Del., 1936; B.S. in L.S., Drexel Inst. Tech., 1937; m. James Harmon Chadbourn, Aug. 16, 1940; children—Marianne (Mrs. A.J. O'Leary), Leslie (Mrs. Donald West), James Harmon, Cataloger, Middlebury (Vt.) Coll., 1937-38; asst. librarian Hunterdon County Library, Flemington, N.J., 1938-39; cataloger Temple U., Library, Phila., 1939-40; curator of manuscripts and archives Harvard Law Sch. Library, Cambridge, Mass., 1966—. Mem. Soc. AM. Archivists, Assn. Am. Law Libraries, Oral History Assn., Internat. Council Archives, New Eng. Archivists, New Eng. Law Librarians. Home: 16 Hartley Rd Belmont MA 02178 Office: Harvard Law School Library Langdell Hall Cambridge MA 02138

CHADBOURNE, CHRISTOPHER DOUGLAS, urban planner, architect; b. West Point, N.Y., Oct. 31, 1942; s. Otto William and Kathryn (Herren) C.; B.Arch. summa cum laude, U. Calif., 1965; M.Arch., U. Pa., 1967. Head urban design Fisher/Jackson Assos., Cons., Harlem Model Cities Program, N.Y., 1968-69; mgr. community planning Levitt & Sons, Lake Success, N.Y., 1969-70; dir. N.Y.C. Planning Commn., Borough of Richmond, 1970-73; partner Ehrenkrantz & Assos., P.C., N.Y.C., 1973-74; pres. Chadbourne Assos., Boston, N.Y.C., 1974—; adj. asso. prof. urban design Columbia U., 1974-75; vis. lectr. in residence Princeton U. Sch. of Arch. and Urban Planning, 1975-77; vis. critic Harvard Grad. Sch. of Design, 1978—; cons. Mideast Devel., 1975—. Rockefeller fellowship, Japan, 1965; recipient AIA citation, residential design awards, 1978. Mem. AIA, Am. Inst. Planners, Nat. Council Archtl. Registration Bds. Author reports on urban design, neighborhood preservation, new town devel. Office: 156 Milk St Boston MA

CHADDA, KUL DEEP, cardiologist; b. India, Aug. 14, 1943; s. Moti Lal and Saraswati C.; came to U.S., 1967; student Ewing Christian Coll., India, 1961; M.B.B.S., Maulana Azad Med. Coll., U. Delhi (India), 1966; m. Usha Nath, Feb. 2, 1973; children—Rishi, Manu. Practice medicine specializing in cardiology, 1973—; chief cardiology labs. Mt. Sinai Hosp. Services, City Hosp. Center, Elmhurst, N.Y., 1974-76; dir. cardiopulmonary lab. Maimonides Med. Center, Bklyn., 1976—; asst. prof. cardiology Mt. Sinai Sch. Medicine, 1975-76; asst. prof. medicine State U. N.Y., Brooklyn., 1976—. Diplomate Am. Bd. Internal Medicine and subsplty. in cardiovascular disease. Fellow A.C.P.; mem. Am. Coll. Cardiology, Am. (council on clin. cardiology), N.Y. heart assns., Am. Soc. Internal Medicine, Am. Fedn. for Clin. Research, Am. Coll. Nutrition, Am. Coll. Angiology, Am. Coll. Chest Physicians. Contbr. articles to med. jours. Office: Maimonides Med Center 4802 10th Ave Brooklyn NY 11219

CHADWICK, DEXTER ANTHONY, educator; b. Washington, Aug. 18, 1950; s. Furney Anthony and Juanita Glen C.; B.A., U. D.C., 1974, U. Ghana, 1973. Chmn. chemistry dept. U. D.C., 1970-74; supr. Nat. Naval Med. Center, Bethesda, Md., 1976—. Mem. D.C. City Council, 1976—, chmn. budget com., 1972—. Mem. Internat. Sch. Assn. (treas. 1972), Phi Beta Kappa. Author: Spirit of God in Africa, 1972; rec.: African Tribal Religions, 1972. Home: 611 Edgewood Med Center Washington DC 20017 Office: NNMC 8900 Wisconsin Ave NW Bethesda MD 20014

CHAFEE, FRANCIS H(ASSELTINE), physician; b. Providence, Dec. 12, 1903; s. Zechariah and Mary Dexter (Sharpe) C.; Ph.B., Brown U., 1927; M.D., Harvard U., 1931; m. Jane Spofford, June 26, 1929; children—Richard S., Mary Deborah, Nathaniel. Intern, Presbyn. Hosp., N.Y.C., 1931-33; pvt. practice medicine, Providence, 1934-75; vis. physician R.I. Hosp., 1939-65, dir. Allergy Clinic, 1938-65, cons. staff, 1966—; mem. div. univ. health Brown U., 1935-61, vis. lectr. medicine, 1973—; cons. allergy Butler Health Center, Miriam Hosp. (all Providence). Served from capt. to maj., U.S. Army, 1942-46, ETO. Fellow A.C.P., Am. Acad. Allergy, (v.p. 1968), Am. Coll. Allergists (award of merit 1977), AMA; mem. Am. Fedn. Clin. Research, Internat. Corr. Soc. Allergists, Providence Med. Assn. (pres. 1955), R.I. Hist. Soc., New Eng. (past pres.), R.I. (pres. 1970-72) socs. allergy. Clubs: Providence Art, University (Man of Yr. award 1975), Hope. Home: 8 Roger Williams Green Providence RI 02904

CHAFEE, JOHN HUBBARD, U.S. senator; b. Providence, Oct. 22, 1922; s. John S. and Janet (Hunter) C.; grad. Deerfield (Mass.) Acad., 1940; B.A., Yale, 1947; LL.B., Harvard, 1950; LL.D., Brown U., 1964, Providence Coll., 1965, U. R.I., 1965, Jacksonville U., 1970, Barrington Coll., 1971; m. Virginia Coates, Nov. 4, 1950; children—Zechariah, Lincoln, Tribbie (dec.), John, Georgia, Quentin. Admitted to R.I. bar, 1950; also Fed. bar; practice in Providence, 1952-62, 73-76; mem. R.I. Ho. of Reps. 3d Dist. Warwick, 1957-62, minority leader, 1959-62; gov. of R.I., 1963-69; U.S. sec. of Navy, 1969-72; mem. U.S. Senate from R.I., 1977—; dir. Hasbro Industries. Vis. Chubb fellow Yale, 1965; chmn. Compact for Edn., 1965; mem. vis. com. J.F. Kennedy Sch. Govt. Harvard, 1967-72; trustee Yale U., Deerfield Acad. Served to capt. USMCR, 1942-45, 51-52. Republican. Home: Rector Ln McLean VA 22101 Office: Post Office Annex Providence RI 02903 also 3105 Dirksen Senate Office Bldg Washington DC 20510

CHAGNON, MARC MARCEL, econ. cons.; b. St. Paul D'Abbotsford, Que., Can., June 18, 1934; s. Dominique and Annette (Beaudry) C.; diploma Royal Mil. Coll., 1956; B.Engring., McGill U., 1957, diploma mgmt., 1963; M.Sc., U. Birmingham (Eng.), 1960; M.Econs., U. Montreal, 1968; m. Odette Charbonneau, Sept. 10, 1960; children—Dominique, Isabelle, Sophie, Philippe. Analytical services officer, indsl. engr. Canadian Nat. Rys., Montreal, 1957-67; partner, project mgr. Belanger, Chabot & Assos., Mgmt. Cons., Montreal, 1967-73; sr. economist Canadian Internat. Devel. Agy., Tanzania, 1973-75; transp. cons. UN, Peru, 1975-76, indsl. economist, Mali, 1976-77; econ. cons. Canadian Internat. Devel. Agy. Latin Am. div., 1977—. Athlone fellow, Eng., 1959-61; registered profl. engr., Que. Mem. Order Mgmt. Cons. Que., Assn. Internat. Devel. Roman Catholic. Club: RMC of Can. Home: 2061-81 Jasmine Crescent Ottawa K1J 7W2 Canada Office: Stock Exchange Bldg Suite 1825 Montreal PQ Canada

CHAI, SOO KYEUNG, psychiat. social worker; b. Seoul, Korea, Dec. 11, 1926; s. Sung Suhk and Min Sook (Park) C.; B.Ed., Plymouth State Coll. of U. N.H., 1960; M.A., U. Detroit, 1962; M.S.W., U. Md., 1966; Ph.D., Catholic U. Am. Sch. Edn., 1977; children—Chris, Shirley. Tchr., Tong Yung Fisheries High Sch., Kyung Nam, Korea, 1948-55; asst. prof. Po Hang Jr. Fisheries Coll., Kyung Buk, Korea, 1955-57; social work program coordinator Crownsville (Md.) Hosp. Center, 1966—. Mem. Nat. Assn. Social Workers, Am. Personnel and Guidance Assn. Home: 349 Burns Crossing Rd Severn MD 21144 Office: Crownsville Hosp Center Crownsville MD 21032

CHAIKEN, BERNARD HENRY, gastroenterologist; b. N.Y.C., Oct. 14, 1927; s. Max and Esther (Golland) C.; student N.Y. U., 1944-45; M.D., U. Tex., 1949; m. Mildred Gilbert, Dec. 5, 1950; children—Barry Glenn, Caryl Chaiken Gordon. Intern, Boston City Hosp., 1949-50; resident internal medicine Cushing VA Hosp., Framingham, Mass., 1950-51; resident internal medicine and gastroenterology Phila. VA Hosp., 1953-54; vis. fellow gastroenterology U. Pa. Hosp., 1954; mem. med. and gastroent. staff Dallas VA Hosp., 1954-55, East Orange (N.J.) VA Hosp., 1955-56; practice medicine specializing in internal medicine and gastroenterology, Short Hills, N.J., 1956—; chief gastrointestinal sect., attending staff Overlook Hosp., Summit, N.J., 1973-75; mem. asso. attending staff St. Barnabas Med. Center, Livingston, N.J.; clin. asst. prof. Seton Hall U. Coll. Medicine, 1965-70, N.J. Coll. Medicine, 1970-75. Served to capt. M.C., AUS, 1951-53. Diplomate Am. Bd. Internal Medicine (gastroenterology). Fellow A.C.P.; mem. Am. Gastroenterol. Assn., Am. Soc. Internal Medicine, AMA, N.J. Gastroent. Soc. (past pres.), N.J., Essex County med. socs., Alpha Omega Alpha, Phi Delta Epsilon. Contbr. med. jours. Home: 35 Kenilworth Dr Short Hills NJ 07078 Office: 58 Chatham Rd Short Hills NJ 07078

CHAIKIN, BARRY HOWARD, market research exec.; b. N.Y.C., Dec. 16, 1941; s. Jack and Sylvia C.; B.S., N.Y.U., 1963; M.B.A., City U. N.Y., 1967; m. Sharon Roth, Nov. 20, 1965; children—Suzanne, Dana. Sr. research analyst R.T. French, Rochester, N.Y., 1968-70; asso. dir. consumer and audit div. Appel, Haley, Fouriezos, N.Y.C., 1970-72; client service rep. Nat. Family Opinion, N.Y.C., 1972-73; dir. mktg. services Commercial Analysts, N.Y.C., 1973-74; pres.

Full-Line Research, Inc., N.Y.C., 1974. Mem. Am. Mktg. Assn., Am. Statis. Assn. Author: Designing Test Market Measurement Programs to Provide National Estimates. Home: 28 Shelby Rd E Northport NY 11731 Office: 211 E 43rd St New York City NY 10017

CHAIKIN, SOL CHICK, labor union ofcl.; b. N.Y.C., Jan. 9, 1918; s. Sam and Beckie C.; B.S., Coll. City N.Y., 1938; LL.B., Bklyn. Law Sch., 1940; m. Rosalind Bryon, 1940; 4 children. Organizer, Local 178, Internat. Ladies' Garment Workers Union, 1940-41, bus. agt. local 281, 1941-43, mgr. local 226, 1946-48, mgr. Western Mass. Dist. Council, 1948-56, dir. Lower SW Region, 1956-59, asst. dir. NE dept., 1959-65, asso. dir. and internat. v.p. NE dept., 1965-73, gen. sec.-treas., 1973-75, internat. pres., 1975—; v.p. AFL-CIO, 1975—, v.p. indsl. union dept., 1973—. Asso. trustee L.I. Jewish-Hillside Med. Center, 1969—; bd. dirs. N.Y. Urban Coalition, 1973—; mem. Gov.'s Task Force on Housing, 1975—; nat. chmn. Am. Trade Union Council for Histadrut, 1967-73. Home: 16 W Terrace Rd Great Neck NY 11021 Office: ILGWU 1710 Broadway New York City NY 10019

CHAISSON, ERIC JOSEPH, astrophysicist, educator; b. Lowell, Mass., Oct. 26, 1946; s. Louis Joseph and Marion Loretta (Brennan) C.; A.B. cum laude, U. Lowell, 1968; A.M., Harvard U., 1969, Ph.D., 1972; m. Lola Judith Eachus, May 1, 1976. Exptl. astrophysicist Smithsonian Astrophys. Obs., Cambridge, Mass., 1969-74, Harvard Obs., Cambridge, 1969-74; asst. prof. astrophysics Harvard U., 1974-78, asso. prof., 1979—. Served to capt. USAF, 1969-73. Nat. Acad. Scis. fellow, 1972-74; Sloan Found. fellow, 1976-79. Mem. Am. Astron. Soc., AAAS, Fedn. Am. Scientists, Am. Assn. Physics Tchrs., Internat. Astron. Union, Union Radio Scientifique Internationale. Contbr. numerous tech. articles to profl. jours. Home: 24 Squire Rd Winchester MA 01890 Office: 60 Garden St Cambridge MA 02138

CHAIT, ARNOLD, radiologist, educator; b. N.Y.C., Jan. 20, 1930; s. Irving and Tillie (Newman) C.; B.A., N.Y. U., 1951; M.D., U. Utrecht, Netherlands, 1957; M.A. (hon.), U. Pa., 1971; m. Joan Lois Oppenheim, Mar. 14, 1965; children—Andrea, Elizabeth, Caroline. Intern, Kings County Hosp., Bklyn., 1958; resident pathology Manhattan Vets. Hosp., N.Y.C., 1959, radiology Kings County Hosp., 1959-62; instr. radiology State U. N.Y., Bklyn., 1962-64, asst. prof. radiology, 1964-67, asso. prof., 1967; asst. prof. radiology U. Pa., Phila., 1967-70, asso. prof., 1970-74, prof., 1974-76, clin. prof., 1976—; chief vascular radiology Hosp. U. Pa., 1969-76, dir. dept. radiology Grad. Hosp., 1976—; cons. radiology Bklyn. VA Hosp., 1962-67, Phila. VA Hosp., 1969—, Phila. Naval Hosp., 1975—. Diplomate Am. Bd. Radiology. Fellow Am. Coll. Radiology, Coll. Physicians Phila.; mem. Pa., Phila. County med. socs., Am., Phila. roentgen ray socs., Radiol. Soc. N.Am., N.Y. Roentgen Soc., AAAS, Assn. U. Radiologists, Soc. Cardiovascular Radiology, Am. Heart Assn. (council on cardiovascular radiology), Soc. Uroradiology, Contbr. numerous chpts. to books, articles to med. jours. Home: 835 Chauncey Rd Narberth PA 19072 Office: Grad Hosp U Pa 19th and Spruce Sts Philadelphia PA 19142

CHAIT, LAWRENCE G., advt. exec.; b. Scranton, Pa., June 27, 1917; s. Perez and Rebecca (Chait) C.; student pub. schs.; m. Sylvia Levine, June 12, 1938; children—Martha, Pamela, George. Direct mail advt. mgr. Dow Jones & Co., Inc., pubs. Wall St. Jour., and Barron's Weekly, N.Y.C., 1945-49; advt. mgr. Arthur Wiesenberger & Co., mem. N.Y. Stock Exchange, 1950-51; circulation exec. Time, Life, Fortune, 1951-55; v.p. R. L. Polk Co., Pubs., 1955-58; pres. Lawrence G. Chait & Co., Inc., counsellors in advt. and sales devel. by mail N.Y.C., 1958-67, chmn., 1968-73; chmn. MMDM, Inc., multi-media direct mktg. counsellors, N.Y.C., 1973-74; treas., sec. Internat. Bus. Devel. Corp., merger, acquisition and corp. funding specialists, 1974-75; mktg. cons. to various corps. and govts., 1975—. Served with U.S. Maritime Service, World War II, chief radio officer U.S.S. Joseph Jefferson, Mitchell Palmer, Sul Ross. Mem. Direct Mail Advt. Assn. (past pres.), Advt. Fedn. Am. (past dir.), Sales Promotion Execs. Assn. (past dir., nat. v.p.), Assn. Direct Mktg. Agencies (founding pres.), L.I. Direct Mktg. Assn., Direct Mktg. Writers Guild, Sales Execs. Club N.Y. (dir., chmn. research com.). Clubs: Mid-Am., Atrium, Hundred Million (past pres.). Author: Those Little Golden Lists, 1955; Purchasing Is Predictable, 1956; Direct Mail-Future Unlimited, 1956; Nine Priceless Ingredients of Success in Selling to Businessmen by Mail, 1958; The Case for Legal Regulation of Advertising, 1962; Targeted Marketing: The New Science of Advertising and Selling, 1966; Six Elements in the Consumer Credit Revolution, 1967; The Problems of Market Management in A New Era of Social Responsibility, 1967; Four Vital Ingredients of the Coming Revolution in Consumer Marketing 1970-2000, 1968; Multi-Media Direct Marketing, 1971; A Businessman's Notes on Opportunities in the South Pacific, 1972. Home and Office: 32 Lynwood Dr Valley Stream NY 11580

CHAIT, ROBERT ABBE, allergist; b. N.Y.C., May 18, 1909; s. Abraham and Anna (Frumerman) C.; B.S., Coll. City N.Y., 1930; M.D., U. Paris, 1935; m. Vivian Levinson, Aug. 18, 1945; children—Allan, Peter. Intern, Fitkin Meml. Hosp., Neptune, N.J., 1936-37; resident in otology and laryngology Sea View Hosp., S.I., N.Y., 1937, in ophthalmology and otology Buffalo Gen. Hosp. and Buffalo Children's Hosp., 1937-40, in allergy Jewish Hosp. Bklyn., 1940-41; practice medicine specializing in allergy, Rockville Centre, N.Y., 1946—; mem. staffs Mid Island Hosp., Lydia E. Hall Hosp. Served to maj., M.C., U.S. Army, 1942-46. Diplomate Am. Bd. Otolaryngology. Fellow AMA, Am. Acad. Allergy, Am. Acad. Ophthalmology and Otolaryngology; mem. N.Y., Kings County, Nassau County med. socs., Nassau Physicians Guild, N.Y., Nassau-Suffolk allergy socs. Contbr. articles to profl. jours.; contbg. author: Fundamentals of Modern Allergy. Office: Medical Bldg 165 N Village Ave Rockville Centre NY 11570 also Medical Bldg 20 Hicksville Rd Massapequa NY 11758

CHAKOIAN, GEORGE, aerospace engr.; b. Providence, June 14, 1924; s. Daniel and Margaret (Derderian) C.; B.S. in Machine Design, R.I. Sch. Design, 1949; B.M.E., Tri-State U., 1950; m. Marion Mahdesian, Aug. 29, 1948; children—Janis, Cynthia, Laura. Engr., B.I.F. Industries, Providence, 1950-55; mech. engr. R.M. Hallam Cons. Engrs., U.S. Naval Underwater Ordnance Sta., Newport, R.I., 1955-56; mech. engr., supervisory mech. engr., asst. tech. dir. U.S. Naval Aircraft Torpedo Unit, Quonset Point, R.I., 1956-66; aerospace engr., supervisory aerospace engr. U.S. Army Natick (Mass.) Research and Devel. Command, 1966—; trustee, v.p. Atlas Assos. Inc. Mem. parish council St. Sahag and Mesrob Armenian Apostolic Ch., 1967-74, vice chmn. parish council, 1972-74, diocesan del., 1975-78. Served with USAAF, 1943-45; PTO. Decorated Air medal with 4 oak leaf clusters and 5 battle stars; recipient Kabakjian Sci. award Armenian Students Assn., 1975; registered profl. engr., R.I., Mass. Mem. Am. Inst. Aeros. and Astronautics, Nat., R.I. socs. profl. engrs. Club: Knights of Vartan. Contbr. articles to profl. jours.; patentee in field. Oud player, leader New Eng. Ararat Orch.; 5 recs. Home: 11 Southwick Dr Lincoln RI 02865 Office: US Army Natick Research and Devel Command Natick MA 01760

CHAKRABARTI, ALOK KUMAR, educator; b. Calcutta, India, Sept. 20, 1942; s. Sachindra Nath and Manimala (Chakrabarti) C.; came to U.S., 1967, naturalized, 1976; B.Chem. Engring. (AEC India fellow), Jadavpur (India) U., 1963; M.B.A., Indian Inst. Mgmt., 1966; Ph.D. (Calcutta U. fellow), Northwestern U., 1971; m. Kabita Majumdar, July 13, 1967. Chem. engr. Dabur Co., Calcutta, 1963, Kanoria Chems., 1964; mgmt. trainee Sahu Jain Co., Calcutta, 1965, exec. asst. 1966-67; systems analyst Continental Can, Chgo., summer 1969; researcher, teaching asst. Northwestern U., Evanston, Ill., 1967-71, research asso., lectr., 1973-74, research cons., 1974—; research asso. U. Hawaii, Honolulu, 1972-73, asst. prof., 1973; asst. prof. mktg. DePaul U., Chgo., 1974-76; asso. prof. mgmt. Drexel U., Phila., 1976—; joint session chmn. Coll. Mktg. and Coll. Research Devel. TIMS-ORSA, 1977; U.S. mem. U.S.-India Conf. Sci. Tech. Info. NSF, project leader and investigator NSF; cons. mgmt. and mktg. East West Center of U. Hawaii fellow, 1972-73. Mem. Am. Mktg. Assn., Acad. Mgmt., Inst. Mgmt. Scis., Sigma Xi. Editorial bd. IEEE Transactions Engring. Mgmt.; contbr. articles to profl. jours. Home: 310 Copples Ln Wallingford PA 19086 Office: Dept Mgmt Drexel Univ Philadelphia PA 19104

CHAKRABARTI, SATYABRATA, elec. engr.; b. Calcutta, India, Aug. 17, 1947; s. Sukhamoy and Uma Debi (Bhattacharyya) C.; came to U.S., 1972; B.Sc. with honors, U. Calcutta (India), 1965, B. Tech., 1967, M. Tech., 1968, D.Sc., 1974. Lectr. dept. electronics Indian Inst. Tech., Kharagpur, 1971-72; post-doctoral research asso. Concordia U., Montreal, Que., Can., 1974-76; research fellow dept. elec. engring. U. Calif., Davis, 1976-77; asst. prof. dept. elec. engring. Rutgers U., New Brunswick, N.J., 1977-78; mem. tech. staff Bell Labs., Holmdel, N.J., 1978—. Mem. IEEE, Am. Math. Soc., AAAS, Soc. Indsl. and Applied Math., Math. Assn. Am., Sigma Xi. Contbr. articles on digital signal processing and mathematical systems to profl. jours. Office: Bldg WB Room IG-204 Bell Labs Holmdel NJ 07733

CHALETZKY, STEPHEN EDWARD, realtor; b. Abilene, Tex., Oct. 23, 1945; s. George S. and Gertrude (Zallen) C.; grad. Manter Hall Sch., 1963; m. Tara Ann Patricia Hilton, Oct. 9, 1976; children from previous marraige—Lisa Ann, Aaron Douglas. Partner, Norge Realty Investment and Mgmt., Boston, 1965—; dir. Hillside Credit Union, Investment Corp. Boston; mgr. Beacon Capitol Corp. Clubs: B'nai B'rith (pres. 1973-75), New Eng. Realty Lodge. Home: 125 Pleasant St Brookline MA 02146 Office: 587 Beacon St Boston MA 02215

CHALMERS, ROBERT CHARLES, sales exec.; b. N.Y.C., Aug. 2, 1924; s. Charles and Estrella Shalmi; student Bklyn. Coll., 1942, N.Y. U., 1942-43; m. Beth Beracha, June 7, 1947; children—Cary, Cheryl. With Carlson Constrn., 1956, salesman, 1963; salesman Swensen Builders, after 1958, sales mgr., designer, estimator, to 1962; with Hobby Center, 1965-67; salesman, designer, estimator Jarro Bldg. Industries Corp., E. Meadow, N.Y., 1968—. Served with USAAF, 1943-45; ETO. Office: 1796 Hempstead Turnpike East Meadow NY 11554

CHALON, JACK, anesthesiologist, educator; b. Cairo, Egypt, July 7, 1920; s. William and Helen (Hirsch) C.; came to U.S., 1965, naturalized, 1972; M.B., B.S., Univs. of London and Edinburgh, 1946; m. Barbara Elizabeth Coombs, Oct. 22, 1948; children—Mary Coombs (Mrs. Robert Weinstein), Jonathan William. Intern, Eastern Gen. Hosp., Edinburgh, 1946-47; resident surgery and anesthesiology Sinai Hosp., N.Y.C., 1965-67; instr. to asst. prof. Albert Einstein Coll. Medicine, Bronx, N.Y., 1968-74; asso. prof. anesthesiology N.Y. U. Med. Center, 1974-78, research prof., 1978—; pvt. practice medicine, Aldershot, Eng., 1949-64; asso. dir. anesthesiology, dir. lab. of pulmonary cytology N.Y. U. Med. Center; cons. anesthesiologist Manhattan VA Hosp. Served with M.C., Royal Army, 1947-49, Territorial Army, 1950-58. Diplomate Am. Bd. Anesthesiology, Soc. Apothecaries of London. Fellow Am. Coll. Anesthesiologists, Royal Soc. Medicine, N.Y. Acad. Medicine (chmn. anesthesiology and resuscitation sect. 1978-79), Am. Coll. Chest Physicians; mem. AMA, Am., N.Y. socs. anesthesiologists, AAAS, Brit., Pan Am med. assns., Internat. Anesthesia Research Soc., Assn. Police Surgeons Gt. Britain, Internat. Acad. Cytology. Asso. editor Survey of Anesthesiology; co-editor: Current Problems in Anesthesiology; contbr. articles to profl. jours. Home: 9 Tarryhill Rd Tarrytown NY 10591 Office: 560 1st Ave New York City NY 10016

CHAMBERLAIN, CARL EUGENE, farm coop. exec.; b. Everett, Pa., Sept. 22, 1925; s. John Thomas and Naomi Ruth (Edwards) C.; student Wittenberg Coll., 1943-44; m. Doris Suzanne Rearick, July 16, 1945; children—Steven Craig, Betsy Ann, Sally Leigh. Br. store mgr. Bedford Farm Bur. Co-op Assn., Everett, 1946-47, asst. assn. mgr., Bedford, Pa., 1947-48; store mgr. Pa. Farm Bur. Co-op. Assn., Indiana, Pa., 1949-51, dist. mgr. Lewistown, 1953-58, petroleum div. mgr., Harrisburg, 1959-61, retail services mgr., 1961-62, dir. distbn., 1962-65; regional mgr. petroleum div. Agway, Inc., Harrisburg, 1965, Ithaca, N.Y., 1966, asst. to dir. distbn., Syracuse, N.Y., 1966-71, ops. mgr. So. retail div., Harrisburg, 1971-73, dir. retail Eastern retail div., West Springfield, Mass., 1973—; pres. Pa. Assn. Farmer Coops., 1961-64; dir. N.Y. Council Retail Mchts., 1969-71. Sec. council St. John's Lutheran Ch., Lewistown, 1955-58; council St. John's Luth. Ch., Hoernerstown, Pa., 1961-64, Liverpool, N.Y., 1968-71; trustee Luth. Student Found., Syracuse U. Served with USAAF, 1943-46, USAF, 1951-53. Mem. West Springfield C. of C. (dir. 1976—). Republican. Club: Masons. Home: 58 Beacon Hill Rd West Springfield MA 01089 Office: 95 Elm St West Springfield MA 01089

CHAMBERLAIN, JOHN LOOMIS, III, pediatrician; b. Balt., July 18, 1930; s. John Loomis and Marie (Brosius) C.; A.B., Amherst Coll., 1953; M.D., U. Va., 1957; m. Marietje Bongers, Apr. 29, 1977; children by previous marriage—Carolyn, Allison, John Loomis IV. Intern, Mary Imogene Bassett Hosp.; resident Vanderbilt U. Hosp., Nashville; practice medicine specializing in pediatrics, Washington, 1966-78; chmn. med. staff Children's Hosp. Nat. Med. Center, 1976-79; mem. staff George Washington U., Sibley hosps.; asso. clin. prof. George Washington U. Med. Sch. Served with M.C., AUS, 1958-60. Decorated Army Commendation medal. Mem. Am. Acad. Pediatrics. Episcopalian. Club: Chevy Chase (Md.). Contbr. to med. jours.; editor Clin. Pros., 1974—. Home: 5015 Hawthorne Pl NW Washington DC 20016 Office: 5301 Westbard Circle Bethesda MD 20016

CHAMBERLAIN, JOSEPH REID, inst. adminstr.; b. Lewistown, Pa., June 21, 1941; s. Robert A. and Virginia M. (Park) C.; B.S. in Edn., U. Del., 1969, M.Ed., 1971. Research advisor, editor Del. Easter Seal Soc., Wilmington, 1966, 74-75; county transp. coordinator Del. Agy. for Specialized Transp., Wilmington, 1971-73; learning disabilities specialist Appoquinimink Sch. Dist., Middletown, Del., 1970-74; Spinal Cord Injury program coordinator Alfred I. DuPont Inst., Wilmington, 1975—. Chmn. archtl. barriers com. Del. Easter Seals Soc.; pres. chpt. Nat. Paraplegia Found., 1976; policy devel. com. mem. Vocat. Rehab. Service, 1977; campaigner for legis. benefiting handicapped state, county, city levels; bd. dirs. Brookside Community, Inc., 1976. Recipient CAP Meritorious Service award, 1966, Search and Rescue award, 1965. Mem. Nat., Del. rehab. assns., Am. Personnel and Guidance Assn., Am. Rehab. Counselors Assn., Nat. Wheelchair Athletic Assn., Am. Radio Relay League. Democrat. Roman Catholic. Author: A Guide to Wilmington for the Handicapped, 1966; A Guide to No. Del. for the Handicapped, 1975. Home: 110 Kenmar Dr Newark DE 19711 Office: PO Box 269 Wilmington DE 19899

CHAMBERLAIN, LLOYD BAXTER, paperboard co. exec.; b. Hudson Falls, N.Y., Oct. 10, 1915; s. Lloyd Oliver and Dorothea (Harvey) C.; B.S., Syracuse U., 1940; m. Margaret Snow Roach, Oct. 11, 1940; children—Lloyd Michael, Mary Margaret. With Container Corp. Am., 1940-65, gen. mgr., Wabash, Ind., 1952-57, gen. mgr. Hoya, W.Ger., then div. gen. mgr. Midwest Mills, Chgo., 1960-65; v.p. New Eng. Mills, Fed. Paper Board Co., Inc. Versailles, Conn., 1965-68, sr. v.p., 1968—; dir. Fed. Paperboard Co., Inc. Past pres. bd. trustees Syracuse U. Recipient award for personal service to Town of Hoya, 1960. Mem. TAPPI, Paper Industry Mgmt. Assn. (past pres.), Boxboard Research and Devel. Assn. (dir.), Fiber Conservation Assn. (past pres.), Nat. Paper Bd. Assn. (chmn. Western div.). Roman Catholic. Home: 73 Fox Hedge Rd Saddle River NJ 07458 Office: 75 Chestnut Ridge Rd Montvale NJ 07645

CHAMBERLIN, MICHAEL ALOYSIUS, publishing co. exec.; b. Merrick, N.Y., Oct. 10, 1933; s. Ross Irving and Dora Theresa (Lynch) C.; A.B., Niagara U., 1955; m. Christine R. Garred, Sept. 21, 1962; children—Michael, Tracy, Kevin, Jeanine. Personnel asst. R. H. Macy, N.Y.C., 1958-61; asst. personnel dir. J. M. Fields Inc., Boston, 1961-62; personnel mgr. MacMillan Co., N.Y.C., 1962-65; personnel dir. Harcourt Brace and World Pub. Co., N.Y.C., 1965-68; v.p. Richard Chess Assos., N.Y.C., 1968-69; v.p. adminstrn. Lebhar Friedman Inc., N.Y.C., 1969—, asst. sec., 1974—. Served to lt. U.S. Army, 1955-57. Mem. N.Y. Advt. Club (pres. 1976—), Am. Soc. Personnel Adminstrs. Club: K.C. Home: 16 Sherwood Rd Ridgefield CT 06877 Office: 425 Park Ave New York City NY 10022

CHAMBERS, HARRY R., accountant; b. Ft. Erie, Ont., Can., Sept. 22, 1923; s. Reed Andrew and Mable Alma (Bain) C. (father Am. citizen); B.S. in Bus. Adminstrn., U. Buffalo, 1953; m. Elizabeth Marie Abel, July 31, 1943; children—Richard, Diane, Gary. Accountant, Reed Chambers, 1949-53; pvt. practice pub. accounting, Buffalo, 1953—; treas. Sord Sunstone Computer Corp. Served with AUS, 1943-45. Mem. Nat. Soc. Pub. Accountants. Republican. Club: Lions (Kensington). Home: 132 Robin Hill Dr Williamsville NY 14221 Office: 3879 Bailey Ave Buffalo NY 14226

CHAMBLISS, HIRAM DARDEN, JR., assn. exec.; b. Columbia, Mo., Aug. 2, 1929; s. Hiram Darden and Florence (Blakemore) C.; student Duke U., 1948-49; B.A. with honors, U. N.Mex., 1956; m. Eleanor Schwarz, Mar. 11, 1954; children—Catherine, David, Elizabeth. Sports editor Oak Ridge Times, 1947; news writer A.P., Albuquerque, 1954-56, Sioux Falls, S.D., 1956-58, Pierre, 1958-61, Mpls., 1961, N.Y.C., 1961-64; pub. affairs v.p. Aluminum Assn., Washington, 1964—. Recipient Loeb Achievement award U. Conn., 1964. Mem. Pub. Relations Soc. Am. (chmn. assn. sect. 1975), Am. Soc. Assn. Execs. Clubs: N.Y. Press, Overseas Press. Home: 9335 Tovito Rd Fairfax VA 22030 Office: 818 Connecticut Ave Washington DC 20006

CHAMPAGNE, JOSEPH STENARD, cons. engr.; b. Altamont, N.Y., Aug. 27, 1933; s. Ralph George and Katherine (Stenard) C.; B.S. in Civil Engring., Rensselaer Poly. Inst., 1955, M.S. in Civil Engring., 1959; certificate in traffic engring. Yale U., 1963; m. Martha Ellen Walsh, Aug. 6, 1960; children—Joseph R., Elizabeth W., Mark P., Christopher R., Daniel W. Project engr. Ralph G. Champagne Assos., Troy, N.Y., 1957-58; asst. civil engr. N.Y. State Dept. Transp., Albany, 1959-60; chief engr. Nat. Fence Co., Meriden, Conn., 1961-62; asso. traffic engr. N.Y. Port Authority, N.Y.C., 1963-66; project engr. Travers Assos. Traffic Engrs., Clifton, N.J., 1966-68; v.p., dir. Pal Jac Installations, Inc., Albany, 1969; exec. v.p., dir. Wallace Champagne Assos., Mechanicville, N.Y., 1970-76; v.p., dir. Greenman-Pedersen Assos., Albany, 1976—; partner Chawa Assos., Troy, N.Y., 1977—; adj. asso. prof. traffic engring. Rensselaer Poly. Inst., 1970-71. Scoutmaster, bd. dirs. Ft. Orange council Boy Scouts Am., 1955-57; bd. dirs. Rensselaer County Jr. Mus. Served with USN, 1955-57. Registered profl. engr., N.Y., Mass., Vt., Fla., N.J., Maine, Conn., Pa.; Automotive Safety Found. fellow, 1962-63. Mem. Nat. Soc. Profl. Engrs., ASCE, Inst. Traffic Engrs., Inst. Transp. Engrs. (vice chmn. dist. bd. 1978—), Nat. Parking Assn. Roman Catholic. Clubs: Troy Country, Uncle Sam Aquatic (pres. 1975-76). Home: 11 Whitman Ct Troy NY 12180 Office: 245 Lark St Albany NY 12210

CHAMPE, MRS. CARLTON G. (MARY FOLSOM CHAMPE), vol. worker; b. N.Y.C., Oct. 14, 1908; d. Clyde Hallett and Thalia (Goddard) Folsom; ed. St. Agatha Sch., N.Y.C.; A.B. cum laude, Smith Coll., 1931; student Columbia, 1937; m. Carlton George Champe, June 9, 1938; children—Nancy (Mra. Merz K. Peters), Jane (Mrs. John W. Payne), David Folsom (dec.). Vol. dir. Yorkville Youth Council, 1958-59; dir. Jobs for Youth, 1959-62. Pres. Episcopal Ch. Women of Ch. of the Epiphany, 1965-66. Treas., dir. Carl Schurz Park Concerts, Inc., 1958-64. Mem. N.Y. Women's Com. United Negro Coll. Fund, 1966-67. Mem. Met. Opera Guild, Soc. Mayflower Descs., Alumnae Assn. Smith Coll (dir. 1963-66), Kimball Family Assn. (treas. 1971-74). Republican. Episcopalian. Clubs: Smith Coll. (dir. 1937-39, pres. 1961-64), Cosmopolitan (N.Y.C.). Home: Rumford Center ME 04278

CHAMPSI, DOLLY, mgmt. exec.; b. Poona, India, Nov. 2, 1937; d. Jaffer Mohamed and Fatmabai Jivraj (Khimji) Kolsawalla; B.A. with honors, Poona U., 1962, M.A. 1965; M. in Sci. of Mgmt., Arthur D. Little Mgmt. Edn. Inst., Inc., 1978; came to U.S., 1974; m. Mir Rashid Ali, Mar. 6, 1977; children—Mumtaz, Jamila, Farah, Tippu. Vocat. counselor Children's Acad., Poona, 1961-64; trading partner H. Jaffer Co., Karachi, Pakistan, 1964-73, overseas rep., 1974-77; dir. Johnny's Trading Co., Pakistan; cons. A. Lalljee Co., India. Mem. Zanzibar Women's Assn. Club: Harvard Neighbours (Cambridge). Home and Office: 222 Pleasant St Brookline MA 02146

CHAMZAS, CHRISTODOULOS, educator; b. Komotini, Greece, Sept. 6, 1951; s. Constantinos and Evanthia (Chamza) C.; diploma Nat. Tech. U. Athens, 1974; M.S., Poly. Inst. N.Y., 1975, Ph.D., 1979. With Nat. Co. of Electricity, Athens, Greece, 1971, Portugal, 1972, Grant Instrument Ltd., Cambridge, Eng., 1973, Bell Telephone Labs., Holmdel, N.J., 1976; research fellow Poly. Inst. N.Y., Bklyn., 1975-77, teaching fellow, 1977-78, academic asso., dept. elec. engring., 1978—. Greek Inst. of Fellowships nat. fellow, 1970-74; Poly. Inst. N.Y. fellow, 1974-77. Mem. Tech. Chamber of Greece, IEEE, Sigma Xi. Home: 2 Carmans Ct Farmingdale NY 11735 Office: PINY Route 110 Farmingdale NY 11735

CHAN, GEORGE MOY, mech. engr.; b. N.Y.C., Mar. 23, 1948; s. George Ink Wah and Shue Mee (Moy) C.; M.Engring., Pa. State U., 1975; B.Engring., Pratt Inst., 1969; m. Virginia Sorio Maneclang, June 25, 1977; 1 dau., Andrea May. Engring. staff RCA, Camden, N.J., 1969-72; mech. systems engr. Sperry Rand Corp., Bluebell, Pa., 1972-73; engring. staff RCA, Camden, 1973-75; project engr. Armament Research and Devel. Command, U.S. Army, Dover, N.J., 1975—. Mem. ASME, Am. Inst. Aeros. and Astronautics, Am. Def. Preparedness Assn., Pa. State Alumni Assn., Laser Inst. Am., Pratt Inst. Alumni Assn., Pi Tau Sigma, Pi Mu Epsilon. Home: Mountain View Manor B6 Richard Mine Rd Wharton NJ 07885 Office: ARRADCOM US Army Dover NJ 07801

CHAN, KAM-FAI, physician; b. Hong Kong; s. Wei-Yeuk and Swee-King (Lui) Chan; M.D., Cheeloo U., China, 1945; M.B., B.S., Hong Kong U., 1946; M.P.H., Columbia, 1950, Dr. P.H., 1952; m. Lau C. Kwan; children—Stephen Han-Chieh, David Han-Seng. Came to U.S., 1947, naturalized 1961. Intern, Cheeloo U. Hosp., 1944-45; resident Lingnan Univ. Hosp., 1946-47; research asso. div. tropical diseases Columbia U. Coll. Physicians and Surgeons, 1952-58; sr. physician, supervising roentgenologist Bur. Tb Control, N.Y. State Dept. Health, 1958-61; staff physician VA Hosp., Bronx, 1961—, chief radiology service, 1967—; clin. instr. radiology N.Y.U. Med. Sch., N.Y.C., 1966-70, clin. asst. prof., 1970-73; asst. prof. radiology Mt. Sinai Med. Sch., N.Y.C., 1973-76, asso. prof., 1976—; cons. radiologist Animal Med. Center, N.Y.C., 1965—. Fellow Am. Coll. Chest Physicians, Am. Coll. Radiology; mem. AMA, Am. Roentgen Ray Soc., N.Y. Roentgen Soc., Radiol. Soc. N.Am., Educators Council for Vet. Radiology. Author articles in field. Address: 130 W Kingsbridge Rd New York City NY 10468

CHAN, PETER WING KWONG, pharmacist; b. Los Angeles, Feb. 3, 1949; s. Sherwin T.S. and Shirley W. (Lee) C.; B.S., U. So. Calif., 1970, D.Pharmacy, 1974; m. Patricia Jean Uyeno, June 8, 1974; children—Kristina Dionne, Kelly Alison, David Shoichi. Clin. instr. U. So. Calif., 1974-76; staff clin. pharmacist Cedars-Sinai Med. Center, Los Angeles, 1974-76; 1st clin. pharmacist in ophthalmology Alcon Labs., Inc., Ft. Worth, 1977—, now in Phila. monitoring patient drug therapy, teaching residents, nurses, pharmacy students; cons. in field; del. Am. Pharm. Assn. House of Dels., 1976-78. Recipient Hollywood-Wilshire Pharm. Assn. spl. award for outstanding service, 1974; licensed pharmacist, Calif. Mem. Am., Calif., Hollywood-Wilshire (bd. dirs. 1972-76) pharm assns., Am. Soc. Hosp. Pharmacists, Am. Pharm. Assn. Acad. of Pharmacy Practice, U. So. Calif. Gen. Alumni Assn., QSAD Centurions. Democrat. Home: 12 Candlewood Terr Medford NJ 08055 Office: Alcon Labs Inc Clin Pharmacy Services 6201 South Freeway Fort Worth TX 76101

CHAN, WALLACE LANE, physician, med. adminstr.; b. San Francisco, Dec. 30, 1923; s. Allan Lam and Rose Elsie (Sue) C.; student U. Calif., 1939-42; A.B., Stanford U., 1947, M.D., 1952; m. Emelda E., Oct. 14, 1948; children—Carolyn, Wallace, Jean, Elaine, Allan. Intern, Tripler Gen. Hosp., Honolulu, 1950-52; research dir. CIA, Washington, 1953-57; asst. research prof. physiology George Washington U. Sch. Medicine, Washington, 1956-57; exec. dir. Med. Scis. Research Found., Stanford, Calif., 1957-65, Bio-Research, Inc., San Mateo, Calif., 1957-59; med. dir., v.p. Resources Research, Inc., Washington, 1959-61; asst. clin. prof. medicine Stanford U. Sch. Medicine, 1957-61, asso. in medicine, Stanford, 1961-63; pres. Asian Exports, Inc. San Francisco, 1958-61; spl. asst. to dep. surgeon gen. and surgeon gen., dir. investigations USPHS, Washington, 1961-62; spl. asst. to chancellor U. Calif., Davis, 1962-63; incorporator Neuroscis. Research Found., Mass. Inst. Tech., Boston, 1962-66; med. dir. Alderson Convalescent Hosp., Woodland, Calif., 1966-67, Sunnydale Convalescent Hosp., Fremont, Calif., 1969-70, Mt. Oliver Convalescent Hosp., Carmichael, Calif., 1968-69, Norwood Hosp., Foxboro (Mass.) Area Health Center, 1977—; mng. dir. Marion Internat., Inc., Kansas City, Mo.; med. dir. Boston Chinese Community Health Services, Inc., Boston, 1974-76; dir. health services Mass. Dept. Corrections, 1974-77; chief exec. officer Norfolk (Mass.) Hosp.; practice family medicine, Pasadena, Calif., 1953, Washington, 1956-57, San Carlos, Calif., 1957-61, Sacramento, 1964-67, Oakland, Calif., 1967-71, Boston, 1974—; staff mem. Lemuel Shattuck Hosp., Norwood Hosp.; asst. clin. prof. Tufts Med. Sch., 1975—; asso. clin. prof. dept. community medicine U. Mass. Med. Sch., Boston, 1975—; dir. Intercommerce of Am., Banmerical; chmn. bd. Internat. Resource Mgmt., Inc., Wellesley Farms, Mass., 1973-74; pres. The Elane Co.; cons. in field. Mem. Mass. Health Policy and Planning Council; mem. pub. health com. Sacramento County C. of C.; adviser Chinese Students Orgn. Served with U.S. Army. 1943-46, 51-53. Charles Murphy scholar U. Calif., 1940; named Man of Achievement, San Francisco C. of C., 1961. Mem. AMA, Pan-Am., Calif., Alameda-Contra Costa County med. assns., Am., Calif. acads. gen. practice, AAAS, Assn. Mil. Surgeons, N.Y. Acad. Sci., Am. Cancer Soc. (dir.). Clubs: Lions Internat. (past pres.), Internat. World Trade. Office: Norwood Hosp 800 Washington St Norwood MA 02062

CHAN, WAN-KANG WILL, mech. engr.; b. Canton, China, Nov. 3, 1946; s. Kin and Pui-Lee (Tam) C.; came to U.S., 1964, naturalized, 1972; B.M.E., N.J. Inst. Tech., 1972; M.S., N.Y. Poly. Inst., 1976. Mech. engr. Phila. Naval Shipyard, 1973-75; design engr. M. Rosenblatt Marine & Naval Architect Inc., N.Y.C., 1975-77, Sanderson & Porter Inc., N.Y.C., 1977; cons. mech. engr. Gibbs & Cox Naval Architects Inc., N.Y.C., 1978—. Initator, promotor Chinese cultural movements, N.Y.C., 1967—; v.p., actor 1st formal Chinese stage play in N.Y.C. (Emperor's Daughter), 1968; vice prin. Chinese Lang. Sch., 1968-70; founder, 1969, since bd. dirs. N.Y. Hong Kong Student Assn.; instr. Tai-Chi-Chuan and Chinese self def., 1970—. Republican. Roman Catholic. Home: 25 Buerum St #137 Brooklyn NY 11206

CHANCE, HENRY MARTYN, II, engring. exec.; b. Pottsville, Pa., Jan. 16, 1912; s. Edwin M. and Eleanor (Kent) C.; B.S. in Civil Engring., U. Pa., 1934; m. Suzanne Sharpless, June 12, 1934; children—Edwin M., Suzanne, Barbara; m. 2d, Elisabeth Reese, Aug. 19, 1944; children—Steven K., James M., Henry Martyn III, Mark Raymond. Chemist, assayer Am. Smelting & Refining Co., 1934-36; with United Engrs. & Constructors, Inc., Phila., 1936—, pres., 1954-71, chmn. bd., 1972-77, cons., dir., 1977—; dir. Pennwalt Corp., Lukens Steel Co., Coatesville, Pa., Girard Trust Bank, Girard Co., Badger Co., Cambridge, Mass. Life trustee, mem. exec. bd. U. Pa.; pres. Haverford Sch., 1962-70, also life dir.; bd. mgrs. Franklin Inst., U. Pa. Mus. Named Engr. of Year, Del. Valley, 1964. Mem. ASCE. Club: Union League (Phila.). Home: PO Box 432 Malvern PA 19355 Office: 30 S 17th St Philadelphia PA 19101

CHANDA, RAJINDER NATH, economist; b. Jhang, India, Feb. 18, 1942; s. Nandlal and Tarawanti C.; B.A., Punjab U., India, 1961; M.S. in Urban Planning, Mass. Inst. Tech. and U. R.I., 1966; M.S. in Econs., Brown U., 1967; postgrad. in Econs., Harvard U., 1963, in Mgmt., George Washington U., 1969-70; m. Jaspreet Majithia, Sept. 30, 1975. Mgr. urban and mgmt. programs NUS Corp., Washington, 1968-72; sr. cons. in charge urban and mgmt. programs Bolt Berenak & Newman, Inc., 1972-73; vis. expert, prof. Sch. Planning and Architecture, New Delhi and cons. Life Ins. Corp. India, Bombay, 1974-75; prin. Environment Research and Design, Inc., Washington, 1975-77; v.p. Pantek, Inc., Washington, 1977—; cons. U.S. Congress, fed. agys, Am. Indian tribes, fgn. govts. Sears Roebuck fellow, 1962-63, F.W. Chandler fellow, 1962-63. Mem. Am. Inst. Planners, Soc. Internat. Devel., Am. Econ. Assn. Hindu. Contbr. articles to profl. jours. Home: 2130 P St NW Washington DC 20037 Office: 1100 17 St NW Suite 1100 Washington DC 20036

CHANDLER, ALFRED DUPONT, JR., educator, historian; b. Guyencourt, Del., Sept. 15, 1918; s. Alfred Dupont and Carol (Ramsay) C.; grad. Phillips Exeter Acad., 1936; B.A., Harvard U., 1940, M.A., 1947, Ph.D., 1952; M.A., U. N.C., 1951; Ph.D. (hon.), U. Leuven (Belgium), 1976; m. Fay Martin, Jan. 8, 1944; children—Alpine Douglass Chandler Bird, Mary Morris Chandler Watt, Alfred Dupont III, Howard Martin. Research asso. Mass. Inst. Tech., Cambridge, Mass., 1950-51, from instr. to prof., 1951-63; prof. history Johns Hopkins U., Balt., 1963-71, chmn. dept., 1966-70, dir. Center Study Recent Am. History, 1964-71; Straus prof. bus. history Harvard Bus. Sch., Cambridge, 1971—; vis. fellow All Souls Coll., Oxford U., 1975; dir. Data Pack, Inc., Landmark Communications, Inc.; cons. Naval War Coll., 1954; mem. Nat. Adv. Council on Edn. Professions Devel., 1970-71; chmn. adv. hist. com. AEC (renamed ERDA 1974), 1969-77. Trustee Park Sch., Brookline, Mass., 1957-63, chmn. bd., 1961-63; trustee Brookline Pub. Library, 1959-63, Roland Park Sch., Balt., 1964-70, Johns Hopkins, 1971—. Served to lt comdr. USNR, 1940-45. Recipient Pulitzer prize in history, 1978. Guggenheim fellow, 1958-59; research fellow Harvard U., 1953. Mem. Econ. History Assn. (trustee 1966-70, pres. 1971-72), Orgn. Am. Historian (exec. bd. 1969-72), Soc. for History Tech. (exec. council 1972-75), Am. Hist. Assn., Soc. Am. Historians, Mass. Hist. Soc. (council 1977—), Bus. History Conf. (pres. 1977-78), Am. Acad. Arts and Scis., Episcopalian. Clubs: St. Botolph (Boston); Nantucket (Mass.) Yacht; Harvard (N.Y.C.); Hamilton Street (Balt.). Author: Henry Varum Poor, 1956; Strategy and Structure (Newcomen award 1964), 1962; Giant Enterprise, 1964; The Railroads, 1965; (with Stephen Salsbury) Pierre S. duPont, 1971; The Visible Hand: The Managerial Revolution in American Business (Bancroft and Pulitzer prizes 1978), 1977. Editor: Papers of Dwight D. Eisenhower, vols. 1 - 5, 1970, co-editor vol. 6, consulting editor vols. 7 - 9, 1978; asst. editor The Letters of Theodore Roosevelt, vols. 1-4, 1950-53. Home: 1010 Memorial Dr Cambridge MA 02138*

CHANDLER, ELISABETH GORDON (MRS. R. K. CHANDLER), sculptor, harpist; b. St. Louis, June 10, 1913; d. Henry Brace and Sara Ellen (Sallee) Gordon; grad. The Lenox School, 1931; pvt. study sculpture and harp; m. Robert Kirtland Chandler, May 27, 1946 (dec.). Exhibited sculptures NAD, Nat. Sculpture Soc., Allied Artists Am., Nat. Arts Club, Pen and Brush, Lyme Art Assn., Mattatuck Mus., Catherine Lorillard Wolfe Art Club, Am. Artists Profl. League, Smithsonian Instn., USIA (overseas); represented in permanent collections Aircraft Carrier USS Forrestal, Gov. Dummer Acad., James Forrestal Research Center of Princeton U., Lenox Sch., James L. Collins Parochial Sch., Tex., Storm King Art Center, Columbia U., Woodrow Wilson Sch. for Pub. and Internat. Affairs of Princeton U., Ga.-Pacific Corp., Bldg., Portland, Oreg., Messiah Coll., Grantham, Pa.; also pvt. collections; performed as concert harpist on stage, radio, TV, 1933-45; mem. Mildred Dilling Harp Ensemble, 1934-46. Bd. dirs. Council Am. Artist Socs., 1971-73; chmn. Asso. Taxpayers of Old Lyme, 1969-72, now advisory council, exec. com.; trustee The Lenox Sch., 1953-55; trustee, instr. Lyme Acad. Fine Arts, 1976—. Served with mus. therapy div. Am. Theatre Wing, 1942-45. Recipient 1st prize Bklyn. War Meml. competition, 1945; 1st prize sculpture Catherine Lorillard Wolfe Art Club, 1951, 58, 63, Anna Hyatt Huntington award, 1969; Founders prize Pen and Brush, 1954, 76, 78, gold medal, 1961, 62, 63, 69, 74; Am. Heritage award, 1968, Solo Exhbn. award, 1969, 75; Thomas R. Proctor prize NAD, 1956, Dessie Greer prize, 1960; gold medal Hudson Valley Art Assn., 1956, 69, 74, 75, Anna Hyatt Huntington award, 1970, 76, Mrs. John Newington award, 1976, 78; sculpture awards Nat. Arts Club, 1959, 60, 62, gold medal, 1971; Am. Artists Profl. League Gold medal, 1960, 69, 73, 75, Harriet Mayer award, 1961; New Netherlands D.A.R. Bicentennial medal, 1976; Tallix Foundry award, 1978. Fellow Nat. Sculpture Soc. (rec. sec. 1973-76, council 1976-79), Am. Artists Profl. League (dir. 1971-73), Internat. Inst. Arts and Letters; mem. Nat. Arts Club, Allied Artists of Am. (Lindsey Morris Meml. award 1973), Pen and Brush, Catherine Lorillard Wolfe Art Club, Lyme Art Assn. (v.p. 1973-75, pres. 1975-78). Home and studio: Mill Pond Ln Old Lyme CT 06371

CHANDLER, JAMES JOHN, surgeon; b. Dayton, Ohio, Nov. 13, 1932; s. James Kapp and Margaret Bertha (Paulson) C.; A.B., Dartmouth Coll., 1954, diploma in medicine, 1955; M.D. cum laude, U. Mich., 1957; m. Fleur Elizabeth Varney, July 23, 1955; 1 dau., Jennifer Fleur. Intern, Harvard Surg. Service, Boston City Hosp., 1957-58, jr. asst. resident, 1958, resident, chief resident in surgery, clin. fellow Am. Cancer Soc., U. Oreg. Hosps., Portland, 1961-64, instr. surgery 1964; attending staff, chmn. surgery Med. Center at Princeton (N.J.) 1972—; clin. prof. surgery Coll. Medicine and Dentistry N.J.-Rutgers Med. Sch., Piscataway, 1975—; cons. in surgery Princeton U. Bd. dirs. Trinity Counseling Service 1968—, chmn., 1968-72; pres. Princeton Day Sch. PTA, 1976-78, trustee, 1976—; active All Saints Episcopal Ch., Princeton, 1965—. Served to lt. comdr. USN, 1958-60, USNR, 1960-61. Diplomate Am. Bd. Surgery. Fellow A.C.S. (pres. N.J. chpt. 1976-77), Soc. for Surgery Alimentary Tract, Am. Coll. Chest Physicians; mem. Pan-Pacific Surg. Assn., Soc. Surgeons N.J., Med. Soc. N.J. (sec., chmn. surgery sect. 1967-69), Mercer County Med. Soc., Collegium Internationale Chirurgiae Disgetivae, Soc. Surg. Oncology, Oncology Soc. N.J., Acad. Medicine N.J., Alpha Omega Alpha. Republican. Episcopalian. Clubs: Nassau Gun, Bedens Brook, Gatineau Fish and Game, Sea Pines. Contbr. chpt. to book, articles to profl. jours. Home: 292 Edgerstoune Rd Princeton NJ 08540 Office: 253 Witherspoon St Princeton NJ 08540

CHANDLER, JOHN WESLEY, coll. pres.; b. Mars Hill, N.C., Sept. 5, 1923; s. Baxter Harrison and Mamie (McIntosh) C.; student Mars Hill Coll., 1941-43; A.B., Wake Forest Coll., 1945, L.H.D., 1968; B.D., Duke, 1952, Ph.D., 1954; LL.D., Hamilton Coll., 1968, Colgate U., 1968, Williams Coll., 1973, Amherst Coll., 1974; m. Florence Gordon, Aug. 25, 1948; children—Alison, John Wesley, Jennifer, Patricia. Instr. philosophy Wake Forest Coll., 1948-51, asst. prof., 1954-55; asst. prof. religion Williams Coll., 1955-60, asso. prof., chmn. dept., 1960-65, Cluett prof. religion, 1965-68, acting provost, 1965-66, dean faculty, 1966-68; pres. Hamilton Coll., 1968-73, Williams Coll., 1973—; trustee Williams Coll., 1969-73; exec. com. New Eng. Colls. Fund, Assn. Ind. Colls. and Univs. in Mass.; pres. New Eng. Assn. Schs. and Colls., 1977-78. Bd. visitors Wake Forest U., 1971—; trustee Sterling Francine Clark Art Inst., Williamstown Theatre. Fulbright fellow, India, 1963; Kent fellow. Mem. Am. Acad. Religion, Soc. For Sci. Study Religion, Assn. Am. Colls. (task force on presdl. selection and career devel.), Soc. for Christian Ethics, Soc. for Religion in Higher Edn., Phi Beta Kappa. Mem. United Ch. of Christ. Clubs: University, Century (N.Y.C.); Williams (N.Y.). Contbg. author: Miscellany of American Religion, 1963; Masterpieces of Religious Literature, 1963; Liberal Education. Home: 936 Main St Williamstown MA 01267

CHANDLER, RICHARD MERRICK, apt. owner and mgr.; b. Lewiston, Maine, Feb. 23, 1935; s. Robert Cummings and Helen Elizabeth (Merrick) C.; B.Marine Sci., Maine Maritime Acad., 1956. Owner, Merrick Estate Apts., Augusta, Maine, 1968—; profl. mcht. marine officer Isthmian Lines, Inc., 1956-66, chief mate, 1962-66. Coordinator Maine Products Show Afloat, Expo 67. Served as ensign USNR, 1956-66. Mem. Navy League U.S. (life), U.S. Naval Inst. (life), Nat. Trust Historic Preservation, Nat. Small Bus. Assn., Franklin Mint Collectors Soc., Internat. Soc. Artists, Maine Maritime Acad. Alumni Assn. (life). Club: Masons. Home and Office: 26 1/2 Sewall St Augusta ME 04330

CHANDLER, ROBERT LESLIE, hosp. exec.; b. Phila., Mar. 3, 1948; s. Joel Leslie and Evelyn Laney (DeLaney) C.; A.S., Atlantic Community Coll., 1969; B.S., Bowling Green State U., 1971; M.S., Ohio U., 1972; postgrad. in hosp. adminstrn. Wagner Coll.; m. Maureen O'Keefe, Mar. 21, 1970. Dir. pub. relations Athens (Ohio) Mental Health Center, 1972; internal communications editor, pub. affairs dept. Owens-Corning Fiberglas Corp., Toledo, 1972-74; dir. community relations Wyandotte (Mich.) Gen. Hosp., 1974-76; dir. pub. affairs Meth. Hosp., Bklyn., 1976—. Mem. budget com. United Way Mich., 1975-76. N.J. State scholar, 1969. Mem. Pub. Relations Soc. Am., Internat. Assn. Bus. Communicators, Hosp. Pub. Relations Soc. Greater N.Y., Sigma Delta Chi, Kappa Tau Alpha. Home: 700 Victory Blvd Parkview House Apt 6C Staten Island NY 10301 Office: Meth Hosp 506 6th St Brooklyn NY 11215

CHANEY, LOUISE BOCKELMAN, water and wastewater treatment plant operator; b. Sioux City, Iowa, Feb. 20, 1926; d. Paul Frederick and Louise Katherine (Lettengarver) Bockelman; student Charles County Community Coll., 1973-74, 75, 76, 77; m. James Louis Chaney, Apr. 24, 1946 (dec.); children—Linda Louise, James William, Louis John, Thomas Edward. Water and wastewater treatment plant operator, Indian Head, Md., 1975—. Bd. dirs. Potomac Heights Mut. Home Owners Assn., Inc.; mem. PTA, 1953-70; active Charles County League Women Voters, bd. 1967-68; advisory bd. Ten Yr. Comprehensive Plan for Charles County, 1969—; dir. mem. Citizens for a Better Charles County Com., 1977-78; mem. Potomac Heights coms. Mem. Am. Water Works Assn. (certified). Democrat. Club: VFW Aux. (pres., 1960-65). Office: 1107 Stafuss Ave Indian Head MD 20640

CHANEY, VERNE EDWARD, JR., surgeon, found. exec.; b. Kansas City, Mo., July 16, 1923; s. Verne Edward and Adelaide (Hafner) C.; B.S., Va. Mil. Inst., 1951; M.D., Johns Hopkins U., 1948, M.P.H., 1972; div.; children—Christopher Edward, Steven Wood. Intern surgery Johns Hopkins, 1948-49, asst. resident, 1949-50, instr. anatomy, 1950-53; surg. resident N.C. Meml. Hosp., Chapel Hill, 1953-56; chief surgery Albert Schweitzer Hosp., Deschappeles, Haiti, 1956-58; practice medicine specializing in thoracic surgery, Monterey, Calif., 1958-61; pres., founder Thomas A. Dooley Found., San Francisco, 1961-76; clin. prof. surgery U. Miami, 1976, clin. prof. epidemiology and public health, 1977; founder, pres. Intermed, Geneva, Switzerland, 1976—. Served from pvt. to capt. M.C., U.S. Army, 1944, 51-53. Decorated Silver Star, Bronze Star medal with V, Purple Heart (U.S.); Croix de Guerre (France); Order of Million Elephants (Laos). Diplomate Am. Bd. Surgery, Am. Bd. Thoracic Surgery. Fellow A.C.S., Am. Coll. Chest Physicians; mem. Calif. med. assns., Nathan A. Womack Surg. Soc., Monterey County Med. Soc. Republican. Episcopalian. Patentee in field. Home: 520 E 76th St Apt 14E New York NY 10021 Office: 420 Lexington Ave Room 2656 New York NY 10017

CHANG, CHIN-AN, chemist; b. Sian, China, June 13, 1943; s. Kuo-When and Kuan-Lun I.C.; came to U.S., 1965; B.S., Chung-Hsing U., Taiwan, China, 1963; M.S., Colo. State U., 1967; Ph.D., U. Calif., Berkeley, 1970; m. I-Chia Hsu, Jan. 1, 1966; children—Betrina Pi-Ju, Janice Mei-Yu, Iris Ay-Shin, Sharon Shuh-Shin. Nat. Sci. Council vis. asso. prof. Nat. Tsing Hua U., Taiwan, China, 1970-71; postdoctoral research asso. chemistry dept. Tex. A. and M. U., College Station, 1971-72; research fellow chemistry dept. Calif. Inst. Tech., Pasadena, 1972-73; chemist Lawrence Berkeley Lab., Berkeley, Calif., 1973-75; mem. research staff Thomas Watson Research Center, IBM, Yorktown Heights, N.Y., 1975—. Mem. Am. Phys. Soc., Electrochem. Soc. Contbr. articles in field to profl. jours. Home: 17 2nd St Quarry Acres Peekskill NY 10566

CHANG, CHING MING, chem. co. exec.; b. Nanking, China, Oct. 13, 1935; s. Wen Pei and Su Hin (Pi) C.; came to U.S., 1968, naturalized, 1976; diploma in engring. Tech. U. Aachen (W. Ger.), 1962, Ph.D., 1967; m. Birdie Shiao-Ching Ku, Dec. 18, 1964; children—Andrew Liang-Ping, Nelson Liang-An. Research asst. Inst. Mechanics, Tech. U. Aachen, 1962-64, instr., 1964-67, research asso., 1967; vis. asst. prof. engring. mechanics N.C. State U., 1968-70, asst. prof., 1970-73; sr. engr. Linde div. Union Carbide Corp., Tonawanda, N.Y., 1973-75, cons., 1975, supr., 1975-78, engring. asso., 1978—; adj. asso. prof. engring. sci., aerospace engring. and nuclear engring. State U. N.Y. at Buffalo, 1975—. Registered profl. engr., N.Y. Mem. AAAS, Am. Phys. Soc., Nat. Soc. Profl. Engrs. (dir. Erie-Niagara chpt. 1975-78, 2d v.p. 1978—) ASME, Air Pollution Control Assn., Sigma Xi, Phi Kappa Phi. Contbr. articles on fluid dynamics, heat transfer, two-phase flows, air pollution control, high-temperature gasdynamics, kinetic theory of gases to profl. jours.; asst. editor Plasma Physics, 1971-72. Home: 171 The Paddock Williamsville NY 14221 Office: Linde Div Union Carbide Corp PO Box 44 Tonawanda NY 14150

CHANG, CHIN-TSE (ROBERT), mfg. co. exec.; b. Hsin-Chu, Taiwan, June 11, 1943; s. Yang-Chueh and Feng-Cheng (Chen) C.; came to U.S., 1968; Ph.D. in Physics, Carnegie-Mellon U., 1976; m. Ping-Yuan Wang, Aug. 10, 1973; children—Frank Hung-Yueh, Patricia Huey-Ming. Research asst. Carnegie-Mellon U., Pitts., 1968-74; computer system programmer Honeywell Corp., Billerica, Mass., 1974-75, computer system analyst, 1976-77, computer sr. analyst, 1977—. Served to 2d lt. ROCAF, 1966. Mem. IEEE, Am. Phys. Soc., Assn. for Computing Machinery. Office: MS 844A 300 Concord Rd Billerica MA 01821

CHANG, DARWIN RAY, civil engr.; b. Jukao, Kiangsu, China, Aug. 1, 1917; s. Wey and Susan (Hsiong) C.; came to U.S., 1945, naturalized, 1962; B.S., Chiao Tung U., Shanghai, China, 1940; M.C.E., Cornell U., 1946;; m. Yen Ma, Dec. 23, 1961; children—Gordon, Susan, Martha, Leslie. Structural engr. Borsari Tank Corp., N.Y.C., 1951; project engr. Ebasco Internat. Corp., N.Y.C. 1956-60; prin. engr. Pub. Service Electric and Gas Co., Newark, 1960—; cons. engr., 1956—. Mem. N.J. Soc. Profl. Engrs., IEEE, Chinese Inst. Engrs. Presbyterian. Club: Masons. Contbr. articles on esthetic transmission structures to trade mags. Home: 108 Green Ave Madison NJ 07940 Office: Pub Service Electric and Gas Co Newark NJ 07101

CHANG, MICHAEL MACHAW, canadian provincial ofcl.; b. India, June 21, 1937; s. Shin Hai and Psi (Chow) C.; B.Com., Calcutta U., 1957; Bombay U., LL.B., 1960; m. Chiao Chen, Nov. 12, 1960; children—Angela, Tommy, David. Insp. customs Govt. India, 1962-65; sr. auditor Glendinning, Jarrett, Gould & Co., Toronto, 1966-70; mgr. financial sect. Ministry Revenue, Toronto, Ont., 1971-72; dir. audit services br. Ministry Agr. and Food Ont., Toronto, 1972—. Mem. Inst. Chartered Accountants Ont., Inst. Internat. Auditors, Pub. Accountants Council. Conservative. United Ch. Can. Home: 128 Edmonton Dr Willowdale ON M2J 3Xi Canada Office: 1200 Bay St Toronto ON Canada

CHANG, PYOUNG RYOUL PETER, surgeon; b. Chonan, Korea, Nov. 20, 1936; s. Chun Won and Chi Ye (Yoo) Chang; came to U.S., 1966, naturalized, 1976; student Yonsei U. Coll. (Korea), 1954-60, M.D., 1960; m. Min Hee Theresa Cho, Mar. 27, 1966; children—Eugene, Andrew, Marian. Intern, Seoul Naval Hosp., 1960-61; resident in neurosurgery U.S. Naval Hosp., Oakland, Calif.,

1962-63, Naval Med. Center, Chinhae, Korea, 1963-66; intern St. Clare's Hosp., N.Y.C., 1966-67; resident in gen. surgery St. Clare's Hosp., 1967-71, surg. research fellow, 1971-72; practice medicine specializing in surgery, Cortland, N.Y., 1972—; attending surgeon Cortland Meml. Hosp., 1972—; clin. instr. surgery Upstate Med. Center, State U. N.Y., Syracuse, 1972—; med. dir. Highgate Manor Nursing Home, Cortland, N.Y., 1972-73. Served with Republic of Korea Navy, 1960-66. Diplomate Am. Bd. Surgery. Fellow ACS; mem. Med. Soc. County of Cortland (v.p. 1977—), Am. Med. Assn., Internat. Coll. Surgeons, Am. Coll. Angiology, Med. Soc. State of N.Y. Club: Cortland Country. Home: 85 N Main St Homer NY 13077 Office: 6 Euclid Ave Cortland NY 13045

CHANG, SHEN CHIN, research chemist; b. China, Oct. 1, 1914; s. Tsu Chun and Shu Chen (Shu) C.; B.S., Chekiang U., 1938; Ph.D. in Entomology, Oreg. State U., 1952; came to U.S., 1948, naturalized, 1961; m. Mei Ling Wu, Aug. 15, 1953; children—Myron Nan, Susan Chang. Research asst. Oreg. State U., 1952-54; research asst. prof. U. Ill., Urbana, 1954-62; research chemist Agrl. Research Service, U.S. Dept. Agr., Beltsville, Md., 1962—. Pres. Washington Insecticide Soc., 1967-68. Mem. AAAS, Am. Chem. Soc. (abstractor), Entomol. Soc. Am. Club: Beltsville Garden. Discover/co-discoverer phosphoramides, s-triazines, dithiobiurets and dithiazolium salts as insect chemosterilants. Home: 11329 Frances Dr Beltsville MD 20705 Office: Agrl Research Center US Dept Agr Beltsville MD 20705

CHANG, TED TEH-LIANG, chemist; b. Tainan, Taiwan, Oct. 6, 1935; s. Shie-Huei and Ou (Chiu) C.; came to U.S., 1961, naturalized, 1972; B.S., Nat. Taiwan U., 1957; M.S., U. Va., 1963, Ph.D., 1965; m. Kay H. Hsu, Jan. 31, 1960; children—Grace, Susan, Diana. Research fellow Calif. Inst. Tech., Pasadena, 1965-66; sr. research chemist Am. Cyanamid Co., Stamford, Conn., 1966-71; dept. supr. Wyeth Lab. Inc., Radnor, Pa., 1971-77; sr. research chemist Celanese Corp., Summit, N.J., 1977—. Francis du Pont fellow, 1963-65. Mem. Am. Chem. Soc., Am. Soc. Mass. Spectrometry, Am. Inst. Chemists, AAAS, Sigma Xi. Contbr. articles to profl. publs. Home: 294 Gates Ave Gillette NJ 07933

CHANG, THOMAS MING SWI, physician, physiologist, educator; b. Swatow, Kwantang, China, Apr. 8, 1933; s. Henry Sue-Yue and Frances Hue-Soo (Lim) C.; B.Sc., McGill U., 1957, M.D., C.M., 1961, Ph.D., 1965; m. Lancy Yuk Lan, June 21, 1958; children—Harvey, Victor, Christine, Sandra. Intern, Montreal (Que., Can.) Gen. Hosp., 1961-62; research fellow, dept. physiology McGill U., Montreal, 1962-65, lectr. faculty medicine, 1965, asst. prof., 1966-69, asso. prof., 1969-72, prof. physiology, 1972—, prof. medicine, 1975—, dir. artificial organs research unit, 1975—; practice medicine specializing in med. scis., Montreal, 1962—; staff Royal Victoria Hosp., Montreal Gen. Hosp.; cons. Montreal Chinese Hosp., 1970—. Med. Research Council fellow, 1962-65, scholar, 1965-68, asso., 1968—. Fellow Royal Coll. Physicians Can.; mem. Biophysic Soc., Am., Canadian physiology socs., Canadian Med. Assn., Am. Nephrology Soc., Internat. Soc. Artifical Internal Organs, Internat. Soc. Nephrology. Author: Artificial Cells, 1972; Biomedical Application of Immobilized Enzymes and Proteins, 1977; Artificial Kidney, Artificial Liver and Artificial Cells, 1978. Mem. editorial bd. Jour. Biomaterial Med. Devices and Artificial Organs, 1972—, Jour. Membrane Sci., 1975—, Jour. Bioengring., 1975—, Internat. Jour. Artificial Organs, 1977—, Artificial Organs Jour., 1977—. Office: Artificial Organs Research Unit McIntyre Med Sci Bldg McGill U 3655 Drummond St Montreal PQ Canada

CHANG, TSUN-YUNG, engring. cons.; b. Shanghai, China, Dec. 12, 1942; s. Jen-Tao and Daisy (Kao) Tsang; came to U.S., 1963, naturalized, 1975; B.S., Taiwan Cheng-Kung U., 1962; M.S., (univ. scholar), Calif. Inst. Tech., 1964; M.A., Princeton U., 1967; Ph.D. (NSF grantee), Poly. Inst. Bklyn., 1972; m. Pei-lan Li Chang, Aug. 20, 1967; children—Walter H.C., Caroline S.H. Research asst. Princeton U., 1965-67; sr. research asst., research and devel. dept. Gen. Tech. Corp., Lawrenceville, N.J., 1967-68; research asso. Poly. Inst. Bklyn., 1968-72; prin. engr. Nuclear Power Plant Project, Stone & Webster Engring. Corps., Boston, 1972—; mem. faculty Poly. Inst. Bklyn., 1968-72. Mem. ASME, Am. Inst. Aeros. and Astronautics, Soc. for Exptl. Stress Analysis, Sigma Xi, Sigma Gamma Tau. Contbr. articles to profl. jours. Office: 245 Summer St Boston MA

CHANG, YUAN, actuary, lawyer, ins. co. exec.; b. Peking, China, July 16, 1934; s. Chung Fu and Shan Fin (Chen) C.; came to U.S., 1947, naturalized, 1961; B.A., Oberlin Coll., 1956; J.D., U. Conn., 1966; m. Mary Han, Oct. 16, 1936; children—Christine, Timothy, Derek, Leslie. Admitted to Conn. bar, 1966; actuarial analyst Travelers Ins. Co., Hartford, Conn., 1956-61, asst. actuary, 1962-66, sec. Personal Lines Systems div., 1966-68, 2d v.p., 1968-71, v.p., 1971-73, v.p. group pension products, 1973—; cons. to Minister Fin., Republic China, 1971-72; vis. prof. actuarial sci. Soochew U., Taipei, Taiwan, 1971-72. Justice of Peace, Hartford, 1970-72; mem. pension commn. City of Hartford, 1969—, chmn., 1977—; mem. Citizens for Quality Edn.; mem. Rep. Town Com., Bloomfield, Conn., 1967-68; corporator Hartford Hosp., 1978—; trustee Kingswood Oxford Sch., 1977; trustee Hartford Conservatory, 1970—, treas., 1971-76; bd. dirs. Producing Guild, chmn., 1975—. Served with AUS, 1957. Recipient Reitmeyer award 826th M.I., Army Res., 1959, Allstate award Allstate Ins. Co., 1966. Fellow Soc. Actuaries, Acad. Actuaries; mem. Conn., Hartford County bar assns., Am. Pension Conf., Am. Council Life Ins. (chmn. valuation subcom. 1977—), Life Office Mgmt. Assn. (chmn. systems research com. 1967-73), Hartford C. of C. (chmn. local govt. com. 1976—). Clubs: Oberlin Alumni (v.p. Central Conn. 1970-73), Hartford Golf. Contbr. articles to profl. jours. Home: 7 Woodside Circle Hartford CT 06105 Office: 1 Tower Sq Hartford CT 06115

CHANG-RODRIGUEZ, EUGENIO, educator; b. Trujillo, Peru, Nov. 15, 1926; Ph.B., U. San Marcos, Peru, 1946; B.A., William Penn Coll., 1949; M.A., U. Ariz., 1950; M.A., U. Wash., 1953, Ph.D., 1956. Instr. Romance langs. U. Wash., 1952-56, dir. La Casa Hispana, 1951-56; asst. prof. Romance langs. U. Pa., 1956-61; from asst. prof. to prof. Romance langs. Queens Coll. of City U. N.Y., Flushing, 1961—, chmn. Latin Am. area studies, 1969-78; vis. prof. U. Miami, 1967-68; chmn. Columbia Seminar on Latin Am., 1974—; adv. editor Charles Scribner's Sons, N.Y., 1965-66. Bd. dirs. Internat. League for Rights of Man, 1962—, also pres. adv. council; mem. White House Conf. Internat Coop., 1966; chmn. organizing com. Nat. Conf. on Linguistics, N.Y., 1967; mem. joint com. Latin Am. studies Social Scis. Research Council, 1976—. Mem. Latin Am. Studies Assn. (exec. council 1972-73), Hispanic Soc. Am. (corr.), Instituto Internacional de Literatura Iberoamericana, N.Am. Acad. Spanish Lang., Clasp (steering com. 1975—), Linguistic Circle N.Y. (exec. council 1967-69), Internat. Linguistic Assn. (pres. 1969-72), Am. Acad. Polit. and Social Scis., Am. Assn. Tchrs. Spanish and Portuguese, N.Y. Acad. Sci., Modern Lang. Assn. Am., AAUP, Latin Am. Studies Assn., Am. Acad. Polit. Social Sci. Author: Literatura Politica, 1957; co-author: Frequency Dictionary of Spanish, 1964; Continuing Spanish, 1969; The Lingering Crisis: A Case Study of the Dominican Republic, 1969; (with C. Smith) Colliers Dictionary of Spanish, 1971. Asso. editor Hispania, 1962-65; co-editor La America Latina de Hoy, 1961; The Hemisphere's Present Crisis, 1963; editor BANLE, 1976—. Contbr. articles to profl. jours. Home: 65-30 Kissena Blvd Flushing NY 11367

CHANG-RODRÍGUEZ, RAQUEL (TORRES), educator; b. Cárdenas, Cuba, Jan. 23, 1943; B.S. with distinction, Mont. State U., 1965; M.A., Ohio U., 1967; Ph.D. (grad. honors scholar), N.Y. U., 1973; m. Eugenio Chang-Rodríguez, Dec. 17, 1966. Teaching fellow Ohio U., Athens, 1965-67; instr. U. Dayton (Ohio) NDEA Spanish Inst., summers 1967, 68; vis. lectr. Yeshiva U., N.Y.C., 1968-69; from lectr. to asso. prof. Spanish, City Coll., City U. N.Y., N.Y.C., 1968-79. Bd. dirs. Pan Am. Women Assn., 1968-74. Recipient Faculty Research award City U. N.Y., 1974-75; Am. Council Learned Socs. travel grantee, 1975. Mem. Modern Lang. Assn. (exec. com. Latin Am. lit.), Am. Assn. Tchrs. Spanish and Portuguese, Instituto Internacional de Literatura Iberoamericana (dir.), Internat. Linguistic Assn. Editor: (with Donald A. Yates) Homage to Irving A. Leonard: Essays on Hispanic Art, History and Literature, 1977; Prosa hispanoamericana virreinal, 1978; contbr. articles in field to profl. jours. Home: 60 Sutton Pl S New York City NY 10022 Office: Romance Langs Dept The City College New York City NY 10031

CHANT, DAVIS RYAN, real estate broker; b. Port Jervis, N.Y., Dec. 15, 1938; s. B. Ryall and Miriam C. (Cathy) C.; B.A., Belmont Abbey Coll., 1960; m. Dorothy Leggett, July 25, 1959; children—Tamara, Holley. Constrn. materials salesman, architect service U.S. Gypsum Co., Chgo., 1960-62; pres. Davis R. Chant, Inc., realtors, Milford, Pa., 1962—, Davis R. Chant Assos., Inc., realtors, Lords Valley, Pa., Davis R. Chant Inc., Realtors of N.Y. Chmn., Econ. Devel. Council NE Pa.; mem. Pres.' com. on Leisure Housing. Bd. dirs. Pike County Conservation Dist.; trustee Milford Reservation, Inc. Recipient nat. award for advt. Nat. Assn. Real Estate Brokers, 1971. Mem. Am. Right of Way Assn., Nat., N.Y. assns. real estate bds., Nat. Inst. Real Estate Brokers, Pa. Vacation Land Developers Assn., Pa., N.Y. assns. realtors, Internat. Real Estate Fedn., Sullivan County, Delaware County bds. realtors, Pike County (past dir.), Wayne County, Port Jervis, N.Y. chambers commerce, NE Soc. Farm Mgrs. and Rural Appraisers, Pike-Wayne County Bd. Realtors (past pres.), Monroe-Pike Builders Assn., Urban Land Inst., Nat. Inst. Farm and Land Brokers, Nat. Assn. Home Builders, Pocomo Mountain Vacation Bur., Community Assn. Inst. Am. (charter, dir.). Mason (32 deg.), Lion. Home: Twin Lakes Milford PA 18337 Office: 106 E Harford St Milford PA 18337

CHAO, HSIN CHENG, anesthesiologist; b. Taiwan, China, Mar. 4, 1938; s. Tien Chie and Chin Chu (Cheng) C.; came to U.S., 1967, naturalized, 1977; M.D., Nat. Taiwan U., 1963; m. Sun Faye Liang, Nov. 29, 1964; children—Erie, Jerome, James. Intern, Nat. Taiwan U. Hosp., Taipei, 1962-63, resident in surgery, 1964-67; intern St. Joseph's Hosp., Paterson, N.J., 1967-68; resident in gen. practice Lower Bucks Hosp., Bristol, Pa., 1968-69; resident in anesthesiology, then asst. dir. div. anesthesiology Westchester County Med. Center, Valhalla, N.Y., 1969-72; sr. attending anesthesiology Phelps Meml. Hosp., N. Tarrytown, N.Y., 1972—. Served as med. officer Chinese Navy, 1963-64; Diplomate Am. Bd. Anesthesiology. Fellow Am. Coll. Anesthesiologists; mem. Am., N.Y. State socs. anesthesiologists, N.Y. State, Westchester County med. socs., N.Y. Soc. Acupuncture for Physicians and Dentists. Home: Country Club Ln Briarcliff NY 10510 Office: Phelps Meml Hosp North Tarrytown NY 10591

CHAO, HUNG-CHI, metallurgist; b. Loyang, Honan Province, China, Nov. 19, 1921; s. Der-Yu Chao and Whoifan Lin Chao; came to U.S., 1959, naturalized, 1971; B.S. Mech. Engring., Central U., Chung King, China, 1946; M.S. in Metallurgy, U. Mo., 1961; Ph.D. in Metallurgy, U. Mich., 1964; m. Yu-E Chen, Jan. 16, 1954; children—Betty Pao-ti, Paul Pao-Ngang. Jr. engr. Shanyang Locomotive & Car Mfg. Co., Shanyang, China, 1946-49; M.E., metallurgy engr. Taiwan Machinery Mfg. Corp., Kaohsiung, Taiwan, China, 1949-59; technologist U.S. Steel Research Lab., Monroeville, Pa., 1964-65, sr. research engr., 1965-68, asso. research cons., 1968-76, research cons., 1976—. Mem. Am. Soc. Metals, Japan Iron and Steel Inst., Am. Powder Metallurgy Inst., Japan Soc. Powder and Powder Metallurgy. Buddhist. Patentee powder-metal and sheet steel products; contbr. to publs. in field. Home: 151 Urick Ln Monroeville PA 15146 Office: 125 Jamison Ln Monroeville PA 15146

CHAPARAS, SOTIROS DEMETRIOS, immunologist, microbiologist; b. Lowell, Mass., May 4, 1929; s. Demetrios Constantine and Panagiota (Pliatska) C.; B.S., Northeastern U., 1951; M.S., U. Mass., 1953; Ph.D., St. Louis U., 1959; m. Alma Rose Monnig, Aug. 18, 1956; children—Mary Paula, James. Instr., St. Louis U. Med. Sch., 1958-59, U. So. Calif. Med. Sch., 1959-60; sect. chief lab. bacterial products, div. biol. standards NIH, Bethesda, Md., 1960-72, faculty chmn. for microbiology and immunology Found. Advanced Studies in Sci., 1965—; br. dir. Bur. Biologics, FDA, 1973—; lectr., Howard U., 1972—; guest lectr. George Washington U. Med. Sch., 1972—. mem. advisory com. Trudeau Inst., Saranac Lake, N.Y., 1968-74, scientist dir. USPHS, 1960—; mem. Tb panel U.S.-Japan Med. Coop. Program, 1975—. Recipient Commendation medal USPHS, 1973; diplomate Am. Bd. Microbiology. Mem. Am. Thoracic Soc. (chmn. sci. assembly 1974), Am. Soc. Microbiology (pres. Washington br. 1971-72), Am. Assn. Immunologists, Internat. Union Against Tb, Internat. Working Group Mycobacterial Taxonomy. Contbr. articles to profl. jours.; developer methods on standardization of biols. Home: 1820 Billman Ln Silver Spring MD 20902 Office: 8800 Rockville Pike Bethesda MD 20014

CHAPIN, DIANE NELSON, pub. relations cons.; b. Chgo., Oct. 2, 1942; d. George Albert and Margaret Eleanor (Larson) Nelson; A.B. in English, U. Miami, 1964; M.A. in Edn., George Washington U., 1972; m. Lewis Mulford Chapin, Feb. 26, 1972; children—Lindsay Margaret, Allison Mulford. With C & P Telephone Cos. (subs. Bell System), Washington, 1965—, traffic adminstrv. asst., 1965-66, group chief operator, 1966-67, tng. asst. AT&T, N.Y.C., 1967-68, staff asst. tng., 1968-73, staff asso. pub. relations, 1973-74, editor Tempo, Mgmt. Reports, 1975-76, asst. producer, dir. audio-visual center, 1977—; free-lance pub. relations cons. Washington Internat. Coll. and C & P Telephone Co. Founding mem. N.W. Community Relations Team, 1973-76. Mem. Internat. Assn. Bus. Communicators (v.p. 1973-75, pres. 1976, Communicator of Year award 1974, award of Excellence 1975, 78), Pub. Relations Soc. Am., Alpha Chi Omega. Editor various co. newsletters and reports; dir. co. films.

CHAPIN, HOMER NEWTON, financial cons.; b. Springfield, Mass., Mar. 4, 1904; s. Newton William and Ella Leanord C.; D. Finance (hon.), Franklin Pierce Coll., 1973; m. Evelyn Boyce, June 17, 1933; children—Carolyn, Joan, Barbara, Robert. With Mass. Mut. Life Ins. Co., Springfield, 1922-69, exec. v.p., 1958-69; fin. cons., Springfield, 1969—; dir. Condec Corp., Grow Chem. Corp., Loral Corp., Novo Corp. Pres., United Fund, 1968; trustee Macduffie Sch. for Girls. Republican. Congregationalist. Clubs: Colony (Springfield); Longmeadow Country; Board Room, Wall St., Marco Polo (N.Y.C.); Masons. Home: 7 Hilltop Dr Wilbraham MA 01095

CHAPLINE, WILLIAM RIDGELY, forestry cons.; b. Lincoln, Nebr., Jan. 10, 1891; s. William Ridgely and Henrietta Rachel (Duncan) C.; B.Sc., U. Nebr., 1913; postgrad. U. Nebr., 1913, U.S. Dept. Agr. Grad. Sch., 1930, 40; m. Eva Mae Behn, Dec. 7, 1921; children—Barbara Ruth Chapline Waldner, Eve Ridgely Chapline Peterson. Grazing asst. Forest Service, U.S. Dept. Agr., 1913-15, grazing examiner, 1915-20, insp. of grazing, 1920-25, chief Office Grazing Studies, sr. insp. of grazing, 1926-35, chief Div. Range Research, 1935-52; chief forest conservation sect. UN FAO, Rome, Italy, 1952-54; prof. 2d Internat. Grad. Course on Pastures, Instituto Interamericano de Ciencias Agricolas, Zona Sur, Montevideo, Uruguay, 1954; cons. to Argentina, Chile, Peru Ministries of Agr., 1955, Spain, Spanish Forest Service, U.S. AID, 1956-57, Charles Lathrop Pack Forestry Found., 1957-59; leader Spanish Forestry Team in U.S.A., 1959; cons. Brazil in range mgmt., 1965; coordinator spl. course in range mgmt. Internationals, Colo. State U., 1967; cons. Forest Service, profl. range mgmt. study, 25 countries, 1967-69; volunteer in internat. tech. asst. Vols. In Tech. Assistance, Mt. Rainier, Md., 1968—; cons. Am. U. African Drought Project, Washington, 1974—. Lectr. numerous univs. and colls., assns, and soc. meetings in U.S.A. and abroad; cons. Civilian Conservation Corps, 1934-36, U.S. Navy, 1944; del. Internat. Congress Soil Sci., Washington, 1927, Interam. Conf. Agr., Forestry and Animal Industry, Washington, 1930, Internat. Grassland Congress, Wales, 1937, The Netherlands, 1949, Pa., 1952, Brazil, 1965, Russia, 1974, German Democratic Republic, 1977, Internat. Conf. Renewable Nat. Resources, Denver, 1948, Lake Success, 1949, 11th Congress Internat. Union of Forest Research Orgns., Rome, Italy, 1953, Internat. Forest Grazing Conf., Rome, Italy, 1954, World Forestry Congress, Seattle, 1960, Internat. Conf. on Water for Peace, Washington, 1967, Interam. Meeting on Sci. and Man in Amers., Mexico City, 1973, Internat. Meeting on Animal Prodn. from Temperate Grassland, Ireland, 1977, 1st Internat. Rangeland Congress, Denver, 1978. Mem. pres.'s adv. com. on waterflow, 1933-34. Fellow A.A.A.S., Soc. Range Mgmt. (certificate of merit 1967); mem. Grassland Soc. So. Africa (hon. mem.), Soc. Am. Foresters (Golden Membership award 1978), Am. Forestry Assn., Washington Acad. Sci., Washington Bot. Soc. (hon.), Bot. Soc. Am., Am. Soc. Agronomy, Am. Soc. for Animal Prodn., S.R., U. Nebr. Alumni Assn., Grange, Sigma Xi, Alpha Zeta. Christian Scientist (first reader 1957-60). Mason. Contbr. articles to profl. jours. Home: 4225 43d St NW Washington DC 20016

CHAPMAN, ERNA MARTA RIEDEL (MRS. RAY F. CHAPMAN), educator; b. Dresden, Germany, May 20, 1909 (brought to U.S. 1914, naturalized 1923); d. Joseph and Elsa (Mueller) Riedel; B.S., U. Md., 1934, M.S., 1936; postgrad. Ind. U., D.C. Tchrs. Coll., U. Md.; m. Ray F. Chapman, Sept. 5, 1942. Sales, acting asst. buyer The Hecht Co., Washington, 1928-30; card punch operator Census Bur., 1930-31; grad. asst. U. Md. Coll. Home Econs., College Park, 1934-36; corr. editor Social Security Bd., Balt. 1936-38; vocational home econs. tchr. D.C. Pub. Schs., Washington, 1938-56, state supr. home econs. edn., 1960-65; asst. prin. Roosevelt High Sch., Washington, 1956-60; state supr., supervising dir. home econs. edn. D.C. Pub. Schs., Washington, 1967-78; acting Dean U. Md., College Park, 1965-67; free-lance home economist, farmer; mem. nat. adv. com. J.C. Penney Co., Inc. Family life cons. Teamwork Found.; mem. Gov.'s com. State of Md., Status of Women in Higher Edn., 1965-67; trustee U. Md., Met. 4-H Club Found., Inc.; chairperson Anne Arundel County Agrl. Preservation Adv. Bd. Mem. NEA, Am. Vocational Assn., Am. Home Econs. Assn., AAUW, Nat. Council Adminstrs. of Home Econs., Assn. Home Econs. Adminstrs., Nat. Assn. State Univs. and Land Grant Colls., D.C. Home Econs. Assn., Md. Farm Bur. (women's com.), Omicron Nu, Phi Kappa Phi, Phi Delta Gamma. Club: Research (D.C.). Contbr. articles to profl. jours. Home and office: Route 1 Box 374 Gambrills MD 21054

CHAPMAN, JO(SEPHINE LAWTON), publishing and pub. relations co. exec.; b. N.Y.C., Apr. 9, 1918; d. Wolcott Pitkin and Etta (Lawton) Chapman; student Breadloaf Writers' Conf., Middlebury Coll., 1948, 59, Pratt Inst. Evening Sch., 1955. Mem. suburban staff gen. news reporter Bridgeport Time-Star, 1934-40; asso. editor Westport-Herald, 1940-43; town hall-polit. writer Greenwich Time, 1943-44; staff writer Port Chester Daily Item, 1944-46, Stamford Adv., 1946-52; corr. N.Y. Times, 1942-52, Asso. Press, 1944-52; own pub. relations bus. 1952—; aide Housing Authority of Town of Greenwich, Conn., 1962-65; owner Community & Pub. Relations Assos., Greenwich, 1966—; sec., dir. Pix Films Service, Inc., Greenwich, 1965-67; editor Greenwich Mail, 1965—, owner, pub., 1968—; owner Chanticleer Publs., 1968—. Past distributive edn. instr. Conn. Dept. Vocat. Edn. Past instr. first aid A.R.C., Fairfield and Greenwich, past dir. Greenwich; mem. fire prevention com. Greenwich C. of C.; pres. Greenwich Stamp and Coin Club, 1955-56, 69-70, com. chmn. Greenwich Citizens Sch. Study, 1949. Nonpartisan mem. Rep. Town Meeting, Greenwich, 1945-57, 60-61, 68—, sec. 8th Dist. delegation, 1968-73, vice chmn., 1974—, vice chmn. rules com., 1976—, sec. Community Devel. Action Program liaison com., 1968-71; mem. Selectmen's Civic Center Adv. Com., 1966-70; mem. Town Claims Com., 1973—; mem. Rep. Town Com., 1976—. Recipient Service award YMCA, Greenwich, 1957, Bravo award, 1978. Mem. D.A.R. (dir. chpt. 1950-52 1968-71), Crispus Attucks Assn. (dir. 1950-73, past treas.). Republican. Club: Soroptimist Internat. (pres. Greenwich 1956-58, 64-65, 73-74, com. chmn. N.E. region 1952-54, 60-62, 66-68, 74-78, chmn. Am. fedn. service objectives com. 1954-56, mem. Fedn. nominating com. 1964, chmn. Fedn. resolution com. 1968-70). Home: 28 Decatur St Cos Cob CT 06807 Office: 283 Greenwich Ave Greenwich CT 06830

CHAPMAN, JOHN HAVEN, lawyer; b. Norfolk, Va., Nov. 7, 1943; s. Norman Franklin and Margaret Mary (Prior) C.; B.A., B.S., Brown U., 1966; J.D., Boston U., 1969; M.B.A., U. So. Calif., 1974; m. Mary Clemence Meeker, June 21, 1967; children—John Jesse, Thomas Norman. Admitted to Mass. bar, 1969, R.I. bar, 1969, Calif. bar, 1975, U.S. Supreme Ct. bar, 1975; law clk., corp. counsel City of Boston, 1968; legal defender, Roxbury, Mass., 1968; atty. Honeywell Information Systems, Waltham, Mass., 1969-71; atty. Xerox Corp., El Segundo, Calif., 1971-75; corp. counsel Calif. Computer Products, Inc., Anaheim, Calif., 1975-77; trial atty. antitrust div. Dept. Justice, N.Y.C., 1977—; mem. comml. panel Am. Arbitration Assn. Treas., Xerox Community Involvement Program, 1974-75. Mem. Calif., Am. bar assns., Computer Law Assn., Beta Gamma Sigma. Home: 50 Bush Ave Belle Haven Greenwich CT 06830 Office: 1 Saint Andrews Plaza 9th Floor New York City NY 10007

CHAPMAN, JOSEPH ALAN, ecologist, educator; b. Salem, Oreg., Apr. 28, 1942; s. Archie Blaine and Ardyth Loraine (Fallin) C.; B.S. in Wildlife Mgmt., Oreg. State U., 1965, M.S., 1967, Ph.D., 1970; m. Gale Roberta Willner. Sci., tech. trainee Oreg. State Game Common., summers 1963-65; wildlife biologist, U.S. Fish and Wildlife Service, Corvallis, Oreg., 1965-67; research asst. Dept. Fisheries and Wildlife, Oreg. State U., 1967-69; faculty research asst. Natural Resources Inst., U. Md., 1969-70, research asst. prof., 1970-74, asso. prof., 1974-78, prof., head Appalachian Environ. Lab., 1978—; adj. prof. wildlife sci. Garrett Community Coll., 1973—; adj. asso. prof. biology Frostburg State Coll.; guest lectr. in wildlife ecology, W. Va. U., Ohio State U., U. Md.; chmn. Interinstitutional Program in Fisheries and Wildlife; cons. U.S. Bur. Power; co-chmn., editor Worldwide Furbearer Conf.; mem. steering com. World Lagomorph Symposium. Fellow Explorers Club; mem. Center Environ. and Estuarine Studies (adminstrv. council), Wildlife Soc., Am. Soc. Mammalogists, Cooper Ornithol. Soc., Ecol. Soc. of Am., Internat. Assn. Fish and Wildlife

Ags. (fur resources com.), Sigma Xi, Phi Sigma Soc. Cons. editor Wildlife Monograph, asso. editor Terrestrial Ecology, Chesapeake Science. Contbr. numerous publs. to profl. jours. Office: U Md Frostburg State Coll Campus Gunter Hall Frostburg MD 21532

CHAPMAN, NORMAN FRANKLIN, JR., educator; b. Hattiesburg, Miss., Apr. 3, 1942; s. Norman F. and Margaret Mary (Prior) C.; A.B. in History, Brown U., Providence, R.I., 1964; M.A.L.S. in Social Scis., Dartmouth, Hanover, N.H., 1974; postgrad. in edn., social scis., learning theory U. N.H., Dartmouth; m. Nancy Eleanor Sovet; children—Alexander Sovet, Susannah Margaret. Tchr. Frances C. Richmond Sch., Hanover, 1966—; cons., program adminstr. on Brit. edn. Scholastic Internat., Scholastic Mags., Inc., N.Y.C., summers 1974-77; mem. accountability task force N.H. Dept. Edn., 1977—; bd. examiners N.H. Office Tchr. Edn. and Profl. Standards, 1978—; grad. tutor Dartmouth Humanities Inst., 1978—. Vice pres. Hanover Credit Union, 1969-71, pres., 1971—; interviewer Brown U. Nat. Alumni Council, 1973—. Cert. N.H., R.I. and Eng. Mem. NEA, N.H. Edn. Assn., Hanover Edn. Assn. (exec. com., past negotiator, past v.p.), Amnesty Internat., N.H., Vt. Councils Social Studies. Pub.: Franconia Notch Controversy: A Simulation, 1977; For Land's Sake: A Land-Use Simulation, 1979; specialist open, outdoor and computer edn., preadolescent devel. Home: 1 Ledge Rd Hanover NH 03755 Office: 6 Lebanon St Hanover NH 03755

CHAPMAN, OSCAR JAMES, educator; b. Stockton, Md., Oct. 2, 1910; s. Henry Charles and Millie Catherine (Purnell) C.; A.B., Lincoln (Pa.) U., 1932; M.A., U. Mich., 1936; Ph.D., Ohio State U., 1940; m. Mary Anne Wheeler, Apr. 2, 1950; 1 son, Oscar. Prof. edn., chmn. dept. A.&T. State U., Greensboro, N.C., 1939-41, Langston (Okla.) U., 1941-44, Tenn. A.&I. State U., Nashville, 1944-47, Morgan State U., Balt., 1947-50; pres. Del. State Coll., Dover, 1950-52; dean instr., chmn. grad. council Lincoln U., Jefferson City, Mo., 1957-73; prof. edn. Salisbury (Md.) State Coll., 1973—. Served as officer USAF, 1952-57; liaison officer Air Force Acad., 1964-67. Mem. AAUP, Am. Assn. Tchr. Assn., Omega Psi Phi. Democrat. Methodist. Clubs: Shriners, Elks. Author: Historical Study of Negro Land-Grant Colleges, 1940; The Thorn in the Flesh, 1945; Student's Outline of Negro Education in the U.S., 1948. Address: 708 Buckingham Circle Salisbury MD 21801

CHAPMAN, ROBERT MAXWELL, research psychologist; b. Chgo., Aug. 29, 1932; s. Maxwell C. and Margaret (Adkinson) C.; B.A., Oberlin Coll., 1954; M.Sc., Brown U., 1956, Ph.D., 1960; m. Susan Erganian, Apr. 20, 1958; 1 son, Eric Robert Ian. Teaching asst. Brown U., 1954-56, research asst., 1958-59; USPHS, NIMH Walter Reed Army Inst. Research fellows, 1960-61, research asso., 1961-73; research scientist Inst. Behavioral Research, 1961-68, Eye Research Found., Bethesda, Md., 1968-74; professorial lectr. Am. U., 1970-71; vis. prof. psychology Northeastern U., 1973-74; prof. psychology and visual scis. U. Rochester, 1974—, also dir. Center Visual Sci.; lectr. mil. medicine and allied sci. course Walter Reed Inst. Research, 1961-62; mem. vision com. NRC. Served with AUS, 1957-58. Internat. Congress EEG and Clin. Neurophysiology grantee, 1961, Internat. Congress Psychology grantee, 1966. Fellow AAAS; mem. Optical Soc. Am., Psychonomic Soc., Animal Behavior Soc., Assn. Research Vision and Opthalmology, Eastern Psychol. Assn., Sigma Xi. Contbr. articles to profl. jours. Home: 310 Canterbury Rd Rochester NY 14607

CHAPMAN, STUART MACDONALD, chem. engr.; b. Montreal, Que., Can., Mar. 6, 1911; s. Thomas S. and Mary (Macdonald) C.; B.Engring., McGill U., 1936; m. Marie Rose Dagenais, Mar. 15, 1969. Research asso. Canadian Pulp and Paper Assn., 1937; forest products engr. Canadian Dept. Mines and Resources, 1942-50; with Pulp and Paper Inst. Can., Pointe Claire, Que., 1950—, asst. to dir., 1969-76, cons., 1976—; mem. Canadian advisory com. to tech. com. 6 Internat. Standard Orgn. Registered profl. engr., Que. Fellow Chem. Inst. Can.; mem. Canadian Pulp and Paper Assn. (chmn. standards com. 1962-63, chmn. optical subcom. 1960—), TAPPI, Engring. Inst. Can., Tech. Assn. Graphic Arts. Club: Whitlock Golf and Country (Hudson, Que.). Research, publs., patents in drying methods, instruments. Home and Office: 115 Acres Rd Beaconsfield PQ H9W 1Y2 Canada

CHAPPELEAR, JOHN MONROE, utility co. exec.; b. Orange, N.J., July 31, 1938; s. Monroe and Elizabeth Marr (Neblett) C.; B.S., Yale U., 1960; m. Ingrid Marie Bergman, Sept. 10, 1960; children—Steven John, Robert Mark, Peter Monroe. Trainee, jr. analyst Kuhn Loeb & Co., N.Y.C., 1960-63; research analyst Lehman Bros., N.Y.C., 1963-64, portfolio mgr., 1964-68, dir. investement mgmt. dept., 1968-75, exec. v.p. investment mgmt. div., 1975-78; mgr. pension fund investments Pa. Power & Light Co., 1978—. Trustee, chmn. fin. com. Morrow Meml. Methodist Ch., 1973-78. Mem. N.Y. Soc. Security Analysts, Internat. Found. Employee Benefit Plans. Clubs: Orange Lawn Tennis, Yale Central N.J. (v.p., chmn. fin. com. 1971-78). Home: 2039 Overhill Rd Allentown PA 18103 Office: 2 N 9th St Allentown PA 18101

CHAPPELL, SANDRA IRENE, real estate broker; b. Tioga Center, N.Y., Nov. 3, 1940; d. John and Leta (Hollenbeck) Niemi; Asso. Sci., Corning Community Coll.; m. James J. Chappell, Nov. 8, 1958; children—Michael, Michelle, Monica, Mark. Bookkeeper Elmira (N.Y.) Star-Gazette, 1958-62; sec. Esquire Homes, Inc., Elmira-Horseheads, N.Y., 1962—; broker Paisley Real Estate, Horseheads, 1969—. Mem. Chemung County (pres.), N.Y. State bds. Realtors, Nat. Assn. Real Estate Bds., Chemung County Homebuilders Assn. Chemung County C. of C., Chemung County Mobile Home Assn. (sec. 1969-70), Horseheads Bus. and Profl. Women's Club. Episcopalian. Address: 4293 Murphy Hill Rd Horseheads NY 14845

CHAPPELL, THOMAS TYE, lawyer; b. Jersey City, Nov. 15, 1926; s. William Nelson and Florence De Chantel (Ryan) C.; B.A. in Econs., Duke, 1947, J.D., 1951; m. Laurel Reichert, Oct. 1, 1949; children—Thomas Tye IV, William N. III. Admitted to N.J. bar, 1952, U.S. Supreme Ct. bar, 1966; asso. firm Emory, Langan, Lamb & Blake, Jersey City, 1952-58; partner firm Lamb, Hutchinson, Chappell, Ryan & Hartung and predecessor firms, Jersey City, 1958—. Served with USNR, 1944-46. Fellow Am. Coll. Trial Lawyers; mem. Am., N.J. State, Hudson County, Morris County bar assns., Am. Arbitration Assn., Am. Judicature Soc., Am. Soc. Law and Medicine, Pitts. Inst. Legal Medicine, Nat. Assn. R.R. Trial Counsel, Trial Attys. of N.J., N.J. Soc. Hosp. Attys. Club: Spring Brook Country. Home: 5 McNab Ave Cedar Knolls NJ 07927 Office: 70 Sip Ave Jersey City NJ 07306

CHAPPEN, EDWARD PETER, psychiatrist, physician, lectr.; b. Carbondale, Pa., July 8, 1925; s. Peter E. and Amelia E. (Kouloumpy) C.; B.S., Pa. State U., 1946; M.D., Jefferson Med. Coll., 1952. Intern Jefferson Med. Coll. Hosp., Phila., 1953; resident in psychiatry Menninger Sch. Psychiatry, Topeka, Kans., 1967-70; practice medicine, Trenton, N.J., 1955—; mem. staff St. Francis Hosp., also chmn. staff; cons. in psychiatry Hamilton Hosp., Union Indsl. Home, Trenton; staff psychiatrist Central Santa Clara County Mental Health Center, San Jose, Calif., 1970-71. Mem. Trenton Mayor's com. for Selection of Trenton Sister City, 1961; Spl. Groups div. Del. Valley United Fund, 1958; treas. local chpt. Am. Assn. UN, 1960-61; exec. bd. Greater Trenton chpt. People to People; exec. council, pub. relations chmn. Parnassos Greek Cultural Soc. of N.Y. Inc., 1963; mem. Trenton Landmarks Commn. for Historic Preservation; mem. Adv. Com. for Study Sociology Death and Dying in Mercer County; mem. fine arts com. Anglican Cathedral of the Trinity, Trenton; bd. govs. Greater Trenton Symphony Assn., 1966-67; bd. mgrs. Donnelly Meml. Hosp. Served to lt. (j.g.) M.C., USN, 1954; with USMC, 1954. Menninger Sch. Psychiatry fellow, 1970. Mem. N.Y. Acad. Scis., Am. Acad. Gen. Practice, A.M.A., Am. Psychiat. Assn., Santa Clara-Monterey Counties Psychiat. Soc., Mercer County Med. Soc. (chmn. physician placement service com.), Navy League U.S., Internat. Platform Assn., Byzantine Fellowship, Pa. Soc., Assn. Mil. Surgeons U.S., UN Assn. U.S.A. (chpt. pres. 1966), Alumni Assn. Menninger Sch. Psychiatry, Nat. Hist. Soc., Hist. Soc. Hamilton Twp., Nat. Trust for Historic Preservation, Trent House Assn., Met. Mus. Art, Friends of Art Mus. Princeton U., Phi Alpha Sigma. Mem. Greek Orthodox Ch. (trustee 1962-64). Mason (32 deg., Shriner), Rotarian. Clubs: Architectoniki (Athens, Greece); Commd. Officers U.S. Naval Base (Phila.). Office: 476 Hamilton Ave Trenton NJ 08609

CHAPPLE, JOHN DONNELL, coll. adminstr.; b. Ashland, Wis., Nov. 14, 1933; s. John B. and Irene (McDonnell) C.; B.A., Northland Coll., 1955; M.A., Mich. State U., 1960; postgrad. Syracuse U.; m. Helen C. Schroeder; children—John, Jeanne, Joseph, Paul, Clare. Admissions counselor, asst. then asso. dir. admissions Franklin (Ind.) Coll., 1963-65; dir. admissions Clarkson Coll., Potsdam, N.Y., 1965-67, dir. admissions and fin. aid, 1967-68, vice provost, dean admissions, 1977—. Trustee, Village of Potsdam, 1977—, dep. mayor, 1978; mem. Potsdam Airport Commn., 1978. NDEA fellow, 1968-69. Mem. Airplane Owners and Pilots Assn., Nat. Assn. Coll. Admissions Counselors, Am. N.Y. State personnel and guidance assns. Democrat. Roman Catholic. Home: 60 Elm St Potsdam NY 13676 Office: Snell Hall Clarkson Coll Potsdam NY 13676

CHARITY, RAYMOND EMMITT, JR., assn. adminstr.; b. Newport News, Va., Apr. 10, 1948; s. Raymond Emmitt and Clara Mae (Price) C.; B.Arch., Hampton Inst., 1973; m. Linda Marciana Mercado, Sept. 28, 1973; children—Audra Nichelle, Tamia Meko. City planner dept. planning Newport News, Va., 1971-73, sr. city planner, 1973-75; dir. edn. programs Am. Inst. Architects, Washington, D.C., 1975—; sales asso. part-time Shannon & Luchs, Realtors, Washington, 1977-78; v.p. Property Restoration Assos., Inc., 1978—. Advisory council mem. Lemuel Penn Vocat. Center, Washington, 1977-78. Recipient IGLeaguer scholarship, 1966-67. Mem. Assembly of Nat. Arts Edn. Orgns. (del.); asso. mem. Smithsonian Inst., Am. Inst. Planners. Democrat. Baptist. Clubs: RCC Sideband Citizens Radio. Home: 3636 16th St NW B1114 Washington DC 20012 Office: 1735 New York Ave NW Washington DC 20006

CHARLES, EARLE VINCENT, JR., educator; b. Kingston, Pa., July 31, 1930; s. Earle Vincent and Thelma Charles (Evans) C.; B.S., Wilkes Coll., 1959; M.Ed., State U. N.Y. at Buffalo, 1963; m. Eva Lou Marks, Aug. 6, 1951; children—Sandra, Earle. Cost estimator Standard Pressed Steel Co., Phila., 1949-50; cost accountant Harrison Radiator Co., Lockport, N.Y., 1950-51; pub. accountant, Denver, 1951; tchr., head Dean Sch. Bus., Wyo. Sem., Kingston, Pa., 1952-60; tchr. bus. Kenmore-Town of Tonawanda (N.Y.) Pub. Schs. Certified tchr., certified curriculum cons., N.Y. Mem. Am. Vocat. Assn., N.Y. State Bus. Tchrs., Nat. Bus. Edn. Assn., N.Y. State United Tchrs., N.Y. State Occupational Edn. Assn., Kenmore Tchrs. Assn. Episcopalian. Clubs: Headmasters of Kenmore, Masons. Contbr. to bookkeeping and accounting syllabus, State of N.Y. Home: 174 Fries Rd Tonawanda NY 14150 Office: 350 Fries Rd Tonawanda NY 14150

CHARLES, HARRY KREWSON, JR., elec. engr.; b. Audubon, N.J., May 29, 1944; s. Harry Krewson and Laura Estelle (Engel) C.; B.S., Drexel U., 1967; Ph.D. (Univ. fellow), Johns Hopkins, 1972; m. Virginia Dorothy Wall, Mar. 28, 1970. Aerospace engring. trainee NASA Goddard Space Flight Center, Greenbelt, Md., 1964-67, aerospace engr., 1967-68; research asso. Johns Hopkins, 1972-73, engr. sr. staff, Applied Physics Lab., 1973—, instr. microwaves, evenings, 1970-71, teaching asst., 1971-72. Regional dir. annual fund raising campaign Drexel U., 1974-78. NDEA fellow, 1967-70, Mem. IEEE, Am. Phys. Soc., Tau Beta Pi, Eta Kappa Nu, Phi Kappa Phi. Contbr. articles to profl. jours. Home: 8259 Vosges Rd Baltimore MD 21207 Office: John Hopkins Rd Laurel MD 20810

CHARLTON, ALEX, obstetrician, gynecologist; b. N.Y.C., Feb. 21, 1912; s. Sidney and Rose (Lipkin) C.; B.Sc., N.Y. U., 1933; M.D., 1938; m. Alice Simon, June 13, 1939; children—Elinore, Valerie, Vickie. Intern Morrisania City Hosp., Bronx, 1939-41; resident L.I. Coll. Hosp., 1941-42, Morrisania City Hosp., 1942-43; practice medicine specializing in obstetrics and gynecology, Bronx, 1946—; asso. prof. obstetrics and gynecology Albert Einstein Coll. Medicine, 1955—; mem. staff Bronx-Lebanon Hosp. Center, Einstein Coll. Hosp. Served as capt., M.C., USAF, 1943-46; ETO. Fellow Am. Coll. Obstetrics and Gynecology, A.C.S., N.Y. Acad. Medicine; mem. AMA, Bronx County, N.Y. State med. assns, Phi Delta Epsilon. Office: 1770 Grand Concourse Bronx NY 10457

CHARLTON, JOHN WOOD, plant pathologist, artist; b. Bklyn., Dec. 11, 1897; s. John M. and E. Lazelle (Wood) C.; B.S., Coll. of Wooster, 1922; postgrad. N.Y. State Coll. Forestry, 1922-23; pvt. study art, oil and watercolor painting; m. Eloise B. Durham, Oct. 22, 1927; 1 dau., Margaret E. (Mrs. Norman Graves). Asst. dept. forest botany and pathology N.Y. State Coll. Forestry, 1922-23; prin. Brookfield (N.Y.) High Sch., 1923-26; agt. bur. plant industry Dept. Agr., Gloversville, N.Y., 1926-35; pathologist Bur. Entomology and Plant Quarantine, U.S. Dept. Agr., 1935-53; agriculturist U.S. Forest Service, 1953-60, pathologist, 1960-63; ret., 1963; exhibited in group shows including Gloversville Ann. Art Show, from 1965, Mansfield (Mass.) Ann. Art Show, 1965-68, Saratoga Springs Casino Show, 1966, Manchester (Vt.) Art Center, from 1966, Rockport (Mass.) Art Assn., 1970-72, various awards; represented in permanent collection Canajoharie (N.Y.) Art Gallery; Manchester Art Center, Paul Smith's Coll. Cons. forest pathology; pvt. art instr. Mem. Gloversville Civil Def. Commn., 1958-63; nat. adv. bd. Am. Security Council, 1970—. Served with U.S. Navy, 1918. Mem. A.A.A.S., Orgn. Profl. Employees Dept. Agr., Fulton County Hist. Soc., Rockport, So. Vt. art assns., Am. Legion. Republican. Episcopalian (warden 1964-65). Mason. Club: Pewter Collectors (Am.). Author manuals. Home: 147 Prospect Ave Gloversville NY 12078

CHARLTON, MAURICE HENRY, physician; b. Lutterworth, Eng., May 3, 1926; s. Henry James and Violet (Wood) C.; B.A., Oxford U., 1950, M.A., 1953; M.D., Columbia, 1958. Came to U.S., 1956, naturalized, 1961 Intern, U. Cal. Hosps., San Francisco, 1958-59; resident Neurol. Inst. N.Y., 1959-62; NIH fellow, 1962-63; practice medicine specializing in neurology N.Y.C., 1963—; asst. neurologist Neurol. Inst. Columbia-Presbyn. Med. Center, N.Y.C., 1963-67, asst. attending neurologist, 1967-72, dir. seizure clinic, 1965-72, chief neurology clinic, 1967-71; sr. asso. attending neurologist Strong Meml. Hosp., 1972—; neurologist N.J. Consultation Service for Neurol. Diseases, 1967-72; asst. in neurology Columbia, 1962-64, instr., 1964-67, asso., 1967-68, asst. prof., 1968-72, asso. prof. neurology, pediatrics U. Rochester, 1972—. Chmn. profl. adv. bd. Rochester chpt. Epilepsy Assn. Am.; adv. bd. Study in Greece, Inc., 1972-77. Served with Royal Navy, 1944-46. Diplomate in neurology Am. Bd. Psychiatry and Neurology. Fellow Am. Acad. Neurology; mem. Assn. for Research in Nervous and Mental Diseases, Eastern Assn. Electroencephalographers (sec.-treas. 1969), N.Y., Oxford U. med. socs., Acad. Aphasia, Am. Epilepsy Soc., Am. Assn. History Medicine, Am. Electroencephalograph Soc., Archaeol. Inst. Am., N.Y. Acad. Medicine. Author: Science at Oxford: in the Twentieth Century, 1955, Psychiatry and Ancient Medicine: in Historic Derivations of Modern Psychiatry, 1967. Editor: Myoclonic Seizures, 1974. Contbr. articles to profl. jours. Home: 84 Sandringham Rd Rochester NY 14610 Office: Box 673 601 Elmwood Rochester NY 14642

CHARPENTIER, DAVID LEO, engring. exec.; b. Central Falls, R.I., Mar. 13, 1931; s. Lionel Joseph and Louise (King) C.; Asso. degree Northeastern U., 1965; Mech. degree U. Conn., 1970; postgrad. in metallurgy Hartford State Tech. U., 1971-73; m. Tillie C. Marchand, May 10, 1953; children—Keith, Lisa. Engring. aide Tex. Instruments, 1954-65; nondestructive test engr. Pratt & Whitney Aircraft, 1965-70; sr. engr., quality control supr. United Nuclear Corp., 1970-75; quality control mgr. to pres. Metals Testing Co., South Windsor, Conn., 1975—; tchr. Hartford State Tech. U., Norwich State Tech. Coll. Head coach Pop Warner Football; scoutmaster Boy Scouts Am., 1969-73. Served with USAF and USNR, 1950-58. Decorated Purple Heart, Bronze Star; recipient certificate of achievement, Attleboro, Mass., 1964; registered profl. engr., Calif. Fellow Am. Soc. Nondestructive Testing; mem. Am. Soc. Quality Control, ASTM, Mountain Lakes Assn. Democrat. Roman Catholic. Club: Portland Golf. Home: 151 Hickory Circle Middletown CT 06457 Office: PO Box 213 South Windsor CT 06074

CHARVES, JAMES MONTEIRO, lawyer; b. West Bridgewater, Mass., Mar. 28, 1918; s. Joseph Charves and Mary (Monteiro) C.; J.D., Suffolk U., 1939; m. Alice Ruark, Feb. 23, 1946; children—Patricia, James, John. Admitted to Mass. bar, 1940; spl. agt. FBI, U.S. Dept. Justice, Seattle, 1946-48, San Francisco, 1948-51, N.Y.C., 1951-52, Boston, 1952-60; atty.-cons. to dir. pub. relations and corporate sec. Polaroid Corp., Cambridge, Mass., 1960-68; pvt. practice law, Arlington and Falmouth, Mass., 1968—; lawyer, investigator, cons. Smithsonian Astrophys. Lab., Cambridge, 1960, clock div. Gen. Electric Ashland, Mass., 1962, Brown Wales Steel Co., Cambridge, 1963. Served with AUS, 1942-46; PTO. Mem. Fed., Mass. bar assns., Internat. Chiefs of Police, Soc. Former Agts. of FBI, Am. Legion. Roman Catholic. Contbr. articles in field to profl. jours. Home: 11 Loop Rd Falmouth MA 02540

CHARYN, JEROME IRWIN, hosp. adminstr.; b. Bklyn., Mar. 6, 1947; s. Maurice Harold and Rose (Brenman) C.; B.B.A., Pace U. of N.Y., 1968, M.B.A., 1974. Adminstrv. resident State U. N.Y., Downstate Med. Center, 1968-69, evening adminstr., 1969-70; evening adminstr. Jewish Hosp. and Med. Center of Bklyn., 1970-71, adminstrv. asst., 1971-72, asst. hosp. dir., 1972—; asso. prof. health care adminstrn. St. Francis Coll., Bklyn., 1973—. Mem. Mill Basin Civic Assn., Bklyn., 1970—. Certified at master level by Hazard Control Mgr. Certification Bd., 1977. Mem. Am., Greater N.Y. hosp. assns., Kings County Med. Soc., Acad. Medicine Bklyn., Soc. for Computer Medicine, Am. Soc. Safety Engrs., Internat. Assn. for Hosp. Security, Hosp. Execs. Club. Author: Physicians Guide to Utilization Review, 1975-77; Establishing Quality Assurance Programs in N.Y.C. Voluntary Hospitals: A Realistic Approach, 1974; A Year at Newboro and Case Studies in Health Care Administration, 1975. Home: 1640 E 51st St Brooklyn NY 11234 Office: 555 Prospect Pl Brooklyn NY 11238

CHASAN, ALEXANDER ANSCHEL, chemist; b. Berne, Switzerland, Apr. 17, 1926; s. Boris and Liuba (Gorsky) C.; came to U.S., 1947, naturalized, 1953; M.S. in Chemistry, Fed. Inst. Tech., Zurich, Switzerland, 1947; m. Betty Louise Heymann, June 1, 1952; children—Alan Bryan, Elise Gail. Chief chemist Balt. Paint & Chem. Corp., 1950-67, J.M. Huber Corp., Havre de Grace, Md., 1967-70; pvt. practice coatings cons., Balt., 1970-71; specifications mgr. paints and coatings Fed. Supply Service, Gen. Services Adminstrn., Washington, 1971—. Fellow Am. Inst. Chemists; mem. AAAS, Steel Structures Painting Council, Am. Brush Mfrs. Assn., Am. Chem. Soc., Balt. Coatings Assn., Balt. Soc. Coatings Tech. (past pres., Washington Paint Tech. Group (Man of Year award 1977, dir., past pres.). Democrat. Jewish. Club: B'nai B'rith. Home: 2706 Summerson Rd Baltimore MD 21209 Office: Crystal Mall Bldg 4 Washington DC 20406

CHASE, ELIZABETH WAGNER JOHNSON (MRS. HAROLD F. CHASE), librarian; b. Susquehanna, Pa., Aug. 14, 1917; d. Charles Tingley and Marion Elizabeth (Dimock) Wagner; B.S., Phila. Coll. Pharmacy and Sci., 1939; M.S. in L.S., Drexel Inst., 1950; m. Elof Fritiof Johnson, Nov. 23, 1939 (dec. Sept. 1962); m. 2d. Harold F. Chase, Sept. 2, 1966. Librarian Phila. Coll. Pharmacy and Sci., 1946-63, 64—, acting dean women, 1946-62, instr. sci. lit., 1950-62; acquisition librarian Drexel Inst. Tech. Library, Phila., 1964-64; instr. library sci., Drexel Library Sch., 1959-62. Mem. Med. Library Assn., Am. Assn. Colls. Pharmacy, Am. Inst. History Pharmacy, Lambda Kappa Sigma. Republican. Episcopalian. Home: 1732 Old Gulph Rd Villanova PA 19085 Office: Joseph W England Library Phila Coll Pharmacy 42d St and Woodland Ave Philadelphia PA 19104

CHASE, KENNETH HUNTINGTON, mutual fund exec.; b. N.Y.C., July 17, 1944; s. Hollis H. and Beverly Huntington (Seaman) C.; A.B., U. Pa., 1966, LL.B., 1969; m. Jeanne-Nicole Ledoux, Feb. 14, 1971. Asst. sec. Am. Investors Fund, Inc., Greenwich, Conn., 1969-70; admitted to N.Y. bar, 1970; asst. sec. Am. Gen. Funds, 1971-77; asst. sec., asst. counsel Am. Gen. Capital Mgmt., Inc., 1972-77; sec., counsel The Res. Fund, Inc., N.Y.C., 1977—. Vice pres., trustee Bar Harbor Festival. Mem. Assn. Bar City N.Y. (com. art), S.R., Soc. Cin., Phila. Art Alliance, Soc. Colonial Wars, St. George's Soc., St. Nicholas Soc., Phi Kappa Psi (historian 1967-72). Republican. Mem. English Neighborhood Ref. Ch. (deacon, clk.). Clubs: Univ. Pennsylvania (bd. govs., v.p., sec.), Liederkranz, Conductors (sec., dir.) (N.Y.C.); Mendelssonn Glee (exec. com.). Home: 8200 Boulevard E North Bergen NJ 07047 Office: 810 7th Ave New York City NY 10019

CHASE, LUCIA, ballet dancer; b. Waterbury, Conn., Mar. 24, 1907; d. Irving Hail and Elizabeth Hosmer (Kellogg) C.; student St. Margaret's Sch., Waterbury, Theatre Guild Sch., N.Y.C.; m. Thomas Ewing, Jr., Dec. 28, 1926; children—Thomas III, Alexander Cochran. Ballerina Mordkin Ballet 1937-39; ballerina The Ballet Theatre, N.Y.C., 1940-60, co-dir., 1945—. Recipient 17th ann. Capezio Dance award, 1968. Home: 720 Park Ave New York City NY 10021 Office: Am Ballet Theatre 888 7th Ave New York City NY 10019*

CHASE, NORMAN BRADFORD, lumber co. exec.; b. Worcester, Mass., Jan. 25, 1924; s. Samuel Harold and Bessie Elizabeth (Bradford) C.; student Worcester Jr. Coll., 1946-47; m. Norma M. Liebmann, June 5, 1949; children—Susan P., Jonathan D., Lawrence A. Pres., owner Chase Industries, Ellington, Conn., 1950—, Brattleboro, Vt., 1970—. Trustee, Brooks Meml. Library, pres., 1974—; corporator Brattleboro Meml. Hosp., 1975—; trustee, mem.

exec. com. Windham Coll., Putney, Vt., 1977—; mem. Vt. Ho. of Reps., 1975—. Served with AUS, 1943-46. Mem. Am. Legion, Auto Club Vt. (v.p., trustee). Clubs: Mason, Shriner, Rotary. Home: Brookside Brattleboro VT 05301 Office: Corner Main St at High Brattleboro VT 05301

CHASE, ROBERT EDWARD, environ. engr.; b. Boston, Nov. 16, 1943; s. Clarence Ernest and Eleanor Waring (MacLeod) C.; B.C.E., Northeastern U., 1967, M.C.E., 1968; m. Gratia Ellen Smead, May 10, 1970; children—Andrew George, Robert Edward. San. engr. Dept. Interior, 1970; environ. engr. EPA, Boston, 1970-75; regional environ. officer U.S. Fed. Energy Adminstrn., Boston, 1975-77; environ. and energy specialist U.S. Dept. Energy, Boston, 1977—. Asst. dist. commr. Boston council Boy Scouts Am., 1952—; mem. Needham Town Meeting, 1972—, mem. Future Sch. Needs Com., 1974—, chmn., 1977—; mem. Needham Parent-Tchr. Club, Town Growth Policy Com., 1976. Served to capt. U.S. Army, 1968-70. USPHS fellow, 1967-68. Mem. Water Pollution Control Fedn., Soc. Am. Mil. Engrs., Needham Hist. Soc. (dir. 1977-79), Northeastern Alumni Assn., Marine Tech. Soc., Internat. Oceanographic Found., Chi Epsilon. Episcopalian. Clubs: Needham Scouter, Ch. Couples (dir.). Home: 74 Washington Ave Needham MA 02192 Office: 150 Causeway St Room 700 Boston MA 02114

CHASE, SAUL ALAN, artist; b. N.Y.C., Apr. 7, 1945; s. Kalman and Adele (Segal) C.; B.A., Coll. City N.Y., 1965; M.A., City U., 1968. One man shows A.C.A. Gallery, N.Y.C., 1971, 73, Andrew Crispo Gallery, N.Y.C., 1978; exhibited in group shows NAD ann., 1969, 72, 74, Am. Acad. Arts and Letters, 1971, 74, Butler Inst. Am. Art., 1972, 74; represented in permanent collections Bklyn. Mus. Art, Detroit Inst. Arts, Ga. Mus. Art, High Mus., Wichita State U. Mus. Art, Canton Art Inst., U. Wyo. Mus. Art; Cleve. Mus. Art, Joseph Hirschorn Collection, Washington. Recipient S.J. Wallace Truman prize NAD, 1969, 72, Salmatundi Club award Audubon Artists Soc., 1972, Julius Hallgarten prize, NAD, 1974, 77. Home: 148 Greene St New York City NY 10012

CHASEMAN, JOEL, broadcasting exec.; b. Trenton, N.J., Feb. 18, 1926; s. lM.H. and Eva (Pondfield) C.; A.B., Cornell U., 1948; m. Marlene Meyerson, Sept. 11, 1955; children—Martha Hope, Joanne Amy. Vice pres. gen. mgr. WBC Prodns., 1961-63, WINS, N.Y.C., 1964-66; pres. Group W Radio, 1967-70, sr. v.p. programming and prodn. radio-TV, 1970-73; pres. Group W Televison, 1973; pres. Post-Newsweek Stas., 1973—; v.p., dir. Washington Post Co., 1973—; Served with USNR, 1944-45. Home: 9908 Bluegrass Rd Potomac MD 20854 Office: 2139 Wisconsin Ave Washington DC 20007

CHASEN, LAWRENCE ISAAC, librarian; b. Phila., Sept. 20, 1924; s. Harris A. and Sarah (Goldstein) C.; A.B., Gratz Coll., Phila., 1943; m. Frankie Vivian Frank, Mar. 21, 1948; children—Jeffrey, John, Keith. Librarian, Phila. Army Signal Corps, 1942-47; adminstrv. officer U.S. Navy Ship's Service, U.S. Naval Base, Phila., 1947-49; chief librarian Vertol div. Boeing Corp., 1949-56; mgr. libraries Space and RESD div., Gen. Electric Co., Phila., 1956—; cons. in field. Lectr., instr. Israel and Abrabism, Main Line Reform Temple, Wynnewood, Pa., 1956—; engring. indexing cons. Chilton Pub. Co. Recipient 1 in a 1,000 award Gen. Electric Co., 1968. Mem. Spl. Libraries Assn., Franklin Inst., Am. Instr. Aeros. and Astronautics. Contbr. articles to profl. jours. Pioneer facsimile communications. Home: 238 Sherbrook Blvd Upper Darby PA 19082 Office: Space and RESD Div Gen Electric Co Library POB 8555 Philadelphia PA 19101

CHASEN, WILLIAM HENRY, physician; b. Augusta, Germany, May 31, 1907; s. Samuel and Leah (Adlerstein) C.; student U. So. Calif., 1926-28; M.D., U. Lausanne, Switzerland, 1937; L.H.D., New Eng. Law Sch., 1970; m. Mignon Charney, Apr. 10, 1942; children—Barbara Zita, Laura Ruth. Intern, Ft. Oglethorpe Gen. Hosp., 1938-39; gen. practice medicine, Lee, Mass., 1939-41; resident Bronx (N.Y.) VA Hosp., 1945-46; chief arthritis clinic Boston VA Hosp., 1947—, also mem. research and edn. com., chmn., 1970-73; asst. clin. prof. medicine Boston U., 1972—; moderator Ask the Doctor program Sta. WBZ, 1960-63; mem. Govs. Task Force on Aging, 1963; mem. Gov.'s Advisory Com. on State Hosps. Bd. dirs. Mass. Cancer Detection Clinic; mem. sci. advisory com. Arthritis Found; trustee Mass. Mental Health Center, 1969-75, New Eng. Arthritis Found., 1971—. Served to lt. col. AUS, 1941-46; col. Res. ret. Decorated Bronze Star, Army Commendation medal. Fellow N.Y. Acad. Scis., Am. Acad. Family Physicians (pres. Mass. chpt. 1953-54); mem. Assn. Mil. Surgeons U.S. (life). Am. Rheumatism Assn., Mass. Med. Soc., AMA Contbr. articles to profl. jours. Home: 9 Chauncy St Cambridge MA 02138 Office: 17 Court St Boston MA 02108

CHASMAN, HERBERT, coll. adminstr.; b. Bklyn., June 26, 1938; s. Al and Ceil (Goldstein) C.; B.A. in Econs., Coll. City N.Y., 1961; J.D., N.Y. U., 1965; m. Rosalind Axelrod, June 30, 1962; children—Marc Ira, Steven Seth. Admitted to N.Y. State bar, 1965, Pa. bar, 1976; practiced in N.Y.C., 1965-70; advanced underwriting cons. N.Y. Life & Home Life Ins. Co., N.Y.C., 1962-70; dean Sch. Advanced Career Studies, prof. taxation and estate planning Am. Coll., Bryn Mawr, Pa., 1970—; cons. tax and estate planning. Mem. Am., Pa. bar assns., Am. Soc. C.L.U.'s, Nat. Assn. Life Underwriters, Montgomery County Estate Planning Council, Assn. Advanced Life Underwriting, Nat. Assn. Estate Planning Councils (pres.). Author: (with Edwin H. White) Business Insurance, 4th edit., 1974; planner, editor: Deferred Compensation, 1978; also ins. handbooks. Address: 270 Bryn Mawr Ave Bryn Mawr PA 19010

CHASNOFF, JULIUS, internist; b. N.Y.C., July 25, 1902; s. Isaac and Pearl (Feinberg) C.; B.S., Coll. City N.Y., 1922; M.D., Cornell U., 1926; m. Nora Feder, July 18, 1933 (dec. Mar. 1962); children—Amy Helen Chasnoff Finkston, Paul Andrew; m. 2d, Julia Warsh, Dec. 30, 1968. Intern, Beth Israel Hosp., N.Y.C., 1926-29; Beth Israel Hosp. fellow, Städt. Krankenhaus am Urban, Berlin, 1929-30, Hospitant Medicine, Wenckebach Klinik, Vienna Austria, 1930; practice medicine specializing in internal medicine, N.Y.C., 1930-73; internist Comprehensive Health Service, Beth Israel Med. Center, N.Y.C., 1973-77, cons., 1971—; cons. medicine Met. Hosp., 1968—; emeritus attending physician Flower and Fifth Ave. Hosp., 1972—; vis. physician emeritus Bird S. Coler Hosp., 1969—; asso. prof. emeritus clin. medicine N.Y. Med. Coll., 1972—; lectr. medicine Mt. Sinai Sch. Medicine, 1971-77. Served to col. AUS, 1942-46. Diplomate Am. Bd. Internal Medicine. Fellow AMA, A.C.P., N.Y. Acad. Medicine; mem. Phi Beta Kappa, Alpha Omega Alpha, Omega Pi Alpha, Phi Delta Epsilon. Jewish. Contbr. articles to profl. jours. Home: 315 E 70th St New York City NY 10021

CHASTANET, DENIS VERNON PETER, ophthalmologist; b. St. Lucia, West Indies, May 31, 1926; s. Arthur L. and Iris (Monplaisir) C.; came to U.S., 1949, naturalized, 1970; B.S., Tufts U., 1949-52; M.D., U. Montpellier, 1959; postgrad. Harvard, 1961-62; m. Joan Culmo, Sept. 30, 1964; 1 son, Denis D.D. Intern, St. Luke's Hosp., New Bedford, Mass., 1960-61; resident Boston City Hosp., 1962-64, VA Hosp., Bronx, N.Y., 1966-67; practice medicine, specializing in ophthalmology, Milford, Conn., 1967—; mem. staff Milford Hosp. Diplomate Am. Bd. Ophthalmology. Mem. Am. Soc. Contemporary Ophthalmology, New Haven County Med. Assn., Conn. Med. Soc., Conn. Soc. Eye Physicians. Home: 18 Winter St Ansonia CT 06401

CHASTULIK, FRANK, air force officer; b. Washington, Pa., Sept. 9, 1943; s. Frank M. and Helen (Zdybicki) C.; B.S. in Secondary Edn., Pa. State U., 1965; M.S. in Secondary Edn. Guidance and Counseling, Central Mo. State U., 1970; postgrad. Ball State U., 1975—; m. Mary T. Dworzecki, July 3, 1965 (div. 1975); 1 dau., Tracy Lynn. Commd. 2d lt. U.S. Air Force, 1965, advanced through grades to capt., 1969; missile, dep. combat crew comdr., Whiteman AFB, Mo., 1966-72; drug and alcohol rehab. counselor, Vietnam, 1972, Korea, 1973, Germany, 1973-75; equal opportunity and treatment counselor, Ramstein AFB, Germany, 1975—; cons. to wing comdr. and civilian personnel office on equal opportunity and treatment; Lompoc community liaison, cons. for mil. and civilian drug and alcohol abuse rehab., 1970-72. Decorated Air Force Commendation medal with 3 oak leaf clusters. Mem. Am. Personnel and Guidance Assn., Assn. Humanistic Psychology. Democrat. Roman Catholic. Home: 8 Pine St Burgettstown PA 15021 Office: Box 2142 APO New York City NY 09009

CHASZAR, EDWARD, polit. scientist, educator; b. Hungary, Sept. 29, 1920; s. Ede and Ilona (Szonyi) C.; came to U.S., 1950, naturalized, 1956; A.B.S., Law Sch. Pazmany U., Budapest, Hungary, 1943; A.B., Western Res. U., 1954, M.A., 1958; Ph.D., George Washington U., 1972; m. Maja Hartmann, July 3, 1964; children—Andre, Julianna; 1 son by previous marriage, Ede. Dir. youth program Kossuth Found., N.Y.C., 1960-63; vis. scholar Sch. Sociology and Politics, Sao Paulo, Brazil, 1963-65; instr. George Washington U., 1966-69; asso. prof. polit. sci. Indiana U. Pa., 1969-73, prof., 1973—; NSF grantee, participant Engring. and Tech. Soc. workshop, 1972. Asso. pres. Hungarian Scouts Assn., 1958—; bd. dirs. Am. Hungarian Fedn., 1968-77. Served with Royal Hungarian Army, 1944-45. Recipient Teleki medal Hungarian Scouts Assn., Garfield, N.J., 1960, Rakoczy medal, 1975; Gold Arpad medal Hungarian Assn., Cleve., 1975; Internat. Devel. Found. fellow, 1963-65; Indiana U. Pa. travel grantee, 1970. Mem. Internat., Pa. polit. sci. assns., Internat. Studies Assn., Latin Am. Studies Assn., Am. Acad. Polit. and Social Sci., Arpad Acad., Conf. Latin Am. History, Pa. Edn. Assn., Assn. Pa. State Coll. and Univ. Faculties, Pi Sigma Alpha. Republican. Contbr. articles to profl. jours.; editorial bd. Studies for a New Central Europe, 1967-74. Home: 1147 School St Indiana PA 15701 Office: Keith Annex 107 Indiana U of Pa Indiana PA 15701

CHATMAN-ROYCE, EDGAR TRUITT, architect; b. Gloucester City, N.J., Sept. 3, 1924; s. Edgar T. Chatman and Gertrude (Hewett) R.; grad. Sch. Fine Arts U. Pa., 1958; m. Barbara Joan Royce, Dec. 24, 1955; children—Edgar T. Chatman III, Vivian M. Chatman (Mrs. Marc Fontainas), Robert C. Chatman-Royce, Mark E. Chatman-Royce. Bank clk., 1941-42; draftsman E. I. DuPont de Nemours, Inc., Wilmington, Del., 1947-51; draftsman-student H. E. Wagoner, Architect, Wallace & Warner, Architects, Phila., 1953-60; pvt. practice architecture, 1960—; lectr. AIA, 1966. Mem. Council Ednl. Facility Planners, 1966—; mem. Meml. Hosp. Chester County Fund Dr., 1967. Served to 1st lt. AUS. 1942-47, 51-53. Mem. Nat. Rifle Assn., Aircraft Owners and Pilots Assn., Exptl. Aircraft Assn., Soc. Am. Registered Architects (dir. Pa. council 1975—). Republican. Episcopalian (supt. Jr. High Sunday Sch. 1965-68, vestryman, lay reader). Home: Hobby Hill Highspire Rd Lyndell PA 19354

CHAUDHARY, BASUDEO, psychiatrist; b. Bihar, India, Jan. 2, 1930; s. Keso and Balchhari (Devi) C.; M.D., Patna U., India, 1957; m. Yvonne Lewis, May 12, 1965; children—Maria, Raj, Neil. Filaria control officer Govt. of Bihar (India), 1957-58; intern Lincoln Hosp., N.Y.C., 1958-59; gen. practice trainee Polyclinic Hosp., Cleve., 1959-61; indsl. health trainee Royal Inst. Pub. Health, London, 1962-63; resident in psychiatry U. Man. (Can.), 1964-67; fellow in social and community psychiatry Tufts U./Boston State Hosp., 1967-68; chief med. staff Ky. State Hosp., Danville, 1968-69; psychiatrist Pilgrim Psychiat. Center, West Brentwood, N.Y., 1970-73, dir. med. edn., 1974-75, dep. dir. clinic, 1976—; asst. clin. prof. State U. N.Y. at Stony Brook, 1975—; v.p. Cooley's Anemia Found., Suffolk County, 1976—; cons. in field. Diplomate Am. Bd. Psychiatry and Neurology. Mem. Brit. Med. Assn., Royal Coll. Psychiatry, Am. Psychiat. Assn., Am. Geriatric Assn., Med. Acad. Suffolk County. Hindu. Address: Box 79 West Brentwood NY 11717

CHAUNCEY, HOWARD HASKELL, dentist; b. Boston, May 25, 1927; s. Albert Bruce and Mollie (Brown) C.; B.S., Tufts U., 1949, D.M.D., 1961; M.A., Boston U., 1952, Ph.D., 1955; m. Elinor Lois Jacobs, Dec. 25, 1953; children—Peter I., Laura G., Louise A. Chief research in oral diseases VA Central Office, Washington, 1965-71; research prof. dept. oral pathology Tufts U. Dental Sch., Boston, 1964-74; asso. prof. dept. oral pathology Harvard Sch. Dental Medicine, Boston, 1974-75; staff VA Outpatient Clinic, St. Petersburg, Fla., 1971-74; asso. chief of staff research and devel. VA Outpatient Clinic, Boston, 1974-75; mem. rev. panel HEW, 1972-75; cons. U.S. Air Force Sch. Aerospace Medicine. Served with USAAC, 1945-46. NSF grantee, 1962-64. Fellow AAAS, Am. Coll. Dentists; mem. ADA, Internat. Assn. Dental Research, Soc. Exptl. Biology and Medicine, N.Y. Acad. Sci., Am. Soc. Cell Biology, AAAS, Am. Assn. Clin. Chemists, Sigma Xi, Omicron Kappa Upsilon. Contbr. articles in field to profl. jours. Home: 30 Falmouth Rd Wellesley Hills MA 02181 Office: VA Outpatient Clinic 17 Court St Boston MA 02108

CHAVEZ, FELIX, artist, tchr.; b. Talavera, Peru, June 11, 1941; s. Gumercindo and Teofila (Gutierrez) C.; came to U.S., 1971; naturalized, 1977; Prof. of Arts, Nat. Sch. of Fine Arts, Lima, Peru, 1968; m. Yolanda Guadarrama, May 20, 1972; 1 child, Maru. Tchr. art history H.H. Lehman Coll. of U. City N.Y., 1977—; one man shows, N.Y.C., 1972, 73, 75; groups shows include 17, N.Y.C.; represented 1968-68; permanent collections numerous museums and galleries in U.S., also numerous pvt. collections. Recipient 1st prize and gold medal from Nat. Sch. Fine Arts, Peru, 1969; Auguston-Wiese prize, Lima, 1970. Roman Catholic. Address: 34-59 89th St Apt 2-E Jackson Heights NY 11372

CHAVEZ, ISMAEL RUPERTO, community relations officer; b. Havana, Cuba, Mar. 27, 1944; s. Eladio (stepfather) and Hilda Amores; came to U.S., 1964; student Havana Bus. Acad., 1958-59, Chandler Coll., 1959-60, So. Conn. State Coll., 1969. Vocat. counseling aide City of New Haven, 1964-67, employment counselor, neighborhood counselor, 1967-68; community relations officer Yale-New Haven Hosp., 1968-78; mem. mutual respect com., 1972-78; dir. Office Handicapped Services City of New Haven, 1978—; mem. U.S. Com. for Handicapped, 1967; chmn. pro tem. Conn. Coordinating Com. for Handicapped, 1975-76; lectr. on archtl. barriers and handicapped services Yale U., 1971, Quinnipiac Coll., 1971; del. White House Conf. on Handicapped, 1977; mem. exec. com. Conn. Gov.'s Com. to Employ the Handicapped, 1970—; chmn. Junta Health Task Com., New Haven, 1973-76; mem. Mayor's Com. on Handicapped, New Haven, 1976; Bd. dirs. P.R. Paralegia Found., 1964-67, So. Conn. Regional Emergency Med. System, 1971-76, So. Conn. Comprehensive Health Planning, 1973-76; Spinal Cord Fund. Recipient Easter Seal Achievement award, 1975, Stanley Berwald award, 1974, Jefferson award, 1978. Mem. Am. Hosp. Assn., Nat. Rehab. Assn., Internat. Soc. for Disabled, Am. Pub. Health Assn., Nat. Orgn. for Handicapped, Easter Seal Soc. for Handicapped, Paralyzed Vets. Am. (hon.), Nat. Hosp. Helping Hands (hon.), Muscular Dystrophy Assn. Roman Catholic. Home: 183 Sherman Ave New Haven CT 06511 Office: Yale New Haven Hospital ERS-PCC 789 Howard Ave New Haven CT 06504

CHAVIANO, HUGO OSVALDO, dentist; b. Cienfuegos las Vilas, Cuba, Jan. 27, 1923; s. Bienvenido L. and Ada H. (Obeso) C.; came to U.S., 1970, naturalized, 1976; B.A., B.S., Inst. de Segunda Ensenanza, Cuba, 1940; D.D.S., U. Havanna, 1944; D.D.S., State U. N.Y. at Buffalo, 1974; m. Theresa Damien, Dec. 12, 1948; children—Ana T., Hugo M., Rosa M. Instr., U. Havana, 1945-48, asst. prof. dentistry, 1948-58, prof., 1960-65, head dept. prosthodontics, 1965-67; vis. prof. U. de Oriente, Cuba, 1965-66; practice gen. dentistry, Havana, Cuba, 1945-68, Elizabeth, N.J., 1975—. Licensed dentist, Cuba, N.Y. and NE Regional Bd. Mem. Radio Club Cuba, Astron. Soc. Cuba, Colegio Estomatologico Nacional, Colegio Estomatologico de La Habana, Cuban, Havana dental socs., Union County (N.J.) Dental Soc. Roman Catholic. Contbr. articles to dental jours. Home: 880 Salem Ave Hillside NJ 07205 Office: 520 Westfield Ave Elizabeth NJ 07208

CHEATHAM, HENRY PLUMMER, III, consumer product mfg. co. exec.; b. Phila., Dec. 1, 1942; s. Henry Bernard and Naomi C.; B.S., U. Pa., 1965, M.B.A., 1969; m. Carole Marie Miceli, Aug. 12, 1977. Asst. product mgr. Colgate-Palmolive Co., N.Y.C., 1969-71, product mgr., 1971-73, export advt. promotion mgr., 1973-74, U.S. export mgr., 1974—. Served to Capt. AUS, 1965-67. Club: St. Bartholomew Community. Home: 1601 3d Ave New York NY 10028 Office: 300 Park Ave New York NY 10022

CHECKE, ROGER AMEDEO, librarian, library adminstr.; b. Hackensack, N.J., May 10, 1944; s. Amedeo and Frances Beatrice (Currao) C.; B.A., Ithaca Coll., 1966; M.A., L.I. U., 1967, M.S. (Univ. scholar), 1974; postgrad. Bowling Green State U., 1967-71; m. Rosemary Andexler, Mar. 22, 1969; children—Joseph Roger, Steven Michael. Teaching fellow Bowling Green State U., 1967-71; reference librarian Thrall Pub. Library, Middletown, N.Y., 1974; library dir. Hackettstown (N.J.) Free Pub. Library, 1974—. Mem. Morris Regional Film Library adv. bd. N.J. State Library Incentive grantee, 1975, 77. Mem. ALA, N.J., Warren County library assns., Hackettstown Local Cable TV Town Com. Reviewer Learning Today, 1976, 77; creator audiovisual collection and film distbn. center children's activity program, also planner library addition at Hackettstown Free Pub. Library, 1974—. Home: 125 Road B Hackettstown NJ 07840 Office: Hackettstown Free Pub Library Church St Hackettstown NJ 07840

CHELLAND, ORPHIA CYNTHIA, psychologist; b. Old Forge, Pa.; d. Michael and Clementine M. (Comita) C.; B.Sc., Marywood Coll.; M.Ed., Temple U., 1959; Ph.D., Heed U., 1973. Tchr., counselor, pub. schs., Cornwells Heights, Pa.; dir., psychologist Home and Sch. Guidance Center, Boothwyn, Pa., 1967-73; supr. pupil services and spl. edn. Springfield (Pa.) Sch. Dist., 1973—; instr. Parent Effectiveness Training, 1971—; lectr. in field. Mem. Am. Personnel and Guidance Assn., Internat. Platform Assn., Council for Exceptional Children, Am. Assn. Sch. Adminstrs., Nat. Assn. Sch. Psychologists, Alpha Delta Kappa. Contbr. articles in field to profl. jours.; contributing author: Development Program for Kindergarten, 1976. Home: 501 N Providence Rd Media PA 19063

CHELSTROM, MARILYN ANN, ednl. inst. exec.; b. Mpls., Dec. 5; d. Arthur Rudolph and Signe (Johnson) Chelstrom; B.A., U. Minn., 1950. Staff asst. Mpls. Citizens Com. Pub. Edn., 1950-57; coordinator, policies and procedures Lithium Corp. Am., Inc., Mpls., N.Y.C., 1957-62; exec. dir. The Robert A. Taft Inst. Govt., N.Y.C., 1962—, exec. v.p., 1977-78, pres., 1978—. Active League Women Voters, Mpls., 1950-60; charter mem. Citizens League Greater Mpls., 1952-60; del. White House Conf. on Edn., 1955. Vice chmn. Minn. Women for Humphrey, 1954. Recipient Certificate of Recognition for Service to Mpls. Pub. Schs., Mpls. Citizens Com., 1957; named Town Topper, Mpls. Star, 1958. Mem. Am. Polit. Assn., Minn. Alumni Assn. (nat. bd. dirs. 1970-74, sec. N.Y. 1963-69, V.P. 1969-71, pres. 1971-73), Nat. Council for Social Studies. Lutheran (treas. councilman). Clubs: Marco Polo (N.Y.C.); Minn. Alumni (Mpls.). Home: 155 E 38th St New York City NY 10016 Office: The Robert A Taft Inst Govt 420 Lexington Ave New York City NY 10017

CHEN, CHIA TING, indsl. hygienist, chemist, govt. ofcl.; b. Amoy, China, Dec. 22, 1935; s. Shih J. and Chi C. (Lee) C.; came to U.S., 1960, naturalized, 1973; B.S. in Chemistry, Taiwan Normal U., 1956; M.S. in Phys. Chemistry, Lehigh U., Bethlehem, Pa., 1965; Ph.D. in Phys. and Analytical Chemistry, U. Houston, 1970; M.P.H., U. Tex., 1973; m. Claudia Alice Bunn, Sept. 10, 1965; children—Loren Yung Hua, Shana Yi Hsiu, Ming Chao Ying. Instr. physics and chemistry Chungyuan Inst. Tech., Taiwan, 1956-58; tchr. math. Chung Hwa High Sch., Muar, Johore, Malaysia, 1960; teaching, research asst. dept. chemistry U. Kans., Lawrence, 1960-61, Lehigh U., 1961-65, U. Houston, 1965-71; vis. scientist L.B. Johnson Spacecraft Center, NASA, Houston, 1972-73; prin. investigator epidemiology and suspended particulate size distbn. Sch. Pub. Health U. Tex., Houston, 1971-73; indsl. hygienist Houston area office Occupational Safety and Health Adminstrn., U.S. Dept. Labor, 1973-74, Directorate of Health Standards Program, Washington, 1974-77, Washington area office, 1977-78, Directorate of Tech. Support, Washington, 1978—; cons. in field; mem. com. on evaluation indsl. hazards NRC, 1975—. Trustee, Potomac Chinese Sch., 1977-78, tchr., 1978—. AEC fellow, 1967-71; NSF scholar, 1970. Mem. Am. Chem. Soc., Am. Phys. Soc., Am. Soc. Mass Spectrometry, Mid-Atlantic States Chinese Med. and Health Assn., Am. Indsl. Hygienist Assn., Am. Conf. Govtl. and Indsl. Hygienists. Buddhist. Contbr. articles to profl. jours. Home: 11616 Flints Grove Ln Gaithersburg MD 20760 Office: Dept Labor Occupational Safety and Health Adminstrn 200 Constitution Ave NW Washington DC 20210

CHEN, CHUAN YUAN, civil engr.; b. Taiwan, Republic of China, Aug. 18, 1936; s. Chia Tsai and Yen (Huang) C.; came to U.S., 1962, naturalized, 1972; B.S. in Civil Engring., Nat. Taiwan U., 1959; M.S. in Civil Engring., W.Va. U., 1964; Ph.D., U. Pitts., 1976; m. Huei Ling Tsung, Sept. 11, 1964; children—Audrey, Patricia. Jr. engr. Taiwan Pub. Works, Taipei, 1961-62; highway, materials engr. Md. State Roads Commn., Brooklandville, 1964-67; successively soils engr., sr. soils engr., chief soils engr. Michael Baker, Jr., Inc., Beaver, Pa., 1967-77, engring. mgr. geotechnical, 1977—; lectr. in civil engring. Geneva Coll., Beaver Falls, Pa. Served with Chinese Marine Corps, 1959-61. Licensed profl. engr., Pa. Mem. ASCE, Transp. Research Bd., Nat. Research Council, Internat. Soc. Soil Mechanics and Found. Engring. Contbr. articles in field to tech. jours. Office: 4301 Dutch Ridge Rd Beaver PA 15009

CHEN, CHUNG-HO, biochemist; b. Kaohsiung, Taiwan, Dec. 1, 1937; s. Chien-Yu and She-Shia (Liu) C.; came to U.S., 1964, naturalized, 1974; B.S., Chung-Hsing U., 1962; Ph.D., Okla. State U., 1969; m. Sumi Chiong-ying Lin, Sept. 11, 1965; children—Annette, Valentina, Connie, Elliott. Faculty, Johns Hopkins Med. Sch., Balt., 1973—. Served to 2d lt. Chinese Air Force, 1962-63. Recipient Myers award, 1975; Nat. Eye Inst. grantee, 1975—, Am. Diabetes Assn.

grantee, 1975—. Mem. Am. Chem. Soc., AAAS, N.Y. Acad. Scis., Assn. Research in Vision and Ophthalmology, Assn. Clin. Scientists, Sigma Xi. Democrat. Presbyterian. Contbr. articles to profl. jours. Address: Johns Hopkins Med Sch 601 N Broadway Baltimore MD 21205

CHEN, CONCORDIA CHAO, mathematician; b. Peiping, China; d. Chun-fu and Kwie Hwa (Wong) Chao; B.A. in Bus. Adminstrn., Nat. Taiwan U., 1954; M.S. in Math., Marquette U., 1958; postgrad. Purdue U., 1958-60, Mass. Inst. Tech., 1961-62; m. Chin Chen, July 2, 1960; children—Marie Hui-mei, Albert Chao. Came to U.S., 1955, naturalized, 1969. Teaching asst. Purdue U., Lafayette, Ind., 1958-60; system analysis engr. electronic data processing div. Mpls.-Honeywell, Newton Highlands, Mass., 1960-63; mgmt. planning asst. Lederle Labs., Am. Cyanamid Co., Pearl River, N.Y., 1964, computer applications specialist, 1967, ops. analyst, 1967; staff programmer IBM, Sterling Forest, N.Y., 1968-73, adv. programmer Data Processing Mktg. Group, Poughkeepsie, 1973—. Mem. Am. Math. Soc., Soc. Indsl. and Applied Maths. Home: Mountain Pass Rd Box 107 RD 6 Hopewell Junction NY 12533 Office: IBM Data Processing Mktg Group Route 55 Poughkeepsie NY 12602

CHEN, EDWARD WEI-I, lawyer; b. Soochow, Kiangsu, China, Jan. 16, 1932; s. Chester T. and Maria C. (Chen) Kiang; came to U.S., 1964, naturalized, 1975; LL.B., Nat. Taiwan U., 1955; LL.M., Nat. Chengehi U., 1957; M.C.L., So. Meth. U., 1965; M.U.R.P., Va. Poly. Inst. and State U., 1967; m. Jean J. C. Chen, Jan. 26, 1956; children—Bessie B., Henry J., May J., Christopher J. Prin. planner Md. Nat. Capital Park and Planning Commn., 1968-70; dep. chief adminstrv. officer Prince George's County, Md., 1970-74, dep. dir. dept. program planning and econ. devel., 1974-77; admitted to D.C. bar, 1977; individual practice law, Washington, 1977—. Recipient Am. Jurisprudence award, 1964; County Achievement awards Nat. Assn. Counties, 1972, 73, 74; certificate of appreciation Prince George's County, 1974, 75. Mem. Am., Fed. bar assns., Bar Assn. D.C., Am. Inst. Planners, Am. Assn. Planning Ofcls., World Peace Through Law Center, Chengchi U. Alumni Assn. (pres. Washington Met. area chpt. 1976-78). Republican. Methodist. Home: 6464 Windermere Circle Rockville MD 20852 Office: Suite 910 1730 M St at Connecticut Ave NW Washington DC 20036

CHEN, HUNG TSUNG, educator; b. Taiwan, China, Aug. 23, 1935; s. Chin Piao and Tie T. (Cheng) C.; came to U.S., 1960, naturalized, 1972; B.S., Nat. Taiwan U., 1958; M.S., Poly. Inst. Bklyn., 1962, Ph.D., 1964; m. Vera Yuh Zong Chen, May 26, 1964; children—Andrew J.C., Carol. Asst., Chungyuan Inst. Tech., 1958-60; teaching, research fellow Poly. Inst. Bklyn., 1960-64; process engr. FMC Corp., 1964-66; asst. prof. N.J. Inst. Tech., 1966-70, asso. prof. chem. engring., 1970-75, prof., asst. chmn. dept., 1975—; cons. Brookhaven Nat. Lab., L.I., N.Y., 1967—, Formica Corp., 1969-70. Recipient awards NSF. Mem. Am. Inst. Chem. Engrs., Soc. Profl. Engrs., Sigma Xi, Omega Chi Epsilon. Author numerous articles. Home: 40 Tilton Dr Freehold NJ 07728 Office: 323 High St Newark NJ 07102

CHEN, JAMES CHING-YIH, physician; b. Taiwan, Oct. 12, 1939; s. Chun-Siang and Rai (Lui) C.; came to U.S., 1968, naturalized, 1976; M.D., Kaohsiung Med. Coll., Taiwan, 1967; m. Patricia P. Hsieh, July 5, 1968; children—Timothy, Carolyn E., Jennifer R. Intern, McKeesport (Pa.) Hosp., 1968-69; resident in obstetrics-gynecology Mercy Hosp., Pitts., 1969-72; mem. staff, vice-chmn. dept. obstetrics-gynecology Indiana (Pa.) Hosp., 1972—. Served with Chinese Army, 1967-68. Diplomate Am. Bd. Obstetrics and Gynecology. Fellow Am. Coll. Obstetricians and Gynecologists; mem. Pa., Indiana County med. socs. Presbyterian. Home: 141 Hamilton St Indiana PA 15701 Office: Ben Franklin Med Center Shelly Dr Indiana PA 15701

CHEN, JANE LEE, educator; b. Kweiyang, China, Aug. 6, 1940; d. Ching-Chieh and Alice Hsiang-Lien (Hsu) Lee; came to U.S., 1958, naturalized, 1967; B.A. cum laude, Radcliffe Coll., 1962; M.A., U. Calif. at Berkeley, 1964; Ph.D. (Woodrow Wilson fellow, Regent's fellow), UCLA, 1966; m. Wei Lai Chen, Aug. 8, 1964; children—Rei-Yun, Rayenne-Alice. Postdoctoral research fellow dept. bot. scis. UCLA, 1966-69; asst. prof. biology Calif. State U., San Jose, 1969-72, asso. prof., 1972—. Mem. AAAS, Am. Assn. Plant Physiologists, Assn. Women in Sci., Soc. Harvard Chemists, N.Y. Acad. Scis., Sigma Xi. Home: 13705 Wendover Rd Silver Spring MD 20904

CHEN, JEFFREY JUINN-IE, environ. engr.; b. Taipei, Taiwan, China, Oct. 21, 1938; s. Ping Pei and Shou (Chin) C.; came to U.S., 1963, naturalized, 1974; M.S., U. Ariz., 1967; Ph.D., Pa. State U., 1971; m. Joy Wen-Huei Yueh, Aug. 31, 1968; children—Melissa Chih-Penn, Patrick Chih-Pitt. Research engr. Infilco Inc., Tucson, 1965-66; project engr. Roy F. Weston, Inc., West Chester, Pa., 1970-72; devel. mgr. Dravo Corp., Pitts., 1972-76, prin. process engr., 1976—; faculty U. Pitts., part-time 1976. Pa. Health Research Inst. fellow, 1969-70; diplomate Am. Acad. Environ. Engrs; registered profl. engr., Pa. Mem. ASCE, Water Polution Control Fedn., Am. Water Works Assn., Internat. Assn. Water Research. Christian Ch. Patentee in field. Home: 102 Sunnyhill Dr Pittsburgh PA 15237 Office: 1 Oliver Plaza Pittsburgh PA 15222

CHEN, JOHN SHANG-LIEN, physician; b. Shanghai, China, Jan. 7, 1933; s. Thomas T. K. and Laura (Zee) C.; M.B.B.S., Nat. Med. Coll. Shanghai, 1956. Came to U.S. 1965. Intern, Lutheran Hosp., Bklyn.; resident Kings County Hosp. Center, Bklyn.; practice medicine, Bklyn., 1967-68; mem. faculty State U. N.Y., Downstate Med. Center, 1962, 67, Cornell U. Med. Coll., 1968-72; sr. med. officer Queen Mary Hosp., Queen Elizabeth Hosp., Hong Kong, 1963-65; vis. attending physician Kings County Hosp. Center, Bklyn., 1967-68; asst. attending physician Meml. Cancer Center, 1968-72; attending anesthesiologist No. Westchester Hosp. Pioneer anesthesiologist to Hong Kong from U.S.A., Am. Soc. Anesthesiologists, 1963. Diplomate Am. Bd. Anesthesiology. Fellow Am. Coll. Anesthesiologists; mem. Am. Soc. Anesthesiologists. Address: RFD 1 Brundage Ridge Rd Bedford NY 10506

CHEN, LIN, food co. exec.; b. Foochow, China, Jan. 7, 1915; s. Chi Kee and Nu Mei (Lin) C.; B.A., Nat. South-West Asso. U., Kunming, China, 1940; M.B.A., N.Y. U., 1948; m. Susie Cheng-Shun Fan, Feb. 12, 1948; 1 dau., Mimi. Came to U.S., 1945, naturalized, 1956. With Summit Import Corp., importer Oriental foods, 1948—, v.p., gen. mgr., 1957—; pres., gen. mgr. Kam Man Food Products, Inc., Kam Kuo Food Corp., China Royal Restaurant, Inc.; dir. Golden Pacific Nat. Bank (all N.Y.C.). Mem. Chinese C. of C. in N.Y.C. (v.p.). Home: 200 E Winston Dr Apt 1214 Cliffside Park NJ 07010 Office: 415-27 Greenwich St New York City NY 10013

CHEN, MIKE CHI-CHING, info. system engr.; b. Taipei, Taiwan, Feb. 5, 1947; s. Shen-Chu and Wei (Lee) C.; came to U.S., 1971; B.S., Nat. Tsing Hau U., Taiwan; M.S., Kans. State U., 1972, Ph.D. in Computer Sci., 1975; m. Hui-Ying Liu, Aug. 18, 1973; children—Kevin, Connie. Teaching asst. Tamkang Coll., Taipei, 1969-70; grad. teaching and research asst. Kans. State U., 1973-75; sr. programmer analyst Ford Aerospace & Communication Corp., Houston, 1975-77, also lectr. U. Houston, Clear Lake City, 1976-77; analyst computer application Gen. Electric Co., Beltsville, Md., 1977-78; mem. tech. staff, info. system engr. MITRE Corp., McLean, Va., 1978—. Mem. Assn. Computing Machinery. Home: 8403 Oak Stream Dr Laurel MD 20811 Office: 1820 Dolley Madison Blvd McLean VA 22102

CHEN, PAUL KUAN YAO, architect; b. Shanghai, China, Aug. 16, 1924; s. Kung Fang and Sung Yuen (Leung) C.; came to U.S., 1948, naturalized, 1954; B.Arch., St. Johns U., Shanghai, 1946; M.Arch., Cornell U., 1949; m. Rosa Lu Wang, Mar. 29, 1958. Designer, Jose Sert, Architect, N.Y.C., 1951; project architect Kelly & Gruzen, Architects, N.Y.C., 1953-59; partner Richard Kelly & Assos., N.Y.C., 1959-62; prin. Paul K.Y. Chen, Architect, N.Y.C., 1962—. Recipient Am. Heritage award John F. Kennedy Library, 1972. Mem. AIA, Illuminating Engring. Soc., Chinese Inst. Engrs., Alpha Lambda. Works include Chinese and Argentine fine arts pavilions at N.Y. World's Fair, 1964-65; Research and Rehab. Center for Mentally Retarded, N.Y.C.; infirmary, Agr. Lab., dormitory bldgs. Alfred Agr. and Tech. Coll., Zum Zum Restaurants (Bard award 1970), Web Offset Publ., Printing and Bindery Plant, Bklyn., Naval Aviation Mus., Naval Air Sta., Pensacola, Fla., Tavern-on-the-Green (Bard award 1978), Canterbury Towers, Worcester, Mass., Symphony Plaza Housing, Boston, Mott Chatham Office Bldg., N.Y.C., Ft. Lee (N.J.) Housing for Elderly, various Benihana restaurants. Home: 200 L Winston Dr Cliffside Park NJ 07010 Office: 1515 Broadway New York City NY 10036

CHEN, ROBERT SENSING, trade co. exec.; b. Canton, China, Oct. 9, 1942; s. Dan L. and Jan (Huan) C.; came to U.S., 1967, naturalized, 1974; B.S., Nat. Taiwan U., 1965; M.S., Ind. State U., 1971; m., Jan. 19, 1973; children—Winnie, Eugene. Bilingual social worker Hamilton Madison House, N.Y.C., 1971-75; instr. Chinese, N.Y. Chinese Sch., N.Y.C., 1971-72; pres. L.L. Trading Co., N.Y.C., 1976—. Bd. dirs. Chinatown Service Center Inc., N.Y.C., 1976—; membership chmn. Chinese-Am. Republican Club N.Y. State, 1976—; asst. to chmn. dept. social sci. edn. Ind. State U., 1970-71. Mem. Eastern Region Acad. and Profl. Assn. Chinese-Ams. Roman Catholic. Kiwanian. Home: 10 Confucius Plaza Apt 16A New York City NY 10002 Office: 345 W Broadway Ave New York City NY 10013

CHEN, STEPHEN SHAU-TSI, psychiatrist, physiologist; b. Tou-Nan, Taiwan, Aug. 18, 1934; s. R-Yeh and Pi-yu (Huang) C.; came to U.S., 1965, naturalized, 1975; M.D., Nat. Taiwan U., 1959; Ph.D. in Physiology, U. Wis., Madison, 1968; m. Clara Chin-chin Liu, Dec. 22, 1965; children—David, Timothy, Hubert. Staff physician Christian Clinic, Taipei, Taiwan, 1964-65; teaching asst. dept. physiology U. Wis., Madison, 1965-66, Wis. Heart Assn. fellow dept. physiology, 1966-68, instr. dept. physiology, 1969-71, asst. prof. dept. physiology, 1971-75; resident psychiatrist, dept. psychiatry and behavioral sci. State U. N.Y., Stony Brook, 1975-78; asst. prof. psychiatry U. Pitts., 1978—. Wis. Heart Assn. grantee, 1966-75; NIH grantee, 1974-75. Mem. Am. Physiol. Soc., Biophys. Soc., Am. Psychiat. Assn., AMA, Midwest Formosan Christian Found. (charter). Presbyterian. Contbr. articles in field to profl. jours. Office: Western Psychiat Inst and Clinic Pittsburgh PA 15261

CHEN, YUH CHING, mathematician, educator; b. nr. Fukien, China, May 20, 1930; s. Jin Lun and Ma (Lin) C.; came to U.S., 1962, naturalized, 1975; B.S., B.Ed., Taiwan Normal U., 1953; M.S., U. Ill., 1963; Ph.D., City U. N.Y., 1966; m. Jane Yung Huang, July 16, 1955; children—Shwu-ming, Yie-ming, Tse-ming. Tchr. schs. and colls., Taiwan, China, 1953-59, Singapore, 1959-60, Kampar Perak, Malaysia, 1960-61; asst. prof. mathematics U. Minn., Morris, 1964-65, Wesleyan U., Middletown, Conn., 1966-71; asso. prof. Fordham U., Bronx, N.Y., 1972—, chmn. dept., 1974—. Mem. AAUP, Am. Math. Soc., Sigma Xi. Home: 79 Chestnut Ave Park Ridge NJ 07656 Office: Math Dept Fordham U Bronx NY 10458

CHEN, YUNG CHUAN, chem. engr.; b. Hsinchu, Taiwan, Apr. 18, 1937; s. Chi Tsen and Chiao (Hsiao) C.; came to U.S., 1964, naturalized, 1972; B.S. (Su-chuan scholar), Nat. Taiwan U., 1960; M.S., Kans. State U., 1966; Ph.D., Northwestern U., 1975; m. Lily Litzu Lin, Feb. 18, 1962; children—Rose Jen-man, James Jen-chuan, Anthony Jenfong. Research engr. Union Indsl. Research Inst., Hsinchu, 1962-64; chem. engr. FMC Chem. Research and Devel. Center, Princeton, N.J., 1966-67; mech. engr. Fluor Pioneer, Inc., Chgo., 1973-74; research engr. Allis-Chalmers Corp., Milw., 1974-75; sr. cons. Gilbert/Commonwealth, Inc., Reading, Pa., 1975—; sr. cons. on coal conversion and utilization to industry Dept. Energy. Bd. dirs. Formosan Assn. Greater Phila., 1977—. Served with Chinese Army, 1960-61. Stauffer Chem. fellow, 1970; Standard Oil of Calif. fellow, 1971; registered profl. engr., Pa. Mem. Am. Inst. Chem. Engrs., Profl. Engrs. Soc., Sigma Xi. Contbr. articles to profl. jours. Home: 1102 Dogwood Dr Whitfield West Lawn PA 19609 Office: PO Box 1498 Reading PA 19603

CHEN-CHI, artist; b. Wusih, China, May 2, 1912; s. Shih-Pei Chen and Shih Tsai; ed. in China; m. Alice Zu-Min Huang, Oct. 5, 1962. Came to U.S., 1947, naturalized, 1964. First one man exhbn., Shanghai, China, 1940; tchr. art St. John's U., Shanghai, 1942-46; artist-in-residence, Ogden, Utah, 1967, Utah State U., Logan, 1971; one man exhbns. U.S. museums, art galleries including N.Y., Phila., Boston, Washington, Chgo., Denver, Dallas, N.Mex., Houston, Ft. Worth, San Antonio, Portland, Maine, New Orleans, LaJolla, Del., Mich., N.H., Vt., Fla., R.I., Ariz., Ohio, Seattle, San Francisco, Los Angeles, Utah, Allentown (Pa.) Art Mus.; group exhbns. Met. Art Mus., Cleve. Art Inst., Nat. Acad., N.Y.C., Butler Inst., Corcoran Gallery, Washington, Whitney Mus., Pa. Acad., Springfield (Mo.) Art Mus., Bklyn. Mus. others; painter series Am. city scenes, Collier's, Sports Illustrated, other publs.; prof. art Pa. State U., summers 1959, 60; represented in permanent collections numerous museums, univs., founds., corps. including Met. Mus. Art, N.A.D., Pa. Acad. Fine Arts, Butler Inst., Cleve. Inst., Smithsonian Instn., also pvt. collections. Jury selection and awards Nat. Acad. Design, Am. Watercolor Soc., Allied Artists, Audubon Artists, Pa. Acad., Conn. Acad., Del. Art Assn., N.J. Art Assn., N.J. Art Assn., Fort Worth Art Ct.; sole judge 6th, 12th ann. N.W. Coast Exhibit, Seattle, Pitts. Watercolor Soc., Butler Inst. Am. Art., Tex. Watercolor Soc., Calif. Watercolor West, Conn. Watercolor Soc., Montclair Art Mus., Alaska Statewide Competition in Watercolor, 1978, others. Recipient 50 awards, 21 gold silver, bronze medals Am. Watercolor Soc., Nat. Arts Club, Audubon Artists, Phila. Watercolor Club, Salmagundi Club, ann. watercolor exhbn. Nat. Arts Club, 1954; Adolh and Clara Obrig prize N.A.D., 1955, Spl. 1,000 award for watercolor of the year 88th Exhbn., Am. Watercolor Soc., 1955; 1st watercolor prize Butler Inst. Art, 1955, Chautauqua Art Assn., 1955; Gold Medal for watercolor 14th ann. Audubon Artists, 1956, gold medal of honor, watercolor, 1960; 1,500 grant Nat. Inst. Arts and Letters; gold medal honor, 47th ann. Allied Artists Am., 1960; John Singer Sargent Meml. award Springfield Art Mus.; Samuel Finley Breese Morse medal N.A.D., 1961; medal of honor Nat. Arts Club, 1966, gold medal of honor, watercolor, 1967; grand award with gold medal of honor Am. Watercolor Soc., 1966; Saltus gold medal N.A.D., 1969; High Winds medal Am. Watercolor Soc., 1974; 109th ann. Bicentennial gold medal Am. Watercolor Soc., 1976; Lena Newcastle Meml. award, 1977; 80th Anniversary Exhbn. medal Nat. Arts Club, 1978; Winslow Homer Meml. award, numerous others. Mem. Internat. Inst. Arts and Letters, N.A.D., Am. Watercolor Soc., Audubon Artists, Allied Artists, Nat. Arts Club (hon.; gov.). Clubs: Salmagundi, Dutch Treat, Century. Author: Watercolors by Chen Chi, 1942; Chen Chi Paintings, 1965; Two or Three Lines from Sketchbooks of Chen Chi, 1969; China from Sketchbooks of Chen Chi, 1974. Home: 23 Washington Sq N New York City NY 10011 Studio: 15 Gramercy Park New York City NY 10003

CHENEVEY, PAUL ROBERT, orch. condr., educator; b. Cleve., July 13, 1938; s. Clarence Sylvester and Stella Irene (Gruber) C.; B. Music Edn., Baldwin-Wallace Coll., 1960; M.Mus. (grad. fellow.) Eastman Sch. Music, 1962; D.M.A., U. Cin., 1976; m. Sandra Jean Helmacy, Aug. 11, 1962; children—Catherine Anne, Stephen Michael. Violist, Rochester Philharmonic Orch., 1962, Milw. Symphony Orch., 1962-65; string tchr. Wauwatosa and Milw. (Wis.) Pub. Schs., 1963-65; asst. prof. Westminister Coll., 1965—, condr., 1965—; faculty Youngstown State U., 1966-68; grad. teaching asst., condr. U. Cin., 1973-74; mus. dir., condr. Butler (Pa.) Symphony Orch., 1975—. J.S. Mack Found. grantee; Buehl Found. grantee. Mem. Am. Musicol. Assn., Am. Symphony Orch. League, Condrs. Guild, String Tchrs. Assn., Viola Research Soc., Phi Mu Alpha Sinfonia (life, gov. province 21), Pi Kappa Lambda. Author: Contemporary Metric Patterns. Composer various mus. compositions including Densities No. 3. Home: Route 2 Bear Tree New Wilmington PA 16142 Office: Music Dept Westminister Coll New Wilmington PA 16142

CHENEY, CHARLES BROOKER, obstetrician, gynecologist; b. New Haven, Mar. 2, 1912; s. Benjamin Austin and Lillian Clarke (Farrel) C.; B.A., Yale U., 1934, M.D., 1941; m. Frances Crandall Wheelock, July 26, 1947; children—Benjamin L., Charles C., Dexter W., Timothy W., Anne A. Intern in surgery, gynecology, obstetrics New Haven Hosp., 1941-42; resident in obstetrics and gynecology Grace-New Haven Community Hosp., New Haven, 1946-49; practice medicine specializing in obstetrics and gynecology, New Haven, 1949—; asst. chief of service Yale-New Haven Hosp., 1956-58, asst. asso. chief obstetrics and gynecology, 1970—; mem. staff Hosp. St. Raphael; instr. Yale Sch. Medicine, New Haven, 1947-49, clin. instr., 1949-52, asst. clin. prof., 1952-69, clin. asso. prof., 1969—; mem. Conn. Med. Examining Bd., 1964-76, pres., 1972-76. Bd. dirs. Planned Parenthood League Conn., chmn. med. com. Served to maj. M.C., AUS, 1942-46. Diplomate Am. Bd. Obstetrics and Gynecology. Fellow Am. Coll. Obstetricians and Gynecologists (founder 1952); mem. Conn. Soc. Am. Bd. Obstetricians and Gynecologists (pres. 1966), New Haven Obstet. Soc. (pres. 1969-70), New Haven (cabinet), New Haven County Med. Assn., New Eng. Obstet. and Gynecol. Soc., Conn. Med. Soc., AMA, Soc. Colonial Wars in State of Conn. (chmn. membership com., past gov.), Mil. Order Loyal Legion U.S., Phi Beta Kappa. Episcopalian (vestryman, lay reader). Clubs: Lawn (New Haven); Sanctum (Litchfield, Conn.). Home: 104 Huntington St New Haven CT 06511 Office: 111 Park St New Haven CT 06511

CHENG, CHENG-YIN, chemist, educator; b. Shinpu, Formosa, Jan. 29, 1930; s. Shu-Hsien and Hsi-Mei (Chen) C.; came to U.S., 1953, naturalized, 1965; B.S., Berea Coll., 1955; M.S., U. Ill., 1956, Ph.D., 1960; m. Hui-Tzu Lai, Sept. 16, 1972. Instr., Wilson Coll., Chambersburg, Pa., 1960-61; asst. prof. chemistry Shippensburg (Pa.) State Coll., 1961-63, asso. prof., 1963-65, prof., 1965; asso. prof. chemistry Ithaca (N.Y.) Coll., 1965-68; prof. analytical chemistry East Stroudsburg (Pa.) State Coll., 1968—, fgn. student adviser, 1971—. Fellow Am. Inst. Chemists; mem. Am. Chem. Soc., Am. Soc. Agronomy, AAUP, Sigma Xi. Research in analytical chemistry, environ. sci. Home: 400 Quentin Rd Stroudsburg PA 18360

CHENG, DAVID HONG, mech. engr., educator; b. I-Shing, China, Apr. 19, 1920; s. Tze Kuen and Tseng Sun (Sheng) C.; came to U.S. 1945, naturalized, 1956; M.S., U. Minn., 1947; Ph.D. (William Richmond Peters, Jr. fellow), Columbia U., 1950; m. Lorraine Hui-Lan Yang, Sept. 4, 1949; children—Kenneth, Gloria. Instr., Rutgers U., 1949-50; structural engr. Ammann & Whitney, N.Y.C., 1950-52; sr. engr. M.W. Kellogg Co., N.Y.C., 1952-55; lectr. Coll. City N.Y., 1955, asst. prof. civil engring., 1955-58, asso. prof., 1959-65, prof., 1966—, dir. grad. studies and exec. officer Ph.D. programs in engring., 1977—; cons. M.W. Kellogg Co., Inst. Def. Analyses, N.Y.C. Transp. Adminstrn., 1976—; hon. research fellow Harvard, 1967. Recipient 125th Anniversary medal Coll. City N.Y., 1973; Am. Soc. Engring. Edn.-NASA Faculty fellow, 1964-65. Mem. ASCE, ASME, Am. Soc. Engring. Edn., Chinese Inst. Engrs. (dir.), Sigma Xi, Tau Beta Pi (Outstanding Tchr. award 1972), Chi Epsilon, Phi Tau Phi. Author: Nuclei of Strain in the Semi-infinite Solid, 1961; Analysis of Piping Flexibility and Components, 1973. Home: 85 Sherman Ave Teaneck NJ 07666 Office: Coll City NY Convent at 139th St New York NY 10031

CHENG, HSUEH-CHING, physician; b. Taikang, Honan, China, Jan. 26, 1927; s. Chih-kuo and Noong (Hou) C.; came to U.S., 1961, naturalized, 1976; M.D., Nat. Def. Med. Center, Taipei, China, 1952; m. Meio Chien, May 19, 1956; children—Wen, Julie, Ken, Gene. Intern or equivalent tng. Buffalo Gen. Hosp., 1961-62; resident Passavant Meml. Hosp., Chgo., 1963-65; cons. physician Gardiner (Maine) Gen. Hosp., 1971—, Augusta (Maine) Mental Health Inst., 1972—; chief div. medicine Augusta State Hosp., 1971-72; chmn. dept. medicine Augusta Gen. Hosp., 1976-77, attending physician, 1972—. Served to maj., M.C., Chinese Nationalist Army, 1952-61. Fellow Royal Coll. Physicians Can.; mem. AMA, Am. Soc. Internal Medicine, Maine Med. Assn., Royal Coll. Physicians and Surgeons Can. Office: 6 Middle St Augusta ME 04330

CHENG, LUNG, mech. engr.; b. Shaohing, Chekiang, China, Mar. 13, 1920; s. Ren Ching and Chi Wan (Chen) C.; came to U.S., 1964, naturalized, 1972; B.M.E., Nat. Chekiang U., 1945; M.Engring., McGill U., 1961; Ph.D., U. Ill., 1969; m. Carol Dzwen-hua Dju, June 23, 1962; 1 dau., Lilie. Instr. mech. engring. Nat. Taiwan U., 1954-59; engr. Combustion Engring. Incorp., Montreal, Que., Can., 1962-64; asst. prof. mech. engring. Christian Bros. Coll., Memphis, 1969-70; supervisory mech. engr. U.S. Dept. Interior, Bur. Mines, Pitts., 1970—. Mem. ASME, AAAS. Contbr. articles to profl. publs. on nature, behavior of dusts, suppression methods. Home: 140 E Highland Dr McMurray PA 15317 Office: Bur Mines US Dept Interior 4800 Forbes Ave Pittsburgh PA 15213

CHENG, PAUL, JR., hosp. collections mgr.; b. N.Y.C., Jan. 29, 1949; s. Paul and So Har (Chu) C.; A.A., U. Hartford, 1969; B.S., St. John's U., 1977; postgrad. C.W. Post Coll.; m. Sharon Goon, Sept. 2, 1973; children—Christine Ann, Allison Rose. Research aide Travelers Research Center, Hartford, Conn., 1968-69; accountant Booth Meml. Med. Center, Queens, N.Y., 1971-74; adminstrv. dir. outpatient and emergency services Interboro Gen. Hosp., Bklyn., 1974-75; asst. mgr. credit and collections Albert Einstein Hosp., Bronx, N.Y., 1975—. Trustee, treas. Internat. Sch. of Parkway Village, N.Y.C. Notary pub., N.Y.; C.P.A. Served with AUS, 1969-71. Mem. Am. Hosp. Assn., Hosp. Fin. Mgmt. Assn., Am. Coll. Hosp. Adminstrs. (asso.), N.Y. Heart Assn., Pi Lambda Phi. Democrat. Presbyterian.

CHENG, TSUNG O., physician, educator; b. Shanghai, China, Mar. 30, 1925; s. Keith S. and Fanny (Wang) C.; B.S., St. John's U. (China), 1945; M.D., U. Pa., 1950, M.S., 1956; m. Marie Ellen Roe, June 18, 1955; children—Mark Dudley, Yvonne Joyce. Came to U.S., 1950, naturalized, 1960. Intern, St. Barnabas Hosp., Newark, 1950-51; resident Cook County Hosp., Chgo., 1952-55; fellow in cardiovascular disease George Washington U. Sch. Medicine, Dist. of Columbia Gen. Hosp., Washington, 1955-56; instr. cardiology Mass. Gen. Hosp., Boston, 1956-57; fellow cardiorespiratory physiology Johns Hopkins U. Sch. Medicine and Hosp., Balt., 1957-59; acad. medicine, specializing in cardiology, Washington, 1970—; asst. prof. medicine U. State N.Y., 1959-70; asso. prof. medicine George Washington U. Sch. Medicine, 1970-72, prof. medicine, 1972—; chief cardiology D.C. Gen. Hosp., Washington, 1971-72; dir. cardiac catheterization lab. George Washington U. Med. Center, Washington, 1972—; asst. physician Cardiac Clinic, Johns Hopkins Hosp., Balt., 1957-59, mem. staff cardiac catheterization lab., 1957-59; dir. cardiopulmonary lab. Bklyn. Hosp., 1959-66, co-chief Pediatric Cardiac Clinic, 1959-66, chief Adolescent Cardiac Clinic, 1961-66, attending physician Adult Cardiac Clinic, 1959-66; chief pediatric cardiac clinic Cumberland Hosp., Bklyn., 1963-66; asst. chief cardiology VA Hosp., Bklyn., 1966-69, chief Cardiovascular Lab., 1966-70; asst. vis. physician Kings County Hosp. Med. Center, Bklyn., 1964-70; attending physician Univ. Hosp., State U. N.Y., 1967-70; chief cardiology VA Hosp., Bklyn., 1969-70; co-chief cardiology George Washington U. Med. div. D.C. Gen. Hosp., 1970-71. Diplomate Nat. Bd. Med. Examiners. Fellow A.C.P., Am. Coll. Chest Physicians, Am. Coll. Cardiology, Am. Heart Assn. Council Clin. Cardiology, Internat. Coll. Angiology; mem. Am. Fedn. Clin. Research, Am. Heart Assn., Washington Heart Assn., A.A.A.S., D.C. Med. Soc., A.M.A. Contbr. numerous articles to sci., med. jours. Home: 7508 Cayuga Ave Bethesda MD 20034 Office: George Washington Univ Med Center 2150 Pennsylvania Ave NW Washington DC 20037

CHERIAN, EDWARD JOHN, research co. exec.; b. N.Y.C., July 10, 1935; s. Leon S. and Eliza H. C.; B.E.E., Rensselar Poly. Inst., 1958, M.S., 1963, Ph.D., 1966; student law Union U., Albany, N.Y., 1963. Sr. research asso. Logistics Mgmt. Inst., Washington, 1965-67; pres. Inst. for Resource Mgmt., Inc., Bethesda, Md., 1967-69; dir. corp. devel. Mech. Tech., Inc., Latham, N.Y., 1970-71; pres. Cherian & Assos., Inc., 1971—; pres., exec. dir. Inst. Research and Analysis, Washington, 1975-77. Pres. Townhouse Mgmt. Two, Inc., 1977—; mem. Rensselaer Poly. Inst. Patrons, 1976—. Ford Found. research fellow, 1964; hon. mem. faculty U.S. Army Logistics Mgmt. Center, 1966-67; cons. to Sec. of HEW, 1967, Def. Industry Adv. Council, 1966. Mem. AAAS, Am. Ednl. Research Assn., NEA, Inst. Mgmt. Sics., Tau Kappa Epsilon. Author: Automation and Health Care: an Overview of Systems Integration, 1967; Cost-Effectivness of Terminated Job Corps Careers, 1968; Five-Year Program Plan, 1971; A Guide to Follow Through, 1973; Specific Learnings Disabilities Program, 1976. Home: 612 G St SW Washington DC 20024 Office: 955 L Enfant Plaza SW Washington DC 20024

CHERNISH, WILLIAM NORMAN, govt. ofcl.; b. Darby, Pa., July 3, 1941; s. William Adam and Ellen Margaret (Scott) C.; B.M.E., Duke U., 1963; M.B.A., U. Pa., 1965; Ph.D., U. Pa., 1968. Research asso., lectr. Wharton Sch., 1965-69; staff asso. Rohm and Haas Co., Phila., 1969-70; asst. to labor counsel Dart Industries, Los Angeles, 1970-72; social sci. adviser Office Asst. Sec. Policy Eval. and Research, Labor Dept., Washington, 1972-73; exec. asst. to dep. adminstr. GSA, 1973-76; dep. dir. Office of Planning, Policy and Evaluation, 1976-77, dir., 1977—; asso. prof. Univ. Coll., U. Md., 1972—. Mem. Am. Compensation Assn., Indsl. Relations Research Assn., Am. Soc. Personnel Adminstrs. Presbyn. Clubs: City Tavern; Washington Area Sailing (commodore 1974). Author: Coalition Bargaining; (with A.J. Thieblot, Jr.) Racial Employment Policies of the Air Transport Industry, 1971. Home: 2355 Ashmead Pl NW Washington DC 20009 Office: General Sers Adminstrn Washington DC 20405

CHERNUCK, DOROTHY, theatre dir. and producer; b. N.Y.C.; d. William and Alice (Mulligan) Chernuck; B.A., magna cum laude, Coll. of Mt. St. Vincent (N.Y.C.); M.A., Catholic U. of Am.; student Columbia U. Artistic dir., producer Arena Theatre, Rochester, N.Y., 1950-56; dir., free lance Inst. for Advanced Studies in Theatre Arts, Houston, N.J., Conn., N.Y.C., 1956-66; artistic dir. Theatre East, Rochester, N.Y., 1966-67; producer, dir. Corning (N.Y.) Summer Theatre, 1953—; co-producer Kennebunkport (Maine) Playhouse; free lance dir., Balt., N.H., off-Broadway (including revival of Fashion and cabaret-musical Dear Piaf), Corning, N.Y., 1968—; dir.-producer prodns. touring major summer theatres, including 1776, No, No, Nannette, Irene, The Price, Sound of Music; dir. Plays for Living. Former instr. Trinity Coll., Washington; former asst. prof. Skidmore Coll., Saratoga Springs, N.Y., acting chmn. drama dept.; lectr. Hunter Coll., N.Y.C., 1965-66; summer workshop in acting State U. N.Y. Coll. at Geneseo. Mem. governing bd., past pres. Theatre Festival Assn. of N.Y. State, 1960—. Mem. Soc. Stage Directors and Choreographers (dir.), Actors Equity, Am. Theatre Assn., Speech Assn. of Am., Eastern States Theatre Assn.; Speech Assn. Eastern States, Inst. for Advanced Studies in Theatre Arts, Council Stock Theatres (dir.), Kappa Gamma Pi. Home: 220 E 52d St New York NY 10022 Office: Box 51 Corning NY 14830

CHERRY, DONALD STEWART, hockey coach; b. Kinston, Ont., Can., Feb. 5, 1934; s. Delmar John and Maude Louise (Palamountain) C.; m. Rosemarie Martini, Mar. 31, 1956; children—Cynthia, Timothy. Profl. hockey player, 16 years; coach Am. Hockey League, 3 years; now coach Boston Bruins; owner, operator, tchr. summer hockey sch. Recipient Coach of Yr. awards (3). Anglican. Office: Boston Bruins 150 Causeway St Boston MA 02114*

CHERRY, EDWARD ATWELL, educator; b. Columbus, Pa., Dec. 18, 1916; s. Pearley Cadwell and Anna Gertrude (Buchmann) C.; student N.Y. State Ranger Sch., 1937; student U. Buffalo, 1958; B.S., Syracuse U., 1959, M.S., 1961; Ph.D., U. Sarasota, 1971; m. Geneva M. Lookenhouse, May 20, 1938; children—Vickey Lee, David Edward. Asst. technician U.S. Forest Service, 1937-38; tree surgeon Davey Tree Experts, 1938; insp. Bell Aircraft, 1939-40; prodn. control and supr. quality control Gen. Motors Co., 1940-45; supt. Crooker-Carpenter-Skaer, 1945-47; owner, operator Starr Cafeteria/Hotel, 1947-67, E.A. Cherry Hardware Co. Inc., 1950-66, E. Atwell Cherry, Mgmt. Cons., 1966—; prof. mgmt. and econs. Jamestown (N.Y.) Community Coll., 1963—. Commr. Chautauqua Utility Dist., 1954-71; mem. Chautauqua County Republican com., 1958-62; chmn. Chautauqua Lake-Chadakoin River Watershed Dist., 1961-67; chmn. Little Hoover Commn. Chautauqua County, N.Y., 1971-72; cons. Mayor Lundene, City of Jamestown N.Y., 1971-72; receiver N.Y. State Supreme Ct.; trustee Chautauqua Instn.; bd. dirs. Chautauqua Regions, Inc., Chautauqua County YMCA. Found. Econ. Edn. fellow, 1968. Mem. Acad. Mgmt., N.Y. State Economist Assn. Methodist (trustee 1954-70). Mason (32 deg.). Club: Internat. Torch (Jamestown). Home: Box 405 Chautauqua NY 14722 Office: Jamestown Community Coll Jamestown NY 14701

CHERRY, PHILIP, fgn. service officer; b. Phila., Aug. 14, 1931; s. Harry and Betty (Tull) C.; B.S., Temple U., 1956; certificate The Hague (Netherlands) Acad. Internat. Law, 1958; LL.B., U. Pa., 1959; m. Barbara Ronelda Clay, June 3, 1961; children—William Clay, John Bradford, Bettina Marguerite, James Douglas. Asst. in statistics Temple U., Phila., 1955-56; fgn. service officer U.S. Dept. State, Rhodesia, 1962-64, Zanzibar, 1964, Kenya, 1964-67, Mauritius, 1969, New Delhi, India, 1971-74, Dacca, Bangladesh, 1974-77, Lagos, Nigeria, 1977—. Served with USN, 1949-53. Mem. Hague Acad., Temple U., U. Pa. Law alumni assns. Clubs: Hare Law Club (U. Pa.); New Delhi Golf; Parklands, Kenya, Salisbury, Rhodesia, Chelmsford, New Delhi and Dacca Sports Clubs; Met., Ikoyi (Lagos). Home: 9422 Locust Hill Rd Bethesda MD 20014 Office: Lagos Dept of State Washington DC 20520

CHERRY, SHELDON H., obstetrician, gynecologist; b. N.Y.C., Mar. 31, 1934; s. Nathan and Fannie (Kasofsky) C.; A.B., Columbia, 1954, M.D., 1958; m. Gloria Barry, Dec. 18, 1955; children—Sabrina, Dana, Pamela, Cara. Intern, Mt. Sinai Hosp., 1958-59; resident in obstetrics and gynecology Columbia Presbyn. Hosp., N.Y.C., 1959-62; practice medicine specializing in obstetrics and gynecology, N.Y.C., 1964—; med. faculty Columbia, 1964-69, Mt. Sinai Med. Sch., N.Y.C., 1969—; asso. prof. obstetrics and gynecology Mt. Sinai Sch. Medicine, 1969—. Served with USAF, 1962-64. Diplomate Am. Bd. Obstetrics and Gynecology. NIH research grantee, 1965-70. Mem. A.C.S., Am. Coll. Obstetricians and Gynecologists, N.Y. Obstet. Soc. Clubs: City Athletic, N.Y. Athletic. Author: Understanding Pregnancy and Childbirth, 1973; The Menopause Myth, 1976; For Women of All Ages, 1979. Contbr. articles to med. jours. Office: 1160 Park Ave New York City NY 10028

CHERTOFF, ALEX, dentist; b. Bayonne, N.J., Sept. 13, 1915; s. Meyer William and Fannie (Dishler) C.; student U. Mich., 1933-35; D.D.S., 1939; m. Mollie Soloway, Dec. 25, 1939; 1 dau., Frances C. Normane. Intern, Jersey City Med. Center, 1939-40; practice dentistry, Bayonne, 1940—; pres. Chertoff, Seidman, Cohen Herman & Normane; clin. asso. prof. Coll. Medicine and Dentistry of N.J., 1964—, mem. continuing edn. faculty; chief restorative dentistry Newark Beth Israel Med. Center; lectr., clinician Am. Dental Assn., Greater N.Y. Dental Meeting. Dir. Plus Ultra Corp., Bayonne. Mem. Mayor's Com. on Drug Abuse, 1968—. Fellow Acad. Gen. Dentistry, Royal Soc. Health, Am., Internat. colls. dentists; mem. ADA, N.J. State, Hudson County, Bayonne (pres. 1969) dental socs., Am. Assn. Dental Schs., Am. Soc. Preventive Dentistry, Am. Prosthodontic Soc., Internat. Assn. Dental Research, Fedn. Prosthetic Orgns., Acad. Operative Dentistry, Robert E. Gillis Dental Study Club (founder, adviser), Phi Eta Sigma, Phi Kappa Phi, Omicron Kappa Upsilon. Contbr. articles to profl. jours. Home: 711 Ave C Bayonne NJ 07002

CHERTOK, BURTON ZANE, mfg. co. exec.; b. Bklyn., Dec. 16, 1934; s. Max and Vivian (Shain) C.; B.S. in Mech. Engring., N.Y.U., 1955; m. Rena Cohen, May 20, 1954; children—Randi, Stephanie, Daniel, Kenneth. Engr., Brookhaven Nat. Lab., 1955-59; engr. Metall. Processing Corp., Syosset, N.Y., 1959-62, v.p. engring., dir., 1962-70, pres., 1970-71, pres. Burton Industries Inc., Aerotronics Inc., North Babylon, N.Y., 1971—. Mason. Patentee piping-fitting, solar heat collection device. Home: Lecluse Ln Huntington Bay NY 11743 Office: 243 Wyandanch Ave North Babylon NY 11704

CHESBRO, GEORGE WASHINGTON, former pub. welfare adminstr., cons.; b. Pennellville, N.Y., Feb. 22, 1909; s. George F. and Clara A. (Sutton) C.; A.B. magna cum laude, Syracuse U., 1931, M.A., 1933; postgrad. N.Y. Sch. Social Work (now div. Columbia U.), 1934-35; m. Maxine Sharpe, June 19, 1937; children—George C., Judith A. Caseworker, Syracuse (N.Y.) Dept. Pub. Welfare, 1933-35; exec. sec. Queen Anne's County (Md.) Welfare Bd., Centreville, 1936-37, Harford County (Md.) Welfare Bd., Belair, 1937-39, Prince George's County (Md.) Welfare Bd., Hyattsville, 1939-41; area dir. N.Y. Dept. Social Welfare, Rochester, 1945-54; dir. welfare field adminstrn., Albany, 1954-63, dep. commr. for welfare adminstrn., Albany, 1963-67; 1st dep. commr. N.Y. State Dept. Social Services, 1967-71; exec. dir. N.Y. State Bd. Social Welfare, 1971-73; mem. advisory com. to dean Sch. Social Welfare, State U. N.Y. at Albany. Bd. dirs. Gateway United Methodist Youth Center; bd. mgrs., trustee Albany United Meth. Soc.; mem. community advisory bd. Jr. League of Albany. Served to lt. col. USAAF, 1941-45; ETO. Decorated hon. officer Order Brit. Empire (Eng.); Croix de Guerre avec Etoile de Vermeil (France); recipient Conspicuous Service Cross, N.Y. State Div. Mil. and Naval Affairs, 1947. Fellow N.Y. Acad. Pub. Adminstrn., Am. Soc. Pub. Adminstrn.; mem. Nat. Assn. Social Workers, Acad. Certified Social Workers, Am. Pub. Welfare Assn., Res. Officers Assn. U.S., N.Y. State Assn. for Human Services, Am. Legion, Mil. Order World Wars, Scabbard and Blade, Phi Beta Kappa, Phi Kappa Phi, Alpha Kappa Delta, Kappa Phi Kappa, Pi Gamma Mu. Home: 23 Brockley Dr Delmar NY 12054

CHESBRO, JOHN SEVERANCE, army officer; b. Williamstown, Mass., June 21, 1931; s. James Alvin and Mildred (Wright) C.; student Williams Coll., 1949-50; B.S., U.S. Mil. Acad., 1954; M.S., U. Mich., 1962; m. Caroline Shepard Woodard, May 21, 1955; children—Nancy Lynn, John Severance, James Blakeslee. Commd. 2d lt. U.S. Army, 1954, advanced through grades to col., 1975; asst. prof. ordnance engring. U.S. Mil. Acad., West Point, N.Y., 1962-65; chief rev. and analysis div. Guided Missile Dept., Fort Sill, Okla., 1966-67; command and gen. staff coll., 1967-68; various assignments, 1968-76; Army War Coll., 1976; dir. research devel. and engring. U.S. Army Armaments Command, Rock Island, Ill., 1976-77; dir. systems evaluation office hdqrs. U.S. Army Armament Research and Devel. Command, Dover, N.J., 1977—. Decorated Legion of Merit, Bronze Star. Mem. Am. Def. Preparedness Assn. (chpt. pres. 1977-78), Assn. U.S. Army, Am. Inst. Aeros. and Astronautics. Home: Quarters 126 Picatinny Arsenal Dover NJ 07801 Office: HQ ARRADCOM Attention DRDAR-SE Dover NJ 07801

CHESNAKAS, JOSEPH LOUIS, electronic mfg. co. exec.; b. Goffstown, N.H., Jan. 14, 1929; s. Frank Joseph and Veronica Anne (Kasputis) C.; B.S., Northeastern U., 1962; M.S., Mass. Inst. Tech., 1963, Sc.D., 1965; m. Helen Rita Peterson, Aug. 28, 1954; children—Joseph Patrick, Christopher James. Tech. cons. in design of spacecraft and computers NASA, Washington, 1965-70; engring. mgr. Raytheon Co., Lexington, Mass., 1955-65, mgmt. cons., 1970-76; tech. editor Sanders Assos., Nashua, N.H., 1976—. Served with Signal Corps., U.S. Army, 1952-54. Decorated D.S.M. Fellow AAAS; mem. Am. Assn. for Arts and Scis., Am. Def. Preparedness Assn. (life), Am. Chem. Soc., Nat. Geog. Soc., Smithsonian Inst., Phi Beta Kappa. Republican. Designed computer for Apollo Moon Lander, 1964, electronics for Viking and Pioneer spacecraft. Home: 32 Danforth Rd Nashua NH 03060

CHESNUT, DOROTHY SILLIMAN, librarian; b. Harrell, Ark., Oct. 10, 1925; d. Walter Norman and Annie (Daniel) Silliman; student Limestone Coll., 1942-44; B.A. cum laude, Montclair State Coll., 1967; M.S. in L. S., Rutgers U., 1968; m. Robert W. Chesnut, Apr. 20, 1946; children—Robert N., Laurie A. Reference and young adult librarian Verona (N.J.) Pub. Library, 1958-68; reference librarian West Orange (N.J.) Pub. Library, 1968-70, part-time reference librarian, 1970—; ednl. media specialist West Essex High Sch., North Caldwell, N.J., 1970—; instr. library sci. Montclair State Coll., 1969—, Caldwell Coll., 1974—. Mem. N.J., Nat. edn. assns., N.J. Library Assn., Beta Phi Mu. Episcopalian. Home: 60 S Prospect St Verona NJ 07044 Office: West Essex High Sch W Greenbrook Rd Caldwell NJ 07006

CHESS, ABRAHAM PAUL, city ofcl., educator; b. N.Y.C., Dec. 10, 1909; s. Charles and Jeanette (Chess) C.; B.A., N.Y. U., 1931; LL.B., Rutgers U., 1934, J.D., 1970; M. Police Adminstrn., Coll. City N.Y., 1961; m. Janet M. Leblang, Apr. 11, 1948. Admitted to N.Y. bar, 1935; atty. Police Dept., N.Y.C., 1935-54, survey officer, 1954-62, dir. research, 1962-64, dir. Bur. of Audits and Accounts, 1966-69, 70-74, mem. civilian complaint rev. bd., 1966-69, 70-71, chmn., 1971-74; prin. legis. fin. analyst City Council, N.Y.C., 1964-66; asst. adminstr. fiscal EPA, N.Y.C., 1969-70; tchr. Evening Elementary Sch. System, N.Y.C., 1935-42; prin., 1942-45; lectr. police sci. and law Baruch Sch. Bus. and Pub. Adminstrn., City Coll. N.Y., 1963-67; lectr. criminal law and evidence N.Y. Inst. Tech., 1975. Mem. Municipal Assn. for Mgmt. and Adminstrn. (past pres.), N.Y. County Lawyers Assn., Am. Soc. for Pub. Adminstrn., Am. Acad. Profl. Law Enforcement, Acad. Police Sci. Contbr. articles in field to profl. jours. Home: 8 Peter Cooper Rd New York City NY 10010

CHESSON, MICHAEL BEDOUT, educator; b. Richmond, Va., Sept. 5, 1947; s. Wesley Earle and Virginia Winborne (Ramsey) C.; A.B. with high honors in History, Coll. William and Mary, 1969; postgrad. (Gilman fellow) Johns Hopkins U., 1972-73; Ph.D. in History (Grad. fellow), Harvard U., 1978; m. June 15, 1974. Clk., R.F. & P. R.R., Richmond, Va., 1966-69; park ranger-historian Colonial Nat. Hist. Park, Nat. Park Service, Yorktown and Jamestown, Va., 1969-70, 72, 73; teaching fellow Harvard U., 1975-78; asst. prof. history U. Mass., Boston, 1978—. Served to lt. (j.g.) USNR, 1969—. Mem. Am., So. hist. assns., Orgn. Am. Historians, Va. Hist. Soc., Naval Res. Assn., ACLU, Common Cause. Democrat. Author: Richmond After the War, 1965-1890, 1980.

CHESSON, THOMAS RICHARD, lawyer; b. East Orange, N.J., Sept. 4, 1939; s. William Dudley and Loretta Mary (Kain) C.; student Cornell U., 1957-58; B.A., Rutgers U., 1962, LL.B., 1967; m. Maureen R. O'Brien, May 20, 1978; children—Diane Denise, Linda Marlene. Admitted to N.J. bar, 1967, U.S. Supreme Ct. bar, 1975; asso. atty. Porzio Bromberg & Newman, Morristown, N.J., 1967-73, partner, 1973—; mem. Med.-Legal Coop. Commn., Morris County, 1969—. Chmn., Morris County Heart Assn., 1968-70; active gubernatorial campaigns. Served to capt. USAF, 1963-66. Mem. Am., N.J. (exec. com. civil procedure sect. 1977—), Morris County (chmn. calendar control com.) bar assns., N.Y. State, N.J. (trustee 1976—) assns. trial attys. Home: Farmhouse Ln Morristown NJ 07960 Office: 163 Madison Ave Morristown NJ 07960

CHESTON, T. STEPHEN, univ. adminstr.; b. Buffalo, July 2, 1941; s. Earl Arthur and Madeleine Louise (Smith) Chesnutt; A.B., Clark U., 1963; Ph.D., Georgetown U., 1972; m. Arleen Stewart, Sept. 2, 1967; children—Aric Cumberland, Thor Cumberland. Asst. dean Grad. Sch., Georgetown U., Washington, 1972-75, asso. dean, 1976—; pres. Inst. Inst. Social Sci. Study of Space, 1978—; cons. in field. Mem. dean's council Consortium of Univs. Washington, 1973—; mem. Council on Power from Space, 1977—; bd. dirs. L-5 Soc., 1975-76; mem. organizing com. Princeton U. Conf. on Space Mfg., 1977, 79. Bd. advisors Space Studies Inst., 1977—. Scholar-diplomat U.S. Dept. State, 1971. Mem. Univ. Space Research Assn. (vice chmn. bd. trustees 1978-79), Phi Alpha Theta. Editor: (with Bernard Loeffke) Aspects of Soviet Policy Toward Latin America, 1974; contbg. editor Handbook of Latin American Studies, 1973, 75. Contbr. book revs. to profl. publs. Office: Office of Dean Grad Sch Georgetown U Washington DC 20057

CHEVRAY, RENE, physicist; b. Paris, Feb. 6, 1937; s. Robert and Marie-Louise (Fracher) C.; came to U.S., 1962; B.S., U. Toulouse (France), 1962; Dipl. Ing. (French Govt. Highest scholar), Ecole Nationale Supérieure d'Electronique, d'Electrotechnique et d'Hydraulique de Toulouse, 1962; M.S. (Alliance Française of N.Y. fellow), U. Iowa, 1963, Ph.D., 1967; m. Keiko Uesawa, Aug. 9, 1964; children—Pierre-Yves Masaki, Veronique Mie. Product and mfg. engr. Centrifugal Pumps Worthington, Paris, 1963-64; research asso. Iowa Inst. Hydraulic Research, Iowa City, 1964-67; postdoctoral fellow, lectr. aeronautics Johns Hopkins U., 1967-69; asst. prof. State U. N.Y. at Stony Brook, 1969-72, asso. prof., 1972—; cons. physics of fluids and instrumentation; vis. prof. Japan Soc. for Promotion Sci., 1975; vis. prof., von. Humboldt fellow U. Karlsruhe, 1975-76. Fulbright scholar, 1962-63; NSF grantee, 1970-73, 1973—; Research Found. State U. N.Y. Faculty Research fellow, 1970-71. Mem. Internat. Assn. Hydraulic Research, Am. Phys. Soc., N.Y. Acad. Scis., Sigma Xi. Research and publs. on transport processes in fluids. Home: 26 Cliff Rd Port Jefferson NY 11777 Office: Dept Mechanics State U NY Stony Brook NY 11790

CHEW, JOHN CARROLLTON, mktg. cons.; b. Indpls., Sept. 6, 1923; s. Tobias Otterbein and Muriel (Brown) C.; B.S., Pa. State U., 1948; M.S., Akron (Ohio) U., 1968; postgrad. U. Tex., William and Mary Coll., U. Pa., Worcester Poly. Inst.; m. Clare McKellogg, June 18, 1949; children—Randall Elwin, Judith Carol, Carleton Blake. Research specialist Phelps Dodge Co., 1949, Gen. Electric Co., 1951-60; indsl. product planner B.F. Goodrich Co., 1960; tchr. Akron Pub. Schs., 1960-66; prof. math. Hudson Valley Community Coll., Troy, N.Y., 1966-70; high sch. prin., N.Y.C., 1970-72; propr. John C. Chew Assos., cons. mktg. research and product planning, Troy, 1972—; psychometrist state correctional instns., 1974-78. Served with USNR, 1942-46. NSF fellow, 1963-78. Mem. Engrs. Joint Council, Metall. Engrs. Assn., Am. Inst. Mining Engrs., Petroleum Engrs. Assn., NEA, Physics, Math., Chem. tchrs. assns. Baptist. Clubs: Elks. Masons. Author high sch. textbooks. Address: 147 Brunswick Rd Troy NY 12180

CHEW, MELVIN LEWIS, travel agt.; b. Millville, N.J., Feb. 6, 1933; s. Preston Joseph and Vera (Doughty) C.; student Goldey Beacom Coll., Wilmington, Del., 1951-53, evening sch. U. Pa., 1953-55; adopted children—Mark, David. Computer operator Pa. R.R., Phila., 1953-64, Sun Oil Co., Phila., 1964-67; site adminstr. Philco-Ford Willow Grove Hdqrs., 1967-70; pres., owner Welcome Aboard Vacation Center, Wilmington, Del., 1970—, Media, Pa., 1976—. Cubmaster Boy Scouts Am., 1966; judge of election 5th Ward Wilmington, 1964-67; mem. Big Bros. Sports Com.; chmn. Del. Valley Christian Service Brigade, 1957-62, Ch. League. Recipient award for service to youth Chapel of Four Chaplains. Mem. Am. Soc. Travel Agts., Phila. Travel Mgrs. Assn. Republican. Club: Rotary. Author: Travel, Transit and Kids, 1973. Home: 121 Chestnut Pkwy Wallingford PA 19086 Office: 1812 Marsh Rd Wilmington DE 19086

CHEW, PAUL ALBERT, museum dir.; b. Norristown, Pa., Apr. 22, 1925; s. William Hiltner and Gertrude Edith (Hollis) C.; B.A., U. Pitts., 1950, M.A., 1952; Ph.D. (fellow), U. Manchester (Eng.), 1957. Dir. Westmoreland County Mus. Art, Greensburg, Pa., 1957—; lectr. fine arts Greensburg campus U. Pitts., 1963—. Trustee So. Alleghenies Mus. Art, Loretto, Pa., 1975; sec. Woods-Marchand Found. Served with USNR, 1943-46. Mem. Am. Assn. Museums, Coll. Art Assn. Republican. Episcopalian. Club: Rotary. Author: Some Recent British Sculpture: A Critical Review, 1957; 250 Years of Art in Pennsylvania, 1959; work represented in permanent collection Westmoreland County Mus. Art; author numerous mus.

exhbn. catalogs. Home: 208 N Maple Ave Greensburg PA 15601 Office: 221 N Main St Greensburg PA 15601

CHEWNING, JUNE SPANGLER, govt. ofcl.; b. Atlanta, July 27, 1925; d. George McClannahan and Esther Miriam (Ward) Spangler; student S.W. La. Tech. Inst., 1942-43, McNeese Coll., 1945-47, La. State U., 1947-48; B.A., Am. U., 1950; m. Bernard Purcel Chewning, June 25, 1955; children—Bernard Peter, Pamela Anne. Edn. and tng. specialist USN, Washington, 1949-52; research analyst Library of Congress, Washington, 1952-63; fgn. research analyst Dept. Def., Washington, 1963-66; edn. and tng. analyst AEC, Germantown, Md., 1966-71, manpower analyst and program mgr. ERDA, 1971-77; manpower assessment program mgr. Dept. Energy, Washington, 1977—. Founder, Federally Employed Women, Inc., 1968, mem. nat. bd., 1969-70; mem. nat. bd. govs. Am. U., 1974-77, v.p., 1976-77; task force chmn. Fed. Interagy. Subcom. on Environ. Edn., 1975-77; mem. Fed. Interagy. Subcom. on Population Edn., 1977; deacon Nat. City Christian Ch. Recipient Superior Performance award Library of Congress, 1960, Spl. award for women's work ERDA, 1976. Mem. Am. Nuclear Soc., AAAS, Women's Equity Action League. Democrat. Disciple of Christ. Contbr. articles to profl. jours. Home: 3637 Appleton St NW Washington DC 20008 Office: Dept Energy Washington DC 20585

CHEY, WILLIAN Y., physician, educator; b. Ki Jang, Korea, Jan. 21, 1930; s. Kee Bok and Myungkwon (Lee) C.; M.D., Seoul (Korea) Nat. U., 1953; M.Sc., U. Pa., 1962, D.Sc., 1966; m. Fan K. Tang, May 21, 1959; children—William D., Donna C., Richard D., Laura H. Came to U.S., 1954. Intern. N.Y.C. Hosp., N.Y.C., 1954-55, resident, 1955-56; resident in pathology Mt. Sinai Hosp., N.Y.C., 1956-57; fellow Seton Hall Coll. Medicine and Dentistry, Jersey City, 1957-58; practice medicine, specializing in gastroenterology, Phila., 1967-71; attending physician Temple U. Med. Center, Phila.; research fellow Samuel S. Fels Research Inst. Temple U. Med. Center, 1959-60, research asso., 1961, instr. medicine, 1961, asso., 1963, asst. prof., 1965, asso. prof., 1968-71; prof. medicine U. Rochester Sch. Medicine, 1971—; attending physician, dir. Isaac Gordon Center for Gastrointestinal Genesee Hosp., 1971—; attending physician Strong Meml. Hosp., Rochester, 1971—. Mem. A.A.A.S., Am. Fedn. Clin. Research, Am. Gastroent. Assn., Am. Physiol. Soc., Am. Assn. Study Liver Disease, Am. Soc. for Gastrointestinal Endoscopy, Sigma Xi. Contbr. articles to profl. jours. and textbooks. Home: 18 Denonville Ridge Rochester NY 14625 Office: 224 Alexander St Rochester NY 14607

CHI, CHIA-DANN, banker; b. Nanking, China, Mar. 3, 1936; s. Lien and Far-Sen (Liu) C.; came to U.S., 1961, naturalized, 1973; B.S. in Agrl. Econs., Nat. Taiwan U., 1958; M.S. in Econs., U. Wis., 1964; m. Catarina Chen, Apr. 29, 1967; 1 son, Victor J. Economist, Thor Eckert & Co. Inc., N.Y.C., 1964; asst. treas. Asso. Maritime Industries Inc., N.Y.C., 1964-67; registered rep. Cohen, Simonson & Rea, Inc., N.Y.C., 1968-70; v.p., dir. research N.J. Bank N.A., Paterson, 1970—. Pres. Chinese Opera Club Am., 1972-75, bd. dirs., 1970—. Fellow Fin. Analysts Fedn.; mem. N.Y. Soc. Security Analysts, Inst. Chartered Fin. Analysts. Address: 10 Laurel Ct Verona NJ 07044

CHIANG, FU-PEN, mech. engr.; b. Checkiang, China, Oct. 10, 1936; s. Chien-Lo and Lien-Yin (Mao) C.; came to U.S., 1961, naturalized, 1973; B.S., Nat. Taiwan U., 1957; M.S., U. Fla., 1963, Ph.D., 1966; m. Charlotte Cheng-Yi Chen, June 1, 1963; children— Brian Feng-Li, Ted Feng-Nan, Michelle Hsiao-Lan. Civil engr. Mil. Constrn. Bur., Taiwan, China, 1958-59, Shihmen Dam Constrn. Commn., Taiwan, 1959-60; research asst. U. Fla., Gainesville, 1962-66; postdoctoral fellow Cath. U., Washington, 1966-67; asst. prof. dept. mechanics State U. N.Y. at Stony Brook, 1967-70, asso. prof., 1970-74, prof., 1974—; vis. prof. Swiss Fed. Inst. Tech., Lausanne, 1973-74; cons. U.S. Army Missile Command, U.S. Army Materials and Mechanics Research Center, U.S. Naval Ship Research and Devel. Center, Grumman Aerospace Corp., Polarizing Instruments Co., Stress Optic, Inc., Sampson Marine Design Enterprises of L.I., Inc., Poly. Inst. Bklyn., Princeton U. NSF grantee, 1968, 70, 76; faculty fellow and grantee-in-aid State U. N.Y. Research Found., 1968, 70, grantee-in-aid State U. N.Y. at Stony Brook Grad. Sch., 1968, 69, 75. Mem. Soc. Exptl. Stress Analysis (vice chmn. paper com. 1972-73), Soc. Photo-Instrumentation Engrs., AAAS, Am. Acad. Mechanics (founder mem.), Optical Soc. Am. Contbr. numerous articles to profl. jours. Home: 27 Cove Ln Port Jefferson NY 11777 Office: Dept Mech Engring State U NY Stony Brook NY 11794

CHIAO, WEILY FONG, materials scientist, biol. engr.; b. China, Sept. 26, 1921; s. Mon-ling and Chen-lian (Lee) C.; B.S., Nat. Northwestern Coll. Engring., 1943; M.S., Ill. Inst. Tech., 1958; Ph.D., Yale U., 1963, Sussex Coll. Tech., 1978; m. Lily S. Hsu, Sept. 19, 1952; children—Jane C., Ingrid C., Henry C. Shift engr., Iron and Steel Works, Chungking, 1943-47; asst. prof. Nat. Northwestern Coll. Engring., Sian, 1947-49; research fellow Ordnance Research Inst., Taipei, 1949-51; prof. Taipi Inst. Tech., 1951-56; research asso. Ill. Inst. Tech., Chgo., 1956-58; research engr. LaSalle Steel Co., Hammond, Ind., 1958-59; research asso. Yale U., 1959-63; sr. research scientist Climaz, Molybdenum Co., Ann Arbor, Mich., 1963-66; dir. research M & R Refractory Metals, Springfield, N.J., 1966-68; sr. scientist Army Materials and Mechanics Research Center, Watertown, Mass., 1968—. Founder (with son), dir. Belmont Acad. for Ideology, 1976; bd. dirs. Greater Boston Chinese Culture Assn., 1971-73; dir. fin. com. Greater Boston Chinese Bible Ch., 1969-72. Mem. Am. Soc. Metals, AAAS, Am. Soc. Physiology. Contbr. articles to profl. jours. Home: 399 Marsh St Belmont MA 02178 Office: Army Materials and Mechanics Research Center Watertown MA 02172

CHIARAMONTE, JOSEPH SALVATORE, physician; b. Bklyn., Mar. 30, 1938; s. Joseph I. and Concetta (Tuttolomondo) C.; B.S., L.I. U., 1960; M.D., U. Padua, Italy, 1965; m. Lucy Conte, Sept. 3, 1961; children—Joseph Vincent, Andrea Concetta. Intern, Bklyn.-Cumberland Med. Center, Bklyn., 1966; resident Brookdale Hosp. and Med. Center, 1967-68; fellow in allergy and clin. immunology L.I. Coll. Hosp., Bklyn., 1970-71; practice medicine specializing in allergy and clin. immunology, Bay Shore, N.Y., 1971—; mem. staffs Good Samaritan, Southside hosps.; asst. prof. clin. pediatrics Stony Brook U., N.Y.C., 1975—. Served to capt. USAF, 1969-70. Diplomate Am. Bd. Pediatrics, Am. Bd. Allergy and Immunology. Fellow Am. Assn. Certified Allergists, Am. Acad. Allergy, Am. Acad. Pediatrics, Am. Coll. Allergists; mem. AMA, Suffolk County, Nassau-Suffolk County med. socs., Nassau-Suffolk Allergy Soc., Suffolk County Pediatric Soc., N.Y. Trudeau Soc., Phi Sigma. Home: 12 Hollister Ln Islip NY 11751 Office: 649 Montauk Hwy Bay Shore NY 11706

CHIASSON, DONAT, archbishop; b. Paquetville, N.B., Can., Jan. 2, 1930. Ordained priest, Roman Catholic Ch., 1956; archbishop of Moncton (N.B.), 1972—. Address: PO Box 248 Moncton NB E1C 8K9 Canada

CHIAVACCI, HARDING ANTHONY (DENO), handicapped services adminstr.; b. Hughestown Boro, Pa., May 12, 1924; s. Leopoldo and Santina (Casseri) C.; B.S., West Chester State Coll., 1948; M.S., U. Scranton, 1973; postgrad. Bucknell U., 1951, Wilkes Coll., 1951, Bloomsburg State Coll., 1971; certificate in spl. edn. Marywood Coll., 1972, supr. for spl. edn. 1976; m. Vera Troback, Nov. 28, 1953; children—Anthony, Rosetta, John, Deno. Ins. adjuster Calvert Fire Ins. Co., Balt., 1953-58. United Security Ins. Co., Washington, 1958-66; supr. vocat. program, White Haven, Pa., 1966-68; vocat. supr. Luzerne Intermediate Unit 18, Kingston, Pa., 1968-73; adminstr. Intermediate. Care Facility Mental Retardation Unit, Clarks Summit, Pa., 1973—. Councilman Hughestown Boro Council, 1964; dir. civil def. Hughestown Boro, 1959—; pres. Hughestown Jr. Teeners Football, Baseball teams, 1976—. Served with inf. U.S. Army, 1943-45. Decorated Bronze Star with oak leaf cluster. Mem. Am. Assn. Mental Deficiency, Am. Personnel and Guidance Assn., Council for Exceptional Children, Am. Fedn. Musicians, Internat. Personnel Mgmt. Assn., VFW, Hughestown Sprots Club (founder 1967). Clubs: Elks, Sons Italy. Home: 25 Griffith St Hughestown PA 18640 Office: LCF/MR Unit Clarks Summit Hosp Clarks Summit PA 18411

CHIBURIS, EDWARD FRANK, geophysicist, educator; b. Omaha, July 31, 1933; s. Christopher Constantine and Emma Bessie (Vodicka) C.; B.S., Tex. A. and M. U., 1960, M.S., 1962; Ph.D., Oreg. State U., 1965; m. Ann Francis Kealey, Oct. 30, 1954; children—Edward, Catharine, Christopher, Stephen, Andrew. Research geophysicist Teledyne Geotech, Alexandria, Va., 1965-68; dir. research, 1968-69; asso. prof. U. Conn., Groton, 1969-77, asst. dir. Marine Scis. Inst., 1970-77; asst. dir. Weston (Mass.) Obs., 1977—; asso. prof. Boston Coll., 1977—. Served with USAF, 1952-55. Soc. Exploration Geophysicists scholar, 1962; NASA fellow, 1964. Mem. Seismol. Soc. Am., Am. Geophys. Union, Soc. Exploration Geophysicists, Sigma Xi, Tau Beta Pi. Home: 589 Concord Rd Sudbury MA 01776 Office: Weston Obs Weston MA 02193

CHICK, LESLIE STEVEN, retail specialist; b. Bklyn., Feb. 10, 1943; s. Albert L. and Florence (Cohen) C.; B.B.A., N.Y. U., 1964; m. Sheila Provost, Mar. 24, 1963; children—Evan, Austin. Mgr. systems and programming S.H. Kress Co., N.Y.C., 1969-71; advance systems specialist Singer Co., L.I., N.Y., 1971; sr. cons., retail specialist S.D. Leidesdorf & Co., N.Y.C., 1972-75; mgr., nat. dir. retail cons. services Touche Ross & Co., Newark, 1975—. Mem. Nat. Mass Retail Inst., Nat. Retail Mchts. Assn., Nat. Assn. Accountants. Club: K.P. Contbr. monthly column Discount Store News, 1978. Home: 94 Munsey Rd Emerson NJ 07630 Office: 111 Madison Ave Morristown NJ 07960

CHILCOTE, ROBERT HARRY, geographer; b. Bradford, Pa., Oct. 28, 1930; s. Dewey Warren and Caroline Freeman (Robbins) C.; B.S., Pa. State U., 1952, M.S., 1953; postgrad. Marshall U., 1957-62, U. Cin., 1962-63, U. Md., 1972-74; m. Lois Jean Barber, Nov. 14, 1953; children—Stephen B., David J., Susan C. Indsl. analyst, indsl. devel. dept. C.&O. Ry., Huntington, W.Va., 1955-64, sr. indsl. analyst, indsl. devel. dept., 1964-66; asst. dir. indsl. research C.&O./B.&O. Railroads, Balt., 1966-74; asst. mgr. research services Chessie System, Balt., 1974—; urban renewal cons. Huntington Urban Renewal Authority, 1962. Pres. Monel Park Civic Assn., Huntington, 1963-67; commr. Monel Park Pub. Service Dist., 1965-67; mem. Howard County (Md.) Citizens' Adv. Bd. Land Use Regulations, 1974. Bd. dirs. Howard County Citizens Assn., 1968—, v.p., 1971, sec., 1970; bd. dirs. Bethany Community Assn., Ellicott City, Md., 1969—; trustee Howard County Community Hosp., 1975—. Served with AUS, 1953-55. Mem. Assn. Am. Geographers, Am. Geog. Soc., Sigma Gamma Epsilon, Gamma Theta Upsilon, Delta Nu Alpha, Alpha Phi Omega. Republican. Methodist. Contbr. articles to profl. jours. Home: 2829 Foxhound Rd Ellicott City MD 21043 Office: 1 Charles Center Baltimore MD 21201

CHILCOTE, THOMAS C., ednl. adminstr.; b. Mt. Union, Pa., June 27, 1920; s. Thomas Chalmers and Bess (Bair) C.; B.S., Shippensburg State Coll., 1942; M.Ed., Temple U., 1955; m. Esther B. Clemens, Jan. 1, 1946. Classroom tchr. Hatfield (Pa.) Joint Schs., 1942-55; dept. head, tchr. N. Penn. Sr. High Sch., Lansdale, Pa., 1955-62, adminstrv. asst., 1962-65; asst. prin. Spring-Ford Sr. High Sch., Royersford, Pa., 1965-69, prin., 1969—; mem. N. Penn Scholarship Com., Spring-Ford Scholarship Com. Mem. Montgomery County Safety Council. Mem. Montgomery County Prins. Assn. (charter), Pa. (exec. bd., pres. 1977-78), Nat. (status and welfare com.) assns. secondary sch. prins., Am. Assn. Sch. Adminstrs. Methodist. Clubs: Rotary (pres. Spring-City-Royersford 1974-75); Masons. Home: 1631 Ridge Rd Perkasie PA 18944 Office: Lower Lewis Rd Royersford PA 19468

CHILDRESS, WILLIAM BRYANT, psychologist; b. Stuart, Va., Feb. 17, 1944; s. Conduff Green and Alice (Bryant) C.; B.A., Davidson Coll., 1966; M.Ed., U. Va., 1970, Ed.D., 1974; m. Beverly Buck, Dec. 27, 1975; children—Marcus Brian, Michael George. Rehab. counselor Va. Dept. Vocat. Rehab., Charlottesville, 1967-68; instr. U. Va., Charlottesville, 1970-71; predoctoral intern in psychology Devereux Found., Devon, Pa., 1971-72, sr. unit psychologist Leo Kanner div., West Chester, Pa., 1972—; practice psychology, West Chester, 1975—; instr. dept. behavioral scis. Bucks County Community Coll., Newtown, Pa., 1976—. Licensed psychologist, Pa.; certified sch. psychologist, Pa. Mem. Am. Psychol. Assn., Nat. Register Health Service Providers in Psychology. Contbr. articles to profl. jours. Home: 304 Astor Ct Downingtown PA 19335 Office: 891 E Boot Rd West Chester PA 19380

CHILDS, JOHN PATRICK, psychotherapist; b. Orange, N.J., May 7, 1930; s. John Wilton and Gertrude Regina (Daley) C.; B.S., Manhattan Coll., N.Y.C., 1957; M.S., Bklyn. Coll., 1967; M.F.A., Cath. U., Washington, 1964; Ed.D., U. Tenn., Knoxville, 1973; student Art Students League, N.Y.C., 1957-60, Gestalt Therapy Tng. Inst. of Fla., 1975-77. Joined Christian Brothers Order, 1948; tchr. parochial elementary and high schs., N.Y.C., 1951-70; counselor, program writer N.Y. State Div. for Youth, Bronx, 1970-71; teaching asst. U. Tenn., 1971-73; adminstrv. dir. Tidelands Community Sch., Midway, Ga., 1973-75; chief therapist Sch. for Emotionally Distrubed Children, 1973-75; coordinator child and family program Community Mental Health Center, Starke, Fla., 1975-77; asst. prof. psychology Salve Regina Coll., Newport, R.I., 1977—; pvt. practice psychotherapy, 1973—; artist. Mem. Am. Psychol. Assn., Am. Personnel and Guidance Assn. Roman Catholic. Home: 27 Everett St Newport RI 02840 Office: Psychology Dept Salve Regina College Newport RI 02840

CHILINGERIAN, HARRY SAMUEL, banker; b. Beirut, Lebanon, Apr. 13, 1928; s. Samuel Garabed and Marie (Der Sahagian) C.; Baccalaureate degree Lebanese U., Beirut, 1968; grad. Internat. Mktg. Inst., Harvard, 1969; m. Sha-key Babikian, Aug. 19, 1951; children—Astrid, Raffy. Came to U.S., 1968. Advt. and pub. relations mgr. Near East Region, Coca-Cola Export Corp., Beirut, 1958-63; adminstrn. mgr. E.R. Squibb & Son, Squibb Middle East, S.A., Beirut, 1964-68; mktg. and sales exec. Fidelity Bank, Phila., 1969—. Mem. Internat. Advt. Assn., Am. Mktg. Assn. Mem. Armenian Ch. (trustee). Knight of Vartan. Club: Rotary Internat. (Upper Darby, Pa.). Office: Fidelity Bank Broad and Walnut Sts Philadelphia PA 19109

CHIMENE, DONALD ROBERT, surgeon; b. Austin, Tex., Apr. 6, 1933; s. Eugene and Bereneice (Rosenwald) C.; A.B., Cornell U., 1954; M.D., U. Chgo., 1958; m. Ellen Barth Berk, June 17, 1956; children—Susan, Jonathan, Karen. Intern, Bronx Municipal Hosp. Center/Albert Einstein Coll. Medicine, 1958-59, resident in surgery, 1959-64; practice medicine specializing in surgery, Greensboro, N.C., 1966-67, Edison, N.J., 1967—; staff John F. Kennedy Med. Center. Served to capt. MC., AUS, 1964-66. Diplomate Am. Bd. Surgery. Fellow A.C.S.; mem. AMA, N.J. State, Middlesex County (past editor bull.) med. socs. Club: Kiwanis (past pres. Edison). Home: 8 Bluebird Ct Edison NJ 08817 Office: 111 James St Edison NJ 08817

CHIN, CAROLYN SUE, telephone co. exec.; b. Washington, Nov. 28, 1947; d. Tin Wah and Oi Tuck (Ho) Chin; B.S. in Mgmt. Engring., Rensselaer Poly. Inst., 1969; M.B.A., Harvard, 1971; m. Gerald Bingham Sweeney, Sept. 18, 1976. Buyer, R.H. Macy's, Inc., N.Y.C., 1972-74, divisional merchandise adminstr. home accessories, 1974-75; mktg. mgr. design line, group product mgr., AT&T, Morristown, N.J., 1976, mktg. mgr. distbn. programs Bell System products, after 1976, merchandising mgr., 1976-78; White House fellow, spl. asst. Sec. HUD, Washington, 1978—. Cons. N.Y. Emergency Fin. Control Bd. Mem. South Orange Econ. Devel. Com. Named one of 10 Outstanding Young Working Women, Glamour mag., Feb. 1977. Mem. NOW, Pacific Asian Coalition, Task Force Asian Women Bus. Owners (chmn.). Home: 349 Montrose Ave South Orange NJ 07079

CHIN, CHARLES LEE DONG, chem. co. exec.; b. N.Y.C., Feb. 4, 1923; s. Lee Dong and Shee (Lee) C.; B.S., Tri-State Coll., 1941; M.Aero. Engring., Poly. Inst. Bklyn., 1948; S.M., Harvard, 1949, Sc.D., 1965; m. Ethel Wa Gew, Sept. 7, 1946; 1 dau., Susan. Stress engr. Curtiss-Wright, Columbus, Ohio, 1941-43; sr. stress engr. Chance Vought Aircraft, Stratford, Conn., 1943-44; asst. prof. aero. engring. U. R.I., Kingston, 1950-52; head analytical research and engring. Jackson & Church Co., Saginaw, Mich., 1952-55; chmn., prof. aerospace engring. Boston U., 1955-68; dir., engring. and research, machines div. Borg-Warner, Fremont, Ohio, 1968-71; sr. engring. specialist Monsanto Plastics & Resins Co., Bloomfield (Conn.) Tech. Center, 1972—. Specialist, N. Am. Aviation, Los Angeles, 1963, 66; cons. AVCO, Wilmington, Mass., 1963; vis. prof. Cheng Kung U., Republic of China, 1968-69; adj. faculty mech. engring. U. Hartford, West Hartford, 1973—. Served with USNR, 1944-46. Mem. Am. Inst. Aeros. and Astronautics, Am. Soc. for Engring. Edn., Soc. Plastics Engrs., Soc. Harvard Engrs. and Scientists, Sigma Xi. Club: Harvard (No. Conn.). Home: 22 Homestead Ln Avon CT 06001 Office: 101 Granby St Bloomfield CT 06002

CHIN, GILBERT YUKYU, metallurgist; b. Kwangtung, China, Sept. 21, 1934; s. George Shee Ng and Liawah (Gee) C. (father Am. citizen); S.B., Mass. Inst. Tech., 1959, Sc.D., 1963; m. Ginie Wong, June 26, 1960; children—Patrick Ken, Michael Philip, Grace Fay, Karen Jean. Mem. tech. staff Bell Telephone Labs., Murray Hill, N.J., 1962—, head phys. metallurgy and crystal growth research dept., 1973-75, head phys. metallurgy and ceramics research and devel. dept., 1975—. Mem. Am. Soc. Metals, Metall. Soc. of Am. Inst. Metall. Engrs. (Mathewson Gold medal 1974), Am. Ceramics Soc., Magnetics Soc. of IEEE, N.Y. Acad. Scis., AAAS, Sigma Xi, Tau Beta Pi, Phi Lambda Upsilon. Episcopalian (vestry). Author, patentee in field. Office: Bell Telephone Labs Mountain Ave Murray Hill NJ 07974

CHIN, RICCARDO FAY, artist; b. Hong Kong, July 16, 1935; s. Lan Den and Mee Yee (Wong) C.; came to U.S., 1951, naturalized, 1966; B.A., State U. N.Y., 1958; m. Helen Leong, Sept. 21, 1959; children—Steven, Deborah. Staff artist Automation Lab., Inc., Mineola, N.Y., 1960-61; asst. art dir. Tech. Illustrators-Omnibus Tech. Industries, Inc., Hempstead, N.Y., 1961-62; free lance artist, 1962-64; pres. Bertrick Asso. Artists, Inc., Seaford, N.Y., 1964-74; lectr. Chinese culture L.I. U., 1971-73; lectr., demonstrator East West style watercolor on rice papers, 1968—; tchr. Chinese cooking with western ingredients, 1964—; exhbns. of watercolors in U.S. and Far East. Served with AUS, 1958-60. Recipient numerous art awards. Mem. Artists Fellowship, Am. Artists Profl. League, Nat. Art League, Art League Nassau County, Long Beach Art Assn. (v.p. 1972—), Sumi-E Soc. Am. Clubs: Salmagundi (N.Y.C.); K.C. Author: Chinese Cooking with an American Touch; Chinese Hors d'Oeuvre With an American Touch, 1976. Home: 3423 Carrollton Ave Wantagh NY 11793

CHINA, ROBERT HENRY, mfg. co. exec.; b. Bronx, N.Y., Feb. 25, 1939; s. Romolo John and Helen Johanna (Fruhauf) C.; B.A., Fairleigh Dickinson U., 1970, M.B.A., 1977; m. Roberta F. Sulick, May 10, 1959; children—Stacey Ann, Lauren. Lab. technician Inmont, Carlstadt, N.J., 1962-66; prodn. supr. Arsynco, Inc. div. Aceto Chem., Carlstadt, 1967, prodn. mgr., 1968-69, mktg. asso., 1970-72, mfg. mgr., 1972-76, asst. v.p. mfg., 1976—. Mem. Am. Inst. Chem. Engrs. Office: Arsynco Inc 13th St Carlstadt NJ 07072

CHINICH, ARNOLD, constrn. co. exec.; b. Newark, June 23, 1915; s. Barnet and Nettie Chinich; certificate in architecture Newark Sch. of Fine Arts, 1937; student Profl. Sch. of Bus., Union, N.J., certificate in pub. adjusting Sch. Bus. Adminstrn. Fairleigh Dickinson U., 1971. Engr., Newark Housing Authority, 1938-40, Jaehing & Peoples, Inc., Newark, 1940-42; archtl. engr. Dept. of Army, Newark, 1942-44; pres. Harvard Constrn. Co., Newark, 1944-69, Vassar Realty Corp., Newark, 1953—, Pitts Realty Corp., Newark, 1953—; self-employed cons., inst. agt., broker, adjuster, Newark, 1969—. Mem. Am. Assn. for Automotive Medicine, Internat. Platform Assn., Internat. Assn. for Accident and Traffic Medicine. Mason. Address: 815 S 11th St Newark NJ 07108

CHINICH, BESSIE (BESSIE CHINICH FEDERBUSH), lawyer, govt. ofcl.; b. Newark; d. Barnet and Nettie (Chinich) Chinich; LL.B., Rutgers U., 1930, J.D., 1970; m. Harry Federbush, May 28, 1933; children—Paul Gerard, Roberta Dianne. Admitted to N.J. bar, 1930; practiced in Newark, 1931-44, 48-51; conferee, salary stblzn. unit U.S. Dept. Treasury, N.Y.C., 1944-46; investigator Civilian Prodn. Authority, N.Y.C., 1946-47; claims examiner War Assets Adminstrn., N.Y.C., 1947-48; sr. investigator Nat. Prodn. Authority, U.S. Dept. Commerce, Newark, 1951-53; contract specialist N.Y. ordnance dist. U.S. Army, 1953-65; adminstrv. contracting officer Def. Supply Agency, Springfield, N.J., 1965—. Atty. Newark Commn. Neighborhood Conservation and Rehab., 1962; active in local orphanages, home for aged, juvenile delinquency. Recipient awards N.Y. ordnance dist. U.S. Army, 1953, 65. Mem. Nat. Council Juvenile Ct. Judges, Essex County Bar Assn., Rutgers U. Alumni Assn., Internat. Platform Assn., Am. Judicature Soc., Nat. Assn. Women Lawyers. Home: 815 S 11th St Newark NJ 07108 Office: 815 S 11th St Newark NJ 07103 also Def Supply Agency Dept Def 240 Route 22 Springfield NJ 07081

CHINMOY, SRI, spiritual leader, author, painter; b. Shakpura, India, Aug. 27, 1931; s. Shashi Kumar and Yogamaya (Bishwas) Ghose. Spiritual head Sri Chinmoy Centres, Queens, N.Y., and worldwide, 1964—; dir. UN Meditation Group, N.Y.C., 1970—; lectr. univs., U.S., Eng., Italy, Sweden, Australia, France, Switzerland, Japan; author numerous books, including Yoga and the Spiritual Life, 1970; Songs of the Soul, 1971; The Inner Promise, 1974; Beyond Within, 1975; Transcendence-Perfection, 1975; one-man art shows: Museo del Arte, Ponce, P.R., 1975, Jharna-Kala Gallery, N.Y.C., 1975, Sch. Visual Arts, N.Y.C., 1975; instrumental soloist, Carnegie Hall, N.Y.C., 1976. Office: Box 32433 Jamaica NY 11431

CHINO, JOHN JAMES, mech. engr.; b. Bklyn., Sept. 8, 1949; s. Augustine Joseph and Joan Theresa (Claro) C.; B.S., Poly. Inst. Bklyn., 1971; M.S., U. Md., 1973; m. Cathyann Elizabeth Thompson, July 31, 1971; 1 son, John Anthony. Asso. mech. engr. Westinghouse Electric Corp., Balt., 1971-73, mech. engr., 1973-75, sr. mech. engr., 1975—. Registered profl. engr., Md. Mem. ASME, Pi Tau Sigma, Tau Beta Pi. Republican. Roman Catholic. Patentee in field. Home: 463 Century Vista Dr Arnold MD 21012 Office: PO Box 746 Mail Stop 463 Baltimore MD 21203

CHIOGIOJI, MELVIN HIROAKI, govt. ofcl.; b. Hiroshima, Japan, Aug. 21, 1939; s. Yutaka and Harumi (Yamasaki) C.; came to U.S., 1939; B.S. in Elec. Engring., Purdue U., 1961; M.B.A., U. Hawaii, 1968; D.Bus. Adminstrn., George Washington U., 1972; m. Eleanor Nobuko Oura, June 4, 1960; children—Wendy A., Alan K. Head, weapons gen. component div. Quality Eval Lab., Oahu, Hawaii, 1965-69; dir. weapons evaluation and engring. div. Naval Ordnance Systems Command, Washington, 1969-73; dir. Office Indsl. Analysis, Fed. Energy Adminstrn., Washington, 1973-75; asst. dir., div. bldg. and community systems Dept. Energy, Washington, 1975—; prof. mgmt. sci. George Washington U., 1972—. Mem. Md. State Advisory Com. on Civil Rights, 1976—; mem. Nat. Naval Res. Policy Bd., 1977—; vestryman Grace Episcopal Ch., Silver Spring, Md., 1977—. Served with USNR, 1961-65. Decorated Navy Commendation medal. Registered profl. engr., Hawaii. Mem. IEEE, Nat. Soc. Profl. Engrs., Acad. Mgmt., Naval Res. Assn., Soc. Am. Mil. Engrs., Armed Forces Mgmt. Assn., Purdue U. Alumni Assn. Contbr. articles to profl. jours. Home: 15113 Middlegate Rd Silver Spring MD 20904 Office: 20 Massachusetts Ave NW Washington DC 20545

CHIOTELLIS, PHILIP NICOS, physician; b. Kyrenia, Cyprus, May 31, 1942; s. Nicholas Philip and Maria P. (Constanides) C.; came to U.S., 1967, naturalized, 1976; M.D., U. Athens, 1966; m. Lavinia Margaret Conroy, Feb. 1, 1970; children—Nicos Philip, Peter Philip, Fiona Mary Lavinia. Intern, Martland Hosp., Newark, 1968; resident in internal medicine N.J. Med. Sch., 1968-71; fellow in cardiology Hahnemann Med. Coll.-Phila. Gen. Hosp., 1971-72; fellow in cardiology Harvard service Boston City Hosp., 1972-73; fellow in cardiology Boston City Hosp. and Mass. Gen. Hosp., 1973-74; research fellow Harvard Med. Sch., 1972-74, instr. medicine, 1974-75; practice medicine specializing in cardiology, Hyannis, Mass., 1975—; mem. staff Cape Cod Hosp. Diplomate Am. Bd. Internal Medicine. Mem. AMA, Am. Heart Assn. (council clin. cardiology), Mass. Med. Soc., Paul Dudley White Med. Soc. Greek Orthodox. Home: 749 S Main St Centerville MA 02632 Office: 52 Park St Hyannis MA 02601

CHISAMORE, DONALD RAYMOND, educator; b. W. Carthage, N.Y., Aug. 28, 1941; s. Raymond W. and Jane (Ornedorff) C.; B.S. in Elementary Edn., State U. Coll., New Paltz, N.Y., 1963, M.S. in Elementary Edn. Adminstrn., 1968; m. Patricia Ann Chisamore; children—Barbara Ann, Brian Edward. Tchr., Wappingers Central Sch. Dist. 1, Wappinger Falls, N.Y., 1963-68, tchr. coordinator, 1968-72, tchr., 1972—, Title I summer sch. coordinator, 1974-76; co-dir. Bay Area Writing Project-East Pace U., 1978. Fellow Bay Area Writing Project-East, summer 1977. Co-author: kindergarten handbook. Certified as tchr., prin., supr., N.Y. Home: 73 Plass Rd Poughkeepsie NY 12603 Office: Vassar Rd Elementary School Vassar Rd Poughkeepsie NY 12603

CHISHOLM, SHIRLEY ANITA ST. HILL, educator, congresswoman; b. Bklyn., Nov. 30, 1924; d. Charles Christopher and Ruby (Seale) St. Hill; B.A. cum laude, Bklyn. Coll.; M.A., Columbia U.; LL.D., Talladega Coll., 1969, Wilmington Coll., 1970; H.L.D., Hampton Inst., 1970, N.C. Central Coll., 1969; m. Conrad Chisholm, Oct. 8, 1949 (div. Feb. 1977); m. 2d, Arthur Hardwick, Jr., Nov. 26, 1977. Former nursery sch. tchr., and dir. nursery sch.; ednl. cons. Div. Day Care, Bur. Child Welfare; mem. N.Y. State Assembly, 1964-68; mem. 91st-96th Congresses from 12th dist. N.Y.; sec. House Democratic Caucus; mem. rules com.; vice chmn. Congl. Black Caucus. Named Alumna of Yr. Bklyn. Coll. Alumni Bull., 1957; recipient award for outstanding work in field of child welfare Women's Council of Blkyn., 1957; key woman of yr. award, 1963; women of achievement award Key Women, Inc., 1965. Mem. Nat. Assn. Coll. Women, Bklyn. Coll. Alumni, League Women Voters. Methodist. Office: 1149 Eastern Pkwy Brooklyn NY 11213 also 2182 Rayburn House Office Bldg Washington DC 20515

CHISOLM, ALVIN JAMES, radiologist; b. Jersey City, Feb. 18, 1943; s. James J. and Ruth (Rooks) C.; B.S., Howard U., 1964; M.D., N.Y. Med. Coll., 1968; m. Gloria Swanson, Sept. 7, 1972; children—Alvin, Gina, Naima. Intern, Met. Hosp., N.Y.C., 1968-69; resident Montefiore Hosp. Med. Center, Bronx, N.Y., 1969-72, adj. attending radiologist, 1974-76; asst. prof. radiology Albert Einstein Coll. Medicine, Bronx, 1974-76; asso. attending radiologist New Rochelle (N.Y.) Hosp. Med. Center, 1976—, chief computed tomography sect., 1976. Served to maj. U.S. Army, 1972-74. Mem. Radiol. Soc. N.Am., Am. Coll. Radiology, Westchester Acad. Medicine, Westchester Radiol. Soc., NAACP, N.Y. Roentgen Soc., Kappa Alpha Psi. Home: 148 Calton Rd New Rochelle NY 10804 Office: New Rochelle Hosp Med Center New Rochelle NY 10801

CHISOLM, JAMES JULIAN, JR., physician, clin. investigator; b. Balt., July 24, 1921; s. James Julian and Eva Aslee (Frierson) C.; A.B., Princeton, 1944; M.D., Johns Hopkins, 1946; m. Sylvia Larsen, Feb. 7, 1948; children—Edward L., James Julian, III. Intern, Johns Hopkins Hosp., 1946-47, resident, 1948, 51-52, now mem. staff; resident Babies Hosp., N.Y.C., 1950-51; practice medicine specializing in pediatrics, Balt., 1953—; asso. chief pediatrics Balt. City Hosps., 1961—; asso. prof. pediatrics Johns Hopkins Med. Sch., 1963—. Cons. USPHS, Bur. Community Environ. Mgmt., 1971-72; mem. panel on lead NRC, 1970-71, chmn. ad hoc lead in paint com., 1974-76. Served as capt. M.C., U.S. Army, 1948-50. Research grantee USPHS, 1953-72, 78—. Diplomate Am. Bd. Pediatrics. Mem. Soc. for Pediatric Research, Am. Acad. Pediatrics (cons. on environ. hazards 1975—), Am. Pediatric Soc., N.Y. Acad. Sci., AAAS, Am. Pub. Health Assn., Johns Hopkins Club. Contbr. to pediatric textbooks, monograph series, jours. Home: 2007 Stringtown Rd Sparks MD 21152

CHISVETTE, DOMINICK, tech. mgr.; b. Newark, May 30, 1925; s. Carmen and Anna (Lardiere) C.; B.S., Newark Coll. Engring., 1948; m. Eda Galietti, June 1, 1947; children—Donna, Mark, Lisa. Chemist, Devoe-Raynolds Co., Newark, 1948-49; lab. mgr. Interchem. Corp. (now Inmont Corp.), Clifton, N.J., 1949-73, mgr. engring. sect. Central Research Labs., 1974—. Served with Chem. Warfare Service, U.S. Army, 1944-46; PTO. Mem. Am. Chem. Soc. Democrat. Roman Catholic. Club: Plainfield Country. Developer emulsion inks for vinyls, plastisol inks for textiles, foams for various uses, topcoats auto upholstery. Home: 9 Overbrook Dr Colonia NJ 07067

CHITTY, ARTHUR BENJAMIN, JR., assn. exec.; b. Jacksonville, Fla., June 15, 1914; s. Arthur Benjamin and Hazel Talitha (Brown) C.; student U. Fla., summer 1934; A.B., U. of South, 1935; M.A., Tulane U., 1952; L.H.D., Canaan Coll., 1970; LL.D., Cuttington Coll., Liberia, 1975; m. Mary Elizabeth Nickinson, June 16, 1946; children—Arthur Benjamin III, John Abercrombie Merritt, Em Turner, Nathan Harsh Brown. Vice pres. Chitty & Co., Jacksonville, 1937-41, chmn. bd. dirs., 1963-67; dir. pub. relations U. of South, 1946-65, 70-73, historiographer, 1955—, exec. dir. Asso. Alumni 1946-65; pres. Assn. of Episcopal Colls., N.Y.C., 1965-70, 74—, sec., dir., 1971-74. Pres. Sewanee Civic Assn., 1948-49; mem. Tenn. Bishop and Council, 1956-65; iconographer hist. windows All Saints Chapel, 1957; nat. convenor Episcopal historiographers, 1961-66, 71-73; nat. council Brotherhood St. Andrew, mem. exec. com., 1966—, v.p., 1968; Am. coordinator Oxford Scholar Program, Keble Coll., Eng. 1970—. Bd. dirs. Living Ch. Found., Ch. Hist. Soc.; trustee St. Augustine's Coll., St. Paul's Coll.; trustee St. Andrew's Sch. Served with USNR, 1942-45. Mem. N.Y. Acad. Scis., St. Georg's Soc., English-Speaking Union (nat. bd. 1973, pres. local chpt. 1972-73), Phi Beta Kappa (pres. local chpt. 1963-64), Pi Gamma Mu, Phi Alpha Theta, Simga Upsilon, Sigma Nu (pres. Ednl. Found. 1969—). Episcopalian. Clubs: Century Assn., Church (N.Y.C.). Author: Reconstruction at Sewanee, 1954; Sewanee Sampler, 1978. Contbr. articles to profl. jours. Editor: Sewanee News, 1946-65; Historiographical Newsletter, 1962-67; Franklin County (Tenn.) Historian, 1965-69. Editor: (with Elizabeth N. Chitty) Ely: Too Black, Too White, 1970. Home: Sewanee TN 37375 Office: 815 2d Ave New York City NY 10017

CHIU, HUNGDAH, lawyer, educator; b. Shanghai, China, Mar. 23, 1936; s. Han-ping and Ming-non (Yang) C.; came to U.S., 1960; LL.B., Nat. Taiwan U., 1958; M.A. with honors, L.I. U., 1962; LL.M., Harvard U., 1962, S.J.D., 1965; m. Yuan-yuan Hsieh, May 14, 1966; 1 son, Wei-hsueh. Asso. in research East Asian Research Center, Harvard U., 1964-65; asso. prof. internat. law Nat. Taiwan U., 1965-66; research asso. in law Harvard U., 1966-70, 72-74; vis. prof. law Nat. Chengchi U., Taipei, Taiwan, 1970-72; asso. prof. law U. Md., Balt., 1974-77, prof., 1977—; del. UN Conf. Law of the Sea, 1976, 77, 78; chmn. Immigration Commn. Asian-Am. Assembly Policy Research. Served to 2d lt. Chinese Army, 1958-60. Named One of 10 Outstanding Young Men, Jr. C. of C. of Republic of China, 1971; social Sci. Research Council fellow, 1968. Mem. Am. Soc. Internat. Law (panel on China and internat. order 1969-74), Assn. for Asian Studies (com. on Asian law 1976-79). Author: The Capacity of International Organizations to Conclude Treaties, 1966; The People's Republic of China and the Law of Treaties, 1972; China and the Question of Taiwan: Documents and Analysis, 1973; (with J.A. Cohen), People's China and International Law, 2 vols., 1974 (certificate of merit Am. Soc. Internat. Law 1976); Normalizing Relations with China: Problems, Analysis and Documents, 1978; gen. editor: Occasional Papers and Reprints Series, Contemporary Asian Studies, 1976—. Home: 6254 Cricket Pass Columbia MD 21044 Office: U Md Law Sch 500 W Baltimore St Baltimore MD 21201

CHIU, JOHN HUNG CHEUNG, radiologist; b. Hong Kong, China, May 14, 1941; s. Paul Kaison and Ling Hok Nin (Chan) C.; came to Can., 1968, naturalized, 1973; M.B., B.S., U. Hong Kong, 1966; m. Yvonne Yan Kiu Tang, June 9, 1968; 1 son, Derrick. Intern, Ottawa (Ont., Can.) Civic Hosp., 1968-69, chief resident dept. radiology, 1972-73; resident staff, dept. radiology Montreal (Que., Can.) Neurol. Hosp., 1973-74; diagnostic radiologist North York Branson Hosp., Willow Dale, Ont., 1974—. Diplomate Am. Bd. Radiology. Fellow Royal Coll. (Can.); mem. Can., Ont. med. assns., Am. Coll. Radiology, Can. Assn. Radiologists, Que. Corp. Physicians and Surgeons, Royal Coll. Medicine, Royal Coll. Physicians and Surgeons Can., Fedn. Chinese Can. Profls. Roman Catholic. Home: 50 Michael Dr Willowdale ON M2H 2A5 Canada Office: North York Branson Hospital Willowdale ON M2R 1N5 Canada

CHIU, WU SHUNG, physician, educator; b. Taiwan, China, Sept. 15, 1933; s. Cheng and Huo (Huong) C.; came to U.S., 1965, naturalized, 1976; M.D., Nat. Taiwan U., 1959; m. Hsiu Hui Kuo, June 19, 1959; children—Dorothy, William, Jane. Intern, Nat. Taiwan U. Hosp., Taipei, 1959, 61, resident, 1961-64, chief resident in internal medicine, 1965; intern St. Joseph's Hosp., Paterson, N.J., 1965, resident in internal medicine, 1966-67; resident in cardiology Met. Hosp., N.Y.C., 1967, in hematology Newark City Hosp., 1968, in rehab. medicine Albert Einstein Coll. Medicine, 1968-71; asst. prof. medicine George Washington U., 1971-76, asso. prof., 1976—; asso. dir. phys. medicine, vice-chmn. rehab. service George Washington U. Med. Center, 1974; asst. dir. patient care George Washington U. Rehab. Research and Tng. Center, 1974—. Diplomate Am. Bd. Phys. Medicine and Rehab. Fellow Am. Acad. Phys. Medicine and Rehab.; mem. Assn. Academic Physiatrists, Assn. Med. Rehab. Dirs. and Coordinators, Med. Soc. D.C. (com. rehab. and prison health), Chinese Med. and Health Assn. (exec. com.), Nat. Taiwan U. Med. Sch. Alumni Assn. (pres.), AMA. Home: 15112 Bauer Dr Rockville MD 20853 Office: 901 23d St NW Washington DC 20037

CHIZEVER, IRWIN, research co. exec.; b. Bklyn., Feb. 25, 1935; s. Henry and Rebecca (Silverman) G.; B.A., Bklyn. Coll., 1956; M.B.A., Coll. City N.Y., 1963; m. Joyce K. Altheimer, Mar. 29, 1959; children—Jeffrey Stewart, Roger Owen, Brian Michael. Sr. project dir. Gilbert Youth Research, N.Y.C., 1963-65; v.p., group head Admar Research Co., N.Y.C., 1965-69, Market Facts, N.Y.C., 1969; sr. v.p. Monroe Mendelsohn Research, Inc., N.Y.C., 1970—; guest lectr. Columbia Sch. Pharmacy, 1968-73; lectr. Adelphi U., 1978—. Trustee Great Neck/Saddle Harbor Estates, 1976—. Mem. Am. Mktg. Assn., Tau Alpha Omega. Home: 29 Elm St Great Neck NY 11021 Office: 352 Park Ave S New York City NY 10010

CHMIELEWICZ, JOSEPH STANLEY, city ofcl.; b. Webster, Mass., Nov. 30, 1915; s. John Alexander and Stefanie Bernice (Skrzypek) C.; grad. high sch. With J.P. Ivascyn Ins. Agy., 1937-43; tax assesor, Webster, 1944-57, treas., 1957—; sports editor Weekly Times, Webster, 1953-57; corporator, trustee Webster Five Cents Savs. Bank. Bd. dirs. Webster-Dudley Boys Club, Nichols Coll. Golf Course, Worcester chpt. A.R.C. Mem. New Eng. States Finance Officers Assn., Mass. Treasurers and Collectors Assn., Mcpl. Treasurers Assn. U.S. and Can., Calvary Retreat League, Polish Am. Youth Fedn. (pres. 1950-53). K.C. (4 deg.), Eagle, Elk (participating mem. Nat. Found.). Clubs: Webster Exchange (pres. 1960-61), Booster Athletic (hon. life mem.). Home: 31 Morris St Webster MA 01570 Office: POB 66 Webster MA 01570

CHO, ALFRED YI, elec. engr.; b. Peking, China, July 10, 1937; s. Edward I-Lai and Mildred (Chen) C.; came to U.S., 1955, naturalized, 1962; B.S. in Elec. Engring., U. Ill., 1960, M.S., 1961, Ph.D., 1968; m. Mona Lee Willoughby, June 16, 1968; children—Derek Ming, Deidre Lin, Brynna Ying, Wendy Li. Research physicist Ion Physics Corp., Burlington, Mass., 1961-62; mem. tech. staff TRW-Space Tech. Labs., Redondo Beach, Calif., 1962-65; research asst. U. Ill., Urbana, 1965-68, vis. prof. dept. elec. engring., research prof. coordinated science lab., 1977-78, adj. prof. dept. elec. engring., adj. research prof. coordinated sci. lab., 1978—; mem. tech. staff Bell Telephone Labs., Murray Hill, N.J., 1968—. Mem. Am. Phys. Soc., Am. Vacuum Soc., Electrochem. Soc. (electronic div. award), N.Y. Acad. Scis., AAAS, Sigma Xi, Tau Beta Pi, Eta Kappa Nu, Sigma Tau. Contbr. articles to profl. jours. Developer molecular beam epitaxy. Home: 11 Kenneth Ct Summit NJ 07901 Office: Bell Telephone Labs Murray Hill NJ 07974

CHO, JUNG HYUN, city ofcl.; b. Kangnaung City, Korea, Apr. 6, 1939; s. Kyu Ho and Zeung Soon (Kim) C.; came to U.S., 1970, naturalized, 1976; D.V.M., Seoul Nat. U., 1964, M.P.H., 1966; D.Sc. in Hygiene, Tulane U., 1974; m. Annja Ko, July 25, 1970; children—Jimmy Young, Young Sean. Environ. health officer Ministry of Health, Seoul, Korea, 1966; chief environ. health advisor Pub. Health Adv. Group, U.S. AID/KOPREM, Vietnam, 1966-70; postdoctoral fellow Hersey Med. Center, Pa. State U., 1973; dir., health officer Twp. of Cherry Hill (N.J.) Health Dept., 1974—. USPHS Gen. Traineeship grantee, 1971-73; licensed health officer N.J.: registered sanitarian, veterinarian. Mem. U.S. Conf. City Health Officers (trustee), N.J. Health Officers Assn., Am. Pub. Health Assn., N.J. Pub. Health Assn., Nat., N.J. environ. health assns., Central Atlantic States Assn. Food and Drug Ofcls., Air Pollution Control Assn. Home: 1108 Crane Dr Cherry Hill NJ 08003 Office: 820 Mercer St Cherry Hill NJ 08002

CHO, SANG YON, pathologist, educator; b. Kunsan, Korea, July 19, 1932; s. Nam Kyu and Kum Chi (Yu) C.; came to U.S., 1968, naturalized, 1974; M.D., Yonsei U. (Korea), 1958; m. Hee Yul Lee, Nov. 28, 1959. Intern, Nat. Naval Med. Center, Bethesda, Md., 1959-60; dir. Naval Research Inst. Pathology, Korea, 1964-68; sr. resident, sr. fellow in pathology Presbyn.-U. Pa. Med. Center, Phila., 1968-70; instr. pathology Jefferson Med. Coll., Phila., 1970-71, asst. prof. pathology, 1971-76, asso. prof. pathology, 1976—; dir. autopsy pathology Thomas Jefferson U. Hosp., Phila., 1970—; cons. in pathology VA Hosp., Coatesville, Pa., 1972—; reviewer manuscript for Archives Pathology and Lab. Medicine, 1976; mem. pathology com. Cancer and Leukemia Group B, 1976—. Diplomate Am. Bd. Anatomic and Clin. Pathology. Fellow Coll. Am. Pathologists; mem. Pathology Soc. Phila., Pa. Med. Soc., Phila. County Med. Soc. Club: Faculty. Contbr. articles to med. jours. Home: 517 Sentinel Rd Moorestown NJ 08057 Office: 1020 Locust St Philadelphia PA 19107

CHO, YOHAN, electronic co. exec.; b. Seoul, Korea, Feb. 17, 1931; s. Euiyuk and Chi poong (Chang) C.; B.S. in Elec. Engring., Mass. Inst. Tech., 1957, M.S. in Elec. Engring., 1959; m. Rumie Youn, Sept. 7, 1958; children—Milyoung, Danyul. With Honeywell Co., Newton, Mass., 1958-61; mem. staff computer research Mitre Corp., Bedford, Mass., 1961-64; digital signal processing research Lincoln Lab., Mass. Inst. Tech., Lexington, 1964-68; pres. Tau-tron Inc., Billerica, Mass., 1968—, also dir. Mem. exec. com. Korean Christian Ch. Boston. Served to capt. Korean Air Force, 1951-53. Mem. IEEE. Methodist. Author: Radio Science, 1953; Digital Engineering, 1959; Digital Instrumentations, 1972; contbr. articles to profl. jours.; patentee in field. Home: 145 Indian Hill Rd Carlisle MA 01741 Office: 11 Esquire Rd North Billerica MA 01862

CHOBANY, JOHN, ednl. adminstr.; b. Portage, Pa., June 30, 1928; s. Joseph and Mary (Lehan) C.; B.S., Ind. State Tchrs. Coll., 1952; M.Ed., U. Pitts., 1959, postgrad. 1960-70; children—Deborah, John, Rodney, Tammy, Matthew, Alexander. Tchr., Laurel Valley Schs., New Florence, Pa., 1953-58, Norwin High Sch., Irwin, Pa., 1958-59; prin. Berlin Bros. Valley Sch. Dist., Berlin, Pa., 1959-66; dist. supt. Conemaugh Twp. Area Sch. Dist., Davidsville, Pa., 1966—; chief sch. adminstr. Greater Johnstown Area Vocat. Tech. Sch. Chmn. Conemaugh Twp. Christmas Parade, 1966. Served with AUS, 1946-48. Mem. Somerset County (Pa.) Secondary Prins., Pa. Interscholastic Athletic Assn. (vice chmn.), Somerset County Sch. Adminstrs. Assn. (pres.). Home: 1217 Maple St Davidsville PA 15928 Office: Conemaugh Township Area School Dist Campus Ave Davidsville PA 15928

CHODOSH, H LOUIS, physician; b. Newark, Mar. 6, 1925; s. Robert and Ida (Shapiro) C.; student U. Va., 1942-44; M.D., N.Y. U., 1948; m. Leona Kovarsky, Mr. 6, 1949; children—Ellen Iris, Eliot Howard. Intern, Morrisania City Hosp., 1948-49; resident in neurology and psychiatry Bellevue Hosp., N.Y.C., 1949-50, Bronx VA Hosp., 1953-55; practice medicine specializing in neurology, Paterson, N.J., 1955-73, Wayne, N.J., 1973—; mem. staff Barnert Meml. Hosp., Paterson, Greater Paterson Gen. Hosp.; cons. Franklin Hosp.; attending neurologist Chilton Meml. Hosp., VA Hosp., East Orange; asso. clin. prof. neuroscis. N.J. Med. Sch., 1975—. Trustee, Greater Paterson Gen. Hosp. Daus. of Miriam Center for Aged, Clifton, N.J. Fellow Am. Psychiat. Assn., Am. Acad. Neurology; mem. AMA, Pan Am., Passaic County, N.J. med. socs., N.J. Psychiat. Soc., Am. Geriatric Soc., Am. Med. EEG Soc., Acad. Medicine N.J. Fellow Royal Soc. Health. Jewish. Club: Odd fellows. Office: 220 Hamburg Tpk Wayne NJ 07470

CHOI, SOONCHAE, orthopedic surgeon; b. Soonchang, Chonra Buk-Do, Korea, Sept. 13, 1941; s. Hanchul and Jungro (Lee) C.; came to U.S., 1966, naturalized, 1977; M.D., Seoul Nat. U., 1966; m. Whami Min, May 13, 1967; children—Michael, Susan. Intern, Albert Einstein Med. Center, Phila., 1966-67; resident gen. surgery St. Peter's Med. Center, New Brunswick, N.J., 1967-69; resident orthopedic surgery Harlem Hosp. Center, N.Y.C., 1969-73; practice medicine specializing in orthopedic surgery, Bound Brook, N.J., 1976—; clin. asst. prof. orthopedic surgery Rutgers Med. Sch., Coll. Medicine and Dentistry N.J., New Brunswick, 1973—. Diplomate Am. Bd. Orthopedic Surgery. Fellow Am. Acad. Orthopedic Surgeons; mem. AMA, N.J., Somerset County med. socs., N.J. Orthopedic Soc., Nat. Pilots Assn. Home: 86 Old Smalleytown Rd Warren NJ 07060 Office: 515 Church St Bound Brook NJ 08805

CHOKAS, WILLIAM VASILIOS, physician; b. Union City, N.J., Sept. 28, 1929; s. Anastasios and Georgia C.; B.S., St. Peter's Coll., Jersey City, 1951; M.D., N.Y. Med. Coll., 1955; m. Mary George, Jan. 31, 1955; children—Georgia, Gail, Ann. Intern, N.Y. Polyclinic Med. Sch. and Hosp., 1955-56; resident in internal medicine Mountainside Hosp., Montclair, N.J., 1956-57, Bronx VA Hosp., 1960-61; clin. asst. prof. medicine N.Y. Med. Coll.-Flower and Fifth Ave. Hosp., N.Y.C., 1968-72, clin. asso. prof., 1972—; individual practice medicine, specializing in internal medicine, Flushing, L.I., N.Y., 1961—. Served with U.S. Army, 1957-59. Diplomate Am. Bd. Internal Medicine. Mem. AMA. Republican. Greek Orthodox. Contbr. articles to profl. publs.

CHOMITZ, NICHOLAS, chem. engring. cons.; b. N.Y.C., Sept. 17, 1921; s. Maxim and Cleopatra (Kono) C.; B.Chem. Engring., N.Y. U., 1953; m. Mary Barbara Ondera, Feb. 26, 1943; children—Nicholas Jr., Christopher Robert, Marcia Stacey. With Am. Cyanamid Co., various locations, 1953-71, project engr. catalyst plants, Michigan City, Ind., 1967-69, Wayne, N.J., 1969-71; owner Chomitz MCN Catalyst Cons., Gillette, N.J., 1971—. Served with USAAF, 1942-46. Mem. Catalyst Club N.Y. Patentee in field. Address: 40 Lacey Ave Gillette NJ 07933

CHON, YU-TAIK, geophysicist; b. Seoul, Korea, Nov. 21, 1941; s. Yong-Hyun and Hae-Sun (Ahn) C.; B.E.E., Seoul Nat. U., 1964; M.S., Ph.D., U. Mass., 1973; m. Young-Ja Moon, June 2, 1969; children—Kyu-sik, Sang-min. Research asso. NASA/Goddard Space Flight Center, Greenbelt, Md., 1973-75; research geophysicist Gulf

Research and Devel. Co., Harmarville, Pa., 1975—. Mem. IEEE, Soc. Exploration Geophysicists, Sigma Xi, Phi Kappa Phi. Contbr. articles in field to profl. jours. Home: 905 Orchard Park Dr Gibsonia PA 15044 Office: Gulf Research and Development Co PO Drawer 2038 Pittsburgh PA 15230

CHONG, LUIS A., engring. co. exec.; b. Paita, Peru, May 14, 1930; s. Isaac and Maria Victoria (Leon) C.; came to U.S., 1948, naturalized, 1960; B.S. in Mech. Engring., U. Ill., 1952; postgrad. U. Mich.; m. Vivian A. Juco, May 23, 1953; children—Ana, Louis, Michael, Mary, Catherine, Paul. Various engring. positions Cummins Engine Co., Columbus, Ind., 1959-65; with Curtiss Wright Corp., Woodridge and Caldwell, N.J., 1966-71; with Otis Elevator Co., N.Y.C., 1972-78, v.p. engring., 1974-78; corporate dir. tech. planning United Techs. Corp., 1978—. Republican. Roman Catholic. Club: Apple Ridge Country. Home: 59 Ethelbert St Ridgewood NJ 07450 Office: United Technologies Bldg Hartford CT

CHOPOORIAN, JOHN ANDREW, mfg. co. exec.; b. Providence, July 18, 1932; s. Andrew H. and Zabell (Adishian) C.; B.S., Brown U., 1954; Ph.D., Fla. State U., 1960; Fulbright scholar U. London, 1960-61; m. Modena Rea Avery, June 12, 1958; children—Gregory R., Jeffrey R., Jason A. Research scientist Am. Cyanamid Co., Stamford, Conn., 1961-63, Washington tech. rep., 1963-65, mgr. tech. sales, internat. div., 1965-67; market mgr. Union Carbide Corp., N.Y.C., 1967-69; pres. Amcon Industries, Inc., New Bedford, Mass., 1969-74; gen. mgr. Centaur Corp., New Bedford, 1974—; asso. prof. Southeastern Mass. U., 1974-77, asso. prof. mgmt. dept., 1977—. Served with USNR, 1954-56. Mem. Am. Chem. Soc. Republican. Presbyn. (elder). Patentee in field. Home: 5 North St Mattapoisett MA 02739 Office: 384 Nash Rd New Bedford MA 02746

CHOU, CHUNG CHI, chemist; b. Koahsiung, Tawian, Dec. 24, 1936; s. Chia Yung and Kua (Tieng) C.; came to U.S., 1965, naturalized, 1975; B.S., Chen-Kung U., 1959; Ph.D., Baylor U., 1968; m. Chiou Yng Chou, Apr. 10, 1961; children—James H.H., Jack H.S., Hubert H.K. Process supt. Taiwan Sugar Corp., 1959-65; research scientist, group leader research and devel. Amstar Corp., N.Y.C., 1968-75, mgr. process devel. Am. cane sugar div., 1975—; mem. exec. com. U.S. Nat. Com. on Sugar Analysis, 1977—. Mem. Am. Chem. Soc., Sugar Industry Technologists (George and Eleanore Meade award 1971), Sci. Research Soc. N.Am., Sigma Xi. Contbr. articles to profl. jours. Home: 103A Pidgeon Hill Rd South Huntington NY 11746 Office: 1251 Ave of Americas New York City NY 10020

CHOU, PEI CHI, mech. engr.; b. Ichang, Hupei, China, Dec. 1, 1924; s. Hung Lieh and Shiu Lan (Kao) C.; B.S., Nat. Central U., China, 1946; M.S., Harvard U., 1949; D.Sc., N.Y. U., 1951; m. Rosalind Chen, June 23, 1956; children—James C.Y., George C.H., Arthur C.P., William C.T. Cons., Budd Co., Phila., 1955-57. Prewitt Aircraft Co., Clifton Heights, Pa., 1957-58, Kellet Aircraft Corp., Willow Grove, Pa., 1958-62, Allegheny Ballistics Lab., Cumberland, Md., 1961-63; Billings prof. mech. engring. Wave Propagation Inst., Drexel U., Phila., 1953—; cons. Air Force Materials Lab., Wright Patterson AFB, Dayton, Ohio, 1966-70, Dyna East Corp., Wynnewood, Pa., 1968—. Pres. Assn. Chinese Schs.; bd. dirs. Rho Psi Found. Mem. Am. Inst. Aero. and Astronautics, ASME, Am. Soc. Engring. Edn., ASTM, Am. Def. Preparedness Assn., Sigma Xi, Phi Tau Sigma, Phi Kappa Phi, Tau Beta Pi, Rho Psi (trustee 1964-71). Republican. Episcopalian. Author: Elasticity: Tensor, Dyadic, and Engineering Approaches, 1967; Dynamic Response of Materials to Intense Impulsive Loading, 1973; asso. editor Jour. Composite Materials. Home: 227 Hemlock Rd Wynnewood PA 19096 Office: 32d and Chestnut Sts Philadelphia PA 19104

CHOUDHARY, SHYAM SUNDAR, civil engr.; b. Gaya, Bihar, India, June 26, 1948; s. Madan Lal and Sharbati Devi C.; came to U.S., 1971; B.C.E., Punjab U., India, 1968, M.C.E., 1970; m. Suman Gupta, Dec. 13, 1974; 1 dau., Preeti. Asst. engr. Pub. Works Dept., Haryana, India, 1970-71; cons. engr., Washington, 1971-75; project engr. structural dept. Dewberry, Nealon and Davis, Fairfax, Va., 1975—; cons. structural engr. for bldgs. and bridges. Registered profl. engr., Pa. Mem. Am. Concrete Inst., Nat. Soc. Profl. Engrs. Hindu. Club: Holiday Health Spa. Author: Effect of Delayed Compaction on Soil Cement, 1970. Home: 6947 Nashville Rd Lanham MD 20801 Office: 8411 Arlington Blvd Fairfax VA 22030

CHOUDHURY, ABDUR RAQUIB, physician; b. Dacca, E. Pakistan (now Bangladesh), Nov. 21, 1939; s. Abdur Rub and Arefa (Khatun) C.; came to Can., 1968, naturalized, 1972; student Notre Dame Coll., Dacca, 1954-56; M.B., B.S., Dacca Med. Coll., 1961; m. Dilruba Ahmed, June 24, 1963; children—Rubina, Sabina, Asif. Intern, Ohio Valley Hosp., Steubenville, 1963-64; resident in internal medicine Columbus Hosp., Chgo., 1964-65, Lewis Gale Hosp., Roanoke, Va., 1965-66; resident Weiss Meml. Hosp., Chgo., 1966-67, fellow in gastroenterology, 1967-68; sr. asst. resident in internal medicine Queen Mary Vet. Hosp., Montreal, Que., Can., 1968-70; fellow in gastroenterology Montreal Gen. Hosp. Program, 1970-72; asso. physician Ste. Anne's Hosp., Ste. Anne de Bellevue, Que., 1972—. Fellow Royal Coll. Physicians Surgeons Can.; mem. Canadian, Que. med. assns., Med. Council Can. Home: 547 Montford Dr Dollard des Ormeaux PQ Canada

CHOWDHURY, MANNY, librarian; b. Calcutta, India, Aug. 1, 1926; s. Muni N. and Usha (Rani) C.; came to U.S., 1960, naturalized, 1972; B.S. in Bus. Adminstrn., Calcutta U., 1948; M.L.S., Pratt Inst., 1963; postgrad. Columbia U., 1967-68. Trainee Bklyn. Pub. Library, 1960-63; intern Fordham U. Library, N.Y.C., 1963-64; asst. librarian N.Y. State Dept. Edn. and Mental Hygiene, Albany, 1964-68; librarian Harlem Hosp. Med. Center health scis. div. Columbia Univ. Libraries, N.Y.C., 1968—. Mem. AAAS, AAUP, ALA, N.Y. Library Club, Am. Soc. for Info. Sci., Med., N.Y., Spl. libraries assns. Home: 506 Lenox Ave KP 6108 New York City NY 10037 Office: Harlem Hospital Med Center Library 506 Lenox Ave New York City NY 10037

CHRIST, DUANE MARLAND, computer systems analyst; b. Lakota, Iowa, Jan. 5, 1932; s. George Andrew and Esther Gertrude (Franke) C.; B.S. in Forestry, Iowa State U., 1953; M.A. in Math., U. Minn., 1960; m. Lily Esther Shih, Sept. 14, 1963. Sci. programmer United Aircraft Corp., East Hartford, Conn., 1960-63; computer systems analyst IBM, N.Y.C., 1963—. Served with USAF, 1953-56. IBM Residence Study fellow, 1966-68. Mem. Soc. Indsl. and Applied Math., Assn. Computing Machinery. Office: 77 Water St New York City NY 10005

CHRIST, LILY ESTHER SHIH (MRS. DUANE MARLAND CHRIST), educator; b. Korea, Sept. 19, 1936; s. Whan-Chang and Shin-Tze (Lin) Shih; B.S., U. Minn., 1960; M.A., Western Res. U., 1962; Ed.D., Columbia, 1967; m. Duane Marland Christ, Sept. 14, 1963. Came to U.S., 1955, naturalized 1968. Tchr. math. Cleve. Pub. Schs., 1960-62; asst. statis. lab. Columbia, N.Y.C., 1964-66; asst. prof. math. and edn. Coll. of Mt. St. Vincent, N.Y.C., 1966-68; asst. prof. math. John Jay Coll. Criminal Justice, City U. N.Y., N.Y.C., 1969-73, asso. prof., 1974—. Vol. math. tutor Task Force, Riverside Ch., 1966-69; vol. math. fair judge L.I. Math. Fair, 1966-69, Greater Met. N.Y. Math. Fair, 1970—. Fulbright-Hays sr. scholar, 1972-73. Mem. Nat. Council Tchrs. Math., Math. Assn. Am. (del. assembly, Met. N.Y. sect. 1966, 67, 71, 72, sec. 1976—), Am. Statis. Assn., Am. Ednl. Research Assn., Lambda Alpha Psi, Kappa Delta Pi. Office: 445 W 59th St New York City NY 10019

CHRISTEN, JOHN PHILIP, cons. engring. co. exec.; b. Mpls., June 14, 1934; s. Philip Gramne and Ruby Rose (Richert) C.; B.S., S.D. Sch. Mines, 1956; m. Ruth Cobb, Dec. 28, 1955 (dec. 1964); children—Barbara, Daniel, Karen, Matthew; m. 2d, Muriel Lansing, Jan. 21, 1965; adopted children—Robert, Larry. Mech. draftsman to asso. partner-project engr. Sargent Webster Crenshaw Folley, architects, engrs., Syracuse, N.Y., 1956-71; owner, operator John P. Christen Profl. Engr., cons. engrs., Liverpool, N.Y., 1971—; pres. R.H. Hopkins Co. Inc., indsl. engrs., Liverpool, 1975—. Mem. zoning bd. appeals Town of Lysander (N.Y.), 1968-77; pres., bd. dirs. Rapha Corp., 1976—. Registered profl. engr., N.Y., N.J., N.H., W.Va., Pa., Conn., Mass., Maine, Vt. Mem. N.Y. State, Nat. socs. profl. engrs. Republican. Rotary (pres. Baldwinsville club 1976-77). Home: 658 Idlewood Blvd Baldwinsville NY 13027 Office: 326 1st St Liverpool NY 13088

CHRISTENSEN, BILLY CROWL, computer co. exec.; b. Chicago Heights, Ill., July 7, 1926; s. Herman Nelson and Alletta Jett (Crowl) C.; student Ill. Inst. Tech., 1944; B.S., Purdue U., 1950; m. Rosamond Grindy, June 17, 1950; children—David Nelson, Jill Marion. With IBM, various locations, 1950—, asst. gen. mgr. operations, data processing group, White Plains, 1971-72, asst. group exec., 1972-73, v.p., gen. mgr. IBM World Trade Corp., 1974—, also v.p., dir., mem. exec. com. IBM World Trade Europe/Middle East/Africa Corp. Bd. dirs. YMCA Center Internat. Mgmt. Studies, Bus. Council Internat. Understanding, Internat. Mgmt. and Devel. Inst.; trustee Dental Clinic Boys Club N.Y., United Way New Canaan. Mem. Am. C. of C. Paris (v.p. 1970-71), White Plains C. of C. (dir., exec. com.), Internat. Assn. Students in Econs. and Mgmt. (dir.), Iran Am. C. of C. (v.p., dir., exec. com.), Belgian Am. C. of C. (dir.). Served with AUS, 1944-46. Episcopalian. Club: American (Paris). Home: 34 Lone Tree Farm Rd New Canaan CT 06840 Office: 360 Hamilton Ave White Plains NY 10601

CHRISTENSEN, ERNEST MARTIN, real estate broker; b. Marblehead, Mass., Aug. 14, 1933; s. Harry Martin and Amy Viola (Snow) C.; A.A., Boston U., 1958, B.S. in Pub. Relations, 1960; M.A. in Psychology and Guidance, N.Y. U., 1963; m. Gail Sandra Bruno, May 17, 1961; children—Hans Martin, Kirsten Amy. Adminstrv. asst. YMCA, Marblehead, 1949-51; asst. dir. student activities Boston U., 1960-62, counselor, 1961-62; adminstrv. asst. Loeb Student Center, N.Y. U., 1962, dir. Religious Center, 1962-63; dir. Coll. Union, Ithaca (N.Y.) Coll., 1963-65, dean of men, 1964-65; asso. prof. U. Man. (Can.), Winnipeg, 1966-71, dir. students union, 1969-71; dir. Stony Brook Union, Faculty Student Assn., State U. N.Y. at Stony Brook, 1971-73; v.p., treas. Over the Bridge, Inc., 1974—, sr. partner, 1978—; bd. dirs., exec. com. Annunity Account A, Great West Life Assurance Co. (Can.), 1967-70; ednl. cons. Brandon U. (Can.), 1967-68, Mt. Royal Jr. Coll. (Can.), 1968—, U. Man., 1966-71, U. Winnipeg, 1969-71, Del. State Coll., 1969-70, Normandale State Jr. Coll., 1969-71. Founding mem. Friends of the Kennedy Center; bd. dirs. Tompkins County (N.Y.) chpt. ARC; advt. mgr. Belfast (Maine) Broiler Festival, 1976; bd. dirs. Belfast Improvement Group, 1976—, v.p., 1976-77, pres., 1977-78; bd. dirs. Waldo County YMCA, treas., 1977-78; exec. bd. Waldo County Extension Service, 1978—; dist. chmn. Waldo dist. Boy Scouts Am., 1978—. Served from pvt. to sgt. USAF, 1952-56. Recipient Judson Rea Butler award Boston U., 1958. Mem. Am. Personnel and Guidance Assn. (abstractor Jour. Am. Coll. Student Personnel 1966-74), Assn. Coll. Unions (nat. v.p., nat. exec. com. 1969-71; chmn. finance, devel. com. 1973-74), Boston U. Alumni Assn. (nat. council 1967—), DAV (life), Scarlet Key, Tau Mu Epsilon. Methodist. Clubs: Belfast Rotary (dir. 1977-78), Masons (32 deg). Author: (with Keith G. Briscoe) Directory of College Unions, 1963; College Unions at Work, 1967; contbr. articles to profl. jours. Home: Searsport Ave Belfast ME 04915

CHRISTENSEN, KATHY WEBER, archtl. designer; b. Buffalo, Oct. 7, 1922; d. Paul S. and Bertha E. (Smith) Weber; m. James A. Christensen, Aug. 11, 1951 (dec.); children—Carol Schaper, Barbara Peets, Jean McPherson. Continuity dir. Ellis Advt. Co., Buffalo, 1943-45, Sta. WBNY, 1945-47; airport mgr., pilot Mutual Aviation, Buffalo, 1948-49; mem. engring. staff Houdaille Co., Buffalo, 1949-50; asst. sales promotion mgr. Carborundum Co. Inc., Niagara Falls, N.Y., 1950's; archtl. designer Barbalato Homes Co., Amherst, N.Y., 1965—; owner, mgr. Carousel Homes, Amherst, 1963—; sec., dir. Forest Heights Estates, Inc., 1969— now pres.; sec., dir. Barbalato Assos., 1973—. Mem. adv. bd. to Amherst Sch. Dist. number 1, 1965-66. Mem. Niagara Frontier Builders Assn. (dir. Home Show 65, 73), Greater Buffalo Bd. Realtors. Democrat. Designer numerous pvt. homes, Amherst. Home: 355 Berryman Dr Amherst NY 14221 Office: 115 Crestwood Ln Amherst NY 14221

CHRISTENSON, WILLIAM NEWCOME, physician; b. Biltmore Forest, N.C., Dec. 2, 1925; s. William Lambert and Beth (Newcome) C.; B.S., U. N.C., 1949; M.D., Johns Hopkins U., 1948; m. Elizabeth Chandler White, Aug. 9, 1957; children—Lisa Ann, Laurie E., Susan. Intern, asst. resident Mass. Gen. Hosp., Boston, 1948-50; asst. resident N.Y. Hosp., N.Y.C., 1953-55; dir. personnel health service, 1960—, asst. attending physician, 1961-64, asso. attending physician, 1964—; tng. Postgrad. Med. Sch. London, Eng., 1955-56; instr. medicine Cornell U. Med. Coll., N.Y.C., 1956-59, asst. prof. medicine, 1959-65, clin. asso. prof. medicine, 1965—; practice of medicine specializing in internal medicine, N.Y.C., 1960—. Served with USNR, 1950-52. Fellow A.C.P.; mem. Am. Fedn. Clin. Research, Am. Soc. Hematology, Am. Occupational Med. Assn., Phi Beta Kappa, Alpha Omega Alpha, Delta Kappa Epsilon. Research in hematology and human ecology. Home: 4 Legget Rd Bronxville NY 10708 Office: 525 E 68th St New York City NY 10021

CHRISTIANO, LORETTA PICARDI, ednl. adminstr.; b. Gloversville, N.Y., Aug. 5, 1938; d. Domenic and Veronica (Chardie) Picardi; student Fulton-Montgomery Community Coll., 1975-77; m. Tony Christiano, Aug. 28, 1958; children—Dianne Ruth, Louis Anthony. With Fulton County Nat. Bank & Trust Co., Gloversville, 1956-58; with Bd. of Edn., Gloversville, 1967—, account clk., 1976—, bus. ofcl./asst. purchasing agt., 1974—; notary pub., Gloversville, 1978—. Mem. Edn. Secs. Assn. (v.p. 1977-79), N.Y. Assn. Ednl. Secs. Republican. Roman Catholic. Home: 21 N Hollywood Ave Gloversville NY 12078 Office: 90 N Main St Gloversville NY 12078

CHRISTIANSEN, KJELL HROAR, surgeon; b. Oslo, Dec. 6, 1927; s. Rolf and Magda N. (Liberg) C.; came to U.S., 1928, naturalized, 1938; B.S., Dickinson Coll., 1948; M.D., Jefferson Med. Coll., 1952; m. Florence H. Horner, July 10, 1950; children—Stephen, Janet, Lois, Sharon, Susan. Intern, Bryn Mawr (Pa.) Hosp., 1952-53, resident in surgery, 1955-59, thoracic surgeon, 1959-61; thoracic surgeon VA Hosp., Oteen, N.Y., 1959-61; cons. VA Hosp., Wilmington, Del.; clin. prof. surgery Jefferson Med. Coll. Served with U.S. Navy, 1953-55. Mem. AMA, A.C.S., Am. Coll. Chest Physicians, A.C.P., Alpha Omega Alpha. Presbyterian. Club: Skytop. Home: Box 200 Glen Mills PA 19342

CHRISTIANSEN, RICHARD LOUIS, orthodontist; b. Denison, Iowa, Apr. 1, 1935; s. John C. and Rosa Katherine (Reissen) C.; student Iowa State U., 1953-55; D.D.S., U. Iowa, 1959; M.S.D., Ind. U., 1964; Ph.D., U. Minn., 1970; m. Nancy Marie Norman, June 24, 1956; children—Mark Richard, David Norman, Laura Marie. Dental intern USPHS Hosp., San Francisco, 1959-60, USPHS Outpatient Clinic, St. Louis, 1960-62; staff orthodontist Nat. Inst. Dental Research, NIH, Bethesda, Md., 1964-66, prin. investigator, 1970-73, chief craniofacial anomalies program, 1973—; lectr. U. Minn., 1966-70, U. Md., 1970—, Georgetown U., 1970—. Mem. ADA, Am. Assn. Orthodontists, Internat. Assn. Dental Research, AAAS, Internat. Union Physiol. Scis., Commd. Officers Assn. USPHS, Phi Eta Sigma, Omicron Kappa Upsilon. Lutheran (pres. ch. council). Contbr. articles to sci. jours.; research on intra-oral pressures and motor function, hemodynamics of oral facial tissues, equilibrium of dentition and biophysics of orthodontic tooth movement; inventor displacement transducer for oral function, 1970. Home: 5608 Alta Vista Rd Bethesda MD 20034 Office: Nat Inst of Dental Research Westwood Bldg Bethesda MD 20014

CHRISTIE, DONALD MELVIN, JR., physician; b. Lewiston, Maine, May 5, 1942; s. Donald Melvin and Dorothy Carolyn (Doble) C.; A.B., U. Rochester, 1964, M.D., 1968; D.L.F.C., U. Paris, 1963. Med. intern U. Iowa Hosps. and Clinics, Iowa City, 1968-69, resident, 1969-70, 73, chief med. resident, 1973-74; asst. prof. preventive medicine and medicine Sch. Medicine, U. Rochester (N.Y.), 1974-77; univ. physician, dir. clin. services Princeton (N.J.) U. Health Services, 1977—; contract escort-interpretor (French), U.S. Dept. State, 1964-70; coordinator Robert Wood Johnson Found. grantee, primary care tng. evaluation U. Rochester, 1974-77. Served with M.C., U.S. Army, 1970-72. Diplomate Am. Bd. Internal Medicine. Mem. Am. Pub. Health Assn., A.C.P., Am. Coll. Sports Medicine. Democrat. Home: 15-07 Deer Creek Dr Plainsboro NJ 08536 Office: Princeton University Health Services Princeton NJ 08544

CHRISTIE, EUGENE ROY, energy research and devel. co. exec.; b. Cleve., Sept. 17, 1926; s. Mathew James and Margaret Pearl (Haight) C.; B.S. cum laude, Ohio U., 1948; M.S., Mass. Inst. Tech., 1955; grad. Naval War Coll., 1964; M.B.A., George Washington U., 1967; m. June Grace Sheppard, Dec. 12, 1946; children—Kim Ellen, Jill Allyn, Pat Allison. Commd. ensign U.S. Navy, 1948, advanced through grades to comdr., 1963, ret., 1967; fighter pilot, 1950-52, test pilot, research and devel. mgr. Naval Air Devel. Squadron 5, China Lake, Calif., 1955-57; research physicist, mgr. U. Calif. Lawrence Livermore Lab., 1958-61; plans officer NATO, Naples, Italy, 1962-64; chief tech. div. atomic energy Office of Sec. Def. Washington, 1964-67; dir. planning Tracor, Inc., Rockville, Md., 1967-72; dir. program devel. Aerojet Nuclear Co., Idaho Falls, Idaho, 1972-75; mgr. solar, geothermal and advanced energy systems TRW, Inc., McLean, Va., 1975—. Mem. Am. Phys. Soc., Am. Nuclear Soc., Am. Soc. Safety Engrs., System Safety Soc., Air Force Assn., U.S. Naval Inst., Sigma Xi. Clubs: George Washington U., Mass. Inst. Tech. (Washington). Home: 508 Great Falls Rd Rockville MD 20850 Office: 7600 Colshire Dr McLean VA 22101

CHRISTIE, GEORGE NICHOLAS, economist; b. Wilmington, N.C., Nov. 2, 1924; s. Nicholas and Helen (Lymberis) C.; B.B.A., U. Miami, 1948; M.B.A., N.Y. U., 1956, Ph.D., 1963; m. Mary Danatos, July 22, 1951; children—Sultana Helen, Stephanie Hope, Susan Adrianne, Sandra Alicia, Gregory Nicholas. With Dun and Bradstreet, Inc., N.Y.C., 1949-61, staff bus. writer, 1959-61; asso. dir. Credit Research Found., asst. dir. edn. Nat. Assn. Credit Mgmt., N.Y.C., 1961-63; asst. sec. credit policy com., small bus. credit com. Am. Bankers Assn., N.Y.C., 1963-64, sec., 1964-67; asso. dir. Grad. Sch. Credit and Fin. Mgmt., dir. Nat. Inst. of Credit, 1967—; v.p., dir. research Credit Research Found. Inst., N.Y. Inst. Credit; lectr. Dartmouth Coll., Stanford U.; asso. prof. L.I. U.; adminstr. 2d year banking course Stonier Grad. Sch. Banking, Rutgers U. Served with AUS, 1943-46. Mem. Am. Econ. Assn., Am. Fin. Assn., Fin. Mgmt. Assn. Contbr. articles to profl. publs. Home: 65 Nassau Rd Great Neck NY 11021 Office: 3000 Marcus Ave Lake Success NY 11040

CHRISTIE, ROBERT SHARROTT, mech. engr.; b. Paterson, N.J., Oct. 25, 1921; s. Thomas Adams and Ethel G. (Sharrott) C.; B.S. in Mech. Engring., U. Mich., 1947; M.S., Stevens Inst. Tech., 1957; m. Carol Jay Hammann, Oct. 1, 1949; children—Claudia Sharrott, Colin McMillan. Mech. engr. Western Electric Co., N.Y.C., 1947-48; specifications engr. Port of N.Y. Authority, N.Y.C., 1949-50; fuze design engr. Picatinny Arsenal, Dover, N.J., 1950-51; instrument engr. Wallace & Tiernan Products Co., Belleville, N.J., 1952-55; mem. sr. staff, head mech. engring. sect. Plasma Physics Lab., Princeton U., 1955—. Mem. vestry All Saints Episcopal Ch., Princeton, N.J., 1967-71; trustee Chapin Sch., Princeton, 1971-76. Served with USAF, 1942-45. Mem. Am. Phys. Soc. Contbr. articles to profl. jours. Home: 276 Dodds Ln Princeton NJ 08540 Office: PO Box 451 James Forrestal Campus PPL Princeton NJ 08540

CHRISTINZIE, ANTHONY JOHN, counselor; b. Phila., June 3, 1951; s. Anthony John and Julia Virginia Christinzie; A.B. in Psychology, Temple U., 1973; M.A. in Counseling, Villanova U., 1975; psotgrad U. Conn., 1977—. Counselor and psychologist Phila. Bd. Edn., 1971-73, Maternity Blessed Virgin Mary Elementary Sch., Phila., 1976-77; pvt. practice counseling psychology, 1975—; lectr. Office of Residential Life U. Conn., 1977—, head resident for undergrad. dormitories, 1977—. Mem. Am., Pa. personnel and guidance assns., Am., Pa. sch. counselors assns., Am. Guild of Authors and Composers, Am. Soc. of Composers, Authors and Publishers. Home: 2118 Orthodox Philadelphia PA 19124

CHRISTLE, GARY E., govt. ofcl.; b. Boston, Nov. 7, 1943; s. Vernon and Margaet (Ryan) C.; B.M.E., Northeastern U., 1968; postgrad. Babson Coll., 1970-71; M.B.A., George Washington U., 1977; m. Linda M. Pleau, Jan. 6, 1968; 1 son, Michael L. Mgmt. intern Army Chief of Staff, Washington, 1971-72; cost analyst Comptroller of Army, Washington, 1972-75; program analyst Office of Asst. Sec. Def. (Comptroller), Washington, 1975—; lectr. on contract cost performance Def. Systems Mgmt. Coll. Served to 1st lt. U.S. Army, 1968-70. Decorated Bronze Star. Roman Catholic. Home: 14458 Filarete St Woodbridge VA 22193 Office: Office Asst Sec Def/Comptroller The Pentagon Washington DC 20301*

CHRISTOFF, KENNETH EUGENE, realtor; b. Pitts., Feb. 5, 1933; s. Emory Edward and Mildred (Bizub) C.; student U. Miami, 1952-53, U. Pitts., 1954-57; m. Suzanne Olcott, Mar. 2, 1957; children—Kenneth E., Cynthia A., Carole S., Cathleen M. Staff appraiser Western Pa. Research Assos., Pitts., 1957-60, v.p., 1960-61; pres., chmn. bd. Real Estate Appraisal Services, Inc., Pitts., 1961—; cons. Pa. Dept. Transp., Redevel. Authority Allegheny County (Pa.), Port Authority Allegheny County, Allegheny County Dept. Aviation, pub. acquiring agys. specializing in eminent domain; guest lectr. real estate appraisal local univs.; chmn. Scott Twp. Planning Commn., 1968-74, Scott Twp. Zoning Hearing Bd., 1970—. Mem. Greater Pitts. Bd. Realtors, Pa. Realtors Assn., Nat. Assn. Real Estate Bds., Am. Right of Way Assn., Nat. Assn. Rev. Appraisers, Nat. Inst. Real Estate Brokers, Am. Assn. Certified Appraisers, Pa. Soc. Roman Catholic. Home: 2 Manorview Rd Pittsburgh PA 15220 Office: 1910 Lawyers Bldg Pittsburgh PA 15219

CHRISTOFFERSON, GEORGE, microbiologist; b. Chgo., Apr. 10, 1936; s. Paul and Catherine (Arnbal) C.; B.S. in Microbiology, U. Wis., 1958, M.S. in Microbiology, 1962; Ph.D., U. N.C., 1967; m. Diane Carol Knerr, Aug. 10, 1963; children—Catherine Anne, Paul Victor, Mark Alan. Sr. virologist Abbott Labs., North Chicago, Ill., 1967-70; mgr. new products Electro-Nucleonics Labs., Inc., Bethesda, Md., 1970-74; v.p., dir. research Indsl. Biol. Labs., Rockville, Md., 1974-77; mgr. infectious disease br. Millipore Corp., Bedford, Mass., 1977—. Served with AUS, 1958-60. Mem. Am. Soc. Microbiology, AAAS, Tissue Culture Assn., Sigma Xi. Mason. Home: 56 Brucewood Rd Acton MA 01720 Office: Millipore Corp Ashby Rd Bedford MA 01730

CHRISTOPHER, ASPASIA COULOUMBIS, bilingual counselor; b. Utica, N.Y., Mar. 12, 1926; d. Fotty E. and Nicky J. (Livadas) Couloumbis; B.A., Hunter Coll., 1950; M.A., City U. N.Y., 1972, postgrad., 1976-77; m. Chris N. Christopher, Nov. 18, 1951; children—Nicholas C., Diane K. Labor researcher Internat. Brotherhood Pulp and Paper Workers, Washington, 1952-53; tchr. N.Y.C. Bd. Edn., 1963-74, counselor, 1974-75, bilingual-Greek counselor, 1976—. Chmn. edn. com. St. Mary's Day Care Center, 1977—, bd. dirs., 1977—; mem. Sunday Sch. com. St. Dimitrios Greek Orthodox Ch., Astoria, N.Y., 1974—. Certified tchr., counselor, City and State of N.Y. Mem. Greek Am. Behavioral Scis. Inst. (exec. bd.; founding), Am. Personnel and Guidance Assn., Hellenic Am. Educators Assn., AAUW, Hunter Coll. Alumni Assn., Smithsonian Instn., Fortune Soc.

CHROSTOWSKI, EDMUND JOSEPH, journalist; b. Stamford, Conn., Sept. 6, 1928; s. Charles Nicholas and Mary (Tisko) C.; B.A., U. Conn., 1949; m. Deanna Jensen, Jan. 6, 1962 (div. June 1978); children—Marjorie, Amy, Michael. Dispatcher, cashier Indsl. Food Services Inc., 1949-50; reporter WNLK, Norwalk, Conn., 1950; reporter Darien (Conn.) Rev., 1951-57; freelance corr. N.Y. Times, Norwalk Hour, Bridgeport (Conn.) Herald, 1951-57; editor Darien (Conn.) Rev., 1957-61, New Canaan (Conn.) Advertiser, 1961—. Bd. dirs. Am. Cancer Soc., Norwalk, 1970. Recipient George Washington medal Freedoms Found., 1963, Best News Story Typewriter award New Eng. Press Assn., 1970, Best Column award Nat. Editorial Assn., 1959. Mem. Conn. Editorial Assn. (v.p. 1971), New Eng. Press Assn., Nat. Editorial Assn., Darien C. of C., Sigma Delta Chi. Republican. Roman Catholic. Home: 59 Leonard St Stamford CT 06906 Office: 42 Vitti St New Canaan CT 06840

CHRUPCALA, MALCOLM WARNER, sch. dist. adminstr.; b. Fall River, Mass., July 15, 1941; divorced. Mus.B. in Edn., Mass. State Coll. at Lowell, 1963; Mus.M. in Edn., U. R.I., 1972. Band dir. North Kingston (R.I.) High Sch., 1963-64; asst. band dir. U. R.I., 1964-66; instr. orch. and chorus Rogers High Sch., Newport, R.I., 1966-72; dir. music Newport Sch. Dist., 1972—; composer, arranger, jazz pianist. Condr., organizer Newport Community Symphony, 1974-75. Mem. NEA, R.I. Edn. Assn., Jazz Educators Assn., Am. Fedn. Musicians. Developed new technique for classroom instruction on piano. Certified tchr., R.I. Home: 16 Bradford Ave Newport RI 02840 Office: Newport Sch Dept Newport RI 02840

CHRYSSAFOPOULOS, HANKA WANDA SOBCZAK (MRS. NICHOLAS CHRYSSAFOPOULOS), civil engr.; b. Porto Alegre, Brazil; d. Stefan and Estacia (Wilkoszynska) Sobczak; C.E., U. Rio Grande do Sul, 1951, Elec.-Mech. Engr., 1952; M.S. in C.E., U. Ill., 1954, Ph.D., 1963; m. Nicholas Chryssafopoulos, Sept. 6, 1956. Engr. in charge research, head soils lab. Soil Mechanics and Found. Engring. Sect., Tech. Inst. of Rio Grande do Sul, 1952-53, 54-55; research asst. U. Ill., 1955-59; research asst. Ill. State Geol. Survey, Urbana, 1959-60; research engr. Woodward, Clyde, Sherard & Assos., soil and found. cons., Kansas City, Mo., 1964-65; asst. prof. civil engring. Calif. State U. at Long Beach, 1965-67; engaged in pvt. research, 1967-77; sr. engr. Dames & Moore, cons. in environ. and applied earth scis., 1978—; research, cons. geotech. engring., coal tech.; cons. UN Devel. Program. Fulbright fellow, 1953. Registered profl. engr. Brazil. Mem. Am. Soc. C.E., Conselho Regional de Engerharia, Agronomia e Arquitetura (Brazil), Internat. Soc. Soil Mechanics and Found. Engring., Am. Arbitration Assn., Soc. Women Engrs., Geol. Soc. Am., Sigma Xi. Contbr. articles on soil mechanics, engring. geology and remote sensing, coal to profl. jours. Research in connection with differentiation of young glacial tills and their engring. properties. Home: 5 Horizon Rd Fort Lee NJ 07024 Office: Dames & Moore 2 Pennsylvania Plaza Suite 1176 New York City NY 10001

CHRYSSANTHOU, CHRYSSANTHOS P., pathologist; b. Salonica, Greece, Oct. 15, 1925; s. Prodromos C. and Despina (Zafiropoulou) C.; came to U.S., 1954, naturalized, 1968; M.D., Aristotelean U., Salonica, 1953; m. Gabriele Franke, Dec. 12, 1970; children—Despina, Helen. Resident in clin. pathology 424th Gen. Hosp. of Edn., Salonica, 1953-54; resident in pathology N.Y.C. Hosp., 1954-56; intern and resident in pathology Beth Israel Hosp., N.Y.C., 1957-58, research fellow in pathology, 1958-59, research asst., 1959-60, research asso., 1960-63, asso. dir. research, asso. pathologist, 1964-68; instr. pathology N.Y. U. Med. Sch., 1957; mem. faculty Beth Israel Hosp. Sch. Nursing, 1958-70; asso. pathologist Beth Israel Med. Center, N.Y.C., 1963-68, attending pathologist, asso. dir. research, 1968-69, attending pathologist, asso. dir. labs. and research, 1969-76, attending pathologist, dir. pathology, 1976—; asso. prof. pathology Mt. Sinai Sch. Medicine, City U. N.Y., 1967—; vis. prof. Claude Bernard Inst., U. Montreal, 1966. Recipient 1st award Annual Clin. Assembly Osteo. specialists, 1976; diplomate Greek Bd. Pathology; research grantee USPHS, NIH, Dept. Navy. Mem. AMA (Phys. Recognition award 1969, 72, 74, 78), Soc. Exptl. Biology and Medicine, Aerospace, Greek med. assns., Am. Soc. Exptl. Pathology, Am. Assn. Pathologists and Bacteriologists, Am. Assn. for Cancer Research, Am. Soc. Zoologists, Am. Assn. Anatomists, Microcirculatory Soc., AAAS, Undersea Med. Soc., Assn. Clin. Scientists, N.Y. Acad. Scis., Pathologists Club, Sigma Xi. Contbr. articles to med. jours. Patentee microscope attachment, process in osmotic hemolysis. Home: 200 Winston Dr Cliffside Park NJ 07010 Office: Beth Israel Medical Center 10 Perlman Pl New York City NY 10003

CHRYSTIE, THOMAS LUDLOW, investment banker; b. N.Y.C., May 24, 1933; s. Thomas Witter and Helen (Duell) C.; B.A., Columbia U., 1955; M.B.A., N.Y. U., 1960; m. Eliza S. Balis, June 9, 1955; children—Thomas W., Alice B., Helen S., Adden B., James MacD. With Merrill Lynch, Pierce, Fenner & Smith Inc., N.Y.C., 1955-75, dir. investment banking div., 1970-75; sr. v.p. Merrill Lynch & Co., 1975-78 chief fin. officer, 1976-78; chmn. Merrill Lynch White Weld Capital Markets Group, 1978—; dir. Merrill Lynch Rubbard, Merrill Lynch Internat., Merrill Lynch, Pierce, Fenner & Smith Inc., Merrill Lynch Internat. Bank, Merrill Lynch Leasing, Family Life Ins. Co. Trustee Columbia U., Am. Health Found., Taft Sch. Served to capt. USAF, 1956-58. Clubs: Down Town Assn. (N.Y.C.); Short Hills (N.J.). Home: 77 Knollwood Rd Short Hills NJ 07078 Office: 1 Liberty Plaza New York City NY 10080

CHRZANOWSKI, WILLIAM JAMES, lab. mgr.; b. Newark, Oct. 15, 1947; s. William Chester and Mildred D. (Stinson) C.; B.A. in Biology, Bloomfield (N.J.) Coll., 1969; m. Maria Isabel Calatraja, Sept. 16, 1972; 1 son, William James. Pilot plant supr. S.B. Denick Co., Newark, 1969-70; microbiologist Schmid Labs., Inc., Little Falls, N.J., 1971-74, pharm. prodn. supr., 1974-76, prodn. mgr.-latex, 1976—. Served in N.G. Home: 1960 Mountainview Ave Union NJ 07083 Office: Schmid Labs Route 46 West Little Falls NJ 07424

CHU, JEFFREY CHUAN, electronic data processing co. exec.; b. Tientsin, China, July 14, 1919; (came to U.S. 1940, naturalized 1948; s. Yao and Van-yi (Tang) C.; student U. Shanghai (China), 1938-40, Ill. Inst. Tech., 1950, Northwestern U., 1952; B.S., U. Minn., 1942; M.S., U. Pa., 1945; m. Loretta Yung, July 14, 1976; children—Lynnet (Mrs. Franz Helbig), Bambi (Mrs. Michael Rae), Deidre (Mrs. Frantisek Kocica). Engr. Philco Corp., Phila., 1942-43, engr. Reeves Instrument Co., N.Y.C., 1947-49; research asso. U. Pa., Phila., 1943-47; sr. scientist Argonne Nat. Lab., Chgo., 1949-56; dir. engring. Univac div. Sperry Rand Corp., Blue Bell, Pa., 1956-62; v.p. Electronic Data Processing div. Honeywell, Inc., Wellesley Hills, Mass., 1962-69, v.p. planning and devel. Honeywell Computer & Communication Group, Waltham, Mass., 1969-70, v.p. strategical planning Honeywell Info. Systems, Inc., Waltham, 1970-73; 1971-73; sr. v.p. N.Am. market ops. Wang Labs., Tewksbury, Mass., 1973-76; partner Chee Clapp & Idzall, 1976—. Mem. vis. com. Harvard. Fellow IEEE; mem. Research Soc. Am., Sigma Xi. Home: 10 Baldwin Circle Weston MA 02193 Office: 393 Totten Pond Rd Waltham MA 02154

CHU, TSANN MING, immunochemist; b. Kaohsiung, Taiwan, Apr. 18, 1938; s. Tsi Fa and Su Lian (Sun) C.; came to U.S., 1963, naturalized, 1971; B.S., Nat. Taiwan U., 1961; M.S., N.C. State U., 1965; Ph.D., Pa. State U., 1967; m. Bonnie Diane Covert, Sept. 28, 1967; children—Nancy, Daniel. Fellow Med. Found. Buffalo, 1967-69, Buffalo Gen. Hosp., 1969-70; asso. chief cancer research scientist, dir. diagnostic immunology and clin. chemistry Roswell Park Meml. Inst., Buffalo, 1970-76, dir. cancer research in diagnostic immunology research and biochemistry, 1976—; asst. prof. exptl. pathology State U. N.Y. at Buffalo, 1970, asso. prof., 1974-77, prof., 1977—; mem. com. cancer immunodiagnosis Nat. Cancer Inst., NIH, 1978—. United Health Found. Western N.Y. fellow, 1968-69. Mem. Am. Chem. Soc., Am. Soc. Clin. Pathologists, Am. Assn. Clin. Chemists, Am. Assn. Cancer Research, Am. Fedn. Clin. Research, Am. Assn. Immunologists, Am. Soc. Biol. Chemists, Phi Lambda Upsilon. Contbr. articles to profl. jours. Home: 117 Old Orchard Dr Williamsville NY 14221 Office: 666 Elm St Buffalo NY 14263

CHU, VALENTIN YUAN-LING, author; b. Shanghai, China, Feb. 14, 1919; s. Thomas V.D. and Rowena S.N. (Zee) Tsu; B.A., St. John's U. (Shanghai), 1940; m. Victoria Chao-yu Tsao, Sept. 25, 1954; 1 son, Douglas Chi-hua. Came to U.S., 1956, naturalized, 1961. Asst., Shanghai Municipal Council, 1940-42; asst. mgr. Thomas Chu & Sons, pub., printer, Shanghai, 1943-45; chief reporter China Press, Shanghai, 1945-49; pub. relations officer Central Air Transport Corp., Shanghai, Hong Kong, 1949; Hong Kong corr. Time & Life mags., 1949-56, with Time Inc., N.Y.C., 1956-76, writer, asst. editor Time-Life Books, 1968-76; asso. editor Reader's Digest Gen. Books, N.Y.C., 1978—; lectr. on China. Recipient spl. award UN Internat. Essay Contest, 1948. Mem. Authors League Am., Authors Guild. Presbyn. Author: Ta Ta, Tan Tan---Fight Fight, Talk Talk, 1963, Thailand Today, 1968; (with others) U.S.A., A Visitor's Handbook, 1969. Contbr. articles to popular mags. Home: 10 O'Connor Ct Montrose NY 10548

CHUANG, MING CHIA, mech. engr.; b. Taiwan, China, Feb. 13, 1937; s. Lou Hsiung and Chu (Lan) C.; came to U.S., 1963, naturalized, 1968; B.Sc., Cheng Kung U., 1959, M.Sc., 1961; Ph.D., U. Rochester, 1967; m. MowChu Hsu, June 30, 1964; children—Albert K.Y., Felix C.T., Richard S.C. Teaching and research fellow Cheng Kung U., Taiwan, 1962-63; sr. research engr. Westinghouse Research and Devel. Center, Pitts., 1966—. Tech. cons., Taiwan, U.S., 1973. Mem. ASME. Home: 4421 Driftman Dr Monroeville PA 15146 Office: Westinghouse Research Labs Pittsburgh PA 15235

CHUCK, HARRY COUSINS, ret. army officer; b. Bklyn., Mar. 10, 1904; s. Harry and Emily (Cousins) C.; B.A., Colgate U., 1926; J.D., N.Y. U., 1930, J.S.D., 1932; m. Amy May Blakeney, Jan. 16, 1943. Admitted to N.Y. bar, 1932; practiced in N.Y.C., 1932-40; commd. 2d lt., U.S. Army Res., 1925, advanced through grades to col., 1944, ret., 1959. Decorated Legion of Merit. Mem. Am. Bar Assn., N.Y. County Lawyers Assn., Assn. U.S. Army, Ret. Officers Assn., Phi Delta Phi, Pi Delta Epsilon. Baptist. Home: 1047 Sandy Ridge Rd Doylestown PA 18901

CHUN, MYUNG KI, physicist; b. Seoul, Korea, Mar. 19, 1932; s. Eung Kyu and Hyo Sun (Lee) C.; came to U.S., 1961, naturalized, 1969; B.S. in Elec. Engring., Yonsei U., Seoul, 1956, M.S., 1958; M.E.E., Yale U., 1962; Ph.D. in Electrophysics, Rensselaer Poly. Inst., 1969; m. Chung Hee Kim, Dec. 22, 1962; 1 son, Gene. From engr. to chief engr. Christian Broadcasting System, Seoul, 1956-61; with Gen. Electric Co., 1962—, physicist Research and Devel. Center, Schenectady, 1966-69, devel. engr. aerospace controls dept., Binghamton, N.Y., 1969-73, sr. physicist electronics lab., Syracuse, N.Y., 1973—; instr. Yonsei U., 1958-61; adj. prof. Sch. Advanced Tech., State U. N.Y. at Binghamton, 1969-70. Mem. IEEE (sr. mem., chmn. Binghamton chpt. electron devices group 1971-72), Am. Phys. Soc., Optical Soc. Am., Sigma Xi, Eta Kappa Nu. Author research papers. Home: 108 Colony Park Dr Liverpool NY 13088 Office: Gen Electric Electronics Lab Electronics Park Syracuse NY 13201

CHUN, SAE-IL, physician; b. Korea, Sept. 25, 1936; s. Jin Kun and Yong Wha (Yoon) C.; came to U.S., 1967, naturalized, 1977; M.D., Yonsei U., Seoul, Korea, 1961; m. Soon Ok Choi, Sept. 18, 1965; children—Joseph, Scott, Sam. Intern, St. Agnes Hosp., Phila., 1967-68, resident, 1968-70; resident Hosp. U. Pa., Phila., 1970-72; sr. attending physician in rehab. service Phila. Gen. Hosp.; med. dir. Del. Curative Workshop, Wilmington, 1974—; asst. prof. phys. medicine U. Pa., 1972—; chmn. World Acupuncture Congress, 1974; mem. Acupuncture Adv. Bd. to N.J., 1977—. Recipient Physician's Recognition award AMA, 1977. Mem. Am. Acad. Phys. Medicine and Rehab., Internat. Acupuncture Assn. (pres.). Editor Acupuncture Research, 1974—. Home: 1421 Vallee Dr Woodbury NJ 08096 Office: 3400 Spruce St Philadelphia PA 19104

CHUNG, ARTHUR FREDERICK, gynecologic oncologist; b. Portland, Jamaica, B.W.I., Dec. 10, 1942; s. Albert A. and Myrtle Maud C.; came to U.S., 1968, naturalized, 1978; M.B., Chir.B., Aberdeen U., 1967. House surgeon, physician Aberdeen (Scotland) U. Med. Sch. Hosps., 1967-68, asst. resident obstetrics-gynecology, 1968-71, resident, 1971-72; resident N.Y. Hosp.-Cornell Med. Center, N.Y.C., fellow gynecologic oncology Meml. Sloan Kettering Cancer Center, N.Y.C., 1972-74; attending physician Roosevelt Hosp., N.Y.C., 1978—, dir. gynecologic oncology, dept. obstetrics-gynecology, 1975—; asst. prof. obstetrics-gynecology Columbia U., N.Y.C., 1974—. Diplomate Am. Bd. Obstetrics and Gynecology (subsplty. gynecologic oncology). Fellow Am. Coll. Obstetrics and Gynecology; mem. N.Y. County, N.Y. State med. socs., Soc. Surg. Oncology, N.Y. Acad. Scis., N.Y. Obstet. Soc. Contbr. articles to profl. publs. Office: 428 W 59th St New York City NY 10019

CHUNG, EDWARD KOO-YOUNG, physician, educator; b. Seoul, Korea, Mar. 3, 1931; s. Il-Chun C.; came to U.S., 1958, naturalized, 1971; B.S., Seoul Nat. U., 1953, M.D., 1957; m. Sang-In Lee, May 26, 1958; children—Linda C., Christopher D. Rotating intern St. Louis City Hosp., 1958-59; resident St. Louis County Hosp., 1959-60, St. Johns Hosp., St. Louis, 1960-62; fellow cardiology Washington U. Sch. Medicine, St. Louis, 1962-64; asst. prof. medicine Meharry Med. Coll., Nashville, 1964-66, dir. Heart Sta., 1964-68, asso. prof., 1966-68; vis. investigator cardiology Vanderbilt U. Sch. Medicine, Nashville, 1965-68; asso. prof. medicine W.Va. U., 1968-70, dir. Heart Sta., 1968-73, prof. medicine, 1970-73; prof. medicine, dir. Heart Sta., Jefferson Med. Coll., Thomas Jefferson U., Phila., 1973—. Fellow A.C.P., Am. Coll. Cardiology (past gov. W.Va.), Philippine Heart Assn. (hon.), Philippine Coll. Cardiology (hon.); mem. AMA, Am. Heart Assn., Am. Fedn. Clin. Research, Korean Med. Assn. Author: Digitalis Intoxication, 1969; Controversy in Cardiology, 1976; Non-Invasive Cardiac Diagnosis, 1976; Quick Reference to Cardiovascular Diseases, 1977; Cardiac Arrhythmias: Self Assessment, 1977; Principles of Cardiac Arrhythmias, 2d edit., 1977; ECG Diagnosis: Self Assessmen, Vol. II, 1977; Exercise Electrocardiography: Practical Approach, 1978; Artificial Cardiac Pacing: Practical Approach, 1978; Ambulatory Electrocardiography: Holter Monitor Electrocardiography, 1978; Cardiac Arrhythmias: Management (tape series), 1973; Cardiac Emergency Care, 2d edit., 1979; Clinical Electrocardiography Parts I through XII, 1972—; editorial bd. Heart and Lung, 1973—, Jour. Electrocardiology, 1975—, Cardiology, 1975—, Primary Cardiology, 1976—, Drug Therapy, 1976—, The Hosp. Physician, 1978—; editorial cons. various pubs.; book and manuscript reviewer; contbr. articles to med. jours. Office: Thomas Jefferson U 111 S 11th St Philadelphia PA 19107

CHURCH, COLIN BARCLAY, govt. ofcl.; b. Cleve., Mar. 1, 1936; s. Henry Clay and Mary Ethel (Dustman) C.; A.B., Harvard, 1958; M.B.A., Wharton Sch., U. Pa., 1962; m. Cornelia Steele Dimmitt, 1958; children—Colin Barclay, Jeffrey Harrison. Cons. mktg. dept. Wharton Grad. div. U. Pa.; mem. mktg. mgmt. program Gen. Electric Co., N.Y.C., 1962-63; specialist distbn. planning and franchising Internat. Gen. Electric, N.Y.C., 1963-66; sales rep. Mediterranean and mil. sales Gen. Electric Co., Syracuse, N.Y., 1966-68, specialist sales support, Bethesda, Md., 1968-69, mgr. sales support, 1969-70, mgr. internat. bus. planning, 1970-73, mgr. internat. market planning, Rockville, Md., 1973-75; impact analysis Consumer Product Safety Commn., Bethesda, Md., 1975-76; strategic planner, 1977; chmn. interagency regulatory liaison group EPA, FDA, OSHA and CPSC, Washington, 1978—. Vice-pres. Greenwich Forest Citizens Assn., 1971-73, pres., 1973-74. Served to lt. USNR, 1958-60. Mem. Am. Mktg. Assn., Assn. M.B.A. Execs., Acad. Internat. Bus., Advanced Mktg. Research Internat., Am. Arab Assn. Commerce and Industry. Clubs: Harvard, Wharton Graduate (Washington). Home: 7805 Overhill Rd Bethesda MD 20015 Office: 5401 Westbard Ave Bethesda MD 20207

CHURCH, FRANCES CONOVER, family advocate; b. Chgo., Dec. 30, 1922; d. Harvey and Sarah Dorothy (Jobson) Conover; certificate Katherine Gibbs Secretarial Sch., 1944; B.A., Manhattanville Coll., 1973; M.S., Columbia U., 1976; m. John Letchworth Church, Oct. 31, 1974; children—Leslie Conover Gagney, Aileen Conover Gagney, Carolyn Conover Gagney, Richard Arthur Gagney; stepchildren—Eileen Virginia, John Letchworth, Sally Elizabeth. Sec.-accountant Miller Marine Decking Co., N.Y.C., 1941-42; benefits clk. Scarsdale (N.Y.) Sch. System, 1971-72; family advocate Family and Children's Services, Stamford, 1976—. Pres., Harrison (N.Y.) chpt. League Women Voters, 1953-56, sec. pub. relations, publicity chmn., Larchmont, N.Y., 1957-59, chmn. social welfare N.Y. State, 1960, chmn. urban crisis, Stamford, 1977-78; chmn. pub. relations Jr. League Larchmont, 1958; active Girl Scouts U.S., 1958-73; Mayor's rep. S.W. Conn. Regional Housing Council, 1978—. Mem. Conn. Assn. Human Services (dir. 1977—, exec. com. 1978-79), Nat. Assn. Social Work. Clubs: Mid-Day, Wainwright House. Home: 32 Flying Cloud Rd Stamford CT 06902 Office: 60 Palmer's Hill Rd Stamford CT 06902

CHURCH, LLOYD EUGENE, denist, educator; b. Littleton, W.Va., Sept. 25, 1919; s. Howard and Mary (Henderson) C.; A.B., W.Va. U., 1942, D.D.S., U. Md., 1944; M.S., George Washington U., 1951, Ph.D., 1959; m. Hildegard Cascio, Apr. 1, 1964; 1 dau., Pamela Gail. Asst. prof. anatomy George Washington U. Sch. Medicine, Washington, 1962-64, asst. prof. dept. anatomy, 1964-67, asso. research prof., 1967—; asst. prof. medicine Sch. Medicine, U. Md.; research scientist Nat. Biomed. Research Found., Washington, 1963-68; vis. prof. anatomy and oral surgery Bangalore (India) U. Dental Coll., 1966. Mem. Pub. edn. com. Am. Cancer Soc., 1967; mem. adv. group Regional Med. Program, Washington, 1967-69; chmn. Montgomery County Crime Prevention Commn., 1967, organizer and pres. conf. on prevention and control vandalism; mem. Nat. conf. Juvenile Delinquency Dept. Health Edn. and Welfare, 1967. Recipient certificate of Distinguished Citizen, Gov. State Md., 1965, plaque Sword of Hope, 1966. Fellow Royal Micros. Soc. Gt. Britian, Am. Coll. Dentists, Internat. Coll. Dentists, Washington Acad. Scis., Internat. Assn. Oral Surgeons (founding fellow, life); mem. Am., Md. dental assns., Assn. Mil. Surgeons U.S., AAAS, Am. Assn. Oral Surgeons, Am. Soc. Exptl. Biology and Medicine, Fed. Dental Assn. Internat., Internat. Soc. Anesthesia Research, Royal Soc. Health, Am. Hist. Assn., AAUP, Internat. Soc. Burn Injuries Washington Acad. Medicine, Philos. Soc. Washington, Montgomery County Med. Soc., So. Soc. Anatomists. Club: Cosmos (Washington). Research on bone devel. and growth. Home: 7005 Glenbrook Rd Bethesda MD 20014

CHURCH, ROBERTA, govt. ofcl.; d. Robert R. and Sara (Johnson) Church; A.B., Northwestern U., 1935, M.A., 1937. Social worker Family and Child Welfare div. Chgo. Welfare Adminstrn., 1940-43, adoption div. Ill. Children's Home and Aid Soc., Chgo., 1943-53; cons. for minority groups U.S. Dept. Labor, 1953-61; cons. Rehab. Services Adminstrn., HEW, 1961—. Mem. Pres.'s Nat. Adv. Council on Adult Edn., 1970-75; mem. Rep. State Exec. Com. Tenn., 1952-53. Recipient Certificate of Merit, Alpha Phi Alpha, 1956. Mem. Nat. Assn. Social Workers, Delta Sigma Theta. Republican. Episcopalian. Co-author: The Robert R. Churches of Memphis. Home: 1629 Columbia Rd NW Washington DC 20009 Office: US Dept Health Edn and Welfare Washington DC 20201

CHURCHILL, EDWARD DELOS, educator; b. Boston, May 5, 1934; s. Edward Delos and Mary Lowell (Barton) C.; A.B., Harvard U., 1956; M.A., U. Pa., 1962; m. Ellen Ellis, children—Eric, Eva. Instr. history Kent (Ohio) State U., 1967-71, Rutgers U., New Brunswick, N.J., 1972-73, St. Joseph's Coll., Phila., 1975—. Leader experiment in internat. living, India, 1963. Served with U.S. Army, 1956-58. NDEA fellow. Mem. Am. Hist. Assn., Assn. Asian Studies. Unitarian. Contbr. articles to profl. jours. Home: 119 Mountwell Ave Haddonfield NJ 08033

CHURCHILL, FREDERICK DEANE, real estate and pub. relations exec.; b. Brockton, Mass., Jan. 5, 1924; s. Lucius Everett and Mildred White (Deane) C.; student Ohio Wesleyan U., 1942-43; B.S. in Bus. Adminstrn., Boston U., 1949; postgrad. in utility mgmt. U. Mich.,

1962; m. Joan Margaret Russell, May 1, 1954; children—Rolfe Russell, Katherine Deane, Lucius Bradford. Radio announcer Sta. WLLH, Lowell, Mass., 1944; newscaster Sta. WCOP, Boston, 1945; night news editor Sta. CBS-WEEI, Boston, 1946-49; dir. advt. and pub. relations Central Vt. Pub. Service Corp., Rutland, 1950-52, asst. sales mgr., exec. asst. to pres., 1952-55; residential sales promotion mgr. Edison Electric Inst., N.Y.C., 1955-57, advt. mgr. Live Better Electrically program, 1957-58, mgr. Light for Living Program, 1958-60; dir. sales promotion and advt. Am. Electric Power Service Corp., N.Y.C., 1960-66, dir. sales promotion and sales tng., 1966-70; pres., treas. Hilda B. Russell Realty, Inc., Windsor, Vt., 1970—; v.p. pub. relations Churchill Co., Windsor, 1970—; v.p. Vt. Sports & Hobby Inc., 1972-76. Mem. design rev. com. Town of Windsor; chmn. Windsor Bicentennial Com., 1977; mem. State of Vt. Com. of 200, 1977. Mem. Nat., Vt. assns. realtors, Windsor County Bd. Realtors, Windsor Area C. of C. (pres. 1974), Hist. Windsor Inc. (founder). Episcopalian. Club: Rotary (pres. 1975). Editor: Carefree Cooking, 1956-58; Food Freezing Facts, 1955-60; Home Management Guidebook to Electric Living, 1962. Home: Box 66 24 Main St Windsor VT 05089 Office: 149 Main St Windsor VT 05089

CHURCHILL, HOWARD JAMES, lawyer; b. Bklyn., Nov. 19, 1909; s. William Alwood and Blodwen Catherine (Davies) C.; M.E., Bklyn. Poly. Inst.; LL.B., N.Y. Law Sch., 1932; LL.M., Bklyn. Law Sch., 1933; m. Elizabeth Ann Ritchie, Mar. 28, 1942; children—Mary Elizabeth, William George. Admitted to N.Y. bar, 1934; partner firm Fraser, Myers & Manley, N.Y.C., 1946-52, Churchill, Rich, Weymouth & Engel, N.Y.C., 1952-57, Byerly, Townsend, Watson & Churchill, N.Y.C., 1958-66, Cooper, Dunham, Clark, Griffen & Moran, N.Y.C., 1967—. Asso. prof. Bklyn. Poly. Inst., 1946-56. Mem. Am. Bar Assn. (patent sect.), N.Y. Patent Law Assn., N.Y. Law Sch. Alumni Assn. (dir.). Republican. Episcopalian. Club: Cherry Valley. Home: 163 Brompton Rd Garden City NY 11530 Office: 30 Rockefeller Plaza New York City NY 10020

CHURCHILL, JOAN RUSSELL (MRS. FREDERICK DEANE CHURCHILL), pub. relations co. exec.; b. Greenfield, Mass., Dec. 9, 1931; d. Rolfe Spaulding and Hilda (Belknap) Russell; B.A., U. Vt., 1953; m. Frederick Deane Churchill, May 1, 1954; children—Rolfe Russell, Katherine Deane, Lucius Bradford. Newspaper reporter, editor Vt. Jour., Windsor, 1952; advt. rep. Rutland (Vt.) Herald, 1953-55; editor Carrier Internat. News, Carrier Corp., N.Y.C., 1955-57, Builders Pub. Co., Mt. Vernon, N.Y., 1956-59; pub. relations dir. Knudsen-Moore Inc., Stamford, Conn., 1959-66; pres. Churchill Co., pub. relations, Windsor, 1966—, Vt. Sports & Hobby Inc., 1973-76; v.p., clk., broker Hilda B. Russell Realty, Inc., Windsor, 1970—; asso. Stevens & Kirwan, Hanover, N.H., 1973-76. Vice pres. Jr. League of Pelham, 1968-70; pres., trustee, Historic Windsor Inc.; pub. relations dir. Mt. Ascutney Hosp. and Health Center, 1974—, regional planning commr., 1973-76; mem. Town Beautification Com., Town Bicentennial Com.; sec., v.p. Windsor Area Vis. Nurse Assn.; bd. dirs. United Fund, Pelham, 1967-70. Home: 24 N Main St Windsor VT 05089 Office: 149 S Main St Windsor VT 05089

CHURG, JACOB, physician; b. Dolhinow, Poland, July 16, 1910; s. Wolf and Gita (Ravich) C.; came to U.S. 1936, naturalized 1943; M.D., U. Wilno, Poland, 1933, M.D. in Pathology, 1936; m. Vivian Gelb, Oct. 18, 1942; children—Andrew Marc, Warren Bernard. Intern, City Hosp., Wilno, Poland, also State Hosp., Wilejka, Poland, 1933-34; asst. in gen. and exptl. pathology U. Wilno. 1934-36; asst. in bacteriology Mt. Sinai Hosp., N.Y.C., 1938, fellow in pathology, 1941-43, research asso., 1946—, attending pathologist, 1966—; resident in pathology Beth Israel Hosp., Newark, 1939-40; pathologist Barnert Meml. Hosp., Paterson, N.J., 1946—; prof. pathology and community medicine Mt. Sinai Sch. Medicine, N.Y.C., 1966—; cons. pathologist VA Hosp., Bronx, N.Y., Nassau County (N.Y.) Med. Center, St. Barnabus Med. Center, Livingston, N.J.; chmn. mesothelioma reference panel Internat. Union against Cancer, 1965—; chmn. com. for histologic classification renal diseases WHO, 1975—; former mem. scientific advisory group NIH, Bethesda, Md. Served to capt. M.C., AUS, 1943-46. ETO. Diplomate Am. Bd. Pathology. Fellow Coll. Am. Pathologists; mem. AMA, Am. Assn. Pathologists, N.Y. Acad. Scis., N.Y. Acad. Medicine, Internat. Acad. Pathology, Harvey Soc., Am. Soc. Clin. Pathologists, Am. Soc. Exptl. Pathology. Author: Renal Disease; Histological Classification of Renal Diseases; editorial bd. Lab. Investigation, Nephron, Histopathology, contbns. to Nephrology. Research in vascular diseases and renal structure, pneumokonioses. Co-describer syndrome of allergic granulomatosis. Address: 711 Ogden Ave Teaneck NJ 07666

CHUTE, MORTIMER HENRY, JR., wholesale co. exec.; b. Bklyn., Sept. 30, 1935; s. Mortimer Henry and Dorothy Catherine (Ketels) Ch.; B.A., Princeton U., 1956; m. Mary Jane Adams, Mar. 23, 1957; children—Catherine, Elizabeth, Dorothy, Margaret. With Bainbridge, Kimpton & Haupt, Inc., N.Y.C., 1958—, sales mgr., 1960-62, v.p., 1962-73, pres., 1973—. Pres., Garden City Community Fund, 1973—; pres. Internat. Student Exchange, Garden City, 1968-71; v.p. Pro Arte Symphony, Nassau County, 1971-72; chmn. 3d Congl. Dist. Young New Yorkers for Rockefeller, 1966; mem. Nat. Fin. Com. for Rockefeller, 1968; trustee Friends World Coll. Served with USMCR, 1956-58. Mem. Nat. Office Products Assn. (dir., exec. com.), Wholesale Stationers Assn. (dir. 1970—, pres. 1977), S.A.R., Alumni Assn. Princeton U. (pres., 1971-73), Princeton Club N.Y. (gov. 1964—, v.p. 1976). Republican. Episcopalian. Clubs: Nassau, Cap and Gown (Princeton); Cherry Valley (Garden City); Coral Beach (Paget, Bermuda). Home: 27 Chestnut St Garden City NY 11530 Office: 263 9th Ave New York City NY 10001

CHYUNG, CHI HAN, mgmt. cons.; b. Seoul, Korea, Jan. 27, 1933; s. Do Soon and Boksoon (Kim) C.; came to U.S., 1954, naturalized, 1963; B.S., Kans. Wesleyan U., 1958; M.B.A., Mich. State U., 1960; postgrad. Mass. Inst. Tech.; m. Alice Yvonne Whorley, Dec. 23, 1961; children—Eric, Diana. Ops. analyst Chevrolet div. Gen. Motors Corp., 1959-61; economist Internat. Harvester Co., 1961-63; sr. analyst market div. Internat. Minerals & Chem. Corp., 1963-66; mgr. market info. and planning Gulf & Western Industries, 1966-68; dir. market planning and devel. Am. Standard, Inc., 1968-71; pres. Oxytech Corp., mgmt. cons., Darien, Conn., 1971—; dir. Korea Hapsum Co. Cons. Govt. Korea, Taisei Constrn. Co., Tokyo, Japan. Served with Korean Army, 1951-53. Mem. Inst. Mgmt. Scis., Am. Mktg. Assn., Ops. Research Soc., Am. Chem. Soc., N.Am. Corporate Planning Soc., Beta Gamma Sigma. Contbr. papers to profl. lit. Address: 433 Boston Post Rd Darien CT 06820

CHYZOWYCH, EUGENE SOTHER, soccer coach, educator; b. Sambir, Ukraine, Jan. 27, 1935; s. Walter and Helen (Silecka) C.; came to U.S., 1945, naturalized, 1955; B.S., Temple U., 1963; m. Anna Elias, July 11, 1964; children—Eugene, Michael. Tchr., Columbia High Sch., Maplewood, N.J., 1969—; owner, dir. All Am. Soccer Camp, Cornwall, N.Y., 1973-74; pres. Am. Profl. Soccer League, 1971-73; coach U.S. World Cup Team, 1973; asst. coach U.S. Olympic Team, 1976; head coach U.S. Nat. Team, 1973-74. Trustee Newark Pub. Library. Served with M.I., U.S. Army, 1953-64. Named Coach of Year, Am. Soccer League, 1969, State N.J., 1974-75, N.J. State Coll. and High Sch. Ofcls. Assn., 1977, N.J. Coach of Year of Volleyball. Mem. Sch. and Coll. Ofcls. Assn., U.S. Soccer Fedn., Nat. Soccer Coaches Assn., Essex County Coaches Assn., Ukrainian Athletic Assn. Newark. Home: 61 Whiteoak Dr South Orange NJ 07079

CIARFELLA, FRANCIS GERALD, ednl. adminstr.; b. Boston, July 28, 1925; s. Frank and Catherine (Sebastian) C.; B.S., U. Mass., 1950, M.S., 1956; postgrad. Boston U., 1960-66; m. Emily R. Hanley, July 11, 1948; children—Catherine Anita, Dennis Francis, Francis Edward, Donna Marie. Prin. schs., Wendell, Mass., 1950-52, Leverett, Mass., 1952-55, Tewksbury, Mass., 1955-61; supt. schs. Rutland-Windsor Dist., Ludlow, Vt., 1961-63, Sch. Supervisory Union 27, Hudson, N.H., 1963-64, Oxford (Mass.) Pub. Schs., 1965-67, Prospect Pub. Schs., Prospect, Conn., 1968-70, Regional Sch. Dist. 16, Prospect-Beacon Falls, Conn., 1970—. Cons. sch. needs studies. Bd. dirs. United Givers Oxford, 1965-68, Prospect, 1968—. Served with USN, World War II; PTO. Mem. Am. Assn. Sch. Adminstrs., New Eng., Conn., assns. sch. supts., Litchfield County, New Haven County supts. assns., Council Ednl. Facilities Planners. Home: 182 Plymouth St Holbrook MA 02343 Office: Community School Center St Prospect CT 06712

CIBELLA, ROSS CASIMIR, mgmt. cons.; b. Rochester, N.Y., Sept. 20, 1911; s. John S. and Grace (Castiglione) C.; B.S., Alfred U., 1934; student Western Res. U., 1934-35, Fenn Coll., 1935-36, U. Pitts., 1951-52; m. Marjorie Alice Sharp, Jan. 15, 1938; children—Richard S., James H., Robert Gordon. Tech. librarian titanium pigment div. Nat. Lead Co., Sayreville, N.J., 1936-37; librarian Calgon Corp. (formerly Hagan Chems. & Controls, Inc.), Pitts., 1937-50, personnel mgr., dir. library, 1950-69, asst. to pres., 1969-72, also dir. employee relations; mgmt. cons., 1972-73; dir. coop. edn. Allegheny Community Coll., Pitts., 1973-74; mgmt. cons. Engring. Works div. Dravo Corp., Neville Island, Pa. Mgr. support services Nat. Alliance Businessmen, 1970 (on loan); pres., dir. Central Blood Bank Pitts., Inc. Part time instr. Pa. State U. Extension, Robert Morris Coll. Pres. Downtown Br. YMCA, Pitts., 1943-44, Pennhills Br., 1953-54; chmn. indsl. council Sta. WQEX-TV, ednl. TV; bd. dirs. Southwestern Pa. Jr. Achievement, Inc., 1960-73; southeastern sect. chmn. United Fund Allegheny County, 1962. Mem. Pitts. Personnel Assn. (dir.), Chartiers Valley Personnel Assn. (dir.), Chartiers Valley Personnel Group, Spl. Libraries Assn. (pres. Pitts. chpt. 1940-42), Am. Chem. Soc., Pitts. Jr. (pres. 1947-48), Pitts. chambers commerce, Am. Soc. Tng. and Devel. (pres. 1972-73, chmn. bd. 1973—). Methodist (bd.). Mason. Author: Directory of Micro-film Sources, 1941; Trade Names Index, 1941. Editor: Calgon News: 1950-61. Home: 1412 Stoltz Rd Bethel Park PA 15102 Office: Dravo Corp Engring Works Div Neville Island PA 15225

CIBLEY, LEONARD JONATHAN, obstetrician, gynecologist; b. Boston, Nov. 21, 1919; s. Nathan L. and Anna (Rosef) C.; A.B., Boston U., 1948, M.D., 1952; m. Shirley Idelson, Nov. 22, 1942; children—Laurence J., Jerold D. Rotating intern Newton-Wellesley Hosp., Newton, Mass., 1952-53; resident obstetrics and gynecology Beth Israel Hosp., Boston, 1953-55, Fordham Hosp., N.Y.C., 1955-57; vol. fellow pathology Free Hosp. Women, Brookline, Mass., 1957; individual practice medicine, specializing in obstetrics and gynecology, Newton Centre, Mass., 1957—; clin. instr. obstetrics and gynecology Harvard Med. Sch., Boston, 1970-78, lectr., 1978—; clin. instr. Boston U., 1965-77, asst. clin. prof. medicine, 1973-77, asso. clin. prof., 1978—, asst. dir. continuing med. edn., 1977—; sr. obstetrician and gynecologist Newton-Wellesley Hosp., 1957-76; asso. obstetrics and gynecology Beth Israel Hosp., Boston, 1957-74, asso. vis. obstetrician gynecologist, 1974—; sr. obstetrician Waltham (Mass.) Hosp., 1962-70, acting chief dept. obstetrics and gynecology, 1970-71, chief, 1971-76; asst. vis. obstetrician-gynecologist Univ. Hosp., Boston, 1964—; asso. vis. gynecologist Boston City Hosp., 1976—; asso. gynecologist Jewish Meml. Hosp., Boston, 1964—; gynecologist Fernald State Sch. Mentally Retarded, Waltham, Mass., 1972—; chief dysplasia and colposcopy clinic Boston City Hosp., 1975—; med. dir. Meducation Inc., Newton Centre, 1970—; cons. in field; one-man shows metal sculpture; filmmaker. Served with USNR, 1942-45. Diplomate Am. Bd. Obstetrics and Gynecology. Fellow Internat. Soc. for Study of Vulvar Disease, Nat. Bd. Med. Examiners, Mass. Med. Soc., Am. Coll. Obstetrics and Gynecology, New Eng. Assn. Obstetrics and Gynecology; mem. N.Y. Acad. Scis., Biol. Photog. Assn., Soc. Sci. Study Sex, Am. Fertility Soc., Am. Assn. Gynecol. Laparoscopists, Am. Soc. Colposcopy and Colpomicroscopy, New Eng. Sculptors Assn., Mass. Physicians Art Soc. Inventor in field. Contbr. articles to med. publs.; producer med. films and TV programs. Home: 251 Grant Ave Newton Centre MA 02159 Office: 683 Beacon St Newton Centre MA 02159 also 20 Hope Ave Waltham MA 02154

CICERO, FIORELLO THOMAS, health services adminstr.; b. S.I., N.Y., Nov. 17, 1933; s. Gerardo S. and Veneranda (Emanuelle) C.; B.A. in Sociology and Psychology, Pacific U., 1964; M.S.W., Fordham U., 1967; postgrad. Grad. Sch. Pub. Affairs N.Y. Sate U., 1973; m. Andrea Vanderzanden, June, 1964; children—Andre, Lawrence. Group supr. Placer County Juvenile Center, Auburn, Calif., 1960-62; group social worker St. Mary's Home for Boys, Beaverton, Oreg., 1963-64; adminstrv. supr. Catholic Charities Archdiocese of N.Y., S.I., 1964-70; asst. dir. Arthur Kill Rehab. Center Drug Abuse Control Commn., S.I., 1970-75; chief services dept. mental hygiene Willowbrook Developmental Center, S.I., 1975—; psychiat. social worker S.I. Mental Health Soc., 1967-68; mem. adv. bd. Cath. Charities Archdiocese N.Y. Chmn. com. health and hosp. S.I. Community Planning Bd. 4, 1970—; vice chmn. Richboro Community Mental Health Council, 1972—. Served with U.S. Army, 1954-56. Recipient Community Merit award pres. Richmond County (N.Y.), 1971, Commendation award Richmond County Supreme Ct. Grand Jury, 1969; Merit award Deborah League S.I., 1974, S.I. chpt. ARC, 1975; certified social worker, N.Y. Mem. Acad. Certified Social Workers, Nat. Conf. Cath. Charities, Am. Assn. Marriage and Family Counselors (certified), Nat. Coordinating Council Drug Coordination, S.I. Family Service Assn., Michael J. Cicero Civic Orgn. (Community Achievement award 1976). Democrat. Roman Catholic. Clubs: Sons of Italy in Am. (founder and charter mem. local lodge), Toastmasters Internat. (dir. Richmond County br.). Home: 166 Shafter Ave Staten Island NY 10308 Office: 2760 Victory Blvd Staten Island NY 10314

CICHANOWICZ, FRANK ANTONE, III, landscape architect; b. Peconic, N.Y., May 7, 1941; s. Frank Antone and Anne Thresa (Krupski) C.; Asso. Arts and Sci., State U. N.Y., 1961; B. Landscape Architecture, U. Ga., 1964; m. Brenda Marie Lynch, Jan. 9, 1965; children—Sara Lynch, Neal James. Founder, Briarcliff Landscape, Cutchogue, N.Y., 1965, pres., 1968—; founder Briarcliff Sod, 1960; v.p. Briarcliff Sod, Inc., Peconic, 1969—; pres. Briarcliff Sprinkler Systems, Inc., Peconic, 1972—, Holly Hollow Nurseries, Peconic, 1974—. Mem. Southold Town Conservation advisory bd., 1971, 72, 73; bd. dirs. Southold Town Republican Club, 1969-73. Mem. Am. Sod Producers Assn., Am. Soc. Landscape Architects, Nat. Landscape Contractors Assn., N.Y. State, L.I. nurserymen's assns., L.I. Sod Growers Assn., Illuminating Engrs. Soc., Cutchogue-New Suffolk C. of C. (dir. 1969-73, corr. sec. 1969-71, pres. 1974-76), Southold Town Businessmen's Assn. (dir. 1971-73). Clubs: Mattituck (N.Y.) Gun; Shinnecock Marlin and Tuna (Hampton Bays, N.Y.). Home: 104 Lupen Dr Cutchogue NY 11935

CIESIELSKI, JANE BETH, ednl. adminstr., county ofcl.; b. N.Y.C., Apr. 7, 1947; d. William John and Mary Emily (Morgan) Martin; B.S., State Coll. N.Y. at Buffalo, 1969; M. Ed., U. Buffalo, 1975; m. Robert Michael, Feb. 16, 1974. Tchr. English, L.I., N.Y., 1969-70, Arlington, Va., 1970-71; employment counselor Am. Personnel Services Assn., Washington, 1971-73; adminstrv. supr. Am. Research Bur., Beltsville, Md., 1973; market researcher Buffalo Courier-Express, 1973-74; dir. comprehensive Employment and Tng. Act, Individual Referral Program, City of Buffalo, 1975-77, dir. applied vocat. edn. tng. program, Erie County, Erie Community Coll., N.Y., 1977—; asst. coordinator equal employment opportunity porgram City of Buffalo, 1976-78. Mem. Buffalo Mayor's Blue Ribbon McKinley Monument Rev. Com., 1977—; mem. Dist. 10 planning com. revenue sharing City of Buffalo, 1976-77; bd. dirs. Everywoman Opportunity Center, sec., acting pres., 1977—; bd. dirs. Polish Community Center, 1976-78, Broadway-Fillmore Area Council., 1975-77, United Way, 1978—. Kosciuszko Found. scholar, 1976. Mem. Am. Vocat. Assn., Nat. Vocat. Guidance Assn., Work Experience Coordinators Assn., Bus. and Profl. Women's Assn., Interclub Council, Am. Personnel and Guidance Assn., Job Placemant Assn., Niagara Frontier Industry Edn. Council, Iota Lambda Sigma, Phi Delta Kappa.

CIFRULAK, S. DAVID, research adminstr.; b. McKees Rock, Pa., Feb. 17, 1944; s. Stephen and Anna Ruth (Oleyar) C.; B.S., U. Pitts. 1967; postgrad. chemistry, Duquesne U., 1971-75; m. Marcia A. Milowicki, May 27, 1966; children—Erika Nadine, Stephen David. Jr. fellow research Mellon Inst., Pitts., 1965-69; chemist U.S.S. Chems., Pitts., 1969-71; group leader Calgon Corp., Pitts., 1971—. Mem. Spectroscopy Soc. Pitts. (sec. 1973-74), Soc. Analytical Chemists Pitts., ASTM (chmn. D-28.03 liquid phase testing activated carbon), Pitts. Conf. Analytical Chemistry and Applied Spectroscopy (chmn. exhibits 1975, chmn. program 1979), Am. Chem. Soc. Researcher analytical chemistry, spectroscopy. Office: Calgon Corp PO Box 1346 Pittsburgh PA 15230

CIMINO, JAMES ERNEST, physician; b. N.Y.C., July 7, 1928; s. Ernest S. and Rose (Gorga) C.; student Syracuse U., 1946-48; A.B., N.Y. U., 1950, M.D., 1954; m. Dorothy Hilary Naperkoski, June 5, 1954; children—James, Ernest, Christopher, Peter, Paul, Maria. Intern, resident E.J. Meyer Meml. Hosp., Buffalo, 1954-58; research fellow physiology U. Buffalo, 1957-58; practice medicine specializing in internal medicine; dir. renal service Bronx VA Hosp., 1960-68; chief medicine, med. dir. Calvary Hosp.; cons. medicine St. Joseph's Hosp., Yonkers, N.Y., Holy Name Hosp., Teaneck, N.J., VA Hosp., Bronx, N.Y.; asst. clin. prof. medicine Mt. Sinai Sch. Medicine, N.Y.C., 1970-73; adj. prof., cons. nutrition N.Y. U.; cons. internal medicine N.Y.C. Dept. Health, 1971-74, also chmn. com. advanced cancer. Served with USAF, 1958-60. Diplomate Am. Bd. Internal Medicine. Fellow A.C.P.; mem. AMA, N.Y. Acad. Scis. Am. Heart Assn., Am., Internat. socs. nephrology. Contbr. med. articles to profl. jours. Office: 1740-70 Eastchester Rd Bronx NY 10461

CIMINO, JOSEPH A., med. service adminstr., physician, educator; b. N.Y.C., Jan. 1, 1934; s. Ernest and Rose (Gorga) C.; B.A. in Am. History, Harvard U., 1956, M.Indsl. Health, 1964, M.P.H., 1965; M.S. in Biology, Fordham U., 1958; M.D., U. Buffalo, 1962. Intern, Grasslands Hosp., Valhalla, N.Y., 1962-63; resident, AEC fellow in environ. medicine Sch. Pub. Health, Harvard, 1963-65; med. officer U.S. Army Arsenal, Watertown, Mass., 1964-65; practice medicine specializing in preventive medicine, Valhalla, N.Y., 1966—; research asso. N.Y.C. Dept. Health, 1965-66, dir. Bur. Community Safety and Occupational Health, 1968-71, dep. commr. health, 1971-72, commr. health, 1972-74; chief med. officer N.Y.C. Dept. Sanitation, 1966-69; chief med. cons. N.Y.C. Civil Service Commn., 1966-71; med. dir. N.Y.C. Poison Control Center, 1966-72; dir. health and safety N.Y.C. Environ. Protection Adminstrn., 1968-71; asso. prof. environ. medicine and pub. health N.Y. U. Sch. Medicine, 1971-77; adj. prof. pub. health and tropical medicine Tulane U. Sch. Pub. Health and Tropical Medicine, New Orleans, 1972-77; lectr. in pub. health Columbia, N.Y.C., 1973—; vis. prof. community health Albert Einstein Coll. Medicine, Bronx, N.Y., 1973-77; mem. med. and profl. affairs com. N.Y.C. Health and Hosp. Corp., 1972-74; commr. Dept. Hosps., Westchester County, N.Y., 1974-77; pres., prof. preventive medicine N.Y. Med. Coll., Valhalla, 1977—; pres., dir. Hudson Valley Health Systems Agy., 1975-77; mem. agy. relations com. Comprehensive Health Planning Agy., 1972-74. Bd. dirs. United Hosp. Fund, Westchester Artificial Kidney Center, Westchester County Med. Center, Community Council Greater N.Y., Health and Hosp. Planning Council of So. N.Y. Diplomate Am. Bd. Preventive Medicine. Fellow Am. Coll. Preventive Medicine; mem. Am. Pub. Health Assn., Westchester County Med. Soc. (dir. 1974-77), AMA, Indsl. Med. Assn., N.Y. State, Aerospace med. assns., Westchester Heart Assn. (dir. 1974-77), Human Factors Soc., Greater N.Y. Hosp. Assn. (gov. 1972-77), Assn. Govtl. Hygienists. Author: Safety: Protection from Injury, 1969; Medical Services Manual, 1971; contbr. articles on pub. health to profl. jours. Home: 50 Willard Ave North Tarrytown NY 10591 Office: Westchester Medical Center NY Med Coll Valhalla NY 10595

CINA, SAVERIO JOSEPH, marine cons. co. exec.; b. Bklyn., July 22, 1927; s. Ignazio and Vita (LaLuce) C.; B.S. in Naval Architecture and Marine Engring., U. Mich., 1951, M.S. in Nuclear Engring., 1959; m. Helene Zakharoff, July 10, 1974. Naval architect Bur. Ships, Washington, 1951-53; program mgr. N.Am. Rockwell, Inc., Los Angeles, 1960-68; sr. analyst Esso Internat., Inc., N.Y.C., 1969-73; staff cons. John J. McMullen Assos., N.Y.C., 1973-76; pvt. practice marine transp. cons., N.Y.C., 1976—; adviser to mng. dir. Arab Maritime Petroleum Transport Co., Kuwait, 1973-74. Served with U.S. Mcht. Marine, 1945-47, USN, 1953-57. Mem. Soc. Naval Architects and Marine Engrs. (Best Paper award 1966), Am. Soc. Naval Engrs., U. Mich. Alumni Assn., U.S. Naval Inst. Patentee air cushion drilling vehicle. Home: 351 E 84th St New York City NY 10028

CINTAS, PIERRE FRANÇOIS DIÉGO, educator; b. Sfax, Tunisia, Feb. 19, 1929; s. Jean Henri Léon and Joséphine Appolonie Victoire(Duprez) C.; came to U.S., 1959; student U. Paris, 1955-57, U. London, 1957; M.A., U. Colo., 1962; Ph.D., Ind. U., 1969; m. Holly May Lea, Jan. 8, 1966; children—Benjamin-Paul, Nicole-Anne. Teaching asst. Colo. U. 1960-62; lectr. U. Grenoble (France), 1962-63; research asst. Ind. U., 1963-65; teaching fellow Harvard U., 1965-69, lectr., 1969-70; asst. prof. French, U. Va., 1970-76, Dalhousie U., Halifax, N.S., Can., 1976-78, Pa. State U., Ogontz campus, 1978—; dir. N.E. Conf. on Teaching Fgn. Langs., 1975-79. Mem. Am. Assn. Tchrs. French (v.p. Atlantic chpt. 1978), Modern Lang. Assn. Am., Linguistic Soc. Am., Am. Council on Teaching Fgn. Langs., Internat. Linguistic Assn., Internat. Phonetic Assn. (life), Société des Professeurs de Français en Amérique. Club: Ind. U. Alumni (life). Contbr. articles to profl. jours.; asso. editor Am. Council on Teaching of Fgn. Langs. Bibliography, 1975—. Home: 300 Hancock Ct North Wales PA 19454 Office: Pa State U Ogontz Campus 1600 Woodland Rd Abington PA 19001

CIOFFARI, ANGELINA GRIMALDI, educator; b. Port Chester, N.Y.; d. Samuel Ludwig and Mary Grace (Corigliano) Grimaldi; B.A., Coll. New Rochelle, 1935; M.A., Columbia, 1940; m. Vincent Cioffari, Dec. 27, 1937; 1 son, Vincent Grimaldi. Asst. prof. Romance langs.

U. Iowa, 1943-44; asst. dir. modern langs. project War Dept., N.Y.C., 1944-45; lectr. Romance langs. Boston U., 1957-61; vis. prof. Harvard, 1961-62; asso. prof. modern langs. Mass. Bay Community Coll., Watertown, 1965—. Sec., Circolo Italiano Boston, 1960-62. Mem. Modern Lang. Assn., AAUP, Italian Tchrs. Assn., Mass. Tchrs. Assn. Dante Soc. Am. Roman Catholic. Clubs: Watertown Yacht; Windsor; Cornell of N.Y.; Harvard Faculty. Author: Italian Operatic Arias, 1951; Beginning Italian I, 1958, II, 1958. Home: 45 Amherst Rd Waban MA 02168 Office: Dept Modern Langs Mass Bay Community Coll 50 Oakland St Wellesley Hills MA 02181

CIOFFARI, VINCENZO, editor, author; b. Calitri, Italy, Feb. 24, 1905; s. Constantino and Antonietta (Armiento) C.; A.B., Cornell U., 1927, M.A., 1928; Ph.D., Columbia U., 1935; m. Angelina Grimaldi, Dec. 27, 1937; 1 son, Vincent Grimaldi. Lectr., Coll. New Rochelle (N.Y.), 1931-35, Hunter Coll., 1938-42, 45-46; asso. prof. State U. Iowa, 1943-44; spl. cons. editorial staff U.S. Armed Forces Inst., 1943; cons. charge Spanish, Italian, Portuguese projects War Dept., 1944-45, Joint Brazil-U.S. Commn., Rio de Janeiro, 1945, modern lang. editor, 1946-67; prof. Romance langs. Boston U., 1967-71, scholar-in-residence, 1971—; nat. chmn. Dante Centenary, 1965. Decorated Cavaliere al Merito della Repubblica Italiana; named to Hall of Fame of Nat. Fedn. Fgn. Lang. Tchrs. Assns. Mem. Mediaeval Acad. Am., Modern Lang. Assn., Italian Tchrs. Assn., Am. Assn. Tchrs. Italian (past v.p.), Am. Assn. Tchrs. French, Am. Assn. Tchrs. Spanish and Portuguese, Linguistic Soc., Dante Soc. Am. (past pres.), AAUP, Società Dantesca Italiana (hon. life), Renaissance Soc. Am., Dante Alighieri Soc. (hon. life), Phi Beta Kappa, Phi Sigma Iota, Phi Kappa Phi. Clubs: Cornell (N.Y.C.); Harvard Faculty; Windsor; Watertown Yacht. Author: Fortune and Fate from Democritus to St. Thomas Aquinas, 1935; Italian Review Grammar and Composition, 1937, rev. 1969; Amici di Scuola, 1938; Raccontini, 1940; Giulietta e Romeo, 1942; The Conception of Fortune and Fate in the Works of Dante, 1940; I Miei Ricordi, di Massimo d'Azeglio, 1943; Spoken Italian, 1944; Istruzioni per La Guida, 1944; Fourteenth Century Commentators of Dante, 1945; Goldoni's Il Ventaglio, 1948; Letture Varie, 1949; Instruccoes ao Guia, 1946; L'Inglese Parlato, 1944; O Ingles Falado, 1945; El Ingles Hablado, 1945; Beginning Italian Grammar, 1958, rev. 1965, 79; (with others) Spoken Portuguese, 1946; Spanish Review Grammar, 1957, rev. 1964, 72, 79, workbook, 1972, 79; Corrierino delle Famiglie, 1962; Il Segreto di Luca, 1964; La nuvola di Smog, 1967; Guido da Pisa's Commentary on Dante's Inferno, 1974; Repaso practico y cultural, 1977; contbr. articles to learned and profl. publs. Home: 45 Amherst Rd Waban MA 02168 Office: Dept Modern Langs Boston U Boston MA 02215

CIOLLI, ANTOINETTE, librarian; b. N.Y.C., Aug. 20, 1915; d. Pietro and Mary (Palumbo) Ciolli; A.B., Bklyn. Coll., 1937, M.A., 1940; B.S. in L.S., Columbia U., 1943. Tchr. history and civics Bklyn. high schs., 1943-44; circulation librarian Bklyn. Coll. Library, 1944-46; instr. history Sch. Gen. Studies, Bklyn. Coll., 1944-50, asst. prof. library dept., 1965-73, asso. prof., 1973—; reference librarian Bklyn. Coll. Library, 1947-59, chief sci. librarian, 1959-70, chief spl. collections div., 1970—. Mem. ALA, Am. Hist. Assn., AAUP, Spl. Libraries Assn. (museum group chpt. sec. 1950-51, 52-54), N.Y. Library Club, Beta Phi Mu. Author: (with Alexander S. Preminger and Lillian Lester) Urban Educator: Harry D. Gideonse, Brooklyn College and the City University of New York, 1970; contbr. articles to profl. jours. Home: 1129 Bay Ridge Pkwy Brooklyn NY 11228

CION, JUDITH ANN, lawyer; b. N.Y.C., June 27, 1943; d. Peter and Ruth Jeannette (Levy) Schneider; student Smith Coll., 1961-63; A.B., Pomona Coll., 1965; LL.B., Harvard Law Sch., 1968. Admitted to N.Y. bar, 1968; asso. Poletti, Freidin, Prashker, Feldman & Gartner, N.Y.C., 1968-71, Lovejoy, Wasson, Lundgren & Ashton, N.Y.C., 1971-75; mem. firm Lovejoy, Wasson, Lundgren & Ashton, P.C., N.Y.C., 1976—. Dir., sec. Light Opera Manhattan, Inc., N.Y.C., 1973—. Mem. Am., N.Y. (com. corp. law of banking corp. and bus. law sect.) bar assns., Assn. Bar City N.Y. Office: 250 Park Ave New York City NY 10017

CIPRIANO, DONALD M., ednl. adminstr.; b. Waterbury, Conn., Jan. 15, 1943; s. Michael C. and Clare (Greene) C.; B.A., St. Michael's Coll., 1964; M.S., So. Conn. State Coll., 1971, C.A.G.S., 1976; m. Mary Ann Donnelly, June 14, 1969; children—Timothy, Kathleen. Tchr. Brigham Acad., Bakersfield, Vt., 1964-65; guidance dir. Sacred Heart High Sch., Waterbury, Conn., 1965-69; dir. admissions Post Coll., Waterbury, 1969-75; prin. St. Mary's Sch., Newington, Conn., 1975—; dir. The Learning Center; mem. grad. faculty St. Joseph's Coll. Mem. Am. Personnel and Guidance Assn., Nat. Catholic Edn. Assn., Phi Delta Kappa. Home: 22 Midwood Ave Waterbury CT 06708 Office: St Mary's Sch Newington CT 06111

CIRESI, ANTHONY DAVID, architect, engr.; b. Bridgeport, Conn., Feb. 24, 1907; s. Anthony A. and Mary G. (Raymond) C.; C.E., Rensselaer Poly. Inst., 1929; m. Astrid L. Bulow, Nov. 16, 1940. Structural draftsman Am. Bridge Co., Phila., 1930-31; civil engr., Bridgeport, 1932-33; city engrs. office, civil engr., chief engr. F.E.R.A. Planning Bd., 1933-37; instr. Bridgeport Engring. Inst., 1937-42; structural engr. Fletcher-Thompson, Inc., 1937-39, Gibbs & Hill, N.Y.C., 1939, State Dept. Pub. Works, Hartford, Conn., 1940; with Fletcher-Thompson, Inc., 1940—, chief structural engr., 1943-48, chief field engr., 1948-56, exec. v.p., dir., chief engr., 1956-76; cons., 1976—. Engring. mem. bridge commn., Bridgeport, 1937-39; mem. Bridgeport Housing Authority 1939-52, vice chmn., 1944-46, chmn., 1946-52; chmn. Redevel. Agy., 1950-52. Registered profl. engr., Conn., Ill., N.Y., N.J., Pa., Mass., N.H., Md., Kan., R.I.; registered architect, Conn., Mich. Mem. Am. Concrete Inst., Nat. Soc. Profl. Engrs., A.I.A., Internat. Assn. Shell Structures, Prestressed Concrete Inst., Conn. Soc. Profl. Engrs. Home and Office: Redding Ridge CT 06876

CIRILLO, ANTHONY FRANCIS, cinematographer; b. Meriden, Conn., Oct. 25, 1922; s. Frank Anthony and Anna Irene (Kuchta) C.; student ornamental design; m. Angeline M. Geremia, Oct. 29, 1955. Animator, Bay State Films, Springfield, Mass., 1949-51; cameraman Paul Peroff Television Screen Prodns., Derby, Conn., 1951-54; free-lance cinematographer, N.Y.C., 1954—, also design engr. spl. electronic or motion picture camera equipment. Cons., Anamorphic, Ltd., Forest Hills, N.Y., 1955—. Mem. Dirs. Guild Am. Office: 37 E 28th St New York City NY 10016

CIULLA, ANDREW JOSEPH, govt. ofcl.; b. Rochester, N.Y., June 20, 1926; s. Francesco and Frances (Arena) C.; B.S., U. Rochester, 1960; M.A., George Washington U., 1965; m. Corrine Margaret Christiano, Oct. 29, 1949; children—Elaine Ciulla Kamarck, Joanne, Frank. Claims rep. Social Security Adminstrn., HEW, Rochester, N.Y., 1955-57, field rep., 1957-60, claims unit supr., 1960-61, mgmt. analyst, Balt., 1961-70, chief ops. analysis staff, 1970-74, acting dir. div. appraisal, bur. dist. office ops., 1974-77, asst. bur. dir. for program evaluation and appraisal Bur. Disability Ins., 1977—. Mem. trustees council U. Rochester, 1978—. Served with AC, USNR, 1944-45. Exec. Devel. fellow, 1970-72. Mem. U. Rochester Alumni Assn. (dir. 1973-75). Home: 1313 Placid Dr Sykesville MD 21784 Office: Social Security Adminstrn HEW Baltimore MD 21241

CIURCA, SAMUEL JOHN, JR., research chemist; b. Rochester, N.Y., Mar. 30, 1940; s. Samuel John and Betty (Keith) C.; B.S., U. Rochester, 1973. Research chemist Eastman Kodak Co., Rochester, 1959—; founder, 1961, geologist, dir. Museum Petrified Wood, Rochester, 1961—. Mem. Paleontological Research Instn., N.Y. Geol. Assn., Am. Chem. Soc., Geol. Soc. Am. Contbr. articles to profl. jours. Patentee in field. Home: 48 Saranac St Rochester NY 14621 Office: Research Labs Eastman Kodak Co Rochester NY 14650

CIURCZAK, EMIL WALTER, chemist; b. Elizabeth, N.J., Apr. 13, 1945; s. Emil and Albina Mary (Matyiunas) C.; B.A., Rutgers U., 1971, M.S., 1973; m. Judith Grosshandler, June 22, 1968; children—Alex, Adam, Alyssa. Jr. chemist Ciba-Geigy Corp., Summit, N.J., 1970-73; sr. chemist Cooper Labs., Cedar Knolls, N.J., 1973-77; mgr. analytical services Henkle Inc., Hoboken, N.J., 1977—. Merit badge councillor Boy Scouts Am., 1970—. Served with inf. U.S. Army, 1967-69. Mem. Am. Chem. Soc., N.Y. Acad. Sci. Club: Hanover Squares. Contbr. articles to profl. jours. Home: 6 Riverside Dr Denville NJ 07834 Office: 1301 Jefferson St Hoboken NJ 07030

CIZANCKAS, VICTOR IAN, city police ofcl.; b. Buffalo, May 4, 1937; s. Victor Ian and Dorothy (Hembrow) C.; A.A., Coll. San Mateo, 1969; student U. Santa Clara, 1969; A.B.S. in Sociology maxima cum laude, Coll. Notre Dame, 1973; m. Gertrude Alice Joe, July 2, 1960; children—Victor Irelan, Matthew Andrew. With Dept. State, 1956-69; criminal investigator City of Menlo Park (Calif.), 1962-68, chief of police, 1968-77; chief of police City of Stamford (Conn.), 1977—; lectr. in field; mem. Calif. Criminal Justice Council, 1975-77. Bd. dirs. Herbert Hoover Meml. Boys Club, Menlo Park, Calif., 1968-72, Sequoia Dist. Golden Gate chpt. ARC, 1970-75, San Mateo County Service League, 1970-75; pres. San Mateo County Law Enforcement Assn., 1969. Mem. Internat. Assn. Chiefs of Police, Alpha Gamma Sigma. Author: (with Donald Hanna) Modern Police Management and Organization, 1977; contbr. articles to profl. jours. Office: Stamford Police Dept Stamford CT 06902

CLAGETT, JOHN WILLIAMS, assn. exec.; b. Potomac, Md., Apr. 29, 1914; s. Carter and Nora Lyle (Williams) C.; student U. Md., 1933; LL.B., George Washington Sch. Law, 1937; m. Martha Evans, Sept. 29, 1937; 1 son, Evans. Exec. positions U.S. Dept. Interior, U.S. Dept. Agr., U.S. Dept. Labor, War Food Commn., to 1955; founding adminstr. Office Investigations and Audits, Chgo. Bd. Trade, 1955-59; pres. N.Y. Mercantile Exchange, N.Y.C., 1959-61; founding pres. Nat. Stock Exchange, N.Y.C., 1961; nat. community sales mgr. E.F. Hutton & Co., Inc., N.Y.C., 1961-63; pres. Assn. Commodity Exchange Firms, Inc. (now Futures Industry Assn., Inc.), N.Y.C., 1969—; guest lectr. N.Y. City Coll., L.I. U., World Trade Inst. Club: Baltusrol Golf (Springfield, N.J.). Home: 14 Timber Acres Rd Short Hills NJ 07078 Office: Suite 7166 4 World Trade Center New York City NY 10048

CLAIR, CAROLYN GREEN, civic worker; b. Boston, Sept. 18, 1909; d. James Maddocks and Marietta Cecelia (Foeley) Green; B.S., Boston U., 1930, postgrad., 1933; m. Miles Nelson Clair, June 16, 1928; children—Cynthia York Clair Norkin, Valerie DeLuce Clair Stelling, Ardith Monroe Clair Houghton. Dir. Thompson & Lei Chtneo Co. Inc., 1956-77; treas. MNCC; Inc., 1977—. Translator, Am. Concrete Inst., Chgo., 1930-37; regent Mass. soc. D.A.R., 1933-35, state and nat. page Mass. soc., 1932-36; pres. Mass. soc. Children Am. Revolution, 1936-38, historian, 1937-39; v.p. Mass. chpt. Daus. Colonial Wars, 1969-71; active Salvation Army Aux., 1970—, v.p. thrift shop, Boston, 1970-72; active Asso. Country Women World, 1968—, lectr., 1972—, alt. to UN, 1974—; mem. bd. service league, lying-in div. Boston Hosp. Women, 1966-76, treas., 1969-71, v.p., 1971-74, pres., 1974-76, trustee bd. overseers Boston Hosp. Woman, 1974—, chmn. patient care advisory com., 1977—; pres. New Eng. Farm Garden Assn., 1968-71; mem. bd. Boston Morning Musicales Tuft U., 1966—; mem. council Boston Symphony Orch., 1969—; pres. Women's Nat. Farm Assn., 1972-74, chmn. adv. bd., 1974—; mem. corp. Affiliated Hosps. Center, Boston, 1975-76; mem. adv. bd. Nat. Arboretum, Washington, 1974-78; exec. bd. Country Women's Council, 1972-74; v.p. Coll. Culb Boston, 1970—, Mass. Hort. Soc., 1970—; lectr. UN, conventions. Recipient Brit. War Relief award, 1945. Mem. New Eng. (life), Mass. hist. socs., Pam Am. Soc., Internat. Platform Assn., People to People, Boston Mus. Fine Arts, Internat. Womens Ednl. Indls. Union, Audubon Soc., Nat. Wildlife Fedn., Nat. Trust Historic Preservation, Bostonian Soc., Arnold Arboretum. Republican. Episcopalian. Contbr. articles to women's Farm Garden Assn. mags. Address: 17 Dorset Rd Waban MA 02168 also Cataumet ME 20534

CLAMAR, APHRODITE J., psychologist; b. Hartford, Conn., Sept. 26, 1933; s. James John and Georgia (Panas) C.; B.A., City Coll. N.Y., 1953; M.A., Columbia U., 1955; Ph.D., N.Y. U., 1978; m. Richard Cohen, June 24, 1973. Mgmt. cons., psychologist Milla Alihan Assos., 1957-62; research psychologist, coordinator Inst. Devel. Studies, N.Y. Med. Coll., 1964; intern psychologist Bellevue Psychiat. Hosp., 1964-66; asso. prof. Fashion Inst. Tech., 1966-69; supervising psychologist Lifeline Center Child Devel., 1966-67; chief psychologist Beth Israel Med. Center, I Spy Health Program, 1967-70; dir. community-sch. mental health programs Soundview Community Services, Albert Einstein Coll. Medicine, Yeshiva U., N.Y.C., 1970-73; dir. treatment program court-related children, dept. child psychiatry Harlem Hosp., mem. faculty dept. psychiatry Columbia U. Coll. Physicians and Surgeons, N.Y.C., 1973-76; pvt. practice as psychotherapist and cons. to pub. health and mental health agys., N.Y.C., 1976—. Fellow AAAS; mem. Soc. Clin. and Exptl. Hypnosis, Am., Eastern, N.J. psychol. assns., Am. Acad. Psychotherapists. Democrat. Greek Orthodox. Research on adoption, personality devel. and feminist issues. Home: 162 E 80th St New York City NY 10021

CLAPP, HERBERT JAMES, martial arts specialist; b. Upper Darby, Pa., Aug. 29, 1948; s. Eric Chester and Lucille B. C.; B.A. in Polit. Sci., West Chester State Coll., 1970; m. Judith Anderson, Aug. 2, 1975. Instr., mgr. Tracy's Karate Studios, Wilmington, Del., 1970-73, owner, operator, 1975—; owner, tchr., operator Am. Karate Studios, Wilmington, 1973—; tchr. pvt., pub. schs.; TV demonstrator. Mem. U.S. Karate Assn. (3d degre black belt), United Martial Arts Referee Assn. (dir., Del. rep.). Instrumental in establishment of U. Del. accredited self def. program, 1972. Office: 16 Polly Drummond Center Newark DE 19711

CLAPP, PHILIP CHARLES, physicist; b. Belleville, Ont., Can., Oct. 14, 1935; s. Charles William and Phyllis Margaret (Wells) C.; B.Sc., Queens U., 1957; Ph.D., Mass. Inst. Tech., 1963; m. Mireille Treuil, June 9, 1961; children—Andre, Lisanne, Michelle. Sr. physicist Ledgemont Lab. Kennecott Copper Corp., Lexington, Mass., 1963-71, staff scientist, 1971-73, head physics and metallurgy research, 1973-77; prof. metallurgy, head dept. U. Conn., Storrs, 1978—; sr. vis. scientist Oxford (Eng.) U., 1969-70; adj. prof. physics Boston Coll., 1973-78; vis. prof. Mass. Inst. Tech., 1977-78. Active Cub Scouts. Mem. Am. Phys. Soc., Am. Metall. Soc., Canadian Assn. Physicists, Am. Inst. Mining, Metall. and Petroleum Engrs., Soc. Arts and Crafts (dir., v.p. 1977—), Friends of Middlesex Squash Club (exec. officer 1965—). Home: 1196 Storrs Rd Storrs CT 06268 Office: U-136 Univ Conn Storrs CT 06268

CLAPPER, THOMAS WESLEY, educator; b. Altoona, Pa., Oct. 29, 1943; s. Ralph Alton and Betty Jane (Patterson) C.; B.S. in Edn. and Chemistry, Pa. State U., 1965, Ph.D. in Curriculum and Supervision, 1978; M.S. in Chemistry, U. Notre Dame, 1971; m. Irene Rose Marie Pucci, May 9, 1969. Tchr. biology and chemistry Paoli (Pa.) High Sch., 1966; tchr. chemistry and math. Great Valley High Sch., Malvern, Pa., 1966-76; supr. asso. teaching Pa. State U., University Park, 1977—. Served with USCG, 1965-66. Mem. Assn. Supervision and Curriculum Devel., Nat., Pa. State edn. assns., Am. Chem. Soc., Am. Fedn. tchrs., Pi Lambda Theta, Phi Delta Kappa. Presbyterian. Home: Linden Manor 1433 Linden Ln West Chester PA 19380 Office: Pennsylvania State U 172 Chambers Bldg University Park PA 16802

CLARE, JAMES HARVEY THOMSON, assn. exec.; b. Toronto, Ont., Can., May 18, 1941; s. James Archibald and Ruth Hunter (Thomson) C.; B.A., Acadia U. (Can.), 1966; m. Deanne May Oliva, July 11, 1970; children—Jodi, James. Salesman, Inter-Collegiate Press, Toronto, 1965-66; salesman, buyer Hudson's Bay Co., Toronto, 1966-67; radio news and sports commentator Evangeline Broadcasting Corp., Kentville, N.S., Can., 1962-66; exec. dir. Automobile Dealer Assn. of Ont., Toronto, 1967-76. Mem. Toronto Bd. Trade, Inst. Assn. Execs., Automotive Trade Assn. Mgrs., Am. Soc. Assn. Execs. Presbyterian. Home: 30 Archerhill Dr Islington ON M9B 5P3 Canada

CLARE, L(ESLIE) PAUL, metall. engr.; b. Allentown, Pa., Mar. 1, 1925; s. Alfred and Emma Pauline (Geiser) C.; B.S. in Metall. Engring., Lehigh U., 1950; m. Betty Jane German, June 26, 1947; children—Barbara Clare O'Brien, Janet Clare Brito, Peggy. Metall. observer Republic Steel Corp., Buffalo, 1950-51; process engr. Westinghouse Electric Corp., Buffalo, 1951-52; devel. and factory engr. GTE Sylvania Inc., Towanda, Pa., 1952-59, project engr., 1959-65, sect. head, 1965-74, engring. specialist metall. div., 1974—. Bd. dirs. Seven Lakes council Girl Scouts U.S.A., 1967-74, treas., 1974— mem. Towanda Area Sch. Authority, 1977—, Bradford County Area Vo Tech Sch. Authority, 1978—. Served with inf. U.S. Army, 1943-46. Decorated Purple Heart, Combat Inf. Badge. Mem. Am. Soc. for Metals, AIME (mem. refractory metals com.), ASTM (chmn. subcom.), Am. Legion. Republican. Lutheran. Club: Masons. Contbr. articles to profl. jours. Patentee in field. Home: 110 Watts St Towanda PA 18848 Office: Chem and Metall Div GTE Sylvania Inc Towanda PA 18448

CLARIE, T. EMMET, fed. judge; b. 1913; Ph.B., Providence Coll.; LL.B., Hartford Coll. Law. Admitted to bar, 1940; now chief U.S. dist. judge Conn. Mem. Am. Bar Assn. Address: 450 Main St Hartford CT 06103*

CLARK, ANDREW LAWRENCE, lawyer; b. Newark, Jan. 5, 1926; s. William Francis and Katherine Ann (Farrell) C.; A.B., Seton Hall U., 1949; J.D., Harvard U., 1954; m. Elizabeth Ann Brady, Apr. 11, 1959; children—Anne, Jacqueline, Peter. With Royall, Koegel & Rogers, N.Y.C., 1954-66; admitted to N.Y. bar, 1955; v.p., gen. counsel L.W. Frohlich & Co. and I.M.S., Internat., Inc., N.Y.C., 1966-72; v.p., sec., gen. counsel IMS Internat., Inc., N.Y.C., 1972—, also dir. Served with AUS, 1945-47, 51-53. Mem. Am., N.Y. State bar assns., Bar Assn. City N.Y. Republican. Roman Catholic. Home: 420 Colony Ct Wyckoff NJ 07481 Office: 800 3d Ave New York NY 10022

CLARK, CHARLES EDWARD, surgeon; b. Wetumpika, Ala., Nov. 18, 1917; s. Edmund Lewis and Claudia Lenora (Welden) C.; A.B., Howard Coll., 1939; M.D., Columbia U., 1943; m. Margaret K. Aymar, Mar. 7, 1943; children—Margaret Ann, Mary Helen, Charles E. Intern, Bellevue Hosp., N.Y.C., 1943; resident St. Luke's Hosp., N.Y.C., 1946-52; practice medicine specializing in surgery, 1952—; dir. surgery Valley Hosp., Ridgewood, N.J., 1965-74; cons. surgeon Bergen Pines Hosp., Paramus, N.J.; attending surgeon Pasack Valley Hosp., Westwood, N.J. Served with AUS, 1944-46. Diplomate Am. Bd. Surgery. Fellow A.C.S.; mem. AMA, N.J. Soc. Surgeons, Pan-Pacific Surg. Assn. Home: 233 Glen Rd Woodcliff Lake NJ 07675 Office: 385 S Maple Ave Ridgewood NJ 07450

CLARK, CHARLES WARFIELD, surgeon; b. Washington, Dec. 6, 1917; s. Charles Henry and Maude Evelyn (Allen) C.; B.S., U. Mich., 1939; M.D., Howard U., 1944; m. Savanna M. Vaughn. Intern Freedmen's Hosp., Washington, 1944; house physician Trinity Hosp., Detroit, 1944-46; preceptor, then chief resident in urology Freedmen's Hosp., 1946-53; practice medicine specializing in urology, Washington, 1946—; sr. attending urologist Howard U. Hosp.; attending Washington Hosp., Children's Nat. med. centers; clin. asst. prof. Howard U. Med. Sch. Served to capt. M.C., AUS, 1953-55. Diplomate Am. Bd. Urology. Fellow A.C.S.; mem. Am. Urol. Assn., Am. Assn. Clin. Urologists, Nat. Med. Assn., Medico-Chirurg. Soc. D.C., Med. Soc. D.C., AMA, Washington Urol. Soc., Am. Fertility Soc., Société Internationale d'Urologie, Chi Delta Mu, Sigma Pi Phi, Omega Psi Phi. Congregationalist. Contbr. articles to med. jours. Home: 1828 Taylor St NW Washington DC 20011 Office: 106 Irving St NW Suite 406 Washington DC 20010

CLARK, DONALD GRAHAM CAMPBELL, physician; b. Airdrie, Scotland, May 9, 1920; s. Archibald C. and Alice G. (Smellie) C.; came to U.S., 1945, naturalized, 1948; B.Sc., St. Andrew's U., Scotland, 1940, M.B., Ch.B., 1944; M.D., Yale U., 1945; m. Ann B. Kiersted, Dec. 9, 1944; children—Donald Graham Campbell, Michael A.C., Alison K.C., Peter F.C. Med. house officer Dundee Royal Infirmary, Scotland, 1944; surgeon Royal Naval Sea Transport, 1944-45; intern New Haven Hosp., 1948-49, asst. resident, 1949-50, sr. asst. resident, 1950-51; trainee USPHS, 1949-51; asst. resident surgery Meml. Hosp., N.Y.C., 1951-52, resident, 1952-55, spl. fellow gynecol. surgery, 1955, clin. asst. surgeon, 1955-66, asso. attending surgeon gynecol. service, 1966-70, attending surgeon, 1970—; asso. vis. surgeon James Ewing Hosp., 1966-68; clin. asso. Sloan Kettering Inst.; cons. gynecology St. Agnes Hosp.; asso. clin. prof. surgery Cornell U. Med. Coll.; cons. oncology Kingston Hosp.; cons. surg. oncology St. Agnes Hosp. Pres., dir. Greenville Community Council. William Harvey Cushing fellow, 1945-46, Henry Hudson Brown sr. fellow, 1946-47, Nat. Research Council fellow, 1947-48, Sloan Kettering Inst. research fellow, 1955-57. Diplomate Am. Bd. Surgery. Fellow A.C.S.; mem. Soc. Surg. Oncology, N.Y. Cancer Soc., N.Y. Gynecol. Soc. (pres. 1968-69), Am. Radium Soc., Soc. Pelvic Surgeons, N.Y. County, N.Y. State med. socs., Am. Soc. Clin. Oncology, Am., Pan Am. med. assns., Sigma Xi. Clubs: St. Andrew's Golf (Hastings, N.Y.); New York Athletic. Contbr. articles to profl. jours. Home: 145 Old Army Rd Scarsdale NY 10583 Office: 1275 York Ave New York City NY 10021

CLARK, ELIZABETH HUGHES, social worker; b. London, Jan. 9, 1925; d. Percy and Maude Elizabeth (Williams) Hughes; came to U.S., 1927, naturalized, 1952; B.A., N.J. Coll. Women, 1945; M.A. in Sociology, Rutgers U., 1966; m. Leonard Hanley Clark, Sept. 6, 1947; children—Darcy Patrick, Elizabeth Lloyd. Group worker adolescent dept. Rochester (N.Y.) YWCA, 1945-47; dir. social service dept. Presbyn.-U. Pa. Med. Center, Phila., also lectr. U. Pa. Med. Sch., 1966-74; dir. social service dept. Nazareth Hosp., Phila., 1974—; lectr. in field, cons. child abuse and terminal illness.; instr. sociology and social welfare Holy Family Coll., Phila. NIMH grantee, 1972-74, United Fund grantee, 1970-71, William Penn Found. grantee, 1971-74. Mem. Soc. Hosp. Social Work Dirs. (pres. Phila. chpt. 1975-77), Am. Sociol. Assn., Nat. Assn. Social Workers, Soc. Hosp. Social Work Dirs. of Am. Hosp. Assn. Co-editor sect. Social Work in Health Care; contbr. articles in field to profl. jours. Home: 125 Lafayette Ave Oreland PA 19075 Office: 2601 Holme Ave Philadelphia PA 19152

CLARK, ELIZABETH JANE, materials engr.; b. Jackson, Mich., Nov. 21, 1946; s. John Lee and Mary Jane (Firth) C.; B.S., U. Dayton, 1968; postgrad U. Md., 1974—. Materials engr. bldg. materials program Center for Bldg. Tech., Nat. Bur. Standards, Washington, 1969—. Mem. Am. Chem. Soc., Am. Soc. Testing and Materials. Contbr. articles to profl. jours. Home: 18617 Walkers Choice Rd Gaithersburg MD 20760 Office: 226 B-348 Washington DC 20234

CLARK, ELLERY HARDING, JR., historian, educator, coach; b. Cohasset, Mass., Aug. 6, 1909; s. Ellery Harding and Victoria Mary (Maddalena) C.; A.B. cum laude in English, Harvard U., 1933; A.M. in History, Boston U., 1950; m. Grace Marion Gelinas, Oct. 24, 1934; children—Grace Victoria, William Ellery, Susan Elizabeth. Commd. ensign U.S. Navy, 1933, advanced through grades to capt., 1957; ret., 1946; mem. sec. navy's com. on reorgn. Navy, 1945-46; asst. prof. dept. history U.S. Naval Acad., Annapolis, Md., 1946-47, asso. prof., 1947, prof., 1947—, head coach cross country track team, 1946—. Bd. dirs. World Series Room, Northeastern U., Boston. Active numerous charity drives. Decorated Navy Commendation with Combat V, also numerous others. Mem. U.S. Naval Inst., N. Am. Soc. Sport History, Soc. Am. Baseball Research. Democrat. Episcopalian. Club: Army and Navy (Washington). Author: Boston Red Sox: 75th Anniversary History, 1975; Red Sox Forever, 1977. Contbr. to Scribner's Dictionary of American History, Collier's Ency., Brassey's Ann. (London), Jour. United Services Inst. Def. Studies (London); founder, contbr. Ann. Rev., U.S. Naval Inst. Home: 25 Franklin St Annapolis MD 21401 also 262 Jerusalem Rd Cohasset MA 02025 Office: History Dept US Naval Academy Annapolis MD 21402

CLARK, ELTON LOYDON, chem. co. exec.; b. Hartford, Conn., Oct. 30, 1919; s. Loydon H. and Nellie Louise (Sandeen) C.; B.S., U. Conn., 1941; M.S., U. Mass., 1947; Ph.D., Cornell U., 1952; m. Ruth M. Clarke, Aug. 29, 1942; children—Peter, Susan (Mrs. Carl Helms), Deborah, Mary Lou, William, Thomas. Group leader, mgr. biol. research Am. Cyanamid Co., 1952-65; dir. pesticide research W.R. Grace & Co., 1965-69; asst. gen. mgr., to v.p., gen. mgr. Chipman div. Rhodia, Inc., N.Y.C., 1969-70, exec. v.p., 1972-75, mem. exec. com., 1973-75, dir. govt. relations, 1975—. Mem. Conn. Citizens Com. on Edn., 1955-59. Served to maj. USAAF, 1941-45. Mem. Entomol. Soc. Am., Sigma Xi. Home: Codfish Hill Bethel CT 06801 Office: 600 Madison Ave New York City NY 10022

CLARK, EVELYN GAEBEL, editor, bus. exec.; b. San Francisco, Aug. 22, 1907; d. Arthur Henry and Maud (Mason) Gaebel; student Louis Chalif Ballet Sch., 1920-24, Hunter Coll. Evening Art Sch., 1946-47; children—Judith (Mrs. Richard N. McVity), Jacqueline (Mrs. James Gilmour Hill). Receptionist, sec. Walker & Gillette, architects, N.Y.C., 1927-31; owner Evelyn Clark Creations, toys, Larchmont, N.Y., 1942-46; editor Med. Soc. N.Y. State, Lake Success, 1947-74; co-owner, pres., dir. Arthur H. Gaebel, Inc., East Syracuse, N.Y., 1946—. Republican vol. worker Larchmont Town Com., 1960-63. Episcopalian. Club: Twenty-five Year of Medical Society State of N.Y. Home: 12 Ervilla Dr Larchmont NY 10538

CLARK, GERALD ROBERT, physician, educator, adminstr.; b. Parr, Alta., Can., Mar. 17, 1918; s. Alfred Francis and Florence Harriet (McRae) C.; student U. Alta., 1936-38; B.A., U. Oreg., 1942, M.D., 1945; M.P.H., Harvard, 1951; children—Gary, Christy, Linda, Jeffrey, Terry, Gregg. Came to U.S., 1938, naturalized, 1943. Intern, U. Wis., Hosp., Madison, 1945-46; with USPHS, 1946-52, dir. Tb and communicable disease control Ariz. Health Dept., Phoenix, 1947-48; pub. health cons. ECA, Athens, Greece, 1949-50; dir. Clackamas County Health Dept., Oregon City, Oreg., 1952-53; health commr. N.Mex. Dept. Health, Santa Fe, 1953-55; mem. psychiat. staff Norristown (Pa.) State Hosp., 1955-58; supt. Somerset (Pa.) State Hosp., 1958-59; dir. Psychiatry Clinics, Jefferson Med. Coll., Phila., 1959-61, asso. prof. psychiatry, 1965-66; supt. Elwyn Sch. and Hosp., Media, Pa., 1960-66; prof. psychiatry and pediatrics U. Pa., 1967—; sr. physician Children's Hosp. Phila., 1967—; commr. mental retardation Commonwealth Pa., 1966. Pres. Elwyn Inst., Media, 1966—. Diplomate Am. Bd. Preventive Medicine, Am. Bd. Neurology and Psychiatry. Fellow A.C.P., Am. Coll. Psychiatrists, Am. Psychiat. Assn.; mem. Am. Assn. on Mental Devel., Am. Coll. Preventive Medicine. Home: 111 Elwyn Rd Elwyn PA 19063 Office: Elwyn Inst Media PA 19063

CLARK, HERBERT SPENCER, diversified cos. exec.; b. Toronto, Ont., Can., Oct. 10, 1903; s. John Ernest and Esther Louisa C.; B.A.Sc., U. Toronto, 1924; postgrad. McMaster U.; m. Rosa Breithaupt Hewetson, Aug. 7, 1932; children—Ruth Hewetson Langley, Dorothy Hewetson Leonard, Rosemary Hewetson Amell, J. Russell Hewetson. Elec. engr. Niagara-Chippewa Power House, Hydro Electric Power Commn. Ont., 1924-26; pres. Hewetson Shoes, Ltd., Brampton, Ont., 1950-55, Guild Inn Ltd., Toronto, 1951—, Ravenna Woods, Ltd., Toronto, 1953—. Guildwood Devels., Ltd., Toronto, 1956—, Folkestone Corp. Ltd., Toronto, 1964—. Clubs: Granite, Royal Canadian Yacht, Arts and Letters, Canadian, Empire. Address: 191 Guildwood Pkwy Scarborough ON M1E 1P5 Canada

CLARK, HERBERT TRYON, JR., banker; b. Glastonbury, Conn., Jan. 7, 1913; s. Herbert Tryon and Alice (House) C.; B.S., U. Conn., 1934; m. Barbara Richmond, Aug. 1, 1936; children—Herbert T. III, LeRoy Richmond, Marjorie Ann. Asst. foremen assembly Royal-McBee Typewriter Co., Hartford, Conn., 1934-41; asst. plant mgr. Buffalo Arms Corp., 1941-44; procurement mgr. Gen. Ry. Signal Co., Rochester, N.Y., 1945; purchasing agt. Frontier Industries div. Houdaille Industries, 1946-49; pres. Geo. C. Field Co., Madison, Conn., 1949-78; pres. Tuxis Lumber, 1957-68, v.p., 1968—; pres. First Fed. Savs. & Loan Assn., 1957-64, chmn. bd., 1964-75; dir. emeritus, 1977—; pres. Wildwood Properties Inc., 1965—; dir. Coginchaug Devel. Corp., Lyman Farms Inc. Mem. Bd. Fin., Madison, 1959-65, sec., 1962-65; active Boy Scouts Am.; mem. Municipal Bldg. Study Com., 1967-69; arbitrator Am. Arbitration Assn., 1975—. Mem. Theta Sigma Chi. Congregationalist. Clubs: Exchange, Masons. Home: Maplewood Ln Madison CT 06443 Office: 107 Bradley Rd Madison CT 06443

CLARK, JOHN ANDREW, JR., design engr.; b. Harrisburg, Pa., Feb. 13, 1924; s. John Andrew and Lavina Catherine (Free) C.; B.Sc. in Chem. Engring., Lehigh U., 1948; student Northwestern U. Sch. Bus., 1956-57; m. Joyce Stella Vallerschamp, Dec. 29, 1962; children—Andrew Scot, Heather Ann; children by previous marriage—John Andrew III, Valarie Jean, Douglas Lawton. With Patterson-Kelley Co., Inc., mfr. heat transfer and process equipment, 1948—, dist. mgr., Chgo., 1956-61, chief design engr., East Stroudsburg, Pa., 1961—. Bd. dirs. East Stroudsburg Sch. Dist. Served with AUS, 1944-46; ETO. Decorated Purple Heart. Registered profl. engr., Pa., N.J. Mem. Am. Inst. Chem. Engrs. (local dir. 1964-65), Am. Soc. Heating, Refrigeration and Air Conditioning Engrs. Republican. Mason (32 deg.). Author, patentee in field. Home: 21 Lions St East Stroudsburg PA 18301 Office: Patterson-Kelley Co Burson St East Stroudsburg PA 18301

CLARK, JOHN FARRELL, banker; b. N.Y.C., Jan. 19, 1927; s. John Ward and Katherine (Coyne) C.; student Am. Inst. Banking, 1947-51, Columbia U., 1952-54, N.Y. U., 1955, Grad. Sch. Bus., N.Y. U., 1965-67. With Mfrs. Trust Co., N.Y.C., 1946-50, Bankers Trust Co., N.Y.C., 1951-56, Comml. Credit Corp., N.Y.C., 1956-59, European-Am. Banking Corp., N.Y.C., 1959-67; with N.J. Bank N.A., Passaic, 1967-78, v.p., 1967-73; pres. Middle States Leasing Corp.. 1972-78; with Bank of Tokyo Trust Co., N.Y.C., 1978—. Trustee Garden State Credit Bur. Served with USNR, 1945-46, 51-52. Mem. Passaic County (past pres.), Dist. I (v.p.) bankers assns., Robert Morris Assos., Bank Credit Assos., N.Y. Credit and Fin. Mgmt. Assn., N.J. Credit Execs. Republican. Roman Catholic. Club: K.C. Home: 555 Gorge Rd Cliffside Park NJ 07010 Office: 1 Garret Mountain Plaza West Paterson NJ 07424

CLARK, JOHN HOLLEY, III, lawyer; b. N.Y.C., May 31, 1918; s. John Holley, Jr. and Mary (Angus) C.; B.A., Princeton, 1939; J.D., Columbia, 1942; M.A., N.Y. U., 1965; m. Eleanor Jackson, June 4, 1964; children—Benjamin Hayden, Christopher Angus. Admitted to N.Y. bar, 1942; asso. firm Cahill, Gordon, Reindel & Ohl, N.Y.C., 1946-54; atty. Antitrust div. U.S. Dept. Justice, N.Y.C., 1954—. Vice Pres. N.Y. Young Republican Club, 1953-54. Served with USAAF, 1942-46; PTO. Mem. Assn. Bar City N.Y., Am. Sociol. Assn., Am. Anthrop. Assn., Law and Society Assn., N.Y. U. Grad. Sch. Arts and Scis. Alumni Assn. (treas. 1976, corr. sec. 1977). Democrat. Episcopalian. Home: 375 Riverside Dr New York City NY 10025 Office: 26 Fed Plaza Room 3630 New York City NY 10007

CLARK, JOHN KAPP, physician, educator; b. Williamsport, Pa., July 17, 1914; s. Melvin Reamer and Julia (Ebert) C.; B.S., Trinity Coll., 1936, D.Sc., 1964; M.D., U. Pa., 1940; m. Mariana Bray Hoffman, July 10, 1971; children by previous marriage—Sara, Margaret, Thomas, John, William. Intern, Hosp. U. Pa., Phila., 1940-42, resident 1942-43, attending physician, 1947—, chief renal sect., 1947-66; practice medicine, also research specializing in internal medicine, Phila.; asst. instr. medicine U. Pa. Sch. Medicine, 1943-47, research fellow pharmacology, 1946-47, instr. medicine, 1947-48, instr. clin. pharmacology, 1947-52, asso. in medicine, 1948-52, asst. prof. clin. medicine, 1952-54, asso. prof. medicine, 1954-76, prof. emeritus, 1976—; pre-clin. physician Smith Kline & French Labs., Phila., 1949-51, dir. research, 1951-60, dir. research and devel., 1960-61, v.p. research, devel., 1961-66, dir., 1962-66; chief U. Pa. unit Greater Delaware Valley Regional Med. Program, 1967-76. Bd. mgrs. Preston Maternity Hosp., Phila., 1956-74; trustee Trinity Coll., Hartford, Conn. Fellow A.C.P.; mem. Am. Fedn. Clin. Research, A.M.A., Am. Physiol. Soc., Am. Soc. Clin. Investigation, Coll. Physicians Phila., John Morgan Soc., Physiol. Soc. Phila., Sigma Xi, Alpha Omega Alpha, Delta Psi, Kappa Beta Phi. Clubs: Saint Anthony, Penn, Philadelphia; Merion Cricket (Haverford, Pa.); Corinthian Yacht (Cape May, N.J.). Contbr. articles to med. jours. Home: 843 Parkes Run Lane Villanova PA 19085

CLARK, JOSEPH ABEL, engring. educator; b. Lancaster, Pa., Jan. 14, 1939; s. Howard Edwin and Kathryn Elizabeth (Abel) C.; A.B. in Physics, U. Notre Dame, 1960; postgrad. U. Gottingen (Germany), 1961-62; M.S., Cath. U. Am., 1967, Ph.D., 1969. Asst. engr. RCA, Lancaster, Pa., summers 1957-59; research asst. Cath. U. Am., Washington, 1965-69, research asso., 1969-71, research scientist, adj. asso. prof. elec. engring., 1971-73, research scientist, adj. asso. prof. mech. engring., 1973—; acoustical cons. Tech. Ops. Inc., 1969-71, Albert Einstein Coll. Medicine, 1977—; vis. prof. Universidad Nacional de Ingenieria, Lima, Peru, 1977. Served with USN, 1960-65. Rotary Internat. fellow, 1961-62; NDEA fellow, 1965-68. Mem. Acoustical Soc. Am. Roman Catholic. Contbr. articles to profl. jours. Patentee in field. Home: 3919 7th St Apt 3 Washington DC 20017 Office: Cath U Am Mech Engring Dept 620 Michigan Ave NE Washington DC 20064

CLARK, LEONARD HILL, educator; b. Guilford, Conn., Nov. 18, 1915; s. Ridgley Colfax and Idella May (Hill) C.; B.A., Wesleyan U., 1937; Ed.M., Boston U., 1949, Ed.D., 1953; postdoctoral studies U. So. Calif.; m. Maria Aleksandra Langowska, Aug. 30, 1947. Tchr., John Fitch High Sch., Windsor, Conn., 1938-42; lectr. Boston U., 1948-49; dean Lyndon Tchrs. Coll., 1949-54; chmn. dept. secondary edn. U. Hartford, 1954-59; prof. secondary edn. Jersey City State Coll., 1959—, chmn. div. adminstrn., curriculum and instruction, 1976-78; adj. staff Rutgers U., U. Bridgeport, R.I. Coll., Utah State U.; free lance editorial and ednl. cons. Served with AUS, 1942-47. Decorated Commendation Medal. Danforth scholar. Mem. Am. Ednl. Research Assn., Assn. Tchr. Educators, World Edn. Fellowship, Nat. Council Social Studies, Middle States Council Social Studies (dir. 1966-69), N.J. Council Edn., Assn. Supervision and Curriculum Devel., Internat. Assn. Ednl. Research, NEA, N.J. Edn. Assn., Phi Delta Kappa. Author: (with I.S. Starr) Secondary School Teaching Methods, 3d edit., 1976; (with R.L. Klein and J.B. Burks) American Secondary School Curriculum, 2d ed., 1972; Strategies and Tactics in Secondary School, 1968; Teaching Social Studies in Secondary Schools, 1973. Editor: Off Campus Experiences in the Megalopolis, 1965; (with J.F. Callahan) Competency Based Teacher Education Series, 1977. Contbr. articles to profl. jours. Home: 193 Watchung Ave Chatham NJ 07928 Office: Jersey City State College Jersey City NJ 07305

CLARK, MERRELL EDWARD, JR., lawyer; b. Bklyn., Apr. 30, 1922; s. Merrell Edward and Eleanor Everest (Wild) C.; grad. Hotchkiss Sch., 1940; B.A., Yale, 1944, LL.B., 1948; m. Hollis Logan, May 22, 1943; children—Julie (Mrs. Zachary Goodyear), Kenyon Wild. Admitted to N.Y. bar, 1948, since practiced in N.Y.C.; mem. firm Winthrop, Stimson, Putnam & Roberts, partner, 1956—. Rep., Town Meeting, Greenwich, Conn., 1952-55. Trustee Pomfret (Conn.) Sch. Served to capt. AUS, 1943-46. Decorated Bronze Star. Mem. Am., N.Y.C. (chmn. centennial com. 1966-72, pres. 1978—) bar assns., Am. Law Inst., Coll. Trial Lawyers. Clubs: River (N.Y.C.); Riverside Yacht (Riverside, Conn.). Home: 45 Sutton Pl S New York City NY 10022 Office: 40 Wall St New York City NY 10005

CLARK, PEGGY, theatrical lighting designer; b. Balt., Sept. 30, 1915; d. Eliot Round (M.D.) and Eleanor (Linton) Clark; A.B. cum laude, Smith Coll., 1935; M.F.A., Yale, 1938; m. Lloyd R. Kelley, Jan. 28, 1960. Designer theatrical costumes, 1938—; designer settings and lighting Gabrielle, 1941, High Ground, 1951, Curtain Going Up, 1952, Agnes de Mille Dance Theatre, 1953-54; designer stage lighting numerous plays, including Beggar's Holiday, 1946, Song of Norway, 1952, Peter Pan, 1954, Will Success Spoil Rock Hunter, 1955, Kiss Me Kate, 1955, No Time for Sergeants, 1956; designer decor Stage Door Canteen; tech. dir. Lunchtime Follies, Am. Theatre Wing; lighting and tech. dir. other plays including Connecticut Yankee, 1942, Brigadoon, 1946, High Button Shoes, 1947, Along Fifth Avenue, 1948, Gentlemen Prefer Blondes, 1949, Pal Joey, 1951, Mr. Wonderful, Auntie Mame, Bells Are Ringing, 1956, N.Y.C. Center Musical Revivals, 1956, 57, 58, 63-67, Say Darling, 1957; prodns. of Carousel, Susannah, Wonderful Town, at Brussels Internat. Expn., 1958; lighting tech. supr. Flower Drum Song, Juno, Goodbye Charlie, 1959, Bye Bye Birdie, Unsinkable Molly Brown, Under the Yum Yum Tree, 1960, Show Girl, Mary Mary, 1961, Sail Away, 1961, Romulus, 1962, The Girl who Came to Supper, 1963, Around the World in 80 Days, Jones Beach, 1964, Bajour, Poor Richard, 1965, Rose Tattoo, 1966, Darling of The Day, 1967; lighting designer South Pacific, Jones Beach, 1968, 69, Sound of Music, Jones Beach, 1970, 1971, Los Angeles Civic Light Opera, 1969, Jimmy, 1969, Last of the Red Hot Lovers, 1970, How the Other Half Loves, 1971, Candide, 1971, The King and I, Jones Beach, 1972, Carousel, Jones Beach, 1973, several prodns. Bill Baird's Marionette Theatre, 1973-77, others; lighting designer Light Opera of Manhattan, 1977—. Mem. bd. counselors Smith Coll., 1961-69, lectr. lighting design, 1967, 69, pres. Class of '35, 1970-75; instr. lighting design Lester Polakov Studio, Forum Stage Design, 1965—; vis. critic lighting design Yale Drama Sch., 1969-70. Recipient Smith Coll. Distinguished Alumnae medal, 1977. Fellow U.S. Inst. Theatre Tech. (dir. 1969-72, vice commr. engring. commn. 1974—); mem. United Scenic Artists (rec. sec. 1942-47, trustee 1948-51, 53-55, pres. 1968-69, v.p. 1974-76, trustee pension and welfare funds 1970-74, 76—), Yale Drama Alumni Assn. (v.p. 1970-77, pres. 1977-80, mem. search com. for new dean Yale Sch. Drama 1978), Mirror Class Assn. U.S.A., Woods Hole Protective Assn. (pres. 1978—), Illuminating Engring. Soc. Clubs: Brooklyn Smith (dir.), New York Smith, French Bulldog of America (dir., v.p. 1968-72, pres. 1972—), Woods Hole Yacht (sec. 1978—). Home: 36 Cranberry St Brooklyn NY 11201

CLARK, STEPHEN C(UTTER), III, ednl. research exec.; b. Salt Lake City, Mar. 21, 1918; s. Stephen Cutter, Jr. and Helen M. (Moodey) C.; student Calif. Inst. Tech., 1935-37; B.A., U. Wash., 1941, M.A., 1945; Ph.D., Yale U., 1949; m. Anne A. Beaudin, Sept. 30, 1945 (dec. Jan. 1962); children—Margaret Andrews, Katherine Moodey Clark Hanberry, Elizabeth Anne; m. 2d, Caroline P. North, Oct. 18, 1972. Lectr. in English, 1st Higher Sch., Tokyo, 1940-41; acting instr. in physics U. Wash., 1943-45; asst. to dir. student personnel U. New Haven, 1947-49; chmn. dept. psychology Alfred (N.Y.) U., 1949-51; prof. psychology John Muir Coll., Pasadena, Calif., 1951-55; test officer Calif. State Coll. at Los Angeles, 1955-60; dir. research info. center, research asso. Calif. Tchrs. Assn., Los Angeles and Burlingame, 1958-62; dir. adminstrv. research San Diego United Sch. Dist., 1962-63; sr. staff ednl. applications IBM Systems Research and Devel. Center, Los Angeles and Irvine, Calif., 1963-66; edn. and social sci. research analyst HEW, Washington, 1966-67, 71—; sr. scientist, prin. investigator Am. U., Washington, 1967-68; sr. ops. analyst, asst. to pres. Pacific Tech. Analysts, Inc., Saigon and Honolulu, 1968-69; sr. scientist computer devel. div. Univac div. Sperry Rand Corp., Washington, 1970; pres. DekaMeter Testing Service, Washington, 1972—; cons. Former bd. dirs. Family Service of San Diego; chmn. bd. trustees Hawthorne Sch. (Washington); lay reader Episcopal Ch., Diocese of Rochester, 1949-51. Served with USNR. Fellow AAAS; life mem. Am. Personnel and Guidance Assn., NEA, Nat. Vocat. Guidance Assn.; mem. Am. Psychol. Assn., Am. Ednl. Research Assn., Smithsonian Assos., Common Cause, Sierra Club, Phi Delta Kappa. Club: Univ. (San Diego). Author: Clark Occupational Knowledge Inventory, 1970; contbr. to College and Life (M.E. Bennett), 1941, 52, 60. Inventor DekaMeter Testing Terminal. Home and Office: 3900 16th St NW Apt 138 Washington DC 20011

CLARK, WILLIAM FRANCIS, ednl. cons.; b. Boston, Mar. 8, 1909; s. William Randall and Katherine F. (Bates) C.; A.A., Tufts Coll., 1933; Ed.M., Boston U., 1954; m. Evelyn R. Farrell, Nov. 26, 1938; children—Virginia, William Randall III. Gen. bldg. contractor, 1933-39; bus. agt. Belmont (Mass.) Pub. Schs., 1939-49; dir. bus. services Newton (Mass.) Pub. Schs., 1949-57; asst. supt. schs., New Britain, Conn., 1957-58; supt. schs., North Attleboro, Mass. 1959-66; asst. supt. schs., Winchester, Mass., 1966-74; mem. firm Ednl. Service Assos., ednl. cons., Boston. Mem. Am. Assn. Sch. Adminstrs., Am., Mass. assns. sch. bus. ofcls. and supts., Assn. Supervision and Curriculum Devel., Phi Delta Kappa. Address: Melvin Village NH 03850

CLARK, WILLIAM HAWLEY, bishop; b. Escanaba, Mich., May 10, 1919; s. William James and Katherine Elsie (Hawley) C.; B.A., U. Mich., 1942; postgrad. Chgo. Theol. Sem., 1942-44; B.D., Episcopal Theol. Sch., Mass., 1945; S.T.M., Yale, 1952; D.D., Berkeley-at-Yale, 1975; postgrad. St. Augustine Coll., Eng., 1960-61; m. Rosemary Ellen Lehman, June 12, 1943; 3 children. Ordained priest, Episcopal Ch., 1946; asst. rector St. Paul's Ch., Flint, Mich. and vicar Trinity Ch., Flushing, Mich., 1945-49; priest-in-charge St. Peter's Ch., Monroe, Conn., 1949-51; rector Trinity Ch., Concord, Mass., 1951-62; asso. sec. World Council Chs., Geneva, 1962-65; rector St. Andrew's Ch., Wellesley, Mass., 1965-73; bishop of Del., Wilmington, 1975—; tutor Episc. Theol. Sem., 1951-57, 65-66; staff Dept. Christian Edn., Diocese of Mass., 1953-59; exchange preacher Brit. Council Chs., 1969; exec. dir. Worcester County Ecumenical Council. Mem. Mass. Clerical Assn. (pres. 1953-54). Address: 2020 Tatnall St Wilmington DE 19802

CLARK, WILLIAM JAMES, educator; b. Masontown, Pa., Aug. 7, 1931; s. Louis Klarik and Margit (Soltesz) C.; B.A. in Edn., Fairmont (W.Va.) State Coll., 1957; M.Ed. in Math. Edn., U. Ga., Athens, 1961; married; Franklin, Roxana, Steven, Louis, Matthew. Profl. baseball player, minor leagues, Bklyn. Dodgers, 1953-55; tchr. math., Madison, Ohio, 1957-60, Euclid, Ohio, 1961-62; head dept. math. Richard Montgomery High Sch., Rockville, Md., 1962-65; adminstr. secondary sch. Montgomery County (Md.) Pub. Schs., Rockville, 1965-67, coordinator math., 1967-75, dir. div. Acad. Skills, 1975—. Mem. NEA, Montgomery County Edn. Assn., Md. State Tchrs. Assn., Nat. Council Suprs. Math., Nat. Council Tchrs. Math., Assn. Supervision and Curriculum Devel., Phi Delta Kappa. Home: 12304 Melody Turn Bowie MD 20715 Office: 850 Hungerford Dr Rockville MD 20850

CLARK-DUFF, ROBERT HUMPSTONE, electronics mfg. co. exec.; b. Bklyn., Apr. 20, 1926; s. William George and Allice (Carey) Clark-Duff; student RCA Inst., 1945-46; m. Ruth J. Harris, May 25, 1952; 1 dau., Gayle L. Clark-Duff McPhail. Salesman, Gen. Electric Corp., N.Y.C., 1946-52; dir. sales Eico Electronic Instrument Co., Inc., Bklyn., 1952-73; Eastern rep. Electra Corp., Met. N.Y.C., No. N.J. area, 1969-74; owner Monitor Radio Sales Co., Flushing, L.I., N.Y., 1970—, B C-D Sales Co., mfrs. rep., Middle Village, N.Y. Mem. Quarter Century Wireless Assn. Club: N.Y. Radio (chmn. bd. dirs. 1965—, pres. 1966-68). Home: 64-63 80th St Middle Village NY 11379 Office: 163-14 Northern Blvd Flushing NY 11358

CLARKE, AUSTIN CHESTERFIELD, former diplomat, novelist; b. Barbados, W.I., July 26, 1934; s. Fitz Herbert and Gladys Irene (Clarke) Luke; U. Toronto, 1955-59; m. Betty Joyce Reynolds, Sept. 14, 1957; children—Janice Elizabeth, Loretta Anne, Mphabelee Soyinka. Freelance broadcaster CBC, Toronto, 1962—; vis. prof. Yale, 1968-71, Brandeis U., 1970-71, Williams Coll., 1971, Duke U., 1971-72, U. Tex., Austin, 1973-74; cultural attaché Barbados embassy, Washington, 1974-75; gen. mgr. Caribbean Broadcasting Corp., Barbados, 1975-76. Trustee R.I. Sch. Design, 1970-74, Met. Toronto Library, 1973-76. Fellow Can. Council, 1968, 72; recipient President's medal U. Western Ont., 1965; Ind. U. Sch. Letters fellow, 1969-73. Author: Survivors of the Crossing, 1964; Amongst Thistles and Thorns, 1965; The Meeting Point, 1967, 72; Storm of Fortune, 1973; When He Was Free and Young, 1973; The Bigger Light, 1974; The Prime Minister (novel), 1977. Mem. editorial bd. Black Lines Jour., U. Pitts., 1970-74. Home: 432 Brunswick Ave Toronto ON Canada

CLARKE, EDGAR HALE, ins. co. exec.; b. Manchester, Conn., Sept. 21, 1916; s. Fayette Butler and Cora P. (Perry) C.; m. Evelyn Ruth Peterson, Aug. 16, 1940; children—Jeffrey P., Christine L., Deborah H., Clarke Stidson. Founder, Clarke Ins. Agency, Inc., Manchester, 1937—; dir. Savs. Bank Manchester. Corporator Manchester Meml. Hosp., Oak Hill Sch. for Blind. Mem. Manchester Assn. Ins. Agts. (past pres.), Conn. Assn. Ind. Ins. Agts. (past pres.), Antique Auto Club Am., Vet. Motor, Classic car clubs, Rolls Royce Owners Club. Congregationalist. Club: Kiwanis (past pres.). Home: Well Sweep Hebron Rd Andover CT 06040 also Lowell Lake Farm Londonderry VT 05148 Office: 237 E Center St Manchester CT 06040

CLARKE, FRANCES MARGUERITE, psychologist; b. Lorain County, Ohio, Nov. 11, 1905; d. Carl Thomson and Miriam E. (Price) Clarke; A.B., Barnard Coll., 1924; A.M., Columbia U., 1925, Ph.D., 1928; postgrad. Yale U., 1931-33; grad. U. Balt. Law Sch., 1953. Practice psychology, New London, Conn., 1931-36, Towson, Md., 1950-60; mem. faculty U. Md. overseas and Western Md. Coll., Westminster; admitted to Md. bar, 1954. Fellow Am. Psychol. Assn.; mem. Conn., Md. psychol. assns., Internat. Applied Psychotherapists, Soc. Mayflower Descendants in Conn., Md. Bar Assn., Women's Bar Assn. Md. Club: Warren Cousins Assn. Home: 506 Locksley Rd Towson MD 21204

CLARKE, FRANK HENDERSON, JR., pharm. research dir.; b. Newcastle, N.B., Can., Dec. 6, 1927; s. Frank Henderson and Elsie Louisa (Scammell) C.; B.Sc., U. N.B., 1949, M.Sc., 1950; Ph.D., Harvard U., 1954; postdoctoral studies Columbia U., 1953-55, Harvard Bus. Sch., 1968; m. Virginia Nicholas, Sept. 4, 1954; children—Susan Virginia, Sarah Ann. Research chemist Schering Corp., Bloomfield, N.J., 1955-62; group leader Geigy Pharms., Ardsley, N.Y., 1962, dir. medicinal chemistry, 1967-71; dep. dir. chemistry CIBA-GEIGY Pharms., Ardsley, 1971—. Lord Beaverbrook scholar, 1945-49; NRC scholar, 1950. Mem. Am. Chem. Soc., AAAS, Chem. Soc. London, Harvey Soc., N.Y. Acad. Scis., Internat. Union Pure and Applied Chemistry (asso. mem. commn. on medicinal chemistry organic chemistry div. 1977—). Editor: How Modern Medicines Are Discovered, 1973; How Modern Medicines Are Developed, 1976; editor in chief Annual Reports in Medicinal Chemistry, 1976, 77, 78. Contbr. articles to sci. jours. Designer color coded skeletal models, models of enzymes; patentee in pharms. Home: 14 Long Pond Rd Armonk NY 10504 Office: CIBA-GEIGY Pharmaceuticals Ardsley NY 10502

CLARKE, JOSEPH BRIAN, mfg. co. exec.; b. Toronto, Ont., Can., Dec. 2, 1938; s. Kirkwood Johnson and Ethel May (Thomas) C.; student Ryerson Inst. Tech., 1957-61; m. Odette Hamel, July 24, 1972; children—Johanna, Krystina. Sales supr. Moore Bus. Forms, Toronto, 1961-65; v.p. mktg. Deluxe Reading Corp., Toronto, 1966; exec. v.p. Coleco (Can.) Ltd., Montreal, 1967-78, pres., 1978—; v.p. mktg. Coleco Industries, Inc., Hartford, Conn., 1970—. Mem. Can. Export Assn., Can. Toy Mfrs. Assn. Office: 4000 St Ambroise St Montreal H4C 2C8 PQ Canada

CLARKE, RAPHAEL SEMMES, chem. co. exec.; b. Charlestown, W. Va., July 20, 1920; s. Richard Henry and Frances (Chew) C.; A.B., Columbia U., 1941; m. Constance Mary Kilbourn, May 3, 1958; children—Richard H., Catherine K. Production supr. product planning, comml. devel. Merck & Co., Rahway, N.J., 1945-54; with Hoffmann La Roche Inc., Nutley, N.J., 1954—, field sales mgr., 1971-73, dir. mktg. food dept., chem. div., 1973-76, dir. mktg. adminstrn. and customer relations chem. div., 1976—. Trustee Loyola Sch., N.Y.C., 1971-73. Served to capt. USAAF, 1942-45. Recipient Top Ten creative salesmanship award Hoffmann-La Roche Inc., 1961. Mem. Am. Chem. Soc., Am. Oil Chemists Assn., Nat. Inst. Food Technologists. Clubs: Pilgrims (N.Y.C.); Glen Ridge (N.J.) Country. Home: 15 Chester Rd Upper Montclair NJ 07043 Office: 340 Kingsland St Nutley NJ 07110

CLARKE, WILLIAM DECKER, lawyer; b. Cleve., July 25, 1925; s. Dr. James H. and Zelma Frances (Clemons) C.; B.A., Samuel Huston Coll., 1946; M.A., Cath. U. Am.; J.D., Howard U., 1952; m. Eleanora Norwood, Nov. 17, 1952; children—Lynda Michelle, Leigh Decker. Admitted to N.Y. State bar, 1959; dep. commr. City of N.Y., 1966-70; gen. counsel Carver Fed. Savs. & Loan Assn., N.Y.C., 1963—; pres. Decker-Clarke Corp., N.Y.C., 1970—; asst. counsel Commonwealth Land Title Ins. Co., N.Y.C., 1973—; pres. Centennial Abstract Corp., 1976—. Chmn. Norwalk (Conn.) Merit Commn., 1952-57; mem. Norwalk Human Rights Commn., 1957-64; chmn. Sickle Cell Found. of Greater N.Y., 1975—. Mem. Am., Nat. bar assns., Am. Land Title Assn., Alpha Phi Alpha. Office: Suite 323 250 W 57th St New York City NY 10019

CLARY, LEON HOWARD, civil engr., land surveyor; b. Norfolk, N.Y., Dec. 16, 1940; s. Edgar John and Velva Margaret (Burls) C.; B.C.E., Clarkson Coll. Tech., 1962; m. Marilyn Gladys Davies, June 29, 1963; children—Karen Lee, Kimberly Jo, Kristi Jacqueline. Jr. hwy. engr. Calif. Div. Hwys., Marysville, 1962-63; surveyor Dickerson Czerwinski & Warneck, Watertown, N.Y., 1963-68; chief surveys, 1968-70; chief surveys Sear-Brown Assos., Rochester, N.Y., 1970-74, asso. firm, 1974-78, dir. site engring., land surveying, 1977—, also dir.; dir. Shoecraft Realty Corp.; lectr. in field. Active YMCA; mem. curriculum adv. com. Nat. Tech. Inst. for Deaf, Rochester Inst. Tech., 1977—. Registered profl. engr. and land surveyor, N.Y. Mem. Genesee Valley Land Surveyors Assn. (pres. 1976), Am. Soc. Photogrammetry, ASCE, Am. Congress Surveying and Mapping, Nat., N.Y. State socs. profl. engrs., N.Y. State Assn. Profl. Land Surveyors, Nat. Assn. Home Builders, Genesee Conservation League, Chi Epsilon. Republican. Home: 50 Mendon Victor Rd Mendon NY 14506 Office: Metro Park Rochester NY 14623

CLASTER, BARBARA LEINER, clin. psychologist; b. Cleve., Feb. 11, 1931; d. Philip A. and Della Florence (Berkowitz) L.; A.B., Ohio U., 1953; M.A., Northwestern U., 1954, Ph.D., 1966; m. Jay B. Claster, Apr. 28, 1963; 1 dau., Saundra Margaret. Counselor Northwestern U., 1953-54, 58-60; tchr. pub. schs., Warrenville Heights, Ohio, 1954-55; counselor Div. Child Welfare, Cuyahoga County, Cleve., 1955-56, Cleve. Coll., Western Reserve U., Cleve. 1956-58; intern, in med. psychology Sch. Medicine, Washington U., St.Louis, 1960-61; psychologist Pa. State U., 1961-64; staff asst., v.p. for student affairs Pa. State U., 1968-71, tutoring coordinator, 1971; candidate Postgrad Center for Mental Health, N.Y.C., 1973—; pvt. practice psychotherapy, State College, Pa., 1976—, N.Y.C., 1977—. Pres. Centre County Council for Human Services, 1970-72. Mem. Pa., Am., Eastern, N.Y. State psychol assns., N.Y. Soc. Clin Psychologists, Pi Lambda Theta. Home and office: 433 Ridge Ave State College PA 16801 also 1065 Park Ave New York City NY 10028

CLASTER, JAY B., retail exec.; b. Lock Haven, Pa., Nov. 6, 1931; s. Aaron H. and Miriam G. (Herr) C.; B.S., Carnegie-Mellon U., 1953; m. Barbara Leiner, Apr. 28, 1963; 1 dau., Saundra Margaret. With M. L. Claster & Sons, Inc., Bellefonte, Pa., 1955—, mgr. Altoona (Pa.) Br., 1958-59, gen. mgr. Claster Steel, Inc., Williamsport, Pa., 1960-64, gen mgr. parent co., Bellefonte, 1965-71, pres., 1972—; chmn. bd. Sawdust Airlines, 1977—. Nat. v.p. Am. Heart Assn., 1969-73, bd. dirs., 1978—; bd. dirs. Pa. Heart Assn., 1958—, bd. chmn., 1964-66; chmn. Centre County, Pa. Airport Authority, 1977—; bd. govs. Pa. Mfrs. Assn., 1978; mem. council Pa. State U. Fund, 1978—. Served with U.S. Army, 1953-55. Mem. Pennsylvanians for Effective Govt. Home: 433 Ridge Ave State College PA 16801 Office: 1 Phoenix Ave Bellefonte PA 18623

CLAUSEN, RALPH THEODORE, marketing research co. exec.; b. Lake Forest, Ill., May 29, 1920; s. Ralph and Christine (Eide) C.; B.S. in Marketing, U. Ill. at Urbana, 1943; postgrad. Northwestern U., 1946-48; M.B.A., N.Y.U., 1969; m. Mariana Nelson; children—Peter T., Christina. Media research analyst A. C. Nielsen Co., marketing research, Chgo., 1945-48, dept. mgr., N.Y.C., 1948-58, sales service exec., 1958-59, sales service account exec., 1959-62, v.p. sales and service, 1962—. Lectr., N.Y. U., and other colls. Committeeman Boy Scouts Am., Tenafly, N.J., 1957-63; mem. storm drainage study com. Town of Tenafly, 1963—. Served to 2d lt. AUS, 1943-45. Mem. Internat. Radio and TV Soc., Assn. Study Bus. Econs., Radio and TV Research Council, Am. Marketing Assn., Alpha Kappa Psi. Republican. Presbyterian. Home: 24 Bliss Ave Tenafly NJ 07670 Office: A C Nielsen Co 1290 Ave of Americas New York City NY 10019

CLAWAR, HARRY JOSEPH, psychologist; b. Phila., May 11, 1938; s. Murrae and Sarah C.; A.B., Temple U., 1960, M.A., 1961, Ph.D., 1966; m. Sybil A. Bartash, Aug. 26, 1961; children—Randi Lynne, Craig Stewart, Leigh Jason. Testing adminstr. Temple U., Phila., 1961-63; asst. prof. psychology Trenton (N.J.) State Coll., 1963-66; dir. tech. services Ednl. Records Bur., N.Y.C., 1966-67; coordinator instl. research Hunter Coll., N.Y.C., 1968-70, asso. prof. psychol. and social founds. of edn., 1967—; chmn. bd. Testing & Evaluation Services Co., Inc., N.Y.C., 1976-78; sec. Suntherm, Inc., N.Y.C., 1977-78; cons. pvt. corps., Mass. Dept. Edn. Mem. AAAS, Am. Ednl. Research Assn., Am. Mgmt. Assn., Am., Eastern psychol. assns., Nat. Council Measurement in Edn. Jewish. Home: 10 Westerly Dr New City NY 10956 Office: 695 Park Ave New York City NY 10021

CLAWSON, HARRY QUINTARD MOORE, bus. exec.; b. N.Y.C., Aug. 8, 1924; s. Harry Marshall and Marguerite H. (Burgoyne) C.; grad. Staunton Mil. Acad., 1943; student N.Y. U., 1951-52, New Sch. for Social Research, 1953; m. (div. June 1964); m. 2d, Annemarie Korntner Thinnes, Dec. 1967. Supr. transp. responsible adminstrn. and liaison with U.S. Army for ARC overseas, 1945-46; asst. to dir. personnel UNESCO, Paris, France, 1947; resident rep. Texas Co., Douala, French Cameroun, West Africa, 1948-50; asst. dir. overseas bus. service McGraw-Hill Pub. Co., 1951-58; dir. client service Internat. Research Assos., N.Y.C., 1958-61; v.p., sec., dir. Frasch Whiton Boats, Inc., gen. mgr. sailboat tng. facility; pres. Harry Q.M. Clawson & Co., Inc., 1961-76; dir. planning and adminstrn. splty. chems. div. Essex Chem. Corp., 1976-78. Pres., Centre Island Assn., 1974-76. Chmn. planning bd. Village of Centre Island, N.Y. Served with inf., AUS, 1943-45, ETO. Decorated Bronze Star medal. Mem. Ex-Mems. Assn. Squadron A. Clubs: Seawanhaka Corinthian Yacht (Oyster Bay); N.Y. Yacht (N.Y.C). Contbr. articles to profl. jours. Home: 1 King St Charleston SC 29401

CLAXTON, JOHN BROOKE, lawyer; b. Montreal, Que., Can., Jan. 13, 1927; s. Brian Brooke and Helen Galt (Savage) C.; B.C.L., McGill U., 1950; m. Patricia Dorothy Carson, June 22, 1951; children—David Frederick, Brian Edward. Called to Que. bar, 1950; mem. firm Dixon, Claxton, Senecal, Turnbull & Mitchell (and successor firms), Montreal, 1950-63; partner firm Lafleur & Brown, Montreal, 1963—; dir. Benson & Hedges (Can.) Ltd.; lectr. Faculty Law, McGill U., 1956-68. Bd. dirs. Atlantic Salmon Assn., 1974. Served with Canadian Army, 1945. Mem. Bar Montreal (council 1972-74), Bar Que. (council 1973-74), McGill Law Grads. Soc. (pres. 1970). Clubs: Univ., Montreal Racket, Hillside Tennis, Canadian, Red Birds Ski, Ski Hawks. Home: 5138 Cote St Antoine Montreal PQ H4A 1N7 Canada Office: 800 Victoria Sq Suite 720 Montreal PQ H4Z 1E4 Canada

CLAYMAN, LAWRENCE HOWARD, dentist; b. N.Y.C., Jan. 12, 1910; s. Samuel and Rose (Schaeffer) C.; student Coll. City N.Y., 1927-30; D.D.S., Tufts U., 1934; m. Edna Levine, June 11, 1938; children—Joel, Stuart, Maxine, Shari. Intern, Montefiore Hosp. and Med. Center, N.Y.C., 1934-35; gen. practice dentistry, N.Y.C., 1935—; mem. staff Montefiore Hosp. and Med. Center; postgrad. instr. Sch. Dental Medicine, Tufts U., 1966-69, Sch. Dental Medicine, U. Pa., 1969-72, Dental Sch., N.Y.U., 1968, Sch. Dentistry, Emory U., 1968-69. Fellow Am. Coll. Dentists, N.Y. Acad. Dentistry, Greater N.Y. Acad. Prosthodontics; mem. ADA (life), Am. Prosthodontia Soc., N.Y. State, First Dist. dental socs., Am. Acad. Periodontology, Tufts U. Sch. Dental Medicine Alumni Assn., Tufts Dental Club N.Y.C. (pres.), Am. Coll. Dentists, N.Y. Acad. Dentistry, Omicron Kappa Upsilon, Eta Sigma Sigma (pres.). Club: Exchange (pres.). Contbr. articles to dental jours. Home: 50 Oxford Blvd Great Neck NY 11023 Office: 37 Park Ave New York City NY 10016

CLAYTON, CONSTANCE MAE, computer systems analyst; b. Bethel Park, Pa., Dec. 4, 1941; s. Condie and Ruth (Clemons) C.; student U. D.C., 1977—. Supr. clk. data automation br. HEW, 1963-66, computer programmer, 1966-75, computer systems analyst, 1975-78, sr. computer systems analyst, 1978—. Mem. NAACP, Data Processing Mgmt. Assn. (Washington chpt). Democrat. Baptist. Home: 4274 E Capitol St NE Washington DC 20019 Office: HEW Parklawn Center 5600 Fishers Ln Rockville MD 20852

CLAYTON, LEWIS BARRINGTON, physician; b. Bradley Beach, N.J., May 6, 1922; s. Lewis Wellington and Irene May (Parker) C.; student Yale U., 1941-43, N.C. State Coll., 1943-44, U. Ky., 1944; M.D., U. Tenn., 1948; M.P.H., Harvard U., 1961. Intern, U.S. Naval Hosp., Phila.; pvt. practice medicine, Ky., 1950-55, Tenn., 1955-58; resident in pub. health Dade County Health Dept., Miami, Fla., 1959-60, dir. div. research, 1961-62, dir. div. research and epidemiology, 1962-64; asst. prof. medicine U. Miami, 1961-62, asst. prof. preventive medicine, 1962-64, coordinator postgrad. med. edn., 1961; dir. div. epidemiology and statistics Am. Lung Assn., N.Y.C., 1964-71, asso. med. dir., 1971-77; dir. med. affairs, 1977—; cons. evaluations of oral polio vaccines, Tampa, Fla. and Brookline, Mass., 1961-62; hon. cons. in pub. health and preventive medicine Bahamas Govt., 1964—; trustee, mem. sci. advisory bd. Infectious Disease Research Inst., VA, 1969—; adminstrv. officer first community-wide use of oral polio vaccine, Miami-Dade County Community Polio Program, 1960. Fellow Am. Pub. Health Assn., Royal Soc. Health; mem. N.Y. Acad. Scis., Am. Thoracic Soc., Am. Coll. Preventive Medicine. Contbr. articles to profl. jours. Home: 2 Lincoln Sq Apt 31A New York City NY 10023 Office: American Lung Assn 1740 Broadway New York City NY 10019

CLEARY, FRITZ, sculptor, writer; b. N.Y.C., Sept. 26, 1914; s. Francis and Minnie (Walsh) C.; student St. John's U., 1932-36, NAD, 1936-37, Beaux Arts Inst., 1937-38; m. Hope Kielland, Oct. 12, 1959; children—Catherine, Christopher, Cyrus. Art critic, travel editor, feature writer Asbury Park (N.J.) Press, 1943-73; editorial adviser Nat. Scuplture Rev., 1972—; exhibited in one-man and group shows at Nat. Acad., 1938-42, 47-48, Pa. Acad., 1938, 39, Bklyn. Art Mus., 1942, Oakland Art Mus., 1952, Newark Art Mus., 1938, Trenton Art Mus., 1939, Montclair Art Mus., 1938-42, 50-53, Monmouth Art Mus., 1965, Princeton Mus., 1941, Amherst Coll. Mus., 1939, Conn. Coll. for Women Mus., 1939, So. Vt. Artists Galleries, N.Y., N.J. Served with F.A., AUS, 1944-45; ETO. Decorated Bronze Star; recipient Gold medal of honor for sculpture Allied Artists Am., 1967, honorable mention, 1974; Warren prize Am. Artists Profl. League, 1938, prizes Oakland Art Mus., 1952, Montclair Art Mus., 1950; award N.J. Soc. Architects, 1972. Fellow Nat. Sculpture Soc.; mem. Asbury Park Soc. Fine Arts (pres., curator mus.), Nat. Sculpture Soc. (rep. to N.Y. Fedn. Arts 1971-78, John Spring award 1974), Allied Artists, Am. Assn. Registered Architects, Hudson Valley Art Assn. (Anna Hyatt Huntington award 1974), Salamagundi Club. Home: 209 Windermere Ave Interlaken NJ 07712 Office: 205 Grassmere Ave Interlaken NJ 07712

CLEARY, JAMES CHARLES, JR., audiovisual producer; b. N.Y.C., Mar. 15, 1921; s. James Charles and Elizabeth Adelaide (Anglin) C.; grad. Scarsdale (N.Y.) High Sch., 1940; m. Adele Lillian Coe, Nov. 28, 1954. Lithographer, cameraman Advt. Lit. Inc., N.Y.C., 1940-41; advt. copy writer Grosset & Dunlap, book pubs., N.Y.C., 1942-44; advt. copy writer, editor Baker & Taylor, book wholesalers, N.Y.C., 1945-46; asst. mgr. sales Camera Craft Inc., retail photog. sales, White Plains, N.Y., 1946-50, Colortone Camera Inc., White Plains, 1950-57; producer, lectr. Ansco div. Gen. Aniline & Film Corp., Binghamton, N.Y., 1959-61; lab. photographer Nevis Lab. Nuclear Research, Columbia U., 1959-75; audio-visual specialist Edgemont Sch. Dist., Scarsdale, 1975—; owner-producer Cleary Sound-Slides, New Rochelle, N.Y., 1950—. Mem. Scarsdale Camera Club (pres. 1948-49), Color Camera Club Westchester N.Y. (dir. 1958-59), Am. Security Council (advisory bd. 1970—), U.S. Air Force Assn. Patentee of complete sound-synchronized, dissolving slide projection control system, 1966; pioneer in use of dissolve projection and synchronized sound in presentation of color slide continuities. Address: Cleary Sound-Slides 28 Pengilly Dr New Rochelle NY 10804

CLEAVER, DAVID CHARLES, lawyer; b. Sunbury, Pa., Dec. 26, 1941; s. Clarence Perry and Gertrude Lillian (Clarke) C.; B.A., U. N.C., 1964; J.D., Dickinson Sch. Law, 1967; m. Patricia Arlene Caputo, Aug. 23, 1974; children—David Clarke, Christopher Perry. Admitted to Pa. bar, 1967, U.S. Supreme Ct. bar, 1971; asso. firm Black & Davison, Chambersburg, Pa., 1967-71; partner firm Sharpe & Sharpe, Chambersburg, 1971—; adj. prof. law Dickinson Sch. Law, Carlisle, Pa., 1971—. Pres. Franklin County (Pa.) ARC, 1971, Chambersburg YMCA, 1974-75. Mem. Am., Pa. bar assns., Am. Arbitration Assn. (nat. panel), Am., Pa. trial lawyers assns. Republican. Author: Cases and Materials on Wills and Decedents Estates, 1975. Home: 455 Overhill Dr Chambersburg PA 17201

CLEAVES, EMERY NUDD, pub. relations cons.; b. N. Scituate, Mass., May 16, 1902; s. Arthur Wadsworth and Mary Elden (Nudd) C.; B.S., Harvard, 1923; m. Ione Marie Page, Aug. 16, 1924; 1 dau., Nancy Watson Cleaves Blaydes. With John Price Jones Corp., 1925-29, N.J. Buttonworks Co., 1929-38, Robert Heller & Assos., 1939-42, Celanese Corp. Am., 1947-64; pub. relations con. Manning, Selvage & Lee, and predecessors, N.Y.C., 1964—. Served with USNR, 1942-46. Mem. Pub. Relations Soc. Am., Pub. Relations Seminar. Republican. Baptist. Clubs: Harvard, Masons (N.Y.C.). Author: Plenty of Searoom—A Yankee Boyhood; Sea Fever—The Making of a Sailor. Home: 1123 Round Hill Rd Fairfield CT 06430 Office: 99 Park Ave New York City NY 10019

CLEAVES, ROBERT E(DWARD), indsl. developer; b. Portland, Maine, June 17, 1920; s. Orman C. and Abbie E. (Dodge) C.; grad. Command and Gen. Staff Coll., 1951; student Armed Forces Indsl. Coll., 1961; m. Lucile K. Cofran, Jan. 1, 1942; children—Roberta Cleaves Gray, Orman, Elizabeth. Technician Maine N.G., 1947-69; comdg. officer Armor Group MEARNG, 1964-68; exec. officer Armored Cavalry Regiment, 1958-63; mgr. Greater Portland Bldg. Fund, 1969—. Pres. Pine Tree Council Boy Scouts Am., 1974-75; chpt. chmn. ARC, 1971-74; trustee, 1st v.p. Osteopathic Hosp. Maine, Inc., 1972-77; pres. Indsl. Devel. Council Maine, 1974. Served with U.S. Army, 1941-46. Decorated Bronze Star. Mem. Soc. Indsl. Realtors, Am. Indsl. Devel. Council (dir.), Nat. Assn. Indsl. Parks, Northeastern Indsl. Developers Assn., Indsl. Devel. Council Maine. Republican. Congregationalist. Clubs: Portland Rotary, Torch, Maine Chpt. Mil. Order World Wars, Mason. Home: 766 Stevens Ave Portland ME 04103 Office: 142 Free St Portland ME 04101

CLEEK, JOHN WILLARD, environ. cons. exec.; b. Lansdowne, Pa., Feb. 25, 1935; s. Willard and Grace Louise (Harnly) C.; B.S. in Communication, Temple U., 1963; m. Constance Mary Kemmerer, Sept. 24, 1960; children—Elizabeth Louise, John W. Jr. News asst. WPTZ-TV, Phila., 1953-57; copyboy Phila. Dailey News, 1957-60; graphic arts supr. INA Corp. Phila., 1960-65; copy writer TV Guide mag., Radnor, Pa., 1965-67; sales promotion supr. ESB, Inc., Phila., 1967-69; mktg. mgr. Iron Age mag., Radnor, 1969-75; corp. communications mgr. Weston Environ. Cons., West Chester, Pa., 1975—. Radnor Twp. Committeeman, 1971-74; pres. Ithan Valley Group, 1972-73; bd. govs. East Radnor Little League, 1973-77; mem. bd. commrs., Radnor Twp., 1974—, v.p., 1976—. Served with Pa. Air N.G., 1959-66. Recipient Best of Yr. award Printing Week, Del. Valley, 1964, 69. Republican. Clubs: Savoy Opera Co., Conestoga Swim. Home: 228 S Spring Mill Rd Villanova PA 19085 Office: Weston Way West Chester PA 19085

CLEETON, GLEN URIEL, psychologist, educator; b. Green City, Mo., July 2, 1895; s. Zina Ambrose and Dora Alice (Ransom) C.; B.S., N.E. Mo. State U., 1917; M.A., State U. Iowa, 1923; m. Jennie Frances Terry, Apr. 12, 1914; children—Mary Frances (Mrs. Roland James White), Glenna (Mrs. William Frank Nesbit), Alan Robert, Merle Morgan. Supt., Hilton Twp. Pub. Schs., Conroy, Ia., 1918-22; prof. to dean humanities and social studies Carnegie-Mellon U., Pitts., 1923-63, spl. asst. to pres., 1963-65, dean emeritus, 1965—; partner Indsl. Personnel Cons., Allison Park, Pa., 1965-70. Cons. psychologist Am. Transit Assn., 1941-47, Doubleday and Co., N.Y., 1946-70. Chief psychol. examiners U.S. Army Induction Sta., Pitts., 1942-43; mem. arbitration panel Commonwealth Pa. Labor-Mgmt. Adv. Com., 1948-58; engaged in study problems of employment mentally restored United Mental Health Services Allegheny County, Pitts., 1965-66. Diplomate indsl. and organizational psychology. Fellow Am. Psychol. Assn.; mem. Sigma Xi, Phi Kappa Phi, Epsilon Pi Tau. Mason. Author: Executive Ability: Its Discovery and Development, 1946, Making Work Human, 1949, General Printing, 1953, The Story of Carnegie Tech, 1965, also articles; cons. editor McGraw-Hill Book Co., N.Y., 1961—. Home and office: 2812 McCully Rd Allison Park PA 15101

CLELAND, ALAN STUART, consultant; b. Bellefonte, Pa., Jan. 10, 1939; s. Ralph Rankin and Elizabeth Anne (Zerby) C.; B.E., Yale U., 1960; S.M., Mass. Inst. Tech., 1966; M.B.A., Harvard U., 1969; m. Carol Elaine Nolte, Sept. 4, 1965. Vice pres. investment banking Shearson Hammill & Co., N.Y.C., 1969-74; v.p. fin. Lehigh Portland Cement Co., Allentown, Pa., 1974-77; cons. Strategic Planning Inst., Cambridge, Mass., 1978—. Served to lt. USNR, 1960-64. Registered profl. engr., Pa. Mem. Fin. Execs. Inst., ASME, Tau Beta Pi. Home: Deer Run Lincoln MA 01773 Office: One Broadway Cambridge MA 02142

CLEMENDOR, ANTHONY ARNOLD, obstetrician, gynecologist, educator; b. Port-of-Spain, Trinidad, West Indies, Nov. 8, 1933; s. Anthony Arnold and Beatrice Hleen (Stewart) C.; came to U.S., 1954, naturalized, 1959; A.B., N.Y. U., 1959; M.D., Howard U., 1963; m. Elaine Browne, May 31, 1958; children—Anthony Arnold, David Alan. Intern, USPHS, S.I., N.Y., 1963-64; resident Met. Hosp. Center, N.Y.C., 1964-68, chief outpatient dept. obstetrics and gynecology, 1969-73; med. dir. family planning Human Resources Adminstrn., N.Y.C., 1973-74; asso. dean, dir. office of minority affairs N.Y. Med. Coll., N.Y.C., 1974—, asso. clin. prof. dept. obstetrics and gynecology. Bd. dirs. Elmcor; mem. N.Y. Urban League; life mem. NAACP. Diplomate Am. Bd. Obstetrics and Gynecology. Fellow Am. Coll. Obstetrics and Gynecology, Am. Pub. Health Assn.; mem. AMA, Nat. Med. Assn., N.Y. State, N.Y. County med. socs. Office: 12 E 72nd St New York City NY 10021

CLEMENT, DONALD LEEDS, JR., accountant; b. Haddonfield, N.J., Aug. 25, 1947; s. Donald Leeds and Anna Matilda (Torr) C.; A.B., Lafayette Coll., 1969; M.B.A., Harvard U., 1971; m. Patricia Louise Nazak, Oct. 3, 1975; 1 son, Andrew Todd. Staff, Coopers & Lybrand, Phila., 1971-76, mgr., 1976—; author and lectr. in field. C.P.A. Mem. Pa. (editor Phila. chpt. newsletter 1975—), Am. insts. C.P.A.'s, Am. Accounting Assn. Clubs: Vesper, Harvard, Harvard Bus. Sch., Lafayette. Home: 610 Mt Vernon Ave Haddonfield NJ 08033 Office: Coopers & Lybrand 1900 Three Girard Plaza Philadelphia PA 19102

CLEMENT, KARL GUSTAV, financial cons.; b. St. Paul, Nov. 10, 1906; s. Henry and Ida (Mueller) C.; grad. Shattuck Sch.; B.S. in Bus., U. Minn., 1928; grad. Command and Gen. Staff Sch.; m. Mavis W. Poole, Feb. 28, 1945; children—Ronalie Ida (Mrs. Thomas Peterson), Karla Marie. With Nat. Park Bank, N.Y.C., 1928-29; accountant Bendix Corp., 1929-33; comptroller, asst. to pres. Vick Chem. Co., 1933-48; comptroller Port of N.Y. Authority, 1949-53; with R.H. Donelley Corp., 1953-72, comptroller, 1953-60, v.p. adminstrn., 1960-70, v.p. and asst. to pres., 1971-72; financial cons. United Presbyn. Found., 1972-78; v.p. finance Rocliff Assos., Inc., N.Y.C., 1974—; sr. v.p. Internat. Execs. Inc., 1978—. Served as col. USAAF World War II; ETO. Mem. Financial Execs. Inst. (dir. N.Y.C.), Beta Gamma Sigma, Alpha Tau Omega. Episcopalian. Clubs: Cloud, University (N.Y.C.); Lyford Cay (Bahamas); Nassau Country (Glen Cove); Shinnecock Hills Golf (Southampton, N.Y.). Home: 89 Fruitledge Rd Glen Head NY 11545 Office: 12 S Mountain Ave 37 Montclair NJ 07042

CLEMENTE, CELESTINO, physician, surgeon; b. Penns Grove, N.J., June 11, 1922; s. Ermanno and Caroline (Friozzi) C.; B.S., Rutgers U., 1942; M.D., U. Pa., 1945; m. Marie Ann Strangio, Nov. 16, 1946; children—Jeffrey, Roderick, Mark, Laurie Ann, Jonathan. Intern, Jersey City Med. Center, 1945-46; resident gen. surgery Martland Med. Center, Newark, 1950-53; dir. surgery Children's Hosp., Newark, 1962-70, cons., 1970—; med. dir. United Hosps. Newark, 1968-75; dir. surgery St. Vincent's Hosp., Montclair, N.J., 1972—; v.p. med. affairs United Hosp. Newark, 1975—; asso. clin. prof. surgery N.J. Med. Sch., Newark, 1975—; individual practice medicine specializing in gen. surgery Newark, 1953—; dir. Montclair Nat. Bank & Trust Co., 1965-69. Nominee Republican party U.S. Congress 10th. Dist. N.J., 1968; Nat. adv. council nurse tng. HEW, 1970-74. Served to lt., M.C., USNR, 1946-48. Diplomate Am. Bd. Surgery. Fellow A.C.S., Internat. Coll. Surgeons, Royal Soc. Health; mem. AMA, AAAS. Roman Catholic. Club: Essex (Newark). Home: 364 Ridgewood Ave Glen Ridge NJ 07028 Office: United Hosps Newark 15 S 9th St Newark NJ 07107

CLEMENTS, GEORGE F., JR., ind. oil and gas producer; b. Waltham, Mass., Sept. 24, 1925; s. George F. and Florence (Pinkerton) C.; student Rensselaer Poly. Inst., 1943; B.S., Mass. Inst. Tech., 1949; m. Betty McDowell, May 23, 1964; children—Lisa M., George F. III, Sallie E. With Empire Trust Co., N.Y.C., 1949-61, v.p. 1959-61; v.p., dir. Empire Resources Corp., N.Y.C., 1954-61; pres., dir. Whitestone Petroleum Corp., N.Y.C., 1961-72; pres., dir. Whitestone Corp. Greenwich, Houston; dir. Whitestone Internat., Inc., Dallas, Barber Oil Corp., N.Y.C. Served to 2d lt. USAAF, 1943-46; 1st lt. USAF, 1950-51. Decorated Air medal. Mem. Am. Inst. Mining, Metall. and Petroleum Engrs. Clubs: N.Y. Yacht, Leash, India House, Sky, Cruising of Am., Storm Trysail (N.Y.C.); Round Hill, Indian Harbor Yacht (Greenwich); Royal Ocean Racing (London); Beach and Tennis, Eastward Ho, Stage Harbor Yacht (Chatham, Mass.); Ramada (Houston). Office: 283 Greenwich Ave Greenwich CT 06830

CLEMENTS, SARAH WHITE, govt. ofcl.; b. Chickasha, Okla., Mar. 11, 1911; d. Ralph Warren and Carrie Etta (Sheets) White; B.A., U. Okla., 1936, postgrad., 1937; m. Forrest E. Clements, Sept. 6, 1941. Weapon system staff officer Office Chief Ordnance, Dept. Army, Washington, 1956-63; program analyst, project mgmt., comptroller, dir. programs U.S. Army Materiel Command, 1963-64, asst. chief Office Project Mgmt., 1964-75; asst. dep. for materiel acquistion Office Asst. Sec. Army, Washington, 1975-77, dep. for materiel acquistion, 1977—. Recipient meritorious civilian service award, 1966, exceptional civilian service award Dept. Army, 1968, distinguished civilian service award Dept. Def., 1975. Mem. Am. Def. Preparedness Assn., Assn. U.S. Army, Am. Soc. Pub. Adminstrn., Fed. Exec. Inst. Alumni Assn. (dir. 1971-77, pres. 1974), Phi Beta Kappa. Episcopalian. Clubs: Internat., Cosmos. Home: 4914 N 34th St Arlington VA 22207 Office: 2E661 The Pentagon Washington DC 20310

CLEMETSON, CHARLES ALAN BLAKE, physician; b. Canterbury, Eng., Oct. 31, 1923; s. Charles Harold and Gwendoline Maud Winefred (Blake) C.; came to U.S., 1961, naturalized, 1972; B.M., B.Ch., Oxford (Eng.) U., 1948; m. Helen Cowan Forster, Mar. 27, 1947; children—Claudia, Charles, David, Andrew. Research asst. Obstetric Hosp., Univ. Coll. Hosp., London, Eng., 1950-52; Nichols research fellow Royal Soc. Medicine, 1951-52; house surgeon obstetrics West Middlesex Hosp., 1952-53; resident med. officer obstetrics Queen Charlotte's Hosp., 1953; house surgeon gynecology Hammersmith Hosp., 1953-54; obstet. and gynecol. registrar Lake Hosp., Ashton-under-Lyne, Lancashire, Eng., 1954-56; lectr. obstetrics and gynecology Univ. Coll. Hosp., London, 1956-58; asst. prof. obstetrics and gynecology Univ. Hosp., Saskatoon, Sask., Can., 1958-61; asst. prof. obstetrics and gynecology U. Calif. Sch. Medicine, San Francisco, 1961-67; dir. dept. obstetrics and gynecology Meth. Hosp., Bklyn., 1967—; asso. prof. obstetrics and gynecology Downstate Med. Center, State U. N.Y., Bklyn., 1967-72, prof. 1972—; mem. obstetric adv. com. Dept. Health, N.Y.C., 1968; cons. dept. obstetrics-gynecology Luth. Med. Center, 1969; mem. med. adv. com. Planned Parenthood N.Y.C., Inc., 1971; mem. physicians rev. com. Blue Cross-Blue Shield N.Y.C., 1975; lectr. obstetrics and gynecology London U., 1956-58; lectr. maternal health, dept. maternal and child health U. Calif. at Berkeley, 1964-65. Served with RAF, 1948-50. Recipient Research Career Devel. award NIH, 1965-67. Fellow Am., Royal colls. obstetricians and gynecologists, Royal Coll. Physicians and Surgeons Can.; mem. British Med. Assn., N.Y. Acad. Scis., N.Y. Obstet. Soc., Bklyn. Gynecol. Soc. (pres. 1977), Med. Soc. County Kings. Contbr. articles to profl. jours. Home: 179 Nassau Ave Manhasset NY 11030 Office: 506 6th St Brooklyn NY 11215

CLEMMONS, CLIFFORD ROBERT, state ofcl.; b. Kansas City, Kans., May 24, 1919; s. H.B. and Constance (Sargent) C.; B.S., Central State U., Wilberforce, Ohio, 1948; M.A. in Social Adminstrn., Ohio State U., 1950; postgrad. Columbia, 1950-56; m. Jimmie E. Hill, June 21, 1941; children—Jennifer M. (Mrs. Richard Johnson), Robert. Probation officer N.Y. State Supreme Ct., Queens Kew Gardens, N.Y., 1951-66, supervising probation officer, 1966—. Bd. dirs. United Vets. Mut. Housing Co., Queens Village, 1967-68, v.p., 1968-69, pres. bd. dirs., 1969-70; pres. Bell Park Manor Terr. Community Council, 1960-63; pres. Counseliers, 1964-68. Bd. dirs. League Consumer Orgns. for Better Dealer Service, Inc., 1971-72, 1st v.p., 1972—; bd. dirs. Municipal Credit Union City N.Y., Greater N.Y. council Nat. Assn. Investment Clubs; pres. Consumer Groups Greater N.Y.; 1st v.p., bd. dirs. Sickle Cell Disease Found. Greater N.Y., Inc., 1972—. Served with AUS, 1941-45. Recipient award Bell Park-Manor Terr. Community Council, 1964, Assn. Black Social Workers (dir. 1967-70), Merit award Counseliers, Inc., 1975, others. Mem. Nat. Assn. Social Workers, NAACP, Nat. Council on Crime and Delinquency, Fedn. Negro Civil Services Orgns. (v.p., chmn. bd. dirs. 1968-77), Urban League, Consumer Group Greater N.Y. (pres. 1972-74), Am. Acad. Polit. and Social Sci., Alpha Phi Alpha (dir. N.Y. State 1971—, awards 1975, 76, 77, 78, Distinguished Alpha Merit award 1976). Democrat. Presbyterian. Home: 221-25 Manor Rd Queens Village NY 11427 Office: Supreme Ct 125-01 Queens Blvd Kew Gardens NY 11415

CLEVELAND, HARLAN, ednl. adminstr.; b. N.Y.C., Jan. 19, 1918; s. Stanley Matthews and Marian Phelps (Van Buren) C.; student (Rhodes scholar), Oxford (Eng.) U., 1938-39; A.B., Princeton U., 1938; m. Lois W. Burton, July 12, 1941; children—Carol Zoe Cleveland Palmer, Anne Moore Cleveland Kalicki, Alan Thorburn. Exec. editor, pub. The Reporter, mag., N.Y.C., 1953-56; dean Maxwell Grad. Sch. Citizenship and Pub. Affairs, Syracuse U., 1956-61; pres. U. Hawaii, Honolulu, 1969-74; dir. program in internat. affairs Aspen Inst. for Humanistic Studies, 1974—. Writer, Farm Security Adminstrn., Washington, 1940-42; ofcl. bd. econ. warfare Foreign Econ. Adminstrn., Washington, 1942-44; exec. dir., econ. sec. Allied Central Commn., Rome, 1944-45, acting v.p., 1945-46; dep. chief of mission UN Relief & Rehab. Adminstrn., Rome, 1946-47, dir., Shanghai, China, 1947-48; dir. China aid program Econ. Coop. Adminstrn., Washington, 1948-49, dep. asst. adminstr., 1949-51; asst. dir. for Europe, Mut. Security Agy., 1952-53, asst. sec. state internat. orgn. affairs State Dept., 1961-65; U.S. ambassador to NATO, 1965-69. Bd. dirs. Honolulu Symphony Soc.; bd. govs. Pacific Asian Affairs Council. Decorated U.S. Army Medal of Freedom; The Order of the Crown of Italy; grand knight officer Gold Star Order of the Brilliant Star of China; recipient Woodrow Wilson award, 1962; book award Princeton, 1938; Claude Moore Fuess award Phillips Acad. Mem. Fgn. Policy Assn. (bd. dirs. 1969-72), New Sch. Social Research (trustee 1954-60), Expt. in Internat. Living, Am. Assn. Rhodes Scholars, Am. Polit. Sci. Assn., Am. Soc. Pub. Adminstrn. (pres. 1970-71). Clubs: Century (N.Y.C.); International (Washington); Waikiki Yacht (Honolulu); Mid-Pacific (Lanikai, Hawaii). Author: The Overseas Americans, 1960; The Obligations of Power, 1966; NATO: The Transatlantic Bargain, 1970; The Future Executive, 1972; The Third Try at World Order: U.S. Policy for an Interdependent World, 1977. Home: 5 Honey Brook Dr Princeton NJ 08540 Office: PO Box 2820 Rosedale Rd Princeton NJ 08540

CLEVELAND, JAMES COLGATE, congressman; b. June 13, 1920; s. Mather and Susan (Colgate) C.; student Deerfield Acad., 1933-37; B.A. magna cum laude, Colgate U., 1941; LL.B., Yale, 1948 ; m. Hilary Paterson, Dec. 9, 1950; children—Cotton Mather, James Colby, David Paterson, Lincoln Mather, Susan Sclater. Admitted to N.H. bar, 1948; practice of law, Concord, also New London, 1949—; sr. partner Cleveland, Waters & Bass, 1960— (on leave); mem. 88th-95th Congresses, 2d. N.H. dist.; organizer, incorporater, officer, dir. New London Trust Co. Mem. of N.H. Senate, 1950-62. Served with AUS, World War II, Korean War. Decorated Bronze Star. Mem. Am. Legion, VFW, Grange, Phi Beta Kappa. Clubs: Elks, Masons, Eagles, Moose, Rotarians, New London Outing. Home: New London NH 03257 Office: Rayburn Bldg Washington DC 20515

CLEVELAND, PRISCILLA RENDELL, counselor; b. Boston, July 14, 1941; d. Bertrum George and Jean Copeland (Avery) Rendell; B.A., Bennington Coll., 1963; M.A. in Teaching, Harvard U., 1964; M.Ed. with distinction, Boston Coll., 1978, postgrad., 1975—; m. Daniel F. Cleveland, Jan. 2, 1977; children by previous marriage—Jean Copeland Haertl, Erica Jane Haertl. Tchr., Walnut Hill Sch., Natick, Mass., 1968-69; dir. personnel New Eng. Instrument Co., Natick, 1966-77; dir. fin. aid Mt. Ida Jr. Coll., Newton, Mass., 1974-77; counselor Framingham (Mass.) S. High Sch., 1978—. Founding mem. Conservation Council of Framingham, 1966. Mem. Am. Personnel and Guidance Assn., Am. Psychol. Assn. Republican. Episcopalian. Home: 110 Prospect St Framingham MA 01701 Office: Flagg Dr Framingham MA 01701

CLEVENGER, ROBERT WILLIAM, physician; b. Chambersburg, Pa., Sept. 26, 1934; s. Herman M. and Evelyn G. (Martz) C.; B.A., Duke, 1956; M.D., George Washington U., 1960; div.; children—Robert William, Julie, Jennifer, Joelle. Intern, Los Angeles County Gen. Hosp., 1960-61; resident in otolaryngology Eye and Ear Hosp., Pitts., 1964-68; pvt. practice specializing in ear, nose and throat Met. ENT Assos., Pitts., 1968—; chmn. dept. surgery North Hills Passavant Hosp., Pitts., 1977—; clin. instr. U. Pitts. Med. Sch., 1968—. Served as capt. M.C., U.S. Army, 1962-64. Recipient Recognition award Indian Health Service, USPHS, 1974-76. Fellow Am. Acad. Ophthalmology and Otolaryngology, A.C.S.; mem. AMA, Pa., Allegheny County med. socs., Pa. Acad. Ophthalmology and Otolaryngology, Pitts. Otolaryngology Soc. Home: 520 Grandview Pittsburgh PA 15211 Office: Suite 142 550 Grant St Pittsburgh PA 15219 also Doctors Office Bldg 9102 Babcock Blvd Pittsburgh PA 15237

CLEVERLEY, MORRIS LESLIE, JR., engring. co. exec.; b. Oneonta, N.Y., Mar. 12, 1937; s. Morris Leslie and Margaret Elizabeth (Mills) C.; B.S., Rose Poly. Inst., 1962; postgrad. Northwestern U., 1963-64; m. Jane Gibson, June 17, 1956; children—Dawn E., Steven M. Div. engring. mgr. N.Y. State div. Mobil Oil Engring., N.Y.C., 1968-70; dir. engring., v.p. Carrols Constrn. Corp., Syracuse, N.Y., 1970-74; pres. Morris L. Cleverley Engring., P.C., Camillus, N.Y., 1972—, Cleverley C.M. Assos., Inc.; chmn. bd. Coman Construction Corp. Mem. ASCE, Nat. Soc. Profl. Engrs., Sigma Nu. Democrat. Lutheran. Clubs: Bellevue Country, Masons. Home: 107 E Gate Rd Camillus NY 13031 Office: 224 Chapel Dr Syracuse NY 13219

CLIFFORD, ARTHUR, former investment co. exec., civic worker; b. Bridgeport, Conn., Feb. 11, 1896; s. Charles and Mary Maud (Matts) C.; student pub. schs., Bridgeport, also spl. courses; Dr. Humanities, Bridgeport Engring. Inst., 1976; m. Mabel Eva Brough, Apr. 14, 1921 (dec. May 1960); children—Arthur Charles, Elizabeth Mabel (Mrs. Sheldon Homer Clark). With efficiency dept. coke plant U.S. Steel Corp., Gary, Ind., 1913-15, Youngstown Sheet & Tube Co., Struthers, Ohio, 1916; foreman LaBelle Ironworks, Steubenville, Ohio, 1917; gen. foreman Donner Union Coke Corp., Buffalo, 1919-22; with A.W. Burritt Co., Bridgeport, Conn., 1922-63, pres., 1955-63, chmn. bd., 1957-63, dir., 1938-63; asst. to pres. Burritt Lumber Sales Co., 1934-56, v.p., 1951-56, pres., 1956-58, chmn. bd., 1957-58, dir., 1944-58; v.p. Investors Capital Corp., Bridgeport, 1962-67, pres., 1967-68, dir., 1962-68. Bd. dirs. Lakeview Cemetery Assn., 1942—, v.p., 1967—; bd. dirs., charter mem. steering com. Bridgeport region Urban Coalition, 1968; adviser, bd. assos. Bridgeport Engring. Inst., 1966—; chmn. bd. Bridgeport chpt. ARC, 1960; pres., dir. YMCA of Greater Bridgeport, 1960-62, trustee, 1964-70; bd. dirs., finance adviser Bridgeport Police Athletic League, 1950—; bd. dirs. Bridgeport Family Welfare Service, 1960-63, Bridgeport Safety Council, 1946-57, Toys for Hosp. Tots, Inc., 1971—, Rehab. Easter Seal Center, 1972-75; chmn. Mayor's Action Com. for Better Bridgeport, 1966-71; chmn. Redevel. Agy. City Bridgeport, 1958-66; mem. organizing com., mem. community forum Fairfield U., 1966-73; life mem. bd. assos. U. Bridgeport, 1966—, adviser Coll. Bus. Adminstrn., 1960—; mem. adv. com., contest judge Brand Names Found., 1953-54, 58-59; trustee Park City Hosp., Bridgeport, 1964-66, life mem., 1967—; chmn. individual gifts com. United Way, Bridgeport, 1974-75; dir. Liturgical Music Festival, 1976—. Served with USMC, 1917-19. Recipient Distinguished Citizens award Bridgeport C. of C., 1961. Sr. Civic Indsl. Bus. Leader, 1970; Outstanding Citizen of Bridgeport award Bridgeport Civitan Club, 1967; statuette for distinguished service 2d Div. Assn. U.S. Army, 1967-69, plaque, 1970, 72, Outstanding Service citation, 1973; Distinguished Citizen award Bridgeport Vol. Bur., 1969; Service to Youth plaque Brideport YMCA, 1970; Wisdom award of Honor, 1970; plaque Bridgeport Police Athletic League, 1971; Certificate of Appreciation, U.S. Marine Corps, 1973. Ky. Col. Mem. Nat. Retail Lumber Dealers Assn. (dir. and mem. edn. com. 1953-56), Northeastern Retail Lumbermens Assn. (hon. life mem.; pres. 1955, mem. exec. com. 1951-57, dir. 1945-57), Lumber Dealers Assn. Conn. (pres. 1945-47, dir. 1940-48), C. of C. U.S. (mem. policy com. 1956-60), New Eng. (hon.), Conn. (hon.) assns. police chiefs, Nat. Police Hall Fame, Greater Bridgeport C. of C. (pres. 1954; dir. 1945-56), Marine Corps League, Am. Legion, VFW. Episcopalian (mem. fin. organist, choir dir. 1942-47, com. 1965-75). Clubs: Masons, Rotary (dir. 1953-59, 68-71; pres. Bridgeport 1957-58; Rotarian of Century award 1971; International Paul Harris fellow), Algonquin (named Sachem of the Year 1975). Home: 45 Hickory St Bridgeport CT 06610

CLIFFORD, FRANCIS JAMES, physician, educator; b. Lockport, N.Y., Feb. 21, 1913; s. John F. and Helen C. (O'Neill) C.; B.A., U. Buffalo, 1934, M.D., 1942; m. Jane D. Ruhlman, June 13, 1942; children—John W., Anne E., Jane F. Intern, Detroit Receiving Hosp., 1942-43; resident Buffalo Gen. Hosp., 1946-48; asso. prof. anatomy State U. N.Y., Buffalo, 1947—; practice medicine specializing in surgery, Lockport, 1948-74; commr. pub. health, Niagara County, N.Y., 1974—. Served with M.C., AUS, 1942-45, 51-53. Decorated Bronze Star. Fellow A.C.S., Royal Soc. Health. Roman Catholic. Home: 8410 Maplewood Dr Gasport NY 14067 Office: 5467 Upper Mountain Rd Lockport NY 14094

CLIFFORD, PATRICK IGNATIUS, ins. co. exec.; b. Glenbeigh, County Kerry, Ireland, Nov. 15, 1933; s. Patrick D. And Eileen (Mahoney) C.; came to U.S., 1954, naturalized, 1959; B.B.A., Manhattan Coll., 1964; M.B.A., St. John's U., 1966; m. Rose E. Walsh, Aug. 29, 1959; children—Patrick, Steven, Peggy, Ann. Asst. mgr. auditing Met. Life Ins. Co., N.Y.C., 1954-70; chief accountant Standard Security Life Ins. Co. of N.Y., N.Y.C., 1970-74; asst. controller Equitable Life Assurance Soc., N.Y.C., 1974—. Served with AUS, 1956-58. Certified internal auditor. Fellow Life Mgmt. Inst.; mem. Inst. Internal Auditors, Accounting and Statis. Assn. Home: 122-20 Ocean Promenade 5H Rockaway Park NY 11694 Office: 1285 Ave of Americas New York City NY 10019

CLIFFORD, STEWART BURNETT, banker; b. Boston, Feb. 17, 1929; s. Stewart Hilton and Ellinor (Burnett) C.; grad. Phillips Acad., 1947; A.B., Harvard U., 1951, M.B.A., 1956; m. Cornelia Park Woolley, Apr. 26, 1952; children—Cornelia Lee Clifford Wareham, Rebecca Lyn, Jennifer Leggett, Stewart Burnett. With Citibank, N.A., N.Y.C., 1956—, asst. cashier, 1958-60, asst. v.p., 1960-63, v.p. in charge planning overseas div., 1967-68, v.p. adminstrn. comml. banking group, 1969-72; exec. v.p., gen. mgr. Merc. Bank Can., Montreal, Que., 1963-67, head world corp. dept., London, Eng., 1973-75, head energy systems dept., 1975-78, sr. v.p. in charge domestic energy div., 1978—; dir. Monumental Corp., Balt. Pres., Woolley-Clifford Found. Trustee, Spence Sch., Brick Ch., N.Y.C. Served to lt. AUS, 1951-54. Presbyterian (elder). Clubs: Union, University (N.Y.C.); Duxbury (Mass.) Yacht. Home: 120 East End Ave New York City NY 10028 Office: 399 Park Ave New York City NY 10022

CLIFFTON, EUGENE E., surgeon; b. Lansdale, Pa., June 26, 1911; s. Eugene Everett and Emma (Wilson) C.; B.S., Lafayette Coll., 1933; M.D., Yale, 1937; m. Madeline Hartwell, June 1937 (dec.); 1 dau., Joanne; m. 2d, Genia Novakowska, Apr. 12, 1941; children—Vala, Ethan, Erica, Kim Eugenia. Instr. surgery N.Y. Hosp.-Cornell U., 1938-43, asst. resident N.Y. Hosp., 1938-43, resident surgery, 1942-44, asst. attending surgeon, 1952-55, asso. attending surgeon, 1955—; asso. surgeon New Haven Hosp., 1949-50; chief gen. surgeon, asst. chief surg. service Wakeman Gen. Hosp., 1946-47; asst. prof. clin. surgery Med. Coll. Cornell U., 1952-55, asso. prof. clin. surgery, 1955-61, asso. prof. surgery, 1961—; asst. vis. surgeon Cornell Surg. Service Bellevue Hosp., N.Y.C., 1952—, James Ewing Hosp., 1952-62; asst. attending surgeon thoracic service Meml. Hosp., 1953-62, attending surgeon, asso. chief thoracic surgery, 1966—. Asso. mem. Sloane Kettering Inst., 1960—, mem. emeritus staff Meml. Sloan Kettering Cancer Center, 1976—; emeritus staff (surgery) Soc. of N.Y. Hosp., 1978—. Mem. Am. Coll. Angiology (pres.), Soc. Univ. Surgeons, James Ewing Soc. Clin. research fibrinolysin, ellagic acid, streptokinase, pulmonary and esophageal surgery. Home: 797 Lake St White Plains NY 10604 Office: 1275 York Ave New York City NY 10021

CLIFTON, ANNE RUTENBER, psychotherapist, educator; b. New Haven, Dec. 11, 1938; d. Ralph Dudley and Cleminette (Downing) Rutenber; B.A., Smith Coll., 1960, M.S.W., 1962; m. Roger Lambert Clifton, Sept. 9, 1961; 1 dau., Dawn Anne Rutenber. Psychiat. case worker for adult psychiatry unit Tufts New Eng. Med. Center, Boston, 1962-68, supr. of students, 1967-68; pvt. practice psychotherapy, 1966—; supr. of med. students and staff social workers in outpatient psychiatry Tufts New. Eng. Med. Center, Boston, 1973—; asst. clin. prof. psychiatry Tufts U. Med. Sch., Boston, 1974—. Mem. Nat. Assn.

Social Workers, Acad. Certified Social Workers, Phi Beta Kappa, Sigma Xi. Clubs: Cambridge Tennis; Mt. Auburn Tennis. Contbr. articles in field to profl. jours. Home: 126 Homer St Newton Centre MA 02159 Office: 51 Brattle St Cambridge MA 02138

CLIFTON, NANCY LYNN, univ. adminstr.; b. Greensburg, Ind., Jan. 20, 1946; d. Max T. and Carol N. (Howe) Clifton; B.S., Ball State U., 1968; M.S., State U. N.Y., 1969. Asst. residence hall dir. State U. N.Y., Albany, 1968-69; head resident Calif. State U., Fullerton, 1969-70; dir. women's residence halls Ball State U., Muncie, Ind., 1970-75, also instr. Edn. Sch.; asst. dir. housing, personnel and programs State U. N.Y., Oswego, 1975-77; asst. dean students Cornell U., Ithaca, N.Y., 1977—. Mem. Am. Personnel and Guidance Assn., Am. Coll. Personnel Assn. (mem. nat. program planning com. 1974, mem. nat. women's task force 1974—), Nat. Assn. Women Deans, Adminstrs. and Counselors, Assn. Coll. and Univ. Housing Officers (co-editor Newsletter-N.E. Region, liaison editor nat. ACUHO News 1975—, ex-officio mem. exec. council N.E. region 1975), Ind. Nat. Women Deans, P.E.O. (chaplain 1972), Sigma Kappa, Kappa Kappa Kappa. Republican. Contbg. editor Nat. ACUHO News Mag., 1977—. Home: 700 Warren Rd Ithaca NY 14850 Office: Cornell Univ North Campus Union Ithaca NY 14850

CLINE, RALEIGH, hosp. adminstr.; b. Selma, Ala., Oct. 24, 1928; s. John Richard and Bessie May (Roberts) C.; B.S., Livingston Coll., 1952; M.B.A., George Washington U., 1965; m. Carolyn Skinner, Aug. 16, 1952; 1 dau., Carol Leigh. Asst. to dir. Balt. City Med. Care Program, 1955-59; program analyst Md. Dept. Health, 1959-63; asst. adminstr. George Washington U. Hosp., 1964-67, asst. professorial lectr., 1970-72; asst. adminstr., then asso. adminstr. Prince George's Gen. Hosp., Cheverly, Md., 1967-73, exec. v.p., 1973—; asso. clin. prof. N.Y. U., 1975-77. Bd. dirs. Family Service Prince George's County, 1968-71, pres., 1972-74; campaign chmn. United Way Prince George's County, 1974, United Community Fund Prince George's County, 1975—; bd. dirs. Md. Resource Center. Served with U.S. Army, 1953-55. Recipient award for contribution to health Md. Med. and Chirurgical Soc., 1976. Mem. Am. Coll. Hosp. Adminstrs., George Washington U. Health Care Alumni Assn. (sec. 1976-77), Assn. Health Care Adminstrs. Nat. Capital Area (past pres.), Md. Hosp. Assn., Assn. Nat. Capital Area. Democrat. Presbyterian. Office: Prince George Gen Hosp Cheverly MD 20785*

CLINE, RUTH ELEANOR HARWOOD, translator; b. Middletown, Conn., Oct. 31, 1946; d. Burton Henry and Eleanor May (Cash) Harwood; A.B., Smith Coll., 1968; M.A., Rutgers U., 1969; certificate translation from French, Georgetown U., 1978. m. William R. Cline, June 10, 1967; children—Alison, Marian. Contract translator U.S. Dept. State, Washington, 1975—. Mem. Am. Translators Assn., Modern Lang. Assn., Internat. Arthurian Soc. Episcopalian. Translator English verse: Chretien de Troyes, Yvain; or the Knight with the Lion, 1975. Home: 5315 Oakland Rd Chevy Chase MD 20015

CLINEDINST, KATHERINE PARSONS, artist; b. Stamford, Conn., July 13, 1903; d. Harold Ashton and Mary Brookfield (Paxson) Parsons; student Jessie Leith, Su-Ling Wong, N.Y.C., 1951-54; degree Pratt. Inst., 1923; m. We,ndel W. Clinedinst, Oct. 24, 1925; 1 son, Richard W. P. Asst. mgr. N.Y. showrooms Boston Soc. Arts and Crafts, 1923-24; exhibited one-person shows: Bronxville (N.Y.) Library, Mamaroneck and New Rochelle brs. 1st Nat. Bank Westchester, Engring. Women's Club, N.Y.C., Eastchester Savs. Bank (N.Y.); group shows: Nat. Gallery, Washington, Monahan Gallery, N.Y.C., Ogunquit (Maine) Art Assn., Hudson Valley (N.Y.) Art Assn., brs. Seaman's Bank Savs., N.Y.C., Acad. Artists Assn., Springfield, Mass., 1962-72, Hammond Mus., N.Y.C., 1966; represented in permanent collections; demonstrator in field. Organizer Outdoor Art Show, Larchmont, N.Y., also co-founder, 1956. Recipient 1st prize Women's Club Larchmont, 1957, 60; graphic award Hudson Valley Art Assn., 1963, Morris Woodrow prize, 1965; 2d prize Westchester Fedn., 1960; 2d prize Mt. Vernon Art Assn., 1967; 1st prize Kent Art Assn., 1968; 1st prize Meridan (Conn.) Arts and Crafts, 1967. Mem. Nat. League Am. Pen Women (pres. Westchester br. 1954-56, nat. chmn. arts and crafts 1958-59), Am. Artists Profl. League, Hudson Valley Art Assn. (dir. 1959-68), Kent (Conn.) Art Assn., Acad. Artists Springfield (Mass.), Meridan Arts and Crafts Assn., Washington (Conn.) Art Assn., Ocean County Artists Guild (N.J.), Monmouth Arts Found. (N.J.), Palette Scholarship Found., Asbury Park (N.J.) Soc. Fine Arts, Miniature Soc. Washington (D.C.). Presbyterian. Address: 951 A Argyll Circle Lakewood NJ 08701

CLINEDINST, WENDEL WATERS, artist; b. N.Y.C., July 23, 1895; s. Benjamin and Emily Gertrude (Waters) C.; M.E., Stevens Inst. Tech., 1921; m. Katherine Parsons, Oct. 24, 1925; 1 son, Richard W.P. With Gen. Motors Corp., N.Y.C., 1919; service and test engr. Payne Dean Ltd., N.Y.C., 1921-23; prodn. engr., field erection and service engr. Aero Pulverizer Co., N.Y.C., 1923-25; with Rust Engring. Co., Pitts., 1925; asst. to mgr. N.Y. dist. C.H. Wheeler Mfg. Co., Phila., 1926-29, dist. engr., N.Y.C., 1929-62; artist, 1962—; one-man shows at Eastchester (N.Y.) Savs. Bank, 1967, 69, Valley Stream (L.I.) Nat. Bank, 1970, others; exhibited in group shows at Hudson Valley Art Assn., 1962—, Allied Artists Am., 1964—, Knickerbocker Soc., 1969-71, Meridan (Conn.) Arts and Crafts, 1964-71, Kent (Conn.) Art Assn., 1963—; Woodmere Art Mus., Germantown, Pa., 1970, others; represented in permanent, pvt. collections. Lectr. bus. side engring. before sales confs., and ednl. orgns.; pres. West Engring. Corp., N.Y.C., 1935-61. Mem. council Boy Scouts Am., Larchmont, N.Y., 1936—. Trustee Stevens Inst. Tech., 1956-75; resident trustee Leisure Village East, Lakewood, N.J., 1972-73. Served with AUS, 1917-19. Recipient alumni honor award Stevens Inst. Tech., 1961, centennial citation, 1970; honor award Iota chpt. Phi Sigma Kappa, 1961; Camp Dad's award Boy Scouts Am., 1963; medal Cath. Fine Arts Soc. Am., 1969. Fellow ASME (life, sec. Met. sect 1933-34, exec. com. 1931-34), Am. Soc. Naval Architects and Marine Engrs. (life), Hudson Valley Art Assn. (pres. 1962-64), Allied Artists Am. (pres. 1968-70, dir.), Am. Artists Profl. League, Meridian Arts and Crafts, Acad. Artists, Am. Vets. Soc. Artists, Kent Art Assn., Stevens Alumni Assn. (exec. com. 1951-59), Artists Fellowship (hon. mem.; treas. 1962-66). Mason. Contbr. articles to profl. publs. Patentee in field. Home: 951-A Argyll Circle Lakewood NJ 08701

CLINGER, WILLIAM FLOYD, JR., congressman; b. Warren, Pa., Apr. 4, 1929; s. William Floyd and Lella May C.; B.A., Johns Hopkins U., 1951; J.D., U. Va., 1965; m. Julia Whitla, Aug. 2, 1952; children—Eleanore, William Floyd, James, Julia. Advt. exec. New Process Co., Warren, 1955-62; admitted to Pa. bar, 1965, U.S. Supreme Ct. bar, 1975; partner firm Stone & Harper, and successor, Warren, 1965-78; mem. 96th Congress from 23d Dist. Pa.; chief counsel Econ. Devel. Adminstrn., 1975-77; del. Pa. Constl. Conv., 1968. Chmn. Kinzua Dam Dedication Com., 1966; del. Republican Nat. Conv., 1972; pres. Warren Library Assn., 1957-62, 67-70, Warren Hosp. Bd., 1971-75. Served with USN, 1951-55. Decorated Spirit of Honor medal; named Man of Year Pa. Jaycees, 1960. Mem. Am. Bar Assn., Pa. Bar Assn., Warren County Bar Assn., Warren Jaycees (pres. 1959-60). Presbyterian. Editorial bd. U. Va. Law Rev., 1964-65. Office: 1221 Longworth House Office Bldg Washington DC 20515

CLINTON, JOHN JOSEPH, info. scientist; b. Phila., Apr. 5, 1947; s. Francis Leonard and Mary Jane (Meighan) C.; B.S. (univ. scholar), Villanova U., 1968; postgrad. (univ. asst.) U. Fla., 1969-70; m. Janet Cirillo. Asso. editor Biosci. Info. Services of Biol. Abstracts, Phila., 1971—, head quality control for editorial dept., 1975—, asst. dept. head, 1976—. Mem. Alpha Epsilon Delta. Democrat. Roman Catholic. Home: 34 Rittenhouse Rd Broomall PA 19008 Office: 2100 Arch St Philadelphia PA 19103

CLINTON, JOSEPH DEWITT, design scientist; b. Bloomington, Ill., June 26, 1940; s. William Milford and Mary Avo (Thorpe) C.; A.S., Joplin Jr. Coll., 1961; B.S., Kans. State Coll., 1963; M.S., So. Ill. U., 1966; postgrad. N.Y. U., 1970—; m. Elberta Faith Spence, Aug. 19, 1962; children—Lynn Marie, Kimberly Jo, Saundra Michelle. Draftsman Pacific Mercury Corp., Joplin, Mo., 1959, Kans. State Coll., 1962-63, A.J. Carginino Constrn. Co., Carbondale, Ill., 1964; instr., NASA grantee So. Ill. U., Carbondale, 1963-70; asst. prof. design/drafting, design coordinator Kean Coll. N.J., 1970—; design cons. J. Clinton Internat. Design Group, Union, N.J., 1970—; v.p. Dome East Corp., 1971-76. Bd. dirs. Elizabethport Presbyterian Center, Elizabeth, N.J., 1971-73, First Baptist Weekday Nursery, Elizabeth, 1974—, Saybrook Civic Assn., Hillside, N.J., 1976—. Recipient Tech. Art award Tech. Illustrators' Mgmt. Assn., 1970, citation for community service YMCA Eastern Union County (N.J.), 1973, ciation for troop enrichment Girl Scout Troop 775, Hillside, 1977. Mem. Nat. Assn. Indsl. Tech., Newark Mineral. Soc., World Future Soc., Phi Delta Kappa, Iota Lambda Sigma (chpt. pres. 1967). Author: Advanced Structural Geometry Studies, Parts I-II, NASA, 1971. Introduced geometric transformation concept as method of expanding structures, 1965; designer Oct-Tet Barrel Truss structural system, 1971. Home: 101 Conant St Hillside NJ 07205 Office: Dept Indsl Studies Kean Coll Morris Ave Union NJ 07083

CLITHEROE, H. JOHN, educator; b. Hornchurch, Eng., Jan. 2, 1935; s. Joseph and Edith (Defty) C.; B.Sc. with honors, Sheffield (Eng.) U., 1959, Ph.D., 1962; M.I.Biol., Inst. Biology London, 1962; m. Janice L. Blasi, July 6, 1968; children—Jonathan, Jennifer. Came to U.S., 1962. Instr. N.J. Coll. Medicine, Newark, 1963-65, asst. prof., 1965-70; clin. asst. prof. obstetrics and gynecology, 1970-76; asso. prof. anatomy and physiology S.I. (N.Y.) Community Coll., 1970-75, prof., 1975—; cons. cytology St. Elizabeth Hosp., Elizabeth, N.J., 1968—; cons. edn. N.J. State Physiotherapy Soc., 1970-72. Served with RAF, 1954-56. Allen & Hanbury's research student U. Cambridge, 1959-60; Johnson & Johnson fellow Bur. Biol. Research, Rutgers U., 1962; NIH fellow N.J. Coll. Medicine, 1963-65. Fellow Royal Soc. Health; mem. Pan Am. Cancer Cytology Soc., Soc. Endocrinology (U.K.), Soc. Study Reproduction, World Population Soc., Am. Assn. Sex Educators and Counselors, Inst. Biology (London), N.Y. Acad. Scis., Eastern Assn. for Sex Therapy. Contbr. articles to profl. jours. Home: 315 Cumberland Rd South Orange NJ 07079 Office: Staten Island Coll Staten Island NY 10301

CLIVE, CRAIG NORMAN, mfg. corp. ofcl.; b. Waltham, Mass., June 10, 1947; s. Craig and Marie Hope (Smith) C.; B.S. in Bus. Adminstrn. with high honors, Northeastern U., 1974; M.B.A., Babson Coll., 1975; m. Charlotte Ann Cranford, Aug. 23, 1970. Wage and salary adminstr. Mitre Corp., Bedford, Mass., 1971-74; personnel adminstr., personnel mgr. Burlington (Mass.) div. High Voltage Engring. Corp., 1974-78; employment mgr. Compugraphic Corp., Wilmington, Mass., 1978—. career, employment counselor. Active Big Bros. Assn. Served with U.S. Army, 1967-69. Decorated Bronze Star, Purple Heart; recipient coop. student award, 1974. Mem. Am. Assn. Indsl. Mgmt. (employer adv. com. D.E.S. Woburn), Am. Soc. Personnel Adminstrn., Electronic Industries Personnel Assn., N.Eng. Soc. Personnel Mgmt. (dir.), Beta Gamma Sigma. Congregationalist. Clubs: Am. Yacht, DAV. Home: 3 Francis Rd Wellesley MA 02181 Office: 80 Industrial Way Wilmington MA 01887

CLIZBE, JOHN ANTHONY, psychologist; b. Council Bluffs, Iowa, June 28, 1942; s. Harold George and Margaret Jane (Fariday) C.; B.A., William Jewell Coll., Liberty, Mo., 1964; Ph.D. (Nat. Def. Edn. Act fellow), Washington U., St. Louis, 1967; m. Rebecca Rose Maddox, Jan. 30, 1965; children—Mark Andrew, Diane Christine. Clin. psychology resident Norfolk (Nebr.) State Hosp. and N.E. Mental Health Clinic, 1967-68; cons. psychologist Nordli, Wilson Assos., Worcester, Mass., 1968—, gen. partner, 1975—. dir., v.p., treas. Student Achievement Inst., Worcester, 1973—; Instr. psychology Washington U., 1967; vis. lectr. Worcester Poly. Inst., 1973—; cons. in field. Pres. Marlboro-Westboro Community Mental Health and Mental Retardation Area Bd., 1970-74; v.p. Mass. Region V Mental Health and Mental Retardation Adv. Council, 1972-73; dir. Dimensions in Human Devel. Series Northboro, 1973—; dir., treas. Nat. Psychol. Consultants to Mgmt.; commentator on mgmt. psychology Sta. WNCR, Worcester. Mem. Am., Mass. psychol. assns., Sigma Xi, Pi Gamma Mu, Pi Kappa Delta. Unitarian (mem. standing com. ch. 1970-73, pres. congregation 1974-76). Research in field. Home: 53 Granby Dr Madison CT 06443 Office: 43 Trumbull St New Haven CT 06510

CLOHESY, STEPHANIE J., adminstr., orgnl. developer; b. Morgantown, W.Va., Sept. 23, 1948; d. Edwar John and Josephine J. (Pytlak) J.; B.A., Loyola U., 1970; m. William W. Clohesy, June 19, 1971. Adminstr., Rome Center of Loyola U., Chgo., 1970-72; adminstrv. dir. Center for Policy Research, N.Y.C., 1972-77; exec. dir. NOW Legal Def. and Edn. Fund and adminstrv. officer Publishing Tng. Inst. for Women, N.Y.C., 1977—. Mem. Soc. Research Adminstrs. Home: 230 W 107th St New York City NY 10025 Office: 36 W 44 St New York City NY 10036

CLONEY, JAMES MAURICE, chem. co. exec.; b. Kalamazoo, Mich., Mar. 5, 1919; s. Maurice Joseph and Edith (Caster) C.; B.A., Kalamazoo Coll. 1941; m. Margaret Reiser, Jan. 24, 1946; children—Sheila, James, Robert. With GAF Corp. (formerly Gen. Aniline & Film Corp.), N.Y.C., 1946—, v.p. internat. div., 1966-71, group v.p. office systems, 1971—, sr. v.p. govt. relations, 1974—. Served with AUS, 1942-46. Mem. Am. Mgmt. Assn., Washington Export Council. Club: Internat. (Washington). Home: 706 Carnoustie Ln Tantallon MD 20022 Office: 1101 15th St NW Washington DC 20005

CLOSE, ELMER HARRY, broadcaster, legislator, lawyer; b. Toledo, July 16, 1937; s. Joseph Kempf and Luette Ruth (Spitzer) C.; A.B. cum laude, Harvard, 1958, LL.B., 1961; m. Margot Pierce, Feb. 26, 1966; children—Josephine, Amanda. Admitted to N.H. bar, 1961, N.Y. bar, 1964; law clk. to Judge Peter Woodbury, 1st Circuit Ct. of Appeals, Boston, 1961-62; asso. Shearman & Sterling, N.Y.C., 1962-66; individual practice law, Keene, N.H., 1966-70; city solicitor City of Keene, 1969; pres., gen. mgr. WKNE Corp., Keene, 1970—, also pres. Greylock Broadcasting Co., Pittsfield, Mass., 1970—. Incorporator, Dublin (N.H.) Sch. Rep. N.H. Ho. of Reps., 1973—, mem. judiciary com., 1973-74, vice chmn. labor, human resources and rehab. com., 1975-76, chmn. exec. dept., adminstrn. com., elections com., 1977—; mem. govt. ops. task force Nat. Conf. State Legislatures. Served with USMCR, 1962-63. Mem. N.H., F.C.C. bar assns., CBS Radio Affiliates Assn. (dir.). Republican. Episcopalian. Clubs: Keene Rotary, Keene Country; Harvard (Boston); Dublin Lake. Home: 22 Airebrook Rd Keene NH 03431 Office: WKNE Corp Box 466 Keene NH 03431

CLOSE, FRED LELAND, JR., army officer; b. Dallas, Oct. 10, 1941; s. Fred Leland and Martha Anna (Plummer) C.; B.B.A. in Accounting, Arlington State Coll., 1966; M.A. in Accounting, U. Ala., 1973; m. Irene Francine Silagyi, May 6, 1978. Staff accountant Patterson, Winfrey & Co., C.P.A.'s, Arlington, Tex., 1965-66; staff auditor Peat, Marwick, Mitchell & Co., C.P.A.s, Dallas, 1966; commd. 2d lt. U.S. Army, 1967; advanced through grades to maj., 1978; aviation maintenance officer and maintenance test pilot, S. Vietnam, 1968-69, S. Korea, 1974-75; dep. comptroller Edgewood Arsenal, Aberdeen Proving Ground, Md., 1975-77, budget officer Chem. Systems Lab., 1977-78; asst. prof. mil. sci. Rutgers U., 1978—, comdt. of cadets, 1978—; acting insp. gen. U.S. Army Armaments Research and Devel. Command Personnel, Aberdeen Proving Ground, 1977-78. Decorated Bronze Star. Mem. Assn. U.S. Army, Am. Soc. Mil. Comptrollership, Alpha Beta Psi, Phu Mu Alpha, Pi Sigma Epsilon. Methodist. Home: 583-5 Auten Rd Somerville NJ 08876 Office: 157 College Ave New Brunswick NJ 08903

CLOUGH, MARY EVALYN, librarian, educator; b. Kansas City, Mo., July 10, 1930; d. Arthur M. and Candace M. (White) Clough; student U. Kans., 1947-50; B.A., U. Calif. at Los Angeles, 1952; M.S., Columbia, 1956; advanced certificate U. Pitts. Grad. Sch. Library and Information Sci., 1967. Med. library cataloger Columbia, N.Y.C., 1954-56; 1st asst. catalog dept. N.Y. Acad. Medicine Library, N.Y.C., 1956-58; sr. tech. librarian, tech. library, Rep. Aviation Corp., Farmingdale, L.I., N.Y., 1958-64; head librarian PPG Industries, Inc., Glass Research Center, Pitts., 1964-75; acting exec. dir. Pitts. Regional Library Center, 1975; vis. lectr. U. Pitts. Grad. Sch. Library and Info. Scis., 1975—, asst. to dean, 1977—. Mem. ALA, Assn. Am. Library Schs., Spl. Libraries Assn. (chmn. engring. div. 1973-74), Am. Soc. Info. Sci., Phi Delta Gamma, Sigma Alpha Iota, Beta Phi Mu. Home: 6813 Penn Ave Pittsburgh PA 15208 also 1233 W 67th St Kansas City MO 64113

CLOUGH, PERRY RANKIN, mktg. exec.; b. Portland, Maine, July 7, 1940; s. Edwin Moody and Sylvia Carolyn (Rankin) C.; student Tufts U., 1958-59; B.A., U. Maine, 1963; m. Susan Ruth Sale, July 1, 1967; children—Jonathan Ingram, Laura Ruth. Exec. trainee Eastman Kodak Co., 1963-65, advt. editor, 1965-67, sr. advt. editor, 1967-69; advt. mgr. Codman div. Johnson & Johnson, Randolph, Mass., 1969-71, dir. advt., 1971-73, dir. mktg. services, 1973—, dir. customer relations, 1977-78, dir. new market opportunities, 1978—; instr. mktg. planning. Recipient Francis W. Hatch award Art Dirs. Boston, 1974, Design I award Biol. Photog. Assn., 1975, award Bus. Profl. Press, 1976. Mem. Indsl. Advt. Assn., Bus. Profl. Press Am., Ophthalmic Photographers Assn. (hon.), Boston Advt. Club, Sigma Chi. Contbr. articles in field to profl. jours. Home: 60 Old Oaken Bucket Rd Scituate MA 02066 Office: 96 Pacella Park Dr Randolph MA 02368

CLOUGH, PHILIP JAMES, chemist; b. Lewiston, Maine, Sept. 3, 1920; s. Fred Augustus and Ellen Mary (Horrigan) C.; B.S., Bowdoin Coll., 1943; M.S., Middlebury U., 1945; postgrad. Mass. Inst. Tech., 1952, Northeastern U., 1960; m. Betsy Allen Batchelder, June 10, 1944. Research chemist Reynolds Metals Co., Cambridge, Mass., 1945-46; asst. dir. research NRC, Cambridge, 1946-62; div. mgr., tech. dir. Norton Metallized Products Co., Winchester, Mass., 1962-69; v.p., dir. tech. devel. Gorham Internat., Inc. (Maine), 1969—; pres. Dirigo Properties; treas. Maine Chem. Corp.; corporator Gorham Savs. Bank; instr. Bowdoin Coll., 1943-44, Middlebury Coll., 1944-45. Mem. personnel bd. Fin. Com. Reading (Mass.), 1963-69; mem. Devel. Council, Gorham, 1973, pres., 1979. Mem. Soc. Mfg. Engrs., Vacuum Metallizers Assn. (past pres.). Republican. Congregationalist. Clubs: Masons; Shriners; Westbrook Rotary (pres. 1978-79); Gorham Golf. Editor: (with Betsy Clough) World Guide to Covered Bridges, 1960; contbr. articles on vacuum processes and surface finishes to profl. jours. Patentee in field. Home: 191 South St Gorham ME 04038 Office: PO Box 8 Gorham ME 04038

CLOUTIER, LEONCE, chem. engr., educator; b. Quebec City, Que., Can., Feb. 5, 1928; s. Napoleon and Eugenie (Langevin) C.; B.Sc.A., Laval U., 1950, D.Sc., 1964; m. Jeannine Fillion, Aug. 4, 1951; children—Denise, Pauline, Gaston. Prodn. engr. Can. Packers Ltd., Montreal, Que., 1950-52; design engr. C.D. Howe Co., Montreal, 1952-55; mem. faculty Laval U., 1955—, prof. chem. engring., 1967—, dir. dept., 1969-75. Tchr. summer courses to engrs. Alcan Co., Arvida, 1965, Demerara Bauxite Co., Guyana, 1968; vis. prof. material sci. and engring. dept. U. Calif., Berkeley, 1975-76; v.p. Valmiro Ltd., 1965-70, Caisse Populaire St. Thomas D'Aquin, 1965-75, 77—, mem. asso. com. automatic control NRC, 1971-75. Local pres., provincial v.p. Quefratec, 1969-72. Recipient Mgr. Vachon prize Faculty Sci., Laval U., 1950. NRC Can. grantee, 1959—. Mem. Chem. Inst. Can. (prize 1949), Corp. Engrs. Que., Soc. Canadienne de Genie Chimique. Research and publs. in mixing, chem. reactors, simulation and control. Home: 880 Lienard St Quebec PQ G1V 2W5 Canada

CLOW, H. ARNOLD, photographer; b. Springfield, N.B., Can., Feb. 27, 1927; s. John William and Bertha Sara (Thorne) C.; student N.B. pub. schs.; m. Marie Alice McVicar, June 10, 1952; children—Michael John Leonard, Margaret Ann, Arnold Peter Gerard. Mem. Royal Canadian Mounted Police, 1947-66; owner, operator Arnold's Studio, Ltd., Moncton, N.B., Can., 1965—. Served with Canadian Army, 1944-45. Mem. Maritime Profl. Photographers Assn. (past pres.), Profl. Photographers of Can., Inc. (Atlantic v.p.), Profl. Photographers of Am. (mem. council), Nat. Press Photographers Assn., Royal Canadian Legion, U. Moncton Alumni Assn., Fed. Retirement Assn., Maritime Gun Collectors Assn. Roman Catholic. Clubs: Mountain Ridge Golf, K.C., Moncton Mens Press, United Comml. Travelers. Home and office: 221 Reade St Moncton NB Canada

CLOYD, ROYAL HARRISON, art center ofcl.; b. Watseka, Ill., May 21, 1925; s. Roy Nelson and Gwen (Harrison) C.; student U. Md., 1943-44, Am. U., 1946; A.B., U. Ill., 1949, M.A., 1955; m. Nancy Jean Evans, Aug. 28, 1948; children—Jay Raymond, Aaron, Bronwen Evans. Edn. services dir. Chanute AFB, Ill., 1951-57; dir. adult programs Council Liberal Chs., 1958-61; dir. adult programs and info. Unitarian Universalist Assn., Boston, 1961-70, Pacific Central dist. exec., 1964-65; pres. Boston Center for Arts, 1970—. Mem Boston bd. Ams. Democratic Action, 1962-63, citizens adv. com. Boston Redevel., 1966; v.p. South End Planning Council, Boston, 1961-64; mem. South End Project Area Council, 1969—; mem. Citizens Housing and Planning Assn. Boston, 1966—; pres. South End Fedn. Citizen's Orgns., 1967-71; bd. dirs. Citizens for Boston Pub. Sch., 1970-71; juror Am. Film Festival, 1969; mem. adv. council arts and humanities Mass. Dept. Edn., 1972-75, vice chmn. Gov.'s Task Force on Arts Facilities in Commonwealth, 1972—. Trustee Beacon Hill Sch., 1967-69; bd. dirs. Met. Cultural Alliance, 1971—; bd. dirs. Ellis Meml., 1973—; chmn. Prudential bd. Arlington St. Ch., 1977—. Served with AUS, 1943-46. Recipient Neighborhood award NCCJ, 1963. Mem. Nat. Trust Historic Preservation, Council Nat. Orgns. (chmn. participation com. 1960), Mass. Adult Edn. Assn. (exec. com. 1963-65), Adult Edn. Assn. U.S. (New Eng. exec. com. 1966), Inst.

Contemporary Art, Nat. Council Crime and Delinquency Internat. Platform Assn., Alpha Sigma Phi, Phi Delta Kappa. Clubs: Boston Press, Harvard Musical Soc., St. Botolph (Boston). Democrat. Unitarian-Universalist. Author hist. play, film, booklets. Editor: New South End. Home: 42 Union Park Boston MA 02118 also High Sorrowful North Berwick ME 03906 Office: 539 Tremont St Boston MA 02116

CLYMAN, MILTON, sci. and tech. cons. co. exec.; b. Phila., Sept. 30, 1935; s. Manuel and Sylvia G. (Kallick) C.; B.S. in Elec. Engring., Drexel U., 1958; M.B.A., Temple U., 1964; m. Barbara C. Zimmerman, Aug. 25, 1963; 1 dau., Stefanie S. Design engr. Philco-Ford Corp., Phila., 1959-60, project engr., Willow Grove, Pa., 1963-65; quality control engr. Gen. Electric Co., Phila., 1960-63; flight systems engr., project test engr., Valley Forge, Pa., 1965-69; with Info. Spectrum Inc., Warminster, Pa., 1969—, exec. v.p., 1973—; resident staff cons. IDA, Arlington, Va., 1973. Served as 1st lt., C.E., U.S. Army, 1958-59. Mem. Nat. Security Indsl. Assn., Am. Def. Preparedness Assn., Soc. Logistic Engrs., Home: 404 S Sterling Rd Elkins Park PA 19117 Office: 955 Louis Dr Warminster PA 18974

CO, BENITO KONG-LENG D., surgeon; b. Manila, Oct. 19, 1938; s. Ah-Yee and Kiat (Dy) Koo; came to U.S., 1965; M.D. cum laude with meritissimus, U. Santo Tomas (Philippines), 1963; m. Katherine T. So, June 17, 1967; children—Patrick, Mark, Michele, Dominic Oliver. Intern, Kings County Hosp. Center, Bklyn., 1965; resident Downstate Med. Center, Bklyn., 1966-69, Franklin Sq. Hosp., Balt., 1969-71; vis. surgeon Mercy Hosp., Balt., 1977—. Md. Gen. Hosp., Balt., 1973—; attending surgeon Franklin Sq. Hosp. Balt., 1973—. Mem. Med. Soc. D.C., Med. and Chirurg. Faculty State Md., Balt. City Med. Soc., AMA. Roman Catholic. Home: 18 Lord Mayors Ct Cockeysville MD 21030 Office: 1224 Race Rd Baltimore MD 21237

COAKLEY, PAUL EUGENE, JR., hosp. ofcl.; b. Chester, Pa., Nov. 25, 1945; s. Paul Eugene and Bernice Leona (Miller) C.; B.S., U. Balt., 1971, M.B.A., 1976; m. Judith Alice Henkel, June 25, 1966; children—Janet Marie, Brian Alan. Investment bookkeeper Mercantile Safe Deposit & Trust Co., Balt., 1964-65; collection mgr. St. Anges Hosp., Balt., 1965-68, asst. to credit mgr., 1968-70, credit mgr., 1970-72, dir. admissions, 1972-74, adminstrv. coordinator ambulatory services, 1974-78, asst. adminstr., 1978—; asst. prof. Catonsville Community Coll., 1976-78, Essex Community Coll., 1978. Vice pres. St. Agnes Employees Fed. Credit Union, 1972—. Served with N.G., 1971-77. Mem. Admitting Officers Assn. Md. Democrat. Lutheran. Home: 608 North Ct Linthicum MD 21090 Office: 900 Caton Ave Baltimore MD 21229

COATES, CHARLES ROBERT, educator; b. Fairview, N.C., Nov. 2, 1915; s. John Wesley and Hattie (Price) C.; B.A. in Econs., Lake Forest Coll., 1955; M.Ed., Coll. William and Mary, 1958; Ed.D., U. Va., 1965; m. Lucille May Blackman, Oct. 30, 1942; children—Charles Robert, John Thomas, Christopher Scott. Edn. specialist U.S. Transp. Sch., Ft. Eustis, Va., 1955-58; dir. guidance Southampton (Va.) pub. schs., 1958-62; edn. adviser U.S. Army Q.M. Sch., Ft. Lee, Va., 1962-65; prof. counseling and guidance Shippensburg (Pa.) State Coll., 1965—. Extension instr. counseling and guidance Coll. William and Mary, also U. Va., 1958-65; cons. in field. Chmn. campus ministry United Ministries for High Edn.; active local Boy Scouts Am., AWARE groups. Served with USNR, World War II. Mem. Am. Ednl. Research Assn., NEA, AAAS, Am. Personnel and Guidance Assn., Phi Delta Kappa (historian 1967). Author: Learning Power, 1964. Contbr. articles to profl. jours. Home: 756 Roxbury Rd Shippensburg PA 17257 Office: Shippensburg State Coll Shippensburg PA 17257

COATES, ROBERT PEARCE, ret. ins. co. exec.; b. N.Y.C., Dec. 11, 1911; s. Ora Beverly and Emily Letitia (Pearce) C.; B.A. summa cum laude, Princeton U., 1933; m. Alice Louise Canoune, Oct. 3, 1936; children—Nancy Pearce (Mrs. Russell Martin Chenoweth, Jr.), Marian Louise. With Equitable Life Assurance Soc. U.S., N.Y.C., 1933-77, 2d v.p., asso. actuary, 1962-67, v.p., asso. actuary, 1967-69, v.p., actuary, 1969-77. Actuarial cons. Trustee, treas. Neighborhood House, Plainfield, N.J., 1965-69. Fellow Soc. Actuaries, mem. Am. Acad. Actuaries, Phi Beta Kappa, Sigma Xi. Republican. Episcopalian (vestryman). Club: Princeton (N.Y.). Contbr. articles to profl. jours. Home: 1011 Edgewood Ave Plainfield NJ 07060

COBLE, ANNA JANE, physicist, educator; b. Raleigh, N.C., July 12, 1936; d. Cecil Nello and Nellie Kate (Brewington) C.; B.S. in Math., Howard U., 1958, M.S. in Physics, 1961; Ph.D. in Biophysics, U. Ill., 1973. Instr., asst. prof. N.C. A. and T. State U., Greensboro, 1960-64; with IBM, Endicott, N.Y., summer 1963, St. Augustine Coll., Raleigh, summers 1964-65; research asso. Washington U., St. Louis, 1969-71; lectr. Howard U., Washington, 1971-74, asst. prof. dept. physics, 1974—. NDEA-Title IV, USPHS trainee. Mem. Am. Assn. Physics Tchrs., AAAS, Sigma Xi. Episcopalian. Home: 1000 Fairview Ave Takoma Park MD 20012 Office: 2355 6th St NW Washington DC 20059*

COBLE, JEAN, nurse; b. San Antonio, Apr. 10, 1930; d. Otis and Ella (Rogers) C.; nursing diploma Hillcrest Bapt. Hosp., Waco, Tex., 1951; diploma Dallas Bible Coll., 1954; B.S. in Nursing, Tex. Christian U., 1964; M.S., Boston U., 1972. adopted children—Timothy Otis, Joseph Michael. Staff nurse, head nurse, then supr. Scottish Rite Hosp. for Crippled Children, Dallas, 1951-54, 59-62; missionary nursing Latin Am. Mission Bd., Peru, 1956-59; dir. nursing services Abilene (Tex.) State Sch. for Mentally Retarded, 1964-68; dir. community evaluation and rehab. clinic for mentally retarded, Paul A. Dever State Sch., Taunton, Mass., 1968-73, asst. supt. for social devel., edn. and tng., 1973-75; community mental health nursing adviser specialist, 1975-77, sr. program analyst, 1977—. USPHS trainee, 1963-64, 71. Mem. Am. Assn. Mental Deficiency. Home: 269 Burt St Taunton MA 02780 Office: POB 631 Taunton MA 02780

COBURN, JOHN BOWEN, priest, ch. ofcl., Episcopal Ch.; b. Danbury, Conn., Sept. 27, 1914; s. Aaron Cutler and Eugenia Bowen (Woolfolk) C.; A.B., Princeton U., 1936, D.D., 1960; B.D., Union Theol. Sem., 1942; D.D., Amherst Coll., 1955, Huron Coll., 1964, Harvard U., 1964, Middlebury Coll., 1970, Bucknell U., 1971; S.T.D., Berkeley Div. Sch., 1958, Hobart and William Smith Coll., 1967, Gen. Theol. Sem., 1968; Sem., 1968; D.C.L., Kenyon Coll., 1968, U. Kent at Canterbury (Eng.), 1978; m. Ruth Alvord Barnum, May 26, 1941; children—Thomas Bowen, Judy C. Coburn Klein, Michael Cutler, Sarah E. Coburn Borgeson. Ordained priest Episcopal Ch., 1943; instr. Robert Coll., Istanbul, Turkey, 1936-39; asst. Grace Ch., N.Y.C., 1942-44; chaplain USNR, 1944-45; rector Grace Ch., Amherst, Mass., 1946-53; chaplain Amherst Coll., 1946-53; dean Trinity Cathedral, Newark, 1953-57; dean Episc. Theol. Sem., Cambridge, Mass., 1957-69; tchr. Urban League St. Acad., N.Y.C., 1968-69; rector St. James Ch., N.Y.C., 1969-75; bishop Diocese of Mass., Boston, 1976—; pres. Ho. of Deps., Gen. Convs. of Episc. Ch., 1967-70, 70-73, 73-76; dir. Corning Glass Works (N.Y.). Trustee Princeton U., Wooster Sch., Union Theol. Sem. Mem. Century Assn. Author: Prayer and Personal Religion, 1957; Minister: Man in the Middle, 1963; Anne and the S and Dobbies, 1964; Twentieth Century Spiritual Letters, 1967; (with Norman Pittinger) Viewpoints, 1959; A Life to Live-A Way to Pray, 1973; A Diary of Prayers, 1975; The Hope of Glory, 1976; Christ's Life: Our Life, 1978. Home: 60 Chestnut St Boston MA 02108 Office: 1 Joy St Boston MA 02108

COBURN, RICHARD JAMES, plastic surgeon; b. Malden, Mass., Sept. 25, 1935; s. Robert Ernest and Marjorie (Lowe) C.; student Tufts U., 1953-55, D.M.D., 1960; M.D., McGill U. (Can.), 1964; m. Marya Thomas, Sept. 25, 1977. Intern, Cornell U. Med. Center-The N.Y. Hosp., 1964-65, resident in gen. surgery, 1965-66; resident in gen. surgery Harvard U. Service-Boston City Hosp., 1966-69; resident in plastic surgery York U. Med. Center, N.Y.C., 1969-71; practice medicine specializing in plastic surgery, N.Y.C., 1971—; sr. clin. instr. Dept. Surgery, Mt. Sinai Sch. Medicine, N.Y.C., 1973—; staff Drs. Hosp., 1973—, Cabrinia Health, 1973—, St. Luke's Hosp., 1976—, Bd. dirs. Nat. Hypertension Inc. Assn., N.Y.C., 1976—. Served with Dental Corps, USN, 1955-57. Fellow ACS; mem. McGill Soc. N.Y.C. (v.p. 1977-78), AMA, Internat. Assn. for Dental Research, Transplantation Soc., Am. Soc. Plastic and Reconstructive Surgeons, N.Y. State, N.Y. County med. socs., Pan Am. Med. Assn., Alpha Omega Alpha. Republican. Club: Harvard. Contbr. articles to med. jours. Address: 6 E 78th St New York City NY 10021

COBURN, ROBERT BOWNE, stock broker; b. Manchester, Conn., May 19, 1906; s. Edward Hewitt and Lena (Carter) C.; grad. Hotchkiss Sch., 1924; B.S., Yale, 1928; m. Elizabeth Mohun, June 15, 1929; children—Edward H., Elenor (Mrs. Lawrence R. Smith), Barry M. Pres. Glastonbury Knitting Co., 1930-33; spl. partner Easland & Co., stock broker, 1932-34; partner Coburn & Middlebrook, 1934-48; treas., chmn. bd. Coburn & Meredith, Inc., Hartford, Conn., 1948—; pres. Coburn Securities Corp., 1947—; pres., dir. Westminster Leasing Ltd., Kensington Leasing Ltd., Burnham Leasing Ltd., Cains Land Ltd.; dir. Plimpton & Hills, Hartford. Mem. Midwest Stock Exchange. Trustee Nettie Bowne Estate; incorporator Mt. Sinai Hosp., Hartford. Congregationalist. (trustee). Clubs: Lawyers, Yale (N.Y.C.); Hartford, Hartford Golf; Coventry Fish and Game. Home: 43 Juniper Rd Bloomfield CT 06002 Office: 17 Lewis St Hartford CT 06103

COBURN, THEODORE JAMES, physicist; b. Newton, Mass., June 11, 1926; s. Charles Arthur and Viola Mabel (Hunter) C.; student U. Louisville, 1944-46; B.Sc. in Physics, Ohio State U., 1947, Ph.D. in Physics, 1957; m. Edith Marshall Banta, June 16, 1949; children—Sue Ellen, Charles Edwin, Joanne Edith. Sr. design engr. Eastman Kodak Co., Rochester, N.Y., 1957-60, sr. research physicist research lab., 1960-68, research asso. in solid state physics, sr. lab. staff, 1968—. Pres. elementary PTA West Irondequoit Sch. Dist., Rochester, 1970-71, life mem., 1974—, pres. High Sch. Parent Tchr. Orgn., 1975-76; chmn. Citizens Com. for Selection Sch. Bd. Candidates West Irondequoit Sch. Dist., 1976—, 78; mem. West Irondequoit Sch. Dist. Civil Service Grievance Rev. Panel, 1971—; ruling elder, deacon, chmn. coms. Summerville Presbyn. Ch., Rochester. Served with USN, 1944-46, 53-55. U.S. Army research fellow, 1951-53; USN research fellow, 1955-57. Mem. IEEE, Am. Phys. Soc., Electrochem. Soc. Author numerous co., Dept. def. classified reports; contbr. articles to sci. jours.; patentee in field. Home: 156 Pinecrest Dr Rochester NY 14617 Office: Eastman Kodak Co Research Labs B-81 Kodak Park Rochester NY 14650

COCCIA, SILVIO DANIEL, pharm. co. exec.; b. Chester, Pa., Aug. 25, 1932; s. Saverio and Chiara (Marchetti) C.; B.S. in Pharmacy, Temple U., 1954; B.S. in Bus. Adminstrn., Widener Coll., 1962; m. Virginia Pasqualini, Apr. 26, 1958; children—Silvio, Mario, Marco, Bernard, Anthony. Pharmacist, Lloyd Pharmacy, Chester, Pa., 1954-57; with Geigy Pharm. div. Ciba Geigy Corp., Ardsley, N.Y., 1957—, salesman, 1957-62, sales tng. instr., 1962-66, sales promotion mgr., 1966-68, product promotion mgr., 1968-70, group product promotion mgr., 1970-72, copy supr., 1972-75, group sales promotion mgr., 1975-77, dir. sales promotion, 1977—. Served with U.S. Army, 1954-56. Mem. Am. Pharm. Assn., Pa. Pharm. Assn., N.J. Pharm. Assn. Phi Delta Chi. Roman Catholic. Home: 20 Lawrence Dr Berkeley Heights NJ 07922 Office: 556 Morris Ave Summit NJ 07901

COCCO, THOMAS DOMENICK BARTHOLOMEW, surgeon, gynecologist; b. Bridgeport, Conn., Feb. 14, 1931; s. Domenick and Mary Prospera (Benedetto) C.; B.S., Georgetown U., 1951; postgrad. U. Paris, 1951; M.D., Rome Med. Coll., 1957; m. Carol Ann Collins, Mar. 1967; children—Thomas, Christopher, Nicole, Justin. Intern, Meriden (Conn.) Hosp., 1958-59; intern St. Raphael's Hosp., New Haven, 1960-61, resident, 1961-62, 63-64; resident Westfield Cancer Hosp., 1963, Norwalk (Conn.) Hosp., 1964-65; teaching fellow Seton Hall Coll. Medicine and Jersey City Med. Center, 1962; attending surgeon Bridgeport (Conn.) Hosp.; courtesy staff Park City Hosp., Bridgeport; practice medicine specializing in surgery, Bridgeport. Diplomate Am. Bd. Surgery. Mem. Am. Soc. Abdominal Surgeons, Am. Trauma Soc., AMA, Mass., Conn., Fairfield County med. socs., Conn. Soc. Surgeons, Am. Proctology Soc. Republican. Roman Catholic. Club: Italian Community Center. Contbr. articles to profl. jours. Address: 388 Brooklawn Ave Bridgeport CT 06604

COCHÉ, ERICH HENRY ERNST, psychologist; b. Nijmegen, Netherlands, June 24, 1941; s. Erich Johannes Maximilian and Frieda Sophie Eliese (Moellmann) C.; came to U.S., 1968; German License in Psychology, U. Bonn, 1966, Ph.D. magna cum laude, 1968; m. Judith Abbe Milner, Oct. 16, 1966. Teaching asst. Tchrs. Coll., Bonn, Germany, 1966-68; clin. psychologist Friends Hosp., Phila., 1969-74, dir. psychol. services and research, 1974—; clin. asst. prof. mental health scis. Hahnemann Med. Coll., Phila., 1974—. Bd. dirs. Mental Health Assn. Southeastern Pa. Diplomate Am. Bd. Profl. Psychology. Mem. Am., Pa. psychol. assns., Am. Group Psychotherapy Assn., Phila. Soc. Clin. Psychologists (pres. 1977-78). Contbr. articles to psychology jours. Home: 2188 Joshua Rd Lafayette Hill PA 19444 Office: Friends Hosp Roosevelt Blvd and Adams Ave Philadelphia PA 19124

COCHIOS, CHARLES AUGUSTUS, librarian; b. Easton, Pa., Mar. 6, 1928; s. Alex and Georgia (Varzakis) C.; B.L.S., Kutztown (Pa.) State Coll., 1960; postgrad. Rutgers U., 1961; M.Ed., Temple U., 1968; postgrad. library sci. Villanova U., 1977—; m. Dec. 28, 1963; children—Bruce, Kristi. Elementary sch. librarian Flemington Raritan (Pa.) Pub. Schs., 1960-61; acting library dir. Phillipsburg (N.J.) Free Pub. Library, 1961-62; librarian Raub Jr. High Sch., Allentown, Pa., 1962-67; classifier, cataloger beginning collection Lehigh County Community Coll., Schnecksville, Pa., 1966; librarian March Elementary Sch., Easton, Pa., 1967-68, Edward Tracy Elementary Sch., 1968—; co-adviser Tracy Times, 1972-73, reference librarian Easton Area Pub. Library, 1958-69. Served with U.S. Army, 1946-48. Named an Outstanding Librarian, Edinboro State Coll., 1968. Mem. Am., Pa. library assns., Nat., Pa. edn. assns., Easton Area Edn. Assn., Am. Fedn. Musicians. Republican. Profl. musician specializing in jazz trombone and other brass instruments. Address: 4611 Bayard St Easton PA 18042

COCHRAN, JAMES AMOS, systems engr.; b. Greene County, Ark., June 3, 1933; s. Ernest Webster and Claris Mayme (Collings) C.; B.E.E., Purdue U., 1958; M.E.E., N.Y. U., 1960; m. Irene Soliozy, Apr. 23, 1955; children—Rebecca Kay, Mark Stephen. With Bell Telephone Labs., Whippany, N.J., 1958—; mem. tech. staff system requirements and future planning Engring. and Devel. Center, 1976—. Served with USN, 1951-55. Mem. IEEE, AAAS, Conf. Profl. and Tech. Personnel. Mem. Ch. of Nazarene. Home: 15 Knoll Dr Rockaway NJ 07866 Office: Bell Labs Whippany Rd Whippany NJ 07981

COCHRANE, DOUGLAS HAIG, fin. exec.; b. Moncton, N.B., Can., Oct. 27, 1919; s. David and Blanche Myra (MacKinnon) C.; Certificate in Econs., Dunfermline Acad., Scotland, 1939; m. Margaret Grace Weaver, Feb. 14, 1945; children—Wayne Douglas, Heather Lynn. With Eastern Can. Savs. and Loan Co., Halifax, N.S., after 1963, asst. gen. mgr., 1963-71, gen. mgr., 1971-73, v.p., gen. mgr., 1973-76; v.p. adminstrn., dir. Central and Eastern Trust Co., Halifax, 1976—; dir. Scotia Covenants Group Ltd., Scotia Covenants (Holdings) Ltd. (both Toronto, Ont.). Mem. Assessment Appeal Ct., City of Dartmouth (N.S.), 1971—; commr. Supreme Ct. N.S., 1971—; lectr. N.S. Tech. Coll., Halifax. Served as flight lt. RCAF, 1940-45. Accredited appraiser, Can., U.S. Mem. Canadian C. of C. Mason. Clubs: Halifax, Saraguay. Home: 12 Louise Ave Dartmouth NS Canada Office: 5151 Terminal Rd Halifax NS Canada

COCKERLINE, ROGER EARLE, chemist; b. Newark, Mar. 31, 1929; s. William Roy and Ellen Agnes (Gordon) C.; B.S., Seton Hall U., 1952; m. Patricia Elsie Torppey, Mar. 15, 1952; children—Deborah Lea, Mark Roger, Glenn Curtis, Dean Gordon, Janet Lynn, Dorothy Ellen. Chemist, M.W. Kellogg & Co., Jersey City, 1952, 54-55; research chemist Coats & Clark Inc., Newark, 1955-65, Union, N.J., 1965—. Served with USNR, 1952-54. Mem. Am. Chem. Soc., Am. Assn. Textile Chemists and Colorists. Home: 16 Linda Ave Colonia NJ 07067 Office: Coats and Clark Inc 785 Rahway Ave Union NJ 07083

COCKETT, ABRAHAM TIMOTHY KEAWEIWI, physician, educator; b. Maui, Hawaii, Sept. 4, 1928; s. J. Patrick and Mary (Kekahu) C.; B.S., Brigham Young U., 1950; M.D., U. Utah, 1954; m. Willia L. Sindahl, Mar. 23, 1951; children—Timothy William, Shannon Adeal, Cathy Mary, John. Intern VA Hosp., Los Angeles, 1954-55; resident in urology U. Calif. at Los Angeles, 1956-60, asso. prof. urology, 1962-69; chief urology Harbor Gen. Hosp., 1962-69; prof., chmn. dept. urol. surgery U. Rochester (N.Y.), 1969—, also urologist in chief Strong Meml. Hosp., Rochester, 1969—; cons. urology VA Hosps., Batavia and Canandaigua, N.Y., Rochester Gen. Hosp., Highland Hosp.; cons., investigator Office of Naval Research; research investigator, mem. Biosatellite II team NASA, 1964-72; attending staff urologist N.Y. State Mental Hosp. Served to capt. M.C., USAF, 1960-62. Recipient grants and contracts from Office Naval Research, NASA, NIH, Regional Med. Program for Kidney Transplantation. Diplomate Am. Bd. Urology. Fellow A.C.S.; mem. Am. Assn. Genito-Urinary Surgeons, Am. Urol. Assn., Soc. Univ. Surgeons, Soc. Univ. Urologists, AMA, Undersea Med. Soc., Am. Fertility Soc., Soc. Pediatric Urology. Club: Genesee Valley (Rochester). Mem. editorial bd. of Lymphology, 1968-74, Contemporary Surgery, 1973—. Contbr. articles to sci. jours., chpts. to books. Home: 168 Grosvenor Rd Rochester NY 14610 Office: 601 Elmwood Ave Rochester NY 14642

CODDON, DAVID REES, neurologist; b. St. Paul, June 9, 1923; s. Nathan Leo and Harriet Ethel (Shanedling) C.; B.A., Macalester Coll., 1945; M.A., U.Minn., 1948; M.D., N.Y. U., 1953; m. Nancy Frank, June 15, 1958; children—Pamela, David, Susan, Jonathan. Intern, Ancker Hosp., St. Paul, 1953-54; resident neurology Mt. Sinai Hosp., N.Y.C., 1954-57, asso. dir. resident training neurology, 1959-61, asso. attending neurologist, since 1969—; practice medicine specializing in neurology N.Y.C., 1960—; chief neurology Manhattan Manhattan VA Hosp., 1961-64; asso. prof. Mt. Sinai Sch. Medicine, N.Y.C., 1969—; dir. headache clinic Mt. Sinai Med. Center, 1971—; cons. neurologist Gracie Square Hosp., N.Y.C., 1962—; impartial expert neurology Supreme Ct. N.Y., 1971—. Served as capt. USAF, 1957-59; maj. Res., ret. Pub. health fellow Inst. Phys. Medicine Rehab., 1955; fellow Stroke Council Am. Heart Assn., 1978. Mem. AMA, Pan Am. Med. Assn. (sec. sect. nuerology 1971—). Am. Acad. Neurology, Assn. for Research in Nervous and Mental Disease, Am. Assn. for Study Headache, Am. Epilepsy Soc., Am. Geriatric Soc., Am. Coll. Angiology, Eastern Assn. Electroencephalographers Soc., N.Y. Acad. Scis., Asso. Alumni Assn. Mt. Sinai Med. Center (pres.). Asso. editor Mt. Sinai Hosp. Jour., 1978. Home: 176 Elm Rd Englewood NJ 07631 Office: 1031 Fifth Ave New York City NY 10028

CODERRE, GERARD MARIE, bishop; b. St. Jacques de Montcalm, Que., Can., Dec. 19, 1904; s. Ovide and Marie Louise (Beliveau) C.; B.A., U. Montreal, 1927, L.Th., 1931, Bachelier en droit Canon, 1931, certificat en Historie Universelle et en langue greeque, 1933. Ordained priest Roman Catholic Ch., 1931; bishop of St. Jean, Que., Can., 1955—. Office: 740 Blvd Ste Foy Longueuil PQ J4K 4X8 Canada

CODISPOTI, ANDRE JOHN, physician; b. Bklyn., Apr. 27, 1938; s. Bruno and Antoinette (Savarese) C.; B.A., Holy Cross Coll., Worcester, Mass., 1959; M.D., U. Bologna (Italy), 1965; m. Miranda Babini, June 14, 1967; children—Rita, Elisa. Intern, L.I. Coll. Hosp., 1966-67, resident in pediatrics, 1967-69, fellow in allergy and immunology, 1971-73; practice medicine specializing in allergy, Suffern, N.Y., 1973—; mem. staff Good Samaritan Hosp., Suffern, Valley Hosp., Ridgewood, N.J., Nyack (N.Y.) Hosp. Served to maj. M.C., U.S. Army, 1969-71. Diplomate Am. Bd. Pediatrics, Am. Bd. Allergy and Immunology. Fellow Am. Acad. Pediatrics, Am. Acad. Allergy, Am. Coll. Allergists, Am. Assn. Certified Allergists; mem. N.Y. Allergy Soc. Roman Catholic. Office: Physicians and Surgeons Bldg Hemion Rd Suffern NY 10901

CODY, BYRON MILLARD, chem. engr.; b. Albany, N.Y., Feb. 11, 1930; s. Millard James and Grace Louise (Thomas) C.; student Stevens Inst. Tech., 1947-49; B.S. in Chem. Engring., Newark Coll. Engring., 1955, M.S., 1958; m. A. Jane Brooks, Sept. 18, 1954; children—Robert Byron, Carol Jane, James Douglas. Chem. engr. Am. Cyanamid Co., 1955-56; research engr. Celanese Corp. Am., 1956-59, Air Reduction Co., 1959-62; project mgr. Hercules, Inc., 1962-65, Am. Cyanamid Co., 1966-67; dir. phys. plant Bloomfield (N.J.) Coll., 1967-69; mgr. maintenance and constrn. BASF Wyandotte, South Kearny Works (N.J.), 1969-72; pres. Christiana Engring. Inc., Dover, N.J., 1972-73, now dir.; mgr. project services dept. Singmaster & Breyer, cons. chem. engrs., N.Y.C., 1973—; mem. Chem. Week Mgmt. Adv. Panel, 1973-74. Dir. civil def. radiation chem. div. Rockaway Twp., N.J., 1960-63; troop com. chmn. Morris-Sussex (N.J.) council Boy Scouts Am., 1969—; foreman N.J. dist. Fed. Grand Jury, 1975-77. Served with AUS, 1952-54. Registered profl. engr., N.J. Mem. Am. Inst. Chem. Engrs., ASME, Nat. Soc. Profl. Engrs., Am. Assn. Cost Engrs. Methodist (trustee 1968-71). Club: Masons. Home: 130 Oak St Dover NJ 07801 Office: 100 Park Ave New York City NY 10017

CODY, WILLIAM FREDERIC, food co. exec.; b. Holyoke, Mass., July 28, 1931; s. John F. and Mary (Scanlon) C.; B.A., U. Mass., 1953; J.D. cum laude, Harvard U., 1956; m. Nancy J.Sebastian, Apr. 21, 1961; children—Peter Sebastian, Elizabeth Wallace. Admitted to N.Y. bar, 1957; asso. firm Dorr & Whittaker & Watson, N.Y.C., 1956-61; corporate atty. CPC Internat. Inc., N.Y.C., 1961-72, exec. asst. to chmn. bd. CPC, 1972-73, v.p., asst. to pres. CPC Europe, 1973-76, v.p., personnel and pub. affairs, 1976—. Bd. dirs. Guiding

Eyes for Blind; trustee Harvey Sch., Katonah, N.Y. Served with U.S. Army, 1957-58. Mem. Am., N.Y. State bar assns. Republican. Episcopalian. Home: Maple Ave Katonah NY 10536 Office: Internat Plaza Englewood Cliffs NJ 07632

COE, NEILE HECTOR, research co. exec.; b. N.Y.C., May 21, 1923; s. Allan C. and Sara Brooke (Beall) C.; grad. Randolph-Macon Acad., 1940; B.S., summa cum laude, U.S. Naval Acad., 1945; m. Evelyn Pannone, June 6, 1945; children—Gloria (Mrs. Sprigg), Mary Beall, Neile Hector. Chmn. bd., pres., dir. Trilon Research Corp., Plainview, N.Y., 1947—, Trilon Ednl. Corp., 1968—, Island Products Corp., N.Y.C., 1950—; dir. Island Products Corp., Toltec Corp. Bd. visitors Tufts U., 1971—. Served to lt. USNR, 1941-47; PTO. Mem. Am. Ordnance Assn., Navy League, S.A.R. Club: Army Navy (Washington). Home: Bruce Park Dr Greenwich CT 06830 Office: 139-30 34th Rd Flushing NY 11354

COE, ROBERT LEWIS, JR., elec. engr.; b. St. Louis, Apr. 26, 1926; s. Robert Lewis and Dorothy (Coates) C.; student Washington U., St. Louis, 1946-51, N.Y. U., N.Y.C., 1952-55; m. Georgianna Arbuckle, June 7, 1973; children by previous marriage—Robert Lewis III, Cynthia; stepchildren—Debra, Steven, and Laura Wise. Draftsman, Westinghouse Electric Co., St. Louis, 1946-47; designer Guarantee Elec. Co., St. Louis, 1948-51; elec. engr. M.W. Kellogg Co., N.Y.C., 1951-59; chief elec. engr. Crawford & Russell Inc., Stamford, Conn., 1959-77, mgr. design engring., 1977—. Served with USAAF, 1944-46. Mem. IEEE, Nat. Soc. Profl. Engrs. Registered profl. engr., Conn. Home: 47 Harvest Moon Rd Easton CT 06425 Office: 17 Amelia Pl Stamford CT 06904

COELHO, LUIZ CARLOS, artist; b. Campinas, Brazil, May 16, 1935; s. Valentim and Jovina Ammes C.; came to U.S., 1963, naturalized, 1969; student Escola Nacional de Bellas Artes, 1956, U. Brazil, 1961; m. Nidia D'Alessandro, Oct. 24, 1959. One man exhbns. include: Galleria Andrea, Sao Paolo, Brazil, 1958, Galleria Heller, Rio de Janeiro, Brazil, 1960, Museo Coloniale, Quito, Ecuador, 1963, Brazilian Center, Caracas, Venezuela, 1963, Brazilian Center, N.Y.C., 1970, Galleria Internazionale, N.Y.C., 1972, Galleria Guiermo, Albuquerque, 1975, Galleria Stimmate, Rome, 1979; group exhbns. include: Nat. Mus. Belas Arts, Rio de Janeiro, 1958, 59, Fairfield Public Library, 1973, Westwood Gallery, Los Angeles, 1978, Brazilian Center, N.Y.C., 1973, Avanti Gallery, N.Y.C., 1972, Museo de Ponce (P.R.), 1977, Hunterdon (N.J.) Art Center, 1977; represented in permanent collections: Municipal Gallery, Campinas, Brazil, Nat. Mus. Contemporary Art, Lisbon, Portugal, Colonial Mus., Quito, Ecuador. Mem. Shelter Island Community of Arts. Address: Lake Dr Shelter Island NY 11964

COEN, ROBERT JOSEPH, advt. exec.; b. Orange, N.J., June 25, 1923; s. John Francis and Mary Elizabeth (Whitford) C.; B.S., Holy Cross Coll., 1947; M.A., Columbia, 1948, postgrad., 1948-52; m. Wanda G. Gonski, Oct. 13, 1956; children—Lisa, Robert, Theodore. Research analyst McCann-Erickson, Inc., N.Y.C., 1948-53, mgr. media research, 1953-59, asso. research dir., 1960-64; dir. applied sci. div. Interpublic, Inc., N.Y.C., 1964-66, pres. Midas div., 1966-68, exec. v.p. Dataplan div., 1968-69. Served with USNR, 1942-46. Mem. TV Radio Research Council, Advt. Research Council, Media Research Council, Cath. Communications Found., Am. Marketing Assn. Contbg. editor Printers Ink mag., 1950-68, Marketing Communications, 1968-71, Advt. Age, 1972—. Contbr. articles to profl. jours. Home: 255 Gregory Ave West Orange NJ 07052 Office: 485 Lexington Ave New York City NY 10017

COFFEY, JOHN LAWRENCE, TV dir.; b. N.Y.C., Aug. 26, 1926; s. John J. and Elizabeth (Caddle) C.; A.S., Walter Hervey Jr. Coll., 1948; m. Alice M. Parker, May 8, 1948; children—Kathleen (Mrs. Joseph Lawlor), Eileen (Mrs. Lawrence Hickey), Alice, John, Patricia, Mary, Thomas, Matthew, Timothy, Terence. Cameraman NBC, Inc., N.Y.C., 1948-52, tech. dir., 1955-72; dir. Somerset, Another World and All My Children daytime dramas ABC, N.Y.C., 1972—. Served with USNR, 1944-46. Mem. Dirs. Guild Am., Nat. Assn. Broadcast Engrs. Roman Catholic. Home and office: 54 Haverford Rd Hicksville NY 11801

COFFEY, JOSEPH EDWARD, JR., environ. engr.; b. Albany, N.Y., Feb. 24, 1950; s. Joseph Edward and Elizabeth Marion (Hine) C.; B.S. in Engring., Boston U., 1972; M. Engring. in Environ. Engring., Rensselaer Poly. Inst., 1974; m. Sharon Ruth McGrath, May 22, 1971; 1 dau., Laura Sharon. Environ. engr. C.T. Male Asso. P.C., Schenectady, 1973—. EPA grantee, 1972-74. Mem. Nat. Assn. Environ. Profls., ASCE, Am. Water Works Assn., Water Pollution Control Fedn., Chi Epsilon. Democrat. Roman Catholic. Author: (with Connor and Tuttle) Water Quality of Saratoga Lake, 1974. Home: 18 Pine St Westmere Albany NY 12203 Office: 3000 Troy Rd Schenectady NY 12309

COFFIN, CHARLES FREDERICK, JR., ins. exec.; b. Ashland, Maine, June 3, 1931; s. Charles Frederick and Annie Grace (Brooks) C.; student U. Maine, 1949-51; m. Diana Brown, July 20, 1958. Ins. agt. C.F. Coffin Ins. Agy., 1952-56; owner C.F. Coffin Ins. Agy., Ashland, 1956—. Treas. local troop Boy Scouts Am., 1965-67; v.p. Ashland Indsl. Devel. Corp., 1969-77, pres., 1977—. Chmn. Ashland Planning Bd., 1971—; mem. Rep. Town Com., Ashland, 1964-66; mem. No. Maine Regional Planning Commn. Bd. dirs. local chpt. ARC, 1963-66, area finance chmn., 1964. Served with AUS, 1952-54. Recipient Leadership award Maine Dept. Econ. Devel., 1972. Mem. New Eng. Mut. Ins. Agts. Assn., Aroostook County Ins. Agts. Assn. (dir. 1963-65, pres. 1966), Ind. Ins. Agts. Assn., Ashland C. of C. (exec. sec. 1954—, pres. 1973-74). Conglist. (trustee 1960-65). Mason, Rotarian (dir. 1960-66, pres. 1962-63). Home: RFD 1 Ashland ME 04732 Office: 4 Main St Ashland ME 04732

COFFIN, DAVID DOUGLAS, classicist, educator; b. N.Y.C., Nov. 26, 1922; s. Henry Sloane and Dorothy Prentice (Eells) C.; B.A., Yale, 1942; M.A., 1947; postgrad. King's Coll., Cambridge (Eng.) U., 1948-49; m. Rosemary Honor Baldwin, Oct. 15, 1949; children—Sarah Douglas, Peter Douglas. Instr. in classics Smith Coll., Northampton, Mass., 1950-53; instr. in classics Phillips Exeter Acad., Exeter, N.H., 1953-66, chmn. classics dept., 1966-71, Cilley prof. of Greek, 1969—; exchange master Eton Coll., Eng., 1959-60; vis. prof. classics Trinity Coll., Hartford, Conn., summer, 1963, 64; mem. Coll. Bd. advanced placement com., Latin, 1969-77, chmn., 1974-77. Served to lt. USNR, 1942-46. Recipient Harvard Coll. Distinguished Secondary Sch. Tchr. award, 1967. Mem. Am. Philol. Assn., Classical Assn. NE, Vergilian Soc. Am., Nat. Assn. of Ind. Schs. (chmn. Latin com. 1971-72), Phi Beta Kappa. Presbyterian. Clubs: Ausable, St. Hubert's (N.Y.). Co-author: A Teacher's Notebook: Latin, 1974; Beginning an Advanced Placement Classics Course, 1975; editor Ovid: Acis, Galatea, and Polyphemus, 1968. Home: Exeter Rd Hampton Falls NH 03844 Office: Phillips Exeter Acad Exeter NH 03833

COFFIN, FRANK MOREY, judge; b. Lewiston, Maine, July 11, 1919; s. Herbert Rice and Ruth (Morey) C.; A.B., Bates Coll., 1940; Indsl. Adminstrn. degree Harvard, 1943, LL.B., 1947; m. Ruth Ulrich, Dec. 19, 1942; children—Nancy, Douglas, Meredith, Susan. Admitted to Maine bar, 1947; law clk. to fed. judge Dist. of Maine, 1947-49, practice in Lewiston, 1947-52; with Verrill, Dana, Walker, Philbrick & Whitehouse, Portland, Maine, 1952-56; mem. 85th-86th Congresses from 2d Dist. Maine, mem. House Com. Fgn. Affairs, Joint Econ. Com.; mng. dir. Devel. Loan Fund, Dept. State, Washington, 1961, dep. adminstr. AID, 1961-64; U.S. rep. devel. assistance com. OECD, 1964-65; judge 1st circuit U.S. Ct. Appeals, 1965—, chief judge, 1972—. Chmn. Maine Higher Edn. Planning Commn., 1969-72. Chmn. Maine Democratic Com., 1954-56. Trustee Bates Coll.; bd. dirs. Overseas Devel. Council. Served from ensign to lt., USNR, 1943-46, Fellow Am. Acad. Arts and Scis.; mem. Examiner Club (pres.). Author: Witness for Aid, 1964. Home: 1 Ocean Rd South Portland ME 04106 Office: 156 Federal St Portland ME 04112

COFFIN, WILLIAM SARGENT, SR., devel. co. exec.; b. Pittsfield, Maine, Dec. 16, 1914; s. Carl Sargent and Grace (Summerbell) C.; A.B., Bates Coll., 1937; postgrad. Am. Inst. Banking, 1947; m. Amelia Amanda Moore, Sept. 7, 1945; children—Thomas Carl, William Sargent. With First Nat. Bank, Pittsfield, 1939-41, 46-47; credit mgr. Sears, Roebuck & Co., Augusta, Maine, 1947-53; with Electric Boat div. Gen. Dynamics, Groton, Conn., 1953-55; examiner Dept. of Banks & Banking, Augusta, 1955-58; mgr. Devel. Credit Corp. Maine, Augusta, 1958-72, exec. dir., 1972-75; owner, gen. mgr. W. S. Coffin & Assos., Manchester, Maine, 1975—. Div. chmn. ARC, Augusta, 1962-65; div. chmn. Community Chest, Augusta, 1965-68; mem. fin. com. Penney Meml. United Bapt. Ch., 1954-67; chmn. bd. deacons Manchester Community Ch., 1970-74; trustee Maine Central Inst., 1972-76; pres. Indsl. Devel. Council of Maine, 1965. Served to capt. AUS, 1941-46. Mem. Nat. Assn. Bus. Devel. Corps. (pres. 1963-73, exec. v.p., sec., treas. 1973—), Maine Bankers Assn., Maine Merchants Assn. Republican. Clubs: Masons, Order Eastern Star. Home: Williamson Rd Manchester ME 04351 Office: PO Box 262 Manchester ME 04351

COGEN, TESS SCHNITTKRAMER, therapist-counselor, educator; b. Russia, Apr. 28, 1904; d. Morris and Minnie (Winarsky) Schnittkramer; came to U.S., 1908, naturalized, 1919; LL.B., Bklyn. Law Sch., 1925; B.A., Hunter Coll., 1959; M.A., Columbia U., 1961, postgrad., 1962; m. Charles Cogen, Feb. 9, 1929; children—Joel, Edward. Admitted to N.Y. State bar, 1927; tchr. Columbia U., 1960-61; marriage and family counselor Marriage Counseling Clinic of Guidance Lab., Columbia U., N.Y.C., 1961-62; psychotherapist Met. Center for Mental Health, N.Y.C., 1962-64; dir. family life edn. Assn. Family Living, Chgo., 1964-68; cons., author Family Life Edn. Program, Follett Pub. Co., Chgo., 1968—; cons., tchr. Inst. Ednl. Devel., Washington, 1970, Quest Edn. Program, United Fedn. Tchrs., N.Y.C., 1971-75; adj. asso. prof. Pace U., N.Y.C., 1972—; mem. tng. com. and supr. Save A Marriage, Inc., 1976—. Mem. City-wide Adv. Council on Sch. Health, 1974—; UN affiliate rep. Internat. Council Social Dem. Women to Office of Pub. Info., 1974—. Certified sex educator, certified sex therapist; psychology fellow State of N.Y., 1962-64. Mem. Am. Psychol. Assn., Am. Bar Assn., Am. Assn. Marriage and Family Counselors, Am. Assn. Sex Educators, Counselors and Therapists, Soc. Sci. Study of Sex, Sex Info. and Edn. Council U.S., Nat. Council Family Relations, Phi Beta Kappa, Psi Chi, Kappa Delta Pi, Pi Lambda Theta, Orgn. for Rehab. Through Tng., Hadassah, Nat. Council Jew. Women. Jewish. Author: Family Life Edn. Program, 1969; contbr. articles to profl. jours. and presentations to profl. and community group meetings. Home: 185 Park Row New York City NY 10038

COGGINS, WADE THOMAS, assn. exec.; b. New Market, N.C., Dec. 12, 1924; s. Charles Lee and Laura Jean (Hinshaw) C.; B.S., Nyack Missionary Coll., 1955, LL.D., 1973; M.A., U. Md., 1965; m. Jane Marguerite Wells, Aug. 18, 1945; 1 son, Robert Charles. Ordained to ministry Christian Missionary Alliance Ch., 1947; minister Norwoodville Ch., Des Moines, 1945-47; missionary, tchr. Christian and Missionary Alliance, Colombia, 1948-55; minister Alliance Ch., Knoxville, Tenn., 1956-58; exec. dir. Evang. Fgn. Missions Assn., Washington, 1958—. Alumni Assn. Nyack Coll. (v.p. 1966-67). Mem. Christian and Missionary Alliance Ch. (elder 1959—). Author: So That's What Missions Is All About, 1975. Editor: (with Clyde W. Taylor) Protestant Missions in Latin America, 1961, Mobilizing for Saturation Evangelism, 1970; Evangelical Missions Tomorrow, 1977; Missionary News Service, 1958—; mem. editorial com. Evang. Missions Quar. Home: 4913 Bangor Dr Kensington MD 20795 Office: 1430 K St NW Washington DC 20005

COGHILL, CARTER LAMBERT, hosp. adminstr.; b. Charleston, W.Va., May 6, 1929; s. Julian Baxter and Ruth Guerrant (Putney) C.; B.A. cum laude, Hampden-Sydney Coll., 1950; M.A. in English, U. Va., 1958; m. Sara Adele Taylor, Oct. 23, 1954; 1 dau., Constance Lambert. Tchr. high schs., Nelson and Albemarle counties, Va., 1950-53; research asst. Va. Electric & Power Co., 1953-56; tech. writer, editor, personnel adminstr. U.S. Instrument Corp., Charlottesville, Va., 1958-61; personnel rep. Mitre Corp., Montgomery, Ala., and Bedford, Mass., 1961-64; personnel mgr. Electro-Tec Corp., Blacksburg, Va., 1964-66; indsl. relations mgr. Dawbarn div. W.R. Grace & Co., Waynesboro, Va., 1966-70; indsl. relations mgr. Landis Tool Co., Waynesboro, Pa., 1970-74; dir. personnel Forbes Health System, Pitts., 1974-76; dep. dir. for human resources John J. Kane Hosp., Pitts., 1976—. Active United Fund. Mem. Am. Soc. Personnel Adminstrn. (chpt. pres. 1973-74), Internat. Platform Assn., Omicron Delta Kappa, Pi Delta Epsilon, Sigma Upsilon, Eta Sigma Phi, Alpha Psi Omega. Republican. Presbyterian. Home: 117 Lammert Dr Glenshaw PA 15116 Office: John J Kane Hosp Vanadium Rd Pittsburgh PA 15243

COGLIANO, FRANCIS DOMINIC, surgeon; b. Everett, Mass., Oct. 4, 1934; s. Dominic Antony and Lavinia C.; B.S. cum laude, Tufts U., 1956; M.D., Yale U., 1960; m. Ann Kelleher, June 1, 1957; children—Elizabeth, Andrea, Sarah, Francis D., David. Intern, resident in surgery Harvard Health Service, Boston City Hosp., 1960-66; teaching fellow Harvard Med. Sch., 1966; practice medicine specializing in surgery, Brockton, Mass., 1968—; mem. staff Brockton Hosp., 1968—, pres. med. staff, 1978—; asso. prof. surgery Boston U. Sch. Medicine, 1977—; trustee People's Savs. Bank. Served with M.C., USNR, 1966-68. Diplomate Am. Bd. Surgery. Fellow A.C.S.; mem. AMA, Mass., Plymouth County (treas.) med. socs., Boston Surg. Soc., New Eng. Soc. Colon and Rectal Surgeons, Phi Beta Kappa, Alpha Omega Alpha. Clubs: Harvard, Mill Pond Tennis, Hanover Swim and Tennis. Office: 61 Libby St Brockton MA 02401

COGSWELL, KARIN I., curriculum devel. specialist; b. N.Y.C., June 25, 1949; d. Arnold C. and Margot E. (Sopp) Lake; B.A., Barrington Coll., 1971; M.A. in Counseling and Community Services, Fairfield U., 1977; m. Edward William Cogswell, Feb. 26, 1972. Asst. registrar Fairfield (Conn.) U., 1972-77; curriculum devel. specialist Post Coll., Waterbury, Conn., 1977—. Mem. Assn. Humanistic Edn. and Devel., Am. Personnel and Guidance Assn., AAUW, Conn. Assn. Continuing Edn. Home: 252 W Elm St New Haven CT 06515 Office: 800 Country Club Rd Waterbury CT 06708

COHELEACH, GUY JOSEPH, artist; b. N.Y.C.; s. Gaetan Guy and Flauia Marie (Aymong) C.; grad. Cooper Union; D.Arts (hon.), Coll. William and Mary, 1975; m. Patricia Arlene; children—George, Coleen, Hugh, Guy Joseph (dec.). One-man shows at A & F Gallery, N.Y.C., Gallery Wildlife Art, Louisville, Am. Mus. Natural History, N.Y.C.; exhibited in group shows at Bird Art of World, Tryon Gallery, London, Bird Artists of Am., Graham Gallery, N.Y.C., Am. Mus. Natural History, Denver Mus., Animal Artists of World, Nairobi, Toronto, Can.; represented in permanent collections White House, Nat. Gallery, Am. Mus. Natural History, Nat. Wildlife Fedn. Gallery, Washington, Nat. Audubon Soc. Gallery. Bd. dirs. Hawk Mountain Sanctuary, Found. for Environmental Edn. Served with AUS. Mem. Soc. Animal Artists Nat. Audubon Soc. (life), Nat. Wildlife Fedn. (life), Clubs: African Safari (named Conservationist of Yr. 1976) (Washington and N.Y.C.); Campfire, Adventurer's Explorers (N.Y.C.). Office: Box 147 Plainview NY 11803

COHEN, ABRAHAM, physician; b. Bogota, Colombia, June 14, 1937; s. Michael and Rosa (Fernandez) C.; came to U.S., 1963, naturalized, 1968; M.D., Universidad Javeriana, Colombia, 1962; m. Sonia, Nov. 17, 1962; children—Sandra, William, David. Intern, Mt. Vernon (N.Y.) Hosp., 1963-64; resident in obstetrics and gynecology Met. Hosp., N.Y.C., 1968-70; practice medicine specializing in obstetrics and gynecology, N.Y.C., 1970—; clin. instr. N.Y. Med. Coll., 1970—; mem. staff Flower and Fifth Ave., Lenox Hill, Bronx-Lebanon hosps. Served with U.S. Army, 1966-67. Diplomate Am. Coll. Obstetricians and Gynecologists. Fellow Am. Coll. Obstetricians and Gynecologists, ACS; mem. Med. Soc. County N.Y., AMA. Jewish religion. Home: 44 Tarry Hill Rd Tarrytown NY 10591 Office: 1065 Park Ave New York City NY 10028

COHEN, ALAN SEYMOUR, physician; b. Boston, Apr. 9, 1926; s. George I. and Jennie (Laskin) C.; A.B. magna cum laude, Harvard, 1947; M.D. magna cum laude, Boston U., 1952; m. Joan E. Prince, Sept. 12, 1954; children—Evan Bruce, Andrew Hollis, Robert Adam. Successively intern, resident, research fellow Thorndike Meml. Labs., Boston City Hosp., 1952-56; exchange registrar medicine Queen's Coll., Dundee, Scotland, 1956; fellow, asst., instr. medicine Mass. Gen. Hosp. and Harvard Med. Sch., 1956-60; mem. faculty Boston U. Med. Center, 1961—, prof. medicine, 1968—, Wesselhoeft prof., 1972—, dir. arthritis and connective tissue disease sect., 1961—; chief medicine Boston City Hosp., also dir. Thorndike Meml. Lab., 1973—. Chmn. arthritis tng. grants com. study sect. HEW, 1970, mem. gen. medicine study sect. A, 1972—; cons. VA Commn. Mass.; past cons. drug effect study NRC-Nat. Acad. Scis.; chmn. med. and sci. com., trustee, mem. trustees exec. com. Mass. chpt. Arthritis Found., also vice chmn. chpt.; Bernadine Becker meml. lectr. N.Y. Acad. Medicine, 1969; Wallace Graham meml. lectr. Queen's U., Ont., Can., 1973; Tyndale lectr. U. Utah Med. Sch., 1978. Served with USPHS, 1953-55. Recipient Maimonides award Greater Boston Med. Soc., 1952; named Outstanding Young Man in Mass., Mass. Jr. C. of C., 1961. Fellow A.C.P.; mem. Am. Rheumatism Assn. (exec. com., bd. dirs. 1962—, pres. 1978—), Am. Soc. Clin. Investigation, Assn. Am. Physicians, Am. Fedn. Clin. Research, Am. Soc. Exptl. Pathology, Soc. Exptl. Biology and Medicine, Electron Microscope Soc. Am., Am. Soc. Cell Biology, N.Y. Acad. Scis., AMA, Mass. Med. Soc., Boston U. Sch. Medicine Alumni Assn. (pres. 1977-78), Phi Beta Kappa, Alpha Omega Alpha. Clubs: Harvard (Boston); Hazel Hotchkiss Wightman Tennis (Weston, Mass.); Newton (Mass.) Squash and Tennis. Author: Laboratory Diagnostic Procedures in Rheumatic Diseases, 2d edit., 1974; also numerous articles. Co-editor: Amyloidosis, 1968; Medical Emergencies, 1977; editorial bd. Arthritis and Rheumatism, 1963—. Home: 54 Winston Rd Newton Centre MA 02159 Office: Boston City Hosp 818 Harrison Ave Boston MA 02118

COHEN, ALLEN, hosp. adminstr.; b. Chelsea, Mass., Jan. 24, 1929; s. Meyer and Lillian (Wolfe) C.; B.S. in Bus. Adminstrn., U. Bridgeport, 1956; M.S.W., U. Conn., 1963; M.P.H., Yale U., 1966; postgrad., N.Y. U., 1969-71; m. Alice Cadieux, Oct. 12, 1974; children—Jeffrey, Suzanne, Jonathan, David. Police officer, Milford, Conn., 1953-58; social worker, state welfare and juvenile ct., State of Conn., 1958-63, state planner mental retardation, 1966-68; mental health planner, Middlesex County, Conn., 1969; hosp. adminstr., Conn. Valley Hosp., Middletown, 1969-71, Elmcrest Psychiat. Inst., Portland, Conn., 1971—; preceptor Yale U. Pub. Health. Mem. bd. dirs. No. Middlesex C. of C., Middletown. Served with USAF, 1951-53. Mem. Fedn. Am. Hosps. (Little Rock, Ark., bd. dirs.), Conn. Hosp. Assn. (council), Am. Coll. Hosp. Adminstrs., Assn. Mental Health Adminstrs, Pi Gamma Mu. Home: 315 Main St Portland CT 06480 Office: 25 Marlborough St Portland CT 06480

COHEN, ALLEN BAILIN, social service adminstr.; b. N.Y.C., May 22, 1935; s. Julius and Jeanette (Bailin) C.; B.A., Bklyn. Coll. of U. City N.Y., 1957; M.S., Case Western Res. U., 1959; m. Marcia Forman, Jan. 27, 1957; children—Cheryl, Scott. Sr. group worker Jewish Community Centers, Cleve., 1959-62; supr. group services Catholic Charities, Trenton, N.J., 1962-64; exec. dir. Neighborhood House, New Brunswick, N.J., 1964-68; exec. dir. Chinatown Planning Council of N.Y.C., 1968—; field instr. Case-Western Res. U., Rutgers U., Stony Brook of U. City N.Y., Hunter Coll. Mem. adv. bd. N.Y.C. Community Planning Bd. 3, 1976—, mem. exec. com., 1977-78; mem. bd. vol. Protestant Welfare Fedn., 1975-76; chmn. legis. adv. com. Borough Pres. of Manhattan's Com. on Day Care, 1971-72; bd. dirs. Children's Lobby, 1973; mem. N.Y. State Advisory Bd. Social Welfare, 1976—. Recipient Michael Bogart award Case-Western Res. U. Mem. Acad. Certified Social Workers, Nat. Assn. Social Workers (exec. com. South Jersey chpt. 1964-68), Tchrs. of English to Students Who Speak Other Langs. Office: Chinatown Planning Council 45 E Broadway New York City NY 10002

COHEN, ARTHUR CHARLES, real estate cons. and appraiser; b. N.Y.C., Jan. 26, 1940; s. Isidor Michael and Mary Frances (Eskew) C.; B.S., U. Wis., 1961; M.B.A., Columbia U., 1971; m. Eve Lorraine Imberman, Mar. 19, 1966; children—Daniel Charles, Alexander Lloyd. Real estate mgmt. positions J.E. Becker Inc., N.Y.C., 1963-65; area coordinator New Eng. HUD, N.Y.C., 1965-69; pres. Arthur Charles Cohen Inc., N.Y.C., 1970—, trustee pension fund, 1972—. Vice-pres. 110-118 Riverside Tenants Corp., 1975—; bd. dirs. Council West Side Coops., 1975—. Served with arty. U.S. Army, 1964-65. Mem. Am. Soc. Appraisers (sr.), Urban Land Inst., Am. Real Estate and Urban Econ. Assn., Nat. Ry. Hist. Soc. Club: Mil. History. Home: 110 Riverside Dr New York City NY 10024 Office: 14 W 55th St New York City NY 10019

COHEN, BEN, industrialist; b. Balt., Jan. 27, 1900; s. Isaac Meyer and Marsha (Pondfield) C.; student Franklin Sch. Accounting, 1919-21; m. Zelda Greenberg, Jan. 29, 1928; children—Rosalee (Mrs. Richard Davison), Charlotte (Mrs. Carroll A. Weinberg). Pres. Silver Hill Apts. Corp., 1947—, C.D. Constrn. Corp., Balt., 1962-76; partner Housing Engring. Co., Balt., 1939—; sec.-treas. Monroe Park Constrn. Corp., Monroe Park Apts. Corp., 1949-72; sec.-treas. Md. Jockey Club, Balt., 1952; v.p. Charg-It Fla., 1965-73; partner Mt. Royal Bldg. Co., 1970—; organizer, pres. WAAM-TV, 1946-57. Breeder race horses. Pres., Herman & Ben Cohen Charitable Found., 1949—. Club: Suburban Country (Balt.). Home: 6701 Park Heights Ave Baltimore MD 21215 Office: 1233 Mt Royal Ave Baltimore MD 21217

COHEN, BENJAMIN, psychiatrist, psychoanalyst; b. Boston, June 3, 1908; s. Jacob and Rose (Dinner) C.; M.D., Tufts U., 1931; grad. Boston Psychoanalytic Inst., 1959; m. Gertrude Sherey, Dec. 25, 1938; 1 son, Ronald Jay. Intern, Salem (Mass.) Hosp., 1931-32; resident, sr. physician, research asso. Grafton (Mass.) State Hosp., 1932-42; practice medicine specializing in psychiatry and psychoanalysis, Boston, 1945—; cons. in counseling and rehab. VA, Boston; sr. staff Univ. Hosp., Boston; past mem. psychiat. faculties Tufts U., Boston U. Served to maj., M.C., U.S. Army, 1942-45; ETO. Recipient research prize New Eng. Soc. Psychiatry, 1936. Diplomate Am. Bd. Psychiatry and Neurology. Life fellow Am. Psychiat. Assn.; mem. Am. Psychoanalytic Assn. Jewish. Contbr. papers in field to profl. med. jours. Home: 177 Bonad Rd Chestnut Hill MA 02167 Office: 60 Charlesgate W Boston MA 02215

COHEN, BERTRAM MALCOLM, corp. exec., accountant; b. Boston, Sept. 30, 1931; s. Myer and Ruth C.; B.S., U. Ariz., 1952, M.B.A., 1955; m. Nina Cohn, May 27, 1956; children—Brenda, Arnold. Accountant, auditor S.D. Leidesdorf, N.Y.C., 1955-58, v.p. Irwin Corp., N.Y.C., 1960-71, pres., 1971-74; v.p. Gt. Am. Plastics, Inc., Nashua, N.H., 1958-71, pres., 1971—; v.p. Gt. Am. Chem. Corp., Fitchburg, Mass., 1958-76, pres., 1977—. Treas., Agudas Achim Endowment Fund, 1975—; bd. dirs. United Fund, Fitchburg; bd. overseers Strubridge (Mass.) Village. Served with U.S. Army, 1952-54. C.P.A., Ariz. Mem. Pres.'s Assn., Am. Inst. C.P.A.'s, Ariz. Soc. C.P.A.'s, Soc. Plastics Industry, Fitchburg C. of C. (dir.). Clubs: Rotary (asst. treas., dir. Fitchburg 1976—), B'nai B'rith. Home: 667 West St Leominster MA 01453

COHEN, BURTON JEROME, fin. exec.; b. Phila., Dec. 8, 1933; s. Alexander David and Esther (Mirrow) C.; B.S. in Accounting, Temple U., 1955; student Exec. Program, Harvard; m. Jane McDowell, Mar. 16, 1968; children—Paul, Joshua, Douglas, Glen. Operations v.p., Cakemasters, Inc., Phila., 1957-61; mgr., IBM, Phila., White Plains, N.Y., N.Y.C., 1961-70; partner Touche & Ross & Co., N.Y.C., 1970-77; partner, nat. dir. fin. and adminstrn. Coopers & Lybrand, N.Y.C., 1977—; adj. prof. Columbia U. Grad. Sch. Bus.; lectr. Am. Mgmt. Assn. seminars. Mem. adv. bd. Borough Manhattan Community Coll. Served with Fin. Corps, AUS, 1955-57. Mem. Fin. Execs. Inst. Mason. Author: Cost Effective Informations Systems, 1971. Contbr. to Info. Systems Handbook, 1975. Home: 63 Adams Ln New Canaan CT 06840 Office: 1251 Ave of Americas New York City NY 10020

COHEN, BURTON MARCUS, physician, clin. investigator; b. Elizabeth, N.J., Dec. 13, 1925; s. Philip and Beatrice (Kaufman) C.; A.B., Columbia, 1945; M.D., U. Rochester, 1948; m. Elaine N. Mohr, Dec. 24, 1950; children—Elizabeth, Hugh, Claire, Suzanne. Intern, resident Maimonides Hosp., Bklyn., 1948-51; resident physician Strong Meml. Hosp., also asst. medicine U. Rochester, 1950-51; research fellow Columbia U. Research Service, Goldwater Meml. Hosp., asst. medicine Columbia Coll. Phys. and Surg., 1954-58; asst. prof. clin. medicine and clin. preventive medicine N.J. Coll. Medicine, 1959-61, clin. asst. prof. medicine, 1961-63; asso. prof. clin. medicine, 1963—; pres. Burton M. Cohen, M.D.; attending physician Jersey City Med. Center; asso. dir. White Cardiopulmonary Inst., Pollak Hosp., Jersey City, 1959-63; sr. attending physician Elizabeth Gen. Hosp., chmn. dept. medicine, 1975-77; med. bd. Deborah Hosp., Browns Mills; asso. U. Rochester. Dir. Clodagh Assos., Ltd., Ireland. Served as midshipman USNR, 1943-44, lt comdr., USPHS, 1952-55; comdr. (sr. surgeon) Res., 1968—. Fellow Am. Coll. Cardiology. Am. Coll. Chest Physicians, Acad. Medicine N.J., A.C.P., Royal Soc. Medicine (London), Royal Soc. Health, Internat. Acad. Sci. and Medicine, Am. Coll. Clin. Pharmacology and Chemotherapy (a founding fellow), Am. Soc. Clin. Radiology; mem. Union County Heart Assn. (past pres.), Am. Fedn. Clin. Research. Internat. Soc. Internal Medicine, Internat. Cardiovascular Soc., A.A.A.S., Am. Therapeutic Soc., AAUP, Mil. Surgeons U.S. Soc. Automotive Historians, Res. Officers U.S., N.J. Acad. Sci., John Jay Soc., George Hoyt Whipple Soc. (charter), Soc. Older Grads. Columbia U. Club: Columbia University (N.Y.C.); Rolls-Royce Owners (U.S.), Rolls-Royce Enthusiast, Rolls-Royce and Bentley Drivers (Eng.). Cardiology editor Medecine et Hygiene (Switzerland), 1961—; editor-in-chief Current Concepts in Pacing. Contbr. articles to profl. jours. Home: 546 Irvington Ave Elizabeth NJ 07202 Office: 230 W Jersey St Elizabeth NJ 07202

COHEN, DAVID, mfg. co. exec.; b. Red Bank, N.J., Apr. 26, 1924; s. Nathan and Ida (Friedman) C.; B.S. in Chem. Engring., Newark Coll. Engring., 1947, M.S. in Chem. Engring., 1951; postgrad. in Math., Rutgers U., 1953-55; E.E., N.C. State U., 1944-45; m. Mildred Zuckerman, June 8, 1947; children—Janice R., Valerie A. Prodn. supr. Nord & Co., Keyport, N.J., 1947-51; process engr. Hercules Inc., Parlin, N.J., 1951-55, quality control supr., 1955-61, tech. supt., 1969—; lectr. Am. Mgmt. Assn. Mayor of Holmdel, N.J., 1969-74, mem. twp. com., 1969-74, mem. planning bd., 1968-74, mem. bd. of health, 1969-70; chmn. Monmouth-Ocean Counties chpt. NCCJ, 1975-78; bd. dirs. Monmouth County United Way, 1974—. Served with inf. U.S. Army, 1943-45. Recipient citation of merit N.J. Conf. Mayors, 1974; Brotherhood award NCCJ, 1978. Mem. Am. Chem. Soc., Am. Inst. Chem. Engrs., Am. Soc. Quality Control. Republican. Jewish. Clubs: Affiliated Republican (v.p.), B'nai B'rith, Masons, Shriners. Contbr. articles to profl. jours. Patentee plastics manufacture and processing. Home: 1 E Parkway Pl Holmdel NJ 07733 Office: Hercules Inc Parlin NJ 08859

COHEN, EDGAR HORACE, real estate cons.; b. Montreal, Que., Can., Oct. 28, 1913; s. Abraham Zebulon and Malca (Vineberg) C.; B.A. cum laude, McGill U., 1934; m. Ruth Goldberg, Apr. 3, 1949; children—Lenore, Judith, Andrew. Pres. L. Cohen & Son Ltd., Montreal, 1937-61; pres. F.A. Price Coal & Oil Ltd., Montreal, 1978—; pres. Yarco Bldg. Corp., Montreal, 1951—. Guest lectr. on radio and TV on 17th Century French social history. Class reunion chmn. McGill U., 1959, 64; sec. Montreal chpt. Canadian Friends of Hebrew U., 1969; past trustee Shaar Hashomayim Jewish Synagogue. Life gov. Montreal Jewish Gen. Hosp. Mem. Internat. P.E.N. (pres. Canadian centre 1978). Author: Mademoiselle Libertine, 1970; also articles on lit., polit. and fin. subjects. Home: 4817 Cedar Crescent Montreal PQ Canada Office: 3535 Queen Mary Rd Suite 417 Montreal PQ Canada

COHEN, EDWARD GEORGE, ednl. adminstr.; b. N.Y.C., Jan. 23, 1925; s. Isaac Noah and Betty (Fuchs-Fox) C.; B.S. in Social Sci., Coll. City N.Y., 1949; M.A. (N.Y. State War Service scholar), Columbia, 1950; Profl. Diploma in Ednl. Research (fellow), Hofstra U., 1969, Ph.D., 1972; m. Annette Henya Fishman, Mar. 5, 1949; children—Joshua Brett, Marnin David, Rafael Zev. Tchr. social studies, math. Long Beach City sch. dist. N.Y., 1953-67; supr. research Nassau Bd. Coop. Ednl. Services, Jericho, N.Y., 1969-72; dir. ednl. research Queensborough Community Coll., City U. N.Y., Bayside, N.Y., 1972—. Tchr. Hebrew lang. and culture, part-time, 1953-70; field dir. summer work camps Am. Jewish Soc. for Service, N.Y.C., 1961-68; adj. lectr. ednl. psychology Hofstra U., Hempstead, N.Y., 1975—. Bd. edn. East End Synagogue, Long Beach, N.Y., 1966-67. Bd. dirs. Am. Jewish Soc. for Service, N.Y.C. Served with USAAF, 1942-46. NSF fellow Columbia U., 1960. Mem. Am. Ednl. Research Assn., Am. Psychol. Assn., Nat. Council Measurement Edn., Phi Delta Kappa. Home: 558 E Park Ave Long Beach NY 11561 Office: Queensborough Community Coll Springfield Blvd and 56th Ave Bayside NY 11364

COHEN, EDWARD I., lawyer; b. N.Y.C., Apr. 30, 1948; s. Alfred and Irma E. (Doris) C.; B.A. in Econs., Cornell U., 1965, M.B.A., 1967, J.D., 1968, postgrad. in Internat. Legal Studies, 1967-68, LL.M. in Taxation, 1972. Admitted to N.Y. bar, 1969, Pa. bar, 1973, U.S. Supreme Ct. bar, 1974; law clk. to atty. gen. State N.Y.; individual practice law, N.Y.C., 1969—; asst. to atty. gen. of N.Y. State, 1966; cons. to Den Danske Provinsbank, Copenhagen, Denmark, 1967; cons. Metal Purchasing Co., Inc., N.Y.C., 1965, v.p., gen. counsel, 1974—; internat. bus. cons., 1974—; pres. Wardwin Enterprises, Ltd., 1974—; v.p. Murwal, Inc., 1974—; bd. dirs., exec. com. AIESEC-U.S., Inc.; U.S. del. Manila Conf. on Laws of World, 1977. Chmn., founder Friends of the Silver Fox, 1965-68; chmn. bd. govs. ASA, Inc. Nat. Merit scholar; N.Y. State Regents scholar. Mem. Am. (com. internat. taxation 1969—), N.Y. State, Pa., Inter-Am. bar assns., Am. Judicature Soc., Am. Soc. Internat. Law, Am. Fgn. Law Assn., Assn. of Bar N.Y.C., Cornell Law Assn., World Frat. Lawyers (spl. internat. mem.), World Peace Through Law Center Assn. for Internat. Exchange of Students in Econs. and Commerce, Omicron Delta Epsilon, Signifer. Author: Scarsdale High School Handbook, 1961; Manpower Recruitment and Development, 1965; editor Cornell Jour. of Internat. Law, 1967-68; The Development of an International Law of Outer Space, 1977. Home: 10 Split Tree Rd Scarsdale NY 10583 Office: 501 W 30th St New York City NY 10001

COHEN, EDWARD MORTON, analytical chemist; b. N.Y.C., May 12, 1936; s. Abraham and Rose C.; B.S., Columbia U., 1957; M.S., Rutgers U., 1960, Ph.D., 1965; m. Sheila Louise Kadish, July 5, 1959; children—Seth, Brian, Samara. Analytical chemist Johnson & Johnson, New Brunswick, N.J., 1962-65; analytical chemist Merck & Co., Inc., West Point, Pa., 1965—, dir. pharm. research, 1975—. NSF fellow, 1959-60. Mem. Am. Chem. Soc., AAAS, Am. Pharm. Assn. Acad. Pharm. Sci., Sigma Xi. Contbr. articles to profl. jours.; editorial bd. Analytical Profiles of Drug Substances, 1974-77; co-editor Pharmaceutical Analysis, 1973; patentee in field. Home: 3008 Eisenhower Dr Norristown PA 19403 Office: Merck & Co Inc Sumneytown Pike West Point PA 19486

COHEN, EUGENE JOSEPH, clergyman; b. N.Y.C., Aug. 22, 1918; s. Philip J. and Rose (Cohen) C.; Rabbi, Yeshiva U., 1942; Ph.D., Boston U., 1954; m. Ada Twersky, Dec. 1, 1948; children—Burton, Bethsheva (Mrs. Michael Goldenhersh), Leeber. Rabbi, Congregation Derech Emunoh, Arverne, N.Y., 1948-66, Internat. Synagogue, Queens, N.Y., 1966—, VA Hosp., Bklyn., 1969—. Active Bricha underground rescue movement, World War II. Served to capt. AUS, 1945-47. Recipient award Fedn. Jewish Philanthropists, 1964. Mem. Religious Zionists Am. (v.p.), Jewish Chaplains U.S. (past pres.), Rabbinical Council, Rabbinical Alumni, N.Y. Bd. Rabbis. Author: Jewish Concepts of the Servant, 1954. Home: 258 Riverside Dr New York City NY 10025 Office: 800 Poly Pl Brooklyn NY 11209

COHEN, GEORGE M., ednl. adminstr.; b. Hartford, Conn., Aug. 5, 1938; s. Abraham and Nell (Blumenthal) C.; B.A., U. Conn., 1962; M.S., City Coll. N.Y., 1970; m. Esta Harris, Oct. 8, 1972; children—Nathan Michael, Rachel Susan. Tchr. 6th grade N.Y.C. Bd. Edn., Bronx, 1962-68, asst. prin., 1968, guidance counselor, 1968, program adminstr., 1969-73; human relations specialist White Plains (N.Y.) Bd. Edn., 1973—; field asso. Educator Tng. Center, 1974—; asst. prof. Pace U., White Plains; instr. Wetchester Community Coll.; cons. Scholarship Edn. Def. Fund for Racial Equality, Inst. for Reality Therapy N.E.; vol. tng. cons. probation dept. Westchester County Youth Div. Mem. outreach com. YWCA, White Plains; cons. youth group Jewish Community Center, White Plains. Served with U.S. Army, 1960. Certified reality therapist, guidance counselor, tchr., N.Y. State. Mem. Am., N.Y. State, Westchester-Putnam-Rockland personnel and guidance assns., Adminstrs. and Suprs. Assn. White Plains. Home: 22 Lenroc Dr White Plains NY 10607 Office: 5 Homeside Ln White Plains NY 10605

COHEN, HARRIS SAUL, govt. ofcl., health services adminstr.; b. Neptune, N.J., Aug. 29, 1941; s. Meyer and Henrietta (Gershman) C.; B.A. summa cum laude, Bklyn. Coll., 1962; M.A. (Alvin Johnson scholar), New Sch. for Social Research, 1965; Ph.D. (NIMH grad. fellow), N.Y. U., 1970; m. Zipora Milner, June 21, 1964; children—Aaron M., Miriam S., David P., Hannah E. Lectr. in polit. sci. Bklyn. Coll., 1967-68; research asso. Center for Study Man, U. Notre Dame-Hunter Coll., N.Y.C., 1967-68; research social scientist, dept. psychiatry Georgetown U. Sch. Medicine, 1968-70; asst. prof. polit. sci. Fed. City Coll., 1968-70; social sci. analyst Nat. Center for Health Services Research, HEW, 1970-72, chief polit. and legal analysis br., 1972-74, chief health resources br. Office of Health Policy, Research and Statistics, Office Asst. Sec. Health, 1974-78, health policy analyst, 1978—; lectr. polit. sci. George Washington U., 1977; adj. prof. govt. Am. U., 1978; cons. NSF, 1974—; cons. profl. orgns. and state agys., 1971—. Mem. bd. edn. Hebrew Acad. Greater Washington, 1973—. Recipient Meritorious Service award HEW, 1972, Spl. Recognition award office Asst. Sec. for Health, 1977. Mem. Com. on Health Politics (exec. bd. 1973—), Phi Beta Kappa, Alpha Sigma Lambda. Co-author: Developments in Health Manpower Licensure, 1973; Credentialing Health Manpower, 1977; contbr. articles in health care regulation and manpower to profl. jours.; editorial bd. Jour. Health Politics, Policy and Law, 1976—. Home: 9105 Woodland Dr Silver Spring MD 20910 Office: Office Asst Sec Health US Dept Health Edn and Welfare 200 Independence Ave SW Washington DC 20201

COHEN, HARRY DAVID, investment co. exec.; b. Cleve., Dec. 6, 1940; s. Ben and Frances (Shatsky) C.; student Brandeis U., 1958-60; B.A., Case Western Res. U., 1962; M.S., Tufts U., 1964, Ph.D., 1966; m. Fern Davis, Sept. 1, 1962; children—Joseph, Susan. Fellow, Albert Einstein Coll. Medicine, 1966-68; investment adviser Hornblower & Weeks, N.Y.C., 1969—, v.p., 1975—; dir. Stuyvesant Asset Mgmt., 1975—, Hornblower Growth Fund, 1975—; lectr. in field. Bd. dirs. Port Youth Activities, Port Washington, N.Y., 1974—. NIH fellow, Harvard Med. Sch., 1964-65. Mem. AAAS, N.Y. Soc. Security Analysts. Clubs: Shore Tennis, Port Washington Tennis Acad. Contbr. articles in field to profl. jours. Home: 5 Angler Ln Port Washington NY 11050 Office: Loeb Rhoades-Hornblower 14 Wall St New York City NY 10005

COHEN, HENRY, coll. dean; b. N.Y.C., June 5, 1922; s. Abraham and Sadie (Sheftel) C.; B.S., Coll. City N.Y., 1942; M.C.P., Mass. Inst. Tech., 1944; postgrad. U. Iowa, 1942, Columbia U., 1947-48; m. Evelyn Fuhrman, Nov. 10, 1948; children—Alison Cohen Abelson, Daniel. Fellow dept. sociology Coll. City N.Y., 1941-42; resident South End Settlement House, Boston, 1942-44; team dir. displaced persons operation UN Relief Rehab. Adminstrn., 1946; lectr. dept. sociology Coll. City N.Y., 1946-47, asso dir. social research lab., 1947-48; research asso. Inst. Urban Land Use and Housing Studies, Columbia U., N.Y.C., 1948—; vis. lectr. sociology U. Birmingham (Eng.), 1949-50; asst. dir. Coventry Sociol. Survey, Eng., 1949-50; dir. research Dept. City Planning N.Y.C., 1950-55; project mgr. Metro Transit Project, Regional Plan Assn., N.Y.C., 1955-56; lectr. in planning Columbia U., 1951-61; cons. Regional Plan Assn., 1961-65; sr. mgmt. cons. Div. Adminstrn., Office of Mayor N.Y.C., 1955-61; dep. city adminstr. N.Y.C., 1961-64; vis. prof. Cornell U., Ithaca, N.Y., 1965-66; staff cons. on urban affairs Inst. Pub. Adminstrn., N.Y.C., 1964-66, dep. dir. human resources study, 1966; first dep. adminstr. Human Resources Adminstrn., N.Y.C., 1966-67; dean, dir. Center for N.Y.C. Affairs, prof. urban affairs New Sch. Social Research, N.Y.C., 1968—, dean Grad. Sch. Mgmt. and Urban Professions, 1978—. Vice chmn. Am. Jewish Com., N.Y.C., 1973—; bd. dirs. Consumer Credit Counseling Service Greater N.Y., 1973—, Fedn. Jewish Philanthropies, N.Y.C., 1978—, United Neighborhood Houses, N.Y.C., 1978—; chmn. human resources com. Citizens Union, 1968-73; governing bd. Council Univ. Insts. Urban Affairs, 1970-79, chmn. governing bd., 1973-75; mem. Conf. on Pub. Service, Brookings Instn., 1965-68; mem. Ford Found. Mission to Venezuela, 1962-63, others. Served with AUS, 1944-45. Chandler scholar, 1942-43. Mem. Am. Soc. Planning Ofcls., Am. Inst. Planners, Am. Soc. Pub. Adminstrn., Nat. Acad. Pub. Adminstrn., Nat. Assn. Schs. Pub. Affairs and Adminstrn., Am. Consortium Internat. Pub. Adminstrn., Phi Beta Kappa. Contbr. articles in field to profl. jours. Home: 37 W 12th St New York NY 10011 Office: 66 Fifth Ave New York NY 10011

COHEN, HERBERT JESSE, physician, educator; b. N.Y.C., Apr. 27, 1935; s. Barnet and Edith (Lepolstat) C.; B.A. (Ford Found. scholar), Columbia, 1955; M.D., State U. N.Y., 1959; m. Marion E. Finger, Aug. 29, 1960; children—Linda Elizabeth, Gerald Daniel, Seth Michael. Intern Bellevue Hosp., N.Y.C., 1959-60; resident N.Y. Hosp., N.Y.C., 1960-62; asst. instr. Cornell Med. Sch., 1961-62; instr. Tulane Med. Sch., 1962-64; NIH fellow Albert Einstein Coll. Medicine, 1964-66, asst. prof. pediatrics and rehab. medicine, 1966-71, asso. prof., 1971-76, prof., 1976—; dir. Children's Evaluation and Rehab. Clinic, Rose F. Kennedy Center for Mental Retardation and Human Devel., Bronx, N.Y., 1968-74; dir. Bronx Developmental Services, N.Y. State Dept. Mental Hygiene, 1971—; dir. Rose F. Kennedy U. Affiliated Facility Tng. Program, 1974—; mem. study sect. devel. behavioral scis. NIH, 1978—. Served with USPHS, 1962-64. United Cerebral Palsy Research and Edn. Found. fellow, 1966-68. Fellow Am. Acad. Pediatrics, Am. Acad. Cerebral Palsy, Am. Assn. Mental Deficiency, AAAS. Contbr. articles to profl. pubs. Office: R F Kennedy Center 1410 Pelham Pkwy S Bronx NY 10461

COHEN, IRVING DAVID, environ. cons. exec.; b. Bklyn., May 12, 1945; s. Harry and Fay (Michenberg) C.; B.E. in Chem. Engring., City. Coll. of N.Y., 1967; M.E., N.Y.U., 1970, postgrad. in Environ. Safety and Health, 1970—; m. Dorothy Ann Joseph, Aug. 21, 1966; children—Miriam Susan, Esther Heidi, Daniel Marc. Sr. process engr. Crawford & Russell, Inc., Stamford, Conn., 1967-71; asso. chem. engr. Hoffmann-LaRoche, Nutley, N.J., 1971-72; sr. project mgr. Woodward-Envicon, Inc., Clifton, N.J., 1972-75; pres. Enviro-Sciences, Inc., Denville, N.J., 1975—, Aero Instrumentation Resources, Inc., 1978—; cons. Environ. Defense Fund, Rockaway Twp. Environ. Commn.; expert environ. witness Rockaway Twp. Planning Bd. Mem. Am. Inst. Chem. Engrs., Am. Indsl. Hygiene Assn., Internat. Assn. for Pollution Control, Scientists Com. for Pub. Info., Air Pollution Control Assn., Nat., N.Y. assns. environ. profls. Jewish. Contbr. environ. impact reports for energy related projects. Home: 19 Copeland Rd Denville NJ 07834 Offices: 32 E 39th St New York City NY 10016 also 19 Copeland Rd Denville NJ 07834

COHEN, IRWIN, fin. economist; b. Bronx, N.Y., Feb. 29, 1936; s. Samuel and Gertrude (Levy) C.; B.S. in Accounting, N.Y. U., 1956, M.B.A. in Finance, 1964, M.A. in Econs., 1969; B.S. in Math., Coll. City N.Y., 1970. Fin. analyst SEC, N.Y.C., 1965-67, Fed. Res. Bank N.Y., N.Y.C., 1967-72; with Prudential Ins. Co. Am., 1973-74, SEC, N.Y.C., 1974—. Mem. Math. Assn. Am., Am. Finance Assn., Econ. History Assn., Internat. Platform Assn. (life). Home: 3555 Bruckner Blvd Bronx NY 10461

COHEN, JERALD LOUIS, computer exec.; b. N.Y.C., July 7, 1935; s. David Michael and Fay (Rosenberg) C.; B.A., N.Y.U., 1962; m. Lorraine Lovecchio, Jan. 30, 1970; children—Jennifer, Michelle. Computer programmer Kennedy Space Ctr., Mercury and Apollo Missions, Cape Kennedy, Fla., 1962-67; mgr. data center City U. of N.Y. 1967-75; mgr. computer ops. Burns & Roe, Inc. Nuclear Engrs., Paramus, N.J., 1975—; cons. in field. Served with U.S. Army, 1954-56. Mem. Data Processing Mgmt. Assn. (pres. Westchester Chpt. 1978, bd. dirs. 1975—), 4-Phase Users Assn. (v.p. 1978), Assn. Computing Machinery. Home: 74 Sarah Ln Middletown NY 10940 Office: 633 Indusl Ave Paramus NJ 07652

COHEN, JEROME, educator; b. Chgo., May 23, 1935; s. Herman and Irene (Gross) C.; A.A., Wright Jr. Coll., 1955; M.A., U. Chgo., 1959; Ph.D., Walden U., 1975; m. Faye Mandel, July 5, 1959; children—Miriam Pearl, David Aaron. Research asst. Indsl. Relations Center, Chgo., 1959-60; chmn. social studies dept. Chgo. Jewish Acad. High Sch., 1960-63; chmn. social sci. dept. Central YMCA Community Coll., Chgo., 1963-67; chmn. sociology dept. Barry Coll., Miami, Fla., 1968-70; adj. faculty in sociology U. Kans., also adminstrv. asst. in charge curriculum St. Luke's Hosp. Sch. Nursing, Kansas City, Mo., 1970-72; asst. prof. sociology, chmn. behavioral sci. dept. Atlantic Community Coll., Mays Landing, N.J., 1972-75; asst. prof. sociology Annhurst Coll., Woodstock, Conn., 1975-78; dir. div. liberal studies South Central Community Coll., New Haven, 1978—. Mem. Am. Sociol. Assn., Nat. Soc. for Study Edn., Center for Study Dem. Instns., Phi Alpha Theta. Author: The Structure of Forms of Human Inquiry, 1972; Foundations of Knowledge and Education: Exploring Epistemology and Education Through The Thought of Leonard Nelson, 1976. Home: 29 Robin Rd West Hartford CT 06119 Office: South Central Community Coll 60 Sargent Dr New Haven CT 06511

COHEN, JOEL MYRON, univ. adminstr.; b. Providence, Mar. 14, 1939; s. William Samuel and Dorothy Sadie (Blum) C.; B.A. in Math., U. R.I., 1960, M.S., 1962; M.P.H. in Biostatistics, Yale, 1965; m. Carolyn Loeb Scherz, June 11, 1961 (div. 1973); children—Rhonda, Lori, Rachelle. Tchr. math. Nathan Bishop Jr. High Sch., Providence, 1961-62; tchr. high sch. and adult edn. math. North Haven (Conn.) Dept. of Edn., 1962-63; statis. cons. Yale Med. Sch., 1964-65; chief statistician Tb chemotherapy analysis, Dept. of Medicine, VA, Washington, 1965-67; chief of research and evaluation sect. adult heath protection and aging br. Nat. Center for Health Services Research and Devel., USPHS, Washington, 1967-69; instr. dept. math. Bryant Coll., Providence, 1969-74; dir. Office of Research Adminstrn., R.I. Hosp., Providence, 1969-74; dir. grant and contract adminstrn. Children's Hosp. Med. Center, Boston, 1974-78; adminstr. mental retardation research center, 1977-78; adminstr. sponsored programs Brandeis U., 1978—. Mem. Am. Statis. Assn., Soc. Research Adminstrs., Biometric Soc., Nat. Council Univ. Research Adminstrn. (chmn. research adminstrs. discussion group 1975-77), AAAS, Kappa Delta Pi, Pi Mu Epsilon, Alpha Epsilon Pi. Office: 300 Longwood Ave Boston MA 02115

COHEN, LEONARD, ednl. adminstr.; b. Phila., Dec. 7, 1927; s. Meyer and Minnie (Nitzberg) C.; B.S. in Edn., Temple U., 1952, Ed.M., 1956, Ed.D., 1972; postgrad. U. Pitts., U. Wis.; m. Louise Mae Dubin, Apr. 3, 1955; children—Robert, Alan. Phys. edn. tchr. Ridley

Twp. Sch. Dist., Folsom, Pa., 1952-55; elementary tchr. Bensalem Twp. Sch. Dist., Cornwells Heights, Pa., 1955-58, Abington Twp. Sch. Dist., Abington, Pa., 1958-60; prin. Marple Newtown Sch. Dist., Newtown Square, Pa., 1960-69; supervising prin. Chester Twp. Sch. Dist., Brookhaven, Pa., 1969-71; asso. prof. East Stroudsburg (Pa.) State Coll., 1972; supt. No. Lehigh Sch. Dist., Slatington, Pa., 1972—. Exec. com. Lehigh County United Way, 1972—; bd. dirs. Lehigh Valley Community Council, 1973—; pres. No. Lehigh Playground Assn., 1972—; instr., trainer Nat. Am. Red Cross, 1953—. Served with USN, 1946-47. Mem. Am., Pa. assns. sch. adminstrs., Pa. Sch. Bds. Assn., Council of Ednl. Facility Planners Internat. Jewish. Club: Slatington Rotary. Home: 1485 N 39th St Allentown PA 18104 Office: 1201 Shadow Oaks Ln Slatington PA 18080

COHEN, LOUIS MARK, ins. specialist; b. Brookline, Mass., Dec. 23, 1948; s. William Cohen and Harriet (Altshuler) Cohen Cronk; B.S.B.A., Northeastern U., 1971. Assigned risk technician Mass. Worker's Compensation Bur., Boston, 1967-73; comml. casualty underwriter, leadline workmen's compensation underwriter Fireman's Fund Am. Ins. Cos., Boston, 1973-75; sales rep. Met. Ins. Co., Norwood, Mass., 1976; sr. underwriter Ins. Co. N. Am., Boston, 1976—; bus. cons. CJS Cons., Norwood; pres. NEHOC Enterprises, Norwood; notary pub., real estate broker, ins. broker. Mem. Am. Soc. Notaries. Club: Elks. Office: PO Box 10 Norwood MA 02062 also PO Box 1793 Boston MA 02105

COHEN, MARTIN GERALD, psychologist; b. Boston, Sept. 19, 1950; s. Aaron Leon and Evelyn Rhoda (Wenetsky) C.; A.A.S., Rochester Inst. Tech., 1974; B.A., Salem State Coll., 1976; M.Ed., Northeastern U., 1977; m. Judyth L. Newman, June 19, 1977. Adminstrv. dir. Inst. for Family and Life Learning, Danvers, Mass., 1973-75; intern sch. counselor Newton (Mass.) Pub. Schs., 1976-77; vocat. counselor U.S. Dept. Labor, Boston, 1977; prin. Merrimack Edn. Center/Mini Sch., Chelmsford, Mass., 1977-78; counselor/coordinator CASE Youth Devel. Program, Concord, Mass., 1978—. Mem. Am. Personnel and Guidance Assn., Outward Bound Alumni Assn., Assn. Counselor Edn. and Supervision. Home: 6 Mayflower Dr Andover MA 01810 Office: Emerson Sch 42 Stow St Concord MA 01742

COHEN, MARTIN HARVEY, architect; b. Bklyn., Apr. 17, 1932; s. Benjamin and Beatrice (Wexler) C.; certificate in architecture Cooper Union Art Sch., 1952; B.Arch., Mass. Inst. Tech., 1954; m. Arline Sitner, Sept. 30, 1956; children—Bruce, Paul, Adam. Designer, Studio Architetti BBPR, Milano, Italy, 1955, Anderson, Beckwith & Haible, architects, Boston, 1955-56; architect Skidmore, Owings & Merrill, Architects, N.Y.C., 1956—, asso., 1963-73, asso. partner, 1973—; mem. N.Y.C. Landmarks Preservation Commn., 1968-73. Mem. adv. council Cooper Union Sch. Art and Architecture, 1967—; mem. adv. council historic Am. bldgs. survey Nat. Parks Service, 1973. Fulbright scholar, Italy, 1954-55; recipient Profl. Achievement citation Cooper Union, 1971. Mem. A.I.A. (awards com., chmn. historic bldgs. com., hosps. and health com., vice chmn. 1973—, urban design commn. N.Y. chpt. 1964—, nat. historic resources com. 1967-68, 71-74, chmn. 1973, nat. com. on architecture for health 1975—), Archtl. League N.Y., N.Y. Soc. Architects, N.Y. State Assn. Architects (com. on architecture for health 1975—, chmn. 1976—), Municipal Arts Soc. (adv. com. 1973—), Tau Beta Pi. Archtl. works include: 1st Nat. Bank, Ft. Worth, 1961; IBM Corp. Hdqrs., Armonk, N.Y., 1961-64; Yale Computer Center, New Haven, 1961; N.Y.C. Terminal Markets, Hunts Point, 1960-66; Beekman-Downtown Hosp., N.Y.C., 1963-66; N.Y. U. Med. Center, N.Y.C., 1965—; Kiewit Computation Center, Dartmouth Coll., Hanover, N.H., 1966; Otis Elevator Co., Yonkers, N.Y., 1973-76, Wausau (Wis.) Hosp., 1975—. Home: 40 Green Valley Rd Armonk NY 10504 Office: 400 Park Ave New York City NY 10022

COHEN, MARY ANN ADLER, psychiatrist; b. N.Y.C., July 2, 1941; d. Carl and Rose (Klipstein) Adler; student Bryn Mawr Coll., 1958-60; A.B., N.Y. U., 1962; M.D., Med. Coll. Pa., 1966; m. Richard Cohen, June 11, 1960; 1 son, Steven. Intern, Hosp. of Med. Coll. Pa., Phila., 1966-67; resident psychiatry Norristown (Pa.) State Hosp., 1971-72, Tremont Crisis Center, Bronx, N.Y., 1972-75; coordinator liaison psychiatry Fordham Hosp., Bronx, 1975-76; fellow in liaison psychiatry Montefiore Hosp., Bronx, 1976-77, attending psychiatrist, 1976—, liaison psychiatrist med. clinic, 1977—; clin. instr. Albert Einstein Coll. Medicine, Bronx, 1975—. Diplomate Am. Bd. Psychiatry and Neurology. Mem. Assn. for Academic Psychiatry, Psychosomatic Soc. Office: 127 W 79th St New York City NY 10024

COHEN, MAURICE, obstetrician, gynecologist; b. Winnipeg, Man., Can., Dec. 26, 1931; s. Max and Thelma (Slawsky) C.; came to U.S., 1958, naturalized, 1962; M.D., U. Man., 1957; m. Oct. 26, 1959; children—Adam, Alec, Nel. Intern, St. Boniface (Man.) Hosp., 1956-57; resident in pathology Albert Einstein Coll. Medicine, 1957-58, instr. in obstetrics and gynecology, 1962-64; resident in obstetrics and gynecology L.I. Jewish-Hillside Med. Center, New Hyde Park, N.Y., 1958-61; fellow in gynecology Columbia-Presbyn. Med. Center, N.Y.C., 1961-62; practice medicine specializing in obstetrics, gynecology and infertility, Bayside, N.Y., 1964—; mem. staff L.I. Jewish-Hillside Med. Center, New Hyde Park, Queens Hosp. Center, Jamaica, N.Y.; asst. prof. clin. obstetrics and gynecology State U. N.Y., Stony Brook. Diplomate Am. Bd. Obstetrics and Gynecology. Fellow A.C.S., Am. Coll. Obstetrics and Gynecology; mem. Am. Assn. Gynecol. Laparoscopists, Am. Fertility Soc., Soc. Study Reprodn., Queens Gynecol. Soc., Am. Assn. Sex Educators, Counselors and Therapists. Home: 69 Bayview Ave Great Neck NY 11021 Office: 223-01 Union Turnpike Bayside NY 11364

COHEN, MAX HARRY, surgeon; b. Macon, Ga., June 8, 1940; s. Harry M. and Rena C. (Cain) C.; A.B. with honors, Columbia Coll., 1961; M.D. with honors, Harvard U., 1965; Ph.D. with honors, George Washington U., 1970; m. Leslie G. Krupsaw, Apr. 23, 1969; children—Adam, Heather, Robyn. Intern, Mass. Gen. Hosp., Boston, 1965-66, resident in surgery, 1966-67, resident in surgery, 1970-72; practice medicine specializing in surgery, Washington; asst. prof. dept. microbiology George Washington U. Sch. Medicine, Washington, 1968-70; surg. scientist designee Mass. Gen. Hosp., 1970-72; sr. investigator Nat. Cancer Inst., NIH, Bethesda, Md., 1973-77; clin. asst. prof. surgery George Washington U., Washington and attending surgeon Washington Hosp. Center, 1977—; mem. staff Washington Hosp. Center, George Washington Univ., Suburban, Holy Cross and Montgomery Gen. hosps.; cons. in surgery Nat. Cancer Inst., Bethesda, Md., 1977—. Pres., Fox Den Civic Assn., 1976-78. Served with USPHS, 1967-69, 73-77. Recipient Nat. Health Found. award, 1957. Diplomate Am. Bd. Surgery. Fellow A.C.S.; mem. Montgomery County, D.C. med. socs., Am. Fedn. Clin. Research, Am. Soc. Microbiology, AMA, Boylston Med. Soc., Dean Van Amringe Hon. Soc., Phi Beta Kappa, Sigma Xi. Author: Beginning Chemistry: A Programmed Instruction Textbook, 1971; contbr. numerous articles on oncology to profl. jours. Home: 11412 Woodington Terr Potomac MD 20854 Office: Suite 402 10215 Fernwood Rd Bethesda MD 20034 also Suite 402 106 Irving St Washington DC 20010

COHEN, MICHAEL EDWARD, pediatric neurologist; b. Buffalo, May 7, 1937; s. Herman Laurence and Mamie Eleanor C.; student (Coll. scholastic scholar) Dartmouth Coll., 1954-57; M.D. with thesis honors, State U.N.Y., Buffalo, 1961; m. Joan Ruth Neuman, June 21, 1959; children—Shari Lynn, Pamela Sue, Nancy Beth. Intern, Univ. Hosp., Cleve., 1961-62, med. resident, 1962-63, resident in neurology, 1963-65; fellow in child neurology Boston Children's Hosp., 1963-65— spl. fellow NIH, Boston, 1965-66; dir. child neurology Children's Hosp. Buffalo, 1966, 68—; head div. child neurology State U. N.Y., Buffalo Sch. Medicine, 1977—, asso. prof. pediatrics and neurology, 1977—; pres. faculty council State U. N.Y. at Buffalo Sch. Medicine, 1978-79. Active United Jewish Fund, allocation com. United Way. Served as capt. M.C., U.S. Army, 1966-68. Diplomate Am. Bd. Psychiatry and Neurology in adult and child neurology, Am. Bd. Qualification in Electroencyphalography. Mem. AMA, Am. Epilepsy Assn., Am. Acad. Cerebral Palsy, Child Neurology Soc., Am. Acad. Neurology, Alpha Omega Alpha. Republican. Jewish. Contbr. articles to med. publs. Home: 8 Cid-del Way Williamsville NY 14221 Office: Children's Hosp Buffalo NY 14222

COHEN, NEIL, oral and maxillofacial surgeon; b. S.I., N.Y., May 8, 1933; s. Sam and Sylvia (Kirshner) C.; student U. Miami, 1950-53; D.D.S., U. Md., 1957; postgrad. N.Y. U., 1958-59; m. Audrey Phyllis Candor, Aug. 28, 1958 (div. 1972); children—Jane Elizabeth, Jennifer Ann; m. 2d, Cynthia Jane English, June 26, 1976. Intern, Beth Israel Hosp., Boston, 1957-58; resident Harlem Hosp., N.Y.C., 1959-60; practice dentistry specializing in oral and maxillofacial surgery Miami, Fla., 1960, Belmont, Mass., 1961, Burlington, Mass., 1961—; chief oral surgery Winchester (Mass.) Hosp.; mem. staffs Choate Meml. Hosp., Woburn, Mass., New Eng. Meml. Hosp., Stoneham, Mass., Emerson Hosp., Concord, Mass., Mt. Auburn Hosp., Cambridge; oral surgeon Harvard U. Health Services, Cambridge, 1962—; clin. asst. in oral surgery Harvard Sch. Dental Medicine. Fellow Internat. Assn. Oral Surgeons, Royal Soc. Health; mem. New Eng. Soc. Oral Surgeons, Am. Dental Assn., Mass. Dental Soc., Am., Mass. (v.p., 1967-68, pres. 1968-69) dental socs. anesthesiology, Am. Assn. Oral and Maxillofacial Surgeons, Mass. Soc. Oral and Maxillofacial Surgeons, Middlesex Dist. Dental Soc., Greater Boston Dental Soc., Alpha Omega. Club: Harvard (Boston). Contr. articles to profl. jours. Home: 19 Channing St Cambridge MA 02138 Office: 175 Cambridge St Burlington MA 01803

COHEN, PHILIP HERMAN, accountant; b. Bklyn., Dec. 4, 1936; s. David J. and Toby (Jaeger) C.; B.S., N.Y. U., 1957. With firm Touche, Ross, Bailey & Smart, N.Y.C., 1957-69, mgr., 1966-69; partner Touche Ross & Co., 1969—; lectr. in field. Bd. dirs. Alpha Epsilon Pi Found. Inc., Jewish Family Service. C.P.A., N.Y., La., Mich., N.C. Mem. Am. Inst. C.P.A.'s, N.Y. State Soc. C.P.A.'s (mem. faculty Edn. Found.; mem. admissions com. 1968-70; mem. finance and leasing industry com. 1970-72, chmn. com. 1972-74, mem. com. on relations with attys. 1974-76, real estate com. 1976—), Am. Accounting Assn., Nat. Assn. Accountants (dir. N.Y. chpt. 1970-76), Ins. Accountants Statis. Assn., Soc. Ins. Accountants, Am. Jewish Com., Areopagus, Alpha Epsilon Pi (supreme gov. 1966-69, supreme sentinel 1969-70, nat. treas. 1970-71, nat. sec. 1971-72, v.p. 1972-74, nat. pres. 1974-76, mem. fiscal control bd. 1977—), Beta Alpha Psi. Jewish (bd. govs. Synagogue 1964—). Mason. Club: New York Alumni of Alpha Epsilon Pi. Home: 44 W 62d St New York City NY 10023 Office: 1633 Broadway New York City NY 10019

COHEN, RICHARD, librarian; b. Miami, Fla., Feb. 11, 1928; s. Amaziah Melvin and Mamie (Evans) C.; student Morehouse Coll., 1945-46; B.S., Fla. A. and M. U., 1949, M.Ed., 1958; M.L.S., Rutgers State U., 1962. Tchr. pub. shcs. Dade County, Miami, 1950-54; sci. and bus. librarian Bklyn. Pub. Library, 1959-66; librarian Bd. Edn. N.Y.C., 1966—. Reference librarian N.Y. Times, part/time 1967-70. Chmn. 78 Manhattan Ave. Tenants Assn., N.Y.C., 1971—. Mem. N.Y. County Democratic Com., 1973. Served with AUS, 1954-56. Mem. ALA, Spl. Libraries Assn., Fla. A. and M. U. Alumni Assn. (treas. 1972-74, bus. mgr. N.E. region 1974-77). Home: 78 Manhattan Ave New York City NY 10025 Office: 170 Gates Ave Brooklyn NY 11238

COHEN, RONALD GEORGE, corp. exec. and information systems cons.; b. Phila., Oct. 6, 1930; s. Martin A. and Ray (Schwartz) C.; B.S., U. Pa., 1951; m. Gladys L. Miller, Jan. 8, 1955; children—Leslie, Amy, Debra, Joshua. Gen. mgr. Martin & Co., Phila., 1951-62; pres. Computab Assos., Phila., 1963-67, Automatic Data Processing Pa., Phila., 1968-73; pres. R.G.C. Enterprises, 1974—, Datamation Assos., Inc., 1976—, Penn Wax Works, Inc., Phila., 1977—. Troop com. chmn. Boy Scouts Am., 1961-64, instnl. rep., 1965-68; mem. bd. Westgate Hills Civic Assn., Havertown, Pa., 1956-74; chmn. trade council div. Allied Jewish Appeal, 1968-74. Bd. govs. Israel Bond Orgn., 1968; bd. dirs. Am. Friends Hebrew U.; research founder Inst. Immunology, Hebrew U. Named Man of Year Congregation Beth El Suburban, 1960-61; recipient Tribute award State of Israel Bonds, 1973. Mem. Greater Phila. C. of C., Better Bus. Bur., Franklin Inst., Phila. Mus. Art, Sigma Delta. Jewish religion (founder Beth El Suburban 1959; financial sec. 1964-66, pres. 1975-76). Mem. B'nai B'rith. Club: Mens of Congregation Beth El Suburban (pres. 1959-61) (Broomall). Home: 101 Quaker Ln Haverford PA 19041 Office: 5200 Unruh St Philadelphia PA 19135

COHEN, SAMUEL H., research biologist; b. Boston, May 11, 1938; s. Abraham and Esther C.; A.B., Boston U., 1960, M.A., 1963; M.S., Northeastern U., 1972; m. Marilyn Burstein, Nov. 15, 1960; children—Arnold, David. Lab. asst. Children's Cancer Research Found., 1962-64; research biologist, entomology group Pioneering Research Lab., Natick (Mass.) Labs., 1964-74, research biologist Food Sci. Lab., U.S. Army Natick Research and Devel. Command, 1974—. Mem. troop com. Algonquin council Boy Scouts Am., 1976-77. Served with USAR, 1961-66. Recipient Sci. Dir.'s Gold Pin award for research, 1978. Mem. AAAS, Electron Microscopy Soc., Northeastern U., Boston U. alumni assns. Jewish. Contbr. articles to profl. jours. Home: 43 Lohnes Rd Framingham MA 01701 Office: Food Sci Lab US Army Natick Research and Devel Command Natick MA 01760

COHEN, SAMUEL ISRAEL, clergyman, orgn. exec.; b. Asbury Park, N.J., Apr. 17, 1933; s. Meyer and Henrietta (Gershman) C.; B.A., Bklyn. Coll., 1955; M.R.E., Yeshiva U., 1959, Ed.D., 1967; m. Mira Hager, Sept. 5, 1960; children—Baruch Chaim, Michael Nachum, Miriam Rachel. Rabbi, 1956; exec. dir. L.I. Zionist Youth Commn., Queens, N.Y., 1957-61; regional dir. Supreme Lodge B'nai B'rith, Queens, 1961-66, dir. membership dept. 1, N.Y.C., 1966-72; nat. dir. orgn. Am. Jewish Congress, N.Y.C. 1972-74; exec. dir. Am. Zionist Fedn., 1974-77; exec. v.p. Jewish Nat. Fund, 1977—; adj. asst. prof. sociology L.I. U., 1967; lectr. sociology Queensborough Community Coll., 1968, adj. asst. prof., 1971-74; lectr. Borough of Manhattan Community Coll., 1968, adj. asst. prof., 1970-72; adj. asst. prof. John Jay Coll. Criminal Justice, 1973—; lectr. Herzl Inst., N.Y.C., 1974-78. Chmn. edn. adv. bd. Yeshiva Toras Chaim, Woodmere, N.Y., 1971-74; mem. Conf. Jewish Communal Service, 1970—. Bd. dirs. Union Orthodox Jewish Congregations Am., 1973—. Mem. Adult Edn. Assn. (mem. nat. com. on goals and objectives religious edn. sect., 1967-68), Young Israel of Wavecrest and Bayswater (v.p. 1973-75). Mem. B'nai B'rith (v.p. Briarwood Lodge, 1964). Home: 2904 Bayswater Ave Far Rockaway NY 11691 Office: 42 E 69th St New York City NY 10029

COHEN, SAMUEL WILLIAM, ophthalmologist; b. Elizabeth, N.J., Apr. 7, 1931; s. Jacob and Mary (Miller) C.; B.A., N.Y. U., 1951; M.D., U. Geneva, 1956; m. Frances Geldzahler, Aug. 20, 1969; children—Anne, Karen, Chaim-Howard, Rochelle, Shoshana. Intern, Jewish Hosp. and Med. Center, Bklyn., 1956-58, resident, 1958-61; fellow in corneal surgery Bklyn. Eye and Ear Hosp., 1965; practice medicine specializing in opthalmology, Bklyn. and N.Y.C., 1962—; instr. ophthalmology State U. N.Y., Bklyn., 1976—; asst. prof. ophthalmology N.Y. Med. Coll. Diplomate Am. Bd. Ophthalmology. Fellow A.C.S., Internat. Coll. Surgeons, Am. Acad. Ophthalmology and Otolaryngology; mem. AMA, Soc. Eye Surgeons, Pan Am. Assn. Ophthalmology, N.Y. Ophthalmol. Soc., N.Y. State Soc. Surgeons, Phi Beta Kappa. Jewish. Contbr. articles to profl. lit.; patentee sports games. Home: 4401 Beach 44 St Brooklyn NY 11224 Office: 522 Ocean Ave Brooklyn NY 11226

COHEN, SANFORD IRWIN, physician, educator; b. N.Y.C., Sept. 5, 1928; s. George A. and Gertrude C. (Slater) C.; A.B. magna cum laude, N.Y.U., 1948; M.B., M.D., Chgo. Med. Sch., 1952; m. Jean Steinbruecker, Nov. 30, 1952; children—Jeffrey, Debra, John, Robert Intern, Jackson Meml. Hosp., Miami, Fla., 1952-53; resident in psychiatry U. Colo. Med. Center, 1953-54, resident psychiatry Duke Med. Center, 1953-54, 57-58, mem. faculty, 1956-68, prof. psychiatry, 1964-68, head div. psychosomatic medicine and psychophysiol. research, 1964-68, lectr. psychology, 1966-68; instr. Washington Psychoanalytic Inst., 1965-68; prof. psychiatry, chmn. dept. Boston U., 1970—; cons. VA Hosp., Durham, N.C., 1957-68, NIMH, 1963-66. Served to capt., USAF, 1955-57. Recipient Robert Morse award for excellence in sci. writing, 1964; Founds. Fund for Research in Psychiatry fellow, 1958-63; Commonwealth Fund fellow, 1966; named Distinguished Alumnus Chgo. Med. Sch., 1968. Diplomate Am. Bd. Psychiatry and Neurology. Fellow Am. Psychiat. Assn., Am. Coll. Clin. Pharmacology; mem. AAAS, Am. Psychosomatic Soc., [illegible]. Biologic Psychiatry, Am. Psychoanalytic Soc.. Clubs: Union (Boston); New Orleans Jazz. Contbr. articles to profl. jours., chpts. in books. Home: 25 Somerset Rd Lexington MA 02173 Office: Boston University Boston MA 02118

COHEN, SEYMOUR MARTIN, physician; b. N.Y.C., Dec. 19, 1936; s. Harry and Rose (Ehrlich) C.; B.A., Bklyn. Coll., 1957; B.Med. Sci., U. Geneva, 1959; M.D., U. Pitts., 1962; m. Carole J. Pomerantz, Aug. 16, 1976; 1 son, Roger. Intern, Montefiore Hosp., N.Y.C., 1962-63, asst. resident in medicine, 1963-64; resident in medicine Mt. Sinai Hosp., N.Y.C., 1964-65, Am. Cancer Soc. fellow in hematology, 1965-66, mem. staff, 1973—; fellow in hematology L.I. Jewish Hosp., 1968-69; pvt. practice medicine specializing in med. oncology and hematology, N.Y.C., 1969—; physician-in-charge oncology Booth Meml. Hosp., Flushing, N.Y.; clin. asso. in medicine Mt. Sinai Med. Sch., 1969-73, sr. clin. asst. physician in medicine, 1969-73, asst. clin. prof. medicine, 1973-78, asso. clin. prof. medicine, 1979—; mem. Eastern Coop. Oncology Group. Mem. exec. com. Jewish Am. Polit. Action Com., 1975—; bd. govs. State of Israel Bonds, 1979. Served as capt. M.C., USAF, 1966-68. Diplomate Am. Bd. Internal Medicine. Fellow A.C.P.; mem. Am. Soc. Clin. Oncology, Internat., Am. socs. hematology, AAUP, N.Y. Cancer Soc., AMA, New York County Med. Soc. Contbr. articles to profl. publs.; research on malignant melanoma. Office: 1045 Fifth Ave New York City NY 10028

COHEN, STAFFORD IRWIN, cardiologist; b. Boston, May 29, 1934; s. Alfred and Dora (Mittleman) C.; A.B. magna cum laude, Brown U., 1956; M.D., Boston U., 1961; m. Deborah Rosen, May 30, 1960; children—Matthew, Gregory. Intern, Beth Israel Hosp., Boston, 1961, resident, 1962-63, chief resident, 1965; resident in cardiology Mt. Sinai Hosp., N.Y.C., 1964; asso. prof. medicine Harvard Med. Sch., Boston, 1976—; practice medicine, specializing in cardiology, Boston, 1969—; dir. med. intensive care unit Beth Israel Hosp., Boston, 1969—. Served with USPHS, 1966-68. Diplomate Am. Bd. Internal Medicine. Fellow Am. Coll. Cardiology, A.C.P.; mem. Clin. Council Am. Heart Assn., Phi Beta Kappa, Alpha Omega Alpha. Contbr. articles in field to med. jours.; editor: Critical Cardiac Care, 1978. Office: Beth Israel Hosp 330 Brookline Ave Boston MA 02215

COHEN, STANLEY, dentist; b. Bklyn., July 30, 1937; s. Leo and Zina (Hyner) C.; B.A., N.Y. U., 1959, D.D.S., 1963; postgrad. Inst. Grad. Dentists, 1970; m. Joan Bitsky, June 12, 1960; children—Scott Jordan, Jaimi Alison, Stacey Lauren. Practice dentistry, East Brunswick, N.J., 1962—; lectr. Fairleigh Dickinson Coll. Dentistry. Served with Dental Corps, U.S. Army, 1963-64. Fellow Am. Assn. Anesthesia in Dentistry; mem. Am. Dental Soc., N.J. State, Middlesex County dental socs., Internat. Assn. Orthodontics, Royal Soc. Health, Acad. Gen. Dentistry, Dental Arts Profl. Study Group, Am. Inst. Implantology, Am. Soc. Children's Dentistry, East Brunswick C. of C. Jewish. Mem. B'nai B'rith. Home: 50 Sevenoaks Circle Holmdel NJ 07733 Office: 385 Cranbury Rd East Brunswick NJ 08816

COHEN, STEPHEN PAUL, sch. psychologist; b. Gloucester, Mass.; s. Benjamin and Harriet C.; B.A. in Psychology, L.I. U., 1970; M.A. in Psychology, New Sch. Social Research, N.Y.C., 1972; postgrad. Western Colo. U. Psychologist, Neighborhood Youth Corps, Lowell, Mass., 1974; psychol. technician Reiss Mental Health Pavilion, St. Vincent's Hosp., N.Y.C., 1971-72; instr. psychology Mt. Wachusett Community Coll., Gardener, Mass., 1974; sch. psychologist Winthrop (Mass.) Pub. Schs., 1974—; instr. Newbury Jr. Coll.; cons. psychologist. Certified sch. psychologist; certified in learning disabilities, secondary teaching, Mass. Mem. Am. Psychol. Assn., Mass. Sch. Psychologists Assn., Nat., Mass., Winthrop tchrs. assns. Clubs: Lowell Bicycling, Alpine Mountain Climbing. Author: A Sequence of Remedial Skills in the Area of Behavior and Preschool Screening Instrument. Home: 173 Princeton Blvd Lowell MA 01851 Office: Winthrop Public Schools Winthrop MA 01851

COHEN, STEVEN MARK, hosp. exec.; b. Bronx, Nov. 14, 1943; s. Meyer and Pearl C.; B.B.A., Adelphia U., 1965; M. Health Adminstrn., C.W. Post Coll., 1975; m. Cynthia Meisner, July 3, 1965; children—Amy, Heather, Jason. Sr. accountant Haskins & Sells, C.P.A.'s, N.Y.C., 1965-69; asst. dir. fiscal services Beth Israel Med. Center, N.Y.C., 1969-73; dir. fiscal services St. Joseph's Hosp., Yonkers, 1977—. C.P.A., N.Y.; recipient Follmer award Hosp. Fin. Mgmt. Assn., 1976. Mem. Hosp. Fin. Mgmt. Assn. (sec. Met. N.Y.C.), N.Y. State Soc. C.P.A.'s, Am. Inst. C.P.A.'s. Home: Ridge Rd Katonah NY 10536 Office: 127 S Broadway Yonkers NY 10701

COHEN, SYDNEY MORRIS, indsl. engr.; b. Allentown, Pa., Jan. 17, 1924; s. Isador and Sadie Miriam (Miller) C.; B.S. in Indsl. Engring., Lehigh U., 1947; m. Harriet Kremer, Oct. 28, 1956; children—Alan, Nancy. Indsl. engr. Newark Air Force Contract Mgmt. Dist., Newark, 1963-65, resident USAF engr. RCA Space Center, Princeton, N.J.; indsl. engr. prodn. engring. div. Hdqrs. Def. Contract Adminstrn. Services, Cameron Station, Alexandria, Va., 1965-68, U.S. Army Safeguard System Office, Arlington, Va., 1968-73, Hdqrs. USAF, Washington, 1973—. Vice pres. Monticello Woods Civic Assn., Springfield, Va., 1974-76. Served with U.S. Army, 1943-45. Decorated Silver Star, Purple Heart, Bronze Star. Registered profl. engr., Pa., Del. Mem. Res. Officers Assn. (pres. George Washington chpt. 1976—), Am. Def. Preparedness Assn., Air Force Assn., Am. Legion, Jewish War Vets., Nat. Timberwolf Assn. Club:

Mason. Home: 5943 Thomas Dr Springfield VA 22150 Office: HQ USAF-RDCM Washington DC 20330

COHEN, WILLIAM JOHN, urban planner; b. Wilmington, Del., July 30, 1941; s. Edward Joseph and LV Dolores C.; B.A., M.A., U. Del.; children—Edward Joshua, Rebecca Anne. Sr. planner Del. Planning Office, Dover, 1967-71; planning dir. City Newark, Del., 1971-77; pres. William J. Cohen & Assos., planning cons., Newark, 1977—. Mem. Am. Inst. Cert. Planners, Del. Assn. Pub. Adminstrn. (pres. 1976-78). Contbr. planning articles to profl. publs. Office: 342 Paper Mill Rd Newark DE 19711

COHEN, WILLIAM NATHAN, radiologist; b. Balt., Dec. 10, 1935; s. Herbert and Lillian (Goldberg) C.; student Johns Hopkins U., 1952-55; M.D., U. Md., 1959; m. Sylvia Weinstein, Feb. 9, 1964; children—Elaine, Shirah, Jonathan. Intern, U. Mich. Hosp., Ann Arbor, 1959-60; resident in radiology Mallinckrodt Inst., Washington U., St. Louis, 1960-63; chief radiology sect. Gallup Indian Hosp., USPHS, 1963-65; asst. prof. radiology U. Iowa, Iowa City, 1965-69, asso. prof., 1969-73, prof., 1973-76; prof. radiology State U. N.Y. Upstate Med. Center, Syracuse, 1976—. Fellow Am. Coll. Radiology; mem. Radiol. Soc. N. Am., Am. Roentgen Ray Soc., Am. Inst. Ultrasound in Medicine. Contbr. articles in field to med. jours. Office: Dept Radiology Upstate Med Center Syracuse NY 13210

COHEN, WILLIAM SEBASTIAN, senator; b. Bangor, Maine, Aug. 28, 1940; s. Reuben and Clara (Hartley) C.; B.A. cum laude (James Bowdoin scholar 1961-62, Alumni Fund scholar 1962), Bowdoin Coll., 1962; LL.B. cum laude, Boston U., 1965; LL.D., St. Joseph's Coll., Windham, Maine, 1974, U. Maine, 1975, Western New Eng. Coll., 1975, Bodwoin Coll., 1975, Nasson Coll., 1975, m. Diane Dunn, Jan. 6, 1962; children—Kevin, Christopher. Admitted to Maine bar, 1965; partner Paine, Cohen, Lynch, Weatherbee & Kobritz, Bangor, 1966-72; instr. Husson Coll., 1966; instr. U. Maine, 1968-72; asst. county atty. Penobscot County, Maine, 1968-70; mem. 93d-95th Congresses from 2d Maine Dist.; senator from Maine, 1979—. Mem. Zoning Bd. Appeals, 1967-69, Bangor Sch. Com., 1970-71. Mem. Bangor City Council, 1969-72, chmn. finance com., 1970-71; mayor, Bangor, 1972. Trustee Unity Coll.; bd. overseers Bowdoin Coll. Recipient Sewall Latin prize, 1961, Emery Latin prize, 1962, Paul Nixon award for leadership; Distinguished Service award as outstanding young man Jaycees, 1973; named to N.E. Hall of Fame Basketball Team, 1962; named Outstanding Young Man of Year Nat. Jaycees, 1975. James Bowdoin scholar, 1961-62, Alumni Fund scholar, 1962. Mem. Am. (asst. editor-in-chief Jour. 1965-66, co-editor vols. 32 and 33 jour.), Maine (v.p. 1970-72) trial lawyers assns. Author: Of Sons and Seasons (poetry). Home: 1632 Maddux Ln McLean VA 22101 Office: US Senate Washington DC 20510

COHLER, JONAS, psychoanalyst; b. Chgo., July 15, 1934; s. Jonas Robert and Therese Isabell C.; B.A. with honors cum laude, U. Mich., 1956; Ph.D. in Clin. Psychology, Harvard U., 1962; certificate in psychoanalysis William Alanson White Inst. Psychiatry and Psychoanalysis, N.Y.C., 1969; m. Lisa Selsby; children—Eric, Jennifer, Matthew. Lectr. dept. social relations Harvard U., 1961-64; research asso. Mass. Mental Health Center, 1961-64; instr. psychiatry Columbia U., 1964-65; cons. mental health Luth. Ch. Am., N.Y.C., 1964-71; cons. ITT Corp., N.Y.C., 1964—; gen. practice psychoanalysis, N.Y.C., 1969—; clin. asst. prof. psychiatry Cornell Med. Coll., 1977—; clin. asso. Columbia U. Tchrs. Coll., 1977—; supr. low cost clin. services Wm. Alanson White Psychoanalytic Inst., 1978—. Fellow Social Sci. Research Council, 1955, USPHS, 1956-57, 65-66. Mem. Am. Group Psychotherapy Assn., Am. Psychol. Assn., William Alanson White Psychanalytic Soc., Harvard Grad. Soc. (bd. govs.). Clubs: N.Y. Corinthians, Sag Harbor Yacht. Contbr. articles to profl. jours. Address: 126 E 74th St New York City NY 10021

COHN, BERTRAM DOUGLAS, pediatric surgeon; b. N.Y.C., May 7, 1926; s. Isaac H. and Anna (Stein) C.; B.S. cum laude, N.Y. U., 1945, M.D., 1948; m. Rosalie Block, Mar. 17, 1978; children by previous marriage—Jonathan, Mark, Jeanne, Susan. Intern, Bellevue Hosp., N.Y.C., 1948-49, Maimonides Med. Center, Bklyn., 1949-50; resident Montreal (Que.) Children's Hosp., 1950-51, 53-55, VA Hosp., N.Y.C., 1955-56; practice medicine specializing in pediatric surgery, Bklyn., 1956—; dir. pediatric surgery service Maimonides Med. Center; cons. surgeon to hosps.; clin. asso. prof. surgery State U. N.Y. Downstate Med. Center; teaching fellow in surgery McGill U., Montreal, 1954-55. Served with M.C., USAF, 1951-53. NIH grantee, 1960-62; NIH research fellow, 1960-62. Diplomate Am. Bd. Surgery. Fellow A.C.S., Am. Acad. Pediatrics; mem. Am. Pediatric Surg. Assn. (charter), N.Y. Soc. Pediatric Surgery (founder), Phi Beta Kappa, Alpha Omega Alpha. Contbr. articles to med. jours.; patentee caval filter, inserter; inventor slide-rule calculater, surg. instruments. Home and Office: 8420 Ridge Blvd Brooklyn NY 11209

COHN, JAMES RONALD, indsl. hygienist; b. Cin., Oct. 27, 1949; s. Reuben Robert and Leah Jean (Norwich) C.; B.S. in Biology, U. Cin., 1971, M.S. in Environ. Health, 1973. USPHS trainee, 1971-73; research asst. dept. surgery U. Cinn., 1973-74; indsl. hygienist Occupational Safety and Health Adminstrn., U.S. Dept. Labor, Washington, 1974-77; occupational health specialist Allied Chem. Corp., Morristown, N.J., 1977—. Mem. Am. Indsl. Hygiene Assn., Am. Conf. Govtl. Indsl. Hygienists. Research on trace metal metabolism and excretion. Designer govtl. occupational health standards for coke oven emissions. Office: PO Box 1057R Morristown NJ 07960

COHN, MARTIN DAVID, lawyer; b. Hazleton, Pa., Aug. 31, 1925; s. Samuel A. and Hannah (Levine) C.; B.A., Pa. State U., 1945; LL.B., Harvard U., 1950; m. Elsie Bohard, Oct. 6, 1946; children—Lawrence B., Hanna S., Sandra J., Judith T., Joseph S., David C. Admitted to Pa. bar, 1951; instr. polit. sci. Pa. State U., 1947, part-time instr., 1951-61; instr. Tufts U., 1948-50; partner firm Laputka, Bayless, Ecker & Cohn, Hazleton, 1953—. Chmn. Greater Hazleton United Fund Campaign, 1957; spl. asst. atty. gen. Commonwealth of Pa., 1955-63; v.p. Keystone Shortway Assn., 1956—. Mem. nat. bd. United Synagogue of Am.; bd. overseers Jewish Theol. Sem. Am., N.Y.C., 1972—. Served with USAAF, 1945-47. Mem. Pa. (mem. corp. law sect. 1967-71), Am. bar assns., Greater Hazleton C. of C. (pres. 1969-71). Jewish. Mem. B'nai B'rith (mem. nat. commn. on adult Jewish edn. 1961—, nat. chmn. 1971-77, hon. chmn. 1977—). Editorial bd. Jewish Heritage mag., 1961-77. Home: 100 Harding St Hazleton PA 18201 Office: Citizens Bank Bldg Hazleton PA 18201

COHN, NATHAN, bus. exec.; b. N.Y.C., Oct. 24, 1915; s. Jacob and Lillie (Robinson) C.; B.S., Coll. City N.Y., 1937; M.B.A., N.Y. U., 1938; m. Helen Scherer, July 6, 1946; children—Janet Teresa (Mrs. Michael Singer), Barry Howard, Steven Joseph. Instr., N.Y. Inst. Finance, 1938-42; security analyst Mabon & Co., 1938-42, 45-48; auditor C.E. Dept. of War, 1942-45; bus. mgr., controller Saturday Rev., 1948-61, v.p., treas., 1961-72; sr. v.p., treas., dir. Saturday Review World Inc., N.Y.C., 1972-77; sec., treas. Saturday Rev. Mag. Corp., 1977—. Chmn. United Jewish Appeal. Mem. N.Y. Soc. Security Analysts. Jewish (trustee congregation; chmn. budget and fin. com.). Home: 17 Anpell Dr Scarsdale NY 10583 Office: 1290 Ave of Americas New York City NY 10019

COHN, NORMAN UNGER, industrialist; b. Waterloo, Iowa, Jan. 2, 1933; s. Maurice W. and Bess (Unger) C.; B.A., State Coll. Ia., 1957; m. Suzanne Dubiecki, Feb. 14, 1965; 5 children. Chmn. bd. Nat. Bus. Service, Trevose, Pa.,; dir. numerous corps. including Creative Specialty Mfrs., Studio One, Comml. Paper Co., Colorcrafters, Santa Claus Warehouses, Comml. Travel Agy., Nat. Colorcrafters Studios, Retail Grocers, Internat. Mdse. Corp., Twilight Oil Refinery, Royal Windsor China. Chmn. Council Original 13 States. Bd. dirs. Customer Relations Research Found. Served with AUS, 1957-62, Air N.G. Mem. Young Pres. Orgn. (mem. internat. bd.). Home: 200 Pine Tree Rd Radnor PA 19087 Office: NBS Bldg 2d and Clearview Sts Trevose PA 19047

COHN, ROBERT, realtor; b. Binghamton, N.Y., Aug. 25, 1928; s. Myer David and Mollie (Berger) C.; student Siena Coll., 1946-47; B.S., U. Ala., 1950; real estate course Russell Sage Coll., 1953; m. Elaine Janet Frisch, July 10, 1955; children—Debra Ann, Cynthia Lynn. Salesman, O'Connor-Sullivan Real Estate, Albany, N.Y., 1952-55; v.p., co-owner Patroon Agy., real estate and ins., Albany, 1955-60; v.p., sales mgr. Philip E. Roberts Real Estate, Albany, 1960-65; pres., owner Cohn, Yaguda, Cronin Realty, Inc., Albany, 1965—. Instr. Grad. Real Estate Inst. N.Y. Mem. Albany County Bd. Realtors (pres. 1971), N.Y. State (pres. comml. investment div. 1974, chmn. pub. affairs com. 1971-72, trustee real estate polit. edn. com.), Nat. assns. real estate bds., Nat. Inst. Real Estate Bds., Comml.-Indsl. Real Estate Brokers (certified comml. investment mem., pres. capital dist. 1977-78), Albany (dir.), Delmar, chambers commerce, Sigma Alpha Mu. Rotarian (pres. Delmar chpt.); mem. B'nai B'rith. Home: 115 Berwick Rd Delmar NY 12054 Office: 11 N Pearl St Albany NY 12207

COHN, ROBERTA KIMMEL, art dealer, graphic designer; b. Milw., Feb. 1, 1937; d. Maurice David and Helen Theresa (Pollak) Kimmel; student Sophie Newcomb Coll., 1955-56, U. Wis., 1956, 1961; B.F.A., Boston U., 1959; m. Richard A. Cohn., May 28, 1971. Designer, New Am. Library, N.Y.C., 1959-60; art dir. McGraw Hill Co., N.Y.C., 1961-62, McMillan Pubs., N.Y.C., 1964-65, Walker & Co., N.Y.C., 1966-67; owner, designer Roberta Kimmel Advt. Co., N.Y.C., 1967—; partner Kimmel-Cohn Photography Arts, N.Y.C., 1973—. Mem. Soc. Advancement of Judaism N.Y.C. Author: Erste Landung, portfolio of photographs by G. Grosz, 1977; Man Ray, Vintage Photographs, Rayographs & Solarizations, 1977. Home: 41 Central Park W New York City NY 10023 Office: One W 64th St New York City NY 10023

COHN, ROY MARCUS, lawyer; b. N.Y.C., Feb. 20, 1927; s. Albert and Dora (Marcus) C.; B.A., Columbia, 1946, LL.B., 1947. Admitted to N.Y. State bar, 1948; with U.S. dist. atty.'s office, N.Y.C., 1947-52, asst. U.S. atty., 1948-50; confidential asst. to U.S. atty. Saypol, 1950-52; spl. asst. to U.S. atty. gen. McGranery, 1952; chief counsel U.S. Senate Permanent investigations sub-com. 1953-54, partner firm Saxe, Bacon & Bolan, and predecessor firm, N.Y.C., 1959—; prof. law N.Y. Law Sch., 1957—. Pres. Am. Jewish League Against Communism. Regent St. Francis Coll., N.Y.C.; trustee Roy M. Cohn Found. Capt., N.Y. State N.G. Recipient ann. award lawyers div. Fedn. Jewish Philanthropies, 1952; Americanism award Am. Legion N.Y. State, 1956; Patriotism award Cath. War Vets, 1970, award of merit, 1975; award Conservative Party of N.Y. County, 1975, 78. Mem. Am., Bronx County bar assns. Club: Studio 54 (N.Y.C.). Author: McCarthy, 1968; A Fool for a Client, 1971; The Answer to Tail Gunner Joe, 1977. Home: Witherell Dr Greenwich CT 06830 Office: 39 E 68th New York City NY 10021

COHN, SANFORD JAY, educator; b. Hanover, Pa., Nov. 29, 1945; s. Benjamin Kahanovitz and Rose Hilda (Goldman) C.; B.A., Johns Hopkins U., 1967, M.Ed., 1976, M.A., 1978, Ph.D., 1979. Project asso. intellectually gifted child study group Johns Hopkins U., Balt., 1974-76, project asso. study of mathematically precocious youth, 1976, asst. dir. study, 1977—, editor Intellectually Talented Youth, Bull., 1977—; cons. Nat. Interagency Task Force on Gifted and Talented Youth, 1978; speaker in field. Mem. Am., Eastern psychol. assns., Am., Eastern ednl. research assns., Sigma Xi, Phi Delta Kappa, Phi Beta Kappa, Omicron Delta Kappa, Phi Lambda Upsilon, Delta Phi Alpha. Jewish. Club: Johns Hopkins. Contbr. articles to med. and sci. jours. Home: 5953 Western Run Dr #A Baltimore MD 21209 Office: Ames 126 Johns Hopkins U Baltimore MD 21218

COHO, JAMES PRESTON, lawyer; b. Lancaster, Pa., July 6, 1919; s. Ralph W. and Lillie (Eby) C.; A.B., Franklin and Marshall Coll., 1941; J.D., Dickinson Sch. Law, 1944; m. Helene E. Boetzel, Aug. 18, 1945; children—Linda, Jeffrey P. Admitted to Lancaster bar, 1945; asso. G. T. Hambright, Esquire, 1945-48; partner firm Hamaker & Coho, 1949-51; individual practice, 1952—. Dir. Way Oil Co. Law instr. Pub. Service Inst., Pa. Dept. Edn., 1947-68. Trustee Dickinson Sch. Law, 1968-71; pres. advisory bd. St. Joseph Hosp., 1977—. Mem. Am., Fed., Pa. (chmn. appellate rev. com. 1960-63), Lancaster bar assns., Pa., Lancaster chambers commerce, Am. Arbitration Assn., Nat. Assn. Accountants, Lancaster Cemetery Assn. (dir., pres. 1977—), Pa. Soc. N.Y., Pa., Lancaster hist. socs., Soc. Pa. Archaeology, Am. Judicature Soc., Internat. Platform Assn., Chi Phi. Republican. Mem. United Ch. Christ. Rotarian, Mason (Shriner), Elk. Clubs: University (past pres.), Hamilton, Lancaster Country, Lancaster Pirates, Traffic. Home: 23 Glen Moore Circle Lancaster PA 17601 Office: 53 N Duke St Lancaster PA 17602

COLABELLA, CALVIN MICHAEL, architect; b. East Orange, N.J., May 10, 1927; s. Alfred V. and Edith (Colucci) C.; student Stevens Inst. Tech., 1947; B.Arch., Columbia, 1953; m. Jean Mary Tino, Sept. 12, 1953; children—Calvin Michael, Christopher Mark. Architect R.B. Flatt, Bloomfield, N.J., 1953-58; individual practice architecture, 1959-60; partner Colabella & Passaforo, Architects, Newark, 1961-68; prin. Colabella Architects, 1969—; instr. div. tech. N.J. Inst. Tech. Served with USNR, 1945-46. Registered profl. architect, N.J., N.Y., Fla., Ohio, Va., Mass. Mem. Nat. Council Archtl. Registration Bds., A.I.A., Constrn. Specifications Inst., N.J. Soc. Architects (dir., v.p. Newark chpt. 1968, pres. 1969), Caldwell Bus. Community Assn., Unico. Roman Catholic. K.C. Home: 45 Highview Rd Caldwell NJ 07006 Office: 295 Bloomfield Ave Caldwell NJ 07006

COLAIANNI, JOSEPH VINCENT, judge; b. Detroit, Mar. 19, 1938; s. P. and Marie D. (Mastrantonio) C.; B.E.E., U. Detroit, 1956; J.D. with honors, George Washington U., 1961; m. Rita M. Roll, Oct. 13, 1961; children—Marie Elena, Joseph Vincent, Michael Philip, Vincent Gerard. With Burroughs Corp., Detroit, 1956-62, design engr., patent law dept., Washington, 1958-61, atty., Detroit, 1961-62; admitted to Mich. bar, 1961, Ohio bar, 1962, D.C. bar, 1964; asso. firm Marshall, Wilson & Yeasting, Toledo, 1962-63, Fay & Fay, Cleve., 1963-66; trial atty. U.S. Dept. Justice, Washington, 1966-70; trial judge U.S. Ct. Claims, Washington, 1970—; mem. Fed. Sci. Liaison Com. to Establish Sci. Ct. Bd. dirs. Hudson Valley Montessori Sch., Washington; mem. advisory bd. City Dist. Heights (Md.), 1967-72. Mem. Am., Fed., D.C. bar assns. Club: Lido. Home: 6309 Windermere Circle Bethesda MD 20852 Office: 717 Madison Pl NW Washington DC 20005

COLANGELO, DOMENICK ANTHONY, mental health and child guidance center exec.; b. N.Y.C., Sept. 11, 1911; s. Michael and Giulia (Menna) C.; B.A. cum laude, Coll. City N.Y., 1944; M.S.S., Fordham U., 1947; m. Pauline C. Filloramo, Jan. 25, 1942; children—Juliette Colangelo Bryan, Anita Colangelo-Curran, Gloria Colangelo-White. Asst. chmn. social welfare dept. Ben Franklin High Sch., N.Y.C., 1935-38; supr. Dept. Welfare, N.Y.C., 1938-44; caseworker Cath. Guardian Soc., N.Y.C., 1944-47; psychiat. casework cons., supr. Cath. Charities Guidance Inst., N.Y.C., 1947-52; exec. dir. Child Guidance Center of Mercer County, Trenton and Princeton, N.J., 1952-75; pvt. practice, 1975—; dir. devel. Cath. Welfare Bur., Trenton; exec. dir. N.J. Assn. Mental Health Agys.; cons. parent-child relations; lectr. family problems, child guidance; mem. adv. bd. program for adolescent mothers St. Vincent de Paul Soc., 1969—; mem. steering com. N.J. Mental Health Planning Com., 1965; bd. dirs. Bucks County Dept. Child Welfare, Doylestown, Pa., 1963—, v.p., 1966, pres., 1966-68, 77-78; profl. adv. com. Mercer County Mental Health Bd.; mem. Bucks County Crime Commn.; mem. Trenton Diocese Com. on Edn. in Human Sexuality. Pres. Valley Day Sch., Edgewood, Pa., 1958-62, bd. mem., 1958—; pres. Friends of Valley Day Sch., 1975—. Licensed marriage counselor, N.J. Mem. Am. Assn. Psychiat. Clinics for Children (treas. 1965-67, liaison officer com. on regions 1965-67, evaluations visitor membership com. 1962—, chmn. membership com. 1970-72), N.J. Assn. Mental Hygiene Clinics (legis. com. chmn. 1957-61), Mercer County Assn. Mental Health (dir. 1958-70), Nat. Assn. Social Workers (registered clin. social worker, Social Worker of Year award N.J. chpt. 1970, N.J. del. 1972-75), Acad. Certified Social Workers, N.J. Assn. Mental Health Agys. (v.p. 1969-70, pres. 1971-72, exec. dir., editor Newsletter 1970-71), Conf. Agy. Execs. Mercer County (chmn. 1962-64). Democrat. Clubs: Mercer County Social Welfare (Trenton, N.J.). Editor newsletter Am. Assn. Psychiat. Clinics for Children, 1962-65; contbr. articles to various newspapers and mags. Home: 430 W Palmer St Morrisville PA 19067

COLASANTE, JOHN, jewelry co. exec.; b. Providence, Dec. 5, 1932; s. John and Theresa (Thomas) C.; student R.I. Sch. Design, 1952-53; m. Jennie Zanfagna, Sept. 30, 1950; children—David, Deborah, John, Patricia, Michael, Elaina, Phillip. Apprentice model maker Anthony Creations, Jewelry, Providence, 1949-51; dept. foreman, model maker Genser Mfg. Co., jewelry, Providence, 1951-53; designer, model maker in charge prodn. Frank L. Wilmarth Co., 1953-63; v.p., treas. Tru-Art Co., Inc., Jewelry, 1963-69; pres., treas. David Allan Co. and Crestmark Corp., Jewelry, Johnston, R.I., 1963—. Mem. Mfg. Jewelers Sales Assn. (dir.), Mfg. Jewelers and Silversmiths of Am., Providence Jewelers Club, United Comml. Travelers, Internat. Platform Assn., Smithsonian Instn. Club: Quidnessett Country. Home: 109 Winsor Ave Johnston RI 02919 Office: 6 Industrial Ln Johnston RI 02919

COLBURN, NORMA ELAINE WHEELER, city ofcl.; b. St. Johnsbury, Vt., June 26, 1933; d. Clayton Wallace and Ida Minerva (Lang) Wheeler; student Burdett Coll., 1951, Rutgers U., 1968; m. James Austin Colburn, Jan. 19, 1952; children—Candice Margaret, James Austin. Exec. sec. Oswald L. Sanborn C.P.A.'s, Ridgewood, N.J., 1952; exec. sec. archtl. div. Am. Brakeshoe Co., Mahwah, N.J., 1952; postal clk. U.S. P.O., Lyndon Center, Vt., 1956-60; partner Colburn's Store, Lyndon Center, Vt., 1956-60; corr., feature writer Burlington (Vt.) Free Press, 1959-60; dep. borough clk., ct. clk., Allendale, N.J., 1968-70, sec. planning bd., dep. water collector, 1969-70, borough clk., 1970—, borough adminstr., 1972—. Active Girl Scouts U.S.A., 1965-66. Recipient Time Mag. Current Events award, 1950, 51. Mem. Municipal Clks. Assn. N.J., Bergen County Municipal Clks. Assn., Internat. Inst. Municipal Clks. Mem. Order Eastern Star. Home: 310 Brookside Ave Allendale NJ 07401 Office: Office City Clk City Hall Allendale NJ 07401

COLBURN, ROBERT MARSHALL, educator; b. Knoxville, Tenn., July 26, 1937; s. Robert Talbot and Helen (Pearson) C.; B.A., Haverford Coll., 1959; M.S., U. Del., 1963; m. Dorothy Middleton Rowlett, June 17, 1960; children—Robert Dickinson, Bruce Garland, Kathryn St. Clair. Tchr. chemistry, physics and math., baseball and football coach St. Andrews Sch., Middletown, Del., 1960-78, tchr. chemistry, dir. athletics, baseball and football coach, 1978—. Trustee Broadmeadow Sch., Middletown; vestryman St. Anne's Episcopal Ch., Middletown, 1970-72. Mem. Nat. Sci. Tchrs. Assn., Baseball Coaches Assn. Del. (sec.), Del. Athletic Dirs. Assn. Research in carbamates derived from 4-aminopyrimidines, 1960-63. Home and Office: Saint Andrews Sch Middletown DE 19709

COLBY, BARNARD LEDWARD, former newspaper publisher; b. New London, Conn., Feb. 28, 1911; s. Irving and Madelaine (Ledward) C.; A.B., Lafayette Coll., 1933; m. Ruth M. Andrews, Oct. 23, 1937; children—Robert Andrews, David Pierce, Dorothy (Mrs. Michael R. Durham). Reporter, New London Evening Day, 1933-47, city editor, 1947-49, asst. gen. mgr., 1949-59, gen. mgr., 1959-64, pub., 1964-76, pub. emeritus, 1976—; sec. Day Pub. Co., 1950-67, treas., 1959-67, exec. v.p., 1967-73, pres., 1973-76, also dir.; trustee Day Trust, 1959-76; former corporator, trustee Savs. Bank of New London; dir. Meriden Record Co. (Conn.); former mem. New London adv. bd. Hartford Nat. Bank & Trust Co. Chief, New London Census Bur., 1945-47. Trustee Alfred Mitchell Woods Assn., Mitchell Coll., Conn. Pub. Expenditure Council; trustee, corporator, bd. mgrs. Lawrence and Meml. Hosp.; corporator Conn. Blue Cross, bd. dirs., 1969-71. Mem. Navy League, Am. Newspaper Pubs. Assn. (dir. 1960-68, trustee, sec. found. 1962-72, dir., sec. research inst. 1962-70), Inter Am. Press Assn., New Eng. (sec. 1959-66, v.p. 1966-68, pres. 1968-70), Conn. (pres. 1958-60) daily newspapers assns., Southeastern Conn. C. of C. (pres. 1966, dir. 1950-53, 63-66), Acad. New Eng. Journalists, Sigma Delta Chi (Yankee Quill award 1971), Delta Kappa Epsilon. Republican. Episcopalian. Mason, Rotarian (dir. 1956-59). Author: New London Whaling Captains, 1936; Thirty-One Generations, 1947, rev. edit., 1969. Home: 17 Quinnipeag Ave New London CT 06320

COLBY, PAUL, nightclub owner, impressario, music pub. co. exec.; b. Phila., Oct. 4, 1927; s. Isadore and Jennie (Keshdin) C.; student pub. schs., N.Y.C. With Remick Music Co. (Warner Bros. Pub. Co.), Barton Music Co., N.Y.C., 1946-50; custom furniture designer, 1951-59; mgr. Bitter End Cafe, N.Y.C., 1966-68, partner, 1968—; owner, operator Other End Cabaret/Restaurant, N.Y.C., 1974—; pres. Cunhill Road Music Corp., N.Y.C. 1972—. Home: 250 E 51st St New York City NY 10022 Office: 149 Bleecker St New York City NY 10012

COLDWELL, LAWRENCE HOWARD, agriculturalist; b. Port Williams, N.S., Can., Nov. 12, 1917; s. Eldon Edson and Julia Shaw (Illsley) C.; m. Edith Lucy Sutton, Apr. 8, 1947; children—Gregory Ross, Susan Durell, Kathryn Edith, Carol Ann. Farmer, Port Williams, 1935-40, 46-76; pres. Scotian Gold Coop., Kentville, N.S., 1969—; vice-chmn. N.S. Farm Loan Bd., Truro, 1964—; dir. N.S. Resources Devel. Bd., Halifax, N.S., 1972—, N.S. Tobacco Mktg. Bd. Trustee Murdoch Smith Meml. Library, 1970—; commr. Village of Port Williams, 1976 councillor Kings County, 1977—. Served with RCAF, 1942-45. Mem. N.S. Fruit Growers Assn. (pres. 1973), N.S. Potato and Vegetable Growers Assn. (pres. 1967-68), Soil and Crops Assn., Fedn. Agr., Royal Canadian Legion (br. pres. 1952). Mem.

Anglican Ch. Club: Masons. Home: Box 152 Port Williams NS B0P 1T0 Canada

COLE, ELMA PHILLIPSON (MRS. JOHN STRICKLER COLE), social welfare exec.; b. Piqua, Ohio, Aug. 9, 1909; d. Brice Leroy and Mabel (Gale) Phillipson; A.B., Berea Coll., 1930; M.A., U. Chgo., 1938; m. John Strickler Cole, Oct. 3, 1959. Various positions in social work, 1930-42; dir. social service dept. Children's Hosp. of D.C., 1942-49; cons. in pub. cooperation Midcentury White House Conf. on Children and Youth, 1949-51; exec. sec. Nat. Midcentury Com. for Children and Youth, 1951-53; cons. on recruitment Am. Assn. Med. Social Workers, 1953; asso. dir. Nat. Legal Aid and Defender Assn., 1953-56; exec. sec. Marshall Field Awards, Inc., 1956-57; dir. asso. orgns. Nat. Assembly Social Policy and Devel., 1957-73, asso. exec. dir., 1974; project dir. edn. for parenthood Salvation Army, 1974-76, asst. sec. women's and children's social services dept., 1976—, mem. adv. bd., N.Y.C., 1975—, mem. hist. commn., 1978—; cons. to nat. orgns. Golden Anniversary White House Conf. on Children and Youth, 1959-60; mem. adv. council on pub. service Nat. Assn. Life Underwriters and Inst. Life Ins., 1961-74; advisory adv. bd. Sexuality Edn. Project The Population Inst., 1977—; mem. judges com. Louis I. Dublin Pub. Service awards, 1961-74. Mem. com. on pub. relations and fund raising Am. Found. for Blind Commn. on Accreditation, 1964-67; past chmn. personnel and program com. Salvation Army Foster Care and Adoption Service, N.Y.C. Mem. Pub. Relations Soc. Am. (accredited), Nat. Assn. Social Workers (accredited), Nat. Conf. on Social Welfare (com. on pub. relations 1961-66, 69—, vice chmn. 1978—; chmn. adminstrn. sect. 1966-67), Blue Ridge Inst. So. Community Service Execs. (v.p. 1977—), N.Y.C. Advt. Club, Jr. League Washington, Ohio Soc. N.Y., Pi Gamma Mu, Phi Kappa Phi. Club: Women's of N.Y. Contbr. articles to profl. jours., also encys. Home: 19 Washington Sq N New York City NY 10011 Office: 120 W 14th St New York City NY 10011

COLE, FRANCIS VERNON, lawyer; b. Buffalo, June 6, 1906; s. Vernon and Helen Genevieve (Corbett) C.; A.B., Canisius Coll., 1927; LL.B., Yale, 1930; m. Kathleen Mary Griffin, Sept. 15, 1962. Admitted to N.Y. bar, 1933; asso. firm Morey & Schlenker, Buffalo, 1930-33, Killeen & Sweeney, 1933-42; atty. NLRB 3d Region, 1942-43; labor relations mgr. Houdaille-Hershey Corp., Buffalo, 1943-45; mem. firm Phillips Lytle Hitchcock Blaine & Huber (formerly Kenefick Cooke Mitchell & Bass), Buffalo, 1945—; lectr. socio-legal dept. Canisius Coll., 1936-46. Asst. dir. N.Y. State Works Progress Adminstrn., 1935-36; organizer Democratic Lawyers Club, 1954—; trustee St. Louis Roman Cath. Ch. Mem. Am., N.Y. State, Erie County bar assns., Buffalo World Hospitality Assn., Buffalo Hist. Landmark Soc. Clubs: Buffalo, Mid-Day. Home: 10 Brompton Circle Williamsville NY 14221 Office: 3400 Marine Midland Center Buffalo NY 14203

COLE, JOYCE, artist; b. N.Y.C., Sept. 3, 1939; d. David and Ethel Cohn; B.A. in Art History, Finch Coll., 1961; m. Robert Spitzer, Aug. 29, 1963. Exhibited in one-woman shows: Aldrich Mus., N.Y.C., 1974, Tower Gallery, Southampton, L.I., 1974, Susan Caldwell Gallery, N.Y.C., 1977, Gloria Luria Gallery, Fla., 1978; group shows: Andre Emmerich Gallery, N.Y.C., 1972, Whitney Mus., N.Y.C., 1973, Galerie Denise Rene, N.Y.C., 1974, Santa Barbara (Calif.) Mus., 1975, Meadow Brook Art Mus., Calif., 1975, Lehigh U., Pa., 1978. Mem. Art Students League, Archtl. League N.Y., Inst. Archtl. and Urban Studies, Coll. Art Assn., Artists Equity Assn. Clubs: Lexington; Nat. Arts; Lotus.

COLE, LARRY, psychologist; b. Chgo., June 15, 1936; s. Jay Morris and Sally (Goldberg) C.; B.A., Reed Coll., 1958; B.S., U. Oreg., 1959; postgrad. U. Conn., 1959-61; Ph.D., Columbia U., 1965; m. Sharlene Michelle Goldmen, Aug. 30, 1959. Intern psychology VA Hosp., Northampton, Mass., 1960-61; asso. research scientist N.Y. State Dept. Mental Hygiene, Rockland State Hosp., 1961-62; founder, exec. dir. Lower Eastside Action Project, youth orgn., N.Y.C., 1962-73; dir. Inst. for Juvenile Justice, 1969-75; cons. U.S. Senate Com. Juvenile Delinquency, N.Y.C., 1970—; pvt. practice adolescent psychotherapy, N.Y.C., 1963—; mem. faculty Franconia Coll., 1964-65, U. San Francisco, summer 1972. Mem. adv. com. Dist. Sch. Bd., 1968—. Norman Found. fellow, 1969-70; Ford Found. travel and study grantee, 1973. Mem. Eastern Psychol. Assn., Nat. Pilots Assn., Authors Guild, Am. Assn. Humanistic Psychology, Acad. Polit. and Social Sci., Psi Chi. Author: Street Kids, 1970; Our Children's Keepers, 1972; Suburb Kids, 1979. Contbr. articles to jours., mags. Host weekly radio show Growing Up in N.Y., Sta. WRVR, 1970-75. Office: care Lynn Nesbit ICM 40 W 57th St New York NY 10019*

COLE, LEONARD AARON, polit. scientist, dentist; b. Paterson, N.J., Sept. 1, 1933; s. Morris and Rebecca (Harelick) Cohen; student Ind. U., 1951-53; D.D.S., U. Pa., 1957; B.A. with highest honors in Polit. Sci., U. Calif., at Berkeley, 1961; M.A., Columbia, 1965, Ph.D., 1970; m. Ruth L. Gerber, July 7, 1957; children—Wendy Marcia, Philip Arthur, William Edward. Dental extern Children's Hosp. of East Bay, Oakland, Calif., 1960; pvt. dental practice, Hawthorne, N.J., 1961—; lectr. polit. sci. William Paterson Coll., 1970—. Pres. Glen Rock Human Relations Council, 1969-70. Served to capt. Dental Corps, USAF, 1957-59. Mem. Am. Dental Assn., Am. Soc. Dentistry for Children, Am. Polit. Sci. Assn., AAAS, Americans for Dem. Action (mem. N.J. bd. 1965-70), Acad. Polit. Sci., Phi Beta Kappa, Alpha Omega (pres. 1956-57). Author: Blacks in Power, 1976. Contbr. articles to profl. jours.; item writer in polit. sci. Ednl. Testing Service. Home: 381 Crest Rd Ridgewood NJ 07450 Office: 723 Lafayette Ave Hawthorne NJ 07506

COLE, NED, bishop; b. California, Mo., Feb. 6, 1917; s. Ned and Gladys (Walser) C.; B.A., Westminster Coll., Fulton, Mo., 1939, D.D., 1957; postgrad. U. Mo. Law Sch., 1939-40; B.D., Episcopal Theol. Sch., Cambridge, Mass., 1948; m. Martha Elizabeth Dunlap, Dec. 28, 1950 (div. 1977); children—Deborah Anne, Stephen Eberly, Elizabeth Ann, David Brooks. Sec. to Mo. sec. state, 1940-42; ordained to ministry Episcopal Ch.; 1948; curate, Columbia, Mo., 1948-49; rector, Jefferson City, Mo., 1949-56; vicar in Portland, Mo., 1949-56; dean Christ Ch. Cathedral, St. Louis, 1956-64; bishop co-adjutor Diocese Central N.Y., Syracuse, 1964-69, bishop, 1969—. Mem. gen. bd. Nat. Council Chs., 1963-66; mem. com. of nine Episcopal House of Bishops, 1964-73; mem. Bd. Theol. Edn., P.E. Ch., 1970-76, chmn., 1972-76, mem. Joint Com. Constn. and Canons, 1977—; mem. legis. commn. N.Y. Council Chs., 1964-67; Episcopal rep. to Consultation of Ch. Union, 1968-72; rep. exec. council Province II, P.E. Ch., 1967-69; mem. Syracuse div. N.Y. State Commn. Human Rights, 1964-67, Human Rights Commn. Syracuse and Onondaga County, 1965-67, Onondaga Neighborhood Legal Services, 1966-67. Served with USAAF, 1942-46. Home: 107 Parsons Dr Syracuse NY 13219 Office: 310 Montgomery St Syracuse NY 13202

COLE, ROBERT C., vocat. guidance counselor, author; b. Italy, Aug. 12, 1903; s. Nicholas and Philomena Cole; A.B., Syracuse U., 1929; A.M., Clark U., 1935; spl. grad. study in guidance at Columbia, Boston U.; m. Madeleine Burch, July 1, 1929; children—Kimyon, Robert C. Asst. supt. in charge guidance and personnel Boys Club of N.Y., 1929-30; dir. edn. and guidance Worcester (Mass.) Boys Club, 1930-43, asst. exec. dir., dir. edn. and guidance, 1943-54, exec. dir., 1954—; counselor and cons. in vocat. guidance Worcester Acad., 1939—; dir. vocat. guidance Worcester Vets. Service Center, 1943-53; lectr. vocational guidance and problems of boys. Chmn. vocat. guidance com., mem. nat. program com., dir. Boys Clubs Am., Worcester Community Concerts, So. Worcester County Health Assn.; mem. exec. council Worcester YMCA; mem. Worcester Found. Exptl. Biology; mem. Jr. High Sch. Conf., N.Y. U., 1940-41. Bd. dirs. Central Mass. Lung Assn., Mt. St. Ann's Orphanage. Mem. Nat. (profl.), Worcester (pres.) vocat. guidance assns., Am. Personnel and Guidance Assn., Boys Clubs Execs. Assn., Boys Clubs Profl. Assn., Mass. Tb and Health League, Mass. Conf. Social Work, Syracuse U. Alumni Assn., Clark U. Alumni Assn., Worcester County Mus. Assn., Am. Assn. Study Group Work, Pi Mu Epsilon, Kappa Phi Kappa. Methodist. Mason. Clubs: Monday Evening, Torch (Worcester); Green Hill Country. Author: An Evaluation of the Vocational Guidance Program in Worcester Boys Club, 1939; Vocational Guidance for Boys, 1941. Editorial bd.: Profiles mag.; contbr. to Program Service, Jour. of Edn., Vocational Guidance Digest, Keystone, Jour. Boys Clubs Am. Home: 152 Morningside Rd Worcester MA 01602

COLE, SHERWOOD ORISON, psychologist; b. North Scituate, R.I., May 28, 1930; s. Wesley Potter and Ruth Emily (King) C.; B.A. in Psychology, U. Calif., Santa Barbara, 1958; M.A. in Psychology (USPHS grantee), U. Calif., Los Angeles, 1961; Ph.D. in Psychology (USPHS grantee), Claremont Grad. Sch., 1964; m. Dorothy Louise Cole; 2 children. Asst. prof. psychology Calif. State Coll., Fullerton, 1964; asso. prof. Whitworth Coll., 1965-66; asst. prof. Rutgers U. Camden Coll. Arts and Scis., 1966-67, asso. prof., 1967-72, prof., 1972—, acting chmn. dept. psychology, 1966-67, chmn. 1967-74; vis. investigator in psychopharmacology Rutgers Research Council; fellow lab. psycho-biology and psychopharmacology Consiglio Nazionale delle Richerche, Rome, 1971-72. Served with Med. Service Corps, USN, 1951-54. NSF grantee, 1967; USPHS grantee, 1974-75; Rutgers Research Council grantee, 1974-75. Fellow Royal Soc. Health (Eng.); mem. Am., Eastern psychol. assns., AAAS, Psychonomic Soc., N.J. Acad. Sci. (chmn. sect. psychology 1976, 78 meetings), Psi Chi. Contbr. numerous articles to profl. publs.; reviewer for profl. jours. Office: Rutgers U Psychology Dept Camden NJ 08102

COLE, STEPHEN ADAMS, psychiatrist; b. Washington, Dec. 18, 1940; s. Gordon Henry and Malvine (Gescheidt) C.; A.B., Cornell U., 1961; M.A. (NSF fellow in History and Philosophy of Sci.), Harvard U., 1964; M.D., Columbia U., 1970, Robert Wood Johnson Clin. Scholars Program, 1975-77; m. Dalen Lucia Sciarra, Jan. 27, 1974. Intern in psychiatry Roosevelt Hosp., N.Y.C., 1970-71; resident in psychiatry Albert Einstein Coll. Medicine, Yeshiva U., N.Y.C., 1971-74, fellow in social and community psychiatry, 1974-75; extern Child Guidance Clinic, Family Tng. Center, Phila., 1976-77; instr. clin. psychiatry Columbia U., N.Y.C., 1975-77; dir. family therapy unit Manhattan VA Hosp., N.Y.C., 1977—; asst. prof. psychiatry N.Y. U.; asst. attending Univ., St. Luke's hosps.; adj. asst. attending Lenox Hill Hosp. Vol. U.S. Peace Corps, Nepal, 1964-66. Served with USPHS, 1971-75. NIMH Mental Health Career Devel. Program Fellow, 1971-75; recipient Physicians Recognition award AMA, 1978. Diplomate Am. Bd. Psychiatry and Neurology. Mem. Am. Psychiat. Assn., Am. Anthropol. Assn., AAAS, Soc. Med. Anthropology, Soc. Liaison Psychiatry. Democrat. Contbr. articles in field to profl. publs. Home: 652 W 163rd St Apt 6 New York City NY 10032 Office: Psychiatric Service Manhattan VA Hospital 24th St and 1st Ave New York City NY 10010

COLEMAN, BERNELL, physiologist; b. Jefferson County, Miss., Apr. 26, 1929; s. Percy and Julia (Nailor) C.; B.A., Alcorn A. and M. Coll., 1952; Ph.D. (Univ. fellow), Loyola U. Stritch Sch. Medicine, Chgo., 1964; m. Annie C. Richardson, Jan. 30, 1962; children—Rochelle, Ronald. Instr., St. Louis U. Sch. Medicine, 1963-65, asst. prof. physiology, 1965-67; asst. prof. Chgo. Med. Sch., 1967-69, asso. prof., 1969-76, prof., 1976; prof. Howard U. Coll. Medicine, 1976—; lectr. Cook County Grad. Sch. Medicine, U. Ill. Med. Sch.; vis. prof. Rush Med. Coll. Served with U.S. Army, 1953-56; Korea. Recipient research award Chgo. Med. Sch. Bd. Trustees, 1975; NIH research fellow, 1960-61; NIH grantee, 1966-68, 69-74, 74-76; USPHS fellow, 1961-63; Dept. Def. grantee, 1965-67. Mem. AAUP, Am. Physiol. Soc., Am. Heart Assn., AAAS, Fedn. Am. Socs. Exptl. Biology, Sigma Xi, Phi Rho Sigma. Democrat. Research, numerous publs. in cardiovascular physiology. Home: 14200 Myer Terr Rockville MD 20853 Office: 520 W St NW Washington DC 20059

COLEMAN, CATHERINE OFFLEY, headmistress; b. Burlington, Iowa, Feb. 9, 1921; d. Francis A. and Catherine (Robertson) Coleman, Jr.; A.B. magna cum laude, Sweet Briar Coll., 1942; M.A., Mills Coll., 1946; postgrad. State U. Iowa, Ind. U., U. Va., Yale. Sec., math. tchr., asst. dean St. Katharine's Sch., Davenport, Iowa, 1943-45; tchr. St. Anne's Sch., Charlottesville, Va., 1946-50, dormitory head, 1947-50, dean, 1950-56; headmistress, tchr. sacred studies Hannah More Acad., Reisterstown, Md., 1956-64; headmistress St. Paul's Sch., Walla Walla, Wash., 1964-66, St. John's Parish Sch., Olney, Md., 1966-78; mem. NE regional panel secondary sch. cons. Coll. Entrance Exam. Bd., 1962-64. Mem. exec. com. Diocesan Schs. Assn., 1966-78, chmn., 1971-76; mem. Diocesan Council, 1970-72, Diocesan Standing Com., 1973-77, sec., 1976-77, judge Diocesan Ct. Appeals, 1975. Mem. Citizens Planning and Housing Assn., 1957-64. Mem. Assn. Chaplains and Tchrs. Religion in Ch. Schs. (chmn. 1959-60), Episcopal Sch. Assn. (mem. council 1960-66, 71-76, mem. commn. on Old and New Testament curriculum, 1971-78), Assn. Ind. Schs. Greater Washington (sec.-treas. 1973-75), Nat. Assn. Prins. Schs. for Girls, Natural Bridge Conf. (vice chmn. 1952-56), Soc. Bibl. Lit. and Exegesis, Nat. Assn. Bibl. Instrs., Am. Schs. Oriental Research, Cum Laude, Md. Hist. Soc., Religious Edn. Assn., Phi Beta Kappa. Contbr. articles to profl. jours. Address: 3008 Bel Pre Rd Wheaton MD 20906 Died July 5, 1978.

COLEMAN, JAMES EDWARD MARSHALL, naval architect, marine engr.; b. Manila, P.I., Jan. 10, 1935; s. Herbert McClellan and Georgeanne DeRudio (Marshall) C.; B.S. in Marine Engring., Calif. Maritime Acad., 1956; postgrad. Navy War Coll., Indsl. Coll. Armed Forces, Armed Forces Mgmt. Sch. Commd. ensign U.S. Navy, 1958, advanced through grades to comdr., 1972; engring. officer Waterman Corp., S/S Wacosta, 1956-58; active duty, 1958-62; project engr. Vitro Labs., Silver Spring, Md., 1962-66; marine engr. Naval Ship Engring. Center, Hyattsville, Md., 1966-72; ret., 1972; naval architect, program mgr. Naval Sea Systems Command, Washington, 1972—; staff material officer Naval Surface Force Atlantic, Det 606; instr. Emergency Med. Technicians, State of Md.; coach Naval Academy Sailing Squadron; former patrol leader Nat. Ski Patrol. Mem. Soc. Naval Architects and Marine Engrs., Am. Soc. Naval Engrs., Assn. Sr. Engrs., Naval Inst., Navy League, Naval Res. Assn., Res. Officers Assn. Clubs: Ft. Meade Flying. Home: 1A Shipwright St Annapolis MD 21401 Office: Naval Sea Systems Command PMS 383 Washington DC 20362

COLEMAN, JOHN INGRAM, comml. artist; b. Johnstown, Pa., Jan. 19, 1921; s. Carl Frank and Catherine Eleanor (Ingram) C.; student U. Ky., 1942-43; m. Betty Toms, July 29, 1944; 1 son, Keith. By-products engr. coke plant Bethlehem Steel Corp., Johnstown, Pa., 1941-42; asso. editor Army Map Service, Washington, 1946; staff artist Johnstown (Pa.) Tribune Pub. Co., 1947—, editorial cartoonist Tribune-Democrat, 1952—. Adv. com. comml. art Johnstown Area Vo-Tech. Sch. Active YMCA, Boy Scouts Am., United Fund. Served with C.E., AUS, 1942-46; ETO. Republican. Presbyterian. Home: 133 Dahlia St Johnstown PA 15905 Office: 425 Locust St Johnstown PA 15907

COLEMAN, JOHN ROBERT, educator; b. New London, Conn., Sept. 20, 1943; s. Thomas George and Katherine Elinor (Hutchins) C.; B.S. in Mech. Engring., U. Conn., 1966; M.S.I.E., U. Mass., 1968, Ph.D. in Health Systems, 1975; m. Jere Jean Garrett, Aug. 23, 1969; 1 dau., Jennifer Arlene. Research asst. Health Systems Mgmt. Center, Sch. Bus. Adminstrn., U. Conn., 1969-71, research asso., 1971-78; research asso. health systems program, dept. indsl. engring. and ops. research U. Mass., Amherst, 1974-78; asst. prof. dept. mgmt. sci. U. New Haven, 1974-76, asso. prof. dept. pub. adminstrn., 1976—, chmn., 1977-78, dir. Bur. Bus. Research, 1977—; cons. to hosps., group practices, health maintenance orgns., health ins. cos. Legal com. mem. N. Central Conn. Health Systems Agy., 1976-78, vice chmn. Subarea-E, 1976-78. Am. Assembly Collegiate Schs. Bus. Fed. Faculty fellow, 1978-79. Mem. Ops. Research Soc. Am., Am. Inst. Indsl. Engrs., Soc. Advanced Med. Systems, Group Health Assn. Am., Pi Tau Sigma, Alpha Pi Mu, Phi Kappa Phi. Author: Designing Medical Services for Health Maintenance Organizations, 1977; Financial Design and Administration of Health Maintenance Organizations, 1977; contbr. articles to health jours. Home: 820 Hartford Turnpike Vernon CT 06066 Office: Dept Public Administration Univ of New Haven 300 Orange Ave West Haven CT 06516

COLEMAN, JOHN WILLIAM, physicist; b. N.Y.C.; s. John William and Melissa Teresa (Preston) C.; B.S., Howard U., 1950; M.S., U. Ill., 1957; Ph.D., U. Pa., 1963; m. Diane Mea Vaitses, June 5, 1962; children—Melissa Paula, Crystal McCleod. Instr. physics Howard U., Washington, 1957-58; physicist, engr., research leader RCA Corp., Camden, N.J., 1958-69; dir. of engring. Forgflo Corp., Sunbury, Pa., 1969-72; physicist Developmental Electron Optics Lab., Mass. Inst. of Tech., 1972—. Served Beverly Sch. Com., 1976—. Recipient U.S. Fulbright award, 1950, Lucy E. Moten award, 1950; AEC fellow, 1950; David Sarnoff fellow, 1963. Mem. Electron Microscopy Soc. Am., AAAS, Am. Physical Soc. Episcopalian. Contbr. research articles to profl. jours.; patentee electron optics research. Home: 18 Radcliff Rd Beverly MA 01915 Office: Mass Inst of Tech 26 468 77 Massachusetts Ave Cambridge MA 02139

COLEMAN, LOWELL THOMAS, pediatrician; b. Charleston, W.Va., July 9, 1934; s. Audrey C.; B.A., B.S., Medicine, W.Va. U., 1956; M.D., Med. Coll. Va., 1958. Intern, San Francisco Gen. Hosp., 1958-59, Children's Hosp. Cin., 1959-61; fellow in psychol. pediatrics Children's Hosp. Phila., 1963-65; practice medicine specializing in pediatrics; mem. staffs Children's Hosp. Phila., Penn Urban Health Assos., 1973—; asst. prof. pediatrics U. Pa., Phila., 1976-77; cons. in field. Served as capt. U.S. Army, 1961-63. Diplomate Am. Bd. Pediatrics. Mem. Am. Acad. Pediatrics, Am. Acad. Mental Deficiency, Nat. Assn. Edn. Young Children, Phila. Pediatric Soc., Phila. Assn. Retarded Citizens. Democrat. Home: 2409 Pine Philadelphia PA 19103 Office: 415 S 19th St Philadelphia PA 19146

COLEMAN, MARSHALL DONALD, psychiatrist; b. Utica, N.Y., Dec. 27, 1925; s. Jacob and Lucille (Smith) C.; A.B., Harvard U., 1948, M.D., 1952; m. Beverly Sitrin, June 28, 1949; children—Charles Theodore, Jacqueline Sue. Intern, Mass. Meml. Hosp., Boston, 1952-53; resident Boston Psychopathic Hosp., 1953-56; teaching fellow Harvard Sch. Medicine, 1953-56; mem. faculty Albert Einstein Sch. Medicine, 1956—, asst. clin. prof. psychiatry, 1960—; practice medicine specializing in psychiatry and psychoanalysis, N.Y.C., 1956—, Mamaroneck, N.Y., 1968—; mem. staff Jacobi Hosp., N.Y.C.; bd. advs. New Rochelle Guidance Clinic. Served with AUS, 1944-46. Fellow Am. Psychiat. Assn.; mem. N.Y. (trustee), Westchester (pres.-elect 1976) psychoanalytic socs., Internat., Am. psychoanalytic assns., Westchester Psychiat. Soc. Club: Harvard (Westchester, N.Y.). Address: 1030 Greacen Point Rd Mamaroneck NY 10543

COLEMAN, RICHARD PATRICK, sociol. researcher; b. Great Bend, Kans., July 21, 1927; s. Russell Patrick and Fern Jennifer (Wallace) C.; B.A., U. Tulsa, 1948; M.A., U. Iowa, 1949; Ph.D., U. Chgo., 1959. Research asso., com. human devel. U. Chgo., 1952-56; research asso. to v.p. and dir. Social Research, Inc., Chgo., 1957-69; sr. research asso. Joint Center Urban Studies, Mass. Inst. Tech. and Harvard U., 1969—. Cons. to Houston Post, TV and Radio Sta. div. Washington Post, Ind. Research Assos. Washington, Ira Glick & Assos., of Chgo. Mem. Sigma Xi, Lambda Chi Alpha. Club: Quadrangle (Chgo.). Author: (with Lee Rainwater) Workingman's Wife, 1959; TV Guide: A Study in Depth, 1960; (with Bernice Neugarten) Social Status in the City, 1971; (manual) The Index of Urban Status, 1971; (with David Birch) America's Housing Needs: 1970-1980, 1973; (with Lee Rainwater) Social Standing in America, 1978. Contbr. articles to profl. jours. Home: 246 Brattle St Cambridge MA 02138 Office: Joint Center Urban Studies 53 Church St Cambridge MA 02138

COLEMAN, STEPHEN JOEL, psychiatrist; b. Bklyn., May 12, 1942; s. David S. and Ida (Postelnek) C.; B.S., Hofstra U., 1963; M.D., U. Mich., 1967; children—Andrew Tarkin, Rebecca Lynne. Intern, Jackson Meml. Hosp. (Outstanding intern award), Miami, Fla., 1967; resident N.Y. U.-Bellevue Med. Center, 1968-70, chief resident, 1970-71; practice medicine specializing in psychiatry, N.Y.C., 1973—; attending psychiatrist N.Y. U. Med. Center-Bellevue Hosp., Gracie Sq. Hosp., N. Shore Hosp., 1973—; asst. clin. instr. N.Y. U. Med. Center, 1970-71, clin. instr., 1973-77, clin. asst. prof., 1977—. Served to maj. USAF, 1971-73. Diplomate Am. Bd. Psychiatry and Neurology. Mem. Internat. Assn. for Study Pain, N.Y. County Med. Soc., AMA, Am. Psychiat. Assn., Assn. for Advancement Behavior Therapy. Home: 23 Woodland Dr Sands Point NY 11050 Office: 165 E 35th St New York City NY 10016

COLEMAN, STEVEN LAURENCE, hosp. adminsr., air force officer; b. Ft. Wayne, Ind., June 20, 1940; s. Laurence Ferguson and Lois Virginia (McMaken) C.; B.S.B.A., Ohio State U., 1966; M.H.A., Baylor U., 1975; m. Lela Ann Tidwell, Sept. 5, 1964; 1 son, Scott A. Enlisted in USAF, 1962, advanced through grades to maj. 1978; adminstr. 20th Aeromed. Staging Flight, Tachikawa Air Base, Japan, 1970-71; asst. adminstr. resource mgmt. USAF Hosp., Tachikawa Air Base, 1971-73; hosp. adminstr. USAF Hosp., Kincheloe AFB, Mich., 1975-77; dir. base med. services, comdr. USAF Clinic, Ankara, Turkey, 1977—. Decorated Air Force Commendation medal. Mem. Am. Coll. Hosp. Adminstrs., Am. Hosp. Assn. Mem. Christian Ch. (Disciples of Christ). Clubs: Masons, Shriners. Home and Office: TUSLOG Det 37 Box 1401 APO NY 09254

COLETON, STUART HOWARD, periodontist; b. Rockaway, N.Y., May 8, 1938; s. Irving B. and Esther (Engelstein) C.; B.S., City Coll., N.Y., 1961; D.D.S., N.Y. U. Coll. Dentistry, 1964; m. Roberta Nemoytin, June 10, 1961; children—Marci Ilyse, Jodi Lynne, Jamie Allison. Research fellow Guggenheim Inst. for Dental Research,

1963; postgrad. tng. N.Y. U., 1966-68; pvt. practice dentistry specializing in periodontics and oral medicine, White Plains, N.Y., 1968—; attending in periodontics Westchester County Med. Center, Valhalla. Asst. clin. prof. periodontics and oral medicine N.Y. U. Coll. Dentistry, 1968—. Eagle scout Boy Scouts Am. Served to capt., Dental Corps, USAF, 1964-66. Diplomate Am. Bd. Pereodontology, Am. Bd. Oral Medicine. Fellow Royal Soc. Health (Eng.), Internat. Coll. Dentists, N.Y. Acad. Dentistry (asso.); mem. Am. Dental Assn., Sci. Research Soc. Am., Am. Acad. Periodontology, Am. Acad. Oral Medicine, Northeastern Soc. Periodontists, Am. Soc. Preventive Dentistry, Internat. Assn. Dental Research, AAAS, Alpha Omega (pres. N.Y. alumni 1970-71, pres. Westchester County alumni 1974-76), Omicron Kappa Upsilon. K.P., Mason. Founding editor: N.Y. U. Dental Center Faculty Newsletter, 1969. Home: 7 Stone Rd Chappaqua NY 10514 Office: 280 Mamaroneck Ave White Plains NY 10605

COLGAN, SUMNER, reliability engr.; b. Framingham, Mass., Sept. 11, 1934; s. Joseph and Leora C.; student Boston Coll., 1957-61, Boston U., 1961; m. 1 son, Scott Paul. Chem. engr. Beam Tube Corp., Western, Mass., 1962-63; reliability engr. Gen.Motors Corp., Framingham, 1963—. Served in USAF, 1953-57. Mem. Hunting Ravine Avalanche Patrol, 1970-78. Clubs: Appalachian Mountain, Sea Urchins. Home: PO Box 138 Framingham MA 01701 Office: 63 Western Ave Framingahm MA 01701

COLGRASS, MICHAEL CHARLES, composer; b. Chgo., Apr. 22, 1932; s. Michael Clement and Ann (Hand) C.; Mus.B., U. Ill., 1956; scholar Tanglewood (Mass.), 1952, 54, Aspen (Colo.), 1953; pupil Paul Price, Eugene Weigle, Darius Mihand, Lukas Foss, Wallingford Rieger, Ben Weber; m. Ulla Damgaard, Nov. 25, 1966; 1 son, Neal. Free-lance solo percussionist maj. N.Y. mus. orgns., 1956—; narrator Boston Symphony, 1969, Phila. Orch., 1970; dir. Virgil's Dream, Brighton Festival; soloist Danish Radio Orch., 1965; dir. opera Nightingale Inc., U. Ill. Contemporary Music Festival, 1975; author, poet own theatre works, 1966—. Served with U.S. Army, 1954-56. Recipient Fromm award, 1966, Chem. Bank award, 1971, Pulitzer prize for music, 1978; Guggenheim fellow, 1964-65, 68-69; Rockefeller grantee, 1967-69. Composer: Divertimento, 1961; Fantasy Variations, 1961; Wind Quintet, 1962; Light Spirit, 1963; Rhapsody, 1963; Rhapsodic Fantasy, 1965; Sea Shadow, 1966; As Quiet As, 1966; Virgil's Dream, 1967; Three Brothers, 1951; Percussion Music, 1953; Chamber Music for Four Drums and String Quintet, 1954; Chamber Music for Percussion Quintet, 1955; Variations for Four Drums and Viola, 1957; The Earth's Baked Apple, 1968-69; New People for mezzosoprano, viola, piano, 1969; Nightingale, Inc., comic jazz opera, 1971; Auras for Harp and Orch., 1973; Image of Man, 1974; Concertmasters for 3 violins and orch., 1975; Best Wishes U.S.A. for black and white choruses, folk instruments, jazz band and orch., 1976; Theatre of the Universe for solists, chorus and orch., 1976; Wolf for solo cell, 1976; Letter from Mozart for orch., 1976; Deja Vu for Percussion and Orch. (Pulitzer Prize 1978), 1977; Mystery Flowers for Spring for soprano and piano, 1978; The Tower, mus. play for children's theater, 1978; Flashbacks, mus. play for 5 brass, 1979. Works commd. Boston Symphony, Lincoln Center Chamber Music Soc., Fromm Found., Corp. for Pub. Broadcasting, Ford Found., Spokane Symphony Orch., Detroit Symphony Orch., Springfield Symphony Orch., Minn. Orch., Musica Aeterna Orch. N.Y., Young Concert Artists, N.Y., N.Y. Philharm., Can. Broadcasting Corp., works recorded various cos. Contbr. articles to publs. Home: 280 Riverside Dr New York City NY 10025*

COLLARD, THOMAS ALBERT, transp. co. exec.; b. Paterson, N.J., Nov. 9, 1942; s. Albert Garrison and Katherine Barbara (Adams) C.; B.S. in Bus. Adminstrn., U. Buffalo, 1964; m. Cynthia Louise Davis, Nov. 6, 1965; children—Elizabeth, Katherine. Various positions Pa. R.R., Cleve. and Buffalo, 1964-69; service analyst, marketing dept. Penn Central, Phila., 1969-70, supr. service quality control, 1971; mgr. service planning Central R.R. of N.J., Newark, 1972-74, dir. transp. planning, 1974-75, dir. stas. and intermodal operation, 1975; with Conrail Activation Task Force, 1975-76, dir. service planning and performance, 1976—. Active Big Brother Orgn., Willingboro, N.J., 1972—; v.p. Big Bros./Big Sisters of Burlington County (N.J.), 1975-76, pres., 1977-78; vol. juvenile probation counselor, 1978. Mem. Am. Soc. Traffic and Transp. (certified), ICC Practitioners Assn. Episcopalian (vestryman, tchr., dir. ch. edn. 1970—). Author childrens book: Diesels First, 1977; contbr. articles to tech. publs. Home: 30 Topeka Pass Willingboro NJ 08046 Office: Six Penn Center Plaza Philadelphia PA 19104

COLLI, ALBERT JOHN, chem. engr.; b. Bklyn., May 10, 1937; s. Patrick and Rose (Bianco) C.; B.Chem. Engring., Cooper Union Coll., 1959; m. Flora Calabrese, June 4, 1960; children—Jacqueline, Janet, Marisa, Christine, Michael. Chem. engr. Naval Propellant plant, Naval Ordnance Station, Indian Head, Md., 1959-65, branch mgr. chem. processes, 1965—; cons. in field. Registered profl. engr., Md. Mem. Am. Inst. Chem. Engrs., Am. Def. Preparedness Assn. Democrat. Roman Catholic. Inventor pneumatic mix process, 1964; magnetic coal cleaning processes, 1977. Home: 1509 Birchwood Dr Oxon Hill MD 20021 Office: Naval Ordnance Sta Bldg 863 Indian Head MD 20640

COLLIER, THOMAS CLEATON, engr., naval architect; b. Portsmouth, Va., Feb. 18, 1913; s. William Bell and Susan D. (Cleaton) C.; grad. Phillips Exeter Acad., 1931; A.B., Harvard U., 1936. With Bethlehem Shipbldg. Corp., Quincy, Mass., 1936-37, Bur. Ships, Navy Dept., Washington, 1938-55; free lance engr., Silver Spring, Md., 1955—. Patentee in field. Address: 12325 N H Ave Silver Spring MD 20904

COLLINS, A(LBERT) BYRON, surgeon; b. Olean, N.Y., Sept. 10, 1933; s. Albert B. and Clara B. (Satterlee) C.; B.A., U. Buffalo, 1955; M.D., State U. N.Y., Syracuse, 1959; m. Sally Ann Uaine, Dec. 24, 1968 (dec. Jan. 1978); children—Albert B., Karen, Kathy, Kimberly, Colleen, Christopher, Kirstin; m. 2d, Mary Louise Blume, July 22, 1978. Intern, Millard Fillmore Hosp., Buffalo, 1959-60, resident in surgery, 1960-64; practice medicine specializing in surgery, Hornell, N.Y., 1964—; mem. staff, chief surgery Bethesda Community Hosp., St. James Mercy Hosp., cons. in gen. thoracic surgery Cole Meml. Hosp., Coudersport, Pa., 1968—; coroner Steuben County, N.Y., 1964—; Hereford cattle rancher, Canisteo, N.Y. Bd. dirs. Bethesda Community Hosp. Diplomate Am. Bd. Surgery. Fellow Am. Soc. Abdominal Surgeons; mem. AMA, N.Y. State, Steuben County med. socs., Am. (dir.), N.Y. State Hereford assns. Republican. Roman Catholic. Home: RD 2 Canisteo NY 14823 Office: Med Arts Bldg Hornell NY 14843

COLLINS, ALLEN HOWARD, psychiatrist; b. Washington, Sept. 6, 1942; s. Murray and Bertha (Baccalman) C.; A.B., Columbia U., 1964, M.Ph., 1974; M.D., Tufts U., 1968. Intern, USPHS Hosp., Boston, 1968-69; resident in psychiatry N.Y. State Psychiat. Inst.-Columbia Presbyn. Med. Center, N.Y.C., 1969-72; individual practice medicine specializing in gen. psychiatry N.Y.C., 1972—; attending-in-charge psychiatry service Lenox Hill Hosp., N.Y.C., 1978—, coordinator psychiat. edn. Lenox Hill Hosp. undergrad. med. students N.Y. Med. Coll., 1974—; with William A. White Inst. Psychoanalysis, Psychiatry and Psychology, N.Y.C., 1975—; psychiat. cons. NIMH regional office. Served with USPHS, 1968-74. NIMH-Mental Health Career Devel. asso., 1969-74. Diplomate Am. Bd. Psychiatry and Neurology. Mem. Am. Psychiat. Assn., Am. Acad. Psychoanalysis, AAAS, Am. Pub. Health Assn., AMA. Jewish. Home: 25 Pine St Haworth NJ 07641 Office: 15 E 77th St New York City NY 10021

COLLINS, COLLENE, mktg. exec.; b. Leavenworth, Kans., Oct. 11, 1948; d. James Thomas and Vera (Gibson) Collins; student Briar Cliff Coll., 1966-67; B.F.A., Kans. U., 1970; postgrad. Dallas Coll., 1971; M.B.A. (Harriman scholar), Columbia U., 1978, M.D.P.E. in Bus. Policy, 1978. Mem. product mgmt. staff Seven Seas Salad Dressings, Anderson Clayton Foods, Dallas, 1970-72; mem. market research staff Frito Lay Inc., Dallas, 1972-73; investment mgr. Henry S. Miller Companies, Dallas, 1973-75; corporate mktg. staff AT & T, Basking Ridge, N.J., 1976-78; market mgr. N.Y. Telephone Co., N.Y.C., 1978—. Mem. cultural affairs task force Goals for Dallas, 1970-75; patron Mus. Am. Folk Art, N.Y.C., bd. dirs. Dallas Civic Ballet, 1973-76. Mem. Am. Mktg. Assn., Nat. Assn. Real Estate Brokers, Mktg. Sci. Inst., Am. Assembly. Clubs: Dallas Cotillion, Dallas Slipper, Dallas 500 Inc., Dallas Womens, Garden, Jockey, Willow Bend Polo and Hunt; Burnt Mills Polo (Far Hills, N.J.), U.S. Equestrian Team. Home: Dumont Rd Far Hills NJ 07931 also 44 W 62d St New York City NY 10023 Office: 1095 Ave of Americas New York City NY 10036

COLLINS, DOROTHY (MRS. AKIBA EMANUEL), advt. co. exec.; b. Salt Lake City; d. Joseph L. and Dorothy (Frey) Collins; A.B., U. Denver; m. Akiba Emanuel; 1 dau., Lynn Collins. Woman's page editor Rocky Mountain News, Denver; fashion editor NBC, N.Y.C.; pub. relations mgr. Shwayder Bros., Denver; pub. relations account exec. Ellington & Co., N.Y.C.; sr. v.p. Infoplan, N.Y.C.; now v.p. consumer group Burson-Marsteller, N.Y.C. Former nat. dir. women's activities Nat. Jewish Hosp., Denver; cons. Campfire Girls. Mem. Nat. Home Fashions League (pres. 1977-78), Am. Women in Radio and TV, Women's Forum, Women Execs. in Pub. Relations, Nat. Safety Council. Club: Denver Women's Press. Home: Hollis Ln Croton-on-Hudson NY 10520 Office: 866 3d Ave New York City NY 10022

COLLINS, ERIK, ednl. adminstr.; b. Grand Rapids, Mich., May 17, 1938; s. Kreigh Taylor and Theresa (Vanderlaan) C.; student Grand Rapids Jr. Coll., 1957; B.B.A., U. Mich., 1959, M.A., 1963, Ph.D., 1969; m. Judith Arlene Palmer, June 15, 1959 (div. 1971); children—Brett Alan, Brian Edward; m. 2d, Joan Margaret Pause, Feb. 9, 1972 (div. 1978). Tchr., Plymouth (Mich.) Community Schs., 1963-67; vis. lectr. edn. Eastern Mich. U., 1967-69; asst. prof. ednl. psychology State U. N.Y. at Fredonia, 1969-74; dir. Early Childhood Research Center, U. Md. Eastern Shore, Princess Anne, 1974-76; dir. research Geneva Acad., Phila., 1976-77; partner Greeley Collins Assos., 1977—. Cons., N.Y.C. Schs., North Rockland Central Sch. Dist., State U. N.Y. at Brockport. N.Y. State Center for Migrant Studies, N.Y. State Bur. Migrant Edn., Appalachian Regional Commn. Coop. State Research Service grantee. Mem. Am. Ednl. Research Assn., Am. Psychol. Assn., Jean Piaget Soc., Nat. Council Measurement. Home: 4166 Mulberry St Oakford PA 19047 Office: 3222 Douglas Turn Cornwells Heights PA 19020

COLLINS, GEORGE JAMES, physician, army officer; b. Houston, Nov. 19, 1939; s. George James and Joan (Pittman) C.; B.S., Tex. A. and M. U., 1961, M.S., 1963; M.D., U. Tex., 1966; children—Mary Elizabeth, Jennifer. Commd. capt. U.S. Army, 1966, advanced through grades to lt. col., 1973; intern Fitzsimons Army Med. Center, Denver, 1966-67, resident gen. surgery, 1970-74; fellow in peripheral vascular surgery service Walter Reed Army Med. Center, Washington, 1974-75, asst. chief peripheral vascular surgery service, 1975-78, chief, 1978—, asso. investigator, div. surgery and medicine, 1976—; asso. prof. surgery Uniformed Services Univ. of Health Scis., Bethesda, Md., 1977—. Decorated Army Commendation medal. Mem. Soc. Vascular Surgery, Southwestern, Southeastern surg. congresses, Internat. Cardiovascular Soc., Assn. Academic Surgery, Chesapeake Vascular Soc., Mil. Vascular Surgeons, AMA, Tex. A. amd M. U. Alumni Assn., Sigma Xi, Phi Rho Sigma. Republican. Roman Catholic. Home: 8037 Inverness Ridge Rd Potomac MD 20854 Office: Walter Reed Army Hospital OSC Box 144 Washington DC 20012

COLLINS, GEORGE JOSEPH, investment counselor; b. West Haven, Conn., July 31, 1940; s. George Joseph and Orien Frances C.; B.A., Va. Mil. Inst., 1962; M.B.A., Am. U., 1970; m. Maureen Ellen Sullivan, June 15, 1963; children—George Bradford, David Alan, Jonathan Andrew. Fin. analyst Diversified Services, Silver Spring, Md., 1968; sr. security analyst U.S. Fidelity & Guaranty Co., Balt., 1968-71; v.p. T. Rowe Price Assos., Inc., Balt., 1971—; pres., dir. Rowe Price New Income Fund, 1978—, Rowe Price Tax Free Income Fund, 1976—; v.p., dir. Rowe Price Prime Res. Fund Inc., 1978—; professorial lectr. Am. U. Served with USAF, 1963-67. Mem. Chartered Investment Counsel Assn. Am., Bond Portfolio Mgrs. Assn., Municipal Bond Club Belt. Club: Grachur. Home: 12408 Benson Branch Rd Woodmark MD 21043 Office: 100 E Pratt St Baltimore MD 21202

COLLINS, HELEN CLARK (MRS. ARNOLD MILLER COLLINS), ednl. service co. exec.; b. Bklyn.; d. James Alexander and Alice (Van Velzor) Clark; B.S., Columbia U., 1920, M.A., 1921, Ph.D., 1923; m. Arnold Miller Collins, June 28, 1924; 1 son, James Miller. Chem. technician Gen. Chem. Co., 1917-18; patent researcher E.I. DuPont de Nemours & Co., Inc., 1928-30; tutor remedial reading, 1935-45; pres. Ednl. Service, Inc., diagnostic testing, reading cons. for learning disabilities, Wilmington, Del., 1945—, chmn. Ednl. Service Scholarship Found., 1965—. Mem. com. Elementary Sch. Edn. Act Title I, 1965-67. Dir. Kennett Consol. Sch. Bd., Kennett Square, Pa., 1955-71, chmn. pub. relations, 1966-71; chmn. admissions com. Beechwood Sch., 1970—; bd. mgrs. Friends Sch., Wilmington, 1935-55. Recipient award Outstanding Tchr. Learning Disabilities, 1974, award services to handicapped children Coording Council Del. Mem. Internat. Reading Assn., Assn. Learning Disabilities, AAUW (life), Orton Soc., Sigma Xi. Republican. Mem. Soc. of Friends. Author: We Discover Lights, 1935, 2d edit., 1950. Office: 1203 Gilpin Ave Wilmington DE 19806

COLLINS, HERBERT RIDGEWAY, curator; b. Caroline County, Va., Aug. 29, 1932; s. William Joseph and Dorothea Hawes (Campbell) C.; B.S. in Applied Social Sci., Va. Commonwealth U., 1954; postgrad. Am. U., 1958-62. Mem. Presbyn. Com. of Publ., Richmond, Va., 1949-53; with Office of Asst. Chief of Staff for Intelligence, Dept. Army, Pentagon, Washington, 1956-60; curator div. polit. history Smithsonian Instn., Washington, 1960—; chmn. seminar on Am. politics, Landis Valley, Pa., 1968; participant 4th Gulf Coast History and Humanities Conf., Pensacola, Fla., 1972; lectr. ann. meeting Am. Soc. Appraisers, 1972; appeared on numerous radio and TV shows. Vice pres. Smithsonian Employees Credit Union, 1967-69; bd. dirs. Tumbling Waters Mus. Flags, Montgomery, Ala. Served with U.S. Army, 1954-56. Recipient Outstanding Performance award Asst. Chief of Staff for Intelligence, 1960, certificate of award Smithsonian Instn., 1975. Mem. Va. Geneal. Soc. (pres. 1953-55), Va., Arlington County (bd. dirs. 1977—, v.p. 1978), Caroline County (founding; historian) hist. socs., Am. Polit. Items Collectors (bd. dirs. 1968-69), Nat. Trust for Hist. Preservation. Mem. Christian Ch. Author: History and Genealogy of the Collins Family, 1954; The Todds of Virginia, 1960; Presidents on Wheels, 1971; Wills of the Presidents, 1976; contbr. articles to profl. publs. Home: 3510 N Pershing Dr Arlington VA 22201 Office: Div Polit History Smithsonian Instn Washington DC 20560

COLLINS, HOWARD ELISHA, corp. exec.; b. Medina, N.Y., Jan. 5, 1915; s. John Francis and Nina Gertrude (Blount) C.; accounting diploma Bryant and Stratton Bus. Coll., 1935; certificate in basic hosp. adminstrn. Columbia, 1965; m. Florence Jennie Phillips, June 30, 1937; children—Sharon Beth (Mrs. Guy Corriero), Beverly Faye (Mrs. Gerald W. Galloway), John Howard. Gen. mgr. Collins Upholstery Mfg. Co., Silver Creek, N.Y., 1936-54, Silver Creek Motors, 1954-58; practice pub. accounting, Silver Creek, 1958-64; adminstr. Lake Shore Inter-Community Hosp., Silver Creek, 1964-66; adminstr. Mohawk Valley Gen. Hosp. and Nursing Home, Ilion, N.Y., 1966-77; chmn. bd. trustees Chart, Inc., Albany, 1968-77, pres., 1977—. Bd. dirs. Hosp. Underwriters Mut. Ins. Co., 1975-77. Licensed nursing home adminstr., N.Y. State. Fellow Am. Coll. Hosp. Adminstrs.; mem. Hosp. Financial Mgmt. Assn. (advanced mem.), Am., Central N.Y. (chmn. bd. dirs. 1975-77), N.Y. State (trustee) hosp. assns., Hosp. Mgmt. Systems Soc., Assn. Hosp. Adminstrs., Am. Pub. Health Assn., Am. Assn. Hosp. Planning, N.Y. State Assn. Long Term Care Adminstrs., N.Y. State Assn. Homes for Aging, Am. Coll. Nursing Home Adminstrs. Mason, Moose. Home: 8 Summit Park Ballston Lake NY 12019 Office: 20 Computer Park West Albany NY 12207

COLLINS, JAMES ANTHONY, JR., physician; b. Hazleton, Pa., Sept. 5, 1916; s. James A. and Mary E. (Herron) C.; B.S., Pa. State U., 1937; M.D., Jefferson Med. Coll., 1941; m. Virginia T. James, Jan. 24, 1953; stepson, George James. Rotating intern Geisinger Meml. Hosp., Danville, Pa., 1941-42, resident in internal medicine, 1942-43, asso. physician dept. internal medicine, 1943-58, dir. dept. internal medicine, 1958-74, head sect. gastroenterology, 1953-73; chmn. div. med. services Geisinger Med. Center, Danville, 1974—, dir. internal medicine residency tng. program, 1958—, pres. Inst. Edn. and Research, 1976—; corp. mem., bd. dirs. Pa. Blue Shield; med. dir. Maria Joseph Home for Aged, Danville, 1961—; academic staff, clin. prof. medicine Milton S. Hershey Med. Center, Coll. Medicine, Pa. State U. Pres. Danville Bd. Health, 1944—. Diplomate Am. Bd. Internal Medicine. Fellow A.C.P., Pan Am. Med. Assn., Am. Geriatric Soc., Phila. Coll. Physicians; mem. AMA (chmn. joint rev. com. on ednl. programs for asst. to primary care physician), Montour County Med. Soc., Pa., Am. (pres.-elect; trustee 1972—) socs. internal medicine, AAAS, Am. Heart Assn., Am. Soc. Therapeutics and Pharmacology. Republican. Roman Catholic. Clubs: Frosty Valley Country, Elks (Danville). Home: Mill St Riverside PA 17868 Office: Geisinger Medical Center Danville PA 17821

COLLINS, JEAN-PIERRE, dermatologist; b. Montreal, Que., Can., Feb. 12, 1944; s. Raymond Philippe and Jeannine Marie (Charlebois) C.; B.A., U. Montreal, 1963, M.D., 1967; m. Lucie Champagne, May 28, 1966; children—Francois, Sophie. Intern, Hotel Dieu Hosp., Montreal, 1967-68, resident in dermatology, 1968-69, mem. staff, 1973—; resident Skin and Cancer Hosp., Phila., 1969-72; fellow skin and cancer clinic Temple U., Phila., 1969-72, chief resident fellow, 1971-72; practice dermatology Pierrefonds Med. Centre, Roxboro, Que., 1973—; asst. prof. dermatology U. Montreal, 1973—; cons. in field. Certified specialist Coll. Physicians and Surgeons Que. Fellow Royal Coll. Physicians Can., Am. Acad. Dermatology; mem. Royal Soc. Medicine (Eng.), Montreal Dermatol. Soc., Can. Dermatol. Assn., Am. Acad. Dermatology, Soc. Investigative Dermatology, Can. Med. Assn., Assn. Medecins Langue Francaise, Assn. Dermatologues Province Que. Contbg. author, contbr. articles to profl. publs. Home: 171 Les Erables Laval sur le Lac Laval PQ H7R 1A3 Canada Office: 12774 Blvd Gouin W Pierrefonds Roxboro PQ H8Z 1W5 Canada

COLLINS, JOHN GARY, health research exec.; b. Queens, N.Y., Jan. 15, 1941; s. John A. and Gladys (Hufe) C.; B.B.A., Coll. City N.Y., 1962, M.B.A., 1967; m. Carol Ann Walsh, June 12, 1965; children—Michael Alexander, Shawn Brendan. Statistician, N.Y.C. Dept. Health, 1962-65; statis. dir. N.Y. Lung Assn., N.Y.C., 1965-68; dir. evaluation N.J. Med. Regional Program, East Orange, N.J., 1968-73; dist. health mgr. N.Y.C. Dept. Health, S.I., 1973-76; pub. health research analyst Nat. Center Health Services Research, Hyattsville, Md., 1976—; instr. Jersey City State Coll., 1971-76; pub. health cons. to vol. health orgns. Mem. Ops. Research Soc. Am., Am. Pub. Health Assn., Am. Statis. Assn., Coll. City N.Y. Young Alumni Council. Democrat. Home: 14962 Belle Ami Dr Laurel MD 20810 Office: Nat Center Health Services 3700 East West Hwy Hyattsville MD 20782

COLLINS, JOHN JOSEPH, telecommunications exec.; b. Syracuse, N.Y., Dec. 9, 1921; s. Joseph John and Mildred Catherine (Hummel) C.; student Syracuse U., 1940-41; B.S., U.S. Naval Acad., 1945; m. Phyllis Duran Reed, July 5, 1947; children—Cynthia Reed Peters, Priscilla Catherine. With N.Y. Telephone Co., 1947-60, asst. v.p. personnel, to 1960; plant ext. engr. AT&T, 1960-62; gen. plant mgr. N.Y. Telephone Co., N.Y.C., 1962-64, chief engr.-L.I., 1964-66, asst. v.p.-bldgs., 1966-78, gen. mgr. bldg. mgmt. and constrn., 1978—; pres. N.Y. Bldg. Congress. Mayor, Village of Roslyn Harbor (N.Y.), 1976—; mem., pres. North Shore Sch. Bd., Glen Head, N.Y., 1960-69. Served with USN, 1945-47. Named Man of Year, Talbot Perkins Children's Services, 1972. Mem. IEEE, Real Estate Bd. N.Y. (dir.), N.Y. Constrn. Industry Council of Pres.'s (chmn.), N.Y.C. Constrn. Users Council. Republican. Episcopalian. Clubs: Union League (N.Y.C.); North Hempstead Country (Port Washington, N.Y.). Home: 6 Fairway Rd Roslyn Harbor NY 11576 Office: 2 Penn Plaza New York City NY 10001

COLLINS, MALCOLM FRANK, physicist, educator; b. Crewe, Eng., Dec. 15, 1935; s. Bernard and Ethel (Smith) C.; B.A., Cambridge (Eng.) U., 1957, M.A., 1961, Ph.D., 1962; m. Eileen Ray, Apr. 22, 1961; children—Adrian, Andrew, Gillian. Staff scientist Atomic Energy Research Establishment, Harwell, Eng., 1961-69; mem. faculty McMaster U., Hamilton, Ont., Can., 1969—, prof. physics, 1973—, chmn. dept., 1976—. Pres. Canadian Chess Fedn., 1976-77. Sloan fellow, 1970-72. Mem. Canadian Assn. Physicists. Editorial bd. Solid State Communications, 1970—. Research and publs. in solid state physics. Home: 6 Penge Ct Dundas ON L9H 4R4 Canada Office: Physics Dept McMaster Univ Hamilton ON Canada

COLLINS, ROBERT IRA, entertainment mktg. exec.; b. Cleve., Aug. 8, 1948; s. Philip Gilbert and Dorothy (LaVetter) C.; B.S. in Speech, Northwestern U., 1970; M.S. in Pub. Relations, Am. U., 1974; m. Florence Lu Christopher, Feb. 26, 1977. Prodn. asst. Sta. WBBM-TV, Chgo., 1968; asso. dir. Sta. WKYC-TV, Cleve., 1969; regional mktg. dir. Ringling Bros. and Barnum and Bailey Combined Shows, Inc., Washington, 1974—. Served with USCG, 1970-74. Found. for Pub. Relations Research and Edn. grantee, 1974; recipient broadcasting award for pub. service program with KGO radio, Lighthouse for Blind and Ringling Bros. Circus, Ohio State U., 1975. Asso. mem. Pub. Relations Soc. Am. Contbr. articles in field and marine safety to publs. Home: 1700 Treehouse Circle Sarasota FL 33581 Office: 1015 18th St NW Washington DC 20036

COLLINS, ROBERT JOSEPH, physician; b. Olean, N.Y., Apr. 17, 1919; s. Floyd B. and Ethel M. (Miller) C.; B.A., Colgate U., 1940; M.D., U. Buffalo, 1943; m. Jane Ann Kreher, July 5, 1941; children—Dennis Michael, Maureen Ann, Christine Ann, Jacquelyn. Intern, Arnot-Ogden Meml. Hosp., Elmira, N.Y., 1943-44; resident Millard Fillmore Hosp., Buffalo, 1946-49, attending obstetrician and gynecologist, 1958—, chief, dept. obstetrics and gynecology, 1962-66; resident N.Y. Med. Coll., N.Y.C., 1947-48; practice medicine specializing in obstetrics and gynecology, Buffalo, 1948—; asso. clin. prof. obstetrics and gynecology State U. of N.Y., Buffalo, 1974; cons. to Sisters of Charity Hosp., Buffalo, 1963—, San Jorge Hosp., P.R., 1956—. Served to capt., M.C., U.S. Army, 1939-46; ETO. Diplomate Am. Bd. Obstetrics and Gynecology. Fellow Am. Coll. Obstetrics and Gynecology, A.C.S.; mem. N.Y. State, Erie County med. socs., Soc. of Cryobiology, Soc. of Cryosurgery, Heymen Soc. (pres. 1964-65), Buffalo Gynecologic and Obstetric Soc. (pres. 1966-67), Sci. Progress and Research Soc., Buffalo Acad. of Medicine (dir. 1958-62), AMA (Physicians award 1974-77), Am. Assn. of Med. Colls. Republican. Roman Catholic. Clubs: Cherry Hill Country (dir. 1973-76) (Ridgeway, Can.); Frenchmen's Creek Country (Palm Beach, Fla.). Contbr. articles in field to med. jours. Home: 81 Linden Ave Buffalo NY 14214 Office: 4536 Main St Snyder NY 14226

COLLINS, ROBERT YUILLE, computer scientist; b. Waterbury, Conn., Aug. 6, 1944; s. Jack and Dorothy Marie (Miller) C.; M.B.A. U. Md., 1974; grad. Am. U., 1969; m. Alice Elizabeth Fossett, Nov. 19, 1966; children—Kelly Anne, Karen Alexa. Civilian computer programmer Dept. Air Force, 1966-67; civilian mgr. computer systems analyst Dept. Army, 1967-74; computer scientist Am. Mgmt. Systems Co., Washington, 1974-76; mgr. mktg. info. systems Amtrak, Washington, 1976—; cons. in field. Served with USAF, 1962-66. Recipient Civilian commendation Dept. Army (2). Mem. Data Processing Mgmt. Assn., Soc. Mgmt. Info. Systems. Republican. Episcopalian. Author papers in field. Home: 6356 Buffie Ct Burke VA 22015 Office: 400 N Capitol St Washington DC 20001

COLLINS, ROWLAND LEE, educator; b. Bristow, Okla., Sept. 17, 1934; s. John Leland and Velma Grace (Jones) C.; A.B., Princeton U., 1956; M.A., Stanford U., 1959, Ph.D., 1961; m. Sarah Jo Huff, Apr. 10, 1965; children—Robin Elizabeth, Michael John, Catherine Grace. Lectr. in English, Ind. U., 1959-61, instr., 1961-62, asst. prof., 1962-65, asso. prof., 1965-67; prof. English, U. Rochester, 1967—, chmn. dept., 1972—. Academic adviser Montfort Jones and Allie Brown Jones Found., 1961-73, trustee, 1973—, vice chmn., 1974—; mem. Soc. for Preservation of Landmarks in Western N.Y., 1969—, trustee, 1970—, sec., 1974-78, pres., 1978—; bd. dirs. Hillside Children's Center; mem. Rochester Meml. Art Gallery, Rochester Mus. and Sci. Center, Planned Parenthood League; trustee Keuka Coll.; active neighborhood assns. Woodrow Wilson fellow, 1956-57, 59; Guggenheim fellow, 1965-66. Mem. Internat. Assn. Univ. Profs. English, Guild of Scholars, Modern Lang. Assn. (past chmn. Old English group), Medieval Acad. Am., Early English Text Soc., Cambridge Bibliog. Soc., Bibliog. Soc. (London), English Inst., Tennyson Soc. (Am. rep. 1967—). Democrat. Episcopalian. Clubs: Grolier, The Club, Faculty (Rochester). Author: Anglo-Saxon Vernacular Manuscripts in America, 1976; also articles and revs.; editor: Fourteen British and American Poets, 1964; Beowulf, 1965; founding editor: The Year's Work in Old English Studies, 1968—. Home: 16 Arnold Park Rochester NY 14607 Office: U Rochester Rochester NY 14627

COLONY, WILLIAM MANDEVILLE, envrionmentalist, educator; b. Salem, Va., July 27, 1927; s. Clarence Mandeville and Arnie Belle (Goodwin) C.; student Roanoke Coll., 1946-48; B.S. in Civil Engring., Va. Poly. Inst., 1950; M.A. in Pub. Adminstrn., U. Va., 1972; m. Florence Joyce Galbraith, June 21, 1950; children—Margaret Allison, Anne Mandeville, Laura Douglas, Jane Elizabeth. System maintenance engr. Washington Suburban San. Commn., Hyattsville, Md., 1950-58; dir. pub. works City of Rockville (Md.), 1958-60; environ. planner, mgr., 1960-75; dir. Chesapeake-Susquehanna River Basins Project, HEW, 1966-69; dir. planning and evaluation office Region III EPA, 1969-72; prof. urban and environ. planning U. Va., Charlottesville, 1975-77; pub. interest cons., 1975—; planning coordinator, program officer Region III EPA, 1977—. Mem. Charlottesville-Albemarle Civic League, 1962-78; bd. dirs. United Givers Fund, 1969-71. Served with USNR, 1945-46; comdr. Res. ret. Mem. Am. Soc. Pub. Adminstrn., Water Pollution Control Fedn., Am. Soc. Planning Ofcls., Va. Citizens Planning Assn., Citizens for Albemarle, Chi Epsilon, Sigma Chi. Episcopalian. Club: Blue Ridge Swimming. Home: 8703 Waterford Rd Alexandria VA 22308 Office: Room 714 Crystal Mall Bldg 2 Washington DC 20460

COLSON, CHESTER ELMER, educator; b. Boston, June 17, 1917; s. John Elmer and Nellie Elizabeth (Houghton) C.; B.S., Mass. Sch. Art, 1947; M.A., Tchrs. Coll., Columbia, 1950; m. Saralee Cohen, Sept. 15, 1962; With John Hancock Mut. Life Ins. Co., Boston, 1936-43; supr. art pub. schs., Springfield, Vt., 1947-49, Chgo. Tchrs. Coll., 1950-51, pub. schs., Brookline, Mass., 1951-52, Meredith Coll., Raleigh, N.C., 1952-54, Newark State Tchrs. Coll., 1954-56, pub. schs., Burlington, Vt., 1956-58; prof. Wilkes Coll., Wilkes-Barre, Pa., 1958—. Work represented in permanent collection Everhart Mus., Scranton, Pa., also trustee collections. Recipient purchase prize Everhart Mus., 1968, Norwich Mus., Vt., 1970. Mem. Coll. Art assn., Nat. Soc. Painters in Casein and Acrylic, Nat., Pa. art edn. assns., Phila. Water Color Club. Home: 122 Frangorma Dr Trucksville PA 18708 Office: Dept Art Wilkes College Wilkes Barres PA 18704

COLSTON, WILLIAM CARROLL, radiologist; b. Rocky Mount, N.C., Aug. 16, 1935; s. Charles Carroll and Elma Coneley (Melvin) C.; B.S. cum laude, Davidson Coll., 1958; M.D., Duke U., 1962; m. Kathleen Louise Barrett, June 6, 1962; children—Elizabeth Maria, Caroline Louise, Katherine Barrett. Intern, U.S. Naval Hosp., Charleston, S.C., 1962-63; resident in radiology N.Y. Hosp.-Cornell Med. Center, N.Y.C., 1965-68; attending radiologist Morristown (N.J.) Meml. Hosp., 1968—; clin. asst. prof. Coll. Medicine and Dentistry, Rutgers Med. Sch., New Brunswick, N.J.; adj. allied health asst. prof., Fairleigh Dickinson U., Madison, N.J. Served with M.C., USN, 1962-65. Diplomate Am. Bd. Radiology. Mem. Am. Coll. Radiology (certified), AMA, Radiol. Soc. N.J., Med. Soc. N.J., Morris County Med. Soc., N.C. Soc. N.Y., Phi Beta Kappa, Alpha Epsilon Delta, Gamma Sigma Epsilon, Delta Phi Alpha. Roman Catholic. Club: Morris County Golf. Contbr. article in field to profl. conf. Home: 92 Skyline Dr Morristown NJ 07960 Office: 101 Madison Ave Morristown NJ 07960

COLTEN, STERLING IRWIN, counseling psychologist; b. Boston, Sept. 29, 1942; s. Albert Abraham and Bess (Tobins) C.; student U. N.H., 1960-63; B.S., Boston U., 1966, M.Ed., 1968, Ed.D., 1971; m. Patricia Ann Levetin, June 12, 1966; 1 son, Dana Scott. Rehab. counselor Taunton (Mass.) State Hosp., 1968-69, dir. rehab. services, 1969-71, chief psychologist, 1971-74, unit adminstr., 1974-76; mental health program specialist USPHS, 1976-77; individual practice counseling psychology, 1971—; asst. prof. Bridgewater State Coll., 1973-74; psychol. cons. Mass. Rehab. Commn., Mass. Dept. Pub. Welfare; cons. R.I. Div. Retardation, 1970-75. Mem. Am., Mass. psychol. assns., Nat., Mass. (dir.) rehab. assns., Nat., Mass. (pres. 1971-72) rehab. counseling assns., Mass. Teleoanalytic Soc., Mass. Parks and Recreation Soc., Kappa Sigma. K.P. Founder, Pride Sheltered Workshop, 1969, Everett Halfway House, 1971, Union Halfway House. Author 3 books. Contbr. articles to profl. jours. Home: 3 Hampton Rd Brockton MA 02401 Office: 157 Belmont St Brockton MA 02401

COLTOFF, PHILIP, social worker; b. N.Y.C., Feb. 8, 1936; s. Irving and Henrietta (Wieder) C.; B.A., Coll. City N.Y., 1962; M.S.W., N.Y.U., 1964; m. Kay Susan Wishengrad, Mar. 19, 1961; children—Michael, Robert, Julie, Peter. Youth bd. extension worker N.Y.C. Youth Bd. and Boys Club of Queens, 1956; practitioner and youth worker YM & YWHA, Bklyn., 1958-61, youth supr., N.Y.C., 1963, asst. exec. dir., Queens, N.Y., 1964-66; research asst. Nat. Council Crime and Delinquency, N.Y.C., 1965; dir. city and county brs., asso. exec. dir. Children's Aid Soc., N.Y.C., 1966—; adj. prof. social work Adelphi U., Garden City, N.Y., 1967—; cons. Boys Clubs of Am., 1974—, Urban Fellows Program, 1974—, Nat. Inst. for Psychotherapies, 1973-75; trainer Nassau County Mental Health Assn., 1973—. Bd. dirs. Mental Health Materials Center, 1976—. Fedn. Jewish Philanthropies grantee, 1962-63; N.Y. State scholar, 1963. Mem. Nat. Assn. Social Workers, Acad. Certified Social Workers. Co-author: Preventing Child Maltreatment: Begin With the Parent, 1978; contbr. article to profl. jour. Office: Childrens Aid Society 105 E 22d St New York City NY 10010

COLTON, CLARK KENNETH, chem. engr., educator; b. N.Y.C., July 20, 1941; s. Sidney and Goldie (Chases) C.; B.Chem. Engring., Cornell U., 1964; Ph.D. (NIH fellow), Mass. Inst. Tech., 1969; m. Ellen Ruth Brandner, June 20, 1965; children—Jill Erin, Jason Adam, Michael Ross, Brian Scott. Asst. prof. chem. engring. Mass. Inst. Tech., 1969-73, asso. prof., 1973-76, prof., 1976—, dep. head dept. chem. engring., 1977. Cons. NIH, FDA, various indsl. orgns.; mem. advisory bd. mil. personnel supplies NRC, 1971-75 Ford fellow, 1969-70. Recipient Dreyfus Tchr. Scholar award Camille and Henry Dreyfus Found., 1972, Allan P. Colburn award Am. Inst. Chem. Engrs., 1977. Mem. N.Y. Acad. Scis., Am. Inst. Chem. Engrs. (dir. food, pharm. and bioengring. div. 1978—), Am. Soc. Artificial Internal Organs (asso. editor jour.), AAAS, Am. Diabetes Assn., Am. Soc. Engring. Edn., Biomed. Engring. Soc., Sigma Xi, Tau Beta Pi, Phi Lambda Upsilon. Club: Cornell (Boston). Mem. editorial bd. Jour. Membrane Sci., 1975—, Jour. Bioengring., 1976—. Contbr. articles to sci. jours. Home: 279 Commonwealth Ave Newton MA 02167 Office: Dept Chem Engring Mass Inst Tech Cambrige MA 02139

COLTON, RICHARD JOHN, chemist; b. S. Fork, Pa., Dec. 12, 1950; s. George and Carmelina (Ardire) C.; B.S., U. Pitts., 1972, Ph.D., 1976; m. Joanne Sebastian, July 29, 1978. Research asst. U. Pitts., 1972, teaching fellow, 1972-76, dir. electron spectroscopy lab., 1975-76; NRC resident research asso. Naval Research Lab., Washington, 1976-77, research chemist, 1977—. Recipient Pitts. Chemist Club Soc. Tech. Communications Writing award, 1976. Mem. Am. Chem. Soc., AAAS, Phi Lamda Upsilon. Democrat. Roman Catholic. Contbr. articles in field to profl. jours. Office: Chemistry Division Code 6110 Naval Research Lab Washington DC 20375

COLTON, WILLIAM ARTHUR, JR., personnel exec.; b. Queens, N.Y., May 23, 1938; s. William A. and Mildred Marie (Pyle) C.; B.A., Dartmouth Coll., 1960; J.D., Bklyn. Law Sch., 1965; m. Teresa Tranberg, Aug. 1, 1964; children—William Arthur III, Tammie Elizabeth. With Nassau County Probation Dept., 1961-62; with Allstate Ins. Co., Farmington, Conn., 1965-79, div. personnel mgr., 1966-68, personnel mgr., Rochester and Westchester, N.Y., 1968-73, Farmington, Conn., 1973-79; pres. Baxter Reynolds Personnel Consultants, Inc., Hartford, Conn., 1979—. Bd. dirs. Winding Trails, Farmington, 1977—, now pres. Mem. Am. Soc. Tng. Dirs., Conn. Personnel Assn., Dartmouth Alumni Assn. Home: 49 Highwood Rd Farmington CT 06032 Office: Suite 614 111 Pearl St Hartford CT 06103

COLWAY, JAMES ROBERT, silverware mfg. co. exec.; b. Oneida, N.Y., Nov. 12, 1920; s. Joseph William and Mary (Lawler) C.; student Syracuse U., 1945-48, U. Coll., Syracuse, 1946-48; m. Cynthia Frances Townsend, April 17, 1948; children—James Nathan, Mary Thompson. With Oneida Ltd. Silversmiths (N.Y.), 1948—, art dir., 1948-53, creative mgr. sales promotion, 1954-63, mgr. advt. and sales promotion, 1964-67, dir. advt. and sales promotion, 1968-77, v.p., 1977—; numerous one-man shows including Chase Gallery, N.Y.C., St. Lawrence U., Canton, N.Y., Eisenhower Coll., Seneca Falls, N.Y., Utica (N.Y.) Coll., Arvest Galleries, Boston; paintings in many Amer. embassies abroad; represented in various pub. and pvt. collections including Butler Inst. Am. Art, Youngstown, Ohio, Lyman Allyn Mus., New London, Conn., Springfield (Mass.) Coll. Mus., Slater Meml. Mus., Norwich, Conn., Brockton (Mass.) Art Center. Vice pres. Oneida Hosp. Found. Served with 88th Inf. Div., AUS, 1942-45. Mem. Assn. of Nat. Advertisers, Audit Bur. of Circulations, Am. Advt. Fedn., Am. Legion. Club: Oneida Community Golf, Snow Ridge Ski. Home: 101 The Vineyard Oneida NY 13421

COLWELL, RAYMOND CARPENTER, JR., armored vehicle mfg. co. ofcl.; b. Providence, Mar. 3, 1920; s. Raymond Carpenter and Mattie Holmes (Barrows) C.; student U. Md., 1958-61, Mil. Schs. including Command and Gen. Staff Coll., 1961-62; m. Louise Soder, July 2, 1944; children—Raymond Carpenter, Carey Martin, Dana Barrows. With Brown and Sharpe Mfg. Co., Providence, 1941, 46, Gen. Electric Co., Providence, 1946-50; commd. 2d. lt. U.S. Army, 1943, advanced through grades to col., 1970; active duty, 1942-46, 50-70; ret., 1970; asst. project mgr. Bowen McLaughlin York Co. div. Harsco Corp., Iran, 1977—. Mem. Am. Def. Preparedness Assn. (life), Roger Williams Family Assn., Smithsonian Assos., Am. Numismatist Assn., Nat. Assn. Uniformed Services, Nat. Sojourners. Congregationalist. Clubs: Lincoln Continental Owners, Overseas Masons #40 (Providence). Home: 994 Hartford Ave Johnston RI 02919 Office: Box RM APO New York City NY 09202 also Box 335 Masjid I Solyman South Iran

COLYER, RALPH JOSEPH, telephone directory corp. exec.; b. Newark, June 2, 1935; s. Ralph Mitchell and Violet May (Kreideweis) C.; B.S., Rutgers U., 1964; m. Grace Margaret Smith, Dec. 21, 1957; children—Donna Marie, Ralph Joseph, Lisa Rose. Accounting supr. N.J. Bell Telephone Co., Newark, 1953-64; staff accountant Ernst & Ernst, Newark, 1964-66, sr. accountant, 1966-68, supr., 1968-70; comptroller Nat. Telephone Directory Corp., Union, N.J., 1970-72, treas., 1972—. Served with U.S. Army, 1954-56; ETO. C.P.A., N.J. Mem. N.J. Soc. C.P.A.'s, Am. Inst. C.P.A.'s, Nat. Assn. Accountants. Episcopalian. Home: 18 Baldwin Rd Edison NJ 08817 Office: Nat Telephone Directory Corp 1050 Galloping Hill Rd Union NJ 07083

COMBE, IVAN DEBLOIS, drug co. exec.; b. Fremont, Iowa, Apr. 21, 1911; s. Louis Abel and Elsie (Mange) C.; B.S., Northwestern U., 1933, postgrad. Law Sch., 1933-35; m. Mary Elizabeth Deming, Dec. 10, 1938; children—Diana Mary, Juliette Marie, Christopher Bryan. Sales and sales promotion Nat. Dairy Products, Chgo., 1935-36; div. sales mgr. Wilbert Products Co., N.Y.C., 1936-40; merchandising account exec. Young and Rubicam, Inc., N.Y.C., 1940-43; v.p. sales and advt. Pharmacraft Corp., subsidiary Seagram Distillers, N.Y.C., 1944-49; pres. Eastco, Inc., Combe Chem., Inc., White Plains, 1949-70; chmn. bd. Combe Inc., 1970—; dir. Cos-Chem Corp. Chmn. Council on Family Health. Bd. govs., v.p. White Plains Hosp.; Greater N.Y. alumni life regent Northwestern U., trustee, 1967-71. Recipient Alumni Service award Northwestern U., 1962, Merit award, 1970. Mem. World Fedn. Proprietary Medicine Mfrs. (chmn. 1977—). Alpha Delta Phi. Methodist. Rotarian. Clubs: Metropolitan (gov. 1972-76) (N.Y.C.); Ekwanok Golf (Manchester, Vt.); Ocean (Delray, Fla.); Blind Brook (Purchase, N.Y.). Home: 25 Wilshire Rd Greenwich CT 06830 Office: 1101 Westchester Ave White Plains NY 10604

COMBES, RICHARD WILLARD, physician; b. Cleve., July 2, 1926; s. Willard Wetmore and Vivian C. (Kepler) C.; A.B., Oberlin Coll., 1947; M.D., Case Western Res. U., 1951; m. Angela Katryn Wright, Aug. 26, 1949; children—Carol Combes Weimer, Holly Combes Dorst, Willard Wright, Pamela. Intern, St. Lukes Hosp., Cleve., 1951-52; resident, research asst. in neuroanatomy Case Western Res. U., 1952; gen. practice medicine, Oberlin, Ohio, 1954-57; resident in anesthesiology St. Luke's Hosp., Cleve., 1957-59, mem. med. staff, 1959-60; dir. anesthesiology services Booth Meml. Hosp., Salvation Army, Cleve., 1961-70; practice medicine specializing in anesthesiology, Rock Island, Ill., 1970-73, Rutland, Vt., 1973—; med. dir. post anesthesia intensive care units Rutland Hosp.; owner, dir. Oak Research Labs., histochemistry solvent systems, azeotropy, Rutland, 1961—. Bd. dirs. Birthright of Rock Island County, 1972-73. Served to lt. USNR, 1944-45, 52-54. Invited visitor designate to Ch. of Scotland Gen. Assembly from United Presbyn. Ch. U.S.A., 1973. Mem. AAAS, Am. Soc. Anesthesiologists, AMA, Rutland Med. Soc., Brit. Pteridological Soc., Am. Fern Soc. Home and office: 3 Robinwood Ln Rutland VT 05701

COMBS, EARL BURNS, architect; b. Richmond, Va., Feb. 13, 1931; s. Earl Burns and Opal (Earnest) C.; B.Arch., Cornell U., 1954, M.Regional Planning, 1959. Project designer Perkins & Will, White Plains, N.Y., 1954-57; teaching asst. Cornell U., Ithaca, N.Y., 1957-58; Fulbright fellow architecture U. Rome (Italy), 1958-59; designer Ballard, Todd & Snibbe, N.Y.C., 1960-61, Space Design Group, N.Y.C., 1961-63; pvt. practice archtl. design, 1963—; pvt. practice architecture, N.Y.C., 1967—. Vis. critic Cornell U. Coll. Architecture, 1957. Recipient award of excellence for house design Archtl. Record, 1971. Mem. A.I.A. (mem. landmarks preservation com. 1968-69), Gargoyle Soc. Contbr. articles to various jours. Address: 44 W 89th St New York City NY 10024

COMBS, PAUL HOWARD, bus. exec.; b. New Brunswick, N.J., Oct. 23, 1925; s. Howard Leon and Lillian Marie (Knudson) C.; B.A. in Bus. Adminstrn., Rutgers U., 1950; m. Shirley Bertenshaw, July 21, 1962; children—Sharon (Mrs. Louis Martinez), Paul Clifford, Amy B., Debra A.; step-children, Norman Wiseman, Russell Wiseman. Purchasing exec. M.W. Kellogg Co., Houston, 1955-62; exec. v.p. Youngstown Steel Tank Co. (Ohio), 1963-64; mem. corporate staff ITT, N.Y.C., 1965-71; v.p., sec., dir. Chautauqua Hardware Corp., Jamestown, N.Y., 1971-78; pres., dir. Arbor Industries, Inc., Jamestown Lounge Co., 1978—; dir. Jamestown Bd. Pub. Utilities, also chmn. ops. com. Vice pres., sec., dir. CHC Industries, Inc., N.Y.C., Period Brass, Inc., Falconer, N.Y. Decorative Hardware, Inc., Lincolnwood, Ill., 1971-78. Bd. dirs. Chautauqua County Solid Waste Disposal Com.; chmn. adv. bd. Jamestown Gen. Hosp. Served with USAAF, 1943-46. Decorated Air medal with oak leaf cluster: featured in 1973 Newsweek Mag. article for devel. employee compensation. Mem. Mfrs. Assn. Jamestown Area (chmn. utilities com., dir.). Methodist. Mason. Author: Handbook of International Purchasing, 1971, 2d edit., 1976. Home: W Oak Hill Rd Jamestown NY 14701 Office: 40 Winsor St Jamestown NY 14701

COMBS, VAN PIERCEON, scientist, inventor; b. London, Ky., Mar. 16, 1925; s. John Vincent and Ada Pearl (Lovelace) C.; B.A., U. No. Iowa, 1949; m. Margaret Bernedine Meyer, Aug. 21, 1948; children—Joseph Edmund, Nicholas Thomas, Thomas John, Mary Kathryn, James Pierceon. Tchr. high sch. sci. Loras Acad., Dubuque, Iowa, 1949-59, Brighton High Sch., Rochester, N.Y., 1959-62; cons. Xerox Corp., Rochester, 1962-65; founder, pres. KaTee Research Corp., Rochester, 1965-68; founder, chief officer Mega Power Corp., Penfield, N.Y., 1969—, also chmn. bd., dir. research; cons. long range planning and energy devices. Chmn. Penfield Little League, 1964-65; head coach St. Joseph Ch. and Sch., 1963-70; ecumenical minister St. Joseph Ch., 1970—. Served with USAF, 1943-45. Decorated Air medal with clusters, Purple Heart; NSF grantee, 1960, 61. Roman Catholic. Clubs: I (U. No. Iowa), K.C. Contbr. articles to profl. jours. Patentee in field. Home and office: 1617 Scribner Rd Penfield NY 14526

COMEDY, ALAN VAUGHN, coll. adminstr.; b. Canonsburg, Pa., Jan. 2, 1946; s. Harold Douglas and Kathleen Francis C.; B.A., Wilberforce U., 1970; M.A., Antioch Grad. Sch., 1971; m. Deborah Dennise Gardner, Aug. 15, 1970; children—Margaret Ann, Alan Vaughn. Recreation specialist Dayton (Ohio) Recreation Center, 1968-70; counselor-tchr. Phila. Bd. Edn., 1970-72; tchr. D.C. Bd. Edn., 1972-74; dir. Partnership Program, Catholic U. Am., Washington, 1974—; cons. Nat. Urban League, Fed. Bd. Minority and Female Recruitment; advisor Equal Opportunity Bd.; speaker on recruitment and counseling minority students. Receipient Meritorious award D.C. Bd. Edn., 1973; Pub. Service award Black Orgn. Students, 1977. Mem. Am. Personnel and Guidance Assn., Am. Assn. Higher Edn., Personel of Higher Edn. Home: 717 Irving St NE Washington DC 20017

COMER, NATHAN LAWRENCE, psychiatrist; b. Phila., Nov. 10, 1923; s. Rubin L. and Fannie (Cassover) C.; B.A., U. Pa., 1944; M.D., Hahnemann Med. Coll., 1949; certificate Grad. Med. Sch. U. Pa., 1950; m. Rita Ellis, June 19, 1949; children—Robert, Susan Eve, Debra Ruth, Marc Jeremy. Intern, Hahnemann Med. Coll. and Hosp., Phila., 1949-50; resident Grad. Sch. Medicine U. Pa., 1950-51; NIMH fellow, Inst. Pa. Hosp., Phila., 1951-53; practice medicine specializing in psychiatry Phila. and Lower Merion Twp., Pa., 1953—; pres. med. staff Phila. Psychiat. Center, 1975-77, sr. cons. psychiatrist, 1978—; sr. attending psychiatrist Inst. Pa. Hosp., 1958—; chmn. dept. psychiatry West Park Hosp., Phila., 1978—; clin. asst. prof. psychiatry Med. Coll. Pa., 1965-78, clin. asso. prof. psychiatry, 1978—. Bd. dirs. Temple Adath Israel Main Line, 1958—. Diplomate Am. Bd. Psychiatry, also examiner. Fellow Am. Psychiat. Assn.; mem. AMA, Alumni Assn. Hahnemann Med. Coll. (pres. 1973-74). Republican. Jewish. Mem. B'nai B'rith. Contbr. articles to profl. jours. Home: 1100 Hillcrest Rd Penn Valley Narberth PA 19072 Office: Inst Pa Hosp 111 N 49th St Philadelphia PA 19139

COMERFORD, PHILIP MICHAEL, bank exec.; b. Toledo, Apr. 20, 1931; s. L.C. and Regina M. (Heiler) C.; Asso. Sci., Jackson Jr. Coll., 1950; B.B.A., U. Mich., 1952, M.B.A., 1953; m. Diana Lange, Feb. 7, 1953; children—Philip Michael, Cynthia, David, Andrew. Audit mgr. Price Waterhouse & Co., 1957-65; asst. to treas. Standard Pressed Steel Co., Jenkintown, Pa., 1965-68; pres., dir. Eastern Bancorp., Phila., 1969—; pres., dir. State Nat. Bank Md., Rockville, 1976—. Mem. Christ the King Regional Sch. Bd. Edn., finance chmn.,

1972-75; mem. Bd. Edn., Haddonfield, N.J., 1977-78. Served with USCGR, 1953-56; now comdr. Res. C.P.A., D.C., Pa. Mem. Am. Inst. C.P.A.'s, Pa. Inst. C.P.A.'s, Phila. Jaycees (pres. 1965-66, chmn. bd. 1966-67), Pa. Jaycees (state v.p. 1966-67), U. Mich. Alumni Assn. (dir.), Bethesda-Chevy Chase C. of C. (legis. com.). Clubs: University of Mich. Alumni of Phila. (v.p. 1971-73, pres. 1973-75, dist. rep. 1975—, mem. council, sec.-treas. 2d dist. 1976-77, dist. dir. 1977—), Union League (Phila.); Vesper; Tavistock Country; Bethesda Country. Home: 7715 Savannah Dr Bethesda MD 20034 Office: 11616 Rockville Pike Rockville MD 20852

COMPAIN, RITA, educator; b. N.Y.C., Dec. 14, 1926; d. Benjamin and Sarah B. (Modell) Romer; B.S., City U. N.Y., 1947; M.L.S., L.I. U., 1967; advanced degree Columbia U., 1970; postgrad. St. John's U.; m. Ernest A. Compain, Apr. 17, 1948; children—Michael, Daniel, Andrew. Tchr., N.Y.C. Schs., 1956-59; library coordinator Oceanside (N.Y.) Pub. Schs., 1959-61; librarian Franklin Square (N.Y.) Pub. Schs., 1961-71, grade chmn., 1964-71; asst. prof. L.I. U., 1969-77; tchr. tng. program, Nassau County. Ednl. cons., guest speaker Nassau County Jail Pilot Library Project, 1970—; library cons. Great Neck (N.Y.) Pub. Schs. Youth group leader, Elmont, N.Y., 1959-61. Mem. ALA, N.Y. (chmn. service standards com. 1960), Nassau-Suffolk Sch. (pres. 1970-71) library assns., L.I. Ednl. Communication Council, Delta Kappa Gamma. Club: Old Westbury Golf and Country (membership com.). Author: Self-Educators Guide, 1974. Contbr. articles to profl. jours. Home: 118 E 60th St New York City NY 10022

COMPARETTO, JOSEPH, architect, profl. planner; b. Tampa, Fla., Nov. 5, 1923; s. Cosimo and Ignatzia (Zambito) C.; student Fed. Inst. Tech., N.Y.C., 1946, Columbia, 1942; m. Angelina Messina, Feb. 25, 1945; children—Joseph Cosimo, Pamela Ann. Archtl. designer R. Candela, architect, N.Y.C., 1940-42, 45-46; archtl. designer Kelly & Gruzen, architects, N.Y.C., 1946-48; archtl. group leader architecture div. Vitro Corp., N.Y.C., 1948-50; archtl. asso. Mascolo & Masovian, Architects, Jersey City, 1950-56; owner Pvt. Practice Architects & Engrs. Comparetto & Kenny, P.A., Jersey City, 1956-75, Pvt. Practice J. Comparetto, A.I.A., P.A., Architects, 1975—; owner Dellridge Nursing Home, Paramus, N.J., J.F. Kennedy Office Bldg., Jersey City. Served with USAAF, 1942-45. Mem. AIA, N.J. Soc. Architects, Soc. Archtl. Historians, Constrn. Specifications Inst. Clubs: N.Y. Athletic, N.Y. Turf and Field. Works include: Design of Hudson County Court House and Adminstrn. Bldg., Jersey City, 1957; U.S. Postal Mail Handling Depot, Kearny, N.J., 1969; Marine View Plaza Housing Devel., Hoboken, N.J.; numerous schs., office bldgs., housing projects, hosps. Home and Office: 18 Stone Ledge Rd Upper Saddle River NJ 07458

COMPTON, MARY BEATRICE BROWN (MRS. RALPH THEODORE COMPTON), pub. relations exec., writer; b. Washington, May 25, 1923; d. Robert James and Abie Eliza (Stone) Brown; grad. Thayer Acad., Chandler Sch., Leland Powers Sch. Radio, TV and Theatre, Boston, 1942; m. Ralph Theodore Compton, Mar. 18, 1961, step-children—Ralph Theodore, Patricia (Mrs. William R. Schnitzler). Radio program dir. Converse Co., Malden, Mass., 1942-45; head radio continuity dept. Sta. WAAB, Yankee Network, Worcester, Mass., 1945-46; asst. dir. radio Leland Powers Sch. Radio, TV and Theatre, Boston, 1946-49, dir., 1949-51; program asst. Sta. KNBH, Hollywood, Calif., 1951-52; v.p. Acorn Film Co., Boston, 1953-54; dir. women's communications, editor Program Notes, radio interviewer NAM, 1954-61; cons. on women's communications to N.Y. advt. agys., 1961—. Celebrities pub. relations Nat. Citizens for Nixon, 1968. Mem. Soc. Old Plymouth Colony Descs., Magna Carta Dames, Smithsonian Instn. Assos., Corcoran Gallery Assn., Montgomery County Art Assn. Clubs: Congressional Country (Bethesda, Md.); Chesapeake Country (Lusby, Md.). Home: Box 181 Cove Point Beach Lusby MD 20657

COMSTOCK, RICHARD DAVIS, chemist; b. Penn Yan, N.Y., June 7, 1928; s. Robert Monroe and Dorothy (Davis) C.; B.S., U. Rochester, 1958; M.S., Canisius Coll., 1961; m. Barbara Jane Fisher, July 24, 1954 (div. 1977); children—Richard, Susan, Alan. Chem. technician Eastman Kodak Co., Rochester, 1947-55, research technologist, 1955-58, mem. research staff, 1956-58; instr. chemistry and physics Spencerport Central Sch., 1958-60; instr., asst. prof. chemistry Dutchess Community Coll., Poughkeepsie, N.Y., 1960-66; asso. and sr. asso. prof. chemistry Bucks County Community Coll., Newtown, Pa., 1966—, coordinator chemistry programs, 1969—. Pres., Hyde Pk. Sch. PTA, 1965-66; certified lay speaker Genesee Conf., Meth. Ch., 1960-61. NSF grantee, 1961, 62, 64, 65; recipient local coll. grant study computer-assisted instruction U. Pitts., 1975. Mem. Pa. Assn. Coll. Chemistry Tchrs., Am. Chem. Soc., Am. Fedn. Tchrs. Republican. Methodist. Author: (with Muller and Salotto) Lab Experiments in College Chemistry, 1966. Home: 236 Wisteria Dr Churchville PA 18966 Office: Bucks County Community College F-211 Swamp Rd Newtown PA 18940

CONABLE, BARBER B., JR., congressman; b. Warsaw, N.Y., Nov. 2, 1922; s. Barber B. and Agnes G. (Gouinlock) C.; A.B., Cornell U., 1942, LL.B., 1948; m. Charlotte Williams, Sept. 13, 1952. Admitted to N.Y. bar, 1948; practice in Buffalo, 1948-50; partner firm Conable & Conable, Batavia, 1952-62; partner firm Conable & Oshlag, 1962-64; mem, N.Y. State Senate, 1963-64; mem. 89th-96th Congress from 35th N.Y. Dist.; mem. ways and means com., budget com., joint com. on internal revenue taxation. Past pres. Genesee United Fund, Genesee Health Found.; chmn. Rep. Task Force on Seniority in Congress, 1970. Served with USMCR, 1942-46, 50-52; col. Res. ret. Rotarian (pres. Batavia). Editor Cornell Law Quar., 1947-48. Home: 10532 Alexander Rd Alexander NY 14005 Office: Rayburn House Office Bldg Washington DC 20515

CONARY, DAVID ARLAN, investment co. exec.; b. South Paris, Maine, Mar. 3, 1937; s. Wilfred Grindle and Arline (Whitney) C.; A.B., Bowdoin Coll., 1959; postgrad. Northeastern U., 1965-66, Mass. Inst. Tech., 1966-67; Boston U., 1967; m. Frances Jane Harrison, June 8, 1957; children—Lee Harrison, Neil Whitney. Securities trader H.C. Wainwright & Co., Boston, 1959-60; securities trader May & Gannon, Boston, 1960-65, v.p., 1968-71; securities analyst, adminstr. The Boston Co., Boston, 1965-68; mgr. instl. trading Fahnestock & Co., Boston, 1971-72; resident mgr. G.A. Saxton & Co., Boston, 1972-75; instl. trader Baker, Weeks & Co., N.Y.C., 1975; mgr. trading State St. Research & Mgmt. Co., Boston, 1976—; lectr. in field. Dist. dir. Mass. Bay United Fund, 1966. Mem. Nat. Security Traders Assn., Boston Securities Traders Assn. (gov. 1972-73), Boston Investment Club, Bowdoin Club of Boston (dir. 1965-66, dir. 175th anniversary campaign 1973-74), Mensa, Theta Delta Chi. Club: Weymouth Sportsmen's (sec. 1965-66, 71-72). Republican. Home: 79 Atlantic Ave North Hampton NH 03862 Office: 225 Franklin St Boston MA 02110

CONDICT, EDGAR RHODES, med. instrument mfg. exec., med. center exec., inventor; b. Boston, Apr. 27, 1940; s. Clinton Adams and Elizabeth May (Lane) C.; B.S., Bucknell U., 1962; m. Judith Pond, June 9, 1962; children—Edgar Rhodes, Robert Adams. Chmn. bd., pres. Bio-Tronics Research, Inc., New London, N.H., 1962—; pres. Medel Corp., patent devel. investment, N.Y.C., 1965—; founder, chmn. Kearsarge Rehab. Med. Center, 1979—; cons. U. Tex. Med. Sch., 1969; cons. in med. electronics, electronics, biophysics, telecommunications, environ. health and welfare. Active Boy Scouts Am. Recipient various grants in neuro-brain scis.; numerous med. awards from fgn. countries; named Outstanding Young Man of Am., 1971. Mem. Neuroelectric Soc., Sigma Chi. Baptist. Author: A Theory of Anesthesia; Feedback Anesthesia; others. Patentee in fields med. electronics, telecommunications. Address: Main St New London NH 03257

CONDON, CHARLES FRANCIS M., psychologist; b. Quincy, Mass.; s. Charles Francis and Helen (Wassell) C.; A.B., Boston Coll., 1962; M.S., Purdue U., 1964. Staff psychologist Elec. Boat div. Gen. Dynamics, Groton, Conn., 1965-67, head human factors sect. Quincy div., 1967-69; v.p. Systems Operations Support, Inc., 1967-74; sr. staff scientist Matrix Research Co., 1969-73, dir. systems research div., 1973-74; sr. scientist Bradford Computer & Systems, Inc., Rockville, Md., 1974—. Mem. Am., Eastern psychol. assns., Human Factors Soc. (dir. New Eng. chpt. 1969), Nat. Mgmt. Assn., Mensa (treas. Met. D.C. chpt. 1969-72, pres. 1972-74), ACLU, Am. Platform Assn., Nat. Speleological Soc. Contbr. numerous articles to profl. jours. Home: 271 Belmont St Wollaston MA 02170 Office: 2 Research Pl Rockville MD 20850

CONDRATE, ROBERT ADAM, SR., spectroscopist, educator; b. Worcester, Mass., Jan. 19, 1938; s. Adam Vincent and Angela Marian (Talacka) C.; B.S., Worcester Poly. Inst., 1960; Ph.D., Ill. Inst. Tech., 1965; m. Judith Campbell, Aug. 13, 1960; children—Barbara Louise, Robert Adam, Laura Angela. Research asso. U. Ariz., Tucson, 1966-67; asst. prof. spectroscopy N.Y. State Coll. Ceramics, Alfred (N.Y.) U., 1967-70, asso. prof., 1970-78, prof., 1978—; vis. prof. Los Alamos Sci. Lab., 1972; cons. ceramic cos. Mem. parents adv. bd. secondary edn. Alfred-Almond Central Sch., 1975—; Danforth Found. asso. for higher edn., 1976—. Recipient spectroscopy award Chgo. Sect. Soc. Applied Spectroscopy, 1964, Scholes award Alfred U., 1972. Grantee Inland Steel-Ryerson Found., 1963-64, NSF, 1966-67, Coll. Center Finger Lakes, 1969, Alfred U. Research Found., 1971, Corning Glass Works, 1975; NIH fellow 1964-65. Fellow Am. Inst. Chemists; mem. Am., Can. ceramic socs., Am. Chem. Soc., Soc. Applied Spectroscopy, Am. Phys. Soc., Coblentz Soc., N.Y. Acad. Scis., AAAS, Sigma Xi, Phi Kappa Phi, Phi Lambda Upsilon, Sigma Alpha Epsilon. Mason. Contbg. author, contbr. articles to profl. publs. Home: Random Rd Alfred Sta NY 14803

CONDRELL, WILLIAM KENNETH, lawyer; b. Buffalo, Sept. 19, 1926; s. Paul Kenneth and Celia Olga (Schinas) C.; B.S., Yale U., 1946; S.M., Mass. Inst. Tech., 1947; LL.B., Harvard U., 1950; children—Paul, William, Alexander. Admitted to N.Y. bar, 1951, D.C. bar, 1964; asst. econ. adviser Exec. Office Pres., Washington, 1951-54; mgmt. cons. McKinsey & Co., Chgo., 1954-55; mgr. budgets Hotpoint div. Gen. Electric Co., Chgo., 1955-59; practiced law, Washington, 1959—; chmn. bd. dirs. Timber Engrng. Co.; gen. counsel Soc. Am. Foresters, Am. Wood Preservers Inst., Forest Industries Com. on Timber Valuation and Taxation; lectr. Duke U. Chmn. bd. Center for Continuing Edn., Wroxeter-on-Severn Sch.; bd. dirs. Renewable Natural Resources Found. Served with USNR, 1944-46. C.P.A., Ill. Mem. Am. Bar Assn., Am. Inst. C.P.A.'s, Soc. Am. Foresters. Greek Orthodox (chmn. parish council 1965-69). Clubs: Univ. (Washington), Congl. Country. Editor-in-chief Timber Tax Jour., 1965—. Home: 6601 Michaels Dr Bethesda MD 20034 Office: 1250 Connecticut Ave NW Washington DC 20036

CONE, GERTRUDE ELLEN MARY, historian, librarian; b. Syracuse, N.Y.; d. William Horton and Persis (Mather) Cone; A.B., U. Rochester, 1931; M.A., U. Vt., 1945; postgrad. Fordham U. Grad. Sch. Edn., 1960-61, Sch. Social Service, 1964; Canisius Coll., 1963-64, State U. N.Y. Coll. at Geneseo, summers 1931-33, 35. Tchr., librarian Moira (N.Y.) High Sch., 1931-34, Ft. Edward (N.Y.) High Sch., 1934-35, Sr. High Sch., Bristol, Conn., 1939-42; librarian Jr.-Sr. High Sch. Plattsburgh, N.Y., 1942-44; asst. coll. librarian State U. Coll., Plattsburgh, 1945-61, asst. librarian emeritus, 1966—; tchr. librarian Nardin Acad., Buffalo, 1961—. Active A.R.C.; mem. steering com. Sisters Assembly of Diocese of Buffalo, 1971-73, now mem. exec. com.; del. to U.S. Provincial Assembly of Soc. Daus. of Heart of Mary, also mem. planning bd. Mem. Am., N.Y., Catholic library assns., Western N.Y. Catholic Libraries Conf. (sec. 1963-64), N.Y. State Tchrs. Assn., N.E.A., Am. Assn. U. Women, Theta Alpha Epsilon. Democrat. Roman Catholic. Author: Selective Bibliography of Publications on the Champlain Valley, 1959. Asso. editor York State Tradition, 1948—. Contbr. articles on Champlain Valley to hist. jours. Home: 135 Cleveland Ave Buffalo NY 14222

CONE, JOHN FREDERICK, educator; b. Salem, Ohio, Oct. 10, 1926. A.B. in English, Rutgers Coll., New Brunswick, N.J., 1948, A.M. in English, 1953; Ph.D. in Dramatic Arts, N.Y. U., N.Y.C., 1964. Acad. dean N.C. Sch. of the Arts, Winston-Salem, 1966-67; adjunct asst. prof. Fordham U., Bronx, N.Y., 1967—; asst. to dean of students Hunter Coll., N.Y.C., 1969-70; chmn. dept. English, and fine arts Red Bank Regional High Sch., LIttle Silver, N.J., 1970—. Mem. NEA, N.J. Edn. Assn., Phi Delta Kappa. Author: Oscar Hammerstein's Manhattan Opera Company. Editor: The World's Love Poetry; The Civil War in Poetry; Shakespeare's Macbeth. Home: 7 Twin Lights Terr Highlands NJ 07732

CONETTA, JOSEPH ANTHONY, environ. geologist, med. research technologist; b. N.Y.C., Nov. 21, 1941; s. Vincent Corrado and Esther C.; M.L.T., M.T., Manhattan Med. Asst. Sch., 1960-61; B.A., Queens Coll., 1976. Jr.-sr. technologist clin. pathology Caledonia Hosp., 1960-64, supr., 1966-67; med. research technologist, research asst. N.Y. Med. Coll., 1967—; cons., research asst. N.Y. Zool. Soc., 1971-75. Served with AUS, 1964-66. Mem. Soc. Applied Spectroscopy, AAAS, East African Wild Life Soc. (life), Queens Coll. Alumni Assn. (com. of 1000), Sigma Xi. Roman Catholic. Contbr. articles to profl. jours. Home: 154 68 26th Ave Flushing NY 11354

CONGDON, PAUL UBERT, coll. dean; b. Fitchburg, Mass., Aug. 24, 1922; s. James Leonard and Margaret Louise (Parmenter) C.; B.S., Springfield Coll., 1943; M.A. in Edn., Ariz. State U., 1949; Ed.D., Boston U., 1961; m. Phyllis Irene Young, Apr. 22, 1949; children—James Leonard II, Karen Elizabeth. Tchr.-coach Lunenburg (Mass.) Jr.-Sr. High Sch., 1947, 49, 52, Townsend (Mass.) Jr.-Sr. High Sch., 1948-49; elementary sch. prin. South Fitchburg (Mass.) Sch., 1952-54; prin. 1-12, Ashby (Mass.) schs., 1954-57; prin. Littleton (Mass.) Jr.-Sr. High Sch., 1957-59; teaching fellow, then instr. Boston U. Sch. Edn., 1959-61; mem. faculty Springfield Coll., 1961—, dean students, asso. prof. edn., 1963-65, acad. dean, prof. edn., 1965—. Co-founder Springfield Free U., 1970; cons. in field. Served with USNR, 1944-47. Mem. Am. Assn. Supervision Curriculum Devel. (nat. bd. 1973—), Assn. High Edn., Mass. Assn. Supervision and Curriculum Devel. (pres. 1977-79). Rotarian (pres. Springfield 1974—, dist. chmn. found.). Home: 444 Springfield St Wilbraham MA 01095 Office: Box 1765 Springfield MA 01109

CONGER, CLEMENT ELLIS, fgn. service officer, curator; b. Rockingham, Va., Oct. 15, 1912; s. Clement E. and Hallie (Ramsay) C.; grad. Strayer Coll.; postgrad. George Washington U., 1933-34; grad. Adj. Gen. Officer Candidate Sch., Ft. Washington Md., 1943; m. Lianne Hopkins, May 29, 1948; children—William Ramsay, Jay Alden, Shelley Louise. Asst. finance examiner PWA, 1933-34; officer mgr., corr. Chgo. Tribune, Washington 1934-41; office mgr. U.S. Rubber Co., Washington, 1941-42, pub. relations asst., N.Y.C., 1946-47; staff asst., asst. exec. dir. Bur. German Affairs, 1949-54, asst. chief protocol, 1955-57, dep. chief protocol, 1958-61; spl. asst. to dir., exec. sec. ACDA, State Dept., Washington, 1962-69; dep. chief protocol, 1969-70; protocol asst. to chmn. Nixon-Agnew Inaugural, 1968-69; curator Diplomatic Recreation Rooms State Dept., 1962—, White House curator, 1970—. Producer color motion picture travel films, lectr. on diplomatic reception rooms Dept. State and White House Chmn. Alexandria (Va.) Hist. Restoration and Preservation Commn., 1968—; mem. Com. for Preservation White House; mem. men's adv. com. Gunston Hall Plantation, Va.; vice chmn. Com. on Gov.'s Mansion, Richmond, Va.; mem. Supreme Ct. Hist. Commn. Trustee Va. Mus. Fine Arts, Richmond; bd. dirs. Historic Alexandria Found.; v.p. Va. Trust Historic Preservation. Served from 2d lt. to maj. AUS, 1942-46; asst. sec. combined civil affairs com. Combined Chiefs Staff. Episcopalian. Clubs: Metropolitan, Chevy Chase, City Tavern (Washington). Contbr. articles, illustrations to various publs. radio, TV programs. Home: 320 Mansion Dr Alexandria VA 22302 Office: Dept State Washington DC 20525 also The White House Washington DC 20500

CONGLETON, HOWARD, JR., ins., real estate agency exec.; b. Beaufort, N.C., Dec. 26, 1935; s. Howard and Nellie Christine (Spear) C.; m. Carolyn Ann Gibeau, Jan. 12, 1957; children—Kim Ann, Keith Anthony, Kyle Andrew, Kara Ann. Agt., Met. Life Ins. Co., Plattsburgh, N.Y., 1961-63; agency mgr. Paul W. Calkins Inc., Peru, N.Y., 1963-67; owner Congleton Agency, Chazy, N.Y., 1967—; pres. Clinton County Bd. Realtors, 1972-73. Chmn., Clinton County Traffic Safety Bd., 1974—, Chazy Youth Commn., 1970-75. Served with U.S. Army, 1955-58. Mem. Clinton County Agts. Assn. (pres. 1971-73), N.Y. State Ind. Agts. Assn. (chmn. safety com. 1973—, (dir. 1976—), Nat. Ins. Agts. Assn. (vice-chmn. safety com. 1974—), Chazy C. of C. (chmn. 1974—), Nat. Assn. Realtors, N.Y. State Bd. Realtors, N.Y. State Ind. Agts. Assn., Nat. Soc. Real Estate Appraisers. Roman Catholic. Club: Elks. Home: North Farm Rd Chazy NY 12921 Office: Main St Chazy NY 12921

CONIGLIARO, SALVATORE ALFRED, electronics co. exec.; b. N.Y.C., Sept. 17, 1924; s. Anthony and Mary (Yodice) C.; B.E.E., Poly. Inst. Bklyn., 1949, M.E.E., 1954; m. Sarah Billitteri, July 20, 1945; children—Maryann, Anthony, Peter. With Sperry Rand Corp., 1949—, mgr. Polaris program Sperry Gyroscope Co., Great Neck, N.Y.C., 1961-64, group mgr. programs, 1964-66, v.p. systems mgr. Sperry Gryroscope Co., Great Neck, 1966-67, v.p., gen. mgr. Sperry Systems Mgmt. div., Great Neck, 1967-71, pres. Sperry div., Great Neck, 1971—. Chmn., L.I. Met. chpt. Nat. Alliance of Businessmen, 1975-76; trustee Poly. Inst. N.Y. Named Citizen of Yr., N.Y. Profl. Engrs. Mem. Navy League (life), IEEE (sr.), Inst. Nav., Am. Soc. Naval Engrs. Club: Huntington (N.Y.) Crescent. Devel. and prodn. Sparrow I missile, Polaris submarine nav. systems, devel. integrated avionic systems, deep submergence electronic systems. Home: 11 Janes Ln Huntington NY 11743 Office: Marcus Ave Great Neck NY 11020

CONKLIN, EVERETT LAWSON, environ. horticulturist; b. Farmingdale, N.Y., Jan. 11, 1908; s. George and Grace (Williams) C.; student N.Y. U.; m. Ruth Purick, June 20, 1931; children—Everett George, Patricia (Mrs. Thomas Clinton, Jr.), Betty Jane (Mrs. William Baxter III). Partner, Oostrom & Conklin, Syosset, N.Y., 1936-38; div. mgr. Bobbink & Atkins, East Rutherford, N.J., 1938-54; div. mgr., dir. Bobbink Nurseries, Inc., East Rutherford, 1954-57; pres. Everett Conklin & Co., Inc., Montvale, N.J., 1957—, Everett Conklin-West, Inc., East Irvine, Calif., 1974—, Everett Conklin Can., Ltd., Montreal, Que., 1975—. Hort. cons. Sterling Forest Gardens, Tuxedo, N.Y., 1958-69; ann. designer, stager R.H. Macy & Co. Annual Flower Show, N.Y.C., 1975—; designer, stager floral decorations Four Seasons Restaurant, N.Y.C., 1959—; designer, planter interior gardens Frick Mus., N.Y.C., 1969-77; planter interior gardens Ford Found. Bldg., N.Y.C., 1967—, Crown Center Hotel, Kansas City, 1973—; lectr. in field. Mem. N.J. Rural Adv. Commn., 1955-60; pres. Bergen County Bd. Agr., 1957-58; chmn. floral decorations com. Pres. Nixon Inaugural Ball, 1969, 73; advisor U.S. Dept. Agr., 1971—. Bd. dirs. Internat. Flower Show, N.Y.C., 1958-73. Recipient numerous hort. awards including Nat. AAN Landscape award, 1960, 61, 68, 69, 71, 72, 73, 75, 76, 77, Internat. Floral Achievement award, 1965, Florists' Transworld Delivery Assn. award, 1971, Florafax award, 1971, Teleflora award, 1971, 75, Golden Flower award, 1971, Asso. Landscape Contractors Am. nat. award, 1971-76, Am. Inst. Interior Designers ann. Man of Year award, 1973, Nat. Environ. Awareness award, 1976, Fla. State Landscape award; spl. award Am. Soc. Landscape Architects, 1968. Mem. N.J. State Florists Assn. (pres. 1954-55, Man of Yr. award 1974), Am. Acad. Florists (trustee, awards 1967-72), N.Y. Florists Club (pres. 1958, Eminent Merit award 1966, 69), Met. Retail Florists Assn. (pres. 1966), Soc. Am. Florists (pres. 1971-73, Endowment Trustee Safegardian award 1971-74, 77, Nat. award of recognition 1968, Spl. award of recognition 1971), Am. Hort. Soc. (dir. 1977—), Soc. Archtl. Historians, Am. Forestry Assn. Author: A Guide to Interior Planting, 1970. Home: 319 W Passaic Ave Rutherford NJ 07070 Office: 7 Brook Ave Montvale NJ 07645 also 6600 Marine Way E Irvine CA 92650 also 1253 Ave McGill Coll Montreal PQ H3B 2Y5 Canada

CONKLIN, RICHARD NEWTON, elec. engr.; b. Hasbrouck Heights, N.J., Dec. 17, 1932; s. Richard Wardwell and Jessie Frieda (Miller) C.; B.E.E., Union Coll., 1954; m. Susan Edith Gelhaar, Nov. 28, 1973; children—Stephen Peter, Nancy Lee, Robert Wayne, Jason Richard. Adv. engr. IBM Corp., Poughkeepsie, N.Y., 1954—. Vol., Mental Health Club, 1970-73, Coffeehouse, 1972-73; leader Decatur (Ala.) Recovery Inc. Group, 1973-74, Hopewell Junction Recovery Group, 1974—; Mid Hudson Valley dist. leader Recovery Inc. Served to 1st lt. USAF, 1955-58. Recipient grant-in-aid Gen. Electric Co., 1953-54. Mem. I.E.E.E., Mensa. Clubs: Aquarius, Agora (Huntsville, Ala.). Patentee in field. Home: RD 2 Box 497 Guerney Dr Hyde Park NY 12538 Office: Dept 551 Bldg 004-1 IBM Corp Poughkeepsie NY 12602

CONLEY, BERNARD EDWARD, pharmacologist; b. Medina, N.Y., Jan. 28, 1919; s. George Robert and Margaret Loretta (O'Reilly) C.; B.S., Duquesne U., 1942; S.M., U. Chgo., 1951, Ph.D., 1956; m. Veronica M. Lucey, June 30, 1945; children—Colleen, Brian, Kevin, Barry. Dir. toxicology AMA, 1947-60; pharmacologist U.S. Pharmacopeia, 1961-64, NIH, 1964-66; chief drug studies program Nat. Center Health Service Research, Rockville, Md., 1968—. Served to lt. USNR, 1942-46. Recipient Outstanding Pub. Service award Nat. Safety Council, 1955. Fellow AAAS, Am. Pub. Health Assn.; mem. AMA (affiliate), Pharm. Soc. Can. Clubs: University (Chgo.); Manor Country (Rockville). Author: Drug Utilization Research: 1960-75, 1976. Contbg. author various books. Home: 14706 Crossway Rd Norbeck MD 20853 Office: 3700 East-West Hwy Hyattsville MD 20782

CONNANT, CHARLES ELLIS, physician; b. Athens, Greece, Jan. 14, 1922; s. Ellis Charles and Anne Lisa (Economo) C.; came to U.S., 1950, naturalized, 1959; B.A., Marist Fathers Coll. St. Denis, Athens, 1939; M.D., U. Athens, 1949; postgrad. N.Y. U., 1953-54, 54-55, U. Pa., 1955-56; m. Evelyn Gieves, Feb. 24, 1951; children—Pamela

Ann, Charles Ellis, Susan Patricia. Intern, Jersey City Med. Center, 1950-51, Fitkin Meml. Hosp., Neptune, N.J., 1956-57; resident in medicine Jersey City Med. Center, 1951-53; resident in obstetrics and gynecology Bellevue Med. Center, N.Y.C., 1957-58, St. Francis Hosp., Bronx, N.Y., 1958-61; practice medicine specializing in obstetrics and gynecology, Bronx, N.Y., 1961-63, N.Y.C., 1962-63, Jersey City, 1963—; asst. attending physician St. Barnabas Med. Center, Livingston, N.J., 1968—; attending physician Margaret Hague Maternity Hosp., Jersey City, 1963-75, sr. attending physician, 1975—; sr. attending physician Fairmount Hosp., Jersey City, 1968—; sr. attending physician Christ Hosp., 1975—, asst. dir. obstetrics and gynecology, 1976—; asst. clin. prof. dept. obstetrics and gynecology Coll. Medicine and Dentistry, Newark, 1977—. Served as lt. comdr. M.C., Royal Hellenic Navy, 1949-50. Diplomate Am. Bd. Obstetrics and Gynecology. Mem. AMA, Am. Fertility Soc., N.J. Med. Soc., Hudson County Med. Soc., Am. Assn. Gynecol. Laparoscopists, A.C.S., Am. Coll. Obstetrics and Gynecology, Obstet. and Gynecol. Soc. N.J. Home: 321 Long Hill Dr Short Hills NJ 07078 Office: 10 Huron Ave Jersey City NJ 07306

CONNARE, WILLIAM GRAHAM, bishop; b. Pitts., Dec. 11, 1911; s. James J. and Nellie T. (O'Connor) C.; B.A., Duquesne U., 1932, Litt.D., 1961; M.A., St. Vincent Coll., Latrobe, Pa., 1934, L.H.D., 1962; LL.D., Seton Hill Coll., 1960. Ordained priest Roman Catholic Ch., 1936; named domestic prelate, 1955; asst. pastor St. Canice, Pitts., 1936-37, St. Paul's Cathedral, 1937-49; adminstr. St. Richard's Ch., Pitts., 1949-55, pastor, 1955-60; chaplain Univ. Cath. Club. Pitts., 1947-60, Cath. Interracial Council Pitts., 1953-60; dir. Soc. Propagation of Faith, 1950-59; vicar for religious as rep. Bishop of Pitts., 1959-60; consecrated bishop of Greensburg (Pa.), 1960—. Bd. dirs., chmn. community services com. Urban League Pitts., 1950-60; mem. Pitts. Commn. Human Relations, 1953-60; mem. Allegheny County Council Civil Rights, 1953-60, bd. dirs., 1958-60; bd. dirs. Pitts. br. NAACP, 1959-60; Episcopal chmn. Nat. Cath. Com. on Scouting, Boy Scouts Am., 1962-70; Episcopal moderator div. youth activities U.S. Cath. Conf., 1968-70; mem. Bishop's Commn. for Liturgical Apostolate, 1967-72; chmn. commn. on missions Nat. Conf. Cath. Bishops, 1967-71, mem. adminstrv. bd., 1967; mem. Bishop's Com. on Missions, 1971; mem. council Christian Assos. Southwest Pa., 1972; chmn. Am. Bd. Cath. Missions, 1972; mem. Episcopal adv. bd. Word of God Inst., 1974; Episcopal adviser Nat. Cath. Stewardship Council, 1974. Office: 723 E Pittsburgh Greensburg PA 15601

CONNELL, FRANCES JANE, lawyer; b. Phila., Oct. 13, 1946; d. Joseph P. and Frances J. (Rutherford) C.; B.A. cum laude, Duquesne U., 1968; J.D., Dickinson Sch. Law, 1971. Admitted to Pa. bar, 1971; staff atty. Neighborhood Legal Services, Pitts., 1971-72; atty. PPG Industries, Inc., Pitts., 1972-77, sr. atty., 1977—. Sec. bd. mgrs. Toner Inst., 1976-78; bd. dirs. Catholic Social Service Allegheny County, Health and Welfare Planning Assn. Mem. Am., Allegheny County bar assns. Roman Catholic. Office: PPG Industries One Gateway Center Pittsburgh PA 15222

CONNELL, LOUISE FOX, author, mem. Democratic Nat. Com.; b. Bayonne, N.J.; d. Hugh Francis and Virginia (Herrick) Fox; A.B., Barnard Coll., 1914; m. Richard Connell, Nov. 8, 1919 (dec. 1949). Advt. writer J. Walter Thompson Co., 1915-20; asso. editor Delineator mag., 1920-23; asso., then mng. editor Charm, Newark, 1923-25; West Coast editor You, 1936-41; contract writer Conde Nast, 1941-43; free lance writer 1943—. Vol. Lenox Hill Hosp., N.Y.C., 1953-55; vol. Fordham Hosp., N.Y.C., 1955-60, mem. exec. com. of adv. bd. Fordham Hosp., 1964-71. Mem. Dem. Nat. Com. from N.Y. Mem. vol. staff U.S. Food Adminstrn. posters, World War II; ghost writer radio speeches by screen stars on food conservation, World War II. Mem. NAACP, Internat. Council Women, Am. Assn. UN, League Women Voters, ACLU, Citizens Union, Inter-Faith Neighbors New York, Council for a Sane Nuclear Policy, Nat. Council Negro Women, Women's Internat. League Peace and Freedom. Unitarian (deacon). Club: Query (N.Y.C.). Co-author: (play) The Queen Bee, 1929. Contbr. numerous articles to nat. mags. Home: 240 E 82d St New York City NY 10028 Office: care Brandt & Brandt 101 Park Ave New York City NY 10017

CONNELL, WILLIAM FRANCIS, diversified co. exec.; b. Lynn, Mass., May 12, 1938; s. William J. and Theresa (Keaney) C.; B.S. magna cum laude, Boston Coll., 1959; M.B.A., Harvard, 1963; m. Margot C. Gensler, May 29, 1965; children—Monica Cameron, Lisa Terese, Courtenay Erin, William Christopher. Controller, Olga Co., Inc., Van Nuys, Calif., 1963-65; asst. treas. Litton Industries, Inc., also pres. div. Marine Tech., Inc., 1965-68; treas. Ogden Corp., N.Y.C., 1968-71, v.p., 1969-71, sr. v.p., 1971—, also dir.; pres., chief exec. officer Ogden Leisure, Inc., 1972—; chmn., chief exec. officer Ogden Food Service Corp., Ogden Recreation, Inc., Ogden Security, Inc. Active fund raising, trustee Boston Coll.; trustee St. Elizabeth's Hosp., Boston; bd. dirs. Boston 200 Corp. Served to 1st lt. AUS, 1959-61. Mem. Greater Boston C. of C. (dir.), Beta Gamma Sigma, Alpha Sigma Nu, Alpha Kappa Psi. Roman Catholic. Clubs: Univ.; Algonquin; Tedesco Country. Home: 111 Ocean Ave Swampscott MA 01907 Office: 111 Waldemar Ave East Boston MA 02128

CONNELLEY, EARL JOHN, JR., water and waste treatment co. exec.; b. Covington, Ky.; s. Earl John and Grace (Muzzio) C.; B.S., U. Cin., 1947, M.S., 1948; m. Eileen L. O'Connor, Feb. 20, 1965; children—Ann Lloyd, Carol Jeanne, Cynthia Jane. Research engr. Eckey Research Labs., Cin., 1946-47; process engr. Permutit Co. subsidiary Zurn Corp., N.Y.C., 1948-49, sales engr., East Orange, N.J., 1949-50, Chgo., 1951-52, dist. engr., Cin., 1952-62, regional mgr., Chgo., 1962-66, sales mgr., Paramus, N.J., 1966—. Instr., U. Cin., 1947-48. Mem. industry com. Ann. Am. Power Conf.; mem. adv. com. Ann. Internat. Water Conf. Served with AUS, 1943-46, 50-51. Decorated Silver Star, Purple Heart. Registered profl. engr. Ohio, Ill., N.J., Ind., Mich., Mo., Wis., Ky., Iowa, Tex., Minn., N.Y., Pa., Mass., Ky. Mem. Am. Water Works Assn., Waste Pollution Control Fedn., Alpha Chi Sigma, Phi Kappa Theta, Roman Catholic. Club: University (Cin.). Contbr. articles in field to profl. jours. Home: 8 Split Rock Rd Upper Saddle River NJ 07458 Office: E 49 Midland Ave Paramus NJ 07652

CONNELLY, JOHN EDWARD, III, mortgage brokerage co. exec.; b. N.Y.C., Apr. 13, 1935; s. John Edward and Margaret (Scholl) C.; B.A., U. Va., 1958; m. Judith Ellen Moore, Sept. 21, 1977; children by previous marriage—Michael A., Christopher L. Mortgage officer Manufacturers Hanover Trust Co., N.Y.C., 1960-66; asst. v.p. D.H. Overmeyer Co., N.Y.C., 1966-67; dir. mergers and acquisitions Gregory & Sons, N.Y.C., 1967-70; v.p., treas. G.A. Thompson & Co., N.Y.C., 1970-74; v.p., treas., dir. Gregory Capital Corp., N.Y.C., 1974—; pres., dir. Gregory Realty Corp., N.Y.C., 1974—. Trustee, Childrens Aid Soc., 1967—; mem. exec. council Allen-Stevenson Sch., 1962—. Served with AUS, 1958-60. Decorated Commendation medal. Mem. Sigma Phi. Republican. Roman Catholic. Clubs: Leash, Mason. Home: 12 Crestwood Dr Fort Salonga NY 11768 Office: 745 Fifth Ave New York City NY 10022

CONNERS, KENNETH WRAY, author, lay theologian; b. Minotola, N.J., Nov. 12, 1909; s. William Henry and Evelyn Burr (Brown) C.; B.S. in Econs., U. Pa., 1930, A.M., 1932, postgrad., 1941-42; postgrad. Mansfield Coll., Oxford (Eng.) U., 1966, 77, St. Andrews (Scotland) U., 1970; m. Christine Rosenberger, Aug. 10, 1940. Free-lance writer, 1932-34; with Leeds & Northrup Co., North Wales, Pa., 1934-74, advt. mgr., 1947-69, dir. pub. relations, 1969-74. Spl. lectr. journalism U. Pa., 1954-60; artist mem. Phila. Art Alliance, 1961—; conductor retreats and seminars for ministers and laymen, U.S., Can., Eng. Pres. Covenant House, Phila., 1970—; v.p. Phila. Sci. Council, 1963—; bd. dirs. Germantown (Pa.) YMCA, 1968—, v.p., 1971-75; bd. dirs. Kirkridge Study Center, 1974—; mem. exec. bd. jr. com. Phila. Orch., 1946-50, 58-63, chmn., 1962; asso. Lycoming (Pa.) Coll., 1970—; bd. dirs. Phila. Methodist Missionary Soc., 1953-64, Greater Phila. Council Chs., 1965-68, Wellsprings Ecumenical Renewal Center, 1965-71, Met. Boys Clubs Phila., 1976—. Mem. English Speaking Union. Methodist (lay leader). Author: Pro, Con and Coffee, 1942; Stranger in the Pew, 1970; Who's in Charge Here?, 1973; Lord, Have You Got a Minute?, 1979; contbr. chpts. to The Church Creative, 1966, Upper Room Disciplines, 1975; also articles. Home: 1601 Meadowbrook Rd Meadowbrook PA 19046

CONNERY, JOSEPH EDWIN, JR., accountant; b. Phila., Jan. 18, 1947; s. Joseph E. and Marjorie M. Campbell) C.; B.S., LaSalle Coll., 1968; m. Theresa Rachel Gambone, Feb. 12, 1972; children—Michelle, Susan. Sr. accountant Haskins & Sells C.P.A.'s, Phila., 1968-70; sr. auditor UGI Corp., Phila., 1970-73; sr. auditor INA Corp., Phila., 1973-77, mgr. corporate auditing INA Reinsurance Co., Phila., 1978—. Mem. tutorial program Sch. Dist. Phila. Served with USAR, 1968-74. C.P.A., Pa. Mem. Am., Pa. insts. C.P.A.'s, Nat. Assn. Accountants, Alpha Epsilon. Home: 163 Sutcliffe Ln Conshohocken PA 19428 Office: 1600 Arch St Philadelphia PA 19101

CONNOLLY, JOHN DOLAN, investment banker; b. N.Y.C., Oct. 28, 1943; s. Thomas Michael and Ann Dorothy (Dolan) C.; A.B. in Economics, Holy Cross Coll., 1965; M.B.A., Stanford, 1967; m. Elizabeth Pell Frazier, Jan. 18, 1975. Securities analyst First Natl. City Bank, N.Y.C., 1967-69; Nat. Securities & Research Corp., 1969-71; v.p. Faulkner, Dawkins & Sullivan, 1971-77, sr. v.p., 1977; 1st v.p. White, Weld & Co., 1977—. Chartered fin. analyst, N.Y. Mem. Fin. Analysts Fed., N.Y. Soc. of Security Analysts, Stanford Alumni Assn. Club: Downtown Athletic. Contbr. article in field to profl. jour. Home: 240 E 76th New York City NY 10021 Office: White Weld & Co 1 Liberty Plaza New York City NY 10006

CONNOLLY, JOHN JOSEPH, ednl. adminstr.; b. Worcester, Mass., Feb. 4, 1940; s. Nicholas John and Margaret Anne (Flynn) C.; B.S. in Edn., Worcester State Coll., 1962; M.A. in Counseling and Student Personnel Work, U. Conn., Storrs, 1963; Ed.D. in Coll. and Univ. Adminstrn., Columbia U., 1972; m. Ingrid Schlemminger, Apr. 10, 1964; children—Sean Timothy, Cheryl Ann. Dir. admissions, registrar Sullivan County Community Coll., Loch Sheldrake, N.Y., 1965-67; asst. to pres., dir. community and extension services Mercer County Community Coll., Trenton, N.J., 1967-69; dean of coll. Harford Community Coll., Bel Air, Md., 1969-72; pres. Dutchess Community Coll., Poughkeepsie, N.Y., 1973—. Chmn., Dutchess County Indsl. Devel. Agy.; pres., dir. United Way Dutchess County; chmn. bd. trustees St. Francis Hosp., Poughkeepsie; trustee N.Y. Med. Coll.; bd. dirs. Poughkeepsie Area Fund; indsl. adv. com. Hudson Valley Opportunities Industrialization Center; trustee John Carroll Sch.; adv. bd. Dutchess County Commn. on Aging. Mem. Am. Assn. Community and Jr. Colls. (govtl. affairs commn., dir.), N.Y. State Assn. Pres.'s Pub. Community Colls. (pres.), Assn. Colls. and Univs. N.Y. (exec. com.), Associated Colls. Mid Hudson Area (pres., exec. com.), Phi Delta Kappa. Address: 57 Pendell Rd Poughkeepsie NY 12601

CONNOLLY, MICHAEL JOSEPH, III, state ofcl.; b. West Roxbury, Mass., Apr. 20, 1947; s. Michael Joseph and Florence C.; A.B., Holy Cross Coll., 1969; J.D., New Eng. Sch. Law, 1976; m. Lynda Murphy, Aug. 4, 1971; children—John Ronan, Justin. Tchr. math. Boston Latin Sch., 1972; mem. Mass. Ho. of Reps., 1973-79, mem. joint com. on edn., chmn. spl. legis. com. on commuter traffic; sec. of state Commonwealth of Mass., Boston, 1979—. Charter mem. Health Planning Council Greater Boston, 1973; legis. aide Boston City Council. Served with U.S. N.G. Mem. Internat. Brotherhood of Brewery Workers. Club: Holy Cross (class agt. 1970—) (Boston). Home: 122 Montclair Ave Roslindale MA 02131 Office: State House Room 340 Boston MA 02133

CONNOLLY, VIRGINIA STRAUGHAN, state legislator, epidemiologist; b. Manchester, Conn., June 25, 1914; d. Wayland Kemper and Ruth Elizabeth (Wright) Straughan; R.N., Hartford Hosp. Sch. Nursing, 1934; B.S., St. Joseph Coll., 1951; postgrad. Boston U., 1951-53, Harvard extension, 1951-54, Nat. Communicable Disease Center Dept. HEW, 1968-69; m. James Cyril Connolly, Aug. 10, 1935; children—Pamela Connolly Bartlett, James Patrick. Adminstr., Simsbury (Conn.) Vis. Nursing Assn., 1950-65; interim exec. dir. Am. Cancer Soc., Hartford, 1966; head epidemiology services St. Francis Hosp., Simsbury, 1968—; mem. Conn. Gen. Assembly, 1970—, chmn. pub. health and safety com.; dir. Simsbury Bank and Trust Co. Sec. Welfare Salvation Army, 1955—; chmn. Simsbury Voluntary Social Service Dept., 1960-65; mem. legis. com. Conn. Hosp. Assn., 1970—; chmn. Simsbury Com. on Aging; sec. Simsbury Housing Authority, 1967-71; bd. dirs. Simsbury Hist. Soc. Fellow Royal Soc. Health (London); mem. Hartford Hosp., St. Joseph Coll. alumnae assns. Contbr. articles to profl. jours. Home: 91 Old Farms Rd West Simsbury CT 06092

CONNOR, LEO EDWARD, educator; b. Phila., Sept. 5, 1922; s. Leo A. and Margaret (McMahon) C.; B.A., La Salle Coll., 1945; M.A., U. Pitts., 1949; Ed.D., Columbia U., 1955; m. Frances Partridge, June 5, 1952. Tchr. secondary schs., Pitts., 1945-50; elementary prin. Clarkstown Central Sch. Dist., New City, N.Y., 1950-51, dir. elementary edn., 1951-56; asst. supt. Lexington Sch. for Deaf, N.Y.C., 1956-67, exec. dir., 1967—. Instr., N.Y. U., 1963-64; lectr. Tchrs. Coll., Columbia U., 1964—. Research grantee Vocational Rehab. Adminstrn., 1960-62, Nat. Inst. Neurol. Disease and Blindness, 1963-66, Office Edn., 1964-67. Mem. Council for Exceptional Children (pres. 1967-68, exec. com. 1967-67, governing bd. 1961-64, pres. div. children communication disorders 1964-65), Alexander Graham Bell Assn. for Deaf (pres. 1970-72). Contbr. articles to profl. jours. Address: 30th Ave and 75th St Jackson Heights NY 11370

CONNOR, MICHAEL RODNEY, lawyer; b. Phila., Nov. 6, 1942; s. Rodney Morton and Lois (Reckard) C.; B.A., U. Del., 1964; J.D., Dickinson Sch. Law, 1967; m. Brooke S. Amole, Aug. 28, 1965; 1 son, Timothy Charles. Admitted to N.J. bar, 1967; asso. firm Lloyd, Megargee & Steedle, Weinstein & Horn, Atlantic City, 1967-70; partner Lloyd, Megargee, Steedle & Connor, Atlantic City and Pleasantville, N.J., 1970—; instr. Inst. for Continuing Legal Edn., Rutgers U./N.J. Bar Assn., 1970—; trustee, v.p. Cape Atlantic Legal Services, Inc., Atlantic City, 19—; city solicitor Ocean City (N.J.), 1975—; municipal ct. judge Borough Beach Haven (N.J.), 1974-76. Pres. Linwood (N.J.) Bd. Health, 1973-76; mem. Atlantic County Mental Health Advisory Bd.; trustee Sarah West Leeds Found. Recipient State of N.J. Dept. Institutions and Agencies certificate of appreciation for service in Vols. in Parole Program, 1975. Mem. Am., N.J., Atlantic County (trustee 1975—) bar assns., Am. Judicature Soc., Comml. Law League, N.J. Inst. Municipal Attys., Trial Attys. N.J., N.J. Def. Assn., Def. Research Inst., Am. Arbitration Assn. (panel 1970—). Club: Rotary. Bd. editors Dickinson Law Rev., 1966-67; contbr. articles in field to profl. jours. Home: 1301 Franklin Blvd Linwood NJ 08221 Office: PO Box 850 600 Fire Rd Pleasantville NJ 08232

CONNOR, PAUL EUGENE, social worker; b. Atchison, Kans., Aug. 11, 1921; s. Samuel Walters and Juanita Marie (Fry) C.; B.S., Columbia U., 1962; M.A., 1963; grad. certificate in social work, Fordham U., 1973; m. Louise Dorothy Schiddel, June 28, 1959 (div. 1964). Lectr. Am. History Rutgers State U., 1966-67; lectr. S.E. Asian history New Sch. Social Research, 1967-68; caseworker Bergen Center, South Bronx, N.Y., 1970-73; caseworker Protective Services, Bur. of Child Welfare, Bronx, 1973-75; caseworker Preventive Services Spl. Services for Children, N.Y.C., 1975—; tchr. The Internat. Center, 1977—. Served with USN, 1941-42. Mem. Internat. Council Social Welfare, Asia Soc., Am. Hist. Assn., S.C. Hist. Soc., N.C. Lit. and Hist. Assn. Democrat. Home: 88 W 197th St Bronx NY 10468 Office: 80 Lafayette St New York City NY 10013

CONNOR, ROBERT T., govt. ofcl., former borough pres.; b. Washington, 1919; ed. Boston Coll., U.S. Naval Acad.; B.A., City U. N.Y.; LL.D., St. Johns U. Operations Officer CIA, 1946-49; staff officer Fgn. Service, Dept. State, 1949-51, vice consul Mexico City; councilman-at-large, N.Y.C., 1963-65, borough pres. S.I., 1965-77; mem. N.Y.C. Bd. of Estimate, 1965-77; dep. asst. sec. Navy, 1977—. Trustee former Notre Dame Coll., N.Y.C. Served to capt. USNR (ret.). Recipient Outstanding Service award Salvation Army, Distinguished Citizens award B'nai B'rith. Mem. Navy League (past pres. N.Y. council). Roman Catholic. Home: 4545 N 25 Rd Arlington VA 22207 Office: Pentagon Washington DC

CONNOR, TERRENCE POWELL, radiologist; b. Moulmein, Burma, Oct. 14, 1928; s. George Powell and Florence Maud (Terry) C.; came to Can., 1958; M.B.B.S., London U., 1954; D.M.R.D., McGill U., Montreal, Que., Can., 1963; m. Hazel Constance Dewbury, May 9, 1959; 1 son, Quentin Powell. Radiologist, St. Mary's Hosp., Montreal, 1963-66; radiologist Women's Coll. Hosp., Toronto, Ont., Can., 1966—, radiologist in chief, 1975—; asso. prof. diagnostic radiology U. Toronto, 1975—. Diplomate Am. Bd. Radiology; licensed physician, Que.; certificate Royal Coll. Physicians (Can.). Home: 140 Clifton Rd Toronto ON M4T 2G6 Canada Office: 76 Grenville St Toronto ON Canada

CONNOR, THOMAS MARTIN, pediatric cardiologist; b. Nyack, N.Y., Aug. 28, 1939; s. Thomas John and Sara Mary (Gleason) C.; B.S., St. Francis Coll., 1961; M.D., U. Bologna, 1966; m. Patricia Ann O'Hara, July 25, 1964; children—Thomas Patrick, Coleen Patricia, Peter Christian. Intern, Grasslands Hosp., Valhalla, N.Y., 1967-68; resident in pediatrics, 1967-70; pediatric cardiology fellow Yale New Haven Med. Center, 1970-72; practice medicine specializing in pediatric cardiology, Bethesda, Md., 1972—; dir. pediatric cardiology Nat. Naval Med. Center; asst. prof. academic pediatric cardiology, pediatrics Nat. Med. Center Children's Hosp., Washington, 1974, Nat. Naval Med. Center and U.S. Uniformed Health Services Med. Sch., 1975. Served to comdr. M.C., USNR, 1975—. Diplomate Am. Bd. Pediatrics. Fellow Am. Acad. Pediatrics, Am. Coll. Cardiology. Roman Catholic. Club: K.C. Home: 1706 Crestview Dr Potomac MD 20854 Office: Box 114 Wisconsin Ave Bethesda MD 20014

CONNORS, JOHN JOSEPH HAYWARD, health services cons.; b. Manchester, Eng., June 27, 1918; s. John Joseph and Nora (Hayward) C.; student Regiopolis Coll., 1932-34, Balliol Coll., Oxford U., 1945; LL.B., LaSalle U., 1958; M. Hosp. Adminstrn., Baylor U., 1960; m. Doreen Mary Goodall, Jan. 27, 1940; children—John J.G., Michael A., M. Anne T. Entered Canadian Regular Army, 1935, advanced through grades to maj., 1966, ret., 1966; chief hosp. cons. Man. Hosp. Commn., 1966, asst. dir. hosp. services, 1966-68; exec. dir. Misericordia Gen. Hosp., Winnipeg, 1968-76; health services cons., 1976—. Chmn., Man. Medico-Moral Com., 1970-76, Man. Com. on Human Experimentation; tchr. med. jurisprudence and human relation in med. and para-med. fields. Mem. adv. com. Red River Community Coll. Bd. dirs. Canadian Council Christians and Jews; chmn. bd. dirs. Sisters of Providence of Kingston in Man. Decorated 1939-45 Star, France and Germany star, Defence medal, Canadian Vol. Service medal with clasp; War medal 1939-45, Canadian Forces Decoration with clasp; mentioned in Despatches. Fellow Royal Soc. Health; mem. Canadian Coll. Health Service Execs., Winnipeg Regional Hosp. Council, Royal Canadian Legion, United Services Inst., Cath. Hosp. Assn. Can. (pres. 1972-73), Cath. Hosp. Conf. Man. (pres. 1969-73), Def. Med. Assn. (pres. 1978), Cath. Hosp. Assn. (U.S.), Man. Medico-Legal Soc. Contbr. to publs. in field. Home and office: 1488 Lassiter Terr Ottawa ON K1J 8N3 Canada

CONNORS, MARY ANN, pub. relations, arts mgmt. exec.; b. Hartford, Oct. 18, 1930; d. Richard Thomas and Mary Prudence (Gaghan) Connors; B.S., St. Joseph Coll., 1952; postgrad. Georgetown U., 1953-57, U. Hartford, 1966—. Campaign sec., office mgr. Washington and Conn. offices U.S. Senator William A. Purtell, 1953-59; asst. to pub. relations dir. Conn. Rep. State Hdqrs., Hartford, 1959-61; advt. rep. Farmington Valley Herald, Simsbury, Conn., 1961-62; dir. music and art info. U. Hartford, 1962-73; dir. pub. relations and mktg. Hartford Symphony Orch., 1973-76; pub. relations, arts mgmt. cons., 1976—. Sec., Greater Hartford coordinating Council for Arts, 1964-67, v.p., 1968; mem. nat. com. Conn. Young Republicans, 1962-63; state co-chmn. Conn. Young Reps., 1963-64; pres. Hartford Women's Rep. Club, 1966-67; governing bd. Hartt Opera-Theater Guild. Mem. Women in Communications, AAUW, Am. Symphony Orch. League. Editor: New Eng. region newsletter Am. Coll. Pub. Relations Assn., 1972-73. Contbr. articles to profl. jours. and mags. Home and office: 249 Lowrey Pl Newington CT 06111

CONNORS, WILLIAM FRANCIS, JR., community coll. dean, psychologist; b. Bklyn., Mar. 31, 1945; s. William Francis and Ethel Lucille (Sester) C.; A.B., St. Anselm's Coll., 1966; M.Ed., Springfield Coll., 1967; m. Susan Edwards, Nov. 20, 1971; children—Corinne Elizabeth, Kristin Michelle. Counselor, Suffolk Community Coll., 1967-72; asst. prof. psychology Suffolk County Community Coll., Selden, N.Y., 1972-73, asso. prof., 1974—, asst. dean instrn., 1973—. Mem. Sch. Bd., Sts. Philip and James Sch., St. James, L.I., 1974—. Mem. Am. Psychol. Assn., AAUP, Am. Personnel and Guidance Assn. Democrat. Roman Catholic. Home: 4 Balfour Ln Stony Brook NY 11790 Office: Suffolk County Community College Selden NY 11784

CONOBY, JOSEPH FRANCIS, chemist; b. Albany, June 12, 1930; s. Joseph Francis and Helen Emma (Brucker) C.; B.S., Union Coll., 1952; m. Mary Joan A. Ryan, June 21, 1958; children—James Francis, Mark Joseph. Sr. tech. service engr. Allied Chem. Corp., Syracuse, N.Y., 1956-66; research chemist Conversion Chem. Corp., Rockville, Conn., 1966-69; environ. engr., indsl. hygienist, Boston computer ops. Honeywell Info. Systems, Brighton, Mass., 1969—; cons. exptl. project course Mass. Inst. Tech., 1977. Served to lt. USN, 1952-56. Mem. Am. Electroplaters Soc. (chmn. project com.), Am. Inst. Plant Engrs., Am. Indsl. Hygiene Assn. Patentee in field, U.S.,

Germany. Home: 5 Samuel Parlin Dr Acton MA 01720 Office: 38 Life St Brighton MA 02135

CONOLE, RICHARD CLEMENT, mgmt. exec.; b. Binghamton, N.Y., Dec. 7, 1936; s. Clement V. and Marjorie E. (Anable) C.; student U. Pa., 1955, 60, Clarkson Coll., 1956-57; m. Sharyn Stafford, Apr. 18, 1969; children—Margaret Ann, Linda Elizabeth, Samantha Erin. Data processing dept. Campbell Soup Co., Inc., Camden, N.J., 1954; draftsman Gannett, Fleming, Corddry & Carpenter, Inc., Ardmore, Pa., 1955-56; plant mgr., office mgr. Tabulating Card Co., Inc., Princeton, N.J., 1957-59, asst. to pres., asst. sec.-treas., sec., 1959; pres., dir. Data Processing Supplies Co., Inc., Princeton, 1959; sec., dir. Whiting Paper Co., Inc., Princeton, 1959. pres. 1961-62; pres., dir. Mercer-Princeton Realty Co., Inc., Princeton, 1959-61; pres. Am. Bus. Investment Co. Inc., Princeton, 1960; pres., dir. Business Supplies Corp. Am., Skytop, Pa., 1962-65; chmn. bd. Nat. Productive Machines, Inc., Elkridge, Md., 1965-72; pres., chmn. bd. Gen. Bus. Supplies Corp., Ardmore, Pa., 1965-72; pres. Autoberfest, Inc., 1973—, World Series Auto Racing Corp., 1973—; dir., sr. v.p., chmn. finance com. Pocono Internat. Raceway, 1965-74; sales cons. Hess & Barker, 1972-76; pres., dir. Tex. World Speedway Inc., 1976—. Mem. Pa. Soc., U.S. Auto Club, U.S., Phila. (life) squash racquets assns. Clubs: Skytop (Pa.); Philadelphia Country, Merion Cricket (Haverford, Pa.); Pocono Manor. Home: PO Box 9191 College Station TX 77840 also 230 Conshohocken State Rd Gladwyne PA 19035 Office: PO Box AJ College Station TX 77840

CONOVER, WALTER KAY, JR., elec. utility exec.; b. New Castle, Pa., Feb. 17, 1917; s. Walter Kay and Julia Augusta (Cotton) C.; student Youngstown U., 1939-40, Akron U., 1947; m. Betty Jean Campbell, Aug. 9, 1941; children—Julia A., Janice K. Advt. mgr. New Castle Dry Goods, 1940-41; advt. asst. Pa. Power Co., New Castle, 1946-53; gen. supr. advt. and publicity Pa. Power Co., New Castle, 1953-62, in charge of advt., publicity and display, 1962-73, v.p. pub. relations, 1973—. Former chmn. Lawrency County Ind. Devel. Council, Neshanock Sch. Bldg. Authority, 1966—; bd. dirs. ARC, 1948-55, Crippled Children's Assn., 1958-64, Hoyt Inst. Fine Arts, 1968—. Served with U.S. Army, 1941-46, 51-52. Recipient Brotherhood award Temple Israel, 1964. Mem. Pub. Utilities Communicators Assn. (v.p., dir., past regional chmn.), Pa. Electric Assn. (chmn.). Presbyterian. Clubs: New Castle Lions, New Castle Country, New Castle Toastmasters, Masons. Home: 122 Decker Dr New Castle PA 16105 Office: 1 E Washington St New Castle PA 16103

CONOVER, WILLIAM SHELDRICK II, ins. broker; b. Richmond, Va., Aug. 27, 1928; s. Albert W. and Marion (Kline) C.; B.S., Northwestern U., 1950; m. Nancy Jeanne Toel, Dec. 30, 1950; children—David Wesley, Susan Limerick, Patricia Kline, Ann Sheldrick, Katherine Abbott. Asst. v.p. Lannan & Co., ins. brokers, Pitts., 1954-59, v.p., 1959-62, pres., owner, 1962-73, pres., owner Conover & Assos., Inc. (name changed 1969); mem. 92d Congress from 27th Pa. Dist., mem. Armed Services Com. Pres., Mt. Lebanon Young Republicans, 1960, Upper St. Clair Twp. Rep. 1966, Rep. state committeeman, 1978; bd. dirs. Divine Providence Hosp. of Pitts. Served to lt. (j.g.), USNR, 1952-54. Mem. Ind. Ins. Agts. and Brokers Assn. Greater Pitts. (pres. 1966), Pa. Assn. Ins. Agts. (past state dir.), Kappa Sigma. Methodist (dir. ch. 1960—). Clubs: Duquesne, St. Clair Country, Allegheny (Pitts.). Home: 2012 Murdstone Rd Pittsburgh PA 15241 Office: 931 Penn Ave Pittsburgh PA 15222

CONRAD, MORTON SEYMOUR, accountant; b. N.Y.C., Sept. 21, 1899; s. Leon and Mary (Salem) C.; B.C.S., N.Y.U., 1921; m. Mae Schoenfeld, Oct. 28, 1924; children—Eleanor Marcia (Mrs. Marc Sarner Wittlin), Edith Helen (Mrs. Melvyn Leonard Halbert). Partner, Jablow and Conrad, 1927-30; pvt. practice, 1930-55; partner Conrad and Zachary, 1956—. C.P.A., N.Y. State. Mem. N.Y. State Soc. C.P.A.'s, Nat. Assn. Accountants, Am. Inst. C.P.A.'s, Delta Mu Delta. Contbr. articles to tax and accounting jours. Home: 67-76 Booth St Forest Hills NY 11375 Office: 10-5 Granada Crescent White Plains NY 10603

CONRAD, WILLIAM EDWARD, JR., former brokerage firm exec., city ofcl.; b. Newark, Sept. 25, 1928; s. William Edward and Ruth Caroline (Fonda) C.; B.S. in Mgmt., Rutgers U., 1955; m. Mary Rachel Ferry, Nov. 4, 1950 (dec. June, 1972); children—William Edward III, Elyse Lenore; m. 2d, Constance Vallorani, Feb. 2, 1974; children—Scott William, Kurt Edward. Agt., Household Finance Corp., Newark, 1949-50; mgr. investment dept. Nat. Newark & Essex Banking Co., Newark, 1950-55; salesman, Merrill, Lynch, Pierce, Fenner & Smith, Inc., N.Y.C., 1955-58, asst. to div. dir., 1958-68, v.p., adminstrv. mgr., 1968-76; investment counselor, mgmt. cons., 1976—. Mayor, Borough of Kenilworth (N.J.), 1970-75; chmn. bd. dirs. Meml. Gen. Hosp., Union, N.J., 1977—. Served with AC, USN, 1946-48. Mem. Alpha Chi Rho, Phi Epsilon. Club: Suburban Golf (Union, N.J.). Home: 42 Dorset Dr Kenilworth NJ 07033

CONROY, THOMAS JOSEPH, educator; b. N.Y.C., Nov. 29, 1940; s. Frederick and Amelia (Sands) C.; B.A., Fairleigh Dickinson U., 1963; M.A., N.Y. U., 1968; m. Lillian Mathisen, July 3, 1965; children—Christian, Eric, Brian. Instr. Mt. Carmel Sch., Ridgewood, N.J., 1964-65, Cardinal Hayes High Sch., N.Y.C., 1965-66; instr. Pascack Hills High Sch., Montvale, N.J., 1966—, master tchr. U.S. history honors program, 1975—; NDEA fellow, tchr. advanced placement students, Coll. City N.Y., 1967; asso. program dir. cultural forum seminars NDEA, 1968-70; sec. North Jersey Debate League, 1974-78. Mem. Am. Acad. Polit. Social Scis., Am. Polit. Sci. Assn., Nat. Council Social Studies, NEA, N.J. Edn. Assn., World Future Soc. Home: Mine Hill Rd Cornwall NY 12518 Office: Pascack Hills High Sch Montvale NJ 07645

CONROY, WILLIAM THOMAS, JR., educator, author; b. Middletown, Conn., Apr. 14, 1943; s. William Thomas and Frances Marie (Monnes) C.; B.S., Holy Cross Coll., 1965; diploma U. Clermont (France), 1966; Ph.D., Princeton, 1972. Lectr., Queens Coll., 1970-72, asst. prof. depts. Romance langs. and comparative lit., 1972—, chmn. library com., 1975-76. Mem. Citizens for McGovern, 1972, Holy Cross Young Democrats, 1961-65; mem. London Terr. Towers Tenant Assn., 1975-76. Fulbright scholar, 1965-66; Woodrow Wilson fellow, 1966-67. Mem. Modern Lang. Assn., Société française d'Etude du XVIIIe siècle, Am. Assn. Tchrs. of French, N.Y. State United Tchrs., Am. Comparative Lit. Assn., Delta Epsilon Sigma. Roman Catholic. Author: Diderot's Essai sur Sénèque, 1975; Villiers de l'Isle Adam, 1978; also translations, art and lit. revs., articles. Home: 21 Prince St New York City NY 10012

CONSTANTELOS, DEMETRIOS JOHN, educator; b. Spilia, Messinia, Greece, July 27, 1927; s. Joannes B. and Christine J. (Psilopoulos) C.; came to U.S., 1955, naturalized, 1959; B.A. Th., Holy Cross Greek Orthodox Theol. Sch., 1958; M.Th., Princeton, 1959; M.A. (Lane Cooper fellow, Univ. fellow), Rutgers U., 1963, Ph.D., 1965; m. Stella Croussouloudis, Aug. 15, 1954; children—Christine, John, Helen, Maria. Ordained to ministry Greek Orthodox Ch., 1955; pastor St. Demetrios Greek Orthodox Ch., Perth Amboy, N.J., 1955-64; teaching asst. Rutgers U., 1961-62; asst. prof. history Hellenic Coll., Brookline, Mass., 1965-67, asso. prof., 1967-71, chmn. dept. history, 1967-71, dean arts and scis., 1971; prof. history Stockton State Coll., Pomona, N.J., 1971; vis. lectr. history Boston Coll., 1967-68. Recipient jr. fellowship Dumbarton Oaks, Harvard, 1964-65. Mem. Am. Hist. Assn., Soc. Ch. History, Medieval Acad. Am., Soc. Neo-Hellenic Studies, Orthodox Theol. Soc. Am. (pres. 1968-71). Author: The Greek Orthodox Ch., 1967; Byzantine Philanthropy and Social Welfare, 1968; Marriage, Sexuality, Celibacy, 1975. Editor: The Greek Orthodox Theol. Rev., 1966-71; Encyclicals and Documents of the Greek Orthodox Archdiocese of America, 1976. Contbr. articles to profl. jours. Home: 304 Forest Dr Linwood NJ 08221 Office: Dept History Stockton State Coll Pomona NJ 08240

CONSTANTINO, JOSEPH GERALD, physician, co. exec.; b. N.Y.C., Oct. 13, 1914; s. John and Antoinette (Attanasio) C.; B.A., N.Y. U., 1935; M.D., Marquette U., 1940; m. Helen Adela Vilella, Aug. 15, 1962. Intern, Flushing (N.Y.) Hosp., 1939-40; resident in internal medicine, 1940-41; practice medicine specializing in aerospace medicine, tropical diseases and internal medicine, N.Y.C., 1946-69; med. officer Pan Am. World Airways, Jamaica, N.Y., 1947-73, corp. med. dir., 1973—; cons. fed. air surgeon U.S. Dept. Transp., 1967—; clinician Bur. Preventive Diseases, N.Y.C. Dept. Health, 1956—. Served with USAAF, 1941-46. Recipient Pres.'s award Pan Am. World Airways, 1970, profl. service citation FAA Dept. Transp., 1976. Diplomate Am. Bd. Preventive Medicine. Fellow Aerospace Med. Assn. (Howard K. Edwards award 1970), Am. Coll. Preventive Medicine; mem. Internat. Acad. Aviation and Space Medicine, Internat. Air Transport Assn. (med. com.), Airline Med. Dirs. Assn. (pres. 1964-65; award outstanding contbn. to aviation medicine 1978). Contbr. numerous articles to med. jours. Home: 79-10 34th Ave Jackson Heights NY 11372 Office: Pan Am World Airways Internat Airport Jamaica NY 11430

CONTE, SILVIO OTTO, congressman; b. Pittsfield, Mass., Nov. 9, 1921; s. Ottavio and Lucia (Lora) C.; LL.B., Boston Coll., 1949; LL.D., Williams Coll., Hampshire Coll., U. Mass., North Adams State Coll., Amherst Coll., Boston Coll., Georgetown U.; m. Corinne Duval, Nov. 11, 1947; children—Michele, Sylvia (Mrs. Nicholas Certo), John, Gayle. Admitted to Mass. bar, 1949; mem. 86th-95th Congresses, 1st Dist. Mass. Mem. Mass. Senate, 1950-58, chmn. coms. on ins., constl. law, judiciary, chmn. legis. research council, chmn. spl. coms. for investigation health and welfare trust funds, vice chmn. Fgn. Policy subcom. of Platform M Com. Del. Republican Nat. Conv.; mem. platform com. Rep. Nat. Conv., 1960, 64, 68, 72, 76. Named outstanding young man of year Mass. C. of C., 1954. Mem. Fed., Mass., Berkshire bar assns., Am. Legion, VFW, DAV, Pi Sigma Alpha (hon.), Phi Delta Phi. Home: Blythewood Dr Pittsfield MA 01210 Office: 2300 Rayburn House Office Bldg Washington DC 20515

CONTRONI, GUIDO, microbiologist; b. Colon, Republic of Panama, Aug. 19, 1932; s. Ugo and Evangelina (Melendez) C.; came to U.S., 1957, naturalized, 1965; B.S. in Chemistry U. of Panama, 1955; M.S. in Bacteriology, Fla. State U., 1959; m. Martha Posey, Oct. 3, 1959; 1 son, Guido Christopher. Lab. technician Santo Tomas Hosp., Panama City, Panama, 1954-55; teaching asst. Fla. State U., Tallahassee, 1957-59; bacteriologist WHO, Guatemala, 1950-60; instr. and chief bacteriologist U. Fla., Gainesville, 1960-66; dir. clin. microbiology Children's Hosp. Nat. Med. Center, Washington, 1966—, mem. lab. rev. com., 1975—; cons. to various mfg. and sci. cos., 1975—; guest lectr. various hosp. and schs., 1974—. Mem. Am. Inst. Biol. Scis., Am. Soc. Microbiologists, Am. Soc. Clin. Pathologists, Sigma Xi. Contbr. articles on clin. microbiology to sci. jours. Home: 8415 Queen Anne's Dr Silver Spring MD 20910 Office: Children's Hosp Nat Medical Center 111 Michigan Ave NW Washington DC 20010

CONVERSE, JOHN MARQUIS, surgeon; b. San Francisco, Sept. 29, 1909; s. George Marquis and Adele (Clot) C.; student Ecole Gerson, 1920-26; A.B., Lycee Janson de Sailly, 1928; M.D., U. Paris, France, 1935; Dr. honoris causa, U. Bordeaux (France), 1978; m. Sheila Paull-Delany, Nov. 12, 1932 (div.); 1 son, John Marquis; m. 2d, Veronica Balfe Cooper, June 28, 1964. Lawrence D. Bell prof. plastic surgery N.Y. U. Sch. Medicine, dir. Inst. Reconstructive Plastic Surgery, N.Y. U. Med. Center, 1957—; gov., chmn. med. adv. bd. Am. Hosp. of Paris; cons., VA Hosp., N.Y.C.; Med. cons. to Armed Forces; plastic surgeon Am. Hosp. Brit. Unit. 1940-42; cons. French Army North Africa, 1943. Served as hon. maj. French Army, North Africa, 1943-44; maj. U.S. Army, 1944-46. Decorated Croix de Guerra with palms, comdr. Legion of Honor, comdr. Order Sci. Merit (France). Diplomate Am. Bd. Plastic Surgery. Fellow A.C.S., Am. Soc. Plastic and Reconstructive Surgery (Spl. Hon. award 1978), Am. Acad. Ophthalmology and Otolaryngology, N.Y. Acad. Medicine, N.Y. Acad. Scis.; mem. Soc. Rehab. Facially Disfigured, Inc. (v.p. 1951—, founder), Am. Assn. Plastic Surgeons (hon. fellowship award 1976), Transplantation Soc. (founder 1966, pres. 1967-68), Am. Cleft Palate Assn., Am. Assn. Maxillofacial Surgeons, Am. Acad. Maxillofacial Prosthetics (hon.); hon. mem. plastic surgery socs. Brazil, Czechoslovakia, France, Gt. Britain, Mexico, Uruguay, Venezuela, Italy, Spain. Author: (with Dr. V.H. Kazanjian) Surgical Treatment of Facial Injuries, 2d edit., 1959, 3d edit., 1974; author, editor Reconstructive Plastic Surgery, 1964, 2d edn., 1977; also numerous sci. articles. Address: 722 Park Ave New York NY 10021 also Inst Reconstructive Plastic Surgery 560 1st Ave New York NY 10016

CONWAY, ALBERT E(DWARD), real estate agt.; b. West Chester, Pa., Mar. 22, 1918; s. Albert E. and Elsie (Smith) C.; B.S., West Chester State Coll., 1940; M.A., U. Pa., 1941; m. June V. Rider, Dec. 16, 1950; children—James Albert, Charles Albert. Guidance counselor Def. Tng. Program, Berks, Chester, and Lancaster counties, Pa., 1941-42; head, sci. dept. Nether Providence High Sch., Wallingford, Pa., 1942-46; asst. prof. psychology St. Lawrence U., Canton, N.Y., 1946-47, Lafayette Coll., Easton, Pa., 1947-54; life underwriter Sun Life Can., Phila., 1954-56; asst. supr. spl. edn. Northampton County Schs., Nazareth, Pa., 1956-57; supr. spl. edn. Lycoming County Schs., Williamsport, Pa., 1957-60; dir. psychol. services Mt. Pleasant Sch. Dist., Wilmington, Del., 1960-74; practice gen. psychology, 1946-76; instr. psychology continuing edn. div. Pa. State U., Phila. area, 1968—, U. Del., 1975—; real estate salesman, 1975—. Mem. Delmarva Ornithol. Soc., Acad. Natural Scis. of Phila., West Chester Bird Club (pres. 1948-52), Hawk Mountain Sanctuary Assn., Eastern Bird Banding Assn. (editor EBBA News 1952-56), Delaware Valley Ornithol. Club (editor Cassinia 1968). Presbyterian. Address: 713 Woodsdale Rd Wilmington DE 19809

CONWAY, ALVIN JAMES, hosp. adminstr.; b. N.Y.C., Aug. 18, 1925; s. James and Florence (Farbman) C.; B.B.A. in Mgmt., Coll. City N.Y., 1952; M.S. in Hosp. Adminstrn., Columbia U., 1954; m. Eileen Cummins, Aug. 31, 1947; children—James, John, Susan, Christopher. Exec. dir. Knickerbocker Hosp., N.Y.C., 1960-70; dir. div. health and Hosp. of Catholic Charities, Diocese Bklyn., 1970—; exec. v.p. Catholic Med. Center Bklyn. and Queens, Inc., Jamaica, N.Y., 1970—; preceptor Cornell U., Sloan Inst. Hosp. Adminstrn., 1960—, Columbia U. Sch. Pub. Health, 1975—; lectr. in field. Served with U.S. Army, 1943-46. Fellow Am. Coll. Hosp. Adminstrs., Royal Soc. Health, Am. Pub. Health Assn.; mem. Greater N.Y. Hosp. Assn. (gov. 1970—), Queensboro Council for Social Welfare (dir. 1973—), Hosp. Assn. N.Y. State (trustee 1972-75). Roman Catholic. Club: Princeton. Contbr. articles on hosp. adminstrn. to profl. jours. Home: 293 Concord Rd Yonkers NY 10710 Office: 88-25 153d St Jamaica NY 11432

CONWAY, ARTHUR JAMES, psychologist; b. Everett, Mass., Aug. 20, 1908; s. William J. and Mary E. (Delaney) C.; A.B., Boston Coll., 1931; Ed.M., Boston U., 1939; certificate in Psychology, U. Calif., Los Angeles, 1939; postgrad. Harvard U., 1946-49; m. Elizabeth Walsh Delaney, June 30, 1941; children—Christopher, Kevin, Carolyn, Robert, Arthur James, Mark, William, Elizabeth, Richard. Tchr. math. and English, Everett Pub. Schs., 1935-40, dir. guidance and student services, 1940—; asso. prof. guidance and psychology Salem (Mass.) State Coll., 1957-68; prof. secondary edn. Regis Coll., Weston, Mass., 1960-68; asso. prof. research and evaluation Bridgewater (Mass.) State Coll., 1969-73; asso. prof. pupil personnel services Fitchburg (Mass.) State Coll., 1973—; pvt. practice psychology, Everett, 1965—; cons. clin. psychologist; lectr. on The 4 D's. Adv. bd. Aquinas Jr. Coll., Milton, Mass., 1972—; dir. Boys and Girls Camps Inc., 1955-57; dist. chmn. Middlesex council Boy Scouts Am., 1933-40, chmn. nat. def., 1939-41. Served to lt. comdr. USNAF, 1942-45. Recipient award of distinction E Club of Everett, 1977; certified psychologist. Mem. Am. Assn. Clin. Counselors (diplomate; exec. bd. 1965—), Am. Personnel and Guidance Assn., Mass. Sch. Counselors Assn., Nat. Vocat. Guidance Assn., Harvard Tchrs. Assn., Parent Counseling Assn. N. Eng. Clubs: Kiwanis (Everett, life), DAV, VFW, Boston Coll. Varsity (pres., 1977-78). Contbr. articles to publs. Home: 72 Washington St Belmont MA 02178 Office: 10 Trapelo Rd Belmont MA 02178

CONWAY, JAMES FRANCIS, JR., printing co. exec.; b. Lowell, Mass., Apr. 25, 1924; s. James Francis and Ellen Elizabeth (McQuade) C.; A.B., Harvard U., 1947, M.B.A., 1949; m. Grace Reilly, Nov. 3, 1951; children—James Francis, Peter Reilly, Michael Grace, Stephen McQuade, Ruth Grace, John Andrew. With Courier-Citizen Co., Lowell, 1952—, gen. mgr., 1963-66, pres., 1966—, chmn., 1976—; dir. State St. Boston Corp., State St. Bank & Trust Co., Boston; chmn. Graphcomm U.S.A., 1975; dir. Comprint U.S.A., Amsterdam, 1976. Trustee Lowell Gen. Hosp.; campaign mgr. United Fund Greater Lowell. Served with F.A., AUS, 1942-46; ETO. Mem. Printing Industries Am. (chmn.), Internat. Bus. Forms Industries (pres.), Graphic Arts Tech. Found. (v.p., dir.), Associated Industries Mass. (v.p., dir.). Republican. Roman Catholic. Clubs: Racquet and Tennis, Sky (N.Y.C.); Harvard, Comml. (Boston); Spee, Vesper Country Lowell. Home: 823 Andover St Lowell MA 01852 Office: 165 Jackson St Lowell MA 01852

CONWAY, KENNETH JAMES, glass co. exec.; b. Queens, N.Y., May 20, 1948; s. James Donald and Marie Agnes (Murray) C.; B.S., Rutgers U., 1969; postgrad. Syracuse U., 1971; m. Carol Ann Krupka, Aug. 30, 1969; children—Kristen Jamie, Kenneth James. With Corning Glass Works, Big Flats, N.Y., 1971—, prodn. supt., 1977—. Mem. council of partners Orgn. to Increase Black Grads. in Engring. and Arch. at Okla. State U., 1974-77, chmn. summer employment com., 1976-77. Served with U.S. Army, 1969-71. Decorated Army Commendation medal. Mem. Am. Ceramic Soc., Am. Mgmt. Assn. Republican. Roman Catholic. Club: Elks. Home: 11 Churchill Pl Big Flats NY 14814 Office: Corning Glass Works Big Flats NY 14813

CONWAY, WILLIAM GAYLORD, zoologist; b. St. Louis, Nov. 20, 1929; s. Frederick Eldridge and Alice Harriet (Gaylord) C.; A.B., Washington U., 1951. Curator birds St. Louis Zool. Park, 1950-56; curator birds N.Y. Zool. Park, N.Y.C., 1956-72, asso. dir., 1960-61, gen. dir., 1966—. Bd. dirs. Am. Sect. Internat. Council for Bird Protection, Internat. Union for Conservation of Nature, Cornell Lab. Ornithology, World Wildlife Fund, Asa Wright Nature Center. Fellow N.Y. Zool. Soc.; mem. Brit. Avicultural Soc. (hon.), Am. Ornithologists Union (elective), Cooper Ornithol Soc., Internat. Wild Waterfowl Assn. (dir.), Wilson Ornithol. Club, Am. Conservation Assn. (dir.), Am. Assn. Zool. Parks and Aquariums (past pres. chmn. accreditation commn.), Internat. Survival Service Commn., Am. Am. Conservation Assn. (dir.), Soc. Ichthyologists and Herpetologists. Contbr. articles to profl. jours. Expdns. to Trinidad, Argentina, Bolivia. Office: NY Zool Park New York City NY 10460

CONYNGHAM, WILLIAM JOSEPH, polit. scientist, educator; b. Wilkes-Barre, Pa., Aug. 13, 1924; s. William Joseph and Margaret Amelia (Jordan) C.; A.B., Cath. U. Am., 1950; A.M., U. Notre Dame, 1952; Ph.D., Columbia, 1969; m. Margaret Francis Hennessy, Sept. 3, 1955; children—William Joseph, Monica E., Michael E., Maura F. Intelligence officer, Washington, 1952-57; politics Manhattanville Coll., 1957-65; asso. prof. Cath. U. Am., 1965—, subsequently asso. dean Sch. Arts Scis.; cons. Inst. Def. Analysis, 1969-71; sr. fellow Hoover Instn. for War, Revolution and Peace, Palo Alto, Calif., 1971, St. Anthony's Coll. Oxford (Eng.) U., 1972-73. Mem. Am. Assn. Advancement Slavic Studies, Am. Polit. Sci. Assn. Roman Catholic. Author: The Role of the Communist Party in Industrial Decision-making, 1969; Industrial Management in the Soviet Union, 1973. Home: 12907 Goodhill Rd Wheaton MD 20906 Office: Dept of Politics Cath U Am Washington DC 20064

COOK, ALBERT SAMUEL, lawyer; b. Balt., Mar. 24, 1921; s. Albert and Helen (Earnshaw) C.; A.B., Princeton, 1943; J.D., U. Md., 1946; children—Bryson L., Cathy T. Admitted to Md. bar, 1946; individual practice law, Balt., 1947-50; trial atty. U.S. Dept. Labor, Washington, 1950-52; staff atty., office of gen. counsel NLRB, Washington, 1953-54; labor relations mgr. Davison Chem. div. W.R. Grace & Co., Balt., 1955-58; partner firm Cook & Cluster, Balt., 1959-69, Venable Baetjer & Howard, Balt., 1970—; mem. health care industry labor-mgmt. adv. com. to nat. dir. Fed. Mediation and Conciliation Service, 1975—; cons. Am. Hosp. Assn., U.S. C. of C.; lectr. Johns Hopkins U.; gen. counsel Nat. Asso. Builders and Contractors, Inc., 1974—; mem. Gov.'s Task Force on Pub. Employee Labor Relations, 1968-69, Md. Gen. Assembly Task Force on Pub. Sector Collective Bargaining, 1976—; dir. pub. sector Labor Relations Conf. Bd. Md., 1973—. Mem. Am. Arbitration Assn. (adv. council), Balt. (past chmn. labor law com.), Md. State, Fed. (chmn. labor relations com.), Am. bar assns. Republican. Episcopalian. Clubs: Masons, Elkridge, Mchts. Center. Home: 44 Olmsted Green Village of Cross Keys Baltimore MD 21210 Office: 2 Hopkins Plaza 1800 Mercantile Bank & Trust Bldg Baltimore MD 21201

COOK, ALFREDA MARY, educator, bus. exec.; b. Chengtu, China, Sept. 4, 1913; d. Alfred Thomas and Isabella Park (Paton) Crutcher; came to U.S., 1956, naturalized, 1962; B.A., U. Toronto (Can.), 1936, M.A., 1937; m. Leslie G. Cook, Dec. 26, 1940; children—Patricia Joan, Leslie Pamela, Andrew George. Prof. math. and physics Women's Christian Coll., U. Madras (India), 1938-40; lectr. computer scis. State U. N.Y., Albany, 1965-69; v.p. L.G. Cook Assos., Inc., 1977—; lectr. physics Skidmore Coll., Saratoga Springs, N.Y., 1961-63. Mem. Am. Phys. Soc., AAUW. Home: 25 Whittredge Rd Summit NJ 07901 Office: 98 Hobart Ave Summit NJ 07901

COOK, BENJAMIN HOPSON, mfg. co. exec.; b. Shreveport, La., Apr. 7, 1926; s. Tom W. and Eva (Hopson) C.; B.S. in Bus. Adminstrn., La. State U., 1948; m. Irene Haden Owen, Aug. 20, 1948; children—Lura Haden Norman, Terry Ellen Slater, Paul Stuart. Mgr., Free Flow Muffler Co., Toronto, Ohio, 1948-51; partner Stemco Mfg. Co., St. Charles, Mo., 1951-59, gen. mgr., sec.-treas., dir., Longview,

Tex., 1959-65, pres., 1965-69; group v.p. Garlock Inc., 1969-72, pres., Rochester, N.Y., 1972-76, chmn., chief exec. officer, 1976—; dir. Longview Nat. Bank, Security Trust Co., Rochester, Schlegel Corp., Rochester. Served with AUS, 1944-45. Mem. Soc. Automotive Engrs., Longview C. of C. Methodist. Home: 10 Old Landmark Dr Rochester NY 14618 Office: 50 Midtown Tower Rochester NY 14604

COOK, BENJAMIN LEWIS, psychologist, hypnotherapist; b. Pitts., Sept. 13, 1937; s. Benjamin Lewis and Kathleen Klotz (Johnson) C.; B.A., U. Pitts., 1961, M.Ed., 1965, Ph.D., 1969. Tchr. math. and sci. East End Luth. Sch., Pitts., 1961-62; pvt. practice tutoring, Pitts., 1962-65; pvt. practice counseling psychology, Pitts., 1965-69; pvt. practice clin. psychology and hypnotherapy, Pitts., 1969—; cons. in psychology and UFO field investigator Aerial Phenomena Research Orgn., Tucson, 1973—; cons. psychology Dektor Counterintelligence and Security, Springfield, 1977—; specialist in audio stress analysis, Pitts., 1977—; research cons. radionics Mankind Research Unltd., Silver Springs, Md., 1978—; pvt. research analyst and operative in intelligence, counterintelligence and security communities, 1978—. County committeeman Constitutional party of Allegheny County, Pa., 1971-73; asst. scoutmaster Boy Scouts Am., 1957-59. Fellow Pa. Psychol. Assn.; mem. Am. Psychol. Assn., Am. Personnel and Guidance Assn., Am. Ednl. Research Assn., Am. Security Council, Security and Intelligence Fund, Am. Soc. Clin. Hypnosis, Internat. Soc. Hypnosis, Greater Pitts. Psychol. Assn., SAR (Life), Nat. Rifle Assn. (benefactor), Pa. Rifle and Pistol Assn. (life), Bethany Luth. Home Assn. (life), Doctoral Assn. Educators U. Pitts. (life). Lutheran. Author: Freemasonry Versus Christianity, 1965; The Phallic Worship of Freemasonry Unveiled, 1977; The Cook Educational Theory Inventory, 1971; The Cook Weltanschaaung Inventory, 1971. Home and Office: 930 Washington Rd Mt Lebanon Pittsburgh PA 15228

COOK, CHARLES WINANT, educator; b. Spring Lake, N.J., May 25, 1921; s. John Curtis Borden and Beatrice (Winant) C.; A.B., Princeton U., 1942; M.A., Columbia U., 1954; m. Jean Laurethel Johnson, Mar. 24, 1945; children—Charles Winant, Beatrice Jean, John Curtis. Asst. headmaster Browning Sch., N.Y.C., 1948-52, headmaster, 1952—. Trustee Algernon Sydney Sullivan Found., 1970—. Served with AUS, 1943-46. Mem. Guild Ind. Schs. N.Y.C. (treas. 1966-68). Republican. Presbyterian. Mason. Clubs: University, Princeton (N.Y.C.). Home: 357 Oxford Dr Short Hills NJ 07078 Office: 52 E 62d St New York City NY 10021

COOK, DOUGLAS NEILSON, educator; b. Phoenix, Sept. 22, 1929; s. Neil Estes and Louise Y. (Wood) C.; student Phoenix Coll., 1948-49, U. Chgo., 1949-50, U. Calif. at Los Angeles, 1950-52, Los Angeles Art Inst., 1948; B.F.A., U. Ariz., 1953; M.A., Stanford, 1955; postgrad. Lester Polakov Studio Stage Design, 1966-67; m. Joan Stafford Buechner, Aug. 11, 1956; children—John Richard, Peter Neilson, Stephen Barton. Actor, Corral Theatre, Tucson, 1952-53, Orleans (Mass.) Arena Theatre, 1953; dir., designer Palo Alto (Calif.) Community Theatre, 1954, Millbrae Community Theatre, 1955-57, Peninsula Children's Theatre, 1956-57; instr. San Mateo (Calif.) Coll., 1955-57, Nat. Music Camp, Interlochen, Mich., 1961; asst. prof. drama U. Calif., Riverside, 1957-66; asso. prof., 1967-70; prof. theatre and film Pa. State U., University Park, 1970—. Asso. producer Utah Shakespearean Festival, Cedar City, 1966—; producer, Pa. State Festival Theatre, State College, 1970—. Instl. rep. Juniata Valley council Boy Scouts Am., 1973—. Bd. dirs. Central Pa. Festival Arts, 1970-75. Humanities grantee U. Calif., 1964-65; Arts fellow U. Calif., 1966-67. Mem. Am. Theatre Assn., U.S. Inst. Theatre Tech., AAUP, Am. Soc. Theatre Research, Am. Nat. Theatre Assn., Univ. Resident Theatre Assn. (dir. 1971—, v.p. 1973-77, pres. 1977—), Theatre Assn. Pa. (dir. 1972-76). Home: 526 Westview Ave State College PA 16801 Office: Pa State U University Park PA 16802

COOK, EARL CLINTON, JR., mech. engr.; b. Clinton, Mass., Feb. 16, 1917; s. Earl Clinton and Frances Jones (Danford) C.; Asso. in Engring., Lincoln Tech. Inst., 1952; B.B.A., Northeastern U., 1954, M.B.A., 1957; m. Yvonne Mary Moge, Feb. 1, 1942; children—Shirley Jean (Mrs. Robert Howard), Earl Clinton III, Robert Allen, Ronald Bradford. Mech. draftsman Eureka Mfg. Co., Taunton, Mass., 1938-39; machine operator Stedfast Rubber Co., North Easton, Mass., 1939-41; machine designer H.& B. Am. Machinery Co., South Attleboro, Mass., 1941-43, Cumberland Engring. Co., Inc., Pawtucket, R.I., 1946-50; devel. engr. Gen. Electric Co., Providence, 1950-72; mech. engr., South Attleboro, 1972—. Neighborhood commr. Anawon council Boy Scouts Am., 1954-63. Mem. Dale Carnegie Alumni Assn. (div. gov. 1965—). Mason (Shriner). Served with USNR, 1943-45. Address: 48 Seven Mile River Dr South Attleboro MA 02703

COOK, GEORGE PETER, dentist; b. Ticonderoga, N.Y., Aug. 10, 1915; s. George Oscar and Florence (Joubert) C.; student U. Buffalo, 1936-38; D.D.S., U. Md., 1943; m. Marjorie Werther, Mar. 27, 1943; children—Dean, Bonnie, Susan, Marjorie. Intern USPHS Marine Hosp., Brighton, Mass., 1943-44; practice dentistry, Ticonderoga, 1946—; staff Moses Ludington Hosp; dental dir. Medicaid N.Y. State Dept. Health, 1969—. Guest lectr. hypnodontics Green Mountain Coll., 1961—; mem. cons. group for dentistry Albany Regional Med. Program, 1967-77; dental cons. Warren Co. Westmount infirmary. Gen. chmn. constrn. sch. gym and elementary sch., Ticonderoga, 1956-57. Pres. bd. dirs. Ticonderoga Community Bldg. Served with Dental Corps, USNR, 1944-46. Fellow Internat. Coll. Dentists; mem. Navy League, Am. Dental Assn., N.Y. State (chmn. council on relief 1973-77, gen. chmn. ann. meeting 1973), 4th Dist. (pres. 1963-64) dental socs., Am. Dental Soc. Anesthesiology, Am. Soc. Pub. Health Dentists, N.Y. State Soc. Professions, Am. Soc. Dentistry for Children, Am. Soc. Psychosomatic Dentistry and Medicine, Acad. Gen. Dentistry, Pierre Fauchard Acad., Am. Legion, Internat. Oceanographic Found. Home: Heart Bay Ticonderoga NY 12883 Office: 2 Mount Defiance St Ticonderoga NY 12883

COOK, HARLAND LAWRENCE, educator; b. Milford, Mass., Jan. 7, 1945; s. Ralph Walter and Mary Winifred (Lawrence) C.; A.B., Providence Coll., 1966; M.A., Mich. State U., 1968; certificate Boston U., 1969; m. Barbara Audree Blanchard, Aug. 12, 1967; children—Harland Lawrence, Jennifer Ann, Jeffrey Scott, Douglas Paul. Tchr. math. Bath (Mich.) High Sch., 1967-69, head dept. math., 1968-69; tchr. math. Walpole (Mass.) High Sch., 1969-78; guidance counselor Walpole West Jr. High Sch., 1978—; mgr. Ralph W. Cook Sons, Franklin, Mass., 1955—. Mem. NEA, Mass. (county dir. 1974-77), Norfolk County (Service award 1977; v.p. 1971-75, pres. 1975-76, treas. 1976—), Walpole (pres. 1971-73, negogiations team 1970-73, scholarship chmn. 1973-75) tchrs. assns., Nat. Council of Tchrs. Math. (conv. del. 1975, 76, 77). Home: 1225 Washington St Walpole MA 02081 Office: Common St Walpole MA 02081

COOK, JEANNINE SALVO (MRS. DONALD CARTER COOK), librarian; b. N.Y.C., Apr. 11, 1929; d. Ernest August and Edith Agatha (Lombardo) Salvo; A.B., Hunter Coll., 1951; M.L.S., Columbia U., 1958, advanced library degree, 1973; m. Donald Carter Cook, June 9, 1962; 1 son, Carter Steven. Chemist, Charles Pfizer & Co., Inc., Bklyn., 1951-56; lit. chemist, 1956-58; central med. librarian Am. Cyanamid Co., N.Y.C., 1958-60; sr. profl. adminstr. Columbia U. Engring. and Phys. Scis. Library, N.Y.C., 1960-62; asso. librarian State U. N.Y., Stony Brook, 1962-63; dir. Emma S. Clark Meml. Library, Setauket, N.Y., 1967—. Co-chmn. ednl. com. Assn. Community/Univ. Coop., 1973-74; bd. dirs. Council Ministries Setauket United Methodist Ch., 1978—; bd. dirs. Three Village Community and Youth Council, 1977—. Mem. Spl. Libraries Assn., Med. Library Assn., Am. Chem. Soc., League Women Voters, Suffolk County Library Assn., (chmn. pub. libraries sect.) Brookhaven Dirs. Assn. (pres. 1976—), Pub. Library Dirs. Assn. Suffolk County (exec. bd. 1976—). Methodist (trustee 1971-73). Home: 40 Seabrook Lane Stony Brook NY 11790 Office: 120 Main St Setauket NY 11733

COOK, JOHN ALFRED, psychoanalyst; b. N.Y.C., Oct. 31, 1910; s. Alfred A. and Ruth B. (Meyer) C.; grad. Choate Sch., 1928; A.B., Yale, 1932, M.B.A., Harvard, 1934; M.D., Columbia, 1949; m. Margaret Hirschman, Sept. 28, 1949; 1 dau., Mariana. Investment banker Kuhn Loeb & Co., N.Y.C., 1934-41; with WPB and U.S. Bur. Budget, Washington, 1941-44; intern Grasslands Hosp., Valhalla, N.Y.; resident N.Y. State Psychiat. Inst., N.Y.C.; practice medicine specializing in psychoanalysis, N.Y.C., 1950—; asso. attending psychiatrist Presbyn. Hosp., N.Y.C.; asst. prof. psychiatry Columbia Coll. Phys. and Surg., 1970-76, spl. lectr., 1976—; supervising psychoanalyst Columbia Psychoanalytic Center Tng. and Research, 1977—. Trustee Council on Law Related Studies, 1967-75; bd. dirs. Chamber Music Soc. of Lincoln Center. Fellow. Am. Psychiat. Assn., N.Y. Acad. Medicine; mem. Am., N.Y. psychoanalytic assns. Clubs: Century Assn., Yale (N.Y.C.). Home: 1040 Fifth Ave New York City NY 10028 Office: 815 Park Ave New York City NY 10021

COOK, JOHN BARTLEY, ins. co. exec.; b. Camden, N.J., June 28, 1912; s. Alfred Thompson and Maude Ellen (Shaw) C.; B.S., B.A., Drexel U., 1936; m. Christine Thomas, Sept. 17, 1938; children—David Alfred, Christine E. With N.J. Mfrs. Ins. Co., Trenton, 1941-75, sr. v.p., 1966-75, dir., 1968-77, sec., 1971-75. Served to capt. U.S. Army, 1943-45. Decorated Bronze Star (3), Purple Heart. Republican. Episcopalian. Home: 1208 West Ave Beach Haven NJ 08008

COOK, JOYCE FRALIC DECHMAN, ednl. specialist; b. Butler, Ala., July 5, 1937; d. Alpha Paul and Marthey Irene (Morris) Fralic; B.S. (Gen. Tchrs. scholar 1954), Fla. State U., 1959; M.Ed., U. Fla., 1969; postgrad. Nova U., 1975—; m. Daniel Woodworth Dechman, Mar. 15, 1961; 1 son, John; m. 2d, David Hall Cook, Dec. 20, 1972; 1 son, David Hall. Tchr., coordinator coop. edn. Duval County (Fla.) Pub. Schs., 1959-65; guidance counselor, Jacksonville, 1965-69; edn. program specialist U.S. Office Edn., Washington, 1969-78, br. chief, 1978—; cons. local sch. dists. and state depts. edn. on career edn. and vocat. edn. Troop com. mem. Boy Scouts Am., 1972-73; bldg. rep. Duval Tchrs. Assn., 1959-69. Recipient certificates of appreciation, Bernallilo Pub. Schs., N.Mex., 1973, State of Ill. Dept. Edn., 1977. Mem. Am. Vocat. Assn., Am. Personnel and Guidance Assn., Nat. Assn. for Adminstrv. Women in Edn., Smithsonian Assos., U.S. Office of Edn. Vocat. Assn. (pres. 1977), Phi Dleta Kappa. Episcopalian. Clubs: Woods Swimming and Tennis (Martinsburg, W.Va.). Contbr. articles to profl. jours.; planned and conducted nat. confs. on career edn. Home: 6217 Dana Ave Springfield VA 22150 Office: Room 5652 ROB 7th and D Sts SW Washington DC 20202

COOK, PAUL WILLIAM, JR., mgmt. cons.; b. Frostburg, Md., Dec. 4, 1950; s. Paul William and Helen Louise (Settle) C.; student Potomac State Coll., 1969-71; B.A., cum laude, Frostburg State Coll., 1973; postgrad. W.Va. U., 1974. Indsl. mgmt. cons. Norman Jaspan Assos., N.Y.C., 1974-75; mgmt. cons. Ridgeley, W.Va., 1973—; tchr. pub. schs., Md. and W.Va., 1976—. Student cons. Health Planning Council Appalachia, Cumberland, Md., 1973. Mem. Am. Polit. Sci. Assn., Young Democrats Allegany County (Md.), Internat. Platform Assn. Democrat. Home: 13913 Briarwood Dr Laurel MD 20810

COOK, RICHARD KELSEY, aerospace co. exec.; b. White Plains, N.Y., Nov. 14, 1931; s. Albert James and Frances Elizabeth (Butler) C.; A.B., George Washington U., 1959; m. Marjorie A. Shellabarger, Sept. 5, 1959; children—Geoffrey S., Patrick K., Sarah E., Catherine E. Legis. research asst. Am. Trucking Assn., Washington, 1958-61; adminstrv. asst. to Congressman Edwin P. Dooley, 1961-62; legis. asst. to Congressman Oliver P. Bolton, 1963-64; mem. minority staff House Banking and Currency Com., 1964-69; spl. asst. to pres., 1969-71, dep. asst. to pres., 1971-73; v.p. Lockheed Aircraft Corp., Washington, 1973—. Served with USAF, 1949-55. Mem. Nat. Security Indsl. Assn. Republican. Episcopalian. Clubs: Met., Federal City, Aero (1st v.p.) (Washington). Office: 900 17th St NW Suite 414 Washington DC 20006

COOK, SANFORD LEE, mech. engr.; b. Newark, July 26, 1940; s. George and Rose (Shwam) C.; M.E., Okla. U., 1960; Bus. Mgmt. degree Rutgers U., 1972; seminars in engring. N.Y. U., 1972, Mass. Inst. Tech., 1976; m. Harriet Jo Friend, Oct. 28, 1961; children—Mark Steven, Margo Lynn. Mem. tech. staff Airtron div. Litton Industries, Morris Plains, N.J., 1961-66; advanced devel. engr. Am. Standard Inc., Piscataway, N.J., 1966-69; chief engr. Clark Door Co. Inc., Cranford, N.J., 1969-77; dir. engring. Standard Keil Co., Allenwood, N.J., 1977—; tech. cons. to cos.; tchr. fire protection, acoustics, electromech. tech. Mgr. Little League, Edison, N.J., 1971-75; committeeman, outdoors chmn. Troop 122, Thomas A. Edison council Boy Scouts Am., 1975-77. Served with Army N.G., 1961-67. Recipient certificate of appreciation Plant Engring. Conf. Acoustics Seminar, 1974. Mem. Soc. Fire Protection Engrs., Soc. Plastics Engrs., Nat. Fire Protection Assn. (letter of appreciation 1974, 76), World Trade Assn. Contbr. articles to profl. jours.; patentee in field. Home: 13 Shirley Ann Dr Ocean NJ 07712 Office: Route 34 and Allenwood Rd Allenwood NJ 08720

COOK, SY, communications co. exec.; b. N.Y.C., Oct. 12, 1923; s. Benjamin and Sarah Cook; student Bklyn. Coll., 1941-42, Drexel Inst. Tech., 1942-43, Cooper Union, 1958, Valparaiso Inst. Tech., 1964; m. Annette Wolper, Mar. 9, 1947; children—Robert Ian, Mindy, Alan Ira. Vice pres. ITV, Inc., N.Y.C., 1955-67; pres. Continuous Progress Edn. Co., Norwalk, Conn., 1967-69, Riker Info. Systems, Inc., N.Y.C., 1969-71, NetCom Corp., N.Y.C., 1971-73, Indsl. Communications Adv. Group, N.Y.C., 1973-74, Sy Cook, Inc., Spring Valley, N.Y., 1974-77; v.p. TeleSessions Corp., N.Y.C., 1977—; communications cons., 1973-77. Served with AUS, 1943-46; PTO. Mem. Soc. Motion Picture and TV Engrs., IEEE (sr.). Home: 37 Williams Ave Spring Valley NY 10977 Office: 475 Fifth Ave New York NY 10017

COOK, WILLIAM HOLMES, fed. judge; b. Carbondale, Ill., June 2, 1920; s. Rex Holmes and Mary Dola (Carter) C.; student So. Ill. U., 1938-40; J.D., Washington U., St. Louis, 1947. Admitted to Ill. bar, 1947; individual practice law, Charleston, 1949-52; atty. FTC, Washington, 1954-59, asst. to chmn., 1957-59; asso. counsel for property and spl. matters Bur. Aeros., Dept. Navy, 1959-63; counsel Armed Services Com., U.S. Ho. of Reps., 1963; judge U.S. Ct. Mil. Appeals, Washington, 1974—. Served with U.S. Army, 1942-46. Mem. Am., Fed. (hon.) bar assns. Republican. Episcopalian. Home: 2501 Calvert St NW Apt 204 Washington DC 20008 Office: US Ct Mil Appeals 450 E St NW Washington DC 20442

COOK, WILLIAM SUTTON, business exec.; b. Duluth, Minn., Sept. 6, 1922; s. Ellis Ray and Marjorie (Sutton) C.; B.B.A., U. Minn., 1948; m. Rosemary Jeanne Bonnett, June 28, 1946; children—Virginia Ann, William Sutton, James J., Andrew J. Various fin. positions Gen. Electric Co., 1948-62; comptroller, then v.p. and comptroller Pa. R.R./Pa. Central Co., 1962-68; v.p., comptroller Ebasco Industries, Inc., 1968-69; v.p. fin., then exec. v.p. Union Pacific Corp., N.Y.C., 1969-77, pres., 1977—, also dir.; dir. U.P. R.R., Champlin Petroleum Co., Rocky Mountain Energy Co., Upland Industries Corp.; trustee Dry Dock Savs. Bank. Served to capt. AUS, 1943-46. Mem. Fin. Execs. Inst. Clubs: Links, Brook, Economic, Board Room (N.Y.C.); Sleepy Hollow Country (pres. 1976-78) (Scarborough, N.Y.). Home: 2 Woodlea Ln Scarborough NY 10510 Office: 345 Park Ave New York City NY 10022

COOKE, GILBERT DAVID, architect; b. S.I., N.Y., Nov. 13, 1937; s. George H. and Evelyn (Eilenberg) C.; student Rensselaer Poly. Inst., 1954-56; B.Arch., U. Cin., 1962; M.Arch., Cranbrook Acad., 1964; m. Marie Elaine Fischer, Feb. 14, 1969; children—Jason Garner, Geoffrey Aaron. Project designer Tippetts, Abbott, McCarthy, Stratton, N.Y.C., Balt., 1964-67; partner Marks & Cooke, Towson, Md., 1967—; pres., 1973—; sec. Rumsey Townhouse Corp. Instr. archtl. design Md. Inst. Mem. sch. bd. Montessori Soc. Central Md. Mem. AIA (recipient Balt. Design award 1972, pres. elect Balt. chpt. 1976), Md. Soc. Architects (dir.), Nat. Assn. Home Builders, Am. Inst. Planners, Hampton HO Assn. (dir.), Am. Arbitration Assn. (panel), Delta Phi. Home: 1403 Ellenglen Rd Hampton MD 21204 Office: 219 W Joppa Rd Towson MD 21204

COOKE, HELEN PAXTON, guidance counselor; b. Nyack, N.Y., Sept. 20, 1925; d. Osmond William and Helen (Paxton) C.; B.S., N.Y. U., 1947, M.A., 1950; M.A.L.S. in History, Conn. Wesleyan U., 1974, certificate advanced study in history, 1978. Tchr. math. Nanuet and Nyack pub. schs., 1947-53; guidance counselor Nyack pub. schs., 1953-58; dir. pupil personnel Nanuet pub. schs., 1958-61; guidance counselor Farmingdale (N.Y.) Sr. High Sch., 1961—; instr. math. Rockland Community Coll., Suffern, N.Y., eves, 1968—; supr. Coll. Entrance Exam. Bd. and Am. Coll. Testing Programs, 1964-74; mem. chs. coms. Wesleyan U., 1975—; pres. Rockland County Tchrs. Assn., 1957-58. Mem. Am. Personnel and Guidance Assn. (life), Middle State Assn. (edn. com. 1975), Farmingdale Tchrs. Assn., alumni assns. N.Y. U., Wesleyan U. Republican. Episcopalian. Author articles.

COOKE, LAWRENCE HENRY, judge; b. Monticello, N.Y., Oct. 15, 1914; s. George L. and Mary (Pond) C.; B.S. cum laude, Georgetown U., 1935; LL.B., Albany Law Sch., Union U., 1938, LL.D. (hon.), 1975; LL.D. (hon.), Siena Coll., 1964; m. Alice McCormack, Nov. 25, 1939; children—Edward M., George L., II, Mary L. Admitted to N.Y. bar, 1939; children—Edward M., George L., II, Mary L. Admitted to N.Y. bar, 1939; individual practice law, Monticello, 1939-53; Sullivan County judge, Monticello, 1954-61; Supreme Ct. justice 3d Jud. Dist., 1962-68; asso. justice Appellate div. 3d Dept., Albany, 1969-74; asso. judge N.Y. State Ct. Appeals, Albany, 1975-79, chief judge, 1979—. Supr., Town of Thompson, N.Y., 1946-49; chmn. Sullivan County Bd. Suprs., 1947-48. Recipient Torch of Liberty award B'nai B'rith, 1967. Mem. Am., N.Y. State (past chmn. young lawyers sect.), Sullivan County (pres.) bar assns. Democrat. Roman Catholic. Home: 415 Broadway Monticello NY 12701 Office: Ct of Appeals Hall Eagle St Albany NY 12207 also Courthouse Monticello NY 12701

COOKE, ROBERT JOHN, educator; b. Kingston, N.Y., Apr. 12, 1923; s. Harry and Anna (Hyland) C.; B.S., State U. N.Y., 1949; A.M., Columbia, 1950; Ph.D., Syracuse U., 1964; m. Barbara Dexter, 1951 (div. 1973); children—Kathleen Anne, Christian Sean, Kevin Michael, Deborah Gaye, Brian Patrick; m. 2d, Nancy K. Shimer, 1977. Asst. Am. civilization Columbia, 1949-50; tchr. social studies, English, Goshen (N.Y.) Central Sch., 1950-54; mem. staff Citizens Edn. Project, Carnegie Found., 1950-54; mem. faculty Ball State U., Muncie, Ind., 1954-59; faculty Syracuse (N.Y.) U., 1960-65, dir. Chautauqua Center, 1960-62; social sci. asso. Inter-Univ. project Project I, Ford Found., 1963-65; prof. history and Am. studies, dir. Am. studies program Southampton (N.Y.) Coll., 1965—, chmn. history dept., 1965-70, dir. humanities div., 1970-73; vis. lectr. Trinity Coll., Dublin, 1974-75; Legislative affairs com. N.Y. Democratic State Com. Served to lt. USMC, 1942-46; PTO. Mem. Sinn Fein (provo), Am. Studies Assn., Am. Hist. Assn., Nat. Council for Social Studies (chmn. standing com. on research 1961-63, dir. 1966-69), Orgn. Am. Historians. Book rev. editor Social Edn., 1964-70. Contbr. to profl. jours., books. Home: 68 Ridge Rd Southampton NY 11968

COOKE, TERENCE JAMES CARDINAL, archbishop; b. N.Y.C., Mar. 1, 1921; s. Michael and Margaret (Gannon) C.; student Cathedral Coll., N.Y.C.; B.A., St. Joseph's Sem., Yonkers, N.Y., 1945; M.S. in Social Work, Cath. U., 1949. Ordained priest Roman Cath. Ch., 1945; asst. pastor St. Athanasius Ch., Bronx, N.Y., also chaplain St. Agatha Home, Nanuet, N.Y., 1946-47; asst. dir. C.Y.O., also dir. youth activities, N.Y.C., 1949-54; procurator St. Joseph's Sem., Yonkers, N.Y., 1954-57; sec. to Cardinal Spellman, 1957-58; named papal chamberlain, vice chancellor Archdiocese N.Y., 1958, domestic prelate, chancellor, 1961-65, named vicar gen., 1965, titular bishop of Summa and aux. bishop N.Y., 1965; archbishop, N.Y., 1968—; elevated to cardinal, 1969. Home: 452 Madison Ave New York City NY 10022 Office: 1011 1st Ave New York City NY 10022

COOKE, THOMAS H., JR., educator, mayor East Orange, N.J.; b. S.C., Oct. 13, 1929; s. Thomas H. and Julia Melinda (McLeod) C.; B.S. in Health and Phys. Edn., N.Y. U., 1954, M.A. in Guidance and Personnel Admnstrn., 1974; postgrad. Mich. State U., 1956, Seton Hall U., 1957; m. Audrey E. Wilson, Apr. 2, 1955; children—Bonnye, Julie, Michael, Thomas, Michael. Tchr. Newark Pub. Sch. System, 1958-77, community and pub. relations officer for exptl. sch., 1969-77, coach swimming and football, 1963-64, recreation admnstr., 1968-77; coordinator Newark-Victoria Plan, Cleve. Exptl. Sch. in Newark, 1969-77; mem. East Orange City Council, 1962-71, chmn., 1968; mayor City of East Orange, founder, mem. East Orange Better Human Relations Council, 1965—, chmn., mem. numerous coms.; elected mem. Essex County (N.J.) Bd. of Chosen Freeholders, 1970-76, chmn. pub. works and engring. coms., 1971-72; trustee Integrity House Drug Rehab. Residential Facility, East Orange, 1971—; community planning and devel. com. United Way Drive, 1974—; chmn. human resources dir. United Way of Essex County, 1975-76, chmn. govt. fund raising, 1974-75; dep. dir., chmn. fin. com. Essex County Bd. Chosen Freeholders, 1973, dir., 1974. Served with USNR, 1954-56; Korea, Recipient Community Service award Bd. Realtors of Oranges and Maplewood, N.J., 1964; Outstanding Young Man of Yr. award East Orange Jaycees, 1965; Man of Yr. award Frontiers Internat. Club of Oranges and Maplewood, 1968, Optimist Internat., East Orange, 1968, NAACP of Oranges and Maplewood, 1968; award East Orange Central Parent Council, 1978, Newark Tchrs. Union, 1978, East Orange Seventh-Day Adventist Ch., 1978, East Orange Family Devel. Center, 1978. Mem. Nat. Assn. County Ofcls. (chmn. sub-com. on welfare reform, 1974, chmn. sub-com. on income maintenance, 1975-76), Met. Regional Council on TV (chmn. 1976). Address: East Orange NJ

COOL, RODNEY LEE, physicist; b. Platte, S.D., Mar. 8, 1920; s. George E. and Muriel (Post) C.; B.S., U. S.D., 1942; M.A., Harvard U., 1947, Ph.D., 1949; m. Margaret E. MacMillan, June 21, 1949; children—Ellen Cool Kwait, John, Mary Lee, Adrienne. Research physicist Brookhaven Nat. Lab., Upton, N.Y., 1949-59, dept. chmn. high energy physics, 1960-64, asst. dir., 1964-66, asso. dir., 1966-70; prof. physics Rockefeller U., N.Y.C., 1970—; mem. policy com. Stanford Linear Acclerator Center, 1962-67, 76—; asso. univs. high energy panel Assos. Univs., Inc., 1963-70; mem. Walker panel com.sci. and pub. policy Nat. Acad. Sci., 1964; high energy physics adv. panel AEC, 1967-70; chmn. high energy adv. com. Brookhaven Nat. Lab., 1967-70; adv. panel physics NSF, 1970-73; chmn. physics adv. com. Nat. Accelerator Lab., 1967-70; trustee Univ. Research Assos., 1977—. Served to maj. AUS, World War II. Decoraled Bronze Star. Fellow Am. Phys. Soc.; mem. Nat. Acad. Scis.. Phi Beta Kappa, Sigma Xi. Co-editor: Advances in Particle Physics, vols. I and II, 1968. Contbr. articles to prof. jours. Home: 450 E 63d St New York City NY 10021 Office: Rockefeller Univ New York City NY 10021

COOLEY, JAMES KEATS, physician; b. Herkimer, N.Y., May 20, 1930; s. Ernest Lester and Mary Alice (Gilchrist) C.; B.S. in Biology, Hartwick Coll., 1952; M.D., Loma Linda U., 1958; m. Vivien Joyce Ormsbee, Feb. 8, 1952; 1 dau., Diane Jean. Intern, E.J. Meyer Meml. Hosp., Buffalo, 1958-59; gen. practice medicine Russellton Med. Group, Apolla, Pa., 1959-64; pvt. practice medicine, Delanson, N.Y., 1964—; mem. staff Ellis Hosp., St. Clares Hosp., Schenectady; courtesy staff Cobleskill Hosp.; health officer Town of Princeton (N.Y.), 1964—, Town of Duanesburg (N.Y.), 1965—; sch. physician Duanesburg Central Schs., Schalmont Central Schs., 1964—. Mem. Utilization Com., Eden Park; mem. Apollo (Pa.) Sch. Bd., 1961-64. Diplomate Am. Bd. Family Practice. Mem. Am. Acad. Family Practice, AMA, Med. Soc. N.Y., Schenectady Med. Soc. Club: Elks. Home and Office: Delanson NY 12053

COOLEY, JAMES LAWRENCE, aerospace mathematician; b. Northampton, Mass., Apr. 17, 1938; s. Edward Ericson and Evelyn Viola (Avery) C.; B.S., U. Mass., 1960; M.A., Pa. State U., 1962; postgrad. U. Md., 1962-66; m. Brenda Ruth Brizzolari, Sept. 9, 1961; children—Deborah Celeste, Andrew Ericson. Aerospace mathematician NASA Goddard Space Flight Center, Greenbelt, Md., 1963—, head mission design sect., 1973—. Treas. Jaycees, Greenbelt, 1966-67. Mem. Math. Assn. Am., Am. Inst. Aeros. and Astronautics, Sigma Xi, Phi Kappa Phi, Pi Mu Epsilon. Home: 232 Lastner Ln Greenbelt MD 20770 Office: Goddard Space Flight Center Greenbelt MD 20771

COOLIDGE, NICHOLAS JEFFERSON, investment banking co. exec., lawyer; b. Brookline, Mass., Feb. 12, 1932; s. Harold J. and Helen Carpenter (Isaacs) C.; grad. Groton Sch., 1950; A.B., Harvard, 1954, LL.B., 1959; m. Elisha Anne Hasek, June 26, 1977; children by previous marriage—Nicole Rousmaniere, Peter Jefferson. Admitted to N.Y. bar, 1959; practiced in N.Y.C.; asso. firm Sullivan & Cromwell; with Kidder, Peabody & Co. Inc., N.Y.C., 1965-78, v.p. corporate finance dept., also dir., head leasing and asset finance group, real estate finance group and Can. finance group; pres. Nicholas Coolidge Inc., N.Y.C., 1978—. Served to lt. USMRC, 1954-56. Mem. Council on Fgn. Relations. Home: 706 Watergate South 700 New Hampshire Ave Washington DC 20037 Office: Suite 20D 800 Fifth Ave New York City NY 10021

COON, DANIEL WEBSTER, lawyer; b. Towanda, Pa., Dec. 23, 1935; s. Robert Joseph and Alice (Markvad) C.; A.B., Lafayette Coll., 1957; J.D., Georgetown U., 1962; m. Deanna Hicks, Feb. 7, 1959; children—Daniel Webster, Dana Michele. Admitted to D.C. bar, 1962, U.S. Supreme Ct. bar, 1965, Md. bar, 1968; practiced in Washington, 1962—; mem. firm Douglas, Obear & Campbell, 1962-76, Jackson, Campbell & Parkinson, 1976—. Served to lt. U.S. Army, 1957-59. Mem. Am., Md. bar assns., Bar Assn. D.C., Phi Delta Phi. Club: Barristers (Washington). Home: 4516 Hornbeam Dr Rockville MD 20853 Office: So Bldg 15th and H Sts Washington DC 20005 also 414 Hungerford Dr Rockville MD 20850

COONCE, SUSAN MASON, career counselor; b. San Diego, Calif., Apr. 27, 1949; d. James Moody and Kathryn (Tribble) Mason; B.S., Tenn. Tech. U., 1971, M.A., 1972; postgrad. Dept. Agr. Grad. Sch., 1977-78, George Washington U., 1977—; m. Thomas Joseph Coonce, Sept. 4, 1971. Mental health technician Plateau Mental Health Center, Cookeville, Tenn., 1971-73; tchr. Psychiat. Inst., Washington, 1973; instr. Fitness, Inc., Washington, 1973-75; tchr. Arlington County Pub. Schs., Arlington, Va., 1975-76; cons., career counselor Grad. Sch. Dept. Labor, Washington, 1976—; also counselor Southeastern U., Washington, 1977—. Mem. Am. Soc. Trainers and Developers, Am. Personnel and Guidance Assn., Phi Delta Kappa, Kappa Delta Pi, Mortar Bd. Home: 5412 Bradford Ct #31 Alexandria VA 22311 Office: 200 Constitution Ave Dept of Labor N4423 Washington DC 20210

COONEY, JOHN GORDON, lawyer; b. Bklyn., Jan. 21, 1930; s. John Philip and Josephine (Gordon) C.; A.B., St. John's U., 1951, LL.B., 1953; m. Patricia Ruth McEwen, June 8, 1957; 1 son, J. Gordon. Admitted to N.Y. bar, 1953, Pa. bar, 1962; asso. firm Patterson, Belknap & Webb, N.Y., 1953-55; staff counsel U.S. Industries, N.Y., 1956-57; atty. SEC, Washington, 1957-59, FTC, 1959-61; partner firm Schnader, Harrison, Segal & Lewis, Phila., 1963—; dir. Delta Data Systems Corp. Arbitrator, Am. Arbitration Assn., 1964—. Dir., pres. Strafford Village Assn., 1969-70; bd. govs. N.Y.C. Young Republican Club, 1957. Recipient Superior Service award FTC, 1961. Mem. Am. Law Inst., Am. (chmn. Conf. on Broker-Dealer Regulation of Am. Bar Assn.-Am. Law Inst. 1968, chmn. Nat. Conf. on New Perspectives in Securities Regulation 1969; chmn. subcom. on ins. problems, com. fed. securities regulation), N.Y. State, Pa., Phila. bar assns., Catholic Philopatrian Soc. Clubs: Union League (Phila.), Midday (Phila.); Overbrook Golf (Bryn Mawr, Pa.); Marion Cricket (Haverford, Pa.). Home: 320 Gatcombe Ln Bryn Mawr PA 19010 Office: Packard Bldg Philadelphia PA 19102

COOPER, ALAN ROBERT, optometrist; b. Newark, June 28, 1942; s. Herbert and Freda (Edelman) C.; student Mich. State U., 1960-63, Seton Hall U., 1963; B.S., Ill. Coll. Optometry, 1965, O.D., 1966; Pvt. practice optometry specializing in contact lenses, Paterson, N.J., 1969—; clin. investigator soft contact lenses FDA. Served to capt. AUS, 1967-69. Diplomate Nat. Bd. Examiners in Optometry. Mem. Nat. Eye Research Found., Better Vision Inst., Internat. Eye Found., Alumni Assn. Ill. Coll. Optometry, Nat. Assn. Professions, U.S. Power Squadrons, Smithsonian Assos., ACLU. Home: 151 Pine Brook Rd Montville NJ 07045 Office: 45 Church St Paterson NJ 07505

COOPER, CHARLES JASPER, lawyer; b. Tampa, Fla., Mar . 20, 1929; s. Harry Alva and Ruth (Smith) C.; A.B., Brown U., 1951; J.D., Harvard, 1954; Ph.D., Bryn Mawr Coll., 1967; m. Sally Ann Hill, Sept. 8, 1951; children—Carol, Douglas, Charles, Elizabeth, Kate. Admitted to Pa. bar, 1955; asso. counsel Montgomery, McCracken, Walker & Rhoads, Phila., 1954-55, Bellwoar, Rich & Mankas, Phila., 1956-60; lectr. polit. sci. Bryn Mawr (Pa.) Coll., 1961-63; lectr. polit. sci. U. Pa., Phila., 1964-67, asst. prof., 1967-68, vis. lectr., 1968-69; asso. gen. counsel ARA Services, Inc., Phila., 1968-71; v.p., sec.-treas., dir. InterAx, Inc., 1971-72; individual practice, Bryn Mawr, 1972—. Trustee, treas. Friends Central Sch., 1970-74; chmn. Harold and Ida Hill Charitable Fund, 1969—; bd. mgrs., treas. Friends Pub. Corp., 1972—; bd. dirs. Phoenix House, 1973—; trustee, treas. Ardmore Ave. Community Center-Soul Shack, 1975—; bd. dirs., treas. Family Support Center, 1976—; trustee Bryn Mawr Coll., 1978—. Mem. Am., Pa., Phila. bar assns., Am. Polit. Sci. Assn., Am. Acad. Polit. and Social Sci., Ams. for Democratic Action (dir. S.E. Pa. 1955—, nat. bd. del. 1967—), Phi Beta Kappa. Democrat. Home: 310 Caversham Rd Bryn Mawr PA 19010 Office: 14 Elliott Ave Bryn Mawr PA 19010

COOPER, CLEMENT THEODORE, lawyer; b. Miami, Fla., Oct. 26, 1930; s. Benjamin Leon and Louise Bethel C.; A.B., Lincoln U. (Mo.), 1952; postgrad. Boston U., 1954-55; J.D., Howard U., 1958; m. Nannie Coles, Aug. 8, 1964; children—Stephanie L., Bridgette L., Stacie L. Admitted to D.C. bar, 1960, Mich. bar, 1960, U.S. Supreme Ct. bar, 1963, also other fed. ct. bars; individual practice law, Washington, 1960—. Mem. pub. welfare adv. council, Washington, 1966; active ACLU. Served with U.S. Army, 1952-54. Mem. Am. Nat., D.C., Washington bar assns., Mich. State Bar, U.S. Ct. Mil. Appeals, Am. Trial Lawyers Assn., Am. Judicature Soc. Anglican Episcopal. Clubs: Internat. Platform Assn., Alpha Phi Alpha Author: Sealed Verdict, 1964; contbr. articles to publ. Home: 728 Dahlia St NW Washington DC 20012 Office: 918 F St NW #300 Washington DC 20004

COOPER, DAVID YOUNG, scientist; b. Henderson, N.C., Aug. 14, 1924; s. James Allison and Frances (Chatham) C.; student Woodbury Forest Sch., 1941-42; student, U. N.C., 1943-44, Med. Sch., 1944-46; M.D., U. Pa., 1948; m. Cynthia Laughlin, Aug. 6, 1955; children Lucy C., Allison Y. Intern U. Pa. Hosp., 1948-49, resident in surgery, 1950, 53-57, surg. researcher Harrison Dept., 1957-59, asst. prof., 1959-64, asso. prof., 1964-68, prof., 1968—. Served with USNR, 1944-46, 50-52. Recipient Career Div. award Am. Heart Assn., 1959-64; Career Div. award USPHS, 1964-74. Charles O. Findley fellow A.C.S., 1957-59. Mem. Am. Soc. Biol. Chemistry, Am. Physiol. Soc., Am. Soc. Pharm. and Exptl. Theraputics, Endocrine Soc., Phila. Coll. Physicians, John Morgan Soc. Episcopalian. Clubs: Racquet (Phila.), Merion Golf. Home: 424 Colebrook Ln Bryn Mawr PA 19010 Office: 5013 Ravdin Courtyard Building Hosp University Pennsylvania 34th and Spruce Sts Philadelphia PA 19104

COOPER, DORIS JEAN, market research coding service co. exec.; b. N.Y.C., Dec. 17, 1934; d. James and Georgina (Cassidy) Breslin; student N.Y. U. Sch. Commerce, 1953-55, Hunter Coll., 1956-57; m. Samuel James Cooper, June 17, 1956; 1 son, David Austin. Asst. coding supr. Crossley-S-D Surveys, N.Y.C., 1955-57; asst. field supr. Trendex, Inc., N.Y.C., 1957-59; coding dir. J. Walter Thompson Co., N.Y.C., 1960-63, Audits & Surveys, N.Y.C., 1964-65; cons., N.Y.C., 1965-73; pres. Cooper Services, Hastings-on-Hudson, N.Y., 1973—. Vol. spl. com. Hastings-on-Hudson Drug Guidance Council; unit coordinator Westchester-Putnam council Boy Scouts Am. Mem. Am. Mktg. Assn., Nat. Assn. Women Bus. Owners. Republican. Episcopalian. Office: 419 Warburton Ave Hastings-on-Hudson NY 10706

COOPER, DOUGLAS JAMES, jewelry co. exec.; b. Bryn Athyn, Pa., Sept. 19, 1931; s. Fred J. and Aurora (Synnestvedt) C.; A.B., U. Pa., 1962; m. Diene Pitcairn, Jan. 9, 1960; children—Heather Diene, Lochlin Douglas, Christopher Ian. Pres., F.J. Cooper Inc., Phila., 1958—, F.J. Cooper Internat. Co., Phila., and Jamaica, 1964—; chmn. bd. Internat. Gem Investors, Inc., Phila. Chmn. Ann. Giving, evening sch. U. Pa., 1963-66; exec. bd. Opera Co. Phila.; pres. Singing City of Phila., 1963-66; trustee, chmn. oriental art com. Phila. Mus. Art; bd. dirs. Settlement Mus. Sch. (hon.), Beneficia Found., Elwyn Inst.; chmn. bd. dirs. Pa. Ballet Mem. Beta Nu, Delta Sigma Pi, Sigma Kappa Phi. Republican. Swedenborgian. Clubs: Union League, Racquet (Phila.). Home: 1820 Rittenhouse Sq Philadelphia PA 19103 also El Cerro Tamarind Hill Montego Bay POB 306 Jamaica West Indies Office: 1416 Chestnut St Philadelphia PA 19102 also POB 306 2 Orange St Montego Bay Jamaica West Indies

COOPER, EDWARD JOHN WADDELL, artist, art critic, educator; b. Letchworth, Eng., Oct. 10, 1914; s. John Charles and Mathida Elizabeth (Waddell) C.; came to U.S., 1946, naturalized, 1949; student City of London Coll., 1938-40, Northwestern U., Chgo., 1949-50, Grande Chaumière, Paris, France, 1952; m. Mabel Henderson, July 13, 1946 (dec. June 1970). Med. illustrator Dover Clinic, Boston, 1950-58; art critic Boston Univ.'s Radio Sta., WBUR, 1952—; asst. dir. Joint Center Urban Studies, Harvard U. and Mass. Inst. Tech., Cambridge, 1967-69; exec. dir., instr. painting and drawing Cambridge Art Assn., 1970-74; lectr. Boston Arts Festival, 1954-63; instr. Danforth Mus. Sch., Framingham, Mass. Exhibited in one-man shows at Boston U., 1955, Galerie de Baune, Paris, 1956, Paul Schuster Gallery, Cambridge, 1957, Newton Coll., 1963; exhibited in group shows at De Cordova Mus., 1953, Inst. Contemporary Art, Boston, 1955, Stonehill Coll., Mass., 1973; represented in permanent collections Art Inst. Boston, Union Hosp. Lynn, Salem (Mass.) Hosp., others. Served to lt. Royal Navy, Eng., 1941-46. Fellow Internat. Inst. Arts and Letters. Home: 14 Little's Point Swampscott MA 01907

COOPER, HARRY JAMES, trade assn. exec.; b. Kingsville, Ont., Can., Apr. 13, 1917; s. Harry James and Josephine Mildred (Bertrand) C.; student Queen's U. (Can.), 1935, Northwestern U., 1950; m. Nancy Tuck Keeping, Nov. 24, 1940; children—Sandra (Mrs. David Phillips), Deeju (Mrs. Alan Edwards), Bradley Kent. Came to U.S., 1949, naturalized, 1955. Accountant Royal Bank Can., Kingsville, 1936-40; dist. sales mgr. Air Can., Chgo, N.Y.C., 1940-49; passenger and cargo sales mgr. Northeast Airlines, Boston, 1949-51; dist. sales mgr. S.A.S., Chgo, 1951-53; dir. pub. relations Lions Internat., Chgo., 1953-60, Acme Steel Co., Chgo., 1960-61; asst. exec. dir. CARE Inc., N.Y.C., 1961-66; asst. to pres. Am. Field Service, N.Y.C., 1966-67; exec. dir. Internat. Center, N.Y.C., 1967-69; dir. greeting card program UNICEF, N.Y.C., 1969-71; exec. dir. Greeting Card Pubs. Assn., N.Y.C., 1971-74; exec. v.p. Fedn. Nat. Assns., N.Y.C., 1974—. Mem. traffic and transp. conf. Nat. Safety Council, 1953-61; mem. nat. pub. relations com. Boy Scouts Am., 1952-68; mem. nat. pub. relations com. Girl Scouts U.S.A., 1952-68; mem. bd. edn. Rich Twp. High Sch., Park Forest, Ill., 1958-61; mem. Citizens Sch. Com., Greenwich, Conn., 1961-68. Bd. dirs. CARE Inc., 1957-61; adv. bd. Pub. Relations News, 1963-68; exec. bd. Community Council, Park Forest, 1949-51. Served with RAF, 1943-45. Mem. Air Transport Assn., Pub. Relations Soc. Am., Am. Soc. Assn. Execs., U.S. C. of C. Congregationalist. Lion (dist. gov. 1965-66). Clubs: Chicago Press; N.Y. Overseas Press. Editor Our World, 1966-67. Home and Office: 68 Florence Rd Riverside CT 06878

COOPER, JAMES MICHAEL, mental health adminstr.; b. Troy, N.Y., June 8, 1929; s. John Vernon and Margaret Pauline (Snipes) C.; B.A. in Sociology, Siena Coll., 1954; M.S.W., St. Louis U., 1956; m. Geraldine Constance Baxter, May 15, 1965; children—Marc A., Adam M. Dir. Woodland Counseling Center, West Philadelphia Consortium, 1972-75; dir. Partial Hosp. Center, West Philadelphia Mental Health Consortium, 1975-79; dir. base service unit and adult outpatient services Catchment Area 4, Inc., Phila., 1979—. Mem. West Mt. Airy Neighbors, Phila. Mem. Nat. Assn. Social Workers, Acad. Certified Social Workers. Roman Catholic. Home: 616 W Hortter St Philadelphia PA 19119 Office: 4900 Wyalusing Ave Philadelphia PA 19131

COOPER, JOEL JAY, obstetrician, gynecologist; b. N.Y.C., June 10, 1938; s. Philip H. and Lottie (Rabinowitz) C.; student U. Buffalo, 1956-58, N.Y. U., 1958-59; M.D., U. Mich., 1963; m. Rochelle Ginsberg, June 12, 1960; children—Jill, Tracy. Intern, L.I. Jewish Hosp., 1963-64, resident in obstetrics and gynecology, 1966-68, chief resident in obstetrics and gynecology, 1968-69; practice medicine specializing in obstetrics and gynecology, Bayside, N.Y., 1969—; asst. clin. prof. state U. N.Y. at Stoneybrook Med. Campus. Served to capt. USAF, 1964-66. Diplomate Am. Bd. Obstetrics and Gynecology. Fellow Am. Coll. Obstetrics and Gynecology, A.C.S.; mem. Am. Fertility Soc., Am. Lararoscopic Soc., Med. Soc. N.Y. State, Queens Gynecol. Soc., Queens County (N.Y.) Med. Soc. Jewish. Home: 8 Piper Dr Searingtown NY 11507 Office: 223-01 Union Turnpike Bayside NY 11364

COOPER, JOHN MCGILL, JR., mfr's. reps. orgn. exec.; b. Phila., Aug. 9, 1912; s. John McGill and Jane (Williams) C.; B.S. in Indsl. Engring., Lafayette Coll., 1934; m. Lydia Elizabeth Brooks, Oct. 23, 1937; children—John McGill III, Elizabeth Jane. Sales asst. to gen. dept. mgr. refinery dept. Swift & Co., Chgo., 1943-44, regional product mgr., refinery, Newark, 1944-56; nat. sales mgr. Hermes Tyw. Div. Paillard Inc., N.Y.C., 1956-61; mgr. nat. mktg. Kalart Co., Plainfield, Conn., 1961-62; owner Mfr's. Rep. Orgn., W. Hartford, Conn., 1962—; v.p. sales Stony Ridge Silico Corp., Emco Corp. Exec. bd., treas. World Affairs Center, Hartford, Conn.; bd. dirs. Daycroft Sch., Greenwich, Conn. Mem. Am. Mktg. Assn., Field Sales Mgmt. Inst. Republican. Christian Scientist. Home and Office: 11 Beacon Hill Dr West Hartford CT 06117

COOPER, JOY MCCORMICK RHODES (MRS. ROBERT L. COOPER), educator; b. Chgo., July 10, 1927; d. Willard and Lillian (Hansen) Rhodes; B.S., Columbia, 1949; M.A., Columbia, 1951; m. Robert L. Cooper, Apr. 9, 1959; children—Lawrence Michael, Patricia Jane. Materials specialist Bur. Indian Affairs Dept. Interior, Brigham City, Utah, 1951-54; materials specialist Puerto Rican study Ford Found. N.Y.C. Bd. Edn., 1954-55; program specialist Girl Scouts Am., N.Y.C., 1955-59; ind. edn. cons., 1965—. Bd. dirs., 2d v.p. Overseas Edn. Fund League Women Voters, 1971-78, Overseas Edn. Fund rep. to UN, 1978—; bd. dirs. Bancroft North, 1975-78; bd. trustees Bancroft Sch., 1972—. Mem. C.A.P., Aircraft Owners and Pilots Assn., Air Force Assn., Navy League, Nat. Oceanography Assn., Internat. Oceanographic Found., Oceanic Soc., Internat. Platform Assn. Club: Croton Dam Yacht (past commodore) (Ossining, N.Y.). Author: series spl. vocat. textbooks, 1951-54. Home: 9 Taconic Rd Ossining NY 10562

COOPER, LEON N., physicist, educator; b. N.Y.C., Feb. 28, 1930; s. Irving and Anna (Zola) C.; A.B., Columbia U., 1951, A.M., 1953, Ph.D., 1954, D.Sci., 1973; D. Sc., U. Sussex (Eng.), 1973, U. Ill., 1974, Brown U., 1974, Gustavus Adolphus Coll., 1975, Ohio State U., 1976, U. Pierre et Marie Curie, Paris, 1977; m. Kay Anne Allard, May 18, 1969; children—Kathleen Ann, Coralie Lauren. NSF postdoctoral fellow, mem. Inst. for Advanced Study, Princeton, N.J., 1954-55; research asso. U. Ill., 1955-57; asst. prof. Ohio State U., 1957-58; asso. prof. Brown U., Providence, 1958-62, prof., 1962-66, Henry Ledyard Goddard U. prof., 1966-74, Thomas J. Watson Sr. prof. sci., 1974—; lectr. Summer Sch. Varenna, Italy, 1955; vis. prof. Brandeis Summer Inst., 1959, Bergen Internat. Sch. Physics, Norway, 1961, Scuola Internazionali Di Fisica, Erice, Italy, 1965, L'Ecole Normal Supericure, Centre Universitaire Internationale, Paris, 1966, Cargese Summer Sch., 1966, others; cons. indsl., ednl. orgs. NSF fellow, 1954-55; Alfred P. Sloan Found. research fellow, 1959-66, John Simon Guggenheim Meml. Found. fellow, 1965-66. Recipient Comstock prize, Nat. Acad. Scis., 1968, Nobel prize, 1972. Fellow Am. Phys. Soc., Am. Acad. Arts and Scis.; mem. Am. Philos. Soc., Nat. Acad. Scis., Soc. for Neurosci., AAAS, Phi Beta Kappa, Sigma Xi. Author: Introduction to The Meaning and Structure of Physics, 1968. Contbr. articles to profl. jours. Home: 49 Intervale Rd Providence RI 02906

COOPER, MICHAEL ROY, indsl., organizational psychologist; b. Bklyn., Mar. 8, 1946; s. Sam and Shirley (Boris) C.; B.A. in Psychology, Hofstra U., 1968; M.A. in Exptl. Psychology, C.W. Post Center, L.I. U., 1970; Ph.D., in Indsl. Psychology, Ohio State U., 1972; m. Ruth Mines, Sept. 7, 1969; 1 dau., Carolyn. Research asst., dept. psychology L.I. U., Brookville, N.Y., 1968-70; research analyst N.Y. State Div. Youth, N.Y.C., 1970; teaching and research asso. dept. psychology Ohio State U., 1970-72; head of behavioral sci. research GTE Labs., Waltham, Mass., 1972-74; pres. Cooper Assos., Sudbury, Mass., 1974-76; asst. prof. mgmt. and organizational behavior Grad. Sch. Adminstrn. Suffolk U., Boston, 1975-76; v.p., dir. employee relations programs Opinion Research Corp., an Arthur D. Little Co., Princeton, N.J., 1976—; adj. prof. organizational behavior U. New Haven, 1973, Boston U., 1973-74; cons. Dept. Army, Ft. Ord, Calif., organizational devel. directorate, 1973-74, Am. Tel. & Tel., 1974-75. Served to 1st lt., Med. Service Corp., AUS, 1973. Mem. AAAS, N.Y. Acad. Scis., Internat. Congress Applied Psychology, Am. (com. indsl. and organizational psychology and consumer psychology 1972-78), Mass., Eastern psychol. assns. Contbr. articles in field to Harvard Bus. Rev., Jour. Applied Psychology, Am. Psychologist, Internat. Tech. Coop. Center Rev. Home: Liberty Bell Ct Belle Mead NJ 08502 Office: Opinion Research Corp N Harrison St Princeton NJ 08540

COOPER, PAULETTE MARCIA, author; b. Antwerp, Belgium; d. Theodore S. and Stella Rose (Toepfer) Cooper; came to U.S., 1948, naturalized, 1950; B.A. with honors, Brandeis U., 1964; M.A., City U. of N.Y., 1968. Writer, analyst Schwerin Research Corp., N.Y.C., 1965-66; copywriter Batten Barton Durstine & Osborn, N.Y.C., 1966-67; copywriter Norman Craig & Kummel Co., N.Y.C., 1967-68; free lance writer, 1968—. Mem. Soc. Mag. Writers, Author's League, Am. Med. Writers Assn., Mystery Writers Am., Nat. Acad. TV Arts and Scis. Author: The Medical Detectives, 1973; Growing Up Puerto Rican, 1972; The Scandal of Scientology, 1971; Halloween, 1972. Contbr. numerous articles to periodicals. Address: 300 E 40th St New York City NY 10016

COOPER, RICHARD HOUGHTON, interior designer, cabinet maker; b. Orange, N.J., Apr. 26, 1928; s. Everard Jason and Maibelle Cooper (Houghton) C.; student Wharton Sch., U. Pa.; D.B.A. (hon.), Pacific Western U.; m. Elizabeth Brenner, Nov. 17, 1952; children—Carol B., Douglas B. Pvt. investor, 1950-57; pres. Houghton Spltys., Inc., Paoli, Pa., 1957-77, Cooper Spltys., Inc., Willow Grove, Pa., 1977—; dir. Courier-Hooks Eng., Inc. Mem. Am. Soc. Interior Designers, Amateur Trapshooting Assn., SAR, Sons of Revolution, Nat. Rifle Assn. Clubs: Masons, Del. County Field & Stream. Home and Office: 415 Davisville Rd Willow Grove PA 19090 and 2150 Snook Dr Royal Harbor Naples FL 33940

COOPER, ROBERT LEO, garment co. exec.; b. N.Y.C., Apr. 30, 1921; s. Leo M. and Frances (Bogen) C.; student Lafayette Coll., 1939-40; B.A., Cornell U., 1942; m. Joy McCormick Rhodes, Apr. 9,

1959; children—Lawrence Michael, Patricia Jane. With White Swan Uniforms, Inc., Yonkers, N.Y., 1946—, v.p., 1951-56, exec. v.p., 1956-66, pres., 1966—; dir. R.L. Trucking Corp., pres. 1968—. Trustee Yonkers YMCA; bd. dirs. Yonkers Gen. Hosp., treas. 1960-68, 72—, vp.p 1960-73, 76—; bd. dirs. Yonkers Rehab. Center, pres., 1976—; bd. dirs. Bailey Hall Sch. Served with AUS, 1942-46, to 1st lt. USAAF, 1946. Mem. Navy League. Rotarian (pres. 1967). Clubs: City (Yonkers); Boston Yacht; Corinthians, N.Y. Yacht, Explorers (N.Y.C.). Home: 9 Taconic Rd Ossining NY 10562 Office: 21 St Casimer Ave Yonkers NY 10702

COOPER, WILLIAM MARION, physician, educator; b. Pitts., Jan. 12, 1919; s. Lardin Monroe and Sophia Antionette (Swartz) C.; B.S., Pa. State U., 1939; M.D., Hahnemann Med. Coll., 1943; m. Sara Georgia Thomas, Jan. 19, 1942; children—Mikell Lee (Mrs. A. William Schenck III), William Marion, Jr., Thomas L., George Robert. Intern Shadyside Hosp., Pitts., 1943; resident U. Pitts. Sch. Medicine, 1946-48, Cleve. Clinic Found., 1948; practice medicine, specializing in internal medicine and hematology, Pitts., 1948—; mem. staff Presbyn.-Univ. Hosp., Shadyside Hosp., Western Pa. Hosp., Magee Woman's Hosp.; mem. faculty U. Pitts. Sch. Medicine, 1948—, clin. prof. medicine, 1958—, dir. div. continuing edn., 1970—, asso. dean continuing edn., 1974—, asst. vice chancellor U. Pitts. Health Center; dir. continuing edn. Univ. Health Center of Pitts., 1975—. Bd. dirs. Central Blood Bank, Pitts., 1951-60, Pitts. Skin and Cancer Found., 1958-65. Served with M.C., AUS, 1944-45. Diplomate Am. Bd. Internal Medicine, Am. Bd. Hematology. Mem. A.M.A., Pa., Allegheny County med. socs., Am., Internat. socs. hematology, A.C.P. (gov. 1965-71), Am. Assn. Med. Colls., Am. Soc. Internal Medicine, AAAS. Clubs: Oakmont (Pa.) Country; University (Pitts.). Contbr. articles to profl. jours. Home: 813 W Waldheim St Pittsburgh PA 15215 Office: Mellon Pavilion 4815 Liberty Ave Pittsburgh PA 15224

COPE, ALFRED HAINES, educator; b. Oakbourne, Pa., May 29, 1912; s. Joseph and Ellen (Fussell) C.; A.B., Earlham Coll., 1934; Ph.D., U. Pa., 1948; m. Ruth Balderston, Aug. 23, 1937; 1 dau., Joan. Agt., Equitable Life Ins. Co., 1934-36; dir. Am. Friends Service Co., Chgo., 1936-38, War Relief Administrn., Spain, 1938-39; administrv. asst. Inst. Local and State Govt. U. Pa., 1940-42, instr., 1946-48; sr. administrv. aid. U.S. Civil Service Commn., Phila., 1942-43; asst. prof. Syracuse (N.Y.) U., 1949-51, asso. prof., 1951-56, asst. dean Coll. Liberal Arts, 1960-70, prof. citizenship, 1960-75, prof. polit. sci., 1962-75, prof. emeritus, 1975—, registrar, mgr. student data systems, 1970-74; asst. dean, prof. citizenship Utica Coll., 1956-60. Pres. bd. dirs. Child and Family Service, 1963-66; trustee Oakwood Sch., Poughkeepsie, N.Y., 1974-77, treas., 1977—, chmn. treas. sect. of Ams., Friends World Com., 1976—, mem. world finance group, 1976—; bd. dirs. Friends Com. Economic Responsibility, 1977—; mem. central com. Friends Gen. Conf., 1978—. Served to capt. AUS, 1943-46. Fellow AAAS; mem. Am. Acad. Polit. and Social Sci., Acad. Polit. Sci., Am. Arbitration Assn. (mem. pub. employee disputes settlement panel Nat. Center for Disputes Settlement), Am. Judicature Soc., N.Y. Welfare Conf., Am., Soc. Pub. Administrn., Friends Hist. Soc., Pi Gamma Mu, Phi Delta Kappa. Club: Torch (pres. Syracuse 1969-70). Author: Administrators of Civil Service in Cities of the Third Class in Pa., 1948; (with Fred Krinsky) Franklin Roosevelt and the Supreme Court, 1952, rev. edit., 1969; Current Defense of the U.S., 1954; (with E.E. Palmer) The Dixon Yates Contract and the National Power Policy, 1955; The Basis for a New Legal System, 1973; Managing World Resources, 1975. Home: 201 Houston Ave Syracuse NY 13224

COPELAND, AMORITA MURIEL (SESINGER), pub. relations/fundraising cons., civic worker; b. Phila.; d. Charles Franklin and Pauline Elizabeth (Beckler) Sesinger; B.A., Bucknell U., 1922, certificate in voice Dept. Music, 1924; m. Charles Edward Copeland, June 18, 1927 (dec. 1947). Asst. to registrar Bucknell U., 1918-22; tchr. English, French, history and comml. studies Pitman (N.J.) High Sch., 1922-23; tchr. comml. courses Bronx Bus. Coll., N.Y.C., 1927; exec. sec., N.Y.C., 1932-42; vol. salvage program War Prodn. Bd., N.Y.C., 1942-47; personal sec. to Mrs. Cornelius Vanderbilt Whitney, Westbury, N.Y., 1948-49; asst. gen. sec. Columbia U., N.Y.C., 1948-49; asst. to dir. fundraising Planned Parenthood Fedn. Am., N.Y.C., 1949; dir. women's div. hosp. fund-raising campaign N.Y. Infirmary, N.Y.C., 1950; dir. nat. devel. Girl Scouts U.S.A., N.Y.C., 1950-57; dir. pub. relations Fairleigh Dickinson U., Madison, N.J., 1958, dir. admissions, 1957-58; coordinator pub. relations N.Y. U., N.Y.C., 1958-67; field dir. five-county rural health demonstration project in central Pa., Pa. Dept. Health, 1967-71; staff Task Force, Union County, Pa., 1976—; cons. in pub. relations and fundraising, 1971—. Hostess radio show Sta. WMCA, N.Y.C.; ch. soloist, Pitman, 1925-27; soloist with Antonia Brico Choral and Orch., 1945-55; appeared as singer in various radio programs, 1928-30, including Sta. WPG, Atlantic City, 1929; mem. Susquehanna Valley Chorale, 1968—; appeared as actress in plays with the Green Door Players, Madison, N.J., Florham Park (N.J.) Players, 1958-67; pres. Jackson Heights (N.Y.) Community Fedn., 1947-49; trustee Bucknell U., 1962-67. Recipient Bronze medal of Good Citizenship, D.A.R., 1943, Gold award of Recognition, Am. Pub. Relations Assn., 1961, award Girl Scouts U.S.A., Outstanding Service plaque Interagy. Council Central Susquehanna Valley, 1975. Mem. Pub. Relations Soc. Am. (chmn. edn. com., dir. N.Y. chpt.), Nat. Soc. Fund Raisers, Theta Alpha Phi, Mu Phi Epsilon. Clubs: Order Eastern Star, N.Y. U. Faculty, Campus, Bison Century. Address: 1130 Washington Ave Lewisburg PA 17837

COPELAND, LOIS JACQUELINE (MRS. RICHARD A. SPERLING), physician; b. Malden, Mass., Sept. 16, 1943; d. Arnold Alan and Ann (Goldfarb) Copeland; B.A. magna cum laude, Cornell U., 1964, M.D., 1968; m. Dr. Richard A. Sperling, June 7, 1970; children—Mark Edward, Larissa Lynn. Intern N.Y. Hosp., N.Y.C., 1968-69, resident, 1969-70; resident Bellevue Hosp., N.Y. U. Med. Center, 1970-72; teaching asst. internal medicine, N.Y. U. Med. Center, 1971—; asso. attending staff Pascack Valley Hosp., Westwood, N.J., 1974—. Mem. Phi Beta Kappa, Phi Kappa Phi, Alpha Lambda Delta. Home: 25 Sparrowbush Rd Upper Saddle River NJ 07458 Office: 47 Central Ave Hillsdale NJ 07642

COPELAND, NATHANIEL HAWTHORNE, internist; b. Newport News, Va., June 17, 1921; s. Lorenzo and Eva Lucy (Wynne) C.; A.B., Lincoln U., 1942; M.D., Howard U., 1945; children—Nathaniel, Nathan, Paulette. Intern, Harlem Hosp., N.Y.C., 1945-46; resident Mercy-Douglass Hosp., Phila., 1946-47, U. Pa. Grad. Hosp., Phila., 1969-70; practice medicine specializing in internal medicine, Phila., 1947—; mem. staffs Hahnemann, St. Lukes, West Park, St. Josephs hosps.; asst. prof. dept. medicine Hahnemann Med. Coll., 1974—; clin. dir. for family med. care City of Phila., 1971—; med. dir. Mercy-Douglas Human Services Center, 1977—. Bd. dirs. Family Service Phila., 1966-76, Y's Mens Club, Phila., 1957-76. Served with M.C., U.S. Army, 1943-45. Recipient Outstanding Humanitarian award Consistory 1, DeMolay, 1977. Diplomate Am. Bd. Family Practice. Fellow Am. Acad. Family Physicians; mem. A.C.P., Am. Pub. Health Assn., Am. Acad. Health Adminstrn., AMA, Am. Geriatrics Soc., Pa. Med. Soc. Methodist. Office: 4622 Kingsessing Ave Philadelphia PA 19143

COPELAND, TERRY DUANE, chemist; b. Lamar, Colo., Sept. 17, 1937; s. Ray Wesley and Estellyne Laura (Bloyd) C.; B.S., U. Tex., 1961; postgrad. U. Md., 1966-71. Research asso. Flow Labs., Inc., Rockville, M.D., 1971-76; scientist Frederick Cancer Research Center, Litton Bionetics, Inc., Frederick, Md., 1976—; teaching asst. chemistry U. Md., 1966-71; instr. U.S. Power Squadron, 1973—. Served with U.S. Army, 1963-66. Petroleum Research Fund fellow U. Tex., 1961-63; recipient Sr. Mem. award U.S. Power Squadron, 1978. Mem. Am. Chem. Soc., U.S. Power Squadron, Inst. Navigation. Home: 13111 Twinbrook Pkwy Rockville MD 20851 Office: PO Box B Frederick MD 21701

COPLEN, RON, librarian; b. Des Moines, Aug. 2, 1936; s. Kenneth and Marcella (Smith) C.; B.F.A., Drake U., 1959. Librarian N.Y. Pub. Library, N.Y.C., 1960-63, Columbia U. Libraries, N.Y.C., 1963-67; with Oceana Pubs., Dobbs Ferry, N.Y., 1965-67, Fred B. Rothman, S. Hackensack, N.J., 1967-70; librarian Harcourt Brace Jovanovich Inc., N.Y.C., 1970—; library cons. Pres. New Dem. Assembly, 1972; campaign mgr. Al Blumenthal, 1972; campaign coordinator Bella Abzug, 1970, John Lindsey, 1966. Mem. Spl. Libraries Assn. (conf. chmn. 1977, pres. chpt. 1978, chmn. pub. div. 1975-76). Club: N.Y. Library. Contbr. articles in field to profl. jours. Home: 84 Horatio St New York City NY 10014 Office: 757 Third Ave New York City NY 10017

COPPA, ANTHONY PATRICK, cons. engr.; b. Phila., Mar. 22, 1927; s. Nicola and Felicia (Migliaccio) C.; B.M.E., Villanova U., 1948; M.S. in Engring. Mechanics, U. Pa., 1959, postgrad., 1959-62; m. Mary Concetta Cimorelli, July 4, 1952; children—Loretta, Clare, Nicholas, Anthony, Mary Ann, Joan, Jean, Felicia, David, Justin. Mech. devel. engr. Westinghouse Electric Corp., 1949-56; engr. Gen. Electric Missile and Space div. Gen. Electric Co., 1956-59, research engr. Gen. Electric Space Scis. Lab., 1959-67, cons. engr. structural systems and materials, 1967—; cons. Gen. Electric Aircraft Engine Group, Gen. Electric Corporate Research and Devel. Lab., Louis I. Kahn, Architect. Served with USNR, 1944-46. Recipient Ralph J. Cordinar award Gen. Electric Co., 1962; Barnwell Gold pin Tau Beta Pi. Mem. Am. Inst. Aeronautics and Astronautics, AAAS, Internat. Assn. for Shell Structures, Elfun Soc., Nat. Geog. Soc., Men of Malvern. Roman Catholic. Contbr. articles in field to profl. jours. Patentee. Author: Songs and Shadows (poems), 1971. Home: 748 S Highland Ave Merion PA 19066 Office: Gen Electric Co PO Box 8555 Philadelphia PA 19101

COPPA, FRANK JOHN, educator; b. N.Y.C., July 18, 1937; s. Peter Paul and Fanny Rafaella (Coppa) C.; B.A. (Generoso Pope scholar), Bklyn. Coll., 1960; M.A. (K.C. fellow), Catholic U., 1962, Ph.D., 1966; postgrad. (Fulbright fellow) U. Rome, 1964-65; m. Rosina Genovese, Aug. 7, 1965; children—Francesca, Melina. Instr. St. John's U., Jamaica, N.Y., 1965-66, asst. prof., 1966-70, asso. prof., 1971—. Guest lectr. TV series NBC and CBS, 1972-78. Mem. legis. advisory com. 49th Assembly Dist., 1973-74; mem. nat. com. U.S.A. Bicentennial-The Italian Contbn., 1975-76. Grantee Nat. Endowment Humanities, summer 1977. Mem. Am., Am. Catholic hist. assns., Soc. for Italian Hist. Studies, N.Y. Assn. European Historians, Columbia Seminar on Modern Italy. Author: From Vienna to Vietnam: War and Peace in the Modern World, 1969; Economics and Politics in the Giolittian Age, 1971; Camillo di Cavour, 1973; Cities in Transition: From the Ancient World to Urban America, 1974; Religion in the Making of Western Man, 1974; The Immigrant Experience in America, 1976. Contbr. articles to profl. jours. Office: Dept History St John's U Jamaica Queens NY 11439

COPPER, WALTER LOGAN, JR., chem. co. exec.; b. Trenton, N.J., Feb. 19, 1934; s. Walter Logan and Jessie Elizabeth (Gunning) C.; B.A. in Bus. Adminstrn., Duke U., 1956; M.S. in Transp., U. Tenn., 1960; m. Barbara Dena Van Gulik, June 27, 1965; children—Thomas and Douglas (twins), Christine. Transp. analyst Scott Paper Co., Phila., 1960-65; corporate transp. and warehouse mgr. Richardson-Merrell, Inc., Phila., 1965-70; phys. distbn. services mgr. Vick Chem. Co., Phila., 1970—; pres. Woodlock Distbn. Co., Chgo., 1969—; dir. Dalfort Distbn. Co., Arlington, Tex. Bd. dirs. Worcester (Pa.) Civic Assn. Served as capt. USNR, 1978. Mem. Am. Soc. Traffic and Transp., Nat. Indsl. Traffic Conf., Drug and Toilet Preparation Traffic Conf., Nat. Council Phys. Distbn. Mgmt. Home: Box 324 Crest Terrace Dr Worcester PA 19490 Office: PO Box 8155 Philadelphia PA 19101

COPPERMAN, STUART MORTON, pediatrician; b. Bklyn., June 5, 1935; s. Irving and Anne (Reisfield) C.; B.A. cum laude, Bklyn. Coll., 1956; M.D., State U. N.Y. Downstate Med. Center, Bklyn., 1960; m. Renee Stein, Aug. 17, 1959; children—Beth, Alan, Cara. Rotating intern L.I. Jewish Hosp., New Hyde Park, 1960-61, resident in pediatrics, 1961-63; practice medicine specializing in pediatrics, Merrick, N.Y., 1965—; mem. staff L.I. Jewish Hillside Med. Center, New Hyde Park, Nassau County Med. Center, East Meadow, Hempstead Gen. Hosp., Hempstead, N.Y.; clin. asst. prof. pediatrics State U. N.Y., Med. Sch. at Stony Brook, 1972—, asst. prof. clin. health studies Sch. Allied Health, 1977—; clin. instr. in pediatrics physicians asst. program Stony Brook Med. Center, 1972—; med. adviser Assn. Children with Down's Syndrome, 1971—; mem. com. for handicapped Bellmore Sch. Dist., 1976—; mem. ad. hoc com. on community as sch. Merrick/Bellmore Schs., 1976—; preceptor in pediatrics Physicians Asst. Program; lectr., cons. in field; mem. Am. Physicians Fellowship for Isreal Med. Assn., 1974—; mem. doctor's adv. com. Shaare Zedak Hosp., Jerusalem, 1974—; mem. profl. adv. bd. Assn. for Children with Learning Disabilities, La Leche Soc., Latin Am. Parents Assn. Mem. sch. bd. Temple Beth Am, Merrick, 1972—, mem. exec. com., 1973-74, chmn. com. on Israel and World Affairs, 1976-78; mem. sch. com., 1976-78, mem. ritual com., 1976—, mem. temple bd., 1976-77; mem. legis. adv. com. 8th Senatorial Dist. N.Y., 1975—; mem. profl. adv. bd. So. Shore div. YM/YWHA. Served with U.S. Army, 1963-65. Recipient Physicians Recognition award AMA, 1966-69, 69-72, 72-75, 75-78, testimonial dinner and plaque Assn. Children with Down's Syndrome, 1972; diplomate Am. Bd. Pediatrics. Fellow Am. Acad. Pediatrics (chmn. com. TV effects on children 1976—), Internat. Coll. Pediatrics; mem. N.Y. State, Nassau County (N.Y.) med. socs., AMA, Nassau Pediatric Soc. (exec. bd. 1972—, chmn. com. on mental health 1972—), Alpha Epsilon Pi (chancellor Phi Theta chpt. 1955-56), Phi Delta Epsilon (consul Zeta chpt. 1960). Club: B'nai B'rith. Contbr. articles to profl. publs.; research on hetacillin, 1966, pyridoxine effect on serotonin level and performance in children with Down's syndrome, 1970-75, Alice in Wonderland syndrome as presenting symptom of infectious mononucleosis, 1976-77, on transmission of group A Beta hemolytic strep infection from pet reservoirs to children, 1963-78. Office: 3137 Hewlett Ave Merrick NY 11566

COPPOC, WILLIAM JOSEPH, chemist; b. Cumberland, Iowa, July 14, 1913; s. James Sunderland and Winifred (Fowler) C.; B.S., Ottawa U., 1935, D.Sc. (hon.), 1955; M.A., Rice Inst., 1937, Ph.D. in Phys. and Colloid Chemistry, 1939; m. Eleanor Louise Lister, July 2, 1939; children—Teresa Anne DeNies, William Edmund. With Texaco Inc., 1939-78, successively chemist grease research, asst. to asst. chief chemist, Port Arthur, Tex., acting supr. grease research asst. dir. research, Beacon, N.Y., asso. dir. research, N.Y.C., 1939-53, dir. research, N.Y.C., 1953-54, mgr. research, N.Y.C. and Beacon, 1954-57, mgr. research and devel., Beacon, 1957-60, mgr. sci. planning and info., 1960-65, gen. mgr. research and tech. dept., 1965-68, v.p. research and tech. dept., 1968-71, v.p. environ. protection dept., 1971-78; mem. environ. studies bd. NRC. Fellow Am. Inst. Chemists; mem. Am. Chem. Soc., Soc. Automotive Engrs., Am. Petroleum Inst., AAAS, Sci. Research Soc. Am. (chmn. 1960-63), N.Y. Acad. Scis., Dirs. Indsl. Research (chmn. 1971-72), Gordon Research Confs. (chmn. bd. trustees 1970), Soc. Chem. Industry (hon. treas. Am. sect. 1972-76), Sigma Xi, Phi Lambda Upsilon. Home: 14 Kingwood Park Poughkeepsie NY 12601 Office: PO Box 509 Beacon NY 12508

COPPOLA, DOMINICK ANTHONY, librarian; b. N.Y.C., Feb. 23, 1914; s. John and Catherine (Affronti) C.; A.B., Bklyn. Coll., 1935; M.S., Columbia, 1955; m. Esmeralda Cravanzola, Jan. 9, 1949; children—Rita (Mrs. Anthony Santucci), Catherine (Mrs. William Ward), Laura Linda. Head dept. Romance langs. Stechert-Hafner, Inc., N.Y.C., 1935-58, asst. v.p., 1958-64, exec. v.p., 1964-66, pres., 1966-71; chief librarian, asso. prof. Coll. S.I., Library, S.I., 1971—. Co-founder, Latin Am. Coop. Acquisitions Program, 1960; mem. Seminar on Acquisition Latin Am. Library Materials, 1955—, mem. exec. bd., 1969-70. Mem. ALA. Contbr. articles to library jours. Home: 1 Thicket Dr Cold Spring Harbor NY 11724 Office: Coll SI Library 130 Stuyvesant Pl Staten Island NY 10301

COPULSKY, WILLIAM, chem. co. exec.; b. Zhitomir, Russia, Apr. 4, 1922; s. Boris and Betty (Bruman) C.; brought to U.S., 1924, naturalized, 1929; B.A., N.Y.U., 1942, Ph.D., 1957; m. Ruth Brody, Dec. 26, 1948; children—Stephen, Jonathan, Lewis. Asst. to pres. R.S. Aries & Assos., N.Y.C., 1946-51; v.p. W.R. Grace & Co., 1951—; adj. asso. prof. Baruch Coll., 1967—. Served with AUS, 1942-46. Mem. Am. Chem. Soc. Am. Statis. Assn., Chemists Club. Club: New York University (N.Y.C.). Author: Molasses and Its Products, 1949; Marketing Chemical Products, 1950; Forecasting Demand for Chemical Commodities, 1962; Practical Sales Forecasting, 1971; Enterprise and the Corporation, 1974. Home: 23-35 Bell Blvd Bayside NY 11360 Office: 1114 Ave of Americas New York City NY 10036

CORATOLA, JOSEPH JOHN, dentist; b. Bristol, Conn., Jan. 5, 1931; s. Joseph Anthony and Rose Marie (Piccola) C.; B.A., U. Conn., 1952; D.D.S., Georgetown U., 1956; m. Nell Frommelt, Aug. 4, 1956 (dec. Sept. 1960); 1 dau., Rosemarie; m. 2d, Carmine V. Colapinto, Apr. 4, 1964; children—Joseph John, John. Practice dentistry, Bristol, 1957—; mem. staff Bristol Hosp., chief dental staff, 1967—. Active Bristol Assn. Retarded Children. Served with USNR, 1956-57. Recipient Creativity in Dentistry award Johnson & Johnson, 1970. Mem. Acad. Gen. Dentistry, Inst. Advanced Dental Research, Am. Dental Assn., Bristol Dental Soc. (pres. 1970, treas. 1977, sec. 1978), Am. Acad. Implant Dentistry, Implant Study Group Conn., New Eng. Soc. Oral Implantology, Conn. Dental Assn. (quality of care com. 1975-78, ho. of dels.), Omicron Kappa Upsilon. Lion. Home: Plymouth Rd Harwinton CT 06790 Office: 789 Farmington Ave Bristol CT 06010

CORAZZINI, ROBERT FRANK, lawyer; b. Greenport, N.Y., Nov. 22, 1936; s. Henry Anthony and Mildred Mae (Berry) C.; B.S. cum laude, Mt. St. Mary's Coll., 1958; J.D., Georgetown U., 1961; m. Elizabeth Marie Schwilk, Aug. 24, 1963; 1 dau., Lisa Marie. Admitted to D.C. bar, 1962; asso. atty. Smith & Pepper, 1962-63, 65-69, partner, 1969—. Served to capt., USAF, 1963-65. Mem. Am., Fed. Communications, D.C. bar assns. Republican. Roman Catholic. Home: 9513 Falls Rd Potomac MD 20854 Office: 1776 K St NW Washington DC 20006

CORBATO, FERNANDO JOSE, educator; b. Oakland, Calif., July 1, 1926; s. Hermenegildo and Charlotte (Jensen) C.; student U. Calif. at Los Angeles, 1943-44; B.S., Calif. Inst. Tech., 1950; Ph.D., Mass. Inst. Tech., 1956; m. Isabel Blandford, Nov. 24, 1962 (dec. July 7, 1973); children—Carolyn Suzanne, Nancy Patricia; m. 2d, Emily Susan Gish, Dec. 6, 1975; stepchildren—David Lawrence Gish, Jason Charles Gish. With Computation Center, Mass. Inst. Tech., Cambridge, 1955-66, dep. dir., 1963-66, head computer systems research group project MAC, 1963-72, co-head div., 1972-73, co-head automatic programming div., 1972-73, faculty mem., 1962—, prof. elec. engring. and computer sci., 1965—, asso. dept. head for computer sci. and engring., 1974—. Mem. computer sci. and engring. bd. Nat. Acad. Sci., 1971-72. Served with USNR, 1944-46. Fellow IEEE (W.W. McDowell award 1966), Nat. Acad. Engring., Acad. Arts and Scis.; mem. Assn. Computing Machinery (council 1964-66), Am. Phys. Soc., AAAS, Sierra Club, Sigma Xi. Co-author: The Compatible Time Sharing System, 1963; Advanced Computer Programming, 1963. Home: 88 Temple Street W Newton MA 02165 Office: 545 Technology Sq Cambridge MA 02139

CORBETT, RICHARD LEWIS, computer systems adminstr.; b. Stoughton, Mass., Oct. 9, 1937; s. George P. and Mary R. (Callan) C.; student Northeastern U., Boston, 1960-61, N.Y. Tech. Inst., 1961, Benjamin Franklin U., Washington, 1964-66, Frederick (Md.) Community Coll., 1972-73; m. Sheila Mary Ruby, Oct. 6, 1962; children—Richard Lewis, Lynne Anne, Laura Anne, Ross Peter. Instr. data processing Programming and Systems Inst., Washington, 1962-63; computer programmer Litton Systems, Inc., College Park, Md., 1963-64, Giant Foods, Inc., Landover, Md., 1964-65; analyst programmer Punch Care Processing Co., Takoma Park, Md., 1965-67; supervisory computer specialist Walter Reed Army Inst. Research, Washington, 1967-73, dep. dir. div. biometrics, 1973—, mgr. automatic data processing civilian career program, 1969-77. Served with USMC, 1957-60. Named an Outstanding Young Man Am.; recipient Outstanding Performance award Walter Reed Army Inst. Research, 1974, 75, 78. Mem. Aircraft Owners and Pilots Assn., Forum Control Data Users Group (pres. 1977-79; chmn. spl. interest group biomed. applications 1970-74), Walter Reed Army Med. Center Mixed Duckpin Bowling League (pres. 1978-79). Club: Walter Reed Officers. Address: Route 4 Box 382 Woodville Rd Mount Airy MD 21771

CORBIN, HERBERT LEONARD, pub. relations exec.; b. Bklyn., Mar. 30, 1940; s. H. Dan and Lillian Corbin; B.A., Rutgers U., 1961; m. Carol Heller, June 2, 1963; children—I. Jeffrey, Leslie Faith. Staff corr. Newark News, 1961-63; asst. dir. pub. relations dept. News Service of Rutgers U., New Brunswick, N.J., 1963-65; account exec. A.A. Schechter Assos., N.Y.C., 1965-66, Barkas & Shalit Inc., N.Y.C., 1965-66; sr. account exec. Daniel J. Edelman, Inc., N.Y.C., 1967-69; pres., founder Kanan, Corbin, Schupak & Aronow, Inc., N.Y.C., 1969—. Served with N.G., 1961-67. Mem. Pub. Relations Soc. Am., Pub. Relations Soc. N.Y., Sigma Delta Chi. Clubs: Williams, Hudson Hills Country. Home: 31 Hathaway Ln White Plains NY 10605 Office: 99 Park Ave New York City NY 10016

CORBIN, ROBERT GLENN, engring. co. exec.; b. Huntingdon, Pa., Aug. 23, 1912; s. James Wesley and Bertha Lillian (Showalter) C.; student pub. schs., Huntingdon; home study courses in elec. and electronic engring.; m. Josephine Filson, Mar. 25, 1938. With John R. Wald Co., Huntingdon, 1931—, v.p., dir., 1948—, treas., 1964—. Mem. Am. Correctional Assn., Correctional Industries Assn., Am. Def. Preparedness Assn., Am. Radio Relay League, Quarter Century Wireless Assn. Republican. Methodist. Clubs: Kiwanis Internat.

(Legion of Honor), Elks. Holder patent on reciprocating press and work feed mechanism, conveyorized roller coating machine. Home: 1510 Mifflin St Huntingdon PA 16652 Office: Industrial Park PO Box 392 Huntingdon PA 16652

CORBLEY, JOHN JAMES, ins. exec.; b. N.Y.C., Nov. 20, 1926; s. John Patrick and Rose Josephine (Gagan) C.; A.B., Iona Coll., 1950; J.D., N.Y. Law Sch., 1962; m. Renee M. Buck, Aug. 22, 1953 (dec.); m. 2d, June Audrey Ferris, July 24, 1971; children—John Roger, James Brian, Jeanne Marie. Admitted to N.Y. State bar, 1963, Md. bar, 1974; claim supr. Kemper Ins., N.Y.C., 1950-62; sec., mgr. Motor Vehicle Accident Indemnification Corp., N.Y.C., 1963-72; exec. dir. Md. Automobile Ins. Fund, Annapolis, 1973-76, chmn. bd. trustees, 1976—; guest lectr. bar assns. Served with USN, 1944-46; Recipient Outstanding Achievement award in govt. Iona Coll., 1973. Mem. Def. Research Inst., Am., N.Y. State, Md. State, Anne Arundel County, Bronx County (3d v.p.) bar assns., N.Y. Claim Assn. (2d v.p.), Am. Arbitration Assn., N.Y. Law Sch. Alumni Assn. Home: 475 Fair Oak Dr Severna Park MD 21146 Office: 1750 Forest Dr Annapolis MD 21401

CORCORAN, EDWARD DALTON, electric co. exec.; b. Springfield, Ohio, Apr. 20, 1924; s. William Joseph and Gertrude Johanna (Arnold) C.; student Mt. San Antonio Coll., 1958-59; m. Irma K. Dottavio, Oct. 17, 1953; 1 dau., Teresa Ann. Expediter-buyer Gen. Electric Co., Pittsfield, Mass., 1948-54; buyer Gen. Dynamics, Pomona, Calif., 1954-62; gen. sales mgr. Kings Electronics, Tuckahoe, N.Y., 1962-78, v.p. sales, 1978—. Chmn. exhibits com. Electro 79. Served with AUS, 1942-45. Elk, K.C. Home: 463 Bonnie Ct Yorktown Heights NY 10598 Office: 40 Marbledale Rd Tuckahoe NY 10707

CORCORAN, ELIZABETH ANNE, nurse, adminstr.; b. Balt., June 21, 1930; d. J. Neil and Bess (Daily) C.; R.N. diploma Mercy Hosp. Sch. Nursing, Balt., 1951; B.S. Nursing, Loyola Coll.-Mt. St. Agnes Coll., Balt., 1953. Entered Religious Sisters of Mercy, Roman Catholic Ch., 1953; with Mercy Hosp., 1953-58, 65—, asst. dir. recruitment, nursing service, 1965-70, asso. dir. dept. nursing, 1970-76, dir. dept. nursing, 1976—; instr. St. Joseph's Infirmary Sch. Nursing, Atlanta, 1958-65; faculty asst.-adminstr. U. Md. Sch. Nursing; mem. bd. Mercy Hosp. Aux. Mem. Am., Md. (pres. elect 1978—) socs. nursing service adminstrs., Am., Md. (mem. bd. dist. 2) nurses assns., Nat. League for Nursing, Mercy Hosp. Sch. Nursing Alumnae Assn. (moderator). Democrat. Home and Office: 301 Saint Paul Pl Baltimore MD 21202

CORCORAN, JOSEPH EDWARD, real estate exec.; b. Boston, Mar. 14, 1936; s. John Joseph and Mary (Merrigan) C.; B.S., Boston Coll., 1959; m. Rosemarie Gildea, Oct. 24, 1959; children—Joseph Jude, Suzanne, Michael, Patricia, Kathryn, Sean, Patrick. Sales dir. John M. Corcoran & Co., real estate, Boston, 1960-65; partner John M. and P. Leo Corcoran Co., 1968-71; pres. Corcoran, Mullins, Jennison, Inc., Quincy, Mass., 1971—; chmn. Mass. Bd. Registration of Real Estate Brokers and Salesmen, 1971-75. Mem. Boston Ward 16 Democratic Com., 1972-74. Served with AUS, 1954-56. Mem. Nat. Assn. Realtors, Greater Boston Real Estate Bd., Nat. Homebuilders Assn., Boston and S. Shore C. of C., Boston Citizens Housing and Planning Assn. (treas., dir.). Roman Catholic. Clubs: Wollaston Country; Blue Hill Tennis. Home: 51 Highland Ln Milton MA 02186 Office: 1776 Heritage Dr Quincy MA 02171

CORDA, ANTHONY EDWARD, pen co. exec.; b. Hamden, Conn., June 13, 1936; s. John G. and Rose (Santoro) C.; student New Haven State Tchrs. Coll., 1954-55, Stone Bus. Coll., 1956; m. Jean Collins, Apr. 15, 1961; children—John Collins, Christine Lynn. Salesman, Narragansett Brewing Co., Cranston, R.I., 1956-63; with sales dept. Bic Pen Corp., Milford, Conn., 1964—, zone mgr., 1978—. Mem. Democratic Town Com. of Cheshire, 1969-73; coach Charles Heath Little League, 1973-76. Recipient Distinguished Salesmans award Sales and Marketing Execs. Internat., 1976. Mem. R.I. Traveling Men's Assn. Romath Catholic. Clubs: K.C., Elks (Hamden, Conn.). Home: 87 Country Club Rd Cheshire CT 06410 Office: Wiley St Milford CT 06460

CORDE, GEORGE E., ins. co. exec.; b. N.Y.C., Aug. 8, 1932; s. Raymond and Dorothy (Tucker) C.; A.A., Bklyn. Coll., 1957; m. Joan M. Proscia, Oct. 20, 1956; children—George, Richard, Daniel, Gary, Angela. Office mgr. Kaschel Kes & Spies, N.Y.C., 1956-63; unit mgr. Parker & Co. Internat., Inc. (merged with Frank B. Hall Co., 1971, name now Frank B. Halls & Co. Inc.), N.Y.C., 1963-65, 2d v.p.-new bus. devel. devel., 1965-68, v.p.-mgr. N.Y.C. office, 1968-71, corporate v.p.-nat. services div., Briarcliff Manor, N.Y., 1971-76, corporate sr. v.p. Hall services and internat. ops., 1976—; chmn. bd. Frank B. Hall Mgmt. Co., TRIM, Inc., dir. Parker & Co. Interocean Ltd., Union Internat., Union Indemnity Ins. Cos. Served with AUS, 1951-53. Mem. Am. Mgmt. Assn. Clubs: K.C., Union League. Home: 117 Ampel Ave North Bellmore NY 11710 Office: 549 Pleasantville Rd Briarcliff Manor NY 10510

CORDELL, JOSEPH EDWARD, electric co. exec.; b. N.Y.C., June 10, 1914; s. John Joseph and Mary Theresa (Purcell) C.; B.S., St. Johns U., 1935; M.A., Niagara U., 1936; postgrad. N.Y. U., 1947-48; m. Catharine Imelda Scully, Mar. 28, 1942; children—Lynn, Robert, Joan, Douglas. Vice pres. marketing So. States, Inc., Hampton, Ga., 1953-67; chmn. bd., chief exec. Memco, Inc., Atlanta, 1967—; chmn., chief exec. officer, treas. A&A Foundries, Inc., Linden Hurst, N.Y., 1969—, Memco Mfg., Inc., Commack, N.Y., 1967—. Chmn. Spalding County Republican Com., 1962-66. Served with USNR, 1940-46, 1951-53. Fellow A.I.M.; mem. Huntington C. of C., IEEE (sr.), Am. Soc. Mil. Engrs., Lambda Chi Alpha. Roman Catholic. Clubs: Northport (N.Y.) Yacht; Marco Polo (N.Y.C.). Home: 1 Ardendale Rd East Northport NY 11731 Office: Memco Mfg Inc Larkfield Rd Commack LI NY 11725

CORDERO, JULIO, physicist; b. San Jose, Costa Rica, Jan. 10, 1923; s. Julio R. and Maria C. (Fonseca) C.; came to U.S., 1944, naturalized, 1951; B.S. in Meteorology, Inter-Am. Meteorol. Inst., 1943; B.S. in Aero. Engring., Wayne State U., Detroit, 1948; M.S. in Aerodynamics, U. Minn., 1951; m. Claire Cox, Oct. 26, 1963; 1 dau., Astrid Cox. Meteorologist, Pan Am. World Airways, 1944; scientist, U. Minn., 1951-53; sr. scientist FluiDyne Engring. Corp., Mpls., 1953-61; sr. scientist ballistic missiles advanced research and devel. div. AVCO, Wilmington, Mass., 1961-68; sr. systems analyst strategic weapons Analytic Services, Inc., Falls Church, Va., 1969-75; mem. research staff magnetohydrodynamics Mass. Inst. Tech., 1975-76, chief engr. magnetohydrodynamics research facilities, 1976—; owner J. Cordero & Co. Ltd., 1966—; cons. in field. Mem. Am. Astronautical Soc. (sec. 1969-70), Sci. Research Soc., Am. Oceanic Orgn., Am. Meteorol. Soc., Am. Phys. Soc., Am. Inst. Aeros. and Astronautics, AAAS, Internat. Soc. Tech. Assessment, Sigma Xi, Theta Tau. Clubs: Nat. Space (Washington); Mass. Inst. Tech. Faculty. Contbr. articles to profl. jours. Home: 5 Hemlock St Danvers MA 01923 Office: Energy Lab Mass Inst Tech 77 Massachusetts Ave Cambridge MA 02139

CORDREY, RICHARD STEPHEN, state senator Del.; b. Millsboro, Del., Sept. 8, 1933; s. John A. and Rachel S. (Smith) C.; A.B.A., Goldey Bacom Sch.; m. Mary Jane Bowen, Dec. 5, 1953, children—Richard J., Stephen B. Partner, John A. Cordrey & Co., poultry and farming; mem. Del. Ho. of Reps. from 41st Dist., 1971-73, Del. Senate from 20th Dist., 1972—. Trustee Del. Valley Eye Bank. Served with AUS, 1954-56. Democrat. Club: Lions (dist. gov. 1969-70). Home: River Dr Millsboro DE 19966

CORDWELL, MIRIAM, hair stylist, author; b. Bklyn., Jan. 6, 1908; d. Thomas J. and Sarah Ellen (Lynch) Bradley; grad. Baur's Beaty Acad., 1933; m. Richard Cordwell, Apr. 17, 1926; children—Miriam Ann (Mrs. Richard Kurisko), Dorothy Lorraine (Mrs. Robert Yarsinsky). Owner, operator beauty shop, 1934—; mem. faculty Inst. Cosmetology, U. Md., summers, 1950-59; tchr. cosmetology inst. Ohio State U., summers 1960-62, State U. N.Y., Alfred Tech., summers 1962-64; tchr. U. Ark., Fayetteville, 1964; tchr. hair design, fashion, coordinator speech and platform devel. Sec. Hairdressers Bd. Trade, N.Y., 1940-48, chmn. styles com., 1949-50; adv. bd. cosmetology Ednl. Commn. Vocat. and Extension Edn., N.Y.C.; bd. dirs. Essex County Mental Hygiene Assn. Named Woman of Distinction, Soroptimist Fedn. Ams. North Atlantic region, 1962, Woman of Yr., Bus. and Profl. Women's Club, 1965. Mem. Nat. Hairdressers and Cosmetologists Assn. Charles award; past styles dir., past chmn. ofcl. hair fashion com. mem. Hall of Renown 1975), Catholic Big Sisters, New City Fireman's Aux., Bus. and Profl. Women's Club. Club: Soroptimist, Author: (with Marion Rudoy) Hair Design and Fashion, 1956, 6th rev. edit., 1977; The Complete Book of Hair Styles, Beauty and Fashion, 1971; The Complete Book of Men's Hairstyles and Hair Care, 1974. Home: Box 31 Wilmington NY 12997 Office: 254 N Main St New City NY 10956

COREY, SAMUEL CALDWELL, ins. co. exec.; b. Ft. Washington, Pa., Nov. 8, 1917; s. William Butcher and Emma (Richardson) C.; B.S., U. Ga., 1940; postgrad. U. Pa., 1946-48, Rutgers U., 1955-57; m. Elizabeth H. Gnann, Oct. 18, 1941; children—Samuel C., Teena, James William. Asst. forester Ala. Power Co., Birmingham, 1940-42; forester Wood Lumber Co., 1942-45; with Provident Indemnity Life Ins. Co., Norristown, Pa. 1946—, successively agt., div. mgr., v.p., 1946-50, sec. 1950-61, exec. v.p., 1961-64, sec.-treas., 1964—, now chmn. bd., pres.; regional dir. Am. Trust & Trust Co. Chmn. Upper Dublin Zoning Bd. of Adjustment, 1955-64; mem. Upper Dublin Twp. Commn., 1964-73, pres., 1969-70; dist. chmn. Boy Scouts Am., 1959-64, past pres., mem. exec. bd. Valley Forge council, 1964—; treas. Montgomery City Hosp. Authority, 1968—. Del., Pa. Constl. Conv., 1967-68. Served with AUS, 1945-46. Mem. Nat. Assn. Life Underwriters, Internat. Assn. Health Underwriters, Health Ins. Assn. Am. (dir.), Life Insurors Conf. (exec. com.), Ins. Fedn. Pa. (dir.), Am. Legion, Pa. Soc., Highlands Hist. Soc. (dir.), Union League, U.S. Power Squadron, U.S. Coast Guard Aux., Pi Kappa Alpha, Xi Sigma Pi. Lutheran. Mason (32 deg, Shriner, K.T.), Kiwanian. Clubs: Manufactures Country (Oreland, Pa.); Corinthian Yacht, Union League (Phila.); Dunwoody-Big Bear; N.Y. Yacht; Plymouth Country; Kiwanis (past pres. Upper Dublin). Home: 900 Spring Ave Fort Washington PA 19034 Office: 2500 DeKalb Pike Norristown PA 19406

CORI, CARL FERDINAND, educator, biochemist; b. Prague, Czechoslovakia, Dec. 5, 1896; s. Carl I. and Maria (Lippich) C.; student Gymnasium, Trieste, Austria, 1906-14; M.D., German U. Prague, 1920; Sc.D., Yale, Western Res. U., 1947, Boston U., 1948, Cambridge (Eng.) U., 1949, U. Granada (Spain), 1966, Brandeis U., 1965; hon. degrees Monash U., Melbourne, Australia, 1966, Washington U., St. Louis, 1967, St. Louis U., 1967, Gustavus Adolphus Coll., 1963; m. Gerty Theresa Radnitz, Aug. 5, 1920 (dec. 1957); 1 son, Carl Thomas; m. 2d, Anne FitzGerald Jones, Mar. 23, 1960. Came to U.S., 1922; naturalized, 1928. Asst. in pharmacology U. Graz (Austria), 1920-21; biochemist State Inst. for Study Malignant Disease, Buffalo, 1922-31; prof. pharmacology and biochemistry Washington U. Sch. Medicine, 1931-66; cons. biochemistry, vis. lectr. Mass. Gen. Hosp., Boston, 1966—. Recipient Nobel Prize in medicine and physiology, 1948; Willard Gibbs medal Am. Chem. Soc., 1948; Sugar Research Found. award, 1947, 50; Lasker award, 1946; Squibb Award, 1947; St. Louis award. Mem. Nat. Acad. Scis.; hon. mem. Harvey Soc.; mem. Am. Soc. Biol. Chemists, Am. Chem. Soc. (Mid-West award 1946), AAAS, Royal Soc. London, Am. Philos. Soc., Sigma Xi. Contbr. articles, chiefly on carbohydrate metabolism and enzymes of animal tissues to Am. sci. jours. Mem. editorial bd. Jour. Biol. Chemistry, Biochimica et Biophysica Acta. Home: 1010 Memorial Dr Cambridge MA 02138

CORIATY, GEORGE MICHAEL, clergyman, cultural center exec.; b. Sao Paulo, Brazil, Jan. 1, 1931; s. Michael A. and Marie (Nassif) C.; came to Can., 1960, naturalized, 1967; B.A., St. Savior's Sem., Saida, Lebanon, 1950; Ph.D. in Sociology, Pacific So. U., 1976; Ps.D., Uniformed Services U. Am., Washington, 1977. Ordained priest Roman Catholic Ch., 1956; prof. St. Savior's Sem., Lebanon, 1952-56; asst. pastor Our Lady Annunciation Ch., Boston, 1957-60; pastor St. Savior's Ch., Montreal, Que., Can., 1960—; apostolic visitor, patriarchal vicar for Melkites in Can., 1972—; vice-regional superior Basilian Order Can.; founder Our Lady Assumption Parish, Toronto, Ont., Can., Our Lady of Lebanon Parish, Quebec City, Que., St. George's Parish, Vancouver, B.C., Can., 1976; founder Middle-East Immigrant Aid Soc. Can., 1963; mem. multiculturalism Council Can., Que. Region; founder, pres. Centre Multicultural Bois de Boulogne, 1973—; mem. Immigration Council Ministry Immigration Que., 1978; mem. ecumenical movement. Decorated Star Coptic Patriarchate of Alexandria (Egypt); named First Citizen of Montreal, 1973. Mem. House of Trade of Montreal, Canadian and Am. Hist. and Geog. Assn. Founder, pub., editor Trait D'Union Rev., 1964; founder Byzantine Mus., 1975. Office: 329 Viger St Montreal PQ H2X 1R6 Canada

CORISH, JOSEPH RYAN, artist, lawyer; b. Somerville, Mass., Apr. 9, 1909; s. John W. and Sarah (Ryan) C.; J.D., Boston U., 1932; Adj. in Arts, Harvard, 1938; m. Cecelia F. Moore, Nov. 6, 1935; 1 dau., Nancy M. (Mrs. William H. Vincent). Admitted to Mass. bar, 1932; practiced in Mass., 1932—; art dir. Castle Hill Found., 1958-62; artist-in-residence U.S. Navy 1st Naval Dist.; exhibited one-man shows at Harvard, Yale, Boston U., other univs., U.S. Naval Acad. Mus., Columbus (Ohio) Mus. Art, Birmingham (Ala.) Mus. Art, Jasper Rand Mus. Barcelona (Spain) Mus., Deutsches Mus., Bergen (Norway) Mus.; exhibited in group shows at The Salon, Paris, Boston Mus. Fine Arts, Busch Reisinger Mus., Olympic Exhbn., Kiel, Germany, Conn. Coll., Royal Soc. Marine Artists, London, Jordan Exhbn. Contemporary New Eng. Artists, Bertrand Russell Centennial, London; represented in permanent collections museums U.S. and abroad, fgn. embassies, state capitols, U.S. Naval Acad., U.S. Naval War Coll., Boston U. Lectr. painting Harvard, Brooks, Regis, Conn. colls., art assns., 1958—; lectr. law bar assns., others, 1932—. Asst. city colicitor Somerville, 1935; counsel Somerville Housing Authority, 1954-58. Served to lt. (j.g.) USNR, World War II. Mem. Am. Trial Lawyers Assn. (dir.), Mass. Acad. Trial Lawyers (gov.), New Eng. Assn. Pub. Authority Counsel (pres. 1954), North Shore Arts Assn. (dir.). Contbr. articles to profl. jours. Home: 86 Lawson Rd Winchester MA 01890 Office: 421 Highland Ave Somerville MA 02144

CORLEY, NORA TERESA, librarian; b. Montreal, Que., Can.; d. John Kevin and Anna Sara (Magnusdottir) Corley; B.A. with honors in Geography, McGill U., Montreal, 1951, B.L.S., 1952, M.A. in Geography, 1961; m. John T. Murchison, 1972. Asst. librarian Law Library, McGill U., 1952-54; librarian-in-charge Arctic Inst. N.Am., Montreal, 1954-72, fellow, 1972—. Mem. Que. Library Assn. (English sec. 1958-59, editor Bull. 1963-64), Spl. Libraries Assn. (editor Montreal 1961-62, pres. Montreal chpt. 1964-65, chmn. geography and map div. 1969-70), Corp. Profl. Librarian of Province of Que., Canadian Trotting Assn., Canadian Assn. Geographers. Compiler, editor: Polar and Cold Regions Library Resources, a Directory, 1975. Editor The Arctic Circular, 1976—; compiler: Index to Bulletins 71-102, 1968-75, 1978. Contbr. articles, book revs. to geog. and library jours. Home: 185 Kamloops Ave Ottawa ON K1V 7E1 Canada

CORLISS, JOHN MICHAEL, chemist; b. Balt., Sept. 21, 1922; s. John Joseph and Adeline Anna (Witzke) C.; B.S., Loyola Coll., Balt., 1949; postgrad. Johns Hopkins U., 1955-65; m. Rosalie G. Patti, Aug. 14, 1948; children—Michael J., Patricia M., Rita G. Analytical chemist Edgewood Arsenal, Aberdeen Proving Ground, Md., 1949-53, microanalytical chemist, 1953-72, chief microanalytical lab., 1972-77; cons., 1977—. Served with USAAF, 1943-45; ETO. Fellow Chem. Soc. (London); mem. Am. Chem. Soc., AAAS, Am. Microchem. Soc., Soc. Analytical Chemistry, Assn. Ofcl. Analytical Chemists, Sigma Xi. Democrat. Roman Catholic. Home and Office: 1211 W Old Cold Spring Ln Baltimore MD 21209

CORMAN, JAMES C., mech. engr.; b. Rebersburg, Pa., Dec. 16, 1939; s. James George and Adah Elizabeth (Rossman) C.; B.S., Pa. State U., 1961; M.S., Carnegie Mellon U., 1963, Ph.D., 1966; m. Mary Maroney Corman, Dec. 4, 1966; children—Elizabeth Marie, Jennifer Mary. Thermal engr. Westinghouse Electric Co., Pitts., 1963-65, heat transfer engr. Gen. Electric Research and Devel. Center, Schenectady, 1966-74, mgr. energy conversion unit, 1974-75, mgr. power generation tech. br., 1975—. Served with USAF, 1961-62. Mem. ASME (chmn. advanced energy system tech. com.; George Westinghouse medal 1977), Am. Soc. Heating Refrigeration and Air Conditioning Engrs. Patentee in field. Contbr. articles to profl. jours. Home: 5 Herrick Dr Scotia NY 12302 Office: PO Box 8 Schenectady NY 12301

CORMANY, ROBERT BARMONT, sch. adminstr.; b. Chambersburg, Pa., Nov. 26, 1941; s. Robert Ever and Phoebeann Katherine (Barmont) C.; B.S., Shippensburg State Coll., 1963, M.Ed., 1965; Ed.D., Pa. State U., 1973; postgrad. U. Md., 1966, Boston U., 1967; m. Sharlene Rae McAllister, Sept. 24, 1961; children—Cory, Bobbette. Tchr. chemistry Chambersburg (Pa.) Area Sch. Dist., 1963-65; counselor Big Spring Sch. Dist., 1965-69; guidance specialist Pa. Dept. Edn., 1970-72; coordinator spl. services West Shore Sch. Dist., LeMoyne, Pa., 1972—. Mem. Sch. Bd. South Middleton Dist., 1973—; chmn. council Otterbein United Meth. Ch., 1973—. Gen. Electric fellow, 1967; NDEA fellow, 1966. Mem. Am. Personnel and Guidance Assn. (senator 1976—), Am. Sch. Counselors Assn. (del. 1973—), Assn. Counselor Edn. and Supervision (exec. com. 1976—), Pa. Sch. Counselors Assn. (pres. 1976-77), West Shore Adminstrs. Assn. (v.p. 1977-78). Republican. Methodist. Author: The Pennsylvania Guide for Curriculum Improvement Through Career Education, 1977. Editor The Pa. Counselor, 1977—. Home: RD 1 Boiling Springs PA 17007 Office: 1000 Hummel Ave LeMoyne PA 17043

CORMIER, ALBERT LOUIS, counselor; b. Putnam, Conn., July 24, 1943; s. Louis Victor and Eva Anna (Marion) C.; A.B., St. Francis Coll., 1967; M.A., Assumption Coll., 1973; postgrad. Worcester State Coll., 1978; m. Joyce Helen Jewell, Nov. 30, 1974. Admissions counselor St. Francis Coll., Biddeford, Maine, 1968-70; acad. dean, dir. athletics, tchr. Marianapolis Prep Sch., Thompson, Conn., 1970-77; head soccer coach Nichols Coll., Dudley, Mass., 1977; gen. mgr. Cormier C-P, Inc., Putnam, Conn., 1977—. Served with U.S. Army, 1967-69. Decorated Bronze Star medal. Mem. Am. Personnel and Guidance Assn., Nat. Vocat. Guidance Assn., Am. Sch. Counselor Assn., Am. Rehab. Counseling Assn., Assn. for Measurement and Evaluation in Guidance, Nat. Cath. Guidance Conf., Assn. for Humanistic Edn. and Devel. Clubs: Model A Ford, Model A Restorers, Vet. Motor Car. Home: Lake Pkwy RD 4 Webster MA 01570 Office: Route 44 RFD 1 Putnam CT 06260

CORNELIS, JOHAN MARCEL LOUISE, plastic surgeon; b. Gent, Belgium, Jan. 3, 1935; came to Can., 1964; M.D., U. Louvain, 1961. Resident in gen. surgery Med. Coll. Pa., Phila., 1960-64; resident in plastic surgery Royal Victoria Hosp., McGill U., Montreal, 1964-66; practice medicine specializing in plastic surgery, St. John, N.B., Can., 1966—; mem. staff St. John Gen. Hosp., St. Joseph's Hosp., St. John. Fellow Royal Coll. Physicians and Surgeons Can.; mem. Am. Soc. Plastic and Reconstructive Surgeons, Internat. Am. socs. aesthetic plastic surgery, Am. Burn Assn., Canadian Soc. Plastic Surgeons, Am. Assn. Hand Surgery, Canadian Soc. Surgery of Hand. Roman Catholic. Home: 70 Orange St Saint John NB E2L 1M3 Canada

CORNELL, ALBERT, physician; b. N.Y.C., Feb. 13, 1910; s. Isreal and Tillie Cohen; B.S. (Joseph Johnson scholar 1927, Edward Coles scholar 1929), Coll. William and Mary, 1930; M.D., N.Y. U., 1934; m. Phyllis Levine, June 22, 1941; children—Leslie Karen, Jan Ellen, Wendy Lynne. Analytical chemist Eastern Research Lab., E. I. Du Pont Co., Gibbstown, N.J., 1930; intern Montefiore Hosp., N.Y.C., 1934-35; intern in pathology Will Rogers Meml. Hosp., Saranac Lake, N.Y., 1936-37; resident Mt. Sinai Hosp., N.Y.C., 1937-38; practice medicine specializing in internal medicine and gastroenterology, N.Y.C., 1938—; mem. staff 5th Ave. Flower Hosp., Mt. Sinai Hosp.; cons. physician gastroenterology Mt. Sinai Med. Center, 1978—; mem. adj. faculty Columbia U., 1941-63; asso. clin. prof. medicine N.Y. Med. Coll., 1944—, Mt. Sinai Med. Center, N.Y.C., 1966—; mem. advisory com. Chemotherapy Found. Class agt. Coll. William and Mary, 1930—; mem. coms. health and hosp., environ. protection and safety Community Planning Bd. 8, Manhattan, N.Y.C., 1962—; mem. Jewish Theol. Sem. fund-raising com. Park Ave. Synagogue, N.Y.C. Served to maj. USPHS, 1943-46. Recipient John Garland Pollard Hist. prize Coll. William and Mary, 1928, Jacobi medal Mt. Sinai Hosp., 1966; Wyeth and Co. co-grantee, 1938-40; diplomate Am. Bd. Internal Medicine. Fellow Am. Coll. Gastroenterology; mem. Am., N.Y. gastro-enterol. assns., N.Y. County, N.Y. State med. socs., AMA, Am. Digestive Disease Found., Mt. Sinai Hosp. Alumni Assn. (exec. com. 1964—, pres. 1964-65), Phi Beta Kappa, Theta Chi Delta, Phi Kappa Phi, Phi Sigma, Chi Beta Phi. Club: Park Ave. Synagogue Men's. Asso. editor Jour. Mt. Sinai Hosp., 1943-52; mem. abstract editorial staff Am. Jour. Digestive Diseases, 1939-43; research in cancer, 1943-46, in gastroenterology, 1943-61; developer improvement for continuous drip therapy apparatus for treatment peptic ulcer, 1942; developer insulin test for vagal secretion of stomach, 1940. Home: 1175 Park Ave New York NY 10028 Office: 950 Park Ave New York NY 10028

CORNELL, JOHN WHITING, JR., civil engr.; b. Phila., Aug. 16, 1899; s. John Whiting and Ida (Dyer) C.; grad. Germantown Acad., 1917; B.S., C.E., U. Pa., 1922; LL.D., Beaver Coll., 1963; m. Frances Pancoast Doriss, June 7, 1927; children—John William, Ann Cornell

Swalm. Civil engr. J.S. Cornell & Son, Phila., 1922-26; v.p. partner J. S. Cornell & Son, Inc. 1926—, subsequently pres.; now retired. Trustee Beaver Coll.; trustee, elder Presbyterian Ch. Profl. engr. Pa. Mem. Franklin Inst., Phila. C. of C. (panel mem. forecasting conf. 1960), Pa. Soc. Profl. Engrs., Carpenters Co. City and Co. of Phila., Pa. Hort. Soc.. Clubs: Philadelphia Cricket, Union League (Phila.); Highland Park (Fla.); Skytop. Author: History of a Philadelphia Builder. Home: 122 Nottoway Dr Penllyn PA 19422 Office: 1528 Cherry St Philadelphia PA 19102

CORNELL, JOHN WILLIAM, builder; b. Phila., June 6, 1929; s. John W. and Frances (Doriss) C.; grad. Germantown Acad., 1946; B.S. in Civil Engring., U. Pa., 1950; m. Nancy Fleming, Sept. 8, 1956; 1 dau., Nina Frances Draftsman, Howard, Needles, Tamen & Bergendoff, Kansas City, Mo., 1950-51; engr., estimator J. S. Cornell & Son Inc., Phila., 1951-63, v.p., 1963-77, chmn. bd., 1977—; dir. Cathedral Village, Inc.; cons. Phila. area. Mem. Bldg. Advisory Bd., Pa. Dept. Labor and Industry, 1964—, mem. Carpenters Co. City and County Phila., 1959—, pres., 1971—; bd. dirs. Carson Valley Sch., Young Women's Boarding Home Assn. Served with AUS, 1954-56. Registered profl. engr., Pa. Mem. ASCE, Gen. Bldg. Contractors Assn. (dir. 1973-75), Franklin Inst. Republican. Episcopalian (vestryman). Club: Union League. Home: 1107 Chestnut Ln Flourtown PA 19031 Office: 1528 Cherry St Philadelphia PA 19102

CORNELY, KURT WILLY, devel. lab. exec.; b. Stuttgart, Germany, Dec. 24, 1921; s. Julius Herman and Gertrude (Ebert) C.; came to U.S., 1925, naturalized, 1944; B.A., Adelphi Coll., 1949; M.S., Pa. State Coll., 1951; m. Else Maria Knapp, Sept. 20, 1950; children—Norman William, Erich Kurt. Research chemist Nat. Starch and Chem. Co., N.Y.C., 1950-52, Nat. Dairy Research Labs. Oakdale, N.Y., 1952-55, Refined Sugars & Syrups Co. Yonkers, N.Y., 1955-58; chief chemist Am. Thermocatalytic Corp., Mineola, N.Y., 1959-62; sr. chemist, mgr. Catalyst Devel. Lab. Engelhard Industries, Newark, 1962—. Scoutmaster Watchung council Boy Scouts Am., 1962-67. Served with USN, 1942-46. Recipient certificate Center for Profl. Advancement Catalyst Evaluation and Selection. Fellow Am. Inst. Chemists; mem. Catalysis Soc. N.Y., Organic Reaction Catalysis Soc. Republican. Lutheran. Patentee in field. Home: 403 Beechwood Pl Westfield NJ 07090

CORNETTE, ROBERT JOSEPH, process and product devel. exec.; b. Green Bay, Wis., Aug. 27, 1938; s. Cyril Florian and Arletta Agnes (Van Oss) C.; B.S. in Bacteriology, U. Wis., 1961; postgrad. Hunter Coll., 1967; m. Mary Margaret Grobusky, June 29, 1968; children—Thomas Michael, Jacqueline Renee, James Edward. Chief bacteriologist Larsen Co., Green Bay, Wis., 1961-62; quality control supr., Pfizer Diagnostics Co., N.Y.C., 1964-69; dir. process, product devel. dept. Tech. Corp., Tarryton, N.Y., 1969—; voting del. Nat. Com. Clin. Lab. Standards. Served with U.S. Army, 1961-63. Mem. Nat. Registry Clin. Chemistry, Clin. Chem. Techs. Republican. Roman Catholic. Home: 113 Salem Rd Fishkill NY 12524 Office: 511 Benedict Ave Tarrytown NY 10591

CORNICK, DELROY LEON, educator; b. Springfield, Ill., Aug. 22, 1928; s. Leon H. and Leola (Gibbs) C.; B.A., Ripon Coll., 1952; M.A. in Pub. Adminstrn., Am. U., 1969; D.P.A. in Pub. Adminstrn., U. So. Calif., 1978. Asso. supt. for budget and exec. mgmt. D.C. Pub. Schs., Washington, 1968-72; nat. program dir. tng. program in goal-oriented social service system Sch. Social Services, Catholic U., Washington, 1972-73; asso. prof. econs. and bus. adminstrn. Morgan State U., Balt., 1973—. Advisor Pub. Affairs Intern Programs NASA-USC-Washington Pub. Affairs Center. Mem. fiscal adv. commn. Howard County (Md.) Council, 1976; cons. U.S. Civil Service Commn. Mgmt. Tng. Seminars; adviser budget practices fed., state and local govts. Served with USNR, 1946-48. Mem. Am. Soc. for Pub. Adminstrn., Am. Soc. Tng. and Devel., Municipal Finance Officers Assn. Contbr. articles to profl. jours. Home: 8929 Footed Ridge Columbia MD 21045 Office: Morgan State U McMechen 517 Baltimore MD 21239

CORNISH, EDWARD SEYMOUR, editor; b. N.Y.C., Aug. 31, 1927; s. George Anthony and Elizabeth Furniss (McLeod) C.; diplome d'etudes U. Paris (France), 1948; A.B., Harvard U., 1950; m. Sally Woodhull, Oct. 12, 1957; children—George Anthony, Jefferson Richard Woodhull, Blake McLeod. Copy boy, cub reporter Evening Star, Washington, 1950-51; staff corr. U.P. Assn., Richmond, Va., 1951-52, Raleigh, N.C., 1952-53, London, Eng., 1953-54, Paris, 1954-55, Rome, Italy, 1956; staff writer Nat. Geog. Soc., 1957-69; founder, pres., World Future Soc., Washington, 1966—, creator, editor The Futurist Jour., 1966—, editor World Future Soc. Bull., 1968—. Cons. to other govt., bus., ednl. orgns. Bd. dirs. World Watch Inst., 1974—. Advisory bd. Inst. for Alternative Futures. Mem. Soc. Internat. Devel., Internat. Sci. Writers Assn. Author: The Study of the Future, 1977. Editor: Resources Directory for America's Third Century, 1977; The Future: A Guide to Information Sources, 1977. Editorial cons. Nat. Goals Research Staff, 1970, White House report Toward Balanced Growth, 1970; mem. editorial bd. Assn. Vol. Action Scholars. Home: 5501 Lincoln St Bethesda MD 20034 Office: World Future Soc 4916 St Elmo Ave Washington DC 20014

CORNUTE, ROBERT LEROY, univ. adminstr.; b. Huntington, W.Va., June 14, 1932; s. Lacey Leon and Willie Mae (Hamiter) C.; student U. Md., 1959-61, U. Nev., Las Vegas, 1961-62; Asso. Applied Sci. in Police Sci., Hudson Valley Community Coll., 1968; student Russell Sage Coll., 1970-72; B.A. in Criminal Justice, Empire State Coll., 1973; M. Pub. Affairs, SUNY, Stony Brook, 1978; postgrad. in Pub. Adminstrn., Am. Internat. Open U., 1978; m. Carmen May Dunkley, Dec. 19, 1959; children—Robert Scott, Antoinette Renee. Enlisted in U.S. Air Force, 1950, advanced through grades to sgt., 1958, separated 1962; operating room technician St. Peters Hosp., Albany, N.Y., 1962-66; mem. Capital Police, State of N.Y., 1966-68; investigator N.Y. State Crime Victims Compensation Bd., 1968-70; tech. supr., police traffic services N.Y. State Bur. for Municipal Police, 1970-73; sr. staffing services rep. N.Y. State Dept. Civil Service, 1973-76; dir. pub. safety State U. N.Y., Stony Brook, 1976—; expert examiner N.Y. State Dept. Civil Service; exec. sec. N.Y. State Personnel Council, 1973-74. Committeeman troop 12 Boy Scouts Am., Albany, 1966-70, mem. tng. com. Saratoga County council, 1973-76, mem. exec. com. Suffolk County, 1978; cub master Pack 15, Saratoga, 1973-75. Mem. Am. Mgmt. Assn., Internat. Assn. Chiefs of Police, N.Y. State Assn. Chiefs of Police, Internat. Assn. Coll. and Univ. Security Dirs., Hudson/Mohawk Tng. and Devel. Soc., Am. Acad. for Profl. Law Enforcement, Nat. Orgn. Black Law Enforcement Execs., 369 Vets. Assn., Am. Legion. Republican. Methodist. Clubs: Masons (33 deg.), Shriners. Home: RD 3 Locust Grove Rd Saratoga Springs NY 12866 Office: Room 144 Adminstrn Bldg State U NY Stony Brook NY 11794

CORNWELL, WILLIAM SAMUEL, ret. radiographic tech. cons.; b. Penn Yan, N.Y., May 19, 1910; s. Henry Baldwin and Fanny (Hotchkin) C.; B.A., Colgate U., 1932; M.A. in Zoology, Duke, 1936; m. Isabel Claire Strickland, Dec. 22, 1933; children—Patricia Claire (Mrs. Werner Leopold Sassenhausen), Elizabeth Ann (Mrs. William Francis Brainerd). Asst. biology Duke, 1932-33; asst. human anatomy U. Rochester (N.Y.), 1933-34, asst. radiology, 1946-49, asso., 1949-59, clin. asso., 1959—; radiography markets div. Eastman Kodak Co., Rochester, N.Y., asst., 1937-41, acting editor, 1941-46, editor Med. Radiography and Photography, 1946-65, tech. asso., 1965-75; ret., 1975; Jerman Meml. lectr. Am. Assn. Radiologic Technologists, 1974. Recipient spl. award honor Am. Coll. Radiology, 1973. Fellow Rochester Mus. and Sci. Center, Rochester Acad. Sci., Co. Mil. Historians, N.Y. State Archeol. Assn.; mem. Radiol Soc. N.Am., Rochester Roentgen Ray Soc., Am. Assn. Phys. Anthrologists, Am. Coll. Radiology (quality control com. task force on pneumocomiosis 1970—), Rochester Civil War Round Table (past pres.), Rochester Hist. Soc. (past treas.), Sigma Xi. Contbr. articles to profl. jours. Research in field. Home: 27 Vick Park B Rochester NY 14607

CORONETZ, MELANIE ANN, pattern co. adminstr.; b. N.Y.C., Feb. 15, 1944; d. Walter D. and Kathryn B.; B.S., Boston Coll., 1966; postgrad. Sorbonne, 1966-67; M.A., Hunter Coll., 1973; M.B.A. (Mellon Found. scholar), Pace U., 1976. Tchr. French, Long Island, N.Y., 1968-72; internat. coordinator McCall Pattern Co., N.Y.C., 1976—. Mem. Women's Fashion Fabrics Assn., Am. Mktg. Assn. Home: 1200 5th Ave New York City NY 10029 Office: 230 Park Ave New York City NY 10017

CORR, ELEANOR NELSON, computer specialist; b. New Bedford, Mass., July 11, 1932; d. George M. and Elsie M. (Vincent) Nelson; A.A., Keystone Jr. Coll., La Plume, Pa., 1976; m. Robert L. Corr, June 24, 1965; children—Rodman, Deborah, Clayton, Susan. Various legal sec. positions, 1951-52; exec. sec. to dean of coll. Keystone Jr. Coll., 1967-71, asst. to computer center dir., 1971-72, dir. center, 1972—; instr. data processing, careers editor Creative Computing mag. Mem. Data Processing Mgmt. Assn. (chpt. pres. 1978-79). Republican. Author articles. Home: 218 Butternut Ln Clarks Summit PA 18411 Office: Keystone Jr Coll La Plume PA 18440

CORRADINO, GANDOLFO (DOLPH), psychologist; b. Passaic, N.J., Sept. 1, 1942; s. Joseph and Rose (Viviano) C.; B.A. (N.J. State scholar), Seton Hall U., 1964; M.A. (fellow), George Washington U., 1971, Ed.S., 1976, postgrad., 1977—; m. Frances A. LaCorte, Aug. 22, 1964; 1 dau., Leah Joy. Asst. buyer Brooks Bros., N.Y.C., 1964-66; instr. psychology/resident dir. George Washington U., Washington, 1970-72; resident counselor N.Y. U., N.Y.C., 1972-73; counselor No. Va. Community Coll., Annandale, 1974; counseling psychologist D.C. Dept. Corrections, Lorton, Va., 1974; personnel mgmt. specialist Naval Sea Systems Command, Washington, 1974-76, Hdqrs. Naval Material Command, Washington, 1976-78; employee devel. specialist U.S. Dept. Agr., Washington, 1978—. Vol. counselor Hopkins House, Alexandria, Va., 1973-74; vol. host Internat. House, Washington, 1974—; chmn. communications com. Lake Braddock Community Assn., Burke, Va., 1973-75, editor community paper, 1973-75. Served with USAF, 1966-69. Mem. Am. Personnel and Guidance Assn., Nat. Vocat. Guidance Assn., Internat. Personnel Mgmt. Assn., Classification and Compensation Soc. Home: 5512 Kendrick Ln Burke VA 22015 Office: USDA Office of Personnel Career Devel Div 14th and Independence Ave SW Washington DC 20250

CORRADO, FRED, food co. exec.; b. Mt. Vernon, N.Y., May 20, 1940; s. Anthony E. and Rose V. (Capone) C.; B.B.A., Manhattan Coll., 1961; m. Josephine Ann Gonda, July 4, 1962; children—David, Paul, Christopher. Sr. auditor Arthur Andersen & Co., N.Y.C., 1961-65; accounting mgr. Romney Cosmetics, Stamford, Conn., 1965-68; sr. budget analyst ITT, N.Y.C., 1968-69; v.p. fin. specialty div. Kenton Corp., N.Y.C., 1969-73; asst. corporate controller Standard Brands Inc., N.Y.C., 1973-74; dir. fin. planning, controller, v.p., controller Standard Brands Foods, 1974-76, v.p. fin. and planning U.S. consumer products group, 1976-78, v.p.-corporate mgmt. info. systems, 1977—, v.p. corporate planning and systems parent co., 1978—. C.P.A., N.Y. Mem. Am. Inst. C.P.A.'s, N.Y. Soc. C.P.A.'s. Home: 9 Coventry Ct Croton on Hudson NY 10520 Office: 625 Madison Ave New York City NY 10022

CORREA, ALONSO V., physician; b. Copacabana, Colombia, Feb. 12, 1939; s. Bernardo and Bertha (Velez) C.; came to U.S., 1964, naturalized, 1968; M.D., Javeriana U. (S.Am.), 1963; m. Patricia Vullo, Nov. 20, 1965; children—Sonya, Yvonne. Intern, Maimonides Hosp., Bklyn., 1964-65, resident in gen. surgery, 1965; resident Flower and Fifth Ave. Hosp., N.Y.C., 1967-68; resident in neurology VA Hosp., Bronx, 1968-69; resident in neurosurgery Mt. Sinai Hosp., N.Y.C., 1969-74; practice neuro surgery, S.I., N.Y., 1975—; dir. neurosurgery USPHS, S.I., 1975—; cons. neurosurgeon Bronx VA Hosp., 1976—; clin. asst. neurosurgeon Mt. Sinai Sch. Medicine, N.Y.C., 1974—; attending neurosurgeon Beth Israel Med. Center, N.Y.C., Queens Hosp. Center, Jamaica, N.Y., Bklyn. Jewish Hosp.; commd. USPHS, 1975, advanced through grades to capt., 1978—. Served with U.S. Army, 1965-67. Diplomate Am. Bd. Neurol. Surgery. Home: 63 Essex Ave Montclair NJ 07042 Office: USPHS Hosp Staten Island NY 10304

CORREDERA, ROBERT SOCRATES, steel products co. exec.; b. Madrid, Spain, Apr. 19, 1922; s. Manuel Fernandez and Patrocinio C.; came to U.S., 1949, naturalized, 1960; student schs. in various countries completing equivilant of M.S. in Engring.; student officers sch. U.S. Navy, Newport, R.I., 1949-50; m. Betty Marie Krett, Feb. 22, 1952; 1 son, Barton Krett. Dir. foreign sales McCabe Powers Body Co., St. Louis, 1957-62; managing dir. Willys de Venezula, Kaiser Jeep Corp., Oakland, Calif., 1962-70; pres. foreign ops. div. SPS Techs., Jenkintown, Pa., 1970—; chmn. or pres. of subsidiaries or affiliate cos.; lectr. Pre-Columbian archeology; hon. art counselor. Served to lt., 1944-57. Mem. Am. Mgmt. Assn., Soc. Automotive Engrs., Latin Am. Free Trade Assn., Trade Relations Coms., Internat. Bus. Forum. Republican. Clubs: Huntingdon Valley Country. Home: 809 Pardee Ln Wyncote PA 19095

CORRELL, JAMES WILLIAM, physician, educator; b. Bklyn., Dec. 6, 1919; s. Charles Daniel and Florence Oliver (Ritter) C.; B.A., Brown U., 1971; M.D., Cornell U., 1944; m. Cynthia Cannon Hewitt, Aug. 7, 1948; children—Catherine Hewitt, James William. Intern in surgery New Haven Hosp.; asst. in surgery Yale U. Sch. Medicine, 1944-45; intern in pathology N.Y. Hosp., N.Y.C., 1946, asst. resident pathologist, 1947-48; asst. pathology Cornell U. Med. Coll., N.Y.C., 1947-48, instr. pathology, 1948-49; research fellow neurosurgery Coll. Phys. & Surg., Columbia, 1949, instr. neurol. surgery, 1955-60, asso., 1960-61, asst. prof. clin. neurol. surgery, 1961-64, asso. prof., 1964-76, prof., 1976—; asst. resident neurologist Neurol. Inst. N.Y. Columbia-Presbyn. Med. Center, 1950, asst. resident neurosurgeon, 1951-53, asst. and asso. neurosurgeon, 1957-64, neurosurgeon, 1964—; resident neurosurgeon Francis Delafield Hosp., N.Y.C., 1952, clin. asst. vis. neurosurgeon, 1955—; asst. neurosurgeon Valley Hosp., Ridgewood, N.J., 1956-60, neurosurgeon, 1960—; mem. staff Bergen Pines County (N.J.) Hosp., 1957-59, Paterson (N.J.) Gen. Hosp., 1958—, St. Francis Hosp., N.Y.C., 1957-62, N.Y. Psychiat. Inst., N.Y.C., 1955—; cons. Englewood (N.J.) Hosp., 1956—. Served with M.C., USN, 1953-55. Diplomate Nat. Bd. Med. Examiners, Am. Bd. Neurol. Surgeons. Mgm. Am., Pan Am. med. assns., Med. Soc. County N.Y., Bergen County Med. Soc., Am. Acad. Neurology and Neurol. Surgery, A.C.S., Am. Assn. Neurol. Surgeons, Congress Neurol. Surgeons, Assn. Research Nervous and Mental Disorders, Am. Epilepsy Soc., N.Y. Acad. Scis., Soc. Italiana Per Lo Studio Dell'Arteriosclerosi, Soc. Exptl. Biology and Medicine, West Side Clin. Soc., Soc. Neurosci., Am. Heart Assn. (stroke council). Contbr. articles to med. jours. and textbooks. Home: 21 Timber Trail Suffern NY 10901 Office: 710 W 168th St New York City NY 10032

CORRIERE, DONALD BLAISE, county ofcl., lawyer; b. Easton, Pa., June 1, 1939; s. Joseph N. and Rose A. (Ponsetto) C.; B.A., U. Mich., 1962; J.D., U. Mich., 1965; m. Carol Anne Kroenig, Apr. 24, 1964; children—Michael F., Julie Anne, Christina M. Admitted to Pa. bar, 1965; asso. firm Haber & Corriere, Bethlehem, Pa., 1966, partner firm, 1966—; asst. dist. atty. Northampton County (Pa.), 1966; solicitor Boroughs of Hellertown, also Twps. Lower Saucon, Lehigh, 1966—; instr. bus. law Moravian Coll., 1968-73. Commr. Northampton County 1976-77; pres. Northampton County Council, 1978; co-chmn. county Shapp for Gov. com., 1970. Mem. Northampton County, Pa. bar assns. Democrat. Roman Catholic. Home: Raders Ln RD 7 Bethlehem PA 18015 Office: 433 E Broad St Bethlehem PA 18018

CORRIGAN, JOHN PATRICK, govt. ofcl.; b. Fall River, Mass., July 21, 1928; s. John Martin and Phyllis Madelaine (Plunkett) C.; B.A., Providence Coll., 1952; postgrad. Johns Hopkins, 1954-55, U. Md. Sch. Law, 1955-57, Boston Coll. Sch. Law, 1957-58, Northeastern U. Grad. Sch. Bus. Adminstrn., 1965; m. Mary Louise Sullivan, Aug. 23, 1953; children—John, Mary, Christopher, Kathleen, Carol. Group engr. leader, air arm div. Westinghouse Electric Corp., Balt., 1952-57; sr. mem. tech. staff, airborne systems lab. RCA, Waltham, Mass., 1957; asst. chief test integration, missile space and vehicle systems AVCO Research and Advanced Devel. Div., Wilmington, Mass., 1957-65; dir. ops. job corps center AVCO Econ. Systems Corp., Washington, 1966-67, dir. tng. center, 1967-68, corp. dir. adminstrn., 1968-70, dir. program planning, human resources devel., 1970-71; program dir. human resources and tech. services mgmt. AVCO Internat. Services Div., Washington and Cin., 1971-74; program mgr. JRB Assos., Inc., McLean Va., 1974-77; human devel. services program analyst Office of Sec., Office Human Devel. Services, HEW, Wahsington, 1977—. Mem. Sch. Com., Burlington, Mass., 1962-67. Served with AUS, 1946-48. Named Man of Year, Burlington Jaycees, 1965. Mem. IEEE, Am. Mgmt. Assn., Smithsonian Assos., Airline Passenger Assn., Mass. Soc. Washington (pres. 1974-76), Nat. Conf. State Socs. (regional dir. 1977—), Pi Kappa Phi. Roman Catholic. K.C. Project engr. for 1st successful flight test and recovery of ballistic missile re-entry vehicle. Home: 6402 Crane Terr Bethesda MD 20034 Office: 400 6th St SW PO Box 1182 Washington DC 20013

CORSON, DALE RAYMOND, univ. chancellor, physicist; b. Pittsburg, Kan., Apr. 5, 1914; s. Harry Raymond and Alta (Hill) C.; A.B., Coll. Emporia, Kans., 1934, L.H.D., 1970; M.A., U. Kans., 1935; postgrad. Ohio State U., 1935-36; Ph.D., U. Calif., 1938; LL.D., Columbia U., 1972, Hamilton Coll., 1973; Sc.D., U. Rochester, 1975; D.Sc. honoris causa, Elmira Coll., 1977; m. Nellie Elizabeth Griswold, June 17, 1938; children—David, Bruce, Richard, Janet. Instr., research fellow U. Cal., 1938-40; asst. prof. U. Mo., 1940-43, asso. prof., 1943-45; mem. staff Radiation Lab., Mass. Inst. Tech., 1941-43; tech. adviser War Dept., 1943-45; mem. staff Los Alamos Sci. Lab., 1945-46; asst. prof. Cornell U., 1946-47, asso. prof., 1947-52, prof., 1952—, chmn. dept. physics, 1956-59, dean coll. engring., 1959-63, provost, 1963-69, pres., 1969-77, chancellor, 1977—; dir. K Mart Corp., Internat. Minerals & Chem. Corp. Gov. N.Y. Hosp. Recipient Presdl. Certificate of Merit, 1948; Outstanding Alumnus of Year award Coll. Emporia, 1971; Distinguished Service citation U. Kans. Alumni Assn., 1972. Fellow Am. Phys. Soc., N.Y. Acad. Scis., Am. Acad. Arts and Scis.; mem. Council on Fgn. Relations, Phi Beta Kappa, Sigma Xi, Tau Beta Pi. Clubs: Cosmos, Century, Cornell, Univ. Home: 144 Northview Rd Ithaca NY 14850

CORSON, PETER DEXTER, computer co. exec.; b. Lockport, N.Y., Dec. 26, 1945; s. Peter and Hildred Louise (Lammerts) C.; B.S., State U. N.Y., Buffalo, 1974, M.B.A., 1977; children—Christian Peter, Sara Woodburn. Asst. dir. info. and research N.Y. State Senate, Albany, 1970-73; newsman Sta. WBEN-TV, Buffalo, 1973-74; bur. chief Buffalo Evening News, 1974-77; pres. Corson Computer Corp., Inc., Buffalo, 1977—. Served with U.S. Army, 1967-70. Decorated Bronze Star, Silver Star, Air medal, Purple Heart. Mem. Sigma Chi, Sigma Delta Chi, Omicron Delta Epsilon. Republican. Episcopalian. Club: Saturn (Buffalo). Office: 1016 Niagara Falls Blvd Buffalo NY 14150

CORTES, ENGRACIO PADILLA, physician; b. Iloilo City, Philippines, Jan. 9, 1938; s. Felix Francisco and Felly Ledesma (Padilla) C.; came to U.S., 1965; M.D., Far Eastern U. (Philippines), 1964; m. Lilia S. Gonzales, June 7, 1969; children—Engcarlo, Marissa, Alfonso. Intern, Cambridge (Mass.) City Hosp., 1965-66; resident asst. in medicine Lemuel Shattuck Hosp., Boston, 1966-67, sr. med. resident, 1967-68; teaching fellow in medicine Tufts U., Boston, 1967-68; asst. prof. medicine State U. N.Y., Stony Brook, 1975—; research fellow med. oncology Roswell Park Meml. Inst., Buffalo, 1968-71, attending dept. medicine, 1971-72; physician-in-charge oncology service Queens Hosp. Center, L.I. Jewish-Hillside Med. Center, 1972—, physician-in-charge of tumor registry, 1977—; cons. in oncology Jewish Inst. Geriatric Care, 1977—. Am. Cancer Soc. grantee, 1969-70; Nat. Cancer Inst. grantee, 1976—; Adria Labs. Inc. grantee, 1975-76; diplomate Am. Bd. Internal Medicine and Med. Oncology. Mem. Am. Soc. Clin. Oncology, Am. Assn. Cancer Research, Osteogenic Sarcoma Study Group, Internat. Lung Cancer Study Group, Am. Fedn. Clin. Oncologic Socs. Contbr. articles to med. jours. Home: 64 Fairfield Ln Roslyn Heights NY 11577 Office: 270-05 76th Ave New Hyde Park NY 11040

CORTES, LUIS EDUARDO, physician; b. Bogota, Colombia, June 17, 1936; s. Louis Eduardo and Ana (Bernal) C.; came to U.S., 1965; student Instituto de la Salle, 1949-54; M.D., Nat. U., Bogota, 1960; m. Tara Ann Siegal, Jan. 22, 1972; 1 son, Louis Edward. Fellow cardiovascular surgery U. Ky., Lexington, 1965-66; asst. research scientist N.Y. U., N.Y.C., 1966-68; resident in cardio-thoracic surgery, 1968-70, clin. instr. surgery, 1973—; resident in gen. surgery N.Y. Med. Coll., 1971-73, asst. prof. surgery, 1978—; asst. attending surgery Bellevue Hosp., N.Y.C., 1973—; practice medicine specializing in thoracic surgery, N.Y.C., 1973—. Mem. Am. Soc. Artificial Internal Organs, N.Y. Heart Assn., Surg. Soc. N.Y. Med. Coll. Roman Catholic. Contbr. articles to profl. publs. Home: 515 E 84th St New York City NY 10028 Office: 515 E 84th St New York City NY 10028

CORTES, MICHAEL JOSEPH, ins. co. exec.; b. Bklyn., Apr. 6, 1945; s. Michael Edward and Marie Teresa C.; B.S., Hofstra U., 1966; C.L.U., Am. Coll. Chartered Life Underwriters, 1972; m. Paulette A. Gruss, July 16, 1966; children—Melissa, Danielle, Paulette, Jessica. Agent, asst. mgr. Mutual of N.Y., Huntington, 1968-73, agency mgr., Melville, N.Y., 1973—. Served to 1st lt. U.S. Army, 1966-68. Mem. Suffolk Life Underwriters Assn. (dir. 1977—, chmn. tng. council 1977, 78), Gen. Agent and Mgrs. Assn. (Nat. Mgmt. award 1977, 78, 79). Home: 86 Stillwater Rd Saint James NY 11780 Office: One Huntington Quad Melville NY 11746

CORTES-HWANG, ADRIANA, educator; b. Valparaíso, Chile, Nov. 9, 1928; d. Luis and Sofia (Garces) Cortes; came to U.S., 1963, naturalized, 1969; B.A., U. Chile, 1963; B.A., Portland State U., 1965; M.A., U. Oreg., 1966; m. John Hwang, Mar. 17, 1966; 1 dau., Veronica. Instr. in Spanish, Portland (Oreg.) State U., 1963, U. Oreg., Eugene, 1965-67, Wilson Coll., Chambersburg, Pa., 1967; asst. prof. modern langs. Shippensburg (Pa.) State Coll., 1968—, adviser internat. studies, 1971—, Fulbright adviser, chmn. Latin Am. studies, 1970—; instr. Spanish, Pa. State U., Mont Alto, Recipient Gold medal Ateneo Cervantes, Valparaíso, Chile, 1947. Mem. Modern Lang. Assn., AAUP, Latin Am. Studies Assn. Contbr. articles in field to profl. jours. Home: 221 Horst St Chambersburg PA 17021 Office: POB 424 Shippensburg State Coll Shippensburg PA 17257

CORTEZ, JEANETTE SCHLANGER, interior designer, cons.; b. U.S.A.; d. William and Anna (Abramovitz) Berkowitz; student N.Y. Sch. Social Research, 1957-60; diploma N.Y. Sch. Interior Design, 1960; postgrad. N.Y. Phoenix Sch. Design, 1966-68; m. Jose Cortez, Sept. 19, 1973; children by previous marriage—Steven Jay Bergerson, Tina Robin Bergerson Plesset. Showroom designer Berge-Norman Assos., N.Y.C., 1952-57; pvt. practice cons. interior design, N.Y.C., 1959-70; interior cons. and design Ethan Allen Showcase, Astoria, N.Y., 1969-74; asst. dir., instr. Met. Inst. Interior Design, Plainview, N.Y., 1974—; com. mem. Elmer Bopst Library event; design for N.Y. Inst. Consumer Edn., 1970; lectr. in field. Recipient Ethan Allen Model Apts. award, 1970; full page spread House Beautiful Mag., 1973. Mem. Inst. Bus. Designers, Nat. Home Fashion League, Women's Archtl. Aux., AIA, Allied Bd. Trade. Office: 116 Central Park S Suite 4-D New York City NY 10019

CORY, PAUL RICHARD, nursing adminstr.; b. Fall River, Mass., May 2, 1933; s. Charles W. and Olive (Taylor) C.; B.S. in Nursing, U. Kans., 1964; M.S., U. Colo., 1967; m. Anna Mae Miller, July 21, 1961; children—Grace Anne, David C., Sharon L., Christine S. Various positions in profl. nursing, Mo., Kans., Colo., 1960-66; dir. nursing St. Lukes Hosps., Fargo, N.D., 1966-68; asso. prof., chmn. nursing dept. Jamestown (N.D.) Coll., 1968-69; dir. nursing High Point (N.C.) Meml. Hosp., 1969-72; dir. nursing service H.J. Thomas Meml. Hosp., S. Charleston, W.Va., 1972-76; dir. nursing Pottsville (Pa.) Hosp. and Warne Clinic, 1977—; chmn. Nursing Dirs. of Charleston, W.Va. Area, 1974-75. Named Distinguished Lt. Gov., Kiwanis Internat., W.Va. Dist., 1976. Mem. Pa., Am. nurses assns., Nat. League Nursing, Internat. Hosp. Fedn., Am. Soc. Nursing Service Adminstrs., Ry. Hist. Soc. Democrat. Methodist. Club: Kiwanis (club pres., lt. gov. 1973-74, 75-76). Home: 312 Highland Dr Pottsville PA 17901 Office: 420 S Jackson St Pottsville PA 17901

COSGRIFF, STUART WORCESTER, physician; b. Pittsfield, Mass., May 8, 1917; s. Thomas F. and Frances DeFord (Worcester) C.; B.A., Holy Cross Coll., 1938; M.D., Columbia U., 1942, D.Med.Sci., 1948; m. Mary Shaw, Jan. 23, 1943; children—Mary, Thomas, Stuart Worcester, Richard, Robert. Intern, Presbyn. Hosp., N.Y.C., 1942-43; asst. resident medicine 1943, 46-47, chief resident, 1947-48; instr. medicine Columbia U., N.Y.C., 1948-50, clin. asst. prof. medicine, 1951-63, clin. asso. prof. medicine, 1963-73, clin. prof. medicine, 1973-78; attending physician Presbyn. Hosp., N.Y.C., 1948—; individual practice medicine, specializing in internal medicine and vascular disease, N.Y.C., 1948—; cons. in medicine Silver Hill Found., New Canaan, Conn., Phelps Meml. Hosp., North Tarrytown, N.Y., Vassar Bros. Hosp., Poughkeepsie, N.Y.; cons. internal medicine to Dir. Selective Service, N.Y.C., 1957-73; dir. thrombo-embolic clinic Vanderbilt Clinic, N.Y.C., 1948-78. Served to capt. M.C., U.S. Army, 1943-45; ETO. Diplomate Am. Bd. Internal Medicine. Fellow A.C.P., Pan Am. Med. Assn.; mem. AMA, Am. Heart Assn., Alpha Omega Alpha. Roman Catholic. Club: Knickerbocker Country (Tenafly, N.J.). Contbg. author, contbr. articles to profl. publs. anticoagulant therapy, thromboembolic diseases, 1943-78. Home: 11 Park St Tenafly NJ 07670 Office: 161 Ft Washington Ave New York City NY 10032

COSGROVE, MARTIN JOSEPH, radiologist; b. Phila., Nov. 17, 1938; s. Martin Michael and Hilary Ann (Andreczyczk) C.; A.B. cum laude, St. Joseph's Coll., 1960; M.D., Jefferson Med. Coll., 1964; m. Noriss Lee Ennis, Dec. 13, 1969; children—Martin Joseph, Michael, Noriss. Intern, Queen of Angels Hosp., Los Angeles, 1964-65; pvt. family practice, So. Calif. Permanente, Los Angeles, 1967-70; resident in radiology U. Md., College Park, 1970-73; instr. radiology U. Md. Hosp., 1973-74; radiologist Rosewood State Hosp., Reisterstown, Md., 1973-74; staff radiologist, chief radiology Nanticoke Meml. Hosp., Seaford, Del., 1974—; dir., pres. Nanticoke Radiology Assos., Seaford, 1977—; sec. med. staff Nanticoke Meml. Hosp., 1977-78. Served with USN, 1965-67. Recipient Physicians Recognition award AMA, 1977; Christian Schmidt Scholar, 1956; diplomate Am. Bd. Radiology, Am. Bd. Med. Examiners. Mem. Med. Soc. Del., AMA, Sussex County Med. Soc., Am. Coll. Radiology, Soc. Nuclear Medicine, Am. Coll. Nuclear Physicians, VFW. Roman Catholic. Home: 1600 Camden Ave Salisbury MD 21801 Office: Nanticoke Meml Hosp Dept R Seaford DE 19973

COSMAN, BARD, plastic surgeon; b. Bklyn., Nov. 10, 1930; s. Max and Cornelia (Kaps) C.; A.B., Columbia, 1952, M.D., 1955; m. Madeleine Pelner, Sept. 7, 1958; children—Marin, Bard Clifford. Intern Roosevelt Hosp., N.Y.C., 1955-56, resident plastic surgery Presbyn. Hosp., N.Y.C. 1959-61; practice medicine specializing in plastic surgery, N.Y.C. and Ridgewood, N.J., 1963—; attending surgeon Presbyn. Hosp.; asso. attending plastic surgeon St. Elizabeth's Hosp.; prof. clin. surgery Columbia cons. plastic surgeon Blythedale Children's Hosp., Valhalla, N.Y. Served as lt. comdr. USNR, 1961-63. Diplomate Am. Bd. Plastic Surgeons. Fellow A.C.S.; mem. Am. Soc. Plastic and Reconstrv. Surgeons, Am. Assn. Plastic Surgeons, Am. Cleft Palate Assn. N.Y. Regional Soc. of Plastic and Reconstructive Surgeons, N.Y. Acad. Medicine, N.Y. County Med. Soc., A.M.A., Bergen County Med. Soc., N.Y. Acad. Scis. Contbr. articles in field to profl. jours. Home: 32 Knickerbocker Rd Tenafly NJ 07670 Office: 161 Fort Washington Ave New York City NY 10032

COSNOTTI, RICHARD LOUIS, clergyman; b. Pitts., Jan. 27, 1952; s. Frank Paul and Mary Louise (Paich) C.; B.S. in Sociology, Brigham Young U., 1973; M.Div., Princeton Theol. Sem., 1976. Dir. youth programs Orem and Am. Fork Community Chs., Utah, 1971-73; asst. to minister Reformed Protestant Dutch Ch. of Flatbush, Bklyn., 1973-75, Hebron United Presbyterian Ch., Pitts., 1976; ordained to ministry Presbyterian Ch., 1976; asst. minister The Brick Presbyn. Ch., N.Y.C., 1976; Presbytery rep. Presbytery N.Y.C. Greater N.Y. Scouting Council, 1976—; chaplain East Midtown Chaplaincy, N.Y.C., 1976—; liaison East Harlem Tutorial Project, N.Y.C., 1976—, Met. N. Community Narcotics Prevention Program, 1977—; mem. social concerns com., ecumenical relations com. N.Y.C. Presbytery, 1977—. Mem. Soc. for Bibl. Lit., Hymn. Soc. Am. Am. Sociol. Assn., Presbyn. Assn. Musicians, Am. Acad. Religion, Council Religion and Internat. Affairs, Alpha Kappa Delta, Alpha Phi Omega (Eta Omicron chpt.). Republican. Clubs: Princeton, Knickerbocker Rep. (N.Y.C.); Univ. (Pitts.). Composer hymn music. Home: 62 E 92d St New York City NY 10028 Office: 1140 Park Ave New York City NY 10028

COSSA, JOHN PAUL, surgeon; b. Exeter, Pa., June 17, 1933; s. Gino Joseph and Theresa Agnes (Bell) C.; B.S., Muhlenberg Coll., 1954; M.D., Hahnemann Med. Coll., Phila., 1958; m. Arlene Melinchock, Aug. 30, 1958; children—Caryl, Corinne, John, Carla. Intern, Hahnemann Hosp., Phila., 1958-59, resident in gen. surgery, 1959-63, 63-64; asso. in surgery St. Agnes Hosp., Phila., 1963-74; jr. attending dept. surgery Hahnemann Hosp., 1964-66, sr. attending, 1966—; sr. attending in surgery St. Agnes Med. Center, Phila., 1974—, v.p. med. affairs, 1974—; instr. surgery Hahnemann Med. Coll., 1963-64, asst. in surgery, 1964-65, sr. instr., 1965-66, asst. prof., 1968-73, asso. prof., 1973—. Diplomate Am. Bd. Surgery. Am. Cancer Soc. fellow, 1963-64. Fellow A.C.S., Am. Coll. Geriatric Surgery, Phila. Coll. Physicians, Phila. Acad. Surgery; mem. Pan Am. Med. Assn., Am. Assn. Hosp. Educators, Am. Coll. Utilization Rev. Physicians, Am. Acad. Med. Dirs. Roman Catholic. Home: 11 Rabbit Run Rd Malvern PA 19355 Office: 1900 S Broad St Philadelphia PA 19145

COSTA, ALLEN RONALD, mgmt. exec.; b. N.Y.C., Mar. 25, 1937; s. William F. and Shirley Costa; B.S., N.Y. U., 1958; M.B.A., Coll. City N.Y., 1967; m. Marsha Cole, Aug. 16, 1959; children—Donna, Richard, Steven, Emily. With Oppenheimer & Co., Inc., N.Y.C., 1958—, now v.p. ops. Chmn. citizens adv. com. on budget Bd. Edn., 1977-78; trustee, treas. Temple Israel of South Orange; v.p. Citizens Party League. Mem. Am. Mgmt. Assn., Wall St. Communications Assn., Adminstrv. Mgmt. Soc., Am. Soc. Personnel Adminstrs., Office Future Panel. Club: Village South Orange. Home: 356 Harding Dr South Orange NJ 07079 Office; 1 New York Plaza New York City NY 10004

COSTA, CONSTANCE ELAINE, counselor; b. S.I., N.Y., Jan. 3, 1948; d. Joseph Thomas and Lillian Marie (Antilla) Costa; B.S. in Biology, Wagner Coll., 1969; postgrad. in Guidance and Counseling, Coll. S.I., 1975-79. Tchr. biology and chemistry Francis Sch., 1974-75; program dir. counseling and remedial math., tchr. articulation Coll. S.I., 1975-78; dir. higher edn. opportunity program Poly. Inst. N.Y., Bklyn., 1978—. Recipient service key Wagner Coll., 1969, Bd. Higher Edn. grants for remedial edn., 1975, 76, 77. Mem. Am. Personnel and Guidance Assn., Assn. Specialists in Group Work. Home: 80 Muller Ave Staten Island NY 10314 Office: Poly Inst NY 333 Jay St Brooklyn NY 11201

COSTA, HELIO, TV journalist; b. Barbacena, Minas Gerais, Brazil, Aug. 17, 1939; s. Jose Calixto and Renata (Fiorino) C.; came to U.S., 1967; student State Coll. Minas Gerais, 1955-60, U. Md., 1969-73; children—Roberto John, Helio Jose, Marcus Theobaldo. With Associados, newspaper chain, Brazil, 1960-67; press asst. USIA, Belo Horizonte, Brazil, 1961-67; news writer Voice of Am., Washington, 1967-73; bur. chief, sr. fgn. corr. Globo TV Network, Starlight Communications, N.Y.C., 1973—. Served with Brazilian Army, 1958. Recipient Gold medal World Press Assn., 1970; Internat. Communicators award Met. N.Y. chpt. Nat. Assn. Media Women, 1975; Golden TV Athena award TV Critics Assn., 1978. Mem. N.Y. Press-Fgn. Corrs. Center, Newspaper Guild Brazil. Roman Catholic. Club: Connought Tower. Home: 300 E 54th St New York City NY 10022 Office: Starlight Communications 909 3d Ave 21st Floor New York City NY 10022

COSTA, JOSEPH ALFRED, pediatrician; b. Yonkers, N.Y., Nov. 5, 1909; s. Giovanni Salvatore and Consiglia Francesca (Broncati) C.; B.S. (Regents scholar), N.Y. U., 1930; M.D., U. Bellevue Hosp. Med. Coll., 1933; m. Helen Susan Latinka, July 21, 1935; children—Concelia Margaret, John Louis, Ilona Nancy. Intern, St. Agnes Hosp., White Plains, N.Y., 1933, St. John's Riverside Hosp., Yonkers, N.Y., 1933-34; resident in pediatrics Fifth Ave. Hosp., N.Y.C., 1934-35; practice medicine specializing in pediatrics, Bedford Hills, N.Y., 1935-69, South Harwich, Mass., 1969—; hon. dir. pediatrics No. Westchester Hosp.; mem. staff Cape Cod Hosp. Mem. profl. adv. bd. Harwich (Mass.) Home Nursing Service, 1976—, Monomoy Services, Chatham, Mass., 1977—. Recipient Dante Aleghieri medal Order Sons of Italy in Am., 1926; Valentine Mott medal U. and Bellevue Hosp. Med. Coll., 1933. Diplomate Am. Bd. Pediatrics. Fellow Am. Acad. Pediatrics; mem. Mass., Barnstable, Westchester med. socs., Columbia-Presbyterian Med. Center 25 Year Club, CAP (maj. Cape Cod chpt. 1973—), N.Y. U. Sch Medicine, Babies Hosp. alumni assns., Omega Upsilon. Roman Catholic. Club: K.C. Author: Tick Paralysis on the Atlantic Seaboard, 1952. Home and Office: 88 Uncle Venies Rd South Harwich MA 02661

COSTA, JOSEPH JAMES, librarian; b. Frackville, Pa., July 31, 1932; s. Joseph and Rose (Griscavage) C.; B.S. in Edn., Bloomsburg State Coll., 1959; postgrad. Kutztown State Coll., 1961-63; M.S. in L.S., Villanova U., 1966; M.Ed., Kutztown State Coll., 1973; m. Marie A. Pribish, May 25, 1957; children—Joseph A., John L., Anita Marie, Andrew J. Tchr., coach Nativity High Sch., Pottsville, Pa., 1959-66, Kulpmont (Pa.) High Sch., 1966-61; librarian, tchr., coach Frackville High Sch., 1961-66; head librarian North Schuylkill Sch. Dist., Frackville, 1966-68, dir., 1976-77; head librarian Schuylkill campus Library, Pa. State U., Schuylkill Haven, 1968—; mem. Pa. Library Devel. Gov.'s Council, 1976—. Active Boy Scouts Am., 1966—; chmn. Crippled Children's Fund. drive, 1970, 71; active Little League, Midget Football, Biddy Basketball; sec.-treas. Frackville Men's Softball League, 1967-72, statistician, 1969-73. Trustee Frackville Free Pub. Library Bd. Served with USAF, 1952-56. Mem. ALA, Pa. Library Assn., VFW, Amvets, Holy Name Soc., Chi Gamma Iota, Delta Kappa, Epsilon Delta Chi. Roman Catholic. Elk, K.C. (grand knight); mem. Frackville Council. Author: Child Abuse and Neglect: Legislation, Reporting and Prevention, 1978. Home: 494 W Pine St Frackville PA 17931 Office: Schuylkill Campus Library Pa State U Schuylkill Haven PA 17972

COSTAGLIOLA, FRANCESCO, govt. ofcl.; b. Cranston, R.I., Aug. 24, 1917; s. Luigi and Rose (Lubrano) C.; student U. R.I. 1935-37; B.S. in E.E., U.S. Naval Acad., Annapolis, Md., 1941; postgrad. Naval Postgrad. Sch., 1946-47, Mass. Inst. Tech., 1947-49, Cath. U. Am., 1967-71; M.B.A., Am. U., Washington, 1974; m. Agnes Mary Ross, June 14, 1952; children—Francesca Illia, Marisa Pia, Antonia Gabriella, Rose Ann. Commd. ensign U.S. Navy, 1941, advanced through grades to capt., 1960; served in U.S.S. Phoenix in 24 operations PTO, 1941-46; comdg. officer U.S.S. Halsey Powell, Korea, 1951-52; various positions naval sea and shore assignments involving atomic energy, 1952-64; mil. asst. to Asst. to Sec. of Def., 1964-67; ret., 1968; commr. AEC, 1968-69; engr. RCA, 1974-76; staff mem. Joint Congl. Com. on Atomic Energy, Washington, 1967-68, 69-71, 76-77; staff mem. Office of Sec. of Senate, Washington, 1977—; mem. Md. Radiation Control Adv. Bd., 1973-77. Decorated Legion of Merit, Bronze Star medals with Combat V. Mem. Am. Nuclear Soc., Ops. Research Soc. Am., U.S. Naval Inst., Pearl Harbor Survivors Assn., Naval Acad. Alumni Assn., Mass. Inst. Tech. Alumni Assn. Roman Catholic. Club: Army and Navy (Washington). Contbr. articles profl. jours. Home: 307 Gibbon St Alexandria VA 22314

COSTANTINO, JAMES, govt. ofcl.; b. Braintree, Mass., Mar. 20, 1930; s. John and Susan (Marendo) C.; B.S. in Mech. Engring., U. Mass., 1958; M.E.A., George Washington U., 1961; Ph.D., Am. U., Washington, 1971; m. Dolores Ann Billek, Aug. 23, 1966; children—Christopher, Jeffrey. Mech. engr. FAA, Washington, 1958-63; aero. engr. Office Manned Space Flights NASA, Washington, 1963-65, chief tech. support, 1965-69, dir. tech. and mgmt. support, 1969-71; secretarial rep. Dept. Transp., Phila., 1971-73, exec. asst. to dep. sec., Washington, 1974-76; dir. Transp. Systems Center, Cambridge, Mass., 1976—. Mem. advisory council Fed. City Coll., Boston State Coll.; mem. policy com. Boston Fed. Exec. Bd.; chmn. Minority Bus. Opportunity Tech. Commercialization Com. Served with USN, 1949-53. Recipient NASA Apollo Achievement award, 1970, Meritorious Achievement medal Dept. Transp., 1974. Registreed profl. engr., Mass. Mem. Nat., Mass. socs. profl. engrs., Am. Astronautical Soc., Soc. Automotive Engrs., Am. Arbitration Assn., Naval Res. Officers Assn. Home: 96 Sagamore Rd Wellesley Hills MA 02181 Office: Transp Systems Center Dept Transp Kendall Sq Cambridge MA 02142

COSTANZO, RAPHAEL J., elec. engr., inventor; b. Bridgeport, Conn., Oct. 19; s. Arthur and Martha (Scuteri) C.; ed. U. Naples; 1944, Bullard Haven Tech., 1947, U. Bridgeport, 1951. Test engr. quality control labs. CASCO Products, Bridgeport, Conn., 1952-56; mgr. research and devel. Harvey Hubbell, Inc., Bridgeport, 1956-63; pres. Stanzo Electronics, Inc., Bridgeport 1963-66; self employed inventor, Bridgeport and Roxbury, Conn. 1966—; patentee U.S. and abroad, devices including electrically heated sock, belt and sleeping bag, atomic warning device, pressure sensitive switch, electronic dimmer control. Served with U.S. Army, 1943-45. Mem. IEEE, Menco Parapsychology Assn. (pres.). Address: 119 Park St Bridgeport CT 06608

COSTELLO, DANIEL WALTER, fin. services co. exec.; b. Toledo, June 17, 1930; s. Walter William and Rose Angela (Dimond) C.; B.S. in Engring. Sci., Purdue U., 1952; m. Billie Jean Hartz, Jan. 24, 1959; children—Michael Joseph, Colleen Marie. Sales, mktg. positions Shell Oil Co., 1955-63; dir. real estate devel. and constrn. Ford Motor Land Devel. Co., Dearborn, Mich., 1963-74; corporate v.p. real estate, constrn. purchasing, gen. services Am. Express Co. and subs., N.Y.C., 1975—; chmn. Am. Express Realty Mgmt. Co.; cons. real estate appraisal. Served with U.S. Army, 1952-54. Mem. Nat. Bldg. Owners and Mgrs. Assn., Downtown N.Y.C. Owners and Mgrs. Assn., Nat. Assn. Purchasing Agts., Theta Xi. Clubs: Tuxedo (N.Y.) Country, Brookside Tennis, Allendale, N.J. Dir. real estate projects which received archtl. and/or civic awards. Home: 15 Princeton Rd Allendale NJ 07401 Office: Am Express Plaza New York City NY 10004

COSTELLO, DOUGLAS WARREN, newspaper editor; b. St. John, N.B., Can., Nov. 16, 1917; s. Peter and Mary (McKay) C.; came to U.S., 1958, naturalized, 1978; student pub. schs., St. John; m. Violet Leona Connor, Dec. 24, 1940; children—Marcia Costello O'Rourke, Douglas J., Ralph M. Editor, N.B. Pub. Co., St. John, 1937-58, Caribou (Maine) Pub. Co., 1958-66; news editor Northeast Pub. Co., Presque Isle, Maine, 1966-70, v.p., 1966-70; editor Pottsville (Pa.) Republican, J.H. Zerbey Newspapers, Inc., 1970-78; editorial page editor, editor, pub. Aroostook Republican, 1960-70, Loring AFB Limelite, 1966-70. Mem. Maine USO Council, 1960-70, Loring AFB Community Council, 1960-70, Caribou Centennial Com., 1958-59; chmn. City Celebration Com., Caribou, 1968; bd. dirs. United Fund, Caribou, 1959-62. Served with Canadian Army, 1941-46. Recipient numerous awards New Eng. Press Assn., numerous others. Mem. Nat. Newspaper Assn. (vice chmn. promotion com. 1968-69), Northeastern U.S. Press Assn. (pres. 1961-63), Pa. Soc. Newspaper Editors, Nat., Pa. asso. press mng. editors. Methodist. Clubs: Kiwanis (lt. gov. 1969-70, pres. 1964, plaque award 1965). Home: 10 Overlook Dr E Pottsville PA 17901 Office: PO Box 563 Pottsville PA 17901

COSTIKYAN, EDWARD NAZAR, lawyer; b. Weehawken, N.J., Sept. 14, 1924; s. Mibhran Nazar and Berthe (Muller) C.; student Horace Mann Sch. Boys, 1941; A.B., Columbia U., 1947, LL.B., 1949; m. Barbara; children—Gregory John, Emilie Berthe. Admitted to N.Y. State bar, 1949, U.S. Supreme Ct. bar, 1964; law sec. to U.S. Judge Harold R. Medina, N.Y.C., 1949-51; partner firm Paul, Weiss, Rifkind, Wharton & Garrison, N.Y.C., 1960—; lectr. New Sch. Social Research. Chmn., N.Y. State Task Force on N.Y.C. Structure and Jurisdiction, 1971-72; vice chmn. State Charter Revision for N.Y.C., 1972—. Democratic dist. leader, 1955-65, county leader Dem. County Com. N.Y. County, 1962-64; presdl. elector Dem. Party, 1964; bd. dirs. Fund City N.Y., Municipal Art Soc., 42d St Redevel Corp., Pub. Edn. Assn. Served to lt. AUS, 1942-46. Fellow Am. Coll. Trial Lawyers; mem. Assn. Bar City N.Y. (mem. com. character and fitness 1st judicial dept.), Am., N.Y. State bar assns. Unitarian (trustee, 1967-71, pres. bd. trustees 1968-69), Columbia Law Alumni. Club: Century. Author: Behind Closed Doors: Politics in the Public Interest, 1966; co-author: Re-Structuring the Government of New York City, 1972; New Strategies for Regional Cooperation, 1973. Research editor Columbia Law Rev.; bd. editors: N.Y. Law Jour., 1976—; contbr. articles field legal, polit. subjects periodicals and profl. jours.; orchestral condr., oratorio. Home: 50 Sutton Pl South New York City NY 10022 Office: 345 Park Ave New York City NY 10022

COTE, DONALD BERNARD, coll. ofcl.; b. Biddeford, Maine, Feb. 5, 1951; s. Leo Rene and Dolores (Beaulieu) C.; student St. Michaels Coll., 1969-71; B.S., U. Maine, 1973, M.Ed., 1975; m. Pamela J. Hunter, Nov. 19, 1977. Intern, grantee Nat. Tchr. Corps, 1973-75; mem. faculty psychology, counseling staff U. Maine, Machias, 1975-76; dir. residence Salem (Mass.) State Coll., 1976-77, dir. housing, 1977—; cons. Milestone Found., 1973—, recreation counseling, Gorham, Maine, 1973—. Mem. Am. Personnel and Guidance Assn., Am. Coll. Personnel Assn., Boston Assn. Coll. Housing Adminstrs., Am. Coll. and U. Housing Officers. Democrat. Roman Catholic.

COTE, ELEANOR M. MURANO, educator; b. Westerly, R.I., Feb. 28, 1948; d. Michael A. and Elena L. (Notarantonio) Murano; student Rivier Coll., Nashua, N.H., 1966-67; A.A., R.I. Jr. Coll., 1969; B.S., Mt. St. Joseph Coll., 1971; postgrad. U. R.I., 1972-77, R.I. Coll., 1973-76; m. Stephen R. Cote, Aug. 5, 1978. Tchr. sci. Westerly (R.I.) Sch. System, 1971—. Mem. NEA, R.I. Edn. Assn., Westerly Tchrs. Assn., Nat. Sci. Tchrs. Assn. Democrat. Roman Catholic. Home: 7 Joshua St Westerly RI 02891 Office: Highland Ave Westerly RI 02891

CÔTÉ, JOSEPH JULIEN JEAN-PIERRE, lt. gov. Que.; b. Montreal, Que., Can., Jan. 9, 1926; s. Joseph Emile and Cedia (Roy) C.; ed. Longueuil Coll., Tech. Sch., Sch. Dental Tech.; m. Germaine Tremblay, July 31, 1949; children—Andrée, Gilbert, Danielle, Robert, Paul, Hélène, Jocelyne, Isabelle. Former dental technician; elected mem. House of Commons, 1963; mem. Privy Council, apptd. Postmaster gen., 1965; minister nat. revenue, 1968-70, minister without portfolio, 1970-71, postmaster gen., 1971-72, summoned to Senate, 1972; lt. gov. Que., 1978—. Liberal. Roman Catholic. Office: Office Lt Gov Govt Bldgs Quebec PQ Canada*

COTHRAN, RAYMOND JOHN, lawyer; b. Arlington, N.J., Dec. 2, 1911; s. John C. and E. Belle (Cochran) C.; A.B., Cornell U., 1933, J.D., 1937; m. Thelma L. Ramsey, Oct. 9, 1948; children—Elaynne C. Koechling, Carole R., Anne J. Admitted to N.Y. State bar, 1938, U.S. Supreme Ct. bar, 1970; practice law, Lockport, 1938-42, 46-62; asst. counsel to N.Y. State Joint Legislative com. on Mil. Law, 1951-53; acting city judge, Lockport, 1950-53, city judge, 1953, corp.

counsel, 1954-55, mayor, 1958-61; town atty. Town of Somerset, N.Y., 1962. Dir. Republican Club of Lockport, 1962. Co-chmn. steering com. N.Y. State Conf. of Mayors, 1961-62, exec. dir., 1963-78, exec. dir. emeritus, 1978—; mem. N.Y. State Local Govt. Adv. Bd., 1962-75, N.Y. State Employees Retirement System Adv. Council, 1963-78, N.Y. State Tech. Adv. Com. on Emergency Health Services, 1970-75, N.Y. State Emergency Med. Services Council, 1975—; adv. com. on pub. employment for extension and pub. service div. N.Y. State Sch. Indsl. and Labor Relations, 1971—; chmn. State Adv. Council Continuing Higher Edn., 1966-77. Bd. dirs. State Traffic Safety Council, 1963-76. Served from 1st lt. to maj. U.S. Army, 1942-46; lt. col. Res. (ret.). Mem. N.Y. State Bar Assn., Am. Judicature Soc., Nat. League of Cities (exec. com. 1963-65), Phi Beta Kappa. Baptist. Mason. Home: 42 Patroon Pl Loudonville NY 12211

COTTER, JOHN PATRICK, judge; b. Hartford, Conn., Mar. 2, 1911; s. Edward J. and Rose (Doughty) C.; B.S., Trinity Coll., Hartford, 1933, also LL.D.; LL.B., Harvard U., 1936; m. Jeannette Zegger, Mar. 1939; children—Patricia R. Cotter Moller, John Patrick, Elizabeth A. Cotter Vasta. Admitted to Conn. bar, 1936; pros. atty. Ct. Common Pleas, Hartford County, 1949-50; judge Hartford City and Police Ct., 1950, Ct. Common Pleas, 1950-55, Superior Ct. Conn., 1955-65; asso. justice Supreme Ct. Conn., also chief ct. adminstr., 1965-79, chief justice, 1979—. Co-chmn. Conn. Planning Commn. Criminal Adminstrn.; del. 1st Nat. Conf. Crime Control; mem. Conn. Bd. Pardons. Mem. Conn. Ho. of Reps., 1947-50, floor leader, 1947-50, chmn. legis. council, 1947-48. Bd. dirs. Hartford Hosp.; trustee Inst. Ct. Mgmt.; bd. fellows Trinity Coll., 1965-68. Mem. Am., Conn. Hartford County bar assns., Am. Judicature Soc. (dir.), Inst. Jud. Adminstrn. Club: Hartford Golf. Home: 38 Wardwell St West Hartford CT 06107 Office: 231 Capitol Ave Hartford CT 06101

COTTER, WILLIAM R., congressman; b. Hartford, Conn., July 18, 1926; s. William and Mary E. (O'Loughlin) C.; B.A., Trinity Coll., 1949. Treas., Hartford Democratic Town Com., 1953-60; mem. council, Hartford, 1954-55; exec. aide to Gov. Ribicoff, 1955-57; dep. ins. commr., 1957-64, commr., 1964-70; mem. 92d-96th congresses from 1st Dist. Conn. Treas. Conn. State Dem. Central Com., 1962-76; del. Dem. Nat. Conv., 1964. Home: 247 Fairfield Ave Hartford CT 06114 Office: Rayburn House Office Bldg Washington DC 20515

COTTING, JAMES CHARLES, forest products co. exec.; b. Winchester, Mass., Oct. 15, 1933; s. Edward L. and Mary Ellen (Worrell) C.; B.A. cum laude, Ohio State U., 1955; m. Marjorie A. Kirsch, Feb. 8, 1963; children—James Charles, Steven Robert, Brenda Ann-Marie. Accounting supr. U.S. Steel Corp. Pitts., 1959-61; mgr. profit analysis Ford Motor Co., Dearborn, Mich., 1961-63; mgr. devel. planning A.O. Smith Corp., Milw., 1963-66; asst. controller Gen. Foods Corp., White Plains, N.Y., 1966-71; v.p. planning Internat. Paper Co., N.Y.C., 1971-76, v.p., controller, 1976—; dir. Internat. Stanley Corp., Davol, Inc., Am. Central Corp. Served with USN, 1955-58. Mem. Phi Beta Kappa, Alpha Tau Omega. Club: Montclair Golf. Home: 3 S Mountain Terr Montclair NJ 07042 Office: 220 E 42d St New York City NY 10017

COTTLE, ELEANOR CRAY (MRS. EDGAR WILLIS COTTLE), lumber exec.; b. Quincy, Mass., Oct. 13, 1891; d. John D. and Mary Ann (Sullivan) Moriarty; student Boston U.; m. Edgar Willis Cottle, Jan. 17, 1929. Credit mgr. Quincy Lumber Co., Quincy, Mass. 1924-28, pres., treas., 1944—; pres., treas. Rhines Lumber Co., Weymouth, Mass., 1944—. Trustee Edgar W. Cottle Found., Boston. Home: The Crossways Harvard MA 01451 summer West Tisbury Martha's Vineyard MA 02575 Office: 176 Newbury St Boston MA 02116

COTTLE, THOMAS JOSEPH, sociologist; b. Chgo., Jan. 22, 1937; s. Maurice Hiam and Gitta Gradova (Weinstock) C.; B.A., Harvard, 1959; M.A., U. Chgo., 1963, Ph.D., 1968; m. Kay Mikkelsen, June 28, 1964; children—Claudia Mari, Jason Edwin. Asst. prof. sociology Harvard, 1965-69; fellow Center for Advanced Study U. Ill., 1969-70; mem. div. edn. and dept. psychiatry Mass. Inst. Tech., Cambridge, 1970-73; researcher, writer Children's Def. Fund of Washington Research Project, 1973—. NIMH fellow, 1962-64, Guggenheim fellow, 1975. Recipient Young Psychologist award Am. Psychol. Assn., 1966. Mem. Am. Sociol. Assn., PEN, Author's Guild, Soc. for Study Social Problems, Mass. Psychol. Assn., Nat. Soc. Lit. and Arts. Author: Time's Children, 1971; The Present of Things Future (with Stephen Klineberg), 1974; The Prospect of Youth, 1972; (with Craig Eisendrath and Laurence Fink), Out of Discontent, 1972; The Abandoners, 1973; The Voices of School, 1973; Perceiving Time, 1976; Black Children, White Dreams, 1974; A Family Album, 1974; Busing, 1976; Barred from School, 1976. Editorial bd. Social Problems, Urban Edn., Sch. Rev. Contbr. articles to profl. publs. Licensed clin. psychologist Mass. Home: 12 Beaconsfield Rd Brookline MA 02146

COTTON, WILLIAM ROBERT, naval officer, research dentist; b. Miami, Fla., Nov. 29, 1931; s. Robert Lee and Mamie Belle (Daniel) C.; student U. Miami, Fla., 1949-51; D.D.S., U. Md., 1955; certificate Naval Dental Sch., Bethesda, Md., 1959-60; M.S., Northwestern U., 1963; M.A., Roosevelt U., 1973; m. Marye Ruth Hartz; 1 dau., Caroline Ruth; children by previous marriage—William Robert, David Michael, Lynn Cathryn. Commd. lt. (j.g.) USN, 1955, advanced through grades to capt., 1972—; head exptl. pathology div., dental research dept. Naval Med. Research Inst., Bethesda, 1963-67; chief histopathology div. Naval Dental Research Inst., Great Lakes, Ill., 1969-76, exec. officer, 1972, dep. comdg. officer, 1973-76; chmn. dept. dental scis. Naval Med. Research Inst., Bethesda, 1976—. Mem., cons. com. on biol. testing of dental materials Commn. on Dental Materials, Instruments, Equipment and Therapeutics, Fedn. Dentaire Internationale and Internat. Standards Orgn.; mem., cons. adv. com., dental lab. technology Sch. Tech. Careers, So. Ill. U.; contbr. permanent exhibits Mus. Sci. and Industry. Field Mus. Natural History (both Chgo.). Recipient certificate of recognition as Outstanding Young Scientist, D.C. area, 1964. Mem. Internat. Assn. for Dental Research, Am. Dental Assn., Am. Assn. Dental Schs., U. Md. Dental Sch. Alumni Assn., Gorgas Odontological Soc., Beta Beta Beta, Alpha Epsilon Delta. Contbg. author: Biology of the Dental Pulp Organ; Art and Science of Dental Caries Research; also numerous articles in profl. jours. Developed tl (toothless) rat, animal model for bone studies, 1974. Home: 105 Summerfield Rd Chevy Chase MD 20015 Office: Naval Med Research Inst Bethesda MD 20014

COTTRELL, JAMES EDWARD, physician; b. Charleston, W.Va., Nov. 9, 1942; s. Guy and Geraldine L. (Burnside) C.; B.S. cum laude, Morris Harvey Coll., 1964; M.D., W.Va. U., 1968; postgrad. Duquesne U., 1968-69. Intern, Allegheny Gen. Hosp., Pitts., 1968-69; resident Mercy Hosp., Pitts., 1969-71, Children's Hosp., Pitts., 1972; respiratory research fellow Mercy Hosp., 1971-72; practice medicine specializing in anesthesiology, Pitts., 1968-72, Phila., 1973-74, N.Y.C., 1974—; asst. attending in anesthesiology Bellevue Hosp. Center, N.Y.C., 1974-77, asso. attending, 1977—, asso. dir. anesthesiology, 1975—; asso. attending in anesthesiology U. Hosp., N.Y.C., 1977—, Manhattan Vets. Hosp., N.Y.C., 1974—; asst. prof. anesthesiology N.Y. U. Sch. Medicine, N.Y.C., 1974-78, asso. prof., 1978—; vis. prof. Temple U., 1977, U. Calif., San Francisco, 1977, Albert Einstein Coll. Medicine, 1977, Mercy Hosp., U. Pitts., 1977, 78, Vanderbilt U., 1978, also U. Tenn.; guest lectr. N.Y. Acad. Medicine, 1978, A.C.S., Am. Assn. Neurol. Surgeons, also anesthesiol. socs. Served with USN, 1972-74. Diplomate Nat. Bd. Med. Examiners, Am. Bd. Anesthesiology (Ir. examiner 1976—). Fellow Am. Coll. Anesthesiologists (examiner 1977, 78), Am. Heart Assn.; mem. N.Y. State Soc. Anesthesiologists (subcom. sci. exhibits 1975—, del. dist. 11 1976), Internat., Eastern (treas.) Regional assns. study of pain, Soc. Neurol. Anesthesia and Neurologic Supportive Care (chmn. edn. com. 1976—, sec.-treas.), Am. Soc. Anesthesiologists (com. subsplty. representation, com. on panels, com. med. student preceptorship), N.Y. State, N.Y. County med. socs., Internat. Anesthesia Research Soc., N.Y. Acad. Medicine, AMA, Assn. Faculty of Nurse Anesthesia Schs., Chi Beta Phi. Author: Anesthesia and Neurosurgery, also monographs, chpts. Contbr. articles on anesthesiology to profl. jours. Home: 11 Fifth Ave New York NY 10003 Office: NY U Sch Medicine 550 First Ave New York NY 10016

COUGHLIN, FRANCIS RAYMOND, JR., surgeon; b. N.Y.C., Feb. 22, 1927; s. Francis Raymond and Isabel (Archibald) C.; B.S., Fordham U., 1948; M.D., Yale, 1952; M.S. (Hosmer Teaching fellow), McGill U., Montreal, Que., Can., 1955, diploma in surgery, 1959; m. Barbara Ann Blunt, June 9, 1951; children—Hilary, Mary, Patricia, Christopher Francis, Geoffrey Blunt, Daniel Taylor, Isabel, David Carleton. Intern, N.Y. Hosp., N.Y.C., 1952-53; resident in surgery McGill U. Teaching Hosp., Montreal, 1953-57; resident in thoracic surgery Overholt Thoracic Clinic, Boston, 1958-60; practice medicine, specializing in thoracic surgery, Stamford, Conn., 1960—; teaching fellow Harvard U., 1958; dir. div. thoracic and vascular surgery Stamford Hosp., 1970-73; dir. thoracic and vascular surgery St. Josephs Hosp., Stamford, 1970-73, asso. chief surgery, 1971-73, chief surgery, 1973-77; mem. staff Norwalk Hosp., Greenwich Hosp. Served with U.S. Maritime Service, 1944-46. Recipient Encaenia award Fordham U., N.Y.C., 1958. Diplomate Am. Bd. Surgery, Am. Bd. Thoracic Surgery. Fellow Royal Coll. Surgeons (Can.), A.C.S. (Conn. sec.-treas. 1966-70), Am. Coll. Cardiology, Am. Coll. Chest Physicians, Royal Soc. Health, Royal Soc. Medicine; mem. Soc. Thoracic Surgeons (founding mem.), N.Y. Acad. Medicine, Conn. Heart Assn. (dir. 1961-64), Conn. Tb Assn. (dir. and exec. com. 1963-69, v.p. 1967-69), Tb Assn. So. Fairfield County (pres. 1963-68, dir. 1960-70), English-Speaking Union, Scottish-Am. Found., Canadian Soc. Republican. Roman Catholic. Club: Stamford Yacht. Home: 40 Rogers Rd Stamford CT 06902 Office: 144 Morgan St Stamford CT 06905

COUGHLIN, R. LAWRENCE, congressman; b. Wilkes-Barre, Pa.; s. R.L. and Evelyn (Wich) C.; A.B., Yale U., 1950; M.B.A., Harvard U., 1954; LL.B., Temple U., 1958; m. Elizabeth Poole Sellers Worrell; children—Lisa, Lynne, Sara, Larry. Admitted to Pa. bar; former partner law firm Saul, Ewing, Remick & Saul, Phila.; former mfg. foreman and asst. to mfg. v.p. Heintz Mfg. Corp.; mem. Pa. Ho. of Reps., 1965-66; mem. Pa. Senate, 1966-68; mem. 91st-96th Congresses from 13th Pa. Dist.; mem. House Appropriations com., fgn. ops., legis. subcoms. Bd. dirs. Easter Seal campaign, Rosemont-Villanova Civic Assn. Mem. devel. council Villanova U. Served to capt., USMCR, 1950-52. Named Outstanding Young Man of 1965, Main Line Jaycees. Mem. Am., Pa., Phila. bar assns., Big Bro. Assn., Friendly Sons of St. Patrick. Republican. Episcopalian. Home: 856 Mount Moro Rd Villanova PA 19085 Office: 306 Cannon House Office Bldg Washington DC 20515*

COUILLARD, JOSEPH WILLIAM, constrn. and realty co. exec.; b. New London, Conn.; s. Joseph and Harriet Catherine (Tyler) C.; grad. high sch.; m. Maria Sterchele, Nov. 27, 1958; children—Joseph V., John W., M. Christina. Sales corr. Arwood Precision Casting Co., Groton, Conn., 1959-67; pres. Joval Enterprises, Inc., East Lyme, Conn., 1967—. Served wtih AUS, 1956-59. Mem. Nat., Conn. home builders assns., Southeastern Conn. Builders Assn. (pres. 1974, dir.), Home Builders Assn. Southeastern Conn. (pres. 1974-75, named Builder of Yr. 1975), Nat. Assn. Realtors. Home: 10 Brookfield Dr East Lyme CT 06333 Office: 126 Boston Post Rd East Lyme CT 06333

COULOUMBIS, THEODORE ALEXANDER, polit. scientist, educator; b. Thessaloniki, Greece, June 14, 1935; s. Alexander T. and Angela A. (Tsafos) C.; came to U.S., 1952, naturalized, 1958; B.A., U. Conn., 1956, M.A., 1958; Ph.D., Am. U., 1964; m. Zoe Papadopoulou, June 2, 1968; children—Alexander T., Angela T. Ops. research analyst U.S. Dept. Navy, Washington, 1960-65; asst. prof. internat. relations Am. U. Washington, 1965-68, asso. prof., 1968-72, prof., 1973—, asso. dean grad. studies, 1968-70. Served with U.S. Army, 1958-60. Mem. Am. Polit. Sci. Assn., Internat. Studies Assn., Modern Greek Studies Assn., Am. Hellenic Inst. (trustee 1974—), Center for Mediterranean Studies (v.p. 1972—), AAUP, Author: Greek Political Reaction to American and NATO Influences, 1966; (with James H. Wolfe) Introduction to Internation Relations: Power and Justice, 1978; (with Sallie M. Hicks) U.S. Foreign Policy Toward Greece and Cyprus, 1975. Contbr. articles to profl. jours., chpts. to books on internat. relations. Contbg. editor Greek World, 1977; fgn. affairs editor USA Today. Home: 6216 Starwood Way Rockville MD 20852 Office: American Washington DC 20016

COULSON, JOHN L., banker; b. Bayonne, N.J., Nov. 21, 1916; s. William H. and Miriam (Guthrie) C.; A.B., Dartmouth, 1939; postgrad. Stonier Grad. Sch. Banking, 1965; m. Mary A. Bill, June 27, 1942; children—Douglas B., Jeffrey L., Dara V. Credit trainee Mfrs. Trust Co., N.Y.C., 1940-42; credit mgr. J. H. Throp & Co., Inc., N.Y.C. 1946-58; v.p. Franklin Nat. Bank, L.I. N.Y., 1958-69; spl. asst. to commr. Bur. Indian Affairs, Dept. Interior, Washington, 1969-70; adminstrv. v.p. Security Nat. Bank L.I., 1970-75; v.p. Chem. Bank, Melville, N.Y., 1975—. Treas., bd. dirs. Bay Hills Property Owners, Inc., 1965-69; v.p. Suffolk County council Boy Scouts Am., 1965-71, chmn. adv. bd., 1975-78, also mem. exec. bd., chmn. nominating com.; mem. profl. advisory com. Huntington Youth Bur.; treas. Village of Huntington Bay, 1977-78. Served to lt. comdr. USNR, 1942-46. Mem. Greater Bay Shore (v.p., dir. 1959-65), Huntington (neighborhood stblzn. com.) chambers commerce, Robert Morris Assn., Dartmouth Alumni Assn. L.I. (pres. 1951-52), New Eng. Soc. N.Y., Suffolk County Grand Jurors Assn., St. Andrews Soc. (former chmn., bd. mgrs., now 2d v.p.), Huntington C. oc C. (dir.), Zeta Psi (past pres., sec., trustee ednl. found. 1965—). Republican. Presbyterian (ruling elder, deacon). Clubs: Bay Shore Rotary (pres. 1963), Dartmouth College (N.Y.C.); Good Fellows; Club at Point O'Woods. Home: 25 Soundview Dr Huntington NY 11743 Office: 31 W Main St Babylon NY 11702

COULSON, LOUIS ANTHONY, orthopedic surgeon; b. Bklyn., Nov. 10, 1921; s. William and Mary (Peters) C.; student St. John's U., Bklyn., 1946-48; M.D., State U. N.Y. Downstate Med. Center, 1952; m. Frances J. Lipp, Apr. 1, 1950; children—Louis F., Susan E., Carolyn F. Intern, Ind. U. Hosp., 1952-53; asst. resdient in gen. surgery Lawrence Hosp., New London, Conn., 1953-54; asst. resident in orthopedic surgery Yale-New Haven Hosp., 1954-55, resident in orthopedic surgery, 1955-56; asst. resident in orthopedic surgery Newington (Conn.) Children's Hosp., 1956, resident in orthopedic surgery, 1957; practice medicine specializing in orthopedic surgery, New London, 1957—; mem. staff Lawrence Meml. Hosp., New London, Newington Children's Hosp.; cons. Seaside Regional Center, Waterford, Conn. Served to 1st lt. inf. U.S. Army, World War II; NATOUSA. Decorated Bronze Star medal, Purple Heart with oak leaf cluster; diplomate. Am. Bd. Surgery, Am. Bd. Orthopaedic Surgery. Fellow Am. Acad. Orthopaedic Surgeons; mem. AMA, Conn. State Med. Soc. (ho. of dels.), Alpha Omega Alpha. Episcopalian. Office: 397 Ocean Ave New London CT 06320

COULSON, MERLE FRANCIS, assn. exec.; b. York Springs, Pa., Oct. 23, 1919; s. George Washington and Alice Grace (Albert) C.; M.Ed., Pa. State U., 1951; m. Grace Ione Kindig, Nov. 27, 1952; children—Gail Joann, Jeffrey Kindig. Tchr., Tyrone Twp., Adams County (Pa.) schs., 1938-44; tchr., prin. Upper Adams schs., Biglerville, Pa., 1944-52; dir. elementary edn. W. Shore Schs., Lemoyne, Pa., 1952-57; county supr. Adams County (Pa.) schs., Gettysburg, 1957-71; sch. adminstr. Lincoln Intermediate Unit, New Oxford, Pa., 1971-76; exec. sec. Pa. Retired Pub. Sch. Employees Assn., Harrisburg, 1976—; mem. research and evaluation teams Pa. Dept. Edn.; dir. S. Central Pa. Ednl. Broadcasting Council. Served with U.S. Army, 1946-47. Recipient Recognition award for Service, Pa. Dept. Edn., 1965; Pa. Future Farmer Honor award for Service to Agr. Edn., 1970. Mem. Am., Pa. assns. sch. adminstrs., NEA, Pa. State Edn. Assn., Pa. Congress Parents and Tchrs. Republican. Lutheran. Clubs: Lions (sec. 1948-50), Gettysburg Adams County Torch (pres. 1971-72), Mason. Home: 130 Rice Ave Biglerville PA 17307 Office: Box 1724 400 N 3d St Harrisburg PA 17105

COULTER, GLENN RICHARD, coating and laminating co. exec.; b. Worcester, Mass., Dec. 18, 1950; s. Richard A. and Carolyn L. (Baylies) C.; B.S. in Chem. Engring., Lowell Tech. Inst., 1972, B.S. in Paper Engring., 1972; m. Dale Brote, June 23, 1973; children—Christopher, Seth. Product engr. Beloit Corp., Dalton, Mass., 1974; quality control mgr. Custom Coating & Laminating Corp., Worcester, 1974-78, product mgr., 1977-78, tech. mgr. plastic and related products, 1977—; tchr. chemistry Lowell (Mass.) High Sch., nights 1970-72. Mem. Soc. Plastic Engrs., Am. Soc. Quality Control, ASTM. Author: Method for Recovery of Copper Foil from Circuit Board Waste Etchant, 1973-74. Home: Boston Rd Sutton MA 01527 Office: 717 Plantation St Worcester MA 01605

COULTER, HOWARD ALTON, banker; b. Williamstown, Mass., Feb. 26, 1927; s. Alton Numan and Wilmetta (Marsh) C.; student Bliss Bus. Coll., 1947-48, Sch. Banking, Williams Coll., 1957-58; m. Camille Elise Chenail, June 26, 1954; children—Scott A., Stuart R., Tracy H. Purchasing agt. Noel, Inc., 1948-52; with Williamstown Nat. Bank, 1953—, pres., 1965—, trust officer, 1966—, also dir.; propr. Taconic Bus. Service, Williamstown, 1954—. Vice chmn. Williamstown Housing Com., 1968-70; dep. sheriff Berkshire County (Mass.), 1963—. Corporator North Adams Regional Hosp., 1966—, trustee, 1968-70; bd. dirs. Williamstown Boys' Club, 1965-72, pres., 1969-70; bd. dirs. Williamstown Community Chest, 1967-73, pres., 1969-71; bd. dirs. Williamstown Taxpayers Assn.; trustee Williams Coll. Sch. Banking, 1971-75. Mem. Williamstown Republican Com., 1968-76; mem. Williamstown Long Range Financial Planning Commn., 1974—; bd. dirs. No. Berkshire Mental Health Assn., 1975—, treas., 1977—; Served with USNR, 1945-47, 52-53. Certified comml. lender; registered pub. accountant. Mem. Berkshire County Clearing House Assn. (past pres.), Berkshire County Safe Deposit Assn. (past pres.), Bank Adminstrn. Inst., Am. Inst. Banking, Williamstown Bd. Trade (past pres.), Am. Legion, V.F.W. Episcopalian. Mason, Rotarian. Club: Williams College Faculty. Home: Stratton Rd Williamstown MA 01267 Office: 57 Spring St Williamstown MA 01267

COULTER, WILLIAM GODDARD, editor, publisher; b. Clinton, Mass., Feb. 12, 1928; s. Craven Houghton and Barbara (Goddard) C.; A.A., Boston U., 1949, B.J., 1951; m. Joyce I. Mallar, Feb. 28, 1954; children—James, Carolyn, Constance, Candace, Christopher, Catherine. Reporter, Quincy (Mass.) Patriot Ledger, 1953-55; editor Clinton Daily Item, 1955—, co-pub., 1969—; prof. journalism Hudson Inst., 1970-74. Vestryman, Sunday sch. tchr., lay reader Episcopal Ch.; pres. Clinton Citizens Council, 1973-75; chmn. Clinton Bicentennial Book Com., editor book, 1977. trustee Clinton Hosp., 1971—. Served with U.S. Army, 1951-53. Mem. Sigma Delta Chi. Clubs: Mason, Rotary (past pres. Clinton). Home: George Hill Rd Lancaster MA 01523 Office: 156 Church St Clinton MA 01510

COULTHARD, ROBERT, psychiatrist; b. County Durham, Eng., Aug. 14, 1935; s. Joseph Walker and Mary (Wells) C.; M.B., Ch.B., U. St. Andrews, Scotland, 1960; m. Margot Johanna Schlenker, Dec. 12, 1962; children—Jacqueline Ann, Rosalind Jane. Intern, Bishop Auckland Gen. Hosp., County Durham, Eng., 1960; intern Dundee (Scotland) Royal Infirmary, 1961, resident, 1964-68; resident Royal Dundee (Scotland) Liff Hosp., 1964-68, sr. registrar, 1967-68; clin. dir. Oakridge, Maximum Security Div., Mental Health Centre, Penetanguishene, Ont., Can., 1968-70; psychiatrist in charge forensic inpatient service Clarke Inst. Psychiatry, Toronto, Ont., Can., 1970-77, chief forensic service, 1977—; asst. prof. dept. psychiatry U. Toronto, 1971—. Diplomate Royal Coll. Physicians and Surgeons Can. Fellow Royal Coll. Physicians Can.; mem. Royal Coll. Psychiatry, Eng., Ont. (chmn. forensic sect. 1974-76), Canadian, Ont. med. assns. Home: 1398 Shadowa Rd Mississauga ON L5H 2N7 Canada Office: 250 College St Toronto ON M5T 1R8 Canada

COUNCILOR, JAMES ALLAN, accountant; b. Washington, Feb. 19, 1914; s. James Allan and Vesta Nora (Crane) C.; A.B., Cornell U., 1935; children—Pamela, James A., III, Suzanne. Jr. accountant Councilor & Buchanan, Washington, 1935-37; jr. partner James A. Councilor & Co., D.C., 1937-45; sr. partner Councilor, Buchanan & Mitchell, Bethesda, Md., 1945—. Bd. dirs. D.C. chpt. ARC; bd. dirs. Met. Police Boys and Girls Club; past pres. Met. Police Boys Club, President's Cup Regatta Assn.; comptroller, Presdl. Inauguration Coms., 1953-73. C.P.A., D.C., Md., Ill., Ariz. Mem. D.C., Am. insts. C.P.A.'s. Episcopalian. Club: Columbia Country. Home: 5420 Audubon Rd Bethesda MD 20014 Office: 7101 Wisconsin Ave Bethesda MD 20014

COUPER, RICHARD WATROUS, library adminstr.; b. Binghamton, N.Y., Dec. 16, 1922; s. Edgar W. and Esther (Watrous) C.; A.B., Hamilton Coll., Clinton, N.Y., 1944, LL.D., 1969; A.M. in Am. History, Harvard, 1948; L.H.D., N.Y. U., 1974; m. Patricia Pogue, Sept. 24, 1946; children—Frederick Pogue, Barrett Williams, Thomas Hayes, Margaret Channing. With Couper-Ackerman-Sampson, Inc., and predecessor, Binghamton, 1948-62; adminstrv. v.p. Hamilton Coll., 1962-65, v.p., 1965-66, acting pres., 1966-68, v.p., provost, 1968-69, charter trustee, 1967—; dep. commr. higher edn. N.Y. State Edn. Dept., 1969-71; pres., chief exec. officer N.Y. Pub. Library, N.Y.C., 1971—; dir. Security Mut. Life Ins. Co., Binghamton. Chmn. Link Found., Fort Pierce, Fla.; trustee Wesleyan U., John Simon Guggenheim Meml. Found., N.Y.C.; bd. dirs. Communities Aid Assn., N.Y.C., 1962—, pres., 1972-77. Served to capt. AUS, 1942-46. Mem. Orgn. Am. Historians, Am., N.Y. State hist. assns., Phi Beta Kappa. Clubs: Harvard, Grolier, Coffee House, Century Assn. (N.Y.C.); Sadaquada Golf, Ft. Schuyler (Utica, N.Y.). Home: 17 Sunset Dr North Chappaqua NY 10514 Office: NY Pub Library Fifth Ave and 42d St New York City NY 10018

COURAGE, ALEXANDER, advt. and pub. relations exec.; b. Kharkow, USSR, Apr. 18, 1938; s. Serhij and Lidia (Kopeicka) Holubnyczyj; came to U.S., 1950, naturalized, 1957; student N.Y. U., 1958-60; children—Lena, Nadia. Newspaper promotion writer L.I. Press, Jamaica, N.Y., 1960-62; copywriter Ysalbel Sandler Advt., N.Y.C., 1962-64; account exec. Richmond Advt. Service, N.Y.C., 1964-65; account supr. Aladdin Advt. Agy., N.Y.C., 1965-70; pres. Alexander Holub Advt. Agy., N.Y.C., 1970-74; advt. dir. Exposition Press, Inc., Hicksville, N.Y., 1974-76; pres. Alexander Courage Assos./Duma Advt. Agy., Massapequa, N.Y. Recipient profl. soccer awards. Office: 25 E Chestnut St Massapeque NY 11758

COURCHAINE, ARMAND JOSEPH, clin. chemist; b. Swansea, Mass., Mar. 27, 1913; s. Euclide and Elizabeth (Martin) C.; B.S. in Chemistry and Biology, Providence Coll., 1937; m. Sue Stevenson, Oct. 9, 1939; children—Joan, Dorothy, Kathryn, Suzanne, Jean, Mary. Sci. instr. Hahnemann Hosp. Nursing Sch., Phila., 1942-53; instr. in biol. chemistry Hahnemann Med. Coll., 1947-52; clin. chemist The Adams Lab., Phila., 1953-56; lab. supr. and biochemist Phila. Gen. Hosp., 1956-58; clin. chemistry supr. Fitzgerald Mercy Hosp., Darby, Pa., 1957-65; chmn, sci. div. Harcum Jr. Coll., Bryn Mawr, Pa., 1965-68; clin. chemist Sacred Heart Hosp., Chester, Pa., 1968-78. Served with U.S. Army, 1937-38. Nat. registry accredited chemist. Fellow AAAS; mem. Am. Chem. Soc. Am. Assn. Clin. Chemists. Roman Catholic. Author: Chemistry Visualized and Applied, 1956; Basic Human Biochemistry, 1963; Dynamic Aspects of Marriage, 1967. Home: 365 Hutchinson Terr Holmes PA 19043

COURNAND, ANDRE F., physiologist; b. Paris, France, Sept. 24, 1895; s. Jules and Marguerite (Weber) C.; B.A., Sorbonne U., Paris, 1913, P.C.B. in Sci., 1914; M.D., U. Paris, 1930; Dr. h.c., U. Strasbourg, 1957, U. Lyon, 1958, U. Brussels, 1959, U. Pisa, 1960, Columbia U., 1965, U. Brazil, 1965, U. Nancy, 1969; D.Sc., U. Birmingham, 1961, Gustavus Adolphus Coll., 1963; m. Sibylle Blumer (dec. 1959); children—Muriel, Marie-Eve, Marie Claire; m. 2d, Ruth Fabian, 1963 (dec. 1973); m. 3d, Beatrice Bishop Berle, 1975. Came to U.S., 1930, naturalized 1941. Prof. emeritus medicine Coll. Phys. & Surg., Columbia. Served with French Army, 1915-19. Decorated Croix de Guerre (France); recipient Laureate (silver medal), faculty medicine U.Paris; Andrea Retzius, silver medal-Swedish Soc. Internal Medicine; Lasker award USPHS; winner (with Dr. Dickinson W. Richards and Dr. Werner Forssman) of 1956 Nobel Prize in medicine and physiology; recipient Jiminez Diaz prize, 1970. Fellow Royal Soc. Medicine; mem. Nat. Acad. Scis. U.S.A., de l'Academic Nationale de Medecine (fgn.) (France), Academie Royal de Medecine de Belgique, Am. Physiol. Soc., Assn. Am. Physicians, Brit. Cardiac Soc., Swedish Soc. Internal Medicine, Soc. Medicale Hopitaux de Paris, Academie des Sciences, Institut de France (fgn. mem.). Clubs: Century Assn., Am. Alpine. Home: 1361 Madison Ave New York City NY 10028

COURNIOTES, HARRY JAMES, coll. pres.; b. Chicopee Falls, Mass., Aug. 13, 1921; s. James Harry and Chrisanthe (Gardekas) C.; B.S., Boston U., 1942; Indsl. Adminstr. with high distinction, Harvard, 1943, M.B.A. with high distinction, 1947; D.C.S., Western New Eng. Coll., 1976; m. Annette R. Giguere, Sept. 4, 1945; children—James H., Gregory H. Asst. prof. Am. Internat. Coll., Springfield, Mass., 1946-52, asso. prof., 1952-58, prof., 1958-69, dean Sch. Bus Adminstrn., 1960-69, v.p., 1964-69, pres., 1969—; vice chmn. bd., dir. Life Style Cos., Inc., 1969-76. Trustee Springfield Inst. Savs. Mem. exec. com. Springfield Adult Edn. Council, 1972-74; corporator Springfield Girls Club, 1970, Springfield Boys Club, 1972—; mem. adv. bd. World Affairs Council, 1970; com. mem. United Negro Coll. Fund, 1971; mem. exec. com., bd. dirs. Jr. Achievement Western Mass., 1975—; bd. dirs. Springfield Central Bus. Dist., 1976—; corporator Wing Meml. Hosp., 1976—; hon. sponsor Laughing Brook project Mass. Audubon Soc. Trustee Econ. Edn. Council Mass., 1971—. Served to lt. AUS, 1943-46. C.P.A., Mass. Mem. Am. Inst. C.P.A.'s, Greater Springfield C. of C. (dir. 1974-77), Financial Exec. Inst. (chmn. edn. com. 1964-65), Assn. Ind. Colls. and Univs. Mass. (mem. exec. com. 1972-74), Mass. Soc. C.P.A.'s. Clubs: Colony (Springfield); Quaboag Country (Monson, Mass.); University (N.Y.C.). Home: Cote Rd Monson MA 01057 Office: 170 Wilbraham Rd Springfield MA 01109

COURSEN, CHRISTOPHER DENNISON, lawyer; b. Mpls., Dec. 6, 1948; s. Richard Dennison and Helen Wilson (Stevens) C.; B.A., Washington and Lee U., 1970; J.D., George Washington U., 1975; m. Pamela Elizabeth Lynch, June 3, 1978. Admitted to D.C. bar, 1975; legal adviser Met. Police Dept., Washington, 1971-75; individual practice law, Washington, 1975-76; atty. Marmet Profl. Corp., Washington, 1976; asso. firm Bilger & Blair, Washington, 1977—; asso. atty. firm Dempsey and Koplovitz, 1978—. Mem. Am., Fed. Communications bar assns., Bar Assn. D.C., Phi Kappa Psi (pres. 1970). Roman Catholic. Club: Chevy Chase (Md.). Home: 4801 Leland St Chevy Chase MD 20015 Office: 938 Bowen Bldg NW Washington DC 20005

COURSON, ROBERT WYLIE, II, labor relations exec.; b. Washington, Pa., Aug. 24, 1946; s. Robert Wylie and Helen Marie (Vandever) C.; B.A., Coll. Wooster, 1968; postgrad. U, Akron, 1969-72; m. Elizabeth Lou Menhart, July 30, 1966; children—Kelle Lyne, Robert Wylie. Supervisory trainee Timken Co., Canton, Ohio, 1968-69, indsl. relations rep., 1969-70; labor relations rep. Sharon (Pa.) Steel Corp., 1970-72, sr. labor relations rep., 1972-73, supr. personnel and labor relations, 1973; mgr. labor relations Calgon Corp., Pitts., 1973—. Active Big Bros. of Pitts., 1974—. Mem. Jr. C. of C., Am. Soc. for Personnel Adminstrn., Am. Arbitration Assn., Am. Mgmt. Assn. Home: 5807 Southampton Dr Bethel Park PA 15102 Office: PO Box 1346 Pittsburgh PA 15230

COURT, CARL ROGER, hosp. exec.; b. Narragansett, R.I., Oct. 22, 1939; s. Adelino Manuel and Virginia E. (Hazard) C.; ed. Culinary Inst. Am. Asst. to chef Squantum Club, Riverside, R.I., 1972-74; food service cons. Camp War Bonnet for Boys, Cannon, N.H., 1970-74; dir. food service Blakie, Miller and Hines, Stamford, Conn., 1967-70, Marriott Corp., Washington, 1975-77; dir. food service Emma P. Bradley Hosp., Riverside, 1967—; vol. Culinary Arts Program for Emotionally Disturbed Children. Mem. R.I. Hosp. Group Purchasing Assn. (chmn.-elect. 1978—), R.I. Chefs Assn. (pres. 1971-73). Club: Masons. Home: 4 Elliott Pl Newport RI 02840 Office: 1011 Veterans Meml Pkwy Riverside RI 02914

COURTER, JAMES A(NDREW), congressman; b. Montclair, N.J., Oct. 14, 1941; s. Joseph A. and Madeleine (Janis) C.; B.A., Colgate U., 1963; J.D., Duke U., 1966; m. Carmen McCalmen, Dec. 5, 1970; children—Donica, Katrina. Admitted to D.C. bar, 1966, N.J. bar, 1971; with U.S. Peace Corps, Venezuela, 1967-69; asst. corp. counsel City of Washington, 1969-70; atty. Union County (N.J.) Legal Services, 1970-71; first asst. pros. atty. Warren County (N.J.), 1973-77; mem. 96th Congress from N.J. 13th Dist.; bd. dirs. Warren County Legal Services. Mem. civic adv. bd. Hackettstown (N.J.) Community Hosp. Mem. Nat. Dist. Attys. Assn., County Prosecutors Assn. N.J., Asst. Prosecutors Assn. N.J., Trial Attys. N.J., N.J. Inst. Mcpl. Attys., Am. Bar Assn., N.J. Bar Assn., Warren County Bar Assn., D.C. Bar Assn. Republican. Methodist. Club: Rotary (pres. local club 1975-76) (Hackettstown). Home: 19 Reese Ave Hackettstown NJ 07840 Office: 325 Cannon House Office Bldg Washington DC 20515

COURTISS, EUGENE HOWARD, surgeon; b. Boston, Jan. 18, 1930; s. Morris and Rosa (Grace) C.; A.B., Columbia U., 1951; M.D., Boston U., 1955; m. Barbara Faith Block June 9, 1957; children—Gary Block, Linda Sue. Intern, U. Minn. Hosps., Mpls., 1955-56; resident Peter Bent Brigham Hosp., Boston, 1956-57, Christ Hosp., Cin., 1961-63; practice medicine specializing in plastic surgery, Boston, 1963—; mem. staff Newton-Wellesley Hosp., chief div. plastic surgery; mem. Waltham, Boston City, Univ., Leonard-Morse, Falmouth, Glover Meml. hosps.; asso. clin. prof. surgery Boston U., 1970—; lectr. Dir. Mass. Repertory Co., Boston, 1977-78. Served as capt. U.S. Army, 1957-60. Diplomate Am. Bd. Surgery. Fellow A.C.S.; mem. Am. (dir. 1977-78, program com. 1974-75), New Eng. socs. plastic and reconstructive surgeons, Plastic Surgery Coordinating Council, Am. Soc. Aesthetic Plastic Surgery (pres. 1977-78), Mass. Soc. Plastic Surgery (pres. 1977), Mass. Med. Soc., Am. Cleft Palate Assn., Am. Geriatrics Soc. Republican. Contbr. articles in field to med. jours.; editor Aesthetic Surgery Trouble: How to Avoid It and How to Treat It, 1978. Office: 2000 Washington St Newton Lower Falls MA 02167

COURTNEY, IRWIN GREENE, II, police ofcl.; b. Balt., Jan. 31, 1941; s. Irwin Gover and Lucy Virginia (McCormick) C.; ed. high sch.; m. Barbara Ann Mills, Oct. 1, 1967; 1 dau., Susan Louise. City carrier U.S. Postal Service, Annapolis, Md., 1960-69, rural carrier, 1969-71; So. Md. sec. Letter Carriers Rural Nat. Assn., 1970-71; with police marine div. Md. Natural Resources Dept., Annapolis, 1971—, cpl., 1974—; lectr. in field; instr. small boat nav. and piloting. Mem. USCG Res. Mem. U.S. Naval Inst. (asso.), Fraternal Order Police, U.S. Power Squadron (chmn. local bd. advanced grades, chmn. jr. nav. Annapolis squadron 1975—). Home: 992 Hillendale Dr Annapolis MD 21401 Office: Md Natural Resources Dept Police Marine Div Tawes State Office Bldg Annapolis MD 21401

COURTOIS, EDMOND JACQUES, lawyer, business exec.; b. Montreal, Que., Can., July 4, 1920; s. Edmond and Cleophee (Lefebvre) C.; B.A., Coll. de Montreal, 1940; LL.B., Université de Montreal, 1943; m. Joan Miller, Oct. 23, 1943; children—Nicole, Jacques, Marc. Admitted to Que. bar, 1946, created Queen's Counsel, 1963; asso. firm Courtois, Clarkson, Parsons & Tétrault, Montreal, 1946-53, partner, 1953—; chmn. bd., dir. Gaz Metropolitain, inc. Gaz du Que., inc., United N.Am. Holdings Ltd.; pres., dir. Canadian Internat. Investment Trust Ltd., Elican Devel. Co. Ltd., Club de Hockey Canadien, Inc., La Compagnie Foncière du Man. (1967), Limitee; dir. Carena-Bancorp Inc., Eaton Bay Dividend Fund Ltd.; Can.; v.p., dir. Bank N.S.; dir. Can. Life Assurance Co.; vice-chmn. bd. Trizec Corp. Ltd.; dir. BRINCO Ltd., CAE Industries Ltd., Phoenix Steel Corp., Ritz-Carlton Hotel Co. of Montreal Ltd., McGraw-Hill Ryerson Ltd., Norcen Energy Resources Ltd., Rolland Paper Co., Ltd., Que. Iron and Titanium Corp., Eaton Commonwealth Fund Ltd., Eaton Growth Fund Ltd., Eaton/Bay Income Fund, Eaton Internat. Fund Ltd., Eaton Leverage Fund Ltd., Eaton Venture Fund Ltd., Eaton/Bay Viking Fund Ltd., Abitibi Asbestos Mining Co. Ltd. Bd. dirs. Montreal Symphony Orch. Served to lt. Royal Canadian Navy, 1943-45. Mem. Bar Montreal, Bar Province Que. Canadian Bar Assn. Clubs: Mt. Royal, St.-Denis, St. James's (Montreal); York (Toronto); Mt. Bruno (Que.) Country; Forest and Stream (Dorval, Que.). Office: 630 Dorchester Blvd W Montreal PQ H3B 1V7 Canada

COUSIN, DOROTHY MAE, fin. exec.; b. Clinton, N.C., May 22, 1932; d. George Edward and Maggie (Boone) C.; student Va. State Coll., 1952; B.S. Fordham U., 1976; children—Wanda Williamson, Beverly Plaskett. Data processing machine operator N.C. Mutual Life Ins. Co., Durham, 1952-62; supr. data processing dept. Coward Shoe Store, N.Y.C., 1962-69; fin. dir. Opportunities Industrialization Center of N.Y., N.Y.C., 1969—; propr. Dean's Florist Shop, Bronx, 1973—. Bd. dirs. Black Theology Project of Theology in the Ams. Recipient Recognition award Opportunities Industrialization Center, 1972. Mem. Boston Rd. Mchts. Assn. Democrat. Baptist. Clubs: Missionary Circle, Pastor Study. Home: 145 Lindbergh Blvd Teaneck NJ 07666 Office: 460 Park Ave S New York City NY 10016

COUSINS, KATHRYN LAFLER, govt. agency exec.; b. Los Angeles, May 22, 1944; d. Silas Edward and Hazel Irene (Andersen) Lafler; B.A. cum laude, U. Calif., Los Angeles, 1966; M.A., George Washington U., 1972; m. James Cousins, June 11, 1965 (div. 1977). Urban planner Orange County, Calif., 1966-70; regional planner So. Calif. Assn. Govts., Los Angeles, 1970-71; urban planner U.S. Dept. Transp., Washington, 1971; urban planner EPA, Washington, 1971-72; environ. and urban planner Hwy. Users Fedn. for Safety and Mobility, Washington, 1972-75; N. Atlantic regional mgr. Office of Coastal Zone Mgmt., U.S. Dept. Commerce, Washington, 1975—; lectr. in field. Recipient Resolution of Commendation, Orange County Bd. Suprs., 1969; Nat. Assn. Regional Councils Publs. award, 1973. Mem. Am. Inst. Planners (bd. govs. 1974-77, past v.p. D.C. chpt.), Am. Soc Planning Ofcls., Am. Soc. Pub. Adminstrn., Columbia Hist. Soc., Georgetown Citizens Assn. Contbr. articles in field to profl. jours. Home: 3017 Dent Pl NW Washington DC 20007 Office: 3300 Whitehaven St NW US Dept Commerce Washington DC 20235

COUSINS, NORMAN, editor; b. Union Hill, N.J., June 24, 1915; s. Samuel and Sara (Miller) C.; student Columbia U., 1936; Litt.D., Am. U., 1948; L.H.D., Boston U., Colby Coll., 1953, Denison U., 1954, Colgate U., 1958; Litt.D., Elmira Coll., Ripon Coll., Wilmington Coll., 1957, U. Vt., 1957, Newark State Coll., 1958; LL.D., Washington and Jefferson Coll., 1956, Syracuse U., 1956. Albright Coll., 1957, U. R.I., 1965; Ed.D., R.I. Coll. Edn., 1958; Litt.D., Western Mich. State U., Ripon Coll. U. Bridgeport (Conn.); m. Ellen Kopf, June 23, 1939; children—Andrea, Amy Loveman, Candis Hitzig, Sara Kit. Ednl. writer N.Y. Post, 1934-35; lit. editor, mng. editor Current History mag., 1935-40; exec. editor Saturday Rev., 1940-42, editor, 1942-71, 75—; editor World Mag., 1972-73; editor Saturday Rev./World, 1973-74; dir. Saturday Rev./World Inc. Chmn. bd. dirs. Nat. Ednl. TV, 1969-70; chmn. Nat. Programming Council for Pub. TV, 1970—. Editor U.S.A., mem. editorial bd. Overseas bur. O.W.I., World War II; U.S. Govt. lectr. (Smith Mundt) in India, Pakistan, Ceylon, 1951; Japan-Am. Exchange lectr., Japan, 1953. Chmn., Conn. Fact Finding Commn. on Edn., 1948-52; co-chmn. Citizens' Com. for Nuclear Test Ban Treaty; mem. Commn. to Study Orgn. Peace; hon. pres. United World Federalists; chmn. Com. Culture and Intellectual Exchange, Internat. Cooperation Year, 1965, Mayor's Task Force Air Pollution, N.Y.C., 1966—. Mem. Hiroshima Peace Center Assos.; trustee Charles F. Kettering Found., Tchrs. Coll. Columbia; bd. dirs. Samuel H. Kress Found., Ednl. Broadcasting Corp. Recipient Thomas Jefferson award for Advancement of Democracy in Journalism, 1948; Tuition Plan award for outstanding service to Am. Edn., 1951; Benjamin Franklin citation in mag. journalism, 1956; Wayne U. award for nat. service to edn., 1956; Lane Bryant citation for pub. service, 1958; John Dewey award for service to edn., 1958; N.Y. State Citizens Edn. Commn. award, 1959; Publius award N.Y. met. com. United World Federalists, 1964; Eleanor Roosevelt Peace award, 1963; Overseas Press Club award, 1965; Distinguished Citizen award Conn. Bar Assn., 1965; N.Y. Acad. Pub. Edn. award, 1966; Family of Man award, 1968; Aquinas Coll. Ann. award, 1968; nat. mag. award Assn. Deans Journalism Schs., 1969; Peace medal UN, 1971; Carr Van Anda award for contbns. to journalism Ohio U., 1971; Gold medal for lit. Nat. Arts Club, 1972; Journalism Honor award U. Mo., 1972; Irita Van Doren Book award, 1972. Mem. World Assn. World Federalists (pres.), P.E.N., UN Assn. (dir. U.S.), Council Fgn. Relations. Clubs: Coffee House, Nat. Press, Overseas Press; Century. Author: The Good Inheritance; The Democratic Chance, 1942; Modern Man Is Obsolete, 1945; Talks with Nehru, 1951; Who Speaks for Man? 1952; In God We Trust; The Religious Beliefs of the Founding Fathers, 1958; editor: A Treasury of Democreacy, 1941; (with William Rose Benét) and Anthology of the Poetry of Freedom, 1943; Writing for Love or Money, 1949; Doctor Schweitzer of Lambarene, 1960; In Place of Folly, 1961; Present Tense, 1967; The Improbable Triumvirate, 1972; Treasury of Democracy, The Poetry of Freedom, Great American Essays. Editorial supr. March's Dictionary-Thesaurus, 1958. Home: Silvermine Rd New Canaan CT 06840 Office: 488 Madison Ave New York City NY 10022*

COUSINS, RUTH H(UBBARD), assn. exec.; b. Walaska, Ga.; d. Charles T. and Mary Frances (Boston) Hubbard; student Duke U., 1952-53; A.B., George Washington U., 1958, M.A., 1963; postgrad. Am. U., 1965-67; m. James Franklin Cousins, Mar. 1, 1941 (dec. Sept. 1959); children—Carol Ruth Cousins Tracy, Joan Hubbard. Exec. dir. Psi Chi, nat. honor soc. in psychology, Washington, 1958—, editor Psi Chi Newsletter, quar., 1958—, mem. nat. council, 1958—. Licensed psychologist, D.C. Mem. Am., Eastern, D.C. psychol. assns., Am., Washington (dir. 1973-76) socs. assn. execs., Assn. Coll. Honor Socs. (nat. council 1963—), Nat. Press Club Psi Chi, Phi Delta Gamma. Home: 4620 N Park Ave Chevy Chase MD 20015 Office: 1200 17th St NW Washington DC 20036

COUTINHO, JOHN DE S., aero. and mech. engr.; b. Lisbon, Portugal, Aug. 9, 1913; s. Joaquim de S. and Louise (Valet) C.; came to U.S., 1917, naturalized, 1921; M.Aero. Engring., N.Y. U., 1941; Dr.-Ingenieur, Berlin Tech. U., 1970; m. Eleanor Burkarth, Sept. 12, 1942; children—Roy, Alan. With Grumman Aerospace Corp., Bethpage, N.Y., 1939-72, chief reliability control dept., 1958-62, reliability dir. Lunar Module of Apollo, 1962-66, spl. asst. to v.p.-program dir. Lunar Module, 1966-72; chief engring. br. U.S. Army Materiel Systems Analysis Activity, Aberdeen Proving Ground, Md., 1972—; instr., adj. prof. Poly. Inst. N.Y., 1951-61; mem. U.S. Naval Air Systems Effectiveness Adv. Bd., 1958-70; cons. NASA Kennedy Space Center (Fla.), 1970; chmn. Nat. Reliability and Maintenance Confs., 1963, 64, 65, Nat. Transp. Symposium, 1967. Recipient U.S. Navy Rear Adm. Coates award, 1962; N.Y. Acad. Scis. Laskowitz gold medal, 1964; U.S. Naval Air Systems Command Outstanding Service award, 1973; spl. recognition award Am. Inst. Plant Engrs., 1978; registered profl. engr., N.Y., D.C., Md., Fla. Fellow ASME, Am. Soc. Quality Control (Brumbaugh award 1972), N.Y. Acad. Scis. Roman Catholic. Clubs: Cosmos (Washington); Elks (Havre de Grace, Md.). Author: Advanced Systems Development Management, 1977; contbr. articles to profl. jours. Home: 602 Westgate Rd Aberdeen MD 21001 Office: AMSAA DRXSY LM Aberdeen Proving Ground MD 21005

COUTURE, JEAN GUY, bishop; b. Quebec, Que., Can., May 6, 1929; s. Odilon and Eva (Drolet) C.; B.A., Laval U., 1949, B.Ph., 1949, L.Theol., 1953, L.Sc.Phys., 1959. Ordained priest; tchr. math. and sci. St. George Sem., 1953-64, adminstr., 1961-68; adminstr. security plan for Quebec diocesan priests, 1969-75; dir. adminstrv. services Diocese of Quebec, 1973-75; bishop Diocese of Hauterive, Que., 1975—. Home: 468 Pie XII Hauterive PQ G5C 2S8 Canada Office: 639 De Bretagne Hauterive PQ G5C 2S8 Canada

COUTURE, STANISLAS HUBERT, art material dealer; b. St. Jean, Que., Can., Apr. 23, 1931; s. Adrien Eximer and Gertrude Marie (Cote) C.; student Montreal (Que.) Tech., 1950; grad. Institut des Arts Appliques, Montreal, 1954; m. Pierrette G. Poirier, June 28, 1958; children—Diane, Pierre. Interior designer G. Champoux Ltee, Montreal, 1954-55; display designer John Young Designers, Montreal, 1955-56; interior designer Audet-Tremblay-Poulin, Sherbrooke, Que., 1956-71; owner Arthob Distbrs., St. Jean, Que., 1971—, Art and Hobby Registered, St. Jean, 1971—; art material dealer, 1971—. Mem. Nat. Art Materials Trade Assn. Home: 248 Gouin St Jean PQ J3B 3C6 Canada Office: 250 St Jacques St Jean PQ J3B 2K9 Canada

COVAL, NAOMI MILLER, dentist; b. Bayonne, N.J.; d. Jacob Paul and Bertha Miller; student U. Chgo., 1933-36; B.S., N.Y.U., 1939; D.D.S. Columbia, 1943; children—Ilya, Payson, Mark Lawrence. Practice dentistry, specializing in temporomandibular joint dysfunctions, practice ltd. to orthodontics, Lawrence, L.I., N.Y., 1943—. Instr. postgrad. courses for local, nat., internat. dental soc. extension groups; instr. N.Y. Dental Sch.; lectr., U.S. and fgn. countries; staff Peninsula General Hospital; attending dentist N.Y. Infirmary. Chmn., Nassau County for Flouridation, L.I. Fluoridation Com., 1960; del. Oral Hygiene Com. N.Y. Past pres. 5Towns Aux. Peninsula Gen. Hosp.; patron, sponsor Island Concert Hall; active Hull House, Girl Scouts; pres. Lawrence High Sch., P.T.A.; mem. bd. Am. Cancer Soc. Scholar, Art Inst.; v.p. sisterhood Temple Israel, Lawrence; lectr. on travel and flower arranging. Recipient award William Jarvie Soc. Dental Research, 1942. Fellow Soc. Oral Physiology and Occlusion, Royal Soc. Health; mem. Am. Dental Assn., 10th Dist. Dental Soc., Am. Assn. Dental Editors, Columbia Dental Alumni Assn. (exec. bd.), N.Y. State Assn. Professions, Soc. Oral Physiology and Occulsion, Am. Soc. for Study Orthodontics, William Jarvie Soc. for Dental Research, Fedn. Dentaire Internat. Brit. Soc. for Orthodontics, Pan-Am. Med. Assn., Acad. Dental Medicine, Assn. Women Dentists (editor-in-chief bull., v.p., dir. postgrad. courses), Internat. Acad. Orthodontics (editor jour., v.p. Eastern sect., sec.), Fedn. Orthodontic Socs., Rockaway Dental Soc., Nat. Council Jewish Women, Am. Jewish Congress (mem. bd., pres. Five Towns chpt.), Fedn. Am. Orthodontists, AAAS, Am. Assn. Study Psychoanalysis, Am. Acad. Oral Medicine, Am. Soc. Preventive Dentistry, UN Assn., Met. Opera Guild, Nat. Geog. Soc., Am. Mus. Natural History, Internat. Platform Assn. (charter), Am. Red Mogen David Assn., Rapa Nui Soc. for Easter Islands, Fellowship of Reconciliation, Nat. Women's Polit. Caucus (charter dir., v.p. chpt.), NOW, Assn. Women in Sci., Atrium (charter), Common Cause, Pulse of Women (v.p.), Wildlife Soc. Kenya. Mem. B'nai B'rith (v.p.). Clubs: Wayfarers; Nat. Travel. Editor Internat. Jour. Orthodontics. Research and numerous publs. on thyroidectimized rats to determine tooth growth; developed original technique for repositioning mandible. Mem. numerous pvt. anthrop. expdns.; designer and exhibitor gold jewelry; sculptor in bronze and marble; lectr. on aborigines of all continents. Address: 30 Westover Pl Lawrence NY 11559

COVATTA, NICHOLAS JOSEPH, JR., oil co. exec.; b. Troy, N.Y., Sept. 4, 1946; s. Nicholas J. and Lillian C. (Graziade) C.; B.S., Mass. Inst. Tech., 1968; M.B.A., Harvard, 1972. Chmn. bd. dirs., co-founder Logitron, Inc., Cambridge, Mass., 1968-70; exec. v.p., gen. mgr. Bendix Interactive Terminals Corp., Southfield, Mass., 1970-71; cons. Boston Cons. Corp., Inc., 1972-75; v.p. Gulf Oil Corp., Pitts., 1975—. Office: Gulf Bldg Pittsburgh PA 15230

COVI, LINO, psychiatrist; b. Trento, Italy, Mar. 19, 1926; s. Giuseppe and Giuseppina (Mariotti) C.; student in philosophy U. Florence (Italy), 1945-47, Sch. Social Work Trento and Rome, 1949-51; M.D., U. Rome, 1955; m. Beverly A. Yeutsy, Dec. 30, 1958; children—Lisa Martina, Michelle Peppina, Gina Albina, Tina Maria. Came to U.S., 1956, naturalized, 1965. Asst., U. Rome Neuropsychiat. Clinic, 1955-56; intern Albert Einstein Med. Center, Phila., 1956-57; resident fellow psychiatry Johns Hopkins Hosp., 1957-60, dir. outpatient clin. research unit, 1968—; instr. psychiatry Johns Hopkins U., 1960-67, asst. prof., 1967-72, asso. prof., 1972—; vis. psychiatrist Balt. City Hosp., 1960—; staff psychiatrist Patuxent Instn., Jessup, Md., 1960-62; chief out-patient-dept. Gundry Hosp., Balt., 1962—, pres. bd. dirs., 1972—, research dir., 1973—; mem. bd. govs. Central Md. Health Systems Agy., 1978—; research psychiatrist NIMH Collaborative Studies, 1962-64, co-prin. investigator, 1964-65, prin. investigator, 1965—; profl. staff drug evaluation Council on Drugs, AMA, 1968-71; teaching asso. Sheppard and E. Pratt Hosp., 1973—; cons. Pharm. Research Labs., 1971—. Mem. Soc. Neurosci., Am. Assn. Psychoanalytic Physicians, Am. Coll. Neuropsychopharmacology, Md. Psychiat. Soc. (com. mem.), Am. Psychiat. Assn. (editor dist. newsletter, mem. nat. com., dep. rep. Md.), Am. Psychosomatic Soc., AAAS, World Fedn. Mental Health, Johns Hopkins Med. Soc., Am. Group Psychotherapy Assn., N.Y. Acad. Scis., AMA, Md., Balt. (mem. coms.) med. socs., Collegium Internat. Neuropsychopharmacologicum, Italian-Am. Hist. Assn. Democrat. Roman Catholic. Contbr. articles to profl. jours. Home: 502 N Chapelgate Lane Baltimore MD 21229 Office: Johns Hopkins Hosp Baltimore MD 21205 also 2 N Wickham Rd Baltimore MD 21229

COVINGTON, ARTHUR EDWIN, astronomer; b. Regina, Sask., Can., Sept. 21, 1913; s. Joseph Arthur and Isabella (Welch) C.; B.A. in Math. and Physics, U. B.C., Vancouver, 1938, M.A. in Physics, 1940; postgrad. U. Calif. at Berkeley, 1940-42; m. Charlotte Anne Riche, May 23, 1942; children—Nancy Isabel, Eric Donald, Alan Riche, Janet Grace. Lab. asst. cyclotron lab. U. Calif. at Berkeley, 1941-42; jr. research officer radar, Radio br. NRC, Ottawa, Ont., Can., 1942-46, jr. research officer radio astronomy Radio and Elec. Engring. div., 1948-70, sr. research officer Astrophysics br., 1970—. Trustee Riche-Covington Endowment, Queen's U., Kingston, Ont. Mem. Royal Astron. Soc. Can., I.E.E.E., Am., Canadian astron. socs., History Sci. Soc., A.A.A.S., Union Radio Sci. Internat., Internat. Astron. Union. Pioneer in application of radar techniques for observing 2800 megahertz solar radio emissions, developer of compound interferometer to examine details on sun. Home: 269 Pleasant Park Rd Ottawa ON K1H 5M7 Canada Office: Herzberg Inst Astrophysics Nat Research Council Ottawa ON K1A 0R8 Canada

COVINO, BENJAMIN GENE, pharm. co. exec.; b. Lawrence, Mass., Sept. 12, 1930; s. Nicholas and Mary (Zannini) C.; A.B., Holy Cross Coll, 1951; M.S., Boston Coll. Grad. Sch., 1953; Ph.D. (Life Ins. fellow), Boston U. Grad. Sch., 1955; M.D., U. Buffalo Sch. Medicine, 1962; m. Lorraine Gallagher, Aug. 22, 1953; children—Paul, Brian. Teaching fellow Boston U., 1954-55; asst. prof. pharm. Tufts U. Sch. Med., Boston, 1957-59; asst. prof. physiology U. Buffalo Sch. Med., 1959-62; med. dir. Astra Pharm. Products, Worcester, 1962-66, v.p. sci. affairs, 1967—; prof. anesthesiology U. Mass. Med. Sch., 1976—; cons. physiologist St. Vincent's Hosp., Worcester, 1963—. Bd. dirs. St. Vincent's Research Found.; trustee Assumption Coll., Worcester, Mass. Served to 1st lt. USAF, 1955-57. Mem. Am. Physiol. Soc., Am. Heart Assn., Am. Fedn. Clin. Research, Am. Soc. Pharmacology and Exptl. Therapeutics, Am. Soc. Anesthesiology, Alpha Omega Alpha. Contbr. articles to profl. jours. Home: 171 Maple Ave Shrewsbury MA 01545 Office: 7 Neponset St Worcester MA 01606

COWAN, DANIEL ALEXANDER, legal service co. exec.; b. Albany, N.Y., Sept. 11, 1929; s. David Joseph and Ellery Elizabeth (Hawkins) C.; B.S. in Bus., Russell Sage, 1961; children—David, Deborah, Denise, Donna. Asst. mgr. Household Fin., Albany, 1952-55; credit mgr. Montgomery Wards, Albany, 1956-60; founder The Attorney's Service Center (now Alexander Poole & Co., Inc.), Albany, 1960, pres., 1969—; pres. Infosearch, Inc., Albany, N.Y., 1964—. Served with U.S. Army, 1949-52. Decorated Purple Heart. Mem. Internat. Assn. Printing House Craftsmen, Pub. Records Research Assn., Credit Mgmt. Assn. Eastern N.Y. Conservative Republican. Jewish. Office: 170 Washington Ave Albany NY 12210

COWAN, MILTON HOWARD, county agent, educator; b. Talladega, Ala., Feb. 15, 1917; s. Leon and Jennie C.; B.S., Clemson A. and M. Coll., 1936; M.S., Rutgers U., Coll. of Agr., 1946; m. Marie Ina Mackay, June 30, 1950; children—Glenn Allen, Barbara Ann, David Howard. Asst. prof. agr. Rutgers U., 1945-50, asso. prof., 1950-52, prof., 1962, sr. county agent, Extension Service, Cook Coll., 1962—; chmn. Milltown Shade Tree Commn.; mem. Search Com., Dean Cook Coll.; mem. Appointments and Promotions Com., Coll. of Agr. and Environmental Sci.; Com. on Review, Cook Coll.; State Potato Council; past pres. Middlesex County Economics Opportunity. Pres. Cerebral Palsy Hosp., Middlesex County, bd. dirs. Salvation Army, New Brunswick, N.J.; advisory bd. St. Peter's Hosp. Served with U.S. Army, 1944-45; ETO. Decorated with Purple Heart; recipient Distinguished Service Award, Natl. Assn. County Agents, 1967; Merit award Cook Coll. Rutgers U.; named Middlesex County Man of Year George Otlowski's Citizens League, 1977; recipient George H. Cook Meml. award N.J. Agrl. Expt. Sta., 1977. Dow Study Tour, 1955. Mem. N.J. Assn. County Agents (past pres.), Epsilon Sigma Phi (past pres.) Democrat. Lutheran. Club: Kiwanis (New Brunswick), (past pres.), Moderator four weekly radio programs; writer two weekly newspaper columns in field. Home: 101 Van Liew Ave Milltown NJ 08850 Office: 7 Elm Row New Brunswick NJ 08901

COWAN, RUTH BURNS, educator; b. N.Y.C., Apr. 18, 1932; d. Herman L. and Rose (Lauterstein) Burns; B.S., Cornell U., 1953; M.A., U. Ill., 1957; Ph.D., N.Y. U., 1970; m. Morris Cowan, June 27, 1957. Dir. personnel and vol. services Barnert Meml. Hosp., Paterson, N.J., 1955-57; personnel asst. Internat. Ladies Garment Workers Union, 1957-58; editorial asst. Municipal Services, Dun & Bradstreet, 1958-59; ad hoc labor mediator N.J. Pub. Employment Relations Commn., 1976-78, arbitrator nat. labor panel of arbitrators Am. Arbitration Assn., 1974—; chairperson N.Y.C. Commn. on Status of Women, 1976-78, now mem. exec. com.; dir. research and edn. fund Nat. Assn. Commns. for Women, 1977-78; prof. City U. N.Y., 1959—; sr. research asso. Center for Policy Research, 1977—. Mem., pres. adv. council Marymount of Manhattan Coll.; vice-chairperson N.Y. State Internat. Women's Year Conf.; mem. exec. com. N.Y.C. Employment and Tng. Planning Council; past pres. Women's Caucus for Polit. Sci. Penfield fellow, 1968-69, N.Y. State Regents Teaching fellow, 1965-66, Daniel J. Alpern fellow, 1951-52. Mem. Am., Northeastern, N.Y. State polit. sci. assns., Women's Forum, NOW. Club: N.Y.C. Women's City (bd. dirs.). Author articles on women's rights and urban politics. Home: 320 Central Pk W New York City NY 10025

COWAN, WILLIAM MEREDITH, advt. cons., author; b. Havana, Cuba, Nov. 12, 1924; s. William B. and M. Eleanor (Dobbie) C.; came to U.S., 1926, naturalized, 1943; student Northeastern U., 1942-43, 46-47; A.B., Boston U., 1948, M.S., 1949; m. Marion L. MacDonald, July 23, 1955; children—Lesley E., Christina M. Sr. copywriter G.M. Basford Co., N.Y.C., 1956-65; account exec. Fuller & Smith & Ross, Inc., N.Y.C., 1965-73; supr. mktg. services Masoneilan Internat., Norwood, Mass., 1974-77; pres. Cowan Assos., Waban, Mass., 1977—. Served with AUS, 1943-45; ETO. Decorated Purple Heart; recipient numerous advt. awards. Mem. Bus./Profl. Advt. Assn., Word Guild. Republican. Clubs: Scots Charitable Soc. of Boston; St. Andrews Soc. R.I. Author: Adding Room, Saving Energy, 1978; contbg. editor/columnist Ad East mag., 1976—. Home and Office: 1743 Beacon St Waban MA 02168

COWARD, DAVID BRUCE, civil engr.; b. Saratoga Springs, N.Y., Jan. 23, 1933; s. Charles Fred and Agnes Lucille (Greene) C.; B.C.E., Union Coll., 1955; m. Ann Margaret Van Dycke, Aug. 12, 1955; children—Susan, James, Thomas, Sandra, Steven. Jr. track engr. Pa. R.R., Pitts., 1955, asst. supr. track, Cleve., 1958, Jersey City, 1959-60; civil engr. Lummus Co., Newark, 1961-68; dep. city engr. City of Summit (N.J.), 1968-71, city engr., 1971—. Mem. Summit Planning Bd., 1971—. Served with USN, 1955-57. Registered profl. engr., N.J., N.Y. Mem. N.J. Soc. Municipal Engrs., Am. (mem. Inst. for Municipal Engring.), North Jersey pub. works assns. Republican. Presbyterian. Home: 11 Morris Ct Summit NJ 07901 Office: 512 Springfield Ave Summit NJ 07901

COWELL, ROBERT LAWRENCE, indsl. co. ofcl.; b. Cleve., Sept. 3, 1932; s. William Edward and Anna Josephine (Pavlechko) C.; student NCO Acad., 1958; m. Dorothy Lenore Janovac, Oct. 9, 1965; children—Paul Robert, David Mathew, Cathleen Anne. Enlisted in U.S. Air Force, 1950, ret., 1970; mgr. Culligan franchise, Dunkirk, N.Y., 1970-71; safety and tng. mgr. Roblin Steel, Dunkirk, 1971-73; loss control cons. Unigard Ins., Syracuse, N.Y., 1973-75; safety and tng. mgr. Ralston Purina Co., Dunkirk, 1975—; cons. edn1. and bus. insts. Chautauqua County, N.Y.; v.p. Indsl. Mgmt. Assn., Dunkirk, 1973; mem. Am. Mut. Ins. Engrs., Syracuse, 1974-75. Bd. dirs. YMCA Dunkirk, 1972-73; mem. Safety Council Jamestown (N.Y.), 1971-73. Decorated Purple Heart. Mem. Vets. of Safety Internat., Am. Soc. Safety Engrs. (edn. chmn.). Episcopalian. Speaker, instr. various ednl. instns. Home: 283 E Main St Fredonia NY 14063 Office: 3800 Middle Rd Dunkirk NY 14048

COWEN, JAMES, assn. exec.; b. Newark, Oct. 29, 1935; s. Thomas Joseph and May Gertrude (Curtis) C.; M.A., U. So. Calif., 1959; grad. Inst. Orgn. Mgmt., U. Mich. Asst. mgr. United Advt. Corp., Newark, 1959-64; exec. v.p. West Hudson C. of C., 1964-67; exec. v.p. Fall River Area C. of C., 1967-74; pres. Chamber Commerce and Industry No. N.J., 1974—; pub. Commerce mag. Vice pres. West Hudson Boys Club, 1966-67. Bd. dirs. Bergen County Area Devel. Council; adviser Bristol Coll., Mass. Bd. dirs. Found. Free Enterprise, mem. business advisory council Ramapo Coll. Served to capt. USMCR, 1954-56. Mem. Am. Assn. C. of C. Execs., N.J. Assn. C. of C. Execs. (pres. 1971), Mid Atlantic Assn. C. of C. Execs. (dir., pres. 1978), Met. Civic Exec. Conf., U.S. C. of C., N.J. Indsl. Devel. Assn., N.J. Advt. Club (dir). Kiwanian. Club: Optimist (v.p. 1966) (Kearny, N.J.). Office: 411 Hackensack Ave Hackensack NJ 07601

COWEN, NORMAN JAY, hand surgeon; b. Providence, June 7, 1934; s. Everett and Rose C.; A.B. summa cum laude, Brown U., 1956; M.D., U. Pa., 1960; m. Sheila Israel, Dec. 30, 1956; children—Benjamin Ring, Missy. Intern, Del Hosp., Wilmington, 1960, Episcopal Hosp., Phila., 1961; resident in orthopaedics Phila. Naval Hosp., 1963-64, Phila. Gen. Hosp., 1965-68; fellow in hand surgery Thomas Jefferson Med. Center, 1967; Annie C. Kane fellow in hand surgery Columbia Presbyterian Hosp., N.Y.C., 1968-69; practice medicine specializing in hand surgery with spl. interest in birth defects, Pawtucket, R.I., Providence, Fall River, Mass., New Bedford, Mass., 1969-71, Washington, 1971—, McLean, Va., 1972—; dir. hand service Georgetown U. Hosp., 1972-78; head hand clinic Arlington (Va.) Hosp., 1973; mem. staff Washington Hosp. Center, Capital Hill Hosp., Greater Southeast Community Hosp., Hadley Meml. Hosp., Children's Hosp. Nat. Med. Center, Doctor's Hosp., numerous others; lectr. hand surgery Mass. Gen. Hosp., Chelsea Naval Hosp., 1969-71; asst. clin. prof. orthopaedics George Washington U., 1972-73, clin. instr. surgery, 1972-78; cons. hand clinic Truesdale Hosp., Fall River, Mass., 1971-77, Nat. Upper Extremity Rehab. Clinic, 1973—; guest cons. hand surgery Tel Hashomer Med. Center, Tel Aviv, 1975—; program chmn. ann. Georgetown Hand Symposium, 1973—. Pres., chmn. bd. Nat. Hand Research & Rehab. Fund., Inc., Washington, 1973. Served to lt. MC, USN, 1961-65. Diplomate Am. Bd. Orthopaedic Surgery. Fellow Am. Coll. Surgeons; mem. Am. Assn. Hand Surgery (chmn. ad hoc com. resident tng.), Robert E. Carroll Hand Club, Jefferson hand Club, Washington, Va., Arlington County, Fairfax County, Prince George's County med. socs., Va., Washington orthopaedic socs. Contbr. articles in field to profl. jours. Home: 704 A St SE Washington DC 20003 Office: Physicians Office Bldg 106 Irving St NW Washington DC 20010 also 8206 Leesburg Pike Suite 208 McLean VA 22101

COWEN, WILSON, judge; b. nr. Clifton, Tex., Dec. 20, 1905; s. John Rentz and Florence Juno (McFadden) C.; LL.B., U. Tex., 1928; m. Florence Elizabeth Walker, Apr. 18, 1930; children—W. Walker, John E. Admitted to Tex. bar, 1928; pvt. practice Dalhart, 1928-34; county judge Dallas County, 1935-38; dir. for Tex., Farm Security Adminstrn., 1938-40, regional dir., 1940-42; commr. U.S. Ct. Claims, 1942-43, 45-59, chief commr., 1959-64; chief judge, 1964-77, sr. judge, 1977—; asst. adminstr. War Food Adminstrn., 1943-45; spl. asst. to sec. agr., 1945. Past chmn., past trustee Landon Sch. for Boys, Bethesda. Mem. State Bar Tex., Am., Fed. bar assns., Order of Coif, Delta Theta Phi. Presbyterian. Clubs: Masons, Cosmos, Nat. Lawyers (Washington). Home: 2500 Virginia Ave Washington DC 20037 Office: US Court Claims Washington DC 20005

COWETT, RICHARD MICHAEL, neonatologist; b. N.Y.C., Sept. 20, 1942; s. Allen Abraham and Sylvia (Kazan) C.; B.A. cum laude, Lawrence Coll., 1964; M.D., U. Cin., 1968; m. Katherine Manz, June 25, 1966; children—Beth Ellen, Allison Ann, Allen Manz. Intern in pediatrics Cleve. Met. Gen. Hosp.-Case Western Res. U., Cleve., 1968-69, jr. asst. resident in pediatrics, 1969-70; asst. resident in medicine Children's Hosp. Med. Center-Harvard Med. Sch., Boston, 1970-71; teaching fellow dept. pediatrics Harvard Med. Sch., 1970-71; teaching fellow med. sci., div. biol. and med. scis., Brown U., Providence, 1974-75, adj. clin. instr., 1975-76, asst. prof. pediatrics, 1976—; fellow in neonatology Women and Infants Hosp. of R.I.-Brown U., 1973-76, staff neonatologist, 1976—; attending staff Women and Infants Hosp. R.I., R.I. Hosp., Providence; courtesy staff St. Anne's Hosp., Union Truesdale Hosp., Fall River, Mass., Mocton Hosp., Taunton, Mass. Served to maj. M.C., USAF, 1971-73. Nat. Inst. Child Health and Human Devel. fellow, 1974-76. Diplomate Am. Bd. Pediatrics. Mem. Am., R.I. acads. pediatrics, New Eng. Pediatric Soc., R.I., Providence med. socs., AAAS, New Eng. Perinatology Soc. (pres. 1978), Am. Coll. Nutrition, Soc. Pediatric Research. Contbr. articles to med. jours. Home: 125 Woodbury Providence RI 02906 Office: 50 Maude St Providence RI 02908

COWGILL, CAROL ANN, lawyer, assn. exec.; b. Plainfield, N.J., Apr. 21, 1946; d. Daniel E. and Winifred M. (MacQuillan) C.; B.A., Duke U., 1968; J.D. (LaVerne Noyes fellow 1968-71), U. Chgo., 1971. Admitted to D.C. bar, 1971, Ill. bar, 1971, U.S. Supreme Ct. bar, 1975; staff atty. EPA, Washington, 1971-73; atty. Washington office Consumers Union, 1973-75; dir. Washington office Am. Acad. Family Physicians, 1975—. Mem. exec. bd. S.W. Neighborhood Assembly, Washington, 1977—; sec. Potomac Valley Amateur Athletic Union Tae Kwon Do Com., 1977-78; sec.-treas. Nat. Amateur Athletic Union Tae Kwon Do Com., 1978. Mem. D.C. Bar, Fed. (chmn. com. health and welfare), Am. bar assns., Nat. Health Lawyers Assn., Washington Council Lawyers, ACLU. Democrat. Clubs: Potomac Pedalers Touring, YMCA Tae Kwon Do. Home: 239 G St SW Washington DC 20024 Office: 475 L'Enfant Plaza W SW Suite 2970 Washington DC 20024

COWIE, WILLIAM JOHN, advt. agy. exec.; b. Syracuse, N.Y., Oct. 8, 1944; s. William Manns Tufts and Marjorie Joan (Rawlings) C.; B.A. with honors, U. Sussex (Eng.), 1967. Sales mgr. Fairflight Aviation Ltd., Biggin Hill, Kent, Eng., 1968-71; asst. to chmn. bd. Needham, Harper & Steers Advt. Inc., N.Y.C., 1972, account exec., 1972-74; account exec. Compton Advt. Inc., N.Y.C., 1974, v.p., account supr., 1977—. Club: St. Bartholemew's (N.Y.C.). Home: 715 Madison Ave New York City NY 10021 Office: 625 Madison Ave New York City NY 10022

COWLES, CHARLES, publisher; b. Santa Monica, Cal., Feb. 7, 1941; s. Gardner and Jan (Streate) C.; student, Stanford, 1959-65. Asso. pub. Artforum mag., San Francisco, 1964-65; pub., pres. Artforum, Inc., Los Angeles, 1965-67, pub., pres., chmn., N.Y.C., 1967—; curator modern art Seattle Art Mus., 1975—; chmn. Collegiate Press, N.Y.C., 1968-71. Mem. Fine Arts Council Fla. 1972-75; mem. art adv. com. Dade County, Fla., 1974-75; trustee Studio Museum in Harlem, 1967-75, Miami Art Center, 1973-75, San Francisco Art Inst., 1977—. Mem. internat. council Mus. Modern Art, N.Y.C., 1969—. Served with USCG, 1962-70. Office: 667 Madison Ave New York City NY 10021 also Seattle Art Mus PO Box 21228 Seattle WA 98111

COWPER-SMITH, MAURICE A., orgn. exec.; b. Belleville, Ont., Can., Oct. 7, 1913; s. Allan T. and Gladys H. (Good) Cowper-S.; grad. U. Toronto, 1940; m. Elizabeth Laing, July 5, 1941; children—Martha Anne, G. Blair. Supt. agencies Canadian head office Occidental Life Ins. Co. Calif., 1950-74; exec. dir., sec.-treas. Toronto Humane Soc., 1974—. Past chmn. internat. devel. com. Nat. council YMCAs; bd. dirs. N. Toronto Youth Project. Served to capt. Canadian Army, 1942-46. Address: 11 Wellesley St W Toronto ON M4Y 1E9 Canada

COX, ALBERT HARRINGTON, JR., economist; b. St. Louis, Oct. 13, 1932; s. Albert Harrington and Hildegarde (Raab) C.; B.B.A., U. Tex., 1954, M.B.A., 1956; Ph.D., U. Mich., 1965; m. Frances Marie French, Apr. 12, 1960; children—Cynthia, Bruce Harrington. Asst. prof. finance So. Methodist. U., Dallas, 1959; economist First Nat. City Bank, N.Y.C., 1960-61; sec., research com. Am. Bankers Assn., N.Y.C., 1962-64; v.p., economist First Nat. Bank in Dallas, 1965-68, spl. asst. to chmn. President's Council of Econ. Advisers, Washington, 1969-70; exec. v.p., chief economist Lionel D. Edie & Co., N.Y.C., 1970-75, also dir.; sr. econ. adviser Merrill Lynch, Pierce, Fenner & Smith, Inc., N.Y.C., 1970-75; pres. Merrill Lynch Economics, Inc., 1976—; chief economist Merrill Lynch & Co., 1976—; dir. Merrill Lynch Capital Fund. Mem. econ. adv. bd. U.S. Dept. Commerce, 1975—. Mem. Nat. Assn. Bus. Economists (dir.), Am. Econ. Assn., Beta Gamma Sigma, Beta Theta Pi. Clubs: Bronxville Field, Siwanoy Country (Bronxville, N.Y.); Union League (N.Y.C.). Author: Regulation of Interest Rates on Bank Deposits, 1966. Contbg. economist Bankers Monthly, 1971—. Contbr. articles to profl. jours. Home: 80 Tanglewylde Ave Bronxville NY 10708 Office: One Liberty Plaza New York City NY 10006

COX, CORINNE BIRD WOOLARD, club woman; b. Balt., June 26, 1906; d. Leelon F. and Mabel Eugenia (Jones) Woolard; student pub. schs.; m. Merle LeRoy Cox, Nov. 17, 1926 (dec. June 1970); 1 son, Merle LeRoy. Mem. Descs. Lords of Md. Manors (nat. pres. 1947-49), D.A.R. (regent 1946-48), Nat. Soc. Daus. Barons of Runnemede. Order First Families Va. Nat. Soc. Daus. Founders and Patriots Am., Daus. Colonial Wars. D.A.R., Am. Clan Gregor Soc., Md. Hist. Soc., Jamestowne Soc., Brit. Am. Soc., Soc. Descs. William The Conqueror and His Companions at Arms, Huguenot Soc. Washington, Nat. Gavel Soc., Colonial Order of the Crown. Club: Washington. Home: The Kenwood 5101 River Rd Bethesda MD 20016

COX, ELIZABETH LARTER, editor; b. East Orange, N.J., Sept. 20, 1927; d. William H.D. and J. Elizabeth (Larter) Cox; B.A., U. Vt., 1949; M.A., N.Y. U., 1952. Info. analyst Radio Free Europe, 1952-57; editorial asst. Am. City mag., 1958; research librarian Sat. Rev., 1959-72; editorial project coordinator Chicorel Library Pub. Corp., 1973; sales asst. Sta. WMCA N.Y.C., 1974—; free-lance editorial researcher, 1970—. Mem. N.J. Gen. Assembly, 1971; pres. Union County (N.J.) Women's Republican Club, 1972-76; mem. Summit Rep. City Com., 1962—, 2d vice chairwoman, 1970-73, parliamentarian, 1975-76; parliamentarian, chmn. constn. and by-laws, editor newsletter, state del. Union County Women's Polit. Caucus; parliamentarian N.J. Women's Polit. Caucus, 1972—; mem. exec. com. Union County Rep. Com., 1973—; bd. govs., editor newsletter N.J. Fedn. Rep. Women, 1975—; chmn. Summit Civil Rights Commn., 1975—; mem. Adv. Bd. on Status of Women, Union County, 1974—; chmn. hearing panel Summit Housing Authority, 1978—. Mem. Newspaper Guild (past chmn. N.Y. Guild rep. assembly, unit chmn., exec. bd.), Spl. Libraries Assn., Am. Polit. Sci. Assn., U. Vt. Alumni Assn., Coalition Labor Union Women. Episcopalian. Home: 390 Morris Ave Summit NJ 07901 Office: WMCA 888 7th Ave New York City NY 10019

COX, HOUSTON ABRAHAM, JR., investment co. exec.; b. Starkville, Miss., May 21, 1918; s. Houston Abraham and Kathleen (Tidmore) C.; student Miss. State Coll., 1935-38; B.A., U. Mo., 1939, postgrad., 1940, B.J., 1968; m. Margaret Virginia Wray, June 29, 1942; children—Marlys Kimbrough (Mrs. Beetley), Kathleen McCleary (Mrs. Burghardt), Anna Margaret (Mrs. Gregory). News editor KPO, NBC, San Francisco, 1944-45; pres. WCLE, Clearwater Broadcasting Co. (Fla.), 1946-50; mgr. commodity dept. Merrill Lynch, Pierce, Fenner & Smith, Palm Beach, Fla., 1951-58; mgr. nat. commodity dept. Reynolds & Co., N.Y.C., 1963-71; v.p. nat. commodity dept. Reynolds Securities, Inc., 1971-76; v.p. ACLI Commodity Services, Inc., N.Y.C., 1976; 1st v.p. Smith Barney Harris Upham & Co., Inc., 1977—; dir. N.Y. Coffee and Sugar Exchange N.Y., 1971-73; mem. N.Y. Cotton Exchange, 1978—; mem. Chgo. Bd. Trade, 1964—; chmn. N.Y. membership com. Chgo. Bd. Trade, 1972—; mem. Chgo. Merc. Exchange, 1964-76, Kansas City Bd. Trade, 1964-76, mem. N.Y. Cocoa Exchange, 1974—, bd. mgrs., 1974—; Chmn. commodities com. Greater N.Y. council Boy Scouts Am., 1967-68. Bd. dirs. Conn. Young Life. Mem. Futures Industry Assn. (dir. 1965—, chmn. bd. 1971-73), Blue Key, Kappa Sigma, Phi Eta Sigma, Sigma Delta Chi. Methodist (chmn. ofcl. bd. 1966-69), trustee 1966-69. Club: Commodity of N.Y. (pres. 1965-67, dir. 1963-71). Author: Common Sense Approach to Commodity Futures Trading, 1968; Concepts on Profits in Commodity Futures Trading, 1972. Contbr. articles to profl. jours. Office: Smith Barney Harris Upham & Co 120 Broadway 23d Floor New York City NY 10005

COX, JACK CECIL, oceanographer; b. Quincy, Ill., Nov. 16, 1951; s. Arthur C. and Noma Fay (Prater) C.; B.S., Purdue U., 1973, M.S., 1973; postgrad. U. Chgo., 1974, U. Del., 1975-78; m. Margaret Ann Crane, May 10, 1975. Mem. teaching staff applied math. and oceanography Purdue U., 1973, oceanography and meteorology U. Chgo., 1974, fluid mechanics U. Del., 1977; oceanographer Sun Shipbldg. & Dry Dock Co., Chester, Pa., 1974-77, materials corrosion engr., 1977-78; oceanographer Arctec Inc., Columbia, Md., 1978—. Mem. Soc. Naval Architects and Marine Engrs., Am. Geophys. Union, Nat. Assn. Corrosion Engrs., ASCE. Republican. Contbr. articles to profl. publs. Home: 6281 Bright Plume Columbia MD 21044 Office: Arctec Inc Columbia MD 21045

COX, ROBERT GENE, cons. firm exec.; b. Liberal, Kans., June 3, 1929; s. Clarice Elden and Verene (Jones) C.; B.A. with honors, U. N.Mex., 1951, LL.B., 1955, J.D., 1968; postgrad. Fgn. Service Inst., 1956-57, Harvard U. Bus. Sch., 1978; m. Eileen Frances Hinshaw, July 10, 1953; children—Ann Rebecca, Allan Robert. Dept. mgr. Mountain States Investment Corp., Albuquerque, 1955-56; 2d sec. Am. embassy, Panama, 1956-58; Am. consul, Caracas, 1959-61, Korean desk officer Dept. State, Washington, 1961-62; chief of staff for mgmt. planning, 1963-65; officer-in-charge Dept. State Mission to Israel, 1965; staff asst. to Pres., White House, 1966-68; partner William H. Clark Assos., Inc., N.Y.C., Chgo., 1968-71; sr. staff officer UN Secretariat, Vienna and N.Y.C., 1971-72; pres. Hennes & Cox Inc., N.Y.C. and Los Angeles, 1972-75; v.p. Hennes & Cox & Spector Internat. Inc., Washington, 1973-75; prin., nat. dir. human resource systems Ernst & Ernst, 1975-78; partner Human Resource Services, Inc., N.Y.C., 1978—; lectr. U. Nacional de Panama, 1957; vis. instr. history Fla. State U., 1958; cons. to Commn. on U.S.-Latin Am. Relations, 1974; sr. adviser Commn. on Orgn. Govt. for Conduct Fgn. Policy, 1974-75; adviser exec. selection to transition staff Pres.-elect Carter, 1976-77; expert witness on mil. value of Panama Canal, U.S. Ho. Reps., 1977. Dep. to county chmn. Albuquerque Democratic Com., 1954. Served to capt. USMC, 1951-55; Korea. Mem. Royal Econ. Soc., Am. Soc. Internat. Law, Council Fgn. Relations (chmn. study group immigration and U.S. fgn. policy), U.S. Strategic Inst., N. Am. Soc. Corporate Planning, Center for Inter-Am. Relations, Canadian Econs. Assn., Nat. Economists Club, N.Y. Hist. Soc., N.Y. Geneal. and Biog. Soc. Unitarian. Clubs: Union League (N.Y.C.); Harvard Bus. Sch. (Cleve.). Author: Defense Department in Latin America, 1964; Choices for Partnership or Bloodshed in Panama, 1975; The Canal Zone: New Focal Point in U.S.-Latin American Relations, 1977. Home: 225 Central Park W New York City NY 10024 Office: 230 Park Ave New York City NY 10017

COX, WILLIAM JACKSON, bishop; b. Valeria, Ky., Jan. 24, 1921; s. Robert Lee and Ora Ethel (Lawson) C.; grad. Va. Theol. Sem., 1957; m. Betty Drake, Dec. 20, 1941; 3 children. Ordained priest, Episcopal Ch., 1958; vicar Holy Cross Ch., Cumberland, Md., 1957-71, rector, 1971-73; suffragan bishop of Md., 1973—; mem. diocesan standing com., 1968-73, exec. council, 1969-72. Office: 106 W Church St Frederick MD 21701

COX, WILLIAM MARTIN, lawyer; b. Bernardsville, N.J., Dec. 26, 1922; s. Martin John and Nellie (Fotens) C.; A.B., Syracuse U., 1947; J.D., Cornell U., 1950; m. Julia Ann Sebastian, June 14, 1952; children—Janice (Mrs. Mark Walker), William Martin, Joann, Julie Ann. Admitted to N.J. bar, 1950; mem. firm Dolan & Dolan, Newton, N.J., 1950—, partner, 1962—. Mem. Newton Bd. Edn., 1960-65, pres. 1962-65; mem. Sussex County Vocat.-Tech. Sch. Bd., 1965-78, pres., 1968-71, v.p., 1978—; treas. Sussex County Democratic Com., 1952-56; elder Presbyterian Ch., Newton, 1969—; mem. co-adj. staff Rutgers U., 1968—. Served with AUS, 1943-45. Mem. Am., N.J. (chmn. local govt. law sect. 1969-71), Sussex County (pres. 1973-74) bar assns., N.J. Fedn. Planning Ofcls. (dir., gen. counsel), N.J. Inst. Municipal Attys. (1st v.p. 1978—), N.J. Assn. Sch. Attys., Alpha Chi Rho. Clubs: Rotarian (pres. 1978—), Syracuse U., Masons. Author: Handbook on Zoning Administration, 4th edit., 1976. Contbr. articles to profl. jours. Home: 125 Main St Newton NJ 07860 Office: 93 Spring St Newton NJ 07860

COX, WILLIAM VAUGHAN, lawyer; b. Jersey City, Nov. 12, 1936; s. Walter Miles and Emily (McNenney) C.; A.B., Princeton U., 1958; LL.B., Yale U., 1964; m. Lynda Norris, July 27, 1968; children—Millicent Stillwell, Jennifer Vaughan. Admitted to Colo. bar, 1965, N.Y. bar, 1974 sportswriter Colorado Springs Free Press, 1960-61; atty. Continental Oil Co., Denver, 1966-72, Stamford, Conn., 1972-74; v.p., gen. counsel Stromberg-Carlson Corp., Rochester, N.Y., 1974—; mem. advisory bd. Yale Law Sch. Urgent Issues Seminar Series. Served with U.S. Army, 1959-60. Mem. Am., N.Y., Monroe County bar assns., Am. Judicature Soc., Rochester C. of C. Republican. Roman Catholic. Clubs: Genesee Valley, Law (Denver); Dial Lodge. Office: 100 Carlson Rd Rochester NY 14603

COYLE, JOSEPH RICHARD, clergyman; b. Johnstown, Pa., May 26, 1930; s. Joseph Blair and Ada Jean (Wagner) C.; B.A., Otterbein Coll., 1952; B.D., United Theol. Sem., 1958; postgrad. Mich. State U., summers, 1965-68; m. Phyllis Anne Kraft, Aug. 24, 1958; children—Lee Anne, Jeffrey, Janice. Asst. recreational therapist Dayton (O.) Receiving Hosp. for Children, Dayton, 1953-54; group work dir. Montgomery County Juvenile Center, Dayton, 1954-58; ordained to ministry Evang. United Brethern, 1958; pastor Mt. Hope Parish, United Methodist Ch., Clearfield, Pa., 1958-60, 1st United Methodist Ch., Conemaugh, Pa., 1960-64, St. Clairsville Parish, United Ch. of Christ, 1964-68, 1st United Ch. of Christ, Irwin, Pa., 1968—; interim dir. Mountain Reconciliation Center, 1971. Mem. Profl. Counselling Service, 1971-75, Dist. Atty.'s Citizens Adv. Com., 1970-75, Westmoreland County Juvenile Commn., 1974—; exec. sec. Norwin Council Chs., 1974—. Pres., bd. dirs. Norwin YMCA, 1975—. Mem. Quiz and Quill Lit. Soc. (life mem.). Club: Y's Men's International (Johnstown, Pa.). Home and Office: 408 Main St Irwin PA 15642

COYLE, WALTER ANTHONY, food service and health care equipment mfg. co. exec.; b. Watertown, Mass., Aug. 25, 1922; s. Walter Anthony and Adeline Gertrude (Mazone) C.; B.S., Northeastern U., 1947; 1 dau., Karen Marie. Indsl. relations dir. Nat. Pneumatic Co., 1947-52; asst. to pres. Rock Mfg. Co., 1952-53; v.p. ops. Market Forge Co., Everett, Mass., 1953-74; pres. Market Forge Co. div. Beatrice Foods, Everett, 1974—. Mem. Town Meeting, Lexington, Mass., 1964-77. Served with U.S. Army, 1943-46. Mem. Am. Assn. Indsl. Mgmt. (dir.), Mass. Safety Council (dir.), Everett C. of C. (dir. 1965-68, pres. 1968-70). Office: 35 Garvey St Everett MA 02149

COYLE, WILLIAM RADFORD, III, physician; b. N.Y.C., Feb. 11, 1933; s. William Radford and Eleanor Coghlin (Gibbons) C.; A.B., Princeton U., 1955; M.D., N.Y. U., 1960; m. Annamary Monahan, July 13, 1957; children—William Radford IV, James Carroll, Mary Kathleen. Intern, St. Vincents Hosp., N.Y.C., 1960-61, resident in obstetrics and gynecology, 1961-65; practice medicine specializing in obstetrics and gynecology, Derby, Conn., 1965-73, Oxon Hill, Md., 1973—; mem. faculty Georgetown U. Med. Sch. Washington, 1973—; mem. staff Greater S.E. Community Hosp., Georgetown U. Hosp., So. Md. Hosp. Center, Clinton. Fellow ACS, Am. Coll. Obstetricians and Gynecologists; mem. Prince Georges County Med. Soc., Med. Soc. D.C., AMA, Assn. Mil. Surgeons, Am. Assn. Gyncologic Laparoscopists. Clubs: Princeton of Washington and N.Y.; Tantallon Country, Tantallon Yacht. Office: 9401 Indian Head Hwy Oxon Hill MD 20022

CRAFT, DONALD BRUCE, oil co. exec.; b. White Plains, N.Y., Jan. 19, 1935; s. Robert A. and Mary (Blair) C.; B.S., N.Y. U., 1954; M.A., Columbia U., 1956; m. Barbara Blanchard, May 16, 1959; children—Joan, Elizabeth, Kinson, Courtney, Leslie. Regional sales mgr. Tech. Material Corp., Mamaroneck, N.Y., 1956-59; v.p. wholesale sales Wyatt, Inc., New Haven, 1959—. State mgr. Emergency Petroleum and Gas Adminstrn., Dept. of Interior, Washington, 1969—. Mem. Conn. Republican Finance Com., 1969—; mem. Woodbridge (Conn.) Rep. Town Com., 1965—. Served with USNR. Mem. New Eng. Fuel Inst. (pres. 1971-73, chmn. bd. 1973—), Conn. Petroleum Assn. (pres. 1970-72), Nat. Oil Jobbers Council (v.p.), Conn. Petroleum Marketers Assn. (dir.), Greater New Haven Better Home Heat Council (dir.). Home: 37 Hunting Hill Rd Woodbridge CT 06525 Office: 900 Chapel St New Haven CT 06510

CRAFT, JAMES PRESSLEY, JR., educator; b. Louisville, Ga., Nov. 1, 1913; s. James Pressley and Edith (Galphin) C.; student Naval Postgrad. Sch., 1940-42; M.S., Mass. Inst. Tech., 1943; postgrad. Naval War Coll., 1952-53; Ph.D., U. Pa., 1969; m. Carolyn Crockett Martin, July 30, 1937; children—Carolyn Martin, James Pressley III, Frederick Galphin. Commd. ensign USN, 1934, advanced through grades to capt., 1952; head. contingency plans br. of Joint Staff of Joint Chiefs of Staff, 1960-62; comdr. U.S. Destroyers Mediterranean, 1959-60; dean men U. Pa., 1964-67, fellow, 1967-68; asst. prof. Ursinus Coll., Collegeville, Pa., 1968-69, asso. prof. polit. sci., 1969-77, prof., 1977—, asst. dean coll., 1970-77, exec. asst. to pres., 1977—, v.p. for planning and adminstrn., 1977—; vis. scholar U. Mich., summer 1971. Decorated Silver Star, Bronze Star, Purple Heart. NSF fellow Va. Poly. Inst. and State U., 1973. Mem. AAUP, Am. Polit. Sic. Assn., Internat. Studies Assn., Sigma Xi, Pi Gamma Mu. Club: Philadelphia Cricket. Home: 429 Stratford Ave Collegeville PA 19426 Office: Ursinus Coll Collegeville PA 19426

CRAFT, JAMES WILMER, mining co. exec.; b. Edwards, Miss., June 8, 1916; s. Wilmer Earl and Olive Lillian (Musgrove) C.; B.S., Stanford, 1947; m. Frances Carolyn Hall, May 9, 1959. Aero. engr. Pan Am. Airways, San Francisco, 1944-50; mgmt. planner Hughs Aircraft Co., Los Angeles, 1950-55; dir. orgn. Chrysler Corp., Detroit, 1955-66; staff exec. Phelps Dodge Corp., N.Y.C., 1966—; dir. Gainsborough Studios, N.Y.C.; mem. mining and milling com. Atomic Indsl. Forum, Washington. Served with USNR, 1944-45. Mem. N.Y.C. of C., Am. Nuclear Soc., Am. Inst. Aeros. and Astronautics, Inc., Am. Inst. Mining, Metall. and Petroleum Engrs., Am. Soc. Mech. Engrs. Republican. Presbyterian. Clubs: N.Y. Athletic, Rotary, Mining. Home: 45 Grace St Rye NY 10580 Office: 300 Park Ave New York City NY 10022

CRAGIN, CHARLES LANGMAID, lawyer; b. Portland, Maine, Oct. 9, 1943; s. Charles L. and Ruth (Meriam) C.; B.S. cum laude, U. Maine, 1967, J.D. cum laude, 1970; m. Nancy Ann Armbruster, June 5, 1965; children—Christine, Jean, Cathleen. Broadcast announcer, newsman various radio and TV stations, So. Maine, 1964-69; admitted to Maine bar, 1970, U.S. Supreme Ct. bar, 1974, since practiced in Portland; mem. firm Verrill and Dana, 1970-74, partner, 1974-77; candidate for Republican nomination for gov. Maine, 1978; legal cons. to Maine Med. Assn., Maine Psychiat. Assn., Maine Hosp. Assn., Maine Dental Assn., Maine Blue Cross and Blue Shield, Maine Health Facilities Authority; mem. adv. com. on labor relations Am. Hosp. Assn., 1974-78; vis. lectr. U. Maine Sch. of Nursing, 1975; adj. prof. health care law St. Joseph's Coll., Windham, Maine, 1976-77; lectr. Am. Sterilizer Co., Erie, Pa., 1972-77, New Eng. Coll. of Surgeons, Tri-state chpt., 1974—. Mem. Com. for the Protection of Human Research Subjects, Maine Med. Center, Portland, 1972—; mem. Cumberland County (Maine) Mental Health Bd., 1973-75. Mem. Cumberland County Republican. Com., 1972—; chmn. Rep. First Dist. Conv., 1976, chmn., com., 1974—; bd. dirs. Portland Concert Assn., 1973—; chmn. bd. St. Joseph's Manor Nursing Home, 1976-77. Served with USN, 1961-64; lt. comdr. USNR. Recipient Israel Bernstein Meml. award U. Maine, 1970, Citizen-Sailor award Naval Reserve Center, 1975, Outstanding Young Man of Maine award Maine Jaycees, 1975; named Outstanding Young Man of Portland, Portland Jaycees, 1974. Mem. Am., Maine (chmn. pub. relations com. 1972—), Cumberland County bar assns., Am. Soc. of Hosp. Attys., Am. Judicature Soc., Nat. Health Lawyers Assn., U. Maine Alumni Assn (pres. Portland-Gorham 1974-75, Community Service award 1976, mem. adv. council 1975—). Roman Catholic. Contbr. articles on legislation and pub. health to profl. pubs. Home: 349 Gray Rd Falmouth ME 04105 Office: Two Canal Plaza Portland ME 04112

CRAHALL, ADAM CARL, telephone co. ofcl.; b. Wilkes Barre, Pa., Apr. 25, 1943; s. Adam and Stella C.; B.S. in Bus. Adminstrn., King's Coll., 1964; M.B.A., U. Scranton, 1968; m. Patricia A. McHugh, May 20, 1967; children—Adam John, Kathleen Marie, Eric Michael. Mmgt. trainee, comml. rep. mktg. staff asst., traffic mgr. Commonwealth Telephone Co., Dallas and Towanda, Pa., 1967-68, personnel supr., employment mgr., employee relations mgr., personnel mgr., Dallas, 1969—; personnel mgr. Mercy Hosp., Wilkes-Barre, 1968-69; mem. adv. com. for bus. edn. Wilkes-Barre Area Sch. Dist.; co-chmn. employer adv. council Wilkes-Barre Area-Pa. Job Service. Mem. Tri-County Personnel Assn. (pres. 1973-74), Middle Atlantic Placement Assn., Middle Atlantic Career Counseling Assn., Adminstrv. Mgmt. Soc., Am. Soc. Personnel Adminstrn. (certified accredited personnel mgr.). Office: 100 Lake St Dallas PA 18612

CRAIG, CHARLES SAMUEL, educator; b. Atlantic City, May 6, 1943; s. Charles Hays and Catherine Sara (McMullen) C.; B.A., Westminster Coll., 1965; M.S., U. R.I., 1967; Ph.D., Ohio State U., 1971; m. Marilyn Ann Martin, Apr. 3, 1971. Mktg. rep. IBM, Providence, 1966-68; asst. dir. Mechanized Info. Center, Columbus, 1971-73; asst. prof. library adminstrn. Ohio State U., Columbus, 1971-73, asst. prof. mktg., 1972-74; asst. prof. mktg. Grad. Sch. Bus. and Pub. Adminstrn., Cornell U., Ithaca, N.Y., 1974-77, asso. prof., 1977—; dir. Presbyterian and Reformed Pub. Co., Phila., 1973—. NDEA fellow, 1969-71. Mem. Am. Mktg. Assn., Assn. Consumer Research, Phi Kappa Phi, Omicron Delta Epsilon, Psi Chi. Presbyterian. Contbr. articles to profl. jours. Home: 13 Eagle's Head Rd Ithaca NY 14850 Office: 518 Malott Hall Cornell U Ithaca NY 14853

CRAIGMYLE, RONALD M., investment banker; b. Toronto, Ont., Can., June 19, 1896; s. James M. and Jessie (Gregory) C.; A.B., Columbia U., 1920; B.S. in Bus., 1921; m. Louise de Rochemont, Apr. 10, 1923; children—Ronald M., Jr., Mary Louise, Robert de Rochemont. With Minsch, Monell & Co., 1920-24; partner Burley, Peabody & Craigmyle, 1924-26; partner Craigmyle & Co., later Craigmyle, Pinney & Co., mems. N.Y. Stock Exchange, 1926-65; chmn. Giant Portland and Masonry Cement Co.; ltd. partner Fahnestock & Co., mems. N.Y. Stock Exchange, N.Y.C., 1965—. Hon. trustee Green Vale Sch.; mayor Village of Matinecock, N.Y., 1955-67, dep. mayor, 1967-75. Mem. Psi Upsilon. Republican. Episcopalian. Clubs: Piping Rock, Everglades, Bath and Tennis, Creek, Columbia U., Metropolitan, University. Vice pres. Intercollegiate Flying Assn., 1919-21. Home: Box 321 Locust Valley NY 11560 Office: 110 Wall St New York City NY 10005

CRAIN, DARRELL CLAYTON, JR., physician; b. Washington, Mar. 29, 1910; s. Darrell Clayton and Annie (Rau) C.; M.D., George Washington U., 1932; m. Louise Moore, July 12, 1934; children—Barbara (Mrs. Mark Rollinson), Anne (Mrs. Richard Fitzgerald), Darrell Clayton III. Intern, Central Dispensary and Emergency Hosp., Washington, 1932-33, resident, 1933-34; med. officer Walter Reed Gen. Hosp., Washington, 1934-37; practice medicine, specializing in Reumatic diseases, Washington, 1937-42, 45—; mem. staff Georgetown U. Hosp., Drs. Hosp.; past cons. Surgeon Gen. U.S. Army, Surgeon Gen. USPHS: clin. prof. medicine Georgetown U., 1969—. Mem. med. adv. bd. Vis. Nurses Soc., Washington, 1960-73. Bd. dirs. Westminster Found., Annapolis, Md., Arthritis Rehab. Center. Served to maj. M.C., AUS, 1942-45. Diplomate Am. Bd. Internal Medicine. Fellow A.C.P.; mem. Med. Soc. D.C. (pres. 1972, chmn. exec. bd. 1973), A.M.A., Am. Soc. Internal Medicine, Am. Rheumatism Assn., Rheumatism Soc. D.C. (pres. 1946-48; sec.-treas. 1948-52), Am. Therapeutic Soc., Am. Congress Phys. Medicine and Rehab., So. Med. Assn., A.A.A.S., Pan-Am., Internat. med. socs., Washington Acad. Medicine, Am. Med. Authors, Arthritis and Rheumatism Assn. Met. Washington (pres. 1948-52, dir., adv. bd. 1948-72), Assn. Oldest Inhabitants D.C. Contbr. numerous articles to Crain, Darrell Clayton, Jr., profl. jours. Home: 6422 Garnett Dr Kenwood Chevy Chase MD 20015 Office: 1234 19th St NW Washington DC 20036

CRAINE, RALPH B., JR., pharm. co. exec.; b. Altoona, Pa., Nov. 7, 1930; s. Ralph Bryson and Ella Marie (Kern) C.; B.S. in Chemistry, Pa. State U., 1952, postgrad. in Polit. Sci., 1953; student U. Pa. Law Sch., 1954; m. Baerbel K. Chaveriat, Oct. 27, 1957; children—John M., David B., Suzanne C., James G. Announcer, newscaster Sta. WGAL-TV, Lancaster, Pa., 1954; with Merck, Sharp & Dohme Inc. div. Merck & Co., Inc., 1957—, tng. mgr., 1968-70, dist. mgr., N.Y.C., 1970-72, product mgr., West Point, Pa., 1972-75, dir. planning, 1975—. Vice pres. Oxbow Meadows Civic Assn., 1976-77. Served with AUS, 1954-56. Mem. Am. Chem. Soc., Am. Soc. Microbiology. Home: 11 Hickory Ln Chalfont PA 18914 Office: Merck Sharp & Dohme West Point PA 19486

CRAMER, HAROLD, lawyer; b. Phila., June 16, 1927; s. Aaron Harry and Blanche (Greenberg) C.; A.B., Temple U., 1948; LL.B. cum laude, U. Pa., 1951; m. Geraldine Hassuk, July 14, 1954; 1 dau., Patricia Gail. Admitted to Pa. bar, 1951; law clk. Pres. Judge Edwin O. Lewis, Ct. of Common Pleas No. 2, 1953; mem. faculty U. Pa. Law Sch., 1954; asso. firm Shapiro, Rosenfeld, Stalberg & Cook, 1955-56, partner, 1956-67; partner, firm Mesirov, Gelman, Jaffe & Levin, Phila., 1967-73; partner firm Mesirov, Gelman, Jaffe & Cramer, 1974-77, Mesirov, Gelman, Jaffe, Cramer & Jamison, 1977—; instr. Nat. Inst. Trial Advocacy, 1970-77. Chmn. bd. Eastern Pa. Psychiat. Hosp., 1974—, Grad. Hosp., 1975—; trustee Phila. Bar Found., Fedn. Jewish Agys., Jewish Publ. Soc. Served from pvt. to 1st lt., AUS, 1951-53. Decorated Bronze Star medal. Fellow Am. Bar Found.; mem. Am., Pa. (ho. of dels. 1966-75, 78—, gov. 1975-78), Phila. (mem. com. censors 1965, chmn. 1966; gov. 1967-69, chmn. 1969, vice chancellor 1970, chancellor 1972, editor The Shingle 1970—) bar assns., Am. Law Inst., U. Pa. Law Alumni Soc. (mem. bd. mgrs. 1959-64, pres. 1968-70), Order of Coif (chpt. pres. 1965-67, nat. exec. com. 1973-76), Tau Epsilon Rho (chancellor Phila. grad. chpt. 1960-62). Clubs: Locust, Midday; Philmont Country. Co-author: Trial Advocacy, 1968. Contbr. articles in field to profl. jours. Home: 1361 Wright Dr Huntingdon Valley PA 19006 Office: Fidelity Bldg 123 S Broad St Philadelphia PA 19109

CRANDALL, ELIZABETH WALBERT, educator; b. Columbus, Kans., Jan. 18, 1914; d. Stanley and Edna (Daniel) Walbert; B.S., Kans. State Coll., 1935, M.S., 1939; D.Ed., Boston U., 1962; m. Robert Dalton Crandall, Aug. 3, 1946. Tchr. high sch., Cedar Point, Kans., 1935-36, Ellsworth, Kans., 1936-38; instr., asst. prof. home econs. Mich. State Coll., 1939-46; with U. R.I., 1946—, instr., asst. prof., 1948-54, asso. prof., 1954-62, prof. home mgmt., chmn. dept., 1962-74, acting dean Coll. Home Econs., 1973-77, prof. home mgmt. emerita, 1977—. Mem. Nat. Council Family Relations, Internat. Fedn. Home Econs., R.I. (pres. 1950-52, mem. exec. com. 1958-59), Am. (v.p. 1964-67, mem. council for profl. devel. 1971-74, chmn. 1973-74) home econs. assns., AAUW (br. pres. 1967-69, state pres. 1977-79), Omicron Nu (nat. pres. 1957-59, nat. editor 1953-55), League Woman Voters (dir. S. Kingston br. 1955-57), Bus. and Profl. Women's Club (pres. 1971-72), Phi Upsilon Omicron, Phi Kappa Phi (treas. 1959-61, v.p. 1963-65), Zeta Tau Alpha. Author: (with others) Home Management in Theory and Practice, 1947; Management for Modern Families, 1973. Tech. adviser Jour. Home Econs., 1957-60. Home: Indian Lake Shores RFD 3 Wakefield RI 02879 Office: Quinn Hall Kingston RI 02881

CRANDALL, RIEL STANTON, mil. engr.; b. Fairfax, Minn., Oct. 22, 1914; s. Arthur M. and Lydia (Miller) C.; B.S., U.S. Mil. Acad., 1939; M.S., Cornell U., 1947; grad. U.S. Command and Staff Coll., 1951; m. Beatrice M. Mayer, June 28, 1947; children—Adrienne M., Fern L. Commd. 2d lt. U.S. Army, 1939, advanced through grades to col., 1956; co. comdr., Co. B., 65th Engrs., Hawaii, Pearl Harbor, 1941-42; bn. comdr., 300th Combat Engring. Bn., Europe, 1943-45; asst. prof. mil. sci. and tactics City Coll. N.Y., 1947-50; installation operations and planning, communications zone, France, 1951-54; post engr., Ft. Leavenworth, Kans., 1954-57; comdr. 1st training regiment, Ft. Leonard Wood, Mo., 1957-59; chief engring. div., engring. sect., Korea, 1959-60; post engr., Ft. Benning, Ga., 1960-63, U.S. Mil. Acad., West Point, N.Y., 1963-69; engr, Trinity Coll., Hartford, Conn., 1969—. Mem. Wethersfield Flood and Erosion Control Com. Bd. dirs. Hartford Neighborhood Centers. Decorated French Croix de Guerre, Legion of Merit. Registered profl. engr., Ga., N.Y. Mem. Nat. Soc. Profl. Engrs., Am. Soc. Engring. Edn., Assn. Phys. Plant Adminstrs., Soc. Am. Mil. Engrs. Rotarian. Home: 654 Highland St Wethersfield CT 06109

CRANDELL, WALTER BAIN, surgeon; b. N.Y.C., July 26, 1911; s. Walter Solomon and Bess (Bain) C.; A.B., Dartmouth, 1934; M.D., N.Y. U., 1937; m. Eloise Elizabeth Henry, June 22, 1935; children—Anne (Mrs. Eugene Williams), Cynthia, Elizabeth (Mrs. Richard Hutchins), Eloise (Mrs. Keith Bell). Intern, Mary Hitchcock Meml. Hosp., Hanover, N.H., 1937-39; clin. asst. thoracic surgeon Hitchcock Clinic, 1939; instr. anatomy Dartmouth, 1939; resident gen. surgery Mass. Gen. Hosp., 1939-41; thoracic surgery Chest Service Bellevue Hosp., 1941-42, asst. vis. surgeon, 1946-47; instr. surgery N.Y. U., also anatomy and operative surgery, 1946-47; adj. surgeon Lenox Hill Hosp., also attending surgeon thoracic surgery VA Hosp., Bronx, 1946-47; chief surgery VA Hosp., White River Junction, Vt., 1947—, chief staff, 1971-72; asst. clin. prof. surgery Dartmouth, 1947-61, asso. clin. prof. surgery, 1961-68, prof. clin. surgery, 1968-75, prof. surgery, 1975-77, prof. surgery emeritus, 1977—; practice medicine, specializing in surgery, N.Y.C., 1946-47. Served to capt. AUS, 1942-45. Decorated Bronze Arrowhead. Diplomate Am. Bd. Surgery, Am. Bd. Thoracic Surgery. Fellow A.C.S. (gov. 1969-75), mem. Am. Assn. for Thoracic Surgery, New Eng. Surg. Soc. (exec. com. 1972-78), 2d Aux. Surg. Group, N.H.

Med. Soc., Alpha Omega Alpha. Research in metabolic and respiratory problems in surg. patients. Home: 3 Meadow Lane Hanover NH 03755 Office: VA Hosp White River Junction VT 05001

CRANDON, JOHN HOWLAND, surgeon; b. Boston, Apr. 28, 1912; s. LeRoi Goddard and Mina Marguerite (Stinson) C.; A.B., Harvard U., 1933, M.D., 1937; m. Dorothy Katherine Tebbe, July 14, 1940; children—Alan Tebbe, Mary Elizabeth. Intern, Harvard service Boston City Hosp., 1937-39, resident in surgery, 1939-41; asst. prof. surgery Tufts U. Med. Sch., 1947-62, asso. prof., 1962—, chief of surgery Little Company of Mary Hosp., Cambridge, Mass., 1957-62; chief of surgery, Winthrop Hosp., 1971—; past vis. surgeon Boston City Hosp.; courtesy staff Mt. Auburn, Faulkner, Univ., Chelsea, Brooks hosps. Trustee Winthrop Hosp. Served to comdr. M.C., USNR, 1941-45. USPHS grantee, 1957-62. Mem. A.C.S., Am. Bd. Surgery, New Eng. Surg. Soc., Am. Soc. for Surgery of Hand, Mass. Med. Soc. Clubs: Harvard, Cottage Park Yacht. Contbr. chpts. to books, articles to med. jours. Home: 47 Hilltop Rd Chestnut Hill Brookline MA 02167 Office: 520 Commonwealth Ave Boston MA 02215

CRANE, MICHAEL, chem. engr.; b. Newark, June 20, 1931; s. Samuel Lazarus and Anne Sylvia (Goldstein) C.; B.Chem. Engring., Poly. Inst. Bklyn., 1952; M.Nuclear Engring., N.Y. U., 1962, Ph.D. in Chem. Engring., 1974; m. Ziva Raskind, Sept. 5, 1959; children—Charles J., Steven H., Andrew Barry. Engr., Walter Kidde Nuclear Labs., 1956-57; with research dept. N.Y. U., 1958; with nuclear dept. Westinghouse Electric Corp., 1959-61; engr. United Nuclear Corp., White Plains, N.Y., 1961-64; nuclear power plant engr. Burns and Roe Inc., Oradell, N.J., 1964—. Served with C.E., AUS, 1954-56. Recipient certificate Newark Coll. Engring., 1970; grad. seminar award N.Y. U., 1972. Registered profl. engr., N.J., N.Y. Mem. Am. Nuclear Soc., Nat. Soc. Profl. Engrs., Am. Inst. Chem. Engrs. Home: 1 Garfield Ave West Orange NJ 07052 Office: 650 Winters Ave Paramus NJ 07652

CRANKSHAW, JOHN HAMILTON, mech. engr.; b. Canton, Ohio, Aug. 29, 1914; s. Fred. Weir and Mary (Lashels) C.; B.S. in Mech. Engring., Mass. Inst. Tech., M.S., 1940; m. Wilma Chaffee Thurlow, June 5, 1940; children—Wilma Jean, John H., Geoffrey Thurlow. Rotating engr. Gen. Electric Co., 1940-41, sect. engr., mech. design sect. Motor Engr. div. Locomotive Car Equipment, Erie, Pa., 1946-52; exec. engr. J. A. Zurn Mfg. Co., Am. Flexible Coupling Co., 1952-54; v.p. engring., 1954; exec. v.p., dir. Zurn Industries, Inc., mng. dir. Zurn Research and Devel. Div., until 1957; pres. Dynetics, Inc., Erie, 1957—, also dir.; pres., dir. Dynetic Systems, Inc., Erie, 1970—. Mem. adv. council Gannon Coll. Chmn. Erie Sewer Authority. Served to maj. Ordnance Dept., AUS, 1941-46. Registered profl. engr., Pa. Mem. ASME, Soc. Automotive Engrs., Assn. Iron Steel Engrs., Soc. Exptl. Stress Analysis, Soc. Naval Architects and Marine Engrs., Am. Soc. Metals, ASTM, Am. Soc. Lubricating Engrs., Erie Engring. Socs. Council (pres. 1955-57), Pa. Soc. Profl. Engrs., Sigma Xi. Clubs: Mass. Institute of Technology (N.Y.); Erie. Author several tech. papers. Patentee; inventor, designer main propulsion clutches and couplings for nuclear powered ships. Home: 439 Shawnee Dr Erie PA 16505 Office: Commerce Bldg Erie PA 16501

CRAPE, LAMONTE DEEMOR, educator; b. El Dorado, Kans., July 15, 1926; s. Parker LaMonte and Louise Elizabeth Deemor (Brothers) C.; student Thiel Coll., 1944; B.S., Clarion State Coll., 1950; postgrad. Allegheny Coll., 1953-55; M.Ed., U. Pitts., 1957, Ed.D., 1967; m. Marie Gertrude Kohn, July 14, 1951; children—Mark Edward, Christina Louise. Tchr. organ and gifted children Butler (Pa.) Pub. Schs., 1955-60; asso. prof. Slippery Rock (Pa.) State Coll., 1960-66; prof. Butler County Community Coll., Pa., 1966—, dean liberal arts, 1968-69. Concert organist on tours 1955-57; mgr., bd. dirs. Butler County Symphony Orch., 1957-58; vis. prof. Indiana (Pa.) U., 1969-70. County chmn. 1970 White House Conf. Children and Youth; dir. Butler County Saturday Morning Program for Gifted High Sch. Srs., 1968-69. Served with USMC, 1944-46. Mem. Butler Opera Soc. (founder; pres. 1971—), Pa. Council Tchrs. English (past dir.), Pa. Coil. English Assn., Pa. Council Tchrs. English, U. Pitts. Doctoral Assn., Venango Hist. Soc., S.A.R. (pres. local chpt. 1953-55), Lambda Epsilon Delta. Christian Scientist. Author (with Linnie B. James) Geography for Today's Children, 1968; also articles. Home: 412 N Washington St Butler PA 16001

CRATER, THOMAS NEIL, retail trade exec.; b. Pitts., Sept. 11, 1937; s. Quincy M. and Rubye S. (McWilliams) C.; B.A., Brown U., 1959. Trainee, Lord and Taylor Co., N.Y.C., 1959-60; various exec. positions The Joseph Horne Co., Pitts., 1960-67; v.p., fashion dir. John Wanamaker Co., Phila., 1967—; guest lectr. Fashion Inst. of Tech., N.Y.C. 1973—, Moore Coll. of Art, Phila., 1970-74. Trustee Phila. Coll. Art; bd. dirs. Pa. Ballet, Melanoma Found. Mem. Inst. Contemporary Art, Friends Nat. Hist. Parks. Presbyterian. Home: 1420 Locust St Philadelphia PA 19103 Office: John Wanamaker Co Philadelphia PA 19101

CRAUGH, CAROLYN, travel cons.; b. Dallas, May 3, 1929; d. John McAdams and Sara (Thompson) Craugh; B.A. in Psychology, Skidmore Coll., 1950; postgrad. Cornell U., 1951, So. Meth. U., 1954. Travel cons. Sargent Travel Agy., Inc., Rochester, N.Y., 1961—; adminstrv. asst. to pres. Travel Cons., Washington, 1967; spl. assignments Travel-Time Advisors, Dallas, 1969-70, Travelguide, Inc., Hollywood, Calif., 1970-71. Leader, Mayor's Rochester-Sister City tour to Europe, State Dept. People to People Program, 1971, 72. Bd. dirs. Bicentennial Congress Monroe County, Civic Music Assn., Meml. Art Gallery, Rochester Mus. and Sci. Center, Crystal Charity Ball Found., Dallas, Girls Club Dallas, Cystic Fibrosis Found., Dallas. Mem. Jr. League Dallas, Landmark Soc. Western N.Y., Nat. Honor Soc. Clubs: City, Tennis, Oak Hill Country (Rochester). Home: 1132 East Ave Rochester NY 14607 Office: Sargent Travel Agy Inc Midtown Plaza Rochester NY 14604

CRAVATS, MONROE, educator; b. N.Y.C., June 8, 1930; s. Max and Ethel (Fliegelman) C.; B.A., Bklyn. Coll., 1951; M.A., Columbia, 1955, profl. diploma, 1964, Ed.D., 1968. Biology tchr. N.Y.C. schs., also U. City N.Y., 1951—; asso. prof. tchr. preparation York Coll., City U. N.Y., 1970—. Chmn. pub. edn. com. N.Y.C. div. Am. Cancer Soc. Mem. AAAS, N.Y. Acad. Scis., Nat. Sci. Tchrs. Assn. Author books, articles in profl. jours. Home: 3235 Emmons Ave Brooklyn NY 11235 Office: York Coll City U N Y Jamaica Ave Jamaica NY 11451

CRAWFORD, EDWARD E., psychologist; b. Lawton, Ky., July 31, 1929; s. Thurmon Ray and Hazel Mae (Johnson) C.; A.B., W.Va. U., 1956, M.A., 1958; postgrad. U. Pa., 1956-57; Ph.D., Cath. U. Am., 1969; m. Patricia Ann Dulin, Sept. 4, 1954; children—Scott, Susan. Clin. psychologist Rosewood State Hosp., Owings Mills, Md., 1957-67; sr. staff psychologist Montrose Sch. for Girls, Reisterstown, Md., 1967-71; psychol. cons. Md. Dept. Health and Mental Hygiene, Balt., 1971-74, dir. psychol. and developmental services Md. Preventive Medicine Adminstrn., 1974-76, chief psychology programs Dept. Health and Mental Hygiene, 1976—; individual practice psychology, Baltimore County, Md., part time 1961-63; psychol. cons. Kernan Crippled Children's Hosp., 1972, Wicomico County (Md.) Health Dept., 1958-60, Anne Arundel County (Md.) Pub. Schs., 1965-66. Served with AUS, 1948-52. VA trainee, 1956-57. Fellow Md. Psychol. Assn.; mem. Am. Psychol. Assn., Psi Chi. Methodist (bd. stewards 1965-66). Mason. Office: Md Dept Health and Mental Hygiene 201 W Preston St Baltimore MD 21201

CRAWFORD, EDYTHE ROWE, psychotherapist; b. Washington, Dec. 3, 1930; d. Lionel L. and Elizabeth (Wilson) Rowe; B.A., Vassar Coll., 1952; M.A., Fairfield U., 1977; children by former marriage—Kathy, Jean, Sarah. Psychodramatist, Center for Experiential Learning, N.Y.C., 1973; coordinator gestalt program New Haven Center Human Relations, 1973—; pvt. practice psychodrama, gestalt therapy, Rowalton, Conn., 1973—; faculty U. Bridgeport (Conn.), 1976—. Mem. Assn. Humanistic Psychology, Assn. Counselor Edn. and Supervision, Am. Soc. Group Psychotherapy and Psychodrama. Home: 27 Craw Ave Rowayton CT 06853

CRAWFORD, HOMER, lawyer, paper co. exec.; b. St. Louis, Nov. 28, 1916; s. Raymond S. and Mary (Homer) C.; A.B., Amherst Coll., 1938; LL.B., U. Va., 1941; m. Esther Wilkinson, Oct. 4, 1944 (div. 1949); 1 dau., Candace C.; m. 2d, Sara E. Twigg, May 3, 1952; children—Georgianna, William Twigg. Admitted to N.Y. bar, 1942; asso. firm LeBoeuf. Lamb, Leiby & MacRae, 1942-54, partner, 1954-56; sec. St. Regis Paper Co., 1956—, also v.p., dir.; dir. Howard Paper Mills, Inc.; sec., dir. Pinetree Universal Ins. Co. (Bermuda) Ltd.; sec. St. Regis (Alta.) Ltd.; sec., dir. St. Regis Paper Co. (Can.) Ltd., St. Regis Internat. Corp., Strylease Corp.; dir. St. Regis ACI, St. Regis Land Devel. Corp. Mem. Am., N.Y. State bar assns., Am. Soc. Corp. Secs., Theta Delta Chi. Republican. Presbyterian. Home: 1170 Fifth Ave New York City NY 10029 Office: St Regis Paper Co 150 E 42d St New York City NY 10017

CRAWFORD, JOHN MCALLISTER, JR., collector, patron of arts; b. Parkersburg, W. Va., Aug. 6, 1913; s. John M. and Elizabeth (McAllister) C.; A.B., Brown U., 1937, Litt. D. (hon.), 1964; postgrad. Harvard Sch. Edn., 1938-39; L.H.D. (hon.), Syracuse U., 1967. Tchr. European history Mercersburg (Pa.) Acad., 1939-41;v.p., Howell, Soskin Publs., Inc., N.Y.C., 1941-46; co-pub. New Colophon, N.Y.C., 1947-50; collector Chinese painting, Chinese jades, calligraphic works, ceramics, 1945—; exhibited Morgan Library, N.Y.C., 1962, Fogg Art Mus., Harvard, 1963, Nelson Gallery, Kansas City, Mo., 1963, Victoria and Albert Mus., London, Eng., 1965, Nat. Mus., Stockholm, Sweden, 1965, Cernaschi Mus., Paris, France, 1966. Treas. exec. com. Asia House Gallery, N.Y.C., 1965-71; chmn. art com. China Inst., N.Y.C. 1967-77; mem. library com. Brown U., 1958-73; vis. com. Fogg Art Mus., Harvard, 1961-67; adv. council Columbia Libraries, 1967—; fellow, vis. com. Far Eastern art Met. Mus. Art, N.Y.C., benefactor, 1976; trustee Syracuse U. Library. Morgan Library life fellow, 1959—, fellow in perpetuity, 1976—. Mem. Groiller Club (mem. council 1958-76. chmn. arrangements com. 1959-63, chmn. small exhibits, 1965-70), Phi Beta Kappa (hon.). Club: Century Assn. (N.Y.C.). Author (catalogues) William Morris and the Kelmscott Press; Brown U. Library; William Morris and The Art of The Book; Morgan Library; Chinese Calligraphy and Painting in the Collection of John M. Crawford, Jr.; Chinese Painting and Calligraphy: Crawford Collection, Dover, 1978. Address: 46 E 82d St New York City NY 10028

CRAWFORD, SARA E. TWIGG, vol. services exec.; b. Long Beach, Calif., Jan. 29, 1928; d. William C. and Emma (Fitzgerald) Twigg; student Immaculate Coll., 1950-52; m. Homer Crawford, May 3, 1952; children—Georgiana, William Twigg. Asst. media dir. Needham & Grohmann Advt., N.Y.C., 1948-54; acting dir. vol. services N.Y. Hosp-Cornell Med. Center, N.Y.C., 1967-69, dir. vol. services, 1968—. Bd. dirs. Speedwell Services for Children, 1957—, sec. bd., 1960-64, v.p. bd., 1964-73, pres. bd., 1973—; mem. Am. Soc. Dirs. Vol. Services, N.Y. Assn. Dirs. Vol. in Hosps. (dir.), Fedn. Protestant Welfare Agys. (del. 1964—). Republican. Roman Catholic. Home: 1170 Fifth Ave New York City NY 10029 Office: 3 E 29th St New York City NY 10001

CRAWLEY, NORMAN RUSSELL, JR., mktg. co. exec.; b. Beverly, Mass., June 26, 1930; s. Norman R. and Berniece Thruston (Hamblin) C.; B.B.A., Northeastern U. Advt. sales rep. Gloucester (Mass.) Times, 1954-56; editor Yankee Grocer, Boston, 1956-60; account exec. John C. Dowd, Inc., 1961-71; partner Crawley/Pickard; pres. Crawley & Co., Inc., Boston, 1970—; chmn. bd. Mktg. Resources Corp., Palm Beach, Fla., 1975—; instr. North Shore Community Coll., Beverly, 1976-78. Mem. exec. bd. Boston council Boy Scouts Am., 1967-72, United South End Settlements, Boston, 1958-74; trustee Guidance Camps, Inc., Boston, 1974-78. Served to 1st lt., inf. U.S. Army, 1951-54. Mem. Bank Mktg. Assn., Savs. and Mktg. Inst. Contbr. articles to profl. jours. Home and Office: 22 Melrose St Boston MA 02116

CREAGER, CHARLES EDWIN, lawyer, economist, educator; b. Hagerstown, Md., Oct. 20, 1925; s. Charles Edwin and Mary Edith (Bloyer) C.; B.S., U. Balt., 1950, J.D., 1972; M.B.A., Am. U., Washington, 1959, postgrad., 1966-68; m. Alice Eleanor Hollenbach, Oct. 9, 1948 (div. Jan. 1970); children—Charles Edwin, Karen Elaine and Roger Thomas (twins); m. 2d, Dolores Constance Yanuk, Oct. 1970. Admitted to Md., D.C., U.S. Supreme Ct. bars, others; traffic rep. Charlton Bros. Transp. Co., Inc., Balt., 1946-49; gen. freight agt. Novick Transfer Co., Inc., Balt. 1949-58, So. div. sales mgr., Winchester, Va., 1958-59, gen. traffic mgr., 1960-62, v.p. traffic, 1962-64; dir. sales Halls Motor Transport, Sunbury, 1959-60; v.p. traffic Nat. Transport Co., Inc., Bridgeport, Conn., 1964-65, cons., 1965—; partner firm Germelman, Alt & Creager, 1966-68; owner Charles E. Creager & Assos., Hagerstown, Md., 1968-73; individual practice law, Hagerstown, 1974-76; pres. law offices Creager & Button, 1976—; asst. prof., dir. transp. insts. Am. U., 1965-68; adj. asst. prof. mktg. Lord Fairfax Community Coll., Middletown, Va., 1974—; practitioner ICC, 1955—; transp. cons. Served with USAAF, 1943-46. Bd. dirs. Middle Atlantic Conf., Washington, 1963-68. Mem. Eastern Shipper-Motor Carrier Council (pres. 1964-65; chmn. exec. com. 1965-66) traffic clubs N.Y., Balt., Hagerstown, Shenandoah (past pres.), Nat. Shipper Motor Carrier Conf. (exec. com. 1964-66), Am. (com. adminstrv. law), Washington County, D.C., Md. bar assns., Assn. ICC Practitioners, Motor Carrier Lawyers Assn., Phi Alpha Delta. Episcopalian. Clubs: Fountainhead Country; Elks; Rotary of Long Meadows. Home: 133 Overhill Dr Hagerstown MD 21740 Office: Creager & Button 1329 Pennsylvania Ave Hagerstown MD 21740

CREAGER, WILLIAM ARTHUR, mgmt. cons.; b. Columbus, Ohio, Apr. 26, 1932; s. William Arthur and Margaret Annette (Logan) C.; B.S., U.S. Naval Acad., 1954; postgrad. Carnegie Inst. Tech., 1955-59; M. Engring. Adminstrn., George Washington U., 1964; m. Marilyn Louise Jordan, Sept. 22, 1956; children—Matthew Jordan, Anne. Supr. tech. info. office Westinghouse Electric Corp., Pitts., 1954-59; asst. program dir. NSF, Washington, 1959-62; v.p., treas. Herner & Co., Washington, 1962-65; v.p. Wolf Research & Devel. Corp., Washington, 1965-69; pres. Capital Systems Group, Inc., Washington, 1969—, also chmn. bd. Mng. editor Gen. Aviaton Accident Report, Digests of Pipeline Rates on Crude Petroleum and Gasoline. Mem. Am. Soc. Info. Sci., Assn. for Computing Machinery. Contbr. chpt. to book. Home: 11200 Luxmanor Rd Rockville MD 20852 Office: 6110 Executive Blvd Suite 250 Rockville MD 20852

CREAMER, ALICE DUBOIS, artist, sculptress, musician; b. Roadstown, N.J., Apr. 16, 1915; d. Lester Maul and Eva Amy (James) duBois; m. Malcom Kenneth Creamer, Jan. 30, 1934; children—Malcom Kenneth, Alice Virginia (Mrs. Gary Stansell). One man show Bridgeton Art Gallery, 1973; exhibited sculpture and copper enameling, Chgo. and Dallas, 1966; numerous commd. sculpture portraits; performer on recorder and gamba Baroque and renaissance groups. Leader, 4-H Clubs, 1945-55. Mem. Bridgeton Antiquarian League (art gallery com., curator hist. mus. instruments), Christian Art Assos. (charter), Soc. Internat. Harpsichord Builders, Am. Recorder Soc., Viola da Gamba Soc. Am. Home: RD 5 Finley Station Rd Bridgeton NJ 08302

CREAMER, GERALDINE MARGARET, librarian; b. Sayreville, N.J., June 23, 1914; d. Thomas Aloysious and Ann Marie (Johnson) Creamer; student Drakes Bus. Coll., 1930-31. Sample girl, Dupont Photo Products, Parlin, N.J., 1932-34; salesgirl Daylight Bakery, South Amboy, N.J., 1935-40, Berkley Bake Shop, New Brunswick, N.J., 1945-46. Bd. dirs. Sayreville Free Pub. Library, 1946—. Mem. Am., N.J. (co-chmn. room arrangements com.), Cath. library assns. Home: 7 S Minnisink Ave Sayreville NJ 08872 Office: Washington Rd Parlin NJ 08859

CREECH, RICHARD HEARNE, med. oncologist; b. Boston, Apr. 6, 1940; s. Hugh John and E. Marie (Hearne) C.; A.B., Johns Hopkins U., 1961; M.D., U. Pa., 1965; m. Charlotte Elizabeth Goetz, Dec. 28, 1963; children—Susan Marie, Nancy Elizabeth. Intern in medicine Hosp. of U. Pa., Phila., 1965-66, resident in medicine, 1966-67, fellow in immunology and hematology, 1970-71; clin. asso. Nat. Cancer Inst., 1967-70; practice medicine specializing in med. oncology, Phila., 1971—; mem. staff Am. Oncologic Hosp., Phila., 1972—, med. dir. out-patient dept., 1975—, pres. med. staff, 1977—; cons. med. oncology Germantown Hosp. and Dispensary, Phila., Jeanes Hosp., Phila., Mercer Med. Center, Trenton, N.J., St. Mary Hosp., Langhorne, Pa.; asst. prof. clin. medicine Sch. Medicine, U. Pa., Phila., 1973—. Served with USPHS, 1967-70. Diplomate Am. Bd. Internal Medicine (subspltys. med. oncology, hematology). Fellow A.C.P., Coll. Physicians Phila.; mem. AMA, Am. Soc. Clin. Oncology, Eastern Coop. Oncology Group, Pa. Soc. Internal Medicine, Phila. County Med. Soc., Radiation Therapy Oncology Group, Phi Beta Kappa, Alpha Omega Alpha. Republican. Episcopalian. Home: 1135 Goodman Dr Fort Washington PA 19034 Office: Am Oncologic Hosp Central and Shelmire Aves Philadelphia PA 19111

CREED, WILLIAM HOWARD, army officer; b. Siler City, N.C., Mar. 10, 1925; s. Lonnie Wheeler and Alta Elizabeth (Jones) C.; B.S. in Bus. Adminstrn., U. Nebr., Omaha, 1970; M.S. in Mgmt., Fla. Inst. Tech., 1972; m. Katherine Hill, June 22, 1947; 1 son, William Howard. Commd. 2d lt. U.S. Army, 1952, advanced through grades to col., 1973; served in Vietnam, 1967-68; product mgr. Small Arms, Washington, 1969-71; dir. procurement, Joliet, Ill., 1972-73; dir. prodn., Rock Island, Ill., 1973-75; dir. contractor adminstrn. Dept. Def., Garden City, N.Y., 1975—. Decorated Legion of Merit. Mem. coordinating com. Combined Fedn. Campaign, L.I., N.Y., 1975—. Mem. Air Force Assn. (exec. com. Hap Arnold chpt.), Nat. Contract Mgmt. Assn., Am. Def. Preparedness Assn., Am. Legion, VFW. Clubs: Masons, Order Eastern Star.

CREGIER, DON MESICK, educator; b. Schenectady, Mar. 28, 1930; s. Harry Mesick and Marion (Shovea) C.; B.A., Union Coll., 1951; M.A., U. Mich., 1952; m. Sharon Kathleen Ellis, June 29, 1965. Instr. history U. Tenn., Knoxville, 1956-57; asst. prof. history Baker U., Baldwin City, Kans., 1958-61, Keuka Coll., Keuka Park, N.Y., 1962-64, St. John's U., Collegeville, Minn., 1964-65, St. Dunstan's U., Can., 1966-69; asso. prof. history Prince Edward Island U., Charlottetown, 1969—. Mark Hopkins fellow, 1965-66; Can. Council fellow, 1972-73. Mem. Conf. on British Studies, Assn. of Contemporary Historians, Phi Sigma Kappa, Phi Beta Kappa, Phi Kappa Phi, Pi Gamma Mu. Author: Bounder from Wales, 1976; editor, Quest for Edn., 1966-67; contbr. articles in field to profl. jours. Home: 26 York Ln Brighton PE Canada Office: Dept of History Univ of Prince Edward Island Charlottetown PE C1A 4P3 Canada

CREMONA, LEONARD FRANCIS, mfg. co. exec.; b. N.Y.C., Feb. 11, 1922; s. Leonard Francis and Libuse (Senor) C.; B.S. in Applied Math., Poly. Inst. Bklyn., 1958; m. Marie Lanteri, Feb. 19, 1944; children—Thomas, Lynn, Curtis, Wendy, Lisa, Lori. Plant analyst RCA Communications, Inc., N.Y.C., 1947-52; supr. nuclear contracts adminstrn. Combustion Engring., Inc., N.Y.C., 1952-59; mgr. contracts and mktg. adminstrn. ACF Industries, Inc., Paramus, N.J., 1959-64; mgr. corporate contracts and patents Teledyne Isotopes, Inc., Westwood, N.J., 1964-75; mgr. contracts, indsl. process engrs. Aero-jet Gen. Corp., Newark, 1975-77; mgr. contracts Electronic Assos., Inc., W. Long Branch, N.J., 1977—; v.p., dir. Energy Planning Assos. Corp., Hawthorne, N.J., 1977—, Urban Renewal Corp., Newark, 1977—. Served in USMC, 1941-47; PTO. Recipient citation Poly. Inst. Bklyn., 1958, ASME, 1958; medal AEC, 1957; N.Y. state scholar, 1954. Mem. Licensing Execs. Soc., Am. Mgmt. Assn., Internat. Platform Assn., Am. Def. Preparedness Assn., Nat. Contracts Mgmt. Assn. Republican. Roman Catholic. Author articles in field. Home: 231 Nedellec Dr Saddle Brook NJ 07662 Office: 185 Monmouth Pkwy West Long Branch NJ 07764

CREMONA, VINCENT ANTHONY, banking adminstr.; b. Valetta, Malta, Nov. 5, 1925; s. Henry and Jane Mary (Cachia) C.; came to U.S., 1959, naturalized, 1965; B.S., Stella Maris Coll., Maita, 1945; M.S. in Finance, London Sch. Accountancy, 1950. Ships purveyor Peninsular and Oriental Steam Nav. Co., Valetta, 1945-50; asst. supr. Gen. Motors, Oshawa, Ont., Can., 1950-55; accounting supr. Ind. Groceries Assn., Toronto, Ont., Can., 1955-59; asst. accounting mgr. Air India, N.Y.C., 1960-65; dir. adminstrn. and finance Commonwealth Services, Dhahran Internat. Airport, Saudi Arabia, 1965-66; mgr. internal audits Litton Industries, Carlstadt, N.J., 1966-67; v.p. Fashioncade, N.Y.C., 1967-68; staff asst., tng. dir. Fed. Res. System, Washington, 1969—. Certified internal auditor. Mem. Inst. Internal Auditors, Assn. Govt. Accountants. Roman Catholic. Home: Columbia Plaza Envoy 2450 Virginia Ave NW Washington DC 20037 Office: Fed Reserve System Office of Staff Dir for Fed Res Bank Activities Washington DC 20551

CRENSHAW, DAVID ALLEN, psychologist; b. Hannibal, Mo., May 9, 1944; s. Joel V. and Genevieve E. (Meadows) C.; A.B magna cum laude, William Jewell Coll., 1965; Ph.D., Washington U., St. Louis, 1969; m. Mary Lupton, Dec. 27, 1970; children—Stefanie Lee, Gillian Elizabeth. Staff psychologist VA Hosp., St. Louis, 1969-72; asst. clin. prof. psychiatry St. Louis U. Sch. Medicine, 1970-72; dir. clin. services, dir. Rhinebeck (N.Y.) Country Sch., 1972-78; pvt. practice clin. psychology, 1978—; asst. prof. psychology U. Mo., 1969; lectr. Washington U., 1969-72, So. Ill. U., 1967-69; cons. Labor Health Inst., St. Louis, 1970-72. Vol. Parents Without Partners, mental health tng. chaplains and ministers, St. Louis, 1970-71; bd. dirs. Rhinebeck County Vocat. Tng. Center, Inc.; advisory com. Dutchess Community Coll.; mem. community advisory bd. The Gables. Recipient James L. Sullivan award William Jewell Coll., 1965. Mem. Am., Mid-Hudson psychol. assns., Assn. Advancement of Psychology, Dutchess County Mental Health Soc., Rhinebeck Hist. Soc. Phi Epsilon. Club: Rotary (pres. 1978-79). Author film (with Drs.

Waldo Bird and Gary Arthur) on Extended Family Therapy, 1971. Contbr. articles to profl. jours. Home: RD 3 Box 280 Rhinebeck NY 12572 Office: 91-93 Montgomery St Rhinebeck NY 12572

CRENSHAW, MARY ANN, author; b. Montgomery, Ala., Apr. 18, 1929; d. Jack and Catherine (Westcott) Crenshaw; B.A. Vanderbilt U., 1951; student U. Havana, summer 1950, Parsons Sch. Design, 1957. Apprentice, asst. Charles James Inc., N.Y.C., 1957-58; with mdse. dept. Vogue Mag., N.Y.C., 1958-61; mgr. boutique Shangri-La, N.Y.C., 1961-62; publicist Adolfo, Inc., N.Y.C., 1962; fashion coordinator Ohrbach's, N.Y.C., 1962-65; fashion reporter N.Y. Times, 1965-76; pres. M.A.C. Prodns. Ltd., author's corp., N.Y.C., 1972—. Democrat. Episcopalian. Author: The Natural Way to Super Beauty, 1974; Shape Up for Super Sex, 1976. Home and office: 211 E 70th St New York City NY 10021

CRERAR, JOHN DUNCAN MACALLISTER, bronze and silver mfg. co. exec.; b. Providence, Sept. 28, 1928; s. Duncan Haggert and Jean Pratt (MacAllister) C.; student U. R.I., 1947, Brown U., 1948; m. Alice S. Levillie, July 17, 1950; children—Claire M., John Duncan MacAllister. Advt. coordinator Coca Cola Bottling Co., Providence, 1953-58; with Gorham Bronze Textron, 1958—, v.p. mktg. and sales, Washington, 1977—. Advisor, Pres.'s Com. on Olympic Sports. Served with USAF, 1948-52. Mem. Sales and Mktg. Execs. of U.S., Nat. Assn. Cemeteries, Am., So. cemetery assns., Internat. Cemetery Supply Assn. (pres. 1977—), Amateur Hockey Assn. U.S. (dir. 1969—), Southeastern Amateur Hockey Assn. (pres. 1974—). Home: 12504 Two Farm Dr Silver Spring MD 20904 Office: Gorham Bronze Textron Suite 300 1666 K St NW Washington DC 20006

CRESSLER, JOHN CHARLES, former army med. officer, med. adminstr.; b. Wilkes-Barre, Pa., June 17, 1915; s. John Webster and Cora Irene (Reimard) C.; B.S. in Biology, Lafayette Coll., 1937; M.D., Jefferson Med. Coll., 1941; M.H.A. with honors, Northwestern U., 1952; m. Kathleen Hutton Smith, Jan. 18, 1942; 1 son, John Webster II. Commd. 2d lt. U.S. Army, 1937, advanced through grades to col., 1959; rotating intern Walter Reed Gen. Hosp., Washington, 1941-42, gen. surgery tng., 1945-46; gen. surgery tng. Gorgas Gen. Hosp., Panama C.Z., 1946-49; instr. Med. Field Service Sch., Carlisle Barracks, Pa., 1942-43; adminstrv. surgeon, M.C. instr. Anti-Aircraft Sch., Camp Davis, N.C., 1943-44; med. instr. F.A. Sch., Ft. Sill, Okla., 1944; comdg. officer Armored Med. Co., Europe, 1944-45; comdg. officer, chief operating surgeon Sta. Hosp., Ft. Sheridan, Ill., 1949-50; dep. corps surgeon, Korea, 1950-51; comdg. officer Combined Hosp. Facilities, Korea, 1951; dep. comdr. William Beaumont Gen. Hosp., El Paso, Tex., 1952-54; chief M.C. assignment sect. Office Surgeon Gen., Washington, 1954-55, chief officer br. personnel div., 1955-58; asst. Army attache U.S. embassy, London, Eng., 1958-61; chief operations div. Surgeon's Office 2d U.S. Army, Ft. Meade, Md., 1961-62, Army surgeon, 1962-64; comdg. officer Walson Army Hosp., Ft. Dix, N.J., 1964-67, also post surgeon; staff dir. Def. Med. Materiel Bd., Potomac Annex, Washington, 1967-70; ret., 1970; asso. dir. Greater Delaware Valley Regional Med. Program, Haverford, Pa., 1970-74; cons., 1974—. Decorated Legion of Merit with oak leaf cluster. Fellow Am. Coll. Hosp. Adminstrs.; mem. AMA, Am. Hosp. Assn., Assn. Mil. Surgeons, Fed. Hosp. Inst. Assn., Assn. U.S. Army, Soc. Plastic Engrs., Royal Soc. Health Eng. Address: 6011 Bradley Blvd Bethesda MD 20034

CRESSON, JAMES, chem. engr.; b. Jeffersonville, Pa., Jan. 18, 1915; s. James and Mary Wilhomena (Reeb) C.; B.S. Chem. Engring., U. Pa., 1937; m. Marjorie Mulholland, Nov. 21, 1942; children—James L., Carol Elaine. With L.D. Caulk Co., Milford, Del., 1937—, dir. quality assurance, 1960-74, dir. tech. research, 1975—. Sussex County (Del.) chmn. Gov's. Com. for Employment Handicapped, 1961-66; dist. commr. Delmarva council Boy Scouts Am., 1962-64; sr. warden Christ Episcopal Ch., Milford, 1968-72. Mem. Am., Internat. assns. dental research, Am. Chem. Soc., Mil. Order Loyal Legion U.S. Republican. Clubs: Rotary, Shawnee Country. Patentee in field, U.S. and Can. Home: 613 Seabury Ave Milford DE 19963 Office: L D Caulk PO Box 359 Milford DE 19963

CREWS, JAMES ELDON, govt. ofcl.; b. Princeton, Ky., Feb. 15, 1943; s. Evan Eldon and Helen (Pruett) C.; B.S., Tenn. Technol. U., 1965; M.C.E., Cath. U. Am., 1970; m. Ann Suzette Morrow, Feb. 4, 1967. With C.E., U.S. Army, Louisville, 1965-67, Balt., 1967—, chief urban studies br. planning div., 1974—. Pres., Campus Green Community Assn., 1972. Registered profl. engr., D.C. Mem. ASCE, Am. Water Resource Assn., Am. Geophys. Union, Internat. Water Resource Assn., Soc. Am. Mil. Engrs. (pres. 1977; Young Engr. of Year 1977). Democrat. Methodist. Contbr. articles in field to profl. jours. Home: 662 Quail Run Ct Arnold MD 21012 Office: Urban Studies Br Balt Dist Corps Engrs Box 1715 Baltimore MD 21203

CRIARES, NICHOLAS JAMES, obstetrician, gynecologist; b. Bronx, N.Y., Apr. 2, 1934; s. James George and Christina (Brim) C.; B.A., Columbia Coll., 1955; M.D., St. Louis U., 1960; m. Helen Athos, July 3, 1966; 1 son, Peter. Intern, Meadowbrook Hosp., Hempstead, N.Y., 1960-61; resident Met. Hosp., N.Y.C., 1961-62, Misericordia Hosp., Phila., 1962-65, Johns Hopkins Hosp., Balt., 1965-66; practice medicine specializing in obstetrics and gynecology, Hartsdale, N.Y., 1972—; mem. staff Albert Einstein Coll., Bronx-Lebanon hosps.; asst. prof. obstetrics Albert Einstein Coll. Medicine, 1972—; cons. Bronx Peer Systems Rev. Orgn., Kings County Health Care Rev. Orgn. Served to capt. USAF, 1966-68; Vietnam. Mem. AMA (recognition award 1973), Med. Soc. State N.Y., Westchester County Med. Soc., Bronx Obstetrical and Gynecol. Soc., Am. Coll. Obstetricians and Gynecologists, A.C.S., Urban Physicians Soc. Contbr. articles to med. jours.

CRICHTON, NEIL MCCOLLUM, realty and constrn. co. exec.; b. Bklyn., N.Y., Aug. 24, 1932; s. Alexander and Elizabeth Rose (Miller) C.; grad. N.Y. Inst. Tech., 1958; m. Selafani Ceil, June 4, 1955; children—Kevin, Tammie. Engine room engr. Morgan Guaranty Trust Co., N.Y.C., 1955-61; operating engr. Cross & Brown Co., N.Y.C., 1961, chief engr., 1961-64, bldg. mgr., N.Y.C., 1964-70; bldg. mgr. Tishman Realty & Constrn. Co., N.Y.C., 1970-78, area engr., 1974—. Certified fire safety dir. Mem. Nat. Assn. Power Engrs., N.Y. Bldg. Mgrs. Assn. Home: 5 Hearthstone Dr Englishtown NJ 07726 Office: 919 3d Ave New York City NY 10022

CRIDDLE, A. HAWTHORNE, corp. exec.; b. Portsmouth, Va., June 9, 1909; s. Chester A. and Virginia (Hawthorne) C.; student Wharton Sch., U. Pa., 1929-32; m. Josephine Glammer, Sept. 5, 1959; children—A. Hawthorne, Dana C., Priscilla V. With ins. dept. S.A.L. Ry., 1926-29; with Mather and Co., 1929-49, asst. v.p., 1945-49; mgr. gen. ins. dept. Oetheimer Co., 1949-51; v.p., dir., Ostheimer-Walsh, Inc., 1952-57, exec. v.p., 1957-66; pres. OW & Criddle Associates, Inc., Phila., 1966-69; exec. v.p. Fred S. James & Co., Inc. of Pa. (merger with OW & Criddle Assos., Inc.), 1969-76; mng. partner Warren McVeigh & Griffin of Delaware Valley, 1977—. Mem. Ins. Inst. Am. (treas. 1975-77), Soc. Chartered Property and Casualty Underwriters (pres. 1964), Am. Inst. Property and Liability Underwriters (treas. 1975-77, exam. com.), Nat. Assn. Ins. Brokers (pres. 1974), Radley Run Country. Contbg. author Risk management; Property and Liability Insurance Handbook. Contbr. to profl. publs. Lectr., discussion leader various seminars. Home: 1112 Queensway West Chester PA 19380 Office: 845 West Chester Pike West Chester PA 19380

CRIHAN, IOAN G(RIGORE), electronics engr.; b. Romania, Mar. 8, 1932; s. Grigore and Elisabeta (Sarbu) C.; came to U.S., 1969, naturalized, 1974; grad. radar dept. Tech. Mil. Acad., Bucharest, Romania, 1955, utilization of radioisotopes Romanian Acad., Bucharest, 1968; m. Marietta Enescu, Jan. 9, 1964. Electronics engr. Army Lab., Romania, 1956-60, Tarom Radar Dept., Romania, 1961-64, Standards and Inventions Inst., Romania, 1964-66, Bucharest U., 1966-68, Siemens Plant, Nuremberg, W. Ger., 1968-69, N.Y. U. Radiation and Solid State Lab., 1969-71, sci. instrument div. Siemens Corp., Iselin, N.J., 1971-72, dept. cell biology-electronic microscopy Rockefeller U., 1972-73; pres. Art Restoration & Irradiating Preservation, Inc., N.Y.C., 1973—. Mem. IEEE, Am. Phys. Soc., Fedn. Am. Scientists, Assn. Preservation of Tech. Inventor in field. Home and Office: 417 E 64th St Apt 4G New York NY 10021

CRILL, EDWARD L., psychologist, coll. adminstr.; b. North Manchester, Ind., Aug. 13, 1917; s. Jesse J. and Mary M. (Keister) C.; B.A., Manchester Coll., 1946; M. Ed., Johns Hopkins U., Balt., 1952; Ed.D., Temple U., Phila., 1973; m. Helene Blough, May 29, 1943; children—Carol, Linda, Jayk, Anita. Regional field dir. Brethren Service Commn., McPherson, Kans., 1946-48; nat. tng. dir., New Windsor, Md., 1948-51, dir. field services youth div., gen. bd., Elgin, Ill., 1951-59; dean student affairs Elizabethtown (Pa.) Coll., 1959-71, specialist in program devel., 1971-77; pvt. practice counseling and clin. psychology, Harrisburg, Pa., 1975—; communications trainer bus. and industry. Licensed psychologist, Pa. Mem. Am. Soc. Personnel Adminstrn. (accredited personnel specialist), Internat. Transactional Analysis Assn. (certified), Am. Soc. Tng. and Devel. (personnel tng.), Am., Pa. personnel and guidance assns., Am., Pa. coll. personnel assns., Phi Delta Kappa. Democrat. Kiwanian (pres. Elizabethtown 1964, Outstanding Service award 1967). Home: Route 7 Box 344 Manheim PA 17545

CRIMMINS, JAMES JOSEPH, pharmacist; b. Jersey City, Sept. 13, 1947; s. Thomas Lawrence and Wilma Nell (Nobel) C.; student Providence Coll., 1965-67; B.S., Fordham U., 1970; M.S., Bklyn. Coll. Pharmacy, 1976; m. Judith Ann Moritz, May 31, 1969; children—Colleen Lynn, James Brian. Pharmacy intern Pascack Valley Hosp., Westwood, N.Y., 1969-71; staff pharmacist Valley Hosp., Ridgewood, N.J., 1971-73, dispensing supr., 1973-75; dir. pharmacy Riverdell Hosp., Oradell, N.J., 1975-78, S.I. (N.Y.) Hosp., 1978—. Mem. Am., N.J. socs. hosp. pharmacists, Rho Chi. Home: 13 Varnum Ln Manalpan NJ 07726 Office: Castleton Ave Staten Island NY 10301

CRISCI, RICHARD HENRY, psychologist; b. Bklyn., May 3, 1945; s. Clemente and Rose Lucille (Grosswald) C.; B.A., Hofstra U., 1967, Ph.D., 1972; M.A., Bowling Green (Ohio) State U., 1969; m. Barbara Horowski, June 14, 1969. Research asst. psychology Bowling Green State U., 1967, teaching fellow, 1968; instr. psychology Hofstra U., Hempstead, N.Y., 1970-72; psychologist Islip (N.Y.) pub. schs., 1971-72; instr. psychology State U.N.Y., Stony Brook, 1972-73; psychologist Port Washington (N.Y.) pub. schs., 1972—; pvt. practice psychology, Hempstead, 1973—; cons. psychologist Long Beach (N.Y.) Meml. Hosp. Licensed psychologist, N.Y. Mem. Am., N.Y. State, Nassau County (exec. bd.) psychol. assns., Psi Chi. Home: 55 Amherst Rd Albertson NY 11507 Office: 4 Warner Ave Hempstead NY 11550

CRISFAFI, BARTEL ROBERT, cardiologist; b. New Haven, Aug. 9, 1937; s. Anthony J. and Frances Mary (Aversa) C.; B.S., Fairfield U., 1959; M.D., Loyola U., Chgo., 1963; m. Louise Leperi, Sept. 10, 1960; children—Rita, Frances, Julia, Bartel, Louise. Intern, Greenwich (Conn.) Hosp., 1963-64; resident in medicine, 1964-65; cardiology fellow Boston U., 1967-69; practice medicine specializing in cardiology, Greenwich, 1969—; clin. instr. Yale U., New Haven. Served with USAF, 1965-67. Diplomate Am. Bd. Internal Medicine. Fellow Am. Coll. Cardiology, Am. Coll. Chest Physicians, Council Clin. Cardiology of Am. Heart Assn.; mem. Am. Profl. Practice Assn. Roman Catholic. Club: Burning Tree Country (Greenwich). Home: 82 Butternut Hollow Rd Greenwich CT 06830 Office: 49 Lake Ave Greenwich CT 06830

CRISMAN, RONALD EVERETT WILLIAM, state ofcl.; b. Oak Park, Ill., Nov. 2, 1927; s. Wilson Thomas and Anna C. (Johnson) C.; student Ill. Inst. Tech., 1945-46; B.A. in Economics and Bus. Adminstrn., Iowa Wesleyan Coll., 1950; m. JoAnne E. Frick, June 23, 1951; children—Jeffrey T., Candace S., Kevin J. New product analyst Caterpillar Tractor, Chgo., 1950-52, corp. policy planning, Joliet, Ill., 1952-53; ins. and real estate broker, 1953-64; co-owner supermarket chain, Joliet, 1960-64; owner Country Store, Peacham, Vt., 1964-65; asst. budget dir. State of Vt., Montpelier, 1965-68, commr. budget and mgmt., 1968-77, sec. transp., 1977—. Pres. New Lenox (Ill.) Library; mem. New Lenox Sch. Bd. Served with U.S. Army, 1946-47; Japan. Mem. Nat. Assn. State Budget Officers (life; pres. 1974), Am. Assn. State Hwy., Transp. Ofcls., N.E. Assn. Transp. Ofcls., Council State Transp. Dirs., Am. Soc. Pub. Adminstrn. Republican. Unitarian. Home: 5 Liberty St Montpelier VT 05602 Office: Agy Transp 133 State St Montpelier VT 05602

CRISSAN, MICHAEL GEORGE, communications exec.; b. Athens, Greece, June 26, 1922; s. George Michael and Anastasia K.; came to U.S., 1951, naturalized, 1954; B.S., Sup. Coll. Polit. Sci., 1943; student Yale U., 1951, Columbia U., 1952; m. Bonnie R. Munro, July 9, 1966; 1 son, Michael Munro. War corr. Brit. Ministry of Info., Cairo, 1943-46, UP, 1946-48, Time Mag., 1947-49, AP, 1948-51; Fulbright scholar in journalism, 1951-52; dir. communications ITT Grinnell Corp., Providence, 1974—; cons. ITT, Colgate Palmolive, 1966-74. Served to capt. Greek Royal Inf., 1949-50. Mem. Pub. Relations Soc., Overseas Press Club (past gov.). Club: Watch Hill (R.I.) Yacht. Contbr. articles to local and nat. pubs. Home: 182 Shore Rd Westerly RI 02891 Office: 260 W Exchange St Providence RI 02901

CRISSEY, DAVID LEE, counselor vocat. rehab.; b. Tonawanda, N.Y., May 3, 1937; s. Earl Guy and Sadie Kay (Harris) C.; B.A., U. Buffalo, 1959, M.S., 1961; Ph.D., State U. N.Y., Buffalo, 1972. Chief counseling services Buffalo Goodwill Industries Inc., 1969-70; asst. prof. counselor edn. State U. N.Y. at Buffalo, 1971-72, adj. asst. prof., 1973—; counselor vocat. rehab. N.Y. State Office Vocat. Rehab., 1973—; cons. continuing edn. rehab. Served with U.S. Army, 1961-63. Certified rehab. counselor N.Y. Mem. Western N.Y. (pres. 1977-78), Nat. rehab. assns., Western N.Y. Rehab. Counselors Assn. (pres. 1964-65), Am., N.Y. State (rec. sec. 1974-75) personnel and guidance assns., Am. Psychol. Assn. Methodist. Home: 181 Fletcher St Tonawanda NY 14150 Office: NY State Office Vocat Rehab Gen Donovan State Office Bldg 125 Main St Buffalo NY 14203

CRISSMAN, JAMES HUDSON, architect; b. Pitts., Apr. 28, 1937; s. Harold Eugene and Anna Martha (Logan) C.; B.Arch., Carnegie Inst. Tech., 1960; M.Arch. in Urban Design, Harvard U., 1966; m. Louisa Goddard Murray, Dec. 31, 1966; children—Charles Wright McMurtrie, Sarah Wood deCoursey, William Goddard. Architect with Paul Schweikher, architect, Pitts., 1962-63, Ralph R. Drury, architect, Pitts., 1963-64, Skidmore Owings and Merrill, N.Y.C., 1964-66, Victor Gruen Assos., architects, N.Y.C., 1966-67, Sasaki Dawson DeMay Assos., Inc., Watertown, Mass., 1967-70, Crissman & Solomon Architects, Inc., Watertown, 1970—; mem. faculty Boston Archtl. Center, 1968-71; vis. critic, lectr. Harvard Grad. Sch. Design, 1976—; major works include: Crissman House, Hilton Head Island, S.C., 1971, Fenn House, Center Lovell, Maine, 1973, Gill House, West Campton, N.H., 1973, Babcock Kidney Center, Boston, 1975, Curtis House, Millerton, N.Y., 1975, Dickson House, New Vernon, N.J., 1978, Littauer Center, Harvard U., 1978, Sommerville House, Wilson, N.C., 1979. Sec. Watertown Conservation Commn., 1968-70; treas. Sheepscot Valley Conservation Assn., 1970-71; organist and choirmaster Whitehall Ch., Pitts., 1960-64, St. John's Episcopal Ch., Newtonville, Mass., 1972-74; trustee Children's Hosp. Med. Center, Boston; mem. corp. Old North Ch., Boston; chmn. bd. Center Liturgy and The Arts, Newton, Mass. Served with U.S. Air Force Res., 1960-66. Recipient First Prize award Charleston S.C. Mus. Design Competition, 1976; awards Archtl. Record, 1977, 79; registered architect in N.Y., Mass., Maine, Md., N.C., N.H., R.I., S.C., N.J., Vt. Mem. AIA (award of merit New Eng. Regional Council 1976, 78, honor award N.H. chpt. 1976), Mass. State Assn. Architects, Boston Soc. Architects (award of design excellence 1977), Am. Guild Organists. Democrat. Episcopalian. Composer: Carol of the Friendly Beasts, 1965. Home: 3 Brigham St Watertown MA 02172 Office: 44 Hunt St Watertown MA 02172

CRIST, GERTRUDE H. (MRS. HOWARD G. CRIST, JR.), civic worker; b. Barnard, S.D.; d. Jacob H. and Lillian Belle (Freeman) Hartman; student S.D. State Coll., 1936-38; m. Howard Grafton Crist, Jr., Nov. 2, 1940; children—Howard Grafton III, Douglas Freeman. Vice pres. Farm and Home Service, Inc.; dir. Columbia Bank and Trust Co. Chmn., Westmoreland County chpt. A.R.C., 1946—, sec., 1943-45, chmn. vol. spl. services, 1944-45, dir. Howard County chpt. 1973—; past chmn. Cancer drive Howard County; mem. Howard County Bd. Edn., 1953-70, pres., 1963-65; bd. dirs. Howard County Tb Assn.; v.p. Howard Community Coll., 1969-70; adv. council Catonsville Community Coll.; chmn. Emergency Civil Def. Hosp. Howard County; mem, Md. Council for Higher Edn., 1968-77, Md. State Bd. Higher Edn., 1977—; mem. Md. Bd. for Community Colls., 1968-77. Bd. dirs. Central Md. council Girl Scouts U.S.A., Howard County A.R.C. Mem. Nat. Congress Parents and Tchrs. (hon. life), Md. Congress Parents and Tchrs. (life), Md. Assn. Bds. Edn. (sec. 1962-64, pres. 1966, 67), Howard County Council P.T.A.'s, West Friendship PTA (sec. 1949-51), League Women Voters (county sec. 1957-59, dir. 1960-62, pres. 1959), Nat. Schs. Bds. Assn. (bd. dirs. 1968-71); hon. mem. Delta Kappa Gamma state and local chpts. Episcopalian (mem. vestry, chmn. Parish Day Sch. 1970-73). Home: Burnt Woods Rd PO Sykesville MD 21784

CRISTOFER, MICHAEL, actor, author; b. Trenton, N.J., Jan. 22, 1945; s. Joseph Peter and Mary (Muccioli) Procaccino; student Catholic U. Am., 1962-65, Am. U. Beirut, 1968-69. Repertory actor Arena Stage, Washington, 1967-68, Theatre of Living Arts, Phila., 1968, Beirut Repertory Co., 1968-69, N.Y. Shakespeare Festival, 1970, Mark Taper Forum, Los Angeles, 1972-75; stage appearances include The Cherry Orchard, 1977, Conjuring An Event, 1978; TV appearances in The Entertainer, 1975, The Last of Mrs. Lincoln, 1975, Knuckle, 1976; film appearance in Enemy of the People, 1976; author: (plays) The Mandala, 1967, Rienzi, 1968, Dorian, 1969, Plot Counter Plot, 1971, Americomedia, 1972, The Shadow Box (Pulitzer prize for drama 1977, Antoinette Perry award 1977, Los Angeles Drama Critic award best play 1975), 1972, Ice, 1974, Black Angel, 1976. Recipient Theatre World award for performance, 1977, Los Angeles Drama Critics award for acting, 1973. Office: care Morosco Theatre 217 W 45th St New York NY 10036*

CRITCHER, MARGE BERNADINE, ednl. adminstr.; b. Balt., Dec. 17, 1935; d. Joseph Lawrence and Marguerite Cecilia (Flury) Sullivan; student Coll. Notre Dame Md., part-time 1955-69; B.A., Loyola at Balt., 1973, M.S., 1976; postgrad. theology St. Mary Seminary U., 1976—; m. William Anson Critcher, June 17, 1961; children—William Francis, Rosemarie Cecilia, Charlene Marie, Jean Marie. Tchr., Balt. Cath. Elementary and Secondary Schs., 1954—; adult edn. coordinator, St. Michael Parish, Balt., 1976—; chmn. edn. 12 parishes Northeast Baltimore City/County, 1977—. Mem. Am. Personnel and Guidance Assn., Am. Sch. Counselor Assn., Alpha Sigma Nu. Democrat. Roman Catholic. Office: 2 Willow Ave Baltimore MD 21206

CROCKER, JANE LOPES, librarian; b. Wareham, Mass., Sept. 19, 1946; d. Joseoh Barros and Mary (Faria) L.; B.A., Bridgewater State Coll., 1968; M.S. in L.S., Simmons Coll., 1971; m. L. Steven Crocker, Feb. 14, 1976. Library asst. New Bedford (Mass.) Pub. Library, 1968-71; pub. services librarian Simmons Coll., Boston, 1971-73; head librarian Morse-Slanger Library, Boston, 1973-76; dir. library-media center Gloucester County Coll., Sewell, N.J., 1976—; exec. dir. Nat. Library Week in Mass., 1971-72. Mem. ALA, N.J. Library Assn., South Jersey Coll. Library Coop., Gloucester Library Orgn. (pub. relations chair), Camden-Gloucester Area Steering Council, Libraries Unltd. Editor: Bay State Librarian, 1974-76. Office: Tanyard Rd Sewell NJ 08080

CROCKETT, DANIEL JAMES, ambulance service exec.; b. Boston, Dec. 7, 1949; s. David Earl and Wilma Elizabeth (MacKay) C.; student Rockland (Mass.) pub. schs., spl. emergency med. technician tng.; m. Ann Louise Kennedy, Mar. 25, 1972; children—Denise Marie, Katherin Myra. Orderly, Mass. Gen. Hosp., 1967-68; driver, attendant Allied Ambulance Service of Boston, 1968-69; owner, mgr. Shore Ambulance Service, Rockland, 1969—; instr. emergency med. technician courses; sec. Brockton Area Emergency Med. System, 1975—; mem. Mass. Safety Team. Recipient cert. of appreciation Rockland Jaycees, 1976. Mem. Nat. Registry Emergency Med. Technicians, Nat., Mass. emergency med. technician assns., Mass., Southeastern Mass. ambulance assns., Ambulance and Med. Services Assn. Am., Am. Ambulance and Rescue Assn., Wang System Users Soc. Republican. Episcopalian. Office: PO Box 106 Rockland MA 02370

CROCKETT, THOMAS JOHN, III, govt. ofcl.; b. Farmington, Conn., Dec. 4, 1921; s. Thomas John and Agatha Louise (Hollinger) C.; B.A. cum laude, Harvard, 1943; postgrad. (Felix Warburg fellow), N.Y. U., 1944; postgrad. Trinity Coll., George Washington U., Charles U., Prague, Czechoslovakia, U. Bologna (Italy). Columnist, Harford Times, 1943-45; writer 1st Army Spl. Troops, 1945-47; asst. pub. affairs officer Dept. State, Bratislava, Czechoslovakia, 1948, Prague, 1949-50, Florence, Italy, 1950-52, Bologna, 1953-54, with USIA, Milan, Italy, 1955-56, pub. affairs office, Zagreb, Yugoslavia, 1957-58; assigned Rumanian-Russian lang. study Cornell U., 1959; asst. pub. affairs officer, Bucharest, Rumania, 1960; dir. Amerika Haus, Linz, Austria, 1961; policy officer for Eastern Europe, Voice of Am., 1962, chief Czech and Slovak programs, 1963-66; asst. cultural affairs officer, Manila, 1966-69; cultural attache, Tunis, Tunisia, 1969-73, Tel Aviv, 1973-76; dep. dir. Office of Pub. Affairs, Bur. Ednl. and Cultural Affairs, Dept. State, 1976-78; sr. planning officer, policy staff Internat. Communication Agy., Washington, 1978—; North Italian rep. Italo-Am. Commn. Ednl. Exchange, 1955-56. Acting chmn. Philippine-Am. Ednl. Found., 1966-69; chmn. U.S.-Israel Ednl. Found., 1973-74; bd. dirs. Manila Symphony Orch., 1966-69. Mem.

Signet Soc. (Harvard). Editor art catalogues, contbr. short stories and poems to various mags. Home: 3042 Que St NW Washington DC 20007 also PO Box 1 Unionville Farmington CT 06085 Office: Room 606A 1750 Pennsylvania Ave Washington DC 20547

CROFTON, RONALD CHARLES, accountant; b. Bklyn., Feb. 21, 1932; s. Harry Joseph and Grace M. (McDermott) C.; B.S. with honors, Lehigh U., 1954; m. Ruth Elaine Burston, Aug. 17, 1957; children—Michael Gerard, Valerie Ann, Patricia Marie. Partner, Price Waterhouse & Co., Huntington Station, N.Y., 1957—. Bd. dirs. St. Francis Hosp., Roslyn, N.Y.; trustee East Williston Sch. Bd. Served with USAF, 1954-57. Mem. Am. Inst. C.P.A.'s, N.Y. State Soc. C.P.A.'s. Club: Wheatley Hills Golf. Home: 40 Orchard Dr East Williston NY 11596 Office: 1 Huntington Quadrangle Huntington Station NY 11746

CROMBIE, DAVID EDWARD, Canadian govt. ofcl.; b. Toronto, Ont., Can., Apr. 24, 1936; s. Norman and Vera (Beamish) C.; m. Shirley Bowden, May 28, 1960; children—Carrie, Robin, Jonathan. Lectr. econs. and polit. sci. Ryerson Poly. Inst., 1962-71, dir. student services, 1966-71; alderman City of Toronto, 1969-72, mayor, 1972-78; mem. Ho. of Commons from Rosedale, 1978—. Conservative. Office: House of Commons Ottawa ON K1A 0A6 Canada

CROMPTON, CHARLES SENTMAN, JR., lawyer; b. Wilmington, Del., Dec. 30, 1936; s. Charles S. and R. Eugenia (Armstrong) C.; B.A., U. Del., 1958; LL.B., U. Va., 1961; m. Jean W. Ashe, June 15, 1958 (div. 1976); children—Rebecca A., Charles S.; m. 2d, Milbrey Dean Ross, May 21, 1977. Admitted to Del. bar, 1962; law clk. to U.S. Dist. Ct., Wilmington, 1961-62; asso., partner firm Potter, Anderson & Corroon, Wilmington, 1962—. Bd. dirs., sec. Hist. Soc. Del., Wilmington, 1965—; v.p. Critenton Rehab. Center, Wilmington, 1968-70. Mem. Am. (com. on clients security funds), Del. (treas. 1967-69, corp. law com. 1969—, chmn. 1974—) bar assns., Raven Soc., Phi Beta Kappa. Democrat. Clubs: Vicmead Hunt, Wilmington. Home: Box 3946 Greenville DE 19807 Office: 350 Delaware Trust Bldg Wilmington DE 19801

CRON, ANNE MARIE, publisher; b. Hempstead, L.I., N.Y., May 31, 1929; d. Thomas Morgan and Dorothy Josephine (McNally) Bohen; A.A., Mt. Ida Jr. Coll., 1947; m. John Bowes Cron, Apr. 15, 1950; children—Kevin J., Christopher J., Claudia Anne, Ian Morgan. Asst. sales service mgr. Columbia Broadcasting Co., N.Y.C., 1948-50; mgr. directory services, mgr. product info. for schs. Mgmt. Publs., Greenwich, Conn., 1965-66; dir. mktg. services, editor Conover-Nast Purchasing Indsl. Directory, Greenwich, 1966-72, bus. mgr., editor, 1972-73; asst. pub. U.S. Indsl. Directory, Cahners Pub. Co., 1973-75, co-pub., 1975—. Republican. Roman Catholic. Club: Nat. Badminton Assn. Home: 32 Winthrop Dr Riverside CT 06878 Office: 1200 Summer St Stamford CT 06905

CRONAN, DONALD GEORGE, electro-mech. magnetics co. exec.; b. Jamaica, N.Y., Oct. 26, 1924; s. George Daniel and Ethel Grace (Rowlands) C.; student Va. Commonwealth U., 1947-51. Art dir. advt. dept. Am. Bankers Assn., N.Y.C., 1958-72; advt. mgr. IMC Magnetics Corp., Westbury, N.Y., 1973—; dir. Castle & Cronan Inc., 1974. Pres. Manhasset (N.Y.) Young Republicans, 1962-63; commr. Town of North Hempstead (N.Y.) 1974-78. Served with inf. U.S. Army, 1942-46. Decorated Bronze Star. Mem. L.I. Advt. Club, Alden Kindred Am., Nat. Soc. Descendants John, Elizabeth Curtiss, Griswold, Peabody (pres.) family assns., Valley Forge, Conn., Old Saybrook hist. socs., Hist. Soc. Town North Hempstead (charter mem., dir. 1978—), Conn. Soc. Genealogists, S.R., S.A.R., Soc. Desc. Washington's Army at Valley Forge (founder, comdr. in chief), Soc. Mayflower Descs., Vet. Corps. Arty. State N.Y., Am. Legion (Legionaire of Yr. Nassau County 1968-69, chmn. Manhasset Gold Star Meml. com.), Nat. Soc. Old Plymouth Colony Descs., Nat. Soc. Sons and Daus. of Pilgrims, Soc. Descs. of Colonial Clergy, Soc. Descs. Founders of Hartford. Roman Catholic. Clubs: Cath. Alumni of L.I., K.C. Compiler: The Genealogy of Charles Rollo Peabody and Sophia Wilcott Powell of Holland Patent, 1969. Home: 40 Old Estate Rd Manhasset NY 11030 Office: 570 Main St Westbury NY 11590

CRONIE, MERVYN ALLAN, aerospace co. exec.; b. Trail, B.C., Can., June 28, 1938; s. Thomas Albert and Mary (Gripich) C.; came to U.S., 1961, naturalized, 1969; B. Applied Sci. in Metall. Engring., U. of B.C., 1961; m. Doreen Anne Jacobs, Sept. 5, 1959; children—Wendy, Barbara, Scott. Structures engr. Boeing Comml. Airplane Co., Renton, Wash., 1961-63; sr. accident investigator Govt. of Can., Nat. Aero. Establishment, Ottawa, Ont., Can., 1964; sr. analyst sales, mktg. Boeing Comml. Airplane Co., Renton, 1965-69, regional sales mgr., 1969-75, dir. program mgmt. mil. aircraft, 1976; dir. sales and mktg. internat. and comml. Boeing Vertol Co., Phila., 1976—; cons. on loan from Boeing to U.S. Forces on aircraft accident investigations. Brit. Iron and Steel Research Assn. scholar, 1961-63. Mem. Nat. Def. Transp. Assn., Helicopter Assn. Am., Am. Helicopter Soc., Army Aviation Assn., Assn. of the U.S. Army, Fraternal Order of Police. Republican. Clubs: St. James (Montreal). Contbr. tech. papers on airline planning and scheduling. Home: #2 Hunters Ln Chadds Ford PA 19317 Office: PO Box 16858 Philadelphia PA 19142

CRONIN, BONNIE KATHRYN, public relations exec.; b. Mpls., Mar. 11, 1941; d. Edwin Rector and Maude Kathryn (McPherson) Lamb; B.A., U. Mo., 1963, B.S. in Edn., 1964; M.S. in English, Ill. State U., 1970; m. Barry Jay Cronin, Jan. 22, 1963 (div. Feb. 1971); 1 son, Philip Scott. With Neds and Wardlow Advt. Agy., Columbia, 1962-64; tchr. Columbia Sch. System, 1964-68, Coleen Hoose Sch., Normal, Ill., 1968-69; tchr. WGLT Sta., Normal, 1969-70; with WBUR Sta., Boston, 1970—, gen. mgr., 1975-78; dir. public relations The Joy of Movement Center, instr. Boston U., 1973-75. Mem. com. to elect Elaine Noble, 1974; bd. dirs. Nat. Pub. Radio. Mem. Mass. Broadcasters Assn. (dir. 1973-78), NOW, Nat. Assn. Ednl. Broadcasters. Club: Press of Boston. Address: 1111 Boylston St #40 Boston MA 02215

CRONIN, DANIEL A., bishop. Ordained priest Roman Catholic Ch., 1952; aux. bishop of Boston, 1968-70, also titular bishop of Egnatia, 1968-70; bishop of Fall River, Mass., 1970—. Address: Box 2577 Fall River MA 02722

CRONIN, PAUL JOSEPH, dept. store exec.; b. Waltham, Mass., Mar. 19, 1923; s. Grover J. and Helen (Conolly) C.; B.A., Holy Cross Coll., 1944; postgrad. Notre Dame Coll., 1944-45, U. Colo., 1945, State Coll. Mass., 1963-66; m. Anna Moriarty, May 1, 1945; children—Paul Joseph, Anya (Mrs. Alan Ormsby), Philip J., Peter J., Raycliff Mary. Buyer, Grover Cronin, Inc., Waltham, 1947-48, asst. to mdse. mgr., 1948-49, corporate clk., 1949, mdse. mgr., 1950, v.p., 1952-70, pres., 1970—; pres. Frolic Realty & Marine, Martha's Vineyard, Mass., 1965—; trustee H & G Realty Trust, K & M Realty Trust; corporator Newton Savs. Bank, Waltham. Mem. De Cordova Museum, Brockton Art Center. Bd. dirs. Grover Cronin Meml. Found., Boy's Guidance Center. Served to lt. USNR, 1944-46. Mem. Nat. Retail Mchts. Assn., Acad. Polit. and Social Sci., Mass. Bay Yachting Union. Clubs: Corinthian Yacht (Marblehead, Mass.); Blue Water Sailing (Boston). Home: 38 Old Colony Rd Wellesley Hills MA 02181 Office: Moody St Waltham MA 02154

CRONIN, RAYMOND VALENTINE, mining co. exec.; b. Yonkers, N.Y., Feb. 17, 1924; s. Raymond Valentine and Virginia Dolores (Lee) C.; B.S., N.Y. U., 1949, postgrad., 1949-52; m. Gwendoline Mary Tigar, Sept. 21, 1957; children—Kevin, Peter, Brian, Tracie, Courtney. Asst. to comptroller Alexander Smith, Inc., Yonkers, 1949-54; comptroller E.R. Squibb & Son, N.Y.C., 1954-60; v.p. Penick & Ford, Ltd., Cedar Rapids, Iowa, 1960-65, pres., 1965-70; v.p. St. Joe Minerals Corp., N.Y.C., 1971—, v.p. fin., 1973—. Mem. Am. Inst. of Mining, Metall. and Petroleum Engrs., Am. Mining Congress (mem. fin. adv. council exec. com. 1972—), Fin. Execs. Inst., Lead Industries Assn., Zinc Inst. (treas. 1974), U.S. C. of C. (mem. taxation com.). Republican. Roman Catholic. Elk. Clubs: Canadian, Metropolitan, Mining (N.Y.C.). Home: 5 Whippoorwill Rd Chappaqua NY 10514 also 9 Ancona Ave Ocean Park ME 04063 Office: 250 Park Ave New York City NY 10017

CRONIN, TIMOTHY CORNELIUS, computer system mfg. co. exec.; b. Manchester, N.H., Sept. 26, 1927; s. Timothy Cornelius and Ann Frances (Meaney) C.; B.S., U.S. Mil. Acad., 1949; M.B.A., Ohio State U., 1952; m. Gloria Mara; June 8, 1949; children—Gloria Ann, Constance, Timothy, Barbara, Mary, Thomas. Commd. 2d lt. U.S. Air Force, 1949, advanced through grades to capt., 1956; ret., 1956; mgr., v.p. Honeywell, Inc., Mpls. and Wellesley, Mass., 1956-71; exec. v.p. Addressograph Multigraph, Cleve., 1971-74; chmn., chief exec. officer Inforex, Inc., Burlington, Mass., 1974—; dir., vice chmn. Computer and Communications Industry Assn., 1975—; bd. dirs. Asso. Industries Mass., 1976—; bd. dirs. Mass. High Tech. Council, 1977. Decorated Legion of Merit. Republican. Roman Catholic. Home: 65 Juniper Rd Weston MA 02193 Office: 21 North Ave Burlington MA 01802

CROOK, NORRIS CLINTON, educator; b. Speaker, Mich., June 24, 1923; s. Herbert James and Hazel Mildred (Kipp) C.; B.Th., Concordia Theol. Sem., 1947; B.S., U. Omaha, 1953; M.A., Western Res. U., 1959; Ph.D., U. Wis., 1968; m. Bernice Gabram, June 21, 1947. Ordained to ministry Luth. Ch., 1947; minister, Iowa and Ohio, 1947-59; asst. prof. Concordia Coll., Milw., 1959-62; Fulbright Teaching award, Kenya, 1962-64; teaching asst. U. Wis., 1964-66; couselor Madison (Wis.) Pub. Schs., 1962-68; asso. prof. ednl. psychology Slippery Rock (Pa.) State Coll., 1968—. Mem. Pa. Assn. Overseas Educators (pres. 1970-72), Assn. Overseas Educators, Inc. (nat. treas. 1971-72), Aid Assn. Luths. Rotarian (dir. 1971). Home: R F D 1 Box 345A Slippery Rock PA 16057

CROOK, RICHARD GOODRICH, bacteriologist; b. New Haven, July 31, 1934; s. Charles Edward and Bessie Mildred (West) C.; B.S., Moravian Coll., 1956; M.S., South Conn. State Coll., 1973; A.S. in Bus. Adminstrn., NW Conn. Community Coll., 1976; m. Lois Beck Groman, July 4, 1957; children—Kirsten, Charles, Hilary, Noelle. Research asso. dept. radiology and molecular biophysics Yale U., 1966-68; microbiologist Dome Labs. div. Miles Labs., West Haven, Conn., 1968; bacteriologist Becton-Dickinson & Co., Inc., Canaan, Conn., 1968-73, sr. bacteriologist, 1973-75, mgr. bacteriol. and sterilization services, 1975—. Served with USNR, 1956-61. Mem. Soc. Indsl. Microbiology, Am. Soc. Microbiology, Inst. Environ. Scis., Am. Soc. Quality Control, Parenteral Drug Assn. Naval Officers Res. Assn. Contbr. articles to profl. jours. Home: RFD 1 Winsted CT 06098 Office: Route 7 and Grace Way Canaan CT 06018

CROOKS, DONALD LAWRENCE, fin. exec.; b. Jersey City, N.J., Mar. 1, 1946; s. Vincent Lawrence and Dorothy (Blackburn) C.; B.S. in Edn., Wagner Coll., 1969, M.B.A. in Fin., 1972; m. Carol Ann Caldwell, Aug. 26, 1967; children—Donald Edward, Allyson Caldwell, Casey Blackburn. Sr. trader Shearson & Hammill, securities co., N.Y.C., 1969-71; sr. trader Oppenheimer & Co., N.Y.C., 1971-76, special partner, 1971-76; v.p., sr. trader Allen & Co.. Inc., N.Y.C., 1976—; condr. industry seminars. Coach wrestling team Twp. Bernards, Basking Ridge, N.J., 1977—. Mem. Nat. Assn. Security Dealers. Lutheran. Achieved rank of black belt in Okinawan Isshinryn Karate in record time of 8 mos.; instr. Karate for 12 yrs.; holder 4th degree black belt. Home: 56 Canter Dr Basking Ridge NJ 07920 Office: 711 Fifth Ave New York NY 10022

CROSBY, GEORGE FREDERICK, JR., mech. engr.; b. Bayonne, N.J., Mar. 11, 1912; s. George Frederick and Ida May (Evesson) C.; M.E., Stevens Inst. Tech., 1934; m. Josephine Boyd, Oct. 5, 1935 (dec. June 8, 1966); children—Jean Ruth, Jo Ann, George Frederick III, Janice Lee; m. 2d, Florence June Perrilloux Mohn, Feb. 1, 1976. Research engr., engr. in charge of ops. Internat. Nickel Co., Bayonne, 1934-42; mfg. and mgmt. cons. McKinsey Co., N.Y.C., 1942-48; mgr., operator Crosby & Asso., tng. and mfg. reorgn. programs, N.J., N.Y. and Conn., 1948-71; div. mgr. mfg. engring. research and devel. Am. Mgmt. Assn., N.Y.C., 1971-77; mfg. and mgmt. cons., Westport, Conn., 1977—. Active Boy Scouts Am., 50 years, Community Relations Council, Leader Citizenship Forum, others. Recipient Silver Beaver award Boy Scouts Am. Mem. Nat. Soc. Profl. Engrs., ASME, Soc. Advancement of Mgmt., Am. Mgmt. Assn., Am. Soc. for Quality Control, Am. Inst. Indsl. Engrs., others. Contbr. articles to profl. jours. Home and office: 6 Vineyard Ln Westport CT 06880

CROSBY, THOMAS WILLIAM, supermarket exec.; b. Hornell, N.Y., Nov. 12, 1925; s. Hiram Thomas and Gertrude Helen (Stone) C.; diploma bus. adminstrn. Internat. Corr. Schs., 1954; m. Mary Sheila Coleman, Nov. 16, 1947; children—Valerie, Mary Kathleen, Susan Elizabeth, Kimberly Jean, Thomas William, II. With Market Basket Corp., 1947-63, supt. charge stores, Syracuse, N.Y., 1958-63; owner Bayberry Super Duper, Liverpool, N.Y., 1963—; pres. Crosby Markets, Inc., 1963—; dir. O'Connor Mosher, wholesale grocery. Active local Boy Scouts Am. Served with USNR, 1944-46. Recipient Outstanding Citizen award Bayberry Community Assn., 1964-66. Mem. Nat. Assn. Retail Grocers, N.Y. State (chmn. 1978—), Central N.Y. (past pres.) food mchts., Better Bus. Bur., Liverpool C. of C. Conservative. Roman Catholic. Clubs: Beaver Meadows Golf (charter), Lions, Liverpool Rotary, Bellevue Country. Home: 16 Cardinal Path Liverpool NY 10388 Office: 7400 Oswego Rd Liverpool NY 13088

CROSS, JOHN BLAKELY, state ofcl. N.Y.; b. Gloversville, N.Y., June 13, 1935; s. Blakely Elton and Catherine Jane (Gifford) C.; B.A., Cornell U., 1957; J.D., Syracuse U., 1961. Admitted to N.Y. bar, 1961, also U.S. Supreme Ct. bar; lawyer N.Y. State Dept. Law, 1961-63, appellate ct. adv., 1967, lawyer, pension cons. N.Y. State Dept. Civil Ser., 1963-66, supr. lawyer, 1968-71, chief legal counsel, 1971—; spl. dep. atty. gen. to enforce election law, 1964-73. Chmn. Albany Ind. Movement, 1965; sec. Albany County Dist. Atty.'s Readiness Team, 1971-73; pres. Capital Dist. Community Council, 1975. Bd. dirs. UN Assn., 1972-73, Mental Health Assn., 1975-76; bd. mgrs. Woodgate Condominium, 1975-78, pres., 1977-78; trustee Home Aide Service, 1978—. Mem. Am., N.Y. State bar assns., Internat. Personnel Mgmt. Assn. Unitarian-Universalist (Albany treas. 1965-67, trustee 1970-73, canvass dir. 1976, mem. social responsibilities council Albany 1978—). Home: 34 Chestnut Rd Delmar NY 12054 Office: 1220 Washington Ave Albany NY 12239

CROSS, RONALD, musicologist, educator; b. Fort Worth, Feb. 18, 1929; s. John Butler and Verna (Bailey) C.; B.A., Centenary Coll. La., 1950; M.A., N.Y. U., 1953, Ph.D., 1961; postgrad. (Fulbright fellow) U. Florence (Italy), U. Vienna (Austria), 1955-57. Faculty, Notre Dame Coll. S.I., 1958-68; asso. prof. music Wagner Coll., S.I., 1968-75, prof., 1975—, dir. Collegium Musicum, 1968—. Organist, choirmaster various chs. Am. Council Learned Socs. grantee, 1954; recipient Founders Day award N.Y. U., 1962. Mem. Am. Guild Organists (asso.), Internat., Am. musicological socs., Coll. Music Soc., Soc. for Ethnomusicology, Am. Recorder Soc. Author: Matthaeus Pipelare: Opera Omnia, 3 vols., 1966-67. Reviewer Renaissance recs. for Music Quar., 1971—. Contbr. articles to profl. jours. Home: 221 Ward Ave Staten Island NY 10304

CROSTHWAITE, ROBERT HAROLD, clergyman; b. Moncton, N.B., Can., Sept. 14, 1946; s. Samuel Richard and Winifred Zina (Steeves) C.; student Acadia U., Wolfville, N.S., 1964-67, postgrad., 1975-76; B.A., U. Moncton, 1974; m. Barbara Ann Bray, Jan. 20, 1968; children—Todd Robert, Andrew Patrick. Program dir. recreation dept. City of Moncton, 1968-73; mgr. partner Coliseum Enterprises Ltd., Moncton, 1973; exec. dir. Camp Wildwood, Moncton, 1974-75; licensed to ministry Baptist Ch., 1974; pastor Lower Granville Bapt. Ch., Granville Ferry, N.S., Can., 1975-77; founder, pastor Habitation Bapt. Ch. and Living Waters Christian Acad., Port Royal, N.S., 1977; ordained to Christian ministry, 1977. Participant Young Voyageurs, 1969-71; chmn. Maritime Jamboree for Retarded, Moncton, 1972; del. to 5th Internat. Congress Mental Retardation, Montreal, 1972; bd. dirs. Moncton Council Cerebral Palsy Mentally Retarded Children; past pres. Moncton Football Assn., N.B. Amateur Football Union; coach several sports. Recipient Queen's Scout award; Distinction award Moncton High Sch. Mem. Canadian Assn. Mentally Retarded, Nat. Parks Recreation Assn. Home and Office: RR 2 Granville Ferry Annapolis County NS Canada

CROTHERS, J. FRANCES, puppeteer, artist, drama dir., bibliographer; b. Ravenna, Ohio, June 24, 1913; d. William Jerome and Ethel Diadama (Soper) Hinds; B.A., Kent State U., 1935; M.A., Northwestern U., 1949; drama and art studies U. Hartford, Wilimantic Sch. Art, Otis Art Inst., Los Angeles, 1937; m. Thomas Eben Crothers, June 4, 1938; 1 son, Jerome Thomas. With Otis Art Inst., Los Angeles, 1936; asst. dir. Parret Fine Art Research Library, Los Angeles, 1937-38; art dir. Drama Workshop, Los Angeles, 1937-38; sch. art dir., So. Ohio, 1938-41; asst. to dir. Children's Theatre, Northwestern U., also dir. drama and puppetry Evanston (Ill.) Pub. Parks, 1943-44; dir. designer Cain Park Children's Theatre, Cleveland Heights, Ohio, 1943-44; tchr. drama Evanston Pub. Sch., 1943-44, Gary (Ind.) Pub. Schs., 1944-46; speech specialist, Salem, Ohio, 1946; owner puppet touring co., 1946-51; research and pub. speaking, New Eng., 1951-66; art and craft instr., Hartford, 1957-72; producer-dir. Hartford Cast Players, 1964-66. Head women's div. Civil Def., Washingtonville, Ohio, 1941-43. Recipient Meritorious Service award Hartford Bd. Edn., 1972. Mem. Brit. Edn. Puppetry Assn., Internat. Marionnette Assn. (Prague), French Puppetry and Marionette Assn., Nederlandse Vereniging voor het Poppenspel, Puppeteers of Am., Internat. Marionette Assn. (U.S.), Canadian, Ont. Puppetry assns., Alpha Gamma Delta, Phi Alpha Alpha, Alpha Psi Omega, Phi Beta, Lambda Chi. Clubs: Quota (pres. club 1960), Bus. and Profl. Women's. Author: Puppeteer's Library Guide, 6 vols., 1971—; also 5 books poetry, 1935-43. Contbr. to America Singing Poetry Anthology, 1933-35. Home: 81 Flagg Rd West Hartford CT 06117

CROUTHAMEL, ARTHUR WILLIAM, sch. prin.; b. Phila., Apr. 27, 1930; s. John Franklin and Bertha Marie (Nevins) C.; B.S. in Edn., Temple U., 1952, M.Ed., 1959; m. Virginia Arlene Courter, June 25, 1955; children—Judith Ann, David Arthur. Organist, Carmel Presbyn. Ch., Glenside, Pa., 1949-57; tchr. music Abington (Pa.) Jr. High Sch., 1952-67; organist and dir. music Grace Presbyn. Ch., Jenkintown, Pa., 1957-67; asst. prin. Abington (Pa.) Jr. High Sch., 1967-70; prin. Pennridge Central Jr. High Sch., Perkasie, Pa., 1970—; dir. Abington Oratorio Choir, 1969—. Mem. consistory St. Stephen's United Ch. Christ, Perkasie, 1975-77. Served with U.S. Army, 1952-54; Korea. Recipient award of Merit, Pa. Sch. Bds. Assn., 1972. Mem. NEA, Nat., Pa. assns. secondary sch. prins., Am. Guild Organists, Phi Delta Kappa (Kappan of Year 1977). Republican. Clubs: Lions, Masons. Home: 218 Dublin Rd Perkasie PA 18944 Office: 1500 N 5th St Perkasie PA 18944

CROWELL, RALPH GEORGE, govt. ofcl.; b. Rome, Maine, Oct. 29, 1922; s. George Weaver and Mary Charlotte (Yeaton) C.; student pub. schs., Maine; m. Mary Margaret Drechsler, June 18, 1949; children—Charles Drechsler, Margaret Ellen. With GPO, Washington, 1942—, chief gen. specifications sect. comml. printing specifications div., 1971—. Treas., District Heights (Md.) Boys Club, 1964-70; trustee District Heights Presbyn. Ch., 1966-72. Served with AUS, 1943-45; ETO. Decorated Purple Heart, Combat Inf. badge. Mem. GPO Alumni Assn., Franklin Tech. Soc., Am. Legion. Democrat. Home: 2128 Roslyn Ave District Heights MD 20028 Office: GPO N Capitol and H Sts NW Washington DC 20401

CROWL, RICHARD BERNARD, assn. exec.; b. Bklyn., Mar. 25, 1908; s. Thomas Jose and Johanna Anna (Diekmann) C.; Litt.B., Rutgers U., 1930; m. Faith Russell Stevenson, June 15, 1951; 1 son, Richard Bernard. Prin. comml. specialist Dept. Treasury, 1941-45; asst. chief fin. services UNRRA, 1946-48; economist Dept. State, 1949-56; 1st sec., consul U.S. Embassy, Tehran, Iran, 1956-58; 1st sec., comml. attache U.S. Embassy, Ankara, Turkey, 1958-62, The Hague, Netherlands, 1962-66; exec. dir. Rockville (Conn.) C. of C., 1968—. Sec., bd. dirs. Rockville Big Bros., 1969-72; bd. dirs. Indian Valley YMCA, 1969—. Served with U.S. Army, 1941-45. Mem. Alpha Chi Rho. Editor C. of C. newspaper, chamber columnist Manchester (Conn.) Jour. Inquirer, 1969—, Tri-town Reporter, Vernon, Conn., 1969—; contbr. articles to profl. jours. Home: 156 Huntington Dr Vernon CT 06066 Office: Rockville Chamber of Commerce 30 Lafayette Sq Rockville CT 06066

CROWLEY, ARTHUR EDWARD, JR., lawyer; b. Rutland, Vt., Oct. 18, 1928; s. Arthur Edward and Mildred (Gilfeather) C.; student Boston U., 1947-50, 54-56; m. Marcia Colby Smith, July 29, 1961; children—Robert, David, Andrew, Christopher. Admitted to Vt. bar, 1958; practiced in Rutland, 1959; dep. atty. gen. State of Vt., Montpelier, 1960-61; state's atty. for Rutland County, 1961-65; partner Bishop & Crowley, 1965-77; pres. Crowley, Banse & Kenlan, Inc., 1977—; corp. counsel City of Rutland, 1965-67. Mem. Vt. Republican State Com., 1961-71; chmn. Rutland County Rep. Party, 1961-67; chmn. exec. com. Vt. Rep. Party, 1963-67. Served with AUS, 1950-53. Mem. Am., Vt., Rutland County, Vt. Jr. (pres. 1963-64) bar assns., Am. Legion, Rutland Region C. of C. (dir. 1967-71). Roman Catholic. Home: 22 Grandview Terr Rutland VT 05701 Office: 27 S Main St Rutland VT 05701

CROWLEY, EDWARD FRANCIS, plant engr.; b. East Mauch Chunk, Pa., Nov. 1, 1929; s. Edward James and Lottie Wilhelmina (Steidle) C.; degree in electronics, Carbon County Vocat.-Tech. Sch., 1971; m. Cecile Catherine Cossman, Dec. 28, 1949; children—Michael, Daniel, Patrick, Cecile Gerardette. Traffic control maintainer Central R.R. of N.J., Phillipsburg and Scranton, Pa., 1948-72; plant engr., asst. adminstr. Carbon County Home for Aged, Weatherly, Pas., 1972—. Fire marshal of Weatherwood; active ARC.

Mem. Hosp. Engrs. Assn. Eastern Pa., Am. Soc. Hosp. Engring., St. Joseph's Beneficial Assn. Democrat. Roman Catholic. Club: Lehigh Valley Motor. Office: Carbon County Home for the Aged Evergreen Ave Weatherly PA 18255

CROWLEY, HAROLD STERLING, JR., educator; b. Providence, Jan. 23, 1937; s. Harold Sterling and Catherine Bernadette (Shockroo) C.; B.S. in Edn. cum laude, Northeastern U., 1959, Ed.M., 1965. Tchr., Braintree (Mass.) Sch. Dept., 1959-60; tchr. Quincy (Mass.) Pub. Schs., 1962—. Instr. sci. edn. Eastern Nazarene Coll., Quincy, 1971-72. Mem. Quincy Hist. Soc., 1964—, curator, 1970-73, 76—; mem. Quincy Conservation Commn., 1970-76, chmn., 1972-73; active Boy Scouts Am., 1955—. Served to 1st lt. Signal Corps, AUS, 1960-62. Recipient Eagle Scout award Boy Scouts Am., 1952, Blue Granite award, 1972, St. George Emblem, Catholic Com. on Scouting, 1971. Mem. Nat. Sci. Tchrs. Assn. (del. to nat. convs. 1964-68), N.E.A., Mass. Tchrs. Assn., Quincy Edn. Assn. (Tchr. of Year 1969, pres. 1972-73), Germantown Heritage Soc. (pres. 1974—), Massasoit Campers Assn. (pres. 1976—), Kappa Delta Pi. K.C. Home: 3 Flagg St Quincy MA 02170 Office: Snug Harbor Sch 333 Palmer St Quincy MA 02169

CROWLEY, HUBERT CAMERON, advt. exec.; b. White Plains, N.Y., May 7, 1937; s. Hubert Gentry and Mary Estelle (Whitney) C.; B.A., Amherst Coll., 1959; postgrad. in urban planning N.Y. U., 1968-73. Account exec. Doherty, Clifford, Steers & Shenfield Inc., N.Y.C., 1959-64, Needham, Harper & Steers Inc., N.Y.C., 1965-66; product mgr. Lever Bros. Co., N.Y.C., 1966-69; account supr. Ted Bates & Co., Inc., N.Y.C., 1969-74, v.p., 1971—, account dir., 1975—. Served with AUS, 1961-62. Mem. Psi Upsilon. Club: University (N.Y.C.). Home: 113 E 36th St New York City NY 10016 Office: 1515 Broadway New York City NY 10036

CROWLEY, RALPH MANNING, psychotherapist, psychoanalyst; b. Madison, Wis., Nov. 13, 1905; s. Francis Manning and Ada Sophia (Fuller) C.; B.A., U. Wis., 1926; M.A. in Psychology, 1928; M.B., Northwestern U., 1933, M.D., 1934; m. Dorothy A. Walker, June 27, 1927 (div.); 1 son, Stephen Fuller; m. 2d, Margaret Roswitha Anderson, Oct. 3, 1942 (div.); 1 son, Michael Anderson; m. 3d, Mary Bader Yost, July 30, 1960 (div.); children—Daniel Yost, Jonathan Robarts, Patrick Manning. Intern, Cook County Hosp., Chgo., 1933-34; resident psychiatry Sheppard Pratt Hosp., Towson, Md., 1934-37; asst. physician Chestnut Lodge, Rockville, Md., 1937-40; pvt. practice medicine specializing in psychiatry, Washington, 1940-43, N.Y.C., 1946—, Englewood, N.J., 1949-58; asso. vis. psychiatrist Harlem Hosp. Center, N.Y.C., 1974-78; cons. psychiatrist Project Create, N.Y.C., 1974—. hon. mem. staff Sheppard and Enoch Pratt Hosp., Towson, Md. Fellow emeritus W.A. White Inst. Psychiatry, Psychoanalysis and Psychology, N.Y.C., 1948—; cons. psychiatrist Family Service Center Warren County, Belvidere, N.J., 1964—; vis. cons. Roosevelt Hosp., N.Y.C., 1964—; vis. lectr. Albert Einstein Med. Sch., Bronx, 1972—. Trustee Am. Rehab. Com., N.Y.C., 1954-72, W.A. White Inst., N.Y.C., 1957-59, Arts Fund, N.Y.C., 1958-64; bd. dirs. Palisades Nature Assn., Englewood, N.Y., 1956-59. Served with M.C., USNR, 1942-46. Fellow Am. Psychiat. Assn. (life), Am. Acad. Psychoanalysis (pres.) 1966-67), mem. Internat. (life), Am. psychoanalytic assns., Phi Beta Kappa, Alpha Omega Alpha. Contbr. articles to various publs. Address: 7 W 96th St #2E New York City NY 10025

CROWLEY, RICHARD MARR, leasing co. exec.; b. Washington, D.C., Oct. 27, 1935; s. Thomas R. and Frances (Sullivan) C.; B.S., U. Md., 1958; m. Joan Elizabeth Asay, June 12, 1959; children—Stephen F., Paul A. Special rep. REA Express, N.Y.C., 1962-63; asst. to v.p. States Marine Lines, N.Y.C., 1963-64; dir. mktg. Integrated Container Service, N.Y.C., 1965-66; v.p. mktg. Flexi-Van Corp., N.Y.C., 1966-75, group v.p., N.Y.C., 1975—. Served to capt. USAF, 1958-62. Recipient Gold Key award Pub. Relations News, 1974. Mem. Nat. Ry. Intermodal Assn., Am. Trucking Assn., Private Carrier Conf. Author: The State of Containerization, 1972, 74, 77.

CROZIER, RONALD DAVID, chem. co. exec.; b. Antofagasta, Chile, Sept. 9, 1929; s. Hector McIver and Marietta (Rendic) C.; student U. Glasgow (Scotland), 1948-50; B.S. in Metall. Engring., B.S. Engring. in Chem. Engring., U. Mich., 1953, M.S. Engring., 1954, Ph.D. in Chem. Engring., 1956; m. Sabine Slotta, Feb. 2, 1951; children—Ralph, Vanessa, Susan, Janette. Came to U.S., 1950, naturalized, 1965. With Dow Chem. Co., various locations, 1958-68, bus. mgr. Dow Chem. (U.K.) Ltd., London, 1965-66, asst. to bus. dir. Dow Chem. Europe S.A., Zurich, Switzerland, 1966-68; v.p. operations Anglo Lautaro Nitrate Co. Ltd., Santiago, Chile, 1968-72; v.p. Minerec Corp., 1972-74, pres., 1974-76, also dir.; pres., dir. Minerec Internat. Sales Corp., N.Y.C., 1972-75; mng. dir. Tecromin Ltd., Santiago, Chile; cons. in field. Mem. Am. Inst. Chem. Engrs., Am. Chem. Soc., Am. Inst. Mining and Metall. Engrs., Sigma Xi, Phi Kappa Phi, Tau Beta Pi. Club: Mining (N.Y.C.). Patentee in field. Contbr. to profl. jours. Office: Route 2 Box 54 Bedford NY 10506

CRUIKSHANK, ROBERT LANE, investment banker, securities co. exec.; b. Sharon, Pa., Oct. 5, 1936; s. John W. and Jeanette Sprague (Lane) C.; B.A. cum laude, Princeton, 1958; m. Marianne Johnson, Nov. 17, 1962; children—Douglas, Christina. Registered rep. Blyth Eastman Dillon & Co. Inc., N.Y.C., 1958-64, nat. mutual funds mgr., 1964-66, gen. partner, 1966, nat. retail sales partner, 1967, partner-in-charge eastern region, 1968-72, sr. v.p., nat. sales mgr., officer in charge br. offices, dir., 1972—, exec. v.p. securities div., mem. exec. com., 1974—, chief planning officer policy com., 1978—. Bd. dirs. Am. Scottish Found., United Fund Bronxville, N.Y. Served to 1st lt. AUS, 1958-59. Clubs: Quadrangle (Princeton, N.J.); Skytop, Wall Street University (N.Y.C.); Bronxville Field; Ponte Vedra. Home: 40 Elm Ln Bronxville NY 10708 Office: 1221 Ave Americas New York City NY 10020

CRUMB, EDGAR ALVIN, mech. engr.; b. Cape Charles, Va., July 5, 1916; s. Edgar A. and Nell (Howlett) C.; A.A., N.Mex. Sch. Mines, 1938; B.A., George Washington U., 1959, M.B.A., 1961; m. Lois N. Crumb, Nov. 15, 1969. Mech. engr. Eastern Shore Pub. Service Co., Salisbury, Md., 1938-39; mech. engr. Office Chief Chem. Corps, U.S. Army, 1939-43; dept. chief research and devel. Chem. Corps, Edgewood Arsenal, Md., 1947-53, exec. dir. research and engring. command, 1953-55, exec. dir. Chem. Corps, Washington, 1955-62, tech. dir. Edgewood Arsenal, 1962-66, dir. Munitions Command Operations Research Group, Edgewood Arsenal, 1966-73, dir. Chem. Lab., 1973—. Served to 1st lt. USMCR, 1944-47; col. U.S. Army Res. Recipient 3 meritorious civilian service awards, Sec. Army, 1958-73; decorated Legion of Merit. Mem. Am. Chem. Soc., ASME, AAAS, Am. Inst. Mining and Metall. Engrs., Am. Ordnance Assn., Assn. U.S. Army, Armed Forces Chem. Assn., Mil. Order World Wars, Res. Officers Assn., Marine Corps Assn. Methodist. Clubs: Engineers, Chemical Engineers, Kenwood Country, Fort McNair Officers, Army Navy Country (Washington); Baltimore Country; Md. Country; Edgewood Arsenal (Md.) Officers'; Md. Golf and Country (Belair). Home: 600 Banyan Ct Edgewood MD 21040 Office: Dir Chem Lab Edgewood Arsenal MD 21010

CRUMLEY, JAMES ROBERT, JR., clergyman; b. Bluff City, Tenn., Mar. 30, 1925; s. James Robert and Ida (Fine) C.; B.A., Roanoke Coll., Salem, Va., 1948; M.Div., Luth. Theol. So. Sem., Columbia, S.C., 1951; D.D. (hon.), Newberry Coll., 1971, Roanoke Coll., 1973; m. Sara Annette Bodie, May 26, 1950; children—Frances (Mrs. John S. Holman), James Robert, III, Jeanne. Ordained to ministry Lutheran Ch., 1951; pastor Greene County Luth. Parish, Greeneville, Tenn., 1951-53, Grace Luth. Ch., Oak Ridge, 1953-66, Luth. Ch. of Ascension, Savannah, Ga., 1966-74; sec. Luth. Ch. in Am., N.Y.C., 1974-78, pres., 1978—; del. Luth. World Fedn. 6th Assembly, Dar es Salaam, 1977; pres. Luth. World Ministries. Mem. Religion in Am. Life. Author: God and Science, 1965. Home: 2 Drew Ln East Windsor NJ 08520 Office: 231 Madison Ave New York City NY 10016

CRUMP, WALTER MOORE, JR., artist; b. Winston-Salem, N.C., Mar. 18, 1941; s. Walter M. and Dorothy (Clendenin) C.; student Guilford Coll., 1961-64, Harvard U., 1964-66; B.F.A., Boston U., 1970. One-man shows include: Cherry Stone Gallery, Wellfleet, Mass., 1972, 75, 77, Cherrystone Gallery, Wellfleet, Mass., 1972, 75, 77, 5th St. Gallery, Wilmington, Del., 1977, Boston Psychoanalytic Soc., 1977, 1973, Schuster Gallery, Cambridge, Mass., 1971, 72, Chameleon Gallery, Winston-Salem, 1976; two-person show Baak Gallery, Cambridge, 1977; group shows include: Inst. Contemporary Art, Boston, 1972, Connection Gallery, N.Y.C., 1973, Davidson (N.C.) Nat. Print and Drawing Show, 1973, The Show, Nashua, N.H., 1973, S.E. Center Contemporary Art, Winston-Salem, 1976, 78, Silvermine Nat. Printmakers Show, New Cannan, Conn., 1975, 77, N.C. Artists, N.C. Mus. Art, Raleigh, 1974, N.H. Graphics Internat., 1974, Color Print U.S.A., Tex. Tech. U., Lubbock, 1975, Works on Paper, Thayer Acad., Braintree, Mass., 1975, 1st Ann. Crossroads of Am. Art Exhbn., Chgo., 1975, Los Angeles Printmaking Soc. Nat. Exhbns., 1974, 75, Nat. Traveling Exhbn., 1976—, Boston Printmakers Nat. Exhbns., 1975, 76, 77, Pratt Graphics Center, N.Y.C., 1977, Miami (Fla.) Internat. Graphics Biennial, 1977, Brand Library Art Center, Glendale, Calif., 1977, 78, Miami U., Oxford, Ohio, 1977, Spokane (Wash.) Nat. Print Exhbn., 1977, Attleboro (Mass.) Mus., 1977, Nat. Miniature Exhbn., Laramie, Wyo., 1976, Okla. Nat. Print and Drawing Exhbn., 1974, 76, Korean Print Exhbn., Seoul, 1978; represented in permanent collections: Phila. Mus. Art, Boston U., Hampshire Coll., Los Angeles Printmaking Soc., DeCordova Mus., N.Y. Mental Health Center, N.C. Mus. Art, City Savs. Bank, Pittsfield, Mass., Wachovia Bank, Winston-Salem, R. J. Reynolds World Corp. Center; artist in residence Newton Sch. System, 1972-74, Boston Coll., 1969; instr. printmaking Commonwealth Sch., Boston, 1972-78, chmn. art dept., 1973-78; faculty Elma Lewis Sch. Fine Art, Roxbury, Mass., 1967, DeCordova Mus., Lincoln, Mass., 1967, St. Stephens, Boston, 1967-68, Neighborhood Arts, Boston, 1968-69; dir. art dept. Belvoir Terr. Art Center, Lenox, Mass., 1972-74; tchr. Cambridge Center for Adult Edn., 1972-73. Served with USN, 1959-61. Recipient 24 nat. awards, including: purchase prize Boston Printmakers Nat. Exhbn., 1976, 77, 78; purchase prize Minot (N.D.) Nat. Show, 1977; Corning Mus. Purchase award, 1973; Attleboro Mus. award for contemporary painting, 1973, 74; Merit award Okla. Nat. Print Exhbn., 1977; Ingram Merrill fellow, Living and Materials grantee Ingram Merrill Found., 1975-76. Mem. Boston Visual Artists Union, Boston Printmakers (exec. com. 1974—), Los Angeles Printmakers Soc. Address: 59 Delle Ave Roxbury MA 02120

CRUTCHFIELD, SAM SHAW, JR., lawyer, assn. exec.; b. Nashville, July 15, 1934; s. Sam Shaw and Alfreda (Whitworth) C.; B.A., George Washington U., 1960, J.D., 1963; m. Sylvia Ann Dinneen, May 14, 1958; children—Catherine Anne, Firmadge Whitworth, Elizabeth Victoria. Admitted to D.C. bar, 1963; jud. law clk. Hon. Frank H. Myers, D.C. Ct. of Appeals, 1963-64; exec. dir. Va. Commn. Constl. Govt., 1964-67; asso. counsel Am. Enterprise Inst. Pub. Policy Research, Washington, 1967-70, asst. to pres., 1970-73, dir. legal studies, 1973; gen. counsel U.S. Postal Rate Commn., 1973-74; exec. dir. Phi Delta Phi Internat. Legal Frat., Washington, 1974—; cons. Nat. Inst. Law Enforcement and Criminal Justice. Mem. jud. Conf. for D.C. Circuit, 1969. Vice pres. Young Republican Club, Arlington, Va., 1968-69; mem. Arlington County Rep. Com., 1968-70, 74-76; exec. dir. Young Rep. Fedn. Va., 1968-69. Trustee Del. Law Sch., 1972-74. Served with AUS, 1953-56. Mem. Interam., Am., D.C. (asst. editor jour. 1971-73, editor D.C. Bar Report 1973-74) bar assns., George Washington U. Law Assn. (dir. 1977—, exec. council) Am. Judicature Soc., Phila. Soc., Phi Delta Phi. Contbr. articles to profl. jours. Editor: D.C. Young Lawyer, 1968-69. Home: 3528 Gallows Rd Annandale VA 22003 Office: 1750 N St NW Washington DC 20036

CRUZ, A. ERNEST, mgmt. co. exec.; b. N.Y.C., Sept. 6, 1950; s. Abelardo B. and Celica (Lopez) C.; B.A. cum laude, U. Fla., 1973; M.B.A., U. Miami, 1974: J.D., Georgetown U., 1978; m. Dorita Ann Rarouch, May 3, 1969; 1 son, Brandon E. Mgmt. cons. to U.S. Govt., Ednl. Systems Corp., Washington, 1975-76; projects mgr. FAMI Systems, Inc., Washington, 1976-77; exec. v.p. FAMI Service Systems, Washington, 1977—; cons. InterAm. Research Assos., Inc., Washington, 1978—. Address: 1721 DeSales St NW Washington DC 20036

CRUZ, ROBERT, utility co. exec.; b. Pasadena, Calif., July 3, 1933; s. Theodore and Tome (Ramirez) C.; B.A., Calif. State U., 1963, M.A., 1969; m. Florence Nunez, May 26, 1956; children—Robert, Cristina. Tariff analyst Calif. Water & Telephone, Monrovia, 1964-65; mktg. rep. Calif. Water & Telephone, 1965-67; corporate telecommunications cons. Litton Industries, Beverly Hills, Calif., 1967-70; sr. systems cons. Response Communications, Century City, Calif., 1970-71; maj. accounts coordinator Gen. Telephone of Calif., Santa Monica, 1971-72, data and spl. services adminstrn., 1972-73; nat. accounts sales adminstr. GTE Service Corp., Stamford, Conn., 1973-77, bus. systems mgr., 1977, mktg. dir., 1977—. Area campaign mgr. John O'Keef for congress 45th Dist., S. Calif., 1962. Served with USN, 1951-53. Mem. Telecommunications Assn., Petroleum Industry and Electronic Assn., Assn. Coll. and Univ. Telecommunication Adminstrs., Armed Forces Communications and Electronic Assn. Democrat. Roman Catholic. Home: 108 Hillcrest Rd Fairfield CT 06430 Office: 1 Stamford Forum Stamford CT 06904

CRUZE, KENNETH, surgeon; b. Takoma Park, Md., Oct. 10, 1927; s. Conrad Ellis and Claudia Eleanore (Carpenter) C.; B.A., Columbia Union Coll., 1949; M.D., Loma Linda U., 1955; m. Jean Anna Hansen, June 13, 1948; children—Wendy Jean, Lori Ann, Barbara Lee. Intern, Los Angeles County Gen. Hosp., 1955-56; resident in surgery Wadsworth Gen. Med. and Surg. Hosp., West Los Angeles, 1956-60; resident in pediatric surgery Children's Hosp. Los Angeles, 1958-59; fellow in thoracic and cardiovascular surgery U. Fla., Gainesville, 1960-62; practice medicine specializing in thoracic and cardiovascular surgery, Takoma Park, Md., 1962—; mem. staff Washington Adventist Hosp., Takoma Park, 1962—, dir. open heart surgery program, 1970—. Mem. exec. com., bd. trustees D.C. Blue Shield. Served to capt. M.C., U.S. Army, 1956-63. Fellow A.C.S., Am. Coll. Chest Physicians, Am. Coll. Angiology; mem. Am. Thoracic Soc., Am. Trauma Soc., Med. and Chirurg. Faculty Md., Md. Heart Assn., Soc. Thoracic Surgeons. Republican. Clubs: Greencastle Golf and Country, Civitan. Mem. editorial bd. Md. State Med. Jour., 1972-77; contbr. articles to med. jours. Home: 12804 Gaffney Rd Silver Spring MD 20904

CRYAN, EUGENE WHITTY, physician; b. N.Y.C., Oct. 14, 1924; s. Robert R. W. and Eugenie (O'Neill) C.; B.A., Princeton U., 1949; M.D., U. Pa., 1953; m. Alice McAlpin, June 12, 1948; children—Bruce, Kenneth, Richard. Intern, U. Pa. Sch. Medicine, 1954, resident, 1956, cardiology fellow, 1957; practice medicine specializing in internal medicine, King of Prussia, Pa., 1957—; mem. attending staff Bryn Mawr (Pa.) Hosp.; mem. courtesy staff Paoli (Pa.) Hosp., Sacred Heart Hosp., Norristown. Served with USN, 1943-46. Mem. Am. (award 1974), Pa. (v.p. 1971-72), S.E. Pa. heart assns., Am., Pa. socs. internal medicine. Republican. Club: Merion Cricket. Home: 320 Orchard Way Saint David's PA 19087 Office: 491 Allendale Rd King of Prussia PA 19406

CRYAN, MARJORIE ELAINE NIXON, state ofcl.; b. Easton, Pa., Dec. 17, 1922; d. Leroy and Elsie May (Long) Nixon; B.A., U. Pa., 1945; m. James Edward Cryan, Feb. 6, 1951 (dec. Mar. 1964); 1 son, James Nixon. Asst. women's editor The Trentonian, Trenton, N.J., 1948-50; editor Trenton Mag., 1964-70, Mercer County Messenger, Trenton, 1970-74; analyst N.J. Div. Med. Assistance and Health Services, 1974—. Pub. relations dir. Morris Hall Rehab. Center, Lawrenceville, N.J., 1972-74. Mem. N.J. Press Assn., Nat. Newspaper Assn., U. Pa. Alumna Assn., Alpha Omicron Pi. Republican. Home: 17 Mountain View Rd Trenton NJ 08628 Office: 540 State Hwy 33 Trenton NJ 08619

CRYMBLE, JOHN FREDERICK, chem. engr., cons.; b. N.Y.C., Oct. 18, 1916; s. Hugh and Hannah (Knecht) C.; B.A., Columbia, 1938; B.S., 1939, Chem. E., 1940; m. Mary Alenda Smith, June 24, 1944; 1 dau., Joanne Lee (Mrs. Donald L. Gilmore). Prodn. supr. E.I. duPont de Nemours and Co., Chambers Works, Deepwater, N.J., 1940-73, sr. prodn. engr., 1973-76; cons., 1977—. Pres. Salem City Bd. Edn., also rep. N.J. Sch. Bds. Assn. Bd. dirs. Salem Free Library. Mem. Am. Chem. Soc., Am. Inst. Chem. Engrs., John Jay Assos. Columbia, Columbia U. Alumni Assn., Sigma Xi, Phi Lambda Upsilon, Tau Beta Pi. Methodist (trustee, chmn. adminstrv. bd.). Club: DuPont Country (Wilmington, Del.). Home and Office: 22 Chestnut St Salem NJ 08079

CRYSTAL, BORIS, artist; b. nr. Warsaw, Poland, Dec. 25, 1931; s. Shea and Bronislawa (Blumenfeld) C.; came to U.S., 1968, naturalized, 1974; student Plocer's Sch. of Fine Arts, 1962-63, Acad. of Fine Arts, Israel, 1963-64; m. Dalia Gilad, Oct. 6, 1961; children—Julius S., Byron R. One man shows include Katz Art Gallery, Tel Aviv, 1964, Art Gallery 97, Tel Aviv, 1965-66, Journalist House Art Gallery, Tel Aviv, 1967, Lerner Art Gallery, N.Y.C., 1968, Herzl Inst., N.Y.C., 1969, Roerich Mus., N.Y.C., 1970, Crystal Art Gallery, N.Y.C., 1972-76; group shows include Katz Art Gallery, Tel Aviv, 1964-68, Mus. Israel, Tel Aviv, 1964-68, Lerner Art Gallery, N.Y.C., 1968-76, Roerich Mus., N.Y.C., 1968-76, Jewish Mus., N.Y.C., 1968-76, Mus. Modern Art, N.Y.C., 1968-76, LaGalerie Mouffe, Paris; represented in permanent collections Katz Art Gallery, Mus. Israel, Art Gallery 97, Journalist House (all Tel Aviv), Continental Gallery, Crown Art Gallery, Herzl Inst., Lerner Art Gallery, Roerich Mus., Jewish Mus., Mus. Modern Art (all N.Y.C.). Mem. Artists Equity Assn. N.Y. Address: 65-10 108th St Forest Hills NY 11375

CRYSTAL, GRAEF SLATER, mgmt. cons. co. exec.; b. Oakland, Calif., Apr. 30, 1934; s. Louis F. and Esther D. (Harris) C.; A.B., U. Calif. at Berkeley, 1956; M.A., Occidental Coll., 1962; m. Holly Hollingsworth, Apr. 17, 1977; children by previous marriage—David, Allison, Matthew. Mgmt. trainee Sears, Roebuck & Co., Santa Monica, Calif., 1957-59; wage and salary analyst RCA, Van Nuys, Calif., 1959-60; compensation dir. Gen. Dynamics Corp., N.Y.C., 1960-67; dir. compensation Pfizer Internat. Inc., N.Y.C., 1968; sr. asso. Booz, Allen & Hamilton Inc., N.Y.C., 1968-69; v.p. Towers, Perrin, Forster & Crosby Inc., N.Y.C., 1969—; lectr. on exec. compensation. Mem. Am. Compensation Assn. (regional pres. 1968-69). Republican. Methodist. Club: Sky (N.Y.C.). Author: Financial Motivation for Executives; Compensating United States Executives Abroad; Executive Compensation: Men, Money, Motivation and Imagination, 1978; also articles. Home: 60 East End Ave New York City NY 10028 also 1314 Fairway Oaks Kiawah Island SC 29412 Office: Towers Perrin Forster & Crosby Inc 600 3d Ave New York City NY 10016

CSAVINSZKY, PETER JOHN, educator; b. Budapest, Hungary, July 10, 1931; s. Lajos and Ida (Kiss) C.; came to U.S., 1959, naturalized, 1964; Diplom Ing. Chem., Tech. U. Budapest, 1954; Ph.D. in Physics, U. Ottawa (Ont., Can.), 1959; m. Barbara J. Fraser, Oct. 1976. Research physicist Hughes Aircraft Co., Newport Beach, Calif., 1959-60, Gen. Dynamics Corp., Rochester, N.Y., 1960-62, Tex. Instruments Inc., Dallas, 1962-65, TRW Systems, Redondo Beach, Calif., 1965-70; asso. prof. physics U. Maine, Orono, 1970-74, prof., 1974—; vis. lectr. U. Calif. at Berkeley, summer 1971, U. Calif. at Los Angeles, summers 1972, 73, 74, 75, 76, 77, U. So. Calif., 1977-78. Fellow Am. Phys. Soc.; mem. Phys. Soc. Japan, AAUP, AAAS, N.Y. Acad. Scis., Soaring Soc. Am. Contbr. articles to profl. jours. Address: Dept Physics U Maine Orono ME 04469

CSEJKA, DAVID ANDREW, chemist; b. Passaic, N.J., June 9, 1935; s. Anthony Edward and Ann (Pellock) C.; B.S. in Chemistry, Fordham U., 1956; Ph.D. in Phys. Chemistry, Iowa State U., 1961; m. Carol Ann Vorbach, July 10, 1965; children—Andrew, Thomas, Robert, Dianne, Steven. Research chemist Olin Corp., New Haven, 1961-65, sr. research chemist, 1965-74, research asso., 1974-76, group leader, 1976—. Treas. local pack Cub Scouts, 1974-76; bd. dirs. Amity Youth Hockey Assn., 1977—; active Orange (Conn.) Little League, 1978. Mem. Am. Chem. Soc., N.Y. Acad. Scis., Sigma Xi (sec. Olin br. 1973-74). Contbr. articles to sci. jours. Patentee. Home: 495 Derby-Milford Rd Orange CT 06477 Office: 275 Winchester Ave New Haven CT 06511

CSERMELY, THOMAS JOHN, bioengring. physicist; b. Szombathely, Hungary, June 25, 1931; s. Janos and Maria (Szarvas) C.; diploma in engring. Poly. U. Budapest, 1953; Ph.D., Syracuse U., 1968; m. Tiiu Vaharu, June 17, 1962; 1 son, Erik Thomas. Instr., Inst. Theoretical Physics, Poly. U. Budapest (Hungary), 1953-56; nuclear engring. cons. Design Bur. Power Stas., Budapest, 1956; research engr. Carrier Corp., Syracuse, N.Y., 1957-67; research asso. physics Syracuse U., 1967-68, asst. prof. elec. and computer engring., 1976—; asst. prof. physiology State U. N.Y. Upstate Med. Center, Syracuse, 1968-76; asst. prof. physics LeMoyne Coll., Syracuse, 1976-77. Recipient Wolverine Diamond Key award Am. Soc. Heating, Refrigerating and Air Conditioning Engrs., 1965. Mem. Am. Phys. Soc., IEEE, Biophys. Soc., Am. Assn. Physics Tchrs., Am. Nuclear Soc., Soc. Computer Simulation, Am. Soc. Engring. Edn., AAAS, Sigma Xi. Club: Tech. Syracuse. Contbr. articles to profl. publs., papers to profl. orgns. on control, heat exchange dynamics, quantum biochemistry, brain functions and computer simulation neuronal network dynamics. Home: 149 Humbert Ave Syracuse NY 13224

CSICSERY-RONAY, ISTVAN, editor, author, publisher; b. Budapest, Hungary, Dec. 13, 1917; s. Stephen A. and Maria Alexandra (Zichy) C.-R.; came to U.S., 1949; diploma Diplomatische Akademie, Vienna, Austria, 1939; Ph.D. in Polit. Sci., Royal Hungarian U., Budapest, 1940; certificate in agronomy Tech. U., Budapest, 1943; certificate Sch. Diplomacy, Budapest, 1944; M.S.L.S., Cath. U. Am., 1957; m. Elizabeth Tariska, July 27, 1945; children—Elizabeth M., Istvan. Ministerial sec. Fgn. Ministry of Hungary, Budapest, 1944-47; polit. analyst Free Europe Com. Inc. of New York at U.S. Library of Congress, 1949-56; owner, editor-in-chief Occidental Press, Washington, 1953—; sr. cataloger U. Md., 1945-78. Organizer, dir., lectr. on Hungarian fgn. policy between the two wars Sch. Fgn. Affairs, Budapest, 1945-46; scriptwriter Voice of Am., 1954—, Radio Free Europe, 1956—; organizer lecture tours in U.S. for Sandor Veress, 1965, Transylvanian writers, 1973. Acting pres. Teleki Pa'l Munkakozosseg, (Paul Teleki movement), anti-Nazi orgn., Budapest, 1943; head div. fgn. affairs Smallholders' Party, Budapest, 1945-47. Served to 1st lt. (award in 1945 for work in resistance movement), arty., Hungarian Army, 1936-37, 39; Russian front, 1942-43. Recipient Silver medal Nat. Color Slides Competition, Hungarian Assn. Amateur Photographers. Am. Council Learned Socs. grantee, 1961-62. Mem. P.E.N. (del. 1966, 67, 69, 71, 75), Am. Am. Acad. Polit. and Social Sci., Acad. Polit. Sci., Budapest Movie House, McKeldin Library Film Club (organizer 1959, mgr. 1959-60), U.S. Chess Fedn., Phi Kappa Phi. Club: Klub der Absolventen Und Freunde der Diplomatischen Akademie (Vienna). Author: Russian Cultural Penetration in Hungary, 1951, 3rd rev. edit., 1952; Szamuzottek Naptara, 1954 (Calendar of Exiles); (with Ferenc Nagy) Appeal to The Governments of the Free Nations, 1955; First Book of Hungary, 1967; editor and contbg. author: Koltok Forradalma, 1957 (Poets' Revolution); author numerous publs. of Free Europe Com., 1949-56; author TV script: Stephen I: His Life and His Reign, 1969; contbg. author: Collier's Ency., 1962—; Ency. of Poetry and Poetics, 1965; East Central Europe, A Guide to Basic Publications, 1969; Lands and Peoples, 1972. Co-editor Eb Ura Feko, anti-Nazi underground weekly, 1944; editor Hirunk A Vilagban, 1951-64 (Our Reputation in the World), Bibliografia, 1957-64; editor lit. records: Szabadság, szerelem, 1960 (Freedom, Love); Modern magyar költök, 1961 (Modern Hungarian Poets); Magyar költök Balassától Adyig, 1962 (Hungarian Poets from Balassa to Ady); Modern magyar novellák, 1963 (Modern Hungarian Short Stories); Egy mondat a zsarnokságról, 1975 (One Sentence on Tyranny); editor documentary record: A magyar forradalom hangja, 1961 (Voice of the Hungarian Revolution); editor, author introduction of record: Hungarian Folk Songs, 1965. Contbr. articles to lit., library, polit. jours.; exhibited one-man shows color photography U. Md., 1974, Fairfax County Library, Falls Church, Va., 1975. Arrested in 1947 by Communist polit. police; accused of plotting against the state and sentenced to two years imprisonment; released pending appeal after eight months imprisonment, and escaped to Austria, late 1947, then lived in Paris, France, 1948-49. Home: PO Box 1005 Washington DC 20013 Office: McKeldin Library College Park MD 20740

CSOBAJI, SANDOR BELA, architect; b. Budapest, Hungary, Nov. 26, 1936; s. Sandor John and Margaret (Onody) C.; B.S., Rensselaer Poly. Inst., 1960, B.Arch., 1966, M.Arch., 1966; m. Catherine Diane Nelson, July 1960; children—Margaret, Georgette, Stephen, Jennifer. With RTKL Assos. architects, planners, engrs., Balt., 1966—, prin., 1971—; vis. lectr. Johns Hopkins Sch. Medicine, 1976—. Vice pres., 1st Luth. Ch., Towson, Md. Served to 1st lt. USAF, 1960-64. Registered architect, Md., Calif., Ohio, Ky., Mich. Mem. AIA, Am. Inst. Planners, Soc. Am. Mil. Engrs. Contbr. articles to profl. jours. Architect Walter Reed Army Med. Centermaster plan, Washington, St. Elizabeth Hosp., Covington, Ky., Johns Hopkins Hosp. Redevel. (honor award Md. chpt. AIA), Balt. Club: Cosmos (Washington). Home: 2012 Indian Head Rd Ruxton MD 21204 Office: Village Cross Keys Baltimore MD 21204

CUCCI, CESARE ELEUTERIO, pediatric cardiologist; b. Spoleto, Italy, Dec. 22, 1925; s. Otto and Anna (Morelli) C.; came to U.S., 1954, naturalized, 1958; diploma in classics Coll. St. Maria, Rome, 1943; M.D., State U. Perugia (Italy), 1949; m. Gilda Morillo, Oct. 22, 1966; children—Susanna, Gardenia, Otto. Chief pediatric cardiology service Lenox Hill Hosp., N.Y.C., 1963, attending pediatrician, 1973—; cons. pediatric cardiology Flushing Hosp., Queens, N.Y., 1970—, Meth. Hosp., Bklyn., 1966—, Booth Meml. Hosp., Queens, 1964—, Wyckoff Heights Hosp., Bklyn., 1968—; prof. clin. pediatrics N.Y.U., 1977—. Diplomate Am. Bd. Pediatrics also supsplty. Am. Bd. Pediatric Cardiology. Fellow A.C.P., Am. Acad. Pediatrics, Am. Coll. Cardiology, Am. Coll. Chest Physicians. Roman Catholic. Contbr. articles to med. jours. Home: 45 E 62d St New York City NY 10021

CUCCIOLI, ROBERT, civil engr.; b. Bklyn., Mar. 2, 1925; s. Joseph and Emily (Dell'Abate) C.; B.S. in Civil Engring., Mass. Inst. Tech., 1946; s. Ann Barbara Amalfitano, June 15, 1946; children—Barbara Ann, Joan Emily, Patrice Diane, Robert Joseph. Structural engr. with firms in N.Y.C., 1946-52; chief structural engr. Blauvelt Engring. Co., N.Y.C., 1952—, partner, 1966—. Capt., Hempstead (N.Y.) Vol. Fire Dept., 1949-61. Served with USNR, 1943-46. Registered profl. engr. 20 states. Fellow ASCE; mem. Nat. Soc. Profl. Engrs., Am. Welding Inst., Am. Concrete Inst., Internat. Assn. Bridge and Structural Engring., Soc. Am. Mil. Engrs., Am. Rd. and Transp. Builders Assn. (chmn. subcom. 1975—), Am. Arbitration Assn. (panel 1973—). Author articles unique bridge designs. Office: 1 Park Ave New York NY 10016

CUCIN, ROBERT LOUIS, plastic surgeon; b. N.Y.C., Apr. 17, 1946; s.Robert and Julia C.; B.A. magna cum laude, Cornell U., 1967, M.D., 1971; m. Yvonne Schott, June 1969 (div. 1970); m. 2d, Carol Ann Malloy, Nov. 1972 (div. 1975). Intern Cornell-N.Y. Hosp., N.Y.C., 1971-72, resident in gen. surgery, 1972-76, resident in plastic surgery, 1977-78; pres. Esquire Cadillac Limousine Service Inc., N.Y.C., 1977—; individual practice medicine, specializing in plastic surgery, N.Y.C., 1978—; instr. surgery Cornell-N.Y. Hosp., 1978—. Mem. N.Y. County Health Service Rev. Orgn., 1976—. Served to maj. M.C., USAF, 1976-77; Japan. Diplomate Am. Bd. Surgery; licensed physician N.Y. State, Calif., Va. Fellow Internat. Coll. Surgeons; mem. AMA (physicians recognition award 1978), Phi Beta Kappa. Republican. Clubs: Atrium, Regine's, Studio 54, Xenon, N.Y. Athletic, Cornell. Home: 425 E 58th St New York City NY 10022

CUDDY, ROBERT JAMES, JR., iron ore co. exec.; b. N.Y.C., July 29, 1944; s. Robert James and Mary Patricia (O'Toole) C.; B.S. in Accounting, L.I. U., 1966; m. Mary Kathryn Shaver, May 20. 1967; children—Robert James, Richard Joseph, Patrick Michael. Staff auditor Price Waterhouse & Co., N.Y.C., 1966, 69-70; staff auditor Amax Inc., Greenwich, Conn., 1970-71, asst. to dir. accounting, 1971-72, mgr. accounting Iron Ore div., 1972-78, asst. to controller Iron Ore div., 1978—. Mem. Ramapo Valley Ambulance Corps., Suffern, N.Y. Served with U.S. Army, 1967-69. C.P.A. Mem. Am. Inst. C.P.A.'s, N.Y. State Soc. C.P.A.'s, Nat. Assn. Accountants, Phi Kappa Theta. Office: Amax Center Greenwich CT 06830

CUDDY, WILLIAM VINCENT, lawyer; b. Port Chester, N.Y., Jan. 15, 1929; s. William V. and Mary (Murphy) C.; A.B. cum laude, U. Notre Dame, 1952; LL.B., Fordham U., 1956; LL.D., Pace U., 1978; m. Katherine Mahoney, Nov. 24, 1956; children—Maura, William, Patrice, Megan, Christopher. Admitted to N.Y. bar, 1956; partner Close, Griffiths, McCarthy & Gaynor, White Plains, N.Y., 1956-66; v.p., gen. counsel, dir. Bush Universal, Inc., and predecessor cos., 1966-70; partner law firm Cuddy & Feder, White Plains, N.Y., 1971—; city judge, White Plains, 1975-77. Bd. dirs. Westchester County Heart Assn., 1975—; advisory Council Pace U. Sch. Law, 1976—, Coll. White Plains, 1976—. Served with AUS, 1946-47. Named Notre Dame Man of the Year, 1963. Mem. N.Y., Westchester County, White Plains bar assns., Fordham, Notre Dame law assns., Notre Dame Nat. Alumni Assn. (v.p. 1966, dir. 1964-67). Roman Catholic. Clubs: Westchester Country (Rye, N.Y.); Sankaty Head Golf (Nantucket, Mass.); Notre Dame (pres. 1961). Home: 36 Copper Beech Rd Greenwich CT 06830 also 3 Walsh St Nantucket MA 02554 Office: 90 Maple Ave White Plains NY 10601 also 733 Summer St Stamford CT 06904

CUDE, REGINALD HODGIN, architect; b. Greensboro, N.C., May 9, 1936; s. Ernest and Anne (Hodgin) C.; B.Arch., N.C. State U., 1959; m. Nancy V. Worrall, Dec. 31, 1966; children—Jonathan Christopher, Jennifer Elizabeth. Intern with various architects and engrs., N.C. and N.Y., 1957-61; With Marcel Breuer & Assos., N.Y.C., 1962, I.M. Pei & Partners, N.Y.C., 1962-65; asso. Mariani & Assos., Washington, 1966-67, partner, 1968—. Served with U.S. Army, 1960. Registered architect N.Y., D.C., Md., Va. Mem. AIA. Methodist. Prin. works Georgetown U. Med. Library, Green County (Ind.) Gen. Hosp., Community Mental Health Center, Washington, Fine Arts Complex U. D.C. Van Ness Campus, Washington. Home: 5011 14th St N Arlington VA 22205 Office: 1600 20th St NW Washington DC 20009

CUETARA, EDWARD AMADO, architect; b. Boston, Aug. 13, 1924; s. Amado and Martha (Mehnert) C.; B.Arch., Cornell U., 1950; m. Janet Rachel Smith, Jan. 5, 1968; children by previous marriage—John Monroe, James Barry, Virginia Adams, Daniel Underwood. With Walter Gropius and Architects Collaborative, Cambridge, Mass., 1952-56; founder, pres. Core House Corp., Cambridge, 1956-60; with Rome (Italy) office Architects Collaborative, 1960-62; founder, chief architect Interbuild System Corp., Cambridge, 1962-64; pvt. practice architecture, West Tisbury, Mass., 1968—. Bd. dirs. Concerned Citizens of Martha's Vineyard. Served as 2d lt. Ordnance Dept., AUS, 1943-46. Recipient AIA honor award for Woolner Residence, Chilmark, Mass., 1973; Archtl. Record award of excellence for house design, 1974. Mem. AIA, Boston Soc. Architects. Inventor modular residential component system. Address: Box 1262 Edgartown MA 02539

CUETO, AGUSTIN, cable corp. exec.; b. Tampa, Fla., Apr. 10, 1933; s. Agustin and Belia (Cuervo) C.; B.S., U. Tampa. 1959; student U. Bridgeport, 1963; m. Olga Vargas, May 5, 1956; children—Richard, John, Patricia, Robyn, Lisa. With Gen. Cable Corp., Greenwich, Conn., 1956—, mgr. indsl. relations, 1960-61, asst. to pres. subs. corp., 1961-64, asst. dir. personnel, 1964-66, plant mgr., 1966-70, mng. dir. Spanish ops., 1970-77, v.p., gen. mgr. internat. ops., 1977—; pres. Gen. Cable Export Corp.; dir. Cabel (Venezuela), Cables de Communicaciones, (Spain), CEAT Gen. (Colombia), Electrofin. Ltd., Cayman Islands, Gen. Cable CEAT (Spain), Plasmica (Spain), Spenger (Spain). Served with AUS, 1953-55. Mem. Wire Assn. Patentee dual wire extrusion, elec. test equipment, cable sheathing equipment. Home: 11 Ferry Ln Westport CT 06880 Office: 500 W Putnam St Greenwich CT 06830

CUKOR, PETER, chemist; b. Szolnok, Hungary, Aug. 29, 1936; s. Andor and Lili C.; B.Chem. Engring., City Coll. N.Y., 1961; M.S., St. Johns U., N.Y.C., 1963, Ph.D., 1966; m. Adele Bieler, June 6, 1964; children—David, Jeffrey, Barry. Sr. technologist Mobil Oil Co., Bklyn., 1964-67; tech. staff Gen. Telephone and Electronics Inc. labs., Bayside, N.Y., 1967-72, sect. head organic analysis and organic materials, Waltham, Mass., 1972—; vis. prof. chemistry Queens Coll. City U. N.Y., 1967-72. NIH grad. fellow, 1961-64. Mem. Am. Chem. Soc., AAAS, N.Y. Acad. Scis., Sigma Xi. Jewish. Contbr. chpt. to book, articles to profl. publs. analytical chemistry, medicinal chemistry, material sci. Patentee in field. Home: 39 Foxhill Dr Natick MA 01760 Office: 40 Sylvan Rd Waltham MA 02154

CULHANE, SHAMUS, producer of animated films; b. Ware, Mass., Nov. 12, 1908; s. James Henry and Alma (Lapierre) C.; ed. pub. schs.; m. Juana Hegarty, June 30, 1957; children—Brian, Kevin. With J.R. Bray Studios, 1924-29, Krazy Kat Studio, 1929-30, Max Fliescher Studio, 1930-32, 39-41, UB Iwwerks Studio, 1932-34, Van Buerun Prodns., 1934-35, Walt Disney Prodns., 1935-39, Walt Lantz Prodns., 1941-45; dir. Shamus Culhane Prodns., N.Y.C., 1945-58, 67—; producer Paramount Pictures, N.Y.C., 1965-67. Mem. Dirs. Guild Am. Animator of Hi Ho It's Off To Work We Go sequence in Disney's Snow White and the Seven Dwarfs, 1935; producer Saul Bass' titles for Around the World in 80 Days, 1956; co-producer with Frank Capra of Three Bell Telephone Co. sci. spls. on TV, 1954-57; dir. TV spl. The Night the Animals Talked, 1969; writer, dir., producer Noah's Animals, 1974. Address: 325 West End Ave New York City NY 10023

CULLEN, HELEN FRANCES, educator; b. Boston, Jan. 4, 1919; d. James Francis and Letitia Ellen (Johnson) Cullen; A.B., Radcliffe Coll., 1940; M.A., U. Mich., 1944, Ph.D. (fellow), 1950. Asst. prof. math. U. Mass. at Amherst, 1949-56, asso. prof., 1956-71, prof., 1971—. Mem. Am. Math. Soc., Math. Assn. Am., AAUP, Sigma Xi. Author: Introduction to General Topology, 1968; also articles in profl. jours. Office: Dept Math U Mass Amherst MA 01002

CULLEN, LEO FRANCIS, pharm. co. exec.; b. Phila., Mar. 8, 1942; s. Frank J. and Jean Y. (Miraglia) C.; A.B., Temple U., 1964; Ph.D., 1973; m. Mary Louise Sannuti, Sept. 25, 1965; children—Sean, Joanne. Research chemist Wyeth Labs., Inc., Radnor, Pa., 1964-67; supr. analytical and phys. chemistry sect. Wyeth Labs., Inc., Radnor, 1967-74; head of analytical chemistry and microbiol. units of quality assurance dept. Paoli, Pa., 1975-78, mgr. pilot plant sect. of pharmacy research and devel. div., 1978—. Mem. Am. Chem. Soc., Acad. Pharm. Scis. (sec. pharm. analysis control sect. 1977—), AAAS. Contbr. numerous articles on organic analysis, chem. kinetics, immobilized enzyme electrodes, automated continuous-flow analytical techniques, electroanalytical chemistry and pharm. systems to profl. jours. Home: 644 Marydell Dr West Chester PA 19380 Office: PO Box 861 Paoli PA 19301

CULLINAN, WILLIAM EDWARD, JR., airport services adminstr., airport engring. cons.; b. Portland, Maine, Aug. 17, 1907; s. William E. and Mary G. (Connolly) C.; B.S. in Elec. Engring., Mass. Inst. Tech., 1930; m. Janet Gordon, Feb. 25, 1933; children—Carol Ann Cullinan Taylor, William Gordon, Stephen Edward. Resident engr. Dept. of Pub. Works, Portland, Maine, 1930-35; dist. mgr. and dir. ops. of pub. works, various areas of Maine, 1935-40; airport engr. CAA, Boston Dist., 1940-42, dist. airport engr., N.Y.C., 1942-44; dir. N.Y. State Bur. of Aviation, Albany, 1944-46; chief of airports div. eastern region CAA, N.Y.C., 1946-58, 1963-65; dir. Dulles Internat. Airport, Washington, 1961-63; asst. area mgr. FAA, Boston, 1965-67, area mgr., 1967-70; instr. airport engring. Bklyn. Poly. Inst., 1954-56; mgr. Logan Internat. Airport Boston, 1970-72; dir. airport services E.C. Jordan Co., Inc., Portland, Maine, 1972—; airport cons., 1935—; mem. tech. advisory com. on airports, N.Y.C. Planning Commn., 1951-52; vice chmn. Boston Fed. Exec. Bd., 1970. Registered profl. engr., Maine, N.Y. Mem. Am. Inst. Aeros. and Astronautics, Maine Assn. of Engrs., Am. Assn. of Airport Execs., Nat. Aero. Assn., New Eng. Aero Club, Maine Airport Assn. (pres. 1976-77). Roman Catholic. Clubs: Rotary, Purpoodock Golf. Contbr. numerous articles on airport design, planning and ops. to profl. jours. Home: 3 Pilot Point Rd Cape Elizabeth ME 04107 Office: PO Box 7050 Downtown Station Portland ME 04112

CULLINGS, PATRICK ROBERT, union ofcl.; b. Syracuse, N.Y., May 20, 1946; s. Robert Perry and Helen Elizabeth (West) C.; grad. Leland Powers Sch. Speech, Broadcasting and Theatre, 1969; m. Nancy Anne Theodore, Oct. 11, 1969; 1 son, Timothy. Forester's helper N.Y. State Dept. Environ. Conservation, Saratoga, 1970-71; kettle operator Schenectady Chems., Inc. (N.Y.); pres. Varnish Workers Ind. Union, Schenectady, 1974-77. Asst. scoutmaster, Ballston Lake, N.Y., 1971-75. Served with U.S. Army, 1966-68. Roman Catholic. Home: 33 Maplewood Dr Ballston Lake NY 12019

CULVER, EDWARD HOLLAND, JR., advt. agy. exec.; b. Boston, Mar. 28, 1947; s. Edward Holland and Mary Lee (Oliver) C.; B.S., Yale U., 1969. With Culver Advt., Inc., 1972-75, v.p., 1972-75; pres. Culver Advt., Inc., Los Angeles, 1974-75; v.p. Culver Internat., Inc., Boston, London, Seoul, Korea and Tokyo, 1975—. Served to lt. USNR, 1969-72. Mem. Soc. Cincinnati. Episcopalian. Home: 164 Beacon St Boston MA 02116 Office: 535 Boylston St Boston MA 02116

CUMINGS, RICHARD GLENN, electronic engr.; b. Ft. Collins, Colo., Oct. 11, 1926; s. Glenn Arthur and Winifred (Wenkheimer) C.; student U. Md., 1946-49; B.S. in Elec. Engring., Purdue U., 1950; postgrad. U. Md., 1951-59, U. Fla., 1960-64; m. Jane Claggett Gray, May 3, 1952; children—Glenn Arthur, Catherine Anne. Field engr. microwave communication Motorola, Inc., Chgo., 1950-51; electronic scientist Naval Research Lab., Washington, 1951-59; project engr. Electro Mech. Research, Inc., Sarasota, Fla., 1959-64; dir. data products dept. Def. Electronics Inc., 1964-67; expert cons. Bur. Research and Engring., Post Office Dept., Washington, 1967-68; chief special instrumentation sect. U.S. Postal Service Lab., Rockville, Md., 1969-78, program mgr. research and devel. dept., 1975—; owner, cons. engr. E.E. Engring. Services. Served with USN, 1944-46. Mem. IEEE (sr.), Fla. Engrs. Soc., Nat. Soc. Profl. Engrs., Lambda Chi Alpha. Registered profl. engr., Fla. Contbr. articles in field to profl. jours. Inventor in field pulse circuitry. Patentee. Home: 13912 Drake Dr Rockville MD 20853 Office: 11711 Parklawn Dr Rockville MD 20852

CUMMIN, ALFRED S(AMUEL), chemist; b. London, Eng., Sept. 5, 1924; s. Jack and Lottie (Hainesdorff) C.; came to U.S., 1940, naturalized, 1948; B.S. Polytech. Inst. Bklyn., 1943, Ph.D. in Chemistry, 1946; M.B.A., U. Buffalo, 1959; m. Sylvia E. Smolok, Mar. 24, 1945; 1 dau., Cynthia Katherine. Research chemist S.A.M. labs, Manhattan Project, Columbia, 1943-44; plant supr. Metal & Plastic Processing Co., Bklyn., 1946-51; research chemist Gen. Chem. div. Allied Chem. & Dye Corp., N.Y.C., 1951-53; sr. chemist Congoleum Nairn, Kearny, N.J., 1953-54; supr. dielecs-advance devel. Gen. Elec. Co., Hudson Falls, N.Y., 1954-56; mgr. indsl. products research dept. Spencer Kellogg & Sons, Inc. (Textron), Buffalo, 1956-59; mgr. plastics div. Trancoa Chem Corp., Reading, Mass., 1959-62; asso. dir. product devel. service labs. chem. div. Merck & Co., Inc., Rahway, N.J., 1962-69; dir. product devel. Borden Chem. div. Borden Inc., N.Y.C., 1969-72, tech. dir., 1972-73, tech. dir. Borden Inc., 1973—; mem. exec. com. Food Safety Council, 1976—, trustee, chmn. membership com., 1976—; instr., Polytech. Inst. Bklyn., 1946-47; asst. prof. Adelphi Coll., 1952-54; prof. math, sci. U.S. Merchant Marine Acad., 1954; seminar leader Am. Mgmt. Assn.; prof. mgmt. N.Y.U. Sch. Mgmt., 1968—. Recipient certificate award, Fedn. Socs. Paint Tech., 1965. Mem. Am. Chem. Soc. Fedn. Coatings Tech., Inst. Food Tech., Am. Soc. Testing Materials, Paint Research Inst., Delta Sigma Pi, Gamma Sigma Epsilon, Beta Gamma Sigma, Phi Lamda Upsilon. Contbr. to profl. jours. Patentee in field. Research in polymers, electrochemistry, food packaging. Home: 2 Naworth Pass Westfield NJ 07090 Office: 277 Park Ave New York City NY 10017

CUMMING, HUGH SMITH, JR., former govt. ofcl.; b. Richmond, Va., Mar. 10, 1900; s. Hugh Smith and Lucy A. (Booth) C.; student Va. Mil. Inst. Lexington, Va., 1917-20, U. Va., 1920-24; m. Winifred Burney West, Sept. 21, 1935 (dec. Jan. 1978). Mem. Va. bar; banker, London, Bombay, Singapore, Peking, 1924-27; tech. advisor U.S. State Dept., 1928; asst. to U.S. del. Internat. Econ. Conf., London and 7th Pan-Am. Conf., Montevideo, 1933; exec. asst. to Sec. of State, 1934, detailed to U.S. Consulate, Geneva, in connection Italo-Ethiopian affairs, 1935-36; spl. mission to Scandinavia and Netherlands, 1939; mem. exec. com. U.S. Antarctic Service, 1939-41; spl. mission Greenland, 1941; mem. Econ. Warfare Mission, also U.S. del. Internat. Whaling Conf., London, 1943; spl. mission to Sweden, 1943; rep. State Dept. on Anglo-Swedish-Am. Commn. and chief div. No. European Affairs, 1944; polit. liaison officer U.S. del. UN Conf. on Internat. Orgn., San Francisco, 1945; spl. mission Iceland, 1946; counselor of Embassy, Stockholm, 1947-50; counselor of Embassy with personal rank of minister, Moscow, 1950-52; dep. sec. gen. for polit. affairs NATO, Paris, 1952-53; ambassador to Indonesia, 1953-57; spl. asst. to sec. of state, dir. Intelligence, Dept. State, 1957-61, cons., 1961-64; mem. bd. examiners Am. Fgn. Service, 1957-62; adv. bd. Fgn. Service Inst., 1957-62; v.p. West-Wilholt Co., Stockton, Calif., 1961-63. Former mem. bd. govs. Columbia Hosp. for Women, Washington; trustee Washington Inst. Fgn. Affairs, Meridian House Found., Washington, Family and Child Services of Washington; v.p. Overseas Mission Soc., 1963-70; chmn. adv. com. John Foster Dulles Library, Princeton; former mem. adv. council Sch. Internat. Services, Am. U.; trustee Washington Cathedral; bd. dirs. Historic Georgetown, Inc., Bath County Hist. Soc.; adv. bd. Woodrow Wilson House Nat. Trust; pres., chmn. bd. mgrs. Bath County Community Hosp., Hot Springs, Va. Served as 2d lt. U.S. Army, 1918. Mem. U. Va. Law Sch. Assn., Mil. Order World Wars, Bath County Hist. Soc. (dir. 1975—), S.A.R., Nat. Cathedral Assn. (trustee, pres. 1962-65, 73—). Diplomatic and Consular Officers Ret. (past pres.), Com. 100 for Fed. Capital, Raven Soc., Zeta Psi. Episcopalian (vestryman, lay reader). Clubs: Met. (past pres.), Cosmos, Alibi (Washington); Farmington Country (Charlottesville, Va.); Chevy Chase (Md.); Royal Swedish Yacht (life), Sallskapet (life) (Stockholm). Home: 2811 O St NW Washington DC 20007 also Overlook Hot Springs VA 24445 Office: 2811 O St NW Washington DC 20007

CUMMINGS, BENJAMIN EDGAR, mech. engr.; b. Los Angeles, Dec. 21, 1932; s. Elwin Marion and Alexandre Dumas (Bess) C.; B.S., Calif. Inst. Tech., 1955, M.S., 1956, Ae.E., 1957, Ph.D., 1962; m. Patricia Amalina Tola, Nov. 4, 1968; children—Leslie, Hilary, Laird, Heather, Francisco, Tania, Anita, Alejandra. Engr., Aerojet-Gen. Co., Azusa, Calif., 1959-62; sr. staff mem. Inst. Def. Analyses, Washington, 1962-63, 65-66, Gen. Research Corp., Santa Barbara, Calif., 1966-71, Bangkok, Thailand, 1968-69; asst. prof. engring. U. Calif., Los Angeles, 1963-66; br. chief Ballistics Research Labs., Aberdeen Proving Grounds, Md., 1971-77, coordinator Tri-Service Joint Tech. Coordinating Group for Munitions Effectiveness, 1977—; cons. U.

Md. Med. Sch. Troop committeeman Greater Balt. council Boy Scouts Am.; chmn. Ballistics Research Labs. Combined Charities Campaign; active fund raising Calif. Inst. Tech. Served with USAF, 1957-59. Recipient Quality Performance award U.S. Army; Calif. Inst. Tech. scholar, 1951-55, acad. honors, 1955; Ford Found. fellow, 1960-62. Mem. Sigma Xi. Research, publs. on aeroelasticity, structural failure, control of laval flows, turbine projectiles, mil. effectiveness. Home: 804 Earlton Rd Havre De Grace MD 21078 Office: USAMSAA Attention: DRXSY-J Aberdeen Proving Grounds MD 21005

CUMMINGS, HAROLD GREIG, JR., securities co. exec.; b. Washington, July 14, 1934; s. Harold Greig and Annie Pauline (Adams) C.; B.A., Washington and Lee U., 1957; postgrad. N.Y. Inst. Fin., 1959-68; m. Sara Elizabeth Humphrey, Sept. 10, 1960; children—Harold Greig, Elizabeth Ridout. Asst. v.p. Folger Nolan Fleming Douglas, Washington, 1959-67; v.p. Legg Mason Wood Walker, Inc., Washington, 1967—, mem. pres. council, 1971—; v.p. dir. John Hanson Service Corp.; fin. planning cons. Adv. bd. Indsl. Bank of Washington. Past pres., dir. Episc. Ch. Home, Inc., Episc. Ch. Home Friendship, Inc.; bd. dirs. Boys' Clubs Greater Washington. Served to 1st lt. AUS, 1957-59. Lic. ins. field underwriter. Mem. Fin. Analysts Fedn., Washington Soc. Investment Analysts, Bond Club Washington, Beta Theta Pi. Republican. Episcopalian. Club: Rotary (pres. Washington). Home: 5129 Westpath Way Washington DC 20016 Office: 1747 Pennsylvania Ave NW Washington DC 20006

CUMMINGS, MICHAEL JAMES, journalist; b. Williamsport, Pa., Oct. 7, 1941; s. Francis Patrick and Irene Catherine (Williams) C.; A.B., King's Coll., 1964; postgrad., Lycoming Coll., 1964-65, Elmira Coll., 1965-67; grad. Seminar City Editors Am. Press Inst., Columbia U., 1971, Seminar for Mng. Editors, 1976. Tchr. dist. schs., Muncy, Pa., 1964-65, Elmira, N.Y., 1965-68; reporter, state editor, asst. news editor, news editor, asst. to editor, mng. editor Grit Pub. Co., Williamsport, Pa., 1968—. Mem. Pa. Soc. of Newspaper Editors, AP Mng. Editors (dir.). Democrat. Roman Catholic. Home: 907 Louisa St Williamsport PA 17701 Office: 208 W 3rd St Williamsport PA 17701

CUMMINGS, RICHARD HAVEN, leather mfg. co. exec.; b. Woburn, Mass., Jan. 19, 1929; s. Eustace Haven and Eleanor Houston (Ray) C.; studdnt Kimball Union Acad., 1945-47, Norwich U., 1947-50, Pratt Inst., 1950-51; m. Nancy Sutton Brown, Sept., 1954; children—Eleanor Cummings Bowe, Richard Farwell, Andrea Sutton. Pres., gen. mgr. E. Cummings Leather Co., Inc., Lebanon, N.H., 1964—. Mem. Republican Town Com., Grafton County (N.H.) Rep. Exec. Com., N.H. State Rep. Com., N.H. Pub. Employees Labor Relations Bd.; chmn. YMCA Camp Coniston, chmn. N.H. exec. com. Served with U.S. Army, 1951-53. Mem. New Eng. Tanners Club, Am. Leather Chemist Assn., Tanners Council Am., VFW, N.H. Bus. and Industry Assn. Republican. Mem. United Ch. of Christ. Club: Elks. Home: 37 Rip Rd Hanover NH 03755 Office: 10 High St Lebanon NH 03766

CUMMINGS, ROBERT AMBROSE, oceanographer; b. Woodstock, Maine, Feb. 4, 1917; s. Aubrey Otto and Nell (Preble) C.; B.A. in Math., U. Maine, 1941; postgrad. Am. U., 1961-62, George Washington U., 1964-65; m. Mary Pauline Soucie, June 1, 1946; children—Judith Ann, John Frederick. Statis. clk. Bur. Census, Suitland, Md., 1946-47; mathematician and oceanographer U.S. Coast and Geodetic Survey, Dept. Commerce, Washington, 1947-64, Rockville, Md., 1964-74; ret., 1974. Served with USAAF, 1942-45. Recipient Bronze Medal award U.S. Dept. Commerce, 1974. Mem. Am. Geophys. Union. Democrat. Contbr. articles in field to profl. jours. Home: 5100 Oakglen Dr Rockville MD 20852

CUMMINS, FRANCIS MITCHELL, radiologist; b. Balt., Aug. 10, 1921; s. Thomas Joseph and Densey (Mitchell) C.; B.S., Harvard U., 1942; M.D., Columbia U., 1945; m. Rosamond Kane, Nov. 29, 1958; children—Rosamond, Christopher. Intern in medicine Yale U.-New Haven Hosp., 1945-46; intern in surgery N.Y. Hosp., N.Y.C., 1948-49, resident in radiology, 1949-52, asso. attending radiologist, 1959—; asst. attending radiologist Columbia-Presbyn. Med. Center, N.Y.C., 1952-59; clin. asso. prof. radiology Cornell U. Med. Coll., N.Y.C., 1959—. Served as capt. M.C., U.S. Army, 1946-48. Fellow Am. Coll. Radiology, N.Y. Acad. Medicine, N.Y. Acad. Scis.; mem. Radiol. Soc. N.Am., N.Y. Roentgen Soc., AMA, S.A.R. Clubs: Griffin Faculty, Harvard of N.Y., Shenorock Shore. Home: Thistle Ln Rye NY 10580 Office: 50 E 70th St New York City NY 10021

CUNDY, KENNETH RAYMOND, scientist; b. Spearfish, S.D., Dec. 22, 1929; s. Raymond and Letitia (Johnston) C.; B.A., Stanford, 1950, postgrad. Sch. Medicine, 1950-52; M.S. in Microbiology, U. Wash., 1953; postgrad. U. Calif. at Berkeley, 1957-60; Ph.D., U. Calif. at Davis, 1965; m. Elsie Marie Schlachter, Nov. 30, 1957. Research microbiologist U. Calif. at Berkeley, 1957-60; bacteriologist Gerber Products Co., Oakland, Calif., 1960-61; research microbiologist U. Calif. at Davis, 1961-65; instr. microbiology Temple U. Sch. Medicine, Phila., 1966-67, asst. prof., 1967-71, asso. prof. microbiology and immunology, 1971-77, prof., 1977—. Mem. admissions com., 1966-69; dir. clin. microbiology Temple U. Hosp., 1970—. Postdoctoral fellow med. microbiology Temple U., 1965-67; asso. dir. bacteriology St. Christopher's Hosp., Phila., 1967-68, dir. diagnostic microbiology lab., 1968-70. Served with USNR, 1954-57. Diplomate Am. Bd. Med. Microbiology. Fellow Am. Acad. Microbiology; mem. Am. Soc. Microbiology, AAAS, N.Y. Acad. Scis., Coll. Physicians Phila., Sigma Xi. Episcopalian. Mason. Clubs: Phila. Sketch, Commonwealth of California (San Francisco), Pa. Soc. Research in infectious disease process, mechanisms of pathogenicity, anaerobic microbiology, bacterial pathogenesis in cystic fibrosis. Home: 513 Delancey St Philadelphia PA 19106 Office: Temple U Sch Medicine Broad & Ontario Sts Philadelphia PA 19140

CUNEO, JOHN ANDREW, JR., hosp. adminstr.; b. N.Y.C., May 5, 1929; s. John Andrew and Adele (Neive) C.; B.S., Fordham U., 1951; M.S., Columbia U., 1955; m. Gloria F. Britting, June 28, 1952; children—Susan, Richard. Asst. adminstr. Mid Island Hosp., Bethpage, N.Y., 1955-59; adminstr. Pelham Bay Gen. Hosp., Bronx, N.Y., 1959-74; exec. dir. Pkwy Hosp., Forest Hills, N.Y., 1974—. Bd. dirs. N.Y. State Assn. Pvt. Hosps. Inc., 1976-78. Served as officer Med. Service Corp, USAF, 1951-53. Mem. Am. Coll. Hosp. Adminstrs., Am. Hosp. Assn., Am., N.Y.C. pub. health assns., Royal Soc. Health (Eng.), Assn. Alumni Columbia Sch. Pub. Health. Roman Catholic. Home: 650 Meadow Ct Westbury NY 11590 Office: 70-35 113th St Forest Hills NY 11375

CUNEO, LEONARD EUGENE, human service exec.; b. Boston, Mar. 2, 1939; s. Leonard Bartholomew and Mildred (Crosby) C.; B.S., Boston U., 1960, M.A., 1967; grad. Columbia Sch. Bus. Inst. Nonprofit Mgmt., 1977; m. Ann Marie Daley, June 10, 1961; children—Leonard Eugene, Beth Ann, Michael Steven, Amy Lynne, Marc Robert. Health and phys. edn. dir. Dorchester (Mass.) YMCA, 1960-63, Barrington (R.I.) YMCA, 1963-67, Central Queens YMCA, Jamaica, N.Y., 1967-70; exec. dir. Staten Island (N.Y.) YMCA, 1970—; mem. Nat. Council YMCA's, 1974—; dir. Tri-State YMCA, 1972—; faculty health sci. S.I. Community Coll., 1972-75. Mem. council United Way of S.I., 1970—; exec. com. S.I. United Way Agys., 1972—; lector Our Lady of Good Counsel Ch., S.I., 1971—, instr. religious edn. program, 1976—, active fund raising; bd. dirs. Health Sers. Agy., 1972-76. Mem. Assn. Profl. YMCA Dirs. Club: Kiwanis (pres. 1969-70). Home: 27 Silver Lake Rd Staten Island NY 10301 Office: 651 Broadway Staten Island NY 10310

CUNHA, GEORGE MARTIN, conservator; b. Providence, Dec. 25, 1911; s. Anthony Martin and Augusta Elizabeth (Dwyer) C.; student Mass. Inst. Tech., 1930-32, Lowell Inst., 1935-36, USN Line Sch., 1946-47, Naval War Coll., 1958-59; m. Dorothy Bourne Grant, Dec. 31, 1938; 1 stepson, James H. Ryan; children—George Martin, Suzanne Elizabeth. Control chemist Phillips Baker Rubber Co., Providence, 1932-34; devel. chemist Vultex Chem. Co., Cambridge, Mass., 1935-37; apptd. aviation cadet USN, 1938, advanced through grades to capt., 1957, ret., 1963; conservator rare books, documents and works of art on paper Library of Boston Athenaeum, 1963-73; dir. New Eng. Document Conservation Center, 1973-78, dir. emeritus, 1978—; cons. in conservation, writer, lectr., 1963—. Mem. adv. panel Library Binding Inst., Boston, 1972—. Chmn. advancement com. Narragansett council Boy Scouts Am., 1956-59, pres. C.Z. council, 1960-61. Decorated D.F.C., Air medal with star. Recipient Silver Beaver award Boy Scouts Am., 1958; certificate of merit Associacion de Scouts de Panama, 1961. Fellow Royal Soc. Arts, Pilgrim Soc. (editorial com. 1972), Am. Inst. for Conservation; mem. Internat. Inst. for Conservation Historic and Artistic Works, Guild of Book Workers (v.p.-at-large 1971-77), Colonial Soc. Mass. Republican. Mason. Club: Providence Art. Author: The Conservation of Library Materials, 1967, rev. edit., 1971. Editor: Procs. of Boston Athenaeum's 1971 Seminar on The Conservation of Library Materials, 1972, Seminar on Conservation Administration, 1975. Home: 33 High St Topsfield MA 01983 Office: Abbot Hall School St Andover MA 01810

CUNIO, PAUL EDWARD, hosp. engr.; b. Boston, Mar. 10, 1928; s. Thomas Joseph and Agnes Catherine (Bentley) C.; student U. Wis., 1954-55, U. Maine, 1969-70, Chesapeake Coll., 1975-76; m. Rebecca Marie Grover, Mar. 21, 1948; children—Stephanie, Michael, Paul, Jr., Stephen. Enlisted U.S. Navy, 1945, advanced through ranks to chief petty officer, 1958; codes enforcement officer City of Bath, Maine, 1965-71; chief engr. Terry Corp., Virginia Beach, Va., 1971-73; dir. plant ops. Meml. Hosp., Easton, Md., 1973—; tchr., cons. codes enforcement techniques, Maine, N.H., 1968-70. Precinct leader Republican Com., Virginia Beach, 1971-73. Notary public, Md; recipient Nat. Fuel Conservation award Mogul Corp., 1977. Mem. Am. Soc. Hosp. Engring., Internat. Assn. for Hosp. Security, Nat. Fire Protection Assn., VFW, Am. Legion. Republican. Clubs: Elk, Moose. Author: Radiographic Testing with Cobalt 60 and Iridium 197, 1967; contbr. article in field. Home: Box 98-D Route 11 Preston MD 21655 Office: Meml Hosp S Washington St Easton MD 21601

CUNNINGHAM, GEORGE GARRISON, supt. schs.; b. New Brunswick, N.J., Sept. 24, 1936; s. Charles Herbert and Grace Sarah (Shoemaker) C.; B.A., Lebanon Valley Coll., Annville, Pa., 1958; M.S., Hofstra U., Hempstead, N.Y., 1960; Ed.D., Columbia U. Tchrs. Coll., 1969; m. Priscilla Louise Knott, Nov. 29, 1958; children—Alicia Ruth, Reid Knott. Tchr. pub. schs., N.Y. State, 1959-65; grad. asst. Columbia U. Tchrs. Coll., 1965-66; dir. curriculum Milbrook (N.Y.) schs., 1966-68; dir. instrn. Massena (N.Y.) schs., 1968-71; dist. prin., Oppenheim, N.Y., 1971-74; Bd. Coop. Ednl. Services coordinator, Cortland, N.Y., 1974-75; supt. schs., Portland, Conn., 1975—; mem. Conn. Task Career Edn. Recipient Distinguished Educator award Inst. for Devel. Ednl. Activities, 1978. Mem. Am., Conn. assns. sch. adminstrs., Middlesex-Shoreline Supts. Assn., Capitol Region Edn. Council (profl. advisory com.), Phi Delta Kappa, Kappa Delta Pi. Congregationalist. Club: Portland Exchange. Home: 7 Birch Tree Hill Portland CT 06480 Office: PO Box 231 Portland CT 06480

CUNNINGHAM, MARIE (MRS. THOMAS CUNNINGHAM), mfg. co. exec.; b. Dover, N.J., Nov. 15, 1936; d. Joseph and Mina (Sutton) Romano; grad. high sch.; m. Thomas Cunningham, Feb. 12, 1966; children—Thomas III, Nancy Mina. With Precision Mfg. Co., Inc., Dover, 1954—, office mgr., 1960—, asst. to pres., 1965-70, v.p., comptroller, 1970—. Republican. Home: 6 Richards Ave Succasunna NJ 07876 Office: 88 King St Dover NJ 07801

CUNNINGHAM, WILLIAM JOHN, color scientist; b. Phila., Feb. 21, 1922; s. John J. and Emma (Grell) C.; B.A., Temple U., 1955; m. Helen C. Hollenberg, May 10, 1947; children—Vickie E. Cunningham Rowe, Janice L. Cunningham Rackovan, Judith Anne Cunningham Beck, Jeannette Helen. With Rohm & Haas Co., 1941-42, 46—, color coordinator sales dept., Phila., 1964-67, group leader colorimetry, 1967-73, sr. scientist prodn. dept. Bristol, Pa., 1973—. Republican committeeman, NE Phila., 1961-63; pres. PTA Council Rock Secondary Schs. of Bucks County (Pa.), 1966-67; bd. dirs. Bucks County Family Services Assn., 1973-76. Served with Signal Corps U.S. Army, 1942-46; PTO. Decorated Bronze Star. Mem. Soc. Plastics Engrs. (dir. color appearance div. 1973—, treas. 1976—, sec. 1977, chmn. elect 1978—), Inter-Soc. Color Council. Lutheran. Club: Masons (Phila.). Patentee in field. Home: 154 Austin Dr Holland PA 18966 Office: Rohm & Haas Co PO Box 219 Bristol PA 19007

CUNOV, CARL HENRY, chemist; b. Detroit, Feb. 19, 1918; s. Charles Augustus and Hilda (Otto) C.; B.S. in Chemistry, Wayne State U., 1941, Ph.D. In Organic Chemistry, 1951; m. Margaret K. Van Dixon, Oct. 16, 1942; children—Carolyn, Mary, Robert. Drug analyst to chief chemist Jamieson Pharmacal Co., Detroit, 1939-46; chief chemist McKay-Davis Co., Toledo, 1946-47; teaching fellow research fellow Wayne State U., Detroit, 1947-50; asst. plant tech. dir., plant tech. dir., process dept. mgr., mfg. project dir. Smith Kline & French Labs., Phila., 1950-62; asso. prof. chemistry Central Mo. State Coll., Warrensburg, 1962-65; from asso. prof. to prof. chemistry, dept. head Keuka Coll., Keuka Park, N.Y., 1965-68; chem. research supr. Pharm. div. Pennwalt Corp., Rochester, N.Y., 1968—. Cons., translator abstractor, Phila., 1961—. Mem. Am. Chem. Soc., AAAS, NEA, AAUP, Am. Pharm. Assn., Pa. Acad. Sci., Pharm. Mfrs. Assn., Mich. Acad. Pharmacy, Franklin Inst. Phila., Pharm. Prodn. Forum, Christian Businessmen's Assn., Sigma Xi, Phi Lambda Upsilon, Tau Kappa Epsilon. Methodist. Club: Philadelphia Organic Chemists'. Research work in field. Home: 340 Fairwood Circle Rochester NY 14623 Office: Pharm Div Pennwalt Corp Rochester NY 14603

CUOCO, DANIEL A(NTHONY), lawyer, pharm. co. exec.; b. N.Y.C., Oct. 19, 1937; s. Albert and Mary Cuoco; B.A., Iona Coll., 1959; LL.B., Columbia U., 1962; m. Joanne Colavita, July 8, 1961; children—Dana Jean, Mark Alan, Susan Adrienne, Victoria Joanna. Admitted to N.Y. State bar, 1962, U.S. Supreme Ct. bar, 1974; asso. firm Dewey, Ballantine, Bushby, Palmer & Wood, N.Y.C., 1962-71; asso. atty. Squibb Corp., N.Y.C., 1971-74, asst. gen. counsel, 1971—, v.p., 1974—. Mem. Scarsdale (N.Y.) Non-partisan Nominating Com., 1976. Mem. Am. Bar Assn., N.Y. State Bar Assn., City N.Y. Bar Assn. Republican. Roman Catholic. Club: Univ. (N.Y.C.). Home: 10 Overlook Rd Scarsdale NY 10583 Office: 40 W 57th St New York NY 10019

CUOMO, MARIO MATTHEW, lt. gov. N.Y.; b. Queens County, N.Y., June 15, 1932; s. Andrea and Immaculata C.; B.A. summa cum laude, St. John's Coll., 1953; LL.B. cum laude, St. John's U., 1956; m. Matilda Raffa; children—Margaret, Andrew, Maria, Amdeline, Christopher. Admitted to N.Y. bar, 1956, U.S. Supreme Ct. bar, 1960; confidential legal asst. to judge N.Y. State Ct. Appeals, 1956-58; asso. firm Corner, Weisbrod, Froeb & Charles, Bklyn., 1958-63, partner, 1963-75; sec. of state State of N.Y., N.Y.C., 1975-79, lt. gov., Albany, 1979—; faculty St. John's U. Sch. Law, 1963-75; counsel to community groups including Corona Homeowners, 1966-72. Charter mem. 1st Ecumenical Commn. of Christians and Jews for Bklyn. and Queens. Recipient Rapallo award Columbia Lawyers Assn., 1976; Dante medal Italian Govt.-Am. Assn. Tchrs. Italian, 1976; Silver medallion Columbia Coalition, 1976; Public Adminstr. award C.W. Post Coll., 1977. Mem. Am., N.Y. State, Bklyn., Nassau and Queens County bar assns., Assn. Bar City N.Y., Am. Judicature Soc., St. John's U. Alumni Fedn. (chmn. bd. 1970-72), Cath. Lawyers Guild of Queens County (pres. 1966-67), Skull and Circle. Author: Forest Hills Diary: The Crisis of Low-Income Housing, 1974. Contbr. articles to legal publs. Office: Office of Lt Gov State Capitol Albany NY 12224*

CUOMO, THOMAS JOSEPH, JR., physician; b. Bklyn., Aug. 2, 1943; s. Thomas Joseph and Jeanette Rosalie (Gullo) C.; B.A., Fordham U., 1965; M.D., Jefferson U., 1969; m. Jill Rosemarie Sicari, July 8, 1967; 1 son, Thomas Joseph. Intern, St. Vincent's Hosp., N.Y.C., 1969-70; resident medicine Manhattan VA Hosp., Bellevue Hosp., 1970-71, Misericordia Hosp., Fordham Hosp., 1971-72, McGuire VA Hosp., Med. Coll. Va. Hosp., 1972-73; fellow cardiology McGuire VA Hosp., Med. Coll. Va. Hosp., 1973-75; partner Scarsdale Med. Group (N.Y.), 1975—; asso. attending physician White Plains (N.Y.) Hosp., 1975—; asst. attending physician Westchester Med. Center, Valhalla, N.Y., 1976—, St. Agnes Hosp., White Plains, 1975—. Served with U.S. Army, 1970. Diplomate Am. Bd. Internal Medicine (cardiovascular diseases). Mem. ACP, AMA, (Physicians Recognition award). Roman Catholic. Office: 259 Heathcote Rd Scarsdale NY 10583

CUPIDO, RAFFAELLA ELIZABETH, social worker; b. Rochester, N.Y., Apr. 12, 1929; d. Salvatore and Elizabeth (Squilla) C.; B.A. in Sociology, U. Rochester, 1951; M. Social Service, U. Buffalo, 1954. Group worker Lewis St. Center, Rochester, 1951-53; with Baden St. Settlement House, Rochester, 1952-53, Council Social Agys., 1953, Neighborhood House, 1953-54 (both Buffalo); asst. dir. Neighborhood House, Auburn, N.Y., 1954-55; 1st group worker House of Providence, 1955-58, supr. group work Huntington Family Center, 1958-61 (both Syracuse, N.Y.); staff cons. recreation and group work R.I. Council Community Services, Inc., Providence, 1961-65; coordinator pub. and profl. edn. mental retardation Child Health and Devel. Center, faculty Brown U., Providence, 1965-66; exec. dir. Federal Hill House Assn., Providence, 1966-70, Smith Hill Center, Providence, 1970—; field instr. Syracuse U. Sch. Social Work, 1958-61, Boston Coll., 1963-64, U. Conn., 1967; mem. R.I. Bd. Registration Social Workers, 1970—, sec., 1971—. Mem. R.I. Gov.'s Com. on Youth Employment, 1962, Gov.'s Task Force on Youth Employment, 1963; mem. Attys. Gen.'s Youth Adv. Bd., 1967-69, R.I. Youth Council, 1963-65 (award 1964); treas. United Way Execs., 1967-69, vice chmn., 1969-71; mem. capital funds com. United Way, 1971-76, mem. Pres.'s Adv. Com., 1976—; founder Citizens for Preservation Waterman Lake, 1970, v.p., 1970-72, pres., 1972-73, sec., 1976-78; mem. Glocester Democratic Town Com., 1971-73; Mem. Gloucester Conservation Commn., 1974-77, vice-chmn., 1975-77; bd. dirs. Tri-Town Econ. Opportunity Com., 1974-76. Mem. Nat. Assn. Social Workers (chmn. membership Syracuse chpt. 1958-68, editor newsletter R.I. chpt. 1967-70, sec. 1969-73, pres. 1973-75), Acad. Certified Social Workers, Assn. Community Service Execs. Home: Waterman Lake Shore Dr Harmony RI 02829 Office: 110 Ruggles St Providence RI 02908

CUPPELS, NORMAN PAUL, geologist; b. Uxbridge, Mass., Oct. 16, 1916; s. Alphonse L. and Maude May (Greene) C.; B.A., Brown U., 1950; M.S., Rutgers U., 1952; m. Eleanor Hope Riley, Sept. 11, 1941; children—Diane A., Robert A. Geologist, U.S. Geol. Survey, N.C., S.C., S.D., Colo., Wyo., Mass. and Ky., 1952-72; geol. cons. Def. Minerals Exploration Adminstrn., Black Hills, S.D. Served with USCG, 1937-47; PTO. Recipient Scroll of Honor, U.S. Geol. Survey. Fellow Geol. Soc. Am.; mem. Am. Geologic Inst. Contbr. bulls. to U.S. Geol. Survey. Home: Route 5 Hill Farm Rd Coventry RI 02816

CUPRAK, LUCIAN JOHN, biochemist; b. Norwich, Conn., Apr. 2, 1922; s. Lucian and Mary (Humeniuk) C.; B.S., U. Conn., 1943; D.M.D., Tufts U., 1948; Ph.D. in Biochemistry, Brandeis U., 1967; m. Ruth Lois Marvin, June 30, 1945; children—Mary L., Elizabeth E., Gregory T., Dorothy A., Alexander F. Pvt. practice dentistry, New London, Conn., 1948-51; asst. prof. sch. medicine Tufts U., Medford, Mass., 1968-70, asso. dir. dermatology research lab., 1968-70; sci. and research staff New Eng. Med. Center Hosp., Boston, 1968-70; chief dental research tng. program, research dentist Leech Farm VA Hosp., Pitts., 1970-72, adj. asso. prof. pharmacology sch. dental medicine U. Pitts., 1970-72, clin. asst. prof. medicine sch. medicine, 1970-72; asso. chief staff for research VA Center, Togus, Maine, 1973—; lectr. biochemistry dept. U. Maine, Orono, 1973—. Served with U.S. Army, 1943-44, with USN, 1951-62. Decorated UN Service medal. Nat. Inst. Dental Research postdoctoral fellow, 1962-67; recipient Sci. Achievement award R.I. State Dental Assn., 1959. Mem. AAAS, Am. Chem. Soc. (chmn. Maine sect. 1978-80), Am. Tissue Culture Assn., Internat. Assn. Dental Research, N.Y. Acad. Scis., Sigma Xi. Mason. Author publs. in fields of protein chemistry and tissue culture. Home: RD 5 Gardiner ME 04345

CURI, JOSEPH FRANCIS JOHN, pediatrician; s. Humberto and Josephine (Calabrese) C.; B.A. summa cum laude, Colgate U., 1960; M.D., Yale U., 1964; postgrad. Harvard U. Med. Sch., 1970; m. Susannah Evans English, June 1, 1965; children—Anne Josephine, Sarah, Katheryn, J. Michael. Intern, N.Y. Hosp.-Cornell Med. Center, N.Y.C., 1964-65, resident, 1965-67; practice medicine specializing in pediatrics and adolescent medicine, Torrington, Conn., 1970—; mem. staff, chmn. dept. pediatrics Charlotte Hungerford Hosp.; mem. staff Litchfield Hills Med. Center. Bd. dirs. Northwestern Conn. March of Dimes, 1970. Served with USAF, 1967-69. Diplomate Am. Bd. Pediatrics. Mem. Am. Acad. Pediatrics, Soc. Adolescent Medicine (exec. com.), Assn. Yale Med. Alumni, YMCA, Northwestern Conn. C. of C. (dir.), Phi Beta Kappa, Alpha Chi Epsilon, Nu Sigma Nu. Clubs: Litchfield Country, Pinewoods Racquet, Wolcott Athletic. Author: Hypnosis in Medicine, 1958; Indium Photometrics, 1960; Yale Prepared Childbirth, 1964. Home: Knickerbocker Rise Pie Hill Rd Goshen CT 06756 Office: Pediatrics-Adolescent Medicine Litchfield Hills Med Center Torrington CT 06790

CURIALE, SALVATORE BRUCE, acad. counselor; b. Bronx, N.Y., Apr. 14, 1927; s. Joseph and Adeline (Falcomata) C.; B.S., U. Bridgeport (Conn.), 1972, M.S. in Counseling, 1975; m. Phyllis J. Natale, May 7, 1949; children—Adeline Marie, Joseph James, Propr. Joseph Curiale & Son Tailoring, Bridgeport, 1940-60; supr. pricing Avco-Lycoming Co., Stratford, Conn., 1961-70; dir. acad. counseling U. Bridgeport, 1970—. Selectman, City of Bridgeport, 1954-56; chmn. Bridgeport Transit Dist., 1970-73, Bridgeport Civic Service Commn., 1973-75. Recipient Freedom Found. award, 1960, 62, 63, 64, 65, 75; Am. Legion medal, 1966; hon. Dana scholar, 1977. Mem. Am. Personnel and Guidance Assn., Conn. Assn. Continuing Edn., Assn. Continuing Higher Edn., Phi Delta Kappa, Kappa Omega Epsilon.

Democrat. Roman Catholic. Author poems. Home: 459 Savoy St Bridgeport CT 06606 Office: 225 Myrtle Ave Bridgeport CT 06602

CURILLA, JOSEPH, JR., trade assn. exec.; b. St. Clair, Pa., Nov. 24, 1926; s. Joseph and Anna (Halkowicz) C.; B.S. in Edn., Bloomsburg State Coll., 1950; M.Ed., Pa. State U., 1955, postgrad. studies, 1955-62; m. Molly Marie Conner, Aug. 31, 1958; 1 dau. Connie Ann. Tchr. pub. schs., Shamokin, Benton and State Coll., Pa., 1950-64, tchr., prin., State College, 1963-64; retail mcht., The Highland Market, State College, 1964-76; exec. dir. Asso. Builders & Contractors, Inc., State College, 1965-71, Liverpool, N.Y., 1971—. Justice peace, Benton, 1958-59; judge elections, State College, 1969-71. Bd. dirs. Central Pa. Festival Arts, Art Alliance Central Pa. Served with USMCR, 1951-53. Certified assn. exec. Mem. Am. Soc. Assn. Execs. Home: 715 S Manlius St Fayetteville NY 13066 Office: Asso Builders & Contractors Inc Lyndon Office Park 7000 E Genesee St Fayetteville NY 13066

CURKIN, PAULETTE, coll. adminstr.; b. Middletown, Conn., June 1, 1950; d. Harold and Katherine Thelma (Anneberg) Curkin; B.S., So. Conn. State Coll., 1972; M.S. in Higher Edn., So. Ill. U., 1978. Pub. health asst. City of Middletown (Conn.), 1972; tchr. health and phys. edn. Mansfield (Conn.) Middle Sch., 1973; residence hall coordinator So. Ill. U., Carbondale, 1973-75, human sexuality counselor, 1973-75; asst. dir. student housing So. Conn. State Coll., New Haven, 1975—. Mem. Am. Personnel and Guidance Assn., Am. Coll. Personnel Assn., Assn. Coll. and Univ. Housing Officers, Nat. Entertainment and Campus Activities Assn., NOW, Nat. Women's Polit. Caucus. Democrat. Jewish. Home: 320 Fitch St New Haven CT 06515 Office: Housing Office So Conn State Coll New Haven CT 06515

CURLEY, WALTER JOSEPH PATRICK, JR., diplomat; b. Pitts., Sept. 17, 1922; s. Walter Joseph Patrick and Marguerite Inez (Cowan) C.; grad. Philips Acad., Andover, Mass., 1940; B.A., Yale, 1944; M.B.A., Harvard, 1948; LL.D., Trinity Coll., Dublin, 1976; m. Mary Taylor Walton, Dec. 4, 1948; children—Margaret Cowan, Walter Joseph Patrick III, John Walton, James Mellon. Sect. mgr. Cal. Tex. Oil Co., India, Italy, N.Y.C., 1948-57; v.p., dir. San Jacinto Petroleum Co., N.Y.C., 1958-61; partner J.H. Whitney & Co., N.Y.C., 1961-75; dir. Curley Land Co., Pitts., Willers & Sons, Ireland; commr. Dept. Pub. Events, chief protocol City of N.Y., 1973-74; ambassador to Ireland, 1975-77; dir. Fiduciary Trust Co. N.Y., Fairchild Camera and Instrument Corp., Intercontinental Energy Corp., Investment Bank Ireland. Mem. finance com. N.Y.C. Republican Orgn., 1957-59. Bd. dirs. Lenox Hill Neighborhood Assn., 1966-75; trustee Barnard Coll., 1966-75, Buckley Sch., 1960-75, Brooks Sch., 1969-73. Served to capt. USMCR, 1943-46. Decorated Bronze Star (U.S.); Cloud and Banner (China). Republican. Roman Catholic. Author: Letters from the Pacific, 1960; Monarchs in Waiting, 1974. Home: 791 Park Ave New York City NY 10021 Office: 630 Fifth Ave New York City NY 10020

CURLEY, WALTER WILLIAM, bus. exec., librarian; b. Boston, Mar. 29, 1923; s. Walter Christopher and Lillian Elizabeth (Berg) C.; B.S., Northeastern U., 1947; M.S. in L.S., Simmons Coll., 1950; m. Marie Theresa Sullivan, Nov. 9, 1963; children—Celeste, Carolyn, Victoria, Alice. Asst. dir. Providence Pub. Library, 1950-62; dir. Suffolk Coop. Library System, N.Y.C., 1962-67; dir. info. services Arthur D. Little, Inc., Cambridge, Mass., 1967-70; dir. Cleve. Pub. Library, 1970-74; pres. Gaylord Bros., Inc., Syracuse, N.Y., 1974—, Angle-Genessee, Inc., Sanford, N.C., 1974—; chmn. bd. Forest Press, Albany, N.Y. Nat. bd. dirs. Literacy Vols. of Am.; bd. dirs. Mid York Library System; adv. com. White House Conf. on Libraries. Served with AUS, 1943-46. Mem. ALA (council). Home: 51 Forman St Cazenovia NY 13035 Office: PO Box 61 Syracuse NY 13201

CURLINGS, RONALD WAYNE, govt. ofcl.; b. Bklyn., Jan. 8, 1945; s. Chester Louis and Norma C.; A.A., Prince Georges Community Coll., 1973; m. Susan Agnes Boldt, Oct. 21, 1967; children—Scott, Paul, Jeremy. Letter carrier U.S. Post Office, Hyattsville, Md., 1965-69; personnel specialist Dept. Air Force, Andrews AFB, Md., 1969-70; computer specialist Justice Dept., Washington, 1970-75; computer systems analyst Treasury Dept., Washington, 1975—. Treas., Palmer Park (Md.) Boys Club, 1965; pres. Southeastern Christian Ch. League, 1972-73. Served with USAF, 1968-69. Mem. Amateur Basketball Assn. U.S.A., Fedn. Internat. Basketball Amateurs (Va. high sch. basketball ofcl.), Quantico Basketball Ofcls. Assn. Democrat. Lutheran. Office: Dept Treasury Room 220 Annex 1 Pennsylvania Ave Washington DC 20226

CURRAN, FRANK JOSEPH, psychiatrist; b. Mpls., Sept. 17, 1904; s. William T. and Anne (Leonard) C.; B.S., U. Minn., 1926, M.B., 1928, M.D., 1929; m. Charlotte E. Conway, Oct. 1, 1938. Intern, Mpls. Gen. Hosp., 1928-29; resident in psychiatry Boston Psychopathic Hosp., 1929-30; asst. resident and resident in neurology Bellevue Hosp., N.Y.C., 1931, jr. psychiatrist, 1932-34, sr. psychiatrist, 1934-45, in charge dept. child psychiatry, 1932, dir. adolescent ward, 1937-45; dir. psychiat. dept. St. Vincent's Hosp., 1946-47; dir. Children's Service Center, Charlottesville, Va., 1947-58; cons. psychiatrist St. Luke's Hosp.; mem. faculty N.Y. U. Med. Sch., 1932-47; practice child and adolescent psychiatry, N.Y.C., 1958—; asso. prof., prof. psychiatry and neurology U. Va. Med. Sch., 1947-58. Served to lt. USN, 1940-45. Diplomate Am. Bd. Neurology and Psychiatry. Fellow N.Y. Acad. Medicine, Am. Acad. Child Psychiatry (life), Am. Coll. Psychiatrists, Am. Psychiat. Assn. (fellow); mem. Am. Acad. Neurology (life), Am. Soc. Adolescent Psychiatry (life), Assn. Research in Nervous and Mental Disease, Internat. Assn. Child and Adolescent Psychiatry, Schilder Soc. Psychotherapy (past pres.), N.Y. Council Child Psychiatry (past (v.p.), Am. Assn. Psychiat. Services for Children (past pres.), Assn. Research in Nervous and Mental Disease, Med. Correctional Assn. (past pres.), Royal Soc. Medicine (affiliate), N.Y. State (life), N.Y. County (life) med. assns., AMA (life), U. Va. Med. Alumni Assn., Soc. Alumni Bellevue Hosp. Democrat. Roman Catholic. Contbr. numerous articles on various aspects of psychiatry to profl. jours.; contbr. chpts. to books on psychiatry. Office: 11 E 87th St New York NY 10028

CURRAN, KATHRYN, pub. relations exec.; b. N.Y.C., Oct. 7, 1941; d. George A. and Dorothy A. (Stillwell) McKeon; B.A., N.Y. U., 1961; postgrad. Russian Inst. Fordham U.; m. William H. Curran, Oct. 1, 1962. Account exec., pub. relations B.B.D.O., 1969-71; v.p. pub. relations Wisser & Sanchez, Inc., N.Y.C., 1971-75; v.p. Brit. Am. Promotions, N.Y.C., 1976—; cons. in field. Mem. Am. Women in Radio and TV, Am. Women in Communications. Republican. Club: Publicity (N.Y.C.). Home: Plains Rd Moodus CT 06469 Office: Brit Am Prodns 200 Madison Ave New York City NY 10017

CURRAN, MARTIN FRANCIS, chemist; b. Boston, Mar. 31, 1918; s. Joseph Leo and Mary (Lydon) C.; student Lincoln Tech. Inst., 1946-48; B.B.A., Northeastern U., 1950; m. Patricia M. Connors, June 27, 1959. Constrn. laborer, painter, Boston, 1937-42; with Union Bay State Chem. Co., Cambridge, Mass., 1946-51; chemist Angier Adhesive Co., Cambridge, 1951-58; chief chemist Foss Mfg. Co., Haverhill, Mass., 1958—, v.p., 1971-77; ret., 1977. Served with USNR, 1942-45. Mem. Am. Chem. Soc., Am Assn. Textile Tech. Patentee Shoe Stiffeners. Home: 67 North St Georgetown MA 01833 Office: 1 Whitney Ave Haverhill MA 10830

CURRAN, MAURICE FRANCIS, lawyer; b. Yonkers, N.Y., Feb. 20, 1931; s. James F. and Mary (O'Brien) C.; student Cathedral Coll., 1948-50; A.B., St. Joseph Coll. and Sem., 1952; LL.B., Fordham U., 1958; m. Deborah M. Dee, May 7, 1960; children—James, Maurice, Amy, Bridget, Ceara, Sara. Admitted to N.Y. bar, 1958; mem. firm Kelley, Drye, Newhall & Maginnes, N.Y.C., 1958-60, Wilson & Bave, Yonkers, 1960-65; div. counsel Merck & Co., Rahway, N.J., 1965-69; asst. gen. counsel E.R. Squibb & Sons, Inc., N.Y.C., 1967-70; corp. counsel, chief law dept. City of Yonkers, 1970-72; partner firm Bleakley, Platt, Schmidt & Fritz, White Plains, N.Y., 1972—. Mem. Yonkers Urban Renewal Agy., 1970-72; trial commr., dep. comm. pub. safety, Yonkers, 1972-74. Served to capt., USMCR, 1953-55. Home: 388 Bronxville Rd Yonkers NY 10708 Office: 2 William St White Plains NY 10601

CURRIER, MARION WINONA, educator; b. Farmington, N.H., Aug. 10, 1917; d. Fred E. and Abbie (Willey) Currier; B.E., Plymouth Tchrs. Coll., 1939. Bus. tchr. Bridgeton, Maine, 1939-41, Richford, Vt., 1943-44, Agawam, Mass., 1944-46, Webster, Mass., 1946-59, South Yarmouth, Mass., 1959-73; owner, dir. Lake Farm Camp, Inc., Orleans, Mass., 1957—; dir. Cam's Oil Service, Webster; treas., mgr., dir. Orleans Bowling Center and Coin-A-Matic Laundromat, Inc., 1963—. Mem. Town of Orleans Finance Bd., 1972—. Bd. dirs. Quanset Sailing Camps, Inc., South Orleans. Mem. Bus. and Profl. Women's Club, Delta Zeta Gamma. Conglist. Address: 46 Monument Rd Orleans MA 02653

CURRY, THOMAS FORTSON, electronics engr.; b. Thomasville, Ga., Nov. 22, 1926; s. Bostick Underwood and Bertie Eugenia (Cook) C.; B.E.E., Ga. Inst. Tech., 1949; M.S., Pa. State U., 1954; Ph.D., Carnegie Inst. Tech., 1959; m. Mary Ann Kemper, July 2, 1949; children—Bostick U., Thomas Lee, Ruth Ann, David C.K., Laurie F., Clinton M. Research fellow Carnegie Inst. Tech., 1955-57; mem. tech. staff Bell Telephone Labs., Murray Hill, N.J., 1957-58; lab. dir. Syracuse U. (N.Y.) Research Corp., 1958-63; chmn. bd. Curry, McLaughlin and Len, Inc., Syracuse, 1963-65; chief engr. Melpar, Inc., Falls Church, Va., 1965-69; product line dir. LTV-Electrosystems, Inc., Dallas, 1970; tech. adviser to pres. Melpar div. E-Systems, Inc., 1970-74; pres. C-Systems, Inc., Oakton, Va., 1975; v.p., dir. Microwave/Systems, Inc., Syracuse, 1974-75; asst. dir. systems evaluation SIGINT, Office Asst. Sec. Def. (Intelligence), mem. trustees vis. com. elec. engring. Carnegie Mellon U., 1972-74; expert cons. applied communications theory and electronic warfare, 1965-75; Pres. Kemper Park Civic Assn., 1972-73; treas. Centreville Council Civic Assn., Fairfax County, Va., 1973-74. Served to 1st lt. AUS, 1944-47, 50-52. Fellow Gulf Research and Devel. Co., 1955-56; Bell Telephone Lab. fellow in elec. communication, 1956-57. Fellow IEEE (chmn. No. Va. subsect. 1973); mem. Electronics Industries Assn., Assn. Old Crows (papers chmn., pres. 1974-75, nat. dir. 1976-79), Sigma Xi, Tau Beta Pi, Eta Kappa Nu, Alpha Tau Omega. Club: Cardinal Hill Swim and Racquet (Vienna). Tech. editor Electronic Warfare, 1973-74. Home: 2403 Beekay Ct Vienna VA 22180 Office: Room 3C200 The Pentagon Washington DC 20301

CURRY, WILLIAM THOMAS, surgeon; b. Mineola, N.Y., Jan. 4, 1943; s. Alexander James and Celeste Virginia (Starke) C.; B.S., N.Y. U., 1964; M.D., Howard U., 1968; m. Katherine Eloise Lum, Dec. 23, 1967; children—William Thomas, Christian Leigh. Intern, George Washington U. Hosp., Washington, 1968-69; resident in surgery N.Y. Hosp., N.Y.C., 1969-73; practice medicine, specializing in surgery, N.Y.C., 1973—; attending surgeon N.Y. Hosp., 1973—; clin. asst. prof. surgery Cornell U. Med. Coll., N.Y.C., 1976—, med. student advisor, 1976—. Bd. dirs. Music for Westchester Symphony Orch., 1977—. Served with U.S. Army, 1972. Mem. ACS, N.Y., N.Y. County med. socs. Republican. Episcopalian. Clubs: Reveille, Mt. Kisco Country. Office: 342 E 67th St New York City NY 10021

CURTIN, BRIAN JOSEPH, ophthalmologist; b. N.Y.C., July 25, 1921; s. James Joseph and Julia Margaret (Smith) C.; B.S., Fordham U., 1942; M.D., N.Y. U., 1945; m. Claire Margaret Flood, June 18, 1955; children—Edward Brian, James Martin, Thomas Hayes, Deirdre Claire. Intern, St. Vincent's Hosp., N.Y.C., 1945-46; resident surgeon Manhattan Eye, Ear and Throat Hosp., 1950-53, asst. attending surgeon, asso. attending surgeon, 1953-74, surgeon dir., 1974—, pres. med. bd., 1977—; attending ophthalmologist, chief service Misericordia-Lincoln Affiliated Hosps., 1958—; attending ophthalmologist N.Y. Hosp., 1969—; asst. prof. clin. ophthalmology N.Y. U., 1954-70; asst. prof. clin. ophthalmology Cornell Med. Coll., 1970—. Served with U.S. Navy, 1946-48. Diplomate Am. Bd. Ophthalmology. Mem. A.C.S., Am. Ophthalmol. Soc., AMA, N.Y. State N.Y. County med. socs., N.Y. Acad. Medicine, N.Y. Acad. Scis., AAAS, Am. Acad. Ophthalmology and Otolaryngology, Am. Eye Study Club. Roman Catholic. Club: Siwanoy Country. Contbr. chpts. to textbooks, articles to med. jours. Home: 21 Highland Circle Bronxville NY 10708 Office: 133 E 58th St New York City NY 10022

CURTIN, CATHERINE MARY, guidance counselor; b. N.Y.C., June 24, 1917; d. Daniel Francis and Nora Josephine (O'Connor) Curtin; B.S., St. John's U., Jamaica, N.Y., 1941, M.S. in Edn., 1945; Diploma Sacred Sci. cum mentione, Regina Mundi Pontifical Inst., Rome, 1960; M.A., St. Mary's Coll., Notre Dame, Ind., 1960; postgrad. Cath. U. Am., 1962-63. Joined Daus. of Wisdom, 1935; high sch. tchr. in N.Y. and Maine, 1937-57; mem. faculty Seat of Wisdom Coll., Litchfield, Conn., 1960-67; guidance counselor Christ the King Regional High Sch., Middle Village, N.Y., 1965—. Mem. Am. Personnel and Guidance Assn., Assn. for Religious and Value Issues in Counseling. Home: 59-24 70th St Maspeth NY 11378 Office: 68-02 Metropolitan Ave Middle Village NY 11379

CURTIN, JOHN T., fed. judge; b. Buffalo, Aug. 24, 1921; s. John J. and Ellen T. (Quigley) C.; B.S., Canisius Coll., 1945; LL.B., U. Buffalo, 1949; m. Jane R. Good, Aug. 9, 1952; children—Ann Elizabeth, John James, Patricia Marie, Eileen Jane, Mary Ellen, Mark Andrew, William Joseph. Admitted to N.Y. State bar, 1949, U.S. Supreme Ct. bar, 1962; practiced in Buffalo; U.S. atty. Western dist. N.Y., Dept. Justice, 1961-67; judge U.S. Dist. Ct. for Western Dist. of N.Y., from 1967, now chief judge. Served to lt. col. USMC, 1942-45, USMCR, 1952-54. Mem. Am. Bar Assn., N.Y. State Bar Assn., Fed. Bar Assn., Bar Assn. Erie County (nominating com. 1965, 67), Nat. Legal Aid and Defender Orgn. Democrat. Roman Catholic. Office: 624 US Courthouse Buffalo NY 14202*

CURTIN, RAYMOND WILLIAM, engring. librarian; b. Sewickley, Pa., July 22, 1945; s. Raymond William and Madlyn Watson (Laughner) C.; B.A., U. Fla., 1968; M.A., U. Mich., 1972; m. Sally Ricks Barwick, Aug. 28, 1971; children—Sara, Brian, Jennifer. Dir., Dansville (N.Y.) Pub. Library, 1972-76; engring. librarian Eastman Kodak Co., Rochester, N.Y., 1976—. Mem Special Libraries Assn., Am., N.Y. library assns. Home: 105 Westland Ave Rochester NY 14618

CURTIN, WILLIAM JOSEPH, lawyer; b. Auburn, N.Y., Mar. 9, 1931; s. W. Joseph and Edith (Murray) C.; B.S., Georgetown U., 1953, J.D., 1956, LL.M., 1957; m. Helen Bragg White, Aug. 3, 1956; children—Helen Bragg, Caroline Goddard, William Joseph III, Christopher Newport. Admitted to D.C. bar, 1956; asso. firm Morgan, Lewis & Bockius, Washington, 1960-64, partner, 1965—. Pub. mem. Adminstrv. Conf. U.S., 1968-72; chmn. bd. trustees Norwood Sch., 1976—. Recipient Outstanding Service award Am. Arbitration Assn., 1966; John Carroll award Georgetown U., 1973. Fellow Am. Bar Found.; mem. Bar Assn. (chmn. spl. com. to study nat. strikes in transp. industries), Bar Assn. D.C. (labor law com. 1960—, chmn. 1969-70). Editor-in-chief Legal Legislative Reporter of Internat. Found. Employee Benefit Plans. Contbr. to law jour. Home: 11940 Piney Meetinghouse Rd Potomac MD 20854 Office: 1800 M St NW Washington DC 20036

CURTIS, CHARLES RAVAN, plant pathologist; b. Ault, Colo., Oct. 6, 1938; s. Charles Daniel and Lucile Eva (Seibel) C.; B.S., Colo. State U., 1961, M.S., 1963, Ph.D., 1965; m. Louise Johnson Willett, Mar. 23, 1966; children—Robert Parks, Boyd Willett. NSF grantee Colo. State U., 1961-63, NASA fellow, 1963-65; asst. prof. plant pathology U. Md., 1967-72, asso. prof., 1972-77, prof., 1977; prof., chairperson, dept. plant sci. U. Del., Newark, 1978—; Md. Dept. Natural Resources Power Plant Siting Program contract, 1973-78 sci. textbook cons.; cons. EPA, NASA. Served to capt. U.S. Army, 1965-67. Recipient Biomedical Research awards U. Md., 1968, 70, 71, 76; NSF grantee, 1969, 72. Mem. Am. Phytopathol. Soc., Bot. Soc. Am. (chmn. edn. com. 1978, chmn. teaching sect. 1978), Am. Soc. Plant Physiologists, Air Pollution Workshop Steering Com. Contbr. sci. articles to profl. jours. Home: 3 The Horseshoe Covered Bridge Farms Newark DE 19711

CURTIS, DEWEY LEE, found. exec.; b. Arlington, Va., June 20, 1924; s. Dewey Lee and Eula Virginia (Kirby) C.; B.A., Coll. William and Mary, 1949; M.A., U. Va., 1951; postgrad. Sch. Edn. U. Pa., 1951-52. Sales mgr., Wayside Press, Inc., Newport News, Va., 1949-50; asst. dean admissions U. Pa., Phila., 1952-54; exec. dir. Independence Neighborhood Assn., Phila., 1954-56; pres. Curtis Assos. archtl. restoration, Phila., 1956-62; curator Pennsbury Manor Mus., Morrisville, Pa., 1963-77; exec. dir. Decorative Arts Trust, New Hope, Pa., 1977—; archtl. cons. hist. restoration, 1956—. Served with USNR, 1942-45. Mem. Atheneum Phila., Soc. Archtl. Historians, Victorian Soc. Am., S.A.R., Soc. Colonial Wars, Nat. Trust Historic Preservation, Phi Delta Kappa. Republican. Episcopalian. Clubs: Penn, Union League, Rittenhouse (Phila.). Address: Cintra New Hope PA 18938

CURTIS, JAMES THEODORE, lawyer; b. Lowell, Mass., July 8, 1923; s. Theodore D. and Maria (Souliotis) Koutras; B.A., U. Mich., 1948; J.D., Harvard U., 1951; Sc.D., U. Lowell, 1972; m. Kleanthe D. Dusopol June 25, 1950; children—Madelon Mary, Theodore James, Stephanie Diane, Gregory Theodosius, James Theodore. Admitted to Mass. bar, 1951, Fed. bar, 1952; asso. firm Adams & Blinn, Boston, 1951-52; legal asst., asst. atty. gen. Mass., 1952-53; pvt. practice law, Lowell, Mass., 1953-57; partner firm Goldman & Curtis, and predecessor firms, Lowell and Boston, 1957—. Chmn. Lowell and Greater Lowell Heart Fund, 1967-68; mem. Salvation Army Adv. Bd., sec., 1956-58; mem. Bd. Higher Edn. Mass., 1967-72. Del. Democratic Party State Convs., 1956-60. Trustee U. Lowell, 1963-72, chmn., 1968-72, also bd. dirs. U. Lowell Research Found., 1965-72; bd. dirs. Merrimack Valley Health Planning Council. Mem. Lowell Charter Commn., 1969-72. Served with AUS, 1943-46. Decorated knight Order Orthodox Crusade Holy Sepulcher. Mem. Am., Mass., Middlesex County, Lowell bar assns., Am., Mass. trial lawyers assns., Mass. Acad. Trial Lawyers, Am. Judicature Soc., Harvard Law Sch., U. Mich. Alumni assns., Lowell Hist. Soc., D.A.V., AHEPA, Delta Epsilon Pi. Democrat. Greek Orthodox. Mason. Club: Harvard of Lowell (dir., pres. 1969-71). Home: 111 Rivercliff Rd Lowell MA 01852 Office: 8 Merrimack St Lowell MA 01852

CURTIS, JOHN OBED, museum curator; b. Phila., May 1, 1936; s. John Armstrong and Phyllis Leatha (Darch) C.; B.A. in History, Colby Coll., Waterville, Me., 1958; m. Susan Evelyn Sandy, Mar. 29, 1961; children—John Alan, Benjamin Martin. Curator, Ft. Western, Augusta, Me., 1958-59; curatorial asst. Soc. for Preservation New Eng. Antiquities, 1959-60; mem. staff Old Sturbridge (Mass.) Village, 1960—, curator architecture, 1963—, dir. curatorial dept., 1967—; lectr., restoration cons.; cons. Am. Assn. State and Local History, 1977—. Mem. Conn. Nat. Register Rev. Bd., 1973—; chmn. elementary sch. com., vice chmn. bldg. com., Brimfield, Mass., 1969-76. Trustee Brimfield Library, 1969—, chmn., 1973; mem. trustee's adv. com. Westville Mus., Lumpkin, Ga.; adv. bd. Portsmouth (N.H.) Preservation. Old Sturbridge Village grantee, Scandinavia, 1967. Mem. Am. Assn. Museums, Assn. Preservation Tech., Soc. Preservation New Eng. Antiquities, Soc. Archtl. Historians, Company Mil. Historians, Brimfield Hist. Soc. Author: (with W.H. Guthman) New England Militia Accoutrements, 1971; also articles. Home: Brookfield Rd Brimfield MA 01010 Office: Old Sturbridge Village Old Sturbridge MA 01566

CURTIS, RALPH VAN OLINDA, lawyer; b. Bklyn., Aug. 22, 1914; s. Royal Adrian and Elizabeth Judson (Van Olinda) C.; B.A., Mount Union Coll., 1936; LL.B. cum laude, Bklyn. Law Sch., 1942; m. Marjorie Vidoma Sparrow, June 14, 1941; 1 dau., Linda Dorothy (dec.). Mem. new bus. and banking depts. Bklyn. Savs. Bank, 1936-42; admitted to N.Y. State bar, 1942; asso. firm Mendes & Mount, N.Y.C., 1948—, partner, 1968—; dir. Phila. Reins. Corp. Served with AUS, 1943-46, 51. Mem. Am. Bar Assn., Phi Delta Phi. Clubs: Glee of Soc. Friendly Sons of St. Patrick, N.Y., Union League (N.Y.C.); Knickerbocker Field (Bklyn.). Methodist. (trustee). Home: 33-34 Crescent St Long Island City NY 11106 Office: 3 Park Ave New York City NY 10016

CURTIS, THOMAS EDWARD, trust co., food co. exec.; b. Boston, Apr. 25, 1919; s. Thomas L. and Alice (Callahan) C.; student Wofford Coll., 1944; m. Marjorie E. Pearce, June 3, 1944; children—Thomas E., Kathleen M., Brian P., Elizabeth A., Dianne M., Sarah J., Jonathan P. With design dept. Bethlehem Steel Co., Quincy, Mass., 1938-48; pres. Curtis Enterprises, Hingham, Mass., 1948—, Curtis Compacts, Rockland, Mass., 1972—; chmn. bd. Lincoln Trust Co., Hingham, 1968—, Mass. Bank Shares, Inc., Hingham, 1972—; v.p. Angelos Super Markets, Inc., Rockland, 1972—; pres. Five Corners Donuts, Braintree, Mass., Curtis Liquors Inc., Weymouth. Mem. town adv. bd. Hingham, 1959-61; trustee Curtlo Realty Trust, Tobo Realty Trust, South Shore Realty Trust. Served with USAF, 1943-45. Mem. S.Shore C. of C. (v.p. 1976). Clubs: Yacht Racing Union of Mass. Bay (dir., treas. 1964-67, pres. 1967-69), Lincoln Sailing (pres.), Hingham Yacht (Hingham). Home: 21 Bel Air Rd Hingham MA 02043 Office: 400 Lincoln St Hingham MA 02043

CURTIS, WALTER W., bishop; b. Jersey City, May 3, 1913; s. student Fordham U., Seton Hall U., Immaculate Conception Sem. (N.J.), N.Am. Coll. and Gregorian U. (Rome), Cath. U. Am. Ordained priest Roman Catholic Ch., 1937, titular bishop of Bisica and aux. bishop of Newark, 1957-61; bishop of Bridgeport (Conn.), 1961—. Address: 250 Waldemere Ave Bridgeport CT 06604

CURTIS, WILLIAM HENRY, III, educator; b. Phila., June 25, 1939; s. William Henry and Kathryn Helen (McCorkle) C.; B.A., Mt. St. Mary's Coll., 1961; M.Ed., Loyola Coll., Balt., 1964; S.T.B., St.

Mary's U., 1963; Ph.D. equivalent, Cath. U., 1966; Ph.D., Walden U., 1975; clin. behavior therapy trainee Eastern Pa. Psychiat. Inst., 1975-76. Clin. intern Marriage Counseling Center, Cath. U., Washington, 1964-66; instr. Georgetown U., Washington, 1965, Community Coll. of Phila., 1966-67; asst. prof. psychology, sociology Camden County Coll., Blackwood, N.J., 1967—, chmn. div. behavioral scis., 1970-71. Adj. prof. Grad. Sch. Pa. State U., King of Prussia, 1969—; pvt. practice as clin. psychologist, Phila., 1966—; mem. resource subcom. on mental health, alcohol and drug abuse Health Systems Agy. Southeastern Pa., 1978; cons. Cardinal's Commn. on Human Relations Archdiocese of Phila., 1970-74; clin. psychologist N.E. Phila. Community Mental Health Center, 1974—; research cons. Project: Ladder System Approach to Police Tng., 1969-70; cons. AID, 1976—. Mem. Internat. Sci. Commn. on Family, 1969—, mem. N.J. Master Plan for Higher Edn. Phase III Com. on Psychology Programs, 1972-75; mem. group law com. Phila. Consumer Services Coop., 1974-76. Trustee Assn. N.J. County Coll. Faculties, 1969-71. NSF grantee, 1975-76. Certified psychologist, Pa., N.J. Mem. Am., Eastern (conv. com. 1970) psychol. assns., Am. Sociol. Assn. (com. on teaching undergrad. sociology 1971-75, council sect. undergrad. edn. 1972-73, chmn. nominations com. 1970-71), Soc. for Personality Assessment, Soc. Friendly Sons St. Patrick, Pa. Acad. Fine Arts, Camden County Coll. Faculty Assn. (chmn. negotiations com. 1970-71), Am. Fedn. Tchrs. (founding pres. local 1971-72), N.J., N.Y. acads. scis. Club: Peale (Phila). Address: 1011 Dyre St Philadelphia PA 19124

CURTISS, ROBERT STANAGE, real estate counselor; b. Middletown, Ohio, Sept. 15, 1902; s. L. Roy and Helen (Stanage) C.; B.A., Columbia, 1927; m. Esther Perham, June 8, 1929 (dec. Apr. 1965); children—Virginia (Mrs. Bert Langbein), Maybeth (Mrs. Donald E. Collier); m. 2d, Josephine Lake Macdonald, July 28, 1965; 1 stepson, Robert R. Macdonald. Vice-pres. William A. White & Sons, N.Y.C., 1927-43; v.p. real estate Hudson & Manhattan R.R. Co., N.Y.C., 1943-47; dir. real estate Port N.Y. Authority, N.Y.C., 1947-62; pres. Horace S. Ely & Co., N.Y.C., 1962-69; chmn. Ely-Cruikshank Co., N.Y.C., 1969-73; ret. dir. Home Life Ins. Co., Chelsea-Moore Corp.; ret. trustee Prudential Savs. Bank; chmn. Gianopoulos Corps., Pres. Real Estate Bd. N.Y.C., 1957-60. Trustee YMCA Greater N.Y., pres. 1951-61, bd. dirs. 1951—; pres., trustee emeritus Centenary Coll., Hackettstown, N.J., 1971-76; chmn. Asbury Ch. Found. Mem. Alumni Fedn. Columbia (pres. 1962-63), N.Y. State (v.p. 1960), Nat. assns. Realtors, Am. Soc. Real Estate Counselors (nat. pres. 1973). Mason (Shriner). Clubs: Siwanoy Golf (Bronxville); Wall St. (N.Y.C.). Home: 72 Pondfield Rd W Bronxville NY 10708 Office: 200 Park Ave New York City NY 10017

CURTISS, SIDNEY QUINN, lawyer, state legislator; b. Sheffield, Mass., Sept. 4, 1917; s. Roy A. and Ethel (Quinn) C.; A.B., Harvard U., 1940; LL.B., Boston U., 1947; m. Eleanore Leach, Jan. 6, 1946; children—Jonathan Quinn, Melissa J. Admitted to Mass. bar, 1947, D.C. bar, 1965; elected Mass. Gen. Ct., 1948; mem. House of Reps., 1949—; asst. Republican Leader, 1957-61, leader, 1961-71; pub. adminstrn. Berkshire County, 1953-77; examiner Mass. Land Ct., 1951—. Chmn. Republican State Conv., 1964, 66, 70; del.-at-large Rep. Nat. Conv., 1964, 68. Served with AUS, 1941-45. Mem. Am., Boston, Berkshire, Mass. bar assns., City Solicitors Assn., Mass. Moderator's Assn., Am. Legion, Legislator's Assn., V.F.W. Home: Guilder Hollow Rd Sheffield MA 01257 Office: 314 Main St Great Barrington MA 01230

CUSACK, JOHN THOMAS, govt. ofcl.; b. N.Y.C., Mar. 14, 1923; s. Timothy Joseph and Lillian Marie (Kiernan) C.; B.S., Fordham U., 1947; student U. Rochester, 1943-44; m. Mary Josephine Kelly, Jan. 24, 1959; 1 son, Michael Kelly. Narcotic agt. Fed. Bur. Narcotics, N.Y.C., 1947-51, Am. Embassy, Rome, 1951-53, group supr., N.Y.C., 1953-57, dist. supr., Atlanta, 1957-58, dist. supr. for Europe and Mid-East, Am. Embassy, Rome, 1959-63, dist. supr., Kansas City, Mo., 1963-64, spl. advisor to commr. narcotics for internat. affairs, Washington, 1965-67, tech. advisor Am. Embassy on opium control assistance, Ankara, 1967-69, regional dir. Europe and Middle E., Am. Embassy, Paris, 1969-72; dep. chief Drug Abuse Law Enforcement, U.S. Drug Enforcement Adminstrn., Washington, 1972-73, chief internat. ops., 1973-76, chief internat. policy and support, 1976—; advisor U.S. del. U.N. Commn. Narcotic Drugs, Geneva, 1960-63, 69-70, 74-78; mem. U.S. del. Interpol Gen. 73, 75. 1959, 61, 68, 70, 73, 77, chmn. narcotic traffic com., 1961, 73, 75. Served with USN, 1943-46. Recipient Gold medal of Merit, Republic of Italy, 1975; Fordham Coll. Alumni Achievement award, 1973; Gallatin award U.S. Treasury Dept., 1968. Mem. Internat. Assn. Chiefs of Police, Internat. Narcotics Officers Assn., U.S. Naval Inst. Roman Catholic. Clubs: Kenwood Country (Bethesda, Md.). Home: 5910 Wiltshire Dr Bethesda MD 20016 Office: 1405 Eye St NW Washington DC 20537

CUSEO, ALLAN ANTHONY, librarian; b. Rochester, N.Y., Nov. 9, 1940; s. Anthony Joseph and Thelma Anne (O'Grady) C.; student State U. N.Y. at Brockport, 1959-61; B.S., State U. N.Y. at Geneseo, 1963, M.L.S., 1969. Art librarian Rochester Pub. Library, 1963-65; librarian in charge Gates Chili High Sch., Rochester, 1965-69, Greece Athena High Sch., Rochester, 1970-78, Greece Arcadia High Sch., 1978—. Tchr. speech Gates Chili Adult Edn. Sch., 1971-72; vis. faculty Grad. Sch. Library and Info. Sci., State U. N.Y. at Geneseo, 1973; mem. faculty Nazareth Coll. Rochester, 1975—; actor, N.Y.C., 1969. Irish-Am. Cultural Inst. grantee, 1971; NCTE, 1978—. Mem. ALA, NEA, N.Y. Library Assn. (regional rep. 1973-74), Greece Tchrs. Assn., N.Y. State Edn. Assn., Resources (pres. 1972-74), Monroe County Library Club, Ariz. English Tchrs. Assn., ACLU, Greater Rochester Area Sch. Media Specialists, Blackfriars Inc. (pres. 1975-77). Home: 15 Stonewall Ct Rochester NY 14615 Office: 120 Island Cottage Rd Rochester NY 14615

CUSH, RUDOLPH WOODBURY, hosp. exec.; b. Town of Triumph, Guyana, S.Am., Mar. 2, 1930; s. John Lucius and Princess Albertha (Kewley) C.; came to U.S., 1963, naturalized, 1970; B.A., Oakwood Coll., 1966; M.Ed., Loyola Coll., Balt., 1969; C.A.S., Johns Hopkins, 1973; Ph.D., Union Grad. Sch., 1977; m. Lucille Dewdrop Pierce, June 26, 1955; children—Grace C.L., Osbert A.L., Glenna E.I., Charles W.W. Ordained to ministry Seventh-day Adventist Ch., 1955; pastor, Port-of-Spain, Trinidad, 1952-59, Bridgetown, Barbados, 1960-63; dir. edn., supt. youth services Territories of East Caribbean, Bridgetown, 1960-63; rehab. counsellor Md. Dept. Edn., Balt., 1967-70; dir. hosp. improvement Henryton (Md.) Hosp. Center, 1970—; clin. dir. mental retardation unit Highland Health Facility, Balt. City Hosps., 1973-76; dir. Project Exodus, Mental Retardation Adminstrn., 1976—; counselor Family Life Center, Columbia, Md., 1977—. instr. measurement and evaluation Evening Coll., Johns Hopkins, Homewood Campus, Balt., 1973—. Fed. grantee for precommunity tng. of adult retardates, 1970-73. Recipient Brotherhood award WBAL Radio, 1972. Certified spl. educator; licensed nursing home adminstr. Mem. Am. Assn. Mental Deficiency, Phi Delta Kappa. Home: 14565 Dorsey Mill Rd Glenwood MD 21738 Office: Profl Service Adminstrn Herbert R O'Conor Bldg 201 W Preston St Baltimore MD 21201

CUSHING, ARTHUR IRVING, JR., chiropractor; b. Boston, June 21, 1943; s. Arthur Irving and Mary Patricia (Mooney) C.; B.A., McGill U., 1969; D. chiropractic Palmer Coll. Chiropractic, 1975; postgrad. Toftness Post-Grad. Sch. Chiropractic, 1976; m. Lynda Elizabeth Stenson, July 3, 1971; 1 son, Ross Emerson. Social worker Mass. Commn. for the Blind, Boston, 1970-71; sr. counsellor for adult mentally retarded Employment Tng. Center, Toronto, Ont., Can., 1973; pvt. practice chiropractic, Gardiner, Maine, 1973—. Served with U.S. Army, 1964-67. Mem. Am. Chiropractic Assn., Found. Advancement of Chiropractic Research, Inc., Humanitarian Soc. Clubs: Masons, Shriners. Home: 40 Washington Ave Gardiner ME 04345

CUSHING, FRANKLIN SETH, devel. engr.; b. Rochester, N.Y., May 30, 1919; s. John Alden and Marion Thompson (Frankland) C.; B.S., Clarkson Coll. Tech., 1942; postgrad. U. Buffalo, 1944-48; m. Lois Audrey Taylor, Mar. 7, 1942; children—Jon Scott, Wendy Lynn, Eve April. Chemist, devel. engr. Gould, Inc., Depew, N.Y., 1944-58, Mpls., 1959-60; devel. engr. ESB, Inc., Phila., 1960, West Orange, N.J., 1961, 63, Raleigh, N.C., 1964-65, Phila., 1966-69, Yardley, Pa., 1970—; chemist Scott Aviation Corp., Lancaster, N.Y., 1962. Served to 2d lt. U.S. Army, 1942-44. Mem. Am. Chem. Soc., Electrochem. Soc. Protestant Episcopal. Club: Masons. Office: 19 W College Ave Yardley PA 19067

CUSHMAN, ROBERT ARNOLD, wire cable mfg. co. exec.; b. Miami, Fla., Aug. 4, 1918; s. Charles Franklin and Mabel (Rorem) C.; B.S. in Bus. Adminstrn., U. Fla., 1940; M.B.A., N.Y. U., 1951; postgrad. Mich. State U., 1970; m. Helen Merle Baker, June 2, 1945; children—Lucinda, Robert. Adjuster Comml. Credit Corp., Miami, 1941; bus. mgr. research lab Gen. Cable Corp., Greenwich, Conn., 1945-51, purchasing agt., 1951-59, asst. dir. purchases, 1959—. Dist. chmn. Watchung Area council Boy Scouts Am., 1965-75. Served with USN, 1941-45. Recipient Silver Beaver award Boy Scouts Am., 1975. Mem. Purchasing Mgrs. Assn. N.Y. (recipient certificate of honor 1974), Wire Assn., Soc. Mayflower Descs., Delta Tau Delta, Alpha Kappa Psi. Republican. Episcopalian. Home: 266 E Dudley Ave Westfield NJ 07090 Office: 500 W Putnam Ave Greenwich CT 06830

CUSICK, JAMES JOSEPH, JR., dental service co. exec.; b. Cleve., Mar. 20, 1928; s. James Joseph and Lyola (Conklin) C.; A.B., Ohio U., 1952; m. Delores Jean Whatmore, May 5, 1956; children—Kathleen, Colleen, Margaret, Eileen, James Joseph III, Moira, Elizabeth. Sales rep. Singer Sewing Machine Co., Cleve., 1952; New Eng. tech. rep. Ransom and Randolph, Toledo, Ohio, 1954-58; Mid-Atlantic sales rep. Densco Inc., Denver, 1958-61; met. N.Y. tech. rep. J.M. Ney Co., Bloomfield, Conn., 1961-69; founder Servalab, Inc., also United Dental Service, Maywood, N.J., 1969, chmn. bd., 1969—. Guest lectr. N.Y. Sch. Mech. Dentistry, 1965, 66, 67, 68, 69; clinician to dental profession and dental lab. industry, 1958—. Bd. dirs. United Fund, Bogota, N.J., 1963. Served with AUS, 1946-47. Mem. Alpha Kappa Delta. Democrat. Roman Catholic. Home: 623 Franklin Ave Franklin Lakes NJ 07147 Office: 5 Hergesell Ave Maywood NJ 07607

CUSICK, ROBERT EDWARD, psychologist, educator; b. Forest Hills, Boston, Jan. 24, 1922; s. George Edward and Elizabeth (Glawson) C.; B.S., Tufts U., 1950. M.Ed., Boston State Coll., 1967; postgrad. Boston U., 1971—; m. Patricia Josephine Small, Sept. 4, 1950; children—Jane Cusick McMenamy, Polly C., Patricia Ann. Various positions steel, constrn. cos., Boston, 1955-63; New Eng. sales mgr. Nat. Steel Corp., Houston, 1964-66; prof. psychology-sociology Massasoit Community Coll., Brockton, Mass., 1966—, asst. to dir. admissions, 1966-67, dir. vets. counseling program, 1967-69; vis. prof. psychology Quincy (Mass.) Jr. Coll., 1967—; pvt. practice clin. psychology, Brockton, 1973—. Served with USAAF, 1942-46, USAF, 1951-53, 66. Mem. Mass. (asso.), Am. (asso.) psychol. assns., Mass. Tchrs. Assn., NEA. Republican. Roman Catholic. Clubs: Neighborhood Quincy, Tuft U. Alumni. Home: 101 Sims Rd Wollaston MA 02170

CUSTER, JOHN J., phys. scientist; b. Bklyn., Mar. 19, 1911; s. Max M. and Celia (Fast) C.; B.S., Coll. City N.Y., 1931; M.A., N.Y. U., 1937, Bklyn. Coll., 1950; B.Ch.E., Cooper Union, 1956; postgrad. New Sch. for Social Research, Mass. Inst. Tech., U. N.Mex., U. Calif. at Los Angeles, City U. N.Y.; m. Natalie Natelson, June 30, 1935; children—Barbara Grace (Mrs. Uriel J. Goldsmith), Victoria Alice (Mrs. Peter G. Slater), Carol Mae (Mrs. Michael A. Kanthal). Grad. asst. N.Y. U., 1949; asst. mgr. quality engring. lab. Ford Instrument Co., Long Island City, N.Y., 1958; phys. chemist U.S. Army, Picatinny Arsenal, Dover, N.J., 1958-59; gen. engr. U.S. Naval Research and Devel. Facility, Bayonne, N.J., 1959-60; staff engr. sci. and tech. liaison USAF, AFSC, STLO-N.Y., 1960-70; lab. specialist N.Y.C. Bd. Edn., 1971-76; cons. technologist, chem. processing and formulations, 1947-52. Pres. bd. dirs. Franconia Village Coop., Inc.; merit badge counselor Boy Scouts Am., 1950—. Served to lt. comdr. USPHS Res. Fellow N.Y. Acad. Scis. (life mem.); mem. Am. Inst. Aeros. and Astronautics, AAAS, Am. Chem. Soc., Mensa, Res. Officers Assn., Soc. Am. Mil. Engrs., Sci. Research Soc. Am., Sigma Xi. Author: Analytical Chemistry. Home and Office: 148 B Maclura Plaza Cranbury NJ 08512

CUTLER, CLAIRE MINTZ (MRS. MAX CUTLER), lawyer; b. N.Y.C., Jan. 19, 1919; d. Nathaniel I. and Jessie Beatrice (Guttentag) Mintz; B.A., Hunter Coll., 1939; J.D. cum laude, Bklyn. Law Sch., 1942; m. Max Cutler, Oct. 8, 1944; children—William Lewis, John Martin. Admitted to N.Y. bar, 1942; asso. firm William Weisman, N.Y.C., 1942-43, Davis & Gilbert, N.Y.C., 1943-44; partner Cutler & Cutler, N.Y.C., 1944—. Bd. dirs. Citizens Sch. League, Stamford, Conn., 1956-66; exec. bd. North Stamford Democratic Club, 1956-66; exec. bds. P.T.A. assns., N.Y.C., Stamford. Mem. N.Y. State Bar Assn., Hunter Coll., Bklyn. Law Sch. alumni assns., Bklyn. Law Rev. Assn., Pi Alpha Tau. Jewish religion (dir. young married guild 1944-56). Asst. editor Bklyn. Law Rev., 1941-42. Home: 1175 York Ave New York City NY 10021 Office: 150 E 58th St New York City NY 10022

CUTLER, HERBERT WHITNEY, advt. agy. exec.; b. East Orange, N.J., Jan. 26, 1932; s. Herbert Palmer and Florence (Whitney) C.; student Upsala Coll., 1950-52; m. Patricia Wrigley, Dec. 17, 1968; 1 son, David Whitney. Advt. and sales promotion mgr. Forest Lakes Sales Co., Andover, N.J., 1952-58; v.p. Walker, Reilly, Becker, Inc., advt., Sarasota, Fla., 1958-60; v.p. Williams & London Advt., Newark, 1960-61; exec. v.p. Advent Assos., Inc., Livingston, 1961-68, dir., 1965-68; pres., dir. Gilbert, Whitney & Johns, Inc., Morristown, N.J., 1969-71; dir. Terraplan Corp., land planners, cons., developers, Lansdale, Pa., 1969—; chmn., chief exec. officer, dir. H. Whitney Cutler Advt. Co., Fairfield, N.J., 1971—; owner H. Whitney Cutler Co., real estate brokers; pres., dir. Cutler Marine Enterprises, Inc., Wilmington, Del.; v.p., dir. Chambault, Cutler & Assos.; exec. v.p. Wyatt, Kennedy & Assos., advt., Sarasota, Fla., 1978—. Served with USNR, 1950-58. Mem. Bus. and Profl. Advt. Assn., Internat. Star Class Yacht Racing Assn. (life). Clubs: Royal Canadian Yacht; Hackensack Golf; Tarrytown Boat; Fort Comfort Yacht; Palisades Yacht. Home: 857 Pointe Whitecap Circle Venice FL 33595 Office: 389 Passaic Ave Fairfield NJ 07006

CUTLER, KENNETH BURNETT, lawyer; b. Muskegon Heights, Mich., June 19, 1932; s. Stanley and Lucile (Miles) C.; B.B.A., U. Mich., 1954, J.D. 1957; m. Cecelia Bilsly, Mar. 9, 1967; children—Kenneth Burnett, Randall Miles, Cynthia Bilsly, Robert Appleby. Admitted to Mich. bar, 1957, N.Y. bar, 1960; asso. atty. Dewey Ballantine, Bushby, Palmer & Wood, N.Y., 1957-66; v.p., sec. Affiliated Fund, Lord Abbett Income Fund, Lord Abbett Developing Growth Fund, Lord Abbett Bond-Debenture Fund; house counsel Lord, Abbett & Co., N.Y.C., 1966—, partner, 1972—. Served with AUS, 1957-63. Mem. Am. Bar Assn., Phi Delta Phi. Clubs: The Lawyers', Bronxville Field, Winged Foot Golf. Home: 34 Dusenberry Rd Bronxville NY 10708 Office: 63 Wall St New York City NY 10005

CUTLER, LEONARD MYRON, polit. scientist; b. Bklyn., Jan. 1, 1944; s. Jack Isaac and Ann (Schneider) C.; B.A., Coll. City N.Y., 1965; M.A., New Sch. Social Research, 1967, Ph.D., 1970; m. Sheila Moscovice, June 9, 1965; children—Julie Suzanne, Heidi Jo. Instr. polit. sci. Seton Hall U., 1967; asst. prof. polit. sci. Notre Dame Coll., 1967-70; asso. prof. polit. sci. Siena Coll., 1970—; adj. prof. pub. policy Russel Sage Grad. Center for Pub. Adminstrn., 1976—. Grants dir. N.Y. State Senate, Albany, 1972—. Mem. Am. Soc. Internat. Law, Am. Soc. Pub. Adminstrn., World Law Fund. Editor and contbr.: Managing a Way Out: Legislative Action in the Credit Market, 1977; Balanced Growth for the Northeast, 1975; Regional Response to the Energy Crisis, 1974; Cable Communications and the States, 1974. Home: 46 Greenridge Dr Clifton Park NY 12065 Office: Siena Coll Loundville NY 12211 also NY Senate Albany NY 12247

CUTLER, MARSHALL CARL, stock broker; b. San Diego, Nov. 3, 1941; s. David C. and Golde (Goldsmith) C.; B.S. in Bus. Adminstrn., Washington U., 1963; m. Joan Carol Abramson, Aug. 30, 1964; children—Laurie Ann, Diane Elizabeth. Account exec. W.E. Hutton & Co., Washington, 1965-70; v.p. instl. sales Bache Halsey Stuart, Shields, Washington, 1970—. Mem. Soc. Fin. Analysts (Washington), Municipal Fin. Forum (Washington), Bond Club (Washington). Clubs: Woodmont Country. Home: 8200 Lochinver Ln Potomac MD 20854 Office: 1000 16th St NW Washington DC 20036

CUTLER, RHODA, clin. psychologist; b. N.Y.C.; A.B. in Physiology and Psychology, Hunter Coll., N.Y.C.; A.M. in Psychology, N.Y. U., Ph.D., 1967; postgrad. Yeshiva U. Cons. psychologist N.Y. Assn. New Americans, 1947-60; clin. psychol. intern Inst. Phys. Medicine and Rehab., N.Y. U.-Bellevue Med. Center, 1960-61; asst. instr. psychiatry N.Y. Med. Coll., 1961-63; sch. psychologist Bur. Child Guidance, N.Y.C., 1964-65; psychol. cons. div. adoption service Bur. Child Welfare, N.Y.C., 1965—; psychotherapist Mental Health Cons. Center, N.Y.C., part-time 1967-70; research asso. prof. Sch. Edn., N.Y. U., 1966-68; vis. asso. prof. N.Y. U. Sch. Edn., spring 1969; asst. prof. psychiatry N.Y. Med. Coll., 1968-69; research psychologist Child Devel. Center, N.Y.C., 1969-70; asst. clin. prof. Mt. Sinai Coll. Medicine-Beth Israel Med. Center, N.Y.C., 1970—. Contbr. profl. jours. Address: 230 E 88th St Apt 10A New York NY 10028

CUTRONA, MICHAEL PHILLIP, psychologist, psychotherapist, educator; b. Bayonne, N.J.; s. Al A. and Patricia B. (Romano) C.; B.A., Jersey City State Coll., 1967, M.A., 1968; M.A. in Psychology, Jersey City State Coll., 1970; D. Profl. Psychology, 1971; Ed.D., Fordham U., 1973, D. Profl. Edn., 1973. Asst. supr. N.Y. Mission Soc. Reading Inst., N.Y.C., 1966-67; psychoedn. cons. N.J. State Dept. Edn., Trenton, 1968-69; individual practice psychotherapy, hypnotherapy and family therapy, N.Y.C., 1973—; prof. grad. sch. edn. Wagner Coll., S.I., N.Y., 1969—; cons. psychology N.J. Pub. Schs., 1970—; adj. prof. Fordham U., N.Y.C., 1975—; pres. Cutronics Ednl. Inst. Bayonne (psychoednl. cons. and pubs.), N.J., 1970—. Mem. United Way, Widowed Person's Service (founder), Community Services Council, 1973—. Harden E. Goldstein grantee, 1970. Certified psychotherapist, psychologist, N.Y. Fellow Am. Assn. Psychoednl. Therapists (pres. 1975—); mem. Fordham Edn. Doctor's Assn. (v.p.), Am. Psychol. Assn. (chmn. task force on psychoednl. therapy), N.Y. Acad. Scis., Am. Assn. Marriage and Family Counselors (clin.), Am. Soc. Psychosomatic Medicine (clin.), Am. Soc. Clin. Hypnosis, Internat. Soc. Hypnosis, Am. Assn. Clin. Counselors, Am. Orthopsychiat. Assn., Biofeedback Soc. Am., Acad. Psychologist in Marital and Family Therapy (exec. officer), Phi Delta Kappa. Contbr. articles to profl. jours. Author: The Development of Psychoeducational Abilities, 1970; Cutrona Child Study Profile of Psychoeducational Abilities, 1971; Joy of Individual Learning, 1975; Psychoeducational Therapy, 1976; Sociological Foundations of Education, 1976; Divorce Therapy: A New Frontier, The Relationship, 1977; others. Home: 128 W 56 St Bayonne NJ 07002 Office: Wagner Coll Staten Island NY 10301

CUTTER, CURTIS CARLY, cons. co. exec.; b. Sacramento, Oct. 27, 1928; s. Curtis Harold and Leita (Carly) C.; A.B., U. Calif., Berkeley, 1951; certificate U. Geneva, 1955; M.A., Stanford U., 1969; m. Christiane Kühne, Jan. 29, 1965; children—Colette, Curtis Brooks, Lucho Antonio, Kai Kirsten, Sasha Christiana, Knut Carly. Consular officer Am. embassy, Phnom Penh, Cambodia, 1957-59; mem. U.S. delegation to UN and Trusteeship Council, 1959-62; polit. officer Am. embassy, Lima, Peru, 1962-65; chief Office Peruvian Affairs, State Dept., Washington, 1965-67; mem. U.S. del. OAS, 1967-68; prin. officer Am. Consulate, Porto Alegre, Brazil, 1969-70; polit. officer Am. embassy, Madrid, 1970-72; prin. officer, consul gen. Am. Consulate Gen., Seville, Spain, 1972-75; dep. dir. Office UN Polit. Affairs, 1975-77; acting dep. asst. sec. for congressional relations, 1977-78; pres. Interworld Consultants, 1978—; dir. Penn Dixie Industries; lectr. polit. sci. Columbus Coll., 1973—. Bd. dirs. Am. Sch. Madrid, Internat. Sch. Seville; trustee Columbus Internat. Coll. Served as capt. AUS, 1951-53. Recipient State Dept. award for heroism, 1970, State Dept. Meritorious Honor award, 1971. Mem. Am. Fgn. Service Assn., Alpha Delta Phi. Clubs: Pineda, Espanola de Equitation. Address: 2811 Battery Pl NW Washington DC 20016

CUTTING, ALLAN RENWICK, social worker, educator; b. St. Johnsbury, Vt., Feb. 26, 1922; s. Renwick Harrison and Orris (Humphrey) C.; A.B., U. Vt., 1950; M.S.W. (NIMH grantee), Fla. State U., 1962; m. Ethelyn Pratt, Nov. 20, 1942; children—James A., Margaret C., Richard A. Social worker Vt. Dept. Social Welfare, Burlington, 1950-52, juvenile probation counselor, Rutland, 1952-54, probation and parole supr., 1954-60; asst. prof. sociology psychology U. Ala., Tuscaloosa, 1960-67, asso. dir. Texarkana (Tex.) Mental Health Center, 1968; dir. Windham County Mental Health Center, Brattleboro, Vt., 1968-72; dir. Family Services Assn., So. New London County, New London, Conn., 1972—; vis. asst. prof. Conn. Coll., New London, 1972-76. Bd. dirs. Psychiat. Outpatient Centers Am., 1965—, Windsor (Vt.) Sch. Bd., 1966-68; mem. Conn. Commn. Human Service Reorgn., 1977—. Served with AUS, 1942-46. Mem. Acad. Certified Social Workers, Council Social Work Edn., Nat. Council Crime and Delinquency. Democrat. Clubs: Masons, Elks, Rotary. Contbr. articles to profl. jours. Editor: (with Alan Tulipan, M.D.) The Outpatient Patient: Consumer and Client, 1972. Home: PO Box 1084 New London CT 06320 Office: 11 Granite St New London CT 06320

CVACH, PHILIP EDWARD, mortician; b. Balt., July 28, 1927; s. Jerome C. M. and Anna E. (Benda) C.; M.S., Eckels Coll., 1951; m. Mary A. Dolivka, Jan. 24, 1948; children—Phyllis Ann Shand, John J., Jerome J., Philip Edward. Owner, operator Cvach Funeral Home, Balt., 1950—, Rosedale Funeral Home, Baltimore County, Md., 1958—. Bd. advisers Catonsville (Md.) Community Coll. Mortuary

Sch.; pres. Recreation Council Balt., 1959-63. Served with USNR, 1945-48. Recipient Distinguished Service award Balt. Jaycees, 1966, award Baltimore County Youth Commn., 1977. Mem. Nat., Md. (pres. 1973-74) funeral dirs. assns., Automobile Assn. Balt. (pres. 1975-76), Aircraft Owners and Pilots Assn. Democrat. Roman Catholic. Clubs: Lions (charter pres. Rosedale 1960-62), Am. Legion, Alhambra, K.C. Home: 1211 Chesaco Ave Rosedale MD 21237 Office: Cvach Funeral Home Baltimore MD 21237

CYERT, RICHARD MICHAEL, univ. pres., educator, economist; b. Winona, Minn., July 22, 1921; s. Walter Michael and Anne Fostine (Brown) C.; B.S. in Econs., U. Minn., 1943; Ph.D., Columbia, 1951; hon. degree U. Gothenburg (Sweden), 1972, U. Leuven (Belgium), 1973; m. Margaret Shadick, Sept. 8, 1946; children—Lynn Anne Aikin, Lucinda Carol Steffes, Martha Sue. Instr., U. Minn., 1946, Coll. City N.Y., 1948; instr. econs. Carnegie Inst. Tech. (now Carnegie-Mellon U.), Pitts., 1948-49, asst. prof. econs. and indsl. adminstrn. 1949-55, asso. prof. econs. and indsl. adminstr., head indsl. mgmt. dept., 1955-60, prof. econs. and indsl. adminstrn., 1960-62, dean Grad. Sch. Indsl. Adminstrn., 1962-72, pres., 1972—. Dir. Koppers Co., Inc., Lord Corp., 1st Boston Corp., Am. Standard Inc., Allegheny Ludlum Industries, Inc., Copperweld Corp., Regional Indsl. Devel. Corp. Bd. dirs. Presbyn.-Univ. Hosp., WQED-TV; trustee Winchester-Thurston Sch., Com. Econ. Devel.; mem. adv. com. Internat. Inst. Applied Systems Analysis. Served USNR, 1943-46. Recipient Hofstra Distinguished Scholar award, 1973, Outstanding Achievement award U. Minn., 1975; Ford fellow, 1959-60; Guggenheim fellow, 1967-68. Fellow Am. Statis Assn., Econometric Soc.; mem. Am. Econ. Assn., Inst. Mgmt. Scis., Internat. Inst. Mgmt. (adv. council), Phi Beta Kappa, Beta Gamma Sigma. Author: (With R.M. Trueblood) Sampling Techniques in Accounting, 1957; (with H.J. Davidson) Sampling for Accounting Information, 1962; (with J. G. March) A Behavioral Theory of the Firm, 1963; (with K.J. Cohen) Theory of the Firm: Resources Allocation in a Market Economy, 1965. Editor: (with L.A. Welsch) Management Decision Making, 1970; Management of Non-Profit Organizations With Emphasis on Universities, 1975. Contbr. articles to profl. jours. Bd. editors Behavioral Sci. Home: 12 Edgewood Rd Pittsburgh PA 15215

CYLKE, FRANK KURT, librarian; b. New Haven, Feb. 13, 1932; s. Frank Anton and Helen Mary (Callahan) C.; B.A., U. Conn., 1954; M.L.S., Pratt Inst., 1957; postgrad. Fairfield U., 1959, Am. U., 1968-69, Georgetown U., 1978—; m. Mary Elizabeth Zembroski, Dec. 28, 1962; children—Frank Kurt, Mary Amanda, Virginia Ann. Librarian Graham-Eckes Sch., Palm Beach, Fla., 1957-58; reference librarian Bridgeport (Conn.) Pub. Library, 1958-62; head pub. services New Haven Pub. Library, 1962-65; asst. librarian Providence Pub. Library, 1965-68; chief library and information scis. research program U.S. Office Edn., 1968-69; exec. sec. Fed. Library Com., Library Congress, Washington, 1970-73, dir. nat. library service blind and physically handicapped, 1973—. Instr. U. R.I. Grad. Library Sch., 1967-68, Cath. U. Am. Grad. Library Sch., 1974—. Exec. sec. panel on edn. and tng. Com. on Sci. and Tech. Information; chmn. librarians tech. com. Met. Washington Council Govts., 1970-71; sec. U.S. Book Exchange, 1972-74; sec.-treas. Joint Venture Pub. Activity, 1970-74. Mem. East Greenwich (R.I.) Free Library Corp., 1967—; adv. bd. Ednl. Resources Information Center/Clearinghouse on Library and Information Sci., 1970-72. U.S. Office Edn. grantee to develop a survey fed. libraries, 1972. Mem. Am., Spl. library assns., Am. Soc. for Information Sci. (sec. 1974-75), Internat. Fedn. for Documentation, Pvt. Libraries Assn., Spl. Libraries Assn. (pres. D.C. chpt. 1975-76), Am. Assn. Workers for Blind, Internat. Fedn. Library Assns. (chmn. working group for blind), Manuscript Soc., Lewes Hist. Soc. Roman Catholic. Club: Dinghy Cruising Assn. Editor: Captains Shelf, 1964-66, FLC Newsletter, 1970-73. Home: 1032 Harriman St Great Falls VA 22066 Office: Library of Congress Washington DC 20542

CYR, ROB ROY, engring. exec.; b. Parlier, Calif., Jan. 15, 1921; s. William Albion and Jean Lucille (Little) C.; B.S.M.E., U. Calif., 1943; student Calif. Sch. Mech. Arts, 1935-38, Calif. Tech. Inst., 1938-39, San Francisco Jr. Coll., 1939-40, Northeastern U., 1965; m. Verna Florence Demichelli, Nov. 27, 1942; children—Rodney William, Stephen Michael. Tech. supr. Tenn. Eastman Corp., Oak Ridge, 1943-46; research engr. Distillation Products Inc., Rochester, N.Y., 1946-47, tech. sales rep. 1949-51; research engr. U. Calif., Berkeley, 1947-49, lectr. automatic control engring., 1948; pres. Mirra Cote Co., El Segundo, Calif., 1951-57; sales mgr. Optical Coatings Lab, and King Knight Co., San Francisco, 1957-61; v.p., engr. Kinney Vacuum div. Gen. Signal Corp., Boston, 1961-72; dir. engring. Scott Aviation div. ATO, Inc., Lancaster, N.Y., 1972—; lectr. U. Tenn., Oak Ridge, 1944. Cub-master, asst. scoutmaster Boy Scouts Am., Torrance and Mill Valley, Calif., 1953-61; recipient Scouter's award, 1959. Mem. Am. Vacuum Soc., Inst. Environ. Scis., Aerospace Med. Assn., Survival and Flight Equipment Assn., Compressed Gas Assn. Republican. Presbyterian. Clubs: Lancaster Country, Buffalo Aero. Patentee in field. Home: 4883 Winding Ln Clarence NY 14031 Office: 225 Erie St Lancaster NY 14086

DABBS, THERON RANDOLPH, JR., elec. engr.; b. Durham, N.C., Apr. 30, 1940; s. Theron Randolph and Ottis (Allen) D.; student N.C. State Coll., 1959-60, Coll. of Albermarle, 1965-67; B.S., Temple U., 1979; postgrad. Pa. State U., 1979—; m. Betty Lou Hugo, July 12, 1967; children—Vicky Linn, Theron Randolph III. With Philco Ford Corp., 1967—, adviser to S. Vietnam Police, 1967-68, Job Corps instr., Breckenridge, Ky., 1968, communications adviser to Thailand, 1968-70, adviser to Iranian Power Inst., 1970-73, supr. equipment engring., Sao Paulo, Brazil, 1973-76, prodn. engr., Lansdale, Pa., 1976—. Served with USMC, 1960-64. Mem. IEEE, Am. Computer Soc., Solid State Circuits Soc., Info. Soc., Automatic Controls Soc., Soc. Am. Mil. Engrs. Republican. Baptist. Clubs: Masons, Order Eastern Star. Author books on electronics. Home: 1581 Morgan Way Lansdale PA 19446

DACEY, GEORGE CLEMENT, telecommunications co. exec.; b. Chgo., Jan. 23, 1921; s. Clement Anthony and Helen (MacLachlan) D.; B.S. in Elec. Engring., U. Ill., 1942; Ph.D. in Physics, Calif. Inst. Tech., 1951; m. Anne Zeamer, June 20, 1954; children—Donna Lynn, John Clement, Sarah Anne. Research engr. Westinghouse Research Labs., East Pittsburgh, Pa., 1942-45; mem. tech. staff transistor research dept. Bell Telephone Labs., 1952-55, head transistor devel. dept., 1955-58, dir. solid state electronics research, 1958-61, exec. dir. telephones div., 1963-68, v.p. customer equipment devel., 1968-70, v.p. transmission systems, Holmdel, N.J., 1970—; v.p. research Sandia Corp., Albuquerque, 1961-63; dir. Perkin-Elmer Corp., Norwalk, Conn., Colonial 1st Nat. Bank. Mem. exec. bd. Monmouth council Boy Scouts Am., 1970-75. Bd. dirs. Monmouth Mus., 1972—. Recipient Distinguished Alumnus award U. Ill. Elec. Engring. Alumni Assn., 1970. Fellow IEEE, Am. Phys. Soc.; mem. Nat. Acad. Engring., Sigma Xi, Phi Kappa Phi, Tau Beta Pi, Eta Kappa Nu. Contbr. articles on transistor physics, lasers to tech. jours. Patentee transistors. Home: 5 Markwood Ln Rumson NJ 07760 Office: Bell Labs Holmdel NJ 07733

DA CUNHA, JULIO, artist, educator; b. Colombia, Mar. 18, 1929; s. Luis Alberto and Aurora Acuna; naturalized U.S. citizen, 1961; B.Arch., U. Fla., 1952; M.F.A., Cranbrook Acad. Art, Bloomfield Hills, Mich., 1954. Mem. faculty dept. art U. Del., Newark, 1956—, prof., 1970—, acting chmn. dept., 1966-68; vis. prof. East Sydney Tech. Coll., Sydney, Australia, 1968; one man exhbns. include: Galeria El Callejon, Bogota, Colombia, 1962, Zegri Gallery, N.Y.C., 1963, 66, 68, 70, Gallery 252, Phila., 1973, Pleiades Gallery, N.Y.C., 1975, 77, Del. Art Mus., Wilmington, 1977; represented in permanent collections: U. Del., Newark, Del. Mus., Wilmington; vis. artist Yaddo Corp., Huntington Hartford Found. Mem. Colombian Soc. Architects, Phi Kappa Phi. Address: PO Box 893 Newark DE 19711

D'ADAMO, ANTHONY, chemist; b. Newark, Apr. 22, 1919; s. Gabriel and Antoinette (Pagliuco) D'A.; B.A., Rutgers U., 1948; M.A., Columbia U., 1950; m. Connie Pezzino, Sept. 5, 1948; children—Celeste, Anthony, Diane. Research chemist Montrose Chem. Co., Newark, 1950-51, White Labs. Schering, Kenilworth, N.J., 1951-53; dir. analytical research Knoll Pharm. Co., Whippany, N.J., 1968-78, dir. analytical research and chem. prodn., 1968—. Pres. W. Essex Unico nat. chpt., 1977-78. Served with AUS, 1940-45. Decorated Bronze Star. Mem. Acad. Pharm. Scis., Am. Pharm. Assn., Am. Inst. Chemists, Phi Beta Kappa, Phi Lambda Epsilon. Presbyn. Patentee in field. Home: 17 Dillon Rd W Caldwell NJ 07006 Office: 30 N Jefferson Rd Whippany NJ 09871

DADDI, GEORGE, architect; b. Leghorn, Italy, Nov. 14, 1930; s. Guido and Iva (Poggiolini) D.; came to U.S., 1955, naturalized, 1958; recipient high sch. equivalent diploma, 1966; m. Brunett Bianchi, Oct. 30, 1954; children—Sandra, William. Designer S. Serredi & Figli, Leghorn, Italy, 1946-55; designer Marble House, Inc., College Point, N.Y., 1955-57; designer, project mgr., firm Silverman & Cika, N.Y.C., 1957-62; designer, project mgr. firm George J. Sole, N.Y.C., 1962-67; architect Port Authority N.Y. and N.J., 1967—; individual practice, S.I., N.Y., 1970—. Treas. Grasmere Homeowners Assn., 1973-76; chmn. Giuseppe Mazzini Sr. Citizen Center, 1975-76; mem. Community Bd. #2, S.I., 1977. Recipient award achievement S.I. C. of C. Mem. AIA, N.Y. Soc. Architects. Clubs: K.C., Sons of Italy. Important works include St. Charles Open Sanctuary, S.I., N.Y., 1964, Muschello Residence, S.I., 1975, K. of C. Bldg., S.I., 1976, also several dental office interiors. Home: 581 Steuben St Staten Island NY 10305 Office: One World Trade Center New York NY 10048

DADRIAN, VAHAKN NORAIR, educator; b. Istanbul, Turkey, May 26, 1926; s. Hagop and Mayreni (Der Garabedian) D.; cand. rer. pol. U. Zurich (Switzerland); M.A. Wayne State U., 1950; Ph.D., U. Chgo., 1954. Came to U.S., 1947, naturalized, 1961. Asst. prof. sociology Washington Coll., Chestertown, Md., 1955-56; asst. prof. sociology Boston U., 1957-59; research fellow Harvard Center for Middle Eastern Studies, 1961-62; lectr. sociology Boston Coll., 1963-65; asso. prof. sociology Wis. State U., Superior, 1965-67; asso. prof. Fla. Atlantic U., 1967-68, prof., 1968-70; prof. sociology State U. Coll. Arts and Sci., Geneseo, N.Y., 1970—. Vis. scholar Mass. Inst. Tech. Center Internat. Studies, 1960-61; guest researcher Inst. for Research on the Soviet Union, Munich, Germany, summer 1962, Center Documentation USSR, Ecole Pratique des Hautes Etudes, Paris, France, summer 1963; vis. prof. sociology Duke U., summer 1971; dir. genocide study project NSF, 1976-79; lectr. Europe and Soviet Union. Wenner-Gren Found. Anthrop. Research grantee, 1965, 69; NSF grantee, 1968, 73; State U. N.Y. faculty fellow, 1975. Fellow Internat. Soc. for Research on Aggression, Am. Sociol. Assn.; mem. Internat. Sociol. Assn., Am. Philos. Soc., Delta Tau Kappa (hon.). Author: (monographs) Nationalism, Communism and Soviet Industrialization-A Theoretical Exposition, 1972; Nationalism in Soviet Armenia, 1977. Cons. editor Internat. Jour. Contemporary Soc.; translator, editor United and Independent Turania (Zarevand), 1971. Contbr. articles to profl. jours. Address: State U Coll Arts and Sci Geneseo NY 14454

DAENECKE, ERIC, lawyer, former UN advisor; b. Bklyn., Jan. 24, 1914; s. August and Ida (Brosowski) D.; B.S., Am. U., Washington, 1944, M.A., 1947, Ph.D., 1950; J.D., U. Balt., 1954; LL.M. cum laude, U. Manila, 1964; D.C.L., U. Santo Tomas, Manila, 1966; m. G. Alma Schwenn, Apr. 5, 1936; children—William Eric, Maryellen Daenecke Lawlor. Chief of finance GAO and Dept. Labor, Washington, 1935-56; pub. adminstrn. adviser Dept. State, 1957-70; interregional advisor UN, N.Y.C., 1970-77; tchr. Strayer Coll., Washington, 1951-56, U. Md. Far East Br., 1967-70, grad. law U. Santo Tomas, Manila, 1964-66; minister Christian Ch., Washington, 1953-56. Mem. Am. Inst. C.P.A.'s, Fed., Inter-Am. bar assns., Am. Accounting Assn., Rosicrucian Order. Club: Lawyers. Author: Tales of Mullah Nasr-Ud-Din, 1960; More Tales, 1961. Home: 4914 Chesapeake St NW Washington DC 20016

DAFFIN, IRL ALONZO, industrialist; b. Denton, Md., May 28, 1902; s. Alonzo S. and Arkansas Virginia (Dorsey) D.; ed. Md. pub. schs.; m. Nancy W. Davis, Dec. 26, 1975; children—David K., Damaris Rebecca. Sales mgr. Dellinger Mfg. Co., Lancaster, Pa., 1932-40; pres. New Holland Machine Co., 1940-47, New Holland Mfg. Co., Mountville, Pa., 1945-47; exec. v.p. New Holland Metals Co., 1947; sec. Lancaster Engring. Corp. (Pa.), 1946-47, pres., 1947—; pres. Atlas Corp., 1948-49, Hertzier & Zook, Belleville, Pa., 1942-46, Daffin Mfg. Co., Lancaster, 1949-60, Narvon Mines, Ltd., 1962-76, Irl. Daffin Assos., Inc., 1962—, Warwick Corp., 1970—; chmn. Daffin Corp., Hopkins, Minn., 1960-62, Eastern Corp., Federalsburg, Md., 1970—; dir. Hampden Color & Chem. Co. Bd. dirs. Lancaster Gen. Hosp.; trustee Lancaster Country Day Sch. Mem. Newcomen Soc. Eng. C. of C. (dir.). Republican. Presbyterian. Mason (Shriner), Elk. Clubs: National Press; Lake Shore, Lancaster Country, Lancaster County Riding, Hamilton, Rotary, University, Radnor Hunt, Beaufort Hunt, Great Oak Lodge and Yacht, Lyford Cay, Porcupine, Rose Tree Hunt, Talbot Country. Home: Warwick Rd Lititz PA 17543 Office: Lancaster PA 17604

DAGENAIS, YVES, transp. co. exec.; b. Montreal, Que., Can., May 21, 1938; s. Armand and Marguerite (Caron) D.; student Ecole des Hautes Etudes Commerciales, Montreal, 1955-60; m. Louise Mailhot, June 25, 1960; children—Sylvain, Lucie, Celine, Julie. Assessor, Govt. Canada Income Tax, Montreal, 1955-62; with Provincial Transport Enterprises, Ltd., Montreal, 1962—, comptroller, 1968-70, v.p. finance, 1970-77, v.p. parcel express services, 1977—, also dir.; dir. Voyageur Inc., Voyageur Colonial Lt. and other subsidiaries; exec. dir. Canadian Motor Coach Assn. Mem. Certified Gen. Accountants Assn. Home: 1701 Meadowview Crescent Orleans ON K1C-154 Canada Office: 265 Catherine St Ottawa ON Canada

D'AGOSTINO, ANGELO, psychiatrist, clergyman; b. Providence, Jan. 26, 1926; s. Luigi and Julia (Lonardo) D'A.; B.S., St. Michael's Coll., 1945; M.D., Tufts Med. Sch., 1949, M.S. in surgery, 1953; postgrad. Seminary, Woodstock Coll., 1964-67. Intern, R.I. Hosp., Providence, 1949-50, asst. resident, 1950-51; resident New Eng. Center Hosp., Boston, 1951-53; joined S.J., 1955, ordained priest Roman Catholic Ch., 1966; asso. prof. psychiatry George Washington U., Washington, 1969-72, clin. prof., 1972—; dir. Center of Religion and Psychiatry, Washington, 1972—; practice medicine specializing in psychiatry, Washington, 1962—. Mem. Nat. Council for VA Chaplains, 1972—. Bd. dirs. Washington Mental Retarded Group, 1974—, Trinity Cons. Center, 1974-75. Served to capt., USAF, 1953-55. Decorated grand knight Order Merit, Republic of Italy, 1973. Mem. Washington Med. Soc. (chmn. com. on religion and medicine 1971-72), Am. Psychiat. Soc. (vice chmn. task force on religion and psychiatry, 1971-75), Washington Video-Psychiat. Study Soc. (pres. 1971-72), Med. Soc. D.C. (pres. sect. psychiatry 1977—, chmn. medicine and religion com.), Washington Psychiat. Soc. (pres. D.C. chpt.), Italian Execs. Am. (pres. 1975-77), Alpha Omega Alpha, Club: Cosmos (Washington). Editor: Family Community and Church, 1965. Author numerous publs. in field. Home: Georgetown U Hoya Sta Washington DC 20057 Office: 1100 22d St NW Washington DC 20037

D'AGOSTINO, MICHAEL DOMINICK, nuclear research scientist; b. N.Y.C., Mar. 26, 1933; s. Vincent John and Fanny (Memoli) D'A; B.Aero. Engring., N.Y. U., 1954, M.Nuclear Engring., 1967; m. Barbara Ann Notine, Nov. 28, 1957 (dec. 1973); children—Donna, Carol, Linda; m. 2d, Joanne Luther Demarest, Nov. 10, 1974; 1 dau., Nicole. Structures engr. Grumman Aerospace Corp. (formerly Aircraft Engring. Corp.), Bethpage, N.Y., 1954-55; nuclear research scientist, 1957-62, head nuclear and radiation effects group, 1962-71, head nuclear and radiation sci. group, 1971-73, head nuclear and astrophysics lab., 1973-74, dir. nuclear and astrophysics research, 1974—, chmn. Grumman Aircraft Isotopes Com., 1960-62. Guest scientist Brookhaven Nat. Lab., Upton, N.Y., 1961-70; cons. partner Radiation Tech. Assos., Hauppauge, N.Y., 1966—. Served to 1st lt. USAF, 1955-57. Mem. Am. Nuclear Soc. (chmn. isotopes and radiation div. 1975-76, vice chmn. L.I. chpt. 1978-79), Am. Inst. Aeros. and Astronautics, IEEE, Tau Beta Pi. Contbr. articles to profl. jours. Home: 17 Calico Tree Rd Hauppauge NY 11787 Office: Research Center Bldg 26 Gumman Aerospace Corp Bethpage NY 11714

D'AGOSTINO, RALPH BENEDICT, educator; b. Somerville, Mass., Aug. 16, 1940; s. Benedetto and Carmela (Piemonte) D'A.; A.B., Boston U., 1962, M.A., 1964; Ph.D., Harvard U., 1968; m. Leilanie Carta, Aug. 28, 1965; children—Ralph Benedict, Leilanie Maria. Lectr. math. Boston U., 1964-68, asst. prof., 1968-71, asso. prof., 1971-76, prof., 1976—, asso. dean Grad. Sch., 1976—; statis. cons. United Brands, 1968-76, Diabetes and Arthritis Control Unit, Boston, 1971—, City Somerville, Mass., 1972, Ednl. div. Bolt. Beranek & Newman, 1971, Harvard Dental Sch., 1969; cons. biostatistics Lahey Clinic Found., 1973—, Walden research, 1974—, FDA, 1975—, corneal scis., 1976. Mem. Am. Statis. Assn. (pres. Boston chpt. 1972, v.p. 1971, mem. nat. council 1973-75), Inst. Math. Statistics, Phi Beta Kappa, Sigma Xi. Assos. editor Am. Statistician, 1972—; book reviewer Houghton Mifflin, Holden-Day, Duxbury Press, Prentice Hall, 1969—. Contbr. articles to profl. jours. Home: 5 Everett Ave Winchester MA 01890 Office: Grad Sch Boston U 705 Commonwealth Ave Boston MA 02215

DAHAN, FERNAND WILLIAM, architect planner; b. Alexandria, Egypt, June 19, 1933; s. William Choucri and Yolande Michel (Matragi) D.; came to U.S., 1963, naturalized, 1968; B.Arch., Alexandria U., 1959; M.Regional and City Planning, Cath. U. Am., 1968; m. Anita Ansieta, Sept. 5, 1964. Designer archtl. firms, Egypt, Saudi Arabia, Lebanon, 1959-61; prin. Fernand Dahan, architect, Beirut, Lebanon, 1961-63; design, project mgr. archtl. firms, Washington, 1963-68; housing and urban devel. specialist, dep. dir. planning united Planning Orgn., Washington, 1968-71; prin. Fernand W. Dahan, archtl. and planning work, Rockville, Md., 1971—; pres. Dahan Profl. Assn., Rockville, 1974—. Recipient prizes Govt. Lebanon in nat. archtl. competitions. Mem. AIA, Am. Inst. Planners. Author: Subcenters in Growing Metropolitan Areas: The Case of Rockville, Maryland, 1968; co-author: Public Service Careers Program Plan A, Planning Guide and Flow Network, 1971. Address: 5410 Amberwood Ln Rockville MD 20853

DAHILL, THOMAS HENRY, JR., artist, educator; b. Cambridge, Mass., June 22, 1925; s. Thomas Henry and Helen Agnes (Ireland) D.; B.S. in Chemistry, Tufts U., 1949; Dipl. Sch. Mus. Fine Arts Boston, 1953, grad. certificate, 1954; fellow Am. Acad. Rome, 1955-57; A.M. (hon.), Emerson Coll., 1967; postgrad. Harvard, summer 1953. Instr., Sch. Mus. Fine Arts, Boston, 1953—; lectr. fine arts Tufts U., 1954-55, 1959-70, lectr. fine arts Emerson Coll., 1961-64, asst. prof., 1964-66, asso. prof., 1966-69, prof., 1969—, chmn. dept. fine arts, 1966—. Dir. Edward Everett Hale House, Inc.; exhibited drawings one-man shows Boston Mus. Fine Arts, 1963, 66, 67, Siembab Gallery, Boston, 1960-62, Downtown Gallery and Archtl. League, N.Y.C., 1958, Rome, Italy, 1956, 57, Naples, Italy, 1967, Milan, Italy, 1957, Salzburg, Austria, 1959; exhibited group shows numerous cities New Eng. Bd. dirs., v.p. Robbins Inst. Speech Correction. Served with USAAF, World War II. Mem. Soc. Promoting Theol. Edn. (corporator 1969—), Evang. Missionary Soc. Mass., Soc. for Propagating of the Gospel Among Indians (trustee 1966—), Soc. War of 1812 (v.p.), Inst. Contemporary Art, MacDowell Colonists, Alumni Assn. Mus. Sch. (v.p. 1963-65), Gibson Soc. (dir. 1974—). Home: 223 Broadway Arlington MA 02174 Office: 261 Robbins St Milton MA 02186

DAHL, BERNHOFF ALLEN, pathologist; b. Hackensack, N.J., Nov. 3, 1938; s. John Alfred and Alphild Marie (Nilsen) D.; B.S. in Chemistry, Wheaton Coll., 1960; M.D., Cornell U., 1964; children—Sarah, Eric. Intern Mary Fletcher Hosp., Burlington, Vt., 1964-65; resident U. Vt. Hosps., Burlington, 1965-69; practice medicine specializing in pathology, Bangor, Maine, 1971—; chief pathologist Eastern Maine Med. Center, Bangor, 1971—; pres. Dahl-Chase Pathology Assos., Bangor, 1971—; dir. sch. med. tech., U. Maine, 1971—; pres. Am. Geodesic, Inc., Hampden Highlands, Maine, 1974—; exec. v.p. Phi Data, Inc., Bangor. Served with USPHS, 1969-71. Fellow Coll. Am. Pathologists; mem. Am. Soc. Clin. Pathologists, Am. Chem. Soc., Maine Med. Soc., Penobscot County Med. Soc. Address: 489 State St Bangor ME 04401

DAHLE, LELAND KENNETH, cereal chemist; b. Marietta, Minn., June 19, 1926; s. Andrew and Inga (Sortum) D.; B.A., St. Olaf Coll., 1950; M.S., Purdue U., 1952; Ph.D., U. Minn., 1961; m. Sophie Anne Fardal, Aug. 17, 1958; children—Joan, Andrea. Mem. faculty Augsburg Coll., Mpls., 1952-56; researcher Peavey Co., Mpls., 1961-69; cereal chemist, div. head Campbell Soup Co., Camden, N.J., 1969—. Served with AUS, 1944-46. Mem. Inst. Food Tech., Am. Assn. Cereal Chemists (chmn. tech. sessions), Am. Chem. Soc. Lutheran (council). Editoral bd. Cereal Chemistry, Cereal Sci. Contbr. articles to profl. jours. Home: 215 Garfield Ave Cherry Hill NJ 08002 Office: Campbell Soup Co Campbell Pl Camden NJ 08101

DAHLEN, RICHARD LESTER, lawyer; b. Minot, N.D., June 17, 1943; s. Lester and Ragnhild Marie (Dahl) D.; A.B. magna cum laude, Harvard U., 1965; LL.B., Yale U., 1968; m. Anne Carey Phillips, Feb. 8, 1969; 1 son, Christopher B.R. Admitted to Minn. bar, 1970, U.S. Supreme Ct. bar, 1973, Mass. bar, 1976; law clk. Minn. Supreme Ct., 1968-69; asso. firm Johnson, Thompson, Klaverkamp & James, Mpls., 1971-74; litigation atty. E.I. duPont de Nemours & Co., Wilmington, Del., 1974-75; asso. firm Chaplin, Barzun & Casner, Boston, 1976-77, partner, 1978—. Served with U.S. Army, 1969-71. Mem. Am. Bar Assn., Boston Bar Assn., Essex County Bar Assn., Maritime Law Assn. U.S. Republican. Episcopalian. Clubs: Harvard (N.Y.C., Boston); City (Boston). Home: 504 Essex St Hamilton MA 01982 Office: 24 Federal St Boston MA 02110

DAHM, DOUGLAS BARRETT, research co. exec.; b. Buffalo, Apr. 12, 1928; s. J. Earle and Beatrice (Peck) D.; B.S. in M.E., Northwestern U., 1950; postgrad. in engring. mgmt. George Washington U., 1958-63; M. Engring. Sci., State U. N.Y., Buffalo, 1964; m. Jay Goodall, Dec. 24, 1959; children—Doni Lee, Mark Barrett, Douglas Kurt. Asst. chemist Bell & Howell, 1945-46; exec. trainee Caterpillar Tractor Co., Peoria, Ill., 1946-51; staff scientist Calspan Corp. (formerly Cornell Aero. Lab., Inc.), Buffalo, 1955-65, program mgr., 1965-70, head dept. environment, 1970-75; v.p. Info. Scis., Calspan Field Services, 1978—. Served with USAF, 1950-55. Decorated D.F.C., Bronze Star with V device, 3 Air medals. Registered profl. engr., N.Y. Mem. N.Y. Acad. Scis., (past pres. and dir.), U.S. Environment and Resource Council, Internat. Assn. Pollution Control (dir.), Orgn. for Devel. Research (dir. 1975-76), Air Force Assn., Buffalo C. of C., Sigma Alpha Epsilon, Old Crows. Clubs: S. Towns Tennis, New Concord Ski, Wanakah Country. Contbr. numerous articles to profl. jours. Patentee in field. Home: S-5950 Old Lake Shore Rd Lakeview NY 14085 Office: Information Science Services Group PO Box 400 Buffalo NY 14225

DAIGLE, ROSARIO JOSEPH, accountant; b. Ste. Anne-De-Kent, N.B., Can., Mar. 30, 1942; s. Alphonse Joseph and Lina Marie (Richard) D.; B.C.S., Universite de Moncton, 1965; m. Cecile Richard, Aug. 7, 1965; children—Lyne, Carole, Yves. Analyst, Canadian Industries, Montreal, Que., Can., 1967—; chief accountant Stella-Maris-de-Kent Hosp., Ste. Anne-de-Kent, 1972—; lectr. accounting Ecole Polyvalente Clement Cormier; pres. LeFoyer Ste. Anne Inc., Bonbon Carole Anne Candy Inc. Pres. com. Ste. Anne Local Distbn. Services, 1971-77; trustee N.B. Sch. Dist. 12. Mem. N.B. Hosp. Mgmt. Assn. (com. pres. 1973-76). Club: Recratif Ste. Anne (pres.). Home: CP 6 Ste Anne de Kent NB E0A 2V0 Canada Office: CP 9 Ste Anne de Kent NB E0A 2V0 Canada

DAILEY, JEREMIAH ALOYSIUS, med. adminstr.; b. Cranston, R.I., Feb. 3, 1906; s. Jeremiah Francis and Mary Elizabeth (Shippee) D.; student Providence Coll., 1923-25; M.D., Georgetown U., 1930; M.H.A., Baylor U., 1955; m. Blanche M. Taylor, Jan. 25, 1934 (dec. Dec. 1959); children—Barbara A. Dailey O'Neil, Antonia M., Paul G. Intern, St. Joseph's Hosp., Providence, 1930-31, vis. physician out-patient dept., 1931-33, asst. vis. physician, 1933-35; practice medicine specializing in internal medicine, Apponaug, R.I., 1931-34, Las Cruces, N.Mex., 1934-35; Commd. 1st lt. M.C., U.S. Army, 1935, advanced through grades to lt. col., 1950, ret., 1959; dir. health State of R.I., 1959-61; dir. med. research and edn. St. Joseph's Hosp., Providence and Our Lady of Fatima Hosp., North Providence, 1961-65; adminstr. Mercy Hosp., Woonsocket, R.I., 1965-66; asst. dir. curative services R.I. Dept. Social Welfare, 1966-68; cons. physician R.I. State Dept. Health, 1975—; corp. mem. Blue Cross R.I., 1959-75. Mem. AMA, R.I., Providence County med. assns., Ret. Officers' Assn., Catholics United for the Faith. Roman Catholic. Home: 1401 Warwick Ave Apt 320 Warwick RI 02888

DAILEY, MACEO CRENSHAW, JR., historian; b. Norfolk, Va., July 4, 1943; s. Maceo Crenshaw and Marguerite (Britton) D.; B.A., Towson State U., 1967; M.S., Morgan State U., 1971; postgrad. Howard U., 1978—; m. Sandra L. Prettyman, Jan. 13, 1967; children—Michael, Christopher, Maceo Crenshaw III, Cameron. Instr. Towson (Md.) High Sch., 1970-71; instr. Towson State U., 1971-72; instr. Morgan State U., Balt., 1972-73; instr. State U. N.Y., Brockport, 1975-76; instr. history and social scis. Smith Coll., Northampton, Mass., 1976—. Counselor, YMCA, 1965-66. Ford fellow, 1973-74. Mem. Am. Hist. Assn., Assn. Study Negro Life and Culture, Popular Culture Assn. Democrat. Baptist. Home: 108 South St Northampton MA 01060 Office: Dept History Smith Coll Northampton MA 01063

DAILEY, ROGER KENT, tobacco co. exec.; b. Warsaw, Ind., Mar. 29, 1921; s. Roger M. and Estelle I. (Deahl) D.; B.S. in Mech. Engring., U. Colo., 1943; M.B.A., Northwestern U., 1946; m. Charlotte E. Hatler, June 2, 1951; children—Scott, Gregg. With Dailey, Brenner & Schreiber, Chgo., 1947-67, pres., until 67; v.p. fin. U.S. Tobacco Co., Greenwich, Conn., 1967—, also dir.; dir. Union Trust, Greenwich. Served to lt. comdr. U.S. Navy. Mem. Fin. Execs. Inst., Nat. Assn. Accounting. Clubs: County of Darien, Naples Bath and Tennis, Union League, Landmark. Home: 9 Haskell Ln Darien CT 06820 Office: 100 W Putnam Ave Greenwich CT 06830

DAILEY, WILLIAM VINCENT, chemist, mfg. co. exec.; b. Monongahela, Pa., May 18, 1929; s. Paul Herbert and Hazel Mary (Reagan) D.; B.S., U. Pitts., 1952; LL.B., LaSalle Extension U., 1976; children—Michael Paul, Debra Lynn, Alan Robert, Kim Lynn, Jeffrey William. With Mine Safety Appliances Co., Pitts., 1950—, chemist, 1955-56, asst. supr., 1956-58, research engr., 1958-59, application engr., 1959-61, sales engr., 1961-65, sales supr., 1965-75, product line mgr., 1975—. Mem. community advisory com. United Sch. Dist. Bd., Armagh, Pa. Served with USAF, 1950-54. Mem. Instrument Soc. Am. (sr., dir. analysis instrumentation div. 1973), Air Pollution Control Assn., Stack Evaluation Soc., ASTM. Democrat. Home: RD 2 Box 128 New Florence PA 15944 Office: 600 Penn Center Blvd Pittsburgh PA 15235

DAILY, JAY ELWOOD, librarian, educator; b. Pikeview, Colo., June 17, 1923; s. Roy Raymond and Anna Olive (Baker) D.; student So. Colo. State Coll., 1942-43, Grinnell Coll., 1943-44; B.A., N.Y. U., 1951; M.S., Columbia, 1952, D.L.S., 1957; m. Jennifer Mary Hole, Dec. 17, 1960. Adminstrv. officer Am. Edn. Mission Korea, 1952-53; head librarian Wagner Coll., N.Y.C., 1954-55; cons. librarian Office Prime Minister, Rangoon, Burma, 1957-59; adv. librarian U. Mandalay, Burma, 1959-62; library cons. Franklin Books Program, N.Y.C., 1962-65; asst. dir. U. Pitts. Libraries, 1965-66, asso. prof., 1967, prof. library sci., 1968—. Cons. Council Financial Aid Edn., 1953-57, Ford Found., Argentina, Chile, 1963, Rockefeller Found., 1964, U.S. AID, Peru, 1966; library cons. WQED, 1970—. Served with AUS, 1943-46. Recipient Thomas Wolfe Poetry prize Washington Sq. Coll., N.Y. U., 1951; Paula K. Lazrus Meml. fellow NCCJ, 1955-57. Mem. Spl. Library Assn., Assn. Am. Library Schs., AAUP, ALA (exec. bd. cataloging and classification sect. 1967-71). Democrat. Anglican. Clubs: Bibliophiles (Pitts.). Author: (with Mildred Myers) Cataloging for Library Technical Assistants, 1969; (with J. Phillip Immroth) Library Cataloging, 1971; (with James Williams and Martha Manheimer) Classified Library of Congress Subject Headings, 1972; Organizing Nonprint Materials, 1972; The Anatomy of Censorship, 1973—; Cataloging Phonorecordings, 1975; The Looking-Glass Decades, 1977. Editor: (with Harold Lancour and Allen Kent) Ency. Library and Information Sci., 1972—; Practical Books in Library and Information Science. Home: 709 S Negley St Pittsburgh PA 15232

DAKIN, ARTHUR HAZARD, writer; b. Boston, Jan. 25, 1905; s. Arthur Hazard and Emma Frances (Sahler) D.; A.B., Princeton, 1928, M.A., 1929, Ph.D., 1933; D. Phil., Oxford, 1938. Author: Von Hügel and the Supernatural; Man the Measure; chpts. in Audiovisual Aids to Instruction (edited by W. Exton), The Heritage of Kant (edited by G.T. Whitney and D.F. Bowers); A Paul Elmer More Miscellany; Paul Elmer More. Comdr. USNR ret.; exec. officer U.S. Naval Tng. Sch., Hampton, Va., and officer in charge Advance Base Reshipment Depot Battalion, Iroquois Point, Oahu, T.H., World War II. Mem. Am. Philos. Assn., Huguenot Soc., Soc. Colonial Wars, Saint Nicholas Soc. City N.Y., Metaphys. Soc. Am., Phi Beta Kappa. Clubs: Algonquin (Boston); Century, Princeton, University (N.Y.C.). Home: 355 S Pleasant St Amherst MA 01002

DALACK, JOHN DONALD, clin. psychologist; b. Jersey City, Apr. 19, 1933; s. Wakeem and Alice (Kerbawy) D.; B.A., Yale U., 1957; Ph.D., Columbia U., 1964; m. Shamseh Mae Khoury, Sept. 8, 1957; children—Gregory Wakeem, Laila Marie. Intern clin. psychology Walter Reed Gen. Hosp., Washington, 1959-60; chief clin. psychology sect. Patterson Army Hosp., Ft. Monmouth, N.J., 1961-64; supervising staff psychologist Staten Island Mental Health Soc., Staten Island, N.Y., 1964-66, asso. dir. psychol. services, 1966-69, dir. clin. services in psychology, 1969-70, dir. psychol. services and tng., 1970—; dir. day treatment services, dir. psychol. services S.I. Children's Community Mental Health Center, 1973—; asst. instr. Tchrs. Coll. of Columbia, 1960-61; project dir. Louis M. Wakoff Research Center, Staten Island, N.Y., 1965-67, 66-70; cons. psychology Salvation Army Men's Social Service Center, 1965-68; sch. psychologist, cons. evening program N.Y.C. Bd. Edn., 1967-69; lectr. psychology Notre Dame Coll. Staten Island, 1968-70; adj. asst. prof. psychology Richmond Coll. of City U. N.Y., 1970-72; clin. asst. prof. psychiatry in psychology Cornell U. Med. Coll., 1970-74; adj. asst. prof. psychology St. John's U. (S.I.), 1975-76; dir. staff tng. Young People's Info. Service of S.I., 1970-76. Pres. Risq G. Haddad Found., 1972-73, mem., 1968—; trustee Antiochan Orthodox Christian Archdiocese of N.Am., 1970—, sec., 1974—. Served with Signal Corps, U.S. Army, 1953-55, Med. Service Corps, 1959-64. Certified psychologist, N.Y.; licensed substitute sch. psychologist N.Y.C. Bd. Edn. Mem. Am. Psychol. Assn., Eastern, N.Y. State psychol. assns., Assn. Advancement of Psychology, Nat. Register Health Service Providers in Psychology, Sigma Xi. Contbr. articles to profl. jours. Home: 803 Davis Ave Staten Island NY 10310 Office: 657 Castleton Ave Staten Island NY 10301

DAL CORTIVO, LEO A., toxicologist; b. N.Y.C., Sept. 16, 1928; s. Otto and Natalie (Grotto) Dal C.; B.S., Fordham Coll., 1949; M.S., Adelphi U., 1953; Ph.D., Fordham U., 1975; m. Patricia E. Ferrigno, Jan. 5, 1964. Head dept. labs. Hosp. for Spl. Surgery, N.Y.C., 1950-54; sr. toxicologic chemist Office Chief Med. Examiner, N.Y.C., 1956-60, Suffolk County, Hauppauge, N.Y., 1960—; adj. asst. prof. St. Johns U., Jamaica, N.Y. Trustee Forensic Scis. Found., Rockville, Md.; exec. bd. Nat. Safety Council. Served with AUS, 1954-55. Diplomate Am. Bd. Forensic Toxicology. Fellow Am. Acad. Forensic Scis., Am. Inst. Chemists; mem. Am. Bd. Forensic Toxicology (dir.), N.Y. Acad. Scis., AAAS, Am. Chem. Soc., Internat. Assn. Forensic Toxicologists, Soc. Applied Spectroscopy, Forensic Sci. Soc. London, Sigma Xi, Phi Lambda Upsilon, Gamma Sigma Upsilon. Contbr. articles to profl. jours. Home: Miller Place Rd Miller Place NY 11764 Office: Suffolk County Office Bldg Hauppauge NY 11787

DALE, PAUL WORTHEN, physician; b. Moscow, Idaho, May 22, 1923; s. Harrison Clifford and Beulah (Garrard) D.; student Harvard Coll., 1941-43, M.D., 1947; m. Dorothy Jones Dale, Aug. 24, 1946; children—Paul Bradford, Jonathan Winthrop, David Harrison, Dorothy Garrard; Emily Carrington. Intern, King County Hosp., Seattle, 1948; resident Colo. Psychopathic Hosp., Denver, 1948-50; commd. 1st lt. U.S. Army, 1948, advanced through grades to capt., 1954; med. officer Valley Forge Army Hosp.; Phoenixville, Pa.; practice medicine specializing in psychiatry and neurology, Greenwich, Conn., 1954-77; chief mental health Trust Terr. Pacific Islands, 1978, dir. div. med. care, 1978—; faculty Albert Einstein Sch. Medicine, Bronx, N.Y.C., 1956—, asst. clin. prof., 1964—; asst. clin. prof. Med. Sch. U. Hawaii, 1978—; chmn. dept. psychiatry Greenwich (Conn.) Hosp., 1968-74. Served with U.S. Army, 1943-47. Diplomate Am. Bd. Psychiatry and Neurology. Fellow Am. Psychiat. Assn. Author: Seventy North to Fifty South, 1969; Yachtsman's Guide to Dining Out in Maine, 1972; (with C. Bates) Yachtsman's Guide to Dining Out on the Intracoastal Waterway, 1974. Home: 52 Breezemont Ave Riverside CT 06878 Office: Dept Health Trust Territory Pacific Islands Saipan Mariana Islands 96950

DALE, PORTER HINMAN, physician; b. Sherbrooke, Que., Can., Sept. 27, 1922; s. Timothy C. and Emma E. (Hemmig) D.; student Wesleyan U., Middletown, Conn., 1941-42, Yale, 1943; B.S., U. Vt., 1944, M.D., 1947; m. Mary Lois Westover, Oct. 13, 1951; children—Christopher, Peter, Timothy, Susan. Intern, Mary Fletcher Hosp., Burlington, Vt., 1947-48, resident, 1949-51; resident Waterbury (Conn.) Hosp., 1948-49, New Eng. Med. Center, Boston, 1951; pvt. practice medicine specializing in internal medicine, Montpelier, Vt., 1953—; mem. attending staff, dir. coronary care unit Central Vt. Hosp., Berlin. Pres., Vt. Bd. Phys. Therapy Registration, 1957-75; chief med. cons. State Vt. Social Security Disability Agy., 1957—. Served as capt. USAF, 1951-53. Diplomate Am. Bd. Internal Medicine. Fellow A.C.P. (gov. for Vt. 1975—); mem. Vt. Heart Assn. (pres. 1961-63), Vt. Med. Soc. (pres. 1971-72). Rotarian (pres.). Home: 5 McKinley St Montpelier VT 05602 Office: Med Office Bldg RD 4 Montpelier VT 05602

DALEN, JAMES EUGENE, physician, educator; b. Seattle, Apr. 1, 1932; s. Charles A. and Muriel E. (Joanise) Robinson; B.S., Wash. State U., 1955; A.M., U. Mich., 1956; M.D., U. Wash., 1961; M.S., Harvard U., 1972; m. Janice K. Daus, Sept. 17, 1955; children—James E., Angela M. Intern, Boston City Hosp., 1961-62, resident in medicine, 1962-63; sr. resident in medicine New Eng. Med. Center, 1963-64; research fellow in cardiology Peter Bent Brigham Hosp., Boston, 1964-67; instr. Harvard U. Med. Sch., 1967-69, asst. orof. medicine, 1969-74, asso. prof., 1974-75; prof., chmn. cardiovascular medicine U. Mass., 1975-77, chmn. dept. medicine, 1977—; physician-in-chief U. Mass. Hosp., 1977—. Served with USN, 1951-53. Fellow Am. Heart Assn., A.C.P., Am. Coll. Cardiology, Am. Coll. Chest Physicians; mem. Am. Clin. and Climatological Assn., Mass. Hort. Soc. Episcopalian. Mem. editorial bd. Circulation, 1978—; contbr. articles to profl. jours. Home: 15 High St Southboro MA 01772 Office: U Mass Med Center Worcester MA 01602

D'ALESSIO, GREGORY, cartoonist, painter, art educator; b. 1904. Syndicated cartoonist, also lectr. radio, TV, colls. and schs.; cartoons, paintings have appeared in the New Yorker, Look, Saturday Evening Post, Colliers, Esquire, N.Y. Times, others; also published collections; represented in pvt., univ. collections; instr. Art Students League. Recipient awards ann. competition Nat. Graphics Soc. Mem. Art Students League (life, past v.p.), Soc. Classic Guitar (v.p.), Nat. Cartoonists Soc. (past sec., awards), Soc. Illustrators (life). Asso. editor: The Guitar Rev. Address: care Art Students League 215 W 57th St New York City NY 10019

DALEY, JOSEPH T., bishop; b. Connerton, Pa., Dec. 21, 1915; student St. Charles Borromeo Sem., Phila.; D.D. Ordained priest Roman Catholic Ch., 1941; titular bishop Barca and aux. bishop, Harrisburg, Pa., 1963-67; coadjutor bishop with right of succession, 1967-71; bishop of Harrisburg, Pa., 1971—. Address: 4800 Union Deposit Rd PO Box 2153 Harrisburg PA 17105

DALEY, MICHAEL JAMES, educator; b. Boston, June 4, 1940; s. William James and Sally D.; B.S., Boston U., then M.Ed.; m. Martha Roline Allen, June 13, 1964; children—Karen Ann, Michael Allen, Kristine Marie, Karyl Jeanne. Tchr. physics and health, coach Meml. Hihg Sch., Tewksbury, Mass., 1964—. Mem. Tewksbury Bd. Health, 1973—; chmn. Tewksbury Bicentennial Commn., 1973—, Tewksbury Patriotic Activities, 1973—, Growth Policy Com., 1978—; mem. George Kyricos Scholarship Com. Mem. Tewksbury Tchrs. Assn. (pres.). NSF grantee. Home: 61 Carleton Rd Tewksbury MA 01876 Office: Pleasant St Tewksbury MA 01876

DAL FABBRO, MARIO, author; b. Cappella Maggiore, Italy, Oct. 6, 1913; s. Pietro and Luigia Fiorina (Gava) DalF.; B.F.A., Inst. Indsl. Art, Venice, Italy, 1935; M.F.A., Magistero of Art, Venice, 1937; m. Helen Dall'Antonia, May 9, 1944; 1 dau., Sylvia (Mrs. Gerard Nucera). Came to U.S., 1948, naturalized, 1951. Author: Costruzione e funzionalita del mobile moderno, 1950; How to Build Modern Furniture, 1957; Furniture for Modern Interiors, 1954; How to Make Children's Furniture, 1963; Upholstered Furniture: Design and Construction, 1969, and others. One man shows sculpture Meierhans Galleries, Perkasie, Pa., 1969, Allentown (Pa.) Art Mus., 1972; exhbited in group shows Nat. Art Exhibit, Italy, 1969, Allentown Art Mus, 1969-74, Cheltenham Art Center, Phila., 1971-73, Centro Art Italy, Trieste, 1972-73; represented in permanent collection Sant'Andrea, Vittorio Veneto, Italy, Allentown Art Mus., others. Recipient awards Phillips Mill Art Gallery, New Hope, Pa., 1971, Woodmere Art Gallery, Phila., 1974, Centro Art Italy, Trieste, 1975, New Canaan (Conn.) Art Show, 1976. Contbr. to mags., newspapers, encys. Home: 67 Sherman Ct Fairfield CT 06430

DALGAARD, BRUCE RONALD, economist, educator; b. Waukegan, Ill., July 29, 1947; s. Bruce Irving and Lena Alfreda (Pederson) D.; A.B., U. Ill., Urbana-Champaign, 1969, M.S. (Earhart Found. fellow), 1974, Ph.D. (Lincoln fellow), 1976; m. Kathleen Marie Albrecht, Aug. 24, 1968. Instr. social studies Barrington (Ill.) High Sch., 1969-72; lectr. U. Ill., Urbana, 1974-75; asst. prof. econs., dir. Center for Econ. Edn., Lehigh U., Bethlehem, Pa., 1976—; cons. edn. com. Am. Iron and Steel Inst.; cons. NSF Econ. Edn. Program. Mem. Am., Eastern econ. assns., NEA, Nat. Assn. Affiliated Econ. Edn. Dirs., Econ. History Assn., Bus. History Conf., Phi Alpha Theta, Omicron Delta Epsilon. Editor: Proceedings of the Steel Industry Economics Seminar, 1977; contbr. articles to profl. jours. Office: Drown Hall #35 Lehigh U Bethlehem PA 18015

DALGLEISH, LILY MARGARET, nursing supr.; b. Cambridge, Galt, Ont., Can., Nov. 13, 1913; d. Thomas and Lily Ross (Walker) D.; grad. St. Michaels Hosp. Sch. Nursing, Toronto, Ont., 1940; B.S.N., Seton Hall U., East Orange, N.J., 1958. Staff nurse St. Michaels Hosp., Toronto, 1941-42, head nurse, 1947-52, asst. supr., 1952-69; supr. labor and delivery Margaret Hague Hosp., Jersey City, 1969-74, supr. central supply, 1973—; supr. central supply Jersey City Med. Center, 1973—. Served with M.C., Canadian Army, 1942-46. Registered nurse, Ont. N.J. Presbyterian. Home: 270 Henderson St Jersey City NJ 07302 Office: 50 Baldwin Ave Jersey City NJ 07304

DALIANIS, JAMES STEPHEN, learning disabilities cons.; b. Chgo., June 18, 1937; s. Stephen and Evdoxia Dalianis; B.A. in Secondary Edn., Seton Hall U., S. Orange, N.J., 1957; M.A. in Elementary Reading, Rutgers U., New Brunswick, N.J., 1964; M.A. in Adminstrn., Supervision Kean Coll., Union, N.J., 1975; married; children—Dia, Stephanie. Tchr. reading Manalapan (N.J.) Twp. schs., 1959-61; tchr. Irvington (N.J.) Sch. Systems, 1961-69, reading specialist, 1969—, learning disabilities cons., 1978—. Mem. NEA, N.J., Irvington edn. assns. Libensed as reading specialist, N.J. Home: 14 Hickory Rd Nutley NJ 07110 Office: Irvington Sch System Irvington NJ 07111

DALLAS, JOHN R(AYMOND), JR., bus. and fin. info. co. exec.; b. Pitts., Feb. 8, 1950; s. John Raymond and Yvonne (Shearer) D.; student Duquesne U.; m. Cynthia Gray Norris, May 26, 1973; 1 dau., Jennifer Gray. Dir. public relations Jr. Achievement, Inc., Pitts., 1967-70; pres. Dallas Assos., Inc., Pitts., 1970-74, Nat. Bus. Intelligence Corp., N.Y.C., 1974—. Mem. Am. Mgmt. Assn., Pres.'s Assn., Nat. Investor Relations Inst. Republican. Presbyterian. Club: N.Y. Athletic. Office: 200 Park Ave New York NY 10017

DALLAS, ROBERT VALINE, radiologist; b. Methuen, Mass., Dec. 17, 1942; s. Matthew and Hilda Anne Marie (Valine) D.; B.S., Rensselaer Poly. Inst., 1964; M.D., Albany Med. Coll., 1969; m. Margaret McGuirk, July 9, 1966; children—Heather Anne Lee, Robert Matthew. Intern, Albany (N.Y.) Med. Center Hosp., 1969-70, resident in radiology, fellow, 1970-74, attending radiologist, 1977—, head div. diagnostic radiology, 1977—, acting radiologist-in-chief, 1977—; attending radiologist Geneva (N.Y.) Gen. Hosp., 1974-76; acting chmn. dept. radiology Albany Med. Coll., 1977—, asst. prof. radiology, 1977—, exec. faculty, 1977—; advisor Health Systems Agy. of Northeastern N.Y., 1977—; med. bd. Albany Med. Center Hosp., 1977—. Served to capt. USAR, 1970-76. Diplomate Am. Bd. Radiology. Mem. Northeastern N.Y. Radiologic Soc., St. Andrew's Soc. Home: 238 Lenox Ave Albany NY 12208 Office: Albany Med Center Hosp New Scotland Ave Albany NY 12208

DALLOW, THEODORE JULIAN, real estate broker; b. Waterbury, Conn., June 6, 1919; s. Philip D. and Fanny (Winkleman) D.; student Coll. City N.Y., 1939-43, 45-46; m. Phyllis F. Lash, July 30, 1944; children—Ellen S., Richard P., Constance J. Traffic mgr. U.S. Dept. Agr., N.Y.C., 1942-43; mgr. H. Lash Dept. Store, N.Y.C., 1946-50; salesman Curtis Realty, Inc., Elmont, N.Y., 1950-52; pres. Parliament Realty, Inc., Laurelton, N.Y., 1952-60; pres. Theodore J. Dallow, Inc., Lewittown, N.Y., 1960—; sec. Condor Realty Corp., Levittown, 1964—; v.p. Theo. J. Dallow of Farmingdale, Inc. (N.Y.); lectr. real estate N.Y. Inst. Tech., C.W. Post Coll. Extension. Past 1st v.p. Levittown Republican Club; past Rep. committeeman. Served to 1st lt. USAAF, 1943-46. Decorated Air medal. Mem. Columbia Soc. Real Estate Appraisers, L.I. Real Estate Bd. (chpt. pres. 1966-67), Nat. Inst. Real Estate Brokers (councilor 1967-69), Real Estate Exchange Assn. L.I. (past pres.). Mason. Rotarian. Clubs: Optimist (pres. 1962-63, lt. gov. 1963-64). Home: 3638 Richard Ln Wantagh NY 11793 Office: 3076 Hempstead Turnpike Levittown NY 11756 also 392 Conklin St Farmingdale NY 11735

DALRYMPLE, WINDSOR HOWARD, orthopedic surgeon; b. Titusville, Pa., Mar. 4, 1923; s. Windsor Clay and Elisabeth Jane (Wagner) D.; B.S. in Mec. Engring., Cornell U., 1949; M.D., U. Pa., 1953; m. Phyllis Schiffeneder; children—Diana, David, Debra, Mark, Elisabeth, Windsor, Catherine. Intern, Pa. Hosp., Phila., 1953-54; resident in orthopedic surgery Buffalo Gen. Hosp., Buffalo Children's Hosp., Buffalo VA Hosp., 1960-65; practice medicine specializing in orthopedic surgery, Ridley Park, Pa., 1966—; chief dept. orthopedic surgery Taylor Hosp., Ridley Park, 1972—. Served with USMCR, 1942-46. Mem. Am. Acad. Orthopedic Surgery, AMA, Am. Acad. Family Practice. Clubs: Masons, Shrine. Home: 224 N Providence Rd Wallingford PA 19086

DALTON, DENNIS, psychiatrist; b. Waco, Tex., Sept. 23, 1938; s. Martin Alton and Loyce Virginia (Huddleston) D.; B.M., Baylor U., 1959, M.D., 1966; grad. Columbia U. Psychoanalytic Center, 1977. Intern, Methodist Hosp., 1966-67; resident in psychiatry N.Y. State Psychiat. Inst., 1967-70; attending psychiatrist adolescent service Columbia U. Coll. Physicians and Surgeons, 1972-73, supervising psychiatrist N.Y. State Psychiat. Inst., Coll. Phys. and Surgs. Columbia U., 1973—, also collaborating faculty Psychoanalytic Center, 1977—; dir. adolescent unit Harlem Hosp. Dept. Child Psychiatry, 1972-74. Served as lt. comdr. M.C., USNR, 1970-72. Mem. Am. Psychiat. Assn., Am. Soc. Adolescent Psychiatry (treas. N.Y. br.), Eastern Assn. Sex Therapists (charter). Home and office: 240 Central Park S New York City NY 10019

DALTON, EDWARD FRANCIS, accountant, computer systems designer; b. N.Y.C., Apr. 1, 1922; s. John Joseph and Nora Theresa (Angland) D.; B.B.A., Manhattan Coll., 1947; M.B.A., N.Y.U., 1947; 1 son, Edward Francis. Accountant, Haskins & Sells, C.P.A.'s, N.Y.C., 1946-59; cons. computer systems Honeywell, Inc., N.Y.C., 1959-64; mgr. accounting systems Am. Express, N.Y.C., 1964-65; with IBM Corp., White Plains, N.Y., 1967—, adv. market support adminstr., mfg. industry mktg., 1976—. Served with USAF, 1942-46. C.P.A., N.Y. Mem. Inst. C.P.A.'s, N.Y. State Soc. C.P.A.'s, Hosp. Fin. Mgmt. Assn. Republican. Roman Catholic. Author: Hospital Financial Management Systems Concepts, 1975. Home: 32-20 89th St Jackson Heights NY 11369 Office: 1133 Westchester Ave White Plains NY 10601

DALTON, JOHN H., govt. ofcl.; b. New Orleans, Dec. 13, 1941; B.S., U.S. Naval Acad., 1964; M.B.A., Wharton Sch. Fin. and Commerce, U. Pa.; postgrad. U.S. Naval Nuclear Power Sch., 1966. Account exec. Goldman, Sachs & Co., Dallas, 1971-77; pres. Govt. Nat. Mortgage Assn., HUD, Washington, 1977—. Del. to Nat. Democratic Conv., 1976; founding mem. Dallas Dem. Forum. Served with U.S. Navy, 1964-69. Office: 451 7th St SW Washington DC 20410

DALVA, DAVID LEON, II, art dealer; b. N.Y.C., Nov. 8, 1935; s. Leon David and Jean (Casswell) D.; B.S., Villanova U., 1958; m. Margaret Gelinas, Aug. 26, 1960; children—Jean Anne, David Leon III, Peter Curran. With Dalva Bros., Inc., N.Y.C., 1956—, pres., 1972—, chmn., 1974—. With El Diario-La Prensa Inc. newspaper, N.Y.C., 1966—, 1st v.p., asso. publisher, 1972—; also dir.; dir. Dalva Communications, 44 E 57th St Realty Corp. Adv. council Children's Aid Soc.; mem. Commn. for Cultural Affairs, N.Y.C. Life fellow Met. Mus. Art. Served with N.Y. Army N.G., 1956-68; lt. col. Res. Decorated Army Commendation medal. Mem. Appraisers Assn. Am., Nat. Soc. Interior Designers, Art and Antique Dealers League Am. (dir., pres. 1978—), Police Res. Assn. City N.Y. (dir. 1973—, exec. sec. 1975-76), Loyal Legion, Assn. Ex-Members Squadron A, 7th Regiment Rifle Club (dir., 1971—, treas. 1973—), Assos. Engr. Corps (dir. 1971—, v.p. 1977), Loyola Sch. Assn. (dir. 1978). Clubs: N.Y. Athletic, The Leash; Army-Navy (Washington); Southampton Yacht. Office: 44 E 57th St New York City NY 10022

DALY, CHARLES CORNELIUS, educator; b. Stamford, Conn., Nov. 2, 1919; s. Charles Patrick and Margaret (McNamara) D.; B.F.A., Pratt Inst., 1943; M.A., Columbia U., 1947, Ed.D., 1959; postgrad. Syracuse U., 1966, Santa Clara U., 1967; m. Phyllis June Carothers, May 29, 1943; children—Susan Daly Miller (dec.), Owen, Douglas, Christine, Deborah. Prof. art, ednl. media Coll. New Rochelle, N.Y., 1947—; instr. ednl. media Tchrs. Coll., Columbia U., 1958—; dir. ednl. media NDEA Inst., Yeshiva U., summers, 1961, 63, 65; 63, 65, Iona Coll., New Rochelle, summers, 1964, 65; lectr., cons. in field to pub. schs., ednl. systems, bus., industry; prin. Dalarts Co., ednl. media and communications, Mamaroneck, N.Y., 1968. Mem. Bd. Edn., Ryeneck, N.Y., 1971-73. Served with USAF, 1943-46. Mem. N.Y. State Ednl. Communications Assn., Westchester County Ednl. Communications Assn. (pres. 1965-67), Westchester Assn. Ednl. Communications and Tech. (dir. 1964—, pres. 1965-66). Contbr. articles to profl. jours. Home: 115 Osborn Ave Mamaroneck NY 10543 Office: Coll New Rochelle New Rochelle NY 10801*

DALY, WILLIAM JOSEPH, JR., fin. corp. exec.; b. Bklyn., Oct. 2, 1933; s. William Joseph and Gladys Irene (Weidel) D.; student pub. schs., Bklyn.; m. Carol Ann Conzelman, Apr. 8, 1956; children—Susan, Maureen, William Joseph. Supr. stock loan dept. Merrill Lynch, Pierce, Fenner & Smith, Inc., N.Y.C., 1958-63; asst. v.p. stock loan dept. Dean Witter & Co., Inc., N.Y.C., 1963-70; pres. DalGood Instl. Service Corp., N.Y.C., 1971—. Served with U.S. Army, 1952-54. Mem. Assn. Stock Loan Representatives (founder, pres. 1969-70). Home: 3076 Grand Ave Baldwin NY 11510 Office: DalGood Instl Service Corp 99 Wall St New York City NY 10005

DAMAN, HARLAN RICHARD, allergist; b. N.Y.C., Nov. 1, 1941; s. D. Leon and Frances (Weissler) D.; A.B. cum laude, Harvard, 1963; M.D., Albert Einstein Coll. Medicine, 1967. Intern, then resident Yale-New Haven Hosp./Med. Center, 1967-69; fellow in allergy and clin. immunology Nat. Jewish Hosp. Research Center/U. Colo. Med. Center, Denver, 1971-73; staff Albert Einstein Coll. Medicine, N.Y.C., 1974—; mem. teaching staff depts. medicine and pediatrics Mt. Sinai Hosp. and Med. Center/Sch. Medicine, 1976—. Served to maj. M.C., USAF, 1969-71. Diplomate Am. Bd. Pediatrics, Am. Bd. Allergy and Immunology. Fellow Am. Acad. Pediatrics, Am. Coll. Allergists, Am. Coll. Chest Physicians, Am. Acad. Allergy; mem. N.Y., Westchester (ednl. program dir. 1978—) allergy socs., Westchester Acad. Medicine. Office: 769 Kimball Ave Yonkers NY 10704

DAMAST, MELVYN, ophthalmologist; b. Bronx, N.Y., Apr. 18, 1943; s. Joseph and Mary D.; B.S., Coll. City N.Y., 1963; M.D., Albert Einstein Coll. Medicine, 1967; m. Carole Damast, Dec. 27, 1964; 2 children. Intern, USPHS Hosp., S.I., N.Y., 1967-68, resident in ophthalmology, 1968-71, chief dept. ophthalmology, 1972-76; fellow in neuro-ophthalmology Bascom Palmer Eye Inst., U. Miami (Fla.) Sch. Medicine, 1971-72; pvt. practice ophthalmology, White Plains, N.Y., 1976—. Fellow Am. Acad. Ophthalmology and Otolaryngology; mem. Westchester County, N.Y. State med. socs., Am. Assn. Ophthalmology. Office: Greenridge Med Pavilion 12 Greenridge Ave White Plains NY 10605

D'AMATO, ANTONIO GENNARO, univ. adminstr.; b. Brusciano, Italy, Oct. 16, 1937; s. Luigi and Orlanda (Terracciano) D'A.; came to U.S., 1967, naturalized, 1972; student U. Naples, 1961-64; B.A., Columbia U., 1971, M.B.A., 1974, postgrad., 1976—; m. Marie E. Siciliano, Sept. 29, 1969. Successively tchr., research asst., cons. in finance, Italy, 1962-67; programmer Columbia U., N.Y.C., 1969-71, systems analyst, supr. computer ops., 1972-76, asst. dir. computer services, 1976—. Author: Computer Guide Manual, 1974; RSTS/IDA User's Manual, 1977. Home: 819 E 229th St Bronx NY 10466 Office: 201 Uris Hall Columbia U New York City NY 10027

DAMAVANDI, PARVIZ KHATIB, investment co. exec.; b. Tehran, Iran, May 6, 1939; s. Nasrollah Khatib and Moulok (Salehzadeh) D.; came to U.S., 1959; B.M.E., Howard U., 1963; M.S. in Engring., Akron U., 1965; postgrad. N.Y. Inst. Fin. 1968; postdoctoral Columbia, 1969; m. Mary Magill, Nov. 29, 1963; children—Nina, Roya, Lila. Prodn. mgr. Gen. Tire & Rubber Co., Tehran, 1963-65; indsl. engr., Akron, Ohio, 1965-66; sr. indsl. analyst Uniroyal Co., Passaic, N.J., 1966-68; account exec. Blair & Co., Passaic, 1968-69; pres. Kern Investment Co., Passaic, 1969; founder, pres. PARS Securities, Ft. Lee, N.J., 1969—, now also chmn., Tehran, 1973—; dir. Magill & Co., Roya Internat.; cons. in field. Mem. Am. Indsl. Engring., Assn., ASME. Home: 358 Pennington Ave Passaic NJ 07055 Office: 209 Main St Fort Lee NJ 07024 also 129 Khorshid St Tehran Iran

D'AMBOLA, JOSEPH VINCENT, hosp. adminstr.; b. Newark, Oct. 1, 1914; s. Alfonso and Rose (Bancone) D.; B.S. in Pharmacy, Rutgers Coll., 1952; m. Laura Bryson, Aug. 1, 1947; 1 child—Laura Kate. Sec., treas. Vendomat, Inc., Newark, 1947-50; pharmacist Jefferson Med. Coll. Hosp., Phila., 1953-54; dir. pharmacy Hahnemann Med. Coll. and Hosp., Phila., 1954-68, asso. adminstr., 1968—, sr. instr. pharmacy, 1968—; med. advisor Roche Labs., Nutley, N.J., 1970-72; med. cons. West Co., Phoenixville, Pa., 1971-75; sec., treas. Delaware Valley Hosp. Laundry, Inc., 1976—. Served to maj. U.S. Army, 1941-45. Recipient Man of Yr. award Del. Valley Hosp. Pharmacists, 1963, plaque spl. adv. bd. Roche Labs., 1972. Mem. Delaware Valley Hosp. Pharmacists (pres. 1962-63), Am. Soc. Hosp. Pharmacists, Am. Pharm. Assn., Hosp. Assn. Pa., Am. Coll. Hosp. Adminstr., Kappa Psi. Republican. Presbyterian. Club: Mason. Contbr. articles to profl. jours. Home: 1705 Tyson Rd Haverton PA 19083 Office: 230 N Broad St Philadelphia PA 19102

D'AMBROSIO, NICHOLAS, educator; b. Fraine, Italy, Mar. 8, 1929; s. Dominick and Maria Emilia (D'Ambrosio) D.; B.A., Montclair State Coll., 1953, M.A., 1958; postgrad. (Sci. Manpower fellow) Tchrs. Coll., Columbia U., 1959-63; m. Dolores Jean Marino, June 23, 1957; children—Nicholas, Donna Marie. Tchr. chemistry and physics Eastside High Sch., Paterson, N.J., 1955-58; mem. faculty Coll. Education William Paterson Coll., Wayne, N.J., 1958—, now asso. prof. sci. Chem. analyst Internat. Wire, Wykoff, N.J., 1957; cons. sci. and Italian-Am. ethnic culture, 1965—; prin., coordinator Confraternity Christian Doctrine Sch. Religion, Wayne, 1960-72. Treas. PTA, 1965-68. Served with AUS, 1953-55. Fellow N.J. Sci. Tchrs. Assn., AAAS, Am. Inst. Chemists; mem. AAUP, Nat., N.J. (corr. sec. 1959-63) sci. tchrs. assns., Assn. for Edn. Tchrs. Sci., N.E.A., Geol. Soc. Am. K.C. Author: (with James Bufano) Experiments in College Physical Science, 1967; Sourcebook of Selected Resources for Teaching Italian and Italian-American Culture, 1974. Home: 26 Dixon Pl Wayne NJ 07470

DAMERON, DOYLE, pub. relations dir.; b. Catlettsburg, Ky., Apr. 8, 1921; s. Wayne and Jennie (Wigington) D.; student U. Miami, Coral Gables, Fla., 1939-41; B.A. in Journalism, U. Minn., 1944. Advt. copywriter N.W. Daily Press Assn., Mpls., 1946-49; researcher, writer, tech. editor N. Am. Aviation, Inglewood, Calif., 1950-56; mgr. internal communications Gen. Telephone Co. of Calif., Santa Monica, 1956-59; asst. to v.p. pub. relations Gen. Telephone & Electronics Corp., N.Y.C., 1959-65; product researcher, script writer Dale Remington's Kaleidoscope, N.Y.C., 1965-68; dir. communications Blue Cross of N.E. Pa., Wilkes-Barre, 1968—. Recipient Nat. Safety Council award, Los Angeles, 1958, 1st prize for abstract painting Wyoming Valley Spring Art Show, 1973. Mem. Pub. Relations Soc. Am. (asso.) (v.p. N.E. Pa. chpt. 1970-71), Internat. Communications Council, Internat. Council Indsl. Editors, Am. Assn. Indsl. Editors, Internat. Assn. Bus. Communicators, N.Y. Ad Club. Democrat. Presbyterian. Home: 138 E Dorrance St Kingston PA 18704 Office: 15 S Franklin St Wilkes Barre PA 18711

DAMESHEK, H. LEE, physician; b. Balt., Mar. 16, 1937; s. Samuel and Rose (Rudick) D.; B.S. in Chemistry, Franklin and Marshall Coll., 1959; M.D., Tufts U., 1963; m. Michelle Zubasic, Sept. 12, 1965; children—Lynne Rifkin, Amy, David, Deborah. Intern, Presbyn.-Univ. Hosp., Pitts., 1963-64, resident in internal medicine, 1966-68; hematology fellow Ohio State U. Hosp., Columbus, 1968-69; practice medicine, specializing in hematology and oncology, Pitts., 1969—; clin. instr. medicine U. Pitts., 1969-74, clin. asst. prof., 1974—; instr. W. Penn Hosp., Pitts., 1969-77; cons. various hosps. Vice-pres. Leukemia Soc. W. Pa., 1977—. Served to capt. U.S. Army, 1964-66. Diplomate Am. Bd. Internal Medicine. Fellow A.C.P.; mem. Allegheny County, Pa. med. socs., AMA, Pitts. Acad. Medicine (asst. treas.). Jewish. Clubs: Green Oaks Country, Univ. (Pitts.). Contbr. articles to med. jours. Home: 421 Radcliffe Dr Pittsburgh PA 15235 Office: 3600 Forbes Ave Pittsburgh PA 15213

DAMICO, NICHOLAS PETER, lawyer; b. Chester, Pa., June 29, 1937; s. Ralph A. and Mary C. (Ametrane) D.; B.S., St. Joseph's Coll., 1960; LL.B., U. Pa., 1963; LL.M., Georgetown U., 1967; m. Patricia Ann Swatek, Aug. 26, 1967; children—Christine, Gregory. Admitted to Pa. bar, 1963, D.C. bar, 1966; tax law specialist IRS, Washington, 1963-66; asso., partner Silverstein & Mullens, Washington, 1966-76. Adj. prof. Georgetown U., 1973-75. Mem. Am. Bar Assn. Exec. editor: Exec. Compensation Jour., 1973-75. Office: 1819 H St NW Suite 1030 Washington DC 20006

D'AMICO, RICHARD JOSEPH, radiologist; b. Marlborough, Mass., Aug. 7, 1938; s. Frank J. and Pauline G. D'A.; A.B. magna cum laude, St. Anselm's Coll., 1960; M.D., Seton Hall U., 1964; m. Marianne Masiello, Oct. 5, 1963; 1 dau., Paula Ann. Intern, St. Vincent Hosp., Worcester, Mass., 1964-65; Am. Cancer Soc. clin. fellow Meml. Hosp. for Cancer and Allied Diseases, N.Y.C., 1967-69, chief resident diagnostic radiology, 1967-68, chief resident dept. radiation therapy, 1968-69; practice medicine specialzing in radiology, Bayonne, N.J., 1971—; mem. staff Bayonne Hosp., 1971—, asst. dir. dept. radiology and nuclear medicine, 1976—. Pres. Hasbrouck Heights (N.J.) Bd. Health, 1974, Concerned Parents Assn., Corpus Christi Sch., Hasbrouck Heights, 1977-78. Diplomate Am. Bd. Radiology, Nat. Bd. Med. Examiners. Mem. Am. Inst. Ultrasound in Medicine, Am. Coll. Radiology, Soc. Nuclear Medicine, Bayonne, Hudson County med. socs., Med. Soc. State N.J. Roman Catholic. Home: 50 Grandview Blvd Hasbrouck Heights NJ 07604 Office: 29 E 29th St Bayonne NJ 07002

DAMIJONAITIS, VYTAUTAS, psychiatrist; b. Kaunas, Lithuania, Jan. 3, 1913; s. Feliksas and Julija (Tomkeviciute) D.; came to U.S., 1949, naturalized, 1955; M.D., U. Kaunas, 1936, Ph.D., 1942; m. Elena Rekeviclute, Oct. 12, 1935; children—Egle Damijonaitis Pedini, Julius. Intern, Univ. Hosp., Kaunas, 1935-36; resident Hudson River St. Hosp., N.Y. State Psychiat. Ints., Poughkeepsie, 1958-61, supervising Tb physician, 1958-63, supervising psychiatrist, 1963-70, asst. dir., 1970—; adj. prof. Stomatology U. Kaunas, 1942-44; staff physician Gaylord Hosp., Wallingford, Conn., 1949-51; sr. supervising Tb physician J.N. Adam Meml. Hosp., Perrysburg, N.Y., 1951-56; gen. practice medicine Dundee, N.Y., 1956-58; psychiatric service Wallkill (N.Y.) Correctional Facility, 1962—; lectr. in field. Diplomate Am. Bd. Psychiatry and Neurology. Fellow Am. Coll. Chest Physicians; mem. Am. Psychiatric Assn., Med. Soc. State of N.Y., Dutchess County Med. Soc., Am. Lithuanian Med. Fraternity (past pres.). Club: Hudson River Psychiatric Center Golf. Home and Office: Branch B Poughkeepsie NY 12601

DAMON, ALAN WELLS, JR., educator, artist; b. Northampton, Mass., Mar. 25, 1939; s. Alan Wells and Olive Warner (Kellogg) D.; B.F.A. (scholar 1958-61), Mass. Coll. Art, 1961; postgrad. (Max Beckmann fellow), Bklyn. Mus. Art Sch., 1961-62; M.F.A., Pratt Inst., 1964; postgrad. (2 scholarships), Pratt Graphics Center, 1961-64. Instr., asst. prof. art dept. Georgian Ct. Coll., Lakewood, N.J., 1963-71; asst. prof. art and advt. design dept. N.Y.C. Community Coll., City U. N.Y., N.Y.C., 1971—; one-man shows paintings: Mass., N.J., D.C., N.Y., Ward-Nasse Gallery, N.Y.C., 1977-78; also group shows. Daniel Weisberg scholar Provincetown Workshop, Cape Cod, Mass., 1961. Mem. Sch. Art League N.Y., Coll. Art Assn., Ward-Nasse Gallery (coop.). Home: 305 E 24th St New York City NY 10010 Office: 300 Jay St Brooklyn NY 11201

DAMON, CAROLYN ELEANORE, chemist; b. Hancock, Mich., Aug. 16, 1937; d. Glenn Herbert and Laura Eleanore (Gillingham) D.; B.A. (Peabody scholar), Western Coll. Women, 1959; M.S., Purdue U., 1964. Pharm. analyst Am. Pharm. Assn., Washington, 1964-67; chief chemist, drug addiction lab., meat chemistry lab., acting chief, chemistry div. D.C. Govt., Washington, 1967-72; chemist, narcotics specialist U.S. Customs Lab., Savannah, Ga., 1972-77; research chemist Tech. Services Div., U.S. Customs Service, Washington, 1977—; cons. narcotics, fed. cts.; expert govt. witness, narcotics and food additives, criminal litigation. NSF Teaching fellow, 1961-62. Fellow Am. Inst. Chemists; mem. Am. Chem. Soc. (officer), N.Y. Acad. Sci. AAAS, AAUW (exec. bd.), Inst. Food Technologists, Sigma Xi. Lectr. tourist travel Russia to civic groups; interviewee TV news concerning govt. programs; contbr. articles to sci. jours. Home: 3100 S Manchester St Apt 540 Falls Church VA 22044 Office: 1301 Constitution Ave NW Washington DC 20229

D'AMOURS, NORMAN EDWARD, congressman; b. Holyoke, Mass., Oct. 14, 1937; s. Albert L. and Edna (Laplant) D.; A.B., Assumption Coll., 1960; LL.B., Boston U., 1963; m. Helen E. Manning, Sept. 4, 1965; children—Danielle Ann, Susan Ellen, Norman Manning. Admitted to N.H. bar, 1964, practiced in Manchester, 1969—; asst. atty. gen. State N.H., 1966-69; city prosecutor, Manchester, 1970-72; mem. 94th-96th Congresses from 1st N.H. Dist.; instr. St. Anselm's Coll., 1971-73. Alternate del. Democratic Nat. Conv., 1972; chmn. 1st Dist. Dem. Com., 1972—. Served with AUS, 1964-67 Mem. Manchester (dir. 1971-72), N.H., Mass. bar assns. Clubs: Optimists (treas. 1965-67), Elks, Richelieu (Manchester). Home: 617 Collidge Ave Manchester NH 03102 Office: US Ho of Reps Washington DC 20515

DAMSON, BARRIE MORTON, oil and gas exploration co. exec.; b. N.Y.C., Jan. 29, 1936; s. Harry and Ethel (Brody) D.; A.B., Harvard U., 1956; LL.B., N.Y. U., 1959; m. Joan Selig, Feb. 29, 1972; children—Blair, Laura, Bethany. Admitted to N.Y. bar, 1959; practiced in N.Y.C.; pres. Damson Petroleum Corp., N.Y.C., 1963-69; pres. Bronco Oil Corp., Midland, Tex., 1965-69; pres. Delta Minerals Inc., Lake Charles, La., 1967-69; pres., chmn. bd. Damson Oil Corp., N.Y.C., 1969—. Bd. dirs., co-chmn. Children's Blood Found. N.Y. Hosp. Mem. Bar Assn. of N.Y., Oil Investment Inst., Ind. Petroleum Assn. Am. Clubs: Harvard, El Morocco (N.Y.C.). Office: 366 Madison Ave New York City NY 10017

DANA, JEANNE MARIE, corporate mgmt. adviser; b. Los Angeles, Mar. 31. 1941; d. Martin and Anita (Alcala) Lassos; ed. U. Calif., Los Angeles; 1 dau., Pilar Janine. Research asst. Delafield & Delafield Co., N.Y.C., 1965-67; fin. analyst Graham Loving & Co., N.Y.C., 1968; sr. transp. cons. exec. v.p. Connaught Research Corp., N.Y.C., 1969-75; pres. The Dana Group, Inc., N.Y.C., 1975—. Mem. N.Y. Soc. Security Analysts, Conf. Bd., Am. Mgmt. Assn., Fin. Analysts Fedn., Transp. Assn. Am. Club: Met. (N.Y.C.). Office: 645 Madison Ave New York NY 10022

DANAHER, JOHN ANTHONY, judge; b. Meriden, Conn., Jan. 9, 1899; s. Cornelius J. and Ellen (Ryan) D.; A.B., Yale U., 1920; postgrad. Yale Law Sch., 1922; m. Dorothy King, Feb. 3, 1921; children—John A., Robert Cornelius, Jeanne. Law clk. White & Case, N.Y.C., 1921-22; admitted to Conn. bar, 1922, practiced Hartford, Conn., and Washington, 1922-53; asst. U.S. atty., 1922-34; sec. State Conn., 1933-35; U.S. senator, 1939-45; counsel Rep. Senatorial Com., 1946-53; U.S. circuit judge U.S. Ct. Appeals, Washington, 1953-69; sr. U.S. circuit judge, Hartford, Conn., 1969—. Del. Rep. Nat. Conv., 1944, Congl. aide, Rep. Nat. Com., 1945-46; exec. dir. U.S. Senatorial Campaign, 1948. Mem. Pres.'s Commn. Internal Security and Individual Rights, 1951; mem. Pres.'s Conf. Adminstrv. Procedure, 1953-54; dir. div. spl. activities Eisenhower campaign, 1952. Served as 2d lt. F.A., U.S. Army, 1918. Mem. D.C., Conn. Hartford County bar assns., Beta Theta Pi, Elihu. Republican. Roman Catholic. Clubs: Hartford (Conn.); Met. (Washington). Home: 31 Wyndwood Rd West Hartford CT 06107 Office: Fed Bldg Hartford CT 06103*

DANCE, WALTER DAVID, mfg. co. exec.; b. Amherst, N.S., Can., May 13, 1917; s. Walter H. and Gertrude I. (Jones) D.; came to U.S., 1923, naturalized, 1942; A.B., Dartmouth, 1940; m. Jane P. Clune, Mar. 31, 1942; children—Susan P., Peter D., Robert A., Richard M. With Gen. Electric Co., 1948—, gen. mgr. Hotpoint div., 1962-64, v.p., 1964—, gen. mgr. maj. appliance and Hotpoint div., exec. appliance and TV group, 1968, exec. TV group, 1970, sr. v.p. corp. exec. staff, 1970-72, vice chmn. bd., exec. officer, 1972—, also dir.; chmn. bd. Gen. Electric Credit Corps., 1974; dir. Great Atlantic and Pacific Tea Co. Chmn. bd. overseers Amos Tuck Sch., Dartmouth. Served with AUS, 1941-45. Mem. Assn. Home Appliance Mfrs. (dir.), Ky. (dir.), Louisville (dir.) chamber commerce, Nat. Assn. Elec. Mfrs. Assn. (vice chmn. bd. govs.), Com. Econ. Devel. (trustee). Home: 24 Horseshoe Rd Darien CT 06820 Office: Easton Blvd Fairfield CT 06430

DANCHAK, MICHAEL, specialist computer graphics and human engring.; b. Coaldale, Pa., Mar. 28, 1944; s. Michael and Mary (Fedora) D.; B.S., Princeton U., 1965; Ph.D., Rensselaer Poly. Inst., 1974; m. Caroline R. Tomlinson, Feb. 25, 1968. Prin. engr. Combustion Engring. Inc., Windsor, Conn., 1974-78; curriculum chmn. computer and info. sci. Hartford (Conn.) Grad. Center, 1978—, adj. faculty computer sci. dept., 1974—. Served with USMCR, 1965-69. Mem. IEEE Computer Soc., Instrument Soc. Am., Human Factors Soc., Soc. Info. Display, Tau Beta Pi. Russian Orthodox. Home: 62 Prospect St Bloomfield CT 06002 Office: 1000 Prospect Hill Rd Windsor CT 06095

DANCY, NORTH BARRY, clergyman, univ. dean; b. Stamford, Conn., Oct. 5, 1935; s. Archibald North and Ethel Hulda (Swenson) D.; B.A., Baylor U., 1957; M.Div., Princeton, 1960; Ph.D., Temple U., 1972; m. Patcia Laura Anderson, July 29, 1961; children—Peter James, Laura Jeanne. Ordained to ministry Presbyn. Ch., 1960; minister, Unadilla dn Otego, 1960-65; asst. minister 1st Presbyn. Ch., Trenton, N.J., 1965-68; chaplain, instr. religion and philosophy Westminster Choir Coll., Princeton, N.J., 1968-70; dean students Fairleigh Dickinson U., Rutherford, N.J., 1970—; v.p., treas. Alumni Services Inc., 1976—. Exec. dir. Inst. for Applied Christian Ethics, Upper Montclair, N.J., 1973—; pres. Cooper-Summit Assn., Upper Montclair, 1971-73. Trustee Palisades Counseling Center, Rutherford, 1972—. Mem. Palisades Presbytery, Nat. Assn. Student Personnel Adminstrs., Eastern Assn. Coll. Deans and Advisors to Students, Am. Assn. for Higher Edn., Met. Coll. Mental Health Assn., N.J. Personnel and Guidance Assn., Am. Assn. U. Adminstrs. Home: 105 Summit Ave Upper Montclair NJ 07043 Office: Fairleigh Dickinson U Rutherford NJ 07070

DANDES, E. WILLIAM, educator; b. Peabody, Mass., May 3, 1928; s. Samuel and Rose (Weissman) D.; diploma Bentley Coll., 1947, postgrad., 1948-49; B.S., Suffolk U., 1953, M.S., 1954; postgrad.

Harvard, N.Y. U. Mem. faculty Bentley Coll., Boston, 1949—, prof. accounting and taxation, 1961—, v.p. acad. affairs, asso. dean, 1964, dir. grad. programs, 1973—; cons. accounting and mgmt. services U.S. Dept. Def., 1951-53; mgmt. cons. Arthur D. Little, Inc., 1955—; tax cons. Peat, Marwick, Mitchell & Co., 1956—. Served with U.S. Army, 1951-53. C.P.A., Mass. Mem. Am. Accounting Assn., Am. Inst. C.P.A.'s, Mass., Soc. C.P.A's, Nat. Assn. Accountants, Eastern, New Eng. bus. tchrs. assns., Assn. For Higher Edn. Lion. Author: (with Rae P. Anderson) Problems in Auditing, 1962; (with others) Neuner's Cost Accounting Principles and Practice, 1962. Office: Bentley Coll Waltham MA 02154

DANEK, JOSEPH GERARD, found. exec.; b. Astoria, N.Y., Oct. 4, 1941; s. Joseph Robert and Beatrice Marie (Rut) D.; B.S., Mt. St. Mary's Coll., 1963; M.Ed., U. Md., 1966, Ph.D., 1976; m. Marita J. McKenna, June 18, 1966; children—Jody, Jennifer, Geoffrey. Chmn. sci. div. William Wirt Jr. High Sch., Riverdale, Md., 1966-68; with NSF, Washington, 1968—, head spl. project sect., grants and contracts office, 1972-74, program mgr., directorate sci. edn., energy related grad. traineeship, 1974-75, program mgr., directorate sci. edn., research initiation and support, 1975-76, program mgr. minority instns. sci. improvement program, 1976-77, dir. ops. for sci. edn., 1977—. Mem. Nat. Sci. Tchrs. Assn., Nat. Assn. Research in Sci. Teaching, AAAS. Home: 12809 Kernel Circle Bowie MD 20715 Office: 1800 G St Washington DC 20550

DANESH, HOSSAIN BANADAKI, psychiatrist; b. Yazd, Iran, Jan. 15, 1938; s. Jafar and Belqis (Malik-Afsali) D.; M.D., U. Isfahan (Iran), 1961; m. Michele Lynn Bernstein, Dec. 2, 1967; children—Arman Eric, Roshan Phillip. Intern, Univ. Hosps., U. Isfahan, 1960-61; resident in internal medicine Shiraz (Iran) Med. Center, Nemazi Hosp., Shiraz, 1962; resident in psychiatry Ill. State Psychiat. Inst., Chgo., 1964-67, U. B.C. (Can.), Vancouver, 1969-70; pvt. practice psychiatry, 1970-73; asst. chief Michael Reese unit Ill. State Psychiatric Inst., Chgo., 1967; asst. dir. undergrad. edn. in psychiatry and neurology Chgo. Med. Sch. and Univ. Health Scis., 1968; cons. psychiatrist, rehab. and boarding home program B.C. Mental Health Services, Essondale, 1969-70; psychiatrist-in-charge, adolescent services Royal Ottawa (Ont.) Hosp., 1973-77; asst. prof. psychiatry U. Ottawa, 1973—; founder Centre for Studies on Anger, 1975; bd. dirs. family therapy program Ottawa Civic Hosp., dir. thanatology service, 1978—. Fellow Royal Coll. Physicians and Surgeons Can.; mem. Can. Psychiatric Assn., Ont., Can., B.C. med. assns., Am. Suicidology Assn., Am. Group Psychotherapy Assn., Internat. Assn. Suicide Prevention, Can. Assn. Studies on Baha'i Faith. (pres. exec. com.). Mem. Nat. Spiritual Assembly Bahai's Can. Contbr. articles in field to profl. jours. Home: 41 Avonlea Rd Ottawa ON Canada Office: 1053 Carling Ave Ottawa ON K1Y 4E9 Canada

DANFORTH, DANA, investment adviser; b. Cambridge, Mass., Dec. 19, 1924; s. George Newlon and Margaret Clare (Sheehy) D.; A.B. in Econs., Yale U., 1945; m. Franca Scribani-Rossi, Apr. 26, 1947 (div. Jan. 1960); children—David Newlon, Alison Clare, Valerie Laura; m. 2d, Gloria Anne Gould, Sept. 3, 1960; children—Stuart, Robert. Economic consultant Spear & Staff, Inc., Wellesley, Mass., 1945-48; founder, v.p., dir. Danforth-Epply Corp., Wellesley Hills, Mass., 1946, pres., 1952—; pres., dir. Danforth Assos., Inc., Wellesley Hills, 1953—; dir. Bay Bank Norfolk County Trust Co., Brookline, Mass. Trustee Dana Hall Schs., Wellesley Scholarship Found. Mem. N.Y. Soc. Security Analysts. Clubs: Wellesley Country; Yale, Boston Economic, Harvard (Boston). Home: 5 Arlington Rd Wellesley Hills MA 02181 Office: 2 Laurel Ave Wellesley Hills MA 02181

D'ANGELO, JOSEPH FRANCIS, pub. co. exec.; b. Astoria, N.Y., July 4, 1930; s. Frank and Matilda (Oliveri) D'A.; B.B.A., St. John's U., 1952; m. Marcia Elaine Mackie, Mar. 4, 1965; children—Elena, Joseph Francis. Mem. firm Haskins & Sells, C.P.A.'s, N.Y.C., 1952-61; treas., controller internat. operations Borden Co., Panama and P.R., 1961-65; v.p. King Features Syndicate div. Hearst Corp., N.Y.C., 1973-76, pres., 1976—, resident controller, 1965-73, bus. mgr., 1968-73, gen. mgr., 1973-76; pres., dir. King Features Syndicate, Inc., 1973—, Telenews Film Corp., 1973—, KFS Music, Inc., 1973—, Telenews Film Corp., 1973—, King Features TV Prodns., Inc., N.Y.C., 1973—; mem. N.Y. Bd. Trade. Bd. dirs. Saratoga (N.Y.) Perfoming Arts Center, Mus. Cartoon Art and Hall of Fame, Greenwich, Conn.; trustee Emerson Coll., Boston. Mem. Artists and Writers Assn., Nat. Cartoonists Soc., Newspaper Comics Council, N.Y. State Soc. Newspaper Editors, So. Newspaper Pubs. Assn., Inst. Newspaper Controllers and Finance Officers, Nat. Acad. TV Arts and Scis., Sigma Delta Chi. Republican. Roman Catholic. Clubs: Dutch Treat, Friars, N.Y. Athletic, Union League, Overseas Press; Wheatley Hills Golf (East Williston, N.Y.); Strathmore-Vanderbilt Country (Manhasset, N.Y.). Home: 173 Chapel Rd Manhasset NY 11030 Office: 235 E 45th St New York City NY 10017

D'ANGELO, SAMUEL ANTHONY, aircraft co. exec.; b. Buffalo, Apr. 27, 1934; s. Crispino and Mary C. D'A.; B.S., U. Buffalo, 1958; m. JoAnne F. Ventura, Aug. 30, 1958; children—Mary Jean, Charles, Joseph, Albert. Chem. engr. Morrison Steel Corp., Buffalo, 1958-59; chem. and metall. engr. Haliod-Xerox Corp., Rochester, N.Y., 1959-61; tech. dir. Mercury Aircraft, Inc., Hammondsport, N.Y., 1962—; chmn. bd. Crispino Corp., Bath, N.Y., 1971—. Scoutmaster, Boy Scouts Am., 1968-78, bd. mem., 1970—; mem. council St. Mary's Sch. Bd., 1965-67. Mem. Am. Welding Soc., Am. Chem. Soc., Nat. Soc. Plastic Engring., Nat. Soc. Lit. and Arts, AAAS, Am. Soc. Metals, Sons Italy of Am. Republican. Roman Catholic. Clubs: Elks, K.C., Snowmobile Rescue Squad. Patentee in field. Home: 315 Burton St Bath NY 14810

DANGLER, RICHARD REISS, betting co. exec.; b. N.Y.C., Mar. 6, 1940; s. Edward and Gertrude (Reiss) D.; B.A., N.Y. U., 1962; LL.B., Bklyn. Law Sch., 1965, J.D., 1967; m. Lisa Frant, Feb. 1, 1968; children—Ellen Susan, Justin Todd. Asst. to pres. Bogue Electric Mfg. Co., Paterson, N.J., 1965-68; sr. contracts adminstr., mgr. export licensing ITT, N.Y.C., 1968-70; sr. v.p. N.Y.C. Off-Track Betting Corp., 1970—. Sponsor exec. internship program Human Resources Adminstrn., 1972-76. Recipient Norman P. Hefley award, 1968, Blanche White award, 1974, Outstanding Achievement award United Fund N.Y., 1975. Mem. ASME, Practicing Law Inst., Nat. Contract Mgmt. Assn., U.S. Naval Inst., Assn. Old Crows, Nat. Wildlife Fedn., Internat. Game Fish Assn. Clubs: Sea Horses Rod and Gun; Admirals, Contbr. articles to profl. jours. Home: Crow Hill Path Mount Kisco NY 10549 Office: 1501 Broadway New York City NY 10036

DANGREMOND, LUCILLE MARTIN (MRS. HARLEY L. DANGREMOND), civic worker; b. St. Louis; d. George H. and Julia (Blattner) Martin; B.A., Washington U. St. Louis, 1922; M.A., Tchrs. Coll., Columbia, 1940; m. Harley L. Dangremond, June 28, 1924; children—Jack M., Dorothy J. (dec.). Tchr. Bogota (N.J.) High Sch., 1940-43; substitute tchr. Teaneck (N.J.) High Sch., 1943-60; tchr. Englewood (N.J.) High Sch., 1940-55; profl. mag. writer, 1946-48. Mem. adv. com. Sch. Edn., Rutgers U., 1957-59; mem. adv. panel div. environmental engring. and food protection USPHS, 1965-67. Mem. Bergen County Women's Republican Club; bicentennial chmn. N.J. Fedn. Rep. Women, 1974. Named Distinguished Am., Bd. Trustees Dist. Ams. Mem. N.J. Fedn. Women's Clubs (pres. 1960-62, award for distinguished record of leadership 1966, Cecilia Gaines Holland award 1976), Gen. Fedn. Women's Clubs (chmn. religion 1962-64, dir. 1960-70, chmn. home life dept. 1964-66, chmn. consumer trends and home mgmt. 1964-68, chmn. vets. div. 1968-70), Am. Mothers Com., Inc. (dir. 1958-70), Middle Atlantic Conf. Gen. Fedn. Women's Clubs (pres. 1964-66), P.E.O. (pres. chpt. R Teaneck 1967-69). Clubs: Past Presidents' (pres. 1949-51), Washington U. Alumni, Tchrs. Coll. Alumni. Home: 753 Larch Ave Teaneck NJ 07666

DANIEL, ALICE, educator, lawyer; b. N.Y.C.; d. Edwin and Rose (Barnett) Glantz; A.B., Boston U., 1958; LL.B., Columbia U., 1963; 1 son, John. Admitted to N.Y. bar, 1963, Calif. bar, 1971; asso. appellate counsel criminal appeals div. N.Y. Legal Aid Soc., N.Y.C., 1967-70; asso. counsel NAACP Legal Def. and Edn. Fund, San Francisco, 1970-72; asso. prof. law U. Calif. Hastings Coll. Law, San Francisco, 1972—; dep. legal affairs sec. to Calif. Gov. Edmund G. Brown, Jr., 1975; gen. counsel Legal Services Corp., Washington, 1976—. Bd. dirs. No. Calif. Service League. Mem. ACLU (dir. No. Calif.). Editorial adv. bd. Prison Law Reporter, 1973—. Office: 198 McAllister St San Francisco CA 94102

DANIEL, GERARD LUCIAN, physician, drug co. exec.; b. Swanton, Vt., May 6, 1927; s. Edward and Exzilia (Perron) D.; A.B., St. Michaels Coll., 1950; M.D., U. Vt., 1954; m. Armande Renee Messier, Nov. 24, 1949; children—Suzanne Beatrice. Practice medicine, Brattleboro, Vt., 1955-59; chief clin. medicine Dept. Army, Washington, 1959-63, chief life scis. div., 1963-70; med. dir. Pacific Region, Sterling/Winthrop Internat., Minami Azabu, Tokyo, 1970-73, internat. dir. clin. research, Winthrop Products Inc., N.Y.C., 1973-75; corporate med. dir. Rhodia Inc., U.S. affiliate Rhone-Poulenc of France, N.Y.C., 1975-78; exec. v.p. Lipha Chems. Inc. Subs. Air Liquid, France, 1978—; pub. health officer State of Vt., 1958-59; mem. adv. com. Multiple Sclerosis, 1959-60; chmn. Pharm. Dels. Japan, Tokyo, 1972-73. Recipient Achievement award NASA, 1963; Intelligence Merit medal, 1970. Mem. Med. Execs. Assn. N.Y.C., Acad. Medicine. Contbr. sci. and technol. articles to profl. jours. Home: Carnegie House Suite 2Q 100 W 57th St New York City NY 10019 Office: 600 Madison Ave New York City NY 10022

DANIEL-DREYFUS, SUSAN B. RUSSE (MRS. MARC ANDRE DANIEL-DREYFUS), civic worker; b. St. Louis, May 30, 1940; d. Frederick William and Suzanne (Mackay) Russe; student Smith Coll., 1958-60, Corcoran Sch. Fine Arts, 1960-61, Washington U., St. Louis, 1961-62; m. Don B. Faerber, Nov. 27, 1962 (div. 1969); 1 dau., Suzanne Mackay; m. 2d, Marc Andre Daniel-Dreyfus, Aug. 9, 1969. Mem. St. Louis-St. Louis County White House Conf. on Edn., 1966-68; mem. Mo. 1st Gov.'s Conf. on Edn., 1966, 2d Conf., 1968. Bd. dirs. Tunbridge Sch., 1973—, St. Louis Smith Coll.; pres. bd. dirs. Family Counseling Service, Brookline, Mass., 1978—; hon. bd. dirs. New Music Circle. Mem. womans bd. Washington U., Mo. Hist. Soc., New Music Circle, Childrens Art Bazaar, Non-Partisan Ct. Plan for Mo., Young Audiences Inc.; founder St. Louis Opera Theater; chmn. Art. Mus. Bond Issue election St. Louis, 1966. Mem. Colonial Dames, League Women Voters (dir. Boston chpt. 1969-72), Boston Smith Coll. Assn. (dir. 1976—), Boston Jr. League (council 1970-73, dir. 1974—), Soc. Art Historians. Club: Women's City (dir. 1973—), Vincent (dir. 1977-79). Home: 120 Middlesex Rd Chestnut Hill MA 02167

DANIELL, JAMES LACHLAN, mfg. co. exec.; b. Pitts., Apr. 10, 1918; s. Reginald Averell and Euphemia (Machintosh) D.; B.S., Ohio State U., 1942; m. Marcia Wilson Simblest, Jan. 5, 1943; children—James Averell, Susan Wilson Daniell Donaldson, Linda Carol, Deborah Kathleen. With Alloy Mfg. Co., Pitts., 1938-58, beginning as purchasing agt., successively asst. gen. mgr., 1947-48, v.p., gen. mgr., 1950, chmn. bd. 1956; exec. asst. to pres. Jessop Steel Co., Washington, Pa., 1958-63; pres., dir. Green River Steel Corp., Owensboro, Ky., 1959-63; exec. v.p., treas. Daniell-Sapp-Boorn Assos., Inc., Pitts., 1963-67; v.p. mktg. services N. Am. Rockwell Corp. (now Rockwell Internat.), Pitts., 1967-74; asst. to chmn. bd. U.S. Steel Corp., 1974—; pres. RMI Co., 1976—; dir. Youngwood Electronic Metals, Inc., Davison Sand & Gravel Co. Past mem. Pres.'s Council Phys. Fitness; past dir. Mt. Lebanon Twp. Sch. Bd.; past dir. Young Peoples Recreation Center, Young Baseball Programs; founder, past dir. Parents Athletic Council, Mt. Lebanon, Pa.; bd. dirs. Variety Fund Handicapped Children, Pitts., Pitts. chpt. Nat. Football Found. and Hall of Fame. Served to lt., USNR, 1942-45; PTO. Decorated Silver Star, Predsl. Citation with Bronze Star. Mem. Navy League (life), Ohio State U. Alumni Assn., Kappa Sigma. Republican. Clubs: Masons (32 deg.), Jesters, South Hills Country (past pres., bd. dirs.); Allegheny (past pres.), Duquesne, Burning Tree; Youngstown Country. Home: 600 Grandview Ave Pittsburgh PA 15211 Office: 600 Grant St Pittsburgh PA 15230 also 1000 Warren Ave Niles OH 44446

DANIELS, ANTHONY CARL, constrn. co. exec.; b. Meriden, Conn., Oct. 5, 1928; s. Lawrence and Philomen (Ciasulli) D.; B.B.A., Bryant Coll., 1955; m. Joyce M. Dioguardi, May 31, 1954; children—Louis M., Lisa M., Lori A., Lawrence A. Acct. new departure div. Gen. Motors Corp., Bristol, Conn., 1955, data processor, to 1965; controller Stern & Co., Hartford, Conn., 1965-68; sec.-treas. Morris A. Fierberg Co., Hartford, 1968—, also dir.; dir. Indsl. Mech. Corp., Ins. City Sprinkler, Inc., Hartford. Served with AUS, 1950-52. Mem. VFW. Home: 570 Brownstone Ridge Meriden CT 06450 Office: 112 Prospect Ave Hartford CT 06106

DANIELS, DAVID MITCHELL, assn. exec.; b. Evanston, Ill., Apr. 10, 1927; s. Thomas Leonard and Frances (Hancock) D.; grad. Yale, 1948; postgrad. (Marion Szekely-Freschl scholar) Curtis Inst. Music, 1947-50. Soloist Phila. Orch., Am. Opera Co., Phila., St. Paul Opera Co., others, including roles in Call Me Madam, Plain and Fancy nat. co., Carnival nat. co., Oh Kay, N.Y.C., Boys in the Band, N.Y.C.; pres. The Drawing Soc., N.Y.C., 1970—. Mem. vis. com. Met. Mus. Art, N.Y.C., 1973—. Trustee Mpls. Inst. Fine Arts, Skowhegan (Maine) Art Sch. Recipient Theatre World award, 1955, Donaldson award Billboard mag., 1955. Home: 4 Sutton Pl New York City NY 10022 Office: 41 E 65th St New York City NY 10021

DANIELS, LEN D., public relations co. exec.; b. Hudson, N.Y., Sept. 11, 1935; s. Benjamin and Evelyn (Koslow) D.; student N.Y. U., 1951-52; B.A., Alfred U., 1955. With pub. relations dept. N.Y. State Dept. Audit and Control, Albany, 1956-60; pres. Placement Assos., Inc., N.Y.C., 1960—, Len Daniels, Inc., N.Y.C., 1965—. Instr. publicity Publicity Club N.Y., 1969—; adviser to bd. N.Y.C. Jr. C. of C., 1971—. Recipient citation Publicity Club. N.Y., 1969, N.Y.C. Jr. C. of C., 1973. Club: N.Y. Athletic. Home: 400 E 57th St New York City NY 10022 Office: 645 Madison Ave New York City NY 10022

DANIELS, MALCOLM LEON, publisher; b. Providence, Feb. 11, 1926; s. Harry and Mary (Hagopiam) D.; student Amherst Coll., 1944; A.B., Brown U., 1951. Pres., pub., editor Cranston (R.I.) Mirror, 1961—; asso. Z. Daniels & Co., Providence, 1952—; dir., adminstr. Armenian Nursing Home of R.I. Chmn. Cranston City Personnel Appeal Bd.; mem. Cranston City Plan Commn. Served with U.S. Army, 1944-46. Decorated Bronze Star, Purple Heart. Mem. New Eng., R.I. press assns., Providence Club of Printing House Craftsmen (dir.). Republican. Armenian. Clubs: E. Greenwich Yacht, Masons, Shriners, Rotary. Home: 87 Myrtle Ave Cranston RI 02910 Office: 250 Auburn St Cranston RI 02910

DANIELS, MAXINE LOREAT, counselor; b. Columbus, Tex., Oct. 27, 1926; d. Earl Preston and Elizabeth (Wright) Harris; B.A. Music, Prairie View U., 1946; postgrad. U. Iowa, 1947-48, Rutgers U., 1956-58, Newark State Tchrs. Coll., 1957, 67-70; M.S.Ed. magna cum laude, Monmouth Coll., 1974; m. Thomas Edward Daniels, Aug. 8, 1948; children—Michael E., Karen E. Daniels Alston, Kevin E., Daryl E., Larrick E., Danita E., Raun E. Instr. in music Lane Coll., 1948-49, Tillotson Coll., 1949-50; tchr. Neptune Twp. (N.J.) Sch. System, 1956-68, guidance counselor, 1967-70; chmn. dept. guidance Asbury Park (N.J.) Middle Sch., 1970—; tchr. piano, guitar; cons. Head Start. Dist. bd. dirs. Ocean Twp. (N.J.) Democratic Club, 1972—. Recipient certificate of appreciation Whitesville PTA, 1965, 67, N.J. Jaycettes, 1964, Nat. Assn. Negro Bus. and Profl. Women's Clubs, 1977, N.J. Orgn. Tchrs., 1974; letter of appreciation Neptune Supt. Schs., 1969, Brookdale Community Coll., 1969, 70, Bur. Children's Services, Red Bank, N.J., 1969; certified in pupil personnel services, adminstrn., supervision, music, elementary teaching, N.J.; certified tchr., Tex. Mem. NAACP, Nat., N.J., Monmouth County (N.J.) edn. assns., Asbury Park Tchrs. Assn., Asbury Park Study Center, N.J. Orgn. Tchrs., N.J., Am. personnel and guidance assns., Monmouth County Guidance Assn., Nat. Assn. Negro Bus. Prof. Women's Clubs, Monmouth County, Bus. Profl. Women's Council, Continental Socs., U. Iowa (Life), Monmouth Coll. alumni assns., Alpha Kappa Alpha. Mem. African Methodist Episcopal Ch. Research in field. Home: 52 Fredric Dr Oakhurst NJ 07755 Office: 1200 Bangs Ave Asbury Park NJ 07712

DANIELS, ROBERT VINCENT, educator, state senator; b. Boston, Jan. 4, 1926; s. Robert Whiting and Helen Underwood (Hoyt) D.; A.B., Harvard U., 1945, M.A., 1947, Ph.D., 1951; m. Alice May Wendell, July 2, 1945; children—Robert H., Helen L., Irene L., Thomas L. Research asso. M.I.T., 1951-52; mem. social sci. faculty Bennington Coll., 1952-53, 57-58; asst. prof. Slavic studies Ind. U., 1953-55; research asso. Columbia, 1955-56; asst. prof. history U. Vt., Burlington, 1956-57, 58-61, asso. prof., 1961-64, prof., 1964—, chmn. dept., 1964-69, dir. exptl. program, 1969-71; mem. Vt. Senate, 1973—, asst. minority leader, 1977—, vice chmn. com. on energy and natural resources, 1977—. Chmn. Vt. Gov.'s Commn. Med. Care, 1974-75; mem. Vt. Health Policy Corp., 1977—, mem. legis. com. Mem. Chittenden County (Vt.) Democratic Com., 1959—; mem. Burlington City Dem. Com., 1965—; chmn. policy and planning platform com. Vt. Dem. Party, 1962-66, 69-73, 76—; alternate Dem. Nat. Conv., 1968. Bd. visitors USAF Acad., 1965-67. Served to ensign, USNR, 1944-46. U.S.-Soviet Cultural Exchange scholar U. Moscow, 1966; USSR Acad. Scis., 1976; Nat. Endowment for Humanities fellow, 1971-72. Mem. Am. Hist. Assn. (pres. conf. on Slavic and East European History 1976-77), Am. Assn. Advancement Slavic Studies (dir. 1968-71), AAUP, ACLU, Vt. Hist. Soc. (trustee 1968-71), Vt. Council World Affairs. Club: Harvard of Vermont (pres. 1974-75). Author: The Conscience of the Revolution, 1960, Documentary History of Communism, 1960, The Nature of Communism, 1962, Studying History, 1966, Red October, 1967, The Russian Revolution, 1972; Fodor's Europe Talking, 1975; co-editor: Dynamics of Soviet Politics, 1976. Home: 195 S Prospect St Burlington VT 05401

DANIELS, RONALD EARL, elec. engr.; b. Bklyn., May 29, 1948; s. Philip Graden and Edna (Vincent) D.; B.S., N.Y. Inst. Tech., 1970; M.S., Poly. Inst. N.Y., 1977; m. Darlene Teresa Cherry, Sept. 25, 1976. Actuary asst. George B. Buck Co., N.Y.C., 1970-72; systems engr. Sperry Systems Mgmt., Gt. Neck, N.Y., 1972—. Active Greenlawn Civic Assn. Mem. IEEE, Am. Mgmt. Assn., Black Masters Bus. Assn., NAACP. Home: 61 Brand Dr Huntington NY 11743 Office: Great Neck Great Neck NY 11020

DANIELS, THOMAS EDWARD, elec. engr.; b. Ravenna, Ky., Nov. 12, 1926; s. Thomas Edward and Jennie F. (Parks) D.; student Prairie View A. and M. Coll., 1944, U. Kans., 1944, U. Syracuse, 1944, U. Maine, 1945, U. Louisville, 1946-47; B.S. in Elec. Engring., U. Iowa, 1948; postgrad. Rutgers U., 1952-56; M.B.A., Monmouth Coll., 1975; m. Maxine L. Harris, Aug. 8, 1948; children—Michael E., Karen E. Daniels Alston, Kevin E., Daryl E., Larrick E., Danita E., Raun E. Instr. engring. Prairie View A. and M. Coll., 1948-50; electronic engr. Signal Corps Engring. Labs., Ft. Monmouth, N.J., 1950-54, project engr. Electronics Warfare Lab., Signal Corps. Engring. Labs., 1954-59; unit chief Electronic Warfare Lab., Electronics Command, Ft. Monmouth, 1959-66; team leader Avionics Lab., Electronics Command, Ft. Monmouth, 1966-68; div. chief Office Project Mgr. Nav./Control Systems, Ft. Monmouth, 1968-77, dep. project mgr., 1977—; mem. nat. and internat. mil. equipment standardization groups. Pres. Whitesville PTA, 1958-60; v.p. Monmouth Community Action Program, Inc., 1966-68, pres., 1974-76; pres. Inter Community Coordinating Council Inc., 1968; v.p. bd. dirs. St. Stephen Urban Devel. Corp., 1972—; co-chmn. Troop 60, Boy Scouts Am., 1977—; vice chmn. bd. trustees St. Stephen African Methodist Episcopal Zion Ch. Served with U.S. Army, 1945-46. Recipient distinguished service awards for from various community, fraternal and civic orgns. Mem. Army Aviation Assn., Am., IEEE, Inst. of Nav., Wild Goose Assn. (past dir.), Am. Def. Preparedness Assn. (dir.), NAACP (past v.p., dir. Asbury Park br. 1960—), U. Iowa Alumni Assn., Monmouth Coll. Alumni Assn., Kappa Alpha Psi. Democrat. Home: 52 Fredric Dr PO Box 161 Oakhurst NJ 07755 Office: Office Project Mgr Nav/Control Systems Bldg 2525 Fort Monmouth NJ 07703

DANIELS, WHITMAN, park ofcl.; b. Buffalo, July 20, 1910; s. John and Caroline (Dornbach) D.; A.B. (Rufus Choate scholar 1930-31, also sr. fellow), Dartmouth, 1932; postgrad. U. Paris, U. Madrid, Academie Julien, Art Students League, Armed Forces Indsl. Coll., Am. Inst. Banking; m. Dorothy Pitt, Jan. 10, 1942; children—Jocelyn (Mrs. Paul A. Ferguson), Jefferson Pitt. With Household Finance Corp., 1932-33; asst. dir. Park Lodge Sch., Pau, France, 1933-35; extension sec. Child Edn. Found., 1935-36; dir. admissions, head French dept. Riverdale (N.Y.) Country Schs., 1936-38; coll. traveller McGraw-Hill Book Co., 1938-43; pub. relations specialist Chase Bank, N.Y.C., 1946-47; asst. to pres. in charge pub. relations Cornell U., 1947-51; dir. pub. and mem. relations Asso. Industries N.Y. State, Albany, 1951-71, editor Monitor, 1951-71; commr. Adirondack Park Agy., 1971—. Mem. Gov.'s Com. Mgmt. Improvement, 1966—. Mem. bd. edn. Bethlehem Central Sch. Dist., Albany, N.Y., 1959-64, v.p. bd. edn., 1961-62. Bd. dirs. N.Y. State Farm-City Council, N.Y. State Assn. Indsl. Devel. Agys., Schroon Lake Assn., Schroon Lake Council on The Arts. Served to lt. comdr. UNSR, 1943-46. Mem. Pub. Relations Seminar, Am. Coll. Pub. Relations Assn. (mem. exec. bd. 1948-51), Writers Alliance (v.p. 1966-68), Navy League U.S. (founder Upper Hudson council 1963, pres. council 1967-68), N.Y. State Sch. Bds. Assn. (mem. pub. relations com. 1960-64). Home: Severance NY 12872 also Coronado Sta New Smyrna Beach FL 32069 Office: Box 99 Ray Brook NY 12977

DANIELSON, ESKIL STUART, city ofcl.; b. Dover, N.J., Nov. 10, 1942; s. Eskil Lester and Ruth (Hiler) D.; B.A., Lehigh U., 1964; M.A., City U. N.Y., 1975; postgrad. U. Va., 1976; m. Judith Ann Billig, Aug. 15, 1964; children—Eskil Scott, Kevin William, Eric Christopher. Br. mgr. Gen. Electric Credit Co., East Orange, N.J., 1964-65; police officer, detective Chatham Borough (N.J.) Police Dept., 1966-69; law enforcement edn. coordinator County Coll. Morris, Dover, N.J., 1969-71; police chief Byram Twp. (N.J.) Police

Bradstreet, N.Y.C., 1967—; speaker to travel and transp. industry convs., 1959—; mem. mktg. authority Pacific Area Travel Assn., 1975-76; mem. travel adv. bd. U.S. Travel Service, Dept. Commerce, 1978—. Mem. Upper Manhattan Community Planning Bd., 1965. Served with AUS, 1953-55. Recipient nat. travel writing awards. Club: Wings (N.Y.C.). Contbg. travel editor Argosy Mag., 1962-72. Home: 106 Pinehurst Ave New York City NY 10033 Office: 888 7th Ave New York City NY 10019

DEVADASON, CHINNADURAI, physician; b. Gampola, Sri Lanka, Jan. 25, 1940; s. Jesudian Michael and Emily Arulmani (Vedamani) D.; M.D., U. Madras (India), 1965; D.P.H., U. Toronto (Ont., Can.), 1972; m. Annie Maida Lawrence, Sept. 21, 1966; children—Michael, Lawrence, Robert. Tutor faculty medicine Christian Med. Coll., Vellore, South India, 1965-66; med. officer Fed. Ministry Health Malaysia, Sarawak, 1966-70; med. cons. Canadian Exec. Service Overseas, Dominica, B.W.I., 1971; provincial epidemiologist, chief communicable disease control and maternal and child health N.B. (Can.) Dept. Health, Fredericton, 1972—; cons. Family Planning Assn. N.B., N.B. Safety Council. Recipient Most Illustrious Star of Sarawak-Ahli Bintang Sarawak, 1970. Fellow Soc. Med. Officers Eng. Royal Coll. Physicians Can., Am. Coll. Preventive Medicine; mem. Royal Coll. Surgeons (Eng.), U. Toronto Sch. Hygiene Alumni Assn. (past pres.), Royal Coll. Physicians (London) (licentiate), Malaysian Leprosy Relief Assn. (past pres. Sarawak state br.). Anglican. Home: 549 Smythe St Fredericton NB E3B 3E7 Canada Office: Dept Health PO Box 6000 Fredericton NB E3B 5H1 Canada

DEVANE, RICHARD THOMAS, sports cons. co. exec.; b. N.Y.C., May 24, 1955; s. John Patrick and Lorraine Elizabeth (Connolly) D.; A.B. cum laude, Princeton U., 1977. Pres. Found. for Student Communication, Princeton, N.J., 1975-76; mktg. rep. IBM Corp., Armonk, N.Y., 1977-78; exec. dir. Am. Sports Devel. Service, Hilton Head, S.C., 1978—; cons. Whirlpool Corp. Recipient Constn. Speech award N.Y. State Am. Legion, 1973. Mem. U.S.-China People's Friendship Assn., Nat. Catholic Forensic League, Regis Alumni Assn. Republican. Roman Catholic. Club: Cap and Gown, Doubles, Princeton. Author: Issues in US - China Relations, 1977; Entrepreneurs—Endangered Species, 1977; Clains and Assets in Sino-American Relations, 1978. Pub.: Business Today, 1976-77. Home: 65 Haddon Rd New Hyde Park NY 11040 Office: Soldiers Field Park Cambridge MA 02163

DEVEAUGH-GEISS, JOSEPH PAUL, psychiatrist; b. Rochester, N.Y., Apr. 7, 1946; s. Joseph Paul and Gilda (Sposato) Geiss; B.A. cum laude, Syracuse U., 1968; M.D., State U.N.Y. Upstate Med. Center, 1972; m. Joanne DeVeaugh, Aug. 17, 1974; children—Diana, Angela. Resident in psychiatry Upstate Med. Center State U.N.Y., Syracuse, 1972-75, chief resident psychiatry, 1974-75; instr. psychiatry, 1975-77, asst. prof., 1977—; staff psychiatrist Syracuse VA Hosp., 1975—; individual practice medicine, specializing in psychiatry, Syracuse, 1975—. Diplomate Nat. Bd. Med. Examiners, Am. Bd. Psychiatry and Neurology. Mem. Am. Psychiat. Assn. (gen.), AAAS, Am. Assn. Abolition Involuntary Mental Hospitalization. Contbr. articles to profl. jours. Researcher psychopharmcology, movement disorders. Home: 107 Lincklaen St Cazenovia NY 13035 Office: Dept Psychiatry Upstate Med Center State U NY 750 E Adams St Syracuse NY 13210

DEVEREUX, FRANCES CLARK, advt. exec.; b. Bronxville, N.Y.; d. Frederick Leonard and Ruth (Foste) D.; A.A., Mt. Vernon Coll., 1964; postgrad. N.Y. U., Alliance Française, Sorbonne U., Paris. Asst. account exec. Young & Rubicam, N.Y.C., 1965-67; campaign coordinator Stephen C. Hansen, N.Y.C., 1968; v.p. Ogilvy & Mather, N.Y.C., 1969—. Mem. adv. bd. Wildcat Corp. Tng. Center, 1978; coordinator work release program Jr. League N.Y., 1976; mem. woman's adv. com. N.Y. State Legislature, 1975. Mem. Am. Assn. Advt. Agys. (com. edn. 1976, com. equal opportunity employment 1977, 78). Democrat. Home: 17 W 9th St New York NY 10011 Office: 2 E 48 St New York NY 10012

DEVEREUX, FREDERICK LEONARD, JR., author; b. N.Y.C., Apr. 20, 1914; s. Frederick Leonard and Frances Beardsley (Clark) D.; student U. Chgo., 1933-36; m. Ruth Wentworth Foster, June 26, 1936 (dec. 1974); children—Orin Foster, Frances Clark, Frederick Leonard III. Buyer, R.H. Macy & Co., N.Y.C., 1936-39; merchandising exec. Young & Rubicam, Inc., N.Y.C., 1940-41, 45-52; gen. sales mgr. Oneita Knitting Mills, N.Y.C., 1953-55, also lectr. on mktg. N.Y. U. Grad. Sch. Bus. Adminstrn., 1953-54; v.p. Donald Deskey Assos., N.Y.C., 1956-60; mktg. mgr. Allied Stores, N.Y.C., 1961-64; pres. Merit Stores, Inc., N.Y.C., 1965-70; author: Practical Navigation for the Yachtsman, 1972, Ride Your Pony Right, 1974, Horses, 1974, Backyard Pony, 1974, Famous American Horses, 1975, Horseback Riding, 1975, Jump Your Horse Right, 1976, Horse Problems and Problem Horses, 1978; editor The Cavalry Manual of Horsemanship, 1978; contbr. articles to Jour. of Nav., Yachting mag., others. Served from pvt. to lt. col. Gen. Staff Corps, AUS, 1941-45. Mem. Inst. Nav., U.S. Power Squadron (edni. com.), Am. Horse Shows Assn. (past sr. judge, stewards com.), Alpha Delta Phi. Republican. Episcopalian. Clubs: Am. Yacht (Rye, N.Y.); Quechee Polo (v.p.) (Woodstock, Vt.). Home: Fiddler's Green Woodstock VT 05091 Office: 5 Central St Woodstock VT 05091

DEVEREUX, JOSEPH FRANCIS, JR., lawyer; b. St. Louis, Apr. 1, 1949; s. Joseph Francis and Patricia Ann (Leonard) D.; B.S., St. Louis U., 1971, J.D., 1974; m. Susan R. Moutrie, June 12, 1976. With Ralston Purina Co., St. Louis, 1973-74; admitted to Mo. bar, 1974, D.C. bar, 1976; with Dept. Justice, 1974-75; with firm Haight, Gardner, Poor & Havens, Washington, 1975—. Served with AUS, 1974. Mem. Am., Mo., D.C. bar assns., Alpha Sigma Nu. Democrat. Roman Catholic. Mem. staff St. Louis U. Law Jour., 1973. Home: 3495 S Utah St Arlington VA 22206 Office: 1819 H St NW Suite 1050 Washington DC 20006

DEVERS, CHARLOTTE MARGUERITE (MRS. WILLIAM PETER DEVERS), library adminstr.; b. N.Y.C., Aug. 10, 1923; d. Edward C. and Charlotte C. (Wilson) Madison; B.A., Cornell U., 1944; M.S., Columbia, 1958; certificate Ballard Sch., 1956; m. William Peter Devers, Dec. 23, 1967. Research librarian Hearst Publs., N.Y.C., 1954-56; librarian TV Bur. Advt., Inc., N.Y.C., 1956-58; head librarian Compton Advt., Inc., N.Y.C., 1956-58; supr. tech. library Gen. Dynamics/Electronics, Rochester, N.Y., 1963-65; mgr. information services Curtiss-Wright Corp., Woodridge, N.J., 1965-68; dir. North Castle Pub. Library, Armonk, N.Y., 1968—. Cons. to CEIR Corp., N.Y.C., 1967-68; guest lectr. U. Buffalo Grad. Sch. Library and Info. Scis., 1968; panelist Westchester Conf. on Libraries, 1977; del. N.Y. State Gov.'s Conf. on Libraries, 1978. Co-chmn. Town of North Castle Bicentennial Com. Mem. Friends of North Castle Pub. Library, 1968—. Mem. Pub. Library Dirs. Assn. (pres. 1971), Spl. Libraries Assn. (chmn. editorial bd. 1968-70, pres. N.Y. chpt. 1961-63, sec. aerospace div. 1967-68, pres. advt. div. 1960-61), ALA, Green Acres Garden Club, N.Y. Library Assn., North Castle Hist. Soc., League Women Voters. Club: Whippoorwill. Co-editor Guide to Special Issues and Indexes of Periodicals, 1963, 2d edit., 1976. Home: Windmill Farm Armonk NY 10504 Office: 19 Whippoorwill Rd East Armonk NY 10504

DEVINE, C. ROBERT, pub. co. exec.; b. Clarksburg, W.Va., June 13, 1917; s. James J. and Frances M. (Ryan) D.; grad. Princeton U., 1938; D.H.L., Fairleigh Dickinson U., 1976; m. Louise C. Williams, Mar. 27, 1943 (div. 1958); children—Mallory C., Rodney W., Ian C.; m. 2d, Gisele Edenbourgh Lichine, Dec. 23, 1966. Promotion, research dir. U.S. News Pub. Co., 1946-48, asst. advt. dir., 1948-55; exec. bus. dept. Reader's Digest, N.Y.C., 1955-58, advt. dir. internat. edits., 1958-60, asst. gen. mgr., 1960-66, dep. gen. mgr. internat. edits., 1966-68, v.p. Readers Digest Assn., Inc., 1968—. Bd. dirs. Met. Opera Assn., Am. U. in Cairo, Am. Hosp. of Istanbul, Vail-Deane Sch. Mem. pub. affairs research council Nat. Indsl. Conf. Bd. Served from pvt. to maj. AUS, World War II. Decorated Bronze Star medal. Mem. Mil. Order Fgn. Wars, Assn. U.S. Army, Sales Exec. Club (internat. mktg. com.), Internat. Advt. Assn. (pres. 1962-64, dir.-at-large, chmn. 1976—), Internat. C. of C., Mag. Pubs. Assn. (chmn. internat. com. 1964-70), NAM, Pub. Relations Soc. Am., Internat. Fedn. Periodical Press (v.p. 1978—). Republican. Episcopalian. Clubs: Squadron A, River, Pilgrims, Union, Dutch Treat (N.Y.C.). Home: 101 E 69th St New York City NY 10021 Office: 200 Park Ave New York City NY 10017

DEVINE, JAMES JOSEPH, chem. engr.; b. Bklyn., Aug. 14, 1926; s. Peter Charles and Gertrude Marie (Flanagan) D.; B.S. in Chem. Engring., Bucknell U., 1950; M.B.A., Rutgers U., 1959; m. Maud Hearn, Apr. 18, 1953; children—Lynn, Jeffrey, Drew Douglas. Supr., Merck & Co., Elkton, Va., 1950-51, Danville, Pa., 1951-53; asst. plant mgr. Clorox C., Jersey City, 1954-59; coating supt. Natvar Corp., Rahway, N.J., 1959-66; organic plant supt. Vulcan Materials, Newark, 1966-69; mfg. mgr. Shulton Inc., Clifton, N.J., 1969-72; chem. mfg. mgr. Fisher Sci. Co., Fairlawn, N.J., 1972—. Served with USN, 1944-46; PTO. Mem. Am. Chem. Soc., Am. Inst. Clin. Chemistry, Am. Inst. Chem. Engrs., Alpha Chi Sigma, Sigma Chi. Republican. Roman Catholic. Home: 32 Terrill Rd Old Bridge NJ 08857 Office: 1 Reagent Ln Fairlawn NJ 07410

DEVINE, JOANNE FRANCES, nursing adminstr.; b. Jersey City, May 9, 1942; d. Joseph John and Isabel (Spence) D.; diploma St. Mary Sch. Nursing, Orange, N.J., 1963; B.A. in Health Edn. and Nursing, Jersey City State Coll., 1965; M.S. in Nursing Adminstrn., Syracuse U., 1968. Staff nurse St. Mary Hosp., Orange, 1963-65, asso. instr., 1965-66; dir. nursing St. James Hosp., Newark, 1968—. Mem. Am., N.J. nurses assns., Nat. League Nurses, N.J. Soc. Nursing Service Adminstrs. Clubs: Arlington Tennis Players (sec. 1978), St. James Bowling League (v.p. 1978). Home: 8 Davidson St Belleville NJ 07109 Office: 155 Jefferson St Newark NJ 07105

DEVITO, ALBERT KENNETH, musician, composer, editor/publisher; b. Hartford, Conn., Jan. 17, 1919; s. Ralph and Rose (Abronze) DeV.; student Hartford Fed. Coll., 1939-41, Columbia U., 1950-52; B.S., N.Y. U., 1948, M.A., 1950; Ph.D., Midwestern U., 1975; Mus.D. (hon.), E. Nebr. Christian Coll., 1974. Mgr., G. Schirmer, Inc., N.Y.C., 1948-52; instr. Westbury (N.Y.) Pub. Schs., 1952-55; author 11 chord and instruction music books; composer piano sonata, over 15 chorals, 5 organ solos, over 55 piano solos, 2 vocal solos, 2 popular songs; author instruction books 12 for chord organs, 5 organ methods books, 5 piano method books, 1 music terms dictionary, 2 piano arrangements; compiler original works 16 collections for organ, 11 collections for piano; contbr. piano arrangements of sch. music instruction, book series; lectr. and cons. in field. Served with inf., Spl. Services, U.S. Army, 1942-46, Decorated Victory medal, Am., European, African, Middle East theatre campaign ribbons; recipient numerous prizes in music, panel awards, ASCAP; recipient certificate of merit proclaimed throughout world for distinguished service to community Internat. Biography Assn., 1975; Merit award Nat. Fedn. Music Clubs, 1974. Mem. Internat. Platform Assn., Inter-continental Biog. Assn., Am. Choral Dirs. Assn., Am. Music Center, N.Y. State Music Tchr. Assn., ASCAP, Am. Soc. Composers, Author and Pubs. Assn., Asso. Musicians Greater N.Y., Asso. Music Tchrs. League, Music Educators Nat. Conf., Internat. Assos. Organ Tchrs., Piano Tchrs. Congress. Phi Mu Alpha Sinfonic, Piano Tchrs. Congress N.Y.C., N.Y. State Sch. Music Assn., Nat. Geog. Soc. Contbr. over 35 articles in field to profl. jours.; editor, contbr.: Technical Control for the Modern Pianist. Address: 361 Pin Oak Ln Westbury NY 11590

DE VITO, LORENZO, food service exec.; b. Salerno, Italy, Sept. 21, 1936; s. Americo and Tullia (Falivene) DeVito; came to U.S., 1957, naturalized, 1971; B.S., Coll. Agr., Eboly, Italy, 1958; postgrad. Fairfield U., 1970; m. Rosaria Di Feo, Feb. 3, 1960; children—John A., Lorenzo, Santina T. Chef, Waterbury (Conn.) Hosp., 1960-69, asst. food service dir., 1969-72; food service dir. Central Suffolk Hosp., Riverhead, N.Y., 1972—. Served with U.S. Army N.G., 1962. Mem. Nat. Adv. Council. Roman Catholic. Club: Moose. Home: 55 Kings Dr Riverhead NY 11901 Office: 1300 Roanoke Ave Riverhead NY 11901

DEVLIN, ANNE G., newspaper editor; b. Cleve., Apr. 23, 1950; d. Max J. and Elinor D. (Sussman) Gartenberg; B.A., Northeastern U., 1972; m. Robert D. Devlin, May 16, 1976. Reporter, Today's Spirit newspaper, Hatboro, Pa., 1973-74, Souderton Ind. newspaper, Souderton, Pa., 1973-74; editor Greater Phila. Group newspapers and the Gazette newspapers, Phila., 1974—. Bd. dirs. Horrowgate Community Center, Phila., 1977—. Recipient citation City of Phila., 1977; award Palmer Cemetery, Phila., 1976; citation U.S. Congress, 1978. Home: 912 N Pennsylvania Ave Morrisville PA 19067 Office: 250 W Girard Ave Philadelphia PA 19123

DEVLIN, HARRY, artist, writer; b. Jersey City, Mar. 22, 1918; s. Harry George and Amelia Fredrica (Crawford) D.; B.F.A., Syracuse U., 1939; m. Dorothy Louise Wende, Aug. 30, 1941; children—Harry Noel, Wende Elizabeth, Jeffrey Anthony, Alexandria Gail, Brion Phillip, Nicholas Kirk, David Matthew. Editorial cartoonist Colliers mag., 1946-54; editorial cartoonist N.Y. Daily News, 1956; syndicated cartoonist Raggmopp, 1954-57; author 14 children's books including Old Black Witch, 1963; How Fletcher Was Hatched, 1969; To Grandfather's House We Go, 1967; What Kind of House if That?, 1969; Tales of Thunder and Lightning, 1975; Cranberry Christmas, 1976; host, writer 3 films on architecture, 1977; host, narrator documentary To Grandfather's House We Go, 1979. Mem. N.J. State Council on Arts, 1971—, vice chmn., 1977. Served with USN, 1942-46. Recipient Arents medal Syracuse U., 1977. Mem. Soc. Illustrators, Nat. Cartoonist Soc. (pres. 1954), Artists Equity. Republican. Congregationalist. Club: Beacon Hill. Address: 443 Hillside Ave Mountainside NJ 07092

DEVLIN, JOHN FRANCIS, accountant; b. Northampton, Mass., June 18, 1943; s. William Elliot and Catherine Ellen (Meehan) D.; student Northampton Jr. Coll., 1966-68, Am. Internat. Coll., 1968-70; m. Mary C. O'Connor, June 8, 1974; children—Jeremiah F., Brendan M. Accountant, Coopers & Lybrand, Springfield, Mass., 1970—. Served with USN, 1961-66. C.P.A., Mass. Mem. Am. Inst. C.P.A.'s, Mass. Soc. C.P.A.'s, Alpha Chi. Roman Catholic. Club: John Boyle O'Reilly. Home: 53 Park Hill Rd Northampton MA 01060 Office: Coopers & Lybrand 2300 Valley Bank Tower Springfield MA 01101

DEVLIN, ROBERT MARTIN, educator, plant physiologist; b. Albany, N.Y., Oct. 13, 1931; s. Patrick C. and Katherine (Martin) D.; B.S., N.Y. State U. at Albany, 1959; M.S. (Grad. fellow), Dartmouth, 1961; Ph.D., U. Md., 1963; m. Wanda T. Karandy, July 10, 1960; children—William R., Theresa A., Michael P. Grad. teaching asst., botany dept. U. Md., 1961-63; asst. prof. plant physiology N.D. State U., 1963-65; asso. prof. plant physiology U. Mass., 1965-72, prof., 1972—. Instr. grad. courses Northeastern U., 1968—. Town Mem., Barnstable, Mass., 1970-73; Served with AUS, 1952-54. EPA research grantee, 1969-74. Mem. Am. Soc. Plant Physiologists, Am. Soc. Hort. Sci., Internat. Platform Assn., Nat. Council for Environ. Balance, Council for Agrl. Sci. and Tech., Sigma Xi, Phi Sigma. Club: Explorers. Author: Plant Physiology, 1966, 3d edit., 1975; Experiments in Plant Physiology, 1970. Photosynthesis, 1971; Biology of Human Concern, 1972. Contbr. articles to profl. jours. Home: 157 Bristol St Hyannis MA 02601 Office: U Mass East Wareham MA 02538

DE VOID, KENNETH EARL, JR., educator; b. Keene, N.H., Nov. 8, 1945; s. Kenneth Earl and Beverly C. (Bressett) De V.; B.E., Keene State Coll., 1968, M.Ed., 1971. Instr. spl. edn. Keene State Coll., U. N.H., 1970-74, dir. Mental Retardation Clinic, 1971-74; dir. Nashua Center for Multiply Handicapped (N.H.), 1975-77; dir. spl. edn. Fall Mountain Regional Sch. Dist., Charlestown, N.H., 1977—; instr. spl. edn. Rivier Coll., Nashua. Mem. Nat., N.H. edn. assns., Council Exceptional Children, Am. Assn. Mental Deficiency. Author: Six in Depth: Readings for the Prospective Special Educator, 1974. Home: Old Meeting House Rd Walpole NH 03608

DEWEES, DONALD CHARLES, securities co. exec.; b. Phila., Sept. 7, 1931; s. John Coleman and Elva (Burke) DeW.; B.S. in Commerce and Finance, Bucknell U., 1953; M.B.A., Wharton Sch., U. Pa., 1954; m. Martha V. Folk, July 31, 1954; children—Donald C., Suzanne C., Gretchen F. Data processing rep. Nat. Cash Register Co., Wilmington, Del., 1954-62; account rep. Francis I. duPont Co., investments, Wilmington, 1962-67, br. mgr., Balt., 1968; br. mgr. Butcher & Singer, Wilmington, 1969-71, v.p., 1971-76, 1st v.p., 1977, sr. v.p., 1978—, resident mgr., 1969-76, ltd. partner, 1976—; dir. Mgmt. Scis. Inc., Bus. Trends Inc.; cons. in field. Active Wilmington YMCA. Served with AUS, 1954-56, 58-59; Korea. Mem. Fin. Analysts Soc., Am. Philatelic Soc., Phi Kappa Psi. Republican. Methodist. Mason (32 deg., Shriner). Clubs: University (Wilmington); Turf (Delaware Park, Del.). Author sales tng. publs. Home: 6 Harlech Dr Anglesey St Wilmington DE 19807 Office: Suite 1106 Bank of Del Bldg 300 Delaware Ave Wilmington DE 19899

DEWELL, WILBUR, bus. exec.; b. Cushing, Iowa, Dec. 1, 1890; s. George Allen and Agnes Woodside (Moore) D.; student Morningside Coll., Sioux City, Iowa; m. Minna Ehlers, Nov. 24, 1909; 1 son, Lloyd (dec.). Sales mgr. Churchill Drug, Burlington, Iowa, 1922-27; gen. mgr. McKesson & Robbins, Inc., Burlington, 1927-29, Bridgeport, Conn., 1929-57, v.p., 1934-57, dir., 1943-57; gen. mgr. McKesson Labs., Bridgeport, 1929-57; founder, owner Wilbur E. Dewell Assos., mktg. and mergers, Fairfield, Conn., 1957—; chmn. bd. Bishop Industries, mktg. and mergers, 1957-75. Named hon. Ky. col. Mem. Mfrs. Assn. Bridgeport, C. of C. Methodist. Clubs: Masons, Shriners, Rotary; Algonquin (Bridgeport). Home: 494 Hill Farm Rd Fairfield CT 06430 Office: 1424 Post Rd Fairfield CT 06430

DEWEY, CLARENCE FORBES, JR., educator; b. Pueblo, Colo., Mar. 27, 1935; s. Clarence Forbes and Elsie Louise (Hafermalz) D.; B.E., Yale, 1956; M.S. (Douglas fellow), Stanford, 1957; Ph.D. (NSF fellow), Calif. Inst. Tech., 1963; m. Carolyn Miller, Aug. 3, 1963; 1 son, Devan Forbes. Aero. research scientist NASA, Ames, Calif., 1956; mem. tech. staff aeronutronic div. Ford Corp., Newport Beach, Calif., 1957-59; asst. prof. U. Colo., Boulder, 1963-68; faculty fellow, vis. scientist Institut fur Plasmaphysik, Garching, Germany, 1966-67; asso. prof. Mass. Inst. Tech., Cambridge, 1968-76, prof. mech. engring., 1976—; vis. prof. pathology Harvard U. Med. Sch., 1978-79; chmn. bd. Sensoresearch Corp.; cons. in field to numerous engring. and sci. orgns. including Rand Corp., Mass. Gen. Hosp., Avco Corp., Boeing Sci. Research Lab., Faulkner Hosp., Thermo Electron Corp., Allied Chem. Co., Kaye Instruments, Gould, Inc. Trustee, Cardiovascular Trust of Boston, 1974—. Mem. Yale Engring. Assn., Am. Phys. Soc., Coblenz Soc., Sigma Xi, Tau Beta Pi. Contbr. articles in field to profl. jours.; patentee in field. Home: 57 Orne St Marblehead MA 01945 Office: Room 3-250 Mass Inst Tech Cambridge MA 02139

DEXHEIMER, JOHN PATRICK, sch. psychologist; b. Charleston, W.Va., May 11, 1945; s. Robert Donald and Mary Jacqueline (Andersen) D.; B.A., N. Central Coll., 1968; M.S., U. R.I., 1970. Sr. sch. psychologist Attleboro (Mass.) Pub. Schs., 1970—. Mem. Am. Psychol. Assn., R.I. Sch. Psychologists Assn. (dir. 1973-75), R.I. Mental Health Assn. Club: Kent County YMCA Judo (pres. 1976—, sr. instr. 1977—). Home: 28 Cynthia Dr Coventry RI 02816 Office: 28 Sanford St Attleboro MA 02703

DEXTER, CAROLYN R., sociologist, educator; b. Washington; d. Harris Edward and Florence Anna (Isbell) Dexter; B.S., St. Lawrence U., 1948; M.A., Columbia, 1959, Ph.D., 1967. Mgr. safe deposit dept. First Nat. Bank, Poughkeepsie, N.Y., 1948-53; research asst., personnel research IBM, Poughkeepsie, 1953-59; research intern Bur. of Applied Social Research, Columbia, N.Y.C., 1958-60; asst. dir. research Girl Scouts Am., N.Y.C., 1960- 65; cons. marketing program evaluation, N.Y.C., 1965-67; sociologist John Hancock Mut. Life Ins. Co., Boston, 1967-69; asso. prof. Pa. State U., Middletown, 1969—. Lectr. methodology Boston U., 1968-69. Treas., Jr. League of Poughkeepsie, N.Y., 1957-58. Recipient grants Columbia U., Pa. State U., 1971-74. Mem. Internat., Am. sociol. assns., Am. Mktg. Assn. (pres. Central Pa. 1973-74), Pa. Sociol. Soc. (treas. 1976-77, pres. 1977-78), Nat. Assn. State Sociol. Assns. (pres. 1978-79), N.Y. State Safe Deposit Assn. (sec. 1948-53). Asso. editor Pacific Sociol. Rev. Contbr. articles to profl. publs. Home: 660 Boas St Harrisburg PA 17102 Office: Penn State Univ Capitol Campus Middletown PA 17057

DEXTER, MARVIN JUDSON, physician, surgeon; b. Utica, N.Y., Aug. 9, 1919; m. Arnot and Grace Agnes (Loomis) D.; A.B., Syracuse U., 1941, M.D., 1944; m. Barbara Gertrude Tremmel, June 27, 1944; children—Carol, David, Babette. Intern, Ellis Hosp., Schnectady, 1944-45, resident in surgery, 1945-46; gen. practice medicine and surgery, Fulton, N.Y., 1948—; mem. bd. health City of Fulton, 1952-56; mem. bd. mgrs. Oswego County (N.Y.) Mental Health Hosp., Oswego County Lab.; adviser energy conservation U.S. Congress, 1974-75. Served to capt. M.C. U.S. Army, 1946-48. Mem. N.Y., Oswego County med. socs., Assn. Mil. Surgeons. Republican. Baptist. Home: RD 3 Wilobob Terr Fulton NY 13069 Office: 224 Oneida St Fulton NY 13069

DEXTRAZE, JACQUES ALFRED, railway system exec.; b. Montreal, Que., Can., Aug. 15, 1919; s. Alfred and Amanda (Bond) D.; student MacDonald Bus. Coll., Montreal, Columbia U.; Ph.D. in Bus. Adminstrn., Sherbrooke U.; m. Frances Helena Pare, Sept. 2, 1942; children—Jack, Robert, Richard, John. With Dominion Rubber Co., 1938-40; with Singer Mfg. Co., 1945-50, mgr. forestry ops., 1947-50; commd. officer Canadian Armed Forces, advanced through grades to gen.; gen. staff officer, Quebec, 1954-55, chief of staff, 1956-57; comdt. Royal Canadian Sch. Inf., Camp Borden, Ont., 1957-60; comdr. Camp Valcartier, Que., 1960-62, Eastern Que. Area, 1962; chief of staff Hdqrs. UN Ops. in Congo, 1963-64; comdr. 2d

Canadian Inf. Brigrade Group, 1964-66; chief of staff Hdqrs. Mobile Command, 1966-67; dep. comdr. Mobile Command, 1967; dep. chief of personnel Canadian Forces Hdqrs., 1967-69, chief of personnel, 1970-72, chief Def. Staff, 1972-77; ret., 1977; chmn. bd. Canadian Nat. Rys. System, Ottawa, Ont., 1977—; mem. Canadian Com. to Tripartite Mil. Conf., 1957, Internat. Com. for Standardization of Arms and Nat. Mil. Resources, 1957-60; hon. a.d.c. to gov. gen. Can., 1958. Decorated comdr. Order Brit. Empire, Order Mil. Merit, D.S.M., Canadian Forces Decoration; cross of grand officer Order of Crown (Belgium). Roman Catholic. Office: Canadian Nat Rys Systems 935 Lagauchetiere St W Montreal PQ H3C 3N4 Canada*

DEY, LOCHLANN BRUCE, accountant; b. Bristol, Pa., June 2, 1937; s. William and Althea Lucretia (Butt) D.; B.S., Pa. State U., 1960; M.B.A., City U. N.Y., 1968; m. Donna Marie Adams, June 2, 1962; children—Lochlann, Adam, Diana. Sr. accountant Price Waterhouse & Co., N.Y.C., 1960-67; comptroller Met. Opera Assn., Inc., N.Y.C., 1967-71; treas. Am. Home Shield Corp., Paramus, N.J., 1971-73; asst. dir. exams. div. Am. Inst. C.P.A.'s, N.Y.C., 1973—. Mem. Wanaque (N.J.) Bd. Edn., 1972-78, v.p., 1973, pres., 1974; mem. middle mgmt. tenure com. N.J. Sch. Bds. Assn., 1974-75, com. to study tchr. tenure, 1977; bd. dirs. Wanaque Community Center, Inc., 1977—. Served with U.S. Army, 1960-61. C.P.A., N.Y. Mem. Am. Inst. C.P.A.'s, N.Y. State Soc. C.P.A.'s, Alpha Kappa Psi. Home: 13 Morningside Pl Wanaque NJ 07465 Office: 1211 Ave of Americas New York City NY 10036

DEYOE, WARNER STANLEY, health care adminstr.; b. Kinderhook, N.Y., Jan. 3, 1926; s. Frank Searing and Helen Elizabeth (Warner) D.; diploma Albany Bus. Coll.; m. A. Pauline McKay, Apr. 1, 1955; children—George Searing, Helene Ann, Carole Pauline. Purchasing agt. Columbia Meml. Hosp., Hudson, N.Y., 1949-54; purchasing agt., dir. purchases St. Johns Episcopal Hosp., Bklyn., 1954-56; dir. purchasing services N.Y.U. Med. Center, 1956-69, dir. material services, 1969—; lectr. Wagner Coll., Inst. Internat. Med. Edn. Served with U.S. Army, 1944-46. Decorated D.S.C., Bronze Star, Purple Heart with cluster; Croix de Guerre (France). Mem. Nat. Assn. Edn. Buyers, Hosp. Purchasing Agts. Assn. Greater N.Y. (pres. 1975-77), Am. Soc. Hosp. Purchasing (pres. elect 1978, pres. 1979), Am. Hosp. Assn., VFW, 78th Div. Vets. Assn. Contbr. articles to hosp. jours. Office: 550 1st Ave New York City NY 10016

DHAWAN, SWARAN SETH, social worker; b. Simla, Himachel Pradesh, India; d. Kesar Chand and Leela (Khanna) Seth; B.S., Miranda House Delhi U., 1953; M.S.W., M.S. U., Baroda, India, 1958; M.S.W., Smith Coll., 1963; 1 dau., Shubanjali Dhawan. Lectr., psychiat. social worker M.S. U., Baroda, 1958-62; casework supr. Family and Childrens Soc., Balt., 1963—, now dir. profl. services; dir. social service Taylor Manor Hosp., Ellicot City, Md., 1968—; asst. clin. prof. Smith Coll. Bd. dirs. Md. Action for Foster Children, Balt. Recipient Spl. award P.E.O., 1962. Mem. Nat. Assn. Social Workers, Council on Social Work Edn., Family Service Assn. Am., Md. Conf. Social Concern, Am. Soc. for Hosp. Social Work Dirs., Smithsonian Assos. Home: 4 Olmsted Green Baltimore MD 21210 Office: 204 W Lanvale St Baltimore MD 21217

DIAMOND, ALAN SHEVRIN, surgeon; b. Schenectady, Nov. 2, 1936; s. Alexander and Rose D.; B.A., Harvard U., 1958; M.D., Tufts U., 1962; m. Harriet Gorfinkle, June 18, 1961; children—Amy, Lisa, Jill. Intern in surgery Albany (N.Y.) Med. Center, 1962-63; resident in surgery Buffalo Gen. Hosp., 1963-67; practice medicine specializing in surgery, Lynn, Mass., 1969—; mem. staffs Lynn, Union and Saugus Gen. hosps. Trustee N. Shore Health Planning Council, 1976—, chmn. S. Essex sub area council. Served with USAF, 1967-69. Decorated Bronze Star. Diplomate Am. Bd. Surgery. Fellow A.C.S.; mem. Mass. Med. Soc., Essex Surg. Soc., Essex S. Med. Soc. (councillor), Phi Delta Epsilon. Office: Boston St Lynn MA 01904

DIAMOND, DANIEL JOSEPH, editor; b. Bronx, N.Y., Sept. 28, 1936; s. Daniel Joseph and Elizabeth (Curtis) D.; student Kans. State Coll., 1957; certificate in Architecture, Inst. Design and Constrn., N.Y.C., 1960. Asst. supr. Naclerio Contracting, N.Y.C., 1960-63, Gotham Constrn., N.Y.C., 1963-65; supr. Underpinning & Founds., N.Y.C., 1965-68; gen. supr. Welsbach Concrete Systems, Howell, N.J., 1968-74; writer Soho Weekly News, N.Y.C., 1974-75, city hall editor, 1975-77; mng. editor Our Town newspaper, N.Y.C., 1977; mng. editor Yonkers Times Pub. Co., 1977—. Founder, pres. W. Bronx Community Council, 1966-70; trustee S.W. Bronx Civic League, 1969-72. Fund for Investigative Journalism grantee, 1976. Mem. Investigative Reporters and Editors. Democrat. Roman Catholic. Home: 2366 Grand Concourse Bronx NY 10458 Office: 38 Larkin Plaza Yonkers NY 10701

DIAMOND, ISRAEL, physician; b. Flint, Mich., Aug. 1, 1914; s. Leo and Nessie (Jenchelska) D.; B.S., Coll. City N.Y., 1934; M.D., U. Edinburgh (Scotland), 1939; m. Thelma Greenberg, May 6, 1942; 1 son, Jonathan R. Intern, Met. Hosp., N.Y.C., 1940, Lincoln Hosp., N.Y.C., 1941; practice medicine, specializing in pathology, 1942—; resident, Univ. Hosp., Boston, 1946-47; asso. pathologist Childrens Hosp., Boston, 1948-52; dir. labs. Childrens Hosp., Louisville, 1952-60; dir. labs. Lutheran Med. Center, N.Y.C., 1960-68, now cons.; chmn. dept. lab. medicine Roger Williams Gen. Hosp., Providence, also prof. pathology Brown U., 1968—. Cons., VA Hosp., Miriam Hosp., Providence. Served with AUS, 1942-46. Fellow Coll. Am. Pathologists, Am. Soc. Clin. Pathology. Club: University (Providence). Home: 54 Brimmer St Boston MA 02108 Office: 825 Chalkstone Ave Providence RI 02908

DIAMOND, JACK JUDAH, researcher, demographer; b. N.Y.C., June 17, 1917; s. Harry and Sophie (Tannenbaum) D.; B.S., City Coll. N.Y., 1937, M.B.A., 1948; B.H.L., Jewish Theol. Sem., 1941; m. Mildred Greenberg, June 16, 1951 (dec. Sept. 1963); 1 son, Harvey Scott; m. 2d, Judith Gans Cheslow, Aug. 20, 1966; children—Sharon and Elayne Cheslow. Asst. budget officer Am. Export Lines, N.Y.C., 1944-48; free lance research, N.Y.C., 1948-50; research statistician Jewish Edn. Com., N.Y.C., 1950-58, United Hias Service, N.Y.C., 1958-68, Joint Distbn. Com., 1968-70, Meml. Found. for Jewish Culture, N.Y.C., 1970-71, Jewish Child Care Assn. N.Y., 1971-76, Jewish Community Services of L.I., 1976-77, First Investors Corp., 1977—. Mem. Am. Econ. Assn., Am. Hist. Assn. Contbr. articles to profl. jours., encys., books. Home: 14-34 Point Breeze Pl Far Rockaway NY 11691 Office: 2 Pennsylvania Plaza New York City NY 10001

DIAMOND, M. JEROME, atty. gen. Vt.; b. Chgo., Mar. 16, 1942; A.B., George Washington U., 1963; M.A., U. Tenn., 1965, J.D., 1968. Law clk. to U.S. Dist. judge, 1968-69; state's atty. Windham County (Vt.), 1970-74; atty. gen. State of Vt., 1975—; mem. Vt. Criminal Justice Tng. Council. Past pres. Brattleboro (Vt.) Civic Club; chmn. Putney Zoning Bd. Adjustment, 1971-74. Mem. Nat. Assn. Attys. Gen. (v.p. 1978-79), Vt. State's Attys. Assn. (past pres.). Office: Atty Gen of Vt Pavilion Office Bldg 109 State St Montpelier VT 05602*

DIAMOND, MARTIN HOWARD, endodontist; b. N.Y.C., July 26, 1943; s. Samuel and Lillian (Weissman) D.; B.A., Queen's Coll., 1966; D.M.D., U. Pa., 1968; m. Nancy Ruth Golove, Aug. 14, 1966; children—Seth Corey, Greg Adam. Rotating dental intern L.I. Jewish Med. Center, 1968-69, resident endodontics, 1969-71; practice dentistry, specializing in endodontics, Mamaroneck, N.Y., 1971—; attending staff Sloan Kettering Inst. Meml. Hosp., N.Y., Grasslands Hosp., Valhalla, N.Y.; vis. lectr. Columbia U. Dental Sch.; cons. endodontics United Hosp., Port Chester, N.Y. Mem. Am. Assn. Endodontists, Am. Dental Assn., N.Y. State, 9th Dist., Suburban dental socs., Tri State Soc. Endodontists, Westchester Shore Dental Forum, Westchester Acad. Medicine, Alpha Omega. Office: 1600 Harrison Ave Mamaroneck NY 10543

DIAMONDSTONE, LAWRENCE, paper co. exec.; b. N.Y.C., Mar. 27, 1928; s. Harry A. and Sally (Margulies) D.; B.S., U. Ill., 1950; m. Marilyn Dick, Dec. 23, 1960; 1 dau., Cynthia Ann. Founder, pres. Newbrook Paper Corp., N.Y.C., 1958—, Cottonwood Converting Corp., Memphis, 1972—, Garden State Converters Inc., Bayonne, N.J., 1973—, Triangle Mktg. Corp., N.Y.C., 1975—. Mem. Paper Mchts. Assn. N.Y., Phi Epsilon Pi. Home: 650 Park Ave New York City NY 10021 Office: 32 Bleecker St New York City NY 10012

DI AMORE, JOSEPH ROBERT, educator; b. Camden, N.J., Mar. 21, 1948; s. Joseph William and Josephine Marie (Dignazio) Di A.; A.A., Camden County Coll., 1969; B.A. in Biology, Glassboro State Coll., 1977; m. Barbara A. Grigg, Aug. 23, 1969; children—Cynthia Ann Marie, Joseph John. Tchr. Roman Catholic schs., Camden, 1970-72; chief research technician research and devel. Control Research Products, Inc., Cinnamunson, N.J., 1972-74; tchr. sci. St. Teresa Sch., Runnemede, N.J., 1974—. Chmn. bd. Christian edn. St. Maria Gonetti Ch., Runnemede. Mem. Smithsonian Assos., Am. Chem. Soc. Home: 713 Hirsch Ave Runnemede NJ 08078 Office: Evesham Rd Runnemede NJ 08078

DIAS, EARL JOSEPH, educator; b. New Bedford, Mass., Mar. 23, 1916; s. John F. and Virginia (Alexander) D.; A.B. magna cum laude, Bates Coll., 1937; M.A., Boston U., 1938; postgrad. Shakespeare Inst. (Stratford, Eng.), 1957-60, U. London, 1960; m. Edith G. Kenny, Aug. 18, 1951. Tchr. English, dir. student publs. Fairhaven (Mass.) High Sch., 1938-58; prof. English, New Bedford Inst. Tech., 1958-64; prof. English, chmn. dept. Southeastern Mass. U., Dartmouth, 1958—; drama, music critic New Bedford (Mass.) Standard-Times, 1947—. Mem. Fairhaven Town Meeting, 1950—. Chmn. bd. trustees Millicent Library, Fairhaven, Mass.; dir. New Bedford Symphony Orch. Mem. Coll. English Assn., Coll. Entrance Exam Bd., Thoreau Soc., Nat. Council Tchrs. English, Shakespeare Assn., Modern Lang. Assn., AAUP, Nat. Screen Council, Phi Beta Kappa. Author: Melodramas and Farces for Young Actors, 1956; One Act Plays for Teen-Agers, 1961; New Comedies for Teen-agers, 1967; Mark Twain's Letters to the Rogers Family, 1970; Henry Huttleston Rogers: Portrait of a Capitalist, 1974; also various articles pub. in profl. jours. Home: 52 Walnut St Fairhaven MA 02719 Office: Southeastern Mass Univ North Dartmouth MA 02747

DIAZ, CARLOS RICARDO, physician; b. San Juan, P.R., July 23, 1946; s. Alberto and Beverly (Diaz Romero) Diaz Atiles; A.B., Johns Hopkins U., 1968; M.D., George Washington U., 1972; m. Kathleen Fuller Mahagan, Aug. 9, 1969; children—Carlos Alejandro, David Ricardo. Intern, VA Hosp. D.C., 1972-73; resident in internal medicine George Washington U. Hosp., Washington, 1973-75; fellow in infectious diseases VA Hosp. D.C., 1975-77; practice medicine, specializing in internal medicine, Washington, 1977—; asst. dir. dept. emergency services Greater S.E. Community Hosp., Washington, 1977—; cons. internal medicine VA Hosp. D.C., 1977—. Diplomate Am. Bd. Internal Medicine. Mem. AMA, Med. Soc. D.C. Republican. Roman Catholic. Club: Washington Rugby. Contbr. articles in field to med. jours. Home: 124 Cree Dr Forest Heights MD 20021 Office: 1310 Southern Ave Washington DC 20032

DIBBLE, STEPHEN JESSE, clergyman; b. Binghamton, N.Y., Nov. 23, 1923; s. Harry Glenn and Lucy Adella (Callender) D.; student U. N.C., 1943-44; B.A., Adelphi U., 1953, M.A., 1975; M.Div., Nashotah House, 1953; postgrad. N.Y.U., 1977—. With Dun & Bradstreet, N.Y.C., 1946-47; ordained priest Episcopal Ch., 1953; curate Ch. of Ascension, Sierra Madre, Calif., 1953-55; rector Ch. of Transfiguration, Bklyn., 1958-66, St. Andrew's Ch. Astoria, Long Island, N.Y., 1967-78. Served with USNR, 1943-46. Mem. Soc. Colonial Wars, Colonial Lords of Manors in Am., Sons of Revolution, Am. Hist. Assn., Phi Alpha Theta. Home: 82 Ponus Ridge Rd New Canaan CT 06840

DIBBLE, WILLIS ALFRED, JR., human service orgn. exec.; b. Rockville Center, N.Y., Mar. 16, 1946; s. Willis Alfred and Marguerite D.; B.A. in Psychology, Rutgers U., 1968; M.A. in Counseling, Fairleigh Dickinson U., 1972; m. Anne Counselman, Jan. 20, 1979. Project specialist E.R. Johnstone Tng. and Research Center, Bordentown, N.J., 1970-73; psychology cons. United Cerebral Palsy Assn. of Phila. and Vicinity, 1973-75, coordinator children's services, 1975-76, asst. exec. dir., 1976—. Served as ensign, aviator USN, 1968-69. Mem. Am. Psychol. Assn., Assn. Advancement of Behavior Therapy, Am. Assn. Mental Deficiency, Council Exceptional Children. Home: 2611 Swain St Philadelphia PA 19130 Office: 4700 Wissahickon Ave Philadelphia PA 19144

DIBLASI, PAUL JOSEPH, chem. co. exec.; b. Phila., July 18, 1931; s. Gaetano and Angela (Pescatore) D.; B.A., St. Joseph's Coll., Phila., 1953; student U. Pa., 1953-54, 65-66; m. Theresa Annunziato, Apr. 23, 1960; children—Paul Joseph, David, Robert. Plant chemist Dynacolor div. 3M Co., Phila., 1957-59; chief chemist Perfect Photo div. GAF Corp., Phila., 1959-64; salesman McKesson Chem. Co., Phila., 1964-69, br. mgr., Pitts., 1969-73, dist. mgr., Chgo., 1973-75, mktg. mgr., Montvale, N.J., 1976—. Served with U.S. Army, 1954-57. Club: Rotary (past pres.). Mem. Chem. Club Pitts., Sales Execs. Club N.Y., Chemists Club N.J. Republican. Roman Catholic. Home: 49 Huff Terr Montvale NJ 07645 Office: 1 36 Summit Ave Montvale NJ 07645

DIBNER, SUSAN SCHMIDT, sociologist; b. Cin., Apr. 4, 1936; d. Milton Henry and Ruth (Friedlander) Schmidt; student Ind. U., 1954-56; B.A., U. Cin., 1958; Ph.D. (NIMH fellow), Brandeis U., 1973; m. Andrew Sherman Dibner, May 1, 1967; children—Nina S., Lora M. Nat. Inst. Child Health and Devel. fellow Duke Med. Center for Study Aging and Human Devel., 1972-73; faculty U. Mass., Boston, 1973-74; asst. prof. Wellesley Coll., 1974-75; research asso., mem. faculty seminar programs Radcliffe Inst., Cambridge, Mass., 1974—; v.p. Lifeline Systems, Inc. Mem. Am., Mass. (exec. council 1977-80) sociol. assns., Gerontology Soc., Sociologists for Women in Soc. Author: Integration or Segregation for the Physically Handicapped Child, 1973, also articles. Home: 8 Devon Terr Newton Centre MA 02159

DI CARA, C(OSTANTE) JOHN, economist; b. Winsted, Conn., Dec. 31, 1927; s. Salvo P. and Rosalia (Colombi) DiC.; B.A., Yale, 1950; M.A., U. Conn., 1952; postgrad. London Sch. Econs., 1965, Am. U., 1969; . Lolita Mae Lanpher, Sept. 12, 1953; children—Laurie Anna, Andrea Lynn, Dean Adam (dec.). Economist, Conn. Labor Dept., Hartford, 1952, Conf. Bd., N.Y.C., 1953, N.Y. Stock Exchange, 1954-58; officer, economist AID, Kabul, Afghanistan and Washington, 1959-64, aid coordination attaché Embassies London and Bonn., 1965-68; sr. area economist CIA, Washington, 1969—. Participant, U.S. German Aid Confs., Berlin and Bochum, Germany, 1968, Devel. Assistance Com. Confs., Paris, France, 1967-68; lectr. Nat. War Coll., 1973-76. Pres., Great Falls (Va.) Citizens Assn., 1974. Mem. Soc. Internat. Devel., Am. Econ. Assn., Assn. Humanistic Psychology, Key Notes Chorus, Potomac Investment Club (pres. 1978). Democrat. Lion (pres. 1971-72, mem. state adv. com. 1970-72). Unitarian-Universalist. Contbr. articles to profl. pubs. Home: 10605 Good Spring Av Great Falls VA 22066 Mailing Address: Box 46 Great Falls VA 22066 Office: Central Intelligence Agency Washington DC 20505

DI CASPARRO, ERMINE PATRICK, retail lumber exec.; b. Trenton, Ont., Can., Mar. 17, 1925; s. Angelo and Elvira DiC.; came to U.S., 1925, naturalized, 1944; B. Accounting, Hill Coll., Woonsocket, R.I., 1948; postgrad. Brown U., 1956, U. R.I., 1961; m. Romilda G. Truppa, Nov. 28, 1948; children—Gary, Raymond, Donna. Insp., Dept. Agr., Hicksville, N.Y., 1949-50; clk. Dept. Commerce, Great Neck, N.Y., 1950-51; with Big Four Outlet, Mansfield, Mass., 1964—, corporate treas., 1976—. Served with U.S. Army, 1943-45. Mem. New Eng. Retail Lumbermen's Assn., Nat. Assn. Clock Collectors, Aircraft Owners and Pilots' Assn. Roman Catholic. Club: K.C. Home: 20 Brook Farm Rd North Providence RI 02904 Office: 395 Oakland St Mansfield MA 02048

DICENZO, COLIN DOMENIC, educator; b. Hamilton, Ont., Can., July 26, 1923; s. Ferdernado and Kathleen (Quickenden) diC.; B.Sc. in Elec. Engring., U. N.B., 1952; D.I.C., Imperial Coll. Sci. and Tech., London, 1954; M.Sc. in Elec. Engring., U. N.B., 1957; m. Patricia Evelyn Wright, Sept. 12, 1950; children—Colin, Eileen, Brian, Mark, Peter, Pamela. Control engr. Met. Vickers, Eng., 1953-54; lectr. Royal Mil. Coll. Can., 1954-57; dep. head sonar engring. Naval Hdqrs., Ottawa, Ont., 1957-60, head underwater fire control system design group, 1960-62; squadron staff officer 2d Destroyer Squadron, Pacific, 1962-64; project engr. hydrofoil ship HMCS Bras d'Or, Naval Hdqrs., 1964-65; comd. artificer apprentice Canadian Navy, 1941, advanced through grades to comdr., 1964; trans. Naval Res., 1966, Comdg. officer Hamilton Res. div. 1969-71; asso. prof. McMaster U., Hamilton, 1965-72, prof. elec. engring., 1973—, dir. studies faculty of engring., 1968-75, asso. dean engring., 1975—. Decorated Order of Can.; recipient 1952-54; Centennial medal, 1967; Queen's Silver Jubilee medal, 1977; award Pub. Servants invention act; Athlone fellow, 1952-54; Brydon-Jack scholar, 1952. Fellow IEEE (asso. editor transactions 1975-78), Engring. Inst. Can. (Julian C. Smith medal 1977, sr. v.p., pres.-elect 1978); mem. Can. Soc. Elec. Engring. (pres. 1976-78), Assn. Profl. Engrs. Ont. (Engring. medal 1977). Patentee, numerous publs. in field. Home: 28 Millen Ave Hamilton ON L9A 2T4 Canada Office: McMaster U Hamilton ON L8S 4L7 Canada

DICK, CHARLES HOWARD, coll. pres.; b. Hutchinson, Kans., June 11, 1930; s. Charles Otto and Mary Elizabeth (Combs) D.; B.A., U. Kans., 1953; Ph.D., Northwestern U., 1957; M.S., Calif. State U., Fresno, 1971; D.Sc., Hamilton State U., Tucson, 1973; m. Barbarann Deren, June 14, 1969. Dir. pub. edn. Am. Cancer Soc., N.Y.C., 1957-61, Roswell Park Meml. Inst., Buffalo, 1961-67; asst. v.p. SUNY, Buffalo, 1967-69; asst. to pres. Calif. State U., Fresno, 1969-71, prof. health sci., 1970-71; asst. commr. HEW, Washington, 1971-73; v.p. Cornell U. Med. Center, N.Y.C., 1973-76; pres. Centenary Coll., Hackettstown, N.J., 1976—, prof. allied health, 1978-79; trustee Assn. Ind. Colls. and Univs. N.J., 1978-79, N.J. Coll. Fund Assn., 1978-79; chmn. nat. freedom info. task force HEW, 1972-73; chmn. exec. com. Am. Cancer Soc., 1968-69; bd. dirs. Muscular Dystrophy Assn. Am., Buffalo, 1968-69; mem. Nat. Conf. High Blood Pressure, 1972-73. Recipient award Pub. Relations Soc. Am., 1972, Nat. Safety Council, 1972. Mem. Assn. Am. Colls., Am. Council Edn., Council Advancement and Support Edn., Nat. Assn. Sci. Writers. Episcopalian. Author articles, reports, monograph, films. Address: 407 Moore St Hackettstown NJ 07840

DICK, DOUGLAS SHELTON, orthodontist; b. Boston, May 23, 1941; s. Vernon Shelton and Blossom Lydia (Bacon) D.; B.A., Yale, 1963; D.M.D. magna cum laude, Harvard, 1967; m. Eltress Ann Mitchell, June 15, 1963; children—Geoffrey Charles, Nancy Jean. Research fellow in orthodontics Harvard Sch. Dental Medicine, 1969-72, asst. to dean for student affairs, 1971, mem. alumni council, 1971-72; now practice dentistry specializing in orthodontics. Mem. Boxford (Mass.) Bd. Pub. Health. Served with Dental Corps, AUS, 1967-69. Recipient Harvard Odontological Soc. Research award, 1967, Harvard Dental Alumni Silver Medal, 1967. Mem. Am. Dental Assn., Internat. Assn. for Dental Research, Mass., North Shore dental socs., Am. Assn. Orthodontists, Omicron Kappa Upsilon, Phi Gamma Delta. Republican. Mem. Congregational Ch. Club: Rotary. Home: Harris Rd Boxford MA 01921 Office: 2 Orchard Ln Danvers MA 01923

DICK, ROBERT GRANT, steel co. exec.; b. Balt., Apr. 29, 1920; s. Clarance Milton and Anne Marie (Stites) D.; student Balt. City Coll., 1936, U. Md., 1936-37, U. Balt., 1937-38; m. Mary Burton Robinson, Jan. 25, 1941; children—Robert Grant III, Gail (Mrs. Richard H. Keller). Prodn. supt. Koppers Co., Inc., Balt., 1946-53; works mgr. Pusey & Jones Corp., Wilmington, Del., 1953-57; cons. Seaboard Ship, Wilmington, 1957-58; pres. Delaware Valley Steel Works, Inc., Wilmington, 1958—; chmn. bd. Eastern Boiler Assos., Wilmington, Deemer Steel Casting Co., New Castle, Del.; pres. R.G. Dick Ltd., Wilmington, 1955—; partner Whitemarsh Hosp., Phila., 1972—; gen. partner Westminster Assos., Wilmington, 1972—; sec. Ridge Care, Inc., Phila., 1972—. Mem. Del. Racing Commn. Served with M.I., 1943-45. Mem. United Hunt and Steeplechase Assn., Horsemen's Benevolent and Protective Assn. Episcopalian. Club: Delaware Turf. Home: 806 Cheltenham Rd Wilmington DE 19808 Office: PO Box 1085 Wilmington DE 19899

DICKENS, DORIS LEE (MRS. AUSTIN L. FICKLING), psychiatrist; b. Roxboro, N.C., Oct. 12; d. Lee Edward and Delma Ernestine (Hester) D.; B.S magna cum laude, Va. Union U., 1960; M.D., Howard U., 1966; m. Austin L. Fickling. Intern, St. Elizabeth's Hosp., Washington, 1966-67, resident, 1967-70; staff psychiatrist, dir. Mental Health Program for Deaf, St. Elizabeth's Hosp., Washington, after 1970, now chief program; cons. NIMH. Bd. dirs. Nat. Health Care Found. for Deaf. Diplomate Nat. Bd. Med. Examiners. Mem. Am. Psychiat. Assn., Washington Psychiat. Soc., Profl. Rehab. Workers for Adult Deaf, Washington Soc. Adolescent Psychiatry, Alpha Kappa Mu, Beta Kappa Chi. Author: How and When Psychiatry Can Help You, 1972; You and Your Doctor. Home: 12308 Surrey Circle Dr Tantallon MD 20022 Office: 2700 Martin L King Ave Washington DC 20032

DICKEY, CLYDE WILLIAM, physicist, research co. exec.; b. Mahaffey, Pa., Mar. 3, 1921; s. Joseph R. and Laoma A. (Straw) D.; B.S. in Physics, Pa. State U., 1950, M.S. in Physics, 1953; m. Edith Mae Lucy, June 2, 1945; children—Nancy E. (Mrs. Edward S. Ruete), Mary E., Susan E. Research physicist Corning Glass Works (N.Y.), 1953-57, Curtiss Wright Corp., 1957-59; staff engr. HRB Singer Inc., State College, Pa., 1959-61; pres. C.W. Dickey Assos., State College, 1961—. Cons. on acoustics, 1961—; tech. dir. Linden Labs. Inc., 1974—. Served with AUS, 1942-46. Recipient biol., med. and phys. sci. research grants, 1969-71. Mem. Acoustical Soc. Am., Ultrasonic

Mfrs. Assn., Sigma Pi Sigma. Republican. Methodist. Contbr. articles and chpts. to profl. jours. and books. Patentee in field. Home and Office: 705 W Nittany Ave State College PA 16801

DICKEY, JOSEPH LYLE, elec. mfg. co. cons.; b. nr. Sedalia, Mo., Sept. 18, 1910; s. John Logan and Lona Mabel (Shackelford) D.; student Park Coll., 1928-30; B.S., U.S. Naval Acad., 1934; M.S., Harvard, 1942; m. Lillian Belle Morlan, June 24, 1936; children—Diane (Mrs. Robert W. Sherer), Joseph Waldo. Commd. 2d lt. U.S. Marine Corps, 1934, advanced through grades to col., 1949; ret., 1956; operations mgr. Westinghouse Elec. Corp., Balt., after 1956, now cons.; cons. archtl. acoustics, nuclear fall-out protection. Trustee Annapolis Symphony Orch.; bd. dirs. Anapolis Opera. Recipient citation Sec. of Navy, 1945. Mem. I.E.E.E., Inst. Aero. and Astronautical Scientists, Acoustics Soc. Am., U.S. Naval Inst., U.S. Naval Acad. Alumni Assn. (dir.). Presbyn. (life elder). Club: Officers and Faculty (U.S. Naval Acad.). Pioneer devel. of mil. radar. Home: 1863 Lindamoor Dr Annapolis MD 21401 Office: Baltimore Washington International Airport PO Box 746 Baltimore MD 21203

DICKEY, ROBERT, III, mfg., constrn. and engring. co. exec.; b. Pitts., Jan. 28, 1918; s. Robert and Mary Appleby (Hugus) D.; B.M.E., Princeton, 1939; m. Elizabeth P. Beckwith, May 11, 1942; children—Diana B., Susan D., Robert. Engr., United Engring. & Foundry Co., Pitts., 1939-42, H.H. Robertson Co., Ambridge, Pa., 1946-48; with Dravo Corp., Pitts., 1948—, exec. v.p., 1962-64, pres., chief exec. officer, 1964—, chmn. bd., 1974—; dir. Pitts. Nat. Bank, Joy Mfg. Co., Gulf Oil Corp. Chmn., Pitts. Pub. Auditorium Authority; chmn. Allegheny Conf. Community Devel.; bd. dirs. United Way of Allegheny County; trustee E.Liberty Presbyterian Ch., Shadyside Hosp. Served to lt. comdr. USN, 1942-46, 51-52. Decorated Legion of Merit; named Businessman of Year, Pitts. Jaycees, 1972. Mem. Nat. Alliance Businessmen (past chmn.), Am. Iron and Steel Inst., Penn's S.W. Assn. Clubs: Duquesne, Fox Chapel Golf, Laurel Valley Golf, Rolling Rock, Links. Home: 705 Devonshire St Pittsburgh PA 15213 Office: One Oliver Plaza Pittsburgh PA 15222

DICKINSON, DIANE JANE GRAY, real estate broker; b. Balt., Sept. 26, 1946; d. E. Sherwood and Jane (Wagner) Dickinson; student Queens Coll., 1964-66; B.A. in History, U. S.C., 1968, M.A. in History, Geography and Polit. Sci., 1970. Asst. mgr. Russell T. Baker & Co., Inc., Columbia, Md., 1977—, sales asso., 1973-77; tchr. secondary social studies Lexington County (S.C.) pub. schs., 1969-72, Howard County (Md.) pub. schs., 1972-73. Mem. Nat., Md. assns. realtors, Howard County Bd. Realtors. Democrat. Episcopalian. Home: 10326 Twinedew Pl Columbia MD 21044 Office: 3 Sterrett Pl Columbia MD 21044

DICKINSON, JUNE MC WADE, found. exec.; b. Rochester, N.Y., June 26, 1924; d. Howard L. and Esther G. (Benz) McWade; M.F.A.; grad. Women in Mgmt. program Rochester Inst. Tech.; grad. Grantsmanship Tng. Program; m. Edward Dickinson, May 3, 1946. Founder, 1949, since pres. Schumann Meml. Found.; registered music therapist; dir. Casterbridge Village Fine Arts, Conesus, N.Y., 1963—; owner Ink Pen Beacon, weekly newspaper, Conesus, 1962—; dir. pub. relations and communications St. Michael's Episcopal Ch., Genesco, N.Y. Recipient Community Leader of Am. award, 1969; decorated knight's cross Order Merit (Fed. Republic Germany); named Citizen of Day twice in Rochester, N.Y., also Citizen of Week for Livingston County. Mem. Nat. Assn. for Music Therapy (publ. dir. Western N.Y.), Women in Founds./Corp. Philanthropy, Advocates for Arts, ASCAP, Coll. Music Soc., League of Women Composers, Livingston County (N.Y.) C. of C. Clubs: Conesus Lake Water Ski (founder, adviser, sr. mem.); Rochester. Composer: Love's Wine, Sunset Through the Rain, Old Valentines, Glass Balls on a Christmas Tree, High School Memories, My Hand in God's, Happy Pilgrims, My Irish Coleen, In a Bavarian Garden. Address: 2904 E Lake Rd Livonia NY 14487

DICKSON, PAUL WESLEY, JR., nuclear reactor exec.; b. Sharon, Pa., Sept. 14, 1931; s. Paul Wesley and Elizabeth Ella (Trevethan) D.; B.S. in Metall. Engring., U. Ariz., 1954, M.S., 1954; Ph.D. in Physics, N.C. State U., 1962; m. Eleanor Ann Dunning, Nov. 17, 1952; children—Gretchen Ann, Heather Elizabeth, Paul Wesley III. Jr. engr. Gen. Electric Co., Hanford, Wash., 1954-55; sr. scientist astronuclear lab. Westinghouse Electric Corp., Pitts., 1963-64, fellow scientist, 1964-66, mgr. nuclear weapons, 1966-68, mgr. design and analysis, 1968-69, mgr. advanced projects, 1969-72, mgr. liquid metal fast breeder reactor analysis Advanced Reactors div., 1972-77, mgr. reactor analysis and core design, 1977—; mem. adv. com. advanced propulsion systems NASA, 1970-72; mem. adv. com. reactor physics Dept. Energy, 1974—; mem. rev. com. applied physics Argonne Nat. Lab., 1978—. Served to capt. USAF, 1955-63. Mem. Am. Phys. Soc., AAAS, Am. Nuclear Soc., Am. Inst. Mining and Metall. Engrs., N.Y. Acad. Scis., Scabbard and Blade, Sigma Xi, Phi Kappa Phi, Sigma Pi Sigma, Tau Beta Pi, Phi Lambda Upsilon. Republican. Home: 3300 Appel Rd Bethel Park PA 15102 Office: Westinghouse Electric Corp PO Box 158 Madison PA 15663

DICKSTEIN, BENJAMIN, pediatrician; b. Phila., Oct. 28, 1915; s. Harry and Anna (Levitz) D.; A.B., U. Pa., 1936, M.D., 1940; m. Joan Borteck, Dec. 24, 1939; children—Howard, Kenneth, Mary. Intern, Jewish Hosp. Phila., 1940-42; resident pediatrics Childrens Hosp., Phila., 1946-48, now asso. in pediatrics; practice medicine, specializing in pediatrics, Phila., 1948—; asst. prof. U. Pa. Med. Sch.; sr. attending pediatrician Albert Einstein Med. Center; chief pediatrics John F. Kennedy Hosp., Phila., Jeanes Hosp., Phila.; med. dir. Assn. for Jewish Children, 1958—. Chmn., Com. of Responsibility, Phila., 1966—; adviser, bd. dirs. ACLU; trustee Fedn. Jewish Agys. Served to lt. col. USAAF, 1942-46. Decorated Bronze Star, medal, Soldiers medal; recipient Distinguished Service award Hebrew U. Med. Sch., Jerusalem, 1964, Tribute award State of Israel, 1971. Fellow Am. Acad. Pediatrics, Coll. Physicians Phila.; mem. Phila. Pediatric Soc. (pres. 1972), Sigma Xi. Contbr. articles to profl. jours. Home: 8325 Fairview Rd Elkins Park PA 19117 Office: 6810 Castor Ave Philadelphia PA 19149

DICKSTEIN, JACK, chem. co. exec.; b. Phila., Dec. 14, 1925; s. Aaron and Anna (Anselevitz) D.; B.S., Pa. State U., 1946; M.A., Temple U., 1951; Ph.D., Rutgers U., 1958; m. Pauline M. Gothelf, Dec. 24, 1950; children—Jeffrey L., John F., Andrea E. Analytical chemist Lederle Labs., Pearl River, N.Y., 1946-48; research asso. E.R. Squibb & Sons, New Brunswick, N.J., 1951-56; group leader Borden Chem. Co., Phila., 1958-60, mgr. Monomer-Polymer & Dajac Labs., Phila., 1960-61, devel. mgr., Leominster, Mass., 1961-67, dir. research, Phila., 1967-73; group mgr. Haven Chem. Co., Phila., 1974-77; v.p. research and devel. SEAL, Inc., Naugatuck, Conn., 1977—; prof. chemistry Rutgers U., 1955-58, Alma White Coll., 1957-58, Bucks County Community Coll., 1970-72. Mem. Phila. Crime Commn., 1970-72. Mem. Am. Chem. Soc., AAAS, Soc. Plastics Engrs., Franklin Inst., Smithsonian Instn., Internat. Platform Assn., TAPPI, N.Y. Acad. Scis., Phila. C. of C., Sigma Xi, Phi Lambda Upsilon, Phi Eta Sigma. Author: Polyvinyl Alcohol; Manufacture of Plastics, 1964; contbr. articles to profl. jours. Patentee in field. Home: 318 Keats Rd Huntingdon Valley PA 19006

DI CROCE, ANTHONY JOSEPH, physician; b. Newark, Nov. 24, 1924; s. Joseph and Concetta (Cavuoti) Di C.; B.A., Rutgers U., 1958; postgrad. U. Rome, 1959-63; M.D., Duke, 1965; m. Juanita R. Stepp, Dec. 2, 1944; children—Anthony, Dennis, Joseph, Juanita, Michelle. Practice gen. medicine, Point Pleasant Beach, N.J., 1965—; intern Watts Hosp., Durham, N.C., 1965-66; chief med. staff Point Pleasant Hosp., 1976—; pres. N.J. Fedn. Physicians and Dentists, 1974—. Chmn. ann. diabetes dr. Ocean County, 1973-75. Served with USAAF, 1943-45. Decorated Air medal. Mem. N.J. State, Ocean County (pres. 1976—) med. socs., Am. Assn. Physicians and Surgeons, Am. Acad. Family Physicians. Republican. Roman Catholic. Home: 802 Rosewood Ave Point Pleasant Beach NJ 08742 Office: 201 Arnold Ave Point Pleasant Beach NJ 08742

DI CUIO, ROBERT FRANK, psychologist; b. N.Y.C., Feb. 14, 1950; s. Dominick and Natalie (Saitta) DiC.; B.S., Manhattan Coll., 1971; M.Ph., Columbia U., 1976, Ph.D., 1978; m. Susanne Finelli, June 27, 1971. Psychologist, Manhattan Devel. Center, N.Y. State Office Mental Retardation and Developmental Disabilities, N.Y.C., 1973—, dir. edn. and tng., 1978—. Thorndike fellow, 1971—. Mem. Am. Psychol. Assn., Am. Assn. Mental Deficiency, Phi Beta Kappa. Home: 19F Hillside Terr White Plains NY 10601 Office: 75 Morton St New York City NY 10014

DIEFENBACH, MARCIA GAY ANN, interior designer; b. Erie, Pa., Nov. 10, 1941; d. Joseph Michael and Anna Marie (Haibach) Kreger; ed. N.Y. Sch. Interior Design, 1962; m. Thomas Arthur Diefenbach, Sept. 14, 1963; children—Arthur Thomas, Alison Anne. Self-employed interior designer, Erie, 1962—. Mem. Women's Group, Erie Art Center, 1968-77; dist. capt. Heart Fund, Erie, 1975-77, dist. chmn., 1978; bd. incorporators United Way, Erie, 1977, 78; pres. bd. dirs. Florence Crittenton Services, Erie, 1978—; bd. dirs. Mercy Center of the Arts. Mem. Jr. League of Erie. Republican. Roman Catholic. Clubs: Kahkwa Country, Erie Maennerchor, Zonta Internat. Address: 4716 Sunnydale Blvd Erie PA 16509

DIEHL, CAROL SUSAN, juvenile corrections counselor; b. Uniontown, Pa., Dec. 6, 1949; d. Robert Francis and Charlotte Marilyn (Newcomer) Diehl; B.A. in Sociology, Juniata Coll., 1971; M.A. in Counseling and Guidance, W.Va. U., 1976. Counselor, Search Group Home, Betterway, Inc., Elyria, Ohio, 1971-72; youth devel. counselor I, Youth Devel. Center, Waynesburg, Pa., 1972-73, youth devel. counselor II, 1973-75, youth devel. counselor II, supr. crisis intervention team, 1977—; counselor Luther Youngdahl Human Relations Center, Owatonna, Minn., 1976, Valley Comprehensive Community MH/MR Center, Fairmont, W.Va., 1976; student cons. dept. counseling and guidance W.Va. U., 1976. Mem. Am. Personnel and Guidance Assn., Assn. for Specialisits in Group Work. Democrat. Mem. Ch. of the Brethren. Home: 567 E Cherry Alley Waynesburg PA 15370 Office: Youth Devel Center RD 1 Box 67 Waynesburg PA 15370

DIEHL, DONALD WINSTON, broadcasting exec., newspaper pub.-editor; b. Smith Center, Kans., May 30, 1924; s. Claude Winston and Estel (Lull) D.; A.B., U. Kans., 1947; M.B.A., Harvard, 1949; m. Jean E. Mullin, June 5, 1949 (div. 1976); children—Deborah (dec.), Andrea, Lauren, Janet; m. 2d, Marjorie Hansen Schweizer, 1977. Research fellow Harvard U., 1949-50; with Pub.'s Assn. N.Y.C., 1950-52; owner, pub. Florence (Colo.) Citizen, 1952-54; cons. McKinsey & Co., N.Y.C., 1954-56; with Time, Inc., 1956-58; gen. mgr. Endicott (N.Y.) Bull., 1958-60; asst. gen. mgr. Danbury (Conn.) News-Times, 1960-64; with Easton (Pa.) Express, 1964—, pres.-editor, 1967—; pres., dir. WEEX-AM, also WQQQ FM, Easton, 1967—, Hackettstown (N.J.) Gazette, Inc., 1968—, Phillipsburg (N.J.) Pub. Co.; pres. Washington (N.J.) Star, 1967—, The Forum, 1971—; dir. Lafayette Trust Bank, Easton, Easton Pub. Co. (Pa.), State Pub. Co., Hackettstown, N.J., Playboy Enterprises, Inc., 1978—. Mem. exec. com. United Fund, Easton, 1969—; bd. dirs. Parking Authority; mem. Task Force for Pa. Bd. Edn., 1970—; Am. bd. dirs. and vice chmn. Internat. Press Inst., 1978—; bd. advisers Allentown br. Pa. State U., 1969—. Served to lt. (j.g.) USNR, 1943-46. Mem. Am. Newspaper Pubs. Assn. (chmn. pub. affairs com. 1971-77), Am. Soc. Newspaper Editors (future directions com.), Phi Beta Kappa. Sigma Delta Chi. Presbyterian (deacon 1967-69). Clubs: Country of Northampton County, Pomfret. Home: Skyline Dr Easton PA 18042 Office: 30 N 4th St Easton PA 18042

DIEHL, JAMES RAYMOND, JR., hosp. adminstr.; b. Middletown, N.Y., Jan. 25, 1938; s. James Raymond and Julia Marie (Wengenroth) D.; B.A., St. Anslem's Coll., 1960; M.B.A., Rochester Inst. Tech., 1972; m. Egia Marie D'Onofrio, June 8, 1963; children—Scott McLenon, Keith Patrick, Darren Mathew. Sr. adminstrv. analyst Monroe County (N.Y.) Dept. Social Service, Rochester, 1970, dep. dir. adminstrn./income maintenance, 1971-74; dep. commr. Medicaid, N.Y. State Dept. Social Service, Albany, 1974-76; exec. health adminstr. Monroe Community Hosp., Rochester, 1977—. Active Cub Scouts, PTA. Served with USMC, 1961-68; Viet Nam. Decorated D.F.C., Air medal (12). Mem. Am. Mgmt. Assn., Hosp. Fin. Officers Assn., Nat. Assn. Counties, Am., N.Y. State hosp. assns., Aircraft Owners and Pilots Assn. Roman Catholic. Clubs: Irondequoit Little League, Irondequoit Tennis, K.C. Home: 144 Sandoris Circle Rochester NY 14622 Office: 435 E Henrietta Rd Rochester NY 14603

DIEHL, RICK WILLIAM, packaging co. exec.; b. Penn Yan, N.Y., Nov. 5, 1931; s. John Phillip and Virginia Agnes (Mason) D.; B.S., U.S. Naval Acad., 1954; m. Cynthia Ann Barre, June 12, 1954; children—Carole Ann, Nancy Elizabeth, Jane Ellen. Western dist. mgr. Exploratory Research div. Norton Co., Cambridge, Mass., 1959-64; mgr. cons. services Electronic Data Systems Corp., Dallas, 1964-69; dir. market and product planning Continental Can Co., N.Y.C., 1969-71, dir. new bus. devel., 1971-74, gen. mgr. material planning, 1974-78, gen. mgr. corporate tech., 1978—. Mem. staff presdl. candidate, 1968; chmn. Wilton (Conn.) Republican Party, 1972-73. Served in USN, 1954-58. Mem. Am. Econ. Assn., Am. Mgmt. Assn., Assn. Corporate Growth, Nat. Planning Assn., N.Am. Soc. Corp. Planning, World Future Soc., Corp. Develop. Assn. Clubs: Union League (N.Y.C.); Patterson (Fairfield, Conn.); Army-Navy (Washington). Contbr. articles in field to profl. jours. Home: 356 Newtown Turnpike Wilton CT 06897 Office: 633 3d Ave New York NY 10017

DIEHL, RUTHERFORD OLIVER, architect; b. Milw., July 5, 1911; s. Arthur Omer and Lydia (Loehr) D.; student U. Wis., 1933-35, U. Md., 1943-45, Johns Hopkins U., 1955-57, George Washington U., 1961; m. Margaret Hope Badgerow, Aug. 23, 1937; 1 son, Mark Rutherford. Clk., First Wis. Nat. Bank, Milw., 1929-37; mgr. Louise Hand Laundry, Washington, 1937-42; liaison engr. Glen L. Martin Co., Balt., 1942-47; engr. Hall Turpin & Wachter, Balt., 1947-48; architect Lucius R. White, Jr., Balt., 1948-61, Smith & Veale, Balt., 1961-71, Mark Beck Assos., Inc., Towson, Md., 1971-73; dir. Linganore Center for Design, Eaglehead, Frederick, Md., 1973-75. Mem. Christian life and pub. affairs com. Bapt. Conv. Md., 1970-78, Citizens Housing and Planning Assn. Balt., 1960—. Mem. AIA, Historic Annapolis, Balt. Mus. Art. Important works include: auditoriums Wallbrook, Patapsco, Woodlawn, Dundalk sr. high schs. Home: 124 Compass Rd Baltimore MD 21220 Office: 124 Compass Rd Baltimore MD 21220

DIEHL, SAYLOR FLORY, statistician; b. Nokesville, Va., Nov. 8, 1919; s. Daniel Saylor and Vernie (Flory) D.; A.B., Bridgewater Coll., 1943; student George Washington U., 1943-45, Am. U., 1945-50; m. Nettie Ruth Mathison, Aug. 31, 1946; children—Linda Jean, Wayne Bruce. Tchr. Churchville (Va.) High Sch., 1943, Rockville (Md.) High Sch., 1943-44; agrl. statistician Census Bur. Agr. Div., Washington, 1945-47; real estate salesman Max Miller Co., Washington, 1947-48; tchr. Mt. Rainier (Md.) High Sch. 1948-49; specialist Air Intelligence, USAF, Washington, D.C. 1949-51; analyst commodity industry Nat. Prodn. Authority, Washington, 1951-53; analytical statistician Bur. Personnel, U.S. Navy, Washington, 1953-54; head work measurement br. Office Indsl. Relations, exec. office Sec. of Navy, Washington, 1954-57; supervisory survey statistician Census Bur. Washington, 1957-62; ednl. research specialist U.S. Office Edn., Washington, 1962—. Mason (32 deg., Shriner, K.T.). Author: The Presiding Officer, 1969. Home: 11505 Carroll Ct Upper Marlboro MD 20870 Office: US Office Edn Washington DC 20202

DIENER, DEBRA NATALIE, assn. exec.; b. Newark, July 16, 1950; d. Sol and Naomi (Sokler) Diener; B.A. in Polit. Sci. cum laude (Univ. scholar 1971), Syracuse (N.Y.) U., 1972; M.A. in Polit. Sci. and Pub. Policy, U. Pa., 1973; postgrad. Law Sch. George Washington U. Research asso. Syracuse U. Research Corp., Washington, 1973-74; staff asst. to dir. Nat. Inst. Edn., Washington, 1974-76; asst. mgr. for program coordination NEA, Washington, 1976—; cons. in field. Active New Playwrights Theatre, Folger Theatre. Mem. Nat. Women's Polit. Caucus, Pi Sigma Alpha, Eta Pi Upsilon. Address: B-910 500 23d St NW Washington DC 20037

DIERDORFF, LEE HENRY, JR., chem. engr.; b. Moline, Ill., Apr. 29, 1922; s. Lee Henry and Clara Louise (Fisher) D.; student Colo. State U., 1939-41; B.S., Northwestern U., 1943; m. Violet Virginia Schwedt, Apr. 24, 1954; children—Lee Andrew, Deborah Ann. Asst. chem. engr. Tenn. Eastman Corp., Oak Ridge, 1943-45; project engr. Buffalo Electrochem. Co., 1948-49, chief project engr., 1950-57; with FMC Corp., Princeton, N.J., 1958—, research engr., 1961-66, sr. research engr., 1967-73, prin. research engr., 1974—. Active Boy Scouts Am. Served with C.E., AUS, 1945-46. Mem. Am. Inst. Chem. Engrs., Am. Assn. Cost Engrs., Combustion Inst., Nat. Rifle Assn., U.S. Revolver Assn. (dir. 1972—), Sigma Xi, Tau Beta Pi, Phi Lambda Upsilon. Republican. Methodist. Author: Hydrogen Peroxide Physical Properties Data Book, 1955. Contbr. articles to profl. jours. Patentee in field. Co-holder U.S. Nat. Pistol Records, 1968. Home: 433 Walnut Ln Princeton NJ 08540 Office: COGAS Development Co Box 8 Princeton NJ 08540

DIES, DOUGLAS HILTON, assn. exec.; b. St. Paul, Sept. 9, 1913; s. Edward Jerome and Mareeta (Cole) D.; A.B., Harvard, 1934; postgrad. Oxford U., 1934-35; m. Mary Frances Doreen Harding, Nov. 25, 1939; children—Harding Mogridge, Andrea Frances. Editorial staff Grand Forks (N.D.) Herald, summer 1933, Mpls. Star, summer 1934, London Sunday Chronicle, summer 1935; staff London bur. U.P., 1935-38, Knoxville (Tenn.) Jour., 1938-40; pub. relations dept. Westinghouse Electric Co., 1940-41; staff A.P., Cleve., 1941-42; pub. relations staff U.S. Bd. Econ. Warfare, Washington, 1942-43; pub. relations, Washington, 1946—; editor Washington Correspondence, weekly newsletter on oilseeds and fats industry, 1947—; asso. world trading corps, 1947—; asst. to pres. Nat. Inst. Oilseed Products, 1947—; Washington rep. Pillsbury Co., 1956-64, East Asiatic Co., 1956-78, Woodward & Dickerson, Inc., 1958—; asst. sec., bur. raw materials Am. Vegetable Oils and Fats Industries, 1961-62, sec., 1962—; exec. sec. Am. Council Ind. Labs., 1963—; guest lectr. fgn. trade Georgetown U., 1966—; mem. agrl. tech. adv. com. on oilseeds and products for multilateral trade negotiations, 1975; Mem. Republican City Com., Alexandria, 1953-61. Served from ensign to lt. comdr., USNR, 1943-46. Mem. S.R. (gov. D.C. 1965-72), Mil. Order World Wars, Sigma Alpha Epsilon. Episcopalian (vestryman). Clubs: Harvard (N.Y.C., Washington); Metropolitan, University, Oxford-Cambridge (Washington). Editor: Chemurgic Digest, 1950-53. Home: 505 Robinson Ct Alexandria VA 22302 Office: 1725 K St NW Washington DC 20006

DIETHRICK, RUSSELL EDWARD, JR., city ofcl.; b. Patton, Pa., Oct. 9, 1934; s. Russell Edward and Ellen Sophia (Anderson) D.; student pub. schs., Jamestown. Asst. recreation dir. City of Jamestown, 1958-64, dir. recreation, 1964-66, dir. parks and recreation, 1966-72, dir. parks, recreation and conservation, 1972—. Mem. adv. bd. Chautauqua County Office for Aging; treas. Chautauqua County Legal Services; pres. Chautauqua County Adv. Com. of Elderly Orgns.; bd. dirs. Chautauqua Opportunities, Inc.; chmn. spl. gifts Am. Cancer Soc.; chmn. Mayor's Study Commn. on Problems of the Aging. Mem. So. Tier West Recreation and Park Soc. (pres.), Fenton Hist. Soc. Republican. Lutheran. Clubs: Rotary, Masons, Moose. Home: 63 Hallock St Jamestown NY 14701 Office: Municipal Bldg Jamestown NY 14701

DIETRICH, BRUCE LEINBACH, planetarium and museum dir.; b. Reading, Pa., Oct. 10, 1937; s. Harold Richard and Emily Jeanette (Leinbach) D.; B.S., Kutztown State Coll., 1960; M.S., State U. N.Y., 1969; m. Renee Carol Long, Nov. 25, 1959; children—Dodson Bruce, Katie Ellen. Tchr., Reading (Pa.) Pub. Schs., 1960-67; curator space sci. Reading Pub. Mus., 1967-69; dir. Reading Planetarium, 1969—, Reading Pub. Mus. and Art Gallery, 1976—. Astronomy instr. Reading Area Community Coll., 1972-78. Bd. dirs. Reading Music Found. Served with USAF, 1960; now comdg. officer Pa. Air N.G. Mem. Internat. Planetarium Soc., AAAS, Middle Atlantic Planetarium Soc. (v.p.), Association des Planetariums du Can. Mem. United Ch. Christ (deacon 1971-77). Club: Kiwanis. Home: 1546 Dauphin Ave Wyomissing PA 19610 Office: Reading Planetarium Reading PA 19611

DIETZ, WILLIAM RONALD, banker; b. Seattle, Nov. 25, 1942; s. William Phillip and Helen Mae (Wilson) D.; B.A., U. Wash., 1964; M.B.A., Stanford, 1968. Financial cons. 1st Nat. City Bank, N.Y.C., 1968-70; v.p., mgr. Citicorp Subsidiary Mgmt. Office, Citicorp, N.Y.C., 1971-74; chmn. Citicorp Factors, Inc., N.Y.C., 1974-75; v.p., mgr. N.Y., N.J. and Conn. comml. banking Citibank, N.A., N.Y.C., 1976-78, v.p., gen. mgr. Eastern region corporate banking, 1978—; also exec. v.p., dir. Citibank (NYS) N.A.; dir. Citicorp (U.S.A.) Inc. Served to lt. USNR, 1964-66. Mem. Delta Tau Delta. Clubs: Univ. (N.Y.C.); Old Lyme Country. Home: 49 W 76th St New York City NY 10023 also Lieutenant River Ln Old Lyme CT 06371 Office: 399 Park Ave New York City NY 10022

DIETZEL, LOUISE ALVERTA, counselor; b. Canton, Ohio, Nov. 18, 1937; d. Daniel Walter and Velma Irene (Bender) Miller; B.A., Goshen (Ind.) Coll., 1960; M.S., St. Michael's Coll., Winooski, Vt., 1976; m. Cleason Samuel Dietzel, June 18, 1960; children—Laurie Christine, Rebecca Doreen, Beth Ann. Day care dir., then pre-sch. tchr., Mt. Pleasant, Mich., 1965-71; pre-sch. tchr., Winooski, Vt., 1972-73; mem. research staff HEW grant U. Vt., 1976-77; cons. Chittenden Central Sch. Dist., Essex Junction, Vt., 1976-77, home-sch. coordinator, counselor, 1977—; pvt. counselor practice, workshop facilitator. Mem. Am. Personnel and Guidance Assn., Assn.

Humanistic Edn. and Devel., Vt. Assn. Supervision and Devel. Methodist. Home: 37 Prospect St Essex Junction VT 05452

DIFFENDERFER, HOPE ANKER, indsl. specialist; b. Los Angeles, Dec. 28, 1917; d. Herbert and Florence (Immerman) Anker; B.A., U. Redlands, 1938; M.S. in Adminstrn., George Washington U., 1976; m. Henry Earl Diffenderfer, Dec. 26, 1938; children—Niccole, Pieter, Deborah, Kenneth. Counselor, tchr. Seoul (Korea) Fgn. Sch., 1958-61; contract photographer, writer AID, U.S. Dept. State, Sierra Leone, W. Africa, 1962-67; adminstr., tchr. Am. Sch. of Vientiane, Laos, 1967-70; adminstrv. asst. TRACOR, Inc., Washington, 1970-71; coordinator Fed. Women's Program, Washington Naval Yard, 1975-77; indsl. specialist Naval Air Systems Command, Washington, 1972—. Mem. Nat. Contract Mgmt. Assn., Federally Employed Women, Inc., Am. Assn. Fgn. Service Women, Friends of Phi Beta Kappa, Pi Kappa Delta, Delta Alpha, Alpha Phi Gamma, Phi Delta Gamma. Contbr. articles to jours. and mags. Home: 619 Beverley Dr Alexandria VA 22305 Office: Naval Air Systems Command Washington DC 20361

DI GENNARO, JEROME ANTHONY, army officer, mathematician; b. Pitts., Aug. 25, 1953; s. Anthony Dominic and Concetta Mary (Scialabba) DiG.; B.S. in Math., Carnegie-Mellon U., 1976. Commd. 2d lt. U.S. Army, 1976; student U.S. Army, Aberdeen, Md., 1976-77, Redstone Arsenal, 1977, asst. instr. U.S. Army Missile and Munitions Center and Sch., 1977; served as storage platoon leader 69th Ordnance Co., Vicenza, Italy, 1977, asst. ops. officer, 1978—; founder, principle partner ROINC Enterprises, Pitts., 1974—. Life mem. Am. Def. Preparedness Assn.; mem. Assn. of U.S. Army, Delta Tau Delta, Theta Omicron Chi. Republican. Roman Catholic. Clubs: Trinity Lodge, Mason, Liberty Valley Council, Lincoln Commandery, Cahaba Temple, Huntsville AASR Bodies, Philalthies Soc. Contbr. paper on Pa., Ala. freemasonry; contbr. articles in field. Home: 1207 Burchfield Rd Allison Park PA 15101 Office: 69th Ordnance Co APO New York City 09221

DI GEORGE, ANGELO MARIO, physician; b. Phila., Apr. 15, 1921; s. Anthony and Emily (Taraborelli) DiGiorgio; A.B., Temple U., 1943, M.D., 1946, M.S. in Pediatrics, 1952; m. Natalie J. Picarello, May 5, 1951; children—Anthony M., Anita M., Christopher A. Intern, Temple U. Hosp., 1946-47; resident pediatrics St. Christophers Hosp. for Children, Phila., 1949-51, chief pediatric resident, 1951-52, chief sect. endocrinology and metabolism, 1961—, dir. Clin. Research Center, 1963—, dir. tng. program in research pediatrics, 1963-71; practice medicine, specializing in pediatrics, Phila., 1952—; postdoctoral fellow endocrinology Jefferson Med. Coll., 1952-54; instr. Temple U., 1952-57, asst. prof., 1958-61, asso. prof., 1961-67, prof. pediatrics, 1967—; asst. chief pediatrics Phila. Gen. Hosp., 1954-66; cons., lectr. U.S. Naval Hosp., Phila. Bd. dirs. Camp Firefly Diabetic Camp. Served as capt. M.C., AUS, 1947-49. Recipient NIH research grants, 1955-74. Mem. Am. Pediatric Soc., Soc. Pediatric Research, Am., Del. Valley (exec. com.) diabetes assns., Am. Soc. Human Genetics, Am. Fedn. Clin. Research, Am. Acad. Pediatrics, N.Y. Acad. Scis., Endocrine Soc., Lawson Wilkin Pediatric Endocrine Soc., Phila. Endocrine Soc. (Distinguished Service award 1973), Am. Philatelic Soc., Am. Topical Soc., Sigma Xi. Mem. editorial bd. Pediatrics, 1968-74, Jour. Pediatrics, 1975—. Contbr. articles to profl. jours. Home: 3025 W Queen Ln Philadelphia PA 19129 Office: 2600 N Lawrence St Philadelphia PA 19133

DIGERONIMO, ERNEST MICHAEL, dentist; b. Fitchburg, Mass., June 25, 1923; s. Michael and Lena Emilia (Cassinari) DiG.; B.S. in Chemistry magna cum laude, Holy Cross Coll., 1943; M.S. magna cum laude, 1944; D.M.D. magna cum laude, Tufts U., 1949; m. Mary Carbone, Feb. 12, 1945; children—Diane (Mrs. Anthony Champa), Ernest Michael, Thomas, David. Practice dentistry, Fitchburg, 1949—. Pres., Wachusett Enterprises, Inc., Fitchburg, 1961—; treas. Lakeview Nursing Home, Inc., Clinton, Mass., 1966—, pres., 1968—; treas. Mt. Elam Nursing Home, Inc., Fitchburg, 1964—; pres. Canton St. Realty Inc., Fitchburg-Lunenberg, Mass., Geronimo Leathers Inc., Southbridge, Mass. Served to capt. USAF, 1953-55. Recipient award Alpha Omega, 1949. Mem. ADA (pres. Wachusett dist. 1971-72), Am. Soc. Clin. Hypnosis, Pierre Fauchard Acad., Nat. Acupuncture Research Soc., Sons of Italy. Club: Serra (Fitchburg). Home: 239 Mt Elam Rd Fitchburg MA 01420 Office: In Town Profl Bldg 799 Main St Fitchburg MA 01420

DIGGINS, EDWARD PATRICK, accountant; b. Weymouth, Mass., Nov. 11, 1926; s. Joseph L. and Mary (Ryan) D.; B.S. magna cum laude, Rider Coll., 1950; m. Catherine Hulligan, Aug. 8, 1953; children—Therese, Stephen, Matthew, Timothy, Eileen, Claire, Vincent, Bernadette. Staff accountant, Arthur Andersen & Co., N.Y.C., 1950-53, mgr., 1957-64, partner, 1964-68; cons. accounting and fin.; dir. various corps. Served with USNR, 1944-46. C.P.A., N.J., N.Y. Mem. Am. Inst. C.P.A.'s, N.Y. State Soc. C.P.A.'s. Roman Catholic. Home: 2 Deer Trail Old Tappan NJ 07675

DI GIACOMO, WILLIAM ANTHONY, engring. firm exec.; b. N.Y.C., Jan. 12, 1928; s. Salvatore and Lucy (DeBenedetto) DiG.; B.S. in Mech. Engring., N.Y. U., 1948. Sr. engr. with leading archtl. and engring. firms, 1950-56; mng. partner W.A. Di Giacomo Assos., engrs., N.Y.C., 1956—, pres., Los Angeles, also San Francisco, 1968—; cons. Real Estate Bd. N.Y., 1973—; mem. N.Y.C. Bldg. Congress. Served to capt. C.E., AUS, 1948-50. Recipient archtl. and engring. awards for various projects Archtl. Record mag. and Illuminating Engring. Soc. Registered profl. engr., N.Y., Calif. and 14 other states. Mem. Am. Cons. Engrs. Council, Nat. Soc. Profl. Engrs., N.Y. Assn. Cons. Engrs., Cons. Engrs. Assn. Calif., Am. Soc. Heating, Air Conditioning and Refrigeration Engrs., Nat. Assn. Power Engrs. (hon.). Clubs: N.Y. U. (N.Y.C.); Winged Foot Golf (Mamaroneck, N.Y.). Contbg. editor Heating Piping Air Conditioning mag. Contbr. numerous articles to engring. trade jours. Home: 785 Fifth Ave New York City NY 10022 Office: 1133 Ave of Americas New York City NY 10036 also 555 S Flower St Los Angeles CA 90071 and One Maritime Plaza San Francisco CA 94111

DI GIROLAMO, ORLANDO, ednl. adminstr.; b. New Kensington, Pa., Apr. 20, 1924; student in Liberal Arts, N.Y. U., 1949-50, Juilliard Sch. of Music, N.Y.C., 1950-52; Ed.D. in Music and Music Edn., Columbia U.; married; 3 children. Composer, conductor U.S. Army, 1943-46; profl. musician, 1946-54; dir. music Elmwood Park (N.J.) pub. schs., 1954-77; dir. music Ossinig (N.Y.) pub. schs., 1977—. Mem. N.J. Edn. Assn., Am. Fedn. Musicians, N.Y. State Sch. Adminstrs. and Suprs., Nat. Assn. Jazz Educators. Original compositions performed at Town Hall, N.Y.C. Contbr. articles in field to music mag. Office: Ossining Union Free School Dist 83 Croton Ave Ossining NY 10562

DI GREGORIO, GUERINO JOHN, pharmacologist; b. Phila., May 11, 1940; s. Guerino John and Olivera (Fani) Di G.; B.S., Pa. State U., 1962; Ph.D., Hahnemann Med. Coll., 1966, M.D., 1978; m. Mary Ellen Boyle, Aug. 3, 1963; children—Catherine Josephine, Robert Guerino. Asst. prof. pharmacology Hahnemann Med. Coll., 1966-70, asso. prof. pharmacology, dir. toxicology, 1970—. Cons. Phila. div. Bur. Narcotics and Dangerous Drugs, 1969—; cons. VA Hosp., Phila., 1972—. NIMH grantee, 1973—. Mem. N.Y. Acad. Sci., Am. Soc. Pharmacology and Exptl. Therapeutics, Am. Acad. Clin. Toxicology. Research in autonomic effects of commonly abused drugs, also salivary secretion of drugs. Home: 1421 Linden Ln West Chester PA 19380 Office: Hahnemann Med Coll Dept Pharmacology Philadelphia PA 19102

DILENGE, DOMENICO, radiologist; b. Grassano, Italy, June 11, 1925; s. Giovanni and Maria (Lagonigro) D.; M.D., U. Naples (Italy), 1949; m. Jacqueline Galopin, Apr. 17, 1969; children—Marie-Emmanuelle, Thomas. Intern, med. clinics U. Naples, 1947-49, U. Pavia (Italy), 1950-51; resident Hôpital Ste.-Anne, Paris, France, 1959-60; practice medicine specializing in radiology, Paris, 1953-58, Sherbrooke, Que., Can., 1968—; libero docente di neuroradiologia, Pisa, Italy, 1964; maître ès scis. medicales, Paris, France, 1964; professeur agrégé Associé, U. Nantes (France), 1966-68; research asso. prof. Washington U., St. Louis, 1968; prof., chmn. diagnostic radiology, dir. dept. diagnostic radiology U. Sherbrooke, 1968-77. Fellow Royal Coll. Physicians; mem. French Soc. Neurology (hon.), Soc. Radiologie Canadienne Française (hon.) Academia de Ciencias Médicas (mem. de mérito Barcelona), Laureat Académie Nation de Médec de Paris, Am. Soc. Neuroradiology, Am. Coll. Radiology, Canadian Assn. Radiologists, Radiol. Soc. N.Am., N.Y. Acad. Scis. Author: (with M. David) La Selle turcique, Radiologie normal et pathologique, 1957; (with others) Neurochirurgie, 1961; L'angiographie de l'artère carotide interne chez le sujet normal, 1962; (with others) L'angiographie par Soustraction de l'artère ophtalmique et de ses branches, 1965, Recent Advances in The Study of Cerebral Circulation, 1970. Contbr. articles to profl. jours. Home: 427 Victoria St Sherbrooke PQ Canada

DI LEO, JOSEPH HENRY, pediatrician; b. N.Y.C., Nov. 16, 1902; s. Emanuel and Rosa (Cori) DiL.; M.D., U. Bologna, 1927, postgrad., 1928-31; U. Rome, 1931-35; m. Joan LeB. McTague, Nov. 10, 1948; children—Judith, Daniel, Paul. Externe Yale Clinic Child Devel., 1945; dir. developmental clinic N.Y. Foundling Hosp., N.Y.C., 1945-78; asst. clin. prof. pediatrics N.Y. U., N.Y.C., 1955—; lectr. spl. edn. Columbia, 1963—; individual practice medicine, specializing in pediatrics N.Y.C., 1947-76. Chmn. bd. St. Joseph's Sch. for Deaf, N.Y.C., 1962; adv. bd. City of N.Y. Dept. Mental Health and Mental Retardation, 1973—. Diplomate Am. Bd. Pediatrics. Mem. Soc. Research in Child Devel., Am. Acad. Pediatrics, N.Y. Acad. Scis., Internat. Soc. Study Behavioral Devel. Roman Catholic. Author: Physical Factors in Growth and Development, 1970; Young Children and Their Drawings, 1970; Children's Drawings as Diagnostic Aids, 1973; Child Development: Analysis and Synthesis; contbg. author: Exceptional Infant, 1967; Learning Disabilities: Implications for A Responsible Society, 1969; Handbook on Learning Disabilities, 1974. Home: 49 E 86th St New York City NY 10028

DI LEONE, KENNETH ROBERT, accountant; b. Providence, July 13, 1946; s. Leonard O. and Anna (Caldarone) Di L.; A.S., Johnson Wales Coll., 1968; B.S., Husson Coll., 1970; m. Gloria J. Toti, May 5, 1974; children—Amy Bernice, Amanda Gloria. Sr. accountant Kent Nursing Home, Inc., Warwick, R.I., 1970-71; staff accountant Goluses & Brown, C.P.A.'s, Warwick, 1971-74, S. Harry Siperstein, C.P.A., Cranston, R.I., 1975-76; owner, mgr. Profl. Bookkeeping Services, Providence, 1975-76; fin. analyst BIF (div. Gen. Signal Corp.), W. Warwick, 1976—. Mem. Nat. Accounting Assn., Am. Mgmt. Assn., R.I. N.G. Assn. Roman Catholic. Home: 91 Sisson St Providence RI 02909

DI LEVA, ANTHONY JOSEPH, singer, voice tchr.; b. Rocchetta San Antonio, Italy, Jan. 1, 1910; s. Joseph and Luigia (Corbosiero) Di L.; came to U.S., 1913, naturalized, 1935; m. Teresa Castagna, June 28, 1953; 1 son, Charles. Appeared with New Opera Co., N.Y.C., 1939-40, N.Y. Grand Opera Co., 1974-76, others, appered in Broadway musicals, 1944-74, including Billion Dollar Baby, Guys and Dolls, Silk Stockings, Most Happy Fella, Fiddler on the Roof, Whoop-Up, Christine; tchr. vioce devel. and singing techniques, N.Y.C., 1955—, U. Siena, Italy, 1978. Mem. AFTRA, Screen Actors Guild, Actors Equity Assn., N.Y. Singing Tchrs. Assn. (dir., chmn. program com., chmn. composers showcase com.), Am. Guild Mus. Artists, Nat. Assn. Tchrs. of Singing. Home: 174 W 72d St New York City NY 10023 Office: Sherman Sq Studios 160 W 73d St New York City NY 10023

DILLABER, PHILIP ARTHUR, govt. budget analyst; b. Springfield, Mass., Aug. 24, 1922; s. Ralph E. and Grace (Holman) D.; B.A., Am. Internat. Coll., 1949; M.B.A., Ind. U., 1950; postgrad. U. Mich., Ind. U., 1950-54; m. Jacqueline M. Bertin, July 16, 1946; children—Anne Erline (Mrs. Donald Youngblood), Katherine Marie, John Philip, Patricia Elizabeth. Clk. research and devel. div. Springfield Armory, 1946-47; research asst. dept. econs. Ind. U., 1951, lectr. econs., 1955-57; orgn. and methods examiner U.S. Air Force, Gulfports, Miss., 1952-53; mgmt. analyst 5th U.S. Army, Chgo., 1954-61; program progress and resources mgmt. analyst Continental Army Commnad, Ft. Monroe, Va., 1962-66; adminstrv. officer U.S. Army NIKE-X System Office, Alexandria, Va., 1967; program analyst Office Asst. Chief Staff Force Devel., Dept. Army, Washington, 1967-71; budget analyst Office Dep. Chief Staff Logistics Dept. Army, Washington, 1971-74; budget analyst Office Dep. Chief Staff Research, Devel. and Acquisition, 1974—; guest lectr. econs. Purdue U., 1959-61. Served with U.S. Army, 1943-46. Mem. Am. Econ. Assn., Am. Soc. Pub. Adminstrn., Beta Gamma Sigma. Home: 3003 N Arkendale St Woodbridge VA 22193 Office: Dept Army Office Dep Chief Staff Research Devel and Acquisition Pentagon Washington DC 20301

DILLARD, EMIL LEE, educator; b. Langdon, Kans., Mar. 14, 1921; s. Oscar Winfield and Mabel Dollie (Brooks) D.; B.A., Emporia (Kans.) State Coll., 1946; M.A., Columbia, 1948, M. Ph., 1974; m. Leona M. Sneed, Sept. 12, 1942. Instr. in English, Eureka (Kans.) Sr. High Sch., 1946-47, U. Oreg., 1948-50, Hunter Coll., 1952; instr. Adelphi U., 1954-59, asst. prof., 1959-68, asso. prof., 1968-74, prof., 1974—. Served with USAAF, 1942-46. Mem. Modern Lang. Assn., Am. Studies Assn., Nat. Council Tchrs. English, N.Y. State English Council, AAUP (chpt. pres. 1967-70, 72-74, Met. N.Y.C. conf. pres. 1970-72, N.Y. conf. pres. 1974-76.). Unitarian. Author: Nouns and Pronouns (poetry), 1974; contbr. articles to profl. jours. Home: 74 Rutland Rd Hempstead NY 11550 Office: Adelphi U Garden City NY 11530

DILLMAN, HARRY LOUIS, JR., engring. mfg. co. exec.; b. White Plains, N.Y., Jan. 12, 1928; s. Harry Louis and Marguerite Mary (Barlie) D.; student Yale U., 1946-47; Asso. in Bus. Adminstrn., Internat. Accountants Soc., 1948-49; m. Georgiann Barry, Nov. 26, 1953; children—David C., Brian K., Jeffrey L., Amy E., Sheila E. Mgr. accounting and data processing Allstate Ins. Co., White Plains, 1954-64; mgr. data processing Am. Express Co., N.Y.C., 1964-68; dir. computer services Combustion Engring., Inc., Windsor, Conn., 1968—; v.p., dir. Invonics Internat. Corp., Point Lookout, N.Y., 1974-77; cons. in field. Served with A.C., U.S. Navy, 1945-47. Mem. Assn. Systems Mgmt., Data Processing Mgmt. Assn., Guide Internat., Control Data Users Group. Republican. Methodist. Club: Rotary. Home: 30 Laurel Ln Simsbury CT 06070 Office: 100 Lamberton Rd Windsor CT 06095

DILLON, JOHN STANLEY, surgeon, educator; b. Washington, Oct. 19, 1930; s. John Arthur and Alice Zelda (Stanley) D.; B.S., Georgetown U., Washington, 1952, M.D., 1956; m. Mary Frances Kelly, May 29, 1960; children—Patrick Aloysius, Mary Catherine, Margaret Alice, Elizabeth Joan, Anne Frances, John Joseph. Intern Barnes Hosp., St. Louis, 1956-57, asst. resident surgeon, 1957-58, 60-62, resident surgeon, 1962-63; instr., research fellow surgery Washington U., St. Louis, 1962-63; instr. Georgetown U., 1963-67, asst. prof., 1967-72, asso. prof., 1972—, dir. Surg. Metabolic Research Lab., 1963—; practice medicine specializing in surgery, Washington, 1963—; mem. staffs Georgetown U. Hosp., Sibley Meml. Hosp. Clin. asso. br. surgery Nat. Cancer Inst., NIH, 1958-60. Served with USPHS, 1958-60. Fellow A.C.S., Southeastern Surg. Congress; mem. AMA, D.C. Med. Soc., Sigma Xi, Alpha Omega Alpha, Phi Chi. K.C. Home: 1106 Flor Ln McLean VA 22101 Office: 3800 Reservoir Rd Washington DC 20007

DILLON, PAUL WALKER, chemist; b. Westchester, N.Y., Sept. 23, 1944; s. Douglas Franklin and Alice Evangeline (Heidenreich) D.; B.S., Poly. Inst. Bklyn., 1966; postgrad. Fordham U., 1966-67; M.S., N.Y. U., 1969, Ph.D., 1974; m. Jane Hogan, June 11, 1967; children—Karen, Joyce. Chemist, Union Carbide Corp., Tarrytown, N.Y., 1965-70, 73—, N.Y. U., Bronx, 1970-73. Recipient first prize Roon Awards Competition, Fedn. of Socs. for Coatings Tech., 1977; NSF summer research fellow, 1964. Mem. Pi Kappa Phi. Republican. Contbr. articles to profl. jours. Office: Route 100C Tarrytown NY 10591

DILLON, RETTA WALSMITH, clin. psychologist; b. Washington; d. Joseph Scott and Retta (Croghan) Walsmith; A.B., George Washington U., 1934; M.A., Washington Sch. Psychiatry, 1945; m. James Joseph Dillon, Dec. 11, 1934; children—Martin Conboy, Retta Kathleen. Recreation aide D.C. Dept. Recreation, 1920-24; pupil personnel psychologist D.C. Pub. Schs., 1926-68; clin. psychologist Washington Dept. Human Resources, 1968—; pvt. practice psychol. counseling, Washington, 1954—. Recipient Washington Humane Soc. award, 1957; Nat. Best Tchr.'s award, 1947; Outstanding Achievement award Dept. Human Resources, 1977. numerous others. Mem. D.C. Mental Health Assn., Am., D.C. (certificate 1978) psychol. assns., Psi Chi, Chi Sigma. Home: 4330 Blagden Ave NW Washington DC 20011

DILLON, ROBERT MORTON, research exec.; b. Seattle, Oct. 27, 1923; s. James Richard and Lucille (Morton) D.; student U. Ill., 1946-47; B.Arch., U. Wash., 1949; M.A. in Architecture, U. Fla., 1954; m. Mary Charlotte Beeson, Jan. 6, 1943; children—Robert Thomas, Colleen Marie Dillon Brown, Patrick Morton. Draftsman, Williams and Longstreet, Architects, Greenville, S.C., 1949-50; designer William G. Lyles, Bissett, Carlisle & Wolff, Architects, Columbia, S.C., 1950, Robert M. Dillon and Wm. B. Eaton, Architects, Gainesville, Fla., 1952-55; staff architect, project dir. Bldg. Research Adv. Bd., Nat. Acad. Scis.-NRC, Washington, 1955-58, exec. dir., 1959-77, exec. sec. U.S. nat. com. for Conseil Internat. du Batiment, 1962-74. Sec. U.S. Planning Com. 2d Internat. Conf. on Permafrost, USSR, 1973; exec. asst. to pres. Nat. Inst. Bldg. Scis., Washington, 1978—. Asst. prof. architecture Clemson Coll., 1949-50; instr., asst. prof. architecture U. Fla., 1950-55; lectr. civil engring. Catholic U. Am., 1956-62; disting. faculty Acad. Code Adminstrn. and Enforcement, U. Ill., 1972; professorial lectr. engring. George Washington U., 1973—; vis. prof. Grad. Sch. Architecture, U. Utah, 1978. Cons. Ednl. Facilities Labs., N.Y.C., 1958-71. Mem. adv. com., low-income housing demonstration program Dept. HUD, Washington, 1964-67; mem. sub-panel on housing White House Panel on Civilian Tech., Washington, 1961-62; mem. adv. council Basic Homes Program OEO and HUD, 1972-77; mem. steering com. on bldg. and constrn. Am. Nat. Metric Council, 1973—. Served with USNR, 1942-45. Registered architect, Fla. Mem. AIA (mem. com. on research for architecture 1962-67, chmn. 1969; chmn. com. archtl. barriers 1967-68, mem. housing com. 1970-72, nat. adv. council on research in energy conservation 1975—), N.Y. Acad. Scis., AAAS, ASCE (see. 1978—, mem. task com. on cold regions engring. 1977—), Nat. Acad. Code Adminstrn. (trustee 1976—, exec. com. 1978—), Am. Real Estate and Urban Econs. Assn., Sigma Lambda Chi. Author: (with S.W. Crawley) Steel Buildings: Analysis and Design, 1970. Contbr. articles on housing, bldg. and planning to profl. jours.; contbr. to Funk and Wagnall's New Ency., 1972. Home: 811 Arrington Dr Silver Spring MD 20901 Office: 1730 Pennsylvania Ave NW Washington DC 20006

DILLON, STANLEY CLIFTON, sci. programmer analyst; b. Balt., Dec. 2, 1941; s. Howard John and Virginia Mae (Oler) D.; A.A., Catonsville Community Coll., 1962; B.A. cum laude, Loyola Coll., Balt., 1975; M.A.S., Johns Hopkins U., 1979; m. Oct. 5, 1963; children—Kenneth Steven, Bryan, Karyn. Tech. aide Johns Hopkins U., Applied Physics Lab., Laurel, Md., 1963-70, programmer profl. staff, 1970-74, programmer analyst, 1974—; v.p. Dillon Bros. Inc., Balt., 1975—. Mem. Alpha Sigma Nu. Presbyterian. Home: 9530 Lyons Mill Rd Owings Mills MD 21117 Office: Applied Physics Lab Johns Hopkins U Johns Hopkins Rd Laurel MD 20810

DILLON, THOMAS CHURCH, advt. exec.; b. Seattle, Mar. 27, 1915; s. Thomas J. and Clarissa (Church) D.; student Harvard, 1933-36; m. Georgiana Adams, Nov. 8, 1939 (dec. May 1964); children—Thomas Adams, Victoria Caroline, George Anthony; m. 2d, Patricia Doran, 1965. With Batten, Barton, Durstine & Osborn, Inc., 1938—, successively copy writer, Mpls., creative head, San Francisco, Los Angeles, 1938-48, v.p., 1948-59, mgr. Los Angeles office, 1957-58, treas., dir., 1958—, exec. v.p., 1959-64, gen. mgr., 1962—, pres., 1964-75, chief exec. officer, 1967-77, chmn., 1975—; pres., BBDO Internat., Inc., 1971-75, chief exec. officer, 1971-77, chmn. bd., 1975—. Clubs: Advertising of N.Y., Economic, Harvard (N.Y.C.). Home: 870 United Nations Plaza New York City NY 10017 Office: 383 Madison Ave New York City NY 10017

DILLOW, GAYLORD BENJAMIN, aluminum co. exec.; b. Millville, W.Va., Feb. 26, 1940; s. Benjamin Luther and Marie Elizabeth D.; A.B., Shepherd Coll., Shepherdstown, W.Va., 1962; M.S., Va. Commonwealth U., 1969; m. Cherie A. Fitting, June 26, 1966; children—Scott, Steven, Shane. High sch. instr. Washington County Bd. Edn., Hagerstown, Md., 1962-67; counselor-co-ordinator D.C. Govt., Washington, 1968-69; personnel supr. Eastalco Aluminum Co., Frederick, Md., 1969-72; personnel mgr. Howmet Aluminum Corp., Lancaster, Pa., 1972—; cons. Counseling in Indsl. Setting, 1974—. Mem. exec. com., membership chmn. Lancaster County Com. for Employment Handicapped, 1976. Mem. Am. Soc. Personnel Adminstrs. Lancaster County Personnel Assn. (pres. 1978-79), U.S. Jr. C. of C., Lancaster Assn. Commerce and Industry. Republican. Home: Route 1 Box 413 Donegal Springs Rd Mount Joy PA 17552 Office: Box 3167 Lancaster PA 17604

DI LUGLIO, THOMAS ROSS, state ofcl.; b. Providence, Nov. 25, 1931; s. Thomas and Elvira (Rossi) DiL.; A.B., Brown U., 1953; LL.B., Boston U., 1956; m. Loretta A. Migliaccio, Jan. 1, 1951; children—Thomas A., Mark W., Anthony R., Vera H., Beth E. Admitted to R.I. bar, 1956; practiced in Providence, 1956; lt. gov. of R.I., 1976—; pres. True Realty, Inc. Mem. Johnston Democratic Town Com., 1958—, chmn., 1965—; town solicitor, chief prosecutor

Town of Johnston, 1970-76; mem. R.I. Senate, 1960-64; del. Nat. Democratic Conv., 1976; pres. Highland Orchards, Inc. Mem. R.I. Bar Assn., Phi Delta Theta. Roman Catholic. Office: Room 317 State House Providence RI 02903*

DIMANT, JACOB, physician; b. Rehovot, Israel, Apr. 27, 1947; s. Simcha and Ita D.; came to U.S., 1972, naturalized, 1977; M.D., Hadassah Med. Sch., Hebrew U., Jerusalem, 1972; m. Rose Bea Jearolmen, Sept. 11, 1974. Intern, Maimonides Med. Center, Bklyn., 1972-73, resident in medicine, 1973-75, chief resident in medicine, 1975-76; fellow in rheumatology Downstate Med. Center, Bklyn., 1976-78; practice medicine specializing in internal medicine and rheumatology, Bklyn., 1975—; dir. rheumatology div. and asso. dir. dept. med. edn. Maimonides Med. Center, Bklyn., 1978—; med. dir. Prospect Park Nursing Home, Bklyn., 1977—; attending State Univ. Hosp. and Kings County Hosp., Bklyn., 1978—; asst. prof. medicine SUNY, Bklyn., 1978—. Arthritis Found. fellow, 1977-78. Diplomate Am. Bd. Internal Medicine. Mem. A.C.P., Am., N.Y. rheumatism assns., Am. Fedn. Clin. Research, Am. Geriatric Soc. Contbr. articles to med. jours. Office: 4802 10th Ave Brooklyn NY 11219

DIMANTHA, PRIYA CHITTA, analytical engr., mgmt. cons.; b. Sri Lanka, Sept. 17, 1943; s. Kahingalage Wilson De Silva and Catherine Susimawathie (Wickremaratne) DeS.; came to Can., 1966; B.Sc. in Engring., U. Sri Lanka, 1965; M.A. Sci. in Engring. (NRC grantee), U. Waterloo, Can., 1967; diploma in mgmt. McGill U., Can., 1974, M.B.A., 1976; m. D. Amodanie Chula Kumarie Fernando, June 16, 1976. Instr. engring. U. Ceylon, 1965-66; research and teaching asst. U. Waterloo, 1966-67; instr. engring. U. Concordia, Can., 1969-70; analytical engr. Pratt & Whitney Aircraft of Can., Longueuil, Que., 1967-72, sr. analytical engr., 1972—; mgmt. cons., 1974—. Mem. Am. Inst. Aeros. and Astronautics, Order Engrs. Que. Clubs: Ski, Sailing, Golf, Tennis. Contbr. articles in field to profl. jours. Home: 259 Du Dauphine St Lambert PQ J4S 1N6 Canada Office: Pratt & Whitney Aircraft of Can P1 PO Box 10 Longueuil PQ Canada

DIMARIA, FRED JOSEPH, mktg. exec.; b. Paterson, N.J., Feb. 24, 1940; s. Salvatore P. and Concetta T. (Logioco) DiM.; B.S., Fairleigh Dickinson U., 1965, M.B.A., 1972; m. Cecelia T. Skinner, Nov. 18, 1961; children—Lisa, Theresa, Fred Michael. Chemist, Hoffman LaRoche, Nutley, N.J., 1963-67; mgr. techno econ. planning Allied Chem., Morristown, N.J., 1967-71; pres. FAX, Denville, N.J., 1970-74; mgr. sales and comml. devel. Sun Chem., Carlstadt, N.J., 1971-75; dir. planning and mktg. research Roche Chem. div., Nutley, 1975—. Pres. parish council St. Catherine of Sienna Parish, Mountain Lakes, N.J., 1976-78. Mem. Am. Chem. Soc., Comml. Devel. Assn., Chem. Mktg. Research Assn. Inventor in field. Home: 94 Boulevard Mountain Lakes NJ 07046 Office: Hoffman LaRoche Nutley NJ 07011

DIN, HAMEED UD, educator; b. Amritsar, India, July 8, 1915; s. Karim Ud and Hurmat (Begam) D.; came to U.S., 1965; M.A. with honors, Panjab U., 1938; M.A., U. Delhi, 1941; Ph.D., Panjab U., 1954; m. Noor Fatima Husain, Nov. 5, 1944; 1 son, Raza Maabool. Lectr., Panjab U., Pakistan, 1951-55, Govt. Coll., Lahore, Pakistan, 1948-50, Hull (Eng.) U. Coll. Edn., 1960-65; vis. prof. Indo-Muslim and Persian lit. Columbia U., N.Y.C., 1965-66, seminar asso., 1965—; prof. S. Asian History, Syracuse (N.Y.) U., 1966-68; lectr., research asso. Harvard U., Cambridge, Mass., 1967—; advisor and participant S. Asla Hist. Atlas project U. Minn., Mpls., 1969-78. Mem. Am. Hist. Assn. (chmn. conf. on Asian history 1972-73), Asia Soc. (chmn. Pakistan council 1971—), Panjab U. Hist. Soc. (sec. 1951-55), Assn. Asian Studies. Author: Tarikh-i Islam, 1952; Tarikh-i Pak Wa Hind, 1972; The Afghan Sultanate of Delhi; History and Culture of the Indian People, vol. VI, Delhi Sultanate, 1960, co-author 2d edit., 1967; (with others) A Historical Atlas of South Asia, 1978; contbr. articles in field to profl. jours. Address: 124 Winchester Rd Arlington MA 02174

DINBERG, MICHAEL DAVID, indsl. engr.; b. Ogdensburg, N.Y., June 28, 1944; s. Israel and Pauline (Karch) D.; A.S., Broome Community Coll., 1972; B.S. magna cum laude, Syracuse U., 1973; postgrad. Ga. Inst. Tech., 1973-78. Jr. field technician Singer-Link div., Binghamton, N.Y., 1967-69, jr. field engr., 1969-70; health systems specialist, grad. research asst. Ga. Inst. Tech., 1973-74; sr. indsl. engr. Singer-Link div., 1974-75; mgmt. analyst div. research services NIHUSPHS, Bethesda, Md., 1975-77, systems analyst clin. center, 1977-. Served with USNR, 1965-67. Mem. Am. Hosp. Assn., Am. Inst. Indsl. Engrs., Assn. Advance Ethical Hypnosis, Commd. Officers Assn. USPHS, Hosp. Mgmt. Systems Soc., Assn. Mil. Surgeons U.S., Tau Beta Pi. Home: 1901 Stanley Ave Rockville MD 20851 Office: Clin Center NIH Bethesda MD

DINEEN, EUGENE JOSEPH, educator; b. Niagara Falls, N.Y., Nov. 12, 1920; s. Timothy Charles and Margaret Mary (Movnihan) D.; B.S., Niagara U., 1938; M.S., U. Notre Dame, 1948; Ph.D., Ohio State U., 1951. Chemist, Chem. Constrn. Co., Lewiston, N.Y., 1942-43; research asst. Columbia U., N.Y.C., 1943-44; research chemist Hooker Chem. Co., Niagara Falls, 1951-53; research supr. Gen. Mills, Buffalo, N.Y., 1953-54; chief chemist Banite Co., Buffalo, 1955-56; research scientist Allied Chem. Co., Buffalo, 1956-57; asso. prof. W.Va. State Coll., Institute, 1959-63; asso. prof. analytical and phys. chemistries, Niagara U., Niagara University, N.Y., 1963—, mem. research council, 1973. Research dir., pres. Swevco, Inc., Buffalo, 1957-63. Served with AUS, 1944-46. Fellow Am. Inst. Chemists; mem. Am. Chem. Soc., Am. Assn. U. Profs. Home: 1866 Niagara Ave Niagara Falls NY 14305 Office: Dept Chemistry Niagara U Niagara University NY 14109

DINES, ALLEN I., pharm. co. exec.; b. Pitts., Dec. 16, 1929; s. Max W. and Rosalie (Schweiger) D.; B.S., U. Pitts., 1951; M.S., Ohio State U., 1953, Ph.D., 1958; m. Charlotte Weiss, Oct. 18, 1953; children—Howard, Lisa. Asso. dir. Product Devel., Flint, also Eaton, Decatur, Ill., 1958-60; group leader Miles Labs., Inc., Elkhart, Ind., 1960-64; dir. pharm. research Warren-Teed Pharm., Inc., Columbus, Ohio, 1964-69; dir. research Strong, Cobb & Arner, Inc., Cleve., 1969-70; dir. research and devel. Mylan Pharms., Inc., Morgantown, W.Va., 1971-76; tech. mgr. devel. products Vick Internat., Wilton, Conn., 1976—. Fellow Am. Found. Pharm. Edn.; mem. Am. Chem. Soc., Am. Pharm. Assn., Acad. Pharm. Scis., Sigma Xi, Rho Chi, Alpha Zeta Omega. Patentee in field. Office: 10 Westport Rd Wilton CT 06897

DINGEE, JOHN HENRY, JR., pub. co. exec.; b. Phila., Jan. 29, 1940; s. John Henry and Elizabeth (Eisenger) D.; B.A. in English with honors, Dickinson Coll., 1962; m. Gretchen Gastreich, July 4, 1966; children—Harold Albert, Jennifer Elizabeth. Regional mgr. Iron Age Mag., Chilton Co., Chgo., 1965-66, N.Y.C., 1966-68, Boston, 1968-73, sales mgr. Iron Mage Metalworking Internat. mag., Radnor, Pa., 1973-75, dir. internat. ops. Chilton Co., 1975—. Served to 1st lt. U.S. Army, 1963-65. Home: 522 Brookside Ave Saint Davids PA 19087 Office: Chilton Co Chilton Way Radnor PA 19089

DINGLE, JAMES, state ofcl.; b. Summerton, S.C., Sept. 30, 1949; s. Joseph and Martha (Samuel) D.; A.O.S., Collegiate Inst., N.Y.C., 1977; B.S. in Bus. Mgmt., St. Francis Coll., 1978; m. Bernadette Pegues, June 21, 1975. Employment rep. N.Y. State Dept. Labor, N.Y.C., 1976—. Served with U.S. Army, 1968-70. Decorated Purple Heart. Mem. Am. Mgmt. Assn., Civil Service Employee Assn., Amalgamated Transit Union, VFW. Democrat. Baptist. Home: 97-11 Horace Harding Expy Rego Park NY 11368 Office: 2 World Trade Center Room 7260 New York City NY 10047

DINGMAN, MICHAEL DAVID, mfg. co. exec.; b. New Haven, Sept. 29, 1931; s. James Everett and Amelia (Williamson) D.; student U. Md.; m. Jean Hazlewood, May 16, 1953; children—Michael David, Linda Channing, James Clifford. Gen. partner Burnham & Co., N.Y.C., 1964-70; chmn. bd., pres., chief exec. officer, dir. Wheelabrator-Frye Inc., Hampton, N.H., 1970—; dir. Madison Fund Inc., Time Inc., Transway Internat. Corp., Pogo Producing Co.; mem. exec. com. Com. Publicly Owned Cos. Mem. Mus. of Sci. Corp., Boston. Mem. IEEE, N.H. Council World Affairs. Clubs: Recess, Links, Board Room, N.Y. Yacht (N.Y.C.); Lyford Cay (Nassau); Union of Boston; Basin Harbor (Vt.). Home: Moulton Ridge Rd Kensington NH 03833 Office: Liberty Ln Hampton NH 03842

DINMAN, BERTRAM DAVID, aluminum co. exec.; b. Phila., Aug. 9, 1925; s. Meyer and Minnie (Kaufman) D.; student Temple U., 1944-46, 47, M.D., 1951; Sc.D., U. Cin., 1957; m. Gabrielle Stamm, June 11, 1950; children—Stefanie, Jonathan David, Emily, Joshua. Asst. prof. to prof. Ohio State U. Coll. Medicine, 1957-65; prof., dir. Inst. Indsl. Health, U. Mich. Sch. Public Health, 1965-73; corp. med. dir. Aluminum Co. Am., Pitts., 1973-78, v.p.-health and safety, 1978—; cons. U.S. Army, USN, WHO. Served in C.E., U.S. Army, 1944-46. Mem. Permanent Commn. and Internat. Assn. Occupational Health (dir.), Am. Acad. Occupational Medicine (pres. 1973-74; award of Merit), Am. Bd. Preventive Medicine (dir.). Club: Duquesne (Pitts.). Author 3 books, over 90 sci. articles. Office: 1501 Alcoa Bldg Pittsburgh PA 15219

DINSDALE, HENRY BEGG, educator; b. Kingston, Ont., Can., Sept. 22, 1931; s. Harry Hamlin and Doris Eileen (Donnelly) D.; M.D., C.M., Queen's U. (Ont., Can.), 1955; m. Lyla June Yates, June 11, 1955; children—Janice, Scott, Henry, Martha. Resident in medicine Queen's U., 1955-57; registrar Maudsley Hosp., London, 1957-59; Nuffield fellow Queen's Sq., London, 1959-60; resident, research fellow Harvard Neurol. unit Boston City Hosp., 1960-73; lectr.-prof. medicine Div. Neurology, Queen's U., Kingston, Ont., Can., chmn. div. neurology, 1971—; mem. Med. Research Council; chmn. various provincial and fed. research coms. Recipient Brown prize, 1950; Morris prize, 1950; Weil award, 1976; Nuffield fellow, 1959-60; MacLachlan fellow, 1961-62; Bullard fellow, 1962-63. Mem. Royal Coll. Physicians and Surgeons Can., Can., Am. neurol. assns., Am. Acad. Neurology, Can. Med. Assn., Coll. Physicians and Surgeons Ont. and Que., Royal Soc. Medicine. Author: The Nervous System, Structure and Function Disease, 1972; contbr. articles in cerebral circulation and stroke to med., sci. jours. Home: 95 Hill St Kingston ON K7L 2M8 Canada Office: 78 Barrie St Kingston ON K7L 3J8 Canada

DINSMORE, PAUL RICH, psychiatrist; b. Bangor, Maine, Jan. 1, 1932; s. Joseph Smart and E. Marguerite (Rich) D.; B.A., U. Maine, 1954; M.D., George Washington U., 1958; m. Caroline Theresa Cornoni, July 1, 1966; children—Elizabeth Pecce, Paul Rich. Intern, U. Chgo. Clinics, 1958-59; teaching research fellow Harvard U. Sch. Medicine, McLean Hosp., Belmont, Mass., Mass. Gen. Hosp., Boston, 1959-62; asst. psychiatrist McLean Hosp., 1962-73, asst. attending psychiatrist, 1973—; attending physician Mt. Auburn Hosp., 1973—; instr. Harvard Med. Sch., Boston, 1962—; mgmt. cons. Arthur D. Little Inc., Cambridge, Mass., 1975—. Fellow Royal Soc. Health (U.K.), Am. Psychiat. Assn.; mem. AAAS, N.Y. Acad. Scis., Thoreau Soc. and Lyceum, Louisa Mae Alcott Meml. Soc. Republican. Baptist. Contbr. articles to profl. jours. Home: 255 Main St Concord MA 01742 Office: 300 Mount Auburn St Cambridge MA 02138

DINTENFASS, JULIUS, chiropractor; b. Bklyn., Sept. 25, 1910; s. Abraham and Mary (Amsterdam) D.; B.S., Columbia U., 1932; postgrad. U. Heidelberg (Germany), 1932-33, N.Y. U., 1940-41; Dr. Chiropractic, Eastern Chiropractic Inst., 1936; m. Ruth Keisler, Feb. 26, 1939; children—Ellen Joan Dintenfass Berger, Marylyn Sue Dintenfass Katz, Nancy Jill. Pvt. chiropractic practice, N.Y.C., 1936—; faculty mem. depts. pathology and kinesiology Chiropractic Inst. N.Y., 1936-56; dir. chiropractic N.Y.C. Health Dept. Bur. Health Care Services, 1968-76; charter mem. N.Y. State Bd. Chiropractic Examiners, 1963-71, chmn., 1965-66, 69-70. Pres., Norman Sarrett Meml. Found.; trustee Trustee Nat. Coll. Chiropractic, Lombard, Ill. Fellow Internat. Coll. Chiropractors; mem. Am., Met. Dist. (pres. 1946-47), N.Y. State chiropractic assns., Internat. Coll. Applied Nutrition, Internat. Acad. Preventive Medicine, Internat. Acad. Biol. Medicine, AAAS. Author: Chiropractic—A Modern Way to Health, 1966; editor Science Sidelights, 1936-63. Home: 64 Meadow Dr Woodmere NY 11598 Office: 240 Central Park S New York City NY 10019

DION, JOYCE ANN, educator; b. Willimantic, Conn., Sept. 7, 1942; d. Delphis Adelard and Anna May Lilian (Krizanek) D.; B.S., U. Conn., 1964; M.S., Central Conn. State Coll., 1970; M.A., Ball State U., 1976. Tchr. French, Spanish, Windsor (Conn.) High Sch., 1964-67, U.S. Dept. Def. schs., 1967—, Fuchu Middle Sch., Tokyo, 1967-68, Clark High Sch., Philippines, 1968-69, Woodbridge (U.K.) Middle Sch., 1969-72, Torrejon High Sch., Madrid, 1972—. Mem. NEA, Overseas, Madrid edn. assns., Am. Personnel and Guidance Assn. Roman Catholic. Home: 7 Calle Bergantin Madrid Spain Office: Box 4374 APO New York NY 09283

DIONNE, ANDRE CLERMONT, chiropractor; b. St. Dominique, Que., Can., May 23, 1939; s. Joseph and Elise (Lavoie) D.; D.C., Palmer Coll. Chiropractic, 1967; m. Claudette Isella Forget, June 13, 1964; children—Luc, Sylvain. Dir., Assn. Chiropractors of Que., 1971-74; pres. Order of Chiropractors of P.Q., 1974-77. Dir. Caisse d'Entraide Economique, 1971-75; sec., dir. Place le Germoir, 1976; swimming instr. Internat. Red Cross. Named chiropractor of year Province of Que., 1975-76. Mem. Canadian Owner and Pilot Assn. Home: 193 rue de la Gare Montmagny PQ G5V 2T4 Canada

DIPALMA, JOHN CANDIDE, chem. engr.; b. N.Y.C., Nov. 15, 1938; s. Candido and Juliet (Veniero) DiP.; B.S. cum laude in Chem. Engring., Worcester Poly. Inst., 1960; M.S. in Chem. Engring., N.Y. U., 1964; M.B.A., U. Conn., 1970; m. Lenore Estelle Cuneo, Aug. 1961; children—James Michael, Donald John. With Am. Cyanamid Co., 1960—, research engr. Stamford (Conn.) Research Labs., 1960-64, prin. research investigator, Stamford, 1964-67, project leader, Stamford, 1967-70, corp. chem. contract negotiator, purchasing dept., Wayne, N.J., 1970-73, sr. systems analyst, Bound Brook, N.J., 1973-76, sr. energy conservation engr., Wayne, 1976—. Mem. citizens' policy advisory com. N.E. N.J. Water Quality Mgmt. Planning, 1977—; mem. bldg. energy/safety com. West Milford Twp., 1978—. Mem. Am. Inst. Chem. Engrs. (nat., local chpts.). Author, co-author reports for NASA, U.S. Army; patentee reactor design. Home: 135 Green Dale Dr Oak Ridge NJ 07438 Office: Berdan Ave Wayne NJ 07470

DIPAOLA, SALVATORE PAUL, combustion engr.; b. Monongahela, Pa., Apr. 19, 1927; s. Cateno and Anna (Furiga) D.; grad. Lincoln Extension Inst., 1967; m. Eileen T. Koch, June 17, 1948; children—Sherra Lynn, Michael A. With Combustion Engring. Co., Inc., Monongahela, Pa., 1944—, supr. combustion engring., 1968—. Mgr., Little League, Monongahela, 1965—, Pony League Baseball, to 1972. Served with USN, 1945-46. Mem. Cast Metals Inst., Materials Handling Inst. Democrat. Roman Catholic. Clubs: Victory Hill Trap, Elks. Address: 104 Greenridge Dr Monongahela PA 15063

DIPAOLO, GORDON ANTHONY, educator; b. Bklyn., June 22, 1934; s. Dominic and Mary (Novotny) D.; B.A., Bklyn., Coll., 1955; M.B.A. with honors, N.Y.U., 1964, Ph.D. with honors, 1970; m. Lorraine Ann Karam, May 26, 1962. With sales dept. Revlon, Inc., N.Y.C., 1956-59; with sales dept. Lentheric, Inc., Chgo., 1959-60; sales mgr. St. John's U., N.Y.C., 1966-71; asst. prof., now asso. prof. City U. N.Y., 1971—; cons. N.Y.C. Community Council, N.Y. Council for Orthopedic Handicapped, Bklyn. Lacepaper Co., Inc., Power Draulics-Nielsen Co., Inc. Cahs, Inc. Campaign co-mgr. Borenstein for Congress, 1974-76. Recipient Founder's Day award, 1971; Marcus Nadler fellow, 1963; Ford Found. fellow, 1964-65. Mem. Am. Mktg. Assn., Am. Assn. Mktg. Educators. Author: Marketing Strategy for Economic Development, 1976. Contbr. articles to profl. jours. Home: 47 Plaza St Brooklyn NY 11217 Office: 715 Ocean Terr Staten Island NY 10301

DIPASQUALE, EMANUEL PAUL, educator, poet; b. Ragusa, Italy, Jan. 25, 1943; s. Serafino and Giuseppa R. (Scannavino) DiP.; came to U.S., 1957, naturalized, 1964; B.A., Adelphi U., 1965; M.A., N.Y. U., 1966; m. Mari Kula, Feb. 14, 1965; children—Paul, Laura. Instr. Elizabeth City (N.C.) State Coll., 1966-68; asst. prof. English, Middlesex County Coll., Edison, N.J., 1968—. Mem. Am. Fedn. Tchrs. Contbr. poems to various profl. jours., anthologies, study text. Home: 16 Koster Blvd 1B Edison NJ 08817

DI PIERRO, RONALD JOSEPH, mgmt. cons.; b. Bklyn., Oct. 20, 1947; s. Alfonso and Noella Louisenne (Villeneuve) DiP.; A.A., S. I. Community Coll., 1971. Programmer trainee Lombard & Wall Inc., 1971-72; programmer Milady Mfg. Co., 1972; systems analyst, data processing mgr. Sherwood Security Corp., 1972; systems coordinator Matsushita Electric Corp., 1972-74; cons. Stone & Websyer Mgmt. Cons., Inc., N.Y.C., 1974—. Served with USAF, 1967-71. Democrat. Roman Catholic. Club: Z of Am. Home: 20 Cheney Dr RFD 5 Hudson NH 03051 Office: 90 Broad St New York NY 10004

DIPIETRO, G. GUY, supt. schs.; b. N.Y.C., Jan. 1, 1937; s. John and Malfesia (Testa) DiP.; B.S. in Edn., State U. N.Y. at Oneonta, 1961, M.A., 1963; postgrad. N.Y. U.; m. Rose Anne Scavo, Oct. 16, 1959; children—John, Michael, Guy. Mem. faculty, adminstrn. Brentwood (N.Y.) pub. schs., 1963—, dir. personnel, 1971-72, supt., 1972—. Served with AUS, 1955-57. Mem. Am. Assn. Sch. Adminstrs., Kappa Delta Pi. Home: 25 Grayon Dr Dix Hills NY 11746 Office: 3d Ave and 4th St Brentwood NY 11717

DI PRIMIO, ANTHONY, banker; b. Phila., Sept. 14, 1933; s. Aniceto and Angela (Spadea) Di P.; B.S., LaSalle Coll., Phila., 1956; M.A., U. Pa., 1971; Ph.D., Temple U., Phila., 1978; m. Eleanor De Fusco, Sept. 11, 1955; children—Denise, Anthony. Internal productivity cons. Ins. Co. N. Am., Phila., 1967-73; ops. improvement mgr. Fed. Res. Bank Phila., 1973-75, mgr. tng. and devel., 1975—; adj. prof. mgmt. Temple U., LaSalle Coll. Prof. Loman Found. fellow, 1971. Mem. Am. Inst. Banking (dir.), Am. Soc. Tng. and Devel., Indsl. Relations Soc., Assn. Internal Mgmt. Consultants. Author articles. Home: 131 Trent Rd Turnersville NJ 08012 Office: 100 N 6th St Philadelphia PA 19105

DIRCKS, RICHARD JOSEPH, educator; b. N.Y.C., May 22, 1926; s. Curt and Georgette Cecelia (Middleton) D.; A.B., Fordham Coll., 1949, M.A., 1950, Ph.D., 1961; m. Phyllis Ann Toal, Aug. 17, 1963; children—Cathy, Laurie, Deirdre, Richard. Instr., Seton Hall U., 1950-54, asst. prof. English, 1954-56; asst. prof. St. John's U., Jamaica, N.Y., 1956-61, asso. prof., 1961-66, prof., 1966—, chmn. English dept., 1964-67, asso. dean Grad. Sch. Arts and Scis., 1973-75, dir. Humanities Research Center, 1975-77; lectr. Fordham U. Sch. Adult Edn., 1958-68. Served with U.S. Army, 1944-45. Shell grantee, 1966; asso. Danforth Found. Mem. Modern Lang. Assn. Am., N.E. Modern Lang. Assn., AAUP, Am. Soc. 18th-Century Studies, N.Y. State English Council, Conf. Brit. Studies, Internat. Assn. Anglo-Irish Studies, L.I. Brit. Studies Group, Huntington (N.Y.) Hist. Soc., St. John's U. Friends of Library (charter mem., co-founder). Roman Catholic. Author: (with G. Cevasco, J. P. Franzetti) Functional English, 1959; Richard Cumberland, 1976; contbr. articles to profl. jours.; editor: (with J. K. Welcher) An Essay on Fable by Robert Dodsley (1764), 1965. Home: 5 Edwin Ln Huntington NY 11743 Office: St John's U Jamaica NY 11439

DI RENZO, GORDON JAMES, educator; b. N. Attleboro, Mass., July 19, 1934; s. Santo and Giulia (Petti) DiR.; B.A., U. Notre Dame, 1956, M.A., 1957, Ph.D., 1963; postgrad. Harvard U., 1959, Columbia U., 1963-65; m. Mary Kathleen Ryan, July 6, 1968; children—Maria Giulia, Chiara Veronica, Marco Santo. Instr., Coll. of St. Rose, Albany, N.Y., 1957-59, U. Portland (Oreg.), 1961-62, Fairfield (Conn.) U., 1962-66; asso. prof. Ind. U., S. Bend, 1966-70; prof. sociology U. Del., Newark, 1970—; faculty Albany (N.Y.) Med. Center, 1958-59, Coll. of White Plains (N.Y.), 1963-65, Bklyn. Coll. of City U. N.Y., 1965, Western Conn. State Coll., 1964, U. Notre Dame, 1960-61, Siena Coll., N.Y., 1968-69; affiliate mem. med. and dental staff Wilmington (Del.) Med. Center, 1976—; dir. Sociol. Cons. Group, N. Attleboro, 1963—; Fulbright-Hays prof. U. Rome, 1968-69. Certified social psychologist; Ford. Found. grantee, 1960; Italian Ministry of Edn. fellow, 1960; NSF fellow, 1964; Nat. Endowment for Humanities grantee, 1975. Fellow Am. Sociol. Assn.; mem. Am. Psychol. Assn., AAUP, AAAS, Assn. Behavioral Scis. in Med. Edn., Soc. Personality and Social Psychology, Am.-Italian Hist. Assn., Fulbright Alumni Assn., Internat. Sociol. Assn., Internat. Soc. for Polit. Psychology, Soc. for Psychologists in Medicine, Soc. for Study Social Problems, Soc. for Psychol. Study Social Issues, Eastern Sociol. Soc., Alpha Kappa Delta. Contbr. articles to profl. jours.; author: Personality, Power and Politics, 1967; Concepts, Theory and Explanation in the Behavioral Sciences, 1966; Personality and Politics, 1974; We, the People: American Character and Social Change, 1977. Home: 28 Deer Run Little Baltimore Farms Newark DE 19711 Office: Dept Sociology U Del Newark DE 19711

DIRKES, ROBERT FREDERICK, communications cons.; b. N.Y.C., Dec. 3, 1898; s. Herman Frank and Emilie (Back) D.; M.E., Stevens Inst. Tech., 1920; m. Eva Hutchison, June 21, 1924. Joined engring. dept. Western Union Co., N.Y.C., 1920, asst. engr. automatics, 1940, patron system engr., 1945, dir. operations, 1950, asst. v.p. facsimile and pvt. wire services, 1953-62, gen. mgr. systems devel., 1962-63; now communications cons.; dir. Trans Lux Corp.; former dir. Teleprinter Corp., Gray Mfg. Co., Dynametrics Corp., Microwave Assos. Mem. Dept. Def. Exec. Res.; mem. Brookfield Conservation Commn. Served with U.S. Army, 1918. Registered profl. engr., N.Y. Mem. I.E.E.E., Sigma Phi Epsilon. Protestant. Mason. Clubs: Merchants, Stevens Metropolitan. Holder 70 patents on telegraphy, metallurgy, optics. Address: Obtuse Rocks Rd Brookfield Center CT 06805

DI RUGGIERO, MAUREEN ANN, educator; b. Cleve., July 8, 1947; d. Homer Edward and Mariann Lois (Miller) Becks; B.A., Hiram Coll., 1969; M.Ed., Boston Coll., 1973; M.Ed., Providence Coll., 1978; postgrad. Drew U., 1968, Harvard U., 1971; m. Victor Gerard, Jr., Aug. 26, 1972. Tchr., W. Jr. High Sch., Walpole, Mass., 1969-70, E. Jr. High Sch., Walpole, 1970-72; faculty Harvard U. social studies project, Cambridge, Mass., 1971-72; tchr. E. Jr. High Sch., Walpole, 1972-73; guidance counselor Barrington (R.I.) Jr. High Sch., 1973-77; practice marriage and family counseling, Foster, R.I., 1976-77; dir. counseling services Counseling and Family Services, Foster, 1977—; instr. counseling and psychology R.I. Jr. Coll., Lincoln, 1977—; v.p. Eco-Tech, Inc., 1978—. Recipient Greater Cleve. Louis B. Seltzer award, 1965; Hiram Coll. scholar, 1965; St. Thomas Acquinas scholar, 1967-68; Barrington grantee, 1975-76. Mem. Am., R.I. personnel and guidance assns., Am. Psychol. Assn. (asso.), Am. Rehab. Counseling Assn., Nat. Vocat. Guidance Assn., Am. Specialists in Group Work Assn., New Eng. Assn. Group Specialists. Home: RFD 1 PO Box 105 E Killingly Rd Foster RI 02825 Office: Danielson Pike Foster RI 02825

DISALVO, WALTER ANTHONY, chem. engr.; b. Harrison, N.J., Dec. 23, 1920; s. Angelo and Anna (Sylvester) DiS.; B.S. in Chem. Engring., Newark Coll. Engring., 1947, M.S. in Chem. Engring., 1951; m. Yolanda DeCicco, June 8, 1946; children—Carol Ann, Sandra Mary. Sect. head, research and devel. Colgate Palmolive Co., 1965-70, sr. research asso., research and devel., 1970-74; dir. research and devel. Internat. Playtex, Paramus, N.J., 1974—. Pres. North Arlington (N.J.) Bd. Health. Mem. Am. Chem. Soc., Assn. Research Dirs., AAAS, Soc. Cosmetic Chemists. Roman Catholic. Club: K.C. Home: 237 Prospect St North Arlington NJ 07032

DISANTIS, JOHN ANTHONY, material utilization engr.; b. Cleve., May 24, 1920; s. John and Pasqualina (Guarino) D.; B.S. in Metall. Engring., Mich. State U., 1950; postgrad. in engring. adminstrn. Case Inst. Tech., 1952-54; diploma Metals Engring. Inst., 1963; m. Anne M. Pompilli, July 22, 1943; children—John E., James A., Regina A. Mgmt. trainee Gen. Motors Corp., Cleve., 1950; designer F.G. Wade, Inc., Cleve., 1950-52; tech. specialist Sohio, Cleve., 1952-63; sr. metall. engr. Research div. Carrier Corp., Syracuse, N.Y., 1963-74, material utilization engr. Elliott div., Jeannette, Pa., 1975—. Served with USN, 1942-45. Mem. Am. Soc. Metals, Am. Welding Soc. Nat. Mgmt. Assn. (dir. 1971-75), Carrier Mgmt. Assn. (pres. 1970-71), Tech. Club Syracuse (1st v.p. 1974-75), Elliott Mgmt. Club. Republican. Roman Catholic. Club: Toastmasters (gov. dist. 34, 1968-69, named to Hall of Fame 1969). Contbr. articles to profl. publs. Developer automatic tester of expanding tools. Home: 11 Greenview Dr Jeannette PA 15644 Office: Elliott Div Carrier Corp N 4th St Jeannette PA 15644

DI SCIPIO, WILLIAM JOSEPH, psychologist, educator; b. Bronx, N.Y., Feb. 9, 1943; s. Bernard William and Theresa (Rullo) Di S.; B.A. in Psychology, Queens Coll., City U. N.Y., 1964, M.A., 1965; Dip. Psych., U. London, (Eng.), 1966, Ph.D. in Research Psychology, 1968; m. Maria Remenyi, Feb. 22, 1969; children—Aimée, Rebecca. Ward adminstr. Neuropsychiat. Service, Bronx State Hosp., 1968-69, Creedmoor State Hosp., Queens Village, N.Y., 1969-70; research psychologist Clin. Psychopharmacology Service, Bronx State Hosp., 1970, cons. Behavior Therapy Clinic, 1970-72, dir. Evaluation and Research Service, 1972-74, asso. editor hosp. jour. 1972-75; clin. instr. dept. psychiatry Albert Einstein Coll. Medicine, 1970—, asst. clin. prof., 1974—; asst. prof. dept. psychology Coll. New Rochelle (N.Y.), 1973—; dir. psychology Bronx Children's Psychiat. Center, 1974—. Chmn. Larchmont Mararoneck Com. of Family and Youth, 1978; mem. Community Planning Bd. Dist. 10, Bronx, 1972. Clin. fellow Behavior Therapy and Research Soc.; mem. Am. Psychol. Assn., Brit. Psychol. Soc., Royal Coll. Psychiatrists, AAAS. Contbr. articles on behavior therapy and psychiat. disorders to books and profl. jours. Office: 1000 Waters Pl Bronx NY 10461

DI SCIULLO, ANTHONY JOSEPH, physician; b. Boston, Feb. 24, 1943; s. Alfred and Norma Theresa (Balboni) DiS.; A.B. in Biology, Boston Coll., 1964; M.D., New York Med. Coll., 1968; m. Judith Margaret Bottomly, Sept. 28, 1968; children—Elizabeth, John. Intern, S.I. Hosp., N.Y.C., 1968-69; resident R.I. Hosp., Providence Lying In Hosp., 1969-72; Am. Cancer Soc. fellow Beth Israel Hosp., Boston, 1974-75; chief dept. obstetrics and gynecology Mt. Auburn Hosp., Cambridge, Mass., 1975—; instr. Harvard U. Med. Sch. Served to maj., M.C., U.S. Army, 1972-74. Decorated Meritorious Service award. Mem. Am. Coll. Obstetrics and Gynecology, Am. Fertility Soc., Mass. Med. Soc. Roman Catholic. Office: 300 Mt Auburn St Cambridge MA 02138

DISCO, ADRIAN ANTHONY, elec. engr.; b. The Netherlands, Oct. 29, 1915; s. Cornelis Dionisius and Elisabeth (Van De Water) D.; came to U.S., 1954, naturalized, 1959; B.S., Leyden Elec. Engring. Coll. (Netherlands), 1937; m. Adriana Maria Kriek, Sept. 26, 1938; children—Josepha, Cornelis, Elisabeth. With Royal Dutch Airlines, Netherlands, 1936-38; mgr. instrument dept. Royal Dutch Air Force, Indonesia, 1938-47; Japanese prisoner-of-war, 1942-45; research and devel. instr. astronomy dept. U. Leyden, Netherlands, 1947-54; faculty Yale U., New Haven, 1954—, now dir. Sci. Instrumentation Lab.; cons. in field. Mem. Am. Mgmt. Assn., Netherlands Soc. Instrumentation Engring. Home: 111 Hilldale Rd Bethany CT 06525 Office: 260 Whitney Ave New Haven CT 06520

DISKO, MICHAEL DAVID, civil engr.; b. Summit, N.J., Dec. 14, 1936; s. Michael and Amelia (Tomascek) D.; B.S., Newark Coll. Engring., 1959, M.S., 1962; postgrad. Stevens Inst. Tech., 1962-64; Ph.D. (NSF fellow), N.Y. U., 1967; m. Barbara Ann Hassett, Apr. 8, 1961; children—Michael David, Kenneth Robert, Keith Douglas. Asst. prof., instr. Newark Coll. Engring., 1959-65; asst. prof. Drexel Inst. Tech., Phila., 1967-69; project mgr. Quirk, Lawler & Matusky, cons. engrs., N.Y.C., 1969; owner M. Disko Assos., cons. engrs., Union, N.J., 1969—. Adj. asso. prof. Newark Coll. Engring., 1970-75. Registered profl. engr., N.J., Conn., N.Y., Pa., Del. Mem. Water Pollution Control Fedn., N.J. Soc. Profl. Engrs. Home: 2014 Morrison Ave Union NJ 07083 Office: 2035 US Hwy 22 Union NJ 07083

DISNEY, FRANK ALBERT, pediatrician; b. Bklyn., Oct. 1, 1911; s. William Howard and Irma (Tarbell) D.; A.B., Hamilton Coll., 1932; M.D., Columbia U., 1937; m. Rosemary Elizabeth Miller, Oct. 13, 1967; children—Robert, David, Linda, George. Intern, Babies Hosp., N.Y.C., 1938-39; resident Strong Meml. Hosp., Rochester, N.Y., 1939-41; practice medicine specializing in pediatrics, Rochester, 1941—; mem. staff Highland Hosp., Strong Meml. Hosp., Rochester Gen. Hosp., Genesee Hosp.; clin. prof. pediatrics U. Rochester; bd. dirs. Eastman Dental Dispensary, 1961-70, Genesee Valley Med. Care, 1962-69. Trustee Rochester Museum and Sci. Center, 1972-73. Served with U.S. Army, 1943-46. Diplomate Am. Bd. Pediatrics (examiner 1968, sec.-treas. 1977-79, pres.-elect 1979). Mem. AMA, N.Y. State (chmn. and del. pediatric sect. 1962-67), Monroe County (N.Y.) med. socs., Rochester Acad. Medicine, Am. Acad. Pediatrics, Central N.Y. Pediatric Soc. Episcopalian. Club: Monroe Golf. Research, publs. on beta hemolytic streptococcal infections in children, 1954—. Home: 317 Panorama Trail Rochester NY 14625 Office: 1580 Elmwood Ave Rochester NY 14620

DITCH, WILLIAM CLEMENT, electric protection co. exec.; b. Cedar Rapids, Iowa, Dec. 17, 1930; s. William Harold and Veronica Elizabeth (Butler) D.; B.S.M.E., State U. Iowa, 1956; m. Fonda M. Slater, Feb. 21, 1952; 1 son, Stephen C. With AT&T, 1956-73, engring. mgr., N.Y.C., 1971-73; v.p. service Am. Dist. Telegraph Co., N.Y.C., 1973—. Served with Signal Corps, U.S. Army, 1951-53; Korea. Mem. Am. Mgmt. Assn., Central Sta. Electric Protection Assn., Nat. Fire Prevention Assn., Nat. Crime Prevention Assn. Republican. Methodist. Home: 147 Forest Rd Allendale NJ 07401 Office: Suite 9200 One World Trade Center New York City NY 10048

DIVACK, DANIEL MURRAY, obstetrician, gynecologist; b. N.Y.C., July 14, 1931; s. Joseph and Leah (Walker) D.; A.B., Cornell U., 1952; M.D. cum laude, Washington U., 1956; m. Kathe Carol Klatzko, July 30, 1961; children—Joshua, Seth. Intern, Grace New Haven Hosp., 1956; resident in obstetrics and gynecology, Bronx Municipal Hosp., 1959-63; practice medicine, specializing in obstetrics and gynecology, Bayside, N.Y., 1963—; asst. clin. prof. obstetrics and gynecology Einstein Coll. Medicine, 1965-78, State U. N.Y., Stoney Brook, 1975—. Served to lt. comdr., USN, 1957-59. Diplomate Am. Bd. Obstetrics and Gynecology. Fellow Am. Coll. Obstetricians and Gynecologists, ACS. Home: 1629 Bell Blvd Bayside NY 11360 Office: 1629 Bell Blvd Bayside NY 11360

DIXON, ALFRED BURTON, physician; b. Waterbury, Conn., Apr. 18, 1913; s. John Samuel and Florence Mae (Webster) D.; B.S., Trinity Coll., 1934; M.D., C.M., Queens U., Kingston, Ont., Canada, 1939; m. Ella Marion Young, June 10, 1939; children—Alfred Burton IV (dec.), John Millard. Intern, Conn. Gen. Hosp., New Britian; resident Balt. City and Union Meml. hosp., 1940-43; practice medicine specializing in obstetrics and gynecology, Balt., 1943-73; med. dir. surg. clinics Planned Parenthood Assn. Md., Balt., 1973—; asst. in obstetrics Johns Hopkins Sch. Medicine. Past pres. Planned Parenthood Md., also chmn. med. exec. com. Served to capt., AUS, 1943-46. Fellow Royal Soc. Health; mem. Med. and Chirurgical Soc. Md., AMA, Md. Obstet. and Gynecol. Soc. Republican. Episcopalian. Mason (Shriner, 32 deg.), Lion (dist. gov., 1960-61). Home: 10333C Malcolm Circle Cockeysville MD 21030 Office: 610 N Howard St Baltimore MD 21201

DIXON, ANDREW LEE, JR., mgmt. cons. co. exec.; b. Pitts., Apr. 9, 1942; s. Andrew Lee and Dorothy (McCullough) D.; B.S. in Microbiology, Howard U., 1968; M.B.A., Case Western U., 1973; postgrad. Suffolk U. Law Sch., 1978—; m. Jerline Shaw, Oct. 5, 1968; children—Andrew Lee, Chad Leonard. Microbiologist, lab. supr. Calgon Corp., Pitts., 1968-70; personnel mgr., mgr. adminstrn. dept. Polytech, Inc., Cleve., 1970-76, v.p. adminstrn. ECO-Labs., Inc., 1973-76; mgr. compensation, personnel mgr. Arthur D. Little Inc., Cambridge, Mass., 1976—; instr. minority contractors program Cleve. State U., 1963-76. Chmn. bd. dirs. SE Com. Center for Human Services, Cleve., 1968-70; bd. dirs. Program to Aid Citizens Enterprise, Pitts., 1972-76; bd. dirs. Cleve. Aid to Addicts, 1972-76; scoutmaster Nat. Capital Area council Boy Scouts Am., 1968-70; trustee Forest Hills Homeowners Assn., Cleve., 1975-76. Recipient Contbn. to Mgmt. Edn. award Am. Compensation Assn., 1978. Mem. Am. Compensation Assn., Am., New Eng. assns. personnel adminstrn., Soc. Indsl. Microbiology, Boston Indsl. Relations Research Assn., Boston Assn. Black Execs., Soc. Black Engrs. and Techs., Alpha Phi Alpha. Contbr. articles in field to profl. jours. Office: Arthur D Little Inc 20 Acorn Park Cambridge MA 02140

DIXON, DAVID MCFARLAND, lawyer; b. Nashville, July 1, 1932; s. Charles Everett and Frances Medora (Whitsitt) D.; B.A., Vanderbilt U., 1954, LL.B., 1959; m. Jane Hart Holmes, Aug. 6, 1960; children—David McFarland, Edward Holmes, Mary Medora. Admitted to Tenn. bar, 1959, D.C. bar, 1965, U.S. Supreme Ct. bar, 1973; mem. firm Stephenson Lackey & Holman, Nashville, 1959-63; atty. FCC, Washington, 1964, Staff of Com. on Judiciary, U.S. Senate, 1965; partner firm Rhyne & Rhyne, Washington, 1966-76; dept. chief counsel, staff dir. Com. on Judiciary, U.S. Senate, 1977—. Trustee St. Patrick's Episcopal Day Sch., Washington; mem. devel. com. Vanderbilt U. Law Sch.; bd. dirs. Hillcrest Children's Center. Served with AUS, 1954-56. Mem. Am., Tenn., Fed., D.C. bar assns., Nat. Lawyers Club, Phi Delta Phi, Kappa Alpha. Episcopalian (sr. warden). Home: 5218 Edgemoor Ln Bethesda MD 20014 Office: 839 17th St Washington DC 20006

DIXON, HENRY CAMPBELL, JR., educator; b. Hartford, Conn., June 2, 1925; s. Henry Campbell and Ruth Hannah Woodward (Brooks) D.; A.B., Bowdoin Coll., 1949; M.A., Trinity Coll., 1960; certificate advanced grad. specialization Boston Coll., 1960. Instr. math. Mercersburg (Pa.) Acad., 1953-56, George Sch., Bucks County, Pa., 1956-59; chmn. dept. math., alumni dir., editor Berwick (Maine) Acad., 1960-69; chmn. math. dept. Williams Sch., New London, Conn., 1970—; asst. dean, instr. math. Mohegan Community Coll., Norwich, Conn., 1970-72. Pres., Campbell-Dixon Assos., Norwich, 1970—; sr. warden Episcopal Ch. of the Resurrection, Norwich; leader Quaker Work Camp, Germany, 1958. Served with USNR, USMCR, 1943-46. NSF grantee, 1959-60; Gen. Electric fellow, 1955. Mem. Math. Assn. Am., Newcomen Soc. Democrat. Contbr. articles to profl. jours. Home: 46 Palmer St Norwich CT 06360 Office: Williams Sch New London CT 06320

DIZER, JOHN THOMAS, JR., mech. engr., educator; b. Norwood, Mass., Nov. 7, 1921; s. John Thomas and Eunice Haven (Homer) D.; B.S., Northeastern U., 1943; M.S., Purdue U., 1947, Ph.D., 1969; m. Marie Leeramp, Dec. 25, 1947; children—John Thomas III, Jane E., William D., Ann E., Mary L. Standards engr. E.I. du Pont de Nemours & Co., East Chicago, Ind., 1947-50; prodn. engr., supr. Cummins Engine Co., Columbus, Ind., 1952-59; mem. faculty Mohawk Valley Community Coll., Utica, N.Y., 1959—, asso. prof., 1964-66, prof., 1966—, head mech. tech. dept., 1968—. Pres., Salem Community Center, 1963-65; trustee Plymouth-Bethesda United Ch. of Christ; active Boy Scouts Am., 1959—. Served to lt. USNR, 1944-46, 50-52; Korea. Registered profl. engr., certified mfg. engr., N.Y. State. Mem. ASME (chpt. chmn. 1968-69, Outstanding Engr. award 1971), Am. Soc. for Engring. Edn. (tech. coll. council rep.), Mohawk Valley Engring. Execs. Council (chmn. 1976-77, Outstanding Engr. award 1978), Am. Inst. Indsl. Engrs. (edn. com. chmn. 1977-78), Soc. Mfg. Engrs. (chpt. chmn. 1971-72, Outstanding Engr. award 1973), Soc. Indsl. Archaeology, Am. Tech. Edn. Soc., N.Y. State Engring. Tech. Assn. (pres. 1976-78), Oneida Hist. Soc. (bd. mgrs. 1963—), Tau Beta Pi. Club: Masons. Contbr. articles on tech. edn. and juvenile lit. to profl. publs. Home: 10332 Ridgecrest Rd Utica NY 13502 Office: 1101 Sherman Dr Utica NY 13562

DIZIO, STEVEN FRANK, elec. co. exec.; b. Newark, Dec. 15, 1938; s. Frank Lewis and Frances Barbara (Freyer) DiZ.; Ph.D. in Chem. Engring., Rensselaer Poly. Inst., 1964; children—Rochelle Marie, Kathleen Ann. Asso. prof., chmn. biomed engring. Rensselaer Poly. Inst., Troy, N.Y., 1964-69, adj. asso. prof. biomed. engring., 1969—; dir. mktg. Aero Vac Corp, 1969-70, exec. v.p., 1970-72, pres., 1972-74, also dir.; pres., chief exec. officer, dir. SES, Inc., Newark, Del., 1974—. Rep., Upper Hudson Region Comprehensive Health Planning Orgn., Inc., 1969-72. Bd. dirs. St. Marie's Hosp., Troy, Tb and Respiratory Disease Assn., Capital Dist., N.Y. Mem. N.Y. Acad. Sci., Am. Inst. Chem. Engrs., Am. Chem. Soc., AAAS, Am. Soc. Engring. Edn., Assn. Am. Vacuum Equipment Mfrs. (v.p. 1971-73, pres. 1973-74). Contbr. articles to profl. jours. Patentee in field. Office: 1 Tralee Indsl Park Newark DE 19711

DJERASSI, ISAAC, physician; b. Sofia, Bulgaria, July 27, 1925; s. Rahamim and Adela (Tadjer) D.; student Sofia U. Med. Sch., 1944-49; M.D., Hebrew U. Med. Sch., Jerusalem, Israel, 1952; H.H.D. (hon.), Villanova U., 1977; m. Nira Eskenazy, Jan. 31, 1954; children—Ram Isaac, Ady Lynn. Came to U.S., 1954, naturalized, 1962. Intern, Hadassah Hosp., Tel Aviv, Israel, 1951-52, resident, 1953-54; research asso. Harvard Med. Sch., Boston, 1955-60; asst. prof. pediatrics U. Pa. Med. Sch., Phila., 1960-69; dir. research Mercy Cath. Med. Center, Phila., 1969—. Cons. pathology Children's Med. Center, Boston, 1960-73; mem. med. adv. bd. Nat. Hemophilia Found., Phila., 1964—; mem. Leukemia Soc. Med. Adv. Bd., Phila., 1970—. Recipient Albert Lasker award for achievement in med. research Albert and Mary Lasker Found., 1972. Mem. Am. Soc. Cancer Research, Soc. Pediatric Research, Am. Soc. Exptl. Pathology, Am. Assn. Blood Banks. Contbr. articles to profl. jours. Inventor filbration leukopheresis system and machine for white blood cell transfusions, 1970. Office: Mercy Cath Med Center Philadelphia PA 19143

DJINIS, WILLIAM ANTHONY, cons. co. exec.; b. Poughkeepsie, N.Y., Jan. 9, 1922; s. Anthony Charles and Mary (Gourgelli) D.; student Rensselaer Poly. Inst., 1939-42; B.S., USAF Tech. Sch., 1943; B.S., Rensselaer Poly. Inst., 1948, M.S., 1950; Ph.D., N.Y. U., 1952; postgrad. Pratt Inst., 1955-57; m. Mary Telepas, Aug. 22, 1948; children—Anthony William, Peter George, Chrysanthi Maria. Group leader engring. physics group Vitro Corp. Am., West Orange, N.J., 1951-54; engr. Am. Bosch Arma Corp., Garden City, N.Y., 1954-55; sr. project engr. Reeves Instrument Corp., Garden City, 1955-58; head physics research dept. Gen. Bronze Electronics Corp., Garden City, 1958-59; chief engr. Electro Sonic Labs., Long Island City, N.Y., 1959-60; with Grumman Aerospace Corp., Bethpage, N.Y., 1960-67, 69-73, dir. mil. space programs, 1969-73; presdl. appointee as sci. adviser Air Staff, USAF, Pentagon, Washington, 1967-69; mgr. advanced programs Westinghouse Electric Corp., Balt., 1973-78; prin. Booz-Allen & Hamilton, Inc., Bethesda, Md., 1978—; instr. Rensselaer Poly. Inst., Troy, N.Y., 1948-49; v.p., dir. Advance Electronics Corp., North Bellmore, N.Y., 1958-59, Gen. Securities Corp., N.Y.C., 1958-62; dir. Dynatron Electronics Corp., Mineola, N.Y., 1958-65, Cyclomatics Corp., N.Y.C., 1960-63. Mgr. Little League Baseball, Syosset, N.Y., 1960-64; asst. scoutmaster Cub Scouts Am., Syosset, 1959-62; U.S. rep. AGARD NATO Conf., 1964; chmn. man-of-the year com. Solon Cultural Soc., Hempstead, N.Y., 1969-72. Served to capt. USAAF, 1942-46, to col. USAF Res., 1946—. Asso. fellow Am. Inst. Aeros. and Astronautics (mem. com. 1968-72, nat. chmn. tech. com. missile systems 1976—); mem. Am. Def. Preparedness Assn. (gen. conf. chmn. 1973-74, vice chmn. steering com. missiles 1974-76), IEEE (internat. conv. session coordinator 1966, sr. mem.), Am. Astronautical Soc. (sect. vice chmn. 1971-73, sr. mem.), Air Force Assn., Sigma Xi. Republican. Greek Orthodox (mem. Parish Council 1973, 78). Patentee in field. Home: 9704 Conestoga Way Potomac MD 20854 Office: 4330 East-West Hwy Bethesda MD 20014

DJORDJEVIC, VLASTIMIR WALTER, civil engr.; b. Krusevac, Yugoslavia, Apr. 10, 1922; s. Miodrag and Jelena (Jovanovic) D.; came to U.S., 1949, natrualized, 1955; Cand. Ing., C.E., Techniche Hochschule, Braunsweig, Germany, 1949; B.C.E., U. Pitts., 1952, M.S. in Structural Engring., 1957; m. Vera Stankovic, Apr. 28, 1946; children—Helen Djordjevic Morelli, Michael. Structural engr. Am. Bridge Co., 1952-55; cons. engr., 1956-58; from project engr. to dir. engring. Swindell Dressler, Pitts., 1958-70; exec. v.p., gen. mgr. Houser & Carafas Engring. Co., Pitts., 1970—; v.p., gen. mgr. Steel and Iron div. Acres Am. Inc.; dir. Acres Am., Inc.; adj. prof. engring. Geneva Coll.; lectr. Pa. State U. Former bd. dirs. St. Elijah Serbian Orthodox Ch.; former pres. central com. Am. Serbian Nat. Def. Registered profl. engr., Ohio, Ind., Pa., N.J., Calif., Minn., Mich., Colo., Ill., Wis., Del. Mem. Am. Inst. Steel Constrn., Assn. Iron and Steel Engrs., Nat. Soc. Profl. Engrs., Soc. Mil. Engrs., Am. Concrete Inst., Pitts. Engrs. Club, Indsl. Mgmt. Club. Office: 301 5th Ave Pittsburgh PA 15222

D'LAURO, FRANK ANDREW, JR., constrn. co. exec.; b. Phila., Nov. 11, 1940; s. Frank Andrew and Dorothy (Adams) D'L.; B.A., Washington and Lee U., 1962; M.Arch., U. Pa., 1965. Architect, Francis Kaufmann Wilkinson & Pepper, Phila., 1967-68; project mgr. Frank A. D'Lauro Co., Phila., 1968-70, exec. v.p., 1970-71, pres., 1971—; pres. D'Lauro Devel. Corp., Phila., 1973—; mem. regional exec. bd. Continental Bank, Phila., 1972—. Chmn. Montgomery County Young Republican Fedn., 1970-72; bd. dirs. Young Reps. Pa., 1972-74; mem. Montgomery County Rep. Fin. Com., 1972—; bd. dirs., v.p. Big Bros. Assn., Phila.; chmn. Montgomery County Housing Authority, 1976—; trustee Pop Warner Little Scholars, Inc., Phila. Served as capt. AUS, 1965-67. Decorated Bronze Star with oak leaf cluster; recipient award of Merit, Big Bros. of Phila., 1972. Mem. Gen. Contractors Assn. Pa. (bd. govs. 1972—), Pa. Soc. SR, Sigma Nu. Clubs: Union League, Racquet, Phila., Cricket (Phila.). Office: 218 E Willow Grove Ave Philadelphia PA 19118

DLUHY, JOHN MICHAEL, psychiatrist; b. Chgo., Aug. 26, 1937; s. John Michael and Mae (Liska) D.; B.S. with honors, U. Ill., 1959, M.D., 1963; m. Mary Janoff, Nov. 27, 1975; children by previous marriage—Nina Marie, Bartholomew. Intern, Georgetown U. Hosp., Washington, 1963-64, resident in internal medicine, 1964-65; resident in psychiatry Strong Meml. Hosp., Rochester, N.Y., 1965-68; asst. head outpatient psychiatry dept. Main Navy Dispensary, 1968-70; practice medicine, specializing in psychiatry, Washington, 1968—; asst. clin. prof. Georgetown U. Hosp., Washington, 1968—. Served with USN, 1968-70. Mem. Am. Psychiatric Assn., Am. Group Psychotherapy Assn., Washington Psychiatric Assn., Mid-Atlantic Group Psychotherapy Assn. Address: 3709 Ingomar St NW Washington DC 20015

DMOCHOWSKI, JAN RAFAL, surgeon; b. Warsaw, Poland, Aug. 27, 1927; s. Antoni and Teresa (Choloniewska) D.; came to U.S., 1968, naturalized, 1975; M.D., Med. Acad., Lodz, Poland, 1952, Ph.D., 1962, Docent Surgery, 1967; m. Alexandra Zylewicz, Dec. 31, 1953; 1 son, Maciej. Asst., dept. surgery, dept. pathophysiology, Med. Acad. Lodz, 1950-54, sr. asst., 1956-63, adj. prof., 1965-67, docent, 1967-68; research fellow surgery Harvard Med. Sch., 1963-65, 68-70, instr. surgery, 1970-76; asso. in surgery Peter Bent Brigham Hosp., Boston, 1975—, dir. blood bank transfusion service, 1973-77; surg. coordinator S.V. Hosp., Worcester, Mass., 1977—; asso. prof. surgery U. Mass. Med. Sch., 1978. Served with Polish Resistance, Home Army, 1942-45. Fellow A.C.S.; mem. Mass. Assn. Blood Banks, Soc. Cryobiology, Assn. Acad. Surgery. Contbr. papers to sci. jours.

DOBBINS, HOPE JEAN, civic worker; b. Perth, Scotland, May 29, 1915; d. Rainey Munro and Jessie Melville (Brown) Ross; came to U.S., 1947, naturalized, 1947; student Domestic Sci. Coll., Edinburgh,

1938; B.S. in Edn., North Adams State Coll., 1960, M. Edn., 1963; m. Edward L. Dobbins, Sept. 8, 1945; children—Michele, Heather, Holly. Asst. prof. history North Adams (Mass.) Coll., 1963-70. Active ARC, 1942-47, organizer 1st clubmobile unit, Britain, 1942, corps and army supr., 1944-46, field dir., 1946-47, chmn. vols., Berkshire County, 1960-63; pres. Berkshire Art Assn., 1968-72; dir. Trans-Nat. Women's Golf Assn., 1970—, v.p., 1975-77; bd. dirs. YMCA, Pittsfield, Mass., 1976—, Berkshire Garden Center, Stockbridge, Mass., 1976—. Decorated Bronze Star medal. Republican. Home: 252 Grange Hall Rd Dalton MA 01226

DOBBINS, WILLIAM OCTAVIUS, III, physician; b. Phoenix, Oct. 15, 1932; s. William Octavius and Mary (Kimbell) D.; student Davidson Coll., 1950-53; M.D., Med. Coll. Ala., 1957; m. Ellen Scott-Smith, June 29, 1958; children—Laura Diane, Sharon Elene. Resident and fellow U. Wash., Seattle, 1960-65; asst. prof. medicine Duke U., 1965-67, asso. prof., 1967-68; asso. prof. medicine George Washington U., Washington, 1969-73, prof., 1973—; pvt. practice medicine, Washington. Served to capt. U.S. Army, 1958-60. Diplomate Am. Bd. Internal Medicine; USPHS grantee, 1965, 78. Mem. Am. Fedn. Clin. Research (pres. Eastern sect. 1973-74), Am. Digestive Disease Soc. (trustee), AAAS, So. Soc. Clin. Investigation, Am. Gastroenterol. Assn., D.C. Med. Soc., Alpha Omega Alpha. Democrat. Author: (with Shingleton) Malabsorption Syndromes, 1968; contbr. articles to med. jours. Home: 4210 Maple Terr Chevy Chase MD 20015 Office: 2150 Pennsylvania Ave NW Washington DC 20037

DOBBS, CARROLL RAY, chemist; b. Mt. Pleasant, Ark., Jan. 31, 1939; s. Ray Wright and Lenore Margaret (Smith) D.; B.S., Ark. Inst. Tech., 1960; M.S., Ohio State U., 1967; Ph.D., Va. Poly. Inst., 1973. Insp., chemist FDA, New Orleans, 1962-63; commd. lt. USAF, 1962, advanced through grades to maj., 1972; clin. lab. officer USAF Med. Service, Scott AFB, Ill., 1963-67; sr. biomed. scientist USAF Sch. Aerospace Medicine, San Antonio, 1967-74; clin. chemist USAF Hosp., Wiesbaden, W. Ger., 1974-78; research chemist Armed Forces Radiobiology Research Inst., Bethesda, Md., 1978—. Mem. Am. Chem. Soc. (treas. San Antonio sect. 1974), AAAS, Am. Assn. Clin. Chemists, Biochem. Soc. (London), Sigma Xi, Phi Lambda Upsilon. Research and publs. in biochem. effects of physiol. stress, analysis and characterization of steroid hormones. Home: 7618 Clarendon Rd Bethesda MD 20014 Office: Defense Nuclear Agy (AFFRI) Bethesda MD 20014

DOBBS, ROBERT JOSEPH, JR., educator; b. Detroit, Jan. 3, 1944; B.Ed. in L.S., U. Toledo, 1967; M. in L.S., State U. N.Y., Geneseo, 1972; married; 2 children. Library asso. Toledo pub. Library, 1964-67; librarian Ithaca (N.Y.) Sch. Dist., 1967-69; dir. Chili Pub. Library, Rochester, N.Y., 1969-72; coordinator head secondary library Olean (N.Y.) City Sch. Dist., 1972—; owner Horizons Unltd; distbr. Success Motivation Inst., Inc., lectr., cons. in field. Certified media Specialist, N.Y. Mem. N.Y. Library Assn., N.Y. State Ednl. Communications Assn., Nat. Edn. Assn., N.Y. State Educators Assn., Cattaraugus County Librarians Assn. (pres. 1975—), N.Y. Jaycees (state Chaplain 1978-79). Office: 410 West Sullivan Olean NY 14760

DOBELLE, GLADYS KLEINMAN, public relations exec.; b. N.Y.C., Feb. 15, 1943; d. Irving and Sally Kleinman; B.A. with honors, Hunter Coll., 1964; postgrad. Harvard Inst. Arts Adminstrn., 1971; m. William H. Dobelle, Dec. 31, 1972. Mem. faculty Cambridge (Mass.) Center for Adult Edn., Boston Center for Adult Edn., 1968-72; asst. to pub. Boston After Dark, 1968-69; asst. to dir. Newport (R.I.) Romantic Music Festival, summer 1969; exec. dir. Harvard Independent newspaper, Cambridge, 1969-70; pub. relations dir. Boston Center for Arts, 1970-72, Ballet West, Salt Lake City, 1973, San Francisco Opera, 1974, San Francisco Symphony, 1975; pres. Glad Tidings, pub. relations for arts, N.Y.C., 1976—; mem. faculty YMCA, N.Y.C., 1977—, New Sch. for Social Research, N.Y.C., 1977—; cons. Boston Globe, Harvard Inst. Arts Adminstrn.; cons. fine arts devel.; chmn. Dialogue: A Working Woman's Seminar, 1977—. Mem. Citizens Com. for N.Y.C., N.Y.C. Conv./Visitors Bur. Mem. Pub. Relations Soc. Am., Am. Women in Radio and TV, Acad. TV Arts and Sci., Ned D. Frank Philanthropic League. Jewish. Editor: Getting into Ink and Print and On the Air, 1971. Home: One Lincoln Plaza New York City NY 10023 Office: 20 W 64th St New York City NY 10023

DOBKIN, DONALD, metal treating co. exec.; b. N.Y.C., July 9, 1922; s. Isidor and Rebecca (Silverman) D.; B.S., Coll. City N.Y., 1942; postgrad. Lehigh U., 1942, Columbia U., 1946-47; m. Rosalyn Goldberg, June 15, 1956; children—Robert, Lisa. Copywriter, account exec. Wiley, Frazee, Davenport, advt., N.Y.C., 1946-48; copy chief, account exec. Lancaster Advt., N.Y.C., 1948-50; gen. mgr. Ace Metal Treating Corp., Elizabeth, N.J., 1950-59; sales mgr., dir., sec. L-R Metal Treating Corp., Newark, 1959-68; v.p. sales, sec., dir. Thermo Nat. Industries, Inc., Newark, 1968—. Served with U.S. Army, 1942-46; ETO. Decorated Combat Inf. Badge. Mem. Am. Soc. for Metals, Soc. Mfg. Engrs., N.J. Tool and Die Mfrs. Assn., Sigma Alpha Mu. Home: 4 Tilden Ct Livingston NJ 07039 Office: 108-34 Johnson St Newark NJ 07105

DOBKIN, HERBERT, metallurgist; b. N.Y.C., Oct. 31, 1920; s. Isidor and Rebecca (Silverman) D.; Metall. Engr., Stevens Inst. Tech., 1940, M.S., 1943; m. Charlotte Klein, June 15, 1943; one son, Richard. Engr. Standard Oil Co. (N.J.), Elizabeth, 1940-43; metallurgist M.W. Kellogg Co., Jersey City, 1943-47; pres. Thermo Nat. Industries, metal service, Newark, 1947—. Mem. ASME (chmn. N.J. chpt. 1953-54), Am. Soc. for Metals (dir. N.J. chpt. 1956-60). Contbr. articles to profl. publs. Home: 126 Cypress St Millburn NJ 07041 Office: 108 Johnson St Newark NJ 07105

DOBOY, JOSEPH G., radiologist; b. Central City, Pa., Oct. 17, 1918; s. Joseph G. and Mary (Brown) D.; B.S., Juniata Coll., 1937; M.D., B.S., U. W.Va., 1947; M.D., Med. Coll. Va. Instr. chemistry U. W.Va., 1943-45; intern James Walker Meml. Hosp., Wilmington, N.C., 1949-50; med. dir. Semet Solvay Corp. div. Allied Chem. & Dye Corp., Longacre, W.Va., 1952-55; resident in radiology U. Va. Hosp., Charlottesville, 1956-59, vis. fellow Columbia Presbyn. Hosp., N.Y.C., 1962-64; chief radiologist Fairmont (W.Va.) Gen. Hosp., 1960-62; asst. prof. radiology N.J. Coll. Medicine, Newark, 1970—, clin. asso. prof., 1973—; chief, dir. radiology Community Meml. Hosp., Toms River, N.J., 1973—; cons. in field. Diplomate Am. Bd. Radiology. Mem. Ocean County, N.J., Pirquet med. socs., AMA, Phila. Roentgen Ray Soc., N.Y. Roentgen Soc., Soc. Nuclear Medicine, Radiol. Soc. N.Am., Am. Coll. Radiology, Am. Coll. Nuclear Medicine. Lectr. chest disease, diagnostic application nuclear medicine to clinician, also detection of lead poisoning by radiographic computer analysis. Home: 11 Bay Breeze Ave Toms River NJ 08753

DOBRIANSKY, LEV EUGENE, educator, economist; b. N.Y.C., Nov. 9, 1918; s. John and Eugenia (Greshchuk) D.; B.S. (Charles Hayden Meml. scholar), N.Y. U., 1941, Hirshland Polit. sci. fellow, 1943-44, tchg. fellow econ., 1942-43, M.A., 1943, Ph.D., 1951; LL.D., Munich, Germany, 1952; m. Julia Kusy, June 29, 1946; children—Larisa Eugenia, Paula Jon. Faculty mem. N.Y. U., 1942-48; asso. editor Ukrainian Quar., 1946-58, chmn. editorial bd. 1958—; econs. editor Washington Report, Am. Security Council, 1963—; asst. prof. econ. Georgetown U., 1948-52, became asso. prof. econs. 1952, chmn. dept. econs., 1953-54, mem. faculty Nat. War Coll., 1957-58; prof. econs. Georgetown U., 1960—, dir. Inst. Comparative Polit. and Econ. Systems, 1970—; lectr. on Soviet Union; econ. research and cons.; cons. USIA, also State Dept., 1971—; splty. instnl. econs., USSR. Mem. Economists' Nat. Com. on Monetary Policy exec. com., Free World Forum, Pres.'s Commn. on Population, 1974-75; chmn. Nat. Captive Nations Com., 1959—; pres. Am. Council for World Freedom, 1976—; bd. govs. Charles Edison Meml. Youth Fund, 1976. Asst. sec. Republican Nat. Conv., 1952; Rep. Nat. Com. 1956; Rep. Com. Program and Progress, 1959. Col. Res. 352d Civil Affairs. Mem. Acad. Polit. Sci., Nat. Acad. Econs. and Polit. Sci., Am. Assn. U. Profs., Am. Acad. Polit. and Social Sci., Am., Cath. econ. assns., Am. Finance Assn., Nat. Soc. Study Edn., Shevchenko Sci., Soc., Common Cause, Inc. Ukrainian Cong. Com. Am. (chmn.), Fedn. Am. Central and E. European Descent (exec. v.p.), N.Y. U. Alumni Assn., Gold Key Soc. Beta Gamma Sigma, Delta Sigma Pi. Author: A Philosophico-Economic Critique of Thorstein Veblen. 1943; The Social Philosophical System of Thorstein Veblen, 1950; Free Trade Ideal, 1954; Veblenism, A New Critique, 1957; The Great Pretense, 1956; The Crimes of Khrushchev, 1959; Decisions for a Better America, 1960; Nations, Peoples, and Countries in the USSR, 1964; (with others) Peace and Freedom Through Cold War Victory, 1964; The Vulnerable Russians, 1967; U.S.A. and the Soviet Myth, 1971; Editor, contbr. Captive Nations Movement, 1969, the Bicentennial Salute to Captive Nations, 1977; contbr. to Essays on Liberty, 1962, Nationalism in the USSR and Eastern Europe, 1977. Contbr. articles to profl. publs. Radio and TV appearances. Home: 4520 Kling Dr Alexandria VA 22312 Office: Georgetown U Washington DC 20001

DOBROMIL, STANLEY IRWIN, accountant; b. N.Y.C., Apr. 18, 1947; s. Morris Alan and Myrtle Joan (Feinberg) D.; student Corning Community Coll., 1965-67, Tarkio Coll., 1967-68; B.B.A., U. Miami (Fla.), 1971; m. Irene Louise Biggs, Aug. 31, 1968; children—Anita J., Irika L. Staff accountant Rachlin & Co., C.P.A.'s, South Miami, Fla., 1970-71, Dobromil Accounting Co., Corning, N.Y., 1971-72, partner, 1972-73, mng. partner, 1973—; treas. Gelthurst, Inc.; spl. adviser N.Y. State Dep.'s Assn. Treas. Beth Israel Congregation; bd. dirs., treas. Vol. Clearing House; trustee, fin. chmn. Congregation Shomray Hadath. Enrolled agt. IRS. Mem. Nat. Soc. Pub. Accountants (accredited accountant), Accreditation Council Accountancy. Jewish. Club: Corning Lions (treas.). Home: RD #3 Dobby Dr Corning NY 14830 Office: 34-36 E Market St Corning NY 14830

DOBROW, HARVEY ROBERT, ophthalmologist; b. N.Y.C., Sept. 19, 1942; s. Benjamin and Eleanor (Rubin) D.; student Tufts U., 1960-63; M.D., State U. N.Y., 1967; m. Diane Beth Stein, Aug. 20, 1967; children—Lawrence, Julie, Ilyse. Intern, Montefiore Hosp., Bronx, N.Y., 1967-68; resident Manhattan Eye, Ear, Throat Hosp., N.Y.C., 1968-71; practice medicine specializing in ophthalmology, Fair Lawn, N.J., 1973—; asst. attending ophthalmologist Barnert Meml. Hosp., Paterson, N.J., 1973—, Valley Hosp., Ridgewood, N.J., 1974—; asst. attending ophthalmologist Contact Lens Clinic, Manhattan Eye, Ear, Throat Hosp., N.Y.C., 1973—. Served to maj., M.C., U.S. Army, 1971-73. Diplomate Am. Bd. Ophthalmology. Fellow A.C.S., Am. Acad. Ophthalmology and Otolaryngology; mem. Med. Soc. N.J., Eye Inst. N.J., Passaic County Med. Soc., AMA. Contbr. articles to med. jours. Home: 769 Oneida Trail Franklin Lakes NJ 07417 Office: 12-15 Broadway Fair Lawn NJ 07410

DOBSON, BRIAN GREGORY, pub. relations exec.; b. N.Y.C., Jan. 22, 1945; s. James Joseph and Rita Marie (Walsh) D.; B.A., Marist Coll., Poughkeepsie, N.Y., 1967; student N.Y. Inst. Fin., St. John's U. Grad. Sch. Bus.; m. Barbara J. Hodorowski, Nov. 13, 1970; 1 dau., Gweneth Langford. Petroleum news editor Jour. Commerce, N.Y.C., 1969; editor AP-DJ Bus. Newswire, Dow Jones & Co., N.Y.C., 1970; editor-writer Reuters Fin. Newswire, Reuter's Ltd., N.Y.C., 1971; pub. relations rep. N.Y. Stock Exchange, 1973; v.p. pub. relations Iroquois Brands, Ltd., Greenwich, Conn., 1976—. Mem. Greenwich Pro-Am Charity Golf Tournament. Served with AUS, 1967-69. Recipient Best of Industry award for co. ann. report Fin. World Mag., 1979. Mem. Nat. Inst. Investor Relations, Pub. Relations Soc. Am., Greenwich C. of C., Stamford Area Commerce and Industry Assn. Office: 41 W Putnam Ave Greenwich CT 06830

DOBSON, RICHARD HAL, physician; b. Manhattan, Kans., Mar. 23, 1926; s. John Edward and Leana (Smith) D.; B.S., Kans. State Coll., 1949; M.D., George Washington U., 1953; m. Peggy Beatrice Owens, Apr. 4, 1958; children—Karen Lynn, Richard Hal. Intern, Garfield Hosp., Washington, 1953-54; practice medicine, Brandywine, Md., 1954—; mem. staff Prince George's, Providence, Children's Hosps., Washington Hosp. Center; pres., treas., owner Brandywine Waldorf Medicine Dental Clinic, Inc., 1959—, Diversified Investment Corp., 1959—; dir. Bank of Brandywine. Served with USNR, 1943-46, Decorated Purple Heart. Mem. AMA, Md., Prince George County med. assns. Address: Brandywine MD 20613

DOCKSTADER, EMMETT STANLEY, constrn. co. exec.; b. Elmira, N.Y., Nov. 7, 1923; s. Roy S. and Gertrude (Everts) D.; B.C.E. cum laude, Syracuse U., 1947; m. Ruth Norma Emery, May 11, 1946; children—Deborah Ruth, David Stanley. Engr., Am. Bridge Co., Elmira, 1948-50; field engr. Sessinghaus & Ostergaard, Inc., Erie, Pa,, 1950-53, project mgr., 1953-58, v.p., 1958-69; gen. mgr. constrn. div. H.H. Robertson Co., Pitts., 1969-71; sr. v.p., sec. Sessinghaus & Ostergaard Inc., Erie, 1972—. Mem. Erie Port Commn., 1967-69; mem. adv. com. Erie County Tech. High Sch. Bd. dirs. Erie Civic Theatre Assn. Served with USNR, 1944-46. Registered profl. engr., Pa., W.Va., Ga., N.C. Mem. Pa. Soc. Profl. Engrs. (past pres.), Nat. Assn. Purchasing Agts., Erie Mannerchor. Ch. of the Covenant (trustee). Mason (32 deg.), Rotarian. Clubs: Kahkwa, Erie Yacht, Y Mens (past pres.), University (dir. Erie); Edgeworth (Sewickley, Pa.). Home: 326 Shawnee Dr Erie PA 16505 Office: 105 Poplar St Erie PA 16512

DODD, CHRISTOPHER J., congressman; b. Willimantic, Conn., May 27, 1944; s. Thomas J. and Grace (Murphy) D.; B.A. in English Lit., Providence Coll., 1966; J.D., U. Louisville, 1972; m. Susan Mooney. Vol., Peace Corps, Dominican Republic, 1966-68; admitted to Conn. Bar, 1973; mem. 94th-96th Congresses from 2d Conn. Dist. Served with AUS, 1969-75. Democrat. Office: US House of Representatives Washington DC 20515

DODD, DANIEL PHILLIPS, veterinarian; b. St. Louis, July 8, 1919; s. George Deming and Nellie (Phillips) D.; D.V.M., Iowa State U., 1942; m. LaVern Shattuck, June 15, 1946; children—Barbara Ann, Carol Jean. Research asso. Iowa State Coll., 1946-47; pvt. practice vet. medicine, Washington, 1947—. Served from pvt. to maj., U.S. Army, 1942-46 lt. col. Res., ret. Mem. Am., D.C. vet. med. assns., D.C. Acad. Vet. Medicine, Iowa State U. Vet. Assn., Assn. Mil. Surgeons U.S., Iowa State U. Alumni Assn., Sigma Nu. Republican. Methodist. Lion (local pres., zone chmn., dep. dist. gov.). Home: 9806 Ashby Rd Fairfax VA 22031 Office: 317 Massachusetts Ave NE Washington DC 20002

DODDS, RICHARD WILLIAM, pediatrician; b. Sharon, Pa., Sept. 21, 1938; s. Joseph Burns and Julia Elizabeth (Scott) D.; B.S. magna cum laude, U. Pitts., 1960, M.D., 1964; postgrad. U. Mich., 1969-70; m. Mary Katherine Tooker, Sept. 25, 1971; children—Anna Christina, Dorothea Elliot. Pediatric intern Children's Hosp., Pitts., 1964-65; resident, fellow pediatrics Johns Hopkins Hosp., Balt., 1965-67; health program analyst Office of Sec., HEW, Washington, 1970-71; vis. lectr. Harvard Sch. Pub. Health, Boston, 1972-74, asst. prof., 1974-77; chief pediatrics Harvard Community Health Plan, Boston, 1972-74, pediatrician, 1972—; instr. pediatrics Harvard Med. Sch., Boston, 1972—; lectr. health services adminstr. Harvard Sch. Pub. Health, 1977—; asso. medicine, attending physician Children's Hosp. Med. Center, Boston, 1972—; group practice medicine, specializing in pediatrics, Boston, 1972—. Served as capt. M.C., USAF, 1967-69. Smith Kline French fgn. med. fellow Instituto de Nutricion de Central America y Panama, Guatemala City, 1964. Diplomate Am. Bd. Pediatrics. Fellow Am. Acad. Pediatrics; mem. Phi Beta Kappa. Democrat. Congregationalist. Home: 204 Rangeley Rd Chestnut Hill MA 02167 Office: 690 Beacon St Boston MA 02215

DODGE, ALFA DOROTHY MAW (MRS. HAROLD A. DODGE), aircraft tool co. exec.; b. Buffalo; d. Alfred Charles and Lillian (Beyer) Maw; student Chown Bus. Coll., 1916; m. Harold A. Dodge, June 8, 1922; children—Harold A., Dorothy A. (Mrs. Charles L. Plant). Sec. George A. Terry Co., 1941-44, partner, asst. mgr., 1945-62, owner, mgr. 1963—. Trustee Chatauqua Assn. Disciples of Christ; mem. Republican Nat. Com. Mem. Buffalo Philharmonic Women's Com., Albright-Knox Art Gallery Soc., Nat., Buffalo Audubon socs., Am. Forestry Assn., Am. Legion Aux., Am. Mus. Natural History, Buffalo C. of C., Nat. Wildlife Assn., 500 Club WNED-TV, Buffalo Zool. Soc., Cousteau Soc., Soc. Prevention Cruelty to Animals, Nat. Park and Conservation Soc., Nat. Geog. Soc., Mass. Hort. Soc., Buffalo Council Chs., Am. Bible Soc., Amherst Symphony Soc., Better Bus. Bur. Buffalo, Buffalo Goodwill Industries, Nat. Assn. Small Bus., UN Assn. U.S.A. Mem. Disciples of Christ Ch. Club: Zonta (dir.). Home: 4 Mona Dr Buffalo NY 14226 Office: 356 S Elmwood Ave Buffalo NY 14201

DODGE, G. DOYLE, retail chain store exec.; b. Rugby, N.D., Nov. 10, 1930; s. Walter Fred and Faythe Marvel (Brandmeyer) D.; B.S. in Bus., Oreg. State U., 1957; M.B.A., Ind. U., 1959; m. Joan Katherine Bodtker, Aug. 30, 1957. Sr. market research analyst McLouth Steel Corp., Detroit, 1959-67; asst. to pres., dir. pub. affairs Teledyne Continental Motors, Detroit, 1967-72; exec. dir. Mich. Com. for Reelection Pres., 1972; dir. retail services div. GSA, Washington, 1972—; instr. basic econs. Royal Oak (Mich.) Pub. Schs., 1962-68. Scoutmaster, Columbia Pacific council Boy Scouts Am., Westport, Oreg., 1949-50; mem. YMCA Met. Bldg. Fund, Detroit, 1964-68; orgn. dir. Rep. Party, Oakland County, Mich., 1964-68; sec. bldg. com., mem. bd. stewards Beverly Hills (Mich.) Meth. Ch., 1961-66. Served with USN, 1950-54. Mem. Am. Statis. Assn., Detroit Area Econ. Forum, Econ. Club Detroit, Am. Mktg. Assn., Am. Fin. Assn., Nat. Assn. Bus. Economists, Oreg. State Alumni Assn., Ind. U. Alumni Assn., VFW, Sigma Chi. Republican. Methodist. Club: Elks. Contbr. articles to profl. jours. Home: 1119 Randolph Rd McLean VA 22101 Office: Crystal Mall Bldg 4 Rm 412 Washington DC 20406

DODGE, HOMER KINGSLEY, land architect; b. Des Moines, Apr. 14, 1906; s. Herbert Kingsbury and Sarah (Stafford) D.; B.S., Pa. State Coll., 1929; postgrad. Harvard, 1931-32, Mass. Inst. Tech., 1964; m. Ada Evelyn Kosmela, Feb. 16, 1932; children—Carol E. (Mrs. J. Stanford Kirkendall), Kathryn E. (Mrs. John Rapchak), Ann Michele (Mrs. Thomas S. Madigan), Herbert K., Virginia L. Instr. landscape architecture Pa. State U., University Park, 1929-31; supr. CCC, Washington, 1933-34; mgr. landscape dept. Bay State Nurseries, Framingham, Mass., 1934-40; partner Framingham Landscape Co., 1940-58; camouflage designer Army Engrs., Boston, 1944-45; owner Homer K. Dodge Assos., Land Planners, Architects, 1958—. Lectr. landscape and town planning to student and community groups; planning cons. to Dedham, Mass., 1961-69. Mem. Framingham Planning Bd., 1948-61, sec., 1950-54; mem. legis. com. Mass. Fed. Planning Bds., 1956-66. Bd. dirs. Farmers Coop. Exchange, 1956-68, pres., 1962-67. Registered profl. engr., Mass. Mem. Nat. Landscape Assn. (pres. 1953-54, chmn. edn. com. 1947-58), Nat. Soc. Profl. Engrs., Am. Soc. Landscape Architects, Am. Soc. Planning Ofcls., C. of C. Methodist (trustee). Home: 67 Warren Rd Framingham MA 01701 Office: 24 Union Ave Framingham MA 01701

DODSWORTH, ROY WARREN, chemist; b. Norwood, Mass., Sept. 6, 1948; s. James Woodrow and Beulah Grace (Snow) D.; B.A., Drew U., 1970; m. Genevieve Kumpicki, June 26, 1971; 1 dau., Dawn Terri. With Sandoz Inc., East Hanover, N.J., 1970—, supr. for chem. devel. lab., 1977—. Mem. Am. Chem. Soc., Am. Inst. Chemists (asso.) Beta Beta Beta. Democrat. Home: 38G Village Green Budd Lake NJ 07828 Office: Sandoz Inc Route 10 East Hanover NJ 07936

DOEBLER, HAROLD JOSEPH, oceanographer; b. Alamdeda, Calif., Sept. 6, 1933; s. Harold Joseph and Gloria Ann (Cross) D.; B.S., U.S. Naval Acad., 1956; M.S., U. R.I., 1966; postgrad. U.S. Naval War Coll., 1973-74; m. Marie deN. Iselin, Oct. 11, 1958; children—Carl Jay, Sarah Cross, Jonthan Thomas. With Navy Underwater Systems Center, New London, Conn., 1961—, sonar scientist on antisubmarine warfare staff, Naples, Italy, 1969-71, 1976-78. Served with USN 1956-61. Mem. Acoustical Soc. Am., Fed. Profl. Assn. Patentee sonar display.

DOEL, GILBERT HENRY, cons. engring. co. exec., elec. engr.; b. Seymour, Conn., Sept. 7, 1917; s. Albert and Olive (Illingworth) D.; B.S. in Elec. Engring., New Haven Coll., 1949; m. Gretchen; children—Julie, William; children by previous marriage—Stephen, Robert. Draftsman/designer, Westcott and Mapes, cons. engrs., New Haven, 1946-48; designer Hill and Harrigan, cons. engrs., New Haven, 1948-49, Hubbard, Lawless and Blakeley, cons. engrs., New Haven, 1949-50, A. Flynn, cons. engr., Meriden, Conn., 1949; asso. engr. J.F. Mueller & Assos., Hartford, Conn., 1950-62; pres. Tech. Design Assos., Branford, Conn., 1962—. Chmn. Planning and Zoning Commn. Seymour, 1960-62; mem. adv. council SBA, 1967—. Served with AUS, 1942-45; ETO. Registered profl. engr., Conn. Mem. ASME, Am. Pub. Works Assn., Inst. for Municipal Engring., Inst. for Solid Wastes, Constrn. Specifications Inst., AIEE, Illuminating Engring. Soc., Conn. Soc. Profl. Engrs., Conn. Soc. of AIA, U.S. Power Squadron. Clubs: Pine Orchard, Woodbridge, Union League, Lions. Home: 187 Allings Crossing Rd West Haven CT 06516 Office: 388 E Main St Branford CT 06405

DOELL, MARTHA EILEEN, educator, career info. specialist; b. Rochester, N.Y., Jan. 7, 1943; d. William Joseph and Eileen (Hayes) D.; B.S. in Chemistry magna cum laude, Nazareth Coll. of Rochester, 1965; postgrad. Rochester Inst. Tech., 1977—; M.S.T. in Chemistry, Cornell U., 1969; student various summer insts. Tchr. physics and chemistry, curriculum coordinator Notre Dame High Sch., Elmira, N.Y., 1965-68; research chemist Eastman Kodak Co., Rochester, 1969-70; tchr. chemistry and phys. sci. Greece Olympia High Sch., Rochester, 1970-78, career edn. curriculum leader, 1975-78; tchr. Greece Athena High Sch., Rochester, 1978—, coordinator career edn. adv. com., 1977-78; author, developer, instr. secondary level career edn. tchr.-tng. courses; cons. career info. NSF grantee, 1968-69, 73;

Gen. Electric Found. grantee, 1977; certified in chemistry, physics, math., gen. sci., N.Y. State. Mem. Am. Chem. Soc., Sci. Tchrs. Assn. N.Y. State, Nat. Assn. Career Edn., Am. Personnel and Guidance Assn., NEA, N.Y. Edn. Assn., Greece Tchrs. Assn., Cornell U. Alumni Assn. Home: 119 Lake Front Rochester NY 14617 Office: Greece Athena High Sch Long Pond Rd Rochester NY 14612

D'OENCH, RUSSELL GRACE, JR., editor; b. N.Y.C., Feb. 16, 1927; s. Russell Grace and Dorothie Briggs (Sharp) D'O.; grad. Lawrenceville Sch.; m. Ellen Gates, Sept. 10, 1949; children—Peter, Ellen D'Oench Rumierman, Russell Grace. Reporter, Berkshire Eagle, Pittsfield, Mass., 1947-57; editor, pub. Sunnyvale (Calif.) Standard, 1952-56; pres. Sagamore Press, N.Y.C., 1956-58; editor, chmn. bd. Middletown (Conn.) Press, 1959—; dir. Middlesex Assurance Co., Middletown; mem. adv. bd. Hartford Nat. Bank at Middletown, 1960-78. Bd. dirs. Conn. Pub. Expenditure Council, 1965-67, Conn. Humanities Council, 1972-74, Goodspeed Opera House Found., 1970-74; chmn. bd. Middlesex Hosp., Middletown, 1972-74, Conn. Regional Med. Program, New Haven, 1971-74. Served with USMCR, 1945-46. Fellow East Coll. Wesleyan U., 1968-73. Mem. New Eng. Soc. Newspaper Editors (pres., 1965), Sigma Delta Chi. Club: East Haddam (Conn.) Fish and Game. Producer, host Point of View show, ednl. TV, Hartford, 1966-69. Home: Phedon Pky Middletown CT 06457 Office: 472 Main St Middletown CT 06457

DOERFLER, LEO G., audiologist; b. N.Y.C., June 25, 1919; s. Gustav and Anna (Steiner) D.; A.B., N.Y. U., 1939; M.S., Washington U., St. Louis, 1941; Ph.D. (fellow), Northwestern U., 1948; m. Alice Turechak, Dec. 19, 1943; children—Dennis, Donald, David, Ann. Instr., psychologist Iowa State Sch. Deaf, Council Bluffs, 1941-42; instr. Northwestern U., 1947-48; dir. dept. audiology Eye and Ear Hosp., Pitts., 1948-76; mem. faculty U. Pitts. Med. Sch., 1948-76, prof. audiology, 1954-76; chief audiology and speech dept. Latrobe (Pa.) Area Hosp., 1976—; mem. staff Children's Hosp., Pitts., 1965-77; vis. prof. Carlow Coll., Pitts., 1960—; chmn. sensory study sect. Social and Rehab. Services, HEW, 1970-73; pres. Am. Bd. Examiners in Speech Pathology and Audiology, 1960-62; cons. in field. Served to 1st lt. AUS, 1943-46. Fellow AAAS, Am. Speech and Hearing Assn. (pres. 1967; legis. council 1978—, Honors award 1975); mem. Am. Audiology Soc. (exec. com. 1976—), Pitts. Otol. Soc., Am. (com. hearing and equilibrium) Pa. (Community Service citation 1970) acads. ophthalmology and otolaryngology, Acoustical Soc. Am., Am. (dir. 1954-58), Pitts. hearing socs., Am. Pub. Health Assn., Indsl. Med. Assn., United Cerebral Palsy Assn. (dir. 1954—), Am. Indsl. Hygiene Assn., Am. Psychol. Assn., Kappa Delta Pi. Contbr. profl. jours. Editorial bd. Jour. Exceptional Children, 1950-53, Archives of Otolaryngology, 1965-67, Audiology and Hearing Edn., 1975-77, Audiology, 1975—; asso. editor Jour. Speech and Hearing Disorders, 1954-57, Jour. Am. Speech and Hearing Assn., 1961. Home: 4533 Barlind Dr Pittsburgh PA 15227 Office: Audiology and Speech Pathology Dept Latrobe Area Hosp Latrobe PA 15650

DOERR, EDD, assn. exec.; b. Indpls., Dec. 21, 1930; s. Eugene H. and Mary (Burk) D.; B.S., Ind. U., 1956; m. Herenia Isabel Osma, Apr. 21, 1956; children—Eric, Helena. Tchr. pub. schs., Danville, Ind., 1959-60, Plainfield, Ind., 1960-66; ednl. relations dir. Americans United for Separation of Church and State, Silver Spring, Md., 1966—. Mem. exec. com. Nat. Coalition Pub. Edn. and Religious Liberty, 1973—, steering com. Joint Washington Office Social Concern, 1970-75. Musician Paint Br. Pro Musica, Washington. Bd. dirs. ACLU Md. Mem. Horace Mann League, Am. Humanist Assn. (chmn. ch.-state com., bd. dirs.), Phi Delta Kappa. Unitarian. Author: The Conspiracy That Failed, 1968; (novel) Eden II, 1974. Contbg. editor: The Humanist mag., 1972; mng. editor Church and State mag., 1971—. Contbr. more than 1000 articles, short stories, revs. to mags. and jours. Home: 3018 Aquarius Ave Silver Spring MD 20906 Office: 8120 Fenton St Silver Spring MD 20910

DOERSCHUG, LESLIE ROLAND, univ. ofcl.; b. Niagara Falls, N.Y., Apr. 8, 1937; s. Leslie Roland and Delia Melissa (Thomas) D.; B.S., Cornell U., 1959; M.S. in Engring. Sci., U. Ark., 1970; m. Linda Yenner, June 9, 1961; children—Susan Claire, David Thomas. Service engr. John Deere Co., Syracuse, N.Y., 1959-65; asst. prof. Agrl. and Tech. Coll., Alfred, N.Y., 1965-72; acting registrar State U. N.Y. at Alfred, 1971, asst. registrar, 1971-72; registrar Alfred U., 1972—; contbr. Fed. Paperwork Commn., 1976. Asst. fire chief A.E. Crandall Hook & Ladder Co., Alfred, 1974-77, fire chief, 1977—; councilman Town of Alfred, 1976—. Served with Armed Forces, 1960-62. Mem. Am., Middle States assns. collegiate registrars and admissions officers. Republican. Presbyterian. Home: 1834 Water Wells Rd Alfred Station NY 14803 Office: PO Box 805 Alfred NY 14802

DOERSCHUK, ERNEST EDWIN, JR., ret. librarian; b. Sugar Creek, Ohio, Dec. 14, 1914; s. Ernest Edwin and Minnie (Strome) D.; B.A., Oberlin Coll., 1937; B.S., Western Res. U., 1938; m. Helen Elizabeth Monks, Sept. 3, 1938; children—Ernest Edwin, Peter M. Library asst. N.Y. Pub. Library, 1938-46; tech. librarian VA, N.Y.C., 1946-48; librarian Lancaster (Pa.) Free Pub. Library, 1948-57; dir. extension div. State Library Pa., Harrisburg, 1957-63, library devel. dir., 1963-64, state librarian, 1964-78. Mem. Lancaster County Community Council, 1952-57. Served to 1st lt. U.S. Army, 1942-46. Mem. Am., Pa. (past pres.) library assns., Pa. Assn. Adult Edn. (past pres.), Phi Beta Kappa. Mem. United Ch. Christ (sec.). Home: 145 Kready Ave Millersville PA 17551

DOETSCH, RAYMOND NICHOLAS, microbiologist; b. Chgo., Dec. 5, 1920; s. Roman Joseph and Anna (Martin) D.; B.S., U. Ill., 1942; A.M., Ind. U., 1943; Ph.D., U. Md., 1948; postgrad. Rowett Research Inst., Aberdeen, Scotland, 1956; m. Janet Gray Huddle, June 5, 1948; children—Karen, Paul, Jennie. With Nat. Diary Research Lab., Balt., 1943-45; mem. faculty U. Md., College Park, 1945—, prof. microbiology, 1960—; vis. scientist Nat. Inst. Dental Research, NIH, 1964; vis. lectr. Inst. History of Medicine, Johns Hopkins U., 1963. Served to 2d lt. U.S. Army, 1942. Nat. Library of Medicine grantee Brit. Mus., 1977, others. Fellow Am. Acad. Microbiology, AAAS; mem. N.Y. Acad. Sci., Am., Canadian socs. microbiology, Soc. Gen. Microbiology (U.K.), Sigma Xi, Phi Kappa Phi. Democrat. Author: Journey to the Green and Golden Lands, 1976; editor: Microbiology: Historical Contributions 1776-1907, 1960; Optical Deportment of the Atmosphere (John Tyndall), 1965; asso. editor Applied Microbiology, 1962-72, Bacteriol. Revs., 1972-76; contbr. articles to profl. jours. Home: 10429 43d Ave Beltsville MD 20705 Office: Dept Microbiology U Md College Park MD 20742

DOFF, ALFRED FRANK, photographer; b. N.Y.C., July 28, 1926; s. Joseph and Helen (Landau) D.; student Art Center Sch., 1947-50; pvt. study photography with Adolf Fassbender, Richard Averill Smith, Homer English, Peter Nicastro; m. Elayne Millstein, June 30, 1955; children—Jodi Sharane. Studio asst. Vogue Studios, N.Y.C., 1944-46. M. Munkasci, N.Y.C., 1946-47; owner, photographer Frederick Studios, Amityville, N.Y., 1959—. Served with USNR, 1944-46. Recipient State award, L.I. Soc. Photog. Illustrators, 1973, Sect. Chmn. award Profl. Photographers Soc. N.Y., 1970, 1971, service medal, 1970. Mem. L.I. Indsl. Photographers (pres. 1969), L.I. Soc. Photog. Illustrators (pres. 1970, 71), Profl. Photographers Am., Profl. Photographers Soc. N.Y. (dir. 1970, 71). Home: 35 Constellation Rd Levittown NY 11756

DOGGER, ADA RUTH CAROLYN EMDE, educator, author, health sci cons.; b. Milw., Nov. 4, 1925; d. John Henry and Ada Marie-Ruth (Klevenow) Emde; student Milw. Downer Coll., 1942-45; B.S., N.D. State U., Fargo, 1963, M.S., 1965; postgrad. Gallaudet Coll., 1969-70; m. James Russell Dogger, Apr. 12, 1946; children—Allen James, Stuart Jon, Gary Robert. Work-study asst. in Waldorf bio-dynamic agrl. methods Kimberton (Pa.) Farms, 1944; pvt. kindergarten tchr., Madison, Wis., 1946-47, Raleigh, N.C., 1956-57; research asst. in pesticide screening Wis. Alumni Research Found., Madison, 1947; chem. research asst. Am. Machine & Foundry Co., Raleigh, 1955; microbiol. research asst. in viruses, dept. bacteriology N.D. State U., Fargo, 1962, staff asst. teaching radioisotopes, dept. pharm. chemistry, bionucleonics, 1963-65, asst. prof. bionucleonics, radio-pharms., 1968-69, asst. radiol. safety officer for campus, 1969; sci. instr. Fargo jr., sr. pub. high schs., 1965-66, 68; innovative sci. instr. Model Secondary Sch. for the Deaf, Washington, 1969-70; resource, tutorial instr. for hearing-impaired grades 1-6 Montgomery Pub. Schs., Rockville, Md., 1971-72, sci. curriculum innovator for hearing-impaired summer sch. Montgomery Pub. Schs., 1972; innovative, tutorial program developer for hearing-impaired, grades 1-12 Tift County Schs., Tifton. Ga., 1973-74; South Ga. rep. Closer Look, Washington; cons. in field to parents; organizer Tift County Parents of Speech and Hearing Impaired Handicapped; info. coordinator H.E.A.R. Found., Inc., Nat. Info. Center for Quiet, Washington. Mem. steering com. 1st Presbyterian Ch., Cary, N.D., 1953-54, organizer women's group, 1953-55, prin. jr. high dept., Fargo, 1961-62; neighborhood chmn. March of Dimes, Cary, 1954; bd. dirs. Children's Theatre, Raleigh, 1956-57; neighborhood chmn. Obscene Lit. Removal, Fargo, 1962; vol. Alexander Graham Bell Assn. for Deaf, 1976-77. Recipient Certificate of Appreciation, Tifton Lions Club, 1974; NIH fellow 1963-65. Mem. Council for Exceptional Children, Ga. Educators of Hearing Impaired, Am. Soc. Microbiology, Anthroposophical Soc. Am. Clubs: Nat. Women's Book; Faculty Women's (N.D. State U. (Fargo); Okla. State U., (Stillwater); N.C. State U., (Raleigh); Eastern Star. Author: Listen———Please??????, 1974. Home: 710 Winhall Way Silver Spring MD 20904

DOH, BYUNG IL, counselor educator; b. Seoul, Korea, Aug. 13, 1937; came to U.S., 1973; M.A., Yonsei U., 1967; M.Ed., U. Pitts., 1975, Ph.D., 1977; m. Choong Hee, Dec. 2, 1967; children—Hyun-Kyung, You-Joon, You-Kyung. Counselor, instr. religion and edn. Yonsei U., Seoul, 1968-73; dir. human integration, 1973; active chaplain activities NIMH, Washington, 1978—; ordained minister Presbyterian Ch. in U.S.A. Served with Korean Army, 1959-61. Certified counselor Seoul Nat. U. Mem. Korean Counselor Assn., Am. Psychol. Assn., Korean Pastoral Counselor Assn., Am. Personnel and Guidance Assn. Presbyterian. Author: Population Explosion and Man's Future, 1973; Jesus and Logotherapy, 1973. Editor Jour. Yonsei Counseling Rev., 1970-73; Comprehensive Model of the Process of Self-Integration, 1977. Office: Del State Hosp Mental Health Div Newcastle DE 19720

DOHERTY, ANNA MARIE, mag. editor; b. Baldwin, N.Y., Oct. 28, 1929; d. Dennis James and Helen Elizabeth (Koch) D.; A.A., Immaculata Coll., 1949; certificate Traphagen Sch. Interior Design, 1950. Asso. food editor This Week mag., N.Y.C., 1952-66, N.Y. Herald Tribune, 1952-66; acting food editor N.Y. World Jour. Tribune, 1966-67; food editor, columnist Suffolk Sun, L.I., N.Y., 1967-69; with Family Circle mag., N.Y.C., 1970—, sr. editor, dir. editorial services, 1971—, author, editor Family Circle's 429 Great Gifts to Make, 1976; Food industry cons., 1965—; contbr. to Family Circle's Best of the Best Recipes, 1976; free lance food writer, 1966—. Mem. Internat. Fund for Monuments (Venice com.), Nat. Trust Historic Preservation, Met. Opera Guild, Met. Mus. Art. Club: Newswomen's (dir. N.Y.C. 1970-72). Contbr. articles to profl. jours. Home: 154 E 61st St New York City NY 10021 also 4080 Peconic Bay Blvd Laurel NY 11948 Office: 488 Madison Ave New York City NY 10022

DOHERTY, JOHN PATRICK, JR., ednl. cons.; b. Charlestown, Mass., Mar. 10, 1936; s. John P. and Margaret Catherine (Riley) D.; A.B., Boston Coll., 1961, postgrad., 1961-63; postgrad. Boston State U., 1966-69, Harvard U.; m. Geneva C. Murray, July 11, 1970. Tchr., Boston Pub. Schs., 1961-71; pres. Boston Tchr. Union, AFL-CIO, 1971-75, chmn. ednl. com. Greater Boston Labor Council, 1972—; ednl. cons. Lincoln-Filene Center, Tufts U., 1975-78; now asst. supt. schs., Berlin, N.H. Asso. in edn. Harvard Grad. Sch. Edn., 1972—; lectr. Boston Coll., 1972-73, Boston U., 1972-73, Wellesley U., 1971-72. Founder Boston Tchrs. Union Student Scholarship Program. Trustee Boston Tchrs. Health and Welfare Fund. Served with AUS, 1955-57. Mem. Greater Boston Swimming Coaches Assn. (pres. 1966), Mass. Fedn. Tchrs. (exec. bd. 1972— pres. 1976-78), Mass. Football Coaches Assn., Am. Assn. Sch. Adminstrs., Phi Delta Kappa. K.C. Clubs: Drama, Debating, Newspaper (Boston College); Mass. Gridiron (Boston). Home: 17 Williamson Ave Berlin NH 03570 Office: Lincoln-Filene Center Tufts U Medford MA 02155

DOHERTY, JOSEPH FREDERICK, corporate security officer; b. N.Y.C., May 26, 1922; s. Joseph Frederick and Helen (Burnes) D.; B.S., Fordham U., 1946; LL.B., N.Y. U., 1948; M.B.A., Columbia U., 1958; m. Violet Tedlie, Dec. 18, 1965; 1 dau., Diane. Spl. agt. FBI, 1949-54; gen. security coordinator Bell Telephone Labs., N.Y.C., 1954-62; gen. security mgr., long lines dept. AT&T, N.Y.C., 1963-65, dir. corporate security, 1965—; instr. indsl. security N.Y. U., 1964-68. Served with USAF, 1943-46. Decorated D.F.C. Mem. Am. Bar Assn., Am. Soc. Indsl. Security, Phi Delta Phi. Roman Catholic. Home: 8 Drake Rd Mendham NJ 07945 Office: 295 N Maple Ave Basking Ridge NJ 07920

DOHERTY, PATRICIA MCGINN, psychologist; b. Phila., Apr. 11, 1937; d. Joseph Aloysius and Annetta Eleanor (McGinn) Carr; A.B., Trinity Coll., Washington, 1960; M.A., Cath. U., 1964; Ed.D., Boston U., 1976; m. Edward J. Doherty, June 30, 1973. Tchr., Gaithersburg, Md., 1960-62; mem. faculty Trinity Coll., Washington, 1964-70, residence dir., 1966-67; mem. staff Counseling Center, Boston U., 1970-73; practice clin. psychology, Boston and Newton, Mass., 1970—; cons. Human Resource Inst., Brookline, Mass., 1973-78; supr. Boston Inst. Psychotherapies, 1977—, coordinator extern program, 1979—. NDEA fellow, 1967-70. Mem. Am. Personnel and Guidance Assn., Am., Mass. psychol. assns. Office: 520 Commonwealth Ave Boston MA 02215

DOJKA, EDWIN SIGMUND, civil engr., city ofcl.; b. Niagara Falls, N.Y., Dec. 20, 1924; s. Zygmunt Joseph and Felixa (Pasek) D.; B.C.E., Rensselaer Poly. Inst., 1951; m. Jean L. Keller, July 9, 1949; children—Paul, Gail Dojka Rutkowski, Jay. Structures engr. Bell Aircraft Corp., Wheatfield, N.Y., 1951-52; design engr. Hooker Electro Chem. Corp., Niagara Falls, N.Y., 1952-55; civil engr. City of Niagara Falls (N.Y.), 1955-58, asst. city engr., 1958-60, dep. city engr., 1960-63, city engr., 1963—, mem. sewer commn., plumbing bd., 1963—, mem. planning bd., 1963-66, bd. equalization rev., 1963-71; mem. Niagara County Planning Bd., 1978—. Mem. United Fund Community Budget Com., 1962-68; mem. Community Ambassador Gen. Com., 1958, 59; Fleet Safety adv. commr., Niagara Falls, 1960-68; bd. assos. Mt. St. Mary's Hosp., 1969-70. Served with inf. AUS, World War II; ETO. Decorated Bronze Star, Combat Infantryman's badge, Purple Heart. Registered profl. engr., land surveyor, N.Y. Fellow ASCE; mem. Soc. of Am. Mil. Engrs., Am. Pub. Works Assn., Am. Water Works Assn., N.Y. State Assn. of Municipal Engrs., Inst. for Municipal Engring., Am. Arbitration Assn. (comml. panelist 1978), DAV, Am. Legion, Boys Club Alumni Assn., Pulaski Civic League, East Side Profl. and Bus. Mens Assn., Sigma Xi, Chi Epsilon, Tau Beta Pi. Roman Catholic. Clubs: LaSalle Sportsmen's, Echo Sertoma, Elks, First Friday, K.C. Home: 509 80th St Niagara Falls NY 14304 Office: City Hall Niagara Falls NY

DOLAN, CHARLES FRANCIS, communications co. exec.; b. Cleve., Oct. 16, 1926; s. David J. and Corrine Catherine (Henson) D.; student John Carroll U., 1945-49; m. Helen Ann Burgess, July 4, 1950; children—Patrick, Thomas, James, Marianne, Kathleen, Deborah. Pres., Sterling Movies, Inc., N.Y.C., 1956-69, Manhattan Cable TV, N.Y.C., 1961-71, Home Box Office, Inc., N.Y.C., 1971-73, Sterling Communications, Inc., N.Y.C., 1965-73, Cablevision Systems Corp., Jericho, N.Y., 1973—; v.p. L.I. Ednl. TV Council, 1971-72. Trustee Village of Laurel Hollow, 1966-70. Served with USAF, 1945-46. Clubs: Piping, Metropolitan. Home: Cove Neck Rd Oyster Bay NY 11771 Office: 366 N Broadway Jericho NY 11753

DOLAN, GEORGE HENRY, investment co. exec.; b. N.Y.C., Mar. 12, 1911; s. John F. and May D.; student N.Y. U., 1931-33; m. Catherine E. Fernandez, Jan. 31, 1942; 1 son, Dean H. Cashier, Eisele King Libaire Stout & Co., N.Y.C., 1928-44; with Marine Midland Trust Co., N.Y.C., 1944-46; comptroller, office mgr. Kalb Voorhis & Co., N.Y.C., 1946-48; v.p., dir. Axe Houghton Stock Fund Inc., Tarrytown, N.Y., 1973—, chmn. bd. Axe Securities Corp., 1973—, exec. v.p., dir., E. W. Axe & Co., Inc., 1972—, v.p. Axe Houghton Fund A, Inc., Axe Houghton Fund B, 1966—; pres. dir. Emerak Corp., Tarrytown, 1962—. Office: Axe Securities Corp 400 Benedict Ave Tarrytown NY 10591

DOLE, GRACE FULLER, librarian; b. Cambridge, Mass.; d. John Soper and Margaret Fernald D.; B.A., Bryn Mawr Coll., 1944; M.L.S., Columbia U., 1954; m. Paul E. Kohler, Jr., Jan. 22, 1944 (div. May 1946); 1 dau., Margaret Fernold Nicholson. Tchr. French, librarian Low-Heywood Sch., Stamford, Conn., 1948-50; sch. librarian Greenwich (Conn.) Library, 1950-53; with reference dept. N.Y. Pub. Library, N.Y.C., 1954-56; asst. librarian then librarian Benton & Bowles, N.Y.C., 1956-62; reference librarian Ferguson Library, Stamford, 1962-64; librarian U. Conn.-Stamford Br. and Center, 1964-75, asst. librarian, 1975—; mem. Library Adminstrs. Group Fairfield County, 1974-75. Mem. Spl. Libraries Assn. (head com. new library devel. 1962-63, chmn. publicity 1971—, rec. sec. 1972-73), ALA, Am. Artists Profl. League (hon.), Library Group SW Conn. (publicity chmn. 1971-72, co-chmn. newsletter and publicity 1973-73), AAUP, Hudson Valley Art Assn. (rec. sec. 1973-74), Margaret F. Dole Contemporary Art Club (v.p. 1973-74, now pres.), DAR, Colonial Dames XVII Century, Huguenot Soc. Conn., Panhellenic Assn. (chmn. Fairfield br. 1973-74, treas. 1975-76, sec. 1976-77), Catharine Wolfe Art Club (dir. 1975-78). Home: 503 W Lyon Farm Dr Greenwich CT 06830

DOMAN, ELVIRA HAND, educator; b. N.Y.C.; d. Andrew and Lillian (McClary) Hand; B.A., Hunter Coll., 1955; M.S. in Biology, N.Y. U., 1959; M.A. in Biochemistry (Fellow) Columbia, 1960; Ph.D. in Biochemsitry (fellow), Rutgers, 1965; m. John W. Hagan, Jr.; children—Paula, Rodney. Jr. technician Univ. Hosp., N.Y.C., 1955-56; sr. technician Sloan Kettering Inst. for Cancer Research, N.Y.C., 1956-57, research asst., 1960-61; research asst. Columbia Coll. Physicians and Surgeons, 1957-58; research asso. Rockefeller U., N.Y.C., 1965-68; lectr. Douglass Coll., New Brunswick, N.J., 1970-73; asst. prof. Seton Hall U., South Orange, N.J., 1973-77; now with NSF, Washington. Lectr. sickle cell anemia colls., community groups; panelist radio sta. WCTC, New Brunswick, 1973. USPHS pre-doctroal fellow, 1962-64; Sloan-Kettering Inst. fellow, 1965, Rockefeller U., 1965-66. Mem. N.Y., N.J. acads. scis., Am. Chem. Soc., AAAS. Contbr. articles to profl. jours. Home: 1520 Farragut St NW Washington DC 20011 Office: NSF Washington DC 20550

DOMANICO, JOHN PETER, JR., quality engr.; b. Schenectady, Dec. 17, 1949; s. John Peter and Elena Mary (Gabriele) D.; B.S., Clarkson Coll. Tech., 1971; m. Cheryl Ann Schneider, Aug. 22, 1970; children—John Peter III, Gregory Michael. Merchandise mgr. K-Mart, Albany, N.Y., 1971-74; health physicist asst. Morrison-Knudson Co., West Milton, N.Y., 1974; nuclear quality control engr. electric boat div. Gen. Dynamics, West Milton, 1974-77; quality engr. Bard-Parker div. Becton Dickinson & Co., Hancock, N.Y., 1977—. Mem. Am. Soc. Quality Control (certified quality engr.). Roman Catholic. Home: RD 1 Box 175 Hancock NY 13783 Office: Route 97 Hancock NY 13783

DOMARADZKI, THEODORE FELIX, educator, editor; b. Warsaw, Poland, Oct. 27, 1910; s. Joseph and Maria (Tomaszewska) D.; B.A., Polish Coll., Zakopane, 1930; M.A., U. Warsaw, 1939; Litt. D., U. Rome (Italy), 1941; diploma Acad. Polit. Sci., Warsaw, 1936; m. Maria Teresa Dobija, Apr. 22, 1954. Asst. diplomatic history Acad. Polit. Sci., 1936-39; asso. prof. Pontificio Inst. Orientale, Gregorian, U., Rome, 1943-47; prof. Polish lit. and dir. Paderewski Collection, U. Montreal, Que., Can., 1948—, dir. dept. Slavic studies, 1948-63, dir. Polish Research Center, 1963—; vis. prof. Fordham U., 1948-50; prof., dir. dept. Slavic studies U. Ottawa, 1949-53; lectr. Polish lang. State U. Rome, 1941-47. Head demographical div. Warsaw City Hall, 1932-35; chief edn. div. for Poles, Brit. Embassy, Rome, 1945-46; v.p. Can. Inter-Am. Research Inst., Montreal, 1964—; pres. Canadian Com. for Orgn. World U., 1971—; dir. gen. Inst. Comparative Civilizations. Served to maj. with Polish Red Cross, Italy, 1944-46. Mem. Eastern Can. Assn. Slavic and Eastern Europe Specialists (pres. 1950—), Assn. Canadian Writers, Can. Soc. Comparative Study Civilizations (hon. life mem., pres. 1972-76), Can. Internat. Acad. Humanities and Social Scis. (v.p. 1975—), Canadian Assn. Slavists (hon. life), Com. for Canadian-Polish Univ. and Sci. Cooperation (pres. Que. sect. 1969—). Author: Les Considerations de C.K. Norwid sur la liberte de la parole, 1971; Le Symbolism et L'Universalisme de C.K. Norwid, 1974. Editor: Cahiers Culturels. Home: 5601 Ave des Cedres Montreal PQ H1T 2V4 Canada Office: U Montreal Box 6128 Montreal PQ H3C 3J7 Canada

DOMARECKA, SISTER MARY SYLVINA, high sch. prin.; b. Mt. Carmel, Pa., Oct. 28, 1912; d. John and Anna Catherine (Tojza) Domarecki; B.S. in Edn., Seton Hall U., South Orange, N.J., 1946, M.A. in Personnel and Guidance, 1957; postgrad. Cath. U. Am., Fordham U., U. Mass. Joined Felician Sisters, 1930; elementary sch. tchr., N.J., Md., 1932-46; prin. St. Joseph's Elementary Sch., Blackwell, Okla., 1946-53; secondary sch. counselor Immaculate Conception High Sch., Lodi, N.J., 1954-66, Holy Cross High Sch., Dover, Del., 1972-74; prin. Immaculate Conception High Sch., Lodi, N.J., 1967-72, St. Anthony High Sch., Jersey City, 1974—. Mem. Nat. Cath. Edn. Assn., Newark Archdiocesan Assn. Secondary Sch. Prins., Am. Personnel and Guidance Assn., Nat. Cath. Guidance Conf., N.J. Assn. Guidance Counselors, Hudson County Guidance

Counselors. Roman Catholic. Home: 346 6th St Jersey City NJ 07302 Office: 175 8th St Jersey City NJ 07302

DOMBROWSKI, FRANK PAUL, JR., pharmacist; b. Nashua, N.H., May 10, 1943; s. Frank Paul and Yvonne Joan (Paris) D.; B.S., Mass. Coll. Pharmacy, 1965, M.S., 1967; m. Eleanor Cassady, June 15, 1968; children—Michael, Peter, Laura. Pharmacist, Androscoggin Valley Hosp., Berlin, N.H., 1974-75, Eastern Maine Med. Center, Bangor, 1975-77; pharmacist Concord (N.H.) Hosp., 1977—, dir. pharmacy services and central sterile supply, 1977—; cons. nurse anesthetist sch. Concord Hosp. Served with U.S. Army, 1968-74. Decorated Combat Inf. badge, Bronze Star medal, Army Commendation medal. Fellow Am. Acad. Med. Adminstrs.; mem. Am. Pharm. Assn., Am. Soc. Hosp. Pharmacists, Home: Park Ave RFD 1 Contoocook NH 03229 Office: 250 Pleasant St Concord NH 03301

DOMICO, MICHAEL DENNIS, ins. co. exec.; b. Woodbury, N.J., Feb. 3, 1949; s. Michael Angelo and Jeanette Elizabeth (Landolfi) D.; student Wheeling (W.Va.) Coll., 1967-70; m. Jean Lois Hilderbrand, May 29, 1971. With Prudential Ins. Co., 1971—, spl. agt., tng. asst., Vineland, N.J., 1975—. Active local Boy Scouts Am. Mem. S. Jersey Life Underwriters Assn., Nat. Rifle Assn. Home: 515 S 3d St Vineland NJ 08360 Office: 531 N Delsea Dr Vineland NJ 08360

DOMNI, FEJZI ISA, physician; b. Shkoder, Scutari, Albania, Feb. 22, 1922; s. Isa Mahmud and Hajrije (Jenishehri) D.; came to U.S., 1951, naturalized, 1959; M.D., Carola Francisca U., Graz, Austria, 1957; m. Mini Browsh, May 1, 1954; children—Lek, Suzanne. Intern, Women's Hosp., Detroit, 1957-58; resident in gen. medicine Cottage Hosp., Gross Point Farms, Mich., 1958-60; postgrad. tng. in gen. practice Polyclinic Hosp., N.Y.C., 1960-61; gen. practice medicine, Nassau County, N.Y., 1961—. Mem. N.Y., Nassau County, King's County med. socs., Am. Med. Soc. of Vienna (Austria), Albanian-Am. Nat. Orgn., Albanian-Am. Islamic Soc. N.Y. and N.J. (v.p.). Editor religious, cultural jour. Our Effort, 1970—; writer on Albanian culture and religion. Home and Office: 2 Laurae Dr Massapequa Park NY 11762

DOMOVICH, STEPHEN MICHAEL, correctional instn. adminstr.; b. Alexandria, Pa., Dec. 17, 1924; s. Andrew and Catherine (Brokup) D.; B.S. in Health and Phys. Edn., East Stroudsburg State Coll., 1949; M.Ed. in Personnel and Guidance. Rutgers U., 1954; m. Ramona Severance, July 16, 1949. Tchr., counselor Youth Correctional Inst., Annandale, N.J., 1946-56, dir. edn., 1956-64, 65-72, asst. supt., 1972-73, supr., 1973—; program asst. Div. Correction and Parole, Trenton, N.J., 1964-65; tchr. Tng. Acad. for Corrections Officers, Trenton, 1972—. Bd. dirs. water safety, also learn-to-swim program ARC, Hunterdon County (N.J.) 1958-64. Served with AUS, 1943-45. Recipient Outstanding Performance award State of N.J., 1971. Certified in strategic mgmt. in corrections program The Wharton Sch. Mem. Am. Correctional Assn., Correctional Edn. Assn. Clubs: Hunterdon Hills Lions (pres. 1974-75, zone chmn. 1975—), Annandale Officers. Home: Box 231 Annandale NJ 08801 Office: Youth Correctional Instn Annandale NJ 08801

DOMS, KEITH, librarian; b. Endeavor, Wis., Apr. 24, 1920; s. Reinhard Edward and Lillian (Gohlke) D.; B.A., U. Wis., 1942, B.L.S., 1947; m. Margaret Ann Taylor, Apr. 1, 1944; children—Peter Edward, David Laurance. City librarian Concord (N.H.) Pub. Library, 1947-51; dir. Grace A. Dow Meml. Library, Midland, Mich., 1951-56; asso. dir. Carnegie Library, Pitts., 1956-64, dir., 1964-69; dir. Free Library of Phila., 1969—; cons. pub. library devel. programs and pub. library bldgs. U.S. State Dept. specialist and dir. Library Seminar, Pakistan, 1964. Mem. exec. com. United Mental Health Services of Allegheny County, 1959-65, pres., 1963-65; mem. Pa. Bd. Edn., 1976—. Served with AUS, 1942-46. Mem. Am. (chmn. adv. com. library tech. project, 1959-62, pres. 1971-72, pres. library adminstrn. div. 1963-64), Pa. (pres. 1961) library assns., World Affairs Council Phila. (dir.), Internat. Fedn. Library Assns., Internat. Assn. Met. Libraries (past pres.), Beta Phi Mu (pres. 1962-64). Clubs: Pitts. Bibliophiles, Philobiblon, Franklin Inn. Contbr. articles to profl. jours. Home: 3101 W Coulter St Philadelphia PA 19129 Office: Free Library Phila Logan Sq Philadelphia PA 19103

DONAHO, JOHN ALBERT, mgmt. cons.; b. Chgo., Sept. 9, 1917; s. John and Pauline (Langdon) D.; B.A., Central YMCA Coll., 1941; certificate U. Chgo., 1942, M.A., 1943; m. Patricia Ann Maguire, Sept. 23, 1961; children by previous marriage—John William (dec.), Rondi Ann Donaho Reese. Asst. to comptroller Commonwealth Edison Co., Chgo., 1935-43; prin. U.S. Bur. Budget, Washington, 1943-47; v.p. Roosevelt U., Chgo., 1947-48; budget dir., acting city mgr. City of Richmond (Va.), 1948-52; pres. John A. Donaho & Assos., Inc., Balt., 1952—; lectr. U. Chgo., Johns Hopkins, Am. U., U. Wash.; asso. prof. U. Balt., Johns Hopkins; cons. charter commns. Baltimore County, Anne Arundel County, Balt. City, Harford County, Columbia, Md., 1954-75. Chmn., Va. Commn. on Uniform Fin. Reporting, 1950. Fellow Soc. Advancement Mgmt., Am. Soc. Pub. Adminstrn. (sr.); mem. Internat. City Mgrs. Assn., Pub. Personnel Assn., Am. Acad. Polit. and Social Scis., Municipal Fin. Officers Assn., Nat. Municipal League, Am. Polit. Sci. Assn., Am. Soc. Tng. Dirs. Democrat. Clubs: Univ. (pres.), Civitan (pres., dir.) (Balt.); Lakeview (v.p., dir.) (Reisterstown, Md.). Home: 6600 Deer Park Rd Reisterstown MD 21136 Office: Room 320 10 Light St Baltimore MD 21202

DONAHOE, EILEEN O'ROURKE, counselor, educator; b. N.Y.C., Mar. 25, 1942; d. John Thomas and Ellen (Canning) O'Rourke; B.A., Ohio Dominican Coll., 1966; M.S., So. Conn. State Coll., 1977, 6th yr. profl. diploma, 1977; postgrad. Yale U., 1977; m. James Paul Donahoe, Dec. 26, 1973. Joined Dominican Sisters of St. Mary of the Springs, Roman Catholic Ch., 1960; elementary, secondary tchr. Diocese of Columbus (Ohio), 1963-68; chmn. lang. arts dept. St. Timothy Sch., West Hartford, Conn., 1968-71; collateral advisor, researcher 2d New Haven Bank, 1971-73; counselor St. Mary's High Sch., New Haven, 1973-75; project coordinator, cons. career counseling Area Coop. Ednl. Services, Hamden, Conn., 1977—. Equal Rights Ammendment group speaker; counselor, mem. advisory com. Sisters in Transition. Recipient City of New Haven Scholarship award, grant Yale U., 1977; certified guidance counselor, English-Spanish tchr., student personnel counselor, Conn. Mem. NOW, Am. Personnel and Guidance Assn., Am. Coll. Personnel Assn., Assn. Counselor Edn. and Personnel, NEA, Conn. Edn. Assn. Contbr. articles to Dominican Horizons, 1963-65. Author Research papers on edn. Home: 34 Cedar Lake Rd Chester CT 06412

DONAHOE, RITA LOUISE, realtor; b. Boston, Jan. 16, 1930; d. Franklin Augustine and Barbara Rita (Coyne) Bannister; student Boston Coll., 1948-51; m. Robert Francis Donahoe, June 15, 1957; children—Steven Francis, Christopher John. Asst. clk. Suffolk Superior Criminal Ct., Boston, 1948-57; v.p., treas. D&G Constrn. Co., Inc., Merrimack, N.H., 1964-68; broker Fisher Assos., real estate, Nashua, N.H., 1968-71; propr. R. Donahoe Assos., Bedford, N.H., 1971—. Mem. Nashua (v.p. 1975, pres. 1976), Manchester bds. realtors, So. N.H., (v.p. 1975—, award 1973), Greater Manchester multiple listing services, Women's Council Realtors (chpt. pres. 1974), Nat., N.H. (dir. exec. com. 1976—) assns. realtors, Realtors Nat. Mktg. Inst. Manchester C. of C. Club: Manchester Country. Home: Davis Rd Merrimack NH 03054 Office: RFD 5 Daniel Webster Hwy Bedford NH 03102

DONAHUE, IRVING JAMES, JR., mfg. co. exec.; b. Worcester, Mass., Feb. 14, 1922; s. Irving James and Ethel Linnea (Larson) D.; B.S., Worcester Poly. Inst., 1944; M.B.A., Harvard, 1948; m. Barbara May Grant, Sept. 14, 1946; children—Susan (Mrs. Thomas A. Falzoi), Judith. Engaged in mfg. industry, 1948-56; pres. Donahue Industries, Inc., Shrewsbury, Mass., 1957—, I.J.D. Inc., Shrewsbury, 1973—, Donahue Internat., Inc., Wilmington, Del., 1972—; trustee, corp. clk. Consumer Savs. Bank, Worcester; dir. various cos. Chmn. Shrewsbury Bd. Selectmen, 1953-68, chmn. finance com., 1968-76; trustee, exec. com., mem. pres.'s adv. com., also adv. com. mgmt. dept. Worcester Poly. Inst.; trustee, v.p., exec. com. Worcester Meml. Hosp. Served to lt. (j.g.) USNR, 1944-46. Registered profl. engr., Mass. Mem. Central Mass. Employers Assn. (pres., dir. 1971-73), Worcester Area C. of C. (dir.), Small Bus. Execs. Club (chmn.), Worcester Poly. Inst. Alumni Assn. (past pres.), Mass. Finance Com. Assn. (dir.), Phi Sigma Kappa. Republican. Conglist. Mason. Clubs: Worcester (dir.), Worcester Country (bd. govs.), Harvard, Harvard Business School (dir.) (Worcester). Patentee metal-plastic grinding wheel adaptor. Home: 100 Oak St Shrewsbury MA 01545 Office: 5 Industrial Dr Shrewsbury MA 01545

DONAHUE, JOHN JOSEPH, pharm. co. exec.; b. Waterbury, Conn., Feb. 8, 1942; s. John Henry and Gertrude Theresa (Hartigan) D.; B.S., Boston Coll., 1963; M.S., U. Mass., 1968, Ph.D., 1968; m. Priscilla Louise Hartmann, Jan. 14, 1968; children—Kimberley, John. Sr. scientist Hoffmann LaRoche, Nutley, N.J., 1968-72, mgr. analytical research devel., 1972-75, mgr. quality control research products, 1975-77, dir. research quality assurance, 1977—. Vice pres. Nutley Tenants Assn., 1969; pres. Home Sch. Assn., 1977-78; tribal chief Indian Guides YMCA, 1977; tchr. sch. Presbyn. Ch., 1977, mem. bd. stewards, 1978—. Mem. Am. Chem. Assn., Am. Pharm. Assn., N.Am. Thermal Analysis Soc., Soc. Applied Spectroscopy, Sigma Xi. Contbr. articles to profl. jours. Home: 3 Raleigh Ct Morristown NJ 07960 Office: 340 Kingsland St Nutley NJ 07110

DONALD, PATRICK REYNOLDS, army officer; b. Washington, May 17, 1948; s. Walter Godley and Mary Reynolds D.; B.S., U.S. Mil. Acad., 1971; m. Elaine Regina Wick, June 14, 1971; children—Bruce Joseph, Brian Walter. Commd. 2d lt. U.S. Army, 1971, advanced through grades to capt., 1975; unit comdr., Aschaffenburg, Germany, 1976-77; materiel systems staff officer Aberdeen Proving Ground, Md., 1978—. Mem. U.S. Armor Assn., Am. Def. Preparedness Assn., Assn. Grads. U.S. Mil. Acad. Home: 932 Chesapeake Dr Havre de Grace MD 21078 Office: USAOOCS Aberdeen Proving Ground MD 21005

DONALDSON, DOROTHEA AMELIA, airline exec.; b. St. Louis, Oct. 30, 1946; d. James H. and Dola D.; student Skidmore Coll., 1964-66; B.B.A., George Washington U., 1969. Mgmt. trainee Time Inc., 1969, asst. mgr. mdse. sales Time-Life Books, 1969-70, mgr., 1970-72; mgr. spl. mktg. services TWA, N.Y.C., 1972-73, comml. mktg., 1973-75, consumer mktg., 1975-76, dir. automation mktg., 1976-77, automation programs, 1977-78, reservations and automation programs, 1978—. Recipient Tribute to Women in Internat. Industry award YWCA, 1978. Mem. Am. Soc. Travel Agts. Office: TWA 605 3d Ave New York NY 10016

DONALDSON, GERALD KEITH, manpower cons.; b. N.Y.C., Dec. 15, 1933; s. Theodore Roy and Nora (Stern) D.; B.A. in History, Long Island U., 1968. With N.Y.C. Dept. Parks, 1957-61; counselor children Spofford House of Detention, N.Y.C., 1961-64; ednl. counselor, group worker Youth Devel. Agy., N.Y.C., 1964-68; asst. exec. dir. N.Y.C. Mission Soc., 1967-70; cons. Fedn. Protestant Welfare Agencies, N.Y.C., 1969-71; project dir. Nat. Urban League, N.Y.C., 1971-72, asst. coordinator, 1972-73, asst. dir., 1973-78, program specialist, 1978—; cons. Boys Club of Am., 1972; cons., trainer Job Corps, 1977, Phoenix Indian Center, 1977; adj. prof. African and Afro-Am. history N.Y.C. Community Coll., 1972-74; ednl. tour guide, Ghana, Africa, summer, 1974; cons. in field. Served with inf., U.S. Army, 1954-56. Recipient award for outstanding service to youth group, N.Y.C. Mission Soc. Cadet Corps, 1968. Mem. Am. Personnel and Guidance Assn., Carl G. Jung Found., Am. Soc. Training and Devel., Nat. Assn. Human Rights Workers. Home: 48 W 73rd St New York City NY 10023 Office: 500 E 62nd St New York City NY 10021

DONALDSON, PETER SAMUEL, Renaissance scholar; b. N.Y.C., Nov. 21, 1942; s. John Joseph and Constance (Stalberg) D.; B.A., Columbia Coll., 1964; M.A., Clare Coll., Cambridge (U.K.) U., 1970; Ph.D. (NDEA fellow, faculty fellow), Columbia U., 1972; m. Alice Margaret Kaplan, Aug. 22, 1965; children—John Caleb, Ethan Robert, Emily Jean. Preceptor in English, Columbia U., N.Y.C., 1967-69; lectr. comparative lit. Coll. City N.Y., 1967-68; instr. lit. Mass. Inst. Tech., Cambridge, 1969-72, asst. prof., 1973-78, dir. Western tradition program, 1975—, asso. prof., 1978—. Kellett fellow Clare Coll., 1964-66; Old Dominion grantee Mass. Inst. Tech., 1973; Nat. Endowment Humanities Younger Humanist fellow, 1975. Mem. Modern Lang. Assn., New Eng. Renaissance Conf., Renaissance Soc. Am., Am. Hist. Assn., Northeastern Modern Lang. Assn., Internat. Conf. for Study Polit. Thought, Phi Beta Kappa. Editor, translator: A Machiavellian Treatise by Stephen Gardiner, 1975; A Description of England 1556, 1978. Office: 14N422 Mass Inst Tech Dept Humanities Cambridge MA 02139

DONATH, CLARENCE EDGAR, architect; b. Sedalia, Mo., Mar. 10, 1912; s. Otto Arthur and Mary (Page) D.; B.S., U. Ill., 1938; postgrad. Art Inst. Buffalo, 1941-42, State U. N.Y., 1969-71; m. Margaret Young Brown Clark, Nov. 29, 1945; children—Paul Bryan, Ann Susan (Mrs. Andre Meida de Vasconcellos Chaves). Self-employed as architect, East Aurora, N.Y., 1956-65; partner Kideney, Smith, Fitzgerald, Laping Partnership, architects and engrs., Buffalo, 1965—. Served to lt. (j.g.) USNR, 1942-46; PTO, ETO. Recipient Internat. award Galvanizers, 1962. Mem. Mensa, AIA, Creative Edn. Found., N.Y. State Soc. Architects. Prin. archtl. works include Cleveland Heights Christian Ch., Bethany Luth. Ch., Town of Aurora Libraries, St. John's Luth. Ch. of Amherst, Erie Community Coll., Infirmary State U. Coll. Buffalo, Lancaster (N.Y.) Pub. Library. Home: 91 Hillcrest Rd East Aurora NY 14052 Office: 374 Delaware Ave Buffalo NY 14202

DONCHAK, RICHARD MICHAEL, chem. co. exec.; b. Shenandoah, Pa., Oct. 19, 1932; s. Michael and Clara (Zegarsky) D.; B.S., Mount St. Mary's Coll., 1954; m. Shirley Louise Hackenburg, Feb. 25, 1956; children—Elizabeth, Linda, Barbara. With Norwich Pharmacal Co. (N.Y.), 1957—, adminstrv. asst. to dir. quality control, 1971-73, dir. sterile ops., 1973-77, mgr. contract mfg., 1977—; lectr. Center Profl. Advancement, Somerville, N.J., 1972—. Bd. dirs. Parental Drug Assn., Phila., 1970-72. Served with AUS, 1955-57. Mem. Am. Soc. Microbiology, Pharm. Mfrs. Assn. (drug preservation com.). Club: Elks. Patentee in field. Home: 172 N Broad St Norwich NY 13815 Office: 13 Eaton Ave Norwich NY 13815

DONELLI, JOHN JAY, psychologist; b. Lake Mahopac, N.Y., June 14, 1949; s. John Joseph and Mary Jane (Keller) D.; B.A., State U. N.Y., Plattsburgh, 1972; diploma nursing N.Y. State Dept. Mental Hygiene, Middletown, 1971; M.S., State U. Coll. N.Y., Plattsburgh, 1975, certificate adv. studies in counseling, 1976; m. Kathleen Linda Fuller, July 10, 1971. Emergency room nurse, team leader psychiat. treatment unit, asst. head nurse neurol. services CV/PH Med. Center, Plattsburgh, 1971-77; guidance counselor intern Saranac Central and Peru Central Schs., Peru, N.Y., 1975-76; psychologist Merle Cooper program N.Y. State Correctional System, Dannemora, 1977—. Mem. Am. Personnel and Guidance Assn., Am. Sch. Counselors Assn. Democrat. Methodist. Clubs: Shriners, Masons, Elks. Home: 123 N Emmons St Box 272 Dannemora NY 12929 Office: Clinton Correctional Facility Annex Dannemora NY 12929

DONHEISER, WALTER JOSEPH, psychologist; b. N.Y.C., Nov. 23, 1927; s. Sidney and Agnes (Hennessy) D.; Ph.D., Adelphi U., 1959; m. Judith Ann Sachs, Jan. 11, 1969; children—David, Mark. Chief psychologist S.E. La. Hosp., Mendeville, 1959-64; dir. psychol. services S.I. (N.Y.) Mental Health, 1964-66; fellow adult psychoanalysis Postgrad. Center for Psychotherapy, N.Y.C., 1966-69; div. mgr. Am. Mgmt. Psychologists, Chgo., 1969-74; clin. psychologist VA Hosp., Albuquerque, 1975-77; v.p. Mgmt. Resources Devel., San Francisco, 1974-75, dir., 1974-75; asso. dir. psychol. services South Oaks Hosp., Amityville, N.Y., 1977—; asso. clin. prof. psychology Adelphi U., Garden City, N.Y. Served with U.S. Army, 1945-48. Licensed psychologist, Calif., Ohio, N.Y. Diplomate Am. Bd. Profl. Psychology. Mem. Am., Eastern, Western psychol. assns. Address: 400 Sunrise Hwy Amityville NY 11701

DONIKIAN, MARC ROUPEN, physician; b. Harar, Ethiopia, July 2, 1914; s. Roupen Marc and Haigouhie (Patapanian) D.; came to U.S., 1959, naturalized, 1964; Ph.G., Am. U. Beirut (Lebanon), 1937, Ph.C., 1938, certificate pub. analyst, 1943, M.D., 1952; m. Beatrice Jidejian, Sept. 19, 1939; children—Andre, Janine. Mem. faculty Am. U. Beirut Sch. Pharmacy and Arts and Sci., 1938-43; owner, dir. Labs. Dr. Marc, Beirut, 1943-59; sr. research biologist, group leader Sterling-Winthrop Research Inst., Rensselaer, N.Y., 1959-68, dir. clin. pathology labs., 1968—; intern Am. U. Hosp., Beirut, 1951-52. Asst. to dir. forensic medicine Govt. of Lebanon, 1956-57. Mem. Am. Soc. Clin. Pathology, AAAS, N.Y. Acad. Scis. Home: 251 S Manning Blvd Albany NY 12208 Office: Sterling-Winthrop Research Inst Columbia Turnpike Rensselaer NY 12144

DONIO, DOMINIC ANTHONY, physician; b. Phila., Oct. 27, 1910; s. Dominic A. and Catherine (Veneziale) D.; B.S., Hahnemann Coll. Sci., 1930; M.D., Hahnemann Med. Coll., 1934; m. Adeline Eleanor Stravino, Feb. 22, 1936; children—Dominic A., Adeline E., John M., Peter T., Anthony F., David A. Intern, Sacred Heart Hosp., Allentown, Pa., 1934-35; resident dept. rehab. medicine N.Y. U., N.Y.C., 1949-51; rheumatologist Sacred Heart Hosp., Allentown, 1935-49, dir. dept. phys. medicine and rehab., 1952—; cons. phys. medicine and rehab. St. Luke's Hosp., Bethlehem, Pa., 1953-70; med. dir. Reuben Block Health Fund, Allentown, 1973—, Eastern Pa. Health Maintenance Orgn., 1975—, Cedarbrook Hosp. dept. phys. medicine and rehab.; asso. prof. phys. medicine and rehab. Sch. Medicine Temple U.; lectr. in phys. medicine and rehab. Temple U., 1966—. Mem. pres's. council Allentown Coll. of St. Francis de Sales. Fellow Nat. Found. Infantile Paralysis, 1949-51; recipient Distinguished Service award Arthritis and Rheumatism Found., 1962; named Cavalieri of Star of Solidarity, Italian govt., 1969. Diplomate Am. Bd. Phys. Medicine and Rehab. Mem. Am. Acad. Phys. Medicine, Am. Congress Rehab. Medicine, Pa., Lehigh County med. socs. Roman Catholic. Club: Lehigh Country. Contbr. articles in rheumatology to profl. publs. Home: 2720 Chew St Allentown PA 18104 Office: 528 Washington St Allentown PA 18102

DONLEY, BETTIE LOUX, editor, writer; b. Drexel Hill, Pa., Nov. 5, 1931; d. Frank Turner and Elizabeth Ida (Kauffman) Loux; B.S., Pa. State U., 1953; m. Marshall O. Donley, Jr., June 12, 1954 (div. Aug. 1971). Prodn. coordinator, editorial research Nat. Geog. Soc., Washington, 1959-69; editor World Traveler mag., dir. publs. Alexander Graham Bell Assn. for Deaf, Washington, 1969-76; free-lance book editor/writer, 1976—. Mem. forum White House Conf. Children, 1970. Recipient award for picture story Ednl. Press Assn. Am., 1970, award for layout, 1971, award for one-theme issue, 1973, Eleanor Fishburn award for outstanding contbn. to internat. understanding among readers, 1971. Mem. Women in Communications, Ednl. Press Assn. Am., Washington Book Pubs., Washington Ind. Writers, Smithsonian Assos., Alpha Gamma Delta. Democrat. Episcopalian. Club: Silver Spring (Md.) Garden (v.p. 1970-71). Advt. editor Nat. Capital Fedn. Garden Clubs Bull., 1968-73; editor Grace Ch. Messenger, 1971—. Home: 1217 Woodside Pkwy Silver Spring MD 20910

DONLEY, EDWARD, mfg. exec.; b. Highland Park, Mich., Nov. 26, 1921; s. Hugh and Frances (Gavin) D.; B.M.E., Lawrence Inst. Tech., 1943; advanced mgmt. program Harvard, 1959; m. Inez Cantrell, Oct. 24, 1946; children—Martha Donley Robb, Thomas, John. Vice pres. Air Products and Chems., Inc., Allentown, Pa., 1956-66, exec. v.p., 1966, pres., 1966—, chief exec. officer, 1973—, chmn. bd., 1978—, also dir.; dir. Am. Standard Inc. Trustee Dorothy Rider Pool Health Care Trust; mem. corp. Lawrence Inst. Tech.; bd. overseers Coll. Engring. and Sci., U. Pa. Mem. Am. Inst. Chem. Engrs., Mfg. Chemists Assn. (chmn. bd.), Soc. Chem. Industry (exec. com.), Conf. Bd. Home: 326 N 27th St Allentown PA 18104 Office: PO Box 538 Allentown PA 18105

DONLEY, JAMES WALTON, mgmt. cons.; b. Cleve., June 27, 1934; s. Howard Russell and Mary Louise D.; B.A., Denison U., 1958; M.B.A., U. Pa., 1960; m. Frances Elizabeth Jordan, July 5, 1963; children—Dana, Eliza. Asst. to pub. Time mag., N.Y.C., 1960-66; asst. commr. commerce N.Y. City Govt., 1967-68; sr. v.p. Deegan Co., Los Angeles, 1969-71; asst. sec. U.S. Treasury, Washington, 1972-73; pres. Donley Communications Corp., N.Y.C., 1973—. Bd. govs. N.Y. Young Republican Club; vice chmn. Citizen's Union of N.Y.C., Greenwich Health Assn. (dir.), Wharton Alumni Assn. (dir.). Served with U.S. Army, 1954-56. Clubs: Univ. of N.Y.C.; Belle Haven (Greenwich). Home: 51 Dewart Rd Greenwich CT 06830 Office: 405 Park Ave New York City NY 10022

DONLEY, MARSHALL OWEN, JR., edn. editor and writer; b. Christiana, Pa., Mar. 20, 1932; s. Marshall D. and Edna (Detwiler) D.; B.A., Pa. State U., 1954; postgrad. U. So. Calif., 1954-55; M.A., Am. U., 1966, Ph.D., 1971; m. Margaret T. Reagan, Sept. 18, 1971; children—Owen, Susan. Newspaper reporter Lancaster (Pa.) Intelligencer Jour., 1950-52; radio-tv writer WGAL and WGAL-TV, Lancaster, 1953; linguist U.S. Army Security Agy., Ft. Meade, Md., 1955-58; edn. writer, exec. editor N.E.A., Washington, 1958—. Instr. spl. sessions SUNY, Buffalo, summers 1964-65. Served with U.S. Army, 1955-58. Mem. Ednl. Press Assn. (chpt. past pres.), NEA (dept. editorial cons. 1960-67; pres. staff orgn. 1967-68), Phi Kappa Phi, Phi Delta Kappa, Phi Sigma Kappa, Sigma Delta Chi. Author: Power to the Teacher, 1976; The Future of Teacher Power, 1977. Contbr. articles to profl. jours. Home: 10365 May Wind Ct Columbia MD 21044 Office: 1201 16th St NW Washington DC 20036

DONNELLY, BARBARA MAE, med. devices mfg. co. exec.; b. Abington, Pa., Dec. 31, 1946; d. Ross Smith and Marguerite Mae (Wilson) Kirkpatrick; B.S. in Bus. Adminstrn., Pa. State U., 1969; m. Charles Michael Donnelly, Dec. 30, 1977. Engring. adminstr. Philco-Ford Corp., Ft. Washington, Pa., 1965-69; mgr. purchasing and office services Internat. Computaprint Corp., Ft. Washington, 1969-77; purchasing mgr. Extracorporeal Med. Spltys. subs. Johnson & Johnson, King of Prussia, Pa., 1977—; pres. Ft. Washington Mgmt. Assn., 1977-78. Chmn. fund raising Sr. Adults for Greater Adventure, 1977; chmn. Wissahickon br. ARC, 1976; adviser Explorer Scouts, 1976. Recipient certificate achievement ARC, 1976. Cert. purchasing mgr. Mem. Nat. Assn. Purchasing Mgmt., Am. Prodn. and Inventory Control Soc., Phila. Purchasing Mgmt. Assn. (vice chmn. membership 1977-78, dir. 1978-79). Home: 39 Wexford Rd North Wales PA 19454 Office: Extracorporeal Med Spltys Royal and Ross Rds King of Prussia PA 19406

DONNELLY, BRIAN, congressman; b. Boston, Mar. 2, 1946; s. Lawrence and Louise (Kelly) D.; B.S., Boston U., 1970; m. Virginia Norton, Feb. 14, 1976. Tchr., Boston Trade Sch., 1970-72; mem. Mass. Ho. of Reps., 1973-78, asst. majority leader, 1977-78; mem. 96th Congress from Mass. 11th Dist., Recipient Varsity award Boston U., 1970; named Man of Year Dorchester Lower Mills, 1974. Democrat. Roman Catholic. Office: US Ho of Reps Office of Clk of House H-105 The Capitol Washington DC 20515

DONNELLY, WILLIAM LORNE, ophthalmic surgeon; b. Bklyn., July 3, 1915; s. William Henry and Jane (Hoctor) D.; A.B., Columbia, 1939, M.D., 1943; m. Marie Grace Busch, May 3, 1947; children—Laureen Linda, Gregory Lorne, Michael Harold, Kevin William, Christopher Paul. Intern, Kings County Hosp., Bklyn., 1943; resident in ophthalmology N.Y. Postgrad. Med. Sch. and Hosp., N.Y.C., 1944-45; practice medicine specializing in ophthalmology, Rockville Centre, N.Y., 1947—; instr. ophthalmology N.Y. U., 1947-65; dir. ophthalmol. service Mercy Hosp., Rockville Centre, 1964-72; cons. in ophthalmology Mercy Hosp., Hempstead Gen. Hosp., South Nassau Communities Hosp. Mem. exec. council Nassau County council Boy Scouts Am., 1963-67. Served with U.S. Army, 1945-47. Diplomate Am. Bd. Ophthalmology. Fellow A.C.S., Am. Acad. Ophthalmology and Otolaryngology, Nassau Acad. Medicine (past chmn.), Nassau Surg. Soc.; mem. L.I. Ophthal. Soc. (past pres.). Republican. Roman Catholic. Club: Rockville Country. Contbr. articles to med. jours. Home and office: 661 N Long Beach Rd Rockville Centre NY 11570

DONNER, WILLIAM TROUTMAN, psychiatrist; b. Sharon Pa., Jan. 8, 1921; s. Raymond H. and Edna (Troutman) D.; student U. Pa., 1939-42, M.D., 1946; m. Alice Easby Wilkinson, Apr. 12, 1946; children—William W., Marda Elisa, Mary Alice, Margot Ramona. Intern, Allegheny Gen. Hosp., Pitts., 1945-46; resident Friends Hosp., Phila., U. Pa., 1950-51; practice medicine specializing in psychiatry, Abington, Pa., 1951—; psychiatrist Neuropsychiat. Assos. of Old York Rd., Abington, 1962-64; dir. mental health clinic Abington Meml. Hosp., 1958-64; coordinator psychiat. edn., 1964—, program dir. postgrad. course psychiatry for med. practitioners, 1966—; instr. U. Pa., 1951-58, asso. psychiatry, 1958-78; clin. asst. prof. Hahnemann Med. Coll., 1978—. Pres. bd. dirs. Family Service Montgomery County, 1966-67. Served with AUS, 1946-48. Mem. Am., Pa. psychiat. assns., AMA, Pa. State, Montgomery County med. socs., Am. Group Psychotherapy Assn., Acad. Religion and Mental Health. Contbr. articles to tech. jours. Home: 314 Wellington Terr Jenkintown PA 19046 Office: 1245 Highland Ave Abington PA 19001

DONOFRIO, ANTHONY MICHAEL, retail co. exec.; b. Jersey City, Mar. 10, 1918; s. Pasquale and Rose (Izzo) D.; student pub. schs. N.J.; m. Marie Angela Lupinacci, Dec. 13, 1942; children—Anthony Steven, Robert Anthony, Roselyn Marie, James Calahan. With Valley Fair Enterprises, Inc., Irvington, N.J., 1954—, gen. store mgr., 1960-74, personnel dir., 1974—. Mem. adv. bd. Essex County Sheriff's Office, 1976—. Served with USAAF, 1942-45. Mem. N.J. Food Council, Mass Retailing Inst., Valley Fair Credit Union. Republican. Roman Catholic. Clubs: K.C., Optimists, Elks (Elk of Yr. 1975-76), Anchor. Home: 3 Acapulco Dr Bricktown NJ 08723 Office: 15 Jackson Rd Totowa NJ 07512

DONOGHUE, ELIZABETH MARION MACMAHON (MRS. FLORENCE JOSEPH DONOGHUE), mus. curator; b. Castleisland, Kerry, Ireland, Nov. 9, 1896 (parents Am. citizens); d. James and Johanna Mary (Brosnan) MacMahon; B.A., Calvin Coolidge Coll., 1955, M.A., 1956; m. Florence Joseph Donoghue, Apr. 17, 1963 (dec. July 1970). Accountant, Boston Wool Trade, 1914-33; tchr., Everett (Mass.) High Sch., 1934-63; trustee Wenham (Mass.) Hist. Assn. and Mus., Inc., 1956—, curator dolls, 1960—. Driver, Red Cross Motor Corps, Boston, 1939-41, Civilian Def. Motor Corps, Everett, 1941-43. Mem. Antique Toy Collectors Am., Doll Club Gt. Britain, Doll Collectors Am., Emerald Isle, L.I., Ginny doll clubs, League Cath. Women, Mus. Fine Arts Boston, Nat. Ret. Tchrs. Assn., United Fedn. Doll Clubs, Am. Irish Hist. Soc. (life), Christ Child Soc. (life), Soc. Preservation N.E. Antiquities (life), Yesteryears Doll Mus. (life), Eire Soc. Boston (life, editor Bull. 1954-64), Worcester Art Mus., Boston U. Alumni Assn. Contbr. articles to profl. jours. Home: 86 Bradford St Everett MA 02149 Office: 132 Main St Wenham MA 01984

DONOGHUE, KEVIN FRANCIS, ins. co. exec.; b. Cambridge, Mass., Apr. 18, 1940; s. James A. and Margaret M. (Mulrennan) D.; A.B. in Econs., Boston Coll., 1961, M.B.A., 1970; m. Ellen M. Tangney, June 24, 1961; children—Sean, Michael, Coileen, Kerry, Liam. Sales mgr. Liberty Mut. Ins. Co., Boston, 1966-70; pres. Kevin F. Donoghue & Assos., Boston, 1970—. Bd. dirs. Greater Boston Walk for Hunger, 1976—. Served with U.S. Army, 1961-63. Mem. Ins. Cons. Soc. (pres. 1976-78). Home: 31 Brackett St Milton MA 02186 Office: 265 Morrissey Blvd Boston MA 02122

DONOHOE, VICTORIA THERESE, artist and art critic; b. Phila., Mar. 21, 1929; d. Daniel Joseph and Anne (O'Neill) D.; B.A., Rosemont Coll., 1950; M.F.A. (scholar), U. Pa., 1952; postgrad. scholar Pius XII Inst. Fine Arts Grad. Sch., Florence, Italy. Instr. Rosemont Coll. Art Dept., 1950-52, 54-55; columnist of art criticism Standard and Times, Phila., 1959-62, Phila. Inquirer, 1962—; corr. Art News Mag., 1975—, Knight-Ridder Newswire, 1974—. Exhibited group shows, Florence, Italy, Sons of Italy Bldg., and Woodmere Art Gallery, Phila.; represented in permanent collections Villanova (Pa.) U., Merrimack (Mass.) Coll., St. Joseph's Coll., Phila., Holy Child High Sch., Curia bldg. Fiesole, Italy, Vatican Library, Rome, also many pvt. collections. Mem. liturgical commn. Phila. Archdiocese, 1972—; mem. pres.'s assos. LaSalle Coll., 1973-76; dir. selections Liturgical Arts Exhbn., 41st Internat. Eucharistic Congress, Phila., 1976; advisor Phila. Craft Show, 1977; mem. am. crafts exhibit planning com. Vatican Mus. Contemporary Art, Rome, 1978; guest curator exhibit U. Mus., U. Pa., 1974; mem. Mayor's Com. for Neumann Monument for City of Phila. Recipient grant to attend workshop in art criticism Am. Fedn. Arts, N.Y.C., 1968, award Cath. Fine Arts Soc., 1976. Mem. Internat. Assn. Art Critics (Am. sect.), Pa. Acad. Fine Arts, Phila. Mus. Art, America-Italy Soc., Museum Modern Art N.Y., Society of Archtl. Historians, Mediaeval Acad. Am., Hist. Soc. Pa., Genealogical Soc. Pa., Irish Georgian Soc., Met. Mus., N.Y., Fairmount Park Art Assn., Delta Epsilon Sigma (chpt. pres. 1958-66). Contbr. essays to book, nat. mags. and publs. Address: 34 Narbrook Park Narberth PA 19072

DONOHUE, MICHAEL JOSEPH, judge; b. Holyoke, Mass., Dec. 12, 1923; s. David I. and Mary (Fitzgerald) D.; A.B., U. Mass., 1947; J.D., Boston U., 1950; m. Adeline L. O'Neil, Nov. 18, 1950; children—Michael J., Adeline L., Owen Bligh, Anne Carey, Quentin, Maria. Admitted Mass. bar, 1950; pub. adminstr. Commonwealth Mass., 1959-64; judge Dist. Ct. Holyoke, 1963—; asst. city solicitor, Holyoke, Mass., 1959-60. Mem. U. Mass. Bldg. Authority, 1960-63; mem. adv. bd., para-legal studies Salve Regina Coll. Pres., Am. Judges Found., 1977. Served with AUS, 1943-46. Recipient Award for Distinguished Leadership, Boston U. Mem. Am. Judges Assn. (pres. 1978, editor Ct. Rev. 1968-76, exec. dir. 1969-75, award for distinguished leadership). K.C. Editor: Case Law Hilites; mem. editorial rev. bd. Criminal Justice Rev. Office: Dist Ct Holyoke Holyoke MA 01040

DONOVAN, JAMES ROBERT, bus. equipment co. exec.; b. Wichita, Kans., Apr. 11, 1932; s. Karl Genevay and Louise (Silcott) D.; A.B., Harvard, 1954, M.B.A., 1956; m. Ottilie Schreiber, July 2, 1955; children—Amy Louise, Robert Silcott. Mgr. sales adminstrn., market research Hickok, Inc., Rochester, N.Y., 1956-59, regional sales mgr., 1959-62, asst. nat. sales mgr., 1963-65; group program mgr. Xerox Corp., Stamford, Conn., 1965-68, mktg. mgr. spl. products, 1968-70, mgr. copier products, 1970-72, dir. corp. pricing and competitive activity, 1972-78, dir. corporate mktg. strategy and planning, 1978—. Vice pres. Family Service, Rochester, 1971-72; dir. Family and Children's Services, Stamford, 1972—; dir. Rochester Sales Execs. Club, 1966-71; mem. mktg. adv. bd. Columbia Grad. Sch.; dir. Asso. Harvard Alumni, 1978—. Bus. Clubs: Oak Hill Country, Harvard (pres. Rochester 1971-72, pres. Fairfield County 1976-78, Harvard Bus. Sch. (pres. Rochester 1972, chmn. Westchester/Fairfield 1973-74); New Canaan (Conn.) Field; Woodway Country (Darien, Conn.). Home: 111 Glen Dr New Canaan CT 06840 Office: Xerox Corporation Stamford CT 06904

DONOVAN, MAURICE STANTON, psychologist, ednl. adminstr.; b. Brandon, Man., Can., May 4, 1925; s. Maurice S. and Eleanor M. (Griffin) D.; came to U.S., 1955, naturalized, 1964; B.A., U. Toronto, 1948, M.A., 1951; S.T.B., Trinity Coll., Toronto, 1953; Ph.D., Adelphi U., 1969; m. Linda Bueschel, Apr. 2, 1969; 1 son, Michael. Upper sch. master St. Paul's Sch., Garden City, N.Y., 1957-60; clin. psychology intern Creedmoor State Hosp., Queens Village, N.Y., 1963-64; sch. psychologist Jericho (L.I., N.Y.) Pub. Schs., 1964-68, dir. psychol. services, 1968—; faculty Adelphi U., 1963-65; postdoctoral fellow Hofstra U., 1972-73, adj. faculty ednl. psychology, 1973-76; pvt. practice clin. psychology, Port Washington, N.Y., 1969-73. Trustee Nassau County Psychol. Services Inst., 1973—. Served with RCAF, 1944-45, Royal Navy, 1945-46. USPHS fellow, 1961-63. Mem. Am., N.Y. State, Nassau County (pres. 1976-77, chmn. sch. psychology com. 1971-72) psychol. assns., Am. Ednl. Research Assn. Author: The Psychologist in the Schools, 1972; also articles. Editor: Nassau County Psychologist, 1974-75. Home: 38 Amherst Rd Port Washington NY 11050 Office: Psychology Dept Jericho Public Schools Old Cedar Swamp Rd Jericho NY 11753

DONOVAN, PETER MORSE, investment co. exec.; b. Washington, Mar. 1, 1943; s. James Alport and Abbie Dagget (Morse) D.; B.A. in Econs., Goddard Coll., 1965; m. Alexandria Kujan, Nov. 1, 1969; 1 son, Aaron. Cash clk. Jones, Kreeger & Co., Washington, 1965-66; investment and econ. analyst Wright Investors' Service, Bridgeport, Conn., 1966-68; mng. editor investment publs., 1968-69, asst. v.p., 1969-71, v.p., 1971-74, sr. v.p., 1974—; dir., v.p. Wright Investment Shares, Inc., Bridgeport, 1975—; dir. Winthrop Corp. Mem. Fin. Analysis Fedn., N.Y. (sr), Hartford socs. security analysts. Home: 9 Gray Ln Westport CT 06880 Office: 500 State St Bridgeport CT 06604

DONOVAN, RAYMOND EDWARD, utility exec.; b. Lowell, Mass., June 12, 1930; s. Raymond Edward and Gertrude Ursula (Hearn) D.; B.A., Holy Cross Coll., Worcester, Mass., 1951; m. Mary T. Kelley, Oct. 10, 1953; children—Raymond E., Mark S., Mary J., Kevin G. Publicity copywriter Conn. Light & Power, Berlin, 1951-55, advt. and publicity mgr., 1957-66, exec. asst., 1966-68, asst. to pres., 1968-73; dir. corporate devel. N.E. Utilities, Hartford, Conn., 1973-78, v.p.-customer services, 1978—; dir., corporator Central Bank for Savs., Meriden. Mem. Conn. Gov.'s Youth Council, 1969-72; mem. Meriden Bd. Pub. Works, 1963-64, Meriden Redevel. Agy., 1969-72; bd. dirs. Meriden-Wallingford Hosp., 1963—, chmn. bd., 1972-74; pres. Conn. Bible Soc., 1974—; mem. commn. ecumenical affairs Archdiocese of Hartford, 1968-79. Served with Med. Service Corps, U.S. Army, 1952-54. Recipient award United Way, 1963. Mem. Conn. Hosp. Assn. Republican. Roman Catholic. Home: 10 Baldwin St Meriden CT 06450 Office: PO Box 270 Hartford CT 06101

DONOVICK, RICHARD, sci. adminstr.; b. Mpls., July 8, 1911; s. Joseph and Cecelia (Greenstone) D.; B.A., U. Calif. at Los Angeles, 1934, M.A., 1936; Ph.D., U. Ill., 1940; m. Laura Murasko, June 21, 1960; children—Peter, Robin Lynn, Jeffery, Lisa. Schering Corp. postdoctoral fellow Columbia, N.Y.C., 1940-42; with E.R. Squibb & Sons, New Brunswick, N.J., 1944-69, research asso., 1944-50, dir. microbiology, 1950-69; dir. antibiotics research Life Scis., Inc., St. Petersburg, Fla., 1969-73; now cons.; dir. Am. Type Culture Collection, Rockville, Md., 1973—. Mem. Bd. Health, Scotch Plains, N.J., 1954-60, pres., Green Brook, N.J., 1967-69. Fellow Am. Acad. Microbiology (gov. 1972-73); mem. Am. Soc. Microbiology (nat. treas. 1960-64). Patentee in field. Contbr. articles to profl. jours. Home: 16405 Alden Ave Gaithersburg MD 20760 Office: 12301 Parklawn Dr Rockville MD 20852

DOOLEY, JOHN MORSE, vocat. sch. adminstr.; b. Springfield, Mass., Mar. 16, 1922; s. Raymond John and Lucy (Morse) D.; B.S.E., Westfield State Coll., 1964, M.E., 1966; m. Mary Cecelia Cullinane, Apr. 9, 1958; children—Rae, Jean, Scott, Marilyn, Carol. Auto mechanic and auto body man, 1938-53; owner, operator O.K. Garage, Thompsonville, Conn., 1954-55, Dover Garage, Springfield, Mass., 1955-59; tchr. sci. and math. Roger L. Putnam Vocat. Tech. High Sch., Springfield, 1959-75, chmn. math. dept., 1972-74; tchr. United Tech. Sch., Springfield, 1964-65, partner, 1965-66, owner, dir., 1966—; condr. Manpower Devel. Tng. Act pilot program for all-Puerto-Rican class in auto mechanics, 1965. Served with U.S. Army, 1942-46. Mem. Am., Mass., Springfield fedns. tchrs., Am., Mass. vocat. assns., Am. Legion. Roman Catholic. Club: Elks. Home: 120 Hillcrest Ave West Springfield MA 01089 Office: 17 23 Morgan St Springfield MA 01107

DOOLITTLE, SIDNEY BARTOO, gynecologist; b. Binghamton, N.Y., May 8, 1917; s. Luvurn George and Carrie (Walker) D.; A.B., Lafayette Coll., 1939; M.D. cum laude, Syracuse U., 1944; m. Jan. 24, 1943; children—Sidney Bartoo Jr., David Brinton, William Walker. Intern, Presbyn. Hosp. Phila., 1944-45; resident in gynecology Meml. Hosp., Syracuse, N.Y., 1945-49, St. Josephs Hosp., Syracuse, 1949-50; practice medicine specializing in gynecology, Syracuse, 1950—; mem. staff St. Josephs Hosp.; clin. prof. Upstate N.Y. Med. Center. Served to capt. M.C., AUS, 1946-48. Diplomate Am. Bd. Obstetrics and Gynecology. Fellow ACS; mem. Am. Coll. Obstetrics Gynecology, Onondaga County, N.Y. State med. socs., Central N.Y., Interurban obstet. and gynecol. socs., Am. Fertility Soc., Internat. Soc. Obstets. and Gynecology, Alpha Omega Alpha. Republican. Presbyterian. Clubs: Univ., Cavalry, DeWitt Fish and Game, N.Y. Skeet Shooting Assn. Home: RD 2 Sweet Rd Jamesville NY 13078 Office: 612 State Tower Bldg Syracuse NY 13202

D'ORAZIO, DONALD EMIDIO, psychologist; b. Phila., Apr. 2, 1938; s. Emidio J. and Edith L. D'O.; B.A., LaSalle Coll., 1960; M.A., McMurray Coll., 1962; Ph.D., U. Manchester (Eng.), 1966; postgrad. U. Hawaii, 1962-63; m. Andree M. VanLaere, July 29, 1967; children—Claudine, Erik. Staff psychologist Camden County (N.J.) Psychiat. Hosp., 1967-71; mem. faculty Rosemont Coll., 1967-71, St. Charles Sem., 1972-74, Villanova U., 1974-75, Chestnut Hill Coll., 1975—; practice psychology, Wayne, Pa., 1968—; cons. Cabrini Coll., 1973-78. Mem. Nat. Registry Health Service Providers, Am., Pa. psychol. assns., Am. Soc. Psychologists in Pvt. Practice, Psychologists Interested in Religious Issues. Roman Catholic. Contbr. articles to psychol. jours. Home and Office: 444 Louella Ave Wayne PA 19087

DORDEVIC, MIHAILO, educator; b. Belgrade, Yugoslavia, May 10, 1923; s. Vladimir and Jelena (Rasic) D.; came to U.S., 1959, naturalized, 1965; grad. U. Belgrade; M.A., U. Belgrade, 1949; Ph.D., U. Paris, 1958. Asst. prof. Converse Coll., Spartanburg, S.C., 1959-61; asso. prof. Ohio Wesleyan U., Delaware, 1961-65; prof. Cours Dutilleul, Paris, 1965-69; prof. humanities and comparative lit. Pa. State U., Middletown, 1969—; translator publs. into Serbian; mem. adv. bd. Central Coll. Study Abroad Program. Mem. Center Cultural Internat. (France), Modern Lang. Assn., N.E. Modern Lang. Assn., Philol. Assn. Pacific Coast, Assn. Study of Dada and Surrealism in Am. Democrat. Russian Orthodox. Author: Serbian Poetry and Milutin Bojic, 1977. Contbr. revs. on surrealism and comparative lit. to jours. Office: Capitol Campus Pennsylvania State U Middletown PA 17057

DORE, STEPHEN EDWARD, JR., civil engr.; b. Providence, Apr. 1, 1918; s. Stephen Edward and Anna Caroline (Chace) D.; B.S. in Engring., Brown U., 1940; m. Evelyn Mae Andrews, Mar. 14, 1942; children—Linda Jane, Jeffrey Stephen, Sherrill Ann. Surveyor, Met. Dist. Hartford County, Conn., 1940; engring. draftsman U.S. Navy design dept., Quonset Point, R.I., 1940-42; draftsman R.I. Dept. Pub. Works, Providence, 1946; hydraulic engr. U.S. Army, C.E., Providence, 1946; structural designer E.B. Badger Co., Boston, 1946-47; project engr., Coffin and Richardson Inc., Boston, 1947-58, sr. project engr., 1958-62, v.p., chief engr., 1962-73, exec. v.p., 1973—, also dir. Treas. Cedarcrest Civic Assn., Canton, Mass., 1952-55. Served to capt. C.E., U.S. Army, 1942-46. Registered profl. engr., Mass., Maine, N.H., R.I., Conn.; registered surveyor, Maine. Fellow ASCE, Cons. Engrs. Council; mem. Boston Soc. Civil Engrs., Soc. Mil. Engrs., New Eng., Am. water works assns., ASTM. Unitarian. Club: Blue Hills Tennis (Braintree, Mass.). Contbr. papers to confs. and publs. Home: 33 Birchcroft Rd Canton MA 02021 Office: 141 Milk St Boston MA 02109

DOREY, LEONA PIXLEY, psychologist; b. Otter Lake, N.Y., Apr. 19, 1918; d. Stanley Jay and Louise Jackson Pixley; R.N., Utica State Hosp. Sch., 1941; B.S., St. Lawrence U., 1962; M.A., Syracuse U., 1964; m. John James Dorey, Feb. 11, 1942 (dec. Jan. 1961); children—John Patrick, Kathleen Ann. Staff nurse Utica (N.Y.) State Hosp., 1941-42; sch. psychologist Bd. of Coop. Ednl. Services, Onondaga County, N.Y., 1964-74; sch. psychologist Ithaca (N.Y.) Sch. Dist., 1974—. mem. staff St. Joseph's Hosp. Out Patient Psychiat. Clinic, 1965-74. Mem. Nat. Assn. Sch. Psychologists, Am. Psychol. Assn., Delta Kappa Gamma, Psi Chi. Home: 323 Richard Pl Ithaca NY 14850 Office: 400 Lake St Ithaca NY 14850

DORF, PHILIP, pub. relations co. exec.; b. N.Y.C., Mar. 5, 1921; s. Max and Minnie (Siegelbaum) D.; B.A., N.Y. U., 1942; m. Nathalie S. Bernstein, Mar. 30, 1947; children—Robert L., Lewis R., Margaret Sue. Reporter, writer, editor United Press Assn., N.Y.C., 1946-56; account exec. pub. relations dept. N.W. Ayer & Son, Inc., N.Y.C., 1956-58; account supr. Tex McCrary, Inc., N.Y.C., 1958-60; v.p. Rowland Co., Inc., 1960-63, sr. v.p., 1963-70; v.p. Harshe-Rotman & Druck, Inc., pub. relations firm, N.Y.C., 1970-71, sr. v.p. 1971-73, exec. v.p., 1973—. Served to capt. AUS, 1942-46. Decorated Silver Star, Bronze Star, Purple Heart. Mem. Pub. Relations Soc. Am., Nat. Investor Relations Inst., Overseas Press Club Am. Home: 500 E 77th St New York City NY 10021 Office: 300 E 44th St New York City NY 10017

DORFMAN, HOWARD DAVID, pathologist; b. N.Y.C., July 20, 1928; s. Louis and Helen (Weingarten) D.; A.B., N.Y.U., 1947; M.D., State U.N.Y., Bklyn., 1951; m. Esther Novick, June 21, 1952; children—Richard, Peter, Leslie. Intern, Maimonides Hosp., Bklyn., 1951-52; resident in pathology Mt. Sinai Hosp., N.Y.C., 1952-54, Columbia-Presbyn. Med. Center, N.Y.C., 1954-58; asst. pathologist, asso. pathologist, Sinai Hosp., Balt., 1959-64, pathologist-in-chief, 1974—; pathologist, dir. labs. Hosp. for Joint Diseases and Med. Center, N.Y.C., 1964-74; asso. prof. pathology and orthopedic surgery Johns Hopkins U. Sch. Medicine. Served to capt. U.S. Army, 1955-57. Mem. Internat. Acad. Pathology, Internat. Skeletal Soc., Orthopedic Research Soc., Royal Soc. Medicine, N.Y. Acad. Medicine, Am. Soc. Clin. Pathologists, Phi Beta Kappa, Alpha Omega Alpha. Co-author: Tumors of Bone and Cartilege, 1971; contbr. articles on orthopedic pathology to med. jours. Home: 526 E Seminary Ave Towson MD 21204 Office: Pathology Dept Sinai Hosp of Balt Baltimore MD 21215

DORFMAN, WILFRED, psychiatrist; b. N.Y.C., Dec. 14, 1909; s. Benjamin and Bertha (Landau) D.; B.S., N.Y. U., 1930, M.D., 1934; postgrad. N.Y. Sch. Psychiatry, 1956-59; m. Helen Dubroff, July 24, 1943; children—Marjorie Patricia, Jane Dubroff. Intern, Maimonides Hosp., Bklyn., 1934-36; gen. practice internal medicine, Bklyn., 1937-42, 44-46; resident psychiatry Bklyn. State Hosp., 1956-59; pvt. practice psychiatry, Bklyn., 1960—; editor in chief Psychosomatics, 1960—; dir clin. research, cons. psychiatry Brunswick Hosp., Amityville, L.I., 1965-75; cons. psychiatry Gracie Sq. Hosp., N.Y.C., 1960—, Met. Jewish Geriatric Center, Bklyn., 1976—; lectr. psychosomatic medicine. Served with USAAF, 1942-44. N.Y. U. fellow in chemistry, 1929-30. Fellow Acad. Psychosomatic Medicine (pres. 1959-60); mem. Eastern Psychiatric Research Assn. (exec. council 1963-66), ACP, Am. Coll. Psychiatrists, Am. Psychiatric Assn., Acad. Psychosomatic Medicine, Internat. Coll. Psychosomatic Medicine (v.p. N. Am. 1971-75). Author: Closing the Gap Between Medicine and Psychiatry, 1965. Address: 1921 Newkirk Ave Brooklyn NY 11226

DORIA, ANTHONY NOTARNICOLA, educator; b. Savona, Italy, June 2, 1927; s. Vito Sante and Jolanda (Giampaolo) N.; came to U.S., 1949, naturalized, 1954; M. Govt. Adminstrn., U. Pa., 1953; LL.M. equivalent, U. Paris, 1960; J.D., U. Rome, 1962. Adj. prof. history, bus. law and internat. law L.I. U., Southampton, N.Y., 1964-65, State U. N.Y. at Selden, 1960-65; pres., founder Royalton (Vt.) Coll. Sch. Internat. Affairs, 1965-72; founder, 1st. dean Vt. Law Sch., S. Royalton, 1972-74; dean Royalton Coll. Law Study Center, 1974—;

cons. in field. Mem. Vt. Gov.'s Commn. on Student Affairs, 1971-75; active Boy Scouts Am. Served with underground resistance World War II. Decorated UN Certificate of Merit. Mem. Am. Judicature Soc., Internat. Bar Assn., Internat. Law Assn., Am. Soc. Internat. Law, AAUP, Acad. Letters and Sci., Acad. Polit. Sci., Noble Assn. des Chevaliers Pontificaux (life). Mem. Vt. Ind. party. Roman Catholic. Clubs: Pen and Pencil (Phila.); Elysee (Paris). Author: Italy and the Free World, 1945; The Conquest of the Congo, 1947; Influences in the Making of Foreign Policy in the United States of America, Great Britain, and France, 1953; Introduction to International Law, 1976. Home: S Royalton House South Royalton VT 05068 Office: Royalton Coll Law Study Center South Royalton VT 05068

DORIA, JOSEPH VINCENT, JR., coll. adminstr.; b. Bayonne, N.J., June 28, 1946; s. Joseph Vincent and Mary (Doria) D.; B.A., St. Peter's Coll., 1968; M.A., Boston Coll., 1969; postgrad. N.Y. U., 1975—. Chmn. social studies dept., tchr. Holy Family Acad., Bayonne, 1969-72; dir. ednl. services St. Peter's Coll., Jersey City, 1972—. Pres., Bayonne Bd. Edn., 1976—; pres. Hudson County Sch. Bds. Assn., 1976—. Mem. Am. Assn. Higher Edn., Am. Hist. Assn., Am. Acad. Polit. and Social Sci., Jersey City C. of C. Democrat. Roman Catholic. Home: 133 W 26th St Bayonne NJ 07002 Office: 2641 Kennedy Blvd Jersey City NJ 07306

DORKAN, CENAP SUPHI, physician; b. Istanbul, Turkey, Sept. 13, 1928; s. Mehmet S. and H. (Nire) D.; came to U.S., 1957, naturalized, 1973; M.D., U. Istanbul, 1955; m. Linda Bea Watson, June 30, 1964; children—Jale Nuyan, Mehmet Murat. Intern, Swedish Hosp., Mpls., 1957-58, resident in medicine, 1958-59; resident in medicine Harrisburg (Pa.) Hosp., 1959-61; practice medicine specializing in internal medicine, Glen Burnie, Md., 1966—; physician in charge med. services Crownsville (Md.) State Hosp., 1961-63; instr. dept. medicine U. Istanbul (Turkey), 1964-65; mem. adj. active staff South Balt. Gen. Hosp., 1971—; pres. staff North Arundel Hosp., Glen Burnie, 1978—. Mem. Anne Arundel County Med. Soc. (v.p. 1979—), Am. Soc. Internal Medicine, AMA, So. Med. Assn., Med. Chirurg. Faculty Md. Clubs: Masons, Chartwell Country. Home: 19 Saint Ives Dr Severna Park MD 21146 Office: 325 Hospital Dr Glen Burnie MD 21061

DORLAND, JACK ALBERT, assn. exec.; b. Decatur, Ill., Mar. 12, 1910; s. Ralph E. and Edith (Green) D.; B.A., Cornell U., 1931; M.A., Columbia, 1963, diploma, 1964; m. Lillian Byrl Brown, June 11, 1944; children—Lynn Elise, Lee Allison. Salesman Dow Chem. Co., N.Y.C., 1931-48, sr. salesman, 1948-52; mgr. N.Y. office Dow Chem. Export Co., Dow Chem. Internat. S.A. and Dow Chem. Inter-Am. Ltd., 1952-61; cons. Dow Chem., N.Y.C., 1961-65; instr. English, Columbia, 1965-66, Rockland Community Coll., Suffern, N.Y., 1966-72, Dominican Coll., Blauvelt, N.Y., 1972-73. Dir. N.Y. Bd. Trade, 1957-62, chmn. internat. sect. 1954-55, asst. sec., 1961; dir. Export Mgrs. Club, N.Y.C., 1956-59; arbiter Am. Arbitration Assn., 1958—; dir. Found. Study of Cycles, Pitts., 1957-63, pres. N.Y. chpt., sec., 1962-63. Served from 2d lt. to capt., AUS, 1942-45. Mem. Nat. Council Tchrs. of English, Soc. Investigation of Recurring Events (founder, pres.), N.Y. Acad. Scis., Chem. Corps. Assn., Holland Soc., Commerce and Industry Assn., Kappa Delta Pi, Phi Delta Kappa. Clubs: Cornell of N.Y., City Mid-Day, Downtown Athletic. Home: 10 Castle Heights Ave Tarrytown NY 10591

DORMANN, HENRY O., mag. editor, bus. exec.; b. N.Y.C., Mar. 5, 1932; s. Henry Maroni and Ivara (Soberg) D.; m. Alice Andreasen, Apr. 7, 1958; children—Kaari, Kristi. Chmn., Internat. Bd. Indsl. Advisers, 1964—, Haitian Devel. Corp., 1969—, Nat. Enquirer, 1971-72, Sabador, Inc. (Liberia), 1973—; pres., editor-in-chief S.I.P.A. News Service, 1966—; pres. U.S. Tech. Devel. Co., 1969-70; pres., editor-in-chief Holiday Mag., 1976-77, Leaders Mag., 1978—. Mem. adv. council Joint Legis. Com. on Met. and Regional Areas Study of State N.Y., 1969-72; chmn. N.Y. State Assembly Council on Econ. Devel., 1972—. Served with USCG. Address: 988 Fifth Ave New York City NY 10021 also 59 E 54th St New York City NY 10022

DORMER, DEVLIN WILLIAM, publisher, genealogist; b. St. Clair, Pa., July 7, 1903; s. William S. and Anne (Devlin) D.; student pub. schs., St. Clair; m. Mary S. Spadafora, Apr. 10, 1928; children—Devlin W., William S., Mariheln E. Gen. agt. Mut. Guarantee Bldg. and Loan Assn., Phila., 1926, Gen. Accident Assurance Corp., Phila., 1936; owner, mgr. Dormer Agy., Pottsville, Pa., 1928—. Pottsville opinion leader nat. adv. bd. Nat. Security Council. Mem. Valley Forge, Schuylkill County, Am. Irish hist. socs., Am. Irish Bicentennial Com., United Irish Cultural Center, Irish Am. Cultural Inst., Greater Pottsville C. of C., Ancient Order Hibernians (rec. sec.). Editor, pub. Ireland in Pictures 100 Years Ago.; discovered statue of Robert Emment (1778-1803) in U.S. and donated it as a gift to Irish Govt., 1966. Home: 1514 Howard Ave Pottsville PA 17901

DORN, FREDERICK CHRISTIAN, JR., publishing co. exec.; b. Pitts., July 20, 1916; s. Frederick Christian and Margaret Ford (Weaver) D.; certificate Grad. Sch. Bus., U. Pitts., 1940; B.A. in Commerce and Finance, Pa. State U., 1945; m. Rose Marie Crock, Mar. 3, 1946; children—Frederick Christian III, Richard Crock. Employment supr. Kaufmann Dept. Stores, Pitts., 1940-42; personnel cons. Kurt Salmon Assos., Washington, 1945-46; personnel officer Bur. Nat. Affairs, Inc., Washington, 1946-65, bus. mgr., personnel officer, 1965-76, mgr. employees stock plan, asst. treas., 1976—; v.p., dir. BNA-Wash-Inc., Washington, 1972—; treas., trustee, chmn. finance com. Med. Service of D.C. (Blue Shield), 1962—; pres. Nat. Capital Central Fed. Credit Union, 1960—; cons. personnel and labor relations, 1976—. Served with Field Artillery, U.S. Army, 1942-45. Mem. Am. Soc. Personnel Adminstrn. (life), Am. Mgmt. Assn., Washington Personnel Assn., Washington Bd. Trade, Met. Area Credit Union Mgmt. Assn. Methodist. Club: Wally Byam Caravan. Home: 1818 Arcola Ave Wheaton MD 20902 Office: 1231 25th St NW Washington DC 20037

DORN, MICHEL JOHN, author; b. Watertown, S.D., July 11, 1940; s. Wilbur Fred and Margaret Anne (Hjelle) D.; student State U. Iowa, 1959-60, George Washington U., 1960-61, U. Minn., 1960. Canadian editor Bus. Internat., 1963-68; editorial dir. Western Pub. Co., 1968-73; editor-in-chief Random House Enterprises, 1973-75; pres. Food Services Internat., Princeton, N.J., 1975—; lectr. on food; author: Tycoons in the Kitchen, 1969; The 2 in 1 International Collection for Mixed Drinks and Hors D'oeuvre, 1977; Compliments of the Chef, 1978; editor: The Betty Crocker Recipe Card Library, 1974; McCalls Recipe Cards, 1976; Weight Watchers Recipe Cards, 1977. Trustee Princeton Adult Sch., 1975. Address: 652 Kingston Rd Princeton NJ 08540

DORN, PETER KLAUS, graphic designer; b. Berlin, Germany, June 30, 1932; s. Robert and Charlotte D.; came to Can., 1953, naturalized, 1962; student Berufsschule fur Grafisches Gewerbe, 1949-51, Akademic fur Grafik und Buchkunst, Leipzig, 1968, Ont. Coll. Art, 1962-63; m. Charlotte Graffunder, Dec. 24, 1954; children—Gregory, Jennifer, Jefferey. With Howarth & Smith, typographers, Toronto, Ont., 1954-59, Cornish & Wimpenny, Toronto, 1960-63, U. Toronto Press, 1964-70; dir. graphic design unit Queen's U., Kingston, Ont., Can., 1971—; propr. Heinrich Heine Press. Recipient award Am. Inst. Graphic Arts, 1975, AAUP, 1975, Schonste Bucher aus aller Welt, 1977, Design Can., 1977. Can. Council grantee, 1968. Fellow Graphic Designers of Can. (nat. pres. 1978); mem. Royal Canadian Acad. Arts, Guild of Handprinters (dir. Canadian book design com. 1975-78), Canadian Bibliographical Soc. Home: 44 William St Kingston ON K7L 2C4 Canada Office: 72 Queen's Crescent Queen's Univ Kingston ON K7L 3N6 Canada

DORNAN, JAMES EDWARD, JR., educator; b. Bklyn., Jan. 3, 1938; s. James Edward and Florence (Gouch) D.; A.B. magna cum laude, LeMoyne Coll., 1959; Ph.D., Johns Hopkins U., 1968; m. Patricia Ann Capezzuti, June 19, 1959 (div. 1975); children—James Edward, Patrick Francis, Erin Maureen, Kieran Christopher, Mieghan; m. 2d, Diane Sue Schumacher, Apr. 29, 1975; 1 son, Brendan Timothy. Asst. instr. polit. sci. Johns Hopkins U., 1960-61; research asst. Gov.'s Ednl. Commn., Balt., 1961-62; asst. prof. polit. sci. Purdue U., Lafayette, Ind., 1963-67; asst. prof. Inst. Internat. Law and Relations, Cath. U., Washington, 1967-68, asst. prof. politics, 1968-74, asso. prof., 1974—; chmn. dept. politics, 1973—; asst. prof. polit. sci. Johns Hopkins U., evening and summer session 1969-74, asso. prof., 1974—; research and writing Hon. John J. Rhodes, 1970-74; cons. Strategic Studies Center, Stanford Research Inst., 1975, sr. polit. scientist, 1976—; lectr. Utah State U., U.S. Naval Acad., Rockford (Ill.) Coll., numerous others. Republican precinct committeeman Tippecanoe County (Ind.), 1966-68, campaign chmn., 1966, v.p. Critical Issues Council, 1965-67; v.p. Tippecanoe County Rep. Club, 1966, pres., 1967. Recipient Best Instr. award Sch. Humanities Purdue U., 1965, Univ. Tchr. of Year, 1966; Earhart and NATO Research fellow, 1973-74. Mem. Am. Polit. Sci. Assn., AAUP (pres. chpt. 1970-73), Acad. Polit. Sci., Phila. Soc., U.S. Strategic Inst., U.S. Naval Inst., Internat. Inst. Strategic Studies, Royal United Services Inst., Internat. Studies Assn., Arms Control Assn., Pi Sigma Alpha, Omicron Delta Kappa. Editor, co-author: U.S. National Security Policy in the Decade Ahead, 1978; cons., co-author: The U.S. War Machine, 1978; contbg. editor Report mag., N.Y.C., 1964-66, Intercollegiate Rev., 1970—; contbr. numerous articles to profl. jours. Office: Dept Politics Catholic U Washington DC 20064

DORNFEST, BURTON SAUL, educator; b. N.Y.C., Oct. 31, 1930; s. Irving and Yetta (Rosengarten) D.; B.A., N.Y. U., 1952, M.S., 1954, Ph.D., 1960; m. Eveline Drucker, June 13, 1954; children—Michael, Barry. Research asst. dept. biostatistics Sloan-Kettering Inst. and Meml. Hosp., N.Y.C., 1952-53; research asst. dept. biology N.Y. U., 1953-54, 56-58, instr. gen. sci., 1958-63; instr. anatomy N.Y. Med. Coll., 1963-64; instr. anatomy State U. N.Y. Downstate Med. Center, 1964-67, asst. prof., 1967-73, asso. prof., 1973—; adj. asso. prof. City Coll. City U. N.Y., 1974—; adj. prof. Hunter Coll., 1978—. NIH fellow, 1958-60, 61-63; Leukemia Soc., 1960-61; Nat. Inst. Arthritis and Metabolic Diseases grantee, 1964-71; Nat. Cancer Inst. grantee, 1973-75; Mildred Werner League for Cancer Research grantee, 1976-77. Served with U.S. Army, 1954-56. Mem. N.Y. Acad. Scis., AAAS, Reticuloendothelial Soc., Am. Soc. Hematology, Am. Assn. Anatomists, Soc. Experimental Biology and Medicine, Soc. Study Blood, Sigma Xi. Jewish. Contbr. articles in field to profl. jours. Home: 300 Morrow Rd Englewood NJ 07631 Office: Downstate Medical Center 450 Clarkson Ave Brooklyn NY 11203

DORON, ZVI JAY, mfg. co. exec.; b. Jerusalem, Israel, Feb. 11, 1935; s. Paul Herman and Elizabeth (Kirschner) D.; came to U.S., 1971, naturalized, 1977; B.Sc. with first class honors, U. London, 1958, M.Sc., 1959; m. Galia Ben-Gal, Nov. 25, 1956; children—Opher, Yael, Uri; m. 2d Beverly Bloomfield Weisman, May 16, 1976. Engr. Israel AEC, 1958-63, shift supr., 1963-65, reactor operations supt., 1965-66; with Nordostschweiz Kraftwerke AG, Switzerland, 1966-70, sr. rep. in U.S., 1966-68, dep. head Nuclear div., 1968-70; with Westinghouse Electric Corp., Pitts., 1970—, cons., 1970-71, dir. tech. coordination, Brussels, 1971-72, dir. projects dept., Brussels, 1972-74, mgr. projects integration and strategic planning PWR Systems div., Pitts., 1974-76, mgr. strategic planning, Uranium Resources, Pitts., 1976-77, dir. planning and tech., 1977—. Served with Israeli Army, 1952-54. Israel Atomic Energy Commn. grad. study fellow, 1958-59. Contbr. articles to profl. jours. Home: 2333 Marbury Rd Pittsburgh PA 15221 Office: Westinghouse Electric Corp Westinghouse Bldg Pittsburgh PA 15222

DORRIE, CHARLES THEODORE, mfg. co. exec.; b. N.Y.C., June 25, 1925; s. Charles Frederick and Agnes Christine (Andersen) D.; student pub. schs., N.Y.C.; div.; children—Richard Stephen, Suzanne Christine Dorrie McKemie. Chief tool designer and supr. Hilton Tool & Machine Co., Bronx, N.Y., 1947-52; chief design engr. tools and machinery Edwards Engring. Corp., Pompton Plains, N.J., 1952-70; owner, mgr., Karlo Mfg. Co., Wayne, N.J., 1970—. Pres., Pets Poison Protection Assn., Inc. Served with USMC, 1942-45; PTO. Mem. Soc. Mfg. Engrs. (certified mfg. technologist), Nat., N.J. tool, die and precision machining assns. Home: 112 Cedar Ave Pompton Lakes NJ 07442 Office: 825 Black Oak Ridge Rd Wayne NJ 07470

DORSEY, ROBERT FRANCIS, indsl. equipment mfg. co. exec.; b. Worcester, Mass., Jan. 2, 1947; s. Jeremiah E. and Mary (Zelesky) D.; B.S. in Bus. Adminstrn., Nichols Coll., 1973; M.B.A., Babson Coll., 1974; m. Edna Marie O'Brien, July 7, 1967; children—Christopher Robert, Robyn Frances. Mgmt. trainee Ford Motor Credit Co., Southboro, Mass., 1973; regional credit mgr. Ingersoll Rand Equipment Corp., Boston, 1974-75, gen. credit mgr., 1975-78; corp. credit mgr. Lee-Norse Co., Pitts., 1978—. Served with USMC, 1968-70. Mem. Fin. Mgmt. Assn., Nat. Assn. Credit Mgmt., Credit Assn. Western Pa., Nat. Coal Mine Suppliers Credit Group, Nat. Improved Constrn. Practices Com., Nichols Coll. Alumni Assn., Babson Coll. Alumni Assn., Lackawanna County Foster Parents Assn., Am. Legion. Roman Catholic. Home: 343 Sautter Dr Coraopolis PA 15108 Office: 6600 Steubenville Pike Pittsburgh PA 15205

DORTORT, FRANCES K., educator, social worker, mental health cons.; b. Basel, Switzerland; d. Edward K. and Ettie Cirel (Schreiber) Dortort; B.S., Temple U., 1950; M.S.W., U. Pa., 1956, postgrad. 1958. Tchr., counselor, social worker elementary schs., Phila., 1952; instr. social work U. Pa., Phila., 1957-59; prof. psychology, coordinator Psychol. Clinic, Pa. State U., 1963-69; prof. Nat. Coll. Edn., Evanston, Ill., 1959-60; asso. prof. psychology Lock Haven State Coll., cons., supr. Pa. Welfare Dept., 1961-63; adminstr. mental health/mental retardation program, Huntingdon, Juniata and Miflin Counties, Pa., 1969-71. Social work cons. Ford-Wieboldt, Chgo., 1959-62; cons. mental health Fla. Vis. Tchrs. Workshop, Easton Forks Sch. System and Citizens Adv. Com.; lectr. social welfare Temple U., 1968. Mem. Acad. Certified Social Workers, Nat. Assn. Social Workers, AAUP, Am. Profs. for Peace in Middle East, Council Social Work Edn., Soc. Research in Child Devel., Council for Aging, Otto Rank Assn. Contbr. articles to ednl. books, jours. Home: 4878 Roosevelt Blvd Philadelphia PA 19124

DOSIER, LARRY WADDELL, govt. agrl. ofcl.; b. Waynesboro, Va., Mar. 26, 1944; s. Waddell Samuel and Mary Margaret (Showalter) D.; B.S., Coll. William and Mary, 1966; M.A., U. Va., 1971, Ph.D., 1974. Grad. instr. biology U. Va., 1966-73, instr. Sch. Continuing Edn., 1973-74, instr. biology, 1974; plant variety protection jr. examiner U.S. Dept. Agr., Beltsville, Md., 1975-76, asst. plant variety protection examiner, 1976—; mem. Nat. Clover Variety Rev. Bd., 1978-79, Nat. Grass Variety Rev. Bd., 1977-79. NSF predoctoral tng. grantee Mountain Lake Biol. Sta., Pembroke, Va., 1969, 71. Recipient Naturalist award Mountain Lake Biol. Sta., 1971. Mem. AAAS, Am. Inst. Biol. Scis., Bot. Soc. Am., Va. Acad. Scis., Torrey Bot. Club, AAUP, Wedgwood Collectors Soc. Contbr. articles to profl. jours. Home: 3582 Powdermill Rd Apt 104 Beltsville MD 20705 Office: AMS Livestock Poultry Grain and Seed Div Nat Agrl Library Room 205 Beltsville MD 20705

DOSTER, ROSE ELEANOR WILHELM (MRS. JESSE A. DOSTER), artist; b. Balt., May 11, 1938; d. Lewis Milford and Leeanora A. (Naylore) Wilhelm; certificate in illustration and design Art Instruction Sch. Mpls., 1956; certificate in design and painting Md. Inst. Coll. Art, 1960, postgrad., 1960-62; m. Jesse Alfred Doster, Feb. 22, 1958; children—Jeffrey Allen, Roxane Elana. Exhibited in one-woman shows: Hampstead Library Gallery, 1969, 70, Aurora Fed. Gallery, Balt., 1969, Goodman Gallery, Ellicott City, Md., 1971, Central Savs. Gallery, Towson, Md., 1971, Parkville (Md.) Library Gallery, 1972, Equitable Trust Bank Reisterstown Gallery, Balt., 1973, others; exhibited in group shows: St. John's Coll., Johns Hopkins, Goodman Gallery, Slayton House, Columbia, Md., Paynter Gallery, Rehoboth, Del., Hilltop House, Harpers Ferry, W.Va., 1974, Balt. Mus. Art Downtown Gallery, 1976; tchr. drawing, painting and ceramics, 1968—. Active Boy Scouts Am., Girl Scouts U.S.; trustee Balt. Mus. Art; pres. Carroll County Arts Council, 1975-76. Recipient numerous awards including George Peabody award, 1960. Mem. Nat. League Am. Pen Women (br. art chmn. 1970-72, 1st v.p. 1972-74, pres. Carroll br. 1974-76), Rehoboth Art League, Md. Craft Council, Md. Inst. Art Alumni Assns., Hanover Art Guild. Home: Box 403-A Route 3 3913 Shiloh Ave Hampstead MD 21074

DOTEN, HERBERT RUSSELL, engring. firm exec.; b. Brewer, Maine, Dec. 14, 1932; s. Henry Leroy and Cora Francis (Russell) D.; B.S., U. Maine, 1954, M.S., 1966; m. Patricia Alice Fortier, Apr. 14, 1956; children—Debora, Dorothy, Kathleen, Carol, David. Civil engr. Maine State Hwy. Commn., 1958-60; instr. civil engring. U. Maine, 1960-62; civil engr. Maine Hwy. Commn., 1962-69; transp. engr. Edward C. Jordan Co., Portland, Maine, 1969-72; owner cons. engring. firm Doten Assos., Augusta, Maine, 1972—. Served to 1st lt. C.E., AUS, 1955-58; now lt. col. Res. Mem. ASCE (pres. Maine sect. 1977-78), Nat. Soc. Profl. Engrs. (pres. Maine soc. 1971-72), Cons. Engrs. Maine. Congregationalist. Clubs: Masons, Shriners, Kiwanis. Home: 71 Purinton Ave Augusta ME 04330 Office: 10 Summer St Augusta ME 04330

DOTO, PAUL JEROME, accountant; b. Newark, July 22, 1917; s. Anthony and Edith Margaret (Mascellaro) D.; B.S., N.Y.U., 1947. Accountant, exec. asst. John Hewitt Foundry Co., East Newark, N.J., 1941-43; accountant S.D. Leidesdorf & Co., N.Y.C., 1947-56; C.P.A. Peat Marwick Mitchell & Co., N.Y.C., 1956-64; asst. controller Lincoln Center for the Performing Arts Inc., N.Y.C., 1964-69; controller Seton Hall U., South Orange, N.J., 1969-74; v.p., dir. Parkway Ltd.; cons. Controller's Office City N.Y., 1966; accountant N.J. Sch. Bd. Registered mcpl. accountant, N.J. Served with AUS, 1943-46. Mem. N.Y. State Soc. C.P.A.'s (chmn. govtl. acctg. com. 1963-64), Am. Inst. C.P.A.'s Am. Accounting Assn., Catholic Accountants Guild (gov. 1961-64), N.J. Soc. C.P.A.'s, Internat. Platform Assn., Fin. Execs. Inst., Nat. Police Hall Fame. Home: POB 298 Montclair NJ 07042

DOTTER, EUGENE VICTOR, structural engr.; b. Guttenberg, N.J., Sept. 25, 1920; s. Bertram Edward and Katherine (Wiershausen) D.; B.S. with highest honors in Civil Engring., N.J. Inst. Tech., 1941; M.S. in Civil Engring., Mass. Inst. Tech., 1947; postgrad. civil engring. U. Pitts.; m. Elizabeth Jane Wood, Oct. 15, 1949. Draftsman, Bethlehem Steel Co., Pitts., 1941-42; field engr. E. I. DuPont Co., Inc., Wilmington, Del., 1942-43, Walter Kidde, Inc., N.Y.C., 1947-48; constrn. supt. Mellon-Stuart Co., Pitts., 1948-53; structural engr. Leland W. Cook Co., Pitts., 1953-59; staff engr. Aluminum Co. Am., Pitts., 1959-62; asso. Deeter, Ritchey, Sippel, Architects, Pitts., 1962-69; cons. structural engring., Pitts., 1970—; tchr. Pitts. Architects Refresher Course; cons. U.S. Steel Corp., Pitts.; v.p. Allegheny Kiski Engring. Co. Inc.; mem. Pitts. Bd. Standards and Appeals; expert in structural and constrn. engring. for attys. Commr. Penn Hills Twp. (Pa.), 1968-69; Pitts. chmn. Gideons Internat., 1970-74. Served with C.E., U.S. Army, 1943-46. Mem. ASCE (Robert Ridgeway award 1941), Am. Concrete Inst., Internat. Assn. Shell Structures, Internat. Assn. Bridge and Structural Engrs., Christian Bus. Men's Com., Tau Beta Pi. Republican. Research with World Open U., Rapid City, S.D., 1974-75. Home: 2068 Palm Ave Pittsburgh PA 15235 Office: 239 Fourth Ave Pittsburgh PA 15222

DOUCET, NORMAN LEON, mining co. exec.; b. Petit Rocher, N.B., Can., Feb. 19, 1918; s. Leon Joseph and Ida Mary (Doucet) D.; B.C.E., Internat. Corr. Schs., 1942; m. Berthilde Arseneau; children—Ronald, Jean Guy, Maurice, Claudette, Alvin, Zita, Giselle, Murielle, Pierette, Michel. Asst. dist. hwy. engr. Dept. Pub. Works, Bathurst, N.B., 1937-39, dist. hwy. engr., 1945-53; constrn. engr. Dept. Nat. Def., Montreal, Que., Can., 1939-45; mgr., pres. N.L. Doucet Co., Ltd., Bathurst, 1953—; mng. dir. Bathurst Silver Mines, 1963—; pres. Gloucester Mining Corp., Bathurst, 1963—, Profl. Drafting, Ltd., Bathhurst, Can., 1965—. Commr. Bathhurst Planing Commn., 1970—. Mem. Canadian Inst. Mining and Metallurgy, N.B. Land Surveyors Assn. (pres. 1968), N.B. Prospectors and Developers Assn. (pres. 1960), Canadian Inst. Surveyors, Prospectors and Developers Assn., Community Planning Assn. Can. (dir.), Bathurst C. of C. K.C. Home: 1430 St Peter Ave Bathurst NB Canada Office: 1428 St Peter Ave Bathurst NB Canada

DOUD, THOMAS JEFFERSON, JR., lawyer; b. Balt., Sept. 29, 1934; s. Thomas Jefferson and Lillian Marquerite (Croswell) D.; B.S., Loyola Coll., Balt., 1956; LL.B. magna cum laude, U. Balt., 1964; m. Susan Garson, Apr. 23, 1966; children—Thomas Jefferson, Matthew Justin, Amanda Jobst. Admitted to Md. bar, 1964; with James W. Rouse & Co., Inc., Mortgage Bankers, Balt. and Washington, 1961-65; asso. firm Mylander and Atwater, Balt., 1965-68; atty. Fed. Land Bank and Fed. Intermediate Credit Bank, Balt., 1968-71; partner firm Gordon, Feinblatt, Rothman, Hoffberger & Hollander, Balt., 1971—. Served to lt. USN, 1956-59. Mem. Am., Md., Balt. bar assns. Democrat. Roman Catholic. Home: 10106 Daventry Dr Cockeysville MD 21030 Office: 1200 Garret Bldg Baltimore MD 21202

DOUGHERTY, CHARLES F., Congressman; b. Phila., June 26, 1937; B.S. in Polit. Sci., St. Joseph's Coll., 1959; postgrad. in internat. relations U. Pa., 1962-64; postgrad. in polit. sci., Temple U., 1967-68; m. Regina Lavery; children—Regina Rose, Patricia Ann, Mary Katherine, Maureen Theresa, Megan Marie, Charles Kevin. Instr. govt. NW Catholic High Sch., 1962-65; spl. agt. Office Naval Intelligence, 1965-66; asst. dean students Community Coll. Phila., 1966-70; vice-prin., then prin. Tekakwitha High Sch., 1970-72; dir. fin. and devel. Phila. Counseling or Referral Assistance, 1972; mem. Pa. Senate, 1972-79; mem. 96th Congress from 4th Pa. dist. Pres., Resurrection Home and Sch. Assn.; bd. dirs. St. Joseph's Coll.; del. Republican Nat. Conv., 1976. Served with USMC, 1959-62. Republican. Office: 1428 Longworth House Office Bldg Washington DC 20515*

DOUGHERTY, JAMES DOUGLAS, lawyer; b. Baldwin, N.Y., Dec. 29, 1936; s. Thomas Francis and Jean May (Young) D.; A.B., Dartmouth Coll., 1958; LL.B., Columbia U., 1963; m. Nancy Harrington Decker, Dec. 29, 1971. Admitted to N.Y. State bar, 1963; asso. Hughes Hubbard & Reed, N.Y.C., 1963-69, Shea, Gould, Climenko & Casey, N.Y.C., 1969-71; asso. gen. counsel Supermarkets Gen. Corp., Woodbridge, N.J., 1971-72, sec., gen. counsel, 1972-75, v.p., sec., gen. counsel, 1975—. Lectr. Practising Law Inst., N.Y.C., 1970—, Advanced Mgmt. Research, 1976—; pres., dir. 132 E. 19th St., Inc., N.Y.C., 1964-78. Served to lt. (j.g.) USNR, 1958-60. Mem. Am. Bar Assn., Assn. Bar City N.Y. (mem. spl. com. on consumer affairs 1973-77, com. on electronic funds transfer 1976—), Am. Soc. Corp. Secs. Home: 132 E 19th St New York City NY 10003 also Tuthills Hill Shelter Island NY 11964 Office: 301 Blair Rd Woodbridge NJ 07095

DOUGHERTY, JAMES JOSEPH, found. exec.; b. Jim Thorpe, Pa., May 14, 1939; s. Joseph James and Lorraine Ann (Dever) D.; B.A., U. Notre Dame, 1962; Ph.D., U. Md., 1973; m. Mary Agnes Imbriglia, Aug. 21, 1965; 1 son, Michael J. Tchr., St. Edmond's Acad., Wilmington, Del., 1965-66; grad. teaching asst. U. Md., College Park, 1966-70, lectr., 1970—; asst. editor Am. Hist. Rev., Washington, 1973-74, asso. editor, bibliographer, 1974-75; editor Recently Pub. Articles, Washington, 1976-77; humanist, adminstr. Nat. Endowment for Humanities, Washington, 1977—; biblographer U.S. sect. Recently Pub. Articles, Washington, 1977—. U. Md. summer research fellow, 1972. Mem. Am. Hist. Assn., Orgn. Am. Historians, Am. Com. History of Second World War. Clubs: Potomac Valley Srs. Track, Notre Dame Alumni. Author: The Politics of Wartime Aid, 1978; compiler, editor Writings on American History, 1962-77, 8 vols., 1973—. Home: 3219 Tennyson St NW Washington DC 20015 Office: 806 15th St NW Washington DC 20015

DOUGHERTY, JOHN JOSEPH, clergyman, former univ. pres.; b. Jersey City, Sept. 16, 1907; s. John J. and Christina (Farrell) D.; A.B., Seton Hall U., 1930; student U. Propaganda, Rome, 1930-32; S.T.L., Gregorian U., Rome, 1934; student Pontifical Bibl. Inst., Rome, 1934-37, Doctorate Sacred Scripture, 1948; L.H.D. (hon.), U. Detroit, 1960, Seton Hall U., 1969; LL.D., Rutgers U., 1962, St. Peters Coll., 1964, St. Ambrose Coll., 1964. Ordained priest Roman Catholic Ch., 1933, papal chamberlain, 1954, domestic prelate, 1958, consecrated bishop, 1963; apptd. Episcopal vicar of Newark, 1966; prof. sacred scriptures Immaculate Conception Sem., Darlington, N.J., 1937-59; radio broadcasting CBS, NBC, ABC, 1946—; TV broadcasting CBS, NBC, 1951—; regent Inst. Judaeo-Xtian Studies, Seton Hall U., 1954-59, pres. univ., 1959-69, scholar in residence, 1977—; pastor, Short Hills, N.J., 1969-77; mem. Vatican Commn. on Radio and TV, 1956-60; chmn. World Conf. Religion and Peace, 1974—. Bd. dirs. Cath. Bibl. Assn., 1957-59, UNDA (Internat. Assn. Cath. Radio and TV), 1956-59; vice chmn. commn. on religion in higher edn. Assn. Am. Colls.; mem. citizen's com. higher edn. N.J.; mem. Nat. Citizens Commn. Internat. Coop. Yr., 1965, Gov.'s Com. on Civil Disorders, 1967; asst. for UN affairs to chmn. adminstrv. bd. Nat. Cath. Welfare Conf., 1964-71; mem. Nat. Adv. Com. Edn. of Deaf, 1966; mem. Vatican Com. on Peace Studies, 1973-76; chmn. bd. Council Religion and Internat. Affairs, 1974-77, trustee emeritus, 1978—. Recipient Freedoms Found. medal, 1953; award Cath. TV Arts, 1959; U.S. Army Outstanding Civilian award, 1965; Distinguished Service award NCCJ, 1965; Americanism award B'nai B'rith, 1965. Mem. Internat. Assn. Univ. Pres.'s, UN Assn. U.S.A. (dir.). Author: Searching the Scriptures, 1959. Address: Seton Hall U South Orange NJ 07079

DOUGHERTY, MARY ALICE, clergyman; b. Campbellville, Ont., Can., Feb. 21, 1907; d. George Fenton and Margaret E. (Zimmerman) Dougherty; B.A., Victoria Coll., U. Toronto (Ont.), 1937, diploma Covenant Coll., 1938, diploma Emmanuel Coll., 1946; postgrad. London (Eng.) U., 1953-54. With Northwestern Fire Ins. Co., Hamilton, Ont., 1929-34; mission rep. to prin. Wen-Teh Girls Middle Sch., Chungking, China, 1938-44; ordained to ministry United Ch. Can., 1947; parish ministry Lucky Lake, Sask., Can., 1946-51, Underwood, Ont., 1951-53, Tehkummah, Ont., 1954-57, Quyon, Que., Can., 1957-60, Merrickville, Ont., 1960-64, Enniskillen, Ont., 1964-69, Vald'Or, Que., 1970, Coe Hill, Ont., 1970-71, Mountjoy United Ch., Timmin, Ont., 1974. Mem. Internat. Assn. Women Ministers (pres. 1970-72). Home: 74 Hyde Park Ave Hamilton ON L8P 4M7 Canada

DOUGLAS, ARTHUR, electronics and aircraft instrumentation mfg. co. exec.; b. Mpls., Oct. 9, 1928; B.E.E., N.Y. U., 1958; m. Jean Messina, Feb. 10, 1951; children—Denise, Kevin, Brian. Clk., Tele-King Co., N.Y.C., 1952-53; with depts. material control and sales W. L. Maxson, N.Y.C., 1953-56; sales engr. Thomas A. Edison Industries, Orange, N.J., 1957-58; free lance sales rep., 1958; mgr. sales dept. Instrument Systems, Huntington, N.Y., 1959-63; v.p. Ragen Data Systems Inc., Farmingdale, N.Y., 1964-71, pres., 1971—. Served with U.S. Army, 1950-51. Office: 125 Schmitt Blvd Farmingdale NY 11735

DOUGLAS, JOHN JAY, communications co. exec.; b. Chgo., Oct. 4, 1916; s. Charles G. and Martha (Brown) D.; Ph.B., U. Wis., 1939; m. Jeanne M. McGauran, June 3, 1944; children—Charles Gardner, John Jay, Steven Anthony, Thomas Slade, Mary Jeanne, Ann Elizabeth, Patricia Mary. With Gen. Telephone System cos., 1940—; pres. Lenkurt Electric Co., San Carlos, Calif., 1959-63, exec. v.p. finance Gen. Telephone & Electronics Corp., N.Y.C., 1963—, also dir.; pres. Anglo-Canadian Telephone, also dir. several subs. and affiliated cos.; dir. Allendale Ins. Co.; mem. Grand Central adv. bd. Chem. Bank N.Y. Trust Co., N.Y.C. Named Industry Man of Year, San Francisco Peninsula Mfrs. Assn., 1963. Mem. Am. Inst. C.P.A.'s, Delta Upsilon. Republican. Roman Catholic. Clubs: Stanwich (Greenwich, Conn.); Econ. (N.Y.C.). Home: 136 Jonathan Dr Stamford CT 06903 Office: Gen Tel & Tel One Stamford Forum Stamford CT 06904*

DOUGLAS, WILLIAM RICHARD, med. research cons.; b. Indpls., Dec. 16, 1914; s. William Henry and Essie (Woodruff) D.; M.S., U. Chgo., 1939; Ph.D., Columbia, 1957; postgrad. U. Copenhagen, 1963-65; m. Josephine Wheaton, Oct. 13, 1944; 1 dau., Cheri; m. 2d, Ellen Mazur, May, 1, 1952; children—Yvonne, Marilyn. Insp., U.S. Dept. Def. Washington, 1952-53; research group leader Rockland State Hosp., Orangeburg, N.Y., 1953-58; dir. labs. Woman's Hosp., Phila., 1958-60; clin. chemist Rigs Hosp. and Finsen Inst., Copenhagen, 1960-74; dir. research Reference Diagnostics, Inc., Fairfield, Conn., 1974-75; cons. med. research and aerospace medicine, N.Y.C., after 1975; dir. indsl. hygiene and occupational health div. Am. Standards Testing Bur., N.Y.C. Chmn. UN com. Community Ch., N.Y.C., 1974—. Served with AUS, 1941-45. Fellow Am. Inst. Chemists, AAAS; mem. Danish Med. Soc., Danish Soc. Clin. Chemistry, Danish Soc. Cancer Research, European Assn. Cancer Research, Council of Europe, Aerospace Med. Assn. Home: 1020 Grand Concourse Bronx NY 10451 Office: 40 Water St New York City NY 10004

DOUGLAS-HAMILTON, NATALIE WALES (LADY MALCOLM DOUGLAS-HAMILTON), civic, patriotic orgn. exec.; b. Cohasset, Mass., Aug. 8, 1909; d. Nathaniel and Enid Mariner (Scarritt) Wales; student pvt. schs., N.Y.C.; Dr. Humanities (hon.), Rollins Coll., 1942; m. Kenelm Winslow, 1929; children—Natalie Winslow Burnett, Mary Chilton Winslow Mead; m. 2d, Edward Latham, 1937; m. 3d, Edward Bragg Paine, 1947 (dec. 1950); m. 4th, Lord Malcolm Douglas-Hamilton, 1953 (dec. 1964). Founder, pres. Bundles for Britain, 1939-42, Bundles For Am., 1939-42, Bundles for Bluejackets, 1939-42; asst. to publisher N.Y. Times, 1942-47; founder, pres. Common Cause, Inc., 1947-51; founder Citizens for Freedom, Inc., 1956; founder House of Good Taste exhibit N.Y. World's Fair, 1962-64; founder, pres. Center of Am. Living, Inc., 1966-71; pres. Am.-Scottish Found., Inc., N.Y.C., 1965—; founder, pres. Com. to United Am., Inc., 1971—. Decorated Comdr. British Empire. Mem. DAR. Republican. Episcopalian. Home: 174 E 74th St New York City NY 10021 Office: PO Box 537 Lenox Hill Station New York City 10021

DOUGLASS, GORDON KITCHEL, designer and builder sailboats; b. Newark, Oct. 22, 1904; s. George Parsons and Irene Maud (Kitchel) D.; B.S., Dartmouth Coll., 1926; m. Mary Augusta Taylor, May 24, 1933; 1 son, Alan Kitchel. Pres., Gordon Douglass Boat Co., Vermilion, Ohio, 1938-45; v.p. Douglass and McLeod, Ind., Painesville, Ohio, 1946-56; pres. Gordon Douglass Boat Co., Inc., Oakland, Md., 1957-72; designer small sailboats Thistle, 1945, Highlander, 1949, Flying Scot, 1957. Mem. Garrett County Promotion Council; chmn. citizen's com. Garrett County Community Coll.; mem. Oakland Zoning Commn., Oakland Town Council. Mem. Thistle Class Assn. (permanent rear commodore), SPEBSQSA (pres. chpt. 1947-48, 1962-63, mem. internat. judges panel 1947-52), U.S. Internat. Sailing Assn. (life benefactor), Flying Scot Sailing Assn. (permanent gov.). Clubs: Rotary; Royal Canoe of England (hon. life) (Teddington, Middlesex); Hayling Island Sailing (hon. life) (Chichester, Sussex); Gananoque (Ont.) Canoe of Can. (hon. life); Deep Creek Yacht (hon. life) (Oakland, Md.); Vermilion Boat (hon. life); Rudder of Jacksonville (Fla.) (hon. life). Home: 25 W Pennington St Oakland MD 21550 Office: Box 28 Oakland MD 21550

DOUGLASS, JOHN WILLIAM, state legislator; b. Princess Anne, Md., Mar. 19, 1942; s. John and Evelyn Douglass; B.A. cum laude, Lincoln U., 1964; M.A., Johns Hopkins U., 1966; m. Evelyn Archer, Oct. 4, 1971. Salesman, R.L. Johnson Realty Co., Balt., 1967—; mem. Md. Ho. of Dels., 1971—, chmn. joint budget and audit com. Instr. Morgan State Coll., 1966-68; salesman Financial Indsl. Fund, Balt., 1967-68; partner, mgr. D & N Liquors, Balt., 1968-69; indsl. analyst, cons. City Balt., 1970-71. Faculty research grantee Morgan State Coll., 1967; Pa. Senatorial scholar, 1960; Rohm & Hass fellow, 1964; Gilman fellow, 1964. Mem. Businessmen's League Balt. (pres. 1969), Am. Chem. Soc. (pres. 1964), Beta Kappa Chi. Home: 1535 E North Ave Baltimore MD 21213 Office: Md House of Delegates Baltimore MD 21213

DOUGLASS, PAUL F., lawyer, former univ. pres.; b. Corinth, N.Y., Nov. 7, 1904; s. Rev. George C. and Mabel (Parker) D.; A.B., Wesleyan U., 1926, LL.D., 1946; A.M., U. Cin., 1929, Ph.D. (Taft fellow), 1931; student U. Chgo., 1928, U. Berlin, 1931-33. Reporter Cin. Post, 1926-27, ednl. editor, 1927-28; corr. Chgo. bur. Christian Sci. Monitor, 1928-30; dir. study of cts. of ltd. jurisdiction and Cin. Municipal Ct. for Inst. of Law, Johns Hopkins, in Hamilton County, Ohio, 1930-31; ordained to ministry M.E. Ch., 1933; pastor Meth. Ch., Poultney, Vt., 1933-41; pres. Am. U., Washington, 1941-52; prof. polit. sci. Rollins Coll., also dir. Center for Practical Politics (Falk Found.), 1956-71; dir. Mgmt. Corp. of Americas; gen. counsel Nat. League Postmasters, 1971-78, also Middle Americana, Inc. Adviser to pres. of Republic of Korea and counsel to ministry of fgn. affairs, 1952-55; chmn. nat. adv. com. on recruitment, tng. and placement recreation personnel Nat. Recreation Assn., 1952-58; v.p., chmn. finance com. Am. Recreation Found., 1960-65; mem. Pa. Gov.'s Recreation Council, 1956-58; chmn. Settlement Ho. Study Com., United Community Services, Wash., 1951-53; chmn. Christian Friends of Korea; trustee Nat. Recreation and Park Assn., 1965-75; chmn. task force on leisure Nat. Council of Chs., 1965-67; mem. arbitration panel Fed. Mediation and Conciliation Service. Decorated Haakon VII Cross (Norway), 1948; Order of Ascending Star with Rosette (China), 1948; Order of Taiguk (Korea), 1950. Admitted Vt., D.C. bars. Mem. Vt. Ho. Reps., 1937-39, 39-41, Vt. Senate, 1941-43. Mem. numerous profl. assns. and orgns., past officer several. Clubs: National Press, Cosmos (Washington). Author several books, later ones including Six Upon the World, 1954; The Group Workshop Way, 1956; Communication through Reports, 1957; Teaching for Self Education at a Life Goal, 1960; How to be an Active Citizen, 1960; The ABC of Industrial Parks, 1960; Inside Isthmus America, 1971; Black Apostle to Yankeeland, 1972. Editor several books, latest, Recreation in Age of Automation, 1957. Contbr. to Ency. Americana. Home: Grand View Farm Granville NY 12832 Office: West Pawlet VT 05775

DOUKAS, HARRY MICHAEL, univ. adminstr.; b. Washington, July 30, 1919; s. Michael Aristides and Thalia (Fergardis) D.; B.S., U. Md., 1942; M.S., Georgetown U., 1952, Ph.D., 1953; m. Mary Anna Vidos; children—Michael A., Gregory E., David J., Maria T. Head organic chemistry sect. Chem. Corps, U.S. Army, 1955-57, phys. sci. adminstr., 1957-58; program dir. fellowship program NSF, 1958-65; asst. chief career devel. rev. br., div. research grants NIH, 1965-71, chief, 1971-73, chief office of research manpower, 1973-75; dir. Med. Center Sponsored Programs, Georgetown U., Washington, 1975—, asst. dean for research Georgetown U. Med. Sch., 1977—. Served with USAAF, 1942-45. Mem. Assn. Am. Med. Colls., Nat. Assn. Coll. and Univ. Bus. Officers, Soc. Research Adminstrs., Am. Chem. Soc., Research Soc. Am., Nat. Soc. Med. Research, Sigma Xi, Alpha Chi Sigma. Democrat. Greek Orthodox. Contbr. articles to profl. jours. Home: 9920 Brixton Ln Bethesda MD 20034 Office: 3900 Reservoir Rd Washington DC 20007

DOVEL, CLINTON GEORGE, educator; b. Oceanside, N.Y., May 1, 1947; s. George Irenius and Evelyn Cecil (Richmond) D.; student Hofstra U., 1965-66, Nassau Community Coll., 1966-68; B.A., State U. Coll. at Plattsburgh, N.Y., 1970, M.A., 1977; M.S., State U. Coll. at Potsdam, N.Y., 1972; m. Georgette Brandino, Sept. 1, 1968. Tchr. social studies Tupper Lake (N.Y.) High Sch., 1970-72; instr. econs. North Country Community Coll., Saranac Lake, N.Y., 1972-73; spl. edn. teacher Sunmount Developmental Center, Tupper Lake, 1973—; part-time social and econs. instr. North Country Community Coll., 1977—. Chmn., Tupper Lake March of Dimes, 1971-74; mem. Tupper Lake Rescue Squad, 1971-73. Mem. N.Y. Assn. Children with Learning Disabilities, Am. Hist. Assn., Kappa Delta Pi. Republican. Lutheran. Club: Lions (pres.). Home: Dugal Rd Tupper Lake NY 12986 Office: Sunmount Developmental Center Tupper Lake NY 12986

DOW, DONALD DOUGLAS, stockbroker; b. Portland, Maine, Apr. 13, 1942; s. Millard Harding and Marjorie Louise (Gardner) D.; student Boston U., 1961; m. Patricia Molly Towle, Dec. 28, 1968; children—Tracy Dee, Tiffany Georgia. Registered rep. W.E. Hutton & Co., Lewiston, Maine, 1963-69, Dominick & Dominick, Inc., Portland, 1969-73; pres. Dow & Dow Co. div. F.L. Putnam & Co., Inc., Portland, 1973—. Mem. pres.'s council St. Joseph's Coll. Mem. Maine Investment Dealers Assn., Wildlife Conservation Trust, Timber Owners New Eng. Republican. Congregationalist. Clubs: Cumberland, Masons, Shriners. Home: PO Box 955 North Windham ME 04062 Office: 477 Congress St Portland ME 04111

DOW, MILLARD HARDING, broker; b. Rockland, Maine, Feb. 8, 1905; s. George Wright and Georgia Caroline (Harding) D.; grad. Thornton Acad., Hebron Acad.; m. Marjorie Louise Gardner, Nov. 26, 1938; children—Donald Douglas, Patricia Ann. With Montgomery Ward & Co., Barre, Vt., 1933-34, Claremont, N.H., 1934-35, Jamaica, N.Y., 1935-36; with Porteous Mitchell and Braun Co., Portland, Maine, 1936-38; broker, mgr. br. office Townsend Dabney & Tyson, mem. N.Y., Boston stock exchanges, Boston, 1938-68; br. mgr. W. E. Hutton and Co. of N.Y.C., mem. N.Y., Am. stock exchanges, Lewiston, Maine office, 1949-69; registered rep. Dominick & Dominick, mems. N.Y. Stock Exchange, N.Y.C., 1969-73; v.p., sr. analyst Dow & Dow Co. div. F.L. Putnam & Co., Portland, 1973—; v.p. F.L. Putnam Co., Boston, 1973—. Mem. bd. incorporators Central Maine Gen. Hosp. Republican. Conglist. Mason (Shriner). Clubs: Carnation, Cumberland (Portland). Home: 79 Grandview Ave Auburn ME 04210 summer Sebago Lake North Windham ME 04062 Office: 477 Congress St Portland ME 04111

DOW, ROBERT LINCOLN, marine scientist, state ofcl.; b. Jay, Maine, May 2, 1910; s. Wallace L. and Adeline S. (French) D.; A.B., Bowdoin Coll., 1932; m. Ruth R. Campbell, July 20, 1942; children—Pamela Dow Shofner, Bruce C. Lab. technician Internat. Paper Co., 1928, 30-32, mfg. and woodlands divs., 1933-38; secondary sch. tchr., Hallowell, Maine, 1938-42; with Maine Dept. Marine Resources, Augusta, 1946—, in charge research program, 1947—, dir., 1953-77; fishery adviser, alt. mem. New Eng. Regional Fisheries Mgmt. Council, 1977—; chmn. State-Fed. Am. Lobster Sci. Com., 1974—; Wilton Park fellow, 1975; Elliott lectr. in oceanography Bowdoin Coll., 1978. Dir. Research Inst. Gulf of Maine, Maine Partners of the Alliance; mem., chmn. Maine Humanities Council, 1973-78; mem. governing bd. New Eng. Resources Center for Occupational Edn., 1972-75; mem. Maine regional planning commns., 1968-72. Served to maj., C.E., U.S. Army, 1942-46; ETO. Mem. AAAS, Inst. Food Technologists (chmn. Maine sect.), Marine Tech. Soc., Atlantic Fisheries Biologists (pres. 1960), Am. Geophys. Union. Contbr. 200 articles to profl. jours. Home: RFD 1 Augusta ME 04330 Office: State House Dept Marine Resources Augusta ME 04333

DOWD, BENJAMIN S., business exec.; b. Hyde Park, Mass., Feb. 18, 1895; s. John Francis and Mary (Hughes) D.; student Yale and Fordham Law Sch.; m. Gertrude M. McGrane, Oct. 11, 1924; children—Benjamin S., Mary Jane, Joan, Nancy, John Francis, Aaron Higgins, Owen Hughes. Pres., chmn., dir. Chem. Natural Resources, Inc., Venezuelan Sulphur Corp., C.A., Caracas, Carupano, Venezuela. Commd. 2d lt. F.A., U.S. Army 1917, advanced to capt., 1918, with army of occupation in Germany until 1921. Roman Catholic. Clubs: Yale (N.Y.); Westmoreland (Wilkes-Barre, Pa.); Rockville Country Club. Home: 12 Canterbury Rd Rockville Centre NY 11570

DOWD, GEORGE THOMAS, JR., elec. engr.; b. Weymouth, Mass., July 10, 1934; s. George T. and Mary F. (Spence) D.; B.S., Northeastern U., 1958; M.B.A., Suffolk U., 1978; m. Anita C. Mongeon, May 8, 1965; children—George Thomas, Timothy Edwin, Amy Jeanne, Jodi Ellen. Engr., Sylvania Electric Co., Waltham, Mass., 1959-62; engr. E.G. & G., Bedford, Mass., 1962-67; mgr. instrumentation and control engring. Yankee Atomic Electric Co., Westboro, Mass., 1967—. Pub. works commr. Town of Weymouth, 1968-72, exec. ofcl. (selectman), 1972—. Served with U.S. Army, 1959. Mem. Am. Nuclear Soc., IEEE (Sr. Membership award 1976), Mass. Selectmens Assn. Democrat. Roman Catholic. Home: 37 Kingman St Weymouth MA 02188 Office: 20 Turnpike Rd Westboro MA 01581

DOWDEN, ALBERT RICKER, lawyer; b. N.Y.C., Dec. 15, 1941; s. Albert Godfré and Katherine (Ricker) D.; B.A., Middlebury Coll., 1963; J.D., N.Y.U., 1966; m. Carol Marie Nelson, Nov. 3, 1968; children—James Merrill, Christopher Ricker, William Nelson. Admitted to N.Y. Bar, 1967; asso. firm Rogers & Wells, N.Y.C., 1967-74; v.p., sec., gen. counsel Volvo of Am. Corp., Rockleigh, N.J., 1974. Vice pres., trustee, counsel No. Dispensary of N.Y.C., Served with USNG, 1967-71. Mem. Am. Bar Assn. Republican. Club: Shenorock Shore (Rye, N.Y.). Home: 11 Landon Terr Bronxville NY 10708 Office: Rockleigh Industrial Park Rockleigh NJ 07647

DOWDEN, DONALD SMITH, lawyer; b. Louisville, Jan. 15, 1932; s. Charles Merrill and Regina (Popham) D.; B.S. magna cum laude, U. Notre Dame, 1954; LL.B., Harvard, 1960; LL.M., N.Y. U., 1968; m. Shirley Anne Feeney, Aug. 9, 1958; children—Donald Smith, John Merrill, Anne Robertson, Julie Michele. Admitted to N.Y. bar, 1962; practiced in N.Y.C., 1962—; asso. firm Brumbaugh, Graves, Donohue and Raymond, 1960-68, partner, 1968—; adj. asso. prof. L.I. U., 1966; mem. faculty Practicing Law Inst., N.Y.C., 1977—. Served to lt. USNR, 1954-57. Mem. N.Y. State Bar Assn., Assn. Bar City N.Y., Am. Bar Assn., Am., N.Y. patent law assns., Tau Kappa Alpha. Democrat. Roman Catholic. Club: N.Y. Athletic. Home: 2 Viking Rd Glenwood Landing NY 11547 Office: 30 Rockefeller Plaza New York City NY 10020

DOWLER, ROBERT EDWARD, ins. co. exec.; b. Hempstead, N.Y., Oct. 1, 1935; s. James V. and Anna E. (Beekman) D.; A. Arts and Scis., Hofstra U., 1958; m. Allyce M. Bronner, Apr. 4, 1959; children—Christopher Scott, Colleen Yvonne, Clare Marie, Stephen Jay. Sales rep., regional credit mgr. Sinclair Refining Co., N.Y.C., 1954-62; v.p., prin. The Dowler Agency, Inc., Rockville Centre, N.Y., 1963—; cons. in field. Chmn. bd. dirs. Mid-Nassau YMCA, 1974-76; fin. officer Garden City Republican Com., 1971-76; historian Hempstead Fire Dept., 1968-69; mem. Hempstead Planning Bd., 1965-70. Served with U.S. Army, 1955-57. Named Man of Yr., Hempstead C. of C., 1970. Mem. Nat. Assn. Ins. Agts., N.Y. State, Nassau County agts. assns. Club: Kiwanis, Jaycees (pres. 1967-69) (Hempstead). Home: 63-D Signal Hill Rd Madison CT 06443 Office: 450 Sunrise Hwy Rockville Centre NY 11570

DOWLING, JESSIE PENNINGTON, psychiatric social worker; b. Sturgills, N.C., June 15, 1918; d. Rohe V. and Stella (Eller) Pennington; A.B., Berea Coll., 1939; M.S.W., Columbia, 1945. Social work assignments WPA, Ky., 1939-43; social worker ARC, New Orleans, Bklyn., 1943-45, VA, Huntington, W.Va., also Washington, 1946-56; instr. Sch. Social Work, W.Va. U., Morgantown, 1953-54; cons. W.Va. Dept. Mental Health, Charleston, 1954-55; program supr. USPHS Clin. Center, Bethesda, Md., 1956-62; cons. social work Nat. Inst. Mental Health, Chgo., also N.Y.C., 1962-66; asso. regional health dir. Mental Health Programs, N.Y.C., 1966—. Mem. adv. council Columbia U. Sch. Social Work. Mem. Nat. Assn. Social Workers (mem. exec. bd. 1968-70), Columbia U Sch Social Work Alumni Assn. (pres. elect 1978—). Mem. editorial adv. bd. Social Casework, 1968—. Home: 115 E 9th St New York City NY 10003 Office: 26 Federal Plaza New York City NY 10007

DOWLING, LEO JEROME, lawyer; b. Hartford, Conn., Feb. 18, 1898; s. John Francis and Margaret J. (Leary) D.; A.B., Catholic U. Am., Washington, 1920; student Dartmouth (left to enlist World War I); LL.B., Yale, 1925; m. Mary Susan Reidy, Oct. 24, 1929; 1 dau.,

Mary Susan (Mrs. David C. Spencer). Admitted to Conn. bar, 1925, since practiced in Hartford, 1925—; police commr., Hartford, 1931-37; dir. Fowler & Hunting Co., Hartford, Hartford, McNie and Hopkins, Inc., Bloomfield, Conn.; trustee Employees Pension Fund Presto Hartford, Inc., West Hartford, Conn. With Local Draft Board 1-A, also 1, 1940-72; past mem. adv. bd. Diocesan Bur. Social Service; dept. judge advocate Conn. dept. Am. Legion, 1937-44. Served as pvt. AUS, 1918-19. Decorated, Congressional Selective Service Award and Medal. Mem. Hartford County Bar Assn. (past mem. pub. relations com.), Am. Judicature Soc., Yale Law Sch. Assn., Enfield Hist. Soc., Am. Heritage Soc., Book and Gavel (Yale), Smithsonian Assos., Assn. Yale Alumni, Am. Legion (alternate Nat. exec. committeeman, 1944-48), Phi Alpha Delta. Republican. Roman Catholic. Clubs: Yale, Dartmouth, City (Hartford); Golf of Avon. Elk. Home: 281 N Oxford St Hartford CT 06105 also 36 Harmon Dr Suffield CT 06078 Office: 410 Asylum St Hartford CT 06103

DOWNE, EDWARD R., JR., communications and pub. conglomerate exec. Founder Downe Communications, Inc. Home: 834 Fifth Ave New York City NY 10021

DOWNER, CHARLES WEBSTER, investment banker; b. Waco, Tex., Sept. 5, 1940; s. William Webster and Marguerite Helena (Linam) D.; B.A., Harvard U., 1962, M.B.A., 1966; m. Harriette Chalifoux Draper, June 15, 1963; children—Elizabeth Burrage, Charles Webster. Pres., Weaver Internat. Corp., Boston, 1966-75, Robert A. Weaver, Jr. & Assos., Boston, 1972-75, Downer & Co., Boston, 1976—, Downers and Partners Internat., Zurich, Switzerland, 1977—; dir. Bell Western Corp., Eastern Petroleum Co., Halifax Garden Co. Bd. dirs. Big Bro. Assn. of Boston, 1968—; mem. Mass. Minority Bus. Advisory Bd., 1968—, Gov.'s Council on Minority Bus., 1968—. Served with Ordnance Corps, U.S. Army, 1962-63. Republican. Episcopalian. Clubs: Brook (N.Y.C.); Country (Brookline, Mass.); Somerset (Boston). Home: 181 Newton St Weston MA 02193 Office: 175 Federal St Boston MA 02110

DOWNES, EDMUND WILLIAM, newspaper co. exec.; b. Hartford, Conn., Oct. 23, 1920; s. William H. and Katherine L. (Delaney) D.; B.S., Hillyer Coll., 1956; m. Mary Alice Moore, June 5, 1947; children—Donald W., Maryanne M., Elizabeth J. With The Hartford Courant Co., Hartford, 1939—, successively, controller, 1952-56, asst. treas., 1956-59, treas., 1959-61, asst. sec., 1961-62, v.p., bus. mgr., 1962-68, pres., also chief exec. officer, 1968—, also dir.; dir. Conn. Bank and Trust Co., Greater Hartford Corp. Dir., Jr. Achievement Hartford, 1968—; mem. Glastonbury Redevel. Agy., 1967—. Trustee Hartford Courant Found., Inc., Eastern States Expn.; corporator, Hartford Hosp. Served with USAAF, 1942-46. Mem. Conn. Daily Newspaper Assn. (exec. bd.). Home: 39 High Ridge South Glastonbury CT 06073 Office: 285 Broad St Hartford CT 06101*

DOWNEY, THOMAS JOSEPH, congressman; b. Queens, N.Y., Jan. 28, 1949; s. Thomas Anthony and Norma Rita (Morgillo) D.; B.S., Cornell U., 1970; postgrad. St. John's U. Law Sch., 1972—. With personnel dept. Macy's, N.Y.C., 1970-71; mem. 94th-96th Congresses from 2d N.Y. Dist. Del Democratic Nat. Conv., 1972; committeeman N.Y. State Dem. Com., 1972; mem. Suffolk County (N.Y.) Legislature, 1971-74. Mem. Sons of Italy. Methodist. Home: 42 Sequams Ln West Islip NY 11795 Office: 4 Udall Rd West Islip NY 11795 also Ho of Reps Washington DC 20515

DOWNING, JEAN CRAWFORD, town planner; b. Brandon, Man., Can.; d. Albert Bruce and Bertha (Crawford) Downing; B.A., Brandon Coll., 1941; M.A., U. B.C., Vancouver, 1959. Research asst. Met. Plan Greater Winnipeg (Man.), 1945-49; economist Econ. Adv. and Planning Bd. Govt. Sask., Regina, 1949-57; regional planning officer S. Sask, River Devel. Commn., 1959-64; head land use div. Sask. Water Resources Commn., 1964-65; community planner Izumi Arnott and Sugiyama, Regina, 1965-67; asso. Gordon R. Arnott & Asso., Regina, 1968-69; research supr., research and spl. studies Community Planning br. Ont. Dept. Municipal Affairs, Toronto, 1969-72; sr. planner spl. studies sect. Local Planning Policy br. Ministry Treasury, Econs., Intergovtl. Affairs, Toronto, 1972-76, Ministry Housing, Toronto, 1976—. Mem. Regina Community Planning Commn., 1955-57. Bd. dirs. Regina Area Hosps. Planning Council, 1965-67, YWCA, Regina, Mem. Can. Inst. Planners, Assn. Profl. Community Planners Sask., Zonta (pres. 1964-66), Fedn. Ont. Naturalists, Art Gallery Ont., Royal Ont. Mus. Club: Univ. Women's (exec., treas. 1960-62). Home: 322 Eglinton Ave E Apt 1610 Toronto ON M4P 1L6 Canada Office: Queen's Park Toronto ON Canada

DOWNING, WILLIAM SMITH, architect; b. Orange, N.J., Nov. 15, 1920; s. William Smith and Adele (McDonald) D.; B.S. in Architecture, U. Va., 1946; children—William, Elizabeth, Jeanne. Pvt. practice architecture, Charlottesville, Va., 1949-55; asso. Skidmore Owings & Merrill, Architects, N.Y.C., 1955-56; project mgr. Edward Durell Stone, Architect, N.Y.C., 1957-58; sr. partner William Downing Assos., Architects, Ithaca, N.Y., 1959—; pres. Dewitt-Ithaca Corp., real estate devel. co. Mem. Tompkins County (N.Y.) Republican Com., 1960—; chmn. Ithaca Rep. Com., 1963-66. Served to 1st lt. C.E., AUS, 1943-46. Mem. AIA (certificate of merit for excellence in design 1969 for design of Monarch Machine Tool Co. Plant, Cortland, N.Y.; adaptive use award for conversion of Ithaca High Sch. into shopping mall, apt. and office bldg. 1974), Soc. Archtl. Historians. Episcopalian. Clubs: Ithaca Yacht, Country of Ithaca, Rotary. Home: Dewitt Park Apts Ithaca NY 14850 Office: Dewitt Bldg Ithaca NY 14850

DOWNS, JOSEPH HUNTER, II, lawyer; b. Carlisle, Pa., May 17, 1943; s. Joseph Hunter and Margaret (Hornaday) D.; student Depauw U., 1961-63; B.A., Western Res. U., 1964, J.D., 1967; advanced degree Middle East Centre for Arabic Studies, 1969-71; m. Natasha Elise Evans, Aug. 3, 1963; children—Joseph Hunter, Courtney Lee. Admitted to Ohio bar, 1967; atty., U.S. Dept. Defense, Washington, 1967-68; asso. law firm Stephens & Huettig, Washington also Beriut, Lebanon, 1968-71; advisor Middle East affairs Raytheon Corp., Beirut also Jeddah, 1971-73; lawyer Fluor Corp., Los Angeles, 1973—, presently assigned Transvaal, Rep. South Africa, 1976—. Mem. Am., Ohio bar assns., Oceanic Soc., Order of Coif. Clubs: Wanderers (S. Africa), Indonesia Petroleum, Indonesian Executive. Home: 249 Brandyhill Rd Vernon CT 06066 Office: Fluor Corp 3333 Michelson Dr Irvine CA 92730 also PO Box 505 Springs 1560 Transvaal Republic of South Africa

DOYEL, JOHN STEPHEN, mfg. and advt. cos. exec.; b. Winchester, Ind., Nov. 14, 1919; s. Ora G. and Margaret (Watson) D.; student Corcoran Sch. Fine Arts, Washington, 1937-41; m. Rowena Isabelle Diggs, Oct. 5, 1949; 1 dau., Lesley Anne. With Washington Evening Star, 1939-42; ind. indsl. designer, 1946-55; v.p. Kembric Mfg. Corp., Southbury, Conn., 1955—, Bricmar Mfg. Corp., Southbury, 1955—, Southbury Mfg. Corp., 1955—, World Wide Media Corp., Southbury, 1955—. Mem. Chelsea Historic Dist. Exec. Council, 1970-78. Served with Corps Engrs., U.S. Army, 1942-46; ETO. Mem. Met. Mus. Art, Municipal Arts Soc., Nat. Trust for Historic Preservation, Soaring Soc. Am. Democrat. Patentee in U.S. and fgn. countries. Home and Office: 404 W 20th St New York City NY 10011

DOYLE, A(NDREW) GERALD, newspaper editor; b. Boston, Feb. 22, 1907; s. Daniel Patrick and Elizabeth (McGowan) D.; student, N.Y. U., 1929-31; m. Lenis Darrow Downs, Sept. 18, 1942; children—Elizabeth, Gerald C. Jr. account exec. Lord, Thomas & Logan, N.Y.C., 1928-30; with Queens Evening News, N.Y.C., 1931-41, mng. editor, 1936-41; editor Parkchester Press-Review, Bronx, N.Y., 1941-42; wirephoto editor AP, N.Y.C. and Washington, 1942-45; editor, gen. mgr. Bronx Press-Review, 1945—; sec. Parkchester Pub. Co., Bronx, 1948—. Mem. adv. bd. Fordham Hosp., 1960-72; bd. dirs. Bronx council Boy Scouts Am., 1955-70, E. Bronx YMCA, 1964-75; Bronx adv. bd. Salvation Army, 1972-79. Mem. NAACP (chmn. Parkchester com.), Bronx C. of C. (dir. 1975-79), Silurians. Roman Catholic. Home: 1590 Metropolitan Ave New York NY 10462

DOYLE, GERARD FRANCIS, lawyer; b. Needham, Mass., Oct. 25, 1942; s. John Patrick and Catherine Mary (Lawler) D.; B.S. in Indsl. Adminstrn., Yale U., 1966; J.D., Georgetown U., 1972. Group head for operating submarine reactors and reactor tech. Div. Naval Reactors, AEC, Washington, 1970-72; atty. firm Morgan, Lewis & Bockius, Washington, 1972-76; legal counsel Am. Nuclear Energy Council, Washington, 1975-76; partner firm Cotten, Day & Doyle, Washington, 1976—; dir. Western Fin. Corp., Spectrum Leasing Corp, Dubicki & Clarke, Inc.; lectr. in field. Served with USN, 1966-71. Recipient Outstanding Young Man of Year award, 1976. Mem. Am., D.C., Fed. bar assns., Nat. Contract Mgmt. Assn. Republican. Roman Catholic. Clubs: Washington Golf and Country, Washington Area Sailing (dir. 1976-77), Potomac Bachelors (dir. 1974-75). Home: 1566 B Westmoreland St McLean VA 22101 Office: 1899 L St NW Washington DC 20036

DOYLE, JAMES L., clergyman; b. Chatham, Ont., Can., June 20, 1929. Ordained priest Roman Catholic Ch., 1954, consecrated bishop, 1976; bishop Peterborough, Ont., Can., 1976—. Office: 350 Hunter St W Box 175 Peterborough ON K9J 6Y8 Canada*

DOYLE, JOHN THOMAS, fin. co. exec.; b. Kearny, N.J., Jan. 16, 1943; s. Thomas F. and Margaret G. (McCormack) D.; B.A., Rutgers U., 1971; M.B.A., Fordham U., 1973; m. Helga A. Dinzinger, Aug. 10, 1968; children—John Kevin, Kristina Anne. Adminstrv. asst. First Jersey Nat. Bank, Jersey City, 1965-69; asst. treas. Comml. Alliance Corp., N.Y.C., 1969-74; v.p. mktg. Horizon Creditcorp, Morristown, N.J., 1974-78, sr. v.p. domestic and internat. mktg., 1978—. Served with N.G., 1966-77. Mem. Nat. Assn. Equipment Lessors, Nat. Assn. Engine and Boat Mfrs., Am. Boat and Yacht Council. Home: 10 Totty Court Florham Park NJ 07932 Office: 334 Madison Ave Morristown NJ 07960

DRABKOWSKI, ALEX JOSEPH, dentist; b. Detroit, Feb. 25, 1927; s. Stanley Casmir and Josephine (Mysliwiec) D.; B.A., Wayne State U., 1951; D.D.S., U. Detroit, 1955; M.P.H., U. Mich., 1967; m. Laurel Marie Stevens, July 22, 1949; children—Elizabeth, Mark, Michael, Douglas. Mem. dental staff Wayne County (Mich.) Gen. Hosp., Eloise, 1955-58, dir. dental services, 1958-68; dentist in chief Balt. City Hosp., 1968—; chief dental staff Children's Hosp., Inc., Balt., 1974—; dir. dental services Keswick Home for Incurables, Balt., 1974—; clin. prof. U. Detroit, 1966-68; asst. clin. prof. U. Md., Balt. 1968-76, asso. clin. prof., 1976—; lectr. Johns Hopkins U., 1969—; pvt. practice, Dearborn, Mich., 1957-68; ann. trustee Childrens Hosp., Balt., 1977-78. Trustee Wayne State U. Found., 1974—; mem. founders Day Com. St. Mary's Coll. and Seminary, Orchard Lake, Mich., 1967—. Mem. Am., Md. State, Balt. dental assns., Am. Assn. Dental Schs., Am. Pub. Health Assn., Medical Dental Arts Assn. AAAS, Am. Med. Joggers Assn., Omicron Kappa Upsilon. Contbr. articles in field to profl. jours. Home: 4414 Langtry Dr Glen Arm MD 21057 Office: 4940 Eastern Ave Baltimore MD 21224

DRACHMAN, DANIEL BRUCE, physician; b. N.Y.C., July 18, 1932; s. Julian M. and Emily (Deitchman) D.; B.A. summa cum laude, Columbia Coll., 1952; M.D., N.Y. U., 1956; m. Jephta Piatigorsky, Aug. 28, 1960; children—Jonathan Gregor, Evan Bernard, Eric Edouard. Intern internal medicine Beth Israel Hosp., Boston, 1956-57; asst. resident, resident Harvard Neurol. unit Boston City Hosp., 1957-59, resident neuropathology Harvard Neurol. unit and Mallory Inst. Pathology, 1959-60; teaching fellow neurology Harvard U., Cambridge, Mass., 1957-60; clin. instr. neurology Georgetown U., Washington, 1961-63; asst. prof. neurology Tufts U., Boston, 1963-69; asso. prof. neurology Johns Hopkins U., Bslt., 1969-73, prof., dir. neuromuscular unit, 1974—; attending physician Kennedy Inst., Balt., 1969—, Balt. City Hosps., 1970—. Served with USPHS, 1960-63. Recipient Founder's Day award N.Y. U., 1956; grantee NIH, 1964—, Muscular Dystrophy Assn., 1969—, Myasthenia Gravis Foound. since 1970—. Diplomate Am. Bd. Psychiatry and Neurology. Fellow Am. Acad. Neurology, N.Y. Acad. Scis.; mem. AAAS, Am. Neurol. Assn., Phi Beta Kappa, Alpha Omega Alpha. Contbr. articles to profl. pubis. neurology, neuroscis, neuromuscular diseases, notably myasthenia gravis, trophic interactions between nerves and muscles, clubfoot and joint devel., devel. nervous system and muscle diseases. Home: 4006 Stewart Rd Stevenson MD 21153 Office: 1721 E Madison St Baltimore MD 21205

DRAGER, MARVIN, pub. relations exec.; b. N.Y.C., May 10, 1920; s. Harry and Fannie (Katzman) D.; B.S.S., St. John's U., 1940; M.A., Columbia U., 1942; m. Lenore Schwam, June 27, 1943; children—Sharon Drager Katler, Laura, Iris. Reporter, N.Y. Post, 1942; editor AP, 1943; pub. relations exec. Columbia Records, 1946; pres. Marvin Drager, Inc., pub. relations, N.Y.C., 1947—. Author: The Most Glorious Crown, 1975. Contbr. articles to mags. Home: 40 W 86th St New York City NY 10024 Office: Marvin Drager Inc 420 Madison Ave New York City NY 10017

DRAIN, CHARLES SHARER, JR., printing co. exec.; b. Phila., May 7, 1909; s. Charles Sharer and Anna (Scheible) D.; m. Roslyn H. Gibbons, Apr. 20, 1935; children—Donald C., David R. With Strassheim Printing Co., Phila., 1946—, sec-treas., 1950-67, v.p., 1968—. Vice pres. Phila. Assn. Retarded Children; trustee Tennent Coll.; adv. bd. Greater Phila. Salvation Army; moderator Presbytery Philadelphia, 1969; v.p. Presbyn. Children's Village. Mem. Am. Assn. Small Bus. (treas. 1946-48, dir.), Pa. Council Christian Edn. (pres. 1956-61), Pa. Sunday Sch. Assn. (pres. 1956-62), Pa. Christian Endeavor Union (past pres.), Phila. Bible Soc. (pres. 1961-66). Clubs: Lions (past pres. Central Phila.), Friendly Sons St. Patrick (pres. 1974-76), Union League (Phila.). Home: 6753 Rutland St Philadelphia PA 19149 Office: 305 N 15th St Philadelphia PA 19102

DRAKE, JOSEPHINE ELEANOR, publishing co. exec., poet; b. Yellow Frame, N.J., July 20, 1931; d. John Hall and Bertha Ellen (Messler) Stickle; certificate bookkeeping accounting Dover Bus. Coll., 1967; certificate in Basic Insect Sci., Home Lawns, Household Pests and Their Control, Vines, Ground Covers, Espaliers, Soil Fertility and Mgmt., Turf Mgmt., Principles Insect Control, Pa. State U., 1969; certificate in Turf Mgmt., Rutgers U., 1970, Landscape Maintenance, 1971, Home Ground Gardening, 1972, Problems in Community Resource Devel., 1972, Home Grounds Horticulture, 1973, Estate Planning, 1973, Community Planning and Environ. Sci., 1974; m. Paul Edmund Drake, 1952; children—Paul Edmund, Judith Ann, Patricia Ann, Robert Edmund. Pres., Newton (N.J.) Meml. Hosp., 1950-52; co-owner Drake's Nursery, Andover, N.J., 1955—; owner Jo's Book Service, Andover, 1973—. Author: (poetry) Love Speaks, 1974; Drake's Nursery Soliloquy, 1974; Life Races On, 1974; My Lament, 1974; Interference, 1974; The Purpose of Waking in the Morning, 1974; Life's Happenings, 1977; Life's Frustrations, 1977; Life's Passings, 1977; Twenty Five Years Wedded Bliss, 1977; Cerebrations of a Wife, 1977; Evolution, 1977. Certified pesticide application, N.J. Dept. Environ. Protection. Mem. Internat. Platform Assn., Am. Soc. Composers, Authors and Publishers, Nat. Wildlife Fedn., N.J. Turfgrass Assn. Methodist. Clubs: Am. Legion Auxiliary, No. Hills Organic Gardening. Home: Whitehall Rd Andover NJ 07821

DRAKE, ROBERT LEROY, engring. exec.; b. DuBois, Pa., Dec. 26, 1930; s. Wilbur Morris and Lillian Rebecca (White) D.; student in elec. engring. U. Calif. at Ventura; m. Elizabeth Garner King, Apr. 16, 1977; children—Teresa, Bradford, Mallory, Whitney, Debra, Edward. Field engr. Revees Instrument Corp., N.Y.C., 1952-58; engring. program mgr. Raytheon Co., Andover, Mass., 1958—. Served with USN, 1948-52. Recipient commendation Asst. Sec. Def., 1967; certified profl. logistician. Fellow Soc. Logistics Engrs. (dir. 1969—, pres. 1973-74); mem. Am. Def. Prepardness Assn. Republican. Presbyterian. Contbr. research in life cycle engring., econ. analysis, numerous tech, papers in field.

DRAPEAU, JEAN, mayor of Montreal; b. Montreal, Que., Can., Feb. 18, 1916; s. J.N. and Berthe (Martineau) D.; Lic. Soc., Econ. and Pol. Sc., U. Montreal, 1937, Arts degree, 1938, grad. Faculty Law, 1941; hon. degrees U. Moncton, 1956, U. Montreal, 1964, McGill U., 1965, Sir George Williams U., Laval U. 1967, also Boswell Inst. New Orleans; m. Marie-Claire Boucher, June 26, 1945; 3 sons. Admitted to Montreal bar, 1943, apptd. Queen's counsel, 1961, began practice specializing in comml. and corp. law; became mayor Montreal for 1st time, 1954, re-elected, 1960, 62, 66, 70, 74, 78. Founder Montreal Civic Party, 1960. Created Companion Order Can., 1967. Recipient Indsl. Devel. award Trade and Industry Dept. 10 Canadian Provinces, 1965, Gold medal Royal Archtl. Inst. Can., 1967. Mem. Am. Bar Assn. (hon.), numerous other nat. and internat. orgns. Home: 5700 des Plaines Ave Montreal PQ Canada Office: 275 Notre Dame St E Montreal PQ Canada

DRAPER, DAVID WATSON, architect; b. Richmond, Va., Feb. 23, 1940; s. John Thomas and Elizabeth (Knickerbocker) D.; B.Arch. (scholar, AIA fellow), U. Va., 1963; m. Mary Ellen Lytton, June 16, 1962; children—David Watson, Darryl Lytton. Architect, Rawlings & Wilson, architects, Richmond, 1963-65; architect, partner Collins & Kronstadt, architects, planners, engrs., Silver Spring, Md., 1965—; asst. to asso. prof. art dept. U. Va., 1963; asst. to prof. Am. U., Washington, 1969-74. Active William Tyler Page PTA. Mem. AIA (Scholastic Gold medal 1963; mem. Potomac River com. 1969-71, chmn. com. continuing edn. 1973-74, dir., v.p. Potomac Valley chpt. 1973-74, pres. 1975-76, Distinguished Service award 1976), Nat. Trust for Historic Preservation, Md. Soc. Architects (dir. 1974-76, chmn. lecture series U. Md. 1975—, v.p. 1976—), Nat. Council Archtl. Registration Bds., Smithsonian Assos., Sch. Architecture Assn., U. Va. Alumnae Soc., Tamarack Civic Assn., Scarab Soc., Raven Soc., Phi Eta Sigma. Democrat. Methodist. Clubs: Twin Farms (Silver Spring, Md.); University Va. (Washington). Home: 1602 Northcrest Dr Silver Spring MD 20904 Office: 1111 Spring St Silver Spring MD 20910

DRAPKIN, ARNOLD, internist; b. Ridgewood, N.J., Feb. 24, 1930; s. Bennett and Martha (Becker) D.; A.B. magna cum laude, Syracuse U., 1951; M.D. cum laude, State U. N.Y., Syracuse, 1955; m. Ellen Ratine, Dec. 24, 1954; children—Brock, Meredith, Elizabeth. Intern, Mt. Sinai Hosp., N.Y.C., 1955-56; resident in medicine Bronx (N.Y.) Municipal Hosp. Center, 1956-58, chief resident in medicine, 1959-60; fellow in cardiopulmonary medicine Albert Einstein Coll. Medicine, 1958-59, asst. instr. in medicine, 1959-60, instr., 1960-63, asso., 1963-65, asst. prof. medicine, 1965-66, asst. clin. prof., 1966-74, asso. clin. prof., 1974—; practice medicine specializing in internal medicine, N.Y.C., 1960—; mem. staff Montefiore Hosp. and Med. Center, Bronx Municipal Hosp. Center, Hosp. Albert Einstein Coll. Medicine; vol. staff mem. Flower and Fifth Ave. Hosp.; lectr. in field. Diplomate Am. Bd. Internal Medicine. Fellow A.C.P. (life mem.), Clin. Soc. N.Y. Diabetes Assn.; mem. AMA, N.Y. Acad. Scis., Am. Diabetes Assn., Harvey Soc., Am. Soc. Internal Medicine, N.Y. State, Bronx County med. socs., Phi Beta Kappa, Alpha Omega Alpha. Contbr. articles to med. pubs. Home: 5525 Independence Ave Bronx NY 10471 Office: 2 E 86th St New York City NY 10028

DREBUS, RICHARD WILLIAM, pharm. co. exec.; b. Oshkosh, Wis., Mar. 30, 1924; s. William and Frieda (Schmidt) D.; B.S., U. Wis., 1947, M.S., 1949, Ph.D., 1952; m. Hazel Redford, June 7, 1947; children—William R., John R., Kathryn L. Bus. trainee Marathon Paper Corp., Menasha, Wis., 1951-52; tng. mgr. Ansul Corp., Marinette, Wis., 1952-55, asst. to v.p., 1955-58, marketing mgr., 1958-60; dir. personnel devel. Mead Johnson & Co., Evansville, Ind., 1960-65, v.p. corporate planning, 1965-66, internat. pres., 1966-68; v.p. internat. div. Bristol-Myers Co. (merger Mead Johnson Internat. div. with Bristol-Myers Co. Internat. div.), N.Y.C., 1968-77, sr. v.p., 1977-78, v.p. parent co., 1978—. Served with inf. AUS, 1943-45. Decorated Combat Inf. Badge, Purple Heart, Bronze Star. Mem. Am. Psychol. Assn., N.Y. Acad. Scis., Phi Delta Kappa. Clubs: Fox River Hunting and Fishing, Silver Springs Country. Home: 16 Old Driftway Rd Wilton CT 06897 Office: 345 Park Ave New York City NY 10022

DREITLEIN, RAYMOND PAUL, psychologist; b. Bklyn., Sept. 14, 1943; s. Michael George and Madeline (Zimitka) D.; A.A.S., N.Y.C. Community Coll. Applied Arts Scis., 1963; B.A., St. Francis Coll., Bklyn., 1967; M.A., Seton Hall U., 1969; m. Carol Ann Elizabeth Lays, Jan. 23, 1965; children—Raymond, William, Karen, Scott, Adam. Vocat. evaluator Jewish Vocat. Service, Newark, 1967-69; vocat. counselor psychologist VA Guidance Center, 1969-71; group therapist Mt. Carmel Guild Narcotics Rehab. Center, Newark, 1971-72, head dept. counseling and evaluation, 1971-73; asso. dir. alcoholism rehab. unit John E. Runnells Hosp., Berkeley Heights, N.J., 1973-75, dir., 1975-76; project dir. Social Setting Detoxification Center Union County, Inc., 1976—; cons. alcohol control program N.J. Dept. Health; instr. N.J. Police Tng. Commn.; mem. faculty Middlesex County Coll., Edison, N.J., Summer Sch. Alcohol Studies Rutgers U.; lectr. Grad. Sch. Edn., Seton Hall U., South Orange, N.J.; mem. coalition task force Nat. Council Alcoholism. Mem. N.J. Assn. Alcoholism Counselors, Am., N.J. psychol. assns. Roman Catholic. Home: 726 Prospect St Maplewood NJ 07040 Office: John E Runnells Hospital Berkeley Heights NJ

DREMUK, RICHARD, ednl. adminstr.; b. N.Y.C., Nov. 11, 1935; s. Stephen and Mary (Bardygula) D.; B.A., Hunter Coll., 1957; M.A., N.Y. U.; m. Patricia Feraca, Apr. 22, 1961; 1 dau., Justine Ann. Asso. dir. Fgn. Student Center, N.Y. U., 1957-62, instr. English for fgn. students, 1958-65; asst. to dean admissions, 1962-63; head, Office of Admissions and Scholarship Services, Inst. Internat. Edn., N.Y.C., 1963-65; asst. univ. dean grad. and fgn. admissions U. Ill., Urbana, 1965-73, also exec. asso. dir. admissions and records; dir. admissions and records State U. N.Y. at Buffalo, 1973—. Mem. Ill. Com. on Accountancy, 1972-73; examiner, cons. Am. Inst. C.P.A.'s, 1973—.

Dir. Greater N.Y. Council for Fgn. Students, 1963-64; rep. Council on Evaluation Fgn. Credentials, 1965, 75. Trustee World U. Service, Latin Am. Scholarship Program Am. Univs. Mem. Nat. Assn. for Fgn. Student Affairs, Am. Assn. Collegiate Registrars and Admissions Officers. Co-author: Case Studies of Graduate Admissions and Fellowship Selection Policies and Procedures, 1970. Contbr. articles to profl. jours.; contbr. to Coll. Financial Manual of Coll. Scholarship Service, 1963, 65, 70. Home: 49 Heritage Rd E Williamsville NY 14221

DRENNEN, DONALD ARTHUR, educator; b. N.Y.C., Aug. 8, 1925; s. William Michael and Anastasia (Kearney) D.; A.B., Fordham Coll., 1947, M.F.A., 1950, M.A., 1951, Ph.D., 1958; postgrad. Am. U. (Egypt), 1965, Hebrew Union Coll., 1964-65, Columbia, 1965-66, 70, McGill U., 1967; m. M. Eileen Connolly, Aug. 4, 1951; children—Maura, Deirdre, Susan, Eileen, Donald Reid, Maribeth. Lectr., Fordham U., N.Y.C., 1951-53; instr. philosophy Marymont Coll., N.Y.C. and Tarrytown, N.Y., 1952-60, asso. prof., 1960-62; prof. philosophy, chmn. dept. Marist Coll., Poughkeepsie, N.Y., 1962—; vis. scholar Columbia, 1965-66; vis. lectr. Cath. U., Washington, 1966-67; with sales promotion dept. D.X. McMullan, N.Y.C., 1947-48; copy editor Westchester Pub. Co., Tarrytown and White Plains, N.Y., 1948-51; news editor Business Week, N.Y.C., 1952-55; cons. Macmillan-Free Press, N.Y.C., 1960-65, Editions de Paris (France), 1967—, Ednl. Testing, Princeton, N.J., 1968—. Rockefeller grantee, 1952, Carnegie grantee, 1967. Mem. Middle States Assn. Schs. and Colls. (evaluator 1971—), Am. Cath. Philos. Assn. (exec. council 1968-71, chmn. com. on developing philos. resources 1971—), Am. Philos. Assn., Metaphys. Soc. Am., AAUP. Author: Christian Preface to Modern Thought, 1959; Modern Introduction to Metaphysics, 1962; Major Themes in Modern Philosophy, 1963; Philosophy and Theistic Experience, 1965; Methodical Philosophy of Rene Descartes, 1969; Cultural Introduction to Philosophy, 1971; Karl Marx, 1972; Culture, Logic and Science, 1976; Ethical Structures, 1978; Introductory Exercises in Logic, 1978; Science and Scientific Thought, 1978. Asso. editor: Medical Economics, 1955. Book reviewer: America, 1956—. Address: Georgetown Square Poughkeepsie NY 12603

DRESCHER, DENNIS GEORGE, biochemist; b. Milw., Mar. 26, 1942; s. George Gustave and Lillian Frances (Wendlandt) D.; B.S., U. Wis., Madison, 1963, M.Music, 1964; postgrad. Harvard U., 1964-66; Ph.D., U. Wis., 1971; m. Marian Jean Partridge, Feb. 1, 1969; children—David Alan, Andrew Jeremy. Research asso. Central Inst. Deaf, St. Louis, 1971-74; sr. staff fellow NIH, Bethesda, Md., 1974—; lectr., cons. in field. Recipient Vilas grad. award, 1967; Babcock fellow, 1961-63; NIH grad. fellow, 1968-70. Mem. Am. Soc. Neurochemistry, Soc. Neurosci., Assn. Research in Otolaryngology, Acoustical Soc. Am., Found. Advanced Edn. in Scis., AAAS, Sigma Xi, Phi Eta Sigma, Phi Kappa Phi, Phi Lambda Upsilon. Pioneered isolation of inner-ear enzyme. Researcher inner ear, 1971—. Home: 5326 McKinley St Bethesda MD 20014 Office: NIH/Nat Inst Neurol and Communicative Disorders and Stroke Bldg 36 Room 5D32 Bethesda MD 20014

DRESSEL, HENRY FRANCIS, lawyer; b. Bklyn., Apr. 11, 1914; s. Henry Philip and Ernestine (Delmar) D.; A.B., Washington Sq. Coll., N.Y. U., 1943, J.D., 1949; m. Rose Marie Valentine, Nov. 24, 1937; 1 dau., Diana (Mrs. Anthony P. Fradella). Admitted to N.Y. State bar, 1949; asso. corporate law firm Chadbourne, Stanchfield & Levy and successors, N.Y.C., 1933-43; pvt. practice law, N.Y.C., 1950—; partner firm Dressel & Altman, P.C. Served from ensign to lt., USN, 1943-46. Named hon. Okla. Col., 1958, Okie, 1969. Mem. Am., N.Y. State bar assns., Assn. Bar City N.Y., N.Y. County Lawyers, Am. Judicature Soc., Justinian Soc., Internat. Footprint Assn., Phi Delta Phi. Democrat. Episcopalian. Clubs: New York University, Danish Athletic. Home: 8365 Shore Rd Brooklyn NY 11209 Office: 150 Broadway New York City NY 10038

DRESSLER, KENNETH PAUL, clin. chemist; b. Akron, Ohio, Nov. 29, 1942; s. Paul Theodore and Virginia Abigail (Burchill) D.; B.S. magna cum laude, U. Akron, 1964; M.A., Johns Hopkins U., 1966; Ph.D., N.Y. U., 1971; m. Rosalind Brause, Mar. 24, 1968; 1 son, Timothy Kyle. Instr., Mt. Sinai Sch. Medicine, N.Y.C., 1970-71; asst. chemist, 1971-74; chief biochemist Jewish Hosp. of Bklyn., 1974—, coordinator hosp. labs., 1977—; lab. cons. Greenpoint Hosp., 1974—; adj. asst. prof. Mt. Sinai Sch. Medicine, 1974-76. Mem. Am. Assn. Clin. Chemistry, AAAS, Am. Chem. Soc. Democrat. Home: 4 Washington Sq Village New York City NY 10012 Office: 555 Prospect Pl Brooklyn NY 11238

DREVO, JOSEPH CHARLES, archtl. interior designer; b. Balt., Feb. 18, 1908; s. Joseph and Johanna (Lukova) D.; diploma architecture Md. Inst., 1926; certificate City Coll. Balt., 1937; m. Dorothy Jacobs, Dec. 23, 1949; children—Robert J., Charles N. Mfg. shop foreman Ottenheimer Bros., Balt., 1927-37; researcher, designer Moss Mfg. Co., N.Y.C., 1937-38, Stanguard Dickerson Co., N.Y.C., 1938-39; designer, supr. Revere Furniture & Equipment Co., Washington, 1961-69, Kogod Dobb Revere, Inc., Silver Spring, Md., 1969; archtl. interiors specialist Quality Inns Internat., Silver Spring, 1969-74; mgr.-estimator millwork div. Jules H. Van Marken, Inc., Washington, 1974—. Troop leader Boy Scouts Am., 1952-60, Scoutmaster-Leader award, 1952. Recipient Pub. service award D.C., 1944, Community Service award City of Hyattsville, 1957. Mem. Soc. Am. Mil. Engrs., Nat. Wildlife Fedn. Research on marine resource foodstocks protein processing mktg. Home: 6004 Jamestown Rd Hyattsville MD 20782 Office: 950 Upshur St NW Washington DC 20011

DREWSEN, EDMOND TITUS, JR., banker; b. Bklyn., Oct. 29, 1932; s. Edmond Titus and Dorothy W. (MacDonald) D.; B.A., Cornell U., 1954; M.B.A., Columbia, 1958; m. Eunice L. Hull, Aug. 22, 1955; children—Karla H., Edmond Titus. With U.S. Trust Co. of N.Y., N.Y.C., 1958—, sr. v.p., 1976—. Trustee Gould Acad., Bethel, Maine, 1968-76. Served to 1st lt., Adj. Gen. Corps. U.S. Army, 1955-57. Mem. N.Y. Soc. Security Analysts, Fin. Analyst Fedn. Republican. Clubs: Union League of N.Y., Belle Haven (Greenwich, Conn.), St. Andrews Soc. Home: 78 Pecksland Rd Greenwich CT 06830 Office: 45 Wall St New York City NY 10005

DREYER, IRENE STARKEL (MRS. HAROLD E. DREYER), real estate broker; b. nr. Wayne, Nebr., July 4, 1922; d. Henry A. and Elizabeth (Schwindt) Starkel; student Norfolk Coll. Bus., 1942; real estate diploma Lee Inst., 1959; m. Harold E. Dreyer, Feb. 19, 1943; children—Thomas, Douglas, James. Sec., FBI, Justice Dept., Washington, 1942-45; sec. U.S. Army Quartermaster Sch. Ft. Lee, Va., 1945-46; real estate broker, Belmont, Mass., 1959—. Chmn. ways and means com. Locke Sch. PTA, Arlington, Mass., 1951-54, pres., 1954-56; den mother Locke Sch. Cub Scout Pack, 1953-55, sr. den mother, 1955; pack organizer Dallin Sch. Cub Scout Pack, Arlington, Mass., 1956; mem. Belmont Commn. on Suburban Responsibility, 1972—. Mem. League Women Voters (treas. 1959-61), McLean Hosp. Women Aux., Mass. Inst. Tech. Matrons (treas. 1962-65), Parents Music Students (sec. 1971-72), Greater Boston Real Estate Bd., Rental Housing Assn., Nat. Assn. Real Estate Bds. Lutheran. Home: 5 Simmons Ave Belmont MA 02178 Office: 437 Trapelo Rd Belmont MA 02178

DREYFUS, MICHEL ANDRE, physycian; b. Paris, France, May 13, 1916; s. Jacques and Simmonne (Monteaux) D.; M.D., U. Paris, 1943; m. Jan. 18, 1947 (dec.); children—Milan, Simonne; m. 2d, Hélène Briggs; 1 child, Dany. Intern, Ste. Jeanne d'Arc, Montreal, 1954-55, resident in pediatrics, 1955-57; med. officer UNRRA, 1945-47; practice medicine specializing in pediatrics, Beausoleil, Monte Carlo, 1947-53, 75-76, Ottawa, Ont., Can., 1953-74, 76—; mem. staff Eastern Ont. Children's Hosp., Ottawa, Montfort Hosp., Ottawa. Served with French Army, 1939-40, U.S. Army, 1945-46. Decorated chevalier Ordre National du Merite France; recipient Merit medal Am. Legion, Nice, 1976. Mem. Ottawa Acad. Medicine, Ottawa Pediatric Soc. Club: Ambassadors (Monaco). Home: 200 Rideau Terr Champain Towers #603 Ottawa ON K1M 0Z3 Canada Office: 3029 Carling Ave G2 Ottawa ON K2B 7K3 Canada also 405 Maloney E Blvd Gatineau Quebec Canada

DREYFUSS, STEPHEN LEO, health care adminstr.; b. Providence, July 20, 1947; s. Jack B. and Renee (Kahn) D.; B.S., U. R.I., 1969; M.B.A., Providence Coll., 1977; m. Rhoda Lee Hanzel, Dec. 20, 1970; children—Jillian Beth, Emily Ara. Staff announcer, technician and prodn. coordinator for radio outlets Broadcast Communications Radio/CATV, Providence, 1965-71; commd. 2d lt., U.S. Army, 1971, advanced through grades to capt., 1977; health care personnel mgr. 455th Gen. Hosp., Providence, 1971—; adminstrv. asst. Children's Perceptual Achievement Center, Rumford, R.I., 1974—; adminstrv. dir. R.I. Optometric Assn., Rumford, 1976—, cons. to exec. council assn., 1976—, editor newsletter, 1976—. Mem. Internat. Assn. Optometric Execs., Alpha Phi Omega. Office: 428 Pawtucket Ave Rumford RI 02916

DRIGGS, MARGARET (MRS. HOWARD R. DRIGGS), educator; b. Kansas City, Kans., June 30, 1909; d. William Foster and Lillian Edith (Landers) Brazier; A.B., U. Kans., 1930; postgrad. Hofstra Coll., 1960, Grad. Sch. Library Sci., Pratt Inst., 1964-65; m. J.W. Quarrier, Nov. 26, 1933 (div. July, 1945); children—John Chilton, Philip Harrington, Camille Elizabeth; m. 2d, Howard R. Driggs, Sept. 26, 1948 (dec.). Contbr. Kansas City Star and Johnson County (Kans.) Herald, 1930-33; editor Am. Trails Series, filmstrips; nat. dir. pub. relations Am. Pioneer Trails Assn., 1948; chmn. pub. relations N.Y. U. Faculty Women's Club, 1950-54; nat. 1st v.p. Assn. Parents and Friends Kings Point, 1957-58 mem. Nat. Council Coll. Publs. Advisers, 1958; staff adviser Nexus (yearbook), Hofstra Coll., 1961; mem. faculty Westover Sch., Middlebury, Conn., 1964-65; dir. devel. pub. relations, asst. to dean Cathedral Sch. of St. Mary, Garden City, N.Y., 1965, also yearbook adviser; now chmn. guides N.J. Gov.'s Mansion; curator Driggs Collection of Americana. Mem. women's council Hofstra Coll., 1959-60; mem. U.S. Com. for UN Children's Fund, 1957; mem. Friends of Princeton Univ. Library, 1975—; mem. Princeton Med. Center Aux. Recipient Distinguished Service citation Am. Pioneer Trails Assn., 1943; Margaret Brazier Driggs Collection of Americana established at U. Kans., 1953, at Hofstra Coll., 1961; recipient medals Am. Yearbook, Columbia Scholastic Press Assn., 1970; pin for vol. work in Princeton, 1976. Mem. ALA, Internat. Platform Assn., Assn. Coll. and Research Libraries, Princeton Hist. Soc., Met. Mus. Art, Women's Coll. Club Princeton, Pi Delta Epsilon (grand councilman 1960-61). Club: N.Y. U. Faculty (hon. life). Editor: New Light on Old Glory, 1950, Pitch Pine Tales, 1951, Nick Wilson, 1951, George, The Handcart Boy, 1952, The Old West Speaks, 1956, When Grandfather Was a Boy and Western Cowkid, 1957 (all by Howard R. Driggs); contbr. editor Nat. Assn. Ind. Schs. Archives, Harvard, 1965. Home: 135 Princeton Arms S Cranbury NJ 08512

DRIJE, A(NN) CARLA, sociologist; b. Berwyn, Ill., Mar. 10, 1933; d. Arthur Peter and Margaret Elsie (Lofgren) D.; student Millikin U., 1950-52; B.A., U. Mich., 1954; M.A., New Sch. Social Research, 1960, Ph.D., 1974. Research asst. Community Council Greater N.Y., N.Y.C., 1960-62; instr. L.I. U., 1962-64; research asst. Bank St. Coll. Edn., N.Y.C., 1964-71; asst. dir. Office Instl. Research and Program Evaluation, Bklyn. Coll., 1974-76; asso. dir. Martin Luther King Found., 1976—; cons. research and evaluation projects N.Y. Center Ethnic Affairs, New Careers Tng. Lab., Queens Coll., Center for Urban Edn., Coll. Human Services, N.Y.C.; chmn. profl. staff council Bank St. Coll. Edn., N.Y.C. Corr. sec. Phoenix Reform Democratic Club, N.Y.C., 1965-67. Mem. Am. Sociol. Assn., Immigration History Soc., New Sch. Alumni Assn. (v.p., mem. exec. com. 1974—). Contbr. articles to profl. jours. Papers presented profl. assn. confs. Home: 315 E 77th St New York City NY 10021 Office: Martin Luther King Found 309 E 90th St New York City NY 10028

DRINAN, ROBERT FREDERICK, clergyman, congressman; b. Boston, Nov. 15, 1920; s. James Joseph and Ann Mary (Flanagan) D.; A.B., Boston Coll., 1942, M.A., 1947; LL.B., Georgetown U., 1949, LL.M., 1950; Th.D., Gregorian U., 1954; postgrad., Florence, Italy, 1954-55; LL.D., Worcester State Coll., U. R.I., L.I. U., St. Joseph's Coll. Joined Soc. Jesus, 1942, ordained priest Roman Cath. Ch., 1953; admitted to D.C. bar, 1950, Mass. bar, 1956, U.S. Supreme Ct. bar, 1955; asst. dean Boston Coll. Law Sch., 1955-56, dean, 1956-70; mem. 92d-95th congresses from 4th Dist. Mass., mem. house judiciary, govt. ops. coms., select com. on aging; chmn., Mass. adv. com. for U.S. Commn. Civil Rights, 1962-70; vis. prof. U. Tex. Law Sch., 1966-67; mem. exec. com. Assn. Am. Law Schs., 1967-69. Mem. vis. com. Harvard Div. Sch. Fellow Am. Acad. Arts and Scis.; mem. Am. Law Inst. Author: Religion, the Courts and Public Policy, 1963; Democracy, Dissent and Disorder, 1969; Honor the Promise: America's Commitment to Israel, 1977. Editor: The Right To Be Educated, 1968; Vietnam and Armageddon, 1970; editor-in-chief Family Law Quar., 1967-70; corr. editor America, nat. Cath. weekly, 1958-70. Contbr. articles to profl. jours. Address: 140 Commonwealth Ave Newton MA 02167

DRINKWATER, AGNES HILLMAN, artist; b. Bangor, Maine; d. Hiram Madison and Jane (Poore) Hillman; grad. Alandale Art Sch., 1930; student art course Boston U., 1932; m. Alden Drinkwater. Exhibited in Maine, N.Y., Fla., Artists League, Fort Lauderdale, Fla., Sunrise Center. Mem. New Eng. Hist. and Geneal. Soc., LWV, Mass. Civic League, Dedham Hist. Soc., Am. Artists Profl. League, Boston Mus. Fine Arts, Fogg Art Mus., Plimath Plantation Assos., Internat. Platform Assn., DeCordova Mus. and Art Soc., UN Assn., Nat. Trust Historic Preservation, Dedham Community Assn., Nat. Archives U.S., Nat Parks Assn., Soc. Preservation New Eng. Antiquities, Bostonian Soc., World Wildlife Preservation, Wilderness Soc., Smithsonian Instn. Assn., Nat. Hist. Soc. Club: Middlesex. Home: 715 High St Dedham MA 02026

DRISCOLL, DONALD THOMAS, clergyman; b. Bronx, N.Y., Nov. 17, 1931; s. John Francis and Helen Kathleen (McArdle) D.; student St. Jerome's Coll., Kitchener, Ont., Can., 1950-52; A.B. in Philosophy, St. Joseph's Sem. Coll., 1960; M.S. Ed. in Counseling and Personnel, Fordham U., 1977. Ordained priest Roman Catholic Ch., 1964; expediter Ruben H. Donnelly Corp., Mt. Vernon, N.Y., 1953-56; parish minister, S.I., N.Y., 1964-65, Larchmont, N.Y., 1965-68; dir. guidance and counseling Bishop Dubois High Sch. in Harlem, N.Y.C., 1968-76; counselor jr. year students Cardinal Hayes High Sch., Bronx, N.Y., 1976-77; dir. evangelization project Iona Coll., New Rochelle, N.Y., 1977—; cons. unwed mothers shelter, N.Y.C. Served with U.S. Army, 1956-58. Certified neuropsychiat. technician; licensed certified sch. counselor, N.Y. State. Mem. N.Y.C. Personnel and Guidance Assn. (chmn. ethics com, bd. dirs.), Nat. Cath. Guidance Conf. (bd. dirs., awards com., program chmn. N.Y.C. nat. conv. 1975, pres. 1977), Am. Coll. Personnel Assn., Am. Sch. Counselor Assn., Assn. for Measurement and Evaluation in Guidance, Nat. Assn. for Religious and Value Issues in Counseling (pres. 1978), Am., N.Y. State, Fordham personnel and guidance assns., Assn. for Counselor Edn. and Supervision, Nat. Vocat. Guidance Assn., Assn. for Humanistic Edn. and Devel., Am. Rehab. Counseling Assn., Nat. Employment Counselors Assn., Assn. for Non-White Concerns in Personnel and Guidance, Assn. for Specialist in Group Work. Office: Iona Coll 715 North Ave New Rochelle NY 10801

DRISKO, ELLIOT HILLMAN, social service exec., therapist; b. Columbia Falls, Maine, Aug. 19, 1917; s. Eri Haskell and Susie Farnsworth (Allen) D.; B.A. cum laude, Colby Coll., 1939; M.S., Boston U., 1941; Ed.D., Columbia U., 1960; m. Elizabeth Winship, Oct. 17, 1942; children—Elliot Hillman, James Winship. Family counselor Children's Aid Soc., Niagara Falls, N.Y., 1941-42; supr. psychiat. social work Mason Gen. Hosp., Brentwood, N.Y., 1944-46; intake supr. Family Service Soc., Yonkers, N.Y., 1946-49, exec. dir. 1950—; pvt. practice marriage and family therapy, Yonkers, 1965—; founder Yonkers Homemaker Service, 1953, Big-Brother-Big Sister program, 1963, Senior Service Center, 1971; chmn. N.Y. State Council of Family Service Agys. 1959-61, exec. bd., 1974; N.Y. State del. White House Conf. Children and Youth, 1960; mem. adv. council Westchester County (N.Y.) Dept. Social Services, 1975—; Yonkers Youth Bd., Mayor's Com. on Aging; cons. public relations Family Service Assn. Am., 1960-71. Treas., Yonkers Community Planning Council, 1970—; chmn. Yonkers unit Internat. Year of Child, UN Assn./U.S., 1977; bd. dirs. Yonkers council Boy Scouts Am.; mem. Police Athletic League. Served in U.S. Army 1942-46. Recipient Yonkers Community Service award Family Service Soc., 1964; Jenkins Meml. Community Service award Yonkers PTA Council, 1967. Fellow Am. Assn. Marriage and Family Therapists; mem. Acad. Cert. Social Workers (pres. Westchester County chpt. 1971-72), Nat. Assn. Social Workers (chmn. com. third-party payment N.Y. State chpt. 1974—), Westchester Assn. Psychiat. Social Workers, Am. Assn. Sex Educators and Therapists, Soc. for Sci. Study of Sex, NCCJ. Author: Parent-Teen Age Codes in the United States, 1960; contbr. articles to popular magazines. Home: 10 Mitchell Ave Yonkers NY 10701 Office: Family Service Soc 219 Palisade Ave Yonkers NY 10703

DRIVER, PHILIP BROGNARD, JR., lawyer; b. Ridley Park, Pa., Mar. 13, 1910; s. Philip B. and Alice G. (Davison) D.; B.S., U. Pa., 1931, LL.B., 1934. Admitted to Pa. bar. 1934; partner Harper, George, Buchanan & Driver, Phila., 1939—. Served as lt. col. AUS, 1941-46. Mem. Am., Pa., Phila. bar assns., S.R. Mason (33 deg.), Rotarian. Clubs: Union League (Phila.): Seaview Country (Abseacon, N.J.); Rolling Green Golf (Springfield, Pa.). Home: 24 W Ward Ave Ridley Park PA 19078 Office: 1200 Western Sav Bank Bldg Philadelphia PA 19107

DROBENA, THOMAS JOHN, clergyman; b. Chgo., Aug. 23, 1934; s. Thomas and Suzanne (Durec) D.; B.Th., Concordia Theol. Sem., 1961, M.Div., 1974; M.A., Hebrew U., Jerusalem, 1968; Sc.D. (hon.) London Inst., 1972; Ph.D., Calif. Grad. Sch. Theology, 1975. Ordained to ministry Lutheran Ch. Mo. Synod, 1962; priest Emmanuel Ch., Britton, Mich., 1962-67; archeol. researcher Hebrew U. and Inst. Holy Land Studies, Jerusalem, 1967-68; priest Redeemer Luth. Ch., Jerusalem, 1967-68, Ascension Luth. Ch., Binghamton, N.Y., 1969—; adj. instr. Slavic studies State U. N.Y. at Binghamton, 1977-78. Fellow Slovak Inst. Rome; mem. Am. Sci. Affiliation, Am. Assn. Advancement Slavic Studies, Am. Assn. Tchrs. of Slavic and East European Langs., Creation Research Soc., Royal Astron. Soc. Can. Home: PO Box 125 Johnson City NY 13790

DROBILE, JAMES ALBERT, lawyer, chem. engr.; b. Germantown, Pa., Sept. 29, 1927; s. Albert William and Theresa (Janson) D.; B.S. in Chem. Engring., Villanova U., 1949; S.M., Mass. Inst. Tech., 1950; LL.B., Temple U., 1960; m. Dorothy E. McGillicuddy, Oct. 8, 1955; children—Patricia Elizabeth, Margaret Theresa, James Albert, Mary Cornelia, Katharine Frances. Admitted to Pa. bar, 1961, D.C. bar, 1962; various engring. positions, 1950-56; patent agt., then atty. Sun Oil Co., Phila., 1956-61; asso., then partner firm Schnader, Harrison, Segal & Lewis, Phila., 1961—, mng. partner, 1968-71. Mem. adv. bd. lay trustees Villanova U., 1966-67, mem. devel. council, 1967-76, chmn. exec. bd., 1969-70, trustee, 1976—; mem. ednl. council Mass. Inst. Tech., 1972-77; treas. Phila. Engring. Found., 1967—; mem. Radnor Twp. (Pa.) CSC, 1969—. Served with USN, 1945-46, USNR, 1946-50. Recipient Morehouse award Villanova U., 1974, Alumni medal, 1974; registered profl. engr., Pa. Mem. Am., Pa. (spl. task force to rev. work Pa. Atty. Gen. 1971), Phila. bar assns., Am., Phila. (bd. govs. 1965-67, chmn. antitrust and misuse com. 1969-72, 76-77, sec. 1972-74, pres. elect 1978—) patent law assn., Internat. Patent and Trademark Assn., Phila. Jr. Bar Assn. (exec. com. 1962-64), U.S. Trademark Assn. (chmn. state trademark com. 1977—), Licensing Execs. Soc., Nat., Pa. (dir. Phila. chpt. 1970-73, v.p. 1973-74, chmn. state legis. com. 1972-73, mem. task force profl. services procurement 1973-74, task force engrs. registration laws 1975-77) socs. profl. engrs., Am. Inst. Chem. Engrs., Geog. Soc. Phila. (dir. 1971-74, pres. 1978—), Sigma Xi, Phi Alpha Delta, Sigma Nu, Tau Beta Pi. Roman Catholic. Clubs: Engrs. Phila. (v.p. 1968-70, pres. 1970-71, dir. 1971-74), Overbrook Golf, Union League (Phila.); Nat. Lawyers (Washington); Eagles Mere Country. Home: 401 Audubon Ave Wayne PA 19087 Office: Packard Bldg Philadelphia PA 19102

DROEGE, ROBERT CARL, research psychologist; b. Seymour, Ind., July 9, 1924; s. Walter H. and Minna L. (Strasen) D.; B.S., Purdue U., 1949; M.A., U. N.C., 1954; m. Eleanor Baden, Jan. 19, 1957; children—Samuel, Ann, Kenneth, Philip. Psychometrist, Duke U., Durham, N.C., 1950-51; psychologist Dept. Labor, Washington, 1951-53, personnel research psychologist, 1956—; research psychologist Dept. Army, Washington, 1953-55. Served with U.S. Army, 1943-46. Recipient distinguished career service award, U.S. Dept. Labor, 1977. Mem. Am. Psychol. Assn., Am. Personnel and Guidance Assn., Nat. Vocat. Guidance Assn. Lutheran. Contbr. articles on psychol. testing to profl. jours. Home: 6710 West Park Dr Hyattsville MD 20782

DROESCH, VIGEE HALL, retail exec.; b. Los Angeles, Feb. 1, 1950; d. Jerome Lincoln and Elizabeth Lee (Hall) Seelen; A.A., Stephens Coll., 1969; B.J., U. Mo., 1971; M.Ed., Xavier U., 1975; postgrad. Fordham U.; m. Thomas Patrick Droesch, July 8, 1978. Asst. dept. mgr. H & S Pogue Co., Cin., 1975-76; asst. buyer Lord & Taylor, N.Y.C., 1976—; humorous writer Gibson Greeting Cards Co., Cin., 1972; reporter U. Wyo. Communications Service, Laramire, 1972; tchr. Jack and Jill Nursery Sch., 1972; reporter, women's editor Cin. Enquirer, 1973-74; tchr. Sunland Lutheran Sch., Freeport, Bahamas, 1974-75; free lance journalist Cin. newspapers, writer introductory column for evening provisionals Jr. League Newssheet, 1975, 76; publicity chmn. Cin. 4th Ann. Stitchery Fair for benefit Planned Parenthood, 1976; pub. relations writer community relations dept. WCET-TV Pub. Broadcasting, 1975-76. Supr. Freeport Aquanets Swim Group, 1975-76; radio and TV publicity chmn. Ann. Antiques Festival, Cin. Childrens Convalescent Hosp., 1976; admissions alumni adviser Stephens Coll., Cin., 1975, 76,

Northeastern regional rep., 1976—. Mem. Women in Communications, Ohio Newspaper Womens Assn., Nat. Bus. and Profl. Womens Club, Jr. League N.Y.C., D.A.R. (N.Y.C. chpt. (English teaching com.), conservation com.), Freeport Players Guild in Bahamas (nominated Best Actress in Cameo Role and Best Newcomer 1974-75). Author, photographer Sunland Luth. Sch. Yearbook, 1975, playsbills for Freeport Players Guild, 1974-75. Home: 35 Park Ave New York City NY 10016 Office: Lord & Taylor 424 Fifth Ave New York City NY 10018

DROLLETTE, DANIEL DAVID, microbiologist; b. Plattsburgh, N.Y., June 17, 1938; s. Edgar Anthony and Helen (Bates) D.; B.S., Cornell U., 1961; M.S., U. Mass. at Amherst, 1970, Ph.D., 1976; m. Barbara Ann Friedman, Feb. 17, 1962; children—Daniel, Stephen. Bacteriologist virology labs. N.Y. State Dept. Pub. Health, Albany, 1962; microbiologist Holyoke (Mass.) Hosp., 1963—; instr. microbiology Nursing Sch. Holyoke Hosp., 1964-69, dept. organic chemistry Hampden Coll. Pharmacy, Willimansett, Mass., 1970-72. Served with AUS, 1956-57. Mem. Am. Soc. Microbiology, Mycology Soc. Ams., Am. Inst. Biol. Scis., Sigma Xi. Contbr. articles to profl. jours. Home: 12 Pleasant St Granby MA 01033 Office: 575 Beech St Holyoke MA 01040

DROP, LOUIS ROBERT, educator; b. Richeyville, Pa., Aug. 13, 1945; s. John and Helen D.; B.S., Calif. State Coll., 1967; M.S., U. Notre Dame, 1974. Chemist, J & L Steel Corp., 1967; tchr. chemistry Charleroi (Pa.) Sch. Dist., 1968—. NSF grantee, 1971-74. Mem. Pa. State Edn. Assn., NEA, Charleroi Area Tchrs. Assn. (pres.). Home: Box 207 Richeyville PA 15358 Office: Fecsen Dr Charleroi PA 15358

DROWNE, BROTHER LAWRENCE, librarian; b. Malone, N.Y., Jan. 21, 1916; s. George W. and Janet (Jarvo) D.; B.A., St. Francis Coll., 1947; M.L.S., St. John's U., Jamaica, N.Y., 1955. Tchr. grade schs. Bklyn., 1940-45; tchr. French High Sch., St. Francis Prep. Sch., Bklyn., 1947-53; librarian St. Francis Coll., Bklyn., 1955—. Mem. Am., Catholic, N.Y. library assns., Alpha Psi Omega. K.C. Address: 180 Remsen St Brooklyn NY 11201

DROZDOW, STEPHEN ROBERT, mktg. engr.; b. Phila., Feb. 1, 1948; s. Paul Saul and Helen (Neulight) D.; B.S. in Engring., Clarkson Coll. Tech., 1970; M.B.A., Fairleigh Dickinson U., 1978; m. Linda Susan Knott, Nov. 20, 1977. Services analyst Allied Chem. Corp., Morristown, N.J., 1971-72, sales rep., Fla., 1972-74, sr. analyst, Morristown, 1974-77, sr. planning analyst, 1977-78; mktg. engr. Air Products, Inc., Allentown, Pa., 1978—; cons. mgmt. planning and control. Served with Army N.G., 1970-78. Mem. Alpha Kappa Psi, Theta Chi Frat. Alumni Corp. (sec.-treas., Outstanding alumnus award 1976). Home: 2 Lynwood Dr Lebanon NJ 08833 Office: PO Box 538 Allentown PA 18105

DRUCK, KALMAN BRESCHEL, pub. relations counselor; b. Scranton, Pa., Dec. 6, 1914; s. Jacob L. and Mabelle (Breschel) D.; B.S. magna cum laude in Journalism, Syracuse U., 1936; m. Pearl Spiro, Nov. 26, 1936; children—Ellen Druck Mirtz, Nancy Druck Brassam. With Hearst Enterprises, 1936-39, Carl Byoir & Assos., 1939-59; pres. Harshe-Rotman & Druck, Inc., N.Y.C., 1960—, chmn. exec. com., 1973—; supr. courses pub. relations Baruch Sch. Bus., Coll. City N.Y., 1939-55. Mem. advisory com. on communications Syracuse U., Boston U.; bd. dirs. Union Am. Hebrew Congregations, 1956-71, N.Y. Fedn. Jewish Philanthropies, 1957-72, Freedoms Found. at Valley Forge; bd. govs. Am. Jewish Com.; mem. citizens' pub. relations advisory com. U.S. Mil. Acad., West Point, N.Y. Named Pub. Relations Profl. of Year, 1966; recipient Distinguished Alumnus Centennial medal Syracuse U., 1970. Mem. Pub. Relations Soc. Am. (pres. N.Y.C. chpt. 1953-55, nat. chmn. 1972). Clubs: Quaker Ridge Golf (Scarsdale, N.Y.); Banyan (Palm Beach, Fla.). Home: 2 Winding Brook Dr Larchmont NY 10538 also 2780 S Ocean Dr Palm Beach FL 33480 Office: 300 E 44th St New York City NY 10017

DRUCKER, JULES HERBERT, engr., educator; b. Palmer, Mass., Aug. 9, 1921; s. Leo and Gertrude (Riess) D.; M.E., Stevens Inst. Tech., 1941, M.S. in Mech. Engring., 1943; M.S. in Mgmt. Engring., L.I. U., 1971. Exec. sec. Pressure Vessel Research Com., N.Y.C., 1953-57; marine engr., chief safety br. N. Atlantic div. C.E., U.S. Army, N.Y.C., 1957-62; prof. sci. and engring. U.S. Mcht. Marine Acad., U.S. Dept. Commerce, Kings Point, N.Y., 1962—. Cons. engr., 1952—. Served with Mcht. Marine, 1944-46; chief engr. USCG. Registered profl. engr., N.Y., N.J. Mem. Tau Beta Pi. Home: 9 Nagog Hill Rd Acton MA 01720 also 4 Bonnie Ct Hicksville NY 11801 Office: US Merchant Marine Acad Kings Point NY 11024

DRUCKER, TED E., auditor, aerospace co. exec.; b. Fountain Inn, S.C., Nov. 27, 1931; s. Morris and Ida Belle (Andronosky) D.; B.S. magna cum laude, U.S.C., 1956; J.D., George Washington U., 1959; m. Ellen Jeanne Goldenberg, Mar. 24, 1963; 1 son, Martin. With U.S. GAO, Washington, 1956-66, audit supr., 1963; mgr. operational auditing Bell div. Textron Inc., Buffalo, 1967-70, chief auditor, 1970—; admitted to D.C. bar, 1960, U.S. Supreme Ct. bar, 1965. Served with U.S. Army, 1951-53; Korea. Certified internal auditor. Mem. Inst. Internal Auditors (pres. Niagara Frontier chpt. 1976). Democrat. Office: PO Box 1 Buffalo NY 14240

DRUCKMAN, RICHARD ARNOLD, pharm. co. exec.; b. Hartford, Conn., Apr. 4, 1939; s. Harry and Florence (Weinstein) D.; B.A., Trinity Coll., 1961; M.B.A., Columbia U., 1962; m. Joan Phyllis Moskovitz, Aug. 12, 1962; children—Michael Neal, Gregory Wayne, Steven Edward. Mktg. analyst B.F. Goodrich Co., N.Y.C., 1962-63, Merck Internat., N.Y.C., 1963-66; mktg. research mgr. Union Carbide Corp., N.Y.C., 1966-67; dir. mktg. research E.R. Squibb Co., Princeton, N.J., 1967-77, dir. product planning and research, 1977-78, v.p. sales, 1978—. Mgr. Little League; active Boy Scouts Am. Mem. Assn. Internat. Med. Scis. (pres.), Am. Mktg. Assn., Am. Mgmt. Assn., Eastern Pharm. Market Research Group. Jewish. Home: 17 Benford Dr Princeton Junction NJ 08550 Office: PO Box 4000 Princeton NJ 08540

DRUDGE, ROBERT B., social worker; b. Chgo., Sept. 5, 1941; s. James M. and Gladys Drudge; B.S. in Psychology, UCLA, 1965; M.S.W., Howard U., 1969; postgrad. Georgetown U., 1971-72; m. Rachel Stewart, Nov. 5, 1975; 1 son, Matthew; stepchildren—Charles and Thomas Collier. Child welfare caseworker Fairfax (Va.) County Social Services, 1965-71; child protective services and child welfare supr. Montgomery Dept. Social Services, Rockville, Md., 1971-74; asst. dir. Wicomico County Social Services, Salisbury, Md., 1976—; family therapist Cath. Social Services, Salisbury, 1976—. Pres. Wicomico County Children's Council; bd. dirs. Md. H.E.L.P. Resource Project, Md. State Community Coordinated Child Care Com. Mem. Nat. Assn. Social Workers, Acad. Certfied Social Workers. Home: Route 1 Box 143 Tyaskin MD 21865 Office: Box 2298 Salisbury MD 21801

DRUM, JAMES HUNTER, automotive co. exec.; b. Chgo., June 4, 1915; s. Alphonse L. and Jane (Hunter) D.; B.S., U.S. Mil. Acad., 1937; m. Betty Burke, Nov. 16, 1939; 1 dau., Deborah Drum English. Commd. 2d lt. U.S. Army, 1937, advanced through grades to col., 1942, ret., 1946; adminstr. sci. and tech. agys. U.S. govt., 1946-57; tech. adminstrv. exec. Willys Motors Inc., Kaiser Jeep Corp., Washington, 1957-70; v.p. govt. affairs AM Gen. Corp. subs. AM. Motors), Washington, 1970—. Bd. dirs. Internat. Eye Found. Decorated Silver Star, Purple Heart (U.S.); Distinguished Service Order (U.K.). Mem. Am. Legion, Soc. Automotive Engrs., Nat. Secs. Industry Assn., Assn. U.S. Army. Office: 1129 20th St NW Washington DC 20036

DRUM, PEGGI (MARGARET A.), public relations exec.; b. N.Y.C., Aug. 16, 1942; d. Francis and Margaret Mary (Clark) D.; B.S., Fordham U.; M.A., U. Md. Dir. pub. relations Univ. Theatre, U. Md., College Park, 1965-67; asst. publicity dir. Arena Stage, Washington, 1967-68; dir. radio and TV pub. relations George Washington U., Washington, 1968-70; pub. relations mgr. St. Peter's Hosp., Albany, N.Y., 1971-72; advt. promotion/community relations dir. Sta. WAST-TV, Albany, 1972-73; account supr. Madison North Mktg. Communications Agy., Ltd., Schenectady, 1973-76; publicity dir. Saratoga Performing Arts Center, Saratoga Springs, N.Y., 1976; corp. info. specialist J.C. Penney Co., N.Y.C., 1978—. Mem. N.Y. Gov.'s Com. on Discrimination Minority Groups and Women in New Media, 1972-74. Mem. Pub. Relations Soc. Am., Am. Women in Radio and TV (pres. Capital dist. 1975), Women's Press Club N.Y. State (pres. 1972-73). Home: 161 Webb Ave River Edge NJ 07665 Office: JC Penney Co 1301 Ave of Americas New York NY 10019

DRUMM, PHILIP RUSSELL, born-deaf writer, lectr.; b. Bristol, Pa., Jan. 8, 1932; s. Guy Richards and Greta Adelaide (Norton) D.; A.A. cum laude, Lees-McRae Jr. Coll., 1953; 1 son, Kevin Russell. Varied positions, stonemason, carpenter, printer, N.Y. and N.J., 1949-56; mailboy to mktg. services and publicity mgr. Sel-Rex Corp., Nutley, N.J., 1956-66; head Drumm Pub. Relations, N.Y.C., 1967-70; editor and audit reviewer Peat, Marwick, Mitchell and Co., N.Y.C., 1970—; cons. pub. relations, writer, lectr. on deafness, lang. devel.; editor, sec. Alexander Graham Bell Assn., Washington, 1974-76; sec. Thursday's Child Internat., New Orleans; asso. Speakers Forum Internat., N.Y.C.; past editor, Hearing Research Devels., Children's Hearing, Edn. and Research Internat., Yonkers, N.Y.; condr. ednl. seminars McGill U., 1975, U. Houston, 1975; participant radio and TV Talk shows, 1964, 73, 74, 75, 77. Trustee Christ Ch., Paterson, N.J., 1965-66; mem. N.Y.C. Community Bd. #5, 1978—; asso. dep. sheriff, Passaic County, N.J., 1965-68; editor Riverview Towers' Voice of the Towers; committeeman, asst. scoutmaster Altaha council Boy Scouts Am., Paterson, 1964-66, asst. cubmaster, Lincoln Park, N.J., 1962-63; exec. PTA; co-founder, chmn. bd. dirs. Heritage Found., Inc.; mem. housing com. Paterson Task Force for Community Action, Inc. Mem. Internat. Soc. Gen. Semantics, Publicity Club N.Y. (editor Clippings P.R. Jour.; Distinguished Service award 1971), Assn. Indsl. Advertisers (editor Advertalk Jour.), Printing House Craftsmen (Newark), Internat. Typog. Union, Advt. Prodn. Mgrs. Club N.J. Inventor Surfish Pleasureboats. Office: Townhouse 44 120 W 44th St New York City NY 10036

DRUMMOND, JOSEPH JUSTIN, elec. co. exec.; b. Phila., Apr. 15, 1945; s. Justin J. and Mary D.; B.S., La Salle Coll., 1967; m. Suzanne Ochar, Sept. 30, 1967; children—Joseph Justin, Kimberly Ann. Sales, Johnson & Johnson, New Brunswick, N.J., 1967-68; sales mgmt. York, Borg, Warner, Phila., 1968-69; product mgr. Exide Power Systems div. E.S.B., Inc., Horsham, Pa., 1969-71, mgr. mktg., 1971-78, dir. communications and tng., 1972-79; v.p. mktg. emergency lighting Chlorine Systems U.S.A., North Haven, Conn., 1979—. Mem. Warminster Twp. Park and Recreation Bd., 1976-78. Mem. Advt. Research Found. (dir. 1977—), Center Mktg. Communications (dir. 1975—), Internat. Indsl. TV Assn., Material Handling Dealer Assn., Bus. Profl. Advt. Assn., Suburban Bucks Jaycees (pres. 1976). Home: 26 Papermill Madison CT 06443 Office: Mallard Ln North Haven CT 06473

DRUMWRIGHT, THOMAS FRANKLIN, JR., elec. engr.; b. Danville, Va., Sept. 8, 1928; s. Thomas Franklin and Grace Helen (Lamb) D.; B.E.E., Va. Mil. Inst., 1951; M.S., Ohio State U., 1957; m. Patricia Gardner Ryan, Oct. 11, 1958; children—Thomas Franklin, Kathryn R. Staff trainee, welding engr. Newport News (Va.) Shipyard, 1953-55; grad. asst. Ohio State U., Columbus, 1955-57, research engr., 1957-70, sr. research engr., 1970-73; group leader Alcoa Labs., Aluminum Co. Am., Alcoa Center, Pa., 1973-78, engring. asso., 1978—. Sr. warden St. Andrews Episcopal Ch. Served to 1st lt. U.S. Army, 1951-53. Fellow Am. Soc. Nondestructive Testing (past chmn. Pitts. chpt.); mem. ASTM, Sigma Xi. Club: Kiwanis (dir. 1973-75). Home: 790 Kennedy Ave New Kensington PA 15068 Office: Alcoa Tech Center Alcoa Center PA 15069

DRUSKOFF, ELI, accountant, lawyer, educator; b. N.Y.C., Feb. 17, 1923; s. Jacob and Eva (Eventon) D.; B.S., N.Y. U., 1943, M.B.A., 1952; LL.B., Bklyn. Law Sch., 1957, J.D., 1967. Admitted to N.Y. bar, 1957; with Hirschorn, Singer & Brown, C.P.A.'s, N.Y.C., 1947-64; individual practice N.Y.C., 1965—; instr. N.Y. Inst. Tech., 1965-66, asst. prof., 1966-68, asso. prof., 1968—. Served with AUS, 1943-46. C.P.A., N.Y. Mem. Am. Inst. C.P.A.'s, N.Y. State Soc. C.P.A.'s (mems. in field edn. com. 1969-70), Am. Accounting Assn., N.Y. State Bar Assn., Am. Assn. U. Profs., Grand St. Boys Assn., Inc., Bklyn. Law Sch. Alumni Assn. Home: 1151 Brighton Beach Ave Brooklyn NY 11235

DRYER, EDWIN JASON, lawyer, oil industry assn. exec.; b. N.Y.C., Sept. 6, 1916; s. Edwin Jason and Anne (Kennebeck) D.; B.A., Yale U., 1937, LL.B., 1940; m. Dorothea Merrill, Feb. 28, 1942; children—Diana Dryer Wright, Faith Ellen. Admitted to D.C. bar, 1954, N.Y. bar, 1940, Utah bar, 1946, Oreg. bar, 1951, U.S. Supreme Ct. bar, 1950, U.S. Ct. Mil. Appeals, 1954; atty. SEC, 1940-41; asst. to pres. Merrill Co., Salt Lake City, 1946-48; asst. gen. counsel U.S. Bonneville Power Adminstrn., Portland, Oreg., 1948-50; dep. adminstr., gen. counsel U.S. Def. Electric Power Adminstrn., 1950-53; partner firm Meyers & Dryer, and predecessor, Washington, 1955-68; of counsel firm Irons & Sears, Washington, 1970-78; of counsel firm Dunnells, Dewall, Bennett & Porter, Washington, 1978—; exec. sec., gen. counsel Ind. Refiners Assn. Am., Washington. Served to col. U.S. Army Res., 1938-68, U.S. Army, 1941-46. Mem. Am., Fed., D.C., Utah bar assns., Am. Law Inst. (life). Clubs: Army and Navy, Nat. Press (Washington); Alta (Salt Lake City); Yale (N.Y.C.). Home: 5126 Palisade Ln NW Washington DC 20016 Office: 1220 19th St NW Washington DC 20036

DRYMIOTIS, ANDREW DEMETRIOS, psychiatrist, clin. adminstr.; b. Paphos, Cyprus, Oct. 27, 1925; s. Demetrios and Kyriaki (Philippou) D.; came to U.S., 1957, naturalized, 1973; M.D., National U., Athens, Greece, 1953; m. Yvonne Loukides, Jan. 12, 1958; 1 son, James. Chief resident, neurol. div. N.Y. U., N.Y.C., 1958-59, fellow in psychiatry Inst. Rehab. N.Y. U. Med. Center, 1963-64; sr. psychiatrist Creedmoor State Hosp., N.Y.C., 1959-63, chief psychiatrist, adolescent services Creedmoor Psychiat. Center, 1973—; practice medicine specializing in psychiatry, N.Y.C., 1973—; pres. Pancyprian Soc. Mental Health, 1967-69. Diplomate in neurology and psychiatry, Greece, Cyprus. Mem. AMA (Physicians Recognition award 1972, 75), Am. Psychiat. Assn., Med. Soc. N.Y., Nassau County Med. Soc., AAAS, N.Y. Acad. Sci. Contbr. publ. to med. jours. and books. Home: 221 Cherry Valley Ave Garden City NY 11530

DRZEWIENIECKI, WALTER MARIAN, historian, educator; b. Piotrkow Tryb, Poland, Dec. 14, 1914; s. Edward and Zuzanna (Baranowska) D.; B.S., Polish Mil. Acad., 1937; diploma Brit. Army Staff Coll., 1943; B.S. in History, U. Wis. at Stevens Point, 1957; M.A., U. Chgo., 1958, Ph.D., 1963; postgrad. Russian Inst., Columbia, 1965-66; m. Zofia A. Wisniewski, June, 10, 1945; 1 dau., Joanna E. Came to U.S., 1950, naturalized, 1956. Commd. 2d lt. Polish Army, 1937, advanced through grades to maj., 1947, co. comdr., Corps and Army operation officer, div. chief of staff, service in Poland, Middle East, Italy, Eng., ret., 1947; farmer, Can., 1947-50; farmer, also editor Polish lang. weekly Gwiazda Polarna, Stevens Point, Wis., 1954-57; asst. prof. history State U. Coll., Oswego, N.Y., 1959-63; asso. prof. history State U. Coll., Buffalo, 1963-66, prof., 1966—, chmn. East European and Slavic studies program, chmn. dept. history, 1969-71; vis. prof. Elizabeth Gaskell Coll., Manchester, Eng., 1975-76. Pres., Polish Cultural Found., Inc., 1965-71, v.p., 1971-74, pres., 1975—. Decorated Mil. Cross with 3 bars, Silver Cross of Merit with swords, Mil. medal with 1 bar, Cross Monte Cassino (all Poland), Croce al Valor Militare (Italy), Italy Star, Def. medal (Britain), war medal, Africa star, Royal Yugoslav War Cross (Yugoslavia). Recipient State U. N.Y. at Buffalo 125th Anniversary award, 1971; 1st prize for memoirs Polish Acad. Scis., 1977. Mem. Polish Inst. Arts and Sci., J. Pilsudski Hist. Inst., Polish Inst. London, Polish-Am., Am. hist. assns., Am. Assn. Advancement Slavic Studies, Polish Nat. Alliance, Polish Arts Club, Nat. Ethnic Studies Assembly (v.p.) Author: The German-Polish Frontier, 1959; Polonica Buffalonensis, 1976; Wrzesniowe wspomnienie podporucznika, 1978. Contbr. articles to profl. jours. Home: 337 McKinley Ave Kenmore NY 14217 Office: State U NY Coll 1300 Elmwood Ave Buffalo NY 14222

DU, KWEN-MING, paper co. exec.; b. Taiwan, Republic of China, Mar. 24, 1934; s. Wei-chuang and Eng Du; came to U.S., 1964, naturalized, 1978; B.C., Soochow U., 1961; M.B.A., N.Y. U., 1966, Ph.D., 1970; m. Ellen Minlien Li, Aug. 5, 1967; 1 son, Kevin. With Bank of Taiwan (China), 1952-62; auditor U.S. AID Mission to China, Taiwan, 1962-64; ops. research analyst Union Carbide Corp., N.Y.C., 1966-69; ops. research/sci. systems cons. St. Regis Paper Co., N.Y.C., 1969-74; mgr. mgmt. sci. Great No. Nekoosa Corp., Stamford, Conn., 1974—; adj. asst. prof. Pace U., N.Y.C., 1977. Recipient Sustained Outstanding Performance award U.S. AID Mission to China, 1963; Distinction award N.Y. U., 1966; Most Outstanding Alumnus award Soochow U., 1970; Founders Day award N.Y. U., 1971. Mem. Ops. Research Soc. Am., Inst. Mgmt. Sci., Beta Gamma Sigma. Contbr. articles to profl. jours. Home: 30 Nearwater Ln Riverside CT 06878 Office: 75 Prospect St Stamford CT 06901

DUA, FRANK MARTIN, securities broker/dealer; b. Englewood, N.J., Jan. 5, 1923; s. John A. and Isabel G. (Van Nutt) D.; B.A. cum laude, Furman U., 1949; m. Muriel C. Morgan, Oct. 17, 1952; children—Barbara E. Dua Beavers, Connie A., Diane I., Edward M. Mdse. mgr. J.B. White & Co., Greenville, S.C., 1949-51; sr. systems analyst Exxon Corp., N.Y.C., 1951-66; v.p., treas., dir. W.H. Reaves & Co., Inc., N.Y.C., 1966—; allied mem. N.Y. Stock Exchange, 1966—; mem. Detroit Stock Exchange, 1971—. Served with AUS, 1943-46. Mem. N.Y. State Soc. Internat. Medicine (exec. sec. 1960-61), Phi Sigma (treas. 1947-49). Clubs: Lawyers, Monmouth Boat (Red Bank, N.J.), Downtown Athletic, North River Power Squadron (exec. com.) (N.Y.C.). Home: 27 Wardell Ave Rumson NJ 07760 Office: 74 Trinity Pl New York City NY 10006

DUANE, FRANCIS JOSEPH, golf course architect; b. Bronx, N.Y., Aug. 9, 1921; s. James Joseph and Margaret Winifred (Moroney) D.; B.S. in Landscape Architecture, State U. N.Y. Coll. Forestry, 1944; m. Mary Elizabeth Parry, Aug. 13, 1955; children—Mary Elizabeth, Patricia, Olivia, Andrew Francis, Joseph. Landscape architect N.H. Dept. Forestry and Recreation, 1944-45; with firm Robert Trent Jones, golf course architect, N.Y.C., 1945-63; pvt. practice as golf course architect, Port Washington, N.Y., 1963—; dir. Moriches Assos., Rock Hill Golf Club, Apricot Corp. Mem. Am. Soc. Golf Course Architects (pres. 1971-72, gov. 1968-74), Am. Soc. Landscape Architects. Lion (dir. Port Washington 1970-72). Clubs: Port Washington Yacht, Rock Hill Golf. Prin. works include: Half Moon Bay (Calif.) Golf Links; Kapalua Golf (Maui, Hawaii); Marshwood Country Club, Savannah, Ga., Big Sky (Mont.) Golf Club, Brae Burn Country Club, Purchase, N.Y. Home: 11 Monfort Rd Port Washington NY 11050 Office: 1146 Port Washington Blvd Port Washington NY 11050

DUAX, WILLIAM LEO, biophysicist; b. Chgo., Apr. 18, 1939; s. William Joseph and Alice Bernice (Joyce) D.; B.A., St. Ambrose Coll., 1961; Ph.D., U. Ia., 1967; m. Caroline Townsend Dowell, May 6, 1966; children—Julia, Sarah, William, Stephen. Postdoctoral fellow Ohio U., Athens, 1967-68; research asso. dept. biophysics Med. Found. Buffalo (N.Y.), 1968-69, head crystallography lab., 1969-70, head molecular biophysics dept., 1970—. Served with AUS, 1961. NIH Research grantee, 1972—. Mem. Am. Crystallographic Assn., Am. Chem. Soc., Biophys. Soc., N.Y. Acad. Sci., Sigma Xi. Contbr. articles to profl. jours. Office: 73 High St Buffalo NY 14203

DUBARD, WALTER HIGHGATE, oil and gas co. exec.; b. Greenwood, Miss., Dec. 10, 1924; s. Walter Highgate and Maybelle (McDorman) DuB.; student Southwestern Coll., 1942, U. Miss., 1946; B.S., Columbia U., 1949. Owner, realtor W.H. DuBard Real Estate, Greenwood, Miss., 1961—; owner, operator W.H. DuBard Prodn. Co., N.Y.C., 1963—; v.p., dir. Pike Investments Inc., McComb, Miss., 1962-76, chmn. bd. 1976—. Served with M.C., AUS, 1943-45. Decorated Silver Star. Mem. Sigma Alpha Epsilon. Presbyterian. Club: El Morocco. Home: 55 East End Ave New York City NY 10028 Office: PO Box 698 Wall St Station New York City NY 10005

DUBE, JOHN, lawyer; b. Montreal, Que., Can., July 14, 1899; s. Joseph Edmond and Marie-Louise (Quintal) D.; B. Letters and Sci., Montreal (Can.) U., 1920, B.C.L. 1923; Licentiate in Civil Law, Paris U. (France), France, 1924; postgrad. New Coll. at Oxford (Eng.), 1925; 1 son, John Edmund. Came to U.S. 1926, naturalized 1945. Called to Que. bar, 1923; admitted to N.Y. bar 1945; asso. law firm Coudert Bros., N.Y.C. and Paris, 1926-31, Curtis Mallet-Prevost, Colt and Mosle, N.Y.C., 1932-33, Ward & Dube, Nice, France, 1933-36; pvt. practice law, Nice, France, 1936-40, N.Y.C., 1945—; former v.p., dir. Bengue, Inc., Union City, N.J., 1940-64; former pres. Le Moulin Legumes Corp., Wilmington, Del., 1948-64, dirs., 1948—. Consul gen. of Monaco in N.Y.C., 1971—; permanent observer for Monaco at UN. Trustee Soc. Rehab. Facially Disfigured, Inc. Decorated officer Order of Grimaldi (Monaco). Mem. Union Interalliee Paris, Am., N.Y.C. bar assns., Am. Fgn. Law Assn., Internat. Law Assn., Am. Soc. Internat, Law, Soc. Fgn. Consuls, Confrerie des Chevaliers du Tastevin. Clubs: Paris Am.; Ardsley Country. Home: 425 E 58th St New York City NY 10022 Office: 200 Park Ave New York City NY 10017

DUBEY, SATYA DEVA, govt. ofcl.; b. Sakara Bajid, India, Feb. 10, 1930; s. Jagdish Narayan and Sahodara Devi (Mishra) D.; B.Sc. with honors, Patna U., 1951; diploma Indian Statis. Inst., 1953; Ph.D., Mich. State U., 1960; m. Joyce Lura Tubbs, June 18, 1960; children—Jay Dev, Dean Dev, Neal Narayan. Came to U.S., 1956, naturalized, 1963. Sr. math. statistician Procter & Gamble Co., Cin., 1960-65, head statistics sect., 1965-66; prin. statistician, head statistics and operations research group Ford Motor Co., Dearborn, Mich., 1966-68; asso. prof. indsl. engring. N.Y. U., 1968-73; chief statis. evaluation br. Bur. Drugs, HEW, Rockville, Md., 1973—, acting dir. div. biometrics, 1975-76. Cons. on statistics to pvt. and pub. instns.; prin. research investigator statis. reliability; speaker; book reviewer, referee 15 sci. jours. Recipient creativity recognition award Internat. Personnel Research, 1972. Fellow AAAS, Am. Statis. Assn. (pres. Cin. chpt. 1962-63), Washington, N.Y. acads. scis., Royal Statis. Soc.; mem. Internat. Assn. Statistics in Phys. Scis., Internat. Assn. Survey Statisticians (charter), Biometric Soc. (adv. bd. 1974-76), Am. Soc. Clin. Pharmacology, 700 Internat. Club, Full Gospel Bus. Men's Fellowship, Sigma Xi. Mem. editorial bd. Indsl. Mathematics, 1967; bd. editors Jour. Clin. Data and Analysis. Contbr. articles to profl. jours. Home: 7712 Groton Rd Bethesda MD 20034 Office: 5600 Fishers Ln Rockville MD 20852

DUBIN, ISADORE NATHAN, educator; b. Montreal, Que., Can., July 13, 1913; s. Moses Labe and Sarah (Mettarlin) D.; B.Sc., McGill U., 1935, M.D., 1939; m. Alberta Simkevitz, June 21, 1940 (div. May 1969); children—Mary Louise, Elizabeth Simone, William Lyle. Intern medicine Royal Victoria Hosp., Montreal, 1939; asst. resident, resident pathology St. Luke's Hosp., Cleve., 1940-42; asst. resident pathology Duke Hosp., Durham, N.C., 1942-44, asst. pathologist, 1944-45; attendant pathologist John Gaston Hosp., Memphis, 1945-49; pathologist Woman's Med. Coll. Hosp., Phila., 1955—; chief service, pathology Phila. Gen. Hosp., 1955-66; cons. pathology Vets. Hosp., Phila., 1955—; asst. pathology Duke, 1942-43, inst. pathology, 1943-44, asso. pathology, 1944-45; asst. prof. pathology U. Tenn. Coll. Medicine, Memphis, 1945-48, asso. prof., 1948-49; prof. pathology Woman's Med. Coll., Phila., 1955—, chmn., 1955-69. Spl. lectr. U. Miss., 1948-49; spl. research fellow pathology sect. Nat. Cancer Inst., Bethesda, Md., 1949-50; spl. research fellow Nat. Heart Inst., U. Berne, Switzerland, 1970; chief hepatic pathology sect. Armed Forces Inst. Pathology, 1951-55; lectr. pathology U.S. Naval Hosp., Phila., 1961—; mem. ad hoc com. on isoniazid and liver disease Center for Disease Control, USPHS, 1971—. Served to maj. M.C., AUS, 1951-53. Diplomate Am. Bd. Pathology. Fellow A.C.P., AAAS; mem. Am. Assn. Pathologists and Bacteriologists, Am. Soc. Exptl. Pathology, Am. Assn. Study Liver Diseases, Internat. Acad. Pathology, Soc. Exptl. Biology and Medicine, Path. Soc. Phila. Club: Cosmos (Washington). Contbr. articles to profl. jours. Home: 1205 Montgomery St Wynnewood PA 19096 Office: Med Coll Pa Philadelphia PA 19129

DUBIN, MORTON DONALD, advt. videotape and film producer; b. N.Y.C., Sept. 1, 1931; s. Albert and Marla (Suskin) D.; student N.Y. U., 1949-50, Am. U., 1952-53, Coll. City. N.Y., 1953-54; m. Jean Brinning, Jan. 19, 1968. Producer, BIOW Advt. Agy., N.Y.C., 1953-56, Vidicam Pictures, Inc., N.Y.C., 1956-59, Lew Pollack Prodns., N.Y.C., 1956-59; with MPO Videotronics Inc., N.Y.C., 1939-71, producer, 1959-71, v.p., 1965-71; exec. v.p. sales Dirs. Circle, Inc., 1971-75; pres. Jeanmor Enterprises Ltd., N.Y., 1973—, The Best People, Inc., 1975—; lectr. Insp. N.Y.C. Aux. Police; mem. 20th Precinct Community Council N.Y.C.; mem. exec. com. N.Y.C. Mayor's Adv. Council Motion Pictures and TV, 1976-78. Served with USMCR, 1951-53. Recipient Silver Bear award Berlin Film Festival, 1967; awards of merit N.Y.C. Police Dept., 1970, 71; 10 Clio awards; Grand award Atlanta Film Festival, 1973; Golden Reel award Calvin Film Inst.; Grand award Tokyo Art Dirs., 1974; letter of appreciation mayor N.Y.C., 1973, 76. Mem. Videotape Prodn. Assn. (chmn. bd. 1969-78), Dirs. Guild Am. (spl. projects com. 1977-78), Am. Mus. Natural History (asso.), Soc. Motion Picture and TV Engrs., USMC Combat Corrs. Assn., Art Dirs. Club N.Y., Ind. Comml. Producers Assn. Columnist Backstage mag., contbr. articles to profl. and popular mags. Home: 63 W 83d St New York City NY 10024 Office: 63 W 83d St New York City NY 10024 also 7E 48 St New York City NY 10017

DUBIN, SAMUEL, physician; b. N.Y.C., June 17, 1929; s. Morris David and Rose (Gurtler) D.; B.A., N.Y.U., 1950, postgrad., 1950-51; M.D., U. Leiden (Netherlands), 1957; m. Gerdina Eefje Tromp, Dec. 30, 1959; children—Edward John, Stephen Karl. Intern, Univ. and affiliated hosps., Leiden, 1958-60, St. Joseph's Hosp., San Francisco, 1960-61; fellow, resident in psychiatry Menninger Sch., Topeka, 1961-64; staff psychiatrist Med. Center Fed. Prisoners, Springfield, Mo., 1964-65, dep. chief psychiat. service, 1965-66; staff psychiatrist Greene County Guidance Clinic, Springfield, part-time, 1964-65, chief psychiatrist, part-time, 1965-66; candidate in adult and child psychoanalysis Washington Psychoanalytic Inst., 1966—; staff Mental Health Study Center, NIMH, Adelphi, Md., 1966-72, dir., 1968-72; pvt. practice medicine specializing in psychiatry, Bethesda, Md., 1968—; mem. profl. adv. bd. Community Psychiat. Clinic, Bethesda, 1974-75; Vice-chmn. dept. psychiatry Montgomery Gen. Hosp., Olney, Md., 1978; cons. in field. Bd. dirs. Layhill Village Civic Assn.; past merit badge counselor Boy Scouts Am. Served to sr. surgeon, USPHS, 1962-67. Recipient Distinguished Service award Greene County, Mo., 1966. Fellow Am. Psychiat. Assn., Am. Coll. Psychoanalysts (charter), Am. Orthopsychiat. Assn., Am. Pub. Health Assn.; mem. AMA, Am. Psychoanalytic Assn., Washington Psychoanalytic Inst., Washington Psychiat. Soc., Montgomery County Med. Soc., Am. Assn. Sex Educators and Counselors, Am. Soc. Adolescent Psychiatry, Menninger Alumni Assn. Nat. Rifle Assn., Smithsonian Resident Assos. Republican. Clubs: Masonic Book, Bryce Mountain Ski and Country. Home: 2433 East Gate Dr Silver Spring MD 20906 Office: 8212 Wisconsin Ave Bethesda MD 20014

DUBOW, ARTHUR MYRON, bus. exec.; b. Chgo., Sept. 18, 1933; s. David and Matilda D.; A.B., Harvard, 1954, LL.B., 1957; m. Isabella Goodrich Breckinridge, Mar. 2, 1962; children—Charles Stewart, Alexandra Breckinridge. Admitted to N.Y. bar, 1961; mem. firm Webster, Sheffield, Fleischmann, Hitchcock & Chrystie, N.Y.C., 1960-64; v.p., dir. Back Bay-Orient Enterprises, Inc., N.Y.C., 1965-68, pres., 1968-76; pres., dir. Bayorient Holding Corp., 1969-76, dir. Sulpetro of Can., Ltd., 1966-76, chmn. exec. com., 1974-76; dir. Sulpetro Internat., Ltd., 1973-76, chmn. exec. com., 1974-76; dir. Internat. Basic Economy Corp., Castle Convertible Fund, Spectra Fund, Inc., Devel. Resources Inc., Herald Prodns., Inc., Frontier Capital of New York, Inc., vis. fellow Center for Internat. Affairs, Harvard, 1976-77. Co-chmn. New Am. Filmmakers Series, Whitney Mus., 1971-76, vis. com. dept. visual and environ. studies Harvard, 1970-76, vis. com. dept. East Asian langs. and civilizations, 1977—, agt. class of 1954; chmn. bd. dirs. Potomac Assos., Inc., 1975—; trustee Brearley Sch., 1973-76. Served with U.S. Army, 1957-59. Clubs: Harvard of N.Y., Georgica Assn. (Wainscot, N.Y.), Faculty, Harvard (Cambridge, Mass.). Home: Briar Patch Rd East Hampton NY 11937 also 21 Berkeley St Cambridge MA 02138 Office: 1271 Ave of Americas New York City NY 10020

DUBROFF, DIANA D., lawyer; b. N.Y.C., Mar. 4, 1909; d. Meyer and Gussie (Ginsburg) Leibow; B.A., Hunter Coll., 1928; LL.B., Bklyn. Law Sch., 1931, J.D., 1968; m. Alexander DuBroff, June 25, 1936; children—William, Elinor. Tchr., N.Y.C., 1928-61; admitted to N.Y. bar, 1934; pvt. practice law, N.Y.C.; founder, dir. Nat. Orgn. Insure Support Enforcement, N.Y.C., 1971—, N.O.I.S.E. Children of Divorce Fund, N.Y.C., 1973—, N.O.I.S.E. Abused Children Am., Inc., Washington, 1974—; judge Small Claims Ct., N.Y.C., 1968; hearing officer Parking Violations Bur., N.Y.C., 1968; founder Inst. Practical Justice Tng. Center for Mediators, 1977; adj. prof. family law City U. N.Y. Founder, Star Civic League, N.Y.C., 1928; organizer nursery group Forest Hills Jewish Center, N.Y.C., 1942; producer TV show Mini Trials by Mini Judges. Fellow Am. Acad. Matrimonial Lawyers (family law com. 1972, chmn. ct. reform 1973—); mem. Am. Arbitration Assn. (arbitrator 1968—), N.Y. State Bar (family law com. 1973—), N.Y. Trial Lawyers Assn. (chmn. family law com. 1973), Am. (family law com. 1968), N.Y., Bronx women's bar assns., N.Y. Women's Bar, Am. Bar Assn., Internat. Platform Assn., Pres.'s Assn., Am. Soc. Assn. Execs., Gregarians (founder 1949). Author booklet: Not for Women and Children Only, 1972; Humanized Divorce Urged, 1974. Syndicated columnist Let's Look at the Law. Office: 12 W 72 St New York City NY 10023

DU BROFF, SIDNEY JEROME, ednl. inst. adminstr., lawyer; b. Bklyn., Aug. 19, 1905; s. Morris and Bessie (Max) Du B.; B.S., Savage Sch. Phys. Edn., 1925; LL.B., Bklyn. Law Sch., 1929; m. Bernice Horowitz, June 28, 1931; children—Michael, Kenneth, Jane. Tchr. pub. high schs., N.Y.C., 1925-30; admitted to N.Y. State bar, 1931; sr. partner firm DuBroff & DuBroff, 1931—; producer, dir. radio show Bobby Benson & B-Barb, 1949-51, TV shows Big Payoff and Strike It Rich, 1951-59, Haggis Baggis, 1959-60; pres. Lyons Inst., Newark, 1976—; commr. accrediting bur., med. lab. schs.; fin. aid cons., career schs. Mem. Newark Sr. Citizens Commn., 1968-76. Recipient medal of remembrance Work on Behalf of War Orphans, Brussels, 1950. Mem. N.J. Pvt. Career Schs. Assn. (pres.), Nat. Assn. Trade Tech. Schs. Club: B'nai B'rith. Democrat. Jewish. Office: 900 Broad St Newark NJ 07102

DUBUC, CARROLL EDWARD, lawyer; b. Burlington, Vt., May 6, 1933; s. Jerome Joachim and Rose (Bessette) D.; B.S. in Accounting, Cornell U., 1955; LL.B., Boston Coll., 1962; postgrad. N.Y. U., 1966-67; m. Mary Jane Lowe, Aug. 31, 1963; children—Andrew, Steven, Matthew. Admitted to N.Y. bar, 1963, D.C. bar, 1972, U.S. Supreme Ct. bar, 1970, U.S. Ct. Claims bar, 1975; asso. mem. firm Haight Gardner Poor & Havens, N.Y.C., 1962-70, partner, 1970—, resident partner D.C. office, 1975—. Served with USN, 1955-59, now capt. Res. Mem. Am. (com. aviation law) N.Y. State (aviation law com.), D.C., Fed. bar assns., Assn. Bar City N.Y. (aeronautics com.), Maritime Law Assn. U.S., Nav. Aviation Commandery (vice comdr.), Internat. Assn. Ins. Counsel (aviation law com.), Fed. Ins. Counsel, Sigma Chi. Clubs: World Trade Center, Wings (N.Y.C.); Plandome Country (Manhasset, N.Y.); University (Washington); Internat. Town and Country (Fairfax, Va.). Home: 2430 Inglewood Ct Falls Church VA 22043 Office: 1819 H St NW Washington DC 20006

DUCANIS, ALEX JULIUS, educator; b. Pitts., Feb. 18, 1931; s. Alexander J. and Virginia (Vowinkel) D.; B.S., U. Pitts., 1953, M.Ed., 1954, Ed.D., 1961; m. Natalie Jane Taylor, July 1, 1954. Tchr., Lancaster (Pa.) Pub. Schs., 1956-58; lectr., administrv. asst. U. Pitts., 1959-61; research asso. div. research in higher edn. N.Y. State Edn. Dept., Albany, 1961-66; dir. instnl. research State U. N.Y. at Binghamton, 1966-69, project dir. Health Sci. Center Feasibility Study, 1967-68; asso. chmn. dept. higher edn. U. Pitts., 1969—, prof. edn. and health related professions, 1971—, dir. Inst. Higher Edn., 1970-73, chmn. div. specialized profl. devel. Sch. Edn., 1973-75; cons. Coll. Entrance Exam. Bd., 1966-67, GEAR Corp., 1967, Broome County Social Planning Council, 1967-68 (bd. dirs. 1968), Broome County Med. Soc., 1968. Chmn. dist. III regional adv. com. Statewide Rehab. Council, 1967-68; bd. dirs. N.Y.-Pa. Health Planning Council, Inc., 1968. Served with AUS, 1954-56. Mem. Am. Ednl. Research Assn., AAAS, Am. Mgmt. Assn., Am. Acad. Polit. and Social Sci., Assn. Instnl. Research, History Edn. Soc., Nat. Soc. Study of Edn., Am. Pub. Health Assn., Phi Delta Kappa. Contbr. articles to ednl. jours. Home: 230 N Craig St Pittsburgh PA 15213

DUCHARME, CLAIRE PHYLLIS, virologist; b. Irvington, N.J., Feb. 13, 1933; d. Leonide William and Bertha (Brodeur) D.; Asso.Sci., Holyoke Jr. Coll., 1952; B.S., U. Mass., 1954; M.A., Smith Coll., 1959; Med. technologist Holyoke (Mass.) Soldier's Home, 1956-57; bacteriologist div. labs. and research N.Y. State Dept. Health, Albany, N.Y., 1959-67, sr. bacteriologist, 1967—. Mem. Am. Soc. Microbiology, Tissue Culture Assn., A.A.A.S., Sierra Club, Sigma Xi. Roman Catholic. Clubs: Taconic Hiking (Troy, N.Y.), Appalachian Mountain (Berkshire chpt.), Adirondack Mountain, Altrusa (Albany), Tri-City Folk Dancers (Schenectady). Home: Wormer Rd Rural Delivery 1 Voorheesville NY 12186 Office: New Scotland Ave Albany NY 12201

DUCHARME, RAYMOND WALDO, psychologist, educator; b. West Orange, N.J., Oct. 29, 1941; s. Waldo Charles and Josephine D. (Dolce) D.; B.A., U. Hartford, 1964; M.A., U. Conn., 1969, Ph.D., 1973; m. Barbara Dellner, Sept. 16, 1960; children—Robin, Seth. Research adminstr. Project 11-M-4 with Children of Migrant Parents, Bloomfield, Conn., 1968-69; project dir. VAKT program on Child and Family Services and Conn. Research Commn., Hartford, 1969-71; prin. Mansfield (Conn.) Tng. Sch., Longley Sch. Program, 1970-71; research asso. Child and Family Services Hartford, 1971-73, cons., 1975; behavior therapist Diagnostic Treatment Group, Hartford, 1971; mem. Gov.'s Com. on Autism, 1973—, Council on Devel. Mental Disabilities, Hartford, 1974-76; exec. dir. Parent-Child Resources System Council on Human Services, Hartford, 1974-75; dir. spl. services Pomfret (Conn.) Sch. System, 1977-78; lectr. grad. sch. U. Conn. Storrs, 1977—; asst. prof. edn. Brown U., Providence, 1973-77; psychol. cons. pediatric clinic Day Kimbell Hosp., Putnam, Conn., 1974—, U. Conn. Sch. Social Work, Foster Parent Tng. Program, 1975—, autistic unit, Conn. Valley State Hosp., Middletown, 1971-72, 1977-78, Dept. Mental Health Hartford, 1974-75, Conn. State Dept. Health Div. Mental Retardation, 1974, Capital Region Edn. Council, Hartford, 1972-73, Columbus (Ohio) State Hosp. for Retarded, 1972, Nat. Workshop on Behavior Modification, Columbus, 1972, Hartford Community Council for Comprehensive Day Care, 1971, Norwalk (Conn.) Spl. Edn. Dept., 1969; cons. tchr. evaluation Bklyn. (Conn.) Sch. System, 1976-78. Inst. Econ. Edn., U. Conn., Storrs fellow in spl. edn., 1968-69, in ednl. psychology, 1970-72, reading fellow, 1972, grad. sch. award, 1972; selected as rep. for Brown U. Inst. to Dartmouth Conf. Large Group Instrn., Hanover, N.H., 1976, to Ednl. Testing Service Conf., Princeton, N.J., 1976. Cons. editor: Teaching Gifted Children, 1977-78; Learning Disabilities Guide, 1975; contbr. chpts. to textbooks, 35 mm. slide program, research papers, and articles to profl. jours.; developed numerous reading tests and behavior recording methods. Address: Rural Route 1 Elliott Rd Brooklyn CT 06234

DUCK, VIRGINIA ANN, coll. educator; b. Idaville, Pa., Jan. 19, 1919; d. A. Roy and Effie (Murtoff) Delp; B.A., Pa. State U., 1939; M.A., Bucknell U., Lewisburg, Pa., 1965; m. Paul W. Duck; 1 son, Thomas R. Tchr., Coudersport (Pa.) Sch. Dist., 1940-43, Bradford (Pa.) City Schs., 1943-46; substitute tchr. pub. schs., Pa., 1946-58; asst. prof. Bloomsburg (Pa.) State Coll., 1958—. Mem. Nat. Council Tchrs. English, Conf. English Edn., Adolescent Lit. Assembly, NEA, Pa. Edn. Assn., Children's Lit. Assembly, Sigma Tau Delta. Specialized in Am. lit. lit. for children and adolescents. Contbr. articles to profl. jours.; contbg. author: Adventuring with Books. Home: 2391 3d St Bloomsburg PA 17815 Office: Bakeless Center for Humanities Bloomsburg State Coll Bloomsburg PA 17815

DUCK, WILLIAM FRANKLIN, impact aid specialist; b. Greenville County, S.C., Oct. 19, 1921; s. Henry Gomer and Eva Evelyn D.; B.A., Morgan State U., 1950; M.S., U. Utah, 1973; m. Evelyn Nesbia Lillian Blackmore, Feb. 4, 1950; 1 dau., Wyllene Yung Ja Simmons. Project dir. Neighborhood Youth Corps, 1968-69; bus. mgr. N.J. State Prison, 1969-70; manpower coordinator Burlington County Community Action Agy., Inc., 1970-73; fin. specialist Office of Edn., HEW, Phila., 1973-76, mgmt. analyst Office for Civil Rights, Region III, Phila., 1976-78; chief dependent edn. and fed. liaison sect. Sch. Assistance div. U.S. Office Edn., Washington, 1979—. Treas., Southside Baptist Ch., Mt. Holly, N.J., 1972-77; bd. dirs. Burlington County Day Care Center, Merabash Art Mus., Merabash Mus. for Edn. Research of Am. Black Art Sci. and History. Served to maj. U.S. Army, 1942-45, 50-68. Decorated Bronze Star. Mem. Ret. Officers Assn., Nat. Assn. Community Developers, Am. Soc. Notaries, Nat. Assn. Neighborhood Youth Corps Dirs., Assn. U.S. Army, NAACP, Am. Mgmt. Assn., Fed. Bus. Assn., Kappa Alpha Psi, Phi Delta Kappa. Home: 436 Woodlane Rd Mount Holly NJ 08060 Office: 400 Maryland Ave Washington DC 20202

DUCKSWORTH, RUSSELL, dietitian; b. Scotch Plains, N.J., Sept. 26, 1943; s. Worthie and Ann (Jones) D.; B.S., Tuskegee Inst., 1968. Asst. food service dir. St. Elizabeth Hosp., Elizabeth, N.J., 1968-70; food service dir. Senator Convalescent Center, Atlantic City, 1971-74, Burk's Rehab. Center, White Plains, N.Y., 1974-75; dir. dietetics Coll. Medicine and Dentistry N.J., Newark, 1975-77; systems coordinator Therma-Tray Corp., Plainfield, N.J., 1977—. Mem. Am., So. N.J. dietetic assns., Middle Atlantic Soc. Hosp. Dietary Dirs. Baptist. Home: 2418 Park Pl Scotch Plains NJ 07076 Office: 515 Pemberton St Plainfield NJ 07080

DUDANI, NIRANJAN, physician, med. dir.; b. LarKana, Sind, Pakistan, Dec. 31, 1926; s. Gunomal and Chetibai (Jethmalani) D.; came to U.S., 1973; M.B.B.S., Grant Med. Coll., Bombay, India, 1951, D.P.H., 1968; M.D., Comm. Mass., 1974; m. Krishna Dadlani, May 4, 1955; children—Kishore, Mahender. House physician Bombay Hosp., 1951-52; commd. as med. officer Indian Navy, 1952, advanced through grades to comdr., 1970; served in dockyard, survey ship, air stas., and aircraft carrier, 1965-71; certified as flight surgeon, U.S. Navy, Pensacola, Fla., 1962, ret., 1972; hosp. physician, London, 1972-73; sr. physician Middlesex County Hosp., Waltham, Mass., 1973-74; asso. dir. med. sta. Mass. Gen. Hosp., Logan Internat. Airport, Boston, 1974—; founder, vis. physician Alcohol Detoxification Center, East Boston, 1974—; vis. physician Don Orione Nursing Home, East Boston, 1975—. Recipient Gold medal 1st Place Bombay U., 1968. Fellow Am. Coll. Allergists (asso.); mem. Aerospace Med. Assn., Mass. Med. Soc. Editor: Phengoon, 1958; author two novels in Sindhi lang., 1959, 60; Ancestral Agony (poems), 1976. Home: 22 Taft St Marblehead MA 01945 Office: Med Sta Mass Gen Hosp Logan Airport Boston MA 02128 also 214 Ocean St Lynn MA 01902

DUDICK, MICHAEL JOSEPH, bishop; b. St. Clair, Pa., Feb. 24, 1917; s. John and Mary (Jurick) D.; B.A., Ill. Benedictine Coll., Lisle, Ill., 1943; theol. studies St. Procopius Sem., Lisle, 1943-45. Ordained priest Roman Catholic Ch., 1945; vice chancellor Exarchate of Pitts., 1946-55; chancellor Diocese of Passaic (N.J.), 1963-68, bishop, 1968—; mem. Roman Curia-Sacred Congregation for Eastern Cath. Chs. Mem. N.J. Coalition of Religious Leaders; trustee Seton Hall U., 1968—; exec. bd. Nat. Cath. Conf. on Ethnics and Neighborhood. Club: K.C. (4 deg.). Home: 56 Highland Ave Montclair NJ 07042 Office: 101 Market St Passaic NJ 07055

DUDINSKI, CHARLES, civil engr.; b. Chelsea, Mass., May 15, 1933; s. Donald S. and Helen (Strychalski) D.; B.C.E., Northeastern U., 1955; m. Huguette B. Pelletier, May 5, 1956; children—Russell, Douglas, Danielle. Civil engr. Metcalf & Eddy, Inc., Boston, 1953-58; project engr. Anderson-Nichols & Co., Inc., Boston, 1958-67, v.p., 1967-71, sr. v.p., 1971-73, exec. v.p., 1973-75, pres., 1975—; also dir.; v.p. profl. services div. LFE Corp., Waltham, Mass., 1977; dir. Koretsky, King & Assos., Inc., Richmond, Calif., Urban Cons. Assos. Boston, Inc., Moody Group, Inc., Brunswick, Maine, Boston North Assn., Inc. Mem. nat. council Northeastern U. Served with C.E., U.S. Army, 1956. Registered profl. engr., Mass., Maine, R.I., N.H. Mem. ASCE, Am., New Eng. water works assn., Water Pollution Control Fedn., Am. Inst. Indsl. Engrs., Nat. Soc. Profl. Engrs. Roman Catholic. Home: 11 Lindsay Terr Saugus MA 01906

DUDLEY, OFE SARA, ednl. adminstr.; b. Havana, Cuba, Jan. 3, 1941; d. Rubens and Ofelia (Bertematti) Barreto; came to U.S., 1961, naturalized, 1970; grad. summa cum laude Colegio de Las Ursulinas, Cuba, 1957; diploma LaSalle Extension U., 1975; A.A., Brookdale Coll., 1977; student Arts and Crafts Guild, Pitts., 1975, Fla. Atlantic U., 1973; postgrad. Monmouth Coll., 1977—; m. Elbridge Gerry Dudley, Aug. 4, 1973; children—Tony, Dickie, Sally, Eddy. Bilingual exec. sec. Reciprocity Trading Co., Havana, 1957; tchr. art St. Francis of Assisi Sch., Riviera Beach, Fla., 1968-69, tchr. Spanish, 1969-72, social studies, 1970-72; Spanish interpreter for Ct. of Palm Beach, West Palm Beach, Fla., 1970-72, firm Cone, Wagner and Nugent, West Palm Beach, 1970-71; profl. model Carson, Pirie & Scott Co., Peoria, Ill., 1973-74, asst. fashion coordinator, 1974; pres. The World of Ofe Co., Dunlap, Ill., 1973-74; dir. public relations Marforth Showroom subs. Joseph Horne Co., Pitts., 1975; instr. high sch. equivalency courses Monmouth Adult Edn. Commn., Eatontown, N.J., 1977; coordinator bilingual program Monmouth Med. Center, Long Branch, N.J., 1976-77; coordinator edn. and tng. Monmouth Med. Center, 1977—; mem. community services dept. Brookdale Coll., Lincroft, N.J., 1978; one-woman shows paintings: Mellon Bank, Pitts., 1975, Glenshaw (Pa.) Junio Women's Club, 1975, Passavant Hosp., Allison Park, Pa., 1975. Recipient Mansfield State Coll. award in After Dinner Speaking, 1977, Woodrow Wilson Forensic award Monmouth Coll., 1977. Mem. Assn. Adult Edn. N.J., Am. Soc. Tng. and Devel., Middletown Youth Athletic Assn. Democrat. Roman Catholic. Club: Middletown Swim and Tennis. Home: 2 Park Dr Middletown NJ 07748 Office: Monmouth Med Center Dunbar Ave Long Branch NJ 07740

DUER, BEVERLEY CHEW, cons. engr., indsl. consulting co. exec.; b. N.Y.C., Apr. 7, 1928; s. Beverley and Julia Mary (deForest) D.; Geol. Engr., Colo. Sch. Mines, 1953; D.Eng., U. Calif., 1962; advanced profl. certificate in Fin., N.Y. U., 1974; m. Helen Crandell, Feb. 10, 1962; children—John, Alexandra. Staff mem. Arthur D. Little, Inc., 1962-64; supr. Lybrand, Ross Bros. & Montgomery, N.Y.C., 1965-67; mgr. ops. research Corporate Mgmt. Sci., CPC Internat., Inc., Englewood Cliffs, N.J., 1967-75; owner, mgr. B.C. Duer, Indsl. Cons., N.Y.C., 1975—; dir., mem. audit com. Goldfund, Inc., 1978—; mem. bd. Strategic Planning Inst., Cambridge, Mass., 1974-75, research fellow/asst., 1972-75; dir. 1172 Corp., pres., 1973-75. Served with C.E., U.S. Army, 1953-55. Registered profl. engr., N.Y. Mem. Am. Inst. Mining and Metall. Engrs., Am. Inst. Indsl. Engrs. (sr.), Ops. Research Soc. Am., Assn. Computing Machinery, Am. Def. Preparedness Assn., Nat. Soc. Profl. Engrs., Nat. Small Bus. Assn., Marine Tech. Soc., Am. Security Council. Episcopalian. Club: Union. Office: 1172 Park Ave New York City NY 10028

DUFAULT, FATHER NICHOLAS, clergyman; b. Haverhill, Mass., May 23, 1943; s. Francis George and Janice (Skaltsis) D.; B.A., Holy Cross Greek Orthodox Sem., 1967, B.D., 1968, S.T.M. summa cum laude, 1972; m. Katherine Stalikas, Sept. 22, 1968; 1 dau., Angela Elaine. Ordained deacon Greek Orthodox Ch., 1968, priest Greek Orthodox Cathedral, Boston, 1968; adviser, Greater Boston Colls. and Univs., also spiritual adviser Greater Boston Orthodox Youth Groups, 1968-72; priest St. Demetrios Greek Orthodox Parish, Biddeford, Maine, 1972-78, priest, dean Greek Orthodox Cathedral St. George, Manchester, N.H., 1978—. Mem. Diocesan Council, 1971-73; 1st v.p. Biddeford-Saco Council Chs., 1973-74, pres., 1974—. Recipient John C. and Thomas A. Pappas grant, also Peter N. Collatos grant, Rev. Michael Papadopoulos grant Holy Cross Greek Orthodox Sem., 1967. Author: The Doctrine of the Freedom of Will: An Ortho-Point of View, 1972; Orthodox Spirituality, 1972. Translator: Handbook of Byzantine Music, 1963; The Life of Saint Nicholas, 1966; Vachtrage Zum Textbande, 1966. Contbr. articles to profl. jours. Home: 1500 Belmont St Manchester NH Office: 666 Hanover St Manchester NH

DUFF, CHARLES MEREDITH, food co. ofcl.; b. Odessa, Del., June 9, 1935; s. Fred and Mildred Mary (Hanifee) D.; student pub. schs., Smyrna, Del.; m. Ann Cynthia Duff; children—Charles Meredith, Duane Allen, Kim Marie. Office mgr. City Products Corp., Clayton, Del., 1959-60, plant mgr. refrigeration and cold storage, 1960—. Mem. local bd. SSS, 1973—. Mem. Kent County Democratic Com., 1966-71; bd. dirs. Kent County Heart Assn., 1973—. Democrat. Episcopalian. Home: 128 N Bassett St Clayton DE 19938 Office: N Bassett St Clayton DE 19938

DUFF, CLAIR VINCENT, lawyer; b. York, Pa., Nov. 8, 1914; s. Frank A. and Frances A. (Clair) D.; B.A., U. Pitts., 1937, LL.B., 1940; m. Mary McDonald. Jan. 31, 1942; children—Patrick J., James C., Joseph C. Admitted to Pa. bar, 1941; mem. staff U.S. Dept. Labor, 1941-42; atty. War Dept., 1942-44; partner law firm Duff & Doyle, Pitts., 1948-70; sole practice law, Pitts., 1970—, also arbitrator labor mgmt. disputes. Lectr. U. Pitts. Sch. Bus., 1947-62; instr. Duquesne U. Sch. Law, Pitts., 1948-51; asst. dep. atty. gen. Pa., 1951-52; asst. dist. atty. Allegheny County, 1952-56; solicitor Borough Dormont, 1954-58. Mem. Diocesan Sch. Bd., Cath. Diocese Pitts., 1971-74. Served with AUS, 1944-45. Mem. Nat. Acad. Arbitrators, Am., Pa., Allegheny County bar assns. Clubs: Elks, K.C.; Chartiers Country (Allegheny County, Pa.). Home: 986 Summer Pl Pittsburgh PA 15243 Office: 733 Washington Rd Pittsburgh PA 15228

DUFF, LOUIS DUNLAP, real estate broker; b. Kansas City, Mo. May 1, 1929; s. Louis Dunlap and Cyra (Sweet) D.; B.S., U. Kans., 1950; m. Alice Willard Baker, Sept. 4, 1966; children—Elizabeth, Louis D., Alexander Willard. Vice-pres. William Pitt, Inc., Greenwich, Conn., 1971-73; founder, pres. Duff Assos., Inc., Greenwich, 1973—. Mem. Representative Town Meeting, 1973-76. Recipient Port award Realtors Nat. Mktg. Inst., 1975. Mem. Nat., Conn. assns. of realtors, Greenwich Bd. of Realtors. Episcopalian. Clubs: Field Club of Greenwich. Home: 21 Dempsey Ln Greenwich CT 06830 Office: 35 Field Point Rd Greenwich CT 06830

DUFFUS, ROY ALEXANDER, JR., chem. co. exec.; b. Rochester, N.Y., Aug. 27, 1923; s. Roy A. and Lois Margaret (Cooper) D.; A.B., Hiram Coll., 1945; postgrad. U. Rochester, 1946-48; m. Phyllis Margaret Geary, Apr. 12, 1958; children—Carolyn Geary, Joseph Roy. Research engr. Stromberg-Carlson Co., 1946-48; tech. pub. relations rep. Westinghouse Electric Co., Pitts., 1949-53; publicity mgr. Yale & Towne, Phila., 1953; exec. G.M. Basford Co., N.Y.C., 1953-58; v.p. Burson-Marsteller, 1958-63; pres. Roy Duffus Assos., Inc., 1963—. Served with USNR, 1944-46. Mem. Pub. Relations Soc. Am. (accredited), Bus.-Profl. Advt. Assn. Clubs: Overseas Press, Explorers, Overseas Yacht. Home: 27 Dogwood Hill Rd Upper Saddle River NJ 07458 Office: Poppe Tyson Inc 475 Park Ave S New York City NY 10016

DUFFY, BRIAN MICHAEL, banker; b. Elizabeth, N.J., Jan. 5, 1946; s. John Joseph and Margaret Joan (Lambert) D.; student Fordham U., 1963-65; B.A. cum laude, Seton Hall U., 1971; postgrad. Rutgers U., 1977—; m. Barbara Lynne Flannery, Sept. 3, 1965; children—Amy Elizabeth, John Patrick, Michael Edward. With Carteret Savs. & Loan Assn., Newark, 1969—, asst. v.p. gen. services dept., 1975-78, v.p., head adminstrv. services, 1978—. Mem. commerce and industry com. Newark United Way, 1977-78. Served with USAF, 1965-69. Decorated Air Medal with seven oak leaf clusters. Mem. Am. Mgmt. Assn., Nat. Assn. Bus. Economists, St. Benedict's Prep. Sch. Alumni Assn. (treas. 1973—). Home: 530 Clark St Westfield NJ 07090 Office: 866 Broad St Newark NJ 07102

DUFFY, EDWARD W., chmn., chief exec. officer Marine Midland Trust Co. of Mohawk Valley, Utica, N.Y.; vice chmn. Marine Midland Bank-N.Y.; dir. Buffalo Forge Co., Niagara Mohawk Power Corp., Utica Mut. Ins. Office: Marine Midland Banks Inc One Marine Midland Center Buffalo NY 14203

DUFFY, JANET CAMERON DILL, publicity exec.; b. Dayton, Ohio, Apr. 10, 1929; d. Malcolm Howard and Janet (Jordan) Dill; B.A. cum laude, Vassar Coll., 1950; postgrad. (Fulbright scholar) Ecole d'Etudes Politiques, U. Bordeaux (France), 1951-52; postgrad. Johns Hopkins, 1950, Columbia, 1955, N.Y. U., 1959; M.A. in Teaching, U. N.H., 1973; m. Daniel J. Duffy, July 4, 1952 (div. June 1969); children—David Cameron, Robin MacKenzie, Jonathan Reilly, Anne Jordan. Asst. to supt. schs. Baltimore County, 1948-49; asst. to chmn. com. on reading devel. Am. Book Pubs. Council, 1950-51; head women's fund-raising div. N.Y. Legal Aid Soc., 1952-53; exec. sec. to pres. Fgn. Policy Assn., 1958-59; asst. to editor-in-chief Carnegie Endowment for Internat. Peace, N.Y.C., 1959-62; free-lance editor, translator books on internat. affairs Carnegie Endowment, Yale, Columbia presses, 1962-67; tchr. dept. history and current affairs Brearley Sch., N.Y.C., 1965-72; free-lance writer, editor, 1972—; asst. publicity dir. N.H. Pub. TV, Durham, 1974-76, pub. info. dir., 1976—. Mem. Jr. League City N.Y.; mem. exec. com. Am. Friends Service Com. N.Y. Region, 1971-72. Mem. Soc. of Friends. Home: 368 Washington St Dover NH 03820

DUFFY, JOHN LESTER, pathologist; b. Huntington, N.Y., Jan. 26, 1927; s. Lester Maurice and Mildred (Aitken) D.; A.B., Columbia, 1948; M.D., N.Y. Med. Coll., 1952; m. Katherine Dann Smyth, June 21, 1952; children—Mary, Sarah, John. Intern, Nassau County Med. Center (formerly Meadowbrook Hosp.), East Meadow, N.Y., 1952-53, resident, 1953-58, asso. dir. med. tech. program, asso. chmn. dept. pathology and labs.; practice medicine specializing in pathology, East Meadow, 1959—; asst. clin. prof. pathology N.Y. Med. Coll., 1966-70, clin. asso. prof. pathology, 1970-71; asso. prof. pathology State U. N.Y. at Stony Brook, 1971—. Served from 1st lt. to capt. AUS, 1955-57. Diplomate Nat. Bd. Med. Examiners, Am. Bd. Pathology. Fellow Am. Soc. Clin. Pathologists, Nassau Acad. Medicine; mem. AMA, N.Y. State, Nassau County med. socs., N.Y. State Assn. Pub. Health Labs., Assn. Am. Med. Colls., N.Y. Acad. Scis. Office: Nassau County Med Center East Meadow NY 11554

DUFFY, KEVIN THOMAS, fed. judge; b. N.Y.C., Jan. 10, 1933; s. Patrick John and Mary Ellen (McGarrell) D.; A.B., Fordham U., 1954, J.D., 1958; m. Irene J. Krumeich, Nov. 9, 1957; children—Kevin Thomas, Irene Moira, Gavin Edward, Patrick Giles. Law clk. Hon. J. Edward Lumbard, N.Y. Circuit Ct., 1955-58; admitted to N.Y. bar, 1958; asst. chief Criminal div. U.S. Attys. Office, N.Y.C., 1958-61; asso. firm Whitman, Ransom & Coulson, N.Y.C., 1961-66; partner firm Gordon & Gordon, 1966-69; regional adminstr. N.Y. Regional Office, SEC, N.Y.C., 1969-72; judge U.S. Dist. Ct., N.Y.C., 1972—; adj. prof. securities law Bklyn. Law Sch., 1975—. Mem. N.Y. State, Westchester County bar assns., Assn. Bar City N.Y., Fordham Coll. (Achievement award), Fordham U. Law Sch. (trustee 1969-77, v.p. 1977—) alumni assns. Clubs: Friendly Sons St. Patrick, Adventurers. Home: 1436 Roosevelt Ave Pelham Manor NY 10803 Office: US Courthouse Foley Sq New York City NY 10007

DUFFY, THOMAS EDWARD, lawyer; b. Phila., July 24, 1944; s. Edward Brazil and Kathryn Estelle (Solliday) D.; B.A., Lafayette Coll., 1966; J.D., Temple U., 1969. Admitted to Pa. bar, 1969; asst. dist. atty. Montgomery County, Pa., 1971-74; partner firm Duffy, North, Wilson, Thomas & Nicholson, Hatboro, Pa., 1974—. Chmn., Montgomery County Young Rep. Fedn., 1975-77; chaplin Young Reps. of Pa., 1978. Served with U.S. Army, 1970-71. Mem. Montgomery County Bar Assn., Internat., Am., Pa. bar assns., Am. Arbitration Assn., Am., Pa., Montgomery County trial lawyers assns. Republican. Home: 2111 Goodwin Ln North Wales PA 19454 Office: 104 N York Rd Hatboro PA 19040

DUFNER, MARY ELIZABETH, physician, lawyer; b. Phila., July 1, 1921; d. George Francis and Maude (Moore) Dufner; B.S., Temple U., 1943; M.D., Med. Coll. Pa., 1949; J.D., Am. U., 1968. Intern, Aultman Hosp., Canton, Ohio, 1949-50 resident in pathology Akron (Ohio) City Hosp., 1950-52, Phila. Gen. Hosp., 1952-54; practice medicine specializing in pathology, instr. pathology U. Pa. Sch. Medicine, Phila., 1953-54; asso. pathologist Akron City Hosp., 1954-56; asst. pathologist, med. examiner Grasslands Hosp., Valhalla, N.Y., 1957; asso. pathologist Barberton (Ohio) Citizens' Hosp., 1957-59; instr. Akron City Hosp. Sch. Nursing, 1960-62; dir. dept. pathology Harrisburg (Pa.) State Hosp., 1962-65; adj. prof. law and medicine Dickinson Sch. Law, Carlisle, Pa., 1964—; cons. drug regulatory affairs dept., med. research div. Hoffman-La Roche, Inc., 1969-75; med. officer Phila. regional office U.S. Civil Service Commn., 1975—. Chmn. health issues adv. panel HEW Commn. Med. Malpractice, 1973; co-founder, treas., bd. dirs. Windsor Nursing Home, Canton, Ohio, 1960-63; mem. Greater Phila. Vets. and Handicapped Employment Com., Pa. Gov.'s Com. Employment Handicapped. Nat. Endowment Humanities Found. fellow, summer 1974. Diplomate Am. Bd. Pathology. Fellow Coll. Am. Pathology, Am. Soc. Clin. Pathologists, Am. Coll. Legal Medicine, Royal Soc. Health; mem AAAS, Am., World, Pan Am. med. assns., Inst. Soc. Ethics and The Life Scis., Pa., Philadelphia County med. socs., Am. Soc. Law and Medicine, Nat. Health Lawyers' Assn., Fed. Bus. Assn. Phila. Contbr. chpts. Attorney's Textbook of Medicine, 1967-69; feature writer Jour. Legal Medicine, 1973—, also editorial bd. Home: 1008 Spring Garden Rd Box H-240 Ancora Route 2 Hammonton NJ 08037 Office: Ancora Psychiat Hosp Hammonton NJ 08037

DUFOUR, RAYMOND ALBERT, business exec.; b. Haverhill, Mass., Jan. 17, 1907; s. Eli and Elvina (Savignac) DuF.; A.B., Cath. U. Am., 1928; postgrad. Georgetown U., 1928-29; LL.B., Columbus U., 1936; C.L.U., U. Pa. Extension, 1947; J.D., Cath. U. Am., 1972; m. Margaret V. Sheehan, Dec. 26, 1936 (dec. Feb. 1964); children—Margaret E. (Mrs. Paul Macdonald), R. Damian, G. Maurice, Marie Theresa (Mrs. Otto H. Maurer); m. 2d, Kathryn J. Condon, May 13, 1971. Ins. broker, 1930—; pres. Raymond A. DuFour & Co., Inc., gen. ins. agy., Washington, 1954-71, chmn. bd., 1954—, pres., Bethesda, Md., 1957-76; chmn. bd. Integrated Bus. Methods, Inc., Data Processing Center, Washington, 1958—, pres., 1958-68; chmn. bd., pres. DuFour Enterprises, Inc. and divs., 1975—; chmn. bd. Nat. Profl. Group Consultants, Inc., Washington, 1971—; pres. NARCE Services, Inc., Washington, 1957-75, Assn. Group Ins. Adminstrs., Inc., Washington, 1963-75, Naval Acad. Found. Ins. Services, Inc., Bethesda, Md., 1965-75, Compackager Corp., Washington, 1968-75, Maginnis & Assos., Inc., Chgo., 1971-72, vice chmn. bd., 1972-73, chmn. bd., 1973—; chmn. bd. J.B. Johnstone & Assos., Inc., Washington, 1978—; pres. Nat. Union Ins. Co., Washington, 1956—, chmn. bd., 1958—; v.p. Coleman Cadillac Co., Bethesda, 1970-73; v.p. Washington-London Mgmt. Corp., Balt., 1962-75; partner Kenray Assos., Washington, 1968-76; mem. exec. com., dir. Suburban Bancorp., 1972-75; dir. Suburban Trust Co., Hyattsville, Md., 1960-75, exec. com., 1971-75; dir. MIW Advisers, Inc., Bethesda; chmn. exec. com. Variable Annuity Life Ins. Co. Am., Washington, 1963-66. Admitted to Washington bar, 1937, Md. bar, 1952. Mem. Washington Bd. Trade, 1940—, dir., 1949-51; chmn. Econ. Devel. Commn. Montgomery County, Md., 1964-70; chmn. Cardinal's Com. of Laity, 1969; founder Cath. Youth Orgn., 1947, bd. dirs., 1947—, pres., 1951-52; pres. Men of Holy Cross Fgn. Missions, Merrick Boys Camp, 1949-50. Trustee U.S. Naval Acad. Found., Trinity Coll., Washington, 1972-73, Research Found., Doctors Hosp., Washington, Cath. U. Am., Consortium Univs. Washington Met. Area; bd. dirs. United Givers Fund of Nat. Capital Area, Washington. Mem. Bar Assn. D.C., Md. State Bar Assn., Am. Inst. Profl. Assn. Group Ins. Adminstrs. (pres. nat. adv. council 1970-71), Life Ins. Trust Council (founder 1940, pres. 1942-43), D.C. Life Underwriters Assn., Million Dollar Round Table, Nat. Assn. Casualty and Surety Agts., Profl. Ind. Mass-Mktg. Adminstrs., John Carroll Soc., Heroes, Am. Soc. C.L.U.'s, Cath. U. Alumni Assn. (nat. pres. 1951-53). Knight Malta. Clubs: Columbia Country (bd. govs. 1969-72), Congressional Country (Bethesda Md.); University (Washington); Rehoboth Beach Country (Rehoboth, Del.); Pine Tree Golf (Boynton Beach, Fla.); Delray Beach (Fla.); Club International (Chgo.). Home: 16200 Edwards Ferry Rd Poolesville MD 20837 Office: 2135 Wisconsin Ave Washington DC 20007

DUGAS, ROGER ARTHUR, devel. engr.; b. Portsmouth, N.H., June 14, 1949; s. Roger Omer and Rita Mary (Veilleux) D.; B.S. in Mech. Engring., U. N.H., 1972, M.S., 1978; m. Jeneen Sandra Quinlan, July 10, 1971; 1 son, James Eric. Coop. student seawater systems design and nuclear test depts. Portsmouth Naval Shipyard, 1967-70; machine designer Western Electric Co., North Andover, Mass., 1971-76; design devel. engr. Hewlett Packard Co., Waltham, Mass., 1976—; cons. J.R. Banks & Assos., Lee, N.H., 1971-72. Mem. ASME, Tau Beta Pi. Contbr. articles in field to profl. jours. Home: RFD 1 PO Box 140C Chester NH 03036 Office: 175 Wyman St Waltham MA 02154

DUGGAN, DENNIS MICHAEL, editor; b. Detroit, Oct. 12, 1927; s. Michael and Anne D.; B.A., Wayne U., 1951; 1 dau., Nancy Ellen. Reporter, New York Herald Tribune, 1957-60; asst. editor New York Times, 1960-62; New York editor Newsday, 1968—. Mem. The Silurians. Home: 235 W 11th St New York City NY 10014 Office: Room 2201 1500 Broadway New York City NY 10036

DUGGINS, ELIZABETH LAWRENCE, nursing adminstr.; b. Swedesboro, N.J., Nov. 25, 1923; d. Henry Cooper and Greta Sickler (Miller) Lawrence; B.S. in Nursing, Duke U., 1945; M.S. in Nursing, U. Del., 1971; m. Ray Brown Duggins, July 10, 1946; children—Ray Brown, Elizabeth Lawrence. Asst. supr. obstetrics and gynecology Duke Med. Center, Durham, N.C., 1945-46; pvt. duty nurse, Durham, 1946-47; office nurse State College, Pa., 1948-51; head surg. nurse Del. Hosp., Wilmington, 1951-54; instr. Sch. Nursing, 1957-63; inservice edn. coordinator Wilmington Med. Center, 1963-68, staff devel., 1970-71, dir. nursing, 1971—; mem. adv. com. practical nurse program Del. Tech. Community Coll., 1971-78; co-chmn. joint practice com. State of Del.; trustee Nursing Sch. of Wilmington; mem. adv. bd. Del. Cancer Network; bd. dirs. Del. Cancer Soc.; mem. med. adv. bd. Del. March of Dimes; chmn. dirs. of nursing Assn. Del. Hosps. Mem. Am., Del. nurses assns., Am. Soc. Hosp. Nursing Service Adminstrs. of Am. Hosp. Assn., Nat. League Nursing (instl.). Republican. Episcopalian. Office: PO Box 1668 Wilmington DE 19899

DUGUAY, MARTIN ROBERT, psychiatrist, educator; b. Montreal, Que., Can., Dec. 12, 1934; s. Joseph Gerard and Blanche (Rioux) D.; B.A., U. Paris, 1953; M.D., U. Montreal, 1959; m. Marie Saucier, June 11, 1959; children—Marie-Helene, Etienne, Jean-Christophe, Angelique, Jeanne. Intern, l'Hotel-Dieu, Montreal, 1959-60, cons. psychiatrist obstetrics-gynecology dept., clin. supr. med. students, residents, mem. staff 1974—; resident in psychiatry Payne Whitney Clinic Cornell U., N.Y.C., 1960-63; resident in child psychiatry la Salpetriere Hosp., Paris, 1963-64, chief of service, coordinator of med. students, 1966-74, pres., 1973; psychiat. expert Que. Workman Compensation Bd.; asst. prof. psychiatry U. Montreal, 1966-73, asso. prof., 1974—; mem. test com. Royal Coll. of Can.; examiner in psychiatry Royal Coll. Physicians, Surgeons of Can. Mem. Que. Psychiat. Assn. (sec. 1967-70), Canadian, Am. psychiat. assns. Clubs: Clubs des Mycologues Amateurs du Que., Pro Musica Soc. (dir.). Contbr. articles to profl. jours. Home: 44 Maplewood Ave Outremont 915 Montreal PQ Canada

DUKE, VIRGINIA BACON (MRS. H. TRISDOM DUKE III), finance co. exec., civic worker; b. Phila., July 6, 1921; d. Harry Rickards and Dorothy Chappelle (Johnston) Bacon; student Germantown Friends Sch., 1938, Stevens Sch., 1938-40, Pa. Sch. Horticulture for Women, 1940-42; m. H. Trisdom Duke III, Jan. 23, 1942; 1 dau. Susan Chappelle. Office mgr. John Hancock Mut. Life Ins. Co., King of Prussia, Pa., 1961—; v.p. and treas. Profl. Fin. Services, Inc., King of Prussia, 1965—. Vice pres. phys. div. Chestnut Hill Community Assn., 1972-74, bd. dirs., 1972—, mem. land use planning com., 1969—, coordinator, 1969-72, mem. traffic and transp. com., 1972—, mem. nominating com., 1975-76; ch. sch. tchr. Presbyn. Ch. of Chestnut Hill, Phila., 1975-76, now editor newsletter; pres. Chestnut Hill Alliance of Insts. for Achievement Human Potential, Wyndmoor; Pa., 1976; v.p. Chestnut Hill Teenagers, 1968, treas., 1968-71, v.p., 1971, mem. bd. dirs., 1965—; bd. dirs. Chestnut Hill Hist. Soc., 1970—, Chestnut Hill Parking Found., 1970-75. Named John Hancock Office Mgr. Year, Collins Agy., 1973; recipient Ann. Award for Community Service, Chestnut Hill Community Assn., 1974. Home: 8616 Evergreen Pl Philadelphia PA 19118 Office: 150 Allendale Rd King of Prussia PA 19406

DUKELOW, OWEN WARNER, clergyman, philosopher, educator; b. Mpls., Dec. 11, 1922; s. John and Ida Jessa (McCullough) D.; student U. Ala., 1943-44, Johns Hopkins, 1944, Cambridge (Eng.) U., 1945; B.A., U. Minn., 1946, M.A., 1953, Ph.D., 1960; B.D., Union Theol. Sem., 1952; m. Harriet Pauline Stafford, Aug. 26, 1951; children—Ruth Harriet, Deborah Ida, Owen Warner. Ordained to ministry Presbyn. Ch., 1951; asso. dir. Westminster Found., U. Minn., Mpls., 1947-49, Columbia, 1949-51; dir. Westminster Found., U. N.D., Grand Forks, 1951-52; boys' work sec. YMCA, Mpls., 1952-53; instr., dir. religious activities S.D. State Coll., Brooking, 1953-56; freshmen adviser U. Minn., Mpls., 1956-62; prof. philosophy Sir George William U., Montreal, Can., 1962-68; prof., head dept. philosophy, Washington Jefferson Coll., Washington, Pa., 1969—; vis. prof. Macalester Coll., St. Paul, Minn., Hamlin U., St. Paul, Westminster Coll., Fulton, Mo., Eisenhower (N.Y.) Coll. Served with inf., AUS, 1943-46. Mem. Am. Philos. Assn., Canadian Philos. Assn., Archeol. Inst. Am. (charter mem. Minn. chpt., charter mem., dir. Montreal chpt.). Club: Fortnightly (past pres.). Contbr. book revs. to Montreal Gazette, 1966-69, Pitts. Press, 1972—; contbr. to Marginal Rev.; contbr. numerous articles and revs. in philosophy and religion to profl. jours. 109 North Ave Washington PA 15301

DUKES, JERRY LOUIS, educator; b. N.Y.C., Aug. 1, 1943; s. Otto and Elsa (Krumbein) D.; B.A. in Biology, Coll. City N.Y., 1965; M.A. in Biology Edn., N.Y. U., 1967, postgrad., 1968—; m. Linda Schnall, Dec. 18, 1966; children—Philip Laurence, Jeremy Marc. Tchr. biology and microbiology L.D. Brandeis High Sch., N.Y.C., 1966—, also health counselor, 1973—. Microbiologist Roosevelt Hosp., N.Y.C., 1960-77. Pres. Ferris Glen Condominium, Norwalk, Conn., 1970-71; membership chmn. Conn. chpt. Childbirth Assn. Lamaze Method, 1973-75; sch. rep. Jewish Tchrs. Community Chest, 1972—; vol. worker Roosevelt Hosp., 1959-60; mem. ritual com. Temple Shalom, 1975-77. Mem. Am. Soc. Microbiology, Nat. Assn. Biology Tchrs., N.Y. Biology Tchrs. Assn., N.Y. State Registry Med. Technologists, Nat. Sci. Tchrs. Assn., Jewish Tchrs. Assn. (sch. rep.), Am. Sch. Health Assn., Beta Sigma Rho. Jewish (mem. ritual com.). Author: Laboratory Manual in Microbiology for Secondary School students, 1971; co-author: Biology Vocabulary-A Multilingual Approach, 1976. Home: 185 Pell Meadow Fairfield CT 06430 Office: 145 W 84th St New York City NY 10024

DULEEP, KODENDERA SUBBIAH, surgeon; b. Hyderabad, India, Mar. 22, 1934; s. Kodendera Belliappa and Kitty Coravanda (Muthanna) Subbiah; came to U.S., 1971; M.B., Osmania Med. Coll., Hyderabad, India, 1957, B. Chir., 1957; m. Ganga Iychettira Madappa, May 8, 1966, children—Anuradha, Arundathi, Annapurna. Intern Osmania Gen. Hosp., Hyderabad, 1957-58; sr. house officer surgery Chorley Dist. Hosp., Lancashire, Eng., 1960; sr. house officer thoracic surgery City Hosp., Nottingham, Eng., 1961; sr. house officer gen. surgery Kingston Gen. Hosp., Hull, Eng., 1962; registrar in gen. surgery Meml. Hosp., Darlington, Eng., 1962-63; lectr. surgery Christian Med. Coll. and Hosp., Ludhiana, India, 1964-67; practice medicine specializing in surgery, cons. surgery, Hyderabad, India, 1967-69; hon. asst. prof. surgery Gandhi Med. Coll. and Hosp., Hyderabad, 1968; sr. registrar surgery Univ. Hosp. W.I., Jamaica, 1970-71; resident in surgery Norwalk (Conn.) Hosp., 1971-74, mem. staff, 1974—; practice medicine specializing in gen. surgery, Westport and Ridgefield, Conn., 1974—. Diplomate Am. Bd. Surgery. Fellow Royal Coll. Surgeons Edinburgh, Royal Coll. Surgeons Glasgow, A.C.S.; mem. AMA, Conn., Fairfield County (Conn.), Norwalk med. socs. Hindu religion. Home: Brierwood Rd Silvermine Norwalk CT 06850 Office: 125 Kings Hwy N Westport CT 06880

DULEY, WALTER WINSTON, educator; b. Montreal, Que., Can., Oct. 8, 1941; Ph.D., U. London, 1966; D.I.C., Imperial Coll., 1966; B.Eng., McGill U., 1963; m. Irmgardt Zunker, July 3, 1965; children—Nicholas, Mark. Asst. prof. physics York U., Downsview, Ont., Can., 1967-70, asso. prof., 1970-74, prof., 1974—. Pres. Powerlasers Ltd.; cons. on laser applications. Athlone fellow, 1963-66. Fellow Royal Soc. Arts, Royal Astron. Soc.; mem. Internat. Astronom. Union, Am., Canadian astron. socs. Contbr. articles to profl. jours. Office: York U 4700 Keele St Downsview ON M3J 1P3 Canada

DULIN, WILLIAM CARTER, economist, univ. dean; b. Washington, Mar. 15, 1915; s. Edward Milton and Blanche Sothoron (Scott) D.; B.A., Case Western Res. U., 1937; M.B.A., Harvard, 1939;

Ph.D., Am. U., Washington, 1965; m. Phylis Maurine Stuart, Oct. 5, 1940; children—Jacquelyn Scott Dulin Wilson, Patricia Frances, Stuart Milton. Economist, U.S. War Prodn. Bd., Washington, 1941-43, U.S. Dept. Def., Washington, 1946-56; mgmt. cons. Sutherland Co., Peoria, Ill., 1956-58; asst. to chief exec. officer, chmn. bd. Acacia Life Ins. Co., Washington, 1958-68; dir., bus. mgmt. program, Ins. Insts., Sch. Bus. Adminstrn., Am. U., Washington, 1968-74; prof. mgmt., dean grad. bus. pub. adminstrn. Southeastern U., Washington, 1974—; adj. prof. Johns Hopkins, 1970—; dir. Vauxcleuse Devel. Corp., Arlington, Va., Funk, Fletcher & Assos., Balt.; cons. mgmt. orgn., econ. programming; chmn., mem. coll. relations com. Harvard Sch. Bus. Adminstrn., 1961—; mem. Interracial Council Bus. Opportunity, 1965-72. Chmn. suburban com. Nat. Symphony Orch., 1953-60. Served to capt., USAAF, 1943-46. Mem. Acad. Mgmt., Inst. Internal Auditors, AAUP, Corcoran Gallery Art. Republican. Episcopalian. Author economic monographs, 1952-54; contbr. articles to jours. Home: 5612 Grove St Chevy Chase MD 20015 Office: 501 I St SW Washington DC

DULIS, EDWARD JOHN, metals co. exec.; b. Bklyn., Oct. 30, 1919; s. F. and Edith (Swedes) D.; B.S. in Metall. Engring., U. Ala., 1942; M.S., Stevens Inst. Tech., 1950; postgrad. N.Y. U., 1950-52; m. Dorothy Davenport, Sept. 8, 1945; children—Barbara (Mrs. Robert Moody), John, Beverly. Metallurgist, Naval Air Expt. Sta., Phila., 1942-45; research metallurgist, fundamental research lab. U.S. Steel Co., Kearny, N.J., 1945-52, supr. technologist applied research lab., Pitts., 1952-55; with Crucible Steel Co., Pitts., 1955—, pres. Crucible Research Center, Colt Industries, Pitts., 1970—; v.p. Crucible Inc. Fellow Am. Soc. Metals; mem. Am. Inst. Metall. Engrs. (past chmn. Pitts. chpt.), Am. Iron and Steel Inst., (chmn. prodn. subcom.), Am. Soc. Metals. Club: Chartiers Country (Pitts.). Author, patentee in field. Home: 1775 Hastings Hill Rd Pittsburgh PA 15241 Office: Box 88 Pittsburgh PA 15230

DULL, SIDNEY FRANCIS, lumber co. exec.; b. Balt., July 15, 1909; s. Lewis Henry and Janie Sidney (Ballard) D.; B.B.A., Va. Poly. Inst., 1927-31; m. Myrtle Katherine Dix, July 31, 1938; children—Sandra, Robert Sidney. Sales mgr. Sears Roebuck & Co., Newark, 1931-38; sales engr. Penberthy Injector Co., Detroit, 1938-41; v.p. Hardin Chem. Co., Middletown, N.J., 1947-48; pres. Am. Lumber & Supply Co., Middletown, 1948—, Am. Lumber & Bldg. Supply, Atlantic Highlands, N.J., 1964—; br. pres. Jane Roe Inc., Middletown, 1948—; pres. Deepdale Corp., Landholding Corp., Middletown, 1960—, also dir.; dir. N.J. Savs. and Loan, Rumson. Trustee Am. Lumber and Bldg. Supply Profit Sharing Plan, 1954; deacon Baptist Ch., 1953-67. Served to col. USAF, 1941-47. Clubs: Hoo-Hoo (pres. 1973-74), Keylunch, Rootbeer and Checker (Red Bank, N.J.); Navesink Country (Middletown); Beacon Hill Country, Atlantic (Highlands, N.J.); Masons, Shriners, Rotary, Lions (v.p. 1950-53). Home: 52 Woodbine Ave Little Silver NJ 07739 Office: Route 35 Box 447 Middletown NJ 07748

DULLY, FRANK E., lawyer; b. Hartford, Conn., Aug. 27, 1903; s. Joseph F. and Delia A. (Havens) D.; A.B., Holy Cross Coll., 1925, LL.B., Yale Univ., 1928; M.A., Trinity Coll., 1939; m. Monica T. Cooney, June 8, 1931; children—Frank E., Jean (Mrs. John L. Kramer) and Joan (Mrs. Francis F. Graf) (twins), Ann Lalemant (Mrs. William J. Luby), Robert Havens. Admitted to bar 1928; trial counsel Travelers Insurance Co., Hartford, Conn., 1928-68; commr. West Hartford Housing Authority, 1942-48, chmn., 1953-58; chairman Conn. (commr. Uniform State Laws, 1958—, chmn. com. uniform ins. code nat. conf. commrs., 1959-63, chmn. com. amendments uniform acknowledgement act, 1958-69). Chmn., Hartford County Grievance Com., 1969—, chmn., 1971—; mem. pres.'s council Holy Cross Coll., 1968—. Mem. Am. (vice chmn. com. on ins. regulation 1963-73, mem. com. profl. relations 1961-71), Hartford County bar assns., State Bar Assn. Conn. (chmn. com. internat. law 1958-62, chmn. judiciary com. 69), Assn. Conn. Grievance Coms. (chmn. 1974—), Am. Judicature Soc., Yale Law Sch. Assn. (pres. Hartford-Eastern Conn. 1964-65), Internat. Assn. Ins. Counsel, Fedn. Ins. Counsel, Assn. Life Ins. Counsel, Fgn. Policy Assn. Roman Catholic. K.C. (past grand knight. Hartford Council). Elks. Clubs: Univ. Touchdown (v.p.) Hartford, Conn.; Exchange (past dist. gov., past pres.). St. Thomas Men's (past pres.) (West Hartford); Yale (Hartford); World Series (past pres., dir.). Cross and Scroll lectr. on Internat. Relations, Holy Cross Coll., 1941. Author: The Law of Garnishment with Particularity as to the New England States; The Life Insurance Law of Conn. Home: 32 Middlefield Dr West Hartford CT 06107 also Cornfield Point Old Saybrook CT 06475 Office: 80 State St Hartford CT 06103

DUMAINE, MAURICE PHILIPPE, clergyman; b. St. Guillaume d'Upton, Que., Can., July 21, 1916; s. Omer and Emma (Melancon) D.; grad. Theology Scolasticat St. Jean, Cite de Vanier, Ont., Can., 1937-43; Licence Canon Law, Seminaire St. Paul, Ottawa, 1961; Bachillerate Library Sci., Ottawa U., 1965. Ordained priest Roman Catholic Ch.; missionary Haiti, 1943-49, Colombia, S.Am., 1950-56; prof. canon law and moral theology Scolasticat St-Jean, Cite de Vanier, Ottawa, 1956-61; hosp. chaplain Grace Dart Hosp., Montreal, Que., Can., 1963-77; lawyer, defender bond Ch. Tribunal, Montreal, 1965—. Mem. Assn. des Bibliothecaires de Langue Francaise, Assn. des Bibliothecaires profls. du Quebec, Canon Law Soc., Soc. Généalogique Canadienne. Address: 4000 rue Bossuet Montreal PQ H1M 2M2 Canada

DUMBRI, AUSTIN CHARLES, elec. engr.; b. Easton, Pa., Oct. 14, 1947; s. Austin Frank and Helen Ann (Kunigus) D.; A.S. in Elec. Engring., Pa. State U., 1967; B.E.E., Lafayette Coll., 1975; M.E.E., Lehigh U., 1978; m. Sandra Lee Dunlap, Aug. 7, 1971; children—Dori Ann, Charles Austin. Tech. aide materials area Bell Telephone Labs., Allentown, Pa., 1967-70, sr. tech. aide, 1970-76, tech. staff, 1976—. Recipient Easton Area Indsl. Mgmt. Club Merit award, 1965. Mem. Keystone Soc., Phi Beta Kappa, Tau Beta Pi, Eta Kappa Nu, Tau Alpha Pi. Patentee measurement of thickness of hot thin films, forming windows in composite dielectric layers; contbr. papers to sci. pubis. Home: 315 S Watson St Easton PA 18042 Office: 555 Union Blvd Allentown PA 18103

DU MONT, JOHN SANDERSON, mfg. exec.; b. Greenfield, Mass., Oct. 5, 1919; s. Horatio Sanderson and Leila Atkinson (Washburn) duM.; student Deerfield (Mass.) Acad., 1933-35, Salisbury (Conn.) Sch., 1935-37; m. Mary Esther Robinson, June 21, 1941; children—Susanne (Mrs. Curtis Alexander, Jr.), Mary (Mrs. John R. Nelson), Ann Washburn. Prodn. control, asst. prodn. mgr. Millers Falls Co., Greenfield, Mass., 1939-43; v.p., dir. du Mont Corp., Greenfield, 1947-76. Mem. Regional Export Expansion Council, 1969-76. Exec. com. Custer Battlefield Nat. Monument Assn., 1965—; del. N.H. Republican State Conv., 1978, chmn. Rep. town com. Served with inf. AUS, 1943-46. Decorated Bronze Star; knight comdr. Order Saint John of Jerusalem. Hon. fellow Co. Mil. Collectors and Historians; mem. Mass. Arms Collectors (pres., dir. 1951-53). Nat. Rifle Assn. (gun collectors com. 1953-69, 78—), Armor and Arms Club N.Y., SAR, Colonial Wars Soc., SCV, Order Stars and Bars, Soc. War 1812, St. Nicholas Soc., Westerners, Greenfield Library Assn. (pres. 1953-73), Soc. Cin. (pres. N.Y. soc. 1976—, mem. standing com., asst. sec. gen.), Order Founders and Patriots, Soc. Mayflower Descs., SR, Pocumtuck Valley Meml. Assn. (trustee), Mass. Ruffed Grouse Soc. (vice chmn. 1972-76). Club: Wildlife Conservation (trustee). Author: (with John E. Parsons) Firearms in the Custer Battle, 1953; du Mont de Soumagne and Allied Families, 1961; The Custer Battle Guns, 1974; American Engraved Powder Horns, 1978. Contributor articles on antique firearms to Am. Rifleman, Gun Digest, Antiques mag., others. Lectr. on antique firearms. Home: Brimstone Corner Rd Hancock NH 03449

DUMONT, NORMAND EDWARD, librarian; b. Haverhill, Mass., Feb. 9, 1924; s. Edward Louis and Alvinia Marie (Perron) D.; B.A., U. N.H., 1948; M.S., State U. N.Y., 1955. Asst. mgr. J.J. Newberry Co., Woburn, Mass., 1948-51; asst. mgr. Lincoln Stores, Quincy, Mass., 1951-52; raw materials clk. Gen. Ry. Signal Co., Rochester, N.Y., 1952-54; asst. librarian Albany (N.Y.) Med. Coll., 1954-55; adminstrv. asst., br. library head Bklyn. Pub. Library, 1955-65; adminstrv. officer Sinclair Library, U. Hawaii, Honolulu, 1965-68, asso. prof. grad. sch. library studies, 1965-68; asst. dir. Clinton-Essex-Franklin Cos. Library System, Plattsburgh, N.Y., 1968-70; asst. dir. Port Washington (N.Y.) Pub. Library, 1970—. Served with AUS, 1943-44. Mem. ALA, N.Y., Nassau County library assns., Roman Catholic. Club: New York Library (N.Y.C.). Home: 6 Belleview Ave Port Washington NY 11050 Office: 245 Main St Port Washington NY 11050

DUMPER, WILLIAM CLARK, elec. engr.; b. Bklyn., Oct. 28, 1930; s. William Cook and Jessie Edna (Clark) D.; B.E.E., Poly. Inst. Bklyn., 1952, M.E.E., 1953; m. Colleen Green Watts, Feb. 25, 1956; children—William, Lynn, Arlene. Jr. research fellow Bklyn. Poly. Inst., 1952-53; elec. engr. Westinghouse Electric Corp., East Pittsburgh, Pa., 1953-55, Consol. Edison Co., N.Y.C., 1957-71; elec. engr. Gibbs & Hill Inc., N.Y.C., 1971—, chief elec. engr.-nuclear, 1973—. Active Boy Scouts Am., 1965-69. Served with USNR, 1955-57. Mem. IEEE, Power Engring. Soc., Am. Nat. Standards Inst., U.S. Power Squadron (ednl. officer 1975—). Republican. Methodist. Contbg. author Motor Application and Maintenance Handbook, 1969. Home: 19 New Point Pl Amityville NY 11701 Office: 393 7th Ave New York City NY 10001

DUNAIEF, LEAH SALMANSOHN, editor, publisher; b. N.Y.C., Aug. 21, 1940; s. Rudolph and Mollie (Rosenthal) Salmansohn; B.A., Barnard Coll., Columbia U., 1962; m. Feb. 24, 1963; children—Joshua, Daniel, David. With Research Inst. for Medicine and Chemistry, Harvard Med. Sch., Cambridge, Mass., 1962-63; writer, researcher Time-Life Books, Time, Inc., N.Y.C., 1963-67; free-lance writer, 1967-75; co-founder, editor, pub. Village Times, East Setauket, N.Y., 1976—, pres. Village Times, Inc., 1976—. Mem. sub-com. on budget Bd. Edn., Three Village Sch. Dist., Setauket, 1976. Mem. N.Y. Press. Assn. Office: Box 28 185 Route 25A East Setauket NY 11733

DUNBAR, DAVIS TOWNSEND, steel co. exec.; b. Buffalo, Apr. 9, 1918; s. Davis Townsend and Anna (Glenny) D.; B.S., Harvard, 1940; m. Charlotte Shafer, Jan. 14, 1972; children by previous marriage—S. Selden, Peter T., C. Glenny. With Bethlehem Steel Corp. (Pa.), 1940—, asst. v.p. fin., mgr. pension fund, 1967—. Served with USNR, 1943-46. Mem. Am. Bur. Shipping, N.Y. Soc. Security Analysts. Democrat. Episcopalian. Clubs: Saucon Valley Country, Harvard (N.Y.C.). Home: 438 High St Bethlehem PA 18018 Office: Bethlehem Steel Corp Bethlehem PA 18016

DUNBAR, ROBERT EVERETT, writer, editor; b. Quincy, Mass., Nov. 24, 1926; s. Charles Wheeler and Eva Emma (Duquette) D.; B.A. in English, Marietta Coll., 1951; M.S. in Journalism, Northwestern U., 1954; m. Thelma Rose Sally Arseneault, June 26, 1954; children—Yvette Maria, Jesse Robert. Asst. editor publs. Continental Assurance Co., Chgo., 1954-57; dir. pub. relations Jr. Achievement Chgo., 1957-58; editor Selling Sporting Goods, Chgo., 1958-67; dir. communications Am. Soc. Anesthesiologists, Park Ridge, Ill., 1967-70; dir. pub. info. div. Am. Fund for Dental Health, Chgo., 1970-74; partner Dunbar Art and Editorial, Nobleboro, Maine, 1974—; free-lance writer, 1971—; author: Learning to Cope with Arthritis, Rheumatism, and Gout (Beth Fonda Meml. award for Excellence in Med. Feature Writing, Chgo. chpt. Am. Med. Writers Assn.), 1973; A Man's Sexual Health, 1976; Zoology Careers, 1977; Heredity, 1978; Mental Retardation, 1978; adj. asst. prof. sci. communications Univ. Health Scis.-Chgo. Med. Sch., 1974-75. Fellow Am. Med. Writers Assn. (pres. Chgo. chpt. 1970-71, gen. chmn. ann. meeting 1971, co-chmn. edn. com. 1971-75, exec. com., dir. 1971-75, chmn. com. to organize New Eng. chpt. 1975-76, treas. N.E. chpt. 1976-77); mem. Authors Guild, Nat. Assn. Sci. Writers, Sigma Delta Chi. Roman Catholic. Address: Dunbairn E Neck Rd Nobleboro ME 04555

DUNCAN, ARDINELLE BEAN, author; b. Berlin, N.H., Dec. 6, 1913; d. Sylvester James and Mary Ellen (Connors) Bean; student pub. schs., Iroquois Falls, Ont., Can.; m. Robert Leon Duncan, Nov. 23, 1950; children—Carole, Robert Leon, James Bean. Research librarian Abitibi Power and Paper Co., Iroquois Falls, 1930-32; researcher FBI, Washington, 1943-47; editorial staff Television Digest, Washington, 1946-47, Broadcasting-Telecasting Mag., 1947-50; editor Fla. Keys News, Homestead, 1957-58; producer Talk of the Town, Findlay, Ohio, 1969; tchr. creative writing, pub. speaking Catawba Valley Community Coll., Hickory, N.C., 1965-66; guest lectr. in field. Mem. Columbia County (Pa.) Bd. Pub. Assistance, 1972—, sec., 1975; mem. com. one hundred to provide YMCA facility, Bloomsburg, 1976; editor The Record Mental Health Assn. Columbia/Montour counties, 1976-78. Recipient citation for service to mental health, 1977. Mem. Nat. League Am. Penwomen, Bloomsburg State Coll. Woman's Club. Author: Twirly Hurly, the Helicopter Rabbit, 1962. Contbr. articles, stories to ednl. mags., jours. Home: Four Seasons #57 Laconia NH 03246

DUNCAN, CARVILLE DONOVAN, JR., health care adminstr.; b. Balt., Apr. 14, 1942; s. Carville Donovan and Mary Elizabeth (Haywood) D.; B.S.B.A., U. Md., 1965; m. Mary Jennifer Angle, July 28, 1978; children—Kelly Ann, Michael Donovan. Provider relation rep. Md. Blue Cross, Towson, 1970; personnel dir. Dorchester Gen. Hosp., Cambridge, Md., 1970-71; adminstr. House in the Pines-Easton (Md.), 1971—; regional dir. MSC Corp., Towson, 1974—; adviser in long term care Delmarva Found., Easton. Bd. dirs. Talbot County (Md.) YMCA, 1976—; team capt. United Fund of Talbot County, 1976—. Served to capt. Med. Service Corps, USAF, 1966-69. Mem. Am. Coll. Nursing Home Adminstrs. Clubs: Rotary (pres. local club 1977-78), Elks (Easton). Home: Box 66 RD 1 Saint Michaels MD 21663 Office: Route 50 and Dutchmans Ln Easton MD 21601

DUNCAN, ELEANORE KLARI DE BALAGYA DE SZECSANYI, artist; b. Hungary; student Acad. Grande Chaumiere, Paris, Jean Aujaume, Phoenix Sch. Design N.Y. (scholar), Pratt Graphic Center. One person shows Galerie Pierre Charron, S.H.A.P.E., Paris, Galerie Andre Weil, Paris, Salon des Artistes de la Region, Mairie de Mairie Marly-le-Roi, Maitland Art Center (Fla.), 1972, 73, Oklahoma City, 1972, Crespi Gallery, N.Y.C., Cornell Club N.Y., 1975, Nat. Arts Club, N.Y.C., 1978; exhibited in Bremerhaven, Germany, Expo Internati de Monaco, Ecole de France, Paris, Nat. Arts Club, N.Y.C., Artists Equity Assn. N.Y., Irish Pavilion, N.Y.C., Musee de l'art Moderne, Paris, Met. Mus. Art, N.Y.C., Goldsborough Mus.; represented in permanent and pvt. collections. Mem. Nat. Arts Club N.Y.C., Burr Artists, Eleanore Gay lee Found., Artists Equity N.Y., Nat. Soc. Lit. and Arts. Illustrator: Stories of Jesus, Big Big Story Book, and other childrens books 1960-67, also columns of Bishop F.J. Sheen. Address: 342 E 81st St New York NY 10028

DUNCAN, HENRIETTA, career counselor; b. Tuscaloosa, Ala., Aug. 15, 1938; d. Garnett and Frances D.; B.S., Ala. State U., 1960; M.A., Howard U., 1970, postgrad., 1971—. Sec., VA Hosp., Tuskegee, Ala., 1960-62, Area Med. Office, Atlanta, 1962-65, adminstrv. asst. Central Office, Washington, 1965-70; asst. dir., career counselor Career Planning and Placement Services, Howard U., Washington, 1970—; cons. career days, women career seminars, workshops, counselor workshops. Mem. Adv. Neighborhood Council, Woodley Condominium Assn. Recipient job performance award VA, 1968. Mem. Am., Nat. Capital personnel and guidance assns., Am. Coll. Personnel Assn., Nat. Vocat. Guidance Assn., Nat., D.C. assn. non-white concerns in personnel and guidance, Middle Atlantic Placement Assn., Nat., Mid-Atlantic assns. sch., coll. and univ. staffing, Washington Urban League, Howard U. Alumni Club, Ala. State U. Alumni Assn., Delta Sigma Theta, Inc. (Fed. City Alumnae chpt.). Author Howard U. Ednl. Placement Manual, 1971-77. Home: 1851 Columbia Rd NW Washington DC 20009 Office: 2400 6th St NW Washington DC 20059

DUNCAN, MAX CARSON, engring. co. exec.; b. Avondale, N.C., June 17, 1921; s. Amos Carson and May Belle (Goddin) D.; B.S., U.S. Naval Acad., 1941; m. Trilby Gray Hewitt, Dec. 14, 1943; 1 dau., Trilby May. Joined U.S. Navy, 1938, advanced through grades to capt., 1961, ret., 1972; engr. ARINC Research Corp., Annapolis, Md., 1972-73, program mgr., 1973-74, div. mgr., 1974—. Decorated Silver Star, Legion of Merit, Bronze Star. Mem. Am. Assn. Physics Tchrs., Am. Soc. Naval Engrs., Ret. Officers Assn., Am. Def. Preparedness Assn., U.S. Naval Acad. Alumni Assn. Home: 216 Lookout Ln Annapolis MD 21401 Office: 2551 Riva Rd Annapolis MD 21401

DUNCAN, ROBERT CLIFTON, photog. co. exec.; b. Jonesville, Va., Nov. 21, 1923; s. Robley Evans and Selva (Cooney) D.; B.S., U.S. Naval Acad., 1945; B.S., Naval Postgrad. Sch., 1953; S.M., Mass. Inst. Tech., 1954, Sc.D., 1960; m. Rosemary Fleming, Mar. 19, 1949; children—Melissa Duncan Keeney, Babette Duncan Wilson, Robert Clifton, Scott. Commd. ensign USN, 1945, advanced through grades to comdr., 1960, ret., 1965; staff asst. to dir. def. research and engring. Dept. Def., Washington, 1961-64; chief guidance and control div. NASA Manned Spacecraft Center, Houston, 1964-67, asst. dir. Electronics Research Center, Cambridge, Mass., 1967-68; v.p. Polaroid Corp., Cambridge, 1968—; mem. Air Force Sci. Adv. Bd., 1968-69, NASA Research Adv. Com., 1961-68; dir. Charles Stark Draper Lab., Inc. Dist. chmn. Boy Scouts Am., 1969-72. Trustee Forsyth Dental Center, Boston; mem. indsl. and profl. adv. council Pa. State U., 1973-78; corporator Boston Mus. Sci.; pres. Polaroid Found. Decorated Legion of Merit; recipient Norman P. Hays award Inst. Nav., 1967; Exceptional Service medal NASA; Silver Beaver award Boy Scouts Am. Congregationalist. Author: Dynamics of Atmospheric Entry, 1962. Contbr. chpts. to books, articles to profl. pubis. Home: 165 Cherry Brook Rd Weston MA 02193 Office: 565 Technology Sq Cambridge MA 02139

DUNCAN, STANLEY FORBES, hosp. admnstr.; b. Oakland, Calif., Aug. 22, 1944; s. Sheldon Forbes and Dorla May (Powell) D.; B.A., Lake Forest Coll., 1966; M.B.A., U. Chgo., 1968; m. Ethel Marie Bachich, Sept. 12, 1970; children—Robert Forbes, Frank Andrew. Asst. to exec. v.p. Bklyn-Cumberland Med. Ctr., Bklyn., 1968; asst. admnstr. S. Ocean County Hosp., Manahawkin, N.J., 1972-76; asst. admstr. House of Good Samaritan, Watertown, N.Y., 1976-78, exec. dir., 1978—; preceptor Ithaca (N.Y.) Coll., 1976—, St. Lawrence U., Canton, N.Y., 1977. Bd. dirs. Am. Cancer Soc., Jefferson County, 1977—. Served to capt., M.C., U.S. Army, 1968-71. Decorated Army Commendation medal. Mem. Am. Coll. Hosp. Adminstrs. (dir. 1979), Central N.Y. Hosp. Assn., Am. Mgmt. Assn., Hosp. Fin. Mgmt. Assn. Presbyterian. Club: Rotary. Home: 6594 Birch Ln Watertown NY 13601 Office: 830 Washington St Watertown NY 13601

DUNCKEL, ARTHUR ERVIN, utilities adminstr.; b. Manheim, N.Y., June 23, 1939; s. Harvey and Elizabeth (Levi) D.; A.S., Herkimer County (N.Y.) Community Coll., 1976; m. Genevieve Ann Treen, Sept. 9, 1960; children—Jeannine Ruth, Arthur Erivn. With General Electric Co., Utica, N.Y., 1957-71; with firm William Tiel, Engr., Ilion, N.Y., 1971-76; apprentice engring. dept., Village of Ilion, 1971-73, chmn. recycle com., 1972; adminstr. Herkimer County Sewer Dist., Herkimer, N.Y., 1973; mem. water quality problems com. Herkimer and Oneida counties. Mem. adminstrv. bd. Ilion Meth. Ch. Served with U.S. Army, 1963-65. Mem. N.Y. State Conservation Council, N.Y. State Water Pollution Control Fedn., Nat. Audubon Soc., Nat. Wildlife Assn. Republican. Methodist. Club: Masons. Home: 14 S 3d St Ilion NY 13357 Office: Herkimer County Sewer Dist Herkimer NY 13350

DUNFORD, DAVID MARSHALL, ins. co. exec.; b. Providence, Jan. 26, 1949; s. Howard Lee and Jeanne (Thayer) D.; A.B., Princeton U., 1970; M.B.A. (Taggart fellow), N.Y. U., 1972; m. Robin Heather Schulz, June 17, 1972. Fin. analyst Travelers Corp., Hartford, Conn., 1972-75, sr. fin. analyst, 1975-77, asst. investment officer, 1977—. Mem. Simsbury (Conn.) Republican Town Com., 1976. Mem. Am. Fin. Assn., Hartford Soc. Fin. Analysts. Episcopalian. Home: 22 Long View Dr Simsbury CT 06070 Office: 1 Tower Sq Hartford CT 06115

DUNGAN, VICKI LOU, employee benefits cons.; b. Artesia, N.Mex., Mar. 2, 1951; d. Clyde B. and Marinell (Coggin) D.; B.S.Ed. (scholar), Baylor U., 1973; m. Wilson R. Abney, Mar. 12, 1977. Dir. pub. relations Baylor U. Student Found., Tex., 1971-73; asst. dir. Assn. Pvt. Pension and Welfare Plans, Washington, 1973-76; v.p. Schanes Assos., Washington, 1976—; asst. dir. Soc. Prof. Benefit Adminstrs. and Nat. Employee Benefits Inst., 1977—; instr. Certificate Program in Employee Benefit Plan Adminstrn., Georgetown U., Washington, 1979—. Mem. Assn. Pvt. Pension and Welfare Plans (nat. health ins. com., small plans com.), Internat. Found. Employee Benefit Plans, Zeta Phi Eta. Democrat. Baptist. Contbg. editor for legis. Pension World mag., 1978. Home: 737 Tenth St SE Washington DC 20003 Office: 451 New Jersey Ave SE Washington DC 20003

DUNHAM, CHRISTOPHER COOPER, lawyer; b. N.Y.C., Jan. 29, 1937; s. Robert Secrest and Elizabeth Walls (Cooper) D.; B.A., Wesleyan U., 1958; J.D., Columbia, 1961; m. Marjorie Jean Corliss, June 14, 1958; children—Douglas Webber, William Sigler, Anne Corliss. Admitted to N.Y. bar, 1961; practiced in N.Y.C., 1961—; asso. firm Cooper, Dunham, Dearborn and Henninger, 1961-68; mem. firm Cooper, Dunham, Clark, Griffin & Moran, 1968—. Chmn. Westport (Conn.) Democratic Town Com., 1965-66, 67-70; mem. Conn. Dem. State Central Com., 1978—; del. Conn. Dem. State Conv., 1966, 68, 74, 78; alternate Westport Planning and Zoning Commn., 1965; mem. Westport Bd. Finance, 1975, Conn. Safety Commn., 1977—. Mem. N.Y. Patent Law Assn., Phi Beta Kappa, Gamma Psi. Democrat. Conglist. Home: 277 Compo Rd S Westport CT 06880 Office: 30 Rockefeller Plaza New York City NY 10020

DUNHAM, ROBERT SECREST, lawyer; b. N.Y.C., Nov. 15, 1906; s. Sturges Sigler and Stella (Warren) Secrest D.; A.B., Wesleyan U., 1927; LL.B., Columbia, 1930; m. Elizabeth Walls Cooper, June 15, 1934; children—Christopher Cooper, Sally Secrest, Nancy Nicholas. Admitted to N.Y. State bar, 1931, since practiced in N.Y.C.; asso. firm Cooper, Kerr & Dunham, 1930-42, partner, 1942-47, successor firms, 1947-72, Cooper, Dunham, Clark, Griffin & Moran, 1972-73, of counsel, 1973—. Chmn. bd. edn., Westport, Conn., 1955-61; mem. Westport Planning and Zoning Commn., 1963; treas. Westport Community Council 1965-73. Served from lt. to lt. comdr., USNR, 1943-46. Mem. Assn. Bar City N.Y. (chmn. patents com.). Am. Bar Assn., N.Y. Patent Law Assn. (gov. 1968-71), History Sci. Soc., SR, Phi Beta Kappa, Psi Upsilon, Phi Delta Phi. Republican. Conglist. Home: Longview Ln Westport CT 06880 Office: 30 Rockefeller Plaza New York City NY 10020

DUNHILL, HUGO, mailing list co. exec.; b. Los Angeles, May 28, 1932; s. Herbert and Irma (Meyer) Odza; student Adelphi Coll., 1954; m. Priscilla Dunhill, Nov. 9, 1963; children—Adam, Gita, Chris, Liza. Pres., Dunhill Internat. List Co., N.Y.C., 1959-75, Hugo Dunhill Mailing List Co., N.Y.C., 1976—. Served with USCGR, 1956-58. Trustee West Side Montessori Sch. Mem. Nature Conservancy. Democrat. Club: Sheldrake Yacht. Home: 126 W 78th St New York City NY 10024 Office: 630 3d Ave New York City NY 10017

DUNK, RICHARD HARVEY, environ. engr., meteorologist; b. Swedesboro, N.J., Oct. 28, 1944; s. Erwin Samuel and Frances Anna (McKeag) D.; B.A., Glassboro State Coll., 1967; B.S., Rutgers U., 1972, M.S., 1976; m. Beryl Edna Hill, June 24, 1967; children—Richard Scott (Ricky), Rebeka Beryl. Sci. tchr. East Brunswick pub. schs., 1967-68; tech. asst. Research Cottrell Inc., Bound Brook, N.J., 1972-73; grad. asst. meteorology Rutgers U., New Brunswick, N.J., 1973-74; environ. engr. U.S. Metals Refining Co. div. Amax Inc., Carteret, N.J., 1974—, resident meteorologist, 1977—; cons. in field. Active Boy Scouts Am. Served with U.S. Army, 1968-71. Decorated Bronze Star. Mem. Am. Meteorol. Soc., Air Pollution Control Assn., ASTM, Rutgers Alumni Assn., Ducks Unltd., Chi Epsilon Pi. Methodist. Home: 180 Ward Pl Piscataway NJ 08854 Office: 400 Middlesex Ave Carteret NJ 07008

DUNKEL, LAWRENCE, cons. psychologist; b. Paterson, N.J., Apr. 26, 1926; s. Abraham D.; B.A. in Psychology, N.Y. U., N.Y.C., 1948, M.A. in S. Psychology, 1950, Ph.D. in Clin. Psychology, 1967; m. Millicent Dunkel; children—Allan, Stuart, Eloise, Hayley. Cons. psychology N.J. Rehab. Commn., 1960—; dir. spl. services Pompton Lakes (N.J.) Schs., 1967-77; profl. services dir. Family Counselling Assos., Kinnelon, N.J., 1977—. chief psychologists Nat. Inst. Rehab. Engring., Pompton Lakes, 1967—; cons. psychologist North Jersey Mental Health Asso. Oakland, N.J., 1972—. Licensed Marriage and family counselor. Mem. Passaic County Sch. Psychologists Asso. Twin Rivers Spl. Edn. Council (pres.). Inventor field expands eyeglasses, providing 180 degree vision for people with tunnel vision. Licensed psychologist, N.J. Home: 423 Ellis Pl Wyckott NJ 07481 Office: 2 Kiel Ave Kinnelon NJ 07481

DUNLAP, CHARLES JOSEPH, JR., fountain mfg. co. exec.; b. Pitts., June 2, 1925; s. Charles Joseph and Mary Elizabeth (Morrow) D.; student Lynchburg Coll., 1942-43; B.Engring., B.B.A., U. Pitts., 1951; m. J. Patricia Moss, June 14, 1952; children—Jeffrey H., Gregory C. Sales engr. Williams & Co., Inc., Pitts., 1947-51; sales engr., mgr. Crucible Steel Co., Pitts., 1951-59, Cin., 1959-67; pres. Houle Fountain Co., Inc., Pitts., Pa., 1967—. Pres., Falkirk Assos., Inc., Pitts., 1973—. Pres., Pitts. Opera Guild, 1959-61; mem. Nat. Security Council, 1970—. Served with USAAF, 1943-46. Republican. Episcopalian. Mason. Design, engr. water display fountains John F. Kennedy Center for Performing Arts, Washington, 1971, Nat. Geog. Soc., Washington, 1969. Patentee centrifugal pump. Home: 115 Sandhurst Rd Pittsburgh PA 15241 Office: PO Box 12597 Pittsburgh PA 15241

DUNLAP, ESTELLE CECILIA DIGGS (MRS. LEE A. DUNLAP), educator; b. Washington, Sept. 26, 1912; d. John F. and Mary F. (Chasley) Diggs; B.S., D.C. Tchrs. Coll., 1937; M.S., Howard U., 1940; m. Lee A. Dunlap, May 16, 1941; children—Gladys C. (Mrs. Kimbrough), Dolly A. (Mrs. Sparkman). Tchr. math. Garnet-Patterson Jr. High Sch., Washington, 1941-56, head dept. math., 1950-56; tchr. math., sci. MacFarland Jr. High Sch., Washington, 1956-72. Vis. instr. math. D.C. Tchrs. Coll., 1963—. Mem. N.W. Boundary Civic Assn., Washington, 1954—, rec. sec., 1964-66. NSF fellow, 1959. Fellow Intercontintental Biog. Assn.; mem. A.A.A.S., Nat. Edn. Council, Nat. Council Tchrs. Math. Nat. Aviation Edn. Council, Internat. Platform Assn., Washington Performing Arts Soc., Soc. Indsl. and Applied Math., Am. Ordnance Assn., Am. Math. Soc., Math. Assn. Am., Washington Urban League, Washington Opera Soc., UN Assn., Met. Opera Guild, Smithsonian Assos., Fgn. Policy Research Inst., Assos. Nat. Archives, Nat. Ret. Tchrs. Assn., Nat. Trust for Historic Preservation, Nat. Symphony Orch. Assn., Arena Stage Assn., U.S. Olympic Soc., AAUW, Internat. Inst. Community Service. Republican. Clubs: U.S. Senatorial (founding); Stardusters' V.I.P. (Waldorf, Md.). Home: 719 Shepherd St NW Washington DC 20011

DUNLEA, THOMAS ANTHONY, educator; b. Somerville, Mass., July 20, 1917; s. Daniel and Mary (Cotter) D.; A.B. magna cum laude, Tufts Coll., 1939; M.A., Harvard U., 1940; Ph.D., U. Chgo., 1953. Instr. history Loyola U., Chgo., 1946-48, U. Notre Dame (Ind.), 1948-50; asso. prof. Tougaloo Coll., Jackson, Miss., 1953-54; prof. history State Coll., Boston, from 1956, now ret. Served with CIC, AUS, 1942-45; PTO. Decorated Bronze Stars. Mem. Am. Hist. Assn., AAUP. Roman Catholic. Research in history of agrl. edn., role of biography in history, sociol. problems. Address: 74 Chandler Dr Marshfield MA 02050

DUNLEAVY, FRANCIS J., communications co. exec.; b. 1914; B.B.A., Niagara U.; student Wharton Sch. Bus., U. Pa.; married; 4 children. Formerly with Crown Cork & Seal Co., Yale & Towne Mfg. Co., Communications and Control div. RCA; exec. asst. to pres. ITT, N.Y.C., 1962-63; exec. v.p. ITT Europe, Inc., 1963-64, pres., 1965-67; v.p. ITT, N.Y.C., 1964-66, exec. v.p., from 1966, dir., 1967—, mem. Office of Pres., 1968—, pres., chief operating officer, mem. exec. com., 1974-77, vice chmn. bd., vice chmn. exec. com., 1977—. Trustee, Niagara U., LaSalle Coll.; bd. mgrs. Germantown Hosp., Phila.; mem. nat. bds. Morality in Media, Goodwill Industries, United Negro Coll. Fund. Decorated officer Order of Crown (Belgium). Club: Econ. of N.Y. (chmn.). Office: ITT World Hdqrs 320 Park Ave New York NY 10022

DUNMIRE, LESTER ADDISON, physician; b. Duquesne, Pa., Aug. 7, 1925; s. Glenn DeWitt and Bessie Blanche (Botkin) D.; B.S., U. Pitts., 1946, M.D., 1948; m. Enid Jane Mitchell, Sept. 17, 1949; children—Lester Addison, Susan M. Intern, Western Pa. Hosp., Pitts., 1948-49; resident VA Hosp., Aspinwall, Pa., 1949-51, 53-54; practice surgery, Pitts., 1954—; sr. staff div. surgery Western Pa. Hosp., pres. staff, 1972-75. Served in U.S. Army, 1944, 51-53. Diplomate Am. Bd. Surgery. Fellow A.C.S.; mem. Pitts. Acad. Medicine (pres. 1970), County (sec. 1970-73), Pitts. (sec. 1973-75) surg. socs., AMA, Pa., Allegheny County med. socs., Pitts. Athletic Assn. Republican. Presbyterian. Club: Pitts. Athletic. Home: 5903 Fifth Ave Apt 309 Pittsburgh PA 15232 Office: 4815 Liberty Ave Pittsburgh PA 15224

DUNN, BARBARA JANE BAXTER, ins. co. exec.; b. Danbury, Conn., Oct. 24, 1926; d. William Charles and Dorthea (Oestmann) Baxter; B.A., U. Conn., 1948; children—Joanne, Kimberly, James Scott. Tchr. schs., Manchester, Conn., East Hartford, Conn., 1952-58; mem. Charter Revision Commn., E. Hartford 1961, mem. Town Council, 1963-67, mem. Personnel Bd., 1966-67; mem. Conn. Ho. of Reps., 1967-71; commr. Conn. Dept. Consumer Protection, 1971-75; v.p. sales and consumer relations Pepsi-Cola of Hartford, Springfield and New Haven, 1975-76; dir. Women in Bus. and Consumer Affairs, SBA, Washington, 1976-78; mgr. women and minority devel. Aetna Life and Casualty Ins. Co., Hartford, 1978—. Mem. com. to study necessity and feasibility of met. govt. in State of Conn., 1965-67; chmn. Nat. Health Services Industry Com., 1971-73; adv. bd. U.S. Dept. Agr., 1973-75, U.S. Consumer Product Safety Commn., 1974-75. Mem. Gov.'s Cabinet, State Adv. Council on Aging, State Drug Adv. Council, Conn. Comprehensive Health Planning Council, Exec. Com. on Human Rights and Opportunities, Conn. Joint Council on Econ. Edn., Conn. Commn. Boxing. Sec., East Hartford Family Service Soc., 1960; commr. Greater Hartford Emergency Food Bank, 1976-77; v.p. Foursquare, Inc., Newington, Conn., 1976—; vice chmn. sports adv. council Hartford Civic Center, 1978—. Mem. East Hartford Republican Party Town Com., 1952-71, sec., 1955, treas., 1958; trustee Ednl. TV Channel 24. Recipient Distinguished Alumni award U. Conn., 1976. Mem. Assn. Food and Drug Ofcls. U.S., Internat. Narcotics Enforcement Officers Assn., East Hartford League Women Voters (dir. 1961), U. Conn. Alumni Council (sec. 1965-72, dir. 1972—), Hartford Panhellenic Assn. (past pres.), Greater Hartford C. of C. (aviation com. 1975-77), Knights of Grip of Western Mass., Delta Zeta. Episcopalian. Home: 1203 Silver Ln East Hartford CT 06118 Office: 151 Farmington Ave Hartford CT 06156

DUNN, CHARLES THOMAS, banker; b. Phila., Apr. 9, 1930; s. Charles A. and Helen (Courts) D.; B.S., St. Joseph Coll., Phila., 1951; M.B.A., U. Pa., 1955; m. Barbara Helen Long, Sept. 4, 1954; children—Kathleen, Patricia, Charles, Barbara Ann, Rosemary, Carolyn Marie. With Fed. Res. Tng. Program, 1953-55; with Heritage Bank N.A., Cherry Hill, N.J., 1955—, sr. v.p. new bus. dept., 1969—. Mem. Camden County Econ. Devel. Commn., So. N.J. Devel. Council, Del. Valley Council; mem. Camden County council Boy Scouts Am. Trustee United Fund. Served with USMCR, 1951-53. Mem. South Jersey C. of C. (Man of Year award 1957). Rotarian. Club: Tavistock Country. Home: 127 Dumas Rd Cherry Hill NJ 08003 Office: POB 470 Route 70 and Cuthbert Rd Cherry Hill NJ 08002

DUNN, DONALD RICHARD, ordnance research co. exec.; b. Cleve., June 19, 1935; s. Arch and Hortense (Reidenbach) D.; B.S., U.S. Naval Acad., 1959; m. Beverly Joan LeBreton, June 4, 1959; children—Eric Scott, Craig Breton. Commd. ensign USN, 1959, advanced through grades to lt., 1961; stationed on destroyers in Pacific, 1959-61, S.Pole, 1963, Washington, 1964-67; ret., 1967; tech. mgr. CIA, Washington, 1967-70; program mgr. Value Engring. Co., Alexandria, Va., 1970-71; owner H.P. White Lab., Inc., Bel Air, Md., 1971—. Home: Iroquois Rd North East Harbor MD 21901 Office: PO Box 331 Bel Air MD 21014

DUNN, FRANK WILLIAM, metals testing co. exec.; b. Sommerville, Mass., Apr. 13, 1923; s. Frank Stephan and Edith Agnes (Brett) D.; student Bentley Sch. Accounting and Fin., 1941; student U.S. naval service schs., 1947-50, clin. lab. sch., 1947-48, radiol. def. sch., 1949, advanced corps sch., 1950; part-time student Mitchell Coll., 1955-65, Norwich Regional Tech. Sch., 1963. Supr. tech. tng. Electric Boat div. Gen. Dynamics Corp., various tech. and indsl. schs., short-term seminars, 1962-66; m. Hazel Marion Comeau, Dec. 1, 1945; children—Robert William, Gary Francis. Enlisted U.S. Navy, 1941, advanced through grades to chief petty officer, 1944; ret., 1961; biochemist Brookhaven Nat. Labs. (N.Y.), 1961-62; supr. tech. tng. Electric Boat div. Gen. Dynamics Corp., Groton, Conn., 1962-66; nondestructive test engr., group leader Pratt & Whitney Aircraft, East Hartford, Conn., 1966-70; lab. mgr. Metals Testing Co. subs. Walter Kidde, S. Windsor, Conn., 1970-71, gen. mgr., 1971-72, v.p., gen. mgr., 1972-75, pres., 1976-78; sr. quality assurance engr. Stone & Webster Engring. Corp., Boston, 1978—; cons. in field. Decorated 9 Bronze Stars; registered profl. engr., Calif. Fellow Am. Soc. Nondestructive Testing (chmn. Conn. Valley sect.); mem. Health Physics Soc., Am. Technologists Soc., Am. Soc. Quality Control, Am. Soc. Tng. Dirs., Am. Soc. Metals, ASTM. Roman Catholic. Club: Portland (Conn.) Golf. Contbr. articles in field to tech. jours. Home: 11 Winthrop Rd Hingham MA 02043 Office: 245 Summer St Boston MA 02107

DUNN, HENRY THOMAS, lawyer, ins. co. exec.; b. Scranton, Pa., June 12, 1926; s. Anthony J. and Josephine A. (Green) D.; B.A., U. Scranton, 1946; J.D., Temple U., 1948; m. Geraldine A. Lane, Sept. 11, 1951; children—Thomas, Diane. Admitted to Pa. bar, 1948; asso. firm Mauch & Goodman, Bethlehem, Pa., 1948-51; regional mgr. All State Ins. Co., Pitts., 1951-59; v.p. Am. Casualty Ins. Co., Reading, Pa., 1959-62; gen. counsel Prudential-Skandia Co., N.Y.C., 1962-66; pres. Monticello Fin. Co., Holmdel, N.J., 1972—, Monticello Coverage Co., Holmdel, 1972—; pres. Ind. Mgmt. Services, N.Y.C., 1976—; gen. rep. Odyssey Trading Co., Grand Bahamas, 1977—; dir. Underwriters Investment Co. Pres. Red Bank Swim Aux., Holmdel, 1975—. Mem. Fedn. Ins. Counsel, Pitts. Inst. Legal Medicine. Roman Catholic. Clubs: Brant Beach Yacht, Drug and Chem. N.Y., Casualty and Surety N.Y., Ocean Acres. Home: 24 Huntley Rd Holmdel NJ 07733 Office: Suite 605 41 E 42d St New York City NY 10017

DUNN, JAMES JOSEPH, mag. pub.; b. N.Y.C., July 22, 1920; s. James A. and Mary A. (Kelly) D.; B.B.A., Manhattan Coll., 1941; m. Elinor M. Hargesheimer, Aug. 30, 1943; children—Patricia Ann, Kevin James, Gregory John, Sean David, Christopher Kelly. With McCall Corp., 1946-50; with Time, Inc., 1950-66, advt. dir., N.Y.C., 1961-66; pub. Forbes, Inc., 1966—. Served to lt. comdr. USNR, 1941-46. Home: Glenville Rd Greenwich CT 06830 Office: 60 Fifth Ave New York City NY 10011

DUNN, JOHANNA READ, financial communications specialist; b. N.Y.C., Mar. 7, 1946; d. Joseph M. and Anna H. (Judge) Hahnen; B.A. summa cum laude, Barnard Coll., 1965; M.A. summa cum laude, Columbia U., 1967, Ph.D. cum laude, 1970; postgrad. Sorbonne U., Paris, 1969-70; m. G. Leslie Fabian, Feb. 12, 1977; 1 stepdau., Barbara. Editor, McKinsey & Co., Inc., N.Y.C., 1967; mng. editor European Bus., Paris, 1969-70; co-founder, chief bus. editor Tempo Economico, Lisbon, Portugal, 1970-74; chief fin. writer Expresso Lisbon, 1970-74; communications cons. to Citicorp., Norton Simon Inc., Profit Improvement Inc., Council of Americas., Donley Communications Corp., U.S.A., 1975-76; communications specialist N.Y. Stock Exchange, Inc., N.Y.C., 1976-78, exec. asst. to exec. v.p., 1978—; cons. doctoral projects N.Y. State Edn. Dept. Mem. Phi Beta Kappa. Democrat. Author: Counterpoint: A Book of Poetry, 1966; contbr. poems to Anglo-Portuguese News, Lisbon, 1973-75. Home: 1020 Park Ave New York City NY 10028 Office: 11 Wall St New York City NY 10005

DUNN, JOSEPH FRANCIS, ins. co. exec.; b. Cohasset, Mass., Feb. 27, 1924; s. Jesse and Margaret Elizabeth (Flannery) D.; A.B., Syracuse U., 1947; M.A., N.Y. U., 1953; m. Marjorie E. Moore, Dec., 1958; children—Joseph F., Karen. With Prudential Ins. Co. Am., Newark, 1947—, asso. dir. research, 1958-63, dir. planning and research, 1963-74, v.p., 1974—; dir. Prudential Property & Casualty Ins. Co.; cons. Orgn. Dynamics Inc. Lic. psychologist, N.J. Mem. Am. Psychol. Assn., Life Ins. Mktg. Research Assn. (tech. research com.), Agy. Mgmt. Assn. (ins. research dir.'s. group), Am. Coll. Life Underwriters (chartered). Republican. Roman Catholic. Clubs: Mt. Tabor Country. Home: 75 Clearmont Ave Denville NJ 07834 Office: Prudential Ins Co Am Prudential Plaza Newark NJ 07101

DUNN, MARGARET MARY COYNE, journalist; b. Pittsfield, Mass., Sept. 9, 1909; d. Robert Joseph and Margaret Jane (O'Neill) Coyne; student Berkshire Bus. Coll., Pittsfield, Mass., 1928-29; m. John Raymond Dunn, May 29, 1933 (dec.); children—Joyce Dunn Higgins, John Raymond, Joel P. Free-lance contbr. articles to numerous newspapers, including Boston Post, Boston Globe, The Pilot, Beverly Times, Providence Jour., The Tablet, 1937—, to mags. including Better Homes and Garden, Yankee, Conn. Circle, Modern Baby, Family Digest, others; lectr. in field. Mem. Nat. League Am. Pen Women (pres. Boston br. 1968-70, 74-76, rec. sec. 1970-72; nat. charter chmn., 1974-76, Mass. State pres. 1978—; nat. auditor 1978—; co-editor Fifty Year history Boston br.), Boston Authors Club (rec. sec. 1973), Dickens Fellowship (council mem. 1972—), treas. 1977—), Boston Browning Soc. Club: Women's City (heritage com.). Author: (with Barbara B. Reese) Capture of the Johnson Family (hist. pageant for Charlestown, N.H.), 1954. Home: 711 Great Plain Ave Needham MA 02192

DUNN, MARIE EILEEN, educator; b. Hempstead, N.Y., Dec. 8, 1936; d. Timothy Daniel and Mary (Heaney) D.; B.E., Mary Rogers Coll., 1960; A.M., N.Y. U., 1973, Ph.D., 1977. Tchr., St. Bernard's Sch., St. Louis, 1960-61, St. Anthony of Padua, Bronx, N.Y., 1961-64; instr. woodworking, Lima, Peru and Riberalta, Bolivia, 1964-65, Mary Rogers Coll., Ossining, N.Y., 1965-67; tchr. St. Cyril and Methodist Sch., Deer Park, N.Y., 1967, St. Ann's Sch., St. Louis, 1967-68; tchr. educable mentally retarded St. Louis Pub. Schs., 1968-72; tchr. indsl. arts to handicapped N.Y.C. Pub. Schs., 1972-73; tchr. high sch. program for brain injured N.Y.C. Sch. Career Devel., 1973-77; asst. prof. tech. and indsl. edn. Sch. Edn., Health, Nursing and Arts Professions, N.Y. U., N.Y.C., 1977—. Mem. Am., N.Y. State, N.Y.C. indsl. arts assns., Am. Vocat. Assn., Am. Ceramic Soc., Am. Council on Indsl. Arts Tchr. Edn., Phi Delta Kappa, Epsilon Pi Tau (past pres., trustee). Roman Catholic. Home: 23 Waverly Pl New York City NY 10003 Office: 26 Stuyvesant St New York City NY 10003

DUNN, ROBERT FOWLER, educator; b. Mt. Vernon, N.Y., June 22, 1932; s. Elmer Rollins and Helen Louise (Fowler) D.; A.B., UCLA, 1960, Ph.D., 1965; m. Jeanine Anne Robinson, June 11, 1960; 1 son, Michael. Asst. research zoologist, dept. surgery UCLA, 1965-69, asst. prof. surgery, 1969-75, asso. prof. surgery, 1975-76; asso. prof. dept. otolaryngology U. Pitts. Sch. Medicine, 1976—. mem., Jules Stein Eye Inst., 1972-76, U.S. Navy Regional Med. Center, San Diego, 1973—. Served with USN, 1952-56. Mem. So. Calif. Soc. Electron Microscopy (exec. council 1971-73, pres. 1975-76), Electron Microscopy Soc. Am., Am. Assn. Anatomists, Soc. Neurosci., Am. Soc. Cell Biology. Editorial bd. Microstructure, 1971-73. Contbr. to profl. jours. Research on ultrstructure of receptors of inner ear. Home: 365 Backbone Rd Sewickley PA 15143 Office: Dept Otolaryngology U Pittsburgh Sch Medicine Pittsburgh PA 15213

DUNNE, JAMES ROBERT, lab. exec.; b. Cleve., July 8, 1929; s. Carroll Joseph and Wilma Agnes (Sutmore) D.; B.A., Albion Coll., 1951; M.A., State U. N.Y., Albany, 1964, Ph.D., 1972; m. Nancy Anne McSween, Oct. 28, 1952; children—James Robert, Stephen. Sr. publicist Gen. Electric News Bur., Schenectady, 1955-63; pub. info. officer State U. Constrn. Fund, Albany, 1963-68; asst. to chancellor State U. N.Y., Albany, 1968-70, asst. to dir. chancellor's panel on univ. purposes, 1970-71; research dir. Joint Legislative Com. on Higher Edn., N.Y. Legislature, 1971-72; dir. pub. affairs N.Y. State Office Gen. Services, Albany, 1972-74; v.p. mktg. and consumer service N.Y. Higher Edn. Services Corp., Albany, 1974-75; intergovtl. personnel act appointee Office Guaranteed Student Loans, Office Edn., Washington, 1975-76; exec. dir. Cosmetology Accrediting Commn., Washington, 1976-78; dir. govt. relations Wilfred Labs., Inc., N.Y.C., 1978—; lectr. Schenectady County Community Coll., 1969-75. Commr., Capital Dist. Regional Planning Commn., Albany, N.Y., 1969-75. Served with USN, 1952-55. Mem. Am., N.Y. polit. sci. assns. Roman Catholic. Club: Rotary (pres. 1972). Home: 20 Magnolia Dr Fairway Mews Spring Lake Heights NJ 07762 Office: 1700 Broadway New York City NY 10019

DUNNE, MICHAEL CHARLES, fire prevention ofcl.; b. Boston, Nov. 18, 1947; s. Robert Joseph and Mary (Burke) D.; student Northeastern U., 1965-67, Mass. Bay Community Coll., evenings 1970—; m. Dava Miles, Oct. 6, 1978. Firefighter, Sudbury (Mass.) Fire Dept., 1967—; mem. Sudbury Firefighters Assn., 1968—, dir., 1970-71, pres., 1971-75; fire capt. OIC Fire Prevention Bur., 1975—. Pres., Sudbury Fireman's Assn. non-profit social group, 1968-69. Mem. Am. Legion, Mass. Firemen's Assn., Mass. Prevention Assn., Mass. Inst. Fire Dept. Instrs., Internat. Assn. Firefighters, Internat. Assn. Arson Investigators. Democrat. Home: 50 Marlton Dr Marlboro MA 01752 Office: 50 Marlton Dr Marlboro MA 01752

DUNPHY, T.J. DERMOT, corp. exec.; b. Dublin, Ireland, Apr. 15, 1932; s. Phillip Augustine and Marion (Moore) D.; M.A., Oxford U., 1954; M.B.A., Harvard, 1956; m. Joan Steinhardt, July 5, 1974; children—Deirdre Louise, Madeleine Gay, Shannon Beth. Came to U.S., 1954, naturalized, 1962. With air conditioning div. Westinghouse Electric Corp., Staunton, Va., 1956-61, mgr. mktg. services, 1961; pres. Custom-Made Paper Bag Co. and subs., Long Island City, N.Y., 1961-70; pres., chief exec. officer Sealed Air Corp., Saddle Brook, N.J., 1971—, also dir.; dir. Potdevin Machine Co. and subs., Teterboro, N.J., Loctite Corp., Newington, Conn. Mem. Young Pres.'s Orgn. (past chpt. chmn.). Clubs: Harvard; Harvard Bus. Sch. of N.Y.C. (pres.). Home: Layton Rd Far Hills NJ 07931 Office: Park 80 Plaza East Saddle Brook NJ 07662

DUPONG, WILLIAM GREGG, physician; b. Bklyn., Aug. 31, 1911; s. David William and Bertha (Ferris) D.; B.S., Columbia U., 1935; M.D., L.I. Coll., 1939; m. Jessie MacLeman, Feb. 7, 1942. Intern, Norwegian Hosp., Bklyn., 1939-40; resident Swedish Hosp., Bklyn., 1940-41; practice medicine, specializing in occupational medicine and surgery, Bklyn., 1942—; mem. staff Lutheran Med. Center; exam. physician N.Y. Telephone Co., 1943-53, med. dir., L.I., 1953-66, L.I., Upstate N.Y. Telephone, 1966-69, Manhattan, Bklyn., Queens, 1969-75, med. dir. clin. tech., 1975-76; dir. clin. lab. N.Y.C. Dept. Health, 1965-77; cons. Workers' compensation N.Y.C. Law Dept., 1976—; lectr. dept. environ. medicine Coll. Medicine Down-State Med. Center; chmn. indsl. medicine com. Luth. Med. Center; mem. impartial specialist adv. com., mem. rehab. adv. com. N.Y. State Workers' Compensation Bd.; chmn. Council Tb and Health Assns. N.Y. Mem. Park Slope Civic Council, 1958—. Diplomate in occupational medicine Am. Bd. Preventive Medicine; diplomate Am.

Bd. Family Practice; certified instr. cardiopulmonary resuscitation N.Y. Heart Assn. Fellow Am. Coll. Preventive Medicine, Am. Acad. Family Practice, Am. Acad. Compensation Medicine, Indsl. Med. Assn., N.Y. Indsl. Med. Assn., N.Y. Acad. Medicine, Am. Acad. Occupational Medicine, Am. Pub. Health Assn.; mem. N.Y. Pub. Health Assn., Royal Soc. Health, AMA, N.Y. State (sec. sect. occupational medicine 1975; chmn. sect. legal medicine and workers' compensation 1978—), Kings County (chmn. adv. com. on indsl. medicine, chmn. indsl. health com., pub. health com. 1968—, mem. workers' compensation com. 1968-76, chmn. 1976—, peer rev. com. 1971—) med. socs., Am., N.Y. heart assns., Bklyn. Tb and Respiratory Disease Assn. (dir., exec. com., med. adv. com., v.p. 1965-68, pres. 1968-70), Am. Lung Assn. (rep. dir. bd. dirs. 1965—), Assn. Tchrs. Preventive Medicine, N.Y. State Acad. Gen. Practice (indsl. med. adv. com. 1969—), Nat. Council on Alcholism, Am. Acad. Compensation Medicine (gov. 1971—). Methodist. Club: Masons. Contbr. articles to profl. jours. Home: 555 1st St Brooklyn NY 11215

DU PONT, PIERRE S., IV, gov. Del.; b. Wilmington, Del., Jan. 22, 1935; grad. Phillips Exeter (N.H.) Acad., 1952; B.S. in Mech. Engring., Princeton, 1956; LL.B., Harvard, 1963; m. Elise Ravenel Wood, 1957; children—Elise, Pierre, Benjamin, Eleuthere. Admitted to Del. bar, 1964; with photo products dept. E.I. du Pont de Nemours & Co.; mem. Del. Ho. of Reps., 1968-70; mem. 92d-94th Congresses from Del. at large; gov. Del., 1977—. Served with USNR, 1957-60. Office: State Capitol Dover DE 19901

DUPONT, RALPH PAUL, lawyer, educator; b. Fall River, Mass., May 21, 1929; s. Michael William and Gertrude (Murphy) D.; A.B. cum laude, with highest honors in Am. Civilization, Brown U., 1951; J.D. cum laude, Harvard, 1956; children—Ellen O'Neill, Antonia Chafee, William Albert. Admitted to Conn. bar, 1956, U.S. Dist. Ct., 1961, U.S. Ct. appeals, 1967, U.S. Supreme Ct., 1967; asso. firm Davies, Hardy & Schenck, N.Y.C., 1956-57; partner firm Copp and Dupont, New London, Conn., 1957-60; mem. Suisman, Shapiro & Wool, New London, Conn., 1961-63; partner firm Dupont & Dupont and successor firms, New London, Conn., 1963-74; pres. Dupont, Tobin and Williams, P.C., 1974—; instr. Am. history and bus. law Mitchell Coll., New London, 1955, 57-58; vis. prof. Northeastern U. Sch. Law, Boston, 1977-78. Mem. New London Bd. Edn., 1959-61. Mem. Conn. Commn. on Revision of Probate Laws, 1967-69. Democratic candidate for Conn. State Senate, 1960; bd. dirs. Con. Bar Found., 1975—. Served as lt. (j.g.), USNR, 1951-53. Named Outstanding Young Man of Year, Conn. Jr. C. of C., 1960, Distinguished Service award Greater New London Jr. C. of C., 1960. Mem. Am., Conn., New London County bar assns., Assn. Trial Lawyers Am., Delta Sigma Rho, Kappa Sigma. Roman Catholic. Clubs: Spinx of Brown University (Providence). Home: PO Box 58 New London CT 06320 Office: Hartford Nat Bank Bldg US Route 1 New London Shopping Center New London CT 06320

DUPONT, ROBERT LOUIS, JR., physician; b. Toledo, Mar. 25, 1936; s. Robert Louis and Martha Ireton (Lancashire) DuP.; B.A., Emory U., 1958; M.D., Harvard U., 1963; m. Helen Gayden Spink, July 14, 1962; children—Elizabeth, Caroline. Intern, Cleve. Met. Gen. Hosp., 1963-64; resident in psychiatry, teaching fellow Mass. Mental Health Center, Harvard U., Boston, 1964-66; clin. asso. lab. clin. scis. NIH, Bethesda, Md., 1966-68; research psychiatrist and acting asso. dir. community services D.C. Dept. Corrections, 1968-70; adminstr. Narcotics Treatment Adminstrn., Dept. Human Resources, D.C. Govt., 1970-73; dir. White House Spl. Action Office for Drug Abuse Prevention, 1973-75; dir. Nat. Inst. Drug Abuse, HEW, Rockville, Md., 1973-78; pres. Inst. Behavior and Health, Inc., 1978—; health commentator ABC-TV, 1978—; cons. VA, Bur. Drugs of FDA, Spl. Com. on Crime Prevention and Control of Am. Bar Assn., Child Research br. NIH; asso. clin. prof. psychiatry and behavioral scis. George Washington U., 1972—, asst. clin. prof. psychiatry, 1970-72; mem. Coordinating Council on Juvenile Justice and Delinquency Prevention of Dept. Justice, also mem. drug abuse task force Nat. Adv. Commn. on Criminal Justice Standards and Goals; mem. Nat. Adv. Council Drug Abuse Prevention; bd. dirs. Center for Correctional Justice; mem. com. drug abuse Armed Forces Epidemiol. Bd. Bd. dirs. Washington Performing Arts Soc., 1972-76. Served as sr. surgeon USPHS, 1966-68. Recipient Melvin C. Hazen award as Outstanding Young Man in D.C. Govt., 1971-72, meritorious service award D.C. Govt., 1973, Superior Service award USPHS, 1978. Diplomate Am. Bd. Psychiatry and Neurology. Fellow Am. Psychiat. Assn.; mem. D.C. Med. Soc., Washington Psychiat. Soc., Washington Area Council Alcoholism and Drug Abuse, Am. Correctional Assn., Nat. Council Crime and Delinquency, Med. Corrective Assn., Am. Acad. Psychiatry and Law, Am. Pub. Health Assn., Pan Am. Med. Assn. Contbr. articles to profl. jours. Home: 8708 Susanna Ln Chevy Chase MD 20015 Office: 8708 Susanna Ln Chevy Chase MD 20015

DUPORTE, ERNEST MELVILLE, entomologist, educator; b. Nevis, B.W.I., Oct. 24, 1891; s. Daniel Luther and Anna Elizabeth (Hudson) DuP.; B.S.A., McGill U., Montreal, Que., Can., 1913, M.Sc., 1914, Ph.D., 1921; D.Sc. (hon.), Carleton U., Ottawa, Ont., Can., 1963; m. Kathleen Margaret Glen, May 31, 1937. Asst. in biology and bacteriology Macdonald Coll. of McGill U., 1913-15, lectr. entomology, 1915-25, asst. prof., 1925-39, asso. prof., 1939-50, prof., 1950-62, chmn. dept. entomology, 1954-57, prof. emeritus, 1962—. Mem. Inst. Biology London, N.Y. Acad. Sci.; hon. mem. Canadian Soc. Zoologists,Entomol. Soc. Canada, Entomol. Soc. Ont., Entolom. Soc. Que., Que. Soc. Protection of Plants. Author: Manual of Insect Morphology, 1959; contbr. articles to profl. jours. Home: 2A Ste Anne St Ste Anne de Bellevue PQ H9X 1K7 Canada Office: POB 244 Macdonald Coll Ste Anne de Bellevue PQ HOA 1CO Canada

DUPPSTADT, WILLIAM HOMER, farmer, clergyman, botanist, tchr.; b. Buffalo Mills, Pa., May 18, 1919; s. William Oran and Stella (Tomlinson) D.; B.S., Shippensburg State Coll., 1941; M.Ed., Pa. State U., 1960; M.A., W.Va. U., 1967; postgrad. U. Hawaii, 1945-46, Lutheran Theol. Sem., 1946-47, 50-51, U. Pitts., 1957-58, Frostburg State Coll., 1968; m. Esther Irene Ringler, Apr. 20, 1946; children—Joyce Duppstadt Brownfield, Carol Duppstadt Roudabush, Paul L., David A. Minister various Lutheran churches Bedford County (Pa.), 1947—, Mt. Olive Lutheran Church, Fairhope, Pa., 1973—; farmer, Buffalo Mills, 1950—; tchr. sci. Chestnut Ridge High Sch., Fishertown, Pa., 1955-73; herbarium asst. W.Va. U., Morgantown, 1974—, botanist W.Va. Dept. Natural Resources, summers 1977, 78; grad. asst. systemic botany, 1978-79; instr. W. Liberty (W.Va.) State Coll., Spring 1975. Served with U.S. Army, 1942-46; PTO. Mem. NEA, Pa., Chestnut Ridge edn. assns. (pres. local chpt. 1967-69), Nat. Sci. Tchrs. Assn., W.Va., Pa. acads. sci., Am. Soc. Plant Taxonomists, So. Appalachian Bot. Club, Nat. Assn. Biol. Tchrs., Shippensburg Coll., Pa. State U., W.Va U. alumni assns., Phi Delta Kappa, Phi Epsilon Phi. Contbr. articles in to profl. jours. Home: RD 1 Buffalo Mills PA 15534

DUPRE, KATE B., nurse; b. Natick, Mass., Feb. 7, 1944; d. Richard and Grace (Slack) Bigelow; grad. Faulkner Hosp. Sch. Nursing 1966; student in business Massasoit Community Coll. 1968-69; B.S. in Psychology, Bridgewater State Coll. 1978; m. Robert J. Dupre, June 11, 1977; children—Laurie, Janet. Owner, mgr. Jandan Trust Co., Real Estate Co., Middleboro, Mass., 1966; operating room nurse Brockton (Mass.) Hosp., 1966-67; dir. nursing Mildred Alford Nursing Home, Brockton, 1967; head nurse Bridgewater (Mass.) State Hosp. 1967, supr., 1968, acting dir. nursing, 1973, 75, 77; asst. dir. nursing Mass. Dept. Corrections, Boston, 1978—; speaker lectr. in field; pvt. practice counseling, Middleboro, Mass., 1974-75. Recipient scholarships Faulkner Hosp. Sch. Nursing, 1963-64. Mem. Mass. Mental Health Nurses Assn., Am., Mass. nurses assns., Brockton Property Owners Assn., Single Parents of Adoption of Children Everywhere. Author: Faces of Stone, 1972; contbr. numerous unpublished poems. Office: Nursing Office Bridgewater State Hosp Bridgewater MA 02324

DUPREY, EDMOND R., educator; b. Niagara Falls, N.Y., Apr. 17, 1928; A.A.S., Paul Smiths (N.Y.) Coll., 1948; B.S. in Physics and Math., State U. N.Y. at Albany, 1955; M.A. in Edn. Adminstrn., Syracuse (N.Y.) U., 1963; married 2 children. Tchr., Catskill (N.Y.) Central Sch., 1955-56, State U. N.Y. at Morrisville, 1956-58; asst. dist. prin. Onondago Central Schs., Nedrow, N.Y., 1958-64; asst. supt. schs. for bus. East Greenbush (N.Y.) Central Sch. Dist. 1, 1964—. County chmn. ARC, 1965-68. Mem. Am. Assn. Sch. Adminstrs., Am., N.Y. State assns. sch. bus. ofcls. Contbr. articles to ednl. jours. Home: 4 Bellwood Way Castleton NY 12033 Office: Adminstrn Center East Greenbush Central Schs East Greenbush NY 12061

DUPUIS, SYLVIO LOUIS, optometrist, former mayor; b. Manchester, N.H., June 2, 1934; s. Arthur Edward and Alma (Lizotte) D.; student St. Anselm's Coll., 1954; B.S., Ill. Coll. Optometry, 1956, O.D., 1957; D.H.L., Notre Dame Coll., 1975; m. Cecile M. Pellerin, July 14, 1956; children—Jeanne-Marie, Michelle, Marc, Mary. Practice optometry, Manchester, 1957—; mayor Manchester, 1971-75; dir. Manchester Bank. Chmn. state crusade Am. Cancer Soc., 1961-63, bd. dirs.; gen. chmn. United Fund Campaign, 1968-69; v.p. Pine Haven Boys Center, United Community Services Council; mem. N.H. Gov's adv. council Office Econ. Opportunity; mem. Air N.G. Bd. dirs. N.H. Citizens Traffic Safety Com., Spaulding Youth Center, Mid-Merrimac Health Planning Council, NCCJ, Currier Art Gallery, N.H. Performing Arts Center; pres., chief exec. officer Cath. Med. Center, 1975—; adv. bd. Mt. St. Mary Coll., 1976-78; pres. United Health Systems; dir. Manchester Gas Co. Served to lt. Med. Service Corps, USAF, 1957. Named N.H. Optometrist of Year, 1967; recipient Distinguished Service award, 1968; Granite State award U. N.H., 1975; fellowship award NCCJ, 1978. Fellow Am. Acad. Optometry, AAAS; mem. Am. (chmn. com. on pub. information 1967—, trustee, dir. dept. pub. affairs), N.H. (pres. 1969-70) optometric assns., New Eng. Council Optometrists (gen. chmn. 1966, v.p.), Am. Acad. Health Adminstrs. Am. Optometric Found., U.S. Conf. Mayors (human resources com.), N.H. Municipal Assn. (v.p.), Nat. League Cities (com. revenue and finance), Greater Manchester C. of C. (dir.), Beta Sigma Kappa. Club: Exchange (pres. Manchester). Home: 451 Coolidge Ave Manchester NH 03102 Office: 100 McGregor St Manchester NH 03102

DUPUIS, VICTOR LIONEL, educator; b. Chgo., Oct. 30, 1934; s. Edward G. and LaVergne Ann (Brown) D.; B.S., Northwestern U., 1956; M.A., Am. U., 1961; Ph.D., Purdue U., 1965; m. Mary Jean Miles, Aug. 11, 1956; children—Mary Catherine, Victor Edward, Elizabeth Ann. Tchr. jr. high sch., Arlington, Va., 1956-61; tchr. Klondike Sch. Dist., West Lafayette, Ind., 1961-63, curriculum dir., 1962-63; grad. instr. Purdue U., West Lafayette, 1963-65; asst. prof. No. Ill. U., DeKalb, 1965-67; asst. prof. Pa. State U., 1967-70, asso. prof. curriculum, 1970-74, prof. edn., 1974—, also chmn. curriculum and supervision, 1971—; cons. to various pvt. and pub. schs. Chmn. Patton Twp. (Pa.) Park Bd., 1969-70, Patton Twp. Planning Commn., 1971-73; Democratic precinct committeeman, Patton Twp., 1971-76; chmn., twp. supr. Patton Twp., 1973—. Served to 2d lt., inf., U.S. Army, 1957-59. Mem. Am. Ednl. Research Assn., Assn. Supervision and Curriculum Devel., AAUP, Nat. Congress Parents and Tchrs., Phi Delta Kappa. Author: (with others) Introduction to the Foundations of American Education, 1966, Introductory Readings in the Foundations of American Education, 1966, Resource Booklet and Overhead Transparency Masters for the Foundations of American Education, 1966, An Introduction to the Foundations of American Education, 1969, rev. 4th edit., 1979, Foundations of American Education: Readings, 1969, rev. 4th edit., 1979, Resource Booklet: Foundations of American Education, 1970, rev. 4th edit., 1979; also articles in nat., state jours. Home: Rural Route 1 Box 140B Bellefonte PA 16823 Office: Coll Edn Pa State U University Park PA 16802

DUPUY, FRANK RUSSELL, JR., mag. pub.; b. San Antonio, Jan. 30, 1907; s. Frank Russell and Sarah (Tankersley) D.; student Washington and Lee U., 1924-25; m. Nancy Jane McGinley, Oct. 24, 1954; children—Sarah Anne, Frank Russell III. Advt. rep. Los Angeles Examiner, 1930-41; asst. to pub. Good Housekeeping mag., 1946-59; advt. dir. Popular Mechanics, 1960-62; v.p., pub. Cosmopolitan mag., N.Y.C., 1962—. Served with U.S. Army, 1942-46. Home: 45 E 72d St New York City NY 10021 Office: 959 8th Ave New York City NY 10019*

DURAN, HENRY ALFRED, drug co. exec.; b. Guayaquil, Ecuador, Apr. 17, 1917; s. Luis A. and Irma (Salas) D.; brought to U.S., 1924, naturalized, 1943; student Coll. City N.Y., 1935-38; m. Nancy Earl Wilson, July 6, 1951; children—Henry Alfred II, Nina Wilson, Amy Earl. Asst. export mgr. Norwich Pharmacal Co., N.Y.C., 1939-48, pres. Norwich Internat. div. Morton-Norwich Products, Inc., 1963-73; export mgr. Union Pharm. Co., Bloomfield, N.J., 1948-49; field rep. Am. Cyanamid Co., N.Y.C., 1950, Lederle Agrl. div., N.Y.C., 1951-63; now cons. Am. Cyanamid Co., Wayne, N.J. Served with AUS, 1942-46. Home: 60 Oak St Harrington Park NJ 07640 Office: Berdan Ave Wayne NJ 07470

DURAND, EDNA MOTTSHAW, guidance counselor; b. Cranston, R.I., Dec. 11, 1939; d. H. Raymond and Edith H. (Hawkinson) Mottshaw; B.A. in Psychology, Tusculum Coll., 1961; grad. student in guidance and human relations U. Rochester, 1961-62, N.Y. U., 1963-64; M.A. in Student Personnel Service, Montclair State Coll., 1975; dir. student personnel services Seton Hall U. 1977; m. James Harrison Durand, July 27, 1963 (dec. 1974); children—Carolyn Louise, Julia Sara. Admnstr. personnel testing U. Rochester (N.Y.), 1961; asst. program dir. Rochester & Monroe County YWCA, Rochester, 1961-63; teenage program dir. Ridgewood (N.J.) YWCA, 1963-64; substitute tchr. Summit and Chatham Boro, N.J., 1965-75, Chatham Twp., Madison, N.J., 1974-75; dir. Emergency Employment Act for Morris County, N.J., 1974; sales rep. Prudential Ins. Co., Chatham, 1975-76; guidance counselor Hanover Park (N.J.) High Sch., 1976—; v.p. Summit YMCA Girls A Team Parents. Mem. bd. edn. Chatham Boro, 1975-78; chmn. Chatham Boro Bd. Recreation, 1972-74; mem. Newcomers' Bd., pres., co-founder Jr. Women's Club of Chatham, 1965; bd. dirs. LWV, Chatham, 1966-72; mem. Chatham Combined Health Appeal Bd., REACH bd., 1972-74; pres. bd. dirs. Washington Ave. PTO, Chatham, 1973-74, co-v.p., 1972-73, sec., 1971-72, room mother, 1970-71; bd. dirs. Community Ctr. of Chatham, 1972-74. Certified counselor, dir. guidance, N.J. Mem. Tusculum Coll. N.J. Alumni Assn. (v.p. 1977—), Morris County, Am. personnel and guidance assns., N.J. Sch. Bds. Assn., N.J. Edn. Assn., Hanover Pk. Regional Tchrs. Assn., Am. Sch. Counselors Assn. Democrat. Methodist. Clubs: Minisink, Chatham Fish and Game Protection Assn. Home: 115 Chatham St Chatham NJ 07928 Office: Mount Pleasant Ave East Hanover NJ 07936

DURAND, LOUIS MARIUS, mech. engr.; b. Montreal, Que., Can., Nov. 28, 1923; s. Victor and Louise (Salette) D.; B. Applied Scis., Ecole Polytechnique U. Montreal, 1947, Mech. and Elec. Engring., 1947; m. Marielle Desjardins, Sept. 24, 1949; 1 dau., Louise. Engr., supt. tech. div. purchasing dept. City of Montreal, 1947-56; mgr. mktg. Sicard Inc., Ste. Therese, Que., 1956-72; gen. mgr. S.M.I. Industries Ltd., Montreal, 1972—. Mayor, Municipality of Venise-en-Quebec, 1970-76. Mem. Am. Pub. Works Assn., Soc. Automotive Engrs., Corp. Profl. Engrs., Que. C. of C. Home: 3802 de la Peltrie St Montreal PQ H3S 1V3 Canada Office: 2055 Bennett St Montreal PQ H1V 2T3 Canada

DURANT, THOMAS STEPHEN, physician, hosp. adminstr.; b. Jamaica Plain, Mass., July 12, 1928; s. Austin Stephen and Margaret Mary (Faherty) D.; B.S., Boston Coll., 1951; M.D., Georgetown U., 1955; m. Fredericka Theresa Finn, Aug. 23, 1952; children—Stephen, Joseph, Sean. Intern in pathology Boston City Hosp., 1955-56, in medicine, 1956-57, resident in obstetrics and gynecology, 1957-60; practice medicine specializing in obstetrics, Dorchester, Mass., 1960-66; chief pub. health adviser Saigon Prefecture, AID, 1966-68; asst. dir. Mass. Gen. Hosp., 1968—; staff physician N. End Community Health Center, Boston, 1971—; clin. asso. obstetrics and gynecology, Boston U., 1960-66, asst. clin. prof., 1970—; instr. obstetrics and gynecology, Tufts Med. Sch., 1960-66; instr. Harvard Med. Sch., 1969—; cons. U.S. Senate Subcom. on Refugees, 1969. Served with U.S. Army, 1946-48. Diplomate Am. Bd. Obstetrics and Gynecology. Mem. Mass. Hosp. Assn. (chmn. physicians adv. com. 1975—), Mass. Med. Soc., Am. Coll. Obstetricians and Gynecologists, New England Obstetrical Soc., Obstetrical Soc. Boston, Am., Mass. pub. health assns., Mass. Soc. Law and Medicine. Clubs: Beacon Hill Rugby (pres.). Contbr. articles to profl. mags. Home: 28 Melville Ave Dorchester MA 12124

DURANTE, DOMINICK JAMES, systems analyst; b. Passaic, N.J., Aug. 7, 1948; s. Anthony Patrick and Josephine (Sproviero) D.; student Fairleigh Dickinson U., Rutgers U., Bergen Community Coll.; m. Shirley Ruth Friend, Feb. 26, 1972; 1 son, Paul. With M. Grossman & Son, Passaic, 1967-74, data processing mgr., 1973-74; systems analyst Lyle Stuart, Inc., Secaucus, N.J., 1974—. Mem. Wood-Ridge Jaycees (pres. 1978—; named Outstanding New Jaycee 1977, Wood-Ridge Jaycee of Year 1978). Republican. Roman Catholic. Home: 386 Wood-Ridge Ave Wood-Ridge NJ 07075 Office: 120 Enterprise Ave Secaucus NJ 07094

DURDING, WILLIAM WALTER, ret. physicist; b. Balt., Dec. 25, 1911; s. Willis Monroe and Edith (Schaper) D.; A.B., Gettysburg Coll., 1934; Ph.D., Johns Hopkins U., 1946; m. Dorothy Naumann, Sept. 1, 1938; 1 son, Bruce Marshall. Instr. math. Gettysburg Coll., 1938-40; with Applied Phsyics Lab., Johns Hopkins, Silver Spring, Md., 1946-76, sr. physicist, 1946-51, prin. profl. staff, 1951-76, ret., 1976, instr. math. Evening Coll., 1965-69. Served to lt. col. AUS, 1940-46, col. Res. ret. Decorated Legion of Merit. Mem. Phi Beta Kappa. Lutheran. Patentee strain gage operated wing servo. Home: 8910 Chapel Ave Ellicott City MD 21043

DURGIN, FRANK ALBERT, JR., educator; b. Lynn, Mass., Dec. 8, 1923; s. Frank Albert and Dorothy (Smith) D.; B.A., Tufts U., 1949; doctorate and licence en droit, U. Toulouse, 1956; m. Barbara Louise Ann Bright, Feb. 12, 1952; children—Stephen, Brian, Peter, Katie. With U.S. Dept. Def., 1956-57; lectr. U. Md., 1957-59; with USIA, 1959-60; asst. prof. Babson Inst., Babson Park, Md., 1960-64; prof. econs. U. Maine, Portland, 1964—. Served with USAF, 1943-46. Decorated Air Medal (2). Recipient Distinguished Service award USIA, 1960; Ford Found. faculty research grantee, 1964. Mem. Assn. Comparative Econ. Studies, Phi Kappa Phi. Contbr. articles to profl. jours. Home: 974 Sawyer St South Portland ME 04106 Office: 96 Falmouth St Portland ME 04103

DURHAM, JAMES BRYANT, steel co. exec.; b. Tyler, Tex., Apr. 2, 1943; s. Thomas Charles and Dorothy Grace (Harvey) D.; student Tyler Jr. Coll., 1962-64; B.B.A., U. Tex., 1966; m. Mary Louise Bowling, July 4, 1959; children—Laura Louise, James Bryant, Sarah Jane. Owner, mgr. Austin Souvenir Co. (Tex.), 1964-66; mgmt. corr. U.S. Steel Corp., Pitts., 1966-67, service rep., Charlotte, N.C., 1967-69, sales rep., N.Y.C. 1969-72, mgr. sales, Sharon, Pa., 1972-76, asst. mktg. mgr., Pitts., 1976—. Bd. dirs., campaign bldg. chmn. YMCA, Sharon, 1975-76; mem. adv. bd. Mercer County Assn. for Retarded, 1976—; bd. dirs. Christian Assn. Shenango Valley; fin. chmn. and Pres. Ford campaign chmn. Mercer County Republican party, 1976; elder Presbyterian Ch., Sharon, 1975-76; Jr. Achievement cons. for Project Bus., 1977-78; team capt. Nat. Alliance Businessmen, 1978; loaned exec. United Way Pitts., 1978; bd. dirs. Coalition for Christian Outreach, Pitts., 1977—. Mem. Joint Council on Econ. Edn., Steel Shipping Container Inst., Brookings Instn., Shenango Valley C. of C. (dir. 1975-76). Clubs: Aurora Country, Masons. Home: 1825 Tilton Dr Pittsburgh PA 15241 Office: 600 Grant St Pittsburgh PA 15230

DURING, THEOBALD, accountant; b. nr. Wuerzburg, Germany, Dec. 20, 1912; s. Alfred and Maria (Ress) D.; came to U.S., 1934, naturalized, 1943; A.B. cum laude, Bklyn. Coll., 1948; postgrad. N.Y. U. Sch. Law, 1948-50, M.B.A., Grad. Sch. Bus. Adminstrn., 1952; m. Marie Delaunay, Sept. 21, 1945; children—Dennis Charles, Linda Marie. With various import firms, 1934-43; staff mem. Byrnes & Baker, C.P.A.'s, N.Y.C., 1948-52; auditor Army Audit Agency, 1952-54; staff mem. John J. Donohue & Co., N.Y.C., 1952-54; sr. partner Cleary, During & Co., C.P.A.'s, N.Y.C., 1954-75; instr. accounting Bklyn. Coll., 1959-61. Fiscal coordinator, controller Roman Catholic Diocese Bklyn., 1970—. Served to 1st lt. AUS, 1943-46. Decorated Bronze Star; named knight Equestrian Order Holy Sepulchre Jerusalem; C.P.A., N.Y. Mem. Am. Inst. C.P.A.'s, N.Y. State Soc. C.P.A.'s, Am. Accounting Assn., Nat. Assn. Accountants. Home: 4011 Ave R Brooklyn NY 11234 Office: 75 Greene Ave Brooklyn NY 11238

DURKIN, JOHN A., U.S. Senator; b. Mar. 29, 1936; student Holy Cross Coll., 1959, Georgetown U., 1965; m. Patricia Moses, 1965; children—Andrea E., John E., Sheilagh. Admitted to Mass. bar, 1966; ins. commr. State of N.H., 1968-73; asst. atty. gen., 1967-68; mem. U.S. Senate from N.H., 1975—. Served with USN. Mem. Common Cause, Council for Better Schs., Merrimac Valley Navy League. Democrat. Club: Elks. Office: 1409 Dirksen Senate Office Bldg Washington DC 20510

DURLEY, GERALD LEE, chem. co. exec., documentary producer; b. Wichita, Kans., May 11, 1942; s. LeRoy Raymond and Charles (Lee) D.; B.S. in Psychology, Tenn. State U., 1964; M.S. in Community Mental Health, No. Ill. U., 1967; Ph.D. in Urban Edn., U. Mass., 1973; m. Muriel Eleanor West, Aug. 17, 1968; children—Nia Kila, Hasan Jelani. With U.S. Peace Corps, Africa, 1964-66; tchr. psychology U. Neuchatel, Switzerland, 1966; with U.S. Steel Co., Gary, Ind., 1967; head counseling program No. Ill. U., 1968; asst. br. chief, pupil personnel U.S. Office Edn., 1969, br. chief career opportunities program, 1970; dir. div. curriculum and faculty devel.

Inst. for Services to Edn., 1972-77; exec. v.p. United Industries, Inc., Oxon Hill, Md., 1977-78; documentary producer, 1978—; pres., chmn. bd. Perspectives Internat., Inc.; faculty U. D.C.; cons. to coll. presidents and deans. Mem. Am. Personnel and Guidance Assn. (chmn. finance com.), Smithsonian Instn., Inst. Rational Living, Nat. Coordinating Council for Ednl. Opportunity, Am. Assn. Higher Edn., Assn. Supervision and Curriculum Devel., Kappa Delta Pi, Sigma Rho Sigma, Kappa Alpha Psi. Contbr. articles on sociol. and ednl. issues to mags., newspapers and anthologies to books. Home: 6302 Lenham Dr Oxon Hill MD 20022

DURNIAK, JAMES DENNIS, aero. engr.; b. Sewickley, Pa., Oct. 24, 1946; s. Peter Richard and Nell Francis (Routh) D.; B.S., LeTourneau Coll., 1968; M.S., Air Force Inst. Tech., 1977; m. Sharon Marie Moore, Aug. 23, 1969. Heavy equipment engr. R.G. Le Tourneau Inc., Longview, Tex., 1967-68; commd. 2d lt. USAF, 1969, advanced through grades to capt., 1972; navigator Grand Forks AFB, 1974-75; project engr., turbofan engine, Wright Patterson AFB, Ohio, 1977—, F-107 lead engr. with USN, Washington, 1978—. Decorated DFC, Air medal with 4 oak leaf clusters. Mem. Am. Inst. Aeros. and Astronautics, Air Force Assn. Roman Catholic. Home: 205 Yoakum Pkwy #720 Alexandria VA 22304 Office: JCMPO Washington DC 20360

DURNIN, RICHARD GERRY, educator; b. Haverhill, Mass., Mar. 9, 1920; s. William Edward and Ethel (Millett) D.; B.S., Columbia U., 1947; M.Ed., Harvard U., 1950; postgrad. summers U. Nottingham, 1950, U. Oxford, 1956; Ed.D., U. Pa., 1968. Tchr. pub. schs., N.J., Mass., 1946-49; instr. State Coll. at Fitchburg (Mass.), 1949-51; dir. Antioch Sch., Yellow Springs, Ohio, 1951-52; asst. prof. N.Y. State Coll. at Buffalo, 1952-58; vis. lectr. edn. Tufts U., spring 1957; dir. Smith Coll. Day Sch., 1958-59; asst. prof. edn. Rutgers U., 1959-65; asso. prof. social and hist. founds. of edn. Coll. City N.Y., 1965—; instr. U. Nev., U. N.H., Coll. William and Mary, Johns Hopkins U., summers 1951-68. Bd. dirs. Internat. Social Service-WAIF; nat. council Travelers Aid Internat. Social Service, 1972-77; chmn. Middlesex County (N.J.) Cultural and Heritage Commn., 1976—; trustee Proprietary House Assn. N.J., 1977—. Served to 1st lt. USAAF, 1942-46. Mem. History of Edn. Soc., Am. Hist. Assn., New Brunswick (pres. 1969-71), N.Y., N.J., Nat. Ry. hist. socs., Essex Inst., Soc. for Preservation New Eng. Antiquities, SAR, Soc. Mayflower Descs., English-Speaking Union, Kappa Delta Pi, Phi Delta Kappa. Episcopalian. Contbr. articles to profl. jours. Home: 50 Chester Circle New Brunswick NJ 08901 Office: Sch Edn City Coll NY New York City NY 10031

DUROCHER, ARMAND DAVID, accountant; b. Woonsocket, R.I., May 19, 1915; s. Hormisdas D. and Anna L. (Gagnon) DuR.; student Mt. St. Charles Acad., 1930; grad. Sch. of Comml. Sci., 1931; B.B.A., Northeastern U., 1949; m. Teresa F. Leverone, Jan. 15, 1940; children—Frances A., Joan T. (Mrs. Albert P. Brouillard). Pvt. bookkeeping practice, 1932-36; property mgr. Keough & Pratt, Inc., 1936-38; staff accountant F. E. Welch & Co., C.P.A., Providence, 1938-41; city auditor, Woonsocket, R.I., 1941-42; dep. tax adminstr. State of R.I., 1942; state adminstrv. officer O.P.A., 1943; sr. price economist, 1944-45; controller Welch Engring. Co. and Welch Industries, Inc., Pawtucket, R.I., 1945-46; supr., sr. accountant F.E. Welch & Co., C.P.A., Providence, 1946-47; prin. Armand D. DuRocher, C.P.A., 1947-68; mng. partner DuRocher & Arenburgh, 1968-74; pres. Securities Traders, Inc., 1955-78. Mem. R.I. Bd. Accountancy, 1963-69. Mem. North Smithfield School Com., 1956-64, chmn., 1960-64; mem. corp. Roger Williams Coll., Woonsocket Hosp., Fogarty Meml. Hosp., Blue Cross of R.I.; bd. dirs. Marquette Credit Union; pres. Stroke Club, R.I. Heart Assn. Served as pvt. AUS, 1943-44. Recipient Community Service awards Amvets, Franco-Am. War Vets.; Silver Beaver award Boy Scouts Am.; Heart of Yr. award Am. Heart Assn. R.I. affiliate, 1977; C.P.A., N.Y., R.I. Mem. Am. Inst. C.P.A.'s (mem. council 1969-73), R.I. Soc. C.P.A.'s (pres. 1962-63), Nat. Assn. Cost Accountants, Nat. Assn. C.P.A. Examiners, D.A.V., Amvets. Elk. Home: 4 Mitris Blvd Lincoln RI 02865

DURR, BEULAH PATTON, educator; b. Clinton, Miss., Aug. 21, 1938; d. George and Mable (Thompson) Patton; B.S., Tougaloo Coll., 1958; M.S. with high honors, N.Mex. Highlands U., 1963; m. Charles Durr, June 6, 1958; children—Viva Joi, Lori Nicole. Instr., Milw. Inst. Tech., 1958-60; tchr. Liverpool (N.Y.) High Sch., 1965-66; tchr. chemistry William Nottingham High Sch., Syracuse, N.Y., 1966—, head dept. sci., 1972—; mem. N.Y. State Regents Adv. Bd. on Tchrs. Edn., Certification and Practice, 1977—. Mem. edn. com. Am. Cancer Soc. Named N.Y. State Tchr. of Year, N.Y. State Dept. Edn., 1977, Outstanding Tchr. Am. Chem. Soc., 1975. Mem. Nat., N.Y. State sci. tchrs. assns., Links, Inc., Alpha Kappa Alpha, Delta Kappa Gamma. Democrat. Congregationalist. Home: 3400 E Genesee St Syracuse NY 13214 Office: 3100 E Genesee St Syracuse NY 13224

DURSIN, HENRY LOUIS, opinion survey co. exec.; b. Woonsocket, R.I., May 3, 1921; s. Henry and Mary Regina (Butler) B.; A.B. with honors, Brown U., 1942; M.B.A., Harvard, 1948, m. Margaret Alice Smith, Apr. 20, 1943 (dec.); children—Henry Peter, Philomene Louise Resnikoff, Margaret Elizabeth Coello. Supr. corporate research Gen. Electric Co., N.Y.C., 1948-63; supr. corporate research Harper-Atlantic Sales Co., N.Y.C., also dir. research and promotion, 1963-67; dir. research ORC Caravan Surveys Co., Princeton, N.J., 1968-70, pres., 1970—; v.p. Opinion Research Corp., Princeton, 1970-74, sr. v.p., 1974—. Bd. dirs. United Fund No. Westchester, also chmn. agy. com., 1960-68, pres., 1967-68, v.p. Westchester County, co-chmn. agy. com., 1966-67. Served with USAAF, 1942-46. Mem. Am. Assn. Pub. Opinion Research, Am. Mktg. Assn., Assn. Consumer Research, Travel Research Assn. Roman Catholic. Club: Harvard N.Y.C. Home: 42 Bear Brook Rd Princeton Junction NJ 08550 Office: Opinion Research Corp N Harrison St Princeton NJ 08540

D'URSO, JOHN ANTHONY, physician; b. Bklyn., Nov. 6, 1931; s. Joseph Philip and Grace Marie D'U.; B.S., McGill U. (Can.), 1954, M.D., 1958; m. Nadia Zajac, Aug. 17, 1957; children—Steven, Michael, John, Neil, Jennifer. Intern, St. Joseph Hosp., Flint, Mich., 1958-59; resident Bellevue Hosp., N.Y.C., 1959-62; oncology fellow Meml. Hosp., 1962-64; practice medicine, specializing in obstetrics, N.Y.C., 1964—; attending and teaching staff Cornell Lying-In Hosp., N.Y.C., 1964—, Meml. Sloan Kettering, N.Y.C., 1964—, Lenox Hill Hosp., N.Y.C., 1964—. Diplomate Am. Bd. Obstetricians and Gynecologists. Mem. Bellevue Alumni Assn., N.Y. Cancer Soc., N.Y. Acad. Medicine, AMA, N.Y. County, Westchester County med. socs., N.Y. Gynecol. Soc., Royal Soc. Health, A.C.S., Am. Coll. Obstetricians and Gynecologists, Pan Am. Med. Assn., N.Y. State Soc. Surgeons, Soc. Continuing Med. Edn. Office: 17 E 82nd St New York City NY 10028

DURYEA, EDWARD RUSSELL, landscape architect, community planner; b. Passaic, N.J., Mar. 28, 1935; s. James Edward and Priscilla Eleanor (Larlham) D.; B.Landscape Architecture, U. Ga., 1957; m. Edna Anne Hahn, Sept. 9, 1955; children—Russell Duane, Lynn Allison, Susanne Michele, Kim Elizabeth. Landscape architect Div. Architecture, State of N.Y., 1957-59; asso. landscape architect H. Boyer Marx, Atlanta, 1959-60; sr. city planner City of Syracuse (N.Y.), 1960-62; founder, pres. Duryea & Wilhelmi Profl. Corp., Syracuse, 1962—; v.p. 1208 James Property Ltd., 1971—; v.p. Stoneridge Properties Ltd., 1975—; pres. Chatham Woods Ltd., 1978—. Active Vols. in Tech. Assistance. Mem. Am. Soc. Landscape Architects (accreditation bd. 1976), Am. Arbitration Assn. (mem. panel 1970—), World Commerce Assn. Central N.Y., N.Y. State Recreation and Parks Soc., Landmarks Assn. Central N.Y. Author: Unit Cost Index, 1970. Home: 3 Limberlost Ln Manlius NY 13104 Office: 1208 James St Syracuse NY 13203

DURYEA, PERRY BELMONT, JR., state legislator; b. East Hampton, N.Y., Oct. 18, 1921; s. Perry Belmont and Jane (Stewart) D.; B.A., Colgate U.; LL.D., Dowling Coll., Southampton Coll.; L.H.D., Sienna Coll.; m. Elizabeth Ann Weed, Apr. 4, 1944; children—Lynn, Perry Belmont III. Pres., Perry B. Duryea & Son; N.Y. State assemblyman, 1961—, minority leader, 1966-68, 75-78, speaker, 1969-74. Pres., L.I. State Park Commn., 1962-70, Bethpage Park Authority, 1962-70; pres. Jones Beach State Pkwy., 1962-70, mem., 1971-77. Mem. N.Y. State Republican Com.; del. Rep. Nat. Convs., 1968, 72, 76. Bd. dirs. Citizens Conf. on State Legislatures, 1971-77. Served to lt. comdr. USNR, 1942-45. Mem. Nat. Conf. State Legislature (dir., exec. com. 1971—), C. of C., Am. Legion, VFW. Presbyterian. Club: Lions. Office: State Assembly Offices Albany NY 12224

DUSHMAN, ALLAN, elec. engr.; b. Brockton, Mass., June 12, 1934; s. Jacob and Florence (Cohen) D.; B.S., U. Mass., 1956; M.S. (Hughes fellow), U. So. Calif., 1958; M.S., Northeastern U., 1971; m. Carol Saulich, Aug. 12, 1956; children—Richard Joseph, Lawrence Mitchell. Mem. tech. staff Hughes Aircraft Co., Culver City, Calif., 1956-58; systems analyst Melpar, Inc., Watertown, Mass., 1958-60; systems analyst Dynamics Research Corp., Wilmington, Mass., 1960-64, program mgr., 1964-70, mgr. analysis dept., 1970—. Mem. Paint Rock Community Pool Corp., 1968—, treas., 1971-72, pres., 1972-73. Recipient Certificate of Merit for significant contbns. in support of U.S. Navy Fleet Ballistic Missile program, 1974. Mem. IEEE, Inst. Nav., Am. Inst. Aeros. and Astronautics, Ops. Research Soc. Am., Phi Kappa Phi, Tau Beta Pi. Contbr. articles to profl. jours.; research in improvement of inertial nav. systems and devel. of related accuracy and cost models. Home: 8 Partridge Rd Lexington MA 02173 Office: 60 Concord St Wilmington MA 01887

DUSOLD, LAURENCE RICHARD, chemist, computer specialist; b. Chgo., Nov. 15, 1944; s. Henry E. and Collette M. D.; B.S. in Chemistry, Purdue U., 1966; M.S., U. N.C., 1969; m. Karen A. Marsh, Aug. 29, 1970; children—Amy, Lauren, Patty. Research chemist, residue analysis and methods investigation br. Bur. Foods, FDA, Washington, 1971-75, chemist, computer specialist, div. chemistry and physics, 1975—; mem. faculty, evening div. U. Md., 1973—. Recipient Commendable Service award FDA. Mem. Am. Chem. Soc., Am. Soc. Mass Spectrometry, Assn. Computing Machinery, Greater Washington Fed. Agy. APL Users Group (co-chmn.), Alpha Chi Sigma, Phi Lambda Upsilon. Office: FDA 200 C St SW Washington DC 20204

DUSS, WILLIAM ADOLPH, personnel exec.; b. N.Y.C., Nov. 4, 1936; s. William Frederick and Mary (Popoli) D.; B.B.A., Iona Coll., 1958; M.B.A., N.Y. U., 1963; m. Rita Marie McCormack, Nov. 15, 1958; children—Christine, Mark, Holly. Group annuity adminstr. Met. Life Ins. Co., N.Y.C., 1958-60; project controller Greenwich Engring. div. Am. Machine & Foundry, Greenwich, Conn., 1960-61; v.p. adminstrn. Bunker Ramo Corp., Trumbull, Conn., 1961—. Mem. Am. Soc. Personnel Adminstrn. (compensation com. 1971—), Greater Bridgeport Personnel Assn., Indsl. Realtions Dirs. Council Bridgeport. Clubs: K.C., Exchange (Trumbull). Home: 31 Mariner Circle Trumbull CT 06611 Office: 35 Nutmeg Dr Trumbull CT 06609

DUTTA, SISIR KAMAL, educator; b. Bengal, India, Aug. 28, 1928; s. Krishna K. and Satyabati (Chanda) D.; came to U.S., 1956, naturalized, 1974; M.S., Kan. State U., 1958, Ph.D., 1960; m. Minati Roy, July 1, 1955; children—Mahasweta, Basabi. Dir., chief research officer Nat. Pineapple Research Inst., Malaysia, 1961-64; research asso. Rice U., Houston, 1964-65; asst. prof. biology Tex. So. U., Houston, 1965-66; chmn. div. sci. and math., asso. prof. biology Jarvis (Tex.) Christian Coll., 1966-67; prof. molecular genetics dept. botany Howard U., Washington, 1967—. Cons. pineapple industries Formosa, Phillippines, Malaysia, various univs.; collaborator Pasteur Inst., Carnegie Instn.; lectr. univs. U.S. and abroad. Grantee NSF, NIH, Olin Found., EPA, Research Corp. N.Y., Anna Fuller Found., USNR. Mem. AAAS, Genetics Soc. Am., AAUP, Am. Mycol. Soc., Am. Soc. Environ. Mutagen, Sigma Xi, Beta Kappa Chi. Contbr. to profl. jours. Home: PO Box 34864 West Bethesda MD 20034 Office: Dept Botany Howard Univ Washington DC 20059

DUTTON, DAVID BELLAMY, physicist; b. Asheville, N.C., Nov. 19, 1926; s. Teeps B. and Bess (Drumheller) D.; B.S., Case Inst. Tech., 1947; M.S., U. Ill., 1949, Ph.D., 1952. With U. Rochester (N.Y.), 1953—, research scientist in optics, 1974—. Served with USNR, 1945-46. Fulbright scholar Ecole Normale Supérieure, France, 1952-53. Fellow Am. Phys. Soc., Soc. Photo-optical Instrumentation Engrs.; mem. Optical Soc. Am., AAAS, Sigma Xi, Tau Beta Pi. Home: 22 Colebourne Rd Rochester NY 14609 Office: U Rochester Rochester NY 14627

DUTTON, LISLE GEORGE, assn. exec.; b. Bklyn., Mar. 5, 1930; s. Lisle Bertram and Iva Belle (Dockstader) D.; A.B., U. Miami, 1952; m. Isabel Josephine Samul, June 23, 1951; children—Sherree Anne, Pamela Kay. Band leader, Great Barrington, Mass., 1945-48; performer variety show WLCR, Torrington, Conn., 1946-48; head bookkeeping dept. First Nat. Bank, Great Barrington, 1947-48; sales supr. Miami Daily News, Miami Beach, Fla., 1951-52; mgmt. trainee Dairylea Coop., Utica, N.Y., 1956-60; asst. dist. mgr. Pa. Mut. Life Ins., Utica, 1960-61; spl. agt. Companion Life N.Y., Utica, 1961-64; field rep. Dairy Industry, N.Y., Pa., Vt., 1964-69; pub. relations dir. Eastern Milk Producers Coop. Assn., Inc., Syracuse, N.Y., 1969-77, membership and pub. relations mgr., 1977—; mem. June Dairy Month com., banquet, publicity chmn. Onondaga County, N.Y., 1973-78; youth com. rep. N.Y. State Council Farmer Coops., 1972-73; promotion chmn., treas. N.Y. State Farm-City Council, 1973-78. Served with USNR, 1952-56. Recipient On Target award N.Y. State Bus. and Industry Communicators Council, 1971; Companion Life of N.Y. award Pres. Club, 1962. Mem. Am. Agrl. Editors Assn., Nat. Coop. Editorial Assn., Internat. Assn. Bus. Communicators, N.Y., New Eng. press. assns., Pa. Dairy Sanitarians Assn., Twin State Sanitarians Assn., N.Y. State Assn. Milk and Food Sanitarians, Syracuse Bus. and Industry Communicators Council, Sigma Phi Epsilon. Methodist. Clubs: Masons, Rotary. Home: 9654 Mallory Rd New Hartford NY 13413 Office: 6567 Kinne Rd Syracuse NY 13214

DUTTON, ROBERT EDWARD, JR., educator; b. Milford, N.H., Aug. 11, 1924; s. Robert Edward and Mildred Beatrice (Prior) D.; student Gettysburg Coll., 1942-43, The Citadel, 1943-44, Johns Hopkins U., 1944-45; M.D., Med. Coll. Va., 1949; m. Cynthia Baldwin, June 15, 1958; children—Elizabeth Helen, Leila Baldwin. Intern, Boston City Hosp., 1950-51, resident, 1953-54; resident State U. N.Y., Syracuse, 1954-56, instr. medicine, 1956-59; asst. prof. environ. medicine and medicine Johns Hopkins U., 1964-68; asso. prof. physiology Albany Med. Coll., Union U., 1968-74, asso. prof. medicine, 1970-77, prof. physiology, 1974—, prof. medicine, 1977—, also cons. trauma research unit, 1971—; prof. biomed. engring. Rensselaer Poly. Inst., 1972—; cons. pulmonary div. VA Hosps., Balt., Albany, N.Y., 1968-69; prin. investigator grants Nat. Heart and Lung Inst., 1965—. Served with AUS, 1943-46, USAF, 1951-53. Nat. Heart Inst. postdoctoral fellow, 1959-61. Mem. Am. Physiol. Soc., Am. Thoracic Soc., Am. Fedn. Clin. Research, Johns Hopkins Med. and Surg. Assn., Sigma Xi, Sigma Zeta. Contbr. articles to profl. jours. Home: 21 Pinedale Ave Delmar NY 12054 Office: Albany Med Coll Albany NY 12208

DUTTON, THOMAS EUGENE, archtl. photographer; b. Bristol, Conn., Sept. 30, 1936; s. Vernet Ray and Margorie Lillian (Doane) D.; student Hartford State Tech. Inst., 1956-63, Yale U., 1963-65; grad. Famous Photographers Sch., Westport, Conn., 1971; m. Joetta Raye Hammons, July 18, 1971. Jr. archtl. draftsman Factory Ins. Assn., Hartford, Conn., 1957-63; archtl. draftsman Fred Dubin Assos., cons. engrs., Hartford, 1963; archtl. photographer, draftsman Warren Ashley, architect, West Hartford, 1963-65; photographer, archtl. draftsman Lee and Crabtree Assos., architects, Hartford, 1965-68; archtl. photographer, draftsman Malmfeldt Assos., architects, Hartford, 1968-78; asso. architect Conn. Soc. Architects, 1977—; exhbns. pen and ink drawings Mystic Seaport Art Gallery (Conn.), other art galleries. Vol. leader Hartford YMCA, 1953-58; mem. ch. choirs; active Boy Scouts Am. Mem. AIA (asso.), Profl. Photographers Am., Profl. Photographers New Eng., Conn. Profl. Photographers Assn., Am. Youth Hostelers (life; v.p. Hartford council 1960-62), Conn. 33 Group Artists, Nat. Geog. Soc., Sons of DAR. Republican. Congregationalist. Club: Simsbury Ski. Contbr. photographs to YMCA, archtl. publs. Home: 116 W Avon Rd Farmington CT 06032 Office: Glen Locken East 41C Glastonbury CT 06033

DUVAL, MARJORIE ANN, librarian; b. Leominster, Mass.; d. Daniel J., Jr. and Margaret L. (Desmond) Duval; tchr.'s diploma New Eng. Conservatory Music, 1943, B.Mus., 1945; M.S., Simmons Coll., 1962. Music tchr., choral condr. Jeanne D'Arc Acad., Milton, Mass., 1946-51; recreation supr. spl. services div. U.S. Dept. Army, Europe, Far East, New Eng., 1951-61; head librarian U. Maine, Portland, 1962-72, asso. prof. library service, 1965—, univ. archivist U. So. Maine, 1972—. Mem. Altrusa Internat. (pres. chpt. 1973-74, dist. chmn. 1974-76), Maine (sec. 1971-74), New Eng. (sec. coll. librarians sect. 1970-71) library assns., Soc. Am. Archivists, New Eng. Archivists (v.p. 1978-79, pres. 1979-80), Maine Hist. Soc., Oral History Assn., Mu Phi Epsilon. Home: 32 Wildwood Blvd Cumberland Foreside Portland ME 04110 Office: 96 Falmouth St Portland ME 04103

DU VIGNEAUD, VINCENT, ret. educator; b. Chgo., May 18, 1901; s. Alfred Joseph and Mary Theresa (O'Leary) duV.; B.S., U. Ill., 1923, M.S., 1924, Sc.D., 1960; Ph.D., U. Rochester, 1927, Sc.D., 1965; Sc.D., Yale, N.Y. U., 1955, St. Louis U., 1965, George Washington U., 1968; m. Zella Zon Ford, June 12, 1924; children—Vincent, Marilyn Renée Brown. Asst. biochemsit Phila. Gen. Hosp., asst. biochemist U. Pa. Grad. Sch. Medicine, 1924-25; teaching asst. Sch. Medicine U. Rochester, 1925-27; NRC fellow Johns Hopkins Med. Sch., 1927-28, Kaiser Wilhelm Inst., Dresden, Germany, U. Edinburgh Med. Sch., UCH Med. Sch., London, 1928-29; asso. dept. chemistry U. Ill., 1929-30, asst. prof., 1930-32; prof., head dept. biochemistry George Washington U. Sch. Medicine, 1932-38; prof. head dept. biochemistry Cornell U. Med. Coll., N.Y.C., 1938-67, emeritus prof. biochemistry, 1967—; prof. chemistry Cornell U., Ithaca, N.Y., 1967—; lectr. various univs. Mem. Health Research Adv. Council City N.Y., 1958-62; nat. adv. arthritis and metabolic diseases council NIH, 1960-64. Trustee Rockefeller U. Recipient Hillebrand prize Chem. Soc. Washington, 1936; Borden award for Research in Med. Scis., 1947; Lasker award Am. Pub. Health Assn., 1948; Merit award for War Research, 1948; John Scott award, 1954; Sci. award Am. Pharm. Mfrs. Assn., 1955; Passano Found. award, 1955; Nobel prize in Chemistry, 1955; Chandler medal, 1956; Nutrition Found. 20th Anniversary award, 1961; 7th Ann. Hon. Lecture award Albany Med. Coll., 1963; A.C.P. award, 1965; Eli Lilly award Endocrine Soc., 1967. Fellow Am. Acad. Arts and Scis., Royal Soc. Edinburgh (hon.), Chem. Soc. London, Royal Soc. Scis, Upsala (hon.), Royal Inst. Chemistry (London); mem. Am. Inst. Nutrition (Mead Johson vitamin award 1943, Osborne and Mendel award 1953), Am. Soc. Biol. Chemistry (pres. 1951-52), Am. Chem. Soc. (council at large 1943, chmn. N.Y. sect. 1943, Nichols medal N.Y. sect. 1945, Willard Gibbs medal Chgo. sect. 1956), Soc. Exptl. Biology (past chmn. bd.). Harvey Soc., Am. Philos. Soc., Nat., (chmn. sect. biochem. 1958-60), N.Y. acads. scis. Washington Acad. Medicine, Sigma Xi, Alpha Chi Sigma, Phi Lambda Upsilon, Alpha Omega Alpha (hon.). Club: Chemists' (hon., N.Y.C.). Contbr. articles to sci. jours. Home: 200 White Park Rd Ithaca NY 14850

DUZY, FRANK JOSEPH, mining co. exec.; b. Darby, Pa., Apr. 29, 1943; s. Frank Joseph and Elizabeth Ann (Betsch) D.; B.S., Pa. State U., 1965; M.B.A., Northeastern U., 1971; m. Marjorie T. Biro, Aug. 17, 1968. Sr. auditor Ernst & Ernst Pub. Accounting, New Haven, 1970-72; fin. accountant Citizens Utilities Co., Stamford, Conn., 1972-74; asst. treas. Callahan Mining Corp., Darien, Conn., 1974—; instr. accounting Fairfield U.; dir. Guenster Home, Inc. Served to lt. USNR, 1966-69. Licensed real estate broker, Conn.; C.P.A. Mem. Am. Inst. C.P.A.'s, Conn. Soc. C.P.A.'s, Nat. Assn. Accountants. Club: Patterson (Fairfield, Conn.). Home: 300 Half Mile Rd Southport CT 06490 Office: 1120 Post Rd Darien CT 06820

DVARECKA, CHRISTOPHER LAWRENCE, community and pub. relations cons.; b. Newark, Sept. 9, 1919; s. Kris Michael and Mary V. (Sedgewick) D.; student Am. Internat. Coll., 1941-43, U. Alaska, 1944, U. Tokyo, 1950, U. Wis., 1962; m. Edith Evelyn Williams, June 29, 1946; children—Edith Susan, Pamela Ann. Reporter, Springfield (Mass.) Union, 1937-43, 53-54; bur. chief news Manchester (N.H.) Union-Leader, 1951-53; information officer Dept. of Army, Springfield, 1954-69, Hdqtrs. U.S. Army Materiel Command, Washington, 1969-70; community and pub. relations exec., Springfield, 1970—. Cons., pub. relations; lectr., historian 1954—; columnist Springfield Daily News, 1954-70, Springfield Herald, 1970—. Served with AUS, 1943-46, 47-50, col. Res. Mem. Pub. Relations Soc. Am., Pub. Relations Register, Valley Press Club, Indsl. Editors Western Mass., Greater Spring-field Army Adv. Council, Assn. U.S. Army, Zeta Chi. Author: Springfield Armory: Pointless Sacrifice, also bicentennial edit.; The Rifle: Its Birth and Growth; History of the Springfield Armory. Contbr. articles to profl. jours. Address: 12 Hadley Village Rd South Hadley MA 01075

DVOICHENKO-MARKOV, DEMETRIUS, educator; b. Saloniki, Greece, July 10, 1921; s. Vladimir and Eufrosina M. (de Markov) Dvoichenko de Kovalevski; came to U.S., 1942, naturalized, 1943; baccalaureate, German Ev. Lyceum, Rumania, 1941; A.B., U. Calif. at Los Angeles, 1950; M.A., Columbia, 1951; m. Inna Moore, July 18, 1952; children—Vlad, Laria. Translator, research analyst U.S. War Dept., Nurnberg, Germany, 1946-47; research analyst Dept. Def., Washington, 1952-53; asst. field dir. ARC, Alexanderia, Va., 1954-56; tchr. German and Spanish, Wakefield High Sch., Arlington, Va., 1956-57; instr. Russian and social sci., Monmouth Coll., W. Long

Branch, N.J., 1957-61, asst. prof., 1961—; Russian lang. instr., Ft. Monmouth, N.J.; lectr. history and geography Newark State Coll. Served with U.S. Army, 1942-45. Am. Council of Learned Socs. travel grantee, 1971; recipient Dimitrie Cantemir medal, Rumanian Nat. Acad. Sci., 1975. Mem. Am. Hist. Assn., Assn. Am. Geographers, U. Calif. at Los Angeles Alumni Assn., Am. Assn. Advancement of Salvic Studies, Assn. Study of the Nationalities (USSR and Eastern Europe), N.J. Ednl. Assn., Romanian Studies Group, Delta Tau Kappa, Phi Alpha Theta, Gamma Theta Upsilon. Mem. Eastern Orthodox. Ch. Contb. articles and revs. to profl. jours. Home: 359 Lowden Ct Long Branch NJ 07740 Office: Monmouth Coll West Long Branch NJ 07764

DVORNICKY, JOSEPH ANDREW, JR., clin. engr.; b. Balt., Dec. 20, 1950; s. Joseph Andrew and Betty Dolores D.; B.A., Loyola Coll., Balt., 1972; postgrad. Johns Hopkins U. Sch. Medicine; m. Dianne Lynn Krause, Nov. 23, 1974. Research technician div. nuclear medicine Johns Hopkins U. Sch. Medicine, Balt., 1971-74; research asso., 1974-78; sec. Nuclear Medicine Instrumentation Group, cons. engr., 1978; engr., info. display group Tektronix, Inc., Rockville, Md., 1978—. USPHS grantee, 1971-78. Democrat. Roman Catholic. Contbr. to tech. publs. in field. Home: 824-102 Quince Orchard Blvd Gaithersburg MD 20760 Office: Tektronix Inc 2 Research Ct Rockville MD 20850

DWECK, EDWARD JACK, dentist; b. Syracuse, N.Y., Nov. 3, 1933; s. Jack and Sophia Ruth (Bronstein) D.; D.D.S., U. Buffalo, 1957; postgrad., 1964; postgrad. Walter Reed Army Inst. Dental Research, 1968-70; m. Ruth L. McCollough, Dec. 23, 1973; children by previous marriage—Steven Howard, Lisa Anne; stepchildren—Malene, Jeanne, Ami. Biochemist, Roswell Park Meml. Inst., Buffalo, 1954-57; pvt. practice dentistry, Buffalo, 1960-64, Tonawanda, N.Y., 1964—; pres. dental staff Rosa Coplon Jewish Home and Infirmary, 1971-72. Chmn. dental div. United Jewish Appeal, Buffalo, 1966, 70, 76, 77. Served to capt. USAF, 1957-60. Fellow Acad. Gen. Dentistry (chpt. pres. 1974-76, chpt. sec. 1976, chpt. treas. 1976-77); mem. Am. Acad. Dental Practice Adminstrn. (dir. 1977-79), Am. Soc. Preventive Dentistry (dir. N.Y. State chpt. 1975—, treas. 1976, sub-chpt. pres. 1975-76), Alpha Omega (bd. dirs. found. 1972—, exec. bd. 1973-78, treas. 1978; chpt. pres. 1966, editor 1962-63, sec. 1964-65, chmn. internat. com. 1969, 74—, regent Upstate N.Y. 1972-74, internat. trustee 1975-77), Twin City Dental Soc. Jewish. Mem. B'nai B'rith. Home: 2486 Colvin Blvd Tonawanda NY 14150 Office: 884 Brighton Rd Tonawanda NY 14150

DWIVEDI, BASANT KUMAR, food mfg. co. exec.; b. Agra, India, Dec. 25, 1945; s. Brahm Bandhu and Ramrupa Devi D.; came to U.S., 1970, naturalized, 1978; B.S. (Nat. Scholar, Merit Scholar), Panjab (India) U., 1967; M.S., U. Sask. (Can.), 1970; Ph.D., U. Nebr., 1972; m. Pratibha Chaturvedi, June 22, 1965; 1 child, Surekha. Supr., Glaxo Labs., Aligarh, India, 1967-68; research asst. U. Sask., Saskatoon, 1968-70, U. Nebr., Lincoln, 1970-72; research asso. Cornell U., Ithaca, 1972-74; asso. research dir. Booz-Allen & Hamilton, Florham Park, N.Y., 1974-75; v.p. research and devel. and quality control The Estee Corp., Parsippany, N.J., 1975—. U.S. Army Natick grantee, 1974. Mem. Am. Chem. Soc., Inst. Food Technologists, AAAS, Grocery Mfrs. Assn., Nat. Confectioners Assn., Calorie Control Council, Sigma Xi (Grad. Research award 1973). Author: Low Calorie and Special Dietary Foods, 1978. Patentee chewing gum. Home: 3 Farm Rd Randolph NJ 07801 Office: 169 Lackawanna Ave Parsippany NJ 07054

DWORSKY, LEONARD BERNARD, educator; b. Chgo., Jan. 5, 1915; s. Barney J. and Anna G. (Treletsky) D.; B.S., U. Mich., 1936, postgrad., 1955-56; M.A., Am. U., 1955; m. Diana Levin, July 31, 1941; children—Richard, Michael, Andrea, Donald, Barbara. Engr., Ill. Dept. Pub. Health, 1936-40; commd. officer, san. engr. dir. USPHS, 1946-64, sr. staff officer div. water pollution control, 1948-55, regional officer water pollution control Mo.-Columbia River Basins, 1956-62, asst. to chief fed. water pollution program, 1962-64; prof. civil engring., dir. Water Resources and Marine Scis. Center, Cornell U., 1964-74; sr. staff asst. water resources Pres.'s Sci. Adviser, Exec. Office of Pres., Washington, 1967-68, mem. environ. panel, 1968-72; mem. sci. adv. commn. U.S. Ho. Reps. Pub. Works Com., 1972-74; cons. Rockefeller Found., 1972-75, Office Sci. and Tech. of Exec. Office of Pres., 1968-72, Govt. P.R., 1964-73, USPHS, U.S. Adv. Commn. Intergovtl. Relations, Fed. Water Resources Council, UN Water Center, 1975-76, USIA, 1973-75. Mem. Internat. Joint Commn. Great Lakes Research Adv. Bd., cabinet N.Y. State Sea Grant Consortium, 1972-74; co-chmn. Canadian-U.S. Great Lakes Seminar; mem., chmn. Columbia Basin Interagy. Com., 1958-62. Served to lt. col. AUS, 1941-46. Recipient HEW-USPHS commendation medal, 1964. Diplomate Am. Acad. Environmental Engrs. Mem. Am. Soc. C.E., Am. Water Resources Assn., Hudson River Environmental Soc. (v.p.), Pi Sigma Alpha, Chi Epsilon. Jewish (trustee temple). Author: Conservation History Air and Water Pollution in the United States, 1971. Contbr. articles to profl. jours. Home: 8 Winthrop Pl Ithaca NY 14850

DWORZAN, GEORGE R., artist; b. N.Y.C., Mar. 28, 1924; s. Herman and Charlotte (Lepmann) D.; certificate fine arts Cooper Union, 1943; student Art Students League, 1945-48, Atelier Leger (Paris, France), 1949, Academie Grande Chaumiere (Paris), 1947-50; m. Helene Liberman, Nov. 28, 1949. One man shows Grande Galerie, Paris, 1948, 50, Nonogon Gallery, N.Y.C., 1958, Bleecker Gallery, N.Y.C. and Easthampton, N.Y., 1964-65, 70, Westbeth Gallery, N.Y.C., 1972, L.I.U., 1973; exhibited group shows Mus. Modern Art, Paris, 1947, 48, 50, Herron Mus., Indpls., 1964-68, Westmorland (N.J.) Mus., 1969, Bicentennial Religious Art, Cranbrook, Mich., 1969, Fordham U., N.Y.C., 1968, Southampton (N.Y.) Coll., 1966-69, L.I.U., 1973, and others; represented permanent collections U. Mass., N.Y. U., Chase Manhattan Bank, Hinkhouse Coll., Herron Mus., Indpls., Ohio State U.; Conover Nast Publs., numerous others; prof. art N.Y. U., 1970—. Served with AAC, ETO., 1943-46. Decorated 3 Air Medals, Presdl. Citation. Fulbright grantee, 1951. Mem. Art Students League (life mem.). Address: 17 Bleeker St New York City NY 10012

DWORZAN, HELENE, novelist, poet, playwright; b. Paris, France, Mar. 13, 1925; d. Ansjel and Rebecca (Weiripp) Liberman; came to U.S., 1950, naturalized, 1952; student Lycee Victor Hugo, Paris, 1937-43, New Sch. for Social Research, 1952-53; B.A., Richmond Coll., 1974; m. George R. Dworzan; 1 son, Patrice Olivier; m. 2d, Donald H. Reiman, 1975. Translator, Robin Internat./Cinerama, N.Y.C., 1954-59; freelance translator NBC, 1962; asso. editor Chelsea, lit. rev., 1970—; tchr. French, Lang. Inst., N.Y.C., 1970-73, Riverdale Country Sch., N.Y.C., 1973—; founder Continuum, poetry and fiction readings, 1970, since dir. Recipient novel grant Material Jewish Claims against Germany, 1961, Short Story award Dial Press, 1953. Mem. Authors League Am., Dramatists Guild. Author: (novel) Le Temps de la Chrysalide, 1957; also short stories and poems in various publs. Address: 6495 Broadway Riverdale NY 10471

DWYER, EDWARD JAMES, former co. exec.; b. South Norwalk, Conn., Sept. 21, 1906; s. John Augustus and Alura Ann (Waters) D.; B.A., St. Johns Coll., Annapolis, 1930; M.E., Johns Hopkins, 1933; J.D., George Washington U., 1938; m. Elizabeth MacLachlan, Dec. 30, 1933; children—Nancy Elizabeth (Mrs. W. Roy Kolb, Jr.), John Adam. Admitted to D.C. bar, 1938; with Gen. Electric Co., Schenectady, also Washington, 1933-41, patent atty., 1938-41; with ESB Inc. (formerly Electric Storage Battery Co.), Phila. 1941-77, pres., 1959-71, chmn. bd., 1971-77; dir. Armstrong Cork Co., Phila. Mfrs. Mut. Ins. Co., Quaker Chem. Co., Trustee Thomas Jefferson U., Phila., 1973—, Phila. Adv. Council Opportunities Industrialization Center, 1966-76; pres. United Fund Phila., 1969-71. Republican. Presbyn. Clubs: Union League of Phila. (pres. 1973, 74); Huntingdon Valley Country (Abington, Pa.). Home and Office: Grasshopper Ln Gwynedd Valley PA 19437

DWYER, JOHN FRANCIS, physician; b. Bklyn., Dec. 24, 1934; s. John Joseph and Grace Cecelia (Moylan) D.; A.B., Fordham U., 1956; M.D., Cornell U., 1960; m. Barbara F. Frisch, Dec. 4, 1971; 1 son, Thomas. Intern, Bellevue Hosp., N.Y.C., 1960-61; resident in obstetrics and gynecology N.Y. Hosp., 1961-64; practice medicine specializing in obstetrics and gynecology, N.Y.C., 1966—; asst. attending physician Roosevelt Hosp., N.Y.C., 1966-70, asso. attending physician, 1970, attending physician, 1971, chief obstetric service, 1970—; asst. attending Presbyn. Hosp., N.Y.C., 1977—; instr., obstetrics-gynecology Cornell U., 1967-70; clin. asst. prof. obstetrics-gynecology Columbia, 1970-78, asso. clin. prof. obstetrics and gynecology, 1978—. Served to capt. M.C., U.S. Army, 1964-66. Fellow A.C.S., Am. Fertility Soc., Am. Coll. Obstetricians and Gynecologists, N.Y. Gynecol. Soc., N.Y. Obstet. Soc. Home: 205 West End Ave New York City NY 10023 Office: 428 W 59th St New York City NY 10019

DWYER, ROBERT FRANCIS, chem. corp. exec.; b. Utica, N.Y., Feb. 20, 1930; s. Francis Stephen and Margaret Ione (Toy) D.; B.S., Syracuse U., 1951; M.S., Pa. State U., 1953; certificate Oak Ridge Inst. Nuclear Studies, 1954; m. Margaret Mary Kinchellagh, Jan. 31, 1953; children—Mary Elizabeth, Eleanor Margaret. With Union Carbide Corp., 1953—, research chemist, Tonawanda, N.Y., 1953, sr. chemist, 1953-58, group leader, 1965-67, supr., 1967-69, operations mgr., 1969-72, mgr. sci. services Tarrytown (N.Y.) Tech. Center, 1972—. Mem. Buffalo C. of C. (mem. nuclear adv. council 1959-69), Am. Chem. Soc. Roman Catholic (mem. finance com. 1966-73). Contbr. articles to profl. jours. Introduced practical prodn. and transfer of hydrogen slush, 1964. Home: Allison Rd RFD 1 Box 57 Katonah NY 10536 Office: Tarrytown Tech Center Tarrytown NY 10591

DWYER, TERRENCE EDWARD, health assn. exec.; b. Ft. Wayne, Ind., June 6, 1945; s. Michael Kenneth and Maxine Marie (Berkhimer) D.; A.B., Harvard U., 1967; M.P.A., U. Mich., 1968. Teaching fellow in polit. sci. U. Mich., 1968-72, research asso. Sch. Public Health, 1973-74; research asso. Pres.'s Adv. Council. on Exec. Orgn., White House, 1969-70; lectr. in polit. sci. Eastern Mich. U., 1972-73; asso. dir. Mich. Profl. Standards Rev. Orgn. Support Center, East Lansing, Mich., 1974-76; exec. dir. Profl. Standards Rev. Orgn. Central N.Y., Syracuse, 1976. Mem. Am. Assn. Profl. Standards Rev. Orgns. (exec. com. exec. dirs. sect.), Am. Public Health Assn., Am. Soc. Public Adminstrn., Am. Polit. Sci. Assn., Am. Acad. Polit. and Social Scis., Acad. Polit. Sci. Republican. Club: Harvard-Radcliffe of Central N.Y. Office: Profl Standards Rev Orgn Central NY 90 Presidential Plaza Syracuse NY 13202

DWYER, WILLIAM ALOYSIUS, JR., surgeon; b. Paterson, N.J., Apr. 6, 1927; s. William Aloysius and Amelia Mary (Dunn) D.; A.B., Princeton U., 1951; M.D., N.Y. U., 1951; m. Janet Thelma Roberts, July 17, 1954; children—William Aloysius, Karen, Pamela. Intern, Lenox Hill Hosp., N.Y.C., 1951-52; resident in surgery N.Y. U.-Bellevue Hosp., 1954-58; instr. surgery U. Mo., Columbia, 1958-59; practice medicine specializing in surgery, Paterson, 1959—; mem. staff Paterson Gen. Hosp., St. Joseph's Hosp.; clin. asso. prof. surgery Coll. Medicine and Dentistry N.J., Newark, 1974—. Project dir. Passaic Valley Profl. Services Rev. Orgn., 1974—, pres. 1975-77, also mem. N.J. State Council; commr. CD, Paterson, 1967-70. Served with USN, 1944-46, to lt. M.C., 1952-54. Recipient award for achievement in cardio pulmonary resucitation Am. Heart Assn., 1968; diplomate Am. Bd. Surgery. Mem. AMA, N.J., Passaic County (past pres.) med. socs., A.C.S. (chmn. N.J. chpt. com. on trauma 1974-77), Nat. Acad. Scis., Am. Med. Writers Assn. Roman Catholic. Asso. editor Med. Soc. N.J. Jour., 1975—; mem. editoral bd. Surg. Team Mag. (now Jour. Surg. Practice), 1971-74; contbr. articles to profl. jours. Home: 4 Rillo Dr Wayne NJ 07470 Office: 412 Park Ave Paterson NJ 07504

DWYER, WILLIAM DENNIS, printing co. exec.; b. Rochester, N.Y., Sept. 1, 1946; s. John Leo and Francis Helen (Knapp) D.; student U. Wis., Milw., 1965-68; B.S., U. Rochester, 1972; student U. Nev., Las Vegas, 1968; m. Bernadette Walter, Dec. 27, 1971; 1 dau., Amy. Salesman, Burroughs Corp., Las Vegas, 1974-75, Reynolds & Reynolds, North Hollywood, Calif., 1975-76; owner, operator Printing Co., Fairport, N.Y., 1976—. Served with U.S. N.G., 1968-75, 77—. Mem. Irish Hist. Assn., Perinton C. of C. Home: 196 Dover Dr West Seneca NY 14226 Office: 20 Aldrich Rd Fairport NY 14450

DYBNER, RUBEN, physician; b. Buenos Aires, Argentina, Oct. 1, 1937; s. Pedro and Manie (Ocseugoren) D.; came to U.S., 1965, naturalized, 1975; M.D., U. Buenos Aires, 1962; m. Ana Berlante, Jan. 17, 1965; children—Karen, Ariel, Alan. Intern, Buenos Aires U. Hosp., 1962-63, Mt. Sinai Hosp., Elmhurst, N.Y., 1965-66; resident Buenos Aires U. Hosp., 1963-65, VA Hosp., N.Y.C., 1966-67, urology Beth Israel Med. Center, N.Y.C., 1967-70; fellow pediatric urology Columbia Presbyterian Med. Center, N.Y.C., 1970-71; mem. staff Booth Meml. Hosp., Flushing, N.Y., Jamaica Hosp. (N.Y.), Parkway Hosp., Forest Hills, N.Y. Served with Argentinian Army, 1957-58. Diplomate Am. Bd. Urology. Fellow A.C.S.; mem. N.Y. State, Queens County med. socs., Am. Urol. Assn. Jewish. Office: 109-23 71st Rd Forest Hills NY 11375

DYCK, MANFRED F., med. tech. co. exec.; b. Krefeld, Germany, Aug. 16, 1935; s. Anton W. and Maria (Kampschulte) D.; B.S., Tech. Inst. Sch., Krefeld, West Germany, 1960; postgrad. U. Miami, 1965-71; m. Ursula M. Bister, Mar. 2, 1961; children—Martin C., Saskia M., Peter D., Silke T. Lab. mgr. Danske Oliemoellen og Saebefabrikker A/S, Copenhagen, 1960-62; chief chemist Messrs. Polyplex A/S, Copenhagen, 1962-65; mem. staff Cordis Corp., Miami, Fla., 1965-71; head biomed. product devel. Ethicon, Inc., Somerville, N.J., 1971-72; pres. Biosearch, Inc., Raritan, N.J., 1973—. Mem. Am. Soc. Implantable Organs, Assn. Advancement Med. Instrumentation. Patentee in field. Contbr. articles to profl. jours. Office: 77 Tillman St Raritan NJ 08869

DYCK, MARTIN, lit. theoretician, educator; b. Grunfeld, Russia, Jan. 16, 1927; s. Martin and Helene (Peters) D.; came to U.S., 1956; Abitur, Gisela Gymnasium für Jungen, Munich, Germany, 1947; B.A. with double honours in German lit. and pure math., U. Man. (Can.), 1953, M.A. in German and Math., 1954; Ph.D. in German, U. Cin., 1956; m. Marie Wiens, June 12, 1949; children—Vernon George M., Victor Herbert M., Martin Christopher C. and Ingrid Rose Marie (twins). Asst. prof. German and Russian, Mass. Inst. Tech., 1956-58; from asst. prof. to prof. German, U. Mich., 1958-65; prof. German and humanities Mass. Inst. Tech., Cambridge, 1965—. Guggenheim fellow, 1961-62; fellow Am. Council Learned Socs., 1961-62; Taft Meml. fellow, 1954-56; Isbister, McLean scholar, U. Man. traveling fellow, 1952-55, Am. Philos. Soc. grantee, Germany, 1969. Mem. Modern Lang. Assn., Northeast Modern Lang. Assn., Modern Humanities Research Assn., Internat. Vereinigung fur germanische Sprach und Literaturwissenschaft, History of Sci. Soc., Freies Deutsches Hochstift Goethehaus (Frankfurt am Main), Am. Soc. 18th Century Studies, AAUP, Kafka Soc. Am., Lessing Soc. Am. Mennonite. Author: Novalis and Mathematics, 1960, 2d edit., 1969; Die Gedichte Schillers, 1967; also numerous articles. Asso. editor Historia Mathematica, 1972-76. Home: 18 Red Coat Ln Lexington MA 02173 Office: Mass Inst Tech Cambridge MA 02139

DYER, CHARLOTTE LEAVITT (MRS. GEORGE BELL DYER), educator, conservationist, twp. ofcl.; b. N.Y.C.; d. Charles Wellford and Clara Gordon (White) Leavitt; student Scarborough Sch., 1918-19, Rosemary Hall, 1920-22, Wykeham Rise, 1923-24, Finch Sch., 1924-25, U. N.Mex., 1928; B.A. Barnard Coll., 1931; postgrad. Columbia U., 1932; A.M., U. Pa., 1948, Ph.D., 1950; m. George Bell Dyer, June 26, 1930. Instr. anthropology Barnard Coll., 1930-31; field trips to Kutenai Indians, B.C. (Can.), 1928, 31; one of founders Farmers Digest mag., asst. editor, 1937-51; instr. Sch. of Horticulture, Ambler, Pa., 1937-38; instr. Army Gen. Sch., 1950-52, University Pa., 1947-50, 53-67, Yale U., 1957-58; pres. Open Space. Pres. sch. bd. Upper Makefield Twp. Bucks County, Pa., 1957-58; mem. Pa. Citizens Council Better Schs., 1959; mem. council Rock High Sch. Bd., 1955-67; mem. Gov.'s Council for Rural Devel., 1971—; supr. Upper Makefield Twp., 1971-77, chmn., 1974-76; chmn. solid waste com. Bucks County Assn. Twp. Suprs., 1974-77. Enlisted WAAC, 1942; later maj. WAC, U.S. Army Res.; active duty in U.S. and Europe, 1942-46; at Fort Riley, 1950-52. Decorated European Theater and Army Commendation Ribbon with oak leaf cluster. Founder (with George Bell Dyer), asso. dir. The Dyer Inst. of Interdisciplinary Studies, New Hope, Pa., 1952. Fellow Co. Mil. Historians; mem. Alumni Assn. Grad. Sch. Arts and Scis. U. Pa. (co-pres. 1959-62), Acad. Polit. Sci., Am. Acad. Polit. and Social Sci., Colonial Dames Am. (chpt. pres. 1975-78), Bucks County Conservation Fedn. and Open Space (a founder 1969, 1st pres. 1970—), Pi Gamma Mu. Clubs: Cosmpolitan (Phila.); Faculty (U. Pa.); Joint Master; Lanape Hunt. Author: (with George Bell Dyer) The Beginnings of a U.S. StrategicIntelligence System in Latin America, 1950; A Century of Strategic Intelligence Reporting, 1954; A Strategic Intelligence Lesson, 1956; The World Analyst, 1958; Estimating National Power and Intentions, 1960; Exercises on an Assumption of Violence, 1962; The Cruelest War, 1965; Ritualization of War, 1975; co-author numerous monographs profl. journals. Home: Diabase Farm Box 109 RD 2 New Hope Bucks County PA 18938

DYER, DORIS ANNE, nurse; b. Washington, Jan. 14, 1944; d. William Edward and Helen Gertrude (Smith) Swain; R.N., Sibley Nursing Sch., Washington, 1964; B.S., Am. U., 1966, M.A., 1969; m. Robert Francis Dyer, Jr., June 27, 1970; children—Robert Francis, William Edward, Anne-Marie Helen Sallie, Scott Robertson McGavin. Mem. staff emergency medicine dept. George Washington U. Hosp., 1960-69, emergency specialist protective services clinic, 1967-70, adminstr. asst. to dir. clinic, 1970-78. Trinity Coll. scholar, 1960; Lucy Webb Hayes scholar, 1964; recipient Martha Washington award Md. Soc. SAR, 1977. Mem. Am., D.C. nurses assns., Am. U. Grads. Assn., DAR, Washington Assembly. Clubs: Washington, Annapolis Yacht, Kenwood Golf and Country. Author: Say Ah, 1971; also articles. Address: 5608 Albia Rd Bethesda MD 20016

DYER, GEORGE BELL, writer, educator; b. Washington, Apr. 12, 1903; s. George Palmer and Dorothy (Bell) D.; student Oahu Coll. (Honolulu), Phillips Acad., Andover, Mass.; Ph.B., Yale, 1925; M.A. in Polit. Sci., U. Pa., 1948, Ph.D., 1950; m. Charlotte Leavitt, June 26, 1930. Ins. salesman, 1926; reporter San Francisco Examiner, 1929-30; free lance writer, 1930—; organizer, writer, tchr. courses, including nat. intelligence methodology U. Pa., 1947-50, Army Gen. Sch., 1950-52; instr. U. Pa. Grad. Sch. Arts and Scis., 1955-67, Yale, 1957-58. Co-founder Dyer Inst. Interdisciplinary Studies, New Hope, Pa., 1952; chmn. Upper Makefield Twp. Historic Commn., 1972-77. Served to lt. col. U.S. Army, 1940-47, 50-52; ETO. Decorated Bronze Star medal. Fellow Co. Mil. Historians, Am. Mil. Inst. (trustee, life); mem. Nat. Rifle Assn. (life), Soc. Am. Mil. Engrs. (life), Zeta Psi, numerous others. Clubs: Cosmos (Washington); Yale (N.Y.C.); Faculty (Phila.). Author books including: The Three-Cornered Wound, 1931; The Five Fragments, 1932; A Storm Is Rising, 1934; The Catalyst Club, 1936; The Long Death, 1937; Adriana, 1939; The People Ask Death, 1940; XII Corps, Spearhead of Patton's Third Army, 1947; (with Charlotte Leavitt Dyer) The Beginnings of a U.S. Strategic Intelligence System in Latin America, 1950, A Century of Strategic Intelligence Reporting, 1954; A Strategic Intelligence Lesson, 1955; The World Analyst, 1958; Estimating National Power and Intentions, 1960; Exercises on an Assumption of Violence, 1962; Zoe, 1962; Jersey Parallel I, 1964; Operation Ho!, 1964; The Warsaw Story, (The Cruelest War), 1965; City in Extremis, 1966; Jersey Parallel II, 1967; Second Battle of Valcour Island, 1969; Ritualization of War, 1975; Great March to Quebec, 1975; Upper Makefield Days, 1975, 76; Attack on Louisbourg, 1982. Home: Diabase Farm Box 109 Route 2 New Hope PA 18938

DYER, ROBERT FRANCIS, JR., physician; b. Washington, Nov. 18, 1926; s. Robert Francis and Sallie Antoinette (Worley) D.; A.B., U. Mich., 1951; M.D., George Washington U., 1955; certificate Postgrad. Med. Sch. Harvard, 1958; m. Doris Anne Swain, June 27, 1970; children—Robert Francis, William Edward, Anne-Marie Helen Sallie. Intern, George Washington U. Hosp., 1955-56; resident in medicine D.C. Gen. Hosp., 1956-57, VA Hosp., Washington, 1957-58; chief resident physician George Washington U. Hosp., 1958-59; chief of staff Herndon (Va.) Med. Center, 1960-61, U.S. Army Hosp., Ft. Lewes, Del., 1963-65; chief of medicine U.S. Army Hosp., Ft. Indiantown Gap, Pa., 1962-63, dep. comdr., 1964-65; practice medicine specializing in internal medicine, Washington and Chevy Chase, Md., 1965—; mem. staffs George Washington U. Hosp., Washington Hosp. Center, Sibley Meml. Hosp., Drs. Hosp. (all Washington); dir. Research Lab. on Eosinophil Effect of Heparin, Washington, 1959-71; asst. clin. prof. medicine George Washington U., 1963—; dir. clin. research Police and Fire Clinic, Washington, 1964—, acting chief of medicine, 1970, clinic adminstr., 1973-75, clinic dir., 1973—; nat. med. dir. Emphysema Control Com., 1967-70; mem. D.C. Mayor's Adv. Bd. on Emergency Med. Service, 1974-75; lectr. U.S. Park Police Acad., Alexandria, Va., 1964-76, D.C. Fire Tng. Acad., 1964—; chief med. flight surgeon Met. Police, Washington, 1968—, U.S. Park Police Helicopter Corps, 1970—; cons. in medicine D.C. Gen. Hosp., Walter Reed Army Hosp., VA, George Washington U. Hosp. Cardiology Clinic. Bd. dirs. Bd. Police and Fire Surgeons, Washington, 1963—, sec., 1964-71, chmn., 1973—; founder, dir. Police and Fire Surgeons Library, 1976—; chmn. bd. dirs. D.C. Bd. Police and Fire Surgeons, 1973—. Served with M.C., U.S. Army, 1945-47, to col., 1956-65; Korea. Recipient E. H. Hill award U. Mich., 1950, Citizenship award Am. Legion, 1954, Osler award George Washington U., 1954. Diplomate Nat. Bd. Med. Examiners. Fellow Internat., Am. colls. angiology, Am. Geriatrics Soc., Royal Soc. Health; mem. Am. Soc. Clin. Research, George Washington U. Med. Soc., D.C. Med. Soc. (sec.-treas. sect. occupational medicine 1974-75, inter-specialty bd. 1975, vice chmn.

state com. on environ. and occupational health 1975-76, pres.-elect), Nat., Nat. Capital (dir.) occupational med. assns., AMA, Am. Soc. Internal Medicine, Am. Acad. Med. Dirs., U.S. Assn. Mil. Surgeons, So. Med. Assn., Pan Am. Med. Soc., Internat. Assn. Fire Chiefs (sec. med. sect. 1973-76), S.A.R. (v.p. chpt. 1974-76, pres. 1976-77, state pres. 1976-78), Descs. Colonial Physician (gov. gen. 1974—), Washington Assembly, Am. Assn. Police Physicians and Surgeons (founder 1976), Washington Med. and Surg. Soc. (exec. sec. 1977-78), Hippocrates-Galen Med. Soc. (chmn. bd. 1976-77), George Washington U. Faculty Club, Soc. Colonial Wars (gov. chpt. 1969-72, mem. resolutions com. 1972—), Delta Deuteron (pres. 1950), Phi Sigma Kappa (Scholarship award 1950), Phi Chi (v.p. 1965). Clubs: Army and Navy, Univ., Kenwood Golf and Country, George Washington U.; Annapolis Yacht; Royal Health (London). Contbr. articles to profl. jours. Home: 5608 Albia Rd Westwood Bethesda MD 20016 Office: 5530 Wisconsin Ave NW Washington DC 20015

DYER, THOMAS KEANE, civil engr.; b. Medford, Mass., Jan. 28, 1922; s. Michael Andrew and Mary (Cunningham) D.; B.S., Mass. Inst. Tech., 1943; m. Hilda Worrall, June 18, 1949; children—Sharon, Deborah, Pamela, Elaine, Joyce. With B.&M. R.R., Boston, 1946-63, chief engr., 1959-63; pres., also dir. Thomas K. Dyer, Inc., cons. engrs., Lexington, Mass., 1963—; pres., dir. Kencomp, Inc. Served to lt. (j.g.) USNR, 1943-45. Registered profl. engr., Mass., Conn., N.H., Vt., Ont. (Can.). Mem. ASCE, Boston Soc. Civil Engr., Am. Ry. Engring. Assn., Am. Welding Sch., Am. Concrete Inst., Nat. Def. Transp. Assn., Nat. Soc. Profl. Engrs. (cons. engrs. council), Inst. for Rapid Transit, Am. Transit Assn. Club: New England Railroad. Home: 13 Demar Rd Lexington MA 02173 Office: 1762 Massachusetts Ave Lexington MA 02173

DYKA, VITERBIA MARY, psychologist, nun, educator; b. Adams, Mass., Sept. 21, 1909; d. Adam and Thecla (Wojcik) D.; B.A., Catholic U. Am., 1938, M.A. in Math. and Chemistry, 1939; M.S. in Ednl. Psychology, Fordham U., 1963, Ph.D., 1972. Joined Felician Sisters, 1927; prin., tchr. St. Mary Sch., Indian Orchard, Mass., 1940-44; prin. Our Lady of the Angels Acad., Enfield, Conn., 1944-59; instr. Our Lady of the Angels Jr. Coll., 1945-64, dean, 1950-64; pres. Longview Coll. (formerly Our Lady of the Angels Jr. Coll.), 1964-72; prof. psychology Felician Coll., Lodi, N.J., 1972—, dir. psychol. services, 1972—; provincial superior Felician Sisters, Enfield, 1964-70, provincial councilor, 1946-64; dir. higher edn. Felician Sisters of Our Lady of the Angels Province, 1946-64; provincial del. to gen. chpts. Felician Sisters, 1953, 58, 65, 68, 70, 76. Bd. dirs. Religious Educators Found., Washington, 1964-70, St. Joseph Hosp., Bangor, Maine, 1946-70. Mem. Am. Psychol. Assn. Address: 260 S Main St Lodi NJ 07644

DYMICKY, MICHAEL, chemist; b. Synewidsko, Wyzhne, Ukraine, Oct. 1, 1920; s. Nykola and Eva (Andrushkiw) D.; student Chem.-Tech. Sch., 1942-43, Poly. Lwiw, 1942-44; Doctorandum, U. Innsbruck (Austria), 1949; Ph.D., Temple U., 1960; m. Olha Zmurko, Jan. 22, 1943; children—Lida (Mrs. Benjamin Pakula), Oksana (Mrs. Zenon D. Matla). Came to U.S., 1949, naturalized, 1955. Research chemist Wyeth Inst. Med. Research, 1953-56, 59-62, U.S. Dept. Agr., Phila., 1956-59, 66—. Asso. prof. chemistry Kutztown (Pa.) State Coll., 1962-65, Gwynedd-Mercy Coll., 1965-66. Gen. sec. Internat. Student Service, Verschtändigungsrat, 1948-49; adv. bd. Manor Jr. Coll., 1976—. Recipient Citation of Merit, DAV, 1970, Spl. Citation, Chem. Abstracts, 1971. Mem. Am. Chem. Soc., Shevchenko Sci. Soc. (mem. council 1968—), Phila. Organic Chemists Club, Sigma Xi. Home: 9653 Dungan Rd Philadelphia PA 19115 Office: 600 E Mermaid Ln Philadelphia PA 19118

D'ZMURA, THOMAS LEO, psychiatrist; b. Pitts., Sept. 8, 1929; s. Andrew Peter and Elizabeth Ann (O'Rourke) D'Z.; B.S., U. Pitts., 1951; M.D., 1954; m. Justine Mary Rusnock, Jan. 5, 1957; children—Thomas Michael, Stephen Mark, David Andrew, Anne Justine. Intern, St. Francis Gen. Hosp., Pitts., 1954-55; resident in psychiatry Cin. Gen. Hosp., 1957-60; practice medicine specializing in psychiatry, Cin., 1960-61, Phila., 1961-73, Paoli, Pa., 1969—. Served to capt. USAF, 1955-57. Diplomate Am. Bd. Psychiatry and Neurology. Mem. Coll. Physicians Phila., Am. Psychiat. Assn., Chester County Med. Soc. Republican. Roman Catholic. Contbr. articles in field to profl. jours. Home: 944 Summit Rd Narberth PA 19072 Office: Paoli Meml Med Bldg Paoli PA 19301

EADS, LAURA KRIEGER, psychoanalyst; b. Buffalo, Jan. 23, 1902; d. Siegfried and Bertha (Röschke) Krieger; B.S., U. Buffalo, 1924; M.A., Tchrs. Coll., Columbia U., 1926; Ph.D., Columbia U., 1930; postdoctoral N.Y.U., New Sch. Social Research Nat. Psychol. Assn. for Psychoanalysis; m. James K. Eads, Apr. 4, 1942; 1 son, Douglas Kirk. Tchr. elementary schs., Elma and Buffalo, 1919-25, N.Y.C., 1927; part-time tchr. grad. schs., N.S., Can., 1959-65, also Ind. U., Bloomington, U. Va., Indiana (Pa.) State Tchrs. Coll., Yeshiva U., N.Y.C., others; psychologist Friends Sem., N.Y.C., 1928-29, Horace Mann Sch., Columbia U., 1926-27, Erpi Classroom Films, 1930-37, Bklyn. Children's Aid Soc., 1930-31; psychoanalyst and psychoanalytic psychotherapist, Bklyn., 1960—; attending psychologist Stuyvesant Polyclinic, N.Y.C., 1960-77; guest lectr., cons., discussion leader. Recipient numerous certificates of merit and awards for work in field. Mem. N.Y. Acad. Scis., Nat. Psychol. Assn. for Ps-choanalysis, Am., N.Y.State, Bklyn. psychol. assns., N.Y. Soc. Clin. Psychology, Assn. Advancement of Psychology, Am. Assn. Gifted Children, Soc. Clin. and Exptl. Hypnosis, Am. Assn. Psychologists in Pvt. Practice, Council Psychoanalytic Psychotherapists, Assn. for Study of Social Issues, Nat. Council Math. Tchrs., others. Unitarian. Author: Prediction of Success in Professional Courses for Teachers, 1930; Appraisal of the Educational Talking Picture, 1933; Utilization of Talking Pictures in Primary Grades, 1935; The Education of Superior Children, 1945; Guiding Arithmetic Learning, 1954; Getting Meaning in Reading and Arithmetic, 1956; others; contbr. articles to profl. jours. Home: 141 Joralemon St Brooklyn NY 11201 Office: 142 Joralemon St Brooklyn NY 11201

EAGER, MARGUERITE ETHEL, career counselor; b. Kearny, N.J., May 22, 1926; d. George and Edythe Irene (Whittles) Eager; B.S., Rutgers U., 1971. With Pub. Service Electric and Gas Co., Newark, N.J., 1956—, career counselor, 1976—; counselor Rutgers U. Coll., 1971-76; v.p., treas. Entelekia Assos., Vincentown, N.J., 1975-76, pres., 1976-77. Mem. Internat. Assn. Personnel Women, Am. Mgmt. Assn., AAUW, Am. Personnel Guidance Assn., Nat. Employment Counselors Assn., Phi Chi Theta. Home: 91 Beech St Kearny NJ 07032 Office: 80 Park Pl Rm 152 Newark NJ 07101

EAGLER, ROBERT THEODORE, med. service adminstr.; b. Niagara Falls, N.Y., July 9, 1941; s. Francis Edward and Vera (Krigger) E.; grad. Green & Kellogge Sch. Respiratory Therapy, 1970; m. Ann Lee Pole, Jan. 9, 1965; children—Robert A., Michael S., Marc J., Holly A., Jennifer A. Cardiopulmonary technician Buffalo Gen. Hosp., 1961-73; respiratory therapist Emergency Hosp., Buffalo, 1972-73; dir. cardiopulmonary Niagara Falls Meml. Med. Center, 1974—; instr. emergency med. tech. program Niagara Community Coll., 1975-78; asst. prof. Eire County Community Coll., Buffalo, 1977-78, mem. bd. advisers respiratory therapist program, 1977-78. Mem. Nat. Bd. Respiratory Therapy, Am. Assn. Respiratory Therapy, Am. Lung Assn. Western N.Y. (chmn. ad hoc com. 1977-78). Republican. Roman Catholic. Club: Niagara Falls Football (dir. 1978—). Home: 2436 Cleveland Ave Niagara Falls NY 14305

EAMES, WARREN BAKER, interior designer; b. Gardner, Mass., June 3, 1925; s. Harold William and Ruth Sibyl (Baker) E.; A.B. magna cum laude, Harvard U., 1950; diploma in bus. adminstrn. Stevens Bus. Coll., 1953; m. Susan Elizabeth Cliver, Jan. 29, 1961; children—Alan Duane, Holiday. Lab. research asst. Peabody Mus. Archaeology and Ethnology, Cambridge, Mass., 1950-51, asst. archaeologist, 1950-51; asst. archaeologist in site excavation Am. Mus. Natural History N.Y., Belzoni, Miss., 1951; treas. Parker & Eames, Inc., Fitchburg, Mass., 1953-55; pres., treas. Eames Interiors Inc., Fitchburg, 1955—; founder Templeton Church Decorators, 1966—, Eames Interiors, Contract Carpeting, 1966—, Eames Interiors, Auditorium Planners, 1968. Served with inf. AUS, 1943-46. Decorated Purple Heart with oak leaf cluster, Bronze Star; fourragère of Croix de Guerre (Belgium). Mem. Am. Soc. Interior Designers, Soc. 1st Inf. Div., Nat. Rifle Assn., Narragansett Hist. Soc. (asso. historian 1960—), Eastern Jaguar Group, Soc. Preservation New Eng. Antiquities. Club: Harvard (Boston). Home: Whitney Tavern East Templeton MA 01438 Office: 1 Main St East Templeton MA 01438

EARL, DONALD WADSWORTH, stage lighting co. exec.; b. Buffalo, May 14, 1946; s. Elmer Wadsworth and Florence (Siegrist) E.; B.F.A., Carnegie-Mellon U., 1968. Tech. dir. Tyrone Guthrie Theatre's Other Place, Mpls., 1967-68; stage mgr., lighting designer Theatre of Living Arts, Phila., 1968-70; pres. Aladdin Lighting, Inc., Phila., 1970—; sec.-treas. Auburn Devel. Corp., Phila., 1972—; vis. lectr. Towson (Md.) State Coll., 1968; adviser to Phila. '76. Bicentennial Planning Group's Cultural Activities Coordinator, 1973-74; prodn. stage mgr. Famous Artists Series, summers, 1968, 69; gen. mgr. Famous Artists Series, Syracuse, summer 1970. Recipient Grand prize Three Rivers Arts Festival Bridge Sculpture, 1968. Mem. U.S. Inst. Theatre Tech., Illuminating Engring. Soc., Am. Theatre Assn., Actors Equity Assn., Nat. Thespian Soc., Soc. Motion Picture and TV Engrs., Mensa. Home: 510 South St Philadelphia PA 19147 Office: PO Box 1953 Philadelphia PA 19105*

EARLES, DONALD RAY, systems devel. engr.; b. Seminole, Okla., Dec. 1, 1928; s. Artie Ray and Iva Lee (Whiddon) E.; diploma, Mesa Coll., 1950; B.S. in Indsl. Engring., So. Meth. U., 1957; diploma Western Electric Co. Grad. Engring. Sch., 1958; m. Mary Farre Eddins, Apr. 13, 1965; children—Donald Patrick, Renate Elizabeth, Donald Ray, Catherine Mary. Reliability engr. Western Electric Co., Wilmington, N.C., 1957-59; group engr. Martin Co., Denver, 1959-61; reliability engring. mgr. AVCO Corp., Wilmington, Mass., 1961-62; Apollo Program cons. Gen. Electric Co., Daytona Beach, Fla., 1962-64; mgr. design to cost Raytheon Co., Bedford, Mass., 1964—. Mem. logistics adv. com. Dept. of Def., 1970-73; lectr. Def. Systems Mgmt. Sch., 1974-75. Served with USMC, 1946-48, USAF, 1950-54. Fellow Soc. Logistic Engrs. (Armitage award 1968); mem. Nat. Security Indsl. Assn. (chmn. logistics mgmt. com., Greer award 1975), Soc. Reliability Engrs., Am. Def. Preparedness Assn., Am. Aging Assn. Republican. Methodist. Contbr. articles to profl. jours. Home: 89 Lee Dr Concord MA 01742 Office: Raytheon Co Hartwell Rd Bedford MA 01730

EARLEY, DELIA THERESA, nursing supr.; b. Newark, Sept. 25, 1925; d. Nicholas and Carnella (Russolillo) Corsano; grad. Mountainside Sch. Nursing, 1943-46; student Cook County Hosp., Chgo., 1948-49, Seton Hall U., 1958-60; m. John J. Earley, Sept. 8, 1951 (dec.). With Mountainside Hosp., Montclair, N.J., 1946—, supr. emergency dept., 1967-78, supr. central service dept., 1967-78, coordinator ambulatory care, 1978—. Mem. Am. Nurses Assn., Emergency Dept. Nurses Assn., N.J. Emergency Dept. Nurses Assn. (pres.), Am. Soc. Hosp. Central Service Personnel. Roman Catholic. Home: 741 Bloomfield Ave Verona NJ 07044 Office: Mountainside Hosp Bay Ave Montclair NJ 07042

EARLY, JOSEPH DANIEL, Congressman; b. Worcester, Mass., Jan. 31, 1933; s. George F. and Mary V. (Lally) E.; B.S. in Bus. Adminstrn., Coll. of Holy Cross, 1955; LL.D., Central New Eng. Coll. Tech., 1975; m. Marilyn Powers, Apr. 7, 1956; children—Joseph D., Mark, Colleen, Maureen, Lynn, Sean, Eileen, Patrick. Tchr., St. Joseph's Prep. Sch., Shrewsbury, Mass., 1962-65; tchr., coach David Prouty High Sch., Spencer, Mass., 1959-63; mem. Mass. Ho. of Reps., 1963-74; mem. 94th-96th Congresses from 3d Mass. Dist., mem. House Appropriations com.; mem. exec. com. Democratic Nat. Congl. Com. Served as ensign USNR, 1955-57. Roman Catholic. Office: 1032 Longworth House Office Bldg Washington DC 20515 also 34 Mechanic St Worcester MA 01608*

EARNHEART, FRANK JONES, lawyer; b. Salisbury, N.C., June 14, 1924; s. Hilbert F. and Fannie (Jones) E.; B.A. in Chemistry, U. N.C., 1947; postgrad. Duke Law Sch., 1947-48; J.D., George Washington U., 1951; m. Mildred Schulken, Nov. 15, 1923 (div. 1965); children—Laurie Jeanne, Gregory Steven, Barbara Susan; m. 2d, Sonia Keeble, May 1967; 1 stepson, Christopher. Admitted to D.C. bar, 1951, Ark. bar, 1956, Ohio bar, 1958, Pa. bar, 1975; asso. firm Cushman, Darby & Cushman, Washington, 1948-52; asst. patent counsel Beaunit Mills Inc., N.Y.C., 1952-54, Lion Oil Co., El Dorado, Ark., 1954-56; chief patent counsel Gen. Tire & Rubber Co., Akron, Ohio, 1956-67, gen. mgr. Gen. Tire Internat. Co., 1967-69; v.p. adminstrn. Interpace Corp., Parsippany, N.J., 1969-71; asst. to pres., sec., corporate counsel Selas Corp. Am., Dresher, Pa., 1971—. Pres., dir. Interpace Found., 1969-71; pres., counsel Plumstead Civic Assn., 1975—. Served to lt. (j.g.) USNR, 1943-46. Fellow Internat. Acad. Law and Sci.; mem. Am. Bar Assn., Am., Phila. patent law assns., Am. Assn. Mfrs. (mem. patent com.), Delta Theta Phi. Republican. Lutheran. Home: Tall Trees Bergstrom Rd RD 2 Doylestown PA 18901 Office: Limekiln Pike Dresher PA 19025

EASLEY, ROBERT MARSHALL, JR., cardiologist; b. Schenectady, Jan. 21, 1936; s. Robert Marshall and Dorothy Jordan (Webb) E.; A.B., U. Rochester, 1957; M.D., Albany Med. Coll., 1961; m. Norma J. Joss, Sept. 8, 1956; children—Robert M., William A., James D., Timothy B., Steven M. Intern, Genesee Hosp., Rochester, N.Y., 1961-63, med. resident, 1965-66; research fellow in cardiology Rochester Gen. Hosp., 1967-69; practice medicine specializing in cardiology, Rochester, 1969—; cardiologist Rochester Gen. Hosp., 1969—; asst. prof. medicine U. Rochester, 1970-74, clin. asst. prof., 1974-78, clin. asso. prof., 1978—; asso. physician Strong Meml. Hosp. Dir. Genesee Valley Heart Assn., 1970-78, pres., 1974-76; dir. N.Y. affiliate Am. Heart Assn., 1976-78. Served with USAF, 1963-65. Diplomate Am. Bd. Internal Medicine. Fellow A.C.P., Am. Coll. Cardiology, council Clin. Cardiology; mem. Am. Fedn. Clin. Research, Am. Soc. Internal Medicine, AMA. Home: 52 Larchwood Dr Pittsford NY 14534 Office: 1445 Portland Ave Rochester NY 14621

EASTBURN, WILLIAM HENRY, III, lawyer; b. Germantown, Pa., Aug. 26, 1932; s. William Henry and Nancy (White) E.; student Trinity Coll., 1956; LL.B., U. Pa., 1959; m. Constance Allen, Nov. 23, 1960; children—Page, Holly, William Henry, Christopher Ames, Brooke. Admitted to Pa. bar, 1960; asst. dist. atty., Bucks County, Pa., 1962-65; spl. asst. to atty. gen. Commonwealth of Pa., 1963-65, asso. govt. appeal agt., 1967; sr. partner firm Eastburn & Gray, Doylestown, Pa., 1968—. Chmn. bd. dirs. Today, Inc., Newtown, Pa., Bucks County unit Am. Cancer Soc.; bd. dirs. Probational Vol. Services; mem. exec. com., asst. county chmn. Republican party Bucks County, Pa.; rector Warden Trinity Ch. Mem. Am., Pa. trial lawyers assns., Am., Bucks County (pres. 1976-77) bar assns. Home: Happiness Farm Doylestown PA 18901 Office: 60 N Main St Doylestown PA 18901

EASTHAM, THOMAS, journalist; b. Attleboro, Mass., Aug. 21, 1923; s. John M. and Margaret (Marsden) E.; ed. Northwestern U.; m. Berenice J. Hirsch, Oct. 12, 1946; children—Scott Thomas, Todd Robert. Former reporter, feature writer, asst. Sunday editor Chgo. Am.; then news editor San Francisco News Call Bull., then exec. editor; now exec. editor, Washington rep., corr. San Francisco Examiner. Mem. exec. com. Youth Tennis Found. Served with USMC, 1941-45. Mem. Am. Soc. Newspaper Editors, Nat. Press Club, White House Corrs., Am. Press Inst., Inter-Am. Press Assn., Sigma Delta Chi. Home: 2801 New Mexico Ave NW Washington DC 20007 Office: 110 5th St San Francisco CA 94119

EASTLUND, BERNARD JOHN, physicist; b. Salem, Oreg., Aug. 7, 1938; s. Rolin Francis and Grace Victoria (Tracy) E.; B.S., Mass. Inst. Tech., 1960; Ph.D. (AEC spl. fellow nuclear engring.), Columbia, 1965; m. Sherrie Rodman, June 6, 1964; children—Beth, David, Robert. Mem. faculty Hunter Coll., N.Y.C., 1965; cons. Bell Telephone Labs., 1966; physicist AEC, Washington, 1966-75; v.p. research Fusion Systems Corp., Rockville, Md., 1975—. Recipient Spl. Achievement award AEC, 1970. Mem. Am. Phys. Soc., Am. Astrophys. Soc. Contbr. to profl. jours. Co-developer fusion torch concept. Home: 17605 Queen Elizabeth Dr Olney MD 20832 Office: Fusion Systems Corp Rockville MD 20852

EASTON, LOUISE LUMINO, publisher, editor; b. Jersey City, Dec. 27, 1931; d. Frank and Philomena (Sciarra) Lumino; B.A. in Journalism, Bowling Green State U., 1952; m. William Easton Nov. 3, 1962; children—Philip, Peter. Asso. editor Automotive World, N.Y.C., 1952-55; account exec. Worthington Corp., Harrison, N.J., 1955-64; editor Summit (N.J.) Independent, 1969-73; editor-publisher Madison Eagle-Chatham Courier, Chatham N.J., 1973—. Publicity chmn. United Fund Campaign, 1966-69; sec. Madison Eagle Christmas Fund, 1973—; mem. Madison Sr. Citizen's Center Devel. Com., 1973—. Named Woman of Yr., Summit YWCA, 1975; named Suburban Journalist of Yr., Suburban Newspapers Am., 1972, recipient Editorial Columnist award, 1977. Mem. Nat. Newspapers Assn. (McKinney award 1978), N.J. Press Assn. (honorable mention editorial award 1976), AAUW, N.J. Fedn. Women's Clubs (state project chmn. 1959-61), Morris County C. of C. (editorial bd., dir. 1973—). Roman Catholic. Home: 190 Sagamore Dr Murray Hill NJ 07974 Office: 41 Kings Rd Madison NJ 07940

EASTON, VIRGIL JAMES, bookbinder; b. Edelmans, Pa., Oct. 28, 1909; s. Joseph Horne and Alice Mary (Rundle) E.; student Churchman's Bus. Coll., 1946; m. Myrtle Laura Helms, June 15, 1940; 1 dau., Myrna-Faye. Apprentice bookbinder Chem. Pub. Co., 1925-28; knitter Kayser Hosiery Mill, 1928-32; owner, gen. mgr. V.J. Easton Bookbinding Co., Nazareth, Pa., 1938-43, 46—; lectr. in field. Served with U.S. Army, 1943-45; ETO, MTO. Democrat. Home, office: 459 E Center St Nazareth PA 18064

EATON, ALVIN RALPH, research and devel. adminstr.; b. Toledo, Ohio, Mar. 13, 1920; s. Alvin Ralph and Katherine (Hasel) E.; A.B. (Miller scholar), Oberlin Coll., 1941; M.S., Cal. Inst. Tech., 1943; m. Kathleen Steiner, Aug. 15, 1942 (div.); children—Eric Lloyd, Alan Ralph; m. 2d, Ellen Griffiths Phillips, Oct. 3, 1970. Engr., So. Calif. Co-op. Wind Tunnel, Pasadena, 1944-45; with Johns Hopkins Applied Physics Lab., Silver Spring, Md., 1945—, mem. prin. profl. staff, 1950—, supr. aerodynamics, dynamics and guidance analysis groups, 1949-54, program supr. supersonic missile and weapon system programs, 1954-64, supr. missile systems div., 1964-73, faculty evening coll. grad. sch., 1973-75, asst. dir. applied physics lab. for tactical systems, 1973—, supr. fleet systems dept., 1973—, also mem. adv. bd. Chmn. Def. Sci. Bd. Task Force, 1977-78; trustee Howard County (Md.) Gen. Hosp., 1977—. Recipient Meritorious Pub. Service award USN, 1957, Distinguished Pub. Service award USN, 1975. Mem. Washington Philos. Soc., Assn. Old Crows, Phi Beta Kappa, Sigma Xi. Methodist. Clubs: Cosmos (Washington); Explorers. Inventor in field. Home: 6701 Surrey Ln Clarksville MD 21029 Office: Johns Hopkins Rd Laurel MD 20810

EATON, AMOS JORGE, truck co. exec.; b. Asuncion, Paraguay, Feb. 19, 1944; s. Robert James and Dorothy Iris Veronica (Kent) E.; B.A., U. Vt., 1966; m. Susan Yvonne Deslauriers, May 29, 1966; children—Amos Joseph, Catherine Veronica. Sr. programmer Aetna Life & Casualty Co., Hartford, Conn., 1969-71; sr. analyst Royal Typewriter Co. div. Litton Industries, Hartford, 1971-72; project mgr. Zayre Corp., Framingham, Mass., 1972-73; pres. Eaton-Turner, Inc., North Reading, Mass., 1974—. Served to 1st. lt., U.S. Army, 1966-68. Mem. Truck Body and Equipment Assn., Phi Delta Theta. Home: 25 Lee St Stoneham MA 02180 Office: 145 Park St North Reading MA 01864*

EATON, EDGAR PHILIP, JR., indsl. co. exec., mech. engr.; b. Milw., Jan. 17, 1923; s. Edgar P. and Dorothy E. (Morgenthau) E.; B.S. in Mech. Engring., Mass. Inst. Tech., 1944, postgrad., 1945; M.B.A. Boston U., 1948; m. Helen Yansura, Mar. 29, 1960; children—Richard, Randall. Asst. plant mgr. Gen. Dynamics Corp., Groton, Conn., 1944-45; sales engr. New Eng. region Allis-Chalmers Co. Boston, 1945-49; nat. sales mgr. The Carbone Corp., Boonton, N.J., 1949, asst. to pres., 1950-51, exec. v.p., 1951-57, pres., 1957-74; pres. Carbone-Lorraine Industries Corp., Boonton, N.J., 1974—, dir., 1951—; chmn. Carbone-Ferraz Corp., also Phairman Carbons, Inc., 1971—; dir. Adamas Carbide Corp., 1967—; chmn., pres. Cipel & Le Carbone, Ltd., 1972—; dir. Advance Carbon Products, Inc., 1970—. Bd. dirs. N.J. Shakespeare Festival, Glen Kirk Sch., Physicians Service Rev. Orgn. of Morris County (N.J.); bd. dirs. Hosp. and Health Planning Council of Met. N.J., mem. rev. com., 1973—; trustee Morristown Meml. Hosp., mem. personnel com., 1967—, co-chmn. corp. devel. com., 1961—. Served with U.S. Army, 1941-43. Mem. Boonton Area C. of C. (dir. 1975—), Nat. Elec. Mfrs. Assn. (treas. 1968), Met. Presidents Orgn. (pres. 1975—), Employers Assn. of N.J. (dir. 1975—), Boston U. Alumni Council, Bentley Drivers Club. Unitarian. Republican. Clubs: Rockaway River Country. Patentee in field. Home: 30 Colonial Dr Convent Station NJ 07961 Office: Carbone Lorraine Industries Corp 400 Myrtle Ave Boonton NJ 17005

EATON, HAVEN MCCRILLIS, communications co. exec.; b. Youngstown, Ohio, Sept. 26, 1926; s. Gordon Forest and Elsie Marie (Werts) E.; B.B.A., Western Res. U., 1947; J.D., Duquesne U., 1959; m. Mary Ellen Lyman, Mar. 23, 1946; children—Haven McCrillis, John G., Laura M., Kathryn A. Clerical asst. Pitts. Steel Co., 1947-48; v.p., sec.-treas. Kenn Buick, Inc., Pitts., 1949-58; v.p., gen. mgr. S.H. Motors, Pitts., 1958-59; salesman Terryphone Corp., Pitts., 1959-60, asst. sec., Harrisburg, Pa., 1960-61, sec., 1961-62, treas., 1962-63, v.p., Camp Hill, Pa., 1963-64; v.p., chief counsel, sec., dir. ITT Terryphone Corp., 1964—; admitted to Pa. bar, 1959; asso. firm Kirkpatrick, Pomeroy, Lockhart and Johnson, Pitts., 1959-60. Bd. dirs. Paxton

Crossing Home Owner's Assn., 1974—; pres., 1974, 75. Maj., CAP, USAF, Mem. Am., Fed., Pa. (chmn. com. corp. law depts. 1974—), Dauphin County bar assns., N. Am. Telephone Assn. (dir., exec. com. 1973—), Air Force Assn. (state v.p. 1971-73, pres. Olmstead chpt. 1973-74), Nat. Rifle Assn., Am. Mgmt. Assn., Am. Ordnance Assn., Pa., Harrisburg Area C. of C., U.S. Power Squadron, Am. Security Council, Omicron Delta Kappa, Phi Gamma Delta. Republican. Unitarian. Clubs: Masons; Rotary, Tuesday (Harrisburg). Office: 300 E Park Dr Harrisburg PA 17111

EATON, RICHARD GILLETTE, surgeon; b. Forty Fort, Pa., Dec. 3, 1929; s. Walter L. and Ruth (Shaw) E.; B.A., Franklin and Marshall Coll., 1951; M.D., U. Pa., 1955; m. Du Ree Hunter, June 13, 1954; children—Bradford, Holly, Hillary. Intern, U. Pa. Grad. Hosp., 1956; gen. surg. resident Peter Bent Brigham Hosp., Boston, 1957; orthopedic resident Children's Hosp. Med. Center, Mass. Gen. Hosp. and Peter Bent Brigham Hosp., Boston, 1959-62; hand surgery fellow J.W. Littler, Roosevelt Hosp., N.Y.C., 1962, attending orthopedic surgery and reconstrn., chief hand clinic; asso. clin. prof. surgery Columbia Coll. Physicians and Surgeons, N.Y.C. Trustee Huguenot Presbyterian Ch., Pelham, N.Y., 1973-74, ruling elder, 1975—. Served to capt., M.C., U.S. Army, 1957-59. NIH fellow, 1963-64. Diplomate Am. Bd. Orthopedic Surgeons. Mem. Am. Acad. Orthopedic Surgery, Am. Orthopaedic Assn., Am. Soc. Surgery of Hand, A.C.S., Interurban Orthopedic Group, N.Y. Acad. Medicine, J.W. Littler Soc., N.Y. Soc. Surgery of Hand (treas. 1976-78). Author: Joint Injuries of the Hand, 1971; also articles. Home: 640 Ely Ave Pelham Manor NY 10803 Office: Roosevelt Hosp 428 W 59 St New York City NY 10019

EATON, RODERIC LEWIS, ins. co. exec.; b. Utica, N.Y., July 4, 1939; s. Jesse Bennett and Blanche Arlene (Kidney) E.; B.A., Baylor U., 1961, M.B.A., 1964; m. Barbara Ann Taylor, Oct. 18, 1975. Vice-pres., Equitable Life Assurance Soc. U.S., N.Y.C., 1964—; dir. Equico Lessors, Mpls. Served with U.S. Army, 1963-64. Mem. N.Y. Soc. Security Analysts. Republican. Office: Equitable Life Assurance Soc 1285 Ave of the Americas New York City NY 10019

EATON, WILLIAM MELLON, lawyer; b. N.Y.C., Oct. 5, 1924; s. Ernest Risley and Carolyn (Mellon) E.; B.S. Duke U., 1945; J.D., Harvard U., 1949; m. Elizabeth Waring Witsell, Dec. 21, 1956; children—Carolyn, Alexander, Sarah, Lisa. Admitted N.Y. State bar, 1949, U.S. Supreme Ct. bar, 1961, since practiced in N.Y.C.; asso. firm White & Case, 1949-60; mem. firm Hardy, Peal, Rawlings, Werner & Maxwell, 1960-65; sr. partner firm Eaton, Van Winkle, Greenspoon & Grutman, specializing bank, corp., estate and trust law and litigation, 1965—; pres., dir. BT Capital Corp., SBIC of Bankers Trust N.Y. Corp.; trustee, executor pvt. estates, dir. various corps. Trustee Skowhegan Sch. Painting and Sculpture, Hartford Family Fund and other charitable orgns. Served with USNR, 1943-46; PTO. Mem. Internat., Am. (mem. com. investment securities, chmn. 1969-73), N.Y. State (chmn. investment com.), bar assns., Assn. Bar City N.Y., N.Y. County Lawyers Assn., Soc. Colonial Wars (1st dep. gov. 1970-72), St. Nicholas Soc. (gov. 1965-68), Pilgrims. Episcopalian. Clubs: Union, Pinnacle (N.Y.C.); French Alpine; Appalachian Mountain, Profile, others. Office; 600 3d Ave New York City NY 10016

EAVES, JOHN, JR., diplomat; b. Southbridge, Mass., Feb. 11, 1925; s. John and Rhoda (Heathcote) E.; B.A., Clark U., 1944; Ph.D., Columbia U., 1953; student Nat. War Coll., 1969-70; m. Maria Margaret Perry, June 16, 1951; children—Bryan Perry, Susan Heathcote. Fgn. service officer State Dept., Washington, 1956-61; 1st sec. Am. embassy, New Delhi, 1961-65; chief polit. sect. Am. embassy, Colombo, Ceylon, 1965-67; adviser polit. and security affairs U.S. Mission to UN, 1967-69; pub. affairs adviser Bur. Nr. Eastern and South Asian Affairs, 1970-72; consul gen., Madras, India, 1973-76; dep. chief of mission Am. embassy, Kathmandu, Nepal, 1976-78, Am. embassy, Nicosia, Cyprus, 1978—; mem. U.S. del. 22d, 23d, 27th UN Gen. Assemblies; instr. govt. Columbia, 1949-53, lectr. govt., 1955-56; lectr. govt. Cath. U., 1960. Served to lt. (j.g.) USNR, 1943-46. Decorated Purple Heart. Ford Found. fellow, 1953-55. Mem. Am. Fgn. Service Assn. Author: Emergency Powers and the Parliamentary Watchdog, 1957. Office: Nicosia Dept State Washington DC 20520

EBEN, KURT JULIUS, chem. engr.; b. Schoensee, Germany, Feb. 17, 1920; came to U.S., 1934, naturalized, 1941; s. Ernest and Meta (Schaler) E.; B.Chem.Engring., Rensselaer Poly. Inst., 1941; m. Audrey Janice Fitz, July 13, 1958; 1 son, Marc David. Designer, Stone & Webster Engring. Co., Boston, 1941-43, 46; engr. Marbon Corp., Gary, Ind., 1947-51; piping engr. Blaw-Knox Corp., Pitts., 1951-52; sr. process engr. E.I. duPont de Nemours & Co., Wilmington, Del., 1952—. Served with U.S. Army, 1943-46. Registered profl. engr., Del. Mem. Sigma Xi. Tau Beta Pi. Home: 5 Woodley Circle Wilmington DE 19803 Office: Louviers Bldg Wilmington DE 19898

EBERHART, HARRY SIMON, JR., city planner; b. Allentown, Pa., May 21, 1934; s. Harry S.F. and Anna H. Eberhart; B.S., Pa. State U., 1956; M.Pub. Adminstrn., U. Pitts., 1964; m. Adele H. Gregg, Nov. 28, 1959; 1 dau., Karen G. Planning and renewal technician Pa. Bur. Community Devel., Pitts., 1962-63; planning dir. City of Easton (Pa.), 1963-65, City of Meriden (Conn.), 1965-77; planning and community devel. cons., Meriden, 1977—; lectr. Inst. Pub. Service, U. Conn. Pres., Hooker Sch. PTA. Served with USN, 1956-58. Mem. Am. Inst. Planners, Urban Land Inst., Internat. City Mgmt. Assn., Am. Soc. Planning Ofcls. Contbr. articles on planning and community devel. to newspapers. Home: 100 Sandy Ln Meriden CT 06450

EBERHART, RUSSELL CARLEY, elec. engr.; b. Liberal, Kans., Oct. 19, 1942; s. Oliver Roy and Geneva Gladys (Carley) E.; B.S. magna cum laude in Elec. Engring., Kans. State U., 1965, M.S. in Elec. Engring., 1969, Ph.D. in Elec. Engring., 1972; postgrad. Johns Hopkins U., 1965-66; children—Renee Marie, Mark Christopher; m. 2d, SueLynn Eberhart, June 24, 1978. Project engr. Applied Physics Lab., Johns Hopkins U., Laurel, Md., 1972-74, prin. investigator Chesapeake research consortium, 1974-76, acting dir. Md. coastal zone mgmt. program, 1977, supr. energy facility siting and spl. studies sect. Applied Physics Lab., 1977—; mem. advisory bd. Math.-Engring.-Sci. Achievement Program, 1975—; chmn. commn. on energy and environment, mem. U.S. del. Pan Am. Congress of Engring., Sao Paulo, Brazil, 1975. Served to 1st lt. Mil. Intelligence, U.S. Army, 1966-68. Decorated Army Commendation medal. Putnam Scholar, 1960-63; John Sweeney Scholar, 1963-65; NSF fellow, 1968-70. Mem. AAAS, IEEE. Home: 5655 Thicket Ln Columbia MD 21044 Office: Johns Hopkins U Johns Hopkins Rd Laurel MD 20810

EBERLY, WARREN SAMUEL, steel co. exec.; b. West Lawn, Pa., Aug. 19, 1918; s. Samuel E. and Estella (Reedy) E.; B.S., Muhlenberg Coll., 1940; m. Blanche M. Kershner, Aug. 21, 1942; children—Lolita Eberly Pace, Glenn Warren. With Carpenter Tech. Corp., Reading, Pa., 1940—, mgr. electron alloys-metallurgy, 1970-73, mgr. electronic and magnetic alloy metallurgy, 1973—. Mem. Berk County council Girls Scouts, also Great Valley council, 1956-63, recipient Distinguished Service award, 1962; property chmn. Muhlenberg Twp. Sch. Dist. Bd., 1968-73, v.p., 1970-73; pres. Swimming Assn. Muhlenberg, 1970, 75, 76. Mem. Am. Soc. Metals, ASTM, IEEE, Am. Inst. Metall. Engrs. Mem. United Ch. of Christ. Club: Lions. Home: 626 Euclid Ave Temple PA 19560 Office: 102 W Bern St Reading PA 19603

EBERSOLE, J. GLENN, JR., transp. engr.; b. Lancaster, Pa., Feb. 8, 1947; s. J. Glenn and Marie Christine (Stoner) E.; student Ohio No. U., 1965-67; B.C.E., Pa. State U., 1970, M.Engring. in Engring. Sci., 1973; m. Helen Louise Walton, July 11, 1970. Research technician Pa. State U., University Park, 1968-70; civil engr. intern Pa. Dept. Transp., Harrisburg, 1970-71, asst. dist. design liaison engr., 1971, head research and spl. studies, bur. traffic engring., 1971-76; asst. chief engr.-traffic Pa. Turnpike Commn., 1976-78; chief transp. engr. Huth Engrs. Inc., Lancaster, Pa., 1978—; mem. part-time faculty Pa. State U., Capitol campus. Chmn. Rapho Twp. Planning Commn., 1973—; mem. adv. com. local govts. Lancaster County Planning Commn. Registered profl. engr., Pa. Mem. ASCE (past pres. Pa. State student chpt.), Transp. Research Bd., Inst. Transp. Engrs., Nat. Soc. Profl. Engrs., Phi Eta Sigma, Alpha Sigma Phi. Lutheran. Clubs: Masons, Shriners. Home: RD 2 Box 305 Bricker Rd Manheim PA 17545 Office: PO Box 1547 1650 Manheim Pike Lancaster PA 17604

EBERSOLE, WILLIAM JOHN, JR., counselor; b. Pitts., Feb. 16, 1949; s. William John and Helen (Werlinich) E.; B.S., Indiana (Pa.) U., 1971, M.Ed., 1973; m. Judith Irene Koontz, Aug. 11, 1973. Guidance counselor Southmoreland Sch. Dist., Alverton, Pa., 1973-75; vocational counselor Derry (Pa.) Area Sch. Dist., 1975—. Adviser youth group Ch., 1973-75; mem. cons. task force on unemployment Christian Assos. Pa., 1977. Mem. Westmoreland County, Pa. counselors assns., Pa. Edn. Assn., Am. Pa. personnel and guidance assns., Nat., Pa. vocational guidance assns., Westmoreland County Coaches Assn., Kappa Delta Pi. Republican. Home: Rd 5 Box 258 Latrobe PA 15650 Office: Derry Area Sch Dist Box 169 Derry PA 15627

EBIN, LEONARD NED, radiologist; b. Moscow, Oct. 20, 1926; s. Emanuel and Helen (Goldin) E.; came to U.S., 1939, naturalized, 1948; B.A., U. Va., 1946, M.D., 1951; m. Eva Siegel, Nov. 24, 1954; children—Paul J., Jane L., Susan N., Amy L. Intern, Morisania City Hosp., Bronx, N.Y., 1951-52; resident Flower and Fifth Ave Hosp., N.Y.C., 1952-55, fellow, 1955-59, asst. radiologist, 1959-66, asst. physician, 1959—, asst. attending radiologist, 1966—; asst. roentgenologist Met. Hosp., Bird S. Coler Hosp., N.Y.C., 1960-76; asso. attending radiologist Bird S. Coler Hosp., 1976—; clin. instr. radiology N.Y. Med. Coll., 1960-66, asst. prof., 1966-68, clin. instr. medicine, 1959—, asst. clin. prof. radiology, 1968—; practice medicine, specializing in radiology, N.Y.C., 1959—. Nat. Cancer Inst. fellow, 1955-57; diplomate Am. Bd. Radiology, Am. Bd. Internal Medicine, Am. Bd. Nuclear Medicine. Fellow N.Y. Acad. Medicine, Am. Coll. Gastroenterology; mem. Am. Coll. Radiology, Am. Coll. Nuclear Physicians (charter), Radiol. Soc. N. Am., N.Y. Acad. Gastroenterology, AMA, N.Y. State, N.Y. County med. socs., Soc. Nuclear Medicine, N.Y. Acad. Compensation Medicine. Office: 521 Park Ave New York City NY 10021

EBOH, ENOBONG THOMPSON, educator; b. Etinan, Nigeria, Feb. 6, 1927; s. Thompson Umo and Annie (Ekong) E.; tchr.'s certificate Meth. Coll., Nigeria, 1948; B.S., Southeastern U., Washington, 1965; M.B.A., Atlanta U.; m. Bernice Lavern Calhoun, Feb. 6, 1971; children—Abia Thomson, Ekaete Mattie Lisa. Tchr., Qlm Primary Sch., Nigeria, 1949-56; headmaster Ikot Edor High Sch., 1957-61; instr. Fort Valley (Ga.) State Coll., 1968-71; instr. mktg. Morgan State U., Balt., 1971—. Mem. ednl. com. Balt. N.E. Community Orgn. Mem. Am. Marketing Assn., NAACP. Baptist. Home: 1516 Lockwood Rd Baltimore MD 21218 Office: Morgan State U Baltimore MD 21239

EBY, PAUL JOSEPH, program analyst; b. Miami, Fla., July 24, 1921; s. Reuben Joseph and Maude May (Porter) E.; B.S., Eastern Nazarene Coll., 1947; M.Ed., Boston U., 1949, postgrad., 1950-52; m. Ruth Emma Bingler, June 2, 1944; children—Paul Charles, Ronald Joseph, Cheryl Lynne. Instr. math., sci. Boston U., 1949-52; instr. U.S. Army Signal Center and Sch., Ft. Monmouth, N.J., 1952-55, edn. specialist, 1955-63, supervisory edn. specialist, 1963-75; program analyst U.S. Army Communications-Electronics Readiness Command, Ft. Monmouth, 1975—. Lectr. math. Monmouth Coll., 1956-74. Cubmaster, Monmouth council Boy Scouts Am., 1956-57, committeeman, 1957-58, camp counselor, 1968. Served with AUS, 1943-45. Decorated Bronze Star; recipient 2 Sustained Superior Performance awards, 2 Quality Incrase awards, 6 Outstanding Performance awards Dept. Army. Mem. Nat. Council Tchrs. Math., Math. Assn. Am., Ops. Research Soc. Am. Baptist (deacon 1971—). Math. editor Edn. News, 1950-52. Home: 135 Heights Terr Middletown NJ 07748 Office: US Army Communications Electronics Readiness Command Fort Monmouth NJ 07703

ECHEVERRIA, ALFREDO DIEGO, architect; b. Havana, Cuba, Nov. 12, 1935; s. Raul B. and Emma (Merille); came to U.S., 1961, naturalized, 1972; ed. U. Havana, 1953-60, U. of Arts, 1956-58; B.Arch., Catholic U. Am., 1965, M.City and Regional Planning, 1967; m. Mirta E. Ramos Izquierdo, Nov. 22, 1959; children—Luis H., Alfredo J., Mirta M., Elena M., Juan Carlos. Architect, Havana, 1959-61, Washington, 1963-67; urban planner, San Francisco, 1961-63; urban planner, architect, Washington, 1968—; cons. housing devel.; lectr. Bd. dirs. United Way Am., Washington Urban League, NCCJ, Sociedad Pro-Arte y Cultura, Met. Washington Planning and Housing Assn. Recipient awards 1st nat. pub. speaking Havana, 1958, outstanding performance Washington Dept. Environ. Service, 1977. Mem. AIA, Am. Inst. Planners. Roman Catholic. Contbr. articles to profl. jours. Office: 9300 Corsica Dr Bethesda MD 20014

ECHEVERRIA, FEDERICO SERGIO, application engr.; b. Havana, Cuba, July 20, 1940; s. Federico Castor and Sara Ines (Cruz) E.; came to U.S., 1962, naturalized, 1973; B.S. in Mech. Engring., Villanova U., 1966; M.S. in Mech. Engring., Rensselaer Poly. Inst., 1967; m. Maria Elena Fernandez, Aug. 14, 1971; children—Frederick, Marietta, Angeline. Design engr. Gen. Electric Co., Schenectady, 1967-72, ventilation design engr., 1972-73, devel. engr., 1973-76, application engr., 1976—. Mem. ASME, IEEE, Schenectady Gen. Electric Engrs. and Scientists Assn., Tau Beta Pi, Pi Tau Sigma. Roman Catholic. Patentee in field. Home: 2 Dawn Dr RD 1 Scotia NY 12302 Office: 1 River Rd Schenectady NY 12345

ECHOLS, IVOR TATUM, educator; b. Oklahoma City, Dec. 28, 1919; d. Israel E. and Katie (Bingley) Tatum; A.B., U. Kans., 1942; postgrad. (A.R.C. scholar) U. Nebr., 1945-46; M.S. in Social Work (Nat. Urban League fellow, Porter R. Lee fellow), Columbia, 1952, postgrad. (NIMH fellow), U. So. Calif., 19621-62, D.S.W., 1968; m. Kenneth Johnson, Dec. 28, 1948 (div. June 1951); 1 dau., Kalu Helene Wilcox; m. 2d, Sylvester J. Echols June 13, 1954 (div.); 1 son, Kim Arnett. Tchr. social studies high sch., Holdenville, Okla., 1942-43, Geary, Okla., 1943-45; caseworker A.R.C., Chgo., 1946-47; resident group worker, Dosoris House for Teen-Age Grils, Community Services Soc., N.Y.C., 1950-51; supr. group work Walnut Grove Center Neighborhood Clubs, Oklahoma City, 1948-51; program dir. Camp Lookout YWCA, Denver, 1951; dir. program services Presbyn. Neighborhood Services, Detroit, summer 1960, supr. group work Merrill-Palmer Inst., Detroit, 1951-70; asst. dir. Merrill-Palmer Camp, Dryden, Mich., 1951-59; prof. Sch. Social Work, U. Conn., West Hartford, 1970—. Mem. Ad Hoc Com. Citizens Concerned with Equal Ednl. Opportunity, Detroit, 1964—; cons. to NEA, Conf. Family Camping Washington, 1959, ednl. film Scott Paper Co., Phila., 1963-64; summer study skills project Presbyn. Ch. Bd. Nat. Missions, Knoxville, Tenn., 1965—; pres. Protestant Community Services, Detroit, 1969-70. Recipient Sojourner Truth award Detroit chpt. Nat. Assn. Negro Bus. and Profl. Women, 1969. Mem. Nat. Assn. Colored Women's Clubs (participant White House Conf. on Children and Youth 1960), A.M.E. Ministers Wives (Sweetheart award), Acad. Certified Social Workers, Nat. Assn. Social Workers (chmn. nat. com. on minority affairs), Nat. Fedn. Settlements (nat. sec., chmn. nat. com. leadership devel.), Delta Sigma Theta. Mem. A.M.E. Ch. Home: 51 Chestnut Dr Windsor CT 06095 Office: Sch of Social Work U Conn West Hartford CT 06117

ECKERSLEY, ROBERT NEAL, pub. accountant; b. Scranton, Pa., Dec. 18, 1919; s. Jacob and Reba (Jenkins) E.; B.A., U. Pa., 1941; M.B.A., Marywood Coll., 1974; m. Helen Thompson Palmer, June 28, 1941; children—Bruce Loc, Richard Laurence, Tari Louise. Individual practice as pub. accountant Scranton, 1941-64; partner Eckersley Accounting Service, Scranton 1941—; dir. United Penn Bank; asso. instr. U. Scranton, 1946-50; lectr. accounting Keystone Coll., 1966; instr. Grad. Sch. Bus. Marywood Coll., 1966-67. Treas. Episcopal Ch. Pub. Co., Inc. Served to 2d lt. AUS, 1943-45. C.P.A., Pa. Mem. Am., Pa. (council) insts. C.P.A.'s Inst. Internal Auditors, Am. Arbitration Assn. (nat. panel arbitrators). Am. Accounting Assn. Home: Miller Rd RD 4 Waverly PA 18471 Office: Scranton Nat Bank Bldg Scranton PA 18503

ECKERT, WILLIAM GEORGE, realtor, appraiser; b. Erie, Pa., May 16, 1922; s. Henry Martin and Catherine Barbara (Wildnauer) E.; grad. U.S. Mcht. Marine Acad., 1944; student appraising various colls.; m. Rita J. Bolla, Aug. 23, 1944; children—William H., David F. With Gen. Electric Co., Erie, 1940-43, 45-46; shop supr. Pepsi Cola Co., Erie; driver, salesman Firch Baking Co., Erie, 1947-56; realtor and appraiser, Erie, 1952—; partner firm Messenkopf & Eckert, Real Estate & Appraisal, Erie, 1956—; cons. in field; instr. appraising Pa. State U., Erie, 1970-76, Gannan Coll., Mercyhurst Coll.; mem. Erie Bldg. Codes Com., Erie Planning and Zoning Commn., mem. adv. bd. Coastal Zone Mgmt. program Erie Council for Community Affairs. Served with U.S. Mcht. Marine, 1943-45. Certified rev. appraiser Nat. Assn. Rev. Appraisers, sr. real property appraiser Soc. Real Estate Appraisers; licensed real estate broker, Pa. Mem. Am., Pa., Erie assns. realtors, Am. Right of Way Assn., Pa. Soc., Am. Real Estate and Urban Econs. Assn., Am. Appraisers Soc. (asso.), Pa. Soc. Democrat. Roman Catholic. Clubs: Sportsman Athletic, East Erie (life), S. Erie Turners, Marionville Vets. (social mem.), Erie Mannerchor, Zukor, Knights of St. John, Greek Cath. Home: 3320 Oakwood St Erie PA 16508 Office: 926 W 26th St Erie PA 16508

ECKERT, WILLIAM HENRY, lawyer; b. Pitts., Mar. 27, 1900; s. William George and Matilda (Nickel) E.; B.S. in Econs. summa cum laude, U. Pitts., 1921, LL.B. with high honor, 1924; m. Josephine B. Gibson, July 13, 1934; children—Josephine (Mrs. John S. Diggs), Dorothy (Mrs. Paul D. Grannis). Admitted to Pa. bar, 1924, since practiced in Pitts.; partner firm Eckert, Seamans, Cherin & Mellott, and predecessors, 1930-75; parttime prof. law U. Pitts. Law Sch., 1924-48. Mem. Pa. Supreme Ct. Procedural Rules Com., 1945—; chmn. adv. com. law decedents estates and trusts Pa. Joint Govt. Commn., 1945—; chmn. Commonwealth Ct. Rules Com., 1973. Mem. Rosslyn Farms Borough Council, 1942-45, Crafton Sch. Bd., 1936-40. Served with U.S. Army, 1918. Named Man of Yr. in Law, Pitts. Jaycees, 1975. Mem. Am., Pa. (pres. 1969), Allegheny County (pres. 1945-46) bar assns., Am. Law Inst. Republican. Presbyterian. Home: 410 Kings Hwy Rosslyn Farms Carnegie PA 15106 Office: US Steel Bldg Pittsburgh PA 15219

ECKMAN, BERTHA ELIZABETH, educator; b. Berlin, Pa.; d. Frank and Augusta (Olson) Eckman; student California Tchrs. Coll., 1929-31; B.S., U. Pitts., 1940, postgrad., 1950-61; in service tng. Ind. Tchrs. Coll., 1959-61. Tchr., Brothers Valley Twp. Sch., Berlin, 1931-33. Lincoln Twp., Somerset, Pa., 1934, Maple Ridge Sch., 1944—; dir., counselor student tchrs. California (Pa.) State Coll. Exec. sec. Somerset County Council Christian Edn., 1956—, editor yearbooks, 1958-61; youth counselor Somerset County Youth Camp, 1954—, tchr. young people's class, 1929—; campaign chmn. A.R.C., Somerset, 1954-57; promotional sec. Somerset County Sunday Sch. Convs., 1957-68; mem. synodical affairs com. Fgn. Missions West Allegheny Conf. Central Pa.; campaign chmn. Alleghany Luth. Homes Aux., Johnstown, Pa.; pres. Garrett Luth. Parish Joint Council, exec. sec. Garrett Parish Luth. Ch. Am. Pres. Somerset County aux. Allegheny Luth. Home for Aged. Mem. Nat. (del. to centennial conv. 1957, del. to classroom tchrs. conf.), Pa., (pres. Somerset County) edn. assns., United Ch. Women, Nat. Geog. Soc., Educators Beneficial Assn., Internat. Platform Assn., Marquis Biog. Library Soc., Delta Kappa Gamma (pres. Alpha Delta chpt., dir. program work Alpha Delta chpt.). Republican. Lutheran (program co-ordinator spl. spiritual programs 1936-68). Home: RD 4 Berlin PA 15530 Office: Maple Ridge Sch RD 3 Somerset PA 15501

ECKMANN, LEO JAMES, civil engr.; b. Elizabeth, N.J., Dec. 26, 1929; s. Fred William and Mary Angela (Costello) E.; B.S. in Civil Engring., Newark Coll. Engring., 1960; m. Corinne Ann Willoughby, June 22, 1957; children—Stephen, Patricia, Kathleen, Ann, Peter. Asst. engr., Livingston, N.J., also Summit, N.J., 1957-64; borough engr., North Plainfield, N.J., 1964-67; twp. engr., Branchburg, N.J., 1967-71; asst. twp. engr., Maplewood, N.J., 1971-72; dist. engr. Asphalt Inst., East Orange, N.J., 1972—. Chmn., Springfield Flood Adv. Com., 1968—. Served with U.S. Army, 1951-54. Registered profl. engr., N.J., N.Y. Mem. Am. Pub. Works Assn., Assn. Asphalt Paving Technologists, N.J. Soc. Profl. Engrs., N.J. Soc. Municipal Engrs. (sec.-treas.), Union County Pub. Works Adminstrs. (past pres.), Barbershop Quartet Soc. Roman Catholic. Club: Hill City Square Dance (past pres.). Home: 33 Oakland Ave Springfield NJ 07081 Office: 20 Evergreen Pl East Orange NJ 07018

ECKSTEIN, ZVI MULLER, engring. exec.; b. Linz, Austria, Aug. 18, 1946; s. Joseph M. and Ita M. (Grossman) E.; came to U.S., 1968; B.S., Columbia U. 1971, M.S., 1974, also postgrad.; m. Nurit Blum, June 5, 1968; children—Amyt, Ayal. Project engr. IBM affiliated research Dr. Guatelli Assn., N.Y.C., 1968-72; biomed. engr. Columbia U. Med. Center, N.Y.C., 1971-75; v.p. engring. Colorforms, Inc., Norwood, N.J., 1975—. Served with Israeli Air Force, 1964-67. Mem. Assn. for the Advancement of Med. Instrumentation, Am. Inst. Indsl. Engrs., IEEE, Internat. Material Mgmt. Soc. Home: 644 Primrose Ln River Vale NJ 07675 Office: Walnut St Norwood NJ 07648

ECROYD, LAWRENCE GERALD, assn. exec.; b. Montreal, Que., Can., Sept. 14, 1918; s. George Smith and Marie (Guibord) E.; intermediate certificate U. London (Eng.), 1960; M.B.A., Fla. Atlantic U., 1972; m. Dorothy Gertrude Howson, Dec. 26, 1949; children—Lynn (Mrs. Thomas Egan), Claire, Beverly, Bruce. B.C. mgr. Canadian C. of C., Vancouver, 1946-53; exec. dir. Mitchell Press Ltd., Vancouver, 1953-61; exec. v.p. Travel Industry Assn. Can.,

Ottawa, Ont., 1961-73; pres. Canadian Inst. Plumbing and Heating, Montreal, 1973—. Served to lt. comdr. Royal Canadian Navy, 1941-45. Recipient Bota award tourism, 1973. Mem. Am. Soc. Assn. Execs. (Merit award 1971, Certified Assn. Exec. 1974), Inst. Assn. Execs. (Can.). Home: 432 Concord Dr Beaconsfield PQ H9W 5S9 Canada Office: 785 Plymouth Ave Montreal PQ H4P 1B3 Canada

EDBERG, STEPHEN CHARLES, microbiologist; b. N.Y.C., Mar. 13, 1945; s. Jacques and Bella (Schiller) E.; B.A., Lehigh U., 1967; M.A., Hofstra U., 1968; Ph.D. (NIH fellow), State U. N.Y., 1971; m. Miriam M. Kohn, June 22, 1969; children—Michael Alan, Rachael Faye. Operating dir. dept. microbiology Montefiore Hosp. and Med. Center, N.Y.C., 1971—; asst. prof. microbiology Albert Einstein Coll. Medicine, N.Y.C., 1971—, asst. prof. pathology, 1976—; adj. asso. prof. biol. sci. City U. N.Y., 1974—; spl. exam. expert N.Y.C. Dept. Health; cons. The Med. Lette. Diplomate Am. Acad. Microbiology, Am. Bd. Bioanalysis. Mem. Am. Soc. Microbiology, N.Y. Soc. Microbiology (clin. chmn.), AAAS, Reticuloendothelial Soc., Soc. Exptl. Biology and Medicine, N.Y. Acad. Sci. Contbr. articles to profl. jours. Home: 22 Verona Ct New City City NY 10956 Office: 111 E 210th St New York City NY 10467

EDELMAN, GERALD MAURICE, biochemist; b. N.Y.C., July 1, 1929; s. Edward and Anna (Freedman) E.; B.S., Ursinus Coll., 1950, Sc.D., 1974; M.D., U. Pa., 1954; Ph.D., Rockefeller U., 1960; D.Sc., U. Pa., 1973, Gustavus Adolphus Coll., 1975; M.D. (hon.), U. Siena (Italy), 1974; Sc.D., Williams Coll., 1976; m. Maxine Morrison, June 11, 1950; children—Eric, David, Judith. Med. house officer Mass. Gen. Hosp., 1954-55; asst. physician hosp. of Rockefeller U., 1957-60, mem. faculty, 1960—, asso. dean grad. studies, 1963-66, prof., 1966-74, Vincent Astor Distinguished prof., 1974—. Asso., Neuroscis. Research Program; mem. adv. bd. Basel Inst. Immunology, 1970-77, chmn., 1975-77; bd. govs. Weizmann Inst. Sci.; trustee Rockefeller Bros. Fund, 1972—; non-resident fellow, trustee Salk Inst. for Biol. Studies; mem. sci. overseers Jackson Lab.; mem. adv. com. Carnegie Inst. of Washington. Served to capt. M.C., AUS, 1955-57. Recipient Spencer Morris award U. Pa., 1954; Ann. Alumni award Ursinus Coll., 1969; Nobel prize for physiology or medicine, 1972; Albert Einstein Commemorative award Yeshiva U., 1974; Buchman Meml. award Calif. Inst. Tech., 1975; Rabbi Shai Shacknai Meml. prize in immunology and cancer research Hebrew U.-Hadassah Med. Sch., Jerusalem, Israel, 1977. Fellow N.Y. Acad. Scis.; mem. Am. Soc. Biol. Chemists, Am. Assn. Immunologists, Genetics Soc. Am., Harvey Soc. (pres. 1975-76), Am. Chem. Soc. (Eli Lilly award biol. chemistry 1965), AAAS, Am. Acad. Arts and Scis., Am. Philos. Soc., Nat. Acad. Sci., Acad. Scis. Inst. France (fgn.), Am. Soc. for Cell Biology, Soc. Developmental Biology, Japanese Biochem. Soc. (hon.), Sigma Xi, Alpha Omega Alpha. Research structure antibodies. Home: 35 E 85th St New York City NY 10028

EDELMAN, PAUL STERLING, lawyer; b. Bklyn., Jan. 2, 1926; s. Joseph S. and Rose (Kaminsky) E.; A.B., Harvard, 1947; LL.B., 1950; m. Rosemary H. Jacobs, June 15, 1951; children—Peter H., Jeffrey D. Admitted to N.Y. bar, 1951; practice law in N.Y.C.; partner Kreindler & Kreindler, 1953—; speaker on trial practice and procedure Practising Law Inst. Mem. Planning Bd. Hastings-on-Hudson, N.Y., chmn., 1969-78. Chmn. young lawyers div. United Jewish Appeal, 1960-63; chmn. Com. on Ocean Resources; cons. Nat. Council Marine Resources; chmn. Non-partisan Bd. for Sch. Elections; participant Law of Sea Inst. Bd. dirs., counsel Westchester County Planned Parenthood, Westchester and N.Y. chpts. Am. Jewish Com., Hasting, Creative Arts Council. Served with AUS, 1944-46. Mem. N.Y. State Assn. Trial Lawyers (mem. various coms.), Am. Trial Lawyers Assn. (admiralty editor 1960—, chmn. admiralty sect. 1968-70), N.Y. Acad. Trial Lawyers (adminstrv. asso.), N.Y. State Bar Assn. (chmn. marine ins. com. 1972—, asst. editor ins. sect. jour. 1972-73, editor 1973—, exec. com. ins. sect.), Maritime Law Assn. (procedure com.), World Peace Through Law Center, Fed. Bar Council (chmn. admiralty com. 1970—). Club: Riverview Manor Tennis. Democrat. Author: Maritime Injury and Death, 1960. Columnist: N.Y. Law Jour. Contbr. articles to legal jours. Home: 57 Buena Visit Dr Hastings-on-Hudson NY 10706 Office: 99 Park Ave New York City NY 10016

EDELMAN, SAMUEL JOSEPH, mgmt. cons., promotions co. exec.; b. Bklyn., June 9, 1950; s. Harry and Basia (Katz) E.; B.A. cum laude, L.I. U., 1974, postgrad., 1975—. Asst. to dir. pub. relations L.I. U., Bklyn. Center, 1970-74, program asst., 1974-75, cons., 1976—; cons. to exec . bd. Alternative Lifestyles, Bklyn., 1975—; mgr., dir. pub. relations Sports-Time Industries, Bklyn., 1976—. Mem. Publicity Club N.Y., Deadline Club, Sigma Delta Chi, Kappa Tau Alpha. Republican. Jewish. Home: 77 E 55th St Brooklyn NY 11203 Office: 2516 Atlantic Ave Brooklyn NY 11207

EDELSON, LARRY MARK, equipment co. exec.; b. Bklyn., Feb. 7, 1949; s. Irving and Lillian (Resnick) E.; B.Ed., U. Toledo, 1970; m. Dale S. Levinson, Mar. 23, 1969; children—Jeffrey Alan, David Barry. Product and mktg. dir. Air-Shields, Inc., Hatboro, Pa., 1971-74; pres. RE-DE Equipment Corp. of N.J., Edison, 1974—; cons. on intensive care nursery planning State of N.J., 1974—. Mem. Aircraft Owners Pilots Assn. Democrat. Jewish. Research on sudden infant death syndrome. Office: 17 Gross Ave Edison NJ 08817

EDELSTEIN, ALAN MARTIN, lawyer, accountant; b. Boston, May 5, 1926; s. Barney and Gertrude (Lobel) E.; B.S. in Bus. Adminstrn., Boston U., 1947, J.D., 1949; m. D. Sybil Abrams, Apr. 16, 1950; children—Marica S., David R. Practice accounting, Boston, 1947—; admitted to Mass. bar, 1949, U.S. Tax Ct., 1949, U.S. Supreme Ct. bar, 1962; practice law Boston, 1949—; partner Alan M. Edelstein and Co. Mem. profl. liason com. Internal Revenue Service, Mass. Dist., 1964-66. Founder, 1st pres. adv. com. Hillel Founds. New Eng., B'nai B'rith, Boston, 1951-52, treas. Commonwealth Lodge, 1951-53, del. Central New Eng. council, 1951-52; del. Jewish Community Council Met. Boston, 1952; area chmn. ARC, Brighton-Allston, Mass., 1950-51; mem. nat. alumni council Boston U., 1972—, pres. alumni bd. dirs. Sch. Mgmt., 1978—. Bd. trustees, exec. v.p. Temple Emanuel, Newton, Mass., treas., 1972-78; bd. dirs. Asso. Synagogues Mass., 1973—. Served with USN, 1944-45. C.P.A., Mass. Mem. Am., Mass. (pres. 1965-66) assns. attys.-C.P.A.s, Mass. Soc. C.P.A.'S (fed. tax com. 1959-75, relations with fin. instns. com. 1978—), Am. Inst. C.P.A.'s, Boston Bar Assn. (fed. tax. com. 1954—), Am. Arbitration Assn. (nat. panel arbitrators), Jewish War Vets. (past comdr. 1951-52, past nat. dep. judge adv.). Mason (lodge treas. 1959-62), Kiwanian (past dir. Brighton-Allston). Home: 276 Dorset Rd Waban MA 02168 Office: 1 State St Boston MA 02109

EDELSTEIN, ARNOLD NEIL, publisher; b. Jersey City, Mar. 1, 1935; s. Jack and Helen (Lustberg) E.; B.S., Fairleigh Dickinson U., 1958; m. Mary D. Hollender, Jan. 18, 1959 (dec. July, 1974); children—Howard Craig, Steven Lawrence, Mitchell Lewis; 2nd. m. Deanne Gilman Lichtenstein, Oct. 5, 1975; stepchildren—June Michèlle Lichtenstein, Jon David Lichtenstein. Sales rep. Twinboro News, Bergenfield, N.J., 1959-61, No. Jersey Suburbanite, Englewood, N.J., 1961-63; pub. Teaneck (N.J.) News, 1963—. Mem. Teaneck C. of C. Home: 57 Franklin Rd Scarsdale NY 10583 Office: 415 Cedar Ln Teaneck NJ 07666

EDELSTEIN, DAVID NORTHON, judge; b. N.Y.C. Feb. 16, 1910; s. Benjamin and Dora (Mancher) E.; B.S., M.A., LL.B., Fordham U., m. Florence Koch, Feb. 18, 1940; children—Jonathan H., Jeffrey M. Admitted to N.Y. State bar, practiced in N.Y.C.; atty. claims div. Dept. Justice, 1944; asst. U.S. atty., So. Dist. N.Y., 1945-47, spl. asst. to atty. gen. in charge lands div., 1947-48; asst. atty. gen. in charge customs div. Dept. Justice, 1948-51; U.S. dist judge So. Dist. N.Y., 1951—, now chief judge. Assisted Pres.'s Temporary Commn. on Employee Loyalty, chmn. in preparation of its report, 1946. Mem. legis. com. Attys. Gen. Conf. on Crime, 1950. Fellow Am. Bar Found.; mem. Fed. (past pres. Empire chpt., past nat. del.), Am. (past alt. del. ho. of dels. for Fed. Bar Assn.) bar assns., Bar Assn. City N.Y. (jud. mem). Bklyn.-Manhattan Trial Lawyers Assn., Maritime Lawyers Assn. (jud. mem.), Am. Trial Lawyers Assn. (hon.), Nat. Lawyers Club (hon.), Lawyers Assn. Textile Industry (hon.), Met. Conf. Ch. Judges (planning commn.). Clubs: Downtown Athletic, Manhattan. Author: The History and Scope of The Fair Labor Standards Act of 1938, 1941. Home: 1040 Park Ave New York City NY 10028 Office: US Court House Foley Sq New York City NY 10007

EDELSTEIN, DAVID SIMEON, educator, historian; b. N.Y.C., Jan. 19, 1913; s. William and Clara Brener (Gordon) E.; A.B., City U. N.Y., 1932; M.A., Columbia, 1933, Ph.D., 1949; m. Frances Marion Fisher, June 4, 1939; children—Helen Judith (Mrs. Henry Alan Freedman), Henry Franklin, Daniel Louis. High sch. tchr. N.Y.C. Pub. Schs., 1934-38; tchr. acting chmn. dept. social studies N.Y. Sch. Printing, 1938-42, Alfred E. Smith Vocat. High Sch., 1942-45; chmn. acad. subjects Manhattan Vocat. and Tech. High Sch., 1945-51, Grace Dodge Vocat. High Sch., 1951-58; jr. prin. P.S. 13, Bronx, N.Y., 1958; prin. Countee Cullen All-Day Neighborhood Sch., N.Y.C., 1958-67; asst. examiner Bd. Examiners of N.Y.C. Bd. Edn., 1948-75, also field supr. Federally Funded After Sch. Study Center, 1966-67; lectr. history City Coll., City U. N.Y., 1946-47; lectr. Ferkauf Grad. Sch. Humanities and Social Scis., Yeshiva U., 1960-61, Sch. Gen. Studies and grad. div. Sch. Edn., City Coll., summer 1964; vis. lectr. Sch. Edn., U. Colo., 1961; lectr. dept. edn. Hunter Coll., 1964-65; asso. prof. edn. Western Conn. State Coll., Danbury, 1967-76, prof., 1976—; adj. asso. prof. history Fordham U., 1967-70, Lehman Coll. of City U. N.Y., 1970-75. Active Boy Scouts Am., ARC; v.p. Solomon Schechter Day Sch., White Plains, N.Y., 1966-67; pres. Genesis Hebrew Center, Tuckahoe, N.Y., 1972-74, Hattan B'reshit award, 1969; mem. exec. bd. Concerned Democrats of Yonkers, 1969-70. Recipient honor award Fedn. Jewish Philanthropies, 1973. Mem. Am. Assn. Sch. Adminstrs., Am. Hist. Assn., AAUP, Conn. Edn. Assn., Nat., N.Y. State assns. elementary sch. prins., N.Y.C. Elementary Sch. Prins. Assn. (life), Nat. Council Local Adminstrs. Vocat. Edn., Council Chairmen Acad. Subjects, Nat. Soc. Study of Edn., Phi Alpha Theta, Phi Delta Kappa. Jewish. Author: Joel Munsell: Printer and Antiquarian, 1949. Contbr. articles to profl. jours. Home: 84 Avondale Rd Yonkers NY 10710 Office: 181 White St Danbury CT 08810

EDELSTEIN, MARDEE FARNHAM, nurse, counselor, educator; b. Ossining, N.Y., Aug. 19, 1935; d. Frank Gaius and Frances Ruth (Peacock) Farnham; B.A., Rochdale Coll., 1970, M.A., 1971; Litt.D. (hon.), Chgo. Kings. Counsellor, tchr. spl. edn. Lakehead Bd. Edn., Thunder Bay, Ont., Can., 1970; nurse, head emergency room Northville (Mich.) Community Hosp., 1959; recreation specialist, various cities in N.Y., also Can., 1964-71; editor Lakehead Living, weekly newspaper/mag., 1973-75; counsellor, tchr. Aunt Bessie's Open Door, Peekskill, N.Y., 1967-68; pvt. practice counseling, Thunder Bay, Ont., Can., Homer, N.Y., 1971—; adj. prof. Tompkins-Cortland Community Coll., 1977—. Founder, Cortland County Vol. Emergency-Dog Unit. Recipient award ARC, 1978, Press Club, 1976, Moonlight Meldorama Theatre, 1972. Mem. Am. Personnel and Guidance Assn., Am. Rehab. Counsellors Assn., Am. Mental Health Counsellors Assn., Am. Horse Shows Assn., Nat. Sheriffs Assn., Profl. Horsemen's Assn. Am. Clubs: Thunder Bay Kennel and Tng.; Ithaca Dog Tng.; Focus Infinity. Author: Cats in Your Home, 1956; Troubador Prince, 1958; Fragments, 1966; Voices, 1970; Modern Dog Training, 1977; Teaching Dog Training and Instructing, 1978; contbr. articles to various publs. Home and Office: 15 Bedford St Homer NY 13077

EDEN, ALVIN NOAM, pediatrician, author; b. Bklyn., Mar. 21, 1926; s. Emanuel M. and Rae (Taran) Edelstein; B.A., Columbia U., 1948; M.D., Boston U., 1952; m. Elaine Jaffe, Nov. 20, 1952; children—Robert, Elizabeth. Intern, Bellevue Hosp., N.Y.C., 1952-53; resident Univ. Hosp., N.Y.C., 1953-55; practice medicine specializing in pediatrics, Forest Hills, N.Y., 1955—; dir. dept. pediatrics Wycoff Hts. Hosp., Bklyn., 1959—; asso. clin. prof. pediatrics N.Y.U. Sch. Medicine, N.Y.C., 1965—; cons. pediatrician, columnist Am. Baby mag., 1975—. Served with USN, 1944-46. Fellow Am. Acad. Pediatrics; mem. N.Y. Pediatric Soc., AMA, Queens Pediatric Soc. (pres. 1972-73). Author: Growing Up Thin, 1975; Handbook for New Parents, 1978; columnist, Family Weekly, 1977—; contbr. to Ency. Brit. Med. and Health Annual, 1979. Home: 108-25 68th Ave Forest Hills NY 11375 Office: 107-21 Queens Blvd Forest Hills NY 11375

EDENBAUM, MARTIN I., health care co. exec.; b. Bklyn., July 25, 1935; s. Alexander and Dorothy (Rigler) E.; B.S. in Chem. Engring., Princeton U., 1956; m. Ruth Joanna Levin, Apr. 23, 1961; children—James Joshua, Daniel Ethan, Thomas Adam, Sarah Angela. Research scientist Johnson & Johnson, New Brunswick, N.J., 1956-69, dir. quality assurance, 1972-76, nat. dir. technical services, 1976—; dir. mfg. Arbrook Inc., Arlington, Tex., 1969-72. Mem. Am. Inst. Chem. Engrs., Soc. Plastic Engrs. Patentee in field. Office: Johnson & Johnson New Brunswick NJ 08903

EDERMA, ARVO BRUNO, physician; b. Haapsalu, Estonia, May 13, 1928; s. Bruno Immanuel and Erika Alice (Drake) E.; came to U.S., 1949, naturalized, 1956; B.A., Lenoir Rhyne Coll., 1952; M.S. in Pub. Health, U. N.C., 1953; M.D., Bowman-Gray Sch. Medicine, 1957; m. Miriam Maris Kikas, Sept. 25, 1954; children—Karin Erika, Tiina Inge, Erik Arvo. Med. officer in charge U.S. AEC, Washington, 1958-60; med. cons., div. hosps. Fed. Employee Health Program, Washington, 1960-62, dep. chief div. hosps., 1962-66; asst. dir. for clin. services Div. Fed. Employee Health, Bur. Med. Scis., Health Services Adminstrn., USPHS, HEW, West Hyattsville, Md., 1966-75, dir. div. Fed. Employee Health, 1975—. Recipient Distinguished Alumnus award Lenoir Rhyne Coll., 1976; Commendation medal USPHS, 1977; diplomate Am. Bd. Preventive Medicine. Fellow Am. Occupational Med. Assn., Am. Coll. Preventive Medicine, Am. Acad. Occupational Medicine; mem. Assn. Mil. Surgeons U.S., Nat. Capital Occupational Med. Assn. Lutheran. Clubs: Estonian Soc. of Washington, Fratenitas Ucuensis, N.Am. Estonian Acad. Med. Scis. Contbr. articles to profl. jours. Home: 10800 Kirkwall Terr Potomac MD 20854 Office: 6525 Belcrest Rd R330 West Hyattsville MD 20782

EDET, EDNA MARILYN SMITH, musician; b. Boston, Jan. 16, 1924; d. Clement Oscar and Beatrice Louise (Reid) Smith; B.Mus., Manhattan Sch. Music, M.Mus., 1956; M.A., Columbia U. Tchrs. Coll., 1960, Ed.D., 1961; m. Humphry Edet, Sept. 15, 1963; children—Clement Asuguo, Asari Aduni. Bassist, Sweethearts of Rhythm, Burnside's Band, 1945-54; instrumental tchr. N.Y.C. Bd. Edn., 1956-60, music tchr., 1967-70; head music U. Nigeria, 1961-67; prof. music Medgar Evers Coll., 1970—; cons., workshop leader, lectr., TV, radio appearances. Recipient City U. N.Y. Faculty grants, 1975, 76; U. Nigeria Faculty award, 1964, 65, 66. Mem. Music Educators Nat. Conf., Black Music Caucus. Democrat. Episcopalian. Home: 4041 Bruner Ave Bronx NY 10466

EDGAR, ROBERT WILLIAM, Congressman; b. Phila., May 29, 1943; s. Leroy Raymond and Marion Louise (Fish) E.; B.A., Lycoming Coll., 1965; M.Div., Drew U., 1968; m. Merle Louise Deaver, Aug. 29, 1964; children—Robert William, Thomas David, Andrew John. Ordained to ministry United Meth. Ch.; pastor in Pa., 1961-74; wrestling, track and cross country coach Drew U., 1965-67; United Protestant chaplain Drexel U., Phila., 1971-74; mem. 94th-95th Congresses from Pa. Dist.; mem. pub. works and transp., vet. affairs coms.; mem. police-clergy unit in high crime areas of Phila., 1968-71; co-dir., funding coordinator Peoples Emergency Center, Phila., 1971-74. Organizer, writer proposal for East Falls Reconciliation Project, Phila.; organizer, first pres. Human Relations Com. East Falls; vice chmn. Emergency Housing Com., Phila., 1973; vice chmn. Environ. Study Conf.; mem. steering com. Northeast-Midwest Econ. Advancement Coalition. Bd. advisors Close-Up. Recipient NAACP award for courage and humanitarianism, 1975, Jewish War Vets. award for service to vets., VFW of U.S.A. award. Mem. Congress for Peace Through Law, Nat. Adv. Council of No Greater Love. Democrat. Home: 4172 36th St Fairlington Glen Arlington VA 22206 Office: 117 Cannon House Office Bldg Washington DC 20515

EDGAR, WILLIAM DUNLAP, mech. engr.; b. Pitts., Dec. 15, 1929; s. Robert Franklin and Dorothy Cartwright (Dunlap) E.; B.S. in Mech. Engring., U. Pitts., 1950; m. Patricia Lou Hegmann, Aug. 25, 1951; children—William, Gay, Amy. With Koppers Co., various locations, 1950-58, Pitts., 1958—, asst. gen. mgr. operating dept., 1967-70, mgr. pollution control project, devel. and design of equipment, 1970-73, asst. chief engr., coke plant proposal and design, 1973—. Mem. Eastern States (dir.), Western States blast furnace and coke plant assns., Am. Inst. Mining, Metall. and Petroleum Engrs., Assn. Iron and Steel Engrs. Republican. Presbyterian. Patentee coke oven pollution control equipment. Contbr. articles to profl. jours. Home: 1993 Menold Dr Allison Park PA 15101 Office: Koppers Bldg Pittsburgh PA 15219

EDGELL, GEORGE PAUL, lawyer; b. Dallas, Mar. 9, 1937; s. George Paul and Sarah Elizabeth (McDonald) E.; B.S. in Aero. Engring., U. Ill., 1960; J.D., Georgetown U., 1967; m. Karin Jane Williams; 1 son, Scott Rickard. Admitted to Va. bar, 1967, D.C. bar, 1968; patent examiner U.S. Patent Office, Washington, 1963-65; partner firm Schuyler, Birch, Swindler, McKie & Beckett, Washington, 1969—, asso., 1965-69. Vol. tutor Hopkins Ho., 1968-69; officer St. Stephen's Dads Club, 1975-77. Served with USMC, 1960-63. Mem. Am., D.C., Va. bar assns., Am. Patent Law Assn., Licensing Execs. Soc., Am. Mgmt. Assn. Republican. Presbyn. Club: Army Navy Country. Home: 2602 Farm Rd Alexandria VA 22302 Office: 1000 Connecticut Ave Washington DC 20036

EDHORN, ANNA-STINA, micropaleontologist; b. Sundsvall, Sweden; d. Birger and Dagmar Elisabeth Magnusson; came to Can., 1954, naturalized, 1961; student geology U. Toronto, 1965-69; Philosophie Candidate Exam., U. Stockholm, 1974; m. Allard Edhorn, Feb. 9, 1945. Asst. various pharmacies, Sweden, 1940-45; research asst. U. Toronto (Ont., Can.), 1960-70; asso. researcher Brock U., St. Catharines, Ont., 1970—. Served with Swedish Vol. Air Force, 1943-54. Fellow Geol. Assn. Can.; mem. Mineral. Assn. Can., Palentol. Soc. Am., AAAS. Lutheran. Club: Salmagundi (v.p., pres. 1966-70) (Toronto). Author: Fossils from the Animikie, 1973; Early Cambrian Croppers, 1977; Algal Remains in Bonavista Formation, 1977. Home: 582 Davenport Rd Toronto ON M5R 1K9 Canada Office: Dept Geol Scis Brock U Saint Catharines ON L2S 3A1 Canada

EDICK, ALAN DALE, radio/TV exec.; b. Muskegon, Mich., May 16, 1934; s. Marion James and Margaret Veronica (Miner) E.; B.A., U. Md., 1972; M.A., Boston U., 1976; m. Ingrid Wobser, May 2, 1958; 1 dau., Joanne M. Staff announcer Sta. WMUS, Muskegon, 1952-53, Sta. WKNK, Muskegon, 1954-55; program dir. So. European Radio Network, Italy, 1957-67, mgr., 1967-75, chief ops. radio/TV, Vicenza, Italy, 1975—; cons. U.S. Army Edn. Center, Italy for Communicatons, 1975—; counselor U.S. Army Hosp., 1976-77; chmn. curriculum devel. com. U.S. Army Overseas Sch., Vicenza, 1976. Bd. dirs. Vicenza Community Theatre, 1973—. Served with U.S. Army, 1955-57. Recipient Best Actor award Vicenza Community Theatre, 1970; Friend of Edn. award Overseas Tchrs. Assn., 1977; Outstanding Performance award U.S. Army, 1977-78. Mem. Nat. Assn. Broadcasters, Smithsonian Assos., Am. Personnel and Guidance Assn., Nat. Vocat. Guidance Assn., Am. Sch. Counselor Assn., Assn. Measurement and Guidance. Clubs: Toastmasters (pres. 1962-70, outstanding toastmaster award 1968), Red Barons. Office: So European Network APO New York NY 09221

EDINGER, STANLEY EVAN, clin. chemist, govt. ofcl.; b. Bklyn., Aug. 9, 1943; s. Louis and Lenore (Danenberg) E.; B.S. cum laude, Bklyn. Coll., 1964; M.S., N.Y. U., 1969, Ph.D., 1970. Teaching fellow N.Y. U., 1964-66, research asst., 1966-70; self-employed translator, N.Y.C., 1970-71; asst. chemist Mt. Sinai Med. Center, N.Y.C., 1971-76; sr. sci. officer Bur. Quality Assurance, USPHS, Rockville, Md., 1976-77, sr. sci. officer (comdr.), Washington, 1976, sr. scientist, clin. lab. specialist Health Care Financing Adminstrn., 1977—; project officer HEW Proficiency Exam Program, 1977—; subject matter cons. in lab. scis. Profl. Exam. Service, N.Y.C., 1975-76. Mem. Nat. Council on Health Lab. Services. Accredited profl. chemist Am. Inst. Chemists; licensed lab. dir. N.Y. State Dept. Health, N.Y.C. Dept. Health. Fellow Am. Inst. Chemists (chmn. membership com., auditor, councilor N.Y. sect.); mem. Am. Chem. Soc., Bklyn. Coll. Alumni Assn., Bklyn. Coll. Chemistry Alumni Assn. (dir.), AAAS, Am. Assn. Clin. Chemists, Am. Pub. Health Assn., Assn. Mil. Surgeons U.S., Found. for Advanced Edn. in Scis., Annapolis Naval Sailing Assn. Contbr. articles to profl. jours. and books. Research in gypsum chemistry, art conservation, clin. chemistry, lab. automation and computerization, edn. testing in lab. scis., design of clin. labs. and mobile labs., clin. lab. licensure. Home: 12000 Old Georgetown Rd Apt 404 N Rockville MD 20852 Office: Health Standards and Quality Bur Health Care Financing Adminstrn HEW Room 9-A-45 5600 Fishers Ln Rockville MD 20857

EDIS, GLORIA TOBY (MRS. MYRON R. SCHOENFELD), pediatrician; b. N.Y.C., Dec. 6, 1939; d. Murray Alvin and Anne (Goldstein) Edis; student Cornell U., 1956-59; M.D., N.Y. U., 1963; m. Myron R. Schoenfeld, June 14, 1959; children—Bradley, Glenn, Dawn, Melody. Intern, Montefiore Hosp., Bronx, N.Y., 1963-64; gen. practice medicine, Yonkers, N.Y., 1964-66; resident pediatrics Babies Hosp., Columbia-Presbyn. Med. Center, N.Y.C., 1966-68; attending pediatrician Lincoln Hosp., Bronx, 1968-70; chief pediatrics Edward Barsky Med. Group, N.Y.C., 1970—; clin. instr. pediatrics Cornell U. Med. Coll., N.Y.C., 1971-77, clin. asst. prof., 1977—; pediatrician N.Y.C. Health Dept., 1971-73. Fellow Am. Acad. Pediatrics, Westchester Acad. Medicine; mem. A.M.A., Westchester County Med. Assn., Phi Beta Kappa, Alpha Epsilon Delta. Club: Cornell Alumni Assn. (Westchester, N.Y.). Home: 57 Sprain Rd Scarsdale

NY 10583 Office: 123 W 79th St New York City NY 10024 also 2 Overhill Rd Scarsdale NY 10583

EDMAN, WALTER WILLIAM, chem. co. exec.; b. Bklyn., Jan. 12, 1913; s. Edward A. and Olga (Benson) E.; B.S. in Chem. Engring., Cooper Union, 1938; postgrad. Polytech. Inst., 1938-39, Columbia, 1942-44; m. Berta Cohen, Aug. 13, 1939; children—Margot A., Luke A., Nancy A. Analytic chemist Colgate-Palmolive-Peet Co., Jersey City, 1931-37; analytic research chemist M.W. Kellogg Co., Jersey City, 1939-42; project leader Evans Research & Devel. Corp., N.Y.C., 1942-55, asso. research dir., 1955-65; research dir. Zotos Internat. Inc., Darien, Conn., 1965-71, v.p. research and devel., 1972-78, sr. v.p., 1978—. Mem. Am. Assn. Textile Chemists and Colorists, Am. Inst. Chemists, Soc. Dyers and Colourists, Textile Research Inst., Cosmetic, Toiletry and Fragrance Assn., Soc. Cosmetic Chemists. Contbr. articles to profl. jours. Patentee in field. Home: 5 Little Ln Westport CT 06880 Office: 100 Tokeneke Rd Darien CT 06820

EDMONDS, ROGER SIDNEY, educator; b. Boston, Jan. 27, 1937; s. Reginald Whitney and Marietta Viola (Swett) E.; B.S., Yale, 1960; M.A., U. Calif. at Davis, 1963; m. Ruth Dennis Walley, July 5, 1969; children—Reginald Walter, Grant Whitney. Research physicist Stanford Research Inst., Menlo Park, Calif., 1963-67, Tech. Ops., Inc., Burlington, Mass., 1967-68, EG&G, Inc., Bedford, Mass., 1968-70; tchr. math. Ipswich (Mass.) High Sch., 1970-73; prof. physics Middlesex Community Coll., Bedford, 1973—. Pres., Ipswich Environ. Quality, Inc., 1971-73; mem. Ipswich Master Plan Adv. Com., 1972-74. Mem. Am. Phys. Soc., Am. Geophys. Union. Unitarian. Contbr. articles to profl. jours. Home: 38 High St Ipswich MA 01938 Office: Middlesex Community Coll Bedford MA 01730

EDMONDS, WALTER PATRICK, pulp and paper co. exec.; b. South Bound Brook, N.J., Mar. 15, 1940; s. Walter Martin and Margaret (Lundrigan) E.; B.A. in Psychology, Rutgers U., 1973; grad. Internat. Safety Acad., 1976; postgrad. in E.E.O. studies Cornell U., 1977; m. Caroline Marjorie Crandell, Dec. 21, 1963; children—Bret Gordon, Bryce Walter, Kyle David, Megan Caroline. Prodn. foreman A.P. Smith Co., 1966-70; traffic mgr. Mikropul div. U.S. Filter Co., Summit, N.J., 1970-74; exec. asst. to v.p. Alco-Gravure Inc., div. Macmillan Corp., N.Y.C., 1974-78, also dir. safety and dir. equal opportunities; corp. safety dir. Hudson Pulp & Paper Corp.; instr. Essex (N.J.) Coll. Bus., 1973-77. Mem. search com. for new dean univ. coll., Rutgers U., 1972-73; mem. N.J. Gov.'s Conf. on Higher Edn., 1972. Served with AUS, 1959-63. Recipient Outstanding Sr. award Rutgers U. Coll., 1973. Mem. Am. Mgmt. Assn., Raritan Traffic Club, Rutgers U. Alumni Assn. (pres. Newark div. Univ. Coll. 1974). Home: 355 Central Ave New Providence NJ 07974 Office: 477 Madison Ave New York City NY 10022

EDMONDS, WAYNE KING, health adminstr.; b. McDonald, Pa., Oct. 6, 1933; s. Densel and Grace I. (Thornton) E.; B.A., U. Notre Dame, 1956; M.S.W., U. Pitts., 1959; m. Dorothy J. Evans; children—Kim, Kathy, Gina, Laurel. Clin. social worker VA Hosp., Pitts., 1960-64; dir. mental health and mental retardation Centerville Clinic, Fredericktown, Pa., 1964-74; asst. dean Sch. Social Work, U. Pitts., 1968-70; exec. dir. Pa. Council Fitness and Sports, Harrisburg, 1976—; lectr. Pa. State U. Mem. Nat. Assn. Social Workers, Acad. Certified Social Workers, Pa. Public Health Assn. Home: 5907 E Shenaur Dr Harrisburg PA 17112 Office: PO Box 9 Harrisburg PA 17012

EDMONDS, WILLIE, JR., engr.; b. Grand Rapids, Mich., Jan. 9, 1945; s. Willie and Dora Lee (Delbridge) E.; A.A.S., Grand Rapids Jr. Coll., 1971; B.S., Mich. Tech. U., 1974; m. Cynthia Ann Roden, June 26, 1965; children—Yvette Marie, Willie. Service engr. Eastman Kodak Co., Rochester, N.Y., 1974-78, dist. supt., 1978—. Served with U.S. Army, 1966-68. Baptist. Home: 125 Holybrook Rd Rochester NY 14623 Office: 1187 Ridge Rd W Rochester NY 14650

EDMONSTON, WILLIAM EDWARD, JR., educator; b. Balt., Nov. 20, 1931; s. William Edward and Helen (Mallonee) E.; B.A., Johns Hopkins, 1952; M.A., U. Ala., 1956; Ph.D., U. Ky., 1960; m. Nellie Jane Kerley, Aug. 3, 1957; children—Kathryn Nell, Rebecca Jane, Owen William. Instr., asst. prof. Washington U. Sch. Medicine, St. Louis, 1960-64; mem. faculty Colgate U., Hamilton, N.Y., 1964—, dir. neurosci. program, 1971—, prof. psychology, 1973—, chmn. dept., 1973—. Served with U.S. Army, 1952-54; Korea. Recipient Bernard E. Gorton award, 1961; Sloan Found. fellow, 1967, 69; sr. fellow U. Wash., 1971; USPHS grantee, 1964-65; diplomate Am. Bd. Psychol. Hypnosis. Fellow AAAS, Am. Psychol. Assn., Am. Soc. Clin. Hypnosis, Internat. Soc. Clin. and Exptl. Hypnosis; mem. N.Y. Acad. Scis., Eastern Psychol. Assn., Soc. Neurosci., Am. Psychopathol. Assn., Sigma Xi. Editor, Am. Jour. Clin. Hypnosis, 1968-76. Contbr. articles to profl. jours. Home: 30 Maple Ave Hamilton NY 13346 Office: Dept Psychology Colgate U Hamilton NY 13346

EDMUNDS, ARTHUR J., assn. exec.; b. Des Moines, July 4, 1922; B.A., Fisk U., 1943; M.A., Drake U., 1945. Exec dir. Urban League Flint (Mich.), 1952-60, Urban League Pitts., 1960—. Bd. dirs. W. Penn Hosp., Hosp. Council Western Pa. Mem. Acad. Certified Social Workers. Named Man of Yr. in Human Relations, Jaycees, 175. Home: 2337 Haymaker Rd Monroeville PA 15146 Office: 200 Ross St Pittsburgh PA 15219*

EDMUNDS, ROBERT THOMAS, surgeon; b. Toledo, Sept. 14, 1924; s. Marion Kenneth and Frances Ethel (McCauley) E.; B.A., Harvard U., 1947; M.D., Columbia U., 1951; m. Margaret Minka Murray, May 3, 1952; children—Nancy, Priscilla, Elizabeth, Cynthia, Robert. Intern, St. Luke's Hosp., N.Y,C., 1951-52, resident in surgery, 1952-56, asst. attending surgeon, 1956; asst. attending surgeon Knickerbocker Hosp., N.Y.C., 1957-60, St. Barnabas Hosp., N.Y.C., 1972-74; attending surgeon St. Luke's Hosp., N.Y.C., 1963—; asst. clin. prof. surgery Columbia U.; cons. Am. Cancer Soc. Served to lt. j.g. USNR, 1942-46. Diplomate Am. Bd. Surgeons. Fellow Am. Coll. Surgeons; mem. N.Y. Cancer Soc. (treas 1973-78). Republican. Congregationalist. Clubs: Union (N.Y.C.); Rockaway Hunting, Lawrence Beach. Contbr. articles in field to profl. jours. Home: 8 E 96th St New York City NY 10028 Office: 1090 Amsterdam Ave New York City NY 10025

EDSALL, HOWARD LINN, mktg. exec.; b. N.Y.C., Nov. 17, 1904; s. John Linn and Alise (Stoughton) E.; student pub. schs., pvt. tutoring; m. Florence S. Small, July 5, 1930; children—Florence Linn (Mrs. Robert James Whitehouse). With marine div. RCA, 1920-25, advt. and sales promotion mgr. tube div., 1944-47; with Curtis-Martin Newspapers, Inc., 1926; mktg., sales promotion exec., plans writer R.E. Lovekin Corp., 1928-34, Bridge & King, 1934-35. E.F. Houghton Co., 1935-37; co-founder, dir. G.S. Rogers & Co., Chgo., 1937-40, Ajax Metal Co. & Affiliates, 1940-44; v.p., dir. Craven & Hedrick, 1949-53; exec. v.p. Fred Wittner Advt., N.Y.C., 1953-57; sec. dir. Plastomics Products Co., Inc., 1946; pres., founder AIMS, Inc. (counselors to profl. mgrs.), 1959; partner Bonniview Lodge. Lake Penage, Whitfish, Ont., Can. Mem. Re-Employment Planning Assos., 1966; dir. spl. events UN Council, 1944-45. Mem. Am. Soc. Metals (bd. editors 1944-47), Soc. Profl. Mgmt. Cons. (charter, v.p., dir. 1967-69), Inst. Mgmt Cons. (founder-mem.). Clubs: Pen and Pencil (Phila.); Morse Telegraph; Listentome (N.J.). Author: Borrow & Prosper, 1946; Management Consultant and Reporter, 1968; The How You Can Borrow and Prosper Kit, 1972; co-author One To Ten Thousand Copies, 1963. Cons. editorial bd. Jour. Mgmt. and Bus. Consulting, 1976. Contbr. fiction articles to mags. Inventor, Violute, 1940. Home: 39A North Mountain Ave Montclair NJ 07042

EDSON, ANDREW STEPHEN, pub. relations exec.; b. N.Y.C., Jan. 8, 1946; s. Herbert and Frances (Bauling) E.; A.B. (Y scholar), Fairleigh Dickinson U., 1967; M.A. (grad. asst.), Memphis State U., 1969; m. Marilyn Borer, July 22, 1972; 1 son, Garrett Matthew. Account supr. Ruder and Finn, Inc., N.Y.C., 1970-73; asst. dir. pub. relations Anaconda Co., N.Y.C., 1973-74; pub. affairs mgr. Citicorp, 1974-78; v.p. Padilla and Speer, Inc., N.Y.C., 1978—; vis. instr. merchandising and mgmt. Pratt Inst., Bklyn., 1972-75; adj. prof. pub. relations Syracuse U., 1977—. Mem. Pub. Relations Soc. Am., Nat. Investor Relations Inst. Clubs: Publicity (exec. com. N.Y.C. 1973-74); Hertford (London). Contbr. articles to profl. publs. Home: 100 Twin Oaks Dr Fort Salonga NY 11754 Office: 950 3d Ave New York City NY 10022

EDSON, HUBERT, accountant; b. Long Eaton, Eng., Jan. 23, 1913; s. Bertie and Ethel (Islip) E.; came to U.S., 1923, naturalized, 1929; B.B.A., Northeastern U., 1936; m. Eleanor F. Hunter, July 24, 1935; children—Ronald Allan, Janice Ruth, Dale Cameron, Jean Lynne Edson Miller. With Gen. Motors Corp., Providence, 1936-42, Tonawanda, N.Y., 1942-45, Providence, 1945-53; sr. accounting mgr. Lees Baer & Hanover, C.P.A.'s, Providence, 1954-61; comptroller Woonsocket (R.I.) Hosp., 1961-64; sr. accountant Michael T. Federico & Co., Providence, 1964-70; pvt. practice accounting, Providence, 1971—. Leader, 4H Club, 1961-65; chmn. Coventry Easter Seal Campaign, 1967-71; chmn. Bd. Canvassers, Exeter, R.I., 1973—. Served with USCRG, 1943-45. Mem. Northeastern U. Alumni Club R.I. (pres. 1972), Nat. Soc. Pub. Accountants, R.I. Assn. Pub. Accountants, Nat. Assn. Notaries Public, Congregationalist. Clubs: Springhaven Golf, Moosup Valley Grange. Home: West Shore Dr Exeter RI 02822 Office: 849 N Main St Providence RI 02904

EDWARDS, ARTHUR WILLIAM, city planning cons.; b. Trenton, N.J., Feb. 17, 1935; s. Arthur Issac and Marian Frances (Gross) E.; student Pa. State U., 1952-54; B.A., Tulane U., 1960; M. City Planning, Ga. Inst. Tech., 1965; m. Patricia Ann Van Over, Feb. 23, 1963; children—Arthur William, Richard Bennet, Jeremy Van Over. Dir. Ga. Appalachian Devel., Atlanta, 1965-67; regional planner Appalachian Regional Commn., Washington, 1967-68; local liaision officer U.S. Dept. Transp., Washington, 1968-69; treas. Indsl. Devel. Assos., Washington, 1969-71; pres. Arthur W. Edwards Assos., Annapolis, Md., 1971—; chmn. CASE/Edwards Enterprises, Annapolis and Washington, 1971—. Trustee Key Sch., Annapolis, 1976—; mem. rapid transit com. Anne Arundel County, Md., 1976-77. Served with U.S. Navy, 1954-58. Mem. Am. Inst. Planners (membership examiner 1974—), Am. Soc. Planning Ofcls., Nat. Assn. Housing and Redevel. Ofcls. Democrat. Club: Annapolis Yacht. Contbr. articles to profl. jours. Home: 111 Monticello Ave Annapolis MD 21401 Office: 5135 MacArthur Blvd Washington DC 20016

EDWARDS, BERT TVEDT, accountant; b. Washington, Aug. 23, 1937; s. Archie Campbell and Geniana (Rasmussen) E.; B.A., Wesleyan U., 1959; M.B.A., Stanford, 1961; m. Susan Elizabeth Dye, July 18, 1964; children—Christopher Andrew, Stacey Elizabeth. With Arthur Andersen & Co., Washington, 1961-69, 70—, mgr. 1965-69, 70-71, partner, 1971—; fin. v.p. Lesuire Time Industries, Inc. 1969-70. Trustee The Barker Found., 1968-78, treas., 1968-71, 1st v.p., 1971-72, pres., 1972-75; trustee, treas. Population Reference Bur., Inc., 1975—; bd. dirs. Jr. Achievement Met. Washington, Inc., 1973—, treas., 1973-74, sec., v.p., 1974-75, 1st v.p., 1975-77, pres., 1977-78, chmn., 1978—; dir., treas. Heritage Walk Homes Corp., 1976—. Served with AUS, 1962-63. C.P.A., D.C., Va., N.C., La. Victor Royall fellow, 1960-61. Mem. Am., D.C. insts. C.P.A.'s, Va. Soc. C.P.A.'s, Nat. Assn. Accountants, Am. Accounting Assn., Am. Meat Inst., Nat. Ind. Meat Packers Assn., Assn. Sch. Bus. Ofcls., Municipal Fin. Officers Assn., Md. Pub. Fin. Officers Assn., Met. Washington Bd. Trade, Rockville C. of C., Wesleyan U. Alumni Club Washington (treas. 1968-70, pres. 1970-73). Methodist. Club: Univ. Home: 18 Windermere Ct Rockville MD 20852 Office: 1666 K St NW Washington DC 20006

EDWARDS, CARL NORMAND, social scientist; b. Norwood, Mass., Jan. 22, 1943; s. Wilfred Carl and Cecile Marie-Anne (Pepin) E.; student Brdigewater State Coll.; M.Ed., Suffolk U., 1969; postgrad. Harvard; m. Elizabeth Anne Pyper, May 9, 1964. Cons. dept. social relations Harvard, 1966-69, research fellow, 1969-71, lectr. social relations, 1971-72; cons. research psychologist Cambridge Computer Assos. (Mass.), 1966—; cons. social scientist pvt. practice, Medway, Mass., 1967—; asso. clin. prof. psychiatry Tufts U. Sch. Medicine, 1971—, research social psychologist Tufts-New Eng. Med. Center, 1969—; dir. Four Oaks Research Inst., Norfolk, Mass., 1974—; sr. asso. for policy planning and research Justice Resource Inst., 1971—; field faculty grad. program Goddard Coll., Plainfield, Vt., 1972—; tchr. seminars; cons. to major corps., govt. agys. and pub. instns. in human dynamics and pub. policy; lectr., thesis adviser, program devel. cons. schs., colls., insts., New Eng. area. Mem. U.S. N.G., 1963-64. Mem. Am., Mass. psychol. assns., Soc. for Psychol. Study Social Issues, Peace Research Soc., Nat. Pilots Assn., Nat. Trust for Hist. Preservation. Clubs: Harvard (Boston); Appalachian Mountain, Sierra. Author: Drug Dependence: Social Regulation and Treatment Alternatives. Contbr. articles to profl. jours., monographs, revs. Home: Four Oaks PO Box 187 Norfolk MA 02056

EDWARDS, CHARLES CANNON, orthopedic surgeon; b. Silver Spring, Md., Mar. 15, 1942; s. Earl Lester and Martha (Cannon) E.; A.B., Duke U., 1964; M.D., U. Md., 1968; m. Gretchen Schwarting, Dec. 28, 1965; children—Holly Ann, Charles, James, Marianne. Intern, Yale U., New Haven, 1968-69, gen. surgery resident, 1969-70; orthopedic surg. resident Yale-New Haven Hosp., 1972-75; instr. surgery Yale Med. Sch., New Haven, 1974-75; asst. prof. surgery U. Md., Balt., 1975-77, asso. prof., 1978—, chief orthopedic surgery Sch. Medicine and Hosp., 1977—; chief orthopedic surgery Md. Inst. Emergency Medicine, Balt., 1977—; dir. Md. Orthopedic Research Labs., Balt., 1976—; dir. Assocs. in Surgery, Inc., Balt.; owner The Edwards Co., Balt. Served as orthopedic surgeon, M.C., U.S. Army, 1970-72. Diplomate Am. Bd. Orthopedic Surgery. Mem. Orthopedic Research Soc., Assn. Orthopedic Chmn., Yale Orthopedic Assn., Md. Chirurg. Soc., Md. Orthopedic Soc., Am. Med. Assn., Md. Med. Soc. Contbr. articles to profl. jours. Home: 3907 Greenway Baltimore MD 21218 Office: 22 S Greene St Baltimore MD 21201

EDWARDS, CHARLES HENRY, JR., surgeon; b. Goldsboro, N.C., Dec. 22, 1920; s. Charles Henry and Lillie Estelle (Thornton) E.; B.A., U. N.C., 1940, postgrad. in Medicine, 1940-42; M.D., Thomas Jefferson U., 1944; m. Betty Shea, Mar. 11, 1950; children—Charles Henry, Christopher G. Intern, Pa. Hosp., Phila., 1944; resident in gen. surgery Halloran VA Hosp., S.I., 1947-51; surg. resident Martland Hosp., Newark, 1951-52; practice gen. and vascular surgery, Newark, 1951-55, Glen Ridge, N.J., 1955-71, Montclair, N.J., 1971—; mem. surg. staff St. Vincent's, St. James, United Hosp. of Newark, St. Barnabas, Riverside hosps.; med. dir. Riverside Hospice, Boonton, N.J., 1976-78; clin. asst. prof. surgery N.J. Coll. Medicine and Dentistry, Newark, 1966-78; med. dir. Individual Freedom Found. Ednl. Trust, 1976—. Served to capt., M.C., U.S. Army, 1944-47. Diplomate Am. Bd. Surgery. Fellow A.C.S.; mem. AMA, N.J. State, Essex County med. socs. Clubs: Masons (32 deg.), Shriners. Home: 19 Club Rd Upper Montclair NJ 07043 Office: 5 Roosevelt Pl Montclair NJ 07042

EDWARDS, CHARLES MUNDY, JR., mgmt. cons., former univ. dean; b. Richmond, Va., Nov. 2, 1903; s. Charles Mundy and Lelia Le Moyne (Gahagan) E.; B.B.A., U. Richmond, 1925, LL.D. (hon.), 1963; M.S. in Retailing, N.Y. U., 1930, D.C.S., 1936; m. Nancy Blow Rawls, Apr. 2, 1931 (dec. Nov. 1968); children—Charles Mundy, Richard Franklin; m. 2d, Marie Elizabeth Flannery, Oct. 10, 1969. Instr. English, head track coach Staunton Mil. Acad. (Va.), 1925-29; with mgmt. div. James McCreery & Co., N.Y.C., 1929-30; sales promotion exec. Frederick Loeser & Co., Bklyn., 1930-31; faculty N.Y. U., N.Y.C., 1930—, dean Inst. Retail Mgmt., 1946-70, dean and prof. emeritus, 1970—; cons. to retailers and mfrs., 1936—; sr. v.p. Search Assos., Inc., Summit, N.J.; dir. Russ Togs, Inc., Concord Fabrics, Inc., Old Deerfield Fabrics, Inc., Williamhouse Regency, Inc. Served to capt. U.S. Army, 1924-37, organizer, dir. Army Exchange Service Sch., ETO with assimilated rank col., 1945. Decorated Chevalier Ordre Du Merite Commercial (France). Mem. Nat. Retail Assn. (dir. 1951-53, Gold medal 1958, named one of ten All Time Greats in Retail Sales Promotion 1969), Am. Mktg. Assn., Am. Collegiate Retailing Assn. (pres. 1948-49), Kappa Alpha, Omicron Delta Kappa, Eta Mu Pi, Alpha Delta Sigma. Author: (with William H. Howard) Retail Advertising and Sales Promotion, rev. edit., 1943, 3d edit. (with Russell A. Brown), 1959; (with Howard M.Cowee) The Retail Advertising Budget, rev. edit., 1952. Chmn. editorial bd. Jour. Retailing, 1946-73; contbr. articles to profl. jours. Home: 65 Hobart Ave Summit NJ 07901 Office: Tisch Hall NY U Washington Sq New York City NY 10003

EDWARDS, JAMES PERCIVAL, III, indsl. engr.; b. Bronxville, N.Y., June 20, 1939; s. James Percival and Dorothy (Roche) E., Jr.; B.S. in Physics, U. Tex. 1962; postgrad. So. Meth. U., 1965-67; m. Betsy Dianne Hamric, Sept. 9, 1960; children—James, Julia, Richard, Patricia. Tech. staff Tex. Instruments, Inc., Dallas, 1964, program mgr., 1965— mgr. advanced systems engring. div. Gould, Inc., Glen Burnie, Md. 1973-76, mgr. engring., 1976-77, dir., 1977—; instr. advanced signal processing anti-submarine warfare, Washington, 1973-75. Pack chmn. Boy Scouts of Am., 1976. Served to capt. U.S. Army 1962-64. Named distinguished military grad. U. Tex., 1962; recipient grad. studies grant in physics Tex. Instruments, Dallas 1966-68. Mem. Am. Defense Preparedness Assn., Nat. Security Indsl. Assn. Republican. Methodist. Contbr. numerous tech. reports Dept. of Def. Office: 6711 Baymeadow Dr Glen Burnie MD 21061

EDWARDS, RALPH, coll. adminstr.; b. Chgo., Jan. 27, 1931; s. Harold and Ruth (Lurie) E.; B.S., Coll. City N.Y., 1953; M.S., U. Ill., 1954; Ed.D., Tchrs. Coll., Columbia U., 1959; m. Roberta Strauber, Sept. 3, 1955; children—Bruce, Sharon. Instr., U. Ill., Urbana, 1953-54, asso. supr. rehab. center, 1955-56; tutor health edn. Queens Coll., N.Y.C., 1954-55; tchr. N.Y.C. Pub. Schs., 1956-57; asst. prof. child devel. and health edn. Columbia U., 1957-64; prof. health sci. Kingsborough Community Coll., Bklyn., 1964-66, chmn. health sci. dept., 1964-66, dean adminstrn., 1966-69, dean faculty, 1969-70, dean ednl. devel., 1970-71, dean adminstrn. and planning, 1971—; cons. to N.Y. State Dept. Edn., 1966—. Mem. master plan com. Central High Sch. Dist. 2, N.Y.C., 1971—. Recipient Certificate of Appreciation, Union Free Sch. Dist. 17, 1969. Mem. Nat. Council Family Relations, Am. Assn. Sex Educators and Counselors, AAHPER, Am. Assn. History of Medicine, Assn. Schs. Allied Health Professions. Mem. editorial bd. Jour. Drug Edn., 1971—; contbr. articles to profl. jours. Home: 782 Cornell Rd Franklin Sq NY 11010 Office: Kingsborough Community Coll 2001 Oriental Blvd Brooklyn NY 11235

EDWARDS, RAY CONWAY, engring. corp. exec.; b. Belleville, Ont., Can., Sept. 1, 1913; s. Ernest Alfred and Augusta (Fee) E.; B.A., U. Cal. at Los Angeles, 1935; m. Marjorie Baisch; children—David, Douglas, Ruth, Diane, Robert (dec.), Helen. Engr., Carrier Corp., Syracuse, N.Y., 1935-42; physicist Gen. Lab., U.S. Rubber Co. Passaic, N.J., 1942-46; accoustical cons., founder, chmn. bd., pres. Edwards Engring. Corp., mfrs. air conditioning and refrigeration equipment, gas treatment and pollution control equipment for petroleum industry, Pompton Plains, N.J., 1947—; founder, chmn. bd. Spi-Rol-Fin Corp., 1954-58. Licensed profl. engr., N.Y., N.J., Va. Mem. Am. Soc. Heating and Air Conditioning Engrs., Am. Soc. Refrigerating Engrs., Theta Delta Chi. Patentee in field. Home: 396 Ski Trail Smoke Rise Butler NJ 07405 Office: 101 Alexander Ave Pompton Plains NJ 07444

EDWARDS, ROBERT LOMAS, research lab. adminstr.; b. Phila., Aug. 24, 1920; s. Robert Davis and Frances (Lomas) E.; B.S., Colgate U., 1947; M.A., Harvard, 1949, Ph.D., 1951; m. Sylvia Bitler Pierce, May 29, 1942; children—Carol Edwards Senske, Eric, Susan Edwards Frank, Annabel. Instr. Tufts U., 1949-50, Brandeis U., 1950-53; asst. dir. Woods Hole (Mass.) lab. Bur. Comml. Fisheries, 1961-70; asst. dir. planning Nat. Marine Fisheries Service, Washington, 1970-72, dir. 6 research labs. N.E. Fisheries Center, Woods Hole, 1972—; del. Internat. Council Exploration of the Seas, 1975—; mem. working group U.S.-USSR studies biol. productivity and biochemistry of world ocean, 1974—; sci. adviser fishery negotiations with USSR, Poland, Internat. Com. N.W. Atlantic Fisheries. Trustee Boston Ballet Co. Served to maj. USAF, 1941-59. Decorated D.F.C. with oak leaf cluster, Air medal with 3 oak leaf clusters; recipient gold medal Dept. Commerce. Mem. Am. Soc. Mammalogists, Am. Fisheries Soc., Am. Soc. Parasitologists, Canadian Entomol. Soc., Wilson Ornithol. Soc., Sigma Xi, Phi Tau Sigma. Research and publs. in fields of ecology, parasitology and fisheries. Home: Box 505 Woods Hole MA 02543 Office: NE Fisheries Center Woods Hole MA 02543

EDWARDS, ROY LAWRENCE, educator, ecologist; b. Southampton, Eng., Dec. 2, 1922; s. Bertram Frank and Ellen Mary Jane (Hicks) E.; tchrs. certificate Borough Rd. Coll., Isleworth, Eng., 1943; B.A., Keble Coll., Oxford (Eng.) U., 1950, M.A., D.Phil., 1952; m. Joyce Margaret Sanders, Aug. 27, 1949; children—Rachael Elizabeth (dec.), Diana Margaret, Sylvia Anne. Came to Can., 1957, naturalized, 1967. Lectr. entomology U. Hull (Eng.), 1952-57; research fellow Can. Dept. Agr., 1957-58, research officer, 1958-61; asst. prof. biology U. Sask., 1961-64; prof. biology Trent U., Peterborough, Ont., Can., 1964—. Cons. ecologist, 1967—. Mem. water control adv. bd. Otonabee Region Conservation Authority. Served as pilot RAF, 1943-47. Decorated War medal. NRC Can. postdoctoral fellow, 1957. Fellow Royal Entomol. Soc.; mem. Entomol. Soc. Can., Am. Entomol. Soc., Brit. Ecol. Soc., Ecol. Soc. Am. Clubs: Brit. Schools Exploring; Canadian Power Squadrons. Contbr. articles to profl. jours. Home: 553 Homewood Ave Peterborough ON K9H 2N4 Canada

EFFINGER, GEORGE ALEC, author; b. Cleve., Jan. 10, 1947; s. George Paul and Ruth Carolyn (Uray) E.; student N.Y. U., 1968-69, Yale, 1965-66, 69-70. Writer scripts Marvel Comics, N.Y.C., 1972-73; author (novels) What Entropy Means to Me, 1972, Relatives, 1973, Those Gentle Voices, 1976, Felicia, 1976, Death in

Florence, 1978, Teflon, 1979; (with Gardner Dozois) Nightmare Blue, 1975; (short stories) Mixed Feelings, 1974; Irrational Numbers, 1976; Dirty Tricks, 1978; (non-fiction) Blood Pinball, 1979. Instr. sci. fiction Tulane U., evenings 1973-74. Mem. Sci. Fiction Writers Am., Authors Guild. Home: Box 15183 New Orleans LA 70175 Office: care Jane Rotrosen Agency 318 E 51st St New York City NY 10022

EFFINGER, GEROLD JOSEPH, physician; b. Phila., Aug. 19, 1923; s. Louis and Bertha (Splanemann) E.; Certificate Haverford Coll., 1944; M.D., Temple U., 1949; m. Rita Mahoney, Feb. 3, 1951; children—Rita, Eileen, Gerold, Linda, Brian. Intern, Phila. Gen. Hosp., 1949-51; pvt. practice specializing in internal medicine, Penndel, Pa., 1951—; asst. vis. physician dept. chronic diseases Phila. Gen. Hosp., 1951-56; asso. attending Nazareth Hosp., Phila., 1952—; clinician Dept. Health Bucks County, 1958-70; asst. medicine Lower Bucks County Hosp., Bristol, Pa. Treas. Penndel (Pa.) Municipal Authority, 1958-63; deputy coroner, Bucks County, Pa., 1966-72; Tb cons. Phila. State Hosp., 1968—, Bucks County Dept. Health, 1970-73. Mem. Ed Wynn Tent, Circus Saints and Sinners. Served with AUS, 1943-46; served to capt. AUS, 1953-55. Mem. Bucks County Med. Soc., Am. Pa. (mem. exec. com.) thoracic socs., Am. (dir. 1977—), Pa. (pres. 1976—) lung assns., Southeastern Pa. Heart Assn., Bucks County Tb and Health Soc. (pres., mem. bd. dirs. 1965—), Laennec Soc. of Phila., Order Alhambra (spl. asst. supreme organizer). Republican. Roman Catholic. K.C. Home: 1145 Sunny Hill Dr RD 1 Langhorne PA 19047 Office: 142 Bellevue Ave Penndel PA 19047

EFRON, SAMUEL, lawyer; b. Lansford, Pa., May 6, 1915; s. Abraham and Rose (Kaduchin) E.; B.A., Lehigh U., 1935; LL.B., Harvard U., 1938; m. Hope Bachrach Newman, Apr. 5, 1941; children—Marc Fred, Eric Michael. Admitted to Pa. bar, 1938, D.C. bar, 1949; atty. forms and regulations div., also registration div. SEC, 1939-40, office solicitor Dept. Labor, Washington, 1940-42; asst. chief real and personal property sect. Office Alien Property Custodian, Washington, 1942-43; chief debt claims sect., also asst. chief claims br. Office Alien Property, Dept. Justice, Washington, 1946-51; asst. gen. counsel internat. affairs Dept. Def., Washington, 1951-53, cons., 1953-54; partner firm Surrey, Karasik, Gould & Efron, Washington, 1954-61; exec. v.p. Parsons & Whittemore, Inc., N.Y.C., 1961-68; now partner firm Arent, Fox, Kintner, Plotkin & Kahn. Served to lt. (s.g.) USNR, 1943-46. Decorated Knight First Clsss Order of Lion of Finland, 1975. Mem. Am., Fed., Inter-Am. bar assns., Am. Soc. Internat. Law, Phi Beta Kappa. Republican. Clubs: Army-Navy, Capitol Hill, Nat. Press. Nat. Lawyers, Harvard (Washington); New York, Harvard, Lotos (N.Y.C.). Author: Creditors Claims Under the Trading with the Enemy Act, 1948; Foreign Taxes on United States Expenditure, 1954; Offshore Procurement and Industrial Mobilization, 1955. Home: 3537 Ordway St NW Washington DC 20016 Office: Arent Fox Kintner Plotkin & Kahn 600 Federal Bar Bldg 1815 H St NW Washington DC 20006

EFTHYMIOU, CONSTANTINE JOHN, microbiologist, educator; b. Athens, Greece, Apr. 21, 1930; s. Harilaos and Anna (Roda) E.; B.S., Athens Coll. Agr., 1952; M.S., U. Md., 1958, Ph.D., 1961; m. Aglaia Giannatos, Apr. 18, 1964; children—Anna, Barbara, Bette. Came to U.S., 1955, naturalized, 1968. Instr., research asst. dept. microbiology U. Md., 1958-61; asst. prof. Carnegie Inst. Tech., 1961-64; asst. prof. St. John's U., Jamaica, N.Y., 1964-68, asso. prof. biology, 1968—; cons. microbiologist; research asso. in immunology Queens Med. Center, 1968-76. Served to lt. Greek Nat. Army, 1952-54. Mem. Am. Soc. Microbiology, AAAS, Am. Inst. Biol. Scis., Sigma Xi, Mem. Greek Orthodox Ch. Patentee in field. Home: 78-61 222d St Oakland Gardens NY 11364 Office: Dept of Biological Scis St John's University Jamaica NY 11439

EGAN, JOHN FREDERICK, electronics co. exec.; b. Council Bluffs, Iowa, Feb. 25, 1935; s. Frederick Emerson and Ruth Pauline (Russell) E.; A.B. with honors (Baker scholar), Grinnell Coll., 1957; M.S. (Transp. Center fellow), Northwestern U., 1958, Ph.D. (Transp. Center fellow), 1961; m. Anne B. Patterson, June 14, 1958; children—John Frederick, James Michael, Tech. dir. computer systems div. electronics systems USAF, Bedford, Mass., 1964-67; sr. staff specialist Office of Dir. Def. Research and Engring., Washington, 1967-71; chief scientist Office Chief of Naval Operations, Washington, 1971-73; dir. fed. systems group Sanders Assos., Inc., Nashua, N.H., 1973-77, v.p. fed. systems group, 1977-78, v.p. corporate devel., 1978—; mem. Navy Space Advisory Com.; mem. exec. panel Chief Naval Ops. Chmn. alumni fund Grinnell Coll., 1972—; trustee Nashua Symphony Assn., 1976—. Served to capt. USAF, 1961-64. Mem. IEEE, Assn. Computing Machinery, Inst. Aeros. and Astronautics, Sigma Xi, Eta Kappa Nu. Home: 7 Beverlee Dr Nashua NH 03060 Office: Daniel Webster Hwy S Nashua NH 03061

EGAN, MICHAEL JOSEPH, govt. ofcl., lawyer: b. Savannah, Ga., Aug. 8, 1926; s. Michael Joseph and Elise (Robider) E.; B.A., Yale, 1950; LL.B., Harvard, 1955; m. Donna Cole, Apr. 14, 1951; children—Moira, Michael, Donna, Cole, Roby, John. Admitted to Ga. bar, 1955; partner Sutherland, Asbill & Brennan, Atlanta and Washington, 1960—; mem. Ga. Ho. of Reps., 1965-77, minority leader, 1970-77; asso. atty. gen. U.S., 1977—. Home: 4840 Van Ness St Washington DC 20016 Office: Dept Justice Washington DC 20530

EGAN, SHIRLEY ANNE, nursing educator; b. Haverhill, Mass.; d. Rush B. and Beatrice (Bengle) Willard; diploma St. Joseph's Hosp. Sch. Nursing, Nashua, N.H., 1945; B.S. in Nursing Edn., Boston U., 1949, M.S., 1954. Instr. sci. Sturdy Meml. Hosp. Sch. Nursing, Attleboro, Mass., 1949-51; instr. sci. Peter Bent Brigham Hosp. Sch. Nursing, Boston, 1951-53, ednl. dir., 1953-55, asso. dir. Sch. Nursing, 1955-59, med. surg. coordinator 1971-73, asso. dir. Sch. Nursing, 1973—; nurse edn. adviser AID (formerly ICA), Karachi, Pakistan, 1959-67; prin. Coll. Nursing, Karachi, 1959-67; dir. Vis. Nurse Service, Nashua, N.H., 1967-70; exec. dir. Lowell (Mass.) Vis. Nurse Assn., 1970-71; cons. nursing edn. Pakistan Ministry of Health, Labour and Social Welfare, 1959-67; adviser to editor Pakistan Nursing and Health Rev., 1959-67; exec. bd. Nat. Health Edn. Com., Pakistan; WHO short-term cons. U. W.I., Jamaica, 1970-71; mem. Greater Nashua Health Planning Council. Bd. dirs. Matthew Thornton Health Center, Nashua, Nashua Child Care Center; vol. ombudsman N.H. Council on Aging; mem. Nashua Service League. Served as 1st lt., Army Nurse Corps, 1945-47. Mem. Am. Nurses Assn., Trained Nurses Assn. Pakistan, Nat. League for Nursing, St. Joseph's Sch. Nursing Alumnae Assn., Boston U. Alumnae Assn., Brit. Soc. Health Edn., Cath. Daus. Am. (vice regent ct. Bishop Malloy), Sigma Theta Tau, Statis. study grads. Karachi Coll. Nursing. Contbr. articles to profl. publs. Home: 20 Tinker Rd Nashua NH 03060 Office: 721 Huntington Ave Boston MA 02115

EGELSTON, RICHARD LESTER, educator; b. Albany, N.Y., Jan. 9, 1937; s. Lester George and Martha Jane (Albright) E.; B.S., State U. N.Y. at Albany, 1960, M.S., 1963; Ph.D., State U. N.Y., Buffalo, 1969; m. Darlene Marie Lester, May 23, 1975. Tchr. sci. Berlin (N.Y.) Central Sch., 1960-63; asst. prof. No. Mich. U., 1965-67; research asso. State U. N.Y. at Buffalo, 1967-69; asst. prof. psychology State U. Coll. at Geneseo, 1969-74; research asso. The Univ. at Albany, 1975—. Project dir. Upper Peninsula Multi-Dist. Planning Project, Ishpeming, Mich., 1966-67; evaluation specialist Project Innovation, Williamsville, N.Y., 1967-69. State U. N.Y. Research Found. grantee, 1971. Mem. Phi Delta Kappa. Contbr. articles to profl. jours. Home: 420 Sand Creek Rd #201 Albany NY 12205

EGGERS, MELVIN ARNOLD, univ. chancellor; b. Ft. Wayne, Ind., Feb. 21, 1916; s. Frederick Carl and Minnie (Kiel) E.; A.B., Ind. U., 1940, A.M., 1941; Ph.D., Yale U., 1950; m. Mildred Grace Chenoweth, Apr. 5, 1941; children—Nancy Louise, William David, Richard Melvin. Clk., Peoples Trust & Savs. Co., Ft. Wayne, 1934-38; instr. econs. Yale, 1947-50; mem. faculty Syracuse U., 1950—, prof. econs., 1963—, chmn. dept., 1960-70, vice chancellor for acad. affairs, also provost, 1970-71, chancellor, 1971—; dir. First Trust & Deposit Co.; mem. faculty Pacific Coast Banking Sch., 1955-70; cons. fin. instns. Served to lt. USNR, 1942-46. Mem. Phi Beta Kappa. Home: 701 Walnut Ave Syracuse NY 13210 Office: Syracuse U Syracuse NY 13210

EGLI, PETER, radiochemist; b. Maennedorf. Switzerland, Jan. 23, 1933; s. Emil and Hedwig (Isler) E.; came to U.S., 1961; B.Sc., Winterthur Tech. Inst. (Switzerland), 1953; m. Margrith R. Pfister, Nov. 10, 1956; children—Charles Donald, Beatrice Regula. Plant chemist Swiss Soda Works, 1953-56; chemist Merck, Ltd., Montreal, Que., Can., 1956-61; radiochemist Nuclear Research Chems., Inc., Orlando, Fla., 1961-62, New Eng. Nuclear Corp., Boston, 1962-69, E.R. Squibb Co., New Brunswick, N.J., 1970—. Mem. Am. Chem. Soc. Patentee variable speed transmission. Home: Continental Ln RD 1 Titusville NJ 08560 Office: Georges Rd New Brunswick NJ 08903

EGOLF, RALPH JENNINGS, JR., educator, historian; b. Somerset, Pa., Jan. 20, 1931; s. Ralph J. and Emma Grace (Stahl) E.; B.S., Pa. State U., 1952, M.A., 1953; m. Finnette Elizabeth More Barkel, June 5, 1953; children—Karen Elizabeth, Barbara Ann. Tchr., Somerset (Pa.) Area Sr. High Sch., 1953—; historian Fort Necessity Nat. Battlefield, Nat. Park Service, 1956-65; mem. Hist. Commn. Evang. United Brethren and United Meth. chs., 1967-74. Pres. bd. trustees Mary S. Biesecker Pub. Library, Somerset, 1971—. Mem. Nat., Pa. edn. assns., Phi Kappa Phi, Phi Eta Sigma, Kappa Phi Kappa, Pi Gamma Mu. Methodist. Club: IOOF. Author: Quaker Pacificism and the Pennsylvania Militia Act of 1755, 1953; The China Policy, 1946-49, 1955. Contbr. articles to profl. jours. Home: 406 Davis Ave Somerset PA 15501

EGYED, ALEX, retail trade co. exec.; b. Budapest, Hungary, Apr. 23, 1935; s. Sandor and Terez (Eckl); came to U.S., 1957, naturalized, 1962; B.S. in Elec. Engring., Purdue U., 1961; m. Edit Latorcai, Sept. 14, 1957; children—Edith, Christopher, Victoria. Jr. engr. United Engineers & Contractors, Phila., 1961-62; various engring. positions Atlantic Refining Co., Phila., 1962-72; exec. v.p. Basco, Inc., Cherry Hill, N.J., 1972-74, pres., 1974—; chmn. bd. A/W Cons.'s, Inc., Cherry Hill, 1976—; dir. Gamma Telecommunications Systems, London. Registered profl. engr., Pa. Mem. Am. Mgmt. Assn., Nat., Pa. socs. profl. engrs. Home: 480 Pinewood Pl Philadelphia PA 19116 Office: Route 38 and Woods Rd Cherry Hill NJ 08002

EHMER, MARJY ARDUINA NICCOLL, psychologist; b. N.Y.C., Feb. 3, 1927; d. George A. and Ray (Haberman) Niccoll; B.A. cum laude, Bklyn. Coll., 1947; postgrad. N.Y. U., 1947-49; Ph.D., U. Rochester, 1959; m. Richard Ehmer, Jan. 23, 1948 (div. Sept. 1965); 1 son, George; m. 2d, Jess L. Dow, Sept. 1971. Lab. asst. Bklyn. Coll., 1946-48, instr., 1947-48; research asst. U. Rochester (N.Y.), 1948-51, Tufts Coll., Medford, Mass., 1951-54; instr. Brandeis U., Waltham, Mass., 1952; instr. U. R.I., Kingston, 1954-58, asst. prof., 1958-60; asst. prof. U. Bridgeport (Conn.), 1960-61, asso. prof., 1961-62; trainee VA Hosp., West Haven, Conn., 1962-63; asso. prof. So. Conn. State Coll., New Haven, 1963-69, prof., 1969—; asso. fellow Inst. Advanced Study in Rational Psychotherapy, N.Y.C., 1976-77. Mem. Am., Eastern (election com. 1958), New Eng., Conn. psychol. assns., AAAS, YWCA, Sigma Xi, Psi Chi. Clubs: Race Brook Country, Mount Sunapee Ski, John Cain Golf. Contbr. articles to profl. jours. Office: Southern Conn State Coll New Haven CT 06515

EHRENSTEIN, GERALD, biophysicist; b. N.Y.C., Sept. 27, 1931; s. Irving and Adele (Holzer) E.; B.E.E., Cooper Union, 1952; M.A., Columbia U., 1958, Ph.D., 1962; m. Deborah Ploscowe, Dec. 17, 1960; children—Ruth, David, Steven. Engr., Arma Corp., Mineola, N.Y., 1952; research physicist NIH, Bethesda, Md., 1962—, head sect. on molecular biophysics Nat. Inst. Neurol. and Communicative Disorders and Stroke, 1975—; mem. sci. tech. adv. com. Washington Tech. Inst., 1969—. Chmn. community relations com. Congregation Beth El, 1970-72. Served to lt. (j.g.) USCGR, 1952-54. duPont lectr., 1971. Mem. Am. Phys. Soc., Biophys. Soc., Sigma Xi. Home: 7502 Nevis Rd Bethesda MD 20034 Office: 9000 Rockville Pike NIH Bethesda MD 20014

EHRENZWEIG, JOEL, veterinarian; b. Bklyn., Mar. 14, 1943; s. William B. and Malvina (Heisler) E.; B.S., Coll. City N.Y., 1965; D.V.M., Ont. Veterinary Coll., 1970; m. Ellen Beth Rodburg, Oct. 21, 1973; children—Regina, Rachel, Jesse, Julie. Asso. veterinarian Davis Animal Hosp., Stamford, Conn., 1970-72; dir. Animal Hosp. Bklyn., 1972—; coordinator ABC-TV Heartworm Disease Testing Clinic, 1978; mem. com. on vocat. tng. N.Y.C. Dept. Edn. Mem. AVMA, Canadian, N.Y. State veterinary med. assns., Ont., N.Y.C. veterinary assns., Am. Animal Hosp. Assn., Royal Coll. Veterinary Surgeons (London), Veterinary Radiology Soc., Am. Assn. Feline Practitioners, Am. Assn. Animal Welfare Veterinarians, Veterinary Orthopedic Soc. Contbg. editor Pet News mag., 1975—. Contbr. articles to veterinary jours. Office: 2270 Flatbush Ave Brooklyn NY 11234 also 9107 4th Ave Brooklyn NY 11209

EHRLICH, BERNARD HERBERT, lawyer, trade assn. exec.; b. Washington, Apr. 3, 1927; s. Samuel Zachary and Elsie (Klein) E.; LL.B., George Washington U., 1949, J.D., M.A., 1950; m. Edna Kraft, June 17, 1951; children—Vivian Rose, Beverly Denise, Brenda Susan, Lisa Jean. Admitted to D.C. bar, 1949; since practiced in Washington; gen. counsel many corps., industries, 1949—; with Inst. Indsl. Launderers, Washington, 1949—, exec. v.p., 1955—; pres. Behl Assos., 1960—; counsel Nat. Home Study Council, Nat. Assn. Trade and Tech. Schs., Nat. Assn. Cosmetology Schs. Mem. adv. panel on employee recruitment and job devel. U.S. C. of C., 1967—. Served with USNR, 1943-45. Recipient plaque for significant service Am. Inst. Laundering, 1966, Nat. Assn. Trade and Tech. Schs., 1967. Mem. Am. Bar Assn., Bar Assn. D.C., Am. Soc. Interat. Law, Am. Hist. Assn., Am. Soc. Assn. Execs., Soc. Am. Travel Writers, Acad. Polit. Sci., Internat. Classics Press, C. of C., Phi Beta Kappa, Nu Beta Epsilon, Phi Delta Pi. Jewish religion. Home: 507 Bonifant St Silver Spring MD 20910 Office: 919 18th St NW Washington DC 20006

EHRLICH, GEORGE EDWARD, physician; b. Vienna, Austria, July 18, 1928; s. Edward and Irene (Elling) E.; A.B. cum laude, Harvard, 1948; M.B., Chgo. Med. Sch., 1952, M.D., 1952; m. Gail S. Abrams, March 30, 1968; children—Charles Edward, Steven L. Abrams, Rebecca Ann Abrams. Intern, Michael Reese Hosp., Chgo., 1952; resident Francis Delafield Hosp., N.Y.C., 1955, Beth Israel Hosp., Boston, 1956, New Eng. Center Hosp., Boston, 1957; fellow rheumatology NIH, Bethesda, Md., 1958, fellow rheumatology Hosp. for Spl. Surgery, N.Y.C., 1959-61, asst. attending physician, 1960-64; spl. fellow Sloan Kettering Inst., 1960-61; instr. medicine Cornell U., 1960-64; dir. Arthritis Center, chief rheumatology Albert Einstein Med. Center and Moss Rehab. Hosp., Phila., 1964—, asst. prof. medicine, 1964-67, asso. prof. medicine, 1967-72, prof. medicine, 1972—; asso. prof. rehab. medicine Temple U., 1964-74, prof., 1974—; cons. rheumatology U.S. Naval Hosp., Phila., 1964—; vis. lectr. U. Pa., 1964—; cons. bur. drugs FDA. Pres., Eastern Pa. chpt. Arthritis Found., 1970-72; mem. Phila. Mayor's Sci. and Tech. Adv. Council, 1972—. Served to comdr. M.C., USNR, 1953-55. Recipient citations City Phila., 1969, 74; Distinguished Alumnus award Chgo. Med. Sch., 1969; decorated Cavaliere Order of Star of Italian Solidarity. Fellow A.C.P., Royal Soc. Tropical Medicine, Am. Coll. Clin. Pharmacology, N.Y. Acad. Medicine, Am. Geriatric Soc., Phila. Coll. Physicians; mem. Am. Pub. Health Assn., Am. Soc. Clin. Therapeutics, Am. Coll. Rehab., Acad. Sci., AMA (editorial bd. jour.), Am. Fedn. Clin. Research, Am. Soc. Human Genetics, Assn. Mil. Surgeons (Philip Hench award 1971), Am. Rheumatism Assn., Am. Med. Writers Assn., Am. Psychosomatic Assn. (editorial bd.), Alpha Omega Alpha. Clubs: Harvard (Boston, N.Y.C., Phila.). Author: Differential Diagnosis of Rheumatoid Arthritis, 1972; Oculocutaneous Manifestations of Rheumatic Diseases, 1973; Total Management of the Arthritic Patient, 1973. Editor: Jour. Albert Einstein Med. Center, 1966-71, Arthritis and Rheumatic Diseases Abstracts, 1968-71. Editorial bd. Chronic Disease, 1973-76, Inflammation, 1974—, Psychosomatics, 1977—. Contbr. articles to profl. jours. Home: 2223 Delancey Pl Philadelphia PA 19103 Office: Albert Einstein Med Center Philadelphia PA 19141

EHRLICH, HÉLÈNE HEDY, educator, lit. critic, author; b. Lodz, Poland, Feb. 1, 1924; d. Chaim Hercko and Freida (Nirenberg) Scheibe; came to U.S., 1952, naturalized, 1958; B.A., Hunter Coll., N.Y.C., 1958; degré avancé Langue Francaise, Littérature Contemporaine, Sorbonne, Paris, 1961; M.A., Columbia U., N.Y.C., 1962, Ph.D., 1971; m. Irvin Ehrlich, Jan. 2, 1944 and Nov. 18, 1945 (religious); children—Henri Rene, Sylvie Beatrice. Instr. French, Coll. City N.Y., N.Y.C., 1960; asst. and preceptor of French, Columbia U., N.Y.C., 1961-65; instr. French, Fairleigh Dickinson U., 1966-68, chairperson French Club, 1966-67, organizer Interdisciplinary Symposium on Is The Study of Lit. and Langs. Important in Our Tech. Soc.?, 1967, lectr. humanities program, 1966-67; instr. French, Stern Coll. Women, Yeshiva U., N.Y.C., 1968-69; asst. prof. French, Rutgers Coll., Rutgers U., New Brunswick, N.J., 1970—; adj. lectr. French, Hunter Coll., 1970, Queensborough Community Coll., 1969-72, Stern Coll. for Women, Yeshiva U., 1967-68. Recipient fellowship Conf. on Jewish Material Claims Against Germany, Columbia U., 1959-60; grant Rutgers U. Research Council, 1971. Mem. AAUP, Modern Lang. Assn. Am., Société des Amis de Montaigne, Rennaissance Soc. Am., Assn. Internat. pour la Récherche et la diffusion des méthodes audio-visuelles et structuro-globales, Assn. Canadienne de Linguistique Appliquée, Nat. Soc. Lit. and Arts, Société d'Honneur Française, Pi Delta Phi. Author: Montaigne: la critique et le langage, 1972 (partial English translation 1974-75); Etude critique sur les Essais de Michel de Montaigne et la Controverse sur De La Sagesse de son pretendu disciple, Pierre Charron, 1974 (partial English translation 1975); Charron's La Sagesse: A Study in Moral Pragmatism, 1975; also numerous essays; contbr. articles to French and Am. profl. jours. Innovator, original interpreter works of the Renaissance authors Pierre Charron, Rabelais, Montaigne. Home: 265 Riverside Dr New York City NY 10025 Office: Rutgers U Rutgers Coll Dept French New Brunswick NJ 08903

EHRLICH, STANLEY LEONARD, sonar cons. engr.; b. Newark, Jan. 7, 1925; s. Henry Max and Mary (Lichtenstein) E.; B.Sc., Brown U., 1944, M.Sc., 1945; postgrad. Mass. Inst. Tech., 1945-48, U. Conn., 1951-53; m. Louise Dorothy Waldfogel, June 19, 1949; children—Barbara Ellen, Stephen Mark, Michael Alan. Physicist, USN Underwater Sound Lab., New London, Conn., 1948-53; sr. engr., submarine signal div. Raytheon Co., Boston, also Newton, Wayland, Mass., 1953-59, sect. mgr., Waltham, Mass., Portsmouth, R.I., 1959-62, prin. engr., Portsmouth, 1962-70, cons. engr., 1970—. City of Waltham chmn. Brown U. Ann. Fund, 1956-60, head class agt. Class of 1945, 1970—; team capt. Newport Hosp. Bldg. Fund, 1967; mem. Norman Bird Sanctuary, 1968—; mem. Newport Preservation Soc., 1962—. Bd. dirs. R.I. Arts Found. at Newport (sec. 1977—), Soc. Friends of Touro Synagogue, 1975-78. Recipient Freemen award Providence Engring. Soc., 1976. Fellow Acoustical Soc. Am. (chmn. Narragansett chpt. 1965-66, hon. mem., chmn. com. on regional chpts. 1976—), IEEE, (sr. mem., vice chmn. piezoelec. and ferroelec. crystals com. 1962-66), Am. Phys. Soc., Internat. Orgn. Standardization, Nat. Security Indsl. Assn., AAAS, Sigma Xi, Tau Beta Pi, Sigma Pi Sigma. Jewish religion. Mem. B'nai B'rith (pres. Waltham 1957-58). Club: Brown of Newport County (pres. 1969-71). Translator: (with F. Pordes) Fundamentals of Electroacoustics, 1955. Asso. editor Jour. Oceanic Engring., 1975—. Patentee in field. Home: 1 Acacia Dr Middletown RI 02840 Office: Box 360 Portsmouth RI 02871

EHRMAN, LIBERT, cons. industry, econs., social devel.; b. N.Y.C., July 3, 1916; s. David and Helen (Fleischer) E.; B.S.S., Coll. City N.Y., 1951; postgrad. Am. U., 1951; m. Catherine R. James, Jan. 21, 1971; children by previous marriage—David Jonathan, Daniel Joseph. Chief safety analysis CAA, 1945-54; asso. Samuel Weiss Research Assos., 1954-55; v.p. Stuart Rice Assos., Inc., 1955-58; exec. v.p. Surveys & Research Corp., Washington, 1958-64, pres., 1965-71; exec. v.p. Exotech Systems, Inc., 1971-72, pres., 1973—; pres. ERA 2000, Inc.; cons., OEO, HEW, Gen. Electric Co., United Fruit Co., Chilean Nitrate Co., Man-Made Fiber Producers Assn., Glass Container Mfrs. Inst., Nat. Insts. Health, Calumet & Hecla Corp., NSF, AID, FAA, Dept. Transp., AAAS, Chilton Pubs., Kiplinger Washington Editors, Govt. of Ecuador, govts. of Chile, South Korea, Peru, Ho. Reps. Com. on Judiciary, Senate Fgn. Relations Com., U. Md., Joint Congl. Com. on Washington Area Problems. Served with USAAF, 1943-45. Mem. Am. Statis. Assn., Am. Sociol. Assn., Inst. Mgmt. Scis., Nat. Planning Assn., World Assn. Pub. Opinion Research, A.A.A.S., Soc. for Internat. Devel. Club: Cosmos. Contbr. articles to profl. publs. Home: 1731 Crestwood Dr NW Washington DC 20011 Office: 1200 Quince Orchard Blvd Gaithersburg MD 20760

EHRMAN, RAYMOND STRENG, accountant; b. Pitts., Nov. 19, 1915; s. Raymond Streng and Grace (Russack) E.; B.S., U. Pitts., 1936; m. Agnes McIlree, Apr. 18, 1945; children—James S., Victoria G., Philip B. Treas. Clyde Speer Coal Corp., Pitts., 1947-61; pvt. practice pub. accountant Pitts., 1961-64; partner Adler & Co., C.P.A.'s, Pitts., 1964-73; prin. J.K. Lasser & Co., C.P.A.'s, (now Touche Ross & Co.) Pitts., 1973—. Auditor, Ross Twp., Pa., 1967—. Served with USAAF, 1942-45. Mem. Nat. Fuel Credit Assn. (pres. 1951-52), Pitts. Bus. Adminstrn. Alumni Assn. (pres. 1961-62), Pa. (pres. Pitts. chpt. 1971-72), Am. insts. c.p.a.'s. Republican. Lutheran. Clubs: Downtown (founding dir. 1954—), Mason (Shriner). Home: 201 Kinvara Dr Pittsburgh PA 15237 Office: 2 Oliver Plaza Pittsburgh PA 15222

EHRMANN, ROBERT LINCOLN, pathologist; b. Boston, Sept. 2, 1922; s. Herbert B. and Sara Emily (Rosenfeld) E.; A.B., Swarthmore Coll., 1944; M.D., N.Y. U., 1946; m. Janice Lee Panella, Sept. 7, 1958;

children—Lisa Marie, Martha Lee. Intern, Beth Israel Hosp., Boston, 1946-47; USPHS research fellow, then sr. asst. surgeon, div. cell physiology Johns Hopkins Hosp., Balt., 1949-56; sr. asst. resident pathology Peter Bent Brigham Hosp., also West Roxbury VA Hosp., Boston, 1956-58; asst. resident pathology Boston Lying-In Hosp., also Free Hosp. for Women, Brookline, 1958-59; instr. pathology Harvard, 1959-62, clin. asso. pathology, 1962-71, asst. prof., 1971—; pathologist Pkwy. div. Boston Hosp. for Women, 1970—; dir. Boston Sch. Cytotech. at Pkwy. div., 1969—; lectr. health scis., cons. cytotech. Northeastern U., Boston, 1972—; cons. Naval Hosp., Boston, 1972-73. Vice chmn. Boston chpt. Am. Jewish Com., 1969-74. Served with U.S. Army, 1947-49, USPHS, 1951-56. Recipient research grant Nat. Cancer Inst., 1959-69, Am. Cancer Soc., 1970-72. Diplomate Am. Bd. Pathology. Mem. AAAS, Coll. Am. Pathologists, Am. Soc. Cytology, AMA, Internat. Acad. Cytology, Tissue Culture Assn., N.Y. Acad. Sci., New Eng., Mass. socs. pathologists, Mass., Norfolk Dist. med. socs., Obstet. Soc. Boston, ACLU, Americans for Dem. Action, Sigma Xi (asso.). Contbr. articles to profl. jours. Home: 315 Woodward St Waban MA 02168 Office: 245 Pond Ave Brookline MA 02146

EIBER, BERNARD M., lawyer, educator, ins. co. exec.; b. N.Y.C., Oct., 1912; s. Solomon and Frieda (Katzman) E.; B.S. in Bus. Adminstrn., N.Y. U., 1935; J.D., N.Y. Law Sch., 1951; C.L.U., Am. Coll. Life Underwriters, 1937; m. Geraldine Thorner, June 25, 1939; children—Elissa Tessler, Bruce S. Life ins. exec. various cos., 1940-51; admitted to N.Y. bar, 1951, since practiced in N.Y.C., partner Eiber & Garson; faculty N.Y. U., 1957-59; asst. prof. law N.Y. Law Sch., 1959-63, adj. prof. law, 1971—; past pres., counsel Congl. Life Ins. Co., N.Y.C.; dir. Nassau Ins. Co., Jamaica, N.Y.; counsel L.I. chpt. Am. Soc. C.L.U.'s; former mem. N.Y. State 11th Jud. Dist. Temporary Commn. on Estates; spl. lectr. tax and estate planning for attys., life underwriters trust officers accountants Hofstra U., 1963—, past pres. univ. council, mem. univ. adv. bd. Former sec. Nassau-Suffolk region, chmn. speakers bur. L.I. region NCCJ; pres. N.Y. Law Sch. Alumni Assn., 1973-75, N.Y. Law Sch. Alumni Found., 1976—; bd. dirs. Queensboro Soc. Prevention Cruelty to Children, 1971-74; counsel Queens County Art and Cultural Center, Queens Mus., 1972—. Served to ensign U.S. Maritime Service, 1943-45. Fellow Am. Coll. Probate Counsel, Am. Bar Found.; mem. Tax and Estate Planning Council L.I., N.Y. State Bar Assn. (ho. dels.), Queens County Bar Assn. (bd. mgrs., chmn. tax com., mem. com. ins. law, pres. 1969-71), Scribes, Tau Kappa Alpha. Club: K.P. (past asst. chief dep. grand chancellor). Contbr. articles to profl. jours. Home: 123-60 83d Ave Kew Gardens NY also 25 Somerset Dr S Great Neck NY 11020 Office: 123-60 83d Ave Kew Gardens NY 11415 also 20 Squadron Blvd New City NY 10956

EICKELBERG, W. WARREN BARBOUR, educator; b. N.Y.C., Jan. 19, 1925; s. Graham Alexander and Lillian (Hayes) E.; student Harvard U., 1942-43; B.A., Hope Coll., Holland, Mich., 1949; M.A. (Dennison fellow), Wesleyan U. Conn., 1951; m. Nancy Ann Schneider, Sept. 6, 1952; children—William, Margaret, Robert, Janet. Prof., Adelphi U., Garden City, L.I., N.Y., 1952—, dir. devel., v.p., 1958-66, dir. premed. curriculum, 1967—; cons. devel. planning Human Resources Center, Albertson, N.Y., 1958—; mem. biomechanics cons. group Pres.'s Com. on Disabled; mem. ad hoc com. N.Y. State Joint Legis. Com. on Transp. Chmn. Nassau County Museum Council, 1966-67; mem. founding com. Adelphi Suffolk Coll.; nat. cons. Nat. Council Cath. Men, 1969. Served to 1st lt. USAAF, 1943-46. Recipient Flambeau award Adelphi U., 1956, L.I. Gov.'s award, 1966, certificate of distinction Dictionary Internat. Biography, 1968, Wisdom award, 1970. Mem. N.Y. Acad. Scis., Internat. Soc. Biomechanics (charter), Nat. Soc. Fund Raisers, Pub. Relations Soc. Am. (accredited), L.I. Pub. Relations Assn. (past pres., dir.), L.I. Sci. Tchrs. Assn. (past pres., dir.). Sigma Xi, Kappa Eta Nu. Clubs: Lions; Wesleyan (N.Y.C.); Unqua Yacht (Amityville). Home: 38 Unqua Pl Amityville NY 11701 Office: Adelphi U Garden City NY 11530

EICKHOFF, ALAN CRAIG, educator; b. Phila., Aug. 5, 1946; s. Oscar Jr. and Marion (Bryan) E.; B.A., Pa. State U., 1968; M.A., Trenton State Coll., 1973; m. Linda Murray Croasdale, June 13, 1970; children—Rebecca, Jeffrey. Product quality control staff Zieger and Sons, Inc., rose growers, 1964-71, 75—; high sch. history tchr. Springfield Sch. Dist., Phila., 1968—, student council adviser, 1970—, class adviser, 1971—, intramural dir., 1970-75, asst. athletic dir., 1973—, advanced placement instr., 1974—. Mem. Am. Hist. Assn., NEA, Pa. State Edn. Assn., Smithsonian Assos., Nat. Council Social Studies Tchrs. Lutheran. Home: 1190 Cambridge Rd Warminster PA 18974 Office: 1801 E Paper Mill Rd Philadelphia PA 19118

EIDEL, ZENETH, advt. agy. exec.; b. Bklyn., Nov. 30, 1929; s. Nathan and Ellen (Katz) E.; certificate art Cooper Union for Advancement Sci. and Art, 1950, B.F.A., 1976; m. Doris Rabinowitz, June 5, 1955; children—Carey Steven, Michael Lee, Eric Paul. Asst. marketing dir. Bruno-N.Y., N.Y.C., 1950-51; apprentice Marwell Advt., N.Y.C., 1953-54; asst. designer Reba Sochis Design, N.Y.C., 1954-55; partner Graphic Point Studio, N.Y.C., 1955-57; v.p., creative dir. Jerry Lichtman Advt., N.Y.C., 1957-59; with Zeneth Eidel Assos., N.Y.C., 1959-70; pres., creative dir. Z/E/A Mktg. Communications, N.Y.C., 1970—. Mem. adv. com. Briarcliff Boosters, 1973—; trustee Congregation Sons of Israel, Tri-Community Lodge B'nai B'rith. Recipient 1st ann. Youth award B'nai B'rith, 1975. Served with U.S. Army, 1951-53. Recipient Spl. Merit award Printing Industries N.Y., 1964; ACE Merit award Pitts. Creative Soc., 1971; award Am. Mktg. Assn., 1973. Mem. Am. Inst. Graphic Arts, Art Dirs. Club N.Y., Internat. Radio and TV Soc. Office: 240 Madison Ave New York City NY 10016

EIDELHOCH, LESTER PHILIP, physician; b. N.Y., Jan. 7, 1932; s. Abraham David and Ella (Lovinger) E.; B.A., Columbia U., 1952; M.D., N.Y. U., 1956; m. Cecily Ruth Rosenberg, Apr. 28, 1963; children—Alison, Arthur, Meredith. Intern, Strong Meml. Hosp., Rochester, N.Y., 1956-57; resident Boston City Hosp., Harvard U., 1957-62; instr. surgery San Diego Naval Hosp., 1962-64; practice medicine specializing in surgery, Utica, N.Y., 1965-78; mem. staff St. Lukes Hosp., New Hartford, St. Elizabeth Hosp., Utica; instr. Upstate Med. Center, State U. N.Y., Syracuse, 1978—. Bd. dirs. Utica Symphony, Sitrin Home, Jewish Community Center, Am. Cancer Soc. Served with USNR, 1962-64. Fellow A.C.S.; mem. AMA, N.Y. State Soc. Surgeons, Oneida County Med. Soc., Phi Delta Epsilon. Jewish. Clubs: K.P. Home: 6 Old Willow Rd New Hartford NY 13413 Office: 2206 Genesee St Utica NY 13502

EIDSON, ROBERT ANSEL, corp. exec.; b. Topeka, May 30, 1921; s. O. Bain and Agnes (Ray) E.; student Kans. U., 1938-41; B.S., U.S. Naval Acad., 1944, M.S.E.E., 1953; m. Cecil Ruth King, June 10, 1944; children—Susan Lloyd (Barclay), Robert Bain, John Rhodes. Commd. ensign U.S. Navy, 1944; resigned in 1959; now capt. in Res.; mgr. engring. div. Sanders Assos., Inc., Nashua, N.H., 1959-64, v.p., dir. engring. lab. Airtronics, Inc., Washington, 1964-67, dir. spl. systems Fed. Systems Center, IBM, Gaithersburg, Md., 1967-72; pres., chmn. bd. Decisions and Designs, Inc., McLean, Va., 1972—; dir. 70001 Ltd. Mem. nat. security and internat. affairs adv. council Republican Nat. Com.; bd. dirs. Wolftrap Farm Park for Performing Arts; mem. Golden Circle, Kennedy Center for Performing Arts; mem. exec. com. Naval Acad. Found. Mem. IEEE, Am. Def. Preparedness Assn., Armed Forces Communications-Electronics Assn., Res. Officers Assn., Navy League, Wolftrapper, Sigma Chi. Republican. Presbyn. Clubs: Congressional Country (Washington); Regency Racquet (McLean). Home: 4932 Sentinel Dr Apt 106 Sumner MD 20016 Office: Decisions and Designs Inc 8400 Westpark Dr McLean VA 22101

EIDSVOLD, GARY MASON, physician; b. Morris, Minn., Sept. 28, 1938; s. Lyman Woodrow and Julie Magdalene (Mason) E.; B.A. cum laude, St. Olaf Coll., 1960; M.D., U. Minn., 1964; M.P.H., Johns Hopkins U., 1966. Intern, L.I. Coll. Hosp., Bklyn.; resident AID, Washington, 1966-67, Pub. Health Coll., Gondar, Ethiopia, 1967-68; dir. Indian Health Service Hosp., Tuba City, Ariz., 1968-70; health officer N.Y.C. Dept. Health, 1970-73, Bronx and S.I. dir., 1973-78, med. dir. for N.Y.C., 1978—; lectr. Columbia U. Sch. Pub. Health, 1972—; asst. prof. pub. health Downstate Med. Sch., Bklyn., 1972—. Mem. council, chmn. coms. Trinity Ch. City N.Y. Served with USPHS, 1968-70. Fellow Am. Coll. Preventive Medicine, N.Y. Acad. Medicine; mem. Nat. Bd. Med. Examiners (diplomate), Am. Pub. Health Assn. (governing council), Pub. Health Assn. N.Y.C. (dir.), Pub. Health Physicians Assn. N.Y.C. (pres.), Nat. Assn. County Health Officers (dir.). Democrat. Episcopalian. Contbr. articles to profl. jours., 1974-78. Home: 71 Grand St New York City NY 10013 Office: One Penn Plaza New York City NY 10001

EIFERMAN, DEBORAH BERLINGER, coll. adminstr.; b. Bklyn., Jan. 1, 1923; d. Jack and Frieda (Moser) Berlinger; B.A., Bklyn. Coll., 1944; B.H.L., Jewish Theol. Sem., 1945; M.A., Western Res. U., 1946; profl. diploma Fordham U., 1973, Ph.D., 1979; m. Irving Eiferman, Dec. 13, 1947; children—Jack Avi, Leora Frieda, Loren Sue. Asst. to personnel dir. Jewish Child Care Assn., N.Y.C., 1946-51; guidance counselor N.Y.C. Bd. Edn., 1965-69; adj. lectr., counselor Bklyn. Coll., 1965-69, faculty adminstr. acad. affairs, 1969—; cons. guidance; mem. bds. edn. pvt. schs.; mem. pub. high sch. prin.'s consultative council, high sch. adv. com. Co-chmn. Mental Health Com., Bklyn. Recipient Doctoral Scholarship award Doctorate Assn. N.Y. Educators, 1977. Mem. Am., N.Y. personnel and guidance assns., Am. Coll. Personnel Assn., Adult Student Personnel Assn., Bklyn. Assn. Mental Health, AAUP, Am. Profs. for Middle East, Bklyn. Coll. Alumni Assn. (dir., exec. com.), Alpha Sigma Lambda. Club: Bus. and Profl. Women's of Bklyn. (Woman of Achievement award 1975). Editor: The International Kosher Cookbook, 1972; research on moral devel. of adults. Office: Brooklyn Coll Brooklyn NY 11210

EIFFLER, ELMER EDWARD, metall. engr.; b. Bellevue, Pa., Oct. 10, 1926; s. Elmer Christian and Marie Olga (Ober) E.; B.S., U. Pitts., 1950; m. Joan Martha Stamm, Oct. 6, 1950; children—Gary Edward, Jane Lynn, Donna Ann. Metallurgist Standard Steel Spring, Coraopolis, Pa., 1951-55; metall. engr. gearing div. Westinghouse Electric Co., Lawrenceville, Pa., 1955-58, metall. engr. electro-mech. div., Cheswick, Pa., 1958—, fellow engr., 1977—. Served with USAAF, 1944-46. Mem. Am. Soc. Metals, Am. Welding Soc., ASTM. Republican. Office: Westinghouse Electric Corp Cheswick Ave Cheswick PA 15024

EIGENBRODE, RICHARD DANIEL, motel exec.; b. Waynesboro, Pa., Dec. 28, 1933; s. Mark Daniel and Olive Naomi (Flohr) E.; B.S., Shippensburg (Pa.) State Coll., 1955; postgrad. U. Md., 1957-66, Western Md. U., 1957-66; m. Catherine Joann Greenawalt, Sept. 13, 1968; children—Daniel Lee, Debra Sue, Richard Dwight, Donna Jean, Kristina Marie. High sch. tchr., Waynesboro, 1958-65; mgr. Howard Johnson Motor Lodge, Chambersburg, Pa., 1966-70; motel supr. Porter Assos., Inc., Hagerstown, Md., 1970-73; gen. mgr. Holiday Inn, Chambersburg, 1973-78; pres., mgr. F.P.W. Motel Corp., Waynesboro Travelodge, 1978—; sec. Falling Spring Corp., 1966-70. Mem. bd. Waynesboro Area Sch. System, 1975-81; chmn. Franklin County Bicentennial Com., 1976. Served with AUS, 1956-58. Mem. Franklin County Tourist Council (pres. 1974-75), Franklin County Farmers Assn., Am., Pa. hotel-motel assns., Franklin County Motel Assn. (past pres.), S. Pa. Travel Council, Chambersburg C. of C. (dir. 1974-77). Republican. Mem. Ch. of the Apostles. Clubs: Chambersburg, Chambersburg Rotary. Home: Route 4 Box 19 Waynesboro PA 17268 Office: 1095 Wayne Ave Chambersburg PA 17201

EIKERENKOETTER, ROY CORNELIUS, educator; b. Wilkes-Barre, Pa., Oct. 6, 1931; s. Roy and Sadie Justine (Bethel) E.; B.S. (Presser Found. scholar), Temple U., 1955, M.Ed., 1968; postgrad. (univ. fellow), U. Pa., 1967-69; Ed.D. (Ford Found. fellow), Harvard, 1973; m. Flora Aquila James, June 20, 1959; 1 dau., Allison. Tchr., Phila. Sch. Dist., 1955-69, elementary sch. prin., 1969-72, adminstrv. asst. to supt. Dist. 7, 1972-74; supt. schs., Roosevelt, N.Y., 1974-76; dean tech. and applied scis. Cheyney (Pa.) State U., 1976—. Cons., Community Interaction Through Youth, Cambridge, Mass., Center for Urban Studies, Harvard, Center for Law and Edn., Cambridge. Bd. dirs. N.E. Community Mental Health Center, Phila. Served with AUS, 1956-58. Mem. Nat. Assn. Study Edn., Am. Assn. Sch. Adminstrn., Phi Delta Kappa. Home: 735 Pine Ridge Rd Media PA 19063 Office: Cheyney State Coll Cheyney PA 19319

EIN, DANIEL, physician; b. Liege, Belgium, Nov. 26, 1938; s. Max Motel and Sabine (Toeman) E.; came to U.S., 1941, naturalized, 1946; A.B., Columbia U., 1959; M.D., Albert Einstein Coll. Medicine, 1964; children—Mark David, Jon Spencer. Intern, Bronx Municipal Hosp. Center, N.Y.C., 1964-65; resident Mass. Gen. Hosp., Boston, 1968-69; clin. asso. Nat. Cancer Inst., Bethesda, Md., 1965-68; teaching fellow Harvard Med. Sch., Boston, 1968-69; sr. investigator Nat. Cancer Inst., Bethesda, 1969-71; practice gen. medicine and allergy, Washington, 1971—; asst. clin. prof. medicine George Washington U., Washington, 1971-76, asso. clin. prof. medicine, 1976—. Served with USPHS, 1965-71. Diplomate Am. Bd. Internal Medicine, Am. Bd. Allergy. Fellow A.C.P.; mem. Am. Acad. Allergy, D.C. Allergy Soc. (pres. 1978), Am. Fedn. Clin. Research, Am. Assn. Immunologists. Jewish. Office: 2141 K St NW Washington DC 20037

EIN, MELVIN BENNETT, govt. ofcl.; b. Hammond, Ind., Apr. 2, 1932; s. David and Rose (Chayken) E.; A.B., Ind. U., 1955; B.S., State U. N.Y., 1976; M.B.A., Am. U., 1976; m. Connie Chong, Dec. 9, 1957; children—Esther, Deborah, Michael P., Ruth, Nathan S., Sarah. Chief repair parts br. Engr. Sect. 8th. U.S. Army, Seoul, S. Korea, 1958-63; mgr. regional adminstrv. services Fed. Hwy. Adminstrn., Homewood, Ill., 1963-67; supply mgmt. officer U.S. Fgn. Service, U.S. Dept. State, AID, Am. Embassy, Vientiane, Laos, 1967-75; head material br. Naval Research Lab., Washington, 1975-76; chief material br. FAA, Nat. Aviation Facilities Exptl. Center, Atlantic City, 1976-78, emergency preparedness officer, 1978-79; chief material mgmt. br. Dept. Transp., Washington, 1979—; lectr. in field. Served to 1st lt. U.S. Army, 1955-58. Recipient Sustained Superior Performance award Fed. Hwy. Adminstrn., 1965, HUG award FAA, 1978. Mem. Internat. Material Mgmt. Soc. (profl. certified in material mgmt.), Adminstrv. Mgmt. Soc. (certified adminstrv. mgr.), Am. Logistics Assn., Assn. U.S. Army, Am. Mgmt. Assn., Am. Legion, Sigma Alpha Mu. Democrat. Jewish. Clubs: Elks, Toastmasters (Able award 1976). Home: 1509 Beech Ln Mays Landing NJ 08330 Office: Dept Transp M-471 Room 2302 400 7th St Washington DC 20590

EINACH, CHARLES DONALD, advt. agy. exec.; b. Buffalo, July 1, 1929; s. Joseph and Esther Riva (Liner) E.; B.A., U. Buffalo, 1951; M.A., Syracuse U., 1953; m. Elen Simon, Mar. 15, 1971. Broadcast dir. Rumrill Co., Inc., Buffalo, 1954-60; advt. dir. J. Nelson Prewitt, Inc., Rochester, N.Y., 1960-63; v.p., account supr. Grey Advt., Inc., N.Y.C., 1963-71; sr. v.p. account services Nadler & Larimer, Inc., N.Y.C., 1971—. Mem. Nat. Acad. TV Arts and Scis., Mus. City N.Y. Home: 301 E 66th St New York City NY 10021 Office: 1350 Ave of Americas New York City NY 10019

EINARSON, BALDVIN OLIVER, lawyer; b. Boston, Sept. 10, 1934; s. Einar V. and Margret (Johnson) E.; grad. Phillips Exeter Acad., 1952; A.B., Harvard U., 1956; J.D., Columbia U., 1963; m. Susan Moira Mok, Dec. 24, 1957; children—Stefan, Margret. Admitted to N.Y. bar, 1963, D.C. bar, 1969; asso. firm Kirlin, Campbell & Keating, N.Y.C., 1963—, partner, 1970—. Served to 1st lt. U.S. Army, 1957-60. Office: 120 Broadway New York City NY 10005

EINBOND, BERNARD LIONEL, poet, educator; b. N.Y.C., May 19, 1937; s. Hyman and Julia (Parsont) Einbund; A.B., Columbia, 1958, M.A. with high honors, 1960, Ph.D., 1966; m. Linda Saxe, Feb. 20, 1977; 1 son, Aaron Michael. Announcer, disc jockey Sta. WCED, DuBois, Pa., 1958-59; preceptor in English, Columbia, 1961-63; instr. Hunter Coll., 1964-68; asst. prof. Lehman Coll., City U. N.Y., 1968-72, asso. prof., 1973—, chmn. dept. English, 1976—. Recipient Keats Poetry prize (U.K.), 1974. Mem. Haiku Soc. Am. (pres. 1975), AAUP, Modern Lang. Assn. Jewish. Author: Samuel Johnson's Allegory, 1971; The Coming Indoors and Other Poems, 1979. Poems anthologized in Live Poetry, 1971; Invention, 1973; The Haiku Anthology, 1974. Home: 250 Cabrini Blvd New York City NY 10033 Office: Lehman Coll Bronx NY 10468

EINHORN, CARL MURRAY, psychologist; b. N.Y.C., Oct. 21, 1922; s. Albert H. and Florence (Spiegel) E.; B.A., Yeshiva U., 1945; M.A., U. Mich., 1950, Ph.D., 1956; post-doctoral study in clin. psychology N.Y. U., 1957-59. Asso. prof. social sci. and English, Lawrence Inst. Tech., Detroit, 1947-52; social work supr. Jewish Community Center, Detroit, 1952-55; counselor Metuchen (N.J.) High Sch., 1955-57; tchr. English, Jersey Prep. Sch., Jersey City, 1956-57; intern N.J. Diagnostic Center, Menlo Park, 1956, VA Hosp., Lyons, N.J., 1957-58; supr. psychologist VA Hosp., Lyons, 1957-69, unit psychologist, 1970—; cons. psychologist Lab. of Psychology Studies, Stevens Inst. Tech., 1958-69; supr. psychologist reading clinic Fairleigh Dickenson U., Rutherford, N.J., 1962-63; dir. counseling and psychol. services Newark State Coll., Union, N.J., 1969-70; dir. psychology services New Brunswick (N.J.) Rehab. Center, 1975—; pvt. practice psychology, East Brunswick, N.J.; clin. dir. Human Relations Assos., East Brunswick; field supr. Grad. Sch. Applied and Profl. Psychology, Rutgers U.; mem. profl. adv. staff Raritan Valley Sheltered Tng. Center; adj. staff Middlesex Rehab. Hosp.; cons. N.J. Rehab. Commn., Bur. Childrens Services, N.J. Dept. Pub. Safety, East Brunswick. Coordinator social concerns N.J. Gov.'s Conf. on Handicapped; Founding fellow Center for Human Devel., Hebrew U., Jerusalem. Mem. Am., Eastern, N.J. psychol. assns., Am. Personnel and Guidance Assn., Union County Mental Health Assn. (past dir.), Nat. Vocat. Guidance Assn. (profl. certification), Am. Rehab. Counselors Assn. (profl. certification). Jewish. Contbr. articles in field to profl. jours. Home: 44 Yorktown Rd East Brunswick NJ 08816 Office: VA Hospital Lyons NJ 07939

EINHORN, EDWARD HARRY, psychiatrist; b. N.Y.C., Sept. 7, 1919; s. Harry and Alice (Thal) E.; M.D., Chgo. Med. Sch., 1942; m. Bernice Rubin, Aug. 18, 1968; children—Robert, Lewis, Steven. Intern Port Angeles (Wash.) Gen. Hosp., 1942-43; mixed resident St. Joseph Hosp., Far Rockaway, N.Y., 1946-47; gen. practice medicine, Lynbrook, N.Y., 1947-52; resident in psychiatry Bklyn. VA Hosp., 1952-54; practice medicine specializing in psychiatry, Hempstead, N.Y., 1954—; grad. in psychoanalysis N.Y. Med. Coll.-Flower and Fifth Ave Hosp., N.Y.C., 1954-57; attending psychiatrist L.I. Jewish-Hillside Med. Center; asst. prof. psychiatry U. N.Y., Stony Brook; asst. attending dept. psychiatry and psychology Nassau County Med. Center. Served to capt. M.C., U.S. Army, 1944-46; ETO. Decorated Croix de Guerre (France). Fellow Am. Acad. Psychoanalysis; mem. Soc. Med. Psychoanalysts. Home: 2 N Hills Rd East Norwich NY 11732 Office: 230 Hilton Ave Hempstead NY 11550

EINHORN, ROMAN, neurologist; b. Czenstochowa, Poland, July 24, 1931; s. Pinkus and Sarah (Blibaum) E.; came to Can., 1949; M.D., U. Toronto, 1956; m. Mary Rosalind Morrison, Sept. 11, 1959; children—Romi-Paul, David Alan. Intern, Toronto Western Hosp., 1956-57; resident in neurology U. Toronto, 1957-62, Boston Harvard Med. Sch., 1962-64; cons. neurologist, Hamilton, Ont., 1965—; asso. clin. prof. neurology McMaster Med. Sch., Hamilton, 1973—; mem. staff Hamilton Civic Hosp. Fellow Royal Coll. Physicians Can., Am. Acad. Neurology; mem. Am. Acad. Medicine, Canadian Neurol. Soc., Canadian Med. Assn., Royal Soc. Medicine London, Toronto, Hamilton acads. medicine. Club: Hamilton Thistle. Home: 2108 Salisbury Ct Burlington ON L7P 1P4 Canada Office: Med Arts Bld Hamilton ON Canada

EISAMAN, LEO COBURN, electronics co. exec.; b. Canastota, N.Y., Feb. 4, 1925; s. Durward M. and Ethel M. (Harrington) E.; B.E.E., Syracuse U., 1946; postgrad. Poly. Inst. Bklyn., 1948-50; m. Lois G. Schneider, Aug. 7, 1954; children—Katherane, Gail, Trudy. Research engr. Sylvania Electric Co., Bayside, N.Y., 1946-51; sr. engr. Hazeltine Co., Little Neck, N.Y., 1951-55; lab. mgr. Rochester div. Gen. Dynamics Co., Rochester, N.Y., 1955-66; exec. v.p., gen. mgr., treas. Frequency Sources, Inc., North Chelmsford, Mass., 1966-77; mgr. new bus. devel. R.F. Communications div. The Harris Corp., Rochester, 1977—. Mem. IEEE (sr., chmn. Rochester sect. 1965-66), Tau Beta Pi, Sigma Pi Sigma, Pi Mu Epsilon. Home: 960 Gravel Rd Webster NY 14580 Office: Harris Corp 1960 University Ave Rochester NY 14610

EISELE, JOHN ALLAN, physicist; b. Chgo., Oct. 25, 1929; s. Anton Joseph and Anne Josephine (Bodeck) E.; student U. Chgo., 1947-53, U. Pitts., 1953-57; Ph.D. (NSF predoctoral fellow), Ohio State U., 1959; m. Nancy Crisman, Aug. 3, 1957; children—Jeffery Allan, Jane Katherin. Theoretical physicist, Research Lab., Westinghouse Co., Pitts., 1955-56, atomic power dept., 1956-57; asst. prof. physics So. Ill. U., 1959-62; asso. prof. physics Tex. A. and M. U., 1962-65; research physicist Naval Research Lab., Washington, 1965—; vis. research scientist U. Calif. at Berkeley, 1964; asso. prof. physics U. Md., 1965—; astronomy instr. Smithsonian Instn., 1973; pres. Nat. Book Co. Am., Washington, 1965-71. NSF grantee, 1961-62. Fellow Washington Acad. Scis. (dir.), Am. Phys. Soc., Nat. Capitol Astronomers (pres. 1972-74), Astron. Soc. Pacific, Research Engring. Soc. Am., Sigma Xi. Author: Advanced Quantum Mechanics and Particle Physics, 1964; Astrodynamics, Rockets, Satellites, and Space Travel, 1967; Modern Quantum Mechanics with Applications to Elementary Particle Physics, 1969; (with R.M. Mason) Applied Matrix and Tensor Analysis, 1970. Contbr. articles to profl. jours. Home: 3310 Curtis Dr Hillcrest Heights MD 20023 Office: Aerospace Applications Br Space Systems Div U S Naval Research Lab Code 7970 Washington DC 20032

EISEN, ALAN G., pub. relations exec.; b. N.Y.C., Feb. 11, 1929; s. Nathan and Edna Eisen; B.A., Temple U., 1952; m. Joanne F. Moss. Dir. radio and TV, City of Phila., 1951-52; dir. pub. relations Greater N.Y. councils Boy Scouts Am., 1952-53; asst. dir. press relations Music Corp. Am., 1952-53; v.p. Ruder & Finn, N.Y.C., 1956-63; pres. Alan G. Eisen Co., Inc., Glen Cove, N.Y., 1963—. Chmn. pub. relations Glen Cove Bicentennial Commn. Mem. Pub. Relations Soc. Am. (accredited), Nat. Rifle Assn. (life). Club: Matinecock Rod and Gun. Author: Foodbook, 1973. Office: 1188 Round Swamp Rd Old Bethpage NY 11804

EISEN, DAVID MICHAEL, electronics co. exec.; b. Toronto, Ont., Can., Jan. 5, 1923; s. Samuel and Sarah (Rose) E.; B.A. in Engring. Physics, U. Toronto, 1945; m. Ruth Jewel Kert, June 22, 1945; children—Michael, Cliff. Physicist Nat. Research Council Can., Montreal, Que., Can., 1945; mgr. dept. Imperial Optical Co., Toronto, 1947; mgr. quartz crystal dept. Philips Electronics Ltd., Toronto, 1952-57, gen. mgr. electronic tube div., 1957-65, v.p. mfg., 1965-69, exec. v.p., 1969—, dir., 1969—; dir. Philips Acceptance Corp. Ltd., Toronto, 1969—, Philips Electronics Can. Ltd., Toronto, 1969—, Philips Transformer Co. Ltd., St. Jerome, 1971—. Bd. govs. Can. Opera Co. Registered profl. engr., Ont. Mem. IEEE, Can. Mfrs. Assn. (Ont. exec. com.). Clubs: Empire, Queen's, Donalda (Toronto). Home: 30 York Ridge Rd Willowdale ON Canada Office: 601 Milner Ave Scarborough ON M1B 1M8 Canada

EISEN, LEONARD, furniture designer; b. Bklyn., Nov. 27, 1932; s. Jesse and Gussie E.; B. Indsl. Design, Syracuse U., 1956; m. 2d, Joan Perry Oct. 27, 1968; children—Cindi, Jack, Jeff, Michael, Debra, Emily, Jonathan. Human factors designer IBM, Poughkeepsie, N.Y., 1956-57; designer Eisen Bros. Inc. Furniture Co., Hoboken, N.J., 1960-64; free lance furniture designer, Montvale, N.J., 1964—. Served With USAF, 1957-60. Recipient Poly award Soc. Plastics Industries Inc. Furniture Div., 1973, Good Value award Budget Decorating Mag., 1977; named Designer of Year, Hecht Co., Washington, 1977. Jewish. Address: 14 Lomas Ln Montvale NJ 07645

EISENBERG, ALLAN JAY, county ofcl. Tioga County (N.Y.), b. Hudson, N.Y., Aug. 29, 1942; s. Samuel and Dorothy (Liebman) E.; law qualifying certificate State U. N.Y. at Buffalo, 1963; J.D., Buffalo Law Sch., 1969; m. Kathy J. Proller, July 1, 1967; 1 son, Michael D.J. Civil service mng. atty. trainee Office Atty. Gen. Dept. Law, Albany, N.Y., 1970-72; mortgage adminstr. N.Y. State Health Dept., Albany, 1972-73; commr. Tioga County Dept. Social Services, Owego, N.Y., 1973—. Bd. dirs. N.Y. State Human Services Conf. Mem. Am. Pub. Welfare Assn., Western Region Commrs. Assn. (sec.-treas.), N.Y. Pub. Welfare Assn., Nat. Fraud Assn., N.Y. State County Officers Assn., Tioga County C. of C. Clubs: Tioga County Sportsmens, Elks, Kiwanis. Office: RD 3 Box 394 Owego NY 13827

EISENBERG, DONALD HARVEY, hosp. adminstr.; b. Tampa, Fla., Oct. 17, 1928; s. David and Toba (Moss) E.; A.B., Bklyn. Coll., 1949; M.P.A., N.Y. U., 1970; m. Brenda Bernowitz, Nov. 28, 1959; children—Cindy, Lawrence, Robert. Dept. head Mt. Sinai Hosp., N.Y.C., 1961-63, asst. dir., 1963-69, asso. dir., 1969-71; dir. ops. N.Y.C. Health and Hosps. Corp., 1971, sr. v.p., 1971-73, exec. v.p., 1973-74; exec. dir. Nassau County (N.Y.) Med. Center, East Meadow, 1974—; prof. clin. community medicine SUNY, Stony Brook. Scouting coordinator Boy Scouts Am., 1975—; bd. dirs. L.I. div. Am. Cancer Soc., 1976-77; mem. adv. council C.W. Post Center, L.I. U., 1978—. Served with U.S. Army, 1950-52. Mem. Am. Coll. Hosp. Adminstrn., Am. Hosp. Assn., Am. Soc. Public Adminstrn. (award for disting. contbns. to public adminstrn. L.I. chpt. 1977), Royal Soc. Health, Hosp. Soc. N.Y., Nassau-Suffolk Health Systems Agy., Hosp. Assn. N.Y. State. Contbr. articles to profl. jours. Home and office: 2201 Hempstead Turnpike East Meadow NY 11554*

EISENBERG, GERSON GUTMAN, ednl. co. exec., author; b. Balt., Mar. 5, 1909; s. Abram and Helen (Gutman) E.; A.B., George Washington U., 1930; M.B.A., N.Y. U., 1944; postgrad. Johns Hopkins U., 1936-37; m. Sadie Frenkil, Sept. 15, 1967. With bond dept. Stein Bros. & Boyce, Balt., 1930-31; with Am. Oil Co., Balt., 1932-34; economist, statistician U.S. Census Bur., Suitland, Md., 1944-45; v.p. Robinson's Dept. Store, Glen Burnie, Md., 1949-62; partner Plastic & Metals Products Co., Linthicum, Md., 1964-68; pres. Eisenberg Ednl. Enterprises, Balt., 1970—. Pres., Gerson G. Eisenberg Found., 1952—; bd. dirs. Balt. Mus. Art, 1975—, Md. Conf. Social Concern, 1975—, Citizens Planning and Housing Assn. Balt., 1973—, Johns Hopkins Tutorial Program, 1975—, Am. Jewish Com., 1973—, Assoc. Jewish Charities and Welfare Fund, 1974-78, Balt. Hebrew Congregation, 1977—, Ecumenical Inst. of St. Mary's Theol. Sem., Balt., 1974, Hebrew Immigrant Aid Soc., 1971—. Gerson Eisenberg grantee, 1974-75, 76, 77. Mem. Am. Acad. Polit. and Social Sci., Am., Md. hist. socs., Johns Hopkins Assoc., Authors Guild, Jewish Hist. Soc. Md. (dir. 1974-78), Am. Technion Soc. of Israel. Democrat. Jewish. Clubs: Suburban Country, Johns Hopkins Faculty, Towson. Author: Learning Vacations, 1977, 78; contbr. articles to profl. jours. Home: 7940 Stevenson Rd Baltimore MD 21208 Office: 2 Hamill Rd Suite 327 Baltimore MD 21210

EISENBERG, JOHN MEYER, physician; b. Atlanta, Sept. 24, 1946; s. Irvin and Roslyn (Furchgott) E.; A.B. magna cum laude, Princeton U., 1968; M.D., Washington U., St. Louis, 1972; M.B.A. with distinction, U. Pa., 1975; m. DD Rudner, June 15, 1969; 1 son, William R. Intern, Hosp. U. Pa., Phila., 1972-73, resident, 1973-75; Robert Wood Johnson Found. clin. scholar, 1974-77; asst. prof. medicine U. Pa., 1975—, co-dir. primary care residency, 1976—, asso. dir. Leonard Davis Inst. Health Econs. and Nat. Health Care Mgmt. Center, 1976-78, Sol Katz asst. prof. gen. medicine and primary care, 1978—, chief sect. gen. medicine, 1978—. Mem. Soc. for Research and Edn. in Primary Care Internal Medicine (sec. 1978—), A.C.P., Am. Fedn. Clin. Research. Jewish. Contbr. numerous articles on health care delivery to med. jours. Home: 529 Heath Rd Merion Station PA 19066 Office: Hospital of U Pa 3400 Spruce St Philadelphia PA 19104

EISENBERG, JOSEPH, mgmt. cons.; b. N.Y.C., July 3, 1932; s. Herman and Gertrude (Biernoff) E.; B.S., Wharton Sch. U. Pa., 1952, M.B.A., 1953; postgrad. Princeton, 1955-57. Sr. cons. Stevenson, Jordan & Harrison, Inc., N.Y.C.; partner, dir. Wright Assos., N.Y.C.; mgr. McKinsey & Co., N.Y.C.; pres. Profit-Improvement Inc., mgmt. cons., N.Y.C., 1967—. Served with USAF, 1953-55. Mem. Inst. Mgmt. Cons., Am. Arbitration Assn. Clubs: Princeton, Striper Surf. Author: Cost Controls for The Office, 1968; Turnaround Management, 1974. Mem. bd. experts Boardroom Mag. Contbr. articles to profl. jours. Home: Randall Rd Southampton NY 11968 Office: Profit-Improvement Inc 200 Park Ave Suite 303E New York City NY 10017

EISENBERG, PHILLIP, engring. research co. exec.; b. Detroit, Nov. 6, 1919; s. Morris and Ida (Blaizovsky) E.; B.S., Wayne State U., 1941; postgrad. U. Iowa, 1942; C.E., Calif. Inst. Tech., 1948; m. Edith S. Rosenbaum, Nov. 21, 1942; children—Elyse, Jean. Instr. U. Iowa, Iowa City, 1941-42; head research br. David Taylor Model Basin, Navy Dept., Carderock, Md., 1942-44, 46-53; head mechanics br. Office Naval Research, Washington, 1953-59; pres. Hydronautics, Inc., Laurel, Md., 1959-74, chmn. exec. com., 1974—, also dir. Mem. bd. cons. Iowa Inst. Hydraulic Research, 1954-56, 59-61; mem. Md. Ocean Sci. Com., 1969-70; mem. sea grant adv. panel Nat. Oceanographic and Atmospheric Adminstrn., 1969-77. Mem. vis. com. ocean engring. Mass. Inst. Tech., 1974—; mem. Marine Bd., Maritime Transp. Research Bd., NRC; mem. tech. adv. bd. Dept. Commerce; bd. dirs. Am. Bur. Shipping. Served to lt. (j.g.) USNR, 1944-45. Recipient Meritorious Civilian award U.S. Navy, 1944, Distinguished Alumni award Wayne State U., 1958, tech. achievement award Am. Soc. M.E., 1959, Gold medal Nat. Acad. Scis., 1974. Fellow Royal Inst. Naval Architects, Am. Soc. M.E., Soc. Naval Architects and Marine Engrs. (pres. 1973-74, hon. mem., gold medal 1972); mem. Nat. Acad. Engring., Am. Inst. Aeros. and Astronautics, Am. Phys. Soc., Am. Soc. Engring. Edn., AAAS, Washington Acad. Sci., Internat. Assn. for Hydraulic Research, Am. Inst. Physics, Acoustical Soc. Am., Marine Tech. Soc. Clubs: Whitehall (N.Y.C.); Cosmos (Washington). Contbr. articles to publs. in field. Patentee in field. Home: 6402 Tulsa Ln Bethesda MD 20034 Office: Hydronautics Inc Pindell School Rd Laurel MD 20810

EISENPREIS, ALFRED, mktg. exec.; b. Vienna, Austria, June 16, 1924; s. Zygmunt and Claire (Silberman-Günsberg) E.; came to U.S., 1939, naturalized, 1942; A.B., St. Thomas, 1943; M.A., N.Y. Sch. Social Research, 1974; 1 son, Steven. Exec., Pomeroy's, Inc., dept. store, Wilkes-Barre, Pa., 1943-57; with Allied Stores Corp., N.Y.C., 1957-74, v.p. planning and research, 1963-69, v.p. pub. affairs, 1967-69, v.p. mktg., 1970-74; adminstr. Econ. Devel. Adminstrn., N.Y.C., 1974-76; v.p. mktg. Newspaper Advt. Bur., 1977—; pres. A. Eisenpreis Inc., Cons.; dir. Allerton, Berman, Dean, N.Y.C., 82-83d Corp., N.Y.C.; faculty Grad. Sch. Mgmt., New Sch., 1974—. Chmn. bd. Retail Research Inst., 1964-68; mem. Appeals Bd. Selective Service 3d Dist.; mem. com. dept. store statistics Fed. Res. System, 1960-65; mem. Census Adv. Com., 1971-74; pres. N.Y.C. Indsl. Devel. Corp., 1974-76; chmn. adv. com. Center for Econ. Projections, 1965-69; trustee Fed. Statistic Users Conf., 1965-67, N.Y. Met. Region Statis. Center, 1965-68, cons. U.S. Dept. Commerce, 1965-69; mem. Port Devel. Council, 1974-76, Herald Sq. Council, Times Sq. Council, 1974-76; mem. urban transp. dept. Hwy. Research Bd., 1964-69; dir. Jamaica Devel. Adv. Bd., 1965-68; bd. dirs. S. Bronx Overall Devel. Corp., 1974-76; cons. Office Emergency Preparedness, Exec. Office of Pres., 1967-74; chmn. Mgmt. Adv. Com. on Vocat. Edn., 1968-69; exec. com., nat. mktg. adv. com. Dept. Commerce, 1969-71; chmn. Interagy. Rail Freight Com., N.Y.C., 1976. Bd. dirs. N.Y. Conv. and Visitors Bur., 1974-76, N.Y.C. Conv. and Exhbn. Center, 1974-76; trustee Reece School, N.Y.C., 1969-72, French and Polyclinic Hosp., 1972-73, Nat. Retail Mchts. Found. 1965-70, Wilkes Coll., 1966-74; N.Y. Met. Regional Statis. Center, 1965-67, Congregation EmmanuEl, N.Y.C., 1968—; trustee Nat. Found. Jewish Culture, 1973—, treas., 1976—; trustee Union Am. Hebrew Congregations, 1970—, exec. com., 1973-78; exec. com. N.Y. Fedn. Reform Synagogues, 1969—; adv. com. N.Y. Pub. Library, 1970—; co-dir. Mayor's Mgmt. Adv. Bd., 1975-76; mem. Adv. Com. on Human Resource Devel. and Tourism Center for N.Y.C. Affairs, 1976—; mem. president's council N.Y. U. Sch. Social Work, 1977—; mem. exec. com. N.Y. chpt. Am. Jewish Com., 1976—, mem. commn. on community relations, 1977—; mem. N.Y.C. Community Relations Council, 1976-78; mem. nat. exec. res. Fed. Preparedness Agy. Mem. Am. Statis. Assn., Am. Econ. Assn., Met. Economists Assn., Nat. Assn. Bus. Economists, Am. Marketing Assn., Nat. Retail Mchts. Assn. (dir., exec. com. 1968-73, v.p. 1970), N.Y. Acad. Scis., Retail Research Soc. (hon. life), Am. Retail Fedn. (dir. exec. com. 1968-71), N.Y. C. of C. (mems. council), Forecasters (pres. 1973-74), Nat. Planning Assn. (com. on urban policy 1978—). Clubs: University, Grolier (N.Y.C.). Author: The Changing Consumer, 1961; Organization for Multi-Unit Stores, 1962. Home: 40 E 83d St New York City NY 10028 Office: 485 Lexington Ave New York City NY 10017

EISENSTADT, ABRAHAM SELDIN, educator; b. Bklyn., June 18, 1920; s. Ben-Zion and Sarah (Seldin) E.; A.B., Bklyn. Coll., 1940; Ph.D., Columbia, 1955; m. Paulette Smith, Sept. 4, 1949; children—Elizabeth Anne, Laura Jane, Jonathan. Mem. faculty Bklyn. Coll., City U. N.Y., 1956—, asso. prof. history, 1966-67, prof., 1968—. Vis. prof. Johns Hopkins U., Bologna, Italy, 1962-63; mem. Council Am. Studies, Rome, 1963; hist. editor Pitman Corp., N.Y.C., 1965-70. Served with U.S. Army, 1942-46. Recipient grants Am. Philos. Soc., 1966, City U. N.Y., 1966, 67. Mem. Am. Hist. Assn., Orgn. Am. Historians, Am. Studies Assn., Conf. British Studies. Author, editor American History: Recent Interpretations, 2 vols., 1970, Craft of American History, 2 vols., 1966, Charles M. Andrews: A Study in American Historical Writing, 1956. Contbr. to profl. jours. Home: 567 1st St Brooklyn NY 11215 Office: Dept History Brooklyn College Brooklyn NY 11210

EISENSTADT, GERD MICHAEL, fgn. service officer; b. Free City of Danzig, Nov. 16, 1928; s. Isidor and Edith (Lange) E.; came to U.S., 1939; B.A., Queens Coll., 1951; M.A., U. Wis., 1952; postgrad. Russian Inst., Columbia, 1954-56; m. Mary Louise Gories, Aug. 15, 1959; 1 dau., Judith Luzann. Lectr., Queens Coll., 1955-60; assigned Am. embassy, Jot, Belgrade, Yugoslavia, 1960-61; cultural affairs officer Am. consulate gen., Guyaquil, Ecuador, 1962-63; asst. cultural affairs officer Am. embassy, Belgrade, 1964-67; cultural affairs officer Am. embassy, Warsaw, Poland, 1968-71; European policy officer Voice of Am., Washington, 1971, dep. chief Policy Applications br., 1971-73; 1st sec., program officer USIS, Am. embassy, Bonn, Germany, 1973-76, Washington, 1976-77; counselor for press and cultural affairs Am. embassy, Budapest, Hungary, 1977—. Served with AUS, 1952-54. Home: 76-15 35th Ave Jackson Heights NY 11372 Office: Budapest Dept State Washington DC 20520

EISENSTADT, MARVIN ERNEST, mfg. co. exec.; b. Bklyn., Feb. 24, 1933; s. Benjamin E.; B.A., U. Vt., 1954, LL.B., 1973; m. Barbara Leah Buchwald, June 6, 1959; children—Jeffrey, Jill, Deborah, Stephen. Owner, Cumberland Packing Corp., Bklyn., 1956—. Bd. dirs. Peninsula Hosp. Center, Far Rockaway, N.Y. Served with U.S. Army, 1954-56. Offered fellowship U. Vt. to do cancer research; patentee sugar substitute, air operated packing machine. Office: 2 Cumberland St Brooklyn NY 11205

EISENSTEIN, THEODORE DONALD, pediatrician; b. N.Y.C., July 4, 1930; s. Harry and Myra (Drexler) E.; student N.Y. U., 1948-49; A.B., Johns Hopkins U., 1952; M.D., Albany Med. Coll., 1956; m. Ellen Roob, Dec. 9, 1956; children—Janet, Stephen. Pediatric intern Kings County Med. Center, Bklyn., 1956-57; resident in pediatrics N.Y. Hosp., N.Y.C., 1957-59; NIH vis. fellow in pediatric endocrinology Columbia-Presbyn. Med. Center, N.Y.C., 1961-62; practice medicine specializing in pediatrics, West Caldwell, N.J., 1962—; asst. clin. prof. pediatrics Columbia U. Coll. Phys. and Surg., 1970—; clin. asst. prof. pediatrics N.J. Coll. Medicine and Dentistry, Rutgers U., 1970—. Mem. alumni council N.Y. Hosp.-Cornell Med. Center. Served with M.C., USAF, 1959-61. Diplomate Am. Bd. Pediatrics. Fellow Am. Acad. Pediatrics; mem. AMA, Acad. Medicine N.J., Am. Diabetes Assn., AAAS. Jewish. Research on pediatric endocrinology, human growth hormone. Home: 7 Byron Rd North Caldwell NJ 07006 Office: 700 Passaic Ave West Caldwell NJ 07006

EISLER, PAUL ERICH, musician, educator, author; b. N.Y.C., Sept. 3, 1922; s. Paul Joseph and Edith Vail (Ross) E.; B.S., Columbia U., 1953, A.M., 1955; D.M.A., Boston U., 1965; m. Edith Gertrude Nachod, Mar. 23, 1967; children—Judith Edith, Paul Alfred, Karen Erling, Peter Ross. Chmn. dept. music Bennett Coll., Millbrook, N.Y., 1955-60; dean arts and scis., prof. music and German, New Eng. Coll., Henniker, N.H., 1960-65; founder, dir. Acad. Music and Theatre, Eastchester, N.Y., 1965—; faculty Manhattan Sch. Music, 1965—; asso. adj. prof. N.Y. U., 1965—; condr. Acad. Opera Workshops, Westchester, N.Y., 1967-78, Hudson River Choral Soc., 1973-75, Manhattan Repertory Orch., 1974, Acad. Chorale, 1966-70, N.H. State Band, 1964-65, Vt. State Music Festival, 1947-53, N.Y. Youth Symphony, 1937, Met. Opera, 1927-29. Bd. dirs. Scarsdale (N.Y.) Performing Arts Soc., 1976-77; mem. N.H. com. Nelson Rockefeller presdl. campaign, 1963. Served with USAAF, 1941-45. Decorated D.F.C., Air medal (9); N.Y. State Vets. scholar, 1953-55; recipient Service award Kiwanis Club, 1968. Mem. Am. Fedn. Musicians, The Bohemians, Musicians Emergency Found., Musicians Emergency Fund, Goethe Soc. New Eng., Pi Kappa Lambda, Kappa Gamma Psi. Episcopalian. Club: Masons. Author: World Chronology of Music History, vols. 1-5, 1972-78; composer short musical pieces. Home and Office: 84 Siwanoy Blvd Bronxville Manor Eastchester NY 10707 Died Dec. 12, 1978

EISNER, HERMAN, clergyman; b. Kushnitza, Czechoslovakia, July 14, 1918; s. Solomon and Rose (Friedman) E.; student Rabbinical Sem., Czechoslovakia, 1935-39; Rabbi, Rabbinical Sem. Tifereth Jerusalem, N.Y.C., 1949; B.S., Yeshiva U., 1959, M.S., 1959; m. Malvina Gerlich, Aug. 11, 1946; 1 son, Moshe. Came to U.S., 1947, naturalized, 1952. Rabbi, Congregation Ezrath Israel, Ellenville, N.Y., 1949—; chaplain N.Y. State Correctional Facility, Napanoch, N.Y., 1960—; pres. Rabbinical Council Sullivan and Ulster Counties, 1956-60. Sec.-treas. United Jewish Appeal Ellenville Area, 1967—; bd. dirs. Rabbinical Council Am. Named Citizen of Year, Ellenville, 1966. Mem. Am. Chaplains Assn., Am. Joint Distbn. Com., Clergy Assn. Ellenville (pres. 1960-62). Mem. B'nai B'rith. Home: 36 Center St Ellenville NY 12428

EISNER, LEONARD, concert pianist, tchr.; b. Bklyn., June 29, 1920; s. Alex and Esther (Reich) E.; student Inst. of Musical Art, Juilliard Grad. Sch., N.Y. City Coll. Appeared in first recital, Brooklyn Acad. of Music, 1927; continued studying under scholarships, winner Morris Loeb Memorial prize, for highest achievement in piano class, fellowship Juilliard Grad. Sch. Debut as profl. pianist, Town Hall, N.Y., 1946, piano soloist, accompianist Lauritz Melchior, 1949—; asso. with Olin Downes in nationwide series of lecture recitals, 1951—; recital Carnegie Recital Hall, N.Y., 1968; vis. asst. prof. piano music dept. Coll. Fine Arts, Carnegie Inst. Tech., Pitts., 1955-57; mem. faculty Juilliard School Music, 1959—, Usdan Center for Performing and Visual Arts, 1969—; adj. lectr. Hunter Coll. City U. N.Y., 1973—; master classes N.J. Music Educators Assn., 1975, 76, Rockland County chpt. N.Y. Music Tchrs. Assn., 1976, Nihon U., Tokyo, 1975, Musashino Conservatory, Tokyo, 1975. European concert tour, Eng., Sweden, Denmark, Holland, Switzerland, fall 1954; concert Yamaha Hall, Tokyo, 1975. Served with Signal Corps U.S. Army, 1942-46. Recipient Am. Artists' award, 1946-47. Mem. Piano Tchrs. Congress, Asso. Music Tchrs., Bklyn. Piano Tchrs. Guild. Club: Bohemians (N.Y.C.). Address: 1420 Ocean Pkwy Brooklyn NY 11230

EISNER, MICHAEL CARL, corp. exec.; b. N.Y.C., Sept. 23, 1939; s. Martin Bert and Bertie Martha (Roniger) E.; B.S., Syracuse U., 1961; postgrad. taxation Bernard M. Baruch Grad. Sch. Bus.; m. Adrianne Kobell, June 10, 1961; children—Wendy, Todd, Lori. Sr. accountant Price Waterhouse & Co., N.Y.C., 1961-66; sr. financial systems specialist Gen. Foods Corp., White Plains, N.Y., 1966-67; mgr. corporate accounting Revlon, Inc., N.Y.C., 1967-69; audit mgr. Arthur Andersen & Co., Newark, 1969-72; asst. controller Hertz Corp., N.Y.C., 1972-74; v.p., corp. controller Sony Corp. Am., N.Y.C., 1974—; speaker profl. devel. program N.J. Soc. C.P.A.'s. Pres., local civic assn., E. Brunswick, N.J., 1969-76; treas. E. Brunswick Jewish Center, 1976—. C.P.A. Mem. Am. Inst. C.P.A.'s, Controllers Inst., N.Y. Soc. C.P.A.'s, Am. Mgmt. Assn., Nat. Assn. Accountants. Democrat. Home: 2 Guy Dr East Brunswick NJ 08816 Office: 47-47 Van Dam St Long Island City NY 11101

EISOLD, JOHN EDWARD, cons., ret. textile co. exec.; b. Milw., Feb. 11, 1911; s. John Joseph and Elizabeth Sara (Dusold) E.; B.A., U. Rochester, 1933; m. Helen Rae Beggs, June 30, 1938; children—Nancy (Mrs. W. Douglas Lindsay, Jr.), John Francis, Eric David. With Coats & Clark's Sales Corp., 1934-73, supr. Cleve. dist., 1942-46, dist. mgr., Balt., 1946-50, zone mgr., 1950-54, dist. mgr., 1954-68, regional v.p., 1968-73, ret.; counselor ret. execs. SBA. Active Boy Scouts Am., merit badge counselor; mem. Dartmouth parents' com., U. Rochester Fund Com., 1965-68; active Balt. United Way Fund. Served to lt. USNR, 1942-46. Mem. Sales and Mktg. Execs., Theta Chi. Roman Catholic. Home: 812 Ridgeleigh Rd Stoneleigh Baltimore County MD 21212 Office: 75 Varick St New York City NY 10013

EKMAN, SHELDON VICTOR, lawyer; b. Manchester, N.H., Mar. 12, 1920; s. Nathan and Sonia B. E.; A.B., Harvard U., 1939, J.D., 1942; m. Judith Saturen, Aug. 11, 1943; children—Richard H., Joanna K. Admitted to N.H. bar, 1943, N.Y. bar, 1946; spl. atty. Office of Chief Counsel, Bur. Internal Revenue, N.Y.C., 1945-50; tax prin. S.D. Leidesdorf & Co., N.Y.C., 1950-68; partner firm Reavis & McGrath, N.Y.C., 1969—; lectr. N.Y. U. Inst. on Fed. Taxation, 1950—, mem. adv. com., 1962—, chmn., 1976—; lectr. various tax insts. Bd. dirs. Samuel Rubin Found., 1969—. Served to lt. USNR, 1942-45. Mem. Am. (com. on ct. procedure sect. of taxation), Fed. (com. on taxation), N.Y. State (tax sect.) bar assns., Assn. Bar City N.Y. (com. on taxation 1970-73, com. on lectrs. and continuing edn. 1976—). Clubs: Harvard, Wall St. (N.Y.C.). Contbr. articles to profl. jours. Home: 3 Pumpkin Hill Westport CT 06880 Office: 345 Park Ave New York City NY 10022

EKSTRAND, JANICE IRMO, educator; b. Chgo., July 31, 1940; d. Stephen G. and Helen (Greif) Irmo; B.A., Marquette U., 1962; M.A., Kean Coll., 1978; children—Carrie, Christopher, Laurie. Substitute tchr. Coop. Nursery Sch., Urbana, Ill., 1967-68, St. Genevieve's Sch., Elizabeth, N.J., 1968-69; remedial reading tchr. Rahway (N.J.) Pub. Schs., 1969; tchr. English as 2d lang. Wm. Halloran Sch. for Gifted, Elizabeth, 1973—. Active Union County Women's Polit. Caucus, New Democratic Coalition. Recipient Barat Meml. Scholarship Barat Coll., 1958; internship grantee Employment, Vocat., Edn. Office Kean Coll., Union, N.J., 1972. Mem. Am. Personnel and Guidance Assn., Elizabeth Edn. Assn. (polit. action chmn. 1976), AAUW (cultural arts chmn.), Sigma Delta Pi. Roman Catholic. Club: Officers' Wives (pres. 1964). Contbr. article to Woman's Day Mag., 1969. Home: 55 Summit Rd Elizabeth NJ 07208 Office: 447 Richmond Ave Elizabeth NJ 07202

EKSTROM, LINCOLN, chemist; b. Providence, Aug. 21, 1932; s. Claus Emanuel and Marjorie Aliene (Robertson) E.; Sc.B., Brown U., 1953; Ph.D. (NSF fellow), Mass. Inst. Tech., 1957; m. Ruth Elizabeth Burt, Nov. 9, 1957. Mem. tech. staff RCA Labs., Princeton, N.J., 1957—. Recipient David Sarnoff Outstanding Achievement award

RCA, 1963. Fellow Am. Inst. Chemists, AAAS; mem. Am. Chem. Soc., Am. Phys. Soc., mem. Swedish Colonial Soc. Clubs: Sierra, Brown. Contbr. articles in field to profl. jours. Home: 78 Westerly Rd Princeton NJ 08540 Office: RCA Labs Princeton NJ 08540

ELATTAR, ABDEL MONEIM, oral surgeon; b. Port Said, Egypt, June 22, 1935; s. Abdel Salam and Nabawia (Shihata) E.; student Cairo U., B.Dental Surgery, 1959; M.S. in Oral Surg., U. Pitts., 1964, D.M.D., 1974; m. Elizabeth Jane Mortimore, Feb. 27, 1965; children—Suzanne, Deena, Kareem. Intern, Univ. Hosp., Cairo, 1959-60; resident in oral surgery Magee-Womens Hosp., Pitts., 1962-63, Allegheny Gen. Hosp., Pitts., 1963-64; instr. oral surg. Cairo U. Sch. Denistry, 1960-61, asst. prof., 1966-69; fellow oral surgery U. Pitts Sch. Dentistry and Health Center, 1962-63; advance tng. gen. anesthesia Allegheny Gen. Hosp., 1964-65; cons. maxillofacial dept. gen. surg. Univ. Hosp., 1966-69, mem. maxillofacial team dept. plastic surgery, 1967-69; asst. prof. oral surgery U. Pitts. Sch. Dental Medicine, 1971-76, asso. prof., 1976—, asst. chmn. dept. oral surgery, 1975—; mem. staff Magee Womens Hosp., Children's Hosp., Pitts., 1975, Forbes Health System, 1975, Montefiore Hosp., 1976. Diplomate Am. Bd. Oral Surgery. Mem. ADA, Pa. Dental Assn., Am., Great Lakes, Pa., Western Pa. socs. oral surgeons, Am. Soc. Microbiology, Odontological Soc. Western Pa. Contbr. to textbook Oral and Maxillofacial Surgery (W. Harry Archer), 1975. Contbr. articles in field to profl. jours. Research in clin. evaluation of autologous teeth transplantation and etiology of cysts of the oral cavity. Home: 3632 Cal-Ken Dr Murrysville PA 15668 Office: Suite 207 Penn Hills Mall Pittsburgh PA 15235

EL-BAZ, FAROUK, geologist; b. Zagazig, Egypt, Jan. 2, 1938; s. El-Sayed and Zahia (Hammouda) El-B.; came to U.S., 1960, naturalized, 1970; B.S., Ain Shams, Egypt, 1958; M.S., U. Mo., 1961, Ph.D., 1964; doctoral research Mass. Inst. Tech., 1962-63; m. Catherine Patricia O'Leary, 1963; children—Monira, Soraya, Karima, Fairouz. Lab. instr. U. Assiut (Egypt), 1958-60; lectr. U. Heidelberg (W.Ger.), 1964-65; exploration geologist Pan Am.-UAR Oil Co., Egypt, 1966; supr. lunar sci. planning Bellcomm and Bell Telephone Labs., Washington, 1967-72; research dir. Nat. Air and Space Mus., Smithsonian Instn., Washington, 1973—; adj. prof. geology/geophysics U. Utah, 1974—; adj. prof. geology U. Ain Shams, Egypt, 1977—; cons. in field. Recipient Sci. Achievement medal NASA, 1971. Fellow Geol. Soc. Am., Royal Astronom. Soc., Explorers Club; mem. AAAS, Am. Geophys. Union, Am. Soc. Photogrammetry, Deutsche Mineralogische Gesellschaft, Geochem. Soc., Smithsonian Instn. Assos., Mo. Acad. Sci., Mineral Lit. Center, Geologische Vereinigung, Internat. Astron. Union, Meteoritical Soc., Mineral. Soc. Am., Sigma Xi. Author: Say It in Arabic, 1968; The Moon as Viewed by Lunar Orbiter, 1970; Glossary of Mining Geology, 1970; Astronaut Observations from the Apollo-Soyuz Mission, 1977; Spaceflight and Man's Desting (in Arabic), 1977; Apollo over the Moon: A View from Orbit, 1978. Contbr. articles to profl. jours. Cons. editor Jour. Engring. Scis., 1975, KISR Jour., 1976. Address: Nat Air and Space Mus Smithsonian Instn Room 3101 Washington DC 20560

EL-BEHAIRY, MOHAMED MOHAMED, educator; b. Cairo, Egypt, Oct. 30, 1931; s. Mohamed M. and Ihsan (El Quadi) El-B.; B.Commerce, Cairo U., 1953; M.A., U. Minn., 1956; Ph.D., Ohio State U., 1961; m. Sharon C. Botkin, Mar. 24, 1959; children—Carrie Ihsan, Carima Carol, Joseph Muhamed Edward, Jasmine Sharon. Came to U.S., 1954, naturalized, 1964. From instr. to asst. prof. Defiance (Ohio) Coll., 1961-63; prof. polit. sci. State U. Coll., Buffalo, 1963—, chmn. dept. polit. sci., 1966-69. Vis. prof. U. Riyadh (Saudi Arabia), 1976-77. Mem. Am. Polit. Sci. Assn., Am. Acad. Polit. and Social Scis., Islamic Soc. of Niagara Frontier (pres. 1966-69), Arab Am. Fedn. Western N.Y. (pres. 1977-78), Assn. Egyptian-Am. Scholars, Pi Sigma Alpha. Home: 243 Hennepin Rd Grand Island NY 14072 Office: 1300 Elmwood Ave Buffalo NY 14222

ELDER, ALEXANDER STOWELL, mech. engr.; b. Medford, Mass., July 29, 1915; s. Edward Everett and Alice (Stowell) E.; B.A., Harvard, 1938; M.Ed., Boston U., 1940; M.A., U. Del., 1956; m. Barbara Grace LeGallee, Feb. 22, 1947; children—David Stevens, Johnathan Symmes. Technician Niagara, Lockport & Ont. Power Co., Buffalo, 1940-42; physicist Watertown (Mass.) Arsenal, 1946-49; with Ballistic Research Labs., Aberdeen Proving Ground, Md., 1950—, supervisory research mech. engr., 1962-69, chief solid properties group, 1969-76, dep. chief mechanics and structure br., 1976—. Instr. dept. math. Hartford Jr. Coll., Bel Air, Md., 1958-61. Mem. ofcl. bd. Methodist Ch., 1963-66. Served with AUS, 1942-46. Recipient Meritorious Civilian Service award Dir. Army Research, 1973. Mem. Am. Acad. Mechanics, AAAS, Am. Math. Soc., Math. Assn. Am., Soc. Rheology, Pi Mu Epsilon. Republican. Home: 814 Matthews Ave Aberdeen MD 21001 Office: Ballistic Research Labs Aberdeen Proving Ground MD 21005

ELDERFIELD, JOHN, curator; b. Yorkshire, Eng., Apr. 25, 1943; s. Henry and Rhoda May (Risbrough) E.; B.A., U. Leeds (Eng.), 1966, M.Phil., 1970; Ph.D. (J.S. Guggenheim fellow), U. London, 1975; m. Joyce Davey, Jan. 9, 1965; children—Matthew, Jonathan. Lectr. in history of art Winchester (Eng.) Sch. Art, 1966-70; Harkness fellow dept. history of art Yale U., 1970-72; lectr. Leeds U., 1973-75; curator painting and sculpture Mus. Modern Art, N.Y.C., 1975—; adj. prof. art history Hunter Coll. Fellow Royal Soc. Arts; mem. Internat. Assn. Art Critics. Author: Hugo Ball: The Flight Out of Time, 1975; Fauvism, 1976; The European Master Paintings, 1976; Matisse, 1978; The Cutouts of Henri Matisse, 1978; contbg. editor Art Forum, 1972-75, Studio Internat., 1973-75. Office: 11 W 53d St New York NY 10019

ELDERS, JAMES ALAN, quality assurance engr.; b. Raymondville, Tex., Mar. 28, 1936; s. James Wayne and Edna Irene; B.E.E., U.S. Armed Forces Inst., 1958; B.M.E., U. Mo., Joplin Ext., 1974; m. Joan Anne Clifton, Nov. 26, 1955; 1 son, James Shawn. Sr. product engr. Hi-G Inc., Windsor Locks, Conn., 1960-70; engring. div. mgr. Frost Electronics, Inc., N. Bellingham, Mass., 1970; sr. mech. design engr. Crane/Demming Corp., Rogers, Ark., 1971-72; sr. quality assurance engr. Hi-G Co., Inc., Windsor Locks, 1975—. Served with USN, 1955-59. Developer environ. test lab., coaxial relay. Home: 7 Parky Dr Enfield CT 06082 Office: 580 Spring St Windsor Locks CT 06096

ELDRED, GERALD MARCUS, ballet exec.; b. Cambridge, Ont., Can., Oct. 5, 1934; s. Albert Harold and E.E. Hope (Bardwell) E.; Grad. Diploma, Nat. Theatre Sch. Can., 1965; m. Marjorie Christine Kidd, Aug. 4, 1956; 1 son, Peter Marcus. Stage producer, dir., adminstr. Canadian Players, Toronto, Ont., 1965-66, Man. Theatre Centre, Winnipeg, 1966-72, Shaw Festival, Niagara-on-the-Lake, 1967, Expo '67, Montreal, Que., Can., 1967, Rainbow Stage, Winnipeg, 1968, Kawartha Summer Festival, Lindsay, Ont., 1966; producer Commd. Opera, Nat. Arts Centre, Ottawa, Ont., 1969; adminstr. Nat. Ballet of Can., Toronto, 1972—; cons. in field. Mem. Canadian Actors Equity Assn., Assn. Canadian Theatres, Dance Can., Assn. Cultural Execs., Can. Council (adv. arts panel 1970-72), Canadian Assn. Profl. Dance Orgns. Home: 162 Crescent Rd Toronto ON M4W 1V2 Canada Office: 157 King St E Toronto ON M5C 1G9 Canada

ELDRED, NORMAN ORVILLE, cons. engr.; b. Vicksburg, Mich., Sept. 13, 1916; s. Luell P. and Lola L. (Spigelmyer) E.; B.S. in Engring., U. Mich., Ann Arbor, 1938, M.S., 1947. Cons. indsl. and nuclear engr., 1938—; engaged in design and constrn. nuclear power sta. for L.I. Lighting Co., 1977—. Served as lt. (j.g.) USNR, 1943-46; PTO. Decorated Purple Heart, Bronze Star. Registered profl. engr., Ill. Mem. Nat. Soc. Profl. Engrs., ASME, IEEE, Am. Inst. Chem. Engrs., ASTM, Res. Officers Assn., Am. Legion (life), VFW (life), Mil. Order World Wars, Am. Def. Preparedness Assn. Republican. Club: U.S. Naval Officers (Gt. Lakes, Ill.). Author reports on petroleum refinery tech. Home: 1750 W Main St Apt 14P Riverhead NY 11901 Office: PO Box 253 Calverton NY 11933

ELDRIDGE, BRIAN JOHN, indsl. planner; b. Buffalo, Apr. 24, 1951; s. Clayton Francis and Matilda (Calicchia) E.; A.A., Corning Community Coll., 1971; B.A., Indiana U. of Pa., 1973, M.A., 1974; m. Susan A. Budzich, Mar. 3, 1973; children—Brian John, Alia. Grad. teaching and research asst. Indiana U. of Pa., 1973-74; sr. planner Town of Union Planning Dept., Endwell, N.Y., 1974-77; community planning asso. N.Y. State Electric and Gas Co., Binghamton, 1977—; cons. in field; instr. Dept. Civil Tech. Broome Community Coll., Binghamton, 1976—. Mem. Am. Soc. Planning Ofcls., N.Y. State Assn. Indsl. Devel. Agys., Pi Gamma Mu, Gamma Theta Upsilon. Democrat. Roman Catholic. Home: 54 Colville Ave Johnson City NY 13790 Office: 4500 Vestal Pkwy Binghamton NY 13902

ELDRIDGE, GWENDOLYN BERNICE MORAN, dietitian; b. Presque Isle, Maine, Oct. 19, 1927; d. Willis Averill and Alyce Drucilla (Shaw) Moran; Asso. B.S., Bangor U., 1972; B.S., U. Maine, Orono, 1974; m. Carl Linwood Eldridge, Nov. 23, 1944 (dec.); children—Carl Averill, Linda Marie Eldridge Stanley. Dietary asst., supr. Eastern Maine Med. Center, Bangor, 1972-75; dietitian, food service dir. Sebasticook Valley Hosp., Pittsfield, Maine, 1975—. Mem. Am., No. New Eng. socs. hosp. food service dirs. Republican. Baptist. Home: RFD 2 Box 188 Pittsfield ME 04967 Office: Grove Hill Pittsfield ME 04967

ELEAZAR, ROBERTO SALVADOR PANSACOLA, anesthesiologist; b. Manila, Dec. 22, 1934; s. Procopio Ferreras and Josefina Pansacola Pastrana E.; came to U.S., 1965; student U. Philippines, 1951-53, M.D., 1958; m. Anne Fallon Peden, June 23, 1963; children—Jessica, Jennifer, Jonathan, Jeremy. Intern, Kings County Hosp., Bklyn., 1958-59, resident in anesthesia, 1959-62; resident Downstate Med. Center and State U. N.Y., Bklyn., 1962-63; asst. instr. anesthesia Downstate Med. Center, State U. N.Y., Bklyn., 1962-63, instr., 1965-67; instr. U. Philippines, Manila, 1964-65; practice medicine specializing in anesthesiology, Ridgewood, N.J., 1969—; attending anesthesiologist Kings County Hosp. Center, Bklyn., 1967, Fordham Hosp., Bronx, 1967-69, Valley Hosp., Ridgewood, 1969—, dir. dept. anesthesia, 1976—. Diplomate Am. Bd. Anesthesiology. Fellow Am. Coll. Anesthesiologists; mem. Am., N.J. socs. anesthesiologists. Office: Dept Anesthesiology Valley Hosp Ridgewood NJ 07450

ELECCION, MARCELINO, corp. exec., writer, artist; b. N.Y.C., Aug. 22, 1936; s. Marcelino G. and Margaret J. (Krcha) E.; B.A., N.Y.U., 1961; postgrad. Courant Inst. Math. Scis., 1962-64; m. Naomi E. Cor, Jan. 5, 1978; 1 son, Mark. Electromech. draftsman Coll. Engring., N.Y. U., Bronx, 1954-57, chief designer dept. elec. engring., 1957-60, tech. editor lab. for electrosci. research, 1960-62, editor publs. Sch. Engring. and Scis., 1962-67; asst. editor IEEE Spectrum, N.Y.C., 1967-69, asso. editor, 1969-70, staff writer, 1970-76, contbg. editor, 1976—; dir. adminstrn. Internat. Bur. for Protection and Investigation, Ltd., N.Y.C., 1976—; cons. tech. artist, 1953—; music orchestration cons., 1956-70; cons. Ency. Britannica, 1969-70, Time-Life Books, 1973. Recipient Mayor's commendation award N.Y.C., 1971. Mem. IEEE (sr.), Am. Math. Soc., AAAS, Optical Soc. Am., Laser Inst. Am., Smithsonian Assos., Am. Numis. Assn., Nat. Geog. Soc., U.S. Judo Fedn. Home: PO Box 266 FDR Station New York City NY 10022

ELFNER, DALE ELWOOD, realtor; b. Red Lion, Pa., Aug. 7, 1927; s. Paul and Alice Sarah (Craley) E.; student pub. schs., Red Lion; m. Norma Elaine Eline, Oct. 24, 1951; 1 son, Wade Bryant; m. 2d, Doris Ruth Leiphart, Sept. 28, 1978. Partner Elfner's Body & Fender Shop, Red Lion, 1947-50, Elfner's Auto Sales, Red Lion, 1948-55, Kendale Bldg. Co., Red Lion, 1965-68; salesman Earl J. Elfner Lumber Co., Red Lion, 1956-59, Merton A. Poff, Realtor, Red Lion, 1959-61; owner Century 21 Dale Realty Co., Red Lion, 1962—; pres. Colony Projects, Inc., Red Lion, 1967—; v.p., sec. The Leo Shop, Inc., Red Lion, 1970—; pres. W & W, Inc., Red Lion, 1973—, pres. United Tire Co., Inc., Red Lion, 1975—. Mem. Borough Planning Commn., Red Lion, 1961-65; Borough councilman, Red Lion, 1966-70; 3d dist. committeeman, Red Lion, 1971-75. Served with USNR, 1945-46, 50-52. Mem. Nat., Pa. assns. realtors, York County Bd. Realtors, York County Multiple Listing Service, Nat. Fedn. Ind. Bus., Am. Legion. Democrat. Methodist. Clubs: Red Lion Country, Elks. Home: 2160 Suburban Rd York PA 17403 Office: 45 E Broadway Red Lion PA 17356 also 804 Loucks Rd York PA 17404

ELFVIN, JOHN THOMAS, fed. judge; b. Montour Falls, N.Y., June 30, 1917; s. John Arthur and Lillian Ruth E.; B.E.E., Cornell U., 1942; postgrad. Harvard U. Law Sch., 1942-43; J.D., Georgetown U., 1947; m. Peggy Pierce, Oct. 1, 1949. Admitted to D.C. bar, 1948, N.Y. bar, 1949; conf. clk. Hon. E. Barrett Prettyman, U.S. Ct. of Appeals for D.C., 1947-48; asso. firm Cravath, Swaine & Moore, N.Y.C., 1948-51, Dudley, Stowe & Sawyer, Buffalo, 1951-55; asst. U.S. atty. Western Dist. N.Y., 1955-58, U.S. atty., 1972-75; partner firm Lanadowne, Horning & Elfvin, Buffalo, 1958-69, 70-72; justice N.Y. Supreme Ct., 8th Jud. Dist., 1969; judge U.S. Dist. Ct., Buffalo, 1975—. Mem. Erie County (N.Y.) Bd. Suprs., 1962-66, Buffalo Common Council, 1966-69. Republican. Home: 115 Nottingham Terr Buffalo NY 14216 Office: 68 Court St Buffalo NY 14202

ELGART, MERVYN L., dermatologist; b. Bklyn., Aug. 12, 1933; s. Jacob and Sally R. E.; A.B., Bklyn. Coll. 1953; M.D., Cornell U. Med. Coll., 1957; m. Sheila Ruth Cliff, June 13, 1954; children—Brian, George, Paul, Adam, James. Intern, Buffalo Gen. Hosp., 1957-58; resident in dermatology Walter Reed Gen. Hosp., Washington, 1960-63; chief dermatology VA Hosp., Washington, 1966-67; asst. prof. dermatology George Washington U., 1967-71, asso. prof., 1971-74, prof., 1974—, chmn. dept. dermatology, 1975—, prof. child health and devel., 1972—. Served with M.C., USAF, 1958-66. Fellow Am. Acad. Dermatology; mem. Am., So. med. assns., Med. Soc. D.C., Soc. Investigative Dermatology, Internat. Soc. Dermatology, Washington Dermatol. Soc., Phi Beta Kappa, Alpha Omega Alpha. Roman Catholic. Home: 400 Madison St Apt 1802 Alexandria VA 22314 Office: 2150 Pennsylvania Ave NW Washington DC 20037

ELGART, RUTH CYNTHIA, artist; b. Phila., Aug. 5, 1931; d. Hyman and Belle Deborah (Frank); B.F.A., B.S. in Edn., Temple U., 1954; m. Ernest J. Elgart, Dec. 20, 1953; children—Linda, Daniel, Douglas. Tchr. art jr. and sr. high sch., Fort Washington, Pa., 1954-55; art dir. YMCA, Germantown, Pa., 1955, Norristown, Pa., 1956; tchr., lectr. Phila. Systems of Libraries, Wynnefield, 1965-67; tchr. sculpture Main Line Center of Arts, Haverford, Pa., 1973-74; one-woman shows include: Green Hill, Lower Merion, Pa., 1971, Community Arts Center, Wallingford, Pa., 1975; group shows include: Phila. Mus. Art, 1970, Phila. Art Alliance, 1955, Walnut St. Theatre, 1976, Phila. Civic Center, 1978. Mem. Tyler Alumni Assn., Artists Equity Assn. Democrat. Address: 1516 Brinton Pk Dr Wynnewood PA 19096

ELIEL, STEFAN ERICH, metal co. exec.; b. Amsterdam, Netherlands, May 5, 1936; s. Erwin and Hannah (Lissauer) E.; came to U.S., 1947, naturalized, 1953; A.B., Cornell U., 1957; m. Brenda Susan Kraft, June 30, 1963; children—Michael E., Jennifer M. With Associated Metals & Minerals Corp., N.Y.C., 1960—, v.p., 1969—, dir., 1969—. Served to 1st lt., AUS, 1957-58. Jewish. Home: 1 Richbell Rd Scarsdale NY 10583 Office: 30 Rockefeller Plaza New York City NY 10020

ELINSKAS, ROBERT CHARLES, SR., finance co. exec.; b. Manchester, Conn., Nov. 5, 1943; s. Charles John and Grace Bernice (Sullivan) E.; B.S., U. Bridgeport, 1969; M.B.A., 1970; m. Kathleen Cecilia Lesenski, Sept. 26, 1970; children—Brian Edward, Robert Charles. Mem. risk mgmt. staff Hartford Ins. Group, 1970-73, asst. loss control mgr., 1973-76; regional loss control dir. Continental Nat. Am. Finance Corp., N.Y.C., 1976—. Served with USAF, 1963, Conn. Air N.G., 1963-69. Recipient Spl. Outstanding Service award Becker Jr. Coll., 1967. Mem. Am. Soc. Safety Engrs. Roman Catholic. Home: 876 Burr St Fairfield CT 06430 Office: 7 Ridgedale Ave Cedar Knolls NJ 07927

ELIOT, LUCY CARTER, painter; b. N.Y.C., May 8, 1913; d. Ellsworth and Lucy Carter (Byrd) E.; B.A., Vassar Coll., 1935; student Art Students League, 1935-40. Exhibited 1-woman shows: Rochester (N.Y.) Meml. Art Gallery, 1946, Syracuse (N.Y.) Mus. Fine Arts, 1947, Cazenovia Coll., 1962, Ft. Schuyler Club, Utica, N.Y., 1971; nat. exhbns. Pa. Acad. Fine Arts, Phila., 1946, 48, 49, 50, 52, 54, Corcoran Biennial, Washington, 1947, 51, Va. Biennial, Richmond, 1948, Art U.S.A., Madison Sq. Garden, N.Y.C., 1958, Ringling Bros. Mus., Sarasota, Fla., 1958, Audubon Artists, N.Y.C., 1957, 66, 68—, Butler Inst., Youngstown, Ohio, 1965, 67, 69, 70, 72, 74, NAD, N.Y.C., 1971, 78; numerous regional group shows N.Y. State; represented in permanent collections; tchr. Bronx VA Hosp., 1950, 51. Bd. dirs. Artists Tech. Research Inst., 1975—. Recipient Painting of Industry prize Silvermine Guild, New Canaan, Conn., 1957; Purchase prize Munson-Williams-Proctor Inst., 1949; 1st prize in painting Cooperstown (N.Y.) Art Assn., 1978. Mem. Audubon Artists, N.Y. Soc. Women Artists (pres. 1973-75, chmn. painting jury 1977—), Artists Equity Assn. N.Y. Clubs: Cazenovia, Cosmopolitan. Home: 131 E 66th St New York City NY 10021

ELKHADEM, SAAD ELDIN AMIN, educator; b. Cairo, Egypt, May 12, 1932; s. Amin Saad and Zahra Amin (Tharwat) E.; came to Can., 1968, naturalized, 1974; Ph.D., U. Vienna, 1961; m. Madiha Mahmoud, July 16, 1962; 1 dau., Sherifa. Press attache Egyptian Govt., Berne, 1962-65; dir. Office for Cultural Relations, Cairo, 1965-67; asst. prof. U. N.D., Grand Forks, 1967-68; asso. prof. German, U. N.B., Fredericton, 1968-74, prof., chmn. dept., 1974—. Can. Council grantee, 1974-75. Mem. Modern Lang. Assn. Am., Canadian Assn. Univ. Tchrs. Author: Sechs Essays ueber den deutschen Roman, 1969; Ajniha Min Rasas, 1972; Zur Geschichte des deutschen Romans, 1974; Tajarib Laylah Wahidah, 1975; Dictionary of Literary Terms 1976. Editor: Internat. Fiction Rev., 1974—. Contbr. articles to profl. jours. Home: 96 Meadow Green Ct Fredericton NB Canada Office: Dept German and Russian University New Brunswick Fredericton NB Canada

ELKIN, ERNEST, chem. engr.; b. Bklyn., Dec. 8, 1936; s. Albert and Pearl (Dick) E.; B.S., U. Rochester, 1958; m. Sandra Levine, June 24, 1961; children—Stephanie, Richard, Suzanne. Vice pres. Gotham Chem. Co., Inc., Port Chester, N.Y., 1958—, G.C.C., Inc., Miami, Fla., 1975—, G.I. Chem. Co., Port Chester, N.Y., 1973—, Water Cons. Corp., Port Chester, 1960—. Mem. Nat. Assn. Power Engrs. (pres. 1964), Am. Inst. Chem. Engrs., U.S. Power Squadron. Clubs: Calif., Masons. Patentee in field; contbr. articles to profl. jours. Home: 208 Country Ridge Dr Port Chester NY 10573 Office: 27 Traverse Ave PO Box 133 Port Chester NY 10573

ELKIN, PHILIP, educator; b. Phila., June 21, 1915; s. Newton C. and Villette Virginia (Stringer) E.; A.B., Lafayette Coll., 1948; A.M., U. Pa., 1952, Ph.D., 1958; postgrad. (Ford Found. research fellow) U. Chgo., 1961-62; m. Eleanor Scott, Sept. 16, 1939; children—Richard B., Margot (Mrs. deN. Arden). Instr. ins. Wharton Sch. Commerce and Finance, U. Pa., Phila., 1952-57; asst. prof. econs. Temple U., Phila., 1957-59; asso. prof. finance N.Y. U., N.Y.C., 1959-60; prof. econs. Albright Coll., Reading, Pa., 1960-65; prof. bus. adminstrn. Ferris State Coll., Big Rapids, Mich., 1965-66; prof. mgmt. Phila. Coll. of Textiles and Sci., 1966—. Dir. Provident Indemnity Life Ins. Co., Norristown, Pa. Bd. dirs. Inst. for Research in Textile Mktg., Resource Allocation Mgmt. Program. Served with USAAF, World War II; now col. USAF ret. Decorated Bronze Star. C.L.U. Recipient fellowship Am. Risk and Ins. Assn., 1954, 57, 59. Mem. Am. Econ. Assn., Acad. Mgmt., Am. Risk and Ins. Assn., Fin. Analysts of Phila. Presbyn. (elder-at-large 1961—). Author: The Financial Experience of Beneficiaries of INTER-VIVOS Trusts, 1920-1954, 58; Public Policy Toward Accidents in Agriculture, 1963; Experience Rating in Pennsylvania Unemployment Compensation, 1959. Home: 5555 Wissahickon Ave Philadelphia PA 19144

ELKINS, HOWARD FREDERIC, internat. financial co. exec.; b. N.Y.C., Mar. 4, 1934; s. Frank F. and Flora (White) E.; B.A., St. Lawrence U., 1956; m. Helen Grace Elkins, Dec. 21, 1960; children—Gordon, Douglas, Alexandra. Exec. v.p. Travel-Wide-Syndicate, N.Y.C., 1957-60; pres. R.E.T. Internat., N.Y.C., 1960-62; pres. Lloyd's Industries (U.S.A.) Ltd., N.Y.C., 1962—, Holt Lloyd (U.S.A.) Ltd., 1977—, Holt Lloyd (Can.) Ltd., 1977—; chmn. Overseas Trade & Devel. Corp., Del., 1967-77; dep. sec.-gen. Metra Internat., London, Paris, 1966—; pres. Hormel Internat. Corp., 1971—; vice chmn., chief exec. officer Holt Lloyd Americas, London, 1977—; dir. O.P.F. Corp., Okinawa, Japan, Vista Internat. Packaging Co., Kenosha, Wis., Inter-Nation Holding Co., Del., Lloyd's Trading Corp., N.Y.C., L.I. Internat. Holdings Pty. Ltd., Sydney, Australia, Henry Comber Pty. Ltd., Sydney, Hormel-Cerebos Pty. Ltd., Sydney, First Enterprise Corp., Naha, Okinawa, Tarber Nord, Stockholm, Sweden, Lloyds Tarber, Zurich, Switzerland; guest lectr. internat. mktg. Aoyama-Gakuin U., Tokyo, 1960—. Served to 1st lt. U.S. Army, 1956. Mem. Am. Mgmt. Assn., Brit.-Am. C. of C., Omicron Delta Kappa. Club: Naval and Military (London). Contbr. articles to internat. mktg. and world trade business jours. Home: 75 Ivy Way Port Washington NY 11050 also Elingshof #5 Zuidlaren Holland Office: 185 Great Neck Rd Great Neck NY 11021 also Lloyd's House Handforth Winslow Cheshire SK9 3HR England

ELKINS, JACOB BENJAMIN, financial cons.; b. Rogatchev, Russia, Mar. 10, 1899; s. Louis and Bessie (Guzov) E.; B.C.S., N.Y.U., 1920; m. Lee Marcus, Jan. 3, 1939; children—Leonard, Eleanor (Mrs. Arthur Kahn), Robert, Marshall. Owner, Jacob B. Elkins, N.Y.C., 1921—. Cons. corp. orgns., consolidations, trusts, estates. Founder, Met. Opera, N.Y.C. Mem. Nat. Forestry Assn., Am. Inst. C.P.A.'s, Am. Jewish Hist. Soc., Met. Mus. Art, Vt. Natural Resources Council, Am. Mus. Natural History, N.Y. Zool. Soc., Internat. Platform Assn.

Home: 93 Brite Ave Scarsdale NY 10583 Office: Station Plaza Bldg Hartsdale NY 10530

ELKINS, WILSON HOMER, univ. pres.; b. Medina, Tex., July 9, 1908; s. Will and Mae (Stevens) E.; B.A., M.A., U. Tex., 1932; Litt.B., Ph.D., Oxford (Eng.) U., (Rhodes scholar), 1936; LL.D., Washington Coll., 1954, Johns Hopkins, 1955 ; m. Dorothy Blackburn, June 12, 1937 (dec. 1971); children—Carole Ann (Mrs. Edward G. Neal), Margaret Elise (Mrs. Charles T. Frost); m. 2d, Vivian Noh Andrews, Aug. 4, 1972. Instr. history U. Tex., 1936-38; pres. San Angelo (Tex.) Jr. Coll., 1938-49; pres. Tex. Western Coll. (formerly Tex. Coll. Mines and Metallurgy), El Paso, 1949-54, U. Md., College Park, 1954—. Chmn. bd. Fed. Res. Bank of Richmond, 1963-70. Mem. So. regional edn. bd. Edn. Commn. of States; trustee Md. Acad. Sci. Mem. Nat. Assn. State Univs. and Land-Grant Colls., (pres. 1970-71), So. Univ. Conf. (pres. 1971), Middle States Assn. Colls. and Secondary Schs. (past pres.), Am. Assn. U. Adminstrs., Phi Beta Kappa, Omicron Delta Kappa, Phi Alpha Theta, Tau Kappa Alpha. Sigma Nu. Episcopalian. Home: 3618 Campus Dr College Park MD 20740

EL KODSI, BAROUKH MOUSSA, physician; b. Cairo, Egypt, Aug. 24, 1923; s. Moussa and Zohra (Aslan Cohen) El K.; came to U.S., 1957, naturalized, 1963; M.D., Cairo U., 1945; m. Marie Menasha, Mar. 26, 1960; children—Sylvia, Robert, Karen. Intern, Univ. Hosp. Cairo Sch. Medicine, 1946; resident in gen. medicine Jewish Hosp., Cairo, 1947-50, attending physician, 1950-57; intern, Miriam Hosp., Providence, R.I., 1958; resident in internal medicine, Boston City Hosp., 1959-61, chief resident, 1961-62, fellow in gastroenterology, 1962-64; asst. dir. medicine Union Hosp., Framingham, Mass., 1964-65; asso. dir. medicine Maimonides Med. Center, Bklyn., 1965-67, dir. gastroenterology, 1968—; chief gastroenterology Coney Island Hosp., N.Y.C., 1967-68; instr. Boston City Hosp., 1962-65; instr. Downstate Med. Center, State U. N.Y., Bklyn., 1965-69, asst. prof. medicine, 1969-76, asso. prof., 1976—. Fellow Am. Coll. Gastroenterology, A.C.P.; mem. Am. Fedn. Clin. Research, Am. Gastroenterological Assn., Am. Soc. Gastrointestinal Endoscopy, AMA, Nat. Ileitis and Colitis Found. (vice chmn. Bklyn. chpt.), Ostomy Club (mem. exec. council). Contbr. articles in field to profl. jours. Home: 118 Girard St Brooklyn NY 11235 Office: 4802 Tenth Ave Brooklyn NY 11219

ELKORT, RICHARD JAY, surgeon; b. N.Y.C., Oct. 18, 1933; s. Morris and Anne (Sfard) E.; B.A., N.Y. U., 1955, postgrad., 1957-58; M.D. summa cum laude, State U. N.Y., Bklyn., 1962; m. Avril Tweedley, Nov. 4, 1962; children—Michael, Carolyn. Intern, Boston City Hosp., 1962-63; predoctoral research fellow Pub. Health Service, Coll. Medicine, State U. N.Y., Bklyn., 1959-62; resident surgery Boston City Hosp., 1963-67; research asso. Roswell Park Meml. Inst., 1965-66, NIH postdoctoral research fellow, 1965-66; chief resident Boston City Hosp., 1967-68; Am. Cancer Soc. fellow in clin. oncology Boston U. Med. Center, 1969-70, sr. fellow, 1970-71, asst. surgery univ. hosp., 1970—, asst. vis. surgeon, 1975—; cons. oncology Tri-State Regional Med. Program in Cancer, 1970—, co-dir; instr. surgery Boston U. Sch. Medicine, 1970-74, asst. prof. surgery, 1974—, med. dir. enterostomal therapist tng. program Sch. Nursing, 1974-75; mem. eastern coop. oncology group, Nat. Cancer Inst., Bethesda, Md., 1970—; vis. surgeon Boston VA Hosp., 1972—; cons. oncology USPHS Hosp., Brighton, Mass., 1974—; co-dir. Tri-State Regional Med. Program in Cancer. Pres., Blue Hill Civic Assn., 1976—; chmn. bd. Blue Hill Montessori Sch., 1977—. Served with U.S. Army, 1955-57. Diplomate Nat. Bd. Med. Examiners, Am. Bd. Surgery. Mem. ACS, Assn. Acad. Surgery, AAAS, Am. Assn. Cancer Edn., Daland Soc., N.Y. Acad. Scis., Alpha Omega Alpha. Contbr. articles to profl. jours. Home: 249 York St Canton MA 02021 Office: 75 E Newton St Boston MA 02118

ELLEGARD, ROY TAYLOR, indsl. products mfg. co. exec.; b. Hartford, Conn., May 26, 1927; s. Roy Edward and Helen May (Peberdy) E.; A.B., Princeton, 1951; m. Jeanette Louise Whitney, Mar. 20, 1954; children—Roy Whitney, Jan. Pres., Advancement Opportunities Inc., Hartford, Conn., 1956-66; asso. Booz, Allen & Hamilton, Inc., N.Y.C., 1966-70; v.p. Golightly & Co. Internat., Inc., N.Y.C., 1971-72; v.p. Condec Corp., Old Greenwich, Conn., 1972—. Justice Peace, West Hartford, Conn., 1965-67; mem. Republican town com., Weston, Conn., 1973—. Served with AUS, 1946-47. Episcopalian. Home: 10 High Acre Rd Weston CT 06880 Office: 1700 E Putnam Ave Old Greenwich CT 06870

ELLENBERGER, JACK STUART, librarian; b. Lamar, Colo., Sept. 5, 1930; s. Emmert C. and Ruby Fay (Overstreet) E.; B.S., Georgetown U., 1957; M.L.S., Columbia U., 1959. Law librarian HEW, Washington, 1957; librarian Carter, Ledyard & Milburn, N.Y.C., 1957-60, Jones, Day, Cockley & Reavis, Cleve., 1960, Bar Assn. D.C., Washington, 1961-63, Covington & Burling, Washington, 1963-78, Shearman & Sterling, N.Y.C., 1978—; instr. law librarianship U.S. Dept. Agr. Grad. Sch., Washington, 1962-73. Served with USAF, 1951-54. Mem. Am. Assn. Law Libraries (pres. 1976-77), Spl. Libraries Assn. Author: (with E.P. Mahar) Legislative History of the Securities Acts of 1933 and 1934, 1973. Office: 53 Wall St Room 718 New York City NY 10005

ELLIG, BRUCE ROBERT, personnel adminstr.; b. Manitowoc, Wis., Oct. 15, 1936; s. Robert Louis and Lucille Marie (Westphal) E.; B.B.A., U. Wis., 1959, M.B.A., 1960; m. Marie Phillip Claditis, Nov. 20, 1965; 1 son, Brett Robert. With Pfizer, Inc., N.Y.C., 1960—, v.p. compensation and benefits, 1978—; speaker at personnel workshops, seminars and conferences. Mem. Presidential Pay Commn., 1976, N.Y.C. Mayor's Advisory Pay Commn., 1977. Accredited personnel diplomate; named one of top six compensation specialists in U.S., Am. Compensation Assn., 1975. Mem. N.Y. Personnel Mgmt. Assn. (past pres.), N.Y. Assn. of Compensation Adminstrs. (charter pres.), Nat. Assn. of Mfrs., Conf. Bds. Council on Compensation, Am. Soc. for Personnel Adminstrs., Am. Pension Conf., Am. Compensation Assn. (charter pres. Eastern region), Phi Beta Kappa, Phi Eta Sigma, Phi Kappa Phi, Delta Epsilon, Beta Gamma Sigma, Alpha Kappa Psi. Republican. Roman Catholic. Clubs: Shore and Country (Norwalk, Conn.). Author: Compensation and Benefits: Analytical Strategies, 1978; contbg. author: The Encyclopedia of Professional Management, 1978; contbr. articles to profl. jours. Home: 1 Dawn Rd Norwalk CT 06851 Office: 235 E 42nd St New York City NY 10017

ELLINGER, JOHN LEONARD, radio sta. exec.; b. New Rochelle, N.Y., Apr. 6, 1925; s. Charles Leonard and Margaret Veronica (Leonard) E.; student U. Conn., 1942, Yale U., 1943; m. Monique Agnes Bashaw, Sept. 21, 1953 (dec. 1962); m. 2d, Marjorie Ann Chain, May 2, 1970; 1 dau., Ingrid. Asst. comml. mgr. Sta. WWCO, Waterbury, Conn., 1952-54; comml. rep. WATR-TV, 1953-54; gen. mgr. Sta. WNAB, Bridgeport, Conn., 1954—, gen. mgr., 1954-61; gen. mgr. sta. WNHC-FM, New Haven, 1961-64, WRCH-AM/FM, Hartford, Conn., 1964-70, Sta. WMMW, Meriden, Conn., 1970-78, WJMJ-FM, religious sta., Archdiocese of Hartford, 1978—; coordinator, cons. Choate-Rosemary Schs., Wallingford, Conn., 1978—. Bd. dirs. Conn. Symphony Orch., ARC; chmn. Conn. state radio and TV com. Crusade for Freedom, 1953-57; mem. indsl. bd. FCC. Served in AUS, 1945-46. Recipient single citizen's award United Fund, 1960; award Crusade for Freedom, 1953. Mem. Conn. Broadcasters Assn. (pres. 1960, dir. 1957-59). Roman Catholic. Author article "You and Your United Fund", 1961. Home: 181 Old Lane Rd Cheshire CT 06410 Office: Archdiocese of Hartford 134 Farmington Ave Hartford CT 06105

ELLIOT, IAN DOUGLAS, journalist, editor; b. N.Y.C., Nov. 17, 1925; s. Walter and Marjorie (Powell) E.; A.B., Cornell U., 1950; m. Judith Jackson, Aug. 26, 1966; children—Kristin Elliot, Colin Elliot. Feature writer Syracuse (N.Y.) Herald Jour., 1962-66; asso. editor Sch. Mgmt. mag., Greenwich, Conn., 1966-68; sr. editor Grade Tchr. mag., Stamford, Conn., 1968-72; mng. editor Early Years Mag., Darien, Conn., 1972—. Served with U.S. Army, 1943-46. Democrat. Contbr. articles to numerous mags., jours. Home: 15 Wall St Norwalk CT 06850 Office: Hale Ln Darien CT 06820

ELLIOT, JAMES LUDLOW, astronomer; b. Columbus, Ohio, June 17, 1943; s. James Ludlow and Doris Belle (Eckfeld) E.; S.B., S.M., Mass. Inst. Tech., 1965; A.M. (NSF fellow), Harvard U., 1967, Ph.D. (NSF fellow), 1972; m. Elaine Kasparian, Nov. 24, 1967; children—Lyn, Martha. Research asso. Cornell U., 1972-74, sr. research asso., 1974-77, asst. prof. astronomy, 1977-78; asso. prof. astronomy M.I.T., dir. George R. Wallace, Jr. Astrophys. Obs., 1978—. Recipient Exceptional Sci. Achievement medal NASA, 1977. Mem. Am. Astron. Soc., Internat. Astron. Union. Discoverer rings around Uranus, 1977. Home: 1320 Hanshaw Rd Ithaca NY 14850 Office: Bldg 54-612 MIT Cambridge MA 02139

ELLIOTT, B(ROSE) CHARLES, JR., museum adminstr.; b. Grove City, Pa., Apr. 9, 1924; s. Brose Charles and Ruth Catherine (Martin) E., Sr.; B.A., Allegheny Coll., 1947; M.A. (grad. fellow 1952, 53, 55), Syracuse U., 1955. Adminstrv. asst. Lawrence Coll., Appleton, Wis., 1951-52; asst. dean men U. Pitts., 1952-55, asso. dir. nationality com. program, 1955-56, acting dir. cultural exchange program, 1956-59; dir. Reading (Pa.) Pub. Mus. and Art Gallery, 1967-73. Dir. Cheekwood Fine Arts Center, Nashville, 1965. Recipient Methodist Ch. award Allegheny Coll., 1946, 47; Swedish Com. award U. Pitts., 1953, Cultural Exchange Study-Travel grant, 1956; Eben Demarst award Pitts., 1963; named Hon. Citizen of Reading, 1973. Mem. Am. Assn. Museums (accrediatation team 1972, 73), N.E. Museums Conf., Nat. Trust for Historic Preservation. Author mus. catalogues. Contbr. articles to jours. Home and Office: 855 N Park Rd Wyomissing PA 19610

ELLIOTT, BENJAMIN PAUL, architect; b. Washington, Dec. 27, 1920; s. Benjamin Sargent and Marguerite (Plenckner) E.; student Catholic U. Am., 1940-42, B.Arch., 1948; m. Mary Dickenson, July 22, 1943; children—Paul Charles, Sara. Practice architecture, Silver Spring, Md., 1950—. Pres., West Montgomery Citizens Assn., 1956-57. Chmn. bd. trustees Potomac (Md.) Elementary Sch., 1963-64. Served with AUS, 1942-45; ETO. Fellow AIA (mem. nat. com. on religious architecture, 1964-67, pres. Potomac Valley chpt. 1959-60, 73—, pub., founder Potomac Valley Architect 1957-59, Distinguished Service award 1970), Guild for Religious Architecture (dir. 1968-71, hon. chmn. nat. conf. on religious architecture 1968-70, founder, pub., bus. mgr. Faith and Form, 1966-71), Md. Soc. Architects (dir.), Am. Soc. Ch. Architecture, Stained Glass Assn. Am. (asso.). Episcopalian (jr. warden 1968-69, vestryman 1954-57, 65-68, mem. com. on ch. architecture Diocese of Washington). Home: 11000 Dobbins Dr Potomac MD 20854 Office: 8750 Georgia Ave Silver Spring MD 20910

ELLIOTT, DAVID WILLIAM, author; b. New Haven, July 12, 1939; s. Roger and Dorothy (Bouchat) E.; student pub. schs., Payette, Idaho and Ramsey, N.J. Author novels: Listen to the Silence, 1969, Pieces of Night, 1973; author: (with Merle Miller) Plain Speaking—An Oral Biography of Harry S. Truman, 1974. Mem. Authors Guild, N.Y. State Sherriffs Assn. Democrat. Methodist. Home: Sherwood Hill Brewster NY 10509

ELLIOTT, DONALD JOSEPH, educator; b. Ft. Covington, N.Y., Feb. 13, 1923; s. Clarence J. and M. Margaret (Page) E.; B.A., St. Michael's Coll., 1948; M.A., St. Lawrence U., 1953, postgrad., 1959-60; postgrad. Middlebury Coll., 1949-50, U. Vt., 1956; m. Marion Pearl Briggs, June 15, 1947; children—Donald Joseph II, Debbie Jane, Diane June. Tchr., Brighton High Sch., Island Pond, Vt., 1948-49; tchr. Dannemora (N.Y.) High Sch., 1949-56, counselor, 1956-58, vice prin., 1957-58; dir. guidance services Malone (N.Y.) Central Schs., 1958-66, coordinator pupil personnel services, dir. fed. programs, 1966-74, also sch. psychologist, audio-visual dir.; project dir. Massena (N.Y.) Central Sch. Dist. Dir. Northeastern N.Y. Center for Diagnosis and Amelioration Learning Disabilities, 1967-70; cons. pub., pvt. agys., 1970—. Chmn. edn. com. Franklin County unit Am. Cancer Soc.; bd. dirs. Franklin County Mental Health Assn.; founder Student Assistance Fund, Franklin Acad., 1961; mem. adv. council Agr. and Tech. Inst., Canton, N.Y.; adv. council indsl. arts State U. Coll. at Oswego; chmn. Franklin County Mental Health Bd.; adviser to registrants SSS; dir. personnel recruitment S.R. Med. Center; mem. bd. edn. Salmon River Central Sch. Dist., Ft. Covington, N.Y.; chmn. exec. com. N. Country Sch. Bds. Inst.; sole assessor Town of Ft. Covington. Recipient citations for contbns. from local service and ednl. instns. Mem. Am., No. Zone (pres., exec. com.) personnel and guidance assns., Am. Sch. Counselors Assn., N.Y. State Counselors Assn., Nat. Vocational Guidance Assn., N.Y. State Assn. Pupil Personnel Adminstrns., Internat. Guidance Conf. (co-chmn.), Lang. Tchrs. Assn. (zone chmn.), Phi Delta Kappa. K.C., Elk. Address: Malone Rd Ft Covington NY 12937 Office: Malone Rd Ft Covington NY 12937

ELLIOTT, FRANK ABERCROMBIE, physician; b. Cape Town, South Africa, Dec. 18, 1910; s. Arthur Abercrombie and Kathleen (Gosslin) E.; M.B., Ch.B., U. Cape Town, 1936; m. Betty Kathleen Elkington, Oct. 31, 1940; children—Sally Dawn, Gillian Kathleen (Mrs. Richard Andrew); m. Gwladys Hopkins Marvel, 1970. Came to U.S., 1959. Intern, Groote Schuur Hosp., Cape Town, S. Africa, 1936; resident Nat. Heart Hosp., London, Eng., 1937, Queen Sq. Hosp., London, 1938; practice medicine specializing in neurology, London, 1945-59, Phila., 1959—; mem. staffs Pa. Hosp., Phila., dir. neurology, 1959-73; prof. neurology U. Pa., Phila., 1964—; neurologist Charing Cross Hosp., London, 1947-59. Served to lt. col. Brit. Army, 1942-47. Fellow Royal Coll. Physicians, Am. Coll. Physicians, Acad. Neurology; mem. Brit. Neurol. Assn., Assn. Brit. Physicians, Internat. Soc. Internal Medicine. Club: Philadelphian. Author: Clinical Neurology, 1964, 71. Contbr. articles to profl. jours.Home: 232 Philip Pl Philadelphia PA 19106 Office: 807 Spruce St Philadelphia PA 19107

ELLIOTT, INGER MCCABE (MRS. OSBORN ELLIOTT), textile co. exec.; b. Oslo, Norway, Feb. 23, 1933; d. David and Lova (Katz) Abrahamsen; came to U.S., 1941; naturalized, 1946; A.B. in History with honors, Cornell U., 1954; postgrad. Harvard, 1955; A.M. (Jean Birdsall fellow), Radcliffe, 1957; m. Osborn Elliott, Oct. 20, 1973; children by previous marriage—Kari McCabe, Alexander McCabe, Molly McCabe. Editor, E. European Student and Youth Service, N.Y.C., 1957-60; photographer Rapho-Guillumette, U.S. and fgn. countries, 1960-73; pres. China Seas, Inc., N.Y.C., 1972—. Tchr., Newton (Mass.) Pub. Schs., 1955-56. Mem. Am. Soc. Mag. Photographers, Phi Beta Kappa. Author: Women Photographers, 1970; A Week in Amy's World, 1970; A Week in Henry's World, 1971; also portfolio in Infinity mag., 1969. Home: 10 Gracie Sq New York City NY 10028 Office: 427 E 76th St New York City NY 10021

ELLIOTT, JOHN RAYMOND, machinery and adhesives co. exec.; b. Auburn, Nebr., Jan. 4, 1916; s. Elmer Calahan and Ethel Iva (Stoddard) E.; B.S. in Chem. Engring., Iowa State U., 1937; Ph.D. (Allied Chem. fellowship), U. Ill., 1943; m. Violet Ruth Franzen, June 12, 1943; children—Nancy Elliott Mayer, Patricia. With Gen. Electric Co., Pittsfield, Mass., 1937-40, research chemist Research and Devel. Center, Schenectady, 1943-51, mgr. organic chem. research, 1951-66, mgr. advanced materials programs, 1966-69; v.p. research and devel. Am. group Locticte Corp., Newington, Conn., 1969-72, corp. v.p. research and devel., 1972—, mem. office chief exec., 1976—. Mem. AAAS, Am. Chem. Soc. (chmn. polymer div.), Soc. Plastic Engrs., Am. Mktg. Assn., Sigma Xi, Phi Beta Phi. Holder 21 U.S. patents in silicones, boron chem., polymers, and adhesives; contbr. articles to profl. jours. Home: 19 Hillsboro Ln Avon CT 06001 Office: 705 N Mountain Rd Newington CT 06111

ELLIOTT, JOHN T., filmmaker, artist; student Acad. Fine Arts, France, 1947-50, N.Y. U., 1951-54, Sch. Visual Arts, 1958-59. Pres., Graphics for Industry, Englewood, N.J., 1968—; designer, producer numerous television shows and commls., also motion pictures; spl. cons. AT & T, Bell Labs., NASA, Nova, Ltd., Xerox, others; guest lectr. N.Y. U.; head film dept. Art Center No. N.J.; one-man shows: North Shore Ann. Art Exhibit, 1975, River Edge Savs., 1974; group shows: Am. Art Festival, Chgo., 1974, Carnegie Internat., Pitts., 1972, Gt. Neck Art Collectors Council Exhbn., 1969, Kans. Collectors Coop., 1968, Nat. Womens Art Collectors Guild, San Francisco, 1965, N.Y. Advt. Club, 1963, Volkswagon World Hdqrs., Englewood Cliffs, N.J., 1976, Washington Sq. Art Show, 1959; represented in permanent collections: Am. Citizens Art Council, N.Y.C., Artiste Musee Belgique, Brussels, Biblioteque de la Republique Francaise, Paris, Chemtrade Internat., Inc., Fawcett Publs., Henry Strauss, Inc., Italia Academia de Roma, Rome, Nat. Women's Art Collectors Guild, N.Y. Lawyers Art Affiliates, Novo, Ltd., Vassar Alumnae Art Collectors League, Wharton Sch. Finance, U. Pa. Alumni Investment Group Nat. Trust Historic Preservation, Met. Mus. Art, N.Y.C., Fogg Art Mus., Harvard, Nat. Collection Fine Arts, Smithsonian Instn., Detroit Mus. Art; paintings for childrens books include Children's Bible, Children's Day mag., Children's Almanac, The Legend of John Henry, Alexander Hamilton. Recipient 1st prizes Cannes Film Festival, 1965, 72, Gold award, 1973, Grand award, 1975, Spl. award for best film in cinemascope, 1970, all from N.Y. Internat. Film Festival; Chris award, 1970, Gold medal Freedom Found., 1970, Cine awards, 1965, 75, Chgo. Film Festival award, 1973, 1st prizes N.Y. Advt. Club, 1969, L.I. Art Assn., 1976. Mem. Soc. Illustrators, Postal Soc. Am. Address: Graphics for Industry 231 Liberty Rd Englewood NJ 07631

ELLIOTT, RICHARD VERBRYCK, editor; b. Yonkers, N.Y., Sept. 27, 1934; s. George Francis and Eileen (Higgins) E.; B.S. in Engring., Mcht. Marine Acad., 1958; postgrad. Georgetown U., 1959; M.A. in Psychology, New Sch. Social Research, 1973; m. Linda Lou Deinhardt, July 14, 1973; 1 dau., June Louise. Asst. to dir. info. Am. Mcht. Marine Inst., N.Y.C., 1961-63; asst. to pres. Marine Index Bur., N.Y.C., 1963-65; with Port Authority N.Y. and N.J., N.Y.C., 1965—, asso. editor Via Port of N.Y., 1965-67, aviation pub. services rep., 1968-71, supr. personnel communications, 1971-78, energy task force editor, 1978—. Vice chmn. pub. relations marine sect. Nat. Safety Council, 1965. Served to lt. USNR, 1958-61. Recipient Congressman Wainwright award for scholarship in Am. history, govt., 1958; Feature Editor award Mcht. Marine Acad., 1958. Mem. S.S. Hist. Soc. Am. (High Seas editor Steamboat Bill Jour. 1962-68, v.p. Middle Atlantic states 1968-70), Shipwrites, South St. Seaport Mus. (N.Y.C.). Hist. Soc. N.J., N.Y. Geneal. and Biog. Soc., U.S. Mcht. Marine Acad. Alumni Assn. Author: Last of the Steamboats-The Saga of the Wilson Line, 1970. Home: 71 Central Ave Englewood NJ 07627 Office: 61 West One World Trade Center New York City NY 10048

ELLIOTT, SCOTT CAMERON, art gallery exec.; b. Chgo., Aug. 6, 1941; s. Bruce Ainsley and Grace Marie (Cameron) E.; student Art Inst. Chgo., 1959-60, Art Students League, N.Y.C., 1960-61, Yale Drama Sch., 1963-64; m. Dolores Helen Olsavick, Feb. 23, 1975. Pvt. art dealer, N.Y.C., 1965-68; asst. dir. La Boetie, Inc., 1968-72; owner, dir. Scott C. Elliott Inc., 1973-74; dir. Helios Arts, Inc., 1975—. Organized exhbns. and catalogs for Scott Elliott Gallery and La Boetie, Inc., 1974-75; organized 1st one man shows in U.S. for numerous painters, photographers including Modersohn-Becker, Vordemberge-Gidewart, Marcoussis, James Van der Zee; designed scenery for numerous Chgo. area theatre prodns. Expert in German and Austrian Expressionist art, the Bauhaus, Surrealism, Photo-Secession photographers. Office: Helios Arts Inc 18 E 67th St New York City NY 10021

ELLIOTT, SHEILA HOLLIHAN, arts co. exec.; A.B. in Physics, Vassar Coll., 1967; M.S. in Mgmt. Sci., Fairleigh Dickinson U., 1979. Creative dir. Graphic for Industry, Inc., Englewood, N.J., 1967-76. v.p. fin., 1976—; sr. bus. systems analyst Thomas J. Lipton, Inc., 1978—; producer (public service films) American Phenomenon, 1973, Historic Preservation, 1975, Daniel Chester French 1850-1931, 1976; (presentation film) Advertising Council, 1974. Active in the arts, public service, films and hist. preservation; rep. to Federated Art Assns. N.J., 1977. Recipient Gold award N.Y. Internat. Film and TV Festival, 1973, Bronze award, 1974, 75, Silver award, 1977. Mem. Pastel Soc. Am. (spl. advisor to bd. 1978, dir. 1978), Soc. Illustrators, Nat. Trust Hist. Preservation. Contbg. editor: Condensed Computer Encyclopedia, 1968; editor: Pastellogram, 1979. Office: Graphics for Industry 231 Liberty Rd Englewood NJ 07631

ELLIOTT, WILLIAM JOHN, fin. exec.; b. Phila., July 3, 1919; s. Walter Clare and Florence Amanda (Hatzfeld) E.; A.B., Lafayette Coll., 1941; diplome d'etudes Sorbonne, France, 1948; m. Barbara Ann West, Sept. 2, 1950; children—James William, Deborah Kay. Sr. auditor Lybrand & Cooper, 1951-56; internal auditor RCA, Camden, N.J., 1956-59; sr. auditor Peat, Marwick, Mitchell & Co., Phila., 1959-62; audit mgr. N. Tannenbaum & Co., Camden, N.J., 1962-67; audit mgr. Touche, Ross, & Co., Phila., 1967-69; sr. accountant Wolf & Co., Phila., 1969-73; treas. Ind. Newspapers, Dover, Del., 1973—. Served with USNR, 1943-46. C.P.A., Pa. Mem. Am. Inst. C.P.A.'s, Inst. Newspaper Controllers and Fin. Officers. Republican. Lutheran. Club: Maple Dale Country. Home: 874 Wilson Dr Dover DE 19901 Office: Webbs Ln and New Burton Rd Dover DE 19901

ELLIS, A. RALPH, lawyer; b. Pitts., June 15, 1929; s. Albert R. and Miriam Frances (Whitehouse) E.; student Cornell U., 1947-50; B.A. U., Pitts., 1952, J.D., 1955; m. Denese S. Barone, May 9, 1959; children—Pamela Kathleen, Carolyn Denese. Admitted to Pa. bar, 1958; partner firm Alter Wright & Barron, Pitts., 1958—; asst. atty. gen. Commonwealth of Pa., 1963-71. Bd. dirs. Pitts. Testing Lab., sec., 1978—. Served with inf. U.S. Army, 1955-57. Mem. Am. Arbitration Assn., Nat. Assn. Securities Dealers, Am., Pa., Allegheny County bar assns., Am. Judicature Soc. Republican. Presbyterian. Clubs: Duquesne, Univ. (dir. 1977—). Home: 868 Old Hickory Rd Pittsburgh PA 15243 Office: 1100 Union Bank Bldg Alter Wright & Barron Pittsburgh PA 15222

ELLIS, DANIEL BENSON, biochemist; b. Rochdale, Eng., May 15, 1937; s. Daniel and Annie Elizabeth (Thirsk) E.; B.S. with honors, U. Sheffield (Eng.), 1958; Ph.D., McGill U., 1961; m. Dolores Sue Martak, Aug. 10, 1963; children—Susan E., Carolyn A. Naturalized, 1967. Postdoctoral fellow Wistar Inst., U. Pa., 1962-64; biochemist Stanford Research Inst., Menlo Park, Calif., 1964-65; sr. biochemist, sr. investigator Smith Kline Corp., Phila., 1965-74; sect. head Betz Labs. Inc., Trevose, Pa., 1974-76; mgr. biochemistry Hoechst-Roussel Pharms., Inc., Somerville, N.J., 1976—. Mem. Montgomery County (Pa.) Democratic Com., 1970-76; sec. Lower Moreland Twp. Bipartisan Com. for Fair Reapportionment, 1971-72; mem. citizens adv. council Montgomery County Planning Commn., 1971-73; mem. finance study group Lower Moreland Sch. Bd., 1971; mem. Washington Crossing Park Commn., 1973—. NRC Can. fellow, 1958-61. Mem. Am. Soc. Biol. Chemists, Biochem. Soc. (Eng.), Soc. Complex Carbohydrates, AAAS, Am. Chem. Soc. Author articles, chpts. in books. Home: 3907 Brookdale Ave Huntingdon Valley PA 19006 Office: Route 202-206 North Somerville NJ 08876

ELLIS, ELIZABETH MUELLER, psychologist 5, 1925; d. Louis John and Jean (Cunliffe) Mueller, Jr., B.A., U. Chgo., 1942; M.A., George Washington U., 1963; Ph.D., U. Md., 1972; children by previous marriage—Elizabeth Ellis, Jonathan Ellis, Benjamin Ellis, Nancy Ellis; m. 2d. Daniel M. Friedman, Oct. 18, 1975. Staff psychologist Alexandria (Va.) Community Mental Health Center, 1963-70; cons. Community Psychiatric Clinic, Bethesda, Md., 1973—; pvt. practice psychology, Washington, 1973—; adj. prof. child psychology Trinity Coll., Washington, 1974. Mem. Am., D.C. psychol. assns., Psi Chi.

ELLIS, JEANNE HOLLAND (MRS. CORNELL FRANKLIN ELLIS), educator; b. Winston-Salem, N.C., Sept. 17, 1925; d. William and Cora Margaret (Carter) Holland; B.A., N.C. Central U., 1945; M.A., Columbia, 1969; m. Cornell Franklin Ellis, June 10, 1948; children—Cornell Franklin, Larry Tyrone, Michael Bernard. Tchr. J.H. Gunn High Sch., Charlotte, N.C., 1951-55; tchr., counselor John J. Wright High Sch., Fredericksburg, Va., 1957-58; high sch. tchr. Winter Park (Fla.) Bd. Edn., 1958-59; with Child Care Center of Stamford (Conn.) Inc., 1960—, exec. dir. 1966—; exec. dir. Stamford Day Care Program, 1969—; Head Start Program, Stamford, 1971—, Cons. Therapeutic Nursery, 1972—; seminar cons. U. Bridgeport. Chmn. personnel com. Vol. Action Center, Stamford, 1973-75; chmn. nominating com. Child Guidance Clinic, Stamford, 1973; chmn. evaluation com. City Manpower Council, Stamford, 1972—; mem. Mayor's Appointee Title I Adv. Council, Stamford, 1971-73; sec., treas. exec. council United Way, Stamford, 1970-71, pres. exec council, 1978-79, mem. campaign cabinet agy. relations, 1978-79; auditor Norwalk (Conn.) Credit Union, 1970-71; mem. child care adv. council Norwalk Community Coll., 1971—; v.p. State Funded Daycare Centers Adv. Council; treas.-exec. bd. Friends of Norwalk Community Coll., 1976; mem. Conn. Early Childhood Subcom.; chmn. Stamford Manpower Adv. Council; publicity chmn. Links of Fairfield County, 1976; mem. Norwalk Negro Dem. Club, 1973-74. Mem. N.A.A.C.P., Black Adminstrs. in Child Welfare (asst. treas. 1973—), Assn. for Edn. of Young Children (South Fairfield v.p. 1969-70). Mem. Order Eastern Star. Home: 11 Boxswood Rd Norwalk CT 06851 Office: 64 Palmer's Hill Rd Stamford CT 06902

ELLIS, JOHN SPILLMAN, JR., govt. ofcl.; b. Washington, Apr. 12, 1949; s. John Spillman and Helen Marie (Luken) E.; B.S. cum llaude, Mt. St. Mary's Coll., Md., 1971; m. Felicia Elizabeth Mesaros, July 21, 1973; 1 dau., Jessica Ann. With U.S. Postal Inspection Service, various locations, 1971—, insp., Poughkeepsie, N.Y., 1972-74, insp. fraud unit, N.Y.C., 1974-78, team leader, projects coordinator, 1978—. Recipient Community Activities Support award U.S. Postal Service, 1976. Mem. U.S. Jaycees (dir. 1976), Fed., Nat. law enforcement assns., Fed. Criminal Investigators Assn., N.Y. State Sheriffs Assn., Internal Security Fin. Firms Assn. N.Y., Theta Psi, Phi Alpha Theta. Roman Catholic. Club: K.C. Home: 6 Fairview Dr Warwick NY 10990 Office: Church St Station Room 519 New York City NY 10008

ELLIS, LAWRENCE DOBSON, physician; b. Pitts., Oct. 11, 1932; s. Robert S. and Elizabeth (Dobson) E.; B.S., U. Notre Dame, 1954; M.D., U. Pitts., 1958; m. Jacqueline Coogan, June 8, 1954; children—Christine, Thomas, Holly Anne, Jerome. Intern in internal medicine U. Pitts. Health Center Hosps., 1958-59; resident in internal medicine Presbyn.-U. Hosp., Pitts., 1959-60, 62-63; fellow in hematology Presbyn.-U. Hosp., 1963-64; practice medicine specializing in internal medicine, hematology and oncology, Pitts., 1964—; clin. asst. prof. medicine U. Pitts., 1966-71, clin. asso. prof., 1971—; mem. active staff Presbyn.-U. Hosp., sec., treas. med. staff, 1972-76, v.p. med. staff, 1976-78, pres., 1978—; mem. cons. staff Forbes Hosp. System, Divine Providence Hosp., and Shadyside Hosp. (all Pitts.), 1964—. Trustee Leukemia Soc. Am., 1972—, chmn. profl. edn., 1973—. Served to lt., M.C., USN, 1960-62. Diplomate Am. Bd. Internal Medicine. Fellow A.C.P.; mem. Pa. (del. 1974—), Allegheny County (pres. 1976, chmn. bd. 1977, dir. 1970—) med. socs., Pitts. Acad. Medicine, Royal Soc. Medicine, N.Y. Acad. Scis., AMA, Am. Soc. Hematology, Leukemia Soc. Am. (exec. com. 1978—), Alpha Omega Alpha. Republican. Roman Catholic. Clubs: Pitts. Field; Seaview Country, Univ. Contbr. articles on hematology to profl. jours.; contbr. chpts. in field to med. books. Office: 3600 Forbes Ave Iroquois Bldg Suite 305 Pittsburgh PA 15213

ELLIS, LEE ROY, computer systems devel. co. exec.; b. Lewistown, Pa., Feb. 2, 1934; s. Leroy and Eleanor May (Miller) E.; B.S., Old Dominion U., 1978; m. Jean Louise Lutz, Aug. 3, 1955; children—Richard, Jerle, Lee Roy. Enlisted in U.S. Navy, 1951, ret., 1970; programmer, analyst ITT Data Systems, Virginia Beach, Va., 1970-71; computer system specialist System Devel. Corp., Warminster, Pa., 1971—. Mem. Soc. Certified Data Processors, Data Processing Mgmt. Assn. Republican. Home: 6 Kuhn Dr Furlong PA 18925 Office: 65 W Street Rd Warminster PA 18974

ELLIS, RAY GEORGE, artist; b. Phila., Apr. 24, 1921; s. Raymond Grant and Helen (Trappier) E.; student Phila. Mus. Sch. Art, 1939-42; m. Elizabeth Glover Wallace, Sept. 21, 1974; children from previous marriage—R. George, Andrew K., Margaret V., Elizabeth D. Advt. mgr. Sel-Rex Corp., Belleville, N.J., 1950-52; pres. Ray Ellis Advt., N.Y.C. and Madison, N.J., 1952-68; pres. Ellis Assos., P.R., 1962-69; one-man shows: Columbus (Ga.) Mus., Columbia (S.C.) Mus., Pa. Acad. Fine Arts, Phila., Charles Russel Mus., Great Falls, Mont., Morris Mus., Morristown, N.J.; exhibited in group shows: NAD, Nat. Arts Club, N.Y.C., Salmagundi Club, N.Y.C., Hudson Valley Art Assn.; represented in permanent collections: Columbus Mus., Telfair Mus., Morris Mus., Allied Chem. Gallery, Midlantic Bank Gallery, Phila. Mus. Art, Grumbacher Collection; lectr. watercolor technique. Trustee, pres. Artists Fellowship Found. Served with USCG, 1942-45. Recipient Grumbacher award Am. Watercolor Soc., 1969, Gold medal of honor Hudson Valley Art Assn., 1973. Mem. N.J. Watercolor Soc. (pres. 1968-69, trustee 1970-71), Assn. Indsl. Advt. (chpt. pres. 1957-58), Am. Artists Profl. League, Nat. Arts Club, Audubon Artists. Clubs: Salmagundi (trustee 1972—, 1st v.p. 1973—); Edgartown (Mass.) Yacht; Baltusrol Golf (Springfield, N.J.); Sea Pines (Hilton Head, S.C.). Author: Watercolors of Ray G. Ellis, 1972; contbg. author: Master Watercolorists at Work, 1973. Home: Tower Gate Edgartown MA 02539 also E Beach Lagoon Sea Pines Hilton Head SC 29928

ELLIS, ROY ARTHUR, pharmaceutical med. dir.; b. London, Dec. 5, 1927; s. Herbert Walter and Mary Evelyn (Pollard) E.; came to Can., 1970, naturalized, 1975; M.B., B.S., St. Mary's Hosp. Med. Sch. U. London, 1954; m. Patricia Mary Barker, Apr. 4, 1953; children—Simon Dominic, Duncan Charles. Resident in medicine, St. Mary's Hosp., Eastbourne, U.K., 1954-56; gen. practice medicine, London, 1956-57; dep. med. dir. Sandoz Products Ltd., London, 1957-64; head, med. scis. Boots Co. Ltd., Nottingham, U.K., 1964-70; med. dir. Geigy Can. Ltd., Boehringer Ingelheim Ltd., Montreal, Que., Can., 1970-72, med. dir. Ciba-Geigy Can. Ltd., 1972-76; v.p., med. dir. Ciba-Geigy Corp., Summit, N.J., 1976—. Served with Brit. Army, 1946-48. Mem. Pharm. Mfrs. Assn. Can. (chmn. med. sec. sect. 1976-77), Canadian Found. Advancement Clin. Pharmacology (vice chmn. bd.), Canadian Med. Assn., Canadian Found. Research Toxicology, Royal Soc. Medicine. Home: 6 Birch Hill Dr Chatham NJ 07928 Office: 556 Morris Ave Summit NJ 07901

ELLISON, CYRIL LEE, publisher; b. N.Y.C., Dec. 11, 1916; s. John and Rose (Arnott) E. Vice pres. Watson-Guptill Pub. Co., also advt. mgr. Am. Artist, N.Y.C., 1939-69; v.p. Franklin & Joseph, advt. agency, N.Y.C., 1969-70; exec. v.p. Communication Channels, Inc. (pub. mags. Trusts and Estates, Nat. Real Estate Investor, Pension World, Shopping Center World, Fence Industry), N.Y.C., 1970—. Served with USAAF, 1942-46. Mem. Am. Legion (past post comdr.; Gray-Russo Ad Man of Year award Ad Men's Post 1957). Home: 20 W 64th St New York City NY 10023 Office: 461 8th Ave New York City NY 10001

ELLISON, THEODORE, indsl. toxicologist; b. Milw., July 15, 1930; s. Benjamin and Fanny E.; B.S., U. Wis., 1952, M.S., 1956, Ph.D., 1959; M.B.A., Iona Coll., 1975; m. Diana Krugman, June 21, 1953; children—Barbara, Richard M., Mark D. Sr. biochemist, Smith Kline and French Co., Phila., 1959-65; sect. head Riker Labs., Northridge, Calif., 1965-71; sect. head bioavailability Vick Research Co., Mt. Vernon, N.Y., 1971-74; research specialist biomedicine Gen. Foods Corp., White Plains, N.Y., 1974-76; sr. toxicologist Mobil Oil Corp., N.Y.C., 1976—; adj. asso. prof. pharmacology N.Y. Med. Coll., N.Y.C., 1974—; dir. indsl. toxicology Center Profl. Advancement, East Brunswick, N.J., 1976—. Served with Q.M.C., U.S. Army, 1954-56. Mem. Am. Soc. Pharm. and Exptl. Therapeutics, Soc. Toxicology, Soc. Exptl. Biology and Medicine, Am. Nuclear Soc., Am. Pharm. Assn., Acad. Pharm. Sci., Internat. Soc. Biochem. Pharmacologists, N.Y. Acad. Sci., AAAS, Sigma Xi. Contbr. articles to profl. publs.; editorial bd. Jour. Toxicology and Environ. Health, 1977—, Jour. Exptl. Pathology and Toxicology, 1977—. Home: 1216 Yardley Rd Yardley PA 19067 Office: Mobil Oil Corp PO Box 1026 Princeton NJ 08840

ELLISON, THOMAS GRIFFITTS (GRIFF), govt. ofcl.; b. Portsmouth, Va., May 24, 1946; s. Thomas Ballard and Virginia (Griffitts) E.; B.S., in Commerce, U. Va., 1971; m. Pamela Noggle. Bus. mgr., asso. editor The Progressive mag., 1971-73; asso. pub. Harper's mag., 1974-76; pub. Bookletter, 1975-76; mem. press and advance staff Carter presdl. campaign, 1976; mem. presdl. transition staff, 1976; spl. asst. to dir. communications Dept. Commerce, 1977; dep. dir. public affairs AID, Dept. State, 1977-78; dir. public and govtl. affairs Export-Import Bank U.S., Washington, 1978—. Nat. coordinator Vietnam Vets. Against the War, 1968-71; founder, chmn. U.S. Com. for Diversity of Press, 1971-73. Served with USMC, 1966-68; Vietnam. Mem. Sigma Chi, Delta Sigma Phi. Office: Export Import Bank 811 Vermont Washington DC 20571

ELLMS, CARLTON WARREN, III, sales exec.; b. Framingham, Mass., July 9, 1948; s. Carlton Warren and Marilyn Jean (Field) E.; B.S., U. Maine, 1971, certificate of pulp and paper, 1972; m. Sally Duryea Devereux, June 18, 1972; 1 child, Sasha Leigh. With Nalco Chem. Co., Chgo., 1972, tech. salesman, no. N.Y., 1972—. Vol. fireman, Henderson, N.Y., 1975-78; chmn. Hullabaloo, Henderson Field Days, 1977; fire dist. commr., Henderson, 1977—. Recipient Dale Carnegie Sales Course Human Relations award, 1976. Mem. TAPPI (no. dist. chmn. 1976-77), Paper Industry Mgmt. Assn., Am. Chem. Soc., Am. Inst. Chem. Engrs., Republican. Conglist. Clubs: Henderson Harbor Yacht. Tuscarora. Address: 327 Ten Eyck St Watertown NY 13601

ELLSWEIG, PHYLLIS LEAH, psychotherapist; b. Irvington, N.J., Apr. 19, 1927; d. Sumar and Jeanette (Geffner) Schwartz; B.S., East Stroudsburg (Pa.) State Coll., 1947; Ed.M., Lehigh U., 1966, Ed.D., 1972; m. Martin Richard Ellsweig, Dec. 25, 1947; children—Bruce, Steven. Tchr., Stroud Union High Sch., 1963-66; guidance counselor East Stroudsburg Schs., 1966-68; asst. prof. edn. East Stroudsburg State Coll., 1968; staff psychologist, supr. outpatient services Mental Health Center Carbon, Monroe and Pike Counties, Stroudsburg, 1968—; pvt. practice, 1969—. Pub. speaker, cons. to schs., orgns.; mem. staff Pocono Hosp. Monroe County, East Stroudsburg. Bd. dirs. Planned Parenthood Assn., 1954-59. Mem. Am., Eastern, Pa. psychol. assns., Am. Acad. Psychotherapists, Am., Eastern group psychotherapy assns., NOW (profl. cons. 1973—), Internat. Assn. Group Psychotherapy, Am. Soc. Clin. Hypnosis. Home: 58 S Green St East Stroudsburg PA 18301 Office: 804 Sarah St Stroudsburg PA 18360 also 322 Park Ave Stroudsburg PA 18360

ELLSWORTH, ARTHUR WHITNEY, publisher; b. N.Y.C., May 31, 1936; s. Duncan Steuart and Esther Bowes (Stevens) E.; grad. St. Paul's Sch., 1954; B.A., Harvard, 1958; m. Sarah Bingham, Oct. 11, 1958 (div. 1965); 1 son, Barry; m. 2d, Priscilla Wear, July 1, 1967; children—Joshua, Nina. Editorial asso. Atlantic, 1959-63; pub. N.Y. Rev. Books, 1963—. Pres. bd. trustees Harvard Advocate Bd.; pres. bd. dirs. Ellsworth Meml. Clinic, Chester Vt.; treas. Amnesty Internat. U.S.A. Served with AUS, 1958-59. Office: 250 W 57th St New York City NY 10019

ELLSWORTH, STANFORD GRANT, hosp. adminstr.; b. Washington, Apr. 24, 1933; s. German Smith and Adelaide (Grant) E.; B.S., Brigham Young U., 1960; M.A., George Washington U., 1974; m. Judith Ann Malzahn, Aug. 30, 1957; children—Stanford M., Scott M., Linda Elaine, Gregg M. Supr. indsl. engring. Boeing Co., Seattle, 1961-63; rep. computer marketing IBM, Seattle, 1964; mgmt. cons. Albert Ramond & Assos., Chgo., 1965-67; pvt. practice mgmt. cons., McLean, Va., 1968-69; adminstrv. asst. Cafritz Hosp., Washington, 1970-73; asst. adminstr. Anne Arundel Hosp., Annapolis, Md., 1973-75; adminstr. Pocono Hosp., East Stroudsburg, Pa., 1975—. Commr., Youth Athletic Programs, 1970-73; mem. Gov.'s Council for Youth, 1964. Served with U.S. Army, 1955-56. Mem. Am. Coll. Hosp. Adminstrs., Am. Hosp. Assn. Mem. Ch. of Jesus Christ of Latter-day Saints. Home: 1503 Blue Ridge Dr Canadensis PA 18325 Office: 206 E Brown St East Stroudsburg PA 18301

ELMAN, GERRY JAY, lawyer; b. Chgo., Oct. 7, 1942; s. Earl Samuel and Lucille Paulyne (Greenberger) E.; B.S., U. Chgo., 1963, M.S., Stanford U., 1964; J.D. Columbia, 1967; m. Judith Ann Cohen, Feb. 20, 1966; children—Jason Farrel, Floren Haley. Admitted to N.Y. bar, 1967, U.S. Patent Office bar, 1967, Pa. bar, 1969; asso. firm Hubbell, Cohen & Stiefel, N.Y.C., 1967-68; atty. Rohm and Haas Co., Phila., 1968-72; dept. atty. gen. Pa. in civil law, litigation div. Harrisburg, 1972-75, antitrust and pub. utility litigation unit, 1975-76; trial atty. Middle Atlantic Office, Antitrust div. Justice Dept., 1976—; arbitrator Phila. Ct. Common Pleas, 1971-72. Chmn. pub. schs. com. Common Cause of Phila., 1978—; chmn. Three Steps Nursery Sch., 1977. Mem. Am., Phila. (chmn. com. jurimetrics 1975-77) bar assns. Club: B'nai B'rith (charter v.p. Society Hill lodge 1977—). Editor Columbia Jour. Transnat. Law, 1966-67, Trademark Reporter, 1968. Home: 635 Addison St Philadelphia PA 19147 Office: 3430 US Courthouse 601 Market St Philadelphia PA 19106*

ELMAN, HOWARD LAWRENCE, aero engr.; b. N.Y.C., Dec. 18, 1938; s. Dave and Pauline (Reffe) E.; S.B. (Plankinton scholar), Mass. Inst. Tech., 1960; M.Aero. Space Engring. (Univ. Grad. Dean's scholar), U. Okla., 1962; postgrad. Rensselaer Poly. Inst., 1963-65; m. Joan Carter, Dec. 28, 1974; 1 son, David Lawrence. Research engr. United Aircraft Research Labs., E. Hartford, Conn., 1963-68; sr. rotor dynamics engr. Sikorsky Aircraft, Stratford, Conn., 1968-70, sr. analytical engr. Pratt & Whitney Aircraft Co., 1970-71; research engr. Kaman Aerospace Corp., Bloomfield, Conn., 1972-76. Served to 1st lt. USAF, 1960-63. Registered profl. engr., Conn., Tex., Ohio. Mem. Conn. Aero. Hist. Assn. (life, dir. 1968-76, v.p. research 1969-73, exec. v.p. 1973-76), Inst. Aero. Scis., Am. Inst. Aeros. and Astronautics, Am. Helicopter Soc., Nat. Soc. Profl. Engrs., Am. Aviation Hist. Soc., Soc. World War I Aer Historians. Contbr. articles to profl. publs. Home: 187-B Salmon Brook Dr Glastonbury CT 06033

ELMAN, ROBERT, writer, editor; b. N.Y.C., Nov. 14, 1930; s. Dave and Pauline (Reffe) E.; student Rollins Coll., 1947-48, Carnegie Inst. Tech., 1948-51; B.S., Columbia, 1953; children—Natalie Harrington, Thomas Harrington, Daniel Walter. With Maco Pub. Co., N.Y.C., 1960-69, successively as asso. editor, mng. editor, editor-in-chief; editor The Am. Sportsman, The Ridge Press, Inc., N.Y.C., 1969-71, writer in residence, outdoors editor, 1975-77, cons., 1969-71; free lance writer, N.Y.C., 1972-74; asso. editor Winchester Press, Inc., N.Y.C., 1974, editor-in-chief, 1974-75; cons., exec. editor Cord Communications, N.Y.C., 1968-71; spl. projects editor Aqua-Field Publs., N.Y.C., 1975—. Mem. Field & Stream Environ. Action Group, N.Y.C., 1970—. Served with U.S. Army, 1953-55. Mem. Authors Guild and League Am., Outdoor Writers Assn. Am., Wilderness Soc., Nat. Wildlife Fedn., Ducks Unlimited, Columbia Univ. Alumni Assn., Pi Lambda Phi. Author: Discover The Outdoors, 1969, The Great American Shooting Prints, 1972, The Hiker's Bible, 1974, The Hunter's Field Guide to the Game Birds and Animals of N. Am., 1974, The Living World of Audubon Mammals, 1976, The Fisherman's Field Guide, 1977, First in the Field: America's Pioneering Naturalists, 1977, plus several others, many titles in other langs.; contbr. articles to Argosy, Field and Stream, Outdoor Life, Sport, Gray's Sporting Jour., Am. Sportsman, Sports Afield, numerous others.

ELMES, BADGLEY ALLEN, mfg. co. exec.; b. Ridley Park, Pa., Nov. 13, 1920; s. Clyde C. and Ethel (Badgley) E.; B.S. in Bus. Adminstrn., Lehigh U., 1946; m. Elizabeth A. Boyer, Jan. 20, 1945; children—Patricia A. (Mrs. David E. Farley), Robert B., Michael B. Salesman, Armstrong Cork Co., 1946-51; dist. mgr. Pyrene Mfg. Co., 1951-53; with Houdaille Industries Inc., 1953-70, gen. mgr. S.M. Jones Co. div., Toledo, 1962-63, v.p. group exec. Houdaille Industries, Inc., Buffalo, 1963-70; mgmt. cons., 1971; pres., owner Riley Gear Corp., North Tonawanda, N.Y., 1972—. Served to 1st lt. USMCR, 1942-45. Decorated Air medal. Mem. Phi Gamma Delta. Clubs: Orchard Park (N.Y.) Country. Presbyn. Home: 27 Fox Meadow Ln Orchard Park NY 14127 Office: 61 Felton St North Tonawanda NY 14120

ELMORE, RICHARD FRANCIS, coll. ofcl.; b. Medford, Mass., Mar. 25, 1946; s. Frank Rodgers and Anne Giles (Collins) E.; B.A. with honors, Boston State Coll., 1967; M.A. (Univ. fellow), U. Notre Dame, 1970, Ph.D. in History (NDEA fellow), 1975; m. Elizabeth Ann Christopher, Aug. 22, 1970. Asst. research librarian, research grantee U. Notre Dame, 1971-72; tchr. Mainland Regional High Sch., Linwood, N.J., 1972-75, tchr. adult edn. program, 1973—; mem. adj. faculty Stockton State Coll., Pomona, N.J., 1974—, asst. to dean faculty social and behavioral scis., 1975—, mem. faculty dept. continuing edn., 1976—; cons. Pacemaker Corp., 1974. Social studies teaching certificate, Mass. Mem. Am. Hist. Assn., French, Atlantic County hist. socs., Assos. of Nat. Archives, Soc. Wine Educators, So. Bay-Shore Track Ofcls. Assn., Phi Alpha Theta. Republican. Roman Catholic. Home: 18 Meadow Dr RD 1 Linwood NJ 08221 Office: Faculty Social and Behavioral Scis Stockton State College Pomona NJ 08240

ELSAADY, ATYAAT NASHED, counselor; b. Mahala-Elkobra, Egypt, Apr. 6, 1928; d. Abdul-Hamid Hassan and Basima Mohamad (Taha) Nashed; came to U.S., 1969, naturalized, 1976; B.S. in Social Work, Cairo U., 1950; B.A. in Edn., Am. U., Cairo, 1953; M.S. in Counseling (Fulbright fellow), N.Y. State Coll. for Tchrs., 1954, postgrad. (Fulbright fellow), 1954-55; m. Mohamed Elsaady, June 12, 1958; children—Tariq, Mona. Sch. social worker, Cairo, 1950-53; instr. Sch. Social Work, Cairo, 1955-57, asst. prof. social case work, 1957-60, asso. prof., 1960-65, prof. edn., 1965-69; sr. career devel. specialist Newark Comprehensive Manpower Delivery System, 1970-75; social worker Essex County (N.J.) Children's Shelter, Belleville, 1975-76; social worker Orange (N.J.) Div. Youth and Family Services, 1976—; instr. in Arabic, Essex County Coll., 1970—; condr. group sessions for tng. parents, foster parents in communicative skills. Bd. dirs. Am. Egyptian Assos., 1975—. Certified in personnel, guidance, reading, N.J. Mem. Am. Personnel and Guidance Assn., PTA, Assn. for Counselor Edn. and Supervision. Club: N.J. Women's Press. Author: School Social Work, 1965; The Exceptional Child, 1969; contbr. series of articles on youth problems to Scientist, Egypt, 1974-75; research on social work assessment, working definition for social work, manpower tng. as solution to poverty, all 1974. Home: 790 Carpenter Rd North Brunswick NJ 08902 Office: 78 Carroll Pl North Brunswick NJ 08903

EL-SABBAN, MOHAMED ZAKI, ops. research analyst; b. Cairo, Egypt, May 23, 1924; s. Ahmed Mahmoud and Zahira (Abdel-Meguid) El-S.; came to U.S., 1949, naturalized, 1972; B.S. in Physics with 1st class honors, Cairo U., 1944; Ph.D. in Physics, Ill. Inst. Tech., 1952; m. Effat Ismail Ahmed, July 12, 1956; children—Inas, Yosria. Instr. physics Cairo U., 1944-49; head physics div. Agouza Research Labs., Pub. Health Dept. of Egypt, Cairo, 1949-66; research physicist Petroleum Research Center, Bur. Mines, U.S. Dept. of Interior, Bartlesville, Okla., 1966-69, research mathematician Helium Research Center, Amarillo, Tex., 1969-70; mathematician Army Aviation Systems Command, U.S. Dept. of Army, St. Louis, 1970-74; ops. research analyst Naval Telecommunications Command, U.S. Dept. of Navy, Washington, 1974—. Lectr. Cairo U., Alexandria U., Ain-Shams U., 1960-63; sr. research physicist, project leader, div. radioisotopes Atomic Energy Establishment, Cairo, 1960-62, Middle East Regional Center for Radioisotopes for the Arab Countries, 1962-63. Recipient numerous fellowships; Certificate of Achievement award U.S. Dept. Army, 1974. Mem. Egyptian Assn. for Mathematical and Phys. Scis., Am. Phys. Soc., Optical Soc. Am., Soc. for Applied Spectroscopy,

Spectroscopy Soc. Can., Coblentz Soc., Sigma Xi. Contbr. articles to profl. jours. Home: 808 College Pkwy Rockville MD 20850 Office: 4401 Massachusetts Ave NW Washington DC 20390

ELWARD, JAMES JOSEPH, writer; b. Chgo., Nov. 22, 1928; s. Joseph Francis and Daisy Ann (Lenert) E.; A.B., Cath. U. Am., 1950. Served with AUS, 1950-52; Korea. Recipient Best Comedy Script award Writers Guild, 1956. Co-author TV scripts: The Secret Storm, 1963-67; The Young Marrieds, 1964; The Guiding Light, 1968; Love is a Many Splendored Thing, 1968; The Doctors, 1969; Where The Heart Is, 1970. Author: (plays) Best of Friends, 1970, Friday Night, 1965, Hallelujah, 1973; (novels under pseud. R. James) Storm's End, The House is Dark, Tomorrow Is Mine; (opera liberetto) The Man on the Bearskin Rug, 1971. Address: 14 Bank St New York City NY 10014

ELWOOD, GEORGE HADDOW, lawyer; b. Hancock, N.Y., May 19, 1927; s. Vincent N. and Florence (Doyle) E.; B.A., Rutgers U., 1949; LL.B., Fordham U., 1952; m. Ann M. Guild, Dec. 18, 1954; children—Charles D., Thomas V., Barbara A. Admitted to N.Y. bar, 1953, U.S. Supreme Ct. bar. 1958; partner firm Elwood & Elwood, Hancock, 1954—; supr. town of Hancock, 1954-59; atty. State Tax Commn. Delaware County, N.Y., 1959-75, Village of Hancock, 1964—, Village of Walton, N.Y. 1971—. Dir. Blueberry Lake, Inc., Deposit, N.Y.; atty. 1st Nat. Bank of Hancock. Pres., Hancock Bd. Trade, 1968. Dir. Narcotic Guidance Council Delaware County. Bd. dirs. Hancock Indsl. Devel. Corp. Served with USNR, 1945-46. Mem. Am., N.Y. State (exec. com. real property sect.), Delaware County (past pres.) bar assns., Fedn. Bar Assns. (pres. 6th jud. dist.), Lambda Chi Alpha. Methodist (trustee, sec.). Rotarian, Mason; mem. Order Eastern Star. Home: 49 E Main St Hancock NY 13783 Office: 10 W Main St Hancock NY 13783

EMANUEL, HELENE RICH, musician, educator; b. N.Y.C., Mar. 31, 1926; d. Irving Wolf and Annette (Moskowitz) Rich; B.A., U. Mich., 1947; m. Paul Emanuel, 1950; children—Irene, Carol, Ruth. French horn player U. Mich. Concert Band, 1945-47, Bklyn. Philharmonic, 1948; pvt. tchr. of piano, 1948—; tchr. folk dance Bklyn. youth groups, 1948-50; composer, dir. confirmation programs, North Bergen, N.J., 1954-59; choir dir. Temple Israel, Cliffside Park, N.J., 1954-57, Bergenfield (N.J.) Jewish Center, 1960-62. Chmn. Bklyn. Jewish Music Festival, 1949; trustee Bergen Philharmonic; co-chmn. children's concerts Bergen City YMHA. Recipient award Music Edn. League, 1936; Founder's medal Theodore Roosevelt Soc., 1938. Scholar, Brandies Camp Inst., 1948. Mem. N.J. Fedn. Music Clubs (chmn. bd., past pres.), Bklyn. Music Tchrs. Guild, Profl. Music Tchrs. Assn., Interstate Music Tchrs. Assn. Co-author: Tercentenary History of Jews, 1954. Address: 468 Churchill Rd Teaneck NJ 07666

EMBER, NORMAN ALLEN, clothing co. exec.; b. N.Y.C., May 4, 1925; s. Max William and Ida (Tribijovskia) E.; B.S., Columbia, 1950, M.A., 1953; m. Susan Cohen, Feb. 14, 1974; children by previous marriage—Max, Peter, Richard. Pres. Silverstyle Dress Co., Inc., N.Y.C., 1965—, Ember Industries, Inc., N.Y.C., 1969—, The Sew-In Inc., N.Y.C., 1971—, Mannerism Inc., 1975—, Pan Em Industries, 1977—. Served with inf., AUS, 1943-46. Decorated Bronze Star medal, Purple Heart with oak leaf cluster. Clubs: Columbia U. (N.Y.C.); Knickerbocker Yacht (Manhasset, N.Y.). Contbr. articles to profl. jours. Office: 501 7th Ave New York City NY 10018

EMBERLEY, WILLIAM DAVID, owner engring. firm; b. Morristown, N.J., July 6, 1942; s. Charles Walter and Charlotte Augusta (Theiler) E.; B.S., U. Vt., 1964, postgrad., 1966-68; m. Nancy Ann Farr, Dec. 22, 1962; children—David, Christopher, Deanna. Design engr. Webster-Martin, Inc., Cons. Engrs., South Burlington, Vt., 1964-66, project engr., 1966-68, sr. project engr., 1969-70, project mgr., 1970-72; project dir. Donald L. Hamlin, Cons. Engrs., Essex Junction, Vt., 1968-69; chief civil-san. engring. Jennison Engring., Inc., Cons. Engrs., Burlington, Vt., 1972-73, v.p., part-owner, 1973—. An organizer Friends U. Vt. Hockey, Burlington, 1972, mem. exec. com., 1972-73, 75-76; active Little League, 1973-76; pres. XY Bowling League, Burlington, 1972-73. Registered profl. engr., Vt., N.H., Mass. Mem. Am., New Eng., Vt. water works assns., Water Pollution Control Fedn., New Eng. Water Pollution Control Assn., Nat., Vt. socs. profl. engrs., Vt. Soc. Engrs., Alpha Tau Omega Alumni Assn. (treas. 1965-75, v.p., dir., chpt. adviser 1975—). Home: 19 Hullcrest Rd RD 2 Box 102 Shelburne VT 05482 Office: 182 Main St Burlington VT 05401

EMBERSON, RICHARD MAURY, profl. assn. exec.; b. Columbia, Mo., Apr. 2, 1914; s. Richard and Lulu (Guthrie) E.; A.B., U. Mo., 1931, M.A., 1932, Ph.D., 1936; m. Virginia Nicoll, Aug. 23, 1947; children—Cynthia Emberson Irvine, Richard M., Margaret Ann, Heather V. Bemis fellow Harvard Obs., 1936-39; instr. U. Pitts. Sch. Medicine, 1939-40; mem. staff Radiation Lab., Mass. Inst. Tech., Cambridge, 1941-46, Naval Research Lab., Washington, 1946, Research and Devel. Bd., Dept. Def., Washington, 1947-51; asst. to pres., asst. sec. Asso. Univs., Inc., N.Y.C., 1951-62; dir. tech. activities IEEE, N.Y.C., 1963-77, gen. mgr., exec. dir., 1977—. Fellow Am. Phys. Soc., IEEE; mem. Am. Assn. Physics Tchrs., Am. Astronomy Soc., N.Y. Acad. Scis., AAAS, Sigma Xi. Author articles on optics, radiometrics and radio astronomy. Home: 43 Saw Mill Rd Huntington NY 11743 Office: 345 E 47th St New York City NY 10017

EMBODY, DANIEL ROBERT, biometrician; b. Ithaca, N.Y., July 10, 1914; s. George Charles and Mary Madeline (Riceman) E.; B.S., Cornell U., 1938, M.S., 1939, postgrad., 1939-42; postgrad. N.C. State Coll., summer 1940; m. Margaret Constance Gran, Mar. 21, 1946 (dec. Mar. 1961); children—James Michael, Daniel Robert, David Richard. Instr. limnology Cornell U., Ithaca, N.Y., 1940-42; sr. math. analyst Arnold Bernard & Co., N.Y.C., 1947-48; statistician Wash. Water Power Co., Spokane, 1949-53; head statistics sect. E.R. Squibb & Sons-Olin, New Brunswick, N.J., 1953-57, mgr. electronic data processing service center, 1958-63, coordinator sci. computations, 1964-65; math. statistician Bur. Ships, Navy Dept., Washington, 1965-67; biometrician Dept. Agr., Beltsville, Md., 1967-72, staff biometrician animal and plant health inspection service, Hyattsville, Md., 1972—. Cons., Ida. Fish and Game Dept., 1950-60, U.S. Geol. Survey, 1953-58, N.J. Dept. Fish and Game, 1953-60. Served to lt. comdr. USNR, 1942-46: ETO. Mem. Am. Statis. Assn., Biometric Soc., Am. Math. Soc., Entomol. Soc. Am., N.Y. Acad. Scis., Am. Legion, Nat. Rifle Assn., Sigma Xi, Gamma Alpha. Contbr. articles to profl. jours. Home: 5025 Edgewood Rd College Park MD 20740 Office: Fed Bldg Room 602 US Dept Agr Hyattsville MD 20782

EMCH, GEORGE FREDERICK, physicist; b. Washington, June 17, 1925; s. George Henry and Mabel Henrietta (Stutz) E.; B.S., Trinity Coll., 1947; m. Dorothy Elaine Eggen, Nov. 11, 1950; children—Susan Louise, George Frederick. Asso. physicist Applied Physics Lab., Johns Hopkins, Silver Spring, Md., 1948-56, physicist, 1956—, prin. staff, 1962—. Precinct chmn. Republican party, Silver Spring, 1953-56. Served to ensign USNR, 1943-46. Recipient certificate of Merit, U.S. Naval Material Command, 1970. Mem. Am. Phys. Soc., IEEE. Lutheran (mem. ch. council 1963-67, 68-71). Patentee in field. Home: 14616 Peach Orchard Rd Silver Spring MD 20904 Office: Johns Hopkins Rd Laurel MD 20810

EMERALD, ROBERT LOUIS, bus. machine mfg. co. exec.; b. Rochester, N.Y., Apr. 7, 1943; s. Frank Louis and Bessie (Parisi) E.; A.A.S., State U. N.Y., 1964; B.S., U. Rochester, 1968, M.B.A., 1973; m. Karen Lou Schnarr, Feb. 5, 1966; children—Christopher Robert, Jeffrey Michael. Elec. draftsman Gen. Dynamics Co., Rochester, N.Y., 1964; elec. research technician Eastman Kodak Co., Rochester, 1965-66; with Xerox Corp., Rochester, 1966—, sr. physicist, 1972-74, mgr. technology planning, 1974-77, mgr. spl. materials, 1978—. Asst. Webelo leader Boy Scouts Am., 1977, treas., liaison adviser, 1977-78. Nat. Merit scholar, 1961; U. Rochester scholar, 1968. Mem. Soc. Photog. Scientists and Engrs., Webster Newcomers Alumni Group. Contbr. articles to profl. jours. Patentee in field. Home: 1068 Hrezent View Ln Webster NY 14580 Office: 800 Phillips Rd Webster NY 14580

EMERICK, KENNETH FRED, libarian, educator; b. Brookville, Pa., July 19, 1925; s. Fred McKinley and Minnie Mae (Smith) E.; B.S., Clarion State Coll., 1950; M.L.S., Rutgers U., 1960; m. Leona F. Rice, July 25, 1951 (div. 1975); 1 son, Schuyler Stevenson; m. 2d, Maxine Brunet, Aug. 31, 1976. County librarian Mansfield (Ohio) Pub. Library, 1955-57; circulation librarian Denison U., 1957-58; cataloger Massillon (Ohio) Pub. Library, 1958-61; dir. Wadsworth (Ohio) Pub. Library, 1961-63; asst. prof./librarian Clarion (Pa.) State Coll., 1963—. Chmn., Clarion County campaign McCarthy for Pres., 1968. Mem. ACLU, Pa. Library Assn. Unitarian. Author: War Resisters Canada, 1972. Columnist, Clarion News, 1964-65. Home: PO Box 37 Lucinda PA 16235 Office: Clarion State Coll Clarion PA 16214

EMERLING, EDWARD GEORGE, economist, educator; b. Meriden, Conn., May 4, 1924; s. Ignatius William Fochtmann and Anna Rose (Tyczkowska) Emerling; student Colby Coll., 1943 B.B.A., St. Bonaventure U., 1951; M.A., Cath. U. Am., 1954, Ph.D., 1970; m. June Marie Paik, June 1, 1976. Instr. econs. Cath. U. Am., 1953-54, lectr., 1954-57; asst. prof. econs. St. Bonaventure (N.Y.) U., 1957-67, asso. prof., 1967-70, chmn. dept. econs., 1959-74, prof., 1970—. Served to 1st lt. USAAF, 1942-46. Mem. Am., Eastern econ. assns., Assn. for Social Econs., N.Y. Econ. Assn., Pi Gamma Mu. Home: 7 William St Allegany NY 14706 also 918 18th Ave Honolulu HI 96816 Office: PO Box 13 St Bonaventure NY 14778

EMERSON, ANDI (MRS. EMERSON WEEKS), sales and advt. exec.; b. N.Y.C.; d. Willard Ingham and Ethel (Mole) Emerson; student Barnard Coll.; m. George G. Fawcett, Jr. (div.); children—Ann Emerson II, George Gifford III, Christopher Babcock; m. 2d, Kenneth E. Weeks, (div.); 1 dau., Electra Ingham. Account exec. Smith Hagel & Snyder, N.Y.C., 1952-54; pres. Emerson Assos., Inc., N.Y.C., 1954-56; exec. v.p. Eugene Stevens, Inc., N.Y.C., 1956-60; pres. Emerson-Weeks, Inc., N.Y.C., 1960—, dir., 1960—; pres., dir. Emerson-Weeks & Fawcett Corp., Mail Order Operating Co. Ltd., N.Y.C. and London, Ingham Hall Ltd.; instr. N.Y.U., 1960-65. Block chmn. fund raising A.R.C., Multiple Sclerosis, Nat. Found., Crippled Children, Found. for Blind, 1954-63; vol. worker Childrens Ward, Meml. Hosp., 1964-66, Hosp. for Spl. Surgery, 1967; mem. adv. com. African Students League, 1965-67. Mem. bd. dirs. Violet Oakley Meml. Found., Phila., 1964—. Mem. Direct Mail Advt. Assn., Sales Promotion Execs., Mktg. Execs. Club, Mail Order Profls. Group, Soc. Profl. Writers, Direct Mktg. Writers Guild (pres. 1975—). Clubs: Ex-Mems. Squadron A, Hundred Million (treas. 1960-61), N.Y. Jr. League, Barnard. Home: 16 E 96th St New York City NY 10028 Office: 14 W 40th St New York City NY 10018

EMERSON, ELEANOR ANNIE, nurse; b. Haverhill, Mass., Sept. 20, 1918; d. Horace Ellius and Sarah Ellen (Feather) E.; diploma Lawrence (Mass.) Gen. Hosp. Sch. Nursing, 1940; B.S. in Nursing Edn., Boston U., 1944; M. in Nursing Service Adminstrn., Columbia U., 1959. Pvt. duty nurse, staff nurse Lawrence (Mass.) Gen. Hosp., 1940-44; dir. nursing, 1955-58; instr. nursing Hartford (Conn.) Hosp., 1944-45, Brockton (Mass.) Hosp., 1945-50; asst. dir. nursing service Salem (Mass.) Hosp., 1950-53; dir. nursing Woonsocket (R.I.) Hosp., 1953-55; asst. chief nurse West Haven (Conn.) VA Hosp., 1959-61, Manchester (N.H.) VA Hosp., 1961-65, Mpls. VA Hosp., 1967-68; chief nursing service Newington (Conn.) VA Hosp., 1969-78, Northampton (Mass.) VA Med. Center, 1978—; field rep. JCAH, 1979—. Active Myasthenia Gravis Assn. Mem. Am., Conn. nurses assns., Dirs. of Nursing Conf. Group Conn., Consortium Dirs. of Nursing Greater Hartford Area, Am. Soc. Hosp. Nursing Service Dirs., D.A.R. Republican. Congregationalist. Home: 129 Brace Rd West Hartford CT 06107

EMERSON, J MARTIN, union ofcl.; b. Washington, Aug. 12, 1912; s. Harry Pliny and Roberta Estelle Johnson; student pub. schs., Washington; m. Reva B. Emerson, 1944; children—Sharon Emerson Decker, Jay Martin. Sec., Am. Fedn. Musicians, Local 161-170, Washington, 1950-75, mem. internat. exec. bd., 1966—, sec.-treas., 1975—; v.p. Interamerican Fedn. Entertainment Workers. Bd. dirs. Wolf Trap Farm Park, Va. Clubs: Mason (32 deg.), Elks. Office: 1500 Broadway New York City NY 10036

EMERSON, KARY CADMUS, biologist, govt. ofcl.; b. Sasakwa, Okla., Mar. 13, 1918; s. Earle Evans and Diva (Wilkins) E.; B.S., Okla. State U., 1939, M.S., 1940, Ph.D., 1949; m. Mary Rebecca Williams, Aug. 13, 1939; children—William K., James B., Robert E. Joined U.S. Army, 1940, advanced through grades to col., 1962, instr. U.S. Army Command and Staff Coll., 1955-58, ret., 1966; asst. for research to the asst. sec. of the Army, 1961—, acting dep. asst. sec. for research and devel., 1973-75, dep. for sci. and tech., 1975, acting asst. sec. research and devel., 1976—; adj. prof. Okla. State U., 1971—; mem. U.N. Mil. Armistice Commn. in Korea, 1958-59; dir. Biol. Soc. of Washington; research asso. Smithsonian Inst., 1959—; U.S. mem. NATO Panel for long term sci. studies, 1970-76. Decorated Bronze Star, Purple Heart, Legion of Merit; recipient Exceptional Civilian Service award Dept., Army 1973, 77, Meritorious Civilian Service award Dept. of Def., 1978. Fellow Washington Acad. Sci., Entomol. Soc. Am.; mem. Am. Soc. Parasitologists, Am. Soc. Tropical Medicine and Hygiene, Wildlife Disease Assn., Biol. Soc. Wash., Entomol. Soc. Washington, Am. Inst. Biol. Scis., AAAS, Sigma Xi, Alpha Zeta. Club: Cosmos. Contbr. articles to profl. jours. Home: 2704 N Kensington Arlington VA 22207 Office: Office Sec of the Army Washington DC 20310

EMERSON, PAUL CARLTON, assn. exec.; b. Biddeford, Maine, July 21, 1923; s. James E. and Clara (Macomber) E.; student Grove City Coll., 1942-43; m. Marion G. Tanner; 1 dau., Beverly Ann. Exec. dir. Portland (Maine) Vets. Service Center, 1945-46; field mgr. Maine State C. of C., Portland, 1946-47, exec. mgr., 1947-68, exec. v.p., 1968-75, pres., 1975—; mem. Can.-U.S. Commn. U.S. C. of C., 1967—; founder (with others) Maine World Trade Council; mem. regional export expansion council U.S. Dept. Commerce, 1969-73; chmn. Maine Hwy. Users Conf., Commerce and Industry Council. Mem. Maine Com. Youth Opportunities, 1960, Maine Com. Aging, 1960, Maine Com. Vocat. Edn., 1958—, Maine Adv. Council Higher Edn., 1966, 78, mem. Gov.'s Task Force on Maine Environment, 1969; bd. dirs. Vacation Travel Council Maine; trustee Osteo. Hosp. Maine, 1969—, v.p., 1976, pres., 1977; trustee Maine Council Econ. Edn. Served to 1st lt. USAAF, 1943-45; lt. col. Res. ret. Mem. Am., New Eng., Maine (founder, treas.) assns. C. of C. execs. Club: Cumberland (Portland). Home: Spurwink Ave Cape Elizabeth ME 04107 Office: 477 Congress St Portland ME 04111

EMERSON, SIDNEY THOMAS, computer co. exec.; b. Winnfield, La., Mar. 1, 1941; s. Joe Hall and Byrd L. (Nelson) E.; S.B. in Physics, Mass. Inst. Tech., 1963; M.A., Rice U., Houston, 1966, Ph.D., 1968. Research asso. Bonner Nuclear Labs., Rice U., 1968-69, Brookhaven Nat. Lab., 1969-70; v.p. engring. Periphonics Corp., Bohemia, N.Y., 1970-75, v.p. product devel., 1975—. Mem. Am. Phys. Soc., IEEE, AAAS, Sigma Xi. Author, patentee in field. Home: 107 Drexelgate Ct Middle Island NY 11953 Office: 75 Orville Dr Bohemia NY 11716

EMERSON, WILLIAM R., library exec., historian; b. Little Rock; student Hendrix Coll., U. Mo.; B.A. in History, Yale; Ph.D. (Rhodes scholar), Oxford (Eng.) U., 1952; m. Barbara Clogher Woodriff. Formerly mem. history faculty Yale, King Prof. History U.S. Naval War Coll., asst. to pres. Hollins Coll.; dir. research grants Nat. Endowment for Humanities, Washington, 1969-74; dir. Franklin D. Roosevelt Library, Hyde Park, N.Y., 1974—. Served with USAAF, World War II; MTO. Home: Hyde Park NY Office: Albany Post Rd Hyde Park NY 12538

EMERY, DAVID FARNHAM, Congressman; b. Rockland, Maine, Sept. 1, 1948; B.E.E., Worcester Poly. Inst., 1970. Mem. Maine Ho. of Reps., 1971-74, chmn. legal affairs com., 1973-74; mem. 94th-96th congresses from 1st Maine Dist. Fellow John F. Kennedy Inst. Politics, 1974. Mem. Jr. C. of C. Club: Masons. Office: Room 425 Cannon House Office Bldg Washington DC 20515*

EMICH, CLINTON CRAWFORD, constrn. co. exec.; b. Balt., July 24, 1917; s. Charles C. and Julia (Drechsler) E.; student Balt. Poly. Inst., Balt. Coll. Commerce; B.B.A., Johns Hopkins, 1939. With Riggs Distler & Co., Inc., Balt., 1939—, sec.-treas., 1944-71, exec. v.p., 1971-72, pres., 1972—, also dir. Chmn. bd. mgrs. YMCA Schs., 1950. Mem. Am. Inst. C.P.A.'s, Md. Assn. C.P.A.'s, Engrs. Club Balt., Sales and Mktg. Execs. Internat., Bldg. Congress and Exchange Balt. (pres. 1964), Financial Execs. Inst. Democrat. Episcopalian. Rotarian (dir. 1959-60). Clubs: Baltimore Country, Center (Balt.); Gibson Island (Md.). Home: 7833 Ellenham Rd Ruxton MD 21204 Office: 216 N Calvert St Baltimore MD 21202

EMIG, LOIS IRENE MYERS (MRS. JACK W. EMIG), composer; b. Roseville, Ohio, Oct. 12, 1925; d. Earl Francis and Margaret Byrd (Weaver) Myers; B.S. with distinction, Ohio State U., 1946, also postgrad.; postgrad. Queens Coll.; m. Jack Wayne Emig, June 7, 1947; children—Sandra Jill, Keith Jack. Tchr. vocal and instrumental music pub. schs., Ohio and N.Y., 1946-65; pvt. tchr. piano and theory, 1954—; composer and librettist for adult and children's choirs; church organist; works include 9 cantatas, 2 piano books, over 160 varied choral works. Recipient 1st prize W.Va. Women's Clubs, 1954, 1st prize Lorenz Children's Anthem contest, 1964; honored by Ohioana Library Assn., 1964. Mem. ASCAP, Delta Omicron. Contbr. music to profl. jours. Address: 82 Fletcher Ave Valley Stream NY 11580

EMMERICH, FREDERIC EDWARD, lawyer; b. N.Y.C., Oct. 21, 1908; s. Anthony Trabert and Charlotte (Parke) E.; A.B., Columbia U., 1932, LL.B., 1935; m. Rosemarie Stehm, Apr. 27, 1940; children—F. Anthony, Stephenie Veda. Admitted to N.Y. bar, 1936; asso. law firm Barber, Fackenthal, Giddings, N.Y.C., 1935-40, mem. firm Giddings & Wilkins, 1940-42, asst. counsel Gen. Aniline & Film Corp., 1942-49; pvt. practice law, N.Y.C., 1949—. Mem. N.Y. State, Washington County bar assns., Assn. Bar City N.Y., Assn. Ex-Mems. Squadron A, Sons Union Vets. Civil War, Soc. Older Grads. Columbia, Zeta Psi. Episcopalian. Club: Manhattan. Address: Battenville Greenwich NY 12834

EMMERICH, JOHN PATRICK, microcomputer mfg. co. exec.; b. N.Y.C., Feb. 15, 1940; s. Clifford L. and Anna V.E.; B.S., Fla. State U., 1970; M.B.A., Syracuse U., 1974. Vice pres., treas. G.M. Applied Devices Corp., Hauppage, N.Y., 1955-76; v.p., gen. mgr. Ontel Corp., Woodbury, N.Y., 1976—; dir. Muncie Gear Works (Ind.), G.C. Electronics Co., Houston, G.C. Mfg. Co., Houston. Vice pres. N. Creek Property Owners Assn. (N.Y.), 1976. Recipient commendation U.S. Army, 1962, 64. Mem. U.S. Naval Inst., Am. Mgmt. Assn., Nat. Microfilm Assn., Am. Def. Preparedness Assn., Pres. Club, L.I. Assn. Bus. Commerce. Roman Catholic. Contbr. articles to profl. jours. Home: North Creek Rd Eatons Neck NY 11768

EMMS, JOSEPHA MURRAY, poet; b. Jamaica Plain, Mass., Apr. 21, 1894; d. Joseph Howe and Annie Marie (Welfel) Murray; ed. various writing courses; m. Edward Emms, June 12, 1920 (dec.); 1 dau., Marjorie (Mrs. Frank Robert Pote). Former tchr. drama, expression; judge numerous poetry contests. Author: (plays) Her Son's Sweetheart, 1915; Playing the Game, 1915; Under Suspicion, 1925; A Dream Lesson, 1916; (poetry) April Music, 1962, Epigrams 1946-1960. Recipient certificate of merit N.Y. State Poetry Soc., 2d prize Am. Poetry League Ann. Contest, 1972; Dunbar award, 1976; 2d prize Midwest Chaparral Contest, 1976. Mem. Am. Poetry League, Midwest Chaparral, Poet's Haven, Mass. Poetry Soc. (hon.), Agnes Carr Writer's Club (hon.). Conglist. Home: 205 S Huntington Ave Jamaica Plain MA 02130

EMRICH, WALTER, chem. co. exec.; b. Bleichenbach, Germany, Jan. 10, 1922; came to U.S., 1970; s. Otto and Emma (Selzam) E.; B.A., U. Vienna (Austria), 1942; D.Sc., U. Frankfurt (Germany), 1950; m. Hildegard Bremke, Dec. 31, 1954; children—Katja, Annette. Chemist under temporary contract for French cos. in North Africa, 1951; gen. works mgr., dir. personnel Degussa-Frankfurt/Main (Germany), 1952-70; chmn. bd., exec. officer Degussa, Inc., N.Y.C., 1970-76; dir. Degussa Alabama, Inc., Mobile; pres. Carbon Internat., Ltd., Wilmington, Del., 1976—; European rep. Roger Williams Tech. and Econ. Services, Inc., Princeton, N.J., 1976—. Served as capt. German Army, 1939-45. Decorated Iron Cross. Mem. Am. Chem. Soc., Am. Inst. Chem. Engrs., Am. Soc. Metals, Catalysis Soc., Instrument Soc. Am., Soc. Automotive Engrs., Barbeque Industry Assn., Soc. Vacuum Coaters, AAAS, Air Pollution Control Assn. Lion. Contbr. tech. papers to profl. publs. Home: CN 19 Princeton NJ 08540 Office: Buchenring 7 6078 Zeppelinhein West Germany

END, GERARD EDWARD, JR., pub. relations cons.; b. Phila., Sept. 24, 1933; s. Gerard E. and Veronica M. (Rafferty) E.; B.S. in Bus. Adminstrn., LaSalle Coll., 1963; student Tokyo U. (Japan), 1957-58, Northwood U., 1974; m. Dolores Comerford, Oct. 12, 1963. Editor, Moorestown (N.J.) News Chronicle, 1959-61; mng. editor Burlington County (N.J.) Times, 1962-66; pub. relations cons. Ringold/Kalish & Co., Phila., 1966-67, Ketchum, MacLeod & Grove, Pitts., 1968, Beaumont, Heller & Sperling, Reading, Pa., 1968-74, 75—; corporate advt. mgr. Gen. Battery Corp., Reading, 1974-75; dir. Reading (Pa.) Phillies baseball team, 1974—. Charter bd. dirs. Jr. Achievement of Reading and Berks County, 1968-72; pub. relations dir. Hawk Mt. council Boy Scouts Am., 1973-75. Served with U.S. Army, 1956-58. Recipient Distinguished Service citations NSC, 1973, 74, 75, 76, 77, 78; Outstanding Citizen award, Willow Grove Pa., 1959; Outstanding Service award, Willingboro, N.J., 1964. Mem. NSC (exec. com. 1972—), Nat. Alliance of Businessmen, Berks County Pub. Relations Assn. (pres. 1973), Nat. Assn. Stock Car Auto Racing, Am. Auto Racing Writers & Broadcasters Assn., U.S. Auto Club, Sigma Delta Xi. Republican. Roman Catholic. Clubs: K.C. (4 deg.), Iris (dir. 1974—). Producer: (films) For Good Sound Reasons, 1972; The Real

Winners, 1977. Office: 6th and Walnut Sts PO Box 822 Reading PA 19603

ENDAHL, LOWELL JEROME, agrl. engr.; b. Jerauld County, S.D., July 3, 1922; s. John Martin and Olga A. (Bunde) E.; student Augustana Coll., Sioux Falls, S.D., 1941-43; B.S. in Agrl. Engring., S.D. State U., 1948; m. Vronna B. Lee, Oct. 16, 1948; children—John Raymond, Jay Jerome, Mark Arnold. Agrl. engr. Tri-County Elec. Coop., Plankinton, S.D., 1948-51; dir., mem. services dept. Sioux Valley Empire Elec. Assn., Colman, S.D., 1951-54; agrl. engr. Nat. Rural Elec. Co-op. Assn., Washington, 1954-55, feature editor, 1955-58, dir. mem. services, 1958-73, coordinator research and devel., 1973—. Served as aviation cadet USNR, 1943-44, from 2d lt. to capt., USMCR, 1944-46. Mem. Am. Soc. Agrl. Engrs., Am. Indsl. Devel. Council. Home: 8633 Fort Hunt Rd Alexandria VA 22308 Office: 1800 Massachusetts Ave NW Washington DC 20036

ENDERS, JOHN FRANKLIN, educator, immunologist; b. West Hartford, Conn., Feb. 10, 1897; s. John Ostrom and Harriet Goulden (Whitmore) E.; A.B., Yale, 1920, Sc.D. (hon.), 1953; M.A., Harvard, 1922, Ph.D., 1930; Sc.D., 1956; Sc.D., Trinity, 1955, Northwestern, 1956; Sc.D., Western Res. U., 1958, Tufts U., 1960; LL.D., Tulane U., 1958; L.H.D., Hartford U., 1960; D.Sc., Jefferson Med. Coll., 1962, U. Pa., 1964, U. Ibadan, 1968; m. Sarah Frances Bennett, Sept. 17, 1927 (dec.); children—John Ostrom II, Sarah; m. 2d, Carolyn Keane, May 12, 1951; 1 stepson, William Edmund Keane. Asst. dept. bacteriology and immunology Harvard, 1929-30, instr., 1930-32, faculty instr., 1932-35, asst. prof., 1935-42, asso. prof., 1942-56, prof., 1956-62, Univ. prof., 1962-67, emeritus, 1967—. Served from ensign to lt. (j.g.) Naval Res. Flying Corps., 1917-20. Civilian cons. to sec. war on epidemic diseases, 1942-46; mem. Commn. on Viral Infections, Armed Forces Epidemiological Bd.; sci. adv. bd. Armed Forces Inst. Pathology; chief research div. infectious disease Children's Hosp., Boston, 1947-72, chief virus research unit, 1972—. Recipient Passano Found. award for culturing poliomyelitis viruses in living tissues, 1953; Lasker Award, 1954; Nobel Prize in Medicine and Physiology, 1954; Cameron prize U. Edinburgh, 1960, Howard Taylor Ricketts Meml. award U. Chgo., 1962, Diesel Gold medal, 1962, Robert Koch medal, 1962 (Germany), Sci. achievement award AMA, 1963, Presdl. Medal of Freedom, 1963. Fellow Am. Acad. Arts and Scis.; mem. Nat. Acad. Scis., Harvey Soc., Am. Philos. Soc., Soc. Gen. Microbiology (hon.), Soc. Am. Bacteriologists, Am. Assn. Immunologists (pres.), Soc. Exptl. Biology and Medicine, Am. Pub. Health Assn., AAAS, Mass. Med. Soc. (asso.), Royal Soc. (fgn.), Academie des Sciences de l'Institut de France (hon.), Sigma Xi, Alpha Omega Alpha (hon.). Clubs: Harvard (Boston); Brookline (Mass.) Country. Author: (with Hans Zinsser and Leroy D. Fothergill) Immunity: Principles and Application in Medicine and Public Health, 1939. Contbr. to Virus and Rickettsial Diseases, 1958, 64. Editorial bd. Jour. of Immunology, Jour. Bacteriology, Jour. Virology, others. Home: 64 Colburne Crescent Brookline MA 02146 Office: 300 Longwood Boston MA 02115

ENDERS, MARCH, physician; b. Hartford, Conn., March 29, 1929; d. Ostrom and Alice (Talcott) E.; A.B., Oberlin Coll., 1951; M.D., Yale U., 1960; m. Wallace R. Kornack, June 30, 1973; 1 son, Thomas. Intern, Hartford (Conn.) Hosp., 1960-61; research asso. in multiple sclerosis Brooks Hosp., Brookline, Mass., 1962-67; resident, teaching fellow in rehab. medicine Tufts-New Eng. Med. Center, Boston, 1968-72; asst. prof. dept. medicine George Washington U. Med. Sch., Washington, 1973—; staff physician, George Washington U. Med. Center; cons. VA Hosp., D.C. Div. Vocat. Rehab. Career counsellor Yale U., Oberlin Coll.; class agt. Masters Sch. Recipient citation D.C. Rehab. Assn., 1976; diplomate Am. Bd. Phys. Medicine and Rehab. Fellow Am. Acad. Phys. Medicine and Rehab.; mem. AMA, D.C. Med. Soc. Episcopalian. Condr. research in field. Home: 1315 28th St NW Washington DC 20007 Office: 901 23rd St NW Washington DC 20037

ENG, RICHARD PETER, bank exec.; b. Bklyn., Sept. 25, 1950; s. Lung Yew and Yan Ho (Moy) E.; B.S., N.Y. Inst. Tech., 1971; m. Myrna Gee, Sept. 28, 1975. Ops. officer Citibank, N.Y.C., 1971—. Roman Catholic. Home: 2525 E 12 St Brooklyn NY 11235 Office: 399 Park Ave New York City NY 10043

ENG, RICHARD SHEN, laser corp. exec.; b. Canton, China, Dec. 11, 1930; s. Gooy Yu and Tuck Yin (Chin) Ng.; B.S. cum laude, Coll. City N.Y., 1954; M.S., Mass. Inst. Tech., 1955; Ph.D. (NSF fellow), Poly. Inst. N.Y., 1971; came to U.S., 1947, natruralized, 1950; m. Annette Kathleen Chang, Dec. 28, 1958; children—Victor John, Douglas Walter, Patricia Monalan. Sr. engr. Sperry Gyroscope Co., Great Neck, N.Y., 1955-65; research engr. Grumman Aerospace Corp., Bethpage, N.Y., 1965-69; tech. staff mem. Mass. Inst. Tech. Lincoln Lab., Lexington, 1971-76; sr. research scientist Laser Analytics, Inc., Lexington, 1977—. Mem. Newton (Mass.) Taxpayers Assn., 1972—; active PTA. Mem. Optical Soc. Am., IEEE, Chinese Cultural Assn. Greater Boston. Democrat. Roman Catholic. Club: Boston Camera. Contbr. tech. articles to profl. jours. Patentee bi-refringent lenses, InAs spinflip Raman laser. Home: 164 Hartman Rd Newton MA 02159 Office: 38 Hartwell Ave Lexington MA 02173

ENG, YOUNG F., endocrinologist; b. Norfolk, Va., Jan. 10, 1932; s. Chew and Hosey E.; B.S. cum laude, City Coll. N.Y., 1958; M.D., N.Y. U., 1962; m. Judy Chiu, June 29, 1968. Med. intern Med. Coll. Va. Hosps., Richmond, 1962-63; med. resident, U. Hosp. Nebr., Omaha, 1963-65; NIH trainee in endocrinology Mt. Sinai Hosp., N.Y.C., 1965-67, instr. in endocrinology, 1968-73; cons. in endocrinology Willowbrook State Sch., S.I., N.Y., 1967-77; asso. attending endocrinologist, Staten Island, (N.Y.) Hosp., 1967—, St. Vincent's Med. Center, S.I., 1967—; asso. attending in medicine, Richmond Meml. Hosp., S.I., 1971—; attending physician, endocrinology and medicine, Sea View Hosp. and Home, S.I., 1969-77, vis. physician, 1977—; cons. in endocrinology, USPHS, 1967. Med. advisory council Borough of Richmond, 1978. Diplomate Am. Be. Nuclear Medicine. Mem. Richmond County Med. Soc. (chmn. med. econs. com., 1976), N.Y. Diabetes Assn., Am. Soc. Internal Medicine, Am. Coll. Nuclear Physicians, AMA, Am. Soc. Nuclear Medicine, Chinese Am. Med. Soc., Phi Beta Kappa. Club: Chinese-Am. Assn. of Staten Island (pres., 1978). Contbr. articles in field to profl. jours. Address: 1800 Clove Rd Staten Island NY 10304

ENGALITCHEFF, JOHN, JR., aircoil co. exec.; b. Moscow, Russia, July 26, 1907; s. John and Barbara (Nosova) E.; came to U.S., 1925, naturalized, 1937; B.S. in Mech. Engring., Johns Hopkins, 1930; m. Virginia Porter, Sept. 25, 1948. With Balt. Aircoil Co., Inc., 1947—, pres., 1966, chmn. bd., 1966-72, now ret. Served to lt. USNR, 1943-45. Mem. Gibson Island Squadron. Clubs: Gibson Island, Baltimore Country, Maryland, Center (Balt.). Home: Box 265 Round Hill Rd Gibson Island MD 21056 Office: Suite 301 Empire Towers 7300 Ritchie Hwy Glen Burnie MD 21061

ENGBORG, EDWIN CHARLES, JR., elec. engr.; b. N.Y.C., July 28, 1925; s. Edwin Charles and Ida Teresa (Nelson) E.; B.E.E., Poly. Inst. N.Y., 1954; m. Evelyn M. Hanson, May 24, 1947; children—Edwin Charles, Jane Elizabeth. With N.Y. Telephone Co., N.Y.C., 1947—, gen. staff engr., 1969—; instr. electronics N.Y. U. Active Boy Scouts Am. Served with USMC, World War II. Mem. Am. Right of Way Assn. (chpt. pres.), IEEE, Am. Pub. Works Assn. Republican. Lutheran. Clubs: Lake Wallenpaupack Yacht, Swedish Football Power Squadron. Home: 50 Fort Pl Staten Island NY 10301 Office: 1250 Broadway 36th Floor New York City NY 10001

ENGEL, DAVID CHAPIN, lawyer; b. N.Y.C., Oct. 6, 1931; s. Robert Albert and Mabel Gretchen (Eshbaugh) E.; A.B., St. Lawrence U., 1954; LL.B., N.Y.U., 1956; m. Priscilla Gail Stevens, May 26, 1972; children—Karen, Kathleen, Terri, Julie, Peter, Rebecca, Heidi. Admitted to N.H. bar, 1956, Mass. bar, 1967; law clerk, N.H. Atty. Gen.'s Office, Concord, 1956-58; partner firm Shute, Engel & Frasier, Exeter, N.H., 1958—; arbitrator, Am. Arbitration Assn. Bd. dirs. Greenland Community Church, Exeter Competitive Swim Competition; del. Republican nat., state conventions. Mem. Rockingham County, N.H., Mass., Am. bar assns., Assn. Trial Lawyers Am., Exeter (bd. dirs.), Greenland hist. socs., Nat. Trust Historic Preservation, Internat. Platform Assn., Am. Judicature Soc., Soc. for Preservation and Encouragement of Barbershop Quarter Singing in Am. Congregationalist. Home: 47 Park Ave Greenland NH 03840 Office: 1 Center St Exeter NH 03833

ENGEL, GERTRUDE, lobbyist, syndicated columnist, pub. relations exec.; b. Toronto, Ont., Can.; student pvt. schs., Can.; Arts D. Pvt. practice pub. relations, Washington; columnist Liberty News Service, Detroit; lobbyist health practices, Washington. Coordinator numerous Washington receptions and assignments, including those for astronauts, Sec. of State Kissinger, former Pres. Nixon. Home: 2450 Virginia Ave NW Washington DC 20037 also 15501 E Jefferson Ave Grosse Pointe Park MI 48230*

ENGEL, HOWARD DENTON, mech. engr.; b. Bklyn., Mar. 20, 1925; s. Max and Rose (Politzer) E.; B.Adminstrv. Engring. cum laude, Syracuse U., 1950; M.S., L.I. U., 1970; m. Doris Vera Kandel, Jan. 30, 1949; children—Iris Sherry, Carol Ilene. Indsl. engr. Dejur Amsco, Queens, N.Y., 1951-55; sr. engr. Sperry div. Sperry Rand Corp., Great Neck, N.Y., 1955—, instr. profl. engring., 1970—; chief engr., v.p. All Metal Partition Co., Bklyn., part-time, 1959—. Counselor Syracuse (N.Y.) U., 1971—; adviser on continuing engring. edn. N.Y. Inst. Tech., Old Westbury, 1974. Mem. N.Y. State Manpower Planning Council, Albany, 1972-74, mem. steering com., 1973-74; L.I. Assn. rep. L.I. Waste Water Mgmt. Study Adv. Com., 1975—. Served with USAAC, 1943-46. Recipient Engr. in Industry Distinguished Service award N.Y. State Soc. Profl. Engrs., 1972. Registered profl. engr., N.Y. Mem. Soc. Jewish Sci., Nat. (dir. 1974), Nassau County (pres. 1971-73, trustee 1973—) socs. profl. engrs., Assn. L.I. Engrs. and Scientists (chmn. 1973), Nassau County Syracuse Alumni Assn. (v.p. 1957-59), L.I. Assn. Environ. Task Force (vice chmn. 1978). Republican. Home: 11 Beatrice Ln Old Bethpage NY 11804 Office: 196 Dupont St Brooklyn NY 11222

ENGEL, JERRY S., news photographer; b. Bklyn., Oct. 21, 1935; s. Harry and Jeanette (Ripstein) E.; B.A., N.Y. U., 1959; m. Diane Greenaway, Jan. 16, 1965; 1 son, David. Staff photographer N.Y. Post, N.Y.C., 1958—; freelance writer, aviation, aviation photographer, 1970—; aviation writer Queens Tribune, Airport Press' Airport Bull.; cons. med. photography, lectr. in field. Served with N.Y. Air Nat. Guard, 1953-64. Recipient award for gen. news photography N.Y. Times; award for spot news photography N.Y. Daily News, numerous others. Mem. N.Y. Press Photographers Assn. (trustee), N.Y. Newspaper Guild, Aviation/Space Writers Assn. Home: 123-60 83d Ave Kew Gardens NY 11415

ENGEL, JOHN JACOB, communications exec.; b. N.Y.C., June 9, 1936; s. Stewart I. and Beatrice L. (Schapiro) E.; B.A., Adelphi Coll., 1957; M.S., Boston U., 1959; m. Barbara F. Kaplan, Aug. 25, 1957; children—Susan Lisa, Mark Alan. Program dir. WLAD-FM, Danbury, Conn., 1954-57, WBRY-AM, Waterbury, Conn., 1959-62; account exec. WNHC Radio, New Haven, 1962-63; account exec. N. Am. Precis Syndicate, Inc., N.Y.C., 1963-68, exec. v.p., prin., 1968—; guest lectr. Publicity Club of N.Y., 1971. Mem. Manalapan-Englishtown Regional Bd. Edn., 1971—, pres., 1975—; charter mem. Battleground Arts Center, Freehold, N.J. WGBH-TV scholar, 1958; citations, B'nai B'rith, 1969. Mem. Pub. Relations Soc. Am. Jewish. Clubs: B'nai B'rith, Publicity N.Y. Home: 10 Kilmer Dr Englishtown NJ 07726 Office: 201 E 42nd St New York City NY 10017

ENGEL, RALPH MANUEL, lawyer; b. N.Y.C., May 13, 1944; s. Werner Herman and Ruth Fredericke (Friedlander) E.; B.A. with highest honors in Econs., N.Y.U., 1965, J.D., 1968; m. Diane Linda Weinberg, Aug. 10, 1968; children—Eric M., Daniel C. Admitted to N.Y. bar, 1968, U.S. Supreme Ct. bar, 1972; atty. firm Gilbert, Segall and Young, N.Y.C., 1968-71, Trubin Sillcocks Edelman & Knapp, N.Y.C., 1971-76; atty. firm Burns Jackson Miller Summit & Jacoby, N.Y.C., 1976—, partner, 1978—; lectr. Practicing Law Inst., 1976—. Mem. Estate Planning Council Westchester County. Mem. Am. (com. on legal problems of the elderly and their estates 1971-75, com. on adminstrn. expenses 1975—), N.Y. State bar assns., Assn. Bar City N.Y., Am. Arbitration Assn. (arbitrator). Jewish. Contbr. articles to legal jours.; editor-in-chief The Commentator, N.Y.U., 1968. Home: 6 Rockwood Dr Larchmont NY 10538 Office: 445 Park Ave New York City NY 10022

ENGELBRECHT, EUGENE WILLIAM, civil engr.; b. Camden, N.J., Nov. 3, 1927; s. Emil Henry and Gladys Amelia (Imhoff) E.; B.A., U. Pa., 1951; m. Patricia M. McCarty, Nov. 10, 1951; children—Charlene, William. Cartographer, U.S. Geol. Survey, Washington, 1951-56; v.p. Albert C. Jones Assos., Mt. Holly, N.J., 1956-69; engring. mgr. Korman Corp., Phila., 1969-74; profl. engr. R.A. Alaimo Assos., Mt. Holly, 1974—. Constrn. chmn. Cinnaminson Sewerage Authority, 1974; active United Way, Burlington County, 1975-76. Served with U.S. Army, 1945-46. Registered profl. engr., N.J., Pa., Del. Mem. ASCE, Cons. Council Inst. Transp. Engrs., N.J. (recognition award 1976), Pa. socs. profl. engrs., N.J. Soc. Municipal Engrs., Cons. Engrs. Council N.J. Home: 3107 Woodhaven Dr Cinnaminson NJ 08077 Office: 200 High St Mt Holly NJ 08060

ENGELHARDT, DAVID MEYER, educator; b. Austria, June 15, 1912; s. Chaim and Frieda (Beer) E.; came to U.S., 1920, naturalized, 1925; B.S., Coll. City N.Y., 1932; M.D., U. Vienna, 1937; certificate psychoanalysis N.Y. Med. Coll., 1951; m. Jo Ann Zavatsky, June 30, 1952; children—Jo Ann, Nina, Jaime. Intern, Vienna Gen. Hosp. and Polyclinic, 1936-37; resident Bklyn. State Hosp., 1938-39; successively asst. dir., asso. dir., acting dir. Kings County Psychiat. Hosp., 1947-60, dir. clin. services, 1960-64; dir. psychopharmacology treatment research unit State U. N.Y. Downstate Med. Center, Bklyn., 1956—, prof. psychiatry, 1962—, exec. officer dept., 1960-64, mem. faculty Sch. Grad. Studies, 1972—; attending physician psychiatry Kings County Hosp. Center, 1959—. Mem. clin. psychopharmacology research rev. com. Nat. Inst. Mental Health, USPHS, 1967-69, mem. clin. projects research rev. com., 1970-74, chmn., 1972-74; 1st nat. chmn. adv. council childhood mental illness Nat. Assn. Mental Health, 1962-64. Served to lt. col. M.C., USAAF, 1940-46. Fellow Am. Psychiat. Assn., Am. Acad. Psychoanalysis, AAAS, Am. Coll. Neuropsychopharmacology, Sigma Xi. Author reports in field. Home: 208 Marlborough Rd Brooklyn NY 11226

ENGELHARDT, HUGO TRISTRAM, JR., educator, physician; b. New Orleans, Apr. 27, 1941; s. Hugo Tristram and Beulah (Karbach) E.; B.A., U. Tex. at Austin, 1963, Ph.D., 1969; M.D. with honors, Tulane U., 1972; m. Susan Gay Malloy, Nov. 25, 1965; children—Susan Elisabeth, Christina Tristram, Dorothea. Asst. prof. U. Tex. Med. Br., 1972-75, asso. prof. 1975-77, mem. Inst. Med. Humanities, 1973-77; Rosemary Kennedy prof. philosophy of medicine Georgetown U., 1977—; sr. research scholar Kennedy Inst. Center for Bioethics, Washington, 1977—. Mem. bioethics com. Nat. Found. March of Dimes, 1975—; trustee Reproductive Biology Research Found. Fulbright grad. fellow, 1969-70. Fellow Inst. Soc. Ethics and the Life Scis.; mem. Am. Philos. Assn. Author: Mind Body: A Categorial Relation, 1973. Asso. editor Ency. of Bioethics, 1973-78, Jour. Medicine and Philosophy, 1974—. Editorial adv. bd. Teaching Philosophy, 1975—, Forum for Medicine, 1977—, Philosophy of Science, 1977—. Editor: (with others) Philosophy and Medicine Series, 1974—; Evaluation and Explanation in the Biomedical Sciences, 1975; Philosophical Dimensions of the Neuro-Medical Sciences, 1976; Philosophical Medical Ethics, 1977; Mental Health, 1978. Home: 4104 Sycamore St Chevy Chase MD 20015 also Star Route 2 Box 1 New Braunfels TX 78130 Office: Kennedy Inst Center for Bio Ethics Georgetown U Washington DC 20057

ENGELMAN, GERALD, govt. adminstr., economist; b. Slater, Iowa, June 19, 1914; s. Julius Heinrich Theodor and Clara (Lehman) E.; B.S., Iowa State U., 1937; postgrad. U. Minn., 1937-41, Ph.D. in Agrl. Econs., 1948; m. Annabel Dodge Johnson, Dec. 17, 1943; children—John Victor, Janet Lee, Robert Mark, Elizabeth Ann. Instr., U. Minn., Mpls., 1946-47, vis. prof. agrl. econs., 1961; agrl. economist Bur. Agrl. Econs., U.S. Dept. Agr., St. Paul, 1948-50, Washington, 1950-54, head livestock mktg. research sect. Agrl. Mktg. Service, 1954-62, dir. industry analysis staff Packers and Stockyards Adminstrn., 1962-78, staff economist Agrl. Mktg. Service, 1978—; chmn. Am. Swine Study Mission to Can., 1957. Served to 1st lt. AUS, 1942-46. Recipient Superior Service award U.S. Dept. Agr., 1957. Mem. Am., Western agrl. econs. assns., Canadian Econs. Soc., Govt. Regulatory Economists Seminar, Alpha Zeta. Episcopalian. Club: Farmhouse. Contbr. articles to profl. jours. Home: 3924 Rickover Rd Silver Spring MD 20902 Office: US Dept Agr Washington DC 20250

ENGELMAN, IRWIN, corp. exec.; b. N.Y.C., May 9, 1934; s. Max and Julia (Shaoul) E.; B.B.A., Coll. City N.Y., 1955; J.D., Bklyn. Law Sch., 1961; m. Rosalyn Ackerman, Nov. 24, 1956; children—Madeleine F., Marianne L. Admitted to N.Y. bar, 1972; sr. accountant Pub. Accounting, N.Y.C., 1959-62; controller Razdow Labs., Inc., Newark, 1962-65; bus. mgr. Becker & Becker Asso., Inc., N.Y.C., 1965-66; with Xerox Corp., Rochester, N.Y., 1966-78, corporate v.p., 1975-78; v.p., chief fin. officer Singer Co., N.Y.C., 1978—; asso. prof. Monroe Community Coll., 1967-68. Mem. bd. dirs. Citizens Tax League, 1971—. Served with U.S. Army, 1957-58. C.P.A., N.J. Fellow Am. Bar Assn., Am. Inst. C.P.A. Home: 12 Old Hill Rd Westport CT 06880 Office: Singer Co 30 Rockefeller Plaza New York City NY 10020

ENGISCH, RICHARD ALFRED, elec. engr.; b. Elizabeth, N.J., May 25, 1928; s. William George and Minnie (Housley) E.; B.S. in Elec. Engring., Rutgers U., 1953; m. Elaine Sherry Burgess, May 1, 1965; children—George William, Deborah Susan. From technician to dept. supr. Chatham Electronics, 1948-53; plant engr. GTE Sylvania, Towanda, Pa., 1953-67, engr. in charge plant elec. engring., 1967—. Chmn. bd. Meml. Hosp., Towanda, 1973—; chmn. Bradford County (Pa.) PTA, 1962-64. Served with USN, 1946-48. Decorated Victory medal. Mem. IEEE. Republican. Methodist. Clubs: Bridge St. Hill Rod and Gun, Towanda Gun, Elks. Home: Route 2 Box 31A Wysox PA 18854 Office: Sylvania GTE Hawes St Towanda PA 18848

ENGLE, CHARLES DONALD, educator; b. Phila., Oct. 8, 1930; s. Charles Jay and Stella Geraldine (Cullen) E.; B.S., Temple U., 1961, Ph.D., 1971; M.A., U. Pa., 1964; m. Andrea M. Shelfo, Dec. 21, 1963; 1 son, Christopher. Teaching fellow polit. sci. dept. Temple U., 1966-67, adj. asso. prof., 1969—, founder, dir. Center for Adminstrn. Justice, 1971—; lectr. Pa. Morton Coll., Chester, 1968. Mem. Acad. Criminal Justice Scis. (exec. com. 1978-79), Am. Acad. Polit. and Social Sci., Am. Correctional Assn., Am. Polit. Sci. Assn., Am. Soc. Criminology, Am. Soc. Pub. Adminstrn., Crime Commn. Phila., Internat. Assn. Chiefs of Police, Law and Soc. Assn., North Atlantic Assn. Criminal Justice Educators (pres. 1978-79), Phila. Musical Soc. Home: 112 Righters Ferry Rd Bala Cynwyd PA 19004 Office: Temple U Broad and Oxford Sts Philadelphia PA 19122

ENGLE, HAROLD GLENN, JR., chemist; b. Hershey, Pa., Jan. 20, 1930; s. Harold G. and Mildred R. (Wolfersberger) E.; B.S. in Chemistry, Lebanon Valley Coll., 1951; m. Doris Jane Hovis, May 15, 1954; children—Susan Ann, Glenn Allen. With Hershey (Pa.) Foods Corp., 1955—, research specialist, 1970—. Treas. Hershey High Sch. Band Booster Assn., 1972-76; head usher Hershey 1st United Methodist Ch., 1972—; instl. rep. Keystone Area council Boy Scouts Am., 1970—; comdr. Week-end Warrior Naval Air Res., Willow Grove, Pa., 1955-74. Served with USNR, 1952-55. Mem. Am. Chem. Soc., Inst. Food Technologists, Naval Res. Assn., Retired Officers Assn. Clubs: Masons, Shriners. Home: 405 Chestnut Ave Hershey PA 17033 Office: 925 Reese Ave PO Box 54 Hershey PA 17033

ENGLEHART, HARRY AUGUSTINE, III, pub. relations mgr.; b. Johnstown, Pa., Apr. 8, 1947; s. Harry A. and Mercedes (Parsons) E.; A.B., U. Mich., 1969; postgrad. Duquesne U., 1970-71; m. Linda A. Risaliti, Aug. 3, 1968. Staff writer Mellon Bank, Pitts., 1969-71, asst. advt. mgr., 1971-72, pub. relations mgr., 1972—; faculty Am. Inst. Banking, Pitts., 1975—; news media/promotion chmn. 60th Profl. Golf Assn. Championship, 1978. Campaign mgr. W. Pa. Humphrey for Pres., 1972; bd. dirs. Mendelssohn Choir of Pitts. Mem. Pub. Relations Soc. Am., Bank Mktg. Assn. Democrat. Roman Catholic. Clubs: Oakmont (Pa.) Country, Pitts. Advt., Pitts. Press. Home: 131 Old Suffolk Dr Monroeville PA 15146 Office: Mellon Square Pittsburg PA 15230

ENGLERT, HERBERT CHARLES, found. exec.; b. Newark, Feb. 6, 1921; s. Herbert Philip and Catherine Elizabeth (Bantleon) E.; A.B., Dartmouth, 1942, M.Comml. Sci., Amos Tuck Sch. Bus. Adminstrn., 1943; m. Lillian Jean Sigler, Oct. 17, 1942; children—Joyce Elinor Englert Gertmenian, H. Peter. Staff, Haskins & Sells, C.P.A.'s, N.Y.C., 1945-47; pvt. practice accounting, Newark, 1947-70; with Fannie E. Rippel Found., Morristown, N.J., 1955—, treas., 1963—, exec. v.p., 1974—, trustee, 1968—. Served to lt. USNR, 1943-45. C.P.A., N.J. Mem. N.J. Soc. C.P.A.'s. Home: 161 Western Dr Short Hills NJ 07078 Office: 299 Madison Ave Morristown NJ 07960

ENGLISH, MAURICE, author, pub.; b. Chgo., Oct. 21, 1909; s. Michael and Agnes (Sexton) E.; A.B. magna cum laude, Harvard U., 1933; m. Fanita Blumberg, Apr. 25, 1945; children—Jonathan Brian, Deirdre Elena. Journalist, U.S. and Europe, 1933-53; editor, pub. Chicago mag., 1953-57; free-lance writer, 1957-61; mng. editor, sr. editor U. Chgo. Press, 1961-69; founding dir. Temple U. Press, Phila., 1969-76; founder Pulvinar Press, 1976. Trustee, U. Pa. Press, 1978—. Fulbright fellow, France, 1966-67. Mem. Phi Beta Kappa. Author: (anthology writings Louis Sullivan) The Testament of Stone, 1963; (poems) Midnight in the Century, 1964; (translations) Selected Poems of Eugenio Montale, 1966; (play) The Saints in Illinois, 1969; (poems) A Savaging of Roots, 1974. Home: 724 Pine St Philadelphia PA 19106

ENGLISH, ROBERT, legislator, author; b. Cambridge, Mass., Sept. 18, 1903; s. Walter C. and Anna E. (Durfer) E.; A.B., Harvard U., 1926; diploma Universite de Dijon (France), 1925; div.; children—Ann Durfor (Mrs. Gordon Hutchison), Joseph Grew; m. 2d, Margaret B. Sordoni, Apr. 22, 1972. Fgn. service officer U.S. Dept. State, 1927-48; mem. N.H. Legislature, 1949, N.H. Senate, 1955—; candidate senate pres. Mem. corp. Monadnock Hosp.; pres. Monadnock Community Coll.; mem. State Council on Aging, Commn. to Revise Criminal Code, Edn. Evaluation Commn., Pres.'s Adv. Com. on Arts, N.H. Coordinating Bd. Advanced Edn. and Accreditation; vice chmn. Econ. Growth Survey. Chmn. hist. sites adv. com. Del. Republican Nat. Conv., 1952, 56, 60. Mem. Nat. Def. Exec. Res., Grange. Mason, Rotarian. Contbr. articles to various mags. Address: Box 426 Jaffrey NH 03452

ENGLISH, RUTH HILL, artist, educator; b. Andover, Mass., Feb. 7, 1904; d. Herbert Hudson and Ada Jane (Wells) Hill; grad. Abbot Acad., Andover; m. E. Schuyler English, July 4, 1959; children—Susan K. (Mrs. Howard K. Simpson), Katharine K. (Mrs. Christopher R. Barnes). Faculty, Bryn Mawr Art Center (later Main Line Center of Arts), 1945-65, Wayne Art Center, 1947-49; dir. Hedgeabout Studio, Wynnewood, Pa., 1965—; lectr., art cons. throughout East, 1960-70. Past mem. womens bd. Pa. Hosp.; mem. womens bd. Babies Hosp., 1934-39. Mem. Hist. Soc. Early Am. Decoration (pres. William Penn chpt. 1950-51), Pa. Craftsmans Guild (dir. 1952-54). Republican. Eipscopalian. Club: Acorn. Home: 47 E Wynnewood Rd Merion PA 19066 also Skytop PA 18357 Studio: 306 Gypsy Ln Wynnewood PA 19036

ENGLISHMAN, HERBERT NEIL, civil engr.; b. Paterson, N.J., Jan. 20, 1939; s. Herbert Krine and Kathryn Hester Englishman; B.S. in Engring., Davis and Elkins Coll., 1961; student N.J. Inst. Tech., 1976—; m. Elizabeth C. Bartholomew, June 14, 1969; 1 dau., Robyn Adair. Asst. to twp. engr. Twp. of Parsippany-Troy Hills, N.J., 1967-70; project engr., design engr., corporate environ. engr. Houdaille Constrn. Materials, Inc., Morristown, N.J., 1970-77; engr. Storch Engrs., Florham Park, N.J., 1977-78; asst. supt. ops. Montclair (N.J.) Water Bur., 1978—. Mem. Borough of Verona (N.J.) Environ. Council, 1975—. Served with U.S. Army, 1961-63. Licensed supt. and operator pub. water, sewage and water supply systems and treatment plants, N.J. Mem. Am. Pub. Health Assn., Air Pollution Control Assn., Water Pollution Control Fedn., Nat. Solid Wastes Mgmt. Assn., Am. Chem. Soc. Republican. Presbyterian. Office: 54 Watchung Ave Montclair NJ 07043

ENGLUND, ROY EMIL, orthopedic surgeon; b. Trail, B.C., Can., Feb. 10, 1937; s. John Emil and Signe Marie (Anderson) E.; M.D., Dalhousie U. (Can.), 1967; m. Dianne Geraldine Belmore, Dec. 31, 1965; children—Sonja Marie, Kristel Deanna, Leif Erik. Rotating intern Dalhousie U., 1966-67; resident Victoria Gen. Hosp., Halifax, N.S., Can., 1969-72; practice medicine specializing orthopedic surgery, Halifax 1973—; mem. staff Halifax Infirmary Hosp., Camp Hill Hosp., I.W.K. Hosp. for Children, Halifax Civic Hosp.; asst. prof. dept. surgery Dalhousie U., 1973—. Served with M.C., Canadian Armed Forces, 1967-70. Fellow Royal Coll. Surgeons (Can.), A.C.S.; mem. Canadian Med. Assn., N.S. Med. Soc., Candian Sports Medicine Assn. Clubs: Ashburn Golf, Halifax Curling. Home: 33 Fleming Dr Halifax NS B3P 1A8 Canada Office: 5303 Morris St Halifax NS B3J 2H6 Canada

ENGRAM, THOMAS JAMES, coll. dean; b. Sewanee, Tenn., Apr. 20, 1950; s. W. Thomas and Irene Edith (Pope) E.; B.A., Boston U., 1972; M.Ed., U. Md., 1976. Dir. orientation Boston U., 1970-72; residence hall dir., coordinator spl. groups and housing U. Md., College Park, 1972-76; dean student affairs Widener Coll., Chester, Pa., 1977—. Mem. Am., Pa. personnel and guidance assns., Eastern Deans and Advisers of Students Assn., Nat. Assn. Student Personnel Adminstrs. (del.), Am. Assn. Higher Edn., Am. Coll. Personnel Assn. Episcopalian. Mem. adv. council United Way. Office: Office Student Affairs Widener Coll Chester PA 19013

ENHORNING, NORMAN ARTHUR, educator, historian; b. Waterbury, Conn., Sept. 24, 1936; s. Arthur and Doris (Miller) E.; B.A., U. Conn., 1958, M.A., 1959; Ph.D., Rutgers U., 1970; m. Mary O'Donnell, Dec. 26, 1966; 1 dau., Christine. Tchr. history Wappingers High Sch., Wappingers Falls, N.Y., 1959-62; teaching asst. history Rutgers U., New Brunswick, N.J., 1962-64; instr. Adirondack Community Coll., Glens Falls, N.Y., 1964-68, asst. prof., 1968-71, asso. prof., 1971-74, prof., 1974—, chmn. social sci., 1968—. Pres. Washington County Hist. Soc., Hudson Falls, N.Y., 1970-72, trustee, 1972—. Named Tchr. of Year Adirondack Community Coll., 1976. Mem. Am. Hist. Assn., Soc. Am. Historians, Phi Beta Kappa. Democrat. Home: 7 Oakwood Dr Glens Falls NY 12801 Office: Bay Rd Glens Falls NY 12801

ENI, EMMANUEL UKWU, pathobiologist; b. Lagos, Nigeria, Nov. 30, 1935; s. Okoro Ukwu and Rose (Oji) E.; came to U.S., 1958, naturalized, 1970; B.S., Howard U., 1961, M.S., 1963; Sc.D., Johns Hopkins, 1967; m. Barbara J. Dow, Dec. 23, 1965; children—Emmanuel, Udobundu, Ayanna, Johari. Asst. prof. Atlanta U., 1968-69; asst. prof. Morehouse Coll., 1967-69; asst. prof. Bishop Coll., 1969-70; clin. asso. med. affairs Merck Sharp & Dohme Research Lab., Merck & Co., Rahway, N.J., 1970—; instr. Cornell Med. Sch., 1971-73. NSF fellow, 1968. Fellow Royal Soc. Tropical Medicine and Hygiene; mem. Am. Soc. Parasitologists, Am. Soc. Tropical Medicine and Hygiene. Methodist. Home: Paint Island Spring Rd Millstone NJ Office: Med Affairs Merck & Co 126 Lincoln St Rahway NJ 07065

ENKENHUS, KURT REINHOLD, aero. engr.; b. Alta., Can., Oct. 21, 1929; s. Laurits and Eldri (Lund) E.; came to U.S., 1958, naturalized, 1963; B.Sc., Queen's U., 1951, M.Sc., 1953; Ph.D., U. Toronto, 1957; m. Anna Chin, May 4, 1972. Chief aerodynamics div., then chief aerodynamics dept. Naval Ordnance Lab., White Oak, Md., 1961-67; prof. physics, head high enthalpy dept. Von Karman Inst. Fluid Dynamics, Brussels, 1967-70; staff Naval Surface Weapons Center, White Oak, 1971—, head math. dept., acting chief aeros. and hydroballistics, 1974-75, head flight measurements div., 1975-77, head nuclear effects div., 1978—; postgrad. lectr. mech. engring. Cath. U. Am., 1964-66. Recipient Meritorious Civilian Service award, U.S. Navy, 1966, Canadian Gov. Gen.'s medal, 1944, 51, medal in Physics, Queen's U., 1951. Mem. Am. Inst. Aeros. and Astronautics. Contbr. articles to profl. jours. Home: 1601 Rainbow Dr Silver Spring MD 20904 Office: Naval Surface Weapons Center White Oak Silver Spring MD 20910

ENOCH, KURT, book pub. cons.; b. Hamburg, Germany, Nov. 22, 1895; s. Oscar and Rosa (Neumann) E.; came to U.S., 1940, naturalized, 1947; student Friedrich Wilhelm U., Berlin, 1914-15; D. in Polit. Economy, Hamburg U., 1921; m. Hertha Rehse Frischman, Sept. 2, 1921 (dec. 1934); children—Ruth Enoch Gruenthal, Mirjam Enoch Stevens; m. 2d, Margaret M. Heineman, Mar. 24, 1937. Gen. mgr. then partner, propr. Gebrueder Enoch and Oscar Enoch Pub. Co., Hamburg, 1922-36; co-founder The Albatross Modern Continental Library, Hamburg, 1932; founder, dir. Continenta SRL Pub. Co., Paris, Enoch Ltd., London, 1936-40; book pub. cons., N.Y.C., 1940-42; v.p. Penguin Books, Inc. agy. of Penguin Books Ltd. of London, N.Y.C., 1942-45, pres., dir., 1945-47; pres., dir. New Am. Library, 1947-60; v.p., dir. Times Mirror Co., Los Angeles, also pres. book div., 1960-67; book pub. cons., 1967—; dir. Am. Book Pubs. Council, 1961-63; mem. U.S. Book Industry Del. to USSR, 1962; mem. Nat. Bd. of Nat. Book Com., Inc., 1968—; mem. Franklin Book Programs, Inc., 1965—, dir., 1960-65. Mem. nat. advisory council of Hampshire Coll., Amherst, N.H., 1970—. Served to lt., arty., German Army, World War I; served with French Army, 1940. Mem. Am. Inst. Graphic Arts, Pen Club. Home: 812 Fifth Ave New York City NY 10021 Office: 680 Fifth Ave New York City NY 10019

ENTERLINE, JAMES ROBERT, scientist; b. Salunga, Pa., June 29, 1932; s. Robert Andes and Mary Ebersole (Greenly) E.; B.S., Lebanon Valley Coll., 1954; postgrad. N.Y. U., 1955-57; m. Esther Terry Goldstein, Mar. 28, 1965. Planning engr. Western Electric Co., N.Y.C., 1957-59; chief systems scientist Systems Research Group, Gulton Industries, Mineola, N.Y., 1959-63; v.p. Fox Computer Services, N.Y.C., 1963-65; pres. Enterline Automation & Computing, N.Y.C., 1965—; leader Viking History Expedition, Greenland, 1968; independent researcher on Norse Discovery of Am., 1965—; lectr. Norse Explorations various univs., Smithsonian Inst. Served with USNR, 1953. Recipient Lebanon Valley Coll. Alumni Scholarship award, 1954. Mem. Soc. for History of Discoveries, IEEE, Assn. for Computing Machinery. Club: Explorers (fellow). Contbr. articles in field to profl. jours.; author: Design for an Iterative Parallel Computer, 1962; Systems Organization for a CDC-160 Computing Facility, 1962; Viking America, 1972. Address: 144 W 95 St New York City NY 10025

EPPERSON, JAMES ALLEN, III, educator; b. Salt Lake City, Sept. 17, 1931; s. James Allen and Phyllis (Hampton) E.; A.B., San Francisco State Coll., 1960; M.A., U. Calif., Berkeley, 1961, Ph.D., 1966; m. Karen Louisa Read, Mar. 3, 1956; children—Jane, Ann. Asso. U. Calif., Berkeley, 1961-64; instr. Dartmouth Coll., 1964-66, asst. prof., 1966-71, asso. prof. English, 1971—; dir. Dartmouth Alumni Coll., 1975-78. Served with Utah N.G., 1950-52. Dartmouth Faculty fellow, 1968-69. Mem. Renaissance Soc. Am. Author: The King Lear Experience, 1976. Home: Turnpike Rd Norwich VT 05055 Office: Dartmouth Coll 212 Sanborn House Hanover NH 03755

EPPES, WILLIAM DAVID, civic worker, author; b. Goodwater, Ala., Mar. 4, 1918; s. Talmadge Dewitt and Annie Lou (McCord) E.; A.B., Coll. of William and Mary, 1939; B.S. in L.S., George Peabody Coll., 1940; M.A., N.Y. U., 1959. Reference asst. Newark Public Library, 1940-42, George Washington U., 1943-45; reference asst. Calif. State U., San Francisco, 1945-46; head stack personnel Butler Library, Columbia U., N.Y.C., 1954-58; asso. prof. Kean (N.J.) State Coll., 1958-61; asst. librarian Cooper Union, N.Y.C., 1961-70. Founder, Film Classics League, St. Petersburg, Fla., 1950; co-founder Littlebury Eppes Meml. Library, Westover Church, Va., 1976; bd. dirs. St. Petersburg Symphony Orch., 1950-54; mem. exec. bd. Assn. Village Homeowners, N.Y.C., 1969—, Assos. of Earl Gregg Swem Library, Coll. William and Mary, 1973—. Mem. Theatre Hist. Soc. (research and reference com. 1977—), Hist. Assn. So. Fla., Soc. Four Arts, Soc. Descs. Francis Epes I of Va. Corr., Mus. America, 1950-52. Author: The Empire Theatre (1893-1953), 1978; contbr. articles to mags. and hist. jours. Home: 68 Bedford St New York City NY 10014 also 34 Almeria Ave Coral Gables FL 33134

EPPLEY, ROLAND RAYMOND, JR., fin. services exec.; b. Balt., Apr. 1, 1932; s. Roland Raymond and Verna (Garretson) E.; B.A., Johns Hopkins, 1952, M.A., 1953; m. Le Verne Pittman; children—Kim, Kent, Todd. Asst. chief data processing, Bethlehem Steel Co., Balt., 1958-62; pres., dir. Comml. Credit Computer Corp., Balt., 1962-68, Central Info. Processing Corp., Balt., 1968-71, Eastern States Bankcard Assn., Inc., Lake Success, N.Y., 1971—, Omniswitch Corp., Lake Success, 1973—, Nataswitch Corp., Atlanta, 1973—, Eastern States Monetary Services, 1977—, Eastern States Data Services, 1977—; adj. prof. St. Johns U., 1977—. Mem. adv. bd. St. Johns U., 1973—; bd. govs. Served with USCG, 1953-55. Mem. Am. Mgmt. Assn., Data Processing Mgmt. Assn., Electronic Funds Transfer Assn. (chmn. bd. 1978—, bd. govs.), Interbank Card Assn. N.Y. (ops. com.), Assn. for Systems Mgmt., Presidents Assn., Mensa, Phi Beta Kappa, Omicron Delta Epsilon, Beta Gamma Sigma, Sigma Phi Epsilon. Republican. Clubs: Met., Madison Sq. Garden, Masons, Shriners', Hillendale Country, Plandome Country (bd. govs.). Home: 77 Westgate Blvd Plandome NY 11030 Office: 4 Ohio Dr Lake Success NY 11042

EPSTEIN, BENJAMIN ROBERT, assn. exec.; b. N.Y.C., June 11, 1912; s. Hyman and Sadie (Ziess) E.; Ph.B. cum laude, Dickinson Coll., 1933; exchange fellow Inst. Internat. Edn., U. Berlin, 1934-35; traveling fellow U. Pa., 1934, 38, M.A., 1936; LL.D., Talladega Coll., 1957; L.H.D., Dickinson Coll., 1963; m. Ethel Schwartz, Oct. 21, 1935; children—Ellen, David. Instr. German, U. Pa., 1935-36; faculty Coatesville (Pa.) High Sch., 1936-38; staff N.Y. Fedn. Jewish Charities, 1938; staff Anti-Defamation League of B'nai B'rith, 1939-44, dir. Eastern region, 1944-47, nat. dir., 1947—, nat. commr., 1956—; translator. Mem. Bur. Intercultural Edn. (dir.), Nat. Assn. Intergroup Relations Officers, Assn. Jewish Community Relations Workers, Phi Epsilon Pi. Clubs: Harmonie, Friars, B'nai B'rith. Author: The Troublemakers (with Arnold Forster), 1952; Germany—Nine Years Later (with Jacob Alson and Nathan C. Belth); Crosscurrents (with Arnold Forster), 1956; (with Arnold Forster) Some of My Best Friends . . . . . 1962, Danger on the Right, 1964, The Radical Right: Report on the John Birch Society and Its Allies, 1967; (with Arnold Forster) The New Anti-Semitism, 1974. Home: 411 E 53d St New York City NY 10022 Office: 315 Lexington Ave New York City NY 10016

EPSTEIN, BURTON IRWIN, orthodontist; b. Bklyn., Mar. 4, 1933; s. Samuel and Celia (Levy) E.; B.A. magna cum laude, Washington Sq. Coll., 1954; D.D.S. (N.Y. State scholar), N.Y. U., 1957, certificate orthodontics, 1964; m. Elaine Gleicher, Jan. 26, 1958; children—Kenneth, Michael, Susan. Practice dentistry, specializing in orthodontics, Bklyn., 1965-73, Huntington, N.Y., 1969—; attending orthodontist No. Dispensary, N.Y.C., 1964—. Mem. Oral Hygiene Com. Greater N.Y., 1957-65. Bd. advisers East Midwood Jewish Center, 1970. Served to capt., Dental Corps, AUS, 1957-59. Recipient Herbert Hendricks Meml. award, 1954; C.V. Mosby scholar, 1957; recipient N.Y. U. Founders Day award, 1957; diplomate Am. Bd. Orthodontics. Mem. N.Y. U. Orthodontic Soc., Am. Assn. Orthodontists, Northeastern Soc. Orthodontists, Am. Dental Assn., Internat. Assn. Study Dento-Facial Abnormalities, 2d Dist. Dental Soc. (past chmn. sect. preventive orthodontics and dentistry for children), Alpha Omega, Omicron Kappa Upsilon. Club: Century of N.Y U. Coll. Dentistry. Student editor N.Y.U. Jour. Dentistry, 1957. Co-editor-in-chief Dental Violet, 1957. Home: 10 Grouse Ln Lloyd Harbor NY 11743 Office: 124 Main St Huntington NY 11743

EPSTEIN, DAVID WEISS, dentist; b. Indpls., Oct. 16, 1941; s. Maurice Irving and Ruby Bendett (Weiss) E.; student (Alumni scholar), U. Wis., 1959-62; A.B., Ind. U., 1964, D.D.S., 1968, M.S. in Dentistry (Ind. U. Found. fellow), 1970; m. Cheryl Sarah Shmalo, Aug. 9, 1969; children—Michelle Lorie, Jason William. Asst. prof. pediatric dentistry U. Conn., 1970-72, asso. clin. prof., 1970—; pvt. practice pediatric dentistry, West Hartford, Conn., 1972—. Mem. Am. Acad. Pedodontics, Am. Soc. Dentistry for Children, Am., Conn. dental assns., Hartford Dental Soc., Conn. Soc. Dentistry for Children (exec. bd. 1972-73), Pi Lambda Phi, Alpha Omega. Contbr. articles to profl. jours. Home: 1032 Mountain Rd Bloomfield CT 06002 Office: 345 N Main St West Hartford CT 06117

EPSTEIN, EDWARD GEORGE, mktg. research co. exec.; b. N.Y.C., Mar. 29, 1936; s. Samuel and Mary (Neiderman) E.; B.A., Hunter Coll., 1957; M. B.A. (grantee), Columbia, 1959; m. Phyllis Gorin, June 28, 1958; children—Jeffrey Stuart, Sheryl Lynn, Brian David. Asso. research dir. J. Walter Thompson, N.Y.C., 1966-68; dir. mktg. services J. B. Williams Co., N.Y.C., 1969-70; pres. Action Research Centers, N.Y.C., 1970-71; pres., prin. Edward Epstein & Assos., Inc., Syosset, N.Y., 1971—; dir. Knechtel Research Scis., Skokie, Ill.; lectr. on mktg. research C. W. Post for Small Bus. Inst. Mem. religious sch. bd. North Shore Synagogue; co-chmn. Social Action Com.; v.p. Sysosset-Jericho Democratic Club; committeeman, Dem. party. Served with USAF, 1959. Mem. Am. Mktg. Assn., Civil Liberties Union (dir. Nassau County), Phi Beta Kappa, Beta Gamma Sigma. Home: 140 Split Rock Rd Syosset NY 11791 Office: 40 Underhill Blvd Syosset NY 11791

EPSTEIN, HOWARD ALAN, cosmetic chemist; b. Oceanside, N.Y., Oct. 28, 1951; s. Milton and Edna (Stein) E.; B.A. in Natural Scis., Hofstra U., 1973; M.S. in Microbiology, L.I. U., 1979; m. Lu Ellen Holcombe, Sept. 9, 1977. Asst. to dir. tech. services internat. Estee Lauder Cosmetics Co., Melville, N.Y., 1973—. Mem. Soc. Cosmetic Chemists, Am. Soc. Microbiology. Home: 2007 Salisbury Park Dr Westbury NY 11590 Office: 350 S Service Rd Melville NY 11746

EPSTEIN, MILTON A., lawyer; b. Newark, Nov. 14, 1912; s. Julius and Anna (Gomberg) E.; A.B., U. Pa., 1932; LL.B., Rutgers U., 1935; m. Violet J. Brown, Mar. 7, 1937; 1 son, Andrew M. Admitted to N.J. bar, 1935; mem. firm Epstein, Epstein, Brown, Bosek & Turndorf, Elizabeth, N.J.; counsel N.J. Credit Union League, 1948—, Met. Fed. Savs. & Loan Assn., Jersey City and Denville, N.J., 1948—. Trustee Temple B'nai Israel, Elizabeth, 1944——, pres. 1949-50. Recipient Distinguished Service award N.J. Savs. League, 1975, N.J. Credit Union Man of Year award, 1977. Mem. U.S. (attys. com. 1962—), N.J. (mem. attys. com. 1960—, chmn. 1965—) savs. and loan leagues, Am., N.J., Union County bar assns., Am. Acad. Polit. and Social Sci., U. Pa. Alumni Club (pres. N. Jersey 1964-65; chmn. Secondary Sch. com. 1961-64). Mason (Shriner). Home: 600 Union Ave Elizabeth NJ 07201 Office: 33 W Grand St Elizabeth NJ 07202

EPSTEIN, MORTON, physician; b. Newark, June 28, 1925; s. Samuel and Bertha E.; B.A., N.Y.U., 1947, M.D., 1951; m. Barbara Ann Decher, July 26, 1957; children—Karen, David, Rachel. Intern, Newark City Hosp., 1951-52, resident, 1952-53; resident N.Y.U., 1953-57, Montefiore Hosp., N.Y.C., 1957-58; individual practice medicine, specializing in internal medicine East Orange, N.J., 1958—; clin. asso. prof. medicine N.J. Coll. Medicine and Dentistry, Newark, 1975—; dir. cardiology United Hosps. Newark, 1970—, asso. chief staff, 1974—. Served with U.S. Army, 1943-45. Diplomate Am. Bd. Internal Medicine. Mem. N.J., Essex County, med. socs., AMA, A.C.P. Club: Practitioners Newark. Home: 42 S Crescent St Maplewood NJ 07040 Office: 109 S Munn Ave East Orange NJ 07018

EPSTEIN, PAUL ELLIOTT, physician; b. Lynn, Mass., Nov. 20, 1940; s. Morris E. and Marion W. (Weinstein) E.; B.A., Princeton U., 1962; M.D., Tufts U., 1966; m. Marcia Goldschlager, June 12, 1966; children—Amy, Robin. Intern, U. Chgo., 1966-67, resident in internal medicine, 1967-69; fellow in pulmonary disease U. Pa., Phila., 1969-71; dir. clin. pulmonary training program U. Pa., Phila., 1973—. Served to maj., M.C., USAF, 1971-73. Decorated Air Force Commendation Medal. Recipient Pulmonary Acad. award, Nat. Heart-Lung Inst., 1977. Diplomate Am. Bd. Internal Medicine (sec. pulmonary subspecialty com. 1976—). Mem. Am. Thoracic Soc. Asso. editor Annals Internal Medicine, 1978—. Home: 19 Cohasset Ln Cherry Hill NJ 08003 Office: 3600 Spruce St Philadelphia PA 19104

EPSTEIN, RAYMOND, engring. and archtl. exec.; b. Chgo., Jan. 12, 1918; s. Abraham and Janet (Rabinowitz) E.; student Mass. Inst. Tech., 1934-36; B.S., U. Ill., 1938; m. Betty Jadwin, Apr. 7, 1940; children—Gail, David, Norman, Harriet. With A. Epstein Cos., Inc., Chgo., 1938—, chmn. bd., 1961—. Past pres. Young Men's Jewish Council, Jewish Welfare Fund Met. Chgo.; dir. United Israel Appeal; mem. housing com. Mayor's Commn. Sr. Citizens; pres. Nat. Council Jewish Fedn. and Welfare Funds, Inc.; chmn. bd. dirs. Jewish United Fund; mem. exec. com. United Jewish Appeal; bd. govs. Jewish Agy. Trustee Chgo. Med. Sch.; mem. citizens bd. Loyola U.; life dir. Mt. Sinai Med. Research Found.; bd. govs. Jewish Agy.; bd. dirs. Israel Devel. Corp. Registered architect; registered profl. engr. Mem. ASCE, Soc. Am. Registered Architects, Am. Concrete Inst., dir. Yale Rep., 1972-73, asso. dir., 1973—; acting tchr. Yale Drama Sch., 1968—; mem. faculty Salzburg Am. Seminar, 1972. Bd. dirs. Theatre Communications Group, N.Y.C., 1975—. Served with U.S. Army, 1943-46; ETO. Recipient Obie award for Dynamite Tonite, 1968, Brandeis U. Creative Arts award in theatre, 1966. Ford Found. grantee, 1959-60. Fellow Trumbull Coll., Yale. Co-founder, actor Berkshire Theatre Festival, Stockbridge, Mass., 1966, playing Antrobus in Skin of Our Teeth, Shylock in Merchant of Venice, dir. Colette, 1974. Home: 129 Good Hill Rd Oxford CT 06483 Office: Yale Repertory Theatre 222 York St New Haven CT 06520*

EPSTEIN, SARAH GUNY, library media specialist; b. Providence; d. Maurice and May (Guny) Epstein; student R.I. Coll. Edn., 1943-45, U. Miami, Coral Gables, Fla., 1955; B.A., U. R.I., 1957; M.L.S., Pratt Inst., 1958. Asst., catalog dept. Providence Pub. Library, 1946-55; library media specialist George J. West Middle Sch., Providence, 1958—. Mem. ALA, New Eng. Ednl. Media Assn., R.I. Sch. Media Assn. (treas. 1963-65), R.I. Library Assn., Pratt Inst. Grad. Library Sch. Alumni Assn. Jewish religion. Home: 36 Lincoln Ave Providence RI 02906 Office: 145 Beaufort St Providence RI 02908

EPSTEIN, SEYMOUR GERALD, assn. exec.; b. Trenton, Oct. 11, 1935; s. Norton and Ida (Baran) E.; B.S. (Ford Found. scholar), Lafayette Coll., 1955; M.S., Iowa State U., 1958; m. Margery Ann Pitasky, Aug. 9, 1955; children—Bruce, Jeffrey, Sharon. Research asso. Ames Lab., 1955-58, chemist, 1958; prin. metallurgist Battelle Meml. Inst., Columbus, Ohio, 1958-60; asso. metallurgist Brookhaven Nat. Lab., Upton, N.Y., 1961-69; tech. dir. Aluminum Assn., Washington, 1969—. Mem. Am. Soc. Metals (past chmn.), ASTM, Nat. Safety Council (exec. com. metals sect.), Am. Soc. Nondestructive Testing (chmn. aluminum producers com. 1970-74), Am. Inst. Mining, Metall. and Mining Engrs. Contbr. to profl. jours. Home: 11706 Stonington Pl Silver Spring MD 20902 Office: 818 Connecticut Ave NW Washington DC 20006

EPSTEIN, STANLEY WINSTON, physician, educator; b. Sydney, N.S., Can., Dec. 2, 1937; s. Maxwell and Etta Rose (Green) E.; M.D., Dalhousie U., Halifax, N.S., 1962; m. Paula Rivka Epstein, Mar. 21,

1965; children—Eric Martin, Cheryl Rae, Ian Leonard. Jr. rotating intern Victoria Gen. Hosp., Halifax, 1961-62; sr. intern in internal medicine Sunnybrook Hosp., Toronto, Ont., 1962-63, asst. resident in internal medicine, 1963-64; research fellow in allergy immunology Toronto Western Hosp., U. Toronto, 1964-65; asst. resident in internal medicine Toronto Western Hosp., 1965-66, asst. resident in pathology, 1966; sr. house physician chest disease Brompton Hosp., London, Eng., 1967; hon. research asst. respiratory physiology Postgrad. Med. Sch., Hammersmith Hosp., London, 1967-68; asso. dept. medicine U. Toronto, 1968-71, asst. prof., 1971—; chest physician, active attending staff Toronto Western Hosp., 1968—. Served with RCAF, 1957-66. Fellow Royal Coll. Physicians Can., Am. Coll. Chest Physicians; mem. Canadian, Ont. med. assns., Canadian, Ont., Am. thoracic socs., Canadian Soc. Allergy Clin. Immunology, Am. Acad. Allergy. Jewish. Office: 25 Leonard Ave Suite 407 Toronto ON Canada

ERB, ROBERT ALLAN, phys. scientist; b. Ridley Park, Pa., Jan. 30, 1932; s. John Walter and Roma (Chapman) E.; B.S. in Chemistry, U. Pa., 1953; M.S., Drexel Inst. Tech., 1959; Ph.D., Temple U., 1965; m. Doretta Louise Barker, June 27, 1953; children—Sylvia Ann, Susan Doretta, Carolyn Joy. Chemist, Gates Engring. Co., Wilmington, Del., 1953-54; with research labs. Franklin Inst., Phila., 1954—, sr. staff chemist, 1965-68, prin. scientist, 1968—. Mem. Am. Chem. Soc., A.A.A.S., Soc. Rheology, Soc. Plastics Engrs., Internat. Solar Energy Soc., Sigma Xi. Presbyn. Inventor contraceptive systems, solar collectors, permanent systems for dropwise condensation. Home: Jug Hollow Rd PO Box 86 Valley Forge PA 19481 Office: Franklin Inst 20th and The Parkway Philadelphia PA 19103

ERB, TIMOTHY JOHN, guidance counselor; b. Phila., Aug. 12, 1948; s. John James and Eleanor Marie (Booth) E.; B.A. in Psychology, LaSalle Coll., 1970; M.A. in Secondary Sch. Counseling, Villanova U., 1976; m. Joann M. Kelly, May 5, 1973; children—Timothy, Gregory. Tchr. English and social studigs Archbishop Wood High Sch., Warminster, Pa., 1970-75, asst. football coach, 1970-75, guidance counselor, 1975-76, guidance dir., 1976—; asst. football coach Villanova U., 1976—. Certified counselor, Pa. Mem. Am. Personnel and Guidance Assn., Pa., Bucks County sch. counselors assns., Assn. Catholic Tchrs., Am. Football Coaches Assn. Roman Catholic. Club: K.C. Home: 538 Schoolhouse Ln Willow Grove PA 19090 Office: 675 York Rd Warminster PA 18974

ERBE, GARY THOMAS, artist; b. Union City, N.J., Sept. 2, 1944; s. Herman Charles and Florance (Bertone) E.; student pub. schs., Union City; m. Edny Lourdas Chinea, June 6, 1963; children—Kim, Chantell. One man shows Pace Gallery, Houston, 1970. Veldman Gallery, Milw., 1971, New Britain Mus. Am. Art, 1976, Summit (N.J.) Art Center, 1976; exhibited in group shows Newark Mus., 1971, Rutgers U., 1971, Heritage Gallery, N.Y.C., 1972, N.J. State Mus., 1972, 75; represented in permanent collection New Britain Mus. Am. Art. Recipient Julius Hallgarten award NAD, 1975, Gold medal honor Allied Artists Am., N.Y.C., 1975, 1st award Salmagundi Club, N.Y.C., 1975. Mem. Allied Artists Am., Asso. Artists N.J., Salmagundi Club. Developed contemporary approach to Am. Trompe l'oeil called Levitational Realism, and extended this sch. to 3 dimensional compositions, oil on bronze. Office: 539 42d St Union City NJ 07087

ERES, EUGENIA, painter; b. Ucrania, USSR, Apr. 28, 1928; d. Vasily and Maria (Nosikow) Kutusow; student Sao Paulo (Brazil) Fine Art Sch., 1954-58, Famous Artists Sch., Westport, Conn., 1966-69, Nat. Acad. Fine Arts, N.Y.C., 1970-71; m. Ivan Eres, Nov. 24, 1945; children—Ari, Walter, Luba. One-woman exhbns.: Gal. de Artes IV Centenario, Brazil, 1957-58, Ucranian Art and Lit. Club, N.Y.C., 1963, Panoras Gallery, N.Y.C., 1970, Bronxville Library, N.Y., 1970; group exhbns.: Exposition Intercontinentale, Monaco, 1969, Hammond Mus., N.Y., 1968, NAD, N.Y.C., 1971, Grand Nat., Am. Artists Profl. League, 1968-78, Salmagundi Club, N.Y.C., 1977-78; represented in permanent collection Am. Russian Mus., also pvt. collections. Recipient Oscar award Gallerie de IV Centenario, Sao Paulo, 1958; 1st prize Am. Russian Assn., 1975-78; Gold medal Nat. Art League, 1977; 1st prize Pen & Brush, 1977, 78; others. Mem. Am. Artists Profl. League, Nat. Art League, Hudson Valley Assn., Knickerbocker Artists, Catharine Lorillard Wolfe Art Club, Salmagundi Club, Pen and Brush. Greek Orthodox. Address: 84-21 108th St Richmond Hill NY 11418

ERGIN, MUCEDDIT TAHSIN, surgeon; b. Istanbul, Turkey, Feb. 22, 1927; s. Sabri and Hacer (Daryal) E.; came to U.S., 1954, naturalized, 1961; B.S., Trabzon Coll., Turkey, 1943; M.D., Istanbul U., 1950; m. Florence Roman, Aug. 24, 1957; children—Meliha Ellen, Tahsin Mark, Tarik John, Turhan Michael. Rotating intern J.J. McCook Hosp., Hartford, Conn., 1955-56, asst. resident in surgery, 1956, chief resident, 1956-57; resident in surgery Hartford Hosp., 1957-63; practice medicine specializing in surgery, Hartford, 1961—; mem. courtesy staff Hartford Hosp., 1961-63, clin. asst., 1963-65, asst., 1965-69, asso., 1969-76, sr., 1976—; clin. asso. U. Conn. Med. Sch., Farmington, 1976—. Served to lt. Turkish Air Force, 1950-52. Diplomate Am. Bd. Surgery. Fellow A.C.S.; mem. Pan Am., Conn., Hartford med. socs., Am. (dir. Hartford chpt.), New Eng. cancer socs., Hartford County Med. Assn., Internat. Soc. Lymphology, AAU. Clubs: Avon Country, City (Hartford). Contbr. articles to med. jours. Home: 97 Cliffmore Rd West Hartford CT 06107 Office: 85 Jefferson St Hartford CT 06106

ERICKSON, LOWELL LEROY, assn. exec.; b. International Falls, Minn., Mar. 18, 1931; s. Edwin E. and Evelyn (Wold) E.; A.B., Macalester Coll., 1953; student Harvard Law Sch., 1953; B.D., Yale, 1956; student U. St. Andrews (Scotland), 1960; L.H.D. (hon.), U. Dubuque (Ia.), 1968. Ordained to ministry, Congl. Ch., 1956; asso. minister Plymouth Congl. Ch., Mpls., 1956-60; exec. dir. United World Federalist of Midwest, Davenport, Ia., 1963-65, exec. dir. United World Federalists of New Eng., Boston, 1965-69. Exec. dir. Boston Soc. Architects, 1969—, elected hon. mem., 1976; exec. dir. Mass. State Assn. Architects. Profl. staff dir. Research for Congl. campaign Third Congl. Dist. Minn., 1958; arbitrator Div. Conciliation, State Minn., 1961. Bd. dirs. Mass. Half Way Houses, Inc., pres., 1973-76. Served to lt. USNR, 1962. Contbr. articles to mags., newspapers. Home: 36 Gray St Boston MA 02116 Office: 320 Newbury St Boston MA 02115

ERICSON, JOHN WILLIAMSON, lawyer; b. Washington, Nov. 8, 1927; s. George Robert and Mary (Ricker) E.; B.S., U. Ill., 1949; J.D., George Washington U., 1954; m. Susan Lee Kunce, Dec. 26, 1949 (div. 1971); children—George Magruder, Christine Merriweather, Douglas Tyree, Lars Warren; m. 2d, Virginia J. Ericson, Apr. 1, 1972; children—James Allen, June Marie. Examiner, U.S. Patent Office, Washington, 1950-55; admitted to D.C. bar, 1955, Mass. bar, 1960; patent atty. Union Switch & Signal div. Westinghouse Air Brake, Pitts., 1955-60; practiced in Boston, 1960—; asso. firm Kenway, Jenney & Hildreth, 1960-68; partner firm Rich & Ericson, 1968-71; patent atty. Polaroid Corp., Cambridge, Mass., 1971—. Mem. Am., Boston bar assns., Am., Boston patent law assns., Patent Office Soc., Order of Coif, Sigma Xi, Phi Alpha Delta, Tau Beta Pi, Phi Lambda Upsilon, Sigma Tau, Pi Mu Epsilon. Republican. Conglist. Patentee in computer field. Home: 174 Jersey St Marblehead MA 01945 Office: 545 Main St Cambridge MA 02139

ERICSON, KARL INGVAR, pump mfg. co. exec.; b. Stockholm, Feb. 10, 1936; s. Ragnar Karl and Margit I. (Nilsson) E.; Civ.Eng., Royal U. Engring., Stockholm, 1960; m. Kerstin Wangberg, June 19, 1960; children—Bengt, Eva. With DeLaval Co., 1960-62, Flygt Sweden, 1962-64, 67-76, Sonesson Pump Co., 1964-66; mktg. dir. Flygt USA, Norwalk, Conn., 1977—; tchr. mech. engring. Royal U., Sweden, 1960-73. Served with Swedish Army, 1955-57. Mem. Am. Soc. Swedish Engrs. Author articles in field. Home: 219 Wilton Rd Westport CT 06880 Office: 129 Glover Ave Norwalk CT 06856

ERIKSEN, EINAR ANTON, mech. engr.; b. Bklyn., June 10, 1921; s. Einar Bernard and Inga Emilia (Hansen) E.; B.S. in Mech. Engring., Worcester Poly. Inst., 1944; m. Peggy Eriksen, Dec. 5, 1959; children—Kim Elise, Carl Einar, Lisa Marie. Pres., Eriksen Bros., Inc., Valley Stream, N.Y., 1948-65; mgr. mfg. Automation Engring. Lab., Stamford, Conn., 1965-70, asst. v.p. mfg., 1970-72; plant mgr. Waldes Kohinoor, Inc., Long Island City, N.Y., 1972—. Pres., player agt. Valley Stream Little League, 1970—. Served with USNR, 1944-46. Registered profl. engr., Calif. Mem. ASME, Soc. Mfg. Engrs., Naval Res. Assn. Republican. Lutheran. Home: 59 E Saint Marks Pl Valley Stream NY 11580 Office: 47-16 Austel Pl Long Island City NY 11101

ERIM, KENAN TEVFIK, educator, archaeologist; b. Istanbul, Turkey, Feb. 13, 1929; s. Kerim Tevfik and Fahime (Osan) E.; came to U.S., 1947; student Coll. de Geneve, 1941-46; B.A., N.Y. U., 1953; M.A., Princeton, 1955, Ph.D., 1958. Vis. instr. Ind. U., 1957-58; asst. prof. N.Y. U., N.Y.C., 1958-62, asso. prof. classics, 1962-71, prof., 1971—, field dir. research project, 1961—; field dir. Aphrodisias excavations. Recipient Franklin L. Burr award Nat. Geog. Soc., 1973; citation Turkish Govt. com. for 50th Anniversary of Republic, 1973; Guggenheim fellow, 1961-62. Mem. Archaeol. Inst. Am., Royal Numis. Soc., Am. Schs. Oriental Research, Am. Oriental Soc., Turkish Hist. Soc. (corr.). Club: Explorers. Research in field. Home: 48 Nassau St Princeton NJ 08540

ERINAKES, DOROTHY MAY EDEN (MRS. PETER C.H. ERINAKES), educator; b. Pawtucket, R.I., Dec. 18, 1919; d. Richard William and Isabelle May (Pilblad) Eden; student Brown U., 1946; B.S., U. Conn., 1967, M.A., 1970, now postgrad. doctoral program; m. Peter C.H. Erinakes, July 10, 1972; children by previous marriage—Richard Lucius Trayner, Jr., Patricia Florence (Mrs. Hurt), Dorothy Eden (Mrs. Neumann), William Wesgarth, Trayner, Sarah-Anne Eliza Trayner. Tchr., Preston (Conn.) Sch., 1967-70; coordinator spl. edn. town of Preston, 1969-70; tchr. Lisbon (Conn.) Central Sch., 1970-71; resource room tchr. Donald Kramer Sch., Willimantic, Conn., 1971-72, Nelson Aldrich Sch., Warwick, R.I., 1972—. Served dir. workshops Conn. Coll., Annhurst (Conn.) Coll., 1971. Active 4-H Clubs; mem. Nat. P.T.A. Named Miss New Eng., 1935, Miss R.I., 1937. Mem. Council Exceptional Children, Am. Assn. Mental Deficiency, Delta Kappa Gamma. Home: 311 Love Lane Warwick RI 02886*

ERNST, JAMES WALTER, glass mfg. co. exec.; b. Toledo, July 11, 1936; s. Walter Herman and Theresa Clara (Roszak) E.; B.B.A., U. Toledo, 1959, M.B.A. (Page scholar), 1963; m. Rhua Heckart, Apr. 4, 1970; children—Ronald Bruce, Erik Bernard. Spl. accounts rep. Standard Register Co., Toledo, 1959-63; br. mgr. Owens-Ill. Inc., 1963-67, nat. chain store mgr., 1967-68, mgr. design services, 1968-70, Eastern regional mgr., 1970-74; gen. sales mgr. J.G. Durand Internat., Millville, N.J., 1975-76; gen. sales mgr. Interpace Corp., Parsippany, N.J., 1976; v.p. mktg. and design services Wheaton Industries, Millville, 1976-77; v.p. mktg. Stangl Pottery div. Dorchester Industries, Millville, 1976-77; v.p., gen. mgr. Wheaton Consumer Products div. Wheaton Industries Millville, 1977—. Pres., Cumberland County Democratic Com. Mem. Am. Mgmt. Assn., Am. Mktg. Assn., Sigma Alpha Epsilon. Mormon. Home: RD #7 Bridgeton Ave Bridgeton NJ 08302 Office: Wheaton Ave Millville NJ 08332

ERNST, JOHN GILBERT, bus. exec.; b. Balt., Apr. 9, 1929; s. Charles and Mary Henrietta E.; student U. Md., 1954-57; m. Nancy Lucille Deuterman, Apr. 23, 1949; 1 son, David Michael. Sr. buyer Martin Marietta, Middle River, Md., 1958-63; purchasing agt. Fairchild Industries, Germantown, Md., 1963-70; procurement mgr. Comsat Lab., Clarksburg, Md., 1970—. Served with U.S. Army, 1952-54. Certified purchasing mgr. Nat. Assn. Purchasing Mgmt. Mem. Greater Balt. Minority Purchasing Council (dir.), Purchasing Mgmt. Assn. Balt. (dir.). Club: Ventnor Yacht. Home: PO Box 68A Ijamsville MD 21754 Office: 22300 Comsat Dr Clarksburg MD 20734

ERNSTROM, EDWARD KENNETH, govt. ofcl.; b. Essex County, N.J., Dec. 17, 1942; s. Karl Einar and Elsie Ingeborg (Kindmark) E.; student Stevens Inst. Tech., 1960-61; B.S.C.E. cum laude, Newark Coll. Engring., 1966; grad. Indsl. Coll. Armed Forces, 1977; m. Pamela Ross Gwilliam, Nov. 6, 1965; 1 dau., Kristina Lynn. Commd. san. engr. officer USPHS, 1966, regional water supply cons., N.Y.C., 1968-69; project engr. Pandullo, Chrisbacher, Price Assos., Totowa, N.J., 1969-70, Elam & Popoff, Glen Rock, N.J., 1970; chief Office Emergency Ops. and Planning, U.S. EPA, N.Y.C., 1972-74; regional rep. Fed. Preparedness Agy., GSA, N.Y.C., 1974-78, acting regional dir., 1978—. Trustee, treas. Montville Twp. Pub. Library. Recipient Meritorious Performance citation USPHS, 1969; Certificate of award EPA, 1972; Exceptional Service citation Fed. Preparedness Agy., 1978; I.A.E.S.T.E. Engring. Exchange appointment to Swedish Hwy. and Water Adminstrn., 1964. Mem. Am. Water Works Assn., Am. Soc. Swedish Engrs. Club: Vasa Order Am. Contbr. articles to profl. publs. Home: RD 1 Towaco NJ 07082 Office: 26 Federal Plaza New York City NY 10007

ERTEL, ALLEN EDWARD, congressman; b. Williamsport, Pa., Nov. 7, 1936; s. Clarence Valentine and Helen Kathleen (Froehner) E.; B.A., Dartmouth U., 1958, M.S., 1959; LL.B., Yale U., 1965; m. Catharine Bieber Klepper, June 20, 1959; children—Taylor John, Edward Barnhardt, Amy Sara. Admitted to Pa. bar, 1965, also Del., U.S. Supreme Ct. bars; clk. to chief judge Fed. Ct., Wilmington, Del., 1965-66; asso. firm Candor, Youngman, Gibson & Gault, Williamsport, 1968-72; dist. atty. Lycomong County (Pa.), 1968-76; partner firm Ertel & Kieser, Williamsport, 1972-76; mem. 95th-96th Congresses from 17th Pa. Dist. Served with USN, 1959-62. Mem. Dartmouth Soc. Engrs. Democrat. Club: Lions. Home: RFD 2 Box 145 Montoursville PA 17754 Office: 1019 Longworth House Office Bldg Washington DC 20515*

ERTELL, MERTON WILLIAM, univ. adminstr.; b. Buffalo, Jan. 31, 1918; s. William F. and Caroline D. (Meurer) E.; B.S., U. Buffalo, 1938, M.B.A., 1949; Ph.D., U. Chgo., 1955; m. Agnes A. Black, Nov. 20, 1940; children—Carolyn Anne, Richard M. Accountant Chevrolet div. Gen. Motors Corp., 1938-41; sr. bus. specialist OPA, 1941-43; exec. officer Statis. Control Office, Hdqrs. 4th Air Force, USAAF, 1943-46; asst. dean Sch. Bus. Adminstrn., State U. N.Y. at Buffalo (formerly U. Buffalo), 1946-55, asst. vice chancellor for ednl. affairs, 1955-58, asso. prof. econs. and indsl. relations, dean Univ. Coll., 1958-60, Melvin H. Baker prof. Am. enterprise, 1961-69, asst. v.p. ednl. affairs, dir. instnl. studies, 1961-65, acting v.p. acad. affairs, 1974-75; prof. mgmt., 1975—; vice chancellor for univ. wide activities State U. N.Y., 1969-70, dep. vice chancellor, 1970-73, asso. chancellor spl. projects, 1973-74; co-ordinator inter-instnl. coop. research project N.Y. State Edn. Dept., 1957; staff dir. Ill. Gov.'s Commn. to Study Non-Public Higher Edn., 1968-69. Mem. exec. bd. Buffalo area council Boy Scouts Am. Mem. Buffalo Area C. of C. (chmn. econ. affairs com.), Am. Econ. Assn., Econometric Soc., Indsl. Relations Research Assn., AAUP, Buffalo Council Chs., Beta Gamma Sigma, Alpha Phi Omega, Alpha Kappa Psi. Presbyterian (pres. bd. trustees, mem. gen. council; moderator Presbytery Western N.Y. 1967). Home: 308 Old Meadow East Amherst NY 14051 Office: State U NY Buffalo NY 14214

ERUMSELE, ANDREW AKHIGBE, policy analyst; b. Auchi, Nigeria, Nov. 18, 1944; s. Erumsele Bello and Itete (Isadoh) Iyoke; came to U.S., 1966, naturalized, 1971; B.A. cum laude, Loyola U., Los Angeles, 1969; M.P.A. (Univ. scholar, Nigerian Govt. scholar), U. Calif., Los Angeles, 1971; M.A., Am. U., 1974; postgrad. U. So. Calif., 1976-77; m. Mary Catherine Wimbley, Dec. 6, 1969; 1 son, Uwadia Alexis. Leadership fellow Los Angeles County Planning Commn., 1969-70; research fellow UN Inst. for Tng. and Research, 1970; mem. staff U.S. Congl. Commn. on Reorgn. of D.C. Govt., 1972-73; mgmt. and policy analyst U. D.C., Washington, 1973—; cons. Internat. City Mgmt. Assn., Orgn. of African Unity, Inst. for Pub. Adminstrn. Recipient Hall of Nations award Am. U., Washington, 1972. Mem. Am. Soc. for Pub. Adminstrn., Acad. Polit. Sci., Soc. for Internat. Devel., Am. Soc. for Internat. Law, Pi Gamma Mu. Democrat. Moslem. Spl. corr. for various African newspapers. Office: PO Box 39067 Washington DC 20016

ERWAY, CHARLES ALBERT, engring. corp. exec.; b. Wellsboro, Pa., Mar. 12, 1922; s. Charles Fay and Mildred Seely (Lent) E.; B.M.E., Cooper Union Sch. Engring., 1943; postgrad. Stevens Inst. Tech., U. Pitts., 1945-46; m. Helen Lehto, Mar. 4, 1945; children—Leslie J. Erway Wright, Wendy M., Alison H., Tracey M. With power plant design and startup, Ebasco Services, N.Y.C., 1946-53; staff Peter F. Loftus Corp., Pitts., 1965-70; project engr., power projects for industry and govt., including atomic plant under ice cap, Greenland, 1968-70; designer paper mill power plants, Rust Engring. Co., Pitts., 1960-64; cons. engr., pres. Erway Engring. Co., McMurray, Pa., 1971—. Mem. Peters Twp. Sch. Bd., 1966-78, pres., 1974, 76, 77; mem. C. of C. Registered profl. engr., N.Y., Pa., W.Va., Ohio. Mem. Nat. Soc. Profl. Engrs., ASME (bd. dirs., Pitts., 1965-70), Engrs. Soc. Western Pa. Republican. Presbyterian. Home: Church Hill Rd Venetia PA 15367 Office: 203 S Washington Rd McMurray PA 15317

ESAKI, LEO, physicist; b. Osaka, Japan, Mar. 12, 1925; s. Soichiro and Niyoko (Ito) E.; B.S., U. Tokyo, 1947, Ph.D., 1959; m. Masako Araki, Nov. 21, 1959; children—Nina Yvonne, Anna Eileen, Eugene Leo. Came to U.S., 1960. With Sony Corp., Japan, 1956-60; with Thomas J. Watson Research Center, IBM, Yorktown Heights, N.Y., 1960—, IBM fellow, 1967—, mgr. device research, 1965—; dir. IBM-Japan. Recipient Morris N. Liebmann Meml. prize IEEE, 1961; Stuart Ballantine medal Franklin Inst., 1961; Japan Acad. award, 1965; Nobel Prize in physics, 1973; decorated Order of Culture, Govt. of Japan, 1974. Fellow Am. Phys. Soc. (councillor-at-large 1971-74), IEEE, Japan Phys. Soc., Am. Vacuum Soc. (dir. 1973-74), Nat. Acad. Scis. (fgn. asso.), Nat. Acad. Engring. (fgn. asso.). Inventor tunnel diode, 1957. Home: 16 Shady Ln Chappaqua NY 10514 Office: Watson Research Center IBM PO Box 218 Yorktown Heights NY 10598

ESCALLÓN, MARION SCHMIDT, geologist; b. Chgo., July 25, 1912; d. Harry Logan and Helen (Fraser) Schmidt; B.A., U. Mich., 1933, postgrad., 1933-34; m. Carlos Escallón, June 7, 1941; children—Eduardo Carlos, Roberto Juan. Teaching asst., museum asst. dept. geology U. Mich. at Ann Arbor, 1933-34; asst. to chief geologist, translator Consol. (Sinclair) Oil Corp., N.Y.C., 1935-39; office mgr. in charge geology Tex. Petroleum Co., Bogotá, Colombia, 1939-41; asst. to chief geologist fgn. producing dept. Tex. Co., N.Y.C., 1941; geologist exploration dept. Am. Overseas Petroleum Ltd., N.Y.C., 1955-68; exploration analyst producing dept. eastern hemisphere Texaco, Inc., N.Y.C., 1969-77; cons. geologist, 1977—. Mem. Valhalla (N.Y.) High Sch. Curriculum Com. Secondary Edn., 1960. Active Republican primary campaigns, North White Plains, N.Y., 1961, 62. Bd. dirs. A.R.C., North Castle, 1961. Fellow AAAS; mem. Am. Assn. Petroleum Geologists (sec. Eastern sect. 1957-58; treas. 1958-59, 69-71), Soc. Petroleum Engrs. Am. Inst. Mining, Metall. and Petroleum Engrs. (dir. N.Y. sect. 1969-77), Am. Radio Relay League, Assn. Prof. Geol. Scientists, Communications Club New Rochelle (dir. 1970, 71). Home: 5 Dunlap Way North White Plains NY 10603

ESCAVA, NATHAN ISAAC, retail and wholesale exec.; b. Bklyn., Mar. 14, 1936; s. Isaac and Gladys E.; B.A., Bklyn. Coll., 1959; m. Joyce Goodstein, Sept. 18, 1960; children—Jodi, Helene. Pres., dir. Bunnie Shops, N.Y.C., 1965—, Caravelle Fashions, N.Y.C., 1975—. Vice-pres. Ahi Ezer Yeshiva. Mem. Hub Mchts. Assn. (Man of Year 1971, pres. 1972), East Side C. of C. (v.p. 1978-79). Republican. Jewish. Club: Manhattan South Lions (pres. 1978-79). Home: 196 S Barlow Dr Brooklyn NY 11234 Office: 100 Delancey St New York City NY 10002

ESCHEN, ALBERT HERMAN, optometrist; b. N.Y.C., Dec. 3, 1921; s. Samuel and Frances (Lazelle) E.; student Bklyn. Coll., 1940-42; D.Optometry, Ill. Coll. Optometry, 1948; postgrad. Am. Optometric Center, 1949; D.Ocular Sci. (hon.), Internat. Coll. Ocular Sci., 1956; m. Florence Askwyth, Nov. 22, 1950; children—Burt Steven, Andrew Mark. Pvt. practice optometry, Bklyn., 1950—; mem. staff N.Y.C. Dept. Health, 1962—, N.Y. City Health Ins. Program, 1964—, Crown Nursing Home, Bklyn., 1958—, Coronet Nursing Home, Bklyn., 1965—, Optometric Center, N.Y.C., 1960—. Cons. N.Y.C. Dept. Rehab. and Guidance, 1963—; dir. Brownsville Boys Club Optometry Clinic, 1965—; regional dir. N.E. area Ill. Coll. Optometry. Bd. dirs. E. N.Y. Mental Health Clinic, Bklyn. Served to cpl. USAAF, 1942-46. Recipient awards including Service award Bklyn. Optometric Soc., 1958. Fellow Internat. Coll. Ocular Sci.; mem. N.Y. State (mem. sub-normal vision com. 1967-68), Am. Optometric Assn., Bklyn. Optical Soc. (chmn. exec. bd. 1956-58), Ill. Coll. Optometry Alumni Assn. Clubs: Masons, Lions (charter mem.). Office: 2821 Ave U Brooklyn NY 11229

ESHLEMAN, SILAS KENDRICK, III, psychiatrist; b. Gainesville, Fla., June 28, 1928; s. Silas Kendrick and Aileen Hope (McClamroch) E.; B.S. with high honors, U. Fla., 1949; M.D., U. Pa., 1953; m. Judith Wills Cooper, July 3, 1954; 1 dau., Diane Elizabeth. Intern, Hosp. U. Pa., Phila., 1953-54; resident in psychiatry Norristown (Pa.) State Hosp., 1954-55, 57-59; practice medicine, specializing in psychiatry, Lancaster, Pa., 1959—; mem. med. staff St. Joseph Hosp., also chmn. dept. psychiatry; mem. med. staff Lancaster Gen. Hosp.; cons. VA Hosp., Lebanon, Pa. Served with M.C., U.S. Army, 1955-57. Diplomate Am. Bd. Psychiatry and Neurology. Fellow Am. Psychiat. Assn., Coll. Physicians of Phila.; mem. AMA, Pa. Med. Soc., Am., Pa. psychiat. assns., Phi Beta Kappa, Alpha Omega Alpha. Episcopalian.

Clubs: Torch, Lancaster Cliosophic Soc. Home: 1421 Marietta Ave Lancaster PA 17603 Office: 108 E Lemon St Lancaster PA 17602

ESKANDARIAN, EDWARD, advt. agy. exec.; b. Telford, Pa., Nov. 20, 1936; s. Michael and Katherine (Arslanian) E.; B.S. in Mech. Engring., Villanova U., 1958; M.B.A., Harvard U., 1965; m. Nancy R. Boujicanian, June 18, 1965; children—Wendy, Kristin, Jill. Vice pres., account supr. Compton Advt., N.Y.C., 1965-71; pres., dir. Humphrey Browning MacDougall, Boston, 1971—; instr. Babson Coll., 1972-73. Served with USAF, 1959-60. Mem. Am. Mktg. Assn., Am. Assn. Advt. Agys., New Eng. Broadcasters Assn., Ad Club Boston (pres.), Harvard Bus. Sch. Assn. Boston. Home: 21 Decatur Ln Wayland MA 01778 Office: 1 Beacon St Boston MA 02108

ESKENAZI, GERALD, journalist, author; b. N.Y.C., Sept. 12, 1936; s. Elias and Adella (Schneider) E.; B.A., Coll. City N.Y., 1975; m. Rosalind E. Gerszkop, Aug. 17, 1963; children—Ellen, Mark, Michael. With N.Y. Times, 1959—, reporter, 1963—; adj. asso. prof. English dept. and communications dept. St. John's U., Queens, N.Y., 1975-76, Adelphi U., Garden City, L.I., 1978—. Co-recipient pub. service reporting award Deadline Club, 1974; recipient award Ohio State U. Sch. of Journalism, 1965, 66, 67. Mem. Profl. Football Writers Assn., Profl. Hockey Writers Assn., Baseball Writers of Am., N.Y. Newspaper Guild. Jewish. Author: Hockey, 1969; A Year on Ice, 1970; A Thinking Man's Guide to Pro Hockey, 1972; (with Phil Esposito) Hockey Is My Life, 1972; The Derek Sanderson Nobody Knows, 1972; The Fastest Sport, 1974; There Were Giants in Those Days, 1977. Contbr. to encys. Home: 15 Reed Dr Roslyn NY 11576 Office: NY Times 229 W 43d St New York City NY 10036

ESKOW, ALEXANDER BERNARD, periodontist; b. Perth Amboy, N.J., Aug. 11, 1915; s. Isidor and Rose (Klein) E.; student Dana Coll., 1932-33; student N.Y. U., 1933-34, postgrad. Dental Sch., 1941; D.D.S., U. Md., 1938; m. Sylvia Teresa Abrams, Jan. 15, 1938; children—Ronald Stanley, Sandra Ann. Practice dentistry Med. Arts Bldg., Balt., 1939—; cons. dental staff Sinai Hosp., Balt., 1941—; asst. prof. dept. periodonology U. Md. Dental Sch., Balt., 1942-57. Treas., v.p. Overbrook Egg Nog Corp., Balt., 1958-76, pres., 1976—. Dir. Md. Crime Investigating Com., 1962—, pres., 1977—. Bd. visitors Morgan State Coll., bd. dirs. Talmudical Acad. Mem. Am., Md. State dental assns., Balt. City Dental Soc., Am. Acad. Periodontology, Oral Pathology, Dental Medicine, Internat. Assn. Dental Research, Gorgas Odontological Soc., Beth Jacob Brotherhood (past pres.), Omicron Kappa Upsilon, Sigma Epsilon Delta. Mason; mem. B'nai B'rith (bd. mem.). Contbr. numerous papers to profl. lit. Home: 3511 Woodvalley Dr Baltimore MD 21208 Office: Medical Arts Bldg Baltimore MD 21201

ESKOW, ROY LIONEL, periodontist; b. Perth Amboy, N.J., June 15, 1946; s. Jack Meyer and Theodosia (Katz) E.; B.A., U. Md., 1968, M.A., 1971, D.D.S., 1974; certificate in periodontology Boston U., 1976. Practice dentistry specializing in periodontology, Bethesda, Md., and Gaithersburg, Md., 1976—; asst. clin. prof. dept. periodontology U. Md. Sch. Dentistry, Balt. Mem. Am. Acad. Oral Medicine, Am., Md. State, So. Md. dental assns., Am. Acad. Periodontology, Am. Personnel and Guidance Assn., Am. Coll. Personnel Assn., U. Md., Alumni Assn., U. Md. Sch. Dentistry Alumni Assn., Boston U. Sch. Grad. Dentistry Alumni Assn., Alpha Omega (editor). Home: 5225 Pooks Hill Rd Bethesda MD 20014 Office: 10401 Old Georgetown Rd Bethesda MD 20014

ESLAMI, HOSSEIN HOJATOL, physician; b. Tehran, Iran, July 30, 1927; s. Abul-Hassan and Assieh (Ghafari) E.; M.D., Tehran U., 1952; m. Jean Chinigo, Apr. 27, 1956; children—Darius, Cyrus. Intern, Jersey City Med. Center, 1955-56; resident in surgery Newark Beth Israel Med. Center, 1956-60, fellow in vascular surgery, 1960-61; practice medicine specializing in surgery, Newark, 1961-67; mem. faculty N.J. Coll. Medicine and Dentistry, 1969—, dir. organ transplantation, 1958—, dir. surg. edn., 1967—, asso. prof. surgery, 1976—; chief surgery Newark Beth Israel Med. Center. Diplomate Am. Bd. Surgery. Fellow ACS, Acad. Medicine N.J.; mem. Essex County Med. Soc., Med. Soc. N.J., AMA, Am. Soc. Abdominal Surgeons, Am. Soc. Artificial Internal Organs, Nat. Kidney Found., Transplantation Soc., Am. Soc. Transpolant Surgeons, N.J. Nephrology Soc. Research kidney and liver transplantations. Contbr. articles to profl. jours. Office: 62 Jefferson St Newark NJ 07105

ESLER, RICHARD CURRY, poet, former glass co. exec.; b. Tarentum, Pa., Dec. 25, 1909; s. George Scott and Lottie (Curry) E.; B.A., U. Pitts., 1931, M.A., Pa. State U., 1944; m. Cherrilla Mulder, Dec. 19, 1931; children—Derke Scott, Richard Curry II. Grad. asst. instr. U. Pitts., 1931-32; tchr. secondary sch., Tarentum, 1931-44; various exec. positions PPG Industries, Pitts., 1944-73, chief quality control engr., 1968-73; freelance writer for angling and hunting mags., 1937-50; poet, 1932—. Field dir. JOBS program Nat. Assn. Businessmen, 1968-72. Mem. NEA, Nat. Council Tchrs. of English, Am. Mgmt. Assn., Poetry Soc. Am., Acad. Am. Poets, Am. Poets Fellowship Soc. (publ. grantee 1967), Pa. Poetry Soc. (prizes 1959, 62, 63), Nat. Fedn. State Poetry Socs., Haiku Soc. Am., Bookfellows, Kappa Phi Kappa. Republican. Author: (poetry) Exits and Entrances, 1961; Twenty Ballads Stuck About the Wall, 1967; A Various Language, 1970; To Live On The Earth, 1972; The Fields We Know, 1973; Goldengrove Unleaving, 1974; Stopping By Woods, 1975; Stuck Fast In Yesterday, 1976; Travels with Cherry, 1976; Frog and Friends, 1977; The Days That Are No More, 1978; poetry pub. in anthologies; contbr. articles and stories to Field and Stream, Outdoor Life, others. Home: 125 Opal Ct Natrona Heights PA 15065

ESMOND, PATRICK JOHN, dentist; b. Glen Falls, N.Y., Aug. 28, 1949; s. John Frederick and Naomi Elenor (Guernsey) E.; B.S., Siena Coll., 1971; D.D.S., State U. N.Y., Buffalo, 1975; m. Deborah M. Boehlke, Dec. 26, 1971; children—Shaun Patrick, Erin Elizabeth. Gen. practice dentistry, 1975—; mem. staff Glens Falls Hosp. Mem. Town of Kingsbury Bd. Assessment Rev. Certified N.E. Regional dental Bd. Mem. ADA, N.Y. State, Upper Hudson, 4th Dist. dental socs., Hudson Falls C. of C. (dir.). Club: Rotary. Home: 26 Alma Ave Hudson Falls NY 12839 Office: 85 1/2 Main St Hudson Falls NY 12839

ESPENSHADE, MARLIN ALWINE, microbiologist; b. Middletown, Pa., May 28, 1919; s. Allen Shenk and Annie Mae (Alwine) E.; B.S. in Biology and Botany, Lebanon Valley Coll., 1941; M.S. in Biol. Sci., Purdue U., 1943; Ph.D. in Mycology, Botany and Plant Pathology, George Washington U., 1952; m. Betty Louise Geyer, June 24, 1956; children—Mary Anne, Edith Ellen. Sr. research scientist Wyeth Labs., Inc., West Chester, Pa., 1952-70; sr. research microbiologist W.R. Grace & Co., Columbia, Md., 1970—; lectr. mycology and biology West Chester State Coll., 1963-66. NIH fellow, 1946; NIH grantee, 1959-62. Mem. Am. Soc. Microbiology, Am. Chem. Soc., Mycol. Soc. Am., Soc. Indsl. Microbiology, Am. Inst. Biol. Scis., N.Y. Acad. Scis., Sigma Xi. publs. Home: 9708 Riverside Circle Ellicott City MD 21043 Office: 7379 Route 32 Columbia MD 21044

ESPOSITO, DOMINIC SALVATOR, artist; b. New Haven; s. Michael and Adrian (De Pinna) E.; student Whitney Sch. Art, New Haven, 1948-51, Nat. Acad. Design, N.Y.C., 1963-64. Exhibited at Nat. Acad., N.Y.C., 1963, 64, Allied Artists Am., N.Y.C., 1965, 1968-76, Nat. Acad. Design, 1965, 67, 69, 75, Audubon Artists, 1968, 69, Nat. Arts Club, 1968-69; represented in permanent collections Ward Eggleston Gallery (N.Y.C.), Grinell Galleries (Detroit), Okla. Mus. Art, Butler Inst. Am. Art, Youngstown, Ohio. Served with USNR. Winner 16th Ann. Emily Lowe Competition, 1964; recipient Ralph Weiler award for painting, 1964. Nat. Acad. fellow, 1964; Benedictine Art award, 1968; Bronze medal Nat. Arts Club, 1968, also Cash awards, 1969, 70. Mem. Allied Artists Am. Address: 1364 York Ave New York City NY 10021

ESPOSITO, FRANK VINCENT, engring. exec.; b. Boston, Sept. 27, 1942; s. Frank and Yolanda Mary (Coppola) E.; B.S. in Chem. Engring., Northeastern U., 1965, M.B.A., 1971; m. Dolores Ann DeSisto, Apr. 25, 1965; children—Christopher, Dina. Chem. project engr. Polaroid Corp., Waltham, Mass., 1965-69, mfg. supr. of Sesame div., Norwood, Mass., 1969-70, mgr. engring., chem. div., Waltham, 1971-76; mgr. projects Herzog-Hart Corp., Boston, 1976-77, v.p. ops., 1977—. Bd. dirs. Clapboard Tree Nursery Sch., 1974—, chmn., 1977-78. Mem. Am. Inst. Chem. Engrs. Home: 48 Sycamore Dr Westwood MA 02090 Office: 462 Boylston St Boston MA 02116

ESPOSITO, JOHN ANTHONY, educator; b. Bklyn., Jan. 7, 1949; s. Joachim Anthony and Josephine (Patrizio) E.; B.S. in Chemistry, U. City N.Y., 1971, M.S. in Secondary Edn., 1976. Chem. analyst Gotham Pharms., Bklyn., 1971; sci. tchr. Catherine McAuley High Sch., Bklyn., 1971—, dept. chmn., 1973—, also grade advisor and coach. Mem. Cath. Sci. Council of Bklyn., Nat. Sci. Tchrs. Assn. Home: 1397 Schenectady Ave Brooklyn NY 11203 Office: 710 E 37th St Brooklyn NY 11203

ESPOSITO, JOSEPH ANTHONY, research analyst; b. Hazleton, Pa., Mar. 27, 1950; s. James and Mary L. (Sett) E.; A.B. with high distinction and honors in History, Pa. State U., 1972, M.A., 1973; postgrad., U. Pa., 1976—. Info. specialist, Republican Caucus, Senate of Pa., 1973-76, research analyst, Pa. Senate Local Govt. Com., 1976-77, sr. research analyst to Pa. Senate Rep. Whip, 1977—. Alt. Fellow, James A. Finnegan Found., 1971. Mem. Pa. Pub. Relations Soc., Phi Beta Kappa, Phi Kappa Phi, Phi Alpha Theta, Kappa Tau Alpha, Alpha Phi Omega (life). Republican. Roman Catholic. Clubs: Pa. State Alumni Assn., Penn State Drummers, Penn State Club Greater Hazleton. Office: Suite 535 Main Capitol Bldg Harrisburg PA 17120

ESPOSITO, KENNETH JOHN, psychiat. social worker; b. Bridgeport, Conn., Dec. 9, 1938; s. Thomas Samuel and Saleda (Truncone) E.; B.B.A., Washburn U., 1964; M.S.W., Smith Coll., 1966; m. Catherine DeManuel, July 29, 1961; children—Thomas Anthony, Kenneth John, RoseMary. Mem. staff children's div. Menninger Found., Topeka, 1961-64; psychiat. social worker High Meadows Child Study and Treatment Center, Hamden, Conn., 1966-69; program dir. Opengate, Inc., Somers, N.Y., 1969-71; asso. exec., dir., founder Center for Counseling and Guided Learning, Mt. Kisco, N.Y., 1971-72; practice psychiat. social work, Fairfield and Milford, Conn., 1971—; cons. Norwalk Bd. Edn., 1971—. Mem. Nat. Assn. Social Workers, Am. Group Psychotherapy Assn., Am. Assn. Marriage and Family Counselors, Conn. Soc. Clin. Social Work. Roman Catholic. Home: 104 Wintergreen Dr Easton CT 06425 Office: 1210 Post Rd Fairfield CT 06430

ESPOSITO, RONALD PATRICK, educator; b. Staten Island, N.Y., Jan. 5, 1945; s. Giacomo Jack and Domenica Mae (Brocato) E.; B.S., Georgetown U., 1966; M.S., Fordham U., 1969, Ph.D., 1975; m. Catherine Costa, Aug. 2, 1970. Tchr. Oxon Hill (Md.) High Sch., 1966-67; counselor N.Y.C. Youth Bd., 1967-68; research asso. Mayor's Commn. on Runaway Youth, N.Y.C. Youth Bd., 1968; counselor, instr. N.Y.C. Community Coll., 1968-71; counselor U. Md.-Baltimore County, 1971-74; asso. prof., chmn. dept. counselor edn. N.Y. U., 1974—; exec. sec., dir. Tng. Resources for Human Devel., Inc., 1972-76; dir. Adult Career Counseling and Edn. Services, 1977—. Spencer Found. grantee, 1975-76; NIMH grantee, 1974-75; Gen. Mills Found. grantee, 1975-76; N.Y. Times Found. grantee, 1976-77. Mem. Am. Psychol. Assn., Assn. Humanstic Psychology, Am. Personnel and Guidance Assn., Am. Coll. Personnel Assn., Assn. Counselor Educators, Assn. Specialists in Group Work. Democrat. Home: 230 Warren St Brooklyn NY 11201 Office: Dept Counselor Edn New York U 51 W 4th St New York City NY 10003

ESQUERRE, JEAN ROLAND, aircraft co. exec.; b. Yonkers, N.Y., Dec. 28, 1923; s. Jean Bertrand and Marie Agnes (Bates) E.; student Coll. City N.Y., 1946-58, N.Y. U., 1958-59; B.S. in Engring. Tech., Empire State Coll., 1977; m. Maria Elizabet Edman, Sept. 25, 1968; children—Johanna Maria, Malin Elizabet. Draftsman, Splty. Assembling & Packing Co., Bklyn., 1949-52; mech. engring. draftsman N.Y. Transit Authority, Bklyn., 1952-53; prin. design engr. Republic Aviation Corp., Farmingdale, N.Y., 1953-63; design engr. Grumman Aerospace Corp., Bethpage, N.Y., 1963-66, test dir., 1966-67, engring. supr., 1967-68, price analyst, 1968-69, asst. to pres., dir. opportunity devel. dept., 1969—, dir., 1973—; dir. Grumman Ecosystems Corp., Puritech Industries, Inc. Chmn. Youth Devel. Assn., Huntington Station, N.Y., 1971-73; asst. treas. L.I. YMCA; bd. dirs. Suffolk County unit Girl Scouts U.S.A., 1974, Family Service League Nassau County, Huntington Hosp., 1978, United Way L.I., 1978. Served with USAAF, 1943-46. Recipient Community Service award Huntington Twp., 1968; award Suffolk County council Boy Scouts Am., 1972. Mem. NAACP, Urban League (pres. L.I. 1973—, life mem. bd. dirs. L.I.), All Am. Karate Fedn. (chmn. East Coast region 1977—), Huntington C. of C., One Hundred Black Men Inc., Alpha Phi Alpha. Home: 193 Broadway Greenlawn NY 11740 Office: Grumman Aerospace Corp South Oyster Bay Rd Bethpage NY 11714

ESSMAN, WALTER B(ERNARD), physician, educator; b. N.Y.C., Dec. 25, 1933; s. Louis and Elsie (Eisemann) E.; B.A., N.Y. U., 1954; M.A., U. N.D., 1955, Ph.D., 1957; M.D., U. Milan, 1972; m. Shirley Glass, June 10, 1962; 1 son, Eric J. Sr. postdoctoral fellow in neurophysiology Albert Einstein Coll. Medicine, N.Y.C., 1959-61, asst. prof., 1961-63; asst. prof. depts. psychology and biochemistry Queens Coll., City U. N.Y., 1962-64, asso. prof., 1965-66, prof., 1967—; intern Queens Hosp. Center, Jamaica, N.Y., 1972-73; resident L.I. Jewish-Hillside Med. Center, Jamaica, 1963-65, fellow in endocrinology, 1975-77; lectr. medicine State U. N.Y. Sch. Medicine, Stony Brook, 1974—; attending physician L.I. Jewish-Hillside Med. Center, New Hyde Park, N.Y., 1976—. Served to capt. U.S. Army, 1957-59. Recipient Ambrogino d'Oro Municipality of Milan, 1971, gold medal Mario Negri Inst. for Pharm. Research, 1977. Fellow Am. Coll. Nutrition; mem. Am. Psychol. Assn., Am. Physiol. Soc., Coll. Internat. Neuropsychopharmacology, AAAS, Am. Acad. Neurology, N.Y. Acad. Scis. Author: Neurochemistry of Cerebral Electroshock, 1973; Current Biochemical Approaches to Learning and Memory, 1973; Current Developments in Psychopharmacology, Vols. 1-5, 1974-78; Serotonin in Health and Disease, Vols. I-V, 1978. Home: 6 Ashleigh Ct Glen Cove NY 11542 Office: Queens Coll City U NY Flushing NY 11367

ESSRICK, ABRAHAM JOSEPH, judge; b. Phila., Feb. 8, 1914; s. Jacob and Rachel (Pressman) E.; B.A. in Accounting, George Washington U., 1956; J.D. cum laude, Rutgers U., 1940; postgrad. U. Grenoble, France, 1945, Nat. Coll. State Judiciary, U. Nev., 1974, Georgetown U., 1976; m. Riva Krakuzin, Feb. 14, 1943 (dec. Aug. 1959); children—Helene (Mrs. Feldsher), Carol; m. 2d, Pearl Gibel, May 20, 1972; children—Frances H. Gibel, Bonnie (Mrs. Schneider). Admitted to D.C. bar, 1941, U.S. Supreme Ct., 1964; atty. adviser SEC, Washington, 1946-53; atty. advisor ICC, Washington, 1953-59, hearing examiner, 1959-72, adminstrv. law judge, 1972-74; ret., 1974. Mem. Phila. Speakers Council, 1942, Jewish Educators Council, 1958-60; patron Washington Performing Arts Soc. Bd. dirs. govt. div. United Jewish Appeal of Greater Washington, Inc., 1958-74, mem. exec. com., 1964-65, trustee, 1960-61, 64-73, vice chmn. exec. com. govt. div., 1965. Served with Signal Intelligence Div., ETO, 1944-45. Mem. Am., Fed., D.C. bar assns., Am. Judicature Soc., Nat. Lawyers Club, Fed. Adminstrv. Law Judges Conf., Am. Acad. Polit. and Social Sci., Acad. Polit. Sci., Smithsonian Assos., Friends John F. Kennedy Center, Internat. Platform Assn. Jewish. Mem. B'nai B'rith. Clubs: Rutgers, Gaslight (Washington). Home: 905 Kenbrook Dr Silver Spring MD 20902

ESTERHAI, JOHN LOUIS, lawyer; b. Phoenixville, Pa., Jan. 26, 1920; s. Louis and Mary (Wolarik) E.; B.S.C., Temple U., 1940; LL.B., U. Pa., 1946; m. I. Louise Moyer, Nov. 13, 1943; children—John Louis, Louise Clayton (Mrs. William A. Ratcliffe). Admitted to Pa. bar, 1947; law clk. to Hon. Herbert F. Goodrich, 1946-47; asso. legal dept. Philco Corp., Phila., 1947-58; v.p., sec. dir. Philco Finance Corp., 1958-62; asst. counsel Penn Mut. Life Ins. Co., 1962-65, asso. counsel, 1965-69, asso. gen. counsel, 1970—, sec., 1971-77, dir. govt. relations, 1977—; dir. Deptford Properties, Inc., FNC Properties Corp., Penn Mut. Equity Services Inc., Penn Loop South, Inc., Ind. Sq. Properties, Inc., Walnut Properties, Inc., St. James Realty Corp., Colonial Plaza Properties, Inc., 500 Walnut Corp. Bd. mgrs. Meml. Hosp., Roxborough, chmn. 1969-77, hon. chmn., 1977—; trustee del. Am. Hosp. Assn., 1975. Served to lt. (s.g.) USNR, 1942-45. Mem. Assn. Life Ins. Counsel, Pa. Soc., Am., Pa., Phila. bar assns., U.S. Trade Mark Assn. (pres. 1958-60), Internat. Assn. Protection Indsl. Property (treas. 1954-58). Republican. Baptist. Mason. Club: Union League (Phila.). Author: (with others) Trademark Management, 1955. Home: 8423 Pembrook Rd Philadelphia PA 19128 Office: Independence Sq Philadelphia PA 19172

ESTERMAN, BENJAMIN, ophthalmologist; b. Vilna, Poland, May 1, 1906; s. Marcus and Bella (Shirling) E.; B.A., Columbia U., 1927; M.D., Cornell U., 1931; m. Cinnabelle Morris, Dec. 3, 1972; children by previous marriage—Mark, Daniel, Laura; stepchildren—Noel Morris, Errol Morris. Intern, N.Y. Postgrad. Hosp., N.Y.C., 1931-32; resident Knapp Meml. Eye Hosp., N.Y.C., 1932-35; practice medicine specializing in ophthalmology, Lawrence, N.Y., 1937—; dir. emeritus ophthalmology dept. Peninsula Hosp. Center, St. John's Episcopal Hosp., L.I. Jewish Hosp.; cons. surgeon Manhattan Eye and Ear Hosp.; mem. and pres. med. bd. Peninsula Hosp. Center, St. Joseph's Hosp., Far Rockaway, N.Y. Fellow Am. Acad. Ophthalmology (life, research award 1967), A.C.S., Internat. Coll. Surgeons, N.Y. Acad. Medicine; mem. N.Y. Acad. Scis., N.Y. Soc. Clin. Ophthalmology (pres. 1955-56), Manhattan Ophthal. Soc. (pres. 1976-77). Jewish. Author: The Eye Book, 1977; contbr. articles to med. jours. Home and Office: 130 Central Ave Lawrence NY 11559

ESTES, EDNA EVA, educator; b. Jasper, Ala., Nov. 23, 1921; d. F.E. and Ethel Etta (Ford) Estes; student Birmingham So. Coll., 1946-47; B.S., U. Ala., 1948, M.S., 1949, Ph.D., 1957. Asst. prof. biology Flora Macdonald Coll., Red Springs, N.C., 1949-53; instr. U. Ala., Mobile, 1953-54, St. Mary's Jr. Coll., St. Mary's City, Md., 1957-59; asst. prof. Del Mar Coll., Corpus Christi, Tex., 1959-60; asso. prof. biology Salisbury (Md.) State Coll., 1960-64, prof., 1964—. Served with WAC, AUS, 1943-45; PTO. Recipient Graham award U. Ala., 1956. So. Fellowship Fund fellow, 1956-57. Mem. AAAS, AAUW (v.p. Salisbury 1964, pres. 1965-66), Bot. Soc. Am., Am. Assn. Plant Physiologists, Southeastern Assn. Biologists, Ala. Acad. Scis., Sigma Xi, Delta Kappa Gamma. Research in phosphorus 32 uptake and localization correlated with photosynthetic factors in higher plants. Home: 1177 S Division St Salisbury MD 21801

ESTEY, GEORGE FISHER, educator; b. Cody's, N.B., Can., Jan. 21, 1924 (father Am. citizen); s. Clarence A. and Eileen (Fisher) E.; B.A. magna cum laude, Tufts Coll., 1952; M.A., U. Conn., 1954; Ph.D., U. Ill. at Urbana, 1960; m. Barbara Alice Brown, Aug. 25, 1951; children—Roger Scott, Gregory Alan. Instr., U. Conn., Storrs, 1952-54, U. Ill., Urbana, 1954-59; faculty Boston U., 1959—, asso. prof., 1964-68, prof. rhetoric, 1968—. Served with USAAF, 1942-47. Mem. Nat. Council Tchrs. English, Conf. Coll. Composition and Communication, Assn. for Gen. and Liberal Studies, AAUP, Phi Beta Kappa. Author: (with Harry H. Crosby) College Writing, 1968, 2d edit., 1975; Just Rhetoric, 1972. Editor: (with Doris Hunter) NonViolence, 1971; Violence, 1971; editor Interdisciplinary Perspectives, 1976—. Home: 54 Colony Rd Lexington MA 02173 Office: 871 Commonwealth Ave Boston MA 02215

ESTIN, LEONARD ALLEN, med. co. exec.; b. Cornwall, N.Y., June 17, 1936; s. Harry and Clara E.; B.S., Syracuse U., 1957; M.B.A., N.Y. U., 1960; m. Karen Joan Kamen, Sept. 12, 1971; children—Alanna Meredith, Dana Nicole. Vice pres. fin. Am. Doll & Toy Corp., Bklyn., 1962-68; v.p. fin., treas. Fab Industries, Inc., N.Y.C., 1968-74; pres. Sun Floor Co., Inc., Phila., 1974-75; sr. v.p. Nat. Med. Care, Inc. (Erika, Inc.), Rockleigh, N.J., 1975—; dir. N.E. Gen. Corp., Apollo Equities, Inc. Mem. Sigma Iota Epsilon. Home: 38 E 85th St New York NY 10028 Office: 1 Erika Plaza Rockleigh NJ 07647

ESTRA, JORDAN MARK, mining co. exec.; b. New Haven, Mar. 20, 1947; s. Aaron A. and Bertha (Rotman) E.; B.S. with distinction, Babson Coll., 1968; M.B.A., Columbia U., 1971; m. Amy Insler, June 29, 1969; children—Tara Elizabeth, Bradford Russell. Fin. analyst AMAX Inc., N.Y.C., 1971-72, asst. to chmn., 1972-73, mgr. distbn. climax div., Greenwich, Conn., 1973-76, mgr. fin. planning internat. group, 1976-78, dir. bus. planning base metals group, 1978—; dir. Liberia Iron & Steel Corp.; vis. lectr. Columbia U. Grad. Sch. Bus. Served with M.C., U.S. Army, 1968-69. Mem. Am. Inst. Mining, Mettall. and Petroleum Engrs., N. Am. Soc. Corp. Planning, Nat. Assn. Bus. Economists, Stamford Area Commerce and Industry Assn. (govt. affairs council). Club: Lawyers N.Y. Home: 7 Glenbrook Rd Trumbull CT 06611 Office: 2 Greenwich Plaza Greenwich CT 06830

ESTRELLA, LEO EDWARD, govt. ofcl.; b. Fall River, Mass., Feb. 22, 1935; s. George Manuel and Marie Anne (LePage) E.; B.A. in Pub. Adminstrn., Upper Iowa U., 1976; M.A. in Pub. Adminstrn., Central Mich. U., 1978; m. Eileen Kingston, May 17, 1968; 1 dau., Lisa. Mech. draftsman Sperry Gyroscope Corp., Lake Success, N.Y., 1956-59; machine and tool designer Portsmouth (N.H.) Naval Shipyard, 1962-68; project officer Dover AFB, Dover, Del., 1968-72; plumbing and san. systems designer VA, Washington, 1972-75, sr. project leader/health care facilities specialist, 1975—. Vice chmn. Com. on Out-Moded Schs./Bldgs., Charles County, Md., 1978; adv. rep. Citizens Com., Charles County, 1978—; sec. Dr. Mudd Elementary Sch. PTA, Waldorf, Md., 1978—; bd. dirs. Charles County Humane Soc., 1978—. Served with airborne div. U.S. Army, 1953-56. Recipient certificate of merit Dept. Navy, 1967. Certified Inst. for Certification of Engring. Technicians. Mem. Soc. Am. Mil. Engrs., Am. Soc. Plumbing Engrs., Am. Mgmt. Assn.,

Commonwealth Soc. N.Am. Democrat. Episcopalian. Author Navships manual, also tech. and research studies. Home: 319 Barksdale Ave Waldorf MD 20601 Office: 810 Vermont Ave NW Washington DC 20420

ESTRIN, HERMAN ALBERT, educator; b. N. Plainfield, N.J., June 2, 1915; s. Morris I. and Ida Ruth (Bender) E.; A.B., Drew U., Madison, N.J., 1937; M.A., Columbia U., 1942, Ed.D., 1954; m. Pearl Simon, June 26, 1949; children—Robert Keith, Karen Ruth. Instr. social sci. Jr. High Sch., S. Plainfield, 1938-42; mem. faculty N.J. Inst. Tech., Newark, 1946—, prof. English, 1958—. Served to capt. AUS, 1942-46. Recipient Alumni Achievement award in arts Drew U., 1958; Gold Key award Columbia Scholastic Press Assn., 1962; Robert W. Houton award N.J. Inst. Tech. Alumni Assn., 1970; Nat. Distinguished Newspaper Adviser award Nat. Council Coll. Publs. Adviser, 1970; Western Electric Fund award, 1971; Outstanding Tchr. Tech. Writing award Assn. Tech. Writing Tchrs., 1975. Mem. Nat. (past dir.), N.J. (past pres.; Distinguished Tchr. award 1973) councils tchrs. English, N.J. Collegiate Press Assn. (founder), Nat. Council Publs. Advisers (past pres.), Coll. English Assn. (past regional pres.), N.J. Writers Conf. (dir. 1966—), N.J. Authors Luncheons (dir. 1959—), AAUP, Am. Soc. Engring. Edn., Omicron Delta Kappa, Alpha Phi Omega, Phi Delta Kappa, Kappa Delta Pi, Phi Eta Sigma, Pi Delta Epsilon (past pres.). Author: (with Paul Obler) The New Scientist: Essays on the Methods and Values of Science, 1962; Higher Education in Engineering and Science, 1963; Technical and Professional Writing: A Practical Anthology, 1963; (with Delmar Good) College and University Teaching, 1966; (with Arthur Sanderson) Freedom and Censorship of the College Press, 1966; (with Esther Lloyd-Jones) The American Student and His College, 1967, How Many Roads? The 70's, 1970; (with Donald Mehus) The American Language in the 1970's, 1974; editor: (with Donald Cunningham) The Teaching of Technical Writing, 1975; The Best Student Poetry in New Jersey, 1978; author brochures and articles. Home: 315 Henry St Scotch Plains NJ 07076 Office: Student Center NJ Inst Tech Newark NJ 07102

ESTRIN, SHELDON BARUCH, orthodontist; b. Liberty, N.Y., Sept. 29, 1933; s. Harry and Sadie (Listizky) E.; A.B., N.Y.U., 1953, D.D.S., 1957, postgrad., 1961-65; m. Barbara Braver, Aug. 28, 1954; children—Terri Zoe, Wendy Jill, David Ian. Practice dentistry, Bklyn., 1960-61, specializing in orthodontics, Forest Hills, N.Y., 1961-62, N.Y.C., 1962-73, Hempstead, N.Y., 1964—, Hauppague, N.Y., 1966—. Served to capt. Dental Corps, AUS, 1957-60. Mem. Internat. Acad. Orthodontics, N.Y. State Assn. Professions, Am., N.Y. U. orthodontic socs., Alpha Omega. Jewish. Mason. Club: Tam O'Shanter Golf (Brookville, N.Y.). Home: 51 Hofstra Dr Plainview NY 11803 Office: 131 Fulton Ave Hempstead NY 11550 also 111 Smithtown By-Pass Hauppage NY 11788 also 400 W Main St Babylon NY 11702

ETCOVITCH, ALLEN, mgmt. cons.; b. Montreal, Que., Can., Nov. 25, 1939; s. Jack and Mollie (Neelman) E.; M.Ps., McGill U., 1963; m. Thelma Stavitt, Aug. 10, 1960; children—Joy, Andrea, Eric. Vocat. and employment counselor Jewish Vocat. Service, Montreal, 1963-65; dir. personnel Canadian Art Studios, Ltd., Montreal, 1965-66; dir. psychol. services Craimer Assos., Ltd., Montreal, 1966-69; pres. Allen Etcovitch Assos., Ltd., Montreal, 1970—. Mem. Profl. Corp. Psychologists Que., Am., Can., Ont., B.C. psychol. assns. Home: 5600 Redwood Cote St Luc PQ Canada Office: Suite 1707 666 Sherbrooke St W Montreal PQ H3A 1E7 Canada

ETHAN, CAROL BAEHR, psychotherapist; b. N.Y.C., May 30, 1920; d. Irving and Susan (Goldman) Baehr); B.A. in Psychology (Univ. honors scholar), N.Y. U., 1978; student Met. Inst. Psychoanalytic Studies, 1965-70, M.A. candidate; m. 2d, Sy Ethan, Mar. 18, 1955; children—Willa Capraro, Barbara. Writer, Irvington (N.J.) Herald, 1946; staff writer Walt Framer Prodns., N.Y.C., 1949-50; cons., researcher consumer psychology, N.Y.C., 1950-70; instr. tech. writing Queens Coll., 1956-57; motivation analyst J. Walter Thompson, N.Y.C., 1966-67; asso. research dir. Papert, Koenig, Lois, N.Y.C., 1967-68; motivation project dir. Marplan, N.Y.C., 1964-66; project dir. Ogilvy & Mather, N.Y.C., 1956-64; field dir. Dancer, Fitzgerald-Sample, N.Y.C., 1954-56; staff psychotherapist Fifth Ave. Center for Counseling and Psychotherapy, N.Y.C., 1965-70; practice psychoanalytic psychotherapy, N.Y.C., 1967—. Queens County committeewoman Democratic party, 1960; vol. social rehab. program Queens County Mental Health Soc., 1965-66; active Girl Scouts U.S.A. Recipient Founders Day award N.Y. U., 1978. Mem. Nat. Accreditation Assn. Psychoanalysis, Am. Orthopsychiat. Assn., Assn. Humanistic Psychology, Joint Council Mental Health, N.Y. State Assn. Practicing Psychotherapists. Home and Office: 235 W 76th St New York City NY 10023

ETHRIDGE, HARRISON MOSLEY, educator; b. Hopewell, Va., Apr. 5, 1933; s. Harrison and Pauline (Mosley) E.; student Va. Poly., 1950-54; B.A., Millsaps Coll., 1956; M.A. in History, U. Richmond, 1963; postgrad. Am. U. (Cokesbury fellow), 1967-68, Rutgers U., 1970-71, Cath. U., 1975. Commd. ensign USN, 1957, advanced through grades to lt., 1963; communications officer Destroyer Squadron 36 flagship USS New, 1957-60; staff communications CinC US Naval Forces Europe, London, Eng., 1960-62; asst. dir. admissions George Wash. U., Washington, 1963-67; instr. history Frostburg (Md.) State Coll., 1968-70; asst. prof. history Catonsville (Md.) State Coll., 1970-75, asso. prof., 1975—. Mem. community delegation Bicentennial Assembly (chmn. 1974); candidate city council, 1974. Seay, Carnegie fellow, Mem. Va. (life), Am., Md., Columbia hist. socs., Nat. Trust for Historic Preservation, Kappa Sigma. Club: Army-Navy. Author: Three Hundred Years of American Architecture, 1966. Contbr. articles hist. jours. Home: 1835 Upshur St NW Washington DC 20011

ETHRIDGE, NOEL HAROLD, phys. scientist; b. Plains, Ga., Aug. 7, 1927; s. George Paul and Willie Mae (Blackshear) E.; B.S., Ga. Inst. Tech., 1948, postgrad., 1948-50; m. Gloria Elaine Malone, Oct. 26, 1949 (dec. Oct. 1977); children—Patricia Lynne, David Leslie, Jeffrey Noel. Physicist, Ballistic Research Labs., Aberdeen Proving Ground, Md., 1950-58, supervisory physicist, Ballistic 1960—; physicist Oak Ridge Nat. Lab., 1958-60. Army tech. mem. shielding panel Def. Atomic Support Agy., 1961-63; U.S. rep. Tripartite Tech. Cooperation Program, 1962-65; cons. blast effects of nuclear explosions Dept. of Def. agys. Elder Presbyterian Ch., 1971—. Served with U.S. Army, 1946-47. Mem. Am. Phys. Soc., AAAS. Research on nuclear blast effects on mil. equipment, measurement of blast parameters, large-scale HE blast phenomena; patentee spl. whistle. Home: 503 E Lee Way Bel Air MD 21014 Office: Ballistic Research Labs Aberdeen Proving Ground MD 21005

ETMEKJIAN, JAMES, educator; b. Harpoot, Turkey, Jan. 12, 1915; s. Garabed and Arexi (Bagdasarian) E.; came to U.S., 1928, naturalized, 1928; A.B. in Romance Langs., Harvard, 1939, M.A. in Teaching, 1942; Ph.D. (Univ. fellow), Brown U., 1958; m. Lillian Krikorian, June 29, 1952; children—Charles, Roxanne. Chmn. dept. French and Spanish, Dana Hall Sch., Wellesley, Mass., 1941-50; tchr. French, Milton (Mass.) High Sch., 1950-51; lectr. Armenian univ. extension Mass. Dept. Edn., 1954-55; lectr. Armenian lang. and civilization Brown U. Extension, 1955-56; tchr. French, Wellesley Hills, Mass., 1951-61, head dept. fgn. langs. jr. and sr. high schs., Wellesley, 1954-61, dir. fgn. langs., 1959-60, dir. lang. lab., 1960-61; instr. French, Suffolk U., 1960-61; asst. prof. Romance langs. Queens Coll., City U. N.Y., 1961-64; asso. prof. Romance langs. So. Ill. U., 1964-65; prof. French, chmn. dept. fgn. langs. U. Bridgeport (Conn.), 1965-72; lectr. Armenian lang. and civilization Boston U., 1975-; prof. fgn. lang. methodology NDEA Inst., U. Maine, 1959, 61-62, asst. dir. Inst., 1961-62; prof. fgn. lang. methodology Mich. State U., 1960, 2d Level Inst., U. Mass. at Arcahon, France, 1964-65. French Govt. traveling fellow, 1947; Am. Council Learned Socs. grantee, 1959; HEW grantee, 1977. Mem. Soc. Armenian Studies, Nat. Assn. Armenian Studies and Research, Phi Beta Kappa. Author: A Graded West Armenian Reader, 1963; (with Caefer and O'Brien) Speaking French, 1963; Le Francais courant I, 1964, II, 1965; The French Influence on the Western Armenian Renaissance, 1964; Pattern Drills in Language Teaching, 1966; (with Caefer) Spoken and Written French in Review, 1972: Anthology of 19th and 20th Century Western Armenian Literature, 1979. Contbr. articles to profl. jours. Home: 35 Llewellyn Rd West Newton MA 02165

ETTENBERG, EUGENE M(ARTIN), editor, book designer; b. Westmount, Que., Can., Oct. 21, 1903; s. Max and Minnie (Penny) E.; B.F.A., Pratt Inst., 1925; M.A., Columbia U., 1965, Ed.D. in Fine Arts, 1969; m. Suzanne Bethoux, Apr. 24, 1970. Book editor Colton Press, N.Y.C., 1936-41; mgr. Gallery Press, N.Y.C., 1945-61; instr. dept. art Pratt Inst., Bklyn., 1947-52, Columbia, N.Y.C., 1953-68; art editor Voices newspaper, Southbury, Conn., 1973—. Cons. graphics U.S. Dept. Interior, 1970—; fed. graphics judge Nat. Endowment Arts, 1972—; dir. Waterbury Arts Council, 1974—; pres. Pomperaug Valley Art League, 1974—. Recipient Carey-Thomas award New Eng. Book Pubs., 1958, Golden Keys award Craftsmen Club N.Y., 1970. Mem. Am. Inst. Graphic Arts (dir., v.p. 1950-55), Typophiles (pres. 1968-69), Type Dirs. Club (pres. 1965-67), AAUP, Phi Delta Kappa. Clubs: Dutch Treat, Columbia Faculty (N.Y.C.). Author: Type for Books and Advertising, 1947. Editor-in-chief: Advertising and Publishing Production Yearbook, 1936-41; contbg. editor: Am. Artist, 1945-74. Exhibited graphics and books Pierpont Morgan Library, N.Y.C., 1961, Archtl. League, N.Y.C., 1960, 62, 63, Columbia Univ. Library, 1968. Home and office: 435B Heritage Village Southbury CT 06488

ETTER, THOMAS CLIFTON, JR., lawyer; b. Phila., Apr. 7, 1938; s. Thomas Clifton and Mildred Evelyn (Phillips) E.; B.A. in History, U. Pa., 1961; M.B.A. in Fin., Temple U., 1972; J.D. cum laude, Del. Law Sch., 1975. Stockbroker Bioren & Co., Phila., 1962-66; researcher LaBrum and Doak, Phila., 1967-72; admitted to Pa. bar, 1975; atty. SEC, Washington, 1975—; adj. prof. fin. Southeastern U., 1977—; adj. prof. bus. law Benjamin Franklin U., 1977—. Served with U.S. Army, 1961-62. Mem. Am., Fed., Pa., Phila. bar assns., Fin. Analysts Fedn., Washington Soc. Investment Analysts, Soc. Colonial Wars, SAR, Soc. War 1812, Sons of the Revolution, Sons Union Vets., Hereditary Order of Descendants of Loyalists and Patriots of Am. Revolution. Republican. Episcopalian. Clubs: Rittenhouse, Racquet, Union League (Phila.); Merion Cricket (Haverford, Pa.); University (Washington). Home: South Four Towers Apt 1234 4600 S Four Mile Run Dr Arlington VA 22204 Office: U S Securities and Exchange Commn 500 N Captiol St Washington DC 20549

EUERLE, GEORGE WILLIAM, mfg. co. exec.; b. Stratford, Conn., July 17, 1906; s. John William and Margaret (Sichelstiel) E.; B.C.S. cum laude, N.Y. U., 1930; m. Iva Winifred Lanphear, Sept. 19, 1931; children—Barbara (Mrs. Ronald Parsons), Nancy (Mrs. Harry Gladwin). Vice pres. Carter, Milchman & Frank, N.Y.C., 1945-49; with Atlantic Service Co., Inc., Bklyn., 1951-71, pres., chmn. bd., 1971—; instr. N.Y. U., N.Y.C., 1930-31, Packard Sch., N.Y.C., 1934-35. Chmn. bd. edn. Gateway Christian Sch., 1959-60; chmn. bd. dirs. Bklyn. Salvation Army, 1962-65. C.P.A., N.Y. Mem. Bergen County Christian Sch. Assn. (dir. 1954-58), Bklyn. C. of C. (pres. 1970-71, United Saw Service Assn. (pres. 1961-62). Clubs: Bklyn., Rotarian (pres. 1965-66). Home: 963 Soldier Hill Rd Oradell NJ 07649 Office: 711 Caton Ave Brooklyn NY 11218

EURICH, ALVIN CHRISTIAN, educator, psychologist; b. Bay City, Mich., June 14, 1902; s. Christian H. and Hulda (Steinke) E.; B.A., North Central Coll., 1924, Litt.D., 1949; M.A., U. Maine, 1926, LL.D., 1965; Ph.D., U. Minn., 1929; LL.D., Hamline U., 1944, Alfred U., 1949, Clarke U., 1950, Miami U., 1951, Yeshiva U., 1954, Redlands U., 1960; Litt.D., New Sch. Social Research, 1952, Albion Coll., 1965; L.H.D., U. Fla., 1953, U. Miami, 1968, Fairfield U., 1971; Sc.D., Akron U., 1960; m. Nell P. Hutchinson, Mar. 15, 1953; children—Juliet Ann, Donald Alan. Instr., U. Maine, 1924-26; from asst. in edn1. psychology to prof. U. Minn. 1926-37; prof. edn. Northwestern U., 1937-38; prof. edn. Stanford, 1938-48, v.p., 1944-48, acting pres., 1948; 1st chancellor State U. N.Y., 1949-51; v.p. Ford Fund for Advancement Edn., 1951-64, bd. dirs., 1952-68; exec dir., edn. div. Ford Found., 1958-64; pres. Aspen Inst. for Humanistic Studies, 1963-68; vice chmn. bd. Ednl. Facilities Labs., Inc.; vis. fellow Clare Coll. Cambridge (Eng.) U.; formerly trustee Penn. Mut. Life Ins. Co.; bd. dirs. Acad. Ednl. Devel., Aspen, Inst. Humanistic Studies, 1963-72, spl. adviser to bd., 1972—; pres. Acad. Ednl. Devel., 1963—; bd. govs. Lovelace Found.; chmn. adv. com. Heile Selassie U., Ethiopia; adviser U. Patras (Greece); chmn. Stanford Research Inst.; cons. NASA, other U.S. govt. agys. during, following war years; chmn. U.S. nat. commn. UNESCO, 1967-70; chmn. U.S. delegation to UNESCO Gen. Conf., Paris, France, 1968; supr. ednl. surveys; vis. prof. various univs.; mem., cons. various govt. commns. including Hoover Commn., Pres. Truman's Commn. on Higher Edn., Pres. Kennedy's Task Force on Edn., Nat. Commn. on Libraries; chmn. Surgeon Gen.'s Commn. on Nurses. Served from lt. comdr. to comdr. USNR, 1942-44. Recipient Outstanding Achievement award U. Minn., 1951; Times Sq. Club's 4th Ann. award, 1953; Ann. award N.Y. Acad. Pub. Edn., 1963. Fellow AAAS (council 1941-45), Am. Psychol. Assn.; mem. Am. Ednl. Research Assn. (v.p. 1944, pres. 1945), Acad. for Ednl. Devel. (pres.), Sigma Xi, Phi Delta Kappa. Clubs: University, Century (N.Y.C.); Cosmos (Washington); Explorers; Athenaeum (London, Eng.). Author: Reforming-American Education, 1969. Editor: Campus 1980, 1968; High School 1980, 1970. Author, co-author books, studies in edn., psychol. and achievement tests, including current affairs tests for Time. Contbr. articles to profl. jours. and gen. mags. Home: Sherman CT 06784 Office: 680 Fifth Ave New York City NY 10019

EUSTANCE, WILLIAM ERNEST, environ. engr.; b. Ithaca, N.Y., July 25, 1937; s. Arthur William and Ernestine Elizabeth (Pease) E.; B.S. in Zoology (Ford Found. scholarship 1952-56), U. Wis., 1956; postgrad. in Fisheries Ecology, U. Maine, 1956-59; B.S. in Environ. Engring. (Caird prize 1970), Rensselaer Poly. Inst., 1970, M.S., 1974; m. Carol Hazel Price, Dec. 26, 1964; children—Mary Elizabeth, Rebecca Jean, Nicole Carol. Field surveyer Eustance & Horowitz, P.C., Circleville, N.Y., summers 1952-56; quality control chemist Maine Sardine Industries, Bangor, Maine, summer 1957; asst. field biologist Maine Inland Fish and Game, Ashland, summer 1958; survey party chief Eustance & Horowitz, 1959, 62; fish hatchery mgr. U.S. Fish and Wildlife, Mass., W.Va., Ala., 1963-67; sanitary lab. chemist Eustance & Horowitz, Circleville, N.Y., 1968-69, environ. engr., v.p., 1971—. Lay speaker United Methodist Ch.; vice-chmn. Orange County, N.Y. Environ. Control Commn., 1975-77. Served with Arty., U.S. Army, 1959-62. Licensed profl. engr., N.Y. State; certified fisheries scientist. Mem. Nat. Soc. of Profl. Engrs., Am. Fisheries Soc., Water Pollution Control Assn., Am. Water Works Assn., N.E. Soc. Conservation Engrs., Nat. Assn. Envrion. Profls., Am. Inst. Fishery Research Biologists, Tau Beta Pi. Republican. Clubs: Masons, Kiwanis (pres. Town of Wallkill 1977, 78). Home: 7 Oakcrest Dr Goshen NY 10924 Office: PO Box 42 Circleville NY 10919

EUSTIS, RICHARD ALAN, phys. facilities engr.; b. Strong, Maine, Oct. 24, 1932; s. Ralph Emerson and Marion Elizabeth (Richardson) E.; B.S. in Civil Engring., U. Maine, Orono, 1955; m. Elizabeth Currier, Oct. 4, 1958; 1 dau., Deborah Susan. Asst. maintenance engr. U. Maine, Orono, 1958-60, engr. dept. engring. services, 1960-63, asst. dir. engring. services, 1963-67, dir., 1967-69, asst. dir. phys. facilities U. Maine System, Bangor, 1969-74, dir., 1974-76, asst. vice chancellor adminstrn., dir. phys. facilities, 1976—. Mem. Municipal Planning Bd., Old Town, Maine, 1962-67, municipal sch. bd., 1965-69. Served with U.S. Army, 1955-58. Registered profl. engr., Maine; land surveyor, Maine. Mem. ASCE, Constr. Specifications Inst., Nat. Soc. Profl. Engrs., Assn. Phys. Plant Adminstrs., Univ. Risk Mgmt. and Ins. Assn., Am. Arbitration Assn. (constrn. arbitrator). Methodist. Author articles in field. Home: 85 Burnham St Old Town ME 04468 Office: 107 Maine Ave Bangor ME 04401

EVANOFF, GEORGE C., consumer products co. exec.; b. West Deer, Pa., June 5, 1931; s. Christ and Luba (Georgieff) E.; B.S. cum laude, U. Detroit, 1952; M.B.A., 1956; m. Mary Eleanor Yelavich, Nov. 21, 1964; 1 son, Michael. Engr., Gen. Motors, Detroit, 1953-57; marketing and product devel. exec. Ford Motor Co., Dearborn, Mich., 1957-68; v.p. mktg., planning and corp. devel. RCA Corp., N.Y.C., 1968-76; v.p. corp. planning Norton Simon Inc., N.Y.C., 1977—; dir. Nat. CSS Corp., Norwalk, Conn. Served with USAF, 1952-53. Mem. Beta Gamma Sigma. Home: 310 Stanwich Rd Greenwich CT 06830 Office: 277 Park Ave New York City NY 10017

EVANS, ANDERSON PIERCE, JR., broadcasting co. exec.; b. St. Augustine, Fla., July 8, 1924; s. Anderson Pierce and Grace (Crawford) E.; student North State Tex. Tchrs. Coll., 1943-44; B.E.E., U. Fla., 1949; m. Sadie Elizabeth Jury, 1946; children—Sandra, Pamela Evans Kelber. With CBS-TV, N.Y.C., 1949—, asso. dir. plant systems engring., 1964-67, dir. audio and video engring., 1967-78, dir. TV facilities planning, 1978—. Served with Signal Corps, U.S. Army, World War II; ETO. Fellow Audio Engring. Soc.; mem. IEEE (sr.), Soc. Motion Picture and TV Engrs., Sigma Tau. Presbyterian. Contbr. articles to profl. jours. Home: 29 Highfield Dr Dix Hills NY 11746 Office: 51 W 52d St New York City NY 10019

EVANS, BETTY BOLLBACK (MRS. C. HANS EVANS), educator; b. Bklyn., May 28, 1927; d. Anthony J. and Elizabeth (Balzer) Bollback; B.R.E., Nyack Coll., 1949; M.A., N.Y. U., 1951; postgrad. Northwestern U., 1953, Columbia U., 1952-57; m. C. Hans Evans, June 10, 1961. Audiologist, Manhattan Eye, Ear, Nose and Throat Hosp., N.Y.C., 1949-54; tchr. Lexington Sch. for Deaf, N.Y.C., 1954-59; supervising tchr. N.Y. Sch. for Deaf, White Plains, 1959-60; ednl. cons. Pa. Sch. for Deaf, Phila., 1960-68; prin. Middle Sch., Pa. Sch. for Deaf, 1968-71; asst. prof. spl. edn. Pa. State U., University Park, 1962-71; specialist in deaf edn. Chester County Child Devel. Center, Coatesville, 1971-78; asso. dean of students The King's Coll., Briarcliff Manor, N.Y., 1978—; cons. Nat. Com. on Library Standards for Schs. for Deaf, N.Y., 1965-66; lectr. civic religious and profl. groups. Mem. Chester County Health and Welfare Assn., 1962; social dir. Word of Life Summer Confs., N.Y., 1955-60; mem. corp. Lancaster Sch. of Bible, 1973; v.p. Living Word Radio Ministry Internat., 1974-77; bd. dirs. Coatesville Area Deaf Fellowship. Heartsease Home for Woman, N.Y.C.; hon. mem. program agy. United Presbyn. Ch. U.S.A., 1977—. Recipient Outstanding Service award Coatesville Area Council PTA. Mem. Coatesville Hosp. Aux., Westminister Aux. (pres. 1969), Octarara Hist. Soc., Alexander Graham Bell Assn. for Deaf, Conv. Am. Instrs. for Deaf, Presbyterian Women's Assn. (pres. 1976-77), Delta Kappa Gamma. Republican. Presbyn. Club: Coatesville Century. Address: The King's Coll Briarcliff Manor NY 10510

EVANS, BRUCE EUGENE, oral surgeon; b. Bangor, Maine, Oct. 7, 1943; s. R. Miles and Frances E. (Baldwin) E.; student U. Montpellier (France), 1963, U. Paris, 1964, Ecole de Louvre, Paris, France, 1964; B.A., Williams Coll., 1965; D.M.D., Harvard U., 1969. Practice dentistry specializing in oral surgery, N.Y.C., 1969—; asst. attending oral surgeon Mt. Sinai Hosp., N.Y.C.; clin. asso., coordinator internat. tng. center for hemophilia Mt. Sinai Sch. Medicine, N.Y.C.; asst. Beth Israel Med. Center, N.Y.C.; cons. oral surgeon Jewish Home and Hosp., N.Y.C.; mem. med. adv. bd. Met. chpt. Nat. Hemophilia Found. Mem. benefit com. Skowhegan Sch. Painting and Sculpture; bd. dirs. Haitian and Coarts Assn. Mem. ADA, Internat., Am., N.Y. State socs. oral surgery, ADA, N.Y. State Dental Soc. Clubs: Harvard, Williams (N.Y.C.). Home: New York City NY Office: 630 Fifth Ave Suite 1856 New York City NY 10020

EVANS, CLYDE HENRY, educator; b. Birmingham, Ala., Dec. 9, 1943; s. Samuel Lee and Rebecca Helen (Fields) E.; B.S., U. Detroit, 1966; Ph.D., Mich. State U., 1971. Elec. engr. Fairchild Space and Defense Systems, Syossett, L.I., summer 1966, physicist, summer 1967; asst. prof. philosophy Loyola U., New Orleans, 1972-73; asst. prof. U. Mass., Boston, 1973—; cons. N.Y. State Dept. Edn., 1974-76. NASA trainee, 1968-70. Andrew Mellon fellow, U. Pitts., 1971-72. Mem. Am. Philos. Assn. Author: Critical Thinking and Reasoning: A Handbook for Teachers, 1976. Home: 25 Troy Ln Waban MA 02168 Office: Dept Philosophy U Mass Boston MA 02125

EVANS, ERNEST PIPKIN, JR., govt. ofcl.; b. St. Petersburg, Fla., Mar. 6, 1944; s. Ernest P. and Carrie (McLeod) E.; student Jacksonville U., 1963-65; B.A., U. Md., 1970. Exec. dir. Jacksonville (Fla.) Youth Council, 1962-64, Nat. Youth Councils, Washington, 1964-66; profl. staff mem. Urban Am., Inc., Washington, 1966-67, U.S. Senate Select Com. Small Bus., Washington, 1967-74; sr. partner Ernest Evans & Assos., fed. relations cons., Washington and Elkton, Va., 1974-75; legis. asst. Va. Senate, Richmond, 1974-75; dir. advocacy Commn. on Fed. Paperwork, Washington, 1975-77; spl. asst. Immigration and Naturalization Service, 1977—. Mem. Page County Democratic Com. Recipient citation of merit Reader's Digest, 1965; Service to Mankind award Sertoma Internat., 1964; named in resolution for meritorious service Small Bus. Com., U.S. Senate, 1974. Mem. Am. Soc. Assn. Execs., Nat. Com. Children and Youth, Capitol Hill Restoration Soc. Clubs: U.S. Senate Staff, Capitol Hill Young Democrat. Co-author: Environmental Assessment—Approaching Maturity, 1978. Home: Route 1 Box 205 Elkton VA 22827 also 318 10th St SE Washington DC 20003

EVANS, EVAN, petroleum co. exec.; b. N.Y.C., May 19, 1925; s. John William, Jr. and Therese Rosemary (Guilfoyle) E.; student St. Lawrence U., 1942-43, 46, B.S., 1949; B.S., Mass. Inst. Tech., 1951; m. Natalie Coe Holbrook, Feb. 20, 1968; children—Megan, Meredith, Rhys, Valerie, Cynthia, David. Engr., Calif. Tex. Oil Corp., N.Y.C., 1951-55, Bahrain, 1955-57, refinery ops. asst., N.Y.C., 1957-60, Rotterdam, 1960-62, refinery plant mgr., Lebanon, 1963, refinery specialist, N.Y.C., 1963-65, refinery project mgr., King Wilkinson,

Antwerp, 1966-68; v.p. United Refining Co., Warren, Pa., 1971—; dir. Can Am Oil, Syracuse, N.Y., 1969-70, Kiantone Pipeline, 1970-76, United Refining Co., 1974-76, Texoma Pipe Line, 1974-76. Chmn. Am. Sch. Rotterdam, 1961-62. Served with USN, 1943-46. Mem. Warren C. of C. Clubs: N.Y. Athletic, Conewango. Home: 1265 E 5th St Warren PA 16365 Office: Bradley & Dobson Sts Warren PA 16365

EVANS, FLOYD LEE, JR., airline pilot; b. Springfield, Tenn., Jan. 10, 1931; s. Floyd Lee and Josephine Etta (Evans) E.; student Peabody Coll., 1949-52; m. Diana Lola Pedersen, Nov. 27, 1959; children—Denise Linda, Floyd Lee III. News photographer, corr. Nashville Tennessean, 1946-50; supr. flight tng. Tenn. Air NG, Nashville, 1955; pilot Trans World Airlines, Flemington, N.J., 1956—, capt., 1963—; cons. aviation; owner, operator horse farm Hunterdon County, N.J., 1966—, Ev Air Co., Flemington, 1966—. Mayor, Delaware Township, N.J., 1978. Pres. Delaware Twp. (N.J.) Republican Club, 1972-74. Served with USAF, 1950-54. Mem. Air Line Pilots Assn (dir. 1969-70), V.F.W. Baptist. Clubs: Amwell Valley Hounds Fox Hunt, (Hunterdon County, N.J.), Mason (Shriner), Elks. Home: RD 2 Box 280 Flemington NJ 08822

EVANS, FRANKLIN JAMES, JR., chem. engr.; b. Hazleton, Pa., June 1, 1921; s. Franklin James and Gertrude Elizabeth (Trishman) E.; B.S. in Chem. Engring., Lafayette Coll., 1942; M.S., Pa. State U., 1949; Ph.D. (duPont fellow), Ohio State U., 1952; m. Marian Jeanette Williams, Mar. 22, 1947; children—Franklin James, III, Joan Jeanette. With explosives dept. E.I. du Pont de Nemours & Co., Inc., 1942-45, with rayon dept., 1945-47, research asso., textile fibers dept., Wilmington, Del., 1953-77, ret.; cons. Pres. Northwood Civic Assn., 1957; deacon Presbyterian Ch. Mem. Am. Chem. Soc., Am. Inst. Chem. Engrs., Sigma Xi, Tau Beta Pi. Author, patentee in field. Home: 406 Garland Rd Wilmington DE 19803 Office: Du Pont Co Christina Lab Wilmington DE 19801

EVANS, GEORGE PAUL, educator; b. South Plainfield, N.J., Dec. 23, 1943; s. Paul Matthew and Ann Virginia (Rotola) E.; B.A. cum laude, Rider Coll., 1965; M.S., Ohio U., 1966; Ph.D., Syracuse (N.Y.) U., 1975; m. Susan Irene Cavalline. Reporter, Courier-News, Plainfield, N.J., 1965; instr. St. Bonaventure (N.Y.) U., 1966-69, asst. prof. journalism, 1970-76, asso. prof. mass communication, 1977—; reporter-editor Home News, New Brunswick, N.J., summers 1969-72; adj. prof. Syracuse U., 1969-70. Recipient medal of merit Pi Delta Epsilon, 1965, service award Nat. Council. Coll. Publs. Advisers, 1969, Gold Key Columbia U. Scholastic Press Assn., 1977. Mem. Nat. Council Coll. Publs. Advisers (dist. dir. 1966-72), N.Y. Collegiate Press Assn. (dir. 1969-72, exec. dir.), Greater Buffalo Press Radio and TV Assn., AAUP, Am. Assn. for Edn. in Journalism, Nat. Council Coll. Pub. Advisers, Pi Delta Epsilon (mem.-at-large nat. council 1967-73, nat. 1st v.p. 1973-75), Soc. Profl. Journalists. Author: Producing the School Newspaper: Organizing, Editing, Designing. Editor Coll. Publisher, 1967-71. Contbr. articles to profl. jours. Home: 33 Berva Dr Bradford PA 16701 Office: Box J Dept Mass Communication St Bonaventure U St Bonaventure NY 14778

EVANS, GERARD ERWIN, obstetrician and gynecologist; b. Bklyn., May 12, 1922; s. Robert and Frances (Diamond) E.; B.S., U. Ark., 1942; M.D., N.Y. Med. Coll., 1945; m. Adrienne R. Weiss, Dec. 27, 1952; children—Lisa Damon, Stacey Ann. Intern, Cumberland Hosp., Bklyn., 1945-46, resident, 1948-52; practice medicine, specializing in obstetrics and gynecology, Bklyn., 1952—; cons. dept. obstetrics and gynecology St. Johns Episcopal Hosp., Bklyn., 1970—; dir. dept. obstetrics and gynecology Caledonian Hosp., Bklyn., 1970—; instr. obstetrics and gynecology State U.N.Y., Bklyn., 1952-62; instr. L.I. U., 1975—; mem. med. malpractice panel Supreme Ct. of N.Y., 1975—. Served to capt. M.C., U.S. Army, 1945-47. Diplomate Am. Bd. Obstetrics and Gynecology. Fellow ACS, Am. Coll. Obstetricians and Gynecologists; mem. AMA, N.Y. State, Kings County med. socs., Bklyn. Gynecol. Soc. Club: Montauk. Home: 1051 E 24th St Brooklyn NY 11210 also Mere Point Rd Brunswick ME 04011 Office: 33 8th Ave Brooklyn NY 11217

EVANS, HUGH E., pediatrician; b. N.Y.C., July 6, 1934; s. David and Geraldine (Krebs) E.; A.B. cum laude, Columbia, 1954; M.D., State U. N.Y. Downstate Med. Center, 1958; m. Ruth L. Orloff, June 5, 1960; children—Margo Lynn, Marc Douglas. Intern, Johns Hopkins Hosp., Balt., 1958-59, asst. resident, 1959-60; sr. asst. resident NIH, Bethesda, Md., 1960-62, chief resident out-patient dept., 1962-63; practice medicine, Bellaire, Ohio, 1963-66; asso. dir. pediatrics Harlem Hosp. Center, N.Y.C., 1966-73; dir. dept. pediatrics Jewish Hosp. and Med. Center, Bklyn., 1973—; asso. clin. prof. pediatrics Columbia, 1968-73; prof. pediatrics State U. N.Y. Downstate Med. Center, Bklyn., 1973—; cons. Catholic Med. Center, St. John's Episc. Hosp. Trustee Bergen-Passaic County Lung Assn. Served to sr. asst. surgeon USPHS, 1960-62. Mem. Soc. For Pediatric Research, Harvey Soc., Am. Soc. Microbiology, Am. Thoracic Soc., Am. Pediatric Soc., Alpha Omega Alpha. Co-author: Perinatal Medicine, 1976. Contbr. articles to profl. jours. Home: 165 Serpentine Rd Tenafly NJ 07670 Office: 555 Prospect Pl Brooklyn NY 11238

EVANS, JAMES HURLBURT, corp. exec.; b. Lansing, Mich., June 26, 1920; s. James L. and Marie (Hurlburt) E.; A.B., Centre Coll. Ky., 1943; J.D., U. Chgo., 1948; m. Rosemary Hall Colgate, 1972; children by previous marriage—Eric Betram, Carol Ruth, Joan McLeod. Admitted to Ill. bar, 1949; atty., loan officer Harris Trust & Savs. Bank, Chgo., 1948-56; sec.-treas. Ruben H. Donnelly Corp., Chgo., 1956-57, v.p., N.Y.C., 1957-62, also dir.; co. merged in Dun & Bradstreet, Inc., 1961, fin. v.p., 1962-65, dir., 1962-77; pres. Seamen's Bank for Savs., N.Y.C., 1965-68, also chmn. bd., 1968, trustee, 1965—; pres., dir. Union Pacific Corp., 1969-77, chmn. bd., chief exec. officer, 1977—; dir. U.P.R.R., 1965—, vice chmn. bd., 1969-77, chmn., 1977—; dir. Bristol-Myers Co., AT&T, Citicorp. Pres., Nat. Recreation Found., 1971-75; bd. govs. N.Y. Hosp.; trustee Union Pacific Found., Rockefeller Bros. Fund, U. Chgo., Tax Found.; founding chmn., life trustee Nat. Recreation and Park Assn.; trustee, vice-chmn. Centre Coll. Ky.; founding mem. Citizens Adv. Com. on Environ. Quality, 1966-70; bd. govs. ARC, 1970-76, nat. fund chmn., 1974-76; bd. dirs. Josiah Macy Jr. Found., United Fund Greater N.Y.; bd. mgrs. N.Y. Bot. Garden. Served to lt. USNR, 1943-46. Mem. Assn. Am. R.R.'s (exec. com., dir.), Fgn. Policy Assn. (dir.), Am., Chgo. bar assns., Bus. Roundtable, Bus. Council, Pilgrims of U.S., Phi Beta Kappa, Omicron Delta Kappa, Delta Kappa Epsilon. Presbyterian. Clubs: Met. (D.C.); Downtown Assn., River, Racquet and Tennis, Links (N.Y.C.). Office: 345 Park Ave New York City NY 10022

EVANS, JOHN ROBERT, univ. pres., physician; b. Toronto, Can., Oct. 1, 1929; s. William Watson and Mary Evelyn Lucille (Thompson) E., M.D., U. Toronto, 1952; D.Phil. (Rhodes scholar), Oxford U., 1955; LL.D., Dalhousie U., McMaster U., McGill U., 1972, Queen's U., 1974, Wilfred Laurier U., 1975, York U., 1977, Yale U., 1978; D.Sc., Meml. U., 1973, U. Montreal, 1977; D.H.L., Johns Hopkins U., 1978; D.U., U. Ottawa, 1978; m. Jean Gay Glassco, 1954; children—Derek, Mark and Michael (twins), Gillian, Timothy, Willa. Intern Toronto Gen. Hosp., 1952-53, chief resident physician, 1958-59; practice medicine specializing in cardiology, Toronto, 1961—; asso. dept. medicine U. Toronto Med. Sch., 1961-65, prof., 1972—, pres. univ., 1972—; physician Toronto Gen. Hosp., 1961-65; dean Faculty Medicine, McMaster U., Hamilton, Ont., 1965-72, v.p. health scis., 1967-72. Decorated companion Order of Can.; Markle scholar, 1960-65. Fellow Am., Royal colls. physicians. Home: 93 Highland Ave Toronto ON Canada Office: U Toronto Toronto ON Canada

EVANS, JOSEPH HENRY, clergyman, ch. exec.; b. Kalamazoo, Mich., Aug. 15, 1915; s. Charles A. and Etta (Hill) E.; A.B., Western Mich. U., 1939, L.H.D., 1969; B.D., Yale U., 1942; L.H.D., Cedar Crest Coll., Allentown, Pa., 1968; D.D., Chgo. Theol. Sem., 1969; m. Harriette Clark, Oct. 15, 1944; children—Lesley (Mrs. John Christian), Harriette (Mrs. Charles Smith, Jr.), Barbara. Ordained to ministry Congregational Ch., 1942; pastor St. Lukes Congl. Ch., Bklyn., 1942, Grace Congl. Ch., N.Y.C., 1942-46, Mt. Zion Congl. Ch., Cleve., 1947-53, Ch. of Good Shepherd, Congl. United Ch. of Christ, Chgo., 1953-67; sec. United Ch. of Christ, N.Y.C., 1967—; asso. gen. sec. Conn. Council Chs., Hartford, 1946-47. Chmn. hdqrs. com. United Ch. of Christ, 1961-63, pres. Ill. Conf., 1965-67. Mem. Mayor's Com. on New Residents, 1965-69; mem. Citizens Com. Juvenile Ct., Chgo., 1965-66. Pres. Chgo. Urban League; bd. dirs. Community Renewal Found., Community Fund Chgo., Provident Hosp., Chgo.; trustee LeMoyne-Owen Coll., Memphis. Recipient Scroll of Honor, Ch. of Good Shepherd, Chgo., 1963. Urban League and Chgo., 1967. Mem. World Alliance of Reformed Chs. (exec. com.), Kappa Alpha Psi. Home: 112-20 178th Pl St Albans NY 11433 Office: 297 Park Ave S New York City NY 10010

EVANS, PHILIP GORDON, aerospace engr.; b. Scranton, Pa., Jan. 12, 1915; s. William G. and Rachel M. (Thomas) E.; B.A., Pa. State U., 1936; M.A., George Washington U., 1949; m. Constance A. Larson (dec. 1964); children—Judith M., Philip G. Cons. heavy mil. electronics dept. Gen. Electric Co., Syracuse, N.Y., 1963-65, mgr. spl. requirements, aerospace group, Valley Forge, Pa., 1965—. Active Boy Scouts Am.; mem. Chester County Assn. Retarded Citizens. Served to col. USAF, 1942 -63. Fellow Am. Inst. Aeros. and Astronautics (asso.); mem. Mil. Ops. Research Soc., Assn. Old Crows, Phi Kappa Phi, Kappa Phi Kappa, Phi Eta Sigma, Pi Delta Epsilon, Pi Gamma Mu, Alpha Delta Sigma, Delta Upsilon. Republican. Episcopalian. Clubs: Army and Navy, Capitol Hill (Washington). Home: 5 Treemont Dr Malvern PA 19355

EVANS, RICHARD EDELEN, restaurant exec.; b. Balt., May 23, 1941; s. Gustauvus Warfield and Frances (Edelen) E.; B.A., U. Va., 1965. Exec. dir. Jr. Officers and Profl. Assn., Washington, 1966-68; mem. advance staff Senator Edmund S. Muskie, 1968, 70-72; owner Sarsfield's Restaurant, Washington, 1974—, The Crease, Balt., 1972—. Bd. dirs. Towson Bus. Assn., 1972—, Md. chpt. ARC, LaCrose Found. Mem. Nat. Restaurant Assn., Baltimore County C. of C. (dir. 1977). Democrat. Roman Catholic. Home: 521 Dunkirk Rd Baltimore MD 21212

EVANS, ROBERT HAROLD, orthodontist; b. Warren, Ohio, June 10, 1927; s. Robert Harold and Ida (Grainger) E.; B.A., U. Buffalo, 1948, D.D.S., 1952, certificate in orthodontics, 1957; m. Dorothy Harrington Lapp, Aug. 11, 1951; children—Robert L., Nancy M. Intern, Edward J. Meyer Meml. Hosp., Buffalo, 1952-53; practice orthodontics, Williamsville, N.Y., 1957—; v.p., dir. Protective Closure Co., Inc.; dir. Mfrs. & Traders Trust Co. Mem. Williamsville Planning Commn., 1965-70; bd. dirs. Williamsville Cemetary; pres. Hanford Bay Property Owners Assn., 1969. Served from 1st lt. to capt. USAF, 1953-55. Fellow Internat. Coll. Dentists; mem. ADA, N.Y., 8th Dist., Erie County (dir. 1967) dental socs., Am. Assn. Orthodontists, Northeastern Soc. Orthodontists, U. Buffalo Orthodontic Alumni Assn. (v.p. 1967), Buffalo Acad. Orthodontists (sec. 1968), Alumni Assn. U. Buffalo, Phi Kappa Psi, Xi Psi Phi. Republican. Presbyterian. Clubs: Mason, Shrine, Rotary (pres. 1969-70), Antique Automobile Am. Gridiron of University Buffalo, Automobile of Buffalo, Buffalo Country, Hanford Bay Community (pres. 1961). Home: 4 Ledge View Terr Williamsville NY 14221 Office: 5893 Main St Williamsville NY 14221

EVANS, ROBERT MATTHEW, food service mgmt. co. exec.; b. Hamburg, N.Y., Nov. 12, 1937; s. Mendal Matthew and Hazel (Becker) E.; B.S., Fla. State U., 1959; m. Suzanne Stutzman, Oct. 13, 1962; children—Robert Matthew, Tracy. Gen. mgr. Ziegler's Famous Donuts, Buffalo, 1959-62; v.p. Blue Mountain Ski Resort, Arcade, N.Y., 1959-62; trainee, food service mgr. coll. div., N.E. dist. mgr. health care div. Saga Food Service, Geneva, N.Y., 1962-68; pres. Dietary Cons.'s N.Y., Hornell, 1968—, Dietary Cons.'s Fla., Pensacola, 1976—, Am. Med. TV Leasing Corp., Evandale Devel., Inc. Mem. Am. Mgmt. Assn., Nat. Restaurant Assn. (Gt. Menu award 1978), Am. Soc. Hosp. Food Service Adminstrs., Nat. Free Style Skiers Assn., Lambda Chi Alpha. Republican. Presbyterian. Clubs: Hornell Rotary, N.Y. State Adirondack, Masons. Home: 353 Seneca Rd Hornell NY 14843 Office: 347 1/2 Seneca Rd Hornell NY 14843

EVANS, THOMAS ARCHIE, oral dental mktg. researcher; b. Phila., Aug. 31, 1928; s. Thomas F. and Jessie M. (Redcross) E.; B.S. in Biology/Chemistry, Shaw U., 1950; D.D.S., Temple U., 1958; m. Constance Elizabeth Swain, Aug. 31, 1957; children—Karen Elizabeth, Thomas Anthony. Extern oral surgery Mercy Douglas Hosp., Phila., 1958; practice gen. dentistry, Lawnside, N.J. and Phila., 1958-69; sr. clin. scientist Warner-Lambert Co., Morris Plains, N.J., 1969-72; dir. dental affairs Lactona Corp., 1972-75 dir. clin. dentistry, 1975-77, dir. modular denture div., 1978—; dental examiner Phila. Bd. Pub. Edn., 1959-68, N.J. Dept. Health, 1964-68. Dep. dir. community relations Phila. Opportunities Industrialization Center, 1968-69; v.p. Camden County Dental Health Com., 1963-69; v.p. troop 135 com. Boy Scouts Am., 1962-75; past mem. bd. dirs Camden County Council on Econ. Opportunity, Camden County Legal Services Com.; bd. dirs. Morris County Urban League, Morris County United Way; past mem. adv. com. Expanding Horizons, Drexel Inst. Served with Chem. Corps, AUS, 1951-53; maj. Res. Mem. Am. Med. Writers Assn., Internat. Assn. for Dental Research, Nat., Am. dental assns., Tri-County, N.J., So., Commonwealth dental socs., Res. Officers Assn., Omega Psi Phi. Home: West Valley Brook Rd Long Valley Washington Twp NJ 07830 Office: 173 Tabor Rd Morris Plains NJ 07950

EVANS, THOMAS BEVERLEY, JR., congressman; b. Nashville, Nov. 5, 1931; s. Thomas B. and Hannah (Hundley) E.; B.A., U. Va., 1953, LL.B., 1956; m. Mary Page Hilliard, Sept. 23, 1961; children—Thomas B. III, Robert S., Mary Page. Admitted to Va. bar, 1956; pres. Evans & Assos., Wilmington, Del.; mem. 95th Congress from Del. Mem. Gov.'s Task Force on Marine and Coastal Affairs, Gov.'s Council on Vocat. Edn.; dir. Del. State Devel. Dept.; chmn. for Del., Radio Free Europe; chmn. United Negro Coll. Fund, Del.; mem. exec. com., bd. dirs. Wesley Coll.; chmn. region Nixon-Agnew, 1968; dep. fin. chmn. Rep. Nat. Com., 1969; Rep. nat. committeeman from Del., 1970—; co-chmn. Rep. Nat. Com., 1971-73; trustee Woodberry Forest Sch. Recipient citation for aiding in employment of handicapped Am. Legion. Clubs: Wilmington, Wilmington Country; Pine Valley Golf. Home: 1111 Brandon Ln Westover Hills Wilmington DE 19807 Office: 5021 Fed Bldg Wilmington DE 19801

EVANS, THOMAS HADDOCK, natural gas co. exec.; b. Pitts., May 13, 1913; s. Thomas C. and Mazie E. (Erskine) E.; B.A., U. Pitts., 1938; m. Blanche H. Haus, Sept. 15, 1943; 1 dau., Susan Evans Murray. Comml. sales mgr., promotion mgr., asst. gen. sales mgr., asst. v.p. charge ops. Equitable Gas Co., Pitts., 1946-49, v.p. charge sales, 1953-59; v.p. Ky.-W.Va. Gas Co. subs. Equitable Gas Co., Ashland, Ky., 1950-53; v.p. Carnegie Natural Gas Co. subs. U.S. Steel Corp., Munhall, Pa., 1959-60, pres., 1960—. Active Pitts. Civic Light Opera, 1954-59. Served to capt. U.S. Army, 1942-46. Decorated Purple Heart, Bronze Star. Mem. Am., Pa. gas assns., Engrs. Soc. Western Pa., W.Va. Oil & Natural Gas Assn., Am. Petroleum Inst., Mil. Order of World Wars, VFW, Am. Automobile Assn. Am. (dir., sec.; pres. Pa. fedn., trustee found. for traffic safety). Clubs: West Penn Motor (dir., past pres.), Longue Vue Country, Duquesne, Pitts. Athletic, Masons (32 deg., Shriner, Jester). Home: 453 Summit Dr Pittsburgh PA 15228 Office: 3904 Main St Munhall PA 15120

EVANS, WAYNE RUSSELL, photog. co. exec.; b. Utica, N.Y., July 2, 1921; s. Irwin Ray and Lena K. (Hauser) E.; B.S. in Physics, Cornell U., 1943, M.S., 1947; m. Eleanor Ruth Bellosa, Feb. 2, 1946; children—Eleanor Ann, David R. With Eastman Kodak Co., Rochester, N.Y., 1947—, engr. Navy ordnance div., 1947, various assignments apparatus and optical div., 1948-62, asst. program mgr. research and engring., 1963, staff asst. to gen. mgr. apparatus div., 1964-66, asst. mgr. comml. and profl. products, 1966-73, product group mgr. bus. products, 1973—. Teaching asso. U. Rochester, 1947-48. Served with USMCR, 1943-45. Mem. Optical Soc. Am., Soc. Photog. Engrs. and Scientists, Nat. Microfilm Assn., Rochester C. of C., Sigma Xi. Presbyn. (trustee 1971-74). Club: Monroe Golf (Rochester). Home: 265 Inwood Dr Rochester NY 14625 Office: 901 Elmgrove Rd Rochester NY 14650

EVANS, WILLIAM SAMUEL, mgf. co. exec.; b. Dayton, Ohio, Jan. 23, 1918; s. William Lewis and Della (Ferguson) E.; B.A., Harvard, 1948; M.B.A., U. Chgo., 1952; m. Eva Esterhazy, June 7, 1959; children—Alexander, Eva. Instr., Hofstra U., Hempstead, N.Y., 1953-55; economist First Nat. City Bank, N.Y.C., 1957-59; market researcher St. Regis Paper Co., N.Y.C., 1959-66; dir. bus. devel. Phelps Dodge Industries, Inc., N.Y.C., 1966—. Mem. Darien Rep. Town Meeting, 1972—; active worker Republican Com., Darien, Conn., 1970—. Served with USAAF, 1943-46; PTO. Mem. Sales Execs. Club, Pan Am. Soc. (dir. 1975-79), Nat. Assn. Bus. Econs., Darien C. of C., Beta Theta Pi. Clubs: Copper (N.Y.C.); Darien Cotillion; Harvard (New Canaan, Conn.). Home: 105 Hollow Tree Ridge Rd Darien CT 06820 Office: 300 Park Ave New York City NY 10022

EVE, ARTHUR OWEN, state legislator; b. N.Y.C., Mar. 23, 1933; s. Arthur B. and Beatrice (Clark) E.; student W.Va. State Coll., 1950-53, Erie County Community Coll., 1957; m. Lee Constance Bowles, June 3, 1956; children—Arthur O., Leecia R., Eric V., Martin King, Malcolm X. Pres., Buffalo Challenger news weekly, 1965—; mem. N.Y. State Assembly, 1966—, mem. rules, ways and means, social services, elderly coms., dep majority leader, 1977—, chmn. Assembly urban task force, 1978—; chmn. N.Y. Legis. Black and Puerto Rican Caucus, 1975-76; founder, pres. No. (N.Y.) Region Black Polit. Caucus. Democratic candidate for mayor Buffalo, 1977; mem. N.Y. state Dem. com. 1976—; asso. vestryman St. Philips Episcopal Ch., Buffalo. Served with U.S. Army, 1953-55. Named one of ten most influential persons in Buffalo, Buffalo Mag., 1978. Mem. NAACP (life). Home: 184 Jewett Pkwy Buffalo NY 14214 Office: Legis Office Bldg 1303 Fillmore Ave Buffalo NY 14211

EVELYN, GEORGE ELBERT, educator; b. Sapulpa, Okla., Jan. 12, 1943; s. George E. and Dorthea Jane (MacMillian) E.; Mus.B., Okla. Bapt. U., 1968; Mus.M., N. Tex. State U., 1970; m. Judy K. Edwards, Sept. 5, 1964; children—Jeffrey Stephen, Robert Jason. Instr. music Southeastern State U., Durant, Okla., 1971-73; minister of music First United Methodist Ch., Durant, Okla., 1971-73; lectr. music Mount Allison U., Sackville, N.B., Can., 1973—; dir. music Trinity-St. Stephen United Ch., Amherst, N.S., Can., 1973—; choral dir. Mt. Allison U. Summer Music Camp., 1974—; clinician N.S. Choral Fedn., 1977; recitalist CBC, 1977-78; adjudicator Maritime Music Festival, 1978; participant Can. Choral Dirs. Seminar, 1978. Served with USAF, 1961-65. Mem. Nat. Assn. Tchrs. Singing, Am. Choral Dirs. Assn., Canadian Assn. Univ. Schs. Music, Phi Kappa Lambda, Phi Mu Alpha. Home: PO Box 1018 Sackville NB Canada Office: Dept Music Mount Allison University Sackville NB Canada

EVENSON, DONALD PAUL, educator; b. Story City, Iowa, Oct. 30, 1940; s. Harold Martin and Mildred Bodil (Hermanson) E.; B.A., Augustana Coll., S.D., 1964; Ph.D., U. Colo., 1968; m. Carol Oretta Ausland, June 22, 1963; children—Kay Michelle, Paul Harold, Mark Edward. Postdoctoral research fellow Inst. Molecular Biophysics, Fla. State U., Tallahassee, 1968-70; staff scientist Union Carbide Research Inst., Tarrytown, N.Y., 1970-72; asst. prof. Cornell U. Grad. Sch. Med. Sci., 1972—, also asso. Sloan Kettering Cancer Inst., N.Y.C. Mem. Am. Soc. Cell Biology, Am. Soc. Microbiology, AAAS, N.Y. Soc. Electron Microscopy. Home: 21 Larchmont St Ardsley NY 10502 Office: 410 E 68th St New York City NY 10021

EVERETT, JOHN RUTHERFORD, coll. pres.; b. Portland, Oreg., Dec. 27, 1918; s. Monroe Green and Margaret (Johnson) E.; A.B., Park Coll., 1942, LL.D., 1961; B.D., Union Theol. Sem., 1944; A.M., Columbia, 1943, Ph.D., 1945; LL.D., Roanoke Coll., 1960; m. Elizabeth Sloan, June 13, 1942 (div. June 1963); 1 dau., Margaret Elizabeth; m. 2d, Elsie Lievesly, Jan. 21, 1964. Dir. YMCA, USO McBurney br., N.Y.C., 1943-44; instr. philosophy Columbia, 1943-45, asst. prof. philosophy, 1948-50, chmn. dept. philosophy, sch. gen. studies, 1948-59; asst. prof. philosophy Wesleyan U., Middletown, Conn., 1945-48; pres. Hollins Coll., 1950-60; chancellor City U. N.Y., N.Y.C., 1960-62; sr. v.p. Ency. Brit., Inc., also pres. Ency. Brit. Press, mem. bd. editors, 1962-64; pres. New Sch. Social Research, N.Y.C., 1964—; dir. Shenandoah Life Ins. Co. Mem. Conn. Senate Spl. Investigating Com. on Edn., 1945-46; cons. Council For Fin. Aid to Edn., 1956; adviser to Gov. Conn., 1948-50; del. chmn. 3d Ann. UNESCO Conf., Paris, 1952. Bd. dirs. Roanoke Guidance Center, 1951-56, Roanoke Fine Arts Center, 1951-55, Union Theol. Sem., 1961—; trustee New Lincoln Sch., N.Y.C., 1971—. Recipient U.S. Jr. C. of C. award as 1 of 10 Outstanding Young Men of Year, 1950; comdr. Cross of Order Merit, Fed. Republic Germany, 1973. Fellow Nat. Council Religion Higher Edn.; mem. Am. Philos. Assn., Assn. Am. Colls. (commn. liberal edn. 1953-55, commn. finance 1959—), Am. Council Edn. (com. measurement and evaluation 1959—), Va. Edn. Assn. (ednl. policies com. 1959—), Va. Found. for Ind. (trustee 1952—, sec.-treas. 1952-53), Conn. Research Council (chmn. 1946-49), Council Higher Instns. N.Y.C. (pres. 1967-69). Democrat. Presbyn. Author: Religion in Economics, 1946; Religion in Human Experience, 1950. Book editor Jour. Philosophy, 1945-52. Contbr. article religion to Ency. Americana, 1951, 56; articles, revs. to numerous learned jours. Office: 66 W 12th St New York City NY 10011

EVERETT, WOODROW WILSON, JR., elec. engr.; b. Newton, Miss., Oct. 11, 1937; s. Woodrow Wilson and Katherine Elizabeth (Thrash) E.; B.E.E., George Washington U., 1959; M.S., Cornell U., 1965, Ph.D., 1968; m. Cherry Donna Sarff, Aug. 23, 1958;

children—Woodrow, Cherry Leanne. Project engr. Scott Paper Co., Mobile, Ala., 1959; project engr. Atlantic Research Corp., Ithaca, N.Y., 1962-64; dir. postdoctoral program Rome Air Devel. Center, 1964-75; chmn. bd. N.E. Consortium for Engring. Edn., Bridgeport, N.Y., 1975—; chmn. Southeastern Center for Elec. Engring. Edn.; dir. Device Assos. Corp. of N.Y., Masonwood Inc., Data Functions Inc., Groton Community Devel. Corp. Pres. Groton (N.Y.) Youth Center, 1965-68; dir. CO, Town of Groton, 1967-71; pres. Groton Village Bd. Appeals, 1966-71; chmn. Groton Planning Bd., 1968-69. Served with USAF, 1959-62. Fellow IEEE. Democrat. Author 4 books in field. Office: FTU-SORC 7300 Lake Ellenor Dr Orlando FL 32809 also CHERWOOD-Oneida Lake Walnut Rd Bridgeport NY 13030

EVICA, GEORGE MICHAEL JOSEPH, educator; b. Garfield Heights, Ohio, Dec. 8, 1927; s. Marko and Anna (Stipicivich) E.; A.B., Western Res. U., 1949; M.A. with high honors, Columbia, 1955, postgrad., 1957-60; postgrad. Hartford Sem. Found., 1969-70; m. Alycia Brierley, Sept. 15, 1965; 1 dau., Mariana Kemble. Music and effects editor Hearst-Metrotone News, N.Y.C., 1952-55, rec. dir., 1952-55; instr. Rutgers U., New Brunswick, N.J., 1956-57, Columbia, 1957, Bklyn. Coll., 1957-60; asst. prof. San Francisco State U., 1960-64; asst. prof. U. Hartford (Conn.), 1965-75, asso. prof. English, 1976—; writer, dir. radio series and newspaper columns Assassination Jour. Dir. Conn. Citizens Commn. of Inquiry, 1975-76. Fellow Soc. for Arts, Religion and Contemporary Culture; mem. Modern Lang. Assn., AAUP. Author: And We Are All Mortal: New Evidence and Analysis in the J.F.K. Assassination, 1978. Contbr. articles to profl. jours. Home: 107 N Beacon St Hartford CT 06105 Office: U Hartford Dept English West Hartford CT 06117

EVIRS, HOWARD WESLEY, JR., pub. utility exec.; b. Boston, Oct. 3, 1925; s. Howard Wesley and Inez (Harriman) E.; B.S. in Elec. Engring. with honors, Northeastern U., 1951, M.B.A., 1970; m. Helen G. Keefe, Mar. 12, 1949; children—Howard Wesley III, Diane E., Patricia A. Asst. elec. engr. Exeter & Hampton Electric Co., Exeter, N.H., 1951-52; asst. exec. engr. Fitchburg Gas & Electric Light Co. (Mass.), 1952-63, gen. supt., 1963-65, v.p., 1965-69, exec. v.p., 1969, pres., 1970—, also dir.; pres. Fitchburg Area Econ. Devel. Corp., 1971—; dir. Family Fed. Savs. & Loan Assn.; adv. dir. Worcester County Nat. Bank; exec. com. New Eng. Power Pool; instr., chmn. elec. circuit dept. Lincoln Coll., Boston, 1952-65. Bd. dirs. Montachusett Region Jr. Achievement, pres. 1967-69; bd. dirs. Montachusett area United Fund, v.p., 1969-71. Served with USNR, 1943-46. Registered profl. engr., Mass. Mem. Nat. Soc. Profl. Engrs., IEEE (past chmn. Boston sect.), Edison Elec. Inst., Elec. Council N.E. (dir.), New Eng. (dir.), Am. gas assns., Fitchburg C. of C. (pres., chmn. bd. 1974-76), Eta Kappa Nu, Tau Beta Pi. Clubs: Rotary, Fay (pres., dir.) (Fitchburg), Oak Hill Country; Down East Yacht (Maine); Commodores of America (Boston). Home: 10 Hemlock Dr Lunenburg MA 01462 Office: 655 Main St Fitchburg MA 01420

EVISTON, CHARLES LOUIS, therapeutic cons.; b. Fort Worth, Dec. 28, 1934; s. Albert Leon and Marie A. (Trapp) E.; B.S., Mich. State U., 1957; M.S., U. Mich., 1965, D.Sc., 1971; m. Susan Shirley, Sept. 4, 1973; children—Tracy Lynn, Timothy Charles, Todd Christopher, Debra. Dist. mgr. Greyhound Food Mgmt. Inc., Detroit, 1958-69; dietary dir., instr. Houston Baptist U., 1969-74; owner, mgr. Eviston Therapeutic Cons. Service, Miami, Fla., 1974-76; dir. therapeutics Dietary Cons., Inc., Hornell, N.Y., 1976—; mem. U.S. Pres. Council on Nutrition, 1973-74, named among Outstanding U.S. Nutritionists, 1975; mem. U.S. Disaster Team to Nicaragua, 1973. Mem. Am. Soc. Hosp. Food Service Adminstrs., Nat. Acad. Scis., Nat. Assn. Coll. Food Service Dirs., Phi Mu Alpha, Omicron Nu, Kappa Alpha. Presbyterian. Home: 80 Platt St Hornell NY 14843 Office: 353 Seneca Rd Hornell NY 14843

EVSLIN, BERNARD DAVID, author; b. Phila., Apr. 9, 1916; s. Leo Edward and Tillie (Stalberg) E.; student Rutgers U.; m. Dorothy Shapiro, Apr. 18, 1942; children—Tom, Lee, Pamela, Janet. Tchr. drama New Sch., N.Y.C., 1963-66. Served with AUS, 1942-45. Author: (plays) The Bostonians, 1949; Man That Corrupted Hadleyburg, 1951; The Geranium Hat, 1959; Step on a Crack, 1962; Cherry-Tree, Mo., 1974; (books) Merchants of Venus, 1964; Heroes, Gods and Monsters in Greek Myth, 1967; Adventures of Ulysses, 1968; The Trojan War, 1970; The Green Hero, 1975; Gods, Demigods and Demons, 1975; The Dolphin Rider, 1975; Greeks Bearing Gifts, 1977; Heraclea, 1978; Signs and Wonders, 1979. Home: 158 Sutton Manor New Rochelle NY 10805

EWALD, ELIN LAKE, art cons., appraiser; b. Raleigh, N.C.; d. John Marshall and S. Jane (Palmer) Lake; B.S., U. Md.; postgrad. Chgo. Art Inst.; children—Augusta, Patrick. Asso., Gallery Mayer, N.Y.C.; arts crafts editor Pageant mag.; crafts editor Homelife mag.; exec. v.p. O'Toole Assos., Inc., N.Y.C., 1978—; v.p. bd. dirs. 1185 Park Ave. Corp. Mem. Nat. Assn. Review Appraisers, Am. Soc. Appraisers (Asso.), Am.-Irish Hist. Soc., Am. Assn. Museums. Contbr. articles to mags. Home: 1185 Park Ave New York NY 10028 Office: 667 Madison Ave New York NY 10021

EWALD, FREDERICK CONRAD, orthopedic surgeon; b. Detroit, July 26, 1933; s. Frederick Henry and Rachel (Bauer) E.; B.A., Northwestern U., 1955, M.D., 1962; m. Sara Jane Torrison, Dec. 23, 1961; children—Jorand Adrian, Frederick Mandt, Eric Christopher. Intern, Northwestern U. Hosp., Chgo., 1962-63; resident U. Minn. Hosp., 1963-65, Mpls. Children's Hosp. Med. Center, Mass. Gen. Hosp., Boston, 1966-69; practice medicine specializing in orthopedic surgery, Boston, 1971—; mem. staffs Robert B. Brigham Hosp., Peter Bent Brigham Hosp.; asst. clin. prof. Harvard U. Med. Sch., Boston, 1977—. Served to lt. (j.g.) USNR, 1955-57. Mem. Am. Acad. Orthopedic Surgeons, New Eng. Orthopedic Soc., New Eng. Rheumatism Soc., Orthopedic Research Soc., Internat. Soc. Reconstructive Orthopedics and Traumatology. Contbr. articles to profl. jours.

EWALD, JOHN BENTON, JR., indsl. engr., realty co. exec.; b. Charleston, S.C., Nov. 10, 1918; s. John Benton and Charlotte Vanderhorst (Whaley) E.; B.S. in Indsl. Mgmt., Ga. Tech., 1942; m. Virginia Reynolds, May 17, 1942; children—John B., Walter W., Virginia R. Ewald Wich. Indsl. engr. U.S. Govt., Atlanta and Washington, 1946-50; exec. asst. to Asst. Sec. Def., Washington, 1951-56; logistics specialist Nat. Security Agency, Washington, 1956-64; pres. Dalfowe, Inc., Annapolis, Md., 1964—, River Bend Realty, Annapolis, 1965—. Served with U.S. Army, 1942-46; U.S. Navy, 1950-51. Roman Catholic. Clubs: Sherwood Forest (dir.), Spry Island. Home: 1003 Clumber Hill Sherwood Forest MD 21405 Office: 1625 Generals Hwy Annapolis MD 21401

EWALD, PETER K., educator; b. N.Y.C., Sept. 4, 1923; s. George F. and Bettha (Eckert) E.; A.B., N.Y. U., 1945, A.M., 1947, Ph.D., 1955; LL.D., Philathea Coll., 1967; m. Mary Carolyn Madden, Aug. 29, 1951; children—Peter K., Robert Francis. Asst. prof. N.Y. U., 1946-60; dean Coll. Bus., St. John's U., Jamaica, N.Y., 1960-63; dean, dir. evening div. C.W. Post Coll., Brookville, N.Y. 1963-64, provost, Merriweather campus, Brookville, 1964-69; prof. finance Roth Sch. Bus. C.W. Post Center, 1969—. Chmn. tng. com. Dist. 6, Nassau council Boy Scouts Am. Trustee L.I. Theatre Soc. Recipient Eloy Alfaro Grand Cross award. Mem. L.I. Assn. Commerce and Industry (dir.), Sales and Mktg. Execs. L.I., Real Practitioners Inst. L.I. (dir. 1974—), Delta Mu Delta, Delta Sigma Pi, Omicron Chi Epsilon, Sigma Phi Epsilon, Pi Gamma Mu, Tau Epsilon Phi, Phi Delta Kappa. Clubs: University (L.I. and N.Y.). Author: Political Science—A Review; co-author: Principles and Practices of Political Science, The Future of Business Education, New Dimensions in Business Education. Home: 34 Oak Ln Glen Cove NY 11542

EWART, JON ROBERT, lawyer; b. Weymouth, Mass., Oct. 25, 1944; s. Robert Galbraith and Doris Priscilla (Goodwin) E.; B.A. in Bus., Parsons Coll., 1967; J.D., Suffolk U., 1975; m. Elizabeth Ann Bailey, June 13, 1967; children—Jon R., II, Kristin E. Patrol officer Marshfield (Mass.) Police Dept., 1967-74, dept. prosecutor, 1974—, in-service instr. law, 1972—, instr. med. aid, 1978—; admitted to Mass. bar, 1978. Mem. Internat. Assn. Auto-theft Investigators, Mass. Police Assn., Am., Mass. bar assns., Plymouth County Prosecutors Assn. Address: 30 Elm St Marshfield MA 02050

EWEN, IRA, educator; b. Bklyn., May 30, 1931; s. Louis and Nettie (Glickman) E.; B.A., Harvard U., 1952, M.A. in Math., 1953; m. Linda Diane Beltzer, Aug. 26, 1967; children—Rani, Jessica, Lara, Britt. Teaching fellow in math. Harvard, 1953-57; tchr. math. Martin Van Buren High Sch., N.Y.C., 1958-65; chmn. math. dept. Springfield Gardens High Sch., N.Y.C., 1965-69, John Dewey High Sch., N.Y.C., 1969-75, adj. asst. prof. math. Coll. City N.Y., 1972-75; prin. James Madison High Sch., Bklyn., 1975—; vis. asst. prof. math. edn. U. Ill. at Champaign, 1967. Mem. N.Y.C. Standing Com. on Math., 1961-66; mem. N.Y. State Regents Coms., 1967-72. Mem. Assn. Tchrs. Math. (pres. 1964-66), Math. Chmns. Assn. (pres. 1973-75), Math. Assn. Am. (vice chmn. Met. sect. 1971-72), Nat. Council Tchrs. Math., Am. Math. Soc., Sigma Xi, Phi Delta Kappa, Kappa Delta Pi. Editor: Newsletter Assn. Tchr. Math., 1964-65. Home: 86-06 Edgerton Blvd Jamaica NY 11432 Office: James Madison High Sch 3787 Bedford Ave Brooklyn NY 11237

EWING, BLAIR GORDON, govt. ofcl., research adminstr.; b. Kansas City, Mo., Dec. 3, 1933; s. Lynn Moore and Margaret (Blair) E.; A.B., U. Mo., 1954; postgrad. (Rotary Found. fellow), U. Bonn. (Germany), 1957-58; A.M., U. Chgo., 1960; m. Barbara F. Thompson, Jan. 3, 1959; children—Blair Gordon, Chatham Boyd. Reporter, Chgo. City News Bur., 1958-59, UPI, 1959-60, Traffic World Mag., 1960-61; instr. polit. sci. Chgo. City Jr. Coll., 1961-62, State U.N.Y., Binghamton, 1962-67; planning and mgmt. cons. Harold Wise and Assos., Washington, 1967-69; program analyst Office of Asst. Sec. HEW, Washington, 1969-70; dir. criminal justice planning D.C. Govt., 1970-72; dir. dept. pub. safety Met. Washington Council of Govts., 1972-74; dir. planning and evaluation div. U.S. Dept. Justice, Washington, 1974-78; dep. dir. Nat. Inst. Law Enforcement and Criminal Justice, Dept. Justice, 1976—; acting dir., 1977—; adj. prof. Georgetown U. Law Center, 1971-74. Mem. Montgomery County (Md.) Human Relations Commn., 1975-76, Montgomery County Bd. Edn., 1976—. Served with U.S. Army, 1954-56. Woodrow Wilson fellow, 1956-57. Mem. AAAS, Am. Soc. Criminology, Am. Soc. Pub. Adminstrn., Phi Beta Kappa. Democrat. Unitarian. Author: Peace Through Negotiation: The Austrian State Treaty, 1966; mem. editorial rev. bd. Criminal Justice Rev., 1976—; contbr. articles to profl. jours. Home: 4 Park Valley Rd Silver Spring MD 20910 Office: 633 Indiana Ave NW Washington DC 20910

EWING, DONALD SPENCER, clergyman; b. Peoria, Ill., Feb. 26, 1916; s. Joseph Claude and Jennie Irene (Spencer) E.; student Wheaton Coll., 1939-42, No. Bapt. Sem., 1945-47; B.A., Aurona Coll., 1947; postgrad. Boston U., 1947-50; D.D., Portia Law Sch., 1955; m. Irene Kathleen Hollis, Oct. 21, 1941; children—John Calvin, Susan Spencer. Ordained to ministry Baptist Ch.; minister, Weymouth, Mass., 1948-50, Greenfield, N.H., 1951-55; minister Trinitarian Congl. Ch., Wayland, Mass., 1955—; prof. philosophy, asst. to pres. Gordon Coll., Boston, 1949-51; founding pastor Trinity Ch., Bolton, Mass., 1963; cons. minister St. Lawrence Congl. Ch., 1967-69. Trustee Scripture Union U.S.; bd. dirs. Lexington Christian Acad.; trustee, preacher Trinity Pulpit Trust; corp. mem. New Eng. Bapt. Hosp., Boston. Recipient Freedoms Found. Nat. Sermonic award, 1975. Mem. Evangelistic Assn. New Eng. (bd. mem. exec. com., v.p., corp. mem., chmn. finance and program cons.), Internat. Platform Assn. Author: All Things Are Possible. Contbr. articles to various mags. Weekly broadcast sermons stas. WROL, Boston WNAR, Phila., WGMS, AM and FM, Washington, others. Home: 1 Trinity Pl Wayland MA 01778 (summer) Merryhill Farm Greenfield NH 03047 Office: 53 Cochituate Rd Wayland MA 01778

EWING, ROBERT, lawyer; b. Little Rock, July 18, 1922; s. Esmond and Frances (Howell) E.; B.A., Washington and Lee U., 1943; LL.B., Yale U., 1945; m. Elizabeth Smith, May 24, 1947; 1 dau., Elizabeth Milbrey. Admitted to Conn. bar, 1945; asso. Shipman & Goodwin, Hartford, Conn., 1945-50, partner, 1950—; asst. pros. atty. West Hartford (Conn.), 1953-55; dir. Poly Choke Co., Inc. Bd. incorporators Hartford Hosp., Mt. Sinai Hosp.; bd. dirs. Travelers Aid Soc. Hartford, 1951-57, treas., 1954-57; bd. dirs. West Hartford YMCA, 1959-65, Family Service Soc., 1961-65, Hartford Hosp. Assn.; bd. dirs. Greater Hartford chpt. ARC, chmn., 1976-77, chmn., 1979—; trustee Leslie Jayne Meoni Found., vice-chmn., 1978—. Mem. Am., Conn. (chmn. fed. bench-bar relations com.), Hartford County bar assns., Am. Law Inst., Conn. Hist. Soc. (dir.), Newcomen Soc. N.Am. Congregationalist. (sr. deacon 1972-75, chmn. bd. adminstrn. and fin. 1975-78). Rotarian (pres. Hartford 1966-67). Clubs: Twentieth Century (pres. 1975-76), Hartford (bd. govs.), Mory's Assn., Dauntless. Home: 28 Birch Rd West Hartford CT 06119 Office: 799 Main St Hartford CT 06103

EYES, RAYMOND, mag. publisher; b. New Bedford, Mass.; s. Joseph Chester and Florence (Morgan) E.; B.A., U. Conn.; m. Anne Coleman, Dec. 27, 1947; children—Peter, Virginia, David, Edward. Engaged advt. sales N.Y. News, 1950-53, Advt. Agy. mag., 1953-54; with McCall Corp., 1954—, now pres., pub. McCall's mag., pub. Redbook mag., 1966-69; dir. Select Mags., N.Y.C. Bd. dirs. Day Care and Child Devel. Council Am.; trustee Westport Library. Served with U.S. Army, 1944-46. Mem. Mag. Pubs. Assn. (dir.), New Eng. Soc. Club: Cedar Point Yacht (Westport). Home: 4 Orchard Ln Westport CT 06880 Office: 230 Park Ave New York City NY 10017*

FABBRI, REMO, JR., psychiatrist; b. Norristown, Pa., Nov. 6, 1938; s. Remo and Anne Wilde (Butterworth) F.; B.A. in History, magna cum laude, Harvard, 1960; M.D. (Logan Clendening travelling fellow), Yale, 1964; m. Nancy Batson Nisbet Rash, June 27, 1962; 1 son, Gian-Dillman Rash. Intern, Bryn Mawr (Pa.) Hosp., 1964-65; postdoctoral fellow Yale Dept. Psychiatry, 1968-71, clin. asso. Yale New Haven Hosp., 1971—, clin. instr. Yale U. Sch. Medicine, 1971-77; practice medicine specializing in psychiatry and psychosomatic medicine, New Haven, 1971—; asso. in psychiatry U. Conn. Sch. Medicine. Served to capt. M.C., USAF, 1965-67. Fellow Acad. Psychosomatic Medicine; mem. Am. Psychiat. Assn., Conn. Med. Soc., Am. Assn. Clin. Hypnosis, Conn. Psychiat. Soc., New Eng. Assn. Clin. Hypnosis, Sexual Info. Edn. Counsel U.S., Assn. Advancement Behavior Therapy, Assn. Yale Alumni. Republican. Episcopalian. Contbr. articles to profl. jours. Office: 31 High St New Haven CT 06511

FABER, JOHN HENRY, photographer; b. N.Y.C., Feb. 13, 1918; s. John Martin and Jennie (Wacker) F.; B.A., U. Ala., 1941; m. Gertrud M. Jagode, Nov. 24, 1964; children—Erich, Karin (Mrs. Robert Clothier). Pub. relations photographer U. Ala. News Bur., 1937-41; chief photographer Ala. Ordnance Works of E.I. duPont de Nemours & Co., 1941-43, Birmingham Aircraft Modification Center of Bechtel-McCone-Parsons Corp., 1943-46; photog. dir. Birmingham News and WAMF-TV, 1946-50; photo-press rep. Eastman Kodak Co., N.Y.C., 1950—; lectr.; photog. exhibitor U.S. and Europe; adviser Smithsonian Instn.; mem. faculty Sch. Modern Photography. Past trustee Am. Mus. Photography, Phila. Nat. Press Photographers Assn. fellow, 1950, 71; named to Nat. Headliners Club, 1961; recipient pres.'s medal, Nat. Press Photographers Assn., 1961, 67. Joseph A. Sprague Meml. award, 1974. Mem. Photojournalism Soc. (life), Royal Photog. Soc. Great Britain (asso.), Nat. Press Photographers Assn. (life, nat. sec. 1948-50), Soc. Am. Historians, Photog. Adminstrs., Inc., Soc. Am. Travel Writers. Club: Explorers (N.Y.C.). Author: Industrial Photography, 1948; Great Moments in News Photography, 1960; Humor in News Photography, 1961; Travel Photography, 1971; Great News Pictures and Their Stories, 1978. Contbr. articles to profl. jours. Home: 52 Melrose Rd Mountain Lakes NJ 07046 Office: Eastman Kodak Co 1133 Ave of the Americas New York City NY 10036

FABIANO, WILLIAM LOUIS, educator; b. Weehawken, N.J., Mar. 5, 1946; s. Joseph and Dolores Maria (Gabriele) F.; B.A., St. John's U., 1968; M.A., L.I. U., 1970; m. Donna Anne Pepe, June 3, 1972. Instr., Holy Rosary Acad., Union City, N.J., 1968-71, Ednl. Opportunity Fund Program, Fairleigh Dickinson U., Teaneck, N.J., summer 1971, St. Joseph High Sch., West New York, N.J., 1971—; adj. prof. sociology Middlesex County Coll., Edison, N.J., 1971—, Fairleigh Dickinson U., 1971-72, Seton Hall U., South Orange-Paterson, N.J., 1971-73, St. Peter's Coll., Jersey City-Englewood, 1974—, Hudson County Community Coll., Jersey City, 1975—. Chmn., Ann. Thanksgiving Drives for Needy, Union City, 1968-72. Mem. Am., Eastern sociol. assns., Am. Acad. Polit. and Social Sci., N.J. Assn. Secondary Sch. Tchrs., Am. Assn. Tchrs. English. Club: Elks (chmn. West N.Y. ann. mother's day dinner 1976). Home: 113 Abbott Ave Palisades Park NJ 07650 Office: 5400 Broadway St West New York NJ 07093

FABINYI, GEZA THEODORE, ophthalmologist; b. Budapest, Hungary, Oct. 1, 1937; naturalized, 1966; s. Geza T. and Helen (Koczur) F.; B.S., U. Innsbruck (Austria), 1959, M.D., 1963; m. Jan. 12, 1963. Intern, Greensburg, Pa., 1965-66; emergency physician Columbia Hosp., Pitts., Pitts. Hosp., 1966-70; resident in ophthalmology U. Pa., 1970, W.Va. U., 1970-73; retina fellow H. Goldmann Eye Inst., U. Berne (Switzerland), 1974; practice ophthalmology, Altoona, Pa., 1974—; mem. staff Mercy Hosp., Altoona. Diplomate Am. Bd. Ophthalmology. Fellow Am. Acad. Ophthalmology, Internat. Coll. Surgeons, Swiss Ophthalmol. Soc., A.C.S.; mem. AMA, Pa., Blair County med. socs., Am. Coll. Emergency Physicians, World Med. Assn., Internat. Acad. Cosmetic Surgery. Republican. Lutheran. Office: Central Trust Bldg Suite 30G Altoona PA 16603

FABRICANT, NORMAN, mech. engr., inventor; b. Bklyn., June 28, 1934; s. Edward and Bertha (Gerber) F.; B.M.E., Coll. City N.Y., 1956; m. Arlene Susan Roshgolin, Dec. 24, 1972. Mech. engr. Rocketdyne div. N. Am. Aviation Corp., Calif., 1956-57, Sperry Gyroscope Co., Lake Success, N.Y., 1957-60, Potter Instrument Co., Plainview, N.Y., 1962-64, Bendix Aviation, Teterboro, N.J., 1965-70; patentee, inventor games, toys, and dolls, 1970—.

FACCINI, ERNEST CARLO, mech. engr.; b. Livo, Trento, Italy, May 28, 1949; s. Carlo and Elena Agnes (Pancheri) F.; born Am. citizen; A.A., Western Wyo. Community Coll., 1969; B.S., U. Wyo., 1972, M.S., 1976. Engring. technician Laramie (Wyo.) Energy Research Center, 1968-71; field engr. Mountain Fuel Supply Co., Rock Springs, Wyo., 1972; research engr. Aberdeen (Md.) Proving Grounds, 1972-73; research asst. mech. engring. U. Wyo., Laramie, 1973-76; engring. asst. Bridger Coal Co., Rock Springs, Wyo., 1973; mech. engr. Naval Explosive Ordnance Disposal Facility, Indian Head, Md., 1976—. Mem. ASME (chmn. student sect. 1971-72), Am. Phys. Soc., AAAS, Am. Soc. Metals. Roman Catholic. Researcher rapid explosive excavation techniques, underwater non-explosive excavation, surface/subsurface ordnance clearance vehicle design, remote fuse disassembly, aluminum burn bar investigation, multi-fuel combuster investigation. Home: PO Box 62B Rison MD 20681 Office: Code 50 NAVEQDFAC Indian Head MD 20640

FACER, DAVID CHARLES, pharm. co. exec.; b. Hackensack, N.J., Jan. 13, 1943; s. Charles D. and Margaret Helen (Woodworth) F.; B.A., Rutgers U., 1970, mgmt. certificate, 1974; m. Dolores Jean Walters, Oct. 26, 1963; children—Mark, David, Michele. Cons., Mgmt. Sci. Am., Englewood Cliffs, N.J., 1969-70; sr. systems analyst Warner-Lambert Co., Morris Plains, N.J., 1970-74, project leader systems devel., 1974-78, mgr. diagnostics div., mgmt. info. systems, 1978—. Unit commr. Boy Scouts Am., 1971-74; v.p. Byram Babe Ruth Assn., 1978-79; adv. Explorer post Boy Scouts Am., 1978—. Mem. Assn. Systems Mgmt. (chmn. div. 1972-74). Home: RD 2 Brookwood Rd Stanhope NJ 07874 Office: 201 Tabor Rd Morris Plains NJ 07950

FACOS, JAMES FRANCIS, educator; b. Lawrence, Mass., July 28, 1924; s. Chris and Theresa (McAdam) F.; A.B. in English, Bates Coll., 1949; M.A. in English, Fla. State U., 1958; m. Cleo Facos; children—Theresa Katina, Elizabeth, Anthony. Tchr., Vt. Coll., 1959-72, asso. prof. English, 1972—. Mem. Nat. Council Tchrs. English, Acad. Am. Poets, New Eng. Poetry Club. Author: The Piper O'The May; The Legacy; A Day of Genesis, Morning's Come Singing; The Silver Lady; Silver Wood; One Daring Fling. Specialist in English, Renaissance, poetry and the novel, children's lit. Home: 333 Elm St Montpelier VT 05602 Office: Vermont Coll Div of Norwich U Montpelier VT 05602

FADDEN, EILEEN ANN, bus. exec.; b. Delaware County, Pa., Jan. 13, 1943; d. Gerald Bernard and Ruth Catherine (Hart) F.; B.A., Immaculata Coll., 1969; M.A., Villanova U., 1976. Tchr., Archdiocesan Sch. Dist. Phila., 1963-68; editorial asst. Jour. Ecumenical Studies, Temple U., Phila., 1969; tchr. English, Springfield (Pa.) Sch. Dist., 1970-78, mgr. English dept., 1977-78; account exec. Merrill Lynch, Pierce, Fenner & Smith, Bala Cynwyd, Pa., 1978—. Mem. NEA, Pa. Edn. Assn., Springfield Edn. Assn., Am. Personnel and Guidance Assn., Franklin Inst. Home: 2630 W Chester Pike #J4 Broomall PA 19008 Office: Two Bala Cynwyd Plaza Bala Cynwyd PA 19004

FADELEY, HERBERT JOHN, JR., banker, lawyer; b. Ambler, Pa., Feb. 14, 1922; s. Herbert John and Jennie Miller (Lewis) F.; B.S. in Commerce, Drexel U., 1946; J.D., Temple U., 1953; diploma Stonier Sch. Banking, Rutgers U., 1957; m. Eleanor A. Battafarano, Feb. 8, 1947; children—Herbert John III, Brett Duane, Theresa Jane, Scott Lewis. Admitted to U.S. Supreme Ct. bar, 1957; asst. cashier to v.p. 1st Nat. Bank, Media, Pa., 1951; v.p. Boardwalk Nat. Bank, Atlantic City, 1957-60, Indsl. Trust Trust Co., Phila., 1960-62; v.p., trust officer, County Trust Co., White Plains, N.Y., 1963-68; pres. chief exec. officer Troy Savings Bank, (N.Y.), 1969—, also trustee; dir. Uncle Sam Mall Corp.; lectr. banking and law Drexel U., 1962, Rockland Community Coll., Suffern, N.Y., 1964-68, Westchester County chpt. Am. Inst. Banking, 1965-68, also Albany chpt. Vice-chmn. dist. council, Boy Scouts Am., 1969—; mem. Troy Downtown Devel. Com., Tri-county Fifty Group; bd. dirs. Hudson-Mohawk area United Way, gen. fund chmn., 1972; bd. dirs., pres. Rensselaer County unit Am. Cancer Soc.; trustee Russell Sage Coll. Major Old Guard City of Phila., Centennial Legion of Historic Mil. Commands, Inc. Served to lt. (j.g.), USNR, 1942-43, 48-59. Named Outstanding Alumnus, Drexel U., 1961; recipient trust div. sch. awards, N.Y. State Banker's Assn., 1967-68. Mem. Am. Bar Assn., Greater Troy C. of C. (dir. 1969—), Am. Judicature Soc., Assn. U.S. Army, Soc. Friends of St. Patrick (dir., pres.), Internat. Platform Assn., Nat. Rifle Assn., Drexel U., Temple U. alumni assns., Rensselaer County Hist. Soc., Am. Inst. Banking (Albany chpt.), Lambda Chi Alpha, Phi Alpha Delta (named outstanding alumnus 1957; chief justice Dr. Elden S. Magaw Alumni chpt. 1955-56). Episcopalian. Mason (Shriner, Jester). Clubs: Troy, Country (Troy). Home: 37 Brunswick Rd Troy NY 12180 Office: 32 2d St Troy NY 12180

FADER, SEYMOUR J., mgmt. and engring. cons. co. exec.; b. N.Y.C., Feb. 9, 1923; s. Louis and Bertha (Stachel) F.; student Coll. City N.Y., 1938-42; B.S. in Elec. Engring., U. Pa., 1949, M.B.A., in Indsl. Mgmt., 1950; m. Shirley Ruth Sloan, June 26, 1951; children—Susan Deborah, Steven Micah. Mgr. prodn. Bogue Electric Mfg. Co., Paterson, N.J., 1950-56; mgr. planning and control Rowe Mfg. Co., Whippany, N.J., 1956-58; cons. Koor Crafts & Industries, Ltd., Tel Aviv, 1958-59; dir. mfg. ops. ESC Electronics Corp., Palisades Park, N.J., 1959-62; mgr. mfg. Artistic Mfg., Sun Chem. Corp., Carlstadt, N.J., 1962-66; mgr. ops. Fairchild Instrumentation, Fairchild Camera & Instrument Corp., Clifton, N.J., 1966-67; v.p. Graphic Products, Inc., Hackensack, N.J., 1967-69; gen. mgr., v.p. Berkey Tech., Berkey Photo, Inc., Woodside, N.Y., 1969-72; v.p., prin. Suste Assos., Paramus, N.J., 1972—; asst. prof. mgmt. Ramapo Coll., Mahwah, N.J., 1972-75, asso. prof., 1975—. Mem. pub. health study N.J. State Assembly Commn. on Conservation, Natural Resources, Air and Water Pollution, 1972-73; commr. Paramus Environ. Commn., 1973-78, vice chmn., 1977-78, chmn. inventory and land use com., 1974-78. Served with U.S. Army, 1942-45. Mem. Am. Mgmt. Assn. (certificate of achievement 1974), Am. Arbitration Assn. (panelist), Am. Inst. Indsl. Engrs., Soc. Advancement of Mgmt. Author: Fundamentals of Management for First-Line Supervisors, 1974; The Manufacturing Manager, 1975; co-author: Jobmanship, 1979; contbr. articles to profl. jours. Patentee coreless reeler, desk-top copier, photo-copier. Home: 377 McKinley Blvd Paramus NJ 07652 Office: PO Box 422 Paramus NJ 07652

FADER, SHIRLEY SLOAN (MRS. SEYMOUR J. FADER), writer; b. Paterson, N.J., Feb. 24, 1931; d. Samuel Louis and Miriam (Marcus) Sloan; B.S., U. Pa., 1952, M.S., 1953; m. Seymour J. Fader, June 26, 1951; children—Susan Deborah, Steven Micah Kimchi. Writer, journalist, author, Paramus, N.J., 1956—; writer of People and You, Jobmanship columns Family Weekly, 1971—, also contbg. writer; contbg. editor Glamour mag., also writer column How To Get More From Your Job. Mem. Author's Guild, Am. Soc. Journalists and Authors (nat. v.p. 1976-77, nat. exec. council 1976—). Author: The Princess Who Grew Down, 1968; From Kitchen to Career, 1978; Jobmanship, 1979. Contbr. articles to nat. mags. Address: 377 McKinley Blvd Paramus NJ 07652

FADIL, RICHARD SAMUEL, urologist; b. Passaic, N.J., Feb. 15, 1929; s. Samuel Kaplan and Afife F.; B.A., Colgate U., 1950; M.D., N. Y. U., 1954; m. Beatrice Gevas, Jan. 15, 1956; children—Daniel, Lawrence. Intern, St. Vincent's Hosp., N.Y.C., 1954-55; resident in surgery and urology Coll. of Medicine and Dentistry of N.J., 1958-62; practice medicine specializing in urology, Clifton, N.J., 1962—; clin. instr. Columbia Presbyterian Med. Sch. and Center, N.Y.C., 1963—; dir. urology Passaic (N.J.) Gen. Hosp., 1976-79, Beth Israel Hosp., Passaic, 1977-79; sr. attending urologist St. Mary's Hosp., Passaic, 1962—. Served with USNR, 1955-57. Diplomate Am. Bd. Urology. Fellow A.C.S.; mem. AMA (recipient Physicians Recognition award 1977—). Am. Urol. Assn., Passaic County Med. Assn. Club: Masons. Contbr. articles to profl. jours. Office: 975 Clifton Ave Clifton NJ 07013

FAGAN, RAYMOND BERNARD, chem. co. exec., environ. cons.; b. Bklyn., Nov. 23, 1944; s. James and Helen (Gogarty) F.; B.S. in Biology, Fordham U., 1966; M.A. in Teaching, Fairleigh Dickinson U., 1967; Ph.D., N. Y. U., 1977. Tchr. high schs., N.J., 1964-67; aquatic biologist inst. N.E. Regional Tng. Center, Fed. Water Pollution Control Adminstrn., Edison, N.J., 1969-70; ednl. cons. Behavioral Research Lab., N.Y.C., 1970-71; chief evaluation and info. HUD Model Cities Program, Perth Amboy (N.J.) Community Devel. Agy., 1971-73; sr. environ. scientist Woodward-Clyde Cons., Clifton, N.J., 1973-75; pvt. cons., Laurence Harbor, N.J., 1975-77; mgr. tech. tng. and devel. Drew Chem. Corp., Boonton, N.J., 1977—; tech. reviewer McGraw-Hill Publs., N.Y.C., 1974-77; adminstrv. aide on environ. matters N.J. State Assemblyman John J. Froude, 1972-77; chmn. adv. council on environ. protection Middlesex County (N.J.) Bd. Chosen Freeholds, 1970—. Ford Found. intern, 1966-67. Mem. Am. Ednl. Research Assn., Am. Acad. Polit. and Social Sci., Nat. Assn. Research in Sci. Teaching, Phi Delta Kappa. Roman Catholic. Contbr. articles to profl. jours. Home: 25 Bayshore Ave Laurence Harbor NJ 08879

FAHEY, JOSEPH PAUL, JR. (JAY), advt. exec.; b. Wheeling, W.Va., Sept. 23, 1939; s. Joseph P. and Helen (Wingerter) F.; B.A., Allegheny Coll., 1961; m. Susan Ferdon, Apr. 22, 1967; children—William Wingerter, John Adam Blum. Project rep. Urban Redevel. Authority Pitts., 1961-62; copywriter Schwab, Beatty & Porter, Inc., N.Y.C., 1962-64; sr. copywriter Macmillan Co., N.Y.C., 1964-66; account exec. Am. Mgmt. Assn., N.Y.C., 1966-73; promotion mgr. F.W. Dodge div. McGraw-Hill Info. Systems Co., N.Y.C., 1973—, also dir. McGraw-Hill Credit Union. Lay minister St. Gregory's Ch., N.Y.C.; recorder FISH, N.Y.C. Democrat. Home: 201 W 89th St New York City NY 10024 Office: 1221 Ave of Americas New York City NY 10020

FAHY, CHARLES, judge; b. Rome, Ga., Aug. 27, 1892; s. Thomas and Sarah (Jonas) F.; student U. Notre Dame, 1910-11; LL.B., Georgetown U., 1914, LL.D., 1942; m. Mary Agnes Lane, June 26, 1929; children—Charles (Dom Thomas Fahy, O.S.B.), Anne Marie (Mrs. Rourke Sheehan), Sarah Agnes (Sister Sarah Fahy S.N.D.), Mary Agnes (Mrs. John C. Johnson). Admitted to D.C. bar, 1914, practiced in Washington until 1924; practiced in Santa Fe, 1924-33; city atty., Santa Fe, 1932; apptd. 1st asst. solicitor Dept. Interior, Washington, 1933; apptd. mem. Petroleum Adminstrv. Bd., 1933, chmn., 1934-35; apptd. gen. counsel NLRB, 1935; apptd. asst. solicitor gen. U.S., 1940; solicitor gen. U.S., 1941-45; legal adviser, dir. Legal Div. Mil. Govt., Germany (U.S.), 1945-46; apptd. legal adviser Dept. State, 1946. Adviser to Am. Del., San Francisco Conf., 1945; U.S. mem. legal com. Gen. Assembly UN, N.Y.C., 1946; alt. U.S. rep. to Gen. Assembly, UN, 1947, 1949; chmn. Pres.'s com. on Equality of Treatment and Opportunities in Armed Forces, 1948-50; pvt. practice, Washington, 1947-49; chmn. personnel security review bd. AEC, 1949; judge U.S. Ct. Appeals for D.C., 1949—. Served with U.S. Naval Aviation, 1917-19. Decorated Navy Cross, 1918; Medal for Merit, 1946; recipient Robert S. Abbott Meml. award (to President's Com.), 1951; Russwurm award, 1951, John Carroll award Georgetown U. Mem. Am., N.Mex. D.C., Fed. bar assns., Cath. Assn. Internat. Peace (pres. 1949). Democrat. Roman Catholic. Contbr. articles to publs. Home: 5504 Chevy Chase Pkwy NW Washington DC 20015

FAHY, WILLIAM THOMAS, elec. engr.; b. Boston, Jan. 17, 1941; s. Lawrence Henry and Kathleen J. (Spillane) F.; B.E.E., Merrimack Coll., 1963; M.E.E., Northeastern U., 1965, M.B.A., 1972. With Nat. Radio Co., Melrose, Mass., 1962-64; engr. AVCO, Wilmington, Mass., 1964-68, Raytheon Co., Bedford, Mass., 1968-69; mem. profl. staff TRW Systems Co., Bedford, 1969-70; applications cons. Dial-Data/Tymshare Co., Newton, Mass., 1970-73; tech. transfer Naval Underwater Systems Center, Newport, R.I., 1973—; project engr. USAF Hdqrs. Electronic Systems div. DCY, Hanscom AFB, Bedford, 1966—; instr. physics dept. Lowell Tech. Inst. Recipient Ron Prime Meml. Cup, 1976. Mem. IEEE, Mass. Soc. Profl. Engrs., Armed Forces Communications and Electronics Assn., Assn. Old Crows, Soc. History of Tech., New Eng. Rugby Football Union (team mgr.), Boston Rugby Referees Soc. Democrat. Roman Catholic. Clubs: Mystic River Rugby (treas.); Aberbeeg Rugby Football (Gwent, Wales); X-O Rugby (San Francisco). Home: 42 Bratley St Melrose MA 02176

FAILING, GREGORY SCOTT, winemaker; b. Herkimer, N.Y., Apr. 1, 1946; s. Arthur Howard and Edna Rita (Purdon) F.; B.Sc. in Chemistry, Rochester Inst. Tech., 1969; m. Katherine O'Riely, Apr. 11, 1975; 1 dau., Edna Ann. Research technician dept. food sci. N.Y. State Agrl. Research Sta., Geneva, 1969-72; chief chemist, supr. quality control Gold Seal Vineyards, Inc., Hammondsport, N.Y., 1972-75, winemaker, 1975—. Scoutmaster troop 1 Boy Scouts Am., Geneva; mem. Hammondsport Ambulance Corps. Mem. Am. Chem. Soc., Am. Soc. Enologists, Am. Wine Soc. Republican. Baptist. Club: Seneca Sports Car (pres.). Home: 263 Washington St Geneva NY 14456 Office: Route 54A Hammondsport NY 14840

FAILLA, R. ROY, lawyer; b. Newark, Apr. 29, 1934; s. Philip and Elena (Puglisi) F.; A.B., Seton Hall U., 1955, J.D., 1969; m. Sara Diglio, Feb. 12, 1956; children—Marybeth, Philip. Tech. rep. sales and marketing, tech. service Union Carbide Chems. Co., Buffalo, also Tarrytown, N.Y., 1955-61; tech. rep. marketing Shell Chem. Co. div. Shell Oil Co., Newark, 1961-65; sales mgr. East Coast Chem. Co., Little Falls, N.J., 1965-72; admitted to N.J. bar, 1970, practice in West Caldwell, 1972—; prosecutor Borough of West Caldwell, 1973-78; judge Municipal Ct. Borough of West Caldwell, 1978—. Served with AUS, 1955-63. Mem. Am., N.J., Essex County bar assns. Rotarian. Clubs: UNICO (gen. counsel West Essex 1973-77); Gridiron (counsel Caldwell, N.J. 1971—). Home: 21 Martin Rd West Caldwell NJ 07006 Office: 32 Smull Ave Caldwell NJ 07006

FAIRBANKS, DAVID NATHANIEL FOX, surgeon; b. Ann Arbor, Mich., Mar. 31, 1936; s. Avard Tennyson and Beatrice Maude (Fox) F.; B.S., U. Utah, 1959, M.D., 1963; m. Sylvia West, June 17, 1959; children—David Weston, Lisa Marie, Ethan Jeffrey, Galen Jeremy. Intern, Latterday Saints Hosp., Salt Lake City, 1963-64; resident in otolaryngology, fellow Johns Hopkins Hosp., 1964-69; mem. staff and med. bd., chief otolaryngology sect. Project HOPE, Washington, 1971—; bd. dirs. Ear Nose & Throat Med. Group, Washington, 1971—; chmn. div. otolaryngology George Washington U. Hosp., Washington, 1977—, asso. prof. surgery, 1975—; NIH research tng. fellow, 1968. Bishopric, Ch. of Jesus Christ of Latter-day Saints, 1977-78. Served with USPHS, 1969-71. Fellow ACS, Triological Soc.; mem. Am. Council Otolaryngology (dir., mem. exec. com.), AMA, Am. Acad. Ophthalmology and Otolaryngology, ACS, Am. Bd. Otolaryngology, Phi Beta Kappa, Med. Soc. D.C. Republican. Mem. Ch. of Jesus Christ of Latter-day Saints. Club: Country (Bethesda, Md.). Contbr. articles in field to profl. jours. Home: 6600 Bradley Blvd Bethesda MD 20034 Office: 2141 K St NW Washington DC 20037

FAIRCHILD, JOHN PHILLIP, physician; b. Washington, Dec. 25, 1918; s. Iler James and Vera Fae (Ward) F.; A.B., George Washington U., Washington, 1940, M.D., 1943; m. Julia Pearl Printz, Sept. 12, 1945; children—Jean Printz (Mrs. George DeTarnowsky), John Phillip, Jacqueline Patricia, James Patrick, Jerome Paul, Jeffrey Preston. Enlisted U.S. Army, 1944, resigned, 1946, re-enlisted 1948, commd. 1st lt., 1944, advanced through grades to col.; intern Gallinger Municipal Hosp., Washington, 1943, resident pediatrics, 1948-50; chief pediatric services U.S. Army Hosp. Ft. Bragg, N.C., 1950-53, Brooke Gen. Hosp., Ft. Sam Houston, Tex., 1953-58, Tripler Gen. Hosp., Honolulu, 1958-62, Walter Reed Gen. Hosp., 1963-66; dir. HEW U.S. Civil Adminstrn. Ryukyu Islands, 1966-69; dep. comdr. Walter Reed Hosp., 1969-71, ret., 1971; gen. practice medicine Garnett, Kans., 1946-48; dir. field services div. Montgomery County (Md.) Health Dept., 1971-75; chief surgeon U.S. Soldiers and Airmen's Home Hosp., Washington, 1975—; asst. to asso. clin. prof. pediatrics Baylor U., 1954-58; asso. clin. prof. pediatrics Georgetown U., 1963-66, clin. prof., 1973-75; cons. in field. Decorated Legion of Merit; recipient Supreme award Japanese Med. Assn., 1969. Mem. AMA, Med. and Chirurg. Faculty State Md., Montgomery County Med. Soc., Assn. Mil. Surgeons, Am. Pub. Health Assn., Sigma Chi. Presbyterian. Contbr. articles to profl. publs. Home: 9721 Inaugural Way Gaithersburg MD 20760 Office: US Soldiers and Airmen's Home Hosp Washington DC 20317

FAKUNDINY, ROBERT HARRY, environmental geologist; b. Manitowoc, Wis., Feb. 11, 1940; s. Walter P. and Ann (Kakes) F.; B.A., U. Calif. at Riverside, 1962; M.A., U. Tex., 1967, Ph.D. (Hogg fellow), 1970. Sr. scientist environmental geology N.Y. State Mus. and Sci. Service, Albany, 1971-73, asso. scientist environ. geology, 1974-78, head energy/environ. geology sect., 1978—; U.S. Peace Corps vol. to Ghana, 1963-65; adj. asst. prof. geology state U. N.Y. at Albany, 1974—. NASA research grantee in earth resources tech. satellite-1, 1972-74; U.S. Geol. Survey grantee in nuclear waste burial research, fault structure research, Great Lakes pollution research, 1975-77; NSF grantee in effectiveness of natural sci. data for decision making, 1975-78; EPA and U.S. Nuclear Regulatory Commn. grantee in nuclear waste burial research, 1975-78. Mem. Geol. Soc. Am., Am. Assn. Petroleum Geologists, Am. Geophys. Union, Am. Soc. Photogrammetry, AAAS, Sigma Xi. Home: River Rd 9J Rensselaer NY 12144 Office: Edn Bldg Annex Albany NY 12234

FALARDEAU, MAURICE, surgeon; b. Longueuil, Que., Can., Sept. 24, 1934; s. Lucien and Lucienne (Aumais) F.; B.A. summa cum laude, U. Montreal, 1954, M.D. magna cum laude, 1959; m. Marie-Marthe Gagnon, Aug. 22, 1964; children—Nathalie, Patrick, Jean-Francois. Intern, resident in surgery Notre-Dame Hosp., Montreal, 1958-64, attending and jr. staff surgeon, 1966-73, staff surgeon, 1973—, asst. dir. dept. surgery, 1978—; aggregate prof. medicine U. Montreal, 1974—. McLaughlin Found. traveling fellow, 1965; boursier Province of Que., 1964. Fellow Royal Coll. Surgeons, A.C.S.; mem. French Lang. Med. Assn. of Can., Royal Soc. Medicine, Association des Medecines Clinicens Ensignants du Quebec. Roman Catholic. Home: 437 des Bouleaux Saint Bruno PQ J3V 2J7 Canada Office: 1560 Sherbrooke E Montreal PQ H2L 4M1 Canada

FALBAUM, BERTRAM SEYMOUR, govt. ofcl.; b. N.Y.C., July 28, 1934; s. Abraham and Shari (Greenfield) F.; A.A. in Police Sci., Los Angeles City Coll., 1960; B.S. with honors, Los Angeles State Coll., 1962; postgrad. George Washington U., 1967-69; M.P.A., Syracuse U., 1972; m. Roberta Jessie Oberstone, Sept. 1, 1957; children—Vance Leonard, Stacy Lynn. Customs enforcement officer U.S. Customs Service, San Pedro, Calif., 1961-62, customs port investigator, 1962-63, customs agt., Nogales, Ariz., 1963-64, Los Angeles, 1964-66, sr. spl. agt., Washington, 1969-73; instr. Dept. Treasury Law Enforcement Sch., Washington, 1966-69; dep. chief, div. law enforcement U.S. Fish and Wildlife Service, Washington, 1973—; adj. prof. Am. U., 1977—; guest lectr. law enforcement adminstrn., various univs. Recipient Spl. Achievement award, U.S. Customs Service, 1971. Mem. Internat. Assn. Chiefs Police, Assn. Fed. Investigators, Am. Soc. Pub. Adminstrn. Author texts on investigative photography and marksmanship. Home: 14909 Jaslow St Centreville VA 22020 Office: US Fish and Wildlife Service Washington DC 20240

FALCO, THOMAS GILBERT, librarian; b. New Haven, Oct. 19, 1940; s. Thomas and Dorothea Elizabeth (Gilbert) F.; B.A., Yale, 1962; M.S., So. Conn. State Coll., 1971. Research technician chem. and mech. engring. research and devel. Entoleter Inc., Hamden, Conn., 1963-64; accounting asst. treasurer's office Yale U., New Haven, 1965-66, head circulation Yale Med. Library, 1966-70, asst. hist. librarian, 1970—. Asso. Peabody Mus., New Haven, 1963—. Served to 1st lt. M.I., U.S. Army Res., 1963, summers 1963-69. Fellow Berkeley Coll., Yale U., 1977—. Lutheran (church council 1970-73). Club: Yale. Home: 510 Derby Ave West Haven CT 06516 Office: 333 Cedar St New Haven CT 06510

FALCONE, FRANK EMIDIO, civil engr.; b. Camden, N.J., May 16, 1947; s. Frank Anthony and Ada (Zambetti) F.; B.S. in Civil Engring., Villanova U., 1970, M.S., 1973; m. Linda Ann Altadonna, June 6, 1970; children—Jessica and Wendy (twins). Research engr. Villanova (Pa.) U., 1972-73, grad. asst., 1973; design/project engr., dir. computer programming Justin and Courtney Inc., Phila., 1973-77; bus. devel./mktg. staff Obrien and Gere Inc., Phila., 1977—; instr. evening sch. Villanova U. Served to lt. USN, 1970-72, lt. res., 1973—. Recipient prize for undergrad. thesis Princeton U., 1970; registered profl. engr., N.Y., N.J., Pa., Md., Del. Mem. ASCE, Nat. Soc. Profl. Engrs., Soc. for Mktg. Profl. Services, Civil Engrs. Corps. USNR, Tau Beta Pi.

FALCONE, JOSEPH DANIEL, architect; b. Providence, June 10, 1924; s. Constantino and Jennie Barbato F.; student pub. schs.; grad. Providence Coll.; m. Flora D'Ercole, Sept. 11, 1948; children—Donna, Robert, Cynthia, Nancy, Elena. Gen. practice architect, Cranston, 1960—; tchr. Cranston School System, R.I., 1961-62; mem. faculty U. R.I., Providence Coll., Roger Williams Coll.; pres. Architekton Pub. Co., Inc. Mem. nat. council Archtl. Registration Bd.; pres. 1224 Real Estate Corp. Chmn. Cranston City Plan Commn., 1960-64, vice chmn., 1965-71, chmn., 1972—; asst. prof. Wentworth Tech. Inst., Boston. Recipient Sch. Design award Am. Assn. Sch. Adminstrs. Served with AUS, 1942-46. Registered architect, R.I., N.C. Mem. AIA, Notary Pub. State of R.I., Cranston C. of C. (past v.p.), Council Ednl. Facility Planners, U.S. Power Squadrons. Kiwanian (pres. Cranston 1965). Author: How to Design, Build, Remodel and Maintain Your Home. Home: 845 Scituate Ave Cranston RI 02920 Office: 1216 Park Ave Cranston RI 02910

FALCONERO, ROBERT MARIO, accountant; b. New Bedford, Mass., Aug. 10, 1945; s. Mario and Rose (Belli) F.; diploma Hartford Inst. Accounting, 1965; B.S., Bentley Coll., 1969; M.B.A., Southeastern Mass. U., 1977; m. Mary Noversa; 1 dau., Marcie. Internal auditor John Hancock Ins. Co., Boston, 1969-71; accounting mgr. Union Hosp., Fall River, Mass., 1971-73, asst. controller, 1973-76; asst. controller gen. accounting Union Truesdale Hosp., Fall River, 1976; controller Braintree (Mass.) Hosp., 1976-78; now city comptroller Fall River. Chmn. United Way, Union Hosp., 1973-74; treas. 175th Fall River Anniversary Com., 1978. Mem. Hosp. Fin. Mgmt. Assn., Municipal Fin. Officers Assn. Roman Catholic. Address: 164 George St Fall River MA 02720

FALCONIERI, VIRGINIA PATRICIA, painter, educator; b. Paterson, N.J., Mar. 18, 1943; d. Nathan J. and Lena M. (Farruggio) Falconieri; student Entwistle Sch. of Art, Ridgewood, N.J., 1959-61, Ridgewood Sch. of Art, 1961-64. One-woman shows at Paterson Mus., 1963-64, Ridgewood Sch. Art, 1964, Art Workshop and Gallery, Hawthorne, N.J., 1965-66, The Studio, Hawthorne, annually 1966—; exhibited in group shows at Mus. Fine Arts, Springfield, Mass., 1963, 64, Arts Club Washington, 1968—, Ahda Artzt Gallery, N.Y.C., 1968—, Pacem in Terris Gallery, N.Y.C., 1969—, Nat. Arts Club N.Y., 1971—, Jersey City Mus., 1970-72, Paterson Mus., 1963-66, Bergen Community Mus., Paramus, N.J., 1972—, Salmagundi Club N.Y., 1974; represented in permanent collections Paterson Mus., Bergen Community Mus. Art and Sci., Paramus; instr. oil painting Ridgewood Sch. of Art, 1963-66, Fairlawn (N.J.) Cultural Center, 1964-67, Studio of Virginia Falconieri, Hawthorne, 1966—. Asso. curator Paterson (N.J.) Mus. of Art, 1964—. Recipient Gold medal Gotham Painters, 1968, numerous other awards, 1964—. Mem. Miniature Art Soc. of N.J., Am. Artist Profl. League, Ringwood Manor Assn. of Arts (bd. of children 1964-66), Catharine Lorillard Wolfe Art Club, Gotham Painters N.Y., Burr Artist N.Y., Composers, Authors and Artists Am., Miniature Painters, Sculptors and Gravers Soc., Salmagundi Club, Allied Artists Am. (asso.). Home: 58 Mountain Ave Hawthorne NJ 07506 Studio: 228 Lafayette Ave Hawthorne NJ 07506

FALK, ALMA MARTHA, educator; b. Chgo., Apr. 18, 1910; d. Henry and Alma (Wolowski) Weihofen; certificate, Chgo. Tchrs. Coll., 1932; B.A., George Washington U., 1937, M.A., 1957; postgrad. Howard U., 1972, Indsl. Coll. of Armed Forces, 1973; m. James E. Curry, Apr. 28, 1934 (dec. Aug. 1972); 1 dau., Aileen Curry Cloonan; m. 2d, Byron A. Falk. Tchr., Hull House, Chgo., 1930-32, resident tchr., 1935-36; social worker Ill. Relief Com., 1932-35; tchr. elementary schs., Chgo., 1937-38, 46-47; office mgr. law firms, San Juan, P.R., Washington, 1948-53; elementary tchr. Jr. Village Sch., Washington, 1953-57; reading coordinator Washington Pub. Schs., 1957-72; instr. George Washington U. Reading Clinic, 1957-66; pres. Greater Washington Reading Council, 1966-67. Vol. asst. Civil Def. Milk Sta. Program, San Juan, 1942-46; instr. Urban Service Corps of Vols., 1962-66. Recipient citation White House Conf. on Children, 1962. Mem. AAUW (chmn. edn. com. Washington br. 1959-61, dir. 1976—), Nat. Soc. for Study Edn., Internat. Reading Assn., Am. Fedn. Tchrs., Women's Internat. League for Peace and Freedom, Washington Tchrs. Union (rep. reading specialists 1968-70), UN Assn., Am. Humanist Assn., Columbia Hist. Soc., Mil. Wives Assn., Phi Delta Gamma. Club: George Washington U. (charter). Home: 1330 New Hampshire Ave NW Apt 515 Washington DC 20036

FALK, CHARLES DAVID, pharm. exec.; b. Chgo., July 18, 1939; s. Leo Maurice and Mildred Francine (Bloom) F.; student Wright Jr. Coll., 1957-59; B.S., U. Chgo., 1961, Ph.D. (NASA fellow), 1966; m. Diane Sena Miller, July 16, 1965; 1 son, David Andrew. NIH postdoctoral fellow U. Sussex (Eng.), 1966-67; research chemist E.I. duPont de Nemours & Co., Wilmington, Del., 1967-70; tech. dir., mgr. Riverton Labs., Newark, 1970-74; sr. research chemist, mgr. Engelhard Industries, Edison, N.J., 1974—. Mem. Am. Chem. Soc., Chem. Soc. London. Home: RD 1 Box 183 Marlboro NJ 07746 Office: Engelhard Industries Menlo Park Edison NJ 08817

FALKENAU, MARSHA KASTNER, ednl. adminstr.; b. Sidney, Ohio, Feb. 28, 1951; d. Leo and Lilly (Wall) Kastner; B. in Edn., U. Miami, 1973; M. in Guidance and Counseling, Nova U., 1974; m. Lawrence Gordon Falkenau, Nov. 23, 1974. Tchrs. aide S. W. High Sch., Coral Gables, Fla., 1973; counselor U. Sch. of Nova U., Davie, Fla., 1974; dean students Padua Acad., Wilmington, Del., 1974—. Advisor Beth Emeth Sr. Temple Youth, Wilmington, 1975—. Mem. Am. Personnel and Guidance Assn., Assn. Humanistic Edn. and Devel., Am. Sch. Counselors Assn., Mid-Atlantic Temple Youth. Democrat. Jewish. Home: 136 Kirkcaldy Dr Newark DE 19711 Office: 905 N Broom St Wilmington DE 19806

FALKENBURY, JOHN FRANCIS, environ. engr.; b. Bronxville, N.Y., Jan. 18, 1947; s. Francis Eugene and Talitha E. (Hempel) F.; A.A.S., Westchester Coll., 1968; B.E., N.Y. U., 1971; m. Sydney H. Clark, Apr. 24, 1976. Environ. engr. U.S. Atty.'s Office, So. Dist. N.Y., N.Y.C., 1970-71; environ. engr. C.E., U.S. Army, N.Y.C., 1971-73; environ. engr. EPA, N.Y.C., 1973-75; co-owner, asso. engr. Carpenter Assos., Sparkill, N.Y., 1975—. Chmn. Council of Greenburgh Civic Assns. Mem. ASCE, Hudson River Sloop Restoration. Democrat. Methodist. Office: 4 Union Ave Sparkill NY 10976

FALKOWSKI, EDWARD JOHN, mfg. co. exec.; b. Manchester, Conn., Oct. 6, 1942; s. John Edward and Mildred Camille (Mastropietro) F.; B.S. in Chem. Engring., Worcester Poly. Inst., 1965; M.A.B., Western New England Coll., 1969; m. Brenda W. Lisle, Oct. 19, 1963; children—Brenda June, Richard, Lance. Tech. sales rep. photo products E.I. duPont de Nemours, Wilmington, Del., 1965-70, market planning asst., 1970-71, product specialist export sales, 1971-72, product mgr. internat. ops., 1973-77, internat. market planning mgr., 1977—; instr. in field. Counselor Jr. Achievement, Wilmington, 1971; basketball coach St. David's Episcopal Ch., Wilmington, 1973-76. Mem. Nat. Assn. Photo Lithographers, Flexographic Tech. Assn. Club: DuPont Country. Authored and presented tech. seminars for printing industry in Peoples Republic of China, 1977. Contbr. articles to profl. jours. Home: 2422 Allendale Rd Wilmington DE 19803 Office: Wilson Bldg Concord Plaza Wilmington DE 19898

FALLON, ROBERT THOMAS, corp. exec.; b. Boston, May 12, 1937; s. Frederick Eugene and Ethel Katherine (O'Brien) F.; B.S., Northeastern U., 1960; m. Mary Anne F. Moriarty, Nov. 18, 1961; children—Robert M., Daniel F., Brian P., Charles J. Sr. engr., Raytheon Co., Newton, Mass., 1955-60; research engr., Microwave Assos. Inc., Burlington, Mass., 1960-62; staff engr., Sylvania-GTE, Woburn, Mass., 1962-63; chmn. bd., pres. Parametric Industries, Inc., Winchester, Mass., 1963—; chmn. bd. Microwave Internat. Ltd., London, Eng., 1970—. Recipient award for contbn. to Appollo II, Asso. Industries Mass., 1969. Mem. Assn. Old Crows, Milton Town Club. Patentee solid state tech. Home: 1703 Canton Ave Milton MA 02186 Office: 742 Main St Winchester MA 01890

FALOON, WILLIAM WASSELL, physician, educator; b. Pitts., July 6, 1920; s. Joseph Coulter and Martha Louise (Wassell) F.; B.A., Allegheny Coll., 1941; M.D., Harvard, 1944; m. Roberta Jane Emery, Sept. 11, 1948; children—Karen L., William Wassell, Nancy. Intern, Pa. Hosp., Phila., 1944-45; asst. resident medicine Albany (N.Y.) Hosp., 1945-46, resident medicine, 1946-47; research fellow medicine Harvard Med. Sch., Thorndike Meml. Lab., Boston City Hosp., 1947-48; asst. prof. oncology, instr. medicine Albany Med. Coll., 1948-50; instr. medicine State U. N.Y. Coll. Medicine, Syracuse, 1950-51, asst. prof., 1951-56, asso. prof., 1956-64, prof. medicine, 1964-68; program dir. Adult Clin. Research Center, Syracuse, 1965-68; physician-in-chief, dir. clin. research and edn. Santa Barbara (Calif.) Gen.-Cottage Hosps., 1968-69; prof. medicine U. Rochester (N.Y.) Sch. Medicine, 1969—, mem. internship adv. com., 1970-74, Univ. Senate, 1971-74; dir. gastroenterology unit Monroe Community Hosp., 1969-70; chief medicine Highland Hosp., Rochester, N.Y., 1970—; cons. to several hosps., 1960-68; physician Strong Meml. Hosp., Rochester, 1969—. Bd. mgrs. Camp Dudley YMCA, 1962-67, 69-74, chmn. bd., 1966-67, 71-73; bd. dirs. Onondaga County Met. Health Council, Syracuse, 1959-61; mem. adv. com. Onondaga County Health Dept., 1966-68. Diplomate Am. Bd. Internal Medicine. Fellow A.C.P. (chmn. com. 1961), Rochester Acad. Medicine; mem. Am. Fedn. Clin. Research (councilor 1956-59), A.A.A.S., Onondaga County Med. Soc. (exec. com. 1964-66), Am. Assn. for Study Liver Disease, Am. Inst. Nutrition, Am. Soc. Clin. Nutrition, Endocrine Soc., Am. Gastroen. Assn., Western Soc. for Clin. Research, Med. Soc. Monroe County, Internat. Assn. for Study Liver, Monroe County Med. Soc., Sigma Xi, Phi Delta Theta. Presbyn. (deacon 1958-61, elder 1963-65). Clubs: Interurban; Eastern Gut; Oak Hill Country (Rochester). Mem. editorial bd. Am. Jour. Clin. Nutrition, 1970-76. Contbr. articles to profl. jours. Home: 27 Rensselaer Dr Pittsford NY 14534 Office: Highland Hosp South Ave Rochester NY 14620

FALVO, MICHAEL, educator; b. Sewickley, Pa., June 1, 1943; s. Felix and Assunta (Folino Gallo) F.; B.S., Clarion State Coll., 1967; Ed.M., Slippery Rock State Coll., 1971; postgrad. Duquesne U., 1974—; m. Carol Layne DeMoss, July 7, 1973. Tchr. elementary schs. Avonworth Sch. Dist., Pitts., 1967—. Mem. Community Adv. Com., Emsworth, Pa., 1975-77; treas. PTA, Avonworth, 1974-77, faculty adviser, 1977—. Named Outstanding Elementary Tchr., 1972. Mem. NEA, Am. Personnel and Guidance Assn., Pa. State, Avonworth (v.p. 1968-69, pres. 1969-70) edn. assns., Am. Sch. Counselors Assn. Republican. Roman Catholic. Home: 252 Allegheny Ave Pittsburgh PA 15202 Office: Ohio Twp School Roosevelt Rd Pittsburgh PA 15237

FAMADAS, JOSE, educator, journalist, translator; b. Rio de Janeiro, Brazil, April 10, 1908; s. Joao Famadas and Francisca (Herrera) Famadas; B.S. and Lit., Colegio S. Vicente de Paulo and Colegio Pedro II; Curso Leon Say and Instituto Comercial; C.P.A., Dept. Bus. Edn., Ministry of Edn.; Sch. English Lang. and Lit.; extension and grad. courses U. do Rio de Janeiro, U. do Distrito Federal, U. Pa. field course, U. do Brasil, Instituto de Psicologia, Ministry Edn.; A.M., U. Mich., 1942; postgrad. courses U. Wis. and Columbia, 1942-55; 1 son, Nelson. Staff Banco do Brasil, 1928-62; translator-editor United Press, 1938; instr. Tech. Council on Economics and Finance, 1939-40, Instituto Watson de Organizacao do Trabalho, I.B.M., 1939-40; dir. Instituto Britannia, 1937-42; asso. prof Colegio Pedro II, 1939-44; instr. Am. Council Learned Socs., Inst. for Brazilian Studies, U. Vt., 1942, U. Mich. English Lang. Inst., 1942; teacher extension Columbia, 1943-44, instr. faculty philosophy, 1944-47; dir. bibliography, library and cultural archives Hispanic Inst., 1943-47; translator 20th Century Fox, 1950-56, U.S. Dept. of State, 1951-53, USIA, 1953-78, Universal Internat., 1953-74, United Artists, 1956—, Paramount Pictures, 1971-74, also others; instr. City College of N.Y. extension div., 1947-58; editor in chief Brazilian edit. The Reader's Digest, 1947-50; press officer Brazilian Mission to UN, 1950-55; radio commentator and mem. weekly round table discussion programs on networks, 1944-54. Recipient Inst. Internat. Edn. and Rockefeller Found. fellowship awards. Former v.p. N.Y. chpt. Am. Assn. Tchrs. Spanish and Portuguese; former pres. Soc. Lang. Specialists. Life mem. AAAS, Nat. Acad. Econs. and Polit. Sci., Modern Lang. Assn., Associacao Brasileira de Imprensa, Linguistic Soc. Am., Acad. Polit. Sci., Am. Assn. Tchrs. Spanish and Portuguese, Am. Econ. Assn., Am. Topical Assn.; mem. Nat. Geog. Soc., AAUP, Hispanic Inst. U.S., Nat. Travel Club, Am. Mus. Natural History, Smithsonian Instn., others. Contbr. Columbia Dictionary of Modern European Lit., Revista de Filologia Hispanica, The Romanic Review, New Century Cyclopedia of Names, others. Address: PO Box 752 Flushing NY 11352

FAN, CHIN-FU, physician; b. Taiwan, May 14, 1939; s. Dao-Nang and Liao (Pea) F.; M.D., Nat. Taiwan U., 1966; came to U.S., 1967, naturalized, 1976; m. Shin-Chu Lin, June 26, 1966; children—Joel G., Brian S., Grace J. Rotating intern S.I. Hosp., N.Y., 1967-68; resident in anesthesiology St. Vincent's Hosp. and Med. Center, N.Y.C., 1968-71; courtesy, jr. attending, Washington Hosp. Center, 1971-72; asst. attending Maimonides Med. Center, Bklyn., 1972-74, asso. attending, 1974—, attending-in-charge clin. anesthesia, 1977—; clin. asst. prof. anesthesia State U. N.Y. Downstate Med. Center, Bklyn., 1978—. Served with 841st. Field Hosp., M.C., Taiwan Army, 1966-67. Diplomate Am. Bd. Anesthesiologists. Fellow Am. Coll. Anesthesiologists; mem. N.Y. State Soc. Anesthesiologists, N.Y. State Fedn. Anesthesiologists, N.Y. State, Kings County med. socs., Nat. Assn. Residents and Interns, Am. Soc. Anesthesiologists, Am. Acupuncture Research Soc. Republican. Buddhist. Inventor in field. Office: 4802 10th Ave Brooklyn NY 11219

FAN, KUANG HUAN, educator; b. Hsin-tzu, Taiwan, China, Sept. 1, 1932; s. Chao Teng and Twei-Mei (Chen) F.; came to U.S., 1954, naturalized, 1971; A.B., Bethel Coll., 1956; M.A., Bklyn. Coll., 1958; Ph.D., N.Y. U., 1963; m. Sophie Shun Mei Chen, Sept. 10, 1966. Vis. asst. prof. U. Idaho, 1963-64, asst. prof., 1965-68, asso. prof., 1968; asst. prof. Coll. Great Falls, 1964-65; asso. prof. State U. N.Y. Coll. at Cortland, 1968-73, prof., 1973—, dept. chmn., 1972-74; sr. asso. St. Antony's Coll., Oxford U., 1975. Recipient J.F. Kennedy Am. Heritage award, 1974. Fulbright scholar, 1968. Mem. Am. Polit. Sci. Assn., Assn. Internat. Studies. Author: Chinese Cultural Revolution, 1968; La Cultura Di Mao, 1969; La Revolution Cultural China, 1970. Co-editor Politics in A Changing World, 1971; Mao Tsetung and Lin Piao, 1972; From the Other Side of the River: Self-Portrait of China Today, 1975; Life in Socialist China, 1978; mem. editorial bd. Jour. Social Praxis, Third World Rev. Home: 4017 Kinney Gulf Rd Cortland NY 13045 Office: Dept Polit Sci State U NY Cortland NY 13045

FAN, SHOU-SHAN, civil engr.; b. Hsintsai, China, July 1, 1925; s. Hsiao-tsun and Lan-ju (Wang) F.; came to U.S., 1958, naturalized, 1969; Ph.D., U. Calif. at Berkeley, 1968; m. Mary Yu-ying Wang, Apr. 20, 1949; children—Paul, John. Engr. Sino-Am. Rural Reconstrn. Commn., Taipei, Taiwan, 1954-58; engr. planning Harza Engring. Co., Chgo., 1960-64; oceanographer U.S. Coastal Engring. Research Center, Ft. Belvoir, Va., 1969-71; civil engr., rep. interagy. sedimentation com. Fed. Energy Res. Commn. Dept. Energy, Washington, 1971—; instr. water resources U.S. Dept. Agr. Grad. Sch., Washington, 1971—. Yu-jen fellow, 1943-45. Mem. Sino-Am. Cultural Soc. (dir.), Internat. Assn. Hydraulic Research, ASCE (hydraulic model and computer sci. com.), Am. Geophys. Union (mem. sedimentation com.), Washington Acad. Sci. Roman Catholic. Home: 20427 Aspenwood Ln Gaithersburg MD 20760 Office: Office of Regulatory Analysis FERC/DOE 825 N Capitol St Washington DC 20426

FAN, YOU-LING, chemist; b. NanKing, China, Nov. 11, 1934; s. Y.S. and G.I. (Lee) F.; came to U.S., 1958, naturalized, 1972; B.S., Cheng Kung U., 1956; M.S., U. Wis., 1961; Ph.D., Poly. Inst. Bklyn., 1965; m. Roxy Ni, Aug. 25, 1962; children—George, Grace. Summer jr. chemist Gould-Nat. Batteries Inc., Mpls., 1961; chemist Union Carbide Corp., Bound Brook, N.J., 1964-68, project scientist, 1968-73, research scientist, 1973—; prin. Mid-Jersey Chinese Lang. Sch., East Brunswick, N.J., 1972-73. Bd. dirs. Chinese-Am. Cultural Assn., Somert, N.J. Recipient best paper award Soc. Plastics Industry 1970. Mem. Am. Chem. Soc., Am. Inst. Chemists, Chinese Inst. Engrs. (pres., dir.), Am. Inst. Physics, Soc. Mfg. Engrs., Sigma Xi. Contbr. articles to profl. publs. Patentee in field. Office: River Rd Bound Brook NJ 08805

FANCHER, EDWIN CRAWFORD, psychologist; b. Middletown, N.Y., Aug. 29, 1923; s. Frank Dane and Elizabeth (McGarr) F.; student U. Alaska, 1941-42; B.A., New Sch. Social Research, 1949, M.A., 1951; m. Vivian Kramer, Nov. 8, 1969; children—Bruce Daniel, Emily Jill. Psychologist, Linden (N.J.) Mental Hygiene Clinic, 1955-58; co-founder, pub. Village Voice, N.Y.C., 1955-74; co-founder, clin. dir. Washington Sq. Inst. for Psychotherapy and Mental Health, N.Y.C., 1960-70; psychologist, Community Guidance Service, N.Y.C., 1958—; pvt. practice psychol. counseling, N.Y.C., 1958—; mem. faculty Am. Inst. Psychotherapy and Psychoanalysis, 1977—; bd. dirs. Orange County Telephone Co., Middletown, N.Y., 1946-60; cons. Plumsock Fund, 1974—. Founder, past chmn. N.Y. Neighborhoods Council on Narcotics Addiction. Served with U.S. Army, 1943-46. Decorated Bronze star. Mem. Am., N.Y. State psychol. assns., Am. Orthopsychiat. Assn., N.Y. Soc. Clin. Psychologists (past bd. dirs., exec. sec.), Council of Psychoanalytic Psychotherapists (pres. elect). Democrat. Club: Gipsy Trail. Home: 40 Fifth Ave New York City NY 10011

FANCHER, PAULINE MABEL, librarian; b. Jamestown, N.Y.; d. Leon Livermore and Kate (Waters) Fancher; B.A., U. Buffalo, 1934, B.S. in L.S., 1936. Librarian pub. schs., Jamestown, 1938-40, USAF, Washington, 1941-51, Smith meml. Library, Chautauqua, New York, summers, 1961-74; librarian, winters 1966-74, dir. winter program, 1966-75; librarian Chautauqua Collection, 1968-77; dir. Chautauqua Mus., 1974-77; librarian North Palm Beach (Florida) Library, 1964-65; reference librarian James Prendergast Free Library, Jamestown, 1953-56, dir., 1956-63. Mem. AAUW, Internat. Platform Assn., Nat. Trust Historic Preservation, Friends Smith Library, Pi Kappa Phi. Republican. Presbyterian. Author: Chautauqua: Its Architecture and Its People, 1978. Contbr. articles to profl. jours. Home: PO Box 168 Ashville NY 14710 Office: 34 Janes Ave Chautauqua NY 14722

FANG, HSAI-YANG, educator; b. Shanghai, China, Nov. 25, 1926; s. Chi-Chu and Lai-Pao (Wang) F.; came to U.S., 1952, naturalized, 1972; B.S. in Civil Engring., Hangchow U., China, 1947; M.S., Purdue U., 1956; Ph.D., W.Va. U., 1966; m. Julia S. Fang, July 2, 1960; children—Andrew S., Janice S. Instr. dept. civil engring. Nat. Taiwan U., 1947-52; teaching asst., research asst. Sch. Civil Engring., Purdue U., 1953-56; soils engr., asst. chief spl. assignments br. AASHO Road Test, Transp. Research Bd., 1956-62; research engr. Bur. Research and Devel., Ill. Dept. Transp., 1962-63; instr. dept. civil engring., project dir. Engring. Expt. Sta., W.Va. U., 1963-65; research asso., lectr. dept. civil and geol. engring. Princeton, 1965-66; cons. Water Resources Center, U. Del., 1965-70; prof. civil engring., dir. geotech. engring. div. Lehigh U., Bethlehem, Pa., 1966—, chmn. Conf. on Design and Installation Pile Founds. and Cellular Structures, 1970, course dir. analysis and design of bldg. founds., 1975; chmn. bd. Constrn. Materials Tech., Inc. Internat.; chmn. bd., cons. editor geotech. engring. div. Envo Pub. Co., Inc.; partner Fisher, Fang & Assos., Inc., engring. cons. Recipient Outstanding Service award Transp. Research Bd., Nat. Acad. Scis., 1962, Preceptorship award in civil engring. United Engrs. and Constructors, Inc., 1967; named Hon. Citizen Republic of El Salvador. Mem. Am. Geophys. Union, Am. Soc. Engring. Edn., ASTM, ASCE, Internat. Assn. for Hydraulic Research, Internat. Soc. for Rock Mechanics, Earthquake Engring. Research Inst., Internat. Soc. Soil Mechanics and Found. Engring., Sigma Xi. Editor: (with T.D. Dismuke) Design and Installation of Pile Foundations and Cellular Structures, 1970; (with H.F. Winterkorn) Foundation Engineering Handbook, 1975; Analysis and Design of Building Foundations, 1976. Contbr. articles to profl. jours. Home: 1847 Markham Dr Bethlehem PA 18017 Office: Geotechnical Engring Div Bldg 13 Lehigh U Bethlehem PA 18015

FANG, PEN JENG, civil engr., educator; b. Taiwan, July 13, 1931; s. Ten Chuang and WuTien (Su) F.; B.S., Nat. Taiwan U., 1954; M.S., Okla. State U., 1960; Ph.D., Cornell U., 1965; m. Mei Leng Yang, Aug. 4, 1962; children—Ken Zen, Chunyau Terry, Chunliu Shona. Came to U.S., 1958. Engr., Ministry of Econs., Taiwan, 1955-57; instr. Nat. Taiwan U., 1957-58; structural engr. Inar C. Hillman & Assos., Engrs., Chgo., 1960-62; research asst. Cornell U., Ithaca, N.Y., 1963-65; sr. research engr. U.S. Steel Applied Research Lab., Monroeville, Pa., 1965-68; asst. prof. engring. Sir George Williams U., Montreal, Que., Can., 1968-70; asso. prof. engring. U. R.I., Kingston, 1970—; cons. Promon Engenharia S.A., Brazil; vis. prof. Fed. U. Rio de Janeiro, U. Sao Paulo (Brazil), 1976. Registered profl. engr., R.I., structural engr., Ill. Mem. ASCE (Collingwood prize 1967); Soc. for Exptl. Stress Analysis, Am. Soc. Engring. Edn., Am. Concrete Inst., Am. Acad. Mechanics, Nat. Soc. Profl. Engrs. Home: 72 Springdale Rd Kingston RI 02881 Office: Dept Civil and Environmental Engring University of RI Kingston RI 02881

FANNING, WILLIAM HENRY, JR., data systems analyst; b. N.Y.C., Feb. 12, 1917; s. William Henry and Terese Genevieve (Moloney) F.; B.S., Fordham U. Sch. Edn., 1940; postgrad. Catholic U. Am. Grad. Sch. Arts and Scis., 1940-41; m. Mary Major Winter, Sept. 5, 1940; children—Hugh M. (dec.), Helen A. (Mrs. Andrew Koppel), Mary M., Gerard, William Henry III. Instr. Greek and German, Gonzaga High Sch., Washington, 1940-41; reporter, copyreader Nat. Cath. Welfare Conf. News Service, 1941-42, 45-47, news editor, 1947-55; chief Rome news bur. Radio Free Europe, 1955-57, dir. news and information services, Munich, 1957-59, chief Paris news bur., 1959-60; asso. editor Catholic News, weekly, 1960-61, editor, 1961-66; established and headed U.S. Cath. Bishops Press Office, 2d Vatican Council, 1962; v.p. promotion and advt. Diamond Prodns., Ltd., N.Y.C., 1967-69; programmer, analyst CGA Computer Assos., East Orange, N.J., 1969-73; sr. system specialist Equitable Life Assurance Soc. U.S., N.Y.C., 1973—; head Fanning Pub. Relations, 1966—. Lectr. journalism Good Counsel Coll., White Plains, N.Y., 1967-69; writer documentary scripts for TV, also instrnl. TV scripts for pubs. Mem. Pres.'s Com. on Employment Handicapped, 1947-70; mem. Archdiocesan Edn. Com., 1961-68. Bd. dirs. Westchester Catholic Edn. Council, 1963-69. Served to lt. comdr. USNR, 1942-45. Mem. Writers Guild Am. East, N.Y. Acad. Sci., Phi Kappa Theta (hon.). Office: 1285 Ave of Americas New York City NY 10036

FANNING, WINTHROP COIT, II, journalist; b. Mt. Clemens, Mich., July 20, 1918; s. Winthrop Coit and Emily Ruth (Lauver) F.; A.B., Brown U., 1941; m. Dorothy Johnson (div.); 1 dau., Jennifer Gay (Mrs. Douglas Peck); m. 2d, Viktoria Fanning, Sept. 9, 1950. Corr., Pitts. Press, 1941, Stars and Stripes, 1944-50, London Express, Sunday Express, Reuters News Service, 1948-50; critic, columnist, TV-Radio columnist Pitts. Post Gazette, 1951—; TV commentator, 1951—. Served with USAAF, 1942-47. Named Entertainment Man of Year, Pitts. Jr. C. of C., 1971. Mem. Amateur Radio Relay League, Pitts. Press Club. Club: Variety Tent 1. Contbr. articles to mags. Home: Gateway Towers Apt 4-M Pittsburgh PA 15222 Office: Pitts Post-Gazette Pittsburgh PA 15222

FANOS, NICHOLAS G., hosp. exec.; b. New Brunswick, N.J., Aug. 29, 1919; s. Emmanuel N. and Clara (Colias) F.; B.S.M.E., Rutgers U., 1950; postgrad. U. Cin., 1951-53; m. Pauline Dru, Jan. 4, 1942; children—Caroline Fanos Donovan, Jennifer Fanos Howe, Valerie Fanos Horne. Mechanic-machinist, devel. engr. Johnson & Johnson, New Brunswick, N.J., 1946-50; plant. engr., adminstr. Orange (N.J.) Meml. Hosp., 1951-53; adminstrv. dir. Jewish Hosp. Assn., Cin., 1953-57; faculty U. Cin., 1956-57; exec. v.p., gen. mgr. Frederick (Md.) Iron & Steel Co., 1957-64, Kahan & Co., Inc., Weathersfield, Conn., 1964-65; corporate indsl. engr. Standard Screw Co., Winston, Conn., 1966-67; engr., constrn. cons., pres. Phoenix Steel Corp., Claymont, Del., 1967; pres., gen. mgr. Miami (Fla.) Paper Box Mfg. Co., 1967-69; with Hosp. for Joint Diseases, N.Y.C., 1969—, asso. dir., 1973—, cons. Health & Hosp. Plan; cons. in field. Pres., chmn. bd. Frederick Devel. Corp.; bd. dirs. Community Chest of Frederick County, Am. Red Cross (Frederick chpt.), United Appeal of Frederick County, The Vindobona, Inc. (nursing home). Served with USAAF, 1940-45. Decorated Bronze Star. Mem. Am. Hosp. Assn., Am. Mgmt. Assn. (bd. dirs., dist. leader), Hosp. Execs. Club, ASME (chmn. Western Md. group), Frederick C. of C. (pres. bd. dirs.). Home: 351 E 84th St 18 C New York City NY 10028 Office: Hospital for Joint Diseases 1919 Madison Ave New York City NY 10035

FANT, DAVID LUTHER, chemist; b. Titusville, Pa., May 12, 1943; s. Alfred Augustine and MaryBelle (Kriner) F.; B.A. in Chemistry, U. Maine, 1965; M.S., Union Coll., 1972; m. Pamela Gay Carruthers, Aug. 21, 1965; children—Melinda Gay, Melanie Glee. Research chemist Huyck Felt Co., Rensselaer, N.Y., 1965-68, group leader lab. services, 1968-70; quality control chemist Tobin Packing Co., Albany, N.Y., 1970-71; asso. analyst Sterling Drug, Inc., Rensselaer, 1971-75, good mfg. practice coordinator, 1975—. Scoutmaster, Troop 41, Boy Scouts Am., E. Greenbush, N.Y., 1971—, tng. coordinator for adult leaders, 1977. Mem. Am. Chem. Soc., Am. Assn. Textile Chemists and Colorists. Lutheran. Home: 24 Kitty Ln RD 2 Rensselaer NY 12144

FANTI, ROY, aircraft exec.; b. Bklyn., Dec. 23, 1925; s. Mariano and Anna (DeLia) F.; student Brown U., 1944, Mass. Inst. Tech., 1944-45; B.A., Rensselaer Poly. Inst., 1947, M.A., 1948; m. Shirley Mae Baker, Jan. 11, 1947; children—Sharon, David, Craig. With United Techs. Research Center, East Hartford, Conn., 1946—, supr. aeroelasticity, 1952-62, head aeroelasticity and structures, 1962, mgr. materials lab., 1962-74, mgr. mfg. tech. and process research, 1974-77, mgr. tech. coordination, 1977—. Instr. Rensselaer Poly. Inst., Troy, N.Y., 1947-48, Western New Eng. Coll., Springfield, Mass., 1952-58. Served with USNR, 1944-48. Mem. Sigma Xi. Mason. Club: Country (Springfield, Mass.). Author: An Artist's Moods, 1972. Patentee in field. Home: 171 Atwater Rd Springfield MA 01107 Office: Silver Ln East Hartford CT 06108

FANUS, PAULINE RIFE (MRS. WILLIAM EDWARD FANUS), librarian; b. New Oxford, Pa., Feb. 14, 1925; d. Maurice Diehl and Bernice Edna (Gable) Rife; B.S., Pa. State U., 1945; M.S. in L.S., Villanova U., 1961; m. William Edward Fanus, June 20, 1944;

children—Irene (Mrs. Lewis N. Weaver Jr.), Larry William, Daniel Diehl. Periodical librarian Tex. Coll. Arts and Industries, Kingsville, 1945; tchr. nursery sch. Studio Sch., Wayne, Pa., 1953-55; circulation and reference librarian Franklin Inst., Phila., 1963-66; asst. librarian Ursinus Coll., Collegeville, Pa., 1966; catalog librarian, instr. Eastern Coll., St. Davids, Pa., 1967-71; head librarian Agnes Irwin Sch., Rosemont, Pa., 1971—. Mem. AAUP (chpt. sec. Eastern Coll. 1970-71), Pa. Library Assn. Home: Country Club Rd Phoenixville PA 19460 Office: Agnes Irwin School Rosemont PA 19010

FARBER, DONALD CLIFFORD, lawyer; b. Columbus, Nebr., Oct. 19, 1923; s. Charles and Sarah (Epstein) F.; B.S. in Law, U. Nebr., 1948, J.D., 1950; m. Ann Eis, Dec. 28, 1947; children—Seth H., Patricia M. Admitted to N.Y. bar, 1950; individual practice specializing in entertainment and pub., N.Y.C., 1958—; guest lectr. York U., Toronto, Ont., Can., 1970, 72, 73, New Sch. Social Research, 1972—; prof. entertainment law Hofstra U. Law Sch., Hempstead, N.Y., 1974-75. Served with AUS, World War II. Mem. Practising Law Inst. (chmn. seminar theatre law 1973). Author: From Option to Opening, 3 edit., 1977; Producing on Broadway, 2d edit., 1975; Actors Guide-What You Should Know about the Contracts You Sign, 1971; co-author: Producing, Financing and Distributing Film, 1973. Address: 800 3d Ave New York City NY 10022

FARBER, ERICA, radio sta. exec.; b. Denton, Tex., Jan. 1, 1949; d. Harry and Lazelle (Hohenstein) F.; student pub. schs., Calif. Film and graphic designer Don Record & Assos., 1968-69; mem. advt. dept. Communications Trends, 1969-71; account exec. Sta. KIIS, Los Angeles, 1971-72, Sta. KABC-TV, Los Angeles, 1973-74, Sta. KRTH, Los Angeles, 1974; gen. sales mgr. Sta. WROR-FM, Boston, 1975; sta. mgr. Sta. WROR, Boston, 1975-76; v.p., gen. mgr. Sta. WXLO-FM, N.Y.C., 1976—. Mem. Radio Code Bd. for Nat. Assn. Broadcasters (dir.), N.Y. Mkt. Radio Broadcasters (sec.), N.Y. State Broadcasters, Am. Women in TV and Radio, Women in Communications, N.Y. Women in Advt. Republican. Office: 1440 Broadway New York NY 10018

FARBER, JOSEPH, lawyer; b. Bklyn., Jan. 31, 1944; s. David and Hanna (Beckhoff) F.; B.S., L.I. U., 1965; J.D., Bklyn. Law Sch., 1968; m. Evelyn Caspari, Mar. 23, 1967; children—Leslie Hanna, Danna Hillary, Douglas Elliot, Andrew Eric. Tchr., N.Y.C. Bd. Edn., 1968-70; mng. atty. Queens Legal Services Corp., Jamaica, N.Y., 1970-71; partner, atty. Previte, Glasser & Farber, Queens, N.Y., 1971—. Bd. dirs. Queens Legal Services Corp. Mem. Queens County (mem. com. on family law 1970-73), Nassau County bar assns., Am. Jewish Congress. Clubs: Lions, Elks, Brandies Assn., K.P. Home: 2 Henni Ct Syosset NY 11791 Office: 78-27 37th Ave Jackson Heights NY 11372

FARBER, MARTIN JOSEPH, film co. exec.; b. Phila., June 26, 1933; s. Samuel and Mae (Cohen) F.; student pub. schs., Phila.; m. Julia Pusatere, Feb. 5, 1975; children—Mindi, Eric, Tom. Asst. plant mgr. Sun Ray Photo, Phila., 1952-55; v.p., gen. mgr. Perfect Photo, Phila., 1955-61; chmn. bd., chief exec. officer, pres. Film Corp. Am., Phila., 1961—. Trustee, Albert Einstein Med. Center; program funder Inst. Humanistic Medicine, San Francisco, 1969—, funder Pack Med. Found., N.Y.C., 1966—, Martin J. Farber Endowment Fund for Gratz Coll., Phila. Served with U.S. Army, 1949-51. Clubs: Variety Tent #13, Green Valley Country; Locust, Peale (Phila.). Office: Caroline and Charter Rds Philadelphia PA 19176

FARBER, PAUL ALAN, educator; b. Bklyn., Sept. 13, 1938; s. Joseph and Dorothy (Trager) F.; A.B., U. Mich., 1960, D.D.S., 1962; Ph.D., U. Rochester, 1967; m. Judith Goldblatt, Aug. 14, 1960; children—Leslie, Donna Lynn. Grad. research fellow U. Rochester (N.Y.), 1962-67; asst. prof. microbiology Temple U. Sch. Dentistry, 1967-70; guest worker Nat. Inst. Dental Research, NIH, Bethesda, Md., 1970-71, Albert Einstein Med. Center, 1975-76; asso. prof. pathology Temple U. Sch. Dentistry, Phila., 1972-78, prof. pathology, 1978—. Served as maj. Dental Corps, AUS, 1966—. Recipient postdoctoral fellowship USPHS, 1962-67, spl. fellowship NIH, 1970-71, research grant NIH, 1972—. Mem. A.A.A.S., Am. Soc. Microbiology, Am. Assn. Pathologists and Bacteriologists. Home: 21 Glenn Circle Erdenheim PA 19118 Office: 3223 N Broad St Philadelphia PA 19140

FARBER, SAUL JOSEPH, physician, educator; b. N.Y.C., Feb. 11, 1918; s. Isidor and Mary (Bunim) F.; A.B., N.Y. U., 1938, M.D., 1942; m. Doris Marcia Balmuth, Mar. 13, 1949; children—Joshua M., Beth Mina. Intern Sinai Hosp., Balt., 1942-43; research resident Goldwater Meml. Hosp. N.Y.U., 1946-47; asst. resident Bellevue Hosp., N.Y.U., 1947-48; fellow N.Y.U. Sch. Medicine, 1948-49, asst. in medicine, 1949-50, instr., 1950-53, asst. prof. medicine, 1953-57, asso. prof., 1957-62, prof., 1962-66, Nathan Friedman prof. medicine, 1966-75, dean acad. affairs, acting dean, dep. dir., 1963-66, Frederick H. King prof. medicine, 1978—, chmn. dept. medicine, 1966—; dir. N.Y.U. med. div. Bellevue Hosp., 1966-68, dir. medicine, 1968—; cons. VA Hosp.; dir. medicine Univ. (N.Y.U.) Hosp., 1966—. Bd. dirs. N.Y. Heart Assn., 1963, pres., 1973-75; mem. nat. adv. research sources council USPHS, 1967-71; chmn. com. on resource requirements of VA health care systems NRC, 1974-77; adv. council N.Y. Kidney Disease Inst., 1968—; med. fellow council on circulation and council on kidney in cardiovascular disease Am. Heart Assn.; mem. med. adv. com. Hosp. Corp. Task Force N.Y.C., 1969-71; mem. adv. com. Inter-Soc. Commn. for Heart Disease Resources, 1968—; mem. hypertension-renal subcom. N.Y. Met. Regional Med. Program for Heart Disease, Cancer and Stroke, 1968-71; mem. research career program com. Nat. Inst. Arthritis and Metabolic Diseases, USPHS, 1966-67, 71-73; bd. dirs. Russell Sage Inst. Pathology, 1970—, pres., 1976—; mem. task force to recommend goals and objectives for COTH, Assn. Am. Med. Colls., 1971—; mem. med. adv. bd. Found. for Study Wilson's Disease, 1971—; mem., trustee Riverside Research Inst., 1971-78, cons., 1978—; mem. Inst. Medicine, Nat. Acad. Scis., 1975—, mem. adv. com. splty. and geog. distbn. physicians, 1974-75; mem. N.Y. State Health Adv. Council, 1975—. Served from lt. (j.g.) to lt. USNR, 1943-46. Diplomate Am. Bd. Internal Medicine (mem. bd. 1968-76, exec. com. 1972-76, chmn. 1973-76, chmn. liaison com. continuing med. edn. 1976-78). Master A.C.P. (regent 1978—); fellow N.Y. Acad. Medicine; mem. Am. Soc. Clin. Investigation (sec.-treas. 1957-60, councilor 1960-63), Assn. Am. Physicians, Am. Physiol. Soc., Harvey Soc. (treas. 1963-67, v.p. 1967-68, pres. 1968-69, councillor 1969—), Soc. Exptl. Biology and Medicine, Am. Fedn. Clin. Research, Soc. Urban Physicians (pres. 1970-73, governing council 1968-75), Assn. Profs. Medicine (councillor 1970-73, pres. 1972-73), N.Y. Soc. Nephrology, Practicioners Soc. N.Y., Federated Council for Internal Medicine, Interurban Clin. Club, Salt and Water Club, Alpha Omega Alpha, Sigma Xi. Editor: Am. Jour. Med. Scis., 1969—. Contbr. articles to med. jours. Home: 25 Plaza Brooklyn NY 11217 Office: Dept Medicine Sch Medicine NY U 550 1st Ave New York City NY 10016

FARBISH, ALFRED BUCKS, rubber and plastics co. exec.; b. Phila., Sept. 18, 1923; s. Sydney Allmeyer and Rachel Levy (Bucks) F.; student Oxford (Eng.) U., 1945; B.A., U. Pa., 1948; m. Rita Ruth Fayer, Oct. 11, 1951; children—Michael B., Peter B. Civil engr., Phila. Dist. U.S. Army Engrs. Corp., 1955-57; mgr. comml. devel. Barrett div. Allied Chem. Co., N.Y.C., 1957-65; sales mgr. Am. Cyanamid Co., Wakefield, Mass., 1965-71; v.p. gen. mgt. Rubber & Plastics Compound Co., Long Island City, N.Y.C., 1971-74, pres., 1974—. Served with arty. U.S. Army, 1942-46, 48-53. Mem. U. Pa. Alumni Assn., Sales Exec. Club N.Y. Clubs: U. Pa. (N.Y.C.); Milford Yacht; Fencers. Patentee in field. Home: Ledgeview Parmalee Hill Rd Newtown CT 06470 Office: 36-15 23d St Long Island City NY 11106

FARBRO, PATRICK CLAY, indsl. psychologist; b. Drumright, Okla., Aug. 14, 1921; s. George and Hazel (Worrall) F.; B.A., U. Tulsa, 1947; M.S., Purdue U., 1948. Grad. teching asst. Purdue U., 1947-48; personnel research analyst RCA Victor, 1948-49, supr. employment, Lancaster, Pa., 1949-51, mgr. personnel research div., Camden, N.J., 1951-59, mgr. profl. personnel programs, Camden, dir. profl. personnel programs RCA staff, 1959-71, dir. indsl. relations policy and research RCA staff, 1971—. Trustee Fund for Research in Tng. and Devel., 1964-73. Served to lt. (j.g.), USNR, 1942-46. Mem. Am., N.J., N.Y. Met. Applied psychol. assns., Internat. Assn. of Applied Psychology, N.Y. Acad. Sci., Am. Soc. Tng. Dirs. (regional v.p., nat. bd. dirs. 1963-69), Am. Soc. Tng. and Devel. (nat. pres. 1967), Psi Chi, Sigma Xi, Sigma Alpha Epsilon. Club: Poor Richard (Phila.) Home: 433 E 56th St Apt 11 B New York City NY 10022 Office: RCA Corp 30 Rockefeller Plaza Room 4145 New York City NY 10020

FARENTHOLD, FRANCES TARLTON (MRS. GEORGE EDWARD FARENTHOLD), lawyer, coll. pres.; b. Corpus Christi, Tex., Oct. 2, 1926; d. Benjamin Dudley and Catherine (Bluntzer) Tarlton; A.B., Vassar Coll., 1946; J.D., U. Tex., 1949; LL.D., Hood Coll., 1973, Boston U., 1973, Regis Coll., 1976; m. George E. Farenthold, Oct. 6, 1950; children—Dudley Tarlton, George Edward, Emilie, James Dougherty, Vincent Bluntzer (dec.). Admitted to Tex. bar, 1949; mem. Tex. Ho. of Reps., 1968-72; dir. legal aide Nueces County, 1965-67; asst. prof. law Tex. So. U., Houston; pres. Wells Coll., Aurora, N.Y., 1976—. Mem. Tex. adv. com. to U.S. Commn. on Civil Rights, 1968-76; mem. nat. adv. council ACLU; Democratic candidate Gov. Tex., 1972; del. Dem. nat. conv., 1972, 1st woman nominated to be candidate v.p. U.S., 1972; nat. co-chmn. Citizens to Elect McGovern-Shriver, 1972; chairperson Nat. Women's Polit. Caucus, 1973-75, chmn. adv. com., 1975-76; adv. bd. Schlesinger Library, Kadcliff Coll., bd. dirs. Mental Health Law Project. Recipient Lyndon B. Johnson Woman of Year award, 1973. Mem. State Bar Tex. Roman Catholic. Home: Taylor House Aurora NY 13026 Office: Wells Coll Aurora NY 13026

FARGIS, PAUL MCKENNA, editor, pub. co. exec.; b. N.Y.C., Mar. 19, 1939; s. George Bertrand and Elizabeth Harland (McKenna) F.; student Cath. U. Am., 1958; B. Social Sci., Fairfield U., 1961; M.A. (Publs. Tuition scholar), N.Y. U., 1962; m. Elizabeth Hackett, Aug. 22, 1964; children—John Hackett, Alison Kathryn; m. 2d, Dawn Sangrey, Apr. 23, 1977. Editorial asst. Prentice-Hall, Inc., Englewood Cliffs, N.J., 1961-62; editor Hawthorn Books, Inc., N.Y.C., 1963-67, v.p., editorial dir., 1967-71; v.p., editor in chief Thomas Y. Crowell Co. and Funk & Wagnalls divs. Dun-Donnelley Pub. Corp., N.Y.C., 1971-77; mng. dir. Thomas Y. Crowell div. Harper & Row, Inc., N.Y.C., 1977-78; pub., editor-in-chief The Stonesong Press div. Grosset and Dunlap, Inc., 1978—; creator, owner The Biblioswitch, Bedford Hills, N.Y., 1973—; editor in chief Apollo Books, N.Y.C., 1972—. Mem. adv. bd. Grad. Sch. Corp. and Polit. Communication, Fairfield U., 1969—; exec. dir. Harrison (N.Y.) Town Recreation Commn., 1970-72; dir. Harrison Town Forum, 1969-73; bd. dirs. U.S. Cath. Hist. Soc. Mem. Am. Assn. Pubs., Friendly Sons St. Patrick. Clubs: Dutch Treat, Editor's Lunch. Author: The Consumer's Handbook, 1966, rev. edit., 1974; Company's Coming, 1965. Am. editor Twentieth Century Ency. Catholicism, 1963-67; mng. editor Twentieth Century Catholicism, 1964-66. Home: Stonesong 200 Haines Rd Bedford Hills NY 10507 Office: 51 Madison Ave New York City NY 10010

FARHOUDI, HABIB OLLAH, physician; b. Shiraz, Iran, Aug. 28, 1938; s. Mohammad and Mohtaram (Hatami) F.; came to U.S., 1963; M.D., Pahlavi U. (Iran), 1963; m. Farangis Davari, July 4, 1957; children—Farideh, Rosemary, Fasaneh. Intern, Mercy Hosp., Toledo, Ohio, 1964; resident in medicine St. Vincent Hosp., Erie, Pa., 1965, Doctors Hosp., Washington, 1966-68; fellow in infectious disease Howard U., Washington, 1969; med. officer, instr. medicine D.C. Gen. Hosp., Washington, 1969-71; practice medicine, specializing in internal medicine and infectious diseases, Marlow Heights, Md., 1977—; asst. prof. medicine Howard U., Washington, 1971—; dir. infectious disease lab. D.C. Gen. Hosp., Washington, 1970-74; chief infectious disease Greater S.E. Community Hosp., Washington, 1974—, chmn. Dept. Medicine 1975-77; chief infectious disease Hadley Meml. Hosp., Washington, 1973—, So. Md. Hosp. Center, Clinton, 1977—. Recipient Leon Gordon award as outstanding resident of the year, Doctors Hosp., Washington Med. Center, 1968; recipient Physicians Recognition Award, Am. Med. Assn., 1969, 72, 75; diplomate Am. Bd. Internal Medicine, Am. Bd. Infectious Disease. Fellow ACP; mem. D.C. Med. Soc., Fairfax Med. Soc., So. Med. Assn., Am. Med. Assn., Am. Soc. Internal Medicine, Va. Soc. Internal Medicine, Prince Georges County Med. Soc. Contbt. articles in field to med. jours. Home: 12200 Hollybank Dr Tantallon MD 20022 Office: 4400 Stamp Rd Marlow Heights MD 20031

FARIA, SIXDENIEL, engr. research and devel.; b. Vega Baja, P.R., Jan. 31, 1926; s. Antonio and Petra (Rodriguez) F.; B.S. in Chem. Engring., Poly. Inst. Bklyn., 1958; postgrad. phys. chemistry Adelphi Coll., 1959-60, Wilkes Coll., Pa., 1961-62; m. May 17, 1947; 1 son, Daniel. Chem. technician Consol. Edison Co., N.Y.C., 1951-53; sr. technician Sylvania Electric Co., Bayside, N.Y., 1953-58, devel. engr. GTE Sylvania, Towanda, Pa., 1961—, advanced devel. engr., 1977—. Mem. Am. Chem. Soc. (sec. chpt. 1970-72), Internat. Mgmt. Council (ednl. chmn. Bradford County, Pa., chpt. 1977—), Electrochem. Soc. Am., Measurements and Data Soc. Am. Republican. Baptist. Served with U.S. Army, 1945-47. Contbr. articles to profl. publs. luminescent materials (phosphors). Home: 221 N Main St Towanda PA 18848 Office: GTE Sylvania Co Chem and Metall Div Towanda PA 18848

FARKAS, ANN ELIZABETH, archaeologist, educator; b. New Brighton, Pa., Mar. 7, 1931; d. Eli and Rebecca (Balter) Rosenberg; B.A., U. Chgo., 1950; M.A., Columbia U., 1963; Ph.D., (Woodbridge Hon. fellow), 1967; m. Alexander Farkas, Apr. 22, 1950 (div. 1961); 1 son, Allister. Instr. dept. art history and archaeology Columbia, 1967-68, asst. prof., 1968-73; asso. prof. New Sch. Liberal Arts, Bklyn. Coll., City U. N.Y., 1973—. Columbia U. Council for Research in Humanities summer grantee, 1968, 69. Mem. Coll. Art Assn., Archeol. Inst. Am. Am. Schs. Oriental Research, Columbia U. Seminar on Archeology of Eastern Mediterranean, Eastern Europe and Nr. East. Democrat. Clubs: Princeton; Washington. Author: Achaemenid Sculpture, 1974; (introduction) From the Lands of the Scythians, 1975. Contbr. articles to profl. jours. Home: New Preston Hill Rd New Preston CT 06777 Office: Bklyn Coll 210 Livingston St Brooklyn NY 11201*

FARKAS, EMERY, chem. co. exec.; b. Budapest, Hungary, Oct. 28, 1925; s. Imre and Margit (Egerhazy) F.; M.S. in Chem. Engring., Polytech. U. Budapest, 1948; m. Elizabeth Tersztyanszky, Sept. 17, 1949; children—Lillian Theresa, Leonora Marguerite. Came to U.S., 1956, naturalized, 1962. Research engr. State Hygienic Inst., Rockefeller Found., Budapest, 1948-56; asst. of chemistry Harvard U., Cambridge, Mass., 1957; research chemist W.R. Grace & Co., Dewey & Almy Chem. Div., Cambridge, 1957-60, group leader, 1960-65, dir. tech. services, 1965-70; sr. v.p. Materials & Constrn. Mgmt. Consultants, 1970-72; gen. mgr. constrn. products div. W.R. Grace & Co., Cambridge, Mass., 1972-76, v.p., 1976—. Pres., Hungarian Club of Boston, Inc., 1966-67. Mem. Am. Soc. for Testing and Materials, Am. Concrete Inst. Patentee in field. Home: 48 Oakwood Rd Newtonville MA 02160 Office: 62 Whittemore Ave Cambridge MA 02140

FARLEY, JAMES THOMAS, JR., news broadcasting exec.; b. Chgo., Aug. 24, 1948; s. James Thomas and Mary Jean (Powers) F.; B.A., State U. N.Y., 1975; student Fordham U., 1973-75; B.A., State U. N.Y., 1975; m. Johanna Rutan, Dec. 5, 1970; children—James Thomas, Patrick Henry. Vice pres. HIJH Pub. Co., N.Y.C., 1970-75, editor-in-chief 3 weekly newspapers; with WINS Radio, N.Y.C., 1969-75, writer, 1969-73, editor, 1973-75; producer NBC Nat. News and Info. Service, 1975-76, mgr. news programs, 1976-78, exec. producer radio news, 1978—; mem. communications faculty Fordham U., 1977—. Mem. Republican County Com., Queens, N.Y., 1970-72. Bd. dirs. Nat. Com. for Responsible Patriotism, 1968-76. Mem. Writers Guild of Am. East (governing council 1974), Internat. Radio and TV Soc., N.Y. Press Assn. Home: Iroquois Ave Palisades NY 10964 Office: NBC 30 Rockefeller Plaza New York City NY 10020

FARLEY, JENNIE TIFFANY TOWLE, educator; b. Fanwood, N.J., Nov. 2, 1932; d. Howard Albert and Dorothy Jane (Van Wagner) Towle; B.A. in English, Cornell U., 1954, M.S. in Sociology of Devel., 1969, Ph.D. in Sociology and Communications, 1970; m. Donald Thorn Farley, Jr., June 16, 1956; children—Claire Hamlin, Anne Tiffany, Peter Towle. Mem. editorial staff Mademoiselle mag., 1954-55; asst. to asso. editor Seventeen mag., 1955-56; news writer Univ. News Bur., Cornell U., 1956-59; free lance writer, Cambridge, Eng., 1959-60, Goteborg, Sweden, 1960-61, Chaclacayo, Peru, 1961-64; daily columnist La Prensa, Lima, Peru, 1964-67; research asso., lectr., adj. asst. prof. Cornell U., Ithaca, N.Y., 1970-73, asst. prof. indsl. and labor relations, 1973—, co-founder, dir. Women's Studies Program, 1972-76. Bd. dirs. Profl. Skills Roster; mem. chancellors com. on women's studies State U. N.Y., 1974-76. Center for Research on Women in Higher Edn. and Professions grantee Wellesley Coll., 1977-78. Mem. Am. Sociol. Assn., Sociologists for Women in Soc., AAUP, AAUW, NOW. Author: Affirmative Action and the Woman Worker, 1979; contbr. articles on women and work to profl. jours. Home: 711 Triphammer Rd Ithaca NY 14850 Office: 393 Ives Hall Cornell U Ithaca NY 14853

FARLEY, JOHN MICHAEL, steel co. exec.; b. Bklyn., July 10, 1930; s. John F. and Lucile J. Farley; B. Civil Engring. magna cum laude, Syracuse U., 1952; M.S., U. Ill., 1954; m. Dorothy O. Stacy, Nov. 29, 1959; children—Anne L., Joan E., John O. Project engr. Cleve. Works Jones & Laughlin Steel Corp., 1957-64, engring. staff, Aliquippa Pa., 1964-67, with gen. office, Pitts., 1967-71, gen. mgr. planning, engring. and constrn., 1972-73, v.p. research and engring., 1974-75, v.p. raw materials, 1975-77, pres. raw materials div., 1977—; pres. Gateway Coal Co., Pitts., 1975—. Served with USNR, 1954-57. Registered profl. engr., Ohio, Pa. Mem. Am. Iron Ore Assn., Am. Iron and Steel Inst., Am. Inst. Mining, Metall. and Petroleum Engrs. (Iron and Steel Soc.), Assn. Iron and Steel Engrs., Engrs. Soc. Western Pa., Tau Beta Pi. Clubs: Duquesne, Highland Country (Pitts.). Office: Jones & Laughlin Steel Corp 3 Gateway Center Pittsburgh PA 15263

FARMAKIDES, J(OHN) B(ASIL), lawyer, govt. ofcl., educator; b. Symi Island, Italy (parents Am. citizens); B.S., Case Western Res. U., 1950; J.D. with honors, George Washington U., 1957; LL.M., Georgetown U., 1959; m. Maria T. Kambanis, June 12, 1964; children—Basil J., George S. Admitted to D.C. bar, 1957, U.S. Supreme Ct. bar, 1958; research analyst George Washington U. Patent Found., 1954-55; patent examiner U.S. Patent Office, Washington, 1955-59; atty. U.S. Air Force, Washington, 1960-62; supervisory atty. NASA, Washington, 1962-68, mem. bd. contract appeals, 1968-70; asst. gen. counsel NSF, Washington, 1970-72; chmn. atomic safety bds. AEC, 1972-74; mem. appeals bd. Nuclear Regulatory Commn., 1974-75; chmn. bd. contract appeals, contract adjustment bd., fin. assistance appeal bd. Dept. Energy, Washington, 1975—; U.S. del. Internat. Conf. Govt. Computer Experts, 1972; chmn. subcom. legal aspects of computer systems Fed. Council Sci. and Tech., 1970-72; dir. Nat. Conf. Bd. Contract Appeals Mems.; dir. Joint Army, Navy, Air Force Spl. Analytical Div. USAR, 1972-74; part-time professorial lectr. Washington Coll. Law, Am. U., 1963—; mem. U.S.-Chinese workshop on computerized info. systems Nat. Acad. Sci., 1973. Served from pvt. to lt. U.S. Army, 1951-53, to col. Res., 1972. Mem. Am. Judicature Soc., Am., Fed. bar assns., IEEE, Am. Soc. Pub. Adminstrn., Ahepa, PTA, McLean Civic Assn., Phi Delta Phi, Lambda Xi Alpha. Greek Orthodox. Clubs: Washington Golf, Cosmos, Nat. Lawyers. Research on legal aspects of computerized info. systems, tech. data in govt. contracts, copyright, info. scientist and law. Home: 5835 Upton St McLean VA 22101 Office: Dept of Energy Washington DC 20545

FARMER, LEONARD JEROME, indsl. chems. mfg. co. exec.; b. Dalton, Ga., May 27, 1913; s. Oscar Leonard and Alma Frances (Bearden) F.; B.S. in Sci., Mt. St. Mary's Coll., Emmitsburg, Md., 1935; postgrad. U. Chattanooga, 1936, U. Pa., 1936; m. Marie C. Wilson, Dec. 27, 1937 (dec.); children—Leonard J., Michael W., Joseph P., John E., Anne M., Susan L.; m. Kathleen Norris Keating. Tchr., Archmere Sch. for Boys, Claymont, Del., 1935-42; with Hercules Inc., Wilmington, 1942-78, mgr. ordnance sale, 1967-72, personnel staff engring. dept., 1972-77, sr. personnel specialist, tech. sales service, 1946-61; tchr. ballistic course Del. Tech. Jr. Coll. Police commr., fire commr., Roxbury Twp., N.J.; pres. Babe Ruth League. Mem. Nat. Rifle Assn., Am. Def. Preparedness Assn. Democrat. Roman Catholic. Contbr. articles to profl. jours. Home: 110 Oldbury Dr Wilmington DE 19808 Office: Hercules Inc 910 Market St Wilmington DE 19899

FARNHAM, BEVERLY TEWKSBURY, educator; b. Burlington, Vt., Jan. 16, 1926; d. Lawrence Giles and Genevieve Ellen (Flanders) Tewksbury; R.N., Mary Fletcher Sch. Nursing, 1947; student Montpelier City Coll., 1959-60; A.B., Goddard Coll., 1971; M.S., St. Michael's Coll., 1973; m., May 5, 1946; children—David Lee, Nancy E. Farnham Cutler, Cynthia L. Farnham Craig, Robin F., Brent T. Ward coordinator-psychiatric technician specialist, research asst. in alcohol and drug program Vt. State Hosp., Waterbury, 1956-71, group leader, trainer, to 1971; group co-dir., cons., trainer, instr. St. Michael's Coll., Winooski, Vt., 1962—, practicum supr., instr. grad. program, 1970—; adminstrv. asst. in Operation Jobs-the Diversified Occupation Program, Spaulding High Sch., 1976-77; v.p. living, edn. and training services, LETS, Inc., Stowe, Vt., 1971—. Mem. Am. Personnel and Guidance Assn. Republican. Contbr. articles to profl. jours. Co-founder, developer facts of environ. life process, sociometric psychol. assessment and profile. Home: RFD 2 Montpelier VT 05602 Office: PO Box 199 Stowe VT 05672

FARR, HENRY BARTOW, JR., lawyer; b. N.Y.C., June 16, 1921; s. H. Bartow and Mildred (Blair) F.; B.A. magna cum laude, Princeton U., 1943; LL.B. (Stone scholar), Columbia U., 1948; m. Mary

Elizabeth Roberts, Jan. 22, 1972; children—H. Bartow, Preston Putnam, Christopher Blair. Admitted to U.S. Ct. Appeals 2d Circuit, 1950, U.S. Dist. Ct. bar, 1950; mem. firm Sullivan & Cromwell (leave of absence to serve as Asst. Atty. Gen. N.Y. State Crime Commn. 1951-53), 1948-53; asso. firm Willkie, Farr & Gallagher, N.Y.C., 1953-58; mng. atty. IBM, N.Y.C., 1959-64, Armonk, N.Y., 1964-65, group counsel data processing group, Harrison, N.Y., 1965-68, v.p., gen. counsel World Trade Corp., N.Y.C., 1968-72, v.p., gen. counsel, Sec., 1972-74, World Trade Europe, Paris, 1974-77; v.p. and gen. counsel The Singer Co., N.Y.C., 1977—. Served with USN, 1943-46. Mem. Am. Bar Assn., Assn. of Bar of City of N.Y. Episcopalian. Clubs: Racquet & Tennis, Travellers. Home: One E 66th St New York NY 10021 Office: 30 Rockefeller Plaza New York NY 10020

FARR, JAMES FRANCIS, lawyer; b. Ludlow, Mass., Mar. 17, 1911; s. Charles H. and Stella (Greene) F.; A.B., Harvard, 1933, LL.B., 1936. Admitted to Mass. bar, 1937; practiced in Boston, 1937—; partner Haussermann, Davison & Shattuck, 1948—; dir., clk. Durkee-Mower, Inc., Cape Cod Candle & Gift Shops, Inc., Prien Stone Research Labs., Inc., Bowry Assos., Inc., Camp Namequoit, Inc., Therm-O-Lux Internat., Inc.; dir. Newton-Waltham Bank & Trust Co., H F G Co., Chgo., Savogran Co., Cape Cod Mgmt. Inc., J.J. Grimmings Co., Babson Bros. Co., Blumberg Co., Inc., Robert McF. Brown & Sons, Inc., Currier Cons., Inc., Mooney & Co., Inc.; clk. Downs Bros., Inc., Essex Welding Corp.; trustee Anson Wheeler Bristol Trust, Galen Trust, Mooney Real Estate Trust. Bd. dirs., clk. Scottish Rite Mus. and Library; bd. dirs. Cambridge YMCA; chmn. bd. dirs. New Eng. Deaconess Hosp.; treas., bd. dirs. New Eng. Edn. Soc.; bd. dirs. Cambridge Home For Aged People. Served to lt. USCGR, World War II. Methodist (trustee), Mason (33 deg., Shriner). Clubs: Cambridge Economy (past pres.), Cambridge, Harvard (Boston). Author: (with Mayo A. Shattuck) An Estate Planner's Handbook, 1953; Loring, A Trustee's Handbook Farr Revision, 1961; An Estate Planner's Handbook, 1966. Home: 51 Martin St Cambridge MA 02138 Office: 1 Boston Pl Boston MA 02109

FARR, RICHARD CLABORN, food and beverage co. exec.; b. Wynne, Ark., Nov. 2, 1928; s. Jesse William and Francis Adele (Hooper) F.; A.B., Hendrix Coll., 1952; postgrad. Stanford, 1959-60, So. Meth. U., 1961-62; m. Marcille Mullikin, Dec. 25, 1950; children—Denise, Richardson Lloyd, David Randall. Various mfg. and mktg. positions Procter & Gamble Co., Dallas, Sacramento and Cin., 1952-65; v.p. Continental Grain Co., N.Y.C. and Paris, France, 1965-70; dir. Lehman Bros., Inc., N.Y.C., 1970-71; v.p. Heublein, Inc., Farmington, Conn., 1971—; dir. United Vintners, Inc., Air Sunshine, Inc. Bd. dirs. Fairhaven Home and Hosp., Environ. Centers, Inc., Combined Health Appeal, Inc., Am. Platform Tennis Assn. Served with AUS, 1946-48. Clubs: University (N.Y.C.); Hartford, Hartford Golf, Hartford Tennis; Oysters Harbors (Osterville, Mass.). Home: 36 Westwood Rd West Hartford CT 06117 Office: Munson Rd Farmington CT 06032

FARRALL, ROBERT ARTHUR, electronics co. exec.; b. Evanston, Ill., July 2, 1932; s. Arthur William and Luella (Buck) F.; B.S. in Physics, Mich. State U., 1954; m. Nancy Mary Georgi, Dec. 22, 1955; children—John Robert, George William. Mgr. photometric engring. Gen. Electric Co., Lynn, Mass., 1954-63; exec. v.p. Clairex Corp., Mt. Vernon, N.Y., 1963-69, pres., 1969—; dir. Clairex Electronics of PR. Bd. dirs. Mt. Vernon United Fund. Served with AUS, 1954-56. Mem. Am. Phys. Soc., Soc. Photog. Scientists and Engrs., Sigma Pi Sigma, Delta Upsilon. Club: Am. Yacht (Rye, N.Y.). Patentee photoconductive cell circuits. Home: 69 Hewlett Ave Rye NY 10580 Office: 560 S 3d Ave Mount Vernon NY 10550

FARRAND, GEORGE NIXON, JR., advt. and mktg. exec.; b. Bay Ridge, N.Y., Apr. 1, 1936; s. George Nixon and Pauline (Merchant) F.; B.S. in Bus. Adminstrn., Lehigh U., 1958; M.B.A. candidate N.Y. U., 1960; m. Elyn Marie Hallberg, Aug. 26, 1961; 1 dau., Kathryn Elyn. Staff mem. Union Carbide Corp., N.Y.C., 1959-63, McCann-Erickson Co., N.Y.C., 1963-64, Vick Chem. Co., N.Y.C., 1964-65; sr. account exec., supr. Grey Advt. Co., N.Y.C., 1965-66; mgr. products mktg. Hoffmann-LaRoche, Inc., Clifton, N.J., 1966-68; dir. new mkts. and ventures Inmont Corp., N.Y.C. and Clifton, 1968-69; sr. v.p. Bliss Grunewald, Inc., N.Y.C., 1969-72; pres., chmn. bd. Farrand Mktg. Assoc., Inc., Upper Saddle River, N.J., 1972—; chmn. bd. Cognos Corp., N.Y.C., 1972—. Served with U.S. Army, Signal Corps, 1959. Named Mktg. Man of Month, Sales Mgmt. mag., 1968. Mem. Sales Execs. Club N.Y., N.J. Advt. Club, North Jersey Advt. Club, Lehigh U. Alumni Assn. (dir., past pres.). Republican. Presbyterian. Clubs: Holiday Lake and Country, Saddle River Tennis and Swim. Contbr. numerous articles to profl. jours. Address: 70 Ripplewood Dr Upper Saddle River NJ 07458

FARRAR, DONALD LEROY, ednl. adminstr.; b. Jackson County, Ohio, Jan. 17, 1924; B.A. in English and Social Studies, Rio Grande (Ohio) Coll., 1948, B.S. magna cum laude in Edn., 1950; M.A. in Elementary Adminstrn. and Supervision, Ohio State U., Columbus, 1953; Ed.D. in Edn. Adminstrn., Columbia, N.Y.C., 1959; married; 2 children. Prin., Marion City (Ohio) Pub. Schs., 1952-54; prin. Euclid (Ohio) Sch. Dist., 1954-60, dir. elementary edn., 1960-62; dir. elementary edn., Alfred I. duPont Sch. Dist., Wilmington, Del., 1962-78, asst. supt., 1978—. Pres., Angola Property Owners Assn., 1969—. Recipient Outstanding Educator award Phi Delta Kappa, 1970; Distinguished Alumnus award Rio Grande Coll., 1973. Mem. Am. Assn. Sch. Adminstrs., Nat. Del. assns. supervision and curriculum devel., Phi Delta Kappa. Home: 2400 Silverside Rd Wilmington DE 19801 Office: 4 Mt Lebanon Rd Wilmington DE 19803

FARRAR, FREDERIC BREAKSPEAR, newspaper exec.; b. Haworth, N.J., July 24, 1918; s. Gilbert Powderly and Beatrice Christina (Breakspear) F.; B.A., Washington and Lee U., 1941; M.A., Adelphi U., 1975; 1 son, Frederic Douglas. Salesman, O'Mara and Ormsbee, N.Y.C., 1946-54, v.p., N.Y. sales mgr., 1954-57, v.p., Eastern sales mgr., 1957-63; sr. v.p., gen. sales mgr. Cresmer, Woodward O'Mara and Ormsbee, N.Y.C., 1963-68, exec. v.p., dir. mktg. and sales, 1968—, also dir. Served to 1st lt. USAF, 1942-45. Recipient Minute Man award Internat. Newspaper Pub. Assn., 1976. Mem. Internat. Newspaper Advt. Execs., Am. Antiquarian Soc., Newspaper Advt. Bur. (plans and priorities coms.), So. Newspapers Pubs. Assn. Republican. Club: N.Y. Athletic. Author: This Common Channel to Independence - Revolution and Newspapers - 1759-1789, 1975. Office: 485 Lexington Ave New York City NY 10017

FARRAY, MARILYN CECILE, health adminstr.; b. Queens, N.Y., Sept. 10, 1948; d. Jensen O. and Winifred E. (Johns) F.; A.B. cum laude, Coll. City N.Y., 1971; M.H.A. (USPHS trainee), Columbia U. Sch. Pub. Health, 1973; J.D. candidate, Yale U. Law Sch. Adminstrv. resident, N.Y.C. Health and Hosps. Corp., 1972-73; adminstrv. resident Coll. Medicine and Dentistry N.J., Newark, 1973; asst. dir. Queens Hosp. Center, N.Y.C., 1973-75; program officer, dep. dir. municipal health services program Robert Wood Johnson Found., Princeton, N.J., 1975—; cons. health related agencies, orgns., delivery systems. Program dir. Elmcor Civic Assn. Youth Rehab. Program; staff tchr. basic skills enhancement program Queens (N.Y.) Sch. System. Recipient Tony Maranga Meml. award Columbia U., 1973; mem. Nat. Honor Soc., 1970. Mem. Nat. Assn. Health Services Execs., Am. Pub. Health Assn., Am. Coll. Hosp. Adminstrs., Am. Hosp. Assn. Home: 111 Park St New Haven CT 06511 Office: PO Box 2316 Princeton NJ 08540

FARRELL, GREGORY ALAN, biomed. engr.; b. Bklyn., May 12, 1942; s. Edmond William and Edna Florence (Williams) F.; B.S. in Mech. Engring., Cooper Union, 1964; M.S. in Biomed. Engring., Columbia U., 1972, postgrad., 1972—; m. Mary Louise Lupiani, Sept. 3, 1966; children—Juliana Eden, Cristina Elizabeth. Mech. engr. Gen. Dynamics, San Diego, 1964-65, Rochester, N.Y., 1965-67; research asst. Columbia U. Med. Sch., N.Y.C., 1968-69; instr. pathology N.Y. Med. Coll., 1969-72; research engr. Technicon Instruments Corp., Tarrytown, N.Y., 1972—. Mem. N.Y. Acad. Scis., AAAS, Am. Assn. Med. Instrumentation. Democrat. Roman Catholic. Contbr. articles to profl. jours. Home: 1080 Belle Ave Teaneck NJ 07666 Office: Technicon Instruments Corp 511 Benedict Ave Tarrytown NY 10591

FARRELL, HAROLD MARON, JR., biochemist; b. Pottsville, Pa., Sept. 5, 1940; s. Harold Maron and Marie G. (Daley) F.; B.S., Mt. St. Marys Coll., 1962; M.S., Pa. State U., 1965, Ph.D., 1968; m. Susan J. Gares, June 15, 1963; children—Judith A., Jonathan K. NRC postdoctoral fellow Dept. Agr., Phila., 1967-69, research chemist, 1969—. Mem. Am. Chem. Soc., A.A.A.S., Am. Dairy Sci. Assn., Sigma Xi. Contbg. author: Lactation, 1974; Fundamentals of Dairy Chemistry, 1974. Contbr. articles profl. jours. Home: 500 Inman Terr Willow Grove PA 19090 Office: 600 E Mermaid Ln Philadelphia PA 19118

FARRELL, JAMES PATRICK, lawyer; b. Montclair, N.J., Jan. 22, 1903; s. Patrick J. and Martha (Farrell) F.; LL.B., Fordham U., 1926, D.Law, 1976; D.Law, U. R.I., 1973; m. Kathryn Fischer, Oct. 24, 1929; children—James P., Mary Patricia (Mrs. Allan Russell), Kathryn Anne (Mrs. George J. Noumair), Hazel Claire (Mrs. Matthew J. Murray, Jr.). Admitted to N.Y. bar, 1932; mem. firm Frueauff, Farrell, Sullivan & Bryan, N.Y.C., 1926-74, partner, 1936-74; dir. Tiffany & Co., Cities Service Co., 1966-74. Sec.-treas. W. Alton Jones Found., Inc., 1944-71, pres., 1971—; v.p. Charles A. Frueauff Found., Inc. Trustee Trinity Coll., Washington, Madison Square Boys Club, N.Y.C. Decorated Assn. Master Knights, Sovereign Mil. Order Malta U.S.A., 1958, Knights and Ladies Equestrian Order, Holy Sepulchre Jerusalem, 1962. Mem. Assn. Bar City N.Y., N.Y. County Lawyers' Assn., Am., N.Y., bar assns., Gamma Eta Gamma. Home: 132 S Mountain Ave Montclair NJ 07042 Office: 70 Pine St New York City NY 10005

FARRELL, JOHN MERLYN, JR., educator; b. Wilkes-Barre, Pa., Aug. 5, 1936; s. John Merlyn and Viola (Harlacher) F.; A.B., U. Mich., 1958, A.M., 1960; postgrad. Notre Dame U., 1960-61, Brown U., 1960-61, Montclair Coll., 1961—, Rutgers U., 1961—, Columbia, 1961—. Tchr. pub. schs., Berkley, Mich., 1957-60, guidance counselor, Butler, N.J., 1960-66; dir. adult edn. sch., 1964-66, dir. elementary guidance, 1966-70; instr., guidance dir. Devereux Found., 1971-73, dean of students, 1973-74, dir. alternative edn., Kingston, R.I., 1974—; instr. R.I. Jr. Coll. Asst. dir. Camp Hugh Beaver, Easton, Pa., 1963-65; asst. dir. Silver Lake Camp, 1966-70; bus. mgr. Phila. YMCA Camps, 1970-72. Dir. Civil Def., 1966-69. Gen. Electric Guidance fellow, 1962. Mem. Am., R.I. personnel and guidance assns., Council for Exceptional Children. Lion (pres. 1963-64, zone chmn. 1964-65), Mason (32 deg., Shriner). Research in field. Address: PO Box 130 Narragansett RI 02882

FARRELL, LAWRENCE DAVID, banker; b. N.Y.C., May 22, 1947; s. Vincent John and Carmela Marie (Carafo) F.; student Hudson Valley Community Coll., 1970-73, Columbia Greene Community Coll., 1975-78, State U. N.Y., to 1979; m. Kathleen Ann Steele, Sept. 13, 1969; children—Lawrence David, Bridget Marie. Mgr., Protective Loan Corp., Hudson, N.Y., 1969-72; audit examiner, security officer Troy (N.Y.) Savs. Bank, 1972—. Mem. Town of Coeymans and Village of Ravena Planning Bd., 1976—; mem. parish council St. Patricks Roman Catholic Ch., 1977—. Served with USMC, 1965-69: Vietnam. Mem. Inst. Internal Auditors (pres. 1977-78 Albany), Nat. Assn. Accountants, Auditors and Controllers Forum N.Y. State Mut. Savs. Banks. Roman Catholic. Home: 23 McConnell Ave Ravena NY 12143 Office: Troy Savs Bank 2d and State Sts Troy NY 12180

FARRELL, PATRICK FRANCIS, iron mining co. exec.; b. Mineville, N.Y., Dec. 14, 1918; s. Patrick Francis and Mayme Ellen (Connor) F.; student pub. schs., also specializing courses; m. Flora V. Scott, Dec. 30, 1942; children—Susan Farrell Bouchard, John P. Asst. mine surveyor Witherbee Sherman Corp., Mineville, 1937-38; with Republic Steel Corp., Mineville, 1938—, asst. supt. mines, then supt. mines, 1956-72, dist. supt., 1972—; cons. in field. Pres. Moriah Central Sch. Bd., 1972-73, Essex County Sch. Bds. Assn., 1972-74; 2d v.p., trustee Essex County Hist. Soc. Mem. Soc. Mining Engrs., AIME, Am. Mining Congress, Asso. Industries N.Y. State. Republican. Roman Catholic. Club: Westport (N.Y.) Country. Contbr. papers in field. Home: 521 Main St Mineville NY 12956 Office: Republic Steel Corp Adirondack Ore Mines Port Henry NY 12974

FARRELL, ROBERT TERENCE, juvenile counselor; b. Balt., Apr. 14, 1948; s. George Robert and Margaret Elaine Farrell; B.S. in Criminal Justice, U. Balt., 1974; m. Mary Louise Turnbull, Oct. 17, 1971. Youth supr. Md. Tng. Sch., Balt., 1973; cottage mgr. Montrose Sch., Reistertown, Md., 1974-75; juvenile counselor Md. Juvenile Services, Balt., 1975-78, vol. coordinator, 1978—; coordinator speaker's bur. Juvenile Services Adminstrn., 1975—. Bd. govs. Herring Run Democratic Club, 1977-78; mem. Md. Democratic Central Com., 1978; regional vice-chmn. Md. Dem. party, 1978—; chmn. bd. Santa Claus Anonymous, 1977; mem. Inner Harbor Design Rev. Com., 1978; bd. dirs. Vol. Council Equal Opportunity, 1977. Served in USAR, 1968-74. Mem. Md. Pub. Health Assn., Md. Classified Employees Assn., Balt. Jr. Assn. Commerce (chmn. bd. 1978-79), Parkside Improvement Assn. (pres. 1976-77), Md. Jaycees (regional dir. 1978-79; seantor 1978; named Jaycee of Year 1977, Dist. Dir. of Year 1978). Roman Catholic. Address: 2901 Southern Ave Baltimore MD 21214

FARRISSEY, FRANCIS STACK, graphic arts packaging co. exec.; b. Bogota, N.J., May 4, 1931; s. Frank J. and Margaret Agnes (Stack) F.; student Columbia U., 1955, Cargenie Inst. Tech., 1956; B.S., Fairleigh Dickinson U., 1964; m. Barbara Ann Van Kirk, Apr. 30, 1960; children—Jacquelyn, Stephen and Suzanne (twins), Jennifer. Mgr. mktg. service, gen. mgr. Rossotti Lithograph Corp., North Bergen, N.J., 1956-70; v.p. Raymond Eisenhardt & Son, Oakland, N.J., 1970—; internat. packaging cons., 1970—. Served with USNR, 1951-54. Mem. TAPPI, Packaging Inst. (profl.). Office: Raymond Eisenhardt & Son 95 Bauer Dr Oakland NJ 07436

FARRONE, PAT JOSEPH, psychologist, correctional instn. adminstr.; b. New Castle, Pa., July 27, 1935; s. Pat Andrew and Frances Marie (Galiano) F.; B.A., Westminster Coll., 1958, M.S., 1965; postgrad. U. Pitts., 1971-73; m. Justine Reilly, Aug. 17, 1963; children—Michelle A., Patrick Brian, Suzanne Frances. High sch. tchr. Baltimore County (Md.), 1958-61; psychologist George Jr. Republic, Butler, Pa., 1961-65, clin. dir., 1965-70, asst. dir., 1970-73, adminstr., 1974—; cons. mentally retarded, Butler, Crippled Children's Assn., Butler; cons. in psychol. evaluation Pa. Bur. Vocat. Rehab. Mem. Pa. Gov.'s Justice Commn.; bd. dirs. Mercer County Family Guidance. Certified as pub. sch. adminstr., guidance counselor, Pa.; licensed as psychologist, Pa. Mem. Am., Pa. Psychol. assns., Pa. Assn. Probation, Parole and Corrections, Am. Correctional Assn., Nat. Conf. of Supts., Pa. Assn. Children's Instns. (dir.), Mental Health Assn. (dir. Mercer County chpt.), Grove City (Pa.) C. of C. (dir.), Kappa Delta Pi. Club: Grove City Rotary. Home: 526 Forest Dr Grove City PA 16127 Office: Box 471 Grove City PA 16127

FARSACE, DUVERNE KONRICK, poet, sci. fiction writer; b. Jasper, Tex., Aug. 20, 1928; d. Rudolph Joseph and Vera (Bishop) Konrick; grad. St. Mary's Dominican Coll., New Orleans, 1945; m. Larry Farsace, Aug. 8, 1956. Librarian, New Orleans Pub. Library, 1945-56; Rochester Pub. Library, 1956—; sr. advance reader Lawyer's Co-op Pub. Co. Pub. Co., Rochester; poetess, essayist, author sci. fiction short stories; collector, bibliographer (in collaboration with husband) sci. fiction books and mags. Chmn. La. Poetry Day Com., 1956, co-chmn. Rochester World Poetry Day, 1958, 59, 60, 71, asst. dir., 1970—, co-chmn., 1962, 63, 65, 67; asst. N.Y. State chmn. Nat. Poetry Day Com., 1969—; co-judge Rochester World, Nat. poetry day contests, 1958—, Fedn. State Poetry Socs. contest, 1966; asst. dir. World Poetry Day; co-editor Golden Atom Publs. Recipient James C. Doty Meml. award, poem, 1948; cash prize for A Crusader's Prayer, Avalon World Arts Acad., 1951; Velta Myrtle Allen award, 1952; Allison Nichols Prize for best poem of the year, Chromotones, 1952; John Francis Sims Meml. award for poem Pine Cathedral, 1955, for Psyche's Sorcery, 1957; Diploma Greatness and Leadership award as Champion of Poetry Day, United Poets Laureate Internationale, Phillipines, 1967; Diploma Di Benemerenza Medal Honor and Certificate Merit, Centro Studi E Scambi Internat., 1967; medal Pres. Philippines, 1968. Mem. Nat. League Am. Pen Women (sec. Crescent City chpt. 1956), Composers, Authors and Artists Assn., Avalon World Arts Acad. (contbg. editor 1951-53, hon. life mem. 1952, asst. nat. councillor 1951-53, dir., tchr. poetry workshop New Orleans chpt. 1951-56), Sci. Acad. of Rochester, Rochester Poetry Soc., Rochester Astronomy Club, Nat. Poetry Soc. (contbg. editor Stanza 1948), Am. Poetry League, Acad. Am. Poets (founder 1969), Marquis Biog. Soc., Nolacon. Author: (poems) Flames of Freedom, 1952; (with others) Seven Star Poems; contbg. author: Conquerors of Tomorrow, 1947; This Shall Endure, 1955; With No Secret Meaning, 1957; From Sea to Sea in Song, 1966; Flame Annual, 1966; Moon Age Poets, 1970; The Apollo Anthology, 1970; Dr. Etta J. Murfey Meml. Award Book, 1969, Internat. Who's Who in Poetry Anthology, 1972. Co-editor: Golden Atom; Rochester in Poetry, 1958; Lilac City Lyrics, 1970, 71, The Golden Atom Poets of History, 1973, New York State's Flower of Dreams, 1973; contbg. editor Different, Avalon organ. Contbr. poetry, short stories numerous mags. and anthologies; poems transl. and pub. in France, Greek, Spanish newspapers. Office: Lawyer's Co-op Publishing Co Aqueduct Bldg Rochester NY 14614

FARSACI, LITTERIE B. (LARRY FARSACI), poet, bibliographer, sci. fiction writer; b. Rochester, N.Y., Feb. 11, 1921; s. Placido and Rose (Gentile) Farsaci; student pub. schs., Rochester; m. Duverne Vera Konrick, Aug. 8, 1956. Postal clk. Gen. Post Office, Rochester, N.Y., 1946—; research sci. and lit., poet, essayist, song writer and artist; lectr. astronomy U. Rochester, other schs., orgns.; collector and bibliographer sci. fiction books and mags.; editor poetry mags.; pub. Fantastic, sci. fiction mag. containing bibliog. data for collectors, Rochester, 1938, 2d issue Fantasy Collector, 1939, Golden Atom, 1939—, Science Fiction Fandom, 1940; editor Stars poetry mag., 1940—. First chmn. for World Poetry Day, Rochester, 1958, co-chmn. day and contest, 1959—; asst. N.Y. State chmn. Nat. Poetry Day, Inc., 1970—; asst. dir. World Poetry Day, Phila., 1970—; editor, pub. Golden Atom Publs.; co-judge Rochester World, Nat. poetry day contests, 1958—, Wilson MacDonald Soc. poetry contest, Toronto, 1969, Fedn. State Poetry Socs. contest, Baton Rouge, La., 1966. Recipient medal for achievement in poetry from Philippine Pres., 1968; Superior Achievement award Post Office Dept., Rochester, 1968, 70; certificate of recognition for poem Nat. Poetry Day, Inc., 1969. Served with AUS, World War II, writer, editor Army newspapers. Diploma, Greatness and Leadership award, United Poets Laureate Internat. 1967; diploma from station WBUX and WEFG-FM. Fellow Intercontinental Biog. Assn.; mem. Sci. Acad. of Rochester, Sci. Fiction League, New Fandom, Brit. Sci. Fiction Assn., Internat. Sci. Fiction Assn., Fantasy Amateur Press Assn. (charter), Spectator Amateur Press Assn., Am. Poetry League, Nat. Fantasy Fan Fedn. (charter), Avalon World Arts Acad. (hon. life), Rochester Poetry Soc., Rochester Astronomy Club, Acad. Am. Poets (founder), Am. Poetry League, 1st Fandom (charter), Audience UnLtd. Author: (poems) Star-Bound (Best Publ. of Yr. 1944-45), 1944, Enchanting Reveries, 1949, Be With Me and other song lyrics, 1952. Author, compiler: Rochester in Poetry, 1958. Editor local monthly pub. Nat. Fedn. Post Office Clerks; Seven Star Poems. Co-editor: Lilac City Lyrics, 1970, 71, The Triumph of Dreams, 1972, The Timeless Glory, 1972, The Golden Atom Poets of History, 1973, New York State's Flower of Dreams, 1973. Contbr. poems, short stories to mags.; poems to anthologies including Moon Age Poets, 1970, Best Broadcast Poetry, 1970, From Sea to Sea in Song, 1966, Shadows of the Elusive Dream. Office: PO Box 1101 Rochester NY 14603

FARWELL, CHARLES, IV, physician; b. New Orleans, Dec. 1, 1926; s. Charles Alphonzo and Edwa (Stewart) F.; student Va. Mil. Inst., 1944-45, U. Pa., 1945; M.D., Tulane U., 1949; m. Titine Gibert, July 22, 1968; children—Laura Farwell, Samuel Adams III, Pharr Adams. Intern, Charit Hosp., New Orleans, 1949-50; psychiat. resident Springfield Psychiat. Hosp., 1950-51, VA, 1951-52; practice medicine specializing in family practice and psychiatry, Wheaton, Md., 1952—; pres. vis. staff Suburban hosp., Bethesda, Md., 1961; mem. staff Washington Hosp. & Sanitarium, Takoma Park, Md., Suburban Hosp., Bethesda. Med. dir. Planned Parenthood of Montgomery County, 1958. Pres. Univ. Bldg. Fund, Montgomery County, 1967-68; mem. Opera Soc. Washington, Nat. Symphony Assn. Recipient med. econs. awards also awards Wheaton Rescue Squad, Boys Club, Silver Spring, Md. Fellow Am. Acad. Family Practice (charter); mem. Am. Psychiat. Assn., So. Med. Assn. (life), Montgomery County Med. Soc., Med. and Chirurgical Soc. Med., Md. Med. Soc. (jour. rep. 1960-61), Md. Acad. Family Physicians (treas., dir.), S.A.R., Nu Sigma Nu. Optimist (pres. 1955, lt. gov. 1956) (Southern, Md.). Episcopalian (mem. vestry). Clubs: Wheaton (Md.) Chess (founder 1960); Indian Spring Indoor Tennis. Contbr. articles to med. jours. Address: 11406 Veirs Mill Rd Wheaton MD 20902

FASANA, PAUL JAMES, librarian; b. Bingham Canyon, Utah, July 20, 1933; s. Oreste Joseph and Mary Calcio (Rolando) F.; B.A., U. Calif. at Berkeley, 1959, M.L.S., 1960. Systems engr. Itek Labs., Lexington, Mass., 1961-64; head Systems Office, Columbia Libraries, 1964-71; chief preparation services Research Libraries, N.Y. Pub. Library, N.Y.C., 1971—. Lectr. Grad. Sch. L.S., Rutgers U., 1970—, McGill U., Montreal, Que., Can., 1966-69. Bd. dirs. Documentation Abstracts, Inc., 1970—. Served with AUS, 1951-54. Mem. ALA (council 1970-72, pres. resources and tech. services div. 1975—), Am. Soc. for Info. Sci. (council 1969-73), N.Y. Tech. Services Librarians (pres. 1971-72). Contbr. articles to profl. jours. Home: 115 Central

Park W New York City NY 10023 Office: Research Libraries NY Pub Library Fifth Ave and 42d St New York City NY 10018

FASANELLA, ROCKO MICHAEL, ophthalmologist; b. Trenton, Aug. 4, 1916; s. Vito and Cecelia (Tronolone) F.; B.A., Yale, 1939, M.D., 1943; postgrad. U. Pa., 1947-48; m. Marion Levina Henry, Aug. 10, 1944; children—Marion Cecelia, George Michael, Anne Louise, Katherine Lea, Robert Anthony. Intern, Yale-New Haven (Conn.) Med. Center, 1943-44, resident, 1948-49; intern Mercer Hosp., Trenton, 1946-47; practice medicine, specializing in ophthalmology, New Haven, 1949—; mem. staff Yale-New Haven Hosp., St. Raphael Hosp., New Haven, Waterbury (Conn.) Hosp.; mem. faculty Sch. Medicine, Yale, New Haven, 1950-51, 59—, chief ophthalmology sect., 1959-61, asso. clin. prof., 1961—. Cons. Regional Center Retarded, New Haven, 1963—, Archives de Oftalmología del Norte del Perú, Trujillo, 1969—, Atlantic Med. Research Found., 1969—. Co-chmn. selection com. fellowship program Guild Opticians, 1956-62; mem. exec. steering com. Conn. chpt. Nat. Soc. Prevention Blindness, 1959; mem. New Haven unit Recordings for Blind, 1968. Served to capt. M.C., AUS, 1944-46. Diplomate Am. Bd. Opthalmology (asso. examiner surgery 1954—), Pan-Am. Assn. Ophthalmology, Pan-Am. Med. Assn. Fellow Am. Acad. Ophthalmology and Otolaryngology, A.M.A.; mem. Conn. Med. Soc. (mem. exec. eye com. 1955), New Haven Med. Soc., Assn. Research Ophthalmology, N.Y. Soc. Clin. Opthalmology, Peruvian Eye, Ear, Nose and Throat Soc., French Ophthalmology Soc., Oxford (Eng.) Ophthalmol. Soc., Am. Soc. Ophthalmic Plastic and Reconstructive Surgery, Soc. Eye Surgeons (charter mem.), Pan-Am. Ophthalmol. Found., Pan-Pacific Surg. Assn.; hon. mem. Colo. Med. Soc., Inst. Barraquer (Barcelona, Spain), Gonin Soc. (France). Editor: Management of Complications in Eye Surgery, 1957; Modern Advances in Cataract Surgery, 1963; Cataract Operation by Enzmatic Zonulysis (Hans Hofmann), 1965; Eye Surgery: Innovations, Trends, Pitfalls and Complications, 1976. Mem. editorial bd. Advances in Ophthalmology Germany, 1967. Home: 29 Rolling Ridge Rd Orange CT 06477 Office: 842 Howard Ave New Haven CT 06519

FASCETTA, SALVATORE CHARLES, pharm. co. exec.; b. N.Y.C., Oct. 14, 1940; s. Nicholas and Anne (Piedevillano) F.; B.S. in Pharmacy, St. John's U., 1963; m. Mary-Barbara Aprile, Aug. 8, 1964; children—Christopher, Kevin, Timothy. Devel. pharmacist Wallace Labs., Cranbury, N.J., 1967, group leader pharm. devel., 1968-70, mgr. pharm. devel., 1970-74; dir. pharm. devel. Knoll Pharm. Co., Whippany, N.J., 1974-77, prodn. mgr., 1978—. Pres. East Windsor Rescue Squad. 1969-70. Mem. Am. Pharm. Assn. (Lunson Richardson Pharm. award, 1963), Acad. Pharm. Scis., Soc. Chem. Engrs., Parenteral Drug Assn., Nat. Assn. Retail Druggists. Roman Catholic. Club: Lions. Home: 13 Dunbar Dr RD 4 Trenton NJ 08691 Office: 30 N Jefferson Rd Whippany NJ 07981

FASOLI, ALEXANDER EDGAR, ret. judge; b. Paterson, N.J., Jan. 20, 1913; s. Alexander and Cunegonda (Capra) F.; A.B., U. Pitts., 1935; LL.B., John Marshall Coll., Jersey City, 1939; m. Muriel Dorothy Choyce, Oct. 20, 1946; 1 son, Robert Alexander. Admitted to N.J. bar, 1939; pvt. practice law, Hawthorne, 1939—; prof. law John Marshall Coll., 1947-49; counsel Hawthorne (N.J.) Bd. Edn., 1948-73; former municipal prosecutor of Passaic and Bergen counties; judge Municipal Ct., Midland Park, N.J.; assisting judge various Passaic and Bergen county communities. Lectr. constnl. law; civil rights cons. Mem. Republican Nat. Com. Served with A.A.A., AUS, 1942-44; ETO. Recipient outstanding vets. award Borough of Hawthore, N.J., 1948. Mem. N.J. Patrolmen's Benevolent Assn., Am. Legion, V.F.W., DAV, Passaic County Bar Assn., Bergen County Municipal Judges Assn., N.J. Sch. Bd. Attys. Assn. Republican. Episcopalian. Lion. Home: 168 Pasadera Pl Hawthorne NJ 07506

FASSLER, JOAN GRACE (MRS. LEONARD J. FASSLER), psychologist, author, educator; b. N.Y.C., Sept. 23, 1931; d. Jacob V. and Rose (Sandrowitz) Greenberg; B.B.A., Coll. City N.Y., 1953; M.A., Columbia, 1965; Ph.D. (United Cerebral Palsy Research and Edn. Found. grantee), 1969; m. Leonard J. Fassler, July 26, 1953; children—David Gary, Ellen Beth. Editorial asst. Seventeen at School, N.Y.C., 1954-55, Reader Mail editor Seventeen Mag., N.Y.C., 1955-56; research asst. Tchrs. Coll., Columbia U., N.Y.C., 1966-67, project asso., research asso., research cons. Research and Demonstration Center for Edn. Handicapped Children, 1967-72; cons. early childhood programming Videorecord Corp. Am., Westport, Conn., 1970-72; mem. faculty, research asso. Child Study Center, Yale, New Haven, 1972—, chmn. children's lit. adv. com., 1972-75. Psychologist, moderator program series Conversations With the Very Young, WNYC radio, N.Y.C., 1970; lectr. summer research workshop coll. tchrs., Columbia U., 1970; vis. faculty psychology dept. U. N.H., Durham, 1971. Demonstration Program grantee Grant Found., 1972-74. Mem. Author's League Am., Am. Psychol. Assn., Council for Exceptional Children, Nat. Assn. for Edn. Young Children, Am. Orthopsychiat. Assn. (program com. 1975-76), Psi Chi. Author: The Man of the House, 1969; All Alone with Daddy, 1969; One Little Girl, 1969; Don't Worry Dear, 1971; The Boy With a Problem, 1971; My Grandpa Died Today, 1971; Howie Helps Himself, 1974; Helping Children Cope: Mastering Stress Through Books and Stories, 1978. Contbr. articles to profl. jours. Home: 80 Hickory Hill Dr Dobbs Ferry NY 10522 Office: 333 Cedar St New Haven CT 06510

FATSY, GEORGE CHRISTY, engring. and mfg. co. exec.; b. Woonsocket, R.I., Feb. 17, 1939; s. Christ Evangelos and Vichia (Vanghel) F.; B.A., Widener Coll., 1962; M.B.A., U. Bridgeport, 1978; m. Audrey M. Yanka, Nov. 17, 1963; children—Marianne, Kristin Stephanie. Supr. work measurement Burndy Corp., Norwalk, Conn., 1968-72; supr. indsl. engring. Harvey Hubell, Inc., Bridgeport, Conn., 1972-76; mgr. facilities and mfg. engring. Fermont div. DCA, Bridgeport, 1976-78; mgr. mfg. engring. Roberk Co., Parker Hannifin, Shelton, Conn., 1978; supr. indsl. planning analysis Avco Lycoming, Stratford, Conn., 1978—; lectr., cons. in field. Dist. chmn. City of Bridgeport Republican party, 1967-68; Town of Trumbull (Conn.) Sewer Commn., 1972-75; chmn. exec. com. St. Dimitri Romanian Orthodox Ch., Bridgeport, 1973—. Served with U.S. Army, 1962-65. Mem. Am. Inst. Indsl. Engrs. (sr.), YMCA Mgmt. Assn. Elks. Home: 61 Sabina Rd Trumbull CT 06611 Office: Avco Lycoming 550 S Main St Stratford CT 06497

FAUCI, PETER ANTHONY, JR., surgeon; b. N.Y.C., Jan. 13, 1933; s. Peter Anthony and Mary (Mayo) F.; A.B., Columbia Coll., 1953; M.D., Boston U., 1957; m. Teresita Ghirardi, Sept. 18, 1977; 2 sons, George, Peter. Intern, Jersey City Med. Center, 1957-58; resident Bellevue Hosp., Cornell U. Med. Center, N.Y.C., 1958-60; practice medicine specializing in gen. surgery, New Rochelle, N.Y., 1964—; asso. attending surgeon, New Rochelle Hosp. Med. Center; cons. in surgery, Calvary Hosp., asst. clin. prof. surgery, N.Y. Med. Coll. Served to capt. U.S. Army, 1962-64. Diplomate Am. Bd. Surgery, Fellow A.C.S.; mem. Westchester County, N.Y. State med. socs., AMA. Democrat. Roman Catholic. Home: 90 Chatsworth Ave Larchmont NY 10538 Office: 150 Lockwood Ave New Rochelle NY 10801

FAULHABER, THOMAS ALBERT, mgmt. cons.; b. Cin., Jan. 21, 1931; s. Albert John and Vera Rosalia (Schweer) F.; B.S., Mass. Inst. Tech., 1953; M.B.A., Harvard U., 1957; m. Susan Roberta Playfair, June 22, 1974; children—Thomas Albert, Gregory Reid, Lilian Vaughan. Mgmt. engring. cons. Ganteaume & McMullen, Boston, 1957-60, partner, 1961-75; pres. Case and Co., Boston, Inc., Mgmt. Cons.'s, 1975-76; mgmt. cons., fin. intermediary, Boston, 1977—. Served with AUS, 1954-56. Recipient Daniel W. Mead prize ASCE, 1963; registered profl. engr., Conn., D.C., Fla., Ill., Ind., Ky., La., Maine, Md., Mass., Mich., Mo., Nebr., N.H., N.J., N.Y., Ohio, Pa., R.I., S.C., Tex., Vt., Wis. Mem. Inst. Mgmt. Cons.'s (dir. 1978—), N. Am. Soc. Corp. Planning, Am. Inst. Indsl. Engrs., ASCE, Nat. Soc. Profl. Engrs., Tau Beta Pi, Delta Upsilon. Unitarian. Clubs: Algonquin of Boston, Longwood Cricket, Harvard of Boston, Harvard of N.Y.C. Home and Office: 146 Mount Vernon St Boston MA 02108

FAULKENDER, ROBERT EDGAR, educator; b. Altoona, Pa., Jan. 2, 1917; s. Alton Fern and Edna Rebecca (Rickenbaugh) F.; B.S., Franklin and Marshall Coll., 1942; M.A., U. Pitts., 1949, Ph.D., 1954. Instr., U. Pitts., 1946-51, Sharpsville (Pa.) High Sch., 1953-58; headmaster Marvell Acad. for Boys, Rye, N.Y., 1958-63; prof. econs. Windham Coll., Putney, Vt., 1963—, also chmn. social studies div. Served with AUS, 1942-46. Mem. Am. Arbitration Assn., AAUP, Nat. Assn. Journalism Dirs., Am. Econ. Assn., Phi Kappa Tau, Alpha Delta Sigma. Mason (32 deg.). Club: Lions. Home: Route 1 Box 105C Putney VT 05346 Office: Route 1 Box 105 C Putney VT 05346

FAULL, J. HORACE, JR., chemist, ret. ofcl. Navy Dept.; b. Toronto, Ont., Can., Oct. 16, 1904; A.B., Harvard, 1927, A.M., 1929, Ph.D. in Phys. Cehmistry, 1932. Acting prof. chemistry Meml. U. Coll., Nfld., 1931-33; Harvard traveling fellow, U. Munich (Germany), 1933-34; research asso. Harvard, 1934-36; research chemist Kaysam Corp., 1936-38, Firestone Tire & Rubber Co., 1938-41, research dir. Gen. Latex & Chem. Co., 1941-43; tech. supt. synthetic rubber div. Gen. Tire & Rubber Co., Tex., 1943-46; head sci. sect. Office Naval Research, Boston, 1946-48, chem. cons., 1946-60, sr. staff scientist, 1960-70; ret., 1971. Mem. com. Office Rubber Research. Mem. Am. Chem. Soc. Research in halogens, electrolysis of solutions, ion refraction indices, colloids, rubber latex, synthetic rubbers. Address: 72 Fresh Pond Ln Cambridge MA 02138*

FAULSTICH, RICHARD CHARLES, govt. financial analyst; b. Washington, May 10, 1947; s. Albert Joseph and Anna Emily (Collignon) F.; A.A., Strayer Coll., 1968; B.S., Bethel Coll., McKenzie, Tenn., 1970; M.C.S., Benjamin Franklin U., 1977. Accountant, U.S. Treasury Dept., Washington, 1971-72, bank examiner, bank regulator, 1972—, financial analyst, bank corp. practices, 1972—. Mem. Am. Accounting Assn., Assn. Govt. Accountants. Democrat. Roman Catholic. Home: 505 Elderwood Rd Silver Spring MD 20904 Office: 490 L'Enfant Plaza Washington DC 20219

FAUNTROY, WALTER E., congressman; b. Washington, Feb. 6, 1933; s. William T. and Ethel (Vine) F.; B.A. cum laude, Va. Union U., 1955, D.D., 1968; B.D., Yale U. Divinity Sch., 1958, D.D., 1969; hon. degree Muskingum Coll., 1971; m. Dorothy Simms, Aug. 3, 1957; 1 son, Marvin Keith. Ordained to ministry Baptist Ch., 1958; pastor New Bethel Baptist Ch., Washington, 1958—; founder, former dir. Model Inner City Community Orgn. Inc., Washington; mem. 92d to 96th Congresses from D.C. Dir. Washington bur. SCLC, 1960-71; coordinator March on Washington for Jobs and Freedom, 1963; chmn. D.C. Coalition of Conscience, 1965; coordinator Selma to Montgomery March, 1965; vice chmn. White House Conf. to Fulfill these Rights, 1966; nat. coordinator Poor People's Campaign, 1969; mem. Leadership Conf. on Civil Rights, Yale U. Council, 1969-74. Vice-chmn. D.C. City Council, 1967-69; chmn. bd. dirs. Martin Luther King Jr. Center for Social Change, 1969—. Home: 4105 17th St NW Washington DC 20011 Office: Cannon Bldg Washington DC 20515

FAUST, NAOMI FLOWE, educator; b. Salisbury, N.C.; d. Christopher Leroy and Ada Luella (Graham) Flowe; A.B., Bennett Coll.; M.A., U. Mich.; Ph.D., N.Y. U., 1963; m. Roy Malcolm Faust, Aug. 16, 1948. Elementary tchr. Granard Sch., Gaffney, S.C.; tchr. English, French, phys. edn. Atkins High Sch., Winston Salem, N.C.; instr. English, Bennett Coll., Greensboro, N.C., So. U., Scotlandville, La.; asst. prof. English, Morgan State Coll., Balt.; tchr. English, Greensboro Pub. Sch. System, tchr., N.Y.C. Pub. Sch. System; now prof. dept. edn. Queens Coll., City U. N.Y., Flushing. Mem. AAUP, Assn. Tchr. Educators, Nat. Council Tchrs. English, NEA, Women's Nat. Book Assn., World Poetry Soc. Intercontinental, United Negro Coll. Fund, N.A.A.C.P., Alpha Kappa Alpha, Alpha Epsilon, Alpha Kappa Mu. Author: Discipline and the Classroom Teacher, 1977; (poems) Speaking In Verse, 1974. Contbr. poetry to profl. jours. Office: Queens Coll City U NY Flushing NY 11367

FAVA, CATHERINE MAY, educator; b. Paterson, N.J., Mar. 26, 1946; d. Vincent James and Stella Mildred (Cirangle) F.; grad. Capri Inst. Hair Design; student Am. Acad. Dramatic Arts; B.A., Fairleigh Dickinson U., 1970, M.A. summa cum laude, 1976; postgrad. N.Y. U. Beautician, Mark VII Salon, Clifton, N.J., 1965-67, Florentine Coiffures, Garfield, N.J., 1967-68; tchr. English Eastside High Sch., Paterson, N.J., 1970—, class advisor, 1974—, creative writing mag. editor, 1973—. Mem. Paterson Tchrs. Union, N.J. Council English Tchrs., Nat. Council Tchrs. English. Democrat. Roman Catholic. Author: (play) Christ in Purple, 1968. Address: 4 Ryerson Ave Paterson NJ 07502

FAVREAU, DONALD FRANCIS, univ. adminstr.; b. Cohoes, N.Y., Sept. 7, 1919; s. Alphonse E. and Millie (Smith) F.; B.A., Knox Coll., 1949; M.A., State U. N.Y., 1954; m. Helen Patricia Rafferty, June 2, 1945; 1 dau., Susan Debra. Prof. mil. sci. LaSalle Inst., Troy, N.Y., 1949-54; tng. coordinator Ford Motor Co., Cleve., 1954-57; tng. mgr. Am. Bosch Arma, Garden City, N.Y., 1957-59, Royal Metal Corp., N.Y.C., 1959-60, N.Y. Stock Exchange, N.Y.C., 1960-62; manpower coordinator N.Y. State Labor Dept., Albany, 1962-64; asso. dir. Center Exec. Devel., State U. N.Y., Albany, 1964-69, dir., 1969-73, dir. Center Exec. Devel. and Pub. Safety Mgmt., 1973—; exec. dir. Internat. Fire Adminstrn. Inst., State U. N.Y., Albany, 1964-73. Cons. to assns., mgmt., 1964—. Mem. Nat. Adv. Council Higher Edn. Served to 1st lt. AUS, 1943-46; PTO. Named hon. citizen New Orleans; hon. fire chief Denver; recipient commendation Pres. Carter, 1978. Nat. Alliance Businessmen Career Guidance Inst. grantee, 1973—. Mem. AAUP, Am. Mgmt. Assn., N.Y. State Assn. Fire Chiefs (hon.), Soc. Advancement Mgmt., Internat. Platform Assn., Nat. Council Fire Service Orgns., Am. Soc. Tng. dirs., Nat. Fire Protection Assn., Internat. Chiefs of Police, Sigma Nu. Club: Elks. Author: Fire Science Technology Survey, 1966; Management Bibliography, 1966; Fire Service Management, 1969; The Challenge of the Seventies, 1970; Executive Development for Police Officers, 1971; others. Co-author: The Process of Management in a Law Enforcement Setting, 1974; Modern Police Administration, 1978. Home: 32 Hemlock Dr Clifton Knolls Clifton Park NY 12065

FAVREAU, LAWRENCE ROGER, bus. exec., former city ofcl.; b. Cohoes, N.Y., Feb. 4, 1935; s. Omer Edward and Corinne (Miron) F.; B.A., Siena Coll., 1957; postgrad. Albany Law Sch., 1959-60, Russell Sage U., 1965-68; m. Jean Smithrick, June 23, 1957; 1 son, John Laurent. Tchr. LaSalle Inst., Troy, N.Y., 1960-65; dir. Cohoes Neighborhood Youth Corps, 1965-68; exec. adminstr. to the mayor City of Cohoes, 1968-76; owner Pub. Laurent, Cohoes, 1976—. Mem. Cohoes Citizen Party Exec. Com., 1963—; mem. adv. com. Regional Planning Commn., 1967—. Bd. dir. Cohoes Community Center, 1968—. Served to 1st lt. AUS, 1957-59. Roman Catholic. K.C. Home: 6 Leversee Ave Cohoes NY 12047 Office: 201 Columbia St Cohoes NY 12047

FAWCETT, CLIFFORD WILLIAM, mgmt. cons.; b. N.Y.C., Jan. 3, 1930; s. Clifford Arthur and Madeline (Foskett) F.; B.E.E., U. Md., 1958; M.B.A., Am. U., 1970; D.B.A., George Washington U., 1976; m. Lydia Mae Van Allen, Sept. 1, 1951; children—Cheryl Lynn, Glenn Kenneth, Jeffrey Keith, Clifford William, Bradley Allen. Design engr. Naval Weapons Plant, Washington, 1958-63; tech. dir., project mgr. Navy Weapon Systems, Navy Dept., Washington, 1963-68; tech. dir., project mgr., communications and electronic warfare, 1969-72, dir., program mgr. standard surface-to-surface missile systems, 1972-76, dep. dir. med. range missile systems, 1976-77; mgmt. cons., Annapolis, Md., 1978—; program mgr. Value Engring. Co., Alexandria, Va., 1968; adj. prof. George Washington U., 1976-77; asst. prof. mgmt. Pa. State U., 1978. Served with USN, 1950-54. Mem. AAUP, Assn. Scientists and Engrs., Am. Soc. Naval Engrs., Acad. Mgmt. Home: 1628 Winchester Rd Annapolis MD 21401 Office: National Center 2 Washington DC 20362

FAWCETT, HOWARD HOY, mfg. co. exec.; b. McKeesport, Pa., May 31, 1916; s. Harry Garfield and Ada (Deetz) F.; B.S. in Indsl. Chemistry, U. Md., 1940; postgrad. U. Del., 1945-47; m. Ruth Allen Bogan, Apr. 7, 1942; children—Ralph Willard, Harry Allen. Research chemist Manhattan project E.I. DuPont de Nemours & Co., Inc., Chgo., Hanford, Wash., 1944-45, research and devel. chemist organic chemistry div., Deepwater, N.J., 1945-48; cons. engr. Gen. Electric Co., Schenectady, N.Y., 1948-64; tech. sec. com. on hazardous materials Nat. Acad. Scis.-NRC, Washington, 1964-75; staff scientist, project mgr. Tracor Jitco, Inc., Rockville, Md., 1975-78; sr. chem. engr. Equitable Environ. Health, 1978—; mem. adv. com. study on socio-behavioral preparations for, responses to and recovery from chem. disasters NSF, 1977—; cons. to industry and govt. agys. Chief radiol. sect. Schenectady County CD, 1953-63. Bd. dirs. Safety sect. Schenectady C. of C., 1957-64. Recipient Distinguished Service to Safety citation Nat. Safety Council, 1966, Cameron award, 1962, 69. Registered profl. engr., Calif. Mem. Am. Chem. Soc. (sec. com. chem. safety, chmn. council com. on chem. safety 1974-77, chmn. div. chem. health and safety 1977-79, author audio course on hazards of materials 1977), ASTM (membership sec. 1972—), Am. Inst. Chem. Engrs. (com. on occupational health and safety 1977—), Am. Indsl. Hygiene Assn. (dir. Balt.-Washington chpt. 1975-77), Alpha Chi Sigma. Co-editor: Safety and Accident Prevention in Chemical Operations, 2d edit., 1979; mem. editorial adv. bd. Jour. Safety Research, 1968—, Transp. Planning and Tech., 1972—; N. Am. regional editor Jour. Hazardous Materials, 1975—. Home: 12920 Matey Rd Wheaton MD 20906 Office: 6000 Executive Blvd Rockville MD 20852

FAWCETT, JOHN WILLIAM, III, lawyer; b. Oil City, Pa., May 4, 1920; s. John William and Mary (Chambers) F.; B.A., Yale, 1942; LL.B., Temple U., 1950; m. Margaret B. Hoyer, May 30, 1957; children—John William IV, Jennifer Wales, Erik Hoyer. Admitted to Pa. bar, 1950; partner firm Montgomery, McCracken, Walker & Rhoads, Phila. Consul of France for Phila. Decorated chevalier Ordre National de Merite. Mem. Internat. Law Assn., Internat. Fiscal Assn., Am., Phila. bar assns. Clubs: Yale (Phila. and N.Y.); Corinthian Yacht (Phila.); Rittenhouse. Home: 126 Montrose Ave Rosemont PA 19010 Office: 3 Parkway Philadelphia PA 19102

FAWCETT, MARIE ANN FORMANEK (MRS. ROSCOE KENT FAWCETT), civic worker; b. Mpls., Mar. 6, 1914; d. Peter Paul and Mary (Stepanek) Formanek; grad. high sch.; m. Roscoe Kent Fawcett, Mar. 16, 1935; children—Roscoe Kent, Peter Formanek, Roger Knowlton II, Stephen Hart. Vol. chmn. Merry Go Round, Greenwich, Conn., 1948—; corr. sec., 1967-68, also bd. dirs. vol. chmn. Nathaniel Witherell Hosp., Greenwich, 1952-56, chmn. vols., 1956—; chmn. vols. Greenwich Hosp., 1953-54; dist. chmn. ARC, Community Chest, Mental Health, 1946-50; vol. mentally retarded children Milbank Sch., Greenwich, 1958-59. Bd. dirs. Cerebral Palsy, Greenwich Philharmonia, Merry Go Round Mews for Aged, Merry Go Round, Inc. for Sr. Citizens, Nathaniel Witherell Hosp. Aux.; bd. dirs. Multiple Sclerosis Soc., 1948—, corr. sec., 1958—. Active on drives for ARC, Community Chest, Leukemia, Muscular Dystrophy, Mental Health, Mentally Retarded Children Milbank Sch.; participating mem. Huxley Inst. Biosocial Research. Named Woman of Year, Soroptimist Club, 1967; recipient Community Service award United Cerebral Palsy Assn. Fairfield County, 1972, citations Greenwich Hosp., Conn. State Dept. Health for vol. services, 1974. Mem. Internat. Platform Assn., Sovereign Order Hospitallers St. John of Jerusalem, Knights of Malta. Clubs: Greenwich Women's, York (N.Y.C.). Address: North St and Hawkwood Ln Greenwich CT 06830

FAWCETT, MARY ISABEL SANDOE (MRS. RICHARD SELDEN FAWCETT), social worker; b. Columbus, Ohio; d. D. Nevin and Maud (Collins) Sandoe; B.S., Ohio State U., 1930; M.A., Columbia, 1931; postgrad. New Sch. for Social Research, 1959—; m. Richard Selden Fawcett, June 3, 1931; children—Richard N., Joyce, Gay. With Traveler's Aid Soc., N.Y.C., 1931-32; county supr. Emergency Relief Agy., Bergen County, N.J., 1933-34; social worker Children's Aid and Adoption Soc., Orange, N.J., 1935-40, Family and Children's Agy., Montclair, N.J., 1940-44; tchr. adult edn., Livingston, N.J., 1948-49; parent edn. specialist Essex County Coop. Extension Service, U.S. Dept. Agr., Rutgers U., 1950-51; group psychotherapist Essex County Penitentiary, Caldwell, N.J., 1957-61; exec. sec. Family Counseling Service, Belleville, N.J., 1954-64; research specialist Family Service Bur., Newark, 1964-73; individual practice marriage counseling and psychotherapy, 1948-; family psychotherapist Mt. Carmel guild Narcotics Rehab. Center, 1964—. Bd. dirs. Livingston N.J. Coop. Nursery Sch., 1944-46. Mem. Nat. Assn. Social Workers, Acad. Certified Social Workers, Am. Group Psychotherapy Assn. (asso.), Alpha Delta Pi, Sigma Alpha Sigma. Unitarian. Contbr. articles to profl. jours. Home: 321 Lawrence Dr Lanoka Harbor NJ 08734

FAWWAZ, RASHID ADIB, physician; b. Sao Paulo, Brazil, May 19, 1935; s. Adib R. and Salwa (Sabra) F.; came to U.S., 1963, naturalized, 1973; B.S., Am. U. of Beirut (Lebanon), 1957, M.D., 1960; Ph.D. (Donner fellow), U. Calif. at Berkeley, 1968; m. Marcia Mary Cosse, Jan. 30, 1969; 1 son, Adib Marc. Intern, Am. U. Hosp., Beirut, 1960-61, resident in internal medicine, 1961-63; asso. research physician Donner Lab., U. Calif. at Berkeley, 1968-76; with Columbia U., 1976—; cons. in nuclear medicine Highland Hosp., Oakland, Calif., 1968-74. NIH fellow, 1974-75. Diplomate Am. Bd. Nuclear Medicine. Mem. Soc. Nuclear Medicine. Contbr. research articles on nuclear medicine to profl. publs; research on tumor diagnosis immunotherapy. Home: 231 Secor Pelham NY 10803 Office: Columbia Univ Coll of Physicians and Surgeons 630 W 168th St New York City NY 10032

FAY, JOHN HARVEY, publisher; b. Kingston, N.Y., Mar. 30, 1949; s. Frank L. and Evelyn C. (Christina) F.; B.S. in Bus. Adminstrn. with high distinction, Babson Coll., 1970. Owner, Crafco Homeparties, Rensselaer, N.Y., 1970-72; pres. Apt. Publs., Inc., Albany, N.Y., 1972—, pub. Greater Hartford Bus. Rev., 1976—, New Haven Bus. Rev., 1978—. Organizer Caring for Children, Albany, 1972—. Mem. Am. Mktg. Assn. (Hutchinson Meml. award Boston chpt. 1970), Blue Key. Home: 18-4 Woodlake Rd Albany NY 12203 Office: 179 Allyn St Suite 411 Hartford CT 06103

FAY, THOMAS JOSEPH, counselor, psychologist; b. Yonkers, N.Y., Sept. 8, 1944; s. Patrick F. and Rita C. F.; B.A. magna cum laude, Boston Coll., 1968, M.Ed. cum laude, 1969; M.B.A. cum laude, Adelphi U., 1978; m. Jewel E. Scarth, Oct. 18, 1976; children—Dawn, Deborah. Grad. asst. Boston Coll., 1968-69; rehab. counselor Mass. Rehab. Commn. Brockton, 1969-71; employment counselor N.Y. State Employment Service, Bklyn., 1971-75; rehab. counselor Pilgrim Psychiat. Center, West Brentwood, N.J., 1975—; pvt. practice psychotherapy; substitute tchr.; writer. Supr. Comprehensive Employment and Tng. Act grant, 1977-78; Suffolk County Dept. Labor grantee, 1977-78. Mem. Am. Personnel and Guidance Assn., Nat. Vocat. Guidance Assn., Assn. Measurement and Evaluation in Guidance, Am. Rehab. Couseling Assn., Assn. M.B.A. Execs., Delta Mu Delta. Home: 175 Southaven Ave Medford NY 11763 Office: Pilgrim Psychiat Center Bldg 22 Rehab Services West Brentwood NY 11717

FAYEMI, ALFRED OLUSEGUN, pathologist; b. Ifaki Ekiti, Nigeria, July 17, 1941; s. Alfred Ogunyem and Abimbola F.; came to U.S., 1970; M.S., Hebrew U., Jerusalem, Israel, 1967, M.D., 1968; m. Ayodeji Martins, July 22, 1965; children—Bamidele, Oluwole, Olutoyin. Intern, Univ. Coll. Hosp., Ibadan, Nigeria, 1969-70, sr. house officer, 1970; resident Mount Sinai Hosp., N.Y.C., 1971-73, chief resident, 1973-74, fellow in pathology, 1974-75; practice medicine specializing in pathology, Teaneck, N.J., 1975—; asst. pathologist Holy Name Hosp., Teaneck, 1975-77, asso. pathologist, 1978—; asst. clin. prof. pathology Mount Sinai Sch. Medicine, N.Y.C., 1976—. Recipient Jenny Kline Prize, Hebrew U., 1968; diplomate Am. Bd. Pathology. Mem. Internat. Coll. Pathology, Am. Coll. Pathologists. Contbr. articles in field to med. jours. Home: 15 Francine Ct White Plains NY 10607 Office: Dept Pathology Holy Name Hosp Teaneck NJ 07666

FAZZALARI, FRANK ANTHONY, chem. engr.; b. Oakland, Md., Oct. 2, 1923; s. Ilario and Bertie Florence (Turney) F.; B.S., U. Md., 1948, M.S. (Teaching fellow, U.S. Bur. Mines research fellow), 1951; Profl. engr., State U. N.Y., 1971; m. Edith Marie Zavatsky, Sept. 17, 1953; children—Madeline Marie, Laura Sue. Chem. engr. Allegheny Ballistics Lab., Hercules Powder Co., Cumberland, Md., 1951-52; civilian chem. engr. U.S. Army Chem. Corps Materiel Command, Balt., 1952-54; mgr. reactive metals pilot plant Republic Steel Corp., Canton, Ohio, 1954-58; adv. engr. computer controls IBM, Hopewell Junction, N.Y., 1958—; pres. Consumer Chem. Corp., Inc., Poughkeepsie, N.Y., 1971—. Served with USNR, 1943-46. Mem. Am. Inst. Chem. Engrs. (chmn. Mid-Hudson sect. 1971-72), N.Y. State Soc. Profl. Engrs. (pres., v.p., program chmn. Dutchess County chpt. 1973-76), Am. Inst. Chem. Engrs. (vice-chmn., program chmn. 1970-71, membership chmn. 1968-69). Contbr. articles to profl. jours. Patentee. Home: 9 Bridle Ln Poughkeepsie NY 12603 Office: IBM Hopewell Junction NY 12533

FEAGANS, WILLIAM MARION, dentist, univ. adminstr.; b. Fortescue, Mo., Feb. 2, 1927; s. Dane Marion and Ruth Smith (Maier) F.; student U. Kans., 1947-50; D.D.S., U. Mo., Kansas City, 1954; Ph.D., Med. Coll. Va., 1960; m. Iola Elizabeth Webb, Sept. 1, 1950; children—William Christopher, Kevin Winfield, Timothy Laurence. Asst. prof. Sch. Dentistry, U. Mo., Kansas City, 1954-56; asst. prof. anatomy Med. Coll. Va. Sch. Medicine, 1960-63, asso. prof., 1963-66; asso. prof., asso. dean Sch. Dental Medicine, Tufts U., 1966-70; prof., dean Sch. Dentistry, SUNY, Buffalo, 1970—. Served with U.S. Army, 1945-46. Mem. Histochem. Soc., Am. Assn. Anatomists, N.Y. Acad. Scis., Am. Assn. Dental Schs., ADA, AAAS, Internat. Coll. Dentists, Sigma Xi. Office: Sch Dentistry SUNY Buffalo NY 14214

FEARON, BLAIR, physician; b. Farnham, P.Q., Can., Jan 26, 1919; s. John William and Hattie (Hutchinson) F.; B.A., Mt. Allison U., N.B., 1940; M.D., U. Toronto, 1944; m. Joyce Doreen Ball, June 1, 1946; children—Merrill Ann, Judith Evalie, Stanley Blair. Intern St. Michael's Hosp., Toronto, 1944-45; resident Sick Children's Hosp., Toronto, 1946-50; practice medicine specializing in otolaryngology, Toronto, 1950—; sr. surgeon Hosp. for Sick Children; cons. local hosps.; asst. prof. otolaryngology U. Toronto, 1966—; chief surgeon dept. otolaryngology North York Gen. Hosp., Toronto. Trustee, Chevalier Jackson Research Found. Served with Royal Canadian Army, 1942-46; capt. Res. Recipient Chevalier Jackson award, 1976. Fellow A.C.S., Royal Coll. Surgeons, Am. Acad. Pediatrics; mem. Internat. (founder), Am. (council. past pres.) bronchoesophagol. assns., Can., Ont. med. assns., Can. Otolaryngol. Assn., Am. Acad. Ophthalmology and Otolaryngology, Am. Triological Soc., Am. Laryngol. Assn. (v.p.), Toronto Acad. Medicine (chmn. sect. otolaryngology 1963-64), Pan Am. Assn. Otorhinolaryngology. Home: 13 Douglas Crescent Toronto M4W 2E6 ON Canada Office: Medical Arts Bldg Toronto M5R 2M8 ON Canada

FEARON, ROBERT HENRY, JR., banker; b. Watertown, N.Y., June 24, 1927; s. Robert Henry and Ruby (Kilts) F.; B.S., Syracuse U., 1950; postgrad. Stonier Grad. Sch. Banking, Rutgers U., 1962; m. Ada May Marshall, Feb. 21, 1953; children—Robert Henry, III, Zoe Ann, Mary Patricia. Credit investigator Grace Nat. Bank, N.Y.C., 1950-51; with Oneida (N.Y.) Valley Nat. Bank, 1951—, pres., trust officer, 1971—, dir. 1958—; dir. Hosp. Plan, Inc.; dir., sec. Sylvan Spring Water Co.; dir. treas. Oneida Valley Securities Corp. Vice-chmn. Morrisville Agrl. Tech. Coll., State U. N.Y., 1963—; pres. Oneida City Sch. Bd., 1964-74. Served with USMC, 1945, USAF, 1951-56. Recipient Man of Year award Ondeia Jr. C. of C., 1962. Mem. Ind. Bankers Assn. Am. (dir.), Nat. Assn. Bank Dirs. (dir.), Ind. Bankers Assn. N.Y. State (founder, dir.), N.Y. State Bankers Retirement System (past chmn.), Empire State Safe Deposit Assn. (past pres.), Madison-Oneida-Herkimer Bankers Assn., Ondeia C. of C. (dir. 1977—). Republican. Methodist. Clubs: Rotary, Elks (Oneida, N.Y.). Contbr. articles in field to profl. jours. Home: 506 Main St Oneida NY 13421 Office: 160 Main St Oneida NY 13421

FEARONS, GEORGE HADSALL, 3D, travel agt.; b. N.Y.C., Dec. 22, 1927; s. George Hadsall, Jr. and Alice (Janssen) F.; student Los Angeles City Coll., 1947; m. Sandra Walsh, Oct. 31, 1966; 1 son, George Thomas. Pres., owner Vt. Claims Services, ind. ins. adjusters, Stowe, 1955, owner Stowe Travel Service, 1955—. Mem. Parish council Blessed Sacrement Roman Cath. Ch., Stowe. Decorated knight of Malta. Mem. Nat. Assn. Ind. Ins. Adjusters, Am. Soc. Travel Agts., Pacific Area Travel Assn. Republican. Clubs: Stowe Rotary; Lake Mansfield Trout; Mariner Cay Yacht; Stuart (Fla.) Yacht and Country. Home: Box 249 Stowe VT 05672 Office: Maple St Stowe VT 05672

FEATHERSTONE, CHARLES ROBERT, city ofcl.; b. Barker, N.Y., May 26, 1905; s. Franklin A. and May (Dent) F.; B.S. in Bus. cum laude, Miami U., Oxford, Ohio, 1929; m. Virginia Blade, Mar. 15, 1947; 1 dau., Virginia Ann (dec.). Statistician N.Y. Tel. Co., N.Y.C., 1929-31, accountant, 1931-33; city auditor-comptroller City of Hackensack, N.J., 1933-72, treas., 1964-73; custodian of sch. monies Hackensack Bd. Edn., 1964-73; asso. John J. Eccleston & Co., 1974—; borough auditor Borough of Waldwick (N.J.), 1973—; municipal auditing cons. E. T. Boyle & Co. C.P.A., N.J., 1952-70. Served to maj. AUS, 1943-46. Mem. Municipal Finance Officers Assn. U.S. and Can., Am. Soc. for Pub. Adminstrn., Municipal Finance Officers Assn. N.J., Municipal Accountants Assn. N.J., Phi Beta Kappa. Methodist. Elk, Lion (life mem.). Home: 114 Catalpa Ave Hackensack NJ 07601 Office: 27 Madison Ave Paramus NJ 07652

FEDDER, DONALD OWEN, pharmacist, educator; b. Balt., Nov. 20, 1926; s. William Samuel and Rose F.; student Western Md. Coll., 1944-47; Pharm. B.S., U. Md., 1950; M.P.H., Johns Hopkins U., 1978; m. Norma Kolodner, June 27, 1948; children—Debra M. Fedder Goren, Ira Louis. Staff pharmacist Pikesville (Md.) Pharmacy, 1950-51; chief pharmacist, owner Fedder's Pharmacy, Balt., and Fedder Med. Services, Balt., 1951-74; pres. Med. Equipment & Supply Co., Inc., Balt., 1970-76; asst. prof., dir. community pharmacy programs U. Md. Sch. Pharmacy, 1974—; dir. Calvert Drug Co.; cons. in field. Bd. dirs. Dundalk Concert Assn., 1963—; candidate Md. Legis., 1970. Served to sgt. U.S. Army, 1944-45. Recipient Order Double Star, Alpha Zeta Omega, 1972, 75; Beta chpt. award Phi Alpha, 1950. Mem. Am. (dir., chmn. 1976-77), Md. (President's award 1971) pharm. assns., Am. Assn. Colls. Pharmacy, Acad. of Pharmacy Practice (pres. 1973-74), Balt. Met. Pharm. Assn., Rho Chi. Democrat. Jewish. Club: Optimist (pres. local club 1963-64). Contbr. articles to profl. jours. Home: 6703 Chokeberry Rd Baltimore MD 21209 Office: 636 W Lombard St Baltimore MD 21201

FEDDERSEN, MARYANN ODILIA, psychotherapist; b. Wilmington, Del., Nov. 17, 1945; d. Charles Martin and Ann Catherine F.; B.A., Duquesne U., 1967; M.Ed., U. Pitts., 1970, Ph.D., 1975. Counselor, group leader Neighborhood Youth Corps, Pitts., 1967-68; ednl. coordinator Community Action of Pitts., 1968-71; ednl. facilitator Mon-Yough Council on Drug Abuse, McKeesport, Pa., 1971-73; counselor cons. Allegheny Intermediate Unit Pitts., 1973-75; child and family therapist No. Communities Mental Health Program, Pitts., 1974—; psychologist FosterGrandParents/Home Visitor Program, Pitts., 1976—; pvt. practice, 1974—. Mem. Am. Personnel and Guidance Assn., Pitts. Psychoanalytic Center, Pitts. Assn. Arts in Edn. and Therapy, Assn. Counselor Edn. and Supervision, Am. Sch. Counselors Assn. Home: 5800 Elgin Ave Pittsburgh PA 15206 Office: 3 Rivers Plaza Bldg Pittsburgh PA 15212

FEDELE, CHARLES ROBERT, dermatologist; b. Somerville, N.J., June 8, 1942; s. Vincent Francis and Mary Lucille (Sanchini) F.; B.S. in Biology, Villanova U., 1964; M.D., Bologna (Italy) U., 1970; m. Kathleen Ann Fox, June 23, 1972; children—Charles Robert, Kerry Ann. Intern, No. Westchester Hosp., Mt. Kisco, N.Y., 1971-72; resident Univ. Hosps. of Cleve., Case Western Res. Med. Sch., 1972-75; dermatologist asso. Guthrie Clinic, Sayre, Pa., 1977—; mem. staff Robert Packer Hosp., Sayre. Served to maj. U.S. Army, 1975-77. Diplomate Am. Bd. Dermatology. Fellow Am. Acad. Dermatology; mem. Dermatology Found., AMA, Pa., Bradford County med. socs., Pa. Acad. Dermatology. Roman Catholic. Home: RD 2 Sayre PA 18840 Office: Guthrie Clinic Guthrie Sq Sayre PA 18840

FEDELE, FRANK D., art dealer, pub.; b. N.Y.C., May 23, 1936; s. Fred and Eve (Krevoff) F.; m. Valarie Dipinto, May 20, 1960; children—Denise, Claudia. Pres., pub. Frank Fedele Fine Arts, Inc. Address: 42 E 57th St New York NY 10022

FEDER, WALTER, physician; b. N.Y.C., May 11, 1924; s. Samuel and Pauline (Diamond) F.; A.B. magna cum laude, N.Y. U., 1944; M.D., State U. N.Y., 1955; m. Cecile Salwen, Aug. 3, 1952; children—Martin, Roslyn, Carole. Intern. U. Chgo. Clinics-Billings Hosp., 1955-56, resident 1956-59; dir. cardiology Maimonides Med. Center, Bklyn., 1967-77; asst. prof. medicine U. Chgo., 1961-66; asst. prof. and asso. prof. medicine State U. N.Y. Downstate Med. Center, 1967—; vis. scientist Weizmann Inst. Sci. Mem. editorial bd. Fedn. Jewish Philanthropies; dir. bus. game L.I. U. Donner fellow Nat. Acad. Scis., 1958. Recipient Distinguished Physician award, L.I. U., 1971. Fellow Am. Soc. Internal Medicine, N.Y. Acad. Medicine (chmn. sect. biomed. engring.), N.Y. Cardiol. Soc.; mem. Assn. Jewish Scientists (chmn. bd. dirs. 1958, mem. governing bd.), Com. Concerned Scientists (vice chmn. 1974—), Soc. Exptl. Biology and Medicine, Phi Beta Kappa, Sigma Xi. Editor Bioelectrodes, Annals N.Y. Acad. Scis., 1968. Home: 998 E 8th St Brooklyn NY 11230 Office: 1263 Ocean Pkwy Brooklyn NY 11230

FEDERMAN, STEVEN ROBERT, physicist; b. N.Y.C., Nov. 19, 1949; s. Joseph Meyer and Adele Louise (Strome) F.; B.S., Poly. Inst. Bklyn., 1971, M.S., N.Y.U., 1976. Sr. research technician Hosp. for Spl. Surgery, N.Y.C., 1972-75; teaching fellow N.Y.U., N.Y.C., 1975—. Mem. Am. Phys. Soc. Home: 35 Clark St Apt 2A Brooklyn NY 11201 Office: Physics Dept NYU 4 Washington Pl New York City NY 10003

FEDERMANN, EDWARD FRANK, elec. engr.; b. N.Y.C., Oct. 12, 1919; s. Herbert A. and Mary (Ertling) F.; B.E.E., Poly. Inst. Bklyn., 1943; m. Elizabeth Louise Kaufmann, Aug. 31, 1942. With Westinghouse Research and Devel. Center, Pitts., 1943—, fellow engr., 1962—. Registered profl. engr., Pa. Democrat. Lutheran. Contbr. articles on aircraft and missile systems, solar energy to profl. jours. Home: 118 Yosemite Dr Pittsburgh PA 15235 Office: Westinghouse Research and Development Center Pittsburgh PA 15235

FEDERMANN, FRANKLIN HOWARD, financial exec.; b. N.Y.C., Nov. 8, 1939; s. Alfred B. and Rose G. (Grabinsky) F.; B.S., Bklyn. Coll., 1966; M.S., L.I. U., 1971; m. Rochelle L. Seidner, June 15, 1963; children—Barbara, Daniel, Joshua. Sr. staff mem. Eisner & Lubin, C.P.A.'s, N.Y.C., 1966-69; sr. auditor Asso. Univs., Inc., Upton, N.Y., 1969-70, chief internal auditor, 1970—; guest lectr. Inst. Internal Auditors, 1970-76, L.I. U., 1973—; guest lectr. internal auditing U.S. Energy Research and Devel. Adminstrn. workshop, 1969-76. Served with USCG, 1957. C.P.A., State N.Y.; certified internal auditor, N.Y. Mem. Am. Inst. C.P.A.'s, Inst. Internal Auditors, N.Y. Soc. C.P.A.'s, Nat. Assn. Accountants. U.S. Power Squadron (sec. 1977). Club: Port Jefferson Yacht. Home: 20 Hawkins Path Coram NY 11727 Office: Bldg 134A Upton NY 11973

FEDORENKO, EUGENE WILLIAM, educator; b. Odrynka, Ukraine, Jan. 28, 1929; s. William L. and Ulyana (Berlowskyj) F.; came to U.S., 1955, naturalized, 1961; M.A. (Govt. and Univ. scholar), L'Université Catholique de Louvain (Belgium), 1953, Fordham U., 1963; postgrad. N.Y. U., 1962-69; Ph.D., Ukrainische Free U., 1971; m. Aida Raczok, June 8, 1957; children—Oksana, William, Taras. With Bache & Co., N.Y.C., 1956-63; instr. Russian, N.Y. U., N.Y.C., 1963-65; asst. prof. Slavic lang. and lit. Rutgers U., Newark, 1963-77, Jersey City State Coll., 1977—; guest lectr. Ukrainishe Free U., summer 1972, City Coll. N.Y., State U. N.Y., 1973; script-writer Voice of Am., Washington, 1969-76; dir. Sch. Ukrainian Studies, Whippany, N.J., 1974—. Trustee Ukrainian Orthodox Ch. of Holy Ascension, Maplewood, N.J., 1972-76, 78—; mem. nat. council Ukrainian Congress Com. Am., 1976—, v.p. ednl. council, 1977—. Mem. AAUP, Am. Assn. Tchrs. Slavic and East European Langs., Canadian Assn. Slavists, Modern Lang. Assn., Ukrainian Acad. Arts and Scis., Am. Assn. Advancement Slavic Studies, Shevchenko Sci. Soc. (v.p. 1973—), Ukrainian Am. Assn. Univ. Profs. (exec. bd.), Mykhailo S. Hrushevskii Academic Soc. (past pres.), Conf. Am. Ukrainian Profl. Socs. (pres. 1976—). Club: Newark Sitch Sports. Author: The Search for the Literary Style of Mykhailo Kotsivbynsky, 1975. Co-editor: Almanac Odum, 1965; Readings in Ukrainian Literature of the XX Century, 1978; editor Resistance Movement in the Ukraine, 1977; editorial bd. Moloda Ukraina, 1957-59. Contbr. articles to profl. jours. Home: 10 Marston Dr Morris Plains NJ 07950

FEEHAN, JOHN DANIEL, mfg. co. exec.; b. Carteret, N.J., Oct. 4, 1927; s. Dorsey Daniel and Margaret Veronica Feehan; B.S. in Elec. Engring., U. Ky., 1950; M.S., Newark Coll. Engring., 1957; m. Mary Ann Seibert, Aug. 26, 1950; children—Margaret Ann, Susan Marie, Karen Jane, Mary Genevieve, John Daniel. Engr. with various companies, 1950-62; chief engr. tube div. Sperry Electron Tube Div., 1962-67; with tube div. ITT, Easton, Pa., 1967—, v.p., dir. ops., 1972—. Served with USNR, 1945-46; to 1st lt. AUS, 1951-53. Mem. IEEE. Republican. Roman Cath. Club: Country of Northampton County (Easton). Author, patentee in field. Address: 1341 Gaspar Ave Bethlehem PA 18017

FEELINGS, THOMAS, artist, illustrator; b. Bklyn., May 19, 1933; s. Samuel and Anna (Nash) F.; student Cartoonist and Illustrators Sch., 1951-53, Sch. Visual Arts, 1958-61; m. Muriel Grey, Feb. 18, 1968 (div. 1974); children—Zamani, Kamili. Creator, illustrator weekly comic strip Tommy Traveler in the World of Negro History, N.Y. Age, 1958-59; free-lance mag. illustrator for Look, Pagent, Harpers, Liberator, Freedom Ways, 1959-64; illustrator African Rev. Mag., Ghana Govt. Pub. Co., 1964-66, govt. tchr. of illustrators, 1964-66; illustrator children's books, 1967-76; cons. on art to ministry edn. Govt. of Guyana, 1971-74, govt. tchr. of illustrators, 1971-74; author and illustrator: Black Pilgrimage, 1972; Moja Means One (Caldecott Honor Book award), 1972; Jambo Means Hello (Caldecott Honor Book award), 1975. Served with USAF, 1953-57. Recipient Ann. Book award Woodward Sch., 1973; Outstanding Alumni award Sch. Visual Arts, 1974; Boston Globe Horn Book award, 1974. Home and office: 31 W 31st St New York City NY 10001

FEENEY, DONALD FRANCIS, chiropractor; b. N.Y.C., Oct. 4, 1945; s. John James and Mae Theresa (MacNamara) F.; B.S., Manhattan Coll., 1968; Dr.Chiropractic, Columbia Inst. Chiropractic, 1971; m. Nancy Du Bois, Aug. 31, 1968; children—Karen Christine, Scott Christopher, Jessica Michelle. Gen. practice chiropractic, Wilmington, Del., 1971—; mem. diagnostic radiology task force Del. Health Council. Mem. drug council Open Door, Inc. Recipient Vinton F. Logan Meml. award for Chiropractic, 1971, Merit award N.Y. Coll. Chiropractic, 1977. Mem. Del. Assn. Chiropractic Physicians (treas. 1974-77, v.p. 1977—), Am. Chiropractic Assn. (council on radiology, council on nutrition, council on technic), Parker Chiropractic Research Found., Del. Assn. Brown Baggers (pres. 1974-77), Talleycille Jr. C. of C. Democrat. Roman Catholic. Club: Ambassador. Home and office: 3214 Naamans Rd Wilmington DE 19810

FEFFER, PAUL E., pub. co. exec.; b. N.Y.C., June 27, 1921; s. Joseph A. and Eve (Wax) F.; student Cornell U. Sch. Medicine, 1940-42, USCG Acad., 1944; postgrad. N.Y. U., 1963-64; m. Juliette Fein, July 30, 1964; children—Paula, Hilary, Joseph, Alison, Emily, Nicholas. Vice pres. H. M. Synder & Co., N.Y.C., 1946-55; founder Feffer & Simons, Inc., subs. Doubleday & Co., N.Y.C., 1955, pres., 1955—, also dir.; dir. Tabs, Ltd., London, Vakil's Feffer & Simons, Inc., India, Book Club Assos., Australia. Mem. govt. adv. com. Assn. Am. Pubs., 1963—; mem. joint internat. trade com. Assn. Am. Pubs. and Am. Textbook Inst., 1963—. Served to lt. (j.g.) USCGR, 1942-46. Home: 60 Sutton Pl New York City NY 10022 Office: 100 Park Ave New York City NY 10017

FEGLEY, ROBERT LEROY, JR., pub. relations exec.; b. Allentown, Pa., Dec. 2, 1919; s. Robert LeRoy and Mollie Minerva (Weand) F.; A.B., Columbia, 1941; m. Alice Blaine Longfellow, Aug. 30, 1941; children—Molly (Mrs. Jon Gilbert Rayner), Susan P. With Gen. Electric Co., N.Y.C., 1941—, beginning in indsl. advt., successively mgr. visual edn., mgr. institutional advt., mgr. pub. issues analysis, mgr. exec. communications, mgr. pub. relations planning, 1941-73, staff exec., chief exec. officer communications, 1973—; chmn. Pub. Relations Seminar, 1978. Dir. Silvermine Artists Guild, 1958-60, New Canaan United Fund, 1967-68, New Canaan YMCA, 1969-74. Recipient Woodberry poetry prize Columbia, 1941. Mem. Nat. Elec. Mfrs. Assn. (chmn. pub. relations council 1963-66), NAM (pub. relations council 1966-75), Bus. Roundtable (chmn. pub. info. com. 1975—), Pub. Relations Soc. Am. (accredited), Found. Pub. Relations Edn. and Research (dir. 1969-73), Wisemen Soc., Pub. Relations Soc., N.Y., New Canaan Hist. Soc., N.Y. Gen. and Biog. Soc., Stamford Genel. Soc., John Jay Assn. Republican. Methodist. Author: (with R.J. Cordiner) New Frontiers for Professional Managers, 1956. Pub. of GE Forum Mag., 1960-66. Home: 36 Comstock Hill Rd New Canaan CT 06840 Office: 3135 Easton Turnpike Fairfield CT 06431

FEHRING, ROBERT WILLIAM, residential contracting co. exec.; b. Glendale, Calif., Jan. 26, 1944; s. Robert William and Irene Jeanette (Weinmann) F.; B.S., U. So. Calif., 1972, M.B.A., 1973; m. Sandra Lee Green, June 19, 1971. Internat. cons. TRW, El Segundo, Calif., 1972-73; v.p. mktg. Sonnet Internat., Hawthorne, Calif., 1973-75; v.p. finance and mktg. Vista Shelter Industries, Ventura, 1975-76; dir. Robert W. Fehring Inc., Los Angeles, Chemehuevi Inc.; cons., lectr. in field. Served with USNR, 1966-68. Decorated Purple Heart with cluster, Bronze Star. Licensed contractor Calif., Ariz., Nev. Mem. Beta Gamma Sigma. Episcopalian. Proposals econ. devel. Barrio community East Los Angeles, Calif., 1973, ghetto community Pasadena, Calif., 1973. Home: 16 Baltusrol C Lakewood NJ 08701 Office: 1223 E Calaveras St Altadena CA 91002

FEIERSTEIN, SHIRLEY SANDS, adminstrv. materials engrs.; b. N.Y.C., Oct. 24, 1920; d. Samuel and Dorothy (Ropkin) Sands; B.A., Hunter Coll., 1942; M.A., Columbia U., 1958; m. Bernard Feierstein, Oct., 1944; children—Susan Joyce, Alan Joel. Chemist, Lever Bros., Edgewater, N.J., 1942-45; tech. reports librarian Sperry Gyroscope Co., Lake Success, N.Y., 1958-61; tech. service mgr. United Mineral & Chem. Corp., N.Y.C., 1961-75; pres. Polycorp., Great Neck, N.Y., 1975—; sales mgr., v.p. Metalsmart, Great Neck, 1976—. Mem. Am. Chem. Soc., Acad. Sci. N.Y., Am. Soc. Metals, Am. Inst. Metall. Engrs. Jewish. Mem. B'nai B'rith. Office: PO Box 1267 Great Neck NY 11023

FEIGENBAUM, LAWRENCE HUGO, sch. adminstr.; b. N.Y.C., Oct. 21, 1918; s. Philip and Evelyn (Leventhal) F.; B.A., Bklyn. Coll., 1939; postgrad. George Washington U., 1940-42; M.A., N.Y. U., 1947, Ph.D., 1950; m. Gloria Diamond, July 3, 1947; children—Harold, Arthur. Lectr. English, Coll. City N.Y., 1947-68;

cons. editor Globe Book Co., N.Y.C., 1950-71; asst. prin. pub. schs., N.Y.C., 1955-58; chmn. acad. dept. McKee High Sch., S.I., N.Y., 1958-63; prin. Dreyfus Jr. High Sch., S.I., 1963-71, South Shore High Sch., Bklyn., 1971—. Vis. prof. Richmond Coll., 1968-69. Served with AUS, 1942-45. Joint Council on Econ. Instns. fellow, 1951, Financial Instns.-Cornell U. fellow, 1962. Mem. Nat. Council Tchrs. English (dir. 1959), N.Y.C. Assn. Tchrs. of English (v.p. 1958-63), Bklyn. Coll. Alumni Assn. (dir. 1969-71). Author: Effective Reading, 1953; Radio and Television Plays, 1956; Successful Reading, 1958; (with Kalman Seigel) This is a Newspaper, 1965, Israel: Crossroads of Conflict, 1968. Editor: From Earth to Moon, 1958; Four Complete English Novels, 1961; Four Complete Classic Novels, 1962; Four Complete Novels of Drama and Suspense, 1964. Patentee in field. Home: 1737 E 28th St Brooklyn NY 11229 Office: South Shore High School 6565 Flatlands Ave Brooklyn NY 11236

FEIGIN, MARSHA ISABEL, artist; b. N.Y.C., June 17, 1948; d. Max and Ann (Bricker) F.; student in Design, Syracuse U., 1963-65, in Painting, Cooper Union, 1965-66; B.A. in Painting and Art History, Coll. City N.Y., 1968; M.F.A., U. Hawaii, 1971. Exhibited in group shows: Iran-Am. Soc., Tehran, 1977, Venice (Italy) Municipal Galleries, 1977, Whitney Mus., N.Y.C., 1976, Internat. Print Biennale, Cracow, Poland, 1976, Bklyn. Mus., N.Y.C., 1976, Graphikbiennale, Vienna, Austria, 1975, Biennial of Graphic Art, Ljublana, Yugoslavia, 1975, Mus. Modern Art, Rijeka, Yugoslavia, Internat. Bienniel of Graphic Art and Multiples, Segovia, Spain, 1974; represented in permanent collections: Bklyn. Mus., Boston Public Library, Charles Rand Penney Found., N.Y.C., Rochester Inst. Tech., Hawaii State Found. Culture and Arts, Printingmaking Workshop, N.Y.C., Hamilton and Kirkland Colls., Mpls. Inst. Arts, Indpls. Mus. Art, Minn. Mus. Art, DeCordova Mus., Lincoln, Mass., Nat. Mus. Poland, Lodz, USIA, Tokyo, Del. Mus. Art, IBM, N.J.; asst. to dir. Landau-Alan Gallery, N.Y.C., 1968-69; teaching asst. U. Hawaii, Honolulu, 1969-71, instr. interim session, 1971; instr. Art Center Bishop Mus., Honolulu, 1971; master-printer Printmaking Workshop, 1972; guest lectr. Rutgers U., Camden, N.J., 1973; vis. artist Center for Music Drama and Art, Lake Placid, N.Y., 1973; distinguished visitor Fla. Tech. U., 1977; lectr. printmaking and drawing San Jose State U., 1978-79. N.Y. State Council on Arts grantee, 1973-74, 75-76; Nat. Endowment for Arts Fellowship grantee, 1975-76. Mem. Women's Caucus for Art, Coll. Art Assn., Graphic Arts Council N.Y., Phila. Print Club, N.Y. Rd. Runners. Address: 200 E 84 St New York City NY 10028

FEIN, SHERMAN EDWARD, lawyer, psychologist; b. Springfield, Mass., June 17, 1928; s. Samuel Law and Mildred (Sherman) F.; student Vt. Acad., 1943-45; B.A., Bowdoin Coll., 1948; LL.B., Boston U., 1953; M.S., Springfield Coll. 1962; postgrad. U. Conn., 1963-65; Ed.D., U. Mass., 1969; m. Myra Nancy Becker, Nov. 13, 1955; children—Dina Estelle, Julia Louise, Sara Elizabeth. Admitted to Mass. bar, 1953, practiced in Springfield, 1953—; mem. firm Fein & Fein; vis. lectr. Springfield Coll., 1962-63. Pres. Springfield Area Mental Health Bd., 1968-69. Corporator Wesson Meml. Hosp., Springfield Hosp. Med. Center; bd. dirs. Heritage Acad., Springfield, Child Guidance Clinic of Springfield. Served with USAF, 1950-52; lt. col. Civil Air Patrol. Hon. consul Republic Costa Rica. Fellow Internat. Acad. Law and Sci.; mem. Am., Mass., Hampden County bar assns., Am. Trial Lawyers Assn. (asso. editor Jour. 1961—), Am. Personnel and Guidance Assn., Am. Arbitration Assn. (nat. panel), Jewish War Vets., Old Orchard Beach (Maine) C. of C. (exec. sec. 1950—), Tau Epsilon Phi, Tau Epsilon Rho. Jewish. Mason (Shriner). Editor, USNR newspaper, 1948, USAF newspaper, Ft. Ethan Allen, Vt., 1951. Home: 224 Longmeadow St Longmeadow MA 01106 Office: 52 Mulberry St Springfield MA 01105

FEINBERG, JOSEPH GOODMAN, state ofcl.; b. Chgo., Feb. 21, 1928; s. Morris and Margaret (Goodman) F.; B.A., Lake Forest Coll., 1954; postgrad. U. Chgo., 1954-55, Ill. Inst. Tech., 1956-57; m. Dorothy Ann Purtiman, July 22, 1958; children—Matthew, Valerie, Elizabeth, Jessica. Land planner Chgo. Land Clearance Commn., 1955-58; asso. city planner Syracuse (N.Y.) Dept. City Planning, 1958-60; dir. Syracuse office Blair Assos., 1960-61; supervising planner N.J. Div. State Regional Planning, 1961-66; exec. dir. Jersey City Redevel. Agy., 1966-72; dir. div. housing N.J. Dept. Community Affairs, Trenton, 1972-74, chief Housing and Renewal Bur., 1974—; coadj. faculty Rutgers U. Mem. Lawrence Twp. Historic and Aesthetic Commn., 1970-72; mem. Lawrence Non-profit Housing Corp., 1969-72. Served with AUS, 1948-52; Korea; capt. Res. (ret.). Mem. Nat. Assn. Housing and Redevel. Ofcls. (pres. N.J. chpt. 1971-72), Am. Inst. Planners (mem. bd. examiners 1970—), Am. Soc. Planning Ofcls. Contbr. to profl. publs. Home: 11 Lumar Rd Lawrenceville NJ 08648 Office: 363 W State St Trenton NJ 08625

FEINBERG, ROBERT JACOB, sci. adminstr.; b. Chelsea, Mass., Apr. 6, 1931; s. Charles S. and Mary (Melamed) F.; B.S., Boston Coll., 1953, M.S., 1954; M.S. in Radiol. Physics, U. Rochester, 1955; postgrad. Oak Ridge Sch. Reactor Tech., 1955-56; m. Carole I. Young, May 31, 1964; children—Curt M., Mark W. Weapons physicist Picatinny Arsenal, Dover, N.J., 1951; physicist Nat. Bur. Standards, Washington, 1952; astro physicist Cambridge (Mass.) Research Center, U.S.A.F., 1953-54; health physicist Brookhaven Nat. Lab., Upton, N.Y., 1955; physicist Oak Ridge Nat. Lab., 1955-56; with Knolls Atomic Power Lab., Gen. Electric Co., Schenectady, 1956—, cons. nuclear, radiol. safety, 1963-64, mgr. health physics and nuclear safety, 1966—. Instr. physics Boston Coll., 1954-55, Ednl. program, Gen. Electric, 1961-66. AEC fellow, 1953-54, 55-56; certified health physicist Am. Bd. Health Physics, 1961. Mem. Am. Nuclear Soc., Internat. Health Physics Soc. (pres. elect N.E. N.Y. sect. 1968, chmn. admissions com. 1969-71, chmn. membership com. 1971-75, mem. nominating com. 1976—), Atomic Indsl. Forum, Am. Assn. Physics in Medicine, Am. Inst. Physics, Sigma Pi Sigma, Alpha Sigma Nu. Contbr. articles to profl. jours. Home: 1223 Godfrey Ln Schenectady NY 12309 Office: Box 1072 Knolls Atomic Power Lab Schenectady NY 12301

FEINER, DANIEL, optometrist; b. Bklyn., July 15, 1926; s. Hyman and Esther (Lustrine) F.; B.S., L.I. U., 1949, O.D., 1970; student N.Y. U., 1950; m. Marilyn Zalkin, Sept. 5, 1948; children—Lori, Joan, David. Prodn. mgr. Paper Box Mfg. Co., Bklyn., 1952-70; pvt. practice optometry specializing in contact lenses, Howard Beach, N.Y., 1970—; mem. vol. staff Penninsula Hosp., Far Rockaway, N.Y. Served with USNR, 1944-46. Mem. Am., Queens optometric assns., Pa. Coll. Optometry Alumni Assn. Clubs: B'nai B'rith (pres. 1964), Knights of Pythias. Home: 21 Joseph Ln Staten Island NY Office: 158-38 Cross Bay Blvd Howard Beach NY 11414

FEINGOLD, ADOLPH, educator; b. Poltava, USSR, Mar. 8, 1920; s. Michael and Elizabeth (Okun) F.; D. Naval Architecture and Mech. Engring., U. Genoa, Italy, 1953; m. Gila Anatot, Sept. 12, 1964 (div. May 1970); children—Michael, Elizabeth. Head marine engring. Israel Nautical Coll., 1953-63; prof. mech. engring. U. Mo. at Rolla, 1963-66; prof. civil engring. U. Ottawa, Ont., Can., 1966-67, prof. mech. engring., 1967—, gov., 1976—. Chmn. Ontario Com. Student Awards, 1971-74. Alderman City of Acre, Israel, 1959-64. Fellow Inst. Marine Engrs. (London), Engring. Inst. Can.; mem. Canadian Soc. Mech. Engring. (chmn. admissions com. 1969—, v.p. 1977—), ASME, Assn. Profs. U. Ottawa (pres. 1970-71), Israel Soc. Naval Architects and Marine Engrs. (pres. 1960-61), Internat. Soc. Tech. Assessment. Rotarian. Home: 801-330 Driveway Ottawa ON K1S 3M9 Canada Office: Dept Mech Engring U Ottawa ON Canada

FEINGOLD, S. NORMAN, psychologist; b. Worcester, Mass., Feb. 2, 1914; s. William and Aida (Salit) F.; A.B., Ind. U., 1937; M.A., Clark U., 1940; Ed.D., Boston U., 1948; LL.B., Edwards Waters Coll., Saints Coll.; m. Marie Goodman, Mar. 24, 1947; children—Elizabeth Anne, Margaret Ellen, Deborah Carol, Marilyn Nancy. Dir. vocat. service and ednl. and vocat. dir. Hecht Neighborhood House, Boston, 1940-43; exec. dir. Boston Jewish Vocat. Service and Work Adjustment Center, 1946-58; nat. dir. B'nai B'rith Career and Counseling Services, Washington 1958—; exec. adviser Rehab. Services. Boston, 1953-58; dir. ednl. and vocat. workshop United Cerebral Palsy of Greater Boston, Inc., 1957-58; cons. to scholarships, fellowships and loans news service to state and fedn. govts.; instr., spl. lectr. Boston U., 1951-58; vocat. expert Social Security Adminstrn., 1962—; professorial lectr. Am. U. Rehab. Counseling Adv. Panel, 1963-65; mem. Am. Bd. Counseling Services, 1962-65, 70—; chmn. Washington Bus.-Industry Group, 1963-64. Chmn. Mass. Gov.'s Council on Aging, 1956-58; mem. President's Com. on Employment Handicapped, 1950—; mem. Nat. Home Study Accrediting Commn. Served from pvt. to 1st lt. AUS, 1943-46; ETO and PTO. Recipient Community Service award B'nai B'rith, 1957, Brotherhood and Americanization award, 1958. Fellow Am. Psychol. Assn.; mem. Greater Boston (pres. 1952-53), Am. (past pres.) personnel and guidance assns., Mass., Eastern psychol. assns., Nat. Vocat. Guidance Assn. (past pres.), Am. Assn. Adult Edn., AAAS, Am. Coll. Personnel Assn., Am. Gerontol. Assn., Nat. Soc. Study Edn., Nat. Rehab. Assn., Phi Delta Kappa. Club: Torch. Author: Jobs in Unusual Occupations; Scholarships, Fellowships and Loans (6 vols.); How to Choose that Career, Words for Work: How to Get College Scholarships; Finding Part-time Jobs; The Job Finder; It Pays to Advertise; Occupations and Careers, 1969; The Vocational Expert in the Social Security Disability Program, 1969, A Counselor's Handbook, 1972. Editor: Counselors Information Service. Home: 9707 Singleton Dr Bethesda MD 20034 Office: 1640 Rhode Island Ave E Washington DC 20036

FEINSCHREIBER, ROBERT ANDREW, lawyer; b. N.Y.C., Apr. 18, 1943; s. Selven Frederick and Maxine (Borodkin) F.; B.A., Trinity Coll., Hartford, Conn., 1964; M.B.A., Columbia U., 1967; LL.B., Yale U., 1967; LL.M. in Taxation, N.Y. U., 1973; m. Lana Friestater, July 30, 1967; children—Steven, Kathryn. Admitted to N.Y. bar, 1971; asst. prof. Wayne State U. Law Sch., Detroit, 1967-69; taxation supr. Chrysler Corp., 1969-70; dir. taxation and fin. analysis NAM, N.Y.C., 1970; asst. chief accountant Seagrams Co., N.Y.C., 1970-72; pvt. practice law Robert Feinschreiber & Assos., N.Y.C., 1972—; asso. Oppenheim Appel Dixon & Co., 1972-74; guest lectr. in field. Mem. Am., N.Y. State bar assns., N.Y. County Lawyers Assn., Internat. Tax Inst. (dir. 1972—), Key Biscayne C. of C., Pi Gamma Mu. Author: Tax Depreciation, 1975; Tax Incentives for U.S. Exports, 1975; (with Jon Bischel) Fundamentals of International Taxation, 1977; International Tax Planning Today, 1977; Allocation and Apportionment of Deductions, 1978; Domestic International Sales Corporations, 1978. Editor: Internat. Tax Jour., 1974—, Bus. Operation Tax Jour., 1976-77; U.S. editor Tax Haven and Shelter Report, 1977-78; mem. editorial adv. bd. Internat. Tax Report, 1977-78. Address: 823 Park Ave New York City NY 10021 also 1121 Crandon Blvd Key Biscayne FL 33149

FEINSCHREIBER, SELVEN F., lawyer; b. N.Y.C.; s. Joseph I. and Bertha (Apatoff) F.; B.S., L.I. U., 1931; J.D., Bklyn. Law Sch., 1935; m. Maxine Borodkin, Aug. 17, 1940; children—Robert A., Margery E. Admitted to N.Y. bar, 1936; practiced in N.Y.C., 1937—; registered agt. Justice Dept. U.S.A. for Republic of Ghana, 1957; adviser Constn. Drafting Com., Toro, Uganda, 1957; gen. power of atty. from His Majesty-King George III, Toro, Uganda, 1959; econ. adviser and authority to enter into contracts for the Kingdom, Uganda, 1961; adviser Archbishop of Haiti; spl. rep. of Minister of Mines, Uganda; legal adviser to gov. gen. of Eritrea, 1964—, also to atty. gen. of Uganda, to Uganda ambassador to U.S., to govt. of Uganda, co-author Uganda Constn.; adviser to Jomo Kenyatta, Pres. of Kenya; adviser Royal Imperial Council Ethiopia. Adviser NBC Internat. Ednl. TV, NBC Inter-related Corps.; chmn. Instrnl. TV Corp.; mem. nat. adv. council Center for Study Presidency. Mem. N.Y. County Lawyers Assn., L.I. U. Alumni Assn. (past pres.). Office: 15 Park Row New York City NY 10038

FEINSMITH, BURTON MICHAEL, pediatrician; b. Bklyn., Dec. 14, 1926; s. Bernard and Elizabeth (Kremer) F.; B.S., U. Ark., 1949; M.S., U. Miami, 1951; M.D., U. Berne, 1961; m. Seena Lynn Selbst, Aug. 17, 1952; 1 son, Todd Adam. Intern, Newark Beth Israel Hosp., 1961-62; resident Babies Hosp., Newark, 1962-64; chief indsl. hygiene and toxicology Office Surgeon Gen., 1st Army Hdqrs., 1951-55; practice medicine specializing in pediatrics, Westfield, N.J., 1964—; asst. clin. prof. pediatrics Columbia U. Coll. Physicians and Surgeons, 1968—; cons. EPA, Com. on Radiation Protection, 1974—; sec.-treas. med. staff Muhlenberg Hosp., 1974—. Founding mem. YW-YMHA of Union County, 1976; bd. govs. Solomon Schechter Day Sch. of Essex and Union County, 1974—. U. Miami scholar, 1949-51. Diplomate Am. Bd. Pediatrics. Fellow Am. Acad. Pediatrics; mem. AMA (award for continuing med. edn.), Union County Med. Soc. (mem. finance com., chmn. com. on continuing med. edn.), U. Miami, U. Ark., U. Berne alumni assns. Jewish. Clubs: Hillside Camera, Temple Emanu-El Men's, B'nai B'rith. Home: 6 Pine Ct Westfield NJ 07090 Office: 275 Orchard St Westfield NJ 07090

FEINSTEIN, ALAN SHAWN, author, financial adviser; b. Boston, June 25, 1931; s. Louis and Lillian Edith (Pector) F.; B.S., Boston U., 1952; M.S., Boston State Coll., 1956; m. Pratarnporn Chiemwichit, June 2, 1963; children—Ari Jason, Richard Justin, Leila Jane. Tchr. pub. schs., Mass. and R.I., 1956-57; founder English sch., Bangkok, Thailand, 1965; writer syndicated column The Treasure Chest, 1968—, syndicated feature My America, 1971—; author, pub. financial newsletter The Insiders Report. Lectr. on financial opportunities, Bangkok, 1971. Spl. gifts chmn. R.I. Heart Fund, 1972—. Jewish. Author: Triumph, 1960; Folk Tales from Siam, 1969; Folk Tales from Persia, 1971; Folk Tales from Portugal, 1972; Making Your Money Grow, 1972; How To Make Money, 1976; How to Secure Your Financial Future, 1978; The Vanishing Treasure, 1978. Address: 41 Alhambra Circle Cranston RI 02905

FEINSTEIN, ESTELLE FISHER, historian; b. N.Y.C., Dec. 31, 1923; d. Moses and Libby (Kaleko) Fisher; B.A., Vanderbilt U., 1944; M.A. (fellow), U. Wis., 1946; Ph.D., Columbia U., 1971; m. Malcolm Feinstein, Sept. 18, 1949; children—Daniel, Susan, Deborah. Instr. history Bklyn. Coll., 1946-47, U. Conn., Hartford, 1947-49; lectr. U. Conn., Stamford, 1957-60, instr., 1960-71, asst. prof. dept. history, 1971-73, asso. prof., 1973-77, prof., 1977—; mem. Conn. Hist. Commn., Columbia U. Seminar on the City. Xerox Corp. grantee, 1976; Eli Lilly fellow, 1977. Mem. Am. Hist. Assn., Orgn. of Am. Historians, Assn. Study of Conn. History, Stamford Hist. Soc. (v.p. 1977-78), Phi Beta Kappa. Democrat. Jewish. Author: Stamford in the Gilded Age, 1973; Stamford from Puritan to Patriot, 1976. Home: 76 Four Brooks Rd Stamford CT 06903 Office: U Conn Stamford CT 06903

FEINSTEIN, NORMAN BANKS, ins. co. exec.; b. Phila., Aug. 22, 1934; s. Harry and Mary E. (Banks) F.; B.E.E., U. Pa., 1957, M.B.A., 1957; m. Harriet R. Miller, June 10, 1956; children—Lionel J., Robin J. Sect. mgr. Gen. Electric Co., Valley Forge, Pa., 1959-62; pension mgr., ins. agent John Hancock Life Ins. Co., Bala Cynwyd, Pa., 1962-69; pres. Corporate Cons., Inc., Bala Cynwyd, 1969—; v.p. Capital Spectrum Corp., Bala Cynwyd, 1970-72; div. mgr. Shearson Hammill & Co., Bala Cynwyd, 1972-74. Mem. Nat. Assn. Life Underwriters, Am. Soc. C.L.U.'s. Club: Masons. Home: 1301 Drayton Ln Wynnewood PA 19151 Office: 614 GSB Barclay Bldg PO Box 446 Bala Cynwyd PA 19004

FEIT, ELLIOT MICHAEL, lawyer; b. N.Y.C., Jan. 30, 1942; s. Dudley and Hattie (Koenig) F.; B.B.A., City Coll., N.Y., 1963; J.D., Bklyn. Law Sch., 1966; LL.M., N.Y. U. Law Sch., 1969; m. Anitra Johnson, Dec. 11, 1966; children—Laurie Francine, Neal Evan. Real estate salesman Schlang Bros. & Co., N.Y.C., 1963-65; pub. sch. tchr. N.Y.C., 1966-69; admitted to N.Y. bar, 1966; partner Johnson Tannen Katzman Brecher Fishman & Feit, N.Y.C., 1969—. Co-chmn. Community Planning Bd., N.Y.C., 1972-74; bd. dirs. Flatbush Community Council, Bklyn., Midwood Community Council, Bklyn.; mem. adv. bd. Friends Field, Bklyn., 1973—, bd. dirs., 1972—; bd. dirs. Young Israel Flatbush, Bklyn., 1971—, chmn. civic action com., 1972-73; nat. treas. Intercollegiate Council Young Israel, N.Y.C., 1962-63, nat. pres., 1963-64; co-chmn. North Am. Jewish Youth Council, N.Y.C., 1963-64. Sec. Flatbush Dem. Club, Bklyn., 1972-73, v.p., 1973—; del. Jud. Dist. Conv., Bklyn., 1973. Mem. Bklyn. (chmn. workman's compensation com. 1975—), N.Y. State, Nassau County bar assns., N.Y. County Lawyers Assn., N.Y. State Workman's Compensation Bar Assn., 70th Precinct Youth Council, Coll. City N.Y., Baruch Coll., Bklyn. Law Sch., N.Y. U. Law Sch. alumni assns. Home: 1075 Ocean Pkwy Brooklyn NY 11230 Office: 235 Broadway New York City NY 10007

FELBER, NORBERT, hematologist; b. Leipzig, Germany, Jan. 28, 1931; s. Marcus Meyer and Adelheid (Birnbaum) F.; came to U.S., 1941, naturalized, 1952; B.S. cum laude, John Carroll U., 1954; M.D., Western Res. U., 1958; m. Edith R. Laulicht, June 16, 1963; children—Michael, Adam, Susan. Intern, Cin. Gen. Hosp., 1958-59; resident U. Okla. Med. Center, 1959-60, Bronx VA Hosp., 1962-64; USPHS trainee N.Y. Med. Coll., 1964-65; practice medicine specializing in hematology and internal medicine, Westbury, N.Y., 1965—; attending physician Central Gen. Hosp., Plainview, N.Y., Syosset (N.Y.) Hosp.; cons. hematology Mid-Island Hosp., Bethpage, N.Y., 1969—; asst. attending Nassau County (N.Y.) Med. Center; attending, dir. hematology Nassau Hosp., Mineola, N.Y.; asst. prof. clin. medicine State U. N.Y., 1972. Trustee L.I. chpt. Leukemia Soc. Am. Served with USAR, 1960-62. Diplomate Am. Bd. Internal Medicine. Mem. A.C.P., AMA, Am. Soc. Internal Medicine, Soc. Study Blood, N.Y. State, Nassau County med. socs., Am. Soc. Hematology. Jewish. Contbr. articles to profl. jours. Office: 530 Old Country Rd Westbury NY 11590

FELD, ELIOT, dancer, choreographer; b. Bklyn., July 5, 1942; s. Benjamin Noah and Alice (Posner) F.; student High Sch. Performing Arts, N.Y.C., 1954-58. Debut as child prince in The Nutcracker, N.Y.C. Ballet, 1954; mem. cast West Side Story, 1958; with co. I Can Get It for You Wholesale, 1962; began dancing with Am. Ballet Theatre, 1963, later resident choreographer; founder Am. Ballet Co., 1969, subsequently prin. dancer, mgr. chief choreographer, 1969-71; guest choreographer, N. Am., Europe, 1971-73; founder, artistic dir., chief choreographer Feld Ballet, N.Y.C., 1973—; solo dance appearances in Les Noces, Wind in the Mountains, Dark Elegies, Fancy Free, Billy the Kid, Helen of Troy, Giselle; with Bklyn. Acad. Music for two seasons. Choreographer: Harbinger, 1967; At Midnight, 1967; Meadowlark, 1968; Intermezzo, 1969; Cortege Burlesque, 1969; Pagan Spring, 1969; Early Songs, 1970; Cortege Parisien, 1970; The Consort, 1970; A Poem Forgotten, 1970; Romance, 1971; Theater, 1971; The Gods Amused, 1971; A Soldier's Tale, 1971; Eccentrique, 1971; Winters Court, 1972; Jive, 1973; Tzaddik, 1974; Sephardic Song, 1974; The Real McCoy, 1974; Mazurka, 1975; Excursions, 1975; Impromptu, 1976; Variations on America, 1977; A Footstep of Air, 1977; Santa Fe Saga, 1978; La Vida, 1978; Danzon Cubano, 1978; Half Time, 1978. Address: Feld Ballet 890 Broadway New York City NY 10003

FELD, JOSEPH, real estate and constrn. co. exec.; b. N.Y.C., June 25, 1919; s. Morris David and Gussie (London) F.; student Coll. City N.Y., 1946-47; m. Doris Rabinor, Apr. 10, 1948; 1 dau., Elaine Susan. Builder housing, apartment projects, L.I., N.Y.C., N.J., 1948-54; pres. Kohl and Feld, Inc., builder housing developments Rockland County, N.Y., 1955-57; pres. Feld Constrn. Corp., 1957—, Birchland Constrn. Corp., 1957-70, Ramapo Towers, Inc., 1963—; dir. Rockland County Citizen Public Corp., 1959-60, Peoples Nat. Bank of Rockland County, Monsey, N.Y., 1974—. Chmn. housing adv. council Rockland County Legislature, 1976—. Served to staff sgt. AUS, 1941-45. Mem. Rockland County Home Builders Assn. (past pres., dir., chmn. rental housing com.), Builders Econ. Council, Nat. (dir. 1956-60), N.Y. State (dir. 1958-62) assns. home builders, Rockland County Bd. Realtors, N.Y. State Assn. Real Estate Bds., Rockland County Apt. Owners Assn., (pres., dir.), Jewish War Vets. (past comdr. New City post), Rockland County Council, Nat. Inst. Real Estate Brokers, New City C. of C. Mem. B'nai B'rith, Mason. Club: Lions (local pres. 1959-60, zone chmn. 1961-62, pres. New City Jewish Center Mens Club 1960-61). Home: 9 Woodland Rd New City NY 10956 Office: 20 S Main St New City NY 10956

FELDBERG, DANIEL GERALD, guidance counselor; b. Newark, June 1, 1916; s. Michael Abraham and Rose (Marmerstein) F.; B.S. in Edn., Rutgers U., 1938, B.S. in Pharmacy, 1946; M.A. in Personnel and Guidance, Montclair State Coll., 1960. Pharmacist, Stratford Pharmacy, Newark, 1946-56; tchr., counselor Broadway Jr. High Sch., Newark, 1956-68; dir. guidance Weequahic High Sch., Newark, 1968—. Mem. Am., N.J., Essex County personnel and guidance assns., Nat. Vocat. Guidance Assn., Am. Sch. Counselors Assn., Assn. Counselor Edn. and Supervision, Assn. Ednl. Suprs. N.J., Am. Fedn. Sch. Adminstrs., Ethical Culture Soc. Author, editor: Manual for Guidance Counselors, 1975; Curriculum Guide to Selective Service and the Armed Services, 1973; author: Handbook for Guidance Counselors of Weequahic High School, 1977. Home: 25 Courter Ave Maplewood NJ 07040 Office: 279 Chancellor Ave Newark NJ 07112

FELDER, RAOUL LIONEL, lawyer; b. Bklyn., May 13, 1934; s. Morris and Millie (Goldstein) F.; B.A., N.Y. U., 1954, J.D., 1959; postgrad. U. Bern (Switzerland), 1954-55; m. Myrna Dananberg, May 26, 1963; children—Rachel Harris, James Harris. Admitted to N.Y. bar, 1959; practiced in N.Y.C., 1959-61, 64—; asst. U.S. atty., criminal div. U.S. Dept. Justice, 1961-64. Moderator, lectr. N.Y. Acad. Trial Lawyers, 1974-75. Fellow Am. Acad. Matrimonial Lawyers; mem. Assn. Bar City N.Y. (spl. Com. on matrimonial law 1975-77), Am. (sustaining), N.Y. State (family law sect.) bar assns., Am. Arbitration Assn. (mem. arbitrator panel 1970—), Am. Fedn. Police, Nat. Police Officers Assn., Nat. Legal Aid and Defenders Assn., Nat. Council Family Relations, N.Y. State Soc. Med. Jurisprudence, N.Y. State Dist. Attys. Assn. Author: Divorce - The Way Things Are, Not The Way Things Should Be, 1971. Contbr.

articles to profl. publs. Home: 985 Fifth Ave New York City NY 10021 Office: 711 Fifth Ave New York City NY 10022

FELDERMAN, ERIC, author; b. N.Y.C., Oct. 14, 1944; s. Leon and Beatrice F.; A.B. magna cum laude, Columbia U., 1965; M.A., Cornell U., 1966; Ph.D., State U. N.Y., Buffalo, 1969. Instr., then asst. prof. English, Yale U., 1969-74; asst. prof. humanities Cooper Union, 1975; staff analyst N.Y.C. Dept. Cultural Affairs, 1977—; author: Animal Book, 1978; The Dummy's Soliloquy, 1965; Love Poem, 1974; The Book of Lies, 1975; Garden Street, 1976; rep. anthologies. NDEA fellow, 1966-69; Andrew D. White fellow, 1965-66; Nat. Merit scholar, 1960-65; recipient Nat. Scholastic 1st prize poetry, 1960, 61; Am. Acad. Poets award, 1964. Mem. Authors Guild, Modern Lang. Assn., Phi Beta Kappa. Jewish. Home: 20 Metropolitan Oval Apt 11-B New York City NY 10462 Office: Dept Cultural Affairs 830 Fifth Ave New York City NY 10021

FELDMAN, BERTOLD, physician; b. Spule, Czechoslovakia, Mar. 17, 1903; s. Samuel and Emilie (Pollak) F.; M.D., Charles U. at Prague, Czechoslovakia, 1929; m. Vera Bondy, Mar. 3, 1946; 1 son, George Michael. Came to U.S., 1952, naturalized, 1957. Intern, Gen. Hosp., Opoono, Czechoslovakia, 1930, resident in internal medicine Pardubice 1931-34; practice medicine specializing in internal medicine, Klatovy, Czechoslovakia, 1934-41, 45-48, New City, N.Y., 1953—; cons. internal medicine Nyack Hosp., 1963-64, pres. med. staff, 1964-65, chmn. exec. com., 1965-66, chmn. credential com., 1967-71, asso. dir. dept. medicine, chief gastroenterology sect., 1967-72; sch. physician, New City, N.Y., 1954—. Fellow Am. Coll. Gastroenterology; mem. AMA, Rockland County, N.Y. med. Socs., N.Y. Acad. Gastroenterology. Address: 184 N Little Tor Rd New City NY 10956

FELDMAN, BRUCE ALLEN, otolaryngologist; b. Washington, Mar. 22, 1941; s. Irvin and Miriam Thelma (Rothstein) F.; A.B., Dartmouth Coll., 1962, B. Med. Sci., 1963; M.D., Harvard U., 1965; m. Sharon Lee Pearlman, Dec. 25, 1966; children—Kathryn Ellen, Michael Aaron. Intern, Hosp. U. Pa., Phila., 1965-66, surg. resident, 1966-67; resident otolaryngology Mass. Eye and Ear Infirmary, Boston, 1967-70; practice medicine specializing in otolaryngology, Washington, Chevy Chase, Md., 1972—; asso. clin. prof. George Washington U. Sch. Medicine, 1974—. Served to lt. comdr. USN, 1970-72. Mosby scholar Dartmouth Med. Sch., 1963, NIH trainee Mass. Eye and Ear Infirmary, 1967-70. Mem. AMA, Am. Acad. Ophthalmology and Otolaryngology, ACS, Am. Acad. Facial Plastic and Reconstructive Surgeons, Soc. for Ear, Nose and Throat Advances in Children, Met. Washington Area Ear, Nose and Throat Soc. (pres.), D.C. Med. Soc., Med. Soc. Montgomery County, Phi Delta Epsilon, Phi Beta Kappa, Alpha Omega Alpha. Club: Dartmouth (Washington). Home: 12717 Huntsman Way Potomac MD 20854 Office: 1722 Eye St NW Washington DC 20006

FELDMAN, EDWIN BERNARD, constrn. co. exec.; b. N.Y.C., Dec. 2, 1918; s. Jacob Gustav and Rose Eleanor (Weiss) F.; student George Washington U., 1936-39; m. Florence Duncan, July 1, 1944 (dec. 1957); children—James Gary, Peggy Carol, Jack Mason; m. 2d. Margit Berger Kaufmann, Oct. 16, 1958; 1 son, Ronald Lee Kaufmann. Self-employed, Washington, 1946—. Licensed real estate broker, D.C. Mem. Phi Sigma Delta. Office: 3000 7th St NE Washington DC 20017

FELDMAN, GEORGE JOSEPH, govt. ofcl.; b. Boston, Nov. 6, 1903; s. Harry and Bessie (Alpert) F.; LL.B., Boston U., 1925, LL.D., 1968; LL.D. (hon.), Holy Cross Coll., Worcester, Mass., 1967; m. May 29, 1948; children—George J., Margot. Admitted to Mass. bar, 1925, D.C. bar, 1935, N.Y. bar, 1949; adminstrv. asst. to U.S. Senator David I. Walsh, 1926-30; atty. FTC, 1930-32; practiced in Boston, 1932-34; sr. mem. firm Feldman, Kitelle, Campbell & Ewing, Washington, 1935-47; fgn. service officer Dept. State, 1965; U.S. ambassador to Malta, 1965-67, to Luxembourg, 1967-69; mem. Nat. Commn. for UNESCO, Dept. State, N.Y.C., 1974—; litigation atty. Nat. Recovery Adminstrn., 1934-35; dir., chief counsel U.S. Ho. of Reps. Select Com. on Astronautics and Space Exploration, 1958-59; mem. U.S. del. Gen. Assembly UN, 1959, to UN Conf. on Law of Sea, Geneva, 1960; mem. U.S. NATO Citizen's Com., 1961-62; incorporator, dir. Communications Satellite Corp., 1962-64; cons. Dept. State; mem. adv. council Malta Devel. Corp. Mem. pres.'s. council Holy Cross Coll.; bd. fellows Boston U.; bd. dirs. N.Y. Coll. Osteo. Medicine. Served with USAAF, 1942. Mem. Am., N.Y. State bar assns., Am. Fgn. Service Assn. Club: City Athletic. Author books, the most recent being: The Reluctant Space Farers, 1964; contbr. numerous articles to law revs., jours. Home: 1 Sutton Pl St New York City NY 10022 Office: 516 Fifth Ave New York City NY 10036

FELDMAN, HERBERT BYRON, physician, musician; b. N.Y.C., Oct. 6, 1931; s. Leo and Helen I. Feldman; B.A. cum laude, N.Y.U., 1958; M.D., State U. N.Y., Bklyn., 1962; m. Lauretta Mennone, Nov. 7, 1952; children—David, Aaaron, Linda, Emmanuel, Jonathan, Joseph, Deborah. Intern, Kings County Hosp., 1962-63; practice medicine specializing in family practice and internal medicine, Forest Hills, N.Y., 1963—; mem. patient care com. Parkway Hosp., Queens, N.Y.; tchr. viola and violin Juilliard Sch. Music, 1955-57. Recipient Arthritis and Rheumatism award Downstate Med. Center, 1963. Diplomate Am. Bd. Family Practice. Mem. Am. (chpt. pres. 1978), N.Y. (vice chmn. com. legis. 1978), acads. family practice, N.Y. State, Queens med. socs., L.I. Composers Alliance (dir.), Bayview Music Consort (dir.), Phi Beta Kappa. Jewish. Office: 108-21 69th Rd Forest Hills NY 11375

FELDMAN, JOSEPH HERBERT, psychiatrist, educator; b. Boston, June 21, 1923; s. Harry and Frances (Gelb) F.; B.S., Boston U., 1946, M.D., 1949; m. Selma Ruth Steinberger, July 15, 1950; children—Richard Jay, Ronald James. Intern, USPHS Hosp., S.I., 1949-50; fellow in child psychiatry Inst. Pa. Hosp., Phila., 1952-54; resident in psychiatry State U. N.Y. Downstate Med. Center, Bklyn., 1952-54; asst. psychiatrist Hillside Hosp., Glen Oaks, N.Y., 1954-56, adj. attending psychiatrist, 1959-67, tng. supr., child therapy unit, 1967-71; practice medicine specializing in child, adolescent and adult psychiatry, N.Y.C., 1955-65, Woodmere, N.Y., 1965—; cons. psychiatrist, Child Guidance Inst., Jewish Bd. Guardians, N.Y.C., 1954-65, asst. dir. psychiat. tng. program, 1955-62, asst. clin. dir., 1962-65; staff psychiatrist Long Island Jewish Hosp., New Hyde Park, N.Y., 1965-70, psychiatrist in charge children adolescents S. Shore div. Long Island Jewish Hosp. Hillside Med. Center, 1972-76; cons. psychiatrist dept. pediatrics St. John's Episcopal Hosp., 1976—; cons. psychiatrist Nassau County (N.Y.) Med. Center, 1969—; asst. prof. clin. psychiatry State U. N.Y. Sch. Medicine, Stony Brook, 1973—. Served with USPHS, 1949-50. Diplomate Am. Bd. Psychiatry Neurology. Fellow Am. Psychiat. Assn., Am. Acad. Child Psychiatry; Am. Orthopsychiat. Assn.; mem. AMA, N.Y. Med. Soc., Nassau County Med. Soc., Nassau County Psychiat. Soc., N.Y. Council Child Psychiatry, Soc. Adolescent Psychiatry, Nat. Audubon Soc., Nat. Wildlife Fedn. Home: 36 Herrick Dr Lawrence NY 11559 Office: 29 Woodmere Blvd Woodmere NY 11598

FELDMAN, MAURICE MILTON, cons. engr.; b. N.Y.C., May 26, 1915; s. Isidor and Ida (Rabinowitz) F.; B.S., Coll. City N.Y., 1936; postgrad. Bklyn. Coll., 1937-38; B.C.E., N.Y. U., 1941, M.C.E., 1948; m. Ruth Kalish, Dec. 20, 1936; children—Naomi (Mrs. James F. Collins), Eugene. Civil service career, N.Y.C., 1936-71, including engr. in charge Bur. Waste Disposal, N.Y.C. Dept. Sanitation, 1950-64, dep. gen. mgr. Dept. Pub. Works, 1964-67, chief engr., acting commr. N.Y.C. Dept. Sanitation, 1967-68, commr. water resources, N.Y.C., 1968-71; cons. engr. solid waste mgmt., N.Y.C., 1971—; dir. environ. programs L.S. Wegman, engrs., 1975—; mem. Interstate Sanitation Commn., 1978—; cons. adv. com. solid waste mgmt.-bldg. research adv. bd. Nat. Acad. Scis., 1967-74; cons. textbook revision and solid waste seminar Am. Pub. Works Assn., Chgo., 1971—; cons. N.Y. State Dept. Environ. Conservation, 1972-73; adj. prof. N.Y. U. Grad. Sch. Pub. Adminstrn., 1971—. Citizen mem. N.Y.C. Environ. Control Bd., 1973-76. Served to capt. San. Corps, AUS, 1943-46. Diplomate Am. Acad. Environ. Engring. Fellow N.Y. Acad. Scis.; mem. ASCE, Am. Pub. Works Assn., Water Pollution Control Fedn., Am. Water Works Assn., Tau Beta Pi. Home: 142-11 29th Rd New York City NY 11354

FELDMAN, PHILIP, court reporter; b. N.Y.C., Sept. 26, 1941; s. Nathan and Rose (Schultz) F.; student Mchts. and Bankers Sch. Ct. Reporting, 1960-61; m. Muriel Cardia, June 16, 1963; children—Julie A., Felicia L. Ofcl. and freelance ct. reporter N.Y. State and Fed. Ct. systems, 1961—; personal ct. reporter Hon. Nelson A. Rockefeller, Gov. State N.Y., 1969; ofcl. ct. reporter U.S. Dist. Ct., Phila., 1970—; dir., founder Garden State Sch. Ct. Reporting, Westmont, N.J., 1974—. Recipient certificates of Proficiency and Merit, Nat. Shorthand Reporters' Assn., 1973-74; award of Excellence, Md. Shorthand Reporters' Assn., 1975; certified shorthand reporter, N.J., Pa., Md. Mem. Nat., Md. shorthand reporters assns., Animal Welfare Assn. Jewish. Home: 12 Erynwood Ave Marlton NJ 08053 Office: Room 2722 US Courthouse Philadelphia PA 19106

FELDMAN, ROGER DAVID, lawyer, former govt. ofcl.; b. N.Y.C., Apr. 7, 1943; s. Louis and Dora (Goldsmith) F.; A.B., Brown U., 1962; LL.B., Yale, 1965; M.B.A., Harvard, 1967; m. Gail Steg, May 31, 1969; children—Rebecca Danielle, Seth Steg. Admitted to N.Y. bar, 1966, D.C. bar, 1977; ops. research analyst, office of asst. sec. def., Dept. Def., Washington, 1967-68; staff. asst., Office of U.S. Pres., Washington, 1968-69; asso. firm LeBoeuf, Lamb, Leiby & MacRae, N.Y.C., 1969-75, partner, Washington, 1977—; dept. asst. adminstr., finance and environment, Fed. Energy Adminstrn., Washington, 1975-77; dir. Pan Atlantic Group, Inc. Mem. adv. bd. Energy Bur., Inc. Mem. Am. Bar Assn. (chmn. Nat. Inst. Indsl. Energy Choices 1978 vice chmn. energy com. of adminstrv. law sect. 1978—), Fed. Bar Assn. (vice chmn. energy com.). Asso. editor Juris Doctor, 1971-72; editor Yale Law Jour., 1964-65. Home: 18 Oxford St Chevy Chase MD 20015 Office: 1757 N St NW Washington DC 20036

FELDMAN, RONALD LEONARD, speech pathologist, educator; b. Bklyn., July 17, 1932; s. David and Lillian (Goldstein) F.; B.A., Bklyn. Coll., 1960, M.A., 1962; Ph.D., N.Y.U., 1971; m. Phyllis Greenfield, Oct. 18, 1952; children—Michael, Brian, Sharon. Tchr. speech bd. edn., N.Y.C., 1960-67; asso. prof. dept. speech Bklyn. Coll., 1967—, coordinator clin. practice and speech edn. programs. Served with U.S. Army, 1952-54. Licensed and certificate of clin. practice in speech-lang. pathology, N.Y. Mem. Am., N.Y. State speech and hearing assn., Speech Communication of Am. Contbr. articles to profl. jours. Office: Bklyn Coll Dept Speech Brooklyn NY 11210

FELDMAN, STEPHEN, coll. adminstr.; b. N.Y.C., Sept. 11, 1944; s. Harry and Mae (Morris) F.; B.B.A., Coll. City N.Y., 1966, M.B.A., 1968, (fellow) Ph.D., 1971; m. Constance M. Lerudis, June 1, 1969; 1 dau., Jennifer Dawn. Chmn. dept. banking, finance and investments Hofstra U., Hempstead, N.Y., 1969-77, asso. prof., 1974-77; dean Sch. Bus. and Pub. Adminstrn., Western Conn. State Coll., Danbury, 1977—. Pres., SF Planning Corp., Redding, Conn., 1973—; chmn. bd. Macrolease Internat. Corp., 1976—; cons. IBM, N.Y. Telephone Co., Ednl. Reading Aids Corp. Mem. Am. Fin. Assn., Fin. Mgmt. Assn. Editor: Handbook of Wealth Management, 1977. Home: Old Stagecoach Rd Redding CT 06896 Office: Western Conn State Coll Danbury CT 06810

FELDSTEIN, AARON, biochemist; b. Bklyn., May 24, 1922; s. Victor and Tillie (Friedman) F.; B.A., Bklyn. Coll., 1944; Ph.D., U. Kans., 1952; m. Mildred Laken, Jan. 21, 1957; children—Caren, Debra. Sr. scientist Worcester Found. for Exptl. Biology, Shrewsbury, Mass., 1955-74; mgr. biochem. pharmacology Ciba-Geigy Pharm. Co., Summit, N.J., 1974-75; prof. biochemistry Rutgers U., New Brunswick, N.J., 1975—, documentation Center Alcohol Studies, 1975—. Vice pres. Jewish Community Center, Worcester, Mass., 1970-73, B'nai B'rith, Livingston, N.J., 1977—. USPHS grantee, 1957-73. Mem. Am. Chem. Soc., Am. Soc. Neurochemistry, Research Soc. Alcoholism, Soc. Biol. Psychiatry, Soc. Neurosci., Am. Coll. Neuropsychopharmacology, N.Y. Acad. Scis. Contbr. numerous articles on neurobiochemistry of alcohol and drugs to profl. jours. Home: 18 Tanglewood Dr Livingston NJ 07039 Office: Center Alcohol Studies Rutgers U New Brunswick NJ 08903

FELDSTEIN, CARLENE BROOKS, psychologist; b. Memphis, Apr. 24, 1932; d. Carl Raymond and Ruby (Hindman) Brooks; B.A., Fairleigh Dickinson U., Teaneck, N.J., 1959; Ph.D. candidate, N.Y. U. Sch. Edn., 1964—; m. Julian M. Feldstein, May 19, 1965; children—Kent Nicholson Lowry, Aaron Carl Feldstein. Psychology intern Inst. Rehab. Medicine, N.Y. U. Med. Center, 1966-67, staff psychologist, 1968-73; lectr., then asst. prof. psychology City U. N.Y., 1972—; pvt. practice psychology, 1973—; instr. Pace U., Westchester, Pleasantville, N.Y., 1973—; mem. faculty new directions Coll. New Rochelle (N.Y.); cons. indsl. relations. Nat. Def. Edn. Act fellow, 1964-68. Mem. Am. Psychol. Assn., Internat. Transactional Analysis Assn., Nat. Assn. Family Life, Assn. Humanistic Psychology. Address: 32 Hamilton Rd Scarsdale NY 10583

FELICE, PATRICK ELIO, radiation safety ofcl.; b. Derry, Pa., Nov. 2, 1930; s. Luigi and Lydia (Guiliani) F.; A.A., Penn Tech. Inst., 1950; m. Carole Shrum, June 16, 1956; children—Gracienne, Patrick, Robert, Scott, Crystal, Betsy, Melissa. Electronic technician Westinghouse Electric Corp., Pitts., 1955-62, technician radiation and nucleonic lab. Westinghouse Research Lab., 1962-72, engr., 1972—, radiation safety officer Westinghouse Research and Devel. Center, 1970—. Served with USAF, 1950-54. Mem. Health Physics Soc. (nat.), Health Physics Soc. Western Pa., Am. Nuclear Soc. Democrat. Roman Catholic. Eagle. Patentee in field (U.S. and abroad). Home: 19 Painter St Jeanette PA 15644 Office: Beulah Rd Churchill Boro Pittsburgh PA 15235

FELIU, LEOPOLDO, indsl. hygienist; b. Lajas, P.R., Nov. 18, 1925; s. Placido and Rosa (Rivera) F.; B.S. in Chemistry, St. Johns U., 1952; postgrad. N.Y. U. Grad. Sch. Medicine, 1955-58, Alexander Hamilton Inst., 1963-65, Wayne State U., 1972; m. Francoise DeLorimier, July 7, 1950; children—Leopold, Elina Jeannette, Albert, Robert. Research chemist Kellogg Co., Jersey City, 1952-53; cons. indsl. hygiene Continental Ins. Co., N.Y.C., 1954-66; indsl. hygienist Gen. Electric Co., housewares bus. div. plants, Bridgeport, Conn., 1966-77, contractor equipment div. 1977—; guest lectr. U. Bridgeport, 1975-78. Mem. troop com. local council Boy Scouts Am., 1974-77; pres. Notre Dame Boys High Sch. Parents Assn., 1968-69; mem. Air Pollution Bd. Appeals Bridgeport, 1969-72; mem. Sewer Commn. Trumbull (Conn.), 1970-72. Served to sgt. USAF, 1945-48. Recipient Silver award Gen. Electric Co., 1978. Mem. Am. Indsl. Hygiene Assn., Am. Bd. Indsl. Hygiene, Am. Legion (chaplain 1978—). Republican. Roman Catholic. Home: 42 MacArthur Rd Trumbull CT 06611 Office: 1285 Boston Ave Bridgeport CT 06602

FELIÚ-FLORES, CÁNDIDA ELENA, counselor; b. Santurce, P.R., Aug. 24, 1947; d. Jaime and Amparo (Gonzalez) Feliú; B.A. cum laude in Sociology, City Coll. N.Y., 1974; M.S. with honors in Edn., Richmond Coll., City U. N.Y., 1975; m. Andrés Flores-Mangual, June 21, 1968; children—Mia Lisa, Sarito Amparo. Counselor dept. spl. programs City Coll. N.Y., 1975—; cons. Fordham U. Sch. Social Services, P.R. and Region II Office of Adminstrn. on Aging. Vol., Girl Scouts U.S.A.; bd. dirs. Grosvenor Neighborhood House; mem. Dist. 3 Bilingual Parent Bd. Served with WAVES, 1965. U.S. Dept. Labor grantee, 1974-75. Mem. Am. Personnel and Guidance Assn., Am. Coll. Personnel Assn. Democrat. Presbyterian. Research on student input in evaluation bilingual-bicultural programs. Home: 203 W 103d St New York City NY 10025 Office: 138th and Convent Ave New York City NY 10031

FELLER, MARVIN SHELDON, twp. ofcl.; b. Atlantic City, N.J., July 7, 1922; s. Louis William and Gussie (Fingeroth) F.; B.S. in Indsl. Engring., Widener Coll., 1951; M.S. in Mech. Engring., U. Del., 1953; m. Vera Feldman, Dec. 18, 1948; children—Lawrence Wayne, Barbara Elise, David Scott, Joseph Norman. Process design engr. DuPont Co., Wilmington, Del., 1951-53; proj project mgr. ITE-Imperial, Phila., 1953-63; cons. engr. communications Feller Assn., Upper Dublin Twp., Pa., 1963-72; mem. bd. commrs. Upper Dublin Twp., 1968-72, v.p. bd. commrs. 1970-71, mem. pub. library bd., 1971-73, pres. bd. commrs., 1972, twp. mgr., 1973—. Bd. dirs. Jewish Centers, Phila., 1972—. Served with AUS, 1943-45. Mem. Internat. City Mgrs. Assn., IEEE (cons. chmn. standards com.), Soc. Advancement Mgmt., Am. Pub. Works Assn., Water Pollution Control Fedn., Nat. Model Rr. Assn. Republican. Jewish. Clubs: Shriners, B'nai B'rith (Man of Yr. 1973), Kiwanis (Outstanding Community Service award 1971). Home: 501 Martin Ln Dresher PA 19025 Office: 801 Loch Alsh Ave Fort Washington PA 19034

FELLER, RICHARD TABLER, cathedral adminstr.; b. Fairmont, W.Va., Mar. 14, 1919; s. Richard Roeder and Ethel (Tabler) F.; B.S. in Civil Engring., W.Va. U., 1942; m. Wilma Gertrude Stenger, June 1, 1943; children—Richard Stenger, Nancy Carol (Mrs. N.C. Ecklund). Supervising engr. Def. Plant Corp., Indpls., 1942-45; v.p. Huber, Hunt & Nichols, Inc., Indpls., 1945-47; gen. mgr. Richard R. Feller Co., Martinsburg, W.Va., 1947-51; engr. Ceco Steel Products Co., Washington, 1952-53; mgr. purchasing and accounting, Washington Cathedral, 1953-57, clk. of works, 1957—. Owner R. Feller Co., Martinsburg, W.Va., 1972—. Trustee Stone Cutters and Carvers Welfare Fund, 1965-75; dir., treas. Frat. Housing Corp., Washington, 1952-69, exec. v.p., 1969-71, pres., 1975—. Mem. Guild for Religious Architecture, Nat. Sculpture Soc. (patron mem.), Soc. Archtl. Historians, Am. Mgmt. Assn., Nat. Small Bus. Assn., Kappa Alpha (exec. council 1961-71, nat. pres. 1971-73). Episcopalian (sr. warden). Mason. Club: Arts (bd. govs. 1969-71, v.p. 1970-71) (Washington). Author: (with Marshall W. Fishwick) For Thy Great Glory, 1965; Sculpture and Carving at Washington Cathedral, 1976; contbr. articles to religious and art periodicals. Home: 8014 Maple Ridge Rd Bethesda MD 20014 Office; Washington Cathedral Mt St Alban Washington DC 20016

FELLNER, MICHAEL JOSEF, dermatologist; b. N.Y.C., Sept. 15, 1936; s. Stephen and Selma (Ehrlich) F.; A.B. in Chemistry, Cornell U., 1956; M.D., U. Md., 1960; m. Fredda Ginsberg, Aug. 27, 1961; children—Jonathan, Melinda. Intern, Kings County Hosp., State U., Bklyn., 1960-61; resident Mt. Sinai Hosp., N.Y.C., 1961-63; NIH tng. fellow N.Y. U. Med. Center, N.Y.C., 1963-64; NIH research tng. fellow in allergy and immunology, dept. dermatology N.Y. U., N.Y.C., 1964-66; Am. Allergy Found. fellow, 1966-67; practice medicine specializing in dermatology, N.Y.C., 1966—; asso. vis. dermatologist Bellevue Hosp., N.Y.C., 1970-72; asst. attending dermatologist N.Y. U. Hosp., N.Y.C., 1966-70, asso. attending dermatologist, 1970-72; attending dermatologist Flower and Fifth Ave. Hosp. and Met. Hosp., N.Y.C.; dir. dermatology Bird S. Coler Hosp., N.Y.C., 1973—; asst. prof. dermatology N.Y. U. Sch. Medicine, N.Y.C., 1966-70, asso. prof., 1970-72; prof. dermatology N.Y. Med. Coll., N.Y.C., 1973—; reviewer Archives of Dermatology. Recipient Fred Wise Meml. award N.Y. Acad. Medicine, 1963; Gold medal Am. Dermatol. Assn., 1967; award N.Y. State Med. Soc.; NIH grantee, 1967-73, John A. Hartford Found. grantee, 1972-78. Diplomate Am. Bd. Dermatology. Mem. Am. Acad. Dermatology, Am. Acad. Allergy, Dermatologic Soc. Greater N.Y. (Henry Silver award 1964), Am. Fedn. Clin. Research, Soc. Investigative Dermatology, Am. Dermatologic Soc. for Allergy and Immunology (founding mem; sec.-treas. 1976-79, dir. 1976—, pres. 1979-80), N.Y. Acad. Scis., N.Y. State Dermatology Soc., N.Y. County Soc. Medicine, Internat. Soc. Tropical Dermatology, AAAS. Contbr. numerous articles on immunology, allergy and dermatology to med. jours.; corr. editor Internat. Jour. Dermatology, 1976—. Home: 50 E 89th St New York City NY 10028 Office: 30 E 60th St New York City NY 10022

FELLOWS, LAWRENCE PERRY, journalist; b. Detroit, Dec. 24, 1924; s. Perry Augustus and Gladys Marion (Culver) F.; student Am. U., 1942; A.B., Ohio Wesleyan U., 1948; postgrad. U. Md. in Bonn and Wiesbaden, Germany, 1952-53; m. Ruth Bell, Dec. 27, 1952; children—Eva, Robin. Edn. adviser Berlin Mil. Post, U.S. Dept. Army, 1948-50; sec. Mil. Security Bd., U.S. Dept. State, Berlin and Koblenz, W.Ger., 1950-53; N.Y. reporter, mem. UN Bur., fgn. corr. N.Y. Times, 1959-72, chief Conn. Bur., 1972-78. Served with USNR, 1942-45. Methodist. Author: East Africa, 1972. Home and office: 6 Stuart Dr Bloomfield CT 06002

FELMAN, YEHUDI MOSHE, dermatologist; b. Bridgeport, Conn., July 11, 1938; s. Meir and Helen (Kleter) F.; B.A., Yeshiva U., 1959; M.D., Albert Einstein Coll. Medicine, 1963; M.A. in Hebrew Lit. and Jewish History, Columbia U., 1966, M.Phil. in Hebrew Lit. and Jewish History, 1975; m. Brenda Wishengrad., Oct. 10, 1962; children—Nahum, Hillel. Intern, Mt. Sinai Hosp., N.Y.C., 1963-64; resident, Columbia-Presbyn. Med. Center, N.Y.C., 1964-65, chief resident in dermatology, 1965-66, fellow in dermatology, 1966-67; practice medicine specializing in dermatology and venereology, Bklyn., 1967—; asso. clin. prof. dermatology State U. N.Y., Bklyn., 1977—, asst. clin. prof. dermatology, 1970-77; prof. dermatology Touro Coll. Health Scis., 1973—; attending physician Downstate U. Hosp., Bklyn., 1967—, Maimonides Hosp., Bklyn., 1968—, Kings Hwy. Hosp., N.Y.C., 1969—, Flatbush Gen. Hosp., 1969—, Community Hosp., 1969—; asso. attending physician Kings County Hosp., N.Y.C., 1967—; dir. Bur. Venereal Disease Control, N.Y.C. Health Dept., 1976—; mem. Health Systems Agy., Bklyn., 1977—; asst. prof. Hebrew, Yeshiva U., N.Y.C., 1970-75. Bd. dirs. Yeshiva of Flatbush, 1972—; trustee Young Israel of Bklyn., 1975—. N.Y. State Regents Med. scholar, 1959; diplomate Am. Bd. Dermatology. Fellow ACP, Am. Acad. Dermatology; mem. Med. Soc. State N.Y. (del. 1979-80), N.Y. State Soc. Dermatology (bd. dirs. 1977-80), Bklyn. Dermatologic Soc. (pres. 1976-77), Kings County Med. Soc., N.Y. State Med. Soc., Am. Med. Assn., Pub. Health Assn. N.Y., Am.

Venereal Disease Assn. Contbr. articles in field to med. jours. Home: 1810 Glenwood Rd Brooklyn NY 11230 Office: 8100 Bay Pkwy Brooklyn NY 11214

FELMLY, LLOYD MCPHERSON, ret. journalist, educator; b. Flemington, N.J., Jan. 28, 1894; s. Charles Fox and Minnie (Banghart) F.; Ph.B., Lafayette Coll., 1916, Litt.D., 1943; L.H.D., Rutgers, 1956; m. Anna Tallman, Nov. 22, 1919; children—Lloyd McPherson, Janice (Mrs. Wurfel). With Newark News, 1916-59, beginning as reporter, North Jersey editor, 1920-24, state editor, 1924-26, city editor, 1926-33, mng. editor, 1933-44, editor, 1944-59; chmn. English dept. Newark Coll. Engring., 1959-61, prof. English, 1961-64; mem. TV panel Starring the Editors, N.Y.C., 1951-52. Bd. mgrs. Howard Savs. Bank; trustee N.J. Blue Shield; chmn. alumni council Lafayette Coll., 1942-44, alumni trustee, 1946-52, life trustee, 1954-71, pres. bd., 1956-64. Pres. N.J. Safety Council, 1958-61, trustee, 1961—. Served as pvt. to 1st lt. Transp. Corps, AUS, 1918-19; with AEF, 9 months. Mem. Am. Soc. Newspaper Editors, Phi Beta Kappa. Conglist. Club: Down Town (Newark). Home: 592 Ridgewood Ave Glen Ridge NJ 07028

FELO, MATTHEW FRANCIS, JR., utilities co. exec.; b. Binghamton, N.Y., Sept. 26, 1945; s. Matthew Francis and June Ida (Felske) F.; B.B.A., Niagara U., 1968. Accountant N.Y. State Electric & Gas Corp., Ithaca, 1972-74, treasury asst., 1974-76, supv. treasury dept., 1976-77, asst. treas., 1977—. Served with U.S. Army, 1969-71. Mem. Alpha Kappa Psi. Republican. Roman Catholic. Club: Willowbrook Country. Home: 18 Clinton St Homer NY 13077 Office: PO Box 287 Ithaca NY 14850

FELTON, BLANCHE HELEN DIMIN, physiologist; b. Bklyn., Jan. 6, 1923; d. Edward and Florence Dimin; B.S., Bklyn. Coll. Pharmacy, 1943; M.S., St. John's U., 1965; Ph.D., Fordham U., 1972; m. Philip Felton, Dec. 20, 1942; children—Marilyn Felton Fox, Glenn P., Joyce. Chemist research and devel. Am. Pharm. Co., N.Y.C., 1943-45; clin. chemist Bennitt Labs., Dameron Hosp., Stockton, Calif., 1945-46; hosp. pharmacist L.I. Jewish Hosp., 1957; pharmacist-in-charge Queens Gen. Hosp., Jamaica, N.Y., 1958-67; asso. prof. biol. scis., coordinator environ. health program, Queensborough Community Coll., City U. N.Y.; postdoctoral research fellow Mt. Sinai Sch. Medicine. Trustee, bd. dirs. Research Found., City U. N.Y.; bd. dirs. Marine Ecology Environ. Research, Fort Totten, N.Y.; mem. Comprehensive Health Planning Bd., 1973-76; trustee Bayside Hist. Soc., 1970-73. Vocational Ednl. Adminstrn. grantee, Noyes Found. grantee. Mem. Am. Soc. Zoologists, AAAS, Nat. Environ. Health Assn., Am. Malacology Soc., N.Y. Acad. Sci., Am. Pub. Health Assn., Sigma Xi. Office: Queensborough Community Coll Bayside NY 11364

FELTUS, RUSSELL HODGE, assn. exec.; b. N.Y.C., Mar. 2, 1921; s. Russell Hodge and Alice (Olson) F.; B.S., Harwick Coll., 1950; m. Jane Gray, Apr. 28, 1951; children—Christine (Mrs. Richard Marmor), Russell Gray, Joanne, Lynn. Malpractice claims reviewer Employers Mut. of Wausau, 1951-59; exec. dir. Med. Socs. Counties Oneida, Herkimor, Madison and Chenango, New Hartford, N.Y., 1959—, Central N.Y. Acad. Medicine, 1959—, N.Y. State Soc. Surgeons, 1968—, N.Y. State Soc. Orthopedic Surgeons, 1971—. Served with USMCR, 1941-45. Rotarian. Home: 16 Slaytonbush Ln Utica NY 13501 Office: 210 Clinton Rd New Hartford NY 13413

FENCHEL, GERD H., psychologist, educator; b. Berlin, Germany, Mar. 29, 1926; s. Eric Otto and Rosa (Goldschmidt) F.; came to U.S., 1940.; B.Social Sci., Coll. City N.Y., 1949, M.S., 1950; Ph.D., N.Y. U., 1959; certificate Alfred Adler Inst., 1953; m. Dorothy Flapan, May 28, 1971; children (by previous marriage)—Karen Elizabeth, Eric Steven. Fellow psychology dept. Coll. City N.Y., 1946-50; research asst. Bd. Higher Edn., N.Y.C., 1950; psychotherapist Alfred Adler Mental Hygiene Clinic, 1951-55; dir. Inst. for Group Psychotherapy, supr. psychotherapy L.I. Consultation Center, N.Y.C., 1953-60; psychologist Columbia Grammar Sch., 1954-56; faculty Alfred Adler Inst., N.Y.C., 1955-73; fellow, instr. Inst. for Analytic Psychotherapy, N.Y.C., 1960; pres. Council for Psychoanalytic Psychotherapy, N.Y.C., 1966-67; exec. dir. Washington Sq. Inst. Psychotherapy and Mental Health, N.Y.C., 1960—. Fellow Am. Group Psychotherapy Assn., Internat. Council Psychologists, Council of Psychoanalytic Psychotherapists; mem. Am. Psychol. Assn., N.Y. Psychol. Assn., N.Y. Soc. Clin. Psychologists, Easter Group Psychotherapy Soc., N.Y. Acad. Sci. Office: 80 Fifth Ave New York City NY 10011

FENGLER, JOHN PETER, advt. agy. exec.; b. Leipzig, Germany, Dec. 29, 1928; s. Kurt and Norma (Berend) F.; came to U.S., 1939, naturalized, 1952; B.A. in Radio and TV, N.Y. U., 1952; m. Jessica M. Atkins, Dec. 7, 1961; 1 son, John Mark. Producer, dir. NBC, 1950-58; producer Doyle, Dane, Bernbach, advt., N.Y.C., 1965-68; exec. producer N.W. Ayer Co., N.Y.C., 1958-65; dir., exec. producer radio and TV dept. Kurtz & Symon, Inc., N.Y.C., 1969-74; v.p., dir. comml. prodn. dept., exec. producer D'Arcy-MacManus & Masius, N.Y.C., 1974-75; pres. U.S. Television Co., N.Y.C., 1975—. Served with AUS, 1950-52. Mem. Nat. Acad. TV Arts and Scis. (Emmy award best children's program 1957, 58). Home: 132 Edgemont Rd Scarsdale NY 10583 Office: 220 E 54th St New York City NY 10022

FENN, ANTHONY NEVILLE, mfg. co. exec.; b. Birkenhead, Eng., Dec. 14, 1919; s. Leslie Neville and Lilian (Bind) F.; ed. Eng.; m. Erskine Young, Oct. 5, 1946; children—Ronald, Giles. Came to Canada, 1962. Asst. mgr. F.W. Woolworth Co. Ltd., Lichfield and Oxford, Eng., 1937-39, 46-48; dist. officer Colonial Adminstrv. Service, Nigeria, 1950-53; mng. dir. Vivian Younger Bond (Nigeria) Ltd., trading and mfg. Lagos, 1953-62; with Canada Wire & Cable Co. Ltd., Toronto, Ont., 1962—, v.p., 1968—; pres., dir. Can. Wire & Cable (Internat.) Ltd.; dir. Tycan Ltd., Australia, Conductores Monterrey S.A., Mexico, Fadaltec S.A. Colombia, Iconel C.A. Venezuela, others in Nigeria, Iran, New Zealand, Dominican Republic, S. Africa. Mem. Toronto Bd. Trade. Served with Brit. Army and Gurkha Rifles, 1939-46: CBI. Fellow Inst. Dirs. Clubs: Toronto Cricket Skating and Curling, Royal Canadian Military Inst. Office: 147 Laird Dr Leaside Toronto ON M4G 3W1 Canada

FENN, DAN HUNTINGTON, JR., educator, govt. ofcl.; b. Boston, Mar. 27, 1923; s. Dan Huntington and Anna (Yens) G.; A.B. magna cum laude, Harvard U., 1946, student Grad. Sch. Arts and Scis., 1946-48, A.M., 1972; LL.D., Nasson, 1972, New Eng. Coll., 1976; m. Nancy Ring, Dec. 28, 1946 (div. 1965); children—Peter, Anne, David, Thomas O.; m. 2d, Lenore O. Sheppard, Oct. 10, 1969; children—W. Gregory, W. Marie, Christopher G. Asst. dean freshmen Harvard U., 1946-49; exec. dir. World Affairs Council, Boston, 1949-55; asst. editor Harvard Bus. Rev., mem. faculty, also editor Harvard Bus. Sch. Bull., Harvard Bus. Sch., 1955-61; spl. asst. to Senator Smith, 1961; staff asst. to Pres. Kennedy, 1961-63; mem. U.S. Tariff Commn., 1963-67, vice chmn., 1964-65; pres. Center Bus.-Govt. Relations, Inc., Washington, 1967-71; dir. John F. Kennedy Library, Waltham, Mass., 1971—; mem. faculty, lectr. Harvard Grad. Sch. Bus. Adminstrn., also sr. asso. Mass. Inst. Tech.-Harvard Joint Center on Urban Studies, 1969-74. Mem. pres.'s del. Algerian Independence Day, 1963; sec., Lexington (Mass.) Sch. Com., 1957-61; mem. Lexington Town Meeting, 1953-61, 71—; del. Mass. Democratic Conv., 1954, 56, 58, 60; Dem. nominee for Mass. Legislature, 1952; alt. del.-at-large Dem. Nat. Conv., 1960; trustee Browne and Nichols Sch., 1959-61. Served with USAAF, 1943-45; ETO. Decorated by Govt. Morocco, 1952. Mem. Phi Beta Kappa. Unitarian. Author: Citizens Guide to International Relations, 1953. Editor: Management Guide to Overseas Operations, 1957; Management in a Rapidly Changing Economy, 1958; Management's Mission in a New Society, 1959; Business Responsibility in Action, 1960; Managing America's Economic Explosion, 1961; co-author: Cases in Business and Government, 1966; The Social Audit, 1972; co-editor: Planning the Future Strategy of your Business, 1956; Incentives for Executives, 1962; Management of Materials Research, 1962. Home: 130 Worthen Rd Lexington MA 02173 Office: John F Kennedy Library 380 Trapelo Rd Waltham MA 02154 also Harvard Bus Sch Soliders Field Boston MA 02163*

FENN, EUGENE HENRY, lithography co. exec.; b. Hackensack, N.J., Jan. 1, 1930; s. Gustave Charles and Theresa Marie (Oberle) F.; B.S., Bowling Green State U., 1951; m. Thelma Mildred Miller; children—Kathleen Ann, Nancy Jeanne, Ellen Gray. With Fenn & Fenn, Inc., Lithographers, N.Y.C., 1956—; pres., 1966—. Served to 1st lt. USAF, 1952-55. Mem. Printing Industries Met. N.Y. (dir.), Advt. Sportsmen of N.Y., Sigma Chi. Roman Catholic. Clubs: N.Y. Athletic; Ridgewood (N.J.) Country. Home: 50 Edgewood Dr Ho Ho Kus NJ 07423 Office: Fenn & Fenn Inc 75 Varick St New York City NY 10013

FENNEMAN, LAWRENCE BRITTINGHAM, JR., indsl. real estate cons. and appraiser; b. Balt., Jan. 6, 1929; s. Lawrence B. and Helen M. (Martien) F.; student Johns Hopkins U., 1949-50; m. Cary Randolph Sheets, Aug. 2, 1958; children—Cynthia, Carol, Anne. Real estate salesman William Martien & Co., Inc., 1955-59, Balt.; asst. mgr. Charles Center Mgmt. Office, Balt., 1959-63; exec. v.p., cons. indsl. real estate Kornblatt & Fenneman, Inc., Balt., 1963-75; pres. Santa Claus Anonymous, Inc., 1960-61, Balt. Heritage, Inc., 1962-63; dir. Spicer Inc., F. Bowie Smith & Sons, Inc., instr. Grad. Realtors Inst., Md. univs., 1970—. Mem. exec. com. v.p. March of Dimes, Balt., 1974—; mem. Balt. Harbor Planning Com., 1975—; treas. bd. trustees Grace United Methodist Ch., Balt., 1974—; past bd. dirs. Citizens Planning and Housing Assn.; bd. dirs. German Children's Home, 1975—, Balt. Salvation Army, 1976—; mem. Commn. on Govtl. Efficiency and Economy, Balt., 1976—. Served with USN, 1946-48, 50-51. Named Realtor of the Yr., State of Md., 1968. Mem. Soc. Indsl. Realtors (dir. 1973-75, nat. chmn. appraisal com. 1968-69, 74-75), Nat. Inst. Real Estate Brokers, Balt. Jr. C. of C., Real Estate Bd. Greater Balt. (pres. 1970-71), Md. Assn. of Realtors Realtors (dir. 1966-68), Am. Inst. Planning, Md. Hist. Soc., Balt. Mus. Art, Wine and Food Soc., Balt. Investment and Exchange Council (pres. 1967-69), Sales and Mktg. Execs. Internat. (pres. Md. Chpt. 1969-70). Democrat. Clubs: Rotary (dir. 1969-71), Propeller, Merchants, Paint and Powder (dir. 1961-65), Maryland Water Ski (pres. 1962-63), Gibson Island, Gibson Island Yacht Squadron, Rotary Yacht Squadron of Chesapeake Bay. Address: 17 Chiara Ct Baltimore MD 21204

FENTEN, D(ONALD) X., author; b. N.Y.C., Jan. 3, 1932; s. Harry J. and Ethel Esther (Scheinwald) F.; B.A., N.Y. U., 1953, M.A., 1954; postgrad. Columbia U., 1956-57; m. Barbara Doris Levy, Apr. 7, 1957; children—Donna Ruth, Jeffrey Allan. Free lance writer and photographer for various mags. including Weekend Gardener, Newsday, L.I. Mag., 1974—; garden specialist Newsday, 1978—. Served with AUS, 1954-56. Mem. Am. Hort. Soc., Garden Writers Assn. Am., Authors Guild. Author: Flower and Garden Photography, 1966; Better Photography for Amateurs, 1960; Electric Eye Still Photography, 1961; Plants for Pots, 1969; Aviation Careers, 1969; Greenhorn's Guide to Gardening, 1969; Sea Careers, 1970; Harvesting the Sea, 1970; Ms.-M.D., 1973; Ms.-Atty., 1974; Gardening Naturally, 1973; Making of a Police Officer, 1972; The Organic Grow It, Cook It, Preserve It Guidebook, 1972; First Book Indoor Gardening, 1974; The Concise Guide to Natural Foods, 1974; Greenhousing for Purple Thumbs, 1976; TV and Radio Careers, 1976; Ms.-Architect, 1977; Reserving Your Career in Tourism and Hospitality, 1978, others.

FENTON, FRANK HALLOWELL, JR., engr.; b. Rockledge, Pa., Dec. 23, 1924; s. Frank Hallowell and Jeanne Anderson (Dewar) F.; B.S.M.E., Drexel U., 1948, M.S., 1959; m. Marion Mae Doan, 1957; children—Martha Mae, Frank Hallowell. Mech. engr. U.S. Naval Air. Devel. Center, Johnsville, Pa., 1948-51; research engr. Leeds & Northrup Co., North Wales, Pa., 1951-59; electronic engr. U.S. Naval Air Devel. Center, Johnsville, 1959-64; sect. mgr. Combustion Engring., Inc., Windsor, Conn., 1964-76; pres. FPA Corp., Avon, Conn., 1977—. Mem. IEEE, AAAS. Republican. Congregationalist. Club: Hartford Chorale. Home: 54 Fox Den Rd Avon CT 06001 Office: PO Box 698 Avon CT 06001

FENTON, M(ATTHEW) ROBERT, landscape architect; b. Latrobe, Pa., July 19, 1932; s. Matthew Russell and Helen Mae (Reed) F.; B.S., Pa. State U., 1954; M. in Landscape Arch., Harvard, 1958; m. Heidi Brockmann, Mar. 9, 1962; 1 son, Mattias Robin. Prin. landscape architect M. Robert Fenton & Assos., Pitts., 1958—; lectr. Grad. Sch. Urban Design, Carnegie-Mellon U., Pitts., 1964-65. Mem. Pa. State Art Commn., Harrisburg, 1972-77. Recipient Charles Eliot Traveling fellowship Harvard U., 1960. Mem. Am. Soc. Landscape Architects (Merit award 1965, Honor award 1966), AIA, Am. Inst. Planners (asso.), Am. Rhododendron Soc. (chpt. pres. 1969-70), Pitts. Symphony Soc. Clubs: University, Harvard-Yale-Princeton (Pitts). Patentee in field. Home: 445 Olympia Rd Pittsburgh PA 15211 Office: 1115 Arch St Pittsburgh PA 15212

FENTON, MATTHEW CLARK, III, automobile dealer; b. Balt., Dec. 19, 1925; s. Matthew Clark, Jr. and Beatrice (Trail) F.; A.B., Dartmouth Coll., 1949; m. Mary Lou Dodson; children—Matthew Clark, Sally D. With Cheasapeake Cadillac Co., Balt., 1954—, dir., 1959—, v.p., 1960-65, pres., 1966—; v.p., dir., chmn. exec. com. Landau Corp.; dir. Provident Savs. Bank. Chmn., Balt. City Employees Incentive Awards Bd., 1968—; mem. Commn. on Phys. Fitness for State of Md., 1968-72; active YMCA; bd. dirs. Better Bus. Bur. Balt. Served with USAAF, World War II; to capt. USMC, 1949-54. Mem. Automobile Trade Assn. Md. (pres.). Clubs: Rotary, Maryland, Balt. Country, L'Hirondelle, Bachelors Cotillon, Wednesday. Home: 1015 Winding Way Baltimore MD 21210 Office: 2401 N Charles St Baltimore MD 21218

FENVESSY, STANLEY JOHN, mgmt. cons.; b. Rochester, N.Y., Oct. 30, 1918; s. John H.W. and Bessie Ruth (Weber) F.; B.S. in Econs., U. Pa., 1940; LL.B., Georgetown U., 1943; m. Doris Goodman, July 10, 1943; children—Alice Fenvessy Healy, Barbara Fenvessy Reese. With Aldens, Inc., Chgo., 1945-50; admitted to Ill. bar, 1947; prin. Cresap, McCormick and Paget, N.Y.C., 1950-55; exec. v.p. Am. Merchandising div. Rapid Am. Corp., N.Y.C., 1955-60; adminstrv. v.p. Ethan Allen, Inc., Danbury, Conn., 1960-65; pres. Fenvessy Assos., Inc., mgmt. cons., N.Y.C., 1965—; dir. Present Co., Inc., Lillian Vernon Corp. Served to lt. (s.g.) Intelligence Corps, USNR, 1941-45. Mem. Chgo. Bar Assn., Inst. Mgmt. Cons., Assn. Cons. Mgmt. Engrs. (sec., treas., dir.), Am. Arbitration Assn. Republican. Club: University (N.Y.C.). Author: Keep Your Customers and Keep Them Happy, 1976; contbr. to Graphic Arts Manual, Mag. Pub. Mgmt., Direct Mail Advt., Selling for Retailers, also bus. publs.; patentee addressing methods. Home: 205 E 63d St New York City NY 10021 Office: 745 Fifth Ave New York City NY 10022

FENWICK, MILLICENT HAMMOND, congresswoman; b. N.Y.C., Feb. 25, 1910; d. Ogden Haggerty and Mary Picton (Stevens) Hammond; student Columbia, New Sch. for Social Research; hon. degrees, Stevens Inst. Tech., 1975, Jersey City State Coll., 1975, Newark State Coll., 1975, Drew U., 1976; m. 1932 (div.); children—Mary Stevens (Mrs. Kenneth Reckford), Hugh H. Mem. Bernardsville Bd. Edn., 1936-41, Bernardsville Borough Council, 1958-62, Gen. Assembly N.J., 1970-73; mem. 94th-96th Congresses from 5th N.J. Dist.; dir. Div. Consumer Affairs, N.J. Dept. Law and Pub. Safety, 1973-74. Vice Chmn., N.J. Com. for U.S. Commn. on Civil Rights, 1958-70; past pres. Somerset County Legal Aid Soc. Home: Bernardsville NJ 07924 Office: Longworth House Office Bldg Washington DC 20515

FEODOROFF, NICHOLAS VASILIEVICH, educator; b. Imperial, Russia, Nov. 30, 1901; s. Vasiliy Petrovich and Olga Andreevna (Myagkova) F.; came to U.S., 1929, naturalized, 1938; B.S. in Adminstrn., Svobodnya U. (Bulgaria), 1929; B.S., Columbia, 1935, M.C.E., 1936; D.C.E., Sequoia U., 1952. Head research engrs. Research Bd. Water Supply, Honolulu, 1937-38; head research asso. fluid mech., hydraulics Columbia, N.Y.C., 1939-54; vis. prof. Manhattan Coll., N.Y.C., 1941-48, asso. prof. fluid mech., hydraulics, 1948-68, dir. commonwealth edison research project, 1950-51, whirlpool research project, 1952-53; prof. engring. N.Y. U., N.Y.C., 1946-48; adj. prof. Farleigh Dickinson U., Rutherford and Teaneck, N.J., 1955-60; dir. Applied Physics Found., Palo Alto, Calif., 1955; adj. prof. City Coll. N.Y., 1965—; prof. hydraulic engring., Internat. Technol. Inst. for Hydraulic and San. Engring., U. Netherlands, 1960—; cons. W. Briggs Engring. Co., New Rochelle, N.Y., 1939-55, Engring. Research Devel. Corp., Palo Alto, 1947-50. Pres., Gen. Peter Nikolaevich Krasnoh Found., Howell, N.J., 1965-73; v.p. Russian Am. Aid Assn., N.Y.C., 1973—; del. Republican Heritage Congress Washington and Phila., 1972-76; pres. Russian Am. Rep. Club, Howell, 1968-73. Served with White Russian Army, 1917-20. Decorated St. George Medal; officer Nat. Acad. Scis., golden cross Chypre and Jerusalem, comdr. Ordre du Merite pour la Rechereche et l'Invention, Acad. Palm medal, officer Ordre Palmes Academique (France); recipient J.C. Stevens award Am. Soc. Civil Engrs., 1944, medaille d'argent Renaissance Francaise, Pres. and Ministers France, 1953, Meml. Cross of Legion, Nat. Legion of Greek Am. War Vets. Am., 1958, Medaille D'Honneur, Societe d'Encouragement au Progress, 1966, others. Fellow N.Y. Acad. Sci. (hon., sec. 1953-55, chmn. sect. math. and engring. 1955-57), AAAS (hon.), Royal Soc. Eng., ASCE, French Nat. Assn. Croix de Guerre (Am. chpt.); mem. Am. Soc. Engring. Edn. (life), Am. Geophys. Union, Am. Soc. Mil. Engrs., ASME, Nat. Soc. C.E., Nat. Soc. Prof. Engring., Internat. Assn. Hydraulic Research, Soc. Relief Russian War Vets. Outside Russia (pres. 1967—), Cossacks Outside Russia (pres. 1970—), Royal Soc. Arts (England), Russian Scholars in Am. (dir. 1974—, emeritus mem.), Sigma Xi, Chi Epsilon. Russian Orthodox. Club: Faculty Columbia Univ. Author numerous scientific papers. Home and Office: 16 Ford Rd Howell NJ 07731

FERBER, ROMAN, city planner; b. Krakow, Poland, Jan. 25, 1933; s. Leon and Malia (Chilowicz) F.; B.A., Hunter Coll., 1958; M. Pub. Adminstrn., N.Y. U., 1959, Ph.D., 1965; m. Maxine Singer, Sept. 4, 1961; children—Leonard, Andrew, Julie. Instr. polit. sci. Hunter Coll., N.Y.C., 1960; cons. N.Y.C. Dept. City Planning, 1961-63, dept. dir. comprehensive planning, 1963-69, dir. adminstrn., fiscal mgmt., 1969-71; asso. prof. polit. sci. City U. N.Y., 1966-75; asso. prof. politics N.Y. U., 1967—; prof. urban politics Lehman Coll., N.Y.C., 1971. treas. N.Y.C. Indsl. Devel. Corp., N.Y.C. Dept. Commerce and Industry, 1971-75; dir. financial services N.Y.C. Econ. Devel. Adminstrn., 1975—; exec. dir. N.Y.C. Indsl. and Comml. Incentive Bd., 1977—; treas. N.Y.C. Indsl. Devel. Corp.; v.p. Investors Realty Fund, N.Y.C. Mem. Local Planning Bds., N.Y.C., 1964, 65-68. Served with U.S. Army, 1953-55. Recipient N.Y.U. Founders award, 1966; Werner Hegerman Planning fellow, 1959, Bd. Higher Edn. fellow, 1960, N.Y.U. scholar, 1961. Mem. Exec. Bd. Dining Room Employees Union, 1972—. Mem. Am. Inst. Planners, Am. Polit. Sci. Assn., Met. Pub. Personnel Soc., Profl. Assn. Pub. Execs. City of N.Y. Author: Port of New York and the Management of Its Waterfront, 1959; The Lower East Side, A Community Report, 1962; Management Practices in the Planning Profession, 1971; Problems and Pitfalls of Quantitative Methods in Urban Analysis. Contbr. articles to profl. jours. Home: 5 Iroquois Trail Monsey NY 10952

FERBER, SAMUEL, advt. exec.; b. N.Y.C., June 6, 1920; s. Isidor and Sadie (Irgang) F.; B.B.A., Coll. City N.Y., 1941; postgrad. Columbia U., 1946-48; m. Beatrice Ruth Ziman, June 18, 1944; children—Bruce Joseph, Joel David. Promotion dir. Nat. Advt. Service, Inc., N.Y.C., 1946-50, Boys' Life Mag., N.Y.C., 1950-52; promotion dir. Esquire Mag., N.Y.C., 1952-58, advt. mgr., 1959-65, sr. v.p., asso. pub., 1965-70, advt. dir., 1970-74, pub., 1974-76; sr. v.p. Altman, Stoller, Weiss Advt., N.Y.C., 1976—; faculty econs. and advt. Latin Am. Inst., N.Y.C., 1946-49; lectr. in field. Leader, Gt. Books Discussion Group; co-dir. Bus. and the Arts Awards Program; mem. arts adv. bd. N.Y. Bd. Trade, 1969-73. Home: 17 Solar Ln Searingtown NY 11507 Office: New York City NY

FERDINAND, JOSEPH BENNET, found exec.; b. Drifton, Pa., Feb. 19, 1921; s. Louis J. and Grace P. F.; B.S., E. Stroudsburg U., 1942; M.S., U. Pa., 1952, M.S. in Edn.; m. Louise Kerslake, Dec. 28, 1946; children—Paul M., Janet L. Tchr., Devereux Sch., Devon, Pa., 1945-46, prin., 1946-51, dir. edn., 1951-55; dir. adminstrv. services Devereux Found., Devon, 1955-69, dir. adminstrn., 1969-75, pres., 1975—; coll. lectr.; cons. in field. Served with U.S. Army, 1942-45. Decorated Purple Heart, Bronze Star. Fellow Am. Assn. Mental Deficiency; mem. NEA (life), Internat. Assn. Mental Deficiency, Am. Assn. Sch. Adminstrs., Pa. Assn. Residents Retarded, Nat. Assn. Pvt. Schs. for Exceptional Children. Clubs: Elks, Rotary (pres.; regional, nat. offices). Lectr. in therapeutic edn., mental health, habilitation, rehab.; contbr. papers to publs. Home: 300 Kirkland Ave Westchester PA 19380 Office: 19 S Waterloo Rd Devon PA 19333

FERENCZ, WILLIAM ROBERT, coll. adminstr.; b. Blairsville, Pa., May 3, 1925; s. Anton W. and Zuzie (Miko) F.; B.S., Ind. State U. Pa., 1949; M.A., Allegheny Coll., 1955; postgrad. U. Colo., 1958, Syracuse U., 1960, Pa. State U., 1964—; m. Dorothy Louise Sutton, Dec. 28, 1946; children—Lucinda Kay (Mrs. John L. Rollin). Tchr., dept. chmn. Cambridge Springs (Pa.) High Sch., 1955-61; instr., bus. instr. Mohawk Valley Community Coll., Utica, N.Y., 1961-64; grad. asst. Pa. State U., University Park, 1964-65; prof., div. chmn. bus. and mgmt. services div. Harrisburg (Pa.) Area Community Coll., 1965—. Grad. asst. Inst. Life Ins., 1964-65. Served with AUS, 1944-46. Decorated Bronze Star medal, Purple Heart. Mem. Am. Advt. Fedn., Appalachian Financial Mgmt. Assn., Adminstrv. Mgmt. Soc. (pres. Harrisburg chpt. 1970-71), Nat. Assn. Accountants (pres. Harrisburg chpt. 1971-73), Phi Delta Kappa (pres. Utica Field chpt. 1960-61), Delta Pi Epsilon, Iota Lambda Sigma. Home: 4301 Beaufort Hunt Dr

Harrisburg PA 17110 Office: 3300 Cameron St Rd Harrisburg PA 17110

FERENS, MARCELLA (MRS. JOSEPH J. FERENS), educator; b. Pitts.; d. Ignatius and Marcella (Buzas) Slevinskas; student Greensburg Bus. Coll., 1934-35, Maison Frederic Cosmetology, 1936, Kree Inst. Electrolysis, N.Y., 1952; B.S., U. Pitts., 1957; postgrad. Mid-Western U., 1962; M.Ed., Duquesne U., 1964; m. Joseph J. Ferens, Nov. 27, 1937; children—Joseph Ferens, James. Cosmetologist and electrologist, Manor and Darragh, Pa., 1937—; research in hair regrowth, Darragh, 1954—; tchr. algebra, reading and drama dir. Harold Jr. High Sch., Greensburg, Pa., 1958—; tchr. cosmotology Uniontown (Pa.) Vocational High, 1954-55. Insp. Chem. Corps, Dept. of Army, N.Y. 1951. Mem. Nat. Council Tchrs. Math., Nat., Pa. edn. assns. Patentee in field. Home: Box 84 Daragh PA 15625 Office: RFD 6 Greensburg PA 15601

FERET, ADAM EDWARD, JR., dentist; b. Newark, Mar. 5, 1942; s. Adam Edward and Bronislawa Anne (Szorc) F.; B.A. (athletic scholar), Seton Hall U., 1963; D.M.D., Coll. Medicine and Dentistry of N.J., 1967. Pvt. practice dentistry, Westfield, N.J., 1972—. Served with USNR, 1967-70. Mem. Am., N.J. dental assns., Plainfield County Dental Soc., Am. Soc. Preventive Dentistry, Am. Acad. Gen. Dentistry, Bergen Acad. Dental Practice Adminstrn., L.D. Pankey Inst. Advanced Dental Edn. Alumni Assn., L.D. Pankey Study Club, Internat. Coll. Oral Implantologists, Am. Acad. Implant Dentistry, Soc. Oral Physiology and Occlusion, Polish Falcons of Am., Psi Omega. Roman Catholic. Home: 169 Mountain Ave Westfield NJ 07090 Office: 169 Mountain Ave Westfield NJ 07090

FERGUSON, DONALD GUFFEY, radiologist; b. W. Newton, Pa., July 19, 1923; s. Rutherford Hayes and Beulah Cristabel (Guffey) F.; B.S., U. Pitts., 1944, M.D., 1946; m. Anne Benedict Gallagher, Mar. 4, 1961. Intern, S. Side Hosp., Pitts., 1946-47; resident in radiology and radiation therapy Meml. Sloan-Kettering, N.Y.C., 1950-52; Am. Cancer Soc. fellow, staff radiologist Thomas Jefferson U. Hosp., Phila., 1952-55; attending radiologist Mercy Hosp., Pitts., 1955-57; sr. staff S. Side Hosp., Pitts., 1957—, St. Clair Meml. Hosp., Pitts., 1957—; clin. asst. prof. radiology U. Pitts., 1956—. Served with M.C., U.S. Army, 1948-50. Diplomate Am. Bd. Radiology, Am. Bd. Nuclear Medicine. Fellow Am. Coll. Radiology (dist. councilor 1972—, 1st v.p. Pa. chpt. 1977); mem. Soc. Nuclear Medicine (chpt. pres. 1957-58), Pitts. Roentgen Soc. (pres. 1967-68), Am. Med. Assn., Pa. Med. Soc., Radiol. Soc. N. Am., Allegheny County Med. Soc., Pitts. Athletic Assn. Presbyterian. Club: Masons (Shriner). Home: Hidden Valley Rd Canonsburg PA 15317 Office: 1000 Bower Hill Rd Pittsburgh PA 15243

FERGUSON, DOROTHY MARGUERITTE, orgn. adminstr.; b. Dorchester, Mass., Apr. 25, 1912; d. John Robert and Josephine (Friel) Hughes; student U. Pa., 1929-31, U. Md., 1947-48; m. Daniel J. M. Ferguson, Feb. 12, 1938; children—Gail Ferguson Washburn, Diane Ferguson Donaldson. Adminstrv. asst. to pres. Save the Children Fedn., Norwalk, Conn., 1958-61; adminstrv. asst. to pres., adminstr. community devel. tng. program, writer, editor Community Devel. Found., N.Y.C. and Norwalk, Conn., 1962-67, cons., Westport, Conn., 1968—; editor, writer, officer Internat. Soc. Community Devel., 1968—; instr., cons. in field. Precinct chmn. Silver Spring Republican Com., 1950-57; area chmn. Heart Assn., Norwalk, Conn., 1964-65. Mem. Nat. Conf. Social Welfare, Internat. Council on Social Welfare, Internat. Soc. Community Devel. (sec.-treas.). Roman Catholic. Club: Viking Yacht. Author manuals for handling displaced refugees in Vietnam, 1968-69; contbr. articles to newsletters and jours. of Internat. Soc. Community Devel. Home: 43 East Ave Norwalk CT 06851 Office: Internat Soc Community Devel UN Plaza 345 E 46th St New York NY 10017

FERGUSON, GLENN WALKER, broadcasting exec.; b. Syracuse, N.Y., Jan. 28, 1929; s. Forrest Erwin and Mabel Gertrude (Walker) F.; B.A., Cornell U., 1950, M.B.A., 1951; student U. Santo Tomas, Manila, 1952-53, U. Chgo. Law Sch., 1955-56; J.D., U. Pitts., 1957; D.Sc. (hon.), Worcester Poly. Inst., 1973; LL.D. (hon.), Sacred Heart U., 1974; m. Patricia Lou Head, June 22, 1950; children—Bruce Walker, Sherry Lynn, Scott Sherwood. Staff asso. Govtl. Affairs Inst., Washington, 1954-55; asst. editor, asst. sec.-treas. Am. Judicature Soc., Chgo., 1955-56; adminstrv. asst. to chancellor U. Pitts., 1956-57, asst. dean, asst. prof. pub. adminstrn. Grad. Sch. Pub. and Internat. Affairs, 1957-59, asso. dir. Coordinated Edn. Center, 1959-60; with McKinsey & Co., mgmt. cons., Washington, 1960-61; with Peace Corps, 1961-64, dir. Thailand, 1961-63, asso. dir., Washington, 1963-64; dir. Vols. in Service to Am. (VISTA), Washington, 1964-66; U.S. ambassador to Kenya, 1966-69; pres. Clark U., Worcester, Mass., 1970-73; pres. U. Conn., 1973-78; chief exec. officer Radio Free Europe/Radio Liberty, Munich, W. Ger., 1978—; cons. govtl. agys., 1959-64; TV moderator fgn. affairs, Pitts., 1957-60; dir. Equator Bank Ltd. Bd. dirs. Fgn. Policy Assn., Pvt. Export Funding Co.; mem. Cornell U. Council; trustee Cornell U., 1972-76; bd. dirs. Radio Free Europe, Radio Liberty. Served to 1st lt. USAF, 1951-53; Korea. Recipient Arthur S. Flemming award, 1968. Mem. Am. Polit. Sci. Assn., Fed. Bar Assn., Am. Judicature Soc., Council Fgn. Relations, Century Assn., Phi Beta Kappa, Psi Upsilon, Phi Delta Phi. Club: Internat. (Washington). Contbr. articles to profl. jours. Office: Radio Free Europe 1201 Connecticut Ave NW Washington DC 20036

FERGUSON, LAING, educator; b. Dunfermline, Fife, Scotland, Apr. 25, 1935; s. David and Margaret Penman Archibald (Laing) F.; B.S. with honors in Geology, U. Edinburgh, 1957, Ph.D., 1960; m. Katherine Joyce Kirk, Aug. 6, 1960; children—Neil Robert, Andrew David, Kirk. Postdoctoral fellow U. Alta., Edmonton, 1960-62; asst. prof. Mt. Allison U., Sackville, N.B., Can., 1962-68, asso. prof., 1968-78, prof., 1978—, head dept. geology, 1973—, also mem. exec. com. bd. regents, 1972-76, bd. regents, 1976—; postdoctoral fellow U. Edinburgh (Scotland), 1969-70. Chmn. Amnesty Internat. Can. 4, Sackville, 1971-76, anglophone v.p. Canadian nat. sect., 1974-76, pres., 1976-78; mem. N.B. adv. bd. Canadian Scholarship Trust Found., 1973—. Fellow geol. socs. London, Edinburgh, Am., Linnean Soc. London, Geol. Assn. Can. (exec. paleontol. div.); mem. Soc. Econ. Paleontologists and Mineralogists, Paleontol. Soc. U.S., Palaeontol. Assn. U.K., Marine Biol. Assn. U.K., Am. Assn. Petroleum Geologists, Systematics Assn., Palaeontographical Soc., Brit. Micropaleontol. Soc., Atlantic Geosci. Soc. (exec.). Asso. editor Maritime Sediments, 1966—, Geoscience Canada, 1976—. Home: Box 892 156 W Main St Sackville NB E0A 3C0 Canada

FERGUSON, LESLIE LEE, JR., educator; b. Pomona, Calif., Sept. 12, 1940; s. Leslie Lee and Wanda Viola (Wells) F.; B.A., La Sierra Coll., 1965; M.A., Loma Linda U., 1971; m. Bonnie B. Bortel, Aug. 20, 1969; 1 dau., Heather Lynn. Tchr. music So. Calif. Conf. Seventh-day Adventists, Long Beach, 1965; secondary tchr. French, music Highland View Acad., Hagerstown, Md., 1967-71; secondary tchr. French, Pioneer Valley Acad., New Braintree, Mass., 1971—. Mem. curriculum com. N.Am. div. Seventh-Day Adventist Secondary Schs., 1974—, curriculum com. Atlantic Union Conf., 1975—. Served with U.S. Army, 1965-67. Mem. Nat. Assn. Tchrs. French, Nat. Assn. Tchrs. Singing, Aircraft Owners and Pilots Assn., Am. Audubon Soc. Republican. Home: 14 Circle Dr New Braintree MA 01531 Office: Pioneer Valley Acad New Braintree MA 01531

FERGUSON, MARIAN RAND, editor; b. N.Y.C., June 20, 1945; d. Samuel and Marian (Merrill) Ferguson; B.A., Wellesley Coll., 1967; m. Richard Hays Hawkins, III, June 18, 1977. Editorial asst. Worth Pubs., Berkeley, Calif., 1968-70; free lance agt., San Francisco area, 1970-71; coll. text. editor psychology and history Little Brown Co., Boston, 1971—. Mem. Am. Hist. Assn., Am. Psychol. Assn. Office: 34 Beacon St Boston MA 02106

FERGUSON, ROBERT S., film cons.; b. N.Y.C., May 8, 1915; s. Samuel I. and Augusta H. F.; B.S., N.Y. U., 1936; m. Helene B., Aug. 1, 1940; children—Carole Jane, Sandra Joan. With Scripps-Howard Newspapers, 1936-38, Warner Bros. Pictures, 1938-40; v.p. world-wide mktg. Columbia Pictures, Inc., 1940-73; v.p. corp. relations Columbia Pictures Industries, Inc., 1973-74; v.p. world mktg. Am. Film Theatre, 1974-75; v.p. div. entertainment Rosenfeld. Sirowitz & Lawson Advt., 1975-76; v.p. world mktg. Horizon Pictures, 1976-77; pres. Cinema Think Tank, 1977—; instr. in film Adelphi U. Mem. Motion Picture Acad. Arts, Sci., Motion Picture Pioneers, Screen Publicists Guild (pres.), Variety Clubs Internat., Motion Picture Assn. Am. (chmn. com. advt. dirs.). Home: 84 Fulton Ave Atlantic Beach NY 11509

FERGUSON, THEODORE JOHN, JR., physician; b. Oakmont, Pa., Mar. 15, 1923; s. Theodore John and Daisy Mae (Dunlap) F.; A.B., Coll. of Wooster, 1945; M.D., Case Western Res. U., 1948; m. Doris Jean Stoner, Mar. 23, 1946; children—Patricia Ann Ferguson Woltjen, Sharon Jean Ferguson Ehrlich. Intern, St. Margaret Meml. Hosp., Pitts., 1948-49; resident in rheumatology Montefiore Hosp., Pitts., 1949-50; practice medicine specializing in family practice, Verona, Pa., 1950—; mem. referring staff dept. gen. medicine East Suburban Health Center; mem. staff Columbia Hosp., Pitts. Bd. dirs. Monroeville Blood Bank, 1961-64. Served with U.S. Army, 1943, capt. M.C., 1952-54; Korea. Diplomate Am. Bd. Family Practice. Mem. Am. Med. Assn., Pa., Allegheny County med. socs. Republican. Presbyterian. Clubs: Kiwanis (pres. 1959-60) (Verona-Rosedale Pa.); Oakmont (Pa.) Country; Masons. Home: 1063 Wade Ln Oakmont PA 15139 Office: 5802 Verona Rd Verona PA 15147

FERGUSON, WILLIAM HOMER, business inst. exec.; b. Vandergrift, Pa., Jan. 19, 1929; s. Homer V. and Genevieve (Artman) F.; B.S., U. Pitts., 1951; m. Carol B. Finkelhor, Apr. 6, 1963; 2 children. With Pitts.-Des Moines Steel Co., 1953-63; pres. Duff's Bus. Inst., Pitts., 1963—, Duff's Bus. Coll., Jamaica, W.I., 1965—, Duff's Ltd., Barbados, W.I., 1966—, Duff's Internat., 1971—, John Robert Powers Sch., Pitts., 1971—, Fashion Acad. of Pitts., 1971—. Served with AUS, 1951-53. Mem. Pa. C. of C., Theta Chi. Mason. Home: Baldwin Rd Box 468 Pittsburgh PA 15205 Office: Landmark Bldg 209 4th Ave Pittsburgh PA 15222

FERGUSSON, ROBERT LAURENCE, psychiatrist; b. Dallas, Dec. 14, 1925; s. Robert Lawrence and Eula Pearl (Turner) F.; student Princeton, 1944-45, Columbia, 1945; B.A., Harvard, 1950; student So. Methodist U., 1952; M.D., U. Tex., 1956; postgrad. Yale, 1958-60, N.Y. U., 1961-63, U. Pa., 1970-72. Intern St. Elizabeth Hosp., Washington, 1956-57, Providence Hosp., Washington, 1957-58; resident Conn. Valley Hosp., Middletown, Ct., 1958-60; resident Gracie Square Hosp., N.Y.C., 1960-61, sr. staff psychiatrist, 1960-67; dir., Pa. Hosp. at Byberry, 1968-69; dir. Psychiatry, Malvern (Pa.) Inst., 1970—. Numerous teaching, cons. appointments. Served to lt. (j.g.) USNR, 1943-46; PTO. Research grantee in chemotherapy, psychiat. milieus, alcoholism. Mem. AMA, Am. Psychiat. Assn., Am. Group Therapy Assn., Acad. Medicine and Parapsychology, S.A.R., Stars and Bars, Pi Kappa Alpha, Omicron Delta Kappa, Phi Chi. Republican. Episcopalian (mem. ch. bd.). Author: Alcoholism-A Dependency Disease, 1973. Research on librium in psychotics. Home: 922 Montgomery Ave Bryn Mawr PA 19010 Office: Malvern Inst King Rd Malvern PA 19355

FERLAND, ARMAND, musician, educator; b. St. Boniface, Man., Can., Mar. 31, 1926; s. Joseph A. and Anne-Marie (Prendergast) F.; B.A., U. Man., 1947; Premier prix Conservatoire de Musique, Montreal, Que., 1951; diploma Royal Mil. Sch. Music, Twickenham, Eng., 1954, Royal Acad. Music, London, 1953, London Guildhall Sch. Music, 1954; Mus. B., U. Laval (Que.), 1965, Mus.M., 1968; m. Genevieve Lavoie, Feb. 9, 1952; children—François, Pierre, Madeleine, Marc, Louis. Tchr. clarinet and saxophone Coll. Mont-St.Louis, Montreal, 1949-51; clarinettist Que. Symphony Orch., Quebec City, 1949-51, CBC Orch., Montreal, 1949-51, Matinées Symphoniques, Montreal, 1949-50; solo clarinettist Kneller Hall Band, 1952-54; appeared CBC and BBC radio broadcasts; enlisted warrant officer Canadian Army, 1951, advanced through grades to capt. 1959; dir. music, comdg. officer Royal Canadian Horse Arty. Band, Winnipeg, Man., 1955-61, concert tours, Sask., N.W. Ont., U.S., 1955-61; dir. music, comdg. officer Royal 22d Regiment Band, Quebec City, 1961-65; insp. bands in eastern Can., 1965-68; mus. dir. Canadian Armed Forces Tattoo, 1967; ret., 1968; instr. brass and woodwind instruments Greater Winnipeg (Man.) Sch. Dist., 1959; prof. clarinet Internat. High Sch. Music Camp, Internat. Peace Gardens, N.D., 1959; founder Quintette à vent de Québec, 1963; guest condr. Quebec CBC Orch., 1973, All Star Band, 1971; solo clarinettist Quebec CBC Orch., 1961-69; mem. Music Educators Nat. Conf., 1969—; lectr. conducting; mus. dir., prof. Camp Accord Parfait Inc., 1968-72, v.p., 1971-77; condr. Orford Art Centre, Mt. Orford, Que., summer 1973; lectr. clarinet and saxophone U. Laval, 1966-68, asso. prof., 1971-76, prof., 1976—, dir. applied music dept., 1973-78, sec. Sch. Music, 1978—. Mem. Internat. Clarinet Soc., Am. Fedn. Musicians, Canadian Bandmasters Assn. (pres. Man. chpt. 1959-60), Canadian Assn. Univ. Schs. Music (v.p. 1975—). Roman Catholic. Club: K.C. Home: 1196 Eugene Hamel Ste-Foy PQ G1W 4G4 Canada Office: Ecole de Musique U Laval Quebec PQ G1K 7P4 Canada

FERMAN, IRVING, lawyer, educator; b. N.Y.C., July 4, 1919; s. Joseph and Sadie (Stein) F.; B.S., N.Y.U., 1941; J.D., Harvard U., 1948; m. Bertha Paglin, June 12, 1946; children—James Paglin, Susan Paglin. Admitted to La. bar, 1948; partner firm Provensal, Faris & Ferman, New Orleans, 1948-52; v.p. Internat. Latex Corp., 1960-66; pres. Piedmont Theatres Corp., 1966-69; adj. asso. prof. mgmt. N.Y.U., 1964-67; prof. law Howard U. Law Sch., Washington, 1968—; vis. prof. law Am. U., 1971—; dir. Washington office ACLU, 1952-59, vice chmn. Nat. Civil Liberties Clearing House, 1952-54. Mem. citizens advisory com. U.S. Commn. on Govt. Security, 1957; vice chmn. Pres.'s Com. Govt. Contracts, 1959-60; mem. Am. Com. Cultural Freedom, 1954—, D.C. Health and Welfare Council; bd. dirs. New Orleans Acad. Art, 1948-51; mem. Com. of Arts and Scis. for Eisenhower, 1956; chmn. Washington Police Complaint Rev. Bd., 1965—; mem. Reviewing Authority HEW 1969—. Served from cadet to 1st lt. USAF, 1942-46. Mem. Am., Washington, La., New Orleans bar assns., Jewish. Clubs: Capitol Hill, Internat. (Washington); Harvard, Caterpillar (N.Y.C.); Army-Navy Country (Arlington, Va.). Home: 3818 Huntington St Washington DC 20015 Office: Howard U Law Sch 2935 Upton St NW Washington DC 20008 also Route 1 Sullivan Harbor ME 04682

FERN, RUTH KANE (MRS. WALLACE EDWARD FERN), educator; b. Somerville, N.J., May 12, 1919; d. James Aloysius and Marguerite Anne (Carberry) Kane; B.S., Trenton State Coll., 1941; M.A., N.Y. U., 1944; M.A. in Adminstrn., Montclair State Coll., 1953; postgrad. Columbia, 1957-69, New College, Oxford, Bedford Coll., U. London; m. Wallace Edward Fern, Sept. 3, 1960. Tchr. sr. English Flemington (N.J.) High Sch., 1941-44; dept. chmn., tchr. sr. English, Passaic Valley High Sch., Little Falls, 1944-51; instr. Newark State Coll., 1951-55, asst. prof., 1955-57; dir. pub. relations, 1952-57; asso. prof. English, edn., William Paterson Coll. of N.J., Wayne, 1958—. Cons., English Lang. Arts, Pequannock (N.J.) Pub. Schs., spring 1966, secondary sch. reading Pompton Lakes Pub. Schs., winter 1972. Vice-pres. Essex County (N.J.) Council State Employees, 1956-57. Flemington (N.J.) Bd. Edn. grantee, 1942-43. Mem. N.E.A. (life mem.), N.J. Edn. Assn. N.J. Assn. Tchrs. English (exec. bd. 1963—), Nat. Council Tchrs. English, Nat. Assn. Tchr. Educators, N.J. Hist. Soc., Delta Kappa Gamma (chpt. pres. 1970-72), Kappa Delta Pi, Pi Lambda Theta (co-founder, adviser chpt.). Contbr. articles to profl. pubs. Home: 62 Alpine Dr Wayne NJ 07470 Office: 300 Pompton Rd Wayne NJ 07470

FERNALD, CHARLES E., transp. co. exec.; b. Downingtown, Pa., Sept. 28, 1902; s. Joshiah Pennell and Sophia (Weltner) F.; student mech. engring. Drexel Inst. Tech., 1921-24; student Wharton Sch., U. Pa., 1926-30; m. Gertrude Marie Connell, Oct. 17, 1936; 1 son, Charles Edward. With credit dept. Notaseme Hosiery Co., 1919-22; purchasing agt. Haslett Chute & Conveyoı Co., Oaks, Pa., 1922-24; sr. Partner Fernald & Co., Phila., 1924-64; sec., dir., chmn. finance com. Chem. Leaman Tank Lines, Inc., Downington, 1964—. Active in work Republican Com. Past pres., trustee Credit Research Found. Served as lt. (j.g.) on spl. assignments USN, USCGR, World War II. C.P.A., Pa., N.J., N.Y., Ill. Mem. Am. Inst. C.P.A.'s, Pa., N.J., N.Y. Ill. socs. C.P.A.'s, Nat. Assn. Credit Mgmt. (past nat. pres.). Clubs: Poor Richard, Union League (Phila.); Union League (Chgo.); JDM Country (Palm Beach Gardens, Fla.). Home: 2600 N Flager Dr West Palm Beach FL 33407 Office: PO Box 179 Downingtown PA 19335

FERNANDES, JOHN PETER, camping and environ. edn. cons.; b. Cambridge, Mass., Sept. 28, 1941; s. John Matthew and Agnes Rose (Ferreira) F.; A.B., Boston Coll., 1963, M.Ed., 1964; m. Frances Marie Potts, Sept. 7, 1964; children—Leslie, Laurie. Program specialist environ. edn. Green Acres Day Camp, Waltham, Mass., 1968-69, exec. dir., 1969-75; tchr. English, Newton North High Sch., Newtonville, Mass., 1966—, developer curriculum environ. edn., 1974-75; camping cons. Colegio de Leon de Caracas (Venezuela), 1975; cons., day camping and environ. edn., Pilgrim Day Camp, Framingham, Mass., 1975—; mem. camp services children Met. Opportunity Council. Neighborhood commr. Cambridge Council Boy Scouts Am., 1962-63. Served with inf. AUS, 1964-66. Mem. New Eng. Day Camp Assn. (pres.), Am., New Eng. (dir.), Mass. (treas.) camping assns. Roman Catholic. Editor: Environmental Education: The Ashland Conference, 1973. Home and office: 370 Singletary Ln Framingham MA 01701

FERNANDEZ, JULIO ANTONIO, educator; b. Belize, British Honduras, July 27, 1936; s. Antonio and Rosalina (Torres) F.; came to U.S., 1956, naturalized, 1959; B.A., San Diego State Coll., 1963, M.A., 1964; Ph.D., U. Calif. at Santa Barbara, 1967; m. Doris Pearl Wells, Aug. 25, 1962. Instr. Spanish and Latin, St. John's Coll., Belize, Brit. Honduras, 1954-55; lectr. polit. sci. U. Calif. at Santa Barbara, 1966-67; asst. prof. polit. sci. U. Colo., Boulder, 1967-71; asso. prof. polit. sci. State U. N.Y., Cortland, 1971—. Served with USAF, 1956-60. O.A.S. Research fellow, 1966. Mem. Am. Polit. Sci. Assn., AAUP, Internat. Studies Assn., Latin Am. Studies Assn. Author: Political Administration in Mexico, 1969. The Political Elite in Argentina, 1970. Home: 832 N Lamont Dr Cortland NY 13045

FERNANDEZ, SECUNDINO, architect, planner; b. Havana, Cuba, Mar. 24, 1942; s. Secundino and Pilar (Villoria) F.; came to U.S., 1953, naturalized, 1961; B.S., City U. N.Y., 1965, B.Arch., 1966; M.S. in Architecture, Columbia U., 1967, M.S. in Urban Planning, 1970; m. Barbara Piscitello, Aug. 6, 1977. Architect, Hanford Yang Architect, 1964-67, Alexander Gartner Joint Ventures, 1968-71; project coordinator Gruen Assos., 1971-75; pvt. practice architecture and planning, N.Y.C., 1976—; pres. DAT Consultants, Ltd.; award-winning works include Bklyn. Borough Hall Sq., Hunters Point, Washington U. Sch. Law, Birmingham Civic Center, St. Joseph's Village, Roosevelt Island Housing, playground; prof. Pratt Inst., 1976—, City Coll., 1965, 70—; vis. prof. U. Iowa, 1968-70; urban design cons., Iowa City, 1968-70; adv. planner Communities of Chelsea and Arverne (N.Y.C.). Mem. AIA, Am. Inst. Planners, Archtl. League N.Y., Assn. Collegiate Schs. of Architecture, AAUP, Nat. Inst. Archtl. Edn. Author: The Grid-a Comparative Analysis, 1970. Home: 54 W 16th St New York City NY 10011 Office: 257 Park Ave S New York City NY 10010

FERNANDEZ-HERLIHY, LUIS, physician; b. San Diego, Feb. 3, 1926; s. Luis and Graciela (Herlihy) F.; student St. Louis U., 1943-45; M.D., Harvard U., 1949; m. Ruth Annis Stillman, Dec. 3, 1949; children—Christine, Sarah, Katherine, Elizabeth, Martha. Intern, Boston City Hosp., 1949-50, jr. asst. resident, 1950-51; fellow in internal medicine Mayo Found. for Med. Edn. and Research, Rochester, Minn., 1951-54; chief sect. rheumatology Lahey Clinic, Boston, 1957—; lectr. medicine Harvard Med. Sch.; mem. arthritis adv. com. FDA. Served to capt. M.C., U.S. Army, 1955-57. Diplomate Am. Bd. Internal Medicine. Fellow A.C.P.; mem. AMA, Mass., Charles River Dist. med. socs., Am. Rheumatism Assn., New Eng. Rheumatism Soc. (pres.), Arthritis Found. (trustee Mass. chpt.). Contbr. articles to med. jours. Office: Lahey Clinic Boston MA 02215

FERNANDEZ-MARCANE, LEONARDO LUIS, educator; b. Havano, Cuba, Dec. 10, 1937; s. Luis and Carmen (Fernandez) M-F.; LL.B. U. Havana, 1960; B.A. magna cum laude, U. P.R., 1965; M.A., State U. N.Y., Albany, 1967, Ph.D. with honors, 1974; 1 dau., Ana Maria. Sec. Consulate Republic of Colombia, Havana, 1958-60, chancellor, 1960-62; instr. romance langs. State U. N.Y., Albany, 1966-70, asst. prof. Spanish, 1970-74, asso. prof. Spanish, 1974—; vis. prof. Biscayne Coll., Fla., summer 1977; mem. editorial bd. Spanish Today Mag., 1970; book review editor, 1972—; dir. Cuadernos de Literatura. Recipient Nat. Literary award, Cruzada Educativa Cubana, 1975. Mem. Modern Lang. Assn., Am. Assn. Tchrs. Spanish and Portuguese, Circulo de Cultura Panamericano, Am. Literary Assn., State U. N.Y. Alumni Assn., Sigma Delta Pi. Democrat. Roman Catholic. Author: El Teatro de Tirso de Molina, Estudio de Onomatologia, 1973; 10 Anos de Revolucion Cubana, 1970; Prologue in J. Sanchez-Boudy, 1975; Antologia del Cuento Antillano, 1978; 20 Cuentistas Cubanos, 1978. Home: 900 SW 84 Ave Apt 315 Miami FL 33144 Office: Dept Spanish State Univ NY New Paltz NY 12561

FERNICOLA, ANTHONY RALPH, surgeon; b. Newark, Apr. 5, 1917; s. Gerard and Angela (Saracino) F.; B.S., Georgetown U., 1942, MD., 1945; M.Sc., U. Pa., 1950; m. Vera Alice Merlo, Apr. 23, 1955; children—Regina, Gregory, Lorraine, Ronald, Richard, Robert. Intern, Newark City Hosp., 1945-46, ice medicine specializing in urol. surgery, Newark, 1950—; attending urologist St. James Hosp., 1955—, pres. med. staff, 1966-67; attending urologist Clara Maass Meml. Hosp., Belleville, N.J., 1965—, Columbus Hosp., Newark, 1950—. Served to ensign, USNR, 1942-48. Recipient Prize essay award, N.Y. Urol. Soc., 1950; John Carroll award, Georgetown U. Alumni Assn., 1976. Diplomate Am. Bd. Urology. Fellow ACS; mem.

AMA, Am. Urol. Assn., Am. Med. Writers Assn., Georgetown U. Alumni Assn. (bd. govs. 1960-64), Admir al Farragut Acad. Alumni Assn. (pres. 1949-50). Club: Deal Golf and Country. Contbr. articles in field to med., scientific jours. Home: 7 Spier Ave Allenhurst NJ 07711 Office: 402 Mount Prospect Ave Newark NJ 07104

FERRAIOLI, CHARLES JOSEPH, accountant; b. Kearny, N.J., May 26, 1925; s. P. Charles and Anne (Auteri) F.; student Vanderbilt U., 1945-46; B.S., Seton Hall Coll., 1949; m. Grace Garbarino, June 3, 1950; children—Charles J., Brian K., Donald A. Agt., IRS, Dept. Treasury, Newark, 1950-53; sr. accountant Charles M. Yedwab, C.P.A., Paterson, N.J., 1953-56; owner C.J. Ferraioli & Co., C.P.A.'s, Pompton Lakes, N.J., 1956-69; partner Ferraioli, Wesdyk, Freifeld & Co., 1969-73— chmn. Ferraioli, Wesdyk, Freifeld, & Bruskin, 1974-75; pres., chmn. Ferraioli, Wesdyk, Freifeld, P.A., 1975—; sec.-treas., dir. Lakeland Leasing Corp., 1968-73, J.W. Felber, Inc., 1968-74. Chmn., Wanaque Mental Health Fund Drive, 1958, United Givers Fund Drive, Pompton Lakes, 1965; chmn. Passaic County Overall Econ. Devel. Plan Com., 1972-78. Campaign chmn. Wanaque Democratic Club, Wanaque 1956. Served with USNR, 1943-46. C.P.A., N.J. Mem. Am. Inst. C.P.A.'s, N.J. Soc. C.P.A.'s, Municipal Accountants Assn. N.J., Performing and Visual Arts Soc. (treas. 1975—), Awosting Assn. (treas. 1976), Am. Legion. Roman Catholic (former lector, lay leader, tchr.). K.C. Home: 118 Long Pond Rd Awosting Hewitt NJ 07421 Office: 256 Wanaque Ave Pompton Lakes NJ 07442

FERRARA, ANGELO CARMINE, physician; b. Bklyn., July 25, 1931; s. Joseph and Josephine (Gallo) F.; B.S., City U. N.Y., 1953; M.D., U. Rome, 1958; Ph.D., N.Y. U., 1977; m. Joyce Polvere, June 17, 1961; children—Lisa, Angela, Joseph, Carl, Christine. Intern, St. Vincents Hosp., N.Y.C., 1958-59, resident in pediatrics, 1959-61; resident in allergy Roosevelt Hosp., 1962-63; med. coordinator dept. pediatrics, pediatric allergy St. Vincent's Hosp., N.Y.C., 1963-69, attending, dept. pediatrics, 1963-69; dir. pediatric allergy clinics L.I. Coll. Hosp. and Luth. Hosp., Bklyn., 1963-65; dir. pediatric services and community programs St. Mary's Hosp., Bklyn., 1969-71, dir. allergy clinic, regional med. program, 1969-71; asso. attending Univ. and Bellevue Hosps., N.Y.C., 1969—, dir. infant transport service Bellevue Hosp., 1971—; asso. prof. pediatrics N.Y. U. Sch. Medicine; researcher epidemiology of infant transport services; lectr., cons. in field. Roman Catholic. Contbr. articles to profl. publs. Office: NY U Med Center 560 1st Ave New York City NY 10016

FERRARACCIO, FRANCISCO PAOLO, assn. exec.; b. Du Bois, Pa., Jan. 1, 1923; s. Biagio and Grace (DePalma) F.; B.S., Allegheny Coll., 1949, postgrad. econs., 1950; M.B.A., George Washington U., 1960; m. Margaret Louis McCrory, Aug. 27, 1949; children—Blaise Edward, Francis Paul, Christopher Michael. Adminstr. George Washington U. Hosp., Washington, 1950-65; adminstr. Cafritz Hosp., Washington, 1965-68; adminstr. Univ. Clinics George Washington U. Med. Center, Washington, 1968-71; exec. dir. Med. Soc. D.C., 1971—; cons. in field. Exec. bd. dirs. Nat. Capital Med. Care Found.; trustee Med. Service D.C., Nat. Arthritis and Rheumatism Assn. Served with USAAF, 1942-46. Decorated D.F.C., Air medal. Mem. Am. Coll. Hosp. Adminstrs., Am. Assn. Soc. Execs., Am. Hosp. Assn., Phi Delta Theta. Home: 1723 Evelyn Dr Rockville MD 20852 Office: 2007 Eye St NW Washington DC 20006*

FERRARO, GERALDINE ANN, congresswoman; b. Newburgh, N.Y., Aug. 26, 1935; d. Dominick and Antonetta L. (Corrieri) F.; B.A. in English and Edn., Marymount Sch., 1956; LL.B., Fordham U., 1960; postgrad. in law N.Y. U.; m. John Zaccaro, 1960; children—Donna, John, Laura. Tchr. pub. schs., N.Y.C., 1956-61; admitted to N.Y. State bar, 1961, U.S. Supreme Ct. bar, 1978; practice law, 1961-74, 78; chief spl. victims' bur., confidential unit, asst. dist. atty. Borough of Queens (N.Y.) Dist. Atty.'s Office, 1974-78; mem. 96th Congress from N.Y. State 9th Dist.; mem. adv. council for housing Civil Ct. N.Y.C., 1978—. Mem. Columbian Lawyers' Assn. (past pres.), Queens County Bar Assn., Dist. Atty.'s Assn. (dir.), Catholic Lawyers' Guild (dir.), Democrat. Roman Catholic. Club: 31st Assembly Dist. Regular Dem. (dir.). Home: 22 Deepdene Rd Forest Hills NY 11375 Office: 1725 Longworth House Office Bldg Washington DC 20515*

FERRELL, RUTH MORRIS (MRS. FRANK M. FERRELL), lawyer; b. Portsmouth, Va., Apr. 29, 1928; d. Francis Hubert and Ruth (Whitehead) Morris; B.A., Agnes Scott Coll., 1949; M.A., Emory U., 1952; J.D., U. Pa., 1960; m. Frank M. Ferrell, Apr. 7, 1958. Admitted to Del. bar, 1960, also U.S. Supreme Ct., U.S. Dist. Ct., U.S. Circuit Ct. Appeals; practiced in Wilmington, 1960—; asst. regional atty. Phila. Regional Litigation Center U.S. Equal Employment Opportunity Commn., 1973; law clk. judges Del. State Cts., 1961-62; dep. atty. gen. Del., 1963-70; head civil div. Del. Atty. Gen.'s Office, 1967-70. Mem. Gov's Commn. on Status Women, 1963-68; mem. European adv. council U.S. State Dept., 1971-72. Pres., Women's Republican Club Wilmington, 1965-67; Trustee John Marshall House. Recipient award for outstanding pub. service Rep. Nat. Com. N.E. Regional Women's Conf., 1967. Mem. Am. (mem. council, chmn. budget and finance com., chmn. social services com., specialization, advt. and law lists com., state chmn. local govt. sect., ethics in pub. contracting com.), Del. bar assns., Nat. Assn. Women Lawyers (state del.), Christina Bus. and Profl. Womens Club (pres.), Mortar Bd., Phi Beta Kappa. Presbyterian. Contbr. articles to profl. jours. Home: 17 Cragmere Rd Wilmington DE 19809 Office: 912 Market Tower Bldg Wilmington DE 19801

FERRER, ROMEO A., obstetrician, gynecologist; b. Manila, Philippines, Feb. 18, 1941; s. Gavino U. and Geronima (Agravante) F.; came to U.S., 1964, naturalized, 1973; M.D., U. Philippines, 1964; m. Anna E. Severn, Jan. 29, 1966; children—Robin, Roman, Roland. Intern, Franklin Sq. Hosp., Balt., 1964-65; chief resident in obstetrics and gynecology Mercy Hosp., Balt., 1968-69; fellow in obstetrics and gynecology S. Balt. Gen. Hosp., 1969-71; practice medicine specializing in obstetrics, gynecology, Glen Burnie, Md., 1971—. Bd. dirs. N. Arundel County (Md.) unit Am. Cancer Soc. Diplomate Am. Bd. Obstetrics and Gynecology. Fellow Am. Coll. Obstetricians and Gynecologists; mem. Am. Fertility Soc., Am. Assn. Gynecol. Laparoscopists, Med. and Chirurg. Faculty Md., Md. Obstet. and Gynecol. Soc., Filipino Assn. Md. Club: Katipunan. Office: 300 Hospital Dr Glen Burnie MD 21061

FERRIER, BEATRIZ SERRANO, interior decorator; b. Bogota, Colombia, S.Am., Nov. 21, 1932; d. Ramon Serrano and Isabel Reyes (Patria) Luna; came to U.S., 1963; B.A., Pontificia Universidad Javeriana (Bogota), 1953; m. Leslie H. Ferrier, Jan. 3, 1961. With Cath. Charities, Bogota, 1947-67, Opus Dei, Caracas, Venezuela, 1957-63; tchr. art Taunton (Mass.) Girls Club, 1964-70; supr. art gallery Morton Hosp., Taunton, 1968—; corporator Taunton Savings Bank, 1977—; self-employed interior designer, Raynham, Mass., 1974—. Recipient award for spl. service, Morton Hosp., 1975; citation, Taunton C. of C., 1971, Taunton Girls Club, 1970. Mem. Boston Mus. Fine Arts, Brockton Art Mus., Attleboro Art Mus., Old Colony His. Soc. Roman Catholic. Address: 30 Stony Brook Rd Raynham MA 02767

FERRIS, FREDERICK JOSEPH, social work adminstr.; b. Troy, N.Y., June 2, 1920; s. John and Ameila (Deeb) F.; B.A. cum laude, State U. N.Y. at Albany, 1942; M.S., Columbia U., 1949, D.S.W., 1968; m. Ellen J. Walsh, June 12, 1965. Head social studies dept. Heatly High Sch., Green Island, N.Y., 1946-47; sec. Info. Service, Greater N.Y. Fund, N.Y.C., 1949-51; exec. sec. N. Met. div. United Community Services, Boston, 1951-53, mem. Research div. com., 1953-57; dir. community orgn., asst. prof. Boston Coll. Sch. Social Work, 1953-57; dean, prof. Nat. Catholic Sch. Social Service, Cath. U. Am. 1960-69; Am. Assn. Ret. Persons-Nat. Ret. Tchrs. Assn. coordinator White House Conf. on Aging, 1970-72, dir. planning and research dept. and adminstr. Andrus Found., 1972—; adj. asso. prof. Fordham U. Sch. Social Service, 1957-60; lectr. Adelphi and Rutgers univs., 1959-60; social planning cons. Am. Found. for Blind, 1958-59; proposal reviewer NSF; cons. Inst. Community Studies, United Way Am., 1970—, Psychiat. Inst. Found., 1970—; del. White House Conf. on Aging, 1971; tech. rev. panel Nat. Council on Aging; mem. commn. on services to aging Archdiocese of Washington, 1971-76; vice chmn. Joint Legis. Com., Boston, 1954-57; mem. exec. com. Nat. Vol. Orgns. for Ind. Living for the Aging, 1972-74, 77—; mem. commn. on aging Nat. Conf. Cath. Charities, 1972—, chmn., 1978—. Bd. dirs. Social Service Exchange, Boston, 1955-57, Child Welfare League Am., 1966-70, Cath. Internat. Union Social Service, 1967-72, Christ Child Soc. Washington, 1967-73; treas., bd. dirs. Nat. Conf. Catholic Charities, 1971-74; bd. dirs., mem. exec. com. Associated Cath. Charities, Archdiocese of Washington, 1976—; chmn. Washington com. 13th Internat. Conf. Schs. Social Work, 1965-66. Served from pvt. to capt. U.S. Army, 1942-46. Recipient Lasker Doctoral fellowship Columbia U., 1957-58. Mem. Nat. (chpt. treas., 1956-57, task force on services to aging 1973-75), Am. (chmn. div. pub. policy and social work, exec. com. 1953-55) assns. social workers, Mass. Conf. Social Work (dir., chmn. nominating com. 1956-57), Am. Acad. Polit. and Social Sci., Alumni Assn. Columbia U. Sch. Social Work (chpt. chmn. 1954-55, dir. 1956-59), United Community Funds and Councils Am. (nat. adv. com. health and welfare services 1955-57, council planning execs. 1957-59), Nat. Assn. Hearing and Speech Agy. (nat. tng. adv. com. 1963-70), Acad. Certified Social Workers, Council Social Work Edn. (deans adv. com. fed. welfare agys. 1962-64, 66-68; ho. of dels. 1977—), Nat. Conf. Social Welfare, Social Welfare History Group, Nat. Council on Aging, Assn. Gerontology in Higher Edn. (com. interorgnl. relations), Gerontol. Soc. Home: 5101 River Rd Bethesda MD 20016

FERRIS, ROBERT CLARKE, chem. co. exec.; b. Vancouver, B.C., Can., Dec. 28, 1919; s. Robert Chester and Dora Belle (Clarke) F.; came to U.S., 1920, naturalized, 1943; B.S., U. Wash., 1944; M.S., Northwestern U., 1947; Ph.D., U. Utah, 1949; m. Alma Marie Sweatt, Dec. 10, 1965; children—John Mark, Robert Dana. Dir. research Purex Corp., 1951-59; pres. Chem. Lab. Products, 1959-63; mgr. comml. devel. Monsanto Co., 1964-67; dir. material mgmt. Stepan Chem. Co., Northfield, Ill., 1967-73; v.p. Instapak div. Sealed Air Corp., Danbury, Conn., 1974—; instr. U. Calif., Los Angeles, 1958. Served with USNR, 1944-47. Mem. Am. Chem. Soc., Am. Oil Chemist Soc., Comml. Devel. Assn., ASTM, Sigma Xi. Club: Ridgewood Country (Danbury). Contbr. articles to profl. jours.; patentee in field. Home: 57 Fairmount Dr Danbury CT 06810 Office: Old Sherman Turnpike Danbury CT 06810

FERRO, WALTER, artist; b. N.Y.C., Oct. 6, 1925; s. Joseph Salvador and Mary Elizabeth (Potezna) F.; certificate Bklyn. Mus. Art Sch., 1952; m. Lore Gausmann, Sept. 20, 1966; children—Elizabeth, Paula. One-man shows at Wakefield Gallery, N.Y.C., 1960, Dominican Coll., Racine, Wis., 1962, Kings Coll., Briarcliff, N.Y., 1967; exhibited in group shows at Bklyn. Mus., 1952, U. Okla., 1959, Jersey City Mus., 1966, Phila. Mus., 1966; represented in permanent collections at Met. Mus. of Art, N.Y.C. Art cons. Mobil Corp., 1972—. Served with USNR, 1942-44. Recipient Kenneth Hayes Miller Meml. award Audubon Artists, 1953; Kate W. Arms Meml. award Soc. Am. Graphic Artists, 1959; Guggenheim fellow, 1972. Home and studio: Rural Route 2 Hoyt Rd Pound Ridge NY 10576

FERRY, MARTIN FRANK, waste treatment exec.; b. Long Branch, N.J., Sept. 26, 1948; s. Sylvester Henry and Lina (Strollo) F.; diploma Wallace-Tiennan Sch. for Chlorination, 1978; diploma in electronics Fisher-Porter Sch., 1978; diploma in air conditioning and refrigeration, Monmouth County Vocat. Sch., 1968; m. Ann Brockway, Sept. 16, 1972; 1 dau., Lynn Marie. Custodian Long Branch (N.J.) High Sch., 1970-71; apt. supt. Planned Residential Communities, W. Long Branch, N.J., 1972-76; supt. maintenance and purchasing W. Monmouth Utilities Authority, Manalapan, N.J., 1977—; apt. mgr. Raymond Marzullio Co., 1978; propr. A & M Contracting & Coastal Enterprises. Served with USNR, 1965-68. Cert. stationary engr., N.J. Clubs: Zanchin Karate, NASCAR Auto Racing, Wing and Bonnett Sports Car, E. Gate Dunes Sports Car, Greater Rockaway Auto Sports Soc. Qualified internat. navigator and coxswain; research in field. Home: PO Box 280 Englishtown NJ 07726 Office: PO Box 280 Englishtown NJ 07726

FERRY, MIRIAM, coll. adminstr.; b. Hilo, Hawaii, Apr. 7, 1911; d. Joseph S. and Mary (Aguire) F.; student Mount St. Mary's Coll., 1936-39; B.S. in Edn., U. Dayton, 1958; postgrad. Siena Coll., Albany, N.Y., 1964-65; M.A. in Edn., St. Bonaventure U., 1968. Joined 3d Franciscan Order of Syracuse, 1926; tchr. St. Joseph Sch., Hilo, 1931-41; tchr., prin. Sacred Heart Sch., Lahaini, Maui, 1929-31, 41-47; tchr. St. Francis High Sch., Honolulu, 1947-57; tchr. Christian Doctrine Our Lady of Good Counsel Ch., Endicott, N.Y., 1957-58; tchr. St. Peter Sch., Riverside, N.J., 1958-60, St. John Sch., New Brunswick, N.J., 1960-63, St. Theresa Sch., Syracuse, N.Y., 1963-64, Our Lady of Angels Sch., Albany, N.Y., 1964-66, St. Joseph-St. Patrick Sch., Utica, N.Y., 1966-67; dir student personnel Maria Regina Coll., Syracuse, 1967-71, 76—. Mem. N.Y. State Jr. Coll. Assn., Am. Personnel and Guidance Assn., Assn. Humanistic Edn. and Devel., Am. Coll. Personnel Assn., Assn. Measurement and Evaluation, Assn. Counselor Edn. and Supervision, Acad. Polit. Sci., Nat. Vocat. Guidance Assn., Smithsonian Assn. Roman Catholic. Home: 1024 Court St Syracuse NY 13208 Office: 1000 Ululani St Hilo HI 96720

FERRY, ROBERT DEAN (BOB), profl. basketball exec.; b. St. Louis, May 31, 1937; s. Willard Francis and Elsie (Neuman) F.; B.A., St. Louis U., 1959; m. Rita Brooks, June 25; children—Laura, Robert, Daniel. Player, Nat. Basketball Assn., 1959-70; asst. coach, scout Washington Bullets (formerly Balt. Bullets), 1968-73, gen. mgr., 1973—; mem. Md. Phys. Fitness Commn. Active local Big Bros. Mem. Nat. Basketball Assn. Players Assn. Office: care Washington Bullets Capital Centre Landover MD 20786

FESKOE, GAFFNEY JON, banker; b. N.Y.C., Feb. 21, 1949; s. George J. and Mary M. (Gaffney) F.; B.S., Boston Coll., 1971; M.B.A., Fordham U., 1976. With Mfrs. Hanover Trust Co., N.Y.C., 1971-75; asst. treas./mgr. corporate fgn. exchange adv. service European-Am. Banking Corp./European-Am. Bank & Trust Co., N.Y.C., 1975-77; mgr. fgn. exchange corporate counseling dept., world corporate group Citibank, N.A., N.Y.C., 1977—. Roman Catholic. Clubs: Union (N.Y.C.); Apawamis (Rye, N.Y.). Home: 55 East End Ave New York City NY 10028 Office: 399 Park Ave New York City NY 10022*

FESZCZAK, ZENON LUBOMYR, museum ofcl.; b. West Ukraine, Sept. 1, 1930; s. Mykola and Pauline (Ortynsky) F.; came to U.S., 1949, naturalized, 1954; B.A.A. (senatorial scholar), U. Pa., 1957, M.F.A., 1958; m. Olena Maria Mydlowsky, Sept. 17, 1955; children—Eva Sydonia Zarine, Zenon Orest Marco. Exhibit designer Museum Phila. Civic Center, 1958-60, exhibit design supr., 1960-70, design dir., 1970—; free-lance design cons., 1960—. Bd. dirs. Ukrainian Inst. Art, Chgo., also N.Y.C. Recipient J.P. Metheny medal excellence in design. Mem. Am. Assn. Museums, Pa. Acad. Fine Arts, Mus. Council Phila., Phila. Print Club, Ukrainian Mus. Modern Art. Art critic Ukrainian monthly Suchasnist. Home: 754 N 26th St Philadelphia PA 19130 Office: Mus Phila Civic Center 34th St at Civic Center Blvd Philadelphia PA 19104

FETCH, MYRON LESTER, architect; b. Wyoming, Pa., Aug. 12, 1931; s. John Joseph and Mary (Lukesh) F.; B.Arch., Pa. State U., 1954; m. Carla Jeanne Christine, Jan. 3, 1953; children—Paul Kevin, Erik Christopher, Kyra Christine, Lisa Kyle, John Christian. Tactical warfare draftsman Haller, Raymond & Brown, State College, Pa., 1953-54; design architect, project mgr. Edwards & Green, Camden, N.J., 1954-55; chief designer, project architect Micklewright & Mountford, Trenton, N.J., 1955-59, asso. partner, 1959-65; pvt. practice, Doylestown, Pa., 1965—; owner M.L. Fetch Assos., architects and planners; archtl. cons. design, feasibility studies, community land planning. environ. research; dir., adv. bd. Doylestown br. Indsl. Valley Bank; East Coast rep. Duwe Mausoleum Sales Corp., Oskosh, Wis. Chmn. bd. suprs. Buckingham Twp., Bucks County, Pa., 1970-72, vice chmn., 1965-69; sec. Buckingham Twp. Zoning Hearing Bd., 1962-63; pres. Buckingham Twp. Civic Assn., 1964; police commr. Buckingham Twp., 1967-70. Registered architect, Pa., N.Y., Md., Del., N.J., Tenn., Cal. Diplomate Nat. Council Archtl. Registration Bds. Mem. AIA (Pres. Bucks County chpt. 1966), Pa. (dir. 1967-69), N.J. socs. architects, Am. Inst. Interior Designers, N.J. Soc. of Pa. (dir.), Constrn. Specification Inst., Bucks C. of C. Home: RD 2 Buttonwood Dr Doylestown PA 18901 Office: 30 S Pine St Box 67 Doylestown PA 18901

FETTER, ROBERT POLLARD, railroad exec.; b. Princeton, N.J., Oct. 20, 1931; s. Frank Whitson and Elizabeth Garrett (Pollard) F.; B.A. in Econs., Swarthmore Coll., 1953; M.B.A., Harvard U., 1957; m. Elizabeth Ann Hutcheson, June 25, 1960; children—Allen Hutcheson, Elizabeth Pollard. Methods research B.&O. R.R., analyst Balt., 1957-61, indsl. engr. 1962-63, mgr. equipment planning, 1963-64; mgr. planning traffic C.&O. R.R., B.&O. R.R., Balt., 1964-72; dir. market research So. Railway System, Washington, 1972—. Mem. gen. com. Friends Com. Nat. Legislation, Washington, 1975—, also chmn. fin. com. Served with U.S. Army, 1953-55. Mem. Am. Econ. Assn., Transp. Research Forum. Democrat. Quaker. Home: 198 Oakdale Rd Baltimore MD 21210 Office: 920 15th St NW Washington DC 20013

FEUER, MICHAEL, ct. reporter; b. Paterson, N.J., Feb. 10, 1945; s. Paul and Rose (Hack) F.; grad. Hill Sch. Ct. Reporting, 1966; m. Raquel Mangel, Feb. 12, 1966; children—Evan, Tema Jill. Ofcl. ct. reporter Essex County, N.J., 1966-72; owner Construcciones de Barranquilla, Ltd. (Colombia), 1972; free-lance ct. reporter Ft. Lauderdale, Fla., 1973; ofcl. ct. reporter U.S. Cts., Phila., 1973—. Served with USAF, 1962-63. Recipient Certificate of Merit, Nat. Shorthand Reporters Assn., 1969; certificates of merit and proficiency, Md. Award of Excellence, N.J. Distinguished Service award, 1967; certified shorthand reporter, N.J., Pa., Fla., Md. Mem. Nat. Shorthand Reporters Assn., U.S. Ct. Reporters Assn., Pa., Md., N.J. certified shorthand reporters assns. Contbr. articles to profl. jours. Home: 526 Kings Dr Cherry Hill NJ 08003 Office: 2722 US Courthouse 601 Market St Philadelphia PA 19106

FEUER, WILLIAM WALLACE, lawyer; b. Worcester, Mass., July 21, 1925; s. Harold Daniel and Stella Muriel F.; A.B., Harvard U., 1947; J.D., Suffolk U., 1967; m. Marilyn Trombly, Mar. 2, 1952; children—Lauraine, Marlene, Sandra. Asst. dir. Peter Bent Brigham Hosp., Boston, 1967-69; admitted to Mass. bar, 1967, Calif. bar, 1971, Fla. bar, 1971; legal counsel Meml. Hosp. Med. Center, Long Beach, Calif., 1969-71; regional atty. Am. Medicorp, Inc., Los Angeles, 1971-73; asso. dir. Peter Bent Brigham Hosp., Boston, 1973-77; atty. Affiliated Hosps. Center, Boston, 1977—; vis. lectr. U. Calif., Los Angeles, Mass. Coll. Pharmacy, Harvard U. Med. Sch. Served with U.S. Army, 1943-46; PTO. Mem. Am. Bar Assn., Soc. Law and Medicine, Soc. Hosp. Attys., Am. Arbitration Assn. (panel mem.). Clubs: Masons, Shriners. Home: 171 Clinton Rd Brookline MA 02146 Office: 25 Binney St Boston MA 02115

FEUERBURGH, JOSEPH, psychologist; b. N.Y.C., Aug. 4, 1908; s. Nathan and Regina (Frischer) F.; B.A., L.I. U., 1931; M.A., N.Y. U., 1936, Ph.D., 1954; m. Dec. 25, 1941. Psychologist spl. project Bur. Child Guidance, N.Y.C., 1934-35, Adult Guidance Service, N.Y.C., 1935-38, N.Y.C. Spl. Sessions Ct. Probation Bur., 1938-42; clin. psychologist U.S. VA, 1946, USPHS Hosp., Ellis Island, 1946-51, USPHS Hosp., S.I., N.Y., 1951-75; pvt. practice psychology, 1955-69; instr. psychology dept., evening session Bklyn. Coll., 1947-48; cons. psychologist Am. Tech. Tng. Centers, N.Y.C., 1968. Chmn. speakers campaign com. Democratic Party, Ind. Dem. Assn., Bronx, N.Y., 1933. Served with U.S. Army, 1942-46; Res. ret., 1961. Certified clin. psychologist, N.Y., sch. psychologist, N.Y., cons. psychologist, Conn. Mem. Am., N.Y. State psychol. assns., N.Y. Soc. for Clin. Psychologists, Nat. Roster Health Service Providers in Psychology (council), Am. Group Psychotherapy Assn. (asso.). Clubs: Mens, Mr. and Mrs. of Park Ave. Synagogue (N.Y.C.).

FEUERSTEIN, DONALD MARTIN, lawyer; b. Chgo., May 30, 1937; s. Morris Martin and Pauline Jean (Zagel) F.; B.A., Yale 1959; J.D., Harvard, 1962; m. Dorothy Rosalind Sokolsky, June 3, 1962 (dec. Mar. 1978); children—Eliza Carol, Anthony David. Admitted to N.Y. bar, 1962; asso. firm Cleary, Gottlieb, Steen & Hamilton, N.Y.C., 1962-63; law clk. to Hon. Frederick P. Bryan U.S. Dist. Judge, N.Y.C., 1963-65; asso. firm Saxe, Bacon & Bolan, N.Y.C., 1965; asst. gen. counsel, chief counsel institutional investor study SEC, Washington, 1966-71; partner, counsel Salomon Bros., N.Y.C., 1971—, sec. Salomon Bros. Found., Inc., 1971—. Mem. adv. council U. Pa. Center for Study of Fin. Instns., 1973—; mem. adv. bd. U. Calif. Securities Regulations Inst., 1972-76; chmn. bd. dirs. First All Children's Theatre, 1976—. Served with U.S. Army, 1962-63. Mem. Am., N.Y. State bar assns., Assn. Bar City N.Y., Securities Industry Assn., Nat. Assn. Securities Dealers. Club: Harvard. Mem. editorial advisory bd. Securities Regulation Law Jour., 1973—; mem. bd. editors Nat. Law Jour., 1978—. Home: 1155 Park Ave New York City NY 10028 Office: One New York Plaza New York City NY 10004

FEULNER, EDWIN JOHN, JR., found. exec.; b. Ill., Aug. 12, 1941; s. Edwin and Helen (Franzen) F.; B.S., Regis Coll., 1963; M.B.A., U. Pa., 1964; postgrad. London Sch. Econs., 1965, Georgetown U., 1965-68; m. Linda C. Leventhal, Mar. 8, 1969; children—Edwin, III, Emily. Research analyst Ho. of Reps. Republican Conf., 1966-69; confidential asst. to Sec. of Def. Melvin Laird, 1969-70; adminstrv. asst. to U.S. Congressman Philip M. Crane of Ill., 1970-74; exec. dir. Rep. Study Com., U.S. Ho. of Reps., Washington, 1974-77. Campaign mgr. Crane for Congress, 1972; trustee Heritage Found., pres., 1977; trustee Alpha Kappa Psi Found. Mem. Phila. Soc. (treas.), Mont

Pelerin Soc. (trustee), Am. Polit. Sci. Assn., Am., So. econs. assns., Internat. Inst. Strategic Studies, U.S. Strategic Inst., Nat. Economists Club. Roman Catholic. Clubs: University (Washington); Reform (London). Author: (with others) Trading with the Communists, 1968; Congress and the New Internatnional Economic Order, 1976; also articles. Home: 6216 Berkley Rd Alexandria VA 22307 Office: 513 C St NE Washington DC 20002

FEY, CHARLES JOSEPH, coll. adminstr.; b. McKeesport, Pa., Jan. 4, 1950; s. Norbert L. and Mary E. (Kelly) F.; B.A., Pa. State U., 1971, M.Ed., 1972. Dir. residential life Newbury Jr. Coll., 1973-77, dir. counseling and career services, 1974-75, dir. fin. aid, 1975-76; dir. housing and resident life Cath. U. Am., 1977—, instr. in psychology, 1975—. Mgr. Citizens for McGovern/Shriver, McKeesport, 1972. Mem. Mass. Coll. Personnel Assn. (pres. 1974-76), Boston Assn. Coll. Housing Adminstrs. (pres. 1974-75), Mass. (Profl. Service award 1974-76), Am., Greater Boston personnel, guidance assns., Assn. Coll. and Univ. Housing Officers, Kappa Sigma. Independent Democrat. Roman Catholic. Home: PO Box 73 Cardinal Sta Washington DC 20064 Office: St Bonaventure Hall Room 108 Cath U Am Washington DC 20064

FIALKOV, HERMAN, investment banker; b. Bklyn., Mar. 23, 1922; s. Isidore and Pearl (Heinish) F.; student Coll. City N.Y., 1938-41; B.Adminstrv. Engring., N.Y. U., 1951; m. Elaine Dampf, Nov. 25, 1942; children—Carol Fran, Jay Michael. Engrs., Emerson Radio Corp., 1941-47, MBS, 1947-49, Tele-Tone Radio Corp., 1949-51; chief engr. Radio Receptor Co., 1951-54; pres. Gen. Transistor Corp. (merged with Gen. Instrument Corp., 1960), 1954-60; v.p., dir. Gen. Instrument Corp., 1960-70, sr. v.p., 1967-68; partner Geiger & Fiaikov, 1968—; dir. Standard Microsystems Corp., N.Y., dir. Benrus Corp., Ridgefield, Conn., Xynetics, Inc., Microsemicondr. Corp. Panelist Am. Arbitration Assn.; trustee Adelphi U., Garden City, 1959-70. Served with AUS, 1943-46. Decorated Bronze Star with oak leaf cluster; Conspicuous Service Cross, N.Y. Mem. IEEE, Am. Technion Soc. (dir.). Tau Beta Pi, Alpha Pi Mu. Home: 615 Meryl Dr Westbury NY 11590 Office: 1 Rockefeller Plaza New York City NY 10020

FIAROTTA, NOEL JOSEPH, writer; b. Meriden, Conn., Mar. 13, 1944; s. Anthony and Santa (Lentini) F.; B.A. in English, Jersey City State Coll., 1966; M.A. in Psychology, Fairleigh Dickinson U., 1972; m. Beatriz Esteban, Aug. 17, 1975. Tchr. language arts E. Orange, N.J., 1967-74; dir. program for phys. limited and mentally retarded A.H. Moore Summer Camp, High Bridge, N.J., 1973-75; contbg. editor Leisure Craftsman column for King Features Syndicate, N.Y.C.; author (with Phyllis Fiarotta) children's crafts books, including: Confetti, 1978, Pin It, Tack It, Hang It, 1975, The You & Me Heritage Tree, 1976, Be What You Want to Be, 1977, 101 Things to Make, 1968, 101 Gifts for Children, 1970; contbr. TV and media promotional work for various clients, including Workman Publishing Co., 1970—. Address: Brook Way West Orange NJ 07052

FICHTEL, RUDOLPH ROBERT, assn. exec.; b. N.Y.C., Dec. 12, 1915; s. Paul Gotthard and Helen (Szapka) F.; B.B.A. cum laude, Coll. City N.Y., 1938; certificate Am. Inst. Banking, 1941; diploma financial pub. relations Northwestern U., 1950; M.B.A., N.Y. U., 1951; diploma banking Rutgers U. Stonier Grad. Sch. Banking, 1954; m. Elsie E. Terebesy, Dec. 24, 1942; children—Nancy Lynn, Robert Paul, Richard John. Tchr., N.Y.C. Pub. Schs., 1938-39; adminstr. East River Savs. Bank, 1939-42; dir. pub. relations, editor, asst. sec. Savs. Banks Assn. N.Y. State, 1945-53; dir. pub. relations council, savs. and mortgage div. Am. Inst. Banking of Am. Bankers Assn., N.Y.C., Washington, 1953-78; regional v.p. United Student Aid Funds, Inc., N.Y.C., 1978—. Faculty, Am. Inst. Banking, Stonier Grad. Sch. Banking; contbg. editor Am. Inst. Banking textbooks; speaker. Served to capt. AUS, 1942-45; ETO. Recipient highest award citation Internat. Council Indsl. Editors, 1948; Dr. Marcus Nadler award for excellence in finance N.Y. U., 1951. Mem. Beta Gamma Sigma. Contbr. articles to profl. jours. Home: 65 19 170th St Flushing NY 11365 Office: 200 E 42d St New York City NY 10017

FICHTENHOLZ, MILTON, tax cons.; b. Gloversville, N.Y., Feb. 24, 1918; s. Harry B. and Anna (Liska) F.; B.B.A., St. John's U., 1941; m. Matilda Zagon, Aug. 23, 1941; children—Helene Carolyn, Rosalyn Paula. With IRS, 1945-74, mgr. internat. examiners, N. Atlantic region, N.Y.C., 1961-74; mgr. internat. cons. service Coopers and Lybrand, N.Y.C., 1974—. Served with USAAF, 1943-45. Mem. Internat. Tax Inst. (dir.). Home: 2266 Derby Rd Baldwin NY 11510 Office: 1251 Ave of Americas New York City NY 10020

FICKS, ROBERT LESLIE, JR., furniture mfg. co. exec.; b. Cin., Mar. 18, 1919; s. Robert L. and Virginia Willson (Emerson) F.; B.B.A., U. Cin., 1940; m. Virginia D. Upson, Sept. 12, 1942; children—Robert L., Dorsey Upson, Louis Philip. Sales and advt. mgr. Ficks Reed Co., Cin., 1945-54; sales mgr. Salmanson Co., N.Y.C., 1954-56, Ethan Allen Inc., N.Y.C., 1956-66, v.p. advt. and pub. relations, Danbury, Conn., 1966—. Served with USAAF, 1942-45. Mem. Assn. Nat. Advertisers (dir., treas. 1971-75), Nat. Advt. Rev. Bd. (dir. 1972-75). Episcopalian. Clubs: String and Splinter (High Point, N.C.); Cedar Point Yacht (Westport, Conn.); Rotary. Home: 194 Lyons Plain Rd Weston CT 06883 Office: Ethan Allen Dr Danbury CT 06810

FIEDLER, ARTHUR, musical condr.; b. Boston, Dec. 17, 1894; s. Emanuel and Johanna (Bernfeld) F.; student Boston Latin Sch., 1907-10, Royal Acad. of Music, Berlin, 1911-15; hon. M.A., Tufts Coll., 1931; Mus.D., Boston U., 1951, Am. Internat. Coll., 1959, Southeastern Mass. Technol. Inst., 1965, Merrimack Coll., 1969, U. Mass., 1970, Tufts U., 1971, New Eng. Conservatory Music, 1971, Springfield Coll., 1971, Bowdoin Coll., 1973, U. Maine at Portland-Gorham, 1974, Our Lady of Lake Coll., 1974; D.F.A., Ripon Coll., 1960; Northeastern U., 1966; D. Mus., U. Miami, 1963, Music and Arts Inst., San Francisco, 1963, Jacksonville U., 1964; D.Hum., Glassboro State Coll., 1973, Harvard U., Dartmouth Coll.; m. Ellen M. Bottomley, Jan. 8, 1942; children—Johanna, Deborah, Peter. Made concert debut at age of 17; organized Boston Sinfonietta, 1924; organized Esplanade Concerts, Boston, 1929, condr., 1929—; condr. Boston Symphony Pops Concerts, 1930—; former condr. Ceceilia Soc. Boston, U. Glee Club, Providence, MacDowell Club Orch. of Boston; mem. faculty Boston U.; mus. cons. VA, Boston; guest condr. at San Francisco, N.Y. Philharmonic, Mpls., Chgo., 1923, Montreal, Toronto, Dallas, Seattle N.B.C., Symphony, Portland, Phila., Japan, Korea, S. Africa, Australia, N.Z., Europe, S.Am., Eng., others; condr. RCA Victor Broadcast. Served in U.S. Army, World War I and World War II. Awarded Croix de l'Officier d'Academie; chevalier Legion of Honor (France), 1954; named number 8 in classical field Top Artists on Campus Poll, 1968; recipient Presdl. medal of freedom. Col. on staff Gov. of Ky., 1946; hon. Fire Chief in about 400 cities of world. Mem. Harvard Musical Assn., Boston Soc. Recorded Music (pres.). Home: 133 Hyslop Rd Brookline MA 02146

FIELD, BARRY ELLIOT, internist, gastroenterologist; b. Hartford, Conn., Apr. 21, 1947; s. Arnold and Selma (Nechrich) F.; B.A. (scholar), Harvard U., 1968; M.D., Albert Einstein Coll. Medicine, 1972; m. Virginia Eileen Geohegan, July 27, 1975. Intern in pediatrics Montefiore Hosp., Bronx, N.Y., 1972-73; intern medicine Met. Hosp., N.Y.C., 1973-74, resident in medicine, 1974-76; fellow in gastroenterology Harbor Gen. Hosp., Torrance, Calif., 1976-78; practice medicine specializing in internal medicine and gastroenterology, Pleasantville, N.Y., 1978—; mem. staffs Phelps Meml. Hosp., N. Tarrytown, N.Y., Westchester County Med. Center, Valhalla, N.Y.; clin. instr. dept. medicine N.Y. Med. Coll., Valhalla. Mem. Alpha Omega Alpha. Democrat. Jewish. Office: 424 Bedford Rd Pleasantville NY 10570

FIELD, CHARLES HERBERT, JR., editor; b. Hackensack, N.J., July 24, 1942; s. Charles Herbert and Helen Nellie (DeGroot) F.; student U. Wyo., 1960-61; A.A.S., Ulster County Community Coll., 1969; m. Ann Margaret Shore, Oct. 5, 1963; children—Nina Gabrielle, Adrian Anthony, Jason Walter, Bradley Charles. Reporter Catskill (N.Y.) Daily Mail, 1968-71, editor, 1971-77; editorial writer Harrisburg (Pa.) Patriot-News, 1977—. Democratic committeeman, 1967-68. Served with AUS, 1962-65. Recipient N.Y. Asso. Press awards, 1972, 73; Ceiba-Geigy award, 1974; Distinguished State Govt. Coverage award N.Y. State Pubs. Assn., 1974; Distinguished Writing award N.Y. State Pubs. Assn., 1976. Home: Montebello Farm Rd Duncannon PA 17020 Office: 9th and Market Sts Harrisburg PA 17105

FIELD, GARY GEORGE, printing technologist; b. Melbourne, Australia, Feb. 2, 1944; s. Ralph William and Maisie Maud (Gillam) F.; came to U.S., 1970; diploma in printing tech. Trent Poly. U., Nottingham, Eng., 1970; M.B.A., U. Pitts., 1975. Camera operator Robinson Process Engravers, Melbourne, 1960-63, Mentone Offset Reprodns., Melbourne, 1963-65; camera dept. foreman Leigh-Mardon, Melbourne, 1965-67; printing technologist Mardon Packaging Internat., Bristol, Eng., 1968-70; supr. photo and color research div. Graphic Arts Tech. Found., Pitts., 1970-76; area coordinator adminstrn. and mgmt. LaRoche Coll., Pitts., 1976—; tech. and mgmt. cons. to N.Am. cos.; guest coll. lectr. K.D. MacDougall scholar, 1967-70. Mem. Inst. Printing, Tech. Assn. Graphic Arts, Royal Photog. Soc., Inter Soc. Color Council. Anglican. Editor: Advances in Color Reproduction, 1973; contbr. articles in field to profl. jours.; developer systems engring. approach to color reprodns., 1970, math. decision making models for graphic arts industry applications, 1974. Home: 1322 Arch St Pittsburgh PA 15212 Office: 9000 Babcock Blvd Pittsburgh PA 15237

FIELD, HERMANN HAVILAND, educator, architect; b. Zurich, Switzerland, Apr. 13, 1910 (parents Am. citizens); s. Herbert Haviland and Nina (Eschwege) F.; B.A. cum laude, Harvard U., 1933, Grad. Sch. Design, 1932-34; Diplom Architect, Swiss Fed. Polytechnic Inst. at Zurich, 1936; m. Jean Clark, 1932 (div. 1940); m. 2d, Kate Thornycroft, 1940; children—Hugh, Alan, Alison. Resident architect Roche Products, Ltd., Welwyn Garden City, Eng., 1936-38; field rep. Czech Refugee Trust Fund, Krakow, Poland and Windsor Forest, Eng., 1939-40; site planner Tuttle, Seelye, Place and Raymond, N.Y.C., 1941-45; research dir. Raymond and Rado, Architects, N.Y.C., 1945-47; dir. bldg. plans Western Res. U., 1947-49; victim of kidnapping in Cold War incident, secretly held in Polish prison cellar, Miedzeszyn, 1949-54; preparation of prison novels, London, 1955, Boston, 1956-60; planning dir. Tufts-New Eng. Med. Center, Boston, 1961-72; dir. planning project for innovative Boston elementary sch., 1966-72; prof. environ. planning and design, dir. grad. program in social and environ. policy Tufts U., 1972-78, program adviser, prof. polit. sci. emeritus, 1978—. Vice pres. Cambridge Interfaith Housing Corp., 1968-78; mem. Mass. Gov.'s Task Force on Transp., 1969-70; mem. working com. Boston Transp. Planning Rev., 1971-72; mem. Joint Regional Transp. Com., 1973—; adv. bd. Health Facilities Research, Inc., 1972-74; mem. Shirley (Mass.) Conservation Commn., 1970—, Shirley Historic Dist. Commn., 1973—, Cambridge (Mass.) Conservation Commn., 1975—; bd. dirs. Mass. Assn. Conservation Commns., 1976—; non-govt. orgn. del. UN Habitat Conf., Vancouver, 1976. Fellow AIA; mem. Am. Soc. Planning Ofcls., Am. Soc. Hosp. Planning, Internat. Fedn. Housing and Planning, Boston Soc. Architects (sec., bd. mem. 1968-74), Boston Archtl. Center, Harvard Grad. Sch. Design Assn. (council 1969-71, 74-76), Am. Inst. Planners, Soc. Coll. and Univ. Planning, Internat. Hosp. Fedn., AAUP. Author (with Stanislaw Mierzenski): Angry Harvest, 1958 (German version the selection of Europaischer Buchklub, Stuttgart, 1962), (fgn. edits. Eng., Polish, Swedish, German); Duck Lane, 1961; co-author: Problems of Pediatric Hospital Design, 1965; Evaluation of Hospital Design, 1972; contbg. author: Environment and Cognition, 1973. Home: Valley Farm Shirley MA 01464 Office: Brown House Tufts Univ Medford MA 02155

FIELD, LINCOLN ELMER, veterinarian; b. Mt. Vision, N.Y., Dec. 24, 1906; s. Elmer Lincoln and Maggie Delana (Van Buren) F.; D.V.M., Cornell U.-N.Y. State Veterinary Coll., 1930; m. C. Jane Waldo, June 2, 1934; children—Treva, William, Rebecca. Gen. practice vet. medicine Middleburgh, N.Y., 1932-61, Ithaca, N.Y., 1961—; prof. medicine N.Y. State Veterinary Coll., Cornell U., Ithaca, 1961-71. Pres. N.Y. State Bd. Vet. Med. Examiners, 1948-58. Mem. N.Y. State, Am. veterinary med. assns., Phi Zeta (chpt. pres. 1969). Republican. Conglist. Clubs: Rotary (pres. Middleburgh 1955), Masons (past master). Home: 92 Besemer Rd Ithaca NY 14850

FIELD, MAXWELL JOHN, real estate investment co. exec.; b. London, Eng., June 1, 1934; s. Frederick John and Amelia Glasspool Dean (Allford) F.; student Coll. of Estate Mgmt., London, 1952-56; m. June Edith Madeline Martin, Feb. 2, 1957; children—Guy William, Gillian Rosemary, Duncan Maxwell. Came to Can., 1957. Articled pupil Messrs. Howell & Brooks, Chartered Surveyors, London, 1951-55; profl. asst. Messrs. Gerald Eve & Co., Chartered Surveyors, London, 1955-57, Messrs. W.H. Bosley & Co. Ltd., Toronto, Ont., Can., 1957-62; property mgr. MEPC Canadian Properties Ltd., Toronto, 1963-65; devel. mgr. Monarch Investments Ltd., Toronto, 1965-70; sr. v.p. Marathon Realty Co. Ltd., Toronto, 1970—; chmn., dir. Marathon U.S. Realties, Inc., Marathon Devel. Calif., Inc., Marathon Devel. Oreg., Inc.; pres., dir. Place Montreal, Inc., Project 200 Investments Ltd., Project 200 Properties Ltd.; dir. CCCL Properties Ltd., Marathon Aviation Terminals Ltd., Marathon U.S. Holdings Inc., Metro Centre Devels. Ltd. Fellow Royal Instn. Chartered Surveyors; mem. Ont. Land Economists. Clubs: Cambridge, Granite (Toronto); Whitlock Golf and Country (Montreal). Home: 358 Glencairn Ave Toronto ON M5N 1V1 Canada Office: PO Box 375 Toronto-Dominion Centre Toronto ON M5K 1K8 Canada

FIELD, NORMAN J., physicist; b. N.Y.C., Dec. 5, 1922; s. Morris S. and Clara (Edinburg) F.; B.S. cum laude, City U. N.Y., 1942; M.S. in Physics, Polytech. Inst. Bklyn., 1959; m. Gladys Katz, Nov. 23, 1946; children—Joan, Kenneth, Richard, Elaine. Electronic engr. radar lab. Signal Corps, Ft. Monmouth, N.J., 1942-44, physicist, chief, optical microscopy engring. labs., 1946-54, asst. dir. research, 1954-58; asst. dir. Inst. for Exploratory Research, U.S. Army Research and Devel. Lab., Ft. Monmouth, 1958-62; dep. dir. research U.S. Army Electronics Lab., Ft. Monmouth, 1962-64; chief, applied physics div. U.S. Army Electronics Command, Ft. Monmouth, 1964-68, chief office sci. and tech., 1968-70, dir. program mgmt., army area communications system, 1970-74, dir. internat. logistics, 1975—; adj. prof., lectr. physics Monmouth Coll., West Long Branch, N.J., 1956—. Pres., Monmouth Regional High Sch. Bd. Edn., 1957—. Bd. dirs. Friends Monmouth County Library Assn. Served with AUS, 1944-46. Decorated Bronze Star medal with oak leaf cluster, Purple Heart. Mem. Am. Phys. Soc., Optical Soc. Am., Am. Chem. Soc., Am. Assn. Physics Tchrs., N.J. Fedn. Dist. Bds. Edn. (v.p. 1966), Monmouth County Sch. Bds. Assn. (pres. 1972-73), Am. Ordnance Assn., Assn. U.S. Army (pres. 1978—), N.Y. Acad. Scis. Contbr. articles to sci. jours., books. Home: 726 Sycamore Ave Shrewsbury NJ 07701 Office: Hdqrs USAECOM (DRSEL-IL) Fort Monmouth NJ 07703

FIELD, RONALD MARVIN, mfg. co. exec.; b. Bklyn., Jan. 20, 1932; s. Sam and Rose (Lempert) F.; B.A., B.S., Pa. State U., 1956; postgrad. Am. U., 1960; m. Muriel Heller, Dec. 20, 1953; children—Greg, Ruth, Mark. With Honeywell Valve Div., Phila., 1956-58, Vitro Labs., RCA, Moorestown, N.J., 1959-67; with Water Reactor div. Westinghouse Electric Corp., Pitts., 1967—, communications mgr., 1968—; cons. in micrographics and copier systems; vis. tchr. audio visual systems Pa. State U., 1955-56, U. Mich., U. Pitts., 1971-76. Mem. Murrysville (Pa.) 4C Civic Assn., 1971-73, v.p., 1972; bd. trustees, pres. Murrysville Community Library Bd., 1973-76. Served with Signal Corps, U.S. Army, 1949-52. Decorated Purple Heart. recipient 3-M Co. citation for pioneering in graphics, 1969. Mem. Soc. Tech. Communication (dir. 1973-76, liasion to Am. Nat. Standards Inst., standards council 1974—, award for distinguished tech. communications 1974), Nat. Micrographics Assn., Pa. Library Assn. Jewish. Contbr. articles to profl. jours. Home: 3333 Benden Dr Murrysville PA 15668 Office: PO Box 355 Pittsburgh PA 15230

FIELD, VIRGINIA, editor, designer; b. Kansas City, Mo.; d. Freeman and Virginia (Keith) Field; student U. Calif. at Los Angeles, 1928-30; Chouinard Art Inst., Los Angeles, 1933-37, U. Calif. at San Francisco, 1940-48-49. Art dir. Drury Co., Inc., San Francisco, 1939-41; dress designer Diana Hunt, Ltd., Port of Spain, Trinidad, 1941-42; censor U.S. War Dept., Port of Spain, 1942-43; registrar San Francisco Mus. Art, 1944-45; art dir. City of Paris dept. store, San Francisco, 1945-46, Emporium, San Francisco, 1947-48, Smith's Oakland, Calif., 1949-50; gallery dir. Bertha Schaefer Gallery, N.Y.C., 1950-52; sec. for membership Am. Fedn. Arts, N.Y.C., 1953-54, sec. for exhbns. and publs., 1954-58, editor Art Newsletter, 1955-58, sec. for exhbns., 1959-61, head dept. exhbns., 1962-63; asst. dir. Asia House Gallery, Asia Soc., Inc., N.Y.C., 1963-74, asso. dir., 1974-76; free-lance editor, designer, 1977—. Mem. Asia Soc., Japan Soc., Am. Fedn. Arts, Am. Assn. Museums. Address: 135 E 71st St New York City NY 10021

FIELDHOUSE, DONALD JOHN, educator; b. Dodgeville, Wis., Nov. 18, 1925; s. Virgil Elsmere and Elva Marie (Power) F.; B.S. cum laude, U. Wis., 1950, M.S., 1952, Ph.D., 1954; m. Dona Marie Danhouser, June 30, 1949; children—Diane Deborah, Denise Fieldhouse Ferris, Doris Fieldhouse Andersen. Mem. faculty U. Del., Newark, 1954—, asso. prof. hort. sci., 1967-72, prof., 1972—. Vice pres. Fieldhouse Found. hist., Dodgeville, 1970—. Served to cpl. AUS, 1943-46: ETO. Mem. Genealogical Soc. Pa., Pa. German Soc., Am. Soc. Hort. Sci., Plant Growth Regulator Working Group, Sigma Xi, Alpha Zeta. Club: Torch. Patentee seed treatment. Research with plant water relations, air pollution and agrl. climatology. Home: 715 Susquehanna Circle Newark DE 19711 Office: Dept Plant Science Univ Del Newark DE 19711

FIELDING, ALLEN FRED, oral surgeon, educator; b. Paterson, N.J., Jan. 22, 1943; s. Fred W. and Emily Claire (Boehm) F.; B.S., Fairleigh Dickinson U., 1959, D.D.S., 1963; postgrad. in oral surgery N.Y. U., 1965-66. Intern in oral surgery Roosevelt Hosp., N.Y.C., 1966-67; resident in oral surgery Phila. Gen. Hosp., 1967-69; practice dentistry specializing in oral-maxillo facial surgery, Phila., 1969—; asso. prof., asst. dir. dept. oral surgery Temple U., Phila., 1969—, staff asso. prof. univ. hosp.; cons. VA Hosp., Wilmington, Del.; cons. staff Phila. Gen. Hosp.; staff St. Christophers Hosp. for Children, Phila., Quakertown (Pa.) Hosp., Lawndale Hosp., Phila.; lectr. in field. Served to capt. USAF, 1963-65. Diplomate Am. Bd. Oral Surgery. Fellow Am. Dental Soc. Anesthesiology, Royal Soc. Health; mem. AAUP, Assn. Mil. Surgeons, Am. Assn. Dental Schs., Am., Pa., Delaware Valley (com. resident tng. 1973—) socs. oral surgeons, Am. Assn. Hosp. Dentists (sec.-treas. Delaware County chpt. 1972-74, v.p. 1974, pres. 1976), Pa., Phila. County dental socs., Internat. Assn. Maxillo-Facial-Surgery, Great Lakes, Mid-Atlantic socs. oral maxillofacial surgeons, Am. Dental Assn., Temple U. Oral Surgery Honor Soc. (advisor). Contbr. articles to profl. jours. Home: 1203 Rodman St Philadelphia PA 19147 Office: 3223 N Broad St Philadelphia PA 19140 also 3207 Kensington Ave Philadelphia PA 19134

FIELDING, NATALIE, art historian; b. N.Y.C., June 20, 1928; d. Morris and Belle (Marcus) Silverman; B.A., N.Y. U., 1949; M.A., Columbia U., 1968; m. Edward Fielding, July 29, 1950; 1 dau., Barbara. Interior designer for residences and businesses, N.Y.C., 1953-58; vol. research asst. Dept. European Paintings, Metropolitan Mus. Art, N.Y.C., 1969, Domestic Affairs Dept. Am. Jewish Com., N.Y.C., 1971-75; dir. Natalie Fielding Fine Art, Jersey City, 1976—. Founder, Bklyn. Heights br. League Women Voters, N.Y.C., 1953; bd. dirs. Tenafly League Women Voters, 1965—; founder Am. Jewish Com., Bergen County, N.J., 1968, exec. bd., 1968—, co-chmn., 1976, chmn., 1977—, mem. nat. exec. commn., 1970--; mem. exec. com. Tenafly Rep. Club, 1968—; Rep. County committeewoman, 1975—; coordinator Citizens for Tenafly Green Acres Fund, 1976; mem. Tenafly Environmental Commn., 1976, chmn., 1977-78. Recipient Citation, Girl Scouts U.S.A., 1978. Mem. Tenafly Nature Assn., Palisades Nature Assn., Nature Conservancy, Center for Hudson River Valley, N.J. Conservation Found., Assn. N.J. Environmental Commn., Columbia U. Alumni Assn., Coll. Art Assn. Jewish. Club: Tenafly Tennis. Address: 215-14 St Jersey City NJ 07302

FIELDS, DOUGLAS PHILIP, bldg. supply and home furnishings wholesale co. exec.; b. Jersey City, May 19, 1942; s. Douglas Philip and Priscilla (Wagner) F.; B.S. summa cum laude, Fordham U., 1964; M.B.A. with Distinction, Harvard, 1966; m. Paulette Susan Titko; children—Douglas P., Priscilla W. Investment analyst Lehman Bros., N.Y.C., 1966-67; asst. to pres. Talley Industries, Mesa, Ariz., 1968-69; pres. TDA Industries, Inc., N.Y.C., 1969—, chmn. bd., 1970—; founder, chmn. exec. com. Unimet Corp., N.Y.C., 1970-73; chmn. bd. Westco Corp., Hartford, Conn., 1970—; chmn. bd. Cooper Distbrs. Inc., Jacksonville, Fla., 1972—; chmn. bd. Eagle Supply, Inc., Tampa, Fla., 1973—; dir. Park 86 Apt. Corp., N.Y.C., 1973-77. Spl. cons. U.S. Commr. Edn., 1973-74, Fed. Energy Adminstrn., 1974-75. Bd. dirs. Girls Club N.Y., 1971, Friends of Fordham Found., 1966-69. Clubs: Harvard (N.Y.C.); Harvard Business School of Ariz. (Phoenix); Midtown Tennis (pres. 1969—) (N.Y.C.). Office: 122 E 42d St New York City NY 10017

FIELDS, J. JOY, nursing services adminstr.; b. N.Y.C., Oct. 24, 1946; d. Harry Walson and Edna May (Simmons) Holland; A.A.S., Olive Harvey Coll., 1972; B.S., St. Joseph's Coll., 1976; M.H.A., C.W. Post Coll., 1978; m. Carl A. Fields, Jr., May 25, 1965; children—Carl Allen, Craig Anthony. Staff nurse U. Chgo. Hosps. and Clinics, 1972; charge nurse N.Y. Hosp., 1972; clin. coordinator Drug Abuse Clinic

Montefiore-Morrisania Affiliation, 1973-74; asst. adminstrv. coordinator Pilgrim Psychiat. Center, N.Y., 1975-76, adminstrv. coordinator edn. and tng., 1976, dir. nursing services 1976—. Recipient citation of achievement Nat. Council Women of U.S.A., 1978; Highest Profl. Attainment award Nat. Assn. Negro Bus. and Profl. Women's Clubs, 1977. Mem. Nat. Forum Nursing Service Adminstrs., Nat. League Nursing, Facilitators Nursing Service Adminstrs., N.Y. State Nurses Assn., Am. Hosp. Assn., Am. Mgmt. Assn., Nat. Assn. Negro Bus. and Profl. Womens' Club. Home: 531 Main St Roosevelt Island NY 10044

FIELDS, NORA JANET, artist, educator; b. N.Y.C.; d. Alexander and Sara Soling; B.S., N.Y. U., 1942; M.A., Columbia U., 1943; m. Samuel B. Fields, Aug. 8, 1948; children—Melinda Sue, Nanette Gail. Tchr. art high schs.; tchr. N.Y. Bot. Garden, Westchester Art Workshop, White Plains, N.Y., 1963—; prof. Kenobo Art Center, Kyoto, Japan, 1963—; flower show master judge, 1964—; accredited instr. arranging, horticulture and indoor gardening Nat. Council State Garden Clubs; lectr. indoor gardening to various clubs, 1960—; exhibited sculpture, mosaics, watercolors in group shows, N.Y.C., Westchester, N.Y., Conn. Mem. Art Students League, Federated Garden Clubs N.Y. State, Ikebana Internat. (pres. Hudson Valley chpt. 1969-72), LWV (treas. 1960-62). Republican. Mem. United Ch. Christ. Author: New Ideas for Christmas Decoration, 1967, Flowers and Foliage-Creative Compositions, 1973, Flower Arranging for Parties, 1975; contbr. numerous articles on flower arranging and indoor gardening to various mags. Home: Boutonville Rd South Salem NY 10590 Office: 1251 Pleasantville Rd Briarcliff Manor NY 10510

FIELDS, RICHARD JAMES, refrigeration mfg. co. exec.; b. Lincoln, N.H., Oct. 7, 1940; s. Henry James and Anita Irene (Boldue) F.; student Northeast Inst. Indsl. Tech., 1967, N.H. Coll.; m. Nancy Althea Morse, June 23, 1963; children—Richard James, Douglas E. Asst. to mgr. Barney's Ice Cream Plant, Laconia, N.H., 1963-67; owner, operator Fields Refrigeration Co., Laconia, 1967-70; salesman Humphreys Inc., Laconia, 1970-74, ops. and sales mgr., 1974-77; regional mgr. Warren Sherer div. Kysor Indsl. Corp., Laconia, 1977—; instr. refrigeration N.H. Vocat. Sch. Served with USMC, 1959-63. Mem. Refrigeration Service Engring. Soc. (past pres., dir. Granite State chpt.), Nat. Engring. Honor Soc. (life). Methodist. Home: 64 Parker St Laconia NH 03246

FIELDS, ROBERT SANFORD, orthodontist; b. Bridgeport, Conn., Dec. 20, 1929; s. Maurice Robert and Esther Florence (Chiz) F.; student Brown U., 1951; D.M.D. cum laude, Tufts U., 1954, postgrad. specialty certificate, 1959; m. Joan Flax, Oct. 28, 1961; children—Steven, Andrea, Ellen, Kate. Pvt. practice dentistry, Pawtucket, R.I., 1956-58; pvt. practice orthodontics, Stamford, Conn., 1959—; instr. operative dentistry Tufts U., Boston, 1956-59, instr. orthodontics, 1959-63; instr. clin. dentistry U. Bridgeport, 1961-68. Cons. Stamford Headstart Program, 1966-70, Stamford Hosp.; chmn. dental adv. com. Stamford Bd. Edn., 1970-72; chmn. Stanford Community Dental Health Com. Trustee, sec. Temple Beth El, Stamford. Served with USNR, 1954-56. Diplomate Am. Bd. Orthodontics. Fellow Royal Soc. Health; mem. Am., Conn. (chmn. council dental health, ho. dels. 1970—) dental assns., Am. Assn. Orthodontists, N.E. Soc. Orthodontists, Am. Soc. Dentistry for Children, Stamford Dental Soc. (pres. 1972—), Soc. Oral Physiology and Occlusion, Western Fairfield Dental Soc., Edward H. Angle Soc. Orthodontists, Robert R. Andrews Honor Soc., Omicron Kappa Upsilon, Alpha Omega, Pi Lambda Phi. Clubs: Rockrimmon Country (Stamford, Conn.); Rotary. Contbr. articles to profl. jours. Home: 81 Fox Ridge Rd Stamford CT 06903 Office: 125 Strawberry Hill Ave Stamford CT 06902

FIEN, JEROME MORRIS, pub. accountant; b. Hartford, Conn., Dec. 26, 1921; s. Martin Herman and Frances (Chernalk) F.; B.A., Johns Hopkins, 1943; M.B.A., N.Y. U., 1949; m. Ruth Lee Klein, Apr. 3, 1945; children—Mark Allan, Judith Anne. Sr. staff accountant Samuel Klein & Co., Newark, 1946-50, now mng. partner; v.p. N.J. State Bd. C.P.A.'s, 1965-67, pres., 1967, 78—, sec., 1967-72. Vice pres. Northeast region Nat. Assn. State Bds. Accountancy, 1968, pres., 1969-70, regional dir., 1973—, v.p. nat. assn., 1972-73. Vice Pres. Florence Crittenton League, 1965-67, pres., 1967—; overall chmn. Essex County Bonds for Israel, 1963-64, chmn. N.J. council, 1969-70; sec. K-F. Charitable Found.; v.p. Jewish Community Coouncil Essex County, N.J.; adv. council Seton Hall U. Sch. Bus. Adminstrn.; adv. council accounting program Rutgers U.; bd. fellows Upsala Coll. Served with USNR, 1944-46. C.P.A., N.J. Mem. Am. Inst. C.P.A.'s, N.J. Soc. C.P.A.'s, Tax Soc. Municipal Accounts Assn. N.J. Club: Green Brook Country (Caldwell, N.J.). Home: 65 Speir Dr South Orange NJ 07079 Office: 1180 Raymond Blvd Newark NJ 07102

FIER, LOUIS, educator; b. Bklyn., Feb. 18, 1921; s. Harry and Esther (Minsky) F.; B.A., Bklyn. Coll., 1947, M.A., 1949; Ph.D. (Ford Found. fellow), N.Y.U., 1958; m. Jeanne Stein, Mar. 26, 1949; children—Harriet, Richard. Mem. faculty Bklyn. (N.Y.) Coll., 1947—, prof. dept. econs., 1972—. Vice chmn. Community Dist. Planning Bd., 1963-65. Bd. dirs. Cambridge Appreciation Fund, 1971—. Served with AUS, 1942-46. Decorated Bronze Star medal. Recipient Fulbright award Franco-Am. Univ. Exchange Commn., 1965-66. Mem. Phi Beta Kappa. Home: 101 Clark St Brooklyn NY 11201

FIERHELLER, GEORGE ALFRED, computer services co. exec.; b. Toronto, Ont., Can., Apr. 26, 1933; s. Harold Parsons and Ruth Hathaway (Bauld) F.; B.A., U. Toronto, 1955; LL.D., Concordia U.; m. Glenna E. Fletcher, Apr. 17, 1957; children—Vicki Elaine, Lori Ann. With IBM, Toronto, 1955-68, account mgr., 1962-65, marketing mgr., 1966-68; founder, pres. Systems Dimensions Ltd., Ottawa, Ont., 1968—; dir. GBC Capital Ltd., Dominion Scottish Investments, ART Research Assos., Network Data Systems. Gen. chmn. United Appeal Campaign Ottawa, 1972; chmn. campaign Carleton U., 1975-77, also chmn. bd. govs., 1977—; mem. adv. com. Norman Paterson Sch. Internat. Affairs; bd. dirs., v.p. United Way Ottawa, 1975—, Opera Ottawa, 1970-71; trustee, mem. exec. com. Nat. Arts Centre; trustee Royal Ottawa Hosp., 1978—. Mem. Canadian Information Processing Soc. (pres., 1970-71), Assn. Computing Machinery, Young Pres.'s Orgn., Conf. Bd., Canadian Assn. Data Processing Service Orgns. (sec.-treas., dir. 1971-73), Inst. Certification of Computer Profls. (founding com.), Canadian Inst. Internat. Affairs. Clubs: Royal Ottawa Golf, Le Cercle Universitarire, Rideau. Contbr. articles to profl. jours. Home: 3332 Riverside Dr Ottawa ON K1V 8P1 Canada Office: 770 Brookfield Rd Ottawa ON K1V 6J5 Canada

FIESER, ARTHUR HERBERT, metall. services exec.; b. N.Y.C., Mar. 14, 1929; s. Frank J. and Elsie (McGirr) F.; B. Chem. Engring., Rensselaer Poly. Inst., 1950, B. Mgmt. Engring., 1950; M.S. in Engring., Johns Hopkins, 1960; m. Frances L. Taylor, Mar. 4, 1973; children—Thomas K., Martha E., Gretchen J., Nicole M., Frank J. Various positions to chief engr. Bethlehem Steel Corp. (Pa.), 1950-66; asst. v.p. engring. Nat. Steel Corp., Pitts., 1966-70; pres. A.F. Industries, Inc., Pitts., 1970—. Served with Chem. Corps, AUS, 1953-55. Registered profl. engr., Pa., Calif., Tex. Mem. Assn. Iron and Steel Engrs., Nat. Soc. Profl. Engrs., Am. Iron and Steel Inst., Am. Inst. M.E. (iron and steel soc.). Patentee in field. Home: 9888 W Moccasin Trail Wexford PA 15090 Office: A F Industries 9800 McKnight Rd Pittsburgh PA 15237

FIESER, GEORGE WALTER, cons. engring. co. exec.; b. Mt. Vernon, N.Y., Nov. 6, 1926; s. Frank John and Elsie (McGirr) F.; M.E., Stevens Inst. Tech., 1950; m. Muriel A. Spenner, July 21, 1951; children—Jane Elizabeth, George Walter. Staff, F.J. Fieser Co., N.Y.C. 1950-56; project engr. Am. Machine and Foundry, Atomic Energy div., Greenwich, Conn., 1956-57, Dunedin, Fla., 1957-58; group supr. Atomic Energy div., Allis-Chalmers Mfg. Co., Washington, 1958-60, project engr., Elk River, Minn., 1960, Washington, 1960-61; dir. program mgmt. dept. Susquehanna Corp., Atlantic Research div., Alexandria, Va., 1961-67, dep. asst. gen. mgr., 1967-68, dir., plant mgr. West Hanover and Halifax (Mass.) mfg. plants, 1968-69; dept. mgr. MB Assos., San Ramon, Calif., 1969-70; dir. project mgmt. dept. Central Engring. div. Pa. Engring. Corp., Pitts., 1970-71; v.p. project mgmt/project engring., A.F. Industries Inc., Pitts., 1971—, also dir. Served with USNR, 1944-46. Mem. ASME, Nat. Soc. Profl. Engrs., Engrs. Soc. Western Pa., Engrs. Club, Clubs: Fellows, Masons, K.T., Jesters, 32 deg. Registered profl. engr. N.Y., Md., Va. Home: 116 N Harleston Dr Pittsburgh PA 15237 Office: AF Industries Inc 9800 McKnight Rd Pittsburgh PA 15237

FIESER, JOHN BAILEY, econ. geographer; b. Washington, Nov. 29, 1940; s. James Louis and Mary Elizabeth (Bailey) F.; B.S., U. Md., 1964; postgrad. Ind. U. 1964-65; m. Barbara Stuart Guillan, Oct. 15, 1966; children—Catherine Elizabeth, Emily Brouard. Geographer, information systems specialist Econ. Devel. Adminstrn., U.S. Dept. Commerce, Washington, 1966-67, 70—. Served as intelligence officer USNR, 1967-70. Recipient Bronze Medal award Dept. Commerce, 1972, Recognition award, 1978. Mem. Assn. Am. Geographers, Am. Geog. Soc., Inst. Social and Econ. Research, Phi Kappa Tau, Gamma Theta Upsilon. Methodist. Home: 5932 New England Woods Dr Burke VA 22015 Office: Office of Econ Research Econ Devel Adminstrn Main Commerce Bldg Room 6018 Washington DC 20230

FIFE, EARL HANSON, JR., microbiologist; b. Elkton, Ky., Apr. 14, 1915; s. Earl Hanson and Mable (Oldham) F.; B.S., U. Wash., 1948; M.S., U. Md., 1952; m. Mary Marilla Skillings, June 14, 1941; children—Sally (Mrs. Clifton Jordan Johnson), Earl Dennett, Trudy (Mrs. Harold Thomas Golding). Research asst. Swedish Hosp., Seattle, 1947-48; supervisory microbiologist Walter Reed Army Inst. Research, Washington, 1948-65, chief dept. serology, 1965-73, ret., 1973. Cons. Pan Am. Health Orgn., 1966—; cons. to Surgeon Gen. of U.S. Army, 1962—; mem. faculty Walter Reed Army Inst. Research postgrad. tng. program, 1965—. Served with AUS, 1942-47. Recipient Outstanding Performance award Dept. of Army, 1971; certificate of achievement U.S. Army Med. Research and Devel. Command, 1973, Walter Reed Army Inst. Research, 1973, Ann. Research award Am. Assn. Lab. Animal Sci., 1971. Fellow Washington Acad. Sci., Royal Soc. Tropical Medicine and Hygiene, Am. Inst. Chemists; mem. Soc. for Exptl. Biology and Medicine, Am. Soc. for Microbiology, Am. Soc. Tropical Medicine and Hygiene, Theta Xi. Clubs: Edge Creek Boat (Royal Oak, Md.); Miles River Power Squadron (St. Michaels, Md.). Mem. editorial bd. Exptl. Parasitology, 1968-73. Home: Box 122 Royal Oak MD 21662

FIGURELLI, JENNIFER CONSTANCE, pschologist; b. Jersey City, May 11, 1945; d. Francesco Antonio and Jean (Bigler) Figurelli; B.S., St. Lawrence U., 1966; M.A., U. S.C., 1970; postgrad. U. Calgary, Jersey City State Coll., Ph.D., Fordham U., 1977. Research psychologist Alta. (Can.) Mental Hosp., Ponoka, 1967; psychol. research asst. U. Calgary (Alta.), 1968-69; psychologist Columbia (S.C.) Pub. Schs., 1969-70, Jersey City Pub. Schs., 1970—; adj. prof. psychology St. Peter's Coll., Jersey City, 1970—. Mem. S.C. State Com. on Legilization Abortion, 1970. Mem. Nat., Jersey City edn. assns., Nat. Assn. Sch. Psychologists (chmn. ad hoc com. 1972-73 del. 1978-79), Am., N.J., Inter-Am., Southeastern psychol. assns., Internat. Assn. for Applied Psychology, N.J. Assn. for Sch. Psychologists (sec. 1977-78), Soc. for Research in Child Devel., Am. Ednl. Research Assn. Editorial bd. Sch. Psychology Digest. Home: 88 Highland Ave Jersey City NJ 07306 Office: 182 Merseles St Jersey City NJ 07302

FILBERT, HOWARD CONRAD, JR., mech. engr.; b. Balt., Feb. 7, 1917; s. Howard Conrad and Maie (McGowan) F.; B.S., U. Md., 1941, M.E., 1948, M.S., 1953; m. Jeanette M. Reibetanz, Sept. 20, 1941; children—Susan Carol, David Howard, Richard Conrad. Engr. div. mgr. Naval Ordnance Lab., Silver Spring, Md., 1941-52; gen. mgr. MRC Corp., Balt., 1952-54, v.p., gen. mgr., 1954-56, exec. v.p., gen. mgr., 1956-66, pres., 1966—; pres. Scope Electronics Inc., Reston, Va., 1969-71, dir., 1968—. Nat. chmn. Greater U. of Md. Fund. Recipient citations from USN, U.S. Govt. Registered profl. engr., Md. Mem. Am. Def. Preparedness Assn. (dir.), Am. Inst. Aeros. and Astronautics (dir., past pres. Md.), Nat., Md. socs. profl. engrs., AAAS, Tau Beta Pi, Pi Tau Sigma, Phi Kappa Phi, Omicron Delta Kappa. Presbyterian (elder). Author articles in field. Patentee on mil. devices, systems. Home: 515 E Seminary Ave Baltimore MD 21204 Office: 11212 McCormick Rd Hunt Valley MD 21031

FILENE, WILLIAM, JR., personnel cons., educator; b. Cambridge, Mass., Mar. 5, 1933; s. William and Katherine (Jakeman) F.; A.A., Dean Jr. Coll., 1954; B.S., Boston U., 1956, postgrad., 1971; M.S., U. Mass., 1958; postgrad. Tufts U., 1968; m. Marilyn Joan Costello, Nov. 24, 1955; children—Deborah, Donna, Marie, Patricia, Helen, William. Program dir. Reed St. Settlement House, Phila., 1951-52; ednl. adviser Nat. Assn. Real Estate Bds., Chgo., 1964-67; state dir. edn. Mass. Assn. Real Estate Bds., Boston, 1964-67; dir. personnel Belmont (Mass.) Pub. Schs., 1967-74, Greenwich (Conn.) Pub. Schs., 1974-77; self-employed personnel cons., 1977—; mem. faculty Quincy Jr. Coll., Boston State Coll., 1977—; free-lance writer, 1958—; lectr. colls., ch. and civic orgns.; cons. HEW. Mass. Nat. dir. Teenage Ambassadors, 1962-64; chmn. Braintree (Mass.) Sch. Com., 1967. Dean Jr. Coll. Trustees Centennial Adv. Com., 1966. Exec. bd. Mass. Bay Data Study, 1973; pres. St. Clare's Parish Council, 1973-74. Recipient Freedoms Founds. Tchrs. medal, 1961, Jr. C. of C. Distinguished Service award, 1963; Dean Alumni Centennial award, 1966; named Outstanding Young Man of Am. U.S. Jr. C. of C., 1965. Mem. Am. Assn. Sch. Personnel Adminstrs. (nat. com. chmn. 1972, cons. 1973, exec. com. 1976-78), Am. Assn. Sch. Adminstrs., Assn. Supervision and Curriculum Devel., Mass. Adult Edn. Assn., NEA, Mass. Tchrs. Assn., New. Eng. Assn. for Sch., Coll. and Univ. Staffing (exec. com. 1972—, editor newsletter 1972-73, pres. 1974-76), Nat. Migraine Found., Assn. for Humanistic Psychology, Dean Jr. Coll. Alumni Council (life), Nat. Assn. for Mental Health, ACLU, Am. Assn. Sch., Coll., U. Staffing, Pub. Personnel Assn., Internat. Personnel Assn., Am. Personnel Assn., Am. Mgmt. Assn., Am. Soc. Tng. and Devel. Author: Real Estate License Exam Handbook. Home: 156 Cain Ave Braintree MA 02184

FILER, JOHN HORACE, ins. co. exec.; b. New Haven, Sept. 3, 1924; s. Harry Lambert and Ehrma (Green) F.; B.A., DePauw U., 1947, LL.D., 1970; LL.B., Yale, 1950; m. Jean Rogers Fairchild, June 25, 1949; children—Susan, Cynthia, Kathryn, Ann. Admitted to Conn. bar, 1950; practice in New Haven, 1950-58; law clk. Carroll C. Hincks, U.S. dist. judge, 1950-51; asso., partner firm Gumbart, Corbin, Tyler & Cooper, 1951-58; gen. counsel Aetna Life & Casualty Co., Hartford, Conn., 1958-68, exec. v.p., 1968-72, chmn. bd., chief exec. officer, 1972—, also dir.; dir. U.S. Steel Corp. Chmn. Bd. Edn., Farmington, 1963-67; trustee Mt. Holyoke Coll., Miss Porter's Sch., Farmington; mem. Conn. Commn. to Study Met. Govt., 1966-67; mem. Conn. Senate, 1957-58. Served to ensign USNR, 1943-46. Mem. Am., Conn., Hartford County bar assns., Assn. Life Ins. Counsel, Greater Hartford C. of C. (dir.), Conn. Bus. and Industry Assn. (vice chmn.). Episcopalian. Home: Mountain Spring Rd Farmington CT 06032 Office: 151 Farmington Ave Hartford CT 06115*

FILETTI, DANIEL MEDARDO, business exec.; b. Rimersburg, Pa., May 8, 1919; s. Medardo and Erminia (Reverberi) F.; student Dobe Engring. Sch., 1937-41, Clarion (Pa.) State Coll., 1960-61; m. Bettie K. Filetti; children—Mary Denise Filetti Crockett, Emma Lou, Dante M. Engr., architect Foster Wheeler Corp., N.Y.C., 1939-43; owner Daniel M. Filetti Agy., Rimersburg, 1946-74, Filetti Realty Corp., Rimersburg, 1950—; exec. officer Hallmark Ins. Agy., Rimersburg, 1974—; adminstrv. officer Pa. Dept. Gen. Services, Harrisburg, 1975—; v.p., dir. New Bethlehem Bank, 1963—; sec., dir. Summit Mineral Corp., 1956—, Effeness Enterprises, Inc., 1952—. Trustee Lancaster (Pa.) Theol. Sem., 1978—. Served with USNR, 1943-46. Democrat. Mem. United Ch. of Christ (nat. exec. council). Home: 122 E Chestnut St Rimersburg PA 16248 Office: 20 W Broad St Rimersburg PA 16248

FILLER, DOROTHY SANDS (MRS. SAMUEL FILLER), civic worker, bus. exec.; b. Charleston, S.C.; d. Ernest Desi and Hermina (Klein) Sands; B.S. in Edn., Trenton State Coll., 1945; m. Samuel Filler, Feb. 9, 1947; children—Linda Nerine, James Bertram. Tchr., New Hanover Twp. Sch., Wrightstown, N.J., 1945-48; v.p., sec. Filler Farms, Inc., Florence, 1958—, Pine Tree, Inc., Burlington Twp., N.J., 1961—, Samuel Filler Enterprises, Inc., 1964—. Burlington County Library Commr., 1972-75. Trustee Pub. Library Willingboro, 1962-77, Burlington chpt. Deborah Hosp., 1955-57. Mem. ALA, N.J. Library Assn., Am., N.J. library trustee assns., N.J. Assn. Library Commrs., Nat. Council Jewish Women (treas. 1963-64). Rotary Ann. Office: care Pine Tree Inc Sunset Rd Burlington Twp NJ 08016

FILLMAN, HENRY INGERTON, lawyer; b. N.Y.C., June 4, 1896; s. Abraham Noah and Elizabeth (Ginsburg) F.; B.S., Amherst Coll., 1917; postgrad. U. Montpelier, France, 1919; LL.B., Columbia, 1922; m. Miriam Yvette Rubin, Sept. 12, 1930; children—Caryl Elizabeth (Mrs. Stephen I. Kaplan), Jeffrey Andrew. Admitted to N.Y. bar, 1923, Supreme Ct., 1939, U.S. Ct. Appeals, 1923, U.S. Ct. Claims, 1953, U.S. Customs Ct., 1960; partner firm Katz & Sommerich, N.Y.C., 1939-68. Dir. Samincorp S.Am. Minerals & Merchandise Corp. Served to lt. AUS, 1917-19; lt. col. USAAF, 1942-45. Mem. Am., N.Y., City N.Y. bar assns., Am. Soc. Internat. Law, Am. Fgn. Law Assn., Am. Judicature Soc. Clubs: Amherst of N.Y., Lawyers. Home: 1125 Park Ave New York City NY 10028 Office: 299 Park Ave New York City NY 10017

FILTEAU, GARY REED, real estate appraiser; b. Springfield, Mass., Aug. 22, 1938; s. Jerry and Elizabeth F.; student U. N.H., 1959-60; B.S., U. Conn., 1963; m. Sally Jean Carter, June 11, 1960; children—Jay Reed, Liesl Jean. Appraiser, State of N.H., Concord, 1963-64, Sawyer Appraisal Co., Portland, Maine, 1964-67; appraiser, mgr., Marshall & Stevens, Inc., Portland, 1967-68; appraiser, partner, Hyde Assos., Concord, 1968—; chmn. bd. adjustment Town of Hebron (N.H.). Served with USN, 1956-59. Mem. Soc. Real Estate Appraisers (pres. N.H. chpt.), Nat. Assn. Rev. Appraisers, Nat., N.H., Concord assns. realtors. Club: Masons. Home: North Shore Rd East Hebron NH 03232 Office: 45 Airport Rd Concord NH 03301

FINBERG, LAURENCE, pediatrician; b. Chgo., May 20, 1923; s. Joseph and Anne (Malkow) F.; B.S., U. Chgo., 1944, M.D., 1946; m. Harriet Levinson, June 17, 1945; children—Robert, Jeanne, James. Intern, U. Chgo. Clinics, 1946-47; asst. resident pediatrics Balt. City Hosps., 1949-50, resident, 1950-51; practice medicine, specializing in pediatrics, Balt., 1951-63, N.Y.C., 1963—; asst. chief pediatrician Balt. City Hosps., 1951-61, dir. pediatric outpatient dept., 1951-63, dir. premature nursery, 1951-59, asso. chief pediatrics, 1961-63; pediatrician Harriet Lane Home, 1951-63; chmn. dept. pediatrics Montefiore Hosp. and Med. Center, Bronx, N.Y., 1963—; instr. dept. pediatrics Johns Hopkins Sch. Medicine, 1951-56, asst. prof., 1956-63; prof. pediatrics Albert Einstein Coll. Medicine, Bronx, 1963—; pediatric cons. U.S. Children's Bur., 1965—; cons. pediatrician Blythedale Children's Hosp., Valhalla, N.Y., 1970—. Mem. pediatric adv. com. N.Y.C. Dept. Health, 1970—. Served with USPHS, 1947-49. Diplomate Am. Bd. Pediatrics (examiner 1969—, dir. 1974—, pres. 1978). Mem. Am. Pediatric Soc., Soc. Pediatric Research, Am. Acad. Pediatrics (mem. com. on environmental hazards 1968—), Assn. Med. Sch. Pediatric Dept. Chmn., Am. Inst. Nutrition, Assn. Pediatric Ambulatory Services, Am. Soc. Clin. Nutrition, Am. Fedn. Clin. Research, Am. Soc. Nephrology, A.A.A.S., AMA, Sociedad Peruana De Pediatria, Harvey Soc., Med. Soc. State N.Y., N.Y. Acad. Medicine (chmn. pediatric sect. 1967), N.Y. Acad. Sci., N.Y. Diabetes Assn., Bronx Pediatric Soc. (pres. 1969-70), Phi Beta Kappa, Sigma Xi, Alpha Omega Alpha. Research in electrolyte physiology. Home: 57 Walden Rd Tarrytown NY 10591 Office: 111 E 210th St Bronx NY 10467

FINCH, EDWARD RIDLEY, JR., lawyer, diplomat; b. Westhampton Beach, L.I., N.Y., Aug. 31, 1919; s. Edward R. and Mary Livingston (Delafield) F.; A.B. with honors, Princeton, 1941; J.D., N.Y. U., 1947; LL.D. (hon.), Mo. Valley Coll., 1963; m. Elizabeth Johnson, June 1, 1950 (div. 1977); children—Elizabeth L., Edward Ridley III. Admitted to N.Y. State bar, 1948, U.S. Supreme Ct. bar, 1956, D.C. bar, 1978; partner firm Finch and Schaefler, N.Y.C., 1950—; lectr. Princeton, Am. Inst. Aeros. and Astronautics, Am. Bar Assn., others; faculty Nat. War Coll.; commr. N.Y.C., 1955-58; U.S. del. to 4th UN Congress, 1970, 5th UN Congress, 1975; U.S. Spl. Ambassador to Panama, 1972; pres., dir. Finch Corp., N.Y.C., 1965—. Bd. dirs., pres. N.Y. Inst. Edn. of Blind, 1950—, Adams Meml. Fund, Inc.; founder, bd. dirs. St. Hilda's and St. Hugh's Sch., N.Y.C., 1950—. Crippled Children's Friendly Aid Assn., Inc., 1965—; bd. dirs. pres., dir. Hosp. St. Giles the Cripple, 1974—, St. Nicholas Soc. N.Y.C., 1948—; life fellow Met. Mus. Art. Served to col. USAAF, 1941-46. Mem. Assn. Bar City N.Y. (roundtable com. 1952-57, com. on surrogates cts. 1959-62), Am. Law Inst., Am. Judicature Soc., Am., N.Y. State bar assns., Judge Advs. Assn. (pres. 1971-72), Phi Delta Phi. Republican. Episcopalian. Clubs: Univ., Union League, Union, Princeton (bd. govs.). Contbr. articles to legal publs. Home: 860 Park Ave New York City NY 10021 Office: 36 W 44th St New York City NY 10036

FINDLAY, CHARLES WALTER, JR., physician; b. Bridgeport, Conn., Mar. 28, 1917; s. Charles Walter and Helen (Plumb) F.; grad. Lenox Sch., 1935; A.B., Yale, 1939; M.D., Columbia, 1943; m. Peggy Eagle, Aug. 16, 1944; children—Charles Walter, Frederick Eagle, Laurie Brewster. Intern St. Luke's Hosp., N.Y.C., 1943-44; house officer Children's Hosp., Boston, 1944-45; resident Mass. Gen. Hosp., Boston, 1945-46, N.Y. Hosp., N.Y.C., 1946-47, Presbyn. Hosp., N.Y.C., 1947-48; asst. attending surgeon Presbyn. Hosp., 1950-60, asso. attending surgeon, 1960—; attending Surgeon Laurence Hosp., Bronxville, N.Y., 1977—; asso. clin. prof. Coll. Physicians and

Surgeons, Columbia, 1965—. Served with M.C., AUS, 1953-54. Diplomate Am. Bd. Surgery, Am. Bd. Thoracic Surgery. Fellow A.C.S.; mem. Internat., N.Y. surg. socs., A.M.A., Am. Assn. Thoracic Surgery, Am. Soc. Microbiology, N.Y. Soc. Thoracic Surgery, A.O. Whipple Soc., Med. Strollers N.Y.C. (pres. 1978). Episcopalian. Clubs: St. Andrews Golf (Hastings, N.Y.); Acoaxet (Mass.). Contbr. articles to profl. jours. Home: 11 Kraft Ave Bronxville NY 10708 Office: 161 Fort Washington Ave New York City NY 10032

FINDLAY, RAYMOND DAVID, educator; b. Toronto, Ont., Can., Aug. 10, 1938; s. David and Vera (Brown) F.; B.S. in Engring., U. Toronto, 1963, M.A. in Engring., 1965, Ph.D., 1968; m. Donna Lillian Keene, Sept. 9, 1961; children—Glen Andrew, Natalie Anne, Andrew James, Suzanne Marie. Engrs. asst. Corp. Met. Toronto, 1958-60; instr., research asst. U. Toronto, 1963-67; asst. prof. U. N.B., Fredericton, 1967-72, asso. prof. elec. engring., 1973-78, prof., 1978—; project dir. Canadian Gen. Electric Co., 1972-73. Sec. N.B. Provincial Audio Visual Study Com., 1970-74. J. Edgar McAllister fellow, 1965; NRC fellow, 1966-67, grantee, 1967—, sr. indsl. fellow, 1972-73; NSF fellow, 1966; recipient Dow Outstanding Young Faculty award Am. Soc. Engring. Edn., 1972. Registered profl. engr., N.B. Mem. IEEE (student Paper award Canadian region 1963; past chmn. N.B. subsect. 1970-71), Am. Soc. Engring. Edn. (activity coordinator, rep. 1970-73, 76-78, policy com. 1973-76), Assn. Profl. Engrs. N.B. Presbyterian. Club: Y'smen Internat. Author papers in field. Home: 149 Stanley St Fredericton NB E3B 3A2 Canada

FINDLAY, STEPHEN W(ILLIAM), headmaster; b. Newark, July 16, 1911; s. Matthew James and Katheryn Agnes (Warner) F.; student St. Anselm Coll., Manchester, N.H., 1929-31; A.B., St. Vincent Coll., Latrobe, Pa., 1934; J.C.D., Cath. U. Am., 1941. Professed Benedictine monk, 1932, ordained priest, Roman Catholic Ch., 1937; tchr. Greek, history St. Mary's Sem., Morristown, N.J., 1934-38; tchr. English, St. Benedict's Prep. Sch., Newark, 1941-42; headmaster Delbarton Sch., Morristown, 1942-67, dir. devel., 1967—; dir. Camp Delbarton, Morristown, 1950—; procurator for cause of canonization and beatification Sister Miriam Teresa, 1946—; subprior, St. Mary's Abbey, Morristown, 1956-70. Mem. Morris Twp. Bd. Ethics; chmn. N.J. State Mediation Bd., 1973-76. Mem. Canon Law Soc. Am., Nat. Assn. Secondary Sch. Prins., Nat. Soc. for Study Edn., Acad. Polit. Sci., Am. Alumni Council, Sister Miriam Teresa League of Prayer (spiritual dir.). Author: Canonical Norms Governing Deposition and Degradation, 1941. Home: Delbarton Sch Mendham Rd Morristown NJ 07960

FINE, NORMAN LEE, paint co. exec.; b. Scranton, Pa., Aug. 6, 1943; s. Michael and Frimi (Suravitz) F.; B.A. cum laude, Washington and Jefferson Coll., 1965; postgrad. U. Hartford, 1974; certificate, N.Y.U., 1977; m. Cheryl Tow, Mar. 20, 1968; children—Jeffrey George, Alexander Doran. With Clark Paint Co., East Hartford, Conn., 1965-67, gen. mgr., 1967-73; pres., chief exec. officer FMI Corp., Glastonbury, Conn., 1973—; dir. Capitol Ave. Assoc., Hartford, Conn., 1977—; v.p. Hamark Real Estate Partnership, Manchester, Conn., 1976—; dir., head devel. C & C Co., Glastonbury, 1975; cons. U. Hartford Sch. Bus., 1977-78. Served with Conn. N.G., 1965-71. Mem. C. of C. Contbr. articles to Newspapers, Home: One Brookside West Hartford CT 06107 Office: 158 Hartford Rd Manchester CT 06040

FINEBERG, SEYMOUR KOEPPEL, physician; b. N.Y.C., July 28, 1915; s. Henry and Florence (Koeppel) F.; student Coll. City N.Y., 1932-34; B.S., U. Ark., 1936, M.D., 1940; postgrad. N.Y. U. Med. Sch., 1947-48; m. Seena Madeleine Hamilton, Aug. 18, 1950; 1 son, Bryan Scott. Intern, Harlem Hosp., N.Y.C., 1940-42, resident in medicine, 1942, chief resident in medicine, 1946-47; practice medicine specializing in internal medicine N.Y.C., 1947—; asst. clin. cardiologist Jewish Meml. Hosp., N.Y.C., 1947-52; vis. physician Harlem Hosp., 1952-66, chief of metabolic service, 1956-66, asst. dir. medicine, 1961-62, acting dir. medicine, 1962-64; vis. physician Flower-Fifth Ave. Hosp., N.Y.C., 1956—; chief of diabetes and obesity Met. Hosp., N.Y.C., 1968—; dir. medicine and cardiologist Prospect Hosp., Bronx, N.Y., 1961—, pres. med. bd., 1967-68; clin. instr. medicine N.Y. Med. Coll., 1954-56, clin. asst. prof. medicine, 1968-76, clin. asso. prof. medicine, 1976—; cons. to council on drugs AMA, 1969-72. Served to maj., M.C., USAF, 1942-46. Decorated Air medal; diplomate Am. Bd. Internal Medicine. Fellow A.C.P., Am. Coll. Cardiology; mem. N.Y. Cardiol. Soc., Am. Soc. Internal Medicine, Am. Pub. Health Assn., N.Y. State, N.Y. County med. socs., AMA, Am., N.Y. diabetes assns., Am. Med. Writers Assn., Am. Pub. Health Assn., N.Y. State Soc. Internal Medicine. Jewish. Contbr. articles on research in diabetes and metabolic diseases to med. jours. Home: 450 E 63rd St New York City NY 10021 Office: 1056 5th Ave New York City NY 10028

FINEGOLD, RONALD, computer corp. exec.; b. Bklyn., Nov. 17, 1942; s. Herman Hearsch and Ethel (Kanner) F.; B.S., Coll. City N.Y., 1963; m. Ellen Carole Sehr, Mar. 22, 1964; children—Sherry Dawn, Edward Jon. Supr. programming Celanese Chem. Co., N.Y.C., 1962-66; v.p. mktg. Automation Scis., Inc., N.Y.C., 1966-69; pres., dir. Computer Horizons Corp., N.Y.C., 1969—; chmn. bd. Stamford Assos., Inc., N.Y.C., 1969—; pres. Rizons Brokerage, Inc., 1970-71, chmn. bd., 1971-75, also dir.; chmn. bd. Beamer Personnel, Inc., 1972-74; pres., dir. Nutritional Diets, Inc., 1973-74, CH Horizons Ltd. of Can., 1973-77. Mem. Data Processing Mgmt. Assn., Am. Mgmt. Assn., Am. Philatelic Soc., Aircraft Owners and Pilots Assn., Tau Epsilon Phi. Home: 154 Valley Forge Pl Orangeburg NY 10962 Office: 747 3d Ave New York City NY 10017 also 375 Sylvan Ave Englewood Cliffs NJ 07032 also 1000 Brickell Ave Miami FL

FINEGOLD, WILFRED JAY, gynecologist; b. Pitts., July 31, 1909; s. Julius and Celia (Gruber) F.; B.S., U. Pitts., 1930; M.D., U. London (Eng.), 1935; m. Nov. 12, 1937; children—Alan, Nan. Intern, Pitts., 1935-36; resident Chgo. Lying-In Hosp., 1940-44; fellow in obstetrics Montefiore Hosp., Pitts., 1944-45; mem. faculty U. Pitts., 1945-76, asso. prof. obstetrics and gynecology, 1960-76; practice medicine specializing in infertility, Pitts., 1944-78; mem. staffs Magee Women's Hosp., Montefiore Hosp., until 1978; head W.J. Finegold Infertility Corp., Pitts., 1970-78. Fellow Am. Soc. Obstetricians and Gynecologists; mem. Internat., Am., Pacific Coast fertility socs., Pitts.-Allegheny County Med. Soc., Phi Epsilon Pi. Jewish. Clubs: Masons, Westmoreland Country; Concordia (Pitts.). Author: Artificial Insemination, 1972, rev. edit., 1976; Sperm Freezing, 1978. Home: 4940 Bayard St Pittsburgh PA 15213

FINEMAN, ELLIOT NORMAN, bus. services co. exec.; b. N.Y.C., June 26, 1938; s. Allan and Sylvia (Malakoff) F.; B.S., Mass. Inst. Tech., 1959; m. Patricia Berman, Dec. 18, 1959; children—Elissa, Michael. Structural designer Aamann & Whitney Co., N.Y.C., 1960-61; owner Unlimited Limousine Service, N.Y.C., 1961-63; with Benjamin Berman, Inc., Moonachie, N.J., 1963-77, pres., 1973-77; founder Cost Free Internal Profit Systems, Inc., 1977—; vol. cons. Urban Cons. Corp., 1973—. Sec. Found. Child Mental Welfare, 1965—; pres. bd. dirs. Center for Chamber Music at Apple Hill, N.H., 1970—. Mem. Am. Assn. Commodity Traders. Home: 150 E 69th St New York City NY 10021

FINER, DIANA CAROL, sch. counselor; b. Elizabeth, N.J., Dec. 13, 1944; d. Frank John and Lillian Theresa (Faser) F.; B.A., Mich. State U., 1966; M.Ed., Northeastern U., 1974. Program coordinator drug epidemiology study Mass. Gen. Hosp., Boston, 1969-70; grants admnstr. dept. surgery Boston U. Hosp. 1970-74; special needs counselor Methuen (Mass.) Pub. Schs. 1975—, mem. exec. bd. edn. assn. 1976-78. Recipient scholarship State of N.J., Mich. State U., 1962-66. Mem. Am. Personnel and Guidance Assn., Am. Sch. Counselors Assn., Mass. Sch. Counselors Assn., Mass. Personnel and Guidance Assn., NEA, Mass. Tchrs. Assn., Methuen Edn. Assn., Kappa Delta Pi. Unitarian. Contbr. articles to profl. jours. Home: 144 Page Rd Bedford MA 01730 Office: 129 Haverhill St Methuen MA 01843

FINGER, KENNETH JOEL, lawyer; b. N.Y.C., Feb. 16, 1940; s. Philip and Sally Finger; B.A., N.Y. U., 1960; LL.B., Harvard U., 1963; m. Dorothy Jane Miller, Feb. 13, 1965; children—Carl Laurence, Pamela Ann, Daniel Saul. Admitted to N.Y. bar, 1964; partner firm Menagh, Trainor and Finger, Esqs., N.Y.C., 1964-73, Finger and Koss, White Plains, N.Y., 1973-74; prin. Kenneth J. Finger, P.C., White Plains, N.Y., 1974—; arbitrator Am. Arbitration Assn., 1973—; adj. prof. Hofstra U., 1974; fact finder N.Y. State Pub. Employment Relations Bd., 1972—. Chmn., Westchester County Hosp. Bd., 1977—; mem. community adv. bd. Goldwater Meml. Hosp., 1971—, v.p. 1973-74; candidate N.Y. State Senate, 1972. Served with AUS, 1963. Mem. Am., N.Y. State, Westchester County bar assns., Assn. Bar City N.Y., Nat. Health Lawyers Assn., Assn. Hosp. Attys. Democrat. Jewish. Clubs: Scarsdale Town, Builder's Inst. Westchester County, Rotary. Office: 14 Mamaroneck Ave White Plains NY 10601

FINGERHUT, DONNA, counselor; b. Bronx, N.Y., June 23, 1951; d. Norman and Dorothy Rae (Mirchin) Fingerhut; B.S. in Psychology, Lehman Coll., 1973; M.S. in Edn., Hunter Coll., 1977. Asst. projects coordinator Med. Info. Systems, N.Y.C., 1973-74; hygienic therapist Bronx State Children's Hosp., 1974-75; vocat. counselor asst. Personnel Scis. Center, N.Y.C., 1975; program specialist ICD Rehab. and Research Center, N.Y.C., 1975—; group and individual counselor for Hunter Coll. students; vocat. adviser Norman Thomas High Sch. Mem. Am. Personnel and Guidance Assn., Am. Sch. Counselors Assn. Home: 530 E 89th St New York NY 10028 Office: 340 E 24th St New York NY 10010

FINI, FRANK CAESAR, assn. exec.; b. Leominster, Mass., Oct. 3, 1930; s. John and Sarah (Cappasso) F.; ed. pub. schs., service schs., acads.; children—Lili Fini Zana, John. Joined USAF, 1947, advanced through grades to CMS, 1962; ret., 1970; exec. dir. Air Force Sgts. Assn., Marlow Heights, Md., 1970—. Registered lobbyist. Mem. Am. Soc. Assn. Execs., Internat. Platform Assn., Am. Mgmt. Assn., Am. Security Council. Home: 2020 Brooks Dr Suitland MD 20028 Office: 6101 28th Ave Marlow Heights MD 20031

FINK, AARON HERMAN, box mfg. exec.; b. Union City, N.J., Apr. 1, 1916; s. Jacob and Tessie (Dubow) F.; A.B., Johns Hopkins U., 1938; Ph.D. (hon.), Hamilton State U., 1973; m. Roslyn Lamb, Dec. 6, 1942; children—Elliot, Ilene. Treas., Asso. Mills, 1938-45; v.p., gen. mgr. Essex Paper Box Mfg. Co., Newark, 1945-48, pres., 1948—; pres. Internat. Gift Box Co., 1948—, Gen. Packaging System, 1962—; dir. Asso. Mills; U.S. del. Conf. Mfrs., Paris, 1954, Spl. Econ. Mission to Italy, 1954. Fellow Intercontinental Biog. Assn.; mem. N.J. Box Craft Bur. (pres. 1954-55), Am. Soc. Quality Control, Nat. Paper Box Assn. (adv. bd., chmn. plant ops. and manpower com., chmn. met. div.), TAPPI, Am. Geophys. Union, NAM, Am. Mgmt. Assn., AIM (pres.'s council, adv. bd.), Am. Material Handling Soc., Nat. Soc. Bus. Budget (mem. conf.), Soc. Advancement Mgmt., Am. Inst. Aeros. and Astronautics, Math. Soc. Am., Am. Statis. Assn., Nat. Assn. Cost Accountants, Am. Inst. Corp. Controllers, Paper Industry Mgmt. Assn., Planning Execs. Inst., Am. Water Resources Assn., U.S. Naval Inst., Chaine des Rotisseurs, Water Res. Assn. Delaware River Basin. Clubs: Princeton, Johns Hopkins (N.Y.C.); Newark Athletic; Crestmont Country (gov.) (West Orange); Gt. Oak Yacht (Chestertown, Md.); Le Mirador Country (Lake Geneva, Switzerland); Jockey (Miami, Fla.); Boca Raton, Broken Sound Golf (Boca Raton, Fla.). Home: 20 Crestwood Dr Maplewood NJ 07040 Office: 281 Astor St Newark NJ 07105

FINK, MARTIN RONALD, aero. engr.; b. N.Y.C., Apr. 27, 1931; s. David Peter and Etta Alice (Checker) F.; B.S. in Aero. Engring., Mass. Inst. Tech., 1952, M.S., 1953; m. Jacqueline Fay Klein, Aug. 24, 1952; children—Howard Jeffrey, Andrew Charles, Douglas Reuben. Research asst. Mass. Inst. Tech. Transonic Aircraft Control Project, Cambridge, 1952-53; research engr. United Techs. Research Center, East Hartford, Conn., 1953-58, supr. missile aerodynamics, 1959-63, supr. aerodynamics group, 1964-67, sr. cons. engr. aerodynamics, 1967—. Asso. fellow Am. Inst. Aeros. and Astronautics; mem. Acoustical Soc. Am., Tau Beta Pi (pres. Central Conn. alumni br. 1973), Sigma Xi, Alpha Epsilon Pi. Jewish religion. Contbr. numerous articles to profl. jours. Home: 55 Richmond Ln West Hartford CT 06117 Office: 400 Main St East Hartford CT 06108

FINKE, HANS-JOACHIM, museum service agency exec.; b. Koenigsberg, Germany, Nov. 23, 1939; s. Erich Karl Josef and Renate Gertrud (Montzka) F.; came to U.S., 1954, naturalized, 1959; A.B., Temple U., 1962, M.A., 1962, Ph.D., 1970; m. Leslie Chree O'Malley, Oct. 22, 1966; 1 son, Rupert C. Asst. prof. European history Temple U., 1970-74; asst. prof. German and European history Lehigh U., Bethlehem, Pa., 1974-76; asso. prof. European and German immigration history Moravian Coll., Bethlehem, 1976-77; program dir. Regional Conf. Historical Agencies, Manlius, N.Y., 1977—; staff cons. historian Historic Bethlehem and Am. Heritage, Inc., 1976-77. Served with U.S. Army, 1956-69. NDEA Grad. fellow, 1966-67; Henry Lawrence Gipson fellow, 1975-76. Mem. Am. Hist. Assn., Nat. Archives Assn., Eighteenth Century Studies Group, Nat. Preservation League, Assn. European Historians. Republican. Lutheran. Club: Windward Sailing. Contbr. articles in field to hist. jours. Home: 550 Warren St Apt 4B Fayetteville NY 13066 Office: Regional Conf Hist Agencies 314 E Seneca St Manlius NY 13104

FINKEL, BENJAMIN, lawyer; b. Bklyn., Sept. 10, 1905; s. Max A. and Frieda (Shapiro) F.; student N.Y. U., 1923-24; LL.B., Fordham U., 1927; m. Betty F., Sept. 24, 1927; 1 dau., Phyllis Brofman. Admitted to N.Y. bar, 1929, U.S. Supreme Ct. bar, 1950; asso. firm Finkel, Goldstein & Berzow, and predecessors, N.Y.C., 1927—, partner, 1932—; former small claims arbitrator; lectr. trade assns.; counsel N.Y. Paper Mchts. Assn., 1929—. Recipient awards Anti-Defamation League B'nai B'rith. Mem. N.Y. State, Bklyn. bar assns., Am. Judges Assn. Democrat. Jewish. Club: B'nai B'rith. Mem. editorial bd. Met. Star. Home: 2000 Kings Hwy Brooklyn NY 11229 Office: 67 Wall St New York City NY 10005

FINKEL, BERNARD GERALD, mfg. co. exec.; b. N.Y.C., Dec. 26, 1937; s. Harry and Molly (Stern) F.; student Syracuse U., 1954-57; B.A. in Chemistry, N.Y. U., 1959; m. Natalie Peretz, May 31, 1958; children—Michelle, Susan, Karen. Mgr. diagnostics div. Warner-Lambert Pharm. Co., Morris Plains, N.J., 1960-69; pres. Sci. Spltys. Ltd., Garden City N.Y., 1969-73; pres. Clin. Scis., Inc., Whippany, N.J., 1973—; dir. Purex Labs. Instr. lab. mgmt. N.Y.C. Community Coll., 1969—. NIH grantee, 1959. Mem. Am. Assn. Clin. Chemists, Am. Soc. Microbiologists, Am. Chem. Soc. pres. N.Y. U. chpt. 1959), Downstate Soc. Med. Techs. (pres. 1968), Psi Sigma. Patentee in field. Home: 1 Brian Ln Spring Valley NY 10977 Office: 30 Troy Rd Whippany NJ 07981

FINKEL, COLEMAN LEE, cons. conf. centers; b. Balt.; s. Joseph and Dora (Hamburger) F.; A.B. in Econs., U. N.C., 1941; widowed; 1 son, Andrew. Dir. expediting Bendix Radio Corp., Towson, Md., 1941-44, 46-47; factory mgr. Wire Recording Corp. Am., N.Y.C., 1947-49; dir. divs. Am. Mgmt. Assn., N.Y.C., 1949-59; partner James O. Rice Assos., N.Y.C., 1959-72; pres. Nat. Conf. Center, East Windsor, N.J., 1972—; lectr. in field; columnist Successful Meeting mag. Served to lt., USMCR, 1944-46. Mem. Am. Soc. Tng. and Devel. (pres. Mid-N.J. chpt. 1975-76, Torch award 1975). Club: Princeton. Author: How to Plan a Meeting Like a Professional, 1973; Professional Guide to Successful Meetings, 1976. Home: 15 W 72d St New York City NY 10023 Office: Nat Conf Center Monmouth St East Windsor NJ 08520

FINKEL, MARK WILLIAM, hosp. adminstr.; b. N.Y.C., Jan. 5, 1949; s. Paul and Ruth (Swid) F.; B.A., Ohio State U., 1971; M.P.A., N.Y.U., 1973; m. Naomi Bennett, Aug. 19, 1973; 1 son, Jason Scott. Adminstrv. resident Hosp. for Joint Diseases and Med. Center, N.Y.C., 1972-73, adminstrv. asst., 1973, asst. adminstr., 1973-78, sr. adminstr., 1978—; instr. St. Joseph's Coll., Bklyn., 1977—. Served with USAR, 1970-71. Mem. Am. Hosp. Assn., Am. Pub. Health Assn. Democrat. Jewish. Clubs: Jefferson Democrat. Home: 69-21 E 186th Ln Fresh Meadows NY 11365 Office: 1919 Madison Ave New York City NY 10035

FINKELSTEIN, GERALD ARNOLD, orthodontist; b. Yonkers, N.Y., July 18, 1928; s. Louis Charles and Rose Ann (Distenfield) F.; A.B., N.Y.U., 1950; D.D.S., Columbia, 1954, Certificate Orthodontics, 1960; m. Virginia M. Lynch, Apr. 30, 1961; children—Elizabeth, John, Katherine. Pvt. practice dentistry, Hastings, N.Y., 1956-58, pvt. practice orthodontics, 1960—; part time research and lectr. dept. clin. oral physiology Temporomandibular Joint Clinic, Columbia, 1953-64, guest lectr. orthodontic dept., 1975. Active Boy Scouts Am., 1947-67; pub. relations chmn. Am. Field Service, 1961-63; chmn. Hastings Festival, 1960-61; scholarship chmn. Hastings Creative Arts Council Bd., 1964-68; mem. adv. com. Sch. Bd., 1969-71, nominating com., 1964-65; bd. dirs. Com. for Pub. Edn., 1968-71; bd. dirs. Hastings Parent Group on Learning Disabilities, 1974—, chmn., 1976—. Served with Dental Corps, USAF, 1954-56. Recipient Arrowhead Honor, Boy Scouts Am., 1964, Scouter's Key, 1966, Silver Beaver, 1967; recipient Man of Year award Hastings Lions Club, 1962. Mem. Am. Dental Assn., Ninth Dist. Dental Soc., Am. Assn. Orthodontists, Northeastern Soc. Orthodontists, Orthodontic Staff Confs. Columbia U., Orthodontic Alumni Soc. Columbia U., Hastings Hist. Soc. (pres., a founder 1969—, mem. exec. com. 1973-74, dir. 1973—). Jewish (bd. 1968-70, v.p. temple 1971-72, chmn. nominating com. 1975-76). Address: 584 Broadway Hastings-on-Hudson NY 10706

FINKELSTEIN, LEONARD, physician; b. N.Y.C., Aug. 29, 1938; s. Sam and Tillie F.; B.A., Bklyn. Coll., 1960; M.D., Cath. U., Louvain, Belgium, 1966; m. Janet Elizabeth Scheff, June 7, 1966; children—Lorin, Michael, David. Intern, United Hosp., Port Chester, N.Y., 1965-66; resident internal medicine Met. Hosp., N.Y. Med. Coll., N.Y.C., 1966-69, chief med. resident, 1967-68; practice medicine specializing in internal medicine and cardiology, Port Chester, N.Y., 1971—; sect. chief medicine Methadone Maintenance Treatment Program, Port Chester, 1971—; clin. instr. medicine N.Y. Med. Coll. at Westchester County Med. Center, Vahalla, N.Y., 1976—, asst. attending medicine (cardiology) at center, 1972—; attending medicine United Hosp., Port Chester, 1971—. Served to lt. comdr. USNR, 1969-71. Diplomate Am. Bd. Internal Medicine. Mem. Westchester County Med. Soc., Westchester Heart Assn., Am. Soc. Internal Medicine. Office: 19 Rye Ridge Plaza Port Chester NY 10573

FINKELSTEIN, MARK JON, nursing home adminstr.; b. Middletown, Conn., Jan. 24, 1947; s. Sidney and Hulda Louise F.; B.A. in Psychology, C.W. Post Coll., L.I. U., 1970, M.P.S. in Health Care Adminstrn., 1977; m. Donna Lee Groth, Aug. 6, 1978. Asst. adminstr. New Lakeview Convalescent Home, Cheshire, Conn., 1972-74, adminstr., 1974—; asst. clin. faculty Quinnipiac Coll.; cons. adminstrn., mgmt. long term care facilities; corporator Middlesex Meml. Hosp.; mem. adv. bd. Middlesex Community Mental Health Clinic; vice chmn. Middlesex Area mental Health Council. Mem. Portland (Conn.) Bd. Fin., Portland Democratic Town Com. Fellow Am. Coll. Nursing Home Adminstrs.; mem. Am. Health Care Assn., Conn. Assn. Health Care Facilities (dir., chmn. edn. com.), Am. Geriatrics Soc., Conn. Mental Health Assn. Jewish. Clubs: Lions, B'nai B'rith, Elks. Home: Six Joelle Dr Portland CT 06480 Office: 50 Hazel Dr Cheshire CT 06410

FINKELSTEIN, PAUL, urologist, clin. dir.; b. Bklyn., Feb. 1, 1920; s. Sam and Lena (Cohen) F.; B.S., La. State U., 1941, M.D., 1945; m. Doris May Greenberg, Mar. 14, 1954; children—Henry David, Susan Fay, Dru Anne, Lewis Mark. Practice medicine specializing in urology, Bklyn., 1953—; sr. lectr. urology Downstate Med. Center State U. N.Y., Bklyn., 1953—; dir. urology Bklyn.-Cumberland Med. Center, 1972—; trustee Bklyn. Hosp.; bd. dirs. Kings County (N.Y.) Health Care Rev. Orgn. Served with U.S. Army, 1942-47. Diplomate Am. Bd. Urology. Fellow A.C.S., N.Y. Acad. Surgeons; mem. AMA, Am. Urol. Assn., Am. Trauma Soc., Am. Fertility Soc. Democrat. Jewish. Clubs: Unity, Masons. Home: 599 3rd St Brooklyn NY 11215 Office: 1 Hanson Pl Brooklyn NY 11243

FINKELSTEIN, ROBERT, physicist, ops. researcher; b. N.Y.C., Oct. 13, 1942; s. Sam and Rose; B.A. (scholarship), Temple U., 1964; M.S. in Physics (fellow), Lowell Tech. Inst., 1966; postgrad. M.I.T., 1968-70; M.S. in Ops. Research, George Washington U., 1974, P.D., 1977; m. Beverly Karen Sokol, Dec. 5, 1964; children—Marni, Michael, Lori. Staff mem. M.I.T., Cambridge, 1968-70; task leader Computer Scis. Corp., Silver Spring, Md., 1970-72; project mgr. Atlantic Research Corp., Alexandria, Va., 1972-75; sr. analyst Ketron, Inc., Arlington, Va., 1975-76; program mgr. ManTech of N.J. Corp., Rockville, Md., 1976-77; project mgr. Mitre Corp., McLean, Va., 1977—; instr. Central Mich. U., Golden Gate U., George Mason U., Southeastern U., Prince Georges Community Coll., U. Ala., Lowell Tech. Inst. Served with Ordnance, U.S. Army, 1966-68. Recipient certificate of commendation M.I.T., 1970. Mem. Am. Phys. Soc., AAAS, Ops. Research Soc. Am., Washington Ops. Research Council, Inst. Mgmt. Scis., Smithsonian Instn., Omega Rho. Democrat. Jewish. Clubs: Tompkins Karate Assn., B'nai B'rith. Research in antisatellite systems, space vehicle mission analysis, solar and wind energy systems, combat computer models. Home: 10001 Crestleigh Ln Potomac MD 20854 Office: 1820 Dolley Madison Blvd McLean VA 22101

FINLAY, ALLAN RISLEY, financial cons.; b. N.Y.C., May 6, 1907; s. George Nye and Nellie Allen (Risley) F.; A.B., Dartmouth Coll., 1929; m. Lucy Allen Morrill, July 23, 1932; children—Richard R., Stuart A., Allan R., Susan M. With research dept. Scudder, Stevens & Clark, Boston, 1929-73, sr. v.p.-research, 1965-73, cons., 1973—;

dir. H.K. Webster Co., Lawrence, Mass., Grason-Stadler, Inc., Littleton, Mass., Barnstable Water Co., Hyannis, Mass., Edgertown Water Co., Martha's Vineyard, Mass. Chmn. bd. dirs. Inst. Ednl. Services, Bedford, Mass.; mem. Wayland (Mass.) Planning Bd., 1941-44, chmn. sch. bldg. com., 1948-63; mem. Mass. State Bd. Edn., 1966-75, chmn., 1968-71; bd. corporators Simmons Coll. Mem. Fin. Analysts Fedn. (chmn. banking industry subcom. 1966-75). Republican. Episcopalian. Clubs: Country (Brookline, Mass.); Woods Hole Golf (Falmouth, Mass.); Weston Curling (Wayland). Home: 147 Racing Beach Ave Falmouth MA 02540 Office: care Scudder Stevens and Clark 175 Federal St Boston MA 02110

FINLAYSON, JOCK KINGHORN, bank exec.; b. Nanimo, B.C., Can., May 27, 1921; s. John Archibald and Elizabeth (Lister) F.; m. Madeleine Victoria Coussement, Jan. 7, 1976. With Royal Bank Can., 1939—, mgr. main br., Montreal, 1960-64, exec. officer, 1964-67, gen. mgr. internat. div., 1967-69, chief gen. mgr., 1969-72, v.p., dir., 1970-72, dep. chmn., exec. v.p., 1972—, vice chmn., 1977—; dir. Royal Bank Can. (France), Royal Bank Can. Trust Corp., London, Royal Bank Can. Trust Co., N.Y., Roywest Banking Corp. Ltd., Nassau, Hall Corp. Shipping, Macdonald Tobacco, Inc., Trust Corp. of Bahamas, Nassau, Orion Bank Ltd., London, PanCanadian Petroleum Ltd., Royal Ins. Group, Sun Life Assurance Co. Can., United Corp. Ltd. Served with Canadian Armed Forces, 1942-45. Clubs: Mount Royal, Forest and Stream, Mount Bruno Golf, York, Toronto. Office: Royal Bank of Can Royal Bank of Can Bldg 1 Place Ville Marie Montreal PQ H3C 3A9 Canada*

FINLEY, HOWARD JAMES, mus. ofcl., conservationist; b. Hartford, Mich., Dec. 6, 1901; s. William S. and Clara May (Westcott) F.; student Western State Tchrs. Coll., Mich., 1927-28; B.S. in Agr., Mich. State Coll., 1931; postgrad. Cornell U., various times 1931-56; m. Helen L. Miller, Aug. 20, 1929; children—Marilyn Finley McArdle, John Westcott. Clk., Hartford Baking Co., 1920-22; farmer, Dowagiac, Mich., 1924-27; tchr. Miles Dist., Hartford, 1925-26, Daly Dist., Dowagiac, 1926-27; tchr. vocat. agr., Centreville, Mich., 1928-30, Bristol, Vt., 1931-33, Thetford, Vt., 1933-34, Brushton, N.Y., 1934-38, Weedsport, N.Y., 1938-66; adminstr. vocat. agr. Bd. Co-op. Ednl. Services, 1964-66; dir. Cayuga County Soil and Water Conservation Dist., 1967—, chmn., 1976—; adviser Future Farmers Am. chpts., 1931-66; tchr. trainer Cornell U., 1948-50. Clk., Silver Creek Twp., Cass County, Mich. 1926-27; mem. Town of Brutus Planning Bd., 1967—; mem. Central N.Y. Regional Planning and Devel. Bd., 1974-77, mem. water quality adv. com., 1975-77; originator Erie Canal Aqueduct Project, 1960; originator Old Brutus Hist. Soc., 1967, dir. mus., Weedsport, 1972—; leader 4-H Club, 1927-62; co-organizer Weedsport Community Fair, 1949, pres., 1950-51; chmn. steering com. Heartland Resource Conservation and Devel. Project Central N.Y., 1972, v.p. council, 1974-77; Brutus-Weedsport historian, 1960—. Mem. C. of C., N.Y. Soil Conservation Dists. Assn. (dir. N.Y., state sec. 1971-73, state pres. 1975-77), Nat. Assn. Conservation Dists. (council 1975-77). Republican. Roman Catholic. Clubs: Lions; Whittlers (Weedsport). Author: Centennial History of St. Joseph's Parish, 1954; A Developmental History of Cayuga County, New York, 1968; co-author: An Appraisal of Potential Outdoor Recreational Developments in Cayuga County, 1968; Weedsport-Brutus, a Brief Bicentennial History, 1976; also articles, radio scripts. Home: 2695 Bell St Weedsport NY 13166 Office: 8943 N Seneca St Weedsport NY 13166

FINLEY, MURRAY H., labor union ofcl.; b. Syracuse, N.Y., Mar. 31, 1922; B.A., U. Mich., 1946; J.D., Northwestern U., 1949; m. Elaine Auerbach, 1946; 2 children. Mgr., Chgo. Joint Bd., Amalgamated Clothing Workers Am., 1961-72, nat. v.p., 1962-72, mgr. Midwest Regional Joint Bd., 1964-72, gen. pres., 1972—; v.p. AFL-CIO, 1973—. Mem. Com. for Nat. Health Ins.; mem. Greater N.Y. Community Council; hon. vice chmn. Am. Trade Union Council for Histadrut; bd. dirs. A. Philip Randolph Inst.; mem. Sloan Commn. on Govt. and Higher Edn.; trustee Asian-Am. Free Labor Inst., Nat. Planning Assn.; bd. dirs. African-Am. Labor Center. Served with U.S. Army, 1942-45; ETO. Home: 7002 Blvd E Guttenberg NJ 07093 Office: 15 Union Sq New York City NY 10003

FINLON, FRANCIS PAUL, educator; b. Carbondale, Pa., Sept. 2, 1924; s. Hugh J. and Rose M. (Tammany) F.; student U. Scranton, 1942-44; B.S., Pa. State U., 1947, M.S., 1948; m. Mary M. Henzi, Nov. 25, 1947; children—Richard, David, Debra. Teaching, grad. student, Brown U., Providence, 1948-49; mil. research and devel. Pa. State U., 1949-57, 58—, prof. engring. research, 1962—. Cons. U.S. Navy, 1948—, State of Pa., 1960-62. Served with U.S. Army, 1944-46. Mem. IEEE, Inst. Environ. Scis., Sigma Xi, Tau Beta Pi, Pi Mu Epsilon, Eta Kappa Nu. Club: Centre Hills Country. Patentee in field. Home: 1134 William St State College PA 16801 Office: PO Box 30 State College PA 16801

FINN, D(ANIEL) FRANCIS, assn. exec.; b. Norwich, Conn., Aug. 15, 1922; s. Daniel Francis and Elizabeth Anne (Elliott) F.; A.B. cum laude in Econs., Brown U., 1943; postgrad. U. Maine, 1944, U. Nancy (France), 1945, Purdue U., 1957; m. Gabrielle LaFayette Beausoleil, Aug. 26, 1948; children—Daniel, Mark, Chad, Beth, Bart. Asst. purchasing agt. Brown U., 1946-48, purchasing agt., 1948-55, extension course instr. purchasing, 1954; purchasing agt. Purdue U., 1955-61, bus. mgr., asst. treas., 1961-69; exec. v.p. Nat. Assn. Coll. and Univ. Bus. Officers, Washington, 1969—. Instr., Coll. Bus. Mgmt. Inst., Lexington, Ky., 1969, WACUBO Workshop, Santa Barbara, Cal., 1970-71. Vice pres. Class of 1943, Brown U., 1947; chmn. nat. adv. panel Nat. Center Higher Edn. Mgmt. Systems, Boulder, Colo., 1970-72; dir. Coop. Coll. Registry, 1973. Bd. dirs. Center for Research Libraries, Chgo., 1961-69, pres., 1966; mem. exec. bd. Tippecanoe council Boy Scouts Am., Lafayette, Ind., 1963-69, Lafayette Symphony Orch., 1965-69; mem. adv. bd. Coll. and Univ. Bus. mag., Chgo., 1950-60. Served with Q.M.C., AUS, 1943-45. Decorated Croix de Guerre; named Catholic Man of Year, Tippecanoe County, Ind., 1966. Mem. Central Assn. Coll. and Univ. Bus. Officers (pres. 1969), Phi Beta Kappa; hon. life mem. New Eng. Group Nat. Assn. Ednl. Buyers, Ind. Assn. Coll. and Univ. Bus. Officers, Assn. Phys. Plant Adminstrs. Democrat. Roman Catholic. Rotarian. Contbg. author: Purchasing for Educational Institutions, 1961; College and University Business Administration, rev. edit., 1968. Home: 8517 Warde Terr Potomac MD 20854 Office: 1 Dupont Circle Washington DC 20036

FINN, JAMES FRANCIS, cons. engr.; b. Jersey City, July 11, 1924; s. James Aloysius and Helen Edna (Brown) F.; student St. Peters Coll., 1942-43, Stevens Inst. Tech., 1946-49; B.C.E., Newark Coll. Engring., 1953; m. Evelyn Teresa Dobbins, Sept. 9, 1950; children—Deirdre, Robert, John, Kerry, James. Asst. engr., sr. engr. N.J. Dept. Conservation, Newark, 1949-56; hwy. design engr. Howard Needles Tammen & Bergendoff, N.Y.C., 1956-64, engring. mgr., gen. partner, Fairfield, N.J., 1965—; v.p. Howard Needles Tammen & Bergendoff Internat., Inc., Fairfield, 1965—; dir. Frankfurter, Inc., Washington, 1974—. Served as officer, C.E., U.S. Army, 1943-46; ETO. Fellow Am. Cons. Engrs. Council, ASCE; mem. Am. Rd. Builders Assn., N.J. Soc. Profl. Engrs., N.J. Soc. Planners, Internat. Bridge, Tunnel and Turnpike Assn., Nat. Soc. Profl. Engrs., Transp. Research Bd., Moles, Chi Epsilon. Home: 48 Hampshire Rd Washington Twp Westwood NJ 07675 Office: 330 Passaic Ave Fairfield NJ 07006

FINN, JOAN LOCKWOOD, writer; b. Plainfield, N.J., June 6, 1929; d. William Albert and Ada Louise (Dayton) F.; B.A. in Am. History, Radcliffe Coll., 1951; certificate d'attendance U. Paris Sorbonne Coll., 1952; M.A., Columbia U., 1979. Copywriter, J.C. Penney Co., Inc., 1957-58; jr. account exec. Dudley-Anderson-Yutzey, 1958-61; account exec. Theodore R. Sills & Co., 1961-63, Ted Bates & Co., 1963-67; account supr. Henderson & Roll, 1967-69; dir. press relations Motion Picture Assn. Am., N.Y.C., 1969-71; freelance writer, N.Y.C., 1971-73; communications specialist Coopers & Lybrand, N.Y.C., 1973—. Mem. steering com. N.Y. Upbeat. Pub. relations, fgn. affairs com. FDR-Woodrow Wilson Democratic Club, 1965. Mem. Pub. Relations Soc. Am. (accredited). Democrat. Presbyterian. Club: Harvard (N.Y.C.). Author: Heritage of Evil, 1968; Kiss More, or How to Get Across in Writing, 1977; librettist: (operetta) Chicken Little, 1973; editor Diet Ann., 1973; Diet Yearbook, 1973; contbr. articles to Motor Boating, Ideal Romances, Am. Mercury, Jack O'Dwyer's Newsletter, New Ideas for Figure and Diet, Modern Maturity mags. Home: 17 W 54th St New York City NY 10019 Office: 1251 Ave of Americas New York City NY 10020

FINN, JOHN JOSEPH, JR., physician; b. Boston, Mar. 20, 1915; s. John Joseph and Josephine (Killelea) F.; B.S. in Biology, Tufts U., 1937, M.D., 1941. Intern in internal medicine Boston City Hosp., 1941-42, asst. resident medicine, 1946-47, chief resident, 1947-48, assisting physician, 1952—; resident Joseph H. Pratt Diagnostic Hosp., 1948-49, asso. staff, 1949—; pvt. practice internal medicine, 1949—; med. dir. William Filene's Sons Co., 1954—, Boston Herald-Traveler, 1962-63, Bentley Coll. Accounting and Finance, 1963—; courtesy staff Sancta Maria Hosp. (Cambridge), Faulkner Hosp.; sr. clin. instr. medicine med. sch. Tufts U., 1950—, instr. medicine dental sch., 1953—; instr. Boston Sch. Occupational Therapy; asst. physician Boston Dispensary; comdr. 351 Gen. Hosp., Boston Army Base. Boston examiner for Life Extension Inst., 1953—. Col. U.S. Army Res. Diplomate Am. Bd. Internal Medicine. Fellow A.C.P. (asso.); mem. A.M.A., Mass. Med. Soc. (chmn. sect. indsl. medicine 1964), Am. Fedn. Clin. Research, New England Indsl. Med. Assn. (dir. 1959). Author articles in med. jours. Home: 30 Stearns Rd Brookline MA 02146 Office: 1101 Beacon St Brookline MA 02146

FINN, MICHAEL HERBERT PAUL, psychologist; b. Phila., Jan. 16, 1924; s. Charles and Blanche F.; B.S., U. Md., 1948; M.A., N.Y. U., 1949, Ph.D., 1953; m. Lorraine Kathleen Anne Shea, Nov. 18, 1950; children—Kerry Kathleen, Kellee Patricia, Tara Mavourneen, Maeve Fitzpatrick. Psychologist intern Bellevue Psychiat. Hosp., N.Y.C., 1949-50; staff psychologist Springfield State Hosp., Sykesville, Md., 1950-51, dir. psychol. services, 1951-61, cons. psychologist, 1961-68; pvt. practice psychology, Towson, Md., 1953—; cons. psychologist Wesley Theol. Sem., Washington, 1953-73, Western Md. Coll., Westminster, 1953-63, Balt. Psychiat. Day Hosp., 1961-73; cons. psychologist Montebello Hosp., 1968-75; cons. med. staff St. Joseph Hosp., Towson, Md., 1972—, John L. Deaton Hosp., Balt., 1976—, Psychiat. Inst., Washington, 1976—; cons. Md. Gen. Hosp., 1978—, St. Joseph Hosp., 1977—; chief cons. pastoral counseling program Balt. Ann. Conf., 1969—; cons. psychologist Balt. Ann. Conf. United Meth. Ch., 1969—; vis. lectr. Western Md. Coll., 1953-54; instr. psychology Balt. Coll. Commerce, 1953-54; mem. Md. Bd. Examiners Psychologists, 1959-62, chmn., 1961-62. Served with M.C., AUS, 1943-46. Fellow Md. Psychol. Assn., Soc. Projective Techniques; mem. Am. Psychol. Assn., Md. Hist. Soc. Editor: Myokinetic Psychodiagnosis (M.K.P.), 1958; Training for Clinical Psychology, 1959; contbr. articles to profl. jours. Home: 7820 Ellenham Ruxton MD 21204 Office: St Joseph Professional Bldg 7401 Osler Dr Towson MD 21204

FINN, PETER GERARD, clergyman, supt. schs., ednl. adminstr.; b. S.I., N.Y., Oct. 6, 1938; s. Peter J. and Mary Teresa (Powers) F.; B.A. in English, Manhattan Coll., 1960; B.D., St. Joseph Sem., 1965, M.Div., 1965; M.S. in Edn., Richmond Coll., 1971; Ed.M., Columbia U., 1973. Ordained priest Roman Catholic Ch., 1965; parish priest St. Marys Parish Ch., S.I., N.Y., 1965-66, St. Catharine's Ch., Pelham, N.Y., 1966-68; tchr. social studies Monsignor Farrell High Sch., S.I., 1968-76, chmn. social studies, 1970-74, chmn. athletics, 1973-77, supervising prin., 1977—; dist. supt. Catholic schs., S.I., 1974—; chmn. S.I. Priests Area Conf., 1978; vice chmn. S.I. Continuum of Edn. Bd. dirs. S.I. Cath. Youth Orgn., 1977—, S.I. Mental Health Soc. Named Outstanding Citizen of S.I., 1977, 78. Mem. Nat. Cath. Edn. Assn., Am. Assn. Sch. Adminstrs., Cath. Sch. Adminstrs. Assn. N.Y. State, Nat. Council for Social Studies, Assn. for Supervision and Curriculum, Nat. Sch. Pub. Edn. Assn., Assn. Social Studies Tchrs. N.Y.C., Orgn. Am. Historians, Nat. Hist. Soc., Nat. Sch. Pub. Relations Assn., S.I. Council Arts, S.I. Cath. Secondary Prins. Council (chmn. 1974), S.I. Cath. Elementary Prins. Council (chmn. 1974), Chief Adminstrs. of Cath. Edn., Ancient Order Hibernians, S.I. Vicariate Pastoral Council, Manhattan Coll. Alumni Soc. Democrat. Club: K.C. Address: Monsignor Farrell High School 2900 Amboy Rd Staten Island NY 10306

FINN, ROBERT ALAN, mfg. co. exec.; b. Jersey City, Feb. 11, 1949; s. Carl Walter William and Dorothy Isabella (Lyne) F.; B.A., Brown U., 1971; M.B.A., Northeastern U., 1974; m. Carla Watts Gustafson, June 24, 1978. Indsl. engr. Eskimo Pie Corp., 1971-72; bus. planner Rockwell Internat., Hopedale, Mass., 1974, mfg. analyst, 1974-75, supr. fin. analysis, 1976; sr. fin. analyst Hasbro Industries, Pawtucket, R.I., 1976, corp. mgr. bus. planning and fin. analysis, 1976—, also treas., dir. Hasbro Credit Union; mem. mgmt. sci. faculty Bryant Coll. Fin. adviser Jr. Achievement. Served to 1st lt. U.S. Army N.G., 1971-78. Mem. Bus. Planning Inst. Home: 140 Ridge St Millis MA 02054 Office: 1027 Newport Ave Pawtucket RI 02862

FINN, THOMAS M., safety services co. exec.; b. R.I., Dec. 29, 1924; B.A., U. Md., 1952; m. Ann E. Hurson, June 28, 1952; children—Michael, Norine, Nancy, Margaret, Monica, Elizabeth. Police adviser ICA (name now AID), Tehran, Iran, 1958-59, pub. safety adviser, 1959-63; program ops. officer, Washington, 1963-64, regional pub. safety adminstrv. adviser, 1964, chief tech. services div., 1964-69; chief tng. div., dir. Internat. Police Acad., Office Pub. Safety, 1969-72; asst. dir. pub. safety USOM, AID, Bangkok Thailand, 1972-74; dir. planning staff Office of Internat. Tng., State Dept., 1974-75, dep. dir., 1975-77; v.p. Pub. Safety Services, Inc., Washington, 1977—. Served with USCGR, 1942-45. Mem. Former Spl. Agts. FBI. Home: 921 Hyde Rd Silver Spring MD 20902 Office: 1250 Connecticut Ave Suite 329 Washington DC 20036

FINN, WILLIAM FRANCIS, physician; b. Union City, N.J., July 23, 1915; s. Neil Alysious and Catherine Marie (Hearn) F.; A.B. summa cum laude, Holy Cross Coll., 1936; M.D., Cornell U., 1940; m. Doris Ida Henderson, Sept. 21, 1943; children—Neil C., Sharon R., David. Intern, Albany Hosp., 1940-41; resident obstetrics and gynecology N.Y. Hosp., 1941-44, asst. attending obstetrician and gynecologist, 1946-48, asso. attending obstetrician and gynecologist 1948-67; asst. prof. obstetrics and gynecology Cornell Med. Coll., 1948-67, asso. clin. prof., 1967—; attending obstetrics and gynecology North Shore Hosp.; cons. obstetrics and gynecology Mercy Hosp. Bd. mgrs. Ch. C Found., Episcopal Diocese of L.I. J. Withridge Williams fellow, 1947. Diplomate Am. Bd. Obstetrics and Gynecology. Fellow A.C.S., AMA, Am. Coll. Obstetricians, Am. Soc. Gynecol. Laparoscopy, Am. Soc. Colposcopy; mem. N.Y. Obstet. Soc., Queens (pres.), Nassau (pres.) obstet. socs., Am. Acad. Obstetrics and Gynecology, Lying in Alumni Assn., N.Y. Hosp. Alumni Assn., N.Y. State, N.Y. County med. socs., N.Y. Acad. Medicine. Contbr. articles to profl. jours. Home: 3 Aspen Gate Manhasset NY 11030 Office: 535 Plandome Rd Manhasset NY 11030

FINNEGAN, MARCUS BARTLETT, lawyer; b. Morristown, N.J., Sept. 15, 1927; s. George Bernard and Elisabeth (Morgan) F.; B.S., U.S. Mil. Acad., 1949; J.D., U. Va., 1955; LL.M., George Washington U., 1957; m. Betsy Neil Hammer, June 3, 1950; children—Nancy Lee, Susan Bartlett, Katharine Elisabeth. Admitted to Va., D.C. bars, 1955, U.S. Supreme Ct., N.Y. bars, 1960; U.S. patent adviser to Japan, Tokyo, 1957-59; atty. firm Morgan, Finnegan, Durham & Pine, N.Y.C., 1959-63, firm Irons, Birch, Swindler, & McKie, Washington, 1963-65; sr. partner firm Finnegan, Henderson, Farabow & Garrett, Washington, 1965—; professorial lectr. law George Washington U., 1971—; lectr. in field. Cons. UN Indsl. Devel. Orgn., Vienna, Austria, 1971—; cons. on antitrust and licensing to UN, 1972—; cons., adviser on licensing and technology transfer to Govt. Mexico, 1973—; cons. UN Conf. on Trade and Devel. Geneva, 1974—; del. U.S. Dept. State, 1974-75; cons. U.S./USSR Joint Working Group on Intellectual Property, 1974—; adviser White House Council on Internat. Econ. Policy, 1975-77; mem. Panel of Six Experts to Study ERDA Patent Policy, 1975-77; del. numerous internat. confs. Served to capt. U.S. Army, 1949-59. Hon. fellow Harry S. Truman Library; mem. Raven Soc., U.S. C. of C. (patent system advisory panel, antitrust and trade regulations com.), Am. (chmn. patent law com., adminstrv. law sect. regulations com.), Am. (chmn. patent law com., adminstrv. law sect. 1974), Fed., D.C., Va., Inter-Am., Internat. bar assns., Am. Patent Law Assn. (bd. mgrs. 1974—), Inst. Mil. Law, Internat. Legal Soc. Japan, Va. State Bar, Am. Judicature Soc., Assn. Grads. U.S. Mil. Acad., N.Y., N.J. patent law assns., Licensing Execs. Soc. U.S.A. (trustee, v.p., pres.), Licensing Execs. Soc.-Internat. (pres., Internat. Gold medal 1977), Am. Mgmt. Assn., Patent and Trademark Inst. Can., Internat. Patent and Trademark Assn., Inter-Am. Assn. Indsl. Property, World Peace Through Law Center, World Assn. Lawyers, Internat. Studies Assn., Supreme Ct. Hist. Soc., Wisdom Soc., World Assn. Law Profs., Am. Trial Lawyers Assn., Am. Soc. Internat. Law, Internat. Common Law Exchange Soc., Am. Soc. Internat. Law, Ligue Internat. Contre La Concurrence De' Loyale, Army Athletic Assn., Assn. Bar City N.Y., N.Y. County Lawyers Assn., West Point Soc. D.C., Am. Soc. for Metals, U. Va. Law Sch. Found., West Point Alumni Found., Md. State Golf Assn., UN Assn. U.S.A., St. John's Coll. Alumni Assn. George Washington U. Law Assn., Phi Delta Phi, Omicron Delta Kappa, Order of Coif. Episcopalian. Clubs: Congressional Country; Kenwood Country (Bethesda, Md.); Met., Touchdown, Cosmos, Army and Navy, Nat. Lawyers, Patent Lawyers, George Washington Univ., Internat. (Washington); Tamboo (Great Harbour Cay, Bahamas); Clermont (London); Tokyo (Japan) Am. (life); Washington Golf and Country, Army Navy Country (Arlington, Va.); Tabusintac (N.B., Can.); Mt. Kenya Safari (life) (Nanyuki, Kenya); Marco Polo (N.Y.C.). Author: (with Richard W. Pogue) Federal Employee Invention Rights-Time to Legislate, 1957; co-author: Patent-Antitrust: Compliance and Confrontation, 1972; editor and author: The Law and Business of Patent and Know-How Licensing, 2d edit., 1972, 3d edit., 1975; co-editor and author: The Law and Business of Licensing, 1975; author numerous articles on licensing and technology transfer, 1968—; editorial advisory bd. Patent Trademark and Copyright Jour., 1972—; editor-in-chief Licensing Law and Business Report, 1978—; contbg. editor Les Nouvelles Internat. Licensing Jour. Home: 9017 Clewerwall Dr Bethesda MD 20034 Office: 1775 K St NW Washington DC 20006

FINNERTY, FRANK AMBROSE, physician; b. Montclair, N.J., Nov. 3, 1923; s. Fran A. and Agnes (Fitzsimmons) F.; A.B., Georgetown U., 1943, M.D., 1947; m. Frances Martin, July 26, 1975. Intern, D.C. Gen. Hosp., Washington, 1947-48, Boston City Hosp., 1948-49; research fellow in medicine D.C. Gen. Hosp., 1950-51, chief resident in medicine, 1951-52; research fellow Am. Heart Assn., Washington, 1955-57; practice medicine specializing in internal medicine and cardiovascular disease, Washington, 1955—; established investigator Am. Heart Assn., 1957-62; asst. prof. medicine Georgetown U. Med. Center, Washington, 1958-63, asso. clin. prof. pharmacology, 1963-68, asso. clin. prof. medicine, 1963-68, clin. prof. obstetrics, 1969-72, clin. prof. medicine, 1969-72, 77—, prof. medicine, 1972-76, prof. obstetrics and gynecology, 1972-76; prof. clin. medicine George Washington U. Med. Sch., 1977—; chief of cardiovascular research Georgetown U. Med. Div., D.C. Gen. Hosp., 1952-76; chief of medicine Columbia Hosp. for Women, 1963-74; adj. prof. medicine Catholic U. Grad. Sch. of Nursing, 1975—; dir. Hypertension Center of Washington, 1976—; med. cons. Dept. Corrections, D.C. Jail, 1965-77; mem. Medcom, Inc., Faculty of Medicine, 1974; mem. Task Force for Devel. of Drug Protocol, Nat. High Blood Pressure Info. Program, NIH, 1976—; chmn. Task Force of Therapeutics, Southeastern Regional Med. Hypertension Program, 1974-75. Bd. dirs. Nat. Kidney Found., Citizens Com. for Treatment of High Blood Pressure. Served with M.C., U.S. Army, 1953-55. Diplomate Am. Bd. Internal Medicine. Fellow A.C.P., Am. Coll. of Cardiology (trustee 1975—), Am. Coll. of Angiology; mem. Am. Fedn. Clin. Research, Am. Therapeutic Soc., Am. Coll. Clin. Pharmacology and Therapeutics, Am., D.C. heart assns., D.C. Med. Soc., Am. (mem. com. on hypertension 1975—), So. med. assns., Am. Soc. Contemporary Medicine and Surgery, Georgetown U. Alumni Assn. (bd. govs. 1971-75). Contbr. numberous articles on cardiology and hypertension to med. jours. Office: 1341 Pennsylvania Ave SE Washington DC 20033

FINNERTY, JEAN CLARE, educator; b. N.Y.C.; d. John Joseph and Rose Marie (Bonser) F.; B.A., Manhattan Coll., 1941; M.A., St. John's U., 1946; Ph.D., Fordham U., 1959. Elementary sch. tchr. Cath. schs., Bklyn., 1935-41; secondary sch. tchr. math. Bklyn., 1941-59; grad. adviser elementary and secondary schs., over-all supr., curriculum dir., Rockville Centre, N.Y., 1959-66, prin. St. Agnes Acad. High Sch., College Point, N.Y., 1966-68; asst. supt. Woodcliff Lake Pub. Schs., N.J., 1968-71; adj. prof. Montclair State Coll. and Seton Hall U., 1968-71; asso. prof. Seton Hall U. Grad. Div. Adminstrn. and Supervision, South Orange, N.J., 1971-74, prof., 1974—, acting dept. chmn. Grad. Div. Adminstrn., 1978—; cons. several maj. textbook cos. in social studies, 1959-70; instr. coll. math. Manhattan Coll. Extension, 1946-53; instr. and asst. prof. English St. Joseph Coll., summers 1942-54; cons. N.Y. State Bd. Regents and Scholarships Exams., 1964, 69; mem. Carnegie team Notre Dame Study and Research Team, 1962-63; dir. in-service math. Molloy Coll., L.I., 1959-66; condr. workshops for adminstrs., summers 1975—. Mem. panel Gov.'s Conf. NCCJ, 1959-66; mem. Cath. Interracial Council, Nassau Ecumenical Council, Nassau Community Mental Health Assn., Bklyn. Supt. Schs. Adv. Council, 1959-67; ofcl. observer Internat. Ednl. Conf., Geneva, summer 1964. Recipient Woman in Research citation ALA, 1976, Bicentennial Com. citation, 1976. Mem. Nat. Cath. Edn. Assn. (sec. elementary exec. com. 1960-63, chmn. supr. sect. 1966-68, adv. com. 1968—, co-chmn. middle states 1970, exec. com. 1959-65, mem. middle states team 1968), NEA, AAUP (v.p. chpt. 1976-77), Am. Assn. Supervision and Curriculum Devel., Am. Assn. Sch. Adminstrs. (speaker 1978), Internat. Platform

Assn., Am. Assn. Ednl. Psychotherapists (asso.), World Youth Vocat. Edn. Assn. (trustee), N.J. Profs. Ednl. Adminstrn. and Supervision (v.p. 1977—), Alumni Assn. Seton Hall U., Phi Delta Kappa, Kappa Delta Pi (exec. com.). Co-author series 16 geography lessons video-taped for Channel 13 TV, 1960-66; 8 spelling books, Spell Correctly, 1965, Evaluative Criteria for the Elementary Catholic Schools, 1965; author: Revolution in Geography, Too, 1963; contbr. articles to profl. jours. Home: One South Valley Rd West Orange NJ 07052 Office: Seton Hall U South Orange NJ 07079

FINNERTY, WILLIAM ALOYSIUS, chemist; b. Queens, N.Y., July 19, 1951; s. William A. and Marabeth (Fogarty) F.; B.S., Mt. St. Mary's Coll., 1973; postgrad. St. Johns U., Queens, 1973—. Asso. chemist Center Labs., Inc. div. Alcon Labs., Inc., Port Washington, N.Y., 1974-75, sr. chemist, 1975-76, supr. dept. chemistry, 1976-78, asst. quality control dir., 1978; supr. automated analysis Wyeth Labs., Inc., Paoli, Pa., 1978—. Mem. Am. Chem. Soc. Home: 62 Rockcrest Rd Manhasset NY 11030 Office: Dept 8971 PO Box 861 Paoli PA 19301

FIORAVANTI, NANCY ELEANOR, bank ofcl.; b. Gloucester, Mass., Apr. 10, 1935; d. Richard Joseph and Evelyn Grace (Souza) Fioravanti; grad. high sch. Various positions and depts. Cape Ann Bank and Trust Co. (successor to Gloucester Safe Deposit & Trust Co.), Gloucester, 1953—, with trust dept., 1959—, asst. trust officer, 1970—. Mem. Nat. Assn. Bank Women. Home: 19 Harvard St Gloucester MA 01930 Officer: 154 Main St Gloucester MA 01930

FIORE, JAMES LOUIS, JR., pub. accountant; b. Jersey City, Oct. 7, 1935; s. James Louis and Rose (Perrotta) F.; B.S. In Accounting, Seton Hall U., 1957; M.B.A., Colo. Western U., 1978; postgrad. Calif. Western U.; m. Alberta W. Pope, July 21, 1957; children—Carolyn Leigh, James Louis, Toni Lynn. Field auditor, Trenton, N.J., 1959-60; supr. internal auditing Ronson Corp., Woodbridge, N.J., 1960-64; supr. gen. accounting Electronic Assos., West Long Branch, N.J., 1964-65; pvt. practice accounting, 1965—; pres. Bucks County Research Inst. Inc., 1972—. Bd. dirs. Brick Twp. (N.J.) Scholarship Found., 1963-67. Served to 2d lt. U.S. Army, 1957. Named Jaycee of Year, 1962; accredited Accreditation Council for Accountancy, Washington. Mem. Nat., Pa. socs. pub. accountants, South Hunterdon C. of C. Roman Catholic. Club: K.C. Author: (with others) Non-Absorption of Nitrofurazone from the Urethra in Men, 1976, Comparative Bioavailability of Doxycycline, 1974. Home: PO Box 232 New Hope PA also Thompson Mill Rd Upper Makefield Twp PA 18977 Office: General Knox Rd Washington Crossing PA 18977 also 1600 Lehigh Pkwy East Allentown PA 18103 also 287 S Main St Lambertville NJ 08530

FIORVANTI, ALDO FIORINO, civil engr.; b. Woonsocket, R.I., May 1, 1923; s. Palmiro and Giuseppina (Tofani) F.; B.S., Mass. Inst. Tech., 1948; m. Anne June Valentine, Feb. 2, 1948; children—Richard, Joanne, Patricia Anne, Mary Anne. Timekeeper, field engr. Geo. T. Rooney Co., Cambridge, Mass., 1948-49; field engr. Turner Constrn. Co., N.Y.C., 1950-55, asst. supt., 1955-63, supt., 1963-65; asst. dir. phys. plant, plant supt. U. Rochester (N.Y.) Med. Center, 1965—. Served with U.S. Army, 1943-44. Mem. Am. Soc. Heating, Refrigeration and Air Conditioning Engrs. (tech. com., pres. chpt. 1975-76). Roman Catholic. Club: Rotary (bd. dirs. 1976-77). Home: 51 Elmgrove Rd Rochester NY 14626 Office: 601 Elmwood Ave Rochester NY 14642

FIPPHEN, JOHN STANLEY, spectroscopist; b. Worcester, Mass., Dec. 12, 1927; s. Clarence Wyman and Ethel (Dole) F.; B.A., Clark U., 1949; m. Christine Lois Churchill, Oct. 12, 1956; children—Richard Churchill, Peter John. Staff, Wyman Gordon Co., Grafton, Mass., 1948-53, Watertown (Mass.) Arsenal, 1953-54, Baird Atomic Co., Cambridge, Mass., 1954-58; sr. spectroscopist Wyman Gordon Co., 1958—. Mem. Soc. Applied Spectroscopy, New Eng. Historic Geneal. Soc., Northboro Historic Soc. Congregationalist. Home: 226 Howard St Northboro MA 01532 Office: Wyman Gordon Co Worcester St North Grafton MA 01536

FIRST, HELEN G., clin. psychologist; b. N.Y.C., July 1, 1908; d. Samuel I. and Regina H. Gross; A.B., Hunter Coll., 1928; M.A., Columbia U., 1956; Ph.D., Bryn Mawr Coll., 1966; m. Joseph M. First, Dec. 27, 1931; children—Elsa, Abigail First Farber, Jonathan. Book editor Seventeen mag., N.Y.C., 1952-57; research asso. and cons. Vanguard Sch., Haverford, Pa., 1965—; clin. psychologist Schwartz Inst. of Phila. Psychiat. Hosp., 1966; clin. asst. prof. psychiatry and human behavior Thomas Jefferson U. Med. Coll., Phila., 1969-72, clin. asso. prof., 1972-75, hon. clin. asso. prof., 1975—; mem. Pa. State Bd. Psychologist Examiners, 1974-77; mem. Phila. Mental Health and Mental Retardation Advisory Bd. Mem. Am., Pa. psychol. assns., Phila. Soc. Clin. Psychologists, Soc. Clin. and Exptl. Hypnosis, Internat. Soc. Hypnosis, and Acad. Orthomolecular Psychiatry. Jewish. Contbr. articles in field to profl. jours. Home and office: 230 Orchard Way Merion Station PA 19066

FIRST, MERVIN HENRY, electronics co. exec.; b. Bklyn., May 21, 1928; s. Edward Louis and Rose A. (Kaufman) F.; B.E.E., Coll. City N.Y., 1951; postgrad. Poly. Inst. Bklyn., 1952-53; m. Sharon Joan Rosenberg, Dec. 24, 1950; children—Dennis Arthur, Ellen Lori. Chief engr. Filtron Co., Flushing, N.Y., 1951-61; pres. RF Interonics, Bayshore, N.Y., 1961—; pres. Pine Aire Devel. Corp. Mem. adv. com. Bur. Ednl. Studies and Services, Hofstra U., 1976—; trustee Amityville (N.Y.) Union Free Sch. Dist. Bd. Edn., 1970—, v.p., 1973-74, pres., 1974-75. Served with USN, 1946-48. Mem. IEEE (chmn. N.Y.C. chpt. electromagnetic compatability group 1967-68, citation 1970, chmn. com. internat. symposium 1973), Soc. Automotive Engrs. Patentee in field. Home: 25 Dewey Ave Amityville NY 11701 Office: RF Interonics 100-T Pine Aire Dr Bayshore NY 11706

FIRTH, CLIFFORD EDWARD, chem. co. exec.; b. Chelmsford, Mass., Aug. 2, 1920; s. Thomas Edward and Viola Margaret (Fitzpatrick) F.; student Bradshaw Bus. Coll., Lowell, Mass., 1939-40; m. Jean Bell, May 19, 1951; children—Meredith (Mrs. Robert Norton), Nancy (Mrs. Michael Decker), Cheryl (Mrs. Roger Norton), Clifford G., James L. With New Market Mfg., Lowell, 1938-39, Pacific Mills, Lawrence, Mass., 1940-41; welder Bethlehem Steel, Quincy, Mass., 1941-42; with Samuel Cabot, Inc., Boston, 1946—, traffic mgr., 1947—, sec., 1970—; owner Firth's Paint Store, Chelmsford, 1972—. Served with USAAF, 1942-45. Mem. Seacoast Shippers Assn. (2d v.p. 1978—). Mason. Home: 10 Pendleton Rd Chelmsford MA 01824 Office: 1 Union St Boston MA 02108

FISCH, SOLOMON, internist, cardiologist; b. Havana, Cuba, May 30, 1926; came to U.S., 1942; naturalized, 1953; s. Abraham U. and Ida (Rosenwald) F.; B.S., U. Scranton, 1945; Ph.D. (teaching and research fellow), U. Rochester, 1949; M.D., N.Y. U., 1953; m. Lila May Mirkin, Dec. 16, 1951; children—Susan Barbara, Melanie Ann, Amy Margot, Steven Lloyd. Intern, Montefiore Hosp., Bronx, N.Y., 1953-54; resident VA Hosp., Bronx, 1954-56, dir. cardiac therapy research unit, 1958-70; asst. clin. prof. medicine N.Y. Med. Coll., 1969—; asst. attending physician Flower and Fifth Ave. Hosp., Met. Hosp., 1969—. Served with USAF, 1956-62; maj. Res. Recipient multiple grants from various pharm. cos. and Food and Drug Adminstrn., 1958-70. Fellow A.C.P., Am. Coll. Cardiology, Am. Coll. Clin. Pharm. and Therapeutics, Sigma Xi. Home: 172 Wood Rd Englewood Cliffs NJ 07632 Office: 1095 Park Ave New York City NY 10028

FISCHEL, EDWARD ELLIOT, physician, educator; b. N.Y.C., July 29, 1920; s. Joseph L. and Lisa (Herman) F.; B.A., Columbia Coll., 1941, Sc.D. in Medicine, 1948; M.D., Columbia Coll. Phys. and Surg., 1944; m. Pauline Dunieff, Dec. 26, 1943; children—Robert, Janet. Intern Presbyn. Hosp., N.Y.C., 1944-45, asst. resident medicine, 1945-46; asst. in medicine Columbia Coll. Phys. and Surg., N.Y.C., 1947-50, asso. medicine, 1950-55, asso. clin. prof. medicine, 1969-72, lectr. medicine, 1972—; asst. physician Presbyn. Hosp., N.Y.C., 1947-55; asso. clin. prof. medicine Albert Einstein Coll. Medicine, N.Y.C., 1957-69, prof. medicine, 1972—; dir. dept. medicine Bronx-Lebanon Hosp. Center, Bronx, N.Y., 1954—. Mem. exec. com. Health Research Council City N.Y., 1966-75, chmn. allergy and infectious disease panel, 1968-75. Diplomate Am. Bd. Internal Medicine. Fellow A.C.P., N.Y. Acad. Medicine (v.p. 1969-71; trustee 1972—, chmn. com. edn. 1972-73), A.A.A.S. (mem. council 1957-59); mem. Am. Soc. Clin. Investigation, Am. Assn. Immunologists, Am. Rheumatism Assn. (pres. 1968-69), Assn. Am. Med. Colls., Infectious Diseases Soc. Am., Harvey Soc., Soc. Exptl. Biology and Medicine, Am. Fedn. Clin. Research, A.M.A., Bronx County Med. Soc., Am. Heart Assn. (mem. research com. 1954-60), N.Y. Tb and Health Assn. (dir. 1956-66; mem. research com. 1961-63), Phi Beta Kappa, Alpha Omega Alpha. Home: 337 Engle St Tenafly NJ 07670 Office: 1276 Fulton Ave Bronx NY 10456

FISCHER, CHARLOTTE FROESE (MRS. PATRICK CARL FISCHER), educator; b. Nikolaivka, USSR, Sept. 21, 1929; d. John David and Helen (Thiessen) Froese; B.A., U. B.C., 1952, M.A., 1954; Ph.D., Cambridge U., 1957; m. Patrick Carl Fischer, Apr. 2, 1967; 1 dau., Carolyn. Instr. math. U. B.C. (Can.), Vancouver, 1957-59, asst. prof. math. and computing centre, 1959-63, asso. prof., 1963-65, prof., 1965-69; vis. prof. U. Waterloo (Ont., Can.), 1968-69, prof. computer sci., 1969-72, prof. applied math., 1972-75; prof. computer sci. Pa. State U., 1974—. Research fellow Harvard Coll. Obs., 1963-64; cons. Pacific Oceanographic Group, Nanaimo, B.C., 1957-59. Alfred P. Sloan fellow 1964-68; Nat. Research Council Can. grantee, 1964-76; U.S. Dept. Energy grantee, 1977—. Mem. Assn. Computing Machinery, Computer Sci. Assn. (dir. 1972-74), Soc. Indsl. and Applied Math., Can. Info. Processing Soc. (sect. pres. 1965-67). Author: Introduction to Programming the IBM 1620, 1964; The Hartree-Fock Method for Atoms: A Numerical Approach, 1977. Editor: Computing Revs., 1968-78, Computer Physics Communications, 1968—. Contbr. papers to profl. pubis. Home: 413 Waring Ave State College PA 16801 Office: Whitmore Lab University Park PA 16802

FISCHER, GEORGE, educator; b. Berlin, Germany, May 5, 1923 (father Am. citizen, mother Soviet citizen); s. Louis and Bertha Markoosha (Mark) F.; B.A., U. Wis., 1947; Ph.D., Harvard, 1952; m. Elinor Halsted, 1958 (div. 1972); children—Sara, Mark. Asst. prof. Brandeis U., 1953-58, asso. prof., 1958-60; prof. Cornell U., 1961-65; lectr. Columbia, 1965-69; prof. City U. N.Y., 1969—. Served with AUS, 1942-46. Mem. Soc. Fellows Harvard, Phi Beta Kappa (hon.). Author: Soviet Opposition to Stalin, 1952, 70; Russian Liberalism, 1958, 69; The Soviet System and Modern Society, 1968; The Revival of American Socialism, 1971; Urban Higher Education in the United States, 1974; Ways to Self Rule, 1978. Home: 312 W 20th St New York City NY 10011 Office: PhD Program in Sociology Grad Sch City U NY 33 W 42d St New York City NY 10036

FISCHER, HADWIN KEITH, physician; b. Williamsport, Pa., June 6, 1916; s. M. Hadwin and Alice (Gortner) F.; A.B., Gettysburg Coll., 1939; M.D., Temple U., 1943, M.S., 1949; m. Dorothy Steiger, Mar. 11, 1944; children—David H., Ann. F. Fischer Markel, Nancy H. Fischer Thomason. With dept. psychiatry Temple U. Health Sci. Center, 1949—, successively instr., asst. prof., asso. prof., 1949-66, clin. prof. psychiatry, 1966—; chmn. adv. com. Pa. Mental Health, Inc., 1964-72; mem. Pa. State Adv. Com. on Mental Health and Mental Retardation, 1966—; mem. Pa. Bd. Pub. Welfare, 1968—, sec., 1976-77; cons. Lutheran Home for Orphans and Aged, U.S. Naval Hosp., Phila., Ancora Hosp., Trenton Hosp.; cons. Chestnut Hill Hosp., 1977-78, attending, 1978—. Served to lt. M.C., USNR, 1944-46. Diplomate Am. Bd. Psychiatry. Fellow Internat. Coll. Psychosomatic Medicine; mem. Phila. (pres. 1965), Pa. (pres. 1975) psychiat. socs., Acad. Psychosomatic Medicine (pres. 1976), Psychoanalytic Soc. (treas. 1964-65), Drs. Golf Assn. Phila. (pres. 1971), Med. Club Phila. (pres. 1976), Am. Med. Golf Assn. (pres. 1971), Pa. Med. Polit. Action Com. (dir. 1977-78), Phi Gamma Delta, Phi Chi. Lutheran. Clubs: Sci. and Art of Germantown, Phila. Cricket, Union League (Phila.); Seaview Country. Contbr. to profl. jours.; asso. editor Psychosomatics, 1972—. Home: 3037 W Queen Ln Philadelphia PA 19129 Office: 5450 Wissahichon Ave Philadelphia PA 19144

FISCHER, IRVING, optometrist; b. N.Y.C., July 21, 1920; s. Harry and Bessie (Urdang) F.; student Coll. City N.Y., 1948-50; O.D. magna cum laude, No. Ill. Coll. Optometry, 1950; m. Ann Silverman, Jan. 15, 1944; children—Harvey J., Pamela J. Optometrist, Washington, 1955-60, Wheaton, Md., 1960—. Mem. Nat. Eye Research Found., 1965—. Served with AUS, 1943-46. Mem. Masonic Aid Assn., Jewish War Vets., Md. Optometric Assn. Mem. B'nai B'rith. Home: 13405 Dauphine St Silver Spring MD 20906 Office: Optical Dept Montgomery Ward Wheaton Plaza Wheaton MD 20902

FISCHER, JACK MARSHALL, mfg. co. exec.; b. Pitts., July 24, 1937; s. Samuel M. and Beatrice (Stewart) F.; B.S., Mass. Inst. Tech., 1959; M.B.A., U. Pitts., 1966; m. Margaret Griffin, May 13, 1961; children—Janet, Samuel, Douglas. Staff indsl. engr. Jones & Laughlin Steel Co., Pitts., 1959-65; treas. Belmont Industries Inc., Phila., 1966-75, dir., 1972—; treas. Walbar Inc., Peabody, Mass., 1975—, also dir.; dir. Belmont Industries Inc., Old Colony Bank and Trust Co. of Essex County. Served as officer AUS, 1959-62. Mem. Beta Gamma Sigma. Jewish. Club: Kernwood Country (Salem, Mass.). Address: 94 Bradlee Ave Swampscott MA 01907

FISCHER, JEROME MORTON, civil engr.; b. N.Y.C., Mar. 15, 1924; s. Lester and Hilda (Schwartz) F.; B.C.E., N.C. State U., 1948; postgrad. in civil engring. Tex. A. and M. U., 1942-43, postgrad. Engrs. Sch., 1943; m. Rhoda Sha, Sept. 2, 1946; children—Steven, Karen, Michael, Marion. Project and structural engr. Parsons, Brinckerhoff, Hall & McDonald, N.Y.C., 1948-52; project engr. Tippets-Abbett-McCarthy-Stratton, N.Y.C., 1952-54, gen. mgr., office, San Salvador, El Salvador, 1954-60; v.p. Frederic R. Harris, Inc., The Hague, Netherlands, 1960-64, sr. v.p., 1964-66, exec. v.p., dir., N.Y.C., 1966-72, chmn. bd., 1972—; v.p. Internat. Planning Research Corp., Los Angeles, 1974—; exec. v.p. Planning Research Corp., 1977—, also dir. Served with C.E., AUS, 1942-46. Decorated Order of Crown (Belgium); Medal of Honor (Spanish Ministry Pub. Works). Registered profl. engr., N.Y., Vt.; chartered engr., U.K. Fellow ASCE, Instn. Civil Engrs. (Great Brit.); mem. Am. Cons. Engrs. Council (internat. com.), Am. Inst. Cons. Engrs., Am. Concrete Inst., Internat. Rd. Fedn., Internat. Toll Rds., Tunnel and Turnpike Assn., Nat. Soc. Profl. Engrs., Permanent Internat. Congress Rds., Royal Netherlands Inst. Engrs., Soc. Flemish Engrs., Soc. Am. Mil. Engrs. (dir. N.Y.C. chpt.), Bldg. Trades Employers' Assn., U.S. Chambers Commerce in Netherlands and Belgium, Com. Econ. Devel. Club: Petroleum (London). Contbr. articles to profl. jours. Home: 18 Hampton Rd Scarsdale NY 10583 Office: 245 Park Ave 41st Floor New York City NY 10017

FISCHER, JOHN ALBERT, surgeon; b. Dobbs Ferry, N.Y., Aug. 15, 1920; s. Henry and Daisy Euphremia (Wallace) F.; A.B., N.Y. U., 1943; M.D., Albany Med. Coll., 1947; m. Elizabeth Sannino, Sept. 12, 1953; children—Joan, Susan, Beverly, Joyce. Intern, Union Meml. Hosp., Balt., 1947-48, asst. resident in surgery, 1948-49; asst. resident in surgery, resident, asst. chief surgery VA Hosp., Perry Point, Md., 1949-53, cons. surgeon, 1953—; practice medicine, specializing in surgery, Elkton, Md.; chief surgery Union Hosp., Elkton. Bd. dirs. Am. Cancer Soc., Cecil County, Md., 1963. Diplomate Am. Bd. Surgery. Fellow ACS, Southeastern Surg. Assn., Internat. Coll. Surgeons, Am., Internat. colls. angiology, Royal Soc. Health (London); mem. AMA, Med. and Chirurg. Faculty Md., Cecil County Med. Soc. (past pres.). Republican. Presbyterian. Club: N.E. River Yacht. Contbr. articles to profl. jours. Home: PO Box 307 Christiana Turnpike Elkton MD 21921 Office: 166 W Main St Elkton MD 21921

FISCHER, MARVIN JAY, engr., hosp. adminstr.; b. Bklyn., Aug. 3, 1929; s. David and Shevelin (Goldfein) F.; B.E.E., Syracuse U., 1950; M.B.A., Adelphi U., 1977; m. Ruth Maslow, June 14, 1953; children—Michael, Cathi, Wendy. Tech. writer U.S. Signal Corps, Ft. Monmouth, N.J., 1950-51; engr. Western Union Telegraph Co., N.Y.C., 1953-54, various constrn. cos. under one mgmt., N.Y.C., 1954-61, L.I. Lighting Co., Hicksville, N.Y., 1961-63; chief engr., asso. M.P. Zacharius & Assos., N.Y.C., 1963-72; asst. v.p. facilities planning and engring. services Brookdale Hosp. Med. Center, Bklyn., 1972—; faculty State U. N.Y., Stony Brook, 1975-78; lectr. in field. Asst. cubmaster Boy Scouts Am., Woodmere, N.Y., 1963-65; alumni precoll. counsellor Coll. Engring., Syracuse (N.Y.) U., 1972—; exec. com. sch. dist. budget adv. com., N.Y., 1968-71; pres. Hewlett Park Civic Assn., 1966. Served with Signal Corps, U.S. Army, 1951-53. Registered profl. engr., N.Y., N.J., Conn., Pa., Fla.; certified clin. engr., certificate of qualification Nat. Council Engring. Examiners. Mem. Greater N.Y. Hosp. Assn. (chmn. engrs. adv. com. 1975-76), Nat. Fire Protection Assn. (chmn. tech. com. 76A, 1975—), Nat. Soc. Profl. Engrs., Am. Coll. Hosp. Adminstrs., IEEE, Illuminating Engring. Soc., Internat. Assn. Elec. Insps., Am. Hosp. Assn., Am. Soc. Hosp. Engrs., Hosp. Mgmt. Systems Soc., Assn. Advancement Med. Instrumentation, N.Y. State Assn. Professions, Hosp. Engrs. Soc. Club: Masons (master 1962). Contbr. articles to profl. jours.; author: Designing Electrical Systems for Hospitals, 1975. Office: Care Brookdale Hosp Med Center Linden Blvd at Rockaway Pkwy Brooklyn NY 11212

FISCHER, ROBERT ARTHUR, fertilizer co. exec.; b. N.Y.C., July 6, 1921; s. Ernest Otto and Beatrice Henrietta (McCormick) F.; student Am. Inst. Banking, 1937-38; m. Martha Ellen Haines, Feb. 5, 1944 (dec.); children—Donna, Robert Arthur, Richard, Debra A.; m. 2d, Ruth Anita Johnson, Mar. 8, 1975. With Milford Fertilizer Co. (Del.), 1946—, pres., 1958—, dir. 1950—; now also pres., dir. Valliant Fertilizer Co., Laurel, Del.; pres. Fischer Enterprises, Lewes, D.A. Nitrogen Solution Terminal, Lewes, Del., 1970—, dir., 1970—. Pres. Del-Mar-Va Peninsula Fertilizer Assn., 1950-52. Head Del-Mar-Va Boy Scout Council, 1960-62; mem. Sussex County (Del.) Planning and Zoning Bd., 1970-72. Pres. Milford Meml. Hosp., 1966-70. Served with AUS, 1941-46. Mem. Nat. Fertilizer Inst. (dir.), Internat. Oceanographic Found., Aircraft Owners and Pilots Assn. Kiwanian (pres. 1958-59), Odd Fellow. Club: Shawnee County (pres. 1958-62) (Milford); Lewes Yacht. Home: RD 3 Box 752A Milford DE 19963 Office: NE Front St Milford DE 19963

FISCHER, ROBERT E(LBERT), publisher; b. N.Y.C., May 10, 1920; s. Robert Henry and Virginia (Wimmer) F.; student N.Y.U., 1941-43, Northwestern U., 1946-48, U. St. Louis, 1948-49. Owner, pub. The Evansville (Ind.) News, 1949-51; pres. Accurate Advt. Agy., N.Y.C., 1951-53, dir., 1953-58; owner Robert E. Fischer Enterprises, N.Y.C., 1953—; chmn. bd. Allied Industries Corp. of Am., Spray Chems. Corp.; pres. Projectapix, Ltd., 1969—; dir. Most Publs., Ltd., Addressing Lists, Inc., Sabre Records, Most Records, Top Tunes Records, Patricia de Paree, Gag Cards, Inc., Jessica of N.Y., Press & Television News Co. Active Boy Scouts Am., YMCA, Manpower Mgmt. Forum. Recipient Dartnell Gold Medal award, 1940; Mr. New Yorker award, 1940. Mem. Advt. Assn. Am., Amateur Athletic Assn., Am. Book Publ. Council, Am. Legion, A.S.C.A.P., Authors Build, Brand Names Found., Soc. Mil. Engrs., Writer's Guild, V.F.W., Premium Advt. Assn. Am., Registered Photographers Assn., Press Assn., Photographers Soc. Am., Bachelors Soc. Am., Small Bus. Men's Assn. Clubs: Premium, Advertising, N.Y. Athletic, Strongmen's of Am. (N.Y.C.). Author books in field of health and beauty, also Hi-Fi and electronics; various articles trade jours., mags. Writer, producer radio, TV sreeenplays; lyricist popular recordings. Office: Box 3 New York City NY 10023

FISCHER, ROGER RAYMOND, state legislator Pa.; b. Washington, Pa., June 1, 1941; s. Raymond L. and Louise (Gartley) F.; B.A. in Math. and Physics, Washington and Jefferson Coll., 1963; postgrad. Carnegie Inst. Tech., 1963-64; m. Catherine Louise Trettel, Aug. 13, 1972; children—Roger Raymond II, Steven Gregory. Research engr. Jones and Laughlin Steel Co., 1966; mem. Pa. Ho. of Reps. from 47th Dist., 1966—, chmn. basic edn. subcom., 1973-74, minority chmn. mil. and vets. af airs com. Mm. various task forces Joint State Govt. Commn.; chmn. police subcom. Pa. Crime Commn. Regional Planning Council, 1970. Active local YMCA, Boy Scouts Am., ARC. Mem. Washington Sch. Bd., 1965-71. Bd. dirs. Washington City Mission. Mem. Washington and Jefferson Coll. Alumni Assn., Am. Legion (vice chmn. legis. Pa.), 40 and 8, Res. Officers Assn. (chpt. v.p. 1970-71), Appalachian Trail Conf., Potomac Appalachian Trail Club, Western Pa. Conservancy, Warrior's Trail Assn. Republican. Lutheran (lay asst.). Mason (Shriner), Moose. Club: Washington, Canonsburg and Palanka Sportsmen's. Home: Overlook Dr Washington PA 15301 Office: Box 195 Main Capitol Bldg Harrisburg PA 17120

FISCHGRUND, MILTON LEONARD, pediatrician; b. Franklin Boro, Sussex County, N.J., Jan. 31, 1933; s. Isidor and Frances (Konigsberg) F.; B.S., Rutgers U., 1954; M.D., N.Y. Med. Coll., N.Y.C., 1958; m. Sheila Arlene Knoller, Jan. 28, 1973; children—Karen and Alisa Fischgrund, David and Stacy Kane. Intern, Tripler Army Hosp., 1958-59; resident pediatrics Brooke Army Hosp., San Antonio, 1959-61; practice medicine specializing in pediatrics, Elizabeth, N.J., 1963-72; group practice medicine, specializing in pediatrics Union, N.J., 1972—; sec.-treas. Pediatric Med. Group, Union, 1972—. Prin. founder Richard E. Gruen Meml. Scholarship, Coll. Arts and Scis., Rutgers U., New Brunswick, 1971, Rutgers U. Pres.'s Club, 1972; trustee Temple Shomrei Torah, Hillside, N.J., 1970-72. Served with U.S. Army, 1958-63. Diplomate Am. Bd. Pediatrics. Fellow Am. Acad. Pediatrics; mem. N.J. Med. Soc., Phi Delta Epsilon (pres. No. N.J. chpt. 1975-76). Democrat. Jewish. Club: Rutgers U. Founders. Home: 22 Steven Terr West Orange NJ 07052 Office: 381 Chestnut St Union NJ 07083

FISCHLER, BRYANT, lawyer; b. Bklyn., Nov. 15, 1928; s. Alfred and Fannie (Kluger) F.; student L.I. U., 1949-51; LL.B., Bklyn. Law Sch., 1954; children—Deborah Allyn, Lisa Rose, Aimee Lee, Diane Nadine, Scott Harris Fischler; m. 2d, Linda M. Mercer, May 1, 1977. Admitted to New York bar, 1955, U.S. Supreme Ct. bar, 1964; practiced in Bklyn., 1955-61, Newburgh, N.Y., 1961—; mem. firm Bryant Fischler; atty. appeal bd. N.Y. State Dept. Labor, 1960; acting judge City Ct., Newburgh, 1964-66; asst. prof. Orange County Community Coll., 1969-75, Harriman Coll., 1977—; pres., chmn. bd. Tronic Products Inc., 1973-78, Catania Bros. Foods, Inc., 1973-78; mgr. Brylin Capital Corp., fin. brokers; sec. Star Line Promotions, Ltd. Pres., chmn. bd. Leukemia Soc., 1964-68; chmn. local Draft Bd., Newburgh, N.Y.; Democratic candidate dist. atty. Orange Co., N.Y., 1966; Democratic city chmn. City Newburgh. Served with USNR 1946-48. Mem. Orange County, Newburgh bar assns., Jewish War Vets. U.S. Am., Am. Arbitration Assn. Mem. B'nai B'rith. Home: Route 208 S Blooming Grove NY 10914 Office: PO Box 184 Washingtonville NY 10992

FISCINA, PASQUALE R., govt. architect-engr.; b. Bklyn., Feb. 5, 1914; s. Nicola Michael and Domenica (Esposito) F.; B.Arch., N.Y.U., 1940; m. Elizabeth Rainone, Nov. 18, 1944; children—Nicholas Michael, Patrick Joseph, Donna Marie. Chief engring. div. Atlantic Dist., C.E., N.Y.C., 1953-54; asst. chief engring. div. Eastern Ocean Dist., C.E., N.Y.C., 1957-63; asst. chief mil. br. N.Y. Dist. C.E., N.Y.C., 1963-71; project engr. for expansion U.S. Mil. Acad., West Point, N.Y., 1964-71. Gen. chmn. Sch. Settlement Assn. ann. testimonial, 1975, also 75th anniversary, 1976. Registered profl. engr. Vt. Mem. Nat. Soc. Profl. Engrs., Soc. Am. Mil. Engrs. (chief mil. br. North Atlantic div. 1971—), Holy Name Soc. (pres. 1968-70). Roman Catholic (trustee, gen. chmn. centennial com. 1971, pres. parish council 1972-74). K.C. Home: 133 Frost St Brooklyn NY 11211 Office: 90 Church St New York City NY 10007

FISH, EUGENE CHARLES, lawyer, pub. accountant, metals co. exec.; b. Phila., Jan. 2, 1910; s. Michael A. and E. Corinne (Snyder) F.; B.S., U. Pa., 1931, J.D., 1934; m. Marjorie Scheuerle, June 7, 1947; children—M. Alan, Robert E., Shirley. Admitted to Pa. bar, 1937; practiced in Philadelphia, 1937—; pub. accounting, Phila., 1939—; sr. partner Tax Assos., 1940—; pres. Peerless Industries, Inc., Boyertown, Pa.; chmn. bd. Eastern Foundry Co., Boyertown; dir. Estate Cons., Inc., Alex C. Fergusson Co., Amreg Corp., Hull Corp. Pres., Jenkintown (Pa.) Sch. Bd., 1962-64; sec. Washington Crossing Park Commn., 1964. Trustee Reidler Found.; pres., trustee Washington Crossing Found.; trustee Lebanon Valley Coll.; chmn. bd. YMCA. C.P.A. Methodist (trustee). Mason (32 deg.). Home: Washington Ln and Wyncote Rd Jenkintown PA 19046 Office: 215 S Broad St Philadelphia PA 19107

FISH, FREDERICK STUART, accountant, real estate co. exec.; b. Newark, Mar. 15, 1945; s. Nathaniel Ladner and Daisy (Livingston) F.; B.S. in Bus. Adminstrn., Syracuse U., 1967; m. Merle Lynn Weiner, June 11, 1967; 1 dau., Nicole Leslie. Partner N. L. Fish & Co., C.P.A.'s, N.Y., N.J., 1967—; pres. Woodbury Holding Corp., N.Y.C., 1972—; partner, mgr. Plainview Mgmt. Agts., N.Y.C., 1970—, N.L. Fish Mgmt. Co., Englewood Cliffs, N.J., 1970—, Mazzal Operating Co., Englewood Cliffs, 1970—; dir. Woodbury Holding Corp., Harwood Holding Corp., Renwood Holding Corp., Jefferson Lakes Estates, Inc., Jefferson Lakes Camp & Travel Corp. Chmn. Englewood Israel Bond Drive, 1972; bd. dirs. Englewood Jewish Community Center, past bd. dirs. Englewood United Jewish Fund. Served with AUS, 1968-69. Mem. Beta Alpha Psi, Tau Epsilon Psi. Home: 371 Eton St Englewood NJ 07631 Office: 617 Palisade Ave Englewood Cliffs NJ 07632

FISH, HAMILTON, JR., congressman; b. Washington, June 3, 1926; s. Hamilton Fish; grad. Kent (Conn.) Sch.; A.B., Harvard, 1949; LL.B., N.Y. U., 1957; postgrad. John F. Kennedy Sch. Pub. Adminstrn., Cambridge, Mass.; m. Julia Mackenzie (dec. Mar. 1969); children—Hamilton III, Julia Alexandra, Nicholas S., Peter L.; m. 2d, Billy Laster Cline, Apr. 3, 1971. Admitted to N.Y. bar; vice consul for U.S. in Ireland; atty. N.Y. Assembly Judiciary Com., Albany; mem. 91st-93d congresses from N.Y. 28th Dist., mem. 94th-95th congresses from 25th Dist. Dir. Dutchess County (N.Y.) Civil Def., mem. exec. Dutchess County council Boy Scouts Am. Bd. mgrs. Holiday Hills YMCA; past bd. dirs. Dutchess County Com. for Econ. Opportunity. Served with USNR, 1944-46. Mem. Am. Legion, V.F.W., Dutchess, Ulster, Green county hist. socs., N.Y. State, Dutchess County bar assns. Republican. Episcopalian (bd. missions N.Y. diocese). Mason, Elk. Home: Millbrook NY 12545 Office: Rayburn House Office Bldg Washington DC 20515 Washington DC 20515

FISH, HERMAN LEWIS, psychologist; b. Bklyn., June 17, 1919; s. Joseph and Anna (Reiss) F.; B.S. with honors, Queens Coll., 1942; postgrad. Ind. U., 1943-44, N.Y.U., 1945-59, St. John's U., 1966-70; m. Florence B. Rabinowitz, Aug. 19, 1943; children—Victoria Joan, Kenneth John. Indsl. engr. Western Electric Co., 1944-47; psychol. appraiser Bklyn. Coll. Testing and Advisement Unit, 1947-48, instr. psychology coll., 1947-48; instr. psychology Queens Coll., N.Y.C., 1948-51, research asso., 1949-51; sr. project dir., research and devel. dir. V.W. Eimicke Assos., mgmt. cons.'s Bronxville, N.Y., 1951-66; sch. psychologist, field trainer N.Y.C. Bur. Child Guidance, 1965-76; psychologist Evaluation Unit Dist. 25, N.Y.C., 1977—; chief psychologist Center for Growth and Devel., Flushing, N.Y., 1976—; cons. in field, clin. psychologist; adj. asst. prof. psychology Pace U., N.Y.C., 1972-73. Bd. dirs. Alliance for Neurometrics Inc., 1978—. Certified psychologist, sch. psychologist N.Y. State. Mem. Am., Eastern psychol. assns., AAAS. Contbr. articles to profl. publs. Home: 150-05 78th Ave Flushing NY 11367 Office: Center for Growth and Devel 75-09 Main St Flushing NY 11367

FISH, JILL HARRIET CARLSON (MRS. WILLIAM D. FISH, JR.), publisher, editor; b. Ridgway, Pa., Mar. 10, 1923; d. John Algot and Harriet Marie (Martinson) Carlson; B.S., Grove City Coll., 1945; postgrad. Pa. State U., 1946-48, Mansfield State Coll., 1973-74; m. William D. Fish, Jr., Mar. 30, 1946; children—William D. III, John Frederick. Tchr., Coudersport (Pa.) High Sch., 1945-48, No. Potter High Sch., Ulysses, Pa., 1956-57; asso. editor Potter Enterprise, Coudersport, 1957-74, exec. editor, 1974—; corp. sec. Enterprise Pub. Co., Coudersport, 1970-77, pub., exec. editor, 1977—. Co-owner, co-developer Deer Lick Camping Area, Coudersport, Pa., 1964-68; tchr. adult classes Coudersport Area Sch., 1969-71; pvt. tchr. violin, 1949—. Sec., Council Ch. Women, Coudersport, 1952-54, Potter County Child Welfare Adv. Bd., 1960-62, Potter County chpt. ARC, 1972-75; program chmn. Coudersport PTA, 1960-62; mem. Potter County Christian Ministry to Migrants Com., 1959-64. Mem. Enterprise Pub. Assn. (pres. 1977—), Alpha Theta Mu. Presbyterian (finance chmn. 1952-55). Home: 411 N East St Coudersport PA 16915 Office: PO Box 29 Coudersport PA 16915

FISHBONE, HERBERT, lawyer; b. N.Y.C., Aug. 12, 1921; s. Samuel L. and Anna (Blumenkrantz) F.; A.B., Lafayette Coll., 1941; LL.B., Cornell U., 1949; m. Vivian Manperl, Oct. 23, 1966; children—David S., Deborah I., Daniel H. Admitted to Pa. bar, 1950, since practiced in Easton. Mem. procedural rules com. Supreme Ct. Pa. Hon. chmn. adv. council for Pa., Del. and Md., Am. Jewish Com., 1973—; chmn. Lehigh-Del. Devel. Council, 1971-72. Bd. dirs. Eastern Pa. Comprehensive Health Planning Bd., 1973-76, Lehigh Valley Hosp. Planning Council, 1972-73; trustee Easton Hosp., 1960—, pres., 1963-65. Served to lt. USCG, 1942-46. Mem. Am., Pa. (ho. of dels.), Northampton County (pres. 1971) bar assns., Am. Judicature Soc. Home: 423 Paxinosa Rd E Easton PA 18042 Office: PO Box 1099 ENBT Co Bldg Easton PA 18042

FISHEL, HENRY DETLEV, psychotherapist; b. Leipzing, Germany, Sept. 29, 1925; s. Max and Sylvia (Kohs) F.; came to U.S., 1941, naturalized, 1944; B.A., N.Y. U., 1949, M.A. in Psychology, 1951; M.S.S. (Jewish Child Care Assn. fellow), Adelphi U. Sch. Social Work, 1960; m. Sylvia Birnbaum Kolbert, Apr. 6, 1974; children—Allegra, Deirdre; stepchildren—Steven Kolbert, Jason Kolbert, Peter Kolbert, William Kolbert. Family counselor Family Service Assn. Five Towns, Woodmere, N.Y., 1962-65; therapist Hempstead (N.Y.) Consultation Center, 1963-69; adminstrv. supr. Phoenix Sch., Jewish Bd. Guardians, N.Y.C., 1965-67; exec. dir. Nassau Guidance and Counseling Center, Inc., North Bellmore, N.Y., 1968—; practice psychotherapy, 1965—; instr. spl. edn. Hofstra U., 1967-69; clin. instr. Albert Einstein Coll. Medicine, Yeshiva U., 1967-69; lectr. in field; leader pre-marital seminars C.W. Post Center, L.I. U., Brookville. Served with U.S. Army, 1944-46. Mem. Alumni Assn. Sch. Social Work Adelphi U. (pres. 1962-64, exec. com. 1962-66), Nat. Assn. Social Workers (chmn. public relations com. Nassau chpt. 1964-67, mem. chpt. pvt. practice council 1965-74, chmn. chpt. pvt. practice council 1971-72, chpt. exec. com. 1964-67, 71-72), Acad. Cert. Social Workers. Contbr. articles on day treatment and milieu therapy to profl. publs.; work at Phoenix Sch. subject of book: Nine Rotten Lousy Kids (Herbert Grossman), 1972. Home: 17 Intervale Roslyn Estates NY 11576 Office: 1399 Bellmore Ave North Bellmore NY 11710

FISHEL, LEO, physician; b. Freeport, N.Y., Mar. 7, 1917; s. Leo and Laura Elizabeth (Deurstein) F.; B.S., St. Lawrence U., 1938; M.D., Columbia U., 1942; m. Ann Cowles, Sept. 12, 1942; children—Mary Laura, Leo, Rita, Rosemary, Frederick, Sara, Andrew. Intern, Meadowbrook Hosp., E. Meadow, N.Y., 1942-43; resident Goldwater Meml. Hosp., N.Y.C., 1945-46; resident in internal medicine Bronx Meml. Hosp., 1946-48; practice medicine specializing in internal medicine, 1947—; attending physician Meadowbrook Hosp., 1972—; cons. Lydia E. Hall Hosp., 1970-75, Mercy Hosp., 1970—, South Nassau Communities Hosp., 1959—; asst. vis. physician 1st div. Bellevue Hosp., N.Y.C., 1949-61; asso. prof. clin. medicine State U. N.Y., Stony Brook, 1972—; mem. N.Y. State Bd. for Profl. Med. Conduct, 1975—. Vice pres. governing bd. Nassau/Suffolk (N.Y.) Health Systems Agy., 1976-78; trustee Freeport Library, 1966-73, pres., 1973; bd. dirs. Nassau Community Health Services Found., pres., 1974. Served with M.C., inf., U.S. Army, 1943-45. Decorated Bronze star; diplomate Am. Bd. Internal Medicine. Fellow A.C.P., Nassau Acad. Medicine (pres. 1973-74); mem. Am. Soc. of Internal Medicine, N.Y. Soc. of Internal Medicine (mem. pub. relations com. 1960-62), Nassau Soc. of Internal Medicine (pres. 1960-62), Am., Nassau (mem. med. advisory com. 1965-70) heart assns., N.Y. Acad. Medicine, AMA, Nassau County Med. Soc. (pres. 1971-72), N.Y. Acad. Scis. Presbyterian. Clubs: Elks, Columbia University. Home: 28 Amherst Ct Rockville Centre NY 11570 Office: 155 W Merrick Rd Freeport NY 11520

FISHER, ALLAN JERRY, educator, internat. economist, ret. govt. ofcl.; b. Camden, N.J., Sept. 7, 1906; s. Edward Coyle and Emma (Cramer) F.; B.S. in Econs., U. Pa., 1928; postgrad. U. Wis., 1934-35; Litt.M., U. Pitts., 1936, Ph.D., 1937; m. Roanna Kendall Pickering, Sept. 7, 1938. Instr. accounting Carnegie Inst. Tech., 1928-29, U. Pitts., 1929-37; asst. prof. econs. Am. U., 1937-39; asst. prof. bus. adminstrn. U. Md., 1939-41, prof. accounting and finance, 1951-68, professorial lectr., 1968—, mem. and sec. steering com. dept. bus. adminstrn., sec. deptl. assembly; asso. research accountant SEC, Washington, 1941-42; economist, asst. div. chief U.S. Treasury Dept., Washington, 1942-51, adviser, 1951-68; sr. policy analyst, sec. staff com. Nat. Adv. Council on Internat. Monetary and Fin. Policies, 1968-73, cons., 1973-75; fin. cons. Dept. Agr., Washington, 1937-39; lectr. Grad. Sch., Dept. Agr., 1939-45, Am. U., 1946-51; participant 7th Ann. Forum Finance, N.Y.C., 1957, Conf. Application of Quantitative Techniques to Bus. Problems, Tulane U., 1962, nat. credit conf. Am. Bankers Assn., 1964. Civilian fin. specialist U.S. Mil. Govt., Germany, 1945-46. Fellow Royal Econ. Soc.; mem. Am. Econ. Assn., Am. Accounting Assn., Am. Fin. Assn., Beta Gamma Sigma (pres. chpt. 1954-57, sec.-treas. chpt. 1963-66, 67-68), Delta Sigma Pi, Beta Alpha Psi, Pi Gamma Mu. Contbr. to accounting and fin. publs. Home: 2309 Apache St Adelphi MD 20783 Office: U Md College Park MD 20742

FISHER, FLORENCE ANNA, assn. exec., author; b. Bklyn., May 28, 1928; d. Frederick I. and Florence (Goldstein) Fisher; student pub. schs., Phila.; m. Stanley Eigenfeld, Dec. 20, 1953; 1 son, Glenn Mark Love. Founder, pres. The Alma Soc., Inc. (Adoptees' liberty Movement Assn.), N.Y.C., 1971—; mem. Mabon policy adv. bd. Odyssey Inst., N.Y.C., 1976-77. Author: (autobiography) The Search for Anna Fisher, 1973. Office: PO Box 154 Washington Bridge Sta New York City NY 10033

FISHER, FRANK X., hotels exec.; b. N.Y.C., Dec. 18, 1933; s. Frank X. and Juliet Electra (Pieri) F.; B.S., Cornell U., 1954; M.B.A., Harvard U., 1978; m. Eleanore L. Adam, Sept. 7, 1952; children—Laurent Ann, Frank Adam. Asst. v.p., Hilton Hotels, Waldorf Astoria, N.Y.C., 1956-68; v.p., Loew's Hotels, N.Y.C., 1968-70; area mgt. ITT Sheraton, Chgo., 1970-72; pres. Lex Hotels Inc., N.Y.C., 1972-78, dir., chief exec. officer, 1972—, dir., chief exec. officer Lex Hotels Ltd. (U.K.), 1974-78; pres., chief exec. officer Universal Hotels Corp., 1978—. Served to 1st lt. U.S. Army, 1954-56. Mem. Cornell Soc. Hotelmen (dir.), Hotel Sales Mgmt. Assn. (dir.). Home: 1120 Park Ave New York City NY 10028

FISHER, HOWARD SHREVE, JR., lawyer; b. Greenwich, Conn., Apr. 12, 1907; s. Howard Shreve and Jessie Arbon (Nichols) F.; A.B., Princeton U., 1929; J.D., Harvard U., 1932; m. Sarah Postlethwaite Childs, July 25, 1931; children—Howard Shreve III, Sarah Fisher Bennett, Theodora Fisher Baldelli. Admitted to N.Y. bar, 1934, Conn. bar, 1966, Maine bar, 1975; asso. firm Patterson, Eagle, Greenough & Day, N.Y.C., 1932-39, Chadbourne, Parke, Whiteside & Wolff, N.Y.C., 1940-62; tchr. Brunswick Sch., Greenwich, 1962-64; asso. firm Hirschberg, Pettengill, Strong & Nagle, Greenwich, 1964-73; asso. firm Waterhouse, Carroll & Cyr, Biddeford, Maine, 1976—. Town meeting rep., Greenwich, 1955-73; active Boy Scouts Am., recipient Silver Beaver award, 1973. Served with arty. U.S. Army, 1942-45. Mem. Am., Maine bar assns. Democrat. Episcopalian. Clubs: Nassau (Princeton N.J.); Kennebunk River; Arundel Beach. Home: 17 Juniper Knoll Ln Kennebunkport ME 04046 Office: 234 Maine St Biddeford ME 04005

FISHER, HYMAN WENDELL, physician; b. N.Y.C., June 8, 1926; s. Emanuel and Reba (Jarmovsky) F.; B.S., Mass. Inst. Tech., 1947, M.S., 1948; M.D., N.Y. U., 1954; m. Rosalie Joseph, June 28, 1953; children—Edward Abraham, Laura Lani, Naomi Deirdre Lakshmi, David Alexander, Andrea Maile, Daniel Clark, Jonathan Eliot Este. Intern Bellevue Hosp., N.Y.C., 1954-55, resident in internal medicine, 1955-57; resident Queen's Hosp., Honolulu, 1957-58; individual practice internal medicine, Livingston, N.J., 1958-72; med. dir., sr. v.p. Sudler and Hennessey Inc., N.Y.C., 1972—; dir., sr. v.p. Intramed Communications Inc., N.Y.C., 1974—; lectr. in community medicine Mt. Sinai Med. Sch., N.Y.C., 1975—; clin. instr. medicine N.Y. U. Med. Center, 1975—; cons. in field. Co-chmn. Livingston UN Com., 1975; mem. Livingston Research Planning Panel, 1976-77. Served with U.S. Army, 1945-46; ATO, PTO. Fellow A.C.P., Soc. Advanced Med. Systems; mem. Family Service W. Essex (v.p. 1969-71), AMA, N.J. Heart Assn., Sigma Xi, Tau Beta Pi, Alpha Omega Alpha. Jewish. Club: Pharm. Advt. Mem. B'nai B'rith (gov. Dist. III 1971—). Author, contbr. articles to profl. publs. Home: 121 E Northfield Rd Livingston NJ 07039 Office: 130 E 59th St New York City NY 10022

FISHER, JACK CARRINGTON, educator; b. Cortland, N.Y., Aug. 30, 1932; s. William J. and Jeannette (Carrington) F.; B.A., Syracuse U., 1956, M.A., 1958, Ph.D. (Ford Found. fellow), 1961; m. Katherine A. Probasco, June 15, 1957; children—John C., Margaret Lynn. Asst. prof. city and regional planning Cornell U., Ithaca, N.Y., 1962-68; asso. prof., asso. dir. urban studies Wayne State U., Detroit, 1969-72; prof. geography and environ. engring. Johns Hopkins U., Balt., 1972—, dir. Center for Met. Planning and Research. Served with AUS, 1952-55. Mem. Am. Assn. Planning Ofcls., Am. Inst. Planning, Assn. Am. Geographers, Regional Sci. Assn. Office: Center for Met Planning and Research Johns Hopkins U Baltimore MD 21218

FISHER, JANET ELIZABETH, govt. ofcl., computer systems analyst; b. Green Creek Twp., N.C., Dec. 1, 1928; d. William Mack and Venona Lee (Cole) Fisher; B.A., George Washington U., 1964; postgrad. Cath. U., 1965-70, George Washington U., 1971—. Mem. staff identification div. FBI, Washington, 1945-62; mathematician, crystallographer U.S. Naval Research Lab., Washington, 1963-70; mathematician, computer systems analyst, nonexpendable ordnance div. Naval Ordnance Mgmt. Info. Systems, Naval Ordnance Sta., Indian Head, Md., 1970-74; sci./engring. automatic data processing coordinator mgmt. Info./Data Systems div. Naval Sea Systems Command, Washington, 1974-77; computer specialist Policy, Plans and Programs Directorate, Naval Data Automation Command, Washington, 1977—. Mem. Assn. Scientists and Engrs., Am. Math. Soc., Am. Crystallographic Assn., Philos. Soc. Washington, AAAS, IEEE, Sigma Xi. Home: 6117 Greeley Blvd Springfield VA 22152 Office: Policy Plans and Programs Directorate Naval Data Automation Command Washington DC 20374

FISHER, JAY DONALD, scale co. exec.; b. Lancaster County, Pa., Dec. 4, 1931; s. Charles Franklin and Ada (Foreman) F.; student U. N.Mex., 1950-52; m. Frances Jean Smith, Aug. 16, 1962; 1 dau., Judith Alexandra. Promotion specialist Pollack Bros. Circus, 1952-53; announcer WGAL-TV, Lancaster, Pa., 1953-54; copy writer Thalhimers, Richmond, Va., 1954-55; advt. asst. mgr. sales Titmus Optical Co., Petersburg, Va., 1955-60; advt. mgr. R. H. Sheppard Co., Hanover, Pa., 1960-62; account exec. Kamp Advt., Lancaster, 1962-63; sales promotion mgr. Motor Generator Corp., Troy, Ohio, 1963-64; mgr. sales-marketing Pa. Scale Co., Leola, 1964-73; eastern regional mgr. Nat. Controls Inc., Santa Rosa, Calif., 1973-75; regional sales mgr. John Chatillon & Sons, Kew Gardens, N.Y., 1975—; a founder, sec. Family Recreation, Inc., Lancaster, 1972—. Bd. dirs. Lancaster County unit Am. Cancer Soc. Served with USNR, 1949-52. Mem. Sales and Marketing Execs. Club, Nat. Scale Men, Phi Delta Theta. Clubs: Lancaster County Riding and Tennis (dir. 1970), Media Heights Golf (Lancaster, Pa.). Home: 1526 Biltmore Ave Lancaster PA 17601

FISHER, JOHN HENRY, III, county ofcl.; b. Phila., Dec. 2, 1942; s. John H. and Irvine A. (Henninger) F.; B.A., Rutgers U., 1965; m. Teresa Witkowski, Feb. 16, 1974; 1 son, John Henry. Planning dir. Gloucester County, Woodbury, N.J., 1965-72, county adminstr., 1972—; sec., dir. Wenonah Bldg. & Loan Assn., 1967—. Bd. dirs. Abilities Center So. N.J., 1974—. Mem. N.J. County Adminstrs. Assn., N.J. Municipal Mgmt. Assn., Nat. Woodcarvers Assn. Episcopalian. Club: Rotary. Address: 1 N Broad St Woodbury NJ 08096

FISHER, JOHN HERBERT, physician; b. Tipton, Mich., Dec. 19, 1921; s. William Clarence and Alice (Norcross) F.; student U. Mich., 1940-43; M.D., Harvard, 1946; M.S. in Surgery (Charleton fellow), Tufts U., 1953; m. Virginia Chapin Moore, Feb. 15, 1947; children—Carol (Mrs. Albert Curran), Martha, Elisabeth, John Brewster. Intern Peter Bent Brigham Hosp., 1946-47; resident New Eng. Med. Center Hosps., Boston, 1949-54, chief pediatric surgery, 1960—; practice medicine, specializing in pediatric surgery, Boston, 1954—; mem. staff Boston Floating Hosp., Children's Hosp. Med. Center, Boston; asso. prof. surgery Tufts U. Sch. Medicine, Boston, 1960-74, prof., 1974-76; prof. surgery Harvard Med. Sch., 1976—; chmn. bd. Prescription Parents Inc. Mem. Hingham (Mass.) Civic Orch. Served with AUS, 1947-49. Diplomate Am. Bd. Surgery. Fellow Am. Acad. Pediatrics, Am. Urol. Assn. (New Eng. sect.), Am. Soc. Artificial Internal Organs, Boston Surg. Soc.; mem. Mass. Med. Soc. (councilor), Boston, New Eng. surg. socs., ACS, Am. Assn. Pediatric Surgeons, British Assn. Pediatric Surgery, Hingham Hist. Soc., Hingham Baroque Soc., Aesculapian Soc. Mem. New North Ch. (chmn. parish com.). Contbr. to profl. jours. Home: 17 Miles Rd Hingham MA 02043 Office: Childrens Hosp Med Center 300 Longwood Ave Boston MA 02115

FISHER, JOSEPH ALLEN, ednl. adminstr.; b. Wilmington, Del., Mar. 14, 1945; married. B.A. in Social Sci., U. Del., 1967, M.Ed. in Mental Retardation, 1975. Tchr., De La Warr Dist. Schs., Wilmington, Del., from 1970; now Supr. Spl. Services New Castle County Sch. Dist. Area IV, New Castle, Del. Committeeman Republican Pary, 1968-70; bd. dirs. Arundel Swim Club, 1975—; mem. Del. Health Adv. Com. Mem. Internat. Reading Assn. (pres. local council), Council Exceptional Children, Am. Assn. Mental Deficiency, Nat., De La Warr (pres.), New Castle County (Del.) (pres.), Nat. edn. assns., Am. Assn. Sch. Adminstrs., Assn. Supervision and Curriculum Devel. Certified in secondary social studies, elementary, learning disabilities, mental retardation, social and emotional disturbance, spl. edn. supervision; specialist in spl. edn. reading. Home: 2 Galts Ct Arundel Wilmington DE 19808 Office: Dunleith Sch Talladega and Hastie Dr Wilmington DE 19801

FISHER, KENNETH WALTER, educator; b. Heston-Middlesex, U.K., Dec. 30, 1931; s. Walter and Matilda (Hunt) F.; B.Sc., Queen Mary Coll., U. London (Eng.), 1953, M.Sc., 1954, Ph.D., Royal Postgrad. Med. Sch., 1957; m. Mettie Marie Barton, July 17, 1965; children—Sean Hayes, Galen Hunt. Asso. prof. biochem. genetics, dir. grad. research tng. program Kans. State U., Manhattan, 1966-70; prof. biology Rutgers U., New Brunswick, N.J., 1970—, chmn. biology dept., 1972-78, dir. grad. program in microbiology, 1975-78; mem. CAUSE grant rev. panel NSF, 1976, 78; mem. microbial chemistry study panel NIH, 1977. Recipient Spl. award Med. Research Council, 1957-58; research fellow Pasteur Inst., 1957-58, Princeton, 1962-63; Rockefeller travelling fellow, 1962-63; NSF grantee, 1966-69; NIH grantee, 1966-70; grantee Eli Lilly and Co., 1967-69. Fellow Royal Phys. Soc. Edinburgh; mem. N.Y. Acad. Scis., genetics socs. Am., U.K., Am. Soc. Microbiology, Biochem. Soc., Soc. Gen. Microbiology. Contbr. numerous articles to sci. publs. Home: 33

Stuart Close Princeton NJ 08540 Office: Dept Biology Douglass Coll of Rutgers U New Brunswick NJ 08903

FISHER, LAWRENCE ROGER, mgmt. cons.; b. Lakewood, Ohio, June 9, 1942; s. William Rowley and Janice Lucille (Jones) F.; B.A., Ohio Wesleyan U., 1964; M.Urban Planning, Wayne State U., 1966; postgrad. Benjamin Franklin Sch. Accountancy, Washington, 1974-75; m. Loraine Alice Schneider, June 27, 1964; children—Steven Rowley, Audrey Suzanne, Gregory Russell. Project dir. Parkins, Rogers & Assos., Inc., Detroit, 1964-67; sr. cons. Ernst & Ernst, Washington, 1967-70, supr., 1970-72, mgr., 1972—; spl. asst. to chief med. dir. as participant in Pres's. Exec. Interchange Program, VA, Washington, 1973-74. Pres., Jelleff Boy's and Girl's Club, Washington, 1969-73, v.p. fin., 1977-78; v.p. D.C. Found. Vocat. Tng., 1978; treas. Cub Scout Pack 255 Nat. Capitol Area council Boy Scouts Am., 1977-78. Certified planner-in-charge, Ohio; C.P.A., Md. Mem. Presdl. Interchange Exec. Assn. (chmn. 1977-78), Am. Hosp. Assn., Am. Inst. Planners, Am. Inst. C.P.A.'s., Md. Assn. C.P.A.'s., Montgomery County (Md.) C. of C. (v.p. econ. devel., dir.), Phi Gamma Delta. Republican. Methodist. Club: Univ (Washington); Columbia Country. Home: 6909 Ridgewood Ave Chevy Chase MD 20015 Office: 1225 Connecticut Ave Washington DC 20036

FISHER, MARTHA ANN, ret. clin. psychologist; b. Susquehanna, Pa., Oct. 28, 1900; d. Charles Ithura and Verna O. (Cook) Fisher; diploma Bloomsburg State Normal 1925; Mus.B., Susquehanna U., 1933, B.A., 1937; M.A., Bucknell U., 1943; postgrad. Pa. State U., summers 1943-46, 51, 52, 56. Tchr. rural sch., Snyder County, Pa., 1923-24; tchr. elementary schs., Sunbury, Pa., 1925-38, tchr. jr. high sch. music, 1938-40, tchr. mentally retarded classes, 1940-47; dir. guidance Sunbury Area Schs., 1947-59, sch. psychologist, 1947-59; clin. psychologist, dir. treatment, conductor in-service tng. State Correctional Instn., Muncy, Pa., 1947-72. Tchr. advanced psychology Susquehanna U., nights, 1954. Sec. adv. bd. Sunbury Salvation Army, 1930-59. Mem. AAUW, Am. Assn. Retired Persons, Internat. Council for Exceptional Children (Pa. pres. 1946), Am., Pa. psychol. assns., Pa. Assn. Probation Parole and Correction, Med. Correctional Assn., Ednl. Correctional Assn. Pa., Bus. and Profl. Women's Club (pres. 1948), Northumberland-Snyder County Hist. Soc., Delta Kappa Gamma (chpt. pres. 1950). Methodist. Mem. Order Eastern Star. Clubs: Soroptimist, Iris-Literary, Triangle-Civic. Home: Park Rd Box 273 Hummel's Wharf PA 17831

FISHER, OTHEL ARNOLD, indsl. cons.; b. Charleston, W.Va., May 19, 1914; s. Benjamin Walter and Lula Ann (Harris) F.; B.A., Morris Harvey Coll., 1953; B.Sc., W.Va. U., 1955; m. Margaret Jeanete Lyons, May 29, 1947. Shop supt. Am. Fork & Hoe, Charleston, W.Va., 1936-53; research asso., coal gasification U.S. Bur. Mines, Morgantown, W.Va., 1953-55; corporate chief indsl. engr. True Temper Corp., Cleve., 1955-62; project mgr. Stanley Tools, New Britain, Conn., 1962-65; sr. indsl. cons. Day & Zimmerman, Phila., 1965—. Served with USNR, 1944-46. Registered profl. engr., W.Va., Ohio, Pa. Mem. Nat. Soc. Profl. Engrs., Am. Powder Metallurgy Inst., Soc. Mfg. Engrs., Internat. Materials Mgmt. Soc., Am. Soc. for Metals, Franklin Inst., Computer and Automated Systems Assn., Am. Def. Preparedness Assn. Democrat. Home: 310 Edgewood Ave Folsom PA 19033 Office: 1818 Market St Philadelphia PA 19103

FISHER, ROBERT CHARLES, editor; b. Burlington, Iowa, Mar. 3, 1930; s. Ray Erwin and Blanche Columbia (Brolin) F.; B.A. cum laude, Harvard, 1955; postgrad. Columbia Law Sch., 1955-56, Tokyo U., 1957-59. Analyst, adjutant gen 's, office U.S. Army, Kansas City, Mo., 1949-50, Washington, 1950-51; adviser to Takeo Miki, prime minister of Japan, 1957-64; far eastern rep. U.S. Nat. Student Assn., Tokyo, 1956-59, Fodor Travel Guides, Tokyo, 1959-64, exec. editor, N.Y.C., 1964-66, 75-77, London, 1966-74, exec. v.p., 1975-77, pres., editor-in-chief, 1977—; v.p. David McKay Coy, N.Y.C., 1976—. Founder, dir. Kansas City Open Forum, 1949-50; bd. dirs. Internat. Assn. for Med. Assistance to Travelers, 1972—. Served with CIC U.S. Army, 1952-54; Korea. Baltimore Scholarship Fund grantee for study in India and Japan, 1956-59. Mem. Soc. Am. Travel Writers, N.Y. Travel Writers Assn., Japan Soc. (N.Y.), Internat. House of Japan. Clubs: Harvard of N.Y.C., Overseas Press, Squadron A, Am. of Japan. Author: Picasso, 1967; Klee, 1967. Office: Fodor Travel Guides 750 Third Ave New York City NY 10017

FISHER, ROBERT DALE, economist; b. Memphis, July 30, 1924; s. Hollis Weiton and Anna Sue (Parrish) F.; student Tex. Christian U., 1940-44; B.A., Am. U., 1959; m. Joy Lee Chandler, Mar. 30, 1946. Commd. ensign USN, 1944, advanced through grades to comdr., 1963; served with various ships and stas.; tng. officer Polaris Missile program, 1956-59; comdr. U.S.S. McCaffery, 1960-63; ret., 1963; now with Bache, Halsey Stuart Shields Inc., mem. N.Y. Stock Exchange, Washington. Mem. Internat. Platform Assn., Am. Econ. Assn., Naval Inst. Methodist. Kiwanian (pres. Falls Church). Clubs: Army-Navy, Navy League (Washington). Contbr. articles to profl. jours. Home: 6033 Chesterbrook Rd McLean VA 22101 Office: 1211 Connecticut Ave NW Washington DC 20036

FISHER, ROGER SCOTT, mgmt. co. exec.; b. N.Y.C., Jan. 11, 1950; s. Hamilton and Lucille (Greenberg) F.; B.M.E., N.Y.U., 1971; m. Linda Sue Markowitz, Nov. 21, 1972; children—Andrew Hamilton, Lara Brett. Exec., Stes Advt., Great Neck, N.Y., 1971-74; prin. Nationwide Mgmt. Corp., N.Y.C., 1974—; prin., pres. Hi-Rise Laundry Equipment Corp., N.Y.C. and Richmond Hill, N.Y., 1976—; v.p. various realty holding firms. Rep., Archtl. Rev. Bd., Cedarhurst, 1976-77, Parking and Traffic Commn. of Cedarhurst, 1977—; pres. 165th St. Mall Improvement Assn., Jamaica, N.Y., 1977—; asso. trustee Jewish Center of Atlantic Beach, N.Y., 1977—. Mem. Jamaica C. of C. (v.p. comml. devel.), Comml. Property Owners Cedarhurst (chmn. 1976—), Cedarhurst Bus. Assn. (v.p. 1976—). Club: Friars (N.Y.C.). Address: 6 E 46th St New York City NY 10017

FISHER, RUSSELL SYLVESTER, physician; b. Bernie, Mo., Nov. 15, 1916; s. Jacob R. and Russee (Solomon) F.; B.S., Ga. Sch. Tech., 1937; M.D., Med. Coll. Va., 1942; m. Marjorie Parker, Nov. 27, 1937; children—Patricia (Mrs. David McHold), Martha (Mrs. Martha Ryker). Intern, Henry Ford Hosp., Detroit, 1942-43, resident, 1943-44; research fellow Harvard Med. Sch., Boston, 1946-49; chief med. examiner State of Md., Balt., 1949—; prof. forensic pathology U. Md. Med. Sch., 1949—; lectr. forensic pathology Med. Sch., Johns Hopkins, 1949—, asso. in forensic pathology Sch. Hygiene and Pub. Health, 1955—. Mem. Md. State Adv. Council on Comprehensive Planning, 1968-69. Sec. treas., bd. dirs. Md. Med.-Legal Found., Inc. Served with USNR, 1944-46. Diplomate Am. Bd. Pathology (trustee 1969—, treas. 1978). Fellow Am. Acad. Forensic Sci. (pres. 1960-61); mem. AMA (chmn. com. on medicolegal problems 1966-69, del. 1966—, mem. council on med. edn. 1973—, chmn. liaison com. on grad. med. edn. 1977), Med. and Chirurg. Faculty Md. (pres. 1969-70), Balt. City Med. Soc., Am. Soc. Clin. Pathologists, Coll. Am. Pathologists, Nat. Assn. Med. Examiners (chmn. exec. com. 1968-69), Am. Assn. Pathologists, Internat. Acad. Pathologists, Am. Assn. Blood Banks (dir. 1972—). Contbr. articles to profl. jours. Office: 111 Penn St Baltimore MD 21201

FISHER, STEPHEN, mortgage broker, real estate investor; b. N.Y.C., Jan. 10, 1929; s. Robert and Minnie (Moore) F.; B.A., Brown U., Providence, 1950; m. Renee Schlanger, July 8, 1971; children—Alan, Douglas, Bonnie, Jeffrey, Judith. Mortgage trainee Louis Hammerschlag Co., L.I., N.Y., 1953; mortgage broker in pvt. practice N.Y.C., 1954-60; pres. Stephen Fisher Inc., N.Y.C., mortgage brokers, 1960—; commr. real estate City of N.Y., 1977—. Mem. Mortgage Inst. Adv. Council, N.Y. U., Asso. Builders and Owners, Bus. Leaders Adv. Com. to Mayor N.Y.C.; chmn. transp., parking and traffic com. N.Y.C. Electric License Bd., 1971—; mem. city planning com. N.Y.C., 1962—; pres. Citizens Adv. Com. N.Y.C., 1966—; trustee Anti-Defamation League. Served with AUS, 1950-52. Decorated Bronze Star. Named mortgage broker of year Realty Bd., 1962, 63. Mem. Real Estate Bd. N.Y., Mortgage Bankers Assn., Nat. Assn. Real Estate Bds., Soc. Real Estate Appraisers. Clubs: Williams, B'nai B'rith (pres. lodge 1966-70). Home: 71 Park Ave New York City NY 10016 Office: Stephen Fisher Inc 71 Park Ave New York City NY 10016

FISHER, WILLIAM HENRY, librarian; b. Sellersville, Pa., Oct. 30, 1925; s. Raymond Lewis and Pearl (Prall) F.; B.A., Syracuse U., 1950, M.S. in Library Sci., 1951; m. Edith H. Rosenblad, Jan. 27, 1948; children—Robert, Christopher. Reference librarian CIA, Washington, 1951-53; asso. librarian RCA Labs., Princeton, N.J., 1953-65; head librarian Western Electric Co., Princeton, 1965—. Cons. Spl. Libraries Assn., Princeton, 1971—. Served with USNR, 1944-46; PTO. Home: 7 Harvest Dr Pennington NJ 08534 Office: POB 900 Princeton NJ 08540

FISHER, WILLIAM NELSON, guidance counselor; b. New London, Conn., June 20, 1945; s. John Francis and Carolyn (Nelson) F.; B.A., St. Vincent dePaul Sem., 1967, B.D. cum laude, 1970; M.Ed., Suffolk U., 1975; m. Catherine McLeavey, Aug. 12, 1972; 1 dau., Nora McLeavey. Park dir., supt. mobile recreation Hollywood (Fla.) Recreation Dept., summers, 1962-70; community resource coordinator Econ. Opportunity Coordinating Group, Ft. Lauderdale, Fla., 1970-72; instr./counselor Blue Cross/Blue Shield Mass., Boston, 1972-74; sr. dorm housemaster Riverview Sch., E. Sandwich, Mass., 1975-77, tchr./counselor, 1977—. Bd. dirs. Seed Drug Rehab. Program, Fort Lauderdale, 1971-72, Rumney Marsh Players, Revere, Mass., 1973-75; first aid and water safety instr. Recipient various work achievement awards. Mem. Nat. Assn. Salt Water Instrs., Am. Personnel and Guidance Assn., Mass. Sch. Counselor Assn. Home: 152 Wakeby Rd Marstons Mills MA 02648 Office: Riverview School Route 6A East Sandwich MA 02537

FISHMAN, ALFRED PAUL, physician; b. N.Y.C., Sept. 24, 1918; s. Isaac and Anne (Tiner) F.; A.B., U. Mich., 1938, M.S., 1939; M.D., U. Louisville, 1943; M.A. (hon.), U. Pa., 1971; m. Florence Howitz, Aug. 23, 1948; children—Mark, Jay. Intern, Jewish Hosp., Bklyn., 1943-44; Dazian Found. fellow pathology Mt. Sinai Hosp., N.Y.C., 1946-47, asst. resident, then resident in medicine, 1947-48; Dazian Found. fellow cardiovascular physiology Michael Reese Hosp., Chgo., 1948-49; Am. Heart Assn. research fellow Bellevue Hosp., N.Y.C., 1949-50, Am. Heart Assn. established investigator, cardiopulmonary lab., 1951-55; Am. Heart Assn. research fellow, dept. physiology Harvard U. Med. Sch., Boston, 1950-51; instr. physiology N.Y. U. Coll. Medicine, N.Y.C., 1951-53; asso. in medicine Columbia Coll. Physicians and Surgeons, N.Y.C., 1953-55, asst. prof. medicine, 1955-58, asso. prof., 1958-66; prof. medicine U. Chgo., 1966-69; dir. Cardiovascular Inst., Chgo., 1966-69; dir. div. cardiovascular disease, dept. medicine Michael Reese Hosp. and Med. Center, Chgo., 1966-69; prof. medicine U. Pa., Phila., 1969—, William Maul Measey prof. medicine, 1972—, asso. dean Sch. Medicine, 1969-75; dir. cardiovascular-pulmonary div., also dir. Robinette Found., Clin. Cardiovascular Research Center, U. Pa. Med. Center, 1969-76, dir. Specialized Center of Research (Lung), 1973—; attending physician Hosp. U. Pa., 1969—; sr. attending physician Phila. Gen. Hosp., 1970-76; cons. to chancellor U. Mo., Kansas City, 1973-78; cons. to pres. and provost U. Pa., 1977—; vis. prof. Harvard Med. Sch., 1970, Oxford (Eng.) U., 1972, Washington U., St. Louis, 1973, Johns Hopkins U., 1974, Ben Gurion U., Israel, 1975, Emory U., Atlanta, 1976, U. Porto Alegra, Brazilia, Brazil, 1976; cons. Exec. Office of Pres., 1961-69; mem. WHO Expert Panel, Geneva, 1973—; mem. nat. adv. Heart and Lung Council NIH, 1968-71, pulmonary disease adv. com., 1977—; chmn. Gov.'s Com. for Research on Respiratory Diseases in Coal Miners, 1974-76; chmn. Internat. Conf. on Lung, Titisce, Germany and Florence, Italy, 1976. Bd. dirs. Polachek Found., Phila. Zool. Soc., 1977—. Served to capt. M.C., AUS, 1944-46. Diplomate Nat. Bd. Med. Examiners, Am. Bd. Internal Medicine. Fellow Am. Coll. Chest Physicians (hon.), Royal Coll. Physicians, A.C.P.; mem. Am. Physiol. Soc. (chmn. publs. bd. 1975—), Am. Soc. Clin. Investigation, AAAS, Royal Soc. Medicine (London), Assn. Am. Physicians, Am. Heart Assn. (dir. 1973—, chmn. council on cardiopulmonary disease 1972-74, research council 1974—), Am. Coll. Cardiology (hon.), Interurban Clin. Club, N.Y. County Med. Soc., Phila. Coll. Physicians, Heart Assn. Southeastern Pa. (dir.), Alpha Omega Alpha. Editor: (with D.W. Richards) Circulation of Blood, Men and Ideas, 1964; (with H.H. Hecht) The Pulmonary Circulation and Interstitial Space, 1969; Diseases and Disorders of the Lungs, 1978; Handbooks of Physiology, Am. Physiol. Soc., 1967-72, Physiology in Medicine, New Eng. Jour. Medicine, 1969—; editorial bd. Circulation, 1965—, Circulation Research, 1966—, Merck Manual, 1972—, Ann. Rev. Physiology, 1977—. Contbr. articles to profl. jours. Home: 2401 Pennsylvania Ave Philadelphia PA 19130 Office: Hosp U Pa 3400 Spruce St Philadelphia PA 19104

FISHMAN, DAVID ISRAEL, dept. store exec.; b. N.Y.C., July 2, 1948; s. Irving and Helen (Schilsky) F.; B.A., Brandeis U., 1970; M.A., Cornell U., 1973; m. Ellen Horowitz, July 8, 1973. Asst. to dir. Student Center, Brandeis U., Waltham, Mass., 1970; asst. dean non-residential life Rider Coll., Lawrenceville, N.J., 1973-76, asst. dean students, 1976-77, dir. student devel. center, also dir. orientation programs, 1977-78; exec. devel. tng. rep. Abraham & Straus div. Federated Dept. Stores, 1978—. Brandeis U. scholar, 1967-68. Mem. Am. Personnel and Guidance Assn., Am. Coll. Personnel Assn., Am. Assn. Higher Edn., Nat. Orientation Dirs. Assn., Nat. Assn. Student Personnel Adminstrs., Omicron Delta Kappa, Brandeis U. Alumni Assn., Brandeis Nat. Women's Com., UN Internat. Sch. Former Students Assn., Louis D. Brandeis Club. Democrat. Jewish. Home: 7 Amy Dr East Windsor NJ 08520

FISHMAN, JACOB ROBERT, psychiatrist, educator; b. N.Y.C., Aug. 6, 1930; s. Samuel and Fannie (Goldin) F.; A.B., Columbia U., 1952; M.D., Boston U., 1956; m. Tamar Hendel, June 1, 1958; children—Marc Judah, Risa Esther, Zalman Schneur, Rebecca Anne. Intern, medicine Einstein Coll. Medicine, Bronx, N.Y., 1956-57, resident psychiatry, 1957-59; research psychiatrist Nat. Inst. Mental Health, Washington, 1959-62; prof. psychiatry Howard U. Coll. Medicine, Washington, 1962-71; dir. Howard-D.C. Comprehensive Mental Health Center, 1966-68; chmn. bd., pres. Univ. Research Corp., Washington, 1968-78, Am. Health Services, Inc., 1971-78; pres. Center for Human Services, 1968-74, Human Service Group, 1971-78, Human Devel. Group, 1978—; chmn. psychiatry So. Md. Hosp. Center, 1978—; cons. various govtl. agys. including U.S. Dept. Labor, numerous pvt. corps. Bd. dirs. Webster Coll., Washington, 1971-75, Center for Human Services, 1967-75, DePaul Hosp., New Orleans, 1973-78, St. Elizabeth's Hosp., Richmond, Va., 1971-78, Cin. Mental Health Inst., 1971-78, Nat. Capital Day Care Assn., 1966-68; mem. D.C. Pub. Health Adv. Council, 1966-68; attending psychiatrist Freedman's Hosp., Washington Vets. Hosp., D.C. Gen. Hosp., 1962-68. Served with USPHS, 1959-61. Fellow Am. Pub. Health Assn.; mem. Am. Psychiat. Assn., D.C. Psychiat. Soc., Potomac Psychiat. Assn. (pres. 1978—), AAAS, D.C. Pub. Health Assn. Author numerous profl. articles and books. Bd. editors Nat. Jour. Research on Crime and Delinquency, 1965-71. Home: 1717 Poplar Ln NW Washington DC 20012 Office: 200 Little Falls St Falls Church VA 22046

FISHMAN, STANLEY IRVING, physician; b. Cin., Sept. 29, 1922; s. Henry and Eva (Rafalo) F.; B.S., U. Cin., 1944, M.D., 1946; m. Elizabeth Mary Flynn, Mar. 1, 1947; children—William Lee, Ellen Beth. Intern Michael Reese Hosp., Chgo., 1946-47; resident Kings County Hosp., Bklyn., 1949-52; practice medicine, specializing in internal medicine, Bklyn., 1952—; mem. staff Jewish, Kings County, St. Johns Episcopal and Univ. hosps., Brookdale Med. Center, Kingsbrooke Jewish Med. Center; clin. instr. medicine State U. N.Y., Downstate Med. Center, 1956—; physician-in-charge Chest Clinic, Williamsburg-Greenpoint Dept. of Health Center, 1965-67; pres. med. staff Bklyn. Womens Hosp., 1966-67, dir. dept. medicine, 1962—; v.p. med. staff Unity Hosp., 1968-69, pres. med. staff, 1970-71; chief pulmonary function unit Jewish Hosp. and Med. Center, Bklyn., 1960-72, cons., 1973—; chief pulmonary diseases St. Johns Episcopal Hosp., 1970—. Chmn. com. on environmental health and pollution, coordinating council County Med. Socs. N.Y.C.; chmn. council hosp. med. staffs Med. Soc. County of Kings, 1973—; chmn. com. environ. quality Med. Soc. State N.Y., 1973-77; bd. dirs. Kings County Found. Med. Care, 1974—, Kings County Health Care Review Orgn., 1975— N.Y. Blood Center, 1975-77; bd. dirs., mem. exec. com. N.Y. State Study Uniform Hosp. Data System, 1975—; chmn. bd. dirs. Kings County Health Care Rev. Orgn., 1976—. Served to capt. M.C., U.S. Army, 1947-49. Recipient Laurance D. Redway award, medal for med. writing, 1967. Fellow A.C.P., Am. Coll. Chest Physicians, Am. Geriatrics Soc.; mem. AMA, Am. Thoracic Soc., Am. Heart Assn., Pan-Am. Med. Assn., Am. Soc. Internal Medicine, Kings County Med. Soc. (chmn. com. on environ. health and pollution 1970-73), Phi Delta Epsilon. Research drug therapy of heart failure and lung desease and cosmetic aerosols. Home: 236 Harbor Ln E Massapequa Park NY 11762 Office: 20 8th Ave Brooklyn NY 11217

FISKE, FREDERICK, social services adminstr.; b. N.Y.C., Aug. 1, 1930; s. Frederick and Elsa (Lundquist) F.; B.A., U. Pitts., 1970, M.S.W., 1972; m. Virginia Bridges Lowe, Aug. 26, 1961. Asst. dir. social services Western Restoration Center, Pa. Dept. Public Welfare, Pitts., 1973—; mem. U. Pitts. Task Force for W. Pa. Gerontology Center; pres. Mental Health/Mental Retardation Citizens Council, 1975—; mem. Southwestern Pa. Regional Planning Commn. Com. for Transportation for the Elderly and Handicapped; resource mem. Gov.'s Council on Aging for W. Pa. Mem. Nat. Assn. Social Workers (dir. Pa. chpt., chmn. com. for nontraditional careers in social work), Pa. Soc. Clin. Social Workers, Am. Public Health Assn., Pa. Public Health Assn., W. Pa. Public Health Conf., Am. Public Welfare Assn., Pa. Assn. Older Persons. Episcopalian. Home: 909 N Euclid Ave Pittsburgh PA 15206 Office: 2851 Bedford Ave Pittsburgh PA 15219

FITCH, NANCY ELIZABETH, social scientist; b. White Plains, N.Y., June 17, 1947; d. Robert Franklin and Nancy Elizabeth (Harvey) F.; A.B., Oakland U., 1969; A.M. U. Mich., 1971, postgrad., 1971—; postgrad. U. Rochester, 1970. Asst. prof. history and lit. Sangamon State U., 1972-74; analyst congl. research service Library of Congress, 1975—; Danforth Found. teaching intern, U. Mich., 1970. John Hay Whitney Found. opportunity fellow, 1969-70; NDEA fgn. lang. fellow in Hindu-Urdu, 1970; U. Mich. fellow, 1970-71; Ford Found. advanced-study fellow, 1971-72. Mem. Am. Hist. Assn., Assn. Asian Studies, Modern Lang. Assn., Urban League Westchester County (N.Y.), Afro-Am. Found. Westchester (N.Y.), Collegiate Sororsis (hon.). Republican. Episcopalian. Contbr. book revs. to Jour. South Asian Lit., Lit. East and West; editorial asso. Jour. South Asian Lit., 1968—. Home: 267 Bedford Ave Mount Vernon NY 10553 Office: Library of Congress 2d and Independence Ave Washington DC 20540

FITTER, MORRIS, instrumentation engr.; b. Cuba, Mar. 4, 1934; s. Herzel and Pearl F.; came to U.S., 1961, naturalized, 1966; E.E.(sr.), U. Havana, Cuba, 1955; m. Ana Reznik, Mar. 19, 1961; children—Beatrice, Jeffrey Allen, Bryan Kenneth. Instrument engr. Registered profl. engr., Calif. Mem. IEEE, Instrument Soc. Am. Jewish. Home: 214 Elmwood Ave Glen Rock NJ 07452 Office: Ebasco Services 2 Rector St New York NY 10006

FITTI, JOSEPH EDWARD, govt. ofcl.; b. Bryn Mawr, Pa., Mar. 30, 1928; s. Nicholas S. and Mary Louise (Vassallo) F.; B.A. cum laude, Harvard Coll., 1951; M.S. in Public Health, Yale U., 1952. Health educator Middlesex Health Assn., Somerville, Mass., 1952-59; field interviewer Inst. for Motivational Research, Croton-on-Hudson, N.Y., 1959-65; research asso. Harvard Sch. Public Health, Boston, 1960-61; sr. project dir. Chilton Research Services, Radnor, Pa., 1965-78; survey statistician USPHS, HEW, Hyattsville, Md., 1978—. Served with U.S. Army, 1946-48. Nat. TbAssn. grad. fellow, 1952. Mem. Am. Public Health Assn., AAAS, Washington Ops. Research Council. Home: 1606D Beekman Pl NW Washington DC 20009 Office: 3700 East West Hwy Hyattsville MD 20782

FITTS, LEONARD DONALD, ednl. adminstr., psychologist; b. Montgomery, Ala., Aug. 19, 1940; s. William Leonard and Mary Alice (Brown) F.; B.S., Tuskegee Inst., 1961, Ed.M., 1964; postgrad. Boston U., 1965-66, U. Wis., 1966-67; Ed.D., (Watson Kinter scholar), U. Pa., 1972; m. Sherrell Adrienne Thomas, June 4, 1966. Sch. psychometrist Boston U., 1965-66, NDEA fellow, 1965; guidance counselor U. Wis., Madison, 1966-67; chief of guidance counselors RCA, Sparta, Wis., 1968-69; psychologist Fla. Parent Edn. Follow Through, Phila., Bd. of Edn., Phila., 1971-75; dir. spl. services Camden (N.J.) Bd. of Edn., 1975—; vocat. sch. counselor Camden County Vocat. and Tech. Sch., Pennsauken, N.J., 1968-73; psychol. cons. Rutgers U., Camden, 1969, Narcotic Addict Rehab. Center Orgn., Inc., Atlantic City, N.J., 1971-74, Day Care 100, Glassboro (N.J.) State Coll., 1972, Phila. Bd. of Edn., 1973, Urban League Child Care Project, Phila., 1973—; ednl. cons. N.J. Edn. Consortium, Inc., Princeton, 1969-71; group leader human relations. Phila. Bd. of Edn., 1973; parent edn. cons. region III, HEW, Phila., 1974—, Del. Head Start Program, 1974—, Md. Head Start Porgram, 1974—; cons. to Community Orgn. for Mental Health and Retardation, Inc., Phila., 1976—; adj. asst. prof. psychology Rutgers U., Camden, 1971—; mem. adj. faculty Antioch Coll., Phila., 1974—, Columbia Coll., Columbia, Mo., 1975—, Trenton (N.J.) State Coll., 1973, Glassboro (N.J.) State Coll., 1976—; mem. adv. council Learning Resources Center, Pitman, N.J., 1975—. Adv. chmn. Al-Assist Recovery and Counseling Program, Southeast Neighborhood Health Center, Phila., 1971—; bd. dirs. Lincoln Day Nursery, Phila., 1972—. Served to 2d lt. USAF, 1961-63. Recipient Delta Air Line Service award, 1970, Outstanding Citizen award HEW, 1976. Mem. Nat. Assn. of Sch. Psychologists (award 1973), Am. Psychol. Assn., Am. Personnel and Guidance Assn., Camden County Personnel and Guidance Assn., Council for Exceptional

Children, Assn. of Spl. Edn. Adminstrs., N.J. Assn. of Pupil Personnel Adminstrs., Phi Delta Kappa. Baptist. Clubs: Lion. Home: 1105 Hudson Ave Voorhees NJ 08043 Office: Division of Special Services 7th and Cooper St Camden NJ 08107

FITTS, STANTON T., constrn. equipment distbg. co. exec.; b. Brookline, Mass., Apr. 9, 1939; s. Harvey A. and Frances O. (Ockerman) F.; B.S., U. N.H., 1961. Mechanic, Clark Wilcox Co., Boston, 1956-60, parts man, 1960-61, salesman, 1964-71, owner, 1972—; pres. Staf Corp., Manchester, N.H., 1965—; treas. Clark-Craft Marine, Inc., Quincy, Mass., 1970—. Served with AUS, 1961-64. Mem. Asso. Equipment Distbrs. (dir. region 1 1972—), NEEDA (dir. 1972—, pres. 1976—), Am. Power Boat Assn. (regional treas. 1967-73, region chmn. 1973-78, sr. v.p. 1978—, exec. com. 1977—). Club: Lake Sunapee Yacht (Sunapee, N.H.). Home: 200 Maynard Rd Framingham MA 01701 Office: 118 Western Ave Boston MA 02134

FITZ, CAROLINE MOUL, librarian; b. Hanover, Pa.; d. Earl Samuel and Virginia Washington (Lewis) Fitz; A.B., Wilson Coll., 1941; B.S. in Library Scis., Drexel Inst. Tech., 1942. Asst. cataloger library Drexel Inst. Tech. Phila., 1942-43; asst. librarian Chardon (Ohio) Pub. Library, 1943-44; head librarian Louisville (Ohio) Pub. Library. 1944-45; Amityville (N.Y.) Free Library, 1945-49, Norfolk (Va.) Naval Base, 1949-50; library dir. Valley Stream (N.Y.) Pub. Library, 1950-67, Amityville (N.Y.) Pub. Library, 1967—. Trustee Valley Stream Pub. Library, 1974-75. Mem. Am., N.Y., Nassau County (sec. 1954-56) library assns., D.A.R., Club: Zonta (pres. L.I. 1965-67, dist. treas. 1974-78, lt. gov. 1978—). Contbr. articles to profl. jours. Home: 294 S Brixton Rd Garden City NY 11530

FITZGERALD, CLAUDINE PAYER, dietitian; b. Westphalia, Kans., July 24, 1922; d. Victor Hugo and Helen (Strang) Payer; B.S., Kans. State U., 1946; postgrad. Okla. A. & M. U., 1946-47; m. Maurice Frances Fitzgerald, Apr. 22, 1950; children—Maurice Wayne, Dean Scott, Patrick Michael. Dietitian, Okla. A. & M. U., 1947-48, Northeastern State Coll., 1948-49, U. N.H., 1949-50; food prodn. mgr. Rosewood State Hosp., Owings Mills, Md., 1951-62; food service mgr. Towson State Coll., 1962-65; food adminstr. Mt. Wilson (Md.) Center, 1965—. Registered dietitian, Md. Mem. Am., Md. dietetic assns. Methodist. Home: 319 Upland Rd Baltimore MD 21208 Office: Mt Wilson Center Mt Wilson MD 21112

FITZGERALD, CLIFFORD LLEWELYN, advt. exec.; b. St. Louis, Oct. 10, 1903; grad. The Principia, St. Louis, 1923; student Dartmouth Coll., 1923-24; m. Isabel Hanway, Dec. 31, 1924; children—Shirley Hanway Gately, Joan Hughes Gardner, Clifford Llewelyn. Advt. writer, 1924; founder Dancer-Fitzgerald-Sample, Inc., chmn., 1961—. Dir. Advt. Council Inc. N.Y. Pres. Fitzgerald Found. Mem. U.S. Sr. Golf Assn., Alpha Delta Phi. Clubs: Blind Brook (Portchester, N.Y.); Round Hill (Greenwich); Clove Valley Rod and Gun (Lagrangeville, N.Y.); Anglers (N.Y.C.); Dragon (Dartmouth). Home: Field Point Circle Greenwich CT 06830 Office: 347 Madison Ave New York City NY 10017

FITZGERALD, JAY, lawyer; b. Washington, Sept. 6, 1923; s. James V. and Alice (Tarrant) FitzG.; B.S., Georgetown U. Sch. Fgn. Service, 1948, J.D., 1954; postgrad. N. Y. U., 1948-49, Fordham Law Sch., 1949-51; m. Mary Ellen Igoe, July 17, 1948; children—David W., Cynthia E., Brian C., James Andrew, Gerald Claibourne, Melanie, Matthew, Mary Ellen. Economist, fgn. fin. analyst Standard Oil Co. (N.J.), 1948-51; industry specialist Petroleum Adminstrn. for Def., 1951-53; spl. advisor to comdg. gen. Hdqrs. Command, USAF, 1953-57; admitted to Md. bar, 1954; partner law firm Haynes FitzGerald Wanner Haislip MacHale & Yewell, and predecessors, 1957-67, FitzGerald Rideway Wilson & Stein, 1967—; chmn. bd. Community Savs. and Loan Assn.; gen. counsel, dir. Peoples Nat. Bank Md. Mem. bd. Bldg. Savs. and Loan Commn., State of Md. Active ARC, United Givers Fund; bd. mgmt. Bethesda YMCA; mem. Nat. Cherry Blossom Festival com., 1954-56; pres. Montgomery County Young Democrats, 1947-48, vice chmn. N.Y. State, 1949-50; vice chmn. Young Dem. Clubs Am., 1951; mem. Montgomery County Real Estate Bd.; bd. mgmt. Nat. Capital Area USO. Served as ensign U.S. Maritime Service, 1943-46. Recipient Md. Jaycee Distinguished Service award as Md.'s Outstanding Young Man of 1954, Certificate of Distinction for outstanding contbns. to community and state D.C. dept. Am. Legion, 1954. Mem. Am. Soc. Internat. Law, Am., Md., D.C. bar assns., Georgetown Alumni Assn., Bethesda-Chevy Chase C. of C., U.S. (dir. 1956-58), Md. (pres. 1957-58), Bethesda (pres. 1952-54) jr. chambers commerce, Pi Kappa Alpha, Gamma Eta Gamma. Clubs: N.Y. Athletic, Toastmasters Internat., Kenwood Golf and Country. Home: Beall Mountain Potomac MD 20854 Office: One Central Plaza 11300 Rockville Pike Rockville MD 20852

FITZGERALD, JOHN EDWARD, cons. safety engr.; b. New Haven, Sept. 20, 1928; s. William Joseph and Ruth (Geer) F.; B.S. in Civil Engring., U. Conn., 1952; m. Marian Elaine Ek, May 1, 1954; children—John, Richard, Michael, Patricia, James. Sr. safety engr. Liberty Mut. Ins. Co., N.Y.C., Newark and New Haven, 1952-62; engr. Town of Southington (Conn.), 1962-64; cons. safety engr., Cheshire, Conn., 1964—; tech. adviser U.S. Product Safety Commn., 1974-75. Bd. dirs. Cheshire YMCA, 1972-74. Served with AUS, 1946-48. Registered profl. engr., land surveyor, Conn. Mem. Conn. Soc. Profl. Engrs. (pres. nat. dir.). Clubs: 2d company Gov.'s Foot Guard (New Haven); Toastmasters (v.p., area gov. 1962-66). Home and office: 399 Beacon Hill Dr Cheshire CT 06410

FITZGERALD, ROBERT JAMES, physician; b. N.Y.C., July 19, 1934; s. John Jourdan and Frances Elizabeth (Corcoran) F.; A.B., Fordham Coll., 1956; M.D., N.Y. Med. Coll., 1960; m. Susanna Bennett, May 31, 1958; children—John F. and Susanna. Intern, U.S. Naval Hosp., Bethesda, Md., 1960-61; resident N.Y. Lying-in Hosp., N.Y.C., 1964-67; chief resident in obstetrics and gynecology Ellis Hosp., Schenectady, 1967-68; practice medicine specializing in obstetrics and gynecology, Port Washington, N.Y., 1968—; mem. staff North Shore Hosp., Manhasset, N.Y., St. Francis Hosp., Roslyn, N.Y.; cons. physician L.I. Birth Right, 1971—. Served with USN, 1959-64. Diplomate Am. Bd. Obstetrics and Gynecology. Mem. Nassau County Med. Soc., Am. Soc. Psychoprophylaxis in Obstetrics (chmn. L.I. physicians div.), Med. Soc. State N.Y., Am. Coll. Obstetricians and Gynecologists, A.C.S., Am. Fertility Soc. Democrat. Roman Catholic. Club: Port Washington Yacht. Home: 6 Davis Rd Port Washington NY 11576 Office: 105 Port Washington Blvd Port Washington NY 11576

FITZGERALD, TERENCE SEAN, allergist; b. St. Albans, Vt., May 18, 1941; s. Robert George and Jane (Boudreau) F.; B.A., U. Vt., 1963, M.D., 1968; m. Jacqueline Diane Hussey, June 26, 1965; children—Timothy Sean, Carrie Lee, Shannon Dee. Pediatric intern Med. Coll. Va., Richmond, 1968-69, resident in pediatrics, 1969-71, fellow in allergy and immunology, 1970-72; practice medicine specializing in clin. allergy, Stamford, Conn., 1974—; mem. staff Greenwich (Conn.) Hosp., 1975—, Norwalk (Conn.) Hosp., 1975—, St. Joseph's Hosp., Stamford, 1975—; attending physician allergy clinic Stamford Hosp., 1975—; clin. instr. medicine N.Y. Med. Coll., N.Y.C., 1976—. Served with M.C., U.S. Army, 1972-74. Diplomate Am. Bd. Pediatrics, Am. Bd. Allergy and Immunology. Fellow Am. Acad. Pediatrics, Am. Coll. Allergists; mem. Am. Acad. Allergy, Southeastern Allergy Assn., N.Y., New Eng. allergy socs., Fairfield County Med. Assn., Conn., Greenwich, Stamford med. socs. Republican. Roman Catholic. Contbr. articles to med. jours. Home: 26 Pasture Ln Darien CT 06820 Office: 500 Newfield Ave Stamford CT 06905

FITZGIBBONS, GLORIA HELEN, state ofcl.; b. N.Y.C., June 17, 1922; d. Harry and Rae (Kronenthal) Glassman; B.A., U. Pitts., 1964, M. Pub. Adminstrn., 1967; D.P.A., Nova U., 1978; m. David Fitzgibbons, Dec. 23, 1971; children by previous marriage—Glenn, Susan, Robert. Commr., Princeton (N.J.) Housing Authority, 1958-60, dir., 1960-63; grad. asst. U. Pitts. Grad. Sch. Pub. and Internat. Affairs, 1965; dir. rehab. dept. Allegheny County (Pa.) Redevel. Authority, 1966-68; housing analyst Pa. Dept. Community Affairs, Pitts., 1968-70, regional dir., 1970—. Mem. Am. Soc. Pub. Adminstrn. (exec. bd. Pitts., pres. Pitts.), U. Pitts. Grad. Sch. Pub. and Internat. Affairs Alumni Soc. (pres.). Unitarian. Home: 6645 Landview Rd Pittsburgh PA 15217 Office: 300 Liberty Ave Pittsburgh PA 15222

FITZPATRICK, DONALD WILLIAM, mgmt. cons.; b. Newark, Feb. 21, 1945; s. Donald Edward and Norma (Backstrom) F.; B.S. in E.E., Carnegie Mellon U., 1967; Ph.D., Johns Hopkins U., 1977; children—Michelle Marie, Michael Charles. Analyst, Rockwell Internat., Pitts., 1965-69; engr. Westinghouse Elec. Corp., Arlington, Va., 1969-70; program dir. Orkand Corp., Silver Spring, Md., 1973-75; cons. Touche Ross & Co., N.Y.C., 1975-76; dir. information systems Arthur Young & Co., Washington, 1975—; cons. SEC, EPA, Dept. Def. NSF fellow, 1967-68; NDEA fellow, 1970-73. Mem. Assn. Computing Machinery, Assn. Systems Mgmt., Ops. Research Soc. Am., Tau Beta Pi, Eta Kappa Nu, Phi Kappa Theta. Home: 1800 Old Meadow Rd McLean VA 22101 Office: 1025 Connecticut Ave NW Washington DC 20036

FITZPATRICK, JAMES EARL, JR., chemist, govt. ofcl.; b. Phila., Feb. 16, 1938; s. James Earl and Phoebe Myletta (Norris) F., Sr.; B.S., Va. State Coll. 1960; M.S., George Washington U. 1973; m. Helen Fields, June 23, 1962; 1 son, Kevin E. Chemist Edgewood Arsenal, Md., 1966-68; phys. sci. adminstr. Def. Documentation Center, Alexandria, Va., 1968-70; supervisory research chemist Bur. Engraving and Printing, Washington, 1970-75, asst. chief Office Indsl. Services, 1975—. Chmn. bd. dirs. Harper's Choice (Md.) Community Assn. 1975-76; mem. Harper's Choice Middle Sch. PTA, 1978—; charter mem. St. John the Baptist Ch., Columbia, Md., 1971—; active mem. Howard County (Md.) chpt. NAACP, 1975-77, Howard County Alliance Toward Active Community, 1977—; chmn. Columbia Assn. Softball Bd., 1974; coach Columbia Youth Baseball Assn., 1974-78, Basketball Assn., 1976-78. Served as 1st lt. Chem. Corps, U.S. Army, 1960-62. Recipient Spl. Achievement award Bur. Engraving and Printing, 1974; Afro-Am. Achievement award St. John the Baptist Ch., 1974. Mem. Va. State Coll. Alumni Assn., George Washington U. Alumni Assn., Alpha Phi Alpha. Democrat. Baptist. Presenter research papers to profl. orgns.; condr. profl. workshop in field. Home: 5135 Celestial Way Columbia MD 21044 Office: 14th and C Sts NW Washington DC 20228

FITZPATRICK, JUNE BOUTIN, nurse; b. Laconia, N.H., June 3, 1931; d. Joseph Louis and Annie Evelyn (Laflam) Boutin; diploma Mass. Gen. Hosp. Sch. Nursing, 1953; B.S. cum laude in Nursing, St. Anselm's Coll., 1967; M.S., Boston U., 1970; 1 son, Robert Joseph. Office and pvt. scrub nurse, Laconia, 1953-64; med. and surg. supr. Lakes Region Gen. Hosp., Laconia, 1966-67, dir. dept. nursing, 1967—. Bd. dirs. Lakes Regional Mental Health Center, Laconia, 1967-76, sec., 1970-72; bd. dirs. Laconia chpt. ARC, 1970—; mem. adv. council for continuing edn. St. Anselm's Coll., Manchester, 1976—; mem. area 2 Health Systems Agy., 1977—; mem. membership com. United Health Systems Agy., Concord, N.H., 1977—; mem. adv. council N.H. Tech. Inst. Sch. Nursing, Concord, 1977—. Mem. Am., N.H. (pres. dist. 3 1977-78) hosp. assns., Am. Soc. Hosp. Nursing Service Adminstrs. Democrat. Roman Catholic. Home: Concord St Belmont NH 03246 Office: Highland St Laconia NH 03246

FITZPATRICK, MARGARET MARY, pub. relations exec.; b. Indpls., Apr. 29, 1927; d. John Joseph and Mary Jordon (Boyhan) Clifford; student Wheelock Coll., 1945-47, Boston U., 1975, 77; children—Anne, Bernard, John, Dennis, Paula, Michael. Reporter, Suburban Press, Natick, Mass., 1958-66; reporter, asst. bur. chief South Middlesex News, Framingham, Mass., 1966-69; reporter Boston Globe, 1969-70; pub. relations asst. Leonard Morse Hosp., Natick, 1970—. Mem. Pub. Relations Soc. Am. (accredited), (sec. New Eng. chpt.). Club: Boston Press. Home: 75 Park Ave Natick MA 01760 Office: 67 Union St Natick MA 01760

FITZPATRICK, MICHAEL JOHN, clergyman, ednl. adminstr.; b. Jersey City, May 9, 1927; s. Michael John and Mary Rita (Ahearn) F.; A.B., Seton Hall U., 1948, M.A., 1970; S.T.L., Catholic U. Am., 1952; postgrad. Fordham U., 1955-57. Ordained priest Roman Cath. Ch., 1952; asso. pastor St. Mary's Ch., Rutherford, N.J., 1952-53; adminstr. St. Joseph's High Sch., West New York, N.J., 1953-68; headmaster Oratory Prep. Sch., Summit, N.J., 1968-74, 75—; asst. supt. schs. Roman Cath. Archdiocese of Newark, 1974-78, supt. schs., 1978—. Bd. dirs. North Hudson Community Action League, 1964-66. Mem. N.J. Ednl. Assn., Nat. Assn. Secondary Sch. Prins., NEA, Union County Assn. Priests, Guidance Council Archdiocese of Newark, Serra Internat. (chaplain). Club: K.C. (chaplain 1955-68). Author: History of St. Joseph's Parish, West New York, N.J., 1954. Home: 14 Bedford Rd Summit NJ 07901 Office: 300 Broadway Newark NJ 07104

FITZPATRICK, ROBERT CHARLES, univ. adminstr.; b. Port Huron, Mich., Jan. 18, 1926; s. Charles Francis and Callie (Lenk) F.; student Western Mich. Coll., 1944, U. Notre Dame, 1944-46; B.S., U. Mich., 1948, M.S., 1950; m. Norma M. Carosso, Dec. 1, 1956; children—Robert, Brian. Packaging-material handling engr. Kaiser Fraser Corp., 1950-51; tech. officer Office Naval Research, 1951-53; geophysicist, head geodesy sect. Air Force Cambridge Research Center, 1953-56; research asso. Seismics and Acoustics Lab., U. Mich., 1956-59; research adminstr., asso. dir. research adminstrn. U. Mich., 1959-70; mgr. marketing research Datamax Corp., 1970; asst. v.p. research State U. N.Y., Buffalo, 1970-72, acting v.p. research, 1972—. Tech. adv. bd. Greater Buffalo Devel. Found., 1972-74; adviser Buffalo Mus. Sci., 1973—. Served with USNR, 1944-46, 51-53. Mem. Am. Geophys. Union, Niagara Frontier Assn. Research and Devel. Dirs., Soc. Exploration Geophycists, Geol. Soc. Am., Internat. Assn. Great Lakes Research, Nat. Council Univ. Research Adminstrs., Sigma Gamma Epsilon. Home: 99 Parkledge Dr Snyder NY 14226 Office: 3435 Main St Buffalo NY 14214

FITZROY, NANCY DELOYE (MRS. ROLAND VICTOR FITZROY, JR.), chem. engr.; b. Pittsfield, Mass., Oct. 5, 1927; d. Jules Emile and Mabel Winifred (Burr) DeLoye; B.Chem. Engring., Rensselaer Poly. Inst., 1949; m. Roland Victor Fitzroy, Jr., Mar. 24, 1951. With Gen. Electric Co., 1950—; asst. engr. Knolls Atomic Power Lab., Schenectady, 1950-52, devel. engr. Gen. Engring. Lab., 1953-63, thermal engr. Advanced Tech. Labs., 1963-65, heat transfer engr., 1965-71, mgr. heat transfer cons. Corporate Research and Devel., 1971-74, strategy planner, 1974-76, advanced product planner Gas Turbine div., 1976-77, advanced product planner and proposal mgr. Gas Turbine div., 1977—; mem. NSF adv. com. engring., 1972-73, adv. com. research, 1973-75. Mem. archtl. com. West Hill Devel., Schenectady, 1972-75; mem. Rensselaer Council, Rensselaer Poly. Inst., Troy, N.Y., 1972—, mem. trustees com. on honors, 1973—. Recipient Demers medal Rensselaer Poly. Inst., 1975. Registered profl. engr., N.Y. Fellow ASME (chmn. sect. 1963-64, regional activities del. 1962-65, mem. goals conf. 1970, working party equal opportunities 1971, policy bd., edn. 1974—); mem. Am. Inst. Chem. Engrs. (hon., life), Soc. Women Engrs. (nat. exec. com. 1977—, Achievement award 1972), Nat., N.Y. State socs. profl. engrs., Nat. Acad. Engring. (bd. on engring. manpower and ednl. policy 1974-76), Whirly Girls, Ninety-Nines Internat. Club: Northern Lake George Yacht. Author: My Career as a Heat Transfer Engineer, 1972; editor procs. Conf. Career Guidance for Women Entering Engineering, 1973. Home: 2125 Rosendale Rd Schenectady NY 12309 Office: Gen Electric Co Gas Turbine Div Bldg 500 Room 224 Schenectady NY 12345

FITZSIMMONS, FRANK EDWARD, labor union ofcl.; b. Apr. 7, 1908; LL.D. in Public Service (hon.), St. Joseph's Coll., Rensselaer, Ind., 1972; m. Mary Patricia Fitzsimmons; 4 children. Dockworker, Detroit; then truck driver; bus. agt. Teamster Local 299, Detroit, 1937-40, v.p., 1940-61, sec.-treas. Mich. Conf. Teamsters; later co-founder Central States Drivers' Council; gen. exec. bd. Internat. Brotherhood Teamsters, 1961—, v.p., 1961-67, gen. v.p., 1967-71, gen. pres., 1971—, chmn. negotiating com., 1971—. Mem. or former mem. Nat. Commn. on Productivity, Pres.'s Com. on Employment of Handicapped, Labor Dept. Interdepartmental Workers' Compensation Task Force, White House Conf. on Capital Investment and Employment in Am. Economy, Nat. Petroleum Council, Adv. Com. for Trade Negotiations under Trade Act of 1974, Com. of 100 for Nat. Health Ins., Pres.'s Labor-Mgmt. Adv. Com. to Cost of Living Council; former mem. Labor Mgmt. Collective Bargaining Com. in Constrn.; labor mem. Pay Bd. Active fund raising Frank E. Fitzsimmons Med. Research Complex, Little City Found., Palatine, Ill.; mem. nat. vol. service council ACTION; v.p. Muscular Dystrophy Assn. Am.; sponsoring mem. Citizens for Treatment of High Blood Pressure. Recipient Nat. Spirit of Love award, Four Freedoms award, 1972, Silver Anniversary medal State of Israel, 1973. Office: Internat Brotherhood Teamsters Chauffeurs Warehousemen & Helpers of Am 25 Louisiana Ave NW Washington DC 20001

FITZSIMONS, RUTH MARIE, educator; b. Pawtucket, R.I.; d. Leo A. and Helena (Hollis) Fitzsimons; B.Ed., R.I. Coll., 1940; M.Ed., Boston U., 1949, D.Ed., 1955; postgrad Brandeis U., summer 1958, N.Y.U., 1956. Tchr., prin. Warwick (R.I.) Sch. Dept., 1940-49, speech and hearing therapy coordinator, 1949-68; prof. speech and lang. pathology U. R.I., Kingston, 1969—. Lectr., Boston U., 1956, 58, 59, U. Maine, summer 1966; cons. speech and hearing therapy R.I. Dept. Edn., Providence, 1968-69, cons. Meeting St. Sch. Childrens Rehab. Center, Providence, 1969; cons. editor T.J. Denison & Co., Mpls., 1966—. Mem. R.I. (pres. 1964-65), Am. (legislative councillor 1969-71) speech and hearing assns., Am. Psychol. Assn., Am. Acad. Psychotherapists, Soc. for Research in Child Devel. Author: Stuttering and Personality Dynamics, 1960; Christopher Listens, 1966; Make Believe with Mike, 1968. Contbr. articles to profl. jours. Home: 38 Mystic Dr Warwick RI 02886 Office: Dept Speech U of Rhode Island Kingston RI 02881*

FITZSIMONS, VIRGINIA LOUISE BALDWIN, civic worker; b Lynchburg, Va.; d. Bernard Coleman and Mary (Bell) Baldwin; A.B., Randolph-Macon Woman's Coll., 1929; m. William Griffin Morrel, Oct. 8, 1932 (dec. Mar. 1975); children—William Griffin, Bernard Baldwin; m. 2d, Richard Leiter FitzSimons, Aug. 17, 1977. Asst. alumnae sec. Randolph-Macon Woman's Coll., 1931-32, v.p. nat. alumnae assn., 1944-46, pres., 1953-57, 1st chmn. alumnae fund, 1958-60, alumnae adviser to bd. trustees, 1960-65; chmn. Day Nursery Bd., Lynchburg, Va., 1939, vice chmn., Norfolk, Va., 1944-45; mem. bd. Retreat for Sick Hosp., 1936-38, William Byrd Community House, Richmond, Va., 1945-46; founding mem. Women's Com. for Hampton, Balt., 1950; mem. women's bd. Johns Hopkins Hosp., 1957—, chmn. hosp. aux., 1958-62; mem. nominating com. Md. Assn. Hosp. Auxiliaries, 1967-68; bd. dirs. Valleys Planning Council, 1968-71; exec. bd. 2d Presbyterian Ch., Balt., 1968—, bd. deacons, 1976—, pres. Women's Assn., 1970-72. Mem. Zeta Tau Alpha. Republican. Clubs: Mt. Vernon, Green Spring Valley Hunt (Balt.), Cliff Dwellers Garden (Balt.). Address: 6111 Bellinham Ct Baltimore MD 21210

FJORDBOTTEN, ALF LEE, physician; b. Granum, Alta., Can., June 13, 1920; s. Anton C. and Laura (Vik) F.; M.D., U. Alta., 1944; m. Helene J. Hansen, June 26, 1943; children—Allan Harold, Joy Fjordbotten Thompson, Alf Lee. Intern, U. Alta. Hosp., 1944-45; pvt. practice gen. medicine Smith Clinic, Camrose, Alta., 1946-60; resident ophthalmology Washington Hosp. Center, Washington, 1960-63; Bunker fellow Internat. Eye Found. Care-Medico, St. John's Ophthalmic Hosp., Jerusalem, 1963-64; pvt. practice ophthalmology, Arlington, Va., 1965—; staff Arlington Hosp., No. Va. Drs. Hosp. (both Arlington); asst. clin. prof. ophthalmology George Washington U. Med. Sch., Washington, 1965—. Served with M.C., Royal Canadian Army, 1943-46. Diplomate Am. Bd. Ophthalmology. Fellow A.C.S.; mem. AMA, Va., D.C., Arlington County, So., Canadian (affiliate) med. assns., Am. Acad. Ophthalmology, Va. Soc. Opthalmology and Otolaryngology, No. Va. Acad. Surgery, Am. Profl. Practise Assn. Home: 4400 East-West Hwy Bethesda MD 20014 Office: 3801 N Fairfax Dr Arlington VA 22203

FLACK, JULIUS VINCENT, ophthalmologist; b. Syracuse, N.Y., Apr. 14, 1904; s. Joseph and Helena Flack; M.D., Syracuse U., 1931; D.Sc., Columbia U., 1936; m. Mamie Shaw, Oct. 22, 1936; children—Ellen, Vincent, Douglas, David. Intern, Syracuse Meml. Hosp., 1931-32; resident Edward S. Harkness Eye Inst., Columbia-Presbyn. Med. Center, N.Y.C., 1932-36; practice medicine specializing in ophthalmology, N.Y.C., 1946-69, New Rochelle, N.Y., 1946—; asst. prof. ophthalmology Columbia U., 1959-69; attending ophthalmologist Presbyn. Hosp., 1959-69. Served to capt. M.C., USN, 1942-46. Mem. Am. Bd. Ophthalmology, A.C.S., Am. Acad. Ophthalmology. Republican. Presbyterian. Clubs: Pelham Country, Camp Fire of Am. Contbr. chpt. to Textbook of Trauma, 1959. Home: 1064 Esplanade Pelham Manor NY 10803 Office: 650 Main St New Rochelle NY 10801

FLACK, ROBERT LLOYD, lawyer; b. Syracuse, N.Y., Oct. 2, 1926; s. John Brooks and Miriam (Davis) F.; A.B., Princeton, 1948; LL.B., Syracuse U., 1951, postgrad., 1955—; postgrad. Cornell U., 1965-66; m. Helen Jean Brown, Nov. 3, 1956; 1 dau., Meredith A. L. Admitted to N.Y. State bar, 1952; practiced in Syracuse, 1952-62, Watkins Glen, N.Y. 1962—; dist. atty. Schuyler County, 1975-77; N.Y. State estate tax atty. Schuyler County, 1975—. Mem. Zoning Bd. of Appeals, Watkins Glen, 1967-70; village justice Watkins Glen, 1967-73, village atty., 1963-67. Mem. Am., N.Y. State, Onodaga County, Schuyler County bar assns., S.A.R., Soc. Colonial Wars, Mayflower Soc., Phi Delta Phi. Presbyn. Mason (32 deg., Shriner, K.T.). Clubs: Princeton (N.Y.C.); Univ. (Syracuse); M. and M

(Montour Falls, N.Y.); Elks (treas. 1965), Rotary (v.p. 1967-68, pres. 1968-69). Home: 101 Grand View Ave Watkins Glen NY 14891 Office: 113 E 6th St Watkins Glen NY 14891 also 216 William St Elmira NY 14902

FLAHERTY, HUGH CHARLES, cons. environ. engr.; b. Waterbury, Conn., July 3, 1929; s. Michael J. and Josephine M. (Bagley) F.; B.S.C.E., Tri State Coll., Angola, Ind., 1951; m. Dorothy M. Peters, Oct. 1, 1955; children—Paula, Martha, Ann. Project mgr. Cahn Engrs., Inc., New Haven, 1966-69; owner Hugh C. Flaherty Assos., cons. engrs. and land surveyors, North Branford, Conn., 1969-70; partner Flaherty-Giavara Assos., environ. design cons., West Haven, Conn., 1970—; sec.-treas. Environ. Labs., Inc., West Haven, 1973—; pres. Flaherty Giavara Assos., engrs., planners, environ. scientists, 1977—; past mem. Conn. Bd. Registration Profl. Enrs. and Land Surveyors. Served with USAF, 1951-55. Mem. Nat. (nat. dir.), Conn. (pres.) socs. profl. engrs., Conn. Assn. Land Surveyors, Am. Pub. Works Assn., Am. Congress Surveying and Mapping, Water Pollution Control Fedn., Am. Road Builders Assn., Am. Mgmt. Assn., Conn. Assn. Municipal Devel. Commns. Roman Catholic. Home: 6 Crescent Bluff Ave Branford CT 06405 Office: One Columbus Plaza New Haven CT 06510

FLAHERTY, MICHAEL FRANCIS, mem. Mass. Ho. of Reps.; b. South Boston, Mass., Sept. 6, 1936; s. John James and Mary Eleanor (Joyce) F.; A.B., Boston Coll., 1963; LL.B., New Eng. Sch. Law, 1968; m. Margaret Joanne McGlone, Nov. 25, 1961; children—Margaret, Michael, John. Admitted to Mass. bar, 1970; individual practive law South Boston, 1970—; mem. Mass. Ho. of Reps., Boston, 1967—, chmn. com. social welfare, 1971-74, chmn. com. on judiciary, 1974—, asst. majority leader, 1970—. Past treas. South Boston Citizens Assn. Served with USNR, 1955-57. Named legislator of yr. Mass. Bar Assn. and Boston Tchrs. Union, 1976. Mem. Am., Mass., Boston bar assns., Mass. Legislators Assn. Democrat. Roman Catholic. Clubs: K.C., Am. Legion. Home: 833 E 3d St South Boston MA 02127 Office: 520 E Broadway South Boston MA 02127

FLAHERTY, PETE F., govt. ofcl.; b. Pitts., June 24, 1925; s. Pete and Anne (O'Toole) F.; LL.B., Notre Dame U., 1951; M.P.A., U. Pitts., 1967; m. Nancy Houlihan, Aug. 29, 1958; children—Shawn, Pete, Brian, Maggie, Greg. Admitted to Pa. bar; asst. dist. atty. Allegheny County, 1957-64; councilman City of Pitts., 1966-69; mayor, 1970-77; dep. atty. gen. U.S., 1977—. Served to capt. USAAF, 1942-46. Decorated Air medal. Mem. Am., Pa. bar assns. Home: 5033 Castleman St Pittsburgh PA 15232 Office: Dept Justice Constitution Ave and 10th St NW Washington DC 20530

FLAKER, JAMES HENRY, mgmt. cons. co. exec.; b. Midland Park, N.J., Nov. 21, 1915; s. George William and May (Amos) F.; student Columbia Coll., 1934-38; m. Elois Kathryn Pearson, Aug. 27, 1939; children—Philip George, Kathy May. Asst. to quality mgr., Wright Aero. Corp., Paterson, N.J., 1939-46; asst. prodn. mgr. Sipp-Eastwood Corp., Paterson, 1946-51; chief quality engring. Lycoming div. AVCO, Stratford, Conn., 1951-61; supr. quality engring. Kaman Aircraft Co., Bloomfield, Conn., 1961-63; chief quality engring. Lycoming div. AVCO, Stratford, 1963-78; pres. G & F Assos., Milford, Conn., 1978—; cons., lectr. in field. Fellow Am. Soc. Quality Control (R. Shaw Goldthwait award 1975); v.p. sect. affairs 1977—); mem. Nat. Mgmt. Assn. (distinguished recognition award 1976). Milford Yacht Club (dir. 1974—). Republican. Episcopalian. Clubs: Masons, Elks, Order Eastern Star. Home and Office: 107 Greer Circle Milford CT 06460

FLAMM, DONALD, real estate, investments, theatrical producer; b. Pitts., Dec. 11, 1899; s. Louis and Elizabeth (Jason) F.; ed. pub. schs. N.Y. Pub. mags. and books, 1921-30; owner, operator radio sta. WMCA, N.Y., 1925-41, WPCH, N.Y., 1927-32; pres. and operator Intercity Network, 1927-41; co-owner WPAT, Paterson, N.J., 1942-48; now engaged in theatre, real estate and social welfare activities; theatrical producer, N.Y.C., London, Eng.; pres. Flamm Realty Corp., N.Y.; owner, chmn. bd., pres. radio stas. WMMM (AM) WDJF (FM), Westport, Conn.; bd. dirs. Oscar Lewestein Plays, Ltd., London, Eng. Mem. N.Y. exec. com. Anti-Defamation League Am.; past chmn. N.J. Civil War Centennial Commn.; charter founder Eleanor Roosevelt Inst. for Cancer Research. Bd. dirs., v.p. Hebrew Free Loan Soc. N.Y.; past pres., trustee Mt. Neboh Temple, N.Y.C.; trustee, officer Manfred Sakel Inst. Served as spl. liaison officer OWI, World War II; formulated plans for Am. Broadcasting Sta. in Eng. Mem. Royal TV Soc. (London), Internat. Radio and TV Soc., Drama Desk, United Hunts Racing Assn., Pa. Soc. Clubs: Lambs, Rockefeller Luncheon, Catholic Actors Guild, Jewish Theatrical Guild, Friars, Alpine Country; Le Club, El Morocco (N.Y.C.); Annabel's, White Elephant (London). Home: 470 Anderson Ave Closter NJ 07624 Office: 25 Central Park W New York City NY 10023

FLANAGAN, BERNARD JOSEPH, bishop; b. Proctor, Vt., Mar. 31, 1908; s. John B. and Alice (McGarry) F.; student Holy Cross Coll., North American Coll., Rome; J.C.D., Cath. U. Am., 1943. Ordained priest Roman Cath. Ch., 1931; sec. to bishop, chancellor of diocese, Burlington, 1943-53, named 1st bishop Norwich diocese, 1953; bishop of Worcester, Mass., 1959—. Address: Bishop's House Worcester MA 01602

FLANAGAN, EDWARD CHARLES, banker; b. New Rochelle, N.Y., July 19, 1927; s. Matthew E. and Madeline (Brennan) F.; B.B.A., Iona Coll., 1950. With Barclays Bank of N.Y. (formerly 1st Westchester Nat. Bank), New Rochelle, 1950—, asst. cashier, 1956-61, asst. v.p., 1961-64, v.p., 1964—, sr. loan officer, mgr. head office, 1970-76, v.p., sr. regional loan officer, 1976-77, v.p., sec., 1977—. Treas., New Rochelle Com. March of Dimes, 1960-78. Served with USNR, 1945-46. Mem. Nat. Assn. Bank Loan Officers and Credit Officers, Iona Coll. Alumni Assn. (past dir.). Roman Catholic. Club: K.C. Home: 35 Fern St New Rochelle NY 10801 Office: 491 Main St New Rochelle NY 10802

FLANDER, STANLEY, dentist; b. Queens, N.Y., Aug. 31, 1925; s. Herbert and Mary (Solomon) F.; student Coll. City N.Y., 1941-42, N.Y. U., 1943-45; D.D.S., Temple U., 1949. Intern Guggenheim Dental Clinic, N.Y.C., 1949, Mary Immaculate Hosp., Jamaica, N.Y., 1950; pvt. practice dentistry, Jackson Heights, N.Y., 1950-63, Elmhurst, N.Y., 1963—; clin. assisting vis. dentist Queens Gen. Hosp., 1957; instr. periodontics Sydenham Hosp., N.Y.C., 1958; tng. implant surgery and prosthetics Hospital Laribiosiere, France, 1965; instr. implantology Seaview Hosp., S.I., N.Y., 1969—. Guest lectr. N.Y. U. Sch. of Continuing Dental Edn., N.Y.C., 1971—. Active Children's Dental Health Week Programs. Served with AUS, 1943-44. Fellow Royal Soc. Health; mem. Am. Acad. Implant Dentistry (sub. chmn. exhibit com. 1971), Inst. for Endosseous Implants (research com. 1965), Found. for Advancement Implants and Transplants, Am., N.Y., 11th Dist. dental assns., Am. Analgesia Soc., Fed. Dentaire Internat., Sigma Epsilon Delta. Elk, Lion. Contbr. to profl. jours. Patentee in field. Home: 77-10 34th Ave Jackson Heights NY 11372 Office: 81-31 Baxter Ave Elmhurst NY 11373

FLANDERS, FRANK CHESTER, psychiatrist; b. Washington, May 22, 1916; grad. Hesser Bus. Coll., Manchester, N.H., 1935; student U. Pitts., 1955-56, Allegheny Coll., 1956-58; M.D., Western Res. U., 1963; m. Nina Lesczewicz, Sept. 29, 1963; 1 son, Daniel F. Intern, St. Luke's Hosp., Cleve., 1963-64; resident in psychiatry Fairhill Psychiat. Hosp., Cleve., 1964-67; practice medicine specializing in psychiatry Cleve., 1967-68; psychiatrist Letchworth Village Devel. Center, Thiells, N.Y., 1968-70, clin. physician, 1970-75, dep. dir. clinic, 1975-77; dir. med. edn. and residency tng. Marlboro (N.J.) Psychiat. Hosp., 1977—. Served with C.E., AUS, 1942-46, USAR, 1946-76, now ret. Recipient Med. Edn. award AMA, 1969, 72; diplomate Am. Bd. Neurology and Psychiatry; licensed in medicine and surgery, Ohio, N.Y., Conn., N.J. Mem. Am. Psychiat. Assn., Am. Assn. Mental Deficiency, Res. Officers Assn., Nat. Rifle Assn. Am. Clubs: West Point Officers, Ft. Monmouth Officers. Home: 18 Taylor Rd Marlboro NJ 07746 Office: Marlboro Psychiat Hosp Marlboro NJ 07746

FLANNAGAN, BENJAMIN COLLINS, IV, lawyer; b. Richmond, Va., Sept. 7, 1927; s. Benjamin Collins and Virginia Carolyn (Gay) F.; B.A., U. Va., 1947, M.A. in Econs., 1948, J.D., 1951; LL.M., Georgetown U., 1956. Admitted to Va. bar, 1951; trial atty. Justice Dept., Washington, 1955—, sr. trial atty. in charge civil litigation unit, appellate and civil litigation sect., internal security div., 1971-73, internal security sect. criminal div., 1973-74, spl. litigation sect., 1974—. Served to 1st lt. U.S. Army, 1952-55. Recipient Sustained Superior Service award Justice Dept., 1964, 74, Spl. Commendation for Outstanding Service award criminal div., 1976. Mem. Va. Bar Assn., Beta Gamma Sigma. Episcopalian. Clubs: Country of Va., Deep Run Hunt (Richmond). Book rev. editor Va. Law Rev., 1950-51. Home: 4000 Massachusetts Ave NW Washington DC 20016 Office: Dept of Justice 315 9th St NW Washington DC 20530

FLANNERY, DENNIS EDWARD, investment banker; b. Harrisburgh, Pa., Oct. 7, 1946; s. John Leo and Frances Clarena (Kelly) F.; B.S. in Fgn. Service, Georgetown U., 1972. Internat. credit trainee and analyst Chase Manhattan Bank, 1972-74; asst. v.p., Euro dollar loan syndicator Bank of Am., San Francisco, 1974-77; v.p. Kuhn Loeb Lehman Bros. Internat., 1977—. Served with U.S. Army, 1967-70. Democrat. Roman Catholic. Clubs: Down Town Assn., N.Y. Yacht, Univ. (N.Y.C.); South End Rowing, St. Francis Yacht. Home: 956 Fifth Ave New York City NY 10021 Office: 1 William St New York City NY 10004

FLANNERY, JOHN BERNARD, JR., chemist; b. Providence, Mar. 15, 1941; s. John Bernard and Mary Serena (Murray) F.; student U. Richmond, 1959; B.S., St. Vincent Coll., 1962; Ph.D. (NASA fellow), Rensselaer Poly. Inst., 1965; m. Linda Ann Mishanec, July 20, 1968; children—John Barnard, Lynn Marie, Jennifer Anne. With Xerox Corp., Rochester, N.Y., 1965—, sr. scientist, 1971, prin. scientist, research mgr., 1971-74, lab. dir., 1974-78, tech. program mgr., 1978—; sec., dir. 32-34 W. Main Inst. Inc., real estate, Webster, N.Y., 1972—. Mem. Webster Narcotics Guidance Council, 1970-71; solicitor blood drives ARC, 1969-73; Republican committeeman Monroe County, N.Y., 1971-76, campaign mgr. 7th Legis. Dist., 1971; fin. chmn. Webster Town and County Rep. Com., 1973; bd. dirs. Webster Independence Day Com. Mem. Am. Chem. Soc., AAAS, N.Y. Acad. Sci., Soc. Info. Display (exec. com. 1973—, internat. program chmn. 1976-77, gen. chmn. 1978-79, Outstanding Paper award 1976), Sigma Xi, Phi Lambda Upsilon. Roman Catholic. Clubs: Elks (exalted ruler 1970-71 dist. dep. grand exalted ruler 1974-75, N.Y. state scholarship chmn. 1976—), K.C. Contbr. articles to profl. jours. Patentee in field. Home: 1258 Wildflower Dr Webster NY 14580 Office: Xerox Corp Xerox Sq Rochester NY 14644

FLANNERY, ROSEMARY MCCARRON, lawyer; b. Phila., June 11, 1921; d. Francis A. and Sara D. (Sauer) McCarron; A.B., Chestnut Hill Coll., 1943; LL.B., Villanova U., 1965; m. John F. Flannery, Jan. 21, 1950; children—Mary K., Katherine A., John F. Sports reporter Phila. Inquirer, 1944-49; instr. journalism Rosemont (Pa.) Coll., 1945-53; admitted to Pa. bar, 1965; practiced in Norristown, Pa., 1965—; partner Wisler, Pearlstine, Talone, Craig and Garrity, 1973—. Mem. exec. com. Conf. of County Bar Officers of Pa., 1971-74; bd. dirs. Legal Aid Service Montgomery County, Pa., 1973-77. Tchr. Confraternity of Christian doctrine Epiphany of Our Lord Sch. Plymouth Twp., Pa., 1970—; pres. Montgomery County Estate Planning Council, 1978-79; mem. St. Edmund's Home Aux., 1968—; Democratic committeewoman, Whitpain Twp., Pa., 1962—, former chairperson; mem. Selective Service Bd., Norristown, 1972-76; trustee Eastern State Sch. and Hosp., Trevose, Pa. Fellow Am. Bar Found.; mem. Am., Pa., Montgomery County (sec. 1971—) bar assns., Montgomery County Trial Lawyers Assn., St. Francis, St. Vincent's aid assns. Democrat. Roman Catholic. Club: Iris of Phila. (dir. 1968—). Home: 666 Midway Ln Blue Bell PA 19422 Office: 515 Swede St Norristown PA 19401

FLANSBURGH, EARL ROBERT, architect; b. Ithaca, N.Y., Apr. 28, 1931; s. Earl Alvah and Elizabeth (Evans) F.; B.Arch., Cornell U., Ithaca, 1954; M.Arch., Mass. Inst. Tech., 1957; m. Louise Hospital, Aug. 27, 1955; children—Earl Schuyler, John Conant. Job capt., designer The Architects Collaborative, Cambridge, Mass., 1958-62; partner Freeman, Flansburgh and Assos., Cambridge, 1961-63; prin. Earl R. Flansburgh and Assos., Cambridge, 1963-69, pres., dir. design, 1970—; exec. v.p. Environment Systems Internat., Inc.; vis. prof. archtl. design Mass. Inst. Tech., 1965-66; instr. art Wellesley Coll., 1962-65, lectr. art, 1965-69; cons. Arthur D. Little, Inc., Cambridge, 1964—; cons. to architects, engrs. for Boston City Hall, 1962-63; chmn. architecture com. Boston Arts Festival, 1964. Bd. dirs. Cambridge Center Adult Edn.; trustee Cornell U., 1972—, chmn. bldg. and properties com., mem. exec. com., academic affairs com., chmn. archtl. adv. com., 1972—. Served to 1st lt. USAF, 1954-56. Recipient Fulbright research grant Bldg. Research Sta., Eng., 1957-58; design awards Progressive Architecture, 1962, 64, 68, 69, Record Houses, 1965, 66, 67, 68, 73, 75; hon. mention Copley Sq. competition Boston, 1966; spl. 1st prize Buffalo-Western N.Y. AIA competition, 1968. Fellow AIA; mem. Boston Soc. Architects (chmn. program com. 1969-71, commr. pub. affairs 1971-73, commr. design 1973-74), Cornell U. Council, Quill and Dagger Soc., Tau Peta Pi. Archtl. works include Weston (Mass.) Sr. High Sch. Addition, 1965-67, Cornell U. Campus Store, 1967-70, Cumnock Hall, Harvard Bus. Sch., 1973-75, Acton (Mass.) Elementary Schs., 1966-68, 69-71; Peabody High Sch., 1969-71, Wilton (Conn.) High Sch., 1968-71, Marlborough (Mass.) High Sch., 1972-76, 14 Story St. Bldg., 1970; exhibited works: Light Machine I, IBM Gallery, N.Y.C., 1958, Light Machine II, Carpenter Center, Harvard U., 1965, 5 Cambridge Architects, Wellesley Coll., 1969, The Work of Earl R. Flansburgh and Assos., Wellesley Coll., 1969, New Architecture in New England, De Cordova Mus., 1974-75, Residential Architecture, Mead Art Gallery, Amherst Coll., 1976. Works exhibited in following Books: 50 Ville del Nostro Tempo, 1970; Nouve Ville, New Villas, 1970; Vacation Houses, 1970; Interior Design, 1970; Drawings by American Architects, 1973; Interior Spaces Designed by Architects, 1974; New Architecture in New England, 1974; Great Houses, 1976; Architecture Boston, 1976. Author: (with others) Techniques of Successful Practice, 1975. Home: Old County Rd Lincoln MA 01773 Office: 14 Story St Cambridge MA 02138

FLAST, FLORENCE, ednl. adminstr.; b. N.Y.C., June 14, 1918; d. Saul and Matilda (Barker) Fassler; B.A., Hunter Coll., 1938; m. Howard Warren Flast, Aug. 4, 1941; children—Robert Henry, Barry Richard. Asst. dir. personnel Franklin Simon Dept. Stores, N.Y.C., 1938-42, dir. tng. dept., 1938-42; merchandiser Interstate Dept. Stores, N.Y.C., 1942-43; draftsman Western Electric Co., N.Y.C., 1943-44, Jay Allen Tuck Engring. Corp., N.Y.C., 1944-45; sec. United Parents Assn. of N.Y.C., Inc., 1958-59, v.p., 1960-64, pres., 1964-68; mem. Sch.-Community Com. for Ednl. Excellence, Adv. Com. to Supt. of Schs., N.Y.C., 1965-66; spl. asst. to mem. N.Y.C. Bd. Edn. 1968-69; edn. mgr. N.Y. Indsl. Edn. Centers, N.Y.C., 1969-71; adminstrv. v.p. U.S. Research and Devel. Corp., N.Y.C., 1971-73; staff asso. for edn. Community Service Soc. of N.Y., N.Y.C., 1973-78; dir. bur. pupil transp. N.Y.C. Bd. Edn., 1978—; v.p. Nat. Coalition for Pub. Edn. and Religious Liberty, Washington, 1973—; mem. Task Force on Programs for Socially Maladjusted and Emotionally Disturbed Children, N.Y.C. Bd. Edn., 1975-76; chmn. edn. com. Met. council Am. Jewish Congress, 1969-71; chmn. Com. for Pub. Edn. and Religious Liberty, Inc., N.Y. State, 1975—. Mem. Mayor's Commn. on Inflation and Econ. Welfare, 1969; mem. exec. com. TV Center for Bus. and Industry, 1972-73; mem. N.Y. State Edn. Commr.'s Bilingual Adv. Council, 1976-78, Regents Adv. Council on N.Y.C. Project, 1977—. Recipient citation Americans United for Separation of Ch. and State, 1969; elected to Hunter Coll. Hall of Fame, 1975. Mem. Pub. Edn. Assn. (coordinating com. 1960-68), ACLU (ch.-state com. 1972—), Council for Pub. Higher Edn., Phi Beta Kappa. Club: Women's City. Contbr. articles to profl. jours. Home: 170 Park Row New York City NY 10038 Office: 28-11 Queens Plaza N Long Island City NY 11101

FLASTER, DONALD J(OHN), physician, medicolegal cons.; b. N.Y.C., Aug. 29, 1932; s. Murray J. and Theresa (Brenner) F.; A.B. in Biol. Sci., Johns Hopkins U., 1953; M.D., U. Naples (Italy), 1959; LL.B., Blackstone Coll. Law, 1970; m. Rosemary Carr, Dec. 13, 1959; children—Elisabeth, Andrew. Intern, Meyer Meml. Hosp., Buffalo, 1959-60; Mead Johnson Residency fellow Millard Fillmore Hosp., Buffalo, 1960; pvt. practice of medicine, Valley Cottage, N.Y., 1961-67; med. officer in charge of clin. research Pfizer, Inc., N.Y.C., 1967-69, USV Pharm. Corp., Tuckahoe, N.Y., 1969-71, Sandoz Pharm. Co., East Hanover, N.J., 1971-74; pres. Sci. & Regulatory Services Cons., Inc., Morristown, N.J. and Santa Ana, Calif., 1974—; medicolegal cons. various law firms, health product mfrs.; adminstrv. positions Nyack (N.Y.) Hosp.; advisor Nyack Community Ambulance Corps; fire surgeon Valley Cottage (N.Y.) Fire Dept. Active Boy Scouts Am., YMCA Indian Guides, Recs. for the Blind, Inc. Recipient N.Y. State Acad. Family Practice award. Fellow Am. Acad. Family Physicians; mem. N.J., Morris County, Rockland County med. socs., Am. Diabetes Assn., Am. Heart Assn., Am. Soc. Law and Medicine, Am. Soc. Advancement Med. Instrumentation, Rockland County Acad. Family Practice (past pres.). Home: 62 Dean Rd Mendham NJ 07945 Office: Scientific & Regulatory Services 10 Park Pl Morristown NJ 07960

FLAX, LAWRENCE, physicist, educator; b. Bklyn., May 17, 1934; s. Sam and Celia (Schwartz) F.; Ph.D., Colo. State U., 1969; m. Sandra Hurewitz, Sept. 22, 1956; children—Fred, Cheryl, Scott. Theoretical solid state physicist Lewis Research Lab. NASA, Cleve., 1959-72; acoustical physicist Naval Research Lab., Silver Spring, Md., 1972—; instr. physics, math. Cuyahoga Community Coll., Cleve., 1968-72; instr. physics and astronomy Am. U., Washington, 1972—. Recipient Outstanding Performance award Naval Research Lab., 1975, Outstanding Contribution award, 1975. Mem. Am. Phys. Soc., Acoustical Soc. Am., Sigma Xi, Sigma Phi. Contbr. articles to profl. jours. Home: 15909 Narrows Terr Silver Spring MD 20906 Office: Code 8132 Naval Research Lab Washington DC 20906

FLAYDERMAN, EARLE NORMAN, corp. exec.; b. Boston, July 11, 1928; s. Benjamin and Shirley (Bellar) F.; B.A., Boston U., 1952; children—Judy Ruth, Jean Ellen, John David. Owner, pres. N. Flayderman & Co., Inc., weapons adviser, pub., Kennebunk, Me., 1953-58, Greenwich, Conn., 1959-63, New Milford, 1963—; pres. Flayderman-Northeast, Inc.; bd. incorporators, dir. New Milford Bank & Trust Co. Staff arms cons. U.S. Army, Springfield Armory Mus., 1968—; arms cons. to State Conn. for Colt Collection Firearms, USMC Mus., 1975; appraiser Winchester Gun Mus., Olin Corp. Served with USN, 1946-48; from 2d lt. to 1st lt. USAF, 1951-60. Fellow Co. Mil. Historians; mem. Naval Inst., Naval Hist. Soc., Am. Def. Preparedness Assn., Nat. Rifle Assn. Author: Scrimshaw, The Art of the Whaleman, 1969; Scrimshaw and Scrimshanders: Whales and Whalemen, 1972; Collecting Tomorrow's Antiques Today, 1972; Norm Flayderman Guide to American Gun Collecting, 1976; Sporting Firearms, 1976; also profl. articles. Editor Arms Gazette Mag.; mem. adv. staff Gun Report mag., Gun Week newspaper. Home: Squash Hollow Rd New Milford CT 06776

FLECKNER, ALAN NORMAN, obstetrician, gynecologist; b. N.Y.C., May 3, 1934; s. Paul Richard and Martha (Feldmen) F.; B.S. in Pharmacy, Fordham U., 1956; M.D., Jefferson Med. Coll., 1960; M.P.H., Harvard U., 1969; m. Ann McGranachan, Mar. 29, 1976. Intern, Fitzsimmons Gen. Hosp., Denver, 1960-61; resident in obstetrics and gynecology Boston City Hosp., 1964-70; dir. maternal infant care program Boston Dept. Health and Hosps., 1967-69; practice medicine specializing in obstetrics and gynecology, Middlesex, Mass., 1969—; dir. ambulatory care St. Josephs Hosp., Lowell, Mass., 1977—; staff Lowell Gen. Hosp.; v.p. Middlesex GYN-OB, 1969—; adj. asso. prof. med. health scis. Lowell U., 1973—; instr. obstetrics and gynecology Tufts U., 1976—. Mem. Westford (Mass.) Bd. Health, 1973-74, Nashoba Associated Bds. Health, 1973-74. Served with USAF, 1959-64. Decorated Air Force Commendation medal (U.S.), Cross of Gallantry with palm (Vietnam); recipient Outstanding Aerospace Medicine Physician award USAFR, 1976, Flight Surgeon of Yr. award Soc. Air Force Flight Surgeons, 1977; diplomate Am. Bd. Obstetrics Gynecology. Fellow Am. Coll. Obstetrics and Gynecology; mem. Res. Officers Assn. (Mass. state surgeon), Am., Mass. med. assns., Occupational Medicine Assn., Aerospace Med. Assn., Assn. Mil. Surgeons U.S., Air Force Assn., Middlesex North Med. Soc. (chmn. com. pub. health 1975—). Editor: Programmed Guide to Sex Education (Murphy and Quadland), 1969. Home: 94 A Castlehill Rd Pelham NH 03076

FLEISCHER, RENEE ALTMAN, physician; b. N.Y.C., June 9, 1934; d. Ben Zion and Helen (Smulin) Altman; A.B., Barnard Coll., 1955; M.D., N.Y. U., 1961; m. Elliot Fleischer, Dec. 19, 1954; children—Corey Bennet, Deborah Ellen, Joshua Mark. Intern, Bronx (N.Y.) Hosp., 1961-62; resident in internal medicine N.Y. VA Hosp., N.Y.C., 1962-65; asso. attending physician medicine L.I. Jewish Med. Center Affiliation, Queens Hosp. Center, 1965—; practice medicine specializing in internal medicine, Jamaica, N.Y., 1966-72, New Hyde Park, N.Y., 1972—; dir. Methadone Maintenance Treatment Program, Queens Hosp. Center, L.I. Jewish Med. Center, Beth Israel Med. Center, 1970—; rec. sec. LaGuardia Med. Group, 1970—, attending physician in internal medicine La Guardia Hosp., 1967—; staff internal medicine L.I. Jewish-Hillside Med. Center; asst. prof. medicine State U. N.Y. at Stony Brook, 1972—. Diplomate Am. Bd. Internal Medicine. Mem. AAAS, Am. Chem. Soc., Am. Med. Women's Assn., Soc. Urban Physicians, N.Y. Acad. Scis., N.Y. State, Queens County med. socs., Am. Soc. Internal Medicine, Barnard. Coll. Alumni Assn. Office: 82-68 164th St Jamaica NY 11432 also 2035 Lakeville Rd New Hyde Park NY 11040

FLEISCHER, ROBERT, academic-mgmt. center exec.; b. Flushing, N.Y., Aug. 20, 1918; B.S., Harvard U., 1940, fellow, 1942, M.A., 1947, Ph.D., 1949; Steward Obs. fellow U. Ariz., 1940-41; m. 1942; 3 children. Asst. in astronomy Harvard U., Cambridge, Mass., 1941-42; instr. physics and astronomy Rensselaer Poly. Inst., Troy, N.Y., 1946-49, asst. prof., 1949-55, asso. prof., 1955-57, prof. astronomy, head obs., 1958-62; program dir. solar-terrestrial research, coordinator Internat. Years Quiet Sun, NSF, Washington, 1962-66, dep. head Office Internat. Sci. Activities, 1966-68, head astronomy sect., 1968-75, program dir. spl. activities, exec. sec. interagency coordinating com. on astronomy Fed. Council Sci. and Tech., 1975-76; dir. Greylock Center, Washington, 1976—; cons. in field. Fellow AAAS; mem. Internat. Sci. Radio Union, Internat. Astron. Union, Am. Astron. Soc., Am. Geophys. Union, Royal Astron. Soc. Can., Royal Astron. Soc. London, Astron. Soc. Pacific, AAUP, Philos. Soc. Washington, Am. Mgmt. Assn., Soc. Research Adminstrs. Democrat. Episcopalian. Club: Cosmos. Home: 1733 Church St NW Washington DC 20036 Office: The Greylock Center 1346 Connecticut Ave NW Washington DC 20036

FLEISCHMAN, ALAN ISADORE, biochemist; b. Bklyn., Aug. 10, 1928; s. Louis and Sarah (Schloss) F.; B.S., Coll. City N.Y., 1950; M.A., Bklyn. Coll., 1955; Ph.D., St. John's U., 1960; m. Margot Ilse Becker, Feb. 17, 1974; children—Stephen, Jack. Chemist, N.Y.C. Dept. Pub. Health, 1950-52, Liebmann Breweries, Bklyn., 1952-62; supervising biochemist St. Vincent's Hosp., Montclair, N.J., 1962-66; research scientist heart N.J., Dept. Health, Montclair, 1966—; v.p. Fleischman Electronics Inc., Montclair, 1976—; instr. biology Fairleigh Dickinson U., Madison, N.J., 1964—, research asst. Health Research Inst., 1964—. Active Boy Scouts Am. Served to lt. col. U.S. Army Res., 1950-78. Diplomate Am. Bd. Clin. Chemistry. Fellow Am. Inst. Chemists (certified profl. chemist, N.J. pres.-elect 1978-79), Council on Atherosclerosis, Am. Heart Assn., Council on Epidemiology, Nat. Acad. Clin. Biochemistry; mem. Am. Chem. Soc., AAAS, Am. Oil Chemists Soc., Am. Inst. Nutrition, Am. Inst. Biol. Schs., N.Y. Acad. Sci., Am. Soc. Microbiology, Am. Assn. Clin. Chemists (pres. N.J. sect. 1976—, nat. councilor 1977—), Internat. Soc. Cardiology, N.J. Inst. Chemists (pres.-elect 1978—). Jewish. Club: K.P. Contbr. articles to profl. publs. Patentee in field. Home: 36 Hawthorne Pl Montclair NJ 07042 Office: Div Community Health Services NJ Dept Health PO Box 1540 Trenton NJ 08625

FLEISCHMAN, LAWRENCE ARTHUR, art pub., gallery owner; b. Detroit, Feb. 14, 1925; s. Arthur and Stella (Granet) F.; student Purdue U., 1943-44; B.S., U. Detroit, 1948; m. Barbara Greenberg, Dec. 18, 1948; children—Rebecca Howland, Arthur, Martha. Pres., Lawrence Investment Co., Detroit, 1949-66, Lawrence Advt. Agy., Detroit, 1950-60; bd. dirs. Ind. Newspaper, Inc., Detroit, 1952-60, WITI, Channel 6, Milw., 1952-59; v.p., partner Kennedy Galleries, N.Y.C., 1966—; editor Am. Art Jour., N.Y.C., 1967—. Pres., Archives of Am. Art, 1952-66; mem. Fine Arts Commn., USIA, 1956-62; pres. Detroit Arts Commn., 1962-66; adviser Fine Arts Commn., White House, Washington, 1960-62, 64-66; v.p. Com. Religion and Art Am., N.Y.C., 1972—. Treas. Soc. Arts and Crafts Sch., Detroit, 1953-66. Bd. dirs. Hartwell Hedge Fund, N.Y.C., 1966-72, Detroit Inst. Arts, 1956-66, Mannes Coll. Music, N.Y.C., 1967-71; fellow Morgan Library. Served with AUS, 1943-46; ETO. Recipient Spl. City Detroit Resolution award, 1966; Lotos Club Art award, 1967. Mem. Pa. Acad. Fine Arts (life), Pa. Hist. Soc. (life), Art Dealers Assn. Am. Pub. catalogues fine Am. art, including Edward Hopper, 1977, Charles Burchfield, 1977. Home: 870 United Nations Plaza New York City NY 10017 Office: 40 E 57th St New York City NY 10022

FLEISCHMAN, MARK LAWRENCE, anthropologist; b. Newark, Aug. 20, 1940; s. Martin Leonard and Etta (Greenberg) F.; B.A. with honors in Anthropology, U. Pa., 1962; M.A., U. Chgo., 1964; Ph.D., U. Calif., Los Angeles, 1975; m. Judith P. Miller, Aug. 15, 1971. Research asso. Antioch Coll., Yellow Springs, Ohio, 1965; instr. Los Angeles City Coll., 1966; asst. prof. Calif. State Coll., Los Angeles, 1969-70, Syracuse U., 1970—; cons. in field. Heart Fund grantee, 1962-63; Ford Found. grantee, 1967-68. Mem. Am. Assn. Phys. Anthropology (cons. 1964), Human Biol. Council. Office: 500 University Pl Syracuse NY 13210

FLEISCHMANN, PETER FRANCIS, mag. pub. exec.; b. N.Y.C., Jan. 27, 1922; s. Raoul H. and Ruth (Gardner) F.; B.A., Yale U., 1944; m. Nancy Montgomery, 1948 (div.); children—James R., Ruth G., Stephen G.; m. 2d, Jeanne Cowles Wilson, May 1964. Staff New Yorker Mag., Inc., N.Y.C., 1955—, treas., dir., 1956—, exec. v.p., 1965-68, pres., 1968-75, chmn. bd., 1969—. Served as capt. AUS, 1945. Office: New Yorker Magazine Inc 25 W 43d St New York City NY 10036

FLEMING, ALICE CAREW MULCAHEY (MRS. THOMAS J. FLEMING), author; b. New Haven, Dec. 21, 1928; d. Albert Leo and Agnes (Foley) Mulcahey; A.B., Trinity Coll., 1950; M.A., Columbia, 1951; m. Thomas J. Fleming, Jan. 19, 1951; children—Alice, Thomas, David, Richard. Pres. aux., trustee St. Vincent's Hosp. and Med. Center, N.Y.C. Recipient Nat. Media award Family Service Assn. Am., 1973. Mem. P.E.N., Authors Guild. Author: The Key to New York, 1960; Wheels, 1960; A Son of Liberty, 1961; Doctors in Petticoats, 1964; Great Women Teachers, 1965; The Senator from Maine: Margaret Chase Smith, 1969; Alice Freeman Palmer: Pioneer College President, 1970; Reporters At War, 1970; General's Lady, 1971; Highways into History, 1971; Pioneers in Print, 1971; Ida Tarbell, The First of the Muckrakers, 1971; Nine Months, 1972; Psychiatry, What's it All About?, 1972; The Moviemakers, 1973; Trials that Made Headlines, 1974; Contraception, Abortion, Pregancy, 1974; New on the Beat, 1975; Alcohol: The Delightful Poison, 1975; Something for Nothing, 1978. Editor: Hosannah the Home Run!, 1972; America Is Not All Traffic Lights, 1976; Something for Nothing, 1978. Contbr. articles to mags. Address: 315 E 72d St New York City NY 10021

FLEMING, DAVID LEE, probation officer; b. Huntingdon, Pa., Nov. 29, 1950; s. Karl Eugene and Jean (Drye) F.; A.S., Harrisburg Area Community Coll., 1970; B.S., Am. U., 1972; M.S., Shippensburg State Coll., 1977; m. Karen Smoker, May 26, 1973. Usher, Clifton Theatre, Huntingdon, Pa., 1966-71, asst. mgr., 1971-72; juvenile probation officer Huntingdon County Probation Dept., 1972—. Pres. Consistory of Abbey Reformed Ch., 1974-76; profl. employment div. worker United Way. Mem. Am. Personnel and Guidance Assn., Pa. Assn. Probation, Parole and Corrections (exec. com.), Lambda Alpha Epsilon. Republican. Mem. United Ch. Christ. Clubs: United Comml. Travelers, Demolay (life mem.). Contbr. articles in field to profl. jours. Home: 2524 Holland Ave Huntingdon PA 16652

FLEMING, EDWARD J(UDE), clergyman, former univ. pres.; b. Montclair, N.J., Mar. 22, 1920; s. Timothy Joseph and Agnes (Gannon) F.; grad. Seton Hall Prep. Sch., South Orange, N.J., 1936; student Immaculate Conception Sem., 1936-40; A.B., Seton Hall U., 1940, M.A., 1948, LL.D., 1971; S.T.L., Cath. U. Am., 1944; Ph.D., St. John's U., 1955. Ordained priest Roman Cath. Ch., 1944; created papal chamberlain; priest St. Teresa's Ch., Summit, N.J., 1944-49; prof. edn. psychology Seton Hall U., South Orange, N.J., 1949—, dir. student affairs, 1950-69, dean of coll., 1952-69, exec. v.p., 1960-69, pres., 1969-72; rector Blessed Sacrament Ch., Essex Falls, N.J., 1970—; dean Archdiocese of Newark, 1976—; chaplain Friendly Sons of N.J., 1976—; coordinating dean Essex County, 1976—. Rep. to Edn. Commn. States, 1966—; mem. Army adv. panel ROTC affairs. Mem. Archdiocesian Bd. Clergy Examiners; dean West Essex Deanery, Archdiocese of Newark, 1975—. Trustee Greater Newark Black and White Opera Co. Recipient Alpha Epsilon Mu award, 1956; Sapientiae Christianne award, 1956; named Irishman of Yr., Friends Brian Boru, 1970; Unico Man of Year, N.J., 1975. Mem. Eastern Assn. Coll. Deans and Advisers of Men, Nat. Cath. Ednl. Assn. (pres. Eastern Regional unit 1965-66), Theol. Soc. Am. Address: 28 Livingston Ave Roseland NJ 07068

FLEMING, FLORENCE RUTH, ednl. adminstr.; b. St. Paul, Sept. 6, 1930; d. Riley Deskin and Florence (Smith) Schumann; B.S., Kent (Ohio) State U., 1955; M.A., Bank St. Coll. Edn., N.Y.C., 1967; Ed.D., Rutgers U., 1978; divorced; children—Toni Washington, Rhonda Fleming, Desi Washington. Mem. adminstrv. staff N.Y. City Bd. Edn., 1965—, citywide supr. guidance and social services, 1969-71, dir. personnel, placement and scheduling, 1971—. Asso. Commodity Futures Trading Commn. NDEA grantee, 1965-67, Edn. Professions Devel. Act grantee, 1970-72. Mem. Am. Vocat. Assn., United Fedn. Tchrs., N.Y. State Occupational Edn. Assn., N.Y. Consortium Edn. and Tng. (mem. bd.), NEA, Nat. Assn. Pub. Continuing and Adult Edn., Nat. Manpower Tng. Assn., NAACP, Nat. Urban League, Urban League Guild, Manpower Assn. N.Y., Phi Delta Kappa. Methodist. Author publs. in field. Home: 1270 Fifth Ave New York City NY 10029 Office: 347 Baltic St Brooklyn NY 11201

FLEMING, ROBERT DAVID, truck co. exec.; b. N.Y.C., Dec. 19, 1936; s. Oliver Francis and Martha Nicholas (Bean) F.; student Moravian Coll., 1971—; m. Johanna Weber, July 29, 1967. Sr. quality control engr. Mack Trucks, Inc., Allentown, Pa., 1966-70, sect. supr. assembly inspection, 1970-73, quality control mgr., Hayward, Calif., 1973-74, prodn. mgr., 1974-76, quality control mgr., Allentown, 1977—. Registered profl. engr., Calif. Mem. Am. Soc. for Quality Control (sr. mem., chmn. Lehigh Valley sect., certified quality control engr.), Am. Def. Preparedness Assn., Lehigh County C. of C. Republican. Home: 10 Hollins Ln Quakertown PA 18951 Office: 2100 Mack Blvd Allentown PA 18103

FLEMING, RONALD LEE, pub. interest orgn. adminstr., urban cons.; b. Los Angeles, Calif., May 13, 1941; s. Ree Overton and Elizzbeth Ann (Ebner) F.; B.A. cum laude, Pomona Coll., 1963; M. City Planning, Harvard U., 1966; m. Renata von Tscharner, Nov. 9, 1978. Urban planner Marshall, Kaplan, Gans and Kahn, San Francisco, Calif., 1969-71; founder, pres., exec. dir. townscape planner Vision, Inc., Cambridge, Mass., 1972-78; pres. Townscape Vision, Cambridge, 1978—; cons., lectr. townscape and planning issues throughout U.S.; conservation lectr. various communities as well as meeting of Nat. Trust for Hist. Preservation, Md. Hist. Trust, Soc. for Preservation of Long Island Antiquities and others; lectr. Harvard Grad. Sch. of Design, Harvard Bus. Sch., Yale Coll. and Law Sch., Columbia Grad. Sch. of Historic Preservation; legis. chmn. Mass. Roadside Council; founder, chmn. Cambridge Arts Council, 1975—; bd. overseers Castle Hill Concerts. Served to capt., Intelligence, U.S. Army, 1966-68; Vietnam. Environ. Design fellow, U. Wash., 1965; Heritage fellow Heritage Found., Deerfield, Mass., 1963; State Dept. grantee, 1975; Salzberg fellow Seminar on Am. Studies, 1978; recipient First prize Architecture and Planning, Columbia U. Urban Film Competition, 1975. Mem. Am. Inst. of Planners, Am. Soc. Planning Ofcls., Nat. Trust for Historic Preservation, Soc. Archtl. Historians, Soc. for Preservation New Eng. Antiquities (trustee), Mass. Hort. Soc. (trustee), Preservation Action (bd. advs.), Back to the City, Inc. (bd. advs.). Unitarian. Clubs: Somerset, Union Boat, Harvard (Boston). Editor: Censored Laughter, 1976; contbr. articles on townscape conservation and visual pollution to numerous publs. Home and Office: 2 Hubbard Pk Cambridge MA 02138

FLEMING, WILMOT EGERTON, senator; b. Phila., Dec. 20, 1916; s. Wilmot and Lillie (Bains) F.; B.S., U. Pa., 1939; m. Pauline Barnard, Aug. 18, 1939; 1 son, Jeffrey Barnard. Exec. asst. Sears Roebuck & Co., 1939-42; indsl. engr. E.I. duPont de Nemours & Co., 1942-44; partner Wilmot Fleming Engring, Co., Phila., 1944-68; mem. Pa. Ho. of Reps., 1963-64; mem. Pa. Senate, 1964—, minority policy chmn., 1971-72, republican caucas chmn., 1973—. Chmn. bd. dirs. Pa. Higher Edn. Assistance Agy; mem. Jenkintown Bd. Sch. Dirs., 1953-63, pres., 1957-63. Trustee Beaver Coll., 1954—. Recipient Outstanding Jr. award Engrs. Club Phila., 1950. Presbyterian (trustee, elder). Clubs: Jenkintown Rotary (past pres.); Union League (Phila.). Home: 306 Wyncote Rd Jenkintown PA 19046

FLETCHER, BRADY JONES, ednl. research cons.; b. Natchitoches, La., Apr. 17, 1928; d. Louis Benjamin and Isadore Hannah (Stephens) Jones; B.A., Clark Coll., 1950; M.A. (fellow), Howard U., 1953; postgrad. (NDEA fellow) Ind. U., summer, 1965; Ed.S. in Guidance, George Washington U., 1967, Ed.D., 1977; m. Donald Greene Fletcher, Aug. 13, 1950; children—Donald Bruce, Nathan Louis, Debra Patrice. Tchr. math. and sci. Fairmont Heights (Md.) High Sch., 1951-54, Douglas High Sch., Upper Marlboro, Md., 1955-57, Prince George's County (Md.) pub. schs., 1951-59, Banneker Jr. High Sch., Washington, 1959-63; chmn. guidance dept. Garnet/Patterson Jr. High Sch., Washington, 1963-67; counselor Lincoln Jr. High Sch., D.C. pub. schs., 1967-69, Kensington (Md.) Jr. High Sch., 1969-73, Banneker Jr. High Sch., 1975-77; career edn. specialist Montgomery County (Md.) Schs., 1973-75; cons. D.C. pub. schs., 1974, Md. State Dept. Edn., 1973, Balt. City Pub. schs., 1973, Balt. County pub. schs., 1973; project dir. InterAmerica Research Assos., Inc., Rosslyn, Va., 1977—. Mem. Am. (Human Relations Com. award 1974), Md. (award 1975), Nat. Capital (award 1975-76) personnel and guidance assns., Nat. Vocat. Guidance Assn., Assn. Non-White Concerns, Nat. Assn. Career Edn., Nat. Sch. Counselor Assn., Alpha Kappa Alpha. Editor: Career Edn., 1973-75. Home: 1 Waterway Ct Rockville MD 20853 Office: 1500 Wilson Blvd Suite 800 Rosslyn VA 22209

FLETCHER, CLIFTON MAURICE, accountant; b. Belfast, Maine, Aug. 27, 1935; s. Clifton Edison and Hilda Kate (Lufkin) F.; student Gates Bus. Coll., 1959-63, U. Maine, 1969-73; m. Cecile L. Giroux, Aug. 27, 1960; children—Clifton Maurice, Cullen A., Curt R. Sr. accountant Macdonald, Page, Stratford & Strout, C.P.A.'s, Augusta, Maine, 1963-68; controller, asst. dir. Augusta Gen. Hosp., 1968-72; asst. dir. finance Penobscot Bay Med. Center, Rockport, Maine, 1972-76; partner accounting firm, Augusta, 1976—. Treas., ARC, Augusta, 1964-65, Sno-Fest Winter Carnival, Augusta, 1968-76; bd. dirs., treas. YMCA, Augusta, 1976—, Rockland, 1973-76; bd. dirs. Maine Sch. Adminstrv. Dist. II, Gardiner, 1977—; chmn. fin. com., v.p. parish council St. Joseph's Cath. Ch., Gardiner, 1977—. Served with USAF, 1954-58. C.P.A. Mem. Am. Inst. C.P.A.'s, Maine Soc. Pub. Accountants, Hosp. Fin. Mgmt. Assn. (pres. 1972-73). Republican. Club: Kiwanis (dir. 1978—). Home: RFD 5A Windy Acres Gardiner ME 04345 Office: 103 Winthrop St Augusta ME 04330

FLETCHER, DELBERT VAN, chem. co. exec.; b. Tampa, Fla., May 10, 1918; s. William Delbert and Leo Jane (Van Winkle) F.; B.S., Ga. Inst. Tech., 1940; M. Chem. Engring. (Indsl. Research fellow), U. Louisville, 1941; certificate Northwestern U., 1955; m. Juanita Arrowood, Sept. 8, 1943; children—Elizabeth Ellen (Mrs. Charles A. Rosebrock, Jr.), Jacqueline (Mrs. Mage B. Perryman), Vina Jane (Mrs. Alfred J. DiNorscia, Jr.). Process engr. Grasselli chems. dept. E.I. duPont de Nemours & Co., Cleve. and Linden, N.J., 1941-46, tech. supt., Houston, 1946-48, asst. process mgr., process mgr., Wilmington, Del., 1948-50, asst. research dir., 1950-62, asst. planning mgr. indsl. and biochems. dept., 1962-69, comptroller biochems dept., 1969—. Mem. Kennett Area Park and Recreation Bd., 1955-57. Fellow Am. Inst. Chemists; mem. Am. Chem. Soc., Am. Inst. Chem. Engrs., Alpha Chi Sigma. Republican. Presbyn. (elder). Mason. Club: Kennett Square Country (Pa.). Home: RD 3 Kennett Square PA 19348 Office: 14360 Brandywine Bldg Wilmington DE 19898

FLETCHER, DONALD BURNETT, radiologist; b. Providence, Mar. 12, 1912; s. Alfred Wayland and Ethel Congdon (Colley) F.; Ph.B., Brown U., 1934; M.D., Harvard U., 1938; m. Ruth Alberta Button, Oct. 18, 1939; children—Cherry Ann Fletcher Bamberg, Donald Burnett. Med. house officer, Peter Bent Brigham Hosp., Boston, 1938-40; resident, Univ. Hosp., Ann Arbor, Mich., 1940-42; instr. radiology, Med. Sch., U. Mich., Ann Arbor, 1942-43; practice medicine specializing in radiology, Newport, R.I., 1946—; chief of radiology, Newport Hosp., 1946—, mem. staff, 1946—, pres., 1962-64. Pres., Redwood Library and Athenaeum, 1964—; pres. Newport County Chpt. Am. Cancer Soc., 1953-62, del. R.I. Cancer Soc. to Am. Cancer Soc., 1956-61; trustee St. Michael's Sch.; vestryman Emmanuel Episcopal Ch., 1966-68. Served to maj. M.C. AUS, 1943-46. Diplomate Am. Bd. Radiology. Fellow Am. Coll. Radiology; mem. AMA (Physicians Recognition Award, 1978), Newport County (pres., 1964-66), R.I. Med. Socs., N.Eng. Roentgen Ray Soc., R.I. Radiol. Soc., Radiol. Soc. N. Am., Am. Inst. Ultrasound in Medicine, SE N.Eng. Ultrasound Soc., Sigma Xi, Phi Beta Kappa, Phi Gamma Delta. Clubs: Sphinx, Newport Art Assn., Newport Hist. Soc., English Speaking Union, Soc. Colonial Wars, N.Eng. Hist. Geneal. Soc., Inst. Gen. Semantics, Internat. Soc. Gen. Semantics, SAR, Seaport '76 Found. Co-author: Radiology in World War II, 1966. Home: 60 Ayrault St Newport RI 02840 Office: Newport Hospital Newport RI 02840

FLETCHER, RICHARD MUMMA, educator; b. Lancaster, Pa., Jan. 27, 1916; s. Fred and Anna Martha (Mumma) F.; A.B., Franklin and Marshall Coll., 1940; postgrad. Harvard U., 1940-41; Ph.D., Pa. State U., 1955; m. Betty Lide, Mar. 18, 1967; children—John Stephen, Douglas Frederick. Supr. order dept. Columbia Malleable Castings div. Grinnell Corp. (Pa.), 1942-46; asst. to v.p. York Corrugating Co. (Pa.), 1947-49; bus. systems specialist Yoh Engring. Co., Phila., 1950-51; dir. research project in tng. methods Bainbridge (MD.) Tng. Center, USN, Spl. Devices Center, 1955-56; asso. prof. psychology Ursinus Coll., Collegeville, Pa., 1956-61, prof., 1961—, chmn. dept., 1961-74. Mem. Am. Psychol. Assn., Sigma Xi. Presbyterian. Home: 2812 Village Green Ln Norristown PA 19403 Office: Ursinus Coll Collegeville PA 19426

FLETCHER, RONALD DARLING, educator; b. Foxboro, Mass., Jan. 18, 1933; s. Howard Wendel and Ada (Darling) F.; B.S., U. Conn., 1954, M.S., 1959, Ph.D., 1963; m. Barbara Gundersen, Jan. 30, 1954; children—Deborah, Mark Ronald, Christopher Gary. Instr., U. Conn., Storrs, 1959-63; USPHS fellow U. Zurich (Switzerland), 1963-64; research virologist Lederle Labs, Pearl River, N.Y., 1964-67; asso. prof., asso. head dept. microbiology Sch. Dental Medicine, U. Pitts., 1967—; dir. microbiology McKeesport (Pa.) Hosp., 1971-78; exec. officer 339th Gen. Hosp., Pitts., 1973-78. Served with Med. Service Corps, U.S. Army, 1954-57, col. Res. Recipient certificate of achievement in microbiology Surgeon Gen. U.S. Army, 1973. Army Dept. grantee, 1969-72, Am. Cancer Soc. grantee, 1968, NIH grantee, 1975-79. Fellow AAAS, Am. Acad. Microbiology; mem. Nat. Registry Microbiology, Am. Tissue Culture Assn., Internat. Soc. Dental Research (v.p. Pitts. chpt. 1977-78), ADA, Am. Soc. Microbiologists, N.Y. Acad. Scis., Res. Officers Assn. (sec.). Contbr. to profl. jours. Home: 2228 Kingridge Rd Pittsburgh PA 15237 Office: 647-2 Salk Hall Univ Pitts Pittsburgh PA 15261

FLETCHER, THOMAS FRANCIS, pediatrician, hosp. adminstr.; b. Utica, N.Y., Dec. 1, 1920; s. Thomas F. and Mary Elizabeth (Fischer) F.; B.A., N.Y. U., 1942, M.D., 1946; m. Eileen Mary Stuhr, June 23, 1945; children—Mary Anne, Michael, Susan, Teresa, Joseph, Ellen. Intern, Bklyn., Bellevue and N.Y. Foundling hosps., N.Y.C., 1946-47, resident, 1947-49; fellow in pediatric cardiology Bellevue Hosp., 1950; practice medicine specializing in pediatrics, 1950—; asst. prof. pediatrics Hahnemann Med. Coll., Phila., 1964-70; acting dir. pediatrics Pa. State U., Hershey, 1969-70, clin. asso. prof., 1970—; chief pediatric cardiology Harrisburg (Pa.) Hosp., 1963—, v.p. med. affairs, 1977—; dir. Children's Diagnostic Center, Harrisburg, 1962-70; chmn. Dauphin County (Pa.) Mental Health-Mental Retardation Bd., 1971-72; panel leader Gov.'s Council for Human Services, 1971; co-chmn. council on edn. and manpower Susquehanna Valley Regional Med. Program, 1970-75. Served with USAF, 1951-52. Recipient W.J. Siebert award Central Pa. Acad. Medicine, 1963. Diplomate Am. Bd. Pediatrics. Fellow Am. Acad. Pediatrics, Am. Coll. Chest Physicians; mem. Am. Coll. Cardiology, Am. Heart Assn., Pa., Dauphin County med. socs., AMA, South Central Pa. Heart Assn. (past pres.), Central Pa. Acad. Medicine, Pa. Assn. Med. Educators. Republican. Roman Catholic. Contbr. articles to med. jours. Home: 215 Wood St Camp Hill PA 17011 Office: Harrisburg Hosp S Front St Harrisburg PA 17101

FLETCHER, WILLIAM LEON, cons. engr.; b. Hopkinton, N.Y., Nov. 3, 1929; s. Frederic Hassold and Hazel May (Jenne) F.; B.S., New Eng. Coll., 1957; M.S., Northeastern U., 1962; m. Jacquelyn Bailey, Mar. 28, 1956; children—Tara, Ralph, Bryce. Project engr. Camp Dresser & McKee, Boston, 1957-67; asso. san. engr. N.H. Water Supply and Pollution Control Commn., Concord, N.H., 1967-69; pres. Environ. Engrs., Inc., Concord, 1969—; v.p., New Eng. regional mgr. Roy F. Weston, Inc., 1976—; chmn. bd. dirs., treas. Environ. Analysts, Inc., Concord, 1971-74. Mem. tax map com. Town of Salisbury, 1972-73, mem. solid wastes regional com., 1973-74; mem. N.H. Bd. Registration Profl. Engrs., 1975—. Bd. selectmen Town of Salisbury, N.H., 1978—. Served with AUS, 1955-57. Registered profl. engr., N.H., Mass., Vt., Maine, R.I. Diplomate Am. Acad. Environ. Engrs. Mem. New Eng., N.H. water pollution control assns., New Eng., N.H. water works assns., N.H. Soc. Profl. Engrs. (pres. 1975-76), Constrn. Specifications Inst. (charter), New Eng. Coll. Engring. Alumni Assn. (founder). Rotarian. Home: RFD 1 Warner NH 03278 Office: 2 Chenell Dr Concord NH 03301

FLICKER, PAUL LEO, surgeon; b. Phila., Apr. 7, 1935; s. Jacob I. and Sarah H. (Applebaum) F.; student U. Pa., 1953-55; M.D., Jefferson Med. Coll., 1959; m. Eda Z. Gilgore, July 23, 1957; children—Blair, Scott, Jonathan, James. Intern U. Colo. Med. Center, Denver, 1959-50; resident Albert Einstein Med. Center, Phila., 1960-63; resident orthopedic surgery, Cerebral Palsy fellow Hosp. Spl. Surgery, N.Y.C., 1963-64; practice medicine, specializing in orthopedic surgery, 1966—; orthopedic surgeon North Shore Hosp., Manhasset, N.Y., 1966-68, Somerset (N.J.) Hosp., 1968—; asst. med.

dir. Matheny Sch. for Crippled Children, Peapack, N.J.; lectr. prosthetics and orthotics N.Y. U. Sch. Prosthetics and Orthotics, N.Y.C., 1968—. Served with USPHS, 1964-66. Diplomate Am. Bd. Orthopedic Surgeons. Fellow Am. Acad. Orthopedic Surgeons, A.C.S. (mem. com. on trauma N.J. chpt.); mem. AMA, N.J. Orthopedic Soc., Eastern Orthopedic Assn., Am. Acad. Cerebral Palsy, N.J., Somerset County med. socs. Home: PO Box 6065 Bridgewater NJ 08807 Office: 286 E Main St Somerville NJ 08876

FLINN, DAVID GALBRAITH, bus. co. exec.; b. Balt., Feb. 4, 1938; s. William A. and Jane M. (Case) F.; B.A. in Govt., Cornell U., 1960; m. Mary Anne Quick, Apr. 12, 1961; children—Dale William, Glenn David. Propr., mgr. Stellar Industries, Ithaca, N.Y., 1964-66, pres., 1966-72; propr. Starlane Farms, Lansing, N.Y., 1966—; propr. CFP Enterprises, Ithaca, 1971-78, pres., 1978—; sec., treas. CFP Communications, Inc., Horseheads, N.Y., 1977—; v.p., treas. DeWitt Electronics, Inc. Syracuse, N.Y., 1978—, Sonitrol Security Systems of Syracuse (N.Y.), 1975—; dir. Ehrhorn Technol. Ops., Inc., Canon City, Colo., Digicomp Research Corp., Ithaca. Mem. exec. bd. Baden Powell council Boy Scouts Am., 1976—; bd. dirs. Tompkins County (N.Y.) United Way, 1972-75, Ithaca YMCA, 1969-71, 79—. Served to lt. USAF, 1960-64. Mem. Tompkins County Agrl. and Hort. Soc. (pres. 1976-78). Democrat. Congregationalist. Clubs: Rotary (pres. 1972-73), Tompkins County Amateur Radio. Home and Office: 866 Ridge Rd Lansing NY 14882

FLINN, MICHAEL DE VLAMING, stock broker; b. Durham, N.C., June 15, 1941; s. Lawrence and Marion (de Vlaming) F.; B.A. magna cum laude, Yale, 1962; J.D., Harvard, 1965; m. Elizabeth Jamison Folk, Aug. 3, 1962; children—William III, Michael de Vlaming, T. Rex, Randall E. Admitted to Conn. bar, 1968; ltd. partner Ingalls & Snyder, 1970—. Rep., Town Meeting, Greenwich, Conn., 1970—; mem. Conn. Republican Finance Com., 1972, Greenwich Rep. Finance Com., 1977—. Pres., bd. dirs. Greenwich Boys Club Assn.; pres., bd. dirs. Round Hill Assn. Served as capt. U.S. Army, 1966-68. Mem. Am., Conn., Greenwich bar assns., Down Town Assn. Club: Links. Home: PO Box 1309 Greenwich CT 06830 Office: 100 Broadway New York City NY 10005

FLINT, GERTRUDE KINSEE (MRS. WALTER LEVY), journalist; b. Bklyn., Oct. 29, 1909; B.A., Hunter Coll., 1930; M.A., Columbia, 1934; m. Dr. Walter Levy, July 28, 1939; 1 son, James Lewis. Feature writer, soc. editor Greenwich (Conn.) Time, 1937-39; Greenwich corr. N.Y. Herald Tribune, 1937-39; spl. feature writer Bklyn. Eagle Syndicate, 1935-37; free lance writer, 1960—. Mem. Acad. Polit. Sci., Woman's Press Club of N.Y.C. Club: Pen and Brush. Home: 112 Tower Rd Brookfield Center CT 06805 also 130 E 75th St New York City NY 10021

FLINT, JEAN-JACQUES GEORGE, educator; b. le Vesinet, France, Aug. 14, 1943; s. Jacques and Colette (Francois) F.; B.A., Colby Coll., 1966; M.A., State U.N.Y., 1968, Ph.D. (Research Found grantee, Sigma Xi grantee), 1972. Research asst. State U.N.Y., Binghamton, 1966-70; asso. prof. dept. geology Brock U., St. Catharines Ont., Can., 1970—. NRC grantee, 1971-76. Mem. Am. Geophys. Union, Geol. Soc. Am., Internat. Assn. Great Lakes Research, Am. Quaternary Assn., Ont. Assn. Remote Sensing. Office: Brock U St Catharines ON L2S 3A1 Canada

FLOCH, MARTIN HERBERT, physician; b. N.Y.C., July 24, 1928; s. Samuel and Jean (Scheinman) F.; B.A., N.Y. U., 1949; M.S., U. N.H., 1950; M.D., N.Y. Med. Coll., 1956; m. Gladys Wisser, Nov. 24, 1954; children—Jeffrey Aaron, Craig Lawrence, Lisa Suzanne, Neil Robert. Intern, Beth Israel Hosp., N.Y.C., 1956-57, med. resident, 1957-59; fellow in gastroenterology Seton Hall Coll. Medicine, S. Orange, N.J., 1959-60; instr. medicine U. P.R., 1960-62; practice medicine specializing in gastroenterology, Norwalk, Conn., 1962—; asst. attending physician Montefiore Hosp., N.Y.C., 1962-64; attending physician (sr.) Norwalk (Conn.) Hosp., 1970—, chmn. Dept. Medicine, 1970—; clin. prof. medicine Yale U., New Haven, 1976—; courtesy staff San Juan City Hosp., 1960-62. Bd. trustees Aspetock Valley Health Dist., 1974-76; bd. trustees Norwalk Hosp., 1970—. Served with U.S. Army, 1960-62. Conn. Digestive Disease Soc. grantee, 1974-76; NIH grantee, 1975-78; U.S. Army Med. Research grantee, 1964-67. Diplomate Am. Bd. Internal Medicine, Am. Bd. Nutrition, Am. Bd. Gastroenterology. Fellow ACP; mem. Am. Soc. Clin. Nutrition, Am. Inst. Nutrition, Am. Gastroenterology Assn., Am. Soc. Internal Medicine, Am. Fedn. Clin. Research, Am. Soc. Tropical Medicine and Hygiene, Fairfield County Med. Soc., Conn. Med. Soc. (pres. 1972-74), Assn. Am. Med. Colls., Conn. Digestive Disease Soc. (pres. 1972-74). Contbr. articles in field to profl. jours. Home: 32 Woody Ln Westport CT 06880 Office: 24 Stevens St Norwalk CT 06856

FLOOD, DANIEL J., congressman; b. Hazleton, Pa., Nov. 26, 1904; s. Patrick F. and Sarah (McCarthy) F.; A.B., Syracuse U., 1924; postgrad. Harvard, 1925-26; LL.B., Dickinson Sch. Law, 1929, LL.D., 1960; H.H.D. (hon.), King's Coll., 1967; D.Sc. (hon.), Georgetown U., 1970, Hahnemann Med. Coll., 1971, Pa. Coll. Podiatric Medicine, 1971; LL.D., Wilkes-Coll., 1971, Syracuse U., 1972, Misericordia Coll., 1972; m. Catherine Swank, Sept. 24, 1949. Admitted to Pa. bar, 1930, also D.C. bar, U.S. Supreme Ct. bar; mem. 79th, 82d, 84th-96th Congresses from 11th Pa. Dist., past mem. Fgn. Affairs Com., now mem. Appropriations Com., subcom. Def. Appropriations; past chmn. subcom. on Labor; spl. ambassador to Peru, 1945. Active ARC, Civilian Def., War Loan Drives, local draft bd. Trustee Misericodia Coll., Dallas, Pa.; bd. dirs. Wilkes-Barre Cath. Charities, Wyoming Valley AAA Club; bd. visitors U.S. Naval Acad.; mem. pres.' council King's Coll., Wilkes-Barre. Decorated comdr. Cross of Carlos Caspedas (Cuba), Cross of Polonia Restituta (Polish Govt. in Exile London); Distinguished Service award Am. Cancer Soc., 1971; Distinguished Service citation Pres.'s Commn. Employment of Handicapped, 1971; numerous others. Mem. Am., Pa., Luzerne County bar assns., Sigma Alpha Epsilon, Delta Sigma Rho. Clubs: Harvard (Wilkes-Barre); Lions, Elks, Eagles, Moose, K.C. Home: 460 N Pennsylvania Ave Wilkes-Barre PA 18702 Office: United Penn Bank Bldg Wilkes-Barre PA 18701 also 108 Cannon House Office Bldg Washington DC 20515

FLOOD, (HULDA) GAY, mag. editor; b. Plainfield, N.J., Aug. 14, 1935; d. William Edward and Lucy (Dycker) F.; B.A., Smith Coll., 1957. Picture dept. Sports Illustrated, Time Inc., N.Y.C. 1957-58, letters dept., 1958-59, reporter, 1959-60, writer-reporter, 1960-71, asso. editor, 1971—. Life mem. Alumnae Assn. Smith Coll., Inc., Smith Students Aid Soc., Inc. Mem. Dutch Ref. Ch. Club: Smith Coll. (N.Y.C.). Home: 103 Gedney St #3C Nyack NY 10960 Office: Sports Illustrated Time and Life Bldg Rockefeller Center New York City NY 10020

FLORENCE, BARRY THOMAS, research co. exec.; b. Louisville, Aug. 17, 1946; s. Thomas Gerald and Carolyn (Cassady) F.; B.B.A. magna cum laude, U. Ky., 1968; M.A., Mich. State U., 1973. Sr. research asso. Mich. State U., East Lansing, 1971-74; dir. research Ernest H. Short & Assos., Sacramento, 1975-76; v.p. Resource Planning Corp., Washington, 1976—; lectr. Mich. State U., East Lansing, 1971-73, Calif. State U., Sacramento, 1975-76. Served with U.S. Army, 1968-71. Mem. Internat. Communication Assn., Speech Communication Assn., Beta Gamma Sigma, Phi Kappa Phi. Contbr. articles on communications and jud. system to profl. publs. Home: 1718 Corcoran St NW Washington DC 20009 Office: Resource Planning Corp 1401 16th St NW Washington DC 20036

FLORENCE, WILLIAM JAMES, JR., lawyer; b. West Orange, N.J., June 18, 1934; s. William James and Dorothy Clarisse (Mayo) F.; B.A., Lafayette Coll., 1956; J.D., Syracuse U., 1964; m. Judith Copeland Lawson, Nov. 30, 1957; children—Susan Forbes, William James. Admitted to N.Y. bar, 1965; asso. James Dempsey, 1964-68; partner firm Dempsey, McCaffrey & Florence, 1968-69, Dempsey, O'Keeffe & Florence, 1969-70, Dempsey, Spring, O'Keeffe & Florence, 1970-75; individual practice law, Peekskill and Mt. Kisco, N.Y., 1975—; mem. faculty Am. Banking Inst., 1971—; dir., corp. counsel Hipotronics, Inc.; spl. counsel N.Y. Joint Legis. Com. on Ins. Rates and Regulations, 1972—, N.Y. Joint Legis. Com. on Judiciary, 1974—, State of N.Y. Task Force on Ct. Reorgn., 1975—. Chmn. Yorktown United Fund, 1968; v.p., bd. dirs. United Fund of No. Westchester, 1968-70; chmn. Yorktown Conservation Adv. Council, 1968-72; campaign treas. N.Y. State Sen. Bernard G. Gordon, 1973-74; campaign chmn. Congressman Hamilton Fish, Jr., 1974. Served with U.S. Army, 1957-59. Mem. Am., N.Y. State (exec. com. ins., negligence and compensation sect. 1971—), Westchester County, Putnam County, Peekskill bar assns., Am. Trial Lawyers Assn., Lincoln Soc. Peekskill (pres., dir.). Republican. Episcopalian. Club: Bedford Golf and Tennis. Home: Long Meadow Rd Bedford NY 10506 Office: 1045 Park St Peekskill NY 10566

FLORENT, HUGHES VICTOR, physician; b. Nicolet, Que., Can., Oct. 17, 1940; s. Joseph Donat and Monique Marie (Bernier) F.; B.A., Nicolet Coll., 1960; M.D., Laval U., 1966; m. Ghislaine Desjardins, July 24, 1965; children—Marie-Josee, Julie. Base med. officer Canadian Forces Base, Clinton, Ont., 1966, base flight surgeon, St. Hubert, Que., 1967-69; gen. practice medicine, Montreal, Que., 1969—; med. officer Canadian Pacific, Ltd., 1969—. Mem. Coll. Physicians and Surgeons P.Q., Assn. des Medecins de Langue Francaise du Can. Home: 8501 Place Verdelle Anjou PQ H1K 1N1 Canada Office: 7820 Marquette St Montreal PQ Canada

FLORES, FRANK FAUSTO, graphics and printing co. exec.; b. N.Y.C., Sept. 18, 1930; s. Frank E. and Marie (Navarro) F.; m. Elizabeth L. Weekes, Oct. 2, 1948; children—Donald, Stephen, Allen. Sales mgr. Marsden Offset Printing Co., Inc., N.Y.C., 1955-59, treas., 1959—; pres. Marsden Reprodns., Inc., N.Y.C., 1962—. Mem. governing bd. Flatbush YMCA, 1968; mem. adv. bd. Salvation Army, 1977—. Mem. N.Y. Acad. Sci., Soc. Tech. Writers and Publishers (chpt. chmn. 1970), Minority Bus. Council, Nat. Rifle Assn., Internat. Criminal Justice Found. (chmn. exec. com.), AAAS. Cons. on graphics, communications, visual and verbal. Home: 2301 Ave R Brooklyn NY 11229 Office: 30 E 33d St New York City NY 10016

FLORIAN, MICHAEL ALEXANDER, educator; b. Boucharest, Roumania, Jan. 28, 1939; came to Can., 1957, naturalized, 1964; s. Herman and Rachel (Perlmutter) F.; B.Engring., McGill U., 1962; M.S. (Quincy Ward Boese fellow), Columbia U., 1966, Dr. Engring. Sci., 1969; m. Judit Frank, Dec. 17, 1972. Ops. research analyst Can. Nat. Rys., Montreal, Que., 1962-64, Canadian Internat. Paper, 1967-69; asst. prof. U. Montreal, 1969-72, asso. prof., 1972-77, prof., 1977—, dir. Transp. Research Center, 1973—; cons. industry and govt. Recipient numerous grants and fellowships, 1957-67. Mem. Can. Ops. Research Soc., Ops. Research Soc. Am., Inst. Mgmt. Sci. Editor Canadian Jour. Info. Processing and Operation Research, 1972-76; asso. editor Ops. Research, 1973—, Transp. Sci., 1974—; contbr. articles to sci. jours. Home: 83 Dufferin Rd Montreal PQ H3X 2X8 Canada Office: Dept Computer Sci and Ops Research Univ Montreal Box 6128 Montreal 101 PQ Canada

FLORIANI, LAWRENCE PETER, orthopedic surgeon; b. Jersey City, Sept. 24, 1939; s. Joseph August and Constance (LePore) F.; B.S., Georgetown U., 1961, M.D., 1965; children—Paul, Michele. Intern, New Eng. Med. Center Hosp., Boston, 1965-66; resident orthopedic surgery, NIH tng. grantee Georgetown U., 1967-70; practice medicine specializing in orthopedic surgery, sports medicine Morristown, N.J., 1970—; dir. sports medicine clinic N.J. Community Med. Center, Morristown, 1973—; lectr. in field. Pres. med. staff Community Med. Center, 1978—, also trustee. Diplomate Am. Bd. Orthopedic Surgery. Fellow Am. Acad. Orthopedic Surgeons, Orthopedic Research Soc., Am. Coll. Sports Medicine, AMA, N.J. Orthopedic Soc., Royal Soc. Health. Home: 49 Chimney Ridge Dr Convent Station NJ 07961 Office: 98 Maple Ave Morristown NJ 07960

FLORIO, JAMES J., congressman. Mem. 94th-96th congresses from 1st N.J. Dist. Office: Room 1726 Longworth House Office Bldg Washington DC 20515*

FLOSS, WALTER JOHN, JR., state senator; b. Buffalo, Feb. 13, 1923; s. Walter John and Laura C. (Lillis) F.; student Millard Fillmore Coll., 1946-48; m. Grayce H. Thronberry, July 13, 1946; children—John, Robert, Judith, Mary, Walter John III, James, Margaret, Kathleen, Joseph, Therese. Ins. exec. Floss Agy. Inc., Amherst, N.Y., 1946—; mem. Town of Clarence (N.Y.) Republican Com., 1946—, vice chmn., 1958—; mem. Clarence Planning Bd., 1952-59, Clarence Town Council, 1961-65; legislator Erie County, 1967—; mem. N.Y. Senate from 59th dist., 1978—. Vice pres. Niagra Frontier Housing Council, 1973—; chmn. housing com. Erie and Niagara County Regional Planning Bd., 1972—, sec., 1976-77, chmn., 1977—. Bd. dirs. Millard Fillmore Hosp. Served with USNR, 1941-45. Mem. Am. Legion, VFW, Ind. Ins. Agts. N.Y., U.S. Power Squadron (comdr.). Clubs: Aero of Buffalo, K.C. Home: 6221 Transit Rd E Amherst NY 14051 Office: 6465 Transit Rd E Ahmerst NY 14051

FLOWER, ANNETTE CHAPPELL, univ. dean; b. Washington, Oct. 31, 1939; d. Joseph John and Annette B. (Harley) Chappell; B.A. in English, U. Md., 1962, M.A., 1964, Ph.D., 1970; m. Brian Thomas Flower, Sept. 3, 1960. Lectr., U. Md. European div. (Eng.), 1965-66, instr. English, College Park, 1966-69; asst. prof. English, Towson (Md.) State U., 1969-72, asso. prof., 1972—, spl. asst. to pres., affirmative action officer, 1974-77, dean humanistic, social and managerial studies, 1977—. Lay reader, chalicist All Saints Episcopal Ch., Reisterstown, Md., 1973—; pres. Baltimore County Commn. for Women, 1977—; mem. adv. bd. Baltimore County Sexual Assault and Domestic Violence Center, 1978—. Mem. AAUP, AAUW, Modern Lang. Assn., S. Atlantic Modern Lang. Assn., Am. Assn. Higher Edn., Exec. Women's Council Greater Balt. Contbr. articles to profl. jours. and book revs. to Balt. Sunday Sun and Ms. mag. Home: 3831 Black Rock Rd Upperco MD 21155 Office: Towson State U Towson MD 21204

FLOWERS, JAMES PAUL, journalist; b. Sylvester, Ga., Aug. 5, 1918; s. James Paul and MaeBelle (Gordy) F.; A.B. in Journalism, U. Ga., 1949; M.A. in Polit. Sci., Columbia, 1952; m. Jeannette Kent, June 19, 1947 (div. July 1952); 1 dau., Margaret; m. 2d, Irina Andoga, Jan. 20, 1964 (div. Oct. 1970); m. 3d, Helen Kenny, May 28, 1976. Reporter, Columbus (Ga.) Ledger, 1949, Providence Jour.-Bull., 1953; financial reporter Wall St. Jour., N.Y.C., 1949-50, N.Y. Jour.-Am., N.Y.C., 1950-51; feature writer Newspaper Enterprise Assn., Scripps-Howard, N.Y.C., 1953-54; asso. editor King Features Syndicate, N.Y.C., 1955-68; pub. relations cons. to Howard Hughes, 1969; pres. Polaris Productions, Inc., N.Y.C., 1970—. Press aide for Richard M. Nixon, 1960, to Hubert Humphrey presdl. campaign, 1968; spl. asst. as speech writer to Gov. Nelson Rockefeller, 1970; copy writer November Group, Inc. campaign advt. agy. for Pres. Nixon, 1972; press sec. to Sen. John Marchi N.Y.C. Mayoralty campaign, 1973. Served with USAAF, 1942-45; CBI. Mem. Soc. of The Silurians. Clubs: Dutch Treat, Overseas Press (N.Y.C.); Nat. Press (Washington); Artists and Writers, Turf and Field (N.Y.C.). Author: Prince Valiant in the New World; The Three Challenges of Prince Valiant; also 4-part syndicated series Cuba: Columbus to Castro; A Secret Encounter With Ho Chi Minh; So I'm A Square; Queen of the Clowns; Princes, Presidents and Potentates; Jazz at Noon; Handbook on Handbags. Home: 158 E 74th St New York City NY 10021

FLUEK, TOBY KNOBEL (MRS. CHAIM FLUEK), artist; b. Czernica, Poland, Feb. 20, 1926; d. Naftali and Genia (Schwartz) Knobel; pvt. study with Irving Koenig, 1965, Joe Hing Lowe, 1970-72; student Art Students League, 1968; m. Chaim Fluek, Nov. 21, 1949; 1 dau., Lillian. Exhibited in one-man shows at Fellowship Gallery, Queens, N.Y., Concourse br. N.Y. Pub. Library, Bronx, Hanging Pl., New Hope, Pa., Bronx Mus. Community Gallery; exhibited in group shows at Greater N.Y. Outdoor Art Exhibit, Rego Park, N.Y., 1966, 71, 72, Sedgwick Art Assn., Bronx, 1967, 2d Ann. Bronx Showcase Visual Arts, 1968, N.Y. Pub. Library, Bronx, 1969, Bronx Mus., 1972, 74, 75, 76, Lever House, N.Y.C., 1972, 73, 74, 75, 76, Nat. Arts Club, N.Y.C., 1974, 75, 76, 77, Hudson Valley Art Assn., White Plains, N.Y., 1973, 75, 76, 77, 78, Chung Cheng Cultural Center, St. John's U., Jamaica, N.Y., 1978, others; represented in permanent collections Little Gallery, N.Y.C., also pvt. collections, also documentary film Image Before My Eyes; tchr. art class Woodside Jewish Center, 1972. Recipient 1st prize Brush and Palette Soc., 1971, 3d prize Greater N.Y. Outdoor Exhibit, 1972, Best in Show award Fellowship Art Gallery, 1972, 1st prize Brush and Palette Soc., 1973, 75, 2d prize, 1977, others. Mem. Am. Artists Profl. League, Art League of Nassau County (1st prize 1978, 3d prize 1978), Brush and Palette Soc., Catharine Lorillard Wolfe Art Club, Big Six Art League (organizer 1970). Home: 60-10 47th Ave Woodside NY 11377

FLUHR, FREDERICK ROBERT, electronic engr.; b. Omaha, Jan. 7, 1922; s. Frederick R. and Ruby (Wright) F.; student U. Omaha, 1946-47; B.S., Iowa State U., 1949, M.S., 1950; m. Mary Annie Rosser, June 7, 1952; 1 dau., Glynis Ann. Elec. engr., head high energy laser facility US Naval Research Lab., Washington, 1951—. Served with USAAF, 1940-45. Mem. IEEE, V.F.W., AAAS. Patentee in field. Home: 8716 E Fort Foote Terr Oxon Hill MD 20022 Office: Code 5508 Washington DC 20375

FLUKE, JAMES SAMUEL, cons. engr.; b. Saxton, Pa., Aug. 24, 1925; s. Carl Alva and Leila Irene (Stoler) F.; student Juniata Coll., 1943-45, Va. Poly. Inst. Tech., 1945-46; B.S., Pa. State U., 1950; m. Hazel Fern Hemminger, Dec. 29, 1947; children—Susan Lorraine, David James. Jr. engr. Pa. R.R. Co., Altoona and Columbia, Pa., 1950-51; asst. track supr. Pa. R.R., Columbus, Ohio and Derry, Pa., 1951-54, track supr., Marion, Ind., Olean, N.Y. and Crestline, Ohio, 1954-58; project engr. Shaffer, Parrett & Assoc., Cons. Engrs., Mansfield, Ohio, 1958-65, L. Robert Kimball & Assoc., Cons. Engrs., Ebensburg, Pa., 1965—. Mem. tech. adv. com. Admiral Peary Vo-Tech. Sch., Ebensburg, 1972-74; supervisory com. Highland Fed. Credit Union, 1970-73, pres., 1974-75, dir., 1975-77; troop treas. Boy Scouts Am., Ebensburg, 1970-76. Served with U.S. Army, 1945-46. Registered profl. engr., Ohio, Pa., Ill. Mem. Am. Ry. Engring. Assn. (tech. com.), Am. Soc. Hwy. Engrs. (chpt. v.p., dir. 1968-72), Am. Cons. Engrs. Council, Am. Legion. Democrat. Presbyterian. Club: Masons. Home: 112 Elderwood Dr Ebensburg PA 15931 Office: 615 W Highland Ave Ebensburg PA 15931

FLUM, JOSEPH, lawyer; b. Phila., June 13, 1924; student internat. law and fin. sch. fgn. service Georgetown U., 1944-46; B.S., Temple U., 1947, J.D., 1951. Admitted to Pa. bar, 1961, U.S. Supreme Ct. bar, 1967; owner, operator Flum's Dept. Store, Newtown, Pa., 1950—; individual practice law, Newtown, 1961—; lectr. on law-related edn., world travel and cultures. Bd. mem. council Rock Sch. Dist. Pa., 1967—, pres., 1971-73; chmn. legis. com. Bucks County Sch. Dirs., 1967—; mem. com. revisions state sch. code, mem. com. on law-related edn. Pa. Dept. Edn., 1974—, mem. global edn. adv. com., 1978—. Recipient Chapel of Four Chaplains Legion of Honor award. Mem. Pa. Bar Assn. (youth-edn. com.), Bucks County Bar Assn., Am., Phila. anthrop. assns., Smithsonian Instn., Newtown Hist. Assn., Pa. Sch. Bd. Assn., Explorers Club, Phi Alpha Theta. Author multimedia ednl. material on China. Legis. editor Temple Law Quar., 1950-51. Contbr. articles to legal and edn. jours. Approximately 30 yrs. world exploration in over 200 countries and possessions on all 7 continents with avocation of legal cultural, and ednl. anthropology with splty. in early migrations of man. Home: 43 S State St Newtown PA 18940 Office: State St at Centre Ave Newtown PA 18940

FLYNN, CONRAD PETER, banker; b. Colchester, Vt., Feb. 2, 1933; s. Conrad Joseph and Leona Delima (Ashline) F.; student U. Okla., 1974; m. Joan LaPointe, Aug. 22, 1953; 1 son, Joseph Conrad. Bank messenger Chittenden Trust Co., Burlington, Vt., 1951-56, supr., 1956-60, ops. and lending officer, 1960-75, exec. v.p. loans, 1975—. Commr. Montpelier Housing Authority, 1972-76. St. Michael's Coll. scholar, 1950. Mem. Am. Inst. Banking (mem. nat. com. 1957), Am. Bankers Assn., Alumnus of Nat. Comml. Lending Grad. Sch., Vt. Bankers Assn. Republican. Roman Catholic. Club: Ethan Allen (Burlington). Home: 3 Landing Ave RD 2 Winooski VT 05404 Office: 2 Burlington Sq Burlington VT 05401

FLYNN, DANIEL CLARKE, assn. exec.; b. San Francisco, May 10, 1939; s. John Lawrence and Elizabeth Katherine (Stumpf) F.; B.A., U. Santa Clara, 1961; J.D., Georgetown U., 1975; children—Mary Theresa, Daniel Joseph. Job analyst U.S. Naval Ship Research & Devel. Center, Carderock, Md., 1965; salary adminstr. Control Data Corp., Bethesda, Md., 1965-67; sr. personnel rep. Comsat, Washington, 1967-72; personnel adminstr. Library of Congress, Washington, 1972; asst. dir. Bank Personnel Div., Am. Bankers Assn., Washington, 1975—. Chmn., Arlington County (Va.) Civil Service Commn., 1972-76; mem. Arlington County (Va.) Manpower Planning Commn., 1975-76. Served with U.S. Army, 1961-63. Mem. Am. Bar Assn., Am. Compensation Assn., Am. Soc. Personnel Adminstrn., Va. State Bar, Washington Bank Personnel Assn., Washington Personnel Assn. Club: Capitol Hill Tennis. Editor, Bank Personnel News, 1976—; author: International Personnel Resources, 1978; editor: Salary Administration for Community Banks, 1977. Home: 42 S Park Dr Arlington VA 22204 Office: 1120 Connecticut Ave Suite 532 Washington DC 20036

FLYNN, JOHN EDWARD, architect, educator; b. Cin., Jan. 10, 1930; s. John George and Ethel Mary (Brauer) F.; B.Arch., U. Mich., 1953; m. Iris Pumroy, Feb. 1, 1954; children—Sheryl Ann, J. Michael, James P., Shawn Louise. Staff architect for application research Gen. Electric Co., Nela Park, Cleve., 1955-64; prin. John Flynn/Architect & Cons., Cleve., 1964-73; prof. architecture Kent (Ohio) State U.,

1967-73; prof. archtl. engring. Pa. State U., 1973—. Served with U.S. Army, 1953-55. Recipient Arnold Brunner Scholarship award Archtl. League N.Y., 1965; registered architect, Ohio. Fellow Illuminating Engring. Soc. (dir., sr. v.p., pres.-elect 1978—); mem. AIA (energy resource center), Internat. Commn. Illumination (internat. chmn. com.), Inter-Soc. Color Council. Author: Architectural Lighting Graphics, 1962; Architectural Interior Systems, 1970; contbr. articles to profl. publs.; research on effect of light on human judgment and behavior, 1971—. Home: 685 Devonshire Dr State College PA 16801 Office: 101 Engring A Pa State U University Park PA 16802

FLYNN, JOSEPH PETER, JR., govt. adminstr.; b. Phillipsburg, N.J., Feb. 17, 1946; s. Joseph Peter and Agnes Ruth (Stearns) F.; B.A., LaSalle Coll., 1968; M.S.A., George Washington U., 1975; m. Ann Marie Thomas, Oct. 4, 1969; children—Christopher Joseph, Timothy Russell. Tchr., LaSalle High Sch., Pasadena, Calif., 1968-69; manpower devel. specialist Dept. Labor, Washington, 1972; mgmt. intern Office Emergency Preparedness, Exec. Office of Pres., 1972-73; personnel officer, mgmt. analyst HUD, Washington, 1973-76; personnel office dir. FEA, Washington, 1976-77; asst. to dir. adminstr. Dept. Energy, Washington, 1977-78, exec. dir. for mgmt. support, def. programs, 1978—; adj. prof. mgmt. No. Va. Community Coll. Served with U.S. Army, 1969-71; Vietnam. Mem. Am. Soc. Pub. Adminstrn. Home: 2426 Windbreak Dr Alexandria VA 22306 Office: Dept Energy Washington DC 20545

FLYNN, LAWRENCE FRANCIS, elec. engr.; b. Balt., Mar. 20, 1949; s. Francis Xavier and Martha Helen (Brown) F.; student Balt. Poly. Inst., 1963-66; B.S. in E.E., U. Md., 1971; m. Anne Allen, June 12, 1971. Elec. designer Turpin, Wachter & Assos., Balt., 1970; elec. designer Whitman, Requardt & Assos., Balt., 1971-72; elec. design engr. E-B-L Engrs., Inc., Towson, Md., 1973-75, project mgr., Salisbury, Md., 1976—. Mem. adv. bd. Ward Found., Salisbury, Md., 1976-78. Registered profl. engr., Md., Pa., Del., N.J., Va., W.Va., Maine. Mem. Nat. Soc. Profl. Engrs., Engring. Soc. Balt., IEEE. Democrat. Clubs: Green Spring Valley Hunt, Wicomico County Democratic. Designer first modernized athletic field lighting systems in Baltimore County, Md., 1974. Home: 215 S Clairmont Dr Salisbury MD 21801 Office: 216 E Main St PO Box 407 Salisbury MD 21801

FLYNN, RICHARD JAMES, lawyer; b. Omaha, Dec. 6, 1928; s. Richard T. and Eileen (Murphy) F.; student Cornell U., 1944-46; B.S., Northwestern U., 1950, J.D., 1953; m. Kay Elaine House, June 28, 1975; children—Richard McDonnell, William Thomas, Kathryn Eileen, James Daniel. Admitted to D.C. bar, 1953, Ill. bar, 1954; law clk. to Chief Justices Vinson and Warren, 1953-54; asso. Sidley, Austin, Burgess & Smith, Chgo., 1954-63, partner, Washington, 1963-66, Sidley & Austin, 1967—. Served with USN, 1946-48. Mem. Am. (chmn. subcom. transp. antitrust sect. 1971-73), Fed., Chgo. (antitrust com. 1961-63), Fed. Power bar assns., Bar Assn. D.C., Nat. Lawyers Club, ICC Practioners, Washington Lawyers Commn. Civil Rights Under Law (exec. com.), Order of Coif, Phi Beta Kappa, Phi Delta Phi, Sigma Chi. Republican. Presbyn. (deacon, elder). Clubs: Metropolitan (Washington), Economic of Chicago, Legal, Kenwood Golf and Country. Contbr. articles to profl. jours. Home: 2342 S Queen St Arlington VA 22202 Office: 1730 Pennsylvania Ave NW Washington DC 20006

FLYNN, THOMAS ROBERT, mfg. co. exec.; b. Fall River, Mass., Mar. 5, 1940; s. John J. and Rita R. F.; B.S. in Indsl. Engring., Southeastern Mass. U., 1962; postgrad. Wichita State U., 1963-65; m. Sayra Paulette Dion, July 18, 1964; children—Dominic, Bridget. Contract mgr. United Technologies Corp., Windsor Locks, Conn., 1966-68; mktg. mgr. Atkins & Merrill, Inc., Maynard, Mass., 1969-72; account exec. Merrill Lynch, Inc., Boston, 1972-75; mktg. mgr. def. div. Brunswick Corp., Arlington, Va., 1975—. Mem. finance com. Town of Hopkinton (Mass.), 1972—, chmn., 1974-75. Served as lt. USAF, 1962-66. Recipient commendation Boston C. of C., 1974. Mem. Am. Def. Preparedness Assn., Armed Forces Communication-Electronics Assn., Southeastern Mass. U. Alumni Assn. Club: Eastern Ionosphere, Saddle Hill Country. Home: 9 Eastview Rd Hopkinton MA 01748 Office: 2001 Jefferson Davis Hwy Arlington VA 22202

FLYTHE, RUDOLPH, assn. exec.; b. Conway, N.C., Apr. 13, 1932; s. Lloyd Lawrence and Gertrude Ellen (Stancel) F.; A.B., Shaw U., 1955; postgrad. U. N.C., 1955-56; m. Barbara Fennell, Oct. 24, 1959; children—Lisa C., Mark L., Steven P. Dist. exec. Phila. council Boy Scouts Am., 1962-66, dir. activities and pub. relations, 1966-68, asst. dir. internat. relations Nat. Council, New Brunswick, N.J., 1968-69, dir. field service Chgo. council, 1969-72, scout exec. Nat. Capital area, Washington, 1972—. Bd. dirs. Goodwill Industries, 1974—, Meridian House Internat., 1974—. Served with U.S. Army, 1956-58. Mem. Am. Speech and Hearing Assn. (dir.). Presbyterian. Clubs: Internat., Rotary. Home: 7535 Sebago Rd Bethesda MD 20034 Office: 9190 Wisconsin Ave Washington DC 20014

FOA, URIEL GASTON, educator; b. Parma, Italy, Feb. 25, 1916; s. Enea Avraham and Dora Alice (Muggia) F.; came to U.S., 1965, naturalized, 1972; J.D., U. Parma, 1939; Ph.D., Hebrew U., 1947; m. Edna Ben-Jacob, Aug. 14, 1962; children—Gad, Ephraim, Ora Tamar Foa Goldstein, Hagar, Yael, Michelle. Exec. dir., co-founder Israel Inst. Applied Social Research, Jerusalem, 1948-65; asso. prof., chmn. dept. psychology Bar-Ilan U., Ramat Gan, Israel, 1959-62; vis. prof. U. Ill., Champaign-Urbana, 1965-67; prof. U. Mo. at Columbia, 1967-71; prof. psychology Temple U., Phila., 1971—; specialist UNESCO, 1962; cons. AT&T, Fiat, Pirelli, NSF, Nat. Found. for Humanities. Ford Found. grantee, NIMH grantee, NSF grantee. Fellow Am. Psychol. Assn., AAAS; mem. N.Y. Acad. Sci. Republican. Jewish. Author: (with E.B. Foa) Societal Structures of the Mind, 1974, Resource Theory of Social Exchange, 1975; contbr. articles to profl. jours. Home: 228 Roberts Ave Glenside PA 19038 Office: 505 Weiss Hall Temple Univ Philadelphia PA 19122

FOCHLER, ROBERT CHARLES, JR., advt. and public relations co. exec.; b. Latrobe, Pa., Dec. 3, 1937; s. Robert Charles and Evelyn Jane (Hall) F.; grad. high sch.; m. Bonnie Anne Wheeler, Sept. 20, 1958. Mgr., Western Union Telegraph Co., Punxsutawney, Pa., 1957-60, Batavia, N.Y., 1960-63; asst. mgr., program dir. Sta. WBTA, Batavia, 1963-69; exec. v.p. Batavia Area C. of C., 1969-72, Genesee County C. of C., Batavia, 1973-75, Niagara Falls (N.Y.) Area C. of C., 1975-77; owner Total Communications Concepts, Bellefonte, Pa., 1977—. Home and office: RD 3 Box 173 Bellefonte PA 16823

FOGARTY, CHARLES FRANKLIN, mining co. exec.; b. Denver, May 27, 1921; s. Charles Franklin and Mabel (Still) F.; E.M., Colo. Sch. Mines, 1942, D.Sc. in Geology, 1952; m. Wilma Marguerite Wells, Oct. 14, 1943; children—Charles Michael, Harry Wells, Patricia Ann Kappus, Mary Elizabeth, Catherine Sue Fogarty Peterson, Joan Marie, Paul Thomas, Theresa Ellen. Sr. geologist exploration Socony Vacuum Oil Co., Bogota, Colombia, 1946-50; with Texasgulf Inc., 1952—, geologist, asst. mgr. exploration dept., mgr. exploration dept., 1952-57, sr. v.p., mgr. exploration dept., 1957-61, sr. v.p., 1961-64, exec. v.p., 1964-68, pres., 1968-73, chmn., chief exec. officer, 1973—; chmn., dir. Texasgulf Can. Ltd.; dir. Greyhound Corp., Compania Exploradora del Istmo, S.A., Armco Steel Corp., Lehman Corp., Sulphur Export Corp. Trustee Colo. Sch. Mines, also Colo. Sch. Mines Research Inst. Served from 2d lt. to maj. C.E., AUS, 1942-46. Recipient Distinguished Achievement medal Colo. Sch. Mines, 1962. Registered profl. engr., Tex. Mem. Mfg. Chemists Assn. (dir.), Am. Inst. Mining, Metall. and Petroleum Engrs. (Hal Williams Hardinge award 1969), Am. Petroleum Inst., Canadian Inst. Mining and Metallurgy, Am. Assn. Petroleum Geologists, Mining and Metall. Soc. Am. (pres. 1967-68), Soc. Exploration Geophysicists, Copper Devel. Assn. (dir.), Am. Mining Congress (vice chmn., dir.), Sulphur Inst. (dir.), Nat. Acad. Engring., Zinc Inst., Newcomen Soc. in N.Am., Com. Econ. Devel. (dir.), Houston Geol. Soc., Scabbard and Blade, Tau Beta Pi, Sigma Gamma Epsilon, Kappa Sigma. Clubs: Mining, Sky, Univ., Econ. (N.Y.C.); Blind Brook (Port Chester, N.Y.); Westchester Country (Rye, N.Y.); Houston. Home: Wildcat Rd Darien CT 06820 Office: High Ridge Park Stamford CT 06904

FOGARTY, MARGARET MARY, psychologist; b. New Haven, Feb. 17, 1909; d. James Augustine and Grace Marion (Hyland) Fogarty; diploma New Haven Normal Sch., 1928; B.S., New Britain State Tchrs. Coll., 1939; M.A., Yale, 1944. Tchr. West Haven, Conn., 1928-52; sch. psychologist, dir. psychol. services West Haven Schs., 1952—; pvt. practice, West Haven, 1954—; bd. dirs. Clifford Beers Guidance Clinic, 1975—; mem. Catchment area 6 Mental Health Adv. Com., 1975—; mem. West Haven Mental Health Bd., 1974—, v.p., 1975—. Mem. adv. com. West Haven Community Devel. Action Plan, Race Relations Com. Mem. Am., New Eng., Conn. psychol. assns., Conn. Assn. Sch. Psychologists (sec. 1961-63, chmn. role and functions com. 1963-65), NEA (life), West Haven Community Service Assn. (sec. 1969-70), West Haven Adminstrs. Assn. Roman Catholic. Editor: Study of Role and Function of School Psychological Personnel Working in the Public Schools of Connecticut, 1965. Home: 487 Washington Ave West Haven CT 06516 Office: Blake Administration Bldg 25 Ogden St West Haven CT 06516

FOGARTY, WILLIAM EUGENE, mfg. co. exec.; b. N.Y.C., July 4, 1931; s. William Leo and Gertrude Eliose (Costello) F.; B.S. in Physics, Fairfield U., 1957; M.B.A., U. Conn., 1977; m. Nancy Ellen Meehan, Sept. 15, 1956; children—Nancy, Kathleen, William, Terence. Project engr. A.W. Haydon Co., Waterbury, Conn., 1957-63, sales engr., 1963-65; applications engr. Veeder Root Co., Hartford, Conn., 1965-69, asst. sales and mktg. mgr. instrument div., 1969-70, tech. coordinator Internat. div., 1978—; exec. asst. to commr. State of Conn. Dept. Children and Youth Services, Hartford, 1971—. Chmn., Wolcott (Conn.) Town Council, 1969-73, councilman, 1965-73; mem. Wolcott Republican Town Com., 1962—, chmn., 1978—. Served with USMC, 1951-54. Mem. Am. Mktg. Assn., Wolcott Jaycees (charter mem., dir. 1962-63), Wolcott C. of C. (pres. 1968-69), VFW (comdr. Wolcott post 1963-64). Republican. Roman Catholic. Home: 58 Charles Dr Wolcott CT 06716 Office: 28 Sargeant St Hartford CT 06102

FOGEL, IRVING MARTIN, cons. engr.; b. Gloucester, Mass., Apr. 15, 1929; s. Jacob and Ethel (David) F.; B.S., Ind. Inst. Tech., 1954; children—Ethan, Ronit. Civil engr. Ill. Hwy. Dept., Peoria, 1954-55; field engr. Peter Kiewit Sons Co., East Gary, Ind., 1955, field engr., progress engr., cost engr., Ogdensburg, N.Y., 1955-56; supt. grading and paving Merritt, Chapman & Scott, Binghamton, N.Y., 1956; cost engr. Drake-Merritt, Goose Bay, Labrador, 1956-57; constrn. mgmt. engr. Mil. Estimating Corp., Madrid, Spain, also P.I., 1957-58; project mgr. Ministry of Def., State Israel, 1958-59, Frederic R. Harris (Holland) N.V., The Hague, also Tehran, Iran, 1959-61; project mgr. Solel Boneh & Assos., Addis Ababa, Ethiopia, 1961-63; asst. to tech. dir. Frederic R. Harris, Madrid, 1963-64; chief engr. McKee-Berger-Mansueto, Inc., N.Y.C., 1964-65, v.p. constrn. mgmt., 1965-69; pres. Fogel & Assos., Inc., N.Y.C., also Phila., Boston, Detroit, 1969—; lectr. Registered profl. engr., Conn., Del., Ga., Ill., Maine, Md., Mass., N.H., N.J., N.Y., Pa., Vt., D.C., Israel. Fellow Am. Soc. C.E.; mem. Am. Arbitration Assn., Am. Assn. Cost Engrs., Am. Inst. Constructors, Am. Mgmt. Assn., Assn. Engrs. and Architects in Israel, Constrn. Specifications Inst., Nat. Contract Mgmt. Assn., Nat. Soc. Profl. Engrs., N.Y. Bldg. Congress, Project Mgmt. Inst., Soc. Am. Mil. Engrs. Contbr. articles to profl. jours. Home: 525 E 86th St New York City NY 10028 Office: 130 E 40th St New York City NY 10016

FOGEL, SANDER HERBERT, psychiatrist; b. Bklyn., Oct. 22, 1927; s. Jack and Yetta (Cohen) F.; A.B. in English cum laude, N.Y. U., 1949; M.D., U. Buffalo, 1953; m. Natalee S. Saxon, Aug. 22, 1948; children—Jan, Alice, Brian. Intern, Millard Fillmore Hosp., Buffalo, 1953-54, Fairfield State Hosp., Newtown, Conn., 1954-55; resident Boston VA Hosp., 1956, Thom Children's Clinic, Boston, 1956-57; clin. fellow in child psychiatry Albert Einstein Coll. Medicine, Bronx, N.Y., 1957-59; practice medicine specializing in child and family psychiatry, Ossining, N.Y., 1957—; asst. clin prof. psychiatry N.Y. Med. Coll., 1976—, dir. family therapy dept. child psychiatry; med. dir. Family Mental Health Clinic, Westchester Jewish Community Service, 1959-73; cons. in field; lectr. State U. N.Y., 1970-72. Chmn. adv. council Interfaith Council for Action, Ossining, 1969-71; pres. Ossining High Sch. PTA, 1971-72. Served with U.S. Army, 1946-47. Fellow Am. Psychiat. Assn., Am. Orthpsychiat. Assn., Am. Assn. Social Psychiatry; mem. WHO, World Med. Assn., World Fed. Mental Health, Internat. Platform Assn., Westchester Acad. Medicine, Westchester County Med. Soc. (chmn. mental health com., editorial bd. bull.), Westchester Psychiat. Soc. (chmn. legis. com., exec. council, pres., chmn. com. on continuing edn.). Club: N.Y. Univ. Contbg. editor Mother's Manual mag., 1973-77. Home: Quaker Bridge Rd Ossining NY 10562 Office: 14 Church St Ossining NY 10562

FOGEL, SEYMOUR, pub. co. exec.; b. Rochester, N.Y., July 14, 1929; s. Morris and Dora (Bloom) F.; B.S., U. Rochester, 1951; m. Joan Davis, Mar. 30, 1958; children—Linda, Deborah, Robert, David. Accountant, Am. Sugar Refining Co., N.Y.C., 1951-53, Haskins & Sells, C.P.A., Rochester, 1953-59; v.p., treas. Lawyers Coop. Pub. Co., Rochester, 1959—, also dir., mem. exec. com.; dir. Research Inst. Am., Inc., Bancroft Whitney Co., San Francisco, Baker, Voorhis & Co., Mt. Kisco, N.Y.; mem. adv. bd. Lincoln Rochester Trust Co., 1968-71. Bd. dirs. Community Chest Rochester and Monroe County, Inc., 1973-77, Rochester Hosp. Service Corp., Freedom House, N.Y.C., 1972-75, Genesee Hosp., Jewish Community Center of Greater Rochester, Temple Beth El, Jewish Home and Infirmary. C.P.A., N.Y. Mem. Am. Inst. C.P.A.'s, N.Y. State Soc. C.P.A.'s, Fin. Execs. Inst. (pres. 1970-71). Office: Aqueduct Bldg Rochester NY 14603

FOGELMAN, JAMES, sch. adminstr.; b. Havana, Cuba, Jan. 22, 1932; came to U.S., 1939, naturalized, 1944; s. Isadore and Sonia (Lochinsky) F.; B.Ed., Temple U., 1955, M.Ed., 1959; m. Joyce Isaacs, Aug. 18, 1959; children—Rande, Sharyn, Steven, Aron. Tchr., Roxborough High Sch., Phila., 1955-60, Middletown (N.Y.) High Sch., 1960-66; dir. Crystal Run Camp and Sch., Middletown, 1959—; head counselor, swim dir. SGF Camp for Underprivileged Boys, Collegeville, Pa., 1948-56. Parent Fresh Air Fund, 1971—; treas. Occupations, Middletown, 1972—; v.p. PATH, 1964-65; mem. Big Bros.-Big Sisters; in-service lectr. Middletown State Hosp., 1968; mem. Orange County Mental Health Bd. Mem. N.Y. State Assn. for Pvt. Schs. for Mentally Handicapped, N.Y. Assn. for Emotionally Disturbed, N.Y. State Tchrs. of Mentally Handicapped, Am. Schizophrenia Found., Parents and Friends of Exceptional Children, N.Y. Assn. Brain Injured Children, Delta Pi Epsilon. Jewish. Club: B'nai B'rith. Home and Office: RD 2 Middletown NY 10940

FOGLER, RICHARD JEFFREY, surgeon; b. Bklyn., Oct. 3, 1943; s. Sidney and Frances Hilda (Dubin) F.; B.A., Bklyn. Coll., 1964; M.D., N.Y. Med. Coll., 1968; m. Shari Adler, Jan. 23, 1971; children—Jason M., Daniel K. Intern, Met. Hosp., N.Y.C., 1968-69; resident Brookdale Hosp., Bklyn., 1969-73; practice medicine specializing in surgery, Bklyn., 1973—; asso. attending surgeon Brookdale Hosp., Bklyn., 1975—; asst. prof. clin. surgery SUNY Downstate Med. Center, 1978. Diplomate Am. Bd. Surgery. Fellow A.C.S.; mem. Kings County Med. Soc. Office: 625 Rockaway Pkwy Brooklyn NY 11236

FOGLIETTA, NORBERT LOUIS, mfg. co. exec.; b. Italy, Nov. 8, 1931; s. Louis and Settimia (Palombi) F.; Litt.B., Rutgers U., 1953, M.A., 1954; m. Margaret Ann Young, Jan. 7, 1956; 1 dau., Barbara Lynn. Asst. editor South Plainfield (N.J.) News Rev., 1954; asst. mgr. sales promotion Prudential Ins. Co. Am., Chgo., 1956-59; partner Foristall Co., N.Y.C., 1964-70, pres., dir., 1970-78; pres., chief operating officer Dougherty Bros. Co., Buena, N.J., 1978—; lectr. Pace Grad. Sch. Bus., N.Y.C., 1968. Served to capt. USAF, 1954-56. Mem. Pub. Relations Soc. Am., Nat. Investor Relations Inst. (charter), Alpha Chi Rho. Clubs: Princeton, Downtown Athletic (N.Y.C.). Home: 68 Bay View Dr Somers Point NJ 08244 Office: Pine and Tuckahoe Rds Buena NJ 08310

FOGWELL, FRANK DOUGLAS, charitable orgn. exec.; b. Hamilton, Ont., Can., July 19, 1919; s. Albert Percy and Alice Olive (Brett) F.; student Guildford Coll., Eng., 1945; m. Amelia Mary Erridge, Jan. 20, 1946; children—Denise Elaine, Ross Douglas. Copy editor to sales mgr. Radio Sta. CKOC, Hamilton, 1946-58; time buyer F.H. Hayhurst Advt. Co., Toronto, Ont., 1958-59; comml. copy mgr. Radio Sta. CHML, Hamilton, 1959-61; dir. pub. relations Hamilton and Dist. United Way, 1961-68; exec. v.p. Big Bros. of Can., Hamilton, 1968—; vol. committeeman Canadian Welfare Council, Canadian Red Cross, Family Service; com. mem. Nat. Vol. Orgn.; mem. Internat. Yr. of Child Com. Served as officer, inf. Canadian Army, 1941-46. Decorated Queen's Silver Jubilee medal. Mem. Can., Hamilton pub. relations socs., Inst. Assn. Execs. (pres.), Hamilton C. of C. Baptist. Home: 555 Woodland Ave Burlington ON L7R 2S3 Canada Office: PO Box 758 Burlington ON L7R 3Y7 Canada

FOILES, KEITH ANDREW, publisher; b. Genoa, Ill., Mar. 14, 1926; s. Harold Gustus and Harriet Cordelia (Robinson) F.; B.A., Augustana Coll., 1950; M.A., U. Denver, 1954. High sch. tchr. English, Carlmont High Sch., Belmont, Calif., 1955-57; with Harcourt Brace Jovanovich, N.Y.C., 1957—, beginning as coll. salesman, successivley Western region mgr. coll. dept., exec. editor coll. dept., gen. sales mgr. sch. dept., 1957-75, v.p., dir. sch. dept., 1976-78, sr. v.p., head sch. materials and human assessment group, 1978—. Served with USNR, 1943-46. Mem. Am. Numisatic Assn. Club: Vanderbilt Athletic. Home: 300 E 51st St New York City NY 10022 Office: 757 3d Ave New York City NY 10017

FOLAND, DAVID CRATSLEY, mech. engr.; b. Plainfield, N.J., Dec. 11, 1942; s. Jackson Edward and Edith Violet (Cratsley) F.; B.S.M.E., U. R.I., 1965; m. Winola Jane Hammond, Aug. 7, 1965; children—Kim Ann, Daryl Cratsley, Robin Lee. With Pratt & Whitney div. United Aircraft Corp., East Hartford, Conn., 1965-67; with Gen. Electric Co., Lynn, Mass., 1967—, jet engine systems engr., 1967-74, sr. engr., 1974-76, mgr. F 404 performance analysis, 1976—. Named Jaycee of the Month, W. Hartford Jr. C. of C., May, 1966; recipient Gen. Elec. Managerial award, 1974. Mem. Am. Inst. Aeronautics and Astronautics. Congregationalist. Home: 25 Surrey Ln Topsfield MA 01983 Office: 1000 Western Ave Lynn MA 01901

FOLCARELLI, RALPH JOSEPH, educator; b. Phila., Oct. 5, 1928; s. Joseph John and Mary Theresa (DiTullio) F.; B.S., Kutztown State Coll., 1951; M.L.S., Rutgers U., 1958; Ph.D., N.Y. U., 1973; m. Carol H. Field, July 20, 1952; children—Michele, Guy. Tchr., Tri Valley Sch., Grahamsville, N.Y., 1951-54, Pennsbury Schs., Fallsington, Pa., 1954-59, Mansfield (Pa.) State Coll., 1959-60, Cold Spring Harbor (N.Y.) Schs., 1961-65; asso. prof. library sci. C.W. Post Center, L.I. U. Grad. Library Sch., Greenvale, N.Y., 1965-75, prof., 1975—, asst. acad. v.p., 1976-78; tchr. summer sessions W.Va. U., 1959, 61, Syracuse (N.Y.) U., 1968, 70, State U. N.Y. Maritime Coll., 1972; library cons. Trustee Levittown (Pa.) Pub. Library, Friends of Library, Huntington (N.Y.) Pub. Library, L.I. Library Resources Council; dir. Funded Workshop on Role of Librarian in Reading, 1967. Mem. ALA, NEA, N.Y. (pres. library educators sect. 1970-71), Suffolk County (pres. 1973) library assns., N.Y. State and Suffolk County Intellectual Freedom Com. Co-author: Library Learning Laboratory, 1970. Contbr. numerous articles to profl. jours. Home: 117 Bay Dr Huntington NY 11743 Office: Grad Library School CW Post Center LI U Greenvale NY 11548

FOLEN, VINCENT J., physicist; b. Scranton, Pa., Jan. 17, 1924; s. Joseph William and Josephine (Maldonate) F.; B.A., LaSalle Coll., 1949; M.A., U. Pa., 1954; Ph.D., Am. U., 1972; m. Doris Ruth Braun, Feb. 14, 1954. Physicist, U.S. Naval Research Lab., Washington, 1954-59, head ferromagnetism sect., 1959—. Pres. Naval Research chpt. Sigma Xi, 1976-77. Served with USAAF, 1943-46. Recipient award for outstanding performance U.S. Naval Research Lab., 1962, 75; Research Publs. award U.S. Naval Research Lab., 1968, 70; Pure Sci. award Sci. Research Soc. Am., 1971, Navy Meritorious Civilan Service award, 1977. Fellow Am. Phys. Soc.; mem. Research Soc. Am., Philos. Soc. Washington, Alpha Epsilon. Contbr. articles profl. jours. Co-founder magnetoelectric effect, 1961. Patentee in field. Home: 11 Tecumseh Dr Washington DC 20021 Office: US Naval Research Lab Washington DC 20375

FOLEY, ARMUND EVERETT, pub. relations cons.; b. Outlook, Mont., Feb. 13, 1927; s. Louis Joseph and Alice Eleanor (Gessner) F.; B.J., Mont. State U., 1951; m. M. Louise Kirby, Mar. 23, 1967; 1 dau., Barbara Edith Nyholm. Freelance photographer and reporter, 1947-51; pub. relations exec. ABC Radio and TV Networks, 1955-59; account exec. Biderman Tolk & Assos., 1959-60; freelance film prodn. exec., 1960-62; dir. pub. info. N.Y.C. div. Am. Cancer Soc., 1962-66; asso. dir. N.Y. Acad. Scis., 1965-66; freelance writer Young & Rubicam, 1966-68; dir. pub. edn. and info. Leukemia Soc. Am., 1968-70; dir. external relations Coll. Medicine and Dentistry of N.J., 1970-75; prin. Foley Pub. Relations and Promotion, Hawley, Pa., 1975—. Served with AUS, World War II and Korea. Recipient 3d place award spl. bulls. div. Assn. Am. Med. Colls. and Council Teaching Hosps., 1973. Mem. Sigma Phi Epsilon. Episcopalian. Clubs: Lords Valley Country (Hawley); Overseas Press (N.Y.C.), Rotary. Contbr. articles newspapers and nat. mags. Originator radio series Perspectives on Health. Home: Box 1054 Hemlock Farms Hawley PA 18428

FOLEY, AUGUSTA ESPANTOSO, educator; b. Lima, Peru, Oct. 4, 1923; d. Alberto Bergmann and Maria Kluge (Freund) Espantoso; B.A., Immaculata Coll., 1947; M.A., Catholic U. Am., 1956; Ph.D., U. Pa., 1962; came to U.S., 1943, naturalized, 1964; m. Henry R.

Foley, Sept. 5, 1963. Teaching fellow U. Pa., Phila., 1959-62, post doctoral research fellow, 1964-65, faculty, 1965—, asso. prof. Romance langs. and gen. lit., 1972-77, prof., 1977—; asst. prof. Romance langs. Pa. State U., 1962-63; pres. U. Pa. Seminar on Renaissance, 1975—. Am. Philos. Soc. grantee, 1974, research grantee U. Pa., 1972; Jusserand fellow, 1965, U. Pa. fellow, 1961-62, Pepper fellow, 1960—, Caperton-Ratcliff fellow, 1960-61. Mem. Modern Lang. Assn., Renaissance Soc. Am., Assn. Internat. de Hispanistas, Am. Assn. Tchrs. Spanish and Portuguesee, Am. Comparative Lit. Assn. Republican. Roman Catholic. Club: U. Pa. Research. Author: Occult Arts and Doctrine in the Theater of Ruiz de Alarcon, 1972; (with A.G. Reichenberger) El primero Benavides of Lope de Vega, 1973; Critical Guides to Spanish Texts, La Lozana andaluza of Delicado, 1977. Asso. editor Hispanic Rev.; corr. editor Allegorica. Contbr. articles to profl. jours. Home: 269 W Tulpehocken St Philadelphia PA 19144 Office: 505 Williams Hall U Pa Philadelphia PA 19174

FOLEY, EILEEN, state senator; b. Portsmouth, N.H., Feb. 23, 1918; B.A., Syracuse U.; student U. N.H.; married, 3 children. Dir. Portsmouth (N.H.) Rehab. Center; spl. service work USN; former clk. City Portsmouth; former mayor of Portsmouth; mem. N.H. Senate, formerly minority leader; mem. N.H. staff U.S. Senator Tom McIntyre. Mem. Def. Adv. Com. Women in Services; mem. Portsmouth Housing Authority, Portsmouth Ednl. Council, Atlantic States Marine Fisheries Commn.; mem. exec. bd. Council Sr. Citizens. adult council Catholic Youth Orgn., mother's guild St. Thomas Aquinas, Immaculate Conception Altar Soc.; mem. state adv. bd. Swiftwater council Girl Scouts U.S.A. Past chmn. Portsmouth Democratic City Commn.; past chmn. Rockingham (N.H.) County Dem. Orgn.; vice-chmn. N.H. State Dem. Com. Bd. dirs. Portsmouth Rehab. Center, Gt. Bay Sch. for Mentally Retarded, U.S.O., N.H. Civil Air Patrol. Served in WACs, 1944-45. Mem. Women's Aux. Am. Legion, Portsmouth C. of C. (dir.). Roman Catholic. K.C. aux. Address: 39 Sunset Rd Portsmouth NH 03301

FOLEY, JAMES THOMAS, U.S. dist. judge; b. Troy, N.Y., July 9, 1910; s. Thomas David and Mary (Malone) F.; A.B., Fordham U., 1931; LL.B., Albany Law Sch., 1934; m. Eleanor Marie Anthony, July 16, 1953; 1 dau., Mary Jude. Admitted to N.Y. bar, 1934; engaged in private practice law, Troy, 1935-42; sec. to Supreme Ct. Justice William H. Murray, 1939-42, 46-49; judge U.S. Dist. Ct., No. Dist. N.Y., 1949-63, chief judge, 1963—. Served as lt. USNR, 1942-45. Mem. Am., N.Y. bar assns., Vets. Fgn. Wars, Am. Legion. Clubs: K.C., Elks. Home: RFD 1 Renssealer NY 12144 Office: Federal Post Office Bldg Albany NY 12207*

FOLEY, PAUL, advt. exec.; b. Pontaic, Mich., Mar. 12, 1914; s. Raymond M. and Mary (Hautekeur) F.; B.A. magna cum laude, U. Notre Dame, 1937; m. Sophye Balicki, Oct. 31, 1937; children—Susan Mary, Peter Michael, Jane Celeste. Reporter, Chgo. Evening Am., 1937-38; editorial staff Pontiac (Mich.) Press, 1938-39; copywriter Grace & Bement, Inc., advt. agy., 1940-43; exec. v.p., dir. MacManus, John & Adams, Inc., 1946-56; sr. v.p., dir. McCann-Erickson, Inc., N.Y.C., 1956-71, vice chmn. bd. dirs., 1963-65, chmn. bd. dirs., 1965-71, also chief exec. ofcr.; pres., chief exec. officer Interpub. Group Cos., 1971—. With OWI, N.Y.C., 1943, bur. chief, Istanbul, Turkey, 1944-45. Mem. Hist. Soc. Pa., Detroit Hist. Soc. Clubs: Bloomfield Open Hunt (dir. Bloomfield Hills, Mich.); Detroit Athletic, Recess, Players (Detroit). Home: 1211 Willow Ln Birmingham MI 48009 also 6 E 81st St New York City NY 10028 Office: 485 Lexington Ave New York City NY 10017*

FOLEY, ROBERT MATTHEW, lawyer; b. N.Y.C., Aug. 28, 1943; s. Nestor Shea and Jacqueline Victoria (Peers) F.; B.A., Lehigh U., 1966; M.A., George Washington U., 1968; J.D., Am. U., 1972; m. Linda-Adèle Swide, Aug. 2, 1969. Sch. psychologist City of Alexandria (Va.), 1968-70; admitted to D.C. bar, 1973, U.S. Supreme Ct. bar; staff atty. Broadcast Bur., FCC, Washington, 1972; asso. firm Shack & Mendenhall, Washington, 1972-77; individual practice law, Washington, 1977-78; sr. partner firm Foley & Calubra, 1978—; pres. Foley Enterprises, Washington, 1977—. Vestryman All Saint's Episcopal Ch., Chevy Chase, Md., 1973—; mem. exec. com. All Saints' All-Day Child Care Center, Inc., Chevy Chase, 1973—. Mem. Am. Psychol. Assn. (asso.), D.C., Am., Fed. Communications bar assns., Bar Assn. D.C., Assn. Immigration and Nationality Lawyers, U.S. Ct. Appeals for the D.C. Circuit. Episcopalian. Club: Chevy Chase Country. Contbr. articles to legal jours. Home: 4002 W Underwood St Washington DC 20015 Office: Suite 800 1019 19th St NW Washington DC 20036

FOLEY, THOMAS JAMES, accounting firm exec.; b. Rochester, N.Y., May 31, 1928; s. Thomas Edward and Mary Ellen (McNicholl) F.; certificate bus. Rochester Business Inst., 1950; B.B.A., U. Miami, 1953; m. Dorothy Anne D'Amico, Dec. 3, 1966; children—Eileen, Colleen, Thomas J. Accountant Carl D. Thomy & Co., Rochester, 1953-54, sr. accountant, 1954-56; individual practice, Rochester, 1956-73; sr. partner firm Foley & Stoffel, P.C., Rochester, 1974—. Chmn. Gates-Chili Sch. Dist. Career Edn. Advisory Council, 1975-77. CPA, N.Y. State. Mem. Am. Inst. C.P.A.'s, N.Y. State Soc. C.P.A.'s (past treas. Rochester chpt.), Rochester Area C. of C., Washington-Irving PTA, Eagles, Phi Delta Theta (charter). Club: Midtown Toastmasters (charter). Home: 17 Kernwood Dr Rochester NY 14624 Office: 1160 Chili Ave Rochester NY 14624

FOLGER, LEE MERRITT, investment co. exec.; b. Washington, May 5, 1934; s. John Clifford and Mary Kathrine (Dulin) F.; A.B., Harvard U., 1956; m. Nancy McElroy, 1961 (div.); children—Neil, Peter, Nicholas; m. 2d, Juliet Campbell Birmingham, Oct. 1976. Sr. v.p. Folger, Nolan, Fleming, Douglas Investments, Washington, 1959—, vice chmn., 1976—; v.p. Piedmont Mortgage Co., Washington, 1960—; pres. Cumberland Trust Co., Knoxville, Tenn., 1962—; mng. partner H.L. Dulin Co., Knoxville, 1960—; dir. Va. Industries, Rocky Hill, Conn., Washington Star Newspaper. Chmn. D.C. chpt. ARC, 1971-77; bd. govs. Am. Nat. Red Cross, 1976—, vice chmn., 1978; bd. govs. St. Albans Sch., Washington, chmn., 1975-76; trustee, fin. chmn. Corcoran Gallery of Art, Washington; vice chmn. United Way Nat. Capital Area, 1975-78; mem. D.C. Arts Commn., 1972-75; vestryman St. John's Episcopal Ch., 1969-72; v.p. Folger Fund (Washington), 1958—. Served to lt. j.g., USNR, 1956-58. Mem. Nat. Assn. Security Dealers (mem. dist. com. 1971-74, vice chmn. 1973-74). Clubs: Brook, Downtown Assn. (N.Y.C.); Chevy Chase (Md.); Met., 1925 F Street, Fed. City (Washington); Essex County (Boston). Home: 80 Kalorama Circle NW Washington DC 20008 Office: 725 15th St NW Washington DC 20005

FOLKER, DAVID ALAN, hosp. adminstr.; b. Rochester, N.Y., June 17, 1934; s. Harry Willis and Mary Loretta F.; B.S., Fairleigh Dickinson U., 1959; certificate Rutgers U., 1972; M.B.A., Wagner Coll., 1975; m. Joan E. Voorhis, Jan. 27, 1957; children—Lori, Brian. Various engring. positions with industry and health services, 1959-67; dir. mgmt. engring. Englewood (N.J.) Hosp., 1967-71, Mt. Sinai Med. Center, N.Y.C., 1971-76; v.p. gen. services St. Vincents Med. Center, Bridgeport, Conn., 1976-78; asso. exec. dir. ops. Faulner Hosp., Jamaica Plain, Mass., 1978—. Served with USNR, 1953-55. Registered profl. engr., Calif. Mem. Am. Hosp. Assn., Am. Inst. Indsl. Engrs., Am. Acad. Med. Adminstrs., Am. Coll. Hosp. Adminstrs. Home: 45 Tilden Rd Marshfield MA 02050

FOLKERS, GEORGE FULTON, educator; b. Joliet, Ill., Aug. 27, 1929; s. Herbert Peter and Leilia Pearl (Fulton) F.; B.A., Knox Coll., Galesburg, Ill., 1951; M.A., Princeton U., 1960, Ph.D., 1967; postgrad. U. Basle (Switzerland), 1949-50, 52-53; m. Jean Dorothy Kendall, July 14, 1956; children—Gregory Kendall, Katherine Jean, Jonathan Kendall. Instr. German, Williams Coll., 1959-61, Phillips Exeter (N.H.) Acad., 1961-64; asst. prof. U. Mass., Amherst, 1964-68; prof. German, coordinator grad. studies Bucknell U., Lewisburg, Pa., 1968—. Served with AUS, 1953-58. Fulbright-Hays grantee, 1974. Mem. Am. Assn. Tchrs. German, Modern Lang. Assn., AAUP. Editor, translator: The Complete Narrative Prose of Conrad Ferdinand Meyer, vols. I and II, 1976. Home: 417 S 21st St Lewisburg PA 17837 Office: Grad Studies Office Bucknell Univ Lewisburg PA 17837

FOLLANSBEE, HARPER, educator; b. Pitts., Sept. 12, 1914; s. William Uhler and Ruth (Harper) F.; A.B., Princeton, 1937; Ed.M., Harvard, 1954; m. Patience Gibbs Shorey, June 21, 1947; children—Harper, Nathan, Arthur Shorey. With tar and chem. div. Koppers Co., Kearny, N.J., 1937-40; mem. faculty Phillips Acad., Andover, Mass., 1940-77, chmn. biology dept., 1953-74, instr. biology Samuel Harvey Taylor Found., 1966-77. Mem. biology achievement test com. Coll. Entrance Exam. Bd., 1961-67, adv. placement exam. biology test com., 1967-71; reader Coll. Entrance Exam. Bd. Adv. Placement Exam in Biology, 1961-66; mem. NSF Adv. Com. on Coordination Curriculum Studies, 1959-60; mem. audio-visual com. The Am. Biology Tchr.; cons. editor biol. sch. div. Addison-Wesley Pub. Co., Inc., Palo Alto, Calif., 1961-77. Served to capt. AUS, 1941-46. Recipient Sci. Tchrs. Achievement Recognition award Nat. Sci. Tchrs. Assn., 1958. Mem. A.A.A.S., Am. Inst. Biol. Sci., Nat. Sci. Tchrs. Assn., Nat. Assn. Biology Tchrs., Biol. Scis. Curriculum Study (mem. steering com. 1958-60, mem. com. innovation lab. instrn. 1959-66). Author: Animal Behavior, 1965; (with other) Laboratory and Field Studies in Biology, A Sourcebook for Secondary Schools, 1960; Algae (teaching film), 1965. Ednl. cons. for 5 teaching films on animal systems, 1971. Contbr. articles to profl. publs. Home: Old Troy Rd Fitzwilliam NH 03447

FOLMAR, JOHN KENT, historian; b. Foley, Ala., Jan. 26, 1932; s. Herbert Lee and Pauline F.; B.A., Samford U., 1955; M.A., Birmingham-So. Coll., 1961; Ph.D., U. Ala., 1968; m. Rosa Hildred, June 2, 1951; children—John Kent, Tramel Lee, Jeffrey Forrest, Brendan Arthur. Sales analyst Birmingham (Ala.) Slag div. Vulcan Metals Co., 1955-59; tchr. Birmingham Schs., 1959-61; instr. history Univ. Mil. Sch., Mobile, Ala., 1961-63; grad. teaching asst. history U. Ala., Tuscaloosa, 1963-65, instr., 1965-66; asst. prof. history Morehead (Ky.) State U., 1966-69; prof., chmn. history sect. dept. social sci., California State Coll., Pa., 1969-75, chmn. history dept., 1976-78, chmn. dept. history and urban affairs, 1978—, prof., 1976—, chmn. Com. Action in Politics, 1975—. Served with USAF, 1951-52. Mem. Pa. (exec. council 1978—), Ala., Western Pa., Am., So. (membership com. 1976-78) hist. assns., Orgn. Am. Historians, Assn. Pa. State Coll. and Univ. Faculties (sec. chpt. 1976-77, v.p. 1978—). Democrat. Unitarian-Universalist. Author: United States History to 1877: An Outline and Workbook, 1975. Contbr. articles to profl. hist. publs. Office: Dept History and Urban Affairs California State Coll California PA 15419

FOLTIN, EUGENE, physician; b. Bratislava, Czechoslovakia, Sept. 22, 1911; s. Leopold and Anne (Furst) Feher; M.D., State U. Med. Sch., Bratisalava, 1935; m. Eva Miklos, Sept. 11, 1955; children—Anne Catherine and Elizabeth Irene. Intern, Mil. Hosp., Bratislava, 1935-36, asst. physician, 1935-36; resident State Hosp., Zvolen, 1937-38; asst. physician, 1937-38; resident Jewish Hosp., Bratislava, 1938-42, chief resident 1938-42, asst. physician, 1938-42, med. dir., 1942-45; clin. asst. urology, clinic Bratislava Med. Sch., 1945-47; research asst. Curie Found., Paris, 1948-50, Necker Hosp., Paris, 1949-51; chief resident Boulevard Hosp., N.Y.C., 1952-53; pvt. practice medicine specializing in urology, Bratislava, 1947-48; pvt. practice family medicine, Massapequa, N.Y., 1953—; chief of urology Bratislava Social Security Clinic, 1947-48, St. Elizabeth Hosp., Bratislava, 1948; staff Mid-Island Hosp., Bethpage, N.Y., Brunswick Hosp., Amityville, N.Y. Fellow Am. Acad. Family Physicians (charter); mem. Acad. Medicine, World Med. Assn., Nassau County, N.Y. State med. socs., AMA, Smithsonian Assocs. Club: B'nai B'rith. Home: 19 Dogwood Pl Massapequa NY 11758 Office: 800 Hicksville Rd Massapequa NY 11758

FOMUFOD, ANTOINE KOFI, pediatrician; b. Bamenda, Cameroon, Oct. 16, 1940; s. Ngwabi and Elizabeth Agwa (Assa) F.; M.B., B.S., U. Ibadan, 1967; M.P.H., Johns Hopkins U., 1974; 1 son, Antoine Ngwabi. Intern, Univ. Coll. Hosp., Ibadan, Nigeria, 1967-68, resident in pediatrics, 1968-70; resident in pediatrics Johns Hopkins Hosp., 1970-71, fellow in neonatology, 1971-73; asst. prof. pediatrics Howard U., 1974-78, asso. prof., 1978—; neonatologist Howard U. Hosp. Diplomate Am. Bd. Pediatrics. Fellow Am. Acad. Pediatrics; mem. Johns Hopkins Med. and Surg. Soc., D.C. Med. Soc. Contbr. articles to med. jours. Office: 2041 Georgia Ave NW Washington DC 20060

FONER, PHILIP SHELDON, historian; b. N.Y.C., Dec. 14, 1910; s. Abraham and Mary (Smith) F.; B.A., Coll. City N.Y., 1932; M.A., Columbia U., 1933, Ph.D., 1940; m. Roslyn Held, May 1, 1939; children—Liza, Laura. Instr. history Coll. City N.Y., 1932-40; ednl. dir. Internat. Fur and Leather Workers Union, 1941-45; pub. Citadel Press, N.Y.C., 1945-67; prof. history Lincoln (Pa.) U., 1967—; lectr. U. Havana, U. Moscow, U. Tokyo. Columbia U. fellow, 1933; recipient Deems Taylor award for best music book ASCAP, 1975. Mem. Am. Hist. Assn., Orgn. Am. Historians, Assn. Study Afro-Am. Life and History, Soc. Am. Historians, Phi Beta Kappa. Author: Business and Slavery, 1941; Jack London, Aerican Rebel, 1947; The Fur and Leather Workers Union, 1950; History of Labor Movement in the United States, Vol. 1, 1947, Vol. 2, 1955, Vol. 3, 1964, Vol. 4, 1965; The Life and Writings of Frederick Douglass, 1949-52; Mark Twain, Social Critic, 1958; History of Cuba and its Relations with the United States, 2 vols., 1962-63; The Case of Joe Hill, 1965; The Letters of Joe Hill, 1965; The Haymarket Autobiographies, 1969. The Black Panthers Speak, 1970; W.E.B. DuBois Speaks, 2 vols., 1970; American Labor and the War in Indochina, 1971; The Voice of Black America: Major Speeches of Negroes in the United States, 1797-71, 1972; The Spanish-Cuban-American War, and the Birth of American Imperialism, 1895-1902, 2 vols., 1973; When Karl Marx Died: Comments in 1883, 1973; Organized Labor and the Black Worker, 1619-1973, 1974; American Labor Songs of the Nineteenth Century, 1975; History of Black Americans: From Africa to the Emergence of the Cotton Kingdom, 1975; Labor and the American Revolution, 1976; We the Other People, 1976; Antonio Maceo, 1977; Our America by Jose Marti, 1977; The Great Labor Uprising of 1877, 1977; The Factory Girls, 1977; American Socialism and Black Americans, 1978; The Democratic-Republican Societies, 1790-1800, 1978; Paul Robeson Speaks, 1978; Essays in Afro-American History, 1978; The Black Worker: A Documentary History, Vols. 1 and 2, 1978. Compiler writings Thomas Jefferson, Thomas Paine, Abraham Lincoln, George Washington, Frederick Douglass. Office: Dept History Lincoln U Lincoln PA 19352

FONTAIN, GREGORY, educator; b. Colombia, S. Am.; Ph.B., Colegio Sérafico, Maristas, Colombia, 1946, A.B., 1949; S.T.M., Corazonistas Coll., 1949; postgrad. Eastern Theol. Sem., Phila., 1963. Ordained priest Greek Orthodox Ch., now archimandrite; instr. French, Sérafico Coll., also Christobal Colon Coll., Colombia, 1950-52, Episcopal Acad., Phila., 1958-61, Haddonfield (N.J.) Meml. High Sch., 1961-63; asst. prof., Spanish, French, Latin and German, Valley Forge Mil. Acad. and Jr. Coll., Wayne, Pa., 1962—, chaplain, 1976—; spiritual adviser Orthodox Ch. Fellowship, Bryn Mawr Coll., 1971; rector Sts. Peter and Paul Albanian Orthodox Cath. Ch., Phila., 1967-70; chaplain CAP, 77—; rep. chaplaincies commn. Canonical Orthodox Cath. Bishops in Americas; founder Am. Acad. Poets, 1971; bd. dirs. Acad. Leonardo da Vinci, Rome. Recipient Gold medal Order Anthony Wayne, 1967; Gold plaque Broadway Spanish Ch., Camden, N.J., 1959; named Danae, Internat. Clover Poetry Soc. Mem. Classic Soc. Phila., Centro Studi e Scambi Internat., Am. Poetry League, Pa. Poetry Soc., Am. Poet Fellowship Soc., Christian Writers League. Author: Manojo de Ideales, 1949; Seeds of Love, 1971; contbr. poems anthologies, jours. Address: PO Box 139 Wayne PA 19087

FOOTE, WARREN EDGAR, neuro-scientist, psychologist, educator; b. Boston, Nov. 5, 1935; s. Warren Edgar and Edith Irene (Landry) F.; B.A., Hamilton Coll., 1958; M.A., Boston U., 1960; Ph.D., Tufts U., 1965; m. Cynthia Sue Hall, July 21, 1973; children—Pamela Fowler, Sarah Canby., Julia Landry, Christopher Warren. Research asso. Harvard Med. Sch., 1966-67, vis. asst. prof. psychology, 1970-73, asst. prof., 1974—; USPHS postdoctoral fellow Yale, 1967-69; research scientist Norwich (Conn.) State Hosp., 1969-70; sr. Fulbright scholar Max-Planck Inst., Munich, Germany, 1973-74; asso. psychologist Mass. Gen. Hosp., Boston, 1974—; cons. Gen. Foods Corp., 1970-74. Served with M.C., AUS, 1959-60. Recipient McCurdy prize Mass. Soc. Research in Psychiatry, 1962; Sr. Fulbright fellow, 1973-74; Nat. Inst. Neurol. Disease and Stroke grantee, 1974-77; NIMH grantee, 1970-73. Mem. AAAS, N.Y. Acad. Scis., Soc. Neuroscis., Am. Psychol. Assn., Sigma Xi. Contbr. articles, revs. to profl. jours. Home: 15 Highland Circle Wayland MA 01778 Office: PO Box 70 Mass Gen Hosp Boston MA 02114

FORAN, NICHOLAS A., pump co. exec.; b. N.Y.C., Aug. 9, 1922; s. Nicholas Louis and Phyllis (Flemming) Fiorentino; B.M.E., U. N.Mex., 1948; m. Mary Elizabeth Austin, Sept. 10, 1944; 1 son, Andrew Austin. With Worthington Corp., 1948—, engr., Buffalo, 1948-52, sales engr., Phila., 1952-56, sales office mgr., Montreal, Que., Can., 1956-63, mgr. engineered products, Harrison, N.J., 1963-67, regional sales mgr., N.Y.C., 1967-71, v.p.-sales Latin Am., Mountainside, N.J., 1971—; pres. subs. Worthington, Ltd., Mountainside, N.J., 1971—; dir., Worthington Internat. Co., Inc. Served with USNR, 1942-46. Decorated Bronze Stars (2), Purple Heart. Registered profl. engr., N.Y., Can. Mem. Nat. Elec. Mfrs. Assn. Roman Catholic. Clubs: Naval Officers; Roxiticus Golf and Country (Mendham, N.J.); Palm Air Golf and Country (Pompano Beach, Fla.). Home: 114 Glenside Rd Murray Hill NJ 07974 Office: 270 Sheffield St Mountainside NJ 07092

FORBES, CLARENCE LLEWELLYN, govt. ofcl.; b. N.Y.C., May 29, 1923; s. Clarence Llewellyn and Emily Rose (Cowan) F.; student Coll. City N.Y., 1940-42, Prairie View U., 1943-44; B.B.A., U. Md., 1966; 1 son, David Nelson. Cadet, U.S. Army AC, 1942, advanced through grades to lt. col., 1967; mgmt. auditor GAO, Washington, 1967-71, audit mgr., 1972-73, dir. upward mobility programs, 1973-75, asst. dir. personnel, 1975-76, asst. regional mgr. in-charge Albany (N.Y.) office, 1977—. Served with USAF, 1942-45. Decorated Legion of Merit, Bronze Star. Mem. NAACP, Fed. Govt. Accountants Assn., Am. Soc. Pub. Adminstrn., Minority and Female Profl. Recruiting Assn. Roman Catholic. Home: 6 Hampton London Sq Apts Clifton Park NY 12065 Office: 855 Central Ave Albany NY 12206

FORBES, FRANCIS MURRAY, JR., lawyer; b. Boston, Apr. 21, 1904; s. Francis Murray and Marjorie (Cochrane) F.; B.A., Cambridge U., 1927, M.A., 1944; LL.B., Boston U., 1936; m. Elizabeth Livermore, Dec. 10, 1929; children—Diana, Marjorie, Francis Murray, Lorna, Elizabeth Gay; m. 2d, Serita Bartlett Harwood, Oct. 15, 1977. Admitted to Mass. bar, 1937; registered rep. F. S. Moseley, Boston, 1927-30, G. M. P. Murphy, Boston, 1930-32; asso. firm E. Schier Welch, (name later changed to Welch & Forbes) Boston, 1932—, partner, 1937—; mem. adv. com. State St. Bank & Trust Co.; dir. Vt. & Mass. Ry. Vice pres. Boston Athenaeum; trustee Children's Hosp. Med. Center, Fruitlands Mus.; chmn. bd. Mus. Am. China Trade; trustee emeritus Parents and Children's Services. Served with USNR, 1941-45. Decorated Mil. Order Brit. Empire. Mem. Boston Bar Assn., Res. Officers Assn., Mass. Hist. Soc. (treas.). Republican. Unitarian (vestryman 1947-76). Clubs: Tavern, Union Boat, Wednesday Evening of 1776, Essex County, Somerset; Savile (London). Home: Old Neck Rd Manchester MA 01944 Office: 73 Tremont St Boston MA 02108

FORBES, JOHN DEXTER, physician, corp. med. dir.; b. Phila., Sept. 25, 1937; s. J. Wallace and Dora Evelyn (Edwards) F.; B.A., Haverford Coll., 1959; student (Rockefeller Bros. fellow) Yale U. Div. Sch., 1959-60; M.D., Temple U., 1964; M.P.H., U. Mich., 1966; m. Catherine Hartlaub, June 22, 1964. Rotating intern Cooper Hosp., Camden, N.J., 1964-65; resident in occupational medicine U. Mich. Univ. Hosp. and Sch. Pub. Health, Ann Arbor, 1965-68; in-plant trainee Oldsmobile div. Gen. Motors Corp., Lansing, Mich., 1967-68; asso. med. dir. Western Electric Co., Kearny, N.J., 1970-71; corp. med. dir. Uniroyal Inc., Middlebury, Conn., 1971—; cons. occupational medicine Waterbury Hosp., 1972—. Trustee World Health Found., 1974—, pres., 1976. Served to lt. commdr. USNR, 1968-70. Certified in occupational medicine Am. Bd. Preventive Medicine; recipient award Central States Soc. Indsl. Medicine and Surgery, 1968. Fellow Am. Coll. Preventive Medicine, Am. Acad. Occupational Medicine, Am. Occupational Medicine Assn.; mem. Occupational Med. Assn. Conn. (dir.), AMA, New Haven County Med. Assn. Contbr. articles to profl. jours. Office: Uniroyal Inc Oxford Management and Research Center Middlebury CT 06749

FORBES, W(ILLIAM) HARRY, sch. counselor; b. Fayetteville, Pa., June 17, 1921; s. William Henry and Sara Ellen (Shetter) F.; student Wilson Coll., 1946-47; B.S. in Music Edn., Lebanon Valley Coll., 1950; M.Ed. in Guidance and Counseling, Shippensburg (Pa.) State Coll., 1965; m. Ruth Elisabeth Hill, Aug. 8, 1954. Music supr. Lititz (Pa.) Pub. Schs., 1950-52; elementary music supr. Chambersburg (Pa.) Area Sch. Dist., 1952-69, elementary sch. counselor, 1969-74, sch. counselor, chmn. guidance dept. middle sch., 1974—. Active YMCA, United Way, Contact-Teleministry. Served with USAAF, 1942-46. Mem. Am., Pa., Keystone personnel and guidance assns., Pa. Sch. Counselors Assn., NEA (life), Pa. Edn. Assn. (life), Phi Delta Kappa. Democrat. Home: RD 3 Chambersburg PA 17201 Office: 1151 E McKinley St Chambersburg PA 17201

FORD, CHARLES THOMAS, chemist, research adminstr.; b. Luzerne, Pa., June 15, 1936; s. Charles Vincent and Henrietta Frances (Waverka) F.; B.S. in Chemistry, King's Coll., Wilkes-Barre, Pa., 1958; m. Patricia Ann Hall, May 30, 1964; children—Jennifer Ann, Christopher Thomas, Matthew Joseph. Librarian, Naval Research Lab., Washington, 1958-59; research chemist Mellon Inst., Pitts., 1959-67; chemist, dir. of research in water pollution control Bituminous Coal Research, Inc., Monroeville, Pa., 1967—; sci. reviewer EPA. Mem. Level Green Recreation Com.; mem. Bach Choir of Pitts. Recipient S.A. Braley award, 1977. Fellow Am. Inst. Chemists; mem. Am. Chem. Soc., Pitts. Mus. Soc., Am. Fedn. of Musicians. Republican. Roman Catholic. Contbr. articles on methods of chem. analysis to profl. jours. Home: 109 Echo Springs Circle Level Green PA 15085 Office: 350 Hochberg Rd Monroeville PA 15085

FORD, DANIEL FRANCIS, author; b. Arlington, Mass., Nov. 2, 1931; s. Patrick Joseph and Anne Theresa (Crowley) F.; B.A., U. N.H., 1954; Fulbright fellow, U. Manchester (Eng.), 1954-55; m. Sarah Lansing Paine, July 28, 1967; 1 dau., Katharine Serena. Reporter, Overseas Weekly, Frankfurt, Germany, 1958; asst. editor N.H. Profiles mag., Portsmouth, 1959-60; publs. editor U. N.H., 1961-68; corr. The Nation, South Vietnam, 1964. Served with AUS, 1956-57. Recipient Stern Found. Mag. Writers grant, 1964. Mem. Phi Beta Kappa, Phi Kappa Phi. Author: Now Comes Theodora, 1965; Incident at Muc Wa (filmed as Go Tell the Spartans), 1967; The High Country Illuminator, 1971; The Country Northward, 1976; (with Sally Ford) 25 Ski Tours in the White Mountains, 1977, 25 Ski Tours in the Green Mountains, 1978. Editor: Carter's Coast of New England, 1969. Address: Shankhassick Farm Durham NH 03824

FORD, FRED CHARLES, univ. adminstr.; b. Turtle Creek, Pa., Aug. 2, 1911; s. Charles A. and Lydia M. (Beichling) F.; B.S., Carnegie-Mellon U., 1934; M.A., U. Pitts., 1937, Ph.D., 1950; m. Christina M. Allan, June 20, 1945; children—Fred C., Jeannie A., Allan M. Instr. math., physics Turtle Creek and Mt. Lebanon (Pa.) Sch. Dists., 1934-37; dir. testing and research Mt. Lebanon Schs., 1937-48; dir. personnel, asso. prof. edn. U. Miss., Oxford, 1948-54; asso. dir. personnel U. Pa., Phila., 1954-55, dir. personnel, 1955-73; partner Cons. Personnel Assos., 1974—; mgmt. cons., lectr. statistics and personnel adminstrn. Served to capt. AUS, 1942-46. Mem. Am., Pa. psychol. assns., AAUP, AAAS, Phi Delta Kappa, Phi Mu Alpha. Methodist (trustee). Home: 1451 Stirling Dr Wayne PA 19087

FORD, HAROLD EMERY, digital electronic engr.; b. Chehelis, Wash., June 7, 1939; s. Harvey R. and Naomi Hollis (Underwood) F.; ed. high sch.; m. Mary Donelda Middaugh, May 12, 1961; children—H. Emery, Michael Erin, Caroline LyAnne. Sr. electronics technician, Communications Satellite Corp., Clarksburg, Md., 1967-74; digital electronics engr. Digital Communications Corp., Gaithersburg, Md., 1974—. Active Boy Scouts Am. Served to chief petty officer USN, 1958-69. Bd. dirs. Seneca Valley Youth Club. Patentee in field. Home: 19025 Queens Cross Ln Germantown MD 20767 Office: 19 1st Field Dr Gaithersburg MD 20760

FORD, JEREMIAH, III, architect; b. Phila., Apr. 22, 1932; s. Jeremiah and Mary Sterling (Hewitt) F.; A.B., Princeton U., 1954, M.F.A. in Architecture, 1959; m. Elizabeth Dana, Mar. 1, 1975; children—Amanda Hewitt, Katherine Brewster, Amy Sterling, Dana H. Stewardson, Elizabeth Stewardson, Caroline Stewardson. Designer, Harrison & Abramovitz, Architects, 1959-61; job capt. Kenneth Kassler, Architect, 1961-62; designer World Trade Center div. Port of N.Y. Authority, 1962-63; project designer Welton Becket & Assos., 1963-64; pres. Walker Sander Ford & Kerr P.A. Architects and Planners, 1965-73; partner Short & Ford, Architects, Princeton, N.J., 1974—; mem. Preservation Planning Group, 1974—; bd. dirs. Princeton Community Housing, 1972—. Served to capt. USMC, 1954-57. Mem. Nat. Council Archtl. Registration, AIA, N.J. Soc. Architects, Princeton Area Alumni Assn., 1974—. Democrat. Episcopalian. Clubs: Colonial; Princeton U. Prin. works include Princeton Savs. & Loan Assn., 1970, Community Library, Rocky Hill, N.J., 1975, Maark Corp. Tennis Racquet Factory, South Brunswick, N.J., 1975, Offices, Gallup Poll, Princeton, 1975, Montgomery Nat. Bank (N.J.), 1977, Mergentime Corp. hdqrs., Raritan Twp., N.J., 1978, Benson Office Bldg., Princeton, 1979. Home: 635 Snowden Ln Princeton NJ 08540 Office: Mapleton Rd RD 4 Box 864 Princeton NJ 08540

FORD, JOHN CHARLES, broadcasting co. exec.; b. Washington, Oct. 8, 1942; s. Edgar Martin and Mary (Crowley) F.; B.A., U. Md., 1964, student, 1964-65; M.A., N.Y. U., 1966; postgrad. N.Y. Inst. Finance, 1967-68, New Sch. for Social Research, 1969, Crowell-Collier Inst., 1969, Friesen-Kaye Inst., 1971, Inst. Modern Langs., 1971, Sterling Inst., 1974, Forum Corp., 1976, U. Wis., 1977, U. Va., 1977. Librarian Cath. U. Am., 1958-59; immigration clk. U.S. Dept. Justice, 1960-61; TV prodn. asst. USIA, Washington, 1963-65; instr. U. Md., 1965; acct. exec. Ruder & Finn Inc., N.Y.C., 1965-66; asst. to exec. v.p., mgr. ednl. services Am. Stock Exchange, N.Y.C., 1966-70; mgr. communications and audio visual tng. Merrill Lynch, Pierce, Fenner & Smith Inc., N.Y.C., 1970-74; dir. edn. and tng., dir. employee devel. and edn. CBS, Inc., N.Y.C., 1974—; mem. faculty N.Y. Inst. Finance, 1971-72, Katharine Gibbs Sch., 1972-75. Treas., bd. dirs. Archeus Found., 1972—; v.p., bd. dirs. 15 W 81st St. Tenants Corp., 1978—; vol. Rec. for the Blind, 1971-72, United Fund Greater N.Y., 1966-67; publicity chmn. children's party Coop. Am. Relief Everywhere, 1974. Mem. Nat. Acad. TV Arts and Scis. (sec. bd. govs., trustee 1969—), Fin. Industry Tng. Assn. (pres. 1969-71), AAUP, Speech Communications Assn., Eastern Communications Assn., West 70th St. Assn., Fedn. West Side Block Assns., Internat. Radio and TV Soc., Nat. Soc. Programmed Instruction, Nat. Audio-Visual Assn., Am. Soc. Tng. and Devel., N.Y. Personnel Mgrs. Assn., Internat. Platform Assn., N.Y. C. of C., Wall St. Tng. Dirs. Assn., U. Md. Alumni Assn. Greater N.Y. (dir. 1966—), Omicron Delta Kappa, Phi Delta Theta. Home: 15 W 81st St New York City NY 10024 Office: 51 W 52d St New York City NY 10019

FORD, MARK ROBERT, archivist; b. Bethlehem, Pa., July 6, 1923; s. Mark Aloysius and Rose Helen (Csapek) F.; B.A. in History and Govt., Lehigh U., 1950; J.D., New Eng. Sch. Law, 1968; postgrad. U.S. Dept. Agr., 1954; m. Mary Elizabeth Glancy, May 20, 1946; children—Kathleen Anne Ford Jones, Mark Robert, Michael Thomas, Patrick. Chem. analyst Bethlehem Steel Corp. (Pa.), 1942-50; archivist Nat. Archives, Washington, 1951-55; chief accessions br. U.S. Air Force Film Depository, Wright-Patterson AFB, Ohio, 1955-59; audiovisual archivist Aerospace Med. Div., Brooks AFB, Tex., 1959-63; audiovisual prodn. coordinator 3245 Air Base Group, L.G. Hanscom Field, Bedford, Mass., 1964-68; audiovisual staff officer, electronic systems div.. U.S. Air Force, Hanscom AFB, Mass., 1968—; cons. old film data bank. Pres. Charles River Acad. Fathers Assn., 1973. Served with 28th Inf. Div., U.S. Army, 1943-46. Mem. Soc. Am. Archivists, Info. Film Producers Am. (chmn. Boston 1971-72), Air Force Hist. Assn., Air Force Assn., Washington Film Council, Smithsonian Assos., Delta Theta Phi. Republican. Roman Catholic. Editor: (film) Solar Radio Astronomy, 1972. Home: 82 Menotomy Rd Arlington MA 02174

FORD, MORGAN, judge; b. nr. Wheatland, N.D., Sept. 8, 1911; s. Morgan J. and Mary (Langer) F.; B.A., U. N.D., 1935; LL.B., Georgetown U., 1938; m. Margaret Duffy, July 30, 1955; children—William, Patrick and Michael (twins), Mary Ellen. Tchr. pub. schs. Dist. 102, Everest Twp., Cass County, N.D., 1933-34; with mortgage loan dept. Lincoln Nat. Life Ins. Co., summers 1931-38; state mgr. Royal Union Fund, Des Moines, 1938-39; admitted to N.D. bar, 1938; individual practice law, Fargo, 1939-49; pres. Surety Mut. Health & Accident Ins. Co., Fargo, 1939-49; v.p. 1st State Bank of Casselton, 1941-49; city atty., Casselton, 1942-48; mem. bd. for registrants Selective Service, 1942; judge U.S. Customs Ct., N.Y.C., 1949—. Address: US Customs Ct 1 Federal Plaza New York City NY 10007

FORD, ROBERT PROSPERO, banker; b. N.Y.C., June 23, 1947; s. Hugh Jerome and Jennie Therese (Attanasio) F.; B.S. in Math., St. Francis Coll., 1968; M.B.A. in Ops. Research, Bernard Baruch Coll., City U. N.Y., 1974. Math. tchr. Half Hollow Hills Central Sch. Dist. #5, Melville, N.Y., 1968-73; ops. research analyst mfrs. Hanover Trust Co., N.Y.C., 1973-74, asst. v.p., cons. mgr., 1974-78, v.p., group mktg. mgr., 1978—; mem. adv. bd. Cash Mgmt. Inst.; seminar leader Am. Mgmt. assn., Wharton Exec. Seminars. Mem. Am. Inst. Banking, Bank Mktg. Assn., Ops. Research Soc. Am. (asso.). Home: 238 President St Brooklyn NY 11231 Office: 350 Park Ave New York NY 10022

FORD, SHERMAN ALFRED, electronics co. ofcl.; b. Syracuse, N.Y., Dec. 14, 1931; s. Henry Claire and Leota Mary (Willey) F.; student Santa Ana Coll., 1960-63, Cypress Coll., 1968; m. Betty Jane Bailey Wagner, Dec. 5, 1970; children—Robert Michael Wagner, Patricia Lynn Wagner, Nancy Gwen Ford Miller, Melanie Ann Ford Paris, David Craig Wagner. Mgr. product inspection Autonetics div. Rockwell Internat. Co., Anaheim, Calif., 1964-68, sr. quality assurance project adminstr., 1968-71, quality assurance mgr. Maine Electronics subs., Lisbon, 1972—; sr. design assurance engr. Norden div. United Tech. Co., Norwalk, Conn., 1971-72. Treas., St. Matthews Episcopal Ch., 1976, jr. warden, 1977, sr. warden, 1978—; mem. stewardship commn. Episcopal Diocese of Maine, 1977—. Served with USN, 1949-53. Registered profl. engr., Calif. Mem. Am. Soc. Quality Control. Republican. Club: Masons. Home: 67 Frost Hill Ave Lisbon Falls ME 04252 Office: Maine Electronics PO Box 48 Lisbon ME 04250

FORD, WILLIAM BERT, physician; b. West Point, Ind., May 31, 1917; s. William Bert and Bertha (Mae) F.; B.S., Purdue U., 1939; M.D., Ind. U., 1943; m. Yolanda Ford, Mar. 21, 1942; children—Jane, Bill, Kent. Intern, Nat. Naval Med. Center, 1943-44; resident in gen. surgery George Washington U., 1946-49, resident in thoracic surgery, 1949-51; instr. dept. surgery, 1949-51; mem. staff Shadyside, Western Pa., St. Francis Gen., St. Margaret Meml., St. John's Gen., McKeesport, Children's, Suburban Gen. hosps., South Hills, Forbes health systems, North Hills Passavant. Served with USNR, 1944-46. Diplomate Am. Bd. Surgery, Am. Bd. Thoracic Surgery. Fellow A.C.S., Am. Coll. Chest Physicians; mem. Am., Pa., Pan-Am. med. assns., Soc. Thoracic Surgeons, Allegheny County Med. Soc., Am. Assn. Thoracic Surgery, Pitts. Surg. Soc. Contbr. numerous articles to profl. jours. Home: 116 Derwent Dr Pittsburgh PA 15237 Office: Assn Thoracic and Cardiovascular Surgeons Aiken Profl Bldg Suite 400 532 S Aiken Ave Pittsburgh PA 15232

FORDE, COLIN ARLINGTON, psychotherapist, educator; b. Georgetown, Guyana, Dec. 16, 1941; s. Bertie and Jennie (Bowen) F.; B.A., Fla. Internat. U., 1973; M.A., Columbia U., 1974, M.Ed., 1975, Ed.D., 1977; m. Jennifer Elizabeth Cheong; children—Pauline, Maria, Arlie. Internat. cons. The Psychol. Corp., N.Y.C., 1975—; vis. prof., research cons. Queens U., Ont., Can., 1976-78; prof. edn., dir. counseling and remedial services City U. N.Y., N.Y.C., 1978—. Mem. N.Y. Acad. Scis., Am. Personnel and Guidance Assn., Am. Council Anthropology and Edn., Caribbean Studies Assn., Assn. Measurement and Evaluation in Guidance, Assn. Mental Health Counselors. Office: 60 E 42d St New York City NY 10017 also 164-30 Hillside Ave Jamaica NY 11432

FORDYCE, DONALD MICHAEL, ins. co. exec.; b. N.Y.C., Apr. 26, 1936; s. James Paul and Margaret (Monahan) F.; B.A., U. Notre Dame, 1954-58; m. Ann Glascock, June 9, 1956; children—James H., Elizabeth A., Michael D. With U.S. Life Ins. Co., N.Y.C., 1954-58, Kidder, Peabody & Co., N.Y.C., 1958-60; with Manhattan Life Ins. Co., N.Y.C., 1965—, pres., 1973-78; pres. Manhattan Life Corp., chmn., chief exec. officer, 1978—. Trustee Greater N.Y. councils Boy Scouts Am. Trustee Gilmour Acad., 1962-67, mem. bd. govs., 1967-70. Mem. Am. Soc. C.L.U. (dir. 1977—), N.Y. Area Tng. Dirs. Assn. (pres. 1967), N.Y. Life Mgrs. Assn., N.Y. Life Underwriters Assn., N.Y. Bd. Trade (dir. 1973, mem. exec. com. 1973, pres. 1975), Assn. N.Y. State Life Ins. Cos. (dir. 1973, v.p. 1976, pres. 1977), C.L.U. Assn. (exec. v.p. N.Y. chpt. 1975, dir. 1967, pres. 1976), Young Pres.'s Orgn. (exec. com. Metro chpt.). Clubs: Wee Burn Country (Darien, Conn.); Bankers Club of P.R.; University (N.Y.C.); Sky. Home: Wheat Ln Darien CT 06820 Office: 111 W 57th St New York City NY 10019

FORELLE, CONRAD, constrn. exec.; b. N.Y.C., June 19, 1915; B.S. in Engring., 1936, M.C.E., 1939; m. Blanche Pavelka, May 5, 1940; children—John, Anne (Mrs. Richard McCarthy), Jane, Frank . Engr., Arthur A. Johnson Corp., N.Y.C., 1936-44; v.p. Brown & Matthews, engrs. and contractors, N.Y.C., 1944-50; pres. Schumacher & Forelle Inc., planning, engring., constrn., N.Y.C., 1950-76, chmn. bd., 1976—. Decorated knight Equestrian Order Holy Sepulchre Jerusalem. Mem. Nat. Soc. Profl. Engrs., Pres.'s Assn. Clubs: Nassau Country, Union League, Westhampton Country. Home: Muttontown NY Office: 560 Northern Blvd Great Neck NY 11021

FOREMAN, ARLENE RAINA, mut. funds and ins. cons.; b. Detroit, Aug. 19, 1945; d. Shay Edward and Lucille Helen (Mann) F.; A.A., George Washington U., 1965; Asst. to pres. Gene Galasso Assos., Inc., Washington, 1965-67; co-owner, ops. mgr. Efficient Bus. Service, Inc., Washington, 1967-70; saleswoman Mfrs. Life Ins. Co., Washington, 1971—, ManEquity, Inc., Washington, 1971—; ins. cons., Kensington, Md., 1971—; field cons. Manulife, Toronto, Ont., Can., 1978-79; guest lectr. in field, 1975—. Trustee B'nai B'rith Pension Plan.; mem. ins. and investment coms. B'nai B'rith Women, Inc. C.L.U. Mem. D.C. Life Underwriters Assn. (dir.), Nat. Assn. Women Bus. Owners (officer), Am. Soc. C.L.U.'s, D.C., Suburban Md. estate planning councils, Million Dollar Round Table, Leaders Club Washington, Gold Key Soc., Phi Sigma Sigma. Home: 3333 University Blvd W Kensington MD 20795 Office: 1140 Connecticut Ave Washington DC 20036 also 3333 University Blvd W Kensington MD 20795

FOREMAN, JOHN WICKS, mining engr.; b. Johnstown, Pa., Apr. 4, 1922; s. John Francis and Helen Maria (Wicks) F.; B.S. in Mining Engring., Pa. State U., 1948; m. Barbara Ann Gwin, May 9, 1953; children—John G., Diane L. Foreman Good, Stephen A., James P. Asst. mine foreman Bethlehem Mines Corp., Revloc, Pa., 1948-51; mgr. mines Garfield Refractories Co., Bolivar, Pa., 1951-55; mining engr. Cavalier Coal Co., Inc., Altoona, Pa., 1955-56, L.L.Gwin and Assos., Altoona, 1956-63, Gwin Engrs., Inc., Altoona, 1963-70; exec. v.p. Gwin, Dobson & Foremen, Inc., Altoona, 1971—; mining sch. coordinator St. Francis Coll., 1948-49. Mem. exec. bd. Penn's Woods council Boy Scouts Am., 1950—; pres. Altoona chpt. Full Gospel Businessmen's Fellowship Internat., 1976-77; v.p. Blair County Ministries, 1978; vice chmn. adv. bd. Altoona Campus Pa. State U. Served with USMC, 1943-46. Recipient Silver Beaver award Boy Scouts Am., 1963. Registered profl. engr., Pa., W.Va., Md., Ohio. Mem. Nat. Soc. Profl. Engrs., Am. Inst. Mining, Metall. and Petroleum Engrs., Moshannon Coal Mining Inst. (Miner of Yr. award 1976), Pa. Coal Mining Assn., Am. Legion. Presbyterian. Clubs: Rotary, Masons, Jesters (Altoona). Home: 229 E Fairview Ave Altoona PA 16601 Office: 2900 Fairway Dr Altoona PA 16602

FOREMAN, JOHN WILSON, III, appliance store owner; b. Pawtucket, R.I., Feb. 24, 1931; s. John Wilson and Doris Rose (McVay) F.; student Apprentice Sch. U.S. Govt., 1956, Western Ky. U., 1977; m. Edith Everett, Mar. 18, 1951; children—John Wilson IV, Stanley D., Thomas W. With Naval Air Sta., U.S. Govt., Norfolk, Va., 1951-67, Quonset Point, R.I., 1967-71; pres., owner appliance sales and service store, Wakefield, R.I., 1971—. Baptist. Clubs: Moose, Masons, Shriners. Home: 47 High St Wakefield RI 02879

FOREMAN, LAURA, dancer, video artist, choreographer, educator; b. Los Angeles; b. Michael and Gladys (Charnas) F.; student Mills Coll., Oakland, Calif., 1955-56; B.S. in Dance, U. Wis., 1959; m. John Everett Watts, Dec. 5, 1963. Mem. Ann Halprin Workshop Group, San Francisco, 1955, Marion Scott Dance Co., N.Y.C., Tamiris-Nagrin Dance Co., N.Y.C., 1962-64; dir. Laura Foreman Dance Theatre N.Y.C., 1966—; founder, dir. Choreographers Theatre, N.Y.C., 1964—; choreography instr. C.W. Post Coll., L.I., summer 1963; head dance dept. U. Bridgeport, 1960-63; head dance dept. Notre Dame Coll., 1963-70; mem. faculty, dir. dance dept. New Sch. Social Research, N.Y.C., 1967—; commd. dances Channel 31 TV, 1966, Nat. Council Chs., 1967, CAPS, 1970, 73, Choreographers Theatre, 1970-73, Nat. Endowment for Arts, 1971, 73; artist-in-residence Channel 13 TV Lab., N.Y.C., 1978; dance dir. bd. dirs. Composers & Choreographers Theatre, Inc. Cons., Woodstock Center, N.Y. State Council on Arts. Audition winner Contemporary Dance Prodns., Inc., N.Y.C., 1961. Mem. Nat. Dance Guild, Assn. Am. Dance Cos. (dir.). Choreography includes Memorials, Study, A Time, Perimeters, Epicycles, Margins, Signals, glass and shadows, Laura's Dance, songandance, Locrian, city of angels, Spaces (College I-IV), Performance, àdeux, Postludes, Bud, Monopoly, Program, Heirlooms, Entries. Home: 25 W 19th St New York City NY 10011 Office: New Sch Social Research 66 W 12th St New York City NY 10011

FOREMAN, THOMAS ALEXANDER, dentist; b. Tionesta, Pa., Oct. 24, 1930; s. James Aura and May (Lanson) F.; student Grove City Coll., 1948-50; B.S., Allegheny Coll., 1952; D.D.S. cum laude, U. Pitts., 1957, D.M.D., 1970; m. Dorothy Jean Wolf, June 12, 1953; children—Bonnie Jean, Julie Marie, Mary Aleta, Lloyd George. Gen. practice dentistry, Clarion, Pa., 1961—. Mem. Clarion Hosp. Assn., 1965—. Mem. exec. bd. Colonel Drake Council Boy Scouts Am., 1969-72, mem.-at-large French Creek council, 1972—, vice chmn. Indian Trails dist., 1971-73. Served with Dental Corps, USAF, 1957-61. Fellow Royal Soc. Health; mem. Am., Pa. (dir. 8th dist. 1964—, pres. 1974-76) dental Assns., Am. Acad. Gen. Dentistry, AMA (affiliate), Fauchard Acad. Dental Medicine, S.A.R., (pres. Capt. Samuel Brady chpt. 1970-71, 77-79), Soc. Mayflower Descs., Fedn. Dentaire Internationale, Phi Beta Phi, Omicron Kappa Upsilon, Delta Sigma Delta, Theta Chi. Presbyn. (pres. bd. trustees 1966-67, supt. Sunday sch. 1966-67). Mason (Shriner). Club: Oil City (Pa.) Figure Skating (chmn. tests 1969-70). Strattonville Sportsmen's. Home: 147 S 7th Ave Clarion PA 16214 Office: 832 Main St Clarion PA 16214

FOREST, GERARD MAURICE, engring. co. exec.; b. Brockton, Mass., July 8, 1934; s. Gerard John and Irene Alma (Mitchell) F.; student Northeastern U., 1960-62; m. Ann Marie Giglio, Nov. 20, 1954; children—Elizabeth, Cheryl, Jerri, Michelle, Denise, Ann, Gerard, Danielle. Supr. fire control system testing Bethlehem Steel Corp., Quincy, Mass., 1959-62; group supr., project head Vitro Labs., Silver Spring, Md., 1962-71, asst. v.p. ops., 1971-73; pres., dir. Cosmos, Inc., Rockville, Md., 1973—. Served with USAF, 1952-56. Mem. Am. Soc. Naval Engrs., Am. Legion. Republican. Roman Catholic. Clubs: Elk, Eagle. Patentee target apparatus and projectiles. Home: 3802 Greenly St Wheaton MD 20906 Office: 12320 Wilkins Ave 2d Floor Rockville MD 20852

FOREST, JOSEPH GERARD, food bus. exec.; b. Joliette, Que., Can., Oct. 3, 1914; s. Joseph Edward and Marie Diana (Croteau) F.; student Dale Carnegie Sch., 1946, Laval U., 1947-48; came to U.S., 1949, naturalized, 1955; m. Marie Anita Babin, Sept. 5, 1938; children—Jacques, Andre, Monique, Robert, Charles. Owner, Forest & Feeres, elec. appliances, Joliette, 1935-40; machinist war plant, Montreal, Que., 1940-44; salesman asst. sales mgr. Internat. Stock Food Co., Ltd., Toronto, 1944-49; founder Internat. Stock Food Corp., Waverly, N.Y., 1949—, pres., 1949—, chmn. bd., 1960—, treas., 1970—; dir. Internat. Stock Food Co., Ltd., Valley Econ. Devel. Assn. Mem. Am. Inst. Mgmt., Am. Mgmt. Assn. Roman Catholic. Clubs: K.C., Elks. Inventor in field. Home: 303 Chemung St Waverly NY 14892 Office: 533 Broad St Waverly NY 14892

FORESTER, WAYNE ANDREW, assn. exec.; b. Quincy, Mass., Nov. 12, 1932; s. Toivo Andrew and Rose A. (Dolan) Laitinen; A.B., Harvard U., 1954, postgrad. Div. Sch., 1955-57; M.Ed., Mass. State Coll., 1959; postgrad. U. Oreg., 1966-69; m. Loreen Marie Bettencourt, Sept. 5, 1955 (dec. Aug. 1961); 1 dau., Loreen Marie; m. 2d, Mary V. Crowley, June 29, 1966; children—Scott, Alyson. Exec. sec. Am. Assn. Criminology, 1953—; mem. nat. adv. council Am. Acad. Achievement, 1961—; adviser, cons. Nat. Police Officers Assn. Am., 1963-64, Am. Fedn. Police, 1968—, Inst. Applied Psychotherapy, 1970—; fellow Study Center for Criminology and Forensic Medicine, Belgium; hon. prof. Central Police Coll., Republic China; fellow Acad. Univ. Research Studies; mem. nat. voter adv. bd. Am. Security Council, 1972—. Served with USMCR, 1951-59. Named hon. atty. gen. of La., hon. citizen of Tex., hon. Ky. col.; decorated knight comdr. Mil. Order St. Bridget (Sweden); hon. dean Netherlands Laureate Arts; grand cross La Fundacion Internacional Eloy Alfaro (Panama); grand cross Ordre de la Rose et de la Croix de Jerusalem, Fraternité Chevaleresque Internationale des Templiers (Tunisia); grand cross Order St. John Jerusalem (Knights of Malta), Companion of Merit, Chevaliers de la Cross de Lorraine (France), croix patriar-cale Apotre St. Pierre (France), Gold medal Roma Accademia per le Arti, Lettere, Scienze, Cultura, others. Fellow Columbus Assn. Internat. Inst. Culture and Assistance (gold medal), Internat. Criminal Justice Assn., AAAS, Am. Psychotherapy Assn., Royal Soc. Arts, Royal Asiatic Soc.; mem. Internat. Criminology Soc., Acad. Criminal Justice Scis., Assn. Humanistic Psychology, Am. Soc. Group Psychotherapy, Am. Ednl. Research Assn., Royal Canadian Inst., Am. Psychol. Assn., Soc. Psychol. Study Social Issues, AAUP, U.S. Naval Inst., Marine Corps League, Internat. Probation Officers Assn. (founding officer), Am. Judicature Soc., Medico-Legal Soc., Forensic Sci. Soc., Inst. Study and Treatment Delinquency, Execs. Club, Scriblerus Soc. of 1713 (hon.), Hakluyt Soc., Royal Central Asian Soc., Royal African Soc., Nat. Trust for Scotland, Internat. Inst.

Study and Devel. Human Relations (hon. internat. v.p.), Newcomen Soc., 42d Royal Highland Regt. of 1776, Psychosynthesis Found., Am. Acad. Profl. Law Enforcement, Am. Assn. Clin. Counselors, others. Club: Harvard Faculty. Author: Elements of Criminology, 1953; editor The Am. Criminologist, 1954—; adv. editor various biog. publs. and profl. jours. Home: 492 Careswell St Marshfield MA 02050 Office: Box 1115 North Marshfield MA 02059

FORGACS, JOSEPH, mycotoxicologist; b. Nokomis, Ill., Mar. 20, 1917; s. John and Elizabeth (Hallas) F.; B.S., U. Ill., 1940, M.S., 1942, Ph.D., 1944; m. Lillian Pearl Little, June 1, 1945; children—Theresa Maria, Joseph Alan, Lawrence David, Paul Axel, Lillian Pearl Maria. Dir. mycotoxicoses research Fort Detrick, Frederick, Md., 1944-54; sr. research fellow Am. Cyanamid Corp., Pearl River, N.Y., 1954-57; dir. lab. Spring Valley (N.Y.) Hosp., 1957-61; mycotoxicologist, staff microbiologist Good Samaritan Hosp., Suffern, N.Y., 1961-69; dir. clin. microbiology Ramapo Gen. Hosp. and Automated Biochem. Labs., Spring Valley, 1969—. Cons. mycotoxicologist Agrl. Research Service, U.S. Dept. Agr., food and feed industries, 1957—; cons. microbiologist N.Y. State Dept. Mental Hygiene, Letchworth Village, Thiells, 1973—. Served with AUS, 1944-46. Diplomate Am. Acad. Microbiology. Fellow Am. Acad. Microbiology, Inst. Food Technologists, AAAS; mem. N.Y. Acad. Scis., Am. Inst. Biol. Scis., N.Y. Med. Mycology Soc., Phi Sigma, Sigma Xi. Contbr. articles to profl. jours. Patentee in field. Home: 302 N Highland Ave Pearl River NY 10965 Office: Automated Biochem Labs Spring Valley NY 10977

FORGAN, JAMES RUSSELL, investment cons.; b. Lake Forest, Ill., Aug. 4, 1930; s. James Russell and Ada (Johnson) F.; grad. St. Mark's Sch., 1948; A.B., Princeton, 1952. Vice pres. P.K. Macker & Co., N.Y.C., 1957-58; mgr. fgn. dept. W.C. Langley & Co., N.Y.C., 1958-62; asso. broker firm Carlisle-DeCoppet & Co., N.Y.C., 1962-72; partner firm Hamershlag Borg & Co., N.Y.C., 1972; independent broker N.Y. Stock Exchange, 1973-77; asso. P.C.P., Ltd., London, Eng., 1978—. Served to 1st lt. AUS, 1952-54. Clubs: Union, Links, Racquet and Tennis, Pilgrims of the United States (N.Y.C.); Southampton, Meadow, Bathing Corporation of Southampton (N.Y.); White's (London, Eng.). Home: 12 Charles St London W1 England Office: PCP Ltd 14 Pall Mall London SW1 England

FORGET, TIMOTHY PAUL, pub. co. exec.; b. Chgo., Nov. 16, 1920; s. Timothy Andre and Florence (Jockel) F.; student Rochester Bus. Inst., 1946-47, U. Rochester, 1947-50; m. Marie Victoria Beaulieu, May 19, 1945; children—Timothy, Mark, Cheryl, Jonathan, Christopher, Paul. With Consol. Vultee, San Diego, 1940-43, 44-46; asst. data processing mgr. Security Trust Co., Rochester, N.Y., 1946-50; v.p. Data Base Marketing div. Lawyers Coop. Pub. Co., Rochester, 1950—, also dir., mem. exec. com. Mem. adv. bd. Rochester Inst. Technology Computer Sci.; pres. Williamson Central Sch. Bd., 1975-78. Served with USNR, 1943-44. Mem. Data Processing Mgmt. Assn. (past dir.). Home: 44 Menlo Pl Rochester NY 14620 Office: 50 Broad St Rochester NY 14614

FORGETT, HEIDI E. KOBER (MRS. VALMORE JOSEPH FORGETT, JR.), corp. exec.; b. Treuberg, Germany, Feb. 27, 1939; d. Otto and Gertrud (Hearich) Kober; student Columbia Union Coll., 1959-60, Fairleigh Dickinson U., 1960-62; m. Valmore Joseph Forgett, Jr., Apr. 28, 1963; children—Diana Lynn, Susan Lee, Valmore Joseph III. Came to U.S., 1954, naturalized, 1959. Corp. sec., treas. Service Armament Co., Ridgefield, N.J., 1959—, Navy Arms Co., Inc., Ridgefield, 1960—, Gt. Am. Arms Corp., Ridgefield, 1960—, Collectors' Arms, Inc., Ridgefield, 1964—; dir. Ebbs-Forgett Trading Co. Ltd., Birmingham, Eng. Mem. Ohio Gun Collectors Assn. Republican. Home: Eagle's Roost 60 Pinecrest Dr Woodcliff Lake NJ 07675 also Cannon Hill Farm Box 311B Sussex NJ 07641 Office: 689 Bergen Blvd Ridgefield NJ 07657

FORK, DONALD JOSEPH, educator; b. Beaver Falls, Pa., May 27, 1938; s. Herman Peter and Eleanor Antoinette (Mushinski) F.; M.A., Immaculate Heart Coll., Los Angeles, 1970; M.A., Calif. State U., 1970; Ph.D., U. Pitts., 1974; m. Nadine Lois Ensminger, Aug. 5, 1967; children—Eric, Bryan. Tchr., Foothill High Sch., Pasadena, Calif., 1964-67; part-time instr. Pasadena City Coll., 1964-66; resource specialist Woodrow Wilson Jr. High Sch., Pasadena, 1967-70; bus. mgr. Calif. Sch. Libraries, assn. publ., 1969-70; mem. faculty Temple U., Phila., 1972—, chmn. dept. ednl. media, 1977—; cons. in field. Served with USAF (Res.), 1961-67. HEA Title II-B fellow, 1970-73. Mem. Am. Ednl. Research Assn., ALA, Assn. Coll. and Research Libraries, Assn. Ednl. Communications and Tech., Internat. Visual Literacy Assn. (chmn. task force theoretical constructs of visual literacy 1976—, v.p. 1978—), Internat. Assn. Sch. Librarianship (exec. com., editor newsletter). Office: Dept Ednl Media Coll Edn Temple Univ Philadelphia PA 19122

FORK, RICHARD LYNN, physicist; b. Dearborn, Mich., Sept. 1, 1935; s. Lynn Kenneth and Catherine Elizabeth (Harsch) F.; B.S., Principia Coll., 1957; Ph.D., Mass. Inst. Tech., 1962; m. Patricia Alice Green, Aug. 17, 1957 (div. Aug. 1969); children—Carl Richard, Heather Elizabeth, David Kirtland; m. 2d, Shirley June Dowie, July 3, 1971; 1 dau., Katherine Lynne. Research physicist Bell Labs., Murray Hill, N.J., 1962-69, Holmdel, N.J., 1969—. Fellow Am. Phys. Soc.; mem. Optical Soc. Am. Home: 191 Holland Rd Middletown NJ 07748 Office: Room 4D-417 Bell Labs Holmdel NJ 07733

FORLANO, ROBERT JOSE, ceramic engr.; b. Buenos Aires, Argentina, Nov. 5, 1928; s. Bartolome and Maria Clara (Rizzo) F.; B.S., U. Buenos Aires, 1953; M.S., U. Ill., 1962, Ph.D., 1965; m. Ana Clorinda Repetto, Dec. 16, 1968; children—Bartholomew Francis, William Henry. Came to U.S., 1957, naturalized, 1964. Research asso. Argonne (Ill.) Nat. Lab., 1963-65; with Knolls Atom Power Lab., Gen. Electric Co., Schenectady, 1965—, mgr., 1975—. Mem. Am. Ceramic Soc., Am. Soc. Metals, Sigma Xi. Home: 15 Evergreen Blvd Scotia NY 12302 Office: 1 River Rd Schenectady NY 12301

FORMA, WARREN, film maker, author; b. N.Y.C., Nov. 27, 1923; s. David and Rosalind (Rosenblum) F.; student N.Y. U., 1941, 46; m. Belle Rosenthal, Apr. 6, 1946; children—Carol Forma Bickford, Thomas, Suzanne Forma Collins. Founder, Forma Art Assos., films and books, N.Y.C., 1948—; films include: 5 British Sculptors, 1965; Images of Leonard Baskin, 1968; Weapons of Gordon Parks, 1969; Life, Liberty and the Pursuit of Happiness, 1976; Frontier America, 1977; books include: (novel) The Falling Man, 1973; (non-fiction) 5 British Sculptors Work and Talk, 1965, They Were Ragtime, 1976. Served to capt. USAAF, 1942-45. Decorated D.F.C. with 13 oak leaf clusters, Purple Heart, others. Home: 433 Claflin Ave Mamaroneck NY 10543 Office: 141 E 55th St New York City NY 10022

FORMAN, DONALD WALTER, banker; b. Yonkers, N.Y., June 16, 1939; s. William Edward and Kate Dorothy (Mills) F.; student Westchester Community Coll., 1962-64, U. Wis., 1972-74; 1 son, Donald Walter. Trainee, Nat. Bank Westchester, White Plains, N.Y., 1962-64; cost analyst County Trust Co. White Plains, 1964-69; asst. comptroller State Nat. Bank Conn., Briddgeport, Conn., 1969-73; v.p., comptroller Lafayette Bank & Trust Co., Bridgeport, 1973—; cons. Small Constrn., Interconnect Telephone Co.; Project chmn. Jr. Achievement; sponsor North Branford (Conn.) Youth Hockey League. Served with U.S. Army, 1959-60. Recipient United Way Vol. award, March of Dimes Sponsor award. Mem. Bank Adminstrn. Inst., Conn. (ops. com.), Suburban bankers assns., Bridgeport Clearing House Assn. (dir.), Alumni Assn., Internat. Game Fish Assn., Nat. Marine Fisheries Assn. (coop. tagging program), Am. Littoral Soc., Branford Jaycees (treas., state dir.). Republican. Presbyterian. Clubs: Milford Striped Bass, Guilford Indoor Shooting Range, John Dean Coin, Turtle, Holiday Universal. Home: 26 Orange Ave Milford CT 06460 Office: 345 State St Bridgeport CT 06601

FORMAN, EDGAR ROSS, mech. engr.; b. Camden, N.J., Oct 5, 1923; s. Edgar Charles and Annie (Baragwanath) F.; B.M.E., Drexel Inst., 1950, M.B.A., 1953; m. Alma Kuppinger, Sept. 26, 1953; children—Bruce, Dianne. Project engr. Penn Instrument div. Burgess Manning Co., Phila., 1950-55; application engr. Moore Products Co., Phila., 1955-59; chief instrument engr. Catalytic Co., Phila., 1959-67, mgr. mgmt. systems dept., 1967-71; supervising instrument and controls engr. United Engrs. & Constructors, Inc. Phila., 1971-78; mgr. instrument dept. Day & Zimmermann, Inc., Phila., 1978—. Guest lectr. U.S. Naval Acad., Pa. State U., Sun Oil Co., U. Pa. Engrs. Club Phila., U. Del., Drexel U. Active Boy Scouts Am. Served with AUS, 1944-46. Fellow Instrument Soc. Am. (chmn. edn. commn.), Phila. Jr. C. of C., Am. Soc. Mech. Engrs., Nat. Soc. Profl. Engrs., Alpha Phi Omega (pres.), Pi Tau Sigma, Pi Nu Epsilon. Contbr. articles in field to tech. jours. Home: 702 Avondale Rd Erdenheim PA 19118 Office: Day & Zimmermann Inc 1818 Market St Philadelphia PA 19103

FORMAN, ELI MICHAEL SIMON, govt. ofcl., urban psychologist; b. Bklyn., Nov. 28, 1940; s. Charles B. and Shifra (Schifrin) F.; B.H.L., Hebrew Litt. B.A. in Psychology, Yeshiva U., 1962; M.S.Ed. in Clin. Sch. Psychology, Coll. City N.Y., 1965; profl. diploma in urban edn. Fordham U., 1973, Ph.D., 1975; postgrad. Am. Inst. Psychotherapy and Psychoanalysis, 1976—; m. Eleanor Gross, Mar. 31, 1968; children—Michael, Eliza-Greigh, Elan. Part-time psychotherapist, marital and family therapist Bergen Center Psychol. Services, Tenafly, N.J., 1965—; asst. dir. manpower, supervising psychologist counseling and testing Morrisania Community Corp., Bronx, N.Y., 1966-68; program analyst OEO, N.Y.C., 1968-69; asst. to dir. equal opportunity HUD N.Y. Area Office, N.Y.C., 1969—; counseling psychol. cons. N.J. Community Action Tng. Inst., Trenton, 1967; teaching intern in schs., urban minorities Fordham U., summer 1973. Named Community Leader N.Y.C. Div. Human Rights, 1966. Certified sch. psychologist, N.Y., N.J.; licensed marriage counselor, N.J. Mem. Urban Edn. Doctoral Assn. (exec. sec.), Am. Personnel and Guidance Assn., Am. Assn. Psychoednl. Therapists (N.J. chpt.), Am. Assn. Marriage and Family Counselors, Am. Assn. Sex Educators and Therapists (certified), Am., Eastern psychol. assns., Phi Delta Kappa. Democrat. Home: 280 Ninth Ave Apt 8-F New York City NY 10001 Office: HUD 666 Fifth Ave New York City NY 10019

FORMAN, H(ENRY) CHANDLEE, architect, educator; b. N.Y.C.; s. Horace Baker, Jr. and Elizabeth (Chandlee) F.; A.B., Princeton U., 1926; M.Arch., U. Pa., 1931, Ph.D. in Fine Arts, 1942; m. Caroline Biddle Lippincott, Sept. 28, 1929 (dec. June 1975); children—Elizabeth Forman Harrell, Richard Townsend Turner, Lawrence Thorne; m. 2d, Rebecca Anthony Russell, May 26, 1978. Pvt. practice architecture as H. Chandlee Forman, Easton, Md., 1931-35, 52-78; chief architect Jamestown (Va.) Archaeol. Project, 1935-36; editor nat. records Historic Am. Bldgs. Survey, Washington 1936-37; lectr. fine arts Haverford Coll., 1937-38; instr. art Rutgers U., 1939-40; lectr. history art U. Pa., 1940-41; Catherine L. Comer prof. fine arts Wesleyan Coll. Ga., 1941-45; prof. art, head dept. Agnes Scott Coll., 1945-52; cons. architect Ga. Hist. Commn., 1952-60; adviser Md. St. Mary's City Commn., 1965-69; mem. Md. Archaeol. Commn., 1968-77, chmn., 1973-74; sec. bd. dirs. Soc. Preservation Md. Antiquities, 1952-58; mem. corp. bd. Haverford Coll., 1975—; lectr. throughout world for State Dept., 1964; art works exhibited Library of Congress, Washington, Balt. Mus. Art, Art Inst. Chgo., U. Pa., others. Recipient Calvert prize for hist. preservation State of Md., 1976; George Barnard White prize Princeton U., 1926; Carnegie Found. fellow creative painting, 1948. Fellow Explorers, AIA (charter mem.; 1st v.p. Chesapeake Bay chpt. 1965, exec. com. Balt. chpt. 1955-56); mem. Talbot County (Md.) Hist. Soc. (dir., co-organizer, librarian, 1st curator), Soc. Colonial Wars, Princeton Alumni Assn. Eastern Shore (pres. 1960-61, 70-72, 77—), Townsend Soc. Am. (hon.), Md. Hist. Soc. (life), Nantucket Garden Club (hon.). Author, editor numerous books, including: Early Manor and Plantation Houses of Maryland, 1934; Jamestown and St. Mary's, Buried Cities of Romance, 1938; The Architecture of the Old South, The Medieval Style, 1948; Virginia Architecture in the 17th Century, 1957; Early Nantucket and Its Whale Houses, 1966; Old Buildings, Gardens and Furniture in Tidewater Maryland, 1967; The Virginia Eastern Shore and its British Origins, 1975. Donor H. Chandlee Forman Nature Preserve to Nantucket Maria Mitchell Assn., 1973. Address: PO Box 807 Easton MD 21601

FORMAN, HOWARD IRVING, lawyer, govt. ofcl.; b. Phila., Jan. 12, 1917; s. Jacob and Dora (Moses) F.; B.S. in Chemistry, St. Joseph's Coll., 1937; LL.B., Temple U., 1944; M.A., U. Pa., 1949, Ph.D., 1955; m. Ada Pressman, Aug. 2, 1938; children—Kenneth J., Harvey R. Research chemist Frankford Arsenal, Dept. Army, Phila., 1940-44, patent atty., 1944-46, chief patents br., 1946-56; admitted to D.C. bar, 1945, Pa. bar, 1973; patent atty. Rohm and Haas Co., Phila., 1956-66, trademark counsel, 1966-76; dep. asst. sec. U.S. Dept. of Commerce, 1976—; counsel Weiser, Stapler & Spivak, Phila., 1974-76; sec., dir. Rohm & Haas Asia, Inc., 1973-76; v.p., gen. counsel, dir. Brilliant Internat., Inc., Bala-Cynwyd, Pa., 1974—; sec., dir. Far East Chem. Services, Inc., Wilmington, Del., 1973-76, Rohm and Haas GmbH (Zug), 1975-76. Bd. dirs. Lower Moreland Twp. Sch. Bd., Montgomery County, Pa., 1969-75; bd. dirs. Eastern Montgomery County Vocational-Tech. Sch., 1969-75, sec., 1970. Recipient Robert J. Painter Meml. award for meritorious service in field of Standardization Standards Engrs. Soc./ASTM, 1978. Fellow Am. Inst. Chemists; mem. Am., Fed., Phila. (sec. com. on jurimetrics, tech. and patents 1973-74) bar assns., Am. (bd. mgrs. 1970-73), Phila. (pres. 1964-66) patent law assns., Nat. Council Patent Law Assns. (chmn. 1967-68), Am. Chem. Soc., ASTM, Am. Nat. Standards Inst. (dir. 1977—, chmn. interagy. commn. on standards policy 1976—), Sci. Research Soc. Am., AAAS, Licensing Execs. Soc., Sigma Xi. Author: Inventions, Patents and Related Matters, 1957; Patents-Their Ownership and Administration by the U.S. Government, 1957. Editor: Patents, Research and Management, 1961; The Law of Chemical, Metallurgical and Pharmaceutical Patents, 1967. Contbr. to publs. in field. Home: 1033 Corn Crib Dr Huntingdon Valley PA 19006 Office: US Dept Commerce Washington DC 20230

FORMAN, JOSEPH CHARLES, assn. exec.; b. Chgo., Dec. 22, 1931; s. Joseph O. and Marie (Smith) F.; S.B., Mass. Inst. Tech., 1953; M.S., Northwestern U., 1957, Ph.D., 1960; m. Ursula Diane Weston, July 22, 1953; children—Stephen Charles, Diane Brigitte, Mary Erika. Trainee in chem. engring. Dow Chem. Co., Midland, Mich., 1953-54; sr. chem. engr. Abbott Labs., North Chicago, Ill., 1956-63, group leader, 1963-68, sect. mgr., also project mgr. 1968-74, ops. mgr. procurement, 1974-75, dir. mfg. ops., 1975-77, mgr. corporate planning, 1977; asso. exec. dir. Am. Inst. Chem. Engrs., N.Y.C., 1977-78, exec. dir., sec., pub., 1978—; cons. in field; accreditation insp. chem. engring. curricula, 1967—. Mem. ednl. council Mass. Inst. Tech., 1961-74, 78—; mem. Lake Bluff (Ill.) Bd. Edn., 1967-73, pres., 1971-73; pres. Lake County (Ill.) Sch. Bd. Assn., 1969-71; mem. Lake Bluff Plan Commn., 1973-77, chmn., 1976-77. Served with USAF, 1954-56. Registered profl. engr., Ill. Fellow Am. Inst. Chem. Engrs.; mem. Am. Chem. Soc., Am. Soc. Assn. Execs., Council Engring. and Sci. Soc. Execs., Chemists Club, Sigma Xi, Tau Beta Pi, Phi Lambda Upsilon, Alpha Tau Omega. Club: Lake Bluff Yacht. Patentee in field; contbr. articles to tech. jours. Home: 77 Stanton Rd Darien CT 06820 Office: Am Inst Chem Engrs 345 E 47th St New York City NY 10017

FORMAN, STANLEY JOSEPH, photographer; b. Winthrop, Mass., July 10, 1945; s. David and Gertrude (Levy) F.; student Franklin Inst., Boston, 1965-66. Campaign photographer Sen. Edward Brooke, Mass., 1966; news photographer Boston Record Am. (name now Boston Herald Am.), 1966—. Recipient Golden Plate award Am. Acad. Achievement; World Press Photo award, 1976; Pulitzer prizes, 1976, 77; named Photographer of Year region 1 Nat. Press Photographers Am., 1973. Mem. Boston Press Photographers Assn. (v.p., Best of Show 1976, 77), Nat. Headliners (Spot News Photography award 1976-77). Sigma Delta Chi. Office: Boston Herald American Hearst Corp 300 Harrison Ave Boston MA 02106*

FORMAN, STUART IRVING, psychologist; b. Boston, Nov. 20, 1947; s. Isaac and Jeanette (Levin) F.; B.S., U. Mass., 1968; M.Ed., Springfield Coll., 1971; m. Deborah Jean Tomchik, Jan. 6, 1973; children—Adam Michael, Seth Gabriel. Psychiat. social worker Northampton (Mass.) State Hosp., 1968-69; mental health cons. Lakes Region Mental Health Center, Laconia, N.H., 1969-70; dir. Office Intergroup Relations, City of Springfield, Mass., 1971-74; prin. psychologist, dir. alcohol rehab. unit Rutland Heights Hosp., Rutland, Mass., 1975—; teaching asst. Springfield Coll., 1971, instr. intergroup relations, 1973-74. Municipal chmn. Springfield United Way Campaign, 1973-74; brown belt instr. Kenpo Karate, 1975—. Served with USAF Res., 1965-67. Recipient USAF-Arnold Air Soc. Distinguished Service award, 1967. Mem. Am. Personnel and Guidance Assn., Am. Pub. Health Assn., Am. Rehab. Counseling Assn., Psi Chi. Democrat. Jewish. Office: Rutland Heights Hosp Rutland MA 01543

FORMAN, YALE, cons. color and design; b. N.Y.C., Mar. 1, 1921; s. Harry A. and Anna E. (Friedman) F.; student U. Mich., 1938-40; A.B., U. Wis., 1942; m. Frances Selman; 1 dau., Katherine. Pres., Yale Forman Designs Inc., N.Y.C., 1951—; sec. Color Mktg. Group, N.Y.C., 1974-75, v.p., 1975-76, pres., 1976—. Served with Signal Corps. AUS, 1942-46; PTO. Recipient AID Internat. Design award for floor coverings, 1969. Mem. Nat. Soc. Decorative Design (v.p. 1961-63), Can. Soc. Color, Am. Soc. Metals, Inter-Soc. Color Council, Am. Crafts Council, Am. Assn. Textile Chemists and Colorists (asso.), Am. Soc. Interior Designers (design affiliate). Jewish religion. Contbr. articles to profl. publs. Address: 11 Riverside Dr New York City NY 10023

FORNELLI, FRANCIS JOSEPH, lawyer; b. Sharon, Pa., Aug. 1, 1941; s. Louis N. and Quin D. (Ruscio) F.; A.B. magna cum laude, U. Notre Dame, 1963; J.D. (Root-Tilden scholar), N.Y.U., 1966; m. Joann Lyden, June 27, 1970; children—Jill Ann, Nicholas John. Admitted to Pa. bar, 1966; present partner firm Cusick, Madden, Joyce and McKay, Sharon, Pa., 1966—. Bd. dirs. Shenango Valley Home for sr. Citizens, 1971—; bd. dirs. Mercer County Drug Council, 1969—, 1st v.p., 1975—; bd. dirs. N.W. Legal Services, 1977—, also 1st v.p.; mem. exec. com. Mercer County Democratic Party, 1971; mem. St. Bartholomew's Parish Council; mem. Christian Assos. of Shenango Valley; mem. Erie Diocese Review Bd., Diocesan Dept. Community Action. Dougherty Found. grantee, 1964. Mem. Am., Pa., Mercer County (chmn. com. on criminal rules 1977—) bar assns., Pa. Trial Lawyers Assn., Alumni Assn. U. Notre Dame, Shenango Valley C. of C., Sharpsville High Sch. Alumni Assn. (past trustee). Club: K.C. Home: 190 Todd Ave Sharon PA 16146 Office: 1st Fed Bldg Sharon PA 16146

FORONDA, ELENA ISABEL, educator; b. N.Y.C., Jan. 15, 1947; d. Severino Deliso and LaVerne (Ibanez) Foronda; B.S. in Music, Hunter Coll., City U. N.Y., 1969, M.A. in Music Edn., 1971. Tchr. vocal music N.Y.C. Pub. Sch. System, 1970—; asst. dir. tchr. placement Hunter Coll., City U. N.Y. summers 1971-72. Sponsor children in P.I., World Vision Internat. Dist. winner Nat. Piano Playing Auditions, 1965; recipient N.Y. State permanent certification Dept. Edn., 1971. Mem. Music Educators Nat. Conf., N.Y. State Sch. Music Assn., Amateur Chamber Players (Vienna, Va.), Internat. Platform Assn., Nat., N.Y., Manhattan women's polit. caucuses. Democrat. Baptist. Mem. choirs Hunter Coll., 1968-69, 71. Office: NYC Bd Edn East NY Vocat/Tech High Sch 1 Wells St Brooklyn NY 11208*

FORREST, HERBERT EMERSON, lawyer; b. N.Y.C., Sept. 20, 1923; s. Jacob K. and Rose (Fried) F.; B.A., George Washington U., 1948, J.D., 1952; student Coll. City N.Y., 1941, Ohio U., 1943-44; m. Marilyn Lefsky, Jan. 12, 1952; children—Glenn Clifford, Andrew Matthew. Admitted to Va., D.C. bars, 1952, Md. bar, 1959; law clk. Bolitha J. Laws, Chief Judge U.S. Dist. Ct., Washington, 1952-55; practiced in Washington, 1952—; mem. firm Welch & Morgan, 1955-65, Steptoe & Johnson, 1965—; past chmn. D.C. Criminal Justice Act Adv. Bd.; sec. com. admissions and grievances U.S. Ct. Appeals; mem. Title I audit hearing bd. HEW; plate printer Bur. Engraving and Printing, 1942-43, 46-52. Past pres. Whittier Woods PTA. Served with AUS, 1943-46. Mem. George Washington Law Assn., Am. Judicature Soc., Am. (chmn. com. on agy. rule making, past mem. council sect. adminstrv. law, chmn. com. ann. reports), Va. State, Fed., Fed. Commn. (chmn. legal aid com., past sec.; past book editor Jour.) bar assns., Bar Assn. D.C. (past sec., chmn. com. on ct. appointments of counsel, chmn. legal aid com., lawyer referral service com., domestic relations com.), Am. Arbitration Assn. (comml. panel), NAM (telecommunications com.), Washington Council Lawyers, Legal Aid and Pub. Defender Assn., D.C. Unified Bar (bd. govs., chmn. com. on employment discrimination complaint service, chmn. task force on services to pub.), Computer Law Assn., Order of Coif, Phi Beta Kappa, Pi Gamma Mu, Artus, Phi Eta Sigma, Phi Delta Phi. Democrat. Mem. B'nai Brith. Past mem. bd. advisers Duke Law Jour.; contbr. articles to profl. jours. Home: 8706 Bellwood Rd Bethesda MD 20034 Office: 1250 Connecticut Ave Washington DC 20036

FORREST, VIRGINIA OGDEN RANSON (MRS. WILBUR STUDLEY FORREST), civic leader; b. Balt., June 24, 1896; d. Henry Warfield and Nannie Deaver (Cooper) Ranson; ed. Calvert Sch., Arundell Sch.; m. Frederick Beasley Williamson, Jr., July 4, 1917 (dec. July 1957); children—Virginia Williamson Hutton, Beverley Williamson Musser, Frederick Beasley III; m. 2d, Wilbur Studley Forrest, Apr. 20, 1960 (dec. Mar. 1977). Dir., Goodall Rubber Co., hon. dir., 1973—. Pres. Jr. League, Elizabeth, N.J., 1924-26, hon. mem., 1944; mem. hostess com. Franklin Inst., Phila., 1941; mem. N.J. Recreation Soc., Elizabeth, 1934-35, rep. N.J. to nat. conv., Chgo., 1935; chmn. New Hope (Pa.) chpt. A.R.C., 1939-43, head flood disaster chpt., 1955, chmn. home service, 1943-45; hon. v.p. New Hope Art Assos., 1940; mem. adv. com. Jonathan Dickinson State Park, Martin County, Fla., 1970—; organizer adviser Bucks

County Conservation Alliance, Martin County Conservation Alliance, 1966-74; bd. dirs. Honey Hollow Watershed Assn., 1969—, Soc. Prevention Cruelty Children Family Welfare Bd., Elizabeth, 1928, YWCA, Elizabeth, 1928, Abington (Pa.) Meml. Hosp. Women's Bd., 1941, Vis. Nurse Assn., New Hope, 1941-49; bd. dirs., 2d v.p. Garden Club, Stuart, Fla., 1951-60; trustee Egnolf Day Nursery, Elizabeth, 1923-36; trustee Holmquist Sch. for Girls, New Hope, Martin County Pub. Library, Stuart, 1958-61; bd. dirs. Free Pub. Library Elizabeth, 1926-39, sec., 1927-36; bd. dirs. Keep Fla. Beautiful Com. Recipient award Fla. Fedn. Garden Clubs, 1961; Gov.'s gold medal conservation award (1st woman recipient), 1961; Gov. Kirk's Conservation award, 1970; honoree Martin County Audubon Soc., 1976; named hon. Ky. Col., 1978. Mem. Fla. (recipient award 1960, chmn. Bald Eagle project 1959—, mem. wild life com., 1959—, v.p. 1962-69, hon. v.p. 1970—), Martin County (dir. 1957-78, dir. emeritus, 1978—, chmn. exec. com. 1973-74), Bucks County (dir., adviser, citation for conservation, 1972) Audubon socs., New Hope Hist. Soc. (dir. 1959-60, 67—), Fla. Fedn. Garden Clubs (hon. life), Colonial Dames N.J., Woman Fly Fishers Am. Clubs: Mt. Vernon (Balt.); Hartwood (Monticello, N.Y.); Martin County Anglers (dir. 1966—); L.I. (Eastport, N.Y.). Home: The Birches RD 2 New Hope PA 18938

FORSCHER, FREDERICK, cons.; b. Vienna, Austria, May 20, 1918; s. Morris and Cornelia (Berger) F.; B.S.E., Princeton, 1947, M.S., 1947; Ph.D., Columbia, 1953; m. Mia Weiner, Jan. 1, 1944; children—Carri (Mrs. Stewart Fogel), Joan Ellen, Steffi (Mrs. Bernhard Behrend). Instr., Columbia, 1947-52; supr. mech. metallurgy, atomic power div. Westinghouse Electric Corp., Pitts., 1952-57, mgr. advanced fuel nuclear fuel div., 1967-71; v.p. Nuclear Materials and Equipment Corp., Apollo, Pa., 1957-67; pres. Energy Mgmt. Consultants, Inc., Pitts., 1971—. Served with AUS, 1941-46. Mem. Am. Nuclear Soc., ASME, Am. Inst. Mining, Metall. and Petroleum Engrs., Am. Soc. Metals, ASTM, Am. Nat. Standards Inst., Inst. Nuclear Materials Mgmt., Sigma Xi. Home: 6580 Beacon St Pittsburgh PA 15217

FORSHAW, WILLIAM SHERLOCK, librarian; b. N.Y.C., Jan. 28, 1914; s. William Henry and Mary Ellen (Beierstedt) F.; B.A., Columbia, 1934, M.L.S., 1958; m. Alberta Louise Halley, June 29, 1963. Editorial asst. Time, Inc., N.Y.C., 1938-41; retail store mgr. Doubleday & Co., N.Y.C., 1946-56; librarian Enoch Pratt Free Library, Balt., 1958—; cons. rare books. Served to lt. comdr. USNR, 1942-46. Mem. ALA, Theatre Library Assn. (dir.), Am. Soc. Indexers. Club: Columbia College (N.Y.C.). Home: 2624 St Paul St Baltimore MD 21218*

FORSTCHEN, JOHN JOSEPH, chemist; b. N.Y.C., Sept. 9, 1916; s. Emil and Anna (Dennis) F.; B.S., Seton Hall U., 1949, M.B.A., 1965; m. Dorothy E. Semet, June 14, 1942; children—Ann Carole, John, William. Lab. asst. Pub. Service Electric Gas Co., Harrison, N.J., 1936-41; lab. technician Harrison Gas Plant, 1946-56; plant chemist Trenton Gas Plant, 1956-63; plant chemist Trenton and Camden Gas Plants (N.J.), 1963—; instr. Fairleigh Dickinson U., 1965-72; asst. prof. Mercer County Community Coll., 1970-74; instr. E. Windsor Community Sch., 1977-78, Hillsborough Community Sch., 1978. Bd. govs. Am. Cancer Soc., 1973-78; active Boy Scouts Am.; sec. East Windsor Municipal Utilities Authority, 1968-78. Served with U.S. Army, 1941-45. Recipient numerous awards civic and municipal orgns. Mem. AAUP, Am. Chem. Soc., Am. Gas Assn., N.J. Gas Assn., Assn. Advancement Ethical Hypnosis, Seton Hall Alumni Assn., K.C. Democrat. Roman Catholic. Researcher indsl. chem. problems; hypnotherapist. Home: 18 Glenwood Circle East Windsor NJ 08520 Office: PSE & G Co Camden Gas Plant 2d and Spruce St Camden NJ 08103

FORSYTHE, EDWIN B., congressman; b. Westtown, Pa., Jan. 17, 1916; s. Albert H. and Emily (Matlack) F.; m. Mary McKnight, Aug. 24, 1940; 1 dau., Susan. Gen. mgr. Locust Lane Farm Dairy, 1933-60, sec., treas., 1960—; mayor, Moorestown, N.J., 1957-62; mem. N.J. Senate, 1964-70; mem. 91st-96th Congresses from 6th dist. N.J., 1970—. Sec. Moorestown (N.J.) Bd. Adjustment, 1948-52, chmn. Moorestown Planning Bd., 1962-63; del. Republican Nat. Conv., 1968, 76; mem. Moorestown Twp. Rep. Com., 1953-62; pres. bd. dirs. Burlington County YMCA. Mem. S. Jersey Milk Dealers Assn. (pres. 1958-61), N.J. Milk Industry Assn. (pres. 1960-62). Office: 303 Cannon House Office Bldg Washington DC 20515

FORT, WILLIAM LAPHAM, publishing co. exec.; b. Bklyn., Sept. 19, 1904; s. William Lapham and Elsie Knox (Pearson) F.; grad. Rome Acad., 1922, Am. Inst. Banking, Harvard; m. Margaret M. McKenney, Sept. 8, 1925 (dec. Aug. 1968); 1 dau., Barbara Pearson (Mrs. John David Dorsey); m. 2d, Doris A. Preston, Nov. 8, 1969. Reporter, copywriter, 1922-25; bus. devel. mgr. Citizens Trust Co., Utica, N.Y., 1925-28, asst. v.p., 1928-30; mem advt. sales staff McFadden pubs., 1931-32, A.E. Blackett, Sample, Hummert, 1933-34; advt. mgr. Rural Progress mag., 1934-36; mem. staff Am. Weekly mag., 1936-47; advt. dir. Coronet mag., 1947-49; exec. Life mag., N.Y.C., 1949-69; cons. Time, Inc., N.Y.C., 1969—. Mem. So. Vt. Artists Assn. (trustee), S.A.R., Empire State Soc., S.R., Colonial Wars, St. Nicholas Soc., Hugenot Soc., Assn. Former Intelligence Officers, New Eng. Soc., N.Y. Geneal. Soc. Episcopalian. Clubs: Metropolitan, N.Y. Yacht (N.Y.C.); Ekwanok Country (Manchester, Vt.); Capital Hill (Washington); Royal Thames Yacht, American (London, Eng.); Ponte Vedra (Fla.), Mid Ocean (Bermuda); Everglades (Palm Beach); Country of Fla. Home: Fortlands Manchester VT 05254 also 139 E 63d St New York NY 10021 also La Couqville Villas Manalapan FL 33462

FORTIN, JOSEPH RAYMOND, orthopedic surgeon; b. Lauzon, Que., Sept. 30, 1944; s. Richard and Madeleine (Belanger) F.; B.A., U. Laval, 1963, M.D., 1967; m. Suzanne Hamel, Aug. 21, 1971; children—Justin-Pierre, Charles. Intern Hôpital de L'Enfant-Jésus, Québec, 1967-68; resident in gen. surgery Hôtel-Dieu de Québec, 1968-69; resident in orthopedic surgery Cours d'Orthopédie Edouard Samson, Montréal, Que., 1969-72; group practice medicine specializing in orthopedic surgery, Joliette, Que., 1974—; staff mem. Hôpital Gén. Région l'Amiante, Thetford Mines, Que., 1973-74, Centre Hospitalier St-Eusebe, Joliette, Que., 1974—, pres. med. edn. com., 1975—. Certified orthopaedic surgeon Province of Que.; licensed Med. Council Can. Fellow Royal Coll. Surgeons Can.; mem. Assn. Orthopaedic Surgeons Que., Can. Med. Assn., Assn. Médecins de Langue Française Can., Profl. Syndicate Medico-Legal Experts Province of Que. Roman Catholic. Home: 454 Bordeleau Joliette PQ J6E 2J2 Canada Office: 489 Blvd Sainte Anne Joliette PQ J6E 5A3 Canada

FORTON, JOHN ROBERT, social researcher; b. North Tonawanda, N.Y., Aug. 26, 1927; s. Raymond John and Loretta (Welton) F.; student Canisius Coll., 1948, Niagara U., 1960, Niagara Community Coll., 1974-75, State U. N.Y., Buffalo, 1976-77; B.S. in Pub. Adminstrn., Empire State Coll., 1977; children—Ellen, John, Joseph, Margaret, Ann. Personnel unit supr. Equifax Inc., Buffalo, 1953-72; social researcher Niagara County Youth Bur., Lockport, N.Y., 1973—. Ednl. cons. State U. N.Y., Buffalo; sec. Niagara County Planned Parenthood; mem. Erie Niagara Regional Planning Bd., Criminal Justice Task Force; mem. North Tonawanda Planning and Zoning Bd., 1950-52; mem. North Tonawanda Republican Com., 1960-70; group leader Link and Beginning Experience singles orgns. chmn. Concerned Citizens Council, 1974-76; adviser Women's Polit. Caucus, 1978; bd. govs. N.Y. State Fedn. Student-Alumni Assns., 1979. Served with USN, 1945-46, 50-52. Mem. Empire State Coll. Student Alumni Assn. (chmn. 1979), Assn. Human Services, Western N.Y. Assn. Youth Burs. and Youth Bds. Roman Catholic. Club: K.C. Author: Niagara County Profile of Cities and Towns, 1977. Office: care Niagara County Youth Bur 5465 Upper Mount Rd Lockport NY 14094

FORTUNE, MARY K., mgmt. cons.; b. Mechanicville, N.Y.; ed. Columbia U., Union Coll.; B.S. in Psychology. Mgr. personnel and adminstrn. corp. research and devel. Gen. Electric Co., Schenectady, 1955-73, mgr. orgn. and manpower computer services, Rockville, Md., 1975; expert cons. Nat. Bur. Standards, Gaithersburg, Md., 1974-75; dir. Office Profl. Devel., NASA, Washington, 1975-78; pres. Mary K. Fortune Cons., Bethesda, Md., 1978—; chmn. com. adminstrn. and mgmt., mem. adv. council Dept. Agr. Grad. Sch. Recipient plaque NASA. Mem. Am. Soc. Tng. and Devel., Am. Soc. Pub. Adminstrn., Am. Mgmt. Assn., AAUW, Capitol Speakers Club. Home: 5225 Pooks Hill Rd Apt 925N Bethesda MD 20014 Office: 4330 East-West Hwy Bethesda MD 20014*

FORTUNOFF, ALAN MEYER, retail co. exec.; b. Bklyn., Sept. 19, 1932; s. Max and Clara (Wichner) F.; B.S., N.Y. U., 1953, LL.B., 1955, LL.M., 1974; m. Helene Finke, Nov. 25, 1953; children—Esther, Andrea, Rhonda, Louis, Ruth, David. Pres., Fortunoff Silver Sales, Inc., Westbury, N.Y., 1957—; admitted to N.Y. bar, 1956. Chmn., Nassau County Conv. and Visitors Bur., 1976-77; trustee Friends Acad., Dowling Coll.; asso. trustee N. Shore Hosp.; Mem. Action Com. L.I.; bd. dirs. Regional Plan Assn., Better Bus. Bur. Mem. L.I. Assn. Commerce and Industry (v.p., dir.), Victorian Soc. Am., Nat. Trust Historic Preservation, Am. Soc. Legal History, Italy-Am. C. of C., Am. Importers Assn., Fifth Ave. Assn., Soc. Preservation L.I. Antiquities, Union Am. Hebrew Congregations. Jewish. Home: 7 Forte Dr Old Westbruy NY 11568 Office: PO Box 132 Westbury NY 11590

FORTUNOFF, HELENE, retail exec.; b. Paterson, N.J., Mar. 2, 1933; d. Samuel Julius and Tillie (Kraut) Finke; B.S. cum laude, N.Y.U., 1953; m. Alan Fortunoff, Nov. 25, 1953; children—Esther, Andrea, Rhonda, Louis, Ruth, David. With Fortunoff's retail stores, Westbury, N.Y., 1953—, prin. charge jewelry div., 1957—, sec.-treas. parent company, 1957—. Trustee Temple Sinai, Westbury, 1972—; mem. local women's div. United Jewish Appeal, 1970; mem. women's div. NCCJ, 1970—, chmn. women's div. for Nassau-Suffolk counties, 1974. Recipient citation Anti Defamation League, 1972; Israel Trade award Govt. of Israel, others. Home: 7 Forte Dr Old Westbury NY 11568 Office: 1300 Old Country Rd Westbury NY 11590

FORWARD, DAVID FRANCIS, mfg. co. exec.; b. Rochester, N.Y., Oct. 29, 1928; s. Worthy J. and Winifred (Poppert) F.; student Fordham Coll., 1947-49, Albany Law Sch., 1950-51; U. Pitts., 1967-69; m. Mary L. Sippel, Sept. 15, 1951; children—David J., Mary S. Copywriter, Delco div. Gen. Motors Corp., Rochester, 1952-55; sales promotion mgr. Carrier Corp., Syracuse, N.Y., 1956-59; account exec. Scrivener Advt., Rochester, 1959-60; advt. mgr. Cruisers, Inc., Oconto, Wis., 1960-63; merchandising mgr. Marine div. Chrysler Corp., Marysville, Mich., 1964-66; account supr. Burson-Marsteller, Inc., Pitts., 1967-71; mgr. mktg. communications Rockwell Internat., Pitts., 1971-75, dir. communications gen. products ops., 1975—. Bd. dirs. Worcester (Mass.) Concert Choir, 1973-75; Operation Better Block, Pitts., 1978. Served with USN, 1944. Mem. Pub. Relations Soc. Am., Pitts. Press Club. Roman Catholic. Author, dir. films on textile machinery and energy products. Home: 1460 Navahoe Dr Pittsburgh PA 15228 Office: 400 N Lexington Pittsburgh PA 15208

FOSDICK, RAYMOND WARREN, mfg. co. exec.; b. Ansonia, Conn., Jan. 14, 1921; s. Horace George and Maud P. (Buck) F.; student New Haven Sch. Indsl. Engring., 1942-46; m. Dorothy Louise Tingley, May 24, 1941; children—Lynn (Mrs. Frank R. Foster, III), Lois (Mrs. Glenn Onofrio). Lead indsl. engr. Farrel Corp., Ansonia, 1938-63; pres. F.C. Wetherbee Co., Meriden, Conn., 1963-65, Household Brush Co., Meriden, Premium Services, Wallingford, Conn., 1965-70, Am. Archives & Anci Crafts, Framingham, Mass., 1970-72, Fosdick Corp., Meriden, 1972—. Cons. Anci Craft, Div. Heublein, Hartford, Conn., 1973—, Flemington (N.J.) Cut Glass Co., 1974—. Served with inf., AUS, 1943-46. Decorated Bronze Star medal. Mem. Conn. Bus. and Industry Assn., Mfg. Assn. Meriden, Mfg. Assn. Wallingford, C. of C., Milford Power Squadron. Republican. Baptist (bd. deacons 1974). Mason (32 deg.); mem. Order Eastern Star, Order Amarath. Home: 34 Prindle Ave Ansonia CT 06401 Office: 141 Charles St Meriden CT 06450

FOSHAY, MAXINE VALENTINE SHOTTLAND (MRS. ROBERT LETHBRIDGE FOSHAY), civic worker, pub. relations exec.; b. N.Y.C., Feb. 14, 1921; d. Maximillian Stanford and Violet Gertrude (Turner) Shottland; B.A., Royal Acad. Dramatic Arts, London, Eng., 1943; m. Robert Lethbridge Foshay, Mar. 16, 1956. Field rep. Am. Cancer Soc., N.Y.C., div., 1967-68; dir. fund raising and pub. relations Preventive Medicine Inst., Strang Clinic, 1969-71; dir. fund raising and pub. relations Fedn. Handicapped, N.Y.C., 1971-72; exec. dir. Irvington House, 1972-73; chmn. group affiliates Meml. Sloan Kettering, 1960-66; v.p. Meml. Sloan Kettering Soc., 1966-67; vol. Meml. Sloan Kettering Cancer Center, 1956—; prin. Maxine V. Foshay & Assos., pub. relations. Bd. dirs. Elder Craftsmen, N.Y.C. Mem. Nat. Soc. Fund Raisers (dir., v.p. N.Y. chpt. 1971—), Hosp. Pub. Relations Soc. Greater N.Y. Home: 215 E 68th St New York City NY 10021

FOSS, ARTHUR DEGRANGE, educator; b. Haverhill, Mass., Dec. 5, 1934; s. Arthur B. and Edith A. (Degrange) F.; Diploma in silversmithing and goldsmithing Boston Mus. Sch., 1957; M.Ed. in Art Edn., U. N.H., Durham, 1965; m. Eugenie E. Sotiropoulos. Tchr. art Pentucket Regional Sch., West Newbury, Mass., 1959-62; tchr. art Haverhill pub. schs., 1962-65, supr. art edn., 1965—; exhibited Boston Mus., Boston Opera House, Addison Gallery, others; lectr. in field. Mem. NEA, Mass. Tchrs. Assn., Haverhill pub. sch. Adminstrs. and Suprs. Assn., Nat., Mass. art edn. assns., Mass. Art Edn. Dirs. Assn., Greater Haverhill Arts Assn. Contbr. articles to profl. jours. Home: Old Post RD Box 72 Route 2 Wells ME 04090 Office: Summer St Sch Adminstrn Haverhill MA 01830

FOSSEL, SPENCER MARTEL, mfg. co. exec.; b. Elliott, Ill., Dec. 18, 1914; s. George and Ruby M. (Thompson) F.; B.A., St. Olaf Coll., 1937; postgrad. U. Minn., 1941-42, Columbia U., 1943-44, N.Y. U., 1945-46; m. Jane Beverly Nelson, July 2, 1937; children—Eric Thor, Janna Kristine, Chris Martel. With Sandoz Pharm., N.Y.C., 1941-43; dir. clin. research Sandoz Pharm., 1943-48, asst. mgr., 1948-50, gen. mgr. Pharm. div., 1950-53; dir. clin. promotion Organon, Inc., W. Orange, N.J., 1953-56; dir. marketing L.W. Frohlich Inc., N.Y.C., 1956-57; v.p. Warner Chilcott Labs., Morris Plains, N.J., 1957-58; pres. Spencer Labs., Morristown, N.J., 1958-62; pres., dir. Unimed, Inc., Morristown, 1962-72; pres., dir. J. H. Guild Co., Inc., Rupert, Vt., 1967—. Mem. corporate devl. com. Morristown Meml. Hosp.; bd. dirs. N.J. Soc. Crippled Children; budget com. Morristown Community Chest; bd. dirs. Morris County Heart Assn.; Morris County Mental Health Assn. Mem. Am. Acad. Sci., N.Y. Acad. Sci., Am. Assn. for Study of Headache, Newcomen Soc. Republican. Lutheran. Clubs: Internat. Trotting and Pacing Assn., Am. Carriage Soc., New Eng. Carriage Assn., Pharm. Advt. Patentee in field; contbr. articles in field to profl. jours. Home: 10 Dorset Rd Rupert VT 05768 Office: 200 Main St Rupert VT 05768

FOSSHAGE, JAMES LEWIS, psychologist; b. Durango, Colo., Sept. 9, 1940; s. Ernest Willard and Marie (Ochsner) F.; B.A. cum laude, U. Colo., 1962; Ph.D. in Counseling Psychology, Columbia U., 1968; certificate in psychoanalysis Postgrad. Center Mental Health, N.Y.C., 1972; m. Judith W. Dennis, Aug. 29, 1963; 1 son, Mark Christopher. Instr. dept. psychology, also Counseling Center, Hofstra U., Hempstead, N.Y., 1966-68; mem. staff Postgrad. Center Mental Health, 1968-72; pvt. practice, 1969—; co-founder, dir. clin. research, bd. dirs. Nat. Inst. Psychotherapies, N.Y.C., 1970—; dir. tng. Inst. Counseling and Psychotherapy, Ft. Lee, N.J., 1976—. U.S. Rehab. Service fellow, 1963. Mem. Am., N.Y., N.J. psychol. assns., Soc. Psychotherapy Research, Phi Beta Kappa. Co-author: Dream Interpretation: A Comparative Study, 1978; co-editor: Healing; Implications for Psychotherapy, 1978. Home: 16 Poplar Rd Demarest NJ 07627 Office: 330 W 58th St New York City NY 10019

FOSTER, DAVID NEWELL, mkt. research analyst; b. Rochester, N.Y., Apr. 21, 1950; s. John Henry and Marjorie (Newell) F.; B.S. in Chem. Engring., Purdue, 1972; M.S. in Indsl. Adminstrn., Krannert Grad. Sch. Bus., 1973. Facilities mech. engr. Gleason Works, Rochester, N.Y., 1973-75; promotion and membership dept. mem. Bay View YMCA, Rochester, 1976-77; salesman Murphy & Nolan, Inc., Rochester, 1977-78; mkt. research analyst Gleason Works, Rochester, 1978—. Bd. mgmt. Bay View YMCA, 1977-78, chmn. public relations and membership coms., 1977, sec., 1977, chmn. internat. com., 1978. Clubs: Purdue Alumni Club of Rochester (dir. 1974-78, treas. 1976-78), Bay View YMCA Internat. Y's Men's Club (pres. 1977-78), Masons. Home: 97 Owaissa Dr Rochester NY 14622

FOSTER, DWIGHT LIVINGSTONE, anesthesiologist; b. Kingston, Jamaica, W.I., Aug. 31, 1915; s. Cecil L. and Bertha Amanda (Limonius) F.; came to Can., 1956, naturalized, 1965; M.Sc. (Colonial Devel. and Welfare fellow 1944-45), Cornell U., 1945, Ph.D., 1947; M.D., Meharry U., 1956; D.Sc., Sussex Coll. (Eng.), 1976; m. Daisy Louise Robinson, Sept. 18, 1943; children—Sandra Therese Foster Stott, Phyllis Aline. Agrl. officer plant pathology, Kingston, 1937-38; agrl. officer, Belize, British Honduras, 1938-43; Charles Lathrop Pack research asst. Cornell U., Ithaca, N.Y., 1945-47; agrl. chemist Dept. Agr., Jamaica, 1947; prof., chmn. dept. agronomy Fla. Agrl. and Mech. U., Tallahassee, 1947-52; rotating intern Northwestern Gen. Hosp., Toronto, Ont., Can., 1956-57; sr. intern in anesthesia Toronto Gen. and Wellesley hosps., 1957; asst. resident in anesthesia Sunnybrook Hosp., Toronto, 1958; sr. house officer anesthetics Sefton Gen. Hosp., Liverpool, Eng., 1958-59; acting registrar anesthetics Alder Hey Children's Hosp., Liverpool, 1959; fellow Nuffield Dept. Anesthetics, Oxford U., 1960; anesthesiologist Doctors' Hosp., Toronto, 1960-70; asso. anesthesiologist New Mt. Sinai Hosp., Toronto, 1966-71; clin. tchr. U. Toronto, 1966-71; dir. High Park Lab. & X-ray, Toronto, 1972; med. examiner No. Life Ins. Co., 1973—, Can. Immigration Med. Service, Toronto, 1972—; anesthesiologist Ont. Ministry Health, Queen St. Mental Health Centre, Toronto, 1974—; cons. in anesthesiology Ont. Ministry Health, also Queen St. Mental Health Centre, 1975—; vis. prof. St. George's U. Sch. Medicine, Grenada, W.I., 1977—. Served to lt. British Honduras Vol. Guard, 1940-43. Fellow Royal Econ. Soc. London, Royal Coll. Physicians Can.; mem. Liverpool Med. Inst., Brit. Med. Protective Soc., Brit. Med. Assn. (Jamaica chpt.), Can. Anesthetists' Soc. Progressive Conservative. Anglican. Club: Mason. Mem. editorial bd. Tropical Agriculture, 1944-49; Florida Agrl. and Mech. U. Research Bulletin, 1947-52. Home: 23 Burbank Dr Willowdale ON M2K 1M7 Canada Office: 2140 Bloor St W Suite 1 Toronto ON M6S 1N1 Canada

FOSTER, EUGENE HOWARD, psychologist, educator; b. Cin., Jan. 21, 1947; s. Eugene Lewis and Mavis Estelle (Howard) F.; B.A. in Psychology, Barrington Coll., 1969; M.A. in Sch. Psychology, R.I. Coll., 1972; Ed.D. in Spl. Edn., Sch. Psychology, Boston U., 1975; m. Karen Fregeau, Jan. 8, 1976; children—Jason, Bradford, Nicole. Social worker pub. schs., Johnston, R.I., 1970-72; psychology intern pub. sch., Woonsocket, R.I., 1971-72; instr. psychology R.I. Coll., Providence, 1971-74; dir. learning disabilities program, regional dir. psychol. services NW Special Edn. Region, Scituate, R.I., 1972-74; dir. spl. services program, coordinator fed. and state grants N. Smithfield (R.I.) Sch. Dept., 1974-76; asst. prof. spl. edn., project dir. Providence Coll., 1976—. Bd. dirs. No. R.I. Child Abuse Prevention Center; mem. R.I. Bd. Regents for Edn. Task Force on Tchr. Tng. Certified sch. psychologist R.I. Dept. Edn.; licensed profl. psychologist R.I. Dept. Health. Mem. Am. Psychol. Assn., Council for Exceptional Children, Mass. Assn. Children with Learning Disabilities, N.Y. Acad. Sci., Phi Delta Kappa. Contbr. articles on learning disabilities to profl. jours. Office: Providence Coll Providence RI 02918

FOSTER, FAITH SMITH, probation and parole agt.; b. Cleve., Jan. 8, 1942; d. Willie T. and Estelle (Taylor) Smith; B.S., Central State U., 1965; M.Ed., Kent State U., 1970; m. Esau Foster, Aug. 21, 1971; children—Esau, Shani Lynn. Tchr. pub. schs., Cleve., 1965-69, 70-71; residence hall counselor Kent State U., 1969-70; counselor University City (Mo.) Pub. Schs., 1972-75; probation and parole agt. Ct. Common Pleas, Allegheny County, Pitts., 1977—. Mem. Am. Personnel and Guidance Assn., Am. Rehab. Counseling Assn., Assn. for Non-White Concerns, Pa. Assn. Probation-Parole and Correction. Democrat. Methodist. Contbr. to Career Education in Middle School Education, 1974. Home: PO Box 12015 Pittsburgh PA 15240

FOSTER, FRANK HERBERT, JR., elec. engr.; b. Quincy, Mass., July 29, 1925; s. Frank Herbert and Mary Elsie (McClenning) F.; student Erksine Coll., 1944; B.S., Northeastern U., 1952. Vice pres. MacKenzie & Foster Co., Quincy, 1948-59, Borek Assos., Inc., Boston, 1962-78; dir. Lev Zetlin Assos., Boston, 1974—, now v.p. Dep. warden Election Office, Milton, Mass., 1952-60. Served with AC, U.S. Army, 1943-46. Mem. Mass. Charitable Mechanics Assn. Democrat. Congregationalist. Clubs: Am. Legion, Masons (Milton), Furnace Brook Golf, Taleb Grotto (Quincy). Chief engr. Shrine Burns Inst., Boston, 1966, Bristol Community Coll., Fall River, Mass. 1971, Salem (Mass.) High Sch. 1972. Home: 33 Furnace Ave Quincy MA 02169 Office: 131 State St Boston MA 02109

FOSTER, HOLLAND, artist; sculptor; b. Caledonia, Iowa, Feb. 15, 1906; s. Homer A. and Beatrice Cecil (Holland) F.; student fine arts, Eng., Spain, Holland, France; B.A., State U. Iowa, 1936, M.A., 1939; student NAD, 1931-32, Columbia U., 1948; m. Dora Lucinda Ransom, Mar. 4, 1934; children—Norman Holland, John Homer R., Robert Harry, Cappy A.E., Susan Jean Foster Neff. Profl. portrait and landscape painter, Woodstock, N.Y., 1945—; one man shows at Woodstock, Kingston, N.Y., Greenville, Miss., N.Y.C.; exhibited group shows Jefferson Hotel, Iowa City, Iowa, William Alexander Percy Show, Greenville, Geiser & Kleinert Galleries, Woodstock, N.Y.C.; represented in collections at Iowa State Coll., various pvt.

collections. Served with USN, 1926-30. Recipient certificate of merit in painting, 1967; Community Service award Bronze Medal in painting, 1972, certificate of merit in painting, 1973. Mem. Woodstock Guild Craftsmen. Author: The Ghost Town of Caledonia, 1978; (with others) Art in Kingston Schools, 1956. Address: 75 Country Club Ln Woodstock NY 12498 also Palm Springs CA 92262

FOSTER, HOWARD HATHERLY, JR., educator; b. N.Y.C., May 27, 1937; s. Howard Hatherly and Florence St. John (Wilder) F.; B.A., Harvard U., 1959; M. Community Planning, Yale U., 1963; Ph.D., Cornell U., 1970; m. M. Jean Doig, Feb. 3, 1961; children—Kenneth, Jonathan. Asst. prof. community planning U. R.I., Kingston, 1963-70, dir. grad. curriculum in community planning, 1971-73, asso. prof. community planning, 1971—; pres. Communities Found., Inc., Providence, 1973—. Scandinavian Am. Found. Travel grantee, 1975. Mem. Am. Inst. Planners, Phi Kappa Phi. Contbr. articles in field to profl. jours.; producer film: Conflict of Interest for TV, 1976. Home: 24 Whitman Dr N Kingstown RI 02852 Office: Univ of RI Community Planning Curriculum Kingston RI 02881

FOSTER, JOHN HALLETT, investment co. exec.; b. Cleve., May 12, 1942; s. Hallett Phillips and Virginia Crow (Callow) F.; B.A., Williams Coll., 1964; M.A., Ohio State U., 1965; M.B.A., Dartmouth, 1967; m. Laura Laing Burbank, June 24, 1967; children—Laing Phillips, Virginia Burbank. Asst. v.p. Morgan Guaranty Trust Co., N.Y.C., 1967-72; pres. Foster Mgmt. Co., N.Y.C., 1972—; dir. Gen. Energy Corp.; chmn. Nat. Small Bus. Investment Co. Adv. Council to SBA. Trustee, chmn. fin. com., mem. exec. com. Pratt Inst., Bklyn. Mem. N.Y. Soc. Security Analysts, Nat. Assn. Small Bus. Investment Cos., Nat. Venture Capital Assn. Episcopalian. Clubs: Links (N.Y.C.); Wadawanuck (Stonington, Conn.). Home: 1133 Park Ave New York City NY 10028 Office: One Battery Park Plaza New York City NY 10004

FOSTER, JOHN MICHAEL, behavioral scientist, educator; b. Dayton, Ohio, Aug. 20, 1941; s. Richard L. and Maxine L. (Longstreet) Sheffield; B.A., Ohio U., 1967, M.A., 1968; m. Barbara Melanie Litz, Sept. 4, 1966. Asst. prof. behavioral sci. Bay Path Jr. Coll., Longmeadow, Mass., 1968—. Served with USN, 1959-63. Mem. Am., Mass. sociol. assns. Home: 53 Eton St Springfield MA 01108 Office: 588 Longmeadow St Longmeadow MA 01106

FOSTER, PEARL D. (MRS. CHARLES C. HUNT), physician, educator. Asso. in clin. medicine Columbia; former Cancer Research fellow Harlem Hosp., mem. staff. Mem. N.Y. State Council of Environmental Advisers; mem. adv. bd. Health Man Power Devel. program; mem. White House Conf. Children, 1970. Office: 20015 Linden Blvd St Albans NY 11412

FOSTER, ROBERT WILSON, assn. dir.; b. Monticello, Ill., July 22, 1918; s. Thomas J. and Agnes Elaine (Nichol) F.; B.A., Swarthmore Coll., 1940; m. Mary Ellen Sturdevant, Sept. 21, 1940; children—James R., Patricia Foster Haines, Nancy E. With First Nat. Bank, Chgo., 1940-42, 46; mgmt. cons. Cresap, McCormick and Paget Inc., 1946-49; analyst E.A. Wildermuth, Inc., 1949-52; exec. v.p. Single Service Inst., Inc., Washington, 1952—. Served to lt. USN, 1942-46. Mem. N.Y. Soc. Assn. Execs. (past pres.), Am. Soc. Assn. Execs., Nat. Indsl. Council, N.A.M. (exec. com.). Republican. Episcopalian. Clubs: Union League (N.Y., Chgo.) Silvermine Golf (Norwalk, Conn.). Home: 1636 Ridout Rd Amberley Annapolis MD 21401 Office: Single Service Inst Inc 1025 Connecticut Ave Washington DC 20036

FOSTER, ROCKWOOD HOAR, investment co. exec.; b. Boston, May 7, 1923; s. Reginald Candler and Frances Helen (Hoar) F.; A.B., Harvard, 1945; m. Marguerite Peet, June 19, 1948; children—Reginald Candler, Herbert Peet, Adam Rockwood, Charles Orin. With U.S. Fgn. Service, Washington and London, 1948-63; exec. v.p. Foster & Foster, Inc., Washington, 1963-67; with Research Inst. for Def. Analyses, Washington, 1967-68; cons. in investments, Washington, 1968-72; mem. D.C. City Council, 1972-75; v.p. Whitelaw, Dickens & Co., Investment Counselors, Washington, 1975—, dir., 1976—; dir. Aztech Corp., 1970—; gen. partner Retsof Partnership, Boston, 1972—; mem. Met. Washington Bd. Trade, 1973—; mem. Interstate Commn. on Potomac River Basin, 1975—; mem. C & O Canal Nat. Historic Park Commn., 1976—; mem. Mayor's Com. on Internat. Visitors, 1973—; v.p. Met. Washington Council Govts., 1973-75; pres. House of Mercy, Washington, 1972-76; v.p. Traveler's Aid Soc., Washington, 1971-76; trustee Consortium of Univs., 1973—, Meridian House Internat., 1973—, Columbia Hosp., 1973-76. Served with USN, 1943-46. Mem. Washington Soc. Investment Analysts. Episcopalian. Clubs: Somerset (Boston); Union (N.Y.C.); Met., Chevy Chase Country, City Tavern (Washington). Home: 3047 W Lane Keys NW Washington DC 20007 Office: 910 17th St NW Washington DC 20006

FOSTER, SUSAN JANE, telephone co. exec.; b. Painesville, Ohio, Feb. 22, 1941; d. LaVern Edwin and Catherine Jeanette (Fisher) Foster; B.A., Baldwin-Wallace Coll., 1963; M.B.A., Case Western Res. U., 1970. Asst. accountant Ohio Bell Telephone Co., Cleve., 1963-66, asst. statistician, 1966-68, statistician 1968-71, dist. mgr., 1971—, mktg. supr. visual communications services, 1976—. Tchr. Reading Improvement Center, Cleve., 1968—; cons. Ohio Bd. Edn. and WVIZ, 1973—; vol. reader Cleve. Soc. for Blind, 1973—. Mem. Am. Marketing Assn. (corr. sec. 1972-73, newsletter editor 1973-74), Phi Mu. Club: Baycrafters (Bay Village, Ohio), Women's City of Cleve. Home: 61 Greenwood Ave Madison NJ 07940 Office: American Telephone & Telegraph 295 N Maple Ave Room 541062 Basking Ridge NJ 07940

FOULDS, RAYMOND THOMAS, forester; b. Passaic, N.J., Oct. 26, 1914; s. Raymond Thomas and Florence (Magee) F.; B.S., N.Y. State Coll. Forestry, 1938; M.F., U. Mich., 1952; postgrad. Ore. State U., 1971-72; m. Edith Louise Carrier, Feb. 22, 1941; children—Carolyn Lizette, Thomas Edward, Diane Evelyn. Jr. scaler U.S. Forest Service, Fitchburg, Mass., 1939; field scout exec. Boy Scouts Am., Rutland, Vt., 1939-40, asst. scout exec., East Walpole, Mass., 1940-41; county forester Vt. Forest Service, Montpelier, 1946-48; extension forester U. Vt., Burlington, 1948-51, 52—. Served with AUS, 1941-46. Decorated Purple Heart. Recipient pin and certificate U.S. Dept. Agr., 1968. Mem. Soc. Am. Foresters (chmn. New Eng. sect. 1963-64, award 1963-64, chmn. Green Mountain chpt. 1976-77), Am. Forestry Assn., Northeastern Loggers Assn., Vt. Hist. Soc., Vt. Maple Industry Council (sec.-treas. 1956—), Nat., N.H.-Vt. (chmn. silviculture com. 1972—), Christmas tree assns., N.Am. Maple Syrup Council, Nat., Green Mountain Audubon socs., Vt. Assn. Extension Profls., Vt. Natural Resources Council, Nat. Wildlife Fedn., Epsilon Sigma Phi. Home: 393 S Prospect St Burlington VT 05401 Office: U Vt Burlington VT 05401

FOUNDOS, EVELYN, historian; b. Wanstead, Essex, Eng., June 11, 1936; d. Kuval Charles and Sarah Harris; came to U.S., 1957, naturalized, 1963; B.A. with honors, State U. N.Y., Stony Brook, 1973, M.A. (Univ. Traineeship scholar), 1974, postgrad., 1977—; children—Pamela Suzann, Saundra Elaine, Judith Esther. Mgr., window-interior decorator Luclair's, London, 1952-55; teaching and research asst. State. U. N.Y., Stony Brook, 1973-77, instr. in history, 1977; adj., N.Y. Inst. Tech. 1978—; ednl. researcher L.I. div. Nat. Peace Edn., 1974; pres. Eve's Cosmetic Garden Ltd., Stony Brook. Mem. Am. Hist. Assn., Latin Am. Studies Assn., Nat. Trust Hist. Preservation, Phi Alpha Theta (sec.-treas. local chpt. 1972-73). Democrat. Home: 1527 Stony Brook Rd Stony Brook NY 11790 Office: care Dept History State U NY Stony Brook NY 11794

FOUNTAIN, ROBERT JAMES, judo educator; b. Troy, N.Y., May 2, 1938; s. Edmund Phillip and Irma Mae (Agard) F.; student State U. N.Y. at Albany, 1955-57; m. Sharlene Ellen Grant, Apr. 20, 1968; children—Robert James, Christine Marie. Founder, Troy Judo Club, 1962—; instr. Albany State U., 1969-75, Renssalaer Poly Inst., 1972-73, Russell Sage Coll., 1973-74, 76—, Skidmore Coll., 1971-74, Hudson Valley Community Coll., 1968-69; producer judo program WAST, summer, 1965. Served with USMC, 1957-61. Third degree black belt, 1973; class C licence Referee Com., U.S. Judo Fedn., 1977, class A masters certificate, Tchrs. Inst. Mem. Empire State Judo Assn. (founder, pres.), U.S. Judo Fedn. (bd. govs.), Adirondack Assn. AAU (judo chmn.), Kodokan Judo Inst. Tokyo, Marine Corps League, VFW. Roman Catholic. Home: 30 Denison Rd Schenectady NY 12309 Office: 177 River St Troy NY 12180

FOURNIER, ROSAIRE, mfg. co. exec.; b. St. Agapit, Que., Can. Feb. 6, 1932; s. Albert and Regina (Chayer) F.; student pub. schs. Que.; m. Madeleine Lamontagne, Aug. 22, 1954; children—Louis, Johane, Andre, Pierre, Patrick. Accountant Forano Ltee., Plessisville, Que., 1951-53, Garace J.R. Plourde Ltee., Victoriaville, Que., 1956-64; pres. Interprovincial Parts, Inc., Victoriaville, 1964—. Mem. C. of C. Mem. Liberal Party. Roman Catholic. Club: Lions. Home: 13 Ave Des Planes Victoriaville PQ Canada Office: 26 Blvd de Lartisian Victoriaville PQ Canada

FOURNIER, THERESA LORRAINE, historian, polit. scientist; b. Peasleeville, N.Y., Sept. 23, 1927; d. Paul Napoleon and Florence (Sears) F.; B.A., St. Rose Coll., 1966; M.A.T. in History, Middle Tenn. State U., 1971, D.A., 1975. Mem. Sisters of Charity of St. Louis; tchr. elementary grades, 1946-67; tchr. secondary grades, 1967-75; tchr. history North Country Community Coll., Elizabethtown, N.Y., 1976; instr. state and local govt. and introductory philosophy Clinton Community Coll., Plattsburgh, N.Y., 1975-77, asst. prof. history, 1977—. NDEA grantee, 1968. Mem. Am. Hist. Assn., Clinton County Hist. Assn., League of Women Voters (bd. dirs.), Phi Alpha Theta. Democrat. Home: 11 Hillcrest Ave Plattsburgh NY 12901 Office: Clinton Community Coll Plattsburgh NY 12901

FOUT, JOHN CALVIN, educator; b. Omaha, Nov. 11, 1937; s. Karl Fredrich and Fannie Eva (Mitchell) F.; A.B. in History, U. Nebr., Omaha, 1963, M.A., 1964; Ph.D., in Modern European History, U. Minn., 1969; children—Justine, Elizabeth, John. Instr. U. Nebr., Omaha, 1967-68; part time instr. U. Minn., Mpls., 1968-69; asst. prof. history Bard Coll., Annandale-on-Hudson, N.Y., 1969-73, asso. prof. history, 1973—, chmn. dept. history, 1974—; joined order Oblate Companions of St. John of Eucharistic Catholic Church, 1975, ordained deacon, 1976, rector St. John's Theol. Sem., N.Y.C., 1976-77. Served with U.S. Army, 1959-62. Fulbright fellow, Heidelberg, Germany, 1964-65. Fellow Am. Soc. Church History; mem. Am. Hist. Assn., Phi Alpha Theta. Democrat. Contbr. writings ch. jours; editor of bibliography periodical lit. Home and Office: Bard Coll Annandale-on-Hudson NY 12504

FOWLER, CONRAD JOHN, electronics co. exec.; b. Phila., Dec. 23, 1921; s. Charles Thomas and Katherine (Sauter) F.; B.S. in Elec. Engring., U. Pa., 1943; m. Julia Basala, Nov. 24, 1945; children—Deborah Fowler Sanderson, Janet Fowler Grey. Lab. mgr. Moore Sch. Research dept. U. Pa., Phila., 1946-50; co-founder, v.p. Am. Electronic Labs., Inc., Lansdale, Pa., 1950-65, exec. v.p., chmn. bd., 1965—. Bd. dirs. North Penn Hosp., Lansdale, 1967—; trustee Ellen Cushing Jr. Coll., Bryn Mawr, Pa., 1970—. Served to lt. (USNR, 1943-46). Mem. IEEE, (v.p. 1972-74), Nat. Security Indsl. Assn. (trustee 1975—), Sigma Tau, Sigma Xi. Baptist (trustee 1971—). Clubs: Union League (Phila.); Mfrs. Golf and Country (Oreland, Pa.). Patentee in field. Office: Am Electronic Labs Inc PO Box 552 Lansdale PA 19446

FOWLER, DONALD ROBERT, psychiatrist, educator; b. Dallas, Mar. 13, 1935; student Navarro Coll., 1953-55; B.A., U. Tex., 1957; M.D., Southwestern Med. Sch., 1961; M.A. (hon.), Brown U., 1974; m. Elizabeth Allen, June 10, 1961; 1 son, Justin. Intern, Mary Hitchcock Meml. Hosp., Hanover, N.H., 1961-62; resident Duke Med. Sch., 1962-65, 67-68, research fellow, 1965-68; asst. prof. psychiatry, chief adult pub. psychiatry clinic Duke, 1968-72; asso. prof. Brown U., 1972—; dir. edn. Butler Hosp., Providence, 1972-74; psychi artist-in-chief Miriam Hosp., Providence, 1974—. Mem. Gov. R.I. Task Force on Mental Health, 1976—; bd. dirs. Providence Mental Health Center, 1976—. Fellow Am. Physhiat. Assn. (sec.-treas. R.I. dist. br. 1973-76); mem. Am. Psychosomatic Soc., AMA, Pan Am. Med. Assn., World Psychiat. Assn. Contbr. articles to profl. jours. Office: Miriam Hosp 164 Summit Ave Providence RI 02906

FOWLER, H(ORATIO) SEYMOUR, educator; b. Detroit, Mar. 1, 1919; s. Horatio Seymour and Bessie Liona (Ladd) F.; B.S., Cornell U., 1941, M.S., 1946, Ph.D., 1951; m. Kathleen M. Marshall, Nov. 21, 1945; 1 dau., Kathleen Marie Fowler Barto. Tchr. sci. McLean (N.Y.) Central Sch., 1946-47, Dryden (N.Y.) Freeville Central Sch., 1947-49; asst. prof. sci. edn. So. Oreg. Coll., Ashland, 1951-52; asst. prof. biology U. No. Iowa, Cedar Falls, also dir. Iowa Tchrs. Conservation Camp, 1952-57; prof. edn., dir. Pa. Conservation Lab. for Tchrs., Pa. State U., University Park, 1957—, chmn. sci. edn. faculty, 1969—, coordinator div. academic curriculum and instrn., 1974-76; dir. Pa. Gov.'s Sch. for Scis., 1978—. Served with 9th inf. div. AUS, 1942-45; ETO. Fulbright lectr., Korea, 1968-69; recipient citation Pa. Dept. Edn., 1970, Centre County (Pa.) Conservation award, 1973. Fellow AAAS, Iowa Acad. Sci.; mem. Am. Nature Study Soc. (pres. 1967), Nat. Assn. Biology Tchrs. (v.p. 1956, dir. region II, 1971-74, hon. mem. 1974), Nat. Assn. Research in Sci. Teaching, Nat. (Distinguished Service citation 1976), Pa. (dir., Meritorious Service to Sci. Teaching citation 1975, dir. 1971—, v.p. 1975, pres. 1976), Korean sci. tchrs. assns., Royal Asiatic Soc., Phi Delta Kappa (chpt. v.p. 1973, pres. 1974-75), Phi Kappa Phi, Beta Beta Beta, Phi Sigma, Sigma Xi. Clubs: Masons, Shriners, Rotary, Elks. Author: Secondary School Science Teaching Practices, 1964; Las Ciencias en la Esquelas Secundarias, 1968; Fieldbook of Natural History, 1974; contbr. to profl. jours. Home: 1342 Park Hills Ave W State College PA 16801 Office: Sci Edn Dept Pa State Univ University Park PA 16802

FOWLER, LINDSAY ANDERSON, III, cash mgmt. cons.; b. Binghamton, N.Y., Apr. 27, 1952; s. David Anderson and Holly Reynolds (Reid) F.; B.A. in Geology, Williams Coll., 1975. Cash mgmt. cons. Morgan Guaranty Trust Co. N.Y., N.Y.C., 1975; mem. staff, treasury dept. Equitable Life Assurance Soc. U.S., N.Y.C., 1976—; founder, dir. Save the Old Man Inc., Franconia Notch, Franconia, N.H., 1974—. Mem. Geol. Soc. Am. Soc. Econ. Paleontologists and Mineralogists. Presbyterian. Club: Explorers; Racquet and Tennis. Active in legal action to protect Franconia North Park from constrn. of Interstate Route 93, 1972—. Home: 370 Park Ave New York City NY 10022 Office: 1285 Ave of Americas New York City NY 10019

FOWLER, THOMAS JAMES, pharmacist, hosp. exec.; b. Pitts., Jan. 6, 1933; s. Charles T. and Clara Theresa (Zahren) F.; B.S. in Pharmacy, Duquesne U., 1955; m. Joan A. Craig, Sept. 2, 1961; children—Thomas M., John P., Michael C., Julie Ann. Pharmacist in retail store, Pitts. and Kensington, Md., 1957-62; staff pharmacist Mercy Hosp., Pitts., 1962-66, chief pharmacist, 1964-66; dir. of pharmacy services Sewickley Valley Hosp., Pa., 1966—; pharmacist cons. D.T. Watson Home, 1970—; clin. instr. intern program Duquesne U. Sch. Pharmacy, Pitts., 1976—; instr. Sewickley Valley Hosp. Sch. of Nursing, 1966—; mem. pharmacy advisory com. Hosp. Council Western Pa., 1978-79. Counselor Allegheny Trails council Boy Scouts Am. Served with USN, 1955-57. Diplomate Am. Bd. Diplomates in Pharmacy. Fellow Am. Coll. Apothecaries; mem. Am., Western Pa. (pres. 1970-71), Pa. socs. hosp. pharmacists, Am., Pa. pharm. assns. Republican. Roman Catholic. Club: K.C. Contbr. articles on pharmacy to profl. publs. Home: 104 Connie Dr Pittsburgh PA 15214 Office: Sewickley Valley Hosp Blackburn Rd Sewickley PA 15143

FOWLER, WALTER BRUMBY, physicist; b. Cin., May 5, 1926; s. Julian Sabin and Mary Alexander (Brumby) F.; B.S., Miami U., Oxford, Ohio, 1947, M.A., 1956; m. Lillian Elaine DuCharme, June 13, 1959; children—Susan DuCharme, Robert Brumby. Instr. physics Miami U., Oxford, 1956-58; physicist Naval Research Lab., Washington, 1958-60; Physicist Goddard Space Flight Center, Greenbelt, Md., 1960—. Served with USN, 1947-50, USNR, 1952-53. Mem. Am. Geophys. Union, AAAS, Optical Soc. Am., Washington Acad. Scis. Episcopalian. Contbr. articles on satellite measurements to profl. jours. Home: 9404 Underwood St Seabrook MD 20801 Office: Goddard Space Flight Center Greenbelt MD 20771

FOWLER, WILLIAM MORGAN, JR., educator; b. Clearwater, Fla., July 25, 1944; s. William Morgan and Eleanor Louise (Brennan) F.; B.A., Northeastern U., 1967; M.A. (NDEA fellow), U. Notre Dame, 1969, Ph.D., 1971; m. Marilyn Louise Noble, Aug. 11, 1968. Asst. prof. history Northeastern U., Boston, 1971-77, asso. prof., 1977—, acting asso. dean, 1977. Bd. dirs. Reading Antiquarian Soc., Boston. Served to capt. USAR, 1970—. Phi Alpha Theta scholar, 1967-68; Nat. Endowment Humanities summer fellow, 1974; recipient grants Am. Philos. Soc., 1976, Shell Assistance Fund, 1975; recipient prize Phi Alpha Theta. Mem. AAUP (sec.), U.S. Naval Inst., Orgn. Am. Historians, Bostonian Soc., N. Am. Soc. Oceanic Historians, Democrat. Roman Catholic. Author: William Ellery: A Rhode Island Politico and Lord of Admiralty, 1973; Rebels Under Sail, 1976; contbr. articles to profl. jours., newspapers and encys. Home: 323 Franklin St Reading MA 01867 Office: Dept History Northeastern U Boston MA 02115

FOWLKES, EDWARD BYNUM, II, statistician; b. Tarboro, N.C., Dec. 22, 1936; s. Edward Bynum and Ruth Janet (Laney) F.; B.S. (Westinghouse Achievement scholar), U. N.C., 1959; M.S., N.C. State U., 1963. Mem. tech. staff Bell Telephone Labs., Murray Hill, N.J., 1963—; adj. prof. Stevens Inst. Tech., Hoboken, N.J., 1976-77. Served with USCG, 1961. Mem. Am. Statis. Assn., Phi Beta Kappa, Phi Eta Sigma, Beta Gamma Sigma, Phi Kappa Phi. Home: 212 11th St Hoboken NJ 07030 Office: Mountain Ave Murray Hill NJ 07974

FOWLKES, KAREN ENID, counselor; b. Tarrytown, N.Y., Nov. 19, 1943; d. Levi Julius and Edna (Young) Clark; B.S., State U. N.Y., Plattsburgh, 1966; M.S., City Coll. N.Y., 1972; m. Rodney Hudson Fowlkes, Sept. 14, 1968; 1 son, Michael Rodney. Tchr. math. Anne M. Dorner Middle Sch., Ossining, N.Y., 1966-73; guidance counselor Abbott Sch., Union Free Sch. Dist. Greenburgh, Irvington, N.Y., 1973—. Pres. Parents Assn., Day Care Center Tarrytown, 1974-76, bd. dirs. center, 1976-79. Mem. NAACP, Am., N.Y. State personnel and guidance assns., Westchester, Putnam, Rockland Personnel and Guidance Assn., N.Y. State United Tchrs., Abbott Sch. Tchrs. Assn. Baptist. Home:

FOX, ABIJAH UPSON, state legislator Conn.; b. Bklyn., Jan. 20, 1905; s. Abijah Charles and Helen Manlove (Shawhan) F.; Litt.B., Rutgers U., 1926; m. Isabel Place Sullivan, Nov. 26, 1935; children—Abijah Shawhan, Jarvis Powell, Suzanne Angevine. With United Fruit Co., C.Z., 1926, Nat. City Bank, N.Y.C., assigned to Tokyo, also Yokohama, Osaka, Japan, 1926-34; mng. partner Swan, Culbertson & Fritz, investments bankers, Shanghai, also Hong Kong, Manila, Singapore, 1934-41; dep. dir. fgn. funds control Treasury Dept., Washington, 1941-44; with fgn. ops. dept. Lazard Freres & Co., N.Y.C., 1944-45; dep. dir. finance div. Office Mil. Govt. Germany, Treasury Dept., 1945-46; chmn. bd. dirs. Mathieson Alkaki Works, N.Y.C., 1946-48; treas., v.p., dir., sec. Am. Thread Co., 1948-59; gen. partner, v.p. Hayden Stone Inc., investment bankers, N.Y.C., 1959-72, Smith Barney Harris Upham & Co., investment bankers, Norwalk, Conn., 1972—. Mem. Conn. Ho. of Reps. from 152d Dist., 1968-70, from 149th Dist., 1970—, vice chmn. finance com., 1972-74, ranking mem., 1975—. Past pres., dir. Greenwich (Conn.) Taxpayers Assn.; dir., past chmn. budget com., campaign chmn. Greenwich Community Chest; v.p., mem. exec. bd. and finance com., chmn. long range planning com. Greenwich council Boy Scouts Am.; mem. Gov.'s Adv. Council on Aging, 1971-76, Juvenile Justice Commn., 1975-78; vice chmn. Fiscal Reform Commn., 1977-78; mem. Greenwich Republican Town Com., 1957—, dist. leader, mem. exec. com. 7th dist., 1957-71; mem. Greenwich Bd. Estimate and Taxation, 1965-68; mem. Greenwich Town Meeting, 1960-65; chmn. Greenwich Rep. Finance Com., 1968—; past mem. Conn. Rep. finance and budget coms. Bd. dirs., past vice chmn. Greenwich Community Council; trustee Western Conn. chpt. Multiple Sclerosis Soc., 1973—. Mem. Greenwich C. of C. (past chmn. nat. legis. com.), Navy League (past dir., v.p., chmn. membership com. Western Conn.), Am. Arbitration Assn. (panel arbitrators). Clubs: Indian Harbor Yacht. (Greenwich). Home: 50 Lafayette Pl Greenwich CT 06830 Office: 5 Mott Ave Norwalk CT 06850

FOX, EARLE BLAIR, JR., cons. mech. engr.; b. Troy, N.Y., May 2, 1917; s. Earle Blair and Ruth Bullard (Chapman) F.; B.M.E., Rensselaer Poly. Inst., 1939; m. Elsie Hollingsworth Campbell, Mar. 30, 1946; children—Margaret Fox Grant, Earle Blair, Carolyn H. With Calvert Distillery, Relay, Md., 1939-41, Consol. Gas Electric Light and Power Co., Balt., 1941-42; with M.E. Sanderson & Porter, Pine Bluff, Ark., 1942; constrn. insp. Standard Vacuum Oil, East Africa, 1942-43; exptl. geophysicist Socony Vacuum Oil Co., Venezuela, 1943-46; mech. engr. Austin Co., N.Y.C., 1946-51; chief mech. engr. St. John, Platt & Carlson cons. engrs., Binghamton, N.Y. br., 1951-58; exec. adminstr. Delaware County Disposal Dept. Pa., 1958-64; sr. mech. engr. Catalytic Constrn. Co., Phila., 1964-66; solid waste cons., sr. mech. engr. Roy F. Weston Inc., environ. engrs. and scientists, West Chester, Pa., 1967-72, sr. mech. engr., staff indsl. div., cons. Gilbert Assos., Reading, Pa., 1973—. Registered profl. engr., N.J., N.Y., Pa., Md., Del., Va., W.Va., Mass., Conn., Ohio, Miss., N.C., S.C., Tenn., Ga. Mem. Nat. Assn. Power Engrs. (Engr. of Year Phila. 1963), Nat. Soc. Profl. Engrs. (pres. chpt. 1972-73), ASME, Am. Pub. Works Assn., Am. Soc. Heating, Refrigeration and Air Conditioning Engrs., Franklin Inst. Phila., Engrs. Club Phila., Rensselaer Club Phila. Republican. Episcopalian. Club: N.E. River

Yacht. Home: 161 Rose Ln Haverford PA 19041 Office: PO Box 1498 Reading PA 19603

FOX, HERBERT, tech. inst. dean; b. N.Y.C., May 27, 1939; s. Abraham and Pearl (Grabel) F.; S.B., Mass. Inst. Tech., 1960, M.S., Poly. Inst. Bklyn., 1962, Ph.D., 1964; m. Dorothy Aig, Jan. 27, 1962; children—Paul, Seth, Jeffrey. Research asst., then research asso. aerodynamics lab. Poly. Inst. Bklyn., 1959-63, asst. prof., 1964-68; asso. prof. aeros. and astronautics N.Y. U., 1968-70, chmn. dept. mech. engring. tech., 1970-71; dean div. sci. and tech. N.Y. Inst. Tech., Old Westbury, 1971-77; project mgr., dept. head Pope, Evans & Robbins, N.Y.C., 1978—; cons. to industry. Chmn. bd. edn. Solomon Schechter Sch., Westchester, N.Y., 1972-73; trustee, sec. Beth El Synagogue Center, New Rochelle, N.Y., 1971-73. Recipient Nat. Undergrad. award Inst. Aerospace Scis., 1960; Sigma Xi research award N.Y. U., 1966, Lindback Found. award excellence teaching, 1968. Fellow Am. Inst. Aeros. and Astronautics (asso.; dir. 1971-74, v.p. edn. 1976—). Author: Urban Technology: A Primer on Problems, 1973; Urban Technology: A Second Primer on Problems, 1975; also articles. Home: 35 Trenor Dr New Rochelle NY 10804 Office: 1133 Ave of Americas New York City NY 10036

FOX, JAMES FREDERICK, pub. relations counsel; b. Cedar Rapids, Iowa, Feb. 5, 1917; s. Samuel James and Anna L. (Pietz) F.; B.A., U. Iowa, 1940; LL.D., World U., San Juan, 1975; m. Sylvia Porter Collins, 1979. Copywriter, Kohler Co. (Wis.), 1940-41; partner James W. Irwin Assos., N.Y.C., 1945-48; mgr. editorial services Prudential Ins. Co., Newark, 1949-52; dir. pub. relations Congoleum-Nairn, Inc., Kearney, N.J., 1953; mgr. pub. relations chem. divs. Olin Mathieson Chem Corp., N.Y.C., 1954-56; v.p. Chase Manhattan Bank, N.Y.C., 1957-61, dir. pub. relations, 1959-61, indsl. pub relations counsel, 1961—. Dir. Union Pub. Relations Counsels in Europe, Brussels, Belgium. Served to lt. USNR, 1942-45. Mem. Internat. Pub. Relations Assn., Pub. Relations Soc. Am. (nat. pres. 1975, Gold Anvil award, 1978), Nat. Investor Relations Inst., World Future Soc., Sigma Delta Chi, Phi Delta Theta. Republican. Episcopalian. Clubs: University (N.Y.); Metropolitan Opera (N.Y.C.). Contbr. articles to profl. jours. Home: 2 Fifth Ave New York NY 10011 Office: 342 Madison Ave New York NY 10017

FOX, JOHN JOSEPH, JR., historian; b. Pittsfield, Mass., Dec. 20, 1931; s. John J. and Blanche Julia (Pellerin) F.; B.S., North Adams State Coll., 1959; M.A. in History, Lehigh U., 1964; postgrad. Boston U., 1968; m. Marilyn Ann Volin, Feb. 23, 1957; 1 son, John Charles. Tchr. Pittsfield (Mass.) Pub. Sch. System, 1959-61; teaching asst. Lehigh U., Bethlehem, Pa., 1961-64; asso. prof. dept. history Salem (Mass.) State Coll., 1964—; pres. Oral History Research Assos. Del. Democratic State Conv., Mass., 1970, 72; mem. Danvers Democratic Town Com., 1967—; trustee Peabody Inst. Library, Danvers, Mass., 1976—. Served with inf. U.S. Army, 1952-54. Mem. Am. Hist. Assn., Orgn. Am. Historians, Social Sci. History Assn., Essex Inst., New Eng. Assn. of Oral History (pres. 1974-77), Am. Soc. for Legal History. Democrat. Roman Catholic. Author: Oral History: Window to the Past, 1977; compiler of bibliography Up-Date in The Oral History, Rev., 1977. Home: 134 Burley St Danvers MA 01923 Office: Dept of History Salem State College Salem MA 01970

FOX, JOHN WILLIS, educator; b. Folsom, Calif., Nov. 24, 1921; s. James Watson and Jennie (Lett) F.; A.A., Central Jr. Coll., 1942; A.B., Chico State Coll., 1947; M.A., Columbia U., 1951; Ed.D., U. Oreg., 1957; m. Muriel Christine Meyer, Aug. 24, 1942; children—Susan Christine, John Frederick. Tchr., athletic coach San Juan High Sch., Fair Oaks, Calif., 1947-50; El Camino High Sch., Sacramento, 1950-55; doctoral student, teaching asst. U. Oreg., 1955-57; supr. phys. edn., also sch. recreation Inglewood (Calif.) City Schs., 1957-61; vis. prof. Pepperdine Coll., Los Angeles, 1960-61; Eastern Wash. Coll., Cheney, 1961; prof. men's phys. edn. Boston Bouve Coll. Northeastern U., 1961—, chmn. dept., 1961-74. Co-chmn. phys. edn. com. YMCA, Boston, 1963. Served with USNR, 1942-45. Mem. AAHPER (editorial bd. Jour. 1960-63), Mass. Assn. Health, Phys. Edn.; Recreation (exec. bd. 1968, pres. 1972), Phi Delta Kappa, Phi Epsilon Kappa. Baptist (deacon). Club: Rotary. Co-Editor: A Guide for Physical Education in Mass. Home: 46 Wareland Rd Wellesley MA 02181 Office: 360 Huntington Ave Boston MA 12115

FOX, MADLYN ANN, real estate agt.; b. Framingham, Mass., Nov. 11, 1934; d. Frank M. and Rose M. (DeCenzo) Pizzeri; B.S. in Edn., Framingham State Coll., 1964, M.Ed., 1971; children—Karen J., Carolyn R. Elementary tchr. Natick (Mass.) Pub. Schs., 1964-65; remedial reading tchr., dept. head Ashland (Mass.) Pub. Schs., 1965-69; real estate broker, Framingham, 1971-72; prin., operator Madlyn Fox, Real Estate Framingham, 1972—; purchase and sales dir. Ledgemere Land Corp., Framingham, 1976—. Chmn., Municipal Bldg. Com., Ashland, 1965-66; mem. youth advisory group, Ashland, 1965-66. Licensed ins. broker, Mass.; licensed real estate broker, Mass. Mem. Homebuilders' Assn. Greater Boston (chmn. legis. com. 1974-75). Home: 56 Fruit St Ashland MA 01721

FOX, MARVIN IRVING, gastroenterologist, educator; b. Bklyn., May 26, 1928; s. Harry and Sarah F.; B.A., Cornell U., 1948, M.D., 1953; M.S., U. Chgo., 1949; m. Wilma Bernfeld, Oct. 31, 1954; children—Andrew, Keith, Laurie. Intern, Bellevue Hosp., N.Y.C., 1953-54, asst. resident in medicine, 1956-58; fellow in gastroenterology Yale U. Sch. Medicine, New Haven, Conn., 1958-59; asst. clin. prof. medicine; practice medicine specializing in internal medicine and gastroenterology, Milford, Conn., 1959—; chief gastroenterology Milford Hosp. Served to lt. M.C. USN, 1954-56. Diplomate Am. Bd. Internal Medicine, Nat. Bd. Med. Examiners. Fellow Am. Coll. Physicians, Am. Coll. Gastroenterology; mem. Am. Gastroenterol. Assn., Am. Soc. Gastrointestinal Endoscopy. Home: 515 Sportsman Rd Orange CT 06477 Office: 122 Broad St Milford CT 06460

FOX, ROXANNE ELLIOTT, researcher; b. Washington, June 22, 1946; d. William Ralph and Ruth Pauline (Griffith) Elliott; A.A., Bluefield Jr. Coll., 1966; B.S. in Biology, Towson State Coll., 1971; postgrad. George Washington U., 1971; postgrad. in mgmt. Frostburg State Coll., 1977—; m. Raymond Dale Fox, Aug. 31, 1969; 1 son, Rodney Redford. EKG technician Alexandria (Va.) Hosp., 1967-68; lab. asst. to sr. animal technician Hazleton Lab., Falls Church, Va., 1968-71; sr. lab. technician to research asst. Frederick Cancer Research Center, Litton Bionetics, Inc., Frederick, Md., 1972—. Mem. Am. Assn. Lab. Animal Sci., Frederick County Soc. Advancement Med. Tech. Republican. Episcopalian. Home: 110 East H St Brunswick MD 21716 Office: FCRC Litton Bionetics Inc PO Box B Frederick MD 21701

FOX, ROY WARREN, elec. connector mfg. co. exec.; b. N.Y.C., Feb. 3, 1920; s. Robert Roy and Frances Fox; B.S. in Mech. Engring., U. Vt., 1949; m. Harriet Virginia Norton, Oct. 31, 1942; children—Virginia Anne, Roy Warren, Judith Katherine. With Harriman, Ripley Co., 1936-40; instr. math., thermodynamics U. Vt., 1947-49; with Hamilton Standard Co., 1949-63, Fairchild Stratos Co., 1963-64, Chandler Evans Co., 1965-70, Pratt & Whitney Machine Tool Co., W. Hartford, Conn., 1970-73; pres. Middleburg Corp., Canton, Conn., 1973—; dir. New Eng. Indsl. Resource Devel., Inc., Durham, N.H., 1973—. Mem. Canton Bd. Edn., 1960-63, Econ. Devel. Commn., 1977—; mem. Nat. Ski Patrol, 1957—. Served with U.S. Army, 1940-45. Decorated Purple Heart. Mem. Phi Beta Kappa, Sigma Xi. Republican. Episcopalian. Patentee elec. connector, hydraulic, pneumatic, mech. devices. Office: 220 Albany Turnpike Canton CT 06019

FOX, TERENCE J., consumer products mfg. and distbn. co. exec.; b. Bklyn., Jan. 1, 1938; s. Frank and Regina F.; B.S., N.Y.U., 1960, student Grad. Sch. Bus., 1962; student Latin Am. Inst., 1960; 1 dau., Kersten Kiely. Mgr. underwriting dept. Gruntal & Co., mems. N.Y. Stock Exchange, N.Y.C., 1959-63; sales exec. Am. Flange & Mfg. Co., N.Y.C., 1964-65; pres., chief exec. officer Iroquois Brands, Ltd., 1965—; mem. bd. govs. Am. Stock Exchange; trustee Emigrant Savs. Bank; past vice chmn. Lincoln Nat. Bank Buffalo, 1968-71; chmn. bd. Aberdeen Mut. Fund, 1968-71; dir. Intervestors, Buffalo. Past pres., chmn. bd. Henry St. Settlement Jr. Bd. Former trustee Immaculata Coll., Hilbert Coll., Buffalo; chmn. investment bankers com. Rosary Hill Coll.; bd. dirs. Cath. Youth Orgn.; former chmn. council D'Youville Coll.; former mem. council Canisius Coll. Sch. Bus. Adminstrn.; regional coordinator White House Conf. on Children and Youth. Served with U.S. Army, 1960-61. Mem. Young Presidents Orgn., Am. Inst. Banking, Am. Ordnance Assn., Crippled Children's Guild Buffalo (life). Clubs: Goldens Bridge Hunt (North Salem); Palm Bay (Miami, Fla.); Union League, Nat. Arts (N.Y.C.); Greenwich, Stanwick (Greenwich, Conn.). Inventor, designer, patentee Sam Sneed hand strengthener. Office: 41 W Putnam St Greenwich CT 06830

FOX, THOMAS GEORGE, med. adminstr.; b. N.Y.C., Sept. 15, 1942; s. Thomas and Alice Cecilia (Ehler) F.; B.A., Trenton State Coll., 1964; M.Ed., U. Vt., 1966; Ph.D., U. Mich., 1972; m. Eileen Stephenie Baron, Nov. 7, 1965; children—Christopher Adam, Thomas Andrew, Stephen Baron. Asst. to dean of men U. Mass., Amherst, 1966; dir. counseling and student services U. Mich., Ann Arbor, 1966-68, sr. adminstrv. asst. Med. Center, 1968-69, adminstrv. asso., 1969-71; asst. dean Rutgers Med. Sch., Piscataway, N.J., 1972-77, asso. dean, 1977—, asst. prof., 1973-79, asso. prof., 1979—; cons. to govt. agys., univs. and pvt. cos. Mem. exec. budget com. United Way of Central N.J., 1973-77; bd. dirs. Central Jersey Health Planning Council, 1978—. Mem. Am. Acad. Polit. and Social Sci., Am. Assn. Higher Edn., Am. Assn. Med. Colls., Am. Mental Health Counselors Assn., Am. Personnel and Guidance Assn. Contbr. articles to profl. jours. Home: 990 Hoover Dr North Brunswick NY 08902 Office: PO Box 101 Piscataway NJ 08854

FOX, WILLIAM CHARLES, lawyer; b. Auburn, N.Y., Nov. 27, 1941; s. Leo N. and Elizabeth M. (Curtin) F.; B.S., Georgetown U., 1963; J.D., St. Johns U., 1967; m. Sharon O'Brien, July 30, 1966. Admitted to N.Y. bar, 1967; asso. firm Melvin and Melvin, Syracuse, N.Y., 1967-73, partner, 1974—; sec. Syracuse Def. League, 1977, chmn., 1978. Chmn. profl. div. United Fund, 1974, 75, 76. Mem. Am., N.Y., Onondaga County bar assns. Democrat. Office: Melvin & Melvin 700 Merchants Bank Bldg Syracuse NY 13202

FRACKMAN, RICHARD BENOIT, investment banker; b. N.Y.C., Apr. 14, 1923; s. H. David and Ruth (Warren) F.; grad. Pratt Sch. Bus., 1941; student U. Pa., 1941-42, N.Y. U., 1946-48, N.Y. Inst. Finance, 1962-63; m. Noel Stern, July 2, 1950; 1 dau., Noel Dru. Mdse. mgr. R.H. Miller Stores, Inc., N.Y.C., 1946-49; v.p., mdse. mgr. Darling Stores Corp., N.Y.C., 1949-61; stockbroker, sr. security analyst, ltd. partner Burnham & Co., N.Y.C., 1962, v.p., corporate 1972; corporate v.p. Drexel Burnham Lambert, Inc., 1972—. Pres., Greenville Community Council, 1967-70; vice chmn. Town of Greenburgh (N.Y.) Planning Bd., 1970-77; bd. dirs. N.Y. State Planning Fedn., 1975-78; mem. Westchester County Regional Plan Assn., 1970—. Served to capt. USAAC, 1942-46. Recipient Silver Box award Greenville Community Council, 1970. Mem. N.Y. Soc. Security Analysts, Financial Analysts Fedn. Club: Metropolis Country (bd. govs., v.p. 1977-78) (White Plains, N.Y.). Home: 3 Hadden Rd Scarsdale NY 10583 Office: 60 Broad St New York City NY 10004

FRAIDIN, STEPHEN, lawyer; b. Boston, July 29, 1939; s. Morris and Frieda (Rozeff) F.; A.B., Tufts U., 1961; LL.B., Yale, 1964; m. Susan Phyllis Greene, July 4, 1962; children—Matthew Ira, Samuel Neil, Sarah Ann. Admitted to N.Y. bar, 1965; mem. firm Fried, Frank, Harris, Shriver & Jacobson, N.Y.C., 1964—, partner, 1971—; lectr. Practising Law Inst., 1976. Mem. Assn. Bar City N.Y. (sec. com. on securities regulation 1972-74), Am. Bar Assn. (reporter com. on fed. securities regulation 1974-76). Club: Yale (N.Y.C.). Home: 31 Old Lyme Rd Chappaqua NY 10514 Office: 120 Broadway New York City NY 10005

FRALEY, DONALD SYMONS, nephrologist, educator; b. Somerville, N.J., Apr. 1, 1943; s. Donald Symons and Christine (Roberts) F.; B.S., U. Pitts., 1964, M.D., 1968; m. Zella Zeigler, June 15, 1968. Intern, Montefiore Hosp., Pitts., 1968-69; resident U. Pitts., 1969-70, U. Pa. Med. Center, 1972-73; research nephrology fellow Montefiore Hosp., Pitts., 1973-76; asst. prof. medicine U. Pitts., 1976—, asst. chief renal and electrolyte unit, chmn. med. intensive care unit, 1976—; cons. in field. Served with USNR, 1970-72. Decorated Navy Commendation medal; NIH grantee, 1974-76; Health Related Sci. Found. grantee, 1977-78, 78-79. Mem. Am. Fedn. Clin. Research, Am. Bd. Internal Medicine (diplomate), Train Collectors Assn., Nat. Ry. Historic Soc., Sigma Xi. Unitarian. Editor: Lionel Trains - Standard of the World - 1900 to 1943, 1976; contbr. articles to med. jours. Home: 6949 Claridge Pl Pittsburgh PA 15208 Office: 3459 Fifth Ave Pittsburgh PA 15213

FRALIC, MARYANN F., nursing adminstr.; b. McKeesport, Pa., Oct. 12, 1936; d. Peter A. and Catherine A. Belak; R.N., McKeesport Hosp., 1957; B.S. in Nursing, Duquesne U., 1960; M. in Nursing, U. Pitts., 1973, now postgrad.; m. Donald R. Fralic, June 10, 1961; children—Christopher, Jennifer. Nursing service supr. McKeesport Hosp., 1960-62, mem. faculty Sch. Nursing, 1964-65, 68-71; asst. dir. nursing Braddock (Pa.) Gen. Hosp., 1973-74, dir. nursing, 1974—; lectr. and cons. in field. Mem. Nat. League Nursing, Am. Hosp. Assn., Hosp. Assn. Pa., Am. Mgmt. Assn., Soc. Advancement Mgmt., Forum Hosp. Nurse Adminstrs. (pres. 1979), McKeesport Hosp. Alumni Assn. Club: 20th Century. Home: 136 Sharp Rd White Oak PA 15131 Office: 400 Holland Ave Braddock PA 15104

FRANCHEBOIS, PIERRE JEAN, surgeon; b. Bourges, France, Apr. 5, 1922; s. Marcel Joesph and Claire (Schreiber) F.; M.D., Faculty Medicine Montpellier, France, 1953; m. Christiana Mascres, Aug. 23, 1933. Practice medicine specializing in surgery Montpellier, 1958-69, Montreal, Que., Can., 1972—; asso. prof. U. Montpellier, 1958-60, prof., 1960-74; asso. prof. U. Montreal, 1974-77, prof., 1977—; surgeon St. Lukes Hosp., Montreal, 1973—; expert French Ministry Health, 1960-72. Served to capt. French Army. Fellow Royal Soc. Medicine London; mem. Academie des Sciences et Lettres, others. Roman Catholic. Mem. editorial com. L'Union Medicale du Canada, France Medicale, others. Home: 704 Ave Pratt Montreal PQ H2V 2T6 Canada Office: 235 Dorchester St Montreal 129 PQ Canada

FRANCIS, GEORGE WILLIAM, physicist; b. St. Johns, Antigua, B.W.I., Oct. 31, 1934; s. Joseph Conrad and Margaret Dianna (Williams) F.; M.S., Ill. Inst. Tech., 1957; Ph.D., Syracuse U., 1975; m. Elizabeth Cofield, May 2, 1959. Asso. physicist U. Chgo., 1955-60; sr. physicist Gen. Electric Co., Valley Forge Space Center, Phila., 1967-69; sr. physicist, aerospace electronics dept. Gen. Electric Co., Utica, N.Y., 1969—. Mem. Am. Phys. Soc. (div. cosmic physics, div. on particles and fields), AAUP, NAACP. Contbr. articles to profl. jours. Home: 150 Genesee St New Hartford NY 13413

FRANCIS, JOHN BRUCE, educator; b. Houston, Nov. 4, 1939; s. Frederick Kenyon and Veronica Josephine (Boyle) F.; B.A. in Psychology magna cum laude, U. Detroit, 1961; Ph.D., U. Mich., 1960; m. Marlene Jagella, Apr. 4, 1964; children—John Brian, Jeffrey Benedict. Lectr., spl. asst. to dean U. Md.-Munich (Germany) Campus, 1966-68; USPHS trainee U. Mich., 1969-70; asst. prof. higher edn. State U. N.Y., Buffalo, 1970-75, asso. prof., 1975—, asso. dir. survey research center, 1971-73; cons. in field. Tenor soloist Unitarian Universalist Ch. of Buffalo. Recipient Dean's Key, U. Detroit, 1960, John S. Brubacher award U. Mich., 1969. Mem. Am. Assn. Higher Edn. (program coordinator N.E. region 1974), Am. Ednl. Research Assn., Am. Psychol. Assn., Am. Ednl. Studies Assn., Internat. Soc. Tech. Assessment, World Future Soc. Contbr. articles and revs. to profl. jours. Home: 138 Wickham Dr Williamsville NY 14221 Office: 487 Christopher Baldy Hall State U NY at Buffalo Buffalo NY 14260

FRANCIS, NEVILLE ANDREW, civil engr.; b. Barbuda, West Indies, Oct. 10, 1925; s. James Theophilus and Theckla Adina F.; came to U.S., 1952, naturalized, 1963; B.S. in Engring., Hampton Inst., 1957; postgrad. Hofstra U., 1968-69; M. Pub. Adminstrn., C.W. Post Coll., L.I. U., 1976; m. Christobelle Elain Isaac, Dec. 29, 1962; children—Neville Andrew, Houghton David. Researcher Presdl. Anti-Poverty Programs, N.Y. State, 1963-65; supt. hwys. and bridges, 1958-63; with State of N.Y., N.Y.C., 1965—, project. engr., 1968-70, engr. state facilities, 1971-76, resident engr. Office of Gen. Services, 1978—; engring. cons., instr. Pres. bd. dirs. Unity Church of Christianity N.Y.; founder Baldwin Action Group, 1977; mem. neighborhood action groups; Democratic committeeman. Served with RAF, Eng., 1943-47. Mem. Soc. Pub. Adminstrs., Am. Concrete Inst., Soc. Certified Engring. Technicians, Soc. Profl. Engrs. Barbados, West Indies Ofcl. Planners. Contbr. reports to profl. publs. in field. Home: 1133 Cramer Ct Baldwin NY 11510 Office: General Services Two World Trade Center New York City NY 10047

FRANCIS, RICHARD LOUIS, psychiatrist, state sch. dir.; b. Millerton, N.Y., Oct. 10, 1919; s. Champ Carter and Irene Virginia (Harris) F.; B.S., Howard U., 1941, M.D., 1944; m. DeWreathe Valores Green, Sept. 14, 1943; children—DeWreathe Valores Sarah, Irene Daisy. Intern, Sydenham Hosp., 1945; psychiat. resident Vets. Hosp., Tuskegee, Ala., 1947-49, Harlem Valley State Hosp., Wingdale, N.Y., 1955-57; resident physician N.Y.C. Farm Colony, S.I., 1945-47; neuropsychiatrist VA Hosp., Tuskegee, 1947-53; sr. physician Harlem Valley State Hosp., 1955; supervising psychiatrist, 1955-61, asst. dir., 1961-67; dir. Sunmount Developmental Center, Tupper Lake, N.Y., 1968—. Mem. adv. com. North Country Community Coll., Saranac Lake, N.Y., 1968—. Served to capt. M.C., AUS, 1953-55. Mem. Am. Psychiat. Assn. (sec. Mid.-Hudson dist. br. 1963-67), AMA, Nat., Franklin County, N.Y., Saranac Lake med. socs., Am. Assn. Mental Deficiency. Club: Rotary. Address: Sunmount Developmental Center Tupper Lake NY 12986

FRANCISCHELLI, GERALD JOSEPH, author; b. Astoria, N.Y., Nov. 9, 1942; s. Carmine and Caroline (Marzano) F.; B.A., Pace Coll., 1968; m. Linda Grace Donato, Jan. 20, 1964; children—Elizabeth Teresa, Gerald Joseph. Author: The Lovemakers, 1973; Troublemaker, 1974; Cosmic Rape, 1974; Sliding Down the Air!, 1976; It Adds Up to Murder, 1977; contbr. Argosy, Gallery, See mags.; co-founder N.Y. Erotic Arts Collective. Mem. Sci. Fiction Writers Am. Home: 23-12 Steinway St Astoria NY 11105

FRANCKE, ALBERT, III, lawyer; b. N.Y.C., Nov. 10, 1934; s. Albert and Eleanor (FitzGerald) F.; B.A., Yale, 1956; LL.B., Stanford, 1961; m. Linda Tapp Bird, Oct. 7, 1967; children—Caitlin Bird, Tapp FitzGerald. Admitted to N.Y. State bar, 1962; asso. firm Curtis, Mallet-Prevost, Colt & Mosle, N.Y.C., 1962-68, partner, 1968—; lectr. Practicing Law Inst., 1969—. Mem. Bus. Advisory Council Inter-Agy. Task Force, SEC and U.S. Treasury Dept., 1971-72; mem. Council Fgn. Relations; trustee Evelyn Sharp Found. Served to lt. USNR, 1956-58. Mem. Am., N.Y. State, Fed. bar assns., Assn. Bar City N.Y. (com. fgn. and comparative law), Am. Soc. Internat. Law. Home: 4 East 70 St New York City NY 10021 Office: Curtis Mallet-Prevost Colt & Mosle 100 Wall St New York City NY 10005

FRANCOEUR, ROMAINE DAVIS, hosp. adminstr.; b. Bucksport, Maine, Aug. 5, 1938; d. Wheeler David and Rose Anna (Nadeau) Davis; student U. Maine, 1969-74; B.A. in Social Sci., Coll. St. Rose, 1978; 1 son, Paul David. Instr., Pepperell Mfg. Co., Biddeford, Maine, 1960-71; supr. central supply Maine Med. Center Hosp., 1972-74; dept. head central supply Albany (N.Y.) Med. Center Hosp., 1977—; mem. new product evaluation com. Cheseborough Ponds, Inc. Minnesota Mining and Mfg. Co. grantee, 1976; Am. Hosp. Assn. grantee, 1977; North Eastern N.Y. chpt. Central Service Personnel grantee, 1976. Mem. Central Service Personnel (ednl. chmn. North Eastern N.Y. chpt.), Am. Hosp. Assn. Research on shelf-life testing of single wrapped barrier linen, cross-study respiratory care equipment and ethylene oxide sterilization. Office: Albany Med Center Hosp New Scotland Ave Albany NY 12208

FRANCOIS, EMMANUEL SATURNIN, surgeon; b. Port-au-Prince, Haiti, Dec. 23, 1938; s. Saturnin Antoine and Fausta Marie (Laurenceau) F.; came to U.S., 1966, naturalized, 1976; B.S., Coll. St. Louis de Gonzague, 1958; M.D., U. Haiti, 1958-64; m. Edda Gibbs, June 19, 1965; children—Randolph Emmanuel, Herve Daniel, Claire Chantal. Resident in path. anatomy U. Haiti, Port-au-Prince, 1964-66; intern in gen. surgery Harlem Hosp., N.Y.C., 1966-67, resident, 1967-72; asso. chief surgery Provident Hosp., Balt., 1972-73; practice medicine specializing in surgery Balt., 1973—; developer Oldtown Med. Center, 1975-78. Served to maj., U.S. Army, 1969-71. Vietnam. Mem. Assn. Haitian Physicians Abroad (founding mem., pres. 1971-73), Am., Nat. med. assns., Balt. City Med. Soc., Med. and Chirurg. Faculty Md. Roman Catholic. Home: 5039 Whetstone Rd Columbia MD 21044 Office: 1235 Monument St Baltimore MD 21205

FRANCOIS, EWART IAN, valve mfg. co. exec.; b. Trinidad & Tobago, West Indies, July 24, 1935; s. Theodore Agustus and Ellen Honeychurch (Thomas) F.; came to U.S., 1978; sr. sch. certificate Queen's Coll. Cambridge (Eng.) U., 1953; postgrad. Engring. Loyola Coll., 1965-68; certificate Indsl. Mgmt. and Adminstrn. McGill U., 1972; m. Anna Ginette Inniss, Nov. 21, 1959; children—Graham, Mathew, Maxine. Engring. apprentice, B.O.A.C., Trinidad, 1955-60, aircraft maintenance engr., Brit. West Indian Airways, 1955-63; engring. asst., Abex Industries of Can., Aerospace Div., Montreal, Que., Can., 1963-68; staff engr., quality assurance engring., Canadair Ltd., Montreal, 1968-73; mgr. quality assurance, nuclear div., Velan Engring. Ltd., Montreal, 1974-76, corp. mgr. quality assurance,

Montreal, 1976-78, Williston, Vt., 1978—. Mem. ASTM, Canadian Inst. Mgmt., Am. Soc. Quality Control. Anglican. Office: Velan Valve Corp Ave C Griswold Industrial Park Williston VT 05495

FRANGOS, JOHN, chemist; b. N.Y.C., Aug. 18, 1924; s. Basil and Evelyn (Kriaris) F.; B.S., St. John's U., 1950; postgrad. N.Y. U., 1950-51, Bklyn. Coll., 1951-52; m. Lou Joubert, Oct. 31, 1970. Chief prodn. chemist U.S.V. Corp., Yonkers, N.Y., 1951-53; dept. head V.C.A. Corp., Newark, 1953-55; tech. service rep. for U.S. and Can., Allied Chem., 1955-57; tech. dir. Power-Pak, Bridgeport, Conn., 1957-58; group leader Revlon Co., N.Y.C., 1958-68; asst. research dir. F.D. Snell, Floram Park, N.J., 1968-71; tech. dir. C.A.I., Milford, Conn., 1971—; pres. Penconsey Inc., N.Y.C., 1976—. Served with U.S. Army, 1943-46. Decorated Purple Heart, Bronze Star. Mem. Chem. Spltys. Mfrs. Assn., Soc. Cosmetic Chemists, Am. Chem. Soc., Sci. Research Soc. Am. Greek Orthodox. Club: Optimist. Contbr. articles to profl. jours.; patentee in field. Office: 85 Furniture Row Milford CT 06460

FRANK, ALAN I W, corp. exec.; b. Pitts., Mar. 6, 1932; s. Robert Jay and Cecelia F. (Moreell); A.B. cum laude, Harvard U., 1954; LL.B., Columbia U., 1960; children—Darcy Mackay, Kimberly deVou. Spl. agt. CIC, 1955-57; pres., chmn. bd. Alan I W Frank Corp., 1962—. Gen. chmn. Columbia U. $200 Million Campaign, Pitts. area, 1968-70; mem. Nat. Devel. Bd. Columbia U., 1974—; mem. Rensselaer council Rensselaer Poly. Inst., 1974—. Mem. N.Y. Bar. Clubs: Harvard-Yale-Princeton (Pitts.); Mid-Ocean. Office: Alan I W Frank Corp Exton PA 19341

FRANK, BARNEY, mem. Mass. Ho. of Reps.; b. Bayonne, N.J., Mar. 31, 1940; s. Samuel and Elsie (Golush) F.; A.B., Harvard U., 1962, J.D., 1977. Exec. asst. to mayor White of Boston, 1968-71; adminstrv. asst. to U.S. Congressman Michael Harrington, 1971-72; mem. Mass. Ho. of Reps., 1972—; teaching fellow in govt. Harvard U., 1963-67, asst. to dir. Inst. Politics John F. Kennedy Sch., 1966-67. Mem. Ward 5 Boston Democratic com., 1972—. Fellow Inst. Politics, Harvard U., 1971. Mem. nat. bd. Ams. for Democratic Action, 1969—; mem. state adv. bd. ACLU Mass., 1971—; exec. bd. Mass. chpt. Am. Jewish Com., 1975—. Named one of 10 outstanding young men Greater Boston Jr. C. of C., 1970. Club: Examiners Boston. Home: 18 Commonwealth Ave Boston MA 02116 Office: State House Boston MA 02133

FRANK, BERNARD, lawyer; b. Wilkes-Barre, Pa., June 11, 1913; s. Abraham and Fanny F.; Ph.B., Muhlenberg Coll., 1935; J.D., U. Pa., 1938; postgrad. N.Y. U., 1940-42; m. Muriel I. Levy, June 19, 1938; children—Roberta R. Frank Penn, Allan R. Admitted to Pa. bar, 1939, since practiced in Allentown; asst. U.S. atty. Eastern Dist. Pa., 1950-51; asst. city solicitor Allentown, 1956-60; dir., sec. Hess's, Inc. Vice chmn. B'nai B'rith Nat. Commn. on Adult Jewish Edn., 1959-61, chmn., 1961-63. Served as sgt. F.A., AUS, 1943-46; ETO. Mem. Internat. (chmn. com. on ombudsman 1973—), Am. (com. on ombudsman 1967—, chmn. 1970-76), Fed., Pa., Lehigh County bar assns., World Assn. Lawyers, U.S. Assn. Ombudsmen (hon.), Internat. Ombudsman Inst. (dir. 1978—, v.p. 1978—), 94th Inf. Div. Assn. (nat. pres. 1953-54). Author articles on Ombudsman to jours. including Pa. Bar Assn. Quar., Fed. Bar Jour., Adminstrv. Law Rev., Internat. Bar Jour., Nat. Civic Rev., Denver Jour. Internat. Law and Policy, Cumberland-Samford Law Rev., U. Miami Law Rev. Home: 745 N 30th St Allentown PA 18104 Office: 832 Hamilton St Allentown PA 18105

FRANK, GEORGE, psychologist; b. N.Y.C., 1928; s. Jack and Marilyn F.; B.A., N.Y. U., 1949; Ph.D., Fla. State U., 1956. Psychologist, Topeka State Hosp., 1955-58, VA Hosp., Montrose, N.Y., 1958-59; asst. prof. psychology U. Miami, Coral Gables, Fla., 1959-66; chief clin. psychologist VA Hosp., Bklyn., 1966-67; mem. N.Y. U., Columbia U., N.Y.C., 1967-68, 73-76; asso. prof. psychology N.Y. U., 1968-73; area training cons. in psychology VA, N.Y.C., 1968—; asso. prof. psychology St. John's U., N.Y.C., 1976—. Served with USAAF, 1946-47. Fellow Am. Psychol. Assn., AAAS, Soc. for Personality Assessment; mem. AAUP, N.Y. Acad. Scis., Nat. Assn. for Psychological Psychoanalysts. Contbr. articles, chpts., to sci. jours., texts. Office: 257 Central Park W New York City NY 10024

FRANK, LUDWIG MATHIAS, psychiatrist; b. Phila., Apr. 16, 1920; s. Ludwig and Eleanore Emily (Saverwald) F.; A.B. maxima cum laude, LaSalle Coll., 1942; M.D., U. Pa., 1945; m. Marie T. Johnson, Sept. 21, 1946; children—Ludwig Matthew, Terri Frank Terni, Mary Ellen Frank Willsey. Intern, Fitzgerald Mercy Hosp., Darby, Pa., 1945-46; resident in psychiatry Mayo Found., Rochester, Minn., 1948-51; 1st asst. in psychiatry Mayo Clinic, 1948-52; clin. dir. Inst. Living, Hartford, 1952-55; pvt. practice medicine, specializing in psychiatry, West Hartford, 1955—; chief psychiatry St. Francis Hosp., 1955-75; clin. asso. U. Conn. Med. Sch., 1975—; cons. USAF, San Antonio, 1947—; v.p., dir. Swiss Meadows Inc.; v.p., dir. Hatchetts Improvement Co. Mem. Sch. Bd. Archdiocese Hartford, 1969-74. Served to capt., M.C., AUS, 1946-48. Diplomate Am. Bd. Psychiatry. Fellow Am. Psychiat. Assn., ACP; mem. Hartford Psychiat. Soc. (dir.; past pres.), AMA, Conn., Hartford County med. socs., Conn., Hartford psychiat. socs., Assn. Am. Med. Colls., N.Y. Acad. Sci., Piersol Anat. Soc., Mayo Clinic, Inst. Living, U. Pa. alumni assns. Contbr. to profl. jours. Home: 21 Walbridge Rd West Hartford CT 06119 Office: 801 Farmington Ave West Hartford CT 06119

FRANK, MARJORIE HOFHELMER (MRS. CHRISTOPHER GABLE), city health ofcl.; b. N.Y.C., Feb. 25, 1906; d. Arthur and Helen (Milius) Hofheimer; student Columbia Sch. Bus. Adminstrn., 1924; m. Harry Frank, Jr., Oct. 14, 1926 (dec. Mar. 1963); m. 2d, Christopher Gable, Dec. 29, 1969. Dir. service in VA hosps. North Atlantic area ARC, 1945-49; asst. exec. dir. Nat. Assn. Mental Health, N.Y.C., 1949-59; asso. exec. sec. Nat. Family Life Found., 1959-61; asso. exec. dir. Jewish Guild for Blind, N.Y.C., 1961-63; N.Y.C. regional planning rep. N.Y. Dept. Mental Hygiene, 1963-65; asst. to commr. Mental Health Services, N.Y.C. 1965-68; instr. dept. psychiatry Coll. Physicians & Surgeons, Columbia U., 1968—, adminstrv. asso. to chmn. dept. psychiatry, 1968-75; cons. New Sch. for Social Research, 1975—, faculty, 1976—; spl. cons. N.Y.C. Comprehensive Health Planning Agy., 1973-74; coordinator mental health consortium Gouverneur Hosp., N.Y.C. Health and Hosp. Corp., 1973-76; cons. N.Y. State Dept. Mental Hygiene, 1976-78, Health Systems Agy. N.Y.C., 1978—. Dep. comdr. Warren Twp. (N.J.) CD, 1940-45; bd. mem. at large Plainfield Council Social Agys., 1944-47; founder, pres. Union County Mental Hygiene Soc., 1944-49; adv. council on citizen participation Community Chests and Councils of Am., 1951-57; alt. pres. Nathan Hofheimer Found., 1959-75. Fellow Am. Pub. Health Assn., Am. Orthopsychiat. Assn. Unitarian. Home: 1155 Park Ave New York City NY 10028 Office: 2 World Trade Center New York City NY 10047

FRANK, MARTIN, health scientist, govt. adminstr.; b. Chgo., Oct. 22, 1947; s. Edward D. and Ann (Horwitz) F.; A.B. (Evans scholar), U. Ill., 1969, M.S., 1971, Ph.D., 1973; m. Cheryl Lynn Motel, Aug. 19, 1970; 1 dau., Beth Susan. USPHS predoctoral research trainee U. Ill., 1971-73; research asso. Mich. Cancer Found., Detroit, 1973-74, dept. pharmacology Mich. State U., 1974-75; asst. prof. physiology George Washington U., 1975-78; exec. sec. physiology study sect. div. research grants NIH, Bethesda, Md., 1978—. Vice pres., dir. Bennington Community Assn., Gaithersburg, Md., 1976-78. Nations' Capitol Affiliate Am. Heart Assn. grantee-in-aid, 1975-78. Mem. AAAS, Biophys. Soc., Am. Physiol. Soc., Sigma Xi. Contbr. articles to profl. jours. Home: 40 Goodport Ln Gaithersburg MD 20760 Office: Westwood Bldg Div Research Grants NIH Bethesda MD 20014

FRANK, MORTON, newspaper mag. exec.; b. Pitcairn, Pa., June 14, 1912; s. Abraham and Goldie (Friedenberg) F.; A.B., U. Mich., 1933; postgrad. Carnegie Inst. Tech., U. Pitts., Duquesne U.; m. Agnes Dodds, June 2, 1944 (div. 1958); children—Allan Dodds, Michael Robert, Marilyn Morton; m. 2d, Elizabeth Welt Pope, Dec. 31, 1963. Advt. mgr. Braddock (Pa.) Daily News-Herald, 1933-34; editor Braddock Free Press, 1934-35; advt. salesman, writer, rotogravure mgr. Pitts. Press, 1935-42, also writer, commentator, dir. Pitts. radio stas., 1935-42; v.p., bus. mgr. Ariz. Times, Phoenix, 1946; editor, pub. Canton (Ohio) Economist, 1946-58, Lorain (Ohio) Sun. News, 1949-50, Inter-County Gazette, Strasburg, Ohio, 1950-51, Stark County Times, Canton, 1950-58, Farm and Dairy, Salem, Ohio, 1952-53; pres. Tri-Cities Telecasting, Canton, 1953-61; pub. relations dir., v.p. Family Weekly and Suburbia Today, N.Y.C., 1958-65; pub., exec. v.p. Family Weekly, 1966-71, pres., 1971-75, chmn. bd., 1976, pres., pub., 1976—; v.p. Downe Communications Inc., 1973-76; Bd. dirs. Canton Symphony Orch., 1950-56; trustee Alfred U., 1969—; chmn. com. corr. Ind. Univs. and Colls. N.Y. State, 1976—. Served from ensign to lt. USNR, 1942-45. Recipient award for feature writing, N.E.A., 1954. Mem. Fedn. Non-Comml. Theatres (pres.), Retail Mchts. Bd. (dir.), Controlled Circulation Newspapers Am. (dir.; award for Community Service 1954), Pitts. Fgn. Policy Assn., Nat. Newspaper Assn., Am., So., Inland Daily, Internat., Tex., Calif. newspapers pubs. assn., Newspaper Advt. Bur. (plans com.), Internat. Newspaper Advt. Execs. Assn., Circulation Mgrs. Assn., Promotion Mgrs. Assn., Canton Advt. Club, Sigma Alpha Mu, Sigma Delta Chi. Clubs: Players, Sales Executives, Overseas Press (trustee fedn.). Home: 534 Rock House Rd Easton CT 06425 Office: 641 Lexington Ave New York City NY 10022

FRANK, ROBERT ALLEN, advt. corp. exec.; b. Albany, N.Y., Sept. 26, 1932; s. Edward and Marian (Kostelanetz) F.; B.A., Colby Coll., 1954; M.B.A., Amos Tuck Sch. Bus. Adminstrn., 1958. Cost control adminstr. ABC-TV, N.Y.C., 1958-59; corporate auditor CBS, Inc., N.Y.C., 1959-60, TV sales service account exec., 1961, account exec. radio network sales, 1962-69; exec. v.p., co-founder SFM Media Service Corp., N.Y.C., 1969—. Radio-TV cons. Nat. Kidney Found., 1974. Active radio TV for various polit. campaigns including Robert Kennedy for Senator, 1964, Richard Nixon for Pres., 1972, Gerald Ford for Pres., 1976. Served to capt. USAF, 1954-56. Mem. Internat. Platform Assn., Internat. Radio-TV Soc. (membership com. 1973—), Amos Tuck Alumni (sec. N.Y. chpt. 1975-76, pres. 1976—), Pi Gamma Mu. Club: Dartmouth (N.Y.C.). Home: 9 Hackberry Hill Rd Weston CT 06883 Office: SFM Media Service 6 E 43d St New York City NY 10017

FRANK, RONALD EDWARD, univ. ofcl., educator; b. Chgo., Sept. 15, 1933; s. Raymond and Ethel (Lundquist) F.; student U. Ill., 1951-53; B.B.A., Northwestern U., 1955, M.B.A., 1956; Ph.D., U. Chgo., 1960; m. Iris Patrica Donner, June 14, 1958; children—Linda, Lauren, Kimberly. Instr. bus. statistics Northwestern U. Sch. Bus., Chgo., 1956-57; asst. prof. bus. adminstrn. Harvard U., Cambridge, Mass., 1960-63, Stanford (Calif.) U., 1963-65; asso. prof. mktg. The Wharton Sch., U. Pa., 1965-68, prof., 1968—, chmn. dept. mktg., 1971-74, vice-dean, 1974-76, dir. research and doctoral programs, 1974-76; cons. Market Research Corp. Am., Coca Cola Co., J. Schlitz Brewing Co., Nat. Analysts, AT&T. Mem. Am. Mktg. Assn. (dir. 1968-70, v.p. mktg. edn. div. 1972-73), Assn. Consumer Research, Am. Statis. Assn., Inst. Mgmt. Sci., Am. Assn. Pub. Opinion Research, Consumer Research Inst. (research bd. of rev. 1972-73). Author: (with William Massy and Alfred Kuehn) Quantitative Techniques in Marketing Analysis, 1962; (with John Matthews, Robert Buzzell, Theodore Levitt) Marketing: An Introductory Analysis, 1964; (with Paul Green) Quantitative Methods in Marketing, 1967, Manager's Guide to Marketing Research, 1967; (with William Massy and Thomas Lodahl) Purchasing Behavior and Personal Attributes, 1968; (with William Massy) An Econometric Approach to a Marketing Decision Model, 1971; (with William Massy and Yoram Wind) Market Segmentation, 1972; (with Marshall Greenberg) Audience Segmentation Analysis for Public Television, 1976; editor Jour. Consumer Research, 1973-76. Home: 219 Comrie Dr Villanova PA 19085 Office: U Pa Philadelphia PA 19174

FRANK, RUDY, broadcasting exec.; b. New Haven, Apr. 17, 1914; s. William B. and Caroline (Tishler) F.; student Fordham U., 1936; m. Elisa Petrovich, Nov. 20, 1940; children—Rudy, Richard, Elissa. Publicity dir. Horace Heidt, N.Y., Calif., 1937-40; mgr. State Theatre, Hartford, Conn., 1939-42; owner Rudy Frank Publicity Enterprises, 1942-45; v.p. radio sta. WELI, New Haven, 1945-71; nat. sales coordinator Covenent Broadcasting Corp., 1971-77, exec. asst. to sr. v.p., 1977—; pres. Rudy Frank Record Shops, Inc.; treas. GFR Corp. Chmn. Conn. Bd. Fisheries and Game, Atlantic States Marine Fisheries Commn., 1955-70; sec. Conn. Forest and Wildlife Commn., 1955-70; chmn. gov.'s interim com. to make comprehensive study electric power requirements for Conn.; mem. Council Environ. Quality for Conn. Recipient citation for war bond promotion and sales U.S. Dept. Treasury, 1943; asso. fellow Timothy Dwight Coll., Yale U., 1975. Mem. Am. Fisheries Soc., Internat. Assn. Fish and Game Commrs. Democrat. Clubs: Mory's, Yale Faculty; Nat. Press (Washington). Home: 79 Lake St West Haven CT 06516 Office: Radio Towers Park Hamden CT 06514

FRANK, STANLEY JULIUS, gerontologist, ednl. adminstr.; b. Balt., July 7, 1931; s. Louis and Ruth (Neubauer) F.; B.S., U. Md., 1953; doctoral candidate; m. Paula Florence Salganik, Jan. 6, 1957; children—Lawrence Alan, Stephen Jay, Andrew Barry. Vice pres. The Becker Corp., Balt., 1956-72; coordinator Ret. Sr. Vol. Program, Balt., 1973-74; dir. gerontology curriculum Community Coll. of Balt., 1974—; mem. Income Com. Md. Commn. on Aging, 1972-74, Balt. County Commn. on Aging, 1975—; mem. Md. Employees Ret. Rev. Bd., 1974—; mem. employment and ret. com. Gov.'s White House Conf. on Aging, 1971. Mem. community involvement com. Balt. Hebrew Congregation, 1972-77, bd. dirs. Brotherhood; chmn. home maintence service Balt. Hebrew Congregation, 1976—. Served with USAF, 1954-56. Mem. Am. Gerontol. Soc., Nat. Council on Aging, Nat. Council on Sr. Citizens, Am. Assn. Ret. Persons, Assn. to Guarantee Right of Equality to Elderly, Md. Advocates on Aging. Jewish. Contbr. articles on gerontology to profl. publs.; instrumental in establishing first community coll. gerontology curriculum. Home: 7437 Kathydale Rd Baltimore MD 21208 Office: Community Coll Balt 2901 Liberty Heights Ave Baltimore MD 21215

FRANKEL, ARNOLD JUDAH, chem. co. exec.; b. N.Y.C., Mar. 17, 1922; s. Sol and Rose (Blitz) F.; B.S. in Chem. Engring., Coll. City N.Y., 1942; M.S. in Chem. Engring., Bklyn. Poly. Inst., 1949; m. Miriam J. Drexler, Oct. 29, 1949; children—Hinda Frankel Squires, Janet, Alan. Co-founder, chmn., dir. Aceto Chem. Co., Inc., Flushing, N.Y., 1947—; mem. corp. and met. bank adv. bd. Chem. Bank, N.Y.C. Bd. dirs. Flushing Hosp. and Med. Center; v.p., bd. dirs. Queens Child Guidance Center; bd. govs. Jewish Museum, N.Y.C.; chmn. chems., plastics and paint industry group United Jewish Appeal, N.Y.C. Mem. Am. Chem. Soc., AAAS, Am. Inst. Chemists, City Coll. Alumni Assn., Sigma Xi. Club: Chemists (N.Y.C.).

FRANKEL, CLAIRE LYNN, computer systems specialist; b. Norwich, Conn., Feb. 9, 1950; d. Leonard Robert and Estelle(Masloff) F.; student Rensselaer Poly. Inst., 1967-71; B.S. in Physics, Suny, Albany, 1976; Data conversion supr. Montgomary Ward & Co., Albany, N.Y., 1970-74; land surveyor Richard Danskin, P.C., Troy, N.Y., 1974-75; land surveyor, office mgr. Palma Engring. Co., Nassau, N.Y., 1975-76; sales rep. Digital Equipment Corp., 1976-78; systems support specialist Foxboro Co. (Mass.), 1978—. Bd. dirs. Boston Repertory Ballet. Mem. Am. Inst. Physics, Am. Mgmt. Assn., Instrument Soc. Am. Club: Women's City (Boston). Address: 21 Beacon St Boston MA 02108

FRANKEL, EDWARD BENJAMIN, former textile by products co. exec.; b. Rochester, N.Y., July 26, 1920; s. Ezra and Belle Julia (Federbusch) F.; B.S. in Econs., U. Pa., 1942, M.B.A., 1943; m. Ruth J. Neiman, Dec. 26, 1943 (dec. May 1976); children—Charles, Carole Frankel Carlson; m. 2d, Dorothy C. Maidy, July 31, 1977. With Frankel Bros. & Co., Rochester, N.Y., 1943-78, pres. 1972-76, chmn. bd., 1976-78; asso. prof. Empire State Coll., Buffalo, 1977—; cons. fin. and transp. Chmn. Nat. Traffic Com., N.Y.C., 1960-73; active Boy Scouts Am., Rochester, 1954—. Mem. Nat. Indsl. Traffic League, Nat. Accountants Assn., Nat. Council Phys. Distbn. Mgmt. Clubs: Traffic (N.Y.C.); Irondeqoit Country (Rochester); Woodmont Country (Tamarac, Fla.).

FRANKEL, GEORGE JOSEPH, aerospace engr.; b. N.Y.C., Jan. 3, 1923; s. Joseph and Celia (Simon) F.; B.M.E., Coll. City N.Y., 1944; postgrad. Poly. Inst. Bklyn., 1968; m. Miriam Josephson, Apr. 15, 1945; children—Paul Jay, Alice Frankel Pratt, Lee Jeffrey. Product test engr. Arma Corp., 1944-45; chief engr. Metaplast Process, Inc., 1945-60, sec., 1953-60; prodn. mgr. Brillium Metals Corp., Hollis, N.Y., 1960-62; chief space environment Republic Aviation Corp., Farmingdale, N.Y., 1962-65; sect. head engring. dept. Grumman Aerospace Corp., Bethpage, N.Y., 1965—, corporate metrication officer, 1977—; cons. vacuum metalizing, 1960—; gen. chmn. space simulation conf. Am. Inst. Aeros. and Astronautics/ASTM/Inst. Environ. Scis., 1973, tech. program chmn., 1975. Asso. fellow Am. Inst. Aeros. and Astronautics (chmn. L.I. sect. 1976-77; tech. com. on life scis. 1975—); sr. mem. Inst. Environ. Scis.; mem. Nat. Fire Protection Assn. (chmn. tech. com. fire hazards in oxygen-enriched atmospheres 1966—), Am. Vacuum Soc., Am. Nat. Metric Council (chmn. engring. subsector 1976—), Pi Tau Sigma. Contbr. to profl. jours. Home: 26 Fountain Ln Jericho NY 11753 Office: Grumman Aerospace Corp S Oyster Bay Rd Bethpage NY 11714

FRANKEL, HOWARD JONATHAN, nephrologist; b. Orange, N.J., Jan. 10, 1938; s. Oscar L. and Edith (Reichman) F.; B.A., Dartmouth Coll., 1960; M.D., Boston U., 1964; m. Judy Ann Weg, Aug. 17, 1961; children—Alison Lee, Valerie Ann, Jonathan Stuart. Intern, Beth Israel Med. Center, Newark, 1964-65, resident in internal medicine, 1965-66; resident in nephrology N.Y. Hosp., N.Y.C., 1968, St. Luke's Hosp., N.Y.C., 1969; individual practice medicine, specializing in nephrology, Millburn, N.J., 1970—; mem. med. staff East Orange Gen. Hosp., 1970—, sr. attending, 1976—, chmn. dept. medicine, 1978—; mem. dir. Miele Dialysis Unit, East Orange, 1977—; asst. prof. medicine N.J. Coll. Medicine. Newark, 1970—. Mem. N.J. Renal Network Coordinating Council, 1975—. Served with USAF, 1966-68. USPHS fellow, 1968-69; diplomate Am. Bd. Internal Medicine. Mem. Internat., Am. socs. nephrology, AMA, Am. Soc. Artificial Internal Organs, Am. Fedn. Clin. Research, A.C.P., N.J. Acad. Medicine, Alpha Omega Alpha. Jewish. Research in nephrology. Office: 48 Essex St Millburn NJ 07041

FRANKEL, MICHAEL, mech. engr.; b. N.Y.C., Apr. 15, 1937; s. Kermit and Kate (Satloff) F.; Asso. Applied Sci., N.Y.C. Community Coll., 1956; m. Marion Schenker, July 5, 1959; children—Janice Ilene, Steven Neal, Paul Howard, Gail Sandra. Designer, Syska & Hennessy, 1957-60; job capt. Joseph R. Loring & Assos., 1961-63; head san. engring. dept. Bernard F. Greene, 1963-66; asst. plumbing dept. head, project mgr. Frank J. Sullivan & Assos., 1966-71; head san. engring. dept. M.P. Zacharius & Assos., N.Y.C., 1971-75; with Ebasco Services Inc., N.Y.C., 1975—, prin. engr. mech.-nuclear dept., 1975—; mem. faculty N.Y.C. Community Coll. Officer, N.Y. Guard, 1961—. Mem. Nat. Fire Protection Assn., Am. Soc. San. Engrs., Am. Soc. Plumbing Engrs., Nat. Rifle Assn. (life). Democrat. Jewish. Home: 4 Applewood Rd Vernon NJ 07462 Office: 2 Rector St New York City NY 10006

FRANKEL, ROBERT SIDNEY, surgeon; b. E. Orange, N.J., June 24, 1922; s. Henry H. and Beatrice (Solow) F.; B.S. magna cum laude, Harvard Coll., 1943; M.D., Boston U., 1947; m. Jeanne D. Rothblatt, May 5, 1946; children—Richard Harry, Kenneth Nelson, David Henry. Intern, Roosevelt Hosp., N.Y.C., 1947-48, surg. resident, 1948-51; resident in surgery Roswell Park, Buffalo, 1951-52; dir. surgery, Pascack Valley Hosp., Westwood, N.J., 1977—; chief neoplastic surgery, Hackensack (N.J.) Hosp., 19—; practice medicine specializing in gen. surgery, Hackensack, 1969—; asst. prof. surgery, N.J. Coll. Medicine, Newark. Mem. Human Rights Commn., Hackensack; bd. govs. Bergen County YM-YWHA, 1960-70; chmn. United Jewish Appeal, 1963-67. Served with USNR, 1947-50, with USAF, 1952-54. Diplomate Am. Bd. Surgery. Fellow A.C.S.; mem. AMA. Jewish. Club: Edgewood Country. Home: 365 Anderson St Hackensack NJ 07601 Office: 301 Beech St Hackensack NJ 17601

FRANKEL, SIDNEY A., chem. engr.; b. Bridgeport, Conn., Aug. 8, 1925; s. Samuel L. and Regina (Blum) F.; B.Chem.Eng., Pratt Inst., 1946; M.S., N.J. Inst. Tech., 1951; B.S., Rutgers U., 1960; m. Ruth Hoddeson, Dec. 7, 1952; children—Daniel E., Lynn S. Chem. engr. Squibb Inst. Med. Research, New Brunswick, N.J., 1946-52, Gen. Foods Corp., Hoboken, N.J., 1952-54; sr. chemist Am. Cyanamid Co., Bound Brook, N.J., 1954—, occupational-environ. coordinator Organic Chems. div., 1975—, plant resources conservation mgr., 1977—. Treas. Friends of Library of Edison (N.J.), 1963-69, pres., 1969—; pres. Edison Young Democrats, 1962, 64. Named Outstanding Young Dem., N.J. Young Dems., 1964. Fellow Am. Inst. Chemists; mem. Am. Chem. Soc., Am. Inst. Chem. Engrs., Nat. Soc. Profl. Engrs. (asso.). Jewish. Club: Elks. Patentee in field. Home: 2 Roger Rd Edison NJ 08817 Office: American Cyanamid Co Bound Brook NJ 08805

FRANKEL, STANLEY ARTHUR, publishing co. exec., industrialist; b. Dayton, Ohio, Dec. 8, 1918; s. Mandel and Olive (Margolis) F.; B.S. with high honors, Northwestern U., 1940; student Columbia U., 1940, U. Chgo., 1946-49; m. Irene Baskin, Feb. 20, 1946; children—Stephen, Thomas, Nancy. Reporter, Chgo. News Bur., 1940; publicist CBS, 1941; asst. to pres. Esquire and Coronet mags., N.Y.C., 1946-56; pres. Esquire Club, 1956-58; with McCall Corp., N.Y.C., 1958—, asst. to pres. and pub., 1958—, v.p., 1959-61; v.p., dir. corp. devel., Luria Bros. and Co., Inc. subs. Ogden Corp., 1961—, v.p. Ogden Corp., 1962—; dir. Careful Office Service Inc., Internat. Terminal Operating Co., Inc., Ogden-Am. Corp., Western Canners Corp.; guest lectr. N.Y. U., 1974; adj. prof. Baruch Coll., City U. N.Y.,

1974-78. Bd. dirs. Pub. Relations Bd. N.Y., Chgo.; exec. bd. Writers for Stevenson, 1952, 56, for Kennedy, 1960; pub. relations dir. Stevenson-for-Pres., 1956; exec. producer Stevenson Reports TV; mem. pres.'s adv. council Peace Corps, 1965; bd. dirs., vice chmn. Nat. Businessmen's Council; co-dir. pub. relations course Am. Mgmt. Assn., 1971; bd. dirs., exec. com. Nat. Council Crime and Delinquency, chmn. Loeb Award com., 1972; bd. overseers Rutgers U., 1977—; bd. dirs. N.Y. YMCA, 1960-72, Scarsdale PTA, Scarsdale UN Assn.; exec. bd., v.p. YMCA of Greater N.Y., Scarsdale Youth Recreation Council; mem. Pres.'s Youth Opportunity Council, 1966; trustee Scarsdale Adult Sch.; mem. chancellor's panel, chmn. remediation com., long range planning commn. State U. N.Y.; mem. Gov. N.Y. Higher Edn. Task Force; chmn. Writer for Humphrey, 1964; vice chmn. Humphrey for Pres., 1968, McGovern for Pres., 1972. Served to maj. AUS, 1940-46. Decorated Presdl. Citation, 3 Bronze Stars; recipient Alumni Merit award Northwestern U., 1964; recipient Peabody award for Stevenson Reports, 1963. Mem. Phi Beta Kappa Assos. Clubs: Overseas Press (N.Y.C.); Westchester Tennis; Scarsdale Town (gov.). Author: History of the 37th Division, 1947; contbr. articles to popular mags. Home: 109 Brewster Rd Scarsdale NY 10583 Office: 277 Park Ave New York City NY 10017

FRANKENBACH, WILLIAM ALFRED, hort. cons.; b. Southampton, N.Y., Feb. 21, 1929; s. William August and Leona Winafred (Haeger) F.; B.S., Cornell U., 1954; m. Colleen Audrey Moore, June 20, 1953; children—Susan, Lisa, William Alfred. Vice pres. Charles E. Frankenbach & Sons, landscapers, Southampton, N.Y., 1954-62; pres. W.A. Frankenbach Garden Center, Southampton, 1963—. Chmn. fin. com. Southampton Hosp., 1973; chmn. Southampton Town Republican Com., 1972-74, exec. com. Suffolk County, 1972-74; commr. Suffolk County Water Authority, 1975, treas. and asst. sec., 1975—; mem. Southampton Fire Dept., 1964—. Served with USAF, 1947-51. Mem. Am. Legion (comdr. 1968, 76-77, 77-79), N.Y. State Flower Growers (dir. 1969-70), C. of C. (pres. 1971-72), Am. Assn. Nurserymen, Eastern Regional N.Y. State, L.I. nurserymen's assns., N.Y. State Flowers Industries, Suffolk County Coop. Extension, Nat. Fedn. Ind. Business. Episcopalian. Clubs: Rotary (pres. 1970-71, dist. sec. 1977-78), Elks, Good Fellows, Southampton Beach and Tennis. Home: 104 Post Crossing Southampton NY 11968 Office: PO Box 1234 County Rd 39 Southampton NY 11968

FRANKENBERRY, ROBERT RANDALL, marine and dredging co. exec.; b. Pitts., Mar. 3, 1947; s. Robert E. and Kathleen (Marrs) F.; B.A. in Bus. Adminstrn., Parsons Coll., 1970; m. Gemma Jean Chir, Sept. 14, 1974. Payroll supr. Monongahela & Ohio Dreding Co., McKees Rocks, Pa., 1973, asst. sec., treas., dir., 1974—, dir. profit sharing plan, 1977—; sec., treas., dir. M & O Marine, Inc., 1978—, dir. profit sharing plan, 1978—. Chmn. budget and finance com. Pennsbury Village Condominium, 1976; treas. Pennsbury Village Condo. Council, 1977; founder, first chmn. Republican Com., Pennsbury Village, 1977; finance chmn. Borough Transition Com., 1977. Mem. Am. Arbitration Assn., Pitts. Econ. Club, Nat. Fedn. Ind. Bus., Gamma Zeta Alumni Assn., Sigma Pi. Republican. Presbyterian. Home: 1423 Schauffler Dr West Homestead PA 15120 Office: Ohio River at Ohio St McKees Rocks PA 15136

FRANKENFIELD, HENRY MEYERS, mfg. co. exec.; b. Coopersburg, Pa., Nov. 8, 1905; s. Henry B. and Emma (Meyers) F.; B.S., Pa. State U., 1932, M.S., 1934; m. Frances W. Eichler, Aug. 16, 1944. Art dir. pub. schs., Perkase, Pa., 1923-31; art promotion Hunt Mfg. Co., Phila., 1935-41, gen. v.p., 1944—; condr. workshop printmaking, calligraphy, painting in schs., colls. throughout U.S. Served with AUS, 1942-44. Mem. Nat. Art Edn. Assn., Internat. Soc. Art Edn., State Art Edn. Assn. Author: Block Printing with Linoleum, 1934; Block Printing with Color, 1938; Printmaking, 1939-64. Home: 368 W Graibury Ave Audubon NJ 08106 Office: 1405 Loucst St Philadelphia PA 19102

FRANKFURT, MORTON ALLEN, supermarket chain exec.; b. N.Y.C., Jan. 22, 1937; s. Stanley and Mary (Preisner) F.; B.S., N.Y.U., 1958; LL.B., St. John's U., 1961, J.D., 1968; m. Elaine P. Miller, June 26, 1965. Admitted to N.Y. bar, 1961; mem. law firm Margolin & Schekter, N.Y.C., 1962-68; v.p., legal counsel The Bohack Corp., Bklyn., 1968-77, also dir. Mem. N N.Y. State Bar Assn., Alpha Epsilon Pi. Mason.

FRANKL, KENNETH RICHARD, communications co. exec., lawyer; b. N.Y.C., May 23, 1924; s. Hugo Joseph and Sydney (Miller) F.; A.B. cum laude, Harvard U., 1947, LL.B., 1950; m. Jeanne Ritchie Silver, Aug. 6, 1972; 1 dau., Kathryn; 1 son by previous marriage, Keith E. Admitted to N.Y. bar, 1951; asst. dist. atty New York County, 1951-56; practiced with firm Liebman Eulau & Robinson, N.Y.C., 1957-60; asst. gen. atty. CBS, 1960-69; gen. counsel, asst. sec. Bishop Industries, Inc., 1969-70; v.p., gen. counsel, sec. RKO Gen., Inc. and subs.'s, 1970—. Served with Signal Corps, AUS, 1943-46; PTO. Mem. Assn. Bar City N.Y. (all industry radio com.), FCC Bar Assn., Internat. Radio and TV Soc., Dist. Attys. Assn. Jewish. Author: Equal Justice for the Accused, 1969. Home: 45 Christopher St New York City NY 10014 Office: RKO General Inc 1440 Broadway New York City NY 10018

FRANKL, WILLIAM STEWART, physician, educator; b. Phila., July 15, 1928; s. Louis and Vera (Simkin) F.; B.A. in Biology, Temple U., 1951, M.D., 1955, M.S. in Medicine, 1961; m. Razelle Sherr, June 17, 1951; children—Victor S. (dec.), Brian A. Intern Buffalo (N.Y.) Gen. Hosp., 1955-56; resident medicine, health scis. center Temple U. Phila., 1956-57, 1959-61, mem. faculty Sch. Medicine, Phila., 1962-68, dir. EKG sect. dept. cardiology, 1966-68, dir. cardiac care unit, 1967-68; research fellow cardiology U. Pa., Phila., 1961-62; prof. medicine, dir. cardiology div. Med. Coll. Pa., Phila., 1970—; physician-in-chief Springfield (Mass.) Hosp., 1968-70; practice medicine specializing in cardiology, Phila., 1962-68, 70—; cons. cardiology Phila. VA Hosp., 1970—. Served with M.C., AUS, 1957-59. Recipient Golden Apple award Temple U. Sch. Medicine, 1967, Med. Coll. Pa., 1972; Lindback award for distinguished teaching Med. Coll. Pa., 1975. Fogarty internat. fellow NIH, Cardiothoracic Inst., U. London, 1978. Diplomate Am. Bd. Internal Medicine. Fellow A.C.P., Am. Coll. Cardiology, Phila. Coll. Physicians, Am. Coll. Clin. Pharmacology, Am. Heart Assn. council clin. cardiology, (council on atherosclerosis); mem. N.Y. Acad. Scis., Am. Fedn. Clin. Research, AAUP, Assn. Am. Med. Colls., A.A.A.S., Am. Heart Assn. (gov. 1972—), Am. Soc. Clin. Pharmacology and Therapeutics. Contbr. articles to profl. jours. Home: 536 Moreno Rd Wynnewood PA 19096 Office: 3300 Henry Ave Philadelphia PA 19129

FRANKLIN, ALLEN PHILIP, county ofcl.; b. Orange, N.J., June 26, 1948; s. Frank Charles and Raphaela Beatrice (Barbarulo) F.; B.A. in English and Psychology cum laude, Bloomfield Coll., 1970; M.A. in Counseling, U. Conn., 1971; 6th year certificate in counseling N.Y.U., 1978. Head resident counselor U. Conn., 1970-71; activities dir. Orange (N.J.) Youth Services Bur., 1971-72; dir. Nat. Council on Alcoholsim, Morris County (N.J.) Office, Dover, 1973-78; dir. mental health Passaic County, Paterson, N.J., 1978—; mental health profl. Morristown Meml. Hosp.; cons. Morris County After Care Clinic and Center for Psychotherapy. Certified alcoholism counselor N.J. Assn. Alcoholism Counselors; certified rehab. counselor Chgo. Commn. Rehab.; licensed therapist behavioral modification N.J. Dept. Health. Mem. N.J. Task Force on Women and Alcohol, N.J. Alcoholism Assn., Nat. Assn. Social Workers, Am. Personnel and Guidance Assn., Nat. Assn. Rehab. Counselors, Assn. for Labor & Mgmt. Cons. on Alcohol, Assn. Group Psychotherapy and Psychodrama, N.J. Assn. Alcoholism Counselors, Rutgers Univ. Sch. Alcohol Studies Alumni Assn. Roman Catholic. Home: 948 Valley Rd Clifton NJ 07034 Office: Mental Health Dept Preakness Hosp Paterson NJ 07509

FRANKLIN, ARTHUR EDMUND, microbiologist, educator; b. Zealandia, Sask., Can., June 25, 1921; s. Lester and Myrtle Elsie (Fletcher) F.; B.S., McGill U., 1948, Ph.D., 1951; m. Elizabeth Emma O'Neill, June 16, 1951; children—David Bruce, Philip Gordon. With Connaught med. research labs. U. Toronto (Ont.), 1951-54, research asso. Faculty Medicine, 1954-58, now prof. med. microbiology; cons. infectious diseases Wellesley Hosp., Hosp. for Sick Children, Princess Margaret Hosp., Toronto Gen. Hosp. Served with RCAF, 1940-44. Decorated D.F.C. Mem. Am., Canadian socs. microbiology, Canadian Pub. Health Assn., AAAS, N.Y. Acad. Scis., Am. Mus. Natural History, Sigma Chi. Conservative. Contbr. articles to profl. jours. Home: 84 Steeles Ave E Thornhill ON L3T 1A3 Canada Office: 100 College St Toronto ON M5G 1L5 Canada

FRANKLIN, HARDY R., librarian; b. Rome, Ga., May 9, 1929; B.A. in Sociology, Morehouse Coll., 1950; M.L.S., Atlanta U., 1956; Ph.D. (Higher Edn. Act fellow), Rutgers U., 1971; m. Jarcelyn Fields; 1 son, Petey. Tchr., librarian Rockdale County Bd. Edn., Conyers, Ga., 1950-53; various positions Bklyn. Public Library, 1956-64, sr. community coordinator, 1964-68; asst. prof. library sci. dept. Queens Coll., CUNY, Flushing, 1971-74; dir. D.C. Public Library, Washington, 1974—; cons., guest lectr. in field. Pres., Middle Schs. PTA, Hempstead, N.Y., 1973-74; mem. adv. council to supt. schs., Hempstead, 1973-74; mem. adv. bd. D.C. Citizens for Better Edn., 1975—, Streets for People, 1975—; co-chmn. One Fund campaign, 1975, 76. Served with U.S. Army, 1953-55. Recipient award Bklyn. Friends of Library, 1963; Community Leader award Freedom Nat. Bank, 1968; Council Library Resources grantee, 1970-71; Nat. Endowment for Humanities grantee, 1970-71. Mem. Am., D.C. library assns., Am. Film Inst., Assn. Study of Afro-Am. Life and History, Urban League, NAACP, Sigma Pi Phi, Alpha Phi Alpha. Contbr. articles in field to profl. jours. Office: Public Library DC 901 G St NW Washington DC 20001*

FRANKLIN, JOHN BROOKE, ophthalmologist; b. N.Y.C., Mar. 23, 1937; s. Jerome Lester and Jean Sarah (Smith) F.; B.S., Bklyn. Coll., 1957; M.D., N.J., 1961; m. Ellen Rosen, June 11, 1961; children—John, Cynthia, Patricia. Intern, Jersey City Med. Center, 1961-62; resident in ophthalmology Baylor U. Med. Sch., Houston, 1964-68; asst. prof. ophthalmology U. Conn., Hartford, 1968—; staff Hartford Hosp., 1968—; practice medicine, specializing in ophthalmology, Hartford, 1968—. Served with USNR, 1962-64. Fellow A.C.S., Am. Acad. Ophthalmology and Otolaryngology; mem. Contact Lens Assn. Ophthalmologists. Democrat. Unitarian-Universalist. Club: Hartford. Home: 6 Squirrel Hill Ln West Hartford CT 06107 Office: 100 Retreat Ave Hartford CT 06106

FRANKLIN, KENNETH LINN, astronomer; b. Alameda, Calif., Mar. 25, 1923; s. Myles Arthur and Ruth Linn (Houston) F.; A.A., U. Calif. at Berkeley, 1943, B.A., 1948, Ph.D., 1953; m. Beverly J. Matson, Nov. 1949 (dec. Mar. 1956); children—Julie Franklin Jones, Kathleen Franklin Williams, Christine Franklin Redding; 2d, Charlotte Walton, May 18, 1958. Postdoctoral research fellow dept. terrestrial magnetism Carnegie Inst. Washington, 1954-56; mem. staff Am. Museum-Hayden Planetarium, 1956—, atronomer, 1963—, asst. chmn., 1968-72, chmn., 1972-74; mem. faculty City U. N.Y., 1957-58, N.Y. U., 1959-64, Cooper Union, 1968; vis. prof. astronomy Rutgers U., 1969-72; cons. to industry, 1958—; mem. radio astronomy commn. Internat. Sci. Radio Union. Served with AUS, 1943-46. Fellow Royal Astron. Soc., AAAS, Explorers Club; mem. Am. Astron. Soc. (pub. info. officer 1972—), Astron. Soc. Pacific, N.Y. Acad. Scis., IEEE, Sigma Xi. Astronomy editor World Almanac, 1970—; mem. sci. adv. panel Sci. Digest, 1970—. Co-discoverer radio emissions from Jupiter, 1955. Office: Hayden Planetarium 81st St and Central Park W New York City NY 10024

FRANKLIN, MITCHELL, educator; b. Montreal, Que., Can., Feb. 19, 1902; s. Adolphe and Emma (Franklin) F.; A.B., Harvard U., 1922, J.D., 1925, S.J.D., 1928; LL.D., Tulane U., 1978; m. Virginia Frances Wesler, June 25, 1922. Law sec. to Supreme Jud. Ct. Mass., 1925-28; engaged in practice of law, N.Y.C., 1928-30; W.R. Irby prof. law Tulane U., New Orleans, 1930-67, prof. emeritus, 1967—; vis. prof. State U. N.Y. at Buffalo, 1967-68, prof. law and jurisprudence, 1968-74, prof. philosophy, 1968-74, prof. emeritus, 1974—. Served in U.S. Army, World War I; maj., later lt. col., U.S. Army, World War II. Legal adviser UNRRA, Southwestern Europe, Middle East, hdqrs. Rome, 1946; legal officer UN Secretariat, 1948. Rosenwald fellow, Paris, 1939; Guggenheim fellow, 1948-49; tendered Fulbright lectureship in France, 1950. Contbr. to numerous legal and philos. publs. Home: 675 Delaware Ave Apt 710 Buffalo NY 14202 Office: O'Brian Hall State U NY North Campus Buffalo NY 14260 also Tulane Law Sch New Orleans LA 70118

FRANKLIN, PHILIP EARLE, economist; b. Detroit, Jan. 11, 1928; s. Edward Earle and Minnie (Evans) F.; B.A., George Washington U., 1949, M.A., 1955; Ph.D., Am. U., 1968; m. Jacqueline Jo Rogers, Dec. 28, 1949; children—Debora, Janice, Stephanie, Diana, Jennifer. Bus. economist Office Bus. Econs., Dept. Commerce, 1950-51; indsl. analyst Govt. Patents Bd., Exec. Office Pres., 1952-55; gen. economist Bur. Fgn. Commerce, Dept. of Commerce, 1955-56; transp. specialist Commodity Stblzn. Service, Dept. Agr., 1956-57; transp. economist Maritime Adminstrn., Dept. Commerce, 1957-60, gen. economist Office of Area Devel., 1960-61, transp. economist Office of Under Sec. of Commerce for Transp., 1961-62, internat. economist Bur. Internat. Commerce, 1962-64, gen. economist Office Undersec. Transp., 1964-67; coordinator for water resources Office of Sec., Dept. Transp., 1967-70, chief econs. and spl. project div., 1970-73, chief, organizer internat. trans. div., 1973—; fellow Center for Internat. Affairs, Harvard, 1972-73; transp. cons. UN, 1965. Pres. Eastpines Citizens Assn., Riverdale, Md., 1955-57. Served with USAAF, 1945-47. Served as 1st lt. U.S. Army, 1951-52. Mem. Am. Econ. Assn., Council on Fgn. Relations, Am. Water Resources Assn., Soc. Govt. Economists, Regional Sci. Assn., Econ. History Assn., AAAS, Am. Soc. Pub. Adminstrn., Am. Acad. Polit. Social Sci., Delta Phi Epsilon (pres. Washington alumni assn. 1965-66). Home: 3734 Northampton St NW Washington DC 20015 Office: Office of Sec Dept Transp Washington DC 20590

FRANKLIN, ROBERT LOUIS, hotel exec.; b. Mt Pocono, Pa., July 28, 1951; s. Robert Horace and Carolyn Elizabeth (Tillman) F.; B.S. with distinction, Pa. State U., 1973; m. Suzanne Brodt, Apr. 3, 1969; children—Jennifer Elizabeth, Robert Louis II. Dir. food and beverage ops. Marriott Hote. Corp., Washington, 1973, Houston, 1973-74, Dallas, 1974-75; v.p., gen. mgr. Carriage Inn, Inc., Scarborough, Maine, 1975-76; gen. mgr. Harper Hotels Inc./Holiday Inn, Plattsburgh, N.Y., 1976—. Coorinator Christian edn. United Methodist Ch., Plattsburgh. Recipient Silver award United Way Greater Portland; hon. comdr. 380th Bombardment Wing, SAC, USAF. Mem. Pa. Hotel and Restaurant Soc. (pres. 1972-73), Pa. State Club Maine (pres. 1976-78), Am., N.Y. State hotel and motel assns., Plattsburgh and Clinton County C. of C., Clinton County Tourist Bur. (dir.), Sigma Pi Eta. Clubs: Kiwanis, Rotary. Home: 6 Crescent Dr Plattsburgh NY 12901 Office: Holiday Inn I-87 and NY Route 3 Plattsburgh NY 12901

FRANKLIN, ROGER, actor, singer, dir., stage mgr.; b. Boston, Oct. 22, 1926; s. Roger and Hilda Jane (Cann) Krohn; B.S. in Edn., Mass. Coll. Art, 1948; M.A., N.Y. U., 1966, Ph.D., 1975. Broadway debut with Chartock Gilbert & Sullivan Co., 1952; appeared in Broadway plays The Vamp, 1955, West Side Story, 1958-60, Treasure Island, 1966, Canterbury Tales, 1969, No Sex Please, We're British, 1973; with Nat. Touring Co. in Sound of Music, 1961-64, Annie Get Your Gun, 1954, Damn Yankees, 1956-57, Half-A-Sixpence, 1965, The Impossible Years, 1967, Your Own Thing, 1968, George M., 1970-71, Butterflies Are Free, 1971-72, Fiddler on the Roof, 1975, Absurd Person Singular, 1976-77, South Pacific (revival), Man of La Mancha, 1977-78, Dracula, 1978—; critical acclaim for King Arthur in Camelot, 1968, the king in The King and I, 1967; artist-in-residence U. N.C. dept. speech and drama, 1967; guest lectr. ednl. theatre N.Y. U., 1970-71; dir. Siegfried, St. Paul Opera, 1974, Götterdammerung, 1975. Mem. Am. Guild Mus. Artists, Actors Equity Assn., Screen Actors Guild, Am. Theatre Assn., Children's Theatre Conf., Met. Opera Guild, Wagner Soc. London (Am. corr.), Beta Delta Cast, Alpha Psi Omega. Presbyterian (elder). Home: 4 Guy St Dover NJ 07801 Office: 174 W 76th St Suite 12G New York City NY 10023

FRANKLIN, WILLIAM DONALD, cardiologist; b. N.Y.C., July 23, 1923; s. Irving and May (Bisgyer) F.; B.S., Tulane U., 1943, M.D., 1945; m. Josephine Solomon, Nov. 23, 1947 (dec.); children—Deborah, Laurie, Wendy, Amy, Cathy; m. 2d, Elaine Silver, June 6, 1968. Intern, Kings County Hosp., 1945; resident Halloran VA Hosp., 1947, Goldwater Meml. Hosp., 1948-50; practice medicine specializing in cardiology, Bayside, N.Y., 1950—; asso. vis. physician Goldwater Meml. Hosp., N.Y.C., 1950—; instr. N.Y. U. Med. Sch., 1951; mem. staff internal medicine and cardiology L.I. Jewish Hosp., New Hyde Park, N.Y., 1954—, attending physician, 1977, physician-in-charge echocardiography, 1974; mem. staff internal medicine and cardiology Booth Meml. Hosp., Flushing, N.Y., 1957, cardiologist-in-charge EKG, 1963-67; asst. prof. clin. medicine State U. N.Y., Stony Brook, 1971. Chmn. pub. relations Coordinating Council City N.Y., 1969-70; chmn. Heart Fund, 1974. Served to capt. M.C., U.S. Army, 1946-48. Diplomate Am. Bd. Internal Medicine. Fellow ACP (mem. governing council), Am. Coll. Cardiology; mem. Am. Inst. Ultrasound in Medicine Internat., Am. socs. internal medicine, Am. Soc. Echocardiography, L.I. Soc. Echocardiography (pres.), Phi Beta Kappa, Alpha Omega Alpha. Home: Cove Neck Rd Oyster Bay NY 11771 Office: 73-03 Bell Blvd Bayside NY 11364

FRANKLING, SAMUEL ROY, ophthalmologist; b. Saskatoon, Sask, Can., May 8, 1919; s. Charles Percy and Mabel Charlotte (Stannard) F.; B.A., U. Sask., 1947; M.D., U. Toronto (Ont., Can.), 1949, certificate in ophthalmology, 1961; m. Hazel Elizabeth Heney, Aug. 30, 1941; children—Carol Frankling Drovin, Samuel Robert, William Michael. Intern, Toronto Gen. Hosp., 1949-50, resident ophthalmology, 1958-61; gen. practice medicine, Orangeville, Ont., 1950-58; practice medicine, specializing in ophthalmology, Mississauga, Ont., 1961—; chief ophthalmology service Mississauga Hosp., 1966—; clin. tchr. Sunnybrook Hosp., Toronto, 1961—; staff U. Toronto, 1961—. Served with RCAF, 1940-45. Decorated D.F.C. Fellow Royal Coll. Surgeons (Can.), Royal Coll. Physicians and Surgeons (Can.), Am. Acad. Ophthalmology and Otolaryngology; mem. Canadian Med. Assn., Christian Med. Soc., Full Gospel Businessmen's Assn. Mem. Conservative party. Mem. Anglican Ch. Home: 95 Alexandra Blvd Toronto ON M4R 1M1 Canada Office: Suite 4 95 Dundas St W Mississauga ON L5B 1H7 Canada

FRANKLYN, ROY, theatrical producer; b. Phila., July 21, 1922; s. Albert Abraham and Helen (Teitelbaum) G.; grad. high sch. Actor Hedgerow Theatre, Moylan, Pa., 1939-42; actor, dir., mgr. San Francisco Interplayers, also San Francisco Playhouse Repertory Co., 1947-58; dir., producer Mountain Theatre, Braddock Heights, Md., 1960; gen. mgr., producer N.Y.C. off-Broadway shows, including How to Steal an Election, Kiss Mama, I Dreamt I Dwelt in Bloomingdale's, 1958—; producer Millbrook Playhouse, Mill Hall, Pa., 1969-74; pres. regional council ANTA, No. Calif. and Nev., 1957, Roy Franklyn, Inc., N.Y.C., 1970—; asst. box office treas. Shubert Theatre, N.Y.C., 1974-76; box office treas. Ambassador Theatre, N.Y.C., 1977—; judge Stanford Dramatists Alliance Playwrighting Awards, Palo Alto, Calif., 1956, Miss San Francisco Pageant, 1957. Mem. Actors Equity Assn., Screen Actors Guild, AFTRA, Soc. Stage Dirs. and Choreographers. Address: 29 W 65th St New York City NY 10023

FRANKO-FILIPASIC, BORIVOJ RICHARD SIMON, chemist; b. Zagreb, Yugoslavia, Jan. 5, 1922; s. Marko Vincent and Nada Anna (Filipasic) F.; B.S. magna cum laude, Northwestern U., 1943, M.S., 1951, Ph.D. (Swift Research fellow), 1952; m. Ray Lyall Worthley, Mar. 2, 1948; children—Katherine Jane, Mark Strachan, Richard Crawford. Came to U.S., 1923, naturalized, 1927. Chemist, Pitts. Plate Glass Co., Milw., 1952-53; supr. organic research Mathieson Chem. Corp., Niagara Falls, N.Y., 1953-56; mgr. process research and engring. FMC Corp., Princeton, N.J., 1966—. Violinist, Buffalo Chamber Players, 1953-56. Served to lt. USNR, 1943-46. Mem. Am. Chem. Soc., Chem. Soc., Hakluyt Soc., U.S. Naval Inst., Am. Inst. Chem. Engrs. (vice chmn. high pressure com. 1973—), Compressed Gas Assn., ASTM, Catalysis Soc. N.Y., Assn. Internat. L'Avancement la Research des Hautes Pressions, Soc. Chem. Industry, Phi Beta Kappa, Sigma Xi, Phi Lambda Upsilon. Patentee high pressure equipment, catalysis, polymers. Home: 2 Oak Ave Morrisville PA 19067 Office: PO Box 8 Princeton NJ 08540

FRANT, FREDERICK AARON, biol. research co. exec.; b. New Brunswick, N.J., July 23, 1933; s. Jacob and Blanche (Weitzler) F.; B.S., N.Y. U., 1955; m. Joanna M. Pico, Dec. 21, 1966; children—Jennifer Lee, David Aaron. Co-founder Univ. Labs., Inc., Highland Park, N.J., 1959, lab., adminstrv. supr., 1959-64, v.p., treas., 1964—. Served with AUS, 1955-57. Mem. Soc. Research Adminstrs. (co-founder 1967), Am. Assn. Lab. Animal Sci. Home: 42 Camelot Ct Piscataway NJ 08854 Office: 810 N 2d St Highland Park NJ 08904

FRANTZ, ANDREW GIBSON, physician; b. N.Y.C., May 22, 1930; s. Angus Macdonald and Virginia (Kneeland) F.; A.B., Harvard U., 1951; M.D., Columbia U., 1955. Intern, Presbyn. Hosp., N.Y.C., 1955-56, resident dept. medicine, 1956-58; vis. fellow in medicine Columbia U., N.Y.C., 1958-60, asst. prof. medicine, 1966-68, asso. prof., 1968-73, prof., 1973—, chief div. endocrinology, 1971—; asso. in medicine Harvard U., 1962-66; asst. in medicine Mass. Gen. Hosp., Boston, 1962-66; attending physician Presbyn. Hosp., N.Y.C., 1973—; mem. med. adv. bd. Nat. Pituitary Agy., 1970-73; prin. investigator USPHS grants, 1964—; established investigator Am. Heart Assn., 1968-73. Served to lt. comdr. USNR, 1960-62. Mem. Am. Soc. Clin. Investigation, Endocrine Soc., Internat. Soc. for Neuroendocrinology, Harvey Soc., Am. Fedn. for Clin. Research, N.Y. Acad. Medicine, AAAS. Republican. Episcopalian. Clubs:

Union, Century Assn. (N.Y.C.). Contbr. articles to med. and sci. jours. Mem. editorial bd. Jour. Clin. Endocrinology and Metabolism, 1971-76; asso. editor Metabolism, 1969—. Home: 1185 Park Ave New York City NY 10028 Office: 630 W 168th St New York City NY 10032

FRANTZ, ROBERT LEWIS, lawyer; b. Wilkinsburg, Pa., Aug. 24, 1925; s. Charton Christopher and Gladys Baird (Lewis) F.; B.S., U.S. Mil. Acad., 1946; LL.B., Harvard U., 1954; m. Suzanne H. Allen, Nov. 20, 1948; children—Charton Christopher II, Rodgers Allen, Ruth Patterson. Commd. 2d lt. U.S. Army, 1946, advanced through grades to maj. gen. USAR, 1978; armored officer, U.S. and P.R.; judge adv., U.S. and Korea; comdr. 99th Army Res. Command, 1977—; admitted to D.C. bar, 1954, Pa. bar, 1958; partner firm Buchanan, Ingersoll, Rodewald, Kyle & Buerger, Pitts., 1958—; dir. Universal Welding, Inc., Weaver Assos., Inc. Trustee Eye and Ear Hosp., Pitts., 1965—, Valley Forge Mil. Acad. Found., 1973—. Mem. Am., Pa., Allegheny County bar assns., Res. Officers Assn., Assn. U.S. Army, Mil. Order World Wars. Republican. Episcopalian. Clubs: Harvard-Yale-Princeton (Pitts.), Pitts. Golf. Home: 1049 Highmont Rd Pittsburgh PA 15232 Office: 57th Floor US Steel Bldg Pittsburgh PA 15219

FRANTZEN, HENRY ARTHUR, pension fund exec.; b. Orange, N.J., Nov. 28, 1942; s. Henry and Natalie (Johnson) F.; student Hamline U., 1960-62; B.S.B.A., U. N.D., 1964; m. Julie Louise Haverty, Aug. 14, 1965; children—John Blair, Jill Marie, Eric Patrick. Sr. securities analyst Chem. Bank, 1968-71; adminstrv. asst. Coll. Retirement Equities Fund, 1971, asst. investment officer, 1972, investment officer, 1973, asst. v.p., 1974-76, 2d v.p., 1976, v.p., investment mgr., mem. investment com., 1976—. Pres., Eatontown Republican Club, 1970-71. Served to lt. USNR, 1964-68. Fellow Fin. Analysts Fedn.; mem. N.Y. Soc. Security Analysts, Electro-Sci. Analysts Group, Computer Ind. Analysts Group, Sigma Nu, Alpha Kappa Psi. Republican. Episcopalian. Club: Lions. Home: 17 Emory Ct Eatontown NJ 07724 Office: 711 3d Ave New York City NY 10017

FRANZ, EDWARD QUINLISK, clergyman; b. Erie, Pa., June 14, 1918; s. Edward Fredric and Gertrude Ellen (Quinlisk) F.; A.B., Catholic U. Am., 1940, M.A., 1941, Ph.D., 1950. Ordained priest Roman Catholic Ch., 1945; prof. philosophy Gannon Coll., Erie, 1945-61; prof. St. Mary of the Plains, Dodge City, Kan., 1961-63; asst. pastor St. Callistus, Kane, Pa., 1963-65; pastor Sacred Heart Ch., Genesee, Pa., 1965-66; pastor Holy Cross Ch., Brandy Camp, Pa., 1966-72, Immaculate Conception Ch., Clarion, Pa., 1972-73, Our Lady of the Lake Ch., Edinboro, Pa., 1973—; tchr. Elk County Christian High Sch., St. Marys, Pa., 1966-71; prof. Alliance Coll., Cambridge Springs, Pa., 1973-74, Gannon Coll., Erie, Pa., 1975—; dir. continuing edn. of clergy Diocese of Erie, 1976—. Mem. Am. Cath. Philos. Assn., Metaphys. Soc. Am., Cath. U. Alumni Assn. K.C. (4 deg.). Author: Thomistic Doctrine On the Possible Intellect, 1950. Asso. editor: New Scholasticism, 1954-56. Contbr. articles to profl. jours.; contbg. author The New Cath. Ency. Home: 128 Sunset Dr Box 838 Edinboro PA 16412 Office: Our Lady of the Lake Church Edinboro PA 16412

FRANZ, HELMUT, chemist; b. Kahl, Germany, Sept. 22, 1930; s. Otto and Anna (Lederer) F.; came to U.S., 1967, naturalized, 1973; M.S., U. Wurzburg (Germany), 1959, Ph.D., 1962; m. Toni Becker, Feb. 14, 1958; children—Bettina, Jutta, Christine. Scientist, Max-Planck Inst. for Silicate Research, Wurzburg, 1962-67; research asso. Rensselaer Poly. Inst., Troy, N.Y., 1967-69; sr. scientist PPG Industries Inc., Pitts., 1969—. Mem. Am. Ceramic Soc., Am. Chem. Soc. Republican. Roman Catholic. Contbr. articles on phys. chemistry and glass sci. to sci. jours.; patentee in field. Home: 201 Ridge Rd Pittsburgh PA 15238 Office: PO Box 11472 Pittsburgh PA 15238

FRANZ, ROBERT FRANCIS, JR., lab. dir.; b. Cin., Apr. 19, 1929; s. Robert Francis and Myrtle Katherine (Lindemann) F.; B.S., Xavier U., 1951; M.S., U. Wis., 1956; postgrad. Indsl. Coll. Armed Forces, 1971-72; m. Jane Ellen Linehan, Mar. 8, 1952; children—Barbara, Katherine, Mary, Robert Francis, Teresa, Mark, Christine. Commd. 2nd lt., U.S. Army, 1951, advanced through grades to col., 1971, ret., 1974; asst. dir. Gillette Advanced Tech. Lab., Cambridge, Mass., 1974-76, dir. research and devel. support, 1976—. Vice pres. Bryn Mawr PTA, 1965-66; instl. rep. Boy Scouts Am., Edgewood, Md., 1968; chmn. youth activities Civic Assn. of Lakeridge, Va., 1971, chmn. ways and means, 1972; pres. Forest Glen Civic Assn., 1976. Decorated Legion of Merit (2), Air Medal, Army Commendation Medal (3). Mem. Armed Forces Chem. Assn. (chpt. v.p. 1958), Am. Mgmt. Assn., Am. Def. Preparedness Assn. Republican. Roman Catholic. Home: 17 Olde Lantern Rd Acton MA 01720 Office: 252 Third St Cambridge MA 02142

FRANZ, SALLY ANN JOHNSON, nurse, educator; b. Rockford, Ill., Apr. 24, 1923; d. Herbert A. and Aileen (Peyton) Johnson; R.N., Good Samaritan Hosp., 1945; student U. Ill., 1948-49; m. Robert C. Franz, Apr. 29, 1978; children—Ann Elizabeth, Stacey Aileen, Linda Carol Franz. John Robert Powers model, 1946, Coranet model Miami, 1947; nurse obstetrics delivery Women's Hosp., N.Y.C., 1947-49, St. Francis Hosp., Evanston, Ill., 1953; charge, head nurse Broward Gen. Hosp., Ft. Lauderdale, Fla., 1968; night supr. Ashbrook Convalescent and Nursing Hosp., Scotch Plains, N.J., 1968—. Council chmn. Betty Merit Tchrs. Scholarship, 1962; area nat. organizer Girl Scouts U.S.A., 1962-65; Westfield (N.J.) Round-Up and Health chmn., 1962-63; pres. Tamaques Sch., 1965, adviser Parent Tchr. Orgn., 1966, fgn. relationship chmn., 1967-68; exec. bd. chmn. Westfield High Sch. PTA Newsletter, 1968-70; chmn. Nat. Space Edn., Westfield, 1964; Westfield chmn. fgn. nurses Overlook Hosp., Summit, N.J., 1964-69. Recipient scholarship to Harvard U. Coll. Bus. Mem. Am., Nat. Dist. nurses assns., NOW (N.J. co-ordinator 1967-68), Am. Contract Bridge League, Bridge Tchrs. Assn. Republican. Episcopalian. Inventor holder for marking device. Home: 823 Nancy Way Westfield NJ 07090 also 6750 NE 21st Rd Fort Lauderdale FL 33308 Office: 61 Roosevelt Blvd Florham Park NJ 07932

FRASER, CHARLES EDWARD OVID, microbiologist, veterinarian; b. Georgetown, Guyana, Nov. 6, 1926; s. Newton Berthier and Jane Elizabeth (Fraser) F.; came to U.S., 1961, naturalized, 1972; B.Vsc., U. Liverpool (Eng.), 1957, M.R.C.V.S., 1957; D.T.V.M., U. Edinburgh (Scotland), 1961; M.S., U. Wis., 1964, Ph.D., 1966; m. Mary Madeline Jones, July 27, 1957; children—Paul Garth, Parris Britton, Natalie Jane. Vet. officer Govt. Guyana, 1957-61; research asst. dept. vet. sci. U. Wis.-Madison, 1961-66; research asso. Harvard Sch. Pub. Health, Boston, 1966-71, asst. prof., 1971—; owner Southborough (Mass.) Vet. Clinic, 1973—. Pres., Southborough Village Soc., 1971-72; mem. solid waste disposal site selection com., Southborough, 1972-73. Recipient Sci. Research award Am. Assn. Lab. Animal Sci., 1969. Mem. Am. Assn. Immunologists (travel fellow 1974), Royal Coll. Vet. Surgeons, Am. Soc. Microbiologists, AAAS, Mass. Vet. Med. Assn. Episcopalian (sec. vestry 1969-73). Club: Rotary (pres. 1974-75. Contbr. articles and chpts. to profl. jours. and books. Home: 79 Marlborough Rd Southborough MA 01772

FRASER, VIRGINIA I. MANY (MRS. KENNETH W. FRASER), club woman; b. New Brighton, S.I., N.Y., Sept. 12, 1922; d. Charles Reginald and Irene (Hawkins) Many; student Katherine Gibbs Sch., 1941; m. Kenneth W. Fraser, Dec. 2, 1953; children—Virginia Susan, Sally Irene. Sec., A.R.C., Mitchell Field, N.Y., 1943-46; Textron, Inc., N.Y.C., 1946-50; exec. sec. J.P. Stevens & Co., Inc., N.Y.C., 1950-53. Del., Mid Century White House Conf. Children and Youth, 1950; pres. N.Y. Council Save the Children Fedn., 1950-51. Mem. N.Y. State Fedn. Women's Clubs (chmn. jr. dept. 1949-50), Clubwoman Gen. Fedn. Woman's Clubs (bd. 1950-51), D.A.R. Clubs: Flower Hill Garden (pres. 1964-65, 72-73), Port Washington Garden, Sands Point Garden, Manhasset Bay Yacht. Home: 33 Barkers Point Rd Sands Point NY 11050

FRATER, ROBERT WILLIAM MAYO, surgeon, educator; b. Cape Town, South Africa, Nov. 12, 1928; s. Kenneth and Ethel (Barrow) F.; M.B., B. Chir. (Jagger scholar), U. Cape Town Med. Sch., 1952; M.S. in Surgery (Minn. Heart Assn. fellow), U. Minn., 1961; m. Elaine Glynn Nagle, Aug. 27, 1954; children—Hugh R., Dirk A., Phillipa. Came to U.S., 1964, naturalized, 1974. Intern medicine and surgery Groote Schuur Hosp., Cape Town, 1953; resident casualty officer Lewisham Hosp., London, Eng., 1955; fellow gen. and thoracic surgery Mayo Clinic, 1955-61; sr. lectr. cardiothoracic surgery U. Cape Town, 1962-64; asst. prof. surgery Albert Einstein Coll. Medicine, N.Y.C., 1964-68, asso. prof., 1968-72, prof. surgery, 1972—, chief cardiothoracic surgery, 1968—, acting chmn. dept. surgery, 1971-75, also mem. Senate Council, 1971-74; chief cardiothoracic surgery Montefiore Hosp. and Med. Center, 1975—; mem. exec. council Bronx (N.Y.) Municipal Hosp. Center, Albert Einstein Coll. Hosp., 1969—, also mem. staff; staff Lawrence Hosp., Bronxville, N.Y. Recipient award Noble Found., 1961; West Jones scholarship, 1944-46; NIH grants, 1965-70, 1968-70, 74; Am. Heart Assn. grants, 1966, 71. Fellow Royal Coll. Surgeons, A.C.S., Am. Coll. Cardiology; mem. Am. Assn. Thoracic Surgery, Soc. Thoracic Surgeons, N.Y. Soc. Thoracic Surgery (pres. 1978), N.Y. Surg. Soc. (council 1975—), Assn. Acad. Surgeons, Am. Heart Assn. Club: Bronxville Field. Home: 17 Gladwin Pl Bronxville NY 10708 Office: 1300 Morris Park Ave Bronx NY 10461

FRAUENS, MARIE, editor, researcher; b. Kansas City, Mo., July 10, 1902; d. Frank Henry and Amanda Margaret (Stansch) Frauens; A.A., Kansas City (Mo.) Jr. Coll., 1921; B.Journalism, U. Mo., 1924; M.A., Tchrs. Coll., Columbia U., 1947; postgrad. Naval Reserve Officers' Sch., Washington, 1955-64, Indsl. Coll. of Armed Forces, 1964. Swimming instr., Kansas City, Mo., 1919-21; researcher Mo. State Hist. Soc., 1922-24; teaching prin., dir. extra curricular newspaper and dramatics club Wardell (Mo.) High Sch., 1924-27; math. editor, Row Peterson and Co., Evanston, Ill., 1927-35; chief editor high sch. program, McGraw-Hill Book Co., N.Y.C., 1935-43; commd. lt. j.g. USNR, 1943, advanced through grades to permanent commn. as lt. comdr., 1949, liaison officer U.S. Navy-U.S. Armed Forces Inst., 1943-44, tng. officer Bur. Ordnance, 1944-47; tech. writer Tng. Publs. Project, 1947-49; ret. from Res., 1965; tng. dir., John I. Thompson and Co., Washington, 1949-57; tech. writer, Dept. Navy, Washington, 1957; adminstrv. officer Office of Sec. of Defense, Washington, 1958-69; free-lance editor, researcher, Washington, 1969—, messages of Gov. Ky. to gen. assembly for Ky. Hist. Soc., 1974-76; editor The Machine Gun, Vol. II, Part VII for Lt. Col. George Chinn, USMC, 1952; editor reports for, also exec. sec. Spl. Com. Adequacy of Range Facilities, Dept. Def., 1958. Active first aid, health courses ARC, 1917-18; girls' advisor YWCA, Kansas City, 1923; counselor Chgo. settlement house, 1930-35; active Red Cross Fund, D.C., 1949; mem. bd. dirs. Naval Gun Factory Welfare and Recreation Assn., 1947-49; mem. work group to develop Interagency Sci. and Engring. Exhibit The Vision of Man, Office Sec. Def., 1963-65. Decorated mil. medals. Mem. Naval Res. Assn., Ret. Officers Assn., Res. Officers Assn., Am. Def. Preparedness Assn., Washington Film Council, Ky. Hist. Soc., Capitol Hill Restoration Soc., Pi Gamma Mu. Contbr. to Commn. Implications of Armed Services Ednl. Programs. Author manuals, pamphlets in field of naval ops. Home and Office: 923 E Capitol Washington DC 20003

FRAUNBERGER, ROBERT CARL, cons. forester; b. Bridgeport, Conn., May 10, 1912; s. Carl Ernest and Grace Elvira (Sherman) F.; A.B., U. Mich., 1934, B.S. in Forestry, 1935; student bus. adminstrn. U. Chgo., U. Pa.; M.B.A., Temple U., 1950; m. Kathryn I. Hogan, June 17, 1939; 1 dau., Patricia K. With U.S. Forest Service, 1935-41; former logging supt., plant mgr. N.W. Veneer & Lumber Corp., Gladstone, Mich., mgr. forest ops. Atlas Plywood Corp., Boston, gen. mgr forest products div. Philco Corp., v.p., gen. mgr. Southeastern Industries, Inc., exec. v.p. Roddis Lumber and Veneer Co. Can., Sault Ste. Marie, Ont., v.p. mfg. Plywood, Inc.; forest products cons., 1946—; pres. Lumbermens Merchandising Corp., Wayne, Pa., 1955-75, cons., 1975—. Bd. dirs. Youth Orch. Greater Phila. Served as lt. (s.g.) USNR, 1943-46. Registered profl. forester, Mich., Ga. Mem. Phila. Wholesale Lumber Dealers Assn. (dir.), So. Cypress Mfrs. Assn. (dir.), Nat. Hardwood Lumber Assn., Soc. Am. Foresters, Forest Products Research Soc., Canadian Inst. Foresters, Assn. Cons. Foresters, Am., Pa. forestry assns., Middle Atlantic Lumber Dealers Assn., Eastern Lumber Salesmen Assn., Lumberman's Exchange City Phila., SAR, HooHoo, Main Line C. of C. (dir.), Theta Xi. Clubs: Rotary (pres. Wayne); Overbrook Golf. Contbr. articles to profl. jours.; speaker on forest products. Home: 626 Black Rock Rd Bryn Mawr PA 19010 Office: 107 N Aberdeen Ave Wayne PA 19087

FRAUST, CHARLES LAWRENCE, environ. engr.; b. Bronx, N.Y., Apr. 24, 1943; s. Milton Irving and Mildred Ida F.; B.C.E., Cooper Union, 1963; M.S., Northwestern U., 1966, Ph.D., 1969; 1 son, Kelly Joshua. Sr. staff engr. Western Electric Co., Allentown, Pa., 1968—. Past pres. Clean Air Council of Lehigh Valley; adviser Environ. Explorer Post I, 1975—. USPHS trainee, 1963-68. Registered profl. engr., Pa. Diplomate Am. Bd. Indsl. Hygiene. Mem. Am. Indsl. Hygiene Assn., Water Pollution Control Fedn., Air Pollution Control Assn., Pa. Environ. Council, Sigma Xi, Chi Epsilon. Contbr. chpt. to Environmental Control in Electronic Manufacturing, 1973, also articles to profl. jours. Office: 555 Union Blvd Allentown PA 18103

FRAYNE, NATHANIEL ZEBULON, dentist; b. N.Y.C., Oct. 27, 1911; s. Morris E. and Dinah (Sheff) F.; B.S., U. Va., 1934, M.S., 1935, D.D.S., U. Pa., 1939; m. Jeanne R. Olshan, Feb. 1, 1945; children—Heather Susan, Michael Lloyd. Asso. oral surgeon Polyclinic Post Grad. Med. Sch. and Hosp., N.Y.C., 1940-58; adj. oral surgeon Sydenham Hosp., N.Y.C., 1940-53; pvt. practice Jersey City, 1940—. Served from lt. (j.g.) to lt. USNR, 1943-45. Fellow Royal Soc. Health, Intercontinental Biog. Assn.; mem. AAAS, Am. Micros. Soc., ADA, N.J. Dental Assn., Pierre Fauchard Acad., Soc. Advancement Anesthesia Dentistry, Acad. Medicine N.J., Am. Inst. Biol. Scis., N.Y. Acad. Scis., Acad. Gen. Dentistry, Am. Endodontic Soc., Fedn. Am. Scientists. Clubs: Masons, Shriners. Author articles in field. Discovered and described new parasite specimen, U.S. Nat. Mus. Address: 2768 Kennedy Blvd Jersey City NJ 07306

FRAZIER, JOHN EARL, profl. engr.; b. Houseville, Butler County, Pa., July 4, 1902; s. Chauncey E. and Mary Ellen (Gibson) F.; B.S., Washington and Jefferson Coll., 1922, achievement citation award, 1954; grad. student chem. engring. practice, Mass. Inst. Tech., 1922-24, S.M., 1924; D.Sc., U. Brazil, 1938; m. Frances Sprague Lang, June 23, 1936; children—John Earl, Thomas Gibson. Chemist and engr. Berney Bond Glass Co. div. Owens-Illinois Glass Co., 1924-26; fuel engr. Simplex Engring. Co., 1926-28, asst. sec. and asst. treas., 1928-30, sec., treas., 1930-38; v.p. and treas. Frazier-Simplex, Inc., 1938-45, pres. and sec., 1945-67, pres., treas., 1967—; mem. adv. bd. Pitts. Nat. Bank (Washington County br.); past pres., dir. Washington Union Trust Co., Washington County Motor Club; past trustee, pres. bd. Western Center, Canonsburg; trustee, sec. Wash. Hosp., chmn. property com.; past chmn. adv. bd. dept. ceramic engring. U. Ill., Champaign-Urbana; life trustee Washington and Jefferson Coll.; past chmn., mem. Phoenix com. Glass Industry Award Bd.; bd. dirs. Ceramic Camera Club, past pres; past chmn. Pa. Economy League (Washington County br.); past pres. Washington (Pa.) C. of C.; past pres. Nat. Soc. of Am. Comp. Shooters. Recipient Distinguished Citizen award Washington (Pa.) City Council, 1960; Kappa Sigma Fraternity Man of Yr., 1964; Lion of Year, Washington (Pa.) Lions Club, 1970, John Jeppson award Am. Ceramic Soc., 1976. Registered profl. engr., Pa., Ark. Benjamin Franklin fellow Royal Soc. Arts of Eng.; fellow AAAS, Am. Ceramic Soc. (hon. life mem., v.p. 1967-68, treas. 1968-69, pres. 1970-71, chmn. Orton Meml. lecture com. 1968, recipient Bleininger award 1969), Soc. Glass Tech. Eng.; mem. N.Y. Acad. Scis., Pa. Ceramic Assn. (past pres., dir.), Ind. Heating Equipment Assn. Washington (past dir.), Am. Chem. Soc., Pa. Inst. Chemists (charter), Am. Soc. Mil. Engrs., Nat. Soc. Profl. Engrs., Am. Soc. Heating, Refrigeration and Air-Conditioning Engrs., ASTM, Nat. Acad. Engring., Nat. Inst. Ceramic Engrs. (PACE award judge 1962), Pa. Soc. N.Y.C., Nat. Rifle Assn. Am., Am. Legion. Pa. Atomic Scientists, Pa. Acad. Sci., Keramos, Sigma Xi, Phi Beta Kappa, Phi Chi Mu, Kappa Sigma. Republican. Presbyn. Clubs: Masons, Shriners, Jesters; Mass. Inst. Tech. Western Pa., also N.Y.; Druids, Univ. (Pitts.); Chemists (N.Y.C.); Univ., Varsity Lettermens, Fortnightly (pres. 1964); Lions, Elks. Author: Kilns for Nat. Ency.: co-author: Glass Sand and a Glass Industry in Puerto Rico; Glass Industry for Venezuela; also other papers for trade and sci. publs. Frazier-Keramos Library at Pa. State U. named in his honor. Home: 36 Morgan Ave Washington PA 15301 Office: 436 East Beau St Washington PA 15301

FREAD, DANNY LEE, hydrologist; b. Tuscola, Ill., July 17, 1938; s. Harold Sherman and Margaret Evelyn F.; student Carthage Coll., 1956-59; B.C.E., Mo. Sch. Mines and Metallurgy, 1961; M.C.E. (NDEA fellow), U. Mo., Rolla, 1969, Ph.D. in Civil Engring. (NDEA fellow), 1971; m. Helen Juanita Hale, Jan. 30, 1960; 1 dau., Kristin. Sr. engr. Texaco, Inc., Lawrenceville, Ill., 1961-67; research hydrologist, hydrologic research lab. Nat. Weather Service, Silver Spring, Md., 1971—. Registered profl. engr., Ill. Mem. ASCE (Walter L. Huber Civil Engr. Research prize 1976, J.C. Stevens award 1976), Am. Geophys. Union, Am. Water Resources Assn., Sigma Xi, Phi Kappa Phi. Mem. Ch. Jesus Christ of Latter-day Saints. Club: Washingtonian Country. Contbr. articles on hydraulics of rivers and reservoirs to profl. jours. Home: 9417 Bulls Run Pkwy Bethesda MD 20034 Office: 8060 13th St Silver Spring MD 20910

FRECH, RAYMOND JOSEPH, metals co. exec.; b. Jersey City, Apr. 12, 1947; s. Raymond Joseph and Veronica A. (Deetjen) F.; B.S., St. Peter's Coll., 1969; m. Frances Phyllis Cusumano, July 22, 1973; 1 son, Raymond Joseph. Staff accountant Peat, Marwick, Mitchell & Co., Newark, 1969-71, sr. accountant, 1972-73, supervising sr. accountant, 1974-75; controller Alusuisse Metals, Inc., Ft. Lee, N.J., 1975-78, asst. treas. and asst. sec. parent co. Alusuisse Am., Inc., 1978—. Served with AUS, 1969-75. C.P.A., N.J. Mem. Am. Inst. C.P.A.'s, N.J. Soc. C.P.A.'s. Office: Alusuisse Am Inc 299 Park Ave New York NY 10017

FRECHETTE, GERARD CONRAD, ednl. adminstr.; b. Woonsocket, R.I., Nov. 20, 1944; s. Joseph Eugene and Jeannette Alice (Lebrun) F.; B.A., Providence Coll., 1968; M.A., Northwestern State U., 1972; M.Ed., Rivier Coll., 1978; m. Carol Dawn Smith, June 10, 1967; children—Naomi, Erik, Jason, Sarah. Tchr. parochial schs., Taunton, Mass., 1968-69; grad. teaching asst. Northwestern State U., Natchitoches, La., 1971-72; edn. specialist Dept. of Navy, Manchester, N.H., 1973—; armed forces rep. Council of Chief State Sch. Officers in N.H.; chmn. Edn./Mil. adv. com.; com. mem. for writing of State Plan for Career Edn. in N.H. and Vt. Co-dir. Pre-Marital Confs., 1970-72; parent advisor Pembroke Advisory Com., 1976-77. Served with U.S. Army, 1969-70. Recipient Gold Wreath award USN, 1976, 77. Mem. Am., N.H. personnel and guidance assns., Nat., N.H. vocat. assns., Phi Kappa Phi. Roman Catholic. Author: Aid to Private Education in the State of R.I., 1968; GED Requirements in the New England States, 1975; High School Sociology: A Descriptive Statistical Analysis, 1972. Home: RFD 2 Lower Straw Rd Hopkinton NH 03301 Office: 500 Harvey Rd Manchester NH 03103

FRECKLETON, WINSTON EARLE, oceanographer, educator; b. Jamaica, W.I., Jan 21, 1941; s. Stanley A. and Enid V. (Williams) F.; came to U.S., 1971; B.S. in Meteorology and Oceanography, N.Y. U., 1973, M.S. (NSF Grad. fellow), 1975, postgrad. 1975-76; m. Valerie Patricia Hew, Feb. 27, 1965. Tech. officer Jamaica Meterol. Service, 1970-71, Weather Forecaster Jamaica Info. Service, 1970-71, Research asst. Poly. Inst. of N.Y., Bklyn., 1973-74, research asst. dept. of meteorology and oceanography, 1974—; lectr. dept. biology Fordham U., N.Y.C., 1974, oceanographer JAVEMEX, UN Project, Nat. Resource Conservation Dept., Jamaica, 1976—. Vice pres. Jamaica Progressive League, 1974-75. Decorated Queen's Royal Lanyard. World Meteorol. Orgn. Fellow, 1968-70. Mem. Am. Geophys. Union, Am. Meteorol. Soc., Am. Littoral, Am. Mus. Natural History, Chi Epsilon Pi. Contbr. articles to profl. publs. Home: 3021 Heath Ave Bronx NY 10463 Office: Dept Meteorology and Oceanography Poly Inst NY 333 Jay St Brooklyn NY 11201

FREDERIC, MYRON WAYNE, neurologist, internist; b. Washington, Jan. 1, 1936; s. Jerold L. and Grattis E. (Tanzy) F.; B.A., Ohio State U., 1954, M.D., 1958. Intern, Hosp. of U. Pa., Phila., 1958-59, postdoctoral fellow, 1961-62, resident in medicine, 1962-64, resident in neurology, 1964-66; practice medicine, specializing in neurology, Phila., 1966—; dir. dept. neurology Presbyn. U. Pa. Med. Center, 1971—, v.p. med. staff, 1973-74, pres. med. staff, 1975-77; asst. prof. neurology U. Pa. Med. Sch., Phila., 1970-76, asso. prof. neurology, 1976—, asso. prof. medicine, 1976—. Served with USN, 1959-61. Mem. A.M.A., Am. Acad. Neurology, Philadelphia County Med. Soc., Phi Beta Kappa, Alpha Epsilon Delta. Author: Central Vertigo, Causes and Treatment, 1969, 2d edit., 1973; Cerebrovascular Disease, 1971. Home: 4622 Pine St Philadelphia PA 19143 Office: 51 N 39th St Philadelphia PA 19104

FREDERICK, CALVIN JEFF, govt. health adminstr.; b. Muskogee, Okla., Sept. 22, 1917; s. Calvin Jeff and M. Maude (Baker) F.; M.A. (USPHS fellow 1952-54), U. Calif. at Los Angeles, 1954, Ph.D., 1955; m. Frances Eleanor Salino, Sept. 9, 1964; children—Kristina, Jeff; children by previous marriage—Kathryn, Julie, Melinda. Chief psychology services Patton State Hosp., Highland, Calif., 1963-68; dep. chief Center for Studies Suicide Prevention, Div. Spl. Mental Health, NIMH, Chevy Chase, Md., 1968-72, chief tng. and research fellowships Crime and Delinquency Center, Rockville, Md., 1972-74, chief disaster assistance and emergency mental health, 1974—; asst. prof. dept. psychiatry Johns Hopkins U. Med. Sch., 1968—; asso. prof.

George Washington U. Med. Sch., 1969—; mental health adviser Pan Am. Health Orgn., 1973—. Served with USAAF, 1942-43. Calif. Dept. Mental Hygiene grantee, 1963, 65; NIMH grantee, 1963. Diplomate Am. Bd. Profl. Psychology, Am. Bd. Psychol. Hypnosis. Mem. Nat. Register Health Services Providers in Psychology, Am. Psychol. Assn., AAAS, Am. Assn. Suicidology (exec. bd. 1971-75 pres. elect 1978), Am. Psychology Law Soc. (dir. 1970-73), Am. Group Psychotherapy Assn., Internat. Assn. Suicide Prevention. Author: Future of Psychotherapy, 1969; cons. editor Jour. Life Threatening Behavior, 1972—; also pub. health reports; contbr. numerous articles to profl. jours. Home: 10500 Rockville Pike Rockville MD 20852 Office: 5600 Fishers Ln Rockville MD 20852

FREDERICK, JONATHAN ELBERT, army officer; b. Riverside, Calif., Feb. 12, 1941; s. Elva Luther and Madeline Bessie (King) F.; B.S., N.Mex. State U., 1963; M.S., Oreg. State U., 1969; m. Louise Ardell Pendleton, Dec. 27, 1961; children—Cynthia Lynn, Jonathan Christopher. Commd. 2d lt. U.S. Army, 1963, advanced through grades to maj., 1969; served in Europe, 1963-66, Vietnam, 1969-70; with Def. Nuclear Agy., Los Alamos and Albuquerque, N.Mex., 1970-73; served in Europe, 1973-75; instr. physics dept. U.S. Mil. Acad., West Point, N.Y., 1977—. Decorated Bronze Star, Air medal, Commendation medal. Episcopalian. Home: 155 E Gardiner Loop West Point NY 10996 Office: Physics Dept US Military Academy West Point NY 10996

FREDERICK, LAFAYETTE, educator; b. Friarspoint, Miss., Mar. 19, 1923; s. James Davis and Ellen (Johnson) F.; B.S., Tuskegee Inst., 1943; M.S., U. Rhode, 1950; Ph.D., Wash. State U., 1952; m. Antoinette Ariene Reed, Dec. 24, 1950; children—Lewis Reed, Karla Mae, David Warren. Asso. prof., prof. biology So. U., Baton Rouge, 1952-62; prof. biology Atlanta U., 1962-76, chmn. dept. biology 1963-76; prof., chmn. dept. botany Howard U., Washington, 1976—; commr. Commn. on Undergrad. Edn. Biol. Scis., 1970-71; mem. biology achievement test com. Coll. Entrance Exam. Bd., 1971—, chmn., 1975—, discipline com. biology, 1974, com. examiners, 1974; chmn. gen. research support adv. com. NIH, 1975-76. Served with USNR, 1944-46. Recipient 2d Ann. Trustee award for excellence in teaching, 1964. Fellow Ga. Acad. Sci. (pres.-elect 1975); mem. AAAS, Bot. Soc. Am., Mycol. Soc. Am., Am. Phytopathol. Soc., Assn. Southeastern Biologists, So. Appalachian Bot. Club, Am. Inst. Biol. Scis., Fedn. Am. Scientists, Sigma Xi, Phi Sigma, Beta Beta Beta, Phi Kappa Phi. Presbyterian. Home: 6406 Ft Hunt Rd Alexandria VA 22307 Office: 2400 6th St NW Washington DC 20059

FREDERICKS, CARLTON, nutritionist; b. Oct. 23, 1910; s. David C. and Blanche (Goldsmith) Caplan; B.A., U. Ala., 1931; M.A., N.Y. U., 1949, Ph.D., 1955; m. Betty Schachter, Oct. 22, 1949; children—Alice, April, Dana, Spencer, Rhonda. Pvt. cons. in nutrition, edn., research, New City, N.Y., 1942—; broadcaster TV and radio; author, lectr.; prof. edn., nutrition Fairleigh Dickinson U., Rutherford, N.J., 1957—; health edn. cons. to N.J. schs. and communities. Price Pottenger Found. fellow, 1976. Fellow Acad. Med. Preventics (hon. life), Internat. Coll. Applied Nutrition (founding), Internat. Acad. Preventive Medicine (pres. 1975-76); mem. Internat. Acad. Metabiology (past dir.), Acad. Orthomolecular Psychiatry (asso.). Author: Food Facts and Fallacies, 1964; Low Blood Sugar and You, 1969; Psychonutrition, 1976; Breast Cancer—a Nutritional Approach, 1977; High Fiber Way to Total Health, 1977; Cookbook for Good Nutrition, 1977; contbr. articles on clin. nutrition to profl. jours.

FREDIANI, HAROLD ARTHUR, educator; b. N.Y.C., Dec. 23, 1911; s. Hugo John and Mary F. (Ceruti) F.; B.A., State U. Iowa, 1934, M.S., 1935; Ph.D., La. State U., 1937; m. Lois Hough, Sept. 4, 1935; children—Marita I. Frediani Herbold, Judith L. Frediani Yousten, Harold Arthur, Dale Steven; m. 2d, Gloria Maria Griffo, June 26, 1971; stepchildren—Robert Guido Nonni, Arthur James Nonni. Instr., La. State U., Baton Rouge, 1937-39, asst. prof., 1939-40; chief chemist Fisher Sci. Co., N.Y.C., 1940-47; asst. dir. control Merck & Co., Inc., Rahway, N.J., 1947-56; exec. dir. control Bristol Labs., Syracuse, N.Y., 1956-68, asst. v.p. ops., 1968-74, dir. pharm. counselors, 1974-76; sr. research asso. Cornell U., Ithaca, N.Y., 1976—; cons. Milton Roy Contact Lens Corp., Sarasota, Fla., dir. quality assurance, 1976-78; Fulbright prof. Istituto Superiore Sanità, Rome, 1951-52. Dir. Nat. Alliance Businessmen, Syracuse, 1971-72; supr. Town of Pompey (N.Y.), 1964-68. Fellow Am. Inst. Chemists; mem. Am. Chem. Soc., Am. Pharm. Assn., N.Y. Acad. Sci., Am. Assn. Cons. Chemists, Chemists Club, Alpha Chi Sigma, Phi Lambda Epsilon. Contbr. articles to profl. jours. Patentee in field. Home: RD 4 Mark Ln Cazenovia NY 13035

FREDRICK, JEROME F., chem. co. exec.; b. N.Y.C., Feb. 23, 1926; B.Sc. (Tremaine fellow in biology), Coll. City N.Y., 1949; M.Sc., N.Y. U., 1951, Ph.D., 1955; m. Miriam Macklin, June 6, 1946; children—Alan M., Naomi J., Sharona E. Instr. biology Coll. City N.Y., 1948-49; research biochemist N.Y.C. VA Hosp., 1949-51; chemist customs labs. U.S. Treasury Dept., N.Y.C., 1951-53; dir. chem. research Dodge Chem. Co., Boston, N.Y.C., 1954—; prof. Dodge Inst. Advanced Studies, Miami, Fla. and Boston; cons. enzymology NRC, 1957—. Founder, past chmn. Bronx Council Environ. Quality; chmn. Bronx region N-Y. Action for Clean Air Com. Trustee Am. Inst. City N.Y. Served with USNR, 1944-46. Recipient Fuller award Am. Chem Soc., 1944. Fellow Am. Inst. Chemists, N.Y. Acad. Scis.; mem. Am. Chem. Soc., Am. Inst. Biol. Scis., AAAS, Scandinavian, Japanese socs. plant physiologists. Author: Chelation Phenomena, 1960; Gel Electrophoresis, 1964; Plant Growth Regulators, 1967; Phylogenesis in Algae, 1971; Storage Polyglucosides, 1973; contbr. numerous articles on enzyme and chelation chemistry to profl. publs. Patentee in field. Office: 3425 Boston Post Rd Bronx NY 10469

FREDRICKSEN, CLEVE JOHN, mfg. co. exec.; b. Bklyn., Aug. 24, 1917; s. John A. and Laura A. (Olsen) F.; student St. John's U., 1937-40; m. Harriet Ingrid Johnsen, Dec. 7, 1940; children—Cleve Laurance, Brian Harold, Thomas Mark. Asst. sec., asst. treas. AMP, Inc., Harrisburg, Pa., 1941-42, dir., 1942—, sec., asst. treas., 1942-56, sec.-treas., 1956-59, v.p., treas., 1959-68, v.p., chief fin. officer, 1968-71, chmn. fin. com., 1971-75, chmn. bd., 1975—; dir. Pamcor, Inc., San Juan, P.R., 1952—, sec.-asst. treas., 1952-56, sec.-treas., 1956-59, v.p., treas., 1959-68, v.p., chief fin. officer, 1968-71, chmn. fin. com., 1971-75, chmn. bd., 1975—; dir. Dauphin Deposit Bank & Trust Co., Harrisburg, Harsco Corp. Bd. dirs. Polyclinic Med. Center, Harrisburg; trustee Kline Found., Harrisburg, Whitaker Health Sci. Fund, Boston; chmn. com. Whitaker Found. Presbyn. Mem. Pa. Soc. Clubs: West Shore Country (Camp Hill); Coral Beach and Tennis (Paget, Bermuda). Home: 345 N 27th St Camp Hill PA 17011 Office: Eisenhower Blvd Harrisburg PA 17111

FREDRICKSON, DONALD SHARP, physician; b. Canon City, Colo., Aug. 8, 1924; s. Charles Arthur and Blanche (Sharp) F.; Student U. Colo., 1942-43; B.S., U. Mich., 1946, M.D., 1949; M.D. (hon.), Karolinska Institutet, 1977; D.Sc. (hon.), U. Mich., 1977, Mt. Sinai Sch. Medicine, 1978; m. Henriette Priscilla Dorothea Eekhof, Sept. 5, 1950; children—Eric Henderikus, Rurik Charles. Intern Peter Bent Brigham Hosp., Boston, 1949-50; house staff mem., fellow Peter Bent Brigham and Mass. Gen. hosps., 1950-53; mem. sr. research staff lab. cellular physiology and metabolism Nat. Heart and Lung Inst., Bethesda, Md., 1955-61, clin. dir. inst., dir. inst., 1966-68, chief molecular disease br. div. intramural research, 1966, dir. div. intramural research, 1968-74; pres. inst. Medicine, Nat. Acad. Scis., 1974-75, dir. HIH, 1975—; professorial lectr. medicine George Washington U. Sch. Medicine, 1959—; lectr. preventive medicine Georgetown U. Sch. Medicine, 1963—. Served with U.S. Army, 1943-45. Recipient Gold Medal award Am. Coll. Cardiology, 1967, Internat. award James F. Mitchell Found. for Med. Edn. and Research, 1968. Distinguished Achievement award Modern Medicine, 1971; Superior Service award Dept. Health, Edn. and Welfare, 1970, Distinguished Service award, 1971; McCollum award Am. Soc. Clin. Nutrition and Clin. div. Am. Inst. Nutrition, 1971; Modanina prize, 1975; Irving Cutter medal, 1978; Gairdner Found. award, 1978. Jimenez Diaz lectr., 1974. Fellow Am. Coll. Cardiology; life fellow A.C.P.; mem. AAAS, Am. Heart Assn., Am. Physiol. Soc., Am. Soc. Clin. Investigation, Am. Soc. Human Genetics, Assn. Am. Physicians, Harvey Soc. (hon.), Internat. Soc. Cardiology (exec. com.), Med. Soc. Sweden, Nat. Acad. Scis., Soc. Pediatric Research, Washington Soc. Pathologists, Inst. Medicine Brit. Cardiac Soc. (corr.), Phi Beta Kappa, Phi Kappa Phi, Alpha Omega Alpha. Editor: (with others) The Metabolic Basis of Inherited Diseases, 4th edit., 1978. Contbr. articles to profl. jours. Home: 6615 Bradley Blvd Bethesda MD 20034 Office: NIH Bethesda MD 20014

FREE, ANN COTTRELL, writer; b. Richmond, Va.; d. Emmett Drewry and Emily (Blake) Cottrell; grad. Collegiate Sch. for Girls, Richmond, 1934; student Richmond div. Coll. William and Mary, 1934-36; A.B., Barnard Coll., Columbia, 1938; m. James Stillman Free, Feb. 24, 1950; 1 dau., Elissa. Reporter Richmond Times Dispatch, 1938-40; Washington corr., Newsweek, 1940-41, Chgo. Sun, 1941-43, N.Y. Herald Tribune, 1943-46; pub. information dir. UNRRA China Mission, Shanghai, 1946-47; corr. Middle and Nr. East and Europe, 1947-48; writer-photographer Marshall Plan, Washington and Western Europe, 1949-50; contbr. N.Am. Newspaper Alliance Syndicate, Washington Post, Washingtonian Mag., Defenders of Wildlife, Animals Mag.; Washington editor EnviroSouth Quar. Founding Mem. Friends Nat. Zoo, Eleanor Roosevelt Meml. Commn.; mem. adv. com. Council Livestock Protection; assembly mem. Inst. Ecology; cons. expert Rachel Carson Trust for Living Environment. Bd. dirs. Albert Schweitzer Fellowship. Recipient Dodd Mead-Boys' Life Writing award, 1963, Albert Schweitzer medal, Animal Welfare Inst., 1963, Jr. Book award certificate Boys Clubs of Am., 1964; Humanitarian of Yr. awards Washington Animal Rescue League, 1971, Montgomery County Humane Soc., 1971, News Writing award Dog Writers Assn. Am., 1975, 78. Unitarian. Club: Washington Press. Author: Forever the Wild Mare, 1963. Home: 4700 Jamestown Rd (Westmoreland Hills MD) Washington DC 20016

FREE, SPENCER MICHAEL, JR., biostatistician; b. Greensburg, Pa., Jan. 24, 1923; s. Spencer Michael and Eliza Jeanne (Hunter) F.; B.A., Washington and Jefferson Coll., 1947; M.S., N.C. State Coll., 1952, Ph.D. (Moss Tobacco Research fellow), 1954; m. Patricia Louise Floyd, July 9, 1948; children—Patricia Jeanne Free Lynam, Spencer Michael, David Floyd, Donald Kevin. Geophysicist, Seismograph Service Corp., Tulsa, 1947-48; chemist Samuel Roberts Noble Found., Ardmore, Okla., 1948-50; biostatistician Smith Kline & Franch Labs., Phila., 1954—; prof. statistics Wharton Sch., U. Pa., 1977—; prof. biometry Temple Med. Sch., 1957-73; instr. grad. math Villanova U., 1969-74. Active Boy Scouts Am., also youth athletic programs. Served to lt. (j.g.) USNR, 1943-46. Fellow Am. Statis. Assn., Am. Pub. Health Assn.; mem. Biometrics Soc. (chmn. adv. bd. 1957-64), Gordon Research Conf. Statistics Chemistry and Chem. Engring. (chmn. 1966). Home: 420 Midland Ave Wayne PA 19087 Office: 1500 Spring Garden St Philadelphia PA 19101

FREED, ARTHUR, traffic engr.; b. Paris, Dec. 11, 1930 (parents Am. citizens); s. Harry and Mollie (Feinberg) F.; B.C.E., Coll. City N.Y., 1953; m. Judith Lois Kaplan, July 31, 1960; children—Lisa Anne, Andrew Scott. Jr. civil engr. Westchester County (N.Y.) Dept. Pub. Works, 1953-58, asst. civil engr., 1958-60, sr. civil engr., 1960-62, traffic engr., 1962—; exec. dir. Traffic Safety Bd., 1971—. Mem. N.Y. State traffic engring. adv. com. to Dept. Motor Vehicles, 1959-68; mem. Nat. Adv. Com. on Uniform Traffic Control Devices, 1972—; rep. Pres.'s Com. on Traffic Safety; mem. Hwy. Research Bd. Commn. on Motor Vehicle and Traffic Law, 1965-76; v.p. N.Y. State Assn. Traffic Safety Bds., 1972—; mem. adv. bd. on engring. tech. Westchester Community Coll., 1971—. Served with U.S. Army, 1953-55. Recipient award of merit State Traffic Safety Council, 1964; Engr. of Year award Internat. Inst. Transp., 1978. Mem. Inst. Transp. Engrs. (pres. N.Y.-N.J. 1965-66), ASCE, N.Y. Soc. Profl. Engrs., Nat. Acad. Sci., N.Y. State, Greater N.Y. safety councils, Nat. Assn. Counties (chmn. traffic adv. com. 1974—, County Achievement award 1977). Registered profl. engr., N.Y. Contbr. articles to profl. jours. Home: 6 Patricia Ln White Plains NY 10605 Office: County Office Bldg White Plains NY 10601

FREEDMAN, AARON DAVID, physician; b. Albany, N.Y., Jan. 4, 1922; s. Jacob Abraham and Pauline Rebecca (Hoffman) F.; A.B., Cornell U., 1942; M.D., Albany Med. Coll., 1945; Ph.D., Columbia U., 1958; M.A. (hon.), U. Pa., 1972; m. Alice P. Maurer, Sept. 10, 1948; children—Abigail Faith, Jonathan Joel, Jeremy Sholom. Intern, Mt. Sinai Hosp., N.Y.C., 1945-46, resident in internal medicine, 1948-51; asst. prof. medicine biochemistry Columbia U., 1958-65; clin. prof. medicine U. Kans., Kansas City, 1965-69; chmn. dept. medicine Menorah Med. Center, Kansas City, Mo., 1965-69; dir. Danciger Found., Kansas City, 1966-69; asso. dean Sch. Medicine, U. Pa., Phila., 1969-75, prof. medicine, 1969-75, exec. dir. Grad. Hosp., 1972-75; prof. medicine Coll. City N.Y., 1975—, dir. Herman Goldman Inst. Human Biology, 1975—, acting dean Sophie Davis Sch. Biomed. Edn. and acting coll. v.p. for health affairs; sec. med. bd. Delafield Hosp., N.Y.C.; pres. med. bd. Jackson County (Mo.) Hosp.; bd. mgrs. Grad. Hosp., Phila.; trustee Pa. Inst. Contyi Med. Edn.; mem. N.Y. Bd. Med. Examiners; trustee Western Mo. Arthritis Found., Kansas City Kidney Found., 1965-69. Trustee Ardsley (N.Y.) Sch. Bd., 1962-65, Jewish Vocat. Service, Children's Aid. Served to capt. M.C., U.S. Army, 1946-48, to capt. M.C., USAF, 1953. Libman Found. fellow, 1951-54; NIH postdoctoral fellow, 1954-58; NIH grantee, 1962-66. Mem. Am. Soc. Biol. Chemists, Am. Soc. Cell Biology, Harvey Soc., Phi Beta Kappa, Phi Kappa Phi. Jewish. Editor: Seminars in Medicine, 1973; contbr. research papers in biochemistry and medicine to profl. jours., 1952—. Home: 545 West End Ave New York City NY 10024 Office: 137th and Convent Ave New York City NY 10031

FREEDMAN, ABRAHAM E., lawyer; b. Phila., Aug. 25, 1906; s. Barnett and Rebecca (Rowling) F.; LL.B., Temple U., 1933; m. Roz B. Schneider, June 15, 1930; children—Joan Phyllis (Mrs. Herbert C. Meyer), Barbara Dee (Mrs. Andre G. Sassoon). From engr. to asst. sect. engr. transit dept. City Phila., 1925-32; admitted to Pa. bar, 1933, since practiced in Phila.; mem. firm Freedman, Landy and Lorry, 1944-64, Freedman, Borowsky and Lorry, 1964-76, Freedman and Lorry, 1976—. Mem. adv. com. Supreme Ct., U.S. on Admiralty Rules, 1960—, mem. adv. com. Supreme Ct. U.S. on Civil Rules; permanent mem. 3d Jud. Conf.; permanent mem. 4th Jud. Conf.; lectr. Am. Law Inst., 1959, Practicing Law Inst. Fellow Am. Coll. Trial Lawyers, Internat. Acad. Trial Lawyers (pres. 1962); mem. Internat., Am., Pa., Phila., Fed., N.Y. bar assns., Am. Trial Lawyers Assn. (chmn. admiralty sect. 1950-65). Home: 413 Meadow Ln Merion PA 19066 Office: Lafayette Bldg Chestnut St at Fifth Philadelphia PA 19106

FREEDMAN, BERNARD W., lawyer; b. N.Y.C., June 14, 1934; s. Joseph Max and Sylvia (Casif) F.; B.A. with honors, Rutgers U., 1956; LL.B., Seton Hall U., 1966, J.D., 1969; m. Christina Centuori, Aug. 5, 1956; children—Mitchell Jay, Shari Fern. Tchr. govt. and history, Chatham, N.J., 1959-64; dir. welfare, Woodbridge, N.J., 1964-67; admitted to N.J. bar, 1966; asso. firm Hutt & Berkow, Perth Amboy, 1967-68; dep. mayor, bus. adminstr., zoning bd. atty. Twp. of Woodbridge, 1968-71; counsel U.S. Home Corp. of N.J., Freehold, 1971-75; asst. gen. counsel Prel Corp., River Edge, N.J., 1975-76; asst. resident atty. Prudential Ins. Co., Newark, 1976—; tchr. consumer law Woodbridge Adult Sch. Counsel Congregation Ohev Shalom, Colonia, N.J.; pres. Woodbridge Young Democrats, 1968-69, Middlesex County Young Dems., 1970-71; v.p. Colonia Dem. Club, 1968—; mem. exec. bd. Woodbridge Com. for Charter Reform, 1961-63; mem. exec. com. Middlesex County Dem. Orgn., 1970-71. Served with USAF, 1956-59. Recipient Disting. Service award N.J. Jaycees, 1966, Woodbridge Twp. Jaycees, 1966. Mem. Am., N.J., Middlesex County bar assns., Am. Fedn. Musicians. Club: B'nai B'rith. Home: 22 Kristin Ct Colonia NJ 07067 Office: 10 Bank St Newark NJ 07102

FREEDMAN, ELISHA CHAIM, city mgr. Rochester (N.Y.); b. Hartford, Conn., Aug. 12, 1926; s. Joseph D. and Dorothea (Simons) F.; student U. Conn., 1946-48, Trinity Coll., summer 1947; A.B. cum laude, Syracuse U., 1949, M.Pub.Adminstrn., 1955; m. Adeline Kaufman, Feb. 11, 1951; children—Jonathan, Noah, Jeremy, Anne. With Fed. Rent Control Office, Hartford, 1951-52, Conn. Employees Assn., 1951, Hartford Redevel. Agy., 1952-53; supr. budget and research City of Hartford, 1955-59, exec. sec. to city mgr., 1959-63, city mgr., 1963-71; town controller, Manchester, Conn., 1959; chief adminstrv. officer Montgomery County, Rockville, Md., 1971-72; head pub. sector office exptl. research and devel. incentives program NSF, Washington, 1972-74; city mgr. City of Rochester (N.Y.), 1974—. Mem. task force ERDA, 1975-76; mem. Conn. Temporary Commn. for Study Municipal Collective Bargaining, 1964-65, Conn. Planning Com. on Criminal Adminstrn., 1968-71. Recipient Louis Brownlow award for Outstanding Contbn. to Lit. of Pub. Adminstrn., Internat. City Mgmt. Assn., 1967. Mem. Am. Soc. Pub. Adminstrn. (pres. Conn. 1967), Internat. City Mgmt. Assn. (pres. Conn. chpt. 1969, regional v.p. 1976—). Home: 2053 Highland Ave Rochester NY 14610 Office: City Mgr City of Rochester 30 Broad St Rochester NY 14614

FREEDMAN, ELLEN S., health care adminstr.; b. Bklyn., Apr. 14, 1951; d. Willard and Ruth (Harris) F.; B.S. in Nursing, Hunter Coll., 1972; M.P.A., N.Y. U., 1975. Sr. Staff nurse Inst. Rehab. Medicine, N.Y. U. Med. Center, N.Y.C., 1972-75, instr. nursing inservice edn., 1975-77, coordinator research utilization project, 1977—; exec. sec. region II adv. council Research and Tng. Center I 1978; guest faculty Mt. Sinai Hosp., N.Y.C., 1976-78, N.Y. U. Grad. Sch. Pub. Adminstrn., 1978. Recipient Marchal award, 19—. Mem. Am. Pub. Health Assn., Am. Acad. Health Adminstrn., Sigma Theta Tau. Home: 340 E 34 St New York NY 10016 Office: 400 E 34 St New York NY 10016

FREEDMAN, GERALD STANLEY, radiologist; b. Bklyn., May 28, 1936; s. Martin and Adele (Goodman) F.; B.M.E., Cornell U., 1959; M.D., Columbia U., 1964; m. Karen Johnson, May 12, 1972; children—David, Julia. Resident in radiology Columbia-Presbyn. Hosp., N.Y.C., 1965-68; faculty Yale U. Sch. Medicine, New Haven, 1968-77, asso. clin. prof. radiology, 1978—; dir. radiology Temple Med. Center, New Haven, 1978—; indsl. cons. Mem. Conn. Computerized Tomography Task Force, 1978—. Mem. Soc. Nuclear Medicine (trustee), Radiol. Soc. N.Am., Am. Coll. Radiology, Am. Coll. Nuclear Physicians. Editor: Tomographic Imaging in Nuclear Medicine, 1973; Management Concepts in Nuclear Medicine, 1977; contbr. articles to profl. jours. Patentee. Home: 104 Riverview Ave Branford CT 06405 Office: 60 Temple St New Haven CT 06510

FREEDMAN, JEROME KENNETH, ophthalmologist; b. New Haven, Mar. 8, 1930; s. Barnett Philip and Lillian (Levy) F.; A.B., Yale U., 1951; M.D., Tufts U., 1955; M.S. in Surgery, U. Chgo., 1963; m. Carol Ann Rosenburg, June 25, 1956; children—Emily, Elizabeth, Eleanor. Intern, Yale-New Haven Hosp., 1955-56, now attending ophthalmologist, resident in ophthalmology U. Chgo., 1958-61, Nat. Inst. Neurol. Disease and Blindness fellow, instr. ophthalmology, 1961-63; practice medicine specializing in ophthalmology, New Haven, 1963—; asst. attending staff Hosp. St. Raphael; chmn. peer rev. com., trustee Conn. Area II, Profl. Standards Rev. Orgn.; mem. Conn. Statewide Profl. Standards Rev. Council. Served with USAF, 1956-58. Diplomate Am. Bd. Ophthalmology. Mem. AMA, Am. Acad. Ophthalmology and Otolaryngology, Conn. Med. Soc. (jr. asso., asso., sr. councilor 1971-76, v.p. 1976-77, pres.-elect 1977-78, pres. 1978-79), New Haven County Med. Assn., New Eng. Ophthalmology Soc., Assn. Research in Ophthalmology, New Haven Found. Med. Care (dir.). Republican. Jewish. Clubs: Quinnipiack, Mory's Assn., Yale (New Haven). Home: 460 St Ronan St New Haven CT 06511 Office: 1423 Chapel St New Haven CT 06511

FREEDMAN, JONATHAN ANDREW, mental health center exec.; b. Bklyn., Feb. 13, 1936; s. M. Joel and Florence B. Freedman; B.A., Wesleyan U., Middletown, Conn., 1957; M.A., Brandeis U., 1964, Ph.D. (NIMH fellow), 1973; m. Jo Ann Sanders, June 28, 1959; children—Lorin John, Michael James, Noah David. Lectr. Sch. Social Work, Syracuse (N.Y.) U., 1965-71, adj. prof. dept. sociology Maxwell Sch., 1977—; coordinator staff devel. Syracuse Psy. Hosp., 1971-72; dir. edn. and tng. Hutchings Psychiat. Center, Syracuse, 1973—; asst. prof. dept. psychiatry State U. N.Y. Upstate Med. Center, Syracuse, 1973—. Pres. Max Gilbert Hebrew Acad., 1972-74; unit pres. Am. Jewish Com., Syracuse, 1977—; mem. area com. Syracuse Reevaluation Counseling Community, 1975—. Mem. Am. Sociol. Assn. (sect. on sociol. practice), Am. Soc. Tng. and Devel., World Future Soc. Jewish. Co-author: Clinical Sociology, 1978; contbg. editor Colleague, 1977—. Home: 4305 LaFayette Rd Jamesville NY 13078 Office: PO Box 27 Syracuse NY 13210

FREEDMAN, MARION GLICKMAN, counselor; b. N.Y.C., Feb. 3, 1922; d. Edward and Minnie (Tokarsky) Glickman; B.S., N.Y. U., 1942, M.A. in Secondary Edn., 1964, M.A. in Guidance, 1967, postgrad., 1975-77; m. Bernard M. Freedman, Nov. 29, 1941; children—Rochelle Freedman Hassen, Diane Freedman Slatz. Tchr. high sch., guidance counselor Bushwick High Sch., Bklyn., 1965-74; guidance counselor James Monroe High Sch., Bronx, N.Y., 1974-76, 77—; career counselor Walton High Sch., Bronx, 1976-77. Mem. N.Y. U. Alumni Assn., Am., N.Y. State, N.Y.C. personnel and guidance assns., Delta Pi Epsilon. Jewish. Home: 6556 174th St Flushing NY 11365 Office: 1300 Boynton Ave Bronx NY 10472

FREEDMAN, WARREN, lawyer; b. Scranton, Pa., May 2, 1921; s. Samuel Norman and Sarah (Spitz) F.; B.A., Rutgers U., 1943; postgrad. Yale U., 1943, Cornell U., 1944; LL.B., Columbia U., 1949,

J.D., 1949; m. Esther Rosenbluth, May 3, 1944; children—Debby Freedman Stiebel, Douglas, Miriam. Admitted to N.Y. bar, 1949; instr. Rutgers U. Sch. Law, Newark, 1949-52; atty. examiner FTC, N.Y.C., 1951-53; counsel Clairol, Inc., N.Y.C., 1953-63; liability counsel Bristol Myers Co., N.Y.C., 1963—; instr. New Sch. for Social Work, N.Y.C., 1954-63. Mem. B'nai B'rith (dist. bd. govs. 1968—, nat. commr. Anti-Defamation League, vice chmn. nat. civil rights com.). Author: Richards on Insurance, 3 vols., 1952; Freedman on Allergy and Products Liability, 1960; Society on Trial, 1965; New and Unique Rights of the Person, 1966; Sociology and the Law, 1972; Selective Guide for the Jewish Traveler, 1972; World Guide for the Jewish Traveler, 1980. Home: 81 Stratford Rd New Rochelle NY 10804 Office: 345 Park Ave New York City NY 10022

FREELAND, CHARLES, lawyer; b. Balt., July 18, 1940; s. Benjamin and Beatrice (Polakoff) F.; B.S., U. Md., 1962, LL.B., 1965; diploma U.S. Naval Justice Sch., 1966; m. Beverly Klaff, July 15, 1965; children—Stephen Jason, Jennifer Jill, Gwen Nicole, Kimberly Suzanne. Admitted to Md. bar, 1965, U.S. Supreme Ct. bar, 1969; practiced in Pikesville, also Laurel, Balt., Md., 1968—; financial v.p. Collins Electronics Mfg.; dir. financial planning Cellu-Craft, Inc.; controller Braun-Crystal Mfg. Co., Inc., BCN Design Products, Inc.; v.p. Feirstein and Freeland; accountant, Balt., 1964—, Pikesville, Md., 1968—. Served to lt. USNR, 1965-68. C.P.A., Md. Mem. Am. Inst. C.P.A.'s, Am. (taxation and corp., banking and bus. law sects. 1972-78, com. on tax accounting problems 1976-78, subcom. on reporting of income and deductions 1976-78), Prince George's County, Md., Fed. bar assns., Am. Judicature Soc., Am. Assn. Attys.-C.P.A.'s, Am. Arbitration Assn. (nat. panel), Md. Assn. C.P.A.'s (budget, legislative, estate and gift tax, and fed. taxation coms. 1965-68, 74-75, 76-78). Democrat. Jewish. Club: Woodholme Country. Office: 206 Blaustein Bldg Baltimore MD 21201 also First Nat Bank Bldg Baltimore MD 21202 also Stewart Towers 200 Fort Meade Rd Laurel MD 20810 also 4 Timothy Green Ct Brooklandville MD 21022

FREELAND, T. PAUL, lawyer; b. Princeton, Ind., Sept. 26, 1916; s. L. Theodore and Leona (Tryon) F.; A.B., DePauw U., 1937; LL.B., Columbia, 1940; m. Caroline Van Dyke Ransom, July 7, 1941; 1 dau., Caroline Carr. Admitted to N.Y. bar, 1941, D.C. bar, 1948, Mass. bar, 1955; asso. Cravath, deGersdorff Swaine & Wood, N.Y.C., summer, 1939, Dunnington, Bartholow & Miller, 1940-42; atty. Office Chief Counsel, Bur. Internal Revenue, 1945-48; partner Wenchel, Schulman & Manning, Washington, 1949-62, Sharp and Bogan, Washington, 1962-65, Bogan & Freeland, 1965—. Lectr. tax insts., mem. various taxation coms. Trustee Embry-Riddle Aero. U. Served as lt., USCG, 1942-45, ETO. Mem. Inter-Am., Am., Fed., D.C. bar assns., Internat. Fiscal Assn., Phi Delta Phi. Methodist. Home: 5525 Pembroke Rd Bethesda MD 20034 Office: 1000 16th St NW Washington DC 20036

FREEMAN, CLIFFORD LEE, advt. exec.; b. Vicksburg, Miss., Feb. 14, 1941; s. James Evans and Lillian (Penkobeer) F.; B.S., Fla. State U., 1964; m. Susan Jane Kelner, Sept. 3, 1976; 1 son by previous marriage, Clifford Scott. Copywriter, Sears & Roebuck Co., Atlanta, 1965-66, Liller, Neal, Battle & Lindsey, Atlanta, 1966-68, McCann-Erickson, Atlanta, 1968-70; copywriter, v.p., creative group head Dancer-Fitzgerald & Sample, N.Y.C., 1970-78. Served with Ga. N.G., 1964-70. Recipient Clio award Outstanding Creative Accomplishment, Am. TV Radio Commls. Festivals Group, 1976, 78. Mem. Sigma Chi, Alpha Delta Sigma. Composer songs. Office: Dancer Fitzgerald & Sample 347 Madison Ave New York City NY 10017

FREEMAN, DAVID REED, investor; b. Fredericksburg, Va., July 18, 1941; s. George Cephas and Kathryn (Reed) F.; student U. N.C., 1959-60; m. Patricia Harrison Tydings, May 2, 1977; children by previous marriage—Kimberly Rowe, David Reed; 1 stepson, Basil W. Tydings, Jr. Instl. salesman Eastman Dillon, Union Securities & Co., Washington, 1963-71; v.p. sales Blyth, Eastman Dillon, Washington, 1972-74; chmn. bd. Freeman Distributing Co., Inc., Alexandria, Va., 1973-74; pres., owner Freeman Enterprises, Easton, Md., 1974—; chmn. bd. Tidewater Roofing and Bldg. Supply Co., Inc., 1975—; dir. Washington-Lee Savs. & Loan Assn., 1972—, chmn. adv. bd., 1976—. Bd. dirs. Historic Easton, Inc., 1975—, Easton YMCA, 1976—; chmn. bd. deacons First Bapt. Ch., Easton, 1976—, bd. trustees, 1975—. Mem. Early Am. Soc., Talbot County Hist. Soc., Victorian Soc. Am., Nat., Md. trusts for hist. preservation. Republican. Clubs: Commonwealth (Richmond, Va.); Talbot County Country. Home: Waverly Island Farm RD 4 Box 110 Easton MD 21601 Office: 115 Federal St Easton MD 21601

FREEMAN, ISADORE, pianist; b. Paterson, N.J., Sept. 5, 1912; s. Abram and Anna (Katch) F.; student N.Y. Coll. Music, 1939-41; Mus.B., Perfield Music Sch., 1941; m. Sarah Levin, July 10, 1938. Pianist, chamber music artist; performer with mems. N.Y. Philharmonic Orch.; coach, accompanist; pvt. tchr.; instr. Rutgers U., 1973-74; group instr. pvt., pub., adult schs.; chmn. Nat. Music Week, Nat. Assn. Music Clubs for N.J., 1955-71; reviewer arts Fair Lawn Beacon weekly, 1970-71; prof. music Kean Coll., Union, N.J. Founder, Federated Arts Council Fairlawn, 1965—; founder, dir. Flame-Friends of Living Arts and Music Enjoyment, 1960-71; chmn. Cultural Activities in Fairlawn, 1961; bd. dirs. Fairlawn Summer Festival Music, 1961. Recipient Spl. award for cultural contbns. to community Fair Lawn Council, 1965; Nat. Fedn. Music Clubs, 1972. Mem. N.Y. Musicians Club, The Bohemians, Am. Fedn. Musicians (chmn. music trust fund 1969-73, sec. 1974-75). Club: Rotary. Address: 13-08 Bellair Ave Fairlawn NJ 07410

FREEMAN, LEONARD MURRAY, radiologist, physician, educator; b. N.Y.C., Apr. 20, 1937; s. Joseph and Tillie (Krautman) F.; B.A., N.Y. U., 1957; M.D., Chgo. Med. Sch., 1961; m. Marlene Carolyn Held, Apr. 28, 1967; children—Eric Lawrence, David Robert. Intern, Beth Israel Hosp. and Med. Center, N.Y.C., 1961-62; resident in radiology Bronx (N.Y.) Municipal Hosp. Center, 1962-65; asst. attending radiologist Bronx Municipal Hosp. Center and Hosp. of Albert Einstein Coll. Med., N.Y.C., 1965-67, asso. attending radiologist, 1967-77, co-dir. div. nuclear medicine, 1965—; chief nuclear med. Montefiore Hosp. and Med. Center, N.Y.C., 1976—, attending radiologist, 1977—; cons. nuclear medicine USPHS Hosp., S.I., N.Y., 1967—, Fordham Hosp., Bronx, 1970-76, St. Barnabas Hosp. Chronic Diseases, Bronx, 1967—, Beth Israel Hosp. and Med. Center, 1974—; asst. instr. radiology Albert Einstein Coll. Med., Bronx, 1964-65, instr., 1965-67, asst. prof., 1967-72, asso. prof., 1972-77, prof., 1977—; adv. com. Nuclear Med. Program Brookhaven Nat. Labs., Upton, N.Y., 1972—; examiner nuclear med. Am. Bd. Radiology. Fellow Am. Coll. Radiology; mem. Soc. Nuclear Medicine (gov. local chpt. 1973—, chmn. edn. com. 1974—, chmn. award com. 1972-73; nat. trustee 1973-77, rep. Am. Coll. Radiology's Commn. Nuclear Med. 1975-77, chmn. nat. sci. program. com. 1972-73, nat. v.p. 1977-78, nat. pres. 1979-80), Am. Coll. Nuclear Physicians (publs. com., 1974-77, nuclear med. dept. resourses com. 1975—), Assn. Univ. Radiologists, Radiol. Soc. N.Am., N.Y. Roentgen Soc., L.I. Radiol. Soc., AMA, N.Y. State, Nassau County med. socs., Pan Am. Med. Assn. (hon. life), L.I. Soc. Nuclear Med. Technologists (hon. life). Author: Clinical Scintillation Scanning, 1969; Clinical Scintillation Imaging, 1975; co-editor Seminars in Nuclear Medicine, 1970—, Physicians Desk Reference for Radiology and Nuclear Med., 1971—; reviewer Jour. Nuclear Med., 1972—; contbr. numerous articles to jours., also book chpts. Home: 65 Oak Dr E Hills NY 11576 Office: 111 E 210th St Bronx NY 10467

FREEMAN, MILTON V., lawyer; b. N.Y.C., Nov. 16, 1911; s. Samuel and Celia (Gelfand) F.; A.B., Coll. City of N.Y., 1931; LL.B., Columbia, 1934; m. Phyllis Young, Dec. 19, 1937; children—Nancy Lois (Mrs. Gans), Daniel Martin, Andrew Samuel, Amy Martha (Mrs. Malone. Admitted to N.Y. bar, 1934; D.C. bar, 1946, U.S. Supreme Ct. bar, 1943; with gen. counsel's office, S.E.C., 1934-42, asst. solicitor, 1942-46; with securities div., F.T.C., 1934; practice with firm Arnold & Porter and predecessor firms, Washington, 1946—. Lectr. law schs. Hon. chmn. Inst. for Internat. and Fgn. Trade Law; trustee Georgetown U. Mem. Am., D.C., Fed. bar. assns. Contbr. articles to legal Jours. Home: 3405 Woolsey Dr Chevy Chase MD 20015 Office: 1229 19th St NW Washington DC 20036

FREEMAN, RICHARD PAUL, elec. engr.; b. Malden, Mass., Nov. 26, 1931; s. Sylvester Solomon and Gertrude Sylvia (Wies) F.; student Rensselaer Poly. Inst., 1949-52; B.S., Clark U., 1957; m. Sandra Marilyn Goldstone, Aug. 12, 1962; children—Lori Sheryl, Allison Dayle. Service mgt. Picker Corp., Stoughton, Mass., 1958-62, service engr., 1962-68, engring. mgr. custom med. engring. dept., 1968—. Mem. Stoughton Charter Study Com., Stoughton Indsl. Commn.; Stoughton Town Meeting Rep.; pres. PTA, 1976-77. Mem. IEEE, Am. Radio Relay League. Republican. Jewish. Clubs: Mass. Marriage Encounter, Jewish Expression, K.P. Home: 105 Swanson Terr Stoughton MA 02072 Office: 84 Tosca Dr Stoughton MA 02072

FREESE, ERNST, biologist; b. Dusseldorf, Germany, Sept. 27, 1925; s. Hans D.G. and Hedwig (Von Oehmke) F.; Diplom, U. Heidelberg, 1951; Ph.D., U. Gottingen, 1953; postgrad. U. Chgo., 1954, Calif. Inst. Tech., 1955-56, Purdue U., 1957, Harvard, 1957-59; m. Elisabeth G.M. Bautz, June 15, 1956; children—Katherine, Andrew. Came to U.S., 1954, naturalized, 1963. Asso. prof. genetics U. Wis., 1959-62; chief lab. molecular biology, NIH, Bethesda, Md., 1962—. AID fellow, 1954-56, Damon Runyon Meml. Fund fellow, 1956-58. Mem. Am. Soc. Microbiology, Biochem. Soc., Biophys. Soc., Environ. Mutagen Soc., Teratology Soc. Contbr. to books and profl. jours. Home: 8300 Whitman Dr Bethesda MD 20034 Office: NIH Bldg 36-3D02 Bethesda MD 20014

FREIBAND, JAMES MICHAEL, municipal planning and devel. cons.; b. Kansas City, Kans., Feb. 27, 1944; s. Benjamin M. and Julia Agnes (Tomlin) F.; B.S., Ill. Inst. Tech., 1966; M.U.P., N.Y. U., 1972; certificate Environ. and Social Plan (Inst. Internat. Edn. fellow) U. Manchester (Eng.), 1972; m. Willa Felice Braun, Sept. 4, 1966; children—Meredith Joy, Andrew Sayer. Planner, N.Y. State Office Planning Services, N.Y.C. Met. Dist., 1971-72; asso. planning cons. Manuel S. Emanuel Assos., Inc., Nyack, N.Y., 1972—; lectr., speaker on growth mgmt., transfer devel. rights. Mem. Orange Municipal Planning Fedn., Goshen, N.Y., 1975—; v.p. Orange-Rockland chpt. Navy League Sea Cadets, 1977—. Served to lt. comdr. USN, 1966-70; Vietnam. Recipient New Communities Ednl. award HUD, 1971. Mem. Am. Soc. Planning Ofcls., Illuminating Engring. Soc., Navy League U.S. (Ill. chpt. award 1966), Author: Manual on Transfer of Development Rights, 1976. Office: 50 Piermont Ave Nyack NY 10960

FREIDAY, DEAN, ch. ofcl.; b. Irvington, N.J., June 20, 1915; s. William Sidney and Ethel (Deane) F.; B.A., U. Rochester (N.Y.), 1936; m. Esther Dorothea Selke, June 27, 1946; children—Gail Freiday Crockett, William Arthur. Mem. Christian and interfaith com. Friends Gen. Conf., Phila., 1958—, chmn., 1966-72; del. 4th World Conf. on Faith and Order, World Council Chs., Montreal, 1963, mem. consultation on baptism, eucharist and ministry, Switzerland, 1977, mem. Nat. Faith and Order Colloquium, 1967—; observer-cons. 3d World Congress of Lay Apostolate, Vatican, Rome, 1967; ann. conf. cons. World Confessional Families, Geneva, 1968, 69, 72, 73, 74, London, 1976, Rome, 1977; pres. Council Chs., Greater Red Bank (N.J.) Area, 1965-67; mem. central and exec. coms. Friends Gen. Conf., 1966-72; mem. exec. com. U.S. Conf. World Council Chs., 1967-72; sponsor Cath. and Quaker Studies, 1971—. Served with USNR, 1942-45. Mem. Delta Upsilon. Club: Masons (32 deg.). Editor: Barclay's Apology in Modern English, 1967. Home: 1110 Wildwood Ave Manasquan NJ 08736 Office: 1520 Race St Philadelphia PA 19102

FREIDBERG, ALAN ELLIOT, assn. exec.; b. Phila., Dec. 3, 1936; s. Joseph and Kay (Krasick) F.; B.A., Pa. State U., 1957; M.A., Hebrew U., Jerusalem, 1958; postgrad. Hebrew Union Coll., N.Y.C., 1958-60. Dept. mgr., asst. buyer Ohrbach's, N.Y.C., 1960-66; adminstr. Am.-Israel Cultural Found., N.Y.C., 1966-72; regional dir. Am. Jewish Congress, N.Y.C., 1972—, nat. dir. membership and orgn., 1975—. Mem. Friends of N.Y.C. Opera, 1970-76, Jewish Bd. Guardians, 1965—. Recipient Distinguished Service award United Jewish Appeal, 1973. Mem. Met. Mus. Art, Art Student's League, N.Y., Hebrew U. Am. Alumni Assn. (exec. com. 1964-70, 72-76), Alpha Phi Omega, Beta Sigma Rho (nat. exec. bd. 1959-63). Jewish. Home: 70 W 95th St New York City NY 10025 Office: 15 E 84th St New York City NY 10028

FREIFELD, DANIEL JEROME, accountant; b. Bronx, N.Y., June 13, 1943; s. Robert and Rose (Bernstein) F.; B.S., Fairleigh Dickinson U., 1965; m. Nancy Jill Isenberg, Dec. 6, 1963. Partner, Freifeld & Holtzman, Pompton Lakes, N.J., 1968-69, Ferraioli, Wesdyk & Freifeld, Pomptom Lakes, 1969—. C.P.A., N.J. V.P. Jewish Fed. of N.J.; active Council of Jewish Fedns. and welfare funds, nat. com. on leadership devel.; mem. Nat. U.S.A. Young Leadership Cabinet, recipient Philip Diamond Young Leadership Award, 1970. Mem. N.J. Soc. C.P.A.'s. Home: 201 Pompton Ave Pompton Lakes NJ 07442 Office: 256 Wanaque Ave Pompton Lakes NJ 07442

FREIFELD, STEPHEN FRANCIS, otolaryngologist; b. N.Y.C., Dec. 10, 1939; s. Robert and Rose (Bernstein) F.; B.A., Cornell U., 1961; M.D., N.Y. Med. Coll., 1964; m. Gail Fern Grossman, Oct. 9, 1969; children—Jed Alan, Elisha Dawn. Intern in surgery Mt. Sinai Hosp., N.Y.C., 1965-66, resident in gen. surgery, 1967-68; resident in internal medicine Met. Hosp., N.Y.C., 1966-67; resident in otolaryngology Manhattan Eye, Ear and Throat Hosp., N.Y.C., 1969-72; chief sect. otolaryngology Bronx (N.Y.) VA Hosp., 1972-73; asst. attending physician, asst. dir. otolaryngology City Hosp. Center, Elmhurst, N.Y., 1973-75; asso. dir. otolaryngology Hunterdon Med. Center, Flemington, N.J., 1973-75; pvt. practice medicine specializing in otolaryngology, Summit and East Orange, N.J., 1975—; asst. attending Overlook Hosp., Summit; asso. attending United Hosps. Med. Center-Newark Eye and Ear Infirmary, Irvington (N.J.) Gen. Hosp.; asst. prof. clin. otolaryngology Mt. Sinai Sch. Medicine, 1972-75; clin. asst. prof. Coll. Medicine and Dentistry N.J., 1975—; cons. Jewish Home, Hosp. for Aged, Bronx; pres., founder HEAR Found., 1976—; pres. Hearing Safety, Inc. 1976—. Served with Air N.G., 1965-72. Recipient Physician's Recognition award AMA, 1978; diplomate Am. Bd. Otolaryngology. Fellow Am. Acad. Ophthalmology and Otolaryngology, A.C.S.; mem. Acoustical Soc. Am., Am. Audiology Soc., Deafness Research Found., N.J., Essex Essex County med. socs., Am. Physicians Fellowship Israel, Aerospace Med. Assn., Alpha Omega Alpha. Co-author: Application of Signal Processing Concepts to Hearing Aids, 1978; contbr. articles to profl. jours.; co-inventor audio processor for use in high noise environments. Office: 392 Springfield Ave Summit NJ 07901

FREILICH, DENNIS BYRON, retinal surgeon; b. N.Y.C., June 1, 1934; s. Irving and Ida (Mittelpunkt) F.; student N.Y. U., 1952-54; M.D., State U. N.Y. Downstate Med. Center, 1958; postgrad. in Ophthalmology, Harvard Med. Sch., 1961-62; m. Estelle Feld, June 10, 1962; children—Benjamin D., Jonathan M., David E., Elliot A.J. Intern Kings County Hosp., 1958-59; resident in ophthalmology St. Luke's Hosp. Center, N.Y.C., 1962-64; fellow retina services Mass. Eye and Ear Infirmary, Boston, 1964-66; research fellow Retina Found., Boston, 1964-66; trainee Armed Forces Inst. Pathology, Washington, 1965; clin. prof. ophthalmology, dir. retina service Mt. Sinai Sch. Medicine, City U. N.Y., 1966—; asso. in ophthalmology Columbia, 1974—; attending ophthalmologist, dir. retina service Mt. Sinai Hosp., N.Y.C., 1966—; asso. attending ophthalmologist St. Luke's Hosp. Center, N.Y.C., 1965—; asst. attending ophthalmologist Lenox Hill Hosp., N.Y.C.; practice medicine, specializing in retinal diseases and surgery, N.Y.C., 1966—. Served to lt. comdr., USNR, 1959-61. Traveling fellow Heed Ophthalmic Found., 1964-65. Fellow A.C.S., Am. Acad. Ophthalmology and Otolaryngology; mem. N.Y. Acad. Scis., AMA, N.Y. State, N.Y. County med. socs., Assn. Research in Ophthalmology, Instituto Barraquer, N.Y. Soc. Clin. Ophthalmology, Retina Soc., Soc. Eye Surgeons. Jewish. Contbr. articles to profl. publs. Home: 120 E 81st St New York City NY 10028 Office: 20 E 68th St New York City NY 10021

FREILICH, JOHN DOUGLAS, organic chemist; b. N.Y.C., Mar. 20, 1942; s. Sidney Harold and Esther G. (Vear) F.; B.S., St. Lawrence U., 1963; M.S., Ohio U., 1966; Ph.D., U. Conn., 1972. Group leader for devel. new hydantoin chems. Glyco Chems., Inc., Williamsport, Pa., 1973-76; sr. devel. engr. for abrasives Carborundum Co., Niagara Falls, N.Y., 1976-78; research asso. new product devel. organic chems. div. W.R. Grace & Co., Nashua, N.H., 1978—. Mem. Williamsport Bicentennial Com., 1976. Served as capt. F.A., U.S. Army, 1969-71; Vietnam. Decorated Bronze Star, Army Commendation medal. Mem. Am. Chem. Soc. (chmn. com. profl. relations Susquehanna Valley sect. 1975-76), Am. Security Council, Gamma Sigma Epsilon, Phi Lambda Upsilon. Republican. Roman Catholic. Clubs: Carborundum Mgmt., Toastmasters, Masons. Patentee in field. Home: Apt 12 12 Royal Crest Dr Nashua NH 03060 Office: WR Grace & Co Organic Chems Div Poisson Ave Nashua NH 03061

FREILINGER, JAMES EDWARD, ins. agt.; b. Ft. Thomas, Ky., Mar. 11, 1939; s. Otto Peter and Martha Jane (Hancock) F.; B.A., Ill. Benedictine Coll., 1962; B.A., St. Procopius Sem., 1966; postgrad. Rosary Coll., 1966-68; m. Mary Catherine Freilinger, Aug. 15, 1969; children—Sarah Anne, Peter Joseph. Mem. faculty Marmion Mil. Acad., Aurora, Ill., 1958-68; mgr. Continental Bank, Chgo., 1968-69; agt. Northwestern Mut. Life, Chgo. and Portland, Me., 1969-73; partner Cameron, Freilinger & Co., Portland, 1974—. Chmn. bd., bd. dirs. religious edn. Roman Catholic Diocese of Portland; bd. dirs., of exec. com. Me. affiliate Am. Heart Assn., 1976, state fund-raising chmn., 1977-78. C.L.U. Mem. Am. Soc. C.L.U., Nat. Assn. Life Underwritgrs, So. Me. Assn. Life Underwriters (past pres.), Me. Estate Planning Council, Gen. Agts. and Mgrs. Assn., Million Dollar Round Table (life). Roman Catholic. Club: Cumberland (Portland, Me.). Contbr. articles to ins. jours. Home: 1107 Shore Rd Cape Elizabeth ME 04107 Office: 93 Exchange St Portland ME 04101

FREIMAN, ALVIN HENRY, cardiologist; b. N.Y.C., Jan. 26, 1927; s. Maurice and Beatrice (Freeman) F.; B.A., N.Y. U., 1947, M.D., 1953; M.S., U. Ill., 1949; m. Nadine Roehr, June 12, 1959; children—Audrey L., Gail L., Marshall. Intern, Montefiore Hosp., N.Y.C., 1953-54; resident in medicine and cardiology Beth Israel Hosp., Boston 1954-56; fellow in cardiology Meml. Hosp., N.Y.C., 1956-58; individual practice medicine specializing in internal medicine and cardiology, N.Y.C., 1954—; asso. physician Sloan-Kettering Inst., N.Y.C., 1960—; asso. prof. Cornell U. Med. Coll., N.Y.C., 1967—; attending staff cardiology Meml. Hosp., N.Y.C., 1971—, dept. medicine Meml. Sloan-Kettering Cancer Center, N.Y.C., 1971—, dir. clin. info. center, 1974—. Served with USNR, 1945-46. Diplomate Am. Bd. Internal Medicine. Mem. Nat. Cancer Inst., A.C.P., Am. Coll. Cardiology, Am. Coll. Chest Physicians, Am. Coll. Angiology, AAAS, Am. Heart Assn., N.Y. Acad. Sci., Internat. Coll. Angiology, Alpha Omega Alpha, Sigma Xi. Contbr. articles to profl. jours. Home: 74 Homestead Rd Tenafly NJ 07670 Office: 1050 Fifth Ave New York City NY 10028

FREIMUTH, HENRY CHARLES, educator; b. N.Y.C., June 24, 1912; s. Charles Henry and Emma (Marsh) F.; B.S., Coll. City N.Y., 1932; M.S., N.Y. U., 1933, Ph.D., 1938; m. Madeleine McGlynn, Oct. 14, 1939; children—Kenneth, Karen (Mrs. Francis T. Burch, Jr.), Mary (Mrs. Herbert Stevenson, Jr.), Joanne, Judy (Mrs. Eugene F. Baldwin, Jr.). Spl. agt., analytical chemist FBI, Washington, 1939-44; toxicologist, chief Med. Examiner's Office, State Md., 1944-72, ret., 1972; adj. prof. chemistry Loyola Coll., Balt., 1946-72, prof. chemistry, 1972—, dept. chmn., 1977—. Adj. asso. prof. forensic pathology Med. Sch., U. Md., Balt., 1955—, adj. asso. prof. toxicology Sch. Pharmacy, 1970—; cons. toxicologist, lab. cons. Fisher Sci. Co., Silver Spring, Md., 1973—, PRC Systems Scis. Co., McLean, Va., 1973—; asso. instr. Md. State Police Tng. Sch., Pikesville, Md., 1941—. Mem. Woodbridge Valley Civic Assn., Catonville, Md., 1970—; mem. Gov.'s Adv. Council Alcoholism, Balt., 1972—, vice chmn., 1976. Fellow Am. Acad. Forensic Sci. (past sect. chmn.), AAAS; mem. Am. Chem. Soc. (sect. chmn. 1956, Chemist award Md. sect. 1977) Internat. Assn. Forensic Toxicologists, AAUP Soc. Former FBI Agts., Sigma Xi, Phi Lambda Upsilon. Contbr. articles to profl. jours. Home: 1402 Gibsonwood Rd Catonsville MD 21228 Office: 4501 N Charles St Baltimore MD 21210

FREITAG, HARLOW, computer scientist; b. Bklyn., Apr. 17, 1936; s. Abraham and Eva (Levine) F.; B.S., N.Y. U., 1955; M.S., Yale U., 1958, Ph.D., 1959; m. Patricia Daly. With IBM, 1958—, mgr. design automation research div. Yorktown Heights, N.Y., 1962-66, mgr. computer netting research div., 1966-69, mgr. advanced devel. research div., Yorktown Heights, 1969-77, sr. mgr. tech. planning, 1977—. Mem. IEEE Computer Soc. (sr. mem., governing bd. 1970—, chmn. membership 1972-73, sec. 1974-76, exec. com. 1974—, v.p., 1977—), Yale Sci. and Engring. Assn. (v.p. 1977—), Assn. Computing Machinery, Sigma Xi. Contbr. articles to profl. jours. Patentee in field. Home: 444 E 84 St New York City NY 10028 Office: IBM POB 218 Yorktown Heights NY 10598

FREIZER, LOUIS A., journalist, radio sta. exec.; b. N.Y.C., Oct. 10, 1931; s. Morris and Celia (Blumberg) F.; B.S., U. Wis., Madison, 1953; M.A., Columbia, 1964, postgrad., 1965-70; m. Michele Suzanne Orban, July 6, 1968; children—Sabine, Eric. Corr., UPI, Madison, 1953-54; desk asst. CBS News, N.Y.C., 1956-58, news writer, 1958-59, news editor radio sta. WCBS-AM, N.Y.C., 1964-68, sr. news producer, 1968-73, sr. exec. news producer, 1973—; adj. prof. Fordham U.; lectr., cons. in field. Served with U.S. Army, 1954-56, to capt. Res., 1956-59. CBS News Found. fellow, Columbia, 1962-63. Recipient Am. Legion medal for Americanism, 1953; AMA award for radio journalism, 1965; Nat. Headliners Club award for radio journalism, 1965. Mem. Acad. Polit. Sci., Am. Acad. Polit. and Social Sci., Am. Polit. Sci. Assn., Soc. Profl. Journalists, Radio-TV News Dirs. Assn. Home: 400 Central Park W New York City NY 10025 Office: 51 W 52d St New York City NY 10019

FREMONT, RUDOLPH ERIC, physician; b. Vienna, Austria, Dec. 12, 1912; s. Boris and Anna (Reitman) Friedmann; came to U.S., 1938, naturalized, 1943; M.D., U. Vienna, 1936; m. Gloria Zegans, Jan. 15, 1967. Intern, Univ. Hosp., Vienna, 1935-36, Municipal Hosp., Vienna, 1936-37; resident S. Canning Child's Hosp. and Research Inst., Vienna, 1937-38; fellow and research asst. in cardiology Mt. Sinai Hosp., N.Y.C., 1938-42; practice medicine specializing in cardiology, N.Y.C., 1947—; chief dept. of medicine VA, 1947—; chief of cardiovascular sect. Halloran VA Hosp., 1947-51; chief cardiology sect., asst. chief medicine VA Hosp., Albany, N.Y., 1951-53; chief cardiovascular sect. Bklyn. VA Hosp., 1953-68; asso. attending in medicine Jewish Chronic Disease Hosp., 1956-61, Maimonides Hosp., 1959-61; sr. attending cardiologist St. Barnabas Hosp., Bronx, N.Y., 1966-72, dir. cardiology, 1973—; attending cardiologist Jewish Meml. Hosp., N.Y.C., 1969-73; dir. cardiology Midtown Hosp., N.Y.C., 1969-74; dir. cardiac rehab. N.Y. U. Med. Center, N.Y.C., 1970-73; asso. attending in rehab. Bellevue Hosp. Center, N.Y.C., 1970-73; attending cardiologist Met. Hosp. Center, N.Y.C., 1973—, Flower Fifth Ave Hosp., N.Y.C., 1973—; asso. attending physician Kings County Hosp., Bklyn., 1966-73; cons. in medicine Maimonides Hosp., Bklyn., 1961-70; asso. attending in medicine Cabrini Health Center, 1976—, No. Westchester Hosp. Center, Mt. Kisco, 1978—; instr. Albany (N.Y.) Med. Coll., 1951-52, asst. prof. medicine, 1952-53; clin. asst. prof. medicine State U. Coll. Medicine, Downstate Med. Center, Bklyn., 1956-61, clin. asso. prof., 1961-73; clin. prof. clin. med. research and surgery N.Y. Med. Coll., N.Y.C., 1973—; cons. in cardiovascular diseases N.Y.C. Bur. Disability Determination, 1969—, impartial specialist N.Y. State Workmen's Compensation Bd., 1969—; sr. aviation med. examiner, 1969—; U.S. rep. internat. council Internat. Congress Diseases of the Chest, Vienna, 1960. Served from lt. to maj., M.C., U.S. Army, 1944-47. Diplomate Am. Bd. Internal Medicine. Fellow Am. Coll. Cardiology, A.C.P., Am. Coll. Chest Physicians, Am., Internat. (v.p. 1965—) colls. angiology, Am. Coll. Clin. Pharmacology, N.Y. Cardiology Soc., N.Y. Acad. Sci., N.Y. Acad. Medicine, Pan Am. Med. Assn., Am. Geriatric Soc.; mem. AMA, Aerospace Med. Assn., Civil Aviation Med. Assn., N.Y. County and State Med. Soc., AAAS, Assn. Mil. Surgeons, Am. Heart Assn. Jewish. Contbr. numerous articles on cardiovascular diseases to books and med. jours. Home: 219 E 69th St New York City NY 10021 Office: 14 E 60th St New York City NY 10022

FRENCH, BRUCE HARTUNG, economist, lawyer; b. Canton, Ohio, May 2, 1915; s. Garnett Bruce and Marie (Hartung) F.; A.B., Haverford Coll., 1937; A.M., U. Pa., 1940, Ph.D., 1946; postgrad. Princeton, 1941-42; LL.B., Rutgers U., 1945; m. Jeanne Adrienne Aeberhard, June 27, 1942 (div. 1969); children—Robert Adrain, David Adrain; m. 2d, Dorothy Fleming Gorman, Nov. 29, 1969. Asst. in govt. Haverford Coll., 1937-39; instr. politics Princeton, 1941-42, 46-47; asst. prof. econs. U. Coll., Rutgers U., 1947-53, asso. prof. econs., 1953—, chmn. dept. econs., 1951-76; admitted to N.J. bar, 1948; partner law firm French & Cook, Princeton, N.J., 1950-59; pvt. practice law, 1959—. Pres. Estate Owners, Inc., Frenchlands, Inc.; corp. counsel Bar Harbor Property Owners; counsel, also exec. dir. Housing Authority Borough Princeton, 1949-58, Hightstown, 1958-75; pres. Princeton Community Chest, 1950; mem. N.J. Tercentenary Adv. Com., 1960. Mem. corp. Haverford Coll.; trustee, chmn. bd. Am. Inst. Econ. Research, 1976—. Served to lt. comdr. USNR, 1942-46; as liaison officer with fgn. govts., officer-in-charge USN Internat. Aid Office, N.Y.C. Recipient letter commendation U.S. Navy. Mem. N.J., Princeton, Mercer County bar assns., Princeton Hist. Soc. (past pres.), Huguenot Soc., Am. Econs. Assn., Soc. War of 1812, St. Nicholas Soc., Soc. Colonial Wars, S.R. (past pres. N.J.), Phi Beta Kappa. Mem. Soc. of Friends. Republican. Clubs: Rotary; Nassau (past pres.), Pretty Brook Tennis (Princeton); Union, Princeton (N.Y.C.); Athenaeum (Phila.); Pot and Kettle, Bar Harbor (Me.); Founders (Haverford Coll.). Author: Banking and Insurance in New Jersey--A History, 1965. Contbr. articles to profl. jours. Home: 19 Winfield Rd Princeton NJ 08540 Office: 192 College Ave New Brunswick NJ 08901 also 10 Nassau St Princeton NJ 08540

FRENCH, CARL BURTON, industrialist; b. Burlington, Mich.; s. Burton D. and Sarah L. (Stark) F.; B.S., Northwestern U., 1928; J.D., Kent Coll. Law, 1935; m. Ruth Maretta Arnold, June 27, 1931; children—Jean C., Carol M. Adminstr., Chgo. Daily News, 1931-35; admitted to Ill. bar, 1935; practiced in Chgo., 1935-37; sec.-treas., dir. Eldorado Mining & Refining, Ltd., 1937-45; pres., gen. mgr. Ceebee Services, Ltd., 1959—. Bd. dirs., chmn. exec. com. Canadian Cancer Soc., 1953-56, nat. pres., 1957-61, hon. pres. North York unit; chmn. Internat. Conf. Cancer Vols., 1965; mem. nat. program control comm. Union Internationale Contre le Cancer; bd. govs. Nat. Theatre Sch., Montreal. Recipient Vermeil medal Soc. Encouragement Progress, U. Paris, 1967; Merit award Northwestern U., 1971. Mem. Canadian Cancer Soc. (hon. life), Liga Colombiana de lucha Contra el cancer (hon.), Phi Kappa Sigma, Phi Delta Phi, Alpha Kappa Psi. Presbyn. Clubs: Nat., Granite, Variety (Toronto), Eglington Hunt, Turf, York Downs Golf and Country. Author: Manual on Fund Raising, 1972. Address: 263 Dawlish Ave Toronto ON M4N 1J4 Canada

FRENCH, HENRY PIERSON, JR., educator; b. Rochester, N.Y., Nov. 21, 1934; s. Henry Pierson and Genevieve Lynn (Johnson) F.; A.B., U. Del., 1960; M.A., U. Rochester, 1961, M.A. in Edn., 1962, Ed.D., 1968; m. Beverly Anne Bauernschmidt, Aug. 22, 1959; children—Henry Pierson III, Donna Lynn (dec.), William Dean, Susan Gayle, John Douglas. Tchr. Pittsford (N.Y.) Central High Sch., 1962-66; field service asso. U. Rochester, N.Y., 1962-66, asso. lectr., 1967-68, vis. asst. prof. Coll. Edn. and E. Asian Center, 1968-69; asst. prof. history State U. N.Y.-Monroe Community Coll., Rochester, N.Y., 1967-70, asso. prof., 1970-74, prof., 1974—; asst. prof. edn. U. Rochester, 1969-70, asso. prof., 1970-72, lectr. East Asian studies East Asian Center, 1972-74, sr. lectr., 1974—; prof. Canisius Coll., summers 1968, 69, 71, 73, Rochester Inst. Tech., 1969-70, spring 1977, State U. N.Y. Coll. at Brockport, summer 1971; adj. mentor State U. N.Y.-Empire State Coll., 1976; mem. bd. dirs. Robert A. Taft Inst. for Govt., 1962-65; co-dir., adminstr. NDEA insts., 1965-69; bd. dirs. Rochester Assn. UN, 1972—, chmn. policy com., 1972-74, v.p., 1975-77, pres., 1977-78, chmn. bd., 1978-79. Vestryman St. Thomas Episcopal Ch., Rochester, 1965-68, Christ Episc. Ch., Pittsford, 1976—. Served with AUS, 1955-57. Center for Internat. Programs and Comparative Studies grantee, 1970. Mem. Assn. Asian Studies, Am. Acad. Polit. and Social Scis., Orgn. Am. Historians, Torch Clubs Internat. (dir. Rochester chpt. 1973-76, v.p. 1973-74, pres. 1974-75), Rochester Com. on Fgn. Relations, Delta Tau Delta. Episcopalian. Club: University (dir. 1973-76, v.p. 1975-76, chmn. nominating com. for bd. dirs. 1977) (Rochester). Moderator, permanent panelist Fgn. Policy Assn. and Rochester Assn. for UN Great Decisions-1973, 77, 78 series Channel 21 Ednl. TV, Rochester; moderator, host Disciples Within the Social Sciences series, 1968. Contbr. articles to profl. jours. Home: 78 Smith Rd Pittsford NY 14534 Office: U Rochester NY 14627; State U NY-Monroe Community Coll Rochester NY 14623

FRENCH, JOHN, educator; b. Bklyn., Oct. 6, 1908; s. John and Florence (Eldredge) F.; A.B., Williams Coll., 1931; M.A., Columbia U., 1932; French teaching diploma Sorbonne, Paris, 1932; Ph.D., Princeton U., 1961. Tchr. French, Pingry Sch., Elizabeth, N.J., 1932-33; tchr. French, English, European civilization Nutley (N.J.) High Sch., 1936-42; instr. French, Princeton U., 1946-48; tchr. French and Spanish, Hun Sch., Princeton, N.J., 1949-55; asso. prof. modern langs. Rider Coll., Trenton, N.J., 1961-71, prof. emeritus. Served with AUS, 1942-45; ETO. Recipient Benedict prize in French, 1931. Mem. Modern Lang. Assn., Cercle Français de Princeton (past pres.), Manhattan French Inst. in U.S., Amicale de Middlebury, Alliance Française de N.Y. Home: 10 Mercer St Princeton NJ 08540

FRENCH, JUDSON CULL, elec. engr.; b. Washington, Sept. 30, 1922; s. Morrison Brady and Ethel Haviland (Cull) F.; B.S., cum laude, Am. U., 1943; M.S., Harvard, 1949; postgrad. Johns Hopkins U., 1943-44, George Washington U., 1944-45, Mass. Inst. Tech., 1951; m. Julia A. McAllister, Aug. 1, 1951; 1 son, Judson Cull. Instr. physics Johns Hopkins U., 1943-44, George Washington U., 1944-47; sec., bd. dirs. Home Title Ins. Co. D.C., 1956-71; with Nat. Bur. Standards Washington, 1948—, chief electron devices sect., 1968-73, chief electronic tech. div., 1973-78, dir. Center for Electronics and Elec. Engring., 1978—. Fellow IEEE; mem. Am. Phys. Soc., ASTM, Sigma Pi Sigma, Pi Delta Epsilon, Alpha Kappa Pi. Office: Center for Electronics and Elec Engring Nat Bur Standards Washington DC 20234

FRENCH, PAUL THOMAS, office services co. exec.; b. N.Y.C., Nov. 8, 1946; s. James Cecil and Ines Marie (Betancourt) F.; B.A. in English, Queens Coll., 1968; m. Dorothy Ellen Rose, Sept. 27, 1975; children—Christine, Kelly, Paul Thomas. Adminstrv. control supr. Crompton-Richmond Co., N.Y.C., 1965-68; dir. sales adminstrn. Ethan Allen Inc., Danbury, Conn., 1968-78; owner Lord & French Office Services, New Fairfield, Conn., 1978—; cons. in micrographics; chmn. bus. adv. com. New Fairfield schs. Lector, St. Edward's Roman Catholic Ch., New Fairfield, 1977—; coordinator God is Love Prayer Community, New Fairfield, 1977—; mem. Eastern Regional Cath. Charismatic Renewal. Republican. Author poetry. Address: RD 5 Route 37 New Fairfield CT 06810

FRENCH, TRAVIS ARMITAGE, obstetrician and gynecologist; b. Jeffersonville, Ind., June 5, 1910; s. Herbert W. and Laura (Carrier) F.; B.S., Westminster Coll., 1931; M.D., Harvard U., 1935; m. Doris Leavens, May 25, 1937; children—Terrill Ann, Laura Marie. Intern, Mercy Hosp., Pitts., 1935-36; resident Presbyn. Hosp., Chgo., Boston Lying-In Hosp., 1936-38; practice medicine specializing in obstetrics and gynecology, New Castle, Pa., 1938—; mem. staff, emeritus chief obstetrics and gynecology Jameson Meml. Hosp., St. Francis Hosp. Bd. dirs. Pa. div. Am. Cancer Soc., pres. Lawrence County unit. Served with U.S. Army, 1942-46. Diplomate Am. Bd. Obstetrics and Gynecology. Fellow A.C.S., Am. Coll. Obstetrics and Gynecology; mem. Lawrence County Med. Soc., Am., Internat. fertility socs., Pitts., Youngstown obstet. and gynecol. socs. Republican. Episcopalian. Clubs: Lawrence, Univ. (Pitts). Home: 3218 Grenway Rd New Castle PA 16105 Office: 1st Federal Plaza North Mill St New Castle PA 16101

FRENCH, WILLIAM RICHARD, aerospace co. exec.; b. Portsmouth, Eng., Dec. 7, 1931; s. William Edgar and Annie Elizabeth (Davies) F.; came to U.S., 1947, naturalized, 1958; student Northrop U., 1949-52, Rollins Coll., 1964-66, U. Calif. at Los Angeles, 1966-68; m. Lelia Elaine Heintz, Nov. 19, 1960; 1 son, Christopher William. Stress test engr. Convair, San Diego, 1952-53, Northrop Co., Hawthorne, Calif., 1953-54; test engr., mgr. projects Coleman Engring. Co., Inc., Torrance, Calif., 1954-61; project engr., project mgr. asst. test base mgr., Cape Kennedy, then Los Angeles area mktg. mgr. chem. systems div. United Technologies, 1962-71, Eastern regional mktg. mgr., 1971-78, v.p. Washington ops. 1978—. Republican. Episcopalian. Clubs: Nat. Space, Aviation (Washington); Internat. Town and Country (Fairfax, Va.). Office: Suite 500 1125 15th St NW Washington DC 20005

FRENCHMAN, ROBERT HENRY, advt. co. exec.; b. Newark, Feb. 16, 1945; s. Morton and Rose F.; student Bryant Coll., 1965-68, Fairleigh Dickinson U., 1968-69; m. Mimi Cohen, Apr. 20, 1967; children—Lori, Debbie. Staff Reast & Connally, Thomas & Gill, South Orange, N.J., 1966-69; v.p. ops. Maczko Wehner Advt., Fairfield, N.J., 1969-72; founder, pres. D & L Advt., Wayne, N.J., 1972—. Mem. B'nai B'rith. Home, office: 12 Welsh Ct Wayne NJ 07470

FRENKEL, BARBARA ISABEL, musician, educator; b. New Haven, June 3, 1941; d. Alexander and Irene (Lefkoff) Gamm; student Boston U., 1959-61; B.S., Juilliard Sch. Music, 1964; postgrad. Yale, 1967, N.Y. U., 1970—; Mus.M., Manhattan Sch. Music, 1969; postgrad. in social work Yeshiva U., 1978—; m. Richard Eugene Frenkel, Dec. 20, 1970; children—Robert Harold, Joseph Lawrence, Elisabeth Anne. Instrumental coordinator Julia Richman High Sch., N.Y.C., 1968-70; dir. Murray Hill Sch. Music, N.Y.C., 1968-70; pvt. tchr. various instruments, Scarsdale, N.Y., 1971—; vis. lectr. New Sch. for Social Research, N.Y.C., 1972; performer with Honor Orch., Tanglewood Music Festival, 1959; bd. dirs. and mem. Westchester (N.Y.) Symphony Orch., 1975—, Sarah Lawrence Community Orch., N.Y.C., 1975—; exec. adminstrv. asst., fellow Am. Acad. Psychiatry and Neurology, Mu Phi Epsilon. Address: 33 Park Rd Scarsdale NY 10583

FRENKEL, HERBERT MILTON, telecommunications co. exec.; b. N.Y.C., July 28, 1924; s. Herman and Renee Regina (Roth) F.; LL.B., N.Y. Law Sch., 1952; LL.D. (hon.), Philathea Sem., London, Ont., Can., 1969; m. Beverly Vivian Rosenberg, Apr. 2, 1967; 1 son, Charles Robert. Admitted to N.Y. bar, 1972; partner Telecommunications Research Assos., concepts, plans and patents for implementation in commerce, Scarsdale, N.Y., 1965—. Served with AUS, World War II. Mem. N.Y. County Lawyers Assn. Club: Masons. Author: World Peace via Satellite Communications, 1965; (monograph) Mirrow Image Projective Technique, 1966. Address: 205 E 78th St Apt 6H New York City NY 10021

FRENKEL, RICHARD EUGENE, psychoanalyst, psychiatrist; b. N.Y.C., July 28, 1924; s. Herman and Renee (Roth) F.; B.A., N.Y. U., 1949; M.D., Lausanne Med. Sch. (Switzerland), 1957; D.Sc. (hon.), Pilathea Coll. (London, Ont.), 1969; certificate psychoanalysis N.Y. Med. Coll., 1972; m. Barbara Gamm, Dec. 20, 1971; children—Robert Harold, Joseph Lawrence, Elisabeth Anne. Lab. asst. Rockefeller Inst. Med. Research, N.Y.C., 1942-43; research asst. Cornell U. Med. Sch., N.Y.C., 1948-51; intern Kings County Hosp., N.Y.C., 1957-58; resident Bellevue Psychiat. Hosp., 1958-59, Hillside Hosp., N.Y.C., 1959-60; sr. psychiatrist Manhattan State Hosp., N.Y.C., 1960-61; dir. psychiatry Frenkel Telecommunications Research Assos., Scarsdale, N.Y., 1960—; supervising psychiatrist Kirby Psychiat. Hosp., N.Y.C., N.Y. State Dept. Mental Hygiene, 1973-77; med. dir. Arista Center for Psychotherapy, Queens, N.Y., 1971-75; psychiatrist Mt. Vernon Mental Health Clinic, 1972-73, Bronx Psychiat. Center, 1977—; asst. clin. prof. Albert Einstein Coll. Medicine, N.Y.C., 1978—; editorial cons. Psychol. Library Pub., N.Y.C., 1963-71; exec. editor Satellite Communications Research News, 1965—. Served with AUS, 1943-46. USPHS fellow, 1958-59; diplomate Am. Acad. Psychiatry and Neurology. Fellow Am. Acad. Psychiatry and Neurology (editor jour. 1975—); mem. AAAS, Am. Psychiat. Assn., AMA, Am. Acad. Psychoanalysis, Soc. Med. Psychoanalysts. Club: Masons. Author: World Peace Via Satellite Communications, 1965; Mirror Image Projective Technique, 1963. Patentee in field. Home and Office: 33 Park Rd Scarsdale NY 10583

FRETER, KURT RUDOLF, chemist; b. Hamburg, Germany, Jan. 26, 1929; s. Rudolf and Paula (Duhn) F.; Diplom Chemiker, U. Frankfurt (Germany), 1953, Ph.D., 1955; m. Helga Schwahn, Aug. 30, 1958; children—Gudron, Detlef, Barbara, Heike. Research chemist C.H. Boehringer, Ingelheim, Germany, 1957-64; head chem. dept. Pharm. & Research Can., Pointe Claire, Que., Can., 1964—; vis. scientist NIH, 1956-57. Fellow Chem. Inst. Can.; mem. Am. Chem. Soc., Gesellschaft Deutscher Chem. Home: 103 Scodon Dr Ridgefield CT 06877 Office: Research and Devel Boehringer Co Ridgefield CT 06877

FRETWELL, ELBERT KIRTLEY, JR., coll. pres.; b. N.Y.C., Oct. 29, 1923; s. Elbert Kirtley and Jean (Hosford) F.; A.B. with distinction, Wesleyan U., Middletown, Conn., 1944; A.M. in Teaching, Harvard U., 1948; Ph.D., Columbia U., 1953; m. Dorrie Shearer, Aug. 25, 1951; children—Barbara Alice, Margaret Jean, James Leonard, Katharine Louise. Corr., A.P., 1942-44; staff writer ARC, 1944-45; vice consul Am. embassy, Prague, Czechoslovakia, 1945-47; tchr. Brookline (Mass.) Public Schs., 1948, Evanston (Ill.) Twp. High Sch. and Community Coll., 1948-50; adminstrv. sec. John Hay Fellowships, John Hay Whitney Found., 1951-53; asst. prof., asst. to dean Tchrs. Coll., Columbia U., 1955-56, asso. prof., 1956; asst. commnr. for higher edn. N.Y. State Edn. Dept., 1956-64; mem. summer faculty U. Calif. Berkeley, 1964; dean acad. devel. City U. N.Y., 1964-67; pres. SUNY at Buffalo, 1967—; trustee Erie County Savs. Bank. Organizer N.Y.C. meeting White House Conf. Edn., 1955; cons. President's Com. Edn. Beyond High Sch., 1956; assisted in James B. Conant Study Edn. Am. Tchrs., 1962; mem. commn. higher instns. Middle States Assn., 1965-71, trustee, 1st v.p., 1972-73, pres., chmn. bd., 1973-74; vice chmn. Temporary State Commn. to commemorate 200th Anniversary Am. Revolution. Trustee Wesleyan U., 1967-70, Nichols Sch., 1968—, Canisius Coll., 1970—, Carnegie Found. for Advancement Teaching, 1968—; bd. mem. Carnegie Council on Policy Studies in Higher Edn., 1973—, NCCJ; exec. dir. com. on edn. N.Y. State Constl. Conv., 1967. Recipient annual award N.Y. State Assn. Jr. Colls., 1962; Carnegie Corp. grantee, 1964. Mem. Am. Assn. Higher Edn. (exec. com. 1962-66, nat. pres. 1964-65), Am. Assn. State Colls. and Univs. (dir. 1972—, pres.-elect), Nat. Ry. Hist. Soc., Buffalo Soc. Natural Scis. (gov.). Buffalo and Erie County Hist. Soc. (gov.), Am. Acad. Polit. Sci., AAUP, Am. Soc. Pub. Adminstrn. Rotarian. Clubs: Univ. (Albany); Harvard (N.Y.C.); Adirondack Mountain. Author: Founding Public Junior Colleges, 1954; also articles, chpts. in yearbooks. Home: 152 Lincoln Pkwy Buffalo NY 14222 Office: 1300 Elmwood Ave Buffalo NY 14222

FREUDENBERGER, HERBERT JUSTIN, psychoanalyst; b. Frankfurt, Germany, Nov. 26, 1926; s. Joseph and Jenny (Braunschweiger) F.; came to U.S., 1938; B.A., Bklyn. Coll., 1952; M.A., N.Y.U., 1953; Ph.D., 1956; m. Arlene F. Somer, Dec. 24, 1960; children—Lisa, Marc, Lori. Practice of psychoanalysis-group therapy, N.Y.C., 1954—; asst. prof. psychology N.Y.U., 1963-72; asso. attending psychoanalyst Stuyvesant Hosp., 1961-67; cons. Haight Asbury Clinic, 1968-70, Mt. Vernon Drug Abuse Council, 1968-77, S.E.R.A. (hispanic drug therapeutic community), 1970-74, social achons program USAF, 1971-76, Tng. for Living Agy., 1972-76; staff trainor N.Y.C. Addiction Services Agy., 1972-76; clin. tng. cons. Daytop Village, Covenant House, 1973—. Nat. co-chmn. Nat. Council on Grad. Edn., 1968-74. Mem. Mayor's Social Scientists Adv. Com., 1965-68, Dep. Mayor's Chem. Abuse Com., N.Y.C. Bd. dirs. Joint Council for Mental Health, 1968-71, Psychol. Service Center, 1965-68, Jewish Inst. for Blind, 1960—; dir. psychol services St. Marks Free Clinic, 1969-71. Fellow Am. Psychol. Assn. (dir. 1972—), mem. N.Y. Soc. Clin. Psychologist (dir. 1960-68, pres. 1965-67, pres. elect 1978—), Nat. Psychol Assn. Psychoanalysts (dir. 1965-70, sr. mem. faculty), Internat. Council Alcohol and Addictions. Asso. editor Profl. Psychology, 1970—, Jour. Psychotherapy, 1973—; exec. bd. Jour. Psychedelic Drugs, Jour. Selected Documents. Home: 81 Central Pkwy Mount Vernon NY 10552 Office: 890 Park Ave New York City NY 10021

FREUDENHEIM, TOM LIPPMANN, mus. ofcl.; b. Stuttgart, Germany, July 3, 1937; s. Ernest S. and Margot R. (Freund) F.; A.B., Harvard U., 1959; postgrad. Hebrew Union Coll.-Jewish Inst. Religion, 1959-61; M.A., Inst. Fine Arts N.Y. U., 1966; m. Leslie Ann Mandelson, Nov. 15, 1964; children—Alexander Darius, Adam Jeremy. Came to U.S., 1938, naturalized, 1943. Curator, Jewish Mus., N.Y.C., 1962-65; asst. dir. U. Art Mus., U. Calif. at Berkeley, 1966-71; dir. Balt. Mus. Art, 1971-78; dir. mus. program Nat. Endowment for Arts, Washington, 1978—; curator Am. Painting Since 1945 for Nat. Collection Fine Arts, Romania, Czechoslovakia, 1969. U.S. State Dept. lectr., Japan, 1971, USSR, Romania, 1974. Trustee Balt. Hebrew Coll. Mem. Assn. Art Mus. Dirs., Am. Assn. Mus., Coll. Art Assn. Jewish. Club: Johns Hopkins (Balt.). Home: 218 Wendover Rd Baltimore MD 21218 Office: Nat Endowment for Arts Washington DC 20506

FREUNDLICH, RICHARD L., clothing mfg. co. exec.; b. Phila., May 7, 1937; s. Fred R. and Adele (Lowenthal) F.; B.S., Wharton Sch. U. Pa., 1959; m. Bonnie R. Bershad, Mar. 14, 1964; children—Laura Pepi, James Frederic. With Ship 'n Shore, N.Y.C., 1960—, mktg. and adminstrv. dir., 1967-70, pres., 1970-78, chief exec. officer, 1970—, chmn. bd., dir., 1978—; pres., chief exec. officer Gen. Mills Apparel Corp., 1978—. Mem. com. troubled youth Jewish Family Service Phila., 1970—; chmn. young men's service com. Fedn. Jewish Agys., 1969-70, mem. nat. com. leadership devel., 1969-72, mem. exec. com., 1970-71, mem. nominating com., 1970-72, trustee, 1969—; mem. Am. Jewish Com., 1972—; bd. dirs. Moss Rehab. Hosp., Phila., 1971—, Jewish Employment and Vocat. Service, 1971—, Jewish Youth Com.; trustee Acad. Natural Scis., 1973—, Pop Warner Little Scholars; bd. dirs., mem. exec. com. Melanoma Found.; bd. govs. Albert M. Einstein Med. Center; mem. Fed. Thrift Shop Men's Aux. mem. Citizens Crime Commn. Phila. Recipient Myer and Rosaline Feinstein Young Leadership award, 1969. Mem. Young Presidents Orgn., AIM, Am. Apparel Mfs. Assn. (dir. 1978), Phila. C. of C., Internat. Friends Sch. Dental Medicine of U. Pa. Home: 1234 Ridgewood Rd Bryn Mawr PA 19010 Office: 630 Fifth Ave New York City NY

FREWIN, WILLIAM ARTHUR, JR., accounting co. exec.; b. Queens, N.Y., Oct. 5, 1942; s. William Arthur and Rita Grace (Amorese) F.; B.B.A., Pace U., 1966; m. Lillian Veronica Burns, Feb. 15, 1969; 1 son, William Patrick. Mgmt. trainee Chase Manhattan Bank, N.Y.C., 1960-65; pub. accountant Peat, Marwick, Mitchell & Co., 1966-69; asst. corporate controller, subs. controller Athlone Industries, Inc., 1969-70; controller, asst. to chmn. bd. Harvey's Stores, Inc., N.Y.C., 1970-71; controller, chief fin. officer Yankelovich, Skelly & White, Inc. subs. Reliance Group, Inc., N.Y.C., 1971-77; controller Cablevision Systems of L.I., N.J. and Westchester, Jericho, N.Y., 1977—. Active Syosset Civic Assn., 1975—. Served with AUS, 1966-67. C.P.A., N.Y. Mem. Nat. Assn.

Accountants (dir. socio-econ. program 1973—), Am. Inst. C.P.A.'s, N.Y. State Soc. C.P.A.'s (retail accounting com. 1971—, community affairs com. 1974—, cooperation with bankers com. 1973—), Tax Inst. C.W. Post Coll., Am. Mgmt. Assn. Syosset NY Office: Jericho NY

FREY, GLORIA JEAN, printer, union ofcl.; b. Denver, Jan. 6, 1934; d. Emil William and Sophia Marie (Bongers) Schultz; student Newark State Coll., 1968-72; m. Joseph Louis Frey, July 29, 1951; children—Cheryl, Susan, Joel. Keypuncher, Farm Bur. Ins. Co., Columbus, Ohio, 1951-52; typist, 1953-54; gen. clk. Garlock Packing Co., Denver, 1952-53; sec. Kenneth Higgins, Architect, Hackettstown, N.J., 1954-65; clk.-typist Picatinny Arsenal, Dover, N.J., 1955; adjustotypist Redmond Press, Denville, N.J., 1963; clk.-typist Interpace Research Center, Wharton, N.J., 1964-66; sec. Robert Heintz, Architect, Short Hills, N.J., 1965-69; receptionist-sec. Integrated Electronics Co., Wharton, 1966, Philipp Chevrolet-Oldsmobile Co., Boonton, N.J., 1966-67; charge classified ad dept. Morris County News Dover, 1969; teletypesetter Parsippany (N.J.) Daily Record, 1969—; sec.-treas. Morris Union 433 Internat. Typog. Union, 1977—, sec. Daily Record, 1975—, mem. exec. com., 1974—, del. Morris-Sussex Central Labor Union, 1974—, del. to internat. union, 1976—. Mem. Parents Without Partners. Home: 4 Idalroy Trail Hopatcong NJ 07843

FREY, PAUL DOUGLASS, psychologist; b. Balt., Oct. 30, 1939; s. Mark Earl and Elizabeth Eva (Sadtler) F.; B.A., St. Mary's Sem. and U., 1963; M.A., Cath. U., 1969, Ph.D., 1970; m. Aug. 20, 1968 (div.); 1 son, Mark. Sch. psychologist Nat. Cathedral Sch. Girls, Washington, 1968-69; specialist mental health Receiving Home for Children, Washington, 1969; clin. psychologist Child Guidance Clinic, D.C. Juvenile Ct., Washington, 1969-72; clin. adminstr. St. Elizabeth's Hosp., Washington, 1972—; instr. developmental psychology Oblate Coll., Washington, 1972. D.C. Neighborhood Planning Council, 1970-73; vol. resource coordinator Am. Youth Hostels, 1971. Mem. Md. Psychol. Assn. Democrat. Buddhist. Home: 1408 Rollins Ave District Heights MD 20027 Office: 2700 Martin L King Ave Washington DC 20032

FREY, RICHARD LINCOLN, author, editor; b. N.Y.C., Feb. 12, 1905; s. Louis Joseph and Bessie Alice (Butzel) F.; extension student Columbia U.; m. Mabel Amy Planco, July 10, 1935; children—Steven Lewis (dec.), Stephanie Constance. With Fed. Advt. Agy., 1921-25; v.p., account exec. Herald Advt. Agy., N.Y.C., 1925-27; advt. mgr. for clothing mfrs., 1928-34; propr. Triangle Bridge Club, 1933-34; nat. sales mgr. Kem Playing Cards, also asso. editor Bridge World mag., 1935-37; pres. Morehead, Frey & Whitman Advt., N.Y.C., 1938-39; freelance author, 1940-60; editor, pub. relations dir. Am. Contract Bridge League, 1959-78; editor-in-chief Ofcl. Ency. Bridge, 1964—; pres. Internat. Bridge Press Assn., 1969—; author: According to Hoyle, How to Win at Contract Bridge in 10 Easy Lessons; chmn. Goren Editorial Bd., 1970—; world championship chief bridge commentator, 1960-70. Named Leading Am. Bridge Player, 1934, Life Master, 1936. Mem. Am. Soc. Journalists and Authors. Home: 235 E 87th St New York City NY 10028 Office: Goren Internat 110 E 42d St New York City NY 10017

FREYMANN, JOHN GORDON, physician; b. Omaha, Apr. 9, 1922; s. John Joseph and Marion (Wicks) F.; B.S., Yale U., 1944; M.D., Harvard U., 1946; m. Ruth Ellen King, Dec. 16, 1950; children—Amanda Wicks, Martha Gordon, Sarah Hilton, Vance Gordon. Intern, Mass. Gen. Hosp., Boston, 1946-47, resident in medicine, 1950-51; resident in medicine Mayo Found., Rochester, Minn., 1949-50; asst. in medicine Mass. Gen. Hosp., Boston, 1951-59; dir. med. edn. Meml. Hosp., Worcester, Mass., 1959-65; gen. dir. Boston Hosp. for Women, 1965-68; dir. edn. Hartford (Conn.) Hosp., 1969-75; asso. prof. family practice U. Conn., 1969—; pres. Nat. Fund for Med. Edn., Hartford, 1975—. Mem. Bd. Health Wayland (Mass.), 1957-69. Served with USPHS, 1947-49. Diplomate Am. Bd. Internal Medicine; recipient Welch Meml. award Nat. Assn. Blue Shield Plans, 1975. Mem. Ednl. Commn. for Fgn. Med. Grads. (pres. 1970-76), Soc. Med. Adminstrs. (pres. elect 1978), Assn. Hosp. Med. Edn., A.C.P., Am. Soc. Clin. Oncology, Phi Beta Kappa, Alpha Omega Alpha. Club: Harvard of Boston. Author: The American Health Care System: Its Genesis and Trajectory, 1974. Home: 37 Main St Farmington CT 06032 Office: 999 Asylum Ave Hartford CT 06105

FREZZA, JOSEPH MICHAEL, real estate broker; b. Hatboro, Pa., Sept. 4, 1928; s. Michael F. and Theresa M. (Bozzuto) F.; student U. Pa., 1967, N.C. State U., 1969, U. Ga., 1971, Pilot, project mgr. Aero Service Corp., Phila., 1952-59; salesman Bailey & Asso. Inc., Hatboro, Pa., 1959-62; founder Frezza Asso. Inc., Horsham, Pa., 1968—; pres. Galaxy Holding Corp., Horsham, 1970—, F.H. Enterprises, Inc., Horsham, 1967—; founder, owner Frezza Ins. Agency, Horsham, 1962-70. Mem. indsl. adv. bd. Horsham Twp., 1966; pres. Simmons Elementary Sch. and Hatboro Horsham High Sch. PTA's, 1970. Served in USAF, 1948-52; Korea. Decorated Air medal with three clusters. Mem. Horsham C. of C. (pres. 1968-69), Southeastern Council Navy League (v.p. 1973, Outstanding Service award). Republican. Roman Catholic. Clubs: Jaycees (Distinguished Service award 1970) (Hatboro); Rotary (pres. Horsham 1970). Office: 1725 County Line Rd Warrington PA 18976

FRIBUSH, ELLIS MARK, cardiologist; b. Albany, N.Y., Aug. 2, 1934; s. Benjamin S. and Sara L. F.; A.B., Hamilton Coll., 1955; M.D., Albany Med. Coll., 1959; m. Joanna Harris, Apr. 10, 1960; children—Andrea Joyce, Lynn Deborah, David Jonathan. Intern, Phila. Gen. Hosp., 1959-60; resident in internal medicine Hartford (Conn.) Hosp., 1960-63, cardiac fellow, 1963; dir. residency internal medicine Berkshire Med. Center, Pittsfield, Mass., 1967-74, chief of staff, 1975, 76, 77, bd. govs., 1975-77, exec. com. med. staff, 1975—; clin. asst. prof. Albany Med. Coll., 1967—, Med. Sch., U. Mass., Worcester, 1975—; treas., clk. Pittsfield (Mass.) Med. Assos. Inc., 1971—. Diplomate Am. Bd. Internal Medicine. Mem. A.C.P., Berkshire Dist. Med. Soc. Jewish. Office: 510 North St Pittsfield MA 01201

FRICKE, EDWIN FRANCIS, nuclear engr.; b. Mackay, Idaho, July 25, 1910; s. William Henry and Blache Myrtle (Ewing) F.; B.S., U. Idaho, 1935; M.A., U. Calif. at Los Angeles, 1937, Ph.D., 1940; m. Harriet Harmon Gronbeck, Dec. 26, 1942; children—Kathleen, William, Robert, Karen, Edwin, Jr., Kathleen (Mrs. Clifford Wainman), Karen (Mrs. Allen Penrod). Design engr. Stone & Webster, Boston, 1940-43; engr. Manhattan project, N.Y.C., 1943-45; physicist Republic Aviation Corp., Farmingdale, N.Y., 1946-49, sr. devel. engr., chief nuclear analysis, 1959-65; sr. scientist Argonne (Ill.) Nat. Lab., 1950-56; sr. nuclear physicist ACF Industries, Washington; research scientist Bell Aerosystems, Buffalo, 1965-66; sr. engr. Sanders Assos., Nashua, N.H., 1967-68; prin. engr. Jackson Moreland, Boston, 1968-70; engr. Stone & Webster Boston, 1973-78, now ret. Instr. physics St. Francis Coll., Biddeford, Me., 1970-71. Pres. Downers Grove (Ill.) Orch. Soc., 1954-55. Will Rogers fellow. U. Calif. at Los Angeles, 1939-40. Registered profl. engr., Mass., N.H. Mem. Am. Nuclear Soc., Am. Chem. Soc., AAAS, Ill. Acad. Sci., Research Soc. Am., Sigma Xi, Phi Delta Chi. Contbr. articles to profl. jours. Home: County Rd Merrimack NH 03054

FRICKS, ERNEST EUGENE, mech. engr.; b. Knoxville, Tenn., Jan. 16, 1948; s. Ernest E. and Barbara (Griffey) F.; A.B., B.S. in Mech. Engring., Rutgers U., 1970; M.S.Engring., Pa. State U., 1974; m. Dorothy Stanton; children—Natalie, Karen. Lead licensing engr. Atlantic Generating sta., Pub. Service Electric and Gas Co. N.J., Newark, 1972-76; asst. mgr. licensing Stone and Webster Engring. Corp., Cherry Hill, N.J., 1976—; cons. for protection offshore assets U.S. Sec. Navy, 1974-75. Vol. fireman, Bound Brook, N.J., 1974-77, Blackwood, N.J., 1977—. Served with USAF, 1970-72. Named Outstanding Res. Augmentee Officer in Mil. Aircraft Comnd., 1977. Mem. ASME, Soc. Am. Mil. Engrs., Royal Aero. Soc. (asso.), Res. Officers Assn., Am. Philatelic Soc. (v.p., 1977—). Democrat. Baptist. Club: Collectors (bd. govs.). Editor Jour. of N.J. Postal History Soc., 1972—. Office: PO Box 5200 Cherry Hill NJ 08034

FRIDAY, GILBERT ANTHONY, JR., physician; b. Pitts., Apr. 16, 1930; s. Gilbert A. and Susan Dorothy (Kumer) F.; B.S. in Biology, Bucknell U., 1952; M.D., Temple U., 1956; m. Christina Cecilia McShane, Sept. 12, 1959; children—Martin, Peter, Martha, Timothy, Amy, Anne, Robert. Intern Phila. Gen. Hosp., 1956-57; resident in pediatrics Children's Hosp. of Phila., 1960-62; asso. chief resident Childrens Hosp. Pitts., 1962-63, clin. instr., 1962-67; practice medicine specializing in pediatrics, Pitts., 1963—; asst. med. dir. out-patient dept. Children's Hosp. of Pitts., 1963-66, dir. allergy clinic, 1968—; chief div. of allergy and immunology Dept. of Pediatrics, Mercy Hosp. of Pitts., 1968—; clin. asst. prof. pediatrics U. Pitts. Sch. of Medicine, 1968-73, asso. prof., 1974—; cons. Home for Crippled Children, Pitts., 1963-68, St. Clair Meml. Hosp., Pitts., 1963—, St. Francis Gen. Hosp. Bd. dirs. Allergy Found. of Am., southwestern Pa. chpt., 1973—. Served with USN, 1957-59. Wyeth Pediatric scholar, 1960-62; diplomate Am. Bd. Pediatrics, Am. Bd. Allergy. Fellow Am. Acad. Pediatrics, Am. Acad. Allergy; mem. Pa., Allegheny County med. socs., Am. Thoracic Soc., Pa. Allergy Assn., Pitts. Pediatric Soc., Pitts. Allergy Soc., Am. Acad. Allergy, AMA, AAAS, Soc. for Ear, Nose and Throat Advances in Children, Alpha Omega Alpha. Democrat. Roman Catholic. Club: St. Clair Country. Contbr. articles on pediatric allergy to med. jours. Home: 1901 Highgate Rd Pittsburgh PA 15241 Office: 1520 Fifth Ave Pittsburgh PA 15213

FRIDAY, JOHN ERNEST, JR., securities co. exec.; b. Pitts., Oct. 24, 1929; s. John Ernest and Jane Nixon (Herron) F.; B.A., Trinity Coll., 1951; postgrad. N.Y. U., 1954; m. Joan B. Gray Israel, Aug. 6, 1977; children—John Ernest III, Andrew Hansen, Richard Fuller, Elizabeth Herron. Sr. asso. Morgan Stanley & Co., N.Y.C., 1953-67; v.p., dir. Drexel Harriman Ripley, Inc., N.Y.C., 1967-73; sr. v.p., dir., head corp. fin. Drexel Burnham Lambert Inc., N.Y.C., 1973—. Served with USMCR, 1951-53. Mem. Bond Club N.Y., Phi Beta Kappa, Psi Upsilon. Clubs: Recess, Pine Valley Golf, Round Hill. Home: 83 Perkins Rd Greenwich CT 06830 Office: 60 Broad St New York City NY 10004

FRIED, HERBERT GEORGE, advt. agy. exec., sales promotion firm exec.; b. N.Y.C., June 21, 1938; s. Julius and Clara (Schechter) F.; student Hunter Coll., 1956; B.B.A., Coll. City N.Y., 1965; grad. EST Seminar Tng., 1975; m. Priscilla Romeo, June 23, 1962; children—David, Jennifer. With advt. dept. Hoffman Beverage Co., N.Y.C., 1957-62; with Warsaw Studios, N.Y.C., 1962-65; v.p. Beacon Advt., N.Y.C., 1965-70; pres. Davis Fried Krieger, Inc., N.Y.C., 1970-74; v.p. Adelante Advt. Inc., also Fashion Mktg. Internat., DFK Sales Promotions, Inc. (all N.Y.C.), 1972—, DFK Music Pub. Inc.; pres. HSD Advt., Inc., N.Y.C. Trustee, Tng. Inst. for Mental Health Practitioners. Mem. Nat. Acad. Rec. Arts and Scis., Mixed Breed Club Am. (dir.). Club: B'nai B'rith. Office: 588 Fifth Ave New York City NY 10036

FRIED, (HELEN) JANE, student affairs adminstr.; b. Yonkers, N.Y., July 12, 1944; d. Sydney Aronld and Sara (Rappaport) Fried; B.A. cum laude, Harpur Coll., Binghamton, N.Y., 1966; M.A. in Edn., Syracuse (N.Y.) U., 1968; Ph.D., Union Grad. Sch., Yellow Springs, Ohio, 1977. Dir. residence and off-campus housing, instr. edn. and English, Trenton State Coll., 1968-71; tchr. English, Pioneer Valley Regional High Sch., Northfield, Mass., 1971-72; coordinator student devel. and research in div. student affairs, lectr. ednl. psychology U. Conn., Storrs, 1972—. Recipient Henriette Pitler award Harpur Coll., 1966. Mem. Am. Coll. Personnel Assn. (chmn. task force new profls.). Nat. Assn. Student Personnel Adminstrs., Am. Personnel and Guidance Assn., Assn. Humanistic Educators. Office: U-49 Univ Conn Storrs CT 06268

FRIED, JOHN P., food service exec.; b. Buffalo, Apr. 17, 1941; s. Martin B. and Isabel P. Fried; student U. Buffalo, 1959-61; Asso. in Restaurant Mgmt., Erie Community Coll., 1961-63; m. Marsha Siegler, June 28, 1964; children—Robyn, Stacey, Stephen. Service supr. Sky Chefs, J.F. Kennedy Airport, N.Y.C., 1963-65—; asst. mgr. The Park Lane, Buffalo, 1965-66; mgr. The Union News Co., N.Y.C., 1966-67; account mgr. Foodco, N.Y.C., 1967-70; asst. food service dir. Ogden Foods, West Hartford, Conn., 1970-71; food service dir. Middlesex Meml. Hosp., Middletown, Conn., 1972—; guest lectr. U. New Haven, Conn. Hosp. Assn. Mem. Food Service Execs., Am. Hosp. Food Service Adminstrs. Jewish. Home: 32 Foxcroft Rd West Hartford CT 06119 Office: Middlesex Meml Hosp 28 Crescent St Middletown CT 06457

FRIED, ROBERT, psychologist, educator; b. Linz, Austria, July 27, 1935; s. Georg and Alice (Schwartz) F.; came to U.S., 1947, naturalized, 1955; A.B., City Coll. N.Y., 1959; Ph.D., Rutgers U., 1963; m. Barbara Slutsky, Aug. 16, 1975; children—Paul, Steven, Dennis. Lectr., dept. psychology Upsala Coll., East Orange, N.J., 1962-63; sr. research asst. Ednl. Testing Service, Princeton, N.J., 1963-64; cons. Bur. of Research in Neurology and Psychiatry, N.J., 1964-65; research asso. in psychiatry Payne Whitney Clinic, Cornell U. Med. Center, N.Y.C., 1965-69; adj. asst. prof. dept. behavioral scis. Temple U. Med. Sch., Phila., 1966-68; asst. prof. dept. psychology Hunter Coll., N.Y.C., 1967-70, asso. prof., 1970—; mem. doctoral faculty City U. N.Y., N.Y.C., 1967—; vis. prof. dept. psychology Calif. Poly. State U., San Luis Obispo, 1977; co-dir. Proseminar Inst., San Francisco, 1978—; cons. N.Y.C. Bd. Edn., 1964—, Bellevue Sch. Nursing, Hunter Coll., 1970-72; psychologist Naval Air Devel. Center, Johnsville, Pa., 1971. Served with Signal Corps, U.S. Army, 1954-56; Korea. Recipient Research award City U. N.Y., 1967-69, Superior Accomplishment award U.S. Dept. Navy, 1965. Fellow N.Y. Acad. Scis. (mem. psychology advisory council 1970—); mem. Am. Psychol. Assn., Pavlovian Soc. Am., Inst. for Research in Clin. and Child Psychology (dir. 1970—), Assn. for Advancement of Behavior Therapy, (co-founder 1966), Sigma Xi. Author: (with B. Heckman) A Manual of Laboratory Studies in Psychology, 1965; Introduction to Statistics, 1969, rev. edit., 1977; contbr. articles on exptl. and physiol. psychology to sci. jours.; patentee in cardiac rhythm computer and method of analyzing cerebral elec. activity. Home: 1040 Park Ave New York City NY 10028 Office: Dept Psychology Hunter College 695 Park Ave New York City NY 10021

FRIED, SIDNEY, psychologist; b. Atlantic City, Dec. 20, 1922; s. Joseph and Henrietta (Bloom) F.; B.S., Seton Hall U., 1951; M.S., Yeshiva U., 1955, Ph.D., 1958; m. Leona Levine, Sept. 12, 1948; children—Scott, Richard. Pvt. practice psychotherapy, Levittown, N.Y., 1958—; prof. psychology State U. N.Y. at Farmingdale, 1970—; chief psychol. service Brunswick Hosp. Center, Amityville, N.Y., 1970—; pres. Indsl. Quotients, Inc., 1958-60. Served with USAF, 1942-45. Decorated D.F.C., Air medal; certified psychologist, N.Y., N.J., Pa. Mem. Am., N.Y. State, Nassau County psychol. assns., Acad. Psychosomatic Medicine, Soc. Clin. and Exptl. Hypnosis, Internat. Assn. Study Pain. Asso. editor Jour. Psychosomatic Medicine, 1972. Home: 427 Coleridge St Levittown NY 11756

FRIEDEL, BERNARD, mfg. co. exec.; b. N.Y.C., Jan. 26, 1930; s. Joseph and Jeanne (Shoenbach) F.; B.S., Hofstra U., 1951, M.B.A., 1952; m. Rosalie Gertsenstein, Mar. 17, 1951 (div.); children—Steven, Joyce. Pres., David Allison Co., Inc., Woodbury, N.Y., 1957—, chmn. bd., 1959—; pres., chmn. bd. Daco Internat. Corp., 1959—; pres. Kingsley Brass Co., Ltd., Woodbury, 1963-71, chmn. bd., 1963; mgmt. cons. Served to lt. USN, 1952-56. Mem. Mensa, Am. Hardware Mfrs. Assn. Clubs: Woodcrest (Syosset, N.Y.); Jockey (Miami, Fla.). Patentee hardware. Home: 24 Split Rock Dr Kings Point NY 11024 Office: 220 Crossways Park W Woodbury NY 11797

FRIEDENBERG, DANIEL MEYER, realtor; b. Mt. Vernon, N.Y., Feb. 24, 1923; s. Samuel and Rose Abravanel (Klein) F.; B.S., U. Pa., 1943; m. Maria del Carmen Joy, May 1, 1956 (div. June 1964); children—Samuel Clark, Danielle Joy; m. 2d, June Meredith Daniels, Apr. 12, 1965; children—Jay Daniels, Bertrand Russell. With John-Platt Realty Corp., N.Y.C., 1947—, pres., 1957—; curator emeritus coins and medals Jewish Mus., N.Y.C., 1962—; guest lectr. Columbia U., Yale U., Swarthmore Coll. Sec. Young Democrats N.Y.C., 1952; exec. dir. N.Y. County Liberal Party, 1945. Served with AUS, 1943-44. Recipient Spl. Achievement award Loeb mag., 1962, Spl. Achievement award Loeb Newspaper, 1965; Heath Literary award distinguished numismatic achievement, 1969. Fellow Am. Numismatic Soc.; mem. Am. Numismatic Assn., Real Estate Bd. N.Y. Author: Great Jewish Portraits in Metal, 1963; Jewish Medals from the Renaissance to the Fall of Napoleon, 1970; Jewish Mint Masters and Medalists, 1976; contbr. articles to newspapers and mags. Home: 79 Byram Shore Rd Greenwich CT 06830 Office: 45 Beekman St New York City NY 10038

FRIEDENBERG, PINHAS P., univ. ofcl.; b. Jerusalem, Israel, July 8, 1943; s. Jacob and Pnina (Schreibhand) F.; came to U.S., 1958; B.A. in Polit. Sci., Yeshiva U., 1967; m. Helena Rosenwasser, June 9, 1974; 1 dau., Amanda Yvette. Asst. to registrar Yeshiva U., N.Y.C., 1967-70; adminstr. Israel programs Am. Zionist Youth Found., 1970-73; asso. registrar Bklyn. Coll., N.Y.C., 1973-78; registrar L.I. U., Bklyn. Center, Bklyn., N.Y., 1978—. Formation chmn. Ann. Salute to Israel Parade, N.Y.C., 1971-72, 77. Mem. Am., Middle States assns. collegiate registrars and admissions officers, Am., Am. Israel numismatic assns., Alpha Sigma Lambda. Jewish. Club: Masons. Office: Registrar LI U Bklyn Center Brooklyn NY 11201

FRIEDHEIM, STEPHEN BAILEY, assn. exec.; b. Joplin, Mo., Nov. 13, 1934; s. Robert Wray and Virginia Grace (Bailey) F.; B.A., U. Ark., 1956; D.B.A. (hon.), Johnson and Wales Coll., Providence, 1978; m. Maureen Kulpin Mauck, Sept. 16, 1972; children by previous marriage—Neenah Marie Friedheim Schissler, Stephen Bailey, Robert William; stepchildren—Juli Ann, Rene, Paul Adam. Announcer, Sta. KBRS, Springdale, Ark., 1956-57; newsman Sta. KFSB, Joplin, 1957; dir. pub. relations Am. Personnel and Guidance Assn., Washington, 1961-66; exec. v.p. Am. Soc. Med. Tech., Houston, 1966-76; pres. Assn. Ind. Colls. and Schs., Washington, 1976—; mem. task force on transfer credit Council on Postsecondary Accreditation, 1977-78. Served with U.S. Army, 1957-61. Recipient Freedoms Found. award, 1960, 62. Fellow Australasian Coll. Bio-med. Scientists; mem. Am. (certified), Washington socs. assn. execs., Am. Assn. Higher Edn., Nat. Assn. Execs. Club, Nat. Assn. Concerned Vets. Episcopalian. Club: Torch. Home: 4401 Granada St Alexandria VA 22309 Office: Suite 405 1730 M St NW Washington DC 20036

FRIEDLAND, EDWARD CHARLES, orthopedic surgeon; b. N.Y.C., June 23, 1937; s. Solomon and Frances (Goldenberg) F.; B.A., N.Y.U., 1957; M.D., State U.N.Y. Dowstate Med. Center, 1961; m. Kathryn Amy Stern, Sept. 6, 1970; 1 son, Steven Mark. Intern, Maimonides Hosp., Bklyn., 1961-62; resident gen. surgery VA Hosp., Bklyn., 1962-63; resident orthopedic surgery St. Joseph's Hosp., Paterson, N.J., 1965-68; practice medicine, specializing in orthopedic surgery, Paterson, 1968-74, Fair Lawn, N.J., 1975—; asso. attending orthopedic surgery St. Joseph's Hosp., 1968-75; attending orthopedic surgery Barnett Meml. Hosp., Paterson, 1968—, chmn. dept., 1974-75; attending orthopedic surgery Valley Hosp., Ridgewood, N.J., 1975—; clin. asst. prof. orthopedic surgery N.J. Coll. Medicine and Dentistry, Newark, 1970—. Trustee Wyckoff-Franklin Lakes Synagogue, 1977—, v.p., 1978—. Served with M.C., USAF, 1963-65. Diplomate Am. Bd. Orthopedic Surgery. Fellow A.C.S., Am. Acad. Orthopedic Surgery, N.J. Acad. Medicine. Mem. AMA, Eastern Orthopedic Assn., N.J. Orthopedic Soc., Passaic County Med. Soc., Zeta Beta Tau. Clubs: Masons, Shriners, B'nai B'rith. Office: 25-15 Fair Law Ave Fair Lawn NJ 07410

FRIEDLANDER, ARTHUR HENRY, oral and maxillo-facial surgeon; b. Bklyn., Feb. 8, 1942; s. Edward and Nettie Ann (Hardbrod) F.; B.A., Bklyn. Coll., City U. N.Y., 1963; D.D.S., Temple U., 1967; m. Ida Kreinik, June 17, 1967. Intern oral surgery Bklyn. Jewish Hosp. and Med. Center, 1967-68; chief resident oral surgery Bklyn. VA Hosp., 1968-71; chief oral and maxillofacial surgery sect. and dir. residency programs Northport VA Hosp., Clin. Campus Stony Brook Schs. Medicine and Dentistry; asso. prof. surgery Stony Brook Sch. Dental Medicine, lectr. Grad. Sch. Medicine; adj. prof. clin. oral hygiene State U. N.Y. at Farmingdale. Diplomate Am. Bd. Oral and Maxillofacial Surgery. Fellow Am. Coll. Oral and Maxillofacial Surgeons (founding); mem. ADA, Am. Assn. Hosp. Dentists, Am. Assn. Oral and Maxillofacial Surgeons, Sigma Epsilon Delta. Home: 5 Scott Dr Smithtown NY 11787 Office: Northport VA Hosp Northport NY 11768

FRIEDLANDER, JACOB, lawyer; b. N.Y.C., Sept. 10, 1935; s. Morris and Sadie (Lebowitz) F.; B. of Chem. Engring., City U. N.Y., 1957; M.S., Yale, 1960, Ph.D., 1963; LL.B., N.Y. U., 1967. Process devel. engr. Lummus Co., Newark, 1962-65; patent chemist Chas. Pfizer & Co., N.Y.C., 1965-68; admitted to N.Y. bar, 1967; admitted to practice before Patent Office, 1968; exec. asst. to the adminstr. N.Y.C. Environmental Protection Adminstrn., 1968-70; asso. LeBoeuf, Lamb, Leiby & MacRae, 1971-75, partner, 1976—. Mem. Am. Chem. Soc., A.A.A.S., Am., Fed. Energy bar assns., Assn. Bar City N.Y. Home: 95 Christopher St New York City NY 10014 Office: 140 Broadway New York City NY 10005

FRIEDLANDER, ZITTA ZIPORA, physicist; b. Bucharest, Romania, Mar. 24, 1947; d. Aron and Clara Chaja (Haas) Rafailovich; came to U.S., 1960, naturalized, 1966; B.S. magna cum laude, (Honors fellow) Bklyn. Coll., 1967; M.Phil., Columbia, 1974; Ph.D. in Physics, 1975; m. Marc Alex Friedlander, June 19, 1969; 1 son, Jason David. Research asso. (NSF fellow) U. Rochester, 1966; sr. research physicist BDM Corp., Vienna, Va., 1975—. Co-chmn. Bklyn. Coll. Laurel Branch Honor Soc. Com. to Bring Opportunities in Higher Edn. to

Under-privileged Youths, 1966-67. NSF Summer Research fellow, 1966; Columbia univ. Faculty fellow, 1967-74; recipient BDM Corp. Publ. award, 1975. Mem. Am. Phys. Soc., Optical Soc. Am., Soc. Photo-Optical Instrumentation Engrs., Phi Beta Kappa, Alpha Sigma Tau, Sigma Xi, Motarboard. Contbr. research articles to profl. jours. Home: 20217 Darlington Dr Gaithersburg MD 20760 Office: 7915 Jones Branch Dr McLean VA 22101

FRIEDLIEB, LESLIE AARON, mktg. co. exec.; b. Manhattan, N.Y., Sept. 16, 1936; s. Theodore and Gertrude F.; B.S., Queens Coll., 1958; M.B.A., Baruch Coll., City U. N.Y., 1971; m. Rose Teresa, June 12, 1965; children—Katharine, Jennifer. Nat. sales staff Olivetti Co., N.Y.C., 1962-63; mktg. devel. staff Mosler Co., N.Y.C., account exec., asst. to pres. Fifth Ave. Letter, N.Y.C., 1965-66; mktg. services mgr. Weldotron Co., Piscataway, N.J., 1967-74; pres. Leslie Aaron Assos., Union, N.J., 1974—. Served with U.S. Army, 1959-61. Mem. Am. Mgmt. Assn. (editor 1971-72), Queens Coll., Baruch, Sch. Visual Arts alumni assns., N.J. Bus. and Industry Assn., Sigma Alpha Mu. Democrat. Clubs: N.Y. Ad (vice-chmn. steering com. 1965-66). Contbr. articles to profl. publs. Home: 292 Clermont Terr Union NJ 07083 Office: 2235 Morris Ave Union NJ 07083

FRIEDMAN, BARRY HOWARD, physician; b. Joplin, Mo., Mar. 18, 1945; s. Marion and Esther (Lerner) F.; B.A., Western Md. Coll., 1965; M.D., U. Md., 1969; m. Marsha Lee Rosenthal, June 25, 1967; children—Heather Michelle, Jarrod David. Intern, Washington (D.C.) Hosp. Center, 1969-70; resident in radiology Sinai Hosp., Balt., 1970-73; NIH nuclear medicine fellow Johns Hopkins Hosp., Balt., 1973-74; practice medicine specializing in nuclear medicine and computer axial topography, Annapolis, Md., 1974—; mem. staff Anne Arundel Gen. Hosp., Annapolis, Md.; chief dept. nuclear medicine Inst. Radiology, Johns Hopkins Hosp., 1974—. Mem. ancillary services com. So. Md. Profl. Review Standards Orgn., 1977—. Recipient Bronze Medal Soc. Nuclear Medicine, 1974, Silver Medal, 1976. Diplomate Am. Bd. Nuclear Medicine. Fellow Am. Coll. Angiology; mem. Md. Soc. Nuclear Medicine, Md. Soc. Radiology, The Soc. Nuclear Medicine, Rediol. Soc. N. Am., Med. and Chirugual Faculty State Md., Am. Coll. Nuclear Medicine, Anne Arundel County Med. Soc., Computerized Tomography Soc., AMA (physician recognition award 1972-77), Phi Delta Epsilon. Republican. Jewish. Contbr. articles in field to med. jours. Home: 170 Glen Oban Dr Arnold MD 21012 Office: Franklin and Cathedral Sts Annapolis MD 21401

FRIEDMAN, CHARLES WALTER, sales and marketing exec.; b. N.Y.C., Nov. 25, 1931; s. Julius and Tobie L. (Swick) F.; B.A. cum laude, City Coll. N.Y., 1954; m. Jane Virginia Masi, Feb. 14, 1976; children—Mindy, David, Michael. With Acme Quilting Co., Inc., N.Y.C., 1961-69, 71-76, gen. sales mgr., 1971-76; nat. sales mgr. Am. Universal, Inc., N.Y.C., 1969-70; v.p. marketing, dir. LCI Industries, Inc., N.Y.C., 1976—; owner Charles W. Friedman Assos., N.Y.C., 1971—. Industry co-chmn. Fedn. Jewish Philanthropies, N.Y.C., 1967-71, United Jewish Appeal, N.Y.C., 1967-71; dist. leader Queens County Rep. Com., 1959-64. Recipient Award for Outstanding Service, Fedn. Jewish Philanthropies, 1968. Mem. Sales Execs. Club of N.Y., Linens and Domestics Assn. Am. Club: Mensa. Pub., editor: The Decisive Factor, 1976—; author: The Better Way, 1976; contbr.: Sales Action, Research Inst. Am., 1975-76; contbr. articles in field to profl. jours. Home: 515 E 14 St New York City NY 10009 Office: 261 Fifth Ave New York City NY 10016

FRIEDMAN, ESIA BARAN, educator; b. Wilno, Poland, Apr. 27, 1930; d. Isaak and Ida (Shoag) F.; B.S. in Elementary Edn., U. Hartford, 1962, M.Ed. in Elementary Edn., 1966, postgrad. in Urban Edn., 1973; m. Edward L. Friedman; children—Barry, Cary. Tchr. English as second lang. to grades 1 and 5 John Barry and Casimir Pulaski schs., Meriden, Conn., 1962—; adj. instr. Middlesex Community Coll., 1972-73; tchr. English and citizenship Meriden Adult Edn., 1967-68. Vice pres., rep. to Meriden PTA Council John Barry Sch PTA, 1959-62; vice chmn. Meriden Republican Town Com., 1971-76; del. Rep. state and dist. convs., 1972, 74; chmn. Meriden Sr. Citizens' Telephone Project, 1976—; internat. life mem. Am. Red Magen David for Israel. Mem. Conn. Tchrs. English to Speakers of Other Langs., Conn. Council Lang. Tchrs. Specialist in urban edn., English as second lang. Home: 115 Kensington Ave Meriden CT 06450 Office: John Barry Sch 124 Columbia St Meriden CT 06450

FRIEDMAN, EUGENE, oral and maxillo facial surgeon; b. Rochester, N.Y., Apr. 4, 1922; s. Abraham and Eva (Goldman) F.; D.D.S., U. Ill., Chgo., 1945, B.S., 1952; student N.Y. Postgrad. Med. Sch., 1953; m. Muriel Ravitz, April 7, 1946; children—Stuart Andrew, Pamela Sue, Kathy, Craig Douglas. Intern oral surgery, Lenox Hill Hosp., N.Y.C., 1945-46, resident, 1946-47; grad. seminar oral pathology N.Y. U., 1948-50; resident anesthesiology Lenox Hill Hosp., N.Y.C., 1953, asst. oral surgeon, 1952—; pvt. practice oral surgery, Massapequa, N.Y., 1955—; cons. Good Samaritan Hosp., West Islip, N.Y., Southside Hosp., Bayshore, N.Y., Mid-Island Hosp., Bethpage, N.Y.; cons. oral and maxillo-facial surgery Central Islip (N.Y.) State Hosp., South Oaks, Amityville, N.Y.; attending in charge oral surgery L.I. Jewish Hosp., Mid-Island Hosp.; chief oral and dental surg. service Southside Hosp., Bayshore, L.I.; dir. oral surgery, mem. exec. com. Brunswick Hosp. Center, Amityville; asso. prof. clin. oral surgery State U. N.Y. at Stony Brook, also mem. faculty exec. council; vis. prof. Unphu U., Dominican Republic, U Guayaquil, Quito, Ecuador Oral surgery S.S. Hope, Ecuador, also mem. med. staff Project Hope, 1964; oral surgeon S.S. Hope, Africa, 1965; cons. Suffolk Psychiat. Hosp.; hosp. evaluation cons. ADA, 1977-78. Served as capt. USAF, 1950-52. Diplomate Am. Bd. Oral Surgery (adv. commn. 1975-77, examiner 1975-77, adv. com. recognition award 1977). Fellow Am. Soc. Oral Surgeons (founder, chmn. hosp. oral surgery com.), Internat. Assn. Oral Surgeons (founder), Am. Dental Soc. Anesthesiology, Am. Coll. Dentists; mem. Assn. Mil. Surgeons, Suffolk Acad. Medicine, Am. Assn. Oral and Maxillofacial Surgeons (trustee 1977-79), Pan-Am. Med. Assn., Nassau Physicians Guild, N.Y. Acad. Sci., N.Y. Soc. Oral Surgeons (chmn. com. pub. info. 1965; exec. bd. 1968—, v.p. 1972, pres. 1973), AAAS, Am. Cancer Soc. (dir. 1960—, sec. Nassau div., pres. 1968-69), Royal Soc. Health Gt. Britain, Phi Eta Sigma. Author articles in profl. jours. Office: 4770 Sunrise Hwy Massapequa Park NY 11762

FRIEDMAN, EUGENE JEROME, health services co. exec.; b. N.Y.C., June 12, 1923; s. Samuel and Kate (Meyerson) F.; student Northeastern U., 1966-67, Rutgers U., 1967-68; m. Rosemary Kaplon, Sept. 25, 1943; children—Mark, Neil. Adminstr., Convalescent Center, Toms River, N.J., 1969-72; pres. Townco Med. Enterprises Inc., Toms River, 1962—; mem. exec. bd. Group Health Ins. N.J. Mem. N.J. Health Coordinating Council; past chmn. Health Manpower; past adv. bd. Hill-Burton Funds; adv. bd. First Nat. State Bank, Edison, N.J.; past mem. Hosp. Adv. Council; vice chmn. Med. Assistance Adv. Bd. Past bd. dirs. Health Careers, Inc.; pres. bd. dirs. Garden State Rehab. Hosp. Served with AUS, 1943-46. Fellow Am. Coll. Nursing Home Adminstrs.; mem. Am. (bd. govs.), N.J. (past pres.) nursing home assns., Toms River C. of C. (dir.). Club: Masons. Home: Box 292 RD 2 Jackson NJ 08527 Office: 14 Hospital Dr Toms River NJ 08753

FRIEDMAN, GERALD, physician; b. N.Y.C., Mar. 9, 1927; s. Leo and Rose F.; B.S. cum laude, Rutgers U., 1951; Ph.D. in Pharmacology, Syracuse U., 1955; M.D. cum laude, U. Buffalo, 1957; m. Roberta Baliba, Sept. 4, 1955; children—Wendi, Gary. Intern Mt. Sinai Hosp., N.Y.C., 1957-58, resident internal medicine, 1959-60, asso. attending, also asst. clin. prof. medicine, 1962—; resident internal medicine Montefiore Hosp., 1958-59; asso. asst. attending Doctors Hosp., N.Y.C., 1962—. Served with C.E., U.S. Army, 1945-46. Mem. A.C.P., Am. Soc. Internal Medicine, Am. Gastrointestinal Assn., Am. Fedn. Clin. Research, AMA, N.Y. State, N.Y. County med. socs., Royal Soc. Health N.Y. Acad. Gastroenterology, Am., N.Y. State socs. gastrointestinal endoscopy, Sigma Xi, Rho Chi. Contbr. articles to profl. publs. Office: 2 E 85th St New York City NY 10028

FRIEDMAN, IRA HUGH, surgeon; b. N.Y.C., July 17, 1933; s. Leonard Seymour and Ruth (Binder) F.; B.A., N.Y. U., 1953, M.D., 1957; m. Erika Berger, Oct. 22, 1961; children—Richard Lawrence, Joanne Beth. Intern, resident surgery Beth Israel Med. Center, N.Y.C., 1957-59, 61-63; surg. resident Bellevue Hosp., N.Y.C., 1959-60; pvt. practice specializing in surgery, N.Y.C., 1963—; attending surgeon Beth Israel Med. Center; asso. attending surgeon Beekman Downtown Hosp.; asso. clin. prof. surgery Mt. Sinai Sch. Medicine. Med. adviser to N.Y.C. Dir. U.S. Selective Service System, 1968. N.Y. Heart Assn. fellow, 1960-61. Diplomate Am. Bd. Surgery. Fellow A.C.S., Am. Coll. Gastroenterology, Royal Soc. Medicine; mem. AMA, N.Y. Acad. Medicine, N.Y. Surg. Soc., Soc. Surgery of Alimentary Tract, Am. Gastroenterol. Assn., N.Y. Cancer Soc., Am., N.Y. socs. colon and rectal surgeons, Collegium Internationale Chirurgiae Digestive. Contbr. articles to profl. jours. Home: 1175 Park Ave New York City NY 10028

FRIEDMAN, IRWIN, physician; b. N.Y.C., Dec. 15, 1929; s. Dave and Lillie (Shapiro) F.; B.S., Union Coll., Schenectady, 1951; M.D., N.Y.U., 1955; m. Iris Zelikofsky, June 28, 1953; children—Robin, Michael, Scott. Intern, Buffalo Gen. Hosp., 1955-56; med. resident U. Utah Hosp., 1958-59, Mary Imogene Bassett Hosp., 1959-60; postdoctoral fellow NIH, 1960-61; practice medicine specializing in internal medicine, Buffalo, 1961; dir. respiratory services Buffalo Gen. Hosp., 1967—, research asso. surgery, 1971; asso. clin. prof. medicine State U. N.Y. Med. Sch., Buffalo, asso. clin. prof. pharmacy, 1978—. Served to capt. M.C., U.S. Army, 1956-58. Fellow A.C.P., Am. Coll. Chest Physicians. Contbr. articles to med. jours. Home: 4 Fox Chapel Rd Williamsville NY 14221 Office: 85 High St Buffalo NY 14203

FRIEDMAN, MARION, physician; b. Onley, Va., Aug. 15, 1918; s. Jacob and Bertha (Bernstein) F.; B.S., U. Md., 1938, M.D., 1942; m. Esther Lerner, May 29, 1941; 1 son, Barry Howard. Rotating intern U.S. Marine Hosp., Norfolk, Va., 1942-43; asst. health officer Montgomery County (Kans.), 1943-43; health officer Cherokee County (Kans.), 1944-45; asst. health commr. St. Louis County (Mo.), 1945-46; resident internal medicine U.S. Marine Hosp., Balt., 1946-49; fellow medicine Johns Hopkins Sch. Medicine, Balt., 1948-49; individual practice medicine, specializing in family practice, internal medicine, Balt., 1949—; asst. medicine U. Md., Balt., 1954-72; chief dept. gen. practice Doctors Hosp., 1952-54; chief dept. family practice N. Charles Gen. Hosp., Balt., 1972-75, med. dir. ambulatory services, 1972—, asso. chief medicine, 1975—, pres. med. staff, 1964, 68. Chmn. cultural com. Liberty Jewish Center, 1960-62. Served with USPHS, 1942-49. Diplomate Am. Bd. Family Practice (charter). Fellow Am. Acad. Family Physicians (charter); mem. Balt. City Med. Soc., Med. and Chirurg. Faculty Md., AMA, Md. Acad. Family Physicians, Pan-Am. Med. Assn., Md. Heart Assn. Democrat. Home: 7906 Terrapin Ct Baltimore MD 21208 Office: 5211 Harford Rd Baltimore MD 21214

FRIEDMAN, MARK, physician; b. Bklyn., Mar. 25, 1932; s. Samuel and Ann (Sapan) F.; B.A. in Physics, Adelphi U., 1953; M.D., Wake Forest U., 1958; m. Myrna Cohen, Nov. 1, 1959; children—Suzanne, Melanie, Barbara. Intern Maimonides Hosp., Bklyn., 1958-59; resident phys. medicine and rehab. VA Hosp., Coral Gables, Fla., 1961-62, East Orange, N.J., 1962-64; practice medicine specializing in rehab. medicine, 1964—; mem. cons. staff VA Hosp., Lyons, N.J., St. Peters Hosp., New Brunswick, N.J., Middlesex Hosp., New Brunswick, Rahway (N.J.) Hosp., Raritan Valley Hosp., GreenKnoll, N.J.; dir. phys. meidicine and rehab. Muhlenberg Hosp., Plainfield, N.J., 1965—; cons. Multiple Sclerosis Soc., Crippled Children's Found. Served with USAF, 1959-61. Diplomate Am. Bd. Phys. Medicine and Rehab. Fellow Am. Acad. Physical Medicine and Rehab.; mem. AMA, Am. Coll. Angiology, N.J. Med. Soc., N.J. Acad. Medicine, N.J. Soc. Phys. Medicine and Rehab., Am. Geriatric Soc., N.J. Soc. Electromyography and Electrodynamics. Home: 58 Robin Glen Rd Watchung NJ 07060 Office: 2509 Park Ave South Plainfield NJ 07080

FRIEDMAN, MARTHA SCHWABINGER, psychotherapist; b. N.Y.C., Aug. 15, 1915; d. Paul and Mollie (Rothstein) Schwabinger; B.S., Coll. William and Mary, 1937; M.S., Coll. City N.Y., 1958; Ed.D., Columbia U., 1970; m. Julius Friedman, Sept. 23, 1939; children—Michael, Joann Friedman Urquhart, Peter. Reading clinician Great Neck (N.Y.) Pub. Sch., 1952-60; ednl. counselor, partial hosp. program N.Y. Med. Coll., N.Y.C., 1967—, asst. prof. psychiatry, 1970—; coordinator Partial Hospitalization Program Met. Community Mental Health Center, 1974—, family coordinator, 1975—; individual practice as psychotherapist, N.Y.C., 1967—; lectr. Hunter Coll., 1967-68, Bank St. Coll., 1967-68. Mem. Am. Psychol. Assn., Am. Group Therapy Assn., Am. Assn. Marriage and Family Counselors, Kappa Delta Pi. Home: 345 E 30th St New York City NY 10016 also Met Hosp 1900 2d Ave New York City NY 10029

FRIEDMAN, MICHAEL PETER, physician, educator; b. Bklyn., Jan. 17, 1934; s. Morris H. and Ida (Topkin) F.; student Western Md. Coll., 1955-58; M.D., U. Md., 1962; m. Patricia Anne McCaffrey, Sept. 1, 1963; children—Michael Peter, Daniel Thomas. Intern, U. Md. Hosp., 1962-63, resident, 1963-65; postdoctoral fellow U. Pa., 1965-68, asst. prof. microbiology, 1968-69; asst. prof. medicine Cardeza Found. for Hematol. Research, 1969-73; dir., chmn. dept. medicine St. Francis Med. Center, Trenton, N.J., 1973—; prof. medicine Hahnemann Med. Coll., Phila., 1973—, dir. div. hematology/oncology, 1978—. Served with AUS, 1953-55. Mem. Leukemia Soc. (pres. Central N.J., trustee), N.J. Med. Soc., AAAS, Phila. Hematol. Soc., Am. Soc. Hematology, Am. Soc. Clin. Investigation, Phila. Med. Assn. Clubs: Wedgewood Swim, Haddonfield Tennis. Home: 920 Washington Ave Haddonfield NJ 08033

FRIEDMAN, PHILIP HARVEY, psychologist; b. Manhattan, N.Y., Oct. 4, 1941; s. Leonard H. and Miriam Rosalyn (Solomon) F.; B.A., Columbia Coll., 1963; M.A., U. Wis., 1965, Ph.D., 1968; m. Teresa Jean Molinaro, Dec. 22, 1965; 1 son, Matthew Alan. NIMH postdoctoral research fellow Temple U. Med. Sch., 1968-69; clin. psychologist Eastern Pa. Psychiat. Inst., Phila., 1969-73; child psychologist NW Mental Health Center, Phila., 1971-74; sr. family therapist dept. psychiatry Jefferson U. and Community Mental Health Center, Phila., 1973, instr., 1975-77, asst. prof., 1977—, program adminstr., 1978—; pvt. practice psychotherapy, Phila., 1974—. Fellow Am. Orthopsychiatry Assn.; mem. Am. Psychol. Assn., Assn. Marriage and Family Therapists, Am. Acad. Psychotherapists, Assn. Humanistic Psychology, Pa. Psychol. Assn. Jewish. Contbr. articles to profl. jours. Home: 46 Red Rowen Ln Plymouth Meeting PA 19462 Office: 130 S 9th St Jefferson Health Sciences Center Philadelphia PA 19107

FRIEDMAN, PHILLIP, physician; b. Pittston, Pa., Dec. 23, 1930; s. Jack and Rose (Levy) F.; A.B., Syracuse U., 1952; M.D., U. Berne (Switzerland), 1957; m. Sheila Alexander, Oct. 15, 1960; children—Deborah, Louis. Intern, Germantown Hosp., Phila., 1958-59; resident in internal medicine Presbyn. Hosp., Phila., 1959-60; practice family medicine, Langhorne, Pa., 1962—; med. dir. Langhorne Gardens Nursing Home, 1965-75, Woods Sch., Langhorne, from 1970; pres. med. staff St. Mary Hosp., Langhorne, 1976, 77. Served with USAF, 1960-62. Recipient Pres.'s award Woods Sch. for Retarded and Exceptional Children, 1977. Diplomate Am. Bd. Family Practice. Fellow Am. Acad. Family Practice; mem. AMA, Pa., Bucks County (bd. dirs. 1978-79) med. socs., Am. Rheumatism Assn., Phila. Rheumatism Soc., Am. Heart Assn., Arthritis Found. Home: 909 Lanyard Rd Yardley PA 19067 Office: 131 S Bellevue Ave Langhorne PA 19047

FRIEDMAN, RALPH, airplane instrument co. exec.; b. Yonkers, N.Y., Aug. 3, 1922; s. Morris and Bessie (Tavris) F.; B.Aero. Engring., N.Y. U., 1944; m. Shirley Rose Meister, Sept. 11, 1949; children—Lee Elliott, Judith Sue, Howard Steven. Detail designer Chance Vought Aircraft, 1944; design engr. Consol. Vultee Aircraft, 1944-46, Republic Aviation Corp., 1946-48, Gassner Aircraft Corp., 1948-49; chief engr. Safe Flight Instrument Corp., White Plains, N.Y., 1949-52, v.p., 1952—; dir. Aviatron Corp., Safe Flight Instrument Can., Ltd. Neighborhood commr. Orawaupum dist. Boy Scouts Am., 1963-69; sec.-treas. Westchester Sci. Adv. Council, 1960-61, bd. dirs., 1962-67; adviser White Plains High Sch. Sci. Adv. Council, 1961-67. Trustee Chain Scholarship div. Greene Found. Asso. fellow Am. Inst. Aero and Astronautics, Canadian Aero. and Space Inst., Inst. Socioecon. Studies (v.p. 1975—, dir. 1978—). Home: 2 Hubbard Dr White Plains NY 10605 Office: PO Box 550 White Plains NY 10602

FRIEDMAN, ROBERT MC ELHINNEY, dermatologist; b. San Juan, P.R., Aug. 21, 1941; s. Samuel Gregory and Mildred (McElhinney) F.; A.B., Syracuse U., 1963; M.D., U. P.R., 1967; m. Winifred Chapin Parks, Oct. 8, 1966; 1 son, Kent Parks. Intern, Ga. Bapt. Hosp., Atlanta, 1967-68, resident in medicine, 1968-69; resident in dermatology Univ. Hosp. of Cleve., 1971-74; practice medicine specializing in dermatology, Willimantic, Conn., 1974—; asst. prof. medicine U. Conn., Farmington, 1976—; staff Windham Community Meml. Hosp., Willimantic, 1974—, Day Kimball Hosp., Putnam Conn., 1976—, U. Conn. Health Center, Farmington, 1976—; asst. dir. Am. Cancer Soc., Willimantic, 1977—. Served to capt., M.C., U.S. Army, 1967-69. Diplomate Am. Bd. Dermatology. Fellow Am. Acad. Dermatology; mem. New Eng. Dermatol. Soc., Conn., Windham County med. assns. Congregationalist. Home: 49 Ball Hill Rd Storrs CT 06268 Office: 196 Conartville Rd Willimantic CT 06226

FRIEDMAN, SAMUEL, credit union examiner; b. N.Y.C., Mar. 25, 1919; s. Israel and Helen (Zuckerman) F.; student Coll. City N.Y., 1936-38, Nat. Agrl. Coll., 1939-40, Benjamin Franklin U., 1941-42, New Sch. Social Research, 1948-50; m. Sylvia Friedman, June 19, 1949; children—L. Jeanne, Linda R. Asst. messenger Farm Credit Adminstrn., Washington, 1941-42, classifier, 1942; voucher examiner VA, N.Y.C., 1946-48; asst. treas. Bronx (N.Y.) VA Hosp. Fed. Credit Union, 1948-50; fed. credit union examiner Bur. Fed. Credit Unions Dept., HEW, Newark, 1950-69; fed. credit union examiner Nat. Credit Union Adminstrn., Washington, 1969-74, prin. examiner, 1974—. Served with USAAF, 1942-46. Mem. Am. Fedn. Govt. Employees (past pres. local 2426, sec.-treas. 1970—). Home: 19 Merklin Ave West Orange NJ 07052 Office: PO Box 926 Fed Bldg Harrisburg PA 17108

FRIEDMAN, STUART WAYNE, biomed. services co. exec.; b. Chgo., Oct. 25, 1938; s. Louis and Raye (Yablonky) F.; B.S. in Indsl. Engring., U. So. Calif., 1959; M.S. in Indsl. Engring., 1962, M.B.A. in Mktg., 1963; m. Enid Segal, June 29, 1957; children—Gregg, Janice. Engr., Hollywood Plastics, Inc. (now subs. Shell Oil Co., Montclair, N.J.), Los Angeles, 1958-60, mgr. tech. sales, 1960-69; pres. Physiodata, Inc., 1969-71; asso. dir. Health Systems dept. Westinghouse Electric Corp., East Orange, N.J., 1971-72; dir. bus. devel., 1972-74; gen. partner Latin Am. Med. Assos., 1970—; asst. v.p. N.J. Blue Cross Plan, 1974-76, pres. Manhattan Health Plan, 1977—. Cons. indsl. engr. on plant layout, facilities engring., 1959—; cons. health, planning and financing, 1974—. Mem. Dept. Commerce Nat. Def. Exec. Res., 1968—; pres. Mensa Edn. and Research Found. Mem. Am. Assn. Advancement Med. Instrumentation, Soc. Advanced Med. Systems, Internat. Health Evaluation Assn., Mensa (nat. and intern. officer), Alpha Pi Mu, Tau Delta Phi. Home: 37 Warren Pl Montclair NJ 07042 Office: 425 E 61 St New York City NY 10021

FRIEDMANN, ARNOLD ARON, educator; b. Nuremberg, Ger., May 12, 1925; s. Max and Else (Bacharach) F.; came to U.S., 1947, naturalized, 1955; m. Susanne Kirsch, Mar. 10, 1949; children—Daniel Peter, Ronald David. Instr. Pratt Inst., N.Y.C., 1954-56, asst. prof., 1956-59, asso. prof., 1959-64, prof., 1964-72, chmn. dept. interior design, 1970-72; individual practice design cons., N.Y.C., 1954-72; head dept. textiles, clothing and environ. arts U. Mass., Amherst, 1972-73, prof. design div., art dept. and grad. program dir. design, 1973—; cons. in field; past dir. Nat. Council Interior Design Qualifications; com. mem., panelist 2d Fed. Design Assembly, 1974. Served with Brit. Army, 1943-46. Nat. Soc. Interior Designers travel grantee, 1965; Interior Design Educators Council research grantee, 1968; HEW research grantee, 1974-77. Fellow Interior Design Educators Council; mem. AAUP, Am. Soc. Interior Designers. Jewish. Author: Interior Design-an Introduction to Architectural Interiors, 2d edit., 1976; Commonsense Design, 1976; (with others) Environmental Design Evaluation, 1978; contbr. articles to profl. jours. Home: 42 N Maple St Hadley MA 01035 Office: Fine Arts Center U Mass Amherst MA 01112

FRIEDRICHS, ARTHUR MARTIN, former mfg. co. exec.; b. N.Y.C., May 8, 1911; s. Arthur C. and Olga A. (Knoepke) F.; student Union Coll., 1930-31; B.S., N.Y. U., 1935; m. Juanita Elizabeth Barrett, Nov. 2, 1968. Bookkeeper, Corn Exchange Bank, N.Y.C., 1935-37; with E. H. & A.C. Friedrichs Co., 1937-71, pres., 1958-71. Bd. dirs. Wartburg Home and Orphan Farm Sch., Mt. Vernon, N.Y., Hackley Sch. Alumni Assn., Fredrix Artists Canvas, Inc., Lawrenceville, Ga.; mem. Norwalk Hosp. Vols. Served with USCGR, 1944-45. Mem. Pompano Beach Power Squadron, Fraternal Order Police (asso.), Artists Fellowship, Weston Hist. Soc., Met. Opera Guild (sustaining), Art Material Mfrs. Assn. N.Y. (past pres.). Clubs: Salmagundi (life) (N.Y.C.); Lighthouse Point Yacht and Racquet (Fla.); Quiet Birdmen. Home: 14 White Birch Rd Weston CT 06883 also 2510 NE 35th St Lighthouse Point FL 33064

FRIEDSON, BERNARD, ophthalmologist; b. N.Y.C., June 8, 1917; s. Arthur and Annie (Jasper) F.; B.A., U. Louisville, 1937, M.D., 1941; m. Ruth Kopolsky, Apr. 20, 1947; children—Arlene Frances, Michael Richard, Arthur Stuart. Intern Cumberland Hosp., N.Y.C., 1941-42;

resident VA Hosp., Bronx, N.Y., 1946-49, Met. Hosp., N.Y.C., 1950-52; practice medicine specializing in opthalmology, Saratoga Springs, N.Y., 1952—; mem. staffs Saratoga Hosp., pres. med. staff, 1956-57. Trustee Saratoga Springs Bd. Edn., 1964—, pres. 1968-70, 74-75; mem. nat. campaign cabinet United Jewish Appeal, 1976—; bd. dirs. Daus. of Sarah Nursing Home, 1975—; trustee Saratoga Warren Bds. Coop. Ednl. Service, 1969—. Served with U.S. Army, 1941-46. Decorated Bronze Star. Mem. Am. Acad. Ophthalmology and Otolaryngology, Internat. Coll. Surgeons, AMA, Am. Soc. Contemporary Ophthalmology. Clubs: Masons, Shriners, Lions (hon.).

FRIEL, FRED JAMES, JR., space scientist; b. Farmer, Ky., Aug. 17, 1912; s. Fred James and Myrtle (Dooley) F.; B.S., U. Ky., 1934, M.E., 1934, E.E., 1951; postgrad. Mass. Inst. Tech., 1952. Engr. RCA, Oak Mfg. Co., Globe Union, Inc., 1934-41; cons. engr., Portsmouth, Va., 1947-55; chief engr., radar and underwater sound labs. of Navy Dept., 1941-55, participated in Pacific Atomic Bomb Expts., 1945-54; with NASA, Washington, 1955—, radio frequency mgr., 1963—. Chmn. study group space research Internat. Consultative Com. Radio; mem. subcoms. and internat. working group Office Telecommunications Policy, Exec. Office of Pres. Hon. comdr. Air Force of Peru. Registered profl. engr., Va. Mem. Nat., Va. socs. profl. engrs., IEEE, Alpha Sigma Phi, Iota Tau Kappa. Clubs: Gaslight (Washington); Playboy (Balt.). Contbr. articles to profl. jours. Home: PO Box 7 Annapolis Junction MD 20701 Office: 600 Independence Ave SW Washington DC 20546

FRIEL, JAMES REYNOLDS, JR., food processing co. exec.; b. Easton, Md., Oct. 20, 1942; s. James Reynolds and Mary (Parks) F.; B.S. in Econs., Villanova U., 1964; m. Mary Helen Urban, Apr. 8, 1967; children—James Reynolds, Darann Whiting, Robert Urban. With S.E.W. Friel Co., Queenstown, Md., 1964—, ltd. partner 1968-70, owner, full partner, 1970—; owner Friel Lumber Co., Queenstown, 1964—; pres. Queenstown Wholesale Co., 1975—, King Foods, 1975—. Mem. Md. Water and Wastewater Bd. Certification, 1975-76. Chmn. fund dr. Queen Anne's County chpt. A.R.C., 1970-71; mem. Queen Anne's County Hist. Soc. Served with Md. N.G., 1964-70. Recipient Outstanding Queen Anne's County Vol. Year award A.R.C., 1970. Mem. Centreville (Md.) Jr. C. of C. (v.p. 1967), Nat. Canners Assn., Mid-Atlantic Food Processors (chmn. raw products com. 1975, v.p. 1976, pres. 1977). Roman Catholic. Club: Chester River Yacht and Country (Chestertown, Md.); Corsica Yacht (Centreville, Md.); Cross Court Tennis (Easton, Md.). Home: Hope Rd Centreville MD 21617 Office: Box 10 Queenstown MD 21658

FRIEL, PATRICK BRENDAN, psychiatrist; b. Donegal, Ireland, May 16, 1925; s. Francis Coll and Cecelia F. (McAteer) F.; came to U.S., 1952, naturalized, 1962; grad. St. Eunans Coll., 1944; M.D. with honors, U. Coll., Dublin, 1950; m. Gerardine Martin, May 24, 1952; children—Daria, Sharon, Patrick F., Michael. Intern, St. Vincent's Hosp., N.Y.C., 1952-53; resident in psychiatry Norwich (Conn.) Hosp., 1953-58, Inst. of Living, 1955-56; staff psychiatrist Inst. Living, 1956-58; practice medicine specializing in psychiatry, West Hartford, Conn., 1958—; mem. psychiat. staff St. Francis, Hartford hosps.; dir. out-patient psychiat. clinic St. Francis Hosp., 1962-68, chmn., dir. dept. psychiatry, 1968-72; cons. psychotherapy Conn. Dept. Mental Health, 1962-68; clin. asso. U. Conn. Sch. Medicine, 1972—. Mem. Hartford Capitol Region Mental Health Planning Commn., West Hartford Mental Health Commn. Diplomate Am. Bd. Psychiatry and Neurology. Fellow Am. Psychiat. Assn., A.C.P., Royal Coll. Psychiatry, Royal Soc. Medicine; mem. Conn., Hartford (pres. 1968-69) psychiat. assns., AMA, Conn., Hartford med. socs. Contbr. articles to profl. jours. Home: 45 Kirkwood Rd West Hartford CT 06117 Office: 801 Farmington Ave West Hartford CT 06119

FRIEND, BENJAMIN, paper box corp. exec.; b. N.Y.C., Feb. 15, 1918; s. Morris and Becky (Weisselber) F.; B.S. magna cum laude, Coll. City N.Y., 1938; D.B.A. (hon.), Hamilton State U., 1973; m. Betty Shirley Terkell, June 27, 1953. Secondary sch. tchr. N.Y.C., 1939-40; gen. mgr. Value Paper Box Corp., N.Y.C., 1941-48, v.p., 1949-65, 1st v.p., 1965—, also mem. bd.; pres. B & B Realty Assos. Co., Newland Container Corp., 1969—, Glo-Mar Paper Products Co., 1969—; 1st v.p., dir. Ru-Bet Realty Assos. Co., 1968—; 1st v.p., chief ops. officer Lemberger Paper Box Co., Inc., 1975—; 1st v.p. City Wide Carton Co., Inc., 1975—; gen. partner Friendly Realty Assos., Ltd., 1975—; pres. Park Paper Box Co., Inc., Pleasure Realty Corp.; adviser package engring. Manhattan Coll., 1966; cons. F.M.C. Corp.; lectr. Columbia U., N.Y. U.; guest lectr. various groups on set-up paper box problems and technologies, 1967, 68. Trustee Met. Rigid Paper Box Mfrs. Assn. Charter mem. Fair Trade Paper Box Assn., Inc.; mem. Paper Box Standards Bur. (arbitration bd. 1958), Phi Beta Kappa. Patentee in field. Home: 640 W 231st St Riverdale NY 10463 Office: 220 Tonnelle Ave Jersey City NJ 07306

FRIEND, CHAIM H., assn. exec.; b. Atlanta, Oct. 14, 1919; s. David and Celia (Elfenbein) F.; student Coll. City N.Y., 1941; children—Gil Philip, Julie Rachel. Area dir. Nat. United Jewish Appeal, 1950-60; pres. Emerald Printing, 1960-61; exec. vice chmn. Reform Jewish Appeal, 1961-70; nat. dir. devel. Hebrew Union Coll.-Jewish Inst. Religion, N.Y.C., 1970-76, dir. bldg. fund B'nai B'rith Internat., Washington, 1975-77; dir. resources Am. Assn. for Jewish Edn., N.Y.C., 1977; exec. dir. West Point Jewish Chapel Fund, N.Y.C., 1977—. Served with AUS, 1942-45. Mem. Zionist Orgn. Am., Nat. Assn. Temple Adminstrs. (courtesy mem.), Am. Acad. Fund Raising Sci., Nat. Soc. Fund Raisers. Home: 444 E 82d St New York City NY 10028 Office: 342 Madison Ave New York City NY 10017

FRIES, GEORGE, transp. co. exec.; b. N.Y.C., May 11, 1920; s. Max and Ida F.; B.B.A., St. John's U., 1940; m. Jeanne Fisch, July 20, 1944; children—Barry, Nancy, Judith, Laurie (dec.). Asst. treas., ops. mgr. Clairol Inc., Yonkers, N.Y., 1963-70; corporate v.p. planning and internal audits Purolater Services Inc., New Hyde Park, N.Y., 1970-77; sr. v.p. fin. planning Purolator Security Inc., Piscataway, N.J., 1978—. Mem. Nassau County (N.Y.) Democratic Com., 1965—. Served with USAAF, 1942-46. Decorated Air medal. Mem. Planning Inst. N.Y., Adminstr. Mgmt. Soc., Adminstrv./Tech. Mgmt. Soc. Home: RD 1 Chrysler Pond Ancram NY 12502 Office: 255 Old New Brunswick Rd Piscataway NJ 08854

FRIES, HELEN SERGEANT HAYNES (MRS. STUART G. FRIES), civic leader; b. Atlanta; d. Harwood Syme and Alice (Hobson) Haynes; student Coll. William and Mary, 1935-38; m. Stuart G. Fries, May 5, 1938. Bd. mem. Community Ballet Assn., Huntsville, Ala., 1968—; mem. nat. nurses aid com. ARC, 1958-59; dir. ARC Aero Club, Eng., 1943-44; supr. ARC Clubmobile, Europe, 1944-46, mem. women's com. Nat. Symphony Orch., Washington, 1959—; chmn. residential fund drive for apts. Nat. Symphony Orch., 1959; bd. dirs. Madison County Republican Club, 1969-70; mem. nat. council Women's Nat. Rep. Club N.Y., 1963—, chmn. hospitality com., 1963-65; bd. mem. League Rep. Women, 1952-61. Recipient certificate of merit 84th Div., U.S. Army, 1945. Mem. Nat. Soc. Colonial Dames Am., D.A.R., Nat. Trust for Historic Preservation, Va., Nat., Valley Forge (Pa.), Eastern Shore Va., Huntsville-Madison County hist. socs., Am. Preservation, Assn. for Preservation Va. Antiquities, Greensboro Soc. Preservation, Tenn. Valley Geneal. Soc., AIM, Nat. Soc. Lit. and Arts, English Speaking Union, Turkish-Am. Assn. Clubs: Washington, Capitol Hill, Army-Navy Country (Washington); Garden (Redstone Arsenal), Redstone (Ala.) Yacht; Army-Navy (D.C.). Home: care Col Stuart G Fries 577 54 7471 TUSLOG Det 4 Box 642 APO New York NY 09133 also Riza Nur Cadessi 11 Kat 5 Sinop Turkey

FRIESE, JOHN CLARK, food service exec.; b. St. Cloud, Minn., Feb. 3, 1925; s. John Frank and Helen (Clark) F.; B.S. in Home Econs., Pa. State U., 1950; m. Helen Miller, June 12, 1948; children—Diane, David. Asst. mgr. Stouffer Corp., Cleve., 1950-51; dir. food services Edinboro (Pa.) State Coll., 1951-58; dir. food services, asst. prof. home econs. Kent (O.) State U., 1958-72; asso. dir. food services Lumberjack Enterprises, Cal. State U., Humboldt, 1972-73; v.p. Toronto (Ont., Can.) office Bernard & Assos., Inc., internat. food service mgmt. cons., 1973-76, v.p. Montreal (Que., Can.) office, 1973-76; cons., food service systems specialist U.S. Dept. Agr. Food and Nutrition Services, New Eng. region, Burlington, Mass., 1976—. Served with USAAF, 1943-45. Recipient Silver Plate award Internat. Foodservice Mfrs. Assn., 1971, Distinguished Service award Nat. Assn. Coll. and Univ. Food Services, 1972, honor award kitchen design Instns. mag., 1960, 61, 62, Superior Service award U.S. Dept. Agr., 1978, others. Mem. Nat. Assn. Coll. and Univ. Food Services (pres. 1968-69), Nat. Restaurant Assn., Am. Coll. and Univ. Housing Assn., Pa. State U. Home Econs. Alumni Assn. Home: 8 Parkhurst Dr Hudson NH 03051 Office: US Dept Agr Food and Nutrition Services 34 3d Ave Burlington MA 01803

FRIESECKE, RAYMOND FRANCIS, corp. exec.; b. N.Y.C., Mar. 12, 1937; s. Bernhard P.K. and Josephine (De Tomi) F.; B.S. in Chemistry, Boston Coll., 1959; M.C.E., Mass. Inst. Tech., 1961. Product specialist Dewey & Almy chmn. div. W.R. Grace & Co., Inc., Cambridge, Mass., 1963-66; market planning specialist USM Corp., Boston, 1966-71; mgmt. cons., Boston, 1971-74; dir. planning and devel. Schweitzer div. Kimberly-Clark Corp., Lee, Mass., 1974-78; v.p. corp. planning Butler Automatic, Inc., Canton, Mass., 1978—; corp. clk., v.p. Bldg. Research & Devel., Inc., Cambridge, 1966-68. State chmn. Citizens for Fair Taxation, 1972-73; state co-chmn. Mass. Young Republicans, 1967-69; chmn. Ward 7 Rep. Com., Cambridge, 1968-70; vice chmn. Cambridge Rep. City Com., 1966-68; Rep. nominee for Mass. Ho. of Reps., 1964, 66. Served to 1st lt., arty., AUS, 1961-63. Mem. Am. Chem. Soc., N.Am. Soc. Corp. Planning, Am. Mktg. Assn., World Future Soc., Am. Numis. Assn., Am. Rifle Assn., Big Bros. Assn., Boston South End Hist. Soc. (dir. 1971-73). Home: 250 Hammond Pond Pkwy Chestnut Hill MA 02167 Office: Butler Automatic Inc 480 Neponset St Canton MA 02021

FRIGAND, HERMAN JOSEPH, chem. engr.; b. Bklyn., Sept. 4, 1914; s. David and Anna Frigand; B.S., Bklyn Coll., 1942; m. Lillian Davis, June 27, 1943; children—Neil Martin, Dennis Allen. Shift supr. Calco Chem. Co., Bound Brook, N.J., 1942-44; group leader Van Dyk Co., Belleville, N.J., 1944-45; research and devel. Penick & Co., Jersey City, 1945-48; project mgr. Army Research and Devel. Center, Dover, N.J., 1948—; cons. Named Man of Year, Morristown Jewish Community Center, 1972; recipient tech. commendations and awards Dept. of Army. Mem. Am. Def. Preparedness Assn. Jewish. Clubs: Officers, Maccabees, Men's (pres. 1969-70), B'nai B'rith (rep.). Research on propellants and process tech.

FRIGAND, SIDNEY JEROME, publicity exec.; b. N.Y.C., Nov. 29, 1925; s. Aaron and Anna (Krauss) F.; B.A., Bklyn. Coll., 1948, postgrad., 1949-51; m. Evelyn Achenbaum, May 6, 1950; children—Steven A., Lisa, Nancy. Reporter, re-writeman, feature writer Bklyn. Daily Eagle, 1948-55; account exec. Victor Weingarten Pub. Relations, 1955-56; dir. pub. relations N.Y.C. Commn. Intergroup Relations, 1956-59; pub. affairs dir. N.Y.C. Planning Commn., 1959-65, dep. exec. dir., 1965-67; dir. pub. affairs Met. Transp. Authority N.Y. State, 1967-74; press sec. to mayor of N.Y.C., 1974-77; dir. pub. affairs Port Authority N.Y.-N.J., 1978—; vis. instr. Pratt Inst. Sch. Architecture and Planning; vis. lectr. Manhattanville Coll., N.Y. U. Sch. Pub. Adminstrn., Baruch Sch. of City U. N.Y., Bklyn. Coll., L.I. U. Sch. Journalism, Washington and Jefferson Coll.; faculty asso. New Sch. Social Research. Served with AUS, 1944-46. Recipient Page One citation N.Y. Newspaper Guild, 1955; Christopher award Christopher Soc., 1955; Headliners award Lincoln (Mo.) U. Sch. Journalism, 1955. Mem. Pub. Relations Soc. Am., Soc. Silurians, Civic Exec. Assn. N.Y. Jewish. Club: B'nai B'rith. Author articles, reports. Home: 298 Richmond Ave Massapequa NY 11758 Office: 1 World Trade Center New York City NY 10048

FRIM, SUMNER PHILIP, oral surgeon; b. Boston, Jan. 28, 1929; s. Zelman and Jennie (Greenberg) F.; A.B., Boston U., 1950; D.M.D., Tufts U., 1954; B.Jewish Edn., Hebrew Coll., Brookline, Mass., 1949; S.D.M., Tufts U., 1964, certificate oral pathology, 1964, oral surgery, 1968; m. Rosalind Steinhardt, Nov. 11, 1956; children—Edward Z., Gerald S., David M., Sara R. Intern oral surgery Worcester (Mass.) City Hosp., 1956-57; pvt. practice dentistry, Newton, Mass., 1957-66; resident oral surgery Cumberland Hosp., Bklyn., 1966-67; sch. dentist, Lexington, Mass., 1957-60; pvt. practice dentistry, specializing in oral surgery, Newton, 1969—; asst. clin. prof. oral pathology Tufts U. Sch. Dental Medicine, 1968-72, clin. instr. pathology Sch. Medicine, 1968-77, asst. clin. prof. pathology, 1977-78, asst. clin. prof. oral health service, 1972—; clin. instr. oral medicine and oral pathology Harvard, 1972—; fellow in gen. anesthesia Am. Dental Soc. Anesthesiology, 1974; mem. oral surgery staff Beth Israel Hosp., Newton, Wellesley Hosp., Waltham Hosp. Chmn. Bd. Edn., Beth El Community Hebrew Sch., Newton, 1962-72; v.p. United Hebrew Schs. Boston; bd. dirs. Bur. Jewish Edn. Boston; hon. trustee Hebrew Coll. of Brookline. Served to lt. Dental Corps, USNR, 1954-56. Diplomate Am. Bd. Oral Medicine. Fellow Am. Soc. Advancement Gen. Anesthesia in Dentistry; mem. Am. Acad. Oral Pathology, Am. Acad. Oral Medicine, New Eng., Mass. socs. oral surgeons, ADA, Am. Assn. Oral and Maxillofacial Surgeons, Mass. Dental Soc., Am. Dental Soc. Anesthesiology, Hebrew Coll. Alumni Assn. (past nat. pres.), Robert R. Andrews Honor Soc. Dental Research, Omicron Kappa Upsilon. Jewish (bd. dirs. congregation). Home: 327 Dedham St Newton MA 02159 Office: 851 Beacon St Newton MA 02159

FRINK, CHARLES RICHARD, soil chemist; b. Keene, N.H., Sept. 26, 1931; s. Richard Stebbins and Marjory Louise (Oakman) F.; B.S., Cornell U., 1953; Ph.D., 1960; M.S., U. Calif. at Berkeley, 1957; m. Roberta Ely Manchester, June 16, 1953; children—Aletta Louise, Calvin Robert, Richard Orlando. Asst. soil chemist Conn. Agrl. Expt. Sta., New Haven, 1960-64, asso. soil chemist, 1964-67, soil chemist, 1967-70, chief soil chemist, head dept. soil and water, 1970—, vice dir. sta., 1972—; cons. coms. Nat. Acad. Scis. Served to (j.g.) USN, 1953-56. Recipient Research award N.E. br. Am. Soc. Agronomy, 1974; Conservation award Connecticut River Watershed Council, 1976. Mem. N.Y. Acad. Scis., Am. Chem. Soc., Conn. Acad. Sci. and Engring., Sigma Xi, Phi Kappa Phi. Asso. editor Procs. Soil Sci. Soc. Am., 1967-69; contbr. numerous articles to sci. jours. Home: 26 Pawson Landing Dr Branford CT 06405 Office: PO Box 1106 New Haven CT 06504

FRISBIE, JOSEPH AUBREY, JR., electronics co. exec.; b. Jamacia, N.Y., Feb. 6, 1939; s. Aubrey Joseph and Laura Raymond (Thorne) F.; student Fairfield Coll. Prep., 1953-57; A.S., Western Conn. State Coll., 1957-59; student U. Bridgeport, 1960-61, U. Md., 1965-66; B.S., Northeastern U., 1971, M.B.A., 1975; m. Rita Marie Tyrell, Sept. 1, 1962; children—Joseph Aubrey, Suzanne Marie. Asst. chief engr. DeForce Constrn. Co., Bridgeport, Conn., 1959-60; lab. technician Barden Corp., Danbury, Conn., 1960-62; with Sanders Assos., Inc., Nashua, N.H., 1966-77, mgr. corporate systems software, computer scis. div., 1971-77, mgr. corp. engring., mfg. and sci. systems Computer Scis. div., 1978—; mgr. software devel., data communications div. Harris Corp., 1977-78. Served with USAF, 1962-66. Mem. Math. Assn. Am., Assn. Computing Machinery, Northeastern U. M.B.A. Assn. Club: K.C. Home: Mathew Dr Merrimack NH 03054 Office: D W Highway South Nashua NH 03061

FRISCH, IVAN THOMAS, computer, communications co. exec.; b. Budapest, Hungary, Sept. 21, 1937; s. Laszlo and Rose (Balog) F.; came to U.S., 1939, naturalized, 1941; B.S., Queens Coll.. N.Y., 1958; B.S., Columbia U., 1958, M.S., 1958, Ph.D., 1962; m. Vivian Scelzo, June 6, 1962; children—Brian, Bruce. Asst. prof. elec. engring., computer sci. U. Calif. at Berkeley, 1962-65, asso. prof., 1965-69; Ford Found. resident engring practice Bell Labs., Holmdel, N.J., 1965-66; founding mem. Network Analysis Corp., Great Neck, N.Y., 1969—, sr. v.p., 1971—, gen. mgr., 1978—; adj. prof. computer sci. Columbia U., N.Y.C., 1977—, State U. N.Y. at Stony Brook, 1975—; cons. in field. Guggenheim fellow, 1969. Fellow IEEE; mem. N.Y. Acad. Scis., Cable TV Assn. Am., Phi Beta Kappa, Tau Beta Pi, Eta Kappa Nu. Author: (with Howard Frank) Communication, Transmission and Transportation Networks, 1971. Founding editor-in-chief Networks, 1971—. Contbr. articles to profl. publs. Office: Network Analysis Corp 130 Steamboat Rd Great Neck NY 11024

FRITCHEN, DEAN HENRY, communication industry cons.; b. Decorah, Iowa, Aug. 7, 1929; s. Arthur Floyd and Ann (Hiatt) F.; B.S. in Commerce, U. Iowa, 1951. Mktg. trainee Gen. Electric Co., Schenectady, 1951-52; mgr. spl. projects Dudley-Anderson-Yutzy Pub. Relations Agy., Washington, N.Y.C., 1955-58; owner Dean Fritchen Pub. Relations, N.Y.C., 1958-66; with Metromedia, N.Y.C., 1966-71, v.p. mktg., 1970-71; v.p. Advt. Council, Inc., N.Y.C., 1971-76; sr. v.p. Madison Sq. Garden, 1976-77; cons. Syn-Cronamics, Inc., Englewood Cliffs, N.J., 1977—. Served from ensign to lt. USNR, 1952-55. Mem. Beta Theta Pi, Alpha Delta Sigma. Congregationalist. Club: Racquet and Tennis, Doubles (N.Y.C.). Home: 340 E 64th St New York City NY 10021

FRITCHEY, JOHN AUGUSTUS, II, physician; b. Harrisburg, Pa., Mar. 15, 1902; s. Elmer Eugene and Bertha Belle (Maurer) F.; Ph.B., Dickinson Coll., 1924; postgrad. Dartmouth, 1925-27; M.D., U. Pa., 1929; m. Dorotha Amy Warren, Nov. 12, 1932; children—Margaret Ann (Mrs. Henry Voltaire Trahan, Jr.), John Warren. Resident, Harrisburg Hosp., 1929-30; practice medicine, Harrisburg; mem. staff Polyclinic Hosp., Harrisburg, med. chief, 1931-48; state med. adminstr. Pa. Bur. Vocat. Rehab., 1948-63; med. cons. Pa. Dept. Pub. Assistance, 1950-54, Cumberland County Bd. Assistance, 1975—, Dauphin County Bd. Assistance, 1976—; sec.-treas., dir. San Family Washing Co., Harrisburg, 1943-48; insternist Harrisburg Dist. Armed Forces Induction Service, 1942-53; country dep. coroner, 1934-69. Chmn. Harrisburg City Democratic Com., 1942-43, chmn. Dauphin County Dem. Com., 1943-46. Mem. AMA, Dauphin County Med. Soc., Harrisburg Acad. Medicine, Nat. Rehab. Assn. (life), Geneal. Soc. Pa., Gesellschaft fur Familienkunde in Kurhessen und Waldeck, SAR (chpt. pres. 1942-44, state pres. 1948-50, v.p. gen. 1947-49, nat. exec. com. 1949-50, registrar gen. 1950-53, surgeon gen. 1956-57), Palatines to Am. (organizing chmn. Pa. chpt. 1977-78, nat. exec. council 1978-79), S. Central Pa. Geneal. Soc. (charter), The Perry Historians, Sigma Chi, Phi Chi. Mason (32 deg., Shriner). Home: 106 November Dr Camp Hill PA 17011

FRITZ, DONALD THEODORE, indsl. fence co. exec.; b. Balt., Aug. 10, 1927; s. Joshua Theodore and Carolyn Estelle (Griffee) F.; B.A., Johns Hopkins, 1950; m. Patience Gordon Linker, May 10, 1958; children—Mark David, Heather Lee Gordon. Pres., J.T. Fritz & Sons, Inc., Glen Burnie, Md., 1951—; dir. Union Liberty Life Ins. Co. Mem. Balt. County Decency Com. Served to lt. (j.g.), USNR, 1945-46, 50-51. Trustee St. Paul's Sch., St. Paul's Sch. for Girls. Mem. St. Paul's Sch. Alumni Assn. (past pres.), Asso. Builders and Contractors, Inc. (past dir., past nat. v.p.), Page Fence Assn. (past pres.), Md. C. of C., Md. Hist. Soc., SAR, Gen. Soc. Colonial Wars, Co. Mil. Historians. Republican. Baptist. Clubs: Balt. Country, Johns Hopkins, Masons. Home: Mays Chapel Rd Lutherville MD 21093 Office: 117 Wellham Ave NE Glen Burnie MD 21061

FRITZ, JAMES CLARENCE, chemist; b. Berlin, Pa., May 15, 1910; s. Robert Lincoln and Emma Elizabeth (Cober) F.; B.S., Pa. State U., 1929; postgrad. U. N.H., U. Md.; m. Jeanette Moore Blair, July 30, 1933; children—Margaret Fritz Baker, Richard. Jr. biologist, U.S. Dept. Agr., Beltsville, Md., 1930-37, asst. biochemist, 1937; lab. dir. Borden Co., Elgin, Ill., 1937-51; dir. nutrition research Dawe's Labs., Chgo., 1952-65; supervisory research chemist, div. nutrition FDA, Washington, 1965-78; ret., 1978. Mem., officer, Elgin Aux. Police Corps, 1942-65. Mem. Assn. Vitamin Chemists (pres.), Animal Nutrition Research Council (chmn. 1952), Am. Chem. Soc., AAAS, Am. Inst. Nutrition, Am. Inst. Chemists, Soc. Exptl. Biology and Medicine, Poultry Sci. Assn., Am. Soc. Animal Sci. Author: (with H.W. Titus) The Scientific Feeding of Chickens, 1971. Contbr. articles to profl. jours. Home: 12314 Madeley Ln Bowie MD 20715

FRNKA, MICHAEL QUENTIN, indsl. engr.; b. Palacios, Tex., Nov. 28, 1947; s. Victor Quentin and Ella Catherine F.; Asso. Applied Sci., Wharton County Jr. Coll., 1968; B.S. in Indsl. Engring., Tex. A. and M. U., 1970, M.S. in Indsl. Engring., 1972; m. Patricia Ann Thompson, Dec. 31, 1968; children—Michael Quentin, Amy Lynn, Christopher Andrew. Engr., U.S. Army Electronics Command, Fort Monmouth, N.J., 1972; indsl. engr. Corpus Christi (Tex.) Army Depot, 1973-76, U.S. Army Iranian Aircraft Program Field Office, Tehran, Iran, 1976—. Registered profl. engr., Tex. Mem. Nat. Def. Preparedness Assn., Am. Inst. Indsl. Engrs., Army Aviation Assn. Am., Tau Beta Pi, Alpha Pi Mu. Address: Box 701 APO New York City NY 09205

FROBISHER, MARTIN, JR., microbiologist; b. N.Y.C., Jan. 17, 1896; s. Martin and Charlotte Augusta (Biggam) F.; student Cornell U., 1916-17, 21-22; B.S., Johns Hopkins U., 1922, Sc.D., 1925; m. Amy Westervelt Willis, June 3, 1922. Asst. state bacteriologist Md. Health Dept., 1923-24; asso. dept. pathology Johns Hopkins Med. Sch., 1924-28; spl. mem. internat. health div. Rockefeller Found., Yellow Fever Lab., N.Y. and Brazil, 1928-32; asso., asso. prof. bacteriology Johns Hopkins U., 1932-48; chief bacteriology sect. Center for Disease Control, USPHS, 1948-52; prof., head dept. microbiology U. Ga., 1952-53; ret., 1970; cons. Surgeon Gen. of U.S. Army ETO, 1946. Served with U.S. Army, 1917-19. Diplomate Am. Bd. Med. Microbiology. Fellow AAAS, Am. Pub. Health Assn., N.Y. Acad. Scis., Royal Soc. Health (life), Am. Acad. Microbiology; mem. Am. Soc. Microbiology (Hon. Distinguished mem. New Eng. br.), Am. Inst. Biol. Scis., Sigma Xi, Delta Omega. Author: Fundamentals of Microbiology, 1974; Microbiology in Health and Disease, 1978; Rypin's Medical Licensure Examinations, 1975; editor in chief Am.

Jour. Hygiene, 1938-48, Am. Jour. Tropical Medicine and Hygiene, 1955-59, med. health sect. Biol. Abstracts, 1939-47. Home: Wessex House Apt 318 St Davids PA 19087

FROEHLICH, CHARLES ORTH, JR., coll. adminstr.; b. Harrisburg, Pa., Oct. 5, 1936; s. Charles Orth and Sara Virginia (Geer) F.; student Franklin and Marshall Coll., 1954-56; B.A., Dickinson Coll., Carlisle, Pa., 1961; m. Kathryn Johnson, June 1, 1957; children—Charles Orth, Kristen Ann, Laura Jean. Announcer, Sta. WHGB, Harrisburg, 1953-56, Sta. WKBO, 1956-57, WTPA-TV, Harrisburg, 1957-65; adminstrv. asst., instr. Harrisburg Inst. Med. Arts, 1961-64; grant examiner, asst. dir. grants Bur. Higher Edn. Facilities, Pa. Dept. Pub. Instruction, Harrisburg, 1965-68; substitute tchr. Harrisburg Area Pub. Schs. Pres., Shiremanstown PTA, 1967-68; dir. fed. programs Franklin and Marshall Coll., Lancaster, Pa., 1968—, asst. dir. devel., 1968-71, asso. dir. devel., 1971-72, dir. adminstrv. services for devel., 1972-77, dir. devel. services, 1977—, adminstrv. adviser to ednl. broadcasting sta. WFNM, 1975—, coll. liaison to WITF-FM, Hershey, Pa., 1978—. Mem. pub. relations com. Lancaster-Lebanon council Boy Scouts Am., 1975-78, instl. rep. Explorer Scout post, 1976-78; trustee Lancaster County Hist. Soc., 1975-78; mem. budget and planning com. Central Pa. Synod, Lutheran Ch. in Am., 1977—. Mem. Lancaster County Hist. Soc. (treas. 1978—), Sigma Pi, Mu Upsilon Sigma. Club: Masons. Home: 5029 Martin Dr East Petersburg PA 17520 Office: College Ave Lancaster PA 17604

FROEHLICH, EDNA BORG, ednl. adminstr., psychologist; b. Union City, N.J., July 28, 1918; d. Adolph Frank and Anna Lena (Frese) Borg; B.A. cum laude, Montclair (N.J.) State Coll., 1939; M.A. in Psychology, Columbia Tchrs. Coll., 1956, profl. diploma, 1967, Ed.D., 1970; m. Paul Edward Froehlich, June 27, 1942; children—Pauline (Mrs. Joseph S. Stroman), Kathleen (Mrs. LeRoy W. Osborn), Linda (Mrs. Walter K. Schreyer). Tchr., Emerson High Sch., Union City, N.J., 1939-45, Cresskill (N.J.) Pub. Sch., 1958-60; instr. Fairleigh Dickinson U., Teaneck, N.J., 1959-60; specialist learning disabilities, reading cons., Palisades Park (N.J.) Pub. Sch., 1962-65, coordinator child study, sch. Psychologist, 1966-69; clin. psycholoIgist Neurol. Inst., Columbia-Presbyn. Med. Center, summer 1966; instr. Bergen Community Coll., Paramus, N.J., 1970-71; sch. psychologist Glen Rock (N.J.) Pub. Sch., 1970-72, dir. spl. services, 1972—; pvt. practice psychology, 1973—. Mem. Spl. Edn. Adv. Bd. for Region IV, Bergen County, sec., 1973-75, coordinator, 1975-76, 78-79; hon. v.p. Glen Rock Spl. Edn. PTA, 1972—. NIMH grantee, 1965-66. Licensed psychologist, N.J., Nat. Register Health Service Providers in Psychology. Mem. Am., Nat., N.J., Bergen County psychol. assns., Nat., N.J., Bergen County edn. assns., Council Exceptional Children, Assn. Children With Learning Disabilities, N.J., Bergen County (pres. 1972-73) assns. sch. psychologists, N.J. Assn. Pupil Personnel Adminstrs., N.J. Assn. Spl. Edn. Adminstrs., Glen Rock Adminstrs. Assn. (sec. 1975-76). Contbr. articles to profl. jours. Home: 208 Engle St Tenafly NJ 07670 Office: Glen Rock Pub Schs Maple Ave Glen Rock NJ 07452

FROEHLICH, FRITZ EDGAR, physicist; b. Worms a/Rh., W. Ger., Nov. 12, 1925; s. Julius and Ida (Heilborn) F.; B.S. in Physics magna cum laude, Syracuse U., 1950, M.S. in Physics, 1952, Ph.D. in Physics, 1955; m. Eileen Karch, Dec. 25, 1949; children—Laurence Alan, Georgine Kay, Philip Marc. Came to U.S., 1938, naturalized, 1944. Research asst., asst. instr. Syracuse (N.Y.) U., 1950-54; instr. physics Utica (N.Y.) Coll., 1952-54; with Bell Telephone Labs., 1954—, supr. data communications, Murray Hill, N.J., 1956-63, head wide band data, Holmdel, N.J., 1963-67, head new sta. services, Holmdel, 1968-78, head bus. terminal dept., 1978—. Pres. Morristown (N.J.) Cooperation Nursery Sch., 1955-56. Served with AUS, 1944-46. Fellow IEEE (chmn. teller's com. 1971, sect. chmn. 1963—, session chmn. 1963-76); mem. N.Y. Acad. Scis., AAAS, Phi Beta Kappa, Sigma Xi, Pi Mu Epsilon, Sigma Pi Sigma. Jewish (trustee, sec., past v.p.). Contbr. articles to profl. jours. Patentee in field. Home: 25 Nottingham Way Little Silver NJ 07739 Office: Bell Telephone Labs Holmdel NJ 07733

FROEHLICH, WALTER, sci. journalist; b. Worms, W. Germany, Nov. 27, 1921; s. Julius and Ida (Heilborn) F.; came to U.S., 1938, naturalized, 1943; B.S., Syracuse U., 1949; m. Luz Ajero, June 2, 1956; children—David Ben, Lisa Catherine. Editor, Genesee Country Express, Dansville, N.Y., 1949-51; reporter, feature writer Buffalo Courier-Express, 1951-63; sci. editor USIA, Washington, 1963-74, sci. and tech. program officer, 1974—; mem. dedication party U.S. Amundsen-Scott South Pole Sta., 1975, lectr. Sci. Journalism and Social Impact Sci. and Tech. in Africa, Southeast Asia, Europe. Served with U.S. Army, 1943-46. Mem. Nat. Assn. Sci. Writers, Brit. Interplanetary Soc., Royal Soc. Sci. (Thailand), Soc. Tech. Communication, Nat. Press Club, Am. Inst. Aero. and Astronautics, Aviation Space Writers Assn., Am. Med. Writers Assn., Am. Polar Soc., Nat. Space Club, Am. Aero. Assn., Sigma Delta Chi. Author: Man in Space, 1971; Apollo 14: Sci. at Fra Mauro, 1971; Apollo 16 at Descartes, 1972; Apollo Soyuz, 1977. Home: 5531 Warwick Pl Chevy Chase MD 20015 Office: ICA Washington DC 20547

FROIX, MICHAEL FRANCIS, phys. chemist, polymer physicist; b. Trinidad, W. Indies, Jan. 27, 1942; s. Arthur C. and Lorna E. (Lopez) F.; came to U.S., 1962; B.S., Howard U., 1966, M.S., 1968, Ph.D. (Fellow), 1971; children—Cherie-Ann, Renee. Chemist, Texaco Research Labs., Beacon, N.Y., 1966, Gillette Research Inst., Washington, 1968; scientist Xerox Corp., Rochester, N.Y., 1971-77; sr. research chemist Celanese Corp., Summit, N.J., 1977-78; research supr. Celanese Research Co., Summit, 1978—; vis. prof. BEEP Program, Nat. Urban League, 1976-77, 77-78; instr. community edn. div. U. D.C., 1970-71. Mem. Am. Phys. Soc., Am. Chem. Soc., N.Y. Acad. Scis., AAAS. Contbr. articles to profl. jours. Home: 138 North Ave Dunellen NJ 08812 Office: Celanese Research Co Summit NJ 07901

FROLICH, HENRIK STAMPE, import co. exec.; b. Odense, Denmark, Sept. 6, 1923; s. Einar Lorenz and Edith Barfoed (Thrige) F.; came to U.S., 1949; M.S. in Engring., Royal Tech. U., Denmark, 1948; M.B.A., U. Conn., 1951; m. Helen Merion Cass, Mar. 18, 1952; children—Benedicte, Ann Catherine. Design engr. Lone Star Cement Corp., N.Y.C., 1949-51; chief project engr. Bechtel Corp., San Francisco, 1951-52; project engr. Bur. Pub. Roads U.S. Dept. Commerce, Juneau, Alaska, 1952-53; project engr. Danish Arctic Contractors, Denmark, Korea and New Rochelle, N.Y., 1953-62; sales engr. F.L. Smith & Co., N.Y.C., 1962-67; pres. Raaco Corp., Stamford, Conn., 1968-72, also dir.; pres. Nordstrand Co., Darien, Conn., 1972—, also dir.; dir. Pressurized Products, Inc., N.J., Everton Internat., Darien. Served with Danish Navy, 1945-46. Mem. Am. Soc. Danish Engrs. (pres. 1973), Purchase Community Assn. (dir.), Brit. Instn. Naval Architects (asso.). Home: 38 Old Farm Rd Darien CT 06820 Office: 6 Great Hill Rd Darien CT 06820

FROLICK, STANLEY WILLIAM, lawyer; b. Hillcrest, Alta., Can., July 7, 1920; s. George Michael and Mary (Nykyforuk) F.; B.A., U. Toronto, 1952; Barrister-at-law, Osgoode Hall Law Sch., 1958; m. Gloria Kupchenko, May 31, 1947; children—Larry George, Vernon Mark, Deborah Cynthia Anne, Christine Mary. Admitted to Ont. bar, 1958; sr. partner firm Frolick, Frolick & Frolick, Toronto, 1975—. Nat. pres. Ukrainian Can. Profl. and Bus. Fedn., 1970-73; pres. Ukrainian Can. com. Ont. Provincial Council, 1975—; chmn. bd. Can. Inst. Ukrainian Studies Found., Inc., 1975—; Progressive-Conservative candidate for M.P. in fed. elections 1953, 62; dir. Central Ukrainian Relief Bur., London, 1946-47; bd. dirs. Liquor License Bd. Ont., 1976—. Served to capt. Brit. Element, Allied Control Commn. Germany, 1944-46. Queen's Counsel, 1968. Mem. Can., Ont., York bar assns. Clubs: Royal Canadian Legion, Empire, Albany. Home: 105 Russell Hill Rd Toronto ON M4V 2S9 Canada Office: Suite 1401 80 Richmond St W Toronto ON M5H 2A4 Canada

FROMNICK, STEPHEN MICHAEL, elec. engr.; b. Phila., Jan. 21, 1948; s. Paul Michael and Virginia Marie F.; B.E.E., Villanova U., 1969; m. Nancy Jane Vanecek, Dec. 29, 1973. Designer, Ceglia & Schlein Assos., Phila., 1965-69; asso. engr. Consol. Cons.'s, Phila., 1965-69; engr. George C. Lewis Assos., Phila., 1967-69; product mgr. B&F Instruments Co., Cornwells Heights, Pa., 1969-73; sr. staff engr. Sun Oil Co. (Suntech Inc.), Newtown Square, Pa., 1973-79; mgr. advanced mgmt. and methods div. Suntech, Inc. subs. Sun Co., 1979—. Mem. IEEE (exec. com.), Instrument Soc. Am. Patentee in field (7). Office: Bishop Hollow Rd Newtown Square PA 19073

FROSCH, ROBERT ALAN, govt. ofcl., physicist; b. N.Y.C., May 22, 1928; s. Herman Louis and Rose (Bernfeld) F.; A.B., Columbia U., 1947, A.M., 1949, Ph.D., 1952; m. Jessica Rachael Denerstein, Dec. 22, 1957; children—Elizabeth Ann, Margery Ellen. Scientist, Hudson Labs. Columbia, 1951-53, asst. dir. theoretical div., 1953-54, asso. dir., 1954-56, dir. 1956-63; dir. nuclear test detection, Advanced Research Projects Agy., Office Sec. Def., 1963-65, dept. dir. Advanced Research Projects Agy., 1965-66; asst. sec. navy for research and devel., Washington, 1966-73; asst. exec. dir. UN Environment Programme, 1973-75; asso. dir. for applied oceanography Woods Hole (Mass.). Oceanographic Instn., 1975—; chmn. Inter-agy. Com. on Marine Research, Edn. and Facilities, 1967-69; Dept. Def. mem. com. for policy rev. Nat. Council on Marine Resources and Engring. Devel., 1969—; chmn. U.S. del. to Intergovtl. Oceanographic Commn. meetings UNESCO, Paris, 1967, 70. Recipient Arthur S. Flemming award, 1966. Fellow A.A.A.S., Acoustical Soc. Am., I.E.E.E.; mem. Am. Geophys. Union, Seismol. Soc. Am., Soc. Exploration Geophysicists, Marine Tech. Soc. Research and publs. numerous sci. and tech. articles. Office: Woods Hole Oceanographic Instn Woods Hole MA 02543*

FROST, FREDERICK GEORGE, III, metals co. exec.; b. Bronxville, N.Y., Sept. 12, 1941; s. Frederick George and Gwendolyn C. (Corwin) F.; A.B. in Polit. Sci., U. Colo., 1964; m. Elizabeth I. Read, Aug. 11, 1962; children—Peter C., Lucy L., Priscilla W. With mktg. dept. Mobil Oil Co., N.Y.C., 1964-66; asst. to pres. A.T. Wall Co., Warwick, R.I., 1966-69, exec. v.p., 1969-72, pres., 1972—; dir. Narragansett Capital Corp., Outlet Co. Trustee Marathon House. Clubs: Agawam Hunt, Hope (Providence); Dunes (Narragansett, R.I.). Home: 6 Barberry Hill Providence RI 02906 Office: 55 Service Ave Warwick RI 02886

FROST, JOHN ELDRIDGE, librarian; b. Eliot, Maine, Jan. 13, 1917; s. Martin and A. M. (Eldridge) F.; B.A., U. Maine, 1938; S.T.B., Berkeley Divinity Sch., 1941; B.S., Columbia, 1948; M.A., U. N.H., 1948; Ph.D., N.Y.U., 1953. Asst. minister, Worcester, Mass., 1941-42; asso. rector, Westbury, L.I., N.Y., vicar, Carle Place, L.I., 1943-44; asst. librarian Drew U., 1949; asst. librarian N.Y.U. Library, N.Y.C., 1950, now librarian. Served with USNR, 1945-46. Mem. ALA, Bibliog. Soc. Am., Newcomen Soc. Eng. Author: Nicholas Frost Family, 1943; Colonial Village, 1948; Sarah Orne Jewett, 1953; Maine Genealogy, 1976. Editor: Portsmouth Record Book, 1946; Soc. for the Libs Bull., 1958—. Contbr. articles to profl. publs. Office: NY University Library Washington Sq New York City NY 10003

FROST, MARSHALL, civil engr.; b. Freehold, N.J., Apr. 24, 1943; s. Howard Marshall and Lucy Bell (Dittmar) F.; B.S. in Civic Engring., Lehigh U., 1966; M.S. in Transp., Poly. Inst. Bklyn., 1969; m. Linda Ann Minkel, July 16, 1966; children—Jennifer Lynn, Sheri Elizabeth, William Marshall. Asst. civil engr. N.Y.C. Dept. Traffic, 1966-67; sr. engr. planning N.J. Dept. Transp., Trenton, 1967-70; head dept. transp. James P. Purcell Assos., East Orange, N.J., 1970-74; pres. Frost Assos., Chatham, N.J., 1974—; instr. traffic engring. Rutgers U., 1970-75; mem. Nat. Acad. Scis.-Transp. Research Bd., 1966-72. Mem. Planning Bd., Chatham, 1977—; v.p. Ewing Twp. Jr. C. of C., 1969, dir., 1970. Mem. Inst. Transp. Engrs. (N.Y. sect.). Home: 77 Rowan Rd Chatham NJ 07928 Office: PO Box 657 Chatham NJ 07928

FROST, REX ALLEN, psychologist; b. Balt., Oct. 2, 1944; s. Theodore Rex and Mabel Virginia (Taylor) F.; B.A., Thomas Edison Coll., 1967; certificate Rutgers U., 1968; M.A., Towson State Coll., 1972; Ph.D., Johns Hopkins U., 1973. Research asso. Balt. City Hosps., 1967-68; chief psychol. services Md. Tng. Sch., Balt., 1973—; pvt. practice psychotherapy, Balt., 1975—; cons. intensive probation Dept. Juvenile Services, 1975—, Model Cities, 1975—, Social Security Disability Program, 1974—; pres. Windemere Investment Trust, Inc., 1975—. Mem. Am. Psychol. Assn. Democrat. Clubs: Johns Hopkins, Masons. Author: Frost Mood Evaluation Scale, 1975. Home: 54 Windemere Pkwy Phoenix MD 21131 Office: 2400 Cub Hill Rd Baltimore MD 21234 also 322 N Marlyn Ave Baltimore MD 21221

FRUCHER, MEYER SAMUEL, state ofcl.; b. Jersey City, May 25, 1946; s. Aaron and Miriam (Greenspan) F.; B.A. in Govt., Columbia U., 1972; M.P.A., Harvard U., 1974; m. Florence Haines, Sept. 4, 1967; children—Kathryn Ilana, Aaron Marshall. Adminstrv. asst. to Insp. Gen., OEO, Washington, 1965; mem. N.Y.C. Council Against Poverty, 1965-66; with U.S. Research & Devel. Corp., N.Y.C., 1966-72; dir. innovative programs Addiction Services Agy. of N.Y.C., 1972-73; dir. Mass. Supported Work Program, 1974-75; exec. dir. N.Y. State Commn. on Mgmt. and Productivity in Pub. Sector, Albany, 1975-78; dir. N.Y. State Office Employee Relations, Albany, 1978—; faculty State U. N.Y., Stony Brook, Harvard U., Cambridge, Mass., Boston U.; cons. dept. social services Human Resources Adminstrn., N.Y.C., N.Y. State Commn. on Revision N.Y.C. Charter. Bd. dirs. Center for Women in Govt., Albany. Littauer fellow John F. Kennedy Sch. Govt., Harvard U. Mem. Am. Soc. Pub. Adminstrn. Democrat. Jewish. Club: B'nai B'rith. Home: PO Box 163 RD 1 Hudson NY 12534 Office: Agy Bldg 2 Nelson A Rockefeller Empire State Plaza Albany NY 12223

FRUHAUF, HENRY, temple exec.; b. N.Y.C., Jan. 24, 1923; s. Henry and Belle (Sohmer) F.; student Columbia U., 1939, U. Va., 1939-41, New Sch. for Social Research, 1968, N.Y. U., 1969; m. Frances Jaeger Falk, July 3, 1943; 1 son, William Henry. Investigator, Office of Sec., U.S. Treasury Dept., N.Y.C., 1942; chief accounting dept. Seaboard Fruit Co., Inc., N.Y.C., 1946-49; adminstrv. v.p. Congregation Emanu-El, N.Y.C., 1950—. Vice chmn. Community Council, N.Y.C., 1963-69; mem. commn. on synagogue adminstrn. Union Am. Hebrew Congregations-Central Conf. Am. Rabbis, 1973—. Bd. trustees Rabbinical Pension Bd., 1969—. Served with AUS, 1942-45. Mem. Nat. Assn. Ch. Bus. Adminstrs., Nat. Assn. Temple Adminstrs. (pres. 1965-67), Am. Jewish Com. (nat. exec. council 1970—, chpt. v.p. 1969—). Mem. B'nai B'rith (sec. 1959). Author: Temple Finance and Reserve Funds, 1968. Office: 1 E 65th St New York City NY 10021

FRY, ALVIN ABRAM, ednl. and tax cons.; b. Progress, Pa., Aug. 10, 1904; s. John Franklin and Rebecca Esther (Burkholder) F.; B.S., Dickinson Coll., 1926; M.S., Pa. State U., 1932; D.Ed., Columbia, 1948; m. Zella Jeanne Oliver, Dec. 29, 1950. Tchr. sci., athletic coach pub. schs., Matamoras, Pa., 1926-29, Dover, N.J., 1929-45; supt. schs., Hamburg, N.J., 1945-48, Pennsville, N.J., 1951-54, Selbyville, Del., 1955-57; prof. edn. W.Va. Wesleyan Coll., 1948-51; asst. prin. A.L. Johnson Regional High Sch., Clark, N.J., 1957-64; adj. prof. edn. Kean Coll., Union, N.J., 1966-73; ednl. cons., 1965—; mem. Kent State U. Research Center for Study Socialist Edn., 1972—. Basketball ofcl. for North Jersey, 1932-55, hon., 1955—; tax cons. served as lt. AUS, 1942-44. Kent State U. grantee for research study socialist edn., 1971. Mem. Am. Assn. U. Profs., Am. Assn. Sch. Adminstrs., N.J. Edn. Assn. (exec. com. 1940-42), Am. Theatre Assn., Speech and Theatre Assn., Speech Assn. N.J., N.Y. Schoolmasters Club (admissions com.), Union County Ret. Educators (pres. 1976-78, legis. com. 1978—), Kappa Delta Pi, Phi Delta Kappa. Clubs: Masons, Penn State of North Jersey (exec. com.). Home: 6 Edgewood Ct North Plainfield NJ 07060

FRY, JOHAN TRILBY (GIFFORD) (MRS. GILBERT WAYNE FRY), occupational therapist, educator; b. Quincy, Mass., Apr. 27, 1937; d. Paul Albert and Mary (Blunt) Gifford; A.A., Westbrook Coll., 1957; B.S. in Edn., Tufts U., 1960; M.A., Western Mich. U., 1971; m. Gilbert Wayne Fry, Dec. 30, 1967 (div.); children from previous marriage—Eluned Pihl, Erik Pihl, Kari Pihl. Occupational therapist Lemuel Shattuck Hosp., Boston, 1961-62, St. Mary's Hosp., Mpls., 1962-63, Mpls. Soc. for the Blind, 1964-68, Gaylord Hosp., Wallingford, Conn., 1970-72; asst. prof. dept. occupational therapy. Quinnipiac Coll., Hamden, Conn., 1972—. HEW grantee, 1968. Mem. Am., Conn. occupational therapy assns., Am. Assn. Workers for the Blind, New Eng. Occupational Therapy Council Edn., Assn. Rehab. Tchrs. Home: 220 Mansion Rd Cheshire CT 06410 Office: Box 117 Quinnipiac College Hamden CT 06518

FRY, ZELLA JEANNE OLIVER (MRS. ALVIN ABRAM FRY), educator; b. Moyie, B.C., Can., Oct. 30, 1909; d. Walter and Mary (Congdon) Oliver; came to U.S., 1951, naturalized, 1958; B.A., U. Alta., 1931, diploma in secondary edn., 1932, Cert. d'Etudes Francaises, 1936; M.A., Columbia U., 1944, postgrad., 1945-51; postgrad. U. B.C., 1940, U. Wash., 1941; m. Alvin Abram Fry, Dec. 29, 1950. Tchr. Alta. pub. schs., 1932-42; asst. prin. High River (S.D.) High Sch., 1935-38; supervising prin. Lomond (S.D.) Consol. Sch., to 1935, tchr. Edmonton (Alta., Can.) City Schs. and univ. demonstration tchr., Alta., 1938-42; lectr. Alta. Normal Schs., 1942-45; asst. prof. lang. arts and theatre U. Alta., Edmonton, 1945-50, asso. prof., 1951; grad. asst. Tchrs. Coll., Columbia U., N.Y.C., 1951-52; asso. prof. math. and adolescent psychology Glassboro (N.J.) State Coll., 1953; adj. prof. elementary edn. U. Del., Dover extension center, 1955-57; tchr. Selbyville (Del.) Pub. High Sch., 1955-57; asso. prof. speech, theatre, media studies Kean Coll. N.J. (formerly Newark State Coll.), Union, 1958-77; adjudicator Westchester (N.Y.) Community Coll. Theatre Arts Festival, 1975, Pa. Regional High Sch. Festival, 1975, State Drama Festival U. Del., 1978. Kappa Delta Pi grantee Kent State U., 1971, 72. Recipient laureate citation Kean Coll. N.J., 1977; studio theatre of Kean Coll. N.J. named for her, 1978. Mem. Am. Community Theatre Assn., Am. Theatre Assn., AAUP, AAUW (chpt. pres. 1954-55, chmn. state com. on ednl. TV 1954, 55), Nat., N.J., Union County, Somerset County ret. educators assns., Am. Coll. and Univ. Theatre Assn., Nat., N.J. edn. assns., Children's Theatre Assn. Am., Secondary Sch. Theatre Assn., Speech Assn. N.J. (v.p. 1968-70, pres. 1970-72, mem. exec. bd. 1972-74), Horatio Alger Soc., Speech Assn. Eastern States, Speech Communication Assn., Canadian Studies Conf. N.J., Kappa Delta Pi (award 1976), Pi Lambda Theta. Episcopalian. Contbr. to publs. in field, poems to mags. Home: 6 Edgewood Ct North Plainfield NJ 07060

FRYE, PIERRE ARNOLD, lawyer; b. N.Y.C., Jan. 19, 1924; s. Lucius Arnold and Suzanne (Jaladert) F.; B.E.S., U. Paris, 1942; student Harvard U., 1942-43; J.D., Columbia, 1948; LL.M., N.Y. U., 1959; m. Annie-Vera Dysthe, July 24, 1965; children—Pierre-Christian, Vera-Ellen Suzanne. Admitted to N.Y. bar, 1950, U.S. Supreme Ct., other fed. cts.; with Hawkins, Delafield and Wood, 1948-49; asst. to L. Arnold Frye, 1949-50; pvt. practice, 1950-52; with 1st Nat. City Bank, 1952-54; counsel Pyrofax Gas Corp., 1954-59; mem. law dept. Union Carbide Corp., 1959-68; pvt. practice law, 1968-69; mem. law dept. Am. Home Products Corp., 1969-73 (all N.Y.C.); internat. counsel Grumman Corp., 1973-78; sec. Grumman Internat., 1974-78; asst. gen. counsel Warnaco, Inc., Bridgeport, Conn., 1978—. Trustee, officer, counsel Fleming Sch., N.Y.C., 1957-58, 64-70. Served with AUS, 1943-46; now col. USAF Res. Decorated Bronze Star, N.Y. State Conspicuous Service Cross. Mem. Am., N.Y. City bar assns., Am. Legion, SAR (life). Home: 24 Salt Box Ln Darien CT 06820 Office: 350 Lafayette St Bridgeport CT 06602

FRYE, RICHARD CRAIG, mktg. exec.; b. Youngstown, Ohio, Aug. 23, 1943; s. Forrest E. and Virginia L. (Rhoads) F.; B.S., Miami U., 1965; children—Carl Andrew, Matthew Philip. Media buyer Ketchum, MacLeod & Grove, Inc., Pitts., 1965-67; media supr., account exec. Fuller & Smith & Ross, Inc., N.Y.C., 1967-69; advt. and sales promotion mgr. hoisting equipment div. Eaton Corp., Forrest City, Ark., 1969-74, indsl. truck div., Phila., 1974-77, mgr. export sales, 1977—. Served with USCGR, 1965-66. Mem. Internat. Trade Devel. Assn., Bus./Profl. Advt. Assn., Bus. Publs. Audit of Circulations. Republican. Methodist. Contbr. articles to bus. jours.

FRYER, APPLETON, sales exec., lectr.; b. Buffalo, Feb. 25, 1927; s. Livingston and Catherine (Appleton) F.; A.B., Princeton U., 1950; m. Angeline Dudley Kenefick, May 16, 1953; children—Appleton, Daniel Kenefick, Robert Livingston, Catherine Appleton. Head interpreter Hewitt-Robins, Inc., Buffalo, 1950-51; advt. dept. Buffalo Evening News, 1953-55; field rep. Ketchum, MacLeod & Grove, Inc., advt., 1955-56; pres. Duo-Fast of Western N.Y., Inc., Buffalo, 1956—. Dep. sheriff Erie County (N.Y.), 1954-68; co-chmn. Eric Bicentennial Commn., 1974-77; adviser Buffalo Environ. Mgmt. Commn., 1973-75; adv. bd. Children's Hosp. Buffalo; bd. mgrs. Buffalo and Erie County Hist. Soc., 1969—, v.p., 1977—; mem. council Charles Burchfield Center, 1974—; trustee Theodore Roosevelt Nat. Hist. Site Found., 1969—; pres. Landmark Soc. Niagara Frontier, 1969-73; mem. council Central Erie Deanery, Diocese of Western N.Y., 1970; pres. Arboretum of Met. Buffalo, 1977-78; bd. dirs. Zool. Soc. Buffalo, Inc., 1972-78, Erie County Sesquecentennial Commn., 1970-71, Buffalo Fine Arts Acad., Albright-Knox Art Gallery, 1973-76; bd. dirs. Maud Gordon Holmes Arboretum, 1974—, pres., 1977-78; mem. com. Young Life on the Niagara Frontier, 1971-72; mem. Community Welfare Council of Buffalo and Erie County; mem. Erie County Preservation Adv. Bd., 1978—, Buffalo Landmark and Preservation Bd., 1978—; chmn. Buffalo-Kanazawa Sister Cities Com., 1978—. Served with USNR, 1945-46, 1st lt., AUS, 1951-52. Licensed lay reader Diocese Western N.Y., 1973—. Mem. S.R. (pres. Buffalo Assn. 1966-73), Soc. Mayflower Descs. (regent Buffalo Colony 1961-65), Soc. Colonial Wars, Niagara Frontier Indsl. Distbrs. Assn., Holland

Soc. N.Y. (pres. Niagara Frontier br. 1969—), Princeton Alumni Assn. (chmn. alumni schs. com. Western N.Y. Area 1974-77), Buffalo Area C. of C. (Buffalo Beautiful com. 1975—), Buffalo Soc. Natural Scis., Old Ft. Niagara Assn., Order Colonial Lords of Manors. Democrat. Episcopalian (warden 1971-74). Clubs: Masons, Rotary; Princeton (pres. Western N.Y. 1960); Univ. Cottage, Nassau (Princeton, N.J.); Saturn (vice dean 1963) (Buffalo); Princeton (N.Y.C.); Porcupine (gov. 1969-72) (Nassau, Bahamas). 85 Windsor Ave Buffalo NY 14209 Office: 365 Nagel Dr Buffalo NY 14225

FRYER, JOHN ERCEL, psychiatrist, educator; b. Winchester, Ky., Nov. 7, 1937; s. Ercel Ray and Katherine Minnie (Zempter) F.; B.A., Transylvania Coll., 1957; M.D., Vanderbilt U., 1962. Intern, Univ. Hosp., Columbus, Ohio, 1962-63; resident in psychiatry VA Hosp., Topeka, Kans., 1963-64, Norristown State Hosp., 1965-67; practice medicine specializing in psychiatry, Phila., 1965—; asso. prof. psychiatry Temple U., Phila., 1978—, fellow in community psychiatry, 1967-68, career instr. alcoholism and addiction, 1975-78; staff psychiatrist cons. and edn. unit Temple U. Community Mental Health Center, 1968-70; dir. tng. Eagleville (Pa.) Hosp., 1970-73; staff psychiatrist Friends Hosp., Phila., 1972-73; chmn. workshops and seminars in field; cons. in field to numerous schs., hosps. Organist-choirmaster St. Peter's Epis. Ch., Germantown, Pa., 1965—; mem. Germantown (Pa.) Community Council, 1967-72; chmn. Internat. Work Group in Death, Dying and Bereavement, 1974—. Fellow Am. Psychiat. Assn.; mem. Pa. Psychiat. Soc., Am. Med. Soc. on Alcoholism, Inst. on Religion in an Age of Sci. (mem. council), Soc. for Health and Human Values., Phi Kappa Tau. Democrat. Episcopalian. Home: 138 W Walnut Ln Philadelphia PA 19144 Office: Dept Psychiatry Temple U Sch Medicine Philadelphia PA 19140

FRYKHOLM, WALTER LAURIE, optical co. exec.; b. Rhinelander, Wis., Sept. 24, 1931; s. Walter John and Sylvia (Inberg) F.; A.B., Lake Forest Coll., 1953; M.S., Ariz. State U., 1962; m. Jean Louise McMahon, Dec. 29, 1956; children—Laurie Jean, Walter Ryan, Amy Joyce. Personnel rep. Sandia Corp., Livermore, Calif., 1962-66; personnel mgr. Moog, Inc., East Aurora, N.Y., 1966-68; staff cons. Arthur Young & Co., 1968-69; mgr. personnel adminstrn. SCM Corp., Bus. Equipment div., Syracuse, N.Y., 1969-76; dir. human resources Shuron div. Textron Inc., Rochester, N.Y., 1976-78; v.p. human resources Hilti Inc., Stamford, Conn., 1978—. Served with AUS, 1953-55. Mem. Soc. Advancement Mgmt., Am. Soc. Personnel Adminstrn., Indsl. Mgmt. Council Rochester. Club: Univ. Syracuse. Home: 4 Brickston Dr Pittsfield NY 14534 Office: 1 Cummings Point Rd Stamford CT 06904

FRYMANN, HANS KASPAR, cement co. exec.; b. Zurich, Switzerland, Mar. 6, 1927; s. J. Heinrich and Margrit (Schaertlin) F.; Propedentic Mech. Engr., U. Lausanne (Switzerland), 1946-47; M.E.E., Swiss Fed. Poly. Inst., Zurich, 1950; m. Louise Sitterding, Apr. 24, 1954 (div. 1971); m. 2d, Antje L. Luders, 1972. Naturalized Canadian citizen, 1960. Devel. engr. Brown Boveri, Switzerland, 1950-53; chief elec. engr., chief mech. engr. St. Lawrence Cement Co., Clarkson, Ont., Can., 1953-60; mgr. cement and pryo process dept. M.W. Kellogg Co., N.Y.C., 1960-65; v.p. engring. and purchasing Lone Star Cement Corp., N.Y.C., 1965-68, v.p. engring., mfg. and purchasing, 1968-72, v.p. cement and constrn. materials group, 1972—; dir. Citadel Cement Corp.; free lance cons., 1962-65. Served to officer pilot Swiss Air Force, 1947-53. Registered profl. engr., Ont. Mem. Engring. Inst. Can. Home: 27 Surf Rd Westport CT 06880 Office: 1 Greenwich Plaza Greenwich CT 06830

FU, LORRAINE S., mathematician, educator; b. China; d. Kang Lo and Yen Fu; came to U.S., 1953; naturalized, 1973; B.A., Hunter Coll.; M.S., N.Y. U.; Ph.D., Poly. Inst. Bklyn.; m. Lee-Shien Lu, 1967; 1 son, Michael. Lectr. math. Hunter Coll., N.Y.C., 1964-67, asst. prof. math., 1971-76; asst. prof. math. Pace U., N.Y.C., 1977—. Mem. Community Sch. Bd. 13, N.Y.C. Bd. Edn., 1975-77, co-chmn. curriculum com., 1975-77, co-chmn. fin. com., 1975-77; bd. mgrs. Bklyn. central br. YMCA, 1979—. Spl. NSF fellow, 1969-70. Mem. Am. Math. Soc., Math. Assn. Am., Soc. Indsl. and Applied Math., AAAS, Sigma Xi. Contbr. articles to profl. jours. Home: 175 Adams St Brooklyn NY 11201

FU, SHOU-CHENG JOSEPH, educator; b. Peking, China, Mar. 19, 1924; s. W.C. Joseph and W.C. (Tsai) F.; came to U.S., 1946, naturalized, 1957; B.S., M.S., Cath. U. Peking, 1944; Ph.D., Johns Hopkins U., 1949; m. Susan B. Guthrie, June 21, 1951; children—Robert W.G., Joseph H.G., James B.G. Vis. scientist Nat. Cancer Inst., 1951-54; Gustav Bissing fellow Johns Hopkins at Univ. Coll., London, 1955-56; chief enzyme and bioorganic chemistry labs. Children's Cancer Research Found., Boston, also research asso. Children's Hosp. Med. Center and Harvard Med. Sch., 1956-67; prof., chmn. bd. chemistry Chinese U. Hong Kong, 1967-70, univ. dean sci. faculty, 1967-69; vis. prof. Coll. Phys. and Surg., Columbia, 1970-71; prof. biochemistry Coll. Medicine and Dentistry N.J., Newark, 1971—, asst. dean Grad. Sch. Biomed. Scis., 1975-77, acting dean, 1977—; cons. edn. and research VA Hosp., East Orange, N.J., 1971—. Pres. Coll. Medicine and Dentistry N.J. Fed. Credit Union, 1973-74. Served to lt. comdr. USPHS Res., 1959—. Fellow AAAS, Chem. Soc. (London); mem. Asia Soc., Sigma Xi (sec. Newark 1973-75, pres. 1977—). Clubs: Royal Hong Kong Jockey, Am. (Hong Kong). Contbr. numerous articles to internat. sci. jours. Home: 693 Prospect St Maplewood NJ 07040 Office: 100 Bergen St Newark NJ 07103

FUCCI, CHARLES DANIEL, physician; b. Jersey City, Apr. 23, 1921; s. Charles Anthony and Rose Amelia (Buglione) F.; student N.Y. U., 1937-40; B.A., Tex. Christian U., 1942; M.D., Middlesex U., 1945; m. Bernice Czapla, May 7, 1949; children—Frank, Rose, Bernadette. Intern Mary Immaculate Hosp., Jamaica, N.Y., 1945-46, resident, 1946-47, now asso. attending physician; practice medicine specializing in family practice, Queens Village, N.Y. 1948—; attending physician, chmn. pharmacy and utilization coms. Terrace Heights Hosp., Hollis, N.Y. Diplomate Am. Bd. Family Practice. Fellow Am. Acad. Family Practice; mem. AMA (awards 1971, 74, 77), N.Y. State, Queens County med. socs., Am. Acad. Family Physicians, Am. Geriatrics Soc., Pan-Am. Soc., N.Y. Trudeau Soc. Republican. Roman Catholic. Home and Office: 93-41 Springfield Blvd Queens Village NY 11428

FUCHS, HELMUTH HANS, educator; b. Chgo., Aug. 25, 1931; s. Hans and Alycia F.; B.S., Loyola U., 1962; M.S., N.Mex. State U., 1966; Ph.D., Fordham U., 1974. Research asst. Great Lakes Naval Tng. Center, 1960-62; sci. tchr. Franklin High Sch., Somerset, N.J., 1965-67; asst. prof. chemistry State U. N.Y., Farmingdale, 1970—. Served with USN, 1952-54. Mem. Am. Chem. Soc., Soc. Applied Spectroscopy, Sigma Xi, Phi Lambda Upsilon. Composer: Ein Stueck Fuer Susanne, 1976; Lieblichkeit, 1977; Schlummerlied, 1977; others. Home: 804 Front St Dunellen NJ 08812

FUCHS, JEROME HERBERT, mgmt. cons.; b. N.Y.C., Jan. 7, 1922; s. Berthold and Fannie (Neuschotz) F.; B.S. cum laude, Syracuse (N.Y.) U., 1950, M.B.A., 1951; m. Eleanor May DeRoo, May 26, 1945; children—Jerome S. Taylor, Susan Fuchs Decker, Sandra Fuchs Lombino. Systems analyst Carrier Corp., 1951-52; supr. systems and procedures Lukens Steel Co., 1952-54; mgr. systems and procedures Pennwalt Co., 1955-57; mgr. systems and procedures Amax Inc., 1958-60; exec. asst. to pres. Rockbestos Wire & Cable Co., 1960-61; v.p. mfg. United Aircraft Products Co., 1970-71; exec. v.p. Bus. Supplies Corp. Am., 1972; pres. Fuchs Assos., mgmt. cons., Massapequa, N.Y., 1960—; lectr. Syracuse U., 1950-52, Johns Hopkins U., 1953-54, Drexel Inst. Tech., Phila., 1955-57, Queens Coll., 1963-65. Served as 2d lt. USAAF, 1943-46. Mem. Soc. Profl. Mgmt. Cons. (charter, pres. 1977—), Inst. Mgmt. Cons. (a founder). Author: Making the Most of Management Consulting Services, 1975; Management Consultants in Action, 1975; Computerized Cost Control Systems, 1976; Computerized Inventory Control Systems, 1977; Administering the Quality Control Function, 1978. Address: 30 Cabot Rd W Massapeque NY 11758

FUCHS, RUTH, phychiatrist; b. Vienna, Austria; d. Jacob and Renee (Klein) F.; B.A., Harvard U.; M.D., State U. N.Y. at Buffalo. Intern, Montefiore Hosp., N.Y.C.; resident pscyhiatry Kingsbridge VA Hosp., Bronx, N.Y., Hillside Hosp., Glen Cove, N.Y., Mt. Sinai Hosp., N.Y.C.; asst. attending psychiatrist Mt. Sinai Hosp., also Mt. Sinai Services at Elmhurst Hosp., Queens, N.Y.; individual practice medicine, specializing in psychiatry and child psychiatry, N.Y.C. Home and Office: 239 E 79th St New York City NY 10021

FUENTEVILLA, MANUEL EDWARD, chem. engr.; b. Havana, Cuba, Feb. 17, 1923; s. Fernando and Edith Alice (Pira) F.; B.Ch.E., Poly. Inst. Bklyn., 1947; M.S., Drexel U., 1954; m. May Belle Tutwiler, Oct. 18, 1945; children—William F., Diane G., Austin D., Eve J., Inez M. Sr. engr. Catalyic Inc., Phila., 1951-60; chief engr. Stokes Equipment div. Pennwalt Corp., 1960-67; asst. mgr. mfg. Esso Eastern, Tokyo, 1967-69, tech. supt., Okinawa, Japan, 1969-72; project mgr. Jacobs Engring. Co., Cherry Hill, N.J., 1972-75; project mgr. Stauffer Japan Ltd., Tokyo, 1975-77; dir. process devel. Alfa Laval Process, Mt. Laurel, N.J., 1977—. Pres., Woodcrest Assn., Cherry Hill, 1965-66. Served with USNR, 1943-46. Mem. Am. Inst. Chem. Engrs., Phi Lambda Upsilon. Club: Cooper River Yacht (Collingswood). Patentee in indsl. processes. Home: 314 Tearose Ln Cherry Hill NJ 08003 Office: Mount Laurel NJ

FUKAE, KENSUKE, mfg. co. exec.; b. Kanazawa, Japan, May 13, 1926; s. Hajime and Hashiko (Inoyue) F.; came to U.S., 1955, B.S., Tokai Sci. Coll. (Japan), 1947; M.A., U. Tokyo, 1954; m. Roswitha Frey, Dec. 28, 1957; children—Kenneth A., Amy C., Mark T. Reporter internat. news Hokkaido Shinbun, Tokyo, 1952-55; U.S. rep. Minolta Camera Co. Ltd., Osaka, Japan, 1955-60; v.p. Minolta Corp., Ramsey, N.J., 1960—. Cons. mktg. and product planning. Mem. Nat. Microfilm Assn., Optical Soc. Am., Soc. Photo-Optical Instrumentation Engrs. Shinto religion. Home: 1 Fessler Rd Monsey NJ 10952 Office: 101 Williams Dr Ramsey NY 17446

FUKUI, HATSUAKI, elec. engr.; b. Yokohama, Japan, Dec. 14, 1927; s. Ushinosuke and Yoshi (Saito) F.; diploma Miyakojima Tech. Coll. (now Osaka City U.), 1949; D.Eng., Osaka U., 1961; m. Atsuko Inamoto, Apr. 1, 1954 (dec. Apr. 1973); children—Mayumi, Naoki; m. 2d, Kiku Kato, Dec. 12, 1975. Came to U.S., 1962, naturalized, 1973. Research asso. Osaka City U., 1949-54; engr. Shimada Phys. and Chem. Indsl. Co., Tokyo, 1954-55; sr. engr. to supr. Sony Corp., semi-condr. div., Tokyo, 1955-61, mgr. engring. div., 1961-62; mem. tech. staff Bell Telephone Labs., Murray Hill, N.J., 1962-69, supr., 1969-73; v.p. Sony Corp. Am., N.Y.C., 1973, asst. to chmn. Sony Corp., Tokyo, 1973; staff mem. Bell Labs., Murray Hill, N.J., 1974—; lectr. Tokyo Met. U., part time 1962. Mem. Inst. Electronics and Communication Engrs. Japan (Inada award 1959), Inst. TV Engrs. Japan (tech. com. 1973-75), IEEE (sr.; standardization com. 1976—). Author: Esaki Diodes, 1963; Solid-State FM Receivers, 1968; contbr. to Semiconductors Handbook, 1963; patents, publs. in field. Home: 53 Drum Hill Dr Summit NJ 07901 Office: 600 Mountain Ave Murray Hill NJ 07974

FULBRIGHT, FREEMAN, public relations counsel; b. Atlanta, Apr. 26, 1925; s. Ernest Alexander and Lessie (Freeman) F.; student Ohio State U., N.Y. U.; m. Jane Meese, Aug. 4, 1947; children—Carolyn Frances, Cary Freeman. Reporter, Durham (N.C.) Morning Herald, 1941-43, Cin. Post, 1943-45; legis. corr. I.N.S., Columbus, Ohio, 1945-46, news editor, Chgo., 1947-50, Washington corr., 1951-52; night mng. editor, N.Y.C., 1952-55; v.p., gen. mgr. Walker & Crenshaw, Inc., pub. relations, 1955-57; gen. editor Newsweek, 1957-61; exec. editor N.Y. Herald Tribune, 1961-62; exec. v.p. Selvage & Lee, Inc., 1962-68; sr. v.p. Hill and Knowlton, Inc., 1969-73, exec. v.p., 1973—; mng. dir. Hill and Knowlton Can. Ltd., 1976—; cons. in field, 1943—. Mem. Sigma Delta Chi. Presbyterian (elder). Club: Nat. Press (Washington). Home: 277 West End Ave New York City NY 10023 Office: 633 3d Ave New York City NY 10017 also One Yonge St Toronto ON M5E 1N4 Canada

FULLER, BRENT DAVIS, geophysicist; b. Yonkers, N.Y., Jan. 16, 1936; s. Burnett O. and Elizabeth (Davis) F.; B.S., Mich. Tech. U., 1964 (Mobil Oil scholar, Internat. Minerals and Chem. scholar); M.S. U. Calif., Berkeley, 1966, Ph.D. (NSF fellow), 1970; m. Doris A. Hoffmann, Feb. 2, 1974; 1 dau., Kristin Ann. Staff geophysicist Newmont Mining Corp., Danbury, Conn., 1969-75; mem. profl. staff Schlumberger-Doll Research Center, Ridgefield, Conn., 1975—. Served with USCG, 1953-57. Mem. Soc. Exploration Geophysicists, Soc. Petroleum Engrs., Soc. Profl. Well Log Analysts, European Assn. Exploration Geophysicists. Republican. Congregationalist. Clubs: Newtown Fish and Game, Brookfield Gun, Pootstuck Archery. Contbr. articles to profl. jours. Home: Hawthorne Hill Rd Newtown CT 06470 Office: Old Quarry Rd Ridgefield CT 06877

FULLER, EARL CLIFTON, univ. ofcl.; b. Providence, May 9, 1926; s. Earl Clifton and Lillian R. (Fletcher) F.; B.B.A., Bryant Coll., 1964; m. Beatrice E. Collemer, Oct. 6, 1950; children—Anne, Paul, Pamela. Field officer mgr. GSA, Boston, 1960-68; terminal adminstr. Eastern Airlines, Logan Airport, Boston, 1968-70; chief security The World Bank, Washington, 1970-73; chief security and spl. investigations State of Md. Lottery and Auto Ins. Fund, Annapolis, 1973-76, dir. corporate security Appendagez, Inc., Norwood, Mass., 1976—; property adminstr. Office Facilities Mgmt. Systems, Mass. Inst. Tech., 1978—; security cons. World Bank & Monetary Fund Credit Unions; ops. officer U.S. Naval Sea Cadet Corps; pub. info. officer U.S. Naval Sea Cadet Corps, Annapolis. Served with USAF, 1943-46, 1950-51. Decorated Air medal, Purple Heart; recipient U.S. Distinguished Pub. Service award, 1968. Mem. Internat. Assn. Chiefs of Police, Am. Soc. Indsl. Security, Nat. Fire Protection Assn., Indsl. Fire Protection Assn., Am. Judicature Soc., FBI Bomb Data Center, DAV (past comdr.), Navy League (dir.), U.S. Naval Inst. (dir.). Home: 3008 Marlin Dr Annapolis MD 21140 Office: 537 University Ave Norwood MA 02062

FULLER, EARNEST MELVIN, architect; b. Princeton, Ill., June 22, 1905; s. John Edgar and Ida Della (Earnest) F.; B.S., U. Ill., 1928; m. Betty Margaret Mooney, May 4, 1946; children—Donald E., Cheryl E. Fuller Marozas, John Edgar. Salesman, Johns-Manville Sales Corp., Chgo., 1930-36, archtl. rep., 1936-41, product mgr. bldg. materials, N.Y.C., 1941-51, various mgmt. positions, 1951-62, v.p., 1962-70; with State U. Constrn. Fund, Albany, N.Y., 1970-77, dir. tech. and engring., 1972-77; cons., Ballston Lake, N.Y., 1977—. Mem. AIA, N.Y. State Assn. Architects, Constrn. Specifications Inst., Am. Arbitration Assn., Soc. Am. Mil. Engrs., Sigma Chi. Contbr. articles to profl. publs. acoustics, roofing, architecture, sales, other topics. Home and Office: 19 Woodstead Rd Ballston Lake NY 12019

FULLER, GERALD WALLACE, hosp. controller; b. Raton, N.Mex., Dec. 29, 1929; s. Richard Lee and Thelma Delores (Kallman) F.; student Eastern N.Mex. U., 1949; B.S., U. Colo., 1953; m. Jane Busch, May 6, 1954; children—Gwendolyn, Michael. With Shell Oil Co., various locations, 1953-63, systems analyst, Houston, 1962-63; owner, operator Gen. Country Store, West Minot, Maine, 1963-67; controller Thayer Hosp., Waterville, Maine, 1967-75; asst. treas., controller Mid-Maine Med. Center, Waterville, 1975—; mem. Maine Health Facilities Cost Rev. Bd., 1978—; mem. vol. budget rev. orgn. Maine Budget Rev. Panel for Hosps., 1978—; pres. Hosp. Services, Inc., 1975-77. Coach, Little League Baseball, 1959-61, Jr. League Ice Hockey, 1968-69, Pop Warner Football League, 1968-72; bd. dirs. Goodwill Home Assn., 1972-78, treas., 1972-73, chmn., 1973-75. Served with USAF, 1954-57. Fellow Hosp. Fin. Mgmt. Assn. (dir. 1976-78, treas. 1978—), Alpha Tau Omega. Republican. Methodist. Club: Rotary Internat. Home: 4 Martin Ave Waterville ME 04901 Office: Mid-Maine Med Center Chase Ave Waterville ME 04901

FULLER, JAMES RALPH, automobile mfg. co. exec.; b. Boston, Sept. 17, 1938; s. Louis V. and Margaret M. (Donlon) F.; B.S. with honors, Northeastern U., 1966; M.B.A. cum laude, Fairleigh Dickinson U., 1971; m. Georgann F. Oswalt, Mar. 25, 1967; children—Stacey, Christopher. Various field sales and ops. assignments Ford Motor Co., Dearborn, Mich., 1966-72, nat. program devel. mgr. Ford customer service div., Dearborn, 1972-73, nat. car merchandising mgr., 1973-75; v.p. sales Renault U.S.A. Inc., Englewood Cliffs, N.J., 1975-79; gen. mgr. mktg. group ops. Am. Motors Corp., Southfield, Mich., 1979—. Served with USMC, 1957-60. Mem. N.Y. Sales Execs. Club. Presbyterian. Club: Indian Trail. Office: 27775 Franklin Rd Southfield MI 48075

FULLER, JEANNE MOLLOY, titanium pigment co. exec.; b. Bklyn., Mar. 12, 1939; d. James G. and Anne M. (Martin) Molloy; A.B., Rutgers U., 1972; children—Paul, Christine. Credit analyst, then supr. data control John Wiley & Sons, Somerset, N.J., 1973-77; credit asst. Gen. Cigar & Tobacco Co., N.Y.C., 1977-78; asst. credit mgr. titanium pigment div. N/L Industries, South Amboy, N.J., 1978—. Mem. Nat. Micrographics Assn. Home: 10 Academic Rd East Brunswick NJ 08816 Office: 100 Chevalier Ave South Amboy NJ 08879

FULLER, RENEE NUNI, child psychologist, publisher; b. Mannheim, Germany, Apr. 14, 1929; d. Eric W. and Fridel (Henning) Stoetzner; came to U.S., 1938, naturalized, 1944; Ph.D., N.Y. U., 1963. Research scientist N.Y. State Dept. Mental Health, Letchworth Village, 1960-66; project dir. Staten Island Soc. Mental Health, 1966-67; chief psychol. services Rosewood State Hosp., Balt., 1967-74; pres. Ball-Stick-Bird Publs., Inc., Stony Brook, N.Y., 1975—. Certified psychologist, Md. Mem. Am. Psychol. Assn., Am. Psychopath. Assn., Ednl. Research Assn., Behavior Genetics Assn. Author Ball-Stick-Bird reading system. Home: Drawer O Miller Place NY 11764 Office: PO Box 592 Stony Brook NY 11790

FULLER, RICHARD BUCKMINSTER, design scientist, author, geometrician, educator; b. Milton, Mass., July 12, 1895; s. Richard B. and Caroline Wolcott (Andrews) F.; student Harvard U., 1913-15, U.S. Naval Acad., 1917; recipient 40 hon. doctorates in sci., fine arts, humane letters, laws, engring., arts and archtl. engring. from N. Am. univs., 1954-78; fellow St. Peter's Coll., Oxford (Eng.) U., 1970; m. Anne Hewlett, July 12, 1917; children—Alexandra Willets (dec.), Allegra Fuller Snyder. Apprentice machine fitter Richards, Atkinson & Haserick, importers of cotton mill machinery, Boston, 1914-15; various apprentice positions Armour & Co., N.Y.C., 1915-17, asst. export mgr., 1919-21; nat. account sales mgr. Kelly Springfield Truck Co., 1922; pres. Stockade Bldg. System Bklyn., 1922-27; founder 4D Co., Chgo., 1927, pres., 1927-32; asst. to dir. of research Pierce Found.-Am. Radiator Standard San. Mfg. Co., 1930-31; editor, publisher Shelter Mag., N.Y.C., 1930-32; founder Dymaxion Corp., Bridgeport, Conn., 1932, dir., chief engr., 1932-36; asst. to dir. research and devel. Phelps Dodge Corp., 1936-38; tech. cons. Fortune Mag., 1938-40; v.p., chief engr. Dymaxion Co., Inc., Del., 1940-50; chief mech. engr. U.S. Bd. Econ. Warfare, 1942-44; spl. asst. to dep. dir. U.S. Fgn. Econ. Adminstrn., 1944; chief engr., chmn. bd. Dymaxion Dwelling Machine Corp. (later Fuller Houses, Beech Aircraft Co.), Wichita, Kans., 1944-46; chmn. bd. trustees Fuller Research Found., Wichita, 1946-54; pres. Geodesics, Inc., Forest Hills, N.Y., 1949—, Synergetics, Inc., Raleigh, N.C., 1954-59, Plydomes, Inc., Des Moines, Iowa, 1957—; chmn. bd. Tetrahelix Corp., Hamilton, Ohio, 1959; research prof. design sci. exploration So. Ill. U., Carbondale, 1959-71, prof. emeritus, 1971—, also dir. Inventory of World Resources, Human Trends and Needs, 1965—; Charles Eliot Norton prof. poetry Harvard U., 1962-63; architect U.S. Pavilion at Expo 67, Montreal (Can.) World's Fair, 1965-67; pres. Triton Found., Cambridge, Mass., 1967; architect in production of tetrahedronal floating city for HUD, 1967; architect Samuel Beckett Theater, St. Peter's Coll., Oxford (Eng.) U., 1969, St. Peters Theatre, London, 1969, geodesic auditorium, Israel, 1969-70, Project Toronto (Can.), 1971, Religious Center, So. Ill. U., Edwardsville, 1971; chief architect Old Man River Project, East St. Louis, Ill., 1971, completion of the design Internat. Airports at New Delhi, India, 1973, Madras, India, 1973; cons. Design Sci. Inst., 1972—; world fellow in residence for consortium of U. Pa., 1972-78, U. City Sci. Center, Phila., 1972—, Haverford and Swarthmore Colls., 1972-78; prof. emeritus U. Pa., Phila., 1975—; vis. prof., lectr., prin. speaker or research seminar dir. at 431 colls., univs. or ednl. instns. in U.S., Can., Eng., Australia, W. Ger., Italy, Nigeria, S. Am., 1929-79; mem. bd. advisers Internat. U. of Communications, Washington, 1970-74, Internat. Edn., U. Tenn., Knoxville, 1972, Britannica Internat. Ency., Energy Info. Service, N.Y.C., 1975—, Emerging Profls. Internat. Confs., N.Y.C., 1975—; numerous exhibits of designs in U.S. and Europe, 1929-79. Mem. Nat. Citizens Com. for Pub. TV, New Orleans, 1967—; mem. bd. overseers, art, Brandeis U., Walthem, Mass., 1965—; bd. dirs. Harmony Hills Music Found., Hot Springs, Ark., 1966—, pres., 1966-67; bd. dirs. Harlem Theater and Workshop, Inc., N.Y.C., 1968—, The Oceanic Edn. Found., Falls Church, Va., 1969, Coastal Resources Action Com., Portland, Maine, 1970, Ishi Center for Consciousness Studies, Cambridge, Mass., 1974-75; trustee Cancer Research Inst., N.Y.C., 1964—, Nat. Pollution Control Found., 1966—; hon. trustee Boys Brotherhood Republic, N.Y.C., 1966—; trustee Undersea Research Ltd., Toronto, Ont., Can., 1970—, Safe Power for Maine, 1974—, Theatre Royal, London, 1975—. Served from ensign to lt., U.S. Navy, World War I. Recipient R. Buckminster Fuller Chair of Architecture, U. Detroit, 1970, Gran premio award Triennale de Milan, Italy, 1954, 57; award of merit USMC, 1955; Plomado de Oro award Soc. Mexican Architects, 1963; Creative Achievement award Brandeis U., 1965; Royal Gold Medal of Architecture from Her Majesty the Queen, Eng., 1968; citation of merit HUD, 1969; McGraw-Hill award, 1969; President's award U. Detroit, 1971; award of merit Phila. Art Alliance, 1973; 1975 Planetary Citizens award UN; named Humanist of the Year, Am. Assn. of Humanists, 1969. Benjamin Franklin fellow Royal Soc. of Arts (Eng.); Hoyt fellow Yale U., 1969. Fellow AIA (award of merit 1952, Gold medal award 1960, 1st. Archtl. Design award 1968, Gold medal award 1970), Am. Acad. Arts and Scis., World Acad. Arts and Sci., Lincoln Acad. of Ill. (Order of Lincoln medal award 1967), Inst. of Gen. Semantics, AAAS, (hon.) Royal Acad. Fine Art of Netherlands, (hon.) Soc. for Tech. Communication, (hon.) Royal Inst. Brit. Architects, Bldg. Research Inst., Inst. for Advanced Philosophic Research; mem. NAD, Nat. Inst. Arts and Letters (Gold medal award 1968), Soc. Archtl. Historians, Soc. Harvard Scientists and Engrs., Assn. Am. Geographers, World Soc. for Ekistics (v.p. 1966-67, pres. 1975-76),

Inst. Human Ecology, Indsl. Designers Soc. of Am. (hon. mem., 1st award of excellence 1966), Am. Inst. Indsl. Engrs. (hon. mem.), Am. Soc. Metals, Franklin Inst., UN Assn. of U.S.A., Phila. Soc. Preservation of Landmarks, Soc. for Study of Humane Genetic Applications (hon. dir. 1973—), Nat. Soc. Lit. and Arts (bd. govs. 1974—), Internat. Assn. Machinists and Aerospace Workers, Am. Astronautical Soc., AAUP, Deer Isle Stonington Hist. Soc., Internat. Soc. for Sterology (hon.), Costeau Soc., Assn. Am. Indian Affairs, Navy League of U.S., Phila. Mus. Art, Advocates for Arts, Israel Inst. Engrs. and Architects (hon. mem.), Soc. Venezuelan Architects (hon. mem.), Royal Soc. Siamese Architects (hon. mem.), Mexican Coll. and Inst. Architects, Zentralvereiningung Der Architekten Asterreichs (hon. mem.); Sigma Xi, Phi Beta Kappa (hon. mem.), Tau Sigma Delta (hon. mem.), Alpha Rho Xi (master architect), Delta Phi Delta, Mensa (internat. pres. 1974—). Clubs: Somerset (Boston); Coffee House, N.Y. Yacht, Salmagundi, Explorers (N.Y.C.); Cosmos (Washington); Harvard, U. Barge (Phila.); Cliff Dwellers (Chgo.); Seawanhaka Corinthian Yacht (Oyster Bay, N.Y.). Author: 4D Timelock, 1928; Nine Chains to the Moon, 1938; (with Robert W. Marks) The Dymaxion World of Buckminster Fuller, 1960; Education Automation, 1963; Untitled Epic Poem on the History of Industrialization, 1962; Ideas and Integrities, 1963; No More Secondhand God, 1963; World Design Decade Documents, 1965-75; Operating Manual for Spaceship Earth, 1968; Utopia Or Oblivion, 1969; The Buckminster Fuller Reader, 1970; (with Jerome Agel and Quentin Fiore) I Seem to Be a Verb, 1970; Buckminster Fuller to Children of Earth, 1972; Intuition, 1973; Earth, Inc., 1973; Synergetics: Explorations in the Geometry of Thinking, 1975; contbr. numerous articles to various mags. and lit. jours.; contbr. numerous intros. and forewords to various books; contbg. editor to several mags.; inventor Dymaxion House, Chgo., 1927; inventor-discoverer synergetic geometry, geodesic structures and tensegrity structures; designer numerous geodesic domes including: Palais de Sports, Paris, France, 1959, Climatron Botanical Garden, St. Louis, 1960, Cinerama Theater, Hollywood, Calif., 1963, U.S. Pavilion at Canadian Universal and Internat. Exhbn., 1967, Airplane Museum, Amsterdam, Holland, 1969, U.S. Research Sta. Dome, South Pole of Earth, 1972, Weather Radome, Mt. Fuji, Japan, 1973.

FULLER, SUE, artist; b. Pitts.; d. Samuel Leslie and Carrie (Cassedy) F.; B.A., Carnegie Inst. Tech., 1936; M.A., Columbia U., 1939. Exhibited in one-woman shows: Bertha Schaefer Gallery, McNay Art Inst., San Antonio, Norfolk Mus. Currier Gallery, Corcoran Gallery, Smithsonian Instn., others; exhibited in group shows: Aldrich Mus., Corcoran Gallery, Phila. Mus., Whitney Mus., Bklyn. Mus., others; represented in permanent collections: Addison Gallery of Am. Art, Larry Aldrich Mus., Chgo. Art Inst., Des Moines Art Center, Guggenheim Mus., Ford Found., Met. Mus., Whitney Mus. Am. Art, Tate Gallery London, Library of Congress, others; tchr. Pratt Inst., Bklyn., 1964-65. Recipient Alumni Merit award Carnegie-Mellon U., 1974; Louis Comfort Tiffany fellow, 1948; John Simon Guggenheim fellow, 1949; Nat. Inst. Arts and Letters grantee, 1950; Eliot Pratt Found. fellow, 1966, 67, 68; Mark Rothko Found. grantee, 1973. Producer movie String Composition, 1970, 74. Patentee in field. Home: PO Box 1580 Southampton NY 11968 Gallery: Chalette International 9 E 88th St New York City NY 10028

FULLER, TERRY KENNETH, chemist; b. Erie, Pa., Jan. 2, 1952; s. George G. and Jane (Cook) F.; B.A., Boston U., 1973; postgrad. Gannon Coll., 1975, Edinboro State Coll., 1976; m. Leta Helene Sawyer, July 1, 1976; children— Christian Michael, Sharon Renee. Chemist, Hammermill Paper Co., Erie, Pa., 1973-75; quality control chemist GAF Corp., Erie, 1976—. Pres., Blue Dolphin Skin Diver's Inc., 1975, 76, treas., 1977; instr. scuba YMCA. Mem. Ohio Council Skin and Scuba Diver (com. chmn. 1975), Cousteau Soc. (founding), Tappi, Oceanic Soc. Democrat. Presbyterian. Home: 2831 Sterrettania St Erie PA 16506 Office: 140 E 16th St Erie PA 16512

FULLER, WILLIAM JOHN, veterinarian; b. Evanston, Ill., Apr. 10, 1945; s. Richard Joseph and Lillian Margaret (Reichert) F.; B.S., Cornell Coll., 1967; D.V.M., Iowa State U., 1972; M.S., 1973; m. Martha Ruth Rieke, Sept. 2, 1967; children—Katharine, Matthew. Intern, Angell Meml. Animal Hosp., Boston, 1972-73; asso. veterinarian Animal Hosp. of Hollywood (Fla.), 1973-75, Animal Hosp. of Wakefield (Mass.), 1975—. NSF fellow, 1966-67; NDEA fellow, 1967-68. Mem. Am., Mass. veterinary med. assns. Office: Animal Hosp Wakefield MA 01880

FULLERTON, R. DONALD, banker; b. Vancouver, B.C.; s. C.G. and Muriel F. Fullerton; B.A., U. Toronto, 1953. With Canadian Imperial Bank of Commerce, 1953—, sr. v.p., dep. chief gen. mgr., Toronto, 1971-73, exec. v.p., chief gen. mgr., 1973-76, dir., 1974—, pres., chief operating officer, 1976—; dir. Am. Can of Canada Ltd., N.Am. Life Assurance Co., Calif. Canadian Bank, Kinross Mortgage Corp., Canadian Eastern Fin. Ltd. Bd. dirs. Wellesley Hosp., Toronto, 1974—; bd. govs. Crescent Sch., Toronto, 1974—, Stratford Shakespearean Festival Found. Can., 1977—; hon. treas. Royal Ont. Mus., Toronto, 1977—. Mem. Canadian Baners Assn. (v.p. 1975—). Clubs: York, Toronto, Rosedale, Granite, Caledon Ski. Office: Commerce Ct W Toronto ON M5L 1A2 Canada

FULOP, MILFORD, physician; b. N.Y.C., Nov. 7, 1927; s. Herman and Adele (Karl) F.; A.B., Columbia U., 1946, M.D., 1949; m. Christine Lawrence, Aug. 4, 1957; children—Michael Alain, Tamara Ann. Intern, then resident in medicine Presbyn. Hosp., N.Y.C., 1949-51, 53-55; practice medicine specializing in internal medicine, N.Y.C., 1955—; mem. faculty Albert Einstein Med. Coll., Bronx, N.Y., 1956—, prof. internal medicine, 1968—, acting chmn. dept. medicine, 1975—. Served with USAF, 1951-53. Mem. ACP, Assn. Am. Physicians, Phi Beta Kappa, Alpha Omega Alpha. Home: 630 W 246th St New York City NY 10471 Office: 1300 Morris Park Ave New York City NY 10461

FULTON, JOSEPH RAYMOND, hosp. adminstr.; b. Phila., Feb. 20, 1923; s. Joseph Raymond and Wilhelmina Thompson (Plumly) F.; A. in Electronics, Temple U., 1950; B.S. Indsl. Mgmt., LaSalle Coll., 1963; m. Dorothy Sarah Willis, Nov. 2, 1946; children—Carol Ann, Raymond Edward, Wendy Lea. Supr. elec. measuring instruments Leeds & Northrup Co., Phila., 1941-63; mgmt. cons. Alexander Proudfoot Co., Chgo., 1963-65; mgmt. cons. United Research Co., Woodcliff Lake, N.J., 1965-67; v.p. gen. services Overlook Hosp., Summit, N.J., 1967—. Served with USMCR, 1942-46. Mem. Am. Hosp. Amssn., Am. Coll. Hosp. Adminstrs., Hosp. Mgmt. Systems Soc., N.J. Hosp. Assn. Lutheran. Home: 30 Fairmount Rd New Providence NJ 07974 Office: 193 Morris Ave Summit NJ 07901

FULTON, PHILIP RONALD, hosp. adminstr.; b. N.Y.C., May 20, 1950; s. Stanley and Maria Carmen Fulton; B.A. in Psychology, U. Rochester (N.Y.), 1972; M.Mgmt., Northwestern U., 1974; m. Marie Tagert, Apr. 15, 1978; children—Jennifer, Joanna. Evening adminstr., then dir. adminstrv. services Greater Southeast Community Hosp., Washington, 1974-78, asst. adminstr. profl. services, 1978—. Mem. Am. Coll. Hosp. Adminstrs., Assn. Health Care Adminstrs. Nat. Capital Area, Am. Pub. Health Assn., Group Health Assn. Am., Northwestern U. Alumni Assn. Address: 1310 Southern Ave SE Washington DC 20032

FULWEILER, SPENCER BIDDLE, photo processing cons.; b. West Chester, Pa., Aug. 26, 1913; s. Walter Herbert and Lydia (Baird) F.; B.S. in Chemistry, Harvard U., 1937; m. Patricia Louise Platt, Oct. 5, 1946; children—Marie-Louise, Pamela Spencer, Hull Platt, Spencer Biddle. Owner, Color Photolab., Phila., 1938-42; technician Product Service Lab. and Film Quality-Control, Ansco, Binghamton, N.Y., 1946-48; dir. research Photo-Finishing Inst., N.Y.C., 1948-54; dir. process control Berkey Photo Service, N.Y.C., 1954-79. Tchr., St. James Ch. Sch., N.Y.C., 1958-69. Served to lt. comdr. USNR, 1942-46; CBI. Mem. Nat. Assn. Photography Mfrs., Am. Chem. Soc., Soc. Photog. Scientists and Engrs., Soc. Photofinishing Engrs. Republican. Episcopalian. Clubs: Norwalk Yacht, St. Nicholas Soc. Patentee silver recovery from photog. solutions. Home: 158 E 83d St New York City NY 10028

FUNG, KEE WAI, pediatrician; b. Canton, China, Jan. 15, 1934; s. Chiu and Wing Yuk (Leung) F.; M.B., Nat. Def. Med. Center, Taiwan, 1960. Rotating intern Army First Gen. Hosp., Taipei, Taiwan, 1959-60; rotating intern Regina (Sask., Can.) Gen. Hosp., 1961-62, pediatric resident, 1962-63; resident in internal medicine Moncton (N.B., Can.) City Hosp., 1963-64; resident in pediatrics Hosp. for Sick Children, Toronto, Ont., Can., 1964-66, fellow in hematology, 1967-68; resident in internal medicine, fellow in cardiology Sunnybrook Hosp., Toronto, 1966-67; chief pediatric dept. Medicine Hat (Alta., Can.) Gen. Hosp., 1968-71; active staff Guelph (Ont.) Gen. Hosp., St. Joseph's Hosp., Guelph; med. staff Union Hosp., Taiwan, 1975—. Diplomate Am. Bd. Pediatrics. Fellow Royal Coll. Physicians and Surgeons Can., Am. Acad. Pediatrics; mem. Canadian Med. Assn., Canadian Pediatric Soc. Home and office: 125 Delhi St Suite 45 Guelph ON N1E 4J5 Canada

FUNGAROLI, A. ALEXANDER, cons. engr.; b. Phila., June 27, 1932; s. Alfonso and Susan (Caruso) F.; B.S. in Civil Engring., Drexel U., 1954; M.S., Lehigh U., 1956; Ph.D., Rensselaer Poly. Inst., 1964; m. Marilyn L. Schmitt, Sept. 12, 1959; children—Elaine, Janet, Linda, JoAnne. Prof. civil and environ. engring. Drexel U., Phila., 1958-74; pres. Enviro/Earth Ltd., Phila., 1972—; pres. Applied Geotech. Environ. Service Corp., Phila., 1975—; adj. prof. civil engring. U. Pa., 1974-75, Temple U., 1975-76; pres. Applied Tech. Assos., 1975—; dir. Valley Forge Labs., 1969-72. NDEA fellow, 1960-64, registered profl. engr., Pa., N.J., Md., Del., Maine, Conn., Mass. Mem. Am. Arbitration Assn., ASCE, Sigma Xi, Tau Beta Pi, Chi Epsilon, Phi Beta Pi. Contbr. articles to profl. jours. Home: 23 Briarcrest Dr Wallingford PA 19086 Office: 215 S Broad St Philadelphia PA 19107

FUNK, CHARLES EARLE, JR., librarian; b. S.I., N.Y., Oct. 22, 1913; s. Charles Earle and Beulah Messinger (Johnson) F.; B.S. magna cum laude in Chemistry, Poly. Inst. Bklyn., 1950; M.L.S., Columbia U., 1955; m. Alma Wingood Griswold, Feb. 15, 1934; children—Charles Earle, Cynthia Ellen, Dency Cornelia. Chemist, Am. Cyanamid Co., Stamford, Conn., 1936-50, group leader tech. info., 1951-65; head planning, evaluation and research dept. Conn. State Library, Hartford, 1965-73, asso. state librarian reader services div., 1974-75, state librarian, 1975—. Mem. ALA, Spl. Libraries Assn., New Eng., Conn., East Granby (dir. 1967-74) library assns., New Eng. Library Bd., Library Group Southwestern Conn., Token and Medal Soc., Early Am. Coppers Club, Am., New Eng., Hartford numis. assns. Republican. Co-author: Horsefeathers and Other Curious Words, 1957; editor: Directory of Subject Strengths of Connecticut Libraries, 1968; Directory of Cooperating Library Activities in New England, 1971. Office: 231 Capitol Ave Hartford CT 06115

FUNK, HARALD FRANZ, inventor; b. Herzogenburg, Austria, Sept. 20, 1917; s. Franz and Ann (Seifried) F.; Chem. Engr., U. Karlsruhe (Germany), 1940, D.Eng., 1944; m. Karin Maria Plank, Dec. 10, 1952; children—Stephan, Christine. Came to Can., 1951, naturalized, 1956. Research engr. BASF Ludwigshafen, 1940-46; self-employed as cons. engr., Salzburg, Austria, 1946-51; engr. Gulf Oil Can., Toronto, 1952-56; rep. N.Am. Linde A.G., 1956-62; mgr. cryogenic sales and devel. Allied Chem. Corp., 1962-65; pres. Silvichem Corp., 1965; dir. York Consol. Exploration, Toronto; cons. World Bank, Washington. Asst. prof. U. Karlsruhe, 1943-45. Registered profl. engr., Ont. Mem. Am. Inst. Chem. Engrs., Assn. Profl. Engrs. Province Ont., Palato-Sinapia, Verein Deutscher Ingenieure, Deutsche Gesellschaft fuer chemisches Apparatewesen. Club: Chemists (N.Y.C.). Patentee wood saccharification process, activation of carbon, solid waste gasification linked with gas purification; inventor papermaking from bagasse, energy-savings devices. Address: 68 Elm St Murray Hill NJ 07971

FUNK, SHERMAN MAXWELL, govt. ofcl.; b. N.Y.C., Nov. 13, 1925; s. Bernard and Dorothy (Arkin) F.; A.B., Harvard U., 1950; postgrad. Columbia, U. 1956; A.M., U. Ariz., 1958; m. Elaine Myrl Bayer, Mar. 6, 1953 (dec. Sept. 1977); children—Katherine Sara, Bernard Eugene. Salesman, sales exec. Bernard Funk Co., N.Y.C., 1950-54; tchr. history Catskill (N.Y.) High Sch., 1954-57; teaching asst. polit. sci. U. Ariz., Tucson, 1957-58; mgmt. intern Hdqrs. USAF, Washington, 1958, logistics/war planning officer, mgmt. analyst, 1958-63, chief Air Force Cost Reduction Office, 1963-67, chief Air Force Mgmt. Improvement Programs Office, 1967-70; White House detail with Office Minority Bus. Enterprise, 1970, chmn. Washington Minority Bus. Opportunity Com., asst. dir. for adminstrn. and program devel., dir. research and program devel., 1972-76, asst. dir. for planning and evaluation, 1976—; extension tchr. in black history and journalism. Mem. City Council, Bowie, Md., 1963-65, chmn. human relations com., 1964-65, chmn. charter rev. com., 1968. Pres. Friends of Bowie Area Library, 1966-68. Served with inf., U.S. Army, 1943-46. Decorated Purple Heart; recipient Spl. award for outstanding program mgmt. Sec. Air Force, 1968, prizes Washington-Md.-Del. Press Assn., 1970, 71, 73, 75, 76, 77, Silver medal Commerce Dept., 1972. Mem. Nat. Rifle Assn., Am. Polit. Sci. Assn., Wilderness Soc., Md. Pistol and Revolver Club, Bowie Citizens Assn. Jewish. Writer weekly column Bowie Blade and Post-Times, 1969—. Contbr. articles profl. jours. Office: Office Minority Bus Enterprise Commerce Dept Washington DC 20230

FUNKHOUSER, RALPH HENRY, psychologist; b. Orofino, Idaho, Oct. 13, 1921; s. James Roscoe and Nettie Mae (Shriver) F.; student Simpson Coll., 1945-48; B.A., Western Wash. State Coll., 1958, B.Ed., 1958, M.Ed., 1959; Ph.D., Cath. U. Am., 1970; m. Virginia Pauline Blevins, May 25, 1967; 1 dau., Darlene. Ordained to ministry Baptist Ch., 1950; pastor in Preston, Ferndale and Auburn, Wash.; faculty Wheaton (Ill.) Pub. Schs., 1960-62; psychologist Rosewood State Hosp., Owings Mills, Md., 1962-70, dir. human devel., 1965-70; chief psychology Mt. Washington Children's Hosp., Balt., 1970-75; pvt. practice psychology, Catonsville, Md., 1971—; asst. prof. psychology Towson State U., Balt., 1964—, Community Coll. Balt., 1964—. Recipient Gold Medal award State of Md., 1970; Outstanding Faculty Mem. of Year award, student body Towson State U., 1978. Mem. Am. Psychol. Assn., Council for Nat. Register Health Service Providers in Psychology. Baptist. Contbr. articles in field to profl. jours. Address: 307 Frederick Rd Catonsville MD 21228

FUREDY, JOHN J., educator; b. Budapest, Hungary, June 30, 1940; s. Bela and Magda (Gardos) F.; ed. in Australia, 1949-65; came to Can., 1967, naturalized, 1972; B.A. (scholar), U. Sydney, 1963, M.A. (scholar), 1964, Ph.D. (scholar), 1966; m. Christine P.M. Roche, June 30, 1966. Mem. faculty Ind. U., Bloomington, 1965-67; mem. faculty U. Toronto (Ont., Can.), 1967—, asso. prof. psychology, 1969-75, prof., 1975—. Fulbright scholar, 1965-67; recipient grants NRC Can., Med. Research Council Can., Can. Council, Atkinson Charitable Found. Fellow Internat. Coll. Psychosomatic Medicine, Am., Australian, Can. psychol. assns.; mem. Am. Assn. Advancement Tension Control, Pavlovian Soc., Soc. Psychophysiol. Research (dir. 1976—). Clubs: Rosedale Tennis, Jackrabbit Cross-Country Ski, Prince Arthur Bridge. Asso. editor Biological Psychology, 1976; editorial bd. Behavioral and Brain Sciences, 1978; contbr. to profl. jours. Home: 24 Astley Ave Toronto ON M4W 3B4 Canada Office: Dept Psychology Univ Toronto Toronto ON Canada

FURFARO, FRANCIS JOSEPH, clergyman; b. Canastota, N.Y., May 5, 1918; s. Angelo Michael and Rose (Pugliano) F.; B.A., St. Bernard's Sem., 1941; M.S., certificate advanced study, State U. N.Y. at Oswego, 1971. Ordained priest Roman Catholic Ch., 1941, monsignor, 1972; asso. pastor Our Lady Pompei, Syracuse, 1941-49; pastor St. Joseph's Ch., Oswego, 1949—; episcopal vicar, Oswego County, 1972—; psychol. cons. House of Providence, Syracuse, 1973-75. Mem. Bd. Edn. Oswego, 1971-76, 78—, pres., 1975-76; mem. Mental Health Bd., 1973-75; bd. visitors Psychiat. Center, Syracuse, 1976-78; pres. bd. visitors Hutchings Psychiat. Center, Syracuse, 1977—. Named Man of Year, Oswego Jaycees, 1966; recipient Outstanding Service to People award AFL-CIO, 1975; Citizenship award Kiwanis, 1976. Democrat. Home: 178 W 2d St Oswego NY 13126

FURIBONDO, MICHAEL JOHN, mech. engr.; b. Rochester, N.Y., Feb. 24, 1951; s. Nicholas John and Anna Furibondo; B.S. in Mech. Engring. cum laude (Notre Dame scholar), U. Notre Dame, 1973; m. Mary Karen Moriarty, July 10, 1976; 1 dau., Sarah Kathleen. Project engr. Eastman Kodak Co., Rochester, N.Y., 1973—; intern engr. State of N.Y. Mem. ASME, Tau Beta Pi, Pi Tau Sigma. Roman Catholic. Home: 1233 W Sweden Rd Brockport NY 14420 Office: Bldg 23 Kodak Park Rochester NY 14650

FURLAN, ANDREW WASHINGTON, internat. mktg. adminstr.; b. Chgo., Feb. 22, 1930; s. Andrew and Albina (Logar) F.; B.S. in Speech, Northwestern U., 1951; student U.S. Mcht. Marine Acad., 1951-53; B.S. in Fgn. Trade, Am. Grad. Sch. for Internat. Mgmt., 1959; m. Maureen Doris French, June 7, 1963; children—Franklin John, Christopher Andrew. Country bus. mgr. Pfizer Internat., Mexico, Venezuela, Brazil, Chile, Argentina, 1959-66; gen. mgr. Argentina Revlon Internat., 1966-70, v.p. internat., N.Y.C., 1971-75; pres. Seprocom Inc., N.Y.C., 1976; dir. consumer goods mktg. Schering-Plough Internat., Kenilworth, N.J., 1977—; trade cons. to various internat. bus. Served to 1st lt. U.S. Army, 1954-58. Mem. Delta Phi Epsilon. Democrat. Club: Hurlingham (Buenos Aires). Home: 784 Norman Pl Westfield NJ 07090 Office: PO Box 500 Kenilworth NJ 07033

FURLONG, THOMAS FRANCIS, III, economist, mil. officer; b. Bryn Mawr, Pa., July 13, 1940; s. Thomas F. and Ada Frances (Hardt) F.; student Pasadena Playhouse Coll., 1963-65; B.Sc., St. Joseph's Coll., 1966, M.A., 1976; grad. Am. Acad. of Dramatic Arts, N.Y.C., 1960-63; m. Rubin Evan Bond, July 4, 1970. Commd. 2d lt. inf. U.S. Army, 1966, advanced through grades to maj., 1976; served in Ft. Benning, Ga., 1966-68, Vietnam, 1968-70; econ. adminstr. Finance Corps, inf. br., Ft. Benning, 1968—; instr. Temple U., Phila., 1974-76; instr. in finance and mgmt., St. Joseph's Coll., Phila., 1974-76; appeared in various Broadway musicals and dramas, radio & TV, summer stock. Decorated Bronze Star, Purple Heart, Silver Star, Air medal, Army Commendation medal. Mem. Am. Bankers Assn., Union League of Phila., SR, Am. Legion, VFW, Phi Delta Theta. Club: Merion Cricket. Home: 250 Ridge Pike Lafayette Hill PA 19444 Office: 4074 RCPTN Sta Woodhaven and Comley Sts Philadelphia PA

FURMAN, ANTHONY MICHAEL, pub. relations exec.; b. Los Angeles, Nov. 5, 1934; s. Le Roy S. and Geraldine (Priluk) F.; B.A., Bethany Coll., 1957; postgrad. New Sch. Social Research, 1957-58; m. Betty Gayle Morgan, Nov. 1, 1970; 1 son, Michael Jason. Asst. account exec. Jules Beitler, Newark, 1958; account exec. Barber & Baar, N.Y.C., 1959-60; media dir. Sydney S. Baron Pub. Relations Corp., N.Y.C., 1961-66; pres. Anthony M. Furman, Inc., N.Y.C., 1966—; dir. FKP Assos., Lake Placid, N.Y. Mem. Olympic bobsled com. AAU; dir. Woman's Profl. Ski Racing Tour; mem. World Bobsled Championship Com., Jr. World Bicycle Championship Com.; mem. adv. council Assn. Coll. Unions-Internat. Served with M.C., AUS, 1957-58. Mem. Pub. Relations Soc. Am. Democrat. Jewish. Home: New York City NY 10024 also West Stockbridge MA 01266 Office: 527 Madison Ave New York City NY 10022

FURMAN, ROY LANCE, securities brokerage exec.; b. N.Y.C., Apr. 19, 1939; s. Joseph M. and Frances L. (Kurlander) F.; B.A., Bklyn. Coll., 1960; LL.B., Harvard, 1963; m. Frieda Ann Bueler, Nov. 7, 1965; children—Jill Tracy, Stephanie Gail. Admitted to N.Y. State bar, 1965; atty. Western Electric Co., N.Y.C., 1964-67; adminstrv. v.p. Continental Telephone Supply, N.Y.C., 1967-68; with Seiden & de Cuevas, N.Y.C., 1968-73, pres., 1973; pres. Furman Selz Mager Dietz & Birney, N.Y.C., 1973—. Mem. Boston Stock Exchange, Phila. Stock Exchange; mem. small firms adv. com. N.Y. Stock Exchange. Pres. Phoenix Theatre. Mem. N.Y. Bar, N.Y. Soc. Security Analysts. Office: 110 Wall St New York City NY 10005

FURMAN, SAMUEL ELLIOTT, dentist; b. Jersey City, Dec. 13, 1932; s. Sol T. and Cecilia (Berman) F.; A.B., U. Pa., 1953; D.D.S., 1957; m. Margaret Ann Gilardi, Feb. 27, 1971; children—Laurie, Jill. Gen. practice dentistry, Tinton Falls, N.J., 1959—; mem. staff Monmouth Med. Center; mem. N.J. Bd. Dentistry. Served to capt. USAF, 1957-59. Fellow Acad. Gen. Dentistry, Internat. Coll. Dentist; mem. Am. Acad. Oral Medicine, N.J. Soc. Dentistry for Children, Am., N.J. (past trustee) dental assns., Monmouth-Ocean County Dental Soc. (past pres.), Alpha Omega. Mem. B'nai B'rith. Home: 8 Woods End Rd Rumson NJ 07760 Office: 1029 Sycamore Ave Tinton Falls NJ 07724

FURNESS, GEOFFREY, microbiologist, educator; b. Blackburn, Lancashire, Gt. Britain, Aug. 2, 1919; s. James and Edith (Greenbank) F.; came to U.S., 1966; B.Sc., Leeds (Eng.) U., 1948; Diploma in Bacteriology, Manchester (Eng.) U., 1949, Ph.D., 1951; m. Margaret Lilian Booth, July 23, 1941; children—Paul Geoffrey, Peter. Lectr. bacteriology Trinity Coll., Dublin, Ireland, 1952-54; Sir Alexander Fleming fellow Wright-Fleming Inst., London, 1954-59; sr. scientist Med. Research Council Lister Inst., London, 1959-62; head virology Twyford Labs., London, 1962-66; prof. virology U. Tex., 1966-67; prof. microbiology Coll. Medicine and Dentistry N.J., Newark, 1967—, acting chmn. Grad. Sch. Biomed. Scis., 1968-71; vis. prof. Pitts. Med. Sch., 1957-59, Commonwealth Sci. and Indsl. Research Orgn., Melbourne, Australia, 1971. Served with Brit. Navy, 1940-46. NIH grantee, 1968-76. Mem. Soc. Gen. Microbiology, Brit. Soc. Cell Biology, Am. Soc. Microbiology, AAUP (gov. chpt. 1971—, 2d v.p. contract adminstrn. 1977—), Inst. Biology, Louis Rapkine Assn. Mem. editorial bd. Veterinary Microbiology, 1976—; contbr. articles to profl. jours. Office: Dept Microbiology NJ Med Sch 100 Bergen St Newark NJ 07103

FURST, SIDNEY CARL, social psychologist; b. N.Y.C., Dec. 11, 1925; s. Nathan and Anna (Levy) F.; student Princeton U., 1943; B.A., U. Chgo., 1948; B.A., Columbia U., 1948-52; m. Vincenza

DiMaggio, Apr. 9, 1972; children-Anne Betsy, Carl Nathaniel. Project dir. market research Batten, Barton, Durstine & Osborn Inc., N.Y.C., 1952-58; sales presentation writer ABC, N.Y.C., 1958-59; pres. Furst Survey Research Center also Furst Analytic Center, 1959—; instr. Fairleigh-Dickinson Coll. Served with AUS, 1944-46. Author: Business Decisions That Changed Our Lives, 1964; Strategy of Change for Business Success, 1969. Home: 3 Washington Square Village New York City NY 10012 Office: 11 Fifth Ave New York City NY 10003

FURSTMAN, SHIRLEY ELSIE DADDOW, pub. co. exec.; b. Butler, N.J., Jan. 26, 1930; d. Richard and Eva M. (Kitchell) Daddow; grad. high sch.; m. Russell A. Bailey, Oct. 1, 1950 (div. Oct. 1967); m. 2d, William B. Furstman, Dec. 24, 1977. Asst. corporate sec. Hydrospace Tech., West Caldwell, N.J., 1960-62; sec. to pres. R.J. Dick Co., Totowa, N.J., 1962-63, Microlab, Livingston, N.J., 1963; asst. corporate sec. Astrosystems Internat., West Caldwell, N.J., 1963-65; corporate sec. Internat. Controls Corp., Fairfield, N.J., 1965-73; sec. Global Fin., Nassau, Bahamas, 1974-75, Internat. Barter Co., Nassau, 1975-76; corporate sec., sec. to pres. Haas Chem. Corp., Taylor, Pa., 1976-77; asst. to pres. and pub. Am. Home mag., N.Y.C., 1977-78. Home: 16 Leamoor Dr Morris Plains NJ 07950

FURTHERER, CHARLES MATTHEW, surgeon, proctologist; b. Rochester, N.Y.; s. Charles William and Kathryn (Englert) F.; student McGill U., 1930-31; B.A., U. Rochester, 1934; M.D., U. Buffalo, 1938. Intern, St. Mary's Hosp., Rochester, 1938-39, resident in surgery, 1939-30; fellow in surgery Strong Meml. Hosp., Rochester, 1946-48; attending proctologist Rochester Gen. Hosp., 1961—; surgeon Genesee Hosp., Rochester. Served to maj., M.C., USAAF, 1942-46. Diplomate Am. Bd. Colon and Rectal Surgery. Fellow Am. Soc. Colon and Rectal Surgery (asso.); mem. N.Y. State, Monroe County med. socs., Rochester Acad. Medicine, Rochester Path. Soc., Am. Legion, Collie Club Am., Genesee Valley Kennel Club, Theta Chi, Phi Chi. Clubs: Univ., Police Locust (hon.) (Rochester). Home: 330 Selye Terr Rochester NY 14613 Office: 1295 Portland Ave Rochester NY 14621

FUSCO, CONO R., accountant; b. N.Y.C., Dec. 2, 1942; s. Rocco C. and Grace (DeFiore) F.; B.B.A., Manhattan Coll., 1964; M.B.A., Adelphi U., 1967; m. Mary Anne Guccione, June 20, 1964; children—Mark Alexander, Bradley David. With Alexander Grant & Co., N.Y.C., 1967—, personnel mgr., 1973, personnel partner, 1973-75; asst. mng. partner adminstrn., 1975-76, mng. partner, Melville, L.I., 1977—; adj. instr. Fordham U., 1969-70; adj. asst. prof. St. John's U. Grad. Sch. Bus., Jamaica, N.Y., 1971-73. Mem. adv. bd. Coll. Bus. Adminstrn., St. John's U. C.P.A., N.Y. Mem. Am. Inst. C.P.A.'s, N.Y. State Soc. C.P.A.'s, Am. Accounting Assn. Roman Catholic. Club: Nassau Country. Home: Brookville NY 11545 Office: 1185 Ave of Americas New York City NY 10036

FUTTERMAN, BETSY WILCOX, sch. prin., b. Phila., Aug. 20, 1944; d. Paul W. and Doris (Underwood) Wilcox; B.S., Pa. State U., 1966, M.Ed. (scholar), 1968, D.Ed., 1978; m. Noel Brian Futterman, Apr. 1, 1967; 1 dau., Susan Doris. Tchr., Neshaminy Sch. Dist., Langhorne, Pa., 1966-67; acting dir., mem. staff Vol. Service Center, Pa. State U., University Park, summers 1971, 72; supervising prin. 3 elementary schs. Bellefonte, Pa., 1968—. Vol. Centre Community Hosp.; mem. Centre Area Health Council. Class of 1922 Meml. scholar, 1966; Senatorial scholar 1965-66. Mem. Nat. Assn. Elementary Sch. Prins., Nat. Soc. Arts and Lit., Nat., Pa. councils social studies, Pi Lambda Theta, Phi Delta Kappa. Lutheran. Home: 528 Brittany Dr State College PA 16801 Office: Benner Elementary Sch RD 4 Box 170 B Bellefonte PA 16823

FUTTERMAN, PHILIP G., real estate cons. and broker, investor; b. Yonkers, N.Y., July 28, 1933; s. Samuel and Ida (Pearlman) F.; B.A., Ohio State U., 1955; M.A., Sch. Advanced Internat. Studies, Johns Hopkins U., 1957; diploma U. Paris, Sorbonne, 1954; m. Janet Cooper, Aug. 7, 1966; children—Damon Elie, Marcel, Madeleine Ceil. Pres., Futterman Orgn., Inc., N.Y.C., 1966—. Mem. Real Estate Bd. N.Y. Home: 7 W 81st St New York City NY 10024 Office: 581 Fifth Ave New York City NY 10017

FUTTERWEIT, WALTER, physician; b. Vienna, Austria, Sept. 8, 1931; s. Henry and Regina (Sternschuss) F.; B.A., N.Y. U., 1953, M.D., 1957; m. Gloria Renee Zisholtz, Sept. 8, 1957; children—Lorelle Ruth, Stephen Gary, Debra Lynn. Intern, Beth Israel Hosp., N.Y.C., 1957-58; resident Montefiore Hosp., N.Y.C., 1958-60; endocrinology fellow Mount Sinai Hosp., N.Y.C., 1961; steroid trainee Worcester Found. Exptl. Biology, Shrewsbury, Mass., 1962; practice medicine specializing in internal medicine and endocrinology, N.Y.C., 1962—; mem. staff Mount Sinai Hosp., Doctors' Hosp.; attending in medicine Bronx-Lebanon Hosp. Center; cons. endocrinologist Margaret Sanger Research Bur.; asso. attending endocrinology, dept. medicine Mount Sinai Hosp., 1962—; asst. clin. prof. medicine div. endocrinology Mt. Sinai Sch. Medicine, N.Y.C. Diplomate Am. Bd. Internal Medicine, Am. Bd. Endocrinology and Metabolism. Fellow A.C.P.; mem. AMA, N.Y. County Med. Soc., Endocrine Soc., Am. Fertility Soc., Am. Fedn. Clin. Research, Am. Soc. Andrology, N.Y. Acad. Scis. Contbr. articles on endocrinology to profl. jours. Home: 254 Devoe Ave Yonkers NY 10705 Office: 1172 Park Ave New York City NY 10028

GAAL, FRANCIS STEPHEN, therapist; b. Bethlehem, Pa., June 10, 1948; s. Joseph Stephen and Agnes Teresa Gaal; B.A., Moravian Coll., 1973; M.Ed., U. Mo., 1974; m. Linda Mae Lane, Dec. 30, 1967. Child care worker Bethelhem's Treatment Center for Emotionally Disturbed Children, 1972-73; vocat. evaluator, counselor Kurtz Tng. Center, Bethlehem, 1974-76; counselor adv. for juvenile delinquency program nat. office Opportunities Industrialization Centers Am., Phila., 1976—; pvt. practice marriage and family therapy, Bethlehem, 1975—; adj. prof. psychology Northampton County Area Community Coll., 1977—; group therapist Allentown (Pa.) Gen. Hosp; marriage and family cons. May Day Inc. Served with USAF, 1966-70. Aircraft control, warning operator. Mem. Am., Pa. assns. marriage and family counselors, Am. Personnel and Guidance Assn. Address: 2140 Worthington Ave Bethlehem PA 18017

GABBARD, O. GENE, electronic co. exec.; b. Sand Gap, Ky., May 7, 1940; s. Moss and Delta (Cook) G.; B.S.E., U. Ky., 1961; M.S., U. Pa., 1965; m. Judith Snare, Nov. 2, 1963; children—Susan Elaine, David Scott. Staff mem., asst. to project mgr. RCA, Astro Electronics div., 1961-63; sect. head, project mgr. COMSAT Labs., Clarksburg, Md., 1965-71; group v.p. tech. Digital Communications Corp., Gaithersburg, Md., 1971-78; pres. Canadian Digital Communications, Ltd. Served to 1st lt. Signal Corps, U.S. Army, 1963-65. Decorated Army Commendation medal. Mem. IEEE, AIAA, Gaithersburg C. of C., Sigma Xi, Tau Beta Pi, Eta Kappa Nu. Contbr. articles to profl. publs. Patentee in satellite communications. Home: 19101 Plummer Dr Germantown MD 20767 Office: 19 Firstfield Rd Gaithersburg MD 20760

GABEL, PAUL MARTIN, sound equipment co. exec.; b. Newark, Mar. 6, 1947; s. Delbert Paul and Gertrude Catherin (Williams) G.; A.A. in Phys. Sci., County Coll. of Morris, 1977, A.A. in Bus. Adminstrn., 1979; m. Virginia Ann Wilmer, Sept. 13, 1968; children—Jonathan Matthew, Jason Bartholomew. Research asst. ITT Rayonier Co., Whippany, N.J., 1969-71; lab. technician Mennen Co., Morristown, N.J., 1971-72, sr. lab. technician, 1972; owner, operator Gabels', Keene, N.H., 1973; quality control technician Atlas Sound div. Am. Trading and Prodn. Corp., Parsippany, N.J., 1973-75, asst. quality assurance supr., 1975-78, quality control supr., 1978—. Served with U.S. Army, 1966-68; Vietnam. Mem. N.J. Assn. for Children with Learning Disabilities, County Coll. of Morris Alumni Assn. Democrat.

GABELLI, MARIO JOSEPH, investment banking co. exec.; b. N.Y.C., June 19, 1942; s. Joseph and Josephine (Alzapiedi) G.; B.A. summa cum laude, Fordham U., 1965; M.B.A., Columbia U., 1967; m. Elaine Madonna, July 30, 1966; children—Marc, Matthew, Elisa, Michael. Vice pres. Loeb Rhoades & Co., N.Y.C., 1967-75, William D. Witter, N.Y.C., 1975-76, pres. Gabelli & Co., Inc., N.Y.C., 1977—. Pres. Lake Isle Civic Assn., 1975-76; mem. Zoning Bd. Appeals, Eastchester, N.Y., 1976—, Columbus Citizens Com., N.Y.C. Mem. N.Y. Soc. Security Analysts (program chmn. 1974-76), N.Y. Soc. Auto Analysts (pres. 1978). Club: Westchester Country. Office: 44 Wall St New York City NY 10005

GABER, IRVING, garment industry exec.; b. Hlinitz, Austria, May 6, 1905; s. Littman and Rose (Hasenfratz) G.; came to U.S., 1921, naturalized, 1928; m. Mae Dermer, June 19, 1932; children—Norma Lee, Irving, Rhoda Sue. Asst. prodn. mgr. Leading Dress, N.Y.C., 1928-32; partner Allen Dress Co., N.Y.C., 1934-39; prodn. mgr. Milmont Gowns, N.Y.C., 1943-47, 49-52, Maurice Rentner, N.Y.C., 1948; partner, prodn. mgr. Jobere, Inc., N.Y.C., 1952-69; prodn. mgr. Norman Norell, N.Y.C., 1970-72; patternmaker Mollie Parnis div. Parnis-Livingston, Inc., N.Y.C., 1976—. Mem. Prodn. Men's Guild N.Y. (pres. 1963-68). Jewish. Home: 2348 Linwood Ave Fort Lee NJ 07024 Office: Mollie Parnis 530 7th Ave New York City NY 10018

GABER, JOANNE GARTEN, clin. psychologist; b. N.Y.C.; d. Stanley and Hannah Rosalind (Frank) Garten; B.S. in Edn., Adelphi Coll., 1949; M.A. in Ednl. Psychology, Tchrs. Coll., Columbia, 1950, profl. diploma, 1969; m. Morton Gaber, Aug. 20, 1950 (div.); 1 dau., Evelyn Jean. Ednl. therapist, 1963-67; psychology intern North Jersey Tng. Sch., Totowa, N.J., 1967-68, clin. psychologist, 1969—; psychology intern Middlesex County Mental Health Clinic, 1968-69; adj. clin. psychologist N.J. Coll. Medicine and Dentistry, Jersey City, 1971-73. Ednl. therapist Shield of David Inst., Maimonides Inst. for Exceptional Children, 1963-67. Program dir. Play Schs. Assn., 1959, 60. Mem. Am., N.J. psychol. assns., N.J. Assn. for Brain Injured Children, Assn. for Help Retarded Children, Am. Assn. on Mental Deficiency, Assn. N.J. Instl. Psychologists (sec.). Home: 28 Highland Cross Rutherford NJ 07070 Office: NJ Tng Sch PO Box 169 Totowa NJ 07511

GABLE, EDWARD BRENNAN, JR., govt. ofcl.; b. Shamokin, Pa., Mar. 15, 1929; s. Edward Brennan and Kathleen (Welsh) G.; B.S., Villanova U., 1953; J.D., Georgetown U., 1957; m. Dee Sear, Feb. 23, 1963; children—Karen Lynn, Kimberly Ann, Katherine Rebel. Admitted to D.C. bar, 1957; with U.S. Customs Service, Treasury Dept., Washington, 1958—, chief atty. documentation br., 1965-66, chief atty. carrier rulings br., 1966-76, chief penalties br., 1976-78, spl. asst. to asst. commr. Office of Regulations and Rulings, 1978—; mem. U.S. del. Intergovtl. Maritime Cons. Orgn., London, 1973, 74, 75, U.S. rep., inter-sessional meeting, Hamburg, Germany, 1973. Pres., Customs Fed. Credit Union, 1967-69. Recipient Superior Performance award Treasury Dept., 1962, commendation letter from asst. sec. treasury, 1964. Mem. Customs Lawyers Assn. (pres. 1965-66), Fed. Bar Assn., Propeller Club U.S., Delta Theta Phi. Roman Catholic. Club: Elks. Home: 18630 Nutmeg Pl Germantown MD 20767 Office: 14th and Constitution Ave NW Washington DC 20229

GABLE, FRED BURNARD, pharmacist, educator; b. Phila., June 30, 1929; s. Samuel and Mollie (Rayfield) G.; B.S., Temple U., 1951, M.S., 1953; M.A. in Sociology, 1959; children—Tracy, Dana Jack. Faculty Temple U. Sch. Pharmacy, Phila., 1955—, prof., 1974—, asst. dean, 1968—. Served with Med. Service Corps, U.S. Army, 1953-55. Mem. Am. Sociol. Assn., Pa. Prison Soc., Am. Pharm. Assn., Sigma Xi, Rho Chi, Rho Pi Phi, Lambda Kappa Sigma, Phi Delta Chi, Alpha Zeta Omega. Author: Opportunities in Pharmacy Careers, 1964, 4th edit., 1978; Psychosocial Pharmacy: The Synthetic Society, 1974; other books. Editor: The Apothecary, 1959—. Contbr. articles to pharm. jours. Home: 1901 JFK Blvd Suite 2703 Philadelphia PA 19103 Office: Sch Pharmacy Temple U 3307 N Broad St Philadelphia PA 19140

GABLE, MARTHA ANNE, educator; b. Phila.; d. James F. and Stella (Gingrich) G.; B.E., Ind. U., 1942; M.Ed., Temple U., 1935. Tchr., Phila. Pub. Schs., 1926-41, asst. dir. phys. and health edn., Phila., 1942-48, asst. dir. sch. and community relations, 1948-55, dir. radio-TV edn., 1955-68; editor Am. Assn. Sch. Adminstrs., Washington, 1968-73, cons. Editechnology, 1973—; mem. Pa. Gov.'s Adv. Commn. on Edn., 1956-58, White House Conf. on Edn., 1955; cons. Joint Council Ednl. TV, Washington; chmn. adv. com. Pa. Ednl. TV, 1960-68; del. Internat. Conf. Ednl. TV, London, 1954. Judge, Olympic Games, London, 1948, Helsinki, 1952, Melbourne, 1956, Rome, 1960, Tokyo, 1964; bd. dirs. Phila. Home and Sch. Council, 1950-68; v.p. Women for Greater Phila. Mem. Phila. Pub. Relations Assn. (sec.), Am. Women in Radio and TV, NEA, Pub. Relations Soc. Am., TV-Radio Advt. Club, AAUW, Nat. Assn. Ednl. Broadcasters, Am. Assn. Sch. Adminstrs., Ednl. Press Assn. Am., Women in Communications, Phila. Fedn. Women's Clubs (dir.), AAUW, Nat. Press Club, Am. Newspapers Women's Club. Presbyterian. Home: 2601 Parkway Philadelphia PA 19130

GABLEHOUSE, CHARLES JOHN, airport services analyst; b. N.Y.C., Apr. 16, 1928; student Coll. William and Mary, 1957, Fordham U., 1960; m. Marge Holman, June 21, 1964; 1 dau., Stephanie. Co. rep. DeLackner Helicopters, Inc., Mt. Vernon, N.Y., 1956-58; tech. editor, project leader Grumman Aircraft Engring. Corp., Bethpage, N.Y., 1958-61; asso. editor Bus./Coml. Aviation Mag., N.Y.C., 1961-62; with aviation dept. Port of N.Y. Authority, N.Y.C., 1962—, airport services analyst, 1968—. Dir. pub. relations Ethical Culture Soc. of Bergen County, 1975—; active Amnesty Internat.; mem. planning bd. City of Passaic (N.J.), 1978—. Served with U.S. Army, 1950-52. Mem. Am. Inst. Aeros. and Astronautics, Am. Helicopter Soc., Exptl. Aircraft Assn., Aviation/Space Writers Assn. (Nat. Pub. Relations award 1974), ASCE, Soc. Tech. Communications, Am. Fedn. Tech. Engrs. Author: Helicopters and Autogiros, 1967 (nat. award Soc. Tech. Writers and Pubs. 1970). Home: 299 Howard Ave Passaic Park Passaic NJ 07055 Office: Port Authority NY and NJ Aviation Dept Room 65N One World Trade Center New York City NY 10048

GABLER, ROBERT CLAIR, JR., research chemist; b. Phila., June 6, 1933; s. Robert Clair and Mary Elizabeth Cecielia (Allen) G.; B.A. in Chemistry, Johns Hopkins U., 1955; M.S. in Chemistry, Fla. State U., 1957. Analytical chemist E.I. DuPont de Nemours & Co., Inc., Kinston, N.C., 1957, 59-61; research chemist U.S. Bur. Mines, Avondale, Md., 1961—; instr. chemistry Frederick (Md.) Community Coll., 1959. Served with U.S. Army, 1957-59. Mem. Am. Chem. Soc., Soc. Applied Spectroscopy, VFW. Democrat. Roman Catholic. Clubs: Kent Island Yacht, Moose. Contbr. articles to tech. jours. Patentee in field. Home: PO Box 325 Cedar Point Marina Grasonville MD 21638 Office: Avondale Metallurgy Research Center Avondale MD 20782

GABODA, JAMES JAMES, educator, painter; b. Bentleyville, Pa., Feb. 7, 1918; s. James and Sophie Charlotte (Balko) G.; B.F.A., Columbia, 1954, M.A., 1955; m. Olga Yarashuk, Nov. 2, 1946. Asst. prof. Meredith Coll., Raleigh, N.C., 1956-57, Glassboro (N.J.) State Coll., 1957-60; lectr. Queens Coll., N.Y.C., 1960-64; asso. prof. Hofstra U., Hempstead, N.Y., 1964—; one-man painting shows: Meredith Coll., Raleigh, N.C., 1956, Glassboro (N.J.) State Coll., 1959, Bridgeport (Conn.) U., 1965, State U. N.Y., Old Westbury, 1971, Galt's Gallery, Chatham, N.J., 1969; group shows in N.Y.C., Madison, Glassboro, N.J., Chgo. Served with U.S. Army, 1941-45. Mem. Art Students League N.Y. (treas., dir., life mem.), Am. Fine Arts Soc. (trustee), AAUP, Coll. Art Assn., Nat. Art Edn. Assn., Phi Delta Kappa, Kappa Delta Pi. Democrat. Eastern Rite Catholic. Clubs: Hofstra U. Century, Hofstra U., Lions (founding Stanhope, N.J.). Home: 11 New St Box 392 Stanhope NJ 07874 Office: Hofstra Univ Dept Fine Arts Hempstead NY 11550

GABRIEL, CHARLES ELIAS, county ofcl.; b. Syracuse, N.Y., Nov. 3, 1937; s. William Abraham and Nettie Helen (Sopp) G.; B.S. in Bus. Adminstrn., Syracuse U., 1968, M.Pub. Adminstrn., 1974; m. Jewell Khammar, Sept. 25, 1960; children—JoAnne, John, Reneé, Thomas, Tonya. With Onondaga County (N.Y.) Sheriff's Dept., 1958—, adminstrv. officer, 1975—, chief adminstr., 1975—; asst. vis. prof. (part-time) Syracuse U. Sch. Mgmt., 1971—; mem. adj. faculty Onondaga Community Coll., 1968-69; cons. Syracuse Housing Authority, 1971-72, Am. U., 1975, Security Mgmt. Consultants, Inc., 1976, Onondaga County Dist. Atty., 1971-74; spl. cons. on computerized law enforcement systems to Ernst & Ernst, C.P.A.'s, N.Y.C., 1976—; mem. adv. com. N.Y. State Police Info. Network, 1975-76. Mem. Air N.G., 1955-62. Mem. Am., Data Processing, Am. Records mgmt. assns., Assn. Timesharing Users, Assn. Pub. Safety Communications Ops. Contbr. articles on law enforcement to profl. jours. Home: 214 Tilden Dr Syracuse NY 13057 Office: Onondaga County Sheriff's Dept 407 S State St Syracuse NY 13202

GABRIEL, RONALD LEE, govt. ofcl.; b. Bklyn., Nov. 8, 1941; s. Louis and Hazel H. (Peller) G.; B.S., U. N.C., 1963, M.B.A., 1966; Ph.D., Am. U., 1974. Statis. analyst Census Bur., 1964-65; staff asst. Benton & Bowles Advt. Co., N.Y.C., 1966-67; market research analyst Warner Lambert Co., Morris Plains, N.J., 1967-68; econ. statistician Dept. Navy, Washington, 1968-70; sr. mgmt. specialist U.S. Postal Service, Washington, 1970-75; personnel mgr. GSA, Washington, 1975—; lectr. in bus. statistics U. N.C., 1964-65; cons. Postal Service Mgmt. Inst., 1973-75. Mem. Presdl. Inaugural Com., 1964-65, 76-77; mem. Carter-Mondale Transition Group, 1976-77; spl. task force Pres.'s Reorgn. Project, 1977—. Recipient U.S. Postal Service Superior Achievement award. Mem. Am. Soc. Pub. Adminstrn., Internat. Personnel Mgmt. Assn. (chpt. exec. v.p.), Am. Mktg. Assn., Am. Statis. Assn., Assn. M.B.A. Execs., Soc. Am. Baseball Research, Am. U., U. N.C. alumni assns., Beta Gamma Sigma. Democrat. Jewish. Home: 5512 Cornish Rd Bethesda MD 20014 Office: General Services Administration 18th St and F St NW Washington DC 20405

GACCIONE, VINCENT JAMES, mfg. co. exec.; b. Bklyn., Nov. 17, 1942; s. Vincent and Vera (Sicari) G.; B.B.A. in Mktg., St. Johns U., 1965; M.B.A., Baruch Coll., 1972; m. Catherine Sansone, Sept. 16, 1967; 1 dau., Vera Ellen. Market analyst Scandinavian Airline System, Queens, N.Y., 1965-67, Am. Can Co., N.Y.C., 1968-69; market researcher Interroyal Corp., N.Y.C., 1969-72; market planning mgr. Hilti Fastening Systems, Stamford, Conn., 1972—; dir. Hilti Credit Union. Mem. Am. Mktg. Assn., Am. Mgmt. Assn. Republican. Roman Catholic. Club: K.C. Contbr. articles in field to profl. jours. Home: 61 Youngstown Rd Fairfield CT 06430 Office: Hilti Fastening Systems Stamford CT 06904

GADDIS, PAUL OTTO, univ. vice pres.; b. Muskogee, Okla., Mar. 20, 1924; s. Paul James and Ida Rose (Oerter) G.; B.S., U.S. Naval Acad., 1946; M.S., Rensselaer Poly. Inst., 1949; M.B.A., Sloan Sch. Mass. Inst. Tech., 1961; m. Martha Louise Rinker, June 28, 1948; children—Paul James, David Charles, Holly. Mgr. computer systems and finance Westinghouse Electric Corp., Pitts., 1954-68, v.p., corporate devel., Pitts., 1968-72; cons. corporate devel., prof. mgmt. Wharton Sch., sr. v.p., U. Pa., Phila., 1972—; chmn., dir. Globe Ticket Co., Phila., 1975—; mem. exec. com., dir. Western Savs. Bank, Phila., 1976—; chmn. exec. com., dir. UNI-COLL Corp., Phila., 1974—; dir. Wharton Econometric Forecasting Assos., Inc. Pres., La Napoule Art Found. (France). Served with USN, 1946-54. Mem. Soc. Mgmt. Info. Systems, Planning Execs. Inst. Author: Corporate Accountability, 1964; contbr. articles to Harvard Bus. Rev. Home: 840 Mt Moro Rd Villanova PA 19085 Office: U Pa Philadelphia PA 19104

GADSBY, DWIGHT MAXON, economist; b. Dickens, Iowa, Oct. 2, 1932; s. William Maxon and Esther Sofia (Holmberg) G.; B.S., Iowa State Coll., 1954; M.S., Iowa State U., 1960; postgrad. U. Minn., 1961; Fulbright scholar U. Padova, 1961-62; m. Jermaine Mae Folkman, June 17, 1961; children—Winston Maxon, Alessandra Mae. Asso., Iowa State U., Ames, 1961-63; economist div. trade analysis Econ. Research Service, U.S. Dept. Agr., Washington, 1963-65, supervisory agrl. economist, 1965—; substitute instr. Iowa State U., 1957-60; coordinator Seminar on Exec. Devel., U.S. Dept. Agr., 1971-73; sec. Army Section Joint Armed Forces Reserve Assembly, Washington, 1970-71. Mem. fiscal com. Hensen Valley Montessori Sch. Corp., Hillcrest Heights, Md., 1970-74, bd. dirs., 1973-74. Served with AUS, 1955-56. Mem. Orgn. Profl. Employees U.S. Dept. Agr. (pres. econ. research service chpt. 1970, membership v.p. 1975—), AAAS, Am. Agrl. Econ. Assn., Am. Econ. Assn., Soil Conservation Soc. Am., Res. Officers Assn., Am. Overseas Educators. Methodist. Club: Econ. Research Service (pres. 1970) (Washington). Contbr. articles to profl. jours. Home: 4711 Medora Dr Suitland MD 20023 Office: 500 12th St Bldg SW Washington DC 20250

GAERTNER, WOLFGANG WILHELM, research co. exec.; b. Vienna, Austria, July 5, 1929; s. Wilhelm and Maria (Schuetz) G.; Ph.D. in Physics, U. Vienna, 1951; Dipl. Ing., Technische Hochschule, Vienna, 1955; m. Marianne L. Weber, Feb. 22, 1955; children—Marianne P., Karin C., Christopher W. Came to U.S., 1953, naturalized, 1961. Research physicist Siemens Halske, Vienna, 1951-53, chief scientist solid state devices div. U.S. Army Signal Research and Devel. Lab., Ft. Monmouth, N.J., 1953-60; v.p. CBS Labs, Stamford, Conn., 1960-65; pres. W.W. Gaertner Research, Inc., 1966—. Fellow IEEE; mem. Am. Phys. Soc. Author: Transistors: Principles, Design and Applications, 1960; author, editor: Adaptive Electronics, 1972; contbr. numerous articles to profl. publs. Home: 205 Saddle Hill Rd Stamford CT 06903 Office: Merritt Plaza Blvd Stamford CT 06905

GAETA, JOSEPH ROLAND, cardiologist; b. Providence, Jan. 25, 1934; s. Giuseppe and Maria (Russo) G.; student Brown U., 1951-54; M.D. cum laude, Boston U., 1958; m. Carol Ann Scialo, Sept. 9, 1968; children—Joseph Roland, Paul, Stephen. Intern, Univ. Hosp., Boston, 1958-59; practice medicine specializing in internal medicine and cardiology, Providence, 1964—; mem. staff R.I. Hosp.; asst. clin. prof. medicine Brown U. Served as capt. USAF, 1962-64. Diplomate Am. Bd. Internal Medicine. Fellow Am. Coll. Cardiology, Council Clin. Cardiology of Am. Heart Assn.; mem. Am., R.I. socs. internal medicine, R.I., Providence med. assns., Phi Beta Kappa, Alpha Omega Alpha. Roman Catholic. Office: 110 Lockwood St Providence RI 02903

GAFFIELD, CHARLES MITCHELL, librarian; b. Dallas, June 23, 1919; s. Samuel Patterson and Grace Rector (Mitchell) G.; B.S., So. Meth. U., 1941; M.L.S., Pratt Inst., 1969; m. Harriett Aileen Mathias, Aug. 10, 1946; children—Noel, Charles Mitchell. Geologist, Atlantic Refining Co., Dallas, 1937-41; sales exec. Am. Car & Foundry Co., N.Y.C., 1947-51; pres. Gaffield Corp., N.Y.C., 1951-68; sr. prin. librarian, head, bus. and sci. dept. Mid-Manhattan Library, N.Y. Pub. Library, N.Y.C., 1968—. Served with USNR, 1941-45. Mem. ASTM, TAPPI. Republican. Episcopalian. Home: 230 E 71st St New York City NY 10021 Office: 8 E 40th St New York City NY 10016

GAFFNEY, JAMES ANTHONY, motion picture co. exec.; b. N.Y.C., Oct. 18, 1929; s. Thomas and Elizabeth (Heffernan) G.; grad. high sch. Asst. film editor Louis de Rochemont Films, N.Y.C., 1947-49; film editor NBC, N.Y.C., 1949-51, supervisory film editor Flamingo Films, N.Y.C., 1952-53; sec.-treas. Ross Gaffney, Inc., N.Y.C., 1955-69, pres., 1969—. Served with Signal Corps, AUS, 1950-52. Mem. Am. Cinema Editors. Roman Catholic. Clubs: Yale, Racquet. Home: 230 Central Park S New York City NY 10019 Office: 21 W 46th St New York City NY 10036

GAFFNEY, PAUL COTTER, medical educator; b. DuBois, Pa., May 12, 1917; s. John Charles and Anna Catherine (Cotter) G.; B.S. magna cum laude, U. Pitts., 1940, M.D., 1942; m. Lois G. Brown, Oct. 14, 1944; children—Louise A., Paul Cotter, William B., Maureen E., Mary Ellen, Frances J., Michael B. Intern, St. Francis Hosp., Pitts., 1942-43, resident in pathology, 1946-48; resident in pediatrics Children's Hosp., Pitts., 1948-50, now mem. staff; fellow hematology Children's Hosp., Detroit, 1950-51; practice medicine, specializing in pediatrics and hematology, Pitts., 1951-63; mem. faculty U. Pitts. Sch. Medicine, 1951—, prof. pediatrics, 1961—, asso. dean, dir. admissions, 1977—; med. dir. Children's Hosp. Pitts., 1978—; mem. staff Magee-Women's Hosp., Pitts. Served to maj. M.C., AUS, 1943-46; ETO. Decorated Bronze Star with oak leaf cluster. Fellow Am. Acad. Pediatrics; mem. AMA, Pa., Allegheny (dir.) med. socs., Am. Pediatric Soc. (Golden Apple teaching award 1967, 71, 75), Pediatric Travel Club, Phi Beta Pi. Republican. Roman Catholic. Research on treatment of childhood leukemia. Home: 5540 Elgin Ave Pittsburgh PA 15206 Office: Children's Hosp 125 De Sota St Pittsburgh PA 15213

GAGLIARDO, DOMINICK FRANK, architect, engr., educator; b. Bklyn., Dec. 3, 1927; s. Andrew and Margaret (Voci) G.; A.A.S., State U. N.Y. at Farmingdale, 1950; teaching certificate N.Y. U., 1966; m. Angelina H. Maniscalco, Oct. 21, 1951; children—Michael, Paul, Sandra, Regina, Cynthia. Draftsman, Airbore Inst., 1950; designer Dyna Labs, Garden City, N.Y., 1952, Fairchild Co., Deer Park, N.Y., 1953; project leader McLean Devel., 1955; prin. archtl. and engring. firm Designers, Planners & Draftsman Service, Massapequa, N.Y., 1955—; archtl. drafting tchr. Hicksville (N.Y.) and Nassau Vocat. Sch., 1955—. Vice-pres., pres. Plainedge Sch. Bd., 1966-78; pres. Plainedge Kiwanis, 1969. Served with USMC, 1946-48. Mem. Am. Inst. Design and Drafting, Am. Soc. Interior Designers, N.Y. State, Nassau Suffolk sch. bds. assns., N.Y. State (v.p. 1965-66), Nassau Suffolk (pres. 1966-67) vocat. tchrs. assns. Roman Catholic. Home: 578 Suffolk Ave Massapequa NY 11758 Office: 693 Broadway Massapequa NY 11758

GAGNON, FRED LOUIS, instrument co. exec.; b. Aspen, Colo., Aug. 22, 1923; s. Fred L. and Ethel Mae (Olson) G.; B.E.E., U. Calif., Berkeley, 1949; m. Virginia L. Smith, Sept. 5, 1958; children—Cheryl Lee, Sandra Jean. Tech. dir. Hoffman Labs., Los Angeles, 1959-60; v.p. mfg. ops., electronics div. Gen. Dynamics, Rochester, N.Y., 1960-69; gen. mgr. Compactor Corp. div. Carrier Corp., Jersey City, 1969-71; v.p., gen. mgr. Kollsman Instrument Co. div. Sun Chem. Corp., Merrimack, N.H., 1971—; dir. Electronic Nav. Industries, Inc.; lectr. U. Rochester, 1965-67; commr. N.H. Data Processing Dept., 1975—. Served with USNR, 1943-46. Mem. Navy League (pres. 1966-68), Greater Nashua (N.H.) C. of C. (dir.). Republican. Inventor automatic flight control system for high performance aircraft, 1955. Home: 5 Birchwood Dr Nashua NH 03060 Office: Kollsman Instrument Co Daniel Webster Hwy 5 Merrimack NH 03054

GAGNON, LIONEL (LEE), owner diversified bus. enterprises; b. Keegan, Maine, June 4, 1942; s. Lezime and Marie (Lizotte) G.; student pub. schs., Keegan; m. Dorothy E. Krajewski, Apr. 8, 1967; 1 dau., Lisa. Owner Gagnon's Secretarial Service, Bristol, Conn., 1968—, Gagnon's Motorhome Rental Service, Bristol, 1972—, Progressive Realty, Bristol, 1976—, Gagnon's Services, Bristol, 1978—. Served with U.S. Army, 1960-63. Mem. C. of C. (legis. com. 1975—), Conn. Bus. and Industry Assn. (legis. com. 1975—), Nat. Assn. Realtors, Bristol Assns. Realtor, Multiple Listing Service, Democrat. Roman Catholic. Clubs: Rotary, Chippannee Country. Author: Job Hunting Guide, 1977. Home: 46 Ridgecrest Ln Bristol CT 06010 Office: 20 Burlington Ave Bristol CT 06010

GAHEEN, ALFRED FRANCIS, JR., elec. engr., elec. products mfg. co. exec.; b. Chicopee, Mass., Jan. 29, 1937; s. Alfred F. and Stella Dolores (Wojtasiewicz) G.; B.S., U.S. Naval Acad., 1958; children—Michael, Kevin, Patrick, Katherine. Fire control radar engr. Westinghouse Corp., Balt., 1962-66, supervisory engr. radar devel., 1966-69, mgr. advanced radar systems, 1969-73, mgr. emerging radar programs, 1973—. Served to 1st lt. USAF, 1958-62. Mem. Advance Def. Preparedness Assn., U.S. Naval Acad. Alumni Assn. Republican. Roman Catholic. Clubs: Severn Valley Racquet, Big Vanilla Racquet. Patentee in field. Home: 7860 Americana Circle Apt 104 Glen Burnie MD 21061 Office: PO Box 746 MS337 Westinghouse Electric Corp Def and Electronics Systems Center Baltimore MD 21203

GAINES, FRED R., chem. engr.; b. Bklyn., Jan. 13, 1941; s. Jerome J. and Sylvia (Gelber) G.; B.S. in Chemistry, St. Johns U., Queens, N.Y., 1964; M.B.A. in Mktg., Pace U.; m. Gail Sandra Eager; children—Judith, Jill. Mktg. engr. Dorr Oliver Co., Stanford, Conn., 1968-69; v.p. Tracy Engrs., Lansdale, Pa., 1971-74; mgr. client services div., sr. project mgr. Weston Environ. Co., Roslyn, N.Y., 1975—; instr. Montgomery County Community Coll.; commr. New Eng. Interstate Water Pollution Control Commn. Registered profl. engr., Conn., N.Y., Pa. Mem. Water Pollution Control Fedn., Am. Water Works Assn., Am. Inst. Chem. Engrs., Am. Pub. Works Assn. Contbr. to profl. jours. Home: 3228 W Bruce Dr Dresher PA 19025 Office: 1044 Northern Blvd Roslyn NY 11576

GAINES, NATALIE EVELYN, sculptor; b. Detroit, Dec. 11, 1929; d. Michael and May (Mantin) Gaines; student Detroit Soc. Arts and Crafts, 1945-51, Greason Sch., Detroit, 1949-50. Exhibited one-man shows at Crespi Gallery, N.Y.C., 1958, Glassboro (N.J.) State Coll., 1961; exhibited in group shows at Detroit Inst. Art, 1949, 50, Wayne County Artists Show, Detroit, 1950, Creative Gallery, N.Y.C., 1951, Kirk-in-the Hills Outdoor Art Festival, Detroit, 1952, Crespi Gallery, 1958, 59, 60, Allied Artists Am., N.Y.C., 1958, Archtl. League N.Y., 1969; represented in permanent collections at Glassboro State Coll.; also pvt. collections. Pres., Temple Israel Youth Group, Detroit, 1947-48, Young Adult Council, Detroit, 1950-51; leader jr. div. Allied Jewish Campaign, Detroit, 1947-51; mem. exec. com., co-chmn. program com. Nat. Jewish Youth Council, 1948-50; pub. relations dir. Henry St. Camp Fund drive, Henry St. Friends Com., N.Y.C., 1957. Recipient 3d prize Crespi Gallery Ann. Competition Award Show, 1958; 1st prize Temple Emanu-El Men's Club Ann. Art Exhbn., 1959, 2d prize, 1961, 3d prize, 1962. Mem. Archtl. League N.Y., Artists Equity Assn. N.Y. (summer program chmn. 1957—). Address: 65 Marilyn Blvd Plainview NY 11803

GAINES, NATHANIEL, architect; b. Bethayres, Pa., Dec. 18, 1926; s. William Henry and Jennie Louise (Jones) G.; B.Arch. cum laude, Howard U., 1952; m. Jean Catherine Lee, Apr. 28, 1956; children—Lisa Renee, Gary Gordon. Designer, Phila. Naval Shipyard, 1952-53; draftsman Baeder, Young & Schultze, 1953-54, Norman N. Rice, architect, 1954-55; partner, project architect Ewing, Cole, Rizzio Cherry Parsky (formerly Alexander Ewing & Assos.), Phila., 1955—. First v.p. parent council Willow Hill Elementary Sch., Abington, Pa. Served with AUS, 1945-46. Registered architect, Pa., Del.; certified Nat. Council Archtl. Registration Bds. Mem. AIA (dir. Bucks County chpt., v.p. 1974, pres. 1975), Tau Beta Pi. Baptist (former v.p. choir). Home: 1643 Park Ave Willow Grove PA 19090 Office: Ewing Cole Rizzio Cherry Parsky Continental Bank Bldg 400 Market St Philadelphia PA 19106

GAINES, SYLVIA MAUDE, ednl. adminstr.; b. N.Y.C., June 25, 1929; d. Henry Charles and Philippa Alexandra (Thomas) Taylor; licensed practical nurse Central Sch. Practical Nursing, 1952; B.A., State U. N.Y. at Old Westbury, 1972; M.S., L.I. U., 1976; m. James Henry Gaines, Sept. 2, 1950; children—Cynthia Ann, Lorraine April, Laura Jean. Nurses aide Queens Gen. Hosp., N.Y.C., 1950-52, practical nurse, 1952-58; pediatric ward supr. Kew Garden Hosp., N.Y.C., 1958-62; founder, tchr. Tiny Tots Westbury (N.Y.), 1962-64; asst. tchr. Westbury pub. schs., 1964-69, Head Start tchr., asst. dir., 1969-71; lectr. edn. State U. N.Y., Old Westbury, 1971-72, adminstrv. dir. Child Creative Ednl. Center, 1972—; Head Start cons., 1968; bd. dirs. N. Shore Child Guidance Center. Active New Cassel Civic Assn., 1960—; founder Mothers Group of Westbury, 1959—. Recipient Sojourner Truth award Nat. Assn. Negro Bus. and Profl. Club, 1972; certified tchr., sch. counselor, N.Y. Mem. NAACP (charter mem. Westbury branch), Doctoral Assn. N.Y. Educators, Am. Personnel and Guidance Assn., Day Care Council Dirs. Nassau County, Assn. Suprs. and Curriculum Developers, State U. N.Y. at Westbury Alumni Assn. Lutheran. Pub. Directory of Resources for Day Care and Pre-School Programs in Nassau County, N.Y., 1977. Home: 46 3d Ave Westbury NY 11590 Office: PO Box 210 Old Wesbury NY 11568

GAINES, THURSTON LENWOOD, JR., surgeon; b. Freeport, N.Y., Mar. 20, 1922; s. Thurston Lenwood and Albertha R. (Robinson) G.; student Howard U., 1941-43; B.A., N.Y. U., 1948; M.D., Meharry Med. Coll., 1953; m. Jacqueline Eleanor Kelly, Feb. 26, 1944; children—Bevely Gaines Harvey, Terrell Lance, William Wesley. Intern, Meadowbrook Hosp., East Meadow, N.Y., 1953-54, resident, 1954-59; practice medicine specializing in surgery, Hempsted, N.Y., 1959-75; attending surgeon Mercy Hosp., Rockville Centre, N.Y., 1954-76, dir. surg. edn., 1969-74; asso. attending in surgery Nassau County Med. Center, East Meadow, 1954-76; asst. prof. clin. surgery State U. N.Y., 1976-77; asst. dir. surgery Creedmoor State Hosp., Queens Village, N.Y.; dep. med. examiner Nassau County, 1962-77, aviation med. examiner, 1975-77; dir. profl. edn. and tng. S. Nassau Community Hosp., Oceanside, N.Y., 1964-69; chief profl. services Western Mass. Hosp., Westfield. Bd. dirs. Nassau div. Am. Cancer Soc.; pres. Hempstead Community Chest; trustee Catholic Hosp. Assn., 1973-76. Served with USAAF, 1943-47. Decorated Air medal with 3 oak leaf clusters; Purple Heart. Diplomate Am. Bd. Surgery. Fellow A.C.S., Internat. Coll. Surgeons; mem. AMA, Nat. Med. Assn., Mass., Hampden County med. socs., Nassau Acad. Medicine, Nassau Surg. Soc., Royal Soc. Medicine London (affiliate). Democrat. Episcopalian. Club: Alpha Phi Alpha. Author: (with others) Single Stage Treatment of Ano Rectal Abscesses and Fistulas, 1958. Home: 159 Burleigh Rd Wilbraham MA 01095 Office: Western Mass Hosp 91 E Mountain Rd Westfield MA 01085

GAINEY, HARVEY NUETON, trucking co. exec.; b. Nicholls, Ga., Nov. 20, 1942; s. Lloyd F. and Rita Mae (Tanner) G.; student pub. schs., Nicholls, Ga.; m. Annie E. Carter, Nov. 9, 1962; children—Angela Marie, Harvey N. Rate analyst Ryder Truck Lines, Inc., Jacksonville, Fla., 1962-68, rate audit mgr., 1968-71, traffic mgr., 1970-71; dir. traffic Helms Express, Irwin, Pa., 1971-76, v.p. sales, 1976—. Mem. Am. Trucking Assn., Sales and Mktg. Council, Eastern Shipper-Motor Carrier Council, Delta Nu Alpha. Democrat. Home: 143 Monticello Dr Monroeville PA 15146 Office: PO Box 340 Irwin PA 15642

GAITHER, GEORGE MANNEY, mktg. cons.; b. Mineola, N.Y., Sept. 21, 1930; s. Roscoe Bradley and Fanny Bullitt (Williams) G.; B.J., U. Mo., 1952; m. Dorothy W. Streater, Apr. 4, 1953; children—Neal, George, Emee, Bruce. Gen. mgr. Internat. Research Assos., Mexico, 1955-64; v.p. Internat. Research Assos. Latin Am., 1965-68; pres. Internat. Research Assos. U.S.A., 1968-71; pres. Gaither Internat., Stamford, Conn., 1971—. Served with U.S. Army, 1952-55. Mem. European Soc. Mktg. Research, World Assn. Pub. Opinion Research, Market Research Council. Republican. Presbyterian. Home: 1792 Newfield Ave Stamford CT 06903 Office: 2777 Summer St Stamford CT 06905

GAJDUSEK, DANIEL CARLETON, pediatrician, research virologist; b. Yonkers, N.Y., Sept. 9, 1923; s. Karl A. and Ottilia D. (Dobroczki) G.; B.S., U. Rochester, 1943; M.D., Harvard U., 1946; NRC fellow, Calif. Inst. Tech., 1948-49; D.Sc., U. Rochester, 1977, Med. Coll. Ohio, 1977; H.H.D., Hamilton Coll., 1977; Dr.h.c., U. Aix-Marseille, 1977; children—Josede Figirliyong, Ivan Mbagintao, Jesus Raglmar, Jesus Mororui, Mathias Maradol, Jesus Tamel, Yavine Borima, Jesus Salalu, John Paul Runman, Arthur Yolwa, Joe Yongorimah Kintoki, Thomas Youmog, Tone Wanevi, Toname Ikabala, Magame Prima. Intern, resident Babies Hosp., Columbia Presbyn. Med. Center, N.Y.C., 1946-47; resident pediatrics Children's Hosp., Cin., 1947-48; pediatric med. mission, Germany, 1948; resident, clin. and research fellow Children's Hosp., Boston, 1949-51; research fellow pediatrics and infectious diseases Harvard, 1949-52; with Walter Reed Army Inst. Research, Washington, 1952-53, Institut Pasteur, Teheran, Iran and dept. medicine U. Md., 1954-55; vis. investigator Nat. Found. for Infantile Paralysis, Walter and Eliza Hall Inst. Med. Research, Melbourne, Australia, 1955-57; dir. program for study child growth and devel. and disease patterns in primitive cultures and lab. slow, latent and temperate virus infections Nat. Inst. Neurol. and Communicative Disorders and Stroke, NIH, Bethesda, Md., 1958—, chief Central Nervous System Studies Lab., 1970—; chief scientist research vessel Alpha Helix expdn. to Banks and Torres Islands, New Hebrides, South Solomon Islands, 1972. Recipient E. Meade Johnson award Am. Acad. Pediatrics, 1963, Superior Service award NIH, HEW, 1970, Distinguished Service award HEW, 1975, Prof. Lucian Dautrebande prize Belgium, 1976, Nobel prize in physiology and medicine, 1976; Dyer lectr. NIH, 1974, Heath Clark lectr. U. London, 1974, B.K. Rachford lectr. Children's Hosp. Research Found., Cin., 1975, Withering lectr. U. Birmingham (Eng.), 1976, Cannon Elie lectr. Boston Children's Med. Center, 1976, Zale lectr. U. Tex., Dallas, 1976, Langmuir lectr. Center for Disease Control, Atlanta, T. Francis lectr. U. Mich. Diplomate Am. Bd. Pediatrics. Mem. Nat. Acad. Scis., Soc. for Pediatric Research, Am. Pediatric Soc., Am. Soc. Human Genetics, Am. Acad. Neurology, Soc. for Neurosci., Am. Epidemiol. Soc., Infectious Diseases Soc. Am., Société des Oceanistes (Paris), Papua and New Guinea Sci. Soc., Micronesian Acad. Sci., Am. Philos. Soc., Am. Soc. Arts and Scis., Phi Beta Kappa, Sigma Xi. Author: Journals, 22 vols., 1957-76; Hemorrhagic Fevers and Mycotoxicoses in the USSR; Correspondence on the Discovery and Original Investigations of Kuru; Slow Latent and Temperate Virus Infections. Home: 4 Laurel Pkwy Chevy Chase MD 20015 Office: NIH Bethesda MD 20014

GALANE, IRMA ADELE BERESTON, electronic engr.; b. Balt., Aug. 23, 1921; d. Dr. Arthur and Sarah (Hillman) Bereston; B.A., Goucher Coll., 1940; postgrad. Johns Hopkins, 1940-42, Mass. Inst. Tech., 1943, George Washington U., 1945, 65, U. Md., 1958, Army Mgmt. Sch., 1964; 1 dau., Suzanne Felice. Physicist, Naval Ordnance Lab., 1942-43; electronic engr. Navy Bur. Ships, 1943-49, Army Office Chief Signal Officer, 1949-51, Navy Bur. Aeros., 1951-56, Air Research and Devel. Command, USAF, 1956-57, FCC, 1957-60, NASA, 1960-62; supervisory electronic engr. USCG Hdqrs., 1962-64; sci. specialist engring. scis. Library of Congress, 1964-65; project engr. Advanced Aerial Fire Support System, Army Material Command, 1965-66; engr. Naval Air Systems Command, 1966-71; electronic engr. Fed. Communications Commn., Spectrum Mgmt. Task Force, 1971-76, sr. research engr., 1976—. Judge nat. capitol awards for engrs. and architects, 1975. Registered profl. engr., D.C., Mem. IEEE (sr.), Am. Inst. Aeros. and Astronautics, Nat. Soc. Profl. Engrs. (chmn. publs. com. 1959-60, co-chmn. civil def. com. 1965, spl. asst. to pres. 1965), Soc. Women Engrs. (sr. mem.; nat. membership chmn. 1952, nat. dir. 1953, mem. nat. scholarship com. 1958), Armed Forces Communications and Electronics Assn., Fedn. Profl. Assn., Am. Ordnance Assn., Johns Hopkins Alumni Assn., AAAS, U.S. Naval Inst., Marine Tech. Soc., Internat. Platform Assn., Smithsonian Inst. (asso.). Editor: The Met. Washington Profl. Engr., 1958-60. Home: 4201 Cathedral Ave NW Washington DC 20016

GALANT, RAYMOND, journalist; b. Shenandoah, Pa., Aug. 29, 1929; s. Abraham and Sarah (Gussman) G.; B.A., Pa. State U., 1952; m. Shirley H. Gable, Sept. 6, 1953; children—Debra L., Mark E., Ellen J. Reporter, Record American, Mahanoy City, Pa., 1947-48; mng. editor Army Times vets. edit., Washington, 1954-57; dir. pub. relations Am. Waterways Operators Inc., Washington, 1957-58; asso. editor F D C Reports, Washington, 1958-61; mng. editor Food Chem. News, Washington, 1961—, v.p., 1966—. Pres., Wakefield Chapel Estates Civic Assn., 1969; 1st v.p. Temple Rodef Shalom, Falls Church, Va., 1972. Served with U.S. Army, 1952-54. Mem. Ind. Newsletter Assn. (pres.), Nat. Press Club, Sigma Delta Chi. Mem. B'nai B'rith. Home: 4411 Duncan Dr Annandale VA 22003 Office: 777 14th St NW Room 400 Washington DC 20005

GALANTE, NICHOLAS THOMAS, paper mill exec.; b. N.Y.C., Feb. 7, 1918; s. Thomas A. and Mildred A. (Petrillo) G.; B.A., N.Y. U., 1939; m. Violet Brocolli, Sept. 1, 1940; children—Joyce M. Carolann Galante Jacobson, Lana Galante Zanello, Nicholas T. III. Pres., Wallomsac Paper Mills, North Hoosick, N.Y., 1943-55, Warrensburg Bd. & Paper Mills (N.Y.), 1955-63, Thomas A. Galante & Sons, Inc.-Tagsons Papers, Inc., Mechanicville, N.Y., 1963—. Served with U.S. Army, 1939. Mem. Am. Paper Inst., Nat. Paper Trade Assn., Nat. Assn. Recycling Industries (exec. com.), Paper Industry Mgmt. Assn., TAPPI, Am. Logistics Assn., Sons Italy. Clubs: K.C., Elks, Albany Country. Home: 5 Chestnut Hill Loudonville NY 12211 Office: PO Box 150 Mechanicville NY 12118

GALANTOWICZ, THOMAS ANTHONY, elec. engr.; b. Buffalo, June 4, 1942; s. Albin S. and Valerie (Darnowski) G.; B.E.E., U. Detroit, 1964, Ph.D. in Elec. Engring., 1969; M.E.E., Ohio State U., 1966; m. Mary Knotts, Aug. 21, 1965; children—Anne Marie, Judith Lynn, David Thomas. Research asso. Electrosci. Lab., Ohio State U., Columbus, 1966-69, asst. prof. dept. elec. engring., 1969-70; asst. prof. elec. engring. Union Coll., Schenectady, 1970-75, asso. prof., 1975—. NDEA fellow, 1964-67; NASA grantee, 1974-78. Mem. IEEE, Optical Soc. Am., Am. Soc. Engring. Educators, Sigma Xi (chpt. sec. 1972-74, pres. 1976-78). Contbr. articles to sci. jours. Home: 9 Yorkshire Terr Clifton Park NY 12065 Office: Union Coll Schenectady NY 12308

GALBRAITH, WILLIAM LESTER, social worker; b. Greensboro, N.C., Jan. 3, 1925; s. John Bauer and Margaret (Howard) G.; B.A., U. Louisville, 1950, M.S.W., 1957; m. Loretta Williams, Oct. 12, 1946; children—Paula Galbraith Witek, Ellen, John. Tchr., Sebree (Ky.) High Sch., 1950-51; probation officer Juvenile Ct. Louisville, 1951-54, 55, supr., 1958-60; personnel officer E.I. duPont Co., Charlestown, Ind., 1954-55; psychiat. social worker Ind. U. Med. Center, 1957-58; regional dir. Juvenile Placement Bur., Columbus, Ohio, 1960-62; exec. dir. Child & Family Services, Knoxville, Tenn., 1962-66; exec. dir. Family Service Agy., Chattanooga, 1966-69; asst. dir. Baird Children's Center, Burlington, Vt., 1969-76; dir. group homes Hillside Children's Center, Rochester, N.Y., 1976—; instr. U. Tenn. Sch. Social Work, 1963-66; lectr. So. Missionary Coll., 1968-69; instr. U. Chattanooga, 1968-69; mem. child placing standards com. Tenn. Dept. Pub. Welfare. Served with U.S. Army, World War II. Mem. Acad. Certified Social Workers, Nat. Assn. Social Workers. Home: 1183 Monroe Ave Rochester NY 14620

GALDAU, FLORIAN MARIN, clergyman; b. Slobozia-Mandra, Romania, Feb. 27, 1903; s. Marin V. and Ioana (Sitaru) G.; M.S.T., U. Bucharest, 1927, M.A., 1927; postgrad. Columbia U., 1928-31; m. Maria Popescu, Nov. 12, 1933; children—Radu Florin, Alexandru Andrei. Ordained priest Romanian Orthodox Ch., 1934; counsellor Romanian Patriardiate, 1934-44; founder Waifs and Strays Children of Romania, 1942, dir., 1942-45; rector St. Constantin and Helen Romanian Orthodox Ch., London, 1949-55; rector St. Dumitru Romanian Ch., N.Y.C., 1955—; religious broadcaster Radio Free Europe to Romania, 1952—; chaplain Brancovenesc Hosp., Bucharest, 1934-45; mem. met. council Orthodox Ch. in Am., 1971—, mem. dept. canonical affairs, 1971—. Address: 50 W 89th St New York City NY 10024

GALDI, WILLIAM ANDREW, county ofcl.; b. Hoboken, N.J., July 15, 1927; s. Mario and Angelina (Costantino) G.; student Rutgers U., 1965; B.A. in Environ Studies, Ramapo Coll., 1977; m. Angelina Vangelakos, Oct. 11, 1952; children—William, John. Automotive diagnostician Diamond T of Hudson County, Hoboken, N.J., 1938-45, 45-64; pres. Grand Autoservice, Hoboken, 1947-64; dir. motorized equipment Dept. Pub. Works, Hackensack, N.J., 1964—; exec. officer Alpine (N.J.) Bd. Health, 1970—. Served with USN, 1945-46. Licensed san. inspector 1st grade, plumbing inspector 1st grade; certified pesticide applicator. Mem. DAV, Bergen County Health Officers Soc., Am. Pub. Works Assn. Home: 5 Engle St Cresskill NJ 07626 Office: 70 Zabriskie St Hackensack NJ 07602

GALE, JAMES ELWIN, cons. energy and environment; b. Oceanside, N.Y., Dec. 8, 1948; s. James S. and Helen A. (Bruington) G.; B.S., Clarkson Coll. Tech., 1970; M.S., George Washington U., 1974. Engr., Gen. Electric Co., Schenectady, 1970-72; staff Met. D.C. Council Govts., 1973; project leader Wilbur Smith & Assos., Washington, 1974-76; project mgr. Hittman Assos., Inc., Columbia, Md., 1976-78; cons. Logistics Mgmt. Inst., Washington, 1978—. U.S. Dept. Transp. fellow, 1972-74. Mem. Ops. Research Soc. Am., ASME (pres. Clarkson chpt. 1969-70), Am. Inst. Planners, Pi Tau Sigma (v.p. 1969-70), Smithsonian Assos., Sierra Club, Alpha Chi Rho. Contbr. articles on transp. and urban environment to profl. publs. Home: 1608 32nd St NW Washington DC 20007 Office: 4701 Sangamore Rd Washington DC 20016

GALEN, ROBERT SANFORD, pathologist; b. N.Y.C., May 29, 1946; s. Ben and Sylvia (Miller) G.; B.A., Boston U., 1970, M.D., 1970; M.P.H., Columbia U., 1972; m. Amy Susan Feinberg, Dec. 27, 1968; children—Ari David, Tamara Anne. Intern, Columbia-Presbyn. Med. Center, 1970-71, resident in pathology, 1971-74; asso. dir. lab. Metpath Inc., Hackensack, N.J., 1974-76, Overlook Hosp., Summit, N.J., 1976—; asst. prof. clin. pathology Columbia U., N.Y.C., 1974—; practice medicine, specializing in pathology, Summit, 1976—. Mem. Am. Soc. Clin. Pathologists (council clin. chemistry 1977—), AMA, Am. Assn. Clin. Chemistry, Assn. Clin. Scientists, Acad. Clin. Lab. Physicians and Scientists, AAAS, N.Y. Acad. Scis., World Future Soc., Am. Mgmt. Assn., Am. Pub. Health Assn., Soc. Computer Medicine. Author: Beyond Normality, 1975. Med. editor: Diagnostic Medicine, 1977—; Med. Lab. Observer, 1977—; editorial bd. Human Pathology, also Lab. Office: 194 Morris Ave Summit NJ 07901

GALEY, JOHN TAYLOR, geologist, natural gas operator; b. Beaver, Pa., Aug. 30, 1907; s. George Banks and Vera MacDonald (Taylor) G.; B.S., Princeton U., 1932; m. Blanche Georgene Fishback, Nov. 19, 1938; children—Margaret Elizabeth, John Taylor. Cons., ind. producer natural gas, 1935—; mem. adv. com. Beaver Trust Co. (Pa.), 1950-59; chmn. steering com. Nat. Conf. Environ. Geology, 1969; chmn. Nat. Interdisciplinary Conf. Planning A New Town's Environment, 1971; mem. geol. survey adv. bd. Commonwealth Pa., 1967-71, chmn., 1970-71. Mem. mus. com. Carnegie Inst., Pitts., 1971-75. Fellow Geol. Soc. Am.; mem. Engrs. Soc. Western Pa., Am. Petroleum Inst., Ind. Petroleum Assn. Am., Pa. Natural Gas Men's Assn. (pres. 1961-62), Pitts. Geol. Soc. (pres. 1948), Pa. Gas. Assn. (hon. life dir.), Am. Assn. Petroleum Geologists (indsl. adv. com. 1966—, pres. eastern sect. 1969-72, nat. adv. bd. 1970-74, nominating, orgn. and personnel coms. 1970-73, chmn. com. on coms. 1972-74, Distinguished Service award 1974, ho. of dels. 1974—, strategic com. on pub. affairs 1975—), Assn. Profl. Geol. Scientists (chmn. membership qualification com. 1966-68, pres. Pa. 1966-67, exec. com. 1967, pres. 1968, chmn. adv. bd. 1969), Am. Geol. Inst. (ho. of soc. reps. 1968-69, council soc. pres.'s 1969, nat. regulatory and legis. commn. 1976—), Soc. Petroleum Engrs., Am. Tree Farm System, Sigma Gamma Epsilon. Episcopalian. Clubs: Cottage, Nassau (Princeton, N.J.); Rolling Rock (Ligonier, Pa.); Harvard-Yale-Princeton, Duquesne (Pitts.). Discoverer 1st Oriskany sand natural gas prodn. in W. Pa., 1935, also in Bedford County, Pa., 1953; pools in W.Va., Pa., Ohio, Va. Contbr. tech. papers to profl. lit. Home: Galecrest RD 4 Somerset PA 15501 also Office: Route 4 Somerset PA 15501

GALILEA, HERNÁN, educator; b. Santiago, Chile, Oct. 8, 1935; s. Andrés and Maria (Linares) G.; Licentiate in Philosophy and Letters, U. Chile, 1965; Ph.D., Catholic U. Am., 1971; m. Gloria del Rosario Ramires; children—Ivar, Gloria. Prof., Universidad Catolica de Chile, Santiago, 1962-64; staff Research Inst. Comparative Lit., Universidad de Chile, 1964-66; asso. prof. Spanish, Temple U., Phila., 1966—. Mem. Am. Assn. Tchrs. Spanish and Portuguese. Roman Catholic. Author: El Mundo Impresionista de Wallace Stevens, 1965; La Poesia Superrealista de Vicente Aleixandre, 1971; Poesia Esencial de Wallace Stevens, 1974; Poemas Monásticos de Irlanda, 1976. Home: 624 Cresson Ln Morton PA 19070 Office: Spanish Dept Temple Univ Philadelphia PA

GALKIN, EDWIN NEIL, periodontist; b. Newark, Mar. 31, 1936; s. Saul J. and Mollie (Kleinberg) G.; student U. Conn., 1954-57; D.M.D., Tufts U., 1961; certificate in grad. periodontics N.Y. U., 1965; m. Roberta Claire Kimmel, Aug. 27, 1960; children—Michael Jay, Marci Sue. Practice dentistry, specializing in periodontics, Woodbridge, N.J., 1965—; clin. asst. prof. periodontics, anesthesiology and hosp. dental services N.J. Coll. Medicine and Dentistry, Jersey City, 1965—; staff periodontist J.F.K. Community Hosp., Edison, N.J., 1966—, now chmn. dept. periodontics; faculty Middlesex County Coll., Sch. Dental Hygiene, Edison, 1971; mem. dental adv. com. Woodbridge Pub. Health Center, 1967—, Middlesex County Coll., 1970—; mem. N.J. Aviation Adv. Council. Served to capt. Dental Corps, AUS, 1961-63. Certified airplane flight instr. Mem. Am. Acad. Periodontology, N.J. (pres. 1971), Northeastern (com. chmn.) socs. periodontists, ADA, N.J., Middlesex County dental socs., Am. Acad. Oral Medicine, N.J. Council Dental Specialists, Flying Dentists Assn., Airplane Owners and Pilots Assn. Home: 108 Buchanan Rd Edison NJ 08817 Office: 711 Amboy Ave Woodbridge NJ 07095

GALKIN, SAMUEL BERNARD, orthodontist; b. Newark, Feb. 9, 1933; s. Saul J. and Mollie (Kleinberg) G.; student U. Conn., 1951-54; D.D.S., Temple U., 1958; M.S. in Histology, certificate in grad. orthodontics U. Ill., 1963; children—Jamie Michelle, Richard Stewart; m. 2d, Gail Beth Elkin, Feb. 26, 1972; 1 son, Scott David. Group practice orthodontics, Woodbridge, N.J., 1963—; staff orthodontist J.F.K. Community Hosp., Edison, N.J., 1966—, cleft palate com., 1971—, dir. dental dept., 1979—; staff Woodbridge Health Center, 1967—, dental adv. com., 1971—; asst. prof. orthodontics N.J. Coll. Medicine and Dentistry, Jersey City, 1963-73; mem. panel physicians N.J. Crippled Children Program, 1971—. Chmn., Woodbridge Twp. Debutante Ball, 1970; bd. dirs. Woodbridge Twp. YMCA. Served to lt. Dental Corps, USNR, 1958-61. Diplomate Am. Bd. Orthodontics. Mem. Middle Atlantic Soc. Orthodontists (chmn. clinics 1969, 72), N.J., Middlesex County dental socs., ADA, Am. Soc. Dentistry for Children, Am. Assn. Orthodontists, Am. Assn. Dental Schs., Am. Acad. Oral Medicine, Alpha Omega (chpt. v.p. 1969—), Omicron Kappa Upsilon. Home: 3 Dorset Rd Colonia NJ 07067 Office: 711 Amboy Ave Woodbridge NJ 07095

GALLAGHAR, ALBERTA KATHRYN, ins. co. exec.; b. Albany, N.Y., June 1, 1923; d. Weber and Kathryn Elizabeth (Albert) Keator; student Albany Bus. Coll., 1942, Rensselaer Poly. Inst., 1976; m. Kenneth W. VanLoan, May 26, 1957 (dec. July 1963); m. 2d, Robert George Gallaghar, Dec. 4, 1970. Legal sec. to Ernest L. Boothby, 1942-46; sec. Underwriters Rating Bd., 1946-76, also N.Y. Mut. Underwriters, 1951-68; auditor N.Y. Mut. Underwriters, 1968-76, gen. mgr., 1976—; treas. Applied Health Physics, Inc., 1971—. Named Ins. Woman of Yr., N.Y. State Profl. Ins. Agts., 1976; C.P.C.U. Mem. Nat., N.Y. State socs. profl. ins. agts., Nat., Northeastern N.Y. (past pres.) socs. chartered property and casualty underwriters., D.A.R. Lutheran. Home: 17 Park Ave East Greenbush NY 12061 Office: 12 Avis Dr Latham NY 12110

GALLAGHER, ANNE TIMLIN, banker; b. Wilkes-Barre, Pa., Mar. 21, 1943; d. James Joseph and Ruth Brandon (MacGuffie) Gallagher; A.B., Bucknell U., 1964. Presentation analyst A.C. Neilsen, N.Y.C., 1964-65; research asso. Gen. Electric Co., N.Y.C., 1965-67, sr. sales rep., computer time-sharing, 1967-69; mgr. fin. services Rapidata Co., N.Y.C., 1969-70; mgr. fin. markets Computer Scis. Corp., N.Y.C., 1970-73; sr. cons. Arthur Young & Co., N.Y.C., 1973-77; product mgr., asst. v.p. Bankers Trust Co., N.Y.C., 1978—. Asst. chmn. Am. Statis. Assn. Ann. Forecast Conf. N.Y., 1966, 67. Mem. Nat. Assn. Bus. Economists, Met. Econ. Assn., Common Cause, N.Y. Jaycees, Am. Statis. Assn. (chmn. bus./econs. sect. N.Y. chpt.). Democrat. Home: 227 E 66th St New York City NY 10021 Office: 1 Bankers Trust Plaza New York City NY 10015

GALLAGHER, BERNARD PATRICK, editor, pub.; b. N.Y.C., Feb. 25, 1910; s. Bernard A. and Mary Helen (Fitzsimmons) G.; student Columbia U., 1928-29, Akron U., 1941-44; m. Harriet Denning, Oct. 17, 1942; 1 dau., Jill. Single-copy sales mgr. Crowell Pub. Co., 1932-34; sales mgr. charge sales tng. Stenotype Co., Inc., Chgo., 1934-39; pres. Stenotype Co. Ohio, Inc., Cleve., 1939-44, World Wide Publs., Inc., N.Y.C., 1945—; editor-in-chief, pub. The Gallagher Report, 1952—, The Gallagher Presidents' Report, 1965; pres. Gallagher Communications Inc., 1972—. Served with AUS, 1944-45. Mem. Nat. Better Bus. Bur., Central Registry Mag. Pubs. Assn., U.S. C. of C., Cath. Press Assn. Clubs: Canadian; Met., Marco Polo. Home: 325 E 41st St New York City NY 10017 Office: 230 Park Ave New York City NY 10017

GALLAGHER, CHARLES CLIFTON, physicist; b. Boston, Feb. 17, 1937; s. Charles Clement and Marion Cecilia (Halligan) G.; B.S., Boston Coll., 1958, M.S., 1960; M.S., Northeastern U., 1967. Physicist, Naval Ordnance Lab., Silver Spring, Md., 1958-60; physicist Air Force Geophysics Lab., Bedford, Mass., 1960—. Recipient USAF Sci. Achievement award, 1977. Mem. Am. Phys. Soc., Sigma Xi, Sigma Pi Sigma. Roman Catholic. Home: 437 W 4th St South Boston MA 02127 Office: Hanscom AFB Bedford MA 01731

GALLAGHER, DAVID PETER, veterinary cons., lectr., author; b. Phila., Apr. 7, 1939; s. Louis Joseph and Gladys Clara; B.A., Villanova U., 1965; M.A. (research and teaching fellowship), Temple U., 1967; m. Jane Agnes Butterfield, June 28, 1969; 1 son, Colin David. Mem. faculty Villanova U., 1968-71, Temple U., 1971-74, Community Coll., Phila., 1974-76; cons. vet. practice mgmt., adminstrn. and fin., ins. broker, 1974—; pres. Vet. Mgmt. Cons., Phila., 1977—; summer fellow Colonial Williamsburg, 1968—; lectr. vet. schs. and profl. meetings. Episcopalian. Contbr. articles on bus. and career mgmt. to vet. jours. Home and Office: 6018 McCallum St Philadelphia PA 19144

GALLAGHER, JOHN ALOYSIUS, coll. adminstr.; b. Waltham, Mass., Feb. 15, 1938; s. Edward Leo and Margaret Mary (Judge) G.; B.S., So. Conn. State Coll., 1963; M.Ed. in Higher Edn. Adminstrn., Northeastern U., 1966, M.Ed. in Guidance, 1965; m. Marianne Elizabeth Case, Apr. 18, 1966; children—Christopher Lee, Mark Case, Michael Lambert. Tchr., Natick (Mass.) Sch. System, 1963-64; resident dir. Northeastern U., 1965-66; asst. dean students So. Conn. State Coll., 1966-70; dean students St. John's U., Jamaica, N.Y., 1970-74; dean student life Stonehill Coll., 1974—. Trustee Goodard Meml. Hosp., Stoughton, Mass., 1976—, mem. exec. com. bd., 1978—; troop 71 committeeman Old Colony council Boy Scouts Am., 1977—. Mem. Am. Assn. Sch. Adminstrs., Nat. Assn. Student Personnel Adminstrs. (sub-group coordinator), Am. Coll. Personnel Assn., Am. Personnel and Guidance Assn., AAUP, Eastern Assn. Coll. Deans and Advisors to Students, Kappa Delta Pi. Roman Catholic. Clubs: Kiwanis (pres. local club 1973-74) (Flushing, N.Y.); Rotary (pres. local club 1977-78) (Easton, Mass.). Home: 90 Prospect St South Easton MA 02375 Office: 320 Washington St North Easton MA 02356

GALLAGHER, JOSEPH EDWARD, JR., wallcovering wholesaler; b. Worcester, Mass., June 7, 1944; s. Joseph Edward and Marie Genevieve (Casey) G.; student Holy Cross Coll., 1962-65; m. Laura Lappin, July 4, 1969; children—Alex, Lauren, Sybil, Asa. Nat. sales mgr. Bank Travel Club, Boston, 1968-70; exec. v.p. I. Lappin Wallpaper Co., Boston, 1970—; v.p., dir. Wallcovering Bur., 1978; speaker to various wallcovering industry groups. Served with U.S. Army, 1966-68. Mem. Nat. Wallcovering Wholesalers Assn. (founder, pres. New Eng. chpt. 1978, nat. pres. 1978). Roman Catholic. Club: Wellesley (Mass.) Country. Home: 6 Pembroke Rd Weston MA 02193 Office: 282 Congress St Boston MA 02210

GALLAGHER, MICHAEL JOHN, psychologist; b. N.Y.C., Nov. 9, 1945; s. Michael John and Catherine (Vislocky) G.; B.A., Manhattan Coll., 1967; M.A., Columbia U., 1969, Ph.D., 1975; postdoctoral traineeship Am. Inst. for Psychotherapy and Psychoanalysis, 1975-78; m. Mary Ann Dzupin, June 6, 1970. Adj. lectr. Hunter Coll., N.Y.C., 1970-72; asst. prof. N.Y.C. Community Coll., Bklyn., 1971—; adj. asst. prof. Adelphi U., Garden City, N.Y., 1975—; pvt. practice psychology, N.Y.C., 1978—; psychologist Community Guidance Service. NDEA Title I fellow, 1968-70, NIMH asst., 1970-71; certified psychologist, N.Y. Mem. Am. Psychol. Assn., AAUP (pres. N.Y.C. Community Coll. chpt. 1975-76). Roman Catholic. Office: 40 Park Ave New York City NY 10016

GALLAGHER, NORMAN RODNEY, pharmacist; b. Bryn Mawr, Pa., Feb. 13, 1929; s. Laurence Owen (stepfather) and Pauline (Fraim) Densmore; B.S., Albany Coll. Pharmacy, 1954; m. Frances Genevieve Witter, Aug. 24, 1957, children—Norman Rodney, Cheryl Elaine, Lisa Michele. Resident in hosp. pharmacy Jefferson Hosp., Phila., 1954-55; asst. dir. pharmacy Hahnemann Hosp., Phila., 1955-58; chief pharmacist St. James Mercy Hosp., Hornell, N.Y., 1958-61; dir. pharmacy St. Francis Hosp., Port Jervis, N.Y., 1961—; pres. N.Y. State Council Hosp. Pharmacists, 1968-69. Chmn. adminstrv. bd. Drew United Meth. Ch., 1970-73; scoutmaster Troop 78 Boy Scouts Am., 1971-75; v.p. Orange County chpt. Am. Cancer Soc., 1969-71. Served with USMC, 1946-48, 50-51. Mem. Am., Mid Hudson Valley socs. hosp. pharmacists, Port Jervis C. of C. Republican. Home: 93 Orange St Port Jervis NY 12771 Office: 160 E Main St Port Jervis NY 12771

GALLAGHER, PHILIP GEORGE, surgeon; b. Peabody, Mass., Dec. 14, 1929; s. John Joseph and Mary Theresa (O'Neil) G.; B.S., Holy Cross Coll., Worcester, Mass., 1951; M.D., Tufts U., 1955; m. Marie Spellman, May 21, 1956; children—Ellen, Karen, Philip, Celeste, Mark, Dianne. Intern, St. Elizabeths Hosp., Boston, 1960-61, resident, 1961-65; practice medicine specializing in surgery Surg. Vascular Assos., Inc., Boston, 1960—; mem. staff St. Elizabeths Hosp., Boston Hosp. for Women; asso. prof. surgery Tufts Med. Sch., 1975—; instr. surgery Harvard Med. Sch., 1965—. Served with USN, 1959-65. Diplomate Nat. Bd. Med. Examiners, Am. Bd. Surgery. Fellow Am. Coll. Angiology; mem. AMA, A.C.S., New Eng. Med. Soc., Boston Surg. Soc. Home: 10 Nobscot Rd Weston MA 02193 Office: 280 Washington St Brighton MA 02135 also 328 Washington St Wellesley Hills MA 02181

GALLAGHER, THOMAS MARTIN, hosp. and comprehensive health benefit plan exec.; b. Elgin, Ill., Feb. 23, 1936; s. Thomas Anthony and Monica (Hogan) G.; student Coll. St. Thomas, 1954-55, 1959-61; B.S., U. Colo., 1963; M.A., George Washington U., 1973; m. Mary Louise Bennett, Apr. 4, 1961; children—Thomas, Patrick, Ann, Sheila. Controller, Illini Hosp., Silvis, Ill., 1968-70; asst. adminstr., dir. fiscal affairs Morris Cafritz Meml. Hosp., Washington, 1970-73; exec. v.p. Central Med. Health Services, Pitts., 1973-74, pres., 1974—. Vis. lectr. Med. Coll. Va., 1970-71, George Washington U., 1972, preceptor grad. program health care, 1973; cons. HEW, IBM Corp., others. Treas. Rock Island County (Ill.) Half-Way House, 1968-69; bd. dirs. Pa. League Nursing, 1974-79. Served to capt. USAF, 1955-59, 61-67. Licensed nursing home adminstr., Pa. Fellow Hosp. Financial Mgmt. Assn.; mem. Eastern Finance Assn., Am. Hosp. Assn., Med. Group Mgmt. Assn., Hosp. Mgmt. Systems Soc., Am. Coll. Hosp. Adminstrs. Club: Pitts. Field. Home: 6821 Edgerton Ave Pittsburgh PA 15208 Office: Central Med Pavillion Pittsburgh PA 15219

GALLAHUE, WILLIAM MICHAEL, machinery mfg. co. exec.; b. Lawrence, Mass., Aug. 20, 1918; s. Patrick John and Helen (Walsh) G.; student McIntosh Bus. Coll., 1938-39; B.S.M.E. summa cum laude, Tri-State Coll., 1943; postgrad. in engring. Yale U., 1943-44; Ph.D., Calif. State U., 1948; m. Larraine D. Ouelette, Dec. 7, 1968; 1 son, William Michael. Account exec. Merrill Lynch, Pierce, Fenner & Smith, N.Y.C., 1949-53; sales mgr. Am. Machine & Foundry, Boston, 1953-54; exec. v.p. Mt. Hope Machinery Co., Taunton, Mass., 1954—. Served to capt. USAAF, 1943-46. Mem. Paper Industry Mgmt. Assn., T.A.P.P.I., Canadian Pulp and Paper Assn., Sigma Tau. Contbr. articles to profl. jours. Home: 2 Fisher St Taunton MA 02780 Office: PO Box 82 Taunton MA 02780

GALLANT, EDWARD, lawyer, former labor ofcl.; b. N.Y.C., Mar. 23, 1921; s. Louis and Fay (Levitte) G.; B.A., U. Colo., 1948; J.D., U. Conn., 1956; m. Claire Bradoc, Nov. 13, 1944; children—K. Bradoc, Anne Claire. Group leader personnel United Aircraft Corp., 1953-58; exec. dir. Conn. State Employees Assn., 1958-77; admitted to Conn. bar, 1956, U.S. Supreme Ct. bar, U.S. Ct. Appeals bar; since practiced in Hartford; adj. prof. law U. Bridgeport Sch. Law. Served as capt. USAAF, 1941-45, USAF, 1951-52. Decorated D.F.C. with 2 oak leaf clusters, Air medal with 4 oak leaf clusters. Mem. Conn. Bar Assn., Stony Creek Boating Assn. Unitarian-Universalist. Pub., Govt. News. Contbr. articles periodicals. Home: 21 Thimble Island Rd Stony Creek CT 06405 Office: 111 Pearl St Hartford CT 06106 also 1052 Main St Branford CT 06405

GALLEGO, MARCOS BERNARDO, obstetrician, gynecologist; b. Philippines, June 6, 1940; s. Pelagio C. and Marcosa G.; came to U.S., 1968; A.A., U. St. Tomas (Philippines), 1958, M.D., 1965; m. Myrna Solis, May 21, 1970; children—Mark Maurice, Mariel Ann. Intern, V-Luna Gen. Hosp., Quezon City, Philippines, 1964-65; resident dept. ob-gyn Marian Gen. Hosp., Manila, 1965-68; resident in ob-gyn State U. N.Y., Buffalo, 1968-72, fellow in pediatric and adolescent gynecology and corrective gynecol. surgery, 1972-74, clin. asst. instr., 1968-72, clin. instr., 1972-74, asst. prof. ob-gyn, 1974—, dir. teaching program dept. ob-gyn, 1977—; co-chmn. dept. ob-gyn Millard Fillmore Hosp., 1979—; chief resident E.J. Meyer Meml. Hosp., Buffalo, 1972; practice medicine specializing in ob-gyn, pediatric and adolescent gynecology and corrective gynecol. surgery, Buffalo, 1974—; mem. staff Millard Fillmore, Children's, Sisters hosps., Buffalo. Recipient Recognition award Lakes Area Regional Med. Program, Inc., Telephone Lecture Network, 1975. Diplomate Am. Bd. Ob-Gyn. Mem. Buffalo Gynecol. and Obstet. Soc., Erie County (N.Y.), N.Y. State med. socs., AMA, Philippine Med. Assn. Roman Catholic. Contbr. articles to profl. jours. Home: 59 Crestwood Ln Williamsville NY 14221 Office: 3 Gates Circle Buffalo NY 14209

GALLEHER, RICHARD MORSE, union ofcl.; b. Bklyn., Oct. 14, 1943; s. John King and Elizabeth (Morse) G.; B.S., LeMoyne Coll., 1965; M.S., Iowa State U., 1967, postgrad., 1971-72; m. Mari McColl, Feb. 14, 1970; children—Tiffany Kaye, Tricia Annette. Instr. bus. Prince Georges Community Coll., Largo, Md., 1967-69; researcher Comml. Credit Corp., Balt., 1969-71; asst. prof. bus. Upper Iowa U. Fayette, 1971-73; economist research dept. AFL-CIO, Washington, 1973-75, dir. research pub. employees dept., 1975—; chmn. Fed. Employees Pay Council, 1973—; mem. pres.'s prevailing rate adv. com., 1975—. Contbr. articles to profl. jours. Home: 3101 Twig Ln Bowie MD 20715 Office: 815 16th St NW Washington DC 20006

GALLEN, HUGH, gov. N.H. Past mem. N.H. Legislature; gov. N.H., 1979—. Democrat. Office: Office of the Governor State Capitol Bldg Concord NH 03301*

GALLINA, DAVID JOSEPH, JR., physician; b. N.Y.C., May 28, 1940; s. David J. and Ethel (Miller) G.; B.S., Manhattan Coll., 1962; M.D., N.J. Coll. Medicine, 1967; postgrad. psychiatry (N.Y. State scholar medicine and dentistry) Cornell Med. Coll., 1971-73; m. Nancy Teresa Burleigh, Nov. 2, 1968; children—Jessica Blair, Jason Marc. Intern, Martland Med. Center, 1967-68; resident in psychiatry Mt. Sinai Hosp., N.Y.C., 1968-69, N.Y. Hosp.-Cornell Med. Center, 1971-73; individual practice medicine, specializing in psychiatry, Wyckoff, N.J., 1972—; dir. Cedar Hill Learning Disability Center, Wyckoff, 1977—; cons. in field. Served with USNR, 1968-71. Diplomate Am. Bd. Psychiatry and Neurology. Mem. Am. Psychiat. Assn., AMA, Adolescent Psychiatry Soc., Am. Group Therapy Assn. Home: 649 Wishing Well Wyckoff NJ 07481 Office: 541 Cedar Hill Ave Wyckoff NJ 07481

GALLIS, JOHN NICHOLAS, naval officer, health care adminstr.; b. Pitts., Dec. 18, 1944; s. John Vincent Glade and Sylvia (Rizzo) Friedman; B.S. in Health Care Adminstrn., George Washington U., 1977; A.S. in Edn., N.Va. Community Coll., 1975; m. Carole Campbell, June 17, 1967; children—J. Christopher, Robin Noel. Enlisted in USN, 1962, advanced through ranks to lt., 1977; hosp. corpsman USN, Houston, 1962, outpatient services officer Naval Regional Med. Center, New London, Conn., 1974-76, commd. hosp. adminstr., 1977; outpatient services officer Med. Service Corps, Naval Regional Med. Center, Phila., 1977-78; chief patient services service Naval Regional Med. Center, Phila., 1978—. Mem. Parents-Tchrs. Council, Caley Rd. Elementary Sch., King of Prussia, Pa., 1977-78; mem. Sweetbriar Civic Assn., King of Prussia, 1977-78. Decorated Nat. Def. medal, submarine qualification badge, submarine polaris patrol pin with 3 stars. Mem. Assn. Mil. Surgeons U.S., Pa. Interscholastic Athletic Assn., Am. Coll. Hosp. Adminstrs. (asso.). Democrat. Roman Catholic. Home: 727 Suellen Dr King of Prussia PA 19406 Office: Naval Reg Med Center Philadelphia PA 19145

GALLIVAN, GREGORY JOHN, thoracic surgeon; b. Hartford, Conn., Apr. 25, 1938; s. John Norman and Stella (Chmiel) G.; B.S., Tufts U., 1958, M.D., 1962; m. Helen Krawski, Apr. 4, 1964; children—Elizabeth Kerry, Kathleen Holly, Gregory John. Intern, Hartford Hosp., 1962-63; resident in gen. surgery USPHS Hosp., S.I., N.Y., 1963-64, resident in gen. and thoracic surgery, 1964-65; jr. resident internal medicine Hartford Hosp., 1965-66, gen. surg. resident, 1966-67; asst. resident in gen. surgery New Britain (Conn.) Gen. Hosp., 1967-68, chief resident, 1968-69; jr. resident thoracic and cardiovascular surgery U. Tex., Southwestern Med. Sch., Dallas,

1969-70, sr. resident, 1970-71; practice medicine, specializing in thoracic surgery, Springfield, Mass., 1971—; sr. clin. instr. surgery Tufts U., Boston, 1977—; attending thoracic surgeon Baystate Med. Center, Springfield, 1971—, Mercy Hosp., Springfield, 1971—, Holyoke (Mass.) Hosp., 1971—, Providence Hosp., Holyoke, 1971—, Western Mass. Hosp., Westfield, 1971—; cons. in thoracic surgery Noble Hosp., Westfield, 1971—, Holyoke Soldiers Home, 1971—, Ludlow (Mass.) Hosp., 1971—, Wing Meml. Hosp., Palmer, Mass., 1971—, Cooley Dickinson Hosp., Northampton, Mass., 1971—, Northampton State Hosp., 1971—. Baritone soloist Project Opera of Mass., 1976—; pianist, composer; baritone soloist, mem. chorus, mem. chamber chorus, mem. leadership com. Springfield Symphony, 1974-76. Served with USPHS, 1963-65. Diplomate Am. Bd. Surgery, Am. Bd. Thoracic Surgery. Fellow ACS, Am. Coll. Chest Physicians; mem. AMA, Nat. Assn. Residents and Interns, Tex. Thoracic Soc., Mass., Hampden Dist med. socs., Springfield Acad. Medicine, Soc. Thoracic Surgeons. Contbr. articles to med. jours. Home: 108 White Oaks Dr Longmeadow MA 01106 Office: 780 Chestnut St Springfield MA 01107

GALLMAN, RAYMOND FOSTER, photographer; b. Hamilton, N.Y., Aug. 11; s. William Christian and Lyra Clarinda (Kelloway) G.; student Winona Sch. Photography; m. Mary Kozak, July 6, 1940; children—Linda Christine, Carol Marie, Sharon Rae. Lab. mgr. Vantine Studios, Hamilton, N.Y., 1936-41; insp. Savage Arms, Utica, N.Y., 1942-45; lab. mgr. Kane Studios, Hamilton, 1945-47; photographer, br. mgr. Vantine Studios, Utica, 1948-53; pres. Fraternal Composite Service, Inc., Coll. Photographers, Utica, 1954—. Mem. Profl. Photographers Am. Republican. Baptist. Clubs: Elks, Moose. Home: 411 Sunlit Terr Utica NY 13502 Office: 810 Varick St Utica NY 13502

GALLO, ROBERT CHARLES, research scientist; b. Waterbury, Conn., Mar. 23, 1937; s. Francis Anton and Louise Mary (Ciancuilli) G.; B.A., Providence Coll., 1959, D.Sc. (hon.), 1974; M.D., Jefferson Med. Coll., 1963; m. Mary Jane Hayes, July 1, 1961; children—Robert Charles, Marcus. Clin. asso. med. br. Nat. Cancer Inst., NIH, Bethesda, Md., 1965-68, sr. investigator human tumor cell biology br., 1968-69, head sect. cellular control mechanisms, 1969-72, chief lab. tumor cell biology, 1972—. Adj. prof. genetics George Washington U.; cons. M.D. Anderson Hosp. and Tumor Inst., Roswell Park Meml. Inst., U. S.C., Hahneman Med. Sch. Cancer Center. Served with USPHS, 1965-68. Recipient Dameshek award Am. Soc. Hematology, 1974; Superior Service award USPHS, 1975; CIBA-Geigy award for research in biomed. sci., 1977. Mem. Internat. Soc. Hematology, Am. Soc. Clin. Investigation, Am. Soc. Biol. Chemists, Am. Microbiology, Am. Soc. Pharmacology and Exptl. Therapeutics, Biochem. Soc., Am. Assn. Cancer Research, Am. Fedn. Clin. Research, Fedn. Advanced Edn. in Scis., Alpha Omega Alpha. Editorial bd. Jour. Virology, Cancer Research, Life Scis., Biochem. Pharmacology, Year Book of Cancer, Proc. Soc. Exptl. Biology and Medicine, Leukemia Research, Cancer Letters. Research on viruses, biochemistry and leukemia. Home: 8513 Thornden Terr Bethesda MD 20034 Office: Nat Insts Health Bethesda MD 20014

GALLUP, JAMES DAVID, environ. engr.; b. Troy, N.Y., Feb. 18, 1946; s. Irving Frank and Pauline Bernice (Warner) G.; B.S., U. Okla., 1968, M.S., 1970, Ph.D., 1971; m. Jacqueline Price, Dec. 2, 1966; children—Dawn Michelle, Michael Steven. Research asst. U. Okla., Norman, 1969-71; san. engr. EPA Indsl. Pollution Control Research Program, Arlington, Va., 1971-73, supervisory environ. engr. Indsl. Effluent Standards Program, Washington, 1973—, mgr. project, Alexandria, Eygpt, 1977—; cons. Systems Engring. & Research, Inc. Recipient Bronze medal for commendable service EPA, 1973, Silver medal for superior service, 1975; NSF grantee, 1969. Mem. Nat., Fed., Chesapeake water pollution control fedns., Am. Water Works Assn., Am. Textile Chemists and Colorists, Inst. Food Technologists, Sigma Xi, Lambda Tau, Sigma Phi Epsilon. Author: Investigation of Filamentous Bulking in the Activated Sludge Process, 1971. Contbr. articles to profl. jours. Home: 4215 Evergreen Dr Woodbridge VA 22193 Office: 401 M St SW Washington DC 20460

GALONSKY, ROBERT STEVEN, clin. chemist; b. Bklyn., Sept. 28, 1944; s. Harry Benjamin and Sonia (Glassman) G.; B.S. in Chemistry, L.I. U., 1969; m. Leona Bernice Cooper, June 10, 1969; children—Seth Michael, Shara Michele, Aron Chase. Lab. technician Jewish Chronic Disease Hosp., Bklyn., 1961-65; asst. to chief chemist dialysis facilities Downstate Med. Center, Bklyn., 1965-69, chief chemist dialysis facilities Downstate Med. Center and Kings County Hosp., 1969—; lab. technician L.I. Jewish Hosp., 1971; cons. in dialysis. Recipient certificate of reconigition of work in devel. of suitcase kidney Kings County Hosp., 1976; NIH grantee, 1975-77. Mem. Am. Chem. Soc., Am. Assn. Nephrology Nurses and Technicians, Am. Soc. for Artificial Internal Organs. Democrat. Jewish. Bimonthly columnist Dialysis and Transplantation, 1977—, contbg. editor, 1977—; contbr. articles to profl. jours. Home: 3 Pheasant Valley Dr Coram NY 11727 Office: 450 Clarkson Ave Brooklyn NY 11203

GALT, THOMAS MAUNSELL, ins. co. exec.; b. Winnipeg, Man., Can., Aug. 1, 1921; s. George F. and Muriel Julyan (Maunsell) G.; student Queen's U., 1939-41, 45-46, U. Man., 1946-48; m. Helen W. Hyndman, June 15, 1942; children—Lesley Maunsell (Mrs. S.R. Brown), George Hyndman. With Sun Life Assurance Co. Can., Montreal, Que., 1948—, actuary, 1961, chief actuary, 1962, v.p., chief actuary, 1963-68, exec. v.p., 1968-72, pres., chief operating officer, 1972-73, pres., chief exec. officer, 1973—, also dir.; chmn., dir. Sun Life Assurance Co. of Can. (U.K.) Ltd.; pres., dir. other Sun Life subsidiary cos.; dir. Bank of Montreal, Liberty Life Assn. Africa Ltd.; pres., dir. Sun Growth Fund Inc. Mem. adv. bd. Salvation Army Montreal; bd. dirs. Montreal Gen. Hosp. Found., Montreal Symphony Orch., Can. Safety Council; bd. mgmt. Montreal Gen. Hosp. Corp. Served to flight lt., RCAF, 1941-45. Fellow Soc. Actuaries, Can. Inst. Actuaries; mem. Am. Acad. Actuaries, Am. Life Ins. Assn. (provincial v.p.), Better Bus. Bur. Can. (adv. council). Clubs: Mt. Bruno Country, St. James's, Montreal Skeet, Royal Ottawa (Ont., Can.) Golf, Mt. Royal, Nat. Home: 4015 Trafalgar Rd Montreal PQ H3Y 1R1 Canada Office: PO Box 6075 Sta A Montreal PQ H3C 3G5 Canada

GALVIN, THOMAS FRANCIS, architect; b. N.Y.C., Oct. 18, 1926; s. Thomas J. and Ruth (Cronin) G.; B.Arch., Pratt Inst., 1950; m. Margaret Rowland, Sept. 6, 1948; children—Susan Galvin Hall, Stephen; m. 2d, Gladys Lozano, Aug. 1974; children—Thomas Francis, Andrew. With Kokkins & Lyras, architects, N.Y.C., 1950-60, asso., 1956-60; sec. Kolyer Constrn. Corp., N.Y.C., 1956-60; partner Lyras, Galvin & Anaya, architects, N.Y.C., 1960-63, also exec. v.p. Lyras-Adams Ltd. Investment Builders, N.Y.C.; pvt. practice Thomas F. Galvin, AIA, N.Y.C., 1963-64; partner Brown Guenther Battaglia Galvin, architects, N.Y.C., 1965-70; chmn. Bd. Standards and Appeals, City N.Y., 1970-72; exec. v.p. N.Y.C. Conv. and Exhbn. Center Corp., 1972-74; gen. mgr., asst. to chmn. Battery Park City Authority, N.Y.C., 1974—; chmn. bd. Urbanetics Corp.; v.p. United Ams. Devel. and Investment Co., 1977—; adj. prof. architecture Coll. City N.Y., 1971-76; cons. on utilization air rights over govt. owned real property N.Y. Legislature, 1964; mem. archtl. adv. com. N.Y.C. Housing and Redevel. Bd., 1966-67; archtl. adv. com. U. City N.Y., 1967-70, chmn., 1970. Republican candidate Ho. of Reps., 1962, N.Y. Senate, 1965; Rep.-Conservative candidate for Pres. of City Council N.Y.C., 1973; Rep.-Conservative candidate Queens Borough Pres., 1977; Rep. dist. leader 64th Assembly Dist. North Manhattan, 1969-71; lay adv. bd. City Hosp. Center, Elmhurst, N.Y., 1967-70 bd. dirs. West Side Assn. Commerce, N.Y.C., Com. Correspondence for Ind. Higher Edn. in N.Y. State; trustee Manhattan Coll., N.Y.C.; adv. council Booth Meml. Med. Center, Flushing, N.Y., 1977-78. Served with USNR, 1944-46. Registered architect, N.Y., Conn., N.J., Md., Maine; certified Nat. Council Archtl. Registration Bd. Fellow AIA (pres. N.Y. chpt. 1972-73); mem. Queens C. of C., Am. Arbitration Assn., N.Y. Bldg. Congress (gov. 1968-73, 76—), N.Y. State Assn. Architects of AIA (pres. 1972-73). Roman Catholic. Home: 37 Ingram St Forest Hills Gardens NY 11375 Office: 40 Rector St New York City NY 10006

GAMBEE, ROBERT RANKIN, investment banker; b. N.Y.C., Aug. 26, 1942; s. A. Sumner and Eleanor Elizabeth (Brown) G.; A.B., Princeton, 1964; M.B.A., Harvard, 1966. Asso. corporate finance White, Weld & Co., N.Y.C., 1966-71, v.p., 1971-73; v.p. Schroder Capital Corp. affiliate J. Henry Schroder Wagg-London, N.Y.C., 1973-78; v.p. Atlantic Capital Corp. affiliate Deutsche Bank, Frankfort/Dusseldorf, N.Y.C., 1978—; dir. Liberty Communications, Inc. Trustee Dwight-Englewood Sch. Republican. Presbyterian. Clubs: Univ., Princeton, City Midday, Downtown Athletic (N.Y.C.). Author, photographer Nantucket Island, 1973, rev. edit., 1974; Manhattan Seascape, 1975. Home: 1230 Park Ave New York City NY 10028 Office: Atlantic Capital Corp 40 Wall St New York City NY 10005

GAMBINO, S(ALVATORE) RAYMOND, clin. pathologist, educator; b. Bklyn., Oct. 13, 1926; s. Salvatore B. and Rose (Ragona) G.; B.S., Antioch Coll., 1948; M.D., U. Rochester, 1952; m. Madeline Russo, Apr. 5, 1953; children—Catherine, Stephen. Intern, Bellevue Hosp., N.Y.C., 1952-53; resident Columbia-Presbyn., N.Y.C., 1953-55; asso. pathologist St. Lukes Hosp., Milw., 1957-61; dir. labs. Englewood (N.J.) Hosp., 1961-69; dir. Clin. Chemistry Labs., Columbia-Presbyn. Med. Center, 1969-77; asst. prof. pathology Columbia, 1961-69, prof., 1969—, dir. pathology course, 1970-77; chief pathologist, dir. labs. St. Luke's Hosp. Center, 1978—. Trustee Bd. Edn. Englewood Cliffs, N.J., 1966-69. Served with USNR, 1945-46. Mem. Am. Soc. Clin. Pathology (chmn. council on clin. chemistry 1965-69, project dir. 1969—), Am. Chem. Soc. Author: (with R. Galen) Beyond Normality, 1975. Contbg. editor Med. Lab. Observer, 1969—, Clin. Lab. Reference, 1974-77; editorial bd. Am. Jour. Clin. Pathology, 1968-76; editor Lab '78, 1978—. Research in acid-base physiology. Home: 11 Carol Dr Englewood Cliffs NJ 07632 Office: St Luke's Hosp Center Amsterdam at 114th St New York City NY 10025

GAMBLE, (GEORGE) ALVAN, Canadian govt. ofcl.; b. Guelph, Ont., Can., Jan. 10, 1916; s. Hugh Miskelly and Margaret (Quarrell) G.; m. Jean Christeen Melrose, Aug. 3, 1940; children—Stephen John, Timothy Clifford, Lois Rebekah. Mgr., cons., co./union negotiations conciliator, Toronto, Ont., 1945-52; dir. merit employment project Am. Friends Service Com., Indps., 1952-55; exec. asst. to gen. dir., dir. info. Can. Mental Health Assn., Toronto, 1955-62; dir. health services Smith Kline & French (Can.), 1962-68; mktg. analyst Paul Maney Labs. (Can.) Ltd., Toronto, 1968-71; chief market research and immigration fgn. service info. adviser Govt. of Can. Employment and Immigration Commn., Ottawa, Ont., 1971—. Mem. Markham Twp. (Ont.) Planning Bd., 1959; provincial health minister's rep. Bd. of Health Regional Municipality of York, 1965-7k; bd. dirs. Union Villa Sr. Citizens Residence, Markham, 1965-71. Served with RCAF, 1940-45. Decorated Order of Can.; recipient Silver Jubilee medal, 1977. Fellow Am. Public Health Assn.; mem. Profl. Mktg. Research Soc. Baptist. Clubs: Albany (Toronto); Nat. Press (Ottawa). Home: 1097 Bronson Pl Ottawa ON K1S 4H2 Canada

GAMBLE, RICHARD BRADLEY, found exec.; b. Phila., Apr. 9, 1928; s. Clarence James and Sarah Merry (Bradley) G.; B.A., Princeton, 1950; M.A., U. Calif. at Berkeley, 1961; m. Nicki Joe Nichols, Nov. 27, 1976; children by previous marriage—Lincoln Bradley, Thalia Kidder, Ian Potter, Martha Dickinson. Research asso. Internat. Population and Urban Research, U. Calif. at Berkeley, 1959-61; chmn., mng. dir. Enterprise Devel. Co. (Nigeria) Ltd., Lagos, 1961-70; pres. Pathfinder Fund, Boston, 1970—; dir. Academy Press Ltd. (Nigeria), Richware Pottery Ltd. (Nigeria), W. African Book Pubs. Ltd. (Nigeria). Bd. dirs. Planned Parenthood League of Mass. Served with U.S. Army, 1951-52. Mem. Am. Pub. Health Assn., Population Assn. Am., World Population Soc., Soc. for Internat. Devel. Clubs: Princeton N.Y.; Harvard Boston. Home: 72 Sparks St Cambridge MA 02138 Office: 1330 Boylston St Chestnut Hill MA 02167

GAMBUTI, GARY, hosp. adminstr.; b. Paterson, N.J., Sept. 27, 1937; s. Archie and Edith (Santero) G.; B.A., Rutgers U., 1959; M.P.A., Cornell U., 1961. Adminstrv. asst., then asst. v.p. Roosevelt Hosp., N.Y.C., 1961-67; asso. v.p. then sr. adminstrv. v.p. St. Luke's Hosp. Center, N.Y.C., 1967-75, exec. v.p., 1975-78, pres., 1978—. Fellow Am. Coll. Hosp. Adminstrs., N.Y. Acad. Medicine (asso.); mem. Am. Hosp. Assn., N.Y. State Hosp. Assn. (bd. govs. 1979), Greater N.Y. Hosp. Assn. (bd. govs. 1975—, chmn.-elect 1979), Council Hosp. Adminstrs. (pres. 1972-75), Sloan Alumni Assn. Grad. Sch. Bus. and Public Adminstrn. (pres. 1972-74), Order St. John (asso. officer). Office: St Lukes Hosp Center Amsterdam Ave at 114th St New York NY 10025

GAMEROV, IRVING JULIUS, engring. and mfg. exec.; b. Lachina, Que., Can., Apr. 27, 1907; s. Barnet R. and Minnie (Munich) G.; came to U.S., 1919, naturalized, 1941; student St. John's Coll., 1926-28, student law, 1928-30; m. Beatrice Abramson, Sept. 14, 1929; children—Beverly S. Gamerov Cooper, Stuart P. Pres. Ever-Ready Gasoline Sta., Inc., 1928-35; pres., dir. Beverly Concessions, Inc., 1935-37, Seaboard Concessions, Inc., 1937-41, Stuart Machine & Tool Corp., 1941-46; officer, dir. Friscon Motors Inc., 1946-48; pres., dir. Stuart Engring. & Mfg. Co., 1948-58; v.p. 1600 Blvd., Inc., Far Rockaway, N.Y.; pres. Gail Constrn. Corp., 1957-68, dir., 1957-60; also realtor. Pres., dir. Belle Harbor Jewish Center, 1954-58, 66-68, chmn. bd., 1960-65, 69-71; chmn. Rockaway Park United Jewish Appeal, 1958; chmn. Fedn. Jewish Philanthropies, 1959; exec. bd. State of Israel Bonds. Chmn. Naponslt. Belle Harbor, Rockaway Park area council Boy Scouts of Am., 1959, chmn. spl. gifts Rockaway Peninsula, 1964—; pres. Far Rockaway br. Am. Cancer Soc., 1968-73. Dir. Rockaway Democratic Club, 1955—; bd. dirs. Peninsula Gen. Hosp., 1953—. Recipient award Yeshiva U., 1955; service award United Jewish Appeal, 1956; honor award State of Israel bonds, 1956; plaque for service Congregation Chab Zedek, 1957, 68; award Zionist Orgn. Am., 1962; Spl. Achievement award Bonds for Isreal, 1962. Mem. Am. Ordnance Assn. (life), C. of C. of The Rockaways (dir. 1972—), Zionist Orgn. Am. (life; v.p. L.I. zionist region 1965-68, pres. Rockaway Park dist. 1958-64). Mason; mem. B'nai B'rith (past dir.). Home: 181 Beach 135th St Belle Harbor NY 11694 Office: 1600 Central Ave Far Rockaway NY 11691

GAMORAN, ABRAHAM CARMI, mgmt. cons., accountant; b. Cin., Mar. 15, 1926; s. Emanuel and Mamie (Goldsmith) G.; B.B.A., U. Cin., 1948; M.B.A., N.Y. U., 1950; m. Ruth Kump, Apr. 14, 1973; children—Shirley, Mary, Samuel, Benjamin, Joseph. Mem. staff Harris, Kerr Forster & Co., N.Y.C., 1949-52, 56-67, supr. mgmt. adv. services div., 1962-67; mgmt. cons. Burke, Landsberg & Gerber, Balt., 1953-54; dir. systems and research, hospitality div. Helmsley-Spear, Inc., N.Y.C., 1967—; lectr. Hotel Real Estate Inst., N.Y. U., Cornell U., Mich. State U., Okla. State U., Am. Hotel and Motel Assn., others. Recipient medal Wall St. Jour., 1948. Mem. Am. Inst. C.P.A.'s, N.Y. State Soc. C.P.A.'s, Internat. Assn. Hospitality Accountants, Am. Soc. Appraisers (sr.), Nat. Restaurant Assn., N.Y. Real Estate Bd. Democrat. Jewish religion. Contbr. articles to profl. jours. Home: 92-30 56th Ave Elmhurst NY 11373 Office: 420 Lexington Ave Suite 205 New York City NY 10017

GANGSTAD, EDWARD OTIS, botanist; b. Chippewa Falls, Wis., Dec. 18, 1917; s. John Otis and Della Beatrice (Brunberg) G.; B.S., U. Wis., 1942; M.S., Rutgers U., 1947, Ph.D., 1950; m. Ruth Margaret Fletcher, Aug. 22, 1946; children—James Otis, John Erik, Karl Edward, Lillis Marie. Research asst. biochemistry U. Wis., Madison, 1946-47; teaching asst. botany Rutgers U., 1947-50; resident agronomist U.S. Dept. Agr., Belle Glade, Fla., 1950-54; agronomist Tex. Research Found., Renner, 1954-58, sr. agronomist, 1959-61, prin. agronomist, 1962-65; mgmt. agronomist U.S. Army, Washington, 1966-69, botanist, 1970—; sr. scientist natural resources mgmt., AID survey Laos-Thailand, 1969-70. Served to capt., AUS, 1942-45. Fellow AAAS, Am. Inst. Chemists; mem. Am. Soc. Agronomy, Weed Sci. Soc. Am. Aquatic Plant Mgmt. Soc., ASCE. Republican. Unitarian. Contbr. articles to profl. publs. Home: 7909 Greeley Blvd Springfield VA 22152 Office: Office Chief Engrs US Army Washington DC 20314

GANIARIS, NEOPHYTOS, research co. exec.; b. Kallimasia, Chios, Greece, Jan. 1, 1935; s. Michael and Chryssanthe (Rithianos) G.; came to U.S., 1952, naturalized, 1968; student Wagner Coll., 1952-55; B.S. in Chem. Engring., Purdue U., 1957; M.S. in Chem. Engring., N.Y. U., 1960, postgrad. 1961-64; m. Stavroula Metaxas, Feb. 13, 1962; 1 dau., Chryssanthe. Teaching and research asst. N.Y. U., 1957-60, 61-62; research engr. Du Pont Co., Gibbstown, N.J., 1960-61; mgr. process systems div. Struthers Sci. and Internat. Corp., N.Y.C., 1962—. Registered patent agt. Mem. Am. Inst. Chem. Engrs., Am. Chem. Soc., Am. Concrete Inst., United Inventors and Scientists, Am., Phi Lambda Upsilon. Greek Orthodox. Contbr. arrticles to profl. jours. Patentee in freeze concentration, desalination, freeze-drying, crystallization and fluidization. Home: Nettleton Hollow Rd Washington CT 06793 Office: 630 Fifth Ave New York City NY 10020

GANIS, STEPHEN LANE, publisher, editor; b. N.Y.C., Sept. 24, 1951; s. Milton and Beverly (Starkman) G.; B.S. in Journalism, Syracuse U., 1973; m. Claudia S. Harris, Nov. 2, 1974; 1 son, Bret Jason. Editorial asst. N.Y. Daily News, 1973-74; editor-in-chief Bklyn. Graphic, 1974-76; exec. editor, pub. Bklyn. Times, 1976—. Editor: Operation Sail, 1976. Home: 61 Pierrepont St Brooklyn NY 11201

GANNON, ALICE, engring. specialist; b. Boston, July 11, 1940; d. Richard Patrick and Alice Margaret (Woods) G.; B.A. in English, Regis Coll., Weston, Mass., 1968; M.A. in English, Pa. State U., 1970, postgrad., 1970—. Tchr. parochial schs., Boston, Quincy, Norwood, Mass., 1961-69; part-time instr. Pa. State U., 1969-73; free-lance tech. editor, 1969-73; tng. specialist Gilbert Assos., Reading, Pa., 1973-75, engring. specialist, 1975—; mem. adv. bd. on constrn. mgmt. edn. Pa. State U., 1977—. Certified elementary and secondary schs. English tchr., Mass. Mem. Nat. Council Tchrs. English, Am. Soc. Tng. and Devel., Victorian Soc. Am., World Affairs Council. Office: Gilbert Assos PO Box 1498 Reading PA 19603

GANNON, JOSEPH PHILIP, economist, union exec.; b. Scranton, Pa., Mar. 14, 1936; s. Leo William and Catherine (Gallagher) G.; B.A. in Economics, U. Scranton, 1961; M.A. in Economics, Cath. U. Am., 1966; m. Ann Marie Stader, May 5, 1962; children—Michael, Joseph, Daniel, Joann, William, Patricia, Rita, Stephen, Kathleen, Timothy. Economist, Bur. Labor Statistics Dept. Labor, Washington, 1961-62, Manpower Adminstrn., 1962-66; economist NSF, Washington, 1966—; local v.p. Am. Fedn. Govt. Employees Union; expert on immigration of fgn. scientists, engrs., physicians to U.S. Served with AUS, 1956-58. Home: 5510 Lincoln St Bethesda MD 20034 Office: 1800 G St NW Washington DC 20550

GANS, EUGENE HOWARD, pharm. research exec.; b. N.Y.C., Dec. 17, 1929; s. Harry and Sophia (Frankel) G.; B.S., Columbia U., 1951, M.S., 1953; Ph.D., U. Wis., 1956; m. Roslyn Phillips, Jan. 18, 1953; children—Steven Roy, Lois Ellen. Sr. scientist, group leader Hoffmann-LaRoche, Nutley, N.J., 1956-60; head new product devel. sect. Vick Research & Devel. Labs., Richardson-Merrell, Mt. Vernon, N.Y., 1960-64, asst. dir. devel., 1964-67, dir. devel., 1967-71, dir. investigative research, from 1972, now v.p., dir. research and devel. Toiletry div.; asso. dir. Alza Inst. Pharm. Chemistry, Lawrence, Kans., 1971-72; adj. prof. U. Kans. Sch. Pharmacy, 1971—. Mem. Am. Pharm. Assn., Am. Chem. Soc., Soc. Cosmetic Chemists, Soc. Investigative Dermatology, Sigma Xi, Rho Chi, Phi Lambda Upsilon, Columbia U. Coll. Pharmacy and Scis. Alumni Assn. (v.p. 1966). Patentee and author in field. Home: 109 Lincoln Ave Hastings-on-Hudson NY 10706 Office: 1 Bradford Rd Mount Vernon NY 10553

GANS, SAMUEL MYER, temporary employment service exec.; b. Phila., June 10, 1925; s. Arthur and Goldie (Goldhirsh) G.; grad. Peirce Jr. Coll., 1949; m. Ada Zuckerman, Aug. 1, 1948; children—Gary M., Jeffrey R. Pub. accountant, 1949-55; sales exec., 1955-58; franchise owner, pres. Manpower, Inc. Delaware Valley, Pennsauken, N.J., 1958—. Franchise cons.; instr. motivation courses. Active United Fund of Camden County, So. N.J. Devel. Council, Boy Scouts Am., Camden County Bicentennial Com., Score and Ace programs, Camden, YMCA, Allied Jewish Appeal; mem. N.J. Gov.'s Mgmt. Commn., 1971. Trustee Camden County Heart Assn., Camden County Mental Health Assn.; exec. bd. Big Bros. Assn. Camden County; pub. relations com. U.S. Savs. Bonds, Camden and Trenton. Served with USNR, 1943-46. Mem. Nat. Assn. Temporary Services (chpt. relations com. 1973), Nat. Soc. Pub. Accountants, Camden County C. of C., S. Jersey Pub. Relations Assn. (pres. 1967), Better Bus. Bur. Camden County, Adminstrv. Mgmt. Soc., N.J. Assn. Temporary Services (pres. 1970-72), Jewish religion (exec. bd. dirs. congregation). Mason, Lion (pres. Camden 1972-73, Lion of Year 1977). Home: 2128 Glenview St Philadelphia PA 19149 Office: 3720 Marlton Pike Pennsauken NJ 08105

GANT, DUPLAIN RHODES, govt. ofcl.; b. Washington, June 24, 1924; s. Wallace Porter and Carrie (Rhodes) G.; A.B., Dillard U., 1948; M.S.W., Howard U., 1951; D.S.W., Catholic U., 1958; m. Lois Alva Williams, July 24, 1949; children—Adrienne Cecelia, Duplain Rhodes. Supervisory social worker Pub. Assistance Div., D.C. Dept. Pub. Welfare, Washington, 1958-62, chief research sect. planning and research div., 1964-67, chief Bur. Spl. Services, 1967—. Spl. cons. Pres.'s Commn. on Crime in D.C. Chmn. Foundry-Met. Community

Council, Inc., 1968-69. Trustee United Planning Orgn., 1969-74. Served with U.S. Army, 1943-46. Mem. Nat. Assn. Social Workers, Am. Pub. Welfare Assn., D.C. Pub. Health Assn., Am. Pub. Health Assn. Home: 6308 16th St NW Washington DC 20011 Office: 1875 Connecticut Ave NW Washington DC 20009

GANT, JAMES QUINCY, JR., ret. physician; b. Detroit, May 26, 1906; s. James Q. and Alice (Black) G.; A.B., Ohio State U., 1930, M.S., 1931; M.D., Med. Coll. Va., 1935; m. Irene S. Ellis, May 21, 1938 (dec. Feb. 1962); m. 2d, Helen Relic Fentress, June 30, 1962; stepchildren—William George, Carole Ann, Janet Marie Fentress. Intern, Stuart Circle Hosp., Bellevue Hosp.; with USPHS, 1939-46; pvt. practice, 1946—, practice ltd. to dermatology; chmn. skin and allergy service U.S. Vets. Hosp., Washington, 1946-66; emeritus prof. clin. dermatology and syphilology George Washington U. Sch. Medicine. Pres., Assn. Res. Officers USPHS, 1962-65, bd. govs., 1966—. Med. dir. USPHS ret. reserves, 1946-71; active duty D.C. Civil Def., 1959—. Diplomate Am. Bd. Dermatology, Am. Bd. Immunology and Clin. Allergy. Fellow Am. Acad. Dermatology and Syphilology, Am. Acad. Allergy; mem. A.M.A., Med. Soc. D.C., British Astron. Soc., Royal Astron. Soc. Can., Internat. Lunar Soc. (pres. 1958-62, sec. gen. 1963—), Washington Acad. Scis., Assn. Lunar and Planetary Observors (lunar recorder Eastern U.S.), Med. Arts Soc. Greater Washington (pres. 1960-61), Va. Med. Soc., Va. Acad. Sci., Richmond Acad. Medicine, So. Med. Assn., Am. Venereal Disease Assn., Assn. Mil. Surgeons, Washington Acad. Sci., Am. Geophys. Union, Internat. Assn. Planetology. Club: Cosmos (Washington). Author articles. Episcopalian. Home: 4349 Klingle St NW Washington DC 20016

GANZ, VIVIAN HOFF (MRS. ANDREW GANZ), psychologist; b. N.Y.C., May 27, 1944; d. Fred and Joan (Lamm) Hoff; M.A., Columbia, 1965; m. Andrew R. Ganz, June 5, 1971; 1 dau., Elissa Tamara. Sr. research scientist N.Y. State Psychiat. Inst.-Columbia-Presbyn. Med. Center, N.Y.C., 1965-71; staff psychologist Springfield (Mass.) Hosp. Med. Center, 1972-73; psychometrician Hillside div. L.I. Jewish-Hillside Med. Center, Glen Oaks, N.Y., 1973-75; psychol. research, 1975—. Mem. Am., Eastern psychol. assns., Psi Chi. Contbr. research papers to profl. jours. Address: 114 E 72d St New York City NY 10021

GAQUER, JOHN GEORGE, aircraft and missile components mfg. co. exec.; b. Paris, Mar. 24, 1924; s. George Eugene and Leone F. (Cassereau) G.; came to U.S., 1929, naturalized, 1943; student Newark Coll. Engring., 1945-47; m. Denise A. Leroy, July 24, 1948; children—Alain, Denis, Maurice. Staff, Bendix Aviation Co., Teterboro, N.J., 1942-43, 51-52, Air Equipment Co., Paris, 1947-48, Westinghouse Electric Co., Bloomfield, N.J., 1949-50; with George E. Gaquer and Son, Clifton, N.J., 1952—, now v.p. mfg. and research and devel.; lectr. in field. Vice-pres. Tamarack council Boy Scouts Am., Rutherford, N.J., 1974-79. Served with USAAF, 1943-45; ETO. Clubs: Masons, Shriners. Patentee heart resuscitation machine. Office: 10 Austin Pl Clifton NJ 07014

GARBARINO, ROBERT PAUL, lawyer; b. Wanaque, N.J., Oct. 6, 1929; s. Attilio and Teresa (Napello) G.; B.B.A. cum laude, St. Bonaventure U., 1951; J.D. summa cum laude, Villanova U., 1956; m. Joyce A. Sullivan, June 29, 1957; children—Lynn Marie, Lisa Clare, Mark, Steven. Admitted to Pa. bar, 1957; law clk. to chief judge U.S. Dist. Ct., Phila., 1956-57; asst. counsel Phila. Electric Co., 1957-61, asst. gen. counsel, 1961-62; partner firm Kania & Garbarino and predecessor, Bala Cynwyd, 1962—. Trustee in bankruptcy Tele-Troncis Co., 1963; right of way cons. Edison Electric Inst., 1960-62; lectr. appraisal, right of way, utilities, real estate seminars, 1959—; mem. community leadership seminar Fels Inst. Local and State Govt., 1961. Mem., chmn. bd. consultors Villanova U. Law Sch.; mem., chmn. pres.'s council St. Bonaventure U. Served with USMCR, 1951-53. Recipient Most Outstanding Bus. Student award St. Bonaventure U., 1951; Faculty award Villanova Law Sch., 1956. Mem. Am., Fed., Fed. Power, Pa., Phila., Montgomery bar assns., Assn. of Army, Thomas Moore Soc., Order of Coif. Roman Catholic. Club: Lawyers (Phila.). Contbr. articles to profl. publs. Home: 302 Conestoga Rd Wayne PA 19087 Office: Two Bala Cynwyd Plaza Bala Cynwyd PA 19004

GARCIA, CELSO-RAMON, physician, educator; b. N.Y.C., Oct. 31, 1921; s. Celso Ondina and Oliva Menendez (del Valle) G.; B.S., Queens Coll., 1942; M.D., State U. N.Y. Downstate Med. Center, 1945; M.A. (hon.), U. Pa., 1972; m. Shirley Jean Stoddard, Oct. 14, 1950; children—Celso-Ramon, Sarita Stoddard. Intern, Norwegian Hosp., Bklyn., 1945-46; resident Cumberland Hosp., Bklyn., 1948-53; asst. prof. obstetrics and gynecology U. P.R., San Juan, 1953-55; co-dir. Rock Reproductive Study Center, asst. obstetrician and gynecologist Boston Lying-In Hosp., asso. surgeon Free Hosp. for Women, Brooklin, Mass., 1955-65; sr. scientist, dir. tng. program in physiology reprodn. Worcester Found. for Exptl. Biology, Shrewsbury, Mass., 1960-62; asst. surgeon, chief Infertility Clinic, Mass. Gen. Hosp., clin. asso. obstetrics and gynecology Harvard Med. Sch., 1962-65; prof. obstetrics and gynecology U. Pa., Phila., 1965—, William Shippen, Jr. prof. human reprodn., 1970—, also vice-chmn. dept. obstetrics-gynecology. Ayerst lectr. Pacific Coast Fertility Soc., 1974; Pincus lectr. Wayne State U., 1974, Worcester Mem. sci. adv. bd. Inst. Human Reprodn. and Fetal Devel., U. Tel Aviv Med. Sch., 1970; rapporteur com. of experts on clin. aspects oral gestogens WHO, Geneva, Switzerland, 1965; mem. ad hoc adv. com. Nat. Inst. Child Health and Devel., 1971-75. Chmn. nat. med. adv. com. Planned Parenthood World Population, 1971-74. Bd. dirs. Am. Fertility Soc. Served with U.S. Army, 1946-48. Recipient Carl G. Hartman award Am. Soc. Study Sterility, 1961, Sequicentennial award U. Mich., 1967. Sidney Graves fellow in gynecology Harvard Med. Sch., 1955. Mem. Am. Physiol. Soc., Am. Gynecol. Soc., Am. Coll. Obstetricians and Gynecologists, AMA, A.C.S., Coll. Physicians Phila., Boston, Phila. obstet. socs., Alpha Epsilon Delta. Republican. Presbyn. Mason. Mem. original team developing application of progestagen-estrogen combinations for oral contraception (the Pill) developer, dir. 1st formal tng. program in physiology of reprodn. in U.S. Home: 109 Merion Rd Merion PA 19066 Office: 3400 Spruce St Philadelphia PA 19104

GARCIA, FERDINAND LAWRENCE, lawyer, educator; b. Tampa, Fla., Aug. 1, 1909; s. Ferdinand Garcia and Elena (Rodriguez) A.; B.S. cum laude, N.Y. U., 1938; LL.B., Bklyn. Law Sch., 1949, J.D., 1967; LL.M., Nat. U., 1951; M.A., Fordham U., 1967; m. Grace C. Coverley, Jan. 12, 1946. Admitted to N.Y. bar, 1950; practice law, Washington, 1953-61; sr. analyst Hoit, Rose & Troster, N.Y.C., 1930-42; mgr. analytical dept. R.M. Horner & Co., N.Y.C., 1946-49; prof. finance Southeastern U., 1950-56; asst. prof. Georgetown U., 1956-61; asst. prof. to asso. prof. Fordham U., 1961-77, asso. prof. emeritus, 1977—, chmn. dept. finance, 1969-72. Served with AUS, 1942-46, 50-53; lt. col. Res. ret. Fellow Nat. Fedn. Fin. Analysts; mem. Am. Econ. Assn., Am., N.Y. State bar assns., Am. Finance Assn., Assn. for Social Econs., N.Y. Soc. Security Analysts, Mil. Order World Wars, Res. Officers Assn., Beta Gamma Sigma, Phi Delta Phi, Pi Gamma Mu, Delta Sigma Pi. Republican. Roman Catholic. Club: National Press (Washington). Editor: Ency. Bus. and Finance 1949—. Contbr. articles to profl. jours. Home: Thornycroft Garth Rd Scarsdale NY 10583 Office: Fordham U Rose Hill Bronx NY 10458

GARCIA, ROBERT, Congressman; b. Bronx, N.Y., Jan. 9, 1933; s. Rafael and Rosa (Rodrigues) G.; E.E., RCA Inst., 1957; B.A., CCNY; children—Robert, Kenneth. Formerly with IBM, Control Data Corp.; mem. N.Y. State Assembly, 1966-67; mem. N.Y. State Senate, 1967-78, dep. minority leader, mem. select com. on criminal instns., 1975-78; mem. 95-96th Congresses from 21st N.Y. Dist., mem. House Banking, Fin. and Urban Affairs Com. subcoms. on housing and community devel., econ. stblzn., cities, chmn. census and population subcom. of Post Office and Civil Service Com.; mem. N.Y. State Temp. Commn. to Evaluate Drug Laws. Mem. Democratic Charter Commn., 1974, del. Dem. Nat. Conv., 1976; bd. dirs. S. Bronx Overall Econ. Devel. Corp., Ams. for Dem. Action, P.R. Legal Def. and Edn. Fund, Harlem Urban Devel. Corp., Nat. Urban Coalition Com. of Hispanics and Blacks, League for Aid Crippled Children; mem. nat. council LaRaza Hispanic Criminal Justice Adv. Council. Served with AUS, 1951-52. Decorated Bronze Star (2). Mem. NCCJ, NAACP, Urban League, Aspira, Puerto Rican Forum, Puerto Rican Nat. Assn. Civil Rights. Office: US House of Reps Washington DC 20515

GARDINER, WILLIAM DOUGLAS HAIG, bank exec.; b. Chatham, Ont., Can., Apr. 21, 1917; s. William Henry and Elsie May (Armstrong) G.; grad. Kennedy Collegiate Sch., Windsor, Ont.; m. Jean Elizabeth Blatchford, Sept. 5, 1945; children—Donald W.B., Campbell D., Gregory F. With Royal Bank of Can., asst. gen. mgr., Montreal, Que., from 1961, Vancouver, B.C., from 1964, v.p., dist. gen. mgr., from 1967, dep. chmn., exec. v.p., Toronto, Ont., 1973-77, vice chmn., 1977—. Pres., Boys and Girls Clubs of Can., 1976. Served to lt. comdr. RCNVR. Presbyterian. Clubs: York, Toronto, Rosedale Golf (Toronto); St. James (Montreal); Vancouver. Office: Royal Bank of Canada Royal Bank Plaza Toronto ON M5J 2J5 Canada*

GARDNER, ALLAN WILLIAM, photog. mfg. co. exec.; b. Rochester, N.Y., Oct. 20, 1921; s. Harold Arthur and Anna (Bauer) G.; B.Chem.Engring., U. Mich., 1949; postgrad. Rochester Inst. Tech., 1968-70; m. Lorma Elizabeth Shaw, Oct. 26, 1946; children—Craig Shaw, Anne Shaw. Methods engr. Indsl. Engring. div. Eastman Kodak Co., Kodak Park Works, Rochester, 1949-51, chem. engr. Roll Coating div., 1951-59, tng. assignment in personnel, quality control and prodn., 1959-60, coordinating engr., 1960-65, asst. supr. engring. and maintenance, 1965-67, supr. engring. and maintenance, 1967—. Vice pres. Hoover Dr. Sch. PTA, 1958, pres., 1959. Served with AUS, 1944-46. Registered profl. engr., N.Y. Mem. Am. Inst. Chem. Engrs., N.Y. (sec. Monroe chpt. 1968-69, dir. 1970-71, v.p. 1972, pres. 1974, membership chmn. 1975, v.p. area 5, 1976), Nat. (chmn. membership com. 1977-78) socs. profl. engrs. Clubs: Masons, Flower City Toastmasters. Home: 47 Oak Manor Ln Pittsford NY 14534 Office: Roll Coating Div Kodak Park Rochester NY 14650

GARDNER, BERNARD, surgeon, educator; b. Bklyn., Oct. 1, 1931; s. Charles and Selma (Lovenberg) G.; A.B. cum laude, N.Y. U., 1954, M.D., 1956; m. Joan E. Mann, Dec. 18, 1954; children—Karen A., Pamela D., Robert A. Intern, Bellevue Hosp. Center, N.Y.C., 1956-57; resident Mt. Sinai Hosp., N.Y.C., 1957-58, U. Calif. Med. Center, San Francisco, 1961-65; asst. prof. surgery State U. N.Y. Downstate Med. Center, Bklyn., 1965-68, asso. prof., 1968-72, prof., 1972; prof. surgery, dir. Bklyn. Cancer Center, Bklyn., 1973—; cons. VA Hosp., Luth. Med. Center, Swedish Hosp., Meth. Hosp., Kingsbrook Med. Center (all Bklyn.); dir. div. surg. oncology Kings County Hosp., 1971. Served to capt. USAF, 1958-60. Fellow Am. Cancer Soc., 1965-68; Markle fellow, 1968-73; recipient numerous grants, 1962—. Fellow A.C.S.; mem. Soc. U. Surgeons, Assn. Acad. Surgery (chmn. com. on issues 1971—), N.Y. Surg. Soc., N.Y. Cancer Soc., Soc. Exptl. Medicine and Biology. Author: Emergency Surgery, 1974; Basic Surgery: Patient Oriented Text, 1978. Research in metabolic effects of cancer, mechanism of gall stone dissolution. Home: 5 Ivy St Cedarhurst NY 11516 Office: 450 Clarkson Ave Brooklyn NY 11203

GARDNER, CHARLES WESLEY, JR., psychoanalyst, educator; b. Bridgeport, Conn., Oct. 24, 1924; s. Charles Wesley and Edna (Tuttle) G.; student Harvard, 1941-43, U. Wis., 1944; M.D., U. Chgo., 1948; postgrad. N.Y. Psychoanalytic Inst., 1955-61; m. Josephine Elizabeth Sperry, May 15, 1948; children—Charles S., Cynthia R., Jonathan B., Anne E., Sarah S. Intern, Strong Meml. Hosp. U. Rochester, 1948-49; resident Yale U. Sch. Medicine, 1949-51; practice medicine, specializing in psychiatry, New Haven, 1953—; instr. psychiatry Yale Sch. Medicine, 1953-57, asst. clin. prof., 1957-66, asso. clin. prof., 1967-78, clin. prof., 1978—, co-dir. Yale Psychiat. Inst., 1966-69, asso. clin. prof. psychiatry, med. dir. Yale Psychiat. Inst., 1969—; attending psychiatrist Yale-New Haven Hosp., 1957—; faculty Smith Coll. Sch. Social Work, 1975—. Served with AUS, 1943-46, 51-53. Recipient Career Tchr. grant Nat. Inst. Mental Health, 1955-57. Mem. Am. Psychiat. Assn., Western New Eng. Psychoanalytic Soc. and Inst. (trustee inst. 1975—), N.Y. Psychoanalytic Inst. and Soc., Am. Psychoanalytic Assn., Fairfield County, Conn. med. socs., N.Y. Acad. Scis., Sigma Xi. Club: Harvard of So. Conn. (New Haven); Black Rock Yacht (Bridgeport). Contbr. articles to profl. jours. Home: 100 Verna Hill Rd Fairfield CT 06430 Office: Yale Psychiatric Inst Box 12A Yale Station New Haven CT 06520

GARDNER, ELIOT LAWRENCE, psychobiologist, educator; b. Boston, Dec. 31, 1940; s. John Jay and Frances (Albert) G.; A.B., Harvard, 1962; M.A., McGill U., Montreal, Que., Can., 1964, Ph.D. (USPHS-NIMH research fellow), 1966; m. Elizabeth Loomis Barkentin, Dec. 18, 1965. Research fellow pharmacology Albert Einstein Coll. Medicine, N.Y.C., 1969-72, USPHS tng. fellow, 1970-71, 71-72, asso. neurology, 1972—, asst. prof. pharmacology, 1973—, USPHS-NIH research grantee, 1974—; adj. asst. prof. psychobiology N.Y. U., N.Y.C., 1970-73; asso. prof. biopsychology City U. N.Y., 1973—. Served to capt. Biomed. Scis. Corps, USAF, 1966-69. Recipient Career Scientist award Health Research Council N.Y., 1975. Mem. Soc. Neurosci., Am., Eastern psychol. assns., AAAS, Psychonomic Soc., Brit. Brain Research Assn., Sci. Research Soc. N.Am., AAUP, N.Y. Acad. Scis., Sigma Xi. Contbr. articles in field to profl. jours. Home: 69 Auldwood Rd Stamford CT 06902 Office: Dept Pharmacology Albert Einstein Coll Medicine 1300 Morris Park Ave New York City NY 10461

GARDNER, LEONARD BURTON, II, computer instrumentation exec.; b. Lansing, Mich., Feb. 16, 1927; s. Leonard Burton and Lillian Marvin (Frost) G.; B.Sc., U. Calif. at Los Angeles; M.Sc., Golden State U., 1952, Sc.D. summa cum laude, 1954; M.Sc. in Applied Sic., Augustana Coll., 1977; m. Barbara Jean Zivi, June 23, 1950; children—Karen Sue, Jeffrey Frank. In radiation measurements Atomics Internat., Canoga Park, Calif., 1956-59; in Hd radiation effects Litton Systems, Woodland Hills, Calif., 1959-62; scientist-in-charge radiation effects Northrop Space Labs., Hawthorne, Calif., 1962; chief Radioisotope Lab., Naval Civil Engring. Lab., Port Hueneme, Calif., 1963-68; chief Aircraft Weapons Lab., Rock Island, Ill., 1968-77; chief computer instrumentation br. Army Armament Research and Devel. Command, Dover, N.J., 1977—; cons. to industry in instrumentation engring. and mfg. processes. Recipient Army Research and Devel. Achievement award, 1970. Mem. IEEE (sr.), ASTM, Sigma Xi. Contbr. articles to profl. jours. Home: 7 Acorn St North Caldwell NJ 07006 Office: DRDAR-TSI-C Dover NJ 07801

GARDNER, WARREN EDWARD, JR., pub. relations exec., govt. ofcl.; b. N.Y.C., May 23, 1922; s. Warren Edward and Alice (Hill) G.; B.S., Hampton Inst., 1947; M.S. in Journalism, Syracuse U., 1949; m. Oveta Kellogg, Feb. 27, 1949; 1 son, Douglas Wayne. Reporter, Norfolk (Va.) Jour. & guide, 1949; Balt. Afro-Am. newspaper, 1949-50; staff writer Our World Pub. Co., Inc., N.Y.C., 1950-55; asst. pub. relations officer N.Y. Dept. Pub. Works, Albany, 1956-58; newswriter-producer WNEW Radio, N.Y.C., 1958-59, pub. relations rep. Pitney-Bowes, Inc., Stamford, Conn., 1959-60; asst. dir. pub. relations N.Y.C. Commn. on Human Rights, 1960, dir. pub. relations, 1961-62; dir. information asst. to adminstrv. dir. Moblzn. for Youth, Inc., N.Y.C., 1962-66; asst. press sec. to gov. N.Y., 1966-73; pub. affairs officer Fed. Energy Office, N.Y.C., 1974; asst. adminstr. N.Y.C. Parks, Recreation, Cultural Affairs Adminstrn., 1974-75; regional dir. bus. and pub. affairs U.S. Gen. Services Adminstrn., N.Y.C., 1975—. Served with USNR, 1944-46. Mem. Pub. Relations Soc. Am. Democrat. Episcopalian. Home: 280 9th Ave New York City NY 10001 Office: 26 Fed Plaza New York City NY 10007

GARDNER, WILLIAM MICHAEL, sec. state N.H.; b. Manchester, N.H., Oct. 26, 1948; s. William and Mildred (Claus) G.; B.A., U. N.H., 1970; postgrad. London Sch. Econs., 1972; M.E., U. N.C., 1973. Mem. N.H. Ho. of Reps. from Hillsborough County Dist. 30, 1973-76; sec. of state N.H., 1976—. Mem. Hillsborough County Exec. Com., 1973-74. Mem. London Sch. Econs. Soc. Phi Sigma, Phi Mu Delta. Roman Catholic. Address: 204 State House Concord NH 03301

GARDY, THAIS, librarian; b. Danville, Pa., Nov. 23, 1947; d. Francis Peter and Sophia (Leginski) Gardy; B.A., Pa. State U., 1969; M.L.S., U. Pitts., 1971. Reference librarian Carlow Coll., Pitts., 1971, Enoch Pratt Free Library, Balt., 1972-73; librarian Ins. Inst. for Hwy. Safety, Washington, 1974-77; librarian Pub. Utility Commn., Harrisburg, Pa., 1977—. Mem. ALA, Spl. Libraries Assn., Hist. Soc. Pa., Western Pa. Hist. Soc. Contbr. profl. jours. Home: 301 Chestnut St Harrisburg PA 17101 Office: 100 North Office Bldg Harrisburg PA 17120

GAREN, JOHN THEODORE, field service mgmt. exec.; b. Canton, Ohio; s. Isabelle Foster Garen; student comml. tech. schs.; m. Josephine Marie Doebel, June 24, 1967; 1 son, John Theodore. Field engr. ITT/Fed. Electric Corp., Paramus, N.J., 1966-72, ITT/Def. Communications, Nutley, N.J., 1972-73; project engr. Singer Bus. Machines Co., San Leandro, Calif., 1973-75; mgr. tech. ops. customer service div. TRW Co., Fairfield, N.J., 1975—. Served with USAF, 1962-66. Home: 6 Marrianne Terr Ogdensburg NJ 07439 Office: 70 New Dutch Ln Fairfield NJ 07006

GARGAN, JOSEPH EDWARD, camp dir.; b. Simsbury, Conn., July 17, 1900; s. Peter E. and Mary M. (Kelly) G.; B.S., U. Ill., 1924; M.A., Columbia, 1925. Dir. phys. edn. Kingswood Sch., West Hartford, Conn., 1926-45; dir. health and phys. edn. Hartford (Conn.) Bd. Edn., 1945-65; owner, dir., West Hill Camps, New Hartford, Conn., 1945—; cons. Conn. Dept. Health, Hartford, 1965-68. Recipient awards Conn. Assn. Health and Phys. Edn., 1965, No. Conn. Football Ofcls. Assn., 1960, Hartford Bd. Edn., 1965. Recipient gold key Conn. Sportswriters Alliance, 1977. Mem. Am. Camping Assn., Nat. Football Found., Am. Assn. Health and Phys. Edn. Roman Catholic. Clubs: Regents, Rotary. Contbr. articles to Athletic Jour., Am. Camping Assn. Home: 57 Robin Rd West Hartford CT 06107

GARGIRELLO, GABRIEL ANTHONY, publishing co. exec.; b. Paterson, N.J., Aug. 13, 1940; s. Gabriel and Louise (Sirvidio) G.; B.S., Fairleigh Dickinson U., 1964; m. Roberta Ann Sincaglia, Aug. 24, 1975; children—Karen, Christine, Dori, Lori, Gale. High sch. tchr., Paterson, 1964-65; motion picture exhibitor Len-Vera Corp., Denville, N.J., 1965-73; tchr. Sch. #15, Paterson, 1973-74; dist. sales mgr. Field Enterprises Ednl. Corp., Jersey City, 1974-75, div. sales mgr., 1975—. Roman Catholic. Home: 19 Myrtle Ave Caldwell NJ 07006 Office: 774 Manner Rd Suite 211C Staten Island NY 10314

GARLAND, MERRITT FREDERICK, JR., physician; b. Boston, Feb. 25, 1920; s. Merritt Frederick and Alice Fay (Dean) G.; B.A., Middlebury Coll., 1941; M.D., Tufts U., 1946; M.P.H., Johns Hopkins U., 1976; m. Saralou Chaffee, Dec. 19, 1943; children—Leane, Christopher, Laurance, Marc. Intern, Central Maine Gen. Hosp., Lewiston, 1946-47; intern Santa Clara County Hosp., San Jose, Calif., 1949-50, resident, 1950-52; resident Mary Fletcher Hosp.-U. Vt. Sch. Medicine, Burlington, 1952-53; pvt. practice medicine specializing in obstetrics and gynecology, Greenfield, Mass., 1953-72; clinician, family planning sect., div. maternal health and population dynamics Md. Dept. Health and Mental Hygiene, Preventive Medicine Adminstrn., 1972-74, project dir. family planning, Balt., 1974—. Incorporator Star Island Corp. Served with M.C., U.S. Army, 1942-49. Diplomate Am. Bd. Obstetrics and Gynecology. Fellow Am. Coll. Obstetricians, Gynecologists; mem. Inst. on Religion in Age of Sci., Am. Assn. Maternal and Child Health, Am. Fertility Soc., Assn. Planned Parenthood Physicians, Am. Soc. Psychoprophylaxis in Obstetrics, Am. Soc. Psychosomatic Obstetrics and Gynecology, Am. Pub. Health Assn., AMA, Mass. Med. Soc., Internat. Childbirth Edn. Assn., Am. Assn. Sex Educators, Counselors and Therapists, Council for Livable World, Common Cause, SANE, ACLU, Isles of Shoals Assn. Unitarian. Home: 12 Keegan Ln Greenfield MA 01301 Office: Preventive Medicine Adminstrn PO Box 13528 Baltimore MD 21203

GARLEY, RICHARD EDWARD, diversified service co. exec.; b. Jersey City, Sept. 24, 1926; s. Richard Harold and Mary (Scott) G.; B.S., St. Peter's Coll., 1950; J.D., St. John's Law Sch., 1954; LL.M., N.Y. U., 1957; m. Susan Prober, Nov. 25, 1977; children by previous marriage—Kathleen, Scott, Gregory, Kelly, Thomas. With Arthur Andersen & Co., C.P.A.'s, N.Y.C., 1952-55; admitted to N.Y. bar, 1954; with firm Kramer, Marx, Greenlee & Backus, N.Y.C., 1955-58; sr. v.p., treas., sec., gen. counsel Novo Corp., N.Y.C., 1958—. Served with USNR, 1944-46. C.P.A., N.Y. Mem. Am. Bar Assn. Home: 114 E 72d St New York City NY 10021 Office: 31 W 53d St New York City NY 10019

GARMEL, DAVID CHARLES (MELTZER), producer; b. Bklyn.; s. Harry and Eva (Garcia) Meltzer; B.S., Ithaca Coll., 1962; student Northeastern U., 1971—. Actor various stock cos., 1957-61; producer Windham (N.H.) Playhouse, 1961—, Town and Country Playhouse, Salem, N.H., 1970—; speech pathologist Pelham (N.H.) Sch. Dist., 1964—. Bd. dirs. Children's Community Co-op. Center, Salem, N.H.; mem. Merimack Valley Charismatic Prayer Group. Roman Catholic. Home: RFD 2 Box 310 Pelham NH 03076 Office: Sherburne Sch Pelham NH 03051

GAROFALO, THOMAS DON, constrn. co. exec.; b. Waterbury, Conn., Aug. 29, 1922; s. Joseph Thomas and Connie Marie G.; B.A., Am. Internat. U., 1952. With T & C Garofalo Constrn. Co., Waterbury, 1940—, pres., 1952—; cons. NASA. Served with USNR, 1942-46. Mem. Nat. Assn. Home Builders (dir.), New Eng. Council Home Builders, Conn. State Home Builders Assn. (past pres.), Home Builders Assn. Greater Waterbury (pres., editor newsletter), Am.

Mgmt. Assn., VFW. Roman Catholic. Clubs: K.C. Home: 10 Medway Rd Waterbury CT 06708

GARON, JOSEPH DANIEL, lawyer; b. N.Y.C., Jan. 8, 1931; s. Joseph Felix and Margaret (McCarthy) G.; B.A., Fordham U., 1953, LL.B., 1958; m. Claudia A. Blouske, Oct. 24, 1954; children—Cathleen, Susan, Lisa, Kerry. Admitted to N.Y. State bar, 1960; asso. firm Brumbaugh Graves Donohue & Raymond, N.Y.C., 1958-65, partner firm, 1965—; adj. asso. prof. law Fordham U., N.Y.C., 1971—, chmn. alumni fedn., 1975—. Served to 1st lt. U.S. Army, 1954-56. Mem. Am. Patent Law Assn., N.Y. State Bar Assn. Home: 25 Birch Brook Rd Bronxville NY 10708 Office: Brumbaugh Graves Donohue & Raymond 30 Rockefeller Plaza New York City NY 10020

GAROVOY, MARVIN ROBERT, nephrologist; b. N.Y.C., June 14, 1943; s. Nathan and Ann (Braffman) G.; A.B., N.Y. U., 1964, postgrad. Grad. Sch. Arts and Sci., 1964-65; M.D. cum laude, State U. N.Y., Bklyn., 1969; m. Seena Fischer, June 7, 1969; children—Natara, Jocelyn. Intern, Bellevue Hosp., N.Y.C., 1969-70; resident in medicine N.Y. U. Med. Center, N.Y.C., 1970-71; fellow in nephrology Peter Bent Brigham Hosp., Boston, 1971-73, transplant nephrologist, 1973—, asso. dir. tissue typing lab., 1975-78, dir. clin. services tissue typing lab. Inter Hosp. Organ Bank, 1978—; asst. prof. medicine Med. Sch., Harvard U., Boston. Served with USAF, 1973-75. Diplomate Am. Bd. Internal Medicine. Mem. A.C.P., Am., Internat. socs. nephrology, Am. Fedn. Clin. Research, Am. Assn. Clin. Histocompatibility Testing, Alpha Omega Alpha. Contbr. articles to profl. publs. Office: Peter Bent Brigham Hospital 721 Huntington Ave Boston MA 02115

GARRAHY, J. JOSEPH, state ofcl.; b. Providence, Nov. 26, 1930; s. John and Margaret (Neylon) G.; ed. U. R.I., U. Buffalo; hon. degree Salve Regina Coll., Newport, 1974; m. Margherite DiPietro, 1956; children—Colleen, John, Maribeth, Sheila, Seaha. Mem. Coms. to Study Juvenile Delinquency, Drug Addiction; mem. R.I. Senate, 1963-69, dep. majority leader, Democratic State chmn., 1967-68; lt. gov. R.I., 1969-76, gov., 1977—; chmn. Gov.'s Council on Youth Opportunities. Del. Dem. Nat. Conv., 1968. Past gen. chmn. Heart Fund, Cerebral Palsy Drive, Meeting St. Sch. Campaign; div. chmn. United Way; bd. dirs. nat. youth in govt. Project Close-Up; mem. advisory com. Brown U. Med. Sch. Served with USAF. Roman Catholic. Office: Office of Gov State Capitol Bldg Providence RI 02903*

GARRECHT, DAVID ARTHUR, clergyman; b. Bound Brook, N.J., Oct. 16, 1936; s. Arthur Henry and Eleanor Evelyn (Washeleski) G.; B.S., Denison U., 1960; M.Div., Andover Newton Theol. Sch., 1964; m. Jean Elisabeth Condon, Apr. 20, 1963; children—Peter Arthur, Stephen Paul, Christopher John. Interim pastor First Baptist Ch., Nantucket Island, Mass., 1962-63; ordained to ministry Bapt. Ch., 1964; asso. pastor First Bapt. Ch., Brattleboro, Vt., 1964-66; missionary pastor S.E. Vt. Christian Parish, Guilford, Vernon and Halifax, 1967-69; pastor South Hampton (N.H.) Bapt. Ch., 1969-73; minister camping and leadership devel. Am. Bapt. Chs. of Conn., Hartford, 1973-77; adminstrv. minister The Parish Center, Brattleboro, 1977—; mem. N.E. sectional team of Christian educators, mem. ministers council Am. Bapt. Chs., U.S.A. Chmn. U. Vt. in Brattleboro Com., 1965-67; town rep. Windham Regional Planning Commn., 1967-69. Mem. Guilford Hist. Soc., Friends of Music in Guilford, Brattleboro Civic Club. Home: Guilford Center Rd Guilford VT 05301 Office: RFD 3 Box 91 Brattleboro VT 05301

GARRETT, PHILIP LEROY, counseling psychologist; b. Hanover, Pa., Apr. 17, 1927; s. LeRoy Earl and Lilly May (Lohr) G.; A.B. in Math., Gettysburg Coll., 1950; M.A. in Guidance and Counseling, Cath. U., Am., 1968, Ph.D., in Higher Edn. Adminstrn., 1971; m. Peggy Louise Deardorff, June 7, 1967. Master of English, Massanutten Mil. Acad., Woodstock, Va., 1950-52; master of math. and sci. Mercersburg (Pa.) Acad., 1952-63; head phys. sci. dept. Sidwell Friends Sch., Washington, 1963-64; asst. prof. math. and sci. York Coll. of Pa., 1964-68; counseling psychologist, prof. edn. Kutztown (Pa.) State Coll., 1968—; counseling psychologist U. Del., summer 1971. Treas. Central Berks County Joint Sch. Authority; councilman, finance chmn., sch. dir. Borough of Fleetwood; lay pres. Lutheran Ch. Council. Served with USN, 1945-46. Gen. Elec. sci. fellow, 1959; licensed psychologist, Pa. Mem. Am., Lehigh Valley psychol. assns., Am. Personnel and Guidance Assn., Assn. Pa. State Colls. and Univ. Faculities, Berks Area Psychol Soc., NEA, Pa. Edn. Assn., Kappa Phi Kappa, Phi Delta Kappa, Tau Kappa Epsilon. Republican. Lutheran. Clubs: Fleetwood Rotary, Masons, Shriners. Home: 417 Greenway W Fleetwood PA 19522 Office: Kutztown State College Kutztown PA 19530

GARRETT, SAMUEL JUDSON, wholesale steel and hardware co. exec.; b. Clover, Va., July 17, 1930; s. Harry Richard and Kate (Williams) G.; B.S., Pa. Mil. Coll., 1953; m. Ruth Ann Worrilow, July 31, 1954; children—Cynthia, Andrew, Courtenay. Commd. 2d. lt. U.S. Army, 1953, advanced through grades to lt. col., 1968, asst. prof. mil. sci. U. Tex., Austin, 1957-60, office of dep. chief staff personnel U.S. Army Continental Army Command. Ft. Monroe, Va., 1962-65, advisor to Turkish Army Gen. Staff, Ankara, 1965-67, dir. storage U.S. Army Field Depot, Qui Nhon, Vietnam, 1967-68, chief supply div., dep. chief staff logistics Mil. Dist. Washington, 1968-69, post logistics officer Ft. Myer, Va., 1969-70, insp. gen. U.S. Army Materiel Command, Washington, 1970-73, ret., 1973; gen. supt. J.B. Kendall Co., Washington, 1973—. Active Lee Dist. Athletic Assn., Alexandria, Va., 1969-73, football commr., 1973. Decorated Legion Merit, Bronze Star, Air medal, Expert Infantryman's Badge. Mem. Ret. Officers Assn. Republican. Presbyterian. Home: 5444 Broadmoor St Alexandria VA 22310 Office: JB Kendall Co 2160 Queens Chapel Rd NE Washington DC 20018

GARRETTO, LEONARD ANTHONY, JR., ins. co. exec.; b. N.Y.C., Apr. 13, 1925; s. Leonard and Evenia (Egidio) G.; B.E.E., Manhattan Coll., 1951; m. Theresa Cennamo, Aug. 6, 1949; children—Deborah, Mark, Michael, Paula, David. Engr., Gen. Precision Lab. Inc., Pleasantville, N.Y., 1951-53, project adminstr., 1953-55, project mgr., 1955-58, subcontracts mgr., 1958-59; adminstrv. engr. Sperry Systems Mgmt. div. Sperry Rand Corp., Great Neck, N.Y., 1959-61, mgmt. services adminstr., 1961-63, mgmt. services mgr., 1963-65, fin. planning mgr., 1965-66, planning mgr., 1966-68, dir. adminstrn., 1968; agt. First Investors Corp., N.Y.C., 1966-69, dist. mgr., 1969-70; gen. mgr. David Gracer Co., N.Y.C., 1970-72; v.p. regional sales Somerset Capital Corp., N.Y.C., 1972-75; regional dir. Wis. Nat. Life Ins. Co., Oshkosh, 1975-77, regional sales v.p., Englewood Cliffs, N.J., 1977—. Served with U.S. Army, 1943-45; ETO. Mem. Am. Soc. Nataries, Nat. Assn. Life Underwriters, Nat. Assn. Securities Dealers. Democrat. Roman Catholic. Home: 39 Rose Hill Ave New Rochelle NY 10804 Office: 375 Sylvan Ave Englewood Cliffs NJ 07632

GARRITY, HELEN MARIE, educator; b. Haverhill, Mass., Mar. 5, 1922; d. John Joseph and Emma Louise (Lanen) Garrity; B.S. in Edn., State Coll., Lowell, Mass., 1944; Ed.M., Boston U., 1946, Ed.D., 1959. Tchr., Westford (Mass.) Pub. Schs., 1944-45; tchr. health, social studies Manchester (Mass.) Pub. Schs., 1945-46; tchr.-supr. phys. edn. Concord (Mass.) Pub. Schs., 1946-47; tchr. phys. edn. Arlington (Mass.) Pub. Schs., 1947-52; asso. prof. health and phys. edn. State Coll., Lowell, Mass., 1952-68; sr. supr. edn., health and safety Mass. Dept. Edn., 1968-73; exec. officer health edn. dept. Boston-Bouvé Coll., Northeastern U., Boston, 1973—, prof., 1973—, coordinator of courses grad. level, 1973—; instr. Camp Wa-Klo, Jaffery, N.H., summers, 1940-42, Tripp Lake Camp, summers, 1944-48; del. 6th Internat. Health Edn. Conf., Madrid, Spain, 1965. Mem. pub. edn. com. Am. Cancer Soc., 1976—; mem. Growth Policy Com., Groveland, Mass., 1976—; mem. Merrimack Valley Health Planning Council, 1975—; mem. exec. com. Middlesex-Cambridge Lung Assn., 1975—; bd. dirs. Am. Lung Assn. Mass.; mem. basketball com. Boston Bd. Ofcls. for Women's Sports, 1952-60, mem. swimming com., 1950-52. Fellow Am. Sch. Health Assn. (Distinguished Service award 1975); mem. AAHPER (mem. necrology com. 1964-66), Mass. Assns. for Health, Phys. Edn. and Recreation (Honor award 1966, pres. 1967-68), Am., New Eng. pub. health assns., Internat. Union Health Edn. (mem. tech. com. 1965-66), New Eng. Health Edn. Assn. (mem. exec. com. 1969-71), Mass. Sch. Health Assn. (mem. adv. bd. 1974—), Mass. Fedn. Bus. and Profl. Women's Clubs, Boston Bd. Women Ofcls., Pi Lambda Theta. Mem. editorial bd. Achieving High Level Wellness, Sch. Health Forum newsletter. Contbr. chpts. to texts on sch. health. Home: PO Box 151 Bradford MA 01830 Office: Boston-Bouvé College Northeastern Univ Boston MA 02115

GARROW, WALTER DAVID, chemist; b. Niagara Falls, N.Y., Nov. 13, 1950; s. Wilfred Vincent and Julia Virginia (Belkota) G.; B.S. in Chemistry, Canisius Coll., 1972, M.B.A., 1977; postgrad. in Chemistry, State U.N.Y. at Buffalo, 1972-73; m. Sharon Mary Schrader, Sept. 28, 1973; children—Kendra Anne, Ryan Neumann. Analytical chemist Hooker Chem. Corp., Niagara Falls, 1972-77, corporate new bus. devel. specialist, 1977-78, environ. affairs systems mgr., 1978—. Commentator for Mass, St. John de LaSalle Ch., Niagara Falls. Mem. Am. Chem. Soc. (exec. officer Western N.Y. sect. 1975—, analytical subgroup), Soc. Applied Spectroscopy, Assn. M.B.A. Execs., Schoellkopf Geol. Soc. Roman Catholic. Club: K.C. (rec. sec. Niagara council 247). Editor publ. N.Y. sect. Am. Chem. Soc., 1975—. Home: 905 92d St Niagara Falls NY 14304 Office: MPO Box 728 Niagara Falls NY 14302

GARRY, RALPH JOSEPH, educator; b. San Francisco, Aug. 10, 1916; s. Joseph Athanatious and Ida Scott (Smith) G.; B.A., Stanford, 1946, M.A., 1950, Ph.D., 1950; m. Mary Bartow Talcott, Feb. 2, 1962; 1 dau., Amanda. Classification sec., adminstrv. asst. at reception centre, Calif. Dept. Corrections, San Quentin, 1941-49; dir. Psychol. Cons., San Francisco, 1947-50; prof. ednl. psychology Boston U., 1950-69; chmn. curriculum dept. Ont. (Can.) Inst. Studies Edn., Toronto, 1969-73, prof., curriculum dept., 1973—; dir. project Found. Character Edn., Boston, 1954-69; dir. natural sci. research project, Boston, 1958-62; dir. research, modern lang. project, Boston, 1959-64; cons. U.S. Senate Subcom. Juvenile Delinquency, 1961-63; cons. Halton Primary Task Force, 1973-76. Recipient George Peabody award, 1963; Fulbright sr. lectr. Chung-Ang U., Seoul, Korea, 1975. Mem. Am., Canadian psychol. assns., Am. Edn. Research Assn., Soc. Psychoceramicists, Sigma Xi. Author: (with H. Kingsley) Nature and Conditions of Learning, 1963; Guidance Techniques for Elementary Teachers, 1963; editor: Television for Children, 1971. Home: Waterford Springs Lower Waterford VT 05848 Office: 252 Bloor St W Toronto ON Canada

GARTLEY, MARKHAM LIGON, former state ofcl.; b. Mayfield, Ky., May 16, 1944; s. Gerald Arthur and Minnie Lee (Ligon) G.; B.S. in Physics, Ga. Inst. Tech., 1966; m. Sherrel Elaine Wilcox, 1975. With Eastern Airlines, Atlanta, 1972-74; sec. of state Maine, 1975-79. Alt. del. Democratic Nat. Conv., 1976. Served to lt. USN, 1966-73; Vietnam. Decorated Air medal, Navy Commendation medal, Vietnam Cross of Gallantry. Mem. Airline Pilots Assn., Amvets., Am. Legion, DAV, Scabbard & Blade, Beta Theta Pi. Home: Beaver Creek Greenville ME 04441*

GARTNER, ELLEN MAY PHILLIPS, pub. relations and advt. co. exec.; b. Lynn, Mass., May 12, 1932; s. Israel and Eva Rebecca (Bragen) P.; grad. Queens Coll., 1969; children—Susan Abigail, Janet Louise. Account exec. Arthur Schmidt & Assos., N.Y.C., 1969-71; with Doremus & Co., N.Y.C., 1971—, account exec., 1971—, asst. v.p., 1977—. Bd. dirs. Way-Off-Broadway Theatre Group, Bayside, N.Y. Mem. Pub. Relations Soc. Am. (accredited), Publicity Club N.Y. Democrat. Office: 120 Broadway New York City NY 10005

GARVER, ROBERT BRUCE, trucking co. exec.; b. Hagerstown, Md., Oct. 9, 1947; s. Jacob Edward and Fredericka (Angle) G.; B.A., Eastern Ky. U., 1970; postgrad. Frostburg State Coll., 1976—; m. Jane Alexandra Ewing, Mar. 27, 1977; 1 dau., Alexandra Brooke. Asso. planner Washington County Planning Commn., Hagerstown, 1973-77; transp. supr. Ryder Truck Lines, Hagerstown, 1977—. Mem. Am. Inst. Planners, Nat. Geog. Soc. Democrat. Mem. United Ch. Christ. Contbr. articles to econ., environ. and transp. publs. 1973—. Home: 2251 Fairfax Rd Hagerstown MD 21740 Office: Industry Dr Airport Indsl Park Hagerstown MD 21740

GARVER, WALTER RAYMOND, artist; b. Medina, N.Y., Aug. 29, 1927; s. Walter Otto and Victoria Constance (Bush) G.; m. Jane Swanz, Jan. 19, 1957. Tchr. art Amherst Central High Sch., Snyder, N.Y., 1958—; exhibited in one-man shows at Hall of Art, N.Y.C., Albright-Knox Gallery, Lakeview Gallery (both Buffalo); group shows at N.A.D., N.Y.C., Art Inst. Chgo., Butler Inst. (McDonough award 1963), Youngstown, Ohio, Corcoran Gallery, Washington, Minn. Mus., St. Paul, Grand Galleria, Seattle, Meml. Art Gallery, Rochester, N.Y., Silvermine Guild, Pa. Acad., Phila., Albright-Knox Gallery (Gold medal Buffalo Soc. Artists Am. 1965, 67, 69), Erie Art Center, Erie, Pa., others; represented in permanent collections Butler Inst., Charles R. Penney Found., Cin. U., Minn. Mus., numerous pvt. and corporate collections. Recipient numerous awards for paintings, including Bellinger award Chautaqua Nat. Jury Show, 1970, 71, 72, 73, Mainstreams award of distinction Marietta (Ohio) Coll., 1969, Grand prize Nat. Art Exhbn., Cooperstown (N.Y.) Art Assn., 1973. Mem. Buffalo Soc. Artists (pres. 1964), Patteran Soc. Artists. Home: 4230 Tonawanda Creek Rd East Amherst NY 14051

GARVEY, FENWICK HILL, financial research dir.; b. Warner Robins, Ga., Feb. 1, 1945; s. Glenwood and Evelyn Caroline (Hill) G.; B.B.A., U. N.Mex., 1967; postgrad. security analysis N.Y. Inst. Finance, 1967-68; m. Nancy Susan Gwin, Jan. 6, 1968; children—Kelly Gwin, Fenwick. Security analyst St. Louis Union Trust Co., 1967-68; security analyst, research officer M.A. Schapiro & Co., N.Y.C., 1968-69; asst. v.p. John J. Ryan & Co., W. Orange, N.J., 1969, dir. research, 1969—, v.p., 1970-72, dir. Banconomics Corp. subs. John J. Ryan & Co., 1971—, exec. v.p., mem. exec. and finance coms., 1972—; cons. comml. banking orgns., N.J.; qualified bank appraiser, fed. cts., fed. reserve; guest lectr. in field, grad. schs. and banking seminars. Served with USNR, 1962-64. Fellow Financial Analyst Fedn.; sr. mem. N.Y. Soc. Security Analysts, Am. Accounting Assn. (asso.), Nat. Assn. Securities Dealers (registered prin.), Alpha Kappa Psi. Republican. Lutheran. Contbr. articles to banking jours. Home: 326 Sunset Blvd Wyckoff NJ 07481 Office: 80 Main St West Orange NJ 07052

GARVIN, CLIFTON CANTER, JR., petroleum co. exec.; b. Portsmouth, Va., Dec. 22, 1921; s. Clifton Canter and Esther (Ames) G.; B.S. in Chem. Engring., Va. Poly. Inst., 1943, M.S., 1947; m. Thelma Volland, Mar. 15, 1943; 1 son, 3 daus. Engr., exec. ore and chem. ops. Exxon Co., U.S.A., Baton Rouge and Houston, 1947-64; exec. asst. to chmn. Exxon Corp., N.Y.C., 1964-65, dir., v.p., 1968, exec. v.p., 1968-72, pres., 1972, chmn. bd., chief exec. officer, 1975—; pres. Exxon Chem. Co., N.Y.C., 1965-68; dir. Sperry Rand Corp., Citicorp & Citibank, N.A., Pepsi Co., Inc. Chmn., Council for Fin. Aid to Edn.; trustee Com. for Econ. Devel., Joint Council on Econ. Edn., Vanderbilt U., Sloan Kettering Inst. Cancer Research. Mem. Am. Petroleum Inst. (dir.), Am. Chem. Soc., Am. Inst. Chem. Engrs., Bus. Com. for Arts, Inc., Bus. Council, Bus. Roundtable, Nat. Petroleum Council. Home: Greenwich CT 06830 Office: 1251 Ave of Americas New York City NY 10020

GARVY, GEORGE, economist; b. Riga, Russia, May 30, 1913; s. Peter and Sophie (Fichman) G.; student U. Berlin (Germany), 1931-33; License-es-lettres, U. Paris (France), 1937, diploma Inst. Statistics, 1935; PH.D., Columbia, 1951; m. Juliette Francoise Blanc, Oct. 17, 1940; 1 dau., Helen. Came to U.S., 1940, naturalized, 1948. With Nat. Bur. Econ. Research, N.Y.C., 1941-43; with Fed. Res. Bank N.Y., 1943-74, v.p., sr. adviser, to 1974; vis. prof. Columbia, 1959-60, 68, Stanford, 1969; 70; lectr. Econ. Devel. Inst., Washington, 1957-68. Mem. rev. com. balance payments statistics Bur. of Budget, 1963-64, mem. Conf. on Research in Income and Wealth, 1948—; mem. com. internat. travel grants Social Sci. Research Council, 1961-64, chmn., 1964; mem. fgn. missions for Internat. Bank Reconstrn. and Devel., 1951-56; mem. selection com. W.S. Woytinsky Lectureship award U. Mich., 1963—. Fellow Am. Statis. Assn.; mem. Am. Econ. Assn., Am. Finance Assn. (pres. 1965), Council Fgn. Relations. Author books, articles in field. Home: 220 Eakins Rd Manhasset NY 11030

GARY, LAWRENCE EDWARD, social research adminstr.; b. Union Springs, Ala., May 26, 1939; s. William Pride and Ludia Bell Gary; B.S., Tuskegee Inst., 1963; M.P.A., U. Mich., 1964, M.S.W., 1966, Ph.D., 1970; m. Robenia Baker, Aug. 8, 1969; children—Lisa Che, Lawrence Charles Andre, Jason Edward. Lectr. U. Mich., 1968-70, asst. prof., 1970-71, asso. prof. acad. affairs, 1971-75; asst. to v.p. acad. affairs Howard U., 1971-72, dir. Inst. Urban Affairs and Research, 1972—, dir. Mental Health Research Center, 1974—. Group Worker March Center, Chgo., 1961-63; adminstrv. asst. to city controller City of Ann Arbor (Mich.), 1964; staff asst. Mich. Econ. Opportunity Office, Detroit, 1967; dir. Park Pl. Assn., Inc., 1971-75, treas., 1971-74. Recipient research grants, NIMH, 1971-79, NIH, 1974-76, Law Enforcement Assistance, 1973-76, Faculty Research Program, 1973-75, Action Agy., 1971-75; James Found. fellow, 1963; U. Mich. fellow, 1964; NIMH travel grantee, China, 1978. Mem. Am. Pub. Health Assn., Am. Polit. Sci. Assn., Council Social Work Edn., Am. Soc. Pub. Adminstrn. Democrat. Methodist. Editor: Social Research and the Black Community, 1974; Restructuring the Educational Process: A Black Perspective, 1975; Crime and its Impact on the Black Community, 1976; Mental Health: A Challenge to the Black Community, 1978; contbr. articles to profl. jours., also chpts. in books. Home: 1213 Kathryn Rd Silver Spring MD 20904 Office: Institute for Urban Affairs and Research Howard University 2935 Upton St NW Washington DC 20008

GASKINS, FREDERICK HUDSON, rheologist; b. Phila., Apr. 29, 1925; s. Bruce Hudson and Maude Ardeen (Johnson) G.; B.A., U. Pa., 1951; postgrad. Drexel U., 1952, Temple U., 1954-56; m. Selena Howard, Jan. 13, 1973; children—Lawrence Hudson, Monica Roxanne, Kevin Claude, Keith Carlyle. Chemist, Phila. Q.M. Depot, Phila., 1951-52; research engr. Franklin Inst., Phila., 1952-59; project leader Aeroprojects, Inc., West Chester, Pa., 1959-63; rheologist Chem. Systems Lab., Aberdeen Proving Ground, Md., 1964—. Mem. Hartford County (Md.) Human Relations Com., 1973-76, vice chmn., 1973-76. Served with AC, US Army, 1943-46; CBI. Recipient Certificate of Outstanding Achievement, U.S. Army Sci. Conf., West Point, 1966, Certificate of Achievement, Edgewood Arsenal, 1975. Mem. AAAS, Soc. Rheology, Sci. Research Soc. N. Am. (sec. Chesapeake chpt. 1975), Sigma Xi, NAACP, Omega Psi Phi. Patentee in field. Office: Box 26 Edgewood Arsenal Aberdeen Proving Ground MD 21010 Died Oct. 20, 1978

GASPER, DONALD, coal co. exec.; b. Du Bois, Pa., Oct. 3, 1927; s. Joseph and Helen (Palko) G.; student U. Pa., 1945-46; B.S., Pa. State U., 1950, M.S., 1951; m. Dorothy Dryna, June 21, 1952; children—Barbara, Therese, Dorothy, Karla. Bus. analyst Consolidation Coal Co., Pitts., 1951-61, mgr. bus. surveys, 1961-67, dir. econ. studies, 1967—. Cons. staff study Com. on Finance U.S. Senate Steel Imports, 1967, Nat. Fuels and Energy Study, U.S. Senate Study, 1962, Mich. Energy Study, 1966, Nat. Coal Policy Conf., Nat. Coal Assn. Fairmont Coal Bur.; cons. fuel allocation adv. group U.S. Dept. Interior, 1973; cons. emergency fuel preparedness com. Nat. Petroleum Council, 1969, 73-74, 76-77; econ. cons. industrywide wage negotiations Bituminous Coal Operator's Assn., 1974, 77-78. Served with USNR, 1945-46. Mem. Assn. Am. Geographers, Am. Inst. Mining, Metall. and Petroleum Engrs., Am. Econ. Assn., Assn. Iron and Steel Engrs. Roman Catholic. Contbr. articles to profl. jours. Home: 103 White Gate Rd Pittsburgh PA 15238 Office: Consol Plaza Pittsburgh PA 15241

GASS, CHARLES, retail co. exec.; b. N.Y.C., June 12, 1918; s. Benjamin and Sophie (Eberlin) G.; B.B.A., Coll. City N.Y., 1940; m. Rosalyn Becker, June 23, 1945; children—Jeffrey, Marc. With Darling Stores Corp., 1946-62, asst. controller, 1956-62; controller Grayson Robinson Stores Corp., 1962-64; v.p. internal audit MMG Stores div. McCrory Corp., N.Y.C., 1966-71, corp. v.p., 1971—, sr. v.p. ops. S. Klein Dept. Stores div., 1972-74, pres. K.N. Distbrs., Inc., 1972-74, sr. v.p. mgmt. services McCrory Stores div., 1974-77, exec. v.p. div., 1978—. Served with AUS, World War II; ETO. Decorated Silver Star, Bronze Star, Purple Heart, Presdl. citation, Combat Inf. Badge. Mem. Coll. City N.Y. Alumni Assn. Home: 2600-14 Netherland Ave Bronx NY 10463 Office: 245 Fifth Ave New York City NY 10016

GASSERT, MARY ELIZABETH, clin. psychologist; b. Lewistown, Pa., Oct. 3, 1905; d. Samuel P. and Bessie (Muthersbaugh) Gassert; A.B., Juniata Coll., 1928; M.S., Pa. State U., 1936. Tchr. pub. schs., sch. psychologist, Lewistown, 1928-38; dir. guidance, dean girls, sch. psychologist Hershey (Pa.) Pub. Schs., 1939-41; supr. spl. edn. York (Pa.) County Pub. Schs., after 1941; staff psychologist York Hosp., after 1957; psychol. testing Pa. Dept. Welfare, 1960; instr. York campus Pa. State U., after 1963; now psychol. cons. Dir. Children's Service York County, 1956-66, York County Assn. for Retarded Children, 1964—. Diplomate Am. Bd. Examiners in Profl. Psychology. Mem. Am., Pa. psychol. assns., AAUW, Cleft Palate Assn., Phi Lambda Theta, Psi Chi. Home: 926 McKenzie St York PA 17403

GASTEYER, CARLIN EVANS (MRS. HARRY A. GASTEYER), mus. adminstr.; b. Jackson, Mich., Mar. 30, 1917; d. Frank Howard and Marian (Spencer) Evans; student Barnard Coll., 1934-35; m. Harry A. Gasteyer, Jan. 8, 1944; 1 dau., Nancy Catherine. Clk., First Nat. City Bank, 1939-42; statistician Bell Telephone Labs., 1942-45;

dir. asst. S.I. Mus., 1956-61; bus. mgr. Mus. of the City of N.Y., 1961-63; mus. adminstr., 1963-66; asst. dir. Monmouth (N.J.) Mus., 1966-67, Mus. of City of N.Y., 1967-70; vice dir. adminstrn. Bklyn. Mus., 1970-75; dir. planning Snug Harbor Cultural Center, S.I., N.Y., 1975—. Active Girl Scouts. Co-founder, pres. Jr. Mus. Guild, S.I. Mus., 1956-58. Mem. N.Y.C. Local Sch. Bd. 54, 1960-61. Mem. Am. Assn. Mus., Mus. Council of N.Y.C., N.Y. Cultural Instns. Group. Club: Cosmopolitan. Home: 50 Fort Pl Staten Island NY 10301 Office: Snug Harbor Center Staten Island NY 10301

GASTON, LESLIE HOMER, former govt. ofcl.; b. Valparaiso, Ind., Nov. 30, 1906; s. Roscoe C. and Alida (Burt) G.; student Valpariso U., 1924-26; B.S. in Chem. Engring., Purdue, U., 1929; M.S., U. Mich., 1932; LL.B., George Washington U., 1940; m. Rebecca L. Cook, Aug. 6, 1933. Chemist U.S. Steel Corp., Gary, Ind., 1929-31, Lever Bros. Co., Hammon, Ind., 1932-36; admitted to D.C. bar, 1939; with U.S. Patent Office, Commerce Dept., Washington, 1936-76, primary examiner, 1959-63, mgr., 1963-66, mem. Bd. Patent Interferences, 1966-76. Recipient Superior Performance award U.S. Patent Office, 1955; Silver medal Meritorious Ser. award Commerce Dept., 1965. Mem. Patent Office Soc. (treas. 1955-58), Am. Bar Assn. Presbyterian (elder). Home: 2500 Q St NW Washington DC 20007

GASTWIRTH, JOSEPH LEWIS, educator; b. N.Y.C.; s. Paul and Tillie (Scheinert) G.; B.S. summa cum laude, Yale U., 1958; Ph.D., Columbia U., 1963. Research asso. Stanford U., 1963-64; asst. prof., then asso. prof. statistics Johns Hopkins U., 1964-70; vis. asso. prof. Harvard U., 1970-71; vis. faculty adviser Office Mgmt. and Budget, 1971-72; prof. statistics and econs. George Washington U., 1972—; cons. Bur. Labor Statistics, 1972-74; panelist grad. student fellowship com. NSF, 1973; cons. Office Mgmt. and Budget, 1974-77; cons. law firms, 1974—. Fellow Am. Statis. Assn. (chmn. com. on privacy and confidentiality 1975-77), Inst. Math. Statistics, AAAS. Author papers in field. Home: 522 21st St NW Washington DC 20006 Office: 2201 G St NW Washington DC 20052

GATES, ARNOLD FRANCIS, editor; b. Johnstown, Pa., Sept. 12, 1914; s. John Paul and Gizella (Shepherd) G.; student Western Res. U., 1937, Columbia U., 1946-47; L.H.D., Lincoln Meml. U., 1970; m. Georgia Myra Philipps, June 1, 1947; 1 son, Robert Allan. Engr. structural estimating dept. Lehigh Structural Steel Co., Allentown Pa., 1949-61, engring. dept. Bethlehem Steel Co., N.Y.C., 1962-65; asso. steel editor Am. Metal Market, N.Y.C., 1965-67; resident editor Steel mag. Penton Pub. Co., Cleve., 1967-69; mem. mus. staff, supr. village staff tng. Old Bethpage Village Restoration, Nassau County Hist. Mus., 1970—. Editor The Round Table and Round Table yearbook, N.Y.C., 1952-67; editorial staff Lincoln Meml. U. Press, Harrogate, Tenn., 1956-77; lit. editor Lincoln Herald, Harrogate, 1956-77; contbg. editor Civil War Times Illustrated, Harrisburg, Pa., 1978—; columnist The Gates Report: The Civil War Today; book scout Civil War Book Club, Chgo., 1960-61; book judge Civil War Times Illus. Book Service, Gettysburg, Pa., 1962-66. Mem. adv. council U.S. Civil War Centennial Commn., Washington, 1961-66; mem. bibliography com. Lincoln Nat. Life Found., Fort Wayne, Ind., 1956—; sec.-treas. Civil War Round Table N.Y., 1954-67, pres., 1965-66; exec. sec. bd. judges Mil. Order Loyal Legion Lit. Award, Phila., 1962-63; Dept. State Cultural Program lectr. on Lincoln in Lebanon, Jordan, 1963. Trustee Garden City Library, 1963—. Served with U.S. Army, 1941-45. Recipient award of Merit, New Haven Civil War Round Table, 1964; citation N.J. Civil War Centennial Commn., 1965; tribute plaques Civil War Round Table N.Y., 1961, 66; Benjamin Barondess Lincoln award, 1974. Fellow So. Am. Historians; mem. Ill., Nassau County hist. socs., N.Y. Hist. Assn., Lincoln groups N.Y. (dir., charter), Washington, Boston, Wis., Am. Assn. for State and Local History, Am. Soc. Bus. Press Editors, Early Trades and Crafts Soc., Internat. Platform Assn., Acad. Polit. Sci., Air Pollution Control Assn., Creative Edn. Found., Abraham Lincoln Assn., Metal Journalists Soc. (charter), L.I. Early Fliers Club. Author poetry, essays on Lincoln, Civil War; Nassau County in the Civil War. Home: 289 New Hyde Park Rd Garden City NY 11530 Office: Old Bethpage Village Restoration Round Swamp Rd Old Bethpage NY 11804

GATES, EDWARD DWIGHT, coll. pres.; b. Wauwatosa, Wis., Mar. 26, 1921; s. Perez Dickinson and Delia (Dousman) G.; B.A., Beloit Coll., 1943; postgrad. U. Chgo., 1943; B.D., Pacific Sch. Religion, 1945; Ph.D., Bradley U., 1953; LL.D., Hiram Scott Coll., 1969; m. June Elizabeth Rowell, Sept. 10, 1944; children—Pamela (Mrs. Charles E. Tressler II), Geoffrey, James. Ordained to ministry, 1945; asst. minister First Presbyn. Ch., Peoria, Ill., 1947-48, minister, 1948-54; ministerial staff First Congl. Ch., Los Angeles, 1954-56; gen. sec. Macalester Coll., St. Paul, 1956-60; pres. Beaver Coll., Glenside, Pa., 1960—. Co-chmn. nat. and sch. awards, jury Freedoms Found., Valley Forge, 1964, chmn., 1974. Chmn. bd. dirs. Council Protestant Colls. and Univs., 1965-66; mem. exec. com. Presbyn. Coll. Union, 1964-71, 76—; mem. commn. coll. adminstrn. Assn. Am. Colls., 1964-67. Mem. bd. Christian edn. U.P. Ch. U. S.A., 1968-72; bd. dirs. NCCJ of Greater Phila., 1972—; chmn. Lehigh Regional Consortium for Grad. Edn., 1973-74, Delaware Valley Regional Planning Council for Higher Edn., 1973—; vice chmn. Found. for Ind. Colls. of Pa., 1972-73; mem. exec. com. Commn. for Ind. Colls. and Univs. of Pa., 1972-75; mem. govt. relations com. Pa. Assn. Colls. and Univs., 1975—, chmn., 1977—. Served as chaplain USNR, 1944-47. 1st pl. winner Freedoms Found. award, 1950, 2d pl., 1951, 52, others 1953-55. Mem. Beta Theta Pi. Mason. Clubs: Penn, Union League. Home: 1273 Butler Pike Blue Bell PA 19422

GATES, WILFRID LYMAN, JR., landscape architect; b. Providence, Feb. 13, 1942; s. Wilfrid Lyman and Elizabeth Eleanor (Hey) G.; B.S., R.I. Sch. Design, 1965; m. Judith Barnett Sherburne, Aug. 12, 1967; 1 dau., Anne. Landscape architect R.I. Dept. Transp., 1966-72; pvt. practice as landscape architect, Providence, 1972—. Pres. Environment Council R.I., 1973-74, Clean R.I., 1971-73; adv. com. R.I. Bicentennial Commn.; pres. Save The Bay, 1978-79. Bd. dirs. R.I. Arts Festival. Served with R.I. N.G., 1965-69. Mem. R.I. SAR, Am. Soc. Landscape Architects, R.I. Sch. Design Alumni Assn. (pres. 1972-77). Home: 1540 Pawtucket Ave East Providence RI 02916 Office: 653 N Main St Providence RI 02904

GATEWOOD, ROBERT PAYNE, ins. exec.; b. Nebr., Mar. 4, 1923; s. Robert Harvey and Bess (Payne) G.; B.S., U.S. Naval Acad., 1946; C.L.U., Am. Coll. Life Underwriters, 1953; postgrad. La. State U., 1974; m. Marilyn Wengert, June 6, 1946; children—Robert, Lottie, Traber, Cy, Marilyn, Bess, John, Anthony, Judemarie, Anne, Tressa, Joseph, Ruth. Estate planner J.D. Marsh & Assos., 1954-56; pres. estate planning Financial Corp. Am., 1956-61; pres. Robert P. Gatewood & Co., 1961—. Mem. sales execs. adv. bd. Inst. Ins. Mktg. La. State U., bd. dirs. found. Served with USN, 1946-50; PTO. Recipient Bernard L. Wilner Meml. award. Mem. Nat. Assn. Life Underwriters (past pres.), Assn. Advanced Underwriters, Million Dollar Round Table, Am. Soc. C.L.U.s (exec. com. 1972-77). Republican. Roman Catholic. Contbr. articles to profl. jours. Home: 3838 52d St NW Washington DC 20016 Office: 905 16th St NW Washington DC 20006*

GATNER, ELLIOTT SHERMAN MOZIAN, educator; b. N.Y.C., Oct. 24, 1914; s. Abraham Eliot and Tillie (Sherman) G.; B.A., L.I. U., 1936; M.S., Coll. City N.Y., 1939; B.S., Columbia U., 1947, psotgrad., 1948-50, 53-55, 66-74, Ed.D., 1974; m. Shirley Golden, July 13, 1941; children—Alice Roberta, Deborah Ann. Instr. English, L.I. U., 1939-47, instr. history, 1948-52, asst. prof. history and govt., 1953-56, asso. prof., 1956-63, reference librarian, 1953-61, prof. history 1963—, asst. dir. libraries, 1961-64, asso. dir., 1965-76, dir., 1976—, asst. to provost, 1964-65, dir. vets. affairs, 1946-50, asso. dir. L.I. U. Press, 1964-76, dir., 1976—. Served with U.S. Army, 1941-46, 50-52. Decorated Bronze Star medal. Mem. Acad. Libraries of Bklyn. (pres. 1967-69), Modern Lang. Assn., A.L.A., Coll. English Assn., Am., N.Y. State, L.I. hist. assns., Nat. Council Tchrs. English, Am. Soc. for Legal History, Ednl. Studies Assn., Am. Assn. U. Profs., Phi Delta Kappa. Home: 81-07 248th St Bellerose NY 11426 Office: LI U Brooklyn NY 11201

GATTO, ANDREW RONALD, toy co. exec.; b. Hoboken, N.J., June 26, 1947; s. Joseph Arnold and Angela (Caruso) G.; B.A., Rider Coll., 1969; m. Susan Roberta Lamb, June 27, 1970; children—Andrew Ronald, Lisa Ann. Asst. toy buyer J.C. Penny Co., N.Y.C., 1969-70; met. N.Y. area mgr. Fisher Price Toys, East Aurora, N.Y., 1970-72, promotional planning coordinator, 1972-74, merchandising mgr., 1974-75, mgr. merchandising and sales promotion, 1975-77; dir. mktg. Reeves Internat., N.Y.C., 1977—. Mem. bd. dirs. Care-Ring, Buffalo; v.p. bd. trustees Southtowns Montessori Sch. Mem. Am. Mktg. Assn., Internat. Sales and Mktg. Execs. Assn., Toy Mfrs. Am. (com. mem. 1975-76). Republican. Roman Catholic. Home: 416 Upper Blvd Ridgewood NJ 07040 Office: 1107 Broadway New York City NY 10010

GATTO, PAUL ANTHONY, artist, art tchr., art appraiser, art gallery operator; b. Bklyn., Sept. 19, 1929; s. James Vincent and Pauline (Nemia) G.; student St. Johns U., 1953-54; m. Isabelle Ann Favuzzi, Sept. 14, 1957; children—Jeanne Marie, Patrice Alaine. Art trainee Traeger Phillips Studio, N.Y.C., 1947; appraiser trainee Gen. Adjustment Bur., Inc., N.Y.C., 1947-51, appraiser, adjuster, Bklyn. and Hempstead, N.Y., 1953-72; owner, operator Art Loft Art Gallery, Bethpage, N.Y., 1965, Paul Gatto Gallery Inc., Farmingdale, N.Y., 1967—; lectr. in field; judge art competitions; restorer works of art. Trustee Farmingdale Pub. Library. Served with U.S. Army, 1951-53. Mem. Profl. Picture Framers Assn., Farmingdale Merchants Assn., Italian Cultural Soc. (pres.), Internat. Order of the Blue Goose. Roman Catholic. Home: 151 N Maple St Massapequa NY 11758 Office: 286 Main St Farmingdale NY 11735

GATTONE, VINCENT HENRY, pharmacist; b. Phila., Apr. 27, 1908; s. Anthony and Josephine (DiLauro) G.; Ph.G., Phila. Coll. Pharmacy and Sci., 1929, B.Sc., 1932, B.Sc., 1942; postgrad. U. Pa., 1932-33; M.Sc., Temple U., 1945; postgrad. U. Wash., 1945-49; m. Ardita Pizzi, Nov. 23, 1948; children—Antonette, Vincent Henry II, Elvira J. With F.R. Perry's Drug Stores, Phila. and Upper Darby, Pa., 1924-32; asst. in chemistry lab. Phila. Coll. Pharmacy and Sci., 1930-32; analysis and control chemist, indsl. chemistry lab. E.I. duPont de Nemours & Co., Inc., Jackson Lab., Deep Water, N.J., 1932-36; chemist Asthmanefrin-Vaponefrin Co., 1936-51; drug salesman, pharmacist, chemist Shoemaker & Busch, Inc., 1951-58; with Lif-O-Gen., Cambridge, Md., 1958—, tech. dir. lab. and splty. gas mixes, 1976—. Registered pharmacist, Pa., N.J., Md. Mem. Md. Pharm. Assn. (trustee), Eastern Shore Pharm. Soc. Md. (sec. 1972—). Republican. Presbyterian. Clubs: Lions, Elks (Easton, Md.). Contbr. articles to profl. jours. Home: Edgemere Rd Route 4 Box 354 Easton MD 21601 Office: Lif-O-Gen Woods Rd Cambridge MD 21613

GATZOGIANNIS, GEORGE EVANGELOS, restauranteur; b. Lia, Epirus, Greece, Apr. 23, 1947; s. Evangelow Foto and Anastasia Vasiliki (Kouka) G.; came to U.S., 1955, naturalized, 1971; B.A., Wake Forest U., 1971; M.A., Ohio U., 1973. Researcher history dept. Ohio U., Athens, 1971-73; tchr. social studies Worcester (Mass.) pub. schs., 1973-74; hist. researcher Commonwealth of Mass., Boston, 1974-76; owner, pres. chain of restaurants in Ipswich, Mass., Upton, Mass., Crete, Greece, 1976—. Hankins scholar, 1967-71; Bancroft scholar, 1967-70; Ohio U. fellow, 1971-73; Fed. Opportunity grantee, 1967-71. Mem. Cyprus Relief Fund, Soc. of Lia, Greater Jr. C. of C. of Boston, Mass. Tchrs. Assn., Am., Mass. hist. socs., Am. Ind. Businessman's Assn., Balkan Hist. Assn., Greater Mass. Businessmen. Greek Orthodox. Address: 22 Morningside Rd Worcester MA 01602

GAUDINO, MARIO, physician; b. Buenos Aires, Argentina, May 22, 1918; s. Nicolas M. and Maria Teresa (Ferrari) G.; B.A., U. Buenos Aires, 1934, M.D., 1944; Ph.D., N.Y. U., 1950; m. Ann Murray, Sept. 24, 1947; children—David, Brian. Came to U.S., 1946, naturalized, 1966. Asst., Inst. Histology and Embryology, U. Buenos Aires, 1936, asst., research asst. Inst. Physiology, 1937-42, chief of lab. biol. physics, 1944; resident, chief resident Ramos Mejia Hosp., Buenos Aires, 1941-44; Millet and Roux fellow Argentine Assn. for Advancement Sci., 1943; asst., attending physician Inst. Semiology, Nat. Clin. Hosp., Buenos Aires, 1944-46; fellow Argentine Nat. Cultural Commn., 1945; Sauberan fellow Argentine Assn. Advancement Sci., 1946; physiol. research fellow N.Y. U., U.S. State Dept., Dazian Found. Med. Research, 1946-49; asst. prof. Tex. U., 1949; chmn. dept. biol. physics U. La Plata, Argentina, 1950-51; attending physician Central Inst. Cardiology, Buenos Aires, 1950-51; asso. dir. med. writing and advt. Lederle Labs. div. Am. Cyanamid Co., N.Y.C., 1951-52; research asso., prof. dept. surgery N.Y. U., 1952-55, adj. asso. prof. surgery, 1955-57; established investigator Am. Heart Assn., N.Y.C., 1954-57; med. dir. Abbott Labs. Internat. Co., Abbott Universal Ltd., Chgo., 1957-61; asso. dept. medicine Northwestern U., 1959-61; asso. med. dir. Pfizer Internat., Inc., N.Y.C., 1962-67; asso. dir. advanced clin. research Internat. Merck Sharp & Dohme Research Labs., Rahway, N.J., 1967-70, dir., 1970-71, sr. dir. clin. research internat. med. affairs area, 1971-74; dir. med. compliance CIBA-GEIGY Corp., Summit, N.J., 1974—; clin. asst. prof. medicine Cornell U., N.Y.C., 1971-77. Fellow N.Y. Acad. Scis.; mem. Am. Physiol. Soc., Soc. for Exptl. Biology and Medicine, Am. Fedn. Clin. Research, Harvey Soc., Am., Internat. socs. nephrology, Microcirculatory Soc. Clubs: Jockey, Argentine Yacht., University, Buenos Aires Rowing. Home: 515 Morris Ave Summit NJ 07901 Office: 556 Morris Ave Summit NJ 07901

GAUGER, JOHN HARDY, educator; b. Norristown, Pa., Feb. 8, 1937; s. Martin John and Hannah Elizabeth (Hardy) G.; B.A., U. Del., 1958, M.A., 1965; postgrad. (NDEA fellow) Pa. State U., 1965, (NDEA fellow) Ind. State U., 1967, (Nat. Endowment for Humanities fellow) U. Minn., 1974, (Nat. Endowment for Humanities fellow), U. Wis., 1977; m. Sandra D. Calhoun, Aug. 8, 1959; children—Amy M., Julie A., Jeffrey A. Tchr. social studies Newark (Del.) Spl. Sch. Dist., 1958-67; established oral history program U. Del., 1966; mem. faculty Lehigh County Community Coll., Schnecksville, Pa., 1967—, prof. social scis., 1975—, coordinator labor studies, 1976—; part-time instr. Allentown Police Acad., Pa. State U. Mem. South Whitehall Twp. Bicentennial Com., 1975, 76; pres. bd. trustees Asbury United Methodist Ch., 1977, 78. Mem. Am. Hist. Assn., NEA, N.E. Polit. Sci. Assn., Lehigh County Hist. Assn., Pa., New Castle (Del.) County (treas. 1963-64) edn. assns., Lehigh County Community Coll. Faculty Assn., Newark High Sch. Alumni Assn. (pres. 1964-65), Smithsonian Assos. Republican. Home: 3 Briarcliff Rd Allentown PA 18104 Office: 2370 Main St Schnecksville PA 18078

GAUGER, THOMAS FREEMAN, broadcasting personality; b. Memphis, Apr. 29, 1940; s. Paul Charles and Katherine (Freeman) G.; student U.N.C. at Chapel Hill, 1959-61. Staff announcer KYSN radio, Colorado Springs, 1957-58; staff announcer, cameraman WUNC TV and WCHL, Chapel Hill, N.C., 1959-61; host after noon program WIOD, Miami, 1965-68; host mid-day program WMAL radio-TV, also critic, Washington, 1968—; announcer Kennedy Center for Performing Arts, Active support of music in schs., also narrator and host high sch. concerts. Bd. dirs. Fairfax Symphony Orch., 1973—, pres., 1976—; bd. dirs. Spina Bifida Parents sssn., 1974—, Nat. Childrens Choir, 1974—, Fairfax Legacy Action Group, 1975—, Washington Ballet, 1977—, Fairfax Choral Soc., 1977—, Choral Arts Soc. Washington. Served with U.S. Army, 1962-65. Named Citizen of Yr., Fairfax County Council Arts, 1977; recipient commendations for work in improving U.S.-German relations, U.S. Army and Fed. Republic of Germany, commendation A.R.C. Composer The Nativity for orchestra, organ, chorus and narrator, Kennedy Center performance, 1974. Office: WMAL 4400 Jenifer St Washington DC 20015

GAULL, GERALD EDWARD, pediatrician, educator; b. Boston, Sept. 17, 1930; s. Samuel and Alice Charlotte (Berkowitz) G.; B.A. with honors in Philosophy, U. Mich., 1951; M.D., Boston U., 1955; m. Siri von Reis Altschul, Sept. 19, 1975; children—Erik, Stephen. Junior and sr. resident in pathology Peter Bent Brigham Hosp., Boston, 1955-57; NIH postdoctoral research fellow Harvard, 1957-60, NIH research fellow in pediatrics, 1963-64; research asso. Columbia, 1965-67; jr. resident pediatrics Babies Hosp., N.Y.C., 1960-61, attending pediatrician, 1965-67; chief pediatric research N.Y. Inst. Research in Mental Retardation, S.I., N.Y., 1967—, chief Div. Human Devel., dep. dir., 1976—; asso. prof. pediatrics Mt. Sinai Sch. Med., 1967-74, prof., 1974—; attending pediatrician Mt. Sinai Hosp., 1974—. Served with U.S. Army, 1961-62. Recipient Borden award Am. Acad. Pediatrics, 1978. Med. Research Council fellow, 1964. Mem. Am. Soc. Biol. Chemists, Am. Soc. Neurochemistry, Soc. Pediatric Research, Am. Inst. Nutrition, Am. Soc. Clin. Nutrition, Internat. Soc. Neurochemistry, Am. Pediatric Soc., Internat. Brain Research Orgn., Soc. Neurosci., Am. Soc. Human Genetics, Perinatal Research Soc. Author: Biology of Brain Dysfunction, 1973-75; contbr. articles to profl. jours. Home: 1107 Fifth Ave Apt 3N New York City NY 10028 Office: 1050 Forest Hill Rd Staten Island NY 10314

GAULT, MARIAN DORIS, nursing services adminstr.; b. Panama, Canal Zone, Oct. 1, 1934; d. Belville C. and Marcela L. (Anderson) Holness; came to U.S., 1952, naturalized, 1961; grad. St. Agnes Hosp. Sch. Nursing, 1955; B.A., Glassboro State Coll., 1971, M.A., 1978; m. Calvin J. Gault, July 13, 1957; children—Daryl Justin, Taisia Marie. Asst. head nurse St. Agnes Hosp., Phila., 1955-57; head nurse Mercy Douglas Hosp., Phila., 1957-59; supr. Haverford Hosp., Phila., 1959-61, medication nurse (part-time), 1962-63; clinic nurse Dept. Pub. Health Child Health Conf., Phila., 1961-62; supr. West Park Hosp., Phila., 1963-64; nurse Roxborough Meml. Hosp., Phila., 1965; research and teaching nurse Downstate Med. Center, Bklyn., 1966-67; house supr. Kennedy Hosp., Stratford, N.Y., 1967-68, 70-73; sch. nurse Manpower Devel. Tng. Act Skill Center, Camden, N.J., 1968; camp and sch. nurse Archway Sch. Camp Happy Times, Atco, N.J., 1970-72; instr. nursing S.E. Phila. Neighborhood Health Center, 1972-73; dir. nursing services Washington Meml. Hosp., Turnersville, N.J., 1972—; cons. on urban edn. N.J. State Dept. Edn., 1968-69. Sec., Edgewood Boy's Club of Camden County, 1968-69; chairperson com. for health workshop Nat. Conf. for Panamanians, Washington, 1974—. Mem. Am., N.J. nurses assns., Nat. League Nursing, Soc. Nursing Service Adminstrs. South Jersey, St. Agnes Alumnae Assn. Sch. Nursing. Democrat. Roman Catholic. Home: 11 Yale Rd Atco NJ 08004 Office: Washington Memorial Hosp Turnersville NJ 08012

GAULT, WILLIS MANNING, composer; b. Showeil, Md. June 10, 1908; s. James E. and Essel May (Campbell) G.; student violin and harmony with Anton Nimmerrichter, Anton Kasper, Dudley Clark; m. Jan. 5, 1935; 2 children. Violinist, Globe Theatre, Berlin, Md., 1927-29; organizer, dir. Chamber Music Workshop, Washington, D.C., 1946-66; dir. Gault Sch. Bowed Instrument Making, Washington, 1950—; composer: Fantasias No. 1 (D Major), No. 2 (D Minor) for viola d'amore and orch., Suite in A Major for viola d'amore and orch., various other works for viola d'amore. Home: 35-A Ridge Rd Greenbelt MD 20770 Office: 5502 Kenilworth Ave Riverdale MD 20840

GAULTNEY, JOHN ORTON, life ins. co. exec.; b. Pulaski, Tenn., Nov. 7, 1915; s. Bert Hood and Grace (Orton) G.; student Am. Inst. Banking, 1936; diploma Life Ins. Agy. Mgmt. Assn., 1948, Little Rock Jr. Coll., 1950; C.L.U., 1948, Mgmt. C.L.U. Diploma, 1952; grad. sales mgmt. and mktg. Rutgers U., 1957; m. Elizabethine Mullette, Mar. 30, 1941; children—Elizabethine Gaultney McClure, John Mullette, Walker Orton, Harlow Denny. With N.Y. Life Ins. Co., 1935—, regional v.p., Atlanta, 1956-64, v.p., N.Y.C., 1964-67, v.p. in charge group sales, 1967-68; v.p. mktg., 1969—; v.p. N.Y. Life Variable Contracts Corp., 1969—. Chmn. Downtown YMCA, Atlanta, 1963-65; mem. pub. relations com. Nat. Council YMCAs, 1965—; bd. dirs. Vanderbilt YMCA, N.Y.C., 1966-76, chmn., 1969-76; mem. internat. world service com. YMCA, 1968—; bd. dirs. Memphis YMCA, 1939-40, Little Rock YMCA, 1941-55, Atlanta YMCA, 1959-65, Met. N.Y. YMCA, 1976—; mem. Bronxville Bd. Zoning Appeals, 1973—. Served to capt. inf., AUS, 1942-45; Italy. Decorated Bronze Star with 3 clusters, Silver Star, Purple Heart with 2 clusters; recipient Devereux C. Josephs award N.Y. Life Ins. Co., 1954; named Ark. traveler, 1955, hon. citizen Tenn., 1956, Ky. col., 1963. Mem. Am., N.Y. socs. C.L.U.'s, Nat., N.Y. assns. life underwriters, N.Y. Gen. Agts. and Mgrs. Conf., Sales and Mktg. Execs. Internat., N.Y. Sales Execs. Club, N.Y. So. Soc. (trustee), 361st Inf. Assn. World War II (pres. 1967-70), Sons of Revolution, Soc. Colonial Wars, St. Nicholas Soc. N.Y., SAR, Tenn. Soc. in N.Y. (pres. 1971-73), Am. Risk and Ins. Assn. Mem. Reformed Ch. (elder). Clubs: Rotary; Capital City (Atlanta); Am. Yacht (Rye, N.Y.); Siwanoy (Bronxville, N.Y.). Home: 22 Oriole Ave Bronxville NY 10708 Office: 51 Madison Ave New York City NY 10010

GAUSS, WILLIAM FREDERICK, physician; b. Pitts., Sept. 18, 1928; s. William Frederick and Helen Sarah (Maxwell) G.; B.S., U. Mich., 1951; M.S., U. Pitts., 1973; Ed.D., Laurence U., 1974; M.D., U. Juarez, 1978; m. Lynn Elliott Diffenderfer, Dec. 23, 1967. Tech. rep. E.I. duPont Nemours & Co., Wilmington, Del., 1951-61; mgr. foam chems. Mobay Chem. Co., Pitts., 1961-71; dir. biochem. tech. Gulf Oil Chems. Co., Pitts., 1971-76; clin. clk. Forbes Health System, 1977-78; cons. Gulf Oil Chems. Co., 1976—; founding dir. Bio-Research Center Co., Ltd., Japan. Served to capt. Chem. Corps U.S. Army, 1954-56. NIH predoctoral fellow, 1969-71. Fellow Am. (accredited), Pa. insts. chemists. Republican. Contbr. articles in field to profl. socs.; patentee biochem. processes. Home: 725 Maryland Ave Pittsburgh PA 15232

GAUT, MARVIN JOSEPH, environ. scis. co. exec.; b. Mesa, Ariz., Aug. 26, 1911; s. John Alexander and Effie (Mayer) G.; accounting degree Ross Bus. Coll., 1929; m. Alice Doris Goode, Oct. 26, 1957; children by previous marriage—Barton C., Norman E.; 1 stepdau., Patricia C. Patton. Dep. assessor, dep. treas. Eagle County, Colo., 1929-38; bus. mgr. Forbush Co., Grand Junction, Colo., 1939,

Winfield Clark, Grand Junction, 1940; area supr. Goodrich Co., San Diego, 1941-42; foreman supr., supt., div. dir. Northrop Corp., Los Angeles, 1942-56; div. gen. mgr. Otis Elevator Co., N.Y.C., 1957-67; pres. Reflectone Inc., Stamford, Conn., 1968-69; founder, chmn. bd. Environ. Research & Technology Inc., Concord, Mass., 1969—. Mem. Am. Def. Preparedness Assn., Air Pollution Control Assn. Republican. Home: 6 Pheasant Ln Lexington MA 02173 Office: 696 Virginia Rd Concord MA 01742

GAUTHIER, GEORGE JAMES, chemist; b. Franklin, N.H., July 22, 1940; s. Peter Andrew and Lucille (LaCoursiere) G.; B.S., U. Notre Dame, 1962; Ph.D., U. N.H., 1966; M.B.A., U. New Haven, 1975; m. Frances Joy Steenbergen, June 27, 1964; children—Pamela Lee, Mark Gerald, Lisa Marie, Lucas Allen. Research asso. USAF Acad., 1966-69, asst. prof., 1967-69; research chemist Pfizer Inc., Groton, Conn., 1969-71, devel. chemist, 1971—; chem. cons. Kaman Nuclear Corp., Colorado Springs, Colo., 1967-69. Served to capt. USAF, 1966-69. Mem. Nat. Mgmt. Assn. Home: 166 Tyler Ave Groton CT 06340 Office: Pfizer Inc Groton CT 06340

GAUTHIER, NORMAN LEONIDAS, entomologist; b. Marlborough, Mass., Sept. 18, 1938; s. Norman Edward and Bertha Marion (Chagnon) G.; B.S. with honors, U. Mass., 1960; postgrad. (Nat. Def. fellow), U. Nebr., 1962; Ph.D., Cornell U., 1966; m. Bonnie Bell Weber, Aug. 6, 1960; children—Julie Lisa, Beth Michelle, Bonnie Claire. Label registration specialist Geigy Agrl. Chems. (name now CIBA-Geigy), Ardsley, N.Y., 1966-67, field research rep., 1967-70; mgr. entomology devel., sr. research entomologist Agway, Inc., Syracuse, N.Y., 1970—. Active Girl Scouts U.S.A. NSF honors grantee U. Mass., 1959-60; certified profl entomologist, N.Y. Mem. Am. Registry Profl. Entomologists, Entomol. Soc. Am., Am. Inst. Biol. Scis., Pesticide Assn. N.Y. State, Controlled Release Soc. Contbr. articles in field to profl. jours. Home: Box 189 RD 1 Old Seneca Turnpike Chittenango NY 13037 Office: 4933 Syracuse NY 13221

GAVURIN, LESTER L., educator; b. N.Y.C., Sept. 6, 1922; s. Louis and Dora (Benkin) G.; A.B. magna cum laude, Bklyn. Coll., 1943; M.Sc., Brown U., 1944; Ph.D., Columbia U., 1957; m. Esther Amkraut, Oct. 24, 1943; children—David Jacob, Rebecca Ann. Instr., Brown U., Providence, 1943-44; math. physicist NACA, Langley Field, Va., 1944-46; instr. Columbia, 1946-51; tchr., program chmn. Boys High Sch., Bklyn., 1950-62; asst. prof. Bklyn. Coll., 1962-70, asso. prof. math., 1970-75, prof. math., 1975—, chmn. dept., 1973—. Dir. Coop. Coll. Sch. Sci. Projects for Tchrs. Math. sponsored by NSF, 1965—. Mem. Am. Math. Soc., Math. Assn. Am., AAAS, N.Y. Acad. Scis., Am. Assn. U. Profs., Nat. Council Tchrs. Math., Sigma Xi (exec. sec. Bklyn. Coll. chpt. 1967-70, v.p. 1970-71, pres. 1972-73), Pi Mu Epsilon, Alpha Sigma Lambda. Author: (with William Forman) Elements of Arithmetic, Algebra and Geometry, 1972; Elements of Algebra and Trigonometry, 1974. Home: 3546 Bertha Dr Baldwin Harbor NY 11510 Office: Bklyn Coll Brooklyn NY 11210

GAY, WILLIAM ARTHUR, physician, educator; b. Richmond, Va., Jan. 16, 1936; s. William Arthur and Marion Harriette (Taylor) G.; B.A., Va. Mil. Inst., 1957; M.D., Duke, 1961; m. Frances Louise Adkins, Dec. 17, 1960; children—William Taylor, Mason Arthur. Asst. prof. surgery Cornell U. Med. Coll., N.Y.C., 1971-74, asso. prof., 1974-78, prof., 1978—; cardiothoracic surgeon-in-chief N.Y. Hosp., 1976—. Served with USPHS, 1963-65. Recipient Career Scientist award Irma T. Hirschl Charitable Trust, 1972. Mem. A.C.S., Assn. for Acad. Surgery, N.Y. Cardiovascular Soc., N.Y. Surg. Soc., Soc. Thoracic Surgery, Soc. Univ. Surgeons (treas. 1977-80). Contbr. articles to profl. jours. Home: 6 Park Hill Ln Larchmont NY 10538 Office: 525 E 68th St New York City NY 10021

GAYDOS, JOSEPH M., congressman; b. Braddock, Pa., July 3, 1926; s. John and Elona (Magella) G.; student pre-law Duquesne U.; LL.B., Notre Dame U., 1951; m. Alice Ann Gray, Nov. 26, 1955. Admitted to Pa. bar; practice law; asst. solicitor Allegheny County, Pa.: legal counsel United Mine Workers Am. Dist. 50; dep. atty. gen. Pa.; mem. Pa. Senate, 1966-68; mem. 91st-96th Congresses, 20th Dist. Pa. Served in World War II, PTO. Mem. Allegheny County Bar Assn., Am. Legion, Catholic War Vets., V.F.W., Sons of Italy, Croatian Fraternal Union, Jednota, Notre Dame Alumni Soc. Eagle. Club: Am.-Slovak (McKeesport, Pa.). Home: 3000 Valley Ridge Rd McKeesport PA 15133 Office: Rayburn House Office Bldg Washington DC 20515

GAYESKI, EDWARD CHARLES, interior designer; b. Duryea, Pa., May 29, 1919; s. Edward P. and Mary (Fudala) G.; student U. Ky., 1938-40; B.A., Washington and Lee U., 1947; m. Alba Lee Lori, Aug. 5, 1947; 1 dau., Diane. Started bus. House of Rex Craft (name changed to Rex Craft Assos., Inc. 1956), 1957; formed Rex Craft Internat., 1963; added Keystone Video System subsidiary to Rex Craft 1964; started Vilage Ice Cream Parlor chain ice cream stores and Internat. Mgmt. Co., 1965; pres. Village Mgmt. Co., 1964-66; started Rex Craft Realty and Devel. Co., 1966; cons. to George Hanby, Food Service Cons., Phila., ABC Paramount Theatres, New Orleans; dir. 1st Fed. Bank, Pittston, Pa. Mem. Pa. Gov.'s 1001 Com., 1965-67. Bd. dirs. pub. broadcasting sta. WVIA-TV. Served with USAF, 1942-45. Recipient Design award Interior Restaurants, 1966. Fellow Inst. Profl. Designers; mem. Am. Inst. Designers, Am. Legion, Nat. Soc. Interior Designers, Inst. Profl. Designers London, V.F.W., Scranton (city beautification com.), Pittston (dir.), Wilkes-Barre (indsl. com.) chambers commerce, Inst. Bus. Designers Archtl. and design work featured in various mags., jours. Home: 627 Charles Ave Kingston PA 18704 Office: Route 315 at Vine St Avoca PA 18641

GAYNES, BEN, JR., polit. economist; b. N.Y.C., Mar. 26, 1927; s. Ben and Ella (Mendelon) G.; B.A., Yale U., 1947; M.A., Stanford U., 1949; m. Helen B. Menjes, Oct. 13, 1959; children—Christopher, Lucinda, Edward, Beton. Vice-pres. Gaynes, Inc., 1949-55; research dir. Spragnegen & Co., N.Y.C., 1955-61; research specialist Shields & Co., N.Y.C., 1961-62; research dir. Sartorius, N.Y.C., 1962-64; v.p., polit. economist Clark Dodge & Co., N.Y.C., 1964-73; polit. economist J. Segab & Co., London, 1974-76, Morgan, Olmstead, Kennedy & Garnder, Los Angeles, 1976—. Mem. Nat. Assn. Bus. Economists, World Strategic Inst., N.Y. Soc. Security Analysts. Episcopalian. Clubs: Internat., Nat., Aspetuck Valley Country. Home: 40 Lyons Plain Weston CT 06883 Office: 606 S Olive St Los Angeles CA 90014

GAYNOR, ELIZABETH ANNE, editor; b. Balt., Feb. 21, 1946; d. Emanuel A. and Anne K. G.; B.A. cum laude in Psychology, Conn. Coll. for Women, 1967. Asst. translator Interpol, Paris, France, 1967-68; promotional rep., fashion coordinator Boussac of France, N.Y.C., 1968-71; asso. at home editor Glamour mag., N.Y.C., 1971-74, at home editor, 1974-76; home furnishings editor Family Circle mag., 1976—. Mem. Nat. Home Fashion League (press affiliate), Am. Soc. Interior Designers (press affiliate). Office: Family Circle Mag 488 Madison Ave New York City NY 10022

GAYNOR, RICHARD DANA, civil engr., assns. exec.; b. Mobile, Ala., July 13, 1931; s. Leo Harold and Frances Winans (Davis) G.; B.S. in Civil Engring., U. Ala., 1952; M.S. (Nat. Sand and Gravel Assn.-Nat. Ready Mixed Concrete Assn. fellow), U. Md., 1954; m. Margaret J. Bowers, Dec. 7, 1955; children—Deborah, Richard Dana, Patricia Jean, Leo Howard. With Nat. Sand and Gravel Assn.-Nat. Ready Mixed Concrete Assn., Silver Spring, Md., 1954—, dir. engring., 1971-75, v.p. engring. and research, 1975—. Registered profl. engr., Md. Mem. Am. Concrete Inst. (Arthur R. Anderson award 1978), ASTM (Sanford E. Thompson award 1963), Hwy. Research Bd., ASCE, Nat. Soc. Profl. Engrs., Tau Beta Pi, Chi Epsilon. Home: 2433 Countryside Dr Colesville MD 20910 Office: 900 Spring St Silver Spring MD 20910

GAZIANO, JOSEPH SALVATORE, mfg. co. exec.; b. Waltham, Mass., Apr. 2, 1935; s. Salvatore and Carmela (Gangi) G.; B.S.E.E., Mass. Inst. Tech., 1956; m. Anne Marie Bradley, Sept. 8, 1962; children—Christopher, Cara, Mary Elizabeth. Mgr. maj. space systems Raytheon Co., Lexington, Mass., 1960-67; v.p., gen. mgr. Allied Research Assos., Concord, Mass., 1967-69; pres. Prelude Corp., Westport, Mass., 1969-73; chmn. bd., pres. Tyco Labs., Inc., Exeter, N.H., 1973—; dir. Mobil Tyco Solar Energy Corp., New Boston Garden Corp. Republican. Roman Catholic. Home: Plumer Rd Epping NH 03042 Office: Tyco Park Exeter NH 03833

GAZIS, DENOS CONSTANTINOS, elec. engr.; b. Salonica, Greece, Sept. 15, 1930; s. Evangelos George and Lila Constantine (Veniamin) G.; came to U.S., 1953, naturalized, 1960; B.S., Tech. U. Athens (Greece), 1952; M.S., Stanford U., 1954; Ph.D. in Engring. Mechs., Columbia U., 1957; m. Jean Ellen Ryniker, Sept. 15, 1974; children—Paul, Jean, Lynn, Andrew, Carey, Jessie, Alexander. Sr. research scientist Gen. Motors Co., Warren, Mich., 1957-61; with IBM, 1961—, tech. adv. to v.p., chief scientist, Armonk, N.Y., 1975-77, cons. to v.p., dir. research, Yorktown Heights, N.Y., 1977—; vis. prof. Yale U., 1969-70; cons. to govt. agys.; mem. transp. research bd. NRC-Nat. Acad. Scis. Recipient Lanchester prize Johns Hopkins U.-Ops. Research Soc. Am., 1959. Mem. Am. Phys. Soc., Ops. Research Soc. Am., Soc. Natural Philosophy, World Future Soc. Author: Free Vibrations of Circular Cylindrical Shells, 1969; Traffic Science, 1974; asso. editor Transp. Sci., 1970—, Networks, 1971—, Computing, 1969-76; contbr. articles on physics, engring. and ops. research to profl. jours. Home: RD 2 Lake Rd Katonah NY 10536 Office: IBM Research Center Box 218 Yorktown Heights NY 10598

GEBAUER, KURT MANFRED, advt.-mktg. exec.; b. Paterson, N.J., Dec. 12, 1951; s. Werner and Edna Julie (Harris) G.; B.A., Bucknell U., 1974. Gen. mgr. Radio Sta. WUDO, Lewisburg, Pa., 1973-74; v.p. Now Sound Assos., Lewisburg, 1974-75; ops. mgr. Radio Sta. WCRV, Washington, N.J., 1975-76; pres. WTS Corp., Hackettstown, N.J., 1976—; cons. Warren Broadcasting Co. (WFMV-FM), Blairstown, N.J., 1978—. Mem. Asso. Photographers Internat., Pi Delta Epsilon. Home: 274 Alexandria Dr Hackettstown NJ 07840 Office: PO Box 428 Blairstown NJ 07825

GEBELEIN, RICHARD STEPHEN, state ofcl.; b. Darby, Pa., June 8, 1946; s. Walter C. and Margaret Elizabeth G.; B.S. in Math., U. Pitts., 1967; J.D., Villanova U., 1970. Admitted to Pa. bar, 1971, Del. bar, 1971, U.S. Supreme Ct. Bar, 1975; clk. Del. Ct. Chancery, 1970-71; dep. atty. gen State of Del., Wilmington, 1971-74, state solicitor, 1974-75, chief dep. public defender, 1975-76, atty. gen., 1978—; partner firm Wilson & Whittington, P.A., Wilmington, 1976-78; instr. in law Del. Law Sch., 1973—. Mem. Del. Bar Assn., Pa. Bar Assn., Am. Bar Assn., Am. Judicature Soc., Nat. Dist. Attys. Assn., Nat. Assn. Attys. Gen. Republican. Roman Catholic. Clubs: Univ., Whist of Wilmington. Home: 2803 Duncan Rd Wilmington DE 19808 Office: 8th Floor State Bldg 802 French St Wilmington DE 19849

GEE, WILLIAM, vascular surgeon; b. Riverhead, N.Y., Nov. 4, 1931; s. John Eccleston and Agnes Katherine (Shea) G.; student Bklyn. Coll., 1955-57; M.D., State U. N.Y., Bklyn., 1961; m. Beverly Joan Furrow, Aug. 11, 1956; children—Catherine, William, Michael, Patricia, Susan. Enlisted in U.S. Navy, 1951, advanced through grades to capt. M.C., 1975; intern Naval Hosp., St. Albans, N.Y., 1961-62, resident, 1963-67; chief surgery Naval Hosp., Guantanamo Bay, Cuba, 1967-69; fellow U. Calif., San Francisco, chief vascular surgery Nat. Naval Med. Center, Bethesda, Md., 1973-77; ret., 1977; dir. vascular lab. Allentown (Pa.)-Sacred Heart Hosp. Center, 1977—. Mem. A.C.S., Internat. Cardiovascular Soc., Soc. Vascular Surgery, Chesapeake Vascular Soc. Roman Catholic. Contbr. articles to med. pubs.; patentee ocular pneumoplethysmograph. Office: 2200 Hamilton St Suite 212 Allentown PA 18104

GEE, ZILPHIA TONI, speech pathologist; b. Port Arthur, Tex., Dec. 11, 1941; d. Lloyd and Georgiana (Manson) Powell; B.A. in Edn., Huston-Tillotson Coll., Austin, Tex., 1963; M.A. in Speech Pathology and Audiology, Cath. U. Am., Washington, 1973. Tchr., Abilene (Tex.) Ind. Sch. Dist., 1963-65, Roosevelt Sch. Dist., Phoenix, 1965-67, D.C. Pub. Schs., Washington, 1967-71; communications disorders tchr. Grant Sch. Spl. Edn., Washington, from 1973; instr., dir. Speech and Hearing Clinic, Howard U., Washington, 1977—; cons. speech pathology Home Health Services, Inc., Washington. Recipient award for outstanding vol. service to head start project, 1978. Mem. Am., Md. speech and hearing assns., AAUW, Nat. Council Negro Women, Alpha Kappa Alpha. Kappa Alpha. Specialist in voice, speech and lang. disorders. Home: 9900 Georgia Ave Apt 516 Silver Spring MD 20902 Office: Howard Univ Dept Communications Arts and Scis Washington DC 20059

GEESLIN, WILLIAM FLEMING, r.r. exec.; b. Macon, Ga., June 16, 1919; s. William Fleming and Louise (Wynn) G.; B.A., Mercer U., 1940; m. Mary Elizabeth Timmerman, May 18, 1946; children—William Fleming, John W., Christopher. Spl. agt. FBI, 1942-47; account exec. Young & Rubicam, N.Y.C., 1947-60; devel. dir., Manatee County, Fla., 1961-63; v.p. First Nat. Bank, Bradenton, Fla., 1963-64; spl. rep. pub. relations So. Ry. System, Washington, 1964-67, asst. v.p. pub. relations and advs., 1967—. Mem. Pub. Relations Soc. Am., Am. Marketing Assn., Soc. Former Agts. FBI, Phi Delta Theta. Clubs: Chevy Chase, City Tavern. Home: 5351 MacArthur Blvd NW Washington DC 20016 Office: Box 1808 So Ry System Washington DC 20013

GEGENY, THOMAS PAUL, psychiat. social worker; b. N.Y.C., Mar. 9, 1940; s. Joseph and Giselle (Loth) G.; A.A.S., Baruch Coll., 1960; B.B.A., CUNY, 1962; M.S.W., Adelphi U., 1971; Ph.D., Sussex Coll., 1976; m. Rose Ann Theresa Puglisi, Mar. 11, 1970; children—Thomas Paul, II, Theresa Ellen, Mark Elliott, Joseph-Louis Sandor. Social investigator N.Y.C. Dept. Welfare, 1965-69; social worker N.Y.C. Bur. Child Guidance, 1969-70, Community Service Soc., N.Y.C., 1970-71, Bur. Child Welfare, N.Y.C., 1971-72, Agy. for Child Devel., Human Resources Adminstrn., N.Y.C. Area Psychiat. Services, 1972-73; founder dir. Psychait. Cons., New Fairfield, Conn., 1973—; founder, bd. dirs. Nat. Research Inst. for Psychoanalysis; N.Y. State scholar N.Y.C. Dept. Social Services, 1969-71. Founder, Kelly St. Block Assn., N.Y.C. 1966, Cedar Ave. Block Assn., N.Y.C., 1969. Cert. social worker, N.Y. State. Mem. Nat. Assn. Social Workers, Acad. Cert. Social Workers, Register Clin. Social Workers, Profl. Directory Social Workers, Candlewood Hills Assn. (pres. 1972-76). Republican. Roman Catholic. Clubs: Hungarian, William Penn Fraternal Assn. Home: Candlewood Hills New Fairfield CT 06810

GEHRING, CHARLES THEODOR, translator, editor; b. Ft. Plain, N.Y., Apr. 3, 1939; s. Charles Theodore and Esther Anaclata (Stefanacci) G.; student Va. Mil. Inst., 1956-58; B.A., W.Va. U., 1962, M.A., 1964; Fulbright fellow, Albert-Ludwigs Universitat, 1964-65; Ph.D., (NDEA fellow), Ind. U., 1973; m. Jean Ann Matis, Feb. 1, 1962; 1 son, Dietrich Christian. Instr. German and linguistics U. Albany (N.Y.), 1968-74; co-worker Royal Dialect Inst., Amsterdam, The Netherlands, summer 1971; translator, editor 17th Century Dutch records of New Netherland, N.Y. State Library, Albany, 1974—; research fellow Huntington Library, 1976. Trustee, Ft. Klock Historic Restoration, St. Johnsville, N.Y. Editor: New York Historical Manuscripts: Dutch, Delaware Papers, Vols. XX-XXL, 1977. Home: RD 2 Picard Rd Altamont NY 12009 Office: Manuscripts and Spl Collections NY State Library Albany NY 12230

GEHRKE, ROBERT FREDERICK, research and devel. exec.; b. Shawano, Wis., June 7, 1935; s. Herman Andrew and Ruth Hulda (Wendt) G.; B.S. in Math., Valparaiso U., 1957; postgrad. U. Md., 1957-59; m. Ellen Erna Heck, Sept. 13, 1958; children—Diane Marie, David Allen. With Applied Physics Lab., John Hopkins U., Laurel, Md., 1957—, guided missile analysis, 1957-66, missile countermeasures supr., 1966-72, mem. prin. profl. staff, 1970—, supr. test and evaluation project office, 1972—, supr. systems evaluation br., 1978—; cons. in field. Served with U.S. Army, 1959. Mem. Assn. Old Crows, Am. Def. Preparedness Assn. Lutheran. Home: 14208 Sturtevant Rd Silver Spring MD 20904 Office: Johns Hopkins Rd Laurel MD 20810

GEHRON, WILLIAM HENRY, JR., urologic surgeon; b. Williamsport, Pa., Dec. 6, 1918; s. William Henry and Marguerite (McKelvey) G.; student Dickenson Jr. Coll., 1936-38; B.A., Susquehanna U., 1940; M.D., Jefferson Med. Coll., 1944; m. Betty Yvonne Schwoerer, Oct. 7, 1944; children—William Henry, Amelia Reppard, Hope Elizabeth, Timothy Marc. Intern, Williamsport Hosp., 1944, resident, 1946-47; plant physician Bethlehem Steel Corp., Williamsport, 1950-55; instr. surgery U. Pitts., 1955-59; practice medicine specializing in urologic surgery, 1959—; chief urology Williamsport Hosp., Divine Providence Hosp., Williamsport; cons. Soldiers and Sailors Meml. Hosp., Wellsboro, Pa., Muncy (Pa.) Valley Hosp., Jersey Shore (Pa.) Hosp.; pres. 1st Fed. Savs. & Loan Co., 1974-76, also dir. Served with USN, 1942-46. Diplomate Am. Bd. Urology. Mem. AMA, NE Am., Am. urol. assns., Pa., Lycoming County med. socs. Republican. Presbyterian. Clubs: Ross, Larry's Creek Fish and Game, Masons. Contbr. articles to med. jours. Home: 747 Arch St Williamsport PA 17701 Office: 699 Rural Ave Williamsport PA 17701

GEIBEL, EDGAR LEROY, hosp. cons.; b. Butler, Pa., Dec. 12, 1910; s. John S. and Irene (Green) G.; student Carnegie Inst. Tech., 1937-39; B.S., U. Pitts., 1941; M.P.H., Yale U., 1949; m. Dorothy Schorner, Oct. 29, 1942; children—Mary Ellen, Victoria Irene. Dir. health Butler, 1936-43; adminstrv. asst. Genessee Hosp., Rochester, N.Y., 1948-49, asst. dir., 1949-54; adminstr. then exec. v.p. Stamford (Conn.) Hosp., from 1954, pres., chief exec. officer, 1976-78; spl. adviser Conn. Hosp. Assn., 1978—; lectr. Yale Sch. Medicine. Served from 2d lt. to capt. AUS, 1943-47. Fellow Am. Coll. Hosp. Adminstrs. (council regents 1964-67), Am. Pub. Health Assn.; mem. New Eng. Hosp. Assembly (pres. 1968-69), Am. (ho. of dels. 1969-72, trustee 1973-76, chmn. New Eng. regional adv. bd. 1973-76), Conn. (pres. 1964-65, distinguished service award 1976) hosp. assns., Pa. Soc. Clubs: Rotary, Grad. (New Haven). Contbr. articles to profl. jours. Home: 345 Hycliff Terr Stamford CT 06902 Office: PO Box 90 Wallingford CT 06492

GEIGER, GENE EDWARD, educator; b. Castle Shannon, Pa., Oct. 27, 1928; s. Harry and Jessie Jane (Lee) G.; B.S., Carnegie-Mellon U., 1950; M.S., U. Pitts., 1955, Ph.D., 1964; m. Virginia Ann Miller, Jan. 24, 1959; children—Gregg, Amy. Instr. mech. engring. U. Pitts., 1951-55, asst. prof., 1955-65, asso. prof., 1965-71, prof., 1971—. Cons. to various cos. Ford Found. grantee, 1962-64. Registered profl. engr., Pa. Mem. Pa. Soc. Profl. Engrs., ASME, Sigma Xi, Pi Tau Sigma. Contbr. articles to profl. publs. Home: 113 Griendrier Dr Carnegie PA 15106 Office: 645 Benedum Hall Univ Pitts Pittsburgh PA 15261

GEIGER, JEAN W. ROBERTS (MRS. ROBERT LOUIS GEIGER), ins. co. exec.; b. Orange, N.J., Apr. 17, 1919; d. Edmund Weston and Anna (DuBois) Roberts; student Colby Jr. Coll., 1937-38; m. Merritt Lum Budd, Jr., Nov. 1937 (div. Mar. 1946); children—Merritt Lum III, David Weston, Pamela DuBois (Mrs. Robert Lawrence); m. 2d, Robert Louis Geiger, Apr. 15, 1950; children—Stephen Roberts, Mark Charles, Lauren Ann. Reporter, Newark News, 1947-48, editorial bur. chief, 1948-51, feature writer, 1951-57; account exec. Williams & London Pub. Relations, 1957-58; dir. pub. relations United Hosps. Newark, 1958-67, N.J. Coll. Medicine and Dentistry, Newark, 1967-70; cons. A.E. Briod & Assos., Inc., Newark, 1970-72; pub. relations officer Blue Shield N.J., Newark, 1973-74, v.p. communications, 1974—, chmn. pub. relations and advt. Eastern div., 1977—. Chmn. council Newark Mus., 1977-78. Recipient nat. awards MacEachern competitions, 1961, 62 (2), 67. Mem. Am., N.J. hosp. assns., Pub. Relations Soc. Am., N.J. Press Assn., Newark C. of C. (editorial adv. com., chmn. communications com.), Advt. club N.J. (pres. 1977-78). Home: 23 Old Forge Rd Millington NJ 07946 Office: 33 Washington St Newark NJ 07102

GEIGER, LOREN DENNIS, band dir.; b. Buffalo, Jan. 23, 1946; s. Carroll Chester and Edith Lucille (Swedenborg) G.; B.Mus., Eastman Sch. Music, Rochester, N.Y., 1968, M.Mus., 1970; m. Elaine Louise Sivers, Aug. 21, 1976. Band dir. Orchard Park (N.Y.) Central Sch., 1969—; profl. tuba player, 1968—. Mem. Music Educators Nat. Conf., N.Y. State Sch. Music Assn., Erie County Music Educators Assn., Orchard Park Tchrs. Assn., Am. Fedn. Musicians, Internat. Mil. Music Soc., Tuba Universal Brotherhood Assn., Circus World Mus. (life), Circus Fans of Am., Circus Model Builders, Circus Hist. Soc., Circus Windjammers Unltd., Nat. Band Assn., Pi Kappa Lamba. Publisher band musicology newsletters, arranger works for bands. Home: 15 Park Blvd Lancaster NY 14086 Office: Orchard Park Central Sch Orchard Park NY 14127

GEIGER, PHILIP EARL, ednl. adminstr.; b. New Brunswick, N.J., June 12, 1947; s. Philip Murray and Ida May (Danley) G.; B.A., Trenton State Coll., 1970; M.A., Columbia U., 1972; Ed.M., Columbia U., 1973; m. Roseann E. Meade, Mar. 21, 1975; children—Philip Earl, Robert, Jennifer, Abigail Leigh. Tchr., Corpus Christi Sch., S. River, N.J., 1967-69, Crossroads Sch., South Brunswick, N.J., 1969-71; staff asst. Crossroads Sch., 1971-74; asst. prin. Bordentown Twp. (N.J.) pub. schs., 1972-74; dir. adminstrv. services Scotch Plains-Fanwood, N.J. pub. schs., 1974-77; supt. schs. Galloway Twp., N.J., 1977—; labor relations cons. N.J. Assn. Elementary and Secondary Sch. Prins., Trenton. Recipient Distinguished Service award N.J. Elementary Sch. Adminstrs. Assn., 1977; Inst. Devel. Ednl. Ideas fellow, 1978. Mem. N.J. Jr. C. of C. (pres. 1970-72), Galloway Twp. C. of C. (dir. 1978—), Nat. Sch. Pub. Relations Assn. (1st v.p. New Jersey chpt. 1976-77), Am., N.J. assns. sch. adminstrs., Phi Delta Kappa. Editorial bd. Elementary Sch. Guidance and Counseling Jour., 1977. Home: 15 Anthony Ln

Galloway Twp NJ 08240 Office: Pomona Plaza Box 843 Pomona NJ 08240

GEIGER, WALTER CASE, univ. adminstr.; b. Marion, Ohio, Mar. 25, 1912; s. E. Stroh and Ruth (Heckert) G.; B.S., Bucknell U., 1934; postgrad. Pa. State U., 1941-42; m. Lois Frey, May 6, 1941. Asst. chief engr. Armour Co., Williamsport, Pa., 1936-46; dir. phys. plant, univ. engr. planning, design and new constrn. Bucknell U., Lewisburg, Pa., 1946—; dir. Citizens Electric Co., Lewisburg, 1961—, chmn. acting pres. com., 1970-71; spl. cons. Alderson-Broaddus Coll., W.Va. Wesleyan Coll., Susquehanna U., Geisinger Med. Center. Bd. dirs. Evang. Community Hosp., Lewisburg, Pa., 1965—, United Meth. Home, 1970—. Registered profl. engr., Pa. Mem. Am. Soc. Heating, Refrigerating and Air Conditioning Engrs. (exec. com. 1972-76), Assn. Phys. Plant Adminstrs. (treas. 1974—, exec. com. 1968—), ASME (exec. com. 1950-55). Methodist. Club: Lions. Home: College Park Lewisburg PA 17837 Office: Phys Plant Bucknell Univ Lewisburg PA 17837

GEIS, BERNARD, book publisher; b. Chgo., Aug. 30, 1909; s. Harry M. and Bessie (Gesas) G.; B.A., Northwestern U., 1931; m. Darlene Stern, Mar. 28, 1940; children—Peter, Stephen. Newspaper reporter, contbr. mags., 1931-33; editor Apparel Arts Mag., 1933-38; asst. editor Esquire mag., 1938-45; editor Coronet mag., 1939-45; war corr., ETO for Coronet and Esquire mags., 1942-43, editor-in-chief Grosset & Dunlap Pub. Co., 1945-53, v.p., 1949-53; editor Prentice-Hall Pub. Co., 1954-57, editor, pres. Bernard Geis Assos., Inc., N.Y.C., 1958—; pres. subsidiary Ampersand Press Inc., 1963—. Chmn. pubs. group N.Y.C. Salvation Army ann. appeal, 1960-66; mem. dirs. council, fund raising adv. com. N.Y. Heart Assn. Bd. dirs. Ams. Dem. Action, mem. exec. com., 1965—. Home: 1385 York Ave New York City NY 10021 Office: 128 E 56th St New York City NY 10022

GEISS, JACQUELINE SUZANNE, lawyer, certified pub. accountant; b. Evanston, Ill., May 18, 1936; d. Frederick William and Suzanne (La Velle) G.; student U. Colo., 1952-55, Baylor U., 1961-63; LL.B., U. Tex., 1961; m. Charles P. Rothmann, Dec. 2, 1972 (dec. 1974). Admitted to Tex. bar, 1961; practiced law Waco, Tex., 1961-62; accountant Scott-Timmons & Co., C.P.A.'s, Waco, 1962-64; sr. law clk. to U.S. Dist. Judge, San Antonio, 1964-66; tax specialist Peat, Marwick, Mitchell & Co., C.P.A.'s, 1967-69; asst. gen. counsel, asst. corporate sec. Data Automation Co., Inc., Dallas, 1969-70; gen. counsel, corporate sec. Alcorn Combustion Co., N.Y.C., 1970-72; corporate counsel, corporate sec., dir. Titan Group, Inc., Paramus, N.J., 1972-76; asst. corporate sec., sr. atty. The Continental Group, Inc., 1976—; mem. Tex. Bd. Pub. Accountancy. C.P.A., Tex. Mem. Am., San Antonio bar assns., State Bar Tex., Am. Inst. C.P.A.'s, Am. Women's Soc. C.P.A.'s, Am. Soc. Women Accountants, Sigma Alpha Iota (sec. 1952-53), Kappa Beta Pi (pres. 1959-61), Beta Alpha Psi (sec. 1962-63), Beta Gamma Sigma. Presbyterian. Asso. editor Dicta (U. Tex. Law Sch. newspaper), 1960-61. Address: PO Box 998 Darien CT 06820

GEISSBUHLER, ARNOLD, sculptor, educator; b. Delémont, Switzerland, Aug. 9, 1897; s. Frederic and Rosina (Brandenberger) G.; student Arts and Crafts Sch., Zurich, Switzerland, 1914-1919, Acad. Julian, Paris, France, 1919-20, Acad. Grande-Chaumiere, 1920-25; m. Elisabeth Chase, Aug. 15, 1927; children—Mirande Holt, Christine Dupuy. Came to U.S., 1927, naturalized, 1941. One-man shows at Delémont, 1924, Kraushar Gallery, N.Y.C., 1929, Balt. Mus. Fine Arts, 1942, Gallery Seven, Boston, 1965, numerous others; exhibited in group shows at Phila. Internat., 1940, 49, Am. Sculpture, 1951, Met. Mus. N.Y., Art in U.S.A., 1958, New Eng. Art, Boston, 1971; also Sculptors Guild shows, N.Y.C., 1939-73; represented in permanent collections at Art Mus., Bern, Switzerland, Mus. Jurassien, Delemont, Fogg Art Mus., Harvard, Mass., Fansworth Mus., Wellesley (Mass.) Coll., Chester Dale Collection, N.Y.C., Nat. Art Mus., Washington, numerous others. Tchr. drawing and sculpture techniques N.Y. Sch. Design, 1929-30; instr. Stuart Sch. Design Boston, 1936-42, Wellesley Coll., 1937-58; tchr. Scargo Pines Studio, Dennis, Mass., 1959-69. Recipient Bronze medal Acad. Julian, 1919, Cambridge Centennial award, 1946, Outstanding award Art U.S.A., 1958. Mem. Sculptor's Guild N.Y. Address: Scargo Pines Box 202 Dennis MA 02638

GEISSLER, SUZANNE BURR, historian; b. Somerville, N.J., Nov. 12, 1950; d. Alfred Henry and Suzanne Judith (Golembiewski) G.; B.A., Syracuse U., 1971, Ph.D., 1976; M.A., Rutgers U., 1972; postgrad. Worcester Coll., Oxford U., 1973. Asst. to dir., lectr. program in nonviolent conflict and change Syracuse (N.Y.) U., 1972-77; lectr. history dept. State U. N.Y., Cortland, 1975-77, Drew U., Madison, N.J., 1978—. Mem. Morris County Election Bd., 1978—. Noyes Found. grantee, 1968-73. Mem. Am. Soc. Ch. History, Am. Studies Assn., Am. Hist. Assn., Orgn. Am. Historians, Polish Inst. Arts and Scis., Aaron Burr Assn., AAUP, Soc. of Friends of St. George's, Phi Beta Kappa. Republican. Episcopalian. Club: Chatham Squash. Home: 4 Midwood Dr Florham Park NJ 07932 Office: History Dept Drew U Madison NJ 07940

GELARDI, ARTHUR V., advt. co. exec.; b. Lawrence, Mass., Aug. 6, 1928; s. Dionigi and Josephine T. G.; B.S., Boston U., 1952; M.Ed., Salem State Coll., 1971; m. Jean Biancucci, June 10, 1951; children—Mark D., Wayne A. Mem. advt. dept. Jordan Marsh Co., Boston, 1952-54; advt. dir. A.B. Sutherland Co., Lawrence, Mass., 1955-67; asst. v.p., advt. dir. Elliott Stores of N.E., Salem, N.H., 1968-74; pres., treas. AD Services Unlimited, Andover, Mass., 1975—. Home: 33 North St Andover MA 01810 Office: 166 N Main St PO Box 9 Andover MA 01810

GELB, JOSEPH DONALD, lawyer; b. Wilkes-Barre, Pa., Dec. 13, 1923; s. Edward and Esther (Fierman) G.; student Pa. State Coll., 1943; B.S., U. Scranton, 1950; LL.B., George Washington U., 1952; m. Anne Mirman, July 3, 1955; children—Adam, Roger. Adjudicator, War Claims Commn., 1952-54; admitted to D.C. bar, 1954, Md. bar, 1963; practiced in Washington, Md., 1954—; partner Gelb & Pitsenberger, Washington, 1969-74, Bowie, Md., 1969-74; prin. Joseph D. Gelb Chartered, 1974—. Served with USAAF, 1943-46. Mem. Am., Md. bar assns., Bar Assn. D.C., Assn. Plaintiff's Trial Attys. Mason; mem. B'nai B'rith. Club: Bethesda Country. Home: 9620 Annlee Terr Bethesda MD 20034 Office: 1120 Connecticut Ave NW Washington DC 20036 also Belair Profl Village Bowie MD 20715

GELB, JUDITH ANNE, lawyer; b. N.Y.C., Apr. 5, 1935; d. Joseph and Sarah (Stein) G.; B.A. cum laude, Bklyn. Coll., 1955; J.D., Columbia U., 1958; m. Howard S. Vogel, June 30, 1962; 1 son, Michael S. Admitted to N.Y. bar, 1959, U.S. Ct. Mil. Appeals, 1962; confdl. asst. to U.S. atty. Eastern Dist. N.Y., Bklyn., 1959-61; asso. Whitman & Ransom, N.Y.C., 1961-70; partner Whitman & Ransom, 1971—. Mem. Assn. Bar City N.Y., Fed. Bar Council, N.Y. State (com. trusts and estates), N.Y. Women's (com. by-laws, com. taxation 1968-70) bar assns., N.Y. State Dist. Attys. Assn., Assn. Ex-Mems. of Squadron A, Psi Chi. Club: Princeton U. (N.Y.C.). Home: 169 E 69 St New York City NY 10016 Office: 522 Fifth Ave New York City NY 10036

GELB, WILLIAM GARY, health care co. exec.; b. Bklyn., Mar. 11, 1946; s. Harold and Frieda (Rosentsrach) G.; A.A.S., State U.N.Y., 1965; B.S. in Chemistry, Hofstra U., 1967; M.S. (NSF fellow), U. Mass., 1970, Ph.D., 1971; m. Penny Lewow, Sept. 4, 1967; children—Jay, Bruce. Chemist, Lederle Labs., Pearl River, N.Y., 1965, asst. mgr. tech. services Pharmacia Fine Chems., Piscataway, N.J., 1970-72, mgr. tech. services, 1972-74, mktg. mgr., 1974-76, dir. mktg., 1976-77, gen. mgr. Pharmacia Diagnostics, 1977—. Mem. Am. Mgmt. Assn., Am. Chem. Soc., Am. Soc. Clin. Pathologists. Contbr. articles to profl. jours. Home: 270 Dutch Farm Rd Bridgewater NJ 08807 Office: 800 Centennial Ave Piscataway NJ 08854

GELBER, MELVIN WILBUR, cons. mech. engr.; b. Hackensack, N.J., Aug. 14, 1923; s. Isidore Baer and Lillian (Celia) Altman; B.S. in Mech. Engring. magna cum laude, U. Notre Dame, 1944, M.S., 1947; m. Beverly E. Gilman, Aug. 22, 1948; children—Linda, Meryl, Lawrence, Douglas, Darlene. Instr. engring. mechanics U. Notre Dame (Ind.), 1947-48; stress analyst Wright Aircraft Corp., Wood-Ridge, N.J., 1948-49; instr. thermodynamics, heat and power Cooper Union, N.Y.C., 1950-51; owner Melvin W. Gelber, Cons. Engr., Hackensack, 1950—. Served with USNR, 1943-46; PTO. Mem. Tau Beta Pi. Club: Masons. Home: 7 Dover Ct Bergenfield NJ 07621 Office: 31 Mercer St Hackensack NJ 07601

GELDBAUGH, GEORGE RICHARD, architect; b. Arthurdale, W.Va., May 7, 1938; s. George Orr and Elizabeth Francis (Warder) G.; student Fla. So. Coll., 1956-57, Emery Riddle Aero. Coll., 1957-58; B. Arch., U. Fla., 1963; m. Barbara Jane Walker, June 14, 1958; children—Mark Richard, Susan Michele. Archtl. designer, Herbert Johnson & Assos. Architects, Miami, Fla., 1964-66, Adonay Bergamaschi, Architect, Miami, 1966-67; indsl. designer, Travel Coach Recreation Vehicles, Elgin, Ill., 1967-70; architect, G. Richard Geldbaugh, Boca Raton, Fla., 1970-71; architect, product designer G. Richard Geldbaugh, Manchester, Vt., 1976—; indsl. designer Cortez Corp. Recreation Vehicles, Kent, Ohio, 1971-72; design partner Bogart, Geldbaugh, Goldstein, Peters, L.I., N.Y., 1974-76; v.p. and dir., Travel Coach, Inc.; v.p. and dir. Bogart, Geldbaugh, Goldstein and Peters Profl. Corp. Mem. Manchester Village design review bd., 1973; Manchester edn. guide planner, 1974, mem. town planning bd., 1974; Manchester Bicentennial Cons., 1975; dir. Northshire Med. Health Care, 1974. Registered architect, Fla., Vt., N.Y. State. Mem. AIA (corp.), Vt. Chpt. AIA (corp.). Republican. Congregationalist. Patentee recreation vehicle 1971. Office: On the Green Manchester Center VT 05255

GELFMAN, JUDITH SCHLEIN, television producer, author; b. N.Y.C., May 26, 1937; d. Samuel R. and Rose (Friedman) Schlein; student Cornell U., 1954-56; B.F.A. cum laude, Columbia U., 1958, M.A., 1962, Ed.D., 1974; m. Stanley Gelfman, July 14, 1957; children—Debra Dawn, Sari Susanne. Producer, broadcaster Channel 13, WNET, 1962-66; freelance television writer, cons., 1966-71; pres. JSG Prodns., N.Y.C., 1974; producer writer TV series Out of Work, Feeling Female; dir. Justonics Corp., N.Y.C.; instr. Tchrs. Coll., Columbia; adj. prof. communication Hunter Coll., N.Y.C. Mem. Actors Equity Assn., Screen Actors Guild, AFTRA, Nat. Acad. TV Arts and Scis., Internat. Radio and TV Soc., Pi Lambda Theta, Kappa Delta Pi. Clubs: Cornell Women's, Statesmen's. Author: Women in Television News, 1976. Home: 4455 Douglas Ave Riverdale NY 10471 Office: 521 Fifth Ave New York City NY 10017

GELFMAN, ROBERT WILLIAM, lawyer; b. N.Y.C., Jan. 22, 1932; s. Irving and Lillian (Meltzer) G.; B.S., U. Pa., 1953; LL.B., Harvard U., 1956; m. Phyllis A. Trustman, Dec. 18, 1955; children—Lisa Jane, Peter Trustman. Admitted to N.Y., Mass. bars, 1956; partner firm Battle, Fowler, Lidstone, Jaffin, Pierce & Kheel; chmn. bd. Arrow Lock Corp., 1969-72. Mem. exec. bd. New Leadership div. Fedn. Jewish Philanthropies, 1962-64, chmn. Speakers Bur., 1964; trustee, v.p. Jewish Bd. Guardians; trustee Hawthorne Cedar Knolls Sch., also pres. mgmt. com., pres. bd. edn. Served to capt. USAF, 1957-60. Mem. Am. Arbitration Assn., Am. Bar Assn., Assn. Bar City N.Y., N.Y. County Lawyers Assn., Am. Law Inst. Jewish. Clubs: Harvard of N.Y.; Metropolis Country (White Plains, N.Y.). Home: 17 Eton Rd Scarsdale NY 10583 Office: 280 Park Ave New York City NY 10017

GELFMAN, STANLEY, mech., indsl. engr.; b. N.Y.C., Oct. 22, 1927; s. Max and Bessie (Mertz) G.; B.S. in Mech. Engring., Coll. City N.Y., 1949; M.B.A., Columbia, 1950, Certificate Indsl. Design, 1950; m. Judith Marlene Schlein, July 14, 1957; children—Debra Dawn, Sari Susanne. Employed Krischer Metal Products, 1949-61, successively efficiency engr., supr. machine design div., charge research testing and devel. div., partner, 1952—; dir., organized Automation Research Corp., 1956; v.p. Research Casual Living Co., 1958—, organized food and drug div.-splty. sales, 1960; organized, pres. Justonics Corp., N.Y.C., 1961—; chmn. bd., chief exec. officer Air Vectors Corp., N.Y.C., 1967; dir. Rodney Kent Silver Co. Friends Com. Henry Street Settlement House; fellowship supporter Harvard Coll. Obs. Mem. ASME, Pi Tau Sigma. Contbr. articles to profl. pubs. Home: 4455 Douglas Ave Riverdale NY 10471 Office: Justonics Corp 521 Fifth Ave New York City NY 10017

GELINAS, PAUL J., psychologist; b. Woonsocket, R.I., July 17, 1911; s. Edmund J. and Marianne (Desaultnier) G.; Ed.D.; m. 1933; 1 son, Robert. Supt. schs. Setauket, N.Y., 1941-63; clin. psychologist in pvt. practice, Setauket, 1963—; faculty State U. N.Y. at Stony Brook, 1970—; cons. municipalities. Tax receiver, Brookhaven (N.Y.) Town, 1975-77. Jr. high sch. in Setauket named in his honor. Mem. N.Y. State, Suffolk County psychol. assns., N.Y. Tchrs. Assn. Democrat. Presbyterian. Club: Lions (pres. 1962-63). Author books; contbr. articles to profl. publs. Home: 31 W Meadow Rd Setauket NY 11733

GELINEAU, LOUIS EDWARD, clergyman; b. Burlington, Vt., May 3, 1928; s. Leon and Juliette (Baribault) G.; student St. Michael's Coll., Winooski, Vt., 1946-48; B.A., B.Philosophy, St. Paul's U., Ottawa, Ont., Can., 1950, L.S.T., 1954; Licentiate Canon Law, Catholic U. Am., 1959; D.R.E., Providence Coll., 1972. Ordained priest Roman Catholic Ch., 1954; asst. chancellor Diocese Burlington, 1959-61, chancellor, 1961-71, vicar gen., 1968-71; bishop of Providence, 1971—. Home: 34 Fenner St Providence RI 02903 Office: Cathedral Sq Providence RI 02903

GELLEIN, OSCAR STRAND, accountant; b. Milnor, N.D., May 15, 1911; s. Ole Andrew and Gunhild (Sandnes) G.; B.S., Southeastern State Coll., 1932; M.S., Okla. State U., 1939; m. Nettie Belle Harshman; 1 dau., Linda Sue Gellein Cooper. Prof. accounting, treas. U. Denver, 1946-52; partner Haskins & Sells, C.P.A.'s, N.Y.C., 1953-74; mem. bd. Fin. Accounting Standards Bd., Stamford, Conn., 1975—; tchr. accounting Kans. State U., 1939-43. Served to lt. USNR, 1943-46. C.P.A., N.J., N.Y. Mem. Am. Inst. C.P.A.'s (Gold medal for distinguished service 1974), Am. Accounting Assn., N.J., N.Y. socs. C.P.A.'s. Home: 15 Highview Rd Darien CT 06820 Office: Financial Accounting Standards Bd High Ridge Park Stamford CT 06905

GELLER, HERBERT Z., radiologist; b. N.Y.C., Jan. 17, 1931; s. Moses and Rose (Breier) G.; B.A., N.Y. U., Bronx, 1952; M.D., U. Chgo., 1957; m. Udell Fishman, June 1, 1957; children—Mark Eli, Robert Aaron, Paul Stuart, David Jonathan, Amy Lynn. Intern, Kings County Hosp., Bklyn., 1957-58, resident in radiology, 1960-63; USPHS cancer control fellow State U. N.Y. Downstate Med. Center, Bklyn., 1963-64; practice medicine specializing in radiology, Nyack, N.Y., 1964—; mem. staff, dir. radiology dept. Nyack Hosp.; radiology cons. N.Y. State Rehab. Hosp. Founder, v.p. Monsey (N.Y.) Jewish Center; pres. Dellwood Park Civic Assn., N.Y.C., 1970-71; mem. alumni admissions com. U. Chgo. Diplomate Am. Bd. Radiology. Mem. Am. Coll. Radiology, Soc. Nuclear Medicine, Radiol. Soc. N. Am., AMA, N.Y. State Med. Soc., N.Y. State Radiol. Soc., N.Y. Roentgen Soc. Democrat. Home: 20 Woodhaven Dr New City NY 10956 Office: Radiology Dept Nyack Hosp Nyack NY 10960

GELLER, JOSEPH JEROME, psychiatrist; b. Elizabeth, N.J., Feb. 19, 1917; s. Samuel A. and Sara (Zabriskie) G.; B.Sc. in Biology, Rutgers U., 1937; M.D., N.Y.U., 1941; children by previous marriage—Robert S., Anne; m. 2d, Janice Grace Clack, Dec. 23, 1973; 1 dau., Elizabeth Joanne. Intern, Elizabeth Gen. Hosp., 1941-42; resident Central Islip (N.Y.) State Hosp., 1946-48, N.Y. State Psychiat. Inst., N.Y.C., 1946-48; practice medicine, specializing in psychiatry and practice psychoanalysis, N.Y.C., 1948—; psychoanalytic trainee William Alanson White Inst. Psychiatry, N.Y.C., 1946-51, mem. faculty, 1951—; mem.N.J. Mental Health Council, 1964-67; psychiat. examiner USIA, 1958-61, FAA, 1964-70; numerous faculty appointments; cons. pub. schs., N.J. Served to maj. M.C., U.S. Army, 1942-46; PTO. Diplomate Am. Bd. Psychiatry and Neurology. Fellow Am. Psychiat. Assn. (life), Am. Acad. Psychoanalysis (charter), Am. Assn. Mental Deficiency, Am. Group Psychotherapy Assn., Am. Acad. Child Psychiatry; mem. N.J. State Med. Soc., AMA, AAAS, N.J. Acad. Psychoanalysis (co-founder), Soc. Gen. Systems Research, Soc. Gen. Semantics, N.Y. Council Child Psychiatry, William Alanson White Psychoanalytic Soc. Home: 159 Fairmount Rd Ridgewood NJ 07450 Office: 69 W 9th St New York City NY 10011

GELLER, JOSHUA S., supt. schs.; b. June 30, 1933; s. Aaron and Sara (Yollick) G.; B.A., Wayne State U., 1958, M.Ed., 1960; Ph.D., U. Mich., 1968; m. Rose Frank, June 28, 1960; children—David, Aaron, Gary. Tchr. Detroit Pub. Schs., 1958-65, counselor, 1965-68, asst. prin., 1968-70; prin. high sch., Farmington, Conn., 1970-73, Hastings-on-Hudson, N.Y., 1973-75; asst. supt. North Hills Pub. Schs., Pitts., 1975-76, supt., 1976—; adj. prof. Eastern Mich. U., Ypsilanti, 1969-70, Central Conn. State Coll., New Britain, 1970-73. Served with AUS, 1953-55. NDEA grantee, 1961-62; Charles E. Merrill Trust Fund grantee, 1967-68; Inst. for Devel. Ednl. Activities fellow, 1973. Mem. Nat. Assn. Secondary Sch. Prins., Westchester Interscholastic Conf. (pres. 1973-74), Assn. Supervision and Curriculum Devel., Am. Assn. Sch. Adminstrs., Phi Delta Kappa. Home: 499 Woodland Rd Pittsburgh PA 15237 Office: 53 Rochester Rd Pittsburgh PA 15229

GELLER, LAWRENCE DAVID, educator; b. Newark, May 29, 1940; s. Samuel and Beatrice (Weisman) G.; A.B., Middlebury Coll., 1962; M.A., N.Y. U., 1963, postgrad. (teaching fellow), 1963-65; postgrad. U. Grenoble (France), 1962; m. Anne Darling Parnes, Feb. 20, 1964; children—Gordon Cameron, Randall Stafford, Alexandra Nicole. Asst. prof. history Madison Coll., Harrisonburg, Va., 1965-69; dir. Pilgrim Soc., Plymouth, Mass., 1969-77, also dir. Pilgrim Hall Mus., other historic landmarks of soc.; asso. prof. Am. history, hist. mus. mgmt. Bridgewater (Mass.) State Coll., 1969-77; chmn. dept. history Germantown Acad., Ft. Washington, Pa., 1977—. Chmn. Plymouth Historic Dists. Commn., 1973—; mem. design rev. bd. Plymouth, 1973—; mem. Nat. Trust for Historic Preservation, 1969—; trustee Cape Cod Conservatory Music, 1971—. Fellow Pilgrim Soc., Royal Soc. Arts; mem. Colonial Soc. Mass., Soc. Am. Archivists, New Eng. Archivists, Am. Assn. Museums, Soc. Preservation New Eng. Antiquities, Delta Kappa Epsilon. Club: Longfellow. Author: Between Concord and Plymouth: The Transcendalists and the Watsons, 1973; Pilgrims in Eden: Conservation Policy in New Plymouth, 1973; The Architecture of Elegance, 1976; co-author: The Books of the Pilgrims, 1975; editor: They Knew They Were Pilgrims: Essays in Plymouth History, 1970. Home: 13 Vernon St Plymouth MA 02360 Office: The Highlands Sheaff Ln Fort Washington PA

GELLINEAU, VICTOR MARCEL, mktg. exec.; b. N.Y.C., Nov. 3, 1942; s. Victor M. and Marcella (Gonzalez) G.; B.A., Howard U., 1967; M.B.A., Baruch Coll., City U. N.Y., 1974; m. Carole Joy Johnston, June 5, 1965; children—Victor M., Maria M., Carmen E. Salesman, Burlington Industries, N.Y.C., 1967-69; asst. product mgr. Lever Bros., N.Y.C., 1969-71; product mgr. Whitehall Labs. div. Am. Home Products, N.Y.C., 1971-73; v.p., dir. account services Zebra Assos., N.Y.C., 1973-76; mktg. mgr. grocery products group Heublein Inc., Hartford, 1976—. Chmn. cub pack Boy Scouts Am.; bd. dirs. Artist Collective, Hartford; vol. Greater Hartford Arts Council. Mem. Am. Mktg. Assn., Am. Mgmt. Assn. Democrat. Roman Catholic. Home: 145 Sunny Reach Dr West Hartford CT 06117 Office: 330 New Park Ave Hartford CT 06101

GELMAN, BERNARD, journalist; b. Bronx, N.Y., June 16, 1933; s. Irving and Sonia (Berlinsky) G.; B.B.A. cum laude, City Coll. N.Y., 1954; m. Anne Terese Westfield, Dec. 20, 1969. Asst. prodn. mgr. Master Matrix Service Co., N.Y.C., 1954; copywriter, traffic and prodn. mgr. S.T. Seidman & Co., Inc., advt. agy., N.Y.C., 1955; asst. advt. mgr. Olympic Radio & TV, Long Island City, N.Y., 1956-57; advt. and sales promotion mgr. Michael Lith, Inc., N.Y.C., 1958; copy chief Philip I. Ross Co., Inc., advt. agy., N.Y.C., 1959; free-lance writer by-line articles to Parade, Indpls. Star, Winnipeg Free Press, N.Y. Herald Tribune's Sunday mag., Success Unltd., Today, Irish Press, Manchester Evening News, 1959—; owner, editor Gelman Feature Syndicate, N.Y.C., 1962—. Mem. Nat. Writers Club (chpt. pres.), Soc. Am. Magicians, Internat. Brotherhood Magicians, Am. Soc. for Psychical Research, Internat. Guild Prestidigitators, Internat. Platform Assn., Eta Mu Pi. Home: 826 E 14th St Brooklyn NY 11230 Office: POB 1370 Grand Central Sta New York City NY 10017

GELSTEIN, LEONARD MICHAEL, advt. exec.; b. Chgo., Jan. 11, 1941; s. Samuel and Ida (Bass) G.; B.S., U. Ill., 1962; postgrad. bus. adminstrn. U. Chgo., 1963-64; m. Dorothy A. Peterson, May 26, 1967; 1 dau., Megan Elizabeth. Copywriter, Sears Roebuck Co., Chgo., 1963-65, Leo Burnett Co., Chgo., 1965-67; copy group head J. Walter Thompson, N.Y.C., 1967-71; creative supr. Ted Bates, N.Y.C., 1971-76; creative dir., v.p. William Esty, N.Y.C., 1976-78; creative supr. BBDO, N.Y.C., 1978; co-creative dir., v.p. E.T. Howard, N.Y.C., 1979—. Bd. govs. Bklyn. Heights Assn., 1973-77; councilor L.I. Hist. Soc., 1977. Served with USAR, 1962-68. Recipient Clio award for Colgate radio comml., 1973, Prudential and Warner Lambert TV commls., 1977; Andy award for Ford, 1970; Art Dirs. Club award for Phillips 66, 1968, others. Mem. Environ. Def. Fund, Alpha Delta Sigma. Club: Heights Casino. Home: 11 Montague Terr Brooklyn NY 11201 Office: 850 3d Ave New York City NY 10011

GELT, JEANETTE ROSE LEBMAN, state legislator; b. Newburyport, Mass., Aug. 21, 1916; d. Joseph and Agnes (Goldsmith) Lebman; grad. high sch.; m. George Gelt, Nov. 25, 1937; children—Sylvia Gelt Bonaccorso, Gloria Malpica. Del., N.H. Constl. Conv., 1964; mem. N.H. Ho. of Reps., 1965—. Chmn., March of

Dimes, 1962-64. Bd. dirs. Salem (N.H.) Mental Health Assn., 1969-71, Salem Vis. Nurses Assn. Mem. Nat. Soc. State legislators (exec. com. Rockingham County 1967—). Republican. Clubs: Salem Garden, Salem Women. Home: 21 Martin Ave Salem NH 03079

GELTZER, HOWARD E., pub. relations co. exec.; b. Hazleton, Pa., Oct. 23, 1936; s. Nathan and Sally (Harris) G.; B.J., Northwestern U., 1958, M.S. in Journalism, 1959; m. Sheila Simon, Sept. 10, 1967; children—Jeremy, Gabriel. Mem. advt., pub. relations program Gen. Electric Corp., 1960-65; advt., pub. relations supr. Potentiometer div. Litton Industries, Mt. Vernon, N.Y., 1966-67; sales devel. mgr. Modern Mfg. mag. McGraw Hill Co., N.Y.C., 1967-68; promotion mgr. Family Health mag., N.Y.C., 1968-71; v.p. Simon & Geltzer Ltd., pub. relations, N.Y.C., 1971-74; pres. Ries & Geltzer Co., pub. relations, N.Y.C., 1974—; adj. asst. prof. mktg. N.Y. U. Sch. Continuing Edn., 1968—; dir. Ries Cappiello Colwell Advt.; lectr. in field; arbitrator Am. Arbitration Assn. Served with U.S. Army Res., 1960-66. Club: Gipsy Trail (dir. 1977—) (Carmel, N.Y.). Co-author: Positioning in PR; Marketing Strategy for College Admissions in the 1980's. Home: 498 West End Ave New York City NY 10024 Office: 1212 Ave of Americas New York City NY 10036

GEMMA, JOHN PETER, state ofcl.; b. N.Y.C., Apr. 16, 1939; s. Leo and Julia (Famiglietti) G.; student U. Rome, U. Florence, Gregorian Pontifical Acad., 1957-58; B.S. in Social Sci. egregia cum laude, Fordham U., 1959, J.D., 1962; m. Anna Marie Melillo, Aug. 24, 1971; children—Julia Marie, Ann Marie, Marie-Christine. Admitted to N.Y. bar, 1963; law clk. U.S. Dist. Judge John M. Cashin, 1962-64; asso. firm Sage, Gray, Todd & Sims, N.Y.C., 1964-67; asst. counsel to N.Y. Gov. Nelson Rockefeller, 1967-71; dep. supt., gen. counsel N.Y. State Ins. Dept., N.Y.C., 1971-75, acting supt., 1975, spl. counsel to supt., 1975—. Recipient Fed. Practice award Am. Jurisprudence Soc., 1962. Roman Catholic. Mem. staff Fordham Law Rev., 1961-62. Office: 2 World Trade Center New York City NY 10047

GEMMELL, GORDON DOUGLAS, metallurgist; b. Christchurch, N.Z., Sept. 18, 1921; s. Gordon and Grace (McLean) G.; B.Sc., U. N.Z., 1942, M.Sc. with first class honors, 1943; M.S. (Alcoa fellow), Mass. Inst. Tech., 1953, Sc.D., 1956; m. Nancy Kathryn Daddow, June 28, 1958; children—Kathryn Grace, Bruce McLean. Came to U.S., 1951, naturalized, 1961. Staff scientist N.Z. Dept. Sci. and Indsl. Research, 1943-51; indsl. metallurgist E.I. duPont de Nemours & Co., Inc., Wilmington, Del., 1956—. Served with N.Z. Army, 1942. Fulbright scholar, 1951. Mem. Am. Soc. Metals (chmn. Wilmington chpt. 1963-64). Presbyterian. Clubs: Racquets, DuPont Country (Wilmington). Patentee in field. Home: 603 Weldin Rd Wilmington DE 19803 Office: DuPont Exptl Sta Wilmington DE 19898

GENDELL, MARTIN BRUCE, mktg. exec.; b. Forest Hills, N.Y., Oct. 4, 1933; s. Irving and Henrietta (Lund) G.; A.B., U. Chgo., 1954, B.A., 1956; M.B.A., U. Pa., 1960. Mktg. research asso. Schering Corp., Bloomfield, N.J., 1962-64, asst. mgr. mktg. research, 1964-66, product mgr., 1966-69; pres. Visual Communications, N.Y.C., 1969-72, dir., 1969-74; sr. product mgr. Block Drug Co., Jersey City, 1973-76; v.p. Internat. Trading & Commodities Ltd., N.Y.C., 1976—. Served with Q.M.C., AUS, 1956-58. Mem. Am. Mktg. Assn., U. Chgo. Alumni Assn. (pres.). Democrat. Jewish. Contbr. articles to profl. jours. Home: 345 E 52d St New York City NY 10022 Office: 200 Central Park S New York City NY 10019

GENDRON, ODORE JOSEPH, bishop; b. Manchester, N.H., Sept. 13, 1921; s. Francis and Valida (Rouleau) G.; student U. Ottawa, 1942-47. Ordained priest Roman Catholic Ch., 1947; asso. pastor Angel Guardian Ch., Berlin, N.H., 1947-52, Sacred Heart Ch., Lebanon, N.H., 1952-60, St. Louis Ch., Nashua, N.H., 1962-65; pastor Our Lady of Lourdes Ch., Pittsfield, Mass., 1965-67, St. Augustine Ch., Manchester, 1967-71; became monsignor, Manchester, 1970; bishop of Manchester, 1975—; episcopal vicar for religious, Manchester, 1972-74, episcopal vicar for clergy, 1974-75. Home: 67 William St Manchester NH 03102 Office: 153 Ash St Manchester NH 03105

GENEEN, HAROLD SYDNEY, communications co. exec.; b. Bournemouth, Eng., Jan. 22, 1910; s. S. Alexander and Aida (DeCrucian) G.; brought to U.S., 1911, naturalized (derivative), 1918; B.S. in Accounting and Fin., N.Y. U., 1934; grad. Advanced Mgmt. Program, Harvard U.; LL.D. (hon.), Lafayette Coll., PMC Colls.; m. June Elizabeth Hjelm, Dec. 1949. Accountant and analyst Mayflower Assos., 1932-34; sr. accountant Lybrand, Ross Bros. & Montgomery, 1934-42; chief accountant Am. Can Co., 1942-46; controller Bell & Howell Co., Chgo., 1946-50; v.p., controller Jones & Laughlin Steel Corp., Pitts., 1950-56; exec. v.p., dir. Raytheon Mfg. Co., Waltham, Mass., 1956-59; pres. ITT, 1959-73, chief exec., 1959-77, dir., 1959—, chmn. bd., 1964—, chmn. exec. com., 1974—, also dir. fgn. subsidiaries, affiliated cos.; advisory com. Uptown br. Bankers Trust Co. Bd. dirs. Internat. Rescue Com.; mem. nat. council Salk Inst. Biol. Studies, 1977—. Decorated grand officer Order of Merit (Peru); comdr. Order of the Crown (Belgium); Grand Cross of Civil Merit, Grand Cross of Isabella Cath. Mother of the Americas (Spain); co-recipient 5th ann. Communications award ICD Rehab. and Research Center, 1976. C.P.A., N.Y., Ill. Mem. Am. Inst. C.P.A.'s, Fin. Execs. Inst., Soc. C.P.A.'s, Nat. Assn. Accountants, Internat. C. of C. (trustee U.S. council), Voice Found. Episcopalian. Clubs: Duquesne (Pitts.); Links, Oakmont Country, Braeburn Country, Oyster Harbors, Union League (N.Y.C.); Harvard (Boston). Office: ITT World Hdqrs 320 Park Ave New York City NY 10022

GENOVA, THOMAS FRANCIS, microbiologist; b. Newark, Jan. 15, 1950; s. Dorsey Lewis and Marie Clare (Ryan) Finn; A.B., Rutgers U., 1972; M.S., Seton Hall U., 1975; m. Maria Rodriguez, July 15, 1978. Teaching asst. vertebrate physiology Seton Hall U., S. Orange, N.J., 1972-74; bacteriologist N.J. Dairy Lab., New Brunswick, 1973-74; research asso., tissue typing lab., pathology dept., N.J. Med. Sch., Newark, 1974, cons., 1974—; lab. instr. microbiology Union County (N.J.) Coll., Cranford, 1975—; asso. scientist microbiol. research Ethicon, Inc., Somerville, N.J., 1976—. Mem. N.Y. Acad. Sci., Am. Soc. Microbiology, Soc. Indsl. Microbiology, Theobald Smith Soc., Tissue Culture Assn., AAAS, Sigma Xi, Alpha Phi Omega. Roman Catholic. Contbr. articles in field to profl. jours. Home: 11 Dobson Rd Edison NJ 08817

GENTILE, ADRIAN GEORGE, entomologist; b. Capri, Italy, Feb. 11, 1926; s. Vincenzo Miro and Anna (Lauro) G.; Dr.Agr., U. Naples (Italy), 1950; M.Sc., U. Calif. at Davis, 1956, Ph.D., 1966; m. Rebecca B. Rosenbaum, May 9, 1952. Came to U.S., 1952, naturalized, 1956. Research technician dept. vegetable crops U. Calif. at Davis, 1956-65, dept. entomology, 1965-66; entomologist U.S. Dept. Agr., Beltsville, Md., 1966-67; pathogen research leader USPHS, Atlanta, 1967-69; extension entomologist, asst. prof. Waltham (Mass.) Suburban Expt. Sta., U. Mass., 1969-75, adj. asso. prof., 1975—. Mem. Entomol. Soc. Am., Am. Inst. Biol. Scis., Am. Mosquito Control Assn., Tomato Genetics Coop., N.Y. Acad. Scis., Am. Registry Certified Entomologists, Sigma Xi. Democrat. Author: A Revision of the Genus Thrips Linnaeus in the New World with a Catalogue of World Species, 1968; contbr. articles to profl. jours. Home: 4 Hosmer Circle West Newton MA 02165 Office: 240 Beaver St Waltham MA 02154

GENTILE, ANTHONY ALBERT, publisher; b. Bklyn., Sept. 15, 1915; s. Michael J. and Rose (Ferma) G.; grad. high sch.; m. Adelaide Kendrick, Oct. 23, 1938; children—Michael, Robert, Mary, Pamela. Pub., pres., dir. E-Z Telephone Directory Brokers & Banks, N.Y.C., 1946—; founder, pres., dir. E-Z Addressing Service Corp., 1946—; pres., dir. A.A.G. Corp., 1967—. Served with AUS, 1943-46: ETO. Mem. Am. Legion. Roman Catholic. Clubs: Elks, Kiwanis; Downtown Athletic (N.Y.C.); Cherry Valley Country (Garden City, N.Y.). Home: 5 Barnes Ln Garden City NY 11530 Office: 80 Washington St New York City NY 10006

GENTLESK, MICHAEL JOHN, pediatric allergist; b. Haddon Heights, N.J., May 23, 1938; s. Michael Louis and Mary Elizabeth (Burgo) G.; B.S. in Biology, Georgetown U., 1960, M.D., 1964; m. Juraté E. Pauliukonis, Oct. 5, 1973; children—Michael L., Maria T., Philip J., Jurate E., Regina F., Joseph D., Anthony Rocco. Intern, Our Lady of Lourdes Hosp., Camden, N.J., 1964-65; resident in pediatrics St. Christopher's Hosp., Phila., 1967-69, chief resident, 1969-70; fellow in pediatric allergy and clin. immunology Thomas Jefferson U., Phila., 1971-73; practice medicine specializing in pediatric allergy, Phila. and Cherry Hill, N.J., 1973—; dir. pediatrics and patient services Children's Heart Hosp., Phila., 1972-73; v.p. Pediatric Allergy Assocs., Cherry Hill, 1973-78; asst. prof. pediatrics, Thomas Jefferson U., 1973—; attending Our Lady of Lourdes Hosp., Camden, Garden State Hosp., Marlton, N.J., Children's Heart Hosp., St. Christopher's Hosp.; sec. bd. dirs. Community Bank, Sicklerville, N.J., 1974—. Served as Mlt. M.C., USN, 1965-67. Diplomate Am. Bd. Pediatrics, Am. Bd. Allergy and Clin. Immunology. Fellow Am. Acad. Pediatrics, Am. Acad. Allergy and Clin. Immunology, Am. Coll. Allergists, Am. Coll. Chest Physicians, Am. Assn. Certified Allergists, Am. Assn. for Clin. Immunology and Allergy, Acad. Medicine N.J.; mem. Allergy Found. Am., Phila. allergy assns., Phila. Pediatric Soc., N.Y. Acad. Scis., St. George Cancer Soc., Phi Chi. Roman Catholic. Home: 322 Woodland Ave Haddonfield NJ 08033 Office: Old Orchard Bldg 1999 E Marlton Pike Route 70 Cherry Hill NJ 08003

GENTRY, GRANT CLAYBOURNE, retail exec., lawyer; b. Chgo., June 5, 1924; s. Grant Claybourne and Helen (Cooley) G.; J.D., DePaul U., 1949; m. Doris Lorraine Helsten, Sept. 8, 1943; children—Grant Claybourne, Scott Wesley. Admitted to Ill. bar, 1949; asso. firm McKnight, McLaughlin & Dunn, Chgo., 1949-53; tax atty. Internat. Harvester Co., 1953-57; asst. sec., corp. atty. Jewel Cos., Inc., Chgo., 1957-64, v.p., sec., gen. counsel, 1964-70, exec. v.p. adminstrn., gen. counsel, 1970-74, also dir.; pres., dir. Gt. Atlantic & Pacific Tea Co., N.Y.C., 1975—. Mem. Gov.'s Revenue Study Com., 1968-69; lay trustee Loyola U., Chgo. Served with 11th Airborne Div., AUS, World War II. Decorated Purple Heart. Mem. Nat. Assn. Food Chains (chmn. bd. dirs.), Phi Alpha Delta, Phi Kappa Delta. Office: Great Atlantic & Pacific Tea Co 2 Paragon Dr Montvale NJ 07645

GENTZLER, BARRY FREDERICK, mgmt. cons. exec.; b. York, Pa., May 12, 1937; s. Merl Frederick and Margaret (Dvbbs) G.; B.S., Drexel Inst. Tech., 1960; M.B.A., N.Y. U., 1964; m. Jane Clarke Bender, Aug. 27, 1967; children—Michael, Amy Lynn. Marketing mgr. Ingersoll Rand, N.Y.C., 1960-67; mgmt. cons. Peat, Marwick, Mitchell & Co., N.Y.C., 1967-70; v.p. Plywood & Door Mfg. Corp., Union, N.J., 1970-76; prin. The Wood Group Ltd., Morristown, N.J., 1976—. Served to 1st lt., arty. AUS, 1961-62. Mem. Am. Marketing Assn., Am. Mgmt. Assn. Mason (32 deg.). Club: Brianburn Country (Madison, N.J.). Home: 34 Cory Rd Flanders NJ 07836 Office: 125 Morris St Morristown NJ 07960

GEOGAN, ROBERT JOSEPH, lawyer; b. Rockland, Mass., Mar. 23, 1920; s. Francis J. and Hortense (Bowler) G.; A.B., Coll. Holy Cross, 1942; J.D., Boston U., 1946; m. Mary R. Donaher, Dec. 27, 1943; children—Deborah Geogan Sprong, Phillip J., F. Joseph, Robyn P. Admitted to Mass. bar, 1946, since practiced in Rockland; town counsel Duxbury (Mass.), 1959-74, Rockland, 1947-63, 68-73, Hanover and Pembroke, 1947-63; corporator Rockland Savs. Bank; dir. Rockland Co-op. Bank, 1944-70, pres., 1962-70; v.p., dir. Mayflower Co-op. Bank, 1970-75; mem. exec. com., dir. Rockland Trust Co. Trustee Rockland Meml. Library, 1953—, chmn., 1978—; trustee Greater Brockton Cath. Charities. Served with USMCR, 1942. Mem Am., Mass., Plymouth County bar assns., Fenwick Soc. Holy Cross Coll., Pres.'s Council Holy Cross Coll., Am. Judicature Soc. Club: Neighborhood (Quincy, Mass.). Home: 72 Union St Rockland MA 02370 Office: 282 Union St Rockland MA 02370

GEORGE, CHARLES WILLIAM, elec. products co. exec.; b. Shenandoah, Pa., July 9, 1914; s. Robert and Martha (Eberhard) G.; B.S., Ursinus Coll., 1935; M.S., Duke U., 1940; m. Helen Marie Brengel, Sept. 30, 1944; children—Nancy George Hamberger, Kathryn, William. Instr., Pa. State U., 1940-42; various mgmt. and engring. positions Gen. Electric Co., 1946-63, mgr. nuclear engring., 1955-59, mgr. gas turbine engring., 1959-63, gen. mgr. radio guidance dept., Syracuse, N.Y., 1963-64, gen. mgr. aerospace electronics dept., Utica, N.Y., 1964-66, v.p., gen. mgr. def. electronics div., 1966-68, aircraft equipment div., 1968—; dir. Toshiba Electronic Systems Co., Ltd., Tokyo, Gen. Electric Tech. Services Co., Inc., N.Y.C., Marine Midland Bank Central Region, Syracuse. Chmn. Greater Utica United Fund Campaign, 1971-72; met. dir. Nat. Alliance Businessmen, 1971-73; bd. dirs. Asso. Industries N.Y. State, 1972—, mem. exec. com., 1976—; bd. dirs. Greater Utica Community Chest and Planning Council, 1972-75; trustee State U. N.Y. Coll. Tech. at Utica-Rome, 1974—, chmn. council, 1978—; bd. dirs. Ursinus Coll., 1977—, nat. chmn. loyalty fund dr., 1976—. Served to lt. USN, 1942-46. Named Indsl. Man of Year, 1972, Alumnus of Year, Ursinus Coll., 1975. Mem. Nat. Security Indsl. Assn. (trustee 1968—), Greater Utica C. of C. (v.p. 1968-76), Air Force Assn., Assn. U.S. Army, Navy League U.S., Am. Inst. Aeros. and Astronautics, Armed Forces Mgmt. Assn., Electronic Industries Assn. (bd. govs. govt. products div. 1974-75), Am. Def. Preparedness Assn., Aerospace Industries Assn. Home: 42 Lynacres Blvd Fayetteville NY 13066 Office: Aircraft Equipment Div Gen Electric Co French Rd Utica NY 13503

GEORGE, HENRY MITCHELL, clergyman, educator; b. Wilkes-Barre, Pa., Mar. 8, 1917; s. William and Edith (Mitchell) G.; A.B., Nazarene Coll., 1942, Th.B., 1943, Th.M., 1950; Th.D., St. Andrews Coll., 1955, S.T.D., Am. U. Found., 1946; D.D., Dr. Laureatus, Imperial Philo Byzantine U., Madrid, 1963; m. Evelyn Martin, Mar. 17, 1939; children—Donna Lou George Lewis, William David. Ordained to ministry, 1936; pastor Welsh Baptist Ch., Wilkes-Barre, 1936-39, music dir., 1940-41; pastor Miner Congregational Ch., Wilkes-Barre, 1942-53; pres. Chatham Hill Coll. and Div. Sch., 1954-60; pastor First United Ch. Christ, Scranton, Pa., 1960—; prof. Bible and ch. history Savonarola Theol. Sem.; pres. ministerial socs. W.Va., Pa.; founder Evang. Prison Soc.; profl. fund dir. Wells Orgn. Trustee Ridgedale Theol. Sem. Recipient Alfaro medal Republic Panama, 1954; Star and Cross of Honor medal Internat. Acad. Council. Life fellow St. Andrew's Ministerial Tng. Coll., Brit. Sch. Theology; mem. Nat. Council Bus. and Profl. Men (hon. life pres.). Club: Masons (32 deg., Shriner). Home: 128 N Bromley Ave Scranton PA 18504 Office: First United Ch Christ 132 N Bromley Ave Scranton PA 18504*

GEORGE, JOSEPH DAVID, former civil engr.; b. Iran, Mar. 4, 1908; s. David Shaloo and Catherine (Sayad) G.; came to Can., 1924, naturalized, 1931; B.Sc. with distinction (Univ. scholar), U. Sask., Saskatoon, Can., 1933; m. Gladys Helen Willsie, Jan. 1, 1939; children—Peter Daniel, Mary-Ann. Civil engr. Sterling Millwork & Hardware Co. Ltd., 1934-35, Canadian Dept. Pub. Works, 1936-37, Dept. Agr., 1938-39, Dept. Def., 1940-43; resident engr. Imperial Oil Co., Moose Jaw, Sask., 1944; asso. Crumm & Young, Cons. Engrs., Toronto, Ont., 1944-45; sr. design engr. Brazilian Traction, Toronto, 1948-51; asso. R. M. Way, Cons. Engr., Toronto, 1952-53, Chem. Constrn. Engrs., Toronto, 1954-55; with Met. Toronto Dept. Traffic and Rds., 1955-78, chief design engring., 1958-73, chief analytic services, 1974-78; chmn. Met. Toronto Pub. Utilities Coordinating Com., 1960-78. Mem. Ont. Profl. Engrs. Assn., Engring. Inst. Can., Transp. Research Bd., Am. Pub. Works Assn., Am. Concrete Inst., Rds. and Transp. Assn. Can., Canadian Tech. Asphalt Assn., Canadian Standards Assn. Liberal. Presbyterian. Contbr. articles to profl. jours. Patentee in field. Home: 1263 Royal York Rd Islington ON M9A 4C4 Canada Office: 401 Bay St Simpson Tower Toronto ON M5H 2Y4 Canada

GEORGE, ROBERT JACOB, publisher; b. Boston, Aug. 11, 1944; s. George J. and Dorothy E (Glick) G.; B.A., Mo. U., 1967; m. Pamela Jones, June 24, 1968. Founder, pres. United Media Internat., Inc.; pres. HBJ Press; v.p. Harcourt Brace Jovanovich; pres. Nat. Aero. Inst., Inc. Served with USMC, 1967-71. Decorated D.F.C. Episcopalian. Clubs: Somerset, Tennis and Racket (Boston); Knickerbocker (N.Y.C.). Home: 60 Washington Sherborn MA 02116 Office: 306 Dartmouth St Boston MA 02116

GEORGE, SYLVIA JAMES, painter, portraitist, illustrator; b. Syracuse, N.Y., Oct. 13, 1921; d. Samuel B. and Helen (Mastropaulo) James; student Everson Mus. Arts Syracuse, 1937, Pratt Inst., 1941-44, Am. U., 1954; m. Henry Horsefield George, Aug. 5, 1946; children—Deborah, Henry, Janice, Greg, Ron, Steve, Ken, Christine. Illustrator Contempo Artists, N.Y.C., 1943-44; free lance fashion illustrator Tobe, N.Y.C., Nat. Levine, N.Y.C., Littman, N.Y.C., 1944-46; portraits on commission, 1943—, silver plate etchings, 1969—; operator SJG Art Studio; illustrator books, publs. and art studios, Columbia, 1969—; illustrator Johnson Studios, Columbia, 1970-72, Nordika Publs., Co umbia, 1972—; represented in permanent collections: Kennedy Library, Howard High Sch., Ellicott City, Md., Rouse Co., B & O R.R. Mus., Ellicott City, du Fief Elementary Sch., Internat. Soc. Artists; tchr. art Glenelg Sch. Music, also pvt. tchr. Mem. Artists Equity Assn., Columbia Art Assn., Howard County Symphony Soc., Graphic Artist (dir.), Howard County Commn. on Arts, Historic Ellicott City. Democrat. Roman Catholic. Clubs: Sr. Investment, John Hopkins U. Women's, Portrait of N.Y. Home and studio: 6510 Beechwood Dr Columbia MD 21046

GEORGI, WILLIAM HENRY, physician; b. Buffalo, Apr. 14, 1917; s. Oscar Frederick and Florence Louise (Dold) G.; A.B., Williams Coll., 1939; M.D., State U. N.Y., Buffalo, 1943; m. Sharlotte M. Beck, Jan. 12, 1957; children—Peter, Barbara, Frederick. Rotating intern Buffalo Gen. Hosp., 1943-44, resident in internal medicine, 1946-48, dir. dept. rehab. medicine, 1955—; practice medicine specializing in internal medicine, Buffalo, 1948-53; fellow phys. medicine and rehab. N.Y. U., N.Y.C., 1953-55; physiatrist Buffalo Children's Hosp., 1957-75, 78—; acting chmn. dept. rehab. medicine, State U. N.Y., Buffalo, 1975-78; cons. rehab. medicine Buffalo VA Hosp., Wyoming County Hosp., Roswell Park Meml. Inst., Buffalo-Erie County Med Center; clin. asso. prof. rehab. medicine, State U. N.Y., Buffalo. Served to capt. M.C. U.S. Army, 1944-46. Decorated Purple Heart, Silver Star. Diplomate Am. Bd. Phys. Medicine and Rehab. Mem. Am. Acad. Phys. Medicine and Rehab., Am. Congress Rehab. Medicine, AMA, Am. Rheumatism Assn., Assn. Acad. Physiatrists, Internat. Rehab. Soc., med. socs. County of Erie, State N.Y., Am. Assn. Electromyography and Electrodiagnosis, N.Y. Soc. Phys. Medicine and Rehab. Home: 7233 Lower East Hill Rd Colden NY 14033 Office: 100 High St Buffalo NY 14203

GEORGIA, RICHARD CLARK, banker; b. Cooperstown, N.Y., Dec. 31, 1927; s. Leon Milan and Emma G. (Turk) G.; student U. Md., 1952; B.A., Westminster Coll., 1953; postgrad. Stonier Grad. Sch. Banking, Rutgers U., 1961. With Fed. Res. System, Cleve., Pitts., 1953-63; v.p., dir. personnel First Nat. Bank of Toledo, 1963-76; v.p.-personnel resources First Nat. Bank N.J., Totowa, 1976—; instr. Am. Inst. Banking; guest lectr. U. Toledo, Bowling Green State U. Bd. community relations, City of Toledo, 1969-71. Mem. central com. Lucas County Republican Party; exec. bd. Lucas County Rep. Workshops, 1965—, pres., 1967-68. Served with AUS, 1946-48, 51. Mem. Am. Inst. Banking (adv. com. 1965—), Ohio State Bankers Assn. (chmn. edn. com. 1969-71), Toledo Opera Assn. (bd. trustees 1965—), Toledo C. of C., Sigma Nu. Presbyn. Home: 28 Goldfinch Dr Hackettstown NJ 07840 Office: 515 Union Blvd Totowa NJ 07511

GERADTS, BERNARDUS, trading co. exec.; b. The Hague, Holland, July 18, 1932; s. Hendrikus Franciscus J. and Bernardina (Scheelings) G.; Doctoraal Economie, Erasmus U. (Netherlands), 1962; m. Catharina L.H. Dielen, Dec. 28, 1963; children—Dorine, Henny, Bernice. Came to U.S., 1972. Mem. comml. dept. staff Nederlandse Stikstof Maatschappij N.V. Sluiskil, the Netherlands, 1962-72; exec. v.p. Transnitro, Inc., N.Y.C., 1973—, dir., 1973—. Served to capt., Netherlands Army, 1952-55. Home: 131 Lake Shore Dr N Eastchester NY 10707 Office: 410 Park Ave New York City NY 10022

GERARD, JEAN BROWARD SHEVLIN, lawyer; b. Portland, Oreg., Mar. 9, 1938; d. Edwin Leonard and Ella (Broward) Shevlin; B.A., Vassar Coll., 1959; J.D., Fordham U. 1977, postgrad. Internat. Law Forum; postgrad. N.Y.U., Law Sch., 1977—; m. James Watson Gerard, II, June 20, 1959; children—James Watson, Harriet Coster. Admitted to N.Y. State, Fla. bars, 1978; asso. firm Cadwalader, Wickersham & Taft. Area dir. Europe Res. Officers Ladies, 1960-61; sec. aux. Sheltering Arms Children's Service, 1967-68, 69-70; co-chmn. Viennese Opera Ball, N.Y.C., 1967—; bd. govs. Women's Nat. Republican Club, 1967-73, 74—, rec. sec., 1968-70, pres., 1971-73, treas., 1974, chmn. 53d ann. luncheon, 1974; bd. dirs. Knickerbocker Greys, 1968-74; sec. Com. to Unite Am., 1970—; bd. dirs. Youth Found., 1973—, sec., 1973-77. bd. dirs. U.S. Flag Found., 1974—. Recipient medal of appreciation SAR, 1970. Mem. Colonial Dames Am. D.A.R., Nat. Soc. New Eng. Women, Nat. Soc. Magna Carta Dames, France-Am. Soc., Order of Lafayette, Am., N.Y. State, Fla. bar assns., Phi Alpha Delta. Clubs: Governors; Capitol Hill. Home: 201 E 79th St New York City NY 10021 Office: 1 Wall St New York City NY 10005

GERARD, PAUL JEFFREY, investment analyst; b. N.Y.C., May 11, 1948; s. Raymond and Norma (Dallis) G.; B.S. in Mech. Engring., U. Calif., Berkeley, 1971; M.B.A., N.Y. U., 1973. Sr. analyst Equitable Life Assurance Soc., N.Y.C., 1973—; adj. prof. N.Y. Inst. Tech., 1972, 73, 76, 77. Mem. Inst. Chartered Fin. Analysts, N.Y. Soc. Security Analysts, Nat. Assn. Security Dealers, Fin. Analysts Fedn., Calif. Engring. Alumni Assn., N.Y. U. Alumni Assn., Elec. Products Group N.Y. Home: 23 Pine Dr Woodbury NY 11797 Office: 1285 Ave of Americas Suite 33G New York City NY 10019

GERBER, DONALD ALBERT, physician, educator; b. N.Y.C., Apr. 10, 1932; s. J. and Isabel (Globus) G.; A.B., Columbia U., 1953, M.D., 1957; m. Marcia L. Getz, June 13, 1964; children—Susan Eve, Andrew James. Intern, Osler Med. Service, Johns Hopkins Hosp., Balt., 1957-58, asst. resident physician, also asst. in medicine, 1958-59; asst. resident in medicine Presbyn. Hosp., N.Y.C., 1959-60, asst. physician, 1960-64; clin. asst. vis. physician Bellevue Hosp., N.Y.C., 1962-63; postdoctoral fellow Arthritis Found. in dept. medicine Columbia U. Coll. Physicians and Surgeons, 1960-63; instr. medicine State U. N.Y., Downstate Med. Center, Bklyn., 1963-64, asst. prof. medicine, 1964-69, asso. prof., 1969—; spl. investigator Arthritis Found., 1963-66; career scientist Health Research Council N.Y.C., 1965-75; prin. investigator, NIH grantee, also attending physician State U. Hosp., Downstate Med. Center, Bklyn., 1966—; asst. vis. physician Kings County Hosp., Bklyn., 1963-66, asso. vis. physician, 1966-71, active attending, 1971—; med. cons. Bklyn. VA Hosp., 1976-78. Mem. med. and sci. com. N.Y. chpt. Arthritis Found., 1971-74. Diplomate Am. Bd. Internal Medicine. Fellow A.C.P.; mem. Am. Fedn. Clin. Research, Soc. Exptl. Biology and Medicine, Harvey Soc., Internat. Soc. Supramolecular Biology, Am., N.Y. (exec. com. 1971-73, v.p. 1976-77) rheumatism assns. Contbr. articles to profl. jours.; research in metabolic abnormalities in rheumatoid arthritis. Office: State U NY Downstate Med Center 450 Clarkson Ave Brooklyn NY 11203

GERBER, EDWARD FERDINAND, lawyer; b. Houston, Oct. 10, 1932; s. Edward Ferdinand and Lucille (Beaver) G.; B.S., Syracuse U., 1957, LL.B., 1960, J.D., 1968; m. Eileen Healy, Sept. 1, 1956; children—Gretchen, Eric, Nils. Admitted to N.Y. State bar, 1960; mem. firm Grossman and Grossman, Attys., Syracuse, N.Y., 1960-62, Rizzo, Aloi, Grasso & Urcinoli, Syracuse, 1962-63; partner firm Ali & Gerber, Syracuse, 1963-77; pres. firm Ali, Gerber, Pappas, Cox, P.C., Syracuse, 1977—; spl. prosecutor Onondaga County, 1976; dir. Onondaga Council Alcoholism, 1965-66; guest lectr. Vista Program Syracuse U., 1965, trial tactics and moot ct. judge, Coll. Law, 1964—; counsel Mayor's Commn. Law Enforcement and Criminal Procedures, Syracuse, 1966; instr. Municipal Police Tng. Sch., Syracuse. Bd. dirs., Fayetteville-Manlius Young Republican Club, 1961-62; co-chmn. Lawyers Com. Rep. Judicial Candidates, 1962—; bd. dirs. Onondaga County Young Rep. Club, 1962-64; pres. Gen. Herkimer Rep. Club, 1964-66; prin. asst. dist. atty. Onondaga County, 1964-67. Served with USN, 1951-54. Mem. Onondaga County (N.Y.) Bar Assn. (dir. 1970-72), Upstate Trial Attys. Assn. (dir. 1964—, pres. 1978), Am. Judicature Soc., Beta Gamma Sigma, Phi Kappa Phi. Republican. Roman Catholic. Asso. editor Syracuse Law Rev., 1959-60. Home: 202 Scottholm Blvd Syracuse NY 13224 Office: 103 E Water St The Gridley Bldg Syracuse NY 13202

GERBER, LEWIS NATHANIAL, poet, educator; b. Boston, Nov. 29, 1935; s. Irving and Freida (Needel) G.; B.A., N.Y.U., 1960, postgrad., 1964—; m. Carole Inge, Jan. 9, 1972. Tchr. history N.Y.C. Pub. Schs., 1966—. Mem. Poetry Soc. Am., Acad. Am. Poets. Contbr. poems to poetry jours. and anthologies. Home: 300 E 71st St New York City NY 10021

GERBER, MARCIA LYNN GETZ (MRS. DONALD A. GERBER), physician; b. Bronx, N.Y., Feb. 17, 1942; d. George S. and Ruth (Mehlman) Getz; A.B. (Mary Pemberton Nourse fellow), Vassar Coll., 1963; M.D., (N.Y. Arthritis Found. fellow), Columbia, 1967; m. Donald A. Gerber, June 13, 1964; children—Susan Eve, Andrew James. Intern in internal medicine State U. N.Y., Downstate Med. Center, Bklyn., 1967-68, emergency room physician, 1968, instr. Physician-Student Health Service, 1969—. Trustee, Downstate Nursery Sch., 1971-73, pres., 1972-73. Home: 1021 E 24th St Brooklyn NY 11210 Office: 450 Clarkson Ave Brooklyn NY 11203

GERBER, THOMAS WILLIAM, newspaper editor; b. Portland, Oreg., May 2, 1921; s. Thomas W. and Mary Anne (Smith) G.; A.B., Dartmouth, 1948; m. Gail L. Graham, Jan. 20, 1951 (div. 1970); children—Cheryl Ann, Linda Lee; m. 2d, Electra Bilmazes, Dec. 1971. Reporter, U.P.I., Boston, 1948-51, mgr. Providence bur., 1952-53; rewriteman, spl. assignment reporter Boston Herald and Traveler, 1953-56, chief Washington bur., 1956-61; gen. mgr. Concord (N.H.) Monitor, 1961-67, editor, asst. pub., 1968—; dir., sec. Monitor Pub. Co., 1962—; dir. Concord br. Bank N.H., 1962—. Mem. adv. com. N.H. Tech. Inst., 1966-70; chmn. air quality com. N.H. Environmental Council, 1970; mem. Citizens Task Force, 1969; mem. N.H. Judicial Council, 1972-74. Bd. dirs. N.H. Council World Affairs, N.H. Council Better Schs.; pres. bd. Bishop Brady High Sch., Concord, 1969-70. Served with USAAF, 1942-45, USAF, 1951-52. Decorated Air medal with two oak leaf clusters; recipient Heywood Broun award Am. Newspaper Guild, 1955. Mem. New Eng. Daily Newspaper Assn., Am., New Eng. (pres. 1967) socs. newspaper editors, Sigma Delta Chi (Yankee Quill award 1973). Home: Carter Hill Rd Concord NH 03301 Office: 3 N State St Concord NH 03301

GERETY, PETER LEO, archbishop; b. Shelton, Conn., July 19, 1912; s. Peter Leo and Charlotte (Daly) G.; student St. Thomas Sem., Bloomfield, Conn., 1934, Seminaire St. Sulpice, Paris, France, 1939. Ordained priest Roman Catholic Ch., 1939; asst. pastor, New Haven, 1939-42; dir. Blessed Martin de Porres Interracial Center, 1942-56; pastor, New Haven, 1956-66; coadjutor bishop, Portland, Maine, 1966; apostolic adminstr., Portland, Maine, 1967—; bishop Portland, 1969-74; archbishop of Newark, 1974—. Address: 31 Mulberry St Newark NJ 07102

GERFIN, DONALD REED, retail store exec.; b. Batavia, N.Y., Jan. 16, 1930; s. John Leonard and Helen Elizabeth (Reed) G.; student Siena Coll., 1948-49, Union Coll., 1951-52; m. Patricia Joan White, Feb. 5, 1953; children—Donald, Kurt, Kathryn. Self employed contractor, Schenectady, 1952-55; partner Leisure Crafts, 1955-76 owner, 1976—; sec. J.L. Gerfin, Inc., real estate, 1962-66, sec.-treas., 1966—. Adv. bd. Salvation Army, Schenectady; instl. rep. Boy Scouts Am., 1973—. Bd. dirs. Coop. Extension Schenectady County, 1974—, sec., 1975-78. Recipient outstanding citizenship award United Fund, Schenectady, 1970. Mem. Mohawk Hudson Wheelmen (pres. 1972, dir. 1973-75), Republican. Lutheran (deacon youth work 1968-71). Club: Rotary (sgt. at arms 1976—, dir. 1978—). Home: 1087 Wendall Ave Schenectady NY 12308 Office: 456-458 State St Schenectady NY 12305

GERING, ROBERT LEE, research co. exec.; b. Parker, S.D., Feb. 18, 1920; s. John J. and Pauline (Graber) G.; A.B., U. Utah, 1947, M.A., 1948, Ph.D., 1950; m. Rose Elaine Kaufman, Nov. 24, 1945; children—Lee Maxwell, John Charles. Chmn. biology dept., natural sci. div. Bethel Coll., 1948-53; asst. dir. ecol. research Dugway (Utah) Proving Grounds, 1953-54; chmn. biology dept. Wells Coll., 1954-65; pres. Information Applications, Inc., Penfield, 1966—. Vis. prof. biology U. Rochester, 1965-66; prof. biology Rochester Inst. Tech., 1966-68, coordinator computer assisted instrn. Nat. Tech. Inst. for Deaf, 1968-69. Served with AUS, 1940-46. Mem. A.A.A.S., Am. Inst. Biol. Scis., N.Y. Acad. Sci., Nat. Soc. for Programmed Instrn. Former asst. mng. editor Am. Biology Tchr. Home and office: 2169 Baird Rd Penfield NY 14526

GERJOVICH, MICHAEL WILLIAM, artist; b. Bklyn., Dec. 15, 1944; s. Henry John and Dorothy Joan (Contarini) G.; asso. degree York Acad. Art, 1968; B.S., U. Del., 1976; student Cleve. Inst. Art, 1969-72, Cleve. State U., 1970-72. Artist, Am. Greetings Corp., Cleve., 1968-73; one-man shows: Centerville Gallery, Greenville, Del., 1973, Images Gallery, Wilmington, Del., 1976, group shows include: Nat. Arts Club, 1976, NAD, 1977, Salon des Artistes Français, Grand Palais des Champs Elysees, 1977, Salon l'Image Festival Internat. d'Art Contemporain, 1977; group shows include: Musée du Luxemburg, 1977, Wichita Mus. Art, 1970, Canton (Ohio) Mus. Art, 1970, Del. Art Mus., 1977-78, Raymond Duncan Galleries, Paris, 1977, Ligoa Duncan Gallery, N.Y.C., 1977, Pan Am. Gallery, N.Y.C., 1969, Gallery North, Setauket, N.Y., 1976-77, Sandpiper Gallery, Stone Harbor, N.J., 1973-78, Kershaw Gallery, Newark, Del., 1978, Penthouse Gallery, Phila. Sketch Club, 1977-78, Phila. Civic Center Mus., 1978, Ware Gallery, 1978; represented in various pub. and pvt. collections; art tchr. Conrad Jr. High Sch., Wilmington, 1977-78. Recipient medal of Recognition and Excellence at Internat. Festival in Europe, Republic of France, 1977; awards Phila. Sketch Club, 1977-78; Rubens medal of honor Holland, 1978. Mem. Soc. N. Am. Artists, Phila. Sketch Club, Phila. Watercolor Club, Rehoboth Art League, Artists Equity, Council Del. Artists, Soc. N.J. Artists, Internat. Soc. Artists, Chester County Art Assn., Les Surindépendents. Roman Catholic. Home: 263 E Main St Newark DE 19711

GERMAN, DONALD ROBERT, author; b. Phila., Feb. 11, 1931; s. Samuel Edward and Reba Logan (Trimble) G.; B.S., Temple U., 1955; m. Joan Alice Wolfe, Sept. 4, 1954; 1 son, Donald Robert. Mgmt. trainee Central Penn. Nat. Bank, Phila., 1956-60; bus. devel. dir. Indsl. Valley Bank, Phila., 1960-61; creative dir. First Fin. Advt. Group, Boston, 1962; dir. pub. relations Savs. Banks Assn. Mass., Boston, 1963; editor Warren, Gorham & Lamont, Inc., Boston and N.Y.C., 1964—. Vice chmn. Center City Bus. Dist., United Fund, Phila., 1959-60; v.p., treas. Muscular Dystrophy Assns. Am., Phila., 1958-61; pub. dir. Health Edn. com., Hopkinton (Mass.) pub. schs., 1970; sr. warden St. Paul's Episcopal Ch., Hopkinton, 1969-70; vice chmn. Friends of Berkshire Atheneum. Served to 1st lt. U.S. Army, 1954-56. Recipient Certificate of Merit, Leukemia Soc., 1958; award of merit United Fund of Phila., 1959; Citation of Merit, Muscular Dystrophy Assns. Am., 1960. Mem. Am. Soc. Journalists and Authors (dir.-at-large), Authors Guild, Boston Authors Club, Berkshire Poets Workshop. Unitarian. Author: The Banker's Complete Guide to Advertising, 1966; The Bank Employee's Security Handbook, 1972; (juvenile) Money, Banks and You, 1979; (with Joan W. German) The Bank Teller's Handbook, 1970, Successful Job Hunting for Executives, 1974, Bank Employee's Marketing Handbook, 1975, Tested Techniques in Bank Marketing, Vol. I, 1977, Vol. II, 1978, Make Your Own Food, 1979; The Bank Teller's Handbook, rev. edit., 1978; editor (with Joan W. German) Bank Teller's Report, 1969—, The Branch Bankers Report, 1968—; contbr. articles to mags. and profl. jours. Home: West Mountain Rd Cheshire MA 01225

GERMAN, JUDY CARLILE, govt. and communication ofcl.; b. Kansas City, Mo.; d. John Mercer and Mary Almeda (Chapin) Ellis; student Okla. State U., Tulsa U.; B.A., Am. U., Washington, 1960; m. William P.Z. German, Jr., Feb. 24, 1973; 1 son by previous marriage—John Philip Carlile. Chief probation officer Tulsa County Ct., 1947-50; real estate broker United Farm Agy., 1952-58; bldg. fund campaign mgr. AAUW, Washington, 1958-59; govt. and pub. relations ofcl. Nat. Counsel Assos., Washington, 1959-61; congressional liaison Dept. Agr., Washington, 1961-65; pub. information officer OEO, 1965-70, spl. asst. to dept. dir. ops., 1970-73; dir. pub. relations Nat. Assn. Social Workers, Washington, 1973-74; social sci. analyst Congressional Research Service, Library of Congress, Washington, 1976—; co-owner, dir. Fundamental Research Orgn., 1973—. Pres. bd. govs. Agr. Symphony Orch., 1961-64; bd. dirs. A.R.C. and Boy Scouts Am., 1948-50; bd. dirs. Little Theater and radio shows, 1956-57. Recipient 1st place Fed. Editors Blue Pencil award, 1967; certified humanist counselor. Mem. Pub. Relations Soc. Am., Nat. Assn. Govt. Communicators, Am. Humanist Assn., Assn. Humanistic Psychology, Am. U. Alumni Assn., Smithsonian Assos., Library of Congress Profl. Assn., Humanist Assn. Nat. Capital Area (pres. 1977-78), Nat. Congress Am. Indians, D.A.R. Democrat. Club: Women's Nat. Dem. (Washington). Arranger Am. Discovers Indian Art exhibit, Smithsonian Inst., 1967. Home: 2365 N Oakland St Arlington VA 22207 Office: Congressional Research Service Library of Congress Washington DC 20540

GERRISH, HOLLIS G., candy mfg. co. exec.; b. Berwick, Maine, June 23, 1907; s. Perley G. and Grace (Guptill) G.; A.B., Harvard U., 1930, postgrad. Bus. Sch., 1930-31; m. Catherine G. Ruggles, Sept. 10, 1946. With Squirrel Brand Co., mfrs. confections, Cambridge, Mass., 1931—, pres., 1939-42, 46—; trustee Cambridge Savs. Bank. Bd. dirs. Cambridge YMCA, East End House, Cambridge Home for Aged, Cambridge Tb and Health Assn.; trustee Lesley Coll., Cambridge. Served as lt. comdr. USNR, 1942-46. Mem. Am. Assn. Candy Technologists, New Eng. Confectioners Club, Cambridge Hist. Soc., Nat. Tax Assn., Cambridge C. of C. Episcopalian (trustee). Clubs: Rotary, Harvard, Faculty, Cambridge, Economy, Norfolk Trout. Home: 207 Grove St Cambridge MA 02138 Office: 10-12 Boardman St Cambridge MA 02139

GERRITY, EDWARD JOSEPH, JR., communications co. exec.; b. Scranton, Pa., Jan. 3, 1924; s. Edward Joseph and Helen T. (Walton) G.; B.S., U. Scranton, 1946, also LL.D.; M.S., Columbia U., 1948; m. Katharine Casey, Sept. 22, 1956; children—Katharine, Edward Joseph III. Editorial staff, columnist Scranton Times, 1948-58; with ITT, 1958—, v.p., dir. pub. relations, 1961-64, sr. v.p., dir. corporate relations and advt., 1964—, dir. subsidiaries. Chmn. pub. relations com. Cardinal's Com. for Laity of Cath. Charities, Archdiocese of N.Y.; bd. dirs. Cath. Big Bros., Fifth Ave. Assn. Served with U.S. Army, 1942-45; ETO. Decorated Silver Star, Bronze Star with cluster. Named PR Profl. of Year, Pub. Relations News, 1971. Mem. Pub. Relations Soc. Am., Internat. Pub. Relations Assn., Am. Mgmt. Assn., Pa. Soc., Internat. Econ. Policy Assn. (dir.), Advt. Council (dir. at large), Sigma Delta Chi. Clubs: Overseas Press (N.Y.C.); Metropolitan, Federal City, Nat. Press (Washington); Westchester Country (Rye, N.Y.). Knight of Malta. Office: ITT World Hdqrs 320 Park Ave New York City NY 10022

GERRY, ROGER GOODMAN, oral surgeon; b. Far Rockaway, N.Y., Feb. 26, 1916; s. Bernard Abraham and Edith Rose (Goodman) G.; A.B., U. N.C., 1936; D.M.D., U. Louisville, 1940; m. Peggy Newbauer, Nov. 6, 1944. Commd. lt. (j.g.) Dental Corps, USN, 1941, advanced through grades to capt., 1955; stationed U.S.N.T.S., San Diego, 1941-42, U.S.S. Boise, 1942-44, U.S. Naval Hosp., Phila., 1944-49, Naval Med. Center, Guam, 1949-51, U.S. Naval Hosp., St. Albans, 1951-56, Yokosuka, Japan, 1956-59; ret., 1965; dir. dental and oral surgery service Mt. Sinai Hosp. Services, City Hosp. Center, Elmhurst, N.Y., 1965—; attending oral surgeon, head div. oral surgery Mt. Sinai Hosp., N.Y.C. Prof. oral surgery Mt. Sinai Sch. Medicine, City U. N.Y. Chmn., Planning Bd Roslyn, N.Y. 1960-72; pres. Roslyn Landmark Soc., Roslyn Preservation Corp., 1964—; councillor L.I. Hist. Soc. Trustee Bryant Library; chmn. Friends Am. Wing, Met. Mus. Art, 1970—. Trustee inc. Village Roslyn, N.Y. Recipient Howard C. Sherwood award Soc. for Preservation L.I. Antiquities, 1976. Fellow Internat., Am. colls. dentists, Internat. Assn. Oral Surgeons; mem. Am. Dental Soc., Am. Soc. Oral Surgeons, Am. Acad. Oral Pathology, Soc. Archtl. Historians, Brit. Assn. Oral Surgeons, Japan Soc. Author: Catalogue of Japanese Ceramics, 1961. Contbr. articles to profl. jours., Dictionary of Art. Office: City Hosp Center Elmhurst NY 11373

GERSH, ROSEMARIE CECILIA, camp exec.; b. Ellenville, N.Y., Aug. 6, 1933; d. George Peter and Cecilia Marie (Lechner) Halbig; A.A., Orange County Community Coll., 1954; B.A., Miami U., 1956; postgrad. Hunter Coll., 1961-64; M.A., N.Y. U., 1967; m. Edward I. Gersh, Apr. 14, 1963; children—Roxanne Cecilia, Kevin George. Profl. concert pianist, 1952-56; co-ordinator N.Y. U. Alumni Assn., 1956-58; asst. to exec. v.p. Asso. Products, N.Y.C., 1958-60; tchr. N.Y.C. Jr. High Sch. 117, 1960-64; asst. dir. West Hills Day Camp, Huntington, N.Y., 1964-70, dir., 1970—; sec. Sweet Hollow Bus. Co., Inc., 1977-78. Swimming instr. YWCA, N.Y.C., 1957-60. Rep. dist. committeewoman, 1973—. Trustee, founder Wilmington (Del.) Coll., 1967-69; trustee Woodland Acad., Woodbury, N.Y., 1969-74, Crestwood County Day Sch., Melville, N.Y., 1973-74; sec. West Hills Day Camp, Inc., 1975—. Mem. Am. Camping Assn., Organist Guild Am., League Women Voters, L.I. Pvt. Schs. and Day Camp Assn. (sec. 1966-70, mem. exec. bd. 1966-70). Republican. Home: 324 West Hills Rd Huntington NY 11743 Office: Sweet Hollow Rd Huntington NY 11743

GERSHEL, CHRISTOPHER PETER, army officer; b. N.Y.C., Aug. 8, 1942; s. Stanley Louis and Alice (Browne) G.; B.S. (honors scholar 1976), U. Nebr. at Omaha, 1976; M.B.A., L.I. U., 1978; m. Sharon Anne Kirth, May 10, 1966; children—Kevin David, Georgette Ann. Police officer City of Fremont, Calif., 1965-69; joined U.S. Army, 1969, commd. maj. 1978; provost marshal ops. officer U.S. Mil. Acad., West Point, N.Y., 1976—. Bd. dirs. Copperas Cove Exchange Club, 1972-73. Decorated D.F.C., Bronze Star, Air medal (4). Mem. Mensa. Republican. Home: Quarters 3052A West Point NY 10996

GERSHEN, ALVIN EDWARD, profl. planner; b. Bronx, N.Y., July 5, 1926; s. Hyman and Jennie (Gerson) G.; B.C.E., Coll. City N.Y., 1948; M.Pub. Adminstrn., N.Y. U., 1955; m. Mildred Blaine, June 27, 1953; children—Reva Gisele, Ruth Susan, Eta Margolit, Elana Lynn, Deborah Michele, Jonathan Seth. With N.Y.C. Dept. City Planning, 1949-51; planning cons., 1951-56; home builder, 1956-58; chief tech. ops. N.J. Div. State and Regional Planning, 1958-61; pres. Gershen and Coppola Assos., Trenton, N.J., 1961—; pres. Moderate Income Housing Co., Inc., Trenton, 1966—. Faculty, Rutgers U., N.Y. U., Coll. City N.Y.; cons. W.Va. Gov.'s Task Force on Housing, 1966, N.J. Civil Service Commn., 1965-66; mem. N.Y. Met. Com. on Planning, 1952; chmn. N.J. Gov.'s Task Force Housing and Urban Renewal, 1965; mem. N.J. Meadowlands Regional Devel. Agy., 1960—, chmn., 1960-62, 64—; mem. Randolph Twp. Zoning Bd. Adjustment, 1960-61; v.p. Nat. Ramah Commn., past pres. Poconos Remah Com.; mem. N.J. Council on Arts, chmn., 1972-77; mem. N.J. Am. Revolution Bicentennial Celebration Commn., past chmn. arts and humanities com. Bd. dirs. Princeton Jewish Center, 1965-66, 68-70, 70-72, pres., 1972-74; bd. dirs. Dr. Herzl Zion Sch. Served with AUS, 1944-46. Registered profl. engr., N.J., N.Y.; registered profl. planner, N.J., Mich. Mem. Am. Inst. Planners (past v.p. N.J. chpt.), Am. Soc. Planning Ofcls., Nat. Assn. Housing and Redevel. Ofcls., Nat. Soc. Profl. Engrs., Am. Inst. Housing Cons. (nat. v.p. 1966, 72), N.J. Bd. Profl. Planners (pres.), N.J. Fedn. Planning Ofcls. (asso. dir.). Author, editor: Zoning in New Jersey, 1960; Guide to Zoning Boards of Adjustment, 1960. Contbr. numerous articles to profl. jours. Home: 60 Philip Dr Princeton NJ 08540 Office: 126 W State St Trenton NJ 08608

GERSHENFELD, MATTI KIBRICK, psychologist; b. Phila., Mar. 26, 1926; d. Hyman and Esther (Kibrick) Kibrick; A.B., U. Pa., 1946, M.A., 1951; Ed.D., Temple U., 1967; certificate U. Pa. Sch. Medicine, 1972; m. Marvin Aaron Gershenfeld, Mar. 23, 1947; children—Robert, Howard, Richard, Kenneth. City planner Phila. City Plan Commn., 1946-51; exec. dir. Phila. Fedn. Community Councils, 1952-54; moderator Citizens in Action TV program U. of Air, 1954, 56-57; lectr., vis. prof. Temple U., 1967—; founder Inst. of Awareness, Phila., 1968, cons.-dir., 1968-75; founder Couples Learning Center, Jenkintown, Pa., 1976, dir., 1976—; dir. Center Family Life Programs, Pa. State U., Ogontz; vis. lectr. various univs., 1970—; cons. various civic, ednl. and community orgns., 1972—; producer TV series on groups, 1978. Pres., Neighborhood Center, Phila., 1971-74; bd. dirs. Phila. council Girl Scouts U.S., 1976—, B'nai B'rith Youth Orgn., 1976—, Fedn. Jewish Agys., 1975—. Fellow Pa. Psychol. Assn.; mem. Am., Eastern psychol. assns., Am. Assn. Marriage and Family Counsellors, Assn. Women Psychologists, Internat. Transactional Analysis Assn. Democrat. Jewish. Author: Groups: Theory and Experience, 1973; Issues in Human Service, 1974; The Impact of the Changing Roles of Women on Women, 1975; Women in Government, 1975; instrumental in establishing ednl. programs at Temple U. Home: Pepper and Winter Rd Rydal PA 19046 Office: Suite 102 Realty World Plaza Jenkintown PA 19046

GERSON, DONALD JEROME, phys. scientist; b. N.Y.C., Apr. 26, 1934; s. Irwin and Helen (Sacks) G.; B.A. in Meteorology, N.Y. U., 1956; M.S. in Computer Sci., U. Md., 1975; m. Barbara Ann Jaques, Aug. 21, 1960; 1 dau., Laura Melissa. Oceanographer, USN Oceanographic Office, Washington, 1956-78, Def. Mapping Agy., Washington, 1978—; U.S. del. working group on sea ice World Meteorol. Orgn., 1975-77. Fellow Explorers Club; mem. Am. Geophys. Union, Arctic Inst. N.Am., N.Y. U., U. Md. alumni clubs, Sigma Xi. Author: Time Lapse Photography of Sea Ice, 1958; Computer Estimation of the Presence of Sea Ice in Satellites Pictures, 1975; A Numerical Ice Forcasting System, 1975; Pattern Analysis for Automatic Location of Oceanic Fronts in Digital Satellite Imagery, 1977; contbr. articles to sci. jours. Home: 3148 Castleigh Rd Silver Spring MD 20904 Office: Def Mapping Agy 6500 Brooks Ln Washington DC 20315

GERSON, HERMAN, chemist; b. Elizabeth, N.J., May 9, 1912; s. Aaron and Ida (Freidin) G.; B.S., U. Calif., Los Angeles, 1947; m. Sophie Greenberg, 1956; children—Alan Jay, Rena Adele. Research chemist Allied Chem. Corp., Haledon, N.J., 1948-77; cons. Harmon Colors Corp., Haledon, 1977—. Democratic dist. leader Greenwich Village, N.Y.C., 1978—; mem. N.Y. State Dem. Com., 1977. Served with inf. U.S. Army, 1945-47; PTO. Mem. Am. Chem. Soc., N.Y. Pigment Club, New Dem. Coalition, Citizens Union N.Y., Greenwich Village C. of C., Village Ind. Dems. Patentee in field. Address: 505 LaGuardia Pl New York City NY 10012

GERSON, JIMMY MARSHALL, physician; b. Pitts., Dec. 28, 1944; s. Joseph and Pearl (Kaufman) G.; B.A., Washington and Jefferson Coll., 1966; M.D., Jefferson Med. Coll., 1970; m. Linda S. Cohen, June 23, 1968; children—Lisa Dara, Matthew. Intern, Children's Hosp. of Phila., 1970-71, resident in pediatrics, 1971-72; Am. Cancer Soc. fellow in pediatric oncology-hematology Children's Hosp. of Phila.-U. Pa., 1973-75, instr. pediatrics, 1973-76, asst. prof., 1977—; clin. immunologist Nat. Cancer Inst., Bethesda, Md., 1977—. Served to lt. comdr. M.C., USNR, 1975-77. Diplomate Am. Bd. Pediatrics. Fellow Am. Acad. Pediatrics; mem. N.Y. Acad. Scis.

Home: 5204 Glenwood Rd Bethesda MD 20014 Office: Nat Cancer Inst NIH Bethesda MD 20014

GERSON, NOEL BERTRAM, author; b. Chgo., Nov. 6, 1914; s. Samuel Philip and Rosa Anna (Noel) G.; A.B., U. Chgo., 1934. M.A., 1935; m. Marilyn A. Hammond; children—Noel Anne Gerson Brennan, Michele Gerson Myers, Margot, Paul. Reporter, rewriteman Chgo. Herald-Examiner, 1931-36; exec. radio sta. WGN, Chgo., 1936-41, radio and TV scriptwriter over 10,000 scripts, nat. networks, 1936-51. Fellow Internat. Inst. Arts and Letters; mem. Authors Guild Am., Am., Miss. Valley hist. assns., Western Writers Am., Mystery Writers Am., Am. Acad. Polit. and Social Sci., Centro Studi E Scambi Internazionali, Kappa Alpha. Clubs: Players (N.Y.C.); Liquanea (Jamaica, W.I.). Author numerous fiction and non-fiction books under own name, various pseudonyms including: The Yankee from Tennessee; The Hittite; The Queen's Husband; The Naked Maja; The Golden Lyre; The Land Is Bright; Queen of Caprice; The Slender Reed; Old Hickory; Lady of France; Yankee Doodle Dandy; Sex and the Mature Man; Kit Carson; Give Me Liberty; Sex and the Adult Woman; Light-Horse Harry Lee; The Swamp Fox; TR, Sam Houston; By Choice, Not Chance; The Anthem; I'll Storm Hell; Warhead; Island in the Wind; Mirror, Mirror; Double Vision; Temptation to Steal; Jefferson Square; Because I Loved Him; The Prodigal Genius; State Trooper; Daughter of Earth and Water; The Sunday Heroes; Victor Hugo; The Divine Mistress; George Sand; Rebel; The Exploiters; That Eaton Woman; All That Glitters; The Caves of Guernica; I Love You, I Hate You; Harriet Beecher Stowe; Neptune; Special Agent; Vidoco; books also pub. in many fgn. countries. Author numerous mag. articles; contbg. author Ency. Americana. Home: 63 Pratt Ave Clinton CT 06413

GERSON, RAYMOND EDGAR, energy and environ. cons.; b. N.Y.C., Feb. 9, 1945; s. Fred and Ruth (Wolf) G.; B.S. with honors, Lehigh U., 1966; Ph.D., Mass. Inst. Tech., 1970. With Environmental Protection Adminstrn., City of N.Y., 1970-75, asst. to commr., 1971-72, dir. noise abatement, 1972-75; energy and environ. cons., N.Y.C., 1975—. Adj. asst. prof. chemistry York Coll., City U. N.Y., 1973-74. NASA trainee, 1968-69; NSF Research fellow, 1965-66; NIH research asst., 1967-68, 69-70. Home: 39 Gramercy Park New York City NY 10010

GERSONI, DIANE CLAIRE, author, editor; b. Bklyn., Apr. 16, 1947; d. James Arthur and Edna Bernice (Krinski) Gersoni; B.A. cum laude, Vassar Coll., 1967; m. James Neil Edleman, Oct. 5, 1975; 1 son, Michael Lawrence. Asst. editor, then asso. editor Sch. Library Jour. Book Rev., 1968-72; free lance writer, 1972-74; writer, editor Scholastic Mags., Inc., N.Y.C., 1974-78; freelance writer, 1978—; author: Sexism and Youth 1974; cons. speaker in field. Jewish. Club: Vassar (N.Y.C.). Author: Work-Wise: Learning About the World of Work from Books, 1979. Contbr. articles, book revs. to anthologies, newspapers, mags. Home: 301 E 78th St New York NY 11375

GERST, ELIZABETH CARLSEN (MRS. PAUL H. GERST), educator, researcher; b. N.Y.C., June 10, 1929; d. Rolf and Gudrun (Wiborg) Carlsen; A.B. magna cum laude, Mt. Holyoke Coll., 1951; Ph.D., U. Pa., 1957; m. Paul H. Gerst, Aug. 3, 1957; children—Steven Richard, Jeffrey Carlton, Andrew Leigh. Instr. physiology Cornell U. Med. Coll., N.Y.C., 1957-58; instr. Columbia Coll. Physicians and Surgeons, N.Y.C., 1959-61, asst. prof., 1961—, dir. Center Continuing Med. Edn., 1978—. Pres. Citizen's Ednl. Council Tenafly, 1972—; vice chmn. Tenafly Environ. Commn., 1972-77; mem. steering com. Citizens Long-Range Planning Com., Tenafly Bd. Edn., 1971-72, chmn. subcom. extended kindergarten day and pre-kindergarten classes, 1971-72, mem. Tenafly Bd. Edn., 1973-77; mem. curriculum study groups on sci. Tenafly High Sch., 1970-71, Tenafly Middle Sch., 1971-72; trustee Tenafly Nature Center, 1972—; bd. dirs., chmn. environ. quality Tenafly LWV, 1971—. Porter fellow Am. Physiol. Soc., 1956-57. Mem. Soc. Med. Coll. Dirs. of Continuing Med. Edn., Am. Physiol. Soc. (task force Women in Physiology 1973—), Physiol. Soc. Phila., Harvey Soc., Biophys. Soc., AAAS, Bergen County LWV (v.p. 1973-75), Phi Beta Kappa, Sigma Xi, Sigma Delta Epsilon. Unitarian. Home: 141 Tekening Dr Tenafly NJ 07670 Office: 630 W 168th St New York City NY 10032

GERST, PAUL HOWARD, physician; b. Sept. 24, 1927; s. David and Hilde (Werbel) G.; A.B., Columbia, 1948, M.D., 1952; m. Elizabeth Carlsen, Aug. 3, 1957; children—Steven R., Jeffrey C., Andrew L. Intern Columbia-Presbyn. Med. Center, N.Y.C., 1952-53, resident, 1956-62, mem. staff, 1962—; instr. physiology U. Pa., 1955-56; practice medicine specializing in surgery, N.Y.C., 1962—; asst. clin. prof. surgery Columbia, 1964-72; prof. surgery Albert Einstein Coll. Medicine, 1972—; dir. surgery Bronx-Lebanon Hosp. Center, N.Y.C. Served to 1st lt. AUS, 1953-55. USPHS postdoctoral research fellow, 1955-56. Recipient USPHS Research Career Devel. award, 1964-65. Diplomate Am. Bd. Surgery, Am. Bd. Thoracic Surgery. Fellow A.C.S.; mem. Am. Physiol. Soc., N.Y. Soc. for Thoracic Surgery, N.Y. Surg. Soc., N.Y. Soc. for Cardiovascular Surgery, Am. Heart Assn. Contbr. articles to profl. jours. Home: 141 Tekening Dr Tenafly NJ 07670 Office: Bronx-Lebanon Hospital Center 1650 Grand Concourse New York City NY 10457

GERSTEIN, DAVID BROWN, hardware mfg. co. exec.; b. N.Y.C., Jan. 30, 1932; s. Frank and May G.; student Columbia U., 1951-53; B.S., Seton Hall U., 1955; m. Jane Ellen Gerstein, May 4, 1963; children—Mark, James. With Thermwell Products Co., Paterson, N.J., 1955—, sales mgr., 1965-68, v.p., 1968-74, pres., 1974—; owner N.J. Nets basketball team, 1978—; v.p. Lever Mfg. Co., Paterson. Home: 432 Long Hill Dr Short Hills NJ 07078

GERSTEIN, GARY ALLEN, investment co. exec.; b. Bklyn., Sept. 7, 1941; s. John and Tina (Bronstein) G.; B.S., N.Y.U., 1962; M.A., Rutgers U., 1965; m. Elaine Thera Greenfield, Dec. 24, 1966; children—Leila Rebecca, Rachel Beth. Vice pres. Chase Manhattan Bank, N.A., N.Y.C., 1965-72; v.p. Chase Investors Mgmt. Corp., N.Y.C., 1972—; instr. econs., Rutgers U. Certified fin. analyst. Fellow Fin. Analysts Fedn.; mem. N.Y. Soc. Security Analysts, Fin. Analysts Fedn., Soc. Govt. Economists, Nat. Economists Club. Home: 325 E 79th St New York City NY 10021 Office: 1211 Ave of Americas New York City NY 10036

GERSTEIN, JUDAH, biophysicist; b. Tel-Aviv, Israel, Oct. 27, 1940; s. Emanuel and Billhah (Bloch) G.; B.S., City U.N.Y., 1972; m. Renee Solmonsohn, June 7, 1964; children—Steven Robert, Ellen Robin. Asso. research scientist Mt. Sinai Sch. Medicine, N.Y.C., 1968-70; chief toxicology lab. N.Y.U. Med. Center, N.Y.C., 1970-74; supr. dept. nuclear medicine Kingsbrook Jewish Med. Center, Bklyn., 1974—. Commr. environ. control commn. Village of Freeport, N.Y., 1970-73. Mem. Soc. Nuclear Medicine, Am. Chem. Soc., IEEE, N.Y. State Soc. Nuclear Medicine Technologists. Jewish. Home: 370 Rose St Freeport NY 11520

GERSTEIN, MEL, research and marketing exec.; b. N.Y.C., Jan. 30, 1937; s. Frank and May (Brown) G.; B.B.A., Pace Coll., 1955; postgrad. Columbia, 1957; m. Gayle Gerstein; children—Teddy, Madeline, Amy. Vice pres. research and devel. financial marketing and packaging Thermwell Products Co., Inc., N.Y.C., 1957—, Lever Machine Corp., N.Y.C., 1958—; v.p., treas. Woodlowe Realty Corp., Paterson, N.J., Lever Mfg. Corp., Paterson, Thermwell Mfg. Corp., Filmco Industries Inc.; dir. Vogue Studios, Inc., Belleville, N.J., Royal Crown Bottling Co., Newark, Lever Mfg. Corp. Bd. dirs. Paterson Cultural Center; trustee, co-chmn. Barnert Meml. Hosp., Paterson. Exhibited art at Ahda Artzt Art Gallery, N.Y.C., Kiron Art Gallery, N.Y.C.; cartoonist; designer greeting cards. Mem. Am. Mgmt. Assn., N.J., Greater Paterson (dir.) chambers commerce. Developer houseware and hardware products. Home: Buckingham Dr Alpine NJ 07620 Office: 150 E 7th St Paterson NJ 07524

GERSTEN, SANDRA JOAN PESSIN (MRS. AARON L. GERSTEN), lawyer; b. Hartford, Conn.; d. Israel George and Gussie (Marcus) Pessin; student U. Geneva, 1955-56; B.A., Vassar Coll., 1957; LL.B., U. Conn., 1960; m. Aaron L. Gersten, Mar. 29, 1957; children—Peter Samuel, Karen Sue. Admitted to Conn. bar, 1960; individual practice law, West Hartford, 1960—. Past pres. Greater Hartford chpt. Orgn. for Rehab. Through Tng., 1968—; sec. U. Conn. Law Sch. Found. Mem. Conn., Hartford County bar assns., Brandeis Aux. (life), Nat. Assn. Women Lawyers, U. Conn. Law Sch. Alumni Assn. (sec.). Club: Cliffside (Conn.). Address: 25 Pioneer Dr West Hartford CT 06117

GERSTENFELD, JACOB, ophthalmologist; b. Bronx, N.Y., Feb. 26, 1935; s. Moe and Lillian G.; B.S. summa cum laude, Bklyn. Coll., 1956; M.D., Albert Einstein Sch. Medicine, 1960; m. Loretta Neuwirth, June 13, 1959; children—David, Edward. Intern and resident Bronx Municipal Hosp. Center; practice medicine specializing in ophthalmology, S.I., N.Y., 1964—; mem. staffs USPHS, S.I., Richmond Meml., Sea View hosps.; asst. clin. prof. ophthalmology Albert Einstein Med. Sch., 1964-75; v.p. Richmond County Profl. Standards Rev. Orgn., 1975—. Salk Med. scholar, 1956. Mem. Richmond County Med. Soc. (pres. 1973), Phi Beta Kappa, Alpha Omega Alpha. Home: 15 Tiber Pl Staten Island NY 10301 Office: 4303 Hylan Blvd Staten Island NY 10312

GERSTINE, JOHN, author; b. Bklyn., Mar. 8, 1915; s. Louis and Jennie (Martell) G.; student Bklyn. Coll., 1932-33, Coll. City N.Y., 1933-34, New Sch. for Social Research, 1934-37; m. Tina Bronstein, May 6, 1939; children—Gary Allen, Nancy Lee. Past editorial writer Commerce and Industry; financial cons., v.p. Robert D. Eckhouse & Assos., financial pub. relations counsel, N.Y.C.; founder, editor quar. newsletter to edn. community Mood of Youth Notes. Mem. Author's Guild. Author: Play it Cool, 1958; The Speculators, 1963; also articles in financial publs., short stories for lit. quars. Home: 32-22 92d St Jackson Heights NY 11369 Office: 1125 Madison Ave New York City NY 10028

GERSTMAN, JUDITH RITA, psychoanalyst; b. Weehawken, N.J., May 22, 1949; d. Harold and Helen Eva (Zamore) Gerstman; B.A., Bklyn. Coll., 1972; M.S., L.I.U., 1973; postgrad. Manhattan Center for Advanced Psychoanalytic Studies, 1972—. Social work asst. Coney Island (N.Y.) Hosp., 1968-69, analytic intern, 1973-75; childrens counselor L.I.U. Learning Disability Center, 1972-73; therapist Manhattan Center Advance Psychoanalytic Studies, Bklyn., 1974-77; pvt. practice psychoanalysis, Bklyn., 1974—. Mem. Am. Personnel and Guidance Assn., Nat. Accreditation Assn. Psychoanalysis, Joint Counsel Mental Health. Home: 770 Ocean Pkwy Brooklyn NY 11230

GERSTNER, EDNA SUCKAU (MRS. JOHN H. GERSTNER), author; b. Champa, India, Apr. 17, 1914; d. Cornelius H. and Lulu (Johnston) Suckau (parents Am. citizens); A.B. magna cum laude, Wheaton Coll., 1934; M.A., U. Pa., 1936; postgrad. Columbia, summer 1938; m. John H. Gerstner, Sept. 7, 1940; children—Judy Black, Rachel Gwen, Jonathan Neil. Dir. religious edn. 1st Parish Presbyn. Ch., Portland, Maine, 1937; tchr. English and German, Monroe (Ind.) High Sch., 1938-40; lectr. ch. groups, women's clubs on travel, 1930—. Mem. Women's Bd. Missions, U.P. Ch. in U.S.A., 1949-53; vol. Passavant Hosp., Columbia Hosp., Home for Crippled Children. Mem. Ligonier Valley Ft. Ligonier Poetry Soc. Author: (novels) Song by the River, 1960; Idelette, 1963; also poems. Home: RFD 5 Ligonier PA 15658

GERTLER, MENARD M., physician; b. Saskatoon, Sask., Can., May 21, 1919; s. Frank and Clare (Handelman) G.; A.B., U. Sask., 1940; M.D., C.M., McGill U., 1943, M.Sc., 1944; D.Sc., N.Y. U. Sch. Medicine, 1959; m. Anna Paull, Sept. 4, 1943; children—Barbara Paull, Stephanie Jocelyn, Jonathan Paull. Intern Royal Victoria Hosp., Montreal, Que., Can., 1943-44; fellow physiology, instr. McGill Med. Sch. 1945-47; hosp. research fellow medicine Harvard, 1945-47; fellow medicine Columbia-Presbyn. Med. Center, N.Y.C., 1950-51; instr. medicine Coll. Phys. and Surg., 1951-56; attending physician U. Hosp. N.Y. U. Sch. Medicine, 1959; med. dir. Sinclair Oil Corp; asst. medicine Presbyn. Hosp., N.Y.C.; asst. vis. physician Frances Delafield Hosp., N.Y.C., 1951-54, physician in-charge cardiology, 1951-54; Nat. Heart Inst. spl. research fellow dept. biochemistry N.Y. U.-Bellvue Med. Center; prof. Inst. Rehab. Medicine, N.Y. U. Med. Center, 1958—, prof., dir. cardiovascular research, 1966—; cons.-lectr. U.S. Naval Hosp., St. Albans, N.Y.; attending medicine N.Y. U. Med. Center; internat. cons. Social and Rehab. Services, Health Edn. and Welfare. Recipient Founder's Day award N.Y. U. Fellow Am. Cancer Soc.; mem. A.M.A., Can. Med. Assn., Can. Physiol. Soc., Am. Heart Assn., Harvey Soc., Am. Assn. Phys. Anthropologists, A.A.A.S., Am. Physiologic Soc., Sigma Xi. Clubs: Harvard (Boston); University (N.Y.C.); Cosmos (Washington). Contbr. articles to med. publs. Home: 1000 Park Ave New York City NY 10028 Office: 400 E 34th St New York City NY 10016

GERWIN, RONALD HAL, educator; b. N.Y.C., Jan. 21, 1944; s. Solomon and Belle Natalie (Mintzes) G.; B.S., Bklyn. Coll., 1964; M.Ed., Temple U., 1966; Ed.D., Columbia U. Tchrs. Coll., 1977; m. Linda Hope Pine, Apr. 15, 1967; children—Samantha, Elizabeth, Valerie. Substitute tchr. N.Y.C. Bd. Edn., 1964-66; lectr. health and phys. edn. Bklyn. Coll., 1966-67; instr. dept. health, phys. edn. and recreation Kingsborough Community Coll., Bklyn., 1967-70, asst. prof., 1970-72, asso. prof., 1972-76, prof., 1976—, chmn. dept., 1971—, athletic dir., 1971—. Mem. Heartland Village Civic Assn., Mid Island Polit. Action Com. Mem. AAHPER, N.Y. State Fedn. Health Educators, Nat. Jr. Coll. Athletic Assn., Met. Community Coll. Athletic Assn., Japan Karate Assn. Contbr. articles to profl. jours. Office: 2001 Oriental Blvd Brooklyn NY 11235

GESOFF, MARK STONE, dir. computer center; b. Bethlehem, Pa., Jan. 20, 1943; s. Philip and Libby Pearl (Stone) G.; student Muhlenberg Coll., 1960-62; B.P.S., Pace U., 1973; m. Jean Edna Gingerich, Mar. 2, 1974; children—Franklin, Glenn, Julie. Tabulating operator Phoenix of London Assurance Co., N.Y.C., 1963-64; sr. computer operator Dean Witter and Co., N.Y.C., 1964-65; jr. programmer Genesco, Inc., N.Y.C., 1965-66; systems programmer Benton & Bowles Advt. Agency, N.Y.C., 1966-68; asst. v.p. software services Davidsohn Computer Services, N.Y.C., 1968-69; project mgr. Dataplan, Inc., N.Y.C., 1969-70; asst. systems mgr. ASCAP, N.Y.C., 1970; adj. prof. Westchester Community Coll., Valhalla, N.Y., 1971—, computer center supr., 1970-72, dir. computer center, 1972—. Recipient certificate of Achievement in EDP, 1966. Mem. Assn. Computer Programmers and Analysts, Adminstrv. Mgmt. Soc. Home: 5 Duluth Pl Eastchester NY 10709 Office: 75 Grasslands Rd Valhalla NY 10595

GESSNER, PETER K. (PIOTR KAZIMIERZ), educator; b. Warsaw, Poland, May 3, 1931; s. Witold and Maria (Parzych) G.; came to U.S., 1958, naturalized, 1969; B.S., U. London (Eng.), 1955, Ph.D., 1958; m. Teresa Kikal, June 4, 1959; children—Julia Anna, Monica Adrienne. Research asso. research div. Cleve. Clinic, 1958-61, asst. staff mem. research div., 1961-62; asst. prof. pharmacology dept. Sch. Medicine, State U. N.Y. at Buffalo, 1962-67, asso. prof., 1967-75, prof., 1975—. Mem. Am. Soc. Pharmacology and Exptl. Therapeutics, Biochem. Soc. Great Britain, Soc. Neurosci., Internat. Soc. Biochem. Pharmacology, Internat. Soc. Psychoneuroendocrinology, Soc. Biol. Psychiatry, Am. Chem. Soc., N.Y. Acad. Sci., AAAS, Nat. Council Alcholism, Sigma Xi. Home: 4712 Brentwood Dr Williamsville NY 14221 Office: Farber Hall State U NY at Buffalo Buffalo NY 14214

GETTER, GUSTAV, cons. engring. firm exec.; b. N.Y.C., Aug. 3, 1926; s. Joseph and Minnie (Girsh) G.; B.S. in Engring., Brown U., 1946; M.C.E., Poly. Inst. Bklyn., 1949; m. Ruth Groton, Dec. 1, 1951; children—Leslie Charles, Elizabeth Valerie. Tech. ops. mgr. firm Seelye Stevenson Value & Knecht, N.Y.C., 1954-63; founder, pres. firm Gustav Getter Assos., P.C., New Rochelle, N.Y., 1963—; pres. Systems Technics & Graphics, Inc., New Rochelle, 1966—. Dir. Charter League and Citizens Council New Rochelle Inc., 1971; mem. New Rochelle Bd. Standards and Appeals, 1975. Served to lt. USNR, 1944-46, 51-53. Registered profl. engr., N.Y., Conn., N.J., Fla., Mass., Va., Del., Ky., Minn. Fellow ASCE; mem. Am. Cons. Engrs. Council, N.Y. Assn. Cons. Engrs., N.Y. State Soc. Profl. Engrs., Am. Public Works Assn., Soc. Am. Mil. Engrs., ASTM, Sigma Xi, Tau Beta Pi. Clubs: Univ. (Westchester, N.Y.); Brown Univ. (Westchester County). Author: (with others) Seelye's Data Book for Civil Engineers, 1960. Home: 21 Bayberry Ln New Rochelle NY 10804 Office: Penthouse The Mall New Rochelle NY 10801

GETTIS, ALAN, clin. psychologist; b. Newark, July 26, 1944; s. George and Betty Gettis; B.A., Fairleigh Dickinson U., 1967; M.A., Central Mich. U., 1968; postgrad. New Sch. Social Research, 1968-69; Ph.D. Utah State U., 1974; m. Nanette Joan Howie, Nov. 30, 1969. Staff psychologist William Beaumont Gen. Hosp., El Paso, Tex., 1969-70; psychotherapist Bklyn. Center for Psychotherapy and N.J. Center Psychotherapy, 1971-72; instr. psychology Utah State U., 1973-74, Farleigh Dickinson U., Teaneck, N.J., 1975—; chief psychologist W. Bergen Mental Health Center, Ridgewood, N.J., 1974—; pvt. practice clin. psychology, Teaneck, 1974—. Mem. Am. Psychol. Assn., Assn. Humanistic Psychology. Contbr. articles on psychology and psychotherapy to profl. jours.; Haiku poetry. Home: 75 Hazel St Dumont NJ 07628 Office: Teaneck Medical Center 185 Cedar Ln Teaneck NJ 07666

GETTY, RALPH WELLMAN, obstetrician, gynceologist; b. Hudson, N.Y., Nov. 22, 1916; s. Edmond Charles and Norma M. (Church) G.; M.D., Syracuse U., 1941; m. Joyce J. Bahme, Aug. 30, 1941; children—Marcia Gay Getty Chaffee, Linda Sue Getty Randall, Joyce Ann Getty Messenger. Intern, Bklyn. Hosp., 1941-42; resident Syracuse (N.Y.) U. Med. Center, 1946-49; fellow in pathology Free Hosp. for Women, Brookline, Mass.; practice medicine, specializing in obstetrics and gynecology, Auburn, N.Y., 1949—; chief obstetrics and gynecology Auburn Meml. Hosp., 1955-65, active staff, 1950—, pres. med. staff, 1969-70. Mem. Auburn Bd. Edn., 1958-70, pres., 1969; mem. bd. coop. ednl. services, Auburn, 1970-74; bd. dirs. Marine Midland, Auburn, 1969-75. Served with M.C., USNR, 1941-46. Decorated Bronze Star medal; diplomate Am. Bd. Obstetrics and Gynecology. Fellow ACS; mem. Am. Coll. Obstetricians and Gynecologists, AMA, N.Y., Cayuga County med. socs., C. of C. (bd. dirs. 1977—). Presbyterian. Club: Owasco Country. Address: 5 Hamilton Ave Auburn NY 13021

GETTY, WILLIAM PATTON, ret. steel co. exec.; b. Pitts., Mar. 26, 1910; s. William Fleming and Bertha A. (Keefe) G.; B.S., U. Pitts., 1932; m. Betty Ann Cochran, Nov. 23, 1938; children—Judith Ann (Mrs. John Walter Treadwell), William Patton III. With Weirton Steel Co., 1933-36; with Jones & Laughlin Steel Corp., 1936-70, asst. v.p. prodn., 1953-63, v.p. prodn., 1963-67, exec. v.p., 1967-68, pres., chief operating officer, 1968-70, also dir.; v.p. dir. Gateway Coal Co., until 1970; cons. to steel industry, 1970—; dir. H.H. Robertson Co., Salem Corp., Pa Engring. Corp., J.P. Driscoll, Inc. Chmn. trustees Winchester-Thurston Sch., 1961-67; trustee United Fund; mem. exec. council, v.p. Allegheny Trails council Boy Scouts Am. Mem. Am. Iron and Steel Inst., (chmn. mfg. problems com. 1966-68), Metals Soc., Am. Inst. Mining and Metall. Engrs., Am. Soc. Metals, Am. Welding Soc., Soc. Automotive Engrs., Coal Mining Inst. Am., Eastern States Blast Furnace and Coke Oven Assn., Assn. Iron and Steel Engrs., Engrs. Soc. Western Pa. Clubs: Duquesne, Longue Vue Country (Pitts.); Laurel Valley Golf (Ligonier, Pa.); Ponte Vedra, Boca Raton, Quail Ridge (Fla.). Home: 107 Hawthorne Rd Fox Chapel Pittsburgh PA 15238

GETZ, SOLOMON, cons. firm exec.; b. Phila., July 1, 1936; s. Nathan and Virginia (Rice) G.; B.S., Drexel U., 1959, M.S., 1963; m. Vera Greenberg, Mar. 26, 1961; children—Rena Debra, Aaron Michael, Shari Lynn. Aircraft powerplant research engr. Naval Air Turbine Test Sta., Trenton, N.J., 1956-62; ops. research analyst Naval Air Devel. Center, Warminster, Pa., 1962-73; pres., dir. Info. Spectrum Inc., Cherry Hill, N.J., 1973—; v.p. Systems Optimization Corp., 1972-73. Served with USNR, 1960-68. Fellow Am. Inst. Aeros. and Astronautics (asso.); mem. Am. Def. Preparedness Assn. Jewish. Club: B'nai B'rith. Contbr. articles to profl. jours. Office: Information Spectrum Inc 1040 Kings Hwy Cherry Hill NJ 08034

GEVALT, FREDERICK CONRAD, JR., physician; b. Boston, Aug. 27, 1914; s. Frederick Conrad and Nina Marcella (Black) G.; A.B., Harvard U., 1936; M.D., Columbia U., 1940; m. Sally Willits Young, Nov. 10, 1945; children—Frederick Conrad III, Peter Young, Geoffrey Willits. House officer in internal medicine Boston City Hosp., 1940-42; asst. resident in internal medicine Mass. Gen. Hosp., 1942-43, asst. in medicine, 1946-47; asst. in medicine Harvard U. Med. Sch., 1946-47; founding partner, pres. Sharon (Conn.) Clinic, 1947-76, pres. emeritus, dir., chmn. pension trust, 1976—; pres. Sharon Research Inst., 1958-73; attending physician Sharon Hosp., 1947—, chmn. dept. medicine, 1960-74, chief of staff, 1963-64, dir. med. edn., 1977—; cons. in internal medicine Mass. Inst. Tech., Cambridge, U.S. Naval Hosp., Chelsea, Mass., 1946-47; instr. Harvard U. Med. Sch., 1946-47, Columbia U., 1947-49. Served with M.C., USNR, 1943-46. Decorated Purple Heart, Bronze Star; diplomate Am. Bd. Internal Medicine. Fellow A.C.P.; mem. AMA, Pan Am. Med. Assn., Conn. (councillor, alt. councillor 1956-60), Litchfield County (exec. com. 1954-60) med. socs. Home: Wells Hill Rd Lakeville CT 06039 Office: Sharon Clinic Sharon CT 06069

GEWANT, WARREN CHARLES, surgeon; b. N.Y.C., Mar. 19, 1942; s. Sidney and Edythe (Wolf) G.; B.A. with honors, Franklin and Marshall Coll., 1963; M.D., State U.N.Y., 1967; m. Toby Frances Wildstein, June 12, 1967; children—Scott Douglas, Beth Denise. Intern in surgery Hosp. of U. Pa., Phila., 1967-68; asst. resident in surgery Yale-New Haven Hosp., 1968-71, chief resident in surgery,

1971-72; practice medicine, specializing in gen. and vascular surgery, Saratoga Springs, N.Y., 1974—; attending surgeon Saratoga Hosp., Saratoga Springs, 1974—; cons. staff Benedict Meml. Hosp., Ballston Spa, N.Y., 1974—; research asso. in surgery Yale U., 1969-70, instr. dept. surgery, 1971-72; clin. asst. prof. dept. surgery Upstate Med. Coll., Syracuse, 1977—. Pres. Saratoga County chpt. Am. Cancer Soc., 1976-78. Served to maj. USAF, 1972-74. Am. Cancer Soc. fellow, 1966; diplomate nat. Bd. Med. Examiners, Am. Bd. Surgery. Fellow Am. Coll. Angiology, ACS, Internat. Coll. Surgeons; mem. AMA, Alden March Surg. Soc., N.Y. State Soc. Surgeons, Sigma Xi. Jewish. Contbr. articles to med. jours. Home: 4 Victoria Ln Saratoga Springs NY 12866 Office: 16 N Van Rensselaer St Saratoga Springs NY 12866

GEWIRTZ, GERRY (MRS. EUGENE FRIEDMAN), editor; b. N.Y.C., Dec. 22, 1920; d. Max and Minnie (Weiss) Gewitz; B.A., Vassar Coll., 1941; m. Eugene W. Friedman, Nov. 11, 1945; children—John Henry, Robert James. Editor, Package Store Mgmt., 1942-44, Jewelry Mag., 1945-53; freelance editor promotion dept. McCall's Mag., 1953-56; free-lance fashion and gifts editor Jewelers Circular Keystone, N.Y.C., 1955-72; editor, pub. The Fashionables, 1972-75, The Jeweler's Forcast, 1974—; editor Ann. Fashion Guide, Nat. Jeweler, 1976—. Trustee, Central Synagogue; bd. govs. N.Y. div. Israel Bonds; mem. exec. com. Citizens Com. N.Y.; mem. Inner City Scholarship Fund of Cath. Archdiocese N.Y. Mem. Home Fashions League, N.Y. Fashion Group. Clubs: Vassar, Overseas Press (N.Y.C.). Home: 55 E 86th St New York City NY 10028 Office: The Jewelers Forcast 420 Madison Ave New York City NY 10017

GHANOTAKIS, ANESTIS JOHN, state ofcl.; b. Addis Ababa, Ethiopia, Apr. 17, 1935; s. John Anestis and Marika Emmanuel (Papaioannou) G.; B.A. in Commerce, Manchester U., 1957; M.A. in History, Boston U., 1969; postgrad. (UN fellow), Harvard U., 1962-64, Boston U., 1970—; m. Natalie Marcia Ghanotakis, June 27, 1964; children—John Anestis Elias, Alexander Anestis Emmanuel. Econ. analyst Ministry of Coordination of Greece, Athens, 1958-66; sales asso. Kendal Internat., Boston, 1967-68; instr. history, econs. and govt. Cambridge (Mass.) Jr. Coll., 1969-74; program analyst/fiscal analyst, office of state health planning Mass. Dept. Pub. Health, Boston, 1974—; exhibited in group shows Radcliffe Coll., Boston City Hall, St. Nicholas Greek Orthodox Ch. Mem. Council of Arts and Scis., Arlington, Mass., 1977-78; mem. council St. Nicholas Greek Orthodox Ch., Lexington, Mass., 1976-77, tchr. Sunday Sch., 1977-78. Recipient Americanism award D.A.R., 1976. Italian Govt. fellow, 1960; EEC fellow, 1966. Mem. Am. Hist. Assn., Am. Pub. Health Assn. Author: (poetry) Poems 1962-73, 1975; Grey Horizons, 1978; also articles on health system fiscal aspects. 6 Carl Rd

GHENTS, JOHN HENRY, oil co. exec.; b. Bklyn., May 7, 1916; s. Frederick Michael and Mary Cecilia (O'Malley) G.; B.B.A., St. John's U., Bklyn., 1942; m. Ruth Heig, Jan. 10, 1943; children—Pamela May (Mrs. Bulkley), Bonnie Ruth (Mrs. Flaherty), Michelle Ann. With Asiatic Petroleum Corp., N.Y.C., 1936-76, asst. treas., 1954-62, controller, 1962—, treas., 1963—, v.p., dir. 1965—, chmn. exec. com., 1971-74; pres., dir. Shell Funding Corp., Greater N.Y. Terminal, Inc., 1969-74; v.p., dir. Res./2d Res. Terminals, Inc., Scallop Holding Inc., Scallop Nuclear Inc.; dir. Shell & Commonwealth Chems., Inc. Bd. dirs. Nat. Hemophilia Found. Mem. Econ. Club N.Y., Am. Petroleum Inst., Newcomen Soc., Am. Mgmt. Assn., Tax Inst. Clubs: Internat. (Washington); New Canaan (Conn.) Field; Metropolitan, Rockefeller Center Luncheon (gov.) (N.Y.C.). Home: 97 Sturbridge Hill Rd New Canaan CT 06840 Office: 1 Rockefeller Plaza New York City NY 10020

GHERGHEL, RADU OLIMPIU, chem. corp. ofcl.; b. Timisoara, Rumania, Jan. 30, 1943; s. Olimpiu Nicolae and Gordana (Kostic) G.; came to U.S., 1967, naturalized, 1973; M. Chem. Engring., Poly. Tech. Inst. Rumania, Timisoara, 1965; m. Judith Ann Triplett, Apr. 18, 1970; children—Radu Dean, Jason Clifford. Chem. engr. Harte & Co. subs. Diamond Shamrock Corp., N.Y.C. and Mountaintop, Pa., 1967-74; supt. tech., plastics and films dept. Fibers div. Allied Chem. Corp., Pottsville, Pa., 1974—. Mem. Air Pollution Control Assn., Soc. Plastics Engrs. Republican. Greek Orthodox. Home: 41 Crestview Dr Forest Hills Pottsville PA 17901 Office: PO Box 697 Pottsville PA 17901

GHOSH, ANIL CHANDRA, chemist, educator; b. Kamaragon, India, Sept. 1, 1936; s. Surendra and Bhuban Bala G.; came to U.S., 1964; B.Sc., Gauhati U., 1956, M.Sc. 1st class, 1958; Ph.D., Poona U., 1963; m. Sumitra Das, Feb. 8, 1968; 1 dau., Swati. Lectr. chemistry J.B. Coll., Jorhat, Assam, India, 1959; Council Sci. and Indsl. Research sr. research fellow Nat. Chem. Lab., Poona, India, 1960-64; research asso. U. Nebr., Lincoln, 1964-66, N.C. State U., Raleigh, 1966-67; research chemist Swiss Fed. Inst. Tech., Zurich, 1968-69; sr. research asso. Roswell Park Meml. Inst., Buffalo, 1969-71; sr. research asso. John C. Sheehan Inst. for Research, Cambridge, Mass., 1971-72, sr. research scientist, 1972—; sr. research scientist SISA Inc., Cambridge, 1972—; vis. scientist, Japan, 1975, India, 1977. Grantee NIH, 1973-75, FDA, 1974-76, NSF, 1977-78. Fellow Royal Inst. Chemistry; mem. Am. Chem. Soc., N.C. Acad. Sci. Author: Total Synthesis of Steroids, 1974. Patentee in field. Contbr. articles to profl. jours. Home: 8 Minute Man Ln Lexington MA 02173 Office: 767 B Concord Ave Cambridge MA 02138

GHOSH, JAYANTA KUMAR, telecommunications com. exec.; b. Jamshedpur, India, Nov. 8, 1948; s. Bijoy Shankar and Purnima (Goon) G.; came to U.S., 1971; B.S. with Honors in Physics, Calcutta (India) U., 1966; M.S. in Physics, U. North Bengal (India), 1968; M.S. in Engring., Rutgers U., 1975, M.B.A., 1977. Tchr. physics Narikeldanga High Sch., Calcutta, 1969-71; adminstr. student services Grad. Sch. Bus. Adminstrn., Rutgers U., Newark, 1977-78, tchr. bus. adminstrn., 1977—; market planner, corp. product planning div. Western Electric Co., N.Y.C., 1978—; research staff mem. Mayor's Com. on Payment In-lieu of Taxes, Newark, 1976; cons. Dept. Higher Edn., N.J., 1976. Student rep. to bd. govs. Rutgers U., 1975-76, bd. trustees, 1974-75, univ. senator, 1974-76, pres. Internat. Student Assn., 1973-74; mem. exec. com. Friends of India Assn., N.J., 1975-76. Recipient achievement award Grad. Sch. Bus. Adminstrn., Rutgers U., 1977. Mem. Am. Mktg. Assn., Assn. M.B.A. Execs., Assn. Indians in Am., Beta Gamma Sigma. Author (with Dr. H. Eastman) Pilgrim Medical Group case series. Address: 292-A Crowells Rd Highland Park NJ 08904

GIACALONE, JOSEPH ANTHONY, univ. adminstr.; b. Bklyn., Sept. 10, 1938; s. Anthony and Mary (Sciuto) G.; B.A., Columbia U., 1960, Ph.D., 1971; M.B.A., St. John's U., 1962; m. Marianne Veronica Zimmermann, Dec. 29, 1962; children—Joseph, Christine, Linda, Thomas. Instr. econs. St. John's U., Jamaica, N.Y., 1962-66, asst. prof., 1966-72. asso. prof., 1972, asst. to dean, 1969-70, asst. dean, 1970-73, asso. dean Coll. Bus. Adminstrn., 1973—; cons. in field. Pres. St. Andrew Avellino Bd. Edn., 1978—. Mem. Am. Econ. Assn., History of Econs. Soc., Nat. Assn. Bus. Economists, Beta Gamma Sigma, Omicron Delta Epsilon, Alpha Chi Rho. Roman Catholic. Contbr. articles and revs. to profl. pubs. Home: 33-54 167th St Flushing NY 11358 Office: St John's U Coll Bus Adminstrn Jamaica NY 11439

GIACOMI, JACK R., mattress mfg. co. exec.; b. Waterbury, Conn., Aug. 16, 1947; s. Alfio James and Santa Concetta (Tortorici) G.; B.S., U. Conn., 1969, M.B.A., 1972; m. Monica Mary Carpini, Aug. 16, 1969; 1 son, Alan Michael. Mgmt. trainee Sealy Mattress Co., Oakville, Conn., 1973-75, personnel mgr., 1976—. Commr. Waterbury Zoning Bd. Appeals, 1978—; del. Conn. Republican Conv., 1978. Served as officer AUS, 1969-71; Vietnam. Decorated Army Commendation medal, Bronze Star. Mem. Naugatuck Valley Personnel Council, VFW. Republican. Roman Catholic. Clubs: Waterbury Republican; Am.-Italian Civic, Elks. Home: 658 Oronoke Rd Waterbury CT 06708 Office: 25 Hillside Ave Oakville CT 06779

GIACONA, ANTHONY S., retail distbn. service co. exec.; b. Newark, Oct. 11, 1943; s. Joseph V. and Mary A. (Colombrita) G.; B.A., St. Bonaventure U., 1966; M.B.A., Seton Hall U., 1968; m. Patricia Flanagan, Nov. 1, 1970; children—Gianna, Joseph. Distbn. analyst Bambergers Dept. Stores, Newark, 1969-71; traffic mgr. Saks Fifth Ave., N.Y.C., 1971-73; dir. corporate distbn. and transp. Vornado Inc., 1973-78, exec. v.p., 1978—; exec. v.p. Retailers & Mrfs. Distbn. Marking Service, 1978—. Home Rural Delivery 2 Petticoat Ln Lebanon NJ 08833 Office: 112 Lehigh Dr Fairfield NJ 07006

GIAEVER, IVAR, physicist; b. Bergen, Norway, Apr. 5, 1929; s. John A. and Gudrun (Skaarud) G.; Siv. Ing., Norwegian Inst. Tech., 1952; Ph.D., Rensselaer Poly Inst., 1964; m. Inger Skramstad, Nov. 8, 1952; children—John, Anne, Guri, Trine. Came to U.S., 1957, naturalized, 1963. Patent examiner Norwegian Patent Office, 1953-54; mech. engr. Canadian Gen. Electric, Peterborough, Ont., 1954-56; applied mathematician Gen. Electric Co., Schenectady, 1956-58, physicist Research and Devel. Center, 1958—. Served with Norwegian Army, 1952-53. Recipient Oliver E. Buckley prize, 1965, Nobel prize in physics, 1973, Zworykin award, 1974; Guggenheim fellow, 1970. Fellow Am. Phys. Soc.; mem. IEEE, Norwegian Profl. Engrs., Nat. Acad. Scis., Am. Acad. Art and Scis., Nat. Acad. Engring., Norwegian Nat. Acad. Sci., Norwegian Nat. Acad. Tech. Pioneer tunneling into superconductors, 1962. Home: 2080 Van Antwerp Rd Schenectady NY 12309 Office: Research and Devel Center Gen Electric Co PO Box 8 Schenectady NY 12301

GIAIMO, ROBERT NICHOLAS, congressman, lawyer; b. New Haven, Oct. 15, 1919; s. Rosario and Rose (Scarpulla) G.; A.B., Fordham Coll., 1941; LL.B., U. Conn., 1943; m. Marion F. Schuenemann, May 17, 1945; 1 dau., Barbara Lee. Admitted to Conn. bar, 1947, practiced in New Haven, 1947—; mem. 86th-96th Congresses from 3d Dist. Conn., chmn. budget com., sr. mem. com. on appropriations, also subcoms. on def., D.C. and legis. br.; mem. com. budget; mem. Select Com. on Congressional Ops.; New Eng. regional Dem. whip; former chmn. Personnel Appeals Bd. Conn. Served as 1st lt. AUS, World War II; capt. JAGC, U.S. Army Res. Democrat. Home: 139 Washington Ave North Haven CT 06473 Office: 2207 Rayburn House Office Bldg Washington DC 20515

GIAMATTI, ANGELO BARTLETT, univ. pres.; b. Boston, Apr. 4, 1938; B.A., Yale U., 1960, Ph.D. in Comparative Lit., 1964; LL.D. (hon.), Princeton U., 1978, Harvard U., 1978; married; 3 children. Instr. Italian and comparative lit. Princeton U., 1964-66, asst. prof., 1965-66; instr. English, Yale U., New Haven, 1966-68, asso. prof., 1968-71, prof. English and comparative lit., 1971-78, master Ezra Stiles Coll., 1970-72, pres. univ., 1978—; vis. prof. comparative lit. N.Y. U., summer 1966; mem. faculty Bread Loaf Sch. English, summers, 1972—. Guggenheim fellow, 1969-70. Mem. MLA, Renaissance Soc. Am., Dante Soc. Am. (v.p. 1973-74), Am. Comparative Lit. Assn. (treas. 1967-71), Mediaeval Soc. Am. Author: The Earthly Paradise and the Renaissance Epic, 1966; editor: The Songs of Bernard de Ventadorn, 1962; (with others) Ariosto's Orlando Furioso, 1968; A Variorum Commentary on the Poems of John Milton, vol. 1, 1970; Western Literature, 3 vols., 1971; Play of Double Senses: Spencer's Faerie Queene. Office: Office of Pres Yale U New Haven CT 06520*

GIARDINA, DAVID DIEGO, radiologist; b. New Haven, July 5, 1919; s. Vincenzo and Maryann (Alu) G.; B.A., Columbia Coll., 1946; M.D., N.Y. Med. Coll., 1950; m. Charlotte Mantiglia, June 17, 1950; children—David V., Kenneth C., Thomas P., Barbara L. Intern, Bridgeport (Conn.) Hosp., 1950-51; resident in radiology VA Hosp.-Med. Coll. Va., Richmond, 1951-53; fellow in radiotherapy Mt. Sinai Hosp., N.Y.C., 1953-54; asso. attending radiologist St. Joseph Hosp., Stanford, Conn., 1956-66; attending radiologist Norwalk (Conn.) Hosp., 1955—, asst. chmn. dept. radiology, 1978—; instr. radiology Yale-New Haven Hosp., 1954-55. Served with U.S. Army, 1941-45. Diplomate Am. Bd. Radiology, Nat. Bd. Med. Examiners. Fellow Am. Coll. Radiology; mem. AMA, Conn. State Med. Soc. (pres. sect. radiology 1975), Radiol. Soc. Conn. (pres. 1975), Norwalk Med. Soc. (pres. 1968), Alpha Kappa Kappa. Club: Shorehaven Golf. Home: 10 Little Fox Ln Westport CT 06880 Office: Norwalk Hosp Dept Radiology Norwalk CT 06856

GIARDINO, ALFRED A., lawyer; b. Bklyn., May 1, 1913; s. Joseph and Lucy (Tasca) G.; A.B., Bklyn. Coll., 1934; LL.B., Columbia, 1937; postgrad. Inst. Internat. Affairs, Geneva, Switzerland, 1946; m. Lucie Veulliez; two children. Admitted to N.Y. bar, 1937; trial atty., then exec. sec. N.Y. State Labor Relations Bd., 1937-48; mem. firm Lorenz, Finn, Giardino & Lambos, N.Y.C., 1948—. Arbitrator panels Fed. Mediation and Conciliation Service, N.Y. State Mediation Bd., Am. Arbitration Assn.; former tchr. Bklyn. Coll., Columbia, N.Y. U. Law Sch., Cornell U. Extension. Dir. research N.Y. Gov.'s Spl. Commn. on Illegitimacy, 1936-37; pub. mem. Internat. Commn. Labor Experts to Bolivia, 1943; spl. rep. State and Labor Depts. in Brazil, Chile, Argentina, Uruguay, 1942-43; mem. com. character and fitness Jud. Dept., 1st Dept. N.Y., 1960—. Mem. v.p., pres. N.Y.C. Bd. Edn., 1964-68; chmn. N.Y.C. Bd. Higher Edn., 1974-76. Served as officer AUS, World War II. Mem. Am. Bar Assn., Assn. Bar City N.Y., Internat. Soc. Labor and Social Security. Home: 4600 Fieldston Rd New York City NY 10471 Office: 25 Broadway New York City NY 10004

GIBB, ROBERTA LOUISE, lawyer, artist, writer; b. Cambridge, Mass., Nov. 2, 1942; d. Thomas Robinson Pieri and Jean Knox (Davis) G.; student Boston Mus. Fine Arts, 1961-66; B.A. in Philosophy, Math. and Biology, U. Calif., San Diego, 1969; J.D., New Eng. Sch. Law, 1977. Painter, sculptor, 1960—; painter mural U. Calif., San Diego, 1967-69, series of murals M.I.T., 1971-75; long distance runner, 1962—; participant Boston Marathon, 1966-68; writer, 1966—; contbr. article to Runners World, 1978; tchr. math., biology, art, 1968-70; environ. cons. Calif. chpt. Sierra Club, 1971; researcher, writer Mass. Legislature, 1973-74; environ. specialist law firm, Boston, 1975; research asso. in theories of knowledge M.I.T., 1977—; pres., dir. Inst. Natural Systems; v.p., treas., dir. Essex County Ecology Center Film Co.; dir. Nest Egg Homes Assos.; grant-writing cons. to environ. groups. Mem. Mass. Bar Assn., Boston Bar Assn., Essex Bar Assn., Essex County Green Belt Assn.

GIBBONS, ANNE EVANS, real estate holding co. exec.; b. Bklyn., May 17, 1944; d. David O. and Oriola Helen Evans; B.S., Cornell U., 1965, M.B.A., 1966; m., July 9, 1966; children—David, Mimi, Anne Marie. Asst. sec. corp., office mgr. engring. office David O. Evans Inc., Hillside, N.J., 1966-68; asst. mgr. Cranford (N.J.) Motor Lodge, 1969-71; v.p. Elberon Devel. Co., real estate holding co., 1971-77, pres., 1978—; sec. corp. Rocky Mountain Security Systems Inc., Denver, 1977—, also dir.; dir. Garden State Bank, N.A. of N.J. Mem. N.J. Bus. and Industry Assn., Delta Delta Delta (area fin. asst. 1975-77, pres. No. N.J. 1976-77). Republican. Home: 517 High St Stirling NJ 07980 Office: 1439 N Broad St Hillside NJ 07205

GIBBONS, EDWARD F., retail co. exec.; b. Boston, 1919; grad. Bentley Coll., 1948; married. With McCord Corp., 1965-66; v.p. fin. United Brands Co., 1966-73; v.p. fin. F.W. Woolworth Co., N.Y.C., 1973-74, exec. v.p., 1974-75, pres., 1975—, also dir. Home: 67 Woodland Dr Princeton NJ 08540 Office: 233 Broadway New York City NY 10007*

GIBBONS, EUGENE FRANCIS, advt. agy. exec.; b. Youngstown, Ohio, Oct. 10, 1926; s. Edward Joseph and Helen Amelia (Ford) G.; A.B., Cleve. Coll., Case Western Reserve U., 1952; m. Aileen Marie McMahon, Sept. 13, 1947; children—Kathleen Ann, Kevin Edward. With Goodyear Tire & Rubber Co., Akron, Ohio, 1954-56, Ketchum, MacLeod & Grove, Inc., Pitts., 1956-61, Gray & Rogers, Inc., Phila., 1962-69, Schaefer Advt. Inc., Phila., 1969-73; with Wilson, Haight & Welch, Inc., Phila., 1973—, v.p., mgr., 1975—; pres. Gene Gibbons Advt./Pub. Relations, 1978—; lectr. in field. Served with U.S. Army, 1944-46. Mem. Bus./Profl. Advt. Assn. Republican. Roman Catholic. Contbr. articles in field to profl. jours. Home: 56 Crestline Rd Strafford PA 19087 Office: 223 Lancaster Ave Devon PA 19333

GIBBONS, JAMES JOHN, ins. co. exec.; b. Phila., Dec. 23, 1931; s. John Patrick and Catherine Theresa (McCarron) G.; student U. Pitts., 1961-62; m. Catherine Mary Mullaney, May 20, 1953; children—James Andrew, Teresa Ann, Karen Elizabeth, Paul Joseph. Staff adjuster Indsl. Ins. Co., Phila., 1957-58; sr. adjuster United Security Ins. Co., Pitts., 1959-62, Syracuse, N.Y., 1962-65, agy. supv., Providence, 1965-68, underwriting mgr., Washington, 1968-69, regional mgr., 1970-71, resident v.p., 1970-71; sr. v.p. Ins. Co. Africa, and Intrusco Corp., Monrovia, Liberia, 1971-73; pres. Ins. Co. of Africa, Monrovia, 1975—. Served with USAF, 1952-53. Mem. Soc. Chartered Property and Casualty Underwriters (sec. Washington chpt.). Roman Catholic. Contbr. articles to profl. jours. Office: Internat Bank of Washington 1701 Pennsylvania Ave NW Washington DC 20006

GIBBONS, ROBERT CHARLES, metall. cons.; b. Cottage Grove, Wis., July 26, 1903; s. Robert Oliver and Agnes (Pratt) G.; student Knox Coll., 1920-22; A.B., U. Wis., 1926; M.S., Purdue U., 1928; m. Mildred Strain, Aug. 30, 1926; children—Gerald Robert, Charles Bernard. Chem. engr. Fansteel Metall. Corp., North Chicago, Ill., 1928-31; metallurgist Internat. Harvester Co., Milw., 1934-40; asst. chief metall. engr. Bendix Corp., Teterboro, N.J., 1941-51, chief metallurgist, Utica, N.Y., 1951-69; metall. cons. Steel Treaters Inc., Oriskany, N.Y., 1970—. Mem. Am. Soc. Testing and Materials, Am. Soc. Metals, Lambda Chi Alpha. Mason. Author: (with N.E. Woldman) Machinability and Machining of Metals, 1951. Editor 5th edit. Engring. Alloys, 1973. Contbr. articles to profl. jours. Home: 1910 Holland Ave Utica NY 13501 Office: Steel Treaters Inc Oriskany NY 13424

GIBBONS, ROBERT JOSEPH, educator; b. Pitts., Jan. 1, 1945; s. Joseph J. and Hazel (Bisson) G.; A.B., Kenyon Coll., 1967; M.Phil., Yale U., 1969, Ph.D., 1972; m. Kathryn A. Sheldon, Sept. 2, 1967; children—Michael L., Jean G. Mem. faculty St. Joseph's Coll., Phila., 1970-77, asst. prof. history, 1973-77; dir. adminstrv. research and devel. Am. Inst. Property and Liability Underwriters, Malvern, Pa., 1977—. Mem. vestry Trinty Ch., Gulph Mills, Pa., 1974-77. Nat. Merit scholar, 1963-67; NDEA fellow, 1967-70; Yale Internat. Relations Council fellow, 1970. Mem. Am. Econ. Assn., Am. Hist. Assn., Econ. History Assn. Episcopalian. Club: Yale (Phila.). Home: 673 General Scott Rd King of Prussia PA 19406 Office: Providence and Sugartown Rds Malvern PA 19355

GIBBS, JAMES WENRICH, ret. glass co. exec.; b. Canton, Ohio, Dec. 12, 1915; s. Alvin J. and Eva A. (Wenrich) G.; B.A., Yale U., 1938; postgrad. U. Mich. Law Sch., 1938-39, Wharton Sch. U. Pa., 1939-40; m. Mary Jewel Hellwig, Apr. 12, 1941; children—Sandra Ann Gibbs Chambers, Stephen V., David S. Asst. to pres. Safetee Glass Co., Inc., Phila., 1940-41, v.p., 1942-67, pres. 1967-71, vice chmn. bd., 1971, also dir. Mem. advisory com. Med. Coll. Pa.; trustee Am. Clock and Watch Mus., Bristol, Conn. Fellow Royal Soc. Arts, Nat. Assn. Watch and Clock Collectors (museum trustee); mem. Colonial Soc. Pa., Mass., Pa. socs. Mayflower descs., St. Nicholas Soc., Pa. Soc. Colonial Wars, Cleve. Grays, Colonial Order of Acorn, Dutch Colonial Soc. Del., Ky. Cols., Order of Lafayette, Temple of Jerusalem, SR, SAR, Vet. Corps Arty., Royal Soc. St. George, Germantown Hist. Soc., Newcomen Soc., Nat. Soc. Old Plymouth Colony Descs., Am. Def. Preparedness Assn., Huguenot Soc. Pa., New Eng. Soc., Pa. Hist. Soc., Pilgrim John Howland Soc., Sons St. George, Sons Union Vets. N.J., Valley Forge Hist. Soc., Penn Club, Sons Daus. of Pilgrim Soc., Order Ams. of Armorial Ancestry, Hereditary Order Descs. of Colonial Govs., Order of Descs. Colonial Physicians Chirugiens. Clubs: Phila. Cricket, Skytop Lodge, Union League. Author: The Duebner-Hampden Story, 1954; The Life and Death of the Ithaca Calendar Clock Company, 1960; Ohio Clock and Watch Story, 1970; Shaker Clockmakers; Dixie Clockmakers. Contbr. articles to jours. Address: 3201 W Coulter St Philadelphia PA 19129

GIBBS, JUNE NESBITT (MRS. DONALD T. GIBBS), Republican committeewoman; b. Newton, Mass., June 13, 1922; d. Samuel F. and Lulu (Glazier) Nesbitt; B.A., Wellesley Coll., 1943; M.A., Boston U., 1947; m. Donald T. Gibbs, Dec. 8, 1945; 1 dau., Elizabeth. Vice chmn. R.I. Republican State Central Com., 1960-69; nat. committeewoman for R.I., 1969—, sec., 1977—; mem. Middletown (R.I.) Town Council, 1974—. Mem. Def. Adv. Com. on Women in Services, 1970-72, vice-chmn., 1972. Served with WAVES, 1943-46. Address: 163 Riverview Ave Middletown RI 02840

GIBBS, LIPPMAN MARTIN, lawyer; b. N.Y.C., Feb. 27, 1938; s. Harold and Shirley (Marks) G.; A.B., Brown U., 1959; J.D., Columbia U., 1962; m. Dona Lynn Fagg, May 3, 1968; 1 son, Bradford Gibbs. Admitted to N.Y. bar, 1963; atty. Port of N.Y. Authority, N.Y.C., 1963-64, Winer, Neuburger & Sive, N.Y.C., 1964-66, Spear & Hill, N.Y.C., 1966-69; with Finley, Kumble, Wagner, Heine & Underberg, N.Y.C., 1969-72, partner, 1972—; arbitrator Am. Arbitration Assn., 1967—. Trustee Community Unitarian Ch., White Plains, N.Y.; bd. dirs. Gallery of Homes, Inc. Served with U.S. Army, 1962-63. Mem. Am. Bar Assn., Computer Law Assn., Assn. Bar City of N.Y. Democrat. Clubs: N.Y. Yacht, Orienta Beach, Dolphin Yacht (commodore), Univ. Home: 8 Woodland Dr Rye NY 10580 Office: 425 Park Ave New York City NY 10022

GIBBUD, JOHN H(ENRY), stone bldg. cons.; b. New Haven, Conn., Dec. 5, 1911; s. Harold Dayton and Anna Mott (Wells) G.; A.B., Denison U., 1935; M.A., Oberlin Coll., 1940; m. Mae Agnes Ranney, June 11, 1935; children—John Ranney, David Wells, Timothy Guy, Margaret Ann (Mrs. Gordon R. Delong). Physicist, tire engr. U.S. Rubber Co., Detroit, 1940-41; instr. physics Vassar Coll., Poughkeepsie, N.Y., 1941-43; asst. prof. physics Denison U.

Granville, Ohio, 1943-45; physicist and engr., from researcher to dir. tests and specifications Owens-Corning Fiberglas Corp., Ohio and R.I., 1945-58; cons., chief sci. United Engrs. Inc., Boston, 1958-59; mgr. research and devel. Howe Scale Co., Rutland, Vt., 1959-62; research and devel. engr. Vt. Marble Co., Proctor, 1963-69; independent cons. natural bldg. stone, 1969—. Mem. sch. bd. Granville Sch. Dist., 1952-55; pres. Granville Council of Chs., 1949-50. Recipient Naval Ordnance Devel. award U.S. Navy. Registered profl. engr., Ohio, Mass., Vt. Mem. Nat., Vt. socs. profl. engrs., Vt., Rutland County (past pres.) socs. engrs., ASTM (chmn. com. C-18 on natural bldg. stones, mem. com. D-20 on plastics, E-G com. on performance bldg. constrns.), Soc. Plastics Engrs., Nat. Geog. Soc. Home and office: 49 Gorham Bridge Rd Proctor VT 05765

GIBSON, CURTIS CHARLES, JR., telecommunications co. exec.; b. Balt., May 10, 1948; s. Curtis Charles and Lola Charity (Gilliam) G.; B.A., U. Md., 1972; M.Adminstrn. and Bus., Johns Hopkins U., 1978; m. Carole Lucille Wiles, Aug. 12, 1972; 1 son, Sean Michael. Admissions adminstr. U. Md., College Park, Md., 1972-73; staff asso. C & P Telephone Co., Silver Spring, Md., 1973-77; industry analyst A T & T, Morristown, N.J., 1977—. Served with AUS, 1969. Mem. Jr. C. of C. Mt. Olive (external dir. 1978—), Am. Mgmt. Assn. Democrat. Episcopalian. Home: 13 Brookside Dr Budd Lake NJ 07828 Office: 1776 On the Green 3A47 Morristown NJ 07960

GIBSON, DONNA TILLINGHAST, elementary tchr.; b. Lewisburg, Pa., Oct. 27, 1942; married, 5 children. B.S. in Elementary Edn., Keuka Coll. Keuka Park, N.Y., 1966; M.S. in Edn., Elmira (N.Y.) Coll., 1975; Tchr., Dundee (N.Y.) Central Sch., 1966—. Coach girls softball Yates County Recreation 1975—. Home: RD 3 Dundee NY 14837 Office: Dundee Central Sch Dundee NY 14837

GIBSON, ELEANOR BEATRICE, artist, library cons.; b. London, Mar. 8, 1905; d. Harry Hepburn and Anne Elizabeth (White) G.; came to U.S., 1905, derivative citizenship, 1914; A.B., Cornell U., Ithaca, N.Y., 1928; postgrad. St. Joseph Coll., West Hartford, Conn., 1937-38; M.S. in Library Sci., Syracuse U., 1957. With Aetna Life & Casualty Co., Hartford, Conn., 1928-42, librarian research div., 1933-42; librarian in charge Logan Lewis Library, Carrier Corp. Research Center, Syracuse, N.Y., 1947-67, spl. adviser, 1967-70; tech. supr. computerized union catalog project Conn. State Library, Hartford, 1968-71; library cons., 1971—; propr. White Studio, White Art Library, White-Kelly Civilization Collection. Served to 1st lt. (WAAC), WAC, AUS, 1942-46; as capt., 1950-52. Recipient Metals/Materials Honors award, 1968. Mem. Spl. Libraries Assn. (Hall of Fame 1968, pres. Western N.Y. 1959-60, placement chmn. 1961-62, nat. chmn. metals div. 1961-62, John Cotton Dana lectr. U. Toronto 1962), New Britain Mus. Am. Art, Wadsworth Atheneum, Syracuse U. Sch. Library Sci. Alumni Assn. (pres. 1967-68), Conn. Acad. Fine Arts (sustaining), West Hartford Art League, Pi Lambda Sigma (pres. 1958-59), Beta Phi Mu (local pres. 1959-60). Republican. Episcopalian. Contbr. articles to profl. jours.; editor: Guide to Metallurgical Information, 2d edit., 1965. Address: White Studio Leighton Hill Rd Wells River VT 05081

GIBSON, GEORGE WILLIAM, educator; b. Mpls., June 14, 1917; married, 2 children. B.A. in Econs., U. Minn., Mpls., 1948. B.S. in Library Adminstrn., 1949. Dir. audio visual edn. div., mem. faculty Grad. Sch. Bus. Adminstrn. and Ednl. Tech. Harvard, Cambridge, Mass., 1953-72; mgr. instructional resource center Minuteman Tech. Sch., Lexington. Mass., 1973—; cons. in bus. communication; also profl. writer. Justice of the Peace, Mass., 1973—. notary pub. Middlesex County, 1973—. Served with USN, 1940-45, SAC, USAF, 1951-53. Mem. AAUP. Certified as media coordinator, librarian, tchr. Writer, producer numerous ednl. motion pictures; exec. producer of numerous ednl. TV programs. Home: 34 Wagon Wheel Rd Sudbury MA 01776 Office: 758 Marrett Rd Lexington MA 02173

GIBSON, JOHN, III, metal fabricating co. exec.; b. Boswell, Pa., Sept. 3, 1915; s. John, Jr. and Primrose (Dixon) G.; B.S., Yale, 1938; m. Edith Canfield Smith, Jan. 6, 1940; children—John IV, David B. With Pitts. Plate Glass Co., Boston, 1938-41; with McKinney Mfg. Co., Pitts. and Scranton, Pa., 1945—, v.p. prodn., 1950-54, pres., 1954—, chief exec. officer, 1960—, chmn., 1977—; dir. Penn Smokeless Coal Co., Pitts., William G. Johnston Co., Pitts. Bd. dirs., pres. Boys Club Scranton. Served to lt. comdr. USNR, 1941-45. Mem. Am. Hardware Mfrs. Assn. (past pres.), Builders Hardware Mfrs. Assn. (past pres.), Delta Psi. Clubs: Duquesne (Pitts.); Allegheny Country (Sewickley, Pa.); Rolling Rock (Ligonier, Pa.); Country Scranton (Scranton); N.Y. Yacht. Home: RD 2 Church Hill Rd Dalton PA 18414 Office: 820 Davis St Scranton PA 18505

GIBSON, KENNETH ALLEN, mayor Newark; b. Enterprise, Ala., May 15, 1932; s. Willie Foy and Daisy (Lee) G.; B.S. in Civil Engring., Newark Coll. Engring., 1960; m. Muriel Cooke, June, 1960; children—Joyce, Cheyrl, Joann. Engr., N.J. Hwy. Dept., Newark, 1950-60; chief engr. Newark Housing Authority, 1960-66; prin. structural engr. City of Newark, 1966-70; mayor Newark, 1970—; cons. engr., 1960—. Served with C.E., AUS, 1950-58. Mem. Am. Soc. C. E., Frontiers Internat. Office: City Hall Broad St Newark NJ 07102

GIBSON, LEONARD JAMES, engring. co. exec.; b. Acadia Valley, Alta., Can., July 5, 1923; s. John Evan and Elizabeth Dorothy (Morrison) G.; B. Applied Sci., U. B.C., 1951; student advanced mgmt. devel. program Northeastern U., 1970; m. Elizabeth Ethelda McDougall, July 1, 1944; children—James, Patrick, Terrence, Delores Gibson Mothersill, Karl, Laurie, Kelly, Phil. Trainee engr. Atlas Steels, Ltd., Welland, Ont., Can., 1951-55, casting shift foreman; plant supt. Premier Steel Mills, Edmonton, Alta., 1955-58, works mgr., 1958-63; cons. engr. G.R. Heffernan Assos., Whitby, Ont., 1963-64; works mgr., v.p. ops. and devel. Lake Ont. Steel Co., Whitby, 1964-70; v.p. Ferrco Engring. Ltd., Whitby, 1970—; dir. Ferrco Engring. Ltd.; mem. local Liberal Assn.; mem. Natural Resource People of Can. Inc. Served with Canadian Army, 1942-46. Mem. Assn. Profl. Engrs. of Ont., Assn. of Profl. Engrs. Geologists and Geophysiciats of Alta., Assn. Cons. Engrs. of Can., Assn. Iron and Steel Engrs., Am. Inst. of Mining and Metall. Engrs., Am. Soc. for Metals, Canadian Inst. Mining and Metallurgy. Clubs: Oshawa Golf and Country. Home: 314 Lyndeview Dr Whitby ON L1N 3A3 Canada Office: 1400 Hopkins St S Whitby ON L1N 2C3 Canada

GIBSON, ROBERT ELMO, assn. exec.; b. Lake Worth, Fla., Oct. 31, 1927; s. Edwin C. and Bertha (Alderman) G.; A.B., U. Fla., 1952, M.Ed., 1953; m. Laurine Catalano, Aug. 26, 1961; children—Robert Elmo, Anita Laurine, Stephen Vincent. Personnel dir. food service div. U. Fla., 1951-52, instr. P.K. Yonge Lab. Sch., 1953-55, chmn. secondary edn. dept., 1957-58; counselor U.S. Army Dependent Schs., France, Germany, 1955-57; ednl. cons. Nat. Com. For Edn. in Family Finance, N.Y.C., 1958-60, exec. sec., 1961-69; exec. dir. Council for Family Financial Edn., Inc., Silver Spring, Md., 1969-70; pres. Nat. Found. for Consumer Credit, Washington, 1971—; dir. Consumer Edn. Consultants, Inc. Bd. dirs. Am. Youth Hostels. Served with USNR, 1943-46. Named to U. Fla. Student Hall of Fame, 1953. Mem. Am. Assn. Sch. Adminstrs., Commn. Econ. Edn., Assn. for Supervision and Curriculum Devel., Blue Key, Phi Delta Kappa, Phi Delta Theta. Home: 6644 Park Hall Dr Laurel MD 20810 Office: 1819 H St NW Washington DC 20006

GIBSON, ROY DEAN, mfg. co. exec.; b. Childress, Tex., May 9, 1937; s. Roy Melvin and Naomi Ann (Scott) G.; B.S., U. Tex., 1959; M.S., Tex. A. and M. U., 1964; M.B.A., Drexel U., 1974; m. Gail Coles, July 18, 1964. Sr. physicist, supr. electro-optics dept. Melpar, Inc., Falls Church, Va., 1964-70; div. mgr. Judson Research and Mfg. Co., Conshohocken, Pa., 1970-75; pres. Judson Infrared, Inc., Fort Washington, Pa., 1976—. Adviser to infrared working group USIA, 1969-70. Served to 1st lt. U.S. Army, 1962-64. Mem. Am. Phys. Soc. Contbr. articles to profl. jours. Home: 547 Winston Way Berwyn PA 19312 Office: 565 Virginia Dr Fort Washington PA 19034

GIBSON, SAM THOMPSON, physician; b. Covington, Ga., Jan. 1, 1916; s. Count Dillon and Julia (Thompson) G.; B.S. in Chemistry, Ga. Inst. Tech., 1936; M.D., Emory U., 1940; m. Alice Chase, Oct. 31, 1942 (dec. Jan. 1971); children—Lena Gibson Shelhamer, Stephen C., Judith T. Gibson Hammer, Lucy F. Med. house officer Peter Bent Brigham Hosp., Boston, 1940-41, asst. resident medicine, 1946-47, asst. medicine, 1947-49; research fellow medicine Harvard, 1941-42, spl. research asso., 1943, Milton fellow medicine, 1947-49; asso. medicine George Washington U. Med. Sch., George Washington U. Hosp., 1949-63, asst. clin. prof. medicine, 1963—; asst. med. dir. A.R.C. Blood Program, 1949-51, asso. med. dir., 1951-53, asso. dir., 1953-56, dir., 1956-66, sr. med. officer A.R.C., 1957-67; asst. dir. div. biologics standards NIH, Bethesda, Md., 1967-72; asst. dir. FDA bur. biologics, Bethesda, Md., 1972-74, asst. to dir., 1974—, dir. div. biologics evaluation, 1977—. Cons. blood Naval Med. Sch., Nat. Naval Med. Center, Bethesda, 1950-63; mem. med. adv. bd. CARE-Medico, 1962-70, cons., 1970—; chmn. U.S. com. for transfusion equipment for med. use Am. Standards Assn., 1954-66; adviser orgn. blood transfusion services League Red Cross Socs., 1955-66; chmn. tech. adv. group blood transfusion equipment Am. Nat. Standards Inst., 1975—. Served from lt. (j.g.) to comdr. M.C., USNR, 1941-46. capt. Res. Diplomate Am. Bd. Internal Medicine. Mem. A.M.A., A.A.A.S., Internat., Am. socs. hematology, Nat. Health Council (dir. 1957-60, 61-64), Internat. Soc. Blood Transfusion (regional counselor 1962-66), Am. Pub. Health Assn., Am. Fedn. for Clin. Research, N.Y. Acad. Scis., Delta Tau Delta, Alpha Kappa Kappa, Alpha Chi Sigma, Tau Beta Pi, Phi Kappa Phi, Omicron Delta Kappa, Alpha Omega Alpha. Contbg. editor Vox Sanguinis Jour. Blood Transfusion, 1956-65, mem. adv. bd., 1965-76. Home: 5801 Rossmore Dr Bethesda MD 20014 Office: Bur Biologics FDA Bethesda MD 20014

GIBSON, WILLIAM LEE, mfg. co. exec.; b. Newark, Dec. 1, 1949; stepson William Barry Leavens, Jr. and S. Margaret Reynolds Gibson Leavens; B.A., Bucknell U., 1972, B.S. in Chem. Engring., 1972; postgrad. Harvard Bus. Sch., 1977. With Bur. Solid Waste Mgmt., EPA, Cin., 1970-71; chemist Dow Chem. Co., Midland, Mich., 1972-75; mktg. cons. Westvaco, Charleston, S.C., 1976; sales rep. Diamond Shamrock Co., Cleve., 1977—. Mem. Soc. Automotive Engrs., Soc. Plastic Engrs., Harvard Bus. Sch. Club N.Y. Club: Toastmasters. Home: 148 Gillies Ln Norwalk CT 06854 Office: 1415 E Marlton Pike Cherry Hill NJ 08034

GIBSON, WILLIAM MOSES, govt. ofcl.; b. Hackensack, N.J., Sept. 11, 1934; s. James C. and Evelyn M. (Scott) G.; A.B., Rutgers, 1956; J.D., Boston U., 1959, M.S.W., Boston Coll., 1966; grad. Advanced Mgmt. Program, Harvard, 1976; m. Phyllis G. Randolph, Nov. 25, 1961; children—Monica, Wayne, Wesley. Admitted to Mass. bar, 1960; law asso. Edward Brooke, Boston, 1960-61; asst. U.S. atty., Mass., 1961-64; social welfare referral coordinator ABCD, Inc., Boston, 1964-66; law asso. Cardoza & Tucker, Boston, 1964-70; dir. law and poverty project Boston U. Law Sch., 1966-70, asso. prof. Grad. Sch. African Studies, 1969-71; regional counsel, area contracts officer Office Econ. Opportunity, Boston, 1970-72; regional dir. FTC, Boston, 1972—. Prof. law Am. Soc. Summer Insts., Chgo., 1968—; dir. law in social studies project Lincoln Filene Center, Tufts U., 1969-70; chmn. Boston Fed. Exec. Bd., 1975—. Vice pres. Roxbury (Mass.) YMCA Bd., 1965-73, Greater Boston YMCA Bd., 1965—; chmn. Boston Task Force on Student Rights, 1970-72; mem. State Council on Juvenile Behavior, 1970-72; Am. Bar Assn. rep. to Nat. Conf. Lawyers and Social Workers, 1972—. Bd. dirs. Mass. Council Crime and Corrections, 1964-74, Nat. Center Afro-Am. Artists, Law in Am. Soc. Found., 1975—; trustee Cath. Charities Archdiocese Boston. Served with M.C., USAF, 1959-64. Recipient Boston U. Young Lawyer's Chair, 1969, Outstanding Community Service award Roxbury YMCA, 1970; Boston Jr. C. of C. Ten Outstanding Young Men Community Service award, 1968; Bryant Stratton Sch. Law and Community Edn. award, 1968; Office Econ. Opportunity Outstanding Community Service award, 1967; Govt. Service award Boston chpt. NAACP, 1975. Mem. Am. (vice chmn. drug abuse com. 1973—), Mass. (chmn. pub. information com. 1967—), Boston bar assns., Nat. Assn. Social Workers, Nat. Acad. Accredited Social Workers, Nat. Council Social Studies, Assn. Am. Law Sch. Civic Edn. Com. Club: Sharon (Mass.) Fish and Game. Author: Social Welfare Resource Guide, 1965; Due Process of Law, 1969; Lessons in Conflict, 1970; In Search of Justice, 1972; (with Robert H. Ratcliffe, others) Great Cases of The Supreme Court, 1968. Contbr. articles to profl. jours. Office: FTC 150 Causeway St Boston MA 02114

GIDEON, RICHARD WALTER, broadcasting mgmt. cons.; b. Phila., Nov. 23, 1928; s. Walter Richard and Amelia Molly (Ebinger) G.; B.S. in Econs., U. Pa., 1952; m. Yolanda Elena Josefe, Jan. 12, 1957; children—Richard E. and Michael J. (twins). Statis. clk. Triangle Pubs. Inc., Phila., 1952-55, research mgr., 1955-62; asst. dir. media research Young & Rubicam, N.Y.C., 1962-63; with John Blair & Co., N.Y.C., 1963-75, dir. research, 1967-75, v.p., 1969-75, dir. sales strategy, 1973-75; pres. Dick Gideon Enterprises, Cherry Hills, N.J., 1975—. Dist. leader Westchester County Republican Com., 1974-76; mem. adv. com. to N.Y. Assemblyman Gordon Burrows, 1974-76. Served with USMC, 1946-48. Mem. Broadcast Pioneers Assn., Sigma Phi Epsilon. Club: Wharton (Phila.). Editor: Statistical Trends In Broadcasting, 1970—. Home and Office: 113 Antietam Rd Cherry Hill NJ 08034

GIELCHINSKY, ISAAC, cardiac and thoracic surgeon; b. Bogota, Colombia, Oct. 6, 1934; s. Leon and Szeina (Szpitalny) G.; came to U.S., 1958, naturalized, 1969; M.D. summa cum laude, U. Colombia, 1958; m. Janet Fields, Nov. 28, 1965; children—Robert, Karen, David. Intern, Albert Einstein Med. Center, Phila., 1959-61; resident in surgery U. Pa. Grad. Sch., 1959-60, Grasslands Hosp., Westchester County, N.Y., 1960-64; resident in cardiac and thoracic surgery N.Y. Med. Coll., 1964-66; practice medicine specializing in cardiac and thoracic surgery, Newark, 1971—; mem. staff Beth Israel Med. Center; asst. prof. surgery N.J. Sch. Medicine, 1971-78, asso. prof., 1978—. Served with U.S. Army, 1969-71. Decorated Bronze Star. Diplomate Am. Bd. Surgery, Am. Bd. Thoracic Surgery. Fellow Acad. Medicine (N.J. chpt.), A.C.S., Am. Coll. Cardiology, Am. Coll. Chest Physicians; mem. AMA, Assn. Mil. Surgeons, N.J., N.Y., Westchester County med. socs., Soc. Thoracic Surgeons, Westchester Acad. Medicine, N.J. Soc. Thoracic Surgeons. Home: 165 Wyoming Ave Maplewood NJ 07040 Office: 201 Lyons Ave Newark NJ 07112

GIERSBACH, MARION AGNES FISK (MRS. WALTER C. GIERSBACH), educator; b. Oak Park, Ill., July 29, 1900; d. Charles Leon and Marion (Ballou) Fisk; grad. Oberlin Kindergarten Sch. and Coll., 1922; student Bush Conservatory Music and Drama, Chgo., 1925-26, Cleve. Inst. Art, 1929-30; A.B., Pacific U., 1946; m. Walter C. Giersbach, June 28, 1927; children—Charles W., Walter F., William H. Summer play dir. Chautauquas, 1918-22; tchr. pub. schs., Youngstown, Ohio, 1922-26; dir. City Christian Edn. Program, Gypsum, Ohio, 1927-28; tchr. pub. sch., Cleve., 1928-30; tchr. summer confs., Ill., Ohio, Mont., Oreg., 1927-53; drama coach, Modjeska Guild, Ohio, 1929-30; researcher-cartographer Chgo. Theol. Sem. 1930-36; dir. kindergarten Pacific U., Oreg., 1943-45, tchr. dept. history, 1948; lectr. E.C. Brown Trust, Portland, Oreg., 1950-52; asst. sec. wills, trusts United Ch. of Christ, N.Y.C., Phila., 1954-63; tchr., counsellor Christian edn. workshops United Ch. of Christ N.J., 1965-72. Founder Tualatin Plains Hist. Soc., Forest Grove, Oreg., 1948-53, Jr. Hist. Soc. Oreg., 1951; pres. Forest Grove Congl. Women's Fellowhsip, 1949-51; nat. vice moderator Congl. Christian Chs., 1949-51. Bd. dirs. Central Atlantic Conf. United Ch. of Christ. Mem. N.J. Ch. Women United (county dir. 1969-72, chmn. communications 1973-76, v.p. 1976—), Oreg. Ch. Women United (state pres. 1951-53), Cherry Hill Ch. Women United (pres. 1967-69). Contbr. articles to profl. jours. Home: 100 Saw Mill Rd Cherry Hill NJ 08034

GIESE, DONALD EMIL, guidance counselor; b. Balt., Jan. 7, 1932; s. Reynold John and Bertha Elizabeth (Wenger) G.; B.S., Towson State U., 1957; M.Ed., Loyola U., 1966; postgrad. Johns Hopkins U., 1969-70, U. Md., 1973-74. Program dir. Salvation Army Boys' Clubs of Balt., 1956-57, asst. dir., 1957-58, dir., 1958-60; unit dir. Camp Puh'tok, Monkton, Md., 1950-54, asst. camp dir., 1957-59, camp dir., 1959-60; tchr. Baltimore County Pub. Schs., 1960-66, guidance counselor, 1966—. Bd. dirs. Camp Puh'tok. Served with U.S. Army, 1954-56. Mem. Am., Md. personnel and guidance assns., Md. State Tchrs. Assn., Balt. County Counselors Assn., Nat. Edn. Assn., Tchrs. Assn. Baltimore County, Friends of Puh'tok. Roman Catholic (usher 1949, v.p. 1973—, mem. Holy Name Soc., 1946—). Clubs: Lake Holiday Country, Medicine Pipe Soc. Home: 1019 S Clinton St Baltimore MD 21224 Office: 9200 Old Harford Rd Baltimore MD 21234

GIESE, ROBERT JOSEPH, corp. exec.; b. N.Y.C., June 16, 1934; s. Emil Joseph and Noreen (Black) G.; student Bklyn. Coll., 1952-57, N.Y. U., 1968-69; 1 dau., Lara. Archtl. draftsman Ebasco Services, Inc., N.Y.C., 1952-53, adminstrv. asst. to supt. design, 1953-56, engring. coordinator on pulp and paper projects, 1956-57, adminstrv. asst. to engring. mgr., 1957-60, mgr. advt. and publicity, 1960-73, mgr. graphics and communications, 1974-77, mgr. corporate communications, 1977-78, dir. mktg. and corporate communications, 1978—. Spl. investigator N.Y. Atty. Gen.'s office, N.Y.C., 1959-61. Served with USNR, 1951-59. Mem. Advt. Club, N.Y. Alumni Assn., Am. Assn. Indsl. Editors, N.Y. Soc. Indsl. Communications, Sales and Marketing Execs. Internat. Roman Catholic. Home: 314 Pinebrook Rd Englishtown NJ 07726 Office: 2 Rector St New York City NY 10006

GIFFORD, HARRY CORTLAND FREY, hosp. adminstr.; b. N.Y.C., Sept. 21, 1919; s. Frank Dean and Hazel (Frey) G.; B.A. in History, Yale U., 1942; M.S. in Hosp. Adminstrn., Columbia U., 1947; m. Catherine Huber, Sept. 14, 1946; children—Linda (Mrs. Jeffrey Parkin), Frank Dean. Adminstrv. resident Greenwich (Conn.) Hosp., 1947; asst. supt. Hackensack (N.J.) Hosp., 1948-49; adminstr. Community Hosp., Glen Cove, N.Y., 1949-61; exec. dir. Springfield (Mass.) Hosp. Med. Center, 1961-67, exec. v.p., dir., 1967-74; pres. Med. Center Western Mass., Springfield, 1974—; vis. lectr. hosp. adminstrn. Columbia U., 1961—, preceptor hosp. adminstrn. residency, 1953-60; preceptor hosp. adminstrn. residency Yale U., 1973. Mem. Springfield Mental Health Bd.; mem. gov.'s com. Health and Ednl. Facilities Authority, 1970-73. Corporator, Springfield Tech. Community Coll. Served to 1st lt. Med. Services, U.S. Army, 1942-45. Decorated Bronze Star with palm. Fellow Am. Coll. Hosp. Adminstrs. (regents council 1970-71); mem. Am. Hosp. Assn. (trustee 1973—, del. at large 1971-73, del. 1967-70, mem. regional adv. bd. 1971-73), Mass. Hosp. Assn. (pres. 1967-68). Rotarian (pres. Glen Cove club 1958-59). Contbr. articles to profl. jours. Home: 181 Captain Rd Longmeadow MA 01106 Office: 759 Chestnut St Springfield MA 01107*

GIFFORD, J. NEBRASKA (MRS. MELVIN SHESTACK), artist; b. Omaha, Nov. 25, 1939; d. Harold and Mary Elizabeth (Jonas) G.; B.A., Bennington Coll., 1961; m. Melvin Shestack, Feb. 13, 1965; 1 dau., Victoria J. One-woman shows: Mercer St. Gallery, N.Y.C., U. Nebr., Louis Meisel Gallery, N.Y.C.; exhibited in group shows: Whitney Mus. Am. Art, Toledo Mus. Art, Joslyn Art Mus., Aldrich Mus.; represented in permanent collections: N.Y. U., Aldrich Mus., Joslyn Mus., Owens-Corning Collection, Prudential Collection, also pvt. collections; art cons. Old Market Project, Omaha, 1969; art columnist Cue mag., 1976. Trustee Gifford Found. MacDowell fellow, 1976. Editor, Nashville Gospel Mag., 1976-77; co-pub. The New York Artist, 1978; contbr. articles to mags. and profl. jours. Home: 4 Great Jones St New York City NY 10012

GIGLIO, FRANK PHILIP, paper, plastics and stationery mfg. co. exec.; b. Bklyn., May 31, 1939; s. Salvatore J. and Mary A. (Borgese) G.; B.B.A., St. John's U., 1961; m. Patricia E. Broadbent, Aug. 1, 1964; children—Karen, Frank S. Pres., Garrett Wire & Cable Corp., v.p. Fairmont Electronics Corp. subsidiary Instrument Systems Corp., 1965-69; group exec. plastics ops. and dir. mergers and acquisitions Standard Industries, Inc., N.Y.C., 1970-72; pres., chief operating officer Effective Industries, Inc., N.Y.C., 1972-74; exec. v.p., dir., mem. exec. com. Williamhouse-Regency, Inc., N.Y.C., 1974—. Served with U.S. Army, 1961. Mem. Am. Mgmt. Assn. Club: K.C. Home: 16 Nassau Dr New Hyde Park NY 11040 Office: 28 W 23d St New York City NY 10010

GIGLIOTTI, MICHAEL FRANCES XAVIER, tech. mgmt. cons.; b. Utica, N.Y., Jan. 31, 1921; s. Francesco Savero and Mary Bernardine (Caligiure) G.; M.E., Stevens Inst. Tech., 1942; m. Miriam Rose Coombs, Apr. 30, 1951; children—Michael, Chalice, Valerie, Edward, Anne. With Monsanto Co., various locations, 1942-77, dir. process tech. and engring. plastics div., Springfield, Mass. and St. Louis, Mo., 1962-68, spl. project dir. packaging div., St. Louis, 1968-72, dir. research and devel. cycle-safe containers div., Bloomfield, Conn., 1972-77; pres. Michael Gigliotti & Assos., Inc., Gloucester, Mass., 1977—; mem. plastics adv. bd. Underwriters Labs., 1956-61. Trustee Plastic Edn. Found., 1969-73; bd. dirs. Plastics Inst. Am., 1968-73, Bldg. Research Inst. of NAS, 1961-65. Recipient Wendell prize Stevens Inst., 1942. Registered profl. engr., Tex., Mass. Mem. Nat. Soc. Profl. Engrs., Engrs. Council for Profl. Devel., Am. Soc. for Engring. Edn., Am. Soc. Chem. Engrs., Soc. Plastics Engrs., Soc. Plastics Engrs., Soc. Plastics Industry (mem. plastics pioneers 1972), Robot Inst. Am., Plastics Inst. Am. Clubs: Chemists (N.Y.C.); Bass Rocks Golf, Rotary (Gloucester). Contbr. articles to profl. jours. Home: 498 Washington St Gloucester MA 01931 Office: Box 25 Riverdale Station Gloucester MA 01930

GIGLIOTTI, STEVEN PETER, med. and sci. illustrator; b. Utica, N.Y., May 5, 1925; s. Steven and Mary (Perritano) G.; Asso. Applied Sci., Rochester Inst. Tech., 1950; grad. U. Rochester Sch. Medicine, 1953; m. Jane Mary Carcaci, July 17, 1948; children—Steven J., Joseph P., Ann Marie, Joan Marie. Med. artist Wright Patterson AFB

Hosp., Fairborn, O., 1953-54: med. sci. illustrator affiliated with Acad. Natural Scis., Phila., 1955, Hahnemann Med. Coll., 1956-63; cons. sci. illustrator, 1964—; asso. med. illustration U. Pa., Phila., 1963—; prodn. mgr. Jour. Assn. Med. Illustrators, 1964, mng. editor, 1965, editor, 1966-71, chmn. bd. govs., 1969-71; med. illustrations and exhibits displayed ann. meetings AMA, 1957—, A.C.S., 1957-61, 63; illustrator med. books Including The Atlas of General Surgery, 1955; Principles and Methods of Physical Diagnosis, 1957; The Technique of Articulation, 1961; The NEY Articulator Manual, 1962; The Bird Respirator, 1961; Fundamental Procedures in Restorative Dentistry, 1968; Basic Anatomy and Physiology, 1966; Fishes of the Bahamas, 1968; Surgical and Nonsurgical Management of Strobismus, 1969; Surgery of the Chest, 1970; Histology, 1973; Surgery of the Hip, 1973; Best and Taylor's Physiological Basis of Medical Practice, 1973, 78; Taber's Med. Dictionary, 14th edit., 1978. Troop committeeman Boy Scouts Am., 1963-73. Served to 2d lt. USAAF, 1943-45. Mem. AAUP, Acad. Fine Arts Phila., Assn. Med. Illustrators, Providence Water Color Soc., Whiskey Painters Am., Pa. Soc., Phila. Watercolor Club. K.C. Home: 3 Grove Ln Broomall PA 19008 Office: Hosp U Pa Philadelphia PA 19104

GIGNOUX, EDWARD THAXTER, U.S. dist. judge; b. Portland, Maine, June 28, 1916; s. Frederick Evelyn and Katherine (Denison) G.; A.B. cum laude Harvard U., 1937, LL.B. magna cum laude, 1940; LL.D. (hon.), Bowdoin Coll., 1962, U. Maine, 1966, Colby Coll., 1974, Nasson Coll., 1974, Bates Coll., 1977; m. Hildegarde Schuyler Thaxter, June 30, 1938; children—Marie Andrée (Mrs. James F. Grise), Edward Thaxter. Admitted to D.C. bar, 1941, Maine bar, 1946; asso. Slee, O'Brian, Hellings & Ulsh, Buffalo, 1940-41, Covington, Burling, Rublee, Acheson & Shorb, Washington, 1941-42; partner Verrill, Dana, Walker, Philbrick & Whitehouse, Portland, 1946-57; U.S. dist. judge, Portland, 1957—. Former corporator Maine Savs. Bank; mem. adv. com. bankruptcy rules U.S. Supreme Ct.; council mem. Harvard Law Sch., also chmn. vis. com.; past mem. adv. panel internat. law U.S. State Dept.; faculty Salzburg Seminar for Am. Studies, 1972. Asst. corp. counsel City of Portland, 1947-48, mem. city council, 1949-55, chmn., 1952. Pres., bd. dirs. Greater Portland Community Chest, 1955-56, United Fund, 1956-57; corporator, trustee Maine Med. Center; trustee Maine Eye and Ear Infirmary, Portland Symphony Orch.; bd. overseers Harvard Coll. Served as maj. U.S. Army, 1942-46. Decorated Bronze Star, Legion of Merit. Mem. Am. (spl. com. on jud. conduct), Maine, Cumberland County bar assns., Inst. Jud. Adminstrn., Jud. Conf. U.S. (mem. com. on jud. adminstrn.), Am. Judicature Soc. (dir.), Am. Law Inst. (council, 2d v.p.). Episcopalian. Clubs: Harvard (pres. Maine 1957) (Boston, N.Y.C.); Portland Country. Editor Harvard Law Rev., 1939-40. Home: Starboard Ln Cumberland Forside Portland ME 04110 Office: 156 Federal St Portland ME 04112

GILBERG, SHELDON FRANCIS, educator; b. Detroit, Mich., Oct. 14, 1934; s. Alfred Melvin and Rose (Kemper) G.; B.F.A., U. Ariz., 1961; B.F.T., Thunderbird Grad. Sch. Internat. Mgmt., 1962; M.S., U. Bridgeport, 1970; Ph.D., U. Iowa, 1973; m. Linda Johanna Palsrok, Sept. 7, 1965; children—Victoria Anne, Alfred John, Cassandra Jane, Wendy Kathleen. Asst. to dir. pub. relations Sta. KPHO, Phoenix, Ariz.; media dir. Ptak, Mueller, and Assos. Advt. Agy., Phoenix; broadcasting cons. NBC Internat., N.Y.C.; account exec. ABC Films Internat., N.Y.C.; asso. prof. TV, U. Wis., LaCrosse, Newhouse Sch. of Pub. Communications, Syracuse (N.Y.) U.; cons. Internat. Broadcasters, Syracuse U. Pub. info. officer Coast Guard Aux. Served with USMC, 1955-57. Mem. Am. Acad. TV Arts and Scis., Am. Film Inst., Nat. Assn. Ednl. Broadcasters. Republican. Roman Catholic. Author: TV Studio Production Handbook, 1977; contbr. articles to profl. jours. Home: 19 Glenburn Rd Liverpool NY 13088 Office: Room 367 Newhouse School of Public Communications Syracuse Univ Syracuse NY 13210

GILBERT, ARTHUR CHARLES, aero. engr.; b. N.Y.C., Sept. 23, 1926; s. Phillip Saul and Annie (Taishoff) G.; B.Aeros. Engring., N.Y. U., 1947, M.Aeros.Engring. (fellow), 1948, Sc.D. with honors (fellow), 1956; m. Suzanne Teperson, June 18, 1953; children—Pamela, Randi. Engr., various aerospace cos.; program dir., corp. acquisition evaluation com. Bendix Corp., Ann Arbor, Mich.; mem. staff acquisition and planning, dir. BioMed. div. United Aircraft Corp., Farmington, Conn.; chief tech. staff CIA, Washington; v.p. engring. Systems Tech. Lab.; sci. adviser to Chief of Naval Ops., USN; v.p. engring. research and devel. Data Solutions Corp., McLean, Va.; v.p. engring. OAO Corp., Beltsville, Md.; founder AutoTrain Corp., Washington. USAF Engring. Research grantee, 1953-56. Mem. Nat. Soc. Profl. Engrs. Club: Cosmos. Contbr. articles to sci. and tech. jours. Home: 4701 Willard Ave Chevy Chase MD 20015

GILBERT, ARTHUR JOSEPH, bishop; b. Hedley, B.C., Can., Oct. 26, 1915; s. George Miles and Ethel May (Carter) G.; student St. Joseph's Coll., St. Joseph, N.B.; B.A. summa cum laude, St. Francis Xavier U. Ordained priest Roman Cath. Ch., 1943, bishop, 1974; curate St. Andrews, N.B., 1943; sec. to bishop, 1943; chancellor Diocese St. John, 1944-49; dir. St. Patrick's Orphanage, 1949; pastor St. Pius X Parish, St. Joseph's Parish, Loch Lomond, St. Joachim's, Silver Falls, 1949-74; bishop St. John Diocese, 1974—. Home: 9 Bishops Dr Renforth Saint John NB Canada Office: 91 Waterloo St Saint John NB E2L 3P9 Canada

GILBERT, FRANCIS CHARLES, sci. adminstr.; b. Richmond, Calif., May 7, 1928; s. Francis Charles and Mary (Wieneke) G.; B.S. in Engring. Physics with honors (Howard C. Holmes fellow, 1946-47, Levi Strauss fellow, 1948-49), U. Calif. at Berkeley, 1950, M.S. in Elec. Engring., 1952, Ph.D. in Physics, 1954; m. Marilyn Ruth Keiser, June 23, 1950; children—Diane Elizabeth, John Charles. Staff physicist Lawrence Radiation Lab., Livermore, Calif., 1954-59, test adminstr., 1961-71; physicist CTR program Centre d'Etudes Nucleaires, Fontenay-aux-Roses, France, 1959-60; dept. dir. mil. application AEC (now Dept. Energy), Washington, 1971—. Mem. Sigma Xi, Tau Beta Pi. Presbyn. (pres. bd. trustees 1971). Contbr. articles to profl. jours. Patentee in field. Home: 1386 Kersey Ln Rockville MD 20854 Office: Dept Energy Washington DC 20545

GILBERT, FREDERICK SPOFFORD, JR., banker; b. Orange, N.J., Mar. 29, 1939; s. Frederick Spofford and Annis (Stearns) G.; grad. Deerfield Acad., 1957; B.A., Williams Coll., 1961; postgrad. N.Y. U., 1962-66; m. Margaret Andrus Moon, Sept. 6, 1961; children—Malcolm Andrus, Frederick Christopher, Douglas Hamlin. Mgmt. trainee Citibank N.A., N.Y.C., 1961-65, asst. mgr., 1965-69, asst. v.p., 1969-72, v.p., 1972—, exec. v.p. Citibank (N.Y. State) N.A., 1976-77; pres. Citicorp Bus. Credit, Inc., N.Y.C., 1977—. Treas. Darien YMCA Indian Guides, 1972-74. Mem. Republican Town Meeting, Darien, 1971-75. Served with AUS, 1962. Mem. Credit and Financial Mgmt. Alumni Assn., Kappa Alpha Soc. Clubs: University, Williams (N.Y.C.), Wee Burn Country (Darien). Home: 46 Ridge Acres Darien CT 06820 Office: 399 Park Ave New York City NY 10043

GILBERT, HARRY IRMAN, ret. supt. schs.; b. Boyertown, Pa., Nov. 5, 1913; s. Harry Irman and Edna (Dout) G.; B.A., Pa. State U., 1936; M.Ed., U. Pitts., 1938; postgrad. Lehigh U., 1940-43, Temple U., 1950—; m. Wilma Marie Hudson, Sept. 11, 1937; children—Keith Duncan, Michael Hudson, Robert Richard, Harry Allen. Tchr., Boyertown Area Sch. Dist., 1938-46, counselor, 1946-53, asst. prin., 1953-56, high sch. prin., 1956-65, asst. supt., 1965-66, supt., 1966-74; dir. Boyertown Area Multi-Service Council; participant comparative ednl. seminars, Finland, Russia, Czechoslovakia and Spain, 1969, Germany, Eng. and Czechoslovakia, 1970, East Africa, 1972, India, 1974. Bd. dirs. United Way, Boyertown and vicinity; bd. mgrs. YMCA. Served as field dir. ARC, World War II; PTO. Mem. Am., Pa. assns. sch. adminstrs., Phila. Suburban Sch. Study Council (pres. Group B 1969-70), Pa. Sch. Press Assn. (pres. 1962), UN Assn. Common Cause, Smithsonian Assos., Wilderness Soc., Sierra Club, Comparative and Internat. Edn. Soc., Phi Delta Kappa. Rotarian. Lutheran. Home: 115 N Monroe St Boyertown PA 19512

GILBERT, JOAN STULMAN, petroleum co. exec.; b. N.Y.C., May 10, 1934; d. Julius and Paula Stulman; student Conn. Coll. for Women, 1951-53; m. Phil E. Gilbert, Jr., Oct. 6, 1968; children—Linda, Dana, Patricia. Br. coordinator Vol. Service Bur., Westchester, N.Y., 1970-72; pub. relations dir. Westchester Lighthouse, 1972-76; exec. dir. Westchester Heart Assn., 1976-77; community relations mgr. Texaco Inc., White Plains, N.Y., 1977—. Bd. dirs. Teatown Lake Reservation of Bklyn. Bot. Graden, 1975—, Leukemia Soc. Am. Mem. Pub. Relations Soc. Am (chpt. pres. 1977), Advt. Club. Home: The Croft Spring Valley Rd Ossining NY 10562 Office: 2000 Westchester Ave White Plains NY 10650

GILBERT, PHIL EDWARD, JR., lawyer; b. Chgo., Jan. 31, 1915; s. Phil Edward and Florence (Miller) G.; A.B., Dartmouth Coll., 1936; LL.B., Harvard U., 1939; m. Nancy Thompson Merrick, June 24, 1939 (div. 1967); children—Mary Randolph, John Sale, Clinton Merrick; m. 2d, Joan Stulman, Oct. 6, 1968. Admitted to N.Y. bar, 1941, since practiced in N.Y.C.; atty. Donovan, Leisure, Newton & Lumbard, 1939-41, Debevoise, Stevenson, Plimpton & Page, 1941; partner Gilbert, Segall & Young, and predecessor, 1946—; pres. Rolls-Royce, Inc., N.Y.C., 1957-71; dep. chmn. Magnesium Elektron, Inc.; dir. Rolls-Royce Inc., Sanger-Funnell, Inc. Vice-chmn. Westchester County Democratic Com., 1960-72; Dem. candidate for U.S. Ho. of Reps. 26th N.Y. Congressional. Dist., 1958, 60; mem. nat. council Salk Inst., 1976—. Served to maj., inf., AUS, 1941-46; ETO. Decorated Bronze Star, Croix de Guerre. Mem. Am., Fed., Westchester bar assns., Bar Assn. City N.Y., Phi Beta Kappa. Baptist. Home: The Croft Spring Valley Rd Ossining NY 10562 Office: 430 Park Ave New York City NY 10022

GILBERT, RAMON, cantor; b. Detroit, Nov. 4, 1932; s. Irving and Frances (Fields) G.; B.A. in Sacred Music, Hebrew Union Coll., 1968; B.A., Brandeis U., 1954; soloist diploma Longy Sch. Music, 1955; postgrad. Julliard Sch. Music, 1956; m. Joyce Marie Benvie, June 12, 1955; children—Caryn Victoria, Eliot Bruce. Mem. faculty Hebrew Union Coll., N.Y.C., 1977—, U. Bridgeport (Conn.), 1970-71, Interarts High Sch. for Artistically Gifted, Bridgeport, 1976-77; producer Coll. Institute's Musica Hebraica Series, N.Y.C., 1977—; stage dir. Greenwich House Music Sch., Greenwich Village, N.Y.C., 1958-59; founder Bridgeport's Liturgical Music Festival, Inc., 1973, artistic dir., 1973—; founding mem. Cantica Hebraica, 1970-78; mem. Am. Conf. Cantors, 1966—, pres., 1977-79, chmn. convs. in Toronto, Ont., Can., 1972, Israel, 1973, 78, Phila., 1970, Washington, 1969, pres., 1977—; baritone soloist with Detroit Symphony, 1952, Bklyn. Philharmonic, 1956; concert tours of liturgical music, Chgo., 1977, Detroit, 1975, 76, San Francisco, 1976, Israel, 1973, 78, Can., 1972, N.Y.C., 1966, others; guest cantor various congregations U.S., 1966—; appeared on various TV networks including NBC, CBS, Sta. WTNH; appeared in opera houses in N.Y.C., 1956-66, Detroit, 1958, Yellow Springs, Ohio, 1959, Boston, 1950-55; leading roles in Don Giovanni, Marriage of Figaro, Trouble in Tahiti, Cosi Fan Tutte, others; mem. Westchester Music Theatre, White Plains, N.Y., 1963-68; cantor Congregation B'nai Israel, Bridgeport, Conn., 1966—. Bd. overseers Sch. Sacred Music, Hebrew Union Coll. Recipient Fulbright award, 1959, Rockefeller award, 1962, Ben Gurion award, 1976. Mem. Brandeis U. Alumni Assn. (pres. Conn. chpt.). Club: Rotary. Home: 112 Benedict Ave Fairfield CT 06432 Office: 2710 Park Ave Bridgeport CT 06604

GILBERT, RICHARD PAUL, judge; b. Balt., Feb. 5, 1924; s. Paul Reed and Elsa (Huse) G.; A.A., U. Balt., 1947, J.D., 1950, LL.M., 1954; m. Audrey Arlene Rude, Aug. 30, 1944; children—Paul Terryl, Richard Joel. Admitted to Md. bar., 1950; gen. practice law, Balt., 1950-71; spl. asst. people's counsel, 1954; asso. judge Traffic Ct., Balt., 1955-59; asso. judge Ct. Spl. Appeals Md., Annapolis, 1971-76, chief judge, 1976—. Chmn., Off-St. Parking Commn., 1963-65; mem. Bd. Municipal and Zoning Appeals, 1965-71, Mayor's Adv. Com. on City Charter, 1963-65, State War Ballot Commn., 1955-67. Mem., past pres. Md. Fedn. Young Republicans; chmn. Md. Rep. Central Com., Balt., 1958-60; mem. Commn. Jud. Disabitities, 1972-74, chmn., 1974—. Served to 1st lt. AUS, 1943-46, 50-52. Mem. Am., Md., Balt. City bar assns., Sigma Delta Kappa. Lutheran (trustee). Home: 1919 Sleepy Hollow Ln Annapolis MD 21401 Office: Ct Appeals Bldg Annapolis MD 21401

GILBERT, SHELDON IAN, dentist; b. Pitts., Oct. 29, 1935; s. Samuel Baer and Rebecca (Marcus) G.; student U. Pa., 1953-56; B.A., Geneva Coll., 1958; D.D.S., U. Pitts., 1962; m. Shandel Sue Spiro, Dec. 23, 1967; children—John Harrison, Rebecca Jo. Individual practice dentistry, Beaver Falls, then New Brighton, Pa., 1964—; mem. dental staff United Hosp., Beaver Falls, v.p. staff, 1971-72, pres., 1972-73. Served to capt. AUS, 1962-64. Mem. Am. Dental Assn., Beaver Valley Dental Soc. (sec.-treas. 1968-69), Alpha Omega. Mem. B'nai B'rith. Club: Beaver Valley Country. Home: 111 Hillcrest Ave Beaver Falls PA 15010 Office: 701 3d Ave New Brighton PA 15066

GILBERT, WILLIAM HOYT, lawyer; b. Buffalo, Sept. 12, 1928; s. Lester Frederick and Josephine Ballard (Hoyt) G.; A.B., Harvard U., 1950, LL.B., 1953; m. Ann M. Gardner, June 15, 1956; children—Christopher Hoyt, Jean Gardner, Lucy Ballard. Admitted to N.Y. bar, 1954; mem. firm Webster, Sheffield & Chrystie, N.Y.C., 1957-58; mem. firm Ohlin, Damon, Morey, Sawyer & Moot (and predecessor firm), Buffalo, 1958—, partner, 1963—; lectr. U. Buffalo Tax Inst.; dir. B. Elliott, Inc., Petrex Petroleum Corp. Bd. dirs. Planned Parenthood Fedn., Am., 1973—, treas., 1976—; pres. Planned Parenthood Buffalo, 1968-70; div. chmn. United Way, 1964, mem. ho. of dels., 1965—; bd. dirs. Blind Assn. Western N.Y., 1967—, v.p., 1971—. Served with USN, 1953-57. Mem. Am., N.Y. State, Erie County bar assns. Clubs: Buffalo Tennis & Squash (pres. 1975-76), Midday, Hermitage, Magog (Quebec). Home: 282 Middlesex Rd Buffalo NY 14216 Office: 1800 Liberty Bank Bldg Buffalo NY 14202

GILCHRIST, DAVID MALCOLM, agrl. engr.; b. Cambridge, Queens County, N.B., Can., Aug. 16, 1915; s. Robert Earle and Florence Olive (DeMille) G.; B.S. in Agr., MacDonald Coll., 1942; m. Helen Grace Lutwick, Nov. 18, 1944; children—Janet Gilchrist Bouchard, Robert, Margaret Gilchrist Gill, Brent E., James Stewart, Peter. Agrl. engr. in charge farm land breaking equipment N.B. Dept. Agr., Fredericton, 1944-61, in charge subsurface drainage and land clearing and breaking programs 1961—; cons. on drainage. Bd. dirs. Canadian Plowing Council, 1961—, N.B. br. Canadian Mental Health Assn.; Active Baptist ch. work. Mem. Am. Soc. Agrl. Engrs., Soil Conservation Soc. Am., Agrl. Inst. Can., N.B. Plowmens Assn. (sec.-mgr.). Home: 169 Burpee St Fredericton NB E3A 1M6 Canada Office: PO Box 6000 Fredericton NB E3B 5H1 Canada

GILCHRIST, ELIZABETH BRENDA, editor, cons.; b. Coulsdon, Surrey, Eng. (parents Am. citizens); d. Huntington and Elizabeth (Brace) Gilchrist; B.A., Smith Coll. Asst. Durlacher Bros. Art Gallery, N.Y.C., 1954-57; art adminstrn. asst. Brussels World's Fair, Belgium, 1957-58; fund raiser Mus. Modern Art, N.Y.C., 1959-62; reporter Show Mag., N.Y.C., 1962-64; staff writer Am. Heritage Pub. Co., N.Y.C., 1964; sr. editor Praeger Pubs., N.Y.C., 1965-75; pub. cons., 1975-gen. editor Smithsonian Illustrated Library of Antiques, Cooper-Hewitt Mus., N.Y.C., 1976—. Mem. adv. council Continuing Profl. Edn. Program, Museums; Collaborative, Inc., 1977—. Bd. dirs. Drawing Soc., mem. exec. com., 1960—. Mem. Soc. Archtl. Historians, Coll. Art Assn., Am. Assn. Museums, Victorian Soc. in Am. Club: Deer Isle Yacht. Translator: Marc Chagall: The Ceiling of the Paris Opera (Jacques Lassaigne), 1966. Home: 175 W 93d St New York City NY 10025

GILDE, LOUIS CHARLES, JR., environ. engr.; b. Phila., Mar. 23, 1924; s. Louis Charles and Therese May (Albrecht) G.; B.S. in San. Engring., Rutgers U., 1950; m. Patricia Ann Gilde; children—Lisa, Mark, Patty, Susan, Troy, Sam. With Campbell Soup Co., Camden, N.J., 1950—, corporate dir. environ. programs, 1970—; v.p. Technol. Resources Inc. subs. Campbell Soup Co., 1978—; lectr. to univs. and environ. groups; adviser Nat. Indsl. Pollution Control Council, U.S. Dept. Commerce, 1970-72. Commr., Camden City Environ. Commn. Served with U.S. Army, 1943-45. Designer Waste treatment center that was recipient Nat. Gold Medal award Sports Found., 1970. Mem. Am. Water Works Assn., Water Pollution Control Fedn., Phila. Acad. Natural Scis., Nat. Canners Assn. (chmn. environ. research com. 1968-74), Am. Frozen Food Inst., N.A.M., Smithsonian Inst., Nat. Environ. Devel. Assn. (dir.). Author chpts. in environ. engring. handbooks. Patentee in field. Developer overland flow waste water treatment systems. Home: 605 Stratford Dr Moorestown NJ 08057 Office: Campbell Soup Co Campbell Pl Camden NJ 08101

GILDER, RODMAN, psychiatrist; b. N.Y.C., June 18, 1918; s. Rodman and Louise Comfort (Tiffany) G.; B.S., Harvard, 1940; M.D., Columbia, 1944; m. Mary Ellen Bowman, June 30, 1948; children—David, Joshua. Intern Presbyterian Hosp., N.Y.C., 1944-45; resident in psychiatry N.Y. Psychiat. Inst., 1949-50; pvt. practice specializing in psychiatry, N.Y.C., 1954—; asso. clin. prof. psychiatry Columbia, 1975—; asso. attending psychiatrist Columbia-Presbyn. Med. Center, 1975—. Trustee Westchester Adoption Service, 1962-65, Scarsdale Family Counseling Service, 1957-60, Westchester Mental Health Assn., 1966-68. Served with M.C., USNR, 1945-46, 52-54. Fellow Westchester Acad. Medicine, Am. Psychiat. Assn., Am. Acad. Child Psychiatry; mem. N.Y. Psychoanalytic Inst. Democrat. Presbyterian. Club: Century Assn. Contbg. editor to Psychoanalytic Quarterly, 1964—. Home and office: 12 School Ln Scarsdale NY 10583

GILES, CHARLES ELLIOTT, corp. librarian; b. Boston, June 3, 1939; s. Charles Metcalf and Dorothy Eleanor (Elliott) G.; B.S., U. Maine, 1962, M.L.S., 1967; m. Martha Emery, Dec. 20, 1962 (div.); children—Scott Elliott, Hope Emery, Jill Elizabeth. Sch. librarian Wiscasset (Maine) High Sch., 1964-67; reference librarian Union Carbide Corp., South Charleston, W.Va., 1967-69; sr. librarian electric boat div. Gen. Dynamics Corp., Groton, Conn., 1969-70, chief librarian electric boat div., 1970-72, div. records mgmt. adminstr., 1972—, sr. supr. info. service, 1972—. Mem. Nat. Mgmt. Assn., Spl. Libraries Assn., Appalachian Mountain Club, Appalachian Trail Conf. Republican. Home: 55 Crouch St Apt 4 Groton CT 06340 Office: Dept 633 Tech Library Electric Boat Div Groton CT 06340

GILES, SHARON ALTHEA, advt. co. exec.; b. East Orange, N.J., Sept. 12, 1951; d. William R. and Althea B. (Banks) G.; B.S., Morgan State U., 1973; Ed. M., Rutgers U., 1975. Tchr. Camden St. Middle Sch., Newark, 1973-75, Washington Sch., East Orange, 1975-77; pres. E.P.C. Internat., Inc., East Orange, 1977—. Bd. dirs. PUSH, Essex County, N.J., Sunn, Inc., East Orange. Mem. Nat. Urban League, Advt. Splty. Inst., Splty. Advt. Assn., East Orange C. of C., Kappa Delta Pi, NAACP. Home: 43 Edgemont Rd West Orange NJ 07052 Office: 715 Park Ave East Orange NJ 07017

GILINSON, PHILIP JULIUS, JR., elec. engr.; b. Lowell, Mass., July 28, 1914; s. Philip Julius and Anna (Turnquist) G.; B.S., Mass. Inst. Tech., 1936, M.S., 1952; m. Hulda Einars, July 6, 1943; children—Philip Julius III, Robert Alan. Engr., Doelcam Inc., Newton, Mass., 1946-47; mem. staff C.S. Draper Lab., Mass. Inst. Tech., Cambridge, 1947—, asst. dir., 1954-63, dep. asso. dir. lab., 1963—. Mem. Sch. Bldg. Com., Chelmsford, Mass., 1950-55; pres. Chelmsford Little League, 1957-62. Chmn. bd. dirs. Chelmsford Scholarship Fund, 1964; bd. dirs. Lutheran Nursing Home, Brockton, Mass., 1968-71, Luth. Social Service, Worcester, Mass., 1968-71. Served to lt. col. USAAF, 1940-46. Registered profl. engr., Mass. Mem. I.E.E.E., Sigma Xi. Lutheran (past v.p.). Mem. Order Demolay (adv. bd.); Mason. Club: MIT Quarter Century. Author: (with C.S. Draper, others) Air, Space and Instruments, 1963; (with R.H. Frazier, G.A. Oberbeck) Magnetic and Electric Suspensions, 1974. Home: 8 Fuller Rd Chelmsford MA 01824 Office: 555 Technology Sq Cambridge MA 02139

GILKESON, VINCENT STANLEY, mfg. co. exec.; b. Allentown, Pa., Jan. 15, 1916; s. Russel Andrew and Johanna (Huebner) G.; student Pratt Inst., Bklyn., 1935; m. Miriam S. Hammond, Jan. 2, 1943; children—Johanna, Patricia, Susan, Terry. Commd. capt. C.E., U.S. Army, 1939, ret., 1962; pres. Vee Gil Constrn. Co., Somerset, N.J., 1962-67; with Seeley, Stevans, Value & Knecht, N.Y.C., 1967, C.W. Ryan, N.Y.C., 1967, Kiff Voss & Franklin, N.Y.C., 1968-69, Amman & Whitney, N.Y.C., 1969-73; chief of specifications Edwards & Kelcey, Inc., Livingston, N.J., 1973—. Mem. Ret. Officers Assn., Am. Security Council. Republican. Home: 55 Appleman Rd Somerset NJ 08873 Office: 70 S Orange Ave Livingston NJ 07039

GILKEY, KENNETH GEORGE, corp. exec.; b. New Kensington, Pa., Dec. 28, 1942; s. Kenneth Simpson and Betty Ida G.; B.S., Pa. State U., 1964; m. Lisette Jacqueline Denis, Sept. 21, 1968. From staff accountant to mgr. Price Waterhouse & Co., C.P.A.'s, N.Y.C., 1967-72; asst. controller, then asst. v.p., dep. controller W.R. Grace & Co., N.Y.C., 1972-78, v.p., controller, 1978—. Treas. New Providence-Berkeley Heights (N.J.) Jaycees, 1976-77, sec., 1977-78. Served to 1st lt. AUS, 1965-67. C.P.A., N.Y. State. Mem. Am. Inst. C.P.A.'s, N.Y. State Soc. C.P.A.'s. Home: 155 Ridge Rd Watchung NJ 07060 Office: Grace Plaza 1114 Ave Americas New York City NY 10036

GILL, ALEXANDER MENZIES, mfrs. agent, importer, mfr.; b. Sarasota, Fla., Sept. 2, 1936; s. Jo Dozier and Virginia (Menzies) G.; A.B., Harvard Coll., 1961. Asst. to pres. Trade Winds, Inc., Boston, 1962-69; propr. Alexander Gill and Co., Boston, 1969-71; partner Devon Service, Boston, 1971-75, propr., 1975—; partner Gill/Poch Partnership, Boston, 1976—; pres., treas. Naga Co. Inc., Boston, 1978—. Mem. N.Eng. Wholesale Decorative Arts Assn. Club: Harvard (Boston). Office: 420 Boylston St Boston MA 02116

GILL, GARY WESLEY, cytotechnologist; b. Balt., Nov. 18, 1941; s. Howard Hayden and Doris Lorraine (Gosnell) G.; B.A., Western Md. Coll., 1963; certificate (HEW fellow) Johns Hopkins Hosp. Sch. of Cytotech., 1964; spl. student Johns Hopkins Sch. Hygiene and Pub. Health, 1965-68. Sr. research cytotechnologist, dept. cytopathology Johns Hopkins Hosp., Balt., 1964-65; chief research asso., div. cytopathology Sch. Medicine, Johns Hopkins U., Balt., 1966-74; asst. Postgrad. Inst. for Pathologists in Clin. Pathology, Johns Hopkins U. Sch. Medicine and Johns Hopkins Hosp., 1969—; lectr. Johns Hopkins Sch. Cytotech., Balt., 1970—; chief research asso. Johns Hopkins Med. Instns. Cytopathology Labs., 1966—; tech. adminstr., early lung cancer detection program Johns Hopkins Med. Instns.; cons. to labs. and mfg. cos.; cons. cytopreparatory technique teaching films. Mem. Am. Soc. Cytology (asso.), Md. Assn. Cytotechnologists (charter), Internat. Acad. Cytology. Democrat. Roman Catholic. Contbr. articles to profl. jours. Home: 11 Stonewain Ct Baltimore MD 21204 Office: 603 Pathology Bldg Johns Hopkins Hosp Baltimore MD 21205

GILL, MICHAEL DOUD, corp. exec., bus. cons.; b. San Antonio, Dec. 14, 1935; s. Richard and Frances (Doud) G.; ed. U. Va.; m. E. Gay Fletcher; 1 child, Fletcher Doud; children by previous marriage—Julia, Gordon, Michael. Pres., G.M. Homes, Inc., Mgmt. Systems and Sales, Inc., Washington, Michael Doud Gill & Assos., Inc., Washington, Michael Doud Gill Africa, Ltd., Zambia; exec. v.p., United Continental Corp.; bd. chmn., v.p., exec. dir. Wells Industries Corp., North Hollywood, Calif.; asst. to pres. Air Transit Services, Inc.; spl. asst. to adminstr. Housing and Home Fin. Agy., HUD; gen. agt. Am. Heritage Life Ins. Co., Washington, Md., Va. Nat. field rep. Citizens for Eisenhower, 1965, Nat. Rep. Congl. Campaign Com., 1956, Nat. Rep. Senatorial Campaign Com., 1958-60; asst. to chmn., adminstrv. asst. to exec. dir., campaign dir. Rep. Nat. Com., 1960, mem. fin. com., 1976—; dir. spl. events and activities Rep. Nat. Conv., 1968, del., 1976; active numerous other polit. coms. and campaigns; mem. nat. com. Boy Scouts Am., 1964—; mem. diplomatic council People-to-People Sports Com., 1969—; active numerous other civic orgns., 1957—. Served with USMCR. Recipient Outstanding Achievement citation 2d Atlantic conf. NATO, 1960; named One of Ten Outstanding Young Men in Politics in the Nation, Nat. Rep. Women's Club, 1957. Mem. Nat. Found., Heart Found., Bahamas Oceanographic Soc. (gen. mgr.), Jr. C. of C., Internat. Platform Assn., Am. Acad. Polit. and Social Sci., Young Rep. Nat. Fedn. (nat. com. Washington 1956-58, 62-64, nat. exec. com. 1956-64; del. from Washington 1957, 59, 61, 63, 65, 67; chmn. nat. fin. com., 1963-65, spl. project com. 1969-61, speakers bureau 1957-59), Am. Legion, Sigma Alpha Epsilon. Home: 4201 Cathedral Ave NW Washington DC 20016 also Rt 4 Box 5101 Ocean Pines Berlin MD 21811

GILL, THOMAS WILLIAM, govt. ofcl.; b. Erie, Pa., May 30, 1926; s. Phelps Levere and Mabel Frances (Hallifield) G.; B.A., Syracuse U., 1950, M.P.A., 1955; m. Maud Maria Buchanan, Dec. 24, 1954; children—Mary Ann, John Richard. Personnel and tng. specialist U.S. Dept. Navy, Washington, 1955-70; tng. officer OEO and State of Md., Balt., 1970-73; tng. officer U.S. Dept. Agr., Washington, 1973-75, head exec. devel., 1975—. Served with AUS, 1944-46, 51. Recipient Commrs.' award for distinguished service, 1978. Mem. Am. Soc. Tng. and Devel. Contbr. articles to profl. jours. Home: 5151 Thunder Hill Rd Columbia MD 21045 Office: US Dept Agr 14th and Independence Ave SW Washington DC 20250

GILLARY, LEO, sculptor, owner art gallery; b. Detroit, Oct. 18, 1915; s. Charles A. and Lena (Nover) G.; student Yale, 1942-43, 44; B.A., N.Y. U., 1944; postgrad. Columbia, 1946-47; m. Sylvia Rita Levy, June 21, 1953. Exhibited one-man shows at Gillary Gallery, Jericho, N.Y., 1970; exhibited in group shows at Greenwich House Show, 1963, Emily Lowe Gallery, Hofstra U., Hempstead, L.I., 1966, N. Shore 8th Ann. Juried Show, Manhasset, L.I., 1966; represented in numerous pvt. collections. Asst. sales mgr. Couture Fabrics, Ltd., N.Y.C., 1960-66; owner, dir. Gillary Gallery, Jericho, N.Y., 1961—; sec. Gildan Assos., Inc., pub. relations mgmt. young musicians, Jericho, 1971—. Served with USAAF, 1942-46. Recipient Clay award Union Dime Savs. Bank, 1960, honorable mention Greenwich House, 1968, Service award B'nai B'rith, 1968. Mem. Mid-Island Concert Assn. (pres. 1969—). Address: 62 Maiden Ln Jericho NY 11753

GILLEN, JAMES FRANCIS, hosp. adminstr.; b. Newark, July 22, 1943; s. Joseph Ellard and Josephine Natalie (Gayer) G.; B.S. in Bus. Adminstrn., Seton Hall U., 1966; M.S. in Hosp. Adminstrn., Columbia U., 1971; m. Alice R. Catullo, June 7, 1970. Asst. adminstr. St. Clare's Hosp. and Health Center, N.Y.C., 1972-74, French-Polyclinic Med. Sch. and Health Center, N.Y.C., 1974-75; asso. cons. F.J. Walsh, Hoboken, N.J., 1975-76; pres. J.G. Assos., Ocean Grove, N.J. and N.Y.C., 1975-76; exec. dir. Bergen Pines County Hosp., Paramus, N.J., 1977—. Mem. Bergen-Passaic Hosp. Adminstrs. Council, Am., N.J. hosp. assns., Columbia Alumni Assn., LaSalle Mil. Acad., Greater N.Y. Hosp. Assn., Met. Health Adminstrs. Assn. (certified; exec. com.), Am. Mgmt. Assn., Hosp. Assn. N.Y. State, N.Y. Zool. Soc., Am. Mus. Natural History. Roman Catholic. Home: 2 Horizon Rd Fort Lee NJ 07024 Office: East Ridgewood Ave Paramus NJ 07652

GILLEO, MATHIAS ALTEN, chem. co. exec.; b. East Grand Rapids, Mich., May 16, 1922; s. Avery Clare and Eleanore (Alten) G.; Asso. Engring., Grand Rapids Jr. Coll., 1942; B.S., U. Mich., 1944; S.M., Mass. Inst. Tech., 1948, Ph.D. in Electrophysics, 1952; m. Constance Galbraith Brinkman, Nov. 22, 1952 (div. Aug. 1969); m. 2d, Margaret Pfeffer, May 27, 1977. Elec. engr. Bur. Ships, Dept. Navy, Washington, 1944, 45; elec. engr. optics div. U.S. Naval Research Lab., Washington, 1945-46; research asst. Mass. Inst. Tech., Cambridge, 1946-52; mem. tech. staff Bell Telephone Labs., Murray Hill, N.J., 1952-58; staff scientist research labs. Lockheed Missiles & Space Co., Palo Alto, Calif., 1958-61; mem. tech. staff Amelco Semicondr. div. Teledyne Inc., Mountain View, Calif., 1961-64; scientist Monsanto Co., St. Louis, 1964-69; mgr. corporate research Allied Chem. Corp., Morristown, N.J., 1969—; lectr. dept. mech. engring. Stanford U., 1961; faculty dept. elec. engring. U. Calif. Extension, Los Altos, 1962, 63; affiliate prof. elec. engring. Washington U., St. Louis, 1967-69. Fellow Am. Phys. Soc.; mem. IEEE (sr.; chmn. awards Princeton sect. 1976-78, sect. treas. 1978—, chmn. magnetics chpt. Princeton sect. 1975-76), Optical Soc. Am., Am. Crystallographic Assn., N.Y. Acad. Scis., Sigma Xi, Phi Kappa Phi, Tau Beta Pi, Eta Kappa Nu. Contbr. articles to profl. jours. Home: 3 St Clair Rd Morristown NJ 07960 Office: PO Box 1021R (MRC) Morristown NJ 07960

GILLESPIE, CARL MICHAEL, newspaper advt. exec.; b. Johnstown, Pa., Oct. 21, 1914; s. Michael Aloysius and Sue Elizabeth (Kuhn) G.; B.S., U. Pitts., 1947; m. Helen Kathryn Myers, June 13, 1942; 1 dau., Jayne Elizabeth (Mrs. Alan Wayne Anderson). With Johnstown Tribune Pub. Co., 1933—, nat. advt. mgr., 1946—, advt. dir., 1949—, v.p., 1974—. Bd. dirs. Lee Hosp., Johnstown, 1970, U. Pitts. at Johnstown. Served with USNR, 1941-45. Mem. Internat. Advt. Execs. Assn. (dir. 1952-56, state v.p. 1960-62, 76—), Bur. Advt. Am. Newspaper Pubs. Assn. (vice chmn. plan com. 1954). Alpha Delta Sigma, Delta Mu Delta, Beta Sigma Phi. Mason (32 deg., Shriner). Clubs: Sunnehanna Country, Bachelor's (Johnstown). Home: 2245 Crabtree Ln Johnstown PA 15905 Office: 425 Locust St Johnstown PA 15907

GILLESPIE, DOROTHY MURIEL (MRS. BERNARD ISRAEL), artist; b. Roanoke, Va., June 29, 1920; d. Earl Vivian and Lillian (Foster) Gillespie; student Md. Inst. Art, 1938-41, Clay Club, N.Y.C., 1943-44, Stanley William Hayter's Atelier 17, 1945, Art Students League, 1944; D.F.A., Caldwell Coll., 1976; m. Bernard Israel, May 29, 1946; children—Dorien Gillespie, Gary Gillespie, Richard Gillespie. Exhibited one man shows Barzansky Galleries, N.Y.C., Miami (Fla.) Mus. Modern Art, Lowe Art Gallery U. Miami, Inst. Contemporary Art Lima, Peru, Gallerie Das Fenster, Frankfurt, Germany, Coll. St. Marys of Springs, Columbus, Ohio, L.I. U., Gertrude Stein Gallery, 1969, N.Y. U., 1970, 71, 75, 76, Columbia, 1971, Women's Interart Center, 1973, 76, New Sch., 1976, Fordham U., 1976, Aaron Berman Gallery, N.Y.C., 1977, 78, Virginia Miller Gallery, Coral Gables, Fla., San Jose (Calif.) U., Fells Point Gallery, Balt., Jersey City Mus., Fredrick Gallery, Washington, many others; exhibited group shows N.Y. Cultural Center, 1973, Bklyn. Coll., 1973, Suffolk Mus., 1973, Bklyn. Mus., 1976; Art Vance N.Y. U., 1973; represented in numerous permanent collections; own radio show Dorothy Gillespie Show, WHBI, N.Y.C., 1967-73; artist-in-residence Women's Interart Center, 1972, co-coordinator, 1973-74, 74-75; mem. faculty New Sch., N.Y.C., 1975—, coordinator Art and Community Inst., 1977-78. Recipient numerous painting awards, 1931—. Patentee ednl. game, 1967. Address: 135 MacDougal St New York City NY 10012

GILLETTE, WALTER RAY, JR., surgeon; b. Chgo., June 1, 1919; s. Walter Ray and Lennie M. (Johnson) G.; B.A., Lafayette Coll., 1942; M.D., N.Y. U., 1946; m. Lucille Joan Saffell, Apr. 9, 1955; children—Walter Ray, Joann Fredericka, William Robert. Intern, French Hosp., N.Y.C., 1946-47; resident gen. surgery Polyclinic Hosp., Cleve., 1947-48; fellow pathology Cook County Hosp., Chgo., 1949; resident gen. surgery Hamot Hosp., Erie, Pa., 1949-50, Caylor Nickel Clinic, Bluffton, Ind., 1950-51; resident in gen. surgery VA Hosp., Dayton, Ohio, 1953-55; gen. surgeon Tioga Gen. Hosp., Waverly, N.Y., 1956—, pres. med. staff, 1962-63, chief gen. surgery, 1963-78, pres. staff, 1976-77; pub. health officer Village of Waverly, Town of Barton, 1975—; trustee Village of Waverly, 1960-62. Served as capt. USAF, 1951-53. Diplomate Am. Bd. Surgery, Internat. Bd. Proctology. Fellow Royal Soc. Health, Royal Soc. Medicine, Am., Internat. colls. surgeons, Am. Coll. Angiology, Am. Soc. Colon and Rectal Surgeons; mem. Am. Med. Soc. Vienna, AMA, N.Y. State, Tioga County med. socs., Assn. Ry. Surgeons, Assn. Mil. Surgeons, Pan Am. Med. Assn., N.Y. State Soc. Surgeons, Ret. Officers Assn., Assn. U.S. Army, Mil. Order World Wars, Norwegian-Am. Hist. Assn., Nu Sigma Nu, Delta Kappa Epsilon. Clubs: Masons, Shriners, Elks, Moose, Am. Legion, K.T. Home and Office: 12-14 Frederick St Waverly NY 14892

GILLIS, LAURENCE JOSEPH, lawyer, former state legislator N.H.; b. Revere, Mass., June 18, 1942; s. Colin Alphonsus William and Dorothy Mary Louise (Kelley) G.; A.B., Harvard U., 1964; LL.B., Boston U., 1971; m. Margaretta Thompson Archbald, Oct. 29, 1971; children—Margaretta Kelley, Sarah Archbald, Carolyn Mercier. Mem. Hampton (N.H.) Police Dept., 1968-69; admitted to Mass. bar, 1971, N.H. bar, 1972; asso. firm Avery, Dooley, Post & Avery, Boston, 1971-72; partner firm Junkins & Gillis, Hampton, 1972—; pros. atty. Seabrook Municipal Ct., 1973; instr. criminal law U. N.H., 1973-74, 78; mem. N.H. Ho. of Reps., 1975-76, chmn. House Appropriations subcom. on Adminstrn. Justice and Pub. Safety; instr. on criminal code N.H. State Police Acad., 1978; instr. law of arrest, search and seizure St. Anselm's Coll., 1978, 79. Mem. N.H. Democratic State Com., 1974-76; mem. Exec. Com. Rockingham County Conv., 1975-76; mem. com. Conf. on Operating Budget of N.H., 1975; moderator Hampton Sch. Dist., 1977; Dem. nominee for Rockingham County atty., 1976, for state rep. from Exeter, 1978; alt. mem. Exeter Planning Bd.; bd. dirs. Rockingham County Human Services Coordinating Council. Served to capt. M.P., U.S. Army, 1964-67. Mem. Rockingham County Bar Assn., Am. Legion. Democrat. Roman Catholic. Clubs: Harvard of Boston. Home: Route 3 Linden St Exeter NH 03833 Office: 445 Lafayette Rd Hampton NH 03842

GILLIS, RICHARD JAMES, automobile rental and leasing co. exec.; b. Phila., Apr. 5, 1939; s. William Vincent and Cecelia Rita (Moscicki) G.; B.Mech. Engring., Villanova U., 1962; M.B.A., U. Del., 1964; m. Rhonda Cox, Apr. 3, 1977; 1 child. Program mgr. Thiokol Corp., Elkton, Md., 1962-64; research mktg. mgr., Washington, 1964-69; mktg. cons. R.J. Gillis & Assos., Washington, 1969-72; pres. Corporate Fleet Mgmt., Inc., Arlington, Va., 1972—; co. dir. Mem. Car and Truck Renting and Leasing Assn. (bd. dirs. 1976—). Democrat. Roman Catholic. Clubs: Internat. Town and Country, Capital Yacht. Author: External Combustion Engines, 1969; Weather Modification: Problems and Prospects, 1970. Home: 1800 Old Meadow Rd McLean VA 22214 Office: 2600 Jefferson Davis Hwy Arlington VA 22202

GILLOOLY, ROBERT JOSEPH, lawyer; b. Bklyn., Oct. 16, 1932; s. Dennis A. and Loretta V. (Bowen) G.; A.B. cum honore, Trinity Coll., Hartford, 1954; J.D., Yale, 1957; m. Marie Clancy, July 13, 1957; children—Claire, Dennis, Sheila, Ellen, Elisabeth. Admitted to Conn. bar, 1957; asso. firm OKeefe, Johnson & O'Keefe, New Haven, 1957-61; mem. firm O'Keefe, Gillooly & Votto, New Haven, 1961-64, Gillooly, Eastman & McGrail, New Haven, 1964-74, Gillooly & McGrail, New Haven, 1974—; panelist Conn. Trial Lawyers, 1974-75. Bd. dirs. Leukemia Soc. Am., New Haven, 1967; trustee Trinity Coll., 1965, pres. New Haven chpt., 1969-73; v.p. Econ. Devel. Commn., New Haven, 1971; mem. Republican Town Com., New Haven, 1973. Served with U.S. Army, 1957-60. Mem. Am., Conn. bar assns., Fedn. Ins. Counsel, Internat. Assn. Ins. Trial Attys., Phi Beta Kappa, Pi Gamma Mu. Roman Catholic. Clubs: Mory's Assn., New Haven Country, Quinnipiak, High Lane Tennis, New Haven Grays, Knights of St. Patrick, Wilsonian, Sigma Nu. Co-author libretto musical Giants in the Earth, 1951. Home: 16 Crestview Dr North Haven CT 06473

GILMAN, BENJAMIN ARTHUR, congressman; b. Poughkeepsie, N.Y., Dec. 6, 1922; s. Harry and Esther (Gold) G.; B.S., U. Pa., 1946; LL.B., N.Y. Law Sch., 1950; m. Jane Prizant, Oct. 19, 1952; children—Jonathan, Harrison, Susan, David, Ellen (dec.). Admitted to N.Y. bar, 1952; dep. asst. atty. gen. N.Y. Dept. Law, 1952-54, asst. atty. gen., 1954-55; partner firm Gilman & Gilman, Middletown, N.Y., 1955-72; atty. N.Y. Assembly's Com. on Local Finance, 1956-64; N.Y. Assemblyman 95th Dist., 1967-72; mem. 93d-95th Congresses from 26th Dist. N.Y.; mem. internat. relations, post office and civil service coms., select com. on missing in action, select com. on narcotics; congl. rep. UN Law of Sea Conf., 1975-76, IMF Conf., 1975, 76, 77; del. U.S.-Mexican Interparliamentary Conf.; mem. Presdl. Commn. on World Hunger. Mem. adv. com. N.Y. State Div. Youth's Start Center, 1962-67; mem. N.Y. State Southeastern Water Study Com., 1971-73, Lawyer's Com. for Civil Rights Under Law, 1963-75. Vice pres., bd. dirs. Orange County Health Assn.; bd. visitors U.S. Mil. Acad., 1973—; chmn. bd. dirs. Middletown Little League; bd. dirs. Goldenarea Hosp. Fund. Served with USAAF, 1943-45. Decorated D.F.C., Air medal. Mem. VFW (past county comdr.), Am. Legion, Masonic War Vets (lt. comdr.), Jewish War Vets, Air Force Assn., Internat. Narcotics Enforcement Officers Assn., Middletown, Orange County, N.Y. State, Am. bar assns., Assn. Bar City N.Y., N.Y., Am. trial lawyers assns., Grange. Republican. Jewish. Clubs: Masons, Shriners, Elks, Capitol Hill Shrine (pres.). Home: PO Box 358 Middletown NY 10940 Office: US House of Reps 1226 Longworth House Office Bldg Washington DC 20515

GILMAN, COOPER LEE, mfg. co. exec.; b. Tientsin, China, Oct. 3, 1928; s. Frank Shepard and Clare (Cooper) G.; (father Am. citizen); B.S., U.S. Naval Acad., 1951; m. Judith Mathews Partelow, July 29, 1961; children—Scott, Bradley. Indsl. engr. Am. Viscose Corp., Front Royal, Va., 1955-56; financial, engring., mfg. staff and mgmt. positions Gen. Electric Co., Lynn, Mass., 1956-66; asst. controller ITT Semiconductors, West Palm Beach, Fla., 1966-67, controller ITT Gen. Controls, Glendale, Calif., 1967-70, v.p. finance ITT Aetna, St. Louis, 1970-71, corporate mgr. fin. controls ITT, N.Y.C., 1971-72; v.p., controller Reed Tool Co., Houston, 1972-74; v.p. fin. DeLaval Separator Co., Poughkeepsie, N.Y., 1974-78, also dir.; v.p. fin. Am. Biltrite Inc., Cambridge, Mass., 1978—. Served to capt. USMC, 1951-55. Decorated D.F.C., Bronze Star, Air medal (8), Purple Heart. Mem. Am. Mgmt. Assn. Republican. Episcopalian. Home: 8 Highland Circle Wayland MA 01778 Office: 575 Technology Sq Cambridge MA 02139

GILMORE, CHARLES ARTHUR, ednl. adminstr.; b. Columbia, S.C., Sept. 23, 1919; s. Arthur William and Rosa Amelia (Scott) G.; B.S., Temple U., 1949; M.A., U. Pa., 1960; m. Josephine Specter, Oct. 14, 1970; children—Charles, Michael, Martha, James. Adminstrv. officer City of Phila., 1957-62; asst. dir. manpower N.Y. State Dept. Labor, Albany, 1963-64; manpower specialist U.S. Dept. Labor, Washington, 1964-67; dean Community Coll. Phila., 1967-72; higher edn. asso. Pa. Dept. Edn., Harrisburg, 1972—; higher edn. cons., manpower devel. specialist. Chmn. edn. com. Phila. Urban Coalition, 1968-71. Served with AUS, 1941-46, 51-54. Mem. Am. Soc. Tng. and Devel., Am. Acad. Polit. and Social Sci., Am. Soc. Pub. Adminstrn., Acad. Polit. Sci., Nat. Council Community Services for Community/Jr. Colls., Pa. Inst. Law and Justice (dir. 1969-72), Center for Study of Presidency, Wharton Grad. Sch. Alumni (exec. bd.). Office: PO Box 911 Harrisburg PA 17126

GILMORE, DAVID JOHN, internist; b. Newton, Kans., June 8, 1914; s. Alexander and Esther LeVan (Bunstein) G.; B.A. summa cum laude, Washington and Lee U., 1936; M.D., U. Pa., 1940; m. Virginia Worrell Layman, Jan. 1, 1942; children—Alexander David, Bruce Allen, Alfred Curtis, Intern, Abington (Pa.) Meml. Hosp., 1940-42; resident Henry Ford Hosp., Detroit, 1942-44, resident in cardiology, 1944-45, fellow in cardiology, 1945-46; practice medicine, specializing in internal medicine, Salisbury, Md., 1946—; staff dept. medicine Peninsula Gen. Hosp., Salisbury, 1946—; dir. Internal Medicine Assocs., Inc., Salisbury; cons. cardiology Md. Health Dept., 1950—; med. cons. Geriatric Evaluation Service, Wicomico County, Md., 1975—; cons. in cardiology Deers Head Hosp. Center, Salisbury, 1973—. Diplomate Am. Bd. Internal Medicine. Mem. Wicomico County Med. Soc., Med. and Chirurg. Faculty Md., A.C.P. Republican. Presbyterian. Contbr. articles in field to med. jours. Home: 1018 Camden Ave Salisbury MD 21801 Office: 239 Florida Ave Salisbury MD 21801

GILMORE, JOHN C., broadcasting exec.; b. Chgo., Apr. 11, 1917; s. Augustine and Florence (Harris) G.; student pub. schs., N.Y.C.; m. Bess Peterson, Jan. 15, 1949; children—John C., Douglas George, Keith Peter. Stage/radio/TV/film actor, N.Y.C., 1934-42; sales mgr. Sta. WICC, Bridgeport, Conn., 1944-46; owner, mgr. New Eng. Advt., New Eng. Sch. Radio Broadcasting, Bridgeport, 1945-50; various radio sta. mgmt. positions in Albany, N.Y., Oak Ridge, Johnston, Pa., Boston, Norfolk, Va.; pres. Com. Club Awards, Inc., Westport, Conn., 1954—; owner, mgr. TELSTAR, Inc., Westport, 1961—. Chmn. Westport Recall Com. Served in U.S. Army, 1942-44, also with N.Y. N.G. Named Mr. Clubwoman, Md. Fedn. Women's Clubs, 1961. Republican. Roman Catholic. Home: 11 Harding Ln Westport CT 06880 Office: PO Box 151 Westport CT 06880

GILMORE, JUDITH MARIE, physician; b. Houston, Dec. 28, 1942; d. Howard Ray and Mary Gardner (Currier) G.; A.B., U. Maine, 1965; postgrad. Sch. Arts and Sci., N.Y. U., 1966-68; M.D., Med. Coll. Pa., 1972; m. Richard Kelley, June, 1974; 1 dau., Lisa. Med. intern St. Vincent's Hosp., N.Y.C., 1972-73, med. resident, 1973-74; metabolism fellow St. Raphael's Hosp., New Haven, 1974-75; endocrine fellow W. Haven VA Hosp.,-Yale, New Haven, 1975-76; attending physician, instr. St. Vincent's Hosp., Bridgeport, Conn., 1976—; practice medicine specializing in internal medicine, Bridgeport, 1976—. Diplomate Am. Bd. Internal Medicine. Mem. Conn. Endocrine Soc., Bridgeport Diabetes Assn., Fairfield County Med. Soc. Office: 2660 Main St Bridgeport CT 06608

GILMOUR, EDWARD ELLIS, psychiatrist; b. Schenectady, N.Y., May 6, 1930; s. William Ellis and Adeline (Campbell) G.; B.Engring., Yale, 1952, M.A. in Philosophy, 1957; M.D., Boston U., 1961. Intern St. Luke's Hosp., N.Y.C., 1961-62, resident in medicine, 1962-64, resident in psychiatry, 1964-66, child psychiatry, 1966-68, asst. attending, child psychiatry, 1968—, cons. community psychiatry, 1973-75, supr. residents, 1968—; individual practice medicine, specializing in adult, child and adolescent psychiatry and psychoanalysis, N.Y.C., 1968—; psychoanalytic tng. William Alanson White Inst., N.Y.C., 1969-74; attending psychiatrist Columbia U. Health Service, N.Y.C., 1969-74; staff psychiatrist Ittleson Center Child Research, Riverdale, N.Y., 1976—. Diplomate Am. Bd. Psychiatry and Neurology. Fellow Am. Acad. Psychoanalysis; mem. Am. Psychiat. Assn., Am. Acad. Child Psychiatry, AMA, N.Y. County, N.Y. State med. socs., William Alanson White Psychoanalytic Soc., N.Y. Council Child Psychiatry, Soc. Adolescent Psychiatry. Clubs: Bugatti Owners, Am. Bugatti. Home and office: 145 E 74th St New York City NY 10021

GILPATRIC, MADELIN THAYER (MRS. THAYER GILPATRIC), civic worker; b. Boston; d. Albert Wilson and Gertrude (Benjamin) Thayer; student Syracuse U., Mass. Sch. Art; m. Arthur H. Kudner, July 1934 (dec. Feb. 1944); children—Arthur H., Karyl; m. 2d, Roswell L. Gilpatric, Sept. 18, 1958 (div.). Dir. Atlantic Monthly, Boston, 1944—. Bd. dirs. Soc. Meml. Hosp. for Cancer and Allied Diseases, Am. Acad. Dramatic Arts, Med. Coll. Pa.; trustee Calif. Inst. Arts; chmn., N.Y. State, Friends of Kennedy Center, Washington; pres. 62d St. Assn., N.Y.C. Club: Seignory (Can.). Home: 124 E 62d St New York City NY 10021 also Talisman Farm Grasonville MD 21638

GINADER, GEORGE HALL, business exec.; b. Buffalo, Apr. 5, 1933; s. George Edward and Meredith (Hall) G.; B.A., Allegheny Coll., 1955; M.S.S., Drexel U., 1964. Asst. buyer Lord & Taylor, N.Y.C., 1957-59; job analyst Ins. Co. N.Am., Phila., 1959-60; asst. buyer John Wanamaker, Phila., 1960-61; acting curator Thomas McKean Automobile Reference Collection, Free Library Phila., 1961-63; librarian N.Y. C. of C., N.Y.C., 1964-66; chief librarian N.Y. Stock Exchange, N.Y.C., 1966-67; exec. dir. Spl. Libraries Assn., N.Y.C., 1967-70; dir. research library Morgan Stanley & Co. Inc., N.Y.C., 1970—. Mem. Assn. Records Mgrs. and Adminstrs. (treas.

N.Y. chpt. 1975-76), Nat. Trust Historic Preservation, Spl. Libraries Assn. (chmn. bus. and fin. div. 1974-75), Nat. Micrographics Assn., Internat. Platform Assn., N.Y. Geneal. and Biog. Soc., Adminstrv. Mgmt. Soc., SAR, Phi Delta Theta (asst. sect. 1967-68, pres. N.Y. Alumni Club 1970—). Republican. Episcopalian. Home: 45 S Main St Cranbury NJ 08512 Office: 1251 Ave of the Americas New York City NY 10020

GINSBERG, ALLAN ROY, telephone co. exec.; b. Bklyn., Aug. 2, 1940; s. Morris Karl and Anne (Selden) G.; B.E.E., Rensselaer Poly. Inst., 1962; postgrad. Cornell U., 1964-67, Wharton Sch., U. Pa., 1968. With N.Y. Telephone Co., N.Y.C., 1962-78, supervising forecaster, 1968-73, mgr. corp. forecasting staff, 1973-78; supr. forecast planning AT&T, Basking Ridge, N.J., 1978—; dir. Different Drum Prodns., 1977—; partner The Theatre Place, dinner theatre, Pleasantville, N.Y., 1977—. Vice pres., dir. N.Y. State Theatre Assn., 1969—; treas., dir. Queens Council Arts, 1969-74, Queens Community Theatre, 1968—; mem. N.Y. Cultural Council Theatre, 1971-74; fin. dir. Village Mall Condominium, 1974-78; chmn. bd. dirs. Hudson Valley Arts Center, 1976—. Served to maj. USAR. Mem. Ops. Research Soc. Am., Am. Statis. Assn., IEEE, U.S. Inst. Theatre Tech., Alpha Psi Omega, Rho Tau Sigma. Home: 315 Eastview Overlook Village Wharton NJ 07885 Office: 295 N Maple Ave Room 3132B1 Basking Ridge NJ 07920

GINSBERG, ALLEN, poet; b. Newark, June 3, 1926; s. Louis and Naomi (Levy) G.; A.B., Columbia, 1948; m. Peter Orlovsky, Dec. 25, 1954. With various cargo ships, 1945-56; asso. with early Beat Generation prose-poets, 1945—; poetry readings Columbia, Harvard, Yale, numerous other univs. and assembly halls in Chile, Peru, Eng., India, Havana, Prague, Moscow, Warsaw, London, also Corcoran Art Gallery, Washington, 1971; addressed conf. Group Advancement Psychiatry, 1961; collaborated with Timothy Leary anti-war new consciousness activism, 1961—; actor motion picture Pull My Daisy, 1961, Guns of the Trees, 1962. Wholly Communion, 1965, Chappaqua, 1966; dir. Com. on Poetry Found., 1971—; co-dir. Jack Kerouac Sch. Disembodied Poetics, Naropa Inst., Boulder, Colo.; narrated TV film Kaddish, 1977. Guggenheim fellow in poetry, 1965-66. Mem. Am. Inst. Arts and Letters. Buddhist. Author: Howl and Other Poems, 1955; Empty Mirror, 1960; Kaddish and Other Poems, 1960; Reality Sandwiches, 1963; Planet News, poems 1961-1967, 1968; Indian Journals, 1970; The Fall of America: Poems of these States (Nat. Book award 1974), 1973; The Gates of Wrath: Early Rhymed Poems 1948-51, 1973; Allen Verbatim, 1974; First Blues, 1975; Journals Early 50's Early 60's, 1977; Mind Breaths, Poems 1972-1977, 1978; Correspondence A.G. & Neal Cassady 1948-68, 1978; Poems All Over the Place, 1978; Mostly Sitting Haiku, 1978; various vols. pub. in numerous langs. Recorded Songs of Innocence and of Experience by William Blake Tuned by Allen Ginsberg, 1970; composer: Plutonium One, 1978. Address: care Naropa Inst 1111 Pearl St Boulder CO 80302

GINSBERG, STEPHEN PAUL, ophthalmologist; b. Columbus, Ohio, Jan. 15, 1941; s. Isadore and Bertha (Mitnick) G.; A.B., U. Calif., Los Angeles, 1962; M.D., U. Calif., San Francisco, 1966; m. Ruth Golden, June 25, 1967; children—Laura Tracy, Karen Melissa. Intern, Los Angeles County Hosp., 1966-67; resident in ophthalmology U. Calif., San Francisco, 1967-70; Heed Ophthalmic Corneal fellow U. Fla., 1970-71; practice medicine specializing in ophthalmology Washington, 1973-74, Silver Spring, Md., 1974—; physicians adv. bd. Shady Grove Adventist Hosp., Gaithersburg, Md., 1978—; med. adv. bd. Lions Eye Bank, Washington, 1978—; attending physician Washington Hosp. Center, 1973—, Washington Adventist Hosp., 1974—; mem. courtesy staff Holy Cross Hosp. of Silver Spring (Md.); bd. dirs. Washington Ear, Inc.; cons. to DeWitt Hosp., St. Elizabeth's Hosp.; asst. clin. prof. George Washington U., 1971—. Served to maj. U.S. Army, 1971-73. Diplomate Am. Bd. Ophthalmology. Fellow A.C.S.; mem. Med. Soc. D.C., Montgomery County Med. Soc., Assn. Research and Vision in Ophthalmology, Am. Intra-Ocular Implant Soc., Jacoby Med. Soc., Contact Lens Assn. Am., Frederick Cordes Eye Soc., U. Fla. Alumni Soc. Republican. Jewish. Contbr. articles to profl. jours.; contbr. chpts. to texts on ophthalmology. Home: 11901 Winterset Terr Potomac MD 20854 Office: 9801 Georgia Ave Silver Spring MD 20902

GINSBERG-FELLNER, FREDDA VITA, pediatric endocrinologist; b. N.Y.C., Apr. 21, 1937; d. Nathaniel and Bertha S. (Jagendorf) Ginsberg; A.B., Cornell U., 1957; M.D., N.Y. U., 1961; m. Michael J. Fellner, Aug. 27, 1961; children—Jonathan R., Melinda B. Intern, Bronx Municipal Hosp. Center, 1961-62; resident Albert Einstein Coll. Medicine, N.Y.C., 1962-67; asst. prof. pediatrics Mt. Sinai Sch. Medicine, N.Y.C., 1969-75; asso. attending pediatrician Mt. Sinai Hosp., N.Y.C., 1974—; asso. prof. pediatrics Mt. Sinai Sch. Medicine, N.Y.C., 1975—, dir. div. pediatric endocrinology and metabolism, 1977—; research collaborator Brookhaven Nat. Labs., Upton, N.Y., 1969-75; chmn. Camp NYDA for diabetic children, 1977—. Recipient Solomon Silver award in clin. medicine Mt. Sinai Sch. Medicine, 1969. Diplomate Am. Bd. Pediatrics. Mem. Am. Fedn. Clin. Research, Lawson Wilkins Pediatric Endocrine Soc., Am. Acad. Pediatrics, Ambulatory Pediatric Assn., Am., N.Y. (research grants 1972, 74, mem. exec. bd. 1974—) diabetes assns. Club: Cornell (N.Y.C.). Home: 50 E 89th St New York City NY 10028 Office: 11 E 100th St New York City NY 10029

GINSBURG, GERALD JOSEPH, lawyer; b. Poughkeepsie, N.Y., Aug. 29, 1930; s. Abraham and Anna (Murkoff) G.; B.S., Syracuse U., 1952; J.D., Bklyn. Law Sch., 1958; m. Vera Evelyn Curtis, Feb. 2, 1963; children—Jason Andrew, Stephanie Carla. Admitted to N.Y. State bar, 1959; jr. accountant Homes & Davis, N.Y.C., 1954-55; semi-sr. accountant Brach, Gosswein & Lane, C.P.A.'s, N.Y.C., 1955-56; sr. accountant Rubman & Rubman, C.P.A.'s, 1956-59; asst. controller Sheffield Watch Corp., N.Y.C., 1959-60, controller, 1960-63, v.p. finance and operations, 1963-67, v.p. finance and operations, dir., 1967-70; practice law in N.Y.C., 1970—. Served with USNR, 1952-53. Mem. Am. Mgmt. Assn., Am., N.Y. bar assns. Home: 31 Speir Dr South Orange NJ 07079

GINSBURG, MARTIN DAVID, lawyer; b. N.Y.C., June 10, 1932; s. Morris and Evelyn (Bayer) G.; A.B., Cornell U., 1953; J.D. magna cum laude, Harvard U., 1958; m. Ruth Bader, June 23, 1954; children—Jane, James. Admitted to N.Y. bar, 1959, since practiced in N.Y.C.; asso. firm Weil, Gotshal & Manges, 1958-62, partner, 1963—; adj. prof. law N.Y. U., 1967—; lectr. Columbia Law Sch., 1976; vis. prof. law Stanford U., 1978; lectr. various tax insts.; mem. adv. group to commr. IRS, 1978-79; mem. adv. bd. U. Calif. Securities Regulation Inst., 1974—. Served to 1st lt. arty. AUS, 1954-56. Mem. Am. (sect. taxation, com. on corp. stockholder relationships, spl. com. tax simplification, vice chmn. 1978), N.Y. State (exec. com. tax sect. 1969—, chmn. tax sect. 1975, ho. dels. 1976) bar assns., Assn. Bar City N.Y. (chmn. com. taxation 1977-80), Am. Law Inst. (cons. fed. income tax project 1974—). Mem. bd. editors Jour. Corporate Taxation, 1974—; contbr., editor articles to legal jours. Home: 150 E 69th St New York City NY 10021 Office: 767 Fifth Ave New York City NY 10022

GINTELL, HOWARD ALAN, wine and spirits mktg. exec.; b. Bklyn., May 24, 1945; s. William and Lillian Lola (Krieger) G.; B.A. (N.Y. State Regents scholar incentive award, N.Y. State Regents scholar), State U. N.Y., 1972. Market research analyst The Seagram Co., N.Y.C., 1971-72, div. adminstr. Summit Mktg. Co. div., Cleve., 1972-73, div. mktg. mgr. Browne Vintners Co. wine div. of Seagrams, Chgo., 1973; dir. mktg. Internat. Knights Wine, Inc., Parsippany, N.J., 1973-75, L'Aiglon Wine & Spirits Import Co. div. The Am. Distilling Co., N.Y.C., 1975-78; sr. brand mgr. Fleischmann Distilling Co. div. Julius Wile Sons, Inc., New Hyde Park, N.Y., 1978—. Served with M.I., U.S. Army, 1965-68. Decorated Purple Heart. Mem. Am. Mktg. Assn. Home: 145 Hicks St Brooklyn Heights NY 11201 Office: 3003 New Hyde Park Rd New Hyde Park NY 11040

GINTHER, RUTH MARGARET, mus. exec.; b. Niagara Falls, N.Y., July 31, 1903; d. Charles Joseph and Jennie (Engel) McCarthy; student Niagara U., 1944-45, U. Buffalo, 1952-56, 58; m. Joseph G. Ginther, Dec. 13, 1922 (annulled); 1 dau., Jeane M. Ginther Hauth. Dir. specifications div. Carbon Products div. Union Carbide Corp., Niagara Falls, 1924-69; curator costumes Niagara County (N.Y.) Hist. Mus., 1969—; social service worker Health Assn. Niagara County; resource person women's div. N.Y. State Dept. Commerce. Lectr. antique costumes. Mem. Niagara Falls City Commn., 1959—, chmn., 1963; pres. Niagara Council Women's Assns., 1961; sec. Operation Petticoat Progress, 1966; mem. Niagara Falls Meml. Hosp. Aux.; mem. corporate body Niagara Falls Meml. Med. Center, now bd. dirs. Sec. bd. dirs. Niagara Falls ARC, Niagara Falls Philharmonic Orch.; bd. control Niagara Falls festivals; mem. Keep Niagara Beautiful Commn.; treas. bd. Odd Fellow and Rebekah Home Assn., Lockport, N.Y., also treas. nursing home. Mem. Republican Women's Forum. Recipient VIM citation N.Y. State Bus. and Profl. Women's Club, 1964; Key to Lockport Falls (N.Y.); Seal of Niagara Falls; Top Hat award radio sta. WHLD, 1977; named Outstanding Woman Community, 1970. Mem. Niagara Falls Philharmonic Guild (pres.), Niagara Falls (dir.), Niagara County (chmn. women's div. 1966) hist. socs., NCCJ (dir.), Bus. and Profl. Women's Club (pres. chpt. 1946; sec. N.Y. State fedn. 1948-50, distinguished service award), Niagara Area C. of C., Am. Bus. Women's Assn., Profl. Women Writers, Beta Sigma Psi. Presbyn. (pub. relations worker). Mem. Rebekah (dist. dep. pres. Western NY.). Clubs: Quota (pres. 1956, dist. lt. gov. 1964, gov. N.Y. State), Niagara Falls Garden (pres. 1943), Niagara Frontier Country, Social Study (pres.). Home: 1135 Garrett Ave Niagara Falls NY 14305 Office: 3625 Highland Ave Niagara Falls NY 14305

GIOFFRE, JOSEPH DOMINIC, savs. and loan exec.; b. Port Chester, N.Y., June 18, 1943; s. Joseph B. and Rose Gioffre; student U. Vt., 1961-63; diploma Inst. Fin. Edn., 1970; m. Kathryn R. Woodward, Oct. 10, 1964; children—Joseph, Kimberly. Supr. accounting dept. Westcheter Fed. Savs. & Loan, New Rochelle, 1967-69; treas. Greenwich Fed. Savs. & Loan (Conn.), 1969-74, v.p., controller, 1974-76, exec. v.p., 1976—, also dir. Mem. fin. com. ARC, Greenwich, 1977—; bd. dirs. Jr. Achievement, 1977—. Mem. Fin. Mgrs. Soc. (pres. 1973-74). Roman Catholic. Club: Kiwanis. Home: 302 Orchard St Greenwich CT 06830 Office: 28 Havemeyer Pl Greenwich CT 06830

GIOIA, ROBERT E(MANUELE), pediatrician; b. Palermo, Italy, Jan. 2, 1921; s. Agostino ans Provvidenza Maria (Pecoriano) G.; came to U.S., 1954, naturalized, 1958; M.D., U. Palmero (Italy), 1952; m. Maria Anita Guastella, June 22, 1953; children—Christopher Adrian, Richard Flavio. Intern, Wyckoff Heights Hosp., Bklyn., 1954-55, resident in pediatrics, 1955-56, 57-58; resident, Kingston Ave. Hosp. for Contagious Diseases, N.Y.C., 1955, U. Hosp. Bellvue Med. Center, N.Y.C., 1958; first house physician Wyckoff Heights Hosp., 1958-59, attending in pediatrics, 1973—; practice medicine, specializing in pediatrics, Bklyn., 1960—; pediatrics cons. Laguardia, Forest Hills, Queens, N.Y., 1974—. Diplomate Am. Bd. Pediatrics, Pan. Am. Med. Soc. Fellow Am. Acad. Peidatrics; mem. AMA, N.Y. State Med. Soc., Kings County Med. Soc. Home: 33-44 164 St Flushing NY 11358 Office: 139 Stanhope St Brooklyn NY 11237

GIOLITO, CAROLYN HUGHES, mem. senatorial staff; b. Birmingham, Ala., d. Cecil T. and Eunice (Brown) Hughes; B.S., Ala. Coll., 1955; postgrad. George Washington Sch. Law, 1956-58; m. Caesar A. Giolito, Apr. 18, 1959; children—Glenn, Antoinette. Spl. asst. to Sen. Kenneth Keating of N.Y., 1960-65; spl. asst. to Rep. Richard L. Ottinger of N.Y., 1965-66; asst. to Rep. Russell Tuten of Ga., 1966-67; aide to Rep. John Dellenback of Oreg., 1967-68; legis. aide rep. Richard White of Tex., 1968-71; asst. to Rep. G. Elliott Hagan of Ga., 1971-73; adminstrv. asst. Rep. John B. Breckinridge of Ky., 1973-77; staff asst. (projects officer) to Senator Robert C. Byrd, 1977—. Mem. Internat. Platform Assn., Adminstrv. Assts. Assn. U.S. Congress. Presbyterian. Home: 13912 Northgate Dr Silver Spring MD 20906 Office: 133 Russell Senate Office Bldg Washington DC 20510

GIORDANO, NICHOLAS ANTHONY, stock exchange exec.; b. Phila., Mar. 7, 1943; s. Nicola and Aida (Gioiso) G.; B.S., LaSalle Coll., 1965; m. Joanne M. Pizzuto, Oct. 21, 1967; children—Jeannine, Colette and Nicholas (triplets). Staff Price Waterhouse & Co., Phila., 1965-68; with various brokerage cos., Phila., 1968-71; controller stock exchange, stock clearing corp. PBW (later Phila.) Stock Exchange Inc., 1971-72, v.p. ops., 1972-75, sr. v.p., 1975-76, exec. v.p., 1976—; mem. bd. SECTOR; chmn. Intermarket Trading System Operating Com.; chmn. bd. Phila. Depository Trust Co. Mem. bus. adv. council LaSalle Coll., 1976--. Served with Pa. Air Nat. Guard, 1965-70. C.P.A. Mem. Pa., Am. insts. C.P.A.'s, Composite Tape Assn., Council Pres.'s Assos. LaSalle Coll. Club: Kiwanis. Home: 501 Kurt Dr Blue Bell PA 19422 Office: 17th St and Stock Exchange Pl Philadelphia PA 19103

GIORGI, LEWIS ASCENTIO, portrait photographer; b. Waterbury, Conn., Aug. 31, 1919; s. Joseph William and Filomena (Stabile) G.; ed. pub. schs.; m. Sylvia Rita Costantini, Feb. 18, 1950; children—Joseph, Filomena, Sandra, Christopher. Retoucher negatives Dolega Studio, Yonkers, N.Y., 1937-42; printer, photographer various studios, Mt. Vernon, N.Y., White Plains, N.Y., N.Y.C., Yonkers, 1945-47; freelance portrait photographer, owner, operator Giorgi Process Inc., Yonkers, 1947—; inventor photog. reproduction process Relief-o-Chrome; lectr. in field. Chmn. Yonkers Mayor's Adv. Com. Juvenile Crime Prevention, 1975—; mem. adv. bd. Fermi Scholarship Found., Yonkers. Served with Port Bn., 45th Div., U.S. Army, 1942-45. Winner 6 consecutive Court of Honors, N.Y. State Competition, 1970-75. Master's degree Profl. Photographers Am., 1975. Mem. Profl. Photographers Am. (winner Nat. Loan Collection), Profl. Photographers Soc. N.Y., Westchester Profl. Photographers Assn. Club: Italian City. Patentee in field. Home: 17 Normandy Rd Yonkers NY 10701 Office: 286 New Main St Yonkers NY 10701

GIOVACCHINI, ROBERT PETER, toxicologist, mfg. co. exec.; b. Fresno, Calif., June 2, 1928; s. Robert and Olga (Mencarini) G.; B.S., Creighton U., 1948, M.Sc., 1954; Ph.D., U. Nebr., 1958; certificate in bus. adminstrn. Harvard U., 1969; m. Gertrude Joan Stech, June 18, 1949; children—Mary Joan, Diane Marie, Karen Denise. Instr., U. Nebr. Sch. Medicine, Omaha, 1957-58; asso. dept. anesthesia Bishop Clarkson Meml. Hosp., Omaha, 1957-58; research histopathologist biol. dept. Gillette Co., Boston, 1958-60, supr. toxicological evaluations med. dept., 1960-62, asst. med. dir., 1962-64, v.p. corp. product integrity, 1974—; dir. med. evaluations Gillette Med. Research Inst., Washington, 1964-66, v.p., 1967-70, dir. med. evaluations dept., Rockville, Md., 1970-71, v.p., 1970-71; pres. Gillette Med. Evaluation Labs., Rockville, 1971-74; lectr. histopathology of skin Northwestern U. Sch. Medicine and Dentistry, Evanston, Ill., 1960-64. Recipient Gold medal for outstanding contbns. to art and sci. of cosmetics Soc. Cosmetic Chemists, 1976. Mem. Am. Acad. Clin. Toxicology, Am. Acad. Dermatology, Soc. Toxicology, N.Y. Acad. Scis., Va. Dermatol. Soc., Sigma Xi. Clubs: Harvard (Boston and Washington). Home: 2518 Fernwood Dr Vienna VA 22180 Office: 1413 Research Blvd Rockville MD 20850

GIOVANOPOULOS, PAUL ARTHUR, artist; b. Kastoria, Greece, Nov. 11, 1939; s. Arthur T. and Maria (Benjou) G.; came to U.S., 1954, naturalized, 1961; student (Univ. scholar) N.Y. U. Painting Workshop 1958, 59, Sch. Visual Arts N.Y.C., 1961. One-man shows: Larcada Gallery, N.Y.C., 1965, 67, 68; exhibited in group shows: Butler Inst., Youngstown, Ohio, ann. mus. purchase Joslyn Art Mus., Omaha, 1966, Am. drawing biennial Norfolk Mus., 1967, ann. exhbn. NAD, 1966, Phila. Acad. Arts, Corcoran Gallery, Washington, Phila. Mus.; represented in permanent collections: U. Minn., Balt. Mus., Sch. Visual Arts, N.Y. U., N.Y. Pub. Library, Playboy Mag.; tchr. Sch. Visual Arts, 1969, 70, Parsons Sch. Design, N.Y.C., 1970, 71, 72, 73, 74, 75, 76, 77, 78. Recipient Leonard Sansone Meml. award, 1963; awards Artists Guild Chgo., 1967, Soc. Illustrators, 1961; 7 awards Art Dirs. Club Miami, 1967. John Armstrong Chaloner Found. fellow, 1964-65. Illustrator: The Looking Down Game (Leigh Dean), 1968; How Many Miles to Babylon? (Paula Fox), 1967; The Real Tin Flower, 1968; Free as a Frog, 1969. Home: 119 Prince St New York City NY 10012

GIRALDI, ALMERIGO, structural engr.; b. Garwood, N.J., June 6, 1926; s. Antonio and Maria (Sambo) G.; B.C.E., George Washington U., 1955; M.S., U. Md., 1966; m. Lea S. Satti, July 4, 1948; children—Albert E., Eleanor K., Robert R. Structural design engr. Beall & Lemay, structural engrs., Washington, 1955-60, Scullen & Marchigiani, structural engrs., Bethesda, Md., 1960-64, chief structural engr. Daniel, Mann, Johnson & Mendenhall, architects and engrs., Washington, 1964-65; field engr. Paul Weidlinger, cons. engr., N.Y.C., 1965-67; chief engr. M.A. Gurewitz & Assos., Washington, 1967-70; partner Allison & Meyer, structural engrs., Rockville, Md., 1970-74; prin. Almerigo Giraldi, structural engr., Silver Spring, Md., 1974—. Served with C.E., AUS, 1946-49. Registered profl. engr., Md., Va., D.C. Mem. Am. Soc. C.E., Cons. Engrs. Council, Am. Concrete Inst., Constrn. Specifications Inst., Lido Civic Club, Sigma Tau, Theta Tau. Office: 13204 Locksley Ave Silver Spring MD 20904

GIRAUDIER, ANTONIO, artist; b. Havana, Cuba, Sept. 28, 1926; s. Antonio Giraudier y Ginebra and Dulce Maria Milagros y Zorrilla; B.Litt., Belén Jesuits, Havana, 1944, Vedado Inst., Havana, 1944; grad. U. Havana Law Sch., 1949; also pvt. student art. Came to U.S., 1960, naturalized, 1969. One-man exhbns. include Smolin Gallery, N.Y.C., 1965, New Masters Gallery, N.Y.C., 1967, Avanti Galleries, N.Y.C., 1968, 69, 71, 73, 75, Palm Beach (Fla.) Towers, 1969, U. Palm Beach, 1970, Marshall (Ill.) Pub. Library, 1975, Eastern Ill. U., 1975; two-man exhbns. include Welfleet Gallery, Cape Cod, Mass., 1967, Welfleet Gallery, Palm Beach, 1968, Avanti Galleries, 1972; numerous group exhbns., U.S. and Europe, 1964—, latest being Avanti Galleries, 1970-75, French Hosp. Art Show, 1970, Argosy Gallery, Miami, 1970, Am. Acad. Arts and Letters, N.Y.C., 1973; rep. permanent collections Fordham U. at Lincoln Center, N.Y.C. and Bronx, N.Y., U. Palm Beach, Greenville (S.C.) Mus. Art, Maryhill (Wash.) Mus. Fine Arts, Am. Poets Fellowship Soc., Ill., also numerous pvt. collections U.S. and Europe. Recipient Premier Prix de Printemps, Paris, 1959, hon. mention Praire Poet Collection, 1972, hon. mention Maj. Poets Contest, 1972; laureat Margerite d'Or, Paris, 1960, Danae Lit. designate, 1973; certificate of merit Am. Poets Fellowship Soc., 1973. Hon. mem. L'Orientation litteraire, Paris; mem. Smithsonian Instn., Nat. Trust Historic Preservation, Ill. State Poetry Soc. Author numerous books poetry, U.S., Cuba, Europe, Venezula, 1955—. Contbr. poetry to compilations, anthologies. Address: 215 E 68th St New York City NY 10021

GIRDLER, REYNOLDS, JR., art materials mfg. co. exec.; b. N.Y.C., Aug. 15, 1935; s. Reynolds and Barbara (Kitchel) G.; B.A., Yale, 1957; m. Jean Abernathy, Aug. 30, 1958; children—Amy, Faith, Reynolds. With Binney & Smith, Inc., N.Y.C., 1957—, v.p. corporate relations, 1976—, also dir.; dir. Can. Crayon Co., Ltd., Binney & Smith (Europe), Ltd. Rep., Greenwich (Conn.) Town Meeting, 1965-72, chmn. social services com., 1967-72; chmn. social services com. Greenwich Community Devel. Action Program, 1970. Mem. Nat. Sch. Supply and Equipment Assn. (dir.), Edn. Industries Assn. (pres. 1978, dir.). Clubs: Yale (N.Y.C.); Rocky Point (Old Greenwich, Conn.). Author: Crayon Techniques, 1967. Home: Binney Ln Old Greenwich CT 06870 Office: 201 E 42d st New York City NY 10017

GIROUX, ALBERT HENRY, JR., public relations exec.; b. Somerville, Mass., June 2, 1932; s. Albert Henry and Marie Teresa (LaTerza) G.; B.S., Boston Coll., 1954; M.A., Boston U., 1959; postgrad. Harvard Grad. Sch. Bus., summer 1973. Tchr., Wilmington (Mass.) Pub. Schs., 1957-58; tchr.-coach Belmont (Mass.) Pub. Schs., 1959-62; account exec. Reilley, Brown, Tapply & Carr, advt., Boston, also N.Y.C., 1962-64; mgr. pub. relations Wall St. Jour., also Dow Jones & Co., N.Y.C., 1964-68; dir. pub. information Cambridge (Mass.) Pub. Schs., 1968—. Served with AUS, 1954-56. Mem. Pub. Relations Soc. Am., Mass. Sch. Pub. Relations Assn., Mass., Cambridge tchrs. assns. Home: 23 Bay State Rd Belmont MA 02178 Office: 1700 Cambridge St Cambridge MA 02138

GIRVIN, GERALD THOMAS, librarian; b. Rochester, N.Y., Apr. 2, 1929; s. Stanley Frank and Marie Anne (Mulqueen) G.; student LeMoyne Coll., 1947-50; student St. Bernard's Sem., 1950-54; B.A., St. John Fisher Coll., 1956; M.S., State U. Coll. N.Y., 1960; postgrad. U. Rochester, 1960-62. Tchr. secondary English, Edison Tech. and Indsl. High Sch., Rochester, N.Y., 1956-57; librarian McQuaid Jesuit High Sch., Rochester, N.Y., 1957-68; media librarian Frederick Douglass Jr. High Sch., Rochester, 1968-69, Chestnut Ridge Sch., Churchville, N.Y., 1969-71; media specialist Churchville-Chili Jr. High Sch., Churchville, 1971-73, Churchville-Chili Sch. Dist., Churchville, 1973—; asso. editor Besancourt Pubs., Brockville, Ont., Can. Mem. Nat. Com. for Heritage of the March. Mem. Am. N.Y. library assns., N.E.A., N.Y. Edn. Assn., Great Lakes Hist. Soc., Great Lakes Maritime Inst., Steamship Hist. Soc. Am., Toronto Marine Hist. Soc., Detroit Marine Hist. Soc. Home: 108 Delmar St Rochester NY 14606 Office: 139 Fairbanks Rd Churchville NY 14428

GISOLFI, ANTHONY M., educator; b. San Felice a Cancello, Italy, Nov. 13, 1909; s. Ernest E. and Vincenza (Prisco) G.; came to U.S., 1910, naturalized, 1924; A.B., Coll. City N.Y., 1930; M.A., Columbia, 1931, Ph.D., 1959; m. Eleanor Hayes, June 29, 1935; children—Miriam Gisolfi D'Aponte, Diana Gisolfi Pechukas, Peter, Laura. Tchr. Spanish and Italian, High Sch. of Music and Art, N.Y.C., 1937-64; asso. prof. Hispanic and Italian, State U.N.Y., Albany, 1964-76, emeritus 1976—; regional specialist overseas br. Office of War Info., Eng. and Mediterranean, 1944-45; lectr. Italian, Sch. Gen.

Studies, City Coll. N.Y., 1947-63, Columbia, summers 1933, 58, 60-63. Mem. Am. Assn. Tchrs. Italian (v.p. 1959-60), Modern Lang. Assn., Dante Soc. Am. Author: On Classic Ground, 1962; The Essential Matilde Serao, 1968; (with C. Coleman) Classical Italian Songs, 1955. Contbr. to Columbia University Dictionary of Modern European Literature, 1947, also 2d edit.; also contbr. articles to profl. jours. Home and office: PO Box 225 Bronxville NY 10708

GIST, LAWSON, JR., mfg. co. exec.; b. Inkster, Mich., Aug. 29, 1947; s. Lawson and Viola R. G.; M.B.A., U. Detroit, 1975; m. Valeria G. Price, July 4, 1976. With Ford Motor Co., Dearborn, Mich., 1971-74, purchasing coordinator, 1973-74; prodn. planning and control analyst Rockwell Internat., Troy, Mich., 1974-75, systems and procedures analyst, 1975, tng. specialist, 1975-77, materials advisor, 1977; corp. mgr. materials systems Fram Corp., Providence, 1977—. Cert. practitioner Am. Prodn. and Inventory Control Soc. Home: 33 Bishop Rd Sharon MA 02067 Office: 105 Pawtucket Ave Providence RI 02916

GITLIN, PAUL, lawyer; b. Bklyn., June 17, 1915; s. Solomon H. and Jennie (Saffer) G.; B.A., N.Y. U., 1935; J.D., Harvard U., 1938; m. Zelda Kaplan, Jan. 5, 1947; 1 son, Jonathan Steven. Admitted to N.Y. bar, 1938; pvt. practice, N.Y.C., 1938-41; partner firm Ernst, Cane, Berner & Gitlin, N.Y.C., 1948—; lectr. Practising Law Inst. Mem. fin. com. Girls Club Am. Mem. Copyright Soc. U.S. (past pres., hon. trustee). Club: Players and Lambs. Co-author: Copyrights, 1965; Tax Aspects of Patents, Copyrights and Trademarks, 1966. Home: 180 East End Ave New York City NY 10028 Office: 7 W 51st St New York City NY 10019

GITMAN, PAUL ALLAN, physician; b. Bklyn., Dec. 30, 1940; s. Leo and Rose (Bluttal) G.; B.A., Columbia Coll., 1962; M.D., Boston U., 1966; m. Gail Donna Yaeger, June 8, 1963; children—Robin Jane, Linda Beth, Michael David. Intern, Univ. Hosp. Boston, 1966-67, resident internal medicine, 1967-68; resident, internal medicine L.I. Jewish Hosp., N.Y.C., 1968-70, chief med. resident, 1969-70; staff L.I. Jewish-Hillside Med. Center, N.Y.C., 1970—; asst. prof. clin. medicine State U. N.Y. at Stony Brook, 1973—; individual practice medicine, specializing in internal medicine, Hollis, N.Y., 1972—. Served with USAF, 1970-72. Diplomate Am. Bd. Internal Medicine. Fellow A.C.P.; mem. AMA, Soc. Internal Medicine, N.Y. State, Queens County med. socs. Jewish. Club: UN Philatelists. Home: 167 Executive Dr Manhasset Hills NY 11040 Office: 195-04 Hillside Ave Hollis NY 11423

GITTELSON, BERNARD, pub. relations cons., author; b. N.Y.C., June 13, 1918; s. Sam and Gussie (Lefand) G.; B.A., St. Johns U., 1939; m. Rosalind Weinstein, Mar. 1, 1945; children—Louise Barbara, Steven Henry. Cons. on race relations N.Y. State War Council, 1939-41, N.Y. Com. on Industry and Labor Relations, 1941-42; dir. N.Y. State Legislative Com. on Discrimination, 1943-45; asso. coordinator Com. on Community Inter-relations, 1945-46; pres. Roy Bernard Co., Inc., 1946-65; chmn. Roy Bernard Co., Ltd. (London), 1955-65; pres. Biorhythm Computers Inc.; cons. to govts., corps., instns. Chmn. bd. Time Pattern Research Inst., 1965-75. Mem. Authors Guild, Am. Soc. Journalists and Authors. Author: Biorhythm A Personal Science, 1975; Biorhythm Sports Forecasting, 1977; Gittelson Biorhythm Code Book, 1978; pub. Biorhythm Newsletter; syndicated columnist Your Personal Biorhythm. Home: 96 Division Ave Summit NJ 07901 Office: 119 W 57th St New York City NY 10019

GITTLEMAN, ALLAN MORRIS, investment co. exec.; b. Providence, June 23, 1942; s. Sidney Allan and Dorothy Foster (Green) G.; B.S., Northeastern U., 1968; grad. Brown U., 1964; m. Ellen Kaplan, May 28, 1966; children—Danielle, Rachel. Vice pres. Michael Investment Co., Providence, 1966-68, pres., 1968—; v.p. F.L. Putnam & Co., Inc., Boston, 1973—; chmn. bd. Gen. Magnaplate Co., Linden, N.J., 1970-71; pres. Foster, Brown & Ballou, Inc., Providence, 1974—. Mem. exec. com. Nat. Jewish Hosp., Denver. Mem. Am. Numis. Assn., Newcomen Soc., Nat., Boston securities traders assns., Providence Soc. Fin. Analysts. Address: FL Putnam & Co Inc 1104 Turks Head Bldg Providence RI 02903

GITTLER, NORMAN, accountant; b. N.Y.C., Dec. 21, 1931; s. Edward and Dora G.; B.S., N.Y. U., 1953; m. Gilda R. Greenfield, June 14, 1953; children—Steven, Esther. Staff, Grossman & Feder, N.Y.C., 1955-65; pvt. practice as C.P.A., N.Y.C., 1965-72; controller Natek Corp., Hackensack, N.J., 1973-77, also dir.; corp. officer, dir. subsidiaries Amtab Data Co., Health Info. Services & Electronic Accounting Systems Co.; pvt. practice accounting and data processing cons., 1978—. Mem. county com. N.Y. State Liberal party, 1970—; Bd. dirs. Young Israel Kew Gardens Hills, Yeshiva Central Queens. Served with U.S. Army, 1953-55. Recipient Dedicators award Yeshiva High Sch. Queens, 1974. Mem. Am. Inst. C.P.A.'s, N.Y. State Soc. C.P.A.'s, Jewish War Vets. Home: 147-10 70th Rd Flushing NY 11367

GITTLIN, A. SAM, industrialist, banker; b. Newark, Nov. 21, 1913; s. Benjamin and Ethel (Bernstein) G.; B.C.S., Rutgers U., 1938; m. Fay Lerner, Sept. 18, 1938; children—Carol (Mrs. Alan H. Franklin), Regina (Mrs. Peter Gross), Bruce David, Steven Robert. Partner, Gittlin Cos. Inc. (formerly Gittlin Bag Co.), Newark and Charlotte, N.C., 1935-40, v.p., dir., 1954—, chmn., 1963—; v.p., dir. Abbey Record Mfg. Co., Newark, 1958-60; partner Benjamin Mission Co., Los Angeles, 1960-64; chmn. Barrington Industries, N.Y.C., 1963-72; vice chmn., dir., chmn. exec. com. Bishop Industries, Union, N.J., 1969-70; past pres., dir. Falmouth Supply, Ltd., Montreal, Que., Can., Ascher Trading Corp., Newark, Aptex, Inc., Newark; vice chmn. bd. Peninsula Savs. and Loan Assn., San Mateo and San Francisco, 1964-67, chmn., 1967-68; chmn. First Peninsula Cal. Corp., N.Y.C., 1964-68; chmn. Pines Shirt & Pajama Co., N.Y.C., 1960—, Pottsville Shirt & Pajama Co. (Pa), 1960—, Wall-co Imperial, Miami, 1965—, Levin & Hecht, Inc., N.Y.C., 1966-72, Wallco of San Juan (P.R.), Brunswick Shirt Co., N.Y.C., 1966-72, Fleetline Industries, Garland, N.C., 1966-72, All State Auto Leasing & Rental Corp., Beverly Hills, Calif., 1968-72, Packaging Ltd., Newark, 1970—, Kan. Plastics, Inc., Garden City, 1970—, Bob Cushman Distbrs., Inc., Phoenix, 1972—; chmn., treas. Packaging Products & Design Co. (now Wallco West Inc.), Newark and Glendale, Calif., 1959-72, chmn. exec. com., treas., 1972—; chmn. bd., treas. Bob Cushman Painting & Decorating Co. (now Wallco West), Phoenix, 1972—; pres. Covington Funding Co., N.Y.C., 1963—; treas., dir. Flex Pak Industries, Inc. (now PPD Inc.), Atlanta, 1973—, Ploy Plax Films, Inc., Santa Ana, Calif., 1973-76; sec., chmn. exec. com. Zins Wallcoverings, Newark; partner Benjamin Co., N.Y.C., Laurel Assos. (Md.); partner, investors cons. Mission Pack, Inc., Los Angeles; dir. Harris Paint & Wall Covering Super Marts, Miami, Morgan Hill Mfg. Co., Reading, Pa.; dir., financial cons. Ramada Inns, Phoenix, Realty Equities Corp. N.Y., N.Y.C., to 1974. Mem. com. to review dept. of banking and ins. N.J. Commn. on Efficiency and Economy in State Govt., 1967—. Chmn. N.C. Com. B'nai B'rith, 1940; treas. N.C. Fedn. B'nai B'rith Lodges, 1941-43, v.p., 1943-44, pres., 1944-47. Trustee BAMA Master Retirement program, Benjamin Gittlin Charity Found., Newark, Rutgers U. Hillel Found.; bd. visitors Franklin and Marshall U. Jewish religion (trustee, pres. temple). Club: Greenbrook Country (Caldwell, N.J.). Home: 59 Glenview Rd South Orange NJ 07079 Office: 10 E 53d St New York City NY 10022

GIUDICI, RAYMOND ANGELO, pharmacist, educator; b. Pitts., June 23, 1942; s. Raymond Ralph and Nellie (Barnes) G. B.S. in Pharmacy, Duquesne U., 1965, Pharm.D., 1969. Staff pharmacist South Side Hosp., Pitts., 1965-68; resident in hosp. pharmacy Mercy Hosp., Pitts., 1968-69, clin. pharmacist, 1969—; instr. clin. pharmacy Duquesne U., Pitts., 1975—, coordinator Phys. Pharmacy Labs., 1975—; instr. Community Coll. Allegheny County. Recipient Faculty award, Merck award, Strader award, Cater award. Mem. Am., Pa., Western Pa. socs. hosp. pharmacists, Am. Soc. Parenteral and Enteral Nutrition, Am. Pharm. Assn., Nat. Intravenous Therapy Assn., AMA, AAUP, Am. Assn. Colls. Pharmacy, Phi Delta Chi, Phi Sigma, Rho Chi (award 1965). Clubs: Open Ends, Pitts. Ski. Co-author: Physical Pharmacy Laboratory Manual, 1977. Contbr. articles to profl. jours. Home: 1217 Dagmar Ave Pittsburgh PA 15216 Office: Mercy Hospital Pride and Locust Sts Pittsburgh PA 15219

GIULIANI, JOSEPH CARL, architect; b. Hagerstown, Md., Feb. 2, 1931; s. Lawrence John and Faith Margaret (Betti) G.; B.Arch., Cath. U. Am., 1955; m. Patricia Anne Cottom, Sept. 23, 1961; children—Mark Lawrence, Mara Anne. Prin. Giuliani Assos., Washington, 1959—. Mem. AIA, Am. Soc. for Testing Materials, Constrn. Specifications Inst., Nat. Fire Protective Assn., Soc. Archtl. Historians, Columbia Hist. Soc., Washington Bldg. Congress, D.C. Profl. Council. Roman Catholic. Clubs: Kiwanis, Univ. (Washington); Congressional (Bethesda, Md.). Home: 9500 Persimmon Tree Rd Potomac MD 20854 Office: 1000 Connicticut Ave NW Washington DC 20036

GIUSTI, GINO PAUL, natural resources co. exec.; b. New Kensington, Pa., May 31, 1927; s. Peter Paul and Rose (Bonadio) G.; B.S. in Chem. Engring., U. Pitts., 1949, M.S., 1953, Ph.D. in Bus. and Econs., 1959; m. Ruth Marie Greblunas, May 4, 1957; children—Paul, Susan, Patricia, John, Christopher. Texasgulf research fellow Mellon Inst. Indsl. Research, Pitts., 1948-57; asst. to pres. Texasgulf Inc., Stamford, Conn., 1958-61, mgr. market research, 1962-64, corp. personnel mgr., 1965-71, v.p. employee relations and adminstrn., 1972-77, v.p. agrl. chems. div., 1978-79, sr. v.p., 1979—; pres. Texasgulf Chems. Co., 1979—; dir. Union Trust Co., N.E. Bancorp, Inc., Phosphate Chems. Export Corp. Mem. metals and minerals unit Nat. Def. Exec. Res., Dept. Interior, 1962—; bd. dirs. Stamford Mus. and Nature Center, Inc., Potash and Phosphate Inst.; mem. corp. Stamford Hosp. Served with USAAF, 1945-46. Registered profl. engr., Pa. Mem. Am. Chem. Soc., Am. Econs. Assn., Am. Inst. Chem. Engrs., Chem. Market Research Assn., Soc. Mining Engrs., Am. Inst. Mining, Metall. and Petroleum Engrs., Canadian Potash Producers Assn., Newcomen Soc. N.Am. Roman Catholic. Clubs: Woodway Country, Landmark, Sky. Home: 236 W Haviland Ln Stamford CT 06903 Office: High Ridge Park Stamford CT 06904

GIZIOWSKI, RICHARD JOHN, educator; b. Worcester, Mass., Aug. 15, 1946; s. John Peter and Mary Margaret (Mai) G.; B.S.Ed., Worcester State Coll., 1968; M.A., U. Conn., 1969; certificate of study (HEW grantee) U. Mysore (India), summer 1973; Certificate of Advanced Study (Univ. scholar), Wesleyan U., 1978, postgrad., 1978—. Tchr. social studies secondary schs. Auburn (Mass.) Pub. Sch. System, 1971—; head resident Wesleyan U., summers 1975, 76. Recipient Sr. Honor award in history Worcester State Coll., 1968. Mem. Auburn (exec. bd. 1973-78), Mass. tchrs. assns., NEA, Am. Hist. Assn. Roman Catholic. Home: 29 Katahdin St Worcester MA 01606

GJERNES, OSCAR, psychologist; b. Oklee, Minn., Aug. 24, 1914; s. Ellef K. and Borghild (Gjeldaker) G.; B.A., Concordia Coll., 1941; M.S., N.D. State U., 1954; postgrad. U. Minn., 1958, U. N.D., 1965; m. Myrdith L. Kronschandbel, Apr. 13, 1941; 1 dau., Marylou Diane. Counseling psychologist VA, N.D., 1946-49; with N.D. Employment Service, 1941-65; supr. tech. services, Bismarck, 1957-65; employment service adviser Manpower Adminstrn., Dept. Labor, Washington, 1965—. Served with AUS, 1942-45, 51-52. Mem. Nat., N.D. (past pres.) vocat. guidance assns., Nat. Employment Counselor Assn. (pres. 1969-70), N.D. Assn. Personnel in Employment, N.D. Personnel and Guidance Assn. (past pres.). Lutheran (deacon). Research in psychol. field. Home: 9039 Sligo Creek Pkwy Silver Springs MD 20901

GLADDEN, DENNIS WILLIAM, newspaper editor; b. Northampton, Mass., Oct. 5, 1952; s. Otto Leon and Ruth Ellen (Wilson) G.; degree Christian Writers' Inst., 1974, Newspaper Inst. Am., 1972; m. Sandra Jean Bucheri, Mar. 31, 1978. Gen. assignment reporter Tri-Town Reporter newspaper, Rockville, Conn., 1973, asso. editor, 1973-74, editor, 1974—; lectr. in local schs. Vice chmn. Tolland (Conn.) Planning and Zoning Commn., 1977; mem. Tolland Charter Revision Commn., 1976; sec. Tri-Town Vocat. Edn. Adv. Com., 1977-78; publicity chmn. Vernon (Conn.) Heart Fund Dr., 1976-77. Recipient hon. mention for newswriting Nat. Assn. Advt. Pubs., 1977, award for editorial, 1975; 3d pl. award for editorial New Eng. Press Assn., 1975. Methodist. Club: Rotary (treas. Rockville 1978-79, sec. 1979-80). Home: 129 Willie Circle Tolland CT 06084 Office: 130 Old Town Rd Rockville CT 06066

GLADDING, EVERETT BUSHNELL, electronics specialist; b. New Haven, June 27, 1917; s. Daniel H. and Grace (Brown) G.; B.A., Wesleyan U., Middletown, Conn., 1938; M.A., Johns Hopkins U., 1946; m. Harriet Allen Clark, June 7, 1941; children—Nicholas Clark, Brenda Bushnell Gladding Alexander. Joined U.S. Navy, 1941, advanced through grades to capt., 1960; mem. staff Supreme Allied Comdr., Atlantic, 1956-59, chief Nat. Security Agy., Pacific, 1960-63, comdg. officer Communications Sta., Adak, 1963-64, chief staff Naval Security Group, Washington, 1964-66; dir. Naval Security Group Pacific, Honolulu, 1966-68; specialist Greenville div. LTV Electrosystems, Inc., 1968-70; mgmt. analyst State Comn., 1970-72; pres. Everdane, Inc., New Haven, 1972-75; pres. Majors Aviation Service, Inc., 1975—. Mem. IEEE (sr.), Armed Forces Communications and Electronics Assn., Aircraft Owners and Pilots Assn., Quarter Century Wireless Assn., Nat. Pilots Assn. Episcopalian. Clubs: Rotary; Quinniplack; Sakonnet Golf (R.I.). Home: Warren's Point Little Compton RI 02837

GLADFELTER, MILLARD E., univ. chancellor; b. York County, Pa., Jan. 16, 1900; s. Phillip and Ida Jane (Shearer) G.; A.B., Gettysburg Coll., 1925, D.Sc., 1942; A.M., U. Wis., 1930; Ph.D., U. Pa., 1945; LL.D., Muhlenberg Coll., 1947; L.H.D. Lebanon Valley Coll., 1954, Dropsie Coll., 1960, St. Joseph's Coll., 1960; Litt.D., Ursinus Coll., 1956, Eastern Bapt. Coll., 1957, U. Pa., 1960, Drexel Inst. Tech., 1961, Albright Coll., 1964, Delaware Valley Coll. Agr., 1964; Ph.D., LaSalle Coll., 1963; D.C.L., Rider Coll., 1966; D.H.L., Hahnemann Med. Coll., 1967, Thomas Jefferson U., 1977; m. Martha Louise Gaut, Dec. 29, 1931; children—Phillip, Bruce Gaut. Tchr. rural schs. Pa., 1918-22; prin., tchr. history West York High Sch., 1925-28; supervising prin. West York Schs., 1928-30; dir. Temple U. High Sch., 1930-31; registrar Temple U., 1931-41, v.p., 1941-59, provost, v.p., 1946-59, pres., 1959-67, chancellor, 1967—, also trustee; cons. in field. Trustee Phila Free Library; hon. life trustee Temple U.; bd. dirs. Ursinus Coll., Valley Forge Mil. Acad., Phila. Diagnostic and Rehab. Center; mem. nat. bd. Goodwill Industries Am.; 1st corp. bd. Goodwill Industries Phila.; mgmt. com., div. for profl. leadership Lutheran Ch. Am.; chmn. bd. Presbyterian Ministers' Fund. Recipient Silver Beaver award Boy Scouts Am.; Grand Gold badge honor for merits Republic of Austria, 1964; Humanitarian award Phila. 32 Carat Club, 1964; All Pa. Coll. Alumni Assn. award, 1964; Nat. Humanitarian award NCCJ, 1965, B'nai B'rith, 1977; Phila. Pub. Relations Assn. Gold Medal award, 1967; Samuel S. Fels medal, 1967; citation Pa. Community Coll. Pres. Council, 1967; numerous others. Mem. Phila. C. of C. (bd. dirs.), Middle States Assn. Colls. and Secondary Schs. (pres. 1959, now cons.), Pa. Assn. Coll. and Univs., Phi Beta Kappa, Kappa Phi Kappa, Phi Delta Kappa, Phi Delta Theta, Phi Beta Kappa. Assos. Kiwanian. Contbr. articles to ednl. jours. Home: 342 Fisher Rd Jenkintown PA 19046

GLADFELTER, VALERIE GARBER (MRS. DAVID DREWS GLADFELTER), social worker; b. Phila., May 18, 1938; d. Samuel and Beatrice (Gillman) Garber; B.A., Brandeis U., 1959; M.S.W. (NIMH fellow), Rutgers U., 1964; postgrad. (NIMH fellow), U. Pa. Sch. Social Work, 1975-77; m. David Drews Gladfelter, July 13, 1968; children—Stephen Garber, Hannah Rachel. Social worker Norristown (Pa.) State Hosp., 1959-60, Camden (N.J.) Psychiat. Hosp., 1960-62; chief social worker Temple Med. Sch. unit, dir. Phila. Day Treatment Center, Eastern State Sch. and Hosp., Trevose, Pa., 1964-68; regional supr. N.J. Div. Mental Retardation, 1968-70; individual practice marriage and family counseling Marriage and Family Therapy Assos., P.A., Willingboro, N.J., 1970—. Mem. co-adj. faculty Rutgers Grad. Sch. Social Work, 1972-75, 78—, also field instr.; field instr. U. Pa. Grad. Sch. Social Work, 1965-68; instr. Temple U. Med. Sch., 1967-68; cons. Willingboro (N.J.) Police Dept., 1973-74; mem. N.J. Bd. Marriage Counselor Examiners, 1973—, sec. bd., 1974—. Vice-chmn. Willingboro Twp. (N.J.) Human Relations Commn., 1970-72, chmn., 1972-74; bd. dirs. Mercer St. Friends Center, Trenton, N.J., 1965-68, Counselling Center, Willingboro, N.J., 1973. Brandeis Nat. scholar, 1955-56. Mem. Am. Assn. Marriage and Family Counselors, Nat. Assn. Social Workers (mem. council on social work edn. 1965). Mem. Soc. of Friends. Home: 228 Winding Way Moorestown NJ 08057 Office: 215 Sunset Rd C1-B Willingboro NJ 08046

GLADSTONE, SUZANNE PINK, clin. psychologist; b. N.Y.C., Sept. 20, 1935; d. Lester Winthrop and Beatrice Joan (Meister) Pink; B.S., Pa. State U., 1957; Degree Superieur U. Paris, Sorbonne, 1958; M.S., Utah State U., 1962; Ph.D., U. Md., 1971; m. Mark B. Gladstone, Feb. 3, 1957; 1 dau., Leslie Anne. Teaching asst. U. Md., 1965-66; psychology trainee VA Hosp., Washington, Balt., 1966-70; clin. psychologist, chief psychologist out-patient services Area C, Community Mental Health Center, Washington, 1971—; pvt. practice psychology, 1972—; lectr. Montgomery Coll., 1975—. Mem. Nat. Registry for Health Service Producers in Mental Health. Mem. Am., D.C. Md. psychol. assns., ACLU, Am. Humanist Assn., Council for Advancement Psychol. Professions and Scis., Ethical Soc., Assn. Practicing Psychologists (organizational chmn.), Assos. in Clin. Psychology, Psi Chi. Home: 7704 Westfield Dr Bethesda MD 20034 Office: 9041 Comprint Ct Gaithersburg MD 20760

GLADSTONE, VIC S., audiologist; b. Spring Valley, N.Y., Apr. 3, 1946; married, 2 children. B.S. in Speech Pathology, Audiology, Pa. State U., University Park, 1968, M.S. in Audiology, 1969; Ph.D., U. Md., Coll. Park, 1977. Clin. audiologist Pa. Rehab. Center, Johnstown, 1969-70, Greater Balt. Med. Center, 1970; asst. prof., dir. audiol. services Speech and Hearing Clinic Towson State U., Balt., 1970-77, asso. prof., dir. program, 1977—. Mem. Am. (legis. councilor; mem. com. immittance measurements), Md. (mem. com. hearing conservation, indsl. audiology nat. chpt. 1973-75; chmn. liaison com. state chpt. 1971-75), speech and hearing assns., Council Exceptional Children, Acoustical Soc. Am., Wash. Acad. Scis., AAAS, Phi Kappa Phi, Sigma Alpha Eta. Recipient Clinic Service award Pa. State Univ. Speech, Hearing Clinic; Danforth asso. Certified in speech pathology, audiology Md. State Dept. Edn.; specialist in diagnostics, rehabilitation. Office: Speech Hearing Clinic Towson State U Baltimore MD 21204

GLAID, ANDREW J., III, chemist, educator; b. Pitts., July 14, 1923; s. Andrew J. and Barbara E. (Sommer) G.; B.S., Duquesne U., 1949, M.S., 1950; Ph.D. (NIH fellow), Duke U., 1955; m. Mary L. Brown, June 27, 1953; children—Andrew IV, Elaine, Karen, Amy, Mark. Asst. prof. chemistry Duquesne U., 1954-57, asso. prof., 1957-61, prof., 1961—, chmn. dept. chemistry. NSF grantee, NIH grantee. Mem. Am. Chem. Soc., AAUP. Contbr. research publs. to sci. jours. Office: Dept Chemistry Duquesne U Pittsburgh PA 15219*

GLAMAN, MARY LOUISE, educator; b. Chgo., Dec. 29, 1929; d. Otto Temple and Lillian Beatrice (Platt) Glaman; B.A., Lake Forest (Ill.) Coll., 1951; M.Ed., Boston U., 1962. Tchr., Park Ridge (Ill.) pub. schs., 1951-54; tchr. Quincy (Mass.) pub. schs., 1954—, tchr. kindergarten Snug Harbor Sch., 1954-57, 62—, 2d grade tchr., 1958-61; tchr. early childhood edn. Eastern Nazarene Coll., Quincy, 1967-70; dir. rep. Quincy pub. schs. South Shore Day Care, 1970-73; ednl. adviser Headstart, Quincy YWCA. Mem. women's aux. Quincy City Hosp.; mem. coms. Bethany Congl. Ch., Quincy, 1954—, pres. Bethany Players, 1966—; bd. dirs. Protestant Social Service Bur. Recipient Paul Revere bowl New Eng. Home Little Wanderers, 1966; awards March of Dimes, CARE. Mem. Nat. (life), Quincy (past chmn. coms.: elementary dir., parliamentarian 1970—;) edn. assns., Mass. (life). Norfolk County tchrs. assns., Mass. Assn. Elementary Edn., Nat. Kindergarten Assn., Assn. Childhood Edn. Internat., Nat. Assn. Edn. Young Children, Assn. Tchr. Educators, Am. Inst. Parliamentarians, Boston Assn. Edn. Young Children, Gen. Fedn. Women's Clubs (pres. Quincy jr. club 1959-61, jr. dir. Mass. 1964-66, pres. Jr. Past Presidents 1974-76), Quincy Hist. Soc., Germantown Heritage Soc. Club: Quincy Women's. Home: 42 Victoria Rd Quincy MA 02169 Office: 33 Palmer St Quincy MA 02169

GLASBERG, H. MARK, psychiatrist; b. N.Y.C., Oct. 11, 1937; s. Joseph and Elsa (Haber) G.; B.A., Yeshiva U., 1953; M.D., State U. N.Y., 1958; m. Paula Drillman, June 19, 1960; children—Scot Bradley, Hilary Jennifer. Intern Maimonides Hosp. N.Y.C., 1958-59; resident in psychiatry Kings County Hosp., N.Y.C., 1959-60; resident in internal medicine Kingsbridge VA Hosp., N.Y.C., 1960-61; resident Payne Whitney Psychiat. Clin., N.Y. Hosp., 1963-65, fellow, 1965-66; spl. research fellow Nat. Inst. Mental Health, 1966-68; practice medicine specializing in psychiatry, N.Y.C., 1968—; instr. Cornell U. Med. Sch., 1966-68; asst. prof. psychiatry Mt. Sinai Sch. Medicine, 1968—; dir. psychiat. outpatient services Beth Israel Hosp., N.Y.C., 1968-74, asso. attending physician, 1968-74; attending psychiatrist St. Vincent's Hosp., N.Y.C., 1974—, chief psychiat. emergency and cons. services, 1974-75. Cons. mem. panel of ind. psychiatrists N.Y.C. Mental Health Information Service, 1968—. Mem. Manhattan physicians com. United Jewish Appeal, 1970—. Served to capt., M.C., AUS, 1961-63. Mem. Am. Psychiat. Assn., A.A.A.S., Am. Psychosomatic Soc., Soc. for Adolescent Psychiatry. Home: 480 Park Ave New York City NY 10022 Office: 480 Park Ave New York City NY 10022

GLASER, ANTON, educator; b. Worms, Germany, Oct. 11, 1924; s. Anton and Katherina (Susemichel) G.; came to U.S., 1939; naturalized, 1949; A.B., Temple U., 1948, D.Ed., 1969; M.Ed., Pa. State U., 1960; m. Ruth Naomi Moser, Nov. 24, 1960. Tchr. math. Abington (Pa.) High Sch., 1960-62; faculty Pa. State U. Ogontz Campus, Abington, 1962—, chmn. acad. advisers, 1964; lectr. Univ. of Air Program WFIL-TV, Phila., 1964-65; cons. Sci. Research Assos., Chgo. Served with AUS, 1946-47. Recipient Valley Forge Classroom Tchrs. medal Freedoms Found., 1959. Mem. Nat. Council Tchrs. Math., Math. Assn. Am., Del. Valley Programming Assn. (past sec.). Author: The Binary System, 1965; History of Binary and other Nondecimal Numeration, 1971; Neater by the Meter: An American Guide to the Metric System, 1974. Home: 1237 Whitney Rd Southampton PA 18966 Office: Ogontz Campus Abington PA 19001

GLASER, DAVID A., painter, illustrator; b. Bklyn., Sept. 29, 1919; s. Samuel and Jennie (Oiffer) G.; student (scholar) Art Students League, 1936; student Bklyn. Mus. Art Sch., 1948, N.Y. Sch. Contemporary Art, 1949; m. Mildred Sappol, Feb. 19, 1943; children—Susan, Sherry. Profl. painter, illustrator, 1936—; devel. process mosaic reprodn. Mosamics Co., 1946-48; graphic designer, exec. owner Studio Concepts, Wantagh, N.Y., 1957—; tchr. art Center Island Jewish Sch., 1959; one-man exhbn. Heckscher Mus., Huntington, L.I., 1964; group exhbns. Allied Artists, N.A.D., Audubon Artists, Hofstra U., Art Directions, City Center N.Y. Served with AUS, 1942-46. Recipient 1st prize Best Redesigned Levitt House, 1968; award Printing Industries N.Y., 1972, 77; Graphic Excellence award Monadnock Paper Mills, 1975. Mem. Allied Artists Am., Am. Vets. Soc. Artists, Nature Conservancy, Common Cause, Better Edn. League. Author, illustrator: 'Em/Me, 1974. Author illustrator series Superstition, Am. Indian, Crime and Punishment, 1950-54, also Planets, 1961. Contbr. illustrations to mags.; originator cartoon charactor Giggy F. Useless, Army Publs.; creator Bicentennial map of Am. revolution; developer archtl. sculptures of copper, plastics, chem. coloring and electric illumination, 1970-77. Address: 33 Downhill Ln Wantagh NY 11793

GLASER, JOSEPH BERNARD, assn. exec.; b. Boston, May 1, 1925; s. Louis James and Dena Sophie (Harris) G.; A.B., U. Calif. at Los Angeles, 1948; J.D. U. San Francisco, 1951; B.H.L., Hebrew Union Coll., 1954, M.H.L., 1956; postgrad (Merrill Trust grantee) Law Faculty Hebrew U., Jerusalem, 1969-70; m. Agathe Maier, Sept. 23, 1951; children—Simeon, Meyer, Sara, John. Rabbi, 1956; rabbi Temple Beth Torah, Ventura, Calif., 1956-59; regional dir. Union Am. Hebrew Congregatons, San Francisco, 1959-71; exec. v.p. Central Conf. Am. Rabbis, N.Y.C., 1971—. Registrar, Hebrew Union Coll., Los Angeles, 1956-59, instr. homiletics, 1956-59; instr. Bible, Hebrew Union Coll., Cin., 1954-56; vis. scholar Oxford Centre for Postgrad. Hebrew Studies, summer 1978. Vice chmn. San Francisco Conf. Religion and peace, 1964-71, San Francisco Conf. Religion and Race, 1963-68; chmn. Clergy Com. Farm Labor Negotiation, 1967-68; chmn. bd. Religion in Am. Life, 1978—, Ams. United to Save Uganda, 1978—. Served with inf. U.S. Army, 1943-46. Decorated Purple heart with oak leaf cluster. Mem. Central Conf. Am. Rabbis, Synagogue Council Am. Office: 790 Madison Ave New York City NY 10021

GLASER, ROBERT LEONARD, TV exec.; b. Chgo., Jan. 9, 1929; s. Maurice L. and Sara (Ziegler) G.; B.A., U. Miami, 1950; m. Nancy Lehman Field, Jan. 4, 1959; children—Robert Leonard, Jr., Geoffrey L., Douglas L. Midwest mgr. Metromedia, 1960-64; Midwest sales mgr. Am. Broadcasting Co., 1964-66; v.p., gen. mgr. WOR-TV, N.Y.C., 1967-70, v.p., gen. mgr., 1971; corporate v.p., RKO Gen., Inc., N.Y.C., 1971—, pres. RKO Gen. TV Inc., N.Y.C., 1973—, RKO Gen. Pictures, 1976—; chmn. RKO TV Reps., 1973—. Bd. dirs. Learning to Read through Arts, Guggenheim Mus., United Cerebral Palsy Research and Ednl. Found. Served to 1st lt. AUS, 1950-53. Mem. Internat. Radio and TV Soc. (dir.), Nat. Acad. TV Arts and Scis. Clubs: Friars (N.Y.C.); Patterson Country (Fairfield, Conn.). Home: 88 Morningside Dr S Greens Farms CT 06436 Office: 1440 Broadway New York City NY 10018

GLASGOW, ROGER DECOUREY, architect; b. N.Y.C., Jan. 31, 1934; s. Lester and Octavia (Adams) G.; B.Arch., Howard U., 1957; children—Allison Lenore, Roger DeCourey, Michael DeCourey. Architect, Ketchum, Gina & Sharp, 1957-58, Francis Gina & Assos., 1958-61, Victor Gruen & Assos., 1961-62, Lippincott & Margulies, Inc., 1962-64, Roger DeCourey Glasgow, N.Y.C., 1964—. Cons. City Rent and Rehab., N.Y.C., 1964-66, Jersey City Can-Do program Office Econ. Opportunity, 1967. Mem. Civic Central Park North Com., N.Y.C., 1966; sec. Sch. Liaison Com. Minorities Program, 1967—. Trustee Calhoun Sch. Mem. A.I.A., N.Y. Soc. Architects, Am. Arbitration Assn., N.Y. Coalition. Author: Schomburg Collection, A Plan for Growth, 1970. Home: 44 Strawberry Hill Ave Stamford CT 06905 Office: 1200 Summer St Stamford CT 06905

GLASS, HARRY SAUL, health adminstr., govt. ofcl.; b. Boston, July 27, 1938; s. Jacob and Ida (Shor) G.; B.B.A., U. Mass. at Amherst, 1960; M.B.A., George Washington U., 1965; m. Vidula Patel, Sept. 25, 1966; 1 dau., Deborah. Adminstrv. resident Maimonides Med. Center, Bklyn., 1964-65; cons. health care Anthony J.J. Rourke Inc., New Rochelle, N.Y., 1966-69; asst. dir. Norwalk (Conn.) Hosp., 1969-72; dir. health service devel. Md. Health Maintenance, Balt., 1972-74; chief Eastern ops. br. Bur. Quality Assurance, HEW, Rockville, Md., 1974-75, dir. div. data planning and analysis Health Standards and Quality Bur., Health Care Financing Adminstrn., 1976—; cons. in field. Treas., Health Security Action Council Md., 1973-75; co-chmn. Howard County Com. for Sensible Hosp. Planning, 1973-75; bd. dirs. Citizens Health Council Balt., 1974-75; bd. incorporators Howard County Gen. Hosp., 1977—. Served with USAF, Med. Service Corps, 1960-63. USPHS trainee, 1963-64. Mem. Am. Pub. Health Assn., Am. Hosp. Assn., Group Health Assn. Am., Nat. Capitol Squash Racquets Assn. (dir. 1976-78). Home: 5410 Marsh Hawk Way Columbia MD 21045 Office: 1849 Gwynn Oak Ave Baltimore MD 21235

GLASS, JANET LEVINE, guidance counselor; b. Bklyn., Nov. 13, 1947; d. Richard Samuel and Miriam (Kaplan) Levine; B.A., Harpur Coll., State U. N.Y., 1967; student Inter-Am. U., Saltillo, Mex., 1966, U. Madrid, 1969; M.S., Queens Coll., N.Y.C., 1973; m. Charles David Glass, Nov. 2, 1969; children—Jessica Rose (1 dau.). Tchr. English as 2d lang. Spanish Am. Inst., N.Y.C., 1968; tchr. Spanish, Beard Jr. High Sch., Queens, N.Y., 1969-73; tchr. English as 2d lang. Englewood (N.J.) Adult Evening Sch., 1973-76; translator documents Begonia Travel Service, N.Y.C., 1973-75; bilingual guidance counselor Samuel Gompers High Sch., N.Y.C., 1977—. Licensed tchr. Spanish, N.Y.C., N.Y. State, N.J.; licensed bilingual counselor, N.Y.C. Mem. Am. Personnel and Guidance Assn., Am. Assn. Tchrs. Spanish and Portuguese, Am. Translators Assn. Home: 93 Glenwood Ave Leonia NJ 07605 Office: 455 Southern Blvd Bronx NY 10455

GLASS, ROBERT ALLAN, psychologist; b. Bklyn., Mar. 12, 1947; s. William and Alice Lou (Tuberville) G.; B.A., U. Toledo, 1969; M.S., U. Md., 1971, Ph.D., 1974; m. Julia Elizabeth Stephens, Mar. 11, 1977. Grad. research psychologist, dept. psychology U. Md., College Park, 1969-74; research psychologist sensory environment sect. Nat. Bur. Standards, Washington, 1974—; chmn. research subcom. on visual alerting Am. Nat. Standards Inst., 1978; mem. bldg. research adv. bd. com. on directional graphics Nat. Acad. Scis., 1977—. Recipient Spl. Achievement award Nat. Bur. Standards, 1976. Mem. Optical Soc. Am., Human Factors Soc. Contbr. articles to profl. jours. Home: 7912 Lysander Ct McLean VA 22102 Office: Nat Bur Standards Bldg 226 Room A313 Washington DC 20234

GLASS, ROBERT DAVIS, judge; b. Wetumpka, Ala., Nov. 28, 1922; s. Isiah and M.E. (Davis) G.; A.B. magna cum laude, N.C. Central U., 1949, J.D. cum laude, 1951; m. Doris Powell, Dec. 9, 1951; children—Robert Davis, Roberta Diane, Rosalyn Doris. Admitted to N.C. bar, 1951; practiced in Charlotte, 1951-53, New Bern, 1953-60; claims examiner Conn. Labor Dept., 1961-62; admitted to Conn. bar, 1962, practiced in Waterbury, 1962-66; asst. U.S. atty. Dist. Conn., New Haven, 1966-67; judge Conn. Juvenile Ct., Torrington, 1967-78, Conn. Superior Ct., 1978—; bd. corporators Waterbury Savs. Bank, 1973—. Regional vice-chmn. Conn. Council Human Rights, 1964; mem. Waterbury Com. Human Rights, 1964; mem. appeals bd. Conn. Justice Commn.; bd. corporators, sec. Waterbury Hosp., 1972; pres. Conn. State Fedn. Negro Democratic Clubs, 1965-67. Served with AUS, 1943-46. Mem. State Bar Assn. Conn., N.C. Bar, Am., Waterbury, Nat. (life mem., mem. jud. council) bar assns., Am. Judicature Soc., Assn. Study Afro-Am. Life and History, Nat. Council Juvenile Ct. Judges (life), NAACP (Eastern N.C. counsel N.C. conf. brs. 1953-60), Omega Psi Phi. Clubs: Masons (32 deg.), Elks. Home: 365 Buckingham St Oakville CT 06779 Office: 50 Linden St Waterbury CT 06702

GLASSBERG, GWENDOLYN REVILDA KROMAN DARLING, portrait artist, poet; b. Phila., Mar. 19, 1927; d. Hugo Edward Kroman and Mary Marian (Piltz) Darling; grad. high sch.; m. Rubin Glassberg, Apr. 3, 1945; children—Sandra (Mrs. Carl Weil, Evy (Mrs. Barry O. Hodson), Fay (Mrs. Leslie M. Brooks, Jr.). Receptionist, Bishop Studio Photography, West Chester, Pa., 1966-71; portrait artist, West Chester, 1973—. Recipient numerous awards, certificates and medals for poetry. Fellow Internat. Poetry Soc., Internat. Acad. Poets (Cambridge, Eng.) (founding); mem. Pa. Poetry Soc., Am. Poets Fellowship, Accademia Leonardo da Vinci (hon. rep. diploma), Am. Poetry League, World Poetry Soc. (India), Chester County Art Assn. Poems rep. in anthologies. Address: 1119 Carolina Ave West Chester PA 19380

GLASSBERG, KENNETH IRA, pediatric urologist; b. Bklyn., Mar. 18, 1943; s. Abe and Lillian (Brown) G.; B.A., Bklyn. Coll., 1964; M.D., SUNY, Bklyn., 1968; m. Michele Cooper, June 9, 1968; children—Lauren Dana, Andrew David, Lawrence Cooper. Intern, George Washington U. and D.C. Gen. Hosp., Washington, 1968-69; resident Montefiore Hosp., Bronx, N.Y., 1971-72, SUNY Downstate Med. Center, 1972-75; Fritz fellow in pediatric urology Alderly Children's Hosp., Liverpool, Eng. and Hosp. for Sick Children, London, 1975-76; practice medicine specializing in pediatric urology, Bklyn., 1976—; asst. prf. urology SUNY, Bklyn., 1976—; dir. pediatric urology Kings County Hosp. Center., Bklyn., 1976—; Long Island Coll. Hosp., Bklyn., 1978—. Served to lt. comdr. USPHS, 1969-71. Diplomate Am. Bd. Urology. Fellow Am. Urol. Assn., Am. Acad. Pediatrics; mem. AMA, Brooklyn-Long Island Urol. Soc., N.Y. Acad. Medicine, N.Y. Pediatric Soc., Bklyn. Pediatric Soc., Kings County Med. Soc. Contbr. articles in field to profl. jours. Home: 531 Main St Roosevelt Island NY 10044 Office: 450 Clarkson Ave Brooklyn NY 11203

GLASSER, BRIAN M., fin. and mgmt. info. services exec.; b. New Brunswick, N.J., Mar. 17, 1947; s. Alex J. and Rose (Rubel) G.; B.S., Fairmont State Coll., 1970; student Rutgers U., summer 1969; m. Arlene Irene VanDalen, July 31, 1970; children—Seth Robert, Jessica Anne. Sr. accountant Main LaFrentz & Co., N.Y.C., 1970-74; fin. analyst Cadence Industries Corp., West Caldwell, N.J., 1974-76, controller Cadence M.I.S., 1976-78; controller Woodward Ryan Sharp & Davis Inc., N.Y.C., 1978—; mem. partner staff coordinating com. Main LaFrentz & Co., 1973-74. Pres., Prescott Ave. Assn., 1978; bd. dirs. Montclair Community Alliance, 1978. Mem. Computer Security Inst. Jewish. Home: 10 Prescott Ave Montclair NJ 07042 Office: 3 Park Ave 38th Floor New York City NY 10016

GLASSER, ISRAEL LEO, coll. dean; b. N.Y.C., Apr. 6, 1924; B.A., Coll. City N.Y., 1943; LL.B., Bklyn. Law Sch., 1948, LL.D., 1977; m. Grace Gribetz, Aug. 24, 1952; children—Dorothy, David, James, Marjorie. Fellow, Bklyn. Law Sch., 1948-49, instr., 1950-52, asst. prof., 1952-53, asso. prof., 1953-55, prof. law, 1955—, dean, 1977—; judge Family Ct. of N.Y., 1969-77; mem. N.Y. State Exec. Adv. Com. on Sentencing, 1978, Mayor's Com. on Judiciary, 1978, Com. for Modern Cts., Family Ct. Panel, 1978. Mem. adv. council Temple Beth El. Served with AUS, 1943-46. Decorated Bronze Star medal. Mem. Am. Bar Assn. Home: 141 Beach 143 St Neponsit NY 11694 Office: Bklyn Law Sch 250 Joralemon St Brooklyn NY 11201

GLASSMAN, JEROME MARTIN, pharm. mfg. co. exec.; b. Phila., Mar. 2, 1919; s. Martin K. and Dorothea (Largeman) G.; B.A., U. Pa., 1939, M.A., 1942; Ph.D. in Pharmacology, Yale, 1950; m. Justine H. Rizinsky, June 15, 1952; children—Martin J., Lorna R., Gary J. Research asso. applied physiology Yale, New Haven, Conn., 1950-51; head dept. pharmacology Wyeth Labs., Radnor, Pa., 1951-62; dir. biol. research USV Pharm. Corp., Yonkers, N.Y., 1962-69; dir. clin. research, pharmacology Wampole Labs., Stamford, Conn., 1969-75; asso. dir. clin. investigation Wallace Labs., Cranbury, N.J., 1975—. Asst. prof. pharmacology N.Y. Med. Coll., Valhalla, N.Y., 1963-73, asso. prof., 1973—. Active Valley Forge council Boy Scouts Am., 1957-62; chmn. adult leadership tng. Briarcliff Village Capital Improvement Com., 1968. Recipient Scouter's award Boy Scouts Am. Fellow AAAS, Am. Coll. Clin. Pharmacology and Chemotherapy, Am. Coll. Clin. Pharmacology, N.Y. Acad. Scis.; mem. Soc. Toxicology (mem. tech. com. 1961-62), Am. Soc. Pharmacology (chmn. analgesic sect. 1969), Sigma Xi. Patentee in field. Contbr. articles to profl. jours. Home: 280 Sleepy Hollow Rd Briarcliff NY 10510 Office: Half Acre Rd Cranbury NJ 08512

GLASSMOYER, THOMAS PARVIN, lawyer; b. Reading, Pa., Sept. 4, 1915; s. James Arthur and Margaretha (Parvin) G.; A.B., Ursinus Coll., 1936, LL.D., 1972; LL.B., U. Pa., 1939; m. Frances Helen Thierolf, May 9, 1942; children—Deborah Jane Beck, Nancy Parvin Brittingham, Wendy Jean Barber. Law clk. Common Pleas Ct. 6, Phila., 1939-40; admitted to Pa. bar, 1940; asso. Murdoch, Paxson, Kalish & Green, Phila., 1940-42; atty. Dept. Justice and OPA, 1942-43; asso. Schnader, Harrison, Segal & Lewis, Phila., 1946—, partner, 1950—; dir. Jefferies Assos., Inc., Milhart Textiles, Inc., Jefferies Processors, Inc., Charmil Realty Corp.; occasional lectr. N.Y. U. Inst. Fed. Taxation. Past pres. Upper Dublin Twp. PTA Council; mem. Zoning Bd. Adjustment Upper Dublin Twp., Montgomery County, Pa., 1957-59, mem. bd. commrs., 1959-71, pres., 1968-69; mem. Upper Dublin Environ. Control Bd., 1972—; bd. dirs. Ursinus Coll., Collegeville, Pa., 1956—, v.p., 1978; bd. dirs. Wissahickon Valley Watershed Assn., 1974-76. Served to 1st lt. Judge Adv. Gen.'s Dept., AUS, 1943-46. Mem. Lawyers Club, Am. Arbitration Assn., Am., Pa., Phila. (sect. taxation) bar assns., Pa. Folklife Soc. (dir., sec.), Order of Coif. Clubs: Manorlu (pres. 1963-65) (Oreland, Pa.); Mfrs. Golf and Country; Union League, Midday (Phila.). Author: (with Sherwin T. McDowell) Legal Problems in Tax Returns, 1949; editor-in-chief U. Pa. Law Rev., 1938-39. Home: 1648 North Hills Ave Willow Grove PA 19090 Office: Packard Bldg Philadelphia PA 19102

GLASSUER, FRANZ ERNST, neurosurgeon; b. Khoau, Czechoslovakia, Feb. 19, 1930; s. Rudolf and Marie (Eckert) G.; M.D., magna cum laude, U. Heidelberg (Germany), 1955; m. Elizabeth A. Garofalo. Intern St. Mark's Hosp., Salt Lake City, 1955-56; resident in surgery, neurosurgery New Eng. Med. Center, Boston, 1957-61: asst. in neurosurgery Tufts U. Sch. Medicine, Boston, 1960-61; asst. prof. neurosurgery State U. N.Y., Buffalo, 1965-69, asso. prof., 1969-72, prof., 1972—; attending neurosurgeon numerous hosps., Buffalo; cons. Meml. Hosp., Mt. St. Mary's Hosp., Niagara Falls, N.Y. Served with USNR, 1961-63. Diplomate Am. Bd. Neurosurgery. Mem. Congress Neurol. Surgeons, Am. Assn. Neurol. Surgeons, N.Y. Acad. Scis., Found. Internat. Edn. Neurol. Surgery, N.Y. State Neurosurg. Soc. (dir. 1971-73), Internat. Soc. Pediatric Neurosurgery. Contbr. articles to med. jours. Office: 462 Grider St Buffalo NY 14215

GLAVIN, A. RITA CHANDELLIER (MRS. JAMES HENRY GLAVIN III), lawyer; b. Schenectady; d. Pierre Charles and Helen (Fox) Chandellier; A.B. cum laude, Middlebury Coll., 1958; J.D., Union U. Albany Law Sch., 1961; m. James Henry Glavin III, June 1, 1963; children—Helene Elizabeth, James Chandellier, Rita Marie, James Henry. Admitted to N.Y., Fed. bar, 1961, U.S. Supreme Ct. bar, 1978; practiced in Albany, N.Y., 1961—, Schenectady and Waterford, N.Y., 1965—; mem. firm Eugene J. Steiner, 1961-64, Glavin & Glavin, 1965—, Helen Fox Chandellier, 1965-76; confdl. law clk. to judges N.Y. State Ct. Claims, Albany, 1968-73. Co-chmn. Cancer Drive, Waterford, 1964; mem. maternity and pediatric care com. Health Systems Agy. Northeastern N.Y., 1976—; mem. nat. exec. com. to head Albany Law Sch. Expansion Fund, 1967—; spl. lectr. in law Middlebury Coll., 1976, mem. adv. com. bequest program, 1976. Bd. dirs. Bellevue Maternity Hosp., sec., 1975—; bd. dirs. Jr. League Schenectady, 1974, 76; trustee Middlebury Coll., 1978—; mem. exec. com. of pub. affairs com. N.Y. State Jr. League, 1977-78. Mem. N.Y. State Bar Assn., Bar Assn. Schenectady and Saratoga Counties, Phi Beta Kappa, Kappa Kappa Gamma (chpt. v.p. 1958). Editor Albany Law Rev., 1960-61. Home: 66 Saratoga Ave Waterford NY 12188 Office: 1578 Union St Schenectady NY 12309 also 74 State St Albany NY 12207 also 69 2d St Waterford NY 12188

GLAZER, JUDITH S., edn. cons.; b. N.Y.C., Apr. 16, 1933; d. Max and Pauline V. (Grossman) Lager; B.A., Smith Coll., 1953; M.A., N.Y. U., 1973; m. Howard C. Glazer, May 2, 1954; children—Helen Marcy, George Douglas. Asst. to dir. pub. info., coordinator spl. projects State U. N.Y., Purchase, 1970-72, asst. to v.p., 1972-73; asst. dean community services Westchester Community Coll., 1973-75; research asso. N.Y. State Commn. on Future of Postsecondary Edn., 1976-77; cons. edn. and pub. affairs, 1975-78; asso. dir. Inter-Univ. Doctoral Consortia Project, N.Y.C., 1978—; instr. higher edn. N.Y. U., 1978—. Trustee, pres. Blind Brook-Rye Town Bd. Edn., 1963-72; campaign chmn. Rye Town-Port Chester United Way; exec. com. Westchester County Environ. Mgmt. Council, 1973—; bd. dirs. Vol. Service Bur., 1974—. Recipient NACO New County U.S.A. Achievement award, 1975, award Westchester Council for Arts, 1971. Mem. Pub. Relations Soc. Am. (accredited), Am. Assn. Higher Edn., Westchester County Assn., Am. Soc. Pub. Adminstrn., Assn. Study of Higher Edn., Council Interinstl. Leadership, Kappa Delta Pi. Contbr. numerous articles to periodicals and newspapers. Home: 287 N Ridge St Port Chester NY 10573 Office: New York NY 10003

GLEASON, CHAPMAN PATRICK, math. statistician; b. Elmira, N.Y., Oct. 4, 1947; s. Chapman Lewis and Sallie Ruth (Spencer) G.; B.A. with honors, Mansfield State Coll., 1970; M.S., Ohio State U., 1972; m. Betsy Alyce Shay, Sept. 23, 1967; children—Carol Lee, Alan Chapman. Grad. teaching asso. Ohio State U., 1970-72; math. statistician Statis. Reporting Service, Statis. Research div., Washington, 1972—. Mem. Am. Statis. Assn. Home: 9606 Glenarm Ct Burke VA 22015 Office: US Dept Agr SD Bldg 4834 Washington DC 20250

GLEASON, DAVID BRUCE, supply co. exec.; b. Syracuse, N.Y., May 15, 1935; s. George Eugene and Jane Helen B.; A.A.S., State U. N.Y., Alfred, 1959; m. Eunice Lydia Bartholomew, Sept. 1, 1956; children—David Bruce, Kevin Brian, Kethleen Kelly. Applications engr. Lennox Industries, Columbus, Ohio, 1959-61, service mgr., 1961-63; salesman Burns H & C Supply Co., West Babylon, N.Y., 1963-66, pres., 1966—. Active Boy Scouts Am., 1963-73; officer parents club St. John the Baptist Diocesan High Sch. Served with USN, 1954-56. Mem. Am. Soc. Heating, Refrigeration and Air Conditioning Engrs., Nat. Assn. Wholesalers, N. Am. Heating and Air Conditioning Wholesalers, Old Timers Club, Nat. Environ. Systems Contractors Assn. Roman Catholic. Office: 266 Farmingdale Rd West Babylon NY 11704

GLEASON, ROBERT PATRICK, safety engr., indsl. hygienist; b. Northampton, Mass., Mar. 13, 1917; s. Michael Joseph and Anna Marie (Callahan) G.; B.S., U. Mass., 1938, M.S., 1941; m. Dorothy Therese Petillon, July 14, 1951; children—Robert Patrick, Joanne Gleason Borkowski, David, James, Mary Elizabeth. Chemist, Commonwealth Mass. Dept. Labor, Boston, 1941-44; indsl. hygienist Fidelity & Casualty Co., N.Y.C., 1944-47; indsl. hygiene engr. Sylvania Electric Products Co., N.Y.C., 1947-53, chief safety engr., 1953-60; safety engr. Gen. Electric Co., Schenectady, 1960-65, IBM Corp., Essex Junction, Vt., 1965-70; dir. environ. health and safety U. Mass., Amherst, 1970-76; safety and indsl. hygiene cons. Registered profl. engr., Mass., Vt.; certified safety profl., in comprehensive practice, indsl. hygiene. Mem. Am. Chem. Soc., Am. Indsl. Hygiene Assn., Am. Soc. Safety Engrs. Home and office: 95 Middle St Hadley MA 01035

GLEASON, THOMAS, labor union ofcl.; b. N.Y.C., Nov. 8, 1900. Dockworker, longshoreman, N.Y.C., from 1932, later dock supt.; bus. agt., pres. Local 1, Internat. Longshoremen's Assn., organizer, 1947-51, exec. v.p., chief negotiator with waterfront employees, 1951-63; pres. Internat. Longshoreman's Assn., 1963—; v.p. Maritime Trades Dept., AFL-CIO, 1965—; v.p. mem. gen. council Internat. Trade Workers Fedn., 1965—; v.p. AFL-CIO, 1969—. Mem. N.Y.C. Council on Port Devel. and Promotion; v.p. Irish Inst. N.Y.; mem. Pres. Johnson's Maritime Adv. Com.; also del. numerous confs. Recipient citations Am. Legion, VFW, 52 Assn., Cath. War Vets., Jewish War Vets. lMem. Friendly Sons St. Patrick, Ancient Order Hibernians, Irish-Am. Hist. Soc. Home: New York City NY Office: 17 Battery Pl New York City NY 10004

GLEASON, WILLIAM CLARENCE, petroleum engr.; b. Hammond, N.Y., Feb. 26, 1918; s. John David and Lena Edith (Sayer) G.; B.Civil Engring., Clarkson Coll. Tech., 1942; m. Lorraine Ann Davenport, Aug. 29, 1945; children—Diane Marie, John Joseph, Richard William. Constrn. engr. Vanguard Constrn. Co., N.Y.C., 1941, C.E., U.S. Army, 1942; with Austin Co., Cleve., 1945-46; asst. supt. chem. plant div. Blaw-Knox Co., Painesville, Ohio, 1946-47; officer Haes Constrn. Inc., Jamestown, N.Y., 1947-49; constrn. engr. Atlantic Refining Co., Syracuse, N.Y., 1950-56; pvt. practice constrn., Dansville, N.Y., 1956-65; constrn. engr. MTS Archtl. Co., Geneseo, N.Y., 1965-67, Konski Engring., Syracuse, 1967-69; engr. petroleum projects Agway, Inc., Syracuse, 1969—. Served with USAAF, 1942-45. Licensed profl. engr., surveyor, Ohio. Fellow ASCE; mem. Nat. Soc. Profl. Engrs., Nat. Assn. Corrosion Engrs., Am. Soc. Petroleum Operating Engrs. (dir.), Am. Petroleum Inst., Toastmasters Internat. Republican. Presbyterian. Clubs: Elks, Masons. Home: 108 River Rd Baldwinsville NY 13027 Office: 333 Butternut Dr DeWitt NY 13221

GLEESON, RONALD FRANCIS, educator; b. Phila., Dec. 12, 1940; s. Francis Edward and Helen Grace G.; B.S., St. Josephs Coll., Phila., 1962; M.S., U. Pa., 1963, Ph.D., 1969; m. Patricia Ann Kuns, Feb. 17, 1968; children—Bentley, Tamara. Asst. prof. physics Trenton (N.J.) State Coll., 1969—. Mem. Am. Phys. Soc. Democrat. Contbr. articles to profl. jours. Home: 1011 Wakeling St Philadelphia PA 19124

GLEIBER, STUART ANDER, lumber mfr.; b. Bklyn., July 20, 1942; s. Ira and Anita Jean (Ander) G.; B.B.A., N.Y. U., 1964; m. Jill Ann Fairberg, Aug. 30, 1964; children—Joshua Daniel, Gary Stephen, Douglas Ross. Vice pres., sales dir. Am. Metal Spinning & Stamping Co., N.Y.C., 1964-70; pres., chmn. bd. Abbot & Abbot Box Corp., L.I. City, 1970—; pres., dir. Ander Lumber Industries, Inc., N.Y.C.; cons. in packaging. Jewish. Contbr. article to profl. jour. Home: 5 Kristi Ct Greenlawn NY 11740 Office: 28-31 Borden Ave Long Island City NY 11101

GLENDENING, FRANK S., accountant; b. Phila., Nov. 2, 1901; s. John Frank and Emilie Brown (Young) G.; B.S., U. Pa., 1922; m. Marion Hastie Smith, June 3, 1930; 1 dau. With firm Edward P. Moxey & Co., 1922-25, Atwater Kent Mfg. Co., 1925-26; prin. firm Frank S. Glendening, Phila., 1926-41, Frank S. Glendening & Co., 1941—; faculty Girard Coll., 1935-41; lectr. Haverford Coll., 1946. Pres., Pa. Valley Civic Assn., 1957-59. Served to capt. USNR, 1941-45. Recipient certificate of appreciation Pa. State Govt. Commn., 1951; C.P.A., Pa. Mem. Am. Inst. C.P.A.'s, Pa. Inst. C.P.A.s (pres., 1949), Beta Alpha Psi (hon.). Republican. Presbyterian. Clubs: Union League, Peale, Downtown, Lions (pres. Phila. club 1937), Masons. Author: Special Investigations, 1953; Lost Time, Is It Ever Found Again?; contbr. articles to profl. jours. Home: 431 Righters Mill Narberth PA 19072 Office: #3 Penn Center Philadelphia PA 19102

GLENN, DIANE JOHNSON, dir. guidance; b. Dunkirk, N.Y., July 12, 1942; d. Rexford Donald and Rosemary (Goggin) Johnson; B.S. in Edn., Medaille Coll., Buffalo, 1968; M.Ed., State U. N.Y. at Buffalo, 1971; Ed.D., Memphis State U., 1975; m. John W. Glenn, Jr., August 9, 1969. Tchr., Arkon (N.Y.) Central Schs., 1968-71; elementary counselor Keystone Central Sch. Dist., Lock Haven, Pa., 1971-73; teaching asst. guidance and personnel dept. Memphis State U., 1973-75; coordinator of counseling activities U. Tenn. Center for Health Sci., 1975-76; instr. human services Herkimer County Community Coll., 1976-77; dir. guidance Liverpool (N.Y.) Central Schs., 1978—. Mem. exec. com. Council for Social Concerns, 1976-77; mem. Rape Crises Task Force of Greater Utica, 1977-78, Com. for the Handicapped, Liverpool; adv. bd. Infant Simulation Project, 1976-78, counselor edn. dept. Syracuse U. Mem. Am., N.Y. State, Onondaga County (pres.) personnel and guidance assns., Am. Assn. Group Workers, N.Y. State Personnel and Guidance Assn., Am. Sch. Counselors Assn., Phi Delta Kappa, Kappa Delta Pi. Contbr. articles to profl. jours. Home: 239 Higby Rd Utica NY 13501

GLENN, NORMAN ROBERT, publisher, editor; b. Chicago Heights, Ill., Sept. 3, 1909; s. Max and Jennie (Wechsler) Goldman; student U. Chgo., 1927-30; m. Elaine Lee Couper, June 14, 1945 (dec.); children—Robin Day, Geoffrey Merrit; m. 2d, Roberta Hope Brewster, Oct. 27, 1972. Promotion mgr. radio sta. WLS, 1932-36; bus. mgr. Broadcasting mag., Washington, 1937-43; pres., pub. Sponsor mag., 1946-65; pres. Moore Pub. Co., 1963-65; pres., pub., editor Decisions Publs. Inc., N.Y.C., 1966—, also Decisions Presentations Inc., Encyclomedia; vis. lectr. Syracuse U., 1961. Served from pvt. to 1st lt. USAAF, 1943-45. Decorated Army Commendation ribbon; recipient Polk award for distinguished journalism. Christian Scientist. Author: (with Irving Settel) Television Advertising and Production, 1953. Home: Forest Rd North Haven NY 11963 Office: 342 Madison Ave New York City NY 10017

GLENN, PETER KEITH, mfrs. rep.; b. Abington, Pa., Feb. 22, 1940; s. Walter J. and Dorothea (Homiller) G.; A.S., Dean Jr. Coll., 1962; Muhlenberg Coll., 1962-64; m. Evonne Faye Schultz, May 28, 1966; children—Christine Lyn, William Kyle. With McKesson Chem. Co., Phila., 1966-68; tech. rep. Glyco Chem. Co., Greenwich, Conn., 1969-72; owner Glenn Assos., Edgewater, N.J., 1972—. Mem. Am. Def. Preparedness Assn., Nat. Rifle Assn. Home: Rural Delivery 1 Hereford PA 18056 Office: Hudson Harbour River Rd Edgewater NJ 07020

GLENN, ROLAND DOUGLAS, chem. engr.; b. Somerville, Mass., Mar. 22, 1912; s. Charles Rathford and Anna Amanda (Card) G.; B.S. in Chem. Engring., Mass. Inst. Tech., 1933, M.S. in Chem. Engring., 1934, postgrad. bus. adminstrn., 1938-39; m. Eleanor Norwood Greene, June 19, 1939; children—Mary, Nancy (Mrs. Robert L. Hansen), Sara Baker, Rolene (Mrs. Jerry A. Ramsey). With Union Carbide Corp., South Charleston, W.Va., 1934-56, v.p., N.Y.C., 1957-68; v.p. Pope, Evans & Robbins, cons. engrs., N.Y.C., Alexandria, Va., 1969-71; pres. Combustion Processes, Inc., N.Y.C., 1971—. Registered profl. engr., Conn., N.Y. Mem. Am. Chem. Soc., Am. Inst. Chem. Engrs., Assn. Cons. Chemists and Chem. Engrs., Chemists Club. Club: Sandy Bay Yacht of Rockport, Mass. Home: 53 Goodwives River Rd Darien CT 06820 Office: 50 E 41st St New York City NY 10017

GLENNON, JOSEPH RAYMOND, JR., chem. co. exec.; b. New Bedford, Mass., Aug. 18, 1912; s. Joseph Raymond and Nora Mary (Manchester) G.; B.S.C., U. Notre Dame, 1934; m. Kathryn Mary Coffey, June 6, 1936; children—Joseph Raymond III, Katharine Holley (Mrs. Richard A. Fralick), John Gerard, Thomas Manchester. With Comml. Solvents Corp., N.Y.C., 1934-52, asst. mgr. market devel., 1942-45, asst. mgr. pharm. div., 1946-52; with dist. chem. sales dept. Stoney Mueller Inc., Lyndhurst, N.J., 1952-56, sales mgr. New Eng., 1956—; partner Glennon Realty. Pres., Dartmouth (Mass.) High Sch. P.T.A., 1965-66. Mem. Dartmouth Town Meeting, 1968—. Mem. Sales Assn. Am. Chem. Industries, Am. Chem. Soc., Mass., New Bedford assns. realtors, Old Dartmouth Hist. Soc. Clubs: New Bedford Yacht, Anthony Beach Corporation (dir.). Home: 25 Prospect St S Dartmouth MA 02748 Office: Page and Newark Ave Lyndhurst NJ 07071

GLENNON, VINCENT JOSEPH, mathematician, educator; b. Worcester, Mass., Mar. 24, 1915; s. John Joseph and Katherine Agnes G.; B.S., Fitchburg (Mass.) State Coll., 1938; M.Ed., Boston U., 1941; Ed.D., Harvard U., 1948; m. Claire Frances Andrews, Aug. 26, 1950; children—John Robert, David Andrew. Tchr. pub. schs., Mass., 1938-43; supr. student teaching Fitchburg State Coll., 1943-46; teaching fellow Harvard U., 1946-47; prof., dir. math. edn. center Syracuse (N.Y.) U., 1947-69, U. Conn., Storrs, 1969—. Chmn. bd. trustees Maria Regina Coll., Syracuse, 1968-73; cons. in field. Recipient Golden Anniversary award Fitchburg State Coll., 1963. Fellow AAAS; mem. Assn. Supervision and Curriculum Devel., Am. Psychol. Assn., Am. Ednl. Research Assn., Nat. Council Tchrs. Math., Sigma Xi, Phi Kappa Phi, Phi Delta Kappa. Author textbooks, contbr. articles to profl. publs. maths. edn. Home: 147 Hillyndale Rd Storrs CT 06268

GLICK, BARRY (HERBERT), psychologist, health service adminstr.; b. Bklyn., Aug. 8, 1945; s. Harry and Dorothy (Landan) G.; A.B. in Psychology, U. Miami, 1966; M.S. in Counseling, State U. N.Y. at Oswego, 1968; Ph.D. in Counseling Psychology, Syracuse U., 1972; m. Joan Ellen Hart, June 15, 1969; children—Brian Hart, Alyson Leigh, Daniel Evan, Joseph Seth. Sch. counselor Hannibal (N.Y.) Central Sch., 1967-68, Baldwinsville (N.Y.) Central Sch., 1968-69; instr. psychology Maria Regina Coll., Syracuse, N.Y., 1969-70; research asso. Ednl. Research Info. Center Clearinghouse on Adult Edn., Syracuse, 1969-70; asso. prof. psychology Onondaga Coll., Syracuse, 1970-73; adj. prof. State U. N.Y. at Utica, 1973—; counseling psychologist Elmcrest Children's Center, Syracuse, 1973-74, dir. boy's div., 1974-75, asst. exec. dir., 1976-77, cons. psychologist, 1970-73; facility dir. N.Y. State Div. for Youth, Auburn Center, 1977—; cons. Max Gilbert Acad., DeWitt, N.Y., 1971—; mem. planning com., families and children subcom. N.Y. State Welfare Conf., 1975; chmn. comprehensive system of personnel devel. adv. bd. N.Y. State Dept. Edn., 1978—. Bd. dirs. Max Gilbert Acad. Certified Sch. Psychologist, counselor, tchr., N.Y. Mem. Council Adminstrs. Spl. Edn., Am. Personnel and Guidance Assn., Am. Psychol. Assn., Council for Exceptional Children (adv. bd. N.Y. state fedn. chpts. 1971-73, pres. elect 1975-76), Phi Delta Kappa. Jewish. Contbr. articles on counseling to profl. jours.; editor The Forum, 1971-74. Home: 102 Enderberry Circle Syracuse NY 13224 Office: Pine Ridge Rd RD 4 PO Box 375 Auburn NY 13021

GLICK, J. LESLIE, corp. exec.; b. N.Y.C., Mar. 2, 1940; s. Arthur Harvey and Hilda Lillian (Lichtenfeld) G.; A.B., Columbia, 1961, Ph.D., 1964; m. Roberta Helen Drusin, Nov. 23, 1961; children—Geoffrey Michael, Jessica Michele. Nat. Cancer Inst. postdoctoral fellow Princeton, 1964-65; sr., asso. cancer research scientist Roswell Park Meml. Inst., Buffalo, 1965-69; asso. research prof. physiology, acting chmn. Roswell Park div. State U. N.Y. at Buffalo, 1968-70; exec. v.p. Asso. Biomedic Systems, Buffalo, 1969-72, pres., 1972-75, chmn. bd., 1972-77; pres. Inst. Sci. and Social Accountability, Washington, 1975—, Genex Corp., Rockville, Md., 1977—; v.p. Nat. Assn. Life Sci. Industries, 1975-76; chmn. bd. HTI Corp., Buffalo, 1972-75; research prof. biology Niagara (N.Y.) U., Canisius Coll., Buffalo, 1968-70. Exec. com. State U. N.Y. Grad. Sch. at Buffalo, 1968-70; vis. lectr. NATO Advanced Study Inst., Belgium, 1970. Mem. N.Y. Acad. Scis., Am. Assn. Cancer Research, Am. Physiol. Soc., Tissue Culture Assn., Sigma Xi. Contbr. articles to profl. jours. Research in molecular and cell biology. Home: 10899 Deborah Dr Potomac MD 20854 Office: Genex Corp Suite 1090 6110 Executive Blvd Potomac MD 20852

GLICK, MARVIN MICHAEL, accountant, real estate investor; b. Brookline, Mass., Nov. 25, 1943; s. James Phillip and Lillian (Keesan) G.; B.B.A. in Accounting, U. Mass., 1966; postgrad. Babson Coll., 1969-70; m. Diane Hahn, June 19, 1966; children—Jonathan, Steven, Ronna. Accountant, Dana, Carmen & Levensohn, C.P.A.'s, Boston, 1966-67; field auditor IRS, Boston, 1967-68; sr. accountant Alvin C. Joseph, C.P.A., Chestnut Hill, Mass., 1968-71; sr. accountant Cutler & Smoller Co., Chestnut Hill, 1971-73; prin. Marvin M. Glick, C.P.A., Newton, Mass., 1973—; founder, treas., dir. Photoelectron Energy Tech., Newton; prin. in Boston Investment Group, Jamar Properties, Chateau Estates, various other real estate investment, loan, devel. and mgmt. firms. Bd. dirs., mem. exec. bd. Israel Histadrut Com. Served with N.G., 1966-69. C.P.A., Mass. Mem. Am. Inst. C.P.A.'s. Jewish. Home: 95 Baldpate Hill Rd Newton MA 02159 Office: 233 Needham St Newton MA 02164

GLICK, STANLEY, pub. accountant; b. N.Y.C., May 3, 1935; s. Charles I. and Jeanne (Bussell) G.; B.B.A., Barnard M. Baruch Coll., 1957; m. Marilyn Galkin, June 9, 1973; children—Richard, Karen. Accountant, H.S. Merman & Co., N.Y.C., 1955-57, Buchbinder, Stein & Co., N.Y.C., 1957-58; partner Frederick & Goglio Co., N.Y.C., 1958-68; controller Boxwood Assos., Greenwich, Conn., 1968-71; supervising sr. accountant Brout, Isaacs & Co., Bridgeport, Conn., 1972; controller Hall-Brooke Found. Inc., Westport, Conn., 1972-73, Suburban Carting Corp., Mamaroneck, N.Y., 1973-77; accountant, Westport, 1977—. C.P.A. Mem. Am. Inst. C.P.A.'s, N.Y. State, Conn. socs. C.P.A.'s, Bernard M. Baruch Coll. Alumni Assn. Clubs: Rotary, K.P. Home and Office: 28 Cross Hwy Westport CT 06880

GLICKMAN, MICHAEL LESLIE, health care mgmt. cons.; b. Phila., June 24, 1949; s. Ruben Bernard and Lee (Rosen) G.; B.A. in Physics, Temple U., 1970; M.Sci. Engring. in Computer and Info. Sci., U. Pa., 1972; m. Marlyn Elayne Silberstein, Aug. 8, 1971. Lab. instr. physics-computer sci. Temple U., Phila., 1968-70, instr. computer sci. coll. engring., 1970-72; mgr. tech. services Rapidata Inc., Phila. and Washington, 1972-77; program mgr. Libra Tech. Inc., Rockville, Md., 1977—; tech. cons. to various govt. agencies. Vol., Rockville Md. Sr. Citizen Orgn. Mem. Am. Mgmt. Assn., Am. Hosp. Assn., Sigma Pi Sigma (past v.p.). Jewish. Office: 1300 Piccard Dr Rockville MD 20852

GLICKSMAN, ARVIN S(IGMUND), physician, educator; b. Bklyn., Mar. 14, 1924; s. Charles and Myrtle (Fetner) G.; M.B., M.D., Chgo. Med. Sch., 1949; m. Bernice R. Grobstein, Jan. 30, 1956; children—Jonathan, Jane Ellen, Merrylee, Caroline, Jeanette. Intern, Kings County Hosp., Bklyn., 1948-50; AEC Postdoctoral research fellow Duke, 1950-51; postdoctoral research fellow Brookhaven Nat. Labs., Upton, N.Y., 1951-52; jr. asst. resident in medicine Meml. Hosp., N.Y.C., 1952-53, clin. asst. physician in medicine, 1955-64, asst. attending radiation therapist, 1964-65; research fellow Sloan-Kettering Inst., N.Y.C., 1954-60, asso., 1960-65; mem. med. research inst. Michael Reese Hosp., Chgo., 1965-67, asso. chmn. dept. radiation therapy, 1965-67; dep. dir. dept. radiotherapy Mt. Sinai Hosp., N.Y.C., 1967-73; prof. radiotherapy Mt. Sinai Sch. Medicine, 1971-73; dir. radiation oncology R.I. Hosp., Providence, 1973—; prof. med. scis., chmn. sect. radiation medicine Brown U., 1973—; practice medicine specializing in radiation oncology; Dillion fellow Royal Marsden Hosp. Surrey (Eng.) Br., 1961-62, hon. med. cons. NIH Research Career Devel. awardee, 1962-64; mem. cancer clin. investigation rev. com. Nat. Cancer Inst., 1975—, mem. radiation oncology coordinating com., 1976—; mem. exec. com. Am. Cancer Soc.; R.I. chmn. radiotherapy com. Cancer and Acute Leukemia Group B; chmn. task force on info. systems and evaluation of Cancer Control Bd. State R.I. Mem. New Eng. Soc. Radiation Oncologists (pres. 1975—), N.Y. Roentgen Ray Soc. (chmn. sect. therapeutic radiology 1972-73), Am. Soc. Clin. Oncology, Am. Assn. Cancer Edn., Am. Assn. Cancer Research, Am. Coll. Radiology, Am. Radium Soc., Am. Soc. Therapeutic Radiologists, Brit. Inst. Radiology. Editor: (with others) Computers in Radiotherapy, 2 vols., 1970, 73; contbr. numerous articles to profl. publs. Home: Old Blackstone Rd Uxbridge MA 01569 Office: Rhode Island Hosp Providence RI 02902

GLIEDMAN, RICHARD, orthodontist; b. N.Y.C., June 4, 1926; s. Selig and Rose (Tobias) G.; B.S. in Aero. Engring., Mass. Inst. Tech., 1946; D.D.S., Columbia U., 1952, certificate in orthodontics, 1954; m. Carole Y. Freeman, July 28, 1958; children—Shari Beth, Lesley Anne, Pamela Sue. Pvt. practice orthodontics, Scarsdale and New Rochelle, N.Y., 1954—; mem. faculty Sch. Dental ans Oral Surgery, Columbia U., N.Y.C., 1954—, asso. clin. prof., 1972—. Served as lt. (j.g.) Supply Corps, USNR. Fellow Royal Soc. Health, Am. Coll. Dentists, N.Y. Acad. Dentistry, Westchester Acad. Medicine (asso.); mem. ADA, Am. Assn. Orthodontists, N.Y. State, Suburban Scarsdale dental socs., N.Y. State Orthodontic Soc., Columbia Dental Alumni Soc., Columbia Orthodontic Alumni Soc., Northeastern Assn. Orthodontists, Fedn. Dentaire Internationale, Sigma Psi, Omicron Kappa Upsilon, Alpha Omega. Clubs: Metropolis, Town. Home: 98 Brookby Rd Scarsdale NY 10583 Office: 77 Quaker Ridge Rd New Rochelle NY 10804

GLINES, CARROLL VANE, JR., mag. editor, mgr., pubs.; b. Balt., Dec. 2, 1920; s. Carroll Vane and Elizabeth Marion (Cross) G.; student Drexel Inst. Tech., 1938-40, Canal Zone Jr. Coll., 1946-48, U. Munich (Germany), 1948, Oklahoma City U., 1949-50; B.B.A., U. Okla., 1952, M.B.A., 1954; M.A. in Journalism, Am. U., 1969; m. Mary Ellen Edwards, Oct. 1, 1943; children—Karen Ann (Mrs. Claude Keys Hudson), David Edwards, Valerie Jean. Asso. editor Armed Forces Mgmt. mag., Washington, 1969-70; editor Air Cargo mag., Washington, 1970-71; editor, mgr. publs. Air Line Pilot mag., Washington, 1971—. Gen. editor Air Force Acad. series Macmillan Co., N.Y.C., 1970-72; free-lance writer, 1954—; contbr. numerous articles to nat. mags.; tchr. journalism U. Dayton (Ohio), 1959-60, U. Alaska, Anchorage, 1966-68, Am. U., Washington, 1970-72. Served to col. USAF, 1941-68. Decorated Legion of Merit with oak leaf cluster, Air medal, Commendation medal; recipient numerous journalism awards. Mem. Aviation/Space Writers Assn., Air Force Assn., Explorers Club, Nat. Aviation Club, Aero Club of Washington, Sigma Delta Chi. Author: Complete Guide for the Serviceman's Wife, 1956; Grand Old Lady, 1959; Air Rescue!, 1960; Minuteman of the Air, 1966; The DC-3, 1966; Doolittle's Tokyo Raiders, 1964; Four Came Home, 1966; First Book of the Moon, 1968; Jimmy Doolittle, 1972, others. Home: 7212 Warbler Ln McLean VA 22101 Office: Air Line Pilots Assn 1625 Massachusetts Ave NW Washington DC 20036

GLOBERMAN, NORMA PHYLLIS, devel. economist; b. N.Y.C., Jan. 19, 1932; s. Herbert and Rebecca (Mitler) G.; B.A., Hunter Coll., 1952. Info. officer UN, N.Y.C., 1955-59, spl. asst. UN Civilian Ops. in Congo, 1960-61, asst. to chief de cabinet Office Sec.-Gen. UN, N.Y.C., 1961-62, projects officer for Thailand and Mekong Program, 1966-73, chief div. for S.E.-Asia, UN Devel. Program, 1974—; chmn. task force on Women in UN Devel. System; artist rep. in galleries, including Gallery Primitive Art, Southampton Gallery, N.Y.C.; one-woman show: Manhattan Art and Antiques Center, N.Y.C.; represented in ann. UNICEF exhbns. Mem. Council Fgn. Relations. Home: 300 E 56th St New York NY 10022 Office: 1 UN Plaza New York NY 10017

GLOD, STANLEY JOSEPH, lawyer; b. Altoona, Pa., June 28, 1936; s. Andrew and Katherine G.; A.B. with high honors, John Carroll U., 1958; J.D., Georgetown U., 1961; certificate Hague Acad. Internat. Law, Holland, 1964; S.J.D., U. Munich (Germany), 1967; children—Valerie Anne, Stephanie Lee, Leslie Joan, Debra Lynn. Admitted to D.C. bar, 1962, Va. bar, 1970, U.S. Supreme Ct. bar, 1969; maj. JAGC, U.S. Army, 1962-69, adj. instr. bus., internat. and mil. law U. Md., European div., Verdun, France, 1963-65, Munich, 1965-67, asso. prof. internat. and comparative law JAGC Sch., U. Va., Charlottesville, 1968-69; partner firm Sutton & O'Rourke, Washington, 1969-71, Boner & Glod, Washington, 1971-72; individual practice law, Washington, 1972-77; of counsel firm Weitzman & Houser, Washington, 1977—; chmn. 1st and 2d Polonia Press Confs., Washington, 1974, 75; mem. Presdl. Adv. Com. for Trade Negotiations, 1975; mem. Presdl. trade del. to Polish Ministry Fgn. Trade, 1976. Col. USAR, 1977—. Recipient Eisenhower award Rep. Nat. Com., 1978. Mem. Am. (chmn. working group on internat. trade cts. 1970-73), Fed., Internat., Inter-Am. bar assns., D.C. Unified Bar, Va. State Bar, Am. Soc. Internat. Law, Internat. Law Assn., World Peace Through Law Center (Geneva), Assn. Alumni Hague Acad. Internat. Law, Judge Advs. Assn., Polish Inst. Arts and Scis. Am., Internat. Soc. Mil. Law and Law of War, Washington Fgn. Law Soc., Am. Fgn. Law Assn., Grotius Found., Polish-Am. Arts Assn. Washington, Nat. Advs. Soc. (v.p. 1977—), Polish Am. Congress (dir. Washington chpt. 1975-77), Smithsonian Inst. Assos. (faculty mem. 1977), Alpha Sigma Nu, Phi Alpha Delta. Republican. Contbr. articles to profl. jours. Home: 2331 Creek Dr Alexandria VA 22308 Office: 1735 K St NW Washington DC 20006

GLODELL, LEROY MARCUS, educator, lectr.; b. Hartford, Conn., May 24, 1902; s. Leroy Marcus and Agnes (McCarthy) G.; B.S., U. Md., 1954; M.Ed., Worcester State Coll., 1961; postgrad. U. Conn., 1964—; m. Frances Grace Knapton, July 14, 1947; children—David Kenyon, Dwight Marcus. Lab. asst. DeForest Radio Tel. & Tel. Co., 1918-19; service mgr. Western Electric Co., 1922-25; wire chief Cia Tel y Tel Mexicana, 1927-29, Am. Tel. & Tel. Co., 1929-35; dep. sec. Inter-Am. Def. Bd., Washington, 1951-55; adj. prof. Spanish, Assumption Coll., 1961-64; asso. prof. Spanish, Quinsigamond Community Coll., Worcester, Mass., 1964-72, prof. emeritus, 1972—. Lectr. Latin Am. affairs; Spanish lang. cons. New Eng. industries. Past pres. Green Hill (R.I.) Civic Assn. Served to col. AUS, 1941-60. Decorated Order of Condor of Andes, (Bolivia); Order of Vasco Nunez de Balboa, Ciudadano Meritorio de Colón (Panama); Order of Merito Civil (Spain). Mem. Soc. Colonial Wars, Mil. Order World Wars, Ret. Officers Assn., Archaeol. Inst., Am. Assn. Tchrs. Spanish and Portuguese, Soc. Descs. Founders of Hartford, SAR (past v.p. gen. New Eng. dist.), Soc. Descs. Colonial Clergy, Nat. Soc. Old Plymouth Colony Descs., Soc. Wireless Pioneers, DeForest Pioneers (dir. 1972—), Radio Vets. de Argentina, AAUP, Am. Assn. Emeriti. Republican. Conglist. Mason (32 deg., Shriner), Elk. Clubs: The Bohemians (past pres.); University (Worcester); Explorers (N.Y.). Home: 143 Institute Rd Worcester MA 01602 also RFD Green Hill Wakefield RI 02879 Office: Adminstrn Bldg Quinsigamond Community Coll 670 W Boylston St Worcester MA 01606

GLOMAN, NANCY LUTZ, dietitian; b. Hazleton, Pa., July 10, 1931; d. Roy Alfred and Martha Altheda (Troll) Lutz; B.S. in Home Econs., Coll. of Misericordia, 1959; m. Robert W. Gloman, Oct. 22, 1970. Staff dietitian Wilkes-Barre (Pa.) Gen. Hosp., 1959-60, asst. dept. dir., 1960-61, dept. dir., 1961—; mem. adv. com. on food mgmt. Wilkes-Barre Vocat.-Tech. Sch., 1964—, West Side Area Vocat.-Tech. Sch., Kingston, Pa., 1977—. Mem. Am. (registered), Pa., N.E. Dist. dietetic assns., Am. Soc. Hosp. Food Service. Republican. Lutheran. Office: Wilkes-Barre Gen Hospital N River and Auburn Sts Wilkes-Barre PA 19702

GLORIG, OSTOR, artist, b. N.Y.C., Feb. 14, 1919; s. Joseph and Agavni (Markarian) G.; 4-year certificate Am. Art Sch., 1951. One-man shows, Lynn Kottler Galleries, N.Y.C., 1956, 59, 61, 64, 72, Clarksville Galleries, West Nyack, N.Y., 1965, Coll. Mt. St. Vincent, Bronx, N.Y., 1967; represented permanent collections Mark Twain Library and Meml., Hartford, Conn. Served with AUS, 1942-46. Recipient Merit award Grumbacher Co., 1961. Life fellow Royal Soc. Arts (Eng.); mem. Nat. Soc. Arts and Letters (life), Kappa Pi (hon.). Elk. Home and studio: 21-56 47th St Long Island City NY 11105

GLOSSNER, DAVID CHARLES, psychologist; b. Rochester, N.Y., May 27, 1938; s. Edward N. and Mary Louise (Ceniglis) G.; B.S., St. John Fisher Coll., 1960; M.A., U. Rochester, 1961, postgrad., 1961-73, State U. N.Y., 1963-72; m. Linda May Wiegand, June 22, 1963; children—Heather Ann, David Charles. Tchr. social studies Benjamin Franklin High Sch., Rochester, 1961-68; counselor Frederick Douglass Jr. High Sch., Rochester, 1968—; adj. prof. psychology Monroe Community Coll., Rochester, 1973—; adj. lectr. psychology St. John Fisher Coll., Rochester, 1974—. Mem. counselors adv. com. City Sch. Dist., Rochester, 1969-70; co-chairperson Tchr. Unity Com. N.Y. State, 1972-73; bd. dirs. Rochester Sch. Employees Credit Union, 1974—, 2d v.p., 1976—. Mem. Am., N.Y. State personnel and guidance assns., Assn. Measurement and Evaluation in Guidance, Rochester Tchrs. Assn. (pres. 1971-73), Profl. Counselors Assn., Nat. Vocat. Guidance Assn., N.Y. State United Tchrs. (fin. com. 1972-73, del. 1968—), Am. Fed. Tchrs. (del. 1971-73), N.Y. State, Am. sch. counselors assns.; Monroe County, Nat. assns. children with learning disabilities, Monroe County Health Assn., Monroe County Mental Health Assn. Roman Catholic. Home: 166 South Main Fairport NY 14450 Office: 940 Fernwood Park Rochester NY 14609

GLOVER, LAURICE WHITE, psychoanalyst, musician; b. Los Angeles, Oct. 15, 1930; d. Lawrence Francis and Alice Violet (King) White; B.A., Occidental Coll., 1951; M.S. in Social Work, Columbia, 1956; certificate in psychoanalysis and psychotherapy Postgrad. Center Mental Health, N.Y.C., 1971, certificate in supervision of psychoanalysis, 1975; student pipe organ Norman Wright, Robert Owen, Virgil Fox; m. Norman James Glover, Aug. 18, 1956 (div. 1963). Pvt. practice psychoanalysis, N.Y.C., 1968—; faculty psychoanalysis Postgrad. Center Mental Health, N.Y.C., 1971—, supr., 1976—; asst. clin. prof. psychiatry Albert Einstein Coll. Medicine, Yeshiva U., N.Y.C., 1975—; adj. asst. prof. psychology Bronx Community Coll., 1974; tng. analyst Nat. Psychol. Assn. for Psychoanalysis, 1974-76; organist, choir dir. Throggs' Neck Lutheran Ch., Bronx, N.Y., 1964-67; jazz organist Hotel Barbizon for Women, 1965-66; organist, choir dir. 4th Ave. Meth. Ch., Bklyn., 1967-74. Mem. Soc. Clin. Social Workers, Am. Group Psychotherapy Assn., Nat. Assn. Social Workers, Am. Guild Organists, Am. Theatre Organists Soc., Am. Fedn. Musicians. Office: 271 Central Park W New York City NY 10024

GLUCK, JULIUS CALVERTON, physician; b. Rawa-Ruska, Poland, Oct. 20, 1906; s. Israel P. and Sarah (Katz) G.; came to U.S., 1921, naturalized, 1924; Ph.G., U. Md., 1929; M.D., U. Brussels, 1940; m. Edna May Goldstein, June 3, 1937; children—Daniel Sheldon, David Emanuel. Intern, Franklin Sq. Hosp., Balt., 1940-41, asst. resident in medicine and obstretics, 1941-42, resident in medicine, 1942-44; family practice, Balt., 1947—; mem. staff Baltimore County Gen. Hosp. Served to capt. AUS, 1944-47. Mem. Balt. Med. Soc., Med. and Chirurg. Faculty of Md., AMA, Am. Acad. Family Physicians. Bahai religion. Home: 6014 Cross Country Rd Baltimore MD 21215 Office: 5356 Reisterstown Rd Baltimore MD 21215

GLUCK, MELVIN CHARLES, internist, nephrologist; b. N.Y.C., Dec. 4, 1935; s. Jack S. and Rhoda (Blum) G.; B.A. with distinction, Cornell U., 1956; M.D., N.Y. U., 1960; m. Kayla E. Zakarin, Aug. 31, 1957; children—Julie Lauren, Arthur Clifford, Nancy Jennifer. Intern, Bellevue Hosp., N.Y.C., 1960-61, resident, 1961-62, 63-65, chief resident, 1965-66; N.Y. Heart Assn. fellow in nephrology N.Y. U., 1966-69, instr. in medicine, 1965-69, asst. prof. medicine, 1969-74, asso. prof. clin. medicine, 1974—; pvt. practice medicine specializing in internal medicine and nephrology, N.Y.C., 1969—; asso. dir. hemodialysis unit Univ. Hosp., 1969—, asso. attending, 1969—; mem. staff Bellevue Hosp., profl. adv. com. on home care; mem. staff VA Hosp.; lectr. on history of nephritis, renal failure, pathophysiology. Served as capt. M.C., U.S. Army, 1962-63. Diplomate Am. Bd. Internal Medicine. Fellow A.C.P.; mem. Internat., Am., N.Y. socs. nephrology, Am., N.Y. heart assns., Nat. Kidney Found., Am. Fedn. Clin. Research, AMA, N.Y. Acad. Scis., AAAS, New York County Med. Soc., Phi Beta Kappa, Alpha Omega Alpha, Alpha Epsilon Delta. Contbr. articles to med. publs. Home: 285 Central Park W New York City NY 10024 Office: 566 First Ave New York City NY 10016

GLUECK, RAYMOND MYRON, chem. engr.; b. Yonkers, N.Y., Mar. 9, 1924; s. David H. and Ella F. (Fried) G.; B.S., Columbia, 1948; M.S., N.J. Inst. Tech., 1952; m. Helene Mildred Goldstein, June 2, 1946; children—Judith Anne, Susan Wendy. Supervising engr. GAF Corp., Linden, N.J., 1949-59; project mgr. Kordite Co., Macedon, N.Y., 1959-61; chief engr. Otto B. May, Inc., Newark, 1961-68; pvt. practice chem. engring., 1968-71; chief engr. Standard Chlorine Chem. Co., Delaware City, Del., 1971-74, Royce Chem. Co., E. Rutherford, N.J., 1974—. Served as 2d lt. USAAF, 1943-46. Decorated Air medal with oak leaf cluster, Purple Heart. Registered profl. engr. N.Y., N.J. Mem. Am. Inst. Chem. Engrs., Am. Chem. Soc., Nat. Soc. Profl. Engrs., Soc. Plastics Engrs., Instrument Soc. Am., Phi Lambda Upsilon. Club: Mason. Contbr. articles to profl. jours. Home: 1 Rutledge Rd Pine Brook NJ 07058 Office: 17 Carlton Ave East Rutherford NJ 07073

GLYN, MARVIN, design, illustration co. exec.; b. Syracuse, N.Y., June 13, 1917; s. Joseph and Sarah (Comras) G.; B.F.A., Syracuse U., 1947. Founder, pres. Marvin Glyn Assos., Syracuse, archtl., graphic and product design, illustration, 1946—; cons. advt., architecture. Served with U.S. Army, 1941-45; PTO. Recipient Comdr. award Allied Chem. Instns. Design Total Project, 1968. Club: Rotary. Designer Gen. Electric Co. div. hdqrs. TV and radio, 1960, Sturbridge Orchard Inn, 1966, Chateau Madrid, 1968, Horizon Hotel, 1970, Simpkins Rome, 1976. Home: 110 Mineola Dr Syracuse NY 13224 Office: 108 Mineola Dr Syracuse NY 13224

GLYNN, KENNETH PAUL, lawyer; b. Cambridge, Mass., July 7, 1947; s. Paul Edward and Alice (May) G.; B.S. in Chem. Engring. cum laude (Trustee scholar), Northeastern U., 1970; J.D. cum laude, George Washington U., 1975; m. Linda Marie Westlin, Sept. 9, 1967; 1 dau., Vanessa Marie. Admitted to Conn. bar, 1975, N.J. bar, 1977, U.S. Patent and Trademark Office bar, 1973, U.S. Ct. Customs and Patent Appeals bar, 1975; patent examiner U.S. Patent Office, Washington, 1970-72; patent agt. Morton, Bernard, Brown, Roberts & Sutherland, Washington, 1972-75; patent atty. Olin Corp., New Haven, 1975-76; sr. patent atty. Exxon Research and Engring. Co., Linden, N.J., 1976—; cons. patent litigation. Mem. Conn., N.J. Am. bar assns., Conn., N.J., Am. patent law assns., Tau Beta Pi, Omega Chi Epsilon, Delta Theta Phi. Author: U.S. Patent System: Understanding It and Using It, 1975; patentee solar operated motor apparatus.

GLYNN, NEIL HELD, home builder; B.S., U. N.H., 1949; postgrad. Gen. Motors Inst.; married; 2 children. Br. mgr. Mass. div. Gen. Motors Corp., Lowell, 1954-61; salesman, asst. sales mgr., pres., chief exec. officer Hanslin-Glynn Assn., Waquoit, Mass., 1962-73; v.p. charge mktg. Green Co., Inc., Wellesley, Mass., 1973—; lectr. in field. Recipient Nat. Environment Honor award to Falmouth Port, Environment Monthly mag., 1976, Grand award Better Homes and Gardens mag., 1976. Mem. Nat. Assn. Home Builders (charter mem. Inst. Residential Mktg.; Sales Mgr. of Year award 1966, Best Idea of Year award 1971, life mem. Million Dollar Circle, Bill Molster award 1972, Owens-Corning Fiberglas Spl. award 1973; chmn. mktg. com. 1972-73, chmn. sales and mktg. council 1970, mem. industry promotion com.), Nat. Assn. Real Estate Editors, Nat. Assn. Real Estate Bds., Mass. Home Builders Assn. (legis. com.), Am. Forestry Assn., Nat. Parks and Conservation Assn., Mass. Audubon Soc., Cape Cod C. of C. (dir.), Sierra Club. Home: Osterville MA 02655 Office: PO Box 365 W Harwich St MA 02671

GOBLE, ROSS LAWRENCE, coll. dean; b. Davis City, Iowa, May 23, 1922; s. Oscar Lawrence and Ida Christine (Bailey) G.; A.B., Coll. William and Mary, 1951; M.A., U. Richmond, 1963; Ph.D., U. Utah, 1968; m. Marian Yvonne Roberts, Mar. 30, 1946; 1 dau., Stephanie Goble Wilson. Dir. evening programs, asso. prof. mktg. and psychology State U. N.Y., Albany, 1968-72; dean, prof. mktg. and psychology Clarkson Coll., Potsdam, N.Y., 1972—. Pres., Univ. Research Assos., 1970—. Served with USN, 1938-46; ETO. NDEA research grantee, 1969-71. Mem. Acad. of Mgmt., Am. Accounting Assn., Am. Mktg. Assn., Am. Psychol. Assn., Assn. for Consumer Research, Inst. Mgmt. Scis., Ops. Research Socs. Am., Sigma Xi, Phi Kappa Phi, Beta Gamma Sigma. Presbyterian. Clubs: Rotary, Ski, Gourmet. Author: (with Shaw) Controversy and Dialogue in Marketing, 1975; co-author: Management for the Future, 1978. Home: 130 Leroy St Potsdam NY 13676 Office: Clarkson Coll Potsdam NY 13676

GOCEK, MATILDA ARKENBOUT (MRS. JOHN A. GOCEK), librarian; b. Hoboken, N.J., Feb. 18, 1923; d. Jacob Richard and Mathilda (Meyer) Arkenbout; A.A., Orange County Community Coll., 1961; B.A., N.Y. State U. Coll. New Paltz, 1964; M.L.S., N.Y. State U. Coll. Albany, 1967; m. Harry Francis Decker, May 15, 1939 (div. Nov. 1955); children—Ruth Ann (Mrs. Donald Case), Dianne Karen (Mrs. Ralph McKinstrie); m. 2d, John A. Gocek, Nov. 18, 1956; 1 son, John Jacob. Librarian, Monroe (N.Y.) Free Library, 1958-61, Tuxedo Park (N.Y.) Library, 1963-76; historian Town of Tuxedo, 1973-76; dir. Suffern Free Library, 1977—; library cons. Tuxedo Union Free Sch., 1967-69. Vice chmn. Montgomery Expdn. Meml. Observance, 1973. Bd. dirs. Tuxedo Park Sch.; trustee Mus. Village of Orange County (N.Y.). Mem. Orange-Sullivan Pub. (pres. 1967-70), N.Y. Library Assn., Southeastern N.Y. Library Reference Resource Council, Library Assn. Rockland County (N.Y.) (goals com. 1977). Editor: Library Research Assos., 1968. Home: Dunderberg Rd Monroe NY 10950 Office: Tuxedo Park NY 10987

GOCHMAN, JOHN JAY, lawyer; b. Bklyn., Mar. 16, 1933; s. Harry and Jean (Stebman) G.; B.A., Bklyn. Coll., 1954; LL.B., N.Y. U., 1957; M.A., New Sch. Social Research, 1961; m. Barbara S. Lowenstein, June 26, 1955; children—Benjamin P., Janet A. Admitted to N.Y. State bar, 1960; mem. firm Greenbaum, Wolff & Ernest, N.Y.C., 1959-60; asst. controller Allstate Ins. Co., White Plains, N.Y., 1960-68; ins. cons. John W. Benesch Assos., N.Y.C., 1968-74; practiced in Croton-on-Hudson, N.Y., 1965—; pros. atty. Village of Croton-on-Hudson, 1976, 77, 77-78; comml. no fault arbitrator Am. Arbitration Assn., 1977—. Gen. chmn. United Fund, Croton-on-Hudson, 1967, Am. Cancer Soc., Croton-on-Hudson, 1971-74; acting village justice, Croton-on-Hudson, 1966-75; scoutmaster Boy Scouts Am., Croton on Hudson. Served with AUS, 1957-59. Mem. Am., N.Y. State, Peekskill, Westchester County bar assns., N.Y. State Magistrates Assn., Croton C. of C. Republican. Clubs: Masons, Rotary. Home: 19 Piney Point Ave Croton-on-Hudson NY 10520 Office: 36 Oneida Ave PO Box 7 Croton-on-Hudson NY 10520

GODBEY, JAMES ALLEN, mfg. co. exec.; b. San Mateo, Calif., Jan. 3, 1935; s. Ray B. and Jean (McLaughlin) G.; student U.S. Mil. Acad., 1954-58; m. Dale Macgregor, Aug. 2, 1975; children from previous marriage—James Allen, Cary D. Engr., Fairchild Camera & Instrument Corp., Clifton, N.J., 1962-65; mgr. spl. product div. Mosaic Fabrications, Southbridge, Mass., 1965-67; founder, pres. Electro Fiberoptics (Now Valtec Corp.) West Boylston, Mass., 1968—. Served with AUS, 1958-62. Mem. Optical Soc. Am., Soc. Automotive Engrs., Soc. Photographic and Instrumentation Engrs. Republican. Clubs: Tatnuck County, Chief Execs. Home: Princeton MA 01541 Office: 99 Hartwell St West Boylston MA 01583

GODDARD, ESTHER CHRISTINE (MRS. ROBERT HUTCHINGS GODDARD), editor; b. Worcester, Mass.; d. August William and Augusta (Johnson) Kisk; student Bates Coll., 1920-22; B.S., Johns Hopkins U., 1945; M.A., Clark U., 1951, L.H.D., 1972; Sc.D., Nasson Coll., 1961, Worcester Poly. Inst., 1969, Anna Maria Coll., 1970; m. Robert Hutchings Goddard, June 21, 1924 (dec. Aug. 1945). Editor books with Dr. G. Edward Pendray: Rocket Development, 1947, The Papers of Robert H. Goddard, 3 vols., 1970; contbr. articles on space exploration to various publns., 1946—; bd. dirs. Age Center of Worcester (Mass.) Area, Inc., 1963-70; dir. First Fed. Savs. and Loan Assn., 1965-73. Mem. exec. bd. Mass. chpt. Arthritis Found., 1964—; trustee Med. Research Inst. Worcester, 1965-70, Clark U., Worcester, 1964-72; mem. adv. bd. Anna Maria Coll., Paxton, 1965-72; mem. adv. historic landmark com. City of Worcester, 1966-70; hon. mem. dir.'s council Worcester Sci. Center, 1970—. Named Woman of the Year, Worcester Bus. and Profl. Women's Club, 1958, Nat. League Am. Pen Women, 1972. Fellow Am. Astronautical Soc.; mem. Am. Inst. Aero. and Astronautics (hon.), Air Force Assn. (hon.), AAUW (outstanding mem.), Soroptimists (hon. mem. Worcester). Club: Nat. Space (bd. govs. Washington), Boston Authors. Home: 1 Tallawanda Dr Worcester MA 01603

GODDEN, GLENN FREDERICK, real estate broker; b. Redfield, S.D., Mar. 7, 1917; s. John Earl and Emma Frances (Watson) G.; student Emmetsburg (Iowa) jr. coll., 1936-37, U. Iowa, 1935-40; m. Mildred Ann Link, Dec. 6, 1945; children—David, Mark. Pres., Glenn F. Godden Agy., Inc., Charlestown, R.I., 1946—. Mem. Planning Bd., Charleston, 1967-77; pres. Charlestown Action Com., Inc., 1975. Served with Air Corps, USN, 1940-46. Named R.I. Realtor of Year, R.I. Bd. Realtors, 1975. Mem. Nat., R.I. assns. Realtors, Farm and Land Inst., Soc. Real Estate Appraisers, Nat., R.I. home builders assns., Previews Internat. (dir.), Washington County, Newport bds. Realtors, Nat. Wildlife Fedn., Navy League, Am. Legion, VFW, Nat. Rifle Assn. Republican. Episcopalian. Clubs: Rotary, Ducks Unlimited, Masons, Shriners. Home: Fort Ninigret Rd Charlestown RI 02813 Office: Crossland Park Charlestown RI 02813

GODFREY, ALBERT L., SR., civil engr.; b. Augusta, Maine, Apr. 8, 1935; s. Albert and Thelma Eulalie (Mitchell) G.; B.S. in Civil Engring., U. Maine, 1958; certificate Northwestern U. Traffic Inst., 1967; m. Mary M. Gallagher (dec. Oct. 1972); children—Albert L., Lawrence R., Jacqueline E., Regina M.; m. 2d, Constance L. Roy, Sept. 29, 1973. With Maine Hwy. Commn., Augusta, 1958-72, state traffic engr., 1968-72; engr. of traffic Maine Dept. Transp., Augusta, 1972-77, dir. Bur. Safety, 1977—; pvt. cons. engr., Winthrop, Maine, 1958—; bd. corporators 1st Consumers Savs. Bank, 1973—. Mem. Winthrop Planning Bd., 1958-63, Winthrop Fire Dept., 1958-68, Winthrop Finance Bd., 1969-72. Registered profl. engr., Maine; registered land surveyor; registered site evaluator. Fellow Inst. Transp. Engrs. (pres. New Eng. sect. 1978); mem. Am. Pub. Works Assn., Maine Good Rds. Assn., Maine Sight Conservation Assn. (sec. 1978-79), Inst. Transp. Republican. Roman Catholic. Club: Lions (sec. Winthrop 1977-78, treas. 1978-79, dep. dist. gov. 1978-79). Home: 3 Butters Hill Terr Winthrop ME 04364 Office: Dept Transp Bldg Augusta ME 04333

GODFREY, GEORGE CHEESEMAN, II, surgeon; b. Atlantic City, Oct. 15, 1926; s. William M. and Elizabeth (Uzzell) G.; student St. Bonaventure Coll., 1944, U. Ky., 1945; A.B., Colgate U., 1948; M.D., Jefferson Med. Coll., 1952; m. Evelyn Fry, Sept. 20, 1952; children—Cheryl Lynn, George Cheeseman. Intern, Atlantic City Hosp., 1952-53; resident in gen. surgery U.S. VA Hosp., Ft. Howard, Balt., 1953-57; practice medicine specializing in surgery, Somers Point, N.J., 1957—; chief gen. and trauma surgery, dir. dept. surgery Shore Meml. Hosp., Somers Point, 1973-76; instr. surgery Jefferson Med. Coll., Phila., 1958—; cons. in orthopedics N.J. Div. Disability Determinations, N.J. Rehab. Program, 1960—; physician Nat. Aviation Fed. Exptl. Center, FAA, part-time, 1977—. Pres., Bd. Edn., Linwood, N.J., 1972-73. Served with U.S. Army, 1944-46. Recipient Distinguished Service award N.J. Jr. C. of C., 1960. Diplomate Am. Bd. Surgery, Nat. Bd. Med. Examiners. Fellow A.C.S.; mem. AMA, Am. Trauma Soc., Am. Soc. Abdominal Surgeons, Aerospace Med. Assn., N.J., Atlantic County med. socs., Phi Kappa Tau, Phi Beta Pi. Methodist. Clubs: Kiwanis, Masons, (Shriner), K.T. Contbr. articles to profl. jours. Home: 112 Glenside Ave Linwood NJ 08221 Office: 647 Shore Rd Somers Point NJ 08244

GODFREY, JOHN CARL, chemist; b. Cornelius, Oreg., Mar. 11, 1929; s. Carl H. and Ruth Emma (James) G.; B.A. in Chemistry cum laude, Pomona Coll., 1951; Ph.D. (NSF fellow, du Pont fellow) in Organic Chemistry, U. Rochester, 1954; m. Nancy Jane Williams, June 12, 1954; children—Laura Alexis, Helen Rebecca, Sabrina Lee. Research chemist Shell Devel. Co., Emeryville, Calif., 1954-55; postdoctoral fellow Rutgers U., New Brunswick, N.J., 1955-57, instr. chemistry, 1957-59; research scientist Bristol Labs., Syracuse, N.Y., 1959-65, dir. biochem. research, 1965-74, dir. med. chem. process labs., 1974, clin. monitor, asst. dir. med. research, 1975-77, mgr. new ventures, 1977—; owner Harvest Mills of Syracuse, 1975—; with Am. Cyanamid Co., Bound Brook, N.J., 1957 (summer); pres. Godfrey Molecular Models, Inc., New Brunswick, 1958-59; cons. VWR Sci. Corp., Rochester, N.Y., 1959-72. Mem. N.Y. Acad. Scis., AAAS, Am. Chem. Soc. (chmn. Syracuse sect. 1977), Am. Soc. Microbiology, Phi Beta Kappa. Clubs: Syracuse Flying (dir. 1970-71, pres. 1974-75); Technology of Syracuse (dir., v.p.). Editor: The Syracuse Chemist, 1964-75; contbr. articles to profl. jours. Home: 215 Manor Dr Syracuse NY 13214 Office: PO Box 657 Syracuse NY 13201

GODICK, NEIL BARNETT, accountant; b. Phila., Oct. 6, 1942; s. Samuel and Jeanette (Goldman) G.; B.S. cum laude, Villanova U., 1964; children—Gene Sherman, Marc Sherman. Accountant, Haskins & Sells, Phila., 1964-70, mem. staff exec. office, N.Y.C., 1970-72; Pa. treas. McGovern for Pres. campaign, Phila., 1972; adminstrv. partner Rudolph, Palitz & Co., Phila., 1972—; treas. Health Mgmt. services Inc., Bala Cynwyd, Pa., 1975—, also dir.; adj. prof. accounting Temple U., 1974—; treas., dir. Community Accountants Inc., 1974—. Treas. Lou Hill for Mayor campaign Phila., 1975; liaison rep. Villanova U. Admissions Office, 1971—; bd. dirs., pres. Phila. All-Star Forum Series, Inc., 1974—; mem. Phila. Controllers Com. Quality Performance, 1974—; bd. dirs. Southeastern Pa. chpt. Ams. for Democratic Action: treas. Friends of Tel-Aviv U., Phila. chpt., 1974—; bd. dirs. Phila. Fedn. of Settlement. C.P.A., Pa. Mem. Am., Pa. insts. C.P.A.'s, N.Y. State, N.J. socs. C.P.A.'s, Nat. Assn. Accountants (pres. Phila. chpt. 1977—), Accountants of Pub. Interest (dir.). Democrat. Jewish religion. Club: Locust. Home: 1500 Locust St Philadelphia PA 19102 Office: Rudolph Palitz & Co 1845 Walnut St Philadelphia PA 19103

GODIN, EDGAR, bishop; b. Negauc, N.B., Can., May 31, 1911; s. Joseph Albanie and Marguerite (Breau) G.; B.A., Bathurst Coll., 1935; License in Canon Law, Laval U., 1947, Gregorian U., Rome, 1948; Ph.D., U. Moncton; LL.D., St. Thomas U., 1970. Ordained priest Roman Catholic Ch., 1941; dir. Retreat House, Bathurst, N.B., 1942-46; vice chancellor Diocese of Bathurst, 1948-51, chancellor, 1951-69; bishop of Bathurst, 1969—. Mem. Canadian Assn. Cath. Hosps. (pres. 1967-69). Author: Hospital Ethics, 1959. Address: 645 Ave Murray C P 460 Bathurst NB E2A 3Z4 Canada*

GODINO, RINO LODOVICO, petroleum and chem. design co. exec.; b. N.Y.C., Mar. 21, 1925; s. Enrico and Emily (Forneron) G.; B. Chem. Engring., N.Y. U., 1950, M. Chem. Engrig., 1952, postgrad., 1967; m. Dolores E. Pagano, June 12, 1955; children—Diane Carol, Marc Lawrence. Asst. instr. N.Y. U., 1950-51; research chem. engr. Stauffer Chem. Co., N.Y.C., 1951; with Foster Wheeler Corp., Livingston, N.J., 1952—, chief engr., lubricating and heavy oil refineries, 1962-72, dir. petroleum and chem. plant design, 1973—; dir. Fractionation Research Inc. Rep. to Protestant Council Chs. in N.Y., 1954-55. Served with inf. AUS, 1943-46. Decorated Bronze Star, Combat Infantryman's badge. Registered profl. engr., N.J., Ill., Pa. Mem. Am. Inst. Chem. Engrs., Nat. Assn. Profl. Engrs., Soc. Am. Magicians, Internat. Brotherhood Magicians, Tau Beta Pi, Phi Lambda Upsilon. Mem. Waldensian Ch. (elder). Contbr. articles to profl. jours. Patentee in field. Office: 110 S Orange Ave Livingston NJ 07039

GODLESKI, JOHN JOSEPH, JR., pathologist; b. Nanticoke, Pa., July 24, 1943; s. John Joseph and Sophie Pauline (Pretko) G.; B.S. in Biology, King's Coll., 1965; M.D., U. Pitts., 1969; m. Mary Lou Moss, June 14, 1969; children—Teresa Louise, Daniel Peter. Intern, Mass. Gen. Hosp., Boston, 1969-70, resident in pathology, 1970-71; fellow in pathology U. N.C., 1971-73; practice medicine specializing in pathology, Phila., 1973-78, Boston, 1978—; asst. prof. pathology Med. Coll. Pa., Phila., 1973-78; mem. staff Peter Bent Brigham Hosp., Boston, 1978—. Active Merion Civic Assn. Served with USPHS, 1971-73. Recipient Pulmonary Young Investigator award, 1st award Student Am. Med. Assn.-Mead Johnson Sci. Forum, 1967. Mem. AAAS, Internat. Acad. Pathology. Roman Catholic. Contbr. articles to med. jours. Home: 421 Conant Rd Weston MA 02193 Office: 721 Huntingdon Ave Boston MA 02115

GODSOE, JOSEPH GERALD, JR., lawyer; b. Toronto, Ont., Can., Feb. 28, 1942; s. Joseph Gerald and Margaret (Cowperthwaite) G.; B.Sc. with honors, U. Toronto, 1963; B.A. (Rhodes scholar), St. John's Coll., Oxford (Eng.) U., 1963, M.A., 1965; LL.B., Dalhousie U., Can., 1968; m. Dale Anne Sullivan, July 4, 1969; children—Suzanne, Stacey. Called to N.S. bar, 1968; partner firm Stewart, MacKeen & Covert, Halifax, 1974—; dir. Eldorado Nuclear Ltd., C.E. Choat & Co.; cons. energy matters; mem. N.S. Law Reform Adv. Commn.; lectr. Dalhousie Law Sch., 1974—. Sec. Maritime Provinces selection com. Rhodes Scholarship Trust, 1971—; chmn. Halifax br. Canadian Inst. Internat. Affairs, 1974-76; chmn. Coordinating Com. Maritime Provinces on Offshore Resources; v.p. N.S. Liberal Fedn., 1974—, acting pres., 1976; mem. standing com. on policy Liberal Party of Can., 1974—, nat. exec., 1976; bd. dirs. Opera East, Atlantic region Canadian Council Christians and Jews; bd. govs., chmn. fin. com. Mt. St. Vincent U. Mem. N.S. Barristers Soc., Canadian Bar Assn. (council), Atlantic Provinces Econ. Council, Halifax Bd. Trade. Clubs: Halifax, N.S. Liberal Century (sec.-treas. 1974-76). Home: 6560 Geldert St Halifax NS B3H 2C8 Canada Office: PO Box 997 Halifax NS B3J 2X2 Canada

GOEBEL, LAWRENCE ROBERT, ednl. adminstr.; b. N.Y.C., Feb. 13, 1946; s. Englebert and Jennie (Hauser) G.; B.A., Rutgers Coll., 1967; M.A., Seton Hall U., 1969; A.B.D., N.Y. U., 1975; m. Susan Ann Coyle, Aug. 28, 1966; children—Laura Susan, Tara Lynn. Instr. history Rider Coll., Lawrenceville, N.J., 1969-73, asst. dir. admissions, asst. prof. history, 1973-78; dir. admissions Passaic County Community Coll., Paterson, N.J., 1978—; ednl. cons. Thomas A. Edison Coll., Princeton, N.J., 1974—. Vol., Princeton Med. Center. Rotary Internat. fellow, India, 1975. Mem. Assn. Collegiate Registrars and Admission Officers, Am. Hist. Assn., Orgn. Am. Historians. Home: 12 VanderVeer Dr Lawrenceville NJ 08648

GOEL, AMRIT LAL, educator; b. Meerut, India, Mar. 4, 1938; s. Gujjar Mal and Shanti Devi (Mittal) G.; came to U.S., 1962; B.S., Agra (India) U., 1957; B. Engring., U. Roorkee (India), 1961; M.S., U. Wis., Madison, 1963, Ph.D., 1968; m. Norma Lynn Currie, Mar. 27, 1967; children—Alok, Nandita. Asst. mech. engr. AEC, India, 1961-62; instr. mech. engring. U. Wis., Madison, 1965-66, lectr., Milw., 1967-68; asst. prof. indsl. and ops. research Syracuse (N.Y.) U., 1968-71, asso. prof., 1971-77, prof., 1977—; cons. to industry, also Dept. Def. NSF grantee, 1969-72; Nat. Acad. Sci. grantee, 1971. Fellow Royal Statis. Soc. (Eng.); mem. AAAS, IEEE, Ops. Research Soc. Am., Am. Statis. Assn., Assn. for Computing Machinery, Sigma Xi. Contbr. articles in field to profl. jours. Home: 112 Standish Dr Syracuse NY 13224 Office: 427 Link Hall Syracuse Univ Syracuse NY 13210

GOELET, ROBERT GUESTIER, bus. exec.; b. Sandricourt, France, Sept. 28, 1923; s. Robert Walton and Anne Marie (Guestier) G.; A.B., Harvard U., 1945; m. Alexandra Gardiner Creel, Sept. 9, 1976. Chmn., R.I. Corp., N.Y.C., 1955—; pres. Goelet Realty Co., N.Y.C., 1955—; v.p. Goelet Estate Co., N.Y.C., 1950—; dir. Chem. Bank, Chem. N.Y. Corp. Trustee French Inst./Alliance Française de N.Y., 1951—, pres., 1967—; trustee N.Y. Hist. Soc., 1961—, pres. 1971—; trustee N.Y. Zool. Soc., 1951—, pres., 1971-75; bd. dirs. Nat. Audubon Soc., 1956-67, 69-75, treas., 1959-69; trustee Am. Mus. Natural History, N.Y.C., 1958—, pres., 1975—; trustee Phipps Houses, 1959—; bd. dirs. Boscobel Restoration Inc., Garrison-on-Hudson, N.Y., 1976—. Served with USNR, 1943-45. Home: 7 Sutton Pl New York City NY 10022 Office: 425 Park Ave New York City NY 10022

GOERTZ, AUGUSTUS FREDERICK, painter, printmaker, musician; b. N.Y.C., Aug. 15, 1948; s. Augustus Frederick and Esther (Meyer) G.; student Carnegie-Mellon U., 1966; B.F.A. with honors, San Francisco Art Inst., 1971; m. Dione Christensen, Sept. 1978. One-man shows include: N.Y. Law Sch., 1977, Sarah Y. Rentschler Gallery, N.Y.C., 1978, 79, Kiva Gallery, Scarsdale, N.Y., 1979; group shows include: Art Fiera, Bologna, Italy, 1978, Am. Fedn. Arts U.S. Tour, 1976, Aldrich Mus., Ridgefield, Conn., 1978, Soho Center for Visual Arts, 1979; represented in permanent collections: Adrich Museum Contemporary Art, Helmut Hofman Schlangenbad, W. Ger, Leo Guttman Collection Chgo. Art Inst., Harmonious Arts Found., N.Y.C., Hosp. for Joint Disease and Med. Center, N.Y.C.; cons. League Internat. Artists, N.Y.C. Mem. Orgn. Ind. Artists, Works Project Assn. Inc., San Francisco Art Inst. Alumni Assn., Internat. Platform Assn. Democrat. Home: 319 Greenwich St New York NY 10013

GOETCHEUS, JOHN STEWART, orthopedic surgeon; b. Cin., May 14, 1938; s. Federick and Elizabeth (Gibson) G.; B.A. with distinction, DePauw U., 1960; M.D., Western Res. U., 1964; m. Janice Berg, July 13, 1963; children—Amy Lisabeth, Gregory John. Intern and resident in gen. surgery Univ. Hosps., Cleve., 1964-66; resident in orthopedic surgery Yale U., New Haven, 1968-71; individual practice orthopedic surgery, Essex, Conn., 1971—; clin. instr. Yale Sch. Medicine, 1970—; mem. staff Middlesex Meml. Hosp., Yale-New Haven Hosp., West Haven VA Hosp. Served to capt. USAF, 1966-68. Diplomate Am. Bd. Orthopedic Surgery. Fellow Am. Acad. Orthopedic Surgeons, Conn., Middlesex County med. assns., Eastern Orthopedic Assn. Republican. Congregationalist. Club: Rotary (Essex). Home: Partridge Hill Essex CT 06426 Office: Wildwood Med Specialists Middlesex Turnpike Essex CT 06426

GOETTEL, GERARD LOUIS, fed. judge; b. N.Y.C., Aug. 5, 1928; s. Louis and Agnes Beatrice (White) G.; student The Citadel, 1946-48; B.A., Duke U., 1950; J.D. (Harlan Fiske Stone scholar), Columbia U., 1955; m. Elinor Praeger, June 4, 1951; children—Sheryl, Glenn, James. Admitted to N.Y. bar, 1955; asst. U.S. atty. So. Dist. N.Y., N.Y.C., 1955-58; dep. chief Atty. Gen.'s Spl. Group on Organized Crime, Dept. Justice, N.Y.C., 1958-59; asso. firm Lowenstein, Pitcher, Hotchkiss, Amann & Parr, N.Y.C., 1959-62; counsel New York Life Ins. Co., 1962-68; with firm Natanson & Reich, N.Y.C., 1968-69; asso. gen. counsel Overmyer Co., N.Y.C., 1969-71; magistrate U.S. Dist. Ct., So. Dist. N.Y., N.Y.C., 1971-76, judge, 1976—; asst. counsel New York Ct. on Judiciary, 1971. Mem. council Fresh Air Fund, N.Y.C., 1961-64; dir. Community Action Program, Yonkers, N.Y., 1964-66; pres. Sprain Lake Civic Assn., Yonkers, 1966. Served to lt. (j.g.) USCG, 1951-53. Mem. Am., Westchester County bar assns., Nat. Conf. Fed. Ct. Judges, Am. Judicature Soc., Columbia Law Sch. Alumni Assn., Ins. Co. Lawyers (chmn. 1968). Clubs: Rye Golf; Siasconset (Nantucket) Casino; Green Woods Country. Home: 232 Lakeridge Torrington CT 06790 Office: US Dist Ct Foley Sq New York City NY 10007

GOETZ, GUENTHER CONRAD, structural engr.; b. Schwetz, Germany, May 25, 1916; s. Friedrich Wilhelm and Ida Aguste (Kowalleck) G.; came to U.S., 1953, naturalized, 1958; M.S., Koenigsberg/P.R. (Germany), 1939; m. Elsa Martha Schulz, June 25, 1939; children—Ingrid, Hendrik. Constrn. engr. Drost Constrn. Co., Rastenburg, Germany, 1939-41; constrn. supt. N. Sued Bau, Kiel, W. Ger., 1945-50; mgr. Diago Werke, Hamburg, W. Ger., 1950-53; structural engr. Parsons Co., Kohorn-Vitro Engring. Co., N.Y.C., 1953-60; asst. chief structural engr. Gibbs & Hill, Inc., N.Y.C., 1960—. Served with German Army, 1940-45. Decorated Silver Purple Heart; registered profl. engr., N.Y. Mem. Nat. Soc. Profl. Engrs. Lutheran. Home: 28 Brightwater Pl Massapequa NY 11758 Office: 393 7th Ave New York City NY 10001

GOFF, H. DAVID, advt. and pub. relations exec.; b. Corning, N.Y., Oct. 14, 1940; s. Howard Dennis and Dorothy Helen (Hardiman) G.; student Sch. Bank Mktg., Northwestern U., 1967; m. Carolyn C. Slater, Aug. 17, 1963 (div. 1975); children—Deborah Marie, Michael David, Stephanie Ann; m. 2d, Tina C. Rhoda, June 24, 1978. Advt. mgr. Chemung Canal Trust Co., Elmira, N.Y., 1962-67; pres. Howell Advt. Assos., Elmira, 1967-73, Mintz, Hoke, & Goff, Inc., Elmira, 1973-77; pres. Goff Communications, Corning, N.Y., 1977—; dir. Affiliated Advt. Agys. Internat., 1966-67. Served with USAF, 1959-62. Mem. Am. Advt. Fedn. (Crystal Prism award 1977), Public Relations Soc. Am. (sec. chpt. 1978), Elmira-Corning Advt. Club (pres. 1967-68, Adman of Yr. 1977). Democrat. Roman Catholic. Home: 190 Hamilton St Corning NY 14830 Office: 19 Denison Pkwy E Corning NY 14830

GOFFIN, SUMNER J., judge; b. Portland, Maine, June 15, 1919; s. Mitchell and Tena D. (Agger) G.; student U. Iowa; LL.B., Peabody Law Sch., 1942; m. Dorothy M. Maxcy, Oct. 27, 1953; children—David, Sally, Peter. Admitted to Maine bar, 1942. Faculty, U. Portland Law Sch., 1949-57; mem. panel mediators State of Maine, 1956-73; chmn. Maine State Employees Appeals Bd., 1967-73; judge Maine Superior Ct., Portland, 1973—. Chmn., Yarmouth Town Council, 1966-67. Bd. dirs. Community Counseling Center, Portland, 1970-74. Blind Children Resources Center, Portland; life dir. Maine Sight Conservation Assn. Mem. Am. Acad. Polit. and Social Sci., Am. Acad. Polit. Sci., Internat. Relations Research Assn., Nat. Acad. Arbitrators. Home: 45 Eastern Promenade Portland ME 04101 Office: Courthouse 142 Federal St Portland Maine 04111

GOGGIN, JAY, govt. ofcl.; b. Homestead, Pa., Oct. 13, 1935; s. James J. and Jean M. (Knepsheild) G.; B.S. in Indsl. Mgmt., Duquesne U., 1957; m. Mary Jane Gropelli, Jan. 14, 1961; children—Jacqueline, Judith, John, Ava, Erik, Sean, Kate. Metall. trainee U.S. Steel Co., Homestead, 1959; production expediter Mesta Machine Co., West Homestead, Pa., 1960-61; pub. Voice, Inc., Pitts., 1961-64; staff reporter Pitts. Post-Gazette, 1964-65; neighborhood adminstr. Action-Housing, Inc., Pitts., 1965-68; adminstrv. dir. Community Action Pitts., 1968-69; dep. dir. Model Cities, Cambridge, Mass., 1970-71; exec. dir. Urban Redevel. Authority, Pitts., 1971-73, Pitts. Housing Authority, 1973-78; disaster recovery adminstr. Johnstown (Pa.) Redevel. Authority, 1978—. Bd. dirs. Southwestern Pa. Econ. Devel. Dist. Served with U.S. Army, 1957-59. Recipient William Bellamy award 1976. Mem. Inst. Real Estate Mgmt., Nat., Pa. assns. housing and redevel. ofcls. Home: 1116 Luxerne St Extension Johnstown PA 15905 Office: 417 Lincoln St Johnstown PA 15901

GOGGINS, JOHN FRANCIS, health sci. adminstr.; b. Flint, Mich., Oct. 26, 1933; s. King Pierre and Genevieve Adeline (Bouchard) G.; student U. Notre Dame, 1951-54; D.D.S., Marquette U., 1958, M.S., 1965; m. Madeleine Alice Murray, Sept. 17, 1960; children—Patrick, Colleen, William. Practice dentistry, Flint, 1960-63; instr. dept. pathology Marquette U., Sch. Dentistry, Milw., 1963-65; scientist Nat. Inst. Dental Research, NIH, Bethesda, Md., 1965-73, chief periodontal and soft tissue diseases program, 1973-74, asso. dir. for collaborative research, 1974—. Served to capt. USAF, 1958-60, with USPHS, 1966—. USPHS fellow, 1965-66. Mem. ADA, Histochem. Soc., AAAS, Internat. Assn. for Dental Research, Genessee County Dental Soc. (chmn. fluoridation com. 1961-62), Jr. C. of C. Contbr. articles on research in dentistry to profl. pubIs. Home: 7624 Dew Wood Dr Derwood MD 20855 Office: National Institute of Dental Research NIH Bethesda MD 20014

GOGLIA, MICHAEL LINCOLN, auditor; b. Syracuse, N.Y., Feb. 12, 1923; s. Thomas and Fanny (Buzzuto) G.; grad. Am. Inst. Banking, 1964; student Sch. Banking, U. Wis., 1969, Syracuse U., 1945-46, LeMoyne Coll., 1949-51; m. Pauline Frances Testone, May 30, 1944; children—Mary Ann, Thomas Anthony. Dept. head, buyer elec. equipment Alexander Grant Hardware, Syracuse, 1945-50; wholesale hardware salesman Lincoln Supply Co., Syracuse, 1950-56; with audit dept. Syracuse Savs. Bank, 1956—, auditor, 1976—. Served to lt. col., USAFR, 1943-73. Certified internal auditor, N.Y.; chartered bank auditor. Mem. Am. Inst. Banking (pres. 1968-69, bd. govs. 1969-76), Bank Adminstrn. Inst. (chpt. sec. 1976-77, v.p. Central N.Y. chpt.), Inst. Internal Auditors (pres. 1972-73, bd. govs. 1973-75), N.Y. State Auditors and Comptrollers Forum (exec. com. 1977-78, treas. 1978-79), EDP Auditors Assn. (pres. Central N.Y. chpt. 1978-79), Nat. Alumni Assn. Sch. Bank Adminstrn. Republican. Roman Catholic. Club: Kiwanis. Home: 4025 Arrowhead Ln Liverpool NY 13088 Office: 1 Clinton Sq Syracuse NY 13202

GOIZUETA-MIMO, FELIX, educator; b. Havana, Cuba, Nov. 20, 1938; s. Felix Mateo Goizueta and Josefina Mimo; Bachiller, L & C, Colegio de la Salle, 1957; B.S. (Benjamin Franklin scholar), U. Pa., 1963, M.B.A. (OAS fellow), 1964, M.A., 1967, Ph.D., 1971; m. Gelsys Florencia Junco, Dec. 19, 1969; came to U.S., 1960, naturalized, 1972. Prof. mgmt. finance, internat. students adv. Phila. (Pa.) Coll. Textiles and Sci., 1965—, past dir. M.B.A. grad. program; lectr. mgmt. Wharton Sch., U. Pa., Phila., 1972—; researcher, cons. in social scis. Southeastern Pa. Econ. Devel. Corp., 1965, Wharton Entrepreneurial Center, 1973, Phila. Bd. City Trusts, 1976, Pa. Utility Commn., 1977. Mem. World Affairs Council, Phila., 1968—, Internat. House Phila., 1963—. Mem. Econ. Hist. Assn., Eastern Finance Assn., Fin. Mgmt. Assn., Am. Acad. Social and Polit. Sci., Assn. Fgn. Students Affairs, AAUP, Delta Sigma Pi, Pi Gamma Mu. Club: Kiwanis. Author: Effects of Sugar Monoculture on Colonial Cuba, 1971; Azucar Amargo Cubano, 1974; Financial Management Analysis Applied to Capital Budgeting: The Range of Optimal Investment, 1976; contbr. articles to profl. jours. Office: 5555 Wissahickon Ave Suite 1006 Philadelphia PA 19144

GOKBORA, MARY JANE MCKEE, social worker; b. Mankato, Minn.; d. John Cecil and Claire (Nieberle) McKee; B.A., U. Iowa, 1946, M.S.W., 1958; m. Ahmet Gokbora, Jan. 11, 1946 (div. June 1956); children—Gail M. (Mrs. William Hurst), Erol K. Pub. assistance worker Iowa Dept. Social Welfare, Linn County, 1951-56; child welfare worker, Marshall and Tama Counties, 1958-59; psychiat. social worker, mental health team Div. Mental Health, Iowa Bd. Control State Instns., 1959-60; dir. social services Iowa State Tng. Sch. for Boys, Eldora, 1960-62; supt. Mo. State Tng. Sch. for Girls, Chillicothe, 1962-71; social work cons. to Mo. Law Enforcement Assistance Council, Jefferson City, Women in Community Service, Lincoln, Nebr., St. Francis Homes, Albany, N.Y., 1971-75; lectr. sch. Social Welfare State U. N.Y., Albany, 1975—; pvt. practice clin. social work, 1977—. Certified social worker, N.Y. Mem. Nat. Fedn. Bus. and Profl. Womens Clubs, AAUW, U. Iowa Alumni Assn., Nat. Assn. Social Workers (chpt. v.p. 1965-66, sec. 1974—, mem. Clin. Social Work Register 1976—), Nat. Council Crime and Delinquency, Joint Commn. Correctional Manpower and Tng., Nat. Assn. Tng. Schs. and Juvenile Agys. (v.p. 1963-69), Nat. Conf. Supts. of Correctional Instns. for Girls and Women (pres. 1965-66), Acad. Certified Social Workers. Episcopalian. Address: 22 Tulip Terr Clifton Park NY 12065

GOLAB, ALEXANDER, gynecologist; b. Tluszcz, Poland, Mar. 1, 1936; s. Samuel and Anne (Grynes) G.; B.A., U. Sask. (Can.) 1957, M.D., 1962; came to Can., 1948, naturalized, 1952; m. Lucy Anne Adam, May 17, 1962; children—Jonathan, Michael. Intern, St. Micahels Hosp., Toronto, Ont., Can., 1962-63; resident in obstetrics and gynecology New Mt. Sinai Hosp., Toronto, 1963-64, Millard Fillmore Hosp., Buffalo, 1964-67; practice medicine specializing in obstetrics and gynecology Richmond Hill, Ont., 1969—; chief obstetrics and gynecology York Central Hosp. Diplomate Am. Bd. Obstetrics and Gynecology. Fellow Royal Coll. Surgeons Can., Am. Coll. Obstetrics and Gynecology; mem. Soc. Obstetrics and Gynecology Toronto, Soc. Obstetrics and Gynecology Can., Ont. Med. Assn., Royal Coll. Physicians and Surgeons, Am. Assn. Gynecol. Laparoscopists. Conservative. Jewish religion. Home: 20 Alcaine Ct Thornhill ON Canada Office: 22 Richmond St Suite 202 Richmond Hill ON L4C 3Y1 Canada

GOLAN, LAWRENCE PETER, mech. engr.; b. Newark, June 20, 1938; s. Joseph and Frances (Duda) G.; B.M.E., W.Va. U., 1961, M.M.E., 1964; Ph.D. in Mech. Engring., Lehigh U., 1968; m. Helen Imelda Hemko, June 30, 1962; children—Lisa Marie, Wanda Marie, Lawrence Peter. Instr. mech. engring. W.Va. U., Morgantown, 1962-64; mech. engr. spl. weapons br. Picatinny (N.J.) Arsenal, 1961-62; instr. mech. engring. Lehigh U., Bethlehem, Pa., 1964-68; sr. staff engr. Exxon Research and Engring. Co., Florham Park, N.J., 1968—; adj. asso. prof. County Coll. Morris (N.J.), 1972-75. Head coach Randolph Twp. (N.J.) Jr. Track Program, 1974—; prin. St. Virgils Confrat. Christian Doctrine, 1969-72. Mass. Inst. Tech. Ford Found. fellow, 1965. Mem. Am. Inst. Chem. Engrs., ASME, Am. Soc. Engring. Edn., Sigma Xi. Roman Catholic. Contbr. articles in field to profl. jours. Office: Exxon Research and Engring Co Florham Pk NJ 07932

GOLANY, GIDEON, urban and regional planner; b. Jan. 23, 1928; B.A., Hebrew U., Jerusalem, Israel, 1956, M.A., 1962, Ph.D., 1966; M.S. in Environ. Studies, Technion, Haifa, Israel, 1965; diploma comprehensive planning, Inst. Social Studies, The Hague, Netherlands, 1965; came to U.S., 1967, naturalized, 1975; married; 2 children. Lectr., Technion, 1963-67; vis. lectr. Cornell U., 1967-68, research officer Office Regional Resources and Devel., 1968; asso. prof. urban and regional planning Va. Poly. Inst. and State U., Blacksburg, 1968-70; vis. prof. Inst. Desert Research, Ben-Gurion U. of Negev, Beer Sheva, Israel, 1975-76; prof. urban and regional planning, sr. mem. Grad. Sch. faculty Pa. State U., 1970—, chmn. grad. program, 1970-76; propr. Gideon Golany Assos., 1970—; cons. to govt. and industry. Served with Hagana, 1946-48, Israeli Army, 1948-50, 56, 67. Grantee Govt. Netherlands, 1965, NSF, 1972-74; recipient prize Exec. Com. Histradut, Tel-Aviv, 1963. Mem. Am. Inst. Planners, Am. Soc. Planning Ofcls., Canadian Inst. Planners, Assn. Engrs. and Architects Israel. Author, editor books, 1962—, latest being Innovations for Future Cities, 1976; New-Town Planning: Principles and Practice, 1976; International Urban Growth Policies: New-Towns Contributions, 1978; Urban Planning for Arid-Zones: Am. Experiences and Directions, 1978; also numerous articles, plans. Home: 292 Douglas Dr State College PA 16801 Office: 308 Sackett Bldg Pa State Univ University Park PA 16802

GOLD, AARON ALAN, finance co. exec.; b. Phila., Oct. 4, 1919; s. Lewis and Rose (Kroll) G.; student Temple U., 1940; m. Claire Halpern, Oct. 18, 1942; children—R. Michael, Julie B. and Joshua S. (twins). Corporate cons., 1946-50; v.p. Oxford Finance Co., Phila., 1949-51; chmn. bd., pres. Oxford 1st Corp., Phila., 1951—; pres. Gen. Syndicate Corp.; v.p. Middle Dept. Inspection Agy.; dir. Continental Bank and Trust Co., Phila. Exec. lectr. Small Bus. Opportunities Corp., 1964—. Group chmn. Phila. United Fund; chmn. Kensington Hosp., vol. chmn. Allied Jewish Appeal, finance chmn. March of Dimes, 1968-69. Bd. dirs. Am. Jewish Com., Phila., Opportunities industrialization Center; trustee Lower Kensington Environmental Center, Phila., Fedn. Jewish Agys. Served with AUS, 1942-45. Mem. Pa. Consumer Finance Assn., Am. Technion Soc. (dir.). Jewish religion (trustee Synagogue). Clubs: Meadowlands Country (Blue Bell, Pa.); Locust (Phila.). Contbr. monographs on consumer finance. Home: 1200 Ansley Ave Melrose Park PA 19126 Office: 6701 N Broad St Philadelphia PA 19126

GOLD, CAROLYN DINAH, tng. specialist; b. Springfield, Mass., Feb. 3, 1945; s. Arthur and Frances June (Alpert) G.; certificate (fellow) U. Sheffield, 1964; B.A., U. Mich., 1966. Tchr. English, Stoughton (Mass.) High Sch., 1966-69; tng. specialist Chem. Bank, N.Y.C., 1969-70; tng. coordinator Flagship Banks, Miami-Tampa, Fla., 1970-72; st. tng. specialist Ryder Systems, Inc., Miami, Fla., 1972-77; tng. mgr. Sheraton Corp., Boston, 1978—; instr. group dynamics U. Miami, 1973—; active with mktg. and fund raising Ednl. TV, Channel 2, Miami, 1970-72. Recipient membership growth award Miami chpt. Am. Soc. for Tng. and Devel., 1976. Mem. Am. Soc. Tng. and Devel. (dir. 1974-77, pres. Miami chpt. 1976, asst. regional v.p. 1977-78). Contbr. research in interviewing and performance appraisal. Office: Sheraton Corp 60 State St Boston MA 02109

GOLD, DOROTHY WALDEN, guidance counselor; b. Providence, May 2, 1929; d. Warren Sayles and Dorothea (Prendergast) Walden; B.A., U. R.I., 1947, M.A. in Counseling, 1975; postgrad. Boston U., 1965, Providence Coll., 1963, Boston Coll., 1977, R.I. Coll., 1967-68, R.I. Sch. Design, 1944; m. Arthur H. Gold, Jr., Aug. 26, 1947 (div. 1957); children—Warren Walden, Nicholas Paul, Andrea Jacqueline. Program dir. YWCA, Providence, 1957-60; dir. City of Providence Golden Age, 1960; dir. student activities R.I. Hosp. Nursing Sch., Providence, 1960-62; rehab. counselor R.I. Dept. Vocat. Rehab., 1962-67; dir. rehab. Anti Poverty Agy., Providence, 1967, dir. vocat. rehab., East Providence, R.I., 1967; tchr. kindergarten, Warwick, R.I., 1967-76, guidance counselor, elementary schs., 1976—; pvt. counseling, 1976—; counseling cons. Warwick Community Action, 1978; portrait painter; free lance writer. Cert. psychometrist. Mem. R.I., Warwick guidance assns., Am. Personnel and Guidance Assn. One woman shows paintings, 1976; columnist Warwick Beacon, 1967-72. Roman Catholic. Home: 209 Tidewater Dr Warwick RI 02889 Office: Sch Dept Warwick Ave Warwick RI 02888

GOLD, HILARY ALEXANDER, educator, ednl. adminstr.; b. London, Eng., July 10, 1931; s. Frank David and Anne (Joseph) G.; came to U.S., 1949, naturalized, 1954; A.B., Bklyn. Coll., 1955, M.S. (Coll. fellow), 1956; Ed.D. (Bklyn. Coll. fellow), Columbia U., 1960; m. Arlene Jeanne Herman, Apr. 10, 1954; children—Jonathan Marc, Laurence Ian. Faculty dept. edn. Bklyn. Coll., 1960—, asso. prof., 1968-71, prof., 1971—, dean Sch. Gen. Studies, 1969-71, dean students, 1971-73, v.p. student affairs and services, 1973—; cons. in field. Vice pres. bd. dirs. Bklyn. Coll. Student Union Corp.; bd. dirs. Bklyn. Coll. Community Services; mem. exec. com., bd. dirs. Bklyn. Coll. Fund. Recipient Alumnus of Year award Bklyn. Coll., 1976; U.S. Office Edn. grantee, 1962-65. Mem. Phi Delta Kappa, Kappa Delta Pi, Alpha Sigma Lambda (nat. counselor 1969). Author: (with Carl Nordstrom, Edgar Z. Freidenberg) Influence of Ressentiment on Student Experience in Secondary School, 1965; (with Nordstrom, Friedenberg) Society's Children, 1967; contbr. articles to profl. jours. Home: 2321 E 65th St Brooklyn NY 11234

GOLD, LAWRENCE HOWARD, hosp. adminstr.; b. N.Y.C., Apr. 20, 1947; s. Jerry Moses and Natalie (Altschul) G.; B.A., City U. N.Y., 1968; M.B.A., St. John's U., 1975; m. Nancy M. Klapper, Oct. 22, 1968; children—Adam, Rian, Derek. Staff asst. Queens Hosp. Center/L.I. Jewish Hillside Med. Center, New Hyde Park, N.Y., 1968-69, adminstrv. asst., 1969-73, asst. adminstr., 1973-74, asst. adminstr. clin. and diagnostic services, 1974-77, asso. adminstr., 1978—; asst. prof. clin. health scis. State U. N.Y., Stony Brook; adj. asst. prof. C.W. Post Coll., L.I. U., 1976—, mem. radiologic adv. com., 1974—. Mem. exec. com. Children's Med. Center Fund of N.Y.; mem. adv. com. Stony Brook Physician's Asst. Program. Served with USAR, 1968-74. Mem. Am. Hosp. Assn., Am., N.Y.C. pub. health assns., Royal Soc. Health, Am. Assn. Physicians Assts. (nat. adv. bd. 1977—), Am. Coll. Hosp. Adminstrs., Hosp. Execs. Club. Address: 270-05 76th Ave New Hyde Park NY 11042

GOLD, LEONARD MORTON, mech. engr.; b. Phila., Feb. 23, 1940; s. Alexander and Regina (Lenetsky) G.; B.S. in Mech. Engring., Drexel Inst. Tech., 1962, M.S., 1964, Ph.D., 1969; m. Estelle Phyllis Prybutok, Aug. 26, 1962; children—Barri Joyce, Fredric Marc, Heidi Sheryl. Research mgr. Lawrence div. CGS Sci. Corp., Southampton, Pa., 1969; mech. engr. U.S. Army, Frankford Arsenal, Phila., 1969-74; lead engr. Stone & Webster, Pennsauken, N.J., from 1974; sr.

analytical engr., mgr. engring. mechanics and analysis, fluid systems div. Gulf and Western Energy Products Group, Warwick, R.I. Mem. Exec. bd. Woods Civic Assn., Cherry Hill, N.J., 1972; mem. Cherry Hill Task Force Study Sewage Problems, 1972. Served to capt. C.E., AUS, 1964-66. Registered profl. engr., Pa., N.J. Mem. ASME (chmn. applied mechanics div. Phila. chpt. 1971-72), Pi Tau Sigma, Tau Beta Pi. Contbr. profl. jours. Home: 77 Glenmere Dr Cranston RI 02920 Office: 235 Kilvert St Warwick RI 02886

GOLD, MICHAEL, lawyer; b. N.Y.C., Nov. 17, 1935; s. Nat and Sylvia (Price) G.; A.B., Columbia, 1957; LL.B., Rutgers U., 1962; m. Lucienne Kacew, July 14, 1957; children—Pamela, Kathrine, Jennifer. Admitted to N.J. bar, 1963; practiced in Jersey City, Trenton, Flemington; mem. firm Gold and Gold; dep. atty. gen. N.J., Trenton, 1964-67; asst. prosecutor Hunterdon County, 1968-70. Counsel, N.J. Dept. Agr., 1964-67, N.J. Dept. Def., 1965-67; prin. Gold Trust, Flemington, N.J., 1959—; sec. Charles Jaeger Found., 1970, Milk Processors and Distbrs. N.J. Inc., 1970—; treas. Hunterdon County Legal Services Corp. Vice chmn. criminal law sect. N.J. SBA; chmn. Hunterdon County Democratic Com., 1972-77; mem. Dem. State Com., N.J., 1977—; del. Dem. Nat. Conv., 1976; trustee Trenton State Coll. Recipient Am. Jurisprudence prize Lawyer's Coop. Pub. Co., 1962. Mem. N.J., Hunterdon County bar assns., Nat. Conf. Weights and Measures, Rutgers, Columbia alumni assns., N.J. Milk Industry Assn., Alpha Epsilon Pi, King's Bench. Lion (Frenchtown v.p. 1966-68, pres. 1968). Club: Flemington Exchange (trustee). Home: RD 6 Box 252 Flemington NJ 08822 Office: 79 Main St Flemington NJ 08822

GOLD, MILTON, electronic co. exec.; b. Shenandoah, Pa., Aug. 5, 1922; s. Max and Sarah (Lippmanovich) G.; student DeForest Inst., 1946-48; E.E., Wilmington Coll., 1950; m. Shirley A. Spivack, Sept. 5, 1945; 1 dau., Sandra Gold Loveless. Supr. elec. engr. USAF Logistics Command, Dayton, Ohio, 1948-56; mem. tech. staff ITT Communications Corp., Paramus, N.J., 1956-63; regional mktg. rep. Lear Siegler, Inc., Houston, 1963-64; mktg. rep. Philco Corp., Houston, 1964-66; sales mgr. Lockheed Electronics Co., Plainfield, N.J., 1966-67; mgr. field engring. and support services Gen. Instrument Co., Hicksville, N.Y., 1967-68; dir. mktg. and services Datatronics Corp., Plainview, N.Y., 1968-69; dir. mktg. Frequency Engring. Labs., Farmingdale, N.J., 1969-76; dir. new bus. devel. REDM Corp., Wayne, N.J., 1976—. Served with USAF, 1942-45. Mem. Fort Monmouth Indsl. Rep. Assn., Nat. Contract Mgmt. Assn., IEEE, Air Force Assn., Am. Def. Preparedness Assn., Armed Forces Communications and Electronics Assn., Am. Mktg. Assn., Army Aviation Assn. Home: 135 Grandview Ave Edison NJ 08817 Office: 70 Old Turnpike Rd Wayne NJ 07470

GOLD, RICHARD LOUIS, psychiatrist; b. Bklyn., Nov. 30, 1933; s. Peter and Anna (Rabinowitz) G.; B.S., Bklyn. Coll., 1954, M.A., 1955; M.D., Albany Med. Coll., 1959; m. Paula Hyman, June 28, 1958; children—Melissa, David, Steven. Intern, Albany Med. Center, 1959-60, resident, 1960-63; staff psychiatrist U.S. Naval Hosp., Bethesda, Md., 1963-65; pvt. practice psychiatry, Spring Valley, N.Y., 1965—, N.Y.C., 1966-72; cons. psychiatrist Bergen Pines Hosp., Paramus, N.J., 1965-68, Bd. Coop. Ednl. Services, Rockland County, N.Y., 1968-70; attending psychiatrist Community Hosp., Spring Valley, 1966—, Good Samaritan Hosp., Suffern, N.Y., 1966—. Lectr. in biology Bklyn. Coll., 1954-55; instr. psychiatry Albany Med. Coll., 1960-63, Georgetown U. Med. Center, 1968-65. Served to lt. comdr. M.C., USNR, 1963-65. Mem. AMA, Am. Psychiat. Assn., World Med. Assn., Rockland County Med. Soc., N.Y. Acad. Scis. Democrat. Jewish religion. Contbr. articles to profl. jours. Home: 8 Druid Ct Suffern NY 10901 Office: 265 N Main St Spring Valley NY 10977

GOLDBECK, WILLIS BETTS, public policy cons.; b. N.Y.C., July 9, 1942; s. Cecil Hamilton and Edith Thomas (Betts) G.; student Dartmouth Coll., 1960-62, U. Md. in Germany, 1963-64, Hunter Coll., 1966-68. Tchr. polit. sci., coach Collegiate Sch., N.Y.C., 1965-68; correspondent Time mag., N.Y.C., 1968-69; spl. asst. for research and tech. HUD, Washington, 1970-73; cons. HUD, Kettering Found. and others, 1973-74; founder, pres. Public Policy Communications, Washington, 1974—; founder, dir. Washington Bus. Group on Health, 1974—; asso. Va. Knauer Assos.; asst. prof. socio-med. sci. Sch. Medicine, Boston U. Served with U.S. Army, 1962-65. Mem. Am. Health Planning Assn. (dir.), Internat. Health Mgrs. Assn. (exec. dir.), Internat. Health Resource Consortium (mem. policy bd.), Am. Soc. Public Adminstrn., Polit. Sci. Assn., Nat. Assn. Housing and Redevel. Ofcls., Am. Public Health Assn., Washington Ind. Writers Assn. Author: A Business Perspective on Industry and Health Care, 1978. Contbr. articles to profl. jours. Home: 822 Independence Ave SE Washington DC 20003 Office: 605 Pennsylvania Ave SE Washington DC 20003

GOLDBERG, ALECK, educator; b. Phila., Jan. 30, 1924; s. Abraham and Helen (Paul) G.; B.A., Temple, 1947, M.A., 1948, postgrad., 1958-64; children—Mark, Susan. Research scientist Franklin Inst., Phila., 1948-49; physicist Frankford Arsenal, Phila., 1951-59; engr. RCA, Moorestown, N.J., 1959-63; instr. physics Rider Coll., Trenton, N.J., 1963-64; asst. prof. Pa. State U., 1964-66; lectr. evening div. LaSalle Coll., Phila.,1964—; prof. Montgomery County Community Coll., Blue Bell, Pa., 1966—. Mem. Am. Phys. Soc. Democrat. Jewish religion. Home: 1904A Mather Way Elkins Park PA 19117 Office: 340 DeKalb Pike Blue Bell PA 19422

GOLDBERG, ARTHUR ABBA, lawyer, investment banker; b. Jersey City, Nov. 25, 1940; s. Jack Geddy and Ida (Steinberg) G.; A.B. with honors, Am. U., 1962; LL.B., Cornell U., Ithaca, N.Y., 1965; m. Jane Elizabeth Gottlieb, Aug. 10, 1968; children—Ari Matthew, Shoshana Eve, Benjamin Saul, Talia Akiva. Admitted to N.J. bar, 1965, Conn. bar, 1966; intern, staff mem. to senator, 1962; law clk. DeSevo & Cerutti, Jersey City, 1964; practiced in Jersey City, 1965—; asst. prof. law U. Conn. Sch. Law, 1965-67; cooperating atty. NAACP Legal Def. Fund, 1965—; adminstrv. asst. to congressman Ohio, 1966-67; dep. atty. gen. N.J., counsel Dept. Community Affairs and Housing Finance Agy., 1967-70; exec. v.p., mgr. municipal finance dept. Matthews & Wright, Inc., N.Y.C., 1970—; v.p. Alfus Corp., 1958—, Basow Corp., 1965—; dir. Titan Group, Inc.; partner Shayna Enterprises, 1978—; vis. lectr. Rutgers U., Practicing Law Inst.; mem. exec. com. N.J. Commn. Discrimination in Housing; mem. urban adv. council Anti-Defamation League; spl. cons. on exclusionary zoning Nat. Com. Discrimination in Housing; cons. scholarship edn. Def. Fund for Racial Equality; gen. counsel N.J. chpt. Municipal Finance Officers Assn., N.J. chpt. Nat. Assn. Housing and Redevel. Ofcls.; chmn. Com. for Absorption of Soviet Emigrees (CASE), 1975—; pres. CASE-UNA Community Devel. Corp., 1976. Co-pres. New Synagogue, Jersey City, 1974—; bd. dirs. Jersey City Hebrew Free Loan Assn., 1976—; pres. Met. N.Y. Coordinating Com. for Resettlement of Soviet Jewry, 1978—; treas. Hebrew Free Loan N.J., 1977—; mem. bd. edn. Yeshiva of Hudson County, 1977—. Mem. Conn. Assn. Municipal Attys. (exec. com., editor Newsletter), Nat. Housing Conf., Am. (local govt. sect.), N.J. (chmn. com. on housing and urban renewal), Conn., Hudson County bar assns., Am. Polit. Sci. Assn., Nat. Acad. Polit. and Social Sci., Nat. Leased Housing Assn. (nat. pres. 1972-74, chmn. 1975—), Pub. Securities Assn. (legis. com. 1978), Omicron Delta Kappa, Pi Gamma Mu, Pi Sigma Alpha, Pi Delta Epsilon. Author: Financing Housing and Urban Development, 1975; Zoning and Land Use, 1972; adv. bd. Housing and Devel. Reporter; contbr. articles to law revs. Home: 83 Montgomery St Jersey City NJ 07302 Office: Matthews & Wright Inc 14 Wall St New York City NY 10005

GOLDBERG, EDWIN, adminstr., rehab. specialist; student b. Bklyn. Coll., 1954-56; D.C., Columbia Inst. Chiropractic, 1960; postgrad. in spl. edn. Columbia, 1961-63; postgrad. Am. Inst. Psychoanalysis, 1966-67, Alfred Adler Inst., 1967-69; M.A.Ed., Hebrew Union Coll., 1971; postgrad. Fordham U., 1971-73; profl. certificate in crisis mgmt. N.Y. State Sch. Indsl. Labor Relations, 1972; profl. diploma in rehab. mgmt. Cornell U., 1973; postgrad. Antioch Grad. Sch. Edn.; m. June Light, June 21, 1972; children—Paul, Joseph. Exec., Greater N.Y. Councils, Boy Scouts Am., Queens, 1960-63; supr. Charles Pfizer & Co., N.Y.C., 1963-64; asso. dir. Western Mediterranean Ops USO, Nice, France, 1964-65; coordinator rehab. skills Jewish Guild for the Blind, N.Y.C., 1965-68, asst. dir., 1968-77; dir. rehab. services, sect. chief Trenton (N.J.) Psychiat. Hosp., 1977—; coordinator corrective therapy internship program VA-Hunter Coll., 1971-77; adj. asst. prof. adapted phys. edn., Hunter Coll., N.Y.C., 1970-77; rehab. tng. specialist of multiple disabled blind State N.Y. Commn. for Visually Handicapped, Roosevelt Hosp., Yonkers Home for Aged, 1970-77; lectr. rehab. Jewish Home, Hosp. for aged, Zeman Center for Instruction, Dept. Mental Hygiene, State N.Y., 1970—; lectr. Am. Indian medicine and mythology Found. Faith, N.Y.C., 1976—, Heye Found. Mus. of Am. Indian, N.Y.C., 1976—; legis. rep. N.Y. State Fedn. Workers for the Blind, 1973-76, program chmn., 1974. Recipient Dr. Frank E. Dean Meml. Award for outstanding contributions to sci. edn., 1976; diploma magistrale Ordine Militare S. Andrea di Caffa (Rome); certified rehab. counselor, disability examiner, master rehab. therapy specialist; registered rehab. therapist; lic. tchr. human relations, N.Y. State Edn. Dept. Fellow N.Y. Acad. Sci., Royal Soc. Promotion of Health (London); mem. Am. Congress Rehab. Medicine, Am. Soc. Adlerian Psychology, Royal Soc. Health, Royal Soc. Medicine, Royal Inst. Pub. Health & Hygiene, Nat. Rehab. Counseling Assn., Am. Assn. Workers for the Blind; Am. Pub. Health Assn., Am. Assn. Rehab. Therapy, Am. Assn. Mental Deficiency, AAUP, Soc. Study Social History of Medicine. Jewish religion. Author: Mobility Training Manual for Teachers of Visually Impaired Children, 1969; Adapted and Corrective Physical Education Curriculum Handbook, 1972; condr. research in mobility of blind amputees, 1969-72. Office: 15 W 65th St New York City NY 10023

GOLDBERG, FREDERICK IRA, architect; b. N.Y.C., Mar. 11, 1943; s. Morris and Rose (Weinstein) G.; B.Arch., Pratt Inst., 1965, M.S. in Environmental Design, 1972; m. Judith Fellner, June 12, 1965; children—Alan Bradley, Taryn Wendy. Head design dept. D. Salvati & Son, Bklyn., 1965-67; dir. Builderamic Research and Devel. div. Lefrak, Inc., Forest Hills, N.Y., 1967; design architect Dallek Design Group, N.Y.C., 1968; architect Environmental Research and Devel., N.Y.C., 1969; owner Frederick Goldberg Architect, N.Y.C., 1969—; pres. Design Derivatives Inc., 1970; adj. asst. prof. grad. environ. design dept. Pratt Inst., 1969—. Recipient certificate of merit Nat. Inst. Archtl. Edn., 1965. Certified by Nat. Council Archtl. Registration Bds. Mem. AIA. Patentee in field. Home: 86 The Serpantine Roslyn Estates NY 11572 Office: 207 E 56th St New York City NY 10022

GOLDBERG, HARLEAN FADER, weight reduction orgn. exec.; b. Bklyn., June 1, 1932; d. Moe and Marjorie (Cullens) Fader; student Bklyn. Coll., 1949-51; m. Leonard Goldberg, Mar. 30, 1969; children—Terry, Janet, Randi, Warren. Pres. Weight Watchers of S.I. Inc., 1965-69; v.p. Weight Watchers of Syracuse Inc. (N.Y.), 1968—; sec. Select-A-Size Ltd., Syracuse, 1972—; pres. Shape Shoppes Inc., Syracuse, 1974—; v.p. Skeleton Foods, 1976—. Dir. W.W. Franchisee Assn. Inc., N.Y.C., 1972-73, mem. purchasing com., 1971-73, chmn. emergency fund com., 1972-74. Bd. dirs. Jewish Family Service Bur., Syracuse, 1973—; bd. dirs. Inter-Agy. Com. for Diabetes Edn., also co-chmn. finance com., 1975-77; treas. Upstate N.Y. chpt. Am. Diabetes Assn., 1977-78, bd. dirs., 1977—. Club: Syracuse University Hardwood (dir. 1973—, corr. sec. 1972-77, 1st v.p. 1978—). Home: 5263 Jamesville Rd Dewitt NY 13214 Office: Suite 112 5858 E Molloy Rd Syracuse NY 13211

GOLDBERG, HAROLD HOWARD, psychologist, educator; b. Bklyn., Apr. 30, 1924; s. Julius and Fannie (Sommers) G.; B.A., N.Y. U., 1948, M.A., 1949; postgrad. Columbia U., 1966-68; m. Roslyn Jacobowitz, June 26, 1948; children—Barbara Ellen, Susan Andrea, Lisa Carol. Chief psychologist Queens Island Readjustment Centers, 1956-62; pvt. practice psychotherapy, N.Y.C., 1949—; mem. faculty and adv. bd. Am. Inst. Psychotherapy and Psychoanalysis, N.Y.C.; prin. League Sch. and Research Center; supr. psychotherapists Community Guidance Services; panel psychologist Office of Vocat. Rehab., Group Health Ins., Big Sisters, Jewish Child Care Assn.; adv. bd. Save A Marriage. Served with USAF, 1942-46. Recipient Distinguished Service award N.Y. Soc. Clin. Psychologists, 1974; licensed clin. psychologist, N.Y. State. Mem. N.Y. Soc. Clin. Psychologists (past pres., treas., dir.), Am., N.Y. psychol. assns., Am. Inst. Psychotherapy and Psychoanalysis (adv. bd.), Phi Delta Kappa, Kappa Delta Pi, Psi Chi. Editor Jour. Clin. Issues in Psychology, 1971-78; editor Psychol. Newsletter, 1965-71; contbr. articles to profl. jours. Office: 111 E 61 St New York City NY 10021

GOLDBERG, HERMAN KRIEGER, ophthalmologist; b. Balt., Feb. 6, 1911; s. Harry and Bertha (Krieger) G.; B.A., Johns Hopkins U., 1932, M.D., 1936; children—Barbara, Harry, Cece. Resident in ophthalmology Johns Hopkins Hosp.-Wilmer Inst., Balt., 1936-40; practice medicine specializing in ophthalmology, Balt., 1940—; asso. prof. ophthalmology and pediatrics Johns Hopkins Hosp., 1973—; dir. ophthalmology Sinai Hosp., Balt. Served with USNR, 1944-46. Fellow A.C.S.; mem. Am. Assn. Opthalmology, Am. Assn. Ophthalmology and Otolaryngology. Author: Dyslexia Problems of Reading Disabilities, 1972. Home: 3131 Old Court Rd Baltimore MD 21208 Office: 2435 W Belvedere Ave Baltimore MD 21215

GOLDBERG, JAY NEIL, date processing co. exec.; b. N.Y.C., Mar. 25, 1941; s. Arthur and Lillian (Sudnovsky) G.; student U. Mich., 1958-60; B.A., N.Y. U.; m. Ellen Xandria Gussaroff, Sept. 19, 1970; children—Laura, Melissa, Susanne. Programmer, IBM. Armonk, N.Y., 1961-66; analyst Union Carbide Corp., N.Y.C., 1966-67; cons. Auerbach Corp., Phila., 1967-68; pres. Software Design Assos., Inc., N.Y.C., 1968—; lectr. in field. Exec. com. Young Men's div. Albert Einstein Coll. Medicine, 1974—. Mem. Am. Mgmt. Assn., Soc. Advancement Mgmt., Software Industry Assn. (dir.), Young Pres.'s Orgn., Assn. Systems Mgmt. Club: Fenway Golf. Home: 254 E 68th St New York City NY 10021 Office: Software Design Assos Inc 260 Madison Ave New York City NY 10016

GOLDBERG, JOSEPH PHILIP, govt. ofcl.; b. Bklyn., May 1, 1918; s. Max and Fanny (Steltzer) G.; B.S.S., Coll. City N.Y., 1937; M.A., Columbia, 1938, Ph.D., 1950; m. Selma Takiff, Aug. 22, 1943; children—Seth M., Lise A. Instr. econ. history Coll. City N.Y., 1937-39; high sch. tchr., N.Y.C., 1938-42; economist Bur. Labor Stats., Washington, 1942; econ. adviser Nat. War Labor Bd. and Wage Stblzn. Bd., Washington, 1943-46; labor adviser Office of Housing Expediter, 1946-48; staff dir. joint congl. com., 1948; div. chief Bur. Labor Stats., Labor Dept., Washington, 1949-51, spl. asst. to commr. of labor stats., 1954—; with Wage Stblz. Bd., 1951-53. Instr. Am. U., 1948-49, research asso. Harvard, 1957, U. Mich., 1964-69; ILO Inst. Indsl. Relations Studies, 1973—; U.S. del. to 17 ILO maritime and internat. labor confs., 1956-76. Pres. J.F. Kennedy High Sch. PTA, New Hampshire Estates, 1956-57, 68-69. Trustee schs. Montgomery County, 1957-62. Recipient research grants Yale Fund, Harvard, U. Mich., Ford Found.; Meritorious Ser. award Labor Dept., 1963, Commr.'s Eminent Ser. award, 1973. Mem. Indsl. Relations Research Assn. (pres. D.C. chpt. 1963-64, mem. nat. exec. bd. 1973-76), Am. Econ. Assn., AAAS, Phi Beta Kappa. Author: The Martime Story, 1958; (with others) Collective Bargaining and Technological Change in American Transportation, Monograph on Modernization in the Maritime Industry, 1971; Productivity Bargaining in the Private Sector, 1975; The Law and Practice of Collective Bargaining, 1976. Contbr. articles to profl. jours. Home: 707 Stonington Rd Silver Spring MD 20902 Office: GAO Building Wasington DC 20212

GOLDBERG, JOYCE ROE, educator, counselor; b. Bklyn., Aug. 7, 1934; d. David and Kate (Kaplan) Roe; B.A., Bklyn. Coll., 1955, M.A., 1959; m. Maurice Goldberg, Dec. 21, 1958; children—Cari Ellen, Jeffrey Evan, Marc Andrew. Tchr., Alden Terrace (N.Y.) Sch., 19S5-59, Cynwyd (Pa.) Sch., 1959, Spaulding (Mass.) Sch., 1960; counselor N.Y. U., N.Y.C., also N.Y.C. Home Adv. Service Council, 1976-77; substitute tchr. Great Neck (N.Y.) Pub. Schs., 1977—. Mem. Am. Personnel and Guidance Assn., Am. Sch. Counselors Assn., Bklyn. Coll. Guidance Assn., Kappa Delta Pi.

GOLDBERG, MARTIN, physician, educator; b. Phila., Sept. 15, 1930; s. Samuel and Esther (Schreibman) G.; B.A., Temple U., 1951, M.D., 1955; M.A. (hon.) U. Pa., 1971; m. Lynn Taksey, June 17, 1951 (dec. Aug. 1976); children—Meryl I., Karen L., Dara S.; m. 2, Marion Lindblad, May 26, 1978. Intern, Phila. Gen. Hosp., 1955-56, resident, 1957-59, sr. attending physician, 1965-76; resident Cleve. Clinic, 1956-57; fellow nephrology Hosp. U. Pa., Phila., 1959-61, past sr. attending physician, mem. faculty Sch. Medicine, 1960—, prof. medicine, 1970—, chief renal electrolyte sect., 1966—, acting chmn. dept. medicine, 1975-76; sr. attending physician Phila. VA Hosp. Mem. sci. adv. bd. Nat. Kidney Found., 1970-76; chmn. kidney council Am. Heart Assn., 1973-74; study cons. NIH, 1968-72. Recipient Alumni prize Temple U. Sch. Medicine, 1955, Lindback award for distinguished teaching U. Pa., 1972, Research Career Devel. award NIH, 1963-70; research grantee NIH, John Hartford Found. Diplomate Am. Bd. Internal Medicine (chmn. nephrology com.), Nat. Bd. Med. Examiners. Fellow A.C.P.; mem. Assn. Am. Physicians, Am. Soc. Clin. Investigation, Am. Physiol. Soc., Am. Fedn. Clin. Research (chmn. Eastern sect. 1967), Am. Soc. Nephrology (sec.-treas. 1975—), Interurban Clin. Club, Internat. Soc. Nephrology (exec. com. 1975—), Alpha Omega Alpha. Editorial com. Jour. Clin. Investigation, 1969-70, Kidney Internat., 1972-74, Jour. Mineral and Electrolyte Metabolism, 1977—. Research and publs. in renal physiology and disease; devel. of computer assisted diagnostic and teaching programs. Office: Gates Bldg Hospital Univ Pa 3400 Spruce St Philadelphia PA 19104

GOLDBERG, MORRELL, hosp. adminstr.; b. Lawrence, Mass., Oct. 12, 1910; s. Samuel and Jennie (Hartman) G.; B.A., Dartmouth Coll., 1933; postgrad. Columbia U., 1937-39; m. Ruth Lazar, Feb. 22, 1941; children—Susan, Daniel, Jane. Asst. adminstr. Beth-El Hosp., Bklyn., 1937-41, adminstr. Jewish Hosp. Chronic Diseases, 1941-42; exec. v.p. Brookdale Hosp. Med. Center, Bklyn., 1946—; lectr. pub. health Columbia, 1961—. Pres. Hosp. Credit Exchange. Bd. dirs. Mayor N.Y.C.'s Comprehensive Health Planning Agy.; mem. coms. Blue Cross, N.Y. State Dept. Health; trustee Health and Hosp. Planning Council So. N.Y., N.Y. State Urban Devel. Corp. Served to capt. U.S. Army, 1942-46. Fellow Am. Coll. Hosp. Adminstrs., Royal Soc. Health; mem. Greater N.Y. Hosp. Assn. (pres. 1974-75), Hosp. Assn. N.Y. State. Club: Dartmouth (N.Y.C.). Home: 55 E 9th St New York City NY 10003 Office: Brookdale Hosp Med Center Linden Blvd and Brookdale Plaza Brooklyn NY 11212*

GOLDBERG, NATHAN MORRIS, pharmacist, univ. adminstr.; b. Boston, May 3, 1918; s. Samuel P. and Ethel (Baker) G.; B.S., Mass. Coll. Pharmacy, 1939; m. Florence Turransky, Oct. 28, 1945; children—Dorothy, Roberta, Michael. Dir. profl. devel. Coll. Pharmacy and Allied Health Professions Northeastern U., Boston, 1975—; mem. corp. Mass. Coll. Pharmacy; dir. The Apothecary. Registered pharmacist, Mass.; recipient Alumni Achievement award Mass. Coll. Pharmacy, 1975. Mem. Boston Assn. Retail Druggists (exec. sec. 1971—, former pres.), Mass. (Pharmacist of Year 1973, treas.), Am. pharm. assns., Mass. Soc. Hosp. Pharmacists, Nat. Assn. Retail Druggists, Am. Assn. Colls. Pharmacy, Met. Pharm. Secs. Assn. (pres.), Northeastern Univ. Alumni Assn. (advisor), Rho Chi. Jewish. Club: Masons. Editor Boston Assn. Retail Druggists Action-O-Gram, 1970—, Pharmacy Letter, 1974—; originator-RX-Info, 1974. Home: 74 Hopkins St Revere MA 02151 Office: Northeastern U 360 Huntington Ave Boston MA 02115

GOLDBERG, NEAL LEON, summer camp adminstr.; b. Phila., Sept. 1, 1943; s. Julius J. and Marjorie (Shatz) G.; B.A., William Penn Coll., 1969; postgrad. U. Conn., 1970-73. Dir. Oskaloosa (Iowa) Youth Club, 1965-69, SGF Camp., Phila., 1969; dir. Med-O-Lark Camp, Washington, Maine, 1969—, owner, 1971—; lectr. in field. Named YMCA Youth of Month, 1966; recipient Service to Youth award Kiwanis Internat., 1967, Service award Altrusa Internat., 1967. Mem. Am. Camping Assn., Maine Camp Dirs. Assn., Maine Audubon Soc., Nat. Resource Council, Maine Organic Gardeners and Farmers Assn., Soc. Am. Magicians. Home: PO Box 267 Storrs CT 06268 Office: Med-O-Lark Camp Washington ME 04579

GOLDBERG, ROBERT IRVING, indsl. designer, educator; b. Bklyn., Dec. 30, 1919; s. David and Rose (Maslow) G.; B.A., Bklyn. Coll., 1941; M.A., Columbia, 1948; postgrad. Coll. City N.Y., 1941-42, Washington U., St. Louis, 1942-44, N.Y. U., 1948-50; Ph.D., Philathia, 1972; m. Leah Mishkin, Mar. 27, 1949; children—Marsha Sue, Mark George. Sr. indsl. designer Emerson Electric Mfg. Co., St. Louis, 1942-44; chief indsl. designer Display House, Phila., 1946; chief indsl. designer N.Am. Shipbuilding & Repair Corp., N.Y.C., 1946-47; partner, chief indsl. designer Robert I. Goldberg Assos., N.Y.C., 1947-56; pres. Asso. Indsl. Designers, Inc., N.Y.C., 1956—; exhibited in group shows watercolor painting Honolulu Art Mus., Indsl. Designers Inst., Springfield Mus. Fine Art, Am. Inst. Graphic Artists Show, others. Prof. marketing and package design N.Y. U. Sch. Commerce, 1952-69; prof. mktg. and bus. mgmt. St. Francis Coll., Bklyn., 1972—; dir. seminars in Indsl. design, color and package design N.Y. U.; dir. workshop in package design Pratt Inst. Art Sch., 1952-69, also prof. packaging; dir. Center Profl. Packaging Edn., New Sch., N.Y.C., 1967-69; pres. Center for Packaging Edn., Inc., N.Y.C., 1969—; lectr. packaging USIA, Zagreb, Belgrade, Yugoslavia, Budapest, Hungary, 1969, Spain, Scandinavia, Mex., 1971-75, Tel Aviv, 1976; prof. mktg. and bus. mgmt. St. Francis Coll., Bklyn., 1970—. Active Boy Scouts Am. Served to lt. (j.g.) USNR, 1944-46. Fellow Package Designers Council (founding mem.); mem. Indsl. Designers Inst. (exec. bd.), Am. Marketing Assn., Inter Soc. Color Council, Indsl. Designers Soc. Am., Inst. Bus. Designers, Execs. Assn. N.Y. (dir.), AAUP, Chi Beta Nu (founding pres.). Contbg. editor: Modern Packaging Ency., Marketing Handbook; packaging editor Toys and Playthings mags. Contbr. over 100 articles to profl. jours.

Home: 29 Lawrence St New Hyde Park NY 11040 Office: 250 W 57th St New York City NY 10019 also St Francis Coll 180 Remsen St Brooklyn NY 11201

GOLDBERG, STEPHEN JAY, designer, photographer; b. Phila., Feb. 12, 1949; s. Arthur Stanley and Beatrice (Horowitz) G.; B.A. (hon.), Penn. State U., 1970; m. Michele Janis Leibowitz, May 16, 1970 (div. Sept. 1978). Cashier, produce clk. Thriftway Supermarkets, Phila., 1972-75; research chemistry technician U. Penn. Phila., 1972-75; profl. free lance photographer, designer, craftsman, woodworker, Phila., 1974; active planning community workshop redevel. area, Phila. Mem. Am. Crafts Council, Head House Craftsman's Assn. Phila. Home: 303 N 3d St Philadelphia PA 19103

GOLDBERGER, HERBERT HENRY, consumer distbn. co. exec.; b. Providence, Dec. 27, 1917; s. Samuel and Bertha (Steiner) G.; A.B. magna cum laude, Brown U., 1939; M.B.A., Harvard U., 1941; m. Phyllis Finkelstein, June 19, 1941; children—Stephen Allen, Laurie Ann. Buyer, mdse. mgr. Clear Weave Stores Inc., Boston, 1945-50; sec.-treas. Van's Hosiery Stores Inc., Boston, 1950-64, Hills Dept. Stores, Inc., Boston, 1957-64; pres. Hills Dept. dept. stores div. SCOA Industries Inc., Boston, 1964—. Bd. dirs. Nat. Mass Retailing Inst. Served with AUS, 1942-45. Mem. Phi Beta Kappa, Pi Lambda Phi. Home: 49 Edge Hill Rd Chestnut Hill MA 02167 Office: 15 Dan Rd Canton MA 02021

GOLDBLATT, BARRY LANCE, mfg. co. exec.; b. Palo Alto, Calif., July 29, 1945; s. Samuel and Joan Charlotte (Morton) G.; B.S., U. So. Calif., 1967, M.B.A., 1968. Supr. market research for brands Procter & Gamble Co., Cin., 1968-71; mgr. market research Personal Products Co., Milltown, N.J., 1971-74; asst. dir. consumer research Johnson & Johnson Baby Products Co., New Brunswick, N.J., 1974—; Bd. dirs. New Brunswick Hot Line, 1973; vol. Vol. Urban Cons. Group. Mem. U. So. Calif. M.B.A.'s, U. So. Calif. Commerce Assos., Am. Mktg. Assn., Assn. M.B.A. Execs., Zeta Beta Tau. Democrat. Club: U. So. Calif. Alumni N.J. (pres.). Home: 42 Phelps Ave New Brunswick NJ 08901 Office: 501 George St New Brunswick NJ 08903

GOLDBLATT, PHILLIP BRIAN, psychiatrist, educator; b. Phila., Dec. 6, 1939; s. Samuel and Ida (Fox) G.; B.A., U. Pa., 1961, M.D., 1965; m. Arlene Bobroff, July 7, 1962; children—Lisa Ann, Dana Lynne. Intern, Michael Reese Hosp., Chgo., 1965-66; postdoctoral fellow in psychiatry Yale, 1966-70, research asso., 1970-73, asst. prof. clin. psychiatry, 1973—; chief day hosp. West Haven (Conn.) VA Hosp., 1973-77; pvt. practice psychiatry, New Haven, 1970—; pres. Partial Hospitalization Assn. Conn., 1977-78; cons. in field. Served with USNR, 1966-71. Mem. Am., Conn. psychiat. assns., AMA, New Haven County Med. Soc., Phi Beta Kappa. Contbr. articles in field to profl. jours. Home: 592 Whitney Ave New Haven CT 06511 Office: 315 Whitney Ave New Haven CT 06511

GOLDEMBERG, ROBERT LEWIS, cosmetic chemist; b. Passaic, N.J., Sept. 18, 1925; s. Maurice and Elizabeth (Grimberg) G.; B.S., Princeton U., 1948; m. Rose Leiman Schiller, Aug. 25, 1969; children—Sharan Ruth, Kathleen, David Randolph. Liaison chemist United Piece Dye Works, Lodi, N.J., 1948-50; sr. chemist Coty, Inc., N.Y.C., 1950-58; dir. toiletries research Shulton, Inc., Clifton, N.J., 1958-64; research dir. Lanvin-Chas. Ritz, Norwalk, Conn., 1964-68; dir. tech. services Van Dyk & Co., Belleville, N.J., 1968-73; pres. Rakuma Labs., Inc., South Hackensack, N.J., 1973—. Served with inf. U.S. Army, 1944-46. Mem. Soc. Cosmetic Chemists (chmn. bd. 1974, pres. 1973; Medal award 1977), Am. Chem. Soc., N.Y. Acad. Scis. Author: (with Beatrice Traven) Here's Egg on Your Face, 1971, The Complete Book of Natural Cosmetics, 1976; editor Advances in Cosmetic Technology, 1978; monthly columnist in Drug & Cosmetic Industry mag., 1974—, Skin and Allergy News, 1959—; contbr. articles to tech. jours. Home: 548 Martense Ave Teaneck NJ 07666 Office: PO Box 2083 South Hackensack NJ 07606

GOLDEMBERG, ROSE LEIMAN, playwright; b. S.I., N.Y.; d. Louis I. and Esther (Friedman) Leiman; B.A. magna cum laude, Bklyn. Coll.; M.A., Ohio State U.; m. Robert L. Goldemberg; children—Lee, Lisa. Author: (plays) Apples in Eden, 1970, The Rabinowitz Gambit 1971, Rites of Passage, 1972, The Merry War, 1973, Love One Another, 1974, Letters Home, 1979; (film) Doubles, 1978; (TV) Land of Hope, 1975, Memoirs of an Ex-Prom Queen, 1978, (mini-series) A Celebration of Women, 1979, Circles, 1979; (books) Here's Egg on Your Face, 1973, (under name Beatrice Traven) The Complete Book of Natural Cosmetics, 1975, Antique Jewelry, A Practical and Passionate Guide, 1976; also documentary films, TV pilot films, radio scripts. Mem. Writers Guild Am., Dramatists Guild, Eugene O'Neill Playwright. Address: Writers and Artists Agy 162 W 56th St New York NY 10019

GOLDEN, BALFOUR HENRY, food service co. exec.; b. Bangor, Maine, Aug. 23, 1922; s. Samuel Henry and Helen (Rybier) G.; A.B. cum laude, Bowdoin Coll., 1944; postgrad. Columbia U., 1945-47; m. Emma Jane Krakauer, June 22, 1956; children—Peter Balfour, Betsy Jane, Robert Henry. Pres., Golden Food Services Corp. N.Y., 1951-70, N.J., 1951-70, Iowa, 1951-70, Golden Co. of Maine, 1952-70, Gold Base Services Corp., 1952-70, Plaza Eats, Inc., 1958-70, Dubonnet Restaurant Corp., 1960-70, Gold Vending div. Marlboro Cafeteria, 1961-70; food service cons., 1970-74; prs. Guardian Food Service Corp., N.Y.C., 1974—. Served with U.S. Army, 1943-45. Mem. New Eng. Soc. N.Y.C., N.Y. Restaurant Assn., Restaurant League N.Y., Affiliated Restauranteurs, Phi Beta Kappa. Club: Williams. Home: 325 Beechwood Rd Ridgewood NJ 07450 Office: 630 Fifth Ave New York City NY 10020*

GOLDEN, SIBYL LEVY (MRS. WILLIAM T. GOLDEN), civic worker; b. N.Y.C., Sept. 26, 1917; d. Guy Wallace and Sibyl (Hershfield) Levy; B.A., Barnard Coll., 1938; m. William T. Golden, May 2, 1938; children—Sibyl Rebecca, Pamela Prudence. Chmn., Internat. House Festival of Arts, N.Y.C., 1968; chmn. Alumnae Spl. Gifts Com., Barnard Coll., N.Y.C., 1967, 68, 69; founding mem., mem. objectives com. Catskill Center for Conservation and Devel.; chmn. Brearley Sch. Parents Assn., 1966-67, mem. orientation class, 1969-70; mem. Citizens Com. for Children; chmn. Internat. House Festival Arts, 1969; trustee Town of Olive Hist. Soc., 1974—, Catskill Conservancy Commn., 1975—; bd. dirs. Christopher Robin House Nursery Sch., 1975—; mem. women's com. Am. Mus. Natural History; mem. pres.'s council Mus. City N.Y.; mem. Congressman Hamilton Fish's Conservation Task Force; Parents League rep. to Mayor Lindsay's Civic Assembly; bd. dirs. Bklyn. Bot. Garden, 1978—, Bard Coll., Annandale-on-Hudson, N.Y.; mem. Town of Olive (N.Y.) Zoning Bd. Appeals, 1973—; mem. Olive Environ. Conservation Commn. Mem. Pub. Edn. Assn. (Parents League rep.; mem. coordinating, ind. schs., elementary and secondary schs. coms. 1965—, mem. high sch. task force 1969-72), Embroiderer's Guild (dir. Am. br., co-chmn. 5th Biennial Exhbt. 1970, v.p., dir. 1972—). Clubs: Cosmopolitan (pub. interests com.), Women's City (dir., sec., membership com.), Barnard Coll. (dir. 1966-67, 73—) (N.Y.C.); Tongore Garden (West Shokan, N.Y.). Contbr. articles in field of ed-n, botany, embroidery to various publs.; book reviews for The Conservationist mag. Home: 730 Park Ave New York City NY 10021

GOLDENBERG, ARNOLD, rheumatologist; b. Hartford, Conn., Feb. 11, 1927; s. Joseph and Esther (Taylor) G.; A.B. cum laude, Syracuse U., 1949; M.D., Boston U., 1954; m. Bernice Wiencrot, Nov. 5, 1955; children—John, Louise, Emily. Intern, City of Detroit Receiving Hosp., 1954-55; resident Kings County Hosp., Bklyn., 1955-58; postdoctoral fellow Arthritis Found., 1959-60; practice medicine specializing in rheumatology, West Hartford, Conn., 1960—; asso. vis. physician St. Francis Hosp., Hartford; asst. clin. prof. medicine U. Conn. Health Center, Farmington; cons. Newington Children's, Rockville Gen. hosps.; mem. med. and sci. com. Conn. chpt. Arthritis Found. Served with USAF, 1945-47. Diplomate Am. Bd. Internal Medicine. Mem. Am. Rheumatism Assn., AMA, Am. Soc. Internal Medicine, Hartford Med. Soc., Alpha Omega Alpha. Home: 138 Lawler Rd West Hartford CT 06117 Office: 1260 New Britain Ave West Hartford CT 06110

GOLDENBERG, GEORGE, pharm. co. exec.; b. N.Y.C., Mar. 12, 1929; s. Gersh and Rose (Kolpacci) G.; student Bklyn. Coll., 1946-47; B.S., Bklyn. Coll. Pharmacy, L.I. U., 1951; m. Arlene Sandra Yudell, May 22, 1955; children—Steven Alan, Heidi Michele, Jeffrey Evan. Pharmacist, Dolcorts Pharmacy, N.Y.C., 1951-56; export mgr. Chem. Spltys. Co., Inc., N.Y.C., 1956-58; sales mgr. Syntex Chem. Co., Inc., N.Y.C., 1958-60, asst. to pres. Syntex Labs., Inc., 1960-61; gen. sales mgr. Panray-Parlam Corp., Englewood, N.J., 1961-63; v.p. Ormont Drug & Chem. Co., Inc., Englewood, 1963-64, exec. v.p., dir., 1964-66, pres., dir., 1966-76, chmn., dir., 1976—; dir. Goldleaf Pharmacal Co., Inc., Englewood, N.J., Lawton Labs., Inc., Bedford Acme Surg. Co., Inc., Bklyn., Fed. Pharmacal Corp., Fort Lauderdale, Fla., Yorktown Research Inc., South Hackensack, N.J., Am Fre Grant, Inc. Trustee Bklyn. Coll. Pharmacy, L.I. U. Fellow Anti-Defamation League; mem. Bklyn. Coll. Pharmacy Alumni Assn. (pres.), Fedn. Alumni Assns. L.I. U. (pres.), Am. Pharm. Assn., Englewood Jr. C. of C., Am. Mgmt. Assn., Young Pres.'s Orgn., Delta Sigma Theta. Club: B'nai B'rith. Home: 21 Carol Ct Demarest NJ 07627 Office: 520 S Dean St Englewood NJ 07631

GOLDENZWEIG, WILLIAM MARTIN, life ins. agt.; Bklyn., July 8, 1922; s. Jacob and Betty (Riskin) G.; B.S., U. Md., 1943; m. Miriam Novick, Nov. 10, 1946; children—Bernard S., Michael A. Agt., Reliance Life Ins. of Pitts., (merged with Lincoln Nat. Life Ins. Co. 1953), 1946-48, dist. mgr., Washington, 1948-53, dist. agt., 1953—; v.p. C.T. Hellmuth & Assos.; co-developer, instr. life ins. and estate planning George Washington U., 1962-65; instr. courses for C.L.U., 1959—. Served with inf. U.S. Army, 1943-46, col. Res. ret. Decorated Bronze Star, Purple Heart, Combat Infantryman's badge. C.L.U. Miles W. McNally fellow Am. Soc. C.L.U.'s, 1972, W. Elwood Baker ednl. grantee D.C. chpt., 1977. Mem. D.C. Life Underwriters Assn. (pres. 1969-70, Bernard L. Wilner award 1973), Am. Soc. C.L.U.'s (pres. D.C. chpt. 1960-61), Life Ins. Club Washington (pres. 1960-61), Washington Estate Planning Council, Assn. Advanced Life Underwriting, Million Dollar Roundtable (life), Beta Gamma Sigma, Phi Alpha. Jewish. Clubs: Leaders of Washington, Toastmasters (chpt. pres. 1959-60). Home: 1206 Godwin Dr Silver Spring MD 20901 Office: Suite 1245 5454 Wisconsin Ave Chevy Chase MD 20015

GOLDFARB, ALEXANDER A., lawyer; b. Hartford, Conn., Oct. 27, 1927; s. Max and Bella (Kaplan) G.; B.S., Trinity Coll. Conn., 1946; LL.B., Cornell U., 1949; postgrad. Yale, 1950-51. Admitted to Conn. bar, 1949; instr. U. Neb. Sch. Law, 1949-50; sr. partner Goldfarb & Reis, Hartford; counsel Democratic State Central Com., 1954—, Greater Hartford Flood Commn. Conn., 1956-72; asst. corp. counsel City Hartford, 1953-55, corp. counsel, 1972-76. Mem. Wadsworth Atheneum, 1951—. Served with AUS, 1944. Mem. Pi Gamma Mu. Clubs: Yale, Cornell, Trinity, University (Hartford). Home: Bushnell Plaza Hartford CT 06103 Office: 1 Lewis St Hartford CT 06103

GOLDFARB, ARTHUR A., physician; b. N.Y.C., May 29, 1917; s. Charles and Tillie (Konig) G.; B.S. cum laude, N.Y. U., 1938, M.D., 1942; m. June Florence Wax, June 3, 1945; children—Barbara Joan, Susan Lynn. Intern, Cumberland Hosp., Bklyn., 1942-43; asst. resident neuropsychiatry Montefiore Hosp., N.Y.C., 1943-44; asst. resident pediatrics Lincoln Hosp., N.Y.C., 1944-45; chief resident pediatrics and contagion Queens Gen. Hosp., 1945-46; postgrad. tng. in allergy N.Y. Postgrad. Hosp., 1946, Mt. Sinai Hosp., N.Y.C., 1946; practice medicine, specializing in allergy, Teaneck, N.J., 1957—; chief allergy service, attending in medicine Holy Name Hosp., Teaneck; chief allergy service Englewood (N.J.) Hosp.; asst. prof. pediatrics for allergy Albert Einstein Coll. Medicine, N.Y.C., 1957—. Rep., chmn. elect No. N.J. Interprofl. Council, 1967—. Served to maj. USPHS, 1951-52. Diplomate Am. Bd. Pediatrics, Am. Bd. Allergy and Immunology. Fellow Am., Internat. acads. allergy, Am. Coll. Allergy, Am. Acad. Pediatrics, N.J. Acad. Medicine; mem. A.M.A., N.J., Bergen County (past pres., past trustee) med. socs., Bronx Pediatric Soc. (past pres.), N.Y., N.J. (past pres., trustee) allergy socs., Phi Beta Kappa. Contbr. articles profl. jours., allergy textbook. Home: 737 Northumberland Ave Teaneck NJ 07666 Office: 1181 River Rd Teaneck NJ 07666

GOLDFARB, MURIEL BERNICE, gold products mfg. co. exec.; b. Bklyn., Mar. 29, 1920; s. Barnett Goldfarb and May (Steinberg) Goldfarb Oshman; B.A., U. Miami, Coral Gables, Fla., 1942; postgrad. Coll. City N.Y., 1950. Advt. mgr. Majestic Specialities Co., N.Y.C., 1942-43; pub. info. asst. UNESCO, Paris, 1946-47; retail promotion mgr. Glamour Mag., 1955-61; advt. dir. Country Tweeds Co., N.Y.C., 1961-65; advt. dir. S. Augstein & Co., N.Y.C., 1966-72, Feature Ring Co., Inc., Gotham Ring Co., Inc., Fidco Inc., N.Y.C., 1972-78; dir. advt. and promotion Wasko Gold Products Corp., N.Y.C., 1979—. Served to lt. WAVES, 1943-46. Mem. Fashion Group N.Y. Inc. Jewish. Home: 340 52d St New York City NY 10022

GOLDFARB, NATHAN, educator; b. N.Y.C., Apr. 28, 1913; s. Samuel and Pessie (Feldman) G.; Ph.D., N.Y. U., 1955; m. Evelyn Richman, June 17, 1935; children—Louis, Aaron, Johanna. Statis. liaison officer U.S. Bur. Census and Bur. of Old Age Survivor's Ins., Balt., Washington, 1936-51; dir. study in utilization med. care for Commonwealth Fund, Rockefeller Found., N.Y.C., 1951-54; dir. mktg. research R.C. Forbes Pub. Co., N.Y.C., 1954-60; dir. research Center for Research in Childhood Schizophrenia, N.Y.C., 1955-78; prof. Hofstra U., Hempstead, N.Y., 1956—; dir. evaluation and research Rockland Children's Psychiat. Hosp., Orangeburg, N.Y., 1976—. IBM research fellow, 1966. Mem. Am. Statis. Assn. Jewish. Author: Longitudinal Statistical Analysis, 1960; contbr. articles to psychiat. jours. Home: 101 Gedney St Nyack NY 10960 Office: Hofstra U 1000 Fulton Ave Hempstead NY 11550

GOLDFARB, NORMAN, physician; b. N.Y.C., Aug. 2, 1921; s. Samuel H. and Bertha G.; B.A., U. Va., 1942, M.D., 1944; m. Leonie Guttstadt, June 20, 1948; children—Karen Joyce, Madelyn June, Leslie Jana. Intern, City Hosp., Welfare Island, N.Y., 1944-46; resident dermatology skin and cancer unit N.Y. U. Med. Center, N.Y.C., 1948-51, asso. prof. clin. dermatology, 1951—; attending N.Y. U. Hosp., N.Y.C., 1951—; attending L.I. Jewish-Hillside Med. Center, 1953—. Served with M.C., U.S. Army, 1946-48. Diplomate Am. Bd. Dermatology. Mem. Soc. Investigative Dermatology, Am. Acad. Dermatology, AMA, Soc. Internat. Mycology, Phi Lambda Kappa. Jewish. Researcher mycology, drug Griseofulvin. Office: 69-39 Yellowstone Blvd Forest Hills NY 11375

GOLDFIELD, ROBERT SAUL, corp. exec.; b. Phila., Aug. 4, 1927; s. James Edward and Minna (Mellen) G.; B.S., Drexel Inst. Tech., 1948; m. Florence P. Berg, Sept. 14, 1948; children—David S., Burton M., Danny J. Technician elec. photometric research Naval Research Labs., Washington, 1944-45; customer service mgr. lab. and photog. equipment dept. Williams, Brown & Earle, Inc., Phila., 1948-55; sec.-treas., sales mgr. Albern Color Research, Phila., 1955-60; v.p., nat. sales mgr. Perfect Photo, Inc., Phila., 1960-62, asst. to pres., v.p., 1962-66, pres., 1966-71; v.p. GAF Corp., N.Y.C., 1971-72; pres., chief exec. officer CGS Sci. Corp., Concordville, Pa., 1973-76, pres., chief exec. officer, chmn. bd., 1976—. Mem. Phila., U.S. chambers commerce, Sales and Mktg. Execs. Internat., Phi Kappa Phi. Home: 213 Stonehouse Ln Wyncote PA 19095 Office: Concord Indsl Park Lacrue Ave PO Box 222 Concordville PA 19331

GOLDIN, FREDERICK, educator, writer; b. Bklyn., Nov. 3, 1930; s. Samuel and Pauline Rose (Somach) G.; B.A., City Coll. N.Y., 1952; M.A., Columbia U., 1954, Ph.D., 1964; m. Dione Rakita; children—Cheryl, Lisa, Paul. Instr., U. Conn., Stamford, 1958-60, Bklyn. Coll., 1960-61; asst. prof. Rutgers U. Coll., New Brunswick, N.J., 1961-67; prof. City Coll. of City U. N.Y., 1967—. Sr. Fulbright research scholar, 1968-69, 75-76. Mem. Mediaeval Acad. Am., Dante Soc., Modern Lang. Assn., Internat. Courtly Lit. Soc., Internat. Arthurian Soc. Author: The Mirror of Narcissus, 1967; German and Italian Lyrics of the Middle Ages, 1973; Lyrics of the Troubadours and Trouveres, 1973; The Song of Roland, 1978; co-author: In Pursuit of Perfection, 1975. Office: Dept English City Coll City U MY 137th St and Convent Ave New York City NY 10031

GOLDMAN, DAVID HARVEY, bowling center and import co. exec.; b. Auburn, N.Y., Mar. 30, 1929; s. Samuel and Bertha (Winnick) G.; B.B.A., Ohio State U., 1951; m. Marilyn Kenyon, Mar. 5, 1955; children—Marjorie, Robert, Amy. Sales exec. I.C. Issac & Co., Balt., 1952-58; a founder Am. Bowling Enterprises, Rochester, N.Y., 1958, chmn. bd., pres., 1958-63; a founder Rochester Elton Corp., 1963, pres., 1963-72; pres. Reltron Corp., Rochester, 1972—, Vanguard Products, Berkely Springs, W.Va., 1977—; founder, pres. Elton Internat., Hong Kong, 1973—, Spitz 7 Ltd., Hong Kong, 1973—. Patron U. Rochester, 1964—. Club: Irondiquoit Country (Rochester). Home: 200 Georgian Ct Rd Rochester NY 14610 Office: 45 Gould St Rochester NY 14610

GOLDMAN, DAVID STEVEN, cons. indsl. and elec. engr.; b. Bklyn., Oct. 31, 1939; s. Maurice and Sara (Bloom) G.; B.S. in Elec. Engring., Poly. Inst. Bklyn., 1961; M.S. in Engring., Northeastern U., 1966; postgrad. Babson Inst., 1966-68. Design engr. Microwave Assos., Burlington, Mass., 1961-62; engring. program mgr. Raytheon Co., Wayland, Mass., 1962-75; mem. faculty Grad. Sch. Engring., Northeastern U., Boston, 1966—, vis. prof. indsl. engring. and engring. mgmt., 1975-78; cons. engr., pres. David Lee & Assos., Framingham, Mass., 1971—. Cons. Mass. Gov.'s Task Force on Capital Formation for Econ. Devel., 1975-76; notary pub., Mass., 1971—. Registered profl. engr., Mass., Calif. Mem. IEEE, Nat. Soc. Profl. Engrs. (named Outstanding Young Engr. 1974, Distinguished Service award 1976), Am. Inst. Indsl. Engrs., Mass. Soc. of Profl. Engrs. (pres. 1977-78, named Young Engr. of Year 1973). Contbr. articles on indsl. engring. to profl. jours.; editor: Value Management Training Manual, 1974. Home: 988 Pleasant St Framingham MA 01701 Office: PO Box 2218 Framingham MA 01701

GOLDMAN, GERALD, city ofcl.; b. Bklyn., Sept. 14, 1934; s. Max and Rae (Golden) G.; B.S. in Commerce and Econs., U. Vt., 1956; J.D., N.Y. U., 1959; m. Sharon Boyarsky, Sept. 2, 1956 (div. May 1972); children—Keith, Kevin, Kim, Lance; m. 2d, Susan Ann Heiblim, Oct. 21, 1973. Admitted to N.J. bar, 1959; founding partner firm Goldman Carlet Garrison Bertoni & Bitterman, Clifton, N.J., 1961—. Mayor, City of Passaic (N.J.), 1971-77. Served as 1st lt. AUS, 1957-58. Recipient Distinguished Service award Passaic Jr. C. of C., 1963. Mem. U.S. Jr. C. of C. (nat. dir. 1965). Contbr. to profl. jours. Home: 107 Ridge Ave Passaic NJ 07055 Office: 925 Clifton Ave Clifton NJ 07013

GOLDMAN, ISA PADAWER, physician; b. Memphis, Nov. 2, 1947; s. Max Mayer and Sheila (Padawer) G.; B.S., U. Ariz., 1967; M.D., Loma Linda U., 1971. Ordained rabbi, 1963; intern Coney Island Hosp. Maimonides Med. Center, Bklyn., 1971-72; resident in internal medicine, 1972-75; cardiology fellow N.Y. Med. Coll., N.Y.C., 1975-77; asst. attending physician, chief cardiology, dir. heart sta. Flower and Fifth Ave Hosps., N.Y.C., 1977—; asst. prof. medicine, cons. cardiology Mental Retardation Inst., N.Y. Med. Coll., 1977—; asst. attending physician Met. Hosp. Center, 1977—. Diplomate Am. Bd. Internal Medicine. Mem. A.C.P. (asso.), Am. Coll. Cardiology (affiliate), Assn. Orthodox Jewish Scientists, Phi Beta Kappa, Phi Kappa Phi, Beta Beta Beta, Alpha Epsilon Delta. Cons. editor cardiology Hosp. Physician Mag., 1977—. Home: 333 86th St W Apt 216 New York City NY 10024 Office: Div Cardiology 1249 Fifth Ave New York City NY 10029

GOLDMAN, JAMES ALLAN, chemist, ednl. adminstr.; b. Chgo., Nov., 20, 1935; s. Mandel and Katherine (Kaplan) G.; B.A. and B.S. in chemistry, U. Chgo., 1958; Ph.D., Northwestern U., 1962; m. Mary Gilbert Schwartz, Apr. 16, 1978. Instr. chemistry Northwestern U., Evanston, Ill., 1961-62; vis. asst. prof. chemistry Poly. Inst. Bklyn. 1962-63, asst. prof., 1963-71; coordinator tech. and indsl. programs div. continuing edn. N.Y.C. Community Coll. of City U. N.Y., Bklyn., 1971—. Chmn. Continuing Dialogue Convocation, 1970. Recipient Sigma Xi Distinguished Service award Poly. Inst. Bklyn., 1971. Fellow Am. Inst. Chemists; mem. Am. Chem. Soc., AAAS, N.Y. Acad. Scis., AAUP, Am. Assn. Physics Tchrs. Editorial bd. of Jour. Chem. Edn., 1964—, Intellect, 1975—, Chem. Tech., 1973—. Contbr. articles to sci. and profl. jours. Home: 270 Jay St Brooklyn NY 11201 Office: 300 Jay St Brooklyn NY 11201

GOLDMAN, MARTIN JEROME, mech. engr.; b. Bklyn., Aug. 9, 1936; s. Hyman and Shirley (Levine) G.; B.M.E., Coll. City N.Y., 1960; m. Rhea Kraf, Oct. 2, 1960; children—Hali Gaye, Geri Ilene, Beth Dana, Michelle Jean. Mech. engr. Thermal Engring., Islen, N.J., 1960-61, Syska & Hennessy, N.Y.C., 1961, E.U. Markush, N.Y.C., 1961-62; asso., dept. head Benjamin & Flack, N.Y.C., 1962-66; partner A.D. Benjamin, N.Y.C., 1966-68; prin. Martin J. Goldman, N.Y.C., 1968-71; partner Goldman Sokolow Copeland and predecessor, N.Y.C., 1971—. Served with U.S. Army, 1954-56. Registered profl. engr., N.Y., N.J., Md., Mass., Conn. Mem. Am. Soc. Heating, Refrigeration and Air Conditioning Engrs., Am. Soc. Mil. Engrs., Soc. Profl. Engrs. Home: Wixon Pond Rd Mahopac NY 10541 Office: 79 Madison Ave New York City NY 10016

GOLDMAN, ROBERT HARRY, magnet mfg. co. exec.; b. Balt., Jan. 20, 1932; s. Arthur Samuel and Betsy Wilner (Bretzfelder) G.; B.S., Johns Hopkins, 1953, postgrad., 1958; postgrad. U. Md., 1959; m. Nadine Ann Randall, Feb. 21, 1959; children—Jeffrey Alan, Wendy Sue, Amy Beth. Salesman, dept. head, buyer S & N Katz, Balt., 1953-58; salesman, hosp. rep. Parke-Davis Pharms., Detroit, 1960-63; pres. Jobmaster Corp., Randallstown, Md., 1963—. Home: 4501 Maryknoll Rd Baltimore MD 21208 Office: 9010 Liberty Rd Randallstown MD 21133

GOLDMAN, ROBERT HURON, lawyer; b. Boston, Nov. 24, 1918; s. Frank and Rose (Sydeman) G.; A.B., Harvard, 1939, LL.B., 1943; m. Charlotte R. Rubens, July 5, 1945; children—Wendy Eve, Randolph Rubens. Admitted to N.Y. State bar, 1945, Mass. bar, 1951; practiced in N.Y.C., 1945-50, Lowell, Mass., 1951—; law clk. Judge Learned Hand, U.S. Ct. Appeals, 1943-44; partner firm Goldman, Curtis, Adams, and Bell, and predecessor firms, 1951—; columnist Lowell Sunday Sun, 1954-78; v.p., asso. pub. Malden (Mass.) Evening News, Medford (Mass.) Daily Mercury, Melrose (Mass.) Evening News; mem. adv. bd. Baybank Middlesex. Radio commentator on internat. affairs, 1954—. Chmn. Greater Lowell Civic Com., 1952-55, Lowell Hist. Soc., 1957-60, Lowell Devel. and Indsl. Commn., 1959-60. Del. Republican State Conv., 1960-62. Bd. dirs. Boston World Affairs Council, 1960—. Named Citizen of Year Greater Lowell Civic Com., 1956. Mem. Am. (mem. nat. com. on consumer protection 1972-73, Sherman Act com. 1973—), Mass. (chmn. bar-press com. 1973-76), Middlesex County, Lowell bar assns., Phi Beta Kappa. Club: Harvard (dir., Lowell 1968—). Author: A Newspaperman's Handbook of the Libel Law of Massachusetts, 1966, rev., 1974; The Law of Libel—Present and Future, 1969. Editor: Harvard Law Review, 1943. Home: 8 Rolling Ridge Rd Andover MA 01810 Office: 8 Merrimack St Lowell MA 01852 also One Boston Pl Boston MA 02108

GOLDMAN, SHELDON, educator; b. Bronx, N.Y., Sept. 18, 1939; s. Yehuda and Anne (Slochower) G.; B.A. summa cum laude, N.Y.U., 1961; Ph.D. (Woodrow Wilson Dissertation fellow), Harvard, 1965; m. Marcia Liebeskind, June 16, 1963; children—Ellen, Jeremy, Sara. Teaching fellow in govt. Harvard, 1963-64; asst. prof. govt. U. Mass., Amherst, 1965-69, asso. prof., 1970-73, prof. polit. sci., 1974—. Woodrow Wilson fellow, 1961-62; NSF grantee, 1966; Social Sci. Research Council grantee, 1967. Mem. Internat., Am., Northeastern, Midwestern, So. polit. sci. assns., Law and Society Assn., AAUP, Phi Beta Kappa. Author: Roll Call Behavior in the Massachusetts House of Representatives, 1968; The Federal Judicial System, 1968; The Federal Courts as a Political System, 2d edit., 1976; American Court Systems, 1978. Contbr. articles to profl. jours. Home: Route 4 Amherst MA 01002 Office: Dept Polit Sci U Mass Amherst MA 01003

GOLDMAN, STANFORD MILTON, radiologist, nuclear medicine physician; b. Salt Lake City, Utah, Nov. 28, 1940; s. Osher and Miriam (Solomon) G.; B.R.E., B.A., Yeshiva U., 1961; M.D., Einstein Coll. Medicine, 1965; m. Harriet Kaplow, May 2, 1965; children—Etan Boaz, Nava. Intern, Jefferson U. Sch. of Medicine, Phila., 1965-66; resident Einstein Coll. Medicine, N.Y.C., 1966-69, asst. radiologist, asst. prof. radiology, 1971-72; radiologist Sinai Hosp. of Balt., 1973—; cons. Eastern Shore State Hosp., Cambridge, Md., 1973-77; asso. dir. radiology residency program Sinai Hosp., 1975—; asst. prof. radiology Johns Hopkins U. Sch. Medicine, 1974—; clin. asst. prof. radiology U. Md., 1975-78, clin. asso. prof., 1978—; vis. lectr. radiology Armed Forces Inst. of Pathology, 1974—. Mem. Bd. Jewish Edn., Balt., 1973—. Served with USPHS, 1969-71. Diplomate Am. Bd. Radiology, Am. Bd. Nuclear Medicine; recipient Outstanding Sci. Exhibit award Ariz. Med. Assn., 1971; Physicians Recognition award AMA, 1979, Silver award Explorer Boy Scouts Am., 1954; State of Israel scroll, 1973. Mem. Am. Coll. Radiology (alt. counsellor 1976, 77) Soc. Nuclear Medicine, Md. Soc. Nuclear Medicine, Soc. Uroradiology, Radiol. Soc. of N.Am., Am. Roentgen Ray Soc., Md. Radiol. Soc. (sec. 1977—), Einstein Alumni Assn. (bd. dirs. 1971-72), Balt. City Med. Soc., Md. Med. and Chirurgical Faculty, Alpha Epsilon Delta. Democrat. Jewish. Editor Radiol. Case of the Month, Md. State Med. Jour., 1974-75; contbr. articles in field to med. jours., sci. presentations at profl. meetings. Home: 4001 Rouen Rd Randallstown MD 21133 Office: Sinai Hospital of Baltimore Inc Belvedere at Greenspring Sts Baltimore MD 21215

GOLDMAN, THOMAS ADLER, statistician; b. Fort Worth, Dec. 16, 1918; s. Marcus Isaac and Mary Lilly (Ware) G.; A.B., Harvard U., 1939; A.M., George Washington U., 1952; Ph.D., U. Chgo., 1962; m. Teuntje Emma Visser, Mar. 17, 1951; children—Michael Standish, Daniel Ware, Emma Wilhelmina, Beatrice Juliana, Robert Adler. Economist, Rand Corp., Santa Monica, Calif., 1955-58; br. chief CEIR Inc. research, Arlington, Va., 1958-60; analyst Center for Naval Analyses, Arlington, 1961-65; pres. Econ. & Tech. Analysis Co., Washington, 1968-71; chief statistician Fed. Home Loan Bank Bd., Washington, 1971—. Served with USAAF, 1943-45. Mem. Econometric Soc., Am. Statis. Assn., Inst. Mgmt. Scis., Washington Ops. Research Council (trustee, 1963-65), Esperanto Soc. Washington (pres. 1970-74), Harvard Club Washington. Editor: Cost Effectiveness Analysis 1967. Home: 7008 Millwood Rd Bethesda MD 20034 Office: 101 Indiana Ave NW Washington DC 20552

GOLDMAN, WILLIAM, radiologist; b. Bklyn., July 6, 1932; s. Oscar and Millie (Heller) G.; B.A., N.Y. U., 1954; M.D., Chgo. Med. Sch., 1958; m. Phyllis M. Schechter, June 15, 1958; children—Laurie Sue, Robert Steven. Intern, L.I. Jewish Hosp., New Hyde Park, N.Y., 1958-59; resident in radiology and nuclear medicine Bellevue Hosp., N.Y.C., 1961-64; practice medicine, specializing in radiology, Syracuse, N.Y., 1964-76; dir. dept. nuclear medicine Community Gen. Hosp., Syracuse, 1968—; clin. asst. prof. radiology Upstate Med. Center, Syracuse, 1978—; dir. dept. radiology Loretto Geriatric Center, Syracuse, 1976—; med. dir. nuclear medicine tech. Rochester Inst. Tech., 1974—; cons. radiologist USAF, Hancock Field, 1970—. Served to capt. USAF, 1959-61. Diplomate Soc. Nuclear Medicine, Am. Coll. Radiology. Mem. AMA, Radiol. Soc. N. Am., Central N.Y. Radiologic Soc., N.Y. State, Onondaga County med. socs. Home: Woodside Rd Fayetteville NY 13066 Office: Community Gen Hosp Broad St Syracuse NY 13215

GOLDMAN, ZACHARY CHARLES, pharm. and toiletry mfg. co. exec.; b. N.Y.C., Sept. 22, 1929; s. Albert W. and Betty (Levy) G.; B.B.A., Bernard M. Baruch Sch. Bus. and Civic Adminstrn., N.Y.C., 1950; m. Martha Levine, Nov. 18, 1950 (div. Jan. 1972); children—Robert, Richard; m. 2d, Kaycele Greenberg, Feb. 4, 1972; stepchildren—Janice, David. C.P.A., J.K. Lasser & Co., N.Y.C., 1953-55; with J.B. Williams Co., Inc., N.Y.C., 1956—, corporate controller, 1963-67, v.p. adminstrn. internat., 1968-72, v.p. internat. operations worldwide, 1973—. Served to sgt. AUS, 1952-53. C.P.A., N.Y., N.J. Mem. Financial Execs. Inst., Am. Inst. C.P.A.'s, N.Y., N.J. socs. C.P.A.'s. Mason. Home: 2 Gately Ct Cherry Hill NJ 08034 Office: JB Williams Co Inc 767 Fifth Ave New York City NY 10022

GOLDREYER, LAWRENCE LOWE, newspaper exec.; b. Bklyn., Mar. 12, 1915; s. Boris Nathan and Antoinette (Lowe) G.; B.S. in Engring., Coll. City N.Y., 1935, M.E., 1936; m. Sydele Schonhorn, May 19, 1938; 1 son, Bruce Neil. With N.Y. Post Newspaper, 1936—, classified advt. mgr., 1963-64, dir. fin. advt., 1964-77, asso. nat. advt. mgr., 1977—. Mem. Mech. Bank Collectors Am., Am. Mktg. Assn., Fin. Advt. and Mktg. Assn. Met. N.Y. (past pres.), Fin. Communications Soc. Composer for piano. Home: 143-50 Hoover Ave Jamaica NY 11435 Office: NY Post 210 South St New York City NY 10002

GOLDRICH, STANLEY GILBERT, optometrist, psychologist, educator; s. Joseph and Doris (Stelzner) G.; B.A., Queens Coll., 1959, M.A., 1965; Ph.D., City U.N.Y., 1966; O.D., Mass. Coll. Optometry, 1974. Research asso. Primate Center, U. Wis., Madison, 1965-67; asst. prof. psychology Ohio State U., Columbus, 1967-72; asst. prof., research scientist Coll. Optometry, State U. N.Y., N.Y.C., 1974—. Fellow Am. Acad. Optometry; mem. Am. Psychol. Assn., Am. Optometric Assn. Contbr. articles in psychol. and optometric research to profl. jours.; inventor optometric eye control tng. system. Home: 150 Lexington Ave New York City NY 10016 Office: 100 E 24th St New York City NY 10010

GOLDSCHMIDT, LEONTINE, biochemist; b. Arad, Austria, Mar. 9, 1913; s. Maximilian and Anna (Michel) G.; Ph.M., Vienna (Austria) U., 1935, Ph.D., 1937. Came to U.S., 1939, naturalized, 1945. Research asst. Boston U. Sch. Medicine, 1942-45; research biologist U.S. Naval Radiation Lab., San Francisco, 1947-50; mem. staff, chief biochem. research Creedmoor Inst., Queens Village, N.Y., 1954—. Mem. A.A.A.S., Am. Assn. Clin. Chemists, Am. Chem. Soc. Contbr. articles to profl. jours. Home: 103-30 68th Ave Forest Hills NY 11375 Office: Creedmoor Inst PO Box 40 Queens Village NY 11427

GOLDSCHMIED, FABIO RENZO, indsl. scientist and engr.; b. Trieste, Italy, Oct. 25, 1919; s. Rodolfo and Ada (Frankel) G.; came to U.S., 1939, naturalized, 1943; B.S. in Engring., Columbia, 1947, M.S., 1948; m. Marie Perfumo, Mar. 21, 1942; 1 dau., Wanda Ada. Aero. research scientist NACA Lewis Research Center, Cleve., 1948-54; mgr. advanced devel. engring. Westinghouse Electric Corp., Boston, 1954-61; engring. supr. UNIVAC Engring. Center and Sperry Utah div. Sperry Rand Corp., Blue Bell, Pa. and Salt Lake City, 1962-65; research prof. mech. engring. U. Utah, Salt Lake 1965-68; adv. scientist Research Labs., Westinghouse Electric Corp., Pitts., 1968—. Vis. prof. Purdue U., 1968-69. Served with AUS, 1942-46. Registered profl. engr., Pa. Mass., Utah. Fellow Am. Inst. Aeros. and Astronautics (asso.); mem. ASME, AAAS, Sigma Xi. Democrat. Jewish religion. contbr. articles to profl. jours. Patentee in field. Home: 1782 McClure Rd Monroeville PA 15146 Office: Research and Devel Center Westinghouse Electric Corp Pittsburgh PA 15235

GOLDSMITH, EDWARD IRA, surgeon, educator; b. Far Rockaway, N.Y., Nov. 13, 1927; s. Abraham J. and Gertrude (Epstein) G.; A.B., Cornell U., 1947, M.D., 1950; m. Gene Louise French, Aug. 29, 1952; children—Joel Andrew, Jeremy Adam, William Glenn, Daniel French. Intern, N.Y. Hosp., 1950-51, resident, 1954-57, attending surgeon, 1972—; resident Boston Children's Hosp., 1952, U. Colo. Med. Center, Denver, 1957-58; practice medicine specializing in gen. and cardiovascular surgery, N.Y.C., 1958—, faculty dept. surgery Cornell U. Med. Coll., N.Y.C., 1954—, clin. asso. prof., 1966-72, prof., 1972—; mem. adv. com. Joint Legislative Com. Mental Retardation, Physically Handicapped, N.Y. State Legislature, 1960—; chmn. Com. Scientists for Use Primates in Med. Research, 1966—; mem. subcom. on care and use of com. on primates NRC. Bd. dirs. Nassau Center for Emotionally Disturbed Children, Woodbury, N.Y.; bd. visitors Rockland Children's Psychiat. Center. Served to 1st lt. M.C., AUS, 1952-54. Recipient Presdl. Merit medal Philippines, 1968; Trumpeldor medal State Israel, 1971. Diplomate Am. Bd. Surgery. Fellow A.C.S.; mem. Med. Soc. County N.Y., A.M.A., Am. Heart Assn., N.Y. Soc. Cardio-Vascular Surgery, N.Y. Surg. Soc., A.A.A.S., N.Y. Acad. Scis., N.Y. Acad. Medicine, Am. Soc. Artificial Internal Organs, Transplantation Soc., Internat. Primatological Soc., Am. Soc. Tropical Medicine and Hygiene, Royal Soc. Tropical Medicine and Hygiene, N.Y. Cardiol. Soc., N.Y. Soc. Nephrology, Harvey Soc., N.Y. Gastroent. Assn., N.Y. State Soc. Med. Research (v.p.), Phi Sigma Delta, Phi Delta Epsilon. Mem. B'nai B'rith. Club: Explorers (N.Y.C.). Editor: Medical Primatology, 1970, 72; Jour. Med. Primatology, 1972. Contbr. articles to profl. jours. Home: Ridge Rd Katonah NY 10536 Office: 525 E 68th St New York City NY 10021

GOLDSMITH, HARRY SAWYER, surgeon; b. Newton, Mass., Sept. 30, 1929; s. Leo and Dorothy Amy (Appleton) G.; A.B., Dartmouth, 1952; M.D., Boston U., 1956; m. Linda Perry, Dec. 8, 1961; children—John, Robert, Lynne. Intern, Boston City Hosp., 1956-57, resident in surgery, 1957-61; resident in surgery Meml. Sloan-Kettering Inst., N.Y.C., 1963-65; practice medicine specializing in surgery, Phila., 1970-77; cons. staff Meml. Sloan Kettering Center, N.Y.C., White River Junction VA Hosp., 1977—; Samuel D. Gross prof. surgery, chmn. dept. Jefferson Med. Coll., Phila., 1970-77, distinguished prof. surgery, 1977—; prof. surgery Dartmouth Coll. Med. Sch., Hanover, N.H., 1977—; surgeon-in-chief Jefferson U. Hosp., 1970-77; staff surgeon Mary Hitchcock Clinic, Hanover, 1977—. Served as capt. U.S. Army, 1961-63. Mem. A.C.S., Soc. Vascular Surgery, British Assn. Surg. Oncology, A.O. Whipple Surg. Soc., Soc. for Surgery of Alimentary Tract. Editor-in-chief: Goldsmith's Practice of Surgery, 1976. Contbr. articles to profl. jours. Home: 129 Brook Hollow Hanover NH 03755 Office: Dartmouth Coll Med Sch Hanover NH 03755

GOLDSMITH, J. DAVIS, clergyman; b. Van Buren, Ark., July 19, 1913; s. Nathaniel Clark and India Riddle G.; student Coll. of the Ozarks, 1932-33, Ouachita Coll., 1936; Th.M., Central Bapt. Theol. Sem., 1942, Th.D., 1947; postgrad. George Washington U., 1959-61, Washington Sch. Psychiatry, 1961; m. Emma Lucille Riddle, Aug. 26, 1933; children—Sondra Leigh, Harold Davis. Ordained to ministry, Baptist Ch., 1933; pastor, Altus, Ark., 1932-33, Scranton, Ark., 1935-36, Magazine, Ark., 1936-39, Marysville, Kans., 1939-42, Girard, Kans., 1942-46, Iola, Kans., 1948-52; state student sec. Kans. Bapt. Conv., 1946-48; chaplain U.S. Army, Korea and U.S., 1953-56; pvt. practice personal and marriage counseling, Gaithersburg, Md., 1961—; prof. Central Sem. Extension Center, 1950-52; cons. Pastors in Family Relations, 1961—. Recipient Certificate of Appreciation, Gov. Kyoggni Provincial Govt., Republic Korea, 1955. Mem. Am. Personnel and Guidance Assn., Am. Coll. Personnel Assn., Nat. Vocat. Guidance Assn., Nat. Council Family Relations, Am. Assn. Sex Educators, Counselors and Therapists, Am. Legion, DAV. Club: Masons. Home and Office: 121 Rolling Rd PO Box 91 Gaithersburg MD 20760

GOLDSMITH, MAXIMILIAN ORFEVRE, ophthalmologist, ophthalmic surgeon; b. Woodridge, N.Y., Jan. 2, 1916; s. Joseph A. and Jennie (Getz) G.; B.S., N.Y. U., 1936; M.B., M.D., Chgo. Med. Sch., 1943; certificate basic ophthalmology U. Pa., 1951; m. Judith Rudensky, Sept. 2, 1951; children—Meredith, Jason, Elizabeth. Intern, St. Mary's Hosp., Huntington, W.Va., 1943-44; resident in ophthalmology Manhattan Eye, Ear and Throat Hosp., N.Y.C., 1953-55, asso. attending ophthalmologist, 1955-77, attending ophthalmologist, 1977—; asso. attending Flower Fifth Ave. Hosp., and Met. Hosp., N.Y.C., 1966—; chief eye plastic service Hosp. Joint Diseases, N.Y.C., also asso. attending in ophthalmology; vis. prof. surgery ophthalmology Chgo. Med. Sch., 1968—; asso. clin. prof. ophthalmology N.Y. Med. Coll., 1968—. Served with M.C., U.S. Army, 1951-53; Korea. Diplomate Am. Bd. Ophthalmology. Fellow A.C.S., Internat. Coll. Surgeons, Am. Acad. Ophthalmology and Otolaryngology, Soc. Eye Surgeons, Royal Soc. Medicine (London), Soc. Mil. Ophthalmologists, Am. Coll. Cryosurgery; mem. Pan. Am. Med. Assn. (diplomate), N.Y. Soc. Clin. Ophthalmology, Pan Am. Assn. Ophthalmology, Am. Soc. Contemporary Ophthalmology, Pan. Am. Soc. Microsurgery (founding), N.Y. State Med. Soc., Am. Geriatric Soc. Jewish. Club: Lions (pres. L.I. City 1971-72). Home: 17 Burton Ave Woodmere NY 11598 Office: 110-31 72d Dr Forest Hills NY 11375

GOLDSMITH, RICHARD, geologist, govt. ofcl.; b. Salem, Mass., Sept. 30, 1918; s. Chester Arthur and May Preston (Jenkins) G.; B.A., U. Maine, 1940; Ph.D., U. Wash., 1951; m. June Lilian Waterman, Feb. 21, 1955; children—Richard Stuart, Kathryn Holloway, Charles Fraser. Geologist, U.S. Geol. Survey, Denver, 1952-63, econ. geologist, Jiddah, Saudi Arabia, 1964-66, econ. geologist, Bucaramanga, Colombia, S.Am., 1966-69, adminstrv. geologist Beltsville, Md., 1969-73, research geologist, 1973—. Served with AUS, 1942-46. Fellow Geol. Soc. Am. (vice chmn. northeast sect. 1969-70); mem. Geol. Soc. Wash., A.A.A.S., Am. Assn. Quaternary Geologists. Home: 105 E Lenox St Chevy Chase MD 20015 Office: National Center Stop 925 Reston VA 22070

GOLDSMITH, ROBERT LEWIS, mag. exec.; b. N.Y.C., Jan. 9, 1928; s. Arthur and Elizabeth (Kohn) G.; B.S., N.Y. U., 1950; m. Joan M. Hartman, 1976. Advt. promotion mgr. Esquire, Inc., N.Y.C., 1952-53; advt. dir. Schine Hotels, N.Y.C., 1953; promotion dir. Dell Pub. Co., N.Y.C., 1953-58, Outdoor Life Mag., N.Y.C., 1958-65; asso. dir. mag. div. Boy Scouts Am., N.Y.C., 1965—. Mem. N.Y. Sales Execs. Club, Mktg. Communications Execs. Assn., Am. Mktg. Assn., Asia Soc., China Inst. Am., N.Y. Zool. Soc. Club: N.Y. U. (bd. govs., v.p., exec. com.). Office: Boy Scouts Am 271 Madison Ave New York City NY 10016

GOLDSMITH, SILVIANNA, filmmaker, educator; b. N.Y.C.; d. Roy and Anna Lewis (Lefkowitz) Goldsmith; B.A., Bklyn. Coll., 1963; M.A., N.Y. U., 1966, Films include: Orpheus Underground, 1975, Lil, Lil Picard, Art is a Party, 1974, Mexico, 1975, Nightclub, Memories of Havana in Queens, 1975; one-woman shows Millenium, 1975, Goethe House, 1976, Westchester Council on Arts, 1977, S.I. Mus., 1978; film shows include: Calif. Inst. Arts, 1973, Graz Mus., Austria, 1974, Mus. of Modern Art, Vienna, 1974, Modern Mus., Basle, Switzerland, 1975, Paris Mus. Modern Art, 1974, Staten Island Mus., 1975, N.Y. U., 1975, Ashawagh Hall, East Hampton, N.Y., 1975, Second Internat. Festival Women's Films, 1976, Soho Festival Arts, 1976; Berlin Arsenal, 1978; tchr., film coordinator Women's Interart Center, N.Y.C., 1972—. Grantee N.Y. State Council Arts, 1974-77, Nat. Endowment Arts, 1974-76. Mem. Women/Artist/Filmmakers, Inc. (past sec., co-project dir.), Millenium Film Workshop, Women's Salon. Home: 411 E 10th St New York City NY 10009 Studio: 151 W 18th St New York City NY 10011

GOLDSMITH, STANLEY JOSEPH, physician; b. Bklyn., Aug. 17, 1937; s. Jack and Mae (Greenzweig) G.; B.A., Columbia U., 1958; M.D., State U. N.Y. Downstate Med. Center, 1962; m. Miriam Schulman, June 6, 1959; children—Ira, Arthur, Beth, Mark. Intern, State U. N.Y.-Kings County Med. Center, Bklyn., 1962-63, resident, 1965-66, chief resident, 1966-67; fellow in endocrinology Mt. Sinai Hosp., N.Y.C., 1967-68, dir. Andre Meyer dept. physics-nuclear medicine, 1973—; research asso. radioisotope service Bronx (N.Y.) VA Hosp., 1968-69; dir. nuclear medicine, asst. dir. endocrino dept. Nassau County Med. Center, East Meadow, N.Y., 1969-73; asst. prof. medicine, radiology State U. N.Y., Stony Brook Health Sci. Center, 1971-73; asst. prof. medicine Mt. Sinai Sch. Medicine, 1973-76, asso. prof., 1976—; research collaborator Brookhaven Nat. Labs., Upton, N.Y., 1971-75; cons. nuclear medicine. Served as capt. M.C., U.S. Army, 1963-65. Diplomate Am. Bd. Internal Medicine (subsplty. bd. endocrinology and metabolism), Am. Bd. Nuclear Medicine. Fellow Am. Coll. Cardiology, A.C.P.; mem. Am. Coll. Nuclear Physicians, AAAS, Am., N.Y. diabetes assns., Am. Fedn. Clin. Research, Endocrine Soc., N.Y. Acad. Scis., Radiol. Soc. N.Am., Soc. Nuclear Medicine (sec. Greater N.Y. chpt. 1975-78, pres.-elect. 1978—). Contbr. numerous articles to med. jours. Home: 72 Ivy Way Port Washington NY 11050 Office: Mount Sinai Med. Center Fifth Ave and 100th St New York City NY 10029

GOLDSPIEL, SOLOMON, metall. engr.; b. Brody, Poland, June 1, 1913; s. Bernard and Celia (Schwager) G.; B.S., Coll. City N.Y., 1934, Chem. Engr., 1936; M.S. in Physics, Poly. Inst. Bklyn., 1954; m. Fannie Stern, Apr. 2, 1938; children—Gloria Goldspiel Muskat, Alfred A. Metallurgist, physicist, nondestructive test specialist USN, Phila. and Bklyn., 1936-70; nondestructive test cons. Naval Ship Research and Devel. Center, Annapolis (Md.) Lab., 1970-73; sr. metallurgist nondestructive test specialist N.Y.C. Bd. Water Supply, 1970—; tchr. N.Y.C. colls., evenings 1946-76; mem. adv. group on metals, fabrication and inspection Maritime Transp. Research Bd., NRC, 1973-76. Fellow Am. Soc. Nondestructive Testing (Mehl honor lectr., N. A. Kahn Meml. award), ASTM (award of merit 1978; chmn. reference radiograph subcom.); mem. City Coll. N.Y. Engring. and Archtl. Alumni Assn. (pres. 1975-77), Am. Nat. Standards Inst. (chmn. sensitometry of indsl. x-ray films), Sigma Xi (pres. br. 1959-60). Jewish. Contbr. articles in field to profl. jours. Home: 2471 E 26th St Brooklyn NY 11235 Office: 1250 Broadway New York City NY 10001

GOLDSTEIN, DAN NICU, surgeon, educator; b. Bucharest, Rumania, June 27, 1927; s. Leopold and Fanny Goldstein; came to U.S., 1964, naturalized, 1969; M.D., U. Bucharest, 1951. Resident, Children's Orthopedic Hosp., Bucharest, 1952-54; lectr. anatomy U. Bucharest Med. Sch., 1954-57; Surgeon Mil. Hosp. Bucharest, 1957-63; intern White Plains (N.Y.) Hosp., 1964-65, resident in gen. surgery, 1965-66; resident in orthopaedic surgery St. Vincent's Hosp., S.I., 1966-67, N.Y. Polyclinic Hosp., N.Y.C., 1967-68, Giles Hosp., Bklyn., 1968-69; practice medicine specializing in orthopaedic surgery, Flushing, N.Y., 1969—; asso. prof. N.Y. Polyclinic Med. Sch. and Health Center; mem. staff Bronx Lebanon Med. Center, L.I. Coll. Hosp., Bklyn., St. Giles Hosp., Parkway Hosp.; chief orthopedic surgeon Hillcrest Hosp. Diplomate Am. Bd. Orthopaedic Surgery. Fellow Am. Acad. Orthopaedic Surgeons, A.C.S., Internat. Coll. Surgeons; mem. AMA, N.Y. State, Queens med. socs. Home: 260 Wyndcliff Rd Scarsdale NY 11053 Office: 176-60 Union Turnpike Flushing NY 11366

GOLDSTEIN, DANIEL ALAN, assn. exec.; b. N.Y.C., Nov. 11, 1934; s. Matt Moses and Eve Beatrice (Bernstein) G.; student Stanford U., 1952-53; A.B., U. Calif., Berkeley, 1956; M.A., U. Mich., 1959; m. Rona Lee Rosenberg, Sept. 1, 1963; children—Adam, Jonathan, David, Sara, Benjamin. Newsman, AP, Fresno, Calif., 1956-57; instr. Queens Coll., U. City N.Y., 1961-65; tchr. high sch. English, pub. schs. N.Y.C., 1963-65; asst. editor N.Y. Herald Tribune News Service, 1965-66; sr. pub. info. specialist N.Y. State Depts. Civil Service and Labor, 1966-71; asso. research editor, N.Y. State Dept. Labor, 1971-72, dir. pub. relations, 1972-73; dir. pub. relations N.Y. State Bar Assn., Albany, 1973—. Mem. Pub. Relations Soc. Am., Nat. Assn. Bar Execs. Home: 44 Gail Ave Albany NY 12205 Office: 1 Elk St Albany NY 12207

GOLDSTEIN, DANIEL LEON, psychiatrist; b. N.Y.C., Sept. 17, 1914; s. Samuel and Pauline (Kleinman) G.; B.S., N.Y.U., 1935, M.D., 1939; m. Erna Gelber, June 27, 1943; children—Cecily, Jonathan, Richard. Intern, Greenpoint Hosp., Bklyn., 1939-41; resident, fellow in psychiatry N.Y.U. and Bellevue Hosp., N.Y.C., 1946-47; postgrad. N.Y. Med. Coll., N.Y.C., 1946-51; practice medicine specializing in psychiatry and psychoanalysis, Hackensack, N.J., 1948—; mem. staffs Martland Hosp., Newark, Bellevue Hosp., N.Y.C., 1948; Hackensack Hosp., 1957—, dir. dept. psychiatry, 1960—; cons. psychiatrist VA Hosp., East Orange, N.J., Child Guidance Center, Montclair, N.J.; Hackensack Bd. Edn.; Jewish Welfare Council Bergen County (N.J.); dir. Hackensack Hosp. Community Mental Health Center, 1976—; asst. prof. psychiatry, N.Y.U., 1950-67; clin. prof. N.J. Coll. Medicine, Newark, 1965—. Served with USAF, 1941-45. Diplomate Am. Bd. Psychiatry and Neurology (examiner in psychiatry 1951—). Fellow Am. Psychiat. Assn. (life), Am. Acad. Psychoanalysts; mem. N.J. Neuropsychiat. Assn. (pres. 1972-73), AMA, N.J., Bergen County med. socs., Soc. Med. Psychoanalysts, Beta Lambda Sigma, Psi Chi, Phi Lambda Kappa. Club: Masons. Office: Hackensack Hosp Hosp Pl Johnson Hall Hackensack NJ 07601

GOLDSTEIN, DONALD MAURICE, historian; b. N.Y.C., Dec. 15, 1932; s. Max A. and Jean M. Goldstein; B.A., U. Md., 1954, M.A., 1962; M.S., Georgetown U., 1963; M.B.A., George Washington U., 1965; Ph.D., U. Denver, 1970; grad. War Coll., 1973, Air Command and Staff Coll., 1965; m. Mariann Norma Zinck, Aug. 5, 1963; children—Tammie, Timmie, Tommie, Teri. Commd. 2d lt. U.S. Air Force, 1955, advanced through grades lt. col., 1972; comdr. missile site, Taiwan, 1958-59; staff officer U.S. Strike Command, 1961-64; research asso. Airstaff Pentagon; asso. prof. history USAF Acad., 1965-71, asst. track coach, 1965-71; ret., 1977; asso. prof. history Troy (Ala.) State U., 1971-74; prof. aerospace studies U. Pitts., 1975-77, asso. prof. pub. and internat. affairs, 1975—, dir. placement and alumni, 1977—. Decorated Soldiers medal, Meritorious Service medal with 2 oak leaf clusters, Joint Service Commendation medal, Air Force Commendation medal with oak leaf cluster. Mem. Am. Hist. Assn., Internat. Studies Assn., Am. Soc. Pub. Adminstrs., Am. Polit. Sci. Assn., Air Force Assn., Omicron Delta Kappa, Phi Kappa Phi, Phi Alpha Theta, Sigma Nu. Roman Catholic. Club: Toastmasters. Author: Ennis C. Whitehead Aerospace Commander, 1970; Adolph Hitler in the Perspective of the American Press, 1961; Adolph Hitler Adminstrator of a Society, 1965. Asst. editor papers on fgn. policy for House Com. on Internat. Affairs, 1947-54. Contbr. articles on def. policy and nat. security affairs to profl. jours. Home: 233 Wells Dr Bethel Park PA 15102 Office: Placement and Alumni 36-26 Forbes 1 Complex Pittsburgh PA 15260

GOLDSTEIN, ELI, physician, educator; b. Minsk, Russia, May 21, 1897; s. Julius and Yente (Komschutz) G.; came to U.S., 1906, naturalized, 1918; M.D., L.I. Med. Coll., 1922; B.S., Columbia, 1926; postgrad. in medicine U. Vienna, 1926; D.Jewish Lit. (hon.), Jewish Tchrs. Sem., 1973; m. Caroline Kleppner, Apr. 6, 1924; children—Judith (Mrs. Wilbert Minowitz), Naomi (Mrs. Franklin Feldman); m. 2d, Hertzliah Zamereth, Apr. 8, 1968. Intern, Fifth Ave. Hosp., N.Y.C., 1922-24, asst. attending physician 1924-28; fellow pathology City Hosp., 1924; asso. attending physician Flower-Fifth Av. Hosps., 1928-36, attending, 1949—; chief med. clinic Fifth Av. Hosp., 1924-36, chief diabetic clinic, 1927-34; asso. attending physician Sydenham Hosp., N.Y.C., 1939-40; asst. clin. prof. medicine N.Y. Med. Coll., 1944-49, asso. clin. prof. medicine, 1949-55, asso. prof. medicine, 1955-62, prof. clin. medicine, 1962—; vis. physician Met. Hosp., 1954-64, cons. physician, 1964—; vis. physian Bird S. Coler Meml. Hosp., 1954-70; dir. medicine and attending physician Hebrew Home for Aged, N.Y.C., 1950—. Adv. bd. N.Y. Coll. Music; bd. dirs. Hebrew Home for Aged; pres., bd. dirs. Herzliah Hebrew Tchrs. Inst., Jewish Tchrs. Sem., and People's U. Diplomate Am. Bd. Internal Medicine. Fellow A.C.P., N.Y. Acad. Medicine, Am. Geriatrics Soc.; mem. Am. Acad. Jewish Research, A.A.A.S., A.M.A., Med. Soc. County N.Y., N.Y. State, Rudolph Virchow med. socs., N.Y. Acad. Scis. Contbr. articles to profl. jours. Address: 150 E 94th St New York NY 10028

GOLDSTEIN, EMANUEL V., physician; b. N.Y.C., June 13, 1914; s. Michael Vallee and Bessie (Leibowitz) G.; M.D., State U. Ia., 1941; m. Frances Virginia Dearborn, Aug. 3, 1947; children—Anne Brenda, Lawrence Michael. Intern, Hartford (Conn.) Municipal Hosp., 1941-42; practice medicine specializing in vascular diseases, N.Y.C., 1945—; clin. asst. medicine St. Luke's Hosp. Served to capt. AUS, 1942-45; med. dir. USPHS Res. Decorated Purple Heart, Bronze Star medal with 3 oak leaf clusters. Fellow Internat., Am. colls. angiology, Am. Geriatrics Soc., N.Y. Cardiology Soc., Peripheral Vascular Soc. Am.; mem. A.M.A., N.Y. State, N.Y. County med. socs., N.Y. Acad. Scis., Mil. Surgeons U.S., Am. Thoracic Soc., Trudeau Soc., Commd. Officers Assn. USPHS, Royal Health Soc., Phi Delta Epsilon. Contbr. articles to profl. jours. Home: 125 Lake Shore Dr Putnam Lake Brewster NY 10509 Office: 423 W 120th St New York City NY 10027

GOLDSTEIN, FREDRIC ROBERT, geologist, educator; b. Bklyn., May 11, 1944; s. Irving and Bertha (Cohen) G.; B.S. (N.Y. Regents scholar), Bklyn. Coll., 1966; M.S., Miami U., 1968; postgrad. Cornell U., 1968-69; Ph.D., Rutgers U., 1974; m. Barbara Feldman, Dec. 24, 1966; children—Mindy, Laurie. Tchr. earth sci. Lakewood (N.J.) High Sch., 1971-72; prof. geology Western Conn. State Coll., 1972-73; prof. geology Trenton (N.J.) State Coll., 1973—, coordinator earth sci. faculty, 1975—; critical reader grant proposals, polar studies div. NSF, 1976—. Mem. Am. Assn. Stratigraphic Palynologists, Geol. Soc. Am. (Penrose Bequest grant 1969), Palynologists Greater N.Y., AAAS. Contbr. articles to profl. jours. Home: 15 Hopatcong Dr Lawrenceville NJ 08648 Office: Trenton State College PO Box 940 Trenton NJ 08625

GOLDSTEIN, GERALD ALAN, thermal engr.; b. Bklyn., Jan. 31, 1942; s. Abraham and Ceil Molly (Raab) G.; B.E.S. (Regents Scholar), State U. N.Y., Stony Brook, 1963, M.S., 1965; M.B.A., Adelphi U., 1975; m. Jane Gilbert, Jan. 30, 1965; children—Mark Howard, Deborah Ellen. Thermal systems engr. Grumman Corp., Bethpage, N.Y., 1965-72; sr. thermal engr. optical tech. div. Perkin Elmer Corp., Danbury, Conn., 1972—. NSF grantee, 1962-64. Mem. Am. Inst. Aeros. and Astronautics, State U. N.Y. Stony Brook Alumni Assn., Delta Mu Delta. Contbr. articles to sci. jours.

GOLDSTEIN, HAROLD H., psychologist; b. N.Y.C., Apr. 20, 1938; s. Louis and Ida (Pofsky) G.; B.B.A. cum laude, City Coll. N.Y., 1959; M.S., U. Mass., Ph.D., 1963; certificate in community mental health, Harvard U., 1967; m. Carole Joyce Golob, Dec. 22, 1962; children—Deborah Ann, Adam Stuart. Chief psychologist Westfield (Mass.) Area Child Guidance Center, 1963-66; spl. asst. to dir., NIMH, 1967-69, chief community mental health services support br., 1972-75, asso. dir. div. mental health service programs, Rockville, 1975—; asso. prof. Westfield State Coll., 1964-66; vis. lectr. U. Mass., 1965-66; clin. cons. Montgomery County Dept. Health, 1967—; pvt. practice psychology, 1975—. Recipient Gardner Murphy award, 1959, spl. achievement award Alcohol, Drug Abuse and Mental Health Adminstrn., 1976; Grant Found. fellow, 1966-67. Mem. Am. Psychol. Assn., Am. Orthopsychiat. Assn., Psi Chi, Beta Gamma Sigma, Phi Kappa Phi. Home: 14013 Broomall Ln Wheaton MD 20906 Office: 5600 Fishers Ln Rockville MD 20852

GOLDSTEIN, HARRY ABRAHAM, chemist, city adminstr.; b. N.Y.C., Mar. 16, 1916; s. Boris and Tillie (Brownstein) G.; B.A., Bklyn. Coll., 1936; M.Sc. in Edn., Coll. City N.Y., 1938; m. Hilda Gaines, Dec. 10, 1944; 1 son, Lawrence W. Chemist, City of N.Y., 1944-60, chief chemist, 1960-72, dir. labs. dept. gen. services, 1972—; mem. com. hwy. and structural maintenance City of N.Y. Fellow Am. Inst. Chemists (profl.); mem. Am. Chem. Soc., Am. Assn. Asphalt Paving Technologists, Am. Concrete Inst., ASTM, Am. Pub. Works Assn., Am. Assn. Textile Chemists and Colorists, Municipal Engrs. City N.Y., Habonim-Ormyim Jewish Soc., Jewish Center Nachlath Zion, Bklyn. Coll. Alumni Assn., Bklyn. Coll. Chemistry Alumni Soc. (treas. 1967-71). Chem. abstractor Chem. Abstracts Service, 1947—. Home: 4190 Bedford Ave Apt 5-K Brooklyn NY 11229 Office: NYC Dept Gen Services Div Pub Structures 480 Canal St New York City NY 10013

GOLDSTEIN, HARRY HAROLD, dentist; b. N.Y.C., June 19, 1922; s. Michael and Alice (Nochimov) G.; B.S., N.Y.U.,1943, D.D.S., 1945, postgrad. in orthodontics, 1951; m. Mimi Kenzer, Dec. 8, 1945; children—Carol Lynn, Myra Phyllis Hersh. Individual practice dentistry, Bronx, N.Y., 1947—; orthodontist Sydenham Hosp., N.Y.C., 1951-61, Jewish Child Care Assn.; chief dentistry Hebrew Hosp., 1947—. Treas., dir. Lyngold Assos. Inc., Yonkers, N.Y., 1969—; dir. Am. Accident, Health Ins. Co. Gen. chmn. Cleft Palate Center, Israel. Served with USNR, 1945-47. Mem. Am. Dental Assn., Internat. Assn. Orthodontists, 1st Dist. Dental Soc., Jewish War Vets. Sigma Epsilon Delta. Jewish. Mem. B'nai B'rith. Club: Ridge Way Country. Home: 400 Midland Ave Yonkers NY 10704 Office: 1171 Grand Concourse Bronx NY 10452 also 170 E Hartsdale Ave Hartsdale NY 10530

GOLDSTEIN, IRA MARVIN, physician, educator; b. Bklyn., Mar. 30, 1942; s. Morris Sam and Lillian Edith (Uhler) G.; B.S., Bklyn. Coll., 1962; M.D., N.Y. U., 1966; m. Barbara Joyce Kaplan, Mar. 30, 1963; children—Michael Seth, Bethany Cara. Intern, then resident in internal medicine Bellevue Hosp., N.Y.C., 1966-68, 70-72; mem. faculty N.Y. U. Sch. Medicine, 1972—, asso. prof. medicine, 1975—. Served with USPHS, 1968-70. Career scientist Irma T. Hirschl Trust. Diplomate Am. Bd. Internal Medicine. Fellow A.C.P.; mem. Am. Fedn. Clin. Research (council Eastern sect.), Am. Assn. Immunologists, Am. Soc. Clin. Investigation. Home: 100 Bleecker St New York City NY 10012 Office: 550 1st Ave New York City NY 10016

GOLDSTEIN, JOSEPH ALLEN, marketing and advt. research co. exec.; b. N.Y.C., Oct. 17, 1935; s. Alex and Selma (Oberman) G.; B.B.A., Coll. City N.Y., 1957; m. Lynette Silverman, Sept. 8, 1957; children—Jodi Dana, Susan Beth. Project dir. Richard Manville Research Co., N.Y.C., 1957-58; group project mgr. Alfred Politz Research Co., N.Y.C., 1958-60; with Data Devel. Corp., N.Y.C., 1960—, v.p., 1960-68, exec. v.p., 1969-71, pres., 1972—; dir. Field & Facts Inc., N.Y.C., 1967—, Central Location Testing Inc., N.Y.C., 1969—. Mem. Byram Hills (N.Y.) Non-Partisan Sch. Com. Mem. Am. Marketing Assn., Am. Assn. Public Opinion Research. Home: Brett Ln Bedford NY 10506 Office: Data Development Corp 600 3d Ave New York City NY 10016

GOLDSTEIN, LAWRENCE JEROME, security analyst, investment mgr.; b. N.Y.C., Jan. 9, 1936; s. Charles and Edna (Glick) G.; B.A., N.Y.U., 1957; M.B.A. (fellow), U. Mich., 1958; m. Dorothy Levine, Apr. 10, 1965; children—David Howard, Daniel Elliot, Deborah Rachel. Security analyst partner Burnham and Co. (predecessor partnership of Drexel Burnham Lambert, Inc., Investment Bankers', N.Y.C., 1st v.p., 1959—; vis. lectr. New Sch. for Social Research, N.Y.C., N.Y.U. Grad. Sch. Bus.; dir., v.p. Drexel Burnham Fund; dir. Greater Southwest Industries Corp.; cons. various corps. Served with U.S. Army, 1958-59, USNG, 1959-64. Fellow Fin. Analysts Fedn.; mem. N.Y. Soc. Security Analysts, Motor Carrier Analysts Group Inc., Phi Alpha Kappa. Jewish religion. Author: Railroad Car Leasing in the United States, 1963; The Brewing Industry in the United States 1966; Investment Opportunities in the Security Protection and Investigative Services Industry, 1970; Revolution in Toy Retailing, 1973, 75; Coal: Paradise Found-Investing in the Coal and Coal Equipment Industries, 1977. Contbr. articles to profl. jours. Home: 1 Santa Monica Dr Eastchester NY 10709 Office: 60 Broad St New York City NY 10004

GOLDSTEIN, MANFRED, engring. and mgmt. cons.; b. Vienna, Austria, Jan. 30, 1927; s. Isadore and Anna (Hahn) G.; student Manhattan Trade Center, 1947; m. Shirley Marie Lavine, Aug. 27, 1950;children—Cindy Marie, Lynn Alyse. Came to U.S., 1939, naturalized, 1945. Sr. technician Bklyn. Radio, 1953-55, Budd Stanley, Inc., Long Island City, 1955; lead engr. telephone equipment Precision Indsl. Design, Newark, 1955-57; project engr., contract adminstr., sales mgr. Lieco, Inc., Syossett, N.Y. 1957—, v.p., 1964-65; engring. and mgmt. cons. Positive Cons. Inc Wantagh, New York, 1965—, now pres. firm; owner Lake Luzerne Sea Plane Base. Mem. small bus. adv. com. to Congressman Thomas J. Downey. Served with AUS, 1945-46. Mem. IEEE (sr.), Am. Air Force Assn., Soc. Plastics Engrs., Am. Def. Preparedness Assn. (life, exec. bd. mgmt. div.), Nat. Contract Mgmt. Assn., Internat. Platform Assn., Capitol Radio Engr. Inst. Alumni (sr.), Nat. Pilots Assn., Aircraft Owners and Pilots Assn., Civil Air Patrol, Aviation Council L.I., Lake Luzerne C. of C. (chmn. indsl. devel. com.), L.I. Assn. Commerce and Industry (small bus. council). Inventor fire control cable and connectors for submarines, connectors and seals for Polaris antennae, technique for molding neoprene to stainless steel. Address: 2255 Arby Ct Wantagh Bellmore PO NY 11710

GOLDSTEIN, MELVIN, social worker; b. Mar. 18, 1933; s. Louis and Helen (Fox) G.; A.A.S., Bklyn. Coll., 1958; B.S., N.Y. U., 1960, M.A., 1963; M.S.W., Hunter Coll., 1965; m. Barbara Weissman, Dec. 22, 1956; children—Scott, Brett, Erik. Asst. dir. club dept. YM-YWHA, N.Y.C., 1965-67; program dir. Samuel Field YM-YWHA, 1967-71; dir. teen and therapeutic services, 1971-77, dir. adolescent therapy and growth center, 1977—; pvt. practice L.I. Center Transactional Analysis and Gestalt Therapy, Floral Park, N.Y.; asso. clin. prof. Adelphi U. Active various civic orgns. Served with U.S. Army, 1952-54. Cert. social worker, N.Y. Mem. Acad. Cert. Social Workers, Nat. Assn. Social Workers, Assn. Jewish Center Workers (exec. bd.), Nat. Tng. Labs. (asso.), Internat. Assn. Group Psychotherapists, Am. Psychol. Assn., Am. Sociol. Assn., NEA, Soc. Intercultural Relationships, Internat. Transactional Analysis Assn. Jewish. Home: 556 E 82d St Brooklyn NY 11236 Office: LI Center 174 Jericho Turnpike Floral Park NY 11001

GOLDSTEIN, MURRAY, dairy co. exec.; b. N.Y.C., June 17, 1916; s. Israel and Fannie (Kaplan) G.; student St. John's U., 1935-37; certificate in bus. mgmt. U. Md., 1960; M.B.A., Loyola Coll., Balt., 1975; m. Edith Wolkenfeld, Feb. 18, 1940; 1 dau., Susan (Mrs. Paul R. Richter). Sales mgr. Lillian Dairy, N.Y.C., 1945-49; sales mgr. Breakstone Food div. Nat. Dairy, 1949-51; pres. Dairy King, Inc., Balt., 1953—; guest lectr. U. Balt., Johns Hopkins. Active Asso. Jewish Charities, 1965—; bd. dirs. K.I.L.D., fund for police and firemen, 1963—, pres., 1963—; mem. pres.'s council Loyola Coll. Served with AUS, 1943-45; ETO. Decorated Bronze Star medal, Purple Heart. Named hon. citizen, Dallas, 1974. Mem. Grocery Mfrs. Balt. (past pres.), Nat. Food Distbrs. Am. (nat. pres. 1973, Distbr. of year award 1972, chmn. bd. 1974-75), Nat. Assn. Wholesalers (nat. trustee), Am. Jewish Congress, Balt. C. of C., Soc. for Technion-Jewish Inst. Tech. Jewish. Mason, Odd Fellow, Golden Eagle. Clubs: Turf Valley Country (gov. 1970-71) (Ellicott City, Md.); Golden Eagle Square and Compass (gov.). Contbr. articles to trade publs. Home: 3619 Anton Farms Rd Pikeville MD 21208 Office: 703 Nursery Rd Linthicum Heights MD 21090

GOLDSTEIN, PERRY BAILY, architect; b. Bklyn., Apr. 10, 1926; s. Nathan and Pearl (Stuppler) G.; Certificate Architecture, Pratt Inst., 1949; m. Mildred Groman, Aug. 24, 1947; children—Stuart Meredith, Lynne Cheryl, Wendy Sue, Alison Joy. Asso. firm Voorhees Walker Foley & Smith, Architects, N.Y.C., 1950-66; partner firm Bonsignore Brignati Goldstein & Mazzotta, Architects, N.Y.C., 1966-73; archtl. adminstrv. officer Halsey, McCormack & Helmer, Inc., Architects, N.Y.C., 1973-74; pvt. practice, 1975—; pres. Perry B. Goldstein, Architect, Garden City, N.Y. Mem. panel arbitrator Am. Arbitration Assn., 1972; mem. Nat. Council Archtl. Registration Bds., 1964—. Served with USAAF, 1944-45. Registered profl. architect, N.Y., N.J., Pa., Va., Conn., Fla. Mem. AIA (dir., v.p. L.I. chpt.), N.Y. State Assn. Architects. Home: 1188 Albert Rd North Bellmore NY 11710 Office: 600 Old Country Rd Garden City NY 11530

GOLDSTEIN, ROBERT LLOYD, psychiatrist; b. N.Y.C., Aug. 29, 1938; s. Abraham and Miriam (Cohen) G.; B.A. cum laude, N.Y. U., 1960; M.D., Chgo. Med. Sch., 1965; children—Delisa Raphaele, James Hughes. Intern in medicine Beekman Downtown Hosp., N.Y.C., 1966-67; resident in psychiatry Bklyn. State Hosp., 1967-69; fellow adolescent psychiatry Bellevue Hosp., N.Y.C., 1969-70; fellow psychotherapy Hillside Hosp., Glen Oaks, N.Y., 1970-72; dir. forensic psychiatry clinics Manhattan Criminal and Supreme cts., 1972-74; staff psychiatrist, asst. prof. clin. psychiatry N.Y. U.-Bellevue Med. Center, Forensic Psychiatry Services, 1974-76; chief psych. outpatient services, asst. prof. psychiatry VA div. N.Y. U. Sch. Medicine, 1976—; dir. psychiat. services Beekman Downtown Hosp., 1973—; chmn. Trial Judges Inst. seminar series Hunter Coll., 1975—. Recipient Recognition award AMA, 1969, 76, Hosp. Physician mag. citation, 1970. Diplomate Am. Bd. Psychiatry and Neurology. Mem. Am. Psychiat. Assn., Eastern Psychiat. Research Assn., Soc. Adolescent Psychiatry, Am. Acad. Psychiatry and Law, Royal Soc. Health, Phi Beta Kappa. Clubs: Princeton (N.Y.C.); N.Y. U. Address: 390 West End Ave New York City NY 10024

GOLDSTEIN, STANLEY IRVING, podiatrist; b. Bronx, N.Y., Oct. 1, 1925; s. Louis and Eva (Yollis) G.; B.Sc. in Pharmacy, Fordham U., 1949; D.Podiatric Medicine, L.I. U., 1957; postgrad. U. Bologna (Italy) Coll. Medicine and Surgery, 1966; m. Hortense Silverstein, June 4, 1949; children—Jerome Eric, Keith Stuart, Brian Alan. Extern, Mt. Sinai and Beth Israel hosps., N.Y.C., 1956-57; chief med. cons. Helen Hayes Rehab. Hosp., Stony Point, N.Y., 1957-61; dir. podiatric med. and surg. service Local 305, AFL-CIO, 1965; sr. clinician Foot Clinics of N.Y., 1965—; chief cons. podiatrist St. Vincent DePaul Hosp., Spring Valley, N.Y.; lectr. N.Y. Coll. Podiatric Medicine; mem. attending staff Bellevue Hosp.; lectr. med. hypnosis throughout U.S. Founder New City (N.Y.) Jewish Center, 1957. Served with USNR, 1943-46. Charter fellow Am. Acad. Psychosomatic Podiatry; fellow Am. Acad. Foot Specialists, Internat. Coll. Foot Surgeons, Internat. Acad. Law and Sci.; hon. fellow Affiliated Podiatrists; mem. Am., N.Y. State (sec.-treas.), Rockland, Putnam and Westchester County (sec.-treas.) podiatry assns., Royal Soc. Health (Eng.). Clubs: Lions, Rotary, Century, Masons. Contbr. to profl. jours. Address: 561 S Main St New City NY 10956

GOLDSTEIN, WILLIAM, partner accounting firm; b. Rochester, N.Y., July 26, 1933; s. Nathan and Sophie (Eissenstat) G.; student U. Rochester, 1952-53; B.A., Syracuse U., 1959; postgrad. City Coll. N.Y., 1961-64; m. Rhoda Helene Levy, Aug. 28, 1960; children—Sanford, Stuart, Daniel. Sr. accountant Robert Simons & Co., C.P.A.'s, N.Y.C., 1959-64, Lawin, Futter & Gelfand, C.P.A.'s, N.Y.C., 1964-67; sr. accountant Cortland Brovitz & Co., C.P.A.'s, Rochester, N.Y., 1967-68, partner, 1968-69; individual practice, Rochester, 1969-71; partner firm Goldstein & Viele, Rochester, 1971—; guest lectr. Rochester Inst. Tech., 1974-75. Bd. dirs., treas. Jewish Community Center, Rochester; mem. Nat. Jewish Welfare Bd., 1972—; Democratic committeeman Town of Brighton, 1971—. C.P.A., N.Y. State. Mem. N.Y. State Soc. C.P.A.'s (pres. Rochester chpt. 1977-78), Am. Inst. C.P.A.'s, Sigma Alpha Mu. Clubs: Knights Pythias, Irondequoit Country. Home: 16 Terrain Dr Rochester NY 14618 Office: 1 E Main St Rochester NY 14614

GOLDSTEN, ROBERT EMANUEL, real estate developer, savs. and loan exec., lawyer; b. Charlottesville, Va., Oct. 8, 1916; s. Joseph and Rebecca S. (Shapero) G.; B.S. in Commerce, U. Va., 1937, LL.B., 1940; children—Douglas Kahn, Ina Lee. Admitted to Va. bar, 1939, D.C. bar, 1941; partner Goldsten Bros. Developers & Builders, Washington, 1941-72; pres. Gen. Mortgage Corp., Washington, 1948-66, Vero Beach Yacht Basin, Inc. (Fla.), 1957-71, Devel. Funding Corp., Washington, 1972-74; v.p. Allied Fin. Corp., Silver Spring, Md., 1950-58, World Wide Airlines, Burbank, Calif., 1960-62; pres., chief exec. officer McLean Savs. & Loan Assn. (Va.), 1977—; individual practice law, Washington, 1972—; vis. lectr. real estate mgmt. Am. U., 1954-60. Pres. Brotherhood-Washington Hebrew Congregation, 1955-56; treas., dir. Washington Area Council for Alcoholism and Drug Abuse, 1971-77, Carl G. Jung Fund of Washington, 1976—. Recipient award for outstanding contbn. to success of Home Builders Met. Washington, 1966, Spl. Beautification award City of Alexandria (Va.), 1968, Distng. Service award Washington Area Council Alcoholism and Drug Abuse, 1977. Mem. Va., D.C. bars, U. Va. Alumni Club Washington. Democrat. Clubs: Capital Yacht, Woodmont Country, McLean Indoor Tennis, B'ani B'rith. Developer limited dividend, nonprofit housing projects for low and moderate income people under fed. programs, 1961-67. Home and office: 3001 Veazey Terr NW Washington DC 20008 Office: care McLean Savs & Loan Dolley Madison Blvd and Churchill Rd McLean VA 22101

GOLEMBIEWSKI, WALTER GREGORY, psychiatric therapist, clinic adminstr.; b. Fairbanks, Pa., Aug. 10, 1936; s. Steven and Sadie Rose (Kozma) G.; B.S., Cal. State Coll., 1962; M.S.W., W.Va. U., 1965; m. Rosalie Livia Magazine, Dec. 30, 1961; children—Jeffrey, Maria Lana, Carrie Lynn. Teacher biology and sci. Norfolk (Va.) City Schs., 1961-62; counselor delinquent boys Youth Devel. Center, Cannonsburg, Pa., 1965-66; psychiatric therapist, dir. Community Mental Health Center, Fredericktown, Pa., 1967—; child protective worker Fayette County and Child Welfare Assn., Uniontown, Pa., 1966-67; field instr. social work students W.Va. U., 1967-76; guest prof. Calif. State Coll., 1973-76; cons. Area Sch. System, 1967-76; Certified Marriage Counselor. Served with USN, 1954-58. Certified Marriage-Family-Sex counselor; Certified Social Worker; Certified Social Work Supr. Mem. Nat. Assn. Social Workers, Am. Assn. Certified Social Workers, Nat. Assn. Family and Marriage Counselors. Democrat. Roman Catholic. Club: Lions Internat. Home: RD 6 Box 419 Uniontown PA 15401 Office: Yablonski Meml Clinic RD 1 Fredericktown PA 15333

GOLER, PATRICIA ANNE, coll. dean; b. Boston, Apr. 28, 1929; d. Clarence H. and Getrude V. (Thomas) Goler; A.B., Regis Coll., 1950, LL.D. (hon.), 1969; M.A., Boston Coll., 1951, Ph.D., 1957; D.H.L., (hon.), Emmanuel Coll., 1974. Instr. history Xavier U., New Orleans, 1951-53, Boston Coll., 1955-57; prof. history Lowell (Mass.) State Coll., 1957-74; dean Coll. Liberal Arts U. Lowell, 1975—. Trustee

Ednl. Devel. Center, Boston Coll., 1974—. Mem. Boston Archdiocesan Bd. Edn., Freedom House Inst. Edn. Democrat. Roman Catholic. Club: Women in Politics. Home: 33 Webb St Lexington MA 02173 Office: South Campus University of Lowell MA 01854*

GOLINO, FRANK R., govt. ofcl.; b. Erie, Pa., Oct. 26, 1936; s. Dominic F. and Mary (Dober) G.; A.B. cum laude, Gannon Coll., 1957; M.A., Fordham U., 1960; postgrad. (Italian Fng. Ministry fellow) Bologna (Italy) Center Sch. Advanced Internat. Studies, 1958-59; m. Lois Mary Jean Tavani, June 21, 1958 (dec.); children—Fabrizio Raffaele, Louis Raffaele, Frank Ralph (dec.). Instr. history and polit. sci. Marymount Coll., 1959-60; Middle East editor Colliers Ency., N.Y.C., 1960-61; 3d sec. Am. embassy, Mogadiscio, 1962-63; vice consul, Tangier, Morocco, 1964-65; 2d sec. Am. embassy, Tripoli, Libya, 1966-68; chmn. Near East and North African area studies Fgn. Service Inst., Dept. State, Washington, 1968-70, planning office Bur. African Affairs, 1970-72; 2d sec. Am. embassy, Valletta, Malta, 1972-74; 2d sec. Am. embassy, Rome, Italy, 1974-76; consul Am. Consulate, Johannesburg, South Africa, 1976—; prof. Loyola U., Rome, 1975, 76, St. Mary's-Notre Dame, Rome, 1976—. Mem. Am., Internat. polit. sci. assns., Middle East Inst., Contbr. articles to profl. jours. Home: 61 Second Ave Inanda Johannesburg South Africa Office: Am Consulate Johannesburg Care Dept State Washington DC 20521

GOLLADAY, LOY EDGAR, spl. educator; b. St. David's Church, Va., Feb. 27, 1914; s. St. James Edgar and Dollie (Lee) (Wright) G.; B.A., Gallaudet Coll., Washington, 1934, M.A., 1942; M.Ed., U. Hartford, 1957; m. Gladys Annabelle Walford, June 7, 1936; 1 dau., June Regina Golladay Edgerton. Tchr., occupational counsel W.Va. Sch. for Deaf, Romney, 1934-41; editor-pub. Cass County Tribune, 1941-42; tchr., editor American Era; chmn. English dept. Am. Sch. for Deaf, West Hartford, Conn., 1942-69; asso. prof. English, gen. studies Nat. Tech. Inst. for Deaf, Rochester (N.Y.) Inst. Tech., 1969—; workshop on evaluating and captioning Films for the Deaf, 1965, 75, on writing and evaluating Lesson Plans for the Deaf, 1967. Charter dir. Council of Orgns. Serving the Deaf, 1966-69; mem. spl. task force on defining developmental disabilities HEW, 1977, mem. bd. rev. of research for protection human subjects, 1978. Recipient G.M. Teegarden Poetry medal Gallaudet Coll., 1964, NSC staff Humanitarian award, 1975, Eisenhart Outstanding Teaching award, 1976; named outstanding staff mem. Nat. Tech. Inst. for Deaf, 1976. Mem. Nat., Empire State assns. of deaf, Am. Instrs. of the Deaf (nat. dir. 1963-65), Conn. Assn. of the Deaf (pres.), Registry Interpreters for Deaf, Rochester Civic Assn. of Deaf, Nat. Gallaudet Coll. Alumni Assn. (1st v.p., dir., Laurent Clerc service award Conn. chpt. 1969), Kappa Gamma. Episcopalian (lay reader ch. for deaf, nat. advisory coms. missions to deaf 1976—). Spl. editor Dictionary of Idioms for the Deaf, 1966; editor, contbr. many spl. publs. on the deaf. Home: 887 Hidden Valley Rd Rochester NY 14624 Office: 1 Lomb Memorial Dr Rochester NY 14623

GOLLER, HENRY FREDERICK, radiologist; b. Buffalo, July 30, 1935; s. Gustav William and Margaret Katherine (Roedel) G.; A.B., Hamilton Coll., 1957; M.D., U. Buffalo, 1961; m. Margaret Ann Kaegebein, Dec. 27, 1960; children—Eric David, Lisa Margaret, Richard Gustav. Intern, Edward J. Meyer Meml. Hosp., Buffalo, 1961-62; resident in radiology State U. N.Y., Syracuse, 1962-65; mem. staff Deaconess Hosp., Buffalo, 1967—, Buffalo Gen. Hosp., 1978—; clin. asst. prof. radiology State U. N.Y., Buffalo. Served to capt. M.C., U.S. Army, 1965-67. Diplomate Am. Bd. Radiology. Mem. AMA, N.Y. State, Erie County med. socs., Am. Coll. Radiology, Radiol. Soc. N.Am., Buffalo Radiol. Soc., U.S. Power Squadron. Republican. Presbyterian. Club: Masons. Home: 159 Stonehenge Dr Orchard Park NY 14127 Office: 1616 Kensington Ave Buffalo NY 14215 also 1001 Humboldt Pkwy Buffalo NY 14208 also 135 Linwood Ave Buffalo NY

GOLLIN, STUART ALLEN, certified pub. accountant; b. Bronx, N.Y., Aug. 7 1941; s. Samuel and Gussie (Schreiber) G.; B.B.A., Coll. City N.Y., 1963; m. Harriet Joy Friedlander, Aug. 16, 1964; children—Deborah Lynn, Mark David, Adam Douglas, Seth Craig. Partner, nat. dir. retailing Touche Ross & Co., Newark. C.P.A., N.Y., N.J. Mem. Am. Inst. C.P.A.'s, N.Y. State, N.J. (accounting and auditing standards, relations with bankers com.) socs. C.P.A.'s, Nat. Assn. Accountants (dir. Westchester chpt.), Nat. Retail Mchts. Assn., N.J. Retail Mchts. Assn., Met. Controllers Assn., White Plains Jaycees, Bergen County C. of C., Beta Alpha Psi. Club: Ardsley Swim (dir.). Home: 9 Longfellow St Hartsdale NY 10530 Office: Touche Ross & Co Gateway 1 Newark NJ 07102

GOLOB, CHARLES GEORGE, automotive machinery mfg. corp. exec.; b. Plymouth, Pa., Sept. 14, 1919; s. Harry and Gussie Golob; B.S., Pa. State U., 1940; M.E., U. Bridgeport, 1960; Mech. and Indsl. Engr., Drexel Inst. Tech., 1962; m. Louise Helene Meisels, Feb. 12, 1946; children—Martin, Paula Golob Greenfield. Supr. prodn. Calvert-Seagrams Corp., Relay, Md., 1940-43; chmn. engr. Capitol Records, Inc., Scranton, Pa., 1949-54; dept. mgr. Columbia Records Inc., Bridgeport, Conn., 1954-60; chmn. engr. Sonic Rec. Co., Hicksville, N.Y., 1962-65; v.p. prodn. Luger Wire-Bennett Products Co., Scranton, 1965-72; plant mgr. Superior Generator Inc., Scranton, 1972—; cons. MGM Records Inc., 1965-67, plating cos., record mfrs. Served with AUS, 1943-46. Decorated Bronze Star. Mem. Soc. Mfg. Engrs. (sr.), Am. Inst. Indsl. Engrs., DAV (chpt. comdr. 1975—). Jewish. Club: Elks. Home: 1828 Cleveland Ave Scranton PA 18505 Office: 100 Electric St Scranton PA 18509 Died Oct. 15, 1978

GOLOMB, FREDERICK MARTIN, surgeon; b. N.Y.C., Dec. 18, 1924; s. Jacob J. and Hannah (Kaplan) G.; B.S., Yale U., 1945; M.D., U. Rochester, 1949; m. Joan E. Schneider, Nov. 28, 1954; children—James, Susan. Practice medicine specializing in surgery, N.Y.C.; mem. staff N.Y. U. Med. Center, 1950—, dir. surg. chemoimmunotherapy div. tumor service dept. surgery, 1967—; dep. div. dir., chief patient research unit div. II, clin. research div., chief chemotherapy unit div. IV, N.Y. U. Cancer Center, 1975—; attending surgeon Univ., Drs. hosps.; attending in gen. surgery VA Hosp.; asso. attending surgeon Cabrini Health Care Center, N.Y. Infirmary; asso. vis. surgeon Bellevue Hosp.; mem. faculty N.Y. U. Sch. Medicine, 1956—, prof. clin. surgery, 1977—; cons. N.Y.C. div. Am. Cancer Soc., 1968—, chmn. nominating com., 1975-76; mem. clin. trials rev. com. Nat. Cancer Inst., 1976—; chmn. melanoma com. Eastern Coop. Oncology Group, 1978—; prin. investigator Central Oncology Group, 1969-77, exec. com., 1976-77; bd. dirs. N.Y. State Cancer Programs Assos.; mem. met. med. com. Chemotherapy Found. Served with M.C., AUS, 1953-54; Korea. Diplomate Am. Bd. Surgery. Fellow A.C.S.; mem. Soc. Head and Neck Surgeons, Soc. Surgery Alimentary Tract, Am. Assn. Cancer Research, Am. Soc. Clin. Oncology (a founder), AMA, N.Y. Cancer Soc. (pres. 1974-75), N.Y. Surg. Soc., N.Y. State, N.Y. County med. socs., Soc. Surg. Oncology, George Hoyt Whipple Soc., Brit. Assn. Surg. Oncology (editorial adv. panel), Sigma Xi. Clubs: Am. Alpine, Explorers. Editorial adv. bd. Oncology News.

GOLOMB, GEORGE EDWIN, lawyer; b. Newark, Jan. 28, 1947; s. Max and Elizabeth Lillian (Epstein) G.; B.A., Yale U., 1968; J.D., U. Pa., 1972; student Hague Acad. Internat. Law, 1971. Admitted to N.Y. bar, 1974, N.J. bar, 1977; asso. firm Weil, Gotshal & Manges, N.Y.C., 1972-74; law clk. U.S. Dist. Ct., Eastern Dist. N.Y., N.Y.C., 1974-76; asso. firm Donovan Leisure Newton & Irvine, N.Y.C., 1976—. Ford Found. fellow, 1971, Phelps Assn. fellow, 1967. Mem. N.J. Bar Assn. Clubs: Yale Central N.J., U. Pa., Mensa. Home: 181 Norman Rd Newark NJ 07106 Office: Donovan Leisure Newton & Irvine 30 Rockefeller Plaza New York City NY 10020

GOLUB, WILLIAM WELDON, lawyer; b. Bklyn., Oct. 7, 1914; s. Joseph and Sarah (Resnek) G.; A.B., Columbia, 1934, J.D., 1937; m. Barbara Lewis, July 3, 1942; 1 dau., Joan L. Admitted to N.Y. State bar, 1937; practice in N.Y.C., 1937-39, 40—; mem. staff atty. gen.'s com. adminstrv. procedure, 1939-40; staff atty. Trustees of Asso. Gas & Electric Corp., 1940-45; pvt. practice, 1945—; partner firm Rosenman Colin Freund Lewis & Cohen, and predecessor, 1969—; spl. counsel N.Y. State Moreland Commn. on Alcoholic Beverage Control Law, 1966; mem. council Adminstrv. Conf. U.S., 1968-69; cons. N.Y. gov. Adviser on r.r. problems, 1959; spl. cons. N.Y.C. Bd. Edn., 1966. Recipient Alumni medal Columbia, 1972. Mem. Am. Law Inst., Am. Bar Assn., Assn. Bar City N.Y., Fed. Bar Council, Columbia Coll. Alumni Assn. (pres. 1976-78), Columbia Law Sch. Alumni Assn. (pres. 1978—), Phi Beta Kappa. Democrat. Clubs: Friars (N.Y.C.); Nat. Lawyers (Washington). Home: 1148 Fifth Ave New York City NY 10028 Office: 575 Madison Ave New York City NY 10022

GOMBAR, OSCAR JULIUS, chemist; b. Budapest, Hungary, Apr. 6, 1920; came to U.S., 1956, naturalized, 1962; M.S., Tech. U. Budapest, 1951; m. Anna M. Karpaty, Aug. 1, 1948; 1 son, Thomas Lance. Mgr. dyeing and finishing dept. HFSZ, textile mill, Budapest, Hungary, 1950-54; asst. dir. textiles, plastics, paint and ink dept. Ministry of Commerce, Hungary, 1955-56; research asso. Textile Research Inst., Princeton, N.J., 1957-58; research chemist Cities Service Co., Cranbury, N.J., 1959—. Mem. Soc. Plastics Engrs., Hungarian Alumni Assn. Rutgers U. (pres. 1969-72). Author: Application and Test Methods of Pigments and Dyestuffs, 1955. Patentee. Home: 197 Mt Lucas Rd Princeton NJ 08540 Office: Drawer 4 Prospect Plains Rd Cranbury NJ 08512

GOMERY, JOHN HOWARD, lawyer; b. Montreal, Aug. 9, 1932; s. Walter Bertram and Jane Elizabeth (Brook) G.; B.A., McGill U., 1953, B.C.L., 1956; m. Pierrette Rayle, Aug. 18, 1973; 1 dau., Elizabeth; children by previous marriage—Geoffrey, Cymry, Sally. Admitted to P.Q. bar, 1957; asso. Martineau, Walker, Allison, Beaulieu, MacKell & Clermont, Montreal, 1956-66, partner, 1966—; apptd. Queen's Counsel, 1971. Mem. Bar of Montreal (council 1969), Bar P.Q. (council 1969), Canadian Bar Assn. (council 1965-69), Montreal Execs. Assn. (pres. 1974). Anglican. Club: Mt. Stephen. Home: 695 Aberdeen Ave Westmount PQ H3Y 3A9 Canada Office: 3400 Stock Exchange Tower Pl Victoria Montreal PQ N4Z 1E9 Canada

GOMES, ALBERT, high sch. counselor; b. Danbury, Conn., Dec. 26, 1944; s. Albert and Benvinda (Nunes) G.; B.S., Western Conn. State Coll., 1966; M.S., U. Bridgeport (Conn.), 1972, profl. diploma advanced study, 1973; certificate Conn. Inst. Gestalt Tng., 1977; m. Kathleen Johnston, Nov. 18, 1972; 1 dau., Natalie Kate. Instr. biology Brookfield (Conn.) High Sch., 1966-72, head wrestling coach, 1969-71, head track coach, 1968-71; lectr. U. Bridgeport, 1972-73; sch. counselor Trumbull (Conn.) High Sch., 1973—; cons. in field. Bd. dirs. Big. Bros., Newtown, Conn., 1972-74; group leader Elderly and Youth Forum Trumbull, 1976-78, Beacon Center, Trumbull, 1972-73; teaching fellow, grad. asst. U. Bridgeport, 1971. Mem. Nat., Conn., Trumbull edn. assns., Am. Personnel and Guidance Assn., Am. Assn. Secondary Sch. Counselors. Democrat. Roman Catholic. Author curriculum material. Home: Ridge Rd Newtown CT 06470 Office: 72 Strobel Rd Trumbull CT 06611

GOMES, JOSEPH ANTHONY, cardiologist; b. Bombay, India, Feb. 29, 1944; s. Agostinho Sebastiao and Olimpia Aduzinda (Souza) G.; came to U.S., 1970; M.B.B.S., U. Bombay, 1970; M.D., State U. N.Y., 1974; m. Marina Raquel do Carmo Flores, Jan. 10, 1970. Intern, Mt. Sinai Hosp., N.Y.C., 1970-71, resident in medicine, 1972-73; fellow in cardiology VA Bronx Hosp. and Mt. Sinai Sch. Medicine, 1974-75; cardiopulmonary fellow USPHS Hosp., S.I., N.Y., 1976-77, asst. chief cardiology, 1977—; cons. in field. Diplomate Am. Bd. Cardiology. Fellow Am. Coll. Cardiologists. Contbr. articles in field to profl. jours. Home: 193 Slater Blvd Staten Island NY 10305 Office: Cardiology Dept USPHS Hosp Staten Island NY 10305

GOMEZ, RAYMOND VASQUEZ, JR., architect; b. Ft. Worth, Apr. 20, 1939; s. Raymond Gonzales and Helen (Vasquez) G.; B.S., Tex. A. and M. U., 1965, B.Arch., 1964; M.S., Columbia U., 1965; m. Mariette Margret Himes, Nov. 25, 1965; children—Alexander Blake, Alicia Brooke. With Edward Durell Stone & Assos., N.Y.C., 1965-74, asso., 1969—; v.p. Edward Durell Stone Internat., Ltd., Nassau, Bahamas, Tehran, Iran and Riyadh, Saudi Arabia, 1974—; v.p. Edward Durell Stone Assos., P.C., N.Y.C., 1974—; v.p. Prudential Tech. Internat. subs. Prudential Group; archtl. cons. Architect's Renewal Com. in Harlem, 1970-72. Asst. dir. Bklyn. Neighborhood Hist. Assn., 1971-74. Mem. AIA, N.Y. State Soc. Architects, Am. Arbitration Assn. (panel arbitrators), Columbia Archtl. Alumni Assn., Alpha Rho Chi. Home: 241 E 78th St New York City NY 10021 also 5 Washington St Shelter Island NY 11965 Office: 745 Fifth Ave New York City NY 10022 also Asia Bldg Ave Tachte Jamshid Tehran Iran

GONANO, JOHN ROLAND, physicist; b. Winchester, Va., Jan. 21, 1939; s. Lezelle and Mary (Fuss) G.; B.S. in Physics with honors (Sigma Pi Sigma Freshman scholar), W.Va. U., 1960; Ph.D. in Physics (So. Fellowships Fund fellow), Duke U., 1967; m. Joyce E. Dove, Aug. 22, 1959; children—Gina M., Dawn M., John Roland. Postdoctoral fellow U. Fla., 1966-68; physicist Nat. Bur. Standards, Washington, 1968-71; research physicist U.S. Army Mobility Equipment Research and Devel. Command, Ft. Belvoir, Va., 1971—. Elder, trustee Boyds (Md.) Presbyn. Ch. Served with USAF, 1961-62. Recipient Sci. Conf. Achievement award U.S. Army, 1974; NSF Summer fellow, 1960. Mem. Am. Phys. Soc., Sigma Xi, Sigma Pi Sigma, Mensa. Contbr. articles on magnetism, nuclear magnetic resonance, thermometry, explosive detection to profl. jours. Office: MERADCOM DRDME-ND Fort Belvoir VA 22060

GONDELMAN, HAROLD, lawyer; b. Pitts., Dec. 16, 1922; s. Samuel and Mollie (Frishman) G.; A.B., U. Pitts., 1943, LL.B., 1949; m. Ruth G. Mullen, Aug. 14, 1949; children—Larry S., Kathy M., Richard F., Nancy Beth. Admitted to Pa. bar, 1950, U.S. Supreme Ct. bar, 1973; gen. partner firm Baskin, Boreman, Wilner, Sachs, Gondelman & Craig, Pitts., 1968—. Pres., Jewish Community Center, Pitts., 1973—, Israel Bond chmn., 1976. Served with U.S. Army, 1943-46. Mem. Am., Pa., Allegheny County bar assns., Pa. Trial Lawyers Assn., Nat. Assn. Criminal Def. Lawyers. Democrat. Jewish. Club: Green Oaks Country. Home: 1182 Beechwood Blvd Pittsburgh PA 15206 Office: 10th Floor Frick Bldg Pittsburgh PA 15219

GONSALVES, JOHN, JR., counseling psychologist; b. Central Falls, R.I., Apr. 29, 1949; B.A., R.I. Coll., 1971; M.Ed., Suffolk U., 1975; M.A., U. R.I., 1973; Ed.D., Boston U., 1978. Counselor psychol. services Central Falls Sch. System, 1974-75; counselor Brookline (Mass.) Sch. System, 1976-77; pvt. practice counseling psychologist, Central Falls, 1978—; cons. in field. Watson fellow, 1971-72, Title VII fellow, 1976-78. Mem. Am. Personnel and Guidance Assn., Am. Sch. Counselor Assn., Nat. Vocat. Guidance Assn., Am. Coll. Personnel Assn., Phi Delta Kappa, Pi Lambda Theta. Roman Catholic. Home: 71 Madeira Ave Central Falls RI 02863

GONZALEZ, ERNESTO, physician; b. Aguadilla, P.R., Nov. 11, 1938; s. Alfredo and Aurora (Martinez) G.; M.D., U. P.R., 1966; m. Julie Castro, June 2, 1962; children—Rosa Aimee, Ernesto, Phillip Omar. Intern, San Juan (P.R.) City Hosp., 1966-67; resident in dermatology U. P.R., 1969-71, Harvard Med. Sch. and Mass. Gen. Hosp., Boston, 1971-72; clin. instr. dermatology U. P.R. Med. Sch., 1972-76; asst. in dermatology Univ. Hosp., San Juan, 1972-74; dermatologist Indsl. Hosp., San Juan, 1973-76; instr. Harvard Med. Sch., 1976—; chief Dermatology Assos. II, dept. dermatology Mass. Gen. Hosp., 1977—, dir. phototherapy center, 1976—. Served with AUS, 1967-69. Decorated Bronze medal. Mem. Am. Acad. Dermatology, Soc. Investigative Dermatology, Dermatology Found., Sociedad Ibero Americana de Dermatologia, Internat. Soc. Dermatology, Boston Dermatol. Club. Pioneer in photochemotherapy. Home: 143 Withington Rd Newtonville MA 02160 Office: Dept Dermatology Mass Gen Hospital Boston MA 02114

GONZALEZ, VIRGINIA GERARDA, counselor; b. Bethlehem, Pa., Mar. 13, 1950; d. Francisco and Josefa (Sanchez) G.; B.A. in Psychology magna cum laude, (Pa. Bur. for Visually Handicapped scholar), Moravian Coll., 1972; Ed.M. in Adult and Coll. Counseling (Pa. Bur. for Visually Handicapped scholar), Boston U., 1973; postgrad. in counseling psychology Rutgers U., 1976—. Instr., counselor Northampton County Area Community Coll., 1973-77, asst. prof. counseling, 1977—, coordinator career devel. center, 1973—; mem. personnel group, adv. bd. Northampton County (Pa.) Children's Bur., 1973-77. Bd. dirs. YWCA, Easton, Pa., 1977—. Mem. Am. Personnel and Guidance Assn., Nat. Vocat. Guidance Assn., Lehigh Valley Mental Health Assn., Triangle Honor Soc. Mem. Moravian Ch. Home: 617 Center St Bethlehem PA 18018 Office: 3835 Green Pond Rd Bethlehem PA 18017

GOOD, ANNE LEEPER (MRS. JOHN CARTER GOOD), civic worker; b. Jackson, Tenn., Nov. 10, 1923; d. Robert Allen and Ola (Crittenden) Leeper; A.B., B.S. cum laude, Lambuth Coll., 1944; m. John Carter Good, Oct. 28, 1945; children—John Robert, Carter Crittenden, William Allen. Co-chmn. Introduction to Washington com. The Hospitality and Information Service, 1968-71, treas., 1971-75, v.p. adminstrn., 1975-77, pres., 1977—; membership chmn. Spanish Portuguese Study Group, 1968-69, v.p., 1969-70, pres., 1970-71; mem. ladies' bd. House of Mercy, 1970—, treas., 1972-74. Bd. dirs. D.C. br. Nat. Capitol Area YWCA, 1973-78, rec. sec., 1974, treas., 1974-77; bd. dirs. Hannah Harrison Career Sch., 1971—, mem. com., 1971—, chmn., 1976-77; bd. dirs. Nat. Capital Area YWCA, 1973—; bd. dirs. Rosemount Infant Day Care Center, 1972—, v.p., 1974-76; bd. dirs. Washington chpt. Achievement Rewards for Coll. Scientists, 1971-72, Alliance Francaise, Club d'Amitie Franco-Internationale. Clubs: St. Albans School Mothers (pres. Washington 1964-65), Air Force Officers Wives (mem. bd. Washington 1959-61). Home: 3712 Fordham Rd NW Washington DC 20016

GOOD, DONALD SIMMONS, air force officer; b. Columbus, O., Oct. 6, 1935; s. Richard George and Evelyn Jeanette (Simmons) G.; student Oberlin Coll., 1953-55; B.S. in Bus. Adminstrn., Ohio State U., 1958; M.H.A. (A.D. Williams scholar), Med. Coll. Va., 1964. Staff accountant Arthur Andersen & Co., Chgo., 1958-59; commd. 2d lt. U.S. Air Force, 1959, advanced through grades to lt. col., 1975; registrar USAF Hosp., Lincoln AFB, Nebr., 1959-62; resource mgmt. officer USAF Hosp., RAF Lakenheath, Eng., 1964-67; asst. chief fin. programs div., office of surgeon gen. Hdqrs. USAF, Washington, 1967-71; adminstr. USAF Hosp., Forbes AFB, Kans., 1971-73; comdr. USAF Hosp., Iraklion, Greece, 1973-75; chief ops. plans and health care delivery, office of surgeon gen. Hdqrs. USAF, Washington, 1976-78, dir. adminstrv. services Hdqrs. Air Force Systems Command, Andrews AFB, Washington, 1978—. Chmn. finance com. Capitol Hill United Methodist Ch., 1978. Decorated Air Force Meritorious Service medal with oak leaf cluster, Air Force Commendation medal with oak leaf cluster. Fellow Am. Coll. Hosp. Adminstrs. (regent-at-large for uniformed services); mem. Am., Mich. hosp. assns., Assn. Mil. Surgeons U.S. Club: Army and Navy (Washington). Home: 315 12th St SE Washington DC 20003 Office: Hdqrs Air Force Systems Command Office of Surgeon Andrews AFB Washington DC 20334

GOOD, MARY ELIZABETH GROUNDS, librarian; b. Roaring Spring, Pa., Dec. 31, 1916; d. Wilbert Lee and Mary Eleanor (Smith) Grounds; student Ursinus Coll., 1934-35; B.A., Westminster Coll., 1938; M.L.S., U. Pitts., 1969; m. John Gilbert Good, Nov. 25, 1939 (dec.); children—Roberta Lee Good Scott, John Gilbert. Tchr., Roaring Spring (Pa.) Elementary Sch., 1938-39, Claysburg (Pa.) Kimmel High Sch., 1942-43; reference librarian Altoona campus Pa. State U., 1970-76, head librarian, 1976—. Organist First Presbyterian Ch., Hollidaysburg, Pa., 1969—. Mem. ALA, AAUW, Am. Guild Organists, Music Library Assn., Pa. Library Assn. Home: 901 Walnut St Hollidaysburg PA 16648 Office: Eiche Library Altoona Campus Pa State U Altoona PA 16603

GOOD, MILTON SHENK, physician, sculptor; b. Morgantown, Pa., Oct. 10, 1932; s. Noah Gehman and Ella Kaufman (Shenk) G.; B.S., Franklin and Marshall Coll., 1954; M.D., Hahnemann Med. Coll., 1958; m. Ann Augsburger, June 11, 1956; children—Sonja Jeanne, Erika Joan, Don Milton, Judith Annette. Intern, Lancaster (Pa.) Gen. Hosp., 1958-59; gen. practice medicine, Elizabethtown, Pa., 1959—; partner Dr. John Barr, 1959-63; pvt. practice, 1963-71; pres. med. corp., 1971—; mem. faculty dept. family practice Pa. State U., Hershey Med. Center. Recipient various awards for sculpture in juried and non-juried competition, 1967—. Diplomate Am. Bd. Family Practice. Fellow Am. Acad. Family Practice; mem. Am., Mennonite, N.W. Lancaster County (dir. 1973—) med. assns., Pa., Lancaster County med. socs., Am. Physicians Art Assn. (treas. 1976—), Elizabethtown C. of C. (dir. 1963). Republican. Mennonite. Home and office: 610 Highlawn Ave Elizabethtown PA 17022

GOOD, ROBERT BARTON, JR., broadcasting co. exec.; b. New Holland, Pa., Oct. 25, 1939; s. Robert Barton and Lois Elizabeth (Groff) G.; student Franklin and Marshall Coll., 1957-59; B.S., Kent State U., 1967; m. Joy L. Brenner, Sept. 8, 1963. Tech. operator radio and TV div. Triangle Publs. Inc., Phila., 1960-63; with WLYH-TV, 1960—, chief engr., Lebanon, Pa., 1967—. Mem. Soc. Broadcast Engrs., IEEE, Audio Engring. Soc., Soc. Motion Picture and TV Engrs., Kent State U. Alumni Assn., Lancaster, Lebanon chambers commerce, Pi Mu Epsilon. Home: RD 3 Box 117 Manheim PA 17545 Office: WLYH-TV Box 226 Route 5 Lebanon PA 17042

GOODBAR, ISAAC, elec. engr.; b. Buenos Aires, Dec. 6, 1918; s. Maurice and Catalina (Simsilevich) G.; came to U.S., 1956, naturalized, 1961; Civil Engr., U. Buenos Aires, 1942; S.M. in Elec. Engring., Mass. Inst. Tech., 1945; m. Esther Margaret Silverio, May 22, 1946; children—Robert David, Diana Teresa Olga Goodbar

Bigansky. With Holophane Co., 1945, Century Lighting, N.Y.C., 1946; with mfg. companies in Argentina, 1946-56; with New Haven Clock & Watch Co., 1956; pvt. cons. lighting engr., 1956—; chief engr. Edison Price Inc., lighting, N.Y.C., 1956—; tchr. advanced calculus New Haven Coll., 1956; cons. Teatro Auditorium, 1947-48, Teatro San Martin, 1952-56, Buenos Aires Opera House, 1967-71; del. Internat. Commn. Illumination, 1971, 75; cons. street lighting code City of Buenos Aires, 1971-72. Fellow Illuminating Engring. socs. U.S. and Gt. Britain; mem. U.S. Inst. Theatre Tech., IEEE, AAAS, N.Y. Acad. Scis., Mass. Inst. Tech. Alumni Assn., Assn. Univ. Argentino-Norteamericana. Jewish. Author, patentee in field. Home: 93-02 211th St Queens Village NY 11428 Office: Edison Price Inc 409 E 60th St New York City NY 10022

GOODCHILD, ANTHONY ALAN, investment counselor; b. Amesbury, Mass., Sept. 26, 1942; s. Harry Moses and Sally Fielden (Sargent) G.; B.A., Colby Coll., 1964; m. Lynn Denise Wilson, Sept. 4, 1971; children—Paige, Wilson, Brooke Porter. With State St. Bank & Trust Co., Boston, 1968-72; instnl. salesman Hornblower & Weeks, Hemphill, Noyes, Boston, 1972-73; mgr. fixed income Eaton & Howard, Boston, 1973-75; v.p. fixed income Phoenix Investment Counsel of Boston, Inc., 1975—. Served with USNR, 1964-67. Mem. Boston Municipal Bond Club, Boston Security Analysts Soc., Inc., Bond Portfolio Mgrs. Assn. Home: Boardman Ln Hamilton MA 01936 Office: 535 Boylston St Boston MA 02116

GOODE, MORTON JACOB, dentist; b. Washington, Feb. 3, 1924; s. Julius and Sadie (Fleisher) G.; B.S., Georgetown, U., 1942; D.D.S., Temple U., 1946; m. Amy Lou Harris, Dec. 23, 1945; children—Scott, Robert, Jill. Intern, Glendale (Md.) Sanitarium, 1946; asso. Dr. Jack Goldblatt, Washington, 1947-49; individual practice gen. dentistry, Washington, 1949-51, 52-59, gen. dentistry, crown bridge and rehab., 1959—. Pres. Budget Rent-a-Car, Miami Beach, Fla.; dir. Beverage Control, Inc.; lectr.; staff adviser dental dept. Children's Hosp.; chief dental service Hebrew Home for Aged; dental dir. Jewish Social Service Agy. Greater Washington, 1978. Dir. Boy Scouts Am., 1961-62. Served with U.S. Army, 1943-44, as capt. Dental Corps, USAF, 1950-51. Fellow Acad. Gen. Dentistry, Am. Coll. Dentists; mem. Am. Dental Assn., D.C. Dental Soc. (dir. dental program for treatment of mentally retarded children, chmn. peer review 1976-77), D.C. Dental Sci. Club (past pres.). Jewish (dir. congregation). Kiwanian. Contbr. articles to profl. jours. Home: 5504 Uppingham St Chevy Chase MD 20015 Office: 11119 Rockville Pike North Bethesda MD 20014

GOODELL, JOHN CARLETON, aerospace co. exec.; b. Chgo., Nov. 7, 1913; s. Robert Hosea and Ellen (Hanlon) G.; A.B., Princeton, 1937; M.B.A. with distinction, Harvard, 1951; m. Dorothy Coy, Nov. 28, 1945; children—Amy (Mrs. Robert Spitzmiller), Robert Justin. Asst. to pres. Scott Aviation, Lancaster, N.Y., 1953-55; v.p. Firewel Corp., mil. life support systems, Buffalo, 1955-60; founder, pres. Carleton Controls Corp., pneumatic controls, East Aurora, N.Y., 1960—; mem. adv. bd. Mfrs. and Traders Trust Co., East Aurora, 1964-74. Mem. Iroquois Central Sch. Bd., Elma, N.Y., 1963-66. Served to lt. col. USAF, 1941-51. Decorated D.F.C., Air medal, Purple Heart; recipient Apollo Achievement award NASA. Republican. Presbyn. (elder). Clubs: Country of Buffalo, Harvard (Buffalo); Princeton (Buffalo and N.Y.C.). Home: Liberia Rd East Aurora NY 14052 Office: Jamison Rd East Aurora NY 14052

GOODENOUGH, DAVID JOHN, med. physicist; b. Reading, Eng., Oct. 3, 1944; s. Douglas Frank and Irene Hilda (Booth) G.; B.S. in Physics, U. Chgo., 1967, Ph.D. in Med. Physics, 1972; m. Marjorie E. Reed, Sept. 7, 1963; 1 dau., Jennifer Clark. Instr. dept. radiology U. Chgo., 1972-73; vis. asso. Bur. Radiol. Health, Rockville, Md., 1973-74; asst. prof. dept. radiology Johns Hopkins, 1974-75; dir., asso. prof. radiology, div. radiation physics, dept. radiology George Washington U. Med. Center, 1975—, adj. asst. prof., 1973-74; mem. Nat. Adv. Com. Diagnostic Radiology, 1977—, Internat. Commn. Radiation Units, 1978—; adj. asst. prof. Hood Coll., 1973-74. Pres., Community Riding Sch., Inc., Hinsdale, Ill., 1970-72; trustee Buckeystown (Md.) United Meth. Ch., 1976-77. USPHS fellow, 1967-71. Mem. Soc. Photo-Optical Instrumentation Engrs. (Service award 1975), AAUP, U. Chgo. Alumnae Assn. Mem. editorial rev. bd. Jour. Applied Photographic Engring., 1976—; asst. editor Jour. Investigative Radiology, 1976—. Patentee radiologic imaging. Home: Blenheim Mead Farm Route 1 Myersville MD 21773 Office: 901 23d St NW Washington DC 20037

GOODFELLOW, LOUIS DEAL, psychologist; b. Altoona, Pa., Oct. 12, 1905; s. Louis and Mary Caroline (Deal) G.; B.S., Lafayette Coll., 1929; Ph.D., Northwestern U., 1932; m. Alice M. Myers, Sept. 2, 1933; children—Carolyn Mae Goodfellow Tutko, Cynthia Helen Goodfellow Baney. Lectr. psychology Northwestern U., Evanston, Ill., 1933-41; asst. to pres. devel. Trimm Radio Mfg. Co., Chgo., 1941-45; prof. psychology Pa. State U., 1946-71; lectr., group leader Mid-state Oasis Personal Growth Center, Altoona, 1972—. Bd. dirs. Audio-visual Research Found., Character Research Found., Innovative Methods Research Found. Recipient Steinbeck award for teaching, 1971, research grants. Mem. Am. Psychol. Assn., Assn. Humanistic Psychology, Assn. Creative Change, AAAS, AAUP. Republican. Methodist. Contbr. articles to profl. jours. Home: 226 W Southey Ave Altoona PA 16602 Office: Ivy Hall Pa State Univ Altoona PA 16603

GOODHUE, CHARLES THOMAS, photog. products scientist, composer; b. Ames, Iowa, Apr. 30, 1932; s. Lyle David and Helen (Hamaker) G.; B.S. in Chemistry, U. Ill., 1954; Ph.D. in Biochemistry, U. Calif. at Berkeley, 1961; m. Margaret Anne Whitcomb, 1977; children by previous marriage—Sara Beth, Steven Taylor, Thomas Hamaker. Research asso. Eastman Kodak Co., Rochester, N.Y., 1969—. Resident composer Greece (N.Y.) Community Orch., 1969—. Served with USNR, 1954-57. Mem. Am. Chem. Soc., Am. Soc. Microbiology. Home: 89 Hidden Spring Circle Rochester NY 14616 Office: Research Labs Eastman Kodak Co Rochester NY 14650

GOODIER, J. LESLIE, ocean engr.; b. Birkenhead, Eng., Dec. 16, 1920; s. Thomas and Anne (Munslow) G.; came to U.S., 1947, naturalized, 1949; M.E., Holt Tech. Coll., 1941; postgrad. in Ocean Engring., U. Calif. at Berkeley, 1964; m. Nancy Allison Woodward, Nov. 22, 1961; children—Thomas Edward, Paul Woodward, David Dixon. Supervising engr. Travelers Ins. Co., Washington, 1947-62, Marine Mineral Tech. Center, U.S. Bur. Mines, Tiburon, Calif., 1962-66; sr. research engr. United Aircraft Research Labs., East Hartford, Conn., 1966-69; sr. staff engr. Arthur D. Little, Inc., Cambridge, Mass., 1969-78; sr. engr. Battelle Pacific N.W. Labs., Washington, 1978—; lectr. U. Md., U. Calif., Tampa U.; cons. Mass. Inst. Tech. Served to lt. comdr. Royal Navy, 1941-47; PTO, NATOUSA. Mem. Soc. Naval Architects and Marine Engrs., Am. Inst. Mining Engrs., Am. Soc. Safety Engrs., Epsilon Pi Tau (past pres.). Democrat. Author: U.S. Federal and Sea Coastal State Offshore Mining Laws, 1972; Foreign Deepwater Ports - Lessons for America, 1974; contbr. chpt. to Oceans Handbook, 1978. Home: 728 Gleneagles Dr Tantallon MD 20022 Office: 2030 M St NW Washington DC 20036

GOODING, JUDSON, writer; b. Rochester, Minn., Oct. 12, 1926; s. Arthur Faitoute and Frances (Judson) G.; grad. Yale U., 1948; diplome d'Etudes Françaises, U. Paris, 1950; m. Françoise Ridoux, June 21, 1952; children—Anthony, Amelie, Timothy. Staff writer Dept. Army, Hdqrs. EUCOM, Germany, 1950-52; script writer Affiliated Film Producers, N.Y., 1952-53; news writer WCCO-CBS, Mpls., 1953; reporter Mpls. Tribune, 1953-57; reporter Life mag., N.Y.C., 1957-60, fgn. corr., Paris, 1960-62; fgn. corr. Time mag., Paris, 1962-65; bur. chief Time-Life News Service, San Francisco, 1966-68, edn. editor Time mag., N.Y.C., 1968-69, asso. editor Fortune mag., 1969-73; v.p. Urban Research Corp., also editor Trend Report, Chgo., 1973-75; mng. partner Trend Analysis Assos., 1976—; contbr. articles to N.Y. Times, Bus. and Soc., Reader's Digest, Money, Travel and Leisure, Sport, Panorama, also anthologies. Served with USNR, 1944-46. Mem. Common Cause, World Future Soc. Clubs: Elizabethan; Century Assn., Yale (N.Y.C.). Author: The Job Revolution, 1972. Address: Stone Hill Rd Bedford NY 10506

GOODKIN, GEORGE, physician; b. N.Y.C., Oct. 22, 1910; s. Samuel G. and Mary (Federman) G.; B.S., N.Y. U., 1931; M.D., U. Glasgow, 1936; m. Joy Vera Robinson, June 1, 1944; children—William George, Pamela May, Wendy Lee Goodkin Messina, Geoffrey Bosworth. Intern, Carney Hosp., Boston, 1937-38, City Hosp., N.Y.C., 1938-39; resident in medicine York Hosp., N.Y.C., 1939; gen. practice medicine, N.Y.C., 1939-56, specializing in internal medicine, N.Y.C., 1956—; med. examiner Equitable Life Assurance Soc., N.Y.C., 1946-47, asst. med. dir., 1947-51, asso. med. dir., 1951-69, sr. asso. med. dir., 1969-72, asst. v.p., asso. med. dir., 1972-75; med. dir. N. Am. Reassurance Co., N.Y.C., 1975—; med. dir. Union Labor Life Ins. Co., N.Y.C., 1975—; cons. med. dir. Peoples Home Life & Fed. Casualty Ins. Co., 1977—. Served to capt. AUS, 1941-45. Fellow Clin. Soc., N.Y. Diabetes Assn. (dir.); mem. Am. Diabetes Assn. (chmn. ins. com.), Am. Life Conv., Med. Dirs. Assn., Glasgow U. Club Am. (past pres.), Australian Soc. Contbr. to profl. jours. Home: 112 Lee Rd Garden City NY 11530 Office: 245 Park Ave New York City NY 10019

GOODMAN, ABRAHAM, architect; b. Newark, June 18, 1930; s. Max and Ida (Feldman) G.; student Chgo. Inst. Design, 1949-50; B.Arch., Ill. Inst. Tech., 1954; m. Rachelle Marks, June 24, 1954; children—Bruce Edward, Paul David, Shelly Sue. Prin. firm Abraham Goodman, AIA, Architect, Linden, N.J., 1960—. Served with AUS, 1954-56. Mem. AIA, N.J. Soc. Architects, Guild for Religious Architecture. Mason. Designer numerous temples, synagogues N.Y. met. area. Home: 1444 Forest Ct Mountainside NJ 07092 Office: 618 Elizabeth Ave Linden NJ 07036

GOODMAN, ALAN HERMAN, food co. exec.; b. Bronx, N.Y., Nov. 13, 1947; s. Marvin and Dorothy G.; Asso. Applied Sci., SUNY, Farmingdale, 1967; B.S., Ohio State U., 1969; M.B.A., St. John's U., 1977; m. Susan Levitan, Sept. 25, 1971; children—Matthew, Randi. Food technologist Modern maid Food Products, Jamaica, N.Y., 1970-73, sr. food technologist, 1973-76, tech. dir. coating devel. lab., 1976—; lectr. Mercy Coll., Dobbs Ferry, N.Y., Elizabeth Seton Coll., Yonkers, N.Y. Mem. Am. Assn. Cereal Chemists, Inst. Food Technologists. Jewish. Home: 14 E Park Dr Old Bethpage NY 11804 Office: 110-60 Dunkirk St Jamaica NY 11412

GOODMAN, CHARLES CLARKE, psychiatrist, state ofcl.; b. Newport, R.I., May 3, 1923; s. Joseph Lawrence and Genevieve (Clarke) G.; B.S., Providence Coll., 1943; M.D., Jefferson Med. Coll., 1948; m. Joan Marie Fox, Apr. 24, 1965; children—Charles, Gail, Lynn, Ann, Robert, Maureen, John, Thomas. Intern, Meml. Hosp., Pawtucket, R.I., 1948-49; resident State Hosp., Howard, R.I., 1949-52, Butler Hosp., Providence, 1952-53; practice medicine specializing in psychiatry, Providence, 1953-65, East Greenwich, R.I., 1975—; adminstr. Div. Alcoholims, Dept. Social Welfare, Providence, 1955-57; chief clin. psychiatrist Mental Hygiene Services, Providence, 1955-65; asst. commr. mental health Office Mental Health, Pa. Dept. Pub. Welfare, Harrisburg, 1965-70; asst. dir. R.I. Dept. Mental Health, Retardation and Hosps., Cranston, 1970-72, dir., 1972-75; cons. NIMH, 1967—, Lebanon VA Hosp., 1968-70, Bradley Hosp., Riverside, R.I., 1971—, Pa. Dept. Health, 1978—; cons. Butler Hosp., Providence, 1971-75, active staff, 1975—; cons. Kent County Meml. Hosp., Warwick, R.I., 1971-75, active staff, 1975—. Chmn., N.E. State Govts. Conf. Mental Health, 1960, exec. com. mem. for Pa., 1965-70. Fellow Am. Psychiat. Assn. (br. pres. 1964-65), Am. Pub. Health Assn.; mem. AMA, R.I., Kent County med. socs. Home and Office: 76 Middle Rd East Greenwich RI 02818

GOODMAN, EDWIN ALAN, lawyer; b. Toronto, Ont., Can., Oct. 11, 1918; s. David Bertram and Dorothy (Soble) G.; B.L., U. Toronto, 1940; m. Suzanne Gross, Dec. 21, 1953; children—Joanne (dec.), Diane. Called to Ont. bar, 1947; practiced in Toronto, 1947—; mem. firm Goodman & Goodman, 1947—. Dir., John Labatt Ltd., Baton Broadcasting Ltd., Cadillac Fairview Corp., Fin. Trust Co., Ogilvie Mills Ltd. Spl. lectr. polit. economy U. Toronto, 1972-73. Bd. dirs. New Mt. Sinai Hosp., Baycrest Home for Aged, YWHA, Shaw Festival-Nat. Ballet Can. (all Toronto). Chmn. Progressive Conservative Party Can., 1965, 68; v.p., 1957-66. Served to maj. Royal Canadian Army, 1939-45. Mem. Law Soc. Upper Can. (bencher). Clubs: Albany, Primrose, Queens Toronto Lawn Tennis (Toronto). Home: 402 Glenayr Rd Toronto ON Canada Office: 101 Richmond St W Suite 1500 Toronto ON Canada

GOODMAN, HELENE SANDRA, interior designer, educator; b. Long Branch, N.J., Aug. 29, 1948; d. William Angelo and Helen Elinor (Christopher) Grasso; B.A. in Math., Marymount Coll., Tarrytown, N.Y., 1970; certificate N.Y. Sch. Interior Design, 1976; m. Gerald J. Goodman, Aug. 4, 1974. Instr. math. Shore Regional High Sch., West Long Branch, N.J., 1970—, spl. lectr. interior design, 1976-77; owner, operator Goodman Design Studio, Middletown, N.J., 1976—. Certified tchr., N.J., N.Y. Mem. NEA, N.J. Edn. Assn. Text cons.: Geometry, 1974. Home and Office: 28 Packard Dr Middletown NJ 07748

GOODMAN, ISIDORE, lawyer; b. N.Y.C., Mar. 10, 1907; s. Jacob and Kate (Rubinstein) G.; B.C.S., N.Y.U., 1928, M.C.S., 1929, J.D., 1931; m. Bertha Cohen, Feb. 18, 1940; 1 son, Robert. Admitted to N.Y. bar, 1932, U.S. Supreme Ct. bar, 1944, D.C. bar, 1960; practiced in N.Y.C., 1932-35; agt. IRS, Chgo., 1935-38, N.Y.C., 1938-44, tech. adviser, asst. br. chief pension trust div., Washington, 1944-57, chief pension trust br., 1957-74, asst. to asst. commr. employee plans and exempt orgns., 1974-77; practice law, Washington, 1977—; guest lectr. pension and profit-sharing plans N.Y. U., U. So. Calif., U. Tex., Am. U., Ind. U., others. Recipient Employee Benefit Man of Year award Pension and Welfare News Mag., 1972. C.P.A., N.Y., Md. Mem. Am. Bar Assn., Bar Assn. D.C., Beta Gamma Sigma. Author: Goodman on Qualified Pension and Profit-Sharing Plans, 1966, 3d edit., 1975. Contbr. articles to profl. jours. Home: 11275 Columbia Pike Silver Spring MD 20901 Office: CCM-425 13th St NW Washington DC 20004

GOODMAN, JEROME DANIEL, lawyer; b. Annapolis, Md., June 1, 1913; s. Aaron Lee and Jeanette (Isaacson) G.; A.B., St. John's Coll., 1934; LL.B., Harvard, 1937; m. Margery Isobel Rose, Nov. 30, 1941; children—Jane Lois, Carol Sue. Admitted to Mass. bar, 1938; practiced law in Boston, 1938—; asst. dist. atty., Norfolk County, Mass., 1957-59. Pres. Jewish Big Bro. Assn. Boston, 1957-59. Mem. Brookline Rep. Town Com., 1954—, also treas.; mem. Brookline Town Meeting, 1949—, Town Adv. Com., 1958—; mem. Brookline Rent Control Bd., 1952-58; Spl. town Counsel, Brookline, 1963—; govt. appeal agt. Brookline S.S.S., 1969—; pres. Brookline Citizens Com.; corporate mem. Morgan Meml., Boston; chmn. lawyers div. Combined Jewish Philanthropies, 1964, 65, trustee, 1965—; counsel Health and Safety Com., Brookline. Treas., Republican Town Com. Brookline, 1972—. Served with AUS, 1943-46. Recipient Community Service citation Asso. Jewish Philanthropies Boston, 1959; Certificate of Merit, Am. Legion, 1958; Distinguished Service award Nat. Jewish Welfare Bd., 1962. Mem. Am., Mass., Norfolk (mem. council 1966—), Norfolk County, Boston bar assns., Mass. Trial Lawyers Assn., Am. Legion (post comdr. 1957), Jewish War Vets. (post comdr. 1952, nat. judge adv. 1956), Phi Sigma Delta. Jewish religion (temple dir. 1957-60, pres. Brotherhood 1969-70). Author: What Are My Rights?—An Employer's Guide to Labor Relations, 1937; also articles legal periodicals. Home: 100 Shaw Rd Brookline MA 02167 Office: 85 Devonshire St Boston MA 02109

GOODMAN, JEROME DAVID, physician, musician; b. Chester, Pa., Oct. 23, 1933; s. William Henry and Amelia Rose G.; B.A., Swarthmore Coll., 1955; M.D., U. Pa., 1959; m. Gail Theis, Feb. 10, 1961; children—David Hammond, Douglas Andrew. Intern, Chestnut Hill Hosp., Phila., 1959-60; fellow in gen. psychiatry Hosp. U. Pa., 1960-62; fellow in child psychiatry S.I. Mental Health Center and St. Vincent Hosp., N.Y.C., 1962-64; practice adult and child psychiatry, Saddle River, N.J., 1968—; dir. child and adolescent psychiatry Bergen Pines Hosp., Paramus, N.J., 1968-75; dir. cons. services Bd. Spl. Services, Bergen County, N.J., 1975—; asst. clin. prof. psychiatry Coll. Physicians and Surgeons, Columbia U., 1964—; solo cellist with Pierre Monteux, l'école Domaine, Hancock, Maine, 1950-53; composer for piano, strings and orch. Mem. Bergen County Mental Health Bd., 1968-71. Served as capt. U.S. Army, 1966-68. Recipient Presser Music award, 1951-53; Distinguished Service award Bd. of Freeholders, 1971. Diplomate Am. Bd. Psychiatry and Neurology. Mem. Am. Psychiat. Assn. Author: (with John A. Sours) The Child Mental Status Examination, 1967. Home and office: 45 W Saddle River Rd Saddle River NJ 07458

GOODMAN, LAWRENCE, social work adminstr., educator; b. Chelsea, Mass., Sept. 11, 1925; s. Benjamin and Celia (Engle) G.; B.A., U. Miami, 1948; M.S.W., Boston U., 1950; postgrad. Yeshiva U., 1972-76. Social worker Jewish Family Service, Miami, Fla., 1950-52, N.Y.C., 1952-53; psychiat. social work supr. Bellevue Psychiat. Hosp., 1953-57; dir. social work Mental Retardation Inst., N.Y. Med. Coll., N.Y.C., 1957—, asso. dir. Mental Retardation Inst. for Community Services, 1969—; asso. prof. mental retardation N.Y. Med. Coll., N.Y.C., 1973—; clin. asso. prof. Smith Coll. Sch. Social Work, Northampton, Mass., 1974—; adj. asso. prof. Fordham U.; adj. asso. prof. N.Y.U., 1968—. Cons. N.Y. State Dept. Mental Hygiene, 1967-68, N.Y. Guild for Jewish Blind, N.Y.C., 1966-68, div. of hosp. and med. facilities, HEW, 1966-68; mem. N.Y.C. Mayor's Com. on Mental Retardation, 1966-68. Served with USNR, 1943-46. Certified social worker, N.Y. Fellow Am. Assn. on Mental Deficiency (v.p. 1970-72); mem. Am. Sociol. Assn., Am. Group Psychotherapy Assn., Nat. Assn. Social Workers, Internat. Soc. for Disabled, AAUP. Contbr. articles to profl. jours. Home: 1 Washington Square Village New York City NY 10012 Office: NY Med Coll Fifth Ave at 106th St New York City NY 10029

GOODMAN, RICHARD SHALEM, orthopedic surgeon; b. Bklyn., Aug. 4, 1934; s. Samuel S. and Minnie Catherine (Blechschmidt) G.; B.A., Alfred U., 1955; M.D., N.Y. U., 1960; m. Florence Libbey Levine, June 20, 1957; children—Lorraine Susan, Caroline Lucille, Deborah Michelle. Intern, Ind. U. Sch. Medicine, Indpls., 1960-61; resident in surgery Albert Einstein Sch. Medicine, N.Y.C., 1961-62, N.Y. U. Bellevue Med. Center, 1964-67; practice medicine specializing in orthopedic surgery, Smithtown, N.Y., 1967—; mem. staff St. John's Hosp.; pres. med. staff Smithtown Gen. Hosp.; cons. Office Vocat. Rehab. and Supreme Ct. Suffolk County. Trustee Alfred U.; mem. Smithtown Art Council. Served to capt. USAF, 1962-64. Mem. N.Y. State, Suffolk County (dir.) med. socs., Eastern Orthopedic Med. Soc., Am. Coll. Legal Medicine, Internat. Coll. Surgeons, Am. Acad. Orthopedic Surgeons, Am. Rheumatism Assn., Am. Coll. Sports Medicine, Am. Coll. Health Assn. Office: 80 Maple Ave Smithtown NY 11787

GOODMAN, ROY MATZ, state senator, business exec., educator; b. N.Y.C., Mar. 5, 1930; s. Bernard A. and Alice (Matz) G.; A.B. cum laude, Harvard U., 1951, M.B.A with distinction, 1953; grad. Naval Officer Candidate Sch., 1953, Naval Supply Corps Sch., 1954; m. Barbara Christine Furrer, June 28, 1955; children—Claire Barbara, Leslie Alice, Randolph Bernard. Pres., Ex-Lax, Inc., 1962-71, chmn. bd., 1971-75, also dir.; chmn. bd. Ex-Lax Distbg. Co., Inc., 1975-; pres., dir. Roycemore Inc., 1968-70; asso. buying and new bus. dept. Kuhn, Loeb & Co., investment bankers, 1956-60; dir. Manhattan Industries, Inc.; mem. Bklyn. adv. bd. Chem. Bank N.Y. Trust Co., 1963-65; adj. prof. pub. adminstrn. Baruch Coll., City U. N.Y. Mem. N.Y. State Senate, 1968—, chmn. taxation and govt. ops. com., com. on housing and urban devel., 1968-76, mem. finance, cities, edn., crime and corrections, banking coms. Dir. finance, finance adminstr. City N.Y., 1966-68, mem. Mayor's Cabinet and Supercabinet, 1966-68; mem. N.Y.C. Banking Commn., 1966-67; chmn. N.Y. State Charter Revision Commn. for N.Y.C. Trustee Brotherhood-In-Action; past class area agt. Harvard Coll. Fund, mem. 1951 permanent class com., past dir. Asso. Harvard Alumni; past dir. Freedom House, Dalton Sch.; mem. adv. council Inst. Philosophy and Politics of Edn., Columbia U. Tchrs. Coll.; bd. advisers Council Mcpl. Performance; trustee N.Y.C. Police Pension Fund, 1966-67, N.Y.C. Fire Dept. Pension Fund, 1966-67, Heart Research Found. Exec. asst. to chmn. N.Y. State Assembly Jud. Com., 1963-64; asst. to atty. gen. State N.Y., 1960; pres. 9th A.D. Republican Club, 1963-64; treas. N.Y. County Rep. Finance Com., 1965; del. Rep. state convs., 1966, 68, 70, Rep. Nat. Conv., 1972, 76; mem. N.Y. State Rep. Com., 1974—; Rep. candidate Mayor N.Y.C., 1977—. Past trustee or bd. dirs. Carnegie Hall Soc., Barnard Coll., N.Y. Com. Young Audiences; trustee or bd. dirs. United Jewish Appeal Tel Aviv U.; past trustee Columbia Coll. Pharm. Scis., L.I. Coll. Hosp. Served to lt. USNR, 1953-56. Recipient Distinguished Service award (Young Man of Year) Jr. C. of C., 1966; Mt. Scopus citation Hebrew U. Jerusalem, 1968; medal merit City U., 1972; Man of Year Brotherhood-in-Action, 1972; scroll of honor United Jewish Appeal, 1970, Humanitarian award Bronx County Soc. Prevention Cruelty to Children, 1976, Odyssey House Citation, 1976, numerous other awards; named N.Y. State Rep. of Year, Ripon Soc., 1972. Mem. Anti-Defamation League, Am. Arbitration Assn. (nat. panel arbitrators), Soc. Security Analysts, Young Pres. Orgn., Asso. Harvard Alumni Omicron Delta Epsilon (hon.). Republican. Clubs: City, Wall Street, Harvard, Harvard Business School (N.Y.C.); Century Country (Purchase, N.Y.); Fort Orange (Albany, N.Y.). Home: 1035 Fifth Ave New York NY 10028 Office: 270 Broadway New York NY 10007

GOODMAN, SEYMOUR, educator; b. N.Y.C., Nov. 12, 1933; s. Morris and Beckie (Weinberg) G.; B.S. magna cum laude with honors, City Coll. City U. N.Y., 1954; M.S., U. Chgo., 1955; Ph.D., Columbia, 1962. Faculty, Queens Coll. City U. N.Y., Flushing, 1962—, asso. prof. chemistry, 1967-76, chmn. dept. computer sci., 1970-76, prof., 1970—, dir. research and instructional computer center, 1964—, mem. doctoral faculty in computer sci. City U. N.Y. Cons. Lenox Hill Hosp., N.Y.C., 1966-68, Cytek Terminal Corp., N.Y.C., 1968-69, Stuart Bros., N.Y.C., 1969-71, Index Terminals Internat., Inc., N.Y.C., 1973—. Recipient Ward medal in chemistry City Coll., 1954. NSF grantee, 1964-67; Dept. Health, Edn. and Welfare grantee, 1972. Mem. Am. Assn. U. Profs., A.A.A.S., Am. Chem. Soc., Am. Inst. Chemists, Am. Phys. Soc., IEEE, Assn. Computing Machinery, Assn. Orthodox Jewish Scientists, Internat. Soc. Magnetic Resonance, N.Y. Acad. Sci., Pattern Recognition Soc., Soc. for Information Displays, Phi Beta Kappa, Sigma Xi, Phi Lambda Upsilon. Home: 67-44 171st St Flushing NY 11365 Office: Computer Center 65-30 Kissena Blvd Flushing NY 11367

GOODMAN, STANLEY, accountant; b. N.Y.C., Aug. 4, 1932; s. Hyman David and Beatrice (Topper) G.; B.S. in Accounting magna cum laude, L.I. U., 1953, M.S. cum laude, 1955; certificates in advanced study taxation and auditing N.Y. State Soc. C.P.A.'s, 1972; m. Carol Reta Schwed, June 21, 1953; children—Robert Martin, Bruce Howard, Linda Sue. Sr. accountant various C.P.A firms, N.Y.C., 1950-60; practice pub. accounting, Mt. Vernon, N.Y., 1960-63, Dobbs Ferry, N.Y., 1963—; partner Goodman and Lind, Pub. Accountants, Dobbs Ferry, 1970—. C.P.A., N.Y. Mem. Am. Inst. C.P.A.'s, N.Y. State Soc. C.P.A.'s (chmn. accountants practice com. Westchester chpt. 1974-75), Nat. Soc. Pub. Accountants. Address: 7 Beechwood Ct Dobbs Ferry NY 10522

GOODMAN, STANLEY ERWIN, surgeon; b. Norwalk, Conn., May 4, 1926; s. Robert M. and Francine (Cotler) G.; B.S., Trinity Coll., Hartford, 1947; M.A., U. Pa., 1949; M.D., Cornell U., 1953; m. Alice Marie Vanderbecq, June 20, 1962; m. 2d, Francine Joan. Intern, Strong Meml. Hosp., Rochester, N.Y., 1953-54; asst. resident surgery Mt. Sinai Hosp., N.Y.C., 1954-55; asst. resident surgery Kings County Hosp., Bklyn., 1955-58, chief resident surgery, 1958-59, attending surgeon vascular service and breast tumor bd., 1959—; research asst. State U. N.Y. Med. Sch., Bklyn., 1956-57; gen. practice, Norwalk, 1959—; sr. attending surg. staff Norwalk Hosp., also chief sect. neoplastic diseases; asst. instr. State U. N.Y. Med. Sch., 1956-57, instr. clin. surgery, 1959—; dir. First Fed. Savs. and Loan Assn. of Norwalk. Bd. dirs. So. Fairfield County unit Am. Cancer Soc.; mem. regional adv. council Norwalk Tech. Coll.; bd. dirs. Greater Norwalk Community Council. Served with USNR, 1944-46, Diplomate Am. Bd. Surgery. Fellow ACS; mem. AAAS, Royal Soc. Health, Pan Am. Med. Assn., Norwalk Med. Soc. (past pres.), N.Y. Acad. Medicine, Am. Heart Assn. Home: 40 Pequot Trail Westport CT 06880 Office: 160 East Ave Norwalk CT 06851

GOODNER, JOHN TETARD, physician, surgeon; b. Denver, Oct. 29, 1912; s. William R. and Clara G. (Tetard) G.; A.B., Columbia, 1935, M.D., 1940; m. Kathleen W. McAllister, Oct. 16, 1965; children—Marylou Bernadette, John McAllister. Intern, Bellevue Hosp., N.Y.C., 1941-42; surg. resident St. John's Episcopal Hosp., Bklyn., 1946-49; asst. resident surgery Meml. Hosp., N.Y.C., 1949-50, fellow surgery, 1950-52, fellow thoracic surgery, 1952-55; fellow, trainee Nat. Cancer Inst., 1951; practice medicine specializing in surgery, N.Y.C.; cons. in surgery thoracic service Meml. Hosp.; surgeon, Manhattan Eye, Ear and Throat Hosp.; hon. staff Lawrence Hosp., Bronxville, N.Y.; clin. asso. prof. surgery Cornell U. Med. Coll.; cons. thoracic surgery St. Francis Hosp., Poughkeepsie, N.Y. Served to maj. M.C., AUS, USAAF, 1942-45. Diplomate Am. Bd. Surgery, Am. Bd. Thoracic Surgery. Fellow A.C.S.; mem. Royal Soc. Medicine (asso.), AMA, N.Y. State, Westchester County med. socs., Pan Am. Med. Assn., Soc. Head and Neck Surgeons, Soc. Surg. Oncology, Am. Cancer Soc. (dir. Westchester div., med. cons. N.Y.C. div.), Am. Radium Soc., N.Y. Soc. Thoracic Surgery, N.Y. Surg. Soc., A.A.A.S., Alumni Soc. Bellevue Hosp., N.Y. Acad. Scis., Physicians Sci. Soc. Knight of Malta. Home: 5 Sycamore St Bronxville NY 10708

GOODRICH, ISAAC, neurosurgeon; b. Milledgeville, Ga., Sept. 19, 1939; s. Ellis and Frieda (Bergman) G.; A.A., Ga. Mil. Coll., 1959; B.S., U. Ga., 1961; M.D., Med. Coll. Ga., 1964; m. Dianne L. Brittain, Aug. 28, 1965; children—Mindy Anne, Scott David. Intern, Columbia-Presbyn. Med. Center, N.Y.C., 1964-65, resident in neurosurgery, Yale-New Haven (Conn.) Med. Center, 1967-71; practice medicine specializing in neurosurgery, New Haven, 1971—; instr. neurosurgery, Yale, 1970-71; attending neurosurgeon, Yale-New Haven Hosp., Hosp. of St. Raphael; cons. neurosurgeon, Griffin Hosp. Served to capt., U.S. Army, 1965-67. Decorated Bronze Star, Air Medal. Certified, Am. Bd. Neurol. Surgery; recipient AMA Physicians Recognition Award for Continuing Med. Edn., 1969, 72, 75. Fellow A.C.S., Internat. Coll. Surgeons, Royal Soc. Medicine; mem. Congress of Neurol. Surgeons, New Eng. Neurosurg. Soc., Pan Pacific Surg. Assn., Am. Assn. Neurol. Surgeons, AMA, Conn. State Med. Soc., New Haven City, County Med. Assns. Jewish religion. Designated hon. citizen, Boys Town, Nebr., 1971; contbr. articles, papers to med. publs., meetings. Home: 15 Birch Rd Woodbridge CT 06525 Office: 60 Temple St New Haven CT 06510

GOODSTEIN, DANIEL BELA, oral surgeon; b. Bklyn., Oct. 27, 1937; s. Charles Benjamin and Florence Ann (Apfel) G.; B.A., U. Conn., 1959; D.M.D., Tufts U., 1963; postgrad. in oral surgery N.Y. U., 1964-65; m. Celia Beth Abrams, Sept. 8, 1968; children—Kimberly Joy, Kara Hope, Lauren Faith. Intern in oral surgery Queens Hosp. Center, 1963-64, resident, 1965-66, attending oral surgeon, 1968—; practice dentistry, specializing in oral surgery, Hempstead, N.Y., 1969—; staff oral surgeon L.I. Jewish Hillside Med. Center, 1968—; staff oral surgeon Hempstead Med. Center; asso. prof. clin. oral surgery Sch. Dental Medicine, State U. N.Y. at Stony Brook. Served with AUS, 1966-68. Decorated Army Commendation medal. Diplomate Am. Bd. Oral Surgery. Fellow Internat. Assn. Oral Surgeons; mem. Am., N.Y. State (chmn. advanced and continuing edn. com.) socs. oral surgeons, Am. Assn. Dental Schs., ADA, N.Y. State 10th Dist. (bd. dels.) dental socs., Alpha Omega, Phi Epsilon Pi. Club: Masons. Contbr. articles to profl. jours. Research on effect of surg. correction of facial deformities on speech. Home: Linden Ln Muttontown NY 11732 Office: 131 Fulton Ave Hempstead NY 11550

GOODSTEIN, SEYMOUR, ophthalmologist; b. Bklyn., Aug. 16, 1922; s. Joe and Kate (Schwartz) G.; B.S., Tulane U., 1943, M.D., 1945; m. Anita Balsalm, Jan. 28, 1951; children—Janet Dale, Judy Louise. Intern, Greenpoint Hosp., Bklyn., 1945-46; resident in ophthalmology Kings County Hosp., Bklyn., 1950-52; practice medicine specializing in ophthalmology with sub-splty. glaucoma, Bayside, N.Y., 1952—; mem. staff, asst. dir. glaucoma N.Y. Eye and Ear Infirmary, N.Y.C., 1960—; mem. staff, dir. glaucoma L.I. Jewish Queens Hosp. Center, New Hyde Park, N.Y., 1965—; mem. staff Franklin Gen. Hosp., Valley Stream, N.Y.; guest lectr. N.Y. Eye and Ear Postgrad. Inst. Served as capt. M.C., U.S. Army, 1946-48. Mem. Am. Acad. Ophthalmology, A.C.S., Assn. Research in Ophthalmology, N.Y. Soc. Clin. Ophthalmology, Soc. Eye Surgeons. Contbr. articles to med. jours.

GOODWIN, DOROTHY CHENEY, educator, state legislator; b. Hartford, Conn., Sept. 2, 1914; d. Charles Archibald and Ruth (Cheney) Goodwin; A.B., Smith Coll., 1937; Ph.D., U. Conn., 1957. With various agencies Fed. Govt., 1937-45; librarian Food and Agr. Orgn., UN, Washington, 1945-46; agrl. economist Allied Powers in Japan, 1946-52; asso. prof. economics U. Conn., Storrs, 1957-74, asst. provost, dir. instl. research, 1965-74; mem. Conn. Ho. of Reps., 1975—; dir. Natural Gas Corp., 1972—. Chmn. Joshua's Tract Conservation and Historic Trust, Windham Planning Retion, Conn., 1968-74; mem. Mansfield (Conn.) Bd. Tax Rev., 1961-71. Mem. Mansfield Town Council, 1971-74; mem. Dem. Town Com., Storrs, 1965. Former vice chmn., then chmn bd. trustees Hartford Coll. for Women, 1975—; mem. bd. regents U. Hartford, 1971—; bd. dirs. U. Conn. Found., 1966—; trustee Conn. chpt. Nature Conservancy; exec. bd. Indian Trails council Eastern Conn. Boy Scouts Am., 1973; corporator Windham Community Meml. Hosp., 1971—, Hartford Hosp., 1972—; trustee Child and Family Services Greater Hartford. Mem. League Women Voters, Assn. for Instl. Research, Common Cause. Democrat. Episcopalian. Home: 447 Browns Rd Storrs CT 06268

GOODWIN, FREDERICK KING, psychiatrist; b. Cin., Apr. 21, 1936; s. Robert Clifford and Marion Cronin (Schmadel) G.; B.S., Georgetown U., 1958; M.D., St. Louis U., 1963; m. Rosemary Julia Powers, Oct. 19, 1963; children—Kathleen Kelly, Frederick King, Daniel Clifford. Intern, State U. N.Y. Upstate Med. Center, Syracuse, 1963-64; resident in psychiatry U. N.C., Chapel Hill, 1964-65; clin. asso. in psychiatry sect. psychosomatic medicine NIMH, Bethesda, Md., 1965-67, chief clin. research unit sect. psychiatry, 1968-71, chief sect. on psychiatry, 1971-76, chief clin. psychobiology br., 1976—; mem. faculty George Washington U. Med. Sch., 1973—, Washington Sch. Psychiatry, 1970—; vis. prof. Boston U. Med. Sch., U. Wis. Med. Sch., U. Calif., Irvine. Served with USPHS, 1965-67. St. Louis U. fellow, 1958-59; spl. research fellow in biochemistry Nat. Heart Inst., 1967-68; recipient A.E. Bennett award Soc. Biol. Psychiatry, 1970, Hofheimer award Am. Psychiat. Assn., 1971, Internat. Anna Monica prize for research in depression, 1971, Taylor Manor award, 1976, Psychopharmacology research prize Am. Psychol. Assn., 1970. Fellow Am. Psychiat. Assn., Am. Coll. Neuropsychopharmacology; mem. Am. Psychosomatic Soc., Soc. Biol. Psychiatry, Soc. Neurosci., Washington Psychiat. Soc., Am. Acad. Psychoanalysis, Internat. Neuropharmacology Congress. Club: Cosmos. Editorial bd. Archives of Gen. Psychiatry, 1977—, Psychopharmacology, 1975—, Acta Neurologia, 1977—. Pioneer in antidepressant effect of lithium. Contbr. numerous articles to profl. jours. Home: 5712 Warwick Pl Chevy Chase MD 20015 Office: NIH Bldg 10 9000 Rockville Pike Bethesda MD 20014

GOODWIN, GERALD LOUIS, finance co. exec.; b. Elmira, N.Y., Feb. 5, 1943; s. Elmer James and Ervene (Snover) G.; A.B. (acad. scholar), Lafayette Coll., Easton, Pa., 1965; M.B.A. (acad. scholar), N.Y. U., 1968; m. Christine Gail Wilsey, June 21, 1969; children—Alexander Gerald, Carrie Christine. Portfolio mgr. Merrill Lynch, N.Y.C., 1967-68; with F. Eberstadt & Co. Inc., N.Y.C., 1968—, v.p. 1971—, portfolio mgr., 1973—; sr. v.p. Anchor Pension Mgmt. Corp., 1976-77; pres. Goodwin, Alexander Inc., investment advisors and venture capitalists, 1978—. Pres. Knickerbocker Republican Club; mem. N.Y. State Rep. Com., 1974—; staff advanceman Pres. Ford, 1976; mem. com. on compaign services Rep. Nat. Com., 1978—. Certified fin. analyst; registered rep. N.Y. Stock Exchange. Mem. N.Y. Soc. Security Analysts, Nat. Assn. Security Dealers (registered prin.), Phi Kappa Psi. Methodist. Clubs: Univ. (N.Y.C.); Capitol Hill (Washington). Home: 444 E 82d St New York City NY 10028 Office: One W 54 St New York City NY 10019

GOODWIN, HAROLD LELAND, marine affairs exec., author; b. Ellenburg, N.Y., Nov. 20, 1914; s. Frank Elmer and Imogene (Van Arman) G.; student Elliot Radio Sch., 1934-35; m. Elizabeth I. Swensk, Apr. 12, 1947; children—Alan C., Christopher R., Derek V. White House corr. Transradio News, Washington, 1942; press attache U.S. Fgn. Service, Philippines, 1947-50; dir. atomic test operations FCDA, 1951-58; sci. adviser USIA, 1958-62; spl. asst. to adminstr. NASA, 1962-67; asso. dir. Office Sea Grant programs NSF and NOAA, Washington, 1967-74; fellow Oceanic Inst., 1974—; marine affairs cons. Served to 1st lt. USMCR, 1942-45. Decorated Air medal. Recipient Arthur S. Flemming award U.S. Jr. C. of C., 1954. Mem. Am. Littoral Soc. (dir. 1975—, Dugan award 1974), Marine Tech. Soc. (sec. profl. and student sects. 1970-72), Am. Oceanic Orgn. (dir. 1970-72), Antarctican Soc., Am. Sci. Film Assn. (nat. v.p. 1965-67), Underwater Soc. Am., Profl. Assn. Diving Instrs. (internat. dir. 1972—), World Mariculture Soc. (v.p. 1977). Methodist. Author: Rick Brant Science adventure series, 1947-72; Challenge of Seven Seas, 1966; All About Rockets and Space Flight, 1962; Space: Frontier Unlimited, 1964; Images of Space, 1965; (with Joe Hanson) Shrimp and Prawn Farming in the Western Hemisphere, 1977. Editor: Americans and the World of Water, 1977. Home and office: 6212 Verne St Bethesda MD 20034

GOODWIN, HAZEL JEAN THOMAS, utility co. exec.; b. St. Louis, Apr. 15, 1946; d. Albert Wendell and Ollie Bell (Matthews) Thomas; B.S. in Bus., Eastern Ill. U., 1969; m. Arthur Lee Goodwin, Dec. 31, 1972; children—Arthur Lee (dec.), Kevin Michael. Computer programmer, instr. McDonald-Douglas Automation Co., St. Louis, 1968-72; computer programmer, sr. data processing instr. Xerox Corp., Webster and Rochester, N.Y., 1972-74; computer tng. coordinator Potomac Electric Power Co., Washington, 1974—. Active Explorer Scouts, St. Louis, 1970-72. Mem. Am. Soc. for Tng. and Devel. Baptist. Home: 64 Great Neck Rd Waterford CT 06385

GOODWIN, REX DEAN, clergyman; b. Martinsville, Mo., Nov. 30, 1909; s. Charles Morgan and Grace Leola (Pyle) G.; A.B., U. Nebr., 1932; B.D., Andover Newton Theol. Sch., 1934; D.D., Sioux Falls Coll., 1957; m. Almira Drew Wallace, June 24, 1933 (dec. Oct. 1964); 1 son, John Charles; m. 2d, Loree Presnell, June 18, 1966. Ordained to ministry Bapt. Ch., 1934; pastor chs., Oxford, Nebr., 1934-36, Oakland, Calif., 1936-37, Boston, 1941-44; dir. Christian edn. First Bapt. Ch., Oakland, 1937-38; asst. pastor Central Bapt. Ch., Hartford, Conn., 1938-41; dir. pub. relations Am. Bapt. Home Mission Soc., N.Y.C., 1944-51; dir. publicity Am. Bapt. Conv., N.Y.C., 1951-58, exec. dir. conv. div. communication, Valley Forge, Pa., 1958-72; pub. liaison exec. Am. Bapt. Chs. Bd. Ednl. Ministries, Valley Forge, 1972-74; dir. devel. Cushing Jr. Coll., Bryn Mawr, Pa., 1975-77; pastor Pughtown (Pa.) Bapt. Ch., 1977—; chmn. communications com. Bapt. World Alliance, 1972-75, mem., 1970—; mem. communications com. Nat. Council Chs., 1961-72; v.p. Main Line Ministerium. Trustee Andover Newton Theol. Sch. Mem. Religious Pub. Relations Council (pres. 1961-62). Republican. Author: Man-Living Soul, 1952; There Is No End, 1956; editor Cushing Way, 1977-78; contbr. articles to ch. jours. Home: 3307 Windsor Dr Norristown PA 19403 Office: Box 340 RD 1 Spring City PA 19475

GOODWIN, ROBERT DELMEGE, assn. exec.; b. Des Moines, Sept. 14, 1920; s. Charles Otis and Lorraine Lee (Delmege) G.; B.S., Northwestern U., 1941, M.S. in Journalism, 1942; m. June Schuyler Patterson, Feb. 15, 1946; 1 dau., Meredith Lee. Chief historian SAC, Washington, 1946-47; pub. relations exec. N.W. Ayer & Son, N.Y.C., 1948; dir. community program devel. Nat. Assn. Mfrs., 1949-53; dir. pub. relations Carpet Inst., N.Y.C., 1954; dir. press relations Pan Am. Coffee Bur., N.Y., 1955-58; dir. advt. pub. relations Sugar Info. Inc., N.Y.C., 1958-60; dir. Hat Council, N.Y.C., 1960-62; dir. pub. relations Grocery Mfrs. of Am. Inc., N.Y.C., 1963-70; exec. v.p. Nat. Assn. of Credit Mgmt., N.Y.C., 1970—; v.p. Credit Research Found., Lake Success, N.Y., 1972—. Served with USAAF, 1942-46. Mem. Am. Soc. Assn. Execs., Pub. Relations Soc. Am., Sales Execs. Club N.Y., Comml. Law League Am., Internat. Platform Assn., U.S. C. of C. Club: Empire State. Editorial bd. Credit Manual of Comml. Laws, 1971—. Home: 151 Frog Town Rd New Canaan CT 06840 Office: 475 Park Ave South New York City NY 10016

GOODWIN, ROGER EUGENE, architect, engr.; b. Medina, N.Y.; s. Henry H. and Nellie (Thorpe) G.; B.S. in Civil Engring., U. Mich., 1943; postgrad. Bklyn. Inst. Design and Constrn., 1958-59; m. Catherine Reid; children—Carol, Harry, Mark, Philip. Pres., Roger E. Goodwin, Inc., Westwood, N.J.; dir. Atlantic Fin. Corp. Dir. Bergen-Passaic Health Systems Agy. Named Engr. of Year Bergen Soc. Profl. Engrs., 1969. Mem. Nat. (past dir.), N.J. (past dir.), Bergen County (past pres.) socs. profl. engrs., AIA (dir. chpt.), N.J. Soc. Am. Registered Architects (past pres.). Home: 19 Bedford Rd Woodcliff Lake NJ 07675 Office: 126 Fairview Ave Westwood NJ 07675

GOOR, DAN, digital equipment co. exec.; b. Palestine, Jan. 16, 1933; s. Amihud Y. and Shifra (Smilansky) G.; came to U.S., 1951, naturalized, 1958; B.S. in Physics, Colo. State U., 1955; student Sr. Exec. Program, Mass. Inst. Tech., 1969; D.Math., Hebrew U., 1961; A.M., Tufts U., 1973, Ph.D., 1975; m. E. Patricia Robison, Aug. 28, 1953; children—YaDean Asaf Grant, Diana Lynn, Elizabeth Rena, Jacqueline, Sharon Patricia. Project engr., heavy mil. electronics dept. Gen. Electric, Syracuse, N.Y., 1959-63; gen. mgr. advanced components and comml. systems Lab. for Electronics, Inc., Waltham, Mass., 1963-67; pres. Goor Assos., Inc., Lincoln, Mass., 1967-74; mem. faculty Tufts U. Engring Sch., 1973-74; dist. mgr. tech. assessment, mem. corp. research and advanced devel. com. Digital Equipment Corp., Maynard, Mass., 1974-77, tech. assessment mgr. digital equipment, 1977—; cons. in field. Certified mfg. engr. Mem. Iran/Am. C. of C., Nat. Soc. Profl. Engrs., IEEE, N.Y. Acad. Scis., Soc. Automotive Engrs., Am. Inst. Aeros. and Astronautics, Computer Soc. India, Brit. Inst. Mgmt. Jewish. Club: Jewish War Vets. U.S.A. Patentee in field. Home: Box 224 Lincoln MA 01773 Office: Digital Equipment Corp 146 Main St Maynard MA 01754

GOOS, ROGER DELMON, mycologist; b. Beaman, Iowa, Oct. 29, 1924; s. Gus and Georgiana Bertha (Witt) G.; B.A., U. Iowa, 1950, M.S., 1955, Ph.D., 1958; m. Mary Lee Engel, Sept. 21, 1946; children—Marinda Lee, Suzanne Maurine. Mycologist, United Fruit Co., Norwood, Mass., 1958-62; scientist USPHS, NIH, Bethesda, Md., 1962-64; curator of fungi Am. Type Culture Collection, Rockville, Md., 1964-68; asso. researcher, vis. asso. prof. botany U. Hawaii, Honolulu, 1968-70; asso. prof. botany U. R.I., Kingston, 1970-72, prof., chmn. dept. botany, 1972—. Served with U.S. Army, 1944-46, 50-51. Decorated Bronze Star, Purple Heart. Mem. AAAS, Mycol. Soc. Am., Bot. Soc. Am., Am. Soc. Microbiology, Am. Phytopath. Soc., Mycol. Soc. Japan, Brit. Mycol. Soc., Mycol. Soc. India. Home: 4 Tanglewood Trail Narragansett RI 02882 Office: Dept Botany U RI Kingston RI 02881

GOOTZEIT, JACK MICHAEL, assn. exec.; b. N.Y.C., Sept. 27, 1924; s. Morris and Pauline (Genn) G.; B.S. in Phys. Therapy, N.Y. U., 1955, M.A. in Psychology, 1956, Ed.D., 1963; m. Rose Weiss, Mar. 21, 1948; children—Sholom Martin, Elias Steven. Research asst. N.Y. U. Sch. Edn., N.Y.C., 1954; phys. therapy adviser Vis. Nurse Service N.Y., 1957-58; asso. dir. sheltered workshop and tng. center Westchester Assn. for Retarded Children, White Plains, N.Y., 1958-65; dir. habilitation services N.Y.C. Assn. for Help Retarded Children, 1959-67; exec. dir. Insts. Applied Human Dynamics, Bronx, N.Y., 1966—, St. Jude Habilitation Inst., 1966—. Cons. Chapman & Garber, architects for state schs. for retarded, 1965-66; cons. N.Y. State Dept. Mental Hygiene; Bronx chpt. Assn. Brain Injured Children, 1965-66; cons. psychologist Operation Headstart, Ringwood, N.J., 1967; adj. asso. prof. Hunter Coll., 1968-76. Instr. water safety A.R.C., 1941—, staff instr. rehab. swimming, 1950—. Served with AUS, 1942-45; MTO. Decorated Bronze Star, Purple Heart. Fellow Am. Assn. on Mental Deficiency, Am. Soc. Group Psychotherapy and Psychoanalysis; mem. Am. Psychol. Assn., Rehab. Counseling Assn., Am. Phys. Therapy Assn., Am. Acad. Psychotherapy, AAAS, N.Y. Acad. Scis. Author books: Situational Diagnosis and Therapy, 1960; Handbook on Personal Adjustment Training, 1965; Effecting Communication and Interaction in the Mentally Retarded; The Development of Behavior and Its Modification, 1975. Contbr. articles to mags. Home: 120-31 DeKrulf Pl Bronx NY 10475 Office: 3625 Bainbridge Ave Bronx NY 10467 also 26 Legion Dr Valhalla NY

GORCICA, LOUIS HENRY, mgmt. exec.; b. Passaic, N.J., Feb. 26, 1927; s. Louis and Lena (Blandine) G.; B.A.B.A., William Paterson Coll., 1979; m. Mary Alice Wyble, Oct. 20, 1973; 1 son, David Louis. Design engr. Designer's Inc., Totowa, N.J., 1971-72; mgr. engring. services Sweda Internat., N.J., 1972—. Pres. John F. Kennedy Democratic Club, 1972-76; pres. Elm Assn., Paterson, N.J., 1971; mem. bd. elections Passaic County (N.J.) Dem. Party, 1965-76, exec. bd., 1975-76; mem. Center for Study of Presidency, N.Y.C., 1975-76; co-chmn. Bicentennial Ball of Hawthorne (N.J.), 1976. Served with USNR, 1945-46. Mem. Am. Mktg. Assn., SBA Active Corps Execs. Republican. Presbyterian. Home: 167 Passaic Ave Hawthorne NJ 07506 Office: 34 Maple Ave Pinebrook NJ 07058

GORDON, ALAN RICHARD, psychotherapist; b. Chgo., Oct. 14, 1948; s. Morris G. and Goldie G.; A.B., Washington U., St. Louis, 1971; M.A., New Sch. for Social Research, 1974; certified in behavior therapy Temple U. Sch. Medicine, 1974. Intern in counselling and work rehab. Postgrad. Center for Mental Health, 1972-73; pvt. practice individual and family psychotherapy, N.Y.C., 1974—; founder, dir. Stress Workshop, N.Y.C., 1977—; instr. New Sch. Social Research, 1978; cons. N.Y. Met. Mental Hygiene Dept. Mem. Am. Personnel and Guidance Assn., Assn. for Counselor Edn. and Supervision. Author: The Stress Workshop Book: Taking Care of Yourself Emotionally, 1978. Office: 39 Fifth Ave Suite 1A New York NY 10003

GORDON, BARON JACK, stock broker; s. George M. and Rose (Salsbury) G.; B.S., Lynchburg Coll., 1953; m. Ellin Bachrach, Aug. 20, 1954; children—Jonathan Ross, Rose Patricia, Alison. Vice pres. Consol. Ins. Agy., Norfolk, 1948-55; asst. treas. Henry Montor Assos., Inc., N.Y.C., 1956; v.p., sec. Propp & Co., Inc., N.Y.C., 1957-58; partner Koerner, Gordon & Co., N.Y.C., 1959-62; sr. partner Gordon, Kulman Perry (and predecessor firm), N.Y.C., 1962-71, pres., chmn. bd., 1971-74; pres., chmn. bd. Palison, Inc., mems. N.Y. Stock Exchange, N.Y.C., 1974—. Mem. Harrison (N.Y.) Archtl. Rev. Bd., 1970-72, Harrison Planning Bd., 1975—. Served to lt. USNR, in U.S.S. Midway, 1953-55. Mem. U.S. Naval Acad. Alumni Assn. (life). Clubs: N.Y. Stock Exchange Luncheon; Poinciana (Palm Beach, Fla.). Home: Westchester Ave Purchase NY 10577 Office: 5 Corporate Park Dr White Plains NY 10604

GORDON, CHARLES EDWARD, II, bank exec.; b. Waynesboro, Va., July 2, 1939; s. Charles Edward and Frances Alise (Mann) G.; student U. Va., 1957; B.S.C. cum laude, Ohio U., 1961; m. Leslie Ann McCulla, Nov. 11, 1967. Investment analyst Standard Oil Co. of Ind., Chgo., 1966-68; stock mkt. analyst Investors Diversified Services, Mpls., 1968-70; investment statis. analyst Capital Mgmt. Systems, Mpls., 1970-71; investment research officer Pitts. Nat. Bank, 1971-72; sr. investment mgr. Indsl. Valley Bank and Trust Co., Jenkintown, Pa., 1972—, also dir. investment research and strategy; instr. investment research and analysis Pa. Bankers Assn. also trust tng. sch. Bucknell U. Served with USAF, 1962-66. Chartered fin. analyst. Mem. Inst. Chartered Fin. Analysts, Fin. Analysts of Phila., Found. for Study of Cycles, Market Technicians Assn. N.Y., Phila. Options Soc. Republican. Presbyterian. Club: Huntingdon Valley Country. Home: 2355 Willowbrook Dr Huntingdon Valley PA 19006 Office: York Rd and West Ave Jenkintown PA 19046

GORDON, GERALD, metal castings co. exec.; b. Woodhaven, N.Y., Dec. 10, 1927; s. Louis and Ida (Kanofsky) G.; B.S., N.Y. U., 1949; m. Marlene Rabinowitz, Apr. 6, 1952; children—Melanie, Amy, Robert. With Grayson Robinson Stores, N.Y.C., 1949-50; sales mgr. Aluminum Co. Am., Bklyn., 1950-52; v.p. Accurate Casting Co. Inc., N.Y.C., 1952—. Mem. adv. com. Baldwin (N.Y.) Adult Edn., 1970-72. Trustee South Baldwin Jewish Center, 1966-70, sec., 1969-70. Republican committeeman Nassau County (N.Y.), 1966-69. Served with Signal Corps AUS, 1946-47. Mem. Plastic and Metal Mfrs. Assn. (dir. 1969-73) Jewish War Vets., N.Y. U. Alumni, Alpha Epsilon Pi. Mason; mem. B'nai B'rith.

GORDON, HAROLD, book pub. co. exec.; b. Bklyn., Oct. 24, 1926; s. Herman and Beatrice (Posner) G.; B.B.A. cum laude, City U. N.Y., 1956, M.B.A., 1964; m. Madeline R. Tragerman, Apr. 1, 1958; 1 son, Scott Jay. Mgr. accounts receivable Pocket Books Inc., N.Y.C., 1956-60, credit mgr., 1960-65; v.p. Affiliated Publishers Inc., N.Y.C., 1966-67; divisional v.p. Simon & Schuster Inc., N.Y.C., 1967-71, corporate v.p., 1971—, also dir.; pres. Total Warehouse Services Corp., Bristol, Pa., 1976—, also dir. Served with USAAF, 1945-46. Mem. Beta Gamma Sigma. Home: 35 Seacoast Terr Brooklyn NY 11235 Office: 1230 Ave Americas New York City NY 10020

GORDON, HARRY WILLIAM, research co. exec.; b. N.Y.C., Mar. 31, 1924; s. Abraham and Elsie (Cheskin) G.; B.S., L.I. U., 1948; Ph.D. (Teaching fellow), Georgetown U., 1952; m. Rosalind Weinberg, Jan. 22, 1950; 1 dau., Bebe Gail. Dir. exptl. research St. Barnabas Med. Center, Livingston, N.J., 1959-62; v.p., dir., sci. dir. Julius Schmid, Inc., N.Y.C., 1962-76; v.p., sci. dir. Del Labs, Inc., Farmingdale, N.Y., 1976—. Served with AUS, 1943-46. Fellow A.A.A.S.; mem. N.Y. Acad. Scis., Am. Pharm. Assn., Am. Chem. Soc., Soc. Food and Drug Ofcls., Sigma Xi. Contbr. articles to profl. jours. Patentee in field. Home: 210 E 181st St New York City NY 10457 Office: Del Laboratories 565 Broad Hollow Rd Farmingdale NY 11735

GORDON, HENRY ROBERT, mech. engr.; b. Boston, June 7, 1920; s. Samuel Joseph and Frances (Gottlieb) G.; B.A. E., N.Y.U., 1941; M.Mgmt. Sci., Stevens Inst. Tech., 1976; m. Marilyn Jacobus, Dec. 1, 1945; children—Nancy Fern, Jane Robin. Draftsman, Republic Aviation Co., Farmingdale, N.Y., 1946-47; project engr. REF Dynamics, Mineola, N.Y., 1948-56, plant engr., 1957-61; plant mgr. Asso. Mfg. Co., Bklyn., 1961-62, Q-Line Instrument Co., Moonachie, N.J., 1962-65; prodn. mgr. Blickman, Inc., Weehawken, N.J., 1965-66; nuclear mech. engr. Picatinny Arsenal, Dover, N.J., 1967-69, commodity mgr., 1969-71, Pershing missile warhead project engr., 1971-75; phys. scientist U.S. Army Armament Research and Devel. Command, Dover, 1976—. Trustee Barnert Temple, Paterson, N.J., 1970-76, past chmn. religious sch. Served as maj. C.E., U.S. Army, 1941-46. Registered profl. engr., N.Y., N.J. Mem. Am. Def. Preparedness Assn., Profl. Engrs. in Govt., Nat., N.J. (past chmn., Distinguished Service award 1973), Bergen County (pres. 1969-70, Distinguished Engr. award 1970) socs. profl. engrs., No. N.J. Round Dance Leaders Council, Internat. Brotherhood Magicians, No. N.J. Contract Bridge League, Am. Radio Relay League, Sigma Xi (chpt. sec. 1976-77). Republican. Club: Ridgewood Radio Amateur. Home: 123 Fairmount Ave Glen Rock NJ 07452 Office: Program Mgmt Support Office Bldg 151 US Army Armament Research and Devel Command Dover NJ 07801

GORDON, JOE ROBERT, state ofcl.; b. Hartford, Conn., Dec. 27, 1923; s. William and Sophie (Singer) G.; student U. Okla., 1943-44, U. Heidelberg (Germany), 1945; B.S., U. Conn., 1950, M.S., 1953; postgrad. U. Nev., 1957-58; m. Beatrice Miller, Sept. 24, 1948; children—LeAnn Estar, David Arnold. Tchr. math. and sci. Burr Jr. High Sch., Hartford, 1950-54; tchr. math. Weaver High Sch., Hartford, 1954-55, counselor, 1955-57, chmn. guidance dept., 1957-65; guidance dir. City of Hartford, 1965-67; Conn. dir. New Eng. Assessment Project, 1967-69; asst. bur. chief Conn. Bur. Pupil Personnel and Spl. Ednl. Services, Hartford, 1969-73, bur. chief, 1973-75, asso. commr. adminstrv. services, 1975—; project dir. Sch. Fin. Adv. Panel. Adj. faculty measurement and evaluation U. Hartford, 1959—; pres. Hartford Fedn. Tchrs., 1960-62; adj. faculty Central Conn. State Coll., New Britain, 1969-71. Pres., Temple Sinai, Newington, Conn., 1962-63. Served with AUS, 1943-46. Recipient award New Eng. Assn. Pub. Adminstrs., 1975. Mem. Am. Personnel and Guidance Assn. (Conn. senator 1970), Conn. Personnel and Guidance Assn. (pres. 1968-69, Distinguished Service award 1972), Measurement and Evaluation in Guidance, Nat. Council Measurement in Edn., Phi Delta Kappa (program chmn. 1970-71). Author: (with others) A New England Survey of Reading Programs, 1969; (with others) A Five Year Plan for Special Education, 1973. Contbr. articles to profl. jours. Home: 53 Dalewood Rd Newington CT 06111 Office: PO Box 2219 Hartford CT 06115

GORDON, JOY L., art mus. adminstr.; b. N.Y.C., Jan. 31, 1933; d. Charles and Silva Lazar; B.A., N.Y. U., 1957, M.A., 1972; 1 son, Andrew James. Mem. promotion dept. Vogue mag., Conde Nast Publs., 1958-68; curator N.Y. U. Art Collection, 1970-77; acting dir., curator Grey Art Gallery, N.Y.C., 1974-77; dir. Danforth Mus., Framingham, Mass., 1977—; adj. prof. N.Y. U., Framingham State Coll. Mem. Am. Assn. Museums, Internat. Council Museums, Coll. Art Assn., AAUW, Bus. and Profl. Women's Orgn. Home: 1500 Worcester Rd Framingham MA 01701

GORDON, KENNETH PHILIP, hosp. exec.; b. Bronx, N.Y., June 7, 1937; s. Alphonse Benedict and Florence Helen Gentile; B.S. in Cardiopulomnary Tech./Respiratory Therapy, State U.N.Y., Stony Brook, 1972; M.Profl. Studies and Health Care Adminstrn., C.W. Post Center, L.I. U., 1976; m. Dorine Nina Apsel, Aug. 10, 1968; children—Felicia Stacey, David Laurence. Dir. respiratory therapy Peninsula Hosp. Center, Far Rockaway, N.Y., 1963-75, dir. ambulatory services, asst. adminstr., 1975—; asst. prof. dept. health techs. Borough of Manhattan Community Coll., N.Y.C., 1967-75; asst. prof., chmn. respiratory therapy dept. Eugenio Mario De Hostos Community Coll., Bronx, 1975-77. Served with USAF, 1955-58. Mem. Hosp. Execs. Club, Am. Assn. Respiratory Therapy, N.Y. State (pres.), Southeastern Chpt. (pres.) socs. for respiratory therapy, Nat. Soc. Cardio Pulmonary Tech., Nat. Bd. Respiratory Therapy (oral registry examiner). Home: 38 Cedarhurst Ave Cedarhurst NY 11561 Office: 51-15 Beach Channel Dr Far Rockaway NY 11691

GORDON, LOIS GOLDFEIN (MRS. ALAN LEE GORDON), educator; b. Englewood, N.J., Nov. 13, 1938; d. Irving David and Betty (Davis) Goldfein; B.A. (Nat. Merit supplementary scholar, Barbour scholar), U. Mich., 1960; postgrad., Columbia, 1960-61; M.A., U. Wis., 1962, Ph.D. (Dissertation Completion fellow), 1966; m. Alan Lee Gordon, Nov. 13, 1961; 1 son, Robert Michael. Teaching asst. U. Wis., 1962-64; lectr. Coll. City N.Y., 1964-66; asst. prof. U. Mo., Kansas City, 1966-68; asst. prof. English, Fairleigh Dickinson U., Teaneck, N.J., 1968-71, asso. prof., 1971-75, prof., 1975—; cons. U. Mo. Press, 1968-69, Prentice Hall, Kennikat Press. Research grantee U. Mo., 1968. Mem. Internat. Bach Soc., Nat. Assn. Psychoanalytic Criticism (exec. com.), Modern Lang. Assn., Internat. League Human Rights. Jewish. Author: Stratagems to Uncover Nakedness: The Dramas of Harold Pinter, 1969. Asst. editor Lit. and Psychology, 1968-71, bd. adv. editors, 1974—. Contbr. articles to profl. jours. Home: 300 Central Park W New York City NY 10024 Office: Dept English Fairleigh Dickinson U Teaneck NJ 07666

GORDON, MARION C., sch. counselor; b. Bronx, N.Y., Mar. 17, 1926; d. Abraham and Fannie (Momat) Cohen; B.A., Am. Internat. Coll., 1947; M.A. (fellow), Boston U., 1950; children—Lisa, Joshua, James. Asst. curator jr. dept. Mus. Nat. History, Springfield, Mass., 1950-52; tchr. Homer Elementary Sch., Springfield, 1952-55; resident in psychodrama and group psychotherapy St. Elizabeth's Hosp., Washington, 1965; counselor, dept. chmn. Kramer Jr. High Sch., 1966-72; counselor, dept. chmn. H.D. Woodson Sr. High Sch., 1972—; instr. Washington Sat. Coll., 1977; lectr. D.C. Tchrs. Coll., 1970-71; cons. in field; pvt. practice in family, marriage, child and adolescent counselling. Vice pres. adv. bd. B'nai B'rith Career and Counseling Services, 1973—; mem. adult edn. com. Washington Hebrew Congregation, 1972—. Mem. Am., Nat. Capital (mem. exec. bd. 1974-75) personnel and guidance assns., D.C., Am. sch. counselors assns., Nat. Vocat. Guidance Assn., N.Am. Soc. Adlerian Psychology, Individual Psychology Assn. Greater Washington, Internat. Transactional Analysis Assn., Nat. Assn. Coll. Admissions Counselors, Smithsonian Assos., Psi Chi, Phi Delta Kappa. Democrat. Jewish. Home: 1301 Delaware Ave SW Apt N-801 Washington DC 20024 Office: H D Woodson High Sch 55th and Eads St NE Washington DC 20019

GORDON, MARTIN ELI, physician; b. Kiev, Aug. 15, 1921; s. Isadore and Belle (Smolens) G.; B.S., Kent State U., 1943; M.D., Yale, 1946; m. Evelyn Shukovsky, Mar. 17, 1946; children—Jeffrey Ivan, Judy Iris. Intern rotating U. Chgo. Clinics, 1946-47; jr. to chief resident in medicine VA Hosp., Newington, Conn., 1949-52; clin. instr. medicine Yale, 1951-57, asst. clin. prof. medicine, 1957-67, asso. clin. prof. Sch. Medicine, 1967—, cons. dept. univ. health; chief gastroenterology West Haven VA Hosp., 1953-54, now attending physician; lectr. in medicine U. Conn. Health Center; cons. gastroenterologist Meriden (Conn.) Hosp., Middlesex Meml. Hosp., Middletown, Conn., Griffin Hosp., Darby, Conn., Milford Hosp., Waterbury (Conn.) Hosp.; attending physician Yale Med Center, Hosp. St. Raphael; lectr. Rocky Hill VA Hosp. Pres., Med Films, Inc. Served with USPHS, 1947-49. Diplomate Am. Bd. Internal Medicine (recertified 1974), Nat. Bd. Med. Examiners. Fellow A.C.P. (audio-visual com.); asso. fellow Pierson Coll. Yale; mem. Am. Fedn. for Clin. Research, Am. Soc. for Gastrointestinal Endoscopy (chmn. history endoscopy com.), Am. Gastroent. Assn. (exhibits com.), Conn. Soc. Bd. Internists, N.Y. Acad. Sci., Conn. Med. Soc. (past chmn. postgrad. Med. com.), New Haven Med Assn. (com. on hosp.-community-physician relations), Univ. Film Producers Assn., Biol. Photog. Soc., Beaumont Med. Soc. (past sec.-treas.), Am. Soc. Parasitologists, Am. Soc. Tropical Medicine and Hygiene, Sigma Xi. Home: 34 Linsley Lake Rd North Branford CT 06471 Office: 111 Sherman Ave New Haven CT 06511

GORDON, MARVIN, wholesale liquor co. exec.; b. Cambridge, Mass., Sept. 26, 1936; s. Morris Joseph and Anna (Shoolman) G.; A.B. magna cum laude, Harvard U., 1958, M.B.A., 1960; m. Andrea Naomi Gargill, July 3, 1960; children—Pamela, Jessica, Melissa, Susannah. Exec. asst. J. Henry Schroder Banking Corp., N.Y.C., 1960-62; asst. gen. mgr. Whitehall Co., Ltd., Allston, Mass., 1962-65, gen. mgr., 1965—, treas., 1972-75, chmn. bd., 1975—; v.p., dir. Milton (Mass.) Bank and Trust Co., 1972-77, chmn. bd., 1974-77; pres. Ocean State Beverage Co., Providence; treas. Crown Distbrs., Inc., Boston, 1970—, New Eng. Liquor Sales Co., Holyoke, Mass., 1973—. Chmn. for Milton Bay United Fund, 1970; vice chmn. Milton Human Rights Fellowship, 1969-70; chmn. Milton Govt. Study Com., 1969-72; mem. Town of Milton Warrant Com., 1973-76, chmn. phy. edn. study com., 1976—; trustee Blue Hill Montessori Sch., Canton, Mass., treas., 1973-77; pres. Housing Opportunities Milton Elderly, Inc., 1978—. Mem. Milton Jr. C. of C. (pres. 1970-71), Quincy Power Squadron. Democrat. Clubs: Milton Town, Milton Hoosic, Milton Yacht, Blue Water Sailing, Megansett Yacht (Falmouth, Mass.); Harvard of Boston. Home: 163 Gun Hill St Milton MA 02186 Office: 120 Ashford St Allston MA 02134

GORDON, MAURICE BEAR, physician, med. historian and philanthropist; b. Phila., July 8, 1916; s. Benjamin Lee and Dorothy (Cohen) G.; B.A., U. Pa., 1936; M.D., Hahnemann Med. Coll., 1940; m. Muriel Hoffman, Feb. 16, 1939; children—Benjamin Lee II, Susan Joan. Resident physician Atlantic City Hosp., 1940-41; practice medicine, specializing in internal medicine, Ventnor, N.J., 1941-76. Fellow Royal Soc. Health; mem. AMA, N.J., Atlantic County med. socs., World, Aerospace, Civil Aviation med. assns., Am. Assn. History Medicine, Nutrition Today Soc. (charter). Author: Aesculapius Comes to the Colonies: The Early Days of Medicine in the Thirteen Original Colonies, 1949, reprinted, 1970; Naval and Maritime Medicine during the American Revolution, 1978; contbr. to Naval Documents of the American Revolution, Vol. 6, 1973; also articles to med. and hist. jours., with emphasis on thyroid function and alcoholism. Originator The Gordon Medical Scholarship Program; donor The Dorothy Gordon Meml. Lecture; The Dr. Benjamin Lee and Dorothy Gordon Meml. Scholarship. Home: 6917 Atlantic Ave Ventnor NJ 08406 Office: 6917 Atlantic Ave Ventnor NJ 08406

GORDON, MILDRED HARRIET GROSS (MRS. IVAN H. GORDON), hosp. exec.; b. Phila., Mar. 13, 1934; d. Nathan and Kate (Segal) Gross; student U. Pa., 1952-56; B.S., Kutztown (Pa.) State Coll., 1960; M.S. (Falk Found. fellow), Med. Coll. Pa., 1970, Ph.D. in Psychiatry (fellow), 1972; m. Ivan H. Gordon, June 13, 1954; 1 dau., Radene Lara. Tchr. sci. pub. schs., 1961-66; with Family Guidance Center, 1966-70; dir. dept. psychiatry Mental Health Treatement Center, Reading Hosp., West Reading, 1972—; clin. asst. prof. dept. psychiatry Temple U. Med. Sch. Clin. instr. dept. psychiatry Med. Coll. Pa., Phila., 1972—; mem. Pa. Gov.'s Council on Drug and Alcohol Abuse, 1972—. Bd. dirs. Confront, 1971-73, Council on Chem. Abuse, 1971-73. Mem. Am. Psychol Assn. Home: 1850 Oak Ln Reading PA 19604 Office: Reading Hospital K Bldg West Reading PA 19603

GORDON, MONTE JEFFREY, investment counselor; b. N.Y.C., Aug. 19, 1923; s. Louis A. and Geraldine (Halpern) G.; B.A., Bklyn. Coll., 1947; M.A., Columbia, 1948, N.Y.U., 1955; m. Arline Bobrick, Mar. 23, 1946; children—Dale Gordon Bell, Margery Gordon Winters. Statis. clk., research dept. Bache & Co., Inc., N.Y.C., 1948-52, asst. mgr., 1952-54, mgr., 1954-64, gen. partner, 1964-65, v.p., 1965-66, first v.p., 1966-69, sr. v.p., 1969-72, chmn. investment policy com., 1971-72, bd. dirs., 1965-72; sr. gen. partner Sartorius & Co., 1972; v.p., dir. research Dreyfus Corp., 1972—. Bd. dirs. N.Y.C. council on econ. edn., Bklyn. Coll. Alumni Fund. Served with USAAF, 1943-45. Mem. Am. Econ. Assn., Acad. Polit. and Soc. Sci., Am. Polit. Acad., N.Y. Soc. Security Analysts (chmn. press com. 1970-72, chmn. relocation com., dir. 1973-75, v.p. 1975-76), Money Marketeers (gov. 1972-75, v.p. 1975-77, pres. 1977-78). Office: 767 Fifth Ave New York City NY 10022

GORDON, PHILIP CYRIL, mfg. co. exec.; b. Balt., Nov. 7, 1928; s. John Lloyd and Dorothy (Barton) G.; A.A., Balt. Jr. Coll., 1950; B.A., Balt. Coll. Commerce, 1952; m. Mae Bernice Kent, Apr. 19, 1952; 1 son, Philip Cyril. With ASARCO, Inc., 1950—, sr. accountant comptroller's staff, N.Y.C., 1959-62, pension adminstr., 1963-74, mgr. benefit planning and devel., 1975—. Served with U.S. ArmY, 1946-48. Mem. Assn. Pvt. Pension and Welfare Plans, Md. Assn. C.P.A.s', Council Employee Benefits, Am. Soc. Personnel Adminstrn. Democrat. Roman Catholic. Club: K.C. Home: 700 Victory Blvd Staten Island NY 10301 Office: 120 Broadway New York City NY 10005

GORDON, ROBERT ALAN, psychologist; b. Charleston, W.Va., Mar. 13, 1947; s. David Leonard and Esther Libby (Shapiro) G.; B.A. in Psychology, Duquesne U., 1969; M.Ed., Springfield (Mass.) Coll., 1971, certificate of advanced grad. study in clin. counseling, 1971; m. Hilarie Mae Seder, Dec. 23, 1971; 1 son, Shawn Isaac. Staff psychologist Rehab. and Indsl. Tng. Center of York County (Pa.), Inc., 1971—, dir. evaluation services, 1974—, project dir. work-adjustment program for moderately and severely retarded (funded Pa. Bur. Vocat. Rehab.), 1977—. Licensed psychologist, Pa.; certified in psychol. evaluation, Pa. Mem. Am. Psychol. Assn. (asso.), Psi Chi. Jewish. Contbr. articles to profl. jours. Home: 327 Maywood Rd York PA 17402

GORDON, ROY HARRIS, engring. and constrn. co. exec.; b. N.Y.C., Sept. 28, 1926; s. William and Fannie Gordon; B.M.E., Poly. Inst. Bklyn., 1946, M.M.E., 1954; m. Anita Lipschitz, Jan. 2, 1949; children—Neil S., David M., Kara L. With Ebasco Services, Inc., N.Y.C., 1946-73, v.p. projects, 1969-72, pres. Walter Kidde Constructors, Inc., subs., 1972-73; with Gibbs & Hill, Inc., N.Y.C., 1973—, sr. v.p. power and energy div., 1978—; pres. Dravo Cogeneration Co., 1978—; dir. Dravo-Gibbs & Hill, Inc. Mem. Am. Mgmt. Assn. Clubs: Midtown Tennis, Roslyn Racquet. Home: 10 Fox Hunt Ln Great Neck NY 11020 Office: 393 7th Ave New York City NY 10001

GORDON, SAMUEL, biochemist; b. N.Y.C., Feb. 7, 1917; s. Max and Sophie (Vohl) G.; B.A., N.Y. U., 1940, M.S., 1949; Ph.D., Cornell U., 1953; m. Marilyn R. Spinner, Dec. 18, 1977; children by previous marriage—Ronni Bergman, Wayne, Nancy. Chemist, Lederle Labs., Pearl River, N.Y., 1946-49, research scientist, 1953-62, group leader, 1963-73, sr. research scientist, 1973—; adj. prof. Fairleigh Dickinson U., 1956-76. Served with USN, 1944-46. USPHS research fellow, 1949-51; Abbott Labs. fellow, 1951-53. Mem. AAAS, Soc. Toxicology, Sigma Xi. Democrat. Jewish. Contbr. articles to profl. jours.; research on drug metabolism, whole body autoradiography. Home: 146 S Little Tor Rd New City NY 10956 Office: Lederle Lab Pearl River NY 10956

GORDON, SYDNEY LEWIS HOWARD, banker; b. Aldershot, Eng., Aug. 22, 1942; s. Joseph Fenton and Vera Pamela (Garrett) G.; came to U.S., 1958, naturalized, 1968; B.B.A., Hofstra U., 1969; m. Carol Grace Wakefield, July 30, 1966; children—Danielle, Kelly, Jamie. Sr. mktg. officer N.Y. Stock Exchange, 1969-73; asst. v.p. Bradford Shareholder Service Corp., N.Y.C., 1974-75; dir. Depository Trust Co., N.Y.C., 1975-78; 2d v.p. Chase Manhattan Bank, N.Y.C., 1978—; guest lectr. in field. Served with AUS, 1964-66. Mem. Am. Bankers Assn., Sales Exec. Club N.Y., Fin. Advt. and Mktg. Assn. N.Y. Republican. Episcopalian. Club: Rockville Links. Home: 497 N Long Beach Rd Rockville Centre NY 11570 Office: 1 Chase Manhattan Plaza New York City NY 10015

GORDON, WALLACE ELLWOOD, realtor, ins. agt.; b. Scranton, Pa., Oct. 24, 1929; s. Harry Morgan and Leona Louise (Eggert) G.; A.A., Keystone Jr. Coll., 1949; B.S., Susquehanna U., 1954; m. Doris C. Francovitch, Apr. 18, 1958; children—Dwight W., Bruce J. Salesman, G & G Realty Co., Scranton and Clarks Summit, Pa., 1948-68, partner, 1968—; sec. Gordon Estates Inc., Scranton, 1959—, v.p., 1970—. Choir dir. Chinchilla Methodist Ch., 1954-56, Asbury Meth. Ch., Scranton, 1956-57, Chinchilla Ch., 1965-69, Clarks Summit United Meth. Ch., 1969-74; chmn. Lackawanna Arts Festival, 1963; bd. dirs. Lackawanna Arts Council, 1964-67; bd. dirs. Community Concert Assn. Scranton, 1969—, pres., 1973-75; dir. Key Notes Mixed Chorus, 1969—, U. Scranton Singers, 1975—. Served with U.S. Army, 1950-52; ETO. Recipient William L. Connell Jr. award for Contbns. to Cultural Enrichment, 1977. Mem. Scranton, Pa., Nat. assns. realtors, Nat. Assn. Ind. Fee Appraisers, Am. Assn. Certified Appraisers (sr.), Am. Choral Dirs. Assn., Am. Legion, VFW. Club: Masons, Home: 317 Crest Dr Clarks Green PA 18411 Office: 1120 Bank Towers Scranton PA 18503

GORDON, WILLIAM HAROLD, educator; b. Tampa, Fla., July 19, 1948; s. Harold L. and Mary (Rich) G.; B.S. in Edn. and Sci., State U. of N.Y., Pittsburgh, 1970; M. in Ednl. Communications, State U. of N.Y., Albany, 1974. m. Mary Hartpence. Tchr., Lake Placid (N.Y.) Schs., 1970-74, dist. media specialist, 1975-77; communications dir. Lake George (N.Y.) High Sch., 1977—. Troop leader Plattsburgh council Boy Scouts Am., 1967-70. Mem. NEA, Lake George Tchrs. Assn., Nat. Rifle Assn. (life). Kappa Phi Kappa, Gamma Delta Epsilon (pres.) N.Y. Home: 2 Swan St Warrensburg NY 12885 Office: Communications Center Lake George High Sch Lake George NY 12845

GOREN, ARNOLD LOUIS, univ. ofcl.; b. Bklyn., Oct. 26, 1925; s. Harry A. and Anna (Spector) G.; student Bklyn. Coll., 1942, Cornell U., 1943; B.S., N.Y. U., 1947, M.A., 1948; m. Rhoda G. Goldberg, Dec. 23, 1948; L.H.D. (hon.), Canisius Coll., 1977; children—Shelley and Susan (twins). Instr., N.Y. U. Sch. Edn., 1948-55, asst. prof., 1955-59, asso. prof., 1959-64, prof., 1964—, asst. dean, 1962-65, dean, 1965-68, asst. chancellor, 1968-73, vice chancellor, 1973—. Cons. banks, labor unions, TV stas.; bd. dirs. Knickerbocker Fed. Savs. Loan Assn. Adviser N.Y. Legislature Select Com. Higher Edn., other fed. and state agys. Former v.p., gen. campaign mgr. 6th dist. N.Y.C. Democratic Com. Trustee Coll. Entrance Exam. Bd. Served with AUS, 1943-46. Mem. AAUP, Am. Assn. Univs. (council on fed. relations 1976—), Citizen's Union, Anti-Defamation League (higher edn. com.). Club: City. Home: 505 La Guardia Pl New York City NY 10012

GORFIEN, PHILIP CHARLES, med. researcher; b. N.Y.C., Dec. 15, 1929; s. Max and Sara G.; A.B., N.Y. U., 1951; postgrad. U. Utrecht (Holland), 1953; m. Nelly Smoorenburg, July 31, 1954; children—Stephen, Marilyn. Research asst. Sloan-Kettering Inst.,

N.Y.C., 1956-59; dir. nephrology labs. Maimonides Med. Center, Bklyn., 1960—. Instl. rep., scoutmaster Greater N.Y. council Boy Scouts Am., 1969-75, chmn. Jewish Scouting, S.I., 1973-74. Served with M.C., U.S. Army, 1954-56. Recipient awards Boy Scouts Am.; NIH grantee, 1964-68. Mem. Am. Chem. Soc., AAAS, N.Y. Acad. Scis., Assn. Advancement Med. Instrumentation, Am. Assn. Clin. Lab. Suprs. and Adminstrs., Soc. Applied Spectroscopy. Contbr. articles to profl. jours. Office: Maimonides Hosp 4802 10th Ave Brooklyn NY 11219

GORIN, LEONARD JOSEPH, dentist; b. N.Y.C., Dec. 16, 1917; s. Louis and Anna (Hottenstien) G.; B.A., N.Y.U., 1939, D.D.S., 1943. Clin. dir. dental service N.Y.C. Fire Dept., 1952-76; attending dentist Mt. Sinai Hosp., N.Y.C., 1965-76; chief dental research Cabrini Health Care Center, N.Y.C., 1970-76; research fellow N.Y.U. Coll. Dentistry, 1974-76; pvt. dental practice, N.Y.C., 1947—; lectr., clinician micro bio quantum physics of human tissue. Served with USPHS, 1944-47. Recipient commendation sci. contbrn. Faculte de Medicine de Paris, 1969. Knight of Malta. Fellow Royal Soc. Medicine, Royal Soc. Health, Acad. Gen. Dentistry, Collegium Internat. Oris Implantatorum, Internat. Coll. Dentists; mem. Am. Dental Assn., Assn. Mil. Surgeons, Am. Acad. Implant Dentistry, Am. Assn. Hosp. Dentists, Northeastern Soc. Periodontists, Phila. Soc. Periodontology, N. Am., Internat. assns. dental research, Spanish Soc. Stomatology (v.p.).

GORIN, ROBERT MURRAY, JR., educator; b. Mineola, N.Y., Oct. 29, 1948; s. Robert Murray and Vivian Margaret (Schleider) G.; A.B., Xavier U., 1970, M.A., 1970; postgrad. Sch. Law, St. Louis U., 1970-71, 1971—; M.S. in Edn., Hofstra U., 1974; M.A., Fordham U., 1978. Tchr. social studies Bellmore-Merrick (N.Y.) Central High Sch. Dist., 1974-77, 78—, Rockville Centre (N.Y.) Union Free Sch. Dist., 1977-78; fellow Robert A. Taft Inst. Govt., 1976. Certificate N.Y. State Edn. Dept. Mem. Am., So. hist. assns., Orgn. Am. Historians, Acad. Polit. Sci., Center for Study Presidency, Am. Heritage Soc., Soc. for History Edn., Nat., N.Y. State, L.I. councils for social studies, Inst. Society, Ethics and Life Scis., Met. Opera Guild, Civil War Round Table N.Y., Phi Alpha Theta. Republican. Roman Catholic. Home: 51 Somerset Ave Garden City NY 11530

GORKES, RICHARD EDWARD, engring. adminstr.; b. Abington, Pa., Apr. 26, 1928; s. Charles Edward and Loretta Mae (Williams) G.; B.S., Temple U., 1951; m. Janet Delores Volpe, Oct. 22, 1949; children—Richard Edward, Edward Douglas. Mgr. pricing and estimating Elco Corp., Phila., 1952-61; mgr. engring. adminstrn. RCA Corp., Moorestown, N.J., 1961—. Served with AUS, 1946-47. Mem. Am. Inst. Aeros. and Astronautics, Am. Radio Relay League (life), Airplane Owners and Pilots Assn., Delmont Radio Club (pres. 1965). Home: 1822 Brentwood Rd Abington PA 19001 Office: Bldg 101-201 RCA Moorestown NJ 08057

GORMAN, JOHN CRAVEN, ret. tobacco co. exec.; b. Bronxville, N.Y., May 15, 1917; s. Patrick Henry and Marie Louise (Craven) G.; A.B., Princeton, 1939; postgrad. Columbia, 1940. Joined Am. Tobacco Co., 1941, with subsidiary Henry Clay Bock & Co., 1941-43, v.p. subsidiary Am. Suppliers, 1958-65; pres. Cuban Land & Leaf Tobacco, Havana, Cuba, 1960-61; pres. Hatheway-Steane Corp., Hartford, Conn., 1961-73; v.p. Leaf Am. Cigar subsidiary Am. Brands, Inc. N.Y.C., 1955-78. Clubs: Princeton of New York; O'Connor's (Doolin, Ireland); Nassau (Princeton, N.J.); Lake Placid (N.Y.). Home: 2 Sutton Pl S New York City NY 10022

GORMAN, (MIKE) THOMAS FRANCIS, reporter, writer; b. N.Y.C., Dec. 7, 1913; s. Frank and Mary (Naughton) G.; A.B., N.Y.U., 1934, postgrad. 1934-36; m. Ernestine Brown, June 3, 1946 (dec. June 1958); children—Michael, Patricia. Advt., free-lance writer, 1936-41; reporter, cover gen. med. run Daily Oklahoman, 1945; writer numerous news stories and editorials in mental hosp. campaign; pioneered in establishment mental hygiene clin. in Okla., also mental hygiene orgn.; chief writer, dir. pub. hearings President's Commn. on Mental Health Needs of Nation, 1950-53; exec. dir. Nat. Com. Against Mental Illness, Washington, 1953—. Mem. Menninger Found., dir. Pub. Policy Office, Nat. Council Alcoholism, 1972—. Nat. Com. Mental Hygiene; mem. 1st U.S. Mental Health Del. to USSR, 1967; exec. bd. Okla. Com. Mental Hygiene. Served with USAAF, 1942-45. Recipient spl. Lasker award 10 outstanding young men U.S. Jr. C. of C., 1949; Edward A. Strecker Meml. medal, 1962, William C. Menninger Meml. medal, 1971, 1st Dr. Benjamin Rush award, 1976. Fellow Am. Pub. Health Assn., Am. Psychiat. Assn. (hon.), Royal Soc. Health (Eng.), N.Y. Acad. Scis.; mem. Nature Conservancy, Phi Beta Kappa. Clubs: Federal City, City Tavern, Nat. Press (award for med. writing 1972) (Washington). Author: Oklahoma Attacks its Snake Pits, 1948; Every Other Bed, 1956; Community Mental Health: The Search for Identity, 1967; co-author Impressions of Soviet Psychiatry, 1969. Contbr. articles on psychiat. subjects to mags. Home: 2501 Calvert St NW Washington DC 20008 Office: 1101 17th St NW Washington DC 20036

GORMAN, TIMOTHY JOHN, pub. relations exec.; b. Washington, Jan. 19, 1939; s. Clarence Reginald and Mary Evelyn (White) G.; B.S., U. Md., 1961; postgrad. Am. U., 1967-69; m. Mary Louise Daly, Nov. 25, 1961; children—Timothy John, Tara Kathleen, Maureen Daly. With Am. Research Bur., Beltsville, Md., 1964-66; account adminstr. West & Brady Advt., Bethesda, Md., 1966-68; v.p., prin. Adams Group Inc., Silver Spring, Md., 1968—, also dir. Served with USNR, 1961-64. Mem. Am., Washington socs. assn. execs., Pub. Relations Soc. Am., Nat. Press Club, Sigma Delta Chi. Democrat. Roman Catholic. Home: 7000 Georgia St Chevy Chase MD 20015 Office: 905 Silver Spring Ave Silver Spring MD 20910

GORMLEY, JAMES JOSEPH, clergyman, educator; b. Phila., Jan. 17, 1924; s. James Joseph and Julia Marie (Gallagher) G.; B.A., Loyola U., Chgo., 1946; Ph.L., West Baden Coll., 1948; S.T.B., S.T.L., Woodstock Coll., 1955; M.A. in History, U. Scranton, 1962; M.A. in Classics, Pa. State U., 1973. Joined S.J., 1941, ordained priest Roman Catholic Ch., 1954; vice prin. Scranton (Pa.) Prep. Sch., 1956-59; vice prin. St. Joseph's Prep. Sch., Phila., 1959-60, tchr. classics and history, 1965-72, 75—; prof. classics and history Jesuit Sem., Wernersville, Pa., 1960-65; tchr. history Georgetown Prep. Sch., Rockville, Md., 1973-75. Certified tchr. history grades 7-12, Md. Mem. Am. Hist. Assn., Hist. Soc. Pa., Pa. State Alumni Assn., Am. Cath. Hist. Soc., Am. Acad. Polit. and Social Sci. Democrat. Author: History of the University of Scranton, 1888-1942, 1962; History of St. Joseph's Preparatory School, 125 Years, 1851-1976, 1976. Home and office: Saint Joseph's Preparatory Sch 1733 Girard Ave Philadelphia PA 19130

GORROW, CHARLES RICHARD, realtor; b. Potsdam, N.Y., Sept. 11, 1933; s. Charles and Iva (Kibbie) G.; student pub. schs., Ogdensburg, N.Y.; m. Patricia Yusczyk Brusky, Oct. 19, 1974; children—Andrea Kellie, Lori Ann. Agt., Castle Real Estate Co., Buffalo, 1956-57, sales mgr., 1957-61; pres. Continental Realty Co., Buffalo, 1961—; instr. State U. N.Y. at Buffalo. Served with U.S. Army, 1953-56; Korea. Mem. Greater Buffalo Bd. Realtors (dir.), N.Y. State Assn. Realtors, Nat. Assn. Realtors. Roman Catholic. Home: 5795 S Abbott Rd Orchard Park NY 14075 Office: 2959 Genesee St Buffalo NY 14225

GOSIN, STEPHEN, surgeon; b. Phila., Sept. 9, 1938; s. Jack M. and Marcella (Richter) G.; B.A., U. Pa., 1958; M.D., Jefferson Med. Coll., 1962; m. Elaine Frances Freedman, Dec. 20, 1959; children—Jeffrey Stuart, Debra Lynn, Nancy Ruth. Intern, Jefferson Med. Coll. Hosp., Phila., 1962-63; resident in surgery Thomas Jefferson U., 1963-66, chief resident, 1966-67; practice medicine specializing in gen. surgery, trauma surgery and vascular surgery, Atlantic City, also Somers Point, N.J., 1969—; instr. surgery Thomas Jefferson U., 1957—; chief, dir. div. vascular surgery Shore Meml. Hosp., Somers Point, N.J. Vice pres. Hebrew Old Age Center, Atlantic City, 1975-76. Served with USPHS, 1967-69. Named Intern of Year, Jefferson Hosp., 1963. Diplomate Am. Bd. Surgery. Fellow A.C.S.; mem. Atlantic County Med. Soc., Phi Beta Kappa, Alpha Omega Alpha. Club: Boardwalk Toastmasters (v.p.). Contbr. articles to profl. jours. Home: 8003 Lagoon Dr Margate NJ 08402 Office: 4700 Atlantic Ave Atlantic City NJ 08401 also 10 E New York Ave Somers Point NJ 08244

GOSLEE, REBA ELENA, nurse, hosp. adminstr.; b. Salisbury, Md., Nov. 23, 1926; d. George William and Mary Ellen (Jones) Cannon; R.N. diploma Md. Gen. Hosp. Sch. Nursing, Balt., 1945; B.S. in Nursing, U. Md., 1969, M.S. in Nursing, 1975; m. Howard Irwin Goslee, Dec. 20, 1947; 1 dau., Jane LaRue Goslee MacMillan. Staff nurse Sheppard & Pratt Hosp., Towson, Md., 1947, Peninsula Gen. Hosp., Salisbury, 1948-50; staff nurse Deer's Head Hosp., 1950-56, supr., 1956-69, dir. nursing services, 1969—. Mem. Am. Nurses Assn., Md. Soc. Hosp. Nursing Service Adminstrs., U. Md. Alumni Assn., Sigma Theta Tau, Phi Kappa Phi. Home: 736 S Park Dr Salisbury MD 21801 Office: PO Box 2018 Salisbury MD 21801

GOSLINE, ANDREW JACKSON, V, hosp. data processing systems cons.; b. Clearfield, Pa., Apr. 16, 1940; s. Andrew J. and Margaret E. (Gross) G.; B.S., Ind. U. of Pa., 1962; M.M.S., Stevens Inst. Tech., 1970; postgrad. Rutgers U., 1962-64; m. Mary Leffler, Nov. 18, 1961; children—Andrew, Matthew. Mgr. ops. research Fairless Works U.S. Steel Corp., 1964-67; dir. data processing Native Textiles, 1967-73; mgr. hosp. systems System Devel. Corp., Hackensack, N.J., 1973—. Mem. Hosp. Fin. Mgmt. Assn. Home: 51 Abbott Ave Ocean Grove NJ 07756 Office: 401 Hackensack Ave Hackensack NJ 07601

GOSLINE, NORMAN ABBOT, realtor; b. Gardiner, Maine, Nov. 6, 1935; s. Arthur N. and Katherine R. (Wardsworth) G.; B.A., U. Maine, 1957; children—Lee Gosline Fairbairn, Jeffrey Crosman, Mark Abbot; m. 2d, Shirlene Heath Hoch; stepchildren—Jolene Hoch, Ellen Hoch, William K. Hoch, Jr. Pres., gen. mgr. Gosline's Dairy, Inc., Gardiner, Maine, 1957-59; realtor, Gardiner, 1959—; mem. faculty (part-time) U. Maine, Augusta, 1973—; cons. in real estate to various agys. and firms in No. New Eng. area, 1965—. Past mem. Gardiner Planning Bd. Named Outstanding Young Man, Gardiner, Maine, 1965, Realtor of the Year, Kennebec Valley Bd. Realtors, 1967. Mem. Am. Inst. of Real Estate Appraisers (dir. chpt. 1973—), Soc. of Real Estate Appraisers (pres. Maine chpt. 1975-76), Nat. (dir. 1967), Maine (pres. 1967) assns. of realtors, Kennebec Valley Bd. Realtors (pres. 1963-64). Episcopalian. Clubs: Masons, Rotary. Home: 87 W Hill Rd Gardiner ME 04345 Office: 2 Central Plaza Augusta ME 04330

GOSNELL, CHARLES FRANCIS, librarian, educator; b. Rochester, N.Y., July 7, 1909; s. James F. and Alameda (Whipple) G.; A.B., U. Rochester, 1930; B.S., Columbia U., 1932, M.S., 1937; PH.D., N.Y. U., 1943; certificate Centro de Estudios Historicos, Madrid, Spain, 1934; m. Patria Aran-Soler, Mar. 31, 1934; children—Alice, Rita; m. 2d Helen L. Kuhlman, Dec. 29, 1951; children—Marsh K., Deborah R., Susan J., Catherine F. Correspondent, Rochester (N.Y.) Democrat & Chronicle, 1927-30; asst. U. Rochester Library, 1926-31; reference asst. N.Y. Pub. Library, 1932-37; libriarian Queens Coll., 1937-45, also asso. prof.; asso. Columbia U. Sch. Library Service, 1943-47; librarian, asst. commr. edn. State of N.Y., Albany, 1945-62; dir. libraries, prof. library adminstrn. N.Y. U., 1962-74, emeritus, 1974—; chmn. bd. Public Affairs Info. Service, Inc., N.Y.C., 1976—; cons. Interamerican Devel. Bank, Ford Found., U.S. Nat. Archives and Records Service, U. Montreal, U. Brasilia; U.S. delegate Unesco, Brasil, 1951, Colombia, 1959. Trustee Skidmore Coll., 1948-68; bd. dirs. Center for Study of Presidency, 1968—. Benjamin Franklin fellow, Royal Soc. Arts, London, 1960; recipient Good Citizenship Gold medal SAR, 1949; Commdr. Order of Jacques Ignace Fresnel, Haiti, 1970; Grand Cross, Eloy Alfaro Found., 1969; Lafayette medal of Merit, 1977. Mem. ALA (past pres. adminstrn. div.), N.Y. Library Assn. (past pres.), Council of Nat. Library Assns., Nat. Fire Protection Assn., Illuminating Engring. Soc., Bibliog. Soc. Am., Philalethes Soc. Republican. Presbyterian. Clubs: Univ. (Albany); Rotary (Bklyn.); Grolier (N.Y.C.); Masons. Author: Spanish Personal Names, 1977; Obsolescence of Books, 1978; contbr. articles in field to profl. jours. Home: 11 Orchard Circle Suffern NY 10901 Office: 71 W 23d St New York NY 10010 also 11 W 40th St New York NY 10018

GOSS, PATRICIA BELLAMY, educator; b. Montreal, Que., Can., May 21, 1944; d. Clifford J. and May Glenn (Black) Bellamy; naturalized, 1966; A.B., U. Calif., Los Angeles, M.A., 1967; Ph.D., N.Y. U., 1978; m. David J. Goss, Aug. 1, 1973; 1 dau., Jennifer Suzanne. Lectr., dir. forensics, U. Calif., Los Angeles, 1967-73; instr., then asst. prof. dept. speech and theatre, Herbert Lehman Coll., U. City N.Y., N.Y.C., 1973—. Named Debate Coach of Yr., Georgetown U., 1971; recipient H.A. Wichelns Award, Speech Communication Assn., for outstanding article in Free Speech Yearbook, 1975. Mem. Speech Communication Assn., Eastern Speech Communiction Assn., Internat. Communication Assn. Democrat. Editor: Media Ecology Rev. 1975-76; contbr. articles to jours. Home: 96 Crest Dr Tarrytown NY 10591 Office: Dept Speech and Theatre Herbert Lehman Coll Bronx NY 10468

GOSSAGE, WAYNE, library adminstr.; b. Bellingham, Wash., June 13, 1926; s. Coy Dell and Sadie Fay (Campbell) G.; B.S., U. Wash., 1947, postgrad., 1947-49; M.S., Columbia, 1951, M.A., 1969; m. Grace Villella, July 3, 1950; children—Leslie Anne, Gordon. Asst. head adult services East Orange (N.J.) Pub. Library, 1951-54; head adult services Levittown (N.Y.) Pub. Library, 1954-55; dir. Warner Library, Tarrytowns, N.Y., 1956-63; asst. librarian Tchrs. Coll., Columbia, 1964-67; dir. Bank St. Coll. Edn. Library, N.Y.C., 1967—; cons. Harvard Club Library, N.Y.C., 1969-71, Scarsdale (N.Y.) Soc. Friends Library, 1972—, Child Welfare League Library/Info. Service, 1976, Columbia U. Press, 1977, Am.-Scandinavian Found., 1978, Conn. Bd. Higher Edn., 1978, Am. Psychol. Assn., 1978. Vice pres. Hist. Soc. of Tarrytowns, 1960-61, Ralph Shaw award for library lit. jury, 1975-76; trustee Harvard Library in N.Y., 1978—; mem. alumni trustee nominating com. Columbia U., 1974—. Served with USNR, 1944-46. Recipient Distinguished Community Service award of Tarrytowns, 1962; fellow Council on Library Resources, 1978—. Mem. ALA (Notable Books Council 1961-62, chmn. edn. and behavioral scis. sect. 1975-76, chmn. Wilson Indexes com. 1978—), N.Y. Library Assn. (v.p. resources and tech. services sect. 1974-75, mem. legis. com. 1974-75, pres. coll. and univ. libraries sect. 1978—), Spl. Library Assn. (chmn. social sci. div. 1975-76), Columbia U. Sch. Library Service Alumni Assn. (sec.-treas. 1974-76, pres. 1977-78), New York Library Club (council 1976—). Contbr. articles to profl. jours. Home: 382 W Clinton Ave Irvington NY 10533 Office: 610 W 112th St New York City NY 10025

GOSSE, CLARENCE L., lt. gov. N.S., urologist; b. Nfld., Can., Oct. 20, 1912; B.Sc., Dalhousie U., 1933, M.D., C.M., 1939, also LL.D. (hon.); D.C.L. (hon.), Acadia U.; m. Grace Elizabeth Carten; 3 children. Practice medicine, specializing in urology, Halifax, N.S., Can., 1945—; prof. urology Dalhousie U.; head dept. urology Victoria Gen. Hosp., Camp Hill Hosp., Halifax Infirmary; lt. gov. N.S., 1973—; dir., v.p. Atlantic Trust Co.; dir. Maritime Telegraph and Telephone Co., CJCH Radio and TV. Past pres. N.S. Human Rights Fedn.; chmn. N.S. Health Council, 1971-72; bd. govs. Dalhousie U. Served with M.C., Canadian Army, 1942-45. Decorated Knight Order of St. John Knight of Grace. Mem. N.S. (past pres.), Halifax (past pres.) med. socs., Can. Urol. Assn. (past pres.), A.C.S. (bd. govs.), Canadian Paraplegic Assn., Royal Coll. Physicians and Surgeons Can., Internat. Coll. Surgeons, Am. Urol. Assn., Can. Med. Assn. Address: Govt House Halifax NS Canada

GOSSEL, JOHN DIETRICH, physician; b. N.Y.C., July 21, 1915; s. John Dietrich and Elizabeth (Heine) G.; A.B., Columbia, 1937; D.M.D., Harvard, 1940; M.D., N.Y. Med. Coll., 1950; m. Frances Mason, Oct. 24, 1942; children—John Dietrich III, Linda Mary, James Brian. Intern oral surgery Flower and Fifth Ave. Hosps., N.Y.C., 1940-41; rotating intern Fordham Hosp., N.Y.C., 1950-51; fellow Mayo Found., 1951-54; practice medicine specializing in plastic surgery, reconstructive surgery, head and neck surgery, maxillo facial surgery, aesthetic surgery, West Englewood, N.J., 1954—; instr. plastic surgery N.Y. Med. Coll., 1955-64. Served to lt. comdr. USNR, 1941-45. Diplomate Am. Bd. Plastic Surgery. Fellow A.C.S.; mem. AMA, Am. Soc. Maxillo Facial Surgeons, Am., N.J., N.Y. Regional socs. plastic and reconstructive surgery, Pan Pacific Surg. Assn. Home: 550 Eastgate Rd HoHoKus NJ 07423 Office: 141 Ayers Ct West Englewood NJ 07666

GOSSELIN, MICHEL HECTOR, accountant, mgmt. cons.; b. Sturgeons Fall, Ont., Can., Mar. 8, 1936; s. William Alaric and Rita Marie (Janisse) G.; student Coll. St. Frederic, Drummondville, Que., Can., 1953-56; B.C.S., U. Sherbrooke (Que.), 1964, M.Commerce in Adminstrn., 1965, M.Commerce in Accounting, 1966, M.Accounting Sci., 1967; m. Pierrette Houle, July 1, 1972; children—Genevieve, Jean-Francois. With Royal Bank of Can., Montreal, Que., 1955-57; accountant Brit. Petroleum Can. Ltd., Montreal, 1957-62; auditor Cooper, Lybrand & Co., Montreal, 1967-68; partner Audet, Gosselin, Lapointe, Moreau and Assos., Chartered Accountants, Montreal, 1969—, Gosselin, Perrault, Comtois, Guerin and Assos., Mgmt. Cons., Montreal, 1970—. Mem. nat. com. Boy Scouts Can., 1962—. Recipient Gold medal Lt. Gov. of Que., 1965; named Mérite Scout, Boy Scouts Can., 1975. Mem. Order Chartered Accountants Que. (Gold medal 1967), Inst. Mgmt. Cons. Que., Certified Gen. Accountants Assn. Que., Gen. Accountants Assn. Can., Société Canadienne de Sciences Economiques, Inst. Internal Auditors. Research on accounting for non-profit orgns., 1973—. Home: 4358 Gouin Blvd E Montreal North PQ H1H 1E3 Canada

GOSSETT, OSCAR MILTON, advt. exec.; b. N.Y.C., May 27, 1925; s. Oscar Percival and Helen (Deutsch) G.; student Inst. Tech., 1943-44, 46-47, Columbia, 1947-48; m. Anna C. Schied, May 29, 1949; children—Susanne, Michael, Thomas, Lorraine, James M. With Compton Advt., Inc., 1949—, pres., 1968—, also chief exec. officer. Chmn. bus. and advt. sect. Am. Cancer Soc., N.Y.C.; chmn. council ministries United Methodist Ch., Ridgefield, Conn. Served with USNR, World War II. Mem. Am. Assn. Advt. Agencies. Inventor mobile of solar system. Home: RD 1 South Salem NY 10590 Office: 625 Madison Ave New York City NY 10022*

GOTLIEB, JERRY, urologist; b. Cin., May 10, 1939; s. David and Reba (Mandelbaum) G.; student Temple U., 1956-59; M.D., Hahnemann Med. Coll., 1963; m. Barbara Levitsky, June 17, 1962; children—Andrew, Steven, Jill. Intern, Abington (Pa.) Hosp., 1963-64; resident gen. surgery Phila. VA Hosp., 1966-67; resident in urology Hosp. U. Pa., 1967-70; practice medicine, specializing in urology Norristown, Pa., 1970—; chief urology Norristown State Hosp., 1972—; asso. Montgomery Hosp., Norristown; attending Sacred Heart Hosp., Norristown; pvt. practice medicine, specializing in urology Norristown, 1970—. Active Boy Scouts Am., Indian Guides. Served with M.C., USAF, 1964-66. Diplomate Am. Bd. Urology. Fellow A.C.S.; mem. Phila., Am., Mid-Atlantic urologic assns., Pa., Montgomery County med. socs., Sword Soc., Alpha Omega Alpha. Jewish. Home: 214 Jeffrey Ln Newtown Sq PA 19073 Office: 1313 DeKalb St Norristown PA 19401

GOTSCHE, ANTON WILLIBALD, hotel exec.; b. Vienna, Austria, June 30, 1934; s. Anton and Hedwig (Weberndorfer) G.; came to U.S., 1956, naturalized, 1965; B.S., Cornell U., 1959; M.B.A., N.Y. U., 1967, Ph.D., 1970, J.D., 1972; m. Etta Steinmeyer, May 24, 1969. Staff mgr. Food Service, Am. Airlines, N.Y.C., 1960-63; dir. inflight service TWA, N.Y.C., 1963-65; asso. prof. mgmt. Grad. Sch. Bus., L.I. U., Bklyn., 1972-73; asst. v.p. Princess Hotels Internat., N.Y.C., 1973—; instr. hotel mgmt. Cornell U., 1957-59; co-founder, cons. INTERSCIENCE, Center for Interdisciplinary Research, Inc., 1968—. Recipient Spl. Service to the Sch. award Cornell U., 1959; NDEA Title IV fellow, 1967. Mem. Acad. Mgmt., Am. Mgmt. Assn., Am. Mktg. Assn., Am. Statis. Assn., Hotel Sales Mgmt. Assn., Cornell Soc. Hotelmen, U.S. Austrian C. of C. (dir.), Beta Gamma Sigma, Mu Gamma Tau, Omicron Delta Epsilon. Democrat. Roman Catholic. Clubs: N.Y. U. Karate, Masons, Shriners. Contbr. articles to profl. jours. Home: One Sheridan Sq New York City NY 10014 Office: 1345 Ave of Americas New York City NY 10019

GOTTFRIED, BYRON STUART, educator; b. Detroit, May 24, 1934; s. Sidney and Faye (Fradkin) G.; B.S., Purdue U., 1956; M.S., U. Mich., 1958; Ph.D., Case-Western Res. U., 1962; m. Marcia Faye Singer, June 21, 1959; children—Sharon, Gail, Susan. Asso. engr. Westinghouse Electric Corp., Pitts., 1958-59, Lewis Research Center, NASA, Cleve., 1959-62; research engr. Gulf Research & Devel. Co., Pitts., 1962-65, supr., 1968-70; asst. prof. dept. mech. engring. Carnegie-Mellon U., Pitts., 1965-68; asso. prof. dept. indsl. engring. U. Pitts., 1970-75, prof., dir. energy resources program, 1975-76, prof. indsl. engring., 1975—; cons. U.S. Dept. Interior Bur. Mines, Dept. Energy. Served with Signal Corps, AUS, 1958. Mem. Am. Inst. Chem. Engrs., Am. Inst. Indsl. Engrs., Ops. Research Soc. Am. Author: (with Joel Weisman) Introduction to Optimization Theory, 1973; Programming with Fortran IV, 1972; Data Processing, 1974; Programming with Basic, 1975; contbr. articles to profl. jours. Home: 129 Old Suffolk Dr Monroeville PA 15146 Office: U Pitts Pittsburgh PA 15261

GOTTFRIED, EUGENE LESLIE, physician, educator; b. Passaic, N.J., Feb. 26, 1929; s. David and Rose (Chill) G.; A.B., Columbia U., 1950, M.D., 1954; m. Phyllis Swain, Aug. 16, 1957. Intern in medicine Presbyn. Hosp., N.Y.C., 1954-55, asst. resident, 1957-58; resident in medicine Bronx (N.Y.) Municipal Hosp. Center, 1958-59, fellow in medicine, 1959-60; academic medicine specializing in hematology, N.Y.C., 1960—; asst. vis. physician Bronx Municipal Hosp. Center, 1960-66; asso. vis. physician Bronx Municipal Hosp. Center, 1966-69; asst. vis. physician Lincoln Hosp., N.Y.C., 1963-69; dir. lab. of clin. hematology N.Y. Hosp., 1969—, asso. attending physician N.Y. Hosp., 1969—, pathologist, 1975—; attending physician Burke Rehab. Center, White Plains, N.Y., 1975—; asso. prof. medicine Cornell U.

Med. Coll., 1969—, asso. prof. pathology, 1975—; asst. instr. Albert Einstein Coll. Medicine, 1959-60, instr., 1960-61, asso., 1961-65, asst. prof., 1965-69; career scientist Health Research Council, City of N.Y., 1964-72. Served to lt. comdr. USN, 1955-57. Diplomate Am. Bd. Internal Medicine. Fellow A.C.P., Am., Internat. socs. hematology; mem. Am. Fedn. Clin. Research, Harvey Soc., Soc. for Study of Blood, N.Y. Lipid Research Club (chmn. 1975-76), AAAS. Editorial bd. Jour. Lipid Research, 1972-77, asso. editor, 1971-72, 75-77; research in hematology. Office: 525 E 68th St New York City NY 10021

GOTTLIEB, LESTER M., data processing co. exec.; b. N.Y.C., May 3, 1932; s. Samuel and Eva (Schoenfeld) G.; B.A., Coll. City N.Y., 1954; postgrad. N.Y. U.; m. Sarah Dean Tompkins, Dec. 4, 1967; children—Cynthia Anne, Curtis Tompkins; children by previous marriage—Mark, Alyssa, Adine. With IBM, 1956-69, mgr. bus. planning for systems devel. div., 1967-69; chmn. bd., pres., Data Dimensions, Inc., Greenwich, Conn., 1969—; adj. asst. prof. econs. U. Bridgeport (Conn.); dir. Continental Field Service Corp., 1968-75, Technicon Med. Information Systems Corp., 1974-77. Nat. lectr. Assn. Computing Machinery. Pres. Woodlands-Worthington Taxpayers Assn., 1962-68. Bd. dirs. Center for Internat. Mgmt. Studies, Nat. Bd. YMCA's, Greater N.Y. YMCA; bd. dirs. North Greenwich Assn., 1973-74. Served with AUS, 1954-56. Fellow Am. Sociol. Soc.; mem. Pres.'s Assn., Acad. Polit. Sci. Republican. Mason. Clubs: Spartan, Landmark (charter) (Stamford, (Conn.); Bailiwick (Greenwich). Editorial bd. Jour. Computer Operations, 1965-69. Home: Pierson Dr Greenwich CT 06830 Office: 51 Weaver St Greenwich CT 06830

GOTTLIEB, MICHAEL NORMAN, physician; b. Bklyn., July 26, 1943; s. Louis and Grace (Rubin) G.; B.A., State U. N.Y., Harpur Coll., 1964, M.D., Downstate Med. Center, 1968; m. Anne Shirley Appelman, Dec. 25, 1965; children—Brian Stanford, Elizabeth Nicole. Intern in medicine U. Calif., San Diego, 1968-69, resident in medicine, 1969-71, postdoctoral fellow in nephrology, 1971-72; research fellow in medicine Peter Bent Brigham Hosp., Boston, 1972-73, asso. in medicine, 1977—; research fellow in medicine Harvard Med. Sch., 1972-73, instr. medicine, 1974-77, clin. asst. prof., 1977—; sci. adv. bd. Mass. Kidney Found. Served to lt. comdr. USNR, 1973-77. NIH spl. fellow, 1972-73. Diplomate Am. Bd. Internal Medicine. Mem. Am. Soc. Nephrology, Am. Soc. Artificial Internal Organs, Alpha Omega Alpha. Contbr. articles to profl. publs. Office: 1055 Commonwealth Ave Boston MA 02215

GOTTLIEB, MORTON EDGAR, theatrical producer; b. Bklyn., May 2, 1921; s. Joseph William and Hilda (Newman) G.; B.A., Yale U., 1941. Singer charity show Go Home and Tell Your Mother, Bklyn. Acad. Music, 1928; asst. press rep. Theatre Inc., N.Y.C., 1945, bus. mgr., 1946, gen. mgr. Cape Playhouse, Dennis, Mass., 1947; gen. mgr. New Stages, N.Y.C., 1947-48; gen. mgr. Cape Playhouse, 1948, mgr. to Robert Morley during Australian prodn., Theatre Royal, Sydney, 1949; gen. mgr. Gilbert Miller Prodns. and Henry Miller's Theatre, N.Y.C., 1951-53; producer Broadway, London shows, 1954-62; gen. mgr. Sail Away, 1961, The Affair, 1962, The Hollow Crown, 1963; co-producer with Helen Bonfils Enter Laughing, 1963, The Killing of Sister George, 1966, Lovers, 1968, We Bombed in New Haven, 1968, The Mundy Scheme, 1969, Sleuth, 1970; producer film Sleuth, 1972, play Veronica's Room, 1973, Play Same Time, Next Year, 1975, film Same Time, Next Year, 1978; guest lectr. Emerson Coll., Yale U., Columbia U., Queens Coll., Wesleyan U.; treas. Friends of the Theatre and Music Collection of Mus. City of N.Y., 1966—. Mem. League N.Y. Theatres (treas.). Club: Yale (N.Y.C.). Contbr. articles to popular mags. Home: Warren CT 06754 Office: 165 W 46th St New York City NY 10036

GOTTSCHALK, JACK ALLTON, advt. agy. exec., lawyer; b. Orange, N.J., Apr. 10, 1937; s. Herman Ernest and Helen Marie (Beyer) G.; A.B., Fairleigh Dickinson U., 1961; J.D., U. Balt., 1969; m. Kathleen Mary Kubler, Feb. 4, 1972. Pub. affairs mgr. Fed. Industries, Belleville, N.J., 1957-63; asst. to v.p., Rubberset Co., E. Newark, 1963-65; staff cons. Post Assos., Essex Fells, N.J., 1965-69; v.p. Healy Dixcy & Forbes, Montclair, N.J., 1969—, dir. 1976—; pres. Mercury Mgmt. Inc., Montclair, 1976—; lectr. grad. sch. bus. Fairleigh Dickinson U., 1975-77, asso. prof., 1977—; admitted to N.J. bar, 1977. Vice chmn., treas. Livingston (N.J.) Indsl. Devel. Council. Served to capt. U.S. Army, 1970-71, served with USAR, 1971-75. Mem. Pub. Relations Soc. Am. Republican. Episcopalian. Clubs: Rock Spring Country (W. Orange, N.J.), Baronial Order of Magna Charta, Masons. Hon. Dep. Police Commr., City of Passaic (N.J.). Contbr. articles to bus. jours. Home: 12 Cross Brook Rd Livingston NJ 07039 Office: 516 Bloomfield Ave Montclair NJ 07042

GOTTSCHO, ALFRED MORTON, cigar co. exec.; b. Bklyn., Apr. 29, 1919; s. Adolph and Ray (Langer) G.; B.S., in Chem. Engring., Coll. City N.Y., 1940; M.S., Franklin and Marshall Coll., 1954; m. Reba Gordon, Apr. 27, 1941; children—Therese Gottscho Lipman, Steven, Richard. Tech. service engr. Mosstype Corp., Baldwick, N.J., 1940-41; fuel consumption study engr. Corps Engrs., Jefferson Barracks, Mo., and Ft. Belvoir, Va., 1941-42; prodn. foreman explosives Plum Brook Ordnance Works, Sandusky, Ohio, 1942-44; chem. engr. Gen. Cigar Co., Lancaster, Pa., 1946-57, asst. dir. devel., 1956-68, dir. research and devel., 1968-76, also asst. v.p., v.p., dir. research and devel. Gen. Cigar and Tobacco Co. div. Culbro Corp., 1976—. Cubmaster Lancaster County Council Boys Scouts Am., 1960-62. Served with U.S. Army, 1944-46. Decorated Bronze Star. Recipient research award, Cigar Research Council, 1973. Mem. Am. Chem. Soc., AAAS, Am. Inst. Chem. Engrs., ASTM, TAPPI, Soc. Chemistry and Industry, Phytochem. Soc. N.Am., N.Y. Acad. Scis. Jewish religion. Club: Elks. Contbr. articles to profl. jours. Patentee in field. Home: 348 Landis Ave Millersville PA 17551 Office: 602 Charlotte St Lancaster PA 17603

GOTTSEGEN, GLORIA BEHAR, psychologist; b. N.Y.C., Nov. 15, 1930; d. Marco and Flora (Salti) Behar; B.A., N.Y. U., 1950; M.A., City Coll., 1951; Ph.D., N.Y. U., 1967; m. Monroe G. Gottsegen, Apr. 14, 1951; children—Abby Jean, Paul Richard. Postgrad. fellow N.Y. Med. Coll., N.Y.C., 1957-58; remedial psychologist Jewish Child Care Assn., N.Y.C., 1958-61; psychologist Bronx (N.Y.) Consultation Center, 1961-64, supervising psychologist, 1964-68; asst. prof. psychology Hebert H. Lehman Coll., City U.N.Y., Bronx, 1968-75, asso. prof., 1975-79, prof., 1979—, chmn. dept. specialized services edn., 1976—. Pres., Sch. Psychology Educators Council N.Y. State, 1977-78. Licensed psychologist, N.Y. State. Fellow Am. Psychol. Assn. (pres. div. humanistic psychology 1976-77, sec. div. psychotherapy 1975-78); mem. N.Y. (pres. div. sch. psychology 1975-76), Eastern psychol. assns., N.Y. Acad. Scis., Am. Orthopsychiat. Assn., Am. Personnel and Guidance Assn. Editor: Professional School Psychology, Vols. I-III, 1960, 63, 69; Confrontation: Encounters in Self and Interpersonal Awareness, 1971. Asso. editor Psychotherapy: Theory, Research and Practice, 1976—. Office: Herbert H. Lehman Coll City U NY Bronx NY 10468

GOTTSHALL, FRANKLIN HENRY, author; b. Boyertown, Pa., Aug. 26, 1902; s. Frank Bauman and Hannah (Borneman) G.; diploma Indsl. Arts, Rochester Inst. Tech., 1925; student in architecture Boston Architects Club, 1926, 27; B.S., Stout State U., 1932; m. Agnes Hamrick, Aug. 15, 1928; children—Franklin Henry, Bruce Hamrick. Furniture designer The Old Am. Co., Framingham, Mass., 1926-27; tchr. indsl. arts pub. schs., West Lawn, Pa., 1932-34, Scotch Plains, N.J., 1934-39; prof. indsl. arts Martha Berry Coll., Mt. Berry, Ga., 1927-31, 1939-43, U. Fla., summers 1944, 45; tchr. Boyertown Area High Sch., 1943-67; author several books including: Simple Colonial Furniture, 1931: How to Design Period Furniture, 1937; Design for the Craftsman, 1940; (with Amanda W. Hellum) You Can Whittle and Carve, 1942; Making Useful Things of Wood, 1950; Heirloom Furniture, 1957; Wood Carving and Whittling Made Easy, 1963; Furniture of Pine, Poplar and Maple, 1966; How to Make Colonial Furniture, 1971; Reproducing Antique Furniture, 1971; Wood Carving and Whittling for Everyone, 1977. Mem. Boyertown Bd. Health, 1944—. Bd. dirs. Boyertown Area Hist. Soc., Boyertown Vis. Nurses Assn. Recipient Masters equivalent in Indsl. Arts, Pa. Dept. Pub. Instrn., 1949, appreciation certificate Boyertown Hist. Soc., 1972. Mem. Nat. Wood Carvers Assn. (Appreciation award 1971), Pa. Ret. Tchrs. Assn., Henry Lomb Soc., Phi Sigma Phi. Republican. Lutheran. Mason. Address: 604 E 4th St Boyertown PA 19512

GOUDA, GEORGE RIZKALLA, ceramic scientist; b. Cairo, May 30, 1934; s. Rizkalla Gouda and Adiba Boulous; came to U.S., 1970, naturalized, 1976; B.Sc. with honors, Cairo U., 1957; M.S., Pa. State U., 1972, Ph.D., 1975; m. Samia Sami, Sept. 27, 1959; 1 child, Hatem G. Chemist, Arabian Cement Co., Jedda, Saudi Arabia, 1958-59, asst. chief chemist, 1959-60, tech. supr., 1960-62; asst. prodn. mgr. Helwan Portland Cement Co. (Egypt), 1962-66; ofcl. del. to Algerian Govt. as expert in cement industry, mission head, Alger, Algeria, 1966-70; mgr. cement tech. Fuller Co., Catasauqua, Pa., 1975—. NSF, Battele Pacific NW grantee. Mem. ASTM, Am. Ceramic Soc., Am. Chem. Soc., Internat. Inst. Ceramic Engrs., Keramos (profl. ceramic engr.), Egyptian Profl. Sci. Soc. Contbr. articles in field of cement sci. to tech. jours. Obtained highest strength, 100,000 psi, for cement paste in world. Home: 1616 W Cedar St Allentown PA 18102 Office: PO x 29 Catasauqua PA 18032

GOUDIE, RONALD JOSEPH, govt. ofcl.; b. Hull, Que., Can., July 12, 1930; s. Bertyle Launcelot and Aldana (Rainville) G.; m. Lucille Aubin, Sept. 4, 1961; children—Elyse, Richard. Shipping clk. Renfrew Furs Ltd., Ottawa, Ont., Can., 1946-50; office clk. NRC, Ottawa, 1950-61; probation officer Social Welfare Ct., Hull, 1961-66; welfare officer Que. Govt., Hull, 1966-70; asst. ct. clk., Aylmer, Que., 1967-68; group head Welfare Office, Gatinequ, Que., 1970-71; dir. welfare office Que. Govt., 1971-76, welfare specialist, 1976—. Scout leader, commr., 1949-67; publicity agt. Gai Lurons Choir; dir. Les Monferrants, La troupe du Bonheur. Recipient decoration for meritorious service to French-Can. scouting Gov. Gen. of Can. Mem. Canadian Snowshoe Assn. (mem. exec. of internat. Snowshoe com. 1968-77, pres. 1977-78, asst. sec.), Iroquois Snowshoe Club (pres.), Que. Provincial Snowshoe Assn. (lst v.p.), Ottawa Square Dance Assn., Specialized Square Dance Clubs (dir.), Homeowner's Assn., Criminology Soc. Que., C. of C. Roman Catholic. Editor Agimag, 1960-64. Home: 44 Toulon Gatineau PQ J8T 4V6 Canada

GOUGE, SUSAN CORNELIA JONES (MRS. JOHN OSCAR GOUGE), microbiologist; b. Chgo., Apr. 18, 1924; d. Harry LeRoy and Gladys (Moon) Jones; student Am. U., Washington, 1942-43, La. Coll., 1944-45; B.S., George Washington U., 1948; postgrad. Georgetown U., 1956-58, 66-69; m. John Oscar Gouge, Aug. 7, 1943; children—John Ronald, Richard Michael, Claudia Renee (Mrs. Esequiel Carr III). Med. technician Children's Hosp. Research Lab., Washington, 1948-49; bacteriologist George Washington U. Research Lab., D.C. Gen. Hosp., 1950-53; med. microbiologist Walter Reed Army Inst. Research, Washington, 1953-61; research asst. Dental Research, Walter Reed Med. Center, 1961-62; microbiologist antibiotics div. FDA, 1962-63; supr. quality control John D. Copanos Co., Pharms., Balt., 1963-64; research tng. asst. infectious diseases and tropical medicine Howard U. Med. Sch., 1964-65; research asso. Georgetown U. Lab. Infectious Diseases, D.C. Gen. Hosp., 1966-69; mycologist Georgetown U. Hosp. Lab., 1969-70; microbiologist The Research Found. of The Washington Hosp. Center, 1971-73; dir. quality control Bio-Medium Corp., Silver Spring, Md., 1973-76; microbiologist Alcolac, Inc., Balt., 1976—. Sec. to exec. bd. Bethesda Project Awareness, 1970-71; vol. lead poisoning detection testing project, D.C. Office Vols. Internat. Tech. Assistance, 1970-71. Mem. Nat. Capital Harp Ensemble, 1941-65; mem. parish social concerns com. Roman Cath. Ch. Mem. Women's Suburban Democratic Club. Recipient medal community service; registered microbiologist Nat. Registry Microbiologists. Mem. AAAS, Am. Soc. for Microbiology, Am. Inst. Biol. Scis., Am. Chem. Soc., Albertus Magnus Guild, Capital Bus. and Profl. Women's Club (rec. sec. 1973-74, 1st v.p. 1974-75, pres. 1975-76), Pi Kappa Delta. Roman Catholic. Home: 4101 Maryland Ave Washington DC 20016 Office: DC Dept Human Resources Community Health and Hosp Adminstrn Prevention Services Dept Div Labs Microbiology Sect 300 Indiana Ave NW Washington DC 20001

GOUGH, BRUCE C., chiropractor; b. Damariscotta, Maine, Nov. 7, 1938; s. Clarence Alexander and Ruth Elizabeth (Nerborne) G.; D.Chiropractic, Palmer Coll. Chiropractic, 1973; m. Janis Caroline Weaver, Aug. 17, 1964; children—Steve, Sean, Wade. Policeman, store detective, whaling seaman, deep-sea diver, various locations, 1962-69; gen. practice chiropractic, nutritional therapy, phys. therapy, Colebrook, N.H., 1973—. Served with AUS, 1958-61. Recipient Clin. Excellence award Palmer Coll. Chiropractic, 1973. Mem. Am., N.H., Christian chiropractic assns., Council Sports Injuries, Council Roentology. Episcopalian. Home: 1 Sunset Dr Colebrook NH 03576 Office: 5 Middle St Lancaster NH 03576

GOUGH, CAROLYN HARLEY, library dir.; b. Paterson, N.J., Sept. 23, 1922; d. Frank Ellsworth and Mabel (Harrison) Harley; B.A., Coll. William and Mary, 1943; M.L.S., Drexel U., 1966; m. George Harrison Gough, Sept. 21, 1944; children—Deborah Ann Gough Bornholdt, Douglas Alan. Research asst. Young and Rubicam, Inc., N.Y.C., 1943-44; library dir., asst. prof. Cabrini Coll., Radnor, Pa., 1966—. Mem. Tredyffrin Twp. Library Resources Study Com., 1964-65. Mem. Tri-State Coll. Library Coop. (v.p. 1973-74, pres. 1974-75), Assn. Coll. and Research Libraries (dir. 1978—), Cath. Library Assn., AAUP, Beta Phi Mu. Republican. Episcopalian. Clubs: Questers, Inc. (1st nat. v.p. 1964-66), Phila. Curling, Mfrs. Golf and Country, Atlantis Golf, Kappa Delta. Home: 532 Timber Ln Devon PA 19333 Office: Cabrini College Library Radnor PA 19087

GOUIRAN, EMILE, mortgage banker; b. Washington, Mar. 14, 1945; s. Emile F. and Dema G.; baccalaureate Lycee Rodin, (France), 1965; m. Donna J. Ryan, Oct. 27, 1968; children—David, Alan, Steven. Pres., chief exec. officer Nat. Richmond Realty Services, Inc., S.I., N.Y., 1970—; pres., chief exec. officer D. Gouiran Realty Holdings, Inc., S.I., 1969—; chmn. bd., chief exec. officer Empire State Bank, S.I., 1978—; instr. Inst. Real Estate, 1969—. Licensed real estate broker, N.Y., N.J., France, Argentina; licensed ins. broker, N.Y., N.J., Mem. Randall Manor Civic Assn., Italian Am. Rep. Club, Staten Island C. of C., Nat. Profl. Real Estate Brokers Assn., N.Y.C. Home Builders Assn., N.Y. State Assn. Ins. Agts., Nat. Assn. Home Builders, Staten Island Mental Health Assn., Nat. Assn. Disabled Vets. Club: Lions. Home: Staten Island NY 10301 Office: 386 Forest Ave Staten Island NY 10301

GOULD, BURNHAM SYLVESTER, JR., real estate exec.; b. Hartford, Conn., June 9, 1932; s. Burnham Sylvester and Edith Marie (Swendsen) G.; B.A., Princeton, 1954; M.S., Mass. Inst. Tech., 1956; m. Vivian Anne Woods, Sept. 3, 1955; children—Burnham III, Eric, Dana. Indsl. research engr. Eastern Gas & Fuel Assos., Boston, 1956-59; asso. mgmt. scientist Dunlap and Assos., Stamford, Conn., 1959-62; mgr. operations planning Gen. Mills, Inc., Mpls., 1962-68; mgr. information center and operations research CPC Internat., Englewood Cliffs, N.J., 1969-74; v.p. operations Treadway Foods, Newark, 1974-75; v.p. Martin & Vaughn Assos., Woodcliff Lake, N.J., 1975—; lectr. Fairleigh Dickinson U., Teaneck, N.J., 1974—. Asst. dist. commr. Boy Scouts Am., Bergen County, N.J., 1972—. Mem. Inst. Mgmt. Scis. (mem. com. 1973—), Operations Research Soc. Am. (mem. com. 1968-71; chpt. chmn. 1967-69). Conglist. (deacon 1971-73, treas. 1976—). Home: 143 Rose Ave Woodcliff Lake NJ 07675 Office: Martin & Vaughan Assos Woodcliff Lake NJ 07675

GOULD, DONALD EVERETT, chem. co. exec.; b. Concord, N.H., May 19, 1932; s. Everett Luther and Gladys (Wilcox) G.; B.S. in Chem. Engring., U. N.H. 1954; postgrad. math. Rutgers U., 1955-59; m. Marilyn Bachelder, June 13, 1953; children—Barbara, Allen, Douglas. Devel. chem. engr. plastics div. Union Carbide Co., Bound Brook, N.J., 1954-59, tech. service engr., Bound Brook and Wayne, N.J. 1959-64, mgr. tech. service indsl. bag dept., Wayne, 1964-66, mgr. tech. services indsl. fabricated products dept. 1966-67, marketing mgr. indsl. bags, 1967-69, sr. packaging engr., 1969-72, mgr. packaging, 1972-75, mgr. distbn. safety and regulations, 1975—. Mem. Packaging Inst. (vice chmn. films, foils and laminations com. 1962-64, chmn. 1964-66, sect. leader bottle containers, vice chmn. bag com. 1973-75, chmn. 1976-78), Am. Soc. Quality Control, Alpha Chi Sigma. Club: Packanack Lake Country. Contbr. articles profl. jours., also to Ency. Engring. Materials and Processes. Home: 98 Lake Dr E Wayne NJ 07470 Office: River Rd Bound Brook NJ 08805

GOULD, HARRY EDWARD, JR., mfg. exec.; b. N.Y.C., Sept 24, 1938; s. Harry E. and Lucille (Quartucy) G.; student Oxford U., 1958; B.A. cum laude, Colgate U., 1960; postgrad. Harvard Bus. Sch., 1960-61; M.B.A., Columbia U., 1964; m. Barbara Clement Hannan, Apr. 26, 1975; children—Harry Edward, Katharine Elizabeth. Asso. in corporate fin. dept. Goldman, Sachs & Co., N.Y.C., 1961-62; exec. asst. to sr. v.p. ops. Universal Am., N.Y.C., 1964-65; sec., treas. Young Spring & Wire Corp., Detroit, 1965-67, exec. v.p., chief operating officer, 1967-69, also dir.; v.p. adminstrn. and fin. Universal Am. Corp., 1968-69; mem. exec. com., v.p., sec.-treas. Daybrook-Ottawa Corp., Bowling Green, Ohio, 1967-69; dir. mem. exec. com. Am. Med. Ins. Co., N.Y.C., 1966-74; pres., chmn., chief exec. officer, dir. Gould Paper Corp., N.Y.C., 1969—; chmn. bd., dir. Samuel Porritt & Co., East Peoria, Ill., 1969—, Computer Copies Corp., N.Y.C., 1970-73, Ingalls Mfg., Inc., Ceres, Calif., 1971—, McNair Mfg., Inc., Chico, Calif., 1972—, Hawthorne Paper Co., Kalamazoo, 1974—, Weiss Mfg., Inc., Chico, Calif., 1974—, Vrisimo Mfg., Inc., Chico, 1974—; pres., dir. Carlyle Internat. Sales Corp., N.Y.C., 1975—; ltd. partner Hardy & Co., mem. N.Y. Stock Exchange, N.Y.C., 1973-78; dir. Reinhold-Gould GmbH, Hamburg, Germany, Lewis & Gould Paper Co., Inc., Chgo. Co-chmn., Pacesetter's com. Boy Scouts Am., 1966-69; participant as U.S. Pres.'s rep. UN E.-W. Trade Devel. Commn., 1967. Mem. N.Y. Gov.'s Task Force N.Y. State Cultural Life and Arts, 1975—; pres. Harry E. Gould Found., N.Y.C., 1971—; bd. dirs. N.Y. Ophthalmol. Found. Am., Inc., 1973—, United Cerebral Palsy Research and Ednl. Found., 1976—; mem. nat. council Colgate U., 1973-76; trustee Nat. Symphony Orch., Washington, 1978—; mem. Democratic Nat. Fin. Council, 1974—, also vice chmn. exec. com., chmn. budget and audit coms.; treas. N.Y. State Dem. Com., 1976-77; bd. dirs. Nat. Multiple Sclerosis Soc., 1977—, N.Y.C. Housing Devel. Corp., 1977—; trustee Colgate U., 1976—, also chmn. maj. gifts com., 1976—, mem. budget, devel., fin. and student affairs coms. Mem. Nat. Paper Trade Assn. (dir., mem. printing com. 1973—) Paper Mchts. Assn. N.Y. (dir. 1972—), Paper Club N.Y., Fin. Execs. Inst., Young Pres.'s Orgn., Phi Kappa Tau. Clubs: Pres.'s N.Y. (co-chmn. assos. div. 1964-68), City Athletic, Harvard, Harvard Bus., Marco Polo (N.Y.C.); Les Ambassadeurs (London); Rockrimmon Country (Stamford, Conn.). Home: 25 Sutton Pl S New York City NY 10022 also Taconic Rd Greenwich CT 06830 Office: 145 E 32d St New York City NY 10016

GOULD, HOWARD RICHARD, radiologist; b. N.Y.C., May 21, 1931; s. John and Mary R. (Harrigan) G.; student Fordham U., 1952; M.D., State U. N.Y. at N.Y.C., 1956; m. Barbara A. Paretti, Oct. 6, 1956. Commd. capt. U.S. Air Force, 1957, advanced through grades to maj., 1964; intern St. Vincent's Hosp. and Med. Center, 1956-57, resident in radiology, 1957-60, chief radiology service 811th med. group Loring AFB, Maine, 1960-62, chief radiol. service USAF Hosp., Wiesbaden, Ger., 1962-65, resigned, 1965; asst. attending radiologist St. Vincent's Hosp. and Med. Center N.Y., 1965-66, asso. attending radiologist, 1966-67, acting chief radioisotope service, 1967-68, attending radiologist, chief nuclear medicine sect., 1968-76, dir. nuclear medicine resident tng. program, 1976-77, asso. dir. dept. radiology, 1974—, pres. med. staff, 1975-76; clin. asst. prof. N.J. Coll. Medicine, 1965-69; clin. asso. prof. N.Y. U., 1969—. Fellow Am. Coll. Radiology, N.Y. Acad. Medicine; mem. N.Y. Roentgen Soc. (pres. 1977-78), AMA, N.Y. County Med. Soc., Med. Soc. State N.Y., Soc. Nuclear Medicine, Bavarian Am., N. Am. radiol. socs., N.Y. Celtic Med. Soc., Alpha Omega Alpha. Home: 28 Woodmont Rd Upper Montclair NJ 07043 Office: 153 W 11th St New York City NY 10011

GOULD, JAMES EDWARD, geol. engr.; b. Canandaigua, N.Y., Oct. 2, 1943; s. Charles and Flora (Wagner) G.; B.S. in Geol. Engring., U. Ariz., 1970, B.S. in Metall. Engring., 1970, M.S. in Geol. Engring., 1973; m. Suzanne Gail Wilson, Apr. 2, 1965; children—Aaron Leigh, Lara Maureen. Supr., Magma Copper Co., San Manuel, Ariz., 1972-73; rock mechanics engr., mining research dept. The Anaconda Co., Tucson, 1973-74; sr. rock mechanics engr. Seegmiler Asso., Tucson, 1974-76; sr. mining engr. Internat. Salt Co., Clarks Summit, Pa., 1976—. Served with USN, 1961-64. Registered profl. engr. Mem. Am. Inst. Mining, Metall. and Petroleum Engrs., Canadian Inst. Mining and Metallurgy, Internat. Soc. Rock Mechanics, Nat. Soc. Profl. Engrs. Research in field of space photographs for determining geol. features. Home: 11 Hamilton Terr Box 121 Clarks Summit PA 18411 Office: Internat Salt Co Clarks Summit PA 18411

GOULD, MORTIMER DAVID, accountant; b. N.Y.C., Oct. 5, 1908; s. Jacob and Sadie (Wagman) G.; B.C.S., N.Y.U., 1929; m. Augusta Beatrice Waxberg, Nov. 1, 1934 (dec. Sept. 21, 1976); m. 2d, Frances R. Axelrod, Aug. 2, 1978. Prin. Mortimer D. Gould, C.P.A., N.Y.C., 1935-43; partner Mortimer D. Gould & Co., N.Y.C., 1946-74; prin. Mortimer D. Gould, mgmt. cons., 1974—; admitted to U.S. Tax Ct. bar, 1938. C.P.A., N.Y. State, Calif. Served with Q.M.C., U.S., Army, 1943-46. Decorated Army Commendation medal. Mem. N.Y. State Soc. C.P.A.'s, Am. Inst. C.P.A.'s, Nat. Assn. Accountants, Am. Logistic Assn., Geneva Execs. Club, Internat. Geneva Assn. Contbr. articles to profl. jours. Office: 333 W 57th St New York City NY 10019

GOULD, STEPHEN, paper mfg. exec. writer, cons.; b. N.Y.C., Dec. 25, 1909; s. Jacob and Fannie (Schwartz) G.; D.F.A. (hon.), Geneva Theol. Coll., 1969; D.Integral Philosophy (hon.), World U.; m. Marlene Ossias, Aug. 24, 1941; children—Phyllis Jane, Roberta

Louise, Debra Elaine. Columnist, Port & Terminal Publs., 1931-36; dir. Stephen Gould Paper Co., Stephen Gould Paper Co. of N.J., Stephen Gould Corp. and affiliates. Recipient H. De Bellis Sculpture award, 1970; Israel Solidarity award. Mem. indsl. packaging Purdue U. Fellow Royal Soc. Arts (London), Am. Assn. Humanistic Psychology; mem. Am. Humanist Assn., Nat. Soc. Arts and Letters (life), N.Y. Acad. Scis. (life), Soc. Indsl. Packaging and Handling Engrs. Mason. Clubs: Salmagundi, Forsgate Country. Home: 29A Larch Plaza Cranbury NJ 08512 Office: Gould Co Bayonne NJ

GOULDER, CAROLJEAN HEMPSTEAD, sch. psychologist; b. Houston, Minn., Apr. 9, 1933; d. Orson George and Jean (Lischer) Hempstead; B.S., Hamline U., 1956; M.A., R.I. Coll., 1972, certificate of advanced grad. study in sch. psychology, 1975; m. Lloyd Lynton Goulder, Jr., May 26, 1956; children—Jean, David, Ann. Dept. head, instr. Highsmith Hosp. Sch. Nursing, Fayetteville, N.C., 1956-57; instr. New Eng. Deaconess Hosp. Sch. Nursing, Boston, 1957-58; sch. psychologist, dir. psychology Burrillville Pub. Schs., Harrisville, R.I., 1972—. Cons., Mary C. Wheeler Sch., Providence, 1970-73. Mem. Am. (asso.), Mass. (asso.) psychol. assns., Nat. Assn. Sch. Psychologists, Council Exceptional Children, Children with Learning Disabilities. Conglist. Home: 85 Old Farm Ln Attleboro MA 02703 Office: Burrillville Schools Harrisville RI 02830

GOUSE, RICHARD IRA, coll. pres.; b. Boston, Oct. 29, 1946; s. Julian B. and Marcia R. (Tuck) G.; A.B., Brown U., 1968; m. Cheryl Connors, Oct. 13, 1970. Adminstrv. asst. Mass. Trades Shops Sch., Boston, 1969, R.I. Trades Shops Sch., 1970; pres., chmn. bd. New Eng. Inst. Tech., Providence, 1970—; participant Brown U. Alumni interviewing program, 1969-70. Mem. Nat. Assn. Trade-Tech. Schs., Am. Vocat. Assn., R.I. Assn. Career, Tech. Schs., Vocat.-Tech. Educators R.I., Providence Better Bus. Bur., Greater Providence C. of C. Club: Brown of R.I. Office: 184 Early St Providence RI 02907

GOVAN, FRANCIS ANTHONY, energy products mfg. co. exec.; b. Detroit, May 25, 1927; s. Francis Joseph and Agnes Winifred G.; B.S. in Engring., U.S. Mcht. Marine Acad., 1948; B.S. in Marine Engring., George Washington U., 1964; M.Engring. Adminstrn., U. New Haven, 1978; m. Margaret Ann Porter, June 20, 1948; children—Francis J., Robert J., Michael A., Suzanne M. Fuels engr. Washington Gas Light Co., 1948-57; with Nat. Acad. Scis., 1957-69, asst. dir. Bldg. Research Adv. Bd., 1969; pres. York Research Corp., Stamford, Conn., 1969-76, dir., 1976—; corporate v.p. combustion/energy div. Combustion Equipment Assn., Stamford, 1967—. Pres. PTA, 1966-68. Mem. Conn. Pub. Expenditures Council. Served with Submarine Service, USNR, 1950-53. Mem. Am. Soc. Heating, Refrigerating and Air-Conditioning Engrs. (award of merit 1969), ASTM (award of merit 1970), Nat. Soc. Profl. Engrs., Am. Inst. Plant Engrs., Conn. Bus. and Industry Assn. (dir.), Nat. Inst. Bldg. Research, Internat. Standards Assn. (chmn. U.S. del. thermal insulation). Republican. Roman Catholic. Clubs: Landmark, K.C. Home: Brushwood Rd Stamford CT 06903 Office: 61 Taylor-Reed Pl Stamford CT 06906

GOWEN, GEORGE WASHINGTON, lawyer; b. Leghorn, Italy, Sept. 14, 1929; s. Franklin C. and May E. (Klein) G. (parents Am. citizens); A.B., Princeton, 1952; LL.B., U. Va., 1957; m. Marcia A. Fennelly, Jan. 17, 1959; children—Cynthia, Lee. Admitted to N.Y. bar, 1958; with Dunnington, Bartholow & Miller, N.Y.C., 1957—, partner, 1966—. Mem. U.S. del. UN Commn. on Human Rights, 1970; alternate mem. UN Subcom. on Prevention Discrimination and Protection Minorities, 1970, 71, 72, 74; dir. North Am. Royalties, 1975—, Paine Webber Cashfund, 1978—; dir. North Am. Royalties. Chmn., Cloister Inn, Princeton, 1970-75; smoke-jumper U.S. Forest Service, Missoula, Mont., summer 1954. Bd. dirs. Nat. Park Found., chmn. exec. com., 1972—; bd. dirs. Lenox Hill Hosp., 1975—, Retarded Infants Services, 1975-78, Am. Soc. Prevention Cruelty to Animals, 1976—, pres., 1978—. Served from 2d to 1st lt., AUS, 1952-54. Mem. U.S. Tennis Assn. (gen. counsel 1969—), Am. Colony Charities Assn. (dir. 1965-77). Clubs: Metropolitan (Washington); River (N.Y.C.). Home: 122 E 76th St New York City NY 10021 Office: 161 E 42d St New York City NY 10017

GOZDZIEWSKI, CHARLES JAMES, structural engr.; b. Queens, N.Y., Oct. 19, 1950; s. John Thomas and Jennie Julia (Danielik) F.; B.S. in Aerospace Engring., Bklyn. Poly. Inst., 1972; m. Ann Rose Landusky, June 7, 1975. Project engr. Hardesty & Hanover Cons. Engrs., Inc., N.Y.C., 1972—. Mem. legis. adv. com. St. Joseph's Youth Orgn.; mgr. YMCA. Mem. Am. Inst. Aeros. and Astronautics, ASCE, Nat. Soc. Profl. Engrs., Poly. Inst. of N.Y. Alumni Assn. (dir.). Club: Friends (pres.). Patentee toilet seat chair. Home: 28-48 43rd St Astoria NY 11103 Office: Hardesty & Hanover 101 Park Ave New York City NY 10017*

GRABARZ, DONALD FRANCIS, pharm. research adminstr.; b. Jersey City, Sept. 18, 1941; s. Joseph and Frances (Zotynia) G.; B.S. in Pharmacy, St. John's U., 1964; m. Joan Marie Isoldi, Aug. 13, 1965; children—Christine Ann, Robert Charles, Danielle Marie. Mgr.-pharmacist Krivin Pharmacy, N.Y.C., 1965; supr. quality assurance, Johnson & Johsnon, New Brunswick, N.J., 1965-68, mgr. analytical labs., Chgo., 1968-71; dir. quality assurance Jelco Labs., Raritan, N.J., 1971-72; dir. quality assurance and regulatory affairs Bard-Parker div. Becton, Dicksinson & Co., N.J., 1972-76, asst. corporate dir. regulatory and industry affairs, Rutherford, N.J., 1976—. Chmn., Drug Edn. Council, Lisle, Ill., 1970-71. Bd. dirs. N.J. chpt. Am. Lung Assn. Mem. Am. Pharm. Assn., Acad. Pharm. Scis., Am. Soc. Quality Control, Am. Mgmt. Assn., Delta Sigma Theta. Office: Rutherford NJ 07070

GRABER, HARRIS DAVID, aerospace co. exec.; b. Bronx, N.Y., Mar. 31, 1939; s. Charles and Ella (Shapiro) G.; A.S., Quensborough Community Coll., 1973; B.S. cum laude, CUNY, 1975; postgrad. in bus. St. Johns U., 1979—; m. Esther Feldman, Dec. 28, 1957; children—Donald Irwin, Gregory Stuart, Monique Cheryl, Roy Scott. Draftsman, Paramount Designs Co., N.Y.C., 1956-58; design draftsman Milgo Electronic Co., Fla., 1961-62; design engr. Cons. and Designers Co., N.Y.C., 1958-61, 62-64; with Grumman Aerospace Co., Bethpage, N.Y., 1964-78, mktg. and sales engr., 1974-75, group head customer engring. tech. requirements, 1975-78, internat. bus. analyst, 1978; regional sales mgr. Systems-East div. Conrac Corp., West Caldwell, N.J., 1978—. Mem. Assn. M.B.A.'s, Tech. Mktg. Soc. Am. Home: 80-51 249th St Bellerose NY 11426 Office: Conrac Corp West Caldwell NJ 07006

GRABOWSKI, ANN JACQUELINE, speech pathologist; b. Jersey City, July 4, 1948; s. John Joseph and Adela Mary (Hopper) G.; B.A., Cath. U. Am., 1970, M.A., 1972. Speech pathologist, dept. rehab., Monmouth Med. Center, Long Branch, N.J., 1972—; cons. in field. Mem. Am. (certified clin. competence), N.J. (certified speech correction and speech pathologist) speech and hearing assns., Am. Cleft Palate Assn. Roman Catholic. Home: 5 Amherst Pl Parlin NJ 08859 Office: Dept Rehab Monmouth Med Center 3d Ave Long Branch NJ 07740

GRACE, ALONZO GASKELL, JR., computer scientist; b. Bottineau, N.D., June 25, 1923; s. Alonzo Gaskell and Jeannette (Meland) G.; B.S., Trinity Coll., 1949; M.A., Yale, 1955; m. Betty Myers, Sept. 1, 1945; children—Alonzo Gaskell, Alexa, Laurie S., Elizabeth Ann. Instr. math. Trinity Coll., 1949-52; teaching fellow Yale U., 1952-55, instr. physics Trinity Coll., Hartford, 1954-56; asso. head computer dept. Gen. Dynamics, 1956-59; mgr. systems programming devel. RCA, Cherry Hill, N.J., 1959-71; chief computer scientist Travelers Corp., Hartford, 1972-74; pres. A.G. Grace & Co., Glastonbury, Conn., 1974—; adj. prof. computer sci. Trinity Coll., 1974—. Served with AUS, 1942-45. Fellow Brit. Computer Soc.; mem. Assn. Computing Machinery, Phi Beta Kappa, Sigma Pi Sigma, Psi Upsilon. Address: 81 Tall Timbers Ln Glastonbury CT 06033

GRACE, H. DAVID, investment mgmt. exec.; b. Hornell, N.Y., Sept. 27, 1936; s. H.F. III and Alice (Lamp) G.; B.S., Rensselaer Poly. Inst., 1957; M.B.A., U. Cin., 1963. Staff chem. engr. Procter & Gamble Co., N.Y.C., 1957-58, supr. prodn., quality control, 1959-60, bus. analyst, math. cons., Cin., 1961-63; supr. operations research, mgmt. econs. Weyerhaeuser Co., Tacoma, 1963-65; dir. operations research Celanese Corp., N.Y.C., 1965-67; mgr. computer applications Francis I. duPont, N.Y.C., 1968-69, mgr. computer and tech. research, 1969-71, mgr. portfolio analysis and investment adv. depts., 1969-71; v.p., dir. Lenox Capital Mgmt. Corp., N.Y.C., 1971-73, pres., 1973-74; pres., chmn. bd. dirs. Grace-Metro Enterprises, Ltd., 1967—, Grace Capital Inc., 1974—; pres., dir. Dirs. Capital Fund, Inc., 1977—. Tchr., Xavier U., 1962-63, Pacific Luth. U., 1964-65. Area counselor Republican party 1964-65. Mem. Am. Statis. Assn., Operations Research Soc. Am., Econometric Soc., N.Y. Soc. Security Analysts. Phi Sigma Kappa. Home: 1 Sherman Sq New York City NY 10023 Office: One Gulf and Western Plaza New York City NY 10023

GRACE, HAROLD PADGET, ret. chem. engr.; b. Parsons, Kans., Apr. 19, 1919; s. Worthington T. and Flossie (Padget) G.; B.S. in Chem. Engring., U. Pa., 1941; postgrad. Princeton, 1943-44, Mass. Inst. Tech., 1944-45; m. Edith Hultman, Aug. 15, 1942; children—Cynthia P. (Mrs. Joseph Mark), Peter W. Field engr. E.I. duPont de Nemours & Co., Inc., 1941-43, research engr., 1946-50, research project engr., 1950-56, research asso., 1956-66, research fellow, Wilmington, 1966-78, ret., 1978. Served with USNR, 1943-46. Mem. Am. Inst. Chem. Engrs. (Colburn award 1954), Am. Chem. Soc., Am. Inst. Chemists, Franklin Inst. Contbr. articles to profl. jours. Patentee in field. Home: 108 N Concord Ave Havertown PA 19083 Office: EI DuPont Exptl Sta Wilmington DE 19898

GRADIN, LAWRENCE PAUL, elec. engr.; b. Bklyn., June 2, 1945; s. Milton and Ann (Miller) G.; B.S. magna cum laude (N.Y. State Regents scholar), N.Y. Inst. Tech., 1969; m. Helene Ann Fortunah, Aug. 7, 1971; children—Michael Craig, Jennifer Renee, Kevin Mark. With Cons. Edison Co., N.Y.C., 1963-65, Sperry Rand Co., N.Y.C., 1967-68, Met. Transp. Authority, N.Y.C., 1968-69; elec. engring. and lead elec. discipline engr. for fossil and nuclear fueled power plants Ebasco Services Inc., N.Y.C., 1969-77; asst. sect. mgr. elec. instrumentation and control engring. for breeder reactor div. Burns & Roe Inc., Oradell, N.J., 1977—. Mem. IEEE Power Engring. Soc. (working group for nuclear power plant heat tracing standards), Indsl. Applications Soc. (sta. design com., electric process heating com.), Am. Soc. Indsl. Security. Home: 20 Phillips Rd Edison NJ 08817 Office: 700 Kinderkamack Rd Oradell NJ 07649

GRADISAR, HELEN MARGARET, coll. adminstr.; b. Bridgeville, Pa., July 1, 1922; d. Frank Luke and Elizabeth Helen (Pogacnik) G.; B.S. in Bus. Adminstrn., Duquesne U., 1944. Jr. accountant Carnegie-Ill. Steel Corp., Pitts., 1943-50; asst. dir. alumni relations Duquesne U., Pitts., 1950-67; registrar Rosemont (Pa.) Coll., 1967-68; registrar Carlow Coll., Pitts., 1968-78, asst. dean coll., 1974-77, dir. instl. research, 1977—. Mem. Duquesne U. Alumnae Assn. (pres. 1948-49), Cath. Daus. Am., Assn. Instl. Research, NE Assn. Instl. Research, Epsilon Eta Phi. Democrat. Roman Catholic. Home: 657 Chestnut St Bridgeville PA 15017 Office: 3333 5th Ave Pittsburgh PA 15213

GRADY, FRANCIS REDDY, assn. exec.; b. Worcester, Mass., May 8, 1921; s. Frank P. and Louise A. (Reddy) G.; B.S., Coll. Holy Cross, 1946; M.S., Boston U., 1948; m. Martha Mills, Sept. 18, 1948; children—Michael, Stephen, Suzanne, David. Supr., Conn. Dept. Pub. Welfare, Bridgeport, 1948-51; adminstrn. supr. Washington Juvenile Ct., 1951-54; asso. exec. dir. United Way, Elizabeth, N.J., 1954-57; exec. dir. United Way, Meriden, Conn., 1957-62; exec. dir. United Way, York, Pa., 1962-72, Tri County United Way, Harrisburg, Pa., 1972—; lectr. Univ. Center, Pa. State U., Harrisburg, 1972—. Mem. Pa. Gov.'s Justice Commn., 1962-76; pres. N.E. Conf. United Way Am., N.Y.C., 1974-76, mem. N.E. task force, 1976—; mem. Hampden (Pa.) Planning Commn., Harrisburg Crime Commn.; bd. dirs. Tri County Commn. Econ. Action, Regional Detention Service; mem. profl. adv. com. Elizabethtown (Pa.) Coll.; adv. bd. Jr. League Harrisburg. Served with AUS, 1943-45. Decorated Purple Heart. Mem. Nat. Health and Welfare Retirement Assn. (pres. council 1974—), Nat. Assn. Social Workers, Am. Acad. Polit. and Social Sci., Navy League, Am. Acad. Cons., Nat. Soc. Fund Raisers, Harrisburg C. of C. (airport com.). Clubs: Harrisburg Rotary (dir.). West Shore Country (Camp Hill, Pa.); Vesper (Phila.). Contbr. articles to profl. jours. Home: 815 Mandy Ln Camp Hill PA 17011 Office: One United Way Harrisburg PA 17110

GRADY, JAMES JOSEPH, tobacco co. exec.; b. Dobbs Ferry, N.Y., June 16, 1943; s. James J. and Dorothy (Byrd) G.; student Pace U.; m. Pirjo L. Jakko, Sept. 7, 1973; children—Miika, Alexander, Jaimie. Foreman, Jenner Tree Service, Elmsford, N.Y., 1967-70; tractor trailer driver Joseph E. Lenner Trucking, Elmsford, 1967-70; with U.S. Tobacco Co., Greenwich, Conn., 1970—, asst. bldg. supt., 1973-76, supt. hdqrs. facilities, 1976-77, dir. office services and facilities, 1977—. Mem. Bldg. Owners and Mgrs. Assn. Greater N.Y., Am. Mgmt. Assn. Home: 401 S Lexington Ave White Plains NY 10606 Office: 100 W Putnam Ave Greenwich CT 06830

GRADY, JOHN JOSEPH, internat. fin. cons.; b. Long Island City, N.Y., June 23, 1924; s. John Joseph and Amanda (Criqui) G.; B.S. in Chem. Engring., Newark Coll., 1948; M.S., Columbia, 1949; m. Eileen Shields, Mar. 4, 1944; children—Eileen, Jacqueline, Linda, Elizabeth, Nancy, Leslie. Engr., Procter & Gamble, N.Y.C., 1949-54; asst. controller Riegel Paper, N.Y.C., 1954-58; v.p. fin. Garlock Inc., Rochester, N.Y., 1958-76; pres. Grady Co., Rochester, 1976—; dir. Spinco Metal Products, Newark, N.Y., ENI Inc., Rochester, Rochester Instrument Systems, ERICA SA, Barcelona, Spain. Bd. dirs. Monroe County (N.Y.) Assn. Retarded Children. Served with U.S. Army, 1943-45. Decorated Silver Star medal. Mem. Fin. Execs. Inst., Nat. Assn. Accountants, Am. Mgmt. Assn. Republican. Roman Catholic. Author: Effect of Surface Roughness on Heat Transfer, 1949; Financial Measurement of Marketing Management, 1963. Home: 105 Knollwood Dr Rochester NY 14618 Office: 925 Midtown Tower Rochester NY 14604

GRAEBER, RAYMOND CURTIS, research psychologist; b. Buffalo, Nov. 17, 1945; s. Raymond George and Anna Louisa (Perez) G.; student Canisius Coll., 1963-65; B.A., State U. N.Y. at Binghamton, 1967; M.A., U. Va., 1970, Ph.D., 1972; m. Janet Sue Miller, May 16, 1970; children—Russell Gray, Sarah Elizabeth, David Andrew. Vis. scientist Lerner Marine Lab., Am. Mus. Natural History, Bimini, Bahamas, 1970-71; commd. 2d lt. Med. Service Corps, U.S. Army, 1969, advanced through grades to capt., 1971; research psychologist Pioneering Research Lab. (now Food Sci. Lab.), Behavioral Sci. Div., Natick (Mass.) Research and Devel. Command, 1972—, neuropsychiatry div. Walter Reed Army Inst. Research, Washington, 1976—; vis. lectr. Framingham State Coll., 1973-76, George Mason U., 1978—; cons. Office of Naval Research. Mem. Eastern Psychol. Assn., Soc. Neurosci., Internat. Soc. Chronobiology, Am. Assn. Anatomists, U. Va. Alumni Assn., Sigma Xi, Phi Sigma. Democrat. Episcopalian. Contbr. articles in fields of shark behavior and brain function, nutrition, biorhythms to profl. jours. Office: Dept Exptl Psychophysiology Neuropsychiatry Div Walter Reed Army Inst Research Washington DC 20012

GRAESE, CLIFFORD ERNEST, accounting exec.; b. Canova, S.D., Jan. 5, 1927; s. Arthur Edward and Alma M. (Neugebauer) G.; B.S., U. S.D., 1949; m. LaVonne Marie Bohn, May 3, 1953; children—Diane, Sally, Susan, Larry. With Peat, Marwick, Mitchell & Co., Mpls., N.Y.C., 1949—, audit partner, 1958-63, partner in charge mgmt. cons., 1963-75, partner in charge accounting and auditing, 1975-77, vice chmn. accounting and auditing, 1977—. Past v.p. Bd. Edn. Saddle River (N.J.), 1972-78. Served with USNR, 1945-46. C.P.A., Minn., N.Y. Mem. Am. Inst. C.P.A.'s (past chmn. div. profl. ethics), N.Y. Soc. C.P.A.'s, Am. Accounting Assn. Republican. Lutheran. Clubs: Ridgewood Country, Board Room. Office: 345 Park Ave New York City NY 10022

GRAF, JOHN ADAM, lawyer; b. Manchester, N.H., June 19, 1935; s. Kenneth Folsom and Mary (Eaton) G.; A.B., Dartmouth, 1958; LL.B., Boston U., 1961; m. Ann M. Hunt, Sept. 6, 1958; children—Theodore, Peter, Juliana. Admitted to N.H. bar, 1961, to practice before N.H. Supreme Ct., 1961, U.S. Supreme Ct. bar, 1971; asso. McLane, Carleton, Graf, Greene & Brown, Manchester, 1961-67, partner, 1967—. Sec. N.H. com. to Study Laws of Eminent Domain, 1968-72; chmn. Commn. to Codify N.H. Criminal Laws, 1972-75. Del. N.H. Republican Conv., 1966-72; rep. N.H. Gen. Ct., 1967-68; mem. N.H. Ballot Law Commn., 1970-72, chmn., 1972; pres. Manchester YMCA, 1974-76, dir., 1962—; bd. dirs. Manchester Inst. Arts and Scis., 1964-67; bd. dirs. Algonquin Indoor Tennis Ct., 1971-74, pres., 1974; bd. dirs. The Derryfield Sch., 1976—, vice chmn., 1977—; research and devel. com. Elliot Hosp. Mem. Am., N.H., Manchester bar assns., N.H. Lawn Tennis Assn. (pres. 1976, dir. 1974-76). Club: Dartmouth (pres. 1972). Home: 15 Church Rd Bedford NH 03102 Office: 40 Stark St Manchester NH 03101

GRAF, LEONARD GRANT, biochemist; b. Aurora, Ill., Sept. 25, 1918; s. Leonard Herman and Edith Rose (Reynolds) G.; B.A., Lawrence Coll., 1940; M.S., Ind. U., 1944; m. Irene Lolita Gersch, Nov. 21, 1943; children—Cheryl Ann, Kevin Leonard. Biochemist, West Side VA Hosp., Chgo., 1953-56; clin. lab. dir. Meml. Hosp. DuPage County, Elmhurst, Ill., 1956-71; edn. coordinator certified lab. assts., lab. mgr. Androscoggin Valley Hosp., Berlin, N.H., 1973-74, North County Hosp., Newport, Vt. and Northeastern Vt. Regional Hosp., St. Johnsbury, 1974—; mem. faculty Norwich U. Served with AUS, 1942-46; col. Res. (ret.). Recipient grant No. New Eng. Acad. Fellow Am. Inst. Chemists (life); mem. Am. Assn. Clin. Chemists, Biol. Photog. Assn., AAAS, Am. Chem. Soc., Am. Inst. Chemistry, Am. Assn. Blood Banks, Internat. Soc. Clin. Lab. Tech., Clin. Lab. Mgmt. Assn., Am. Def. Preparedness Assn., Conservative Caucus. Mem. Seventh-day Adventists. Clubs: North Country Wet Pets Soc. Home: 40 Prospect St Lancaster NH 03584 Office: POB 500 Lyme NH 03768

GRAF, PETER GUSTAV, lawyer, accountant; b. Vienna, Austria, June 19, 1936; s. Joseph and Mary Anna (Harpner) G.; came to U.S., 1940, naturalized, 1945; B.S. in Econs., U. Pa., 1957; LL.B., N.Y. U., 1960, LL.M., 1962; m. Rosalie Greenbaum, Apr. 6, 1963; 1 son, Paul Evan. Auditor, S.D. Leidesdorf, N.Y.C., 1960; admitted to N.Y. bar, 1960; tax accountant J.K. Lasser & Co., N.Y.C. 1961; with Joseph Graf & Co., C.P.A.'s, N.Y.C., 1962—, partner, 1966—; fin. v.p., founder, dir. AGS Computers, Inc., N.Y.C., 1967—; founder, treas., dir. Nardin Gallery, Inc., N.Y.C. Mem. Am. Inst. C.P.A.'s, N.Y. State Soc. C.P.A.'s, Am., N.Y. State bar assns. Home: 87 Holly Pl Briarcliff Manor NY 10510 Office: 21 E 40th St New York City NY 10016

GRAFF, HAROLD, psychiatrist, psychoanalyst; b. Phila., Apr. 11, 1932; B.S., U. Pa., 1954, M.D., 1958; children—David, Caron. Intern, Phila. Gen. Hosp., 1958-59; resident Inst. of Pa. Hosp., Phila., 1959-62; postdoctoral fellow Inst. Neurol. Sci., U. Pa., 1959-62; psychoanalytic trainee Inst. of Phila. Assn. for Psychoanalysis, Bala Cynwyd, Pa., 1962-67; research scientist, dept. clin. sci. Eastern Pa. Psychiat. Inst., Phila., 1963-74, dir. div. psychoanalytic studies, dept. clin. research and tng., 1974—; dir. adolescent psychiatry Pa. Dept. Pub. Welfare, 1977—; chmn. research and publs. com. Inst. of the Pa. Hosp., Phila., 1968-78, chmn. psychoanalytic research group, 1968—; clin. asso. prof. psychiatry Health Scis. Center Temple U., 1974-77; research asst. prof. psychiatry Hahnemann Med. Coll., Phila., 1963-70, asso. prof., 1970-74, vis. prof., psychiat. cons. Inst. for Human Resource Devel., 1974-76; clin. prof. psychiatry and human behavior Jefferson Med. Coll., 1977—; vis. faculty Inst. of Phila. Assn. for Psychoanalysis, 1971—; pres., research dir. Psychiat. Services, Inc., Wynnewood, Pa., 1969—; staff Inst. of Pa. Hosp., Haverford Gen. Hosp., Phila. Psychiat. Center; spl. cons. Spl. Action Office for Drug Abuse Prevention, Washington, 1973-74. Fellow Am., Pa. psychiat. assns., Phila. Coll. Physicians; mem. Phila. Psychiat. Soc., Am. (chmn. Eastern States liaison com. 1977—), Phila. (pres. 1978—) soc. adolescent psychiatry Am. Assn. Suicidology, AMA, Del., New Castle County med. assns., Internat., Am., Phila. psychoanalytic assns., AAUP, Med. Club Phila., Phila. Coll. Physicians, N.Y. Acad. Sci., AAAS, Phi Beta Kappa. Club: Mensa (Delaware County). Contbr. articles to profl. jours. Home: 7222 Society Dr Claymont DE 19703 Office: 111 N 49th St Philadelphia PA 19139 also 1902 Shipley Rd Wilmington DE 19803

GRAFTON, THURMAN STANFORD, assn. exec.; b. Chgo., Dec. 20, 1923; s. Thurman Stump and Ethel (Anderson) G.; D.V.M., Mich. State U., 1947, postgrad., 1947-48; postgrad. U. Md., 1950, U. N.Mex., 1963-64, U. London, 1972-73; m. Jean Marie Robinson, Dec. 21, 1946; children—T. Scott, Michael W., Donald A., Glynis M. Commd. 2d lt. U.S. Army, 1948, advanced through grades to lt. col. USAF, 1953; sr. scientist Aeromed. Research Lab., Holloman AFB, N.Mex., exec. officer Med. Clin. Lab., London, with Dept. Virus and Rickettsial Diseases, 406th Med. Gen. Lab., Tokyo, Walter Reed Army Inst. Research; ret., 1966; prof., chmn. dept. lab. animal sci., dir. lab. animal facilities State U. N.Y. at Buffalo, 1966-76; exec. dir. Nat. Soc. Med. Research, Washington, 1977—; cons. hosps., colls., univs. Decorated Air Force Commendation medal; recipient Distinguished Faculty award State U. N.Y., Buffalo, 1977; Veterinary Alumni award Mich. State U., 1978; diplomate Am. Coll. Lab. Animal Medicine. Mem. AVMA, Nat. Assn. Exec. Club, Assn. Gnotobiotics, Assn. Schs. Allied Health Professions (charter), Conf. Pub. Health Veterinarians, Am. Soc. Lab. Animal Practitioners (charter pres. 1971-72), Am. Assn. Zoo Veterinarians, Wildlife Disease Assn., Internat. Assn. Aquatic Animal Medicine (charter), Intersoc. Council Biology Medicine. Home: 700 7th St SW Washington DC 20024 Office: 1000 Vermont Ave NW Washington DC 20005

GRAHAM, ARNOLD HAROLD, law sch. adminstr.; b. N.Y.C., Dec. 29, 1917; s. Julius E. and Rose Goldstein; B.S. with honors, N.Y. U., 1945; J.D. with honors, N.Y. Law Sch., 1952; m. Roselle Lesser, Dec. 23, 1939; children—Stuart R., Joel M., Jul E. Practice pub. accounting, N.Y.C., 1945-52; admitted to N.Y. bar, 1952, U.S. Supreme Ct. bar, 1959; individual practice law, N.Y.C., 1952-76; dep. atty. gen. N.Y., 1952-54; cons. N.Y. Law Sch., N.Y.C., 1952-76, asst. dean, prof., treas., 1976-77, vice-dean, prof., treas., 1977—; cons., arbitrator Am. Arbitration Assn., 1952—; law cons. exam. div. Am. Inst. C.P.A.'s, 1976—; bd. visitors Appellate div., 1st dept. Supreme Ct. N.Y. Trustee Ave. R Temple, Kings Hwy. Bd. Trade; bd. advisers United Jewish Appeal. C.P.A., N.Y. Mem. Am. Assn. Attys.-C.P.A.'s (founder), Am., N.Y. State trial lawyers assns., Am. Bar Assn., N.Y. State C.P.A. Soc., N.Y. County Lawyers Assn., Fed. Bar Council, Am. Arbitration Assn. Jewish. Home: 2223 Ave T Brooklyn NY 12229 Office: New York Law Sch 57 Worth St New York City NY 10013

GRAHAM, CHARLES RAYMOND, educator; b. Balt., June 17, 1940; s. Charles Raymond and Mathilda (Laimuntavicius) G.; B.S., Loyola Coll. Balt., 1962; M.S., U. Del., 1964, Ph.D., 1967; m. Patricia Ellen Cole, Jan 20, 1962; children—Charles Raymond III, Kelly Patricia, Michael Emory, Kerri Michelle. Faculty dept. biology Loyola Coll. Balt., 1966—, asst. prof., 1967-71, asso. prof., 1971—, chmn. dept. biology, 1975—. Research asso. U. Md. Med. Sch., 1971—, Eye Bank Md., Balt., 1973—. Chmn. ednl. com. St. Charles Sch., Pikesville, Md., 1972—; mem. community resource bd. Jr. League Balt., 1973-77. NIH postdoctoral fellow Marqette U. Med. Sch., Milw., 1967-69; Nat. Soc. Prevention Blindness grantee, 1972-73. Mem. Am. Assn. U. Profs. (pres. Loyola Coll. chpt. 1969-71), Am. Assn. Tissue Banks, N.Y. Acad. Scis., Md. Acads. Scis., Am. Soc. Zoologists, Sigma Xi. K.C. Contbr. articles to profl. jours. Home: 6 Reservior Rd Pikesville MD 21208 Office: 4501 N Charles St Baltimore MD 21210

GRAHAM, CHESTIE MARIE, counselor; b. Louisburg, N.C., Nov. 7, 1917; d. Andrew Luther and Roberta McKnight; B.S., Fayetteville State U., 1944; M.Ed., Pa. State U., 1952; m. Samuel Dangerfield Graham, Apr. 23, 1959; stepchildren—Samuel Dandergield, Barbara, Karen. Tchr., C.M. Eppes High Sch., Greenville, N.C., 1944-58, Charles Young Elementary Sch., Washington, 1958-65; guidance counselor Edmonds-Peabody Lovejoy Sch., Washington, 1965—. Democratic poll watcher, 1974; mem. Adv. Neighborhood Commn., Washington, 1976—. Mem. Assn. Non-White Concerns in Personnel and Guidance (pres.), Elementary Sch. Counselors Assn. (pres. 1975), NEA (life), Washington Tchrs. Union, D.C. Sch. Counselors Assn., Nat. Capital Personnel and Guidance Assn. (trustee 1978-79), Am. Personnel and Guidance Assn., Bus. and Profl. Women's Club, Nat. Negro Women's Assn., Delta Sigma Theta. Episcopalian. Home: 1827 Mass Ave SE Washington DC 20003

GRAHAM, DEAN MCKINLEY, pharm. co. exec.; b. Santa Ana, Calif., May 9, 1923; s. Howard Edward and Mary (Fernandez) G.; Ph.B., U. Wis., 1945; Ph.D., U. Calif. at Berkeley, 1953; M. Dolores Margaret Uradenburg, July 1, 1947 (div. 1970); children—Barry Denton, Darlene Yvonne, Deborah Michelle, Dorenna Meris; m. 2d, Victoria D. Warren, Apr. 14, 1972. Research scientist AEC, U. Calif. at Berkeley, 1949-53; sr. scientist Upjohn Co., Kalamazoo, 1953-57; dir. pharm. research Stanford Research Ins., Menlo Park, Calif., 1957-58; dir. research White Labs., Kennil-worth, N.J., 1958-60; v.p. K-V Pharm. Co., St. Louis, 1960-67; pres. Graham Labs Inc., 1963—, pres. Graham Sci. Inc., 1964—, Graham AgTech, 1971— (all Hobart, N.Y.); dir. Rexmere Toys, Hobart. Cons. in field. Bd. dirs. Graham Sci. Found. Served with USNR, 1943-47. Mem. A.A.A.S., Am. Pharm. Assn., Am. Assn. Pharm. Sci., N.Y. Acad. Scis., Acad. Pharm. Scis., Am. Chem. Soc., Sigma Xi. Contbr. to profl. jours. Patentee in field. Home: Cornell St Hobart NY 13788 Office: Pearl St Hobart NY 13788

GRAHAM, FRANCIS GLENN, educator; b. Braddock, Pa., June 1, 1951; s. Francis Edward and Shirley Ann (Oberdick) G.; B.A., U. Pitts., 1975; m. Charmaine Barbara Havey, June 3, 1972; 1 dau., Kathryn. Sec. Tripoli Fedn., McKeesport, Pa., 1969—; astronomy instr. Allegheny Community Coll., West Mifflin, Pa., 1975—, sci. instr. Allegheny Opportunities Industrialization Center, McKeesport, 1975—. Mem. Am. Inst. Aeronautics Astronautics, Astronomical League. Russian Orthodox. Editor Tripolitan Jour., 1969-75. Home: 622 Arlington Ave McKeesport PA 15133 Office: Tripoli Federation PO Box 1043 McKeesport PA 15134

GRAHAM, JACK BENNETT, cons.; b. Superior, Nebr., Oct. 16, 1913; s. Robert Arnold and Ethel Anne (Shippen) G.; A.B., York Coll., 1935; B.S., U. Nebr., 1937; M.S., U. Iowa, 1940, Ph.D., 1942; m. Lucy Neylan, Aug. 9, 1941; children—John M., Patricia J., Elizabeth (Mrs. Thomas Reardon), Robert G., Mary C., Andrew B. Hydrogeologist U.S. Geol. Survey, Dept. Interior, Cheyenne, Wyo, 1942-44, Phila., 1944-52, Washington, 1952-54; partner Leggette, Brashears & Graham, N.Y.C., 1955-76; pres. Leggette, Brashears & Graham, Inc., N.Y.C., 1976—; guest lectr. hydrogeology several Eastern univs.; mem. adv. com. on hydrology for com. on space programs for earth observations, Nat. Acad. Sci., 1967-74. Mem. Am. Inst. Profl. Geologists (v.p. 1967), Geol. Soc. Am., Am. Water Works Assn., A.A.A.S., Am. Inst. Mining, Metall. and Petroleum Engrs., Sigma Xi. Editor (with M.F. Burrill) Water for Industry, 1956. Home: 7 Mountain View Dr Weston CT 06883 Office: 55 W State St Westport CT 06880

GRAHAM, KATHARINE, newspaper co. exec.; b. N.Y.C., June 16, 1917; d. Eugene and Agnes (Ernst) Meyer; student Vassar Coll., 1934-36; A.B., U. Chgo., 1938; m. Philip L. Graham, June 5, 1940 (dec. 1963); children—Elizabeth Morris Graham Weymouth, Donald Edward, William Welsh, Stephen Meyer. Reporter, San Francisco News, 1938-39; mem. editorial Sunday and circulation staffs Washington Post, 1939-45, pub., 1968—; pres. Washington Post Co., 1963-73, 77, chmn. bd., 1973—; dir. Bowater Mersey Paper Co., Ltd., Newspaper Advt. Bur. Inc., A.P. Mem. Ind. Com. on Internat. Devel. Issues; trustee U. Chgo., Urban Inst.; trustee, mem. exec. com. Fed. City Council. Mem. Am. Newspaper Pubs. Assn. (dir.), Conf. Bd. (trustee), Am. Soc. Newspaper Editors (dir.), Sigma Delta Chi. Clubs: Cosmopolitan (N.Y.C.); 1925 F St., Nat. Press, Washington Press (Washington). Home: 2920 R St NW Washington DC 20007 Office: 1150 15th St NW Washington DC 20071

GRAHAM, LAURA MARGARET (LAURA GRAHAM FORBES), artist; b. Washington, Ind.; d. Ray Austin and Eugenia Bruce (Winston) G.; student Sacred Heart Convents (Grosse Pointe, Mich., Noroton, Conn., N.Y.C.), Westover and Nightingale Schs.; student art Art Students League, with Bridgman and Frank du Mond., Grand Central Art Sch., Traphagen Art Sch., Phoenix Art Inst.; pvt. study with Mead Schaeffer, Henry Rittenberg, N.A., Edward Dufner, N.A.; grad. Sch. Adult Edn., N.Y. U., 1965; m. Clifford Lee Forbes, 1940 (div.); 1 son. Exhibited paintings John Herron Art Mus., Indpls., N.Y. Water Color Club, Am. Water Color Soc., NAD (youngest artist exhibiting Nov. 1932), Pa. Acad., Boston Art Club, Montclair Art Mus., World's Fair 1940, Contemporary Art Bldg., Conn. Acad. Fine Arts Exhibit, Allied Artists Am., Ogunquit (Maine) Art Center, 50th Anniversary Celebration Westover Sch., Newport Art Assn., Nat. Arts Club, 1978, also traveling exhibits. A sponsor N.Y. U. Chamber Music Concerts, 1954—; concerts in Washington Sq. Park, 1954-55. Active Women's Nat. Republican Club. Recipient Alexander Wall prize, 1943, Allied Artists Am. exhbn., N.Y. Nat. Arts Club, 1st prize for painting, 1939; 2d prize, 1940, 41, hon. mention, 1947, 48, 72; hon. mention Allied Artists, 1948, Art Assn. Ogunquit, Maine, 1948; hon. mention and war bond, Terry Art Exhbn., Miami, Fla., 1952. Mem. Allied Artists Am., Conn. Acad. Fine Arts (artist mem.), Nat. Assn. Women Artists, Am. Artists Profl. League, Art Students League (life), N.Y. Hist. Soc., Museum City N.Y., N.Y. U. Alumni Assn., Nat. Trust Historic Preservation, Friends of the Philharmonic. Clubs: Pen and Brush, (N.Y.C.); Nat. Arts. Address: 10 Washington Sq N New York City NY 10003

GRAHAM, LAURENCE IGNATIUS, mgmt. cons., restaurant specialist; b. N.Y.C., Sept. 1, 1902; s. John Laurence and Kathryn (Foley) G.; student Columbia, 1924, N.Y. U., 1925-30; B.A., Goddard Coll.; M.A., Fairfield U., 1973; m. Teresa Rita O'Reilly, Jan. 19, 1928; children—Rita Ann (Mrs. Victor A. Lofink), Della Ann (Mrs. Ivan Spangenberg III), Kathryn Ann (Mrs. Robert Ross), Margot (Mrs. Walter Grallert), Elizabeth Ann (Mrs. John O'Mara), John Laurence. Commissary mgr., purchasing agt. Childs Co., N.Y.C., 1924-29; pres. Food Services, Inc., restaurant mgmt. specialists, N.Y.C., 1929-54; restaurant cons., 1955-69; vis. prof. polit. sci. U. Bridgeport (Conn.), Fairfield U. Chief restaurant div. War Food Adminstrn., World War II. Mem. Wilton Bd. Edn., 1951-57; mem. Wilton Bd. Finance, 1958-64, chmn., 1962-64; fire commr., Wilton, Conn., 1964-66; mem. Wilton Retirement Bd., 1966-69; 1st selectman, Wilton, 1969-73, treas., 1977—. Address: Chestnut Hill Wilton CT 06517

GRAHAM, LEWIS JAMES, ret. physician; b. West Almond, N.Y., Feb. 27, 1910; s. Frank S. and Bessie (Lewis) G.; B.S., Alfred U., 1932; M.D., U. Rochester, 1939; m. Elberta Frees, Aug. 21, 1934; children—David R., Nancy L. Intern, Henry Ford Hosp., Detroit, 1939-40, resident in surgery, 1940-41, 51-57; gen. practice, Corning, N.Y., 1941-42; med. dir. Corning Glass Works, 1946-47; pvt. practice medicine and surgery, Corning, 1948-75; sr. surg. staff Corning Hosp. Served from lt. (j.g.) to lt. comdr. USNR, 1942-45. Mem. N.Y. State Med. Soc., Internat. Platform Assn., AMA. Republican. Presbyn. Mason (32 deg.), Lion. Home: 541 Br West Hammondsport NY 14840

GRAHAM, MALCOLM SANDFORD, dentist; b. White Plains, N.Y., Oct. 15, 1939; s. Lawrence Elbridge and Mary Baldwin (Fleming) G.; B.A., Colby Coll., 1961; D.D.S., Columbia U., 1965; m. Linda Christensen, Sept. 5, 1964; children—Elizabeth, Scott, Leslie. Intern, Beth Israel Med. Center, N.Y.C., 1965-66; pvt. practice dentistry, N.Y.C., 1966-68, White Plains, 1968—; mem. staff White Plains Hosp., N.Y. Hosp., Cornell U. Licensed dentist, N.Y., Conn. Mem. ADA, N.Y. Acad. Dentistry, Acad. Gen. Dentistry, White Plains Dental Forum. Home: 4 Gracie Lane Darien CT 06820 Office: 170 Maple Ave White Plains NY 10601

GRAHAM, MARTHA, dancer, choreographer; b. Pitts., May 11, 1894; studied with Ruth St. Denis; LL.D., Mills Coll., Brandeis U., Smith Coll., Harvard U., 1966, also numerous others. Soloist, Denishawn Co., 1920, Greenwich Village Follies, 1923; faculty Eastman Sch., 1925; debut as choreographer-dancer 48th St. Theatre, N.Y.C., 1926; founder, artistic dir. Martha Graham Dance Co., Martha Graham Sch. Contemporary Dance; Guggenheim fellow, 1932; choreographer 150 works including Appalachian Spring, Letter to the World, Clytemnestra Tragic Patterns, Frontier, Phaedra, with music composed by Aaron Copland, Paul Hindemith, Carlos Chavez, Samuel Barber, Gian-Carlo Menotti, William Schuman, others; guest soloist leading U.S. orchs. in solos Judith, Triumph of St. Joan; Guggenheim fellow, fgn. tours with Martha Graham Dance Co., 1950, 54, 55-56, 60, 62-63, 67, 68, some under auspices U.S. Dept. State; U.S. tours, 1966, 70, sponsored by Nat. Endowment for Arts. Recipient Aspen award, 1965; Creative Arts award Brandeis U., 1968; Distinguished Service to Arts award Nat. Inst. Arts and Letters, 1970; Handel medallion City of N.Y., 1970; others. Author: Notebooks of Martha Graham, 1973. Address: care Columbia Artists Mgmt Inc 165 W 57th St New York City NY 10019*

GRAHAM, ROBERT SHERMAN, physician, ins. co. exec.; b. Columbus, Ohio, July 24, 1920; s. John Palmer and Helen Marie (Sherman) G.; A.A., Mars Hill Coll., 1940; B.A., Ohio State U., 1942; postgrad. Wake Forest U., 1942-43; M.D., Temple U., 1949. Intern, Columbia (S.C.) Hosp., 1949-50; fellow and resident in neurology Columbia Presbyn. Med. Center, N.Y.C., 1956-59; asst. med. dir. Equitable Life Assurance Soc. U.S., N.Y.C., 1954-56, asso. med. dir., 1959-66, med. dir. bur. employees health, 1966-68, asst. v.p., med. dir., 1968-69, 2d v.p., med. dir., 1969-74, v.p., 1974—, dir. personal concerns program, 1978-—; practice medicine specializing in neurology, N.Y.C., 1959-70; mem. faculty Columbia U., 1958-60; attending physician in neurology St. Luke's Hosp. Center, N.Y.C., 1959—, mem. med. bd., 1965—; bd. trustees Nat. Assn. on Drug Abuse Programs, Inc., 1976—; mem. N.Y. State Drug Abuse Adv. Council, 1976—; mem. N.Y. State Council on Health Research, 1978—; mem. Gov. Carey's Transition Task Force for Reorganization Dept. Mental Health, 1977; chmn. N.Y. State Drug Abuse Conf., 1978; nat. chmn. task force on Drugs in Industry, Nat. Drug Abuse Conf., 1978. Served with U.S. Army, 1943-45; with M.C., USN, 1950-54. Recipient awards Equitable Life Assurance Co., 1977. Mem. Am. Acad. Neurology, Am. Acad. Preventive Medicine, Indsl. Med. Assn., Assn. Life Ins. Med. Dirs., AMA, N.Y. County, N.Y. State med. socs., Sigma Phi Epsilon, Phi Rho Sigma, Gamma Nu Iota. Contbg. author Vocational Rehabilitation of the Drug Abuser, 1973. Home: 115 Central Park W New York NY 10023 Office: 1285 Ave of Americas New York NY 10019

GRAHAM, WILLIAM PIERSON, mgmt. services co. exec.; b. East St. Louis, Ill., Feb. 19, 1935; s. William Schley and Opal Elizabeth (Gray) G.; B.S., U. Ill., 1956; m. Margaret Newton McDowell, Sept. 30, 1961; children—Lisa, Heather, Jennifer. With IBM Corp., 1956-69, asst. to pres., 1967-68, dir. mktg. comml. industries, data processing div., 1968-69; exec. v.p. EDP Tech., Inc., Washington, 1969-71, pres., chief exec. officer, 1971-73; pres. Washington Profl. Group, 1973—, also Capitol Venture Group, Inc., real estate devel., Washington Franchise, Inc.; chmn. bd. Daisy Prodns., Inc., entertainment. Asst. for domestic programs White House, Washington, 1966-67; pres. White House Fellows Found., 1973-74; chmn. bd. dirs. Congressional Mgmt. Found.; mem. fgn. service profl. devel. rev. group Dept. State, 1976; mem. U.S. Adv. Com. Vocat. Edn., 1968-69, U.S. Fed. Adv. Com. Employment Security, 1968-71; panel cons. Edn. Professions Devel. Act, HEW, 1969-71; del. German Am. Forum, Bonn, Berlin, 1975; chmn. parents assn. Sidwell Friends Sch., Washington, 1976-78; vice chmn. fin. adv. com. Nat. Com. for Effective Congress, 1976-77. Served with AUS, 1957. White House fellow, 1966-67. Mem. White House Fellows Assn. (pres. 1973-74). Home: 9030 Congressional Pkwy Potomac MD 20854 Office: 3062 M St Washington DC 20007

GRAHAM-DAVIS, PATRICIA, coll. adminstr.; b. Saluda, S.C., Mar. 9, 1949; d. Eddie Roy and Lillian Leo (Wertz) Graham; student Essex County Coll. 1968-70; B.A. Rutgers U., 1972; M.Ed., Antioch Coll., 1974; m. Richard Arter Davis, Jan. 22, 1977. Counselor vocat. and academic ACTION, Vista Vol., Essex County Rehab. Commn., East Orange, N.J., 1970-71; asst. group leader Sisters of the Good Shepherd Sch. for Girls, Fox Chase, Pa., 1972-74; counselor Widener Coll., Chester, Pa., 1974-77; counselor-coordinator East Stroudsburg (Pa.) State Coll., 1977—, instr. tng. workshops for peer counselor program, 1977—, instr. coll. survival skills to freshmen Equal Opportunity Program, 1977—. Sec. Monroe County br. NAACP, 1977—. Certified in counseling and guidance, secondary level, Pa. Mem. Am. Personnel and Guidance Assn., Assn. Non-White Concerns (treas. div. guidance 1978-79), Inst. for Personal and Organizational Devel. Baptist. Researcher in peer counseling. Home: RD 1 Box 523 Henryville PA 18332 Office: Stroud 106 E Stroudsburg State Coll East Stroudsburg PA 18301

GRAHAME, ORVILLE FRANCIS, lawyer, bus. exec.; b. Palo, Iowa Apr. 2, 1904; s. Samuel G. and Dawn (Booth) G.; B.A., U. Iowa, 1925, J.D., 1929; m. Paula Patton, Nov. 3, 1923; 1 dau., Sarah Jane Cairns. Admitted to Iowa bar, 1929, N.Y. bar, 1932, Mass. bar, 1940, U.S. Supreme Ct., 1954; asso. Guardian Life Ins. Co., 1929-39, asst. sec., 1936-39; cons., formerly v.p., gen. counsel, dir. Paul Revere Life Ins. Co., 1940-67, Mass. Protective Assn., Inc., Worcester, Paul Revere Variable Annuity Ins. Co., Paul Revere Corp. and affiliates; v.p., gen. counsel-ins., dir. AVCO Corp.; arbitrator Am. Arbitration Assn. Nat. adv. com. White House Conf. Aging, 1959-61, 70-72; mem. com. on employment and retirement Nat. Council on Aging; past regional mem. adv. council Mass. Bd. Edn.; mem. Bus. Com. for Tax Reduction, 1963-64; exec. com. Health and Accident Underwriters Conf., 1954-55; mem. Mass. Pension Commn., 1953-55, Mass. Variable Annuity Commn., 1956-60, Zoning Appeals Bd. Worcester, 1958-63; past mem. bd. dirs. U. Iowa Found., ARC, Worcester, Iowa Law Sch. Found.; founder U. Iowa Law Scholarship Fund; asst. mgr. campaign lt. gov. Whittier, Mass., 1952-56; coordinator campaign Lt. Gov. Richardson, 1964; mem. N.Y. County Republican Com., 1934-36. U.S. res. officer Inf., 1925-39. Recipient Distinguished Service award State U. Iowa, 1964. Fellow Ins. Inst. Am.; mem. Am., Mass., Worcester County bar assns., Assn. Bar City N.Y., N.Y. County Lawyers Assn., Assn. Life Counsel, Am. Life Conf., Ins. Econs. Soc. Am. (pres. 1954-55), Ins. Fedn. Mass., Newcomen Soc., Acad. Polit. Sci., Am.-Scottish Found., English Speaking Union, Worcester Hist. Soc., Nat. Trust for Historic Preservation, Harry S. Truman Library Inst., Worcester Music Festival Assn., Phi Alpha Delta, Order of Coif. Unitarian. Clubs: Masons, Shriners, Rotary, Worcester. Author: (with others) The Life Insurance Contract, 1953; editorial bd. Corpus Juris, 1929, Ins. Decision, 1933-37; contbr. articles to profl. jours. Home: 6 Bancroft Tower Rd Worcester MA 01609 Office: 18 Chestnut St Worcester MA 01608

GRAHAME, PAULA PATTON (MRS. ORVILLE FRANCIS GRAHAME), artist, writer; b. Clearfield, Iowa; d. Harry T. and Betsey J. (Jacobs) Patton; B.A., U. Iowa, 1926; m. Orville F. Grahame, Nov. 3, 1923; 1 dau., Sarah G. Grahame Cairns. Artist, sculptor exhibited Ind. Artists, N.Y.C., Worcester Art Mus., Rockport Art Assn. Dir. Protective Assn. Can., 1962-70; corporator Worcester Girls Club, Home for Blind; bd. dirs. Worcester Children's Friends Soc., 1963-67, Edward St. Day Nursery, 1954-60, Worcester Youth Guidance Center, 1963-66. Founder, Art Scholarship Fund U. Iowa. Recipient Distinguished Service award U. Iowa, 1969. Mem. Nat. Soc. Lit. and Arts, Worcester Hist. Soc., Art Mus., Music Festival Assn., Worcester Sci. Mus., Am. Mus. Natural History (asso.), Friends of Fogg Mus., Met. Opera Guild, Worcester Heritage Preservation Soc., Nat., Iowa hist. socs., Assos. Nat. Archives, Smithsonian Assos., Rockport Art Assn., AAUW (pres. 1959-61), Unitarian Universalist Alliance (pres. 1966-68), D.A.R. Republican. Unitarian. Author: Palimpsest Stories; also short stories, poems; editor Meml. Hosp. News, 1951-54. Home: 6 Bancroft Tower Rd Worcester MA 01609

GRAHM, MILTON L., former coll. pres.; b. N.Y.C., Jan. 5, 1910; s. William and Jennie (Schwartz) G.; student U. Mich., 1926-29; A.B. cum laude, Harvard, 1931; Ed.M., Boston U., 1964; Sc.D. (hon.), Ft. Lauderdale U.; m. Edith J. Leavitt, July 5, 1932; children—Nancy (Mrs. Lawrence N. Miller), John L., Wendy. Buyer, mgr. bargain basement Leavitt Co., Manchester, N.H., 1932-35; represented James Talcott, Fidelity Factors, N.Y.C., 1935-40; pres. Acceptance Factors, Inc., Boston, 1936-41; pres. Grahm Jr. Coll., Boston, 1951-71, pres. emeritus, 1971-75, 76—, interim pres., 1975-76. Dir., Autodynamics, Inc., Boston Ednl. Research, 1972, Group 128, Inc., 1971-76, Sesame Travel Agy., 1971-75. Commr., Accrediting Commn. for Bus. Schs., 1968-71. Gen. solicitation Red Feather, 1936-61, advance gifts solicitation, 1961—, capt., 1949-50, maj., 1950-51, asst. center chmn., 1951-52; gen. solicitation Combined Jewish Appeal, 1954-55, chmn. advance gifts, 1955-56, chmn. Newton Center, 1956-57, advt. team, 1957—; dir. Jewish Vocational Service, 1965-70, mem. nat. council Joint Distbn. Com., 1963—; mem. adv. bd. Robert F. Kennedy Action Corps, 1969—. Trustee Combined Jewish Philanthropies, Boston Ballet Co., 1971-76; trustee Opera Co. Boston, 1971-73, bd. dirs., 1973—. Recipient certificate of merit Stevens Coll., 1967. Mem. Boston Credit Bur. (treas. 1939-40), Mass. Council Pvt. Schs. (pres. 1957-58), Am. Philos. Soc., History Edn. Soc., Soc. for Advancement Edn., John Dewey Soc., Philosophy Edn. Soc., Found. Integrative Edn., Comparative Edn. Soc., Assn. Higher Edn. N.E.A., Nat. Bus. Edn. Assn., Eastern Bus. Tchrs. Assn., Am. Soc. Aesthetics, Advt. Club Boston (co-chmn., edn. com.), Radio and TV Execs. Club, Back Bay Devel. Assn., Bus. Men's Council (dir.), Harvard Bus. Sch. Alumni Assn. (hon.), Broadcasting Execs. Club, United Bus. Schs. Assn. (chmn. pub. relations com. 1965-70), Temple Israel Brotherhood. Clubs: Harvard (Boston); Belmont (Mass.) Country. Co-author: Two Hour Shorthand, 1960; Legal Typing Practice, 1964. Contbr. articles to profl. jours. Mem. speakers panel Boost Boston, 1963. Home: 487 Ward St Newton Center MA 02159

GRAINGER, THOMAS HUTCHESON, JR., microbiologist; b. Bethlehem, Pa., Dec. 14, 1913; s. Thomas Hutcheson and Frances Roberts (Williams) G.; B.A., Lehigh U., 1936, M.S., 1938; Ph.D., 1946; postgrad. U. Pa., 1939-41; m. Mary Louise Siverling, Dec. 20, 1941; 1 son, Thomas Hutcheson, Instr., Med. Sch. U. Pa., 1939-41; asso. prof. Lehigh U., Bethlehem, Pa., 1948-59; mgr. control Nat. Drug Co., Swiftwater, Pa., 1959-64; asst. dir. Nat. Drug Co., 1964-71; chief microbiologist Pocono Hosp., East Stroudsburg, Pa., 1971—. Mem. Sch. Bd. Swiftwater. Served to maj. AUS, 1941-46. Fellow AAAS, Am. Pub. Health Assn.; mem. Am. Soc. Microbiology, Am. Med. Writers Assn., History of Sci. Soc., N.Y. Acad. Scis., Pharm. Mfrs. Assn., Am. Forestry Assn., Sigma Xi. Author: (with S. Thomas), Bacteria, 1952; Guide to the History of Bacteriology, 1958; contbr. articles to profl. jours. and popular mags. Home: Swiftwater PA 18370 Office: Pocono Hospital East Stroudsburg PA 18301

GRALA, WILLIAM LEON, pharm. co. exec.; b. Hazleton, Pa., Sept. 29, 1922; s. William Leon and Mary Magdalene (Demschick) G.; B.S., Haverford Coll., 1943; m. June Wilkins, Nov. 5, 1943 (div. Mar. 1961); m. 2d, Babette Liversidge Jensen, Nov. 22, 1963; 1 son, Christopher Wells. Copywriter, John F. Arndt, Inc., Phila., 1946; indsl. relations asst. ACF-Brill Motors Co., Phila., 1946-48; with SmithKline Corp., Phila., 1948—, v.p. corporate pub. relations, 1971-73, v.p. pub. affairs, 1973—. Exec. sec. SmithKline Found., 1970-75, pres., chief exec. officer, 1978—, trustee, 1971—; exec. sec. C. Mahlon Kline Meml. Found., 1970-78. Chmn., Pharm. Info. Com. Greater Phila., 1960-65. Asst. sec. Pennsylvanians for Effective Govt.,

1973—; div. chmn. United Fund, 1973-74; gen. chmn. ann. dr. Phila. Police Athletic League, 1975-76, also vice chmn. bd. dirs. Exec. bd. Phila. council Boy Scouts Am., 1967-69, chmn. pub. relations com.; bd. dirs. Citizens Crime Commn. Phila., Pa. Environ. Council, 1977—, Phila. Urban Coalition, 1977—; trustee Child Study Center Phila., 1965-69; bd. dirs., sec. North City Corp., 1968-75; bd. dirs. Burn Found. Greater Delaware Valley, 1975—, chmn., 1978—; bd. dirs. Hahnemann Med. Coll. and Hosp., 1978—; bd. dirs., vice-chmn. Emergency Med. Services, Council of Phila. Health Mgmt. Corp., 1973—, Del. Valley Council, 1968—, Eastern region Pa. Economy League, 1971—, Phila. Commn. Effective Criminal Justice, 1975-77; bd. dirs. Area Council on Econ. Edn., 1975—, mem. exec. com., v.p., 1976—; bd. dirs. Consumer Council of Greater Phila., 1975-76, NCCJ, 1976-78; mem. internat. sponsors council Howard U., 1976—; mem. pub. relations com. Southeastern Pa. chpt. ARC. Served with AUS, 1943-46. Mem. Pub. Relations Soc. Am. (past dir. Phila. chpt.), Phila. Pub. Relations Assn. (dir.), Am. Acad. Polit. and Social Sci., Acad. Polit. Sci., Am. Pub. Health Assn., Pa. C. of C. (dir. 1976—), Mfrs. Assn. Delaware Valley (dir. 1978—), Am. Trauma Soc. (dir., chmn. Southeastern Pa. unit 1976-78), Pa. Soc. Club: Union League (Phila.). Home: 360 Conestoga Rd Wayne PA 19087 Office: 1500 Spring Garden St Philadelphia PA 19101

GRAMMAS, GUS WILLIAM, educator; b. N.Y.C., Feb. 6, 1942; s. Spyros and Nina (Kines) G.; B.A., Columbia U., 1963, Ph.D., 1972; m. Wendy Berkelhammer, June 26, 1977. Asst. prof. mgmt. scis. Grad. Sch. Bus. Columbia U., N.Y.C., 1972-77; asst. prof. bus. Grad. Sch. Bus. Adminstrn., N.Y.U., 1977—; treas., dir. Statistica Cons., Inc., N.Y.C., 1973—. Recipient Distinguished Teaching award Columbia U., 1970, Outstanding Prof. award, 1973. Mem. AAAS, Operations Research Soc. Am., Am. Statis. Assn., Inst. Math. Statistics, Washington Operations Research Council, Inst. Mgmt. Sci. Contbr. to profl. jours. Home: 55 E 87th St New York City NY 10028 Office: NYU 100 Trinity Pl New York City NY 10006

GRANAHAN, JOHN JOSEPH, mut. fund exec.; b. Phila., Jan. 11, 1936; s. Joseph A. and Mary C. (Corcoran) G.; A.B. in Econs., St. Joseph's Coll., Phila., 1958; grad. fellow in econs. Cath. U. Am., 1958-59; m. Kathryn Lombaer, July 2, 1960; children—John, Kevin, Robert, Brian. Investment analyst 1st Pa. Co., Phila., 1960-62; investment analyst Wellington Mgmt., Phila., 1962-68, v.p., 1968-77, sr. v.p. 1977—; fund mgr. Morgan Growth Fund, 1968—, Ivest Fund, 1974-78, Explorer Fund, 1972—. Mem. Community Chest Budget Com., Concord, Mass., 1973-74. Chartered fin. analyst. Mem. Fin. Analysts Fedn., Pi Gamma Mu. Republican. Roman Catholic. Home: 1385 Old Marlboro Rd Concord MA 01742 Office: 28 State St Boston MA 02109

GRANER, GEORGE WILLIAM, JR., banker; b. Allentown, Pa., Oct. 13, 1944; s. George William and Louise Adel (Applegate) G.; B.S., PMC Colls., 1966; m. Mary Elisabeth Allen, Sept. 3, 1966; children—George Michael, Suzanne Elizabeth. Audit staff Arthur Andersen & Co., Phila., 1966-67, 69-71; controller Felix Spatola & Sons Inc., Phila., 1971; v.p. Lincoln Bank, Phila., 1971—. Served to 1st. lt., U.S. Army, 1967-69; Vietnam. C.P.A., Pa. Mem. Lansdale Jr. C. of C., Am., Pa. insts. C.P.A.'s, Robert Morris Assn. Republican. Methodist. Office: Lincoln Bank PO Box 8590 Philadelphia PA 19102

GRANGER, J(EFFREY) S(OLON), stockbroker; b. N.Y.C., June 21, 1891; s. David and Minnie (Neuburn) G.; student N.Y. Mil. Acad., Cornwall-on-the-Hudson, 1903-05, Phillips-Exeter Acad., 1905-09; Ph.B., Brown U., 1913; J.D., Columbia, 1916; m. Carolyn Sears, Apr. 5, 1921; children—Ann (Mrs. Andrew Laszlo), Jeffrey Sears (dec.). Mng. and sr. partner Granger & Co., 1919—; pres., chmn. bd. Fed. Match Corp., 1928-29; dir. McKesson & Robbins, Inc. (now Foremost McKesson, Inc.), 1941-63; chmn. bd. Harvill Corp., Los Angeles, 1944-56; dir. Dempster Investment Co., Evanston, Ill.; mgr., partner Granger Ranches, Ennis, Mont.; pres. Indian Creek Ditch Co., Cameron Ditch Co., Mont.; dir. No. Cross Lands and Livestock Corp., Australia. Served to 2d lt. U.S. Army, 1917-19. Mem. Am. Stock Exchange, Chgo. Bd. Trade, N.Y. Commodity Exchange, Am. Arbitration Assn. (arbitrator), Mil. Order World Wars, N.E. Soc., St. George's Soc. N.Y., Phillips-Exeter Alumni Assn. Clubs: Brown U. (pres.), Touchdown, Church, Bankers Am. (N.Y.C.); Riverside Country (Bozeman, Mont.); Turf and Field. Home: 1155 Park Ave New York City NY 10028 Office: 111 Broadway New York City NY 10006

GRANICK, LOIS WAYNE, info. scientist; b. Weatherford, Okla., Mar. 5, 1932; d. Johnny Wayne and Lois Bernice (Wells) Cox; student U. N.Mex., 1949-51; m. Robert Eugene Granick, June 6, 1951; children—Bruce, Leslie Knipling, Jeffrey, Andrea. Programmer/systems analyst Documentation Inc., Bethesda, Md., 1961-66; cons. Mex. Govt., Mexico City, 1966-69; info. specialist Autocomp Inc., Bethesda, 1970-72; dir. Autocode, div., 1972-73; exec. editor Psychol. Abstracts, Am. Psychol. Assn., Washington, 1974—, dir. Psychol. Abstracts Info. System, 1974—. Mem. Nat. Fedn. Abstracting and Indexing Services (dir. 1977—), Info. Sci. Abstracts (dir. 1978—), Am. Soc. Info. Sci., Assn. Info. and Dissemination Centers, Internat. Council Sci. Unions Abstracting Bd. Home: 6300 Alcott Rd Bethesda MD 20034 Office: Am Psychol Assn 1200 17th St Washington DC 20036

GRANITE, HARVEY RENWICK, educator; b. Rochester, N.Y., Nov. 23, 1927; s. Albert William and Martha (Potter) G.; A.B., Cornell U., 1949; M.A., U. Rochester, 1956; postgrad. Columbia, 1962-63; Ph.D., U. Pitts., 1974; m. Ursula Lisa Blum, June 18, 1950; children—Deborah Ruth, Tamara Eve. Mem. staff Rochester pub. schs., 1956—, supervising dir. instrn., 1969-71, coordinator urban funded programs, dir. Project UNIQUE, 1971—, also bd. dirs.; sr. lectr. English, U. Rochester, 1957—; cons. in field. Vice pres. Living Arts Center, Rochester, 1967-70. Democratic ward committeemen, 1969—; bd. dirs. Action for a Better Community, 1970-76, John Hay Found., 1960-70, Threshold, 1976-77; exec. bd. Rochester Arts Council, 1976-77; bd. mgmt. Midtown YMCA. John Hay fellow, 1960, 62-63; recipient Fiction award Columbia, 1963; fellow Ednl. Professions Devel. Act, 1970. Mem. Nat., N.Y. State councils tchr. English, N.Y. State Adminstrs. in Compensatory Edn. (pres. 1973-76), Nat. Assn. Adminstrs. State-Fed. Edn. Programs (sec. 1975-77), Am. Fedn. Tchrs., Conf. English Edn., Urban League, Phi Delta Kappa. Author: Themes in World Literature, 1970; Literature from the Old Testament, 1971; Action series, 8 vols., 1970-71, 6 vols., 1978; also articles, short stories, revs. Home: 1571 East Ave Rochester NY 14610 Office: 13 Fitzhugh St S Rochester NY 14614

GRANSTON, DAVID WILFRED, fin. exec.; b. Schenectady, N.Y., Dec. 5, 1936; s. Arnold Andrew and Edna (Nickerson) G.; B.A., Colgate U., 1958; M.B.A., Syracuse U., 1960; m. Priscilla Day, June 10, 1961; 1 son, David Wilfred. Supr. E.I. DuPont De Nemours & Co., Inc., Parlin, N.J., 1961-62; sr. fin. analyst Bendix Corp., N.Y.C., 1963-69; controller Allied Chem. Corp., N.Y.C., 1969-71; v.p. fin. Thomas Borthwick Sons, Ltd., N.Y.C., 1972-78; group controller N.Y. Times Co., 1978—. Served with USCGR, 1960. Colgate U. War Meml. scholar, 1954-58. Mem. Phi Delta Theta. Clubs: Colgate U. Alumni (L.I.) (pres. 1975-76); Creek (Locust Valley, N.Y.); Northport (Maine) Yacht (vice commodore 1978), Windham (N.Y.) Mountain. Home: Box 368 Piping Rock Rd Locust Valley NY 11560 Office: 229 W 43d St New York City NY 10036

GRANT, ALLAN AARON, electronics co. exec.; b. N.Y.C., Oct. 19, 1921; s. Hyman and Ida (Ditor) Goldberg; B.B.A., Pace U., 1951; M.B.A., Hofstra U., 1970; m. Lillian Chyatt, Jan. 4, 1944; children—Craig, Susan. Accountant, A. Klein Co., N.Y.C., 1946-50; controller Litecor, Inc., N.Y.C., 1950-60, Progress Electronics, Inc., Plainview, 1960-66; treas. Optomechanisms, Inc., Plainview, 1966-70; v.p. finance Arco Electronics, Inc., mfr. distbr. electronic components, Great Neck, 1970—, dir., 1973—; v.p. fin. Automatic Connector Inc., Commack, N.Y., 1975—; corp. controller Jack LaLanne Health Spas, Rockville Centre, N.Y., 1977—. Served with USNR, 1942-45; PTO. Mem. Nat. Assn. Accountants, Pace U. Alumni Assn., Hofstra U. Alumni Assn.

GRANT, CLIFFORD M., JR., electric co. exec.; b. Cobleskill, N.Y//,M24N.Y., May 6, 1931; s. Clifford M. and Bernice (Scott) G.; student pub. schs.; m. Georgia K. Nelson, Dec. 23, 1967; children—Barbara Carol, Edward Richard. With Gen. Electric Co., 1953-58, 62—, product service engr., 1968-70, with internat. gas turbine works, 1971—, mgr. mech. and nuclear service Chesapeake dist., Columbia, Md., 1976—. Served with USN, 1949-53, USNR, 1958-62. Mem. Reformed Ch. Author tech. papers. Office: Gen Electric Co Room 543 5565 Sterrett Pl Columbia MD 21044

GRANT, EDWARD VINCENT, hosp. adminstr.; b. Jersey City, May 20, 1918; s. John Joseph and Honoriah (Cody) G.; student parochial schs.; m. Helen Joan Grabowski, Apr. 19, 1942; children—Edward, Richard, Robert, Martin, John, Mary Ellen. Barker, Worlds Fair N.Y., 1939; with Lenox Hill Hosp., N.Y.C., 1939-42, 45-55; adminstr. Hunterdon Med. Center, Flemington, N.J., 1955-67; adminstr. N.Y. Infirmary, N.Y.C., 1967—. Lectr., Columbia Sch. Pub. Health and Adminstrv. Medicine, 1958; dir. Hosp. Bur. N.Y.C., 1950-68; preceptor dept. epidemiology and public health Yale, 1960-65; med. coordinator Hunterdon County (N.J.) Civil Def., 1957-67; preceptor hosp. adminstrn. program Wagner Coll., N.Y.C., 1970-72; guest lectr. Northwood Inst., Midland, Mich. Mem. planning bd. Town of Clinton, 1962-67; chmn. Clinton Citizens Com., 1965-67. Trustee George K. Large Found., Flemington. Served from 2d lt. to maj. AUS, 1942-45. Mem. Am. Coll. Hosp. Adminstrs., Am. (com. home and ambulatory care 1963-66), N.J. (trustee) hosp. assns., Council Hosp. Adminstrs., N.J. Hosp. Adminstrs. Soc., Adminstr. Conf. Group, Adminstrs. Club. Roman Catholic (trustee parish). Mem. adv. bd. Health Instns. Purchasing Mag. Home: 15 Maiden Way Colonia NJ 07067 Office: 321 E 15th St New York City NY 10003

GRANT, EDWIN RANDOLPH, mfg. co. exec.; b. Stoneham, Mass., Oct. 6, 1943; s. Lauris Levi and Dorothy Hall (Lewis) G.; B.F.A., Denison U., 1966; M.B.A., Syracuse U., 1969; m. Ruth Louise Kennedy, June 24, 1967. Trainee, Sears, Roebuck & Co., Springfield, Mass., 1968-69; asst. to pres. Kennedy Bros., Inc., Vergennes, Vt., 1969-70, v.p., 1970-72, exec. v.p., 1972-74, pres., treas., 1974—, partner Vergennes Shopping Center, incorporator and dir. Vergennes Devel. Corp., 1977—; incorporator, dir. Addison County Devel. Corp., 1975—; dir. Vt. Attractions Assn., 1975-77, v.p., 1977-78, pres., 1978—. Served to 2d lt. USAR, 1969-73. Mem. Vergennes Area (pres. 1976—), Vt. State (dir. 1976-78), Addison (dir. 1975-76), Lake Champlain (dir. 1977—) chambers commerce. Clubs: Charlotte-Shelburne (Vt.) Rotary; Green Mountain Transp. (pres. 1976-77); Lake Champlain Yacht. Home: RD 3 Box 284 Shelburne VT 05482 Office: 11 Main St Vergennes VT 05491

GRANT, JOHN HERBERT, steel constrn. co. exec.; b. Akron, Ohio, Dec. 19, 1928; s. Jesse Herbert and Hazel Rose (Enborg) G.; B.S. in Civil Engring., U. Pa., 1950, M.S., 1955; m. Marilyn Ann Mayer, Sept. 16, 1950; children—Jeffrey, Herbert, Elizabeth, Douglas. With G & H Steel Service Inc., Bromall, Pa., 1950—, v.p., 1956-75, treas., 1965—, pres., 1975—, also dir.; officer, dir. G & H Steel Service New Eng., Gen. Steel Constrn. Co.; dir. IPA Products Co. Bd. dirs., pres. Marple Newtown (Pa.) Sch. Bd., 1973—. Mem. Philobiblon Soc., Nat. Assn. Rodsetters (v.p.), Radnor Hist. Soc. (dir.). Republican. Methodist (past chmn. coms.). Rotarian (pres.). Club: Athenaeum (Phila.). Home: 35 Dunminning Rd Newton Square PA 19073 Office: 1101 Sussex Rd Broomall PA 19008

GRANT, RONALD ALFRED, psychiatrist, pastoral counselor; b. Providence, May 28, 1938; s. Alfred Edward and Althea (Walker) G.; A.B., Tufts U., 1959; B.D., Andover Newton Theol. Sch., 1963, S.T.M., 1964, D.Min. (Cutting fellow), 1972; M.D., Boston U., 1969; m. Barbara Farnham, June 16, 1962; children—Andrew Edward, Kathryn Caroline. Ordained to ministry Baptist Ch., 1969; intern Mary Imogene Bassett Hosp., Cooperstown, N.Y., 1969-70, asst. resident psychiatry, 1970-71; resident psychiatry N.Y. State Psychiat. Inst. and Columbia Presbyn. Med. Center, N.Y.C., 1971-72, sr. resident community psychiatry, 1972-73; candidate N.Y. Inst. of C.G. Jung Found. Analytical Psychology, 1973—; psychiat. cons. Family Counseling Service of Ridgewood (N.J.), 1971—; cons. psychiatry, religion and pastoral counseling Community Counseling Service of Pascack Valley, Montclair Counseling Center; pvt. practice specializing in psychiatry and pastoral counseling, 1971—; med. dir. Montclair Counseling Center; tng. therapist Inst. Religion and Health. Deacon Emmanuel Baptist Ch. Mem. Am. Orthopsychiat. Assn., Am. Psychiat. Assn., Assn. Advancement Psychotherapy, Assn. Clin. Pastoral Edn., Insts. Religion and Mental Health, Inst. Soc., Ethics and Life Scis. Club: Masons. Home and Office: 523 High Noon Rd Weston CT 06883

GRANTHAM, ROBERT J., educator; b. Durham, N.C., Aug. 3, 1939; s. John Gurney and Grace Elizabeth (Venable) G.; B.S. in Psychology, Pa. State U., 1963; M.A., Seton Hall U., 1965; Ph.D. in Rehab., State U. N.Y., Buffalo, 1970; m. Regina Brownfield, Sept. 7, 1963; children—Keith, Gabarielle. Asso. dean undergrad. div. State U. N.Y., Buffalo, 1971-77, mental health therapist, asst. prof. div. community psychiatry, 1977—; pres. Venable Builders Supplies, Inc., TEFCO Services, Inc. Bd. dirs. Buffalo Hearing and Speech Center, Planned Parenthood of Buffalo; bd. dirs., adv. com. Transitional Services, Inc., 1975-77. Served with AUS, 1965-67. Mem. Am. Personnel and Guidance Assn., Am. Ednl. Research Assn., Am. Psychol. Assn., Phi Delta Kappa, Kappa Alpha Psi. Club: Kenmore Rotary. Research and publs. on effects of counselor sex, race and lang. style on black students in initial interviews, counselor preference and human services delivery. Home: 244 Argonne St Kenmore NY 14217 Office: 462 Grider St Buffalo NY 14215

GRANVILLE, MAURICE FREDERICK, petroleum co. exec.; b. La Grange, Tex., Oct. 26, 1915; s. Maurice Frederick and Dorathea (von Rosenburg) G.; B.S. in Chem. Engring., U. Tex., 1937; Sc.M. in Chem. Engring., Mass. Inst. Tech., 1939; m. Janet Knotts, Jan. 13, 1945; children—Carol McCoy (Mrs. Peter Blyberg), Frederick Lloyd. With Texaco Inc., 1939—, organizer chem. div., Port Arthur, Tex., 1955-58, gen. mgr. petrochem. dept., 1958-60, v.p. petrochem. dept., 1960-67, v.p. strategic planning and asst. chmn., 1967-70, pres., dir., 1970-71, chmn. bd., 1971—, chief exec. officer, 1972—; dir. Fed. Res. Bank N.Y. Bd. dirs. Am. Petroleum Inst., Met. Opera Assn.; mem. Governing bd. corp. Mass. Inst. Tech.; trustee Presbyterian Hosp. in City N.Y. Fellow Am. Inst. Chem. Engrs.; mem. Conf. Bd., Econ. Club N.Y. (dir.), Tau Beta Pi, Delta Kappa Epsilon, Phi Lambda Upsilon. Congregationalist. Clubs: Country (Darien); Cloud, Links (N.Y.C.); Links Golf (Manhasset, N.Y.). Office: Texaco Inc 2000 Westchester Ave White Plains NY 10650

GRASSO, ANTHONY JOSEPH, structural engr.; b. N.Y.C., Dec. 14, 1921; s. Frank and Mary (Massi) G.; B.Civil Engring. cum laude, Coll. City N.Y., 1942; m. Maria R. Leonessa, Apr. 19, 1952; children—Lisa, Rita, Patricia. Various engring. positions, 1942-48; partner Weiskopf & Pickworth, cons. engrs., N.Y.C., 1948—. Served with C.E., AUS, 1944-46. Mem. ASCE, N.Y. Assn. Cons. Engrs. (pres. 1978), Tau Beta Pi, Chi Epsilon. Structural designer bldgs., including Pitts. Nat. Bank, S. Central Bell Hdqrs. Bldg., N.Y. Telephone Co. Hdqrs. Home: 91 Cobb Ln Tarrytown NY 10591 Office: 200 Park Ave New York City NY 10017

GRASSO, DORIS TEN EYCK (MRS. DOMINIC LAWRENCE GRASSO), artist; b. Sullivan County, N.Y., May 3, 1914; d. Eugene Oscar and Elsie (Ten Eyck) Teschner; student Ednl. Alliance, N.Y.C., 1956-57; student art centers and pvt, art tng.; m. Dominic Lawrence Grasso, Nov. 29, 1933; children—Robert Eugene, Virginia Ann. Art dir., instr. Doris Grasso Sch. Fine Arts, Bayonne, N.J., 1952-66; exhibited in numerous group shows; one man shows Burr Gallery, N.Y.C., Bennett Coll., Bayonne Pub. Library, others; shows at Montclair Mus. Art, Newark Mus. Art, Nat. Arts Club, Thomson Gallery, N.Y.C., N.Y. Bank for Savs.; represented in Paul Whitener Meml. Collection, Hickory (N.C.) Mus. Art, George B. Burr Permanent Collection, N,Y.C., Bambergers Collection Famous People N.J. Trustee Jersey City Mus. Art, 1955-57. Owner, dir. The Doris Ten Eyck Grasso Art Gallery and Studio, Gloucester. Recipient Pauline Wick award, 1961; Winsor Newton awards, 1958, 61; Jersey City Mus. award, 1958; Gold medallion for Art, Jersey Jour. Women of Achievement, 1963; N.J. Ter-centennial award, 1964; named to Bamberger Hall of Fame, 1964; Grand Nat. award Am. Artists Profl. League, 1965; Amita Sister award for Art, in 1966; 1st award for sculpture N.J. Fedn. Womens Clubs, 1970. Fellow Internat. Arts and Letters, Am. Artists Profl. League; mem. Hudson Artists (pres. 1960-62, dir.), Jersey City Mus. Assn., Nat., N.J. (rec. sec., Patron's prize 1964) painters and sculptors socs., Trailside Art Mus. (chartered profl. artist mem.), Essex Watercolor Soc., Bayonne Mus. Arts, Whistler Art Soc., Burr Artists N.Y.C., Burr Galleries, Village Art Center Galleries, Sarosota Mus. Art Assn., Hunterdon Art Center Assn., Newark Art Center, Pen and Brush Club, Elks Aux. (pres. 1950-52), Ch. Guild (pres. 1950-52), Asso. Artists, Rockport Art Assn. Club: Bayonne Women's (art chmn.). Address: 15 Langsford St Gloucester MA 01930

GRASSO, ELLA T. (MRS. THOMAS A. GRASSO), gov. Conn.; b. Windsor Locks, Conn., May 10, 1919; d. James and Maria (Oliva) Tambussi; student pvt. schs.; B.A. magna cum laude, Mt. Holyoke Coll., 1940, M.A., 1942; LL.D., Sacred Heart U., 1972; hon. degree, Smith Coll.; m. Thomas A. Grasso, Aug. 31, 1942; children—Susane, James. Asst. dept. econs. and sociology Mt. Holyoke Coll., 1942; asst. state dir. research War Manpower Commn., 1943-46; mem. Conn. Legislature, 1953, 55, asst. house leader, 1955; state sec. Conn., 1958-70; mem. U.S. Ho. Reps., 1970-74; gov. Conn., 1975—; chmn. New Eng. Govs. Conf., 1977, New Eng. Regional Commn., 1977; vice chmn. Coalition Northeastern Govs., 1978-79, Democratic Govs. Assn., 1978-79. Nat. committeewoman from Conn., Democratic party, 1956-58, chmn. state platform com., 1958, 60, 62, 64, 66, 68, nat. platform com., 1960, co-chmn. resolutions com. Dem. Nat. Conv., 1964, 68; del. Dem. floor leader Constl. Conv., 1965; trustee Soc. for Savs. Bank, Hartford, Conn. Mem. Com. 100 for Hartford U.; mem. Long Lane Farm Study Commn., 1953-55, Hwy. Financing Study Commn., 1953-55; state chmn. Cystic Fibrosis Campaign, 1960, 64; pres. White Sands Beach Assn., 1952-55; mem. bd. Fgn. Scholarships, 1960-66, Com. of 1000 for St. Francis Hosp.; mem. Fed. Council on the Arts and Humanities; mem. Presdl. Commn. on Internat. Women's Year, 1975; bd. dirs. Windsor Locks Pub. Library, Conn. Soc. for Prevention Blindness; hon. dir. Manchester Community Coll. Found., Urban League Greater Hartford; trustee Conn. Coll., New London, Central Conn. Communities Cultural, Civic and Charitable Corp.; hon. trustee Conn. Opera Assn.; mem. adv. bd. Hartford, Am. Com. Italian Migration; hon. chmn. Italian Flood Relief. Recipient Amita award as outstanding women of Italian parentage, 1959; Am. Heritage award, 1961; Americanism award Conn. Valley council B'nai B'rith, 1963; named Woman of Year, Hartford Bus. and Profl. Womens Club, 1964; Silver Apple award Conn. Edn. Assn.; Most Distinguished Service citation Am. Legion Aux.; knight Order Merit Republic Italy, 1968; citation for distinguished service in civic, cultural and community endeavors Wilson Coll. Club of Conn., Knights of Khorassan award for work with Conn. Cystic Fibrosis Found.; Merit award dept. Conn., Italian Am. War Vets. U.S., 1972; Outstanding Service award Conn. Cystic Fibrosis Assn.; Marconi award Order Sons of Italy in Am. and Can., Woman of Yr. award ladies aux. Conn. dept. V.F.W.; Commendation for Outstanding Service and Dedication to Am. Vets., Jobs for Vets. Nat. Com.; Chubb fellow, Yale U. Mem. AAUW, Order Sons of Italy (Italian-Am. Gold Medal Conn. lodge 1963), Regina Elena Soc., Conn. Fedn. Dem. Women, Nat. Assn. Secs. State, Alpha Delta Kappa, Kappa Delta Pi (citation Central Conn. State Coll. chpt. 1960). Roman Catholic (council, dir. Cath. Youth Orgn.). Club: Mt. Holyoke of Hartford. Office: Office of Gov State Capitol Hartford CT 06115

GRASSO, SALVATORE PETER, educator; b. Milford, N.H., July 22, 1914; s. Angelo and Vincenza (Locicero) G.; B.S., U. N.H., 1937, M.C.E., 1940; postgrad. N.Y. U., 1942-44; m. Muriel H. Bowler, July 15, 1940; children—Peter A., Nancy J. (Mrs. William C. Freel). Grad. asst. U. N.H., Durham, 1937-30, instr. civil engring., 1938-40; instr. civil engring. U. Santa Clara (Calif.), 1940-41; tutor civil engring. Coll. City N.Y., N.Y.C., 1941-44; asst. engr. Interstate Sanitation Commn., N.Y.C., 1943-44; supr. pub. works Town Milford, 1946-54; subcontract mgr. Hitchiner Mfg. Co., Inc., 1954-56; civil and san. engr. Anderson-Nichols & Co., Inc., Cons. Engrs., Concord, N.H., 1956-60, chief engr., mgr., 1960-65; prof. engring. New Eng. Coll., Henniker, N.H., 1965—. Pres., Milford Co-op. Holding Co., 1957-60; v.p. Rollins King & McKone, Inc., Cons. Engrs., Manchester, N.H., 1967-69; short term cons. pub. health engring. Pan Am. Health Orgn., WHO, 1972—. Mem. Milford Budget Com., 1955, Milford Sch. Bd., 1958-64, Milford Bd. Selectmen, 1964-70, N.H. Water Resources Bd., 1965—, State Adv. Council Water Resource Research Center, Durham, 1972—; pres. N.H. Municipal Assn., 1965, N.H. Gov.'s Task Force, 1969; mem. adv. bd. St. Joseph's Hosp., Nashua, N.H., 1977—. Bd. dirs. Mid Merrimack Health Planning Council, Manchester. Served to capt. AUS, 1944-46. Named N.H. Engr. of Year, 1978; registered profl. engr., N.H., Me., Mass., Conn., Vt. Fellow Am. Soc. C.E. (sect. pres. 1972); mem. Nat., N.H. (pres. 1973-74) socs. profl. engrs., Am. Soc. for Engring. Edn., Am., N.H. (pres. 1953-54), New Eng. water works assns., Soc. Am. Mil. Engrs., Water Pollution Control Fedn., Boston Soc. C.E., Am. Legion (post comdr. 1953-54). K.C. (grand knight 1950-52). Home: 32 Elm St Milford NH 03055 Office: New Eng Coll Henniker NH 03242

GRAUBARD, SEYMOUR, lawyer; b. N.Y.C., Mar. 8, 1911; s. John and Edna (Kiesler) G.; A.B., Columbia, 1931, LL.B., 1933; m. Blanche Kazon, Aug. 24, 1941; 1 dau., Katherine (Mrs. William Calvin) Admitted to N.Y. bar, 1933; legis. asst. to bd. aldermen, N.Y.C.,

1934-35; partner firm Joseph D. McGoldrick, N.Y.C., 1936-37; law sec. to comptroller N.Y.C., 1937-41; sec. to justice Supreme Ct. N.Y. County, 1942, 45-46; practice in N.Y.C., 1949—; mem. firm Graubard, Moskovitz, McGoldrick, Dannett & Horowitz, 1969—; lectr. municipal govt. N.Y.U., New Sch. Social Research, 1938-40. Mem. N.Y.C. Commn. Govtl. Ops., 1959-61, N.Y.C. Transition Com., 1965, Coordinating Council Criminal Justice, 1967—. Nat. chmn. Anti-Defamation League, B'nai B'rith, 1970-76. Chmn. bd. dirs. Fund for N.Y.C.; bd. dirs. N.Y.C. Pub. Events Com., City Univ. Constrn. Fund. Served to maj. AUS, 1942-45. Mem. Assn. Bar City N.Y. (past chmn. com. city cts.), N.Y. State Bar Assn., N.Y. County Lawyers Assn. Clubs: City (trustee past pres.). Harmonie (N.Y.C.). Co-author: Building Regulation in New York City, 1944; also articles. Home: 993 Park Ave New York City NY 10028 Office: 345 Park Ave New York City NY 10022

GRAUPNER, MICHAEL ERNEST, tire co. exec.; b. N.Y.C., Mar. 17, 1950; s. Ernest Arnold and Gabriella (Ledorf) G.; B.A., Gettysburg Coll., 1972; m. Suzanne Frederick Skeats, Oct. 2, 1976. Supr. advt. and sales promotion Uniroyal Inc., N.Y.C., 1972-74, mgr. brand advt. and sales promotion, 1974-78, advt. dir., 1978—. Served with AUS, 1972-78. Mem. Kappa Delta Rho. Lutheran. Home: 308 Washington Rd Woodbury CT 06798 Office: 1230 Ave of Americas New York City NY 10020

GRAVE, GILMAN DREW, physician; b. Rhinebeck, N.Y., Jan. 3, 1941; s. Thomas Brooks and Elizabeth (France) G.; A.B. magna cum laude, Harvard U., 1962, M.D. magna cum laude, 1966; m. Nancy Jane Christy, Dec. 24, 1970; 1 son, Thomas Wade. Intern, Mass. Gen. Hosp., Boston, 1966-67, resident, 1967-68; instr. medicine Harvard U., 1968; research asso. NIH, Bethesda, Md., 1968-70, sr. staff fellow, 1970-72, med. officer, 1972—; cons. in medicine Washington Med. Center; vis. scientist Lab. Cerebral Metabolism, NIMH, 1972. Chmn. NIMH Combined Fed. Charities, 1970. Served with USPHS, 1968-70, 75—. Recipient Bowdoin prize for lit., 1960. Diplomate Am. Bd. Internal Medicine. Mem. Am. Soc. Neurochemistry, Washington Soc. History of Medicine, Alpha Omega Alpha. Mem. Soc. of Friends. Club: Apsculapian. Editor: Control of the Onset of Puberty, 1974; Chronic Childhood Illness, Assessment of Outcome, 1976; Thyroid Hormones and Brain Development, 1977; contbr. numerous articles to profl. jours. Home: 14 W Argyle St Rockville MD 20850 Office: NICHD Room C-718 7910 Woodmont Ave Bethesda MD 20014

GRAVES, GEORGE GARLAND, indsl. designer; b. Salem, Ind., June 17, 1908; s. John T. J. and Leota (Cauble) G.; B.S., Ind. U., 1930; grad. Nat. Acad. Art, 1930; F.F.A., Art Inst. Chgo., 1935; postgrad. Columbia, 1946-49; m. Estelle Madeline Mull, Sept. 18, 1948 (dec. 1973). Indsl. designer Iannelli Studios, Park Ridge, Ill., 1936, Sterling B. McDonald, Chgo., 1937, Dunbar Furniture Mfg. Co., Berne, Ind., 1938-40, John H. Hopkins, Chgo., 1941-42, Murrill Co., N.Y.C., 1946-57, Simmons Co., N.Y.C., 1957-73; exhibited in group shows Huntington Twp. Art League, Suburban Art League, Friends of L.I. Artists, Nassau Community Coll., Malverne Artists of L.I. Served to lt. comdr. USNR, 1942-46. Mem. Indsl. Designers Soc. Am., Indsl. Design Inst. (past chmn.), Am. Watercolor Soc. (asso.), Internat. Platform Assn., Delta Phi Delta, Delta Sigma Pi, Alpha Tau Omega. Methodist. Contbr. articles to profl. jours. Home and office: 26 Cove Rd Huntington NY 11743

GRAVES, WILLIAM ALBERT, ret. advt. exec.; b. Youngstown, Ohio, Jan. 31, 1913; s. Calvin Thos. and Amelia (Keyser) G.; student U. Pa.; m. Sharon Kimball, Feb. 22, 1956; children—Anita Graves Featherstone, Kim Graves Lafakis, William C. Account exec. Outdoor Advt. Inc., N.Y.C., 1950-58; pres. William A. Graves Assos., Inc., N.Y.C., 1959-60; dir. advt., pub. relations Clupak, Inc. div. Cluett Peabody & Co., N.Y.C., 1960-77. Served with USAAF, 1942-45. Mem. Pub. Relations Soc. Am., Internat. Advt. Assn., N.Y. Bus. Press Editors. Clubs: Press (London and San Francisco), Lambs. Home: 36 Park Circle White Plains NY 10603

GRAY, ALINE KOPLIN, interior designer; b. Chgo., Apr. 1, 1936; d. Harry and Hannah (Libman) K.; student Skidmore Coll., 1954-56, Columbia U., 1956-57; B.F.A., Northwestern U., 1958; m. Walter David Gray, Oct. 6, 1963; children—Adam Louis, Jonas Edward, Rebecca Victoria. Asst. to exec. dir. Democratic Fedn. Ill., Chgo., 1959, Draft Stevenson Regional Hdqrs., Chgo., 1960; asst. fin. dir. Yates for U.S. Senate, Chgo., 1961-62; interior designer Richard E. Baringer, Chgo., 1962-63; pvt. practice interior designing, Narberth, Pa., 1976—; founder, ednl. coordinator, prin. tchr. Childrens' Workshops, Inst. Contemporary Art, U. Pa., 1971-78, mem. advi. bd. 1966-78. Democrat. Jewish. Home: 1519 Flat Rock Rd Narberth PA 19072

GRAY, BENJAMIN, architect; b. N.Y.C., June 2, 1909; s. Max and Sara (Hagine) G.; student Columbia Sch. Architecture, 1933-36; m. Helen Elizabeth Williams, June 27, 1946; 1 dau., Sheila-Lucy. Designing architect Chickasaw (Ala.) Shipyard for USN, J.G. White Engring. Corp., 1940-41, U.S. Army base, Walsh Driscoll Co., Trinidad, B.W.I., 1941-42, Cherokee Ordnance Works, Heyden Chem. Co., 1942, Propulsion Scis. Lab. for NACA, Burns & Roe, Inc., 1948-50; planning coordinator on design power plants for Greek govt., Fla. Power Corp., Atlantic City Elec. Co., aero. testing lab. USN, Burns & Roe, Inc., cons. engrs., 1950-52; asst. v.p. Burns & Roe of Mich., Inc., 1954-58, chief architect, 1958—; dir., asst. v.p. Franklin Engring. Corp., 1958—; sr. partner Gray & Karolyi, architects and engrs., 1966—; cons. M.W. Kellogg Co., World Order St. John Bosco, N.Y. Trap Rock Corp., Bechtel Corp., Orange & Rockland Utilities, Inc., Consol. Edison Co.; environ. cons. Conn. Power Evaluation Council. Served to maj. C.E., AUS, 1942-46. Registered architect, N.Y., N.J., Conn., Mich., Ohio, Ga., Fla., Tenn., Md.; registered profl. engr., Conn. Mem. Res. Officers Assn. U.S., Soc. Am. Mil. Engrs. Author: Remote Automatic Communications Buildings. Home: 167 Grandview Ave Nanuet NY 10954 Office: 265 Little Tor Rd S New City NY 10956

GRAY, CHARLES AUGUSTUS, banker; b. Syracuse, N.Y., Sept. 16, 1928; s. Charles William and Elizabeth Marie (Koch) G.; certificate Am. Inst. Banking, 1958, Sch. Bank Adminstrn., 1961. With Mchts. Nat. Bank & Trust Co. of Syracuse, 1946-77, auditor, 1959-77, v.p., 1970-77; N.Y. State dir. Bank Adminstrn. Inst., 1970-72; regional auditor Central N.Y. Region Charter N.Y. Corp., 1977—. Treas. Upper N.Y. Synod Luth. Ch. in Am., 1966—, Luth. Found. Upper N.Y., 1972—. Chartered internal auditor. Mem. Bank Adminstrn. Inst. (pres. central N.Y. chpt. 1970-72), Inst. Internal Auditors (treas. central N.Y. chpt. 1974-76). Republican. Clubs: Lions (pres. local club 1973-75), Masons, Shriners. Home: 1321 Westmoreland Ave Syracuse NY 13210 Office: 220 S Warren St Syracuse NY 13201

GRAY, CLARENCE CORNELIUS, III, found. exec.; b. Ridge Spring, S.C., July 23, 1917; s. Clarence Cornelius and Maude (Griffin) G.; B.S. in Agrl. Edn., Va. State Coll., 1943; M.S., Mich. State Coll., 1947, Ph.D. in Soil Sci., 1952; m. Shirley Ann Brown, June 1, 1958; children—Michele Diane, Clarence Cornelius, Jennifer Anne. Asst. to asso. prof. agronomy Va. State Coll., 1948-58; agrl. scientist, adminstr. AID, Nepal, 1958-63, Egypt, 1963-64, Jordan, 1964-65, Washington, 1965-67, India, 1967-70; asso. dir. agrl. scis. Rockefeller Found., N.Y.C., 1970-71, dep. dir. agrl. scis., 1971-75, rep. for S.E. U.S., 1975—; cons. UN Devel. Plan, 1974-75; mem. audit hearing bd. HEW, 1974-76. Mem. Adv. council N.Y. State Coll. Agr., 1976—; chmn. bd. trustees Internat. Rice Research Inst., P.I.; dir. Nassau County (N.Y.) Extension Assn., 1976—; trustee Gen. Edn. Bd., N.Y.C. Served with AUS, 1943-46, 50-52. Mem. Am. Soc. Agronomy, Soil Sci. Soc. Am., Internat. Soil Sci. Soc., NAACP. Editor: Strategies for Agricultural Education in Developing Nations, vol. I, 1975, vol. II, 1976. Home: 206 Atlantic Ave Hempstead NY 11550 Office: Rockefeller Found 1133 Ave of the Americas New York City NY 10036

GRAY, DAVID MACDONALD, ednl. adminstr.; b. Richwood, W.Va., Mar. 20, 1931; s. Harry M. and Charlotte (Erhart) G.; B.A., U. Pa., 1952, M.A., 1954, Ph.D. (Penfield scholar), 1965; m. Patricia Ann Delano, June 28, 1952; children—Alison, Jonathan. Instr., U. Pa., Phila., 1956-59, research fellow, 1963-64; asst. prof. Drew U., Madison, N.J., 1959-63; asso. prof., dir. internat. programs Beaver Coll., Glenside, Pa., 1964-68, v.p. adminstrn., dir. internat. programs, 1969-71, exec. v.p., 1972—. Bd. dirs., treas. United Colls. for Fgn. Study and Exchange, 1967-72; exec. v.p., bd. dirs. Spruce Hill Assn., Phila., 1964-67; chmn. bd. dirs. Stevens Sch., 1972-75; trustee Found. for Human Behavior, 1975—. Am. Council Edn. fellow, 1968. Fellow African Studies Assn.; mem. Internat. Polit. Sci. Assn., Internat. Studies Assn., AAUP, Am. Assn. for Higher Edn., Pa. Council for Internat. Edn. (chmn. 1972-75, exec. dir. 1976—), Phila. Art Alliance. Author: Prospectus: Foreign Policy Formulation in Emerging African Nations, 1962. Editor: Rising Influences in Tropical Africa, 1956. Home: 4618 Pine St Philadelphia PA 19143 Office: Beaver Coll Glenside PA 19038

GRAY, EDWARD BARTON, JR., surgeon, educator; b. Newton, Mass., May 22, 1924; s. Edward Barton and Mary Josephine (White) G.; student Harvard, 1946, M.D., 1948; m. Mary Frances Dawson, May 24, 1952; children—Stephen Francis, Catherine Rose, Carol Ann. Intern, Peter Bent Brigham Hosp., Boston, 1949-50, asst. resident surgery, 1950-51, 53-56, chief resident surgeon, 1956-57, sr. asso. in surgery, 1957—; practice medicine specializing in gen. surgery, Stoughton, Mass., 1959—; instr. surgery Harvard Med. Sch., Boston, 1957—; chief of surgery Cardinal Cushing Hosp., Brockton, Mass., 1967-74; mem. staff Goddard Meml. Hosp., Stoughton; pres. Park Surg. Assos., 1969—; asst. clin. prof. surgery Tufts Med. Sch., Boston, 1971—; mem. exec. com. Region VII, Comprehensive Health Planning Agy., Middleboro, Mass., 1972-74; mem. exec. com. Brockton (Mass.) Multi-Service Center. Trustee Packard Manse. Served to capt., M.C., USAF, 1951-53. Diplomate Am. Bd. Surgery. Fellow Am. Coll. Surgeons; mem. AMA, New Eng., Boston surg. socs., Mass. (councilor Plymouth dist.), Plymouth County (Mass.) (v.p., pres. 1973-74) med. socs., Soc. Clin. Vascular Surgery. Roman Catholic. Club: Kiwanis. Contbr. articles in field to profl. jours. Home: 175 Chapman St Canton MA 02021 Office: 966 Park St Stoughton MA 02072

GRAY, HERBERT WALTER, JR., banker; b. North Andover, Mass., Jan. 25, 1921; s. Herbert Walter and Grace (Woodcock) G.; student Boston U., 1946-50; grad. with honors Grad. Sch. Savs. Banking, Brown U., 1963; grad. mgmt. devel. program Dartmouth Coll., 1966; m. Janet Haigh, June 14, 1952; children—David, Stephen, Cynthia, Timothy. Social worker, camp dir. YMCA, Lawrence, Mass., 1953-56; with Suffolk Franklin Savs. Bank, Boston, 1956—, pres., 1972—, chief exec. officer, 1975—, also trustee, mem. bd. investment; dir. Investors Bank and Trust Co.; treas., trustee Gen. Ins. Guaranty Fund Commonwealth of Mass.; pres. Savs. Bank Assn. Mass. Treas. com. mgmt. camping services Greater Lawrence YMCA. Bd. dirs., 2d vice dir. Boston Municipal Research Bur.; trustee Lawrence Gen. Hosp., Mass. Eye Ear Infirmary; trustee donations Episcopal Diocese of Mass. Served with USAF, 1941-45. Decorated Air medal. Episcopalian (lay reader). Clubs: Y's Men (Lawrence); Union (Boston); N. Andover Country. Home: 20 Johnson Circle North Andover MA 01845 Office: 45 Franklin St Boston MA 02110

GRAY, JIMMY (JAMES HARGRAVES), radio personality; b. New Bedford, Mass., May 15, 1945; s. William Edmund and Anna (Bollea) Hargraves; student New Bedford pub. schs., Leland Powers Sch. (Boston); m. Melody Ann Mello, Oct. 16, 1965; children—Katie Marie, Kara Ann. Morning announcer, prodn. dir. Sta. WPEP, Taunton, Mass., 1965-67; asst. program dir., evening personality Sta. WNBH, New Bedford, 1967-69; mid-day personality Sta. WPRO, East Providence, R.I., 1969—. Former tchr. radio Providence Boys Club; mem. asso. bd. Meeting St. Sch. Free lance comedy writer; columnist Night Life Mag. Office: 1502 Wampanoag Trail East Providence RI 02915

GRAY, KENNETH STEWART, electronics engr.; b. Teaneck, N.J., June 28, 1945; s. Stewart Louis and Ann Elizabeth (Bauer) G.; B.S.E.E., Norwich U., 1967; M.S.C.S., U. Vt., 1978; m. Carol Ann Wilcox, June 17, 1967; children—Robert Stephen, Michael Stewart. Engr., IBM, Poughkeepsie, N.Y., 1967-70, Essex Junction, Vt., 1970—. Served with AUS, 1966-67. Registered profl. engr., Vt. Mem. Nat. Soc. Profl. Engrs., IEEE, Tau Beta Pi. Methodist. Club: Masons. Home: RFD Pinehurst Dr Underhill VT 05489 Office: IBM Corp Essex Junction VT 05452

GRAY, OSCAR SHALOM, lawyer; b. N.Y.C., Oct. 18, 1926; s. Samuel Zavl and Esther Malke (Grynberg) G.; Grad. Mercersburg Acad., 1944; B.A., Yale U., 1948, J.D., 1951; m. Sara Sheila Hafter, Apr. 8, 1967. Admitted to Md. bar, 1951, D.C. bar, 1952; atty.-adviser Legal Adviser's Office, U.S. Dept. State, Washington, 1951-57; sec. Nuclear Materials & Equipment Corp., Apollo, Pa., 1957-64, treas., 1957-67, v.p., 1964-71, dir. 1964-67; spl. counsel Pres.'s Task Force on Communications Policy, Washington, 1967-68; cons. telecommunications policy U.S. Dept. Transp., Washington, 1967-68, acting dir. Office Environmental Impact, U.S. Dept. Transp., 1968-70; adj. prof. environmental law, professorial lectr. torts Georgetown U. Law Center, lectr. Cath. U. Am. Sch. Law, Washington, 1970-71; asso. prof. law U. Md. Sch. Law, Balt., 1971-74, prof., 1974—; vis. prof. U. Tenn. Coll. Law, 1977; practice law, Washington, 1970—, Balt., 1971—. Served with USNR, 1945-46. Mem. Md. Bar Assn., Assn. Trial Lawyers Am., Am. Law Inst., Order of Coif, Phi Beta Kappa. Clubs: Harvard-Yale-Princeton (Pitts.); Mory's (New Haven). Author: Cases and Materials on Environmental Law, 1970, 2d edit., 1973, Supplements, 1974, 75, 77; (with Harry Shulman and Fleming James, Jr.) Cases and Materials on the Law of Torts, 3d edit., 1976. Office: 1225 19th St NW Washington DC 20036 also 500 W Baltimore St Baltimore MD 21201

GRAY, ROBERT GORDON, physician; b. Evanston, Ill., June 26, 1945; s. David Clark and Jeanne (Lewis) G.; A.B. magna cum laude, Boston U., 1969, M.D. cum laude, 1969; m. Mary Kathleen Kuehler, Oct. 27, 1969. Intern, U. Miami Hosps. (Fla.), 1969-70, resident, 1970-71, 73-74; practice medicine, specializing in internal medicine, Springfield, Mass., 1976—; attending physician Baystate Med. Center, Springfield, 1976—; physician Rheumatology Assos., 1977—; cons. rheumatology Mercy, Ludlow, Noble, Wing Meml., Providence and Holyoke hosps.; clin. asst. prof. dept. medicine Tufts U. Sch. Medicine, 1976—. Served to maj., M.C., U.S. Army, 1971-73. Diplomate Am. Bd. Internal Medicine, Nat. Bd. Med. Examiners. Mem. Am. Rheumatism Assn., New Eng. Rheumatism Soc., Am. Soc. Internal Medicine, A.C.P., Mass. Med. Soc., Phi Beta Kappa, Alpha Omega Alpha. Contbr. sci. articles to med. jours. Office: 50 Maple St Springfield MA 01103

GRAY, ROBERT HUGH, ednl. adminstr.; b. Dallas, Sept. 22, 1931; s. Harold Kirby and Margarete Lucille G.; B.F.A., Yale U., 1959, M.F.A., 1961; m. Constance Montmenny, Dec. 26, 1957; children—Richard Bailey, Charles Hugh. Instr. art Cooper Union, N.Y.C., 1960-66; dean Silvermine Coll. Art, New Canaan, Conn., 1966-71; head dept. art Pa. State U., University Park, 1972-76; dean div. visual arts State U. N.Y. at Purchase, 1976—; cons. in field. Served with USAF, 1950-54. Named an Outstanding Educator Am., 1973. Exec. com. Neuberger Mus., 1977—, also bd. dirs.; bd. dirs. Empire Studio Sch. N.Y., State U. N.Y. Statewide Com. on the Arts; trustee Bruce Mus.; mem. Greenwich Arts Council. Home: 7 Wallasy Way Greenwich CT 06878 Office: Div Visual Arts State U NY at Purchase Purchase NY 10577

GRAY, SHEILA HAFTER, psychiatrist, psychoanalyst; b. N.Y.C., Oct. 19, 1930; M.D., Harvard U., 1958; Washington Psychoanalytic Inst., 1969; m. Oscar Shalom Gray, Apr. 8, 1967. Intern, St. Elizabeth's Hosp., Washington, 1958-59; resident McLean Hosp., Belmont, Mass., 1959-61; clin. research fellow Mass. Gen. Hosp., Boston, 1961-62; staff psychiatrist Chestnut Lodge, Inc., Rockville, Md., 1962-64; practice medicine, specializing in psychiatry and psychoanalysis, Chevy Chase, Md., 1964-76, Washington, 1972—; clin. asst. prof. psychiatry U. Md. Sch. Medicine, Balt., 1968-75, asso. prof., 1975—; instr. Washington Psychoanalytic Inst., 1971-75, teaching analyst, 1975—; mem. staff U. Md. Hosp., Balt.; physician mem. Commn. on Mental Health, Superior Ct. of D.C., 1972—. Mem. Am. Psychiat. Assn., Am., Washington psychoanalytic socs. Office: PO Box 40612 Palisades Sta Washington DC 20016

GRAY, STEPHEN ASHLEY, municipal ofcl.; b. Barre, Vt., July 2, 1947; s. Max Lynn and Eunice Mae (Hathorn) G.; A. Engring., Vt. Tech. Coll., 1969; m. Judith Ann Bailey, July 5, 1969; children—Jamie Alan, Sarah Ann. Engring. aide City of Montpelier, Vt., 1969-72, asst. dir. pub. works, 1972-74, dir. pub. works, 1974—. Mem. Vt. Soc. Surveyors, Am. Pub. Works Assn. Home: RD2 Plainfield VT 05667 Office: City Hall Main St Montpelier VT 05602

GRAY, WARREN, dentist; b. Newark, Nov. 21, 1931; s. Leonard and Miriam (Wagner) G.; B.A., U. Pa., 1953, D.D.S., 1957; m. Marilyn Dorflaufer, Aug. 1, 1953; children—Lennie Ellen, Scott Alan. Individual practice dentistry, Millburn, N.J., 1959—; dentist Millburn Twp. Sch., 1963—. Founder, 1st pres. Millburn-Short Hills Youth Employment Service, 1965; pres. N.J. Youth Employment Services, 1969; mem. Millburn Bd. Recreation Commn., 1968-75, chmn., 1971-73, recipient Nat. Recreation award, 1972; pres. N.J. State Recreation Commn. Assn., 1972; Millburn chmn. N.J. Tri-Centennial Hist. Landmarks Com., 1965; mem. Millburn Narcotics Commn., 1970—. Trustee Congregation B'nai Israel, Millburn. Founder, dir. Millburn Jr. Basketball Program, 1969—; coach Little League Baseball, 1968-71; coach 8th Grade Basketball Team, 1969-74; mem. N.J. Regional Adv. Bd. Anti-Defamation League, 1968—. Served with USNR, 1957-59. Recipient Man of Year award Millburn-Short Hills lodge B'nai B'rith, 1960, 69, State of Israel Bonds Testimonial, 1971. Mem. Am. Soc. Preventive Dentistry (charter, N.J. chpt. dir.), Soc. Dentistry for Children, Am. Dental Assn., N.J. Essex County dental socs., Internat. Coll. Oral Implantologists, Newark Dental Club. Mem. B'nai B'rith (pres. No. N.J. council 1968, pres. 3d dist. 1976-77, internat. bd. govs. 1976-77). Clubs: Varsity, Northern New Jersey Alumni (U. Pa.). Home: 444 White Oak Ridge Rd Short Hills NJ 07078 Office: 116 Millburn Ave Millburn NJ 07041

GRAY, WILLIAM BOYCE, clergyman, communications dir.; b. Augusta, Ga., Nov. 6, 1927; s. Joseph Dewey and Alta (Boyce) G.; B.J., U. Mo., 1947; M. Div., Ch. Div. Sch. Pacific, 1961; m. Betty Jean Wilkison, June 28, 1952; children—Grace Elizabeth, Amy Durden. Instr. English and journalism U. Ga., Atlanta, 1951-53; asst. mgr. Ga. Press Assn., 1952-53, Kans. Press Assn., 1956-57; news editor Mitchell Co. Press News, Osage, Iowa, 1957-58; ordained priest Episcopal Ch., 1961; asst. rector St. Stephen's Ch., Seattle, 1961-62; rector St. Luke's Ch., Cedar Falls, Iowa, 1962-66; editor, communications officer Diocese of Va., Richmond, 1966-70; dir., office of communications Trinity Ch. Parish, N.Y.C., 1970—; vis. fellow Episc. Theol. Sem., Austin, Tex.; mem. planning com. conf. Nat. Alliance Concerned with Sch. Age Parents, 1975; trustee Am.-Israel Friendship League, 1976—; chmn. Student Exposition on Energy Resources com. Nat. Energy Found., 1977; mem. steering com. Writers Artists for Peace in Middle East. Mem. N.Y. Democratic County Com., 1977-78. Served with U.S. Army, 1954-56. Fellow Coll. Preachers; mem. Pub. Relations Soc. Am., Indsl. Communication Council, World Assn. Christian Communicators, Internat. Communications Assn., Soc. Anthropology of Visual Communication, Acad. TV Arts and Scis., Overseas Press Club. Author: (with Betty W. Gray) The Episcopal Church Welcomes You, 1974; contbr. articles to ch. and secular periodicals; owner, editor McDuffie Progress, 1949-51. Home: 156 E 79th St New York City NY 10021 Office: 74 Trinity Pl New York City NY 10006

GRAY, WILLIAM H., III, Congressman. Mem. 96th Congress from 2d Pa. dist., 1979—. Democrat. Office: 429 Cannon House Office Bldg Washington DC 20515*

GRAYER, MERYL ROMAINE, ins. co. exec.; b. N.Y.C., Mar. 7, 1933; d. Harry and Betty (Hurwick) G.; B.S., N.Y. U., 1948, M.A., 1949; postgrad. N.Y. Sch. Bus., 1958, Sobelsohn Sch., 1958-59, Am. Inst. Property and Liability Underwriters, 1973—; children—Melody Anderson, Morgan Meredyth Held. Exec. asst. Federated Brokerage Group, N.Y.C., 1958; asst. v.p. Standard Security Life Ins. Co. N.Y., N.Y.C., 1959-69; corp. asst. sec. Madison Life Ins. Co., N.Y.C., 1969-71, also corp. sec. Asso. Madison Cos., Inc., N.Y.C., 1969-71; industry liaison cons. Met. Life Ins. Co., N.Y.C., 1972—; adj. asst. prof. Coll. Ins., N.Y.C., 1973—; lectr. in field. Mem. fund-raising com. Alumni Fedn. N.Y. U.; membership enrollment chmn. Greater N.Y. council Boy Scouts Am., 1978; mem. 1979 telethon steering com. Easter Seal Soc. Recipient Outstanding Achievement award Myopia Internat. Research Found., 1977, Women Leaders Round Table, 1974, 77; Explorer award Boy Scouts Am., 1977; Outstanding Achievement award, 1978; C.L.U. Mem. Am. Soc. C.L.U.'s (dir. N.Y. chpt. 1972-75, sec. 1974-75, program chmn. 1976-78, pub. relations chmn. 1978—), N.Y. League Bus. and Profl. Women (dir. 1973-76, pres. 1975-76), Bus. and Profl. Women's Clubs N.Y. State (dir., legis. chmn. 1976-77, rec. sec. 1977-78, 2d v.p. 1978-79), Nat. Fedn. Bus. and Profl. Women's Clubs (mem. legis. platform com. 1976-77), N.Y. Press Women (v.p. 1974-76, 78—), Women in Communications (job chmn. 1977-78), N.Y. Chamber Commerce and Industry, Nat. Council Women U.S., N.Y. U. Alumnae Club (dir. 1976—), Golden Key Soc., Nat. Assn. Life Underwriters, Life Underwriters Assn. N.Y.C. (legis. chmn. 1974—, dir. 1977—), Am. Mgmt. Assn., Assos. Lincoln Center, Friends City Center, Nat. Assn. Female Execs. Clubs: Zonta of N.Y. (dir. 1975-76, rec. sec. and program chmn. 1976-77, pres. 1978—), N.Y. U. Editor: Life Underwriters Bull., 1973—. Contbr. articles to profl. jours. Home: 130 E 18th St New York City NY 10003 Office: 1 Madison Ave New York City NY 10010

GRAYSON, HENRY T., psychoanalyst; b. Atmore, Ala., Oct. 25, 1935; s. Henry T. and Ethel (Sageser) G.; A.B., Asbury Coll., 1957; B.D., Emory U., 1961; S.T.M., Boston U., 1963, Ph.D., 1967; postdoctoral certificate in psychoanalysis Postgrad. Center for Mental Health, N.Y.C., 1971; m. Maria Rios Grayson, July 1, 1971; children—Pegine, Douglas. Instr., dir. counseling Mt. Ida Jr. Coll., Newton, Mass., 1964-67; asso. prof. psychology City U. N.Y., Bklyn. Coll., 1967-78; pvt. practice psychotherapy, N.Y.C., 1965—; founder, exec. dir. Nat. Inst. Psychotherapies, N.Y.C., 1970—; pres. Quezon, Inc., 1978—. Fellow Am. Group Psychotherapy Assn.; mem. Am., N.Y. State psychol. assns., Am. Acad. Psychotherapists. Author: Three Psychotherapies, 1975; Changing Approaches to Psychotherapies, 1977; Short Term Approaches to Psychotherapy, 1978. Home: 265 E Lake Blvd Lake Mahopac NY 10541 Office: 330 W 58th St New York City NY 10019

GRAYSON, MARTIN, publishing co. exec.; b. N.Y.C., Mar. 2, 1928; s. Thomas and Mollie G.; B.A. cum laude, N.Y. U., 1948; Ph.D. in Chemistry (AEC fellow, Standard Oil fellow), Purdue U., 1952; m. Virginia H. Suggs, May 9, 1970; children by previous marriage—Karen Grayson Minshall, Michael D., Richard M. Research chemist Allied Chem. Corp., Hopewell, Va., 1952-56; prin. research chemist Am. Cyanamid Co., Stamford, Conn., 1956-75; co-editor Topics in Phosphorus Chemistry, John Wiley & Sons, Inc., N.Y.C., 1964—, exec. editor Kirk-Othmer Ency. Chem. Tech., 1975—; editor-in-chief Phosphorus and Sulfur, Gordon and Breach Publs., N.Y.C., 1971—; adj. prof. chemistry U. Bridgeport (Conn.), 1968—. N.Y. State Regents scholar, 1944-48; recipient Am. Inst. Chemists medal, 1948. Fellow N.Y. Acad. Sci.; mem. Am. Chem. Soc., AAAS, Phi Beta Kappa, Sigma Xi, Phi Lambda Upsilon. Patentee; contbr. articles to profl. jours. Home: 82 Valleywood Rd CosCob CT 06807 Office: 605 3d Ave New York City NY 10016

GRAYSON, RICHARD STEVEN, legal and polit. cons.; b. Harlingen, Tex., June 21, 1944; s. Bernard Lewis and Lucille Ruth (Klisto) G.; B.A., Bucknell U., 1966; M.A., Sch. Internat. Service, Am. U., 1968; Ph.D., Cambridge (Eng.) U., 1974; m. Katherine Lilian Hunston, June 4, 1971; 1 dau., Karyn Elizabeth. Researcher in internat. law and politics Oxford (Eng.) U., 1970-74; adviser, negotiator 2d Diplomatic Conf., Geneva, mem. secretariat and sec. Round Table Diplomatic Conf., Italy, also research fellow, writer and editor Inst. Henry Dunant, Geneva, 1974; internat. legal and polit. adviser, Geneva, 1974; asso. dir. Inst. World Affairs, 1975, exec. dir., 1976—; internat. legal and polit. cons., N.Y.C. and Washington, 1975—; adviser to various internat. and nat. orgns.; cons.; speaker in field; univ. lectr.; radio programs on fgn. policy, 1976—. Bd. dirs. UNESCO Assn. USA, Center for Farm and Food Research; bd. dirs., corp. mem. Com. for World Univ.; trustee Interfuture; del. Fed. Trust Edn. and Research Conf., Eng., 1969. Avalon fellow, 1966-68; grantee Inst. Henry-Dunant, 1971-73. Mem. Internat. Inst. Strategic Studies, Inst. Hist. Research, Inst. Advanced Legal Studies, Inst. U.S. Studies, Mensa, Am. Soc. Internat. Law, Am. Polit. Sci. Assn., Internat. Law Assn., Internat. Polit. Sci. Assn., Am. Acad. Polit. and Social Sci., Oxford Soc., Brit. Inst. Internat. and Comparative Law, Internat. Inst. Humanitarian Law, Cambridge U. Grad. Soc. (pres. 1969-70), Pi Sigma Alpha, Pi Gamma Mu. Clubs: University (N.Y.C.); United Oxford and Cambridge Univ. (London). Author: Basic Background Study of Southeast Asia, 3 vols., 1968; Political and International Legal Implications of the Problems of Civil War, 1980. Home: 9 Hemlock Circle White Plains NY 10605

GREANEY, WILLIAM J., ednl. adminstr.; b. Bay Shore, N.Y., May 3, 1928; s. Patrick J. and Delia B. (Coen) G.; B.A., Villanova U., 1952; M.L.S., L.I. U., 1966. Instr. English, Hauppauge (N.Y.) High Sch., 1955-58, Brentwood (N.Y.) High Sch., 1958-61, North Vancouver High Sch., Vancouver, B.C., Can., 1961-62; media specialist Brentwood (N.Y.) Pub. Schs., 1962—; cons. library constrn. and planning. Mem. NEA (life), ALA, Nat. Assn. Sch. Librarians, N.Y., Brentwood tchrs. assns., Suffolk Sch. Library and Media Assn. Democrat. Club: Villanova (L.I.). Home: Spring Hollow Rd St James NY 11780 Office Sonderling Bldg Brentwood Pub Schs Brentwood NY 11717 also 212-6020 Vine St Vancouver BC V6M 4A6 Canada

GREAVES, BETTINA BIEN (MRS. PERCY L. GRAVES, JR.), economist; b. Washington, July 21, 1917; d. Van Tuyl Hart and Bertha (Conn) Bien; B.A. Wheaton Coll., 1938; postgrad. Strayer Sch. Bus., 1939, N.Y. U.. 1951-52; M.L.S., Columbia, 1967; m. Percy L. Greaves, June 26, 1971. Various secretarial positions, 1939-42; adminstrv. asst. Fgn. Econ. Adminstrn., La Paz, Bolivia, Vienna, Austria, 1943-46, sec. export dept. Smith, Kline & French, Phila., 1946-47; asst. to exec. dir. Found. for Freedom, Washington, 1947-48; office mgr. Thomas L. Phillips, realtor, Washington, 1948-51; sr. staff mem., dir. debate materials program, contbg. editor The Freeman Found. for Econ. Edn., Inc., Irvington-on-Hudson, N.Y., 1951—. Mem. A.L.A., Am. Econ. Assn., Am. Hist. Assn. Author: Free Market Books, 2 vols., 1975. Compiler: The Works of Ludwig von Mises, 1970; translator On the Manipulation of Money and Credit (Ludwig von Mises), 1978; contbr. Toward Liberty, Mises Festsohrift, 1971, also to profl. jours. Home: 19 Pine Lane Irvington-on-Hudson NY 10533 Office: 30 S Broadway Irvington-on-Hudson NY 10533

GREAVES, PERCY LAURIE, JR., economist; b. Bklyn., Aug. 24, 1906; s. Percy Laurie and Grace I. (Dodge) G.; B.S. in Bus. magna cum laude, Syracuse U., 1929; postgrad. in econs. Columbia, 1933-34, N.Y. U., 1950-69; m. Edith Leslye Platt, Aug. 23, 1930; children—Richard L., Muriel A., Charles Flint; m. 2d, Bettina Herbert Bien, June 26, 1971. Bookkeeper, Am. Trading Co., 1923-24; exec. trainee asst. advt. mgr. Gillette Safety Razor Co., 1929-32; advt. tng. Batten, Barton, Durstine & Osborn, 1930; instr. econs. and fgn. trade YMHA, 1933-34; financial editor, research economist U.S. News, 1934-36; advt. mgr. European subsidiaries Pet and Carnation Milk Cos., 1936-38; advt., pub. relations exec. Met. Life Ins. Co., 1938-43; asso. research dir. Republican Nat. Com., 1943-45; chief minority staff Joint Congl. Com. on Investigation Pearl Harbor Attack, 1945-46; exec. dir. Found. for Freedom, Inc., 1946-48; econ. cons., writer, lectr., 1948—; econ. adviser, columnist Christian Freedom Found., 1950-58; guest lectr. econs. Freedom Sch., Inc., 1957-61, Found. Econ. Edn., Inc., 1961-67; Armstrong prof. econs. U. Plano, 1965-71; pres. Free Market Books, 1974—. Exec. bd. Am. Party, 1976—. Mem. Am. Econs. Assn., Am. Hist. Assn., Beta Gamma Sigma, Phi Kappa Phi. Episcopalian Author: Operation Immigration, 1947; Understanding the Dollar Crisis, 1973; Mises Made Easier: A Glossary for Human Action, 1974; also numerous articles on econs., politics, pub. affairs. Contbr. to Perpetual War for Perpetual Peace, 1952; On Freedom and Free Enterprise, 1956; Toward Liberty, 1971; Free Market Economics: A Basic Reader, 1975. Home: 19 Pine Ln Irvington-on-Hudson NY 10533 Office: Box 298 Dobbs Ferry NY 10522

GREBANIER, BERNARD, author; b. N.Y.C., Mar. 8, 1903; s. Benjamin and Ottillie (von Storenberg) G.; A.B., Coll. City N.Y., 1926; M.A., N.Y. U., 1930, Ph.D., 1935; m. Frances Winwar, Sept. 22, 1925 (div. Dec. 1942). Instr., Coll. City N.Y., 1926-30; faculty Bklyn. Coll., 1930—, prof. English, 1957-63, prof. emeritus, 1963—; Lectr., Pace Coll., 1958-63; lectr. adult edn. Hofstra U. 1971-73, YMHA, 1973-75; lectr. poetry workshop Delbrook Coll., Riverton, Va., 1971, Poetry Soc. Am., 1972-73; dir. plays Off-Broadway including Phaedra, Othello, Merchant of Venice, King Lear, Oedipus the King, The Importance of Being Ernest, Recipient Samuel French award for best teaching in playwriting, 1957, 58. Mem. Poetry Soc. Am., Players Club, P.E.N., Author's Guild, Composers, Authors and Artists Am. (pres. N.Y. chpt. 1972—, nat. v.p. 1973—). Author: (with S. Thompson) English Literature and its Backgrounds, 2 vols., 1939-40; (with H. Hintz) Modern American Vistas, 1941; Fauns, Satyrs and a Few Sages, 1945; Mirrors of the Fire, 1946; Essentials of English Literature, 2 vols., 1948-49; (with V. Hopper) Essentials of European Literature, 2 vols., 1950-51; Bibliography of European Literature in English Translation (with V. Hopper), 1953; The Other Love, 1957; Racine's Phaedra, an English Acting Version in Verse, 1958; (with S. Reiter) College Writing and Reading, 1958; Moliere's The Misanthrope, an English Acting Version, 1959; (with S. Reiter) An Introduction to Imaginative Literature, 1960; The Heart of Hamlet, 1960; Playwriting, 1961; Chaucer, 1962; Milton, 1962; The Truth about Shylock, 1962; Moliere, 1963; Rousseau, 1963; Thornton Wilder, 1963; Shakespeare's Henry IV, Part I, 1964; The Great Shakespeare Forgery, 1965; Armenian Miniatures, 1967; The Uninhibited Byron, 1970; Edwin Arlington Robinson, 1971; The Angel in the Rock, 1971; (with S. Lockwood and A. Marx) Pegasus in the Seventies, 1973; The Enjoyment of Literature, 1975; Then Came Each Actor, 1976; also contbr. to encys., mags. Home: 215 W 88th St New York NY 10024

GREBEN, STANLEY EDWARD, psychiatrist; b. Toronto, Ont., Can., Aug. 6, 1927; s. Abraham and Kitty (Goodman) G.; B.A., U. Toronto, 1949, M.D., 1953; m. Marilyn Elma Scher, Dec. 3, 1929; children—Daniel Howard, Jan Elizabeth. Intern, Kings County Hosp., Bklyn., 1953-54; resident Johns Hopkins, Balt., 1954-56, 57-58; sr. house officer Maudsley Hosp., London, 1956-57; practice medicine, specializing in psychiatry, Toronto, Ont., Can., 1958—; psychiatrist-in-chief Mt. Sinai Hosp., Toronto, 1964—; prof. psychiatry U. Toronto, 1973—; cons. Clarke Inst. Psychiatry, Women's Coll. Hosp; fellow Laidlaw Found., 1979. Diplomate Am. Bd. Psychiatry and Neurology. Fellow Am. Psychiat. Assn., Royal Coll. Physicians Can., Royal Coll. Psychiatry, Am. Coll. Psychiatrists; mem. Can. Med. Assn., Canadian Psychoanalytic Soc. (pres. Toronto br. 1975-77), Internat. Psycho-Analytical Assn., Canadian Psychoanalytic Inst. (tng. and supervising analyst), Canadian Psychiat. Assn. (chmn. bd. dirs.). Contbr. articles to psychiat. jours. Home: 148 Dunvegan Rd Toronto ON M5P 2N9 Canada Office: 600 University Ave Toronto ON M5G 1X5 Canada

GREBSTEIN, SHELDON NORMAN, univ. adminstr.; b. Providence, R.I., Feb. 1, 1928; s. Sigmund and Sylvia (Skotkin) G.; B.A. cum laude, U. So. Calif., 1949; M.A., Columbia U., 1950; Ph.D., Mich. State U., 1954; m. Phyllis Strumar, Sept. 6, 1953; children—Jason Lyle, Gary Wade. Instr., asst. prof. English, U. Ky., 1953-62; asst. prof. U. South Fla., 1962-63; asso. prof. English, State U. N.Y., Binghamton, 1963-68, prof., 1968—, asst. to pres., 1974-75, dean arts and scis. Harpur Coll., 1975—; Fulbright-Hays lectr. U. Rouen (France), 1968-69; vis. lectr. Caen, Hull, Edinburgh univs., 1969. Mem. Am. Studies Assn. (past exec. sec. Ky.-Tenn.), Modern Lang. Assn. Author: Sinclair Lewis, 1962; John O'Hara, 1966; Hemingway's Craft, 1973; editor: Monkey Trial, 1960; Perspectives in Contemporary Criticism, 1968; Studies in For Whom the Bell Tolls, 1971; editorial bd. Studies in Am. Jewish Lit.; editorial cons. Princeton Press, U. Ill. Press, La. State U. Press, State U. N.Y. Press, Harper & Row, Am. Quar., U. N.C. Press; contbr. articles to profl. jours. Home: Brown Rd Box 60 RD 7 Binghamton NY 13903 Office: State U NY Binghamton NY 13901

GRECH, ANTHONY PAUL, librarian; b. N.Y.C., July 16, 1930; s. Annibale H. and Anna Jane (Cassar) G.; B.B.A., Manhattan Coll., 1952; M.L.S., Columbia U., 1961. Asst. reference librarian Assn. Bar City N.Y., 1958-65, ref. librarian, 1965-67, librarian, 1967—. Recipient Joseph L. Andrews Bibliog. award Am. Assn. Law Libraries, 1967. Mem. Am. Assn. Law Libraries (chmn. micro facsimiles com., chmn. publs. com. 1975-76), Law Library Assn. Greater N.Y. (pres. 1967-68), ALA, Spl. Libraries Assn., Bibliog. Soc. U. Va., Beta Phi Mu. Home: 15 W 72d St New York City NY 10023 Office: 42 W 44th St New York City NY 10036

GRECO, ALBERT NICHOLAS, ednl. adminstr., film historian; b. Trenton, N.J., June 15, 1945; s. Albert Charles and Nellie Marie G.; B.A., Duquesne U., 1967, M.A., 1969; postgrad. N.Y.U., 1969—; m. Elaine Ann Rovegno, Aug. 10, 1968; children—Albert, Timothy. Teaching grad. asst. Duquesne U., 1967-68; tchr. Dwight-Englewood (N.J.) Sch., 1968—, chmn. dept., 1970-73, dir. testing, 1973-75, prin. summer sch., 1970—, prin. upper sch., 1975-78, dir. devel., 1978—; adj. instr. Bergen Community Coll., 1970—. Vol. Dumont (N.J.) Program for Retarded Children, 1971-73. Mem. Am. Hist. Assn., Orgn. Am. Historians, Am. Studies Assn., Am. Film Inst., Lincoln Center Film Soc., Cum Laude Soc., Phi Alpha Theta. Roman Catholic. Home: 183 S Queen St Bergenfield NJ 07621 Office: Dwight-Englewood Sch 315 E Palisades Ave Englewood NJ 08631

GRECO, ROSEMARIE BERNADETTE, banker; b. Phila., Mar. 31, 1946; d. John Michael and Marie Carmella (DePaolo) G.; B.S. magna cum laude in Edn., St. Joseph's U., 1975. With Fidelity Bank, Phila., 1968—, tng. dir. ops. dept., 1974-75, bank ops. officer, 1975, acting dep. dir. personnel, 1975, sr. personnel officer, 1975-76, dep. dir. personnel, 1976—, asst. v.p., 1976—. Vol. fund-raising drive YWCA; bd. dirs. Phila. Bus. Acad.; mem. subcom. adv. council for career edn. Sch. Dist. Phila. Mem. Nat. Assn. Bank Women (v.p. and dir. personnel 1978, exec. com.), Internat. Assn. Personnel Women, Am. Soc. Personnel Adminstrn., Am. Soc. Tng. and Devel., Am. Inst. Banking (dir. (Phila.). Home: 866 Hendrix St Philadelphia PA 19116 Office: Fidelity Bank Broad and Walnut Sts Philadelphia PA 19109

GREELEY, WILDER JOSEPH, leasing co. exec.; b. Southington, Conn., Sept. 17, 1906; s. Daniel W. and Elizabeth (Belser) G.; student Bates Coll., 1924-25; m. Benita Pape, July 15, 1933; 1 dau., Benita (Mrs. Peter J. Sherwood). Actor, The Jitney Players, A Trip to Scarborough, The Wonder, Murder in the Red Barn, 1929-30; with So. New Eng. Telephone Co., 1930-44; engr. in charge G-23, U.S. Office War Information, Cambridge, Eng., 1944-45; asst. mgr. radio sta. WBRY, 1946-50; pres., treas. Paper Delivery, Inc., Waterbury, Conn., 1950—, Waterbury Motor Lease, 1960—; treas., gen. mgr. Woodbridge Skating Rink, Inc., Woodbridge, Conn., 1938-72; v.p. auto leasing Catrala of Conn., 1972-76, 78—, pres., 1976-78. Treas., Mental Health Assn. Central Naugatuck Valley, 1966-71; finance com. Conn. Mental Health Assn., 1972—. Mem. Republican Town Com., 1946—; chmn. Woodbridge Bd. Police Commrs., 1972—. Mem. New Eng. Fedn. Men's Glee Clubs (pres. 1964—), Waterbury, Naugatuck chambers commerce. Conglist. Mason (33 deg., K.T.), Kiwanian (past pres., lt. gov. div. 1-West). Club: Waterbury. Home: 826 Fountain St Woodbridge CT 06525 Office: 456 Meadow St Waterbury CT 06702

GREEN, CLIFFORD SCOTT, fed. judge; b. Phila., Apr. 2, 1923; s. Robert Lewis and Alice (Johnson) G.; B.S., Temple U., 1948, J.D., 1951, LL.D. (hon.), 1977; m. Mabel Wood, June 20, 1959; children—Terri Alice, David Scott. Admitted to Pa. bar, 1952; individual practice law, Phila., 1952-64; dep. atty. gen. Pa., 1954; judge County Ct., Phila., 1964-68, Ct. of Common Pleas, 1968-71, U.S. Dist. Ct. for Eastern Dist. Pa., Phila., 1972—; lectr. law Temple U. Chmn., Phila. regional panel Pres.'s Commn. on White House Fellows, 1972; chmn. regional adv. com. Eastern Office Law, Edn. and Participation, 1975; chmn. bd. dirs. Crime Prevention Assn. of Phila.; bd. dirs. Childrens Aid Soc. Pa.; bd. mgrs. Childrens Hosp., Phila. Served with USAAF, 1943-46. Recipient Womens Christian Alliance awards for outstanding service to children Opportunities Industrialization Center, 1967, Health and Welfare Council, 1968. Mem. Am., Fed., Pa., Phila. bar assns., Lawyers Club of Phila., Barristers Club, Socialegal Club, Am. Judicature Soc., Temple U. Law Alumni Assn. (exec. com.), Sigma Pi Phi. Home: 2311 N 50th St Philadelphia PA 19131 Office: 15613 US Courthouse Philadelphia PA 19106

GREEN, GEORGE EDWARD, ornamental iron mfr., bldg. contractor; b. Balt., Apr. 18, 1929; s. George Edward and Hazel Roberta (Dawson) G.; B.S. in Bus. Mgmt., U. Balt., 1950; m. Nancy Christine Fryer, May 27, 1950; children—Mark Edward, Christine Margaret. Founder, owner Imperial Industries, Inc., Glen Arm, Md., 1956—; contractor Stratford Bldg. Co., Inc., Glen Arm, 1969—; founder owner Metalfab, Inc., Ft. Pierce, Fla., 1977—. Mem. Nat. Ornamental Metal Mfrs. Assn., U.S. Power Squadron. Republican. Methodist (trustee 1963-66). Mason (Shriner). Clubs: Baltimore Yacht; Boumi Temple Yacht (dir. 1969-74, commodore 1974). Patentee railing system. Home: 11703 Mohr Rd Kingsville MD 21087 Office: 12238 Long Green Pike Glen Arm MD 21057

GREEN, GERARD LEO, clergyman, educator; b. Batavia, N.Y., July 27, 1928; s. George Leo and Marian (Powers) G.; B.S., Mt. St. Mary's Coll., 1952; M.A., St. Bonaventure U., 1958; postgrad. (NSF fellow) U. Notre Dame, summers 1961, 62, U. Buffalo, 1965-66; Ed.M. State U. N.Y., 1968. Lab. technician Eastman Kodak Co., 1947-48; chemist Xerox Co., 1952; ordained priest Roman Catholic Ch., 1956; parish asst Diocese Buffalo, 1956-59; instr. chemistry Bishop Turner High Sch., Buffalo, 1959-74, dir. sci., 1959-70, 72-74; adminstr. Our Lady of the Rosary Parish, Wilson, N.Y., 1968; adminstr. St. Barnabas Parish and Sch., Depew, N.Y., 1973-75, pastor, 1976—. Mem. sci. curriculum com. Dept. Edn. Diocese Buffalo, 1960-70, chmn. diocesan chemistry textbook evaluation com., 1961-70, mem. diocesan pastoral council for handicapped, 1976—, sec., 1978—; chaplain Hyview Fire Co., 1976—, Cheektowaga Police PBA, 1976—, West End Fire Co., 1977—; mem. Western N.Y. Sci. Congress Com., 1960-74, sec., 1968, co-chmn., 1969, chmn., 1972-73, state chmn., 1970; mem. gen. chemistry exam. com. N.Y. State Edn. Dept., 1970-73; cons. sci. facilities in secondary schs.; mem. local IUE-AFL-CIO Scholarship Fund Com., 1968-71. Mem. dist. com. Boy Scouts Am., Buffalo, 1957—. Served with AUS, 1946-47. Recipient Distinguished Service award in sci. edn., 1975. Mem. N.Y. State Tchrs. Assn., Sci. Tchrs. Assn. N.Y. (dir. 1971-73), Nat. Sci. Tchrs. Assn. (regional com. 1969), Nat. Cath. Edn. Assn., Am. Chem. Soc., Order of Arrow. K.C., Knights St. John. Address: 2049 George Urban Blvd Depew NY 14043

GREEN, HELEN IVY, educator; b. N.Y.C., Sept. 6, 1929; d. Morris and Rose (Brodsky) Green; B.A., Bklyn. Coll., 1957; M.A., N.Y.U., 1968, Ph.D., 1975; m. Michael Henri Levy, Nov. 28, 1957; 1 dau., Michel Carla. Adminstrv. supr. Amalgamated Clothing Workers Am., 1947-58; tchr. spl. edn. and gifted N.Y.C. Bd. Edn., 1958-65; rehab. counselor N.Y.C. Fedn. Employment and Guidance Service, 1968-69; clinician rehab. medicine Mt. Sinai Hosp., N.Y.C., 1970-72; asso. research scientist, clin. asst. prof. rehab. counseling N.Y.U., 1973—, also clinician Fifth Ave Center for Counseling and Psychotherapy, N.Y.C., 1971—; trustee Inst. Study of Drug Misuse, 1975-78; bd. dirs. Joint Council Mental Health, 1976-78. Research Soc. Am./HEW fellow, 1966-68; recipient Dean's Research Devel. grant N.Y.U., 1977. Mem. Nat. (nat. taskforce on licensure), N.Y. (presdl. award for achievement 1977), Met. (treas., bd. dirs. 1976-78) rehab. counseling assns., Am., N.Y. State, N.J. psychol. assns., Nat. Rehab. Assn., Am. Personnel and Guidance Assn., AAUP, Phi Delta Kappa. Author: The Family in Rehabilitation, in process; Drug Misuse/Human Abuse, 1976; The Family vs. Drugs and Alcohol, 1974. Exec. editor Internat. Jour. Addictions, 1975-78. Research on career choice and career edn. Home: 76 Oxford Dr Tenafly NJ 07670 Office: SEHNAP New York University 34 Stuyvesant St New York City NY 10003

GREEN, IRVING MORTON, lawyer; b. Johnstown, Pa., Dec. 3, 1925; s. Abraham H. and Cecilia (Whitten) G.; B.A., U. Pitts., 1948; J.D., Duquesne U., 1952; m. Rita Martin, Feb. 13, 1955; children—Cathy Lynn, Jonathan Joseph. Admitted to Pa. bar, 1953, U.S. Supreme Ct. bar, 1965; individual practice law, New Kensington, Pa., Pitts., 1953—; city solicitor, New Kensington, 1966—; solicitor City of Lower Burrell, Pa., 1958—. Served with AUS, 1943-46. Decorated Bronze Star, Purple Heart. Mem. Pa. Bar Assn., Westmoreland Acad. Trial Lawyers, Am. Trial Lawyers Assn., Nat. Assn. Criminal Def. Lawyers. Democrat. Jewish religion. Home: 5545-A Forbes Ave Pittsburgh PA 15217 Office: 1092 5th Ave New Kensington PA 15068

GREEN, JOHN, JR., lawyer; b. Balt., July 4, 1947; s. John and Mary (McDougall) G.; B.S., U. Md., 1971; J.D., 1974; m. Patricia Ann Weldon, Aug. 3, 1974; 1 dau., Penelope Ann. Pvt. accounting practice, Balt., 1971-74; admitted to Md. bar, 1974; staff atty. for Presdl. Clemency Bd., White House, Washington, 1975; atty. Fed. Election Commn., Washington, 1975-76; individual practice law, Cumberland, Md., 1976—. Pres. S.W. Balt. Community Improvement Assn., 1973-75. C.P.A., Md. Mem. Am., Md., Allegany County, Balt. City bar assns., Am. Inst. C.P.A.'s, Md. Assn. C.P.A.'s. Roman Catholic. Clubs: K.C., Moose. Office: 308 Washington St Cumberland MD 21502

GREEN, JUNE LAZENBY, judge; b. Arnold, Md., Jan. 23, 1914; d. Eugene Hooper and Jessie Thomson (Briggs) Lazenby; J.D., Am. U., 1941; m. John Cawley Green, Sept. 5, 1936. Admitted to D.C. bar, Md. bar; claims atty. Lumbermans Mut. Casualty Co., Washington, 1943-47; pvt. practice law, Washington and Annapolis, Md., 1947-68; judge U.S. Dist. Ct. for D.C., 1968—. Mem. Bar Assn. D.C. (past dir.), Womens Bar Assn. D.C. (past pres.), Am., Md., Inter-Am. bar assns. Clubs: Zonta; Nat. Lawyers. Home: 550 N St SW Washington DC 20024 also 464 Joyce Ln Arnold MD 21012 Office: US Courthouse Washington DC 20001

GREEN, MICHAEL JEFFREY, psychologist; b. Boston, July 9, 1942; s. Bernard and Ruth (Paretsky) G.; B.S. in B.A., Babson Coll., 1964; J.D., Boston U., 1967; M.Ed., Boston Coll., 1971; Ph.D., Heed U., 1979. Asst. athletic dir. Babson Coll., 1966-68; dir. student activities Bryant and Stratton Jr. Coll., Boston, 1968; dir. West campus Boston U., 1969-72, instr., 1970-72; asst. dir. Brockton (Mass.) Area Drug Program, 1973-74; instr. Massasoit Community Coll., 1973-74; dir. mental health clinic Mass. Dept. Mental Health, Brockton, 1975-76; clin. dir. Taunton (Mass.) State Hosp., 1974-77; psychologist, exec. dir. Family Counseling Assos., W. Bridgewater, Mass., 1973—; instr. Southeastern Mass. U., 1974-77. Instr., trainer water safety ARC, 1965—. Mem. Am. Personnel and Guidance Assn., Am., Mass. psychol. assns., Am. Group Psychotherapy Assn. Home and Office: 1413 Plymouth St Middleboro MA 02346 Office: 322 E Center St West Bridgewater MA 02379

GREEN, MICHAEL S., rehab. counselor; b. Brussels, May 8, 1950; s. David and Lola G.; came to U.S., 1950, naturalized, 1956; B.A., L.I. U., 1973, M.S., 1975; m. Evelyn Montalvo, June 13, 1976. Asst. therapist N.Y. State Dept. Mental Hygiene, South Beach Psychiat. Center, N.Y.C., 1972-73; rehab. counselor N.Y. State Office Drug Abuse Services, Arthur Kill Rehab. Center, S.I., 1974-76; supr. S.I. Aid Rehab. Center, 1976—, tchr. weekend recreation program, 1977—. Chmn. Toys for Children campaign L.I. U. Radio Sta., 1971-72, cons. to campaign, 1973. Co-recipient George K. Polk award L.I. U., 1971. Mem. Am. Psychol. Assn. (asso.), Am. Personnel and Guidance Assn. Home: 79 Manchester Dr State Island NY 10312

GREEN, MIRIAM BLAU, psychologist; b. New Castle, Pa., Sept. 21, 1932; d. Jacob Mont and Anne (Levine) Blau; A.B. with high distinction, U. Mich., 1954; Ed.M., Harvard U., 1955; Ed.D., Columbia U., 1960; m. Alvin Green, June 13, 1954; children—Andrew, Marie, Jennifer. Tchr. social studies Maimonides Sch., Boston, 1955-57; psychologist Bur. Child Guidance N.Y.C. Pub. Schs., 1960-61, 63-67; clin. psychologist Albert Einstein Coll. Medicine Jacobi Hosp. Developmental Evaluation Clinic, Bronx, N.Y., 1962; lectr. psychology Queens Coll., N.Y.C., 1962-63; psychologist Great Neck Pub. Schs. (N.Y.), 1967—. NIMH trainee, 1958-60; certified psychologist, N.Y. Diplomate Am. Bd. Profl. Psychology. Mem. Am. Psychol. Assn., Phi Beta Kappa. Jewish. Research on disadvantaged pre-school children. Home: 22 Arleigh Rd Great Neck NY 11021 Office: Great Neck Schools Phipps Bldg Lakeville Rd Great Neck NY 11020

GREEN, RAYMOND S(ILVERNAIL), radio sta. exec.; b. Torrington, Conn., Jan. 1, 1915; s. Percy Alexander and Amy (Silvernail) G.; student Julius Hartt Sch. Music, 1934-37; studied violin with Sarah Newton, 1925-33, voice with Royal Dadmun, 1934-38, Giuseppe Boghetti, N.Y.C., 1938-41, Alfredo Martino, 1942-50, coached with Frederick Kitzsinger, 1946, Stuart Ross, 1947, Dr. Ernst Knoch, 1947-50; m. Rose Basile, June 20, 1942; children—Carol Rae, Raymond Ferguson. Producer, dir. mus. programs NBC, N.Y.C., 1941-47, prodn. mgr., 1948; gen. mgr. radio sta. WFLN, 1949—, pres., 1966—. Hon. pres. Phila. Art Alliance; co-chmn. World Affairs Council; bd. dirs. Phila. Opera Co., Am.-Italy Soc.; exec. v.p. Schuylkill Valley Nature Center. Served as maj. USAAF, 1942-46. Recipient Broadcast Pioneer of Yr. award, 1976. Fellow Royal Soc. Arts; mem. Broadcast Pioneers (dir.). Clubs: Poor Richard, Franklin Inn, Philobiblon, Union League, Phila. Cricket. Home: Manor Rd Route 2824 Philadelphia PA 19128 Office: 8200 Ridge Ave Philadelphia PA 19128

GREEN, ROSE BASILE (MRS. RAYMOND S. GREEN), educator, author; b. New Rochelle, N.Y., Dec. 19, 1914; d. Salvatore V. and Caroline (Galgano) Basile; B.A., Coll. of New Rochelle, 1935; M.A., Columbia U., 1941; Ph.D., U. Pa., 1963; m. Raymond S. Green, June 20, 1942; children—Carol Rae C., Raymond Ferguson S. Asso. prof., registrar U. Tampa (Fla.), 1942-43; free lance radio script writer NBC, N.Y.C., 1945-48; spl. instr. English, Temple U., Phila., 1953-58; prof., chmn. dept. English, Cabrini Coll., Radnor, Pa., 1958-70. Bd. dirs. Opera Co. of Phila., Free Library Phila., Phila. Women for the Bicentennial, Balch Inst., Nat. Italian Am. Found., Women for Greater Phila. Decorated Cavaliere Republic Italy; recipient Humanities award Phila. Nationalities Service Center, 1975; Amita Nat. Bicentennial award for lit., 1976; Nat. Bicentennial award for lit. DAR, 1976; named Woman of Year Pa., Sons of Italy, 1975. Mem. Am.-Italy Soc. Phila. (dir.), AAUW (dir.), Phila. Art Alliance (dir.), Am. Acad. Polit. and Social Scis., Am. Studies Assn., Modern Lang. Assn., Nat. Council Tchrs. English, Pa., Walt Whitman poetry socs., Am. Acad. Poets, Kappa Gamma Pi. Clubs: Phila. Cricket, Cosmopolitan, Athenaeum (Phila.). Author: To Reason Why; The Italian-American Novel; Primo Vino; The Cabrinian Philosophy of Education; 76 for Philadelphia, 1976; Women, The Second Coming, 1977. Home: 308 Manor Rd Rt 2824 Philadelphia PA 19128

GREEN, SAMUEL LOUIS, judge; b. Gadsen, Ala., Feb. 10, 1935; s. Clayton and Bertha (Rogers) G.; B.A., U. Buffalo, 1965, LL.B., 1967, J.D., 1968; L.H.D. (hon.), Canisus Coll., 1977; m. Ernestine Riddick, Sept. 17, 1960; children—Samuel Maurice, Beth Ann. Admitted to N.Y. bar, 1968; mem. firm Serotte, Hoffman, Haley and Green, Buffalo, 1968-73; asso. judge City Ct. Buffalo, 1973—. Bd. dirs. Niagara Frontier Housing Devel. Corp., 1969—, mem. exec. com. 1968-71; bd. dirs. Buffalo Urban League; trustee Sch. Social Work, Daemen Coll., Buffalo. Mem. Nat., Erie County bar assns., Trial Lawyers Assn., Nat. Bar Judges Assn., N.Y. State City Ct. Judges Assn. N.A.A.C.P., Law Alumni Assn. State U. N.Y. at Buffalo (bd. dirs. 1972—). Home: 245 Woodbridge Buffalo NY 14214 Office: 50 Delaware Ave Buffalo NY 14202

GREEN, SEDGWICK WILLIAM, govt. ofcl.; b. N.Y.C., Oct. 16, 1929; s. Louis A. and Evelyn (Schoenberg) G.; A.B. magna cum laude, Harvard, 1950, J.D. magna cum laude, 1953; m. Patricia Freiberg, May 29, 1966; children—Catherine Ann, Louis Matthew. Admitted to D.C. bar, 1953, N.Y. bar, 1954; law sec. Ct. Appeals for D.C., 1955-56; atty. firm Cleary, Gottlieb, Steen & Hamilton, N.Y.C., 1956-66, Paul, Weiss, Rifkind, Wharton & Garrison, N.Y.C., 1966-68; counsel N.Y. Joint Legislative Com. on Housing and Urban Devel., 1961-64; mem. N.Y. State Assembly, 1965-68; regional adminstr. HUD, N.Y.C., 1970-77. Dir. Grand Union Co., Unimin, Inc. Chmn., Fed. Regional Council, 1971-77; mem. 96th Congress from N.Y. 18th Dist.; ex officio mem. Tri-State Regional Planning Commn., 1970—. Del., N.Y. State Republican Conv., 1962, 66. Bd. dirs. N.Y. Cancer Research Inst., Citizens Union Research Found.; bd. overseers Center for N.Y.C. Affairs, New Sch. for Social Research; mem. adv. council N.Y. U. Grad. Sch. Pub. Affairs; trustee Montefiore Hosp. and Med. Center. Served as 1st lt. AUS, 1953-55. Mem. Am., N.Y. State bar assns., Assn. Bar City N.Y. (treas.), N.Y. County Lawyers Assn., Harvard Law Sch. Assn. N.Y.C., Signet Soc, Phi Beta Kappa, Club: Harvard (N.Y.C.). Mem. Harvard Law Rev. Contbr. articles to legal jours. Home: 755 Park Ave New York NY 10021 Office: 1213 Longworth House Office Bldg Washington DC 20515

GREEN, THOMAS HENRY, JR., physician; b. Ligonier, Ind., Jan. 26, 1923; s. Thomas Henry and Helen (Schaab) G.; student Harvard, 1940-43; M.D., Harvard, 1946; m. Rae Nicola Melville Duthie, Mar. 23, 1946; children—Nicola, Betsy, Thomas Henry, III. Intern, Mass. Gen. Hosp., Boston, 1946-47, resident, 1947-53, clin. asst. in surgery, 1953-54, asst. in surgery, 1954-59, asst. surgeon, 1959-63, asso. vis. surgeon, 1963-73, vis. surgeon, 1973—; asst. gynecologist Pondville State Cancer Hosp., Mass. Dept. Pub. Health, 1957-59, chief gynecology, 1959—; clin. asst. gynecology New Eng. Deaconess Hosp., 1953-56, gynecologist, sr. active staff, 1956—; clin. asst. gynecology Harvard Med. Sch., 1953-55, instr. gynecology, 1955-59, clin. asso. gynecology, 1959-63, asst. clin. prof. gynecology, 1963-68, asso. clin. prof., 1968—. Served with M.C., AUS, 1948-50. Diplomate Am. Bd. Surgery. Fellow Am. Assn. Obstetricians and Gynecologists, Am. Coll. Obstetricians and Gynecologists, A.C.S.; mem. A.M.A., Am. Soc. for Study Sterility (asst. sec. 1963), Obstet. Soc. Boston (sec. 1970-72, pres. 1974-75), New Eng. Obstet. and Gynecol. Soc., Mid-Eastern Gynecol. and Obstet. Travel Club (sec. 1960-63), Soc. Pelvic Surgeons (sec.-treas. 1965-68, pres. 1973-74), New Eng. Surg. Soc., Soc. Gynecol. Oncologists, Daland Soc. (pres. 1968-69), New Eng. Cancer Soc., Boston Surg. Soc., Phi Beta Kappa, Sigma Xi, Alpha Omega Alpha. Author: Textbook of Gynecology, 1965, 3d edit., 1977. Contbr. articles to profl. jours. Home: 41 Parker Rd Wakefield MA 01880 Office: 8 Hawthorne Pl Charles River Park Boston MA 02114

GREEN, WALLACE HUGHES, data storage and retrieval systems co. exec.; b. Franklin, Tenn., May 18, 1930; s. James Benton and Claudia Cecil (Finley) G.; certificate Internat. Corr. Sch., 1956, Ben Franklin Sch. Bus., 1959; m. Vada Marlene Gray, July 14, 1951; children—Robert B., Thomas H., Cynthia Marie, Kathleen Dawn, Beverly Ann, Candie Michell. Machinist, Wilks Precision Instrument Co., Rockville, Md., 1951-56; gen. supr.-mfg. Am. Research & Mfg. Corp., Rockville, 1956-62; planner Washington Technol. Assn., 1962-67; dir. mfg. Jonker Corp., Gaithersburg, Md., 1967-70; v.p. Remac Info. Corp., Gaithersburg, 1970-76; pres. Termatrex Products Inc., Gaithersburg, 1976—; v.p. Photo Communication Inc., Rockville, 1976—, also dir. Sec., Potomac Falconers Assn., 1977—. Served with USN, 1947-51. Democrat. Home: 5708 Dun Horse Ln Rockville MD 20855 Office: 26 N Summit Ave Gaithersburg MD 20760

GREEN, WAYNE HUGO, psychiatrist, child psychiatrist, psychoanalyst; b. Schenectady, N.Y., July 23, 1941; s. Albert George and Mildred (Hugo) G.; A.B., U. Chgo., 1963; M.D., N.Y. U., 1967; certificate in Psychoanalysis, William Alanson White Inst. Psychiatry, Psychoanalysis and Psychology, 1977. Intern, Lenox Hill Hosp., N.Y.C., 1967-68; resident in psychiatry N.Y. U.-Bellevue Med. Center, 1970-72, fellow in child psychiatry, 1972-74; asst. dir. Children's Mental Hygiene Clinic, Bellevue Psychiat. Hosp., N.Y.C., 1974-77; unit chief Children's Psychiat. In-patient Service, Bellevue Hosp., N.Y.C., 1978—; asst. clin. prof. psychiatry N.Y. U., 1977—; asst. attending dept. psychiatry N.Y. U. Med. Center, Univ. Hosp., N.Y.C., 1974—; asst. attending psychiatrist Bellevue Hosp. Center, N.Y.C., 1974—. Served with USPHS, 1968-70. Diplomate Am. Bd. Psychiatry and Neurology. Recipient AMA Physician Recognition award, 1975. Mem. Am. Acad. Child Psychiatry, Am. Psychiat. Assn., N.Y. Council Child Psychiatry, Am. Acad. Psychoanalysis. Contbr. articles in field to profl. jours. Home: 600 S Mountain Rd New City NY 10956 Office: 110 Bleecker St New York City NY 10012 also Ward PQ6 Bellevue Psychiatric Hosp First Ave and 30 St New York City NY 10016

GREENAWALT, KENNETH WILLIAM, lawyer; b. Town of Wall Street, Colo., Oct. 9, 1903; s. William Eckert and Cora May (Cornell) G.; LL.B., Cornell U., 1927; m. Martha Frances Sloan, Sept. 3, 1929; children—William Sloan, Robert Kent, Ann Cornell (Mrs. William Beaven Abernathy), Kim Chandler. Admitted to N.Y. bar, 1929, U.S. Supreme Ct. bar, 1933, also various dist. cts. and U.S. cts. of appeal; practiced in N.Y.C., 1929—; asso. firm Sackett, Chapman, Brown & Cross, 1927-30, Davies, Auerbach & Cornell, 1930-39, Davies, Auerbach, Cornell & Hardy, 1939-44, mem. firm, 1944-49, and successor firms including Davies, Hardy Ives & Lawther, also Windels, Marx, Davies & Ives, 1949—. Mem. Edgmont Sch. Dist., Bd. Edn. Scarsdale, N.Y., 1957-62, Met. Opera Guild; mem. gen. council Congl. Christian Chs., 1952-58; regent L.I. Coll. Hosp. Recipient Woodford prize Cornell, 1927; George Washington Honor medal Freedoms Found., 1962. Fellow Am. Coll. Trial Lawyers, Soc. for Values in Higher Edn. (dir.); mem. Am. Acad. Polit. Sci., Am. (various coms., Gavel award 1962), N.Y. State (various coms.) bar assns., Am. Judicature Soc., Bar Assn. City N.Y. (various coms.), Cornell Law Assn., Am. Acad. Polit. and Social Sci., N.Y. State Vet. Med. Soc. (hon.), Vet. Med. Assn. N.Y.C. (hon.), Sigma Delta Chi, Phi Sigma Kappa, Phi Delta Phi, Sphinx Head (Cornell U.). Conglist. (pres. bd. trustees). Clubs: Harbor View, Cornell (N.Y.C.); Westchester Country, Westchester County Tennis (past pres.); Fox Meadow Tennis (Scarsdale, N.Y.). Contbr. to legal publs.; guest participant radio, TV programs. Home: 65 Highridge Rd Hartsdale NY 10530 Office: 51 W 51st St New York City NY 10019

GREENAWALT, MARTHA SLOAN (MRS. KENNETH WILLIAM GREENAWALT), civic worker; b. Clarksburg, W.Va., Sept. 8, 1906; d. Herbert Elias and Louella (Dye) Sloan; A.B., Wilson Coll., 1928; M.A., Columbia, 1929; m. Kenneth William Greenawalt, Sept. 3, 1929; children—William Sloan, Robert Kent, Ann Cornell (Mrs. William Beaven Abernethy), Kim Chandler. Tchr., Berkeley Inst., Bklyn., 1929-33. Pres., Westchester council Women's Coll. Clubs, 1952-53; mem. housing research com., mem. bd. Westchester Council Social Agys.; chmn. Greenburgh Urban Renewal Commn., 1961-75; mem. bd. Westchester Citizens com. Nat. Council on Crime and Delinquency; mem. com. for constl. reform, 2d regional plan com., mem. bd. dirs. Regional Plan Assn.; mem. adv. bd. Greenburgh Neighborhood Health Center, 1974—; mem. Nat. Adv. Com. on Comprehensive Health Planning, 1972-74. Bd. dirs. Westchester County Urban League, 1957-62; mem. bd. United Way of Westchester, 1977—. Mem. AAUW, NOW (dir. central Westchester chpt. 1973-78), League Women Voters (pres. Greenburgh 1953-56, pres. Westchester County 1957-59, pres. N.Y. 1963-67, mem. nat. bd. 1968-74), Women of Westchester, Scarsdale-Hartsdale UN Assn. Address: 65 Highridge Rd Hartsdale NY 10530

GREENAWAY, MILLICENT CENTILIA, day care center tchr. and dir.; b. Antiqua, W.I., Feb. 26, 1921; d. Charles and Theresa Dickenson; certificate in elementary edn. Spring Garden's Tchrs'. Tng. Coll., W.I., 1948; student in early childhood curriculum Fairleigh Dickinson U., 1963, Kean's Coll., 1968, Essex Community Coll., 1970; B.A. in Early Childhood Shaw U., 1974; M.A. in Early Childhood Edn., Internat. Open U., 1978; m. Simon Greenaway children—George Thomas, Aubrey Thomas, Myona Greenaway. Tchr., edn. dept. Leeward Islands, W.I., St. John's Antiqua, 1949-59; tchr., supr. Newark Pre-Sch. Council Headstart Program, 1965-68; dir. Newark Day Care Center, 1968-70; dir., head tchr. New Hope Devel. Day Care Center Inc., Newark, from 1971; now owner, exec. dir. Aunt Millie's Children's Learning Center, Inc., Newark; bd. dirs. Day Care Co-ordinating Council of Essex County. Bd. dirs. Franklin-St. John's United Meth. Ch., 1974—, Dramatic Theatre Guild, 1974—; mem. Emergency Com. to Save Child Care in Newark. Named most outstanding dir. in Essex County, Day Care Co-ordinating Council, 1977; recipient certificate of appreciation Emergency Com. to Save Child Care, award Theta chpt. Phi Delta Kappa, 1978; award Franklin—St. John's United Meth. Ch., 1979; others; certified in elem. and nursery sch. edn. N.J. Dept. Edn. Mem. Nat. Council Negro Women. Home: 219 Wainwright St Newark NJ 07112 Office: 15 E Kinney St Newark NJ 07102

GREENBAUM, CHARLES HIRSCH, dermatologist; b. Phila., Feb. 22, 1925; s. Sigmund Samuel and Rae Shirley (Refowich) G.; A.B., U. Pa., 1948; M.D., Jefferson Med. Coll., 1954; m. Julia Heimowitz, July 3, 1955; children—Steven Samuel, Lynne Carol, Robert David. Intern, Phila. Gen. Hosp., 1954-55; resident U. Pa. Grad. Sch. Medicine, 1955-56, Pa. Hosp., 1956-57, Hosp. U. Pa., 1957-58; practice medicine specializing in dermatology, Phila., 1958—; instr. dermatology Jefferson Med. Coll., Phila., 1958-72, clin. asso. prof., 1972—; attending physician, chief dermatology Holy Redeemer Hosp., Meadowbrook, Pa., 1958—; instr. dermatology U. Pa. Grad. Sch. Medicine, 1958-70; med. advisor Pa. Blue Cross, 1973—. Served with USMC, 1943-46. Diplomate Am. Bd. Dermatology. Fellow Am. Acad. Dermatology, A.C.P.; mem. Soc. Investigative Dermatology, Am. Acad. Dermatology (chmn. adv. bd. council 1977), AMA (mem. sect. on dermatology 1978), Pa. Acad. Dermatology (pres. 1976-77), Phila. Dermatol. Soc. (pres. 1976-77), Coll. Physicians Phila., Solomon Solis-Cohen Med. Lit. Soc. (pres. 1978), Pa., Phila. County (pres. N. br. 1976, dir. 1977) med. socs. Contbr. articles in field to profl. jours. Home: 1237 Imperial Rd Rydal PA 19046 Office: 8220 Castor Ave Philadelphia PA 19152

GREENBERG, ALBERT, art dir.; b. N.Y.C., Mar. 15, 1924; s. Samuel David and Mary (Miller) G.; B.F.A., Cooper Union, 1948; m. Marilyn Hoffner, May 29, 1949; children—Doren Roe, Peter Cooper. Art editor Gentry, Am. Fabrics Mags., N.Y.C., 1951-56; art dir. Gentlemen's Quar. Mag., Esquire, Inc., N.Y.C., 1956-70; sales promotion art dir. Lampert Agy., N.Y.C., 1970-71; v.p., sales promotion art dir. Wells, Rich, Greene Inc., N.Y.C., 1971—; tchr. Pratt Inst., 1964-65, 73-74, Cooper Union, 1967-68, Finch Coll., 73-75, Manhattanville Coll., 1974-75, Parsons Sch. Design, 1975—. Served with USAAF, 1943-45; ETO. Decorated Air medal with silver oak leaf cluster. Recipient over 100 profl. awards; named Alumnus of Year Cooper Union, 1968. Mem. Art Dirs. Club N.Y. (designer 43d ann.), Cooper Union Alumni Council (1st v.p. 1970-71, pres. 1971-73, adminstrv. bd. 1974—). Contbg. editor: Typographic Directions, 1964, Advt. Directions, Photography, 1962, Advt. Directions, Visual Advt., 1961. Address: 51 Fifth Ave New York City NY 10003

GREENBERG, BENJAMIN SAUL, assn. exec.; b. Bklyn., Oct. 22, 1922; s. Joseph and Beatrice (Rivlin) G.; B.A., N.Y. U., 1942; postgrad. U.S. Naval Acad., Annapolis, Md., 1946; Rochester Inst. Tech., 1957; m. Nancy May Bloom, May 1, 1960; children—Stephanie, Dorothy, William, Michael. Pres., Anchor Features Inc., N.Y.C., 1954-58; v.p. Allen d'or Prodns. Inc., N.Y.C., 1958-61; pres. Associated Film Cons.'s, N.Y.C., 1961-72, Adm. Film Prodns., N.Y.C., 1972-74; dir. pub. affairs Advt. Council Inc., N.Y.C., 1974—. Pres., bd. dirs. Midwood Park Property Owners Assn.; v.p., bd. dirs. Nat. Musical Theatre. Served with USNR, 1943-53; PTO, ETO. Recipient gold, silver, bronze awards N.Y. Internat. Film and TV Festival, 1968, 69, 71, 72, 74; silver award Atlanta Film Festival, 1970. Mem. Pub. Relations Soc. Am. (dir. del. N.Y. chpt.), TV Acad. Arts and Scis., Naval Inst., Air Force Assn., L.I. Antique Dealers Assn. Home: 723 E 18th St Brooklyn NY 11230 Office: 825 3d Ave New York City NY 10022

GREENBERG, BERNARD, pediatrician; b. N.Y.C., Jan. 21, 1913; s. Joseph and Gussie (Gans) G.; B.S., Columbia U., 1933; M.D., Rush Med. Coll., 1937; m. Bernice Robbins, Nov. 1, 1942; children—Judith J., Steven R. Intern, Maimonides Hosp., Bklyn., 1937-39; resident in pediatrics Kingston Ave. Hosp., Bklyn., 1938; resident pediatrician Home for Hebrew Infants, Bronx, N.Y., 1940, Morrisiania City Hosp., Bronx, 1941; practice medicine specializing in pediatrics, Bklyn., 1946—; attending pediatrician Maimonides Hosp.; asst. clin. prof. pediatrics State U.N.Y. Downstate Med. Center, 1965—. Served with U.S. Army, 1942-46. Mem. Am. Acad. Pediatrics, AMA. Jewish. Home: 25 Sutton Pl S New York City NY 10022 Office: 755 Ocean Ave Brooklyn NY 11226

GREENBERG, CALVIN LEON, real estate broker; b. Bklyn., June 20, 1921; s. Leon and Minnie (Brein) G.; student Bolles; M.B.A., Jackson State U., 1974; children—Paulette, Carol. Profl. boxer, 1946-48; real estate appraiser, investment cons. Balter & Greenberg, Inc., Merrick, N.Y., 1948—, also chmn. bd. Served with USMC, 1942-45. Mem. Nat. Assn. Real Estate Appraisers, Columbia Soc. Real Estate Appraisers, Nat. Assn. Rev. Appraisers. Jewish. Club: Freeport Tuna. Author: How to Become a Successful Store Leasing Broker, 1971; Profit Opportunities in Real Estate Investments, 1976. Home and Office: 89 Henry St Merrick NY 11566

GREENBERG, CARL, lawyer; b. Newark, Oct. 13, 1934; s. Isadore and Mollie (Starr) G.; A.B., Rutgers U., 1956, J.D., 1959; m. Barbara Fisher, June 9, 1959; children—Jill Robin, Wendy Beth, Deborah Amy. Admitted to N.J. bar, 1960; law sec. to judge N.J. Superior Ct., 1960-61; asso. firm Schreiber, Lancaster & Demos, Newark, 1961-64, partner, 1964-67; asso. firm Samuel A. Gennett, Newark, 1967-68; partner firm Porzio and Bromberg, Morristown, N.J., 1968—; lectr. trial practice and procedure N.J. Inst. Continuing Legal Edn., 1965—; adj. prof. Rutgers Law Sch., 1969—. Served with U.S. Army, 1959. Fellow Am. Coll. Trial Lawyers; mem. Am. Abritration Assn. (panel), Am., N.J., Essex County, Morris County bar assns., N.J. Trial Attys. Assn. Editor Rutgers Law Rev., 1957-59. Home: 5 Lenox Terr South Orange NJ 07079 Office: 163 Madison Ave Morristown NJ 07960

GREENBERG, FRANK JOSEPH, educator; b. Boston, June 15, 1933; s. Benjamin and Mary (Cohen) G.; B.A., Brentwood Coll., 1958; D.D. (hon.), Ph.D., Brantridge Forest Sch., 1963; B.D., Felix Adler Meml. U., 1964; LL.B., Blackstone Sch. Law, 1967; M.Ed., Thomas A. Edison Coll., 1970, Ph.D., 1971, D.Ed., 1971, LL.D. (hon.), 1972, M. Criminology, 1972, D. Criminology, 1972; L.H.D. (hon.) London Inst. for Applied Research, 1972, D.C.S. (hon.), 1973; m. Elizabeth Irene Bowser, July 2, 1956; children—Robin E., Linda A. (dec.), Diana R., Frank Joseph, Anita L., Daniel J. Self-employed tax and security accountant, Beverly, Mass., 1956-59; self-employed psychologist and ednl. counselor, Beverly, 1963-72; substitute tchr. Beverly pub. schs., 1970-71; br. prof., dir. admissions Thomas A. Edison Coll., 1972—, dean adminstrn. and faculty, 1974-76; v.p. Palm Beach Psychotherapy Tng. Center, 1974. Served with USCG, 1950-54. Decorated Imperial Order Constantine (Lisbon, Portugal); Knight comdr. Order St. John Jerusalem; comdr. Internat. Order Sursum Corda (Brussels Belgium). Diplomate Am. Bd. Examiners Psychotherapy. Fellow Am. Assn. Criminology (life), Am. Acad. Behavioral Scis. (life), Am. Coll. Clin. Adminstrs., Am. Biog. Inst. (life, hon. mem. editorial adv. bd.), Internat. Biog. Assn., Assn. Social Psychology, Fla. Psychoanalytic Inst. (life); mem. Criminological Execs. Club (life), Am. Assn. Advancement Criminology (life), D.A.V. (life), Am. Soc. Notaries (charter), Soc. Advancement Edn., Am. Parapsychol. Research Found. (charter), Am. Assn. Higher Edn., Internat. Platform Assn., Nat. Psychol. Assn., Nat. Sci. Tchrs. Assn., Nat. Soc. Study Edn., Nat. Soc. Pub. Accountants (asso.), World Future Soc., Inter-Am. Soc., Soc. Profs. Edn., Thomas A. Edison Coll. Alumni Assn. (pres., life mem.), Cousteau Soc. (charter), Am. Ednl. Research Assn., Am. Studies Assn., Navy League U.S., Acad. Polit. Sci., Am. Assn. U. Adminstrs., Am. Forestry Assn., Am. Studies Research Centre (India), Assn. for Supervision and Curriculum Devel., Change Assos., Internat., New Eng. solar energy assns., Soc. for Internat. Devel., Soc. for Intercultural Edn., Tng. and Research, Am. Film Inst., Assn. Ednl. Communications and Tech. (comprehensive), Bibl. Archaeology Soc., Internat. Assn. Hydrogen Energy (profl.), Measurements and Control Soc. Internat., Med. Electronics and Data Soc. Am., Nat. Ret. Tchrs. Assn., U.S. Naval Inst., Alpha Psi Omega Soc., Lambda Epsilon Chi. Clubs: Masons, Shriners. Research, publs. on unstructured higher edn. Home: 14 Lindsey St Dorchester MA 02124

GREENBERG, HERBERT MARVIN, psychologist, psychol. testing firm exec.; b. Detroit, Sept. 23, 1929; s. Harry and Helen Greenberg; B.S., City Coll. N.Y., 1950, M.S., 1951; Ph.D., N.Y. U., 1955; m. Jeanne LeCrann, July 30, 1967; children—Gary, Mark, Scott, Phillip, Holly. Cons. to N.Y.C. Dept. Welfare, 1952-55; asst. prof. psychology Tex. Technol. Coll., Lubbock, 1955-57, asso. dir. Testing Center, 1955-57; asso. prof. psychiatry Rutgers U., New

Brunswick, N.J., 1957-59; exec. dir. Elizabeth (N.J.) Commn. Human Relations, 1959-60; private practice psychotherapy, Lubbock and New Brunswick, 1952-67; founder Mktg. Survey and Research Corp., Princeton, N.J., 1961, pres., 1961—; co-propr., dir. Sta. WTNJ, Trenton, N.J., 1973—; mem. faculty Fairleigh Dickenson U., Rutherford, N.J., 1959-60, L.I. U., 1960-61. Mem. exec. com. Princeton Community Democratic Orgn., 1975—; mem. Mercer County Overall Econ. Devel. Com., Trenton, N.J., 1977—. Recipient Elizabeth (N.J.) Good Neighbor award, 1960; Am. Found. for the Blind grantee, 1954; OEO grantee, 1965-66. Mem. Am., N.J. psychol. assns., Nat. Assn. Broadcasters, N.J. Assn. Broadcasters, Phi Beta Kappa, Phi Delta Kappa. Democrat. Jewish. Author: Successful Salesman-Man and His Manager, 1972; contbr. over 200 articles on personality evaluation, psychology of successful salesmen and bus. psychology to profl. jours. Home: 99 Ridgeview Circle Princeton NJ 08854 Office: 1101-B State Rd Princeton NJ 08854

GREENBERG, JOSEPH, physician; b. N.Y.C., Oct. 6, 1926; s. Morris and Ruth (Milman) G.; B.A., N.Y. U., 1947, M.D., 1951; m. Barbara Rae Brodoff, Sept. 12, 1954; children—Paula Merle, Janis Ruth. Fellow, Nat. Cancer Inst., USPHS, Bethesda, Md., 1952-54; chief radioisotope lab. U.S. Naval Hosp., St. Albans, N.Y., 1954-56; chief div. nuclear medicine L.I. Jewish Hosp., New Hyde Park, N.Y., 1956-60; prof., dir. dept. nuclear medicine, dept. endocrinology N.Y. Polyclinic Med. Sch. and Hosp., N.Y.C., 1960-63; cons. U.S. Naval Hosp., St. Albans, 1956—, Oak Ridge Nat. Lab., 1961—, U.S. Naval Hosp., Bethesda, 1962—; med. adviser Leukemia Soc., N.Y.C., 1959—; cons. dept. nuclear medicine Med. Arts Center Hosp., N.Y.C., 1969—. A founder L.I. Arts Center; charter mem. fine arts council C.W. Post Coll.; mem. Great Neck (N.Y.) Estates Civic Assn., Great Neck Community Concert Assn. Served to lt. M.C., USNR, 1954-56. Recipient Peoples Hosp. Research Found. prize, N.Y.C., 1951. Fellow AAAS, Am. Coll. Nuclear Medicine (charter, bd. reps., v.p.); mem. Soc. Nuclear Medicine (pres. Greater N.Y. chpt., mem. nat. exec. com., trustee, chmn. com. edn. and research 1962—), Am. Physiol. Soc., Am. Assn. Cancer Research, Am. Nuclear Soc., N.Y. Cancer Soc., N.Y. Acad. Scis., AMA, Nassau Acad. Medicine. Contbr. chpts. to books, numerous tech. papers to med. lit. Home: 106 Clover Dr Great Neck NY 11021 Office: 57 W 57th St New York City NY 10019

GREENBERG, LISA ALICE, hotel exec.; b. Vienna, Austria, Mar. 27, 1927; d. Max and Rose (Trompeter) Konigsberg; naturalized, 1965; B.A., Coll. Fashion and Clothing Tech., London, 1944; B.A., Queens Coll., 1956; student Adelphi U., Garden City, N.Y., 1973; children—Jacqueline Greenberg Levine, Michele Greenberg. Market research analyst Revlon, Inc., N.Y.C., 1961-65; mgr. mktg. research Hilton Internat. Co., N.Y.C., 1965—; bd. dirs. Travel Research Assn., 1970. Democrat. Jewish. Home: 156 11 Aguilar Ave Flushing NY 11367 Office: 301 Park Ave New York City NY 10022

GREENBERG, LORRY, city ofcl. Can.; b. Ottawa, Ont., Can., Dec. 31, 1933; s. Roger and Rose (Bezumny) G.; m. Carol Gardner, Apr. 20, 1958; children—Rhonda, Jeffrey, Roger, Stephanie, Heather. Co-founder, v.p. Minto Constrn. Co., Ltd., to 1962, ret., 1962; civic worker, Ottawa, 1962-69, chmn. fund raising com. for constrn. home for delinquent boys, chmn. steering com. for rehab. female chronic alcoholic offenders, dir. Serenity Home, alcoholism treatment and residential center, chmn. residential care div. Ottawa and Dist. Assn. Mentally Retarded; alderman Wellington Ward City of Ottawa, 1968-69, controller, 1969, sr. controller, dep. mayor, 1972-74, mayor, 1974—. Named an Outstanding Young Man, Ottawa West Jaycees, 1969; recipient award for contbn. towards preservation and devel. Can.'s multicultural heritage Carling Community Arts Found., 1976; Meritas Columbus award K.C., Dist. 34, 1977. Liberal. Jewish. Club: B'nai B'rith (Ottawa Lodge 885 Citizen of Yr. 1977). Home: 1970 Lenester Ave Ottawa ON K2A 1J9 Canada Office: 111 Sussex Dr Ottawa ON K1N 5A1 Canada

GREENBERG, ROBERT BENJAMIN, cosmetic co. exec.; b. Cambridge, Mass., May 5, 1944; s. Samuel and Helen Greenberg; B.B.A., U. Mass., 1965, teaching certificate, 1966; J.D., Boston Coll., 1969; 1 dau., Alison. Admitted to Mass. bar, 1969; pres. Cons. Group, Inc., Boston, 1970, Goldman Assos., Boston, 1971-73; treas. Golden Rae, Inc., Boston, 1972—; pres. Natural Cosmetics Chestnut Hill, Inc., Boston, 1973—, Communications, Ltd., Boston, 1974-75, Natural Cosmetics West Hartford (Conn.), 1974—, Natural Cosmetics Hartford (Conn.), 1975—; exec. v.p. Nutrient Cosmetics Ltd., N.Y.C., 1975—; owner I Natural Cosmetics, Las Vegas, 1978—. Trustee Hampshire Country Sch., Rindge, N.H., 1974-77. Mem. Am., Mass. bar assns., Internat. Council Shopping Centers, Internat. Franchise Assn. Club: Charles River Park Tennis (Boston). Home: 4 Longfellow Pl Boston MA 02114 Office: 595 Madison Ave New York City NY 10022 also 133 Newbury St Boston MA 02116

GREENBERG, SIGMUND ROBERT, physician; b. Trenton, N.J., Sept. 3, 1930; s. Jacob and Ella (Dranoff) G.; B.S. in Biology, Franklin and Marshall Coll., 1952; M.D., Hahnemann Med. Coll., 1956; m. Maxine Weisman, Sept. 5, 1960; children—Erik, Robin, Lori, Evan. Intern in medicine Abington (Pa.) Hosp., 1956-57, resident in internal medicine, 1957-60; resident in internal medicine Grad. Sch. Medicine, U. Pa., Phila., 1958-59; practice medicine specializing in internal medicine, Phila. and Abington, 1966—; instr. in medicine Jefferson Med. Coll., Phila., 1960-64; asso. in medicine Grad. Hosp. U. Pa., Phila., 1960—, Abington Hosp., 1960—, chief of endocrinology, 1971—; asso. clin. prof. medicine Temple U., Phila., 1974—; chief med. outpatient dept. Grad. Hosp. U. Pa., Phila., 1964-68. Diplomate Am. Bd. Internal Medicine, Am. Bd. Endocrinology. Fellow A.C.P.; mem. Am. Fedn. Clin. Research, Am., N.Y. diabetic assns., AMA, N.Y. Acad. Scis., Phila. Endocrine Soc., Pa., Montgomery County med. socs., Alpha Omega Alpha, Phi Beta Kappa. Contbr. articles on endocrinology to med. jours. Home: 1025 Coates Rd Meadowbrook PA 19046 Office: Abington Hospital Abington PA 19001

GREENBERG, WARREN PETER, research co. exec.; b. Phila., Nov. 22, 1940; s. Samuel Rosen and Miriam Joan (Goldberg) G.; A.B., Wilkes Coll., 1962; postgrad. U. Pa., 1963, Temple U., 1964; m. Libby Seitz, June 26, 1966; children—Sharon, Andrew. Lab. technician Phila. Gen. Hosp., 1963-64; biologist Merck Inst. for Therapeutic Research, West Point, Pa., 1965-68, research biologist, 1969-70, data coordinator, 1971-73, systems coordinator, 1974-76, mgr. pre-clin. data systems, 1977—. Vice chmn. Montgomery Twp. Park Bd., 1976-77, sec., 1978; mem. com. on admissions Wilkes Coll., 1978. Served with USAR, 1964-65. Recipient Deans award Wilkes Coll., 1961; Mgmt. award Merck & Co., Inc., 1971. Mem. Drug Info. Assn. Jewish. Club: Beth Or Men's. Contbr. articles to profl. jours. Home: 117 Narcissus Pl North Wales PA 19454 Office: Sumneytown Pike West Point PA 19486

GREENBERGER, HOWARD, writer; b. N.Y.C., Sept. 4, 1924; s. William and Jennie (Hoffner) G.; B.B.A., Coll. City N.Y., 1945; postgrad. in English, Columbia U., 1949-50. Pub. relations dir. Motivational Programmers Inc., N.Y.C., 1948-51; TV-radio writer, producer, dir. Arkwright Advt. Co., N.Y.C., 1955-58; copy and pub. relations dir., TV-radio writer, producer, dir. Robert Whitehill Advt. Agy., N.Y.C., 1951-55, 58-61; TV/radio writer, producer, dir. Am. Cancer Soc., N.Y.C., 1961-66; freelance writer N.Y.C., 1966—. Jewish. Author: Off-Broadway Experience, history Off-Broadway theater, 1971; Bogey's Baby, biography, 1976; writer, producer, dir. numerous plays La Mama Exptl. Theatre Club and Caffé Cino, N.Y.C.; also TV, radio prodns. Home: 404 E 55th St New York City NY 10022

GREENBLOTT, CHARLES TODD, health care adminstr.; b. Binghamton, N.Y., July 19, 1951; s. Robert B. and Rose-edyth (Baken) G.; B.S. in Health Care Adminstrn., Ithaca Coll., 1973; M.S., SUNY, Stony Brook, 1976; m. Ellyn D. Green, Aug. 2, 1975; 1 dau., Marley Fae. Asst. adminstr. Susquehanna Nursing Home, Johnson City, N.Y., 1973-74; adminstr. Our Lady of Lourdes Hosp., Binghamton, 1975-76; supervising adminstr. Residence Nursing Homes, 1978—; adj. prof. Ithaca Coll., 1979—; adminstr. Vestal Nursing Home (N.Y.), 1976—. Licensed nursing home adminstr., N.Y. state. Mem. Am. Coll. Nursing Home Adminstrs. (chmn. long-term care facility adminstrs.), Am. Public Health Assn., N.Y. State Assn. Long Term Care Adminstrs. Author: Institutional Care of Terminal Patients, 1976. Home: 70 Aldrich Ave Binghamton NY 13903 Office: 860 Old Vestal Rd Vestal NY 13850

GREENBURG, JERRY LEE, gastroenterologist; b. Chgo., Mar. 4, 1942; s. Morris D. and Maxine K. (Goldberg) G.; B.S., U. Ill., 1962, M.D., 1966; m. Lydia Joan Morowitz, Feb. 23, 1969; children—Susan Maureen, David Blair, Michael Rexford, Jennifer Laurie. Intern, U. Calif. Affiliated Hosps., Los Angeles, 1966-67; resident in internal medicine Wadsworth VA Hosp., Los Angeles, 1967-70, fellow in gastroenterology, 1970-71; pvt. practice internal medicine and gastroenterology, Thousand Oaks and Westlake Village, Calif., 1971-76, Westport, Conn., 1976—; chmn. dept. medicine Los Robles Hosp., Thousand Oaks, Calif., 1973-74, co-dir. gastroenterology unit, 1971-76; cons. physician Wadsworth VA Hosp., Los Angeles, 1971-76; clin. instr. dept. medicine U. Calif. Los Angeles Sch. Medicine, 1971-74, asst. clin. prof., 1974-76; attending physician U. Calif. Hosp. and Med. Center, 1971-76; attending physician Norwalk (Conn.) Hosp.; asst. clin. prof. Sch. Medicine, Yale, 1977—. Diplomate Am. Bd. Internal Medicine, Nat. Bd. Med. Examiners. Mem. AMA (physicians recognition award 1969-78), A.C.P., Am. Soc. Internal Medicine, Phi Delta Epsilon. Contbr. articles to med. jours. Home: 2 Pilgrim Trail Westport CT 06880 Office: 131 Kings Hwy N Westport CT 06880

GREENE, ABE JAY, editor; b. Paterson, N.J., Nov. 27, 1899; s. Morris and Tinie (Grossman) G.; grad. high sch.; m. Hana Bornstein, June 24, 1928; children—Marna (Mrs. Louis G. Palmisano), Ronne Sue Bernstein. With Paterson News, 1918-75, editor, 1935—; dir. Broadway Bank Paterson. Mediator indsl. disputes. Pres., Nat. Boxing Assn., 1941-48, World Boxing Assn., 1949; life world boxing commr., 1943—; commr. N.J. Athletic Commn., 1971—; commr. Paterson Midget Leagues. Trustee Barnert Meml. Hosp.; bd. dirs. Greater Paterson Jewish Community Center; trustee Shapiro Scholarship Found., 1935-50. Named Outstanding Citizen of Paterson, Civic Symposium, 1933; recipient James J. Walker award N.Y. Boxing Writers Assn., 1940. Mem. N.J. AP (past pres.), VFW (hon.). Mason. Contbr. to mags. Home: 362 17th Ave Paterson NJ 07504

GREENE, ADELE SHUMINER, broadcasting exec.; b. Newark, Sept. 16, 1925; d. Adolph and Sara Semel (Schubert) S.; student N.Y. U., 1942-44, Juilliard Sch. Music, 1942-44, New Sch. for Social Research, 1944-47; certificate in public broadcasting sta. mgmt. Harvard U., 1978. 1 son, Joshua Michael. Asst. to pres. Cobleigh & Gordon, N.Y.C., 1962-63; account coordinator Gaynor & Ducas, N.Y.C., 1963-64; with Ruder & Finn, Inc., N.Y.C., 1964-76, v.p., 1968-72, sr. v.p., 1972-76; v.p. for public affairs Corp. for Public Broadcasting, Washington, 1976-78; pres. TV Program Group, Washington, 1978—; instr. in pub. relations and community affairs N.Y. U., 1974-76. Bd. dirs. Queen Symphony Orch., N.Y.C., 1974, Sci. Program Group, Washington, 1976—; trustee Am. Crafts Council, N.Y.C., 1976—; mem. bd. advisers Duke Ellington Sch. Arts, Washington, 1977—. Mem. Am. Women in Radio and TV, Nat. Assn. Ednl. Broadcasters, Public Relations Soc. Am. (Silver Anvil 1971). Author: (with Charles Mangel) Teen-Age Leadership, 1971. Home: 1250 28th St NW Washington DC 20007 also 30 W 60th St New York NY 10023 Office: 1601 Connecticut Ave NW Washington DC 20009

GREENE, ALAN GUYER, radiologist; b. N.Y.C., May 11, 1935; s. Herman Stuart and Edna Betty (Jaffe) G.; B.S., Union Coll., 1956; M.D., State U. N.Y., Syracuse, 1960; m. Roberta Menter, June 7, 1959; children—Judy, David, Deborah. Intern, Upstate Med. Center Hosps., Syracuse, 1960-61; resident Peter Bent Brigham Hosp., Boston, 1961-64, chief resident radiology, 1964, jr. asso. in radiology, 1964; practice medicine specializing in radiology, Boston, 1964—; asso. radiologist Faulkner Hosp., Boston, 1967-75, asso. chief radiology, 1976—; asst. clin. prof. radiology Tufts U., 1975. Served to capt. USAF, 1965-66. Diplomate Am. Bd. Radiology. Mem. Am. Coll. Radiology, Soc. Nuclear Medicine, New Eng. Roentgen Ray Soc., Mass. Med. Soc. Office: 1153 Centre St Boston MA 02130

GREENE, ALAN STEVEN, printing co. exec.; b. N.Y.C., Mar. 6, 1930; s. Herman L. and Jean O. (Davis) G.; B.S., N.Y. U., 1957, M.B.A., 1960; m. Joyce Rosenthal, June 13, 1965; children—Sanford, Roger, David. Prodn. man L.W. Froelich & Co. Inc., N.Y.C., 1949-51, 54; account exec. Doyle/Dane/Bernbach, N.Y.C., 1954-57; advt. prodn. mgr. Geigy Pharms., N.Y.C., 1957-62; salesman Printing Corp. Am., N.Y.C., 1963-66; founder, pres. Grenex Inc., N.Y.C., 1967-68; with Froelich/Greene Litho Corp., N.Y.C., 1969—, pres., 1973—. Chmn. Bd. of Adjustment of North Caldwell (N.J.), 1973—; mem. planning bd. Borough of North Caldwell. Served as officer. U.S. Army, 1951-54. Mem. Printing Industries Met. N.Y. Met. Lithographers Assn. Republican. Club: Green Brook Country (North Caldwell, N.J.). Home: 253 Park Ave North Caldwell NJ 07006 Office: Froelich/Greene Litho Corp 250 Hudson St New York City NY 10013

GREENE, BARTHOLOMEW ANDREW, real estate exec.; b. Bklyn., Nov. 27, 1902; s. Bartholomew Andrew and Elizabeth Gertrude (Boyle) G.; A.B., Princeton, 1925; m. Constance Wellman, Dec. 27, 1938; 1 son, Bartholomew Andrew. Vice pres. Carstens & Linnekin, Inc., N.Y.C., 1947-71, pres., 1971—; v.p. Vinmont Land Corp., N.Y.C., 1950-74, pres., 1974—. Mem. Am. Inst. Real Estate Appraisers (treas. N.Y. Metropolitan Dist. chpt. 1955-57), Real Estate Bd. N.Y., Nat. Assn. Realtors. Clubs: Princeton of N.Y.; Dial Lodge of Princeton U. (chmn. bd. trustees 1952-55). Home: 5425 Fieldston Rd Bronx NY 10471 Office: 347 Fifth Ave New York City NY 10016

GREENE, CHARLES ROBERT, clergyman; b. Charlotte, N.C., Sept. 14, 1930; s. Walter Forrest and Ava Ann (Parker) G.; B.A., Wake Forest U., 1951; M.S.M., Union Sem., 1953, M.Div., 1956; D.Minn., Drew U., 1977; m. Gloria Jane Iacone, May 20, 1953; children—Claire A., Melissa B. Ordained to ministry Episcopal Ch., 1957; asst. rector St. James the Less, Scarsdale, N.Y., 1956-59; rector St. Bartholomew's Ch., Pittsboro, N.C., 1959-62; dir. program Episcopal Diocese of N.C., Raleigh, 1963-67; rector Grace Episcopal Ch., Nyack, N.Y., 1967—. Mem. faculty Inst. of Theology of Episcopal Diocese of N.Y., 1974, mem. exec. com., 1971, mem. diocesan council, 1971; chmn. Ministries Commn. of N.Y., 1971; mem. adv. com., mem. bd. N.C. Council Chs., 1963-67; mem. diocesan council Diocese of N.C., 1963-67; pres. Nyack Clergy Assn., 1971-73, Rockland Interparish Council, 1969-71. Pres. bd. dirs. Nyack Daycare Center, 1968-73; bd. dirs. Community Narcotics Counseling Service, 1970-73; chmn. instnl. rev. com. Research Center, 1973—. Recipient certificate of recognition Ch. Devel. Bd., 1966. Profl. devel. grantee Diocese of N.Y., 1975-77. Republi can. Clubs: Nyack Field, Rectory (N.Y.C.). Contbr. articles to profl. jours. Home: 112 Birchwood Ave Nyack NY 10960

GREENE, ELIZABETH A., state legislator; b. North Hampton, N.H.; ed. U. N.H.; m. Leroy Greene; 3 children. Mem. N.H. Ho. of Reps., 1961—, now chmn. interim solid waste com., environ. and agrl. com.; mem. Bistate Sea Grant Com. Mem. Order Women Legislators. Republican. Home: 399 South Rd Rye NH 03870

GREENE, HENRY IRVING, periodontist; b. Bklyn., Oct. 24, 1920; s. Morris and Rebecca (Dunitz) Greenberg; B.S., Bklyn. Coll., 1942; D.D.S., Western Res. U., 1945; m. Helen Sally Blumberg, Oct. 2, 1954; children—Emily, Julia, Joshua, Michael. Research, Spies Nutrition Clinic, Birmingham, Ala., 1947-49; practice dentistry, Flushing, N.Y., 1949-60, specializing in periodontia, Flushing and Roslyn-Greenvale, N.Y., 1960—; instr. dept. nutrition and metabolism Sch. Medicine, Northwestern U., 1947-49; clin. asst. prof. dept. periodontia Sch. Dentistry, N.Y. U., 1953-63. Served to lt. (j.g.) USNR, 1945-47. Fellow Soc. Oral Physiology and Occlusion, Am., Internat. colls. dentists; mem. Am. Acad. Periodontology, Am. Acad. Dental Medicine (pres. N.Y. sect. 1960-61), Sci. Research Soc. Am., Alpha Omega. Contbg. author: The Practice of Periodontia, 1960, Anterior Restoration, Fixed Bridgework, and Esthetics, 1976; contbr. short story Bread and Snow to Am. Vanguard, 1950; author play Will the Real Mr. Bressman Please Stand Up, 1967; asso. editor Jour. Dental Medicine, 1961-68. Home: 26 Laurel Ave Sea Cliff NY 11579 Office: 9 Northern Blvd Greenvale NY 11548

GREENE, HOWARD GILBERT, surgeon; b. Bklyn., Nov. 16, 1927; s. Lowell and Estelle (Katz) G.; B.A., N.Y. U., 1948, postgrad. in Biophysics, 1948-50, M.D., 1954; m. Cynthia Davis, Dec. 21, 1953; children—Robin, Meryl, Michael. Surg. intern and resident Univ. Hosps. Cleve., 1954-57; resident in surgery Bronx Municipal Hosp. Center, 1957-60; practice medicine specializing in surgery, Spring Valley, N.Y., 1960-61, Forest Hills, N.Y., 1961—; dir. surgery Hillcrest Gen.-GHI Hosp.; asso. dir. surgery LaGuardia Hosp.; asst. clin. prof. surgery Albert Einstein Coll. Medicine; dir. surgery Central Flushing-Upper Queens Med. Group; medicolegal cons. Served as 2d lt., C.E., AUS, 1946-48. Diplomate Am. Bd. Surgery. Fellow A.C.S. Jewish. Contbr. articles in field to profl. jours. Home: 303 E 57 St New York City NY 10022 Office: 104 20 Queens Blvd Forest Hills NY 11375

GREENE, HOWARD PAUL, communications co. exec.; b. N.Y.C., Mar. 18, 1931; s. Jack and Esther (Platt) Greenberg; B.B.A. cum laude, City Coll. N.Y., 1952; m. Lorna Patrox, Aug. 10, 1952; children—Marc David, Jeffrey Glenn. Publicity dir. Popular Library, Inc., 1956-58; promotion dir. Macfadden Publs., 1958; v.p. Barkas & Shalit Pub. Relations, N.Y.C., 1958-65; pres. Medivox Prodns., N.Y.C., 1965-67, Greene Inc. Communications, N.Y.C., 1965—; exec. v.p., partner Infocom Broadcast Service Inc., N.Y.C., 1976—; cons. seminars. Vol., Cerebral Palsy Nassau County, 1963-64. Served to lt. (j.g.) USNR, 1952-56. Recipient Stroock prize City Coll. N.Y., 1952, Mass Media award NCCJ, 1978. Mem. Nat. Assn. Rec. Arts and Scis. Democrat. Jewish. Producer radio series. Home: 272 Heather Ln Hewlett Harbor NY 11557 Office: 71 Park Ave New York City NY 10016

GREENE, HOWARD RODGER, ednl. cons.; b. New Haven, July 26, 1937; s. Charles and Freda (Miller) G.; B.A. cum laude, Dartmouth Coll., 1959; M.A., N.Y. U., 1962; M.Ed., Harvard, 1964; children—Adam Scott, Matthew West. Teaching fellow Harvard, 1963-64; admissions officer, counselor Princeton U., 1964-68; dep. headmaster The Fieldston Sch., Riverdale, N.Y., 1968-69; dir. Ednl. Cons. Center, Westport, Conn., 1969—; cons. Ethel Walker Sch., Westover Sch., Germantown Friends Sch., Beaver Country Day Sch., Northshore County Sch. Trustee Cushing Acad., Ashburnham, Mass.; trustee Westport Unitarian Ch. Mem. Am. Personnel and Guidance Assn., Internat. Bd. Counseling Services. Club: Harvard (N.Y.C., Fairfield County). Author: (with Robert Minton) Scaling the Ivy Wall, 1975. Home: Tall Trees Ln Wilton CT 06897 Office: 19 S Compo Rd Westport CT 06880

GREENE, JEROME DAVIS, II, marketing research co. exec.; b. Boston, May 27, 1923; s. Jerome Crosby and Mary Carrington (Cram) G.; A.B. cum laude, Harvard, 1945; postgrad. N.Y. U., 1947-49; m. Helen M. Wippich, Sept. 18, 1971; 1 dau. by previous marriage, Sarah Perry. With Alfred Politz Research, Inc., N.Y.C., 1947-64, pres. Alfred Politz Media Studies div., 1956-64, v.p. parent co., 1956-64; founder, owner, pres. Marketmath, Inc., N.Y.C., 1965—, dir., 1965—; adj. asso. prof. Grad. Sch. Bus., Columbia, N.Y.C., 1976—; lectr. Coll. City N.Y., 1965-66. Served with U.S. Maritime Service, 1943-46. Mem. Market Research Council (pres. 1978—), Am. Assn. Pub. Opinion Research, Am. Statis. Assn., Am. Mktg. Assn., Modellers Discussion Group (founder 1970). Democrat. Episcopalian. Club: Harvard (N.Y.C.). Contbr. articles in field to profl. jours. Home: 215 E 79 St New York City NY 10021 Office: 1860 Broadway New York City NY 10023

GREENE, LEHMAN OTHO, aluminum co. exec.; b. Savannah, Ga., Nov. 15, 1924; s. Jeff Otho and Lenora (Glover) G.; B.S., Wake Forest Coll., 1948; postgrad. U. Richmond, 1951-52; m. Ann McCollum, Nov. 24, 1948; children—Ann Robin, Lehman Otho. Pub. accountant Baker, Brydon, Rennolds and Whitt, Richmond, Va., 1951-54; exec. v.p., gen. mgr. Lock Vent, Inc., Richmond, Va., 1954-55; gen. mgr. Orma Corp., Beltsville, Md., 1955-58, Alumaroll, Inc., Rutherford, N.J., 1958-61; exec. v.p., gen. mgr. Security Aluminum Co., Detroit, 1961-67, dir. 1963-67; gen. mgr. constrn. materials div. Phelps Dodge Aluminum Corp., Jackson, Miss., 1967-68; gen. mgr. Bldg. Systems div. Phelps Dodge Copper Co., Yonkers, N.Y., 1969-73, dir. indsl. sales Phelps Dodge Brass Co., Dayton, N.J., 1973-75; v.p. Burnham Corp., Irvington, N.Y., 1976—. Past dir. Aluminum Mfrs. Credit Bur., Nat. Assn. Bldg. Mfrs. Served with USNR, 1943-45. Mem. Aluminum Siding Assn. (dir.), Nat. Assn. Bldg. Mfrs. (dir.), Industrialized Bldg. Congress (adv. com.), AIM (president's council). Presbyterian. Mason (32 deg., Shriner). Home: 158 Locust Rd Briarcliff Manor NY 10510

GREENE, LOUIS LEON, dentist; b. N.Y.C., Sept. 5, 1917; s. Morris and Anna (Horowitz) G.; B.S., Columbia, 1939, postgrad., 1954; D.D.S., Ohio State U., 1943; m. Sarah Shenk, Mar. 21, 1943; children—Judy, Diane, Steven. Practice dentistry specializing in crown and bridge work, N.Y.C., 1946—; dir. research Greene Lab.; v.p. Morris Plastic Co., N.Y.C., 1959-60; vis. dental surgeon Harlem Hosp.; lectr. crown and bridge 1st Dist. Dental Soc. N.Y.; postgrad. lectr. N.Y. U. Sch. Dentistry. Designer comml. plastics, toys. Sec. Saddle Rock P.T.A., 1959. Bd. dirs. Saddle Rock Estates Civic Assn., Saddle Rock Estates Pool Club. Served to capt. AUS, 1943-46. Recipient Interfaith award, 1966; award Fedn. Jewish Philanthropies, 1966, plaque N.Y. Oral Rehab. Study Group. Mem. Am. Dental

Assn., 1st Dist. Dental Soc., Ohio State U. Alumni Assn., Fedn. Dentaire Internationale, Internat. Assn. Anesthesiologists, Internat. Coll. Oral Implantology, Inst. for Advanced Dental Research, Inst. Endosseous Implants, Alpha Omega. Jewish. Mason. Club: Fresh Meadow Golf and Country. Patentee indsl. plastics, toys, dentistry. Home: 6 Ridgeway Dr Kings Point NY 11024 Office: 1 Barstow Rd Great Neck NY 11021

GREENE, RICHARD STEPHEN, educator; b. Bklyn., Sept. 9, 1938; B.S. in Econs., Albright Coll. Reading, Pa., 1960; M.Ed. in Elementary Edn., Springfield (Mass.) Coll., 1961; Profl. diploma in Ednl. Adminstrn., Columbia Tchrs. Coll., N.Y.C., 1964; Ed.D. in Ednl. Adminstrn., State U. N.Y. at Albany, 1972; m. Edythe Green; children—Sheryl, Robert. Tchr., River Street Sch., Red Bank (N.J.) Sch. Dist., 1961-63; elementary prin. Paige Sch., Schenectady City Sch. Dist., 1964-68, prin. Steinmetz Jr. High Sch., 1969-72; asst. to supt. White Plains (N.Y.) Pub. Schs., 1972—. Mem. White Plains City Planning Bd., 1975—; dep. commr. Spring Valley Little League. Recipient Distinguished Service award for work with inner city schs. and disadvantaged students Schenectady Jaycees. Mem. Am. Assn. for Sch. Adminstrs., Nat. Sch. Pub. Relations Assn., NEA, Phi Delta Kappa. Home: 14 Ungava Dr New York City NY 10956 Office: 5 Homeside Ln White Plains NY 10605

GREENE, ROBERT BRUCE, social service facility adminstr.; b. Charleston, S.C., Apr. 30, 1940; s. Walter Lawrence and Lottie (Hudson) G.; B.A., Johnson C. Smith U., 1964; M.S.W., N.Y. U., 1972; postgrad. Columbia U.; m. Dorothy lM. Mitchell, Sept. 14, 1964; children—Reginald M., Robyn M. Children's counselor N.Y.C. Dept. Social Service, 1964-66, caseworker, 1966-74; social work supr. Graham Home for Children, Hastings-on-Hudson, N.Y., 1974-78, St. Dominic's Home for Children, Blauvert, N.Y., 1973-76; dir. social service Leake and Watts Home for Children, Yonkers, N.Y., 1976—; adj. prof. Sch. Social Work, N.Y. U. Vice pres. bd. trustees St. James Presbyterian Ch. Mem. Acad. Certified Social Workers, Nat. Assn. Social Workers, Black Social Workers (pres. Westchester chpt., editor chpt. newspaper), Omega Psi Phi. Presbyterian. Club: Kiwanis (Yonkers). Editor: St. James Presbyterian Newsletter.

GREENE, ROBERT FORD, author, sports cons., coll. ofcl.; b. N.Y.C., May 20, 1931; s. John Joseph and Helen Williamson (Ford) G.; B.S., State U. N.Y., Brockport, 1954; M.A., Columbia U., 1955; D.Ed. with honors, U. Calif., 1970; m. Joan Hope Ewers, Mar. 17, 1962. Instr. phys. edn. U. Calif., Los Angeles, 1966-67; asst. prof. phys. and health edn., varsity tennis coach, then asst. dir. athletics City Coll. N.Y., 1971-75, dir. athletics, 1975-76; commr., pres. Met. Coll. Tennis Conf.; mem. coms. Nat. Collegiate Athletic Assn., Eastern Collegiate Athletic Conf.; cons. U.S. Sports Acad.; dir. nat. sports program Middle East, 1977-78; dir. athletics C.W. Post Coll., 1978—; mem. Lambert Cup Football Selection Com., 1978—. Served with USMCR, 1950-51. Decorated Purple Heart. Named Coach of Year, Met. Tennis Conf. and Coll. City N.Y., 1974; coach championship teams. Mem. U. Calif. at Los Angeles Alumni Assn. (dir.), Internat. House Assn. (dir.), Spuyten Duyvil Assn., Interreligious Found. Community Orgn., Colonial Heights Tennis Club. Episcopalian. Author: Tennis Drills, 1976; Tennis Tactics, 1978. Editor: Middle East Sports Sci. Symposium Jour., 1978. Home: 2500 Johnson Ave Apt 12F Riverdale NY 10463

GREENE, STEPHEN C., commodity broker; b. Newark, Sept. 20, 1937; s. Irving I. and Gertrude G.; B.S. in Edn., N.Y. U., 1959; children—David, Allyson. Floor broker, v.p. Jacobson Commodities, Inc., N.Y.C., 1959-71; potato specialist, nat. commodity dept. E.F. Hutton & Co., N.Y.C., 1971—. Contbr. articles to various mags. and trade publs.

GREENE, STEPHEN CRAIG, lawyer; b. Watertown, N.Y., Apr. 27, 1946; s. Harold Adelbert and Mildred Esther (Baker) G.; A.B., Syracuse U., 1967, J.D., 1970; m. Nancy Jean Adams, Mar. 28, 1965; children—Kathryn, Stephen, Hilary. Admitted to N.Y. bar, 1971, U.S. Tax Ct. bar, 1977; asst. to pres. State U. Coll., Oswego, N.Y., 1970-73; asso. firm Leyden E. Brown, Oswego, 1973-75; partner firm Brown and Greene, 1976—; dir. Found. Corporate Legal Studies, Inc., 1968-70; town atty. Oswego, 1972—; counsel Oswego County Bd. Realtors, 1978—. Mem. Oswego County Rep. Com., 1974—. Recipient Ins. Counsel Jour. award Internat. Assn. Ins. Counsel, 1970. Mem. Am., N.Y., Oswego County bar assns., Phi Delta Phi. Episcopalian. Club: Oswego Country (counsel 1977—). Home: RD 6 Box 219 Route 104 W Oswego NY 13126 Office: 130 E 2d St Oswego NY 13126

GREENE, THEODORE RICHARD, internat. freight forwarding co. exec.; b. Germany, May 7, 1921; s. Richard and Erna (Kaufmann) Gruenebaum; student Coll. City N.Y., 1947-48, Pohs Inst. Ins., N.Y.C., 1948-49; m. Erna Wolf, Oct. 24, 1948; children—Janet, Marian. Export traffic mgr. Boehr Shipping Co., Inc., N.Y.C., 1947-52; co-founder, pres. Triangle Forwarding Corp., N.Y.C., 1952, chmn. bd., 1952—. Vice pres. Temple Emanu-El of Queens Aux., 1964-65; v.p. Brotherhood Habonim, N.Y.C., 1974-76, pres., 1977—. Served with AUS, 1942-46. Mem. Greater N.Y. Ins. Brokers Assn. Inc. Clubs: Foreign Commerce, World Trade N.Y. Inc. (N.Y.C.). Home: 77-11 35th Ave Jackson Heights NY 11372 Office: 11 Broadway St New York City NY 10004

GREENE, WILLIAM CASWELL, accountant; b. Natick, Mass., June 5, 1933; s. Whitney E. and Maud (Larsson) G.; A.B., Princeton, 1954; M.B.A., Babson Coll., 1956; m. Davis Crane, Nov. 27, 1954; children—William Caswell, Bruce Boardmen, Josephine Boardman, Winnie, Amy Larson, Leo Maker. Research asso. bus. adminstrn. Harvard Bus. Sch., 1956-59; cons., auditor Lybrand, Ross Bros. & Montgomery, Boston, 1959-64; partner McCann & Greene, Boston, 1964-66; sr. partner Greene & Vecchi, C.P.A.'s, Wellesley, Mass., 1966—; gen. partner Natick Investments, 1971—; dir. Travel Consultants Internat., Inc., Townsman Pub. Co., others. Instr., Mgmt. Growth Inst. Community dir. United Fund, Dover, Mass., 1963-64. Treas., Dover Republican Town Com., 1968-71; state chmn. Accountants for Nixon-Agnew, 1967-68; mem. Mass. Rep. State Com., 1971-73, auditor, 1972—. Trustee Pine Tree Acres Trust, others. C.P.A., Mass. Mem. Am. Inst. C.P.A.'s, Mass. Soc. C.P.A.'s (chmn. small bus. com. 1964-67, asso. editor CPA 1963-65). Clubs: Harvard Faculty (Cambridge, Mass.); Tennis Natick (Mass.); Campus Princeton (N.J.). Author: Case Problems in Managerial Accounting, 1964; Management of Small Business, 1974. Home: 32 Meadowbrook Rd Dover MA 02030 Office: 2 Summer St Natick MA

GREENFIELD, MEG, journalist; b. Seattle, Dec. 27, 1930; d. Lewis James and Lorraine (Nathan) G.; B.A. summa cum laude, Smith Coll., 1952; Fulbright scholar Newnham Coll., Cambridge (Eng.) U., 1952-53. With Reporter mag., 1957-68, Washington editor, 1965-68; editorial writer Washington Post, 1968-70, dep. editorial page editor, 1970—. Recipient Pulitzer Prize for editorial writing, 1978. Mem. Am. Soc. Newspaper Editors, Phi Betta Kappa. Club: Federal City (Washington). Home: 3318 R St NW Washington DC 20007 Office: 1150 15th St NW Washington DC 20005*

GREENFIELD, RICHARD DAVID, lawyer; b. N.Y.C., Feb. 1, 1942; s. Herman and Dorothy G.; B.S. in Acctg., Queens Coll., 1962; LL.B., Cornell U., 1965, J.D., 1969; M.B.A., Columbia U., 1966; m. Ellen L. Steinberg, May 8, 1965; children—Adam Douglas, Amanda Leigh. Admitted to N.Y. bar, 1967, Pa. bar, 1970, U.S. Supreme Ct. bar; individual practice law, 1965-78; sr. partner firm Greenfield & Schoen, P.C., Bala Cynwyd, Pa., 1978—. Pres. Concerned Citizens for Pub. Edn. in Lower Merion, 1976; bd. dirs. Phila. All-Star Forum. Mem. Pa., Phila. bar assns., Am. Arbitration Assn. (nat. panel arbitrators), Phila. Art Alliance, Phila. Mus. Art. Home: 731 Bedford Pl Merion PA 19066 Office: 110 Montgomery Ave Bala Cynwyd PA 19004

GREENFIELD, VAL SHEA, ophthalmologist; b. N.Y.C., Apr. 20, 1932; s. Frank Lynne and Helen (Meyers) G.; student Brown U., 1948-49, 50-51, St. John's U., N.Y., 1949; B.A. cum laude, Bklyn. Coll., 1952; M.D., Yale, 1956. Intern, Walter Reed Army Hosp., Washington, 1956-57; resident in surgery U. Pa.-Presbyn. Med. Center, Phila., 1963-66; asst. chief U.S. Army Dispensary, Phila., 1957-60, chief, 1959-60; practice medicine specializing in obstetrics, Phila. and Riverside, N.J., 1960-63, specializing in ophthalmology, Phila., 1966—; asst. clin. prof. eye surgery Hahnemann Med. Coll., Phila., 1975—; attending surgeon in ophthalmology Frankford and Rolling Hill hosps., Phila. Bd. deacons Community Ch., Mt. Laurel Chapel, 1974—. Served from lt. to capt., M.C., U.S. Army, 1955-60. Fellow A.C.S., Phila. Coll. Physicians; mem. Am. Judeo-Christian Fellowship, AMA, Christian, Pa., Phila. County med. socs., Am., Pan-Am. assns. ophthalmology, Pa. Acad. Ophthalmology, Soc. Contemporary Ophthalmology. Democrat. Home: 623 S Church St Mount Laurel NJ 08054 Office: 5001 Frankford Ave Philadelphia PA 19124

GREENHALGH, JAMES, finishing equipment co. exec.; b. Lancashire, Eng., July 24, 1913; s. Paul and Elsie (Peake) G.; student Wigan Mining and Tech. Coll., Lancashire, 1931-33; m. Eileen Genever Cookson, Feb. 3, 1940; children—Paul James, Gillian Mary, Patricia Anne. Audit work Wood Jackson & Co., chartered accountants, Salford, Lancashire, 1933-40, 46-52; with Devilbiss (Can.) Ltd., mfrs. finishing equipment, Barrie, Ont., Can., 1953—, v.p. fin., 1967-76, v.p., gen. mgr., 1976—. Com. chmn. corporate div. Barrie United Appeal, 1971-72. Mem. City of Barrie Planning Bd., 1968-75. Bd. dirs. Barrie YMCA, 1967-70. Served with Royal Corps Signals, 1940-46. Decorated Defence medal, Victory medal. Mem. Barrie Mfrs. Assn. (past pres.). Kiwanian (past pres. local club). Home: 9 Campfire Ct Barrie ON L4M 5G9 Canada Office: 50 Wood St Barrie ON Canada

GREENHOLT, WALTER HENRY, graphic arts co. exec.; b. Chgo. Apr. 3, 1919; s. Walter A. and Eleanor (Parbs) G.; B.A., Ill. Coll., 1941; m. Phillis Gwen Cowan, Sept. 6, 1946; children—Pamela Jane (Mrs. Joseph T. Armstrong, Jr.), Wendy Ann. Sales trainee to sales mgr. Ditto, Inc., div. Bell & Howell, Chgo., 1946-62; v.p. Graphic Controls Corp., Buffalo, 1962-77, exec. v.p., chief operating officer, 1977—, dir. various cos. Mexico, Eng., Belgium, France and Spain. Chmn. graphic arts sect. United Way, 1973-74. Served with USNR, 1942-46. Mem. Ill. Coll. Alumni Assn. (pres. 1947), Internat. Sales Exec., Am. Mgmt. Assn., Gamma Nu. Home: 18 Ransom Oaks Dr East Amherst NY 14051 Office: 189 Van Rensselaer St Buffalo NY 14210

GREENHOUSE, NATHANIEL ANTHONY, JR., health physicist; b. Washington, June 20, 1940; s. Nathaniel Anthony and Ruth Agnes (Puryear) G.; B.A., Catholic U. Am., 1961; M.S. (AEC spl. fellow in health physics), U. Rochester, 1966; M.S., State U. N.Y., Stony Brook, 1978. Health physicist Lawrence Livermore (Calif.) Lab., 1966-71; health physicist Brookhaven Nat. Lab., Upton, N.Y., 1971-78, sr. health physicist, 1978—, project dir. Marshall Islands radiol. safety program, 1974—; cons. on radiation safety to industry, effects evaluation group WASH-1400 Reactor Safety Study. Served as 1st lt. USAF, 1961-64. Mem. Am. Bd. Health Physics (certified), Health Physics Soc., N.Y. Acad. Sci., Sigma Xi. Contbr. articles to profl. publs. Office: Bldg 535 Brookhaven Nat Lab Upton NY 11973

GREENHOUSE, RANDEY ROBERT, physician; b. Syracuse, N.Y., Jan. 19, 1949; s. Abraham and Roslyn (Olum) G.; B.A. cum laude, Syracuse U., 1968; M.D., State U. N.Y. Downstate, 1972; m. Sharon Dena Mirochin, Dec. 29, 1973; children—Stacy Jill, Adam Todd. Intern, L.I. Jewish Hillside Med. Center, 1972-73; resident in radiology State U. N.Y. Downstate Med. Center, Kings County, 1973-76; asst. radiologist Elizabeth Gen. Hosp. (N.J.), 1976—; instr. State U. N.Y. Downstate Med. Center, 1973—, Alexian Bros. Hosp., Elizabeth Gen. Hosp. Sch. Radiation Tech. Diplomate Am. Bd. Diagnostic Radiology. Mem. Am., N.J. colls. radiology, Union County Med. Soc., AMA. Home: 199 Western Dr Short Hills NJ 07078 Office: 925 E Jersey St Elizabeth NJ 07281

GREENLEE, MICHAEL JOSEPH, architect; b. Omaha, Mar. 12, 1945; s. Dalton LaVerne and Josephone (Salerno) G.; B.Arch. (scholar 1964-68), Iowa State U., 1968. Project designer, then dir. design Sargent, Webster, Crenshaw & Foley, Syracuse, N.Y., 1972—, design partner, 1976—; instr. basic architecture Onondaga Community Coll., Syracuse, 1976; prin. works include N.Y. State Electric and Gas Customer Service Center, Elmira, City Hall, Lockport, N.Y., Elementary Sch., Pavilion, N.Y., Clarkson Coll. Library, Potsdam, N.Y. Mem. AIA, Nat. Trust Historic Preservation, Landmarks Assn. Central N.Y. Home: 320 Genesee Park Dr Syracuse NY 13224 Office: 2112 Erie Blvd E Syracuse NY 13224

GREENOUGH, WILLIAM BATES, III, educator, physician; b. Providence, Jan. 3, 1932; s. William Bates and Dorothy Garrison (Rand) G.; B.A. (Dow fellow), Amherst Coll., 1953; M.D., Harvard Med. Sch., 1957; m. Jane Cheney Woodruff, Aug. 14, 1954 (dec. 1964); children—William Beckley, Kate, Thomas, Elisabeth; m. 2d, Quaneta Ahmed, Jan. 15, 1965; 1 dau., Zarin. Intern, asst. resident medicine Columbia-Presbyn. Hosp., N.Y.C., 1957-59; research fellow Nat. Cancer Inst. Mary Imogene Bassett Hosp., Cooperstown, N.Y., 1959-61; sr. resident medicine Peter Bent Brigham Hosp., Boston, 1961-62; with clin. research sect. Cholera Research Lab., Dacca, Bangladesh, 1962-64, chief, 1964-65; staff asso. Nat. Heart Inst., Bethesda, Md., 1965-67; practice medicine specializing in internal medicine and infectious disease, Balt., 1967—; mem. staffs Balt. City Hosp., Johns Hopkins Hosp.; mem. faculty Johns Hopkins U. Sch. Medicine, Balt., 1967—, asso. prof. medicine and microbiology, 1970—, asso. prof. health care orgn. and emergency medicine, 1974—, chief infectious diseases div., 1970-75, dir. Robert Wood Johnson clin. scholar program, 1974-77; cons. VA Hosp., Perry Point, Md., 1972-77; sci. dir. Cholera Research Lab., Dacca, Bangladesh, 1977—. Pres. Bangladesh Info. Center, Washington, 1971—, Md. Commn. Phys. Fitness, Balt., 1972-77, Md. Marathon Commn., 1974-77; mem. bacteriology and mycology study sect. Nat. Insts. Allergy and Infectious Diseases, Bethesda, Md., 1972-76, chmn., 1974-76. Served with USPHS, 1962-67. Mem. AAAS, Infectious Diseases Soc. Am., Am. Fedn. Clin. Research, Am. Soc. Clin. Investigation, Am. Soc. Microbiology, N.Y. Acad. Sci., Phi Beta Kappa, Sigma Xi, Alpha Omega Alpha. Editor: Topics in Infectious Diseases, 1974—; editorial asso. Infection and Immunity, 1974—. Contbr. articles to profl. jours. Address: CRL/DACCA care Dept State Washington DC 20520

GREENSEID, DAVID ZANVEL, ophthalmologist; b. N.Y.C., May 24, 1940; s. Max and Rebecca (Marcus) G.; A.B., Bklyn. Coll., 1961; M.D., with honors, U. Rochester, 1966; m. Linda Ban, Aug. 15, 1965; children—Julie Michele, Andrew Mark. Intern, Barnes Hosp., St. Louis, 1966-67; resident Mt. Sinai Hosp., N.Y.C., 1969-72; retina service fellow Retina Found. and Mass. Eye and Ear Infirmary, Boston, 1972-73, now mem. staff; practice medicine specializing in ophthalmology, Boston, 1974—. Served with USPHS, 1967-69. Jonas Salk Med. scholar, 1961-66; Heed Ophthalmic fellow, 1973. Mem. Am. Acad. Ophthalmology and Otolaryngology, Mass. Med. Soc., New Eng. Ophthal. Soc., Mass. Soc. Eye Physicians and Surgeons, Am. Assn. Ophthalmology. Jewish. Office: 225 Boston St Lynn MA 01907

GREENSPAN, ADAM, physician; b. Przemysl, Poland, May 28, 1935; s. Bernard and Eugenia G.; came to U.S., 1967, naturalized, 1973; M.D., Med. Acad. Wroclaw (Poland), 1958, D.Med.Sci., 1965; m. Renata Gelber, May 28, 1971; 1 son, Ludwig Bernard. Intern, L.I. Jewish Hosp., Queens Hosp. Center, N.Y.C., 1969-70; resident in radiology Jewish Hosp. and Med. Center of Bklyn., 1970-73; practice medicine, specializing in radiology, N.Y.C., 1973—; attending radiologist Hosp. for Joint Diseases and Med. Center, N.Y.C., 1974—; asst. prof. radiology Mt. Sinai Sch. Medicine, N.Y.C., 1977—. Recipient AMA Physician's Recognition awards, 1974, 77, 78. Diplomate Am. Bd. Radiology. Fellow N.Y. Acad. Medicine; mem. N.Y. Acad. Sci., N.Y. Roentgen Soc., Am. Coll. Radiology. Contbr. articles in field to profl. jours. Office: 1919 Madison Ave New York City NY 10035

GREENWALD, EDWARD HARRIS, mining cons.; b. Pitts., Mar. 30, 1920; s. Harold Putnam and Sophia (Jones) G.; B.S. cum laude, U. Pitts. Sch. Mines, 1942; m. Charlotte Ann Tomlinson, Apr. 25, 1964; children—Edward Harris, Catherine Davies. Mining engr. Boone County Coal Corp., Sharples, W.Va., 1942-45, chief engr. 1945-47, asst. to v.p. 1947-52, gen. mgr., chief operating officer, 1952-56; partner Eavenson, Achmuty & Greenwald, Mining Cons., Pitts., 1956-57, owner 1967—; pres. Resource Engring. and Mgmt., Pitts., 1974-78; v.p., treas., dir. Spruce River Coal Co., Pitts., 1962-70, Aquitaine of Pa., Inc., Pitts., 1975-78, Kanawha Coal Operators Assn. Charleston, W.Va., 1952-56; mem. Commn. on Mine Safety, State of Pa., 1963-64. Bd. dirs. Logan County chpt. ARC, 1952-56, Logan County Tax Payers Assn., 1952-56; v.p., chief Corn Stock council Boy Scouts Am., Logan, 1954-56. Named Engring. Alumnus of yr. U. Pitts. 1975. Mem. Am. Inst. Mining and Metall. Engrs., Am. Mining Congress, Coal Mining Inst. Am., Nat. Mine Rescue Assn., W.Va. Coal Mining Inst. Nat. Def. Preparedness Assn., Am. Inst. Mining Engrs. (vice chmn. Central Appalachian sect. 1955-56), Coal River Mining Inst. (pres. 1950). Contbr. articles to profl. jours. Home: 92 Nancy Ln McMurray PA 15317 Office: Airport Office Park III 420 Rouser Rd Coraopolis PA 15108

GREENWALD, HAROLD, lawyer; b. Yonkers, N.Y., Apr. 2, 1907; s. Louis and Rose (Schwartz) G.; LL.B., N.Y. U., 1928; m. Dorothy R. Nass, June 26, 1943. Admitted to N.Y. State bar, 1929, since practiced in N.Y.C.; asso. Waldo Grant Morse, 1920-34; atty. Agway, Inc. (Coop. Grange League Fedn. Exchange-Eastern States Farmers), 1934—; counsel Quality Bakers Am., 1943—, Plant Devel. Corp., 1961—, United Foods, Inc., L.I. Duck Farmers Coop., Bakers Research Devel. Corp.; counsel N.Y. State Prisoner War Farm Service Program, 1943-44; conferee N.Y. Legis. Com. for Revision Coop. Corps. Law, 1965. Chmn. fin. com., mem. adminstrv. bd. and nat. exec. com. Zionist Orgn.; bd. dirs. Jewish Nat. Fund, United Jewish Appeal; sec., bd. dirs. Ams. for Energy Independence; trustee Wall St. Synagogue. Served with AUS, 1942-43. Mem. Am. Acad. Polit. and Social Sci., Am. Judicature Assn., Assn. Bar City N.Y., Am., N.Y. State, N.Y. County bar assns., Lawyers Club N.Y., Nat. Lawyers Club. Club: N.Y. U. (N.Y.C.). Home: 345 W 58th St New York City NY 10019 Office: 521 Fifth Ave New York City NY 10017

GREENWALD, HARRY, engring. co. exec.; b. Pitts., Nov. 20, 1912; s. Isadore and Fanny (Weisz) G.; m. Dorothy Luoma, Apr. 17, 1949; children—B. Janet (Mrs. Arnold A. Brown), Kenneth R. Pres., Greenwald Industries, Inc. (formerly H. Greenwald Co.), Bklyn., 1946—. Club: Harlem Yacht (City Island, N.Y.). Pioneer coin meter systems for laundry and dry-cleaning industry, cycle timer actuating mechanism, coin chute for washing machine. Home: 149-47 Powells Cove Blvd Whitestone NY 11357 Office: 1340 Metropolitan Ave Brooklyn NY 11237

GREENWOOD, AUDREY GATES, librarian; b. Buffalo, Mar. 27, 1917; d. Marc Herbert and Genevieve Cecelia (Naab) Gates; B.A., D'Youville Coll., 1939; B.S. in L.S., Cath. U. Am., 1940, M.A., 1944; m. Clayton Edward Greenwood, Sept. 2, 1944; children—Mary Ellen, Nancy Jane, Susan Jean. Head librarian Gonzaga High Sch., Washington, 1940-45, Southeastern U. Evening Sch., 1941-45; reference librarian Cath. U. Am., evenings 1942-43; librarian St. Joseph's Collegiate Inst., Buffalo, 1945-46; head librarian Canisius High Sch., Buffalo, 1949-50; head librarian Eden (N.Y.) Central Schs., 1950—, coordinator state and fed. funds, 1969—, dir. adult edn., 1973—. Mem. Eden Tchrs. Assn. (pres.), Erie County Ednl. Assn. (v.p.), NEA, N.Y. State Tchrs. Assn., N.Y. State United Tchrs., Am. Fedn. Tchrs., Sch. Librarians Assn. Western N.Y. (past pres.), N.Y. Educators Assn., Delta Kappa Gamma. Democrat. Roman Catholic. Home: 194 Columbia Rd Hamburg NY 14075 Office: 3150 Schoolview Eden NY 14057

GREER, DAN BLAKE, JR., coll. adminstr.; b. Washington, May 13, 1946; s. Dan Blake and Mabel Marie (Stone) G.; student Whitman Coll., 1964-65; N. Idaho Jr. Coll., Coeur D'Alene, 1965; B.A. in English, U. Wyo., 1969; M.A. in Counseling, Ball State U., 1972; postgrad. Troy (Ala.) State U., 1974; m. Lorraine Hughes, Nov. 9, 1975. Mem. faculty European div. Big Bend Coll., Moses Lake, Washington, 1972—, acting asst. dean instruction for Europe, Bremthal, W.Ger., 1978—, dir. student records, 1978—. Served with U.S. Army, 1969-72. Mem. Am. Personnel and Guidance Assn. Clubs: Automobil von Deutschland, Wiesbaden Am. Ski. Home: Schillerstrasse 14 6201 Bremthal West Germany Office: BBCC Central Services APO New York NY 09111

GREER, THOMAS VERNON, educator; b. Burnet, Tex., Oct. 13, 1932; s. Vernon Otho and Mattye Ether (Cashen) G.; B.A., U. Tex., 1953, Ph.D., 1964; M.B.A., Ohio State U., 1957; m. Joanne Marie Greer, Apr. 23, 1966; children—Marc Bernley, Carl Mathieu Cashen. Accountant, So. regional hdqrs. J.C. Penney Co., Dallas, 1957-59; planner N.Am. Rockwell, Downey, Calif., 1959-61; asst. prof. La. State U., Baton Rouge, 1964-66, asso. prof., 1967-69; Fulbright prof. Universidad de las Americas, Mexico City, 1966-67; asso. prof. U. Md., College Park, 1969-73, prof., chmn. dept. mktg., 1973—; cons. govt. agys., pvt. corps. Served with U.S. Army, 1954-55. Ford Found. fellow, 1963-64; Frost Found. fellow, Soviet Union, summer 1965, Costa Rica, summer 1966, Panama, summer 1967, Spain, summer 1969. Mem. Am. Mktg. Assn., Acad. Internat. Bus., So. Mktg. Assn. (pres.), Assn. Consumer Research, Product Devel. Assn., Am. Statis Assn. Author: Marketing in the Soviet Union, 1973; Cases in

Marketing: Orientation, Analysis and Problems, 1975, 2d edit., 1979. Contbr. articles in field to profl. jours. Home: 12420 Kuhl Rd Silver Spring MD 20902 Office: Coll Bus U Md College Park MD 20742

GREGG, DAVID, III, business exec.; b. N.Y.C., Jan. 29, 1933; s. David, Jr. and Virginia (Wyckoff) G.; A.B., Yale U., 1955; M.B.A., Columbia U., 1959; m. May Foster Bowers, Dec. 21, 1963; children—Justine Simms, David. With Eastman Dillion Union Securities & Co., N.Y.C., 1959-69, partner, 1967; v.p. Blyth & Co., N.Y.C., 1969-72; 1st v.p. Blyth Eastman Dillon & Co., Inc., N.Y.C., 1972-73; exec. v.p. Overseas Pvt. Investment Corp. (presdl. appointment, confirmed by Senate), 1973-77; sr. advisor Porter Internat. Co., Washington, 1978; exec. v.p., dir. Pierce Internat., Washington, 1978—. dir. 1st Variable Rate Fund. Served with U.S. Army, 1955-57. Mem. N.Y. Soc. Security Analysts, Beta Theta Pi, Alpha Kappa Psi. Republican. Episcopalian. Clubs: Yale of N.Y.C. and Washington; Amateur Ski (N.Y.C.); Onteora. Office: 1776 K St NW Washington DC 20006

GREGG, DOROTHY ELIZABETH (MRS. PAUL HUGHLING SCOTT), educator, bus. exec.; b. Tempe, Ariz.; d. Alfred Tennyson and Mamie (Walker) Gregg; B.A., U. Tex., 1944, M.A. (grad. fellow), 1945; Ph.D. (all-univ. grad. fellow), Columbia, 1951; m. Paul Hughling Scott, 1952; children—Kimberly, Gregg. Student tchr. U. Tex., 1941-44; student tchr. Columbia, 1946-50; asst. prof. econs., 1952-54; tchr. econ. history Barnard Coll., 1953; tchr. evening courses New Sch. for Social Research, N.Y.C., 1956-57; research cons. to mgmt. cons. firms, N.Y.C., Chgo., 1954-58; researcher, pub. relations research sect. U.S. Steel Corp., N.Y.C., 1958-60, asst. staff dir. ednl. services, 1960-68, asst. dir. pub. relations, 1968-74; dir. pub. relations Celanese Corp., N.Y.C., 1974-75, corporate v.p. communications, 1975—; asso. prof. Pace Coll. Grad. Sch. Bus., 1962-64. Spl. research asst., N.Y. coordinator to Sen. Jacob K. Javits, N.Y.C., 1957; spl. cons. ECA, Washington, 1952; spl. research asst. to head, financial div. Nat. Bur. Econ. Research, 1951-52; speaker ednl., profl., polit. groups. Co-chmn. consumer com. woman's council N.Y. State Dept. Commerce, 1963—; bd. dirs. Greater N.Y. Safety Council, N.Y.C., Advt. Women N.Y. Com. Women in Pub. Relations. Named One of N.Y.'s Distinguished Women, N.Y. State Dept. Commerce, 1964; recipient Outstanding Woman of Year award Toastmistress Club, 1968, Top Hat award Nat. Fedn. Bus. Profl. Women's Clubs, 1968, Sound of Success award Theta Sigma Phi, 1969. Mem. Nat. Council Women U.S. (1st v.p.), Pub. Relations Soc. Am. (pres. N.Y. chpt.), Bus. and Profl. Women N.Y.C., Am. Woman's Assn. Grad. Faculties Alumni Assn. Columbia, Am. Econ. Assn., Joint Council on Econ. Edn., Am. Acad. Polit. and Social Sci., Am. Sociol. Assn., Indsl. Relations Research Assn., Phi Beta Kappa, Pi Sigma Alpha. Clubs: Zonta (bd. dirs.), Princeton (N.Y.C.). Biographer businessmen for Men in Business, Harvard Entrepreneurial Studies Center, 1952. Contbr. articles to profl. mags., P.F. Collier & Son Ency. Home: 425 E 58th St New York City NY 10022 Office: 1211 Ave of the Americas New York City NY 10036

GREGG, WILLIAM KIRKER, railway rolling stock mfr.; b. Hackensack, N.J., July 11, 1921; s. Otis Tiffany and Juliette Belle (Kirker) G.; student Lehigh U., 1941-42, Carnegie Inst. Tech., 1943-44; m. Louise Lydecker, June 28, 1947; children—Susan, Juliette, Janet, Dorothy. Sales engr. Gregg Co. Ltd., N.Y.C., 1945-47; adminstr. Societe Gregg d'Europe, S.A., Lot, Belgium, 1947-55, 69—; v.p. Gregg Co., Ltd., Hackensack, 1955-63, pres., 1963—, chmn. bd. dirs., 1969—. Bd. dirs. YMCA of Greater Bergen County (N.J.), pres., 1966-68; trustee, v.p. Hackensack Hosp. Assn., 1975-77; mem. East West Trade Council. Served with U.S. Army, 1942-45. Decorated Bronze Star. Mem. Ry. Progress Inst., N.Y. R.R. Club, N.A.M., Am. Soc. Metals, Soc. Mfg. Engrs. Republican. Clubs: Rotary (pres. Hackensack 1970-71); Lawyers (N.Y.C.); American (Brussels, Belgium); Arcola Country. Home: 15 Hollis Dr Ho-Ho-Kus NJ 07423 Office: 15 Dyatt Pl Hackensack NJ 07602

GREGO, NICHOLAS JOHN, physiologist, educator; b. N.Y.C., Feb. 10, 1945; s. Nicholas John and Helen Theresa (Franki) G.; B.S., Fairfield U., 1966; M.S., Adelphi U., 1968; Ph.D., Thomas Jefferson U., 1974; postgrad. Phila. Coll. Osteopathic Medicine, 1977—. Teaching asst. Adelphi U., 1967-68; instr. physiology Temple U. Sch. Dentistry, 1970-72; asst. prof. physiology Phila. Coll. Osteopathic Medicine, 1972—. Mem. ethnic adv. com. Phila. '76, Inc., recipient certificate of merit, 1976. Mem. AAAS, Phila. Physiol. Soc., Croatian Acad. Am., Sigma Xi. Roman Catholic. Club: Croatian Cath. Union Lodge 47 (v.p.). Home: 109 Lawrence St New Hyde Park NY 11040 Office: 4150 City Ave Philadelphia PA 19131

GREGOIRE, PAUL, clergyman; b. Verdun, Oct. 24, 1911; s. Albert and Marie (Lavoie) G.; student, Seminaire de Sainte-Therese, theol. student Grand Sem. Montreal Que., Can.; Ph.D.; S.T.L.; Litt.L., M.A. in History; diploma in pedagogy; hon. doctorate U. Montreal, 1969. Ordained priest Roman Catholic Ch. 1937; dir. Seminaire de Sainte-Therese; prof. philosophy of edn. l'Ecole Normale Secondaire, also l'Institut Pedagogique; chaplain of students U. Montreal; consecrated bishop, 1961; aux. to Archbishop of Montreal; vicar gen., dir. Office for Clergy; acting adminstr. diocese; apostolic adminstr. archdiocese of Montreal, 1967-68, archbishop, 1968—. Pres. French sect. Episcopal commn. ecumenism Canadian Cath. Conf. 1965; presided over numerous diocesan commns., 1965—. Address: 2000 Sherbrooke St W Montreal PQ H3H 1G4 Canada

GREGORIAN, VARTAN, educator; b. Tabriz, Iran, Apr. 8, 1934; s. Samuel B. and Shushanik (Mirzaian) G.; grad. Coll. Armenien, 1955; B.A., Stanford, 1958, Ph.D., 1964; M.A. (hon.), U. Pa., 1972; m. Clare Russell, Mar. 25, 1960; children—Vahé, Raffi, Dareh. Came to U.S., 1962. Instr. San Francisco State Coll., asst. prof. European and Middle Eastern history, 1964-67, asso. prof., 1967-68; asso. prof. history U. Tex. at Austin, 1968-70, prof. history, 1970-72; prof. history, Tarzian prof. Armenian history and culture U. Pa., 1972—, dean Faculty Arts and Scis., 1974—, provost, 1979—. Mem. Nat. Humanities Faculty, 1970—. Adviser Armenian Relief Soc. Ednl. Program, 1973—; vol. lectr. Armenian Sisters' Acad., 1973—. Chmn. Univ. Profs. for Sissy Farenthold for Gov. Tex., 1972. Bd. dirs. Council-Internat. Visitors, Phila., 1973—, Ford Found. fellow, 1960-62; Social Sci. Research Council fellow, 1960; Am. Council Learned Socs.-Social Sci. Research Council fellow, 1965-66; Am. Philos. Soc. grantee, 1965-66; Guggenheim grantee, 1971. Recipient Danforth Founds. Teaching excellence award, 1970, Cactus award, 1971. Mem. Am. Hist. Assn., Am. Assn. Socia. Scis., Afghanistan Found., Armenian Students Assn. Author: The Emergence of Modern Afghanistan, 1880-1946, 1969. Contbr. numerous articles to profl. jours. Home: 408 Drew Ave Swarthmore PA 19081 Office: 116 College Hall 3417 Spruce St Philadelphia PA 19174

GREGORY, EDWARD HAIG, UN ofcl.; b. Summit, N.J., Dec. 10, 1931; s. Leon H. and Lucy (Simsarian) Goomrigian; B.A., Park Coll., 1956; M.A., U. Pa., 1957; m. Jewell Louann Kirchner, May 31, 1953; children—Susan, Hope. Mgmt. analyst, Office Mng. Dir., City of Phila., 1957-62, asst. to dir. commerce, 1962-64; prin. asso. Jacobs Co., pub. adminstrn. cons., Chgo., 1964-69, v.p. pub. mgmt. services, 1969-72; dir. adminstrn. and finance UN Fund Population Activities, N.Y.C., 1973—; cons. Ford Found. Pub. Adminstrn. Reform Project, Saudi Arabia, 1964-66. Mem. Maine Twp. (Ill.) High Sch. Bd. Edn., 1972-73. Fels scholar, 1963-64. Mem. Am. Soc. Pub. Adminstrn., Soc. Internat. Devel. Editor: A Study of Small Community Needs as Related to Federal Assistance, 1971; Model Cities Management Series, 1971. Home: 36 Elmwood Pl Short Hills NJ 07078 Office: 485 Lexington Ave New York City NY 10017

GREGORY, GARDINER EMERSON, former ednl. adminstr.; b. Standish, Maine, Feb. 27, 1917; s. Arthur Emerson and Mabelle (Linscott) G.; A.B., Colby Coll., 1939; M.A. in Edn., U. Maine, 1946; postgrad., Rutgers U.; m. Ann Church, Nov. 15, 1958; children—Gary Scott, Linda Jane (Mrs. Dwight Patten); stepchildren—Linda (Mrs. Kenneth Leisentritt), Susan (Mrs. Howard Palle). Photography editor Collegiate Digest, 1937-39; classroom tchr., Maine, 1939-43; prin. high schs., Castine, Maine, 1943-44, Eliot, Maine, 1946-48, Epping, N.H., 1948-50; dir. audio-visual edn. pub. schs., North Plainfield, N.J., 1950-56; dir. curriculum materials Hicksville (N.Y.) Pub. Schs., 1956-77; ret., 1977; instr. U. Maine, summers 1941-42. Dir. Somerset County (N.J.) YMCA Summer Camp, 1951-52; scoutmaster, Boy Scouts Am., Belmont, N.H., 1949-50, North Plainfield, 1951-56; pres. Somerset County Film Library, 1953-54; mem. Hicksville Community Council, 1970—. Founder, bd. dirs. Gregory Mus., L.I. Earth Sci. Center, Hicksville. Served with USNR, 1944-46. Recipient numerous prizes for photography; Community Achievement award North Plainfield, 1953, Hicksville K.C., 1970; Mens' Garden Club L.I. award, 1972; Good Neighbor award Nassau County (N.Y.) Press Assn., 1973. Mem. Franklin and Ogdensburg Mineral Soc. (historian 1964—), Town of Oyster Bay Hist. Soc. (trustee), various mineral clubs. Mason. Contbr. articles, photographs to various profl. jours., newspapers. Home: 207 Cottage Blvd Hicksville NY 11801

GREGORY, GUY JOHN, beauty supply co. exec.; b. Bristol, R.I., Feb. 25, 1917; s. Ulisse and Antonetta (Palumbo) De Gregorio; student pub. schs.; m. Yolanda J. Sirotti, Oct. 19, 1940; children—William Richard, Robert Anthony. Pres., treas. Gregory Beauty Supply Co., Inc., Lincoln, R.I., 1952—; pres., sec. Bigby Corp., Providence, 1962—; fin. dir. Certified Computer Services Inc., Cranston, R.I., 1973—; pres. Gregory Beauty Supply Cape Code Inc., 1977—. Chmn. 5th Ward Citizens League Providence, 1961-62, Citizens League Providence, 1963-64. Served with AUS, 1943-46. Mem. New Eng. Full Service Beauty Dealers Assn. (pres.), Amvets (state sr. vice comdr. 1950-51). Club: K.C. Home: 26 Maplecrest Dr Greenville RI 02828 Office: 2 Court Dr Lincoln RI 02865

GREGORY, JAMES MICHAEL, profl. hockey team exec.; b. Port Colborne, Ont., Can., Nov. 4, 1935; s. Henry Joseph and Catherine Cecilia (Gandour) G.; student St. Michael's Coll., Toronto; m. Rosalie Donna Bruno, May, 1959; children—Andrea, David, Valerie, Maureen. Trainer, coach, mgr. various hockey teams; mgr.-coach Vancouver (B.C.) Canucks; gen. mgr. Toronto Maple Leafs, 1969—. Recipient (with team) Meml. Cup, 1961, 64, 67. Office: care Toronto Maple Leafs 60 Carlton St Toronto ON M5B 1L1 Canada*

GREGORY, NAHKETAH BASKERVILLE, counselor; b. Knoxville, Tenn., Feb. 8, 1926; d. Douglass D. and Dolly L. (Warren) Baskerville; B.S., Knoxville Coll., 1947; M.Ed., U. Md., 1966; postgrad. Howard U., summer 1955, Columbia U., summer 1953, Johns Hopkins U., 1967; m. Clarence K. Gregory, July 1, 1949; 1 dau., Cheryl Andrea. Tchr. math. Cook High Sch., Athens, Tenn., 1947-49, Henry County Sch., McDonough, Ga., 1952-56, Clifton Park Jr. High Sch., Balt., 1956-66; guidance counselor Gwynns Falls Jr. High Sch., Balt., 1966-68; head guidance dept. Gwynns Falls, Garrison and Hampstead Hill Jr. High Schs., Balt., 1968-78; head guidance dept. Hampstead Hill Jr. High Sch., Balt., 1978—; cons. in field. Pres., Mondawmin Child Study Group, 1968-70; elder Madison Ave. Presbyterian Ch., Balt., 1971-77. Phelps Stokes Found. fellow Howard U., 1955. Mem. Am., Md. personnel and guidance assns., Am., Md. sch. counselors assns. Home: 3616 Wabash Ave Baltimore MD 21215 Office: 101 S Ellwood Ave Baltimore MD 21224

GREGORY, PHILIP ORSON, physician and surgeon; b. Boothbay Harbor, Maine, Dec. 14, 1909; s. George A. and Gertrude (Dodge) G.; student U. Maine, 1929-32; M.D., U. Md., 1936; m. Grace E. Gregory, June 8, 1935; children—Nancy Gregory, Marjorie Ann. Intern, Bellevue Hosp., N.Y.C., 1936-39; practice medicine specializing in surgery, Boothbay Harbor, Maine, 1939—; chief staff St. Andrews Hosp., Boothbay Harbor, 1946—; med. examiner County of Lincoln (Maine), 1946—; dir. Depositors Trust Co. Bd. dirs. Boothbay Region Community Sch. Dist. Fellow A.C.S.; mem. AMA, Internat. Coll. Surgeons, Internat. Bd. Surgery, Maine Med. Assn. Episcopalian. Contbr. articles to med. jours. Home: 46 School St Boothbay Harbor ME 04538 Office: 3 St Andrews Ln Boothbay Harbor ME 04538

GREGORY, ROBERT, JR., finance co. exec.; b. Balt., Jan. 23, 1952; s. Robert Lee and Mary Elizabeth G.; B.A., Loyola Coll., Balt., 1974, postgrad. in bus.; m. Linda Louise Johnson, Oct. 4, 1975; 1 son, Terrell Anton. Dept. mgr. Bond's Clothes, Inc., Balt., 1968-72; asst. mgr. National Shoes Inc., Balt., 1972-74; tax accountant, internal auditor Monumnetal Life Ins. Co., Balt., 1974-77; sr. auditor Comml. Credit Co., Balt., 1977—; instr. Strayer Bus. Coll., 1977-78. Recipient Advisers award Jr. Achievement, 1974, 75. Mem. Nat. Alliance Businessmen (Appreciation award 1974-75), Nat. Assn. Black Accountants (dir., Distinguished Service award 1978), Nat. Assn. Accountants, Balt. Alert Radio Team. Democrat. Methodist. Club: Masons. Instr. Black Belt Karate, 1970—. Home: 551 Lucia Ave Baltimore MD 21229 Office: 301 Charles St N Baltimore MD 21202

GREIDINGER, B. BERNARD, educator, accountant; b. N.Y.C., Mar. 30, 1906; s. Max and Fannie (Oster) G.; B.B.A., City Coll. N.Y., 1928; M.S., Columbia, 1932, Ph.D., 1939; C.P.A., N.Y., 1930. Partner Beame & Greidinger, C.P.A., 1929-42; prof. accounting grad. sch. bus., N.Y.U., 1948—; sr. partner Greidinger and Co., C.P.A., 1946-70; partner Hertz, Herson & Co., C.P.A.'s, N.Y.C., 1971—; prof. accounting U. Calif. at Los Angeles, summer 1947; lectr. accounting City Coll. N.Y., 1930-39, Rutgers U., 1940-46; cons. N.Y.U.-U.S. AID Bus. Adminstrn. Program, U. Lagos, Nigeria, 1965. Past dir., mem. exec. com. U.S. Hoffman Machinery Corp. Rep. dir. gen. UNRRA at inception Internat. Refugee Orgn., 1946; financial adv., chief financial operations UNRRA, 1946-47; cons. budget adv. com. Army-Air Force Post Exchange Service, 1948; cons. to chief ordnance Dept. Army, N.Y. dist., 1952—; nominated by Pres. Truman mem. Renegotiation Bd., 1952; spl. cons. to comptroller N.Y., 1955; cons. internat. cooperation adminstrn. U.S. State Dept., 1956; coordinator, N.Y. U., U.S. Operation Mission (internat. cooperation adminstrn.), Israel, 1956; mem. Mayor's Temporary Commn. City Finances, City N.Y., 1964-67, chmn. Mayor's Transition Com., 1973; mem. Mayor's Council of Econ. and Bus. Advisers, 1974; mem. Mayor's Com. on Judiciary, 1975; mem. Mayor's Commn. for Cultural Affairs of N.Y.C., 1976; mem. citizens comm. Future U. City N.Y., 1970-71. Served with finance dept. AUS, 1942-44, from maj. to lt. col., USAAF, 1944-46, chief budget fiscal div., 2d Air Force, chief tech. service div., Office Chief Finance AUS, World War II; now col. USAF Res. Mem. Am. Inst. C.P.A.'s, N.Y. State Soc. C.P.A.'s, Am. Accounting Assn., Nat. Assn. Cost Accountants, Acad. Polit. Scis. Mason. Clubs: Columbia, New York Univ. Faculty. Author: Accounting Requirements of the Securities and Exchange Commission, 1941; Preparation and Certification of Financial Statements, 1950; Filings with the Securities and Exchange Commission, 1966; S.E.C. Auditing Requirements, 1971; also numerous articles profl. jours. Contbr. Financial Handbook, 3d rev. edit., 1948; co-author, contbr. Big Business Methods for Small Business, 1952. Home: 2 Washington Sq Village New York City NY 10012 Office: 2 Park Ave New York City NY 10016

GREIF, EDWARD LOUIS, pub. relations co. exec.; b. Bklyn., June 8, 1909; s. Herman and Minnie (Lipschitz) G.; student Coll. City N.Y., 1926-27; LL.B., St. Lawrence U., 1930; m. Mildred Schlamm, Mar. 25, 1939; children—Marion, James David. Sports writer Bklyn. Times, 1926-28; admitted to N.Y. bar, 1932; practice law, N.Y.C., 1932-38; mng. editor Trade Jour. Syndicate, N.Y.C., 1937-38; film critic, columnist Motion Picture Daily, N.Y.C., 1938-42; dir. exploitation NBC, N.Y.C., 1942-45; partner firm Banner & Greif, pub. relations, N.Y.C., 1945-68, pres. Banner & Greif Ltd., 1968—; cons. mass. media edn. USPHS; guest lectr. pub. relations Columbia U., Yale U., Temple U., U. Chgo., Sarah Lawrence Coll. Mem. univ. relations com. Brandeis U., 1948-70, Friend, Harlan Chapel, 1968-70; mem. adv. com. to communications project Nat. Commn. Community Health Services, 1964-67. Mem. Pub. Relations Soc. Am. (chmn. research com. N.Y. chpt.), Overseas Press Club. Author: The Silent Pulpit, 1964; contbr. chpt. Crisis in the Church, 1968. Home: 64 Bradford Rd Scarsdale NY 10585 Office: 369 Lexington New York City NY 10017

GREIF, MARTIN, govt. ofcl.; b. N.Y.C., Feb. 27, 1928; s. Saul M. and Anna (Levy) G.; B.A., N.Y. U., 1949; B.S. summa cum laude, St. John's U., 1952; m. Roberta Mace; children—Steven W., Rodger K., Michele S., Janice E., Linda B. Research chemist, product devel. Lederle Labs. div. Am. Cyanamid Co., Pearl River, N.Y., 1955-58, group leader, product devel., 1958-63, sect. mgr. product research and devel., 1963-66, consumer products div., mgr. clin. research services, Wayne, N.J., 1966-75; asst. to dir. div. cosmetics tech., also br. chief FDA, Washington, 1975—; guest lectr. St. John's U., Jamaica, N.Y. Chmn. coll. liaison com. Chem. Spltys. Mfrs. Assn., 1967-70, aerosol div. exec. bd., 1970-72, legislative and regulatory affairs com., 1973-75, personal and pharm. products com., 1969-75; mem. CTFA standards com. 1972-73. Served with Med. Service Corp, AUS, 1952-55. Fellow Soc. Cosmetic Chemists (program chmn. 1969, 73, chpt. treas. 1970, edn. chmn. 1971-73, gen. chmn. 9th congress Internat. Fedn. 1974-76, nat. merit award 1976, chmn. awards com. 1978); mem. Am. Pharm. Assn., Drug Information Assn. (charter), AAAS, N.Y. Acad. Scis. (chmn. pharmacy congress 1964), Am. Coll. Pharmacy (dir. 1974-76, exec. bd. 1976—), Pharmacy Alumni Assn. St. John's U. (v.p. 1968-70, pres. 1971-72, vice chmn. alumni fedn. dirs. 1971-72, mem. alumni fedn. dirs. 1970-74), Alpha Zeta Omega, Rho Chi. Author: Handbook and Formulary, 1954. Contbr. articles to profl. jours. U.S., fgn. patents in field. Home: 8520 Wilkesboro Ln Potomac MD 20854 Office: FDA Washington DC 20204

GREINER, HARRY SANDT, research engr.; b. Bethlehem, Pa., Apr. 18, 1914; s. Henry Harris and Ida (Sandt) G.; B.Chem. Engring., Lehigh U., 1936; student Villanova U., 1956-58; m. Vera Lillian Volker, Aug. 21, 1943; children—Jack Volker, Jill Thelma. Chemist, Reichard Coulston, Bethlehem, 1936-42; head, powder quality control Devoe Reynolds, Louisville, 1942-43; sr. chem. engr. Keystone Chemurgic, Bath, Pa., 1944; supt. plant Calcamine Co., Grand Rapids, Mich., 1944-51; prodn. mgr. Am. Pigment Co., Pulaski, Va., 1951-54; sr. research engr. Pfizer Inc., Easton, Pa., 1954—. Cons., Dr. Freeman, Allentown, Pa. Pres. City Band of Bethlehem, 1968-70; sec. Bethlehem post Am. Legion Band, 1972-74. Mem. Am. Inst. Chem. Engrs. (chmn. Lehigh Valley sect. 1964), Lehigh Valley Engrs. Club. Mem. Central Moravian Ch. (sec. 1969-73, trustee 1972—). Patentee magnetic iron oxide process. Home: 2347 Huntington St Bethlehem PA 18017 Office: 640 N 13th St Easton PA 18042

GRELECKI, CHESTER, cons. chemist; b. Newton Twp., Pa., June 22, 1927; s. Joseph and Mary (Kuna) G.; B.S., Kings Coll. (Pa.), 1950; M.S., Duquesne U., 1952; Ph.D. in Chemistry, Catholic U. Am., 1956; m. Rose Hudyck; children—Mark, Stephen, Fred, Paul, Sue, Carol, David. Research chemist Thiokel Corp. Denville, N.J., 1956-67, mgr. research ops., 1967-69; founder, pres., chief scientist Hazards Research Corp., Denville, 1970—; dir. Deltronic Crystal Industries Inc.; instr. fire explosion hazards evaluation Am. Inst. Chem. Engrs. Mem. planning bd. Rockaway Boro. Served with USN, 1945-46. Mem. Am. Chem. Soc. Roman Catholic. Contbr. articles to profl. jours. Home: 141 Halsey Ave Rockaway NJ 07866 Office: Hazards Research Corp Denville NJ 07834

GRENDON, DAVID ARTHUR, radiologist; b. Bklyn., June 9, 1903; s. George and Natalie (Sieger) G.; B.S., Coll. City N.Y., 1924; M.D., Harvard, 1928; m. Sally Sachs, Apr. 1, 1935; Intern, Bellevue Hosp., N.Y.C., 1928-30; resident Pondville Hosp., Walpole, Mass., 1930; attending physician Bellevue Hosp., N.Y.C., 1931-35, Bronx Hosp., N.Y.C., 1935-41; chief radiology Sharon (Conn.) Hosp., 1947—, Fairview Hosp., Great Barrington, Mass., 1951-71; cons. Radiology Wassaic (N.Y.) State Sch., 1949—; mem. State of Conn. Commn. on Hosps. and Health Care, 1976—. Bd. dirs. Conn. Hosp. Planning Commn., 1967-73, N.W. Conn. Community Council, 1970—; mem. adv. council U. Conn. Health Center, Farmington, Conn., 1971-74. Served to lt. col., AUS, 1941-46. Decorated Army Commendation ribbon. Fellow Am. Coll. Radiology, N.Y. Acad. Medicine; mem. Conn. State Med. Soc. (pres. 1973), Conn. Radiol. Soc. (pres. 1966), N.E. N.Y Radiol. Soc. (pres. 1967), Conn. Valley Radiological Soc. (pres. 1965). Club: Harvard (Northwestern Conn.). Home: Cleaveland St Lakeville CT 06039 Office: Med Arts Center Sharon CT 06069

GRENIER, JEAN PAUL, radiologist; b. Quebec City, Que., Can., Mar. 25, 1939; s. Joseph Emeric and Germaine (Blais) G.; B.A., Laval U., 1959, M.D., 1964; D.M.R., Queen's U., 1971; m. Gaetane Grenier, Aug. 15, 1964; children—Pascale, Marie-France. Intern, Hotel Dieu de Québec, Quebec City, 1963-64; resident, Kingston (Ont., Can.) Gen. Hosp., 1968-72; physician Canadian Forces, Ont. and West Germany, 1964-68; chief radiologist Canadian Forces Hosp., Valcartier, Que.; cons. radiologist Centre Hospitalier Chauveau, Loretteville, Que. Mem. Societe Canadiene Francaise de Radiologie, Canadian Assn. Radiologists, Assn. des Medecins de langue Francaise du Can., Canadian Med. Protective Assn., Coll. Physicans and Surgeons Ont., Fedn. Med. Specialists Que., Assn. des Radiologistes de la Province de Quebec, Que. Profl. Corp. Physicians. Roman Catholic. Club: Condovac. Home: 58 Gourdeau St Neufchatel Quebec PQ G2A 3E4 Canada Office: 153 Blvd Valcartier PQ G2A 2M4 Canada

GRENNELL, ROBERT LOVELL, educator; b. Irving, N.Y., July 28, 1910; s. John Chapman and Emma (Brehn) G.; student State U. N.Y., 1930; B.S., Pa. State U., 1934; M.A., Cornell U., 1937; Ed.D., N.Y. U., 1950; m. Elinor Thorsen, Aug. 16, 1941; children—Donna Grennell Ringler, Susanne T., John C. Tchr., Morrisville (Pa.) Pub. Schs., 1928-32, Silver Creek (N.Y.) High Sch., 1934-35; tchr., psychologist, research dir. Rockville Centre (L.I., N.Y.) Pub. Schs., 1935-42; vocat. adviser, psychologist-counselor U.S. VA, Buffalo, 1946-47; prof. edn. and psychology State Univ. Coll., Fredonia, N.Y., 1947-74, prof. emeritus, 1974—. Mem. Bd. Edn., Lake Shore Central

Sch. system, Angola, N.Y., 1957-60; mem., chmn. Town of Brant Planning Bd., 1959—. Served to capt. AUS, 1942-46; lt. col. USAF Res., ret. State U. N.Y. Research Found. grantee, 1962-65. Mem. Am. Am., Western N.Y. psychol. assns., Ret. Officers Assn., Air Force Assn. Home: 995 Milestrip Rd Irving NY 14081 Office: 2097 Thompson Hall State Univ Coll Fredonia NY 14063

GRESHAM, GLEN EDWARD, physician; b. Ft. Worth, Dec. 1, 1931; s. Perry Epler and Elsie Inez (Stanbrough) G.; B.A., Harvard Coll., 1953; M.D., Columbia U., 1958; m. Phyllis Elaine Kilmer, Nov. 9, 1957; children—Stephen Deane, David Epler, Elizabeth Anne Kilmer, Jennifer Gordon. Intern, Univ. Hosps. Cleve., 1958-59, resident internal medicine, 1959-60, 62-64; asst. prof. preventive medicine Ohio State U., Columbus, 1964-69; asst. prof. medicine Yale U., New Haven, 1969-70; asso. prof. rehab. medicine, medicine and community medicine Tufts U., Boston, 1970-78; prof., chmn. dept. rehab. medicine State U. N.Y. at Buffalo, 1978—. Served with USPHS, 1960-62. Nat. Found. fellow rehab., 1962-64; recipient Distinguished Service award Mass. Council Orgns. Handicapped, 1972. Fellow A.C.P.; mem. Am. Congress Rehab. Medicine, Am. Rheumatism Assn., Am. Fedn. Clin. Research. Congregationalist. Clubs: Harvard Boston, Univ. Buffalo. Researcher epidemiology chronic disease, disability. Office: 462 Grider St Buffalo St Buffalo NY 14215

GRESSEL, MICHAEL LUDWIG, sculptor; b. Wurzburg, Germany, Sept. 20, 1902; s. Adam and Eva (Keup) G.; student Volks Schule, 1908-18, Holzschnitts Schule, 1921-22, Beaux Art Inst. Design, N.Y., 1930-31; m. Clara Maria Scheder, Sept. 21, 1930; children—Ronald J.M., Arthur J. Came to U.S., 1928, naturalized, 1945. Exhibited in group shows at County Center, White Plains, N.Y., 1944, Armonk Library, 1956, Purchase Community House, 1967, Lever House, N.Y.C., 1966, Allied Artists Am., Nat. Acad. Galleries; represented in permanent collections Met. Mus. Art N.Y.C., Bruckner Mus., Albion, Mich., Anta Theater, Helen Hayes Theater, Lund Fontaine Theater, Nat. Theater Washington, Longines-Wittnauer Watch Co., County Trust Co. Bank, Mt. Kisco, U.S. Bronze Co., Maryknoll, N.Y., Stepinac High Sch., White Plains; executed Centennial monument Legend of Sleepy Hollow. Recipient Gold medal for figure Dancer, 1965, Gold medal for Madonna with Lily, 1972 (both Hudson Valley Art Assn.), Archer Huntington award, 1965. Mem. Hudson Valley Art Assn. (dir.), Nat. Sculpture Soc. Address: Gressell Pl Armonk NY 10504

GRESSLE, LLOYD EDWARD, bishop; b. Cleve., June 13, 1918; s. Edward W. and Olga (Hoppensack) G.; B.A., Oberlin Coll., 1940; B.D., Bexley Hall, 1943; D.D., Kenyon Coll., 1953; m. Marguerite Kirkpatrick, July 12, 1943; 3 children. Ordained priest, Episcopal Ch., 1943, bishop, 1970; rector St. James Ch., Wooster, Ohio, 1943-48, St. John Ch., Sharon, Pa., 1948-56; dean Cathedral of St. John, Wilmington, Del., 1956-69; rector St. James Ch., Lancaster, Pa., 1969-70; bishop coadjutor of Bethlehem (Pa.), 1970-72, bishop, 1972—; mem. exec. council Diocese of Sharon, 1948-56; dep. Gen. Gov. Episc. Ch., 1949, 55-57, chmn. dept. Christian edn., 1950-56; exec. v.p. conf. Hood Coll., 1952-56; mem. standing com. Erie (Pa.) Diocese, 1953-56, del. Diocese, 1956-70; pres. Wilmington Council Chs., 1963-70; Wates-Seabury exchange priest, Portsmouth, Eng., 1965-66. Fellow Coll. Preachers. Address: 826 Delaware Ave Bethlehem PA 18015

GRESSMAN, JOHN WESLEY, III, social worker; b. Bridgeton, N.J., Dec. 12, 1950; s. John Wesley and Margaret Emma (Campbell) G.; student Alderson Broaddus Coll., 1970-73, Rutgers U., 1974—, Glassboro State Coll. Probation officer Cumberland County Probation Dept., Bridgeton, N.J., 1973-78, sr. probation officer, 1975-78, coordinator vol. services, 1976-78. Mem. Cumberland County Alcohol Commn.; com. chmn. Boy Scouts Am.; chmn. Bridgeton Youth Council; Vol. mem. Cumberland County Juvenile Conf. Com., 1973-77; vol. cons. Cumberland County Mental Health Assn., 1977-78, Contact Crisis Hotline. Recipient Law Day award Cumberland County, 1977, Outstanding Law Enforcement Officer award Bridgeton Jaycees, 1977. Mem. Nat. Assn. Social Workers, Am. Rehab. Counselors Assn., Am. Assn. Mental Health Counselors, N.J. Assn. Probation Officers. Republican. Baptist. Club: Masons. Home: 147 West Ave S Bridgeton NJ 08302

GREWAL, MANOHAR SINGH, mfg. co. exec.; b. India, Dec. 1, 1935; s. Ranjit Singh and Sant Kaur (Mangat) G.; came to U.S., 1963, naturalized, 1969; M.S. in Metall. Engring., Rensselaer Poly. Inst., 1965; Sc.D., Mass. Inst. Tech., 1971; m. Gurmit Kaur Gill, July 13, 1966; children—Parminder Kaur, Tejinder Kaur. Research asst. Mass. Inst. Tech., Cambridge, 1967-71; research and devel. scientist Gillette Co., Boston, 1971-73, group mgr., 1974—. Recipient cash award Excellence in Metallography, Internat. Metallographic Exhibit, 1973; NASA research grantee and fellow; mem. Am. Soc. Metals (Lucas award), Internat. Microstructural Soc. (Gold medal), Electron Microscopy Soc. Am., N. Am. Thermal Analysis Soc., Am. Powder Metallurgy Inst., New Eng. Sikh Study Circle (founder 1968, pres. 1968-73). Author numerous articles in field. Home: 114 Larchmont Ln Hanover MA 02139 Office: Gillette Co Gillette Park South Boston MA 02106

GREY, ANTHONY JOSEPH, parasitologist; b. Hoboken, N.J., Mar. 11, 1945; s. Stephen Joseph and Henrietta Marie (Grzybowski) G.; B.S., Boston Coll., 1967; postgrad. N.Y. U., 1968-69; M.S., State U. N.Y., Albany, 1972, Ph.D., 1978; m. Sharon Marie Justen, June 11, 1972. Grad. teaching asst. animal zoology State U. N.Y., Albany, 1969-70, gen. parasitology, 1970-72, animal histology, 1972-74, grad. research asst., 1974-76; workshop grantee W. Alton Jones Cell Sci. Center, Lake Placid, N.Y., 1974. Mem. Am. Soc. Parasitologists, Am. Micros. Soc., Helminthological Soc. Washington, Australian Soc. Parasitology, Nat. Wildlife Fedn., Smithsonian Assos. Contbr. articles in field to profl. jours. Home: 166 Homestead Ave Albany NY 12206 Office: Dept Biological Sci State Univ New York Albany NY 12222

GREYTAK, THOMAS JOHN, physicist; b. Annapolis, Md., Mar. 24, 1940; s. John Joseph and Cecilia Felicia (Schwartz) G.; S.B., Mass. Inst. Tech., 1963, M.S., 1963, Ph.D., 1967; m. Elizabeth Ann Bardeen, June 25, 1966. Instr., Mass. Inst. Tech., Cambridge, 1967, asst. prof. physics dept., 1967-70, asso. prof. 1970-77, prof., 1977—; vis. scientist physics dept. U. Calif., San Diego, 1972-73. Alfred P. Sloan Research fellow, 1971-73. Home: 29 Acacia Ave Chestnut Hill MA 02167 Office: Mass Inst Tech Room 13-2074 Cambridge MA 02139

GRIB, HENRY WALTER, librarian; b. Homestead, Pa., May 9, 1927; s. Peter and Katherine (Kulig) G.; B.A. in English, Alliance Coll., 1953; M.A. in Library Sci., Kent State U., 1954; M.A. in Edn., Queens Coll., 1970; m. Sonia Gezarlian, Mar. 5, 1967; children—Jonathan, Margo, Peter. Sci. and tech. librarian U. Md., College Park, 1956-58; classified librarian U.S. Def. Dept., N.Y.C., Washington, 1958-59; librarian Hicksville (N.Y.) sch. dist., 1959—, Nassau Community Coll., Garden City, N.Y., 1965—. Cubmaster Cub Scouts Am., 1969-70; pres. N.Y. chpt. Alliance Coll. Alumni Assn., Cambridge Springs, Pa., 1963-65. Served with Signal Corps, AUS, 1947-48. Recipient Lit. award Alliance Coll., 1952; Hicksville Tchr. award PTA, 1964. Mem. N.Y. Congress Tchrs., Am. Fedn. Tchrs., NEA, Suffolk Library Assn., Tau Sigma Pi, Sigma Tau Delta. Home: 18 Milldam Rd Smithtown NY 11787 Office: Levittown Pkwy and Stewart Ave Hicksville NY 11801

GRIEBEL, RICHARD H., corp. exec.; b. Liberty, N.Y., Apr. 4, 1924; s. Joseph F. and Libbie R. (Henry) G.; A.B., Dartmouth Coll., 1946; postgrad. Columbia U., 1946; grad. exec. devel. program Ind. U., 1956; m. Elaine A. Gretzkowski, Jan. 26, 1946; children—R. Nelson, Douglas M., Barbara E. With RCA, 1946-53, Farnsworth Electric Co., 1953-58, Raytheon Co., 1958-59; v.p. ITT, 1960-62, pres. Kellogg Telecommunications div., group exec. Comml. Telecommunications group, pres., gen. mgr. Kellogg Switchboard & Supply Co.; pres., chmn. bd., dir. Fairbanks, Morse & Co., N.Y.C., 1963-67; v.p., dir. Fairbanks Whitney Corp., N.Y.C., 1963-64; v.p. group exec., dir. Colt Industries, Inc., 1964-67; chmn. bd. Canadian Locomotive Co., Ltd., Kingston, Ont., Can., 1963-67, Pratt & Whitney Machine Tool Co., Hartford, Conn., 1963-64, Colt Firearms Co., Hartford, 1963-64; pres., chief exec. officer, chmn. bd., dir. P. Ballantine & Sons, Newark, 1967-69; pres., chief exec. officer, mem. exec. com. Lehigh Valley Industries, Inc., N.Y.C., 1969-72, chmn. bd., 1972-73; pres., chief exec. officer Tassaway, Inc., Beverly Hills, Calif., 1973-75; pres., chief exec. officer First Found. Corp. Inc., 1976—; pres., chmn. Allied Investment Co., Allied Surety Co., Comparison Ins. Co. Trustee Football Coaches Found., 1967-70; bd. overseers Hanover Inn at Dartmouth Coll., 1968—; mem. exec. com. All-Am. Collegiate Found., 1968-75. Served to capt. USMCR, 1942-46, 50-52. Mem. Am. Inst. Indsl. Engrs., Am. Soc. Tool Mfg. Cos., Am. Soc. Naval Engrs., Assn. U.S. Army, N.J. C. of C., Armed Forces Communications and Electronics Assn., Nat. Def. Transp. Assn. (dir.), Fgn. Policy Assn. (nat. council), AIM (pres.'s council), Soc. Mfg. Engrs., Am. Ordnance Assn., Dartmouth Coll. Club and Ednl. Assn. Club: Rockaway River Country (pres. 1976—) (Denville, N.J.). Home: Claridge House II Apt 8HE Verona NJ 07044 Office: 122 E 42d St New York City NY 10017

GRIEDER, THEODORE GODFREY, JR., librarian, curator; b. Globe, Ariz., Feb. 25, 1926; s. Theodore Godfrey and Lula (Gooch) G.; B.A., U. So. Calif., 1948; M.A., Stanford U., 1950, Ph.D., 1957; M.L.S., U. Calif., Berkeley, 1962. Asst. prof. English, U. Nev., Reno, 1957-61; spl. librarian U. Calif. libraries system, also Isaac Foot librarian, Santa Barbara, 1962-63; chief bibliographer U. Calif., Davis, 1963-66, N.Y. U., N.Y.C., 1966-69; curator Fales Library and spl. collections N.Y. U., 1969—; cons. in field. Served with USNR, 1943-45. Grantee Am. Philos. Soc., 1965-66, Council Library Resources, 1973-74. Mem. Modern Lang. Assn., Phi Beta Kappa, Phi Gamma Delta. Democrat. Club: Grolier. Author books; editor Gale Info. Series; contbr. articles to profl. publs. Home: 1236 Garden St Hoboken NJ 07030 Office: Fales Library Elmer Holmes Bobst Library NY U 70 Washington Sq S New York City NY 10012

GRIER, DOUGLAS AUDENREID, ednl. adminstr.; b. Altoona, Pa., Oct. 26, 1942; s. Thomas Campbell and Solveig (Berg) G.; A.B., Princeton U., 1964; M.A., U. Mich., 1965, Ph.D., 1968; m. Harriet Curry, July 30, 1966; 1 son, Geoffrey Scott. Instr. history U. Mich., Ann Arbor, 1966-68; headmaster Grier Sch., Tyrone, Pa., 1968—. Treas., Tyrone Hosp. Bd., 1973-77; sec. Pa. Assn. Ind. Schs., 1973-77. Mem. Nat. Assn. Prins. Schs. for Girls, Pa. Soc. Republican. Episcopalian. Rotarian. Home and Office: Grier Sch Tyrone PA 16686

GRIERSON, NORMAN HERBERT, mktg. cons., advt. agency exec.; b. Vernon, B.C., Dec. 21, 1926; s. Quinten and Cecilia (Pettifer) G.; B.Th., Northwest Baptist Coll., 1950; Registered Psychiat. Nurse, Essondale Sch. Nursing, 1953; diploma mktg. mgmt. U. Western Ontario Sch. Bus. Adminstrn., 1967; m. Olive M. Vohman, Aug. 25, 1946; children—Robert, Linda, Carol, Susanne. Sales and advt. exec. CIBA, Montreal, Que., 1954-62; account mgr. BBDO, Toronto, Ont., 1963-65; dir. mktg. promotions F.W. Horner Ltd., Montreal, 1966-71; gen. mgr. Deltakos Can., Toronto, 1971-72; corp. dir. mktg. Canox, Toronto, 1973-76; gen. mgr. Crombie-Wilson Mktg. Service, v.p., dir. Crombie Group, Toronto, 1976—; dir. Canadian Holdings Corp., Scarborough, Can.; cons. and lectr. in field. Counsellor Mississauga (Ont.) Distress Centre, 1974—; dir. Toronto Distress Center, 1977—. Served with Canadian Army, 1944-45. Mem. Bus./Profl. Advt. Assn. (dir. 1978—), Am. Mgmt. Assn., Nat. Sales and Mktg. Assn. (dir. 1977—), Am. Mktg. Assn., Bd. Trade Met. Toronto, Internat. Platform Assn., Ont. Soc. Tng. and Devel. Baptist. Club: Toronto Bd. of Trade Golf and Country. Home: 243 Pinetree Way Mississauga ON L5G 2R4 Canada Office: 111 Richmond St W Toronto ON M5H 2G4 Canada

GRIES, LEONARD TODD, psychologist; b. Bklyn., July 13, 1945; s. Nathan and Lillian (Klein) G.; B.S., Bklyn. Coll., 1967; M.A., Hofstra U., 1969, Ph.D., 1972; m. Susanne L. Simmons, Jan. 25, 1970; children—James, Adam, Matthew. Asso. psychologist Bklyn. Developmental Center, 1972-73, chief psychologist, 1973—; psychotherapist Mid-Nassau Community Guidance Center, Hicksville, N.Y., 1975-77; pvt. practice psychology, East Hills, N.Y., 1974—; dir. Park Ave. Psychol. Service, N.Y.C., 1977—; cons. Fedn. P.R. Orgns., 1977—; faculty research advisor Walden U., 1975-77; profl. affiliate Payne-Whitney Psychiat. Clinic-N.Y. Hosp., 1978. Mem. Am. Psychol. Assn., Am. Assn. Mental Deficiency, Nat. Register Health Service Providers in Psychology. Club: Bedford Athletic. Contbr. papers, articles to profl. jours. Home: 33 South St East Hills NY 11577 Office: 550 Park Ave New York City NY 10021

GRIEST, NORMAN JETT, naval architect; b. Washington, Sept. 14, 1942; s. Archie A. and Hazel B. (Barlow) G.; B.S. in Mech. Engring., Va. Poly. Inst., 1965; m. Barbara A. McCarthy, July 31, 1965; 1 son, Allen. Naval architect Naval Ship Engring. Center, U.S. Navy Dept., 1965—. Registered profl. engr., Va. Mem. U.S. Naval Inst., Soc. Naval Architects and Marine Engrs., Am. Soc. Naval Engrs. Republican. Methodist. Home: 17 Watchwater Way Rockville MD 20850

GRIFFEL, JACK, oil co. exec.; b. Vienna, Austria, Apr. 24, 1938; s. Joseph M. and Klara (Fischer) G.; came to U.S., 1940, naturalized, 1945; B.S., Newark Coll. Engring., 1960; M.S., Columbia U., 1962, Sc.D. (Alfred Sloan Found. fellow), 1965; m. Marsha Zakheim, Jan. 26, 1963; children—Louis Howell, Deborah Joy. With Exxon Research & Engring. Co., Florham Park, N.J., 1964-76, mgr. planning engring. div., 1978—; adviser logistics dept. Exxon Corp., N.Y.C., 1976-78. Recipient Alumni Assn. award Newark Coll. Engring., 1960; NSF fellow, 1961. Mem. Am. Inst. Chem. Engrs., Sigma Xi, Tau Beta Pi, Phi Lambda Upsilon, Omega Chi Epsilon. Contbr. articles to profl. jours.; patentee in field. Home: 457A Franklin D Roosevelt Dr New York City NY 10002 Office: Exxon Research & Engring Co PO Box 101 Florham Park NJ 07932

GRIFFENBERG, GRACE LEWIS, psychotherapist; b. N.Y.C., Feb. 27, 1927; d. Samuel and Ida (Cohen) Lewis; B.A., Bklyn. Coll., 1948; M.A., Columbia U., 1952; m. Robert A. Griffenberg, June 17, 1950; children—Susan, Stuart. Guidance cons. N.Y.C. Bur. Ednl. and Vocat. Guidance, 1959—, spl. assignment Bur. for Mentally Retarded, 1972-76, Bur. for Physically Handicapped, 1976—; cons. Sch.-Hosp. Program; pvt. practice psychotherapy, N.Y.C., 1974—; staff therapist Washington Sq. Inst. for Psychotherapy; co-chairperson Industry-Edn. Conf., 1975; bd. dirs. Health Ins. Plan N.Y., also pres. Joint Consumer Council; bd. dirs. Health Systems Agy. N.Y.C.; mem. adv. council to chancellor N.Y.C. Bd. Edn.; bd. dirs. Center for Urban Employment. Named N.Y. State Counselor of Year, 1975, Woman of Year, Abyssinian Baptist Ch. N.Y., 1975, Woman of Year, NAUW, 1977. Fellow Am. Orthopsychiat. Assn. (chairperson); mem. Am. (coordinator 1975 Conv.), N.Y.C. (treas., trustee) personnel and guidance assns., Vocat. Guidance Inst. (dir.), Assn. Psychoanalytic Psychotherapists. Jewish. Home: 3720 Independence Ave Riverdale NY 10463 Office: 660 W 183d St New York City NY 10033

GRIFFIN, JAMES EDWARD, JR., land devel. exec.; b. Fall River, Mass., Jan. 27, 1941; s. James Edward and Marion Beatrice (Johnson) G.; A.A. with honors, Napa Coll., 1965; B.S. with honors, Calif. State U., 1967; m. Audie Leigh Kilwy, July 21, 1963. Auditor, Arthur Young & Co., San Francisco, 1967-69, Providence, 1969-71; v.p., treas. R.I. Land Co., Providence, 1971—. Served with U.S. Army, 1959-62. Mem. Am. Inst. C.P.A.'s, Calif., R.I. socs. C.P.A.'s, Beta Alpha Psi, Beta Gamma Sigma. Home: 140 Butternut Rd Somerset MA 02726 Office: 908 Hospital Trust Bldg Providence RI 02903

GRIFFIN, JAMES EDWIN, utilities co. exec.; b. Langhorne, Pa., Dec. 11, 1927; s. James Edwin and Freda Martha (Seibeneicher) G.; B.S., Pa. State U., 1952, M.S., 1954; children—James, Bruce, Roger. Research analyst Commonwealth Pa., 1953-55; econ. analyst Pa. R.R., 1955-59; area devel. dir. Central Vt. Pub. Service Co., Rutland, 1958-65, v.p., 1965-71, exec. v.p., 1971, pres., dir., 1972—; pres., dir. Vt. Electric Power Co., Inc., Conn. Valley Electric Co., 1972—; dir., exec. v.p. Vt. Yankee Nuclear Power, 1973, pres. 1974. Chmn. Rutland County chpt. ARC; bd. dirs. Vt. Heart Assn.; trustee Green Mountain Coll.; bd. dirs. Eastern States Exposition; trustee Rutland Devel. Corp., New Industries, Inc.; trustee Green Mountain council Boy Scouts Am. Mem. NAM (com. on natural resources mgmt. and conservation), Electric Council New Eng. (pres.), Edison Electric Inst. (dir.). Republican. Episcopalian. Home: 81 Lincoln Ave Rutland VT 05701 Office: 77 Grove St Rutland VT 05701

GRIFFIN, JO ANN THOMAS, urban educator; b. Dallas, July 20, 1933; d. John Baxton and Joan Marion (Ament) Thomas; B.A., U. Miss., 1955; B.S. magna cum laude, Lamar U., 1964; M.Ed., U. Del., 1972; m. Thomas Reese Griffin, Jan. 25, 1976; children by former marriage—John Barrett Brown Jr., Daniel Thomas Brown. Asst. buyer, bridal cons. Neiman-Marcus Co., Dallas, 1955-57; coordinator student activites So. Meth. U., Dallas, 1957-58; asst. women's editor Beaumont (Tex.) Enterprise, 1958-61; therapist, dir. outpatient counseling service Alcoholism Services, State Del., Wilmington, 1972; statewide rehab. coordinator Del. Alcohol Safety Action Project, Wilmington, 1972-74; tchr. counselor Wilmington Pub. Schs., 1974-76; site mgr. Motivational Center Inc., Wilmington, 1976—. Exec. bd. Jr. League Wilmington, 1968-70; exec. com. Outreach div. Episcopal Diocese Del., 1977—; active Boy Scouts Am., Com. of 39, NAACP. AAUW scholar, 1971. Mem. Nat. Assn. Social Workers, Am. Personnel and Guidance Assn., Mortar Bd., Delta Delta Delta. Democrat. Clubs: DAR, Blue and Gold (Newark). Home: 1604 Riverview Ave Wilmington DE 19806 Office: 800 W 9th St Wilmington DE 19801

GRIFFIN, JOHN I., univ. dean; b. N.Y.C., Oct. 18, 1916; s. John A. and Edith (Bodenstab) G.; A.B. cum laude, Georgetown U., 1934, A.M., 1935, Ph.D., Columbia, 1939; m. Carmela M. Barbuto, Mar. 19, 1966; 1 son, John. Tchr. econs., statistics Bklyn. Coll., 1937-40, Fordham U., 1940-42; statistician U.S. Bur. Labor Statistics, 1945-46; faculty City U. N.Y., Baruch Coll., N.Y.C., 1946-77, prof. statistics, 1966-77, dean grad. studies, 1971-77; dean Sch. Bus., Fairfield (Conn.) U., 1978—. dir. N.Y. Regional Statis. Center, 1966-68; econ. cons. J. Carvel Lange, Inc., 1967-74; dir. N.Y. Statis. Center of N.Y. Clearing House, 1975-77; research asso. Nat. Indsl. Conf. Bd., 1939; faculty St. Louis U., summer 1940; vis. lectr. U. Sydney, Australia, 1961. Mem. economists' adv. com. N.Y.C. Econ. Devel. Adminstrn., 1974-77. Served with M.I., AUS, 1942-45. Fellow Royal Statis. Soc.; mem. Am. Statis. Assn. (mem. council 1965-67, pres. chpt. 1975-77), Nat. Assn. Bus. Economists, Am. Econ. Assn. Author books including The Port of New York, 1959; Statistics, Methods and Application, 1962; (with Jean Namias) Fact Book for New York Metropolitan Region, 1965; Police Training and Performance, 1969, 71. Home: 31 Green Hill Rd North Haven CT 06473 Office: Sch Bus Fairfield U Fairfield CT 06430

GRIFFIN, KATHLEEN MARY, assn. exec.; b. Milw., Oct. 1, 1943; d. Edward P. and Jean E. (Fons) Fleming; B.S. (Scholar), U. Wis., 1965; M.A., Stanford U., 1966; Ph.D., U. Oreg., 1971. Office Vocat. Rehab. trainee Stanford U., 1965-66; Neurol. and Sensory Disease trainee U. Oreg., 1968-71; speech-lang. pathologist, cons. Holiday Center for Crippled Children and U. Oreg. Med. Sch., Portland, 1966-68; dir. speech and audiology dept. Glendale (Calif.) Adventist Med. Center, 1971-74; dir. clinic and hosp. program Am. Speech-Lang.-Hearing Assn., Rockville, Md., 1974-78, dir. research, profl. devel. dept., 1978—; cons., pres. Griffin and Assos. Mem. Am. Speech-Lang.-Hearing Assn., Am. Congress Rehab. Medicine, N.Y. Acad. Sci. Clubs: Altrusa (v.p. Glendale 1973-74, corr. sec. Washington 1975-76, treas 1976-78, v.p. 1978—). Author articles on quality assurance, dysphagia, communicative problems of aged. Home: 3343 Dent Pl NW Washington DC 20007 Office: 10801 Rockville Pike Rockville MD 20852

GRIFFIN, PRISCILLA LORING (MRS. JOHN J. GRIFFIN), wax mfg. co. exec.; b. Winchester, Mass., Apr. 1, 1930; d. John Alden and Madeleine (Libby) Loring; student Pembroke Coll., Brown U., 1947-49, Katherine Gibbs Coll., 1949-50; m. John J. Griffin, Jan. 27, 1951; children—Patricia, Michael, Peter. Sec. to project Mass. Inst. Tech. (now Draper Labs.), 1950-52; adminstrv. asst., asst. treas. Roger A. Reed, Inc., Reading, Mass., 1971-72, pres., treas., 1972—; corporator Reading Savs. Bank, 1977. Chmn., Camp Fire Girls of Reading, 1964-66, mem. state bd., 1966-68; mem. Reading Town Meeting, 1957-68; chmn. League Women Voters, Ipswich, 1969-70; trustee Roger A. Reed, Inc. Profit Sharing and Trust. Mem. Assoc. Industries Mass., Small Bus. Assn. New Eng. Unitarian. Club: Ipswich Bay Yacht. Home: 1 Riverside Dr Ipswich MA 01938 Office: 167 Pleasant St Reading MA 01867

GRIFFIN, THOMAS FRANCIS, JR., cons. engr.; b. Boston, Mar. 7, 1916; s. Thomas Francis and Margaret (Cowan) G.; student Mass. Inst. Tech., 1934-38; B.S., U. Md., 1957; m. Mary Santarelli, 1946 (dec. 1970); m. 2d, Sara Hood Grimm, July 4, 1971; children—Judith Rose, Sonia Mercedes Villalba. Commd. 2d lt. C.E., U.S. Army, 1938, advanced through grades to lt. col., 1959; Prisoner of war, Japan, 1942-45; regional post engr., Kansas City, Mo., 1949-50, assigned to France, 1952-55, Ft. Belvoir, Va., 1955-57, Pakistan, 1957-59, ret., 1960; dir. pub. works, city engr. Alton, Ill., 1960-62, city mgr., 1962-63; dir. pub. works, city engr., Portland, Maine 1963-68; pres. Thomas Griffin Assoc. Co., Portland, 1968—; pres. Griffith Internat. Ltd., Lagos and Calabar, Nigeria. Mem. Maine Environ. Improvement Commn., 1967-70; chmn. Maine Pollution Abatement Task Force, 1969; mem. Maine Bd. Registration for Soil Scientists and Geologists, 1973—; mem. pres.'s council St. Joseph's Coll., Windham, Maine, 1973—. Decorated Purple Heart with 2 oak leaf clusters. Registered profl. engr., Maine, N.H., Ill., Mo. Mem. Nat. Soc. Profl. Engrs. (past state pres.), Maine Assn. Engrs., Maine Charitable

Mechanic Assn., A.A.A.S. Rotarian. Home: 65 Berkeley St Portland ME 04103 Office: 562 Congress St Portland ME 04101

GRIFFIN, THOMAS JOSEPH, JR., coach, ednl. adminstr., city ofcl.; b. Buffalo, Mar. 19, 1928; s. Thomas Joseph and Helen Margaret (O'Brien) G.; B.S., State U. N.Y., 1951, M.S., 1957, D.D., 1972; Ed.D., Edison Coll., 1974; m. Jane Marie Franc, May 1, 1952; children—Jane Marie, Thomas Joseph III. Basketball, baseball and football coach Cuba (N.Y.) Central High Sch., 1952-53; basketball coach, asst. varsity basketball coach State U. N.Y., Buffalo, 1953-54; freshman basketball and varsity baseball coach Cleveland Hill High Sch., Cheektowaga, N.Y., 1954-57, head coach varsity basketball and baseball, 1957-59; head coach, varsity basketball and baseball Cardinal Dougherty High Sch., Buffalo, 1960-66; athletic dir., head coach Bryant and Stratton Bus. Inst., Buffalo, 1966—; commr. City of Buffalo Dept. Parks and Recreation, 1978—. Served with USMC, 1945-47. Named High Sch. Coach of Yr., K.C., 1963, 66; College Coach of Yr., Nat. Little Coll. Athletic Assn., 1974; Citizen of Yr., Fathers Club of Dougherty High Sch., 1963. Mem. Am. Acad. Behavioral Sci., Am. Legion, N.Y. State, Cleveland Hill, Erie County tchrs. assns., Eastern Assn. Inter-Collegiate Football Ofcls., Internat. Assn. Approved Basketball Ofcls., Nat. Assn. Basketball Coaches, Nat. Assn. Collegiate Dirs. of Athletics, NEA, Nat. Jr. Coll. Athletic Assn., N.Y. State Assn. Certified Football Ofcls., State U. Coll. at Buffalo, Thomas A. Edison Coll. alumni assns., Western N.Y. Basketball Coaches Assn. Club: K.C. Contbr. articles to Scholastic Coach, Basketball Clinic, others. Home: 602 S Park Ave Buffalo NY 14210 Office: Commr of Parks City Hall Buffalo NY 14202

GRIFFING, WILLIAM E., scriptwriter, cinematographer, motion picture producer; b. White Plains, N.Y., July 20, 1928; s. Chester E. and Charlotte Blanche (DeHan) G.; student Newark Sch. Fine and Indsl. Arts, 1948; m. Norma Marie Biunno, May 11, 1952 (dec. 1975); 1 son, William Wade. Pres., co-owner Creative Productions, Inc., Orange, N.J., 1953—. Mem. Am. Med. Writers Assn., Am. Mktg. Assn., Pharm. Advt. Club, N.J. Art Dirs. Club, Am. Film Inst. Author: Preparation, Production and Presentation of 16mm Films, 1976. Home: 32 MacLeod Ln Bloomfield NJ 07003 Office: 200 Main St Orange NJ 07050

GRIFFIS, JOHN WILLIAM, JR., lawyer; b. Winston-Salem, N.C., June 26, 1941; s. John William and Kathryn Fidelia (Sexton) G.; B.A., Wake Forest U., 1965, J.D., 1967; LL.M., N.Y. U., 1969. Admitted to N.C. bar, 1967, N.Y. bar, 1969; individual practice law, Denton and Lexington, N.C., 1967-68; asso. firm Rogers, Hoge & Hills, N.Y.C., 1969-74; corp. counsel, sec. Gotaas-Larsen Shipping Corp., N.Y.C. and Oslo, 1974—. Trustee N.C. Soc. N.Y. Served with U.S. Army, 1961-62. Mem. N.Y.C. (com. on admiralty 1978—), Am. bar assns., Maritime Law Assn. U.S. (com. on LNG transp. 1978—). Mem. Ch. of Christ (adminstrv. bd., fin. com.). Clubs: Univ., Amateur Comedy, Murray Hill Racquet. Home: 110 E 36th St New York City NY 10016 Office: 1114 Ave of Americas New York City NY 10036

GRIFFITH, CARL H., JR., realtor; b. Russellton, Pa., May 17, 1936; s. Carl H. and Mary (Carroll) G.; children—David, Kimberly. Partner, Century 21 Schmidt & Griffith Real Estate, Coraopolis, Pa., 1971—. Served with AUS, 1957-59. Mem. Nat. Assn. Realtors, Pitts. Bd. Realtors. Republican. Presbyterian. Club: Kiwanis. Home: 1202 College Park Dr Coraopolis PA 15108 Office: 914 Narrows Run Rd Coraopolis PA 15108

GRIFFITH, EMLYN IRVING, lawyer; b. Utica, N.Y., May 13, 1923; s. William Andrew and Maud (Charles) G.; A.B., Colgate U., 1942; J.D., Cornell U., 1950; m. Mary Louise Kilpatrick, Aug. 13, 1946; children—William Lewis, James Reid. Admitted to N.Y. bar, 1950, U.S. Supreme Ct. bar, 1954; practiced in Lockport, N.Y., 1950-52, Rome, N.Y., 1952—; atty. for various twps. and sch. dists., 1956—. Mem. N.Y. State Bd. Regents, 1973—, N.Y. State Commn. for Postsecondary Edn., 1973—; pres.-elect Nat. Assn. State Bds. Edn., 1978—; mem. Forum Ednl. Orgn. Leaders, 1978—; mem. Colgate U. Nat. Council, 1974—; pres. Colgate U. Alumni Interfraternity Council, 1970-73; pres. Presbyterian Home for Central N.Y., 1964-67, Fynmere Home for Ret. Ministers, 1969-72; pres., trustee Rome Coll. Found., 1969-72; chmn. State Conf. on Professions, 1975-77; mem. N.Y. State Gov.'s Commn. on Libraries, 1976—; pres., trustee Community Concerts Assn., 1955-63. Served with USAAF, 1942-46. Recipient Alumni award for distinguished service Colgate U., 1975. Fellow Am. Bar Found.; mem. N.Y. State, Oneida County (pres. 1976-78) bar founds., Am. (pub. edn. com. 1974—), N.Y. State (ho. of dels. 1974-77), Oneida County (pres. 1974-75) bar assns., Nat. Conf. Bar Pres.'s, State Conf. County Bar Officers (chmn. 1975-78), Am. Judicature Soc., Rome Area C. of C. (pres. 1973-74, dir. 1960-74), Newcomen Soc. Am., St. David's Soc. N.Y., Nat. Soc. Lit. and the Arts, Selden Soc. (Eng.), Phi Gamma Delta (internat. trustee 1978—). Presbyterian (nat. bd. pensions 1966-72; del. gen. assembly; elder, past pres. bd. trustees). Clubs: Rome (N.Y.); Ft. Orange (Albany); Colgate (N.Y.C.). Author: The Public Comes First in Professional Discipline, 1976; Is Now the Time, 1977; Advertising of Professional Services is Here to Stay, 1978; contbr. articles to legal, edn. and library publs. Home: Golf Course Rd Rome NY 13440 Office: Profl Bldg 225 N Washington St Rome NY 13440

GRIFFITH, LAWRENCE STACEY CAMERON, cardiologist; b. Washington, Sept. 16, 1937; s. Ernest Stacey and Margaret Dyckman (Davenport) G.; B.A., Haverford Coll., 1959; M.D. with honors, U. Rochester, 1963; m. Anne Gorman Young, June 20, 1959; children—Lawrence, John, Melinda, Gordon. Intern in medicine and surgery Strong Meml. Hosp., Rochester, N.Y., 1963-64, asst. resident in surgery, 1964-65, asst. and asso. resident in medicine, 1967-69; research fellow in cardiology Johns Hopkins U., 1969-71; research asso. NIH, Bethesda, Md., 1965-67; asst. prof. medicine Johns Hopkins U., Balt., 1971-76, asst. prof. radiology, 1974—, asso. prof. medicine, 1976—. Bd. dirs. Andrus Children's Home, Yonkers, N.Y., 1971—, chmn., pres., 1977—; bd. dirs. John E. Andrus Meml. Home for Aged, Hastings-on-Hudson, N.Y., 1974—; chmn. adv. bd. Balt. Pastoral Counseling Service, 1974—; bd. dirs. Surdana Found., N.Y.C., 1977—. Served with USPHS, 1965-67. Clayton scholar, 1971-76; McClure research fellow, 1977-79. Diplomate Am. Bd. Internal Medicine, Nat. Bd. Med. Examiners. Fellow A.C.P., Council Clin. Cardiology of Am. Heart Assn., Am. Coll. Cardiology; mem. Alpha Omega Alpha. Democrat. Methodist. Contbr. articles to profl. jours. Home: 2211 Forest Ridge Rd Timonium MD 21093 Office: Dept Medicine Johns Hopkins Hosp Baltimore MD 21205

GRIFFITH, MILDRED SULLIVAN (MRS. WILLIAM A. GRIFFITH), educator; b. Cambridge, Mass., Aug. 30, 1907; d. Francis M. and Delcina A. (Braithwaite) Sullivan; B.A. in Oratory, Staley Coll., 1954, M.A., 1956, D.A., 1958; m. William A. Griffith, Mar. 20, 1930. Clerical asst. to head clk., 1925-58; adminstrv. asst. to chief probation officer 3rd Dist. Ct. Eastern Middlesex, East Cambridge, Mass., 1959-63; founder Griffith Sch. Speech, Somerville Mass., 1963—; co-dir. Oral Expression, Cambridge, 1958-63. Recipient Acad. key Staley Coll., 1956. Mem. Inst. Gen. Semantics, Speech Assn. Eastern States, Speech Communication Assn., Boston City Fedn. Orgns., Internat. Platform Assn. Club: Zonta (Medford, Mass.). Home: 21 Locke St Winchester MA 01890 Office: 110 Bristol Rd Somerville MA 02144

GRIFFITH, WILLIAM RUSSELL, dentist; b. Fountain Hill, Pa., June 30, 1930; s. Arthur James and Beatrice Maud (Jones) G.; student Pa. State U., 1948-52; D.D.S., Temple U., 1955; m. Jean Elizabeth Yoder, Aug. 24, 1952; children—Brian, Mark, Drew, Todd. Individual practice dentistry, Washington, N.J., 1959—. Com. chmn. George Washington council Boy Scouts Am., 1967-69; cadre L.D. Pankey Inst., Miami, Fla. Served with Dental Corps, USAF, 1955-59. Mem. ADA, Tri-County, Lehigh Valley dental socs., Pankey Mann Schuyler Study Group, Temple U. Alumni Soc., Omicron Kappa Upsilon, Psi Omega. Methodist (chmn. council on ministries and adminstrv. bd. 1968-72). Clubs: Masons, Shriners. Home: Jonestown Rd Oxford NJ 07863 Office: 113 Belvidere Ave Washington NJ 07882

GRIFFITHS, DONALD WESLEY, JR., environ. horticulturist; b. Norristown, Pa., Nov. 11, 1926; s. Donald Wesley and Frances Allerton (Gleason) G.; B.S., Pa. State U., 1950; M.S., Hofstra U., 1960; postgrad. N.Y. U., 1961-62; m. Grace Detwiler, Dec. 13, 1945; children—Marsha Griffiths Sattenspiel, Pamela Griffiths Costanzo. Landscape architect, supr. Henkels & McCoy, Phila., 1950-52; mgr. landscape design and constrn. Wilkie Bros., Cedars, Pa., 1952-53; retail sales mgr. Del-Mar-Va Nursery, Lincoln, Del., 1953; landscape architect, supr. Richard Schwoebel Co., Ardmore, Pa., 1954-56; prof. horticulture State U. N.Y., Farmingdale, 1956—; mem. hort. adv. com. Nassau Bd. Coop. Ednl. Services. Served with USCGR, 1944-46. Mem. Am. Soc. Landscape Architects, AAUP, N.Y. State Assn. Jr. Colls., Am. Hort. Soc., Am. Soc. Hort. Sci., L.I. Nurserymen's Assn. (adv. mem.) L.I. Golf Course Supts. Assn. (hon.), Am. Assn. Nurserymen (educator), Pa. Turfgrass Council, N.J., N.Y. turfgrass assns., Pa. State U. Alumni Assn. Home: Sayville NY 11782 Office: State Univ Farmingdale NY 11735

GRIGLAK, MARTIN SAMUEL, union ofcl.; b. Pitts., Jan. 13, 1927; s. Martin A. and Fannie R. (Nieberg) G.; student Pa. State U., 1946-47, Waynesburg Coll., 1947-48; m. Rita J. Pernatozzi, Nov. 24, 1949; children—Nancy Ann, Martin J., James R., Janet Lee. Telephone serviceman Bell of Pa., Connellsville, 1950-60; various positions Telephone Workers Pa., 1952—, pres. Western Pa., 1960-76, mem. exec. bd., 1960—; exec. sec. Fedn. Telephone Workers, 1962-66; arbitrator, lectr. in field. Mem. profl. staffs of several Presd. candidates; active gubernatorial and U.S. Senate campaigns; chmn. Connellsville Democratic party, 1969—; pres. bd. trustees Connellsville State Gen. Hosp., 1971—; mem. Planning and Zoning Commn. of Fayette County, 1960-64. Served with USNR, 1944-46. Roman Catholic. Club: K.C. Contbr. articles to labor publs. Home: 206 S 9th St Connellsville PA 15425 Office: 505 Troutman Bldg Connellsville PA 15425

GRIGOROFF, LOUIS, real estate corp. exec.; b. Niagara Falls, Ont., Can., Nov. 19, 1932; s. Grigor Lambeff and Marika (Tsvetcoff) G.; diploma Mexico City Coll., 1957; m. Lidia Cass-Ramirez, June 14, 1958; children—Michael George, Brenda Yvonne. With Norton Abrasives Co., Chippawa, Ont., 1951-55; night editor Mexico City Daily News, 1956-58; supplementary editor, staff writer Niagara Falls Evening Rev. 1958-66, writer column Niagara Outdoors, 1962-66; gen. mgr. N.P.H.B. Land Devels., Ltd., St. Catharines, Ont., 1967-71; sec.-mgr., sec.-treas., bd. dirs. Niagara Peninsula Home Builders Assn., 1967-70; devel. dir. Paramount Properties, St. Catharines, 1971-74; pres. Grigoroff Mgmt. Services Inc., 1975—. Chmn., Mayors Com. on Housing Niagara Falls, 1967-73; past pres. Welland County br. Canadian Mental Health Assn.; mem. Niagara Falls Planning Bd., 1972-75. Served to lt. Royal Canadian Arty. 1960-65. Recipient B.F. Goodrich award Western Ont. Newspaper Awards, 1962. Mem. Internat. Platform Assn., Nat. Geog. Soc., Nat. Travel Club, C. of C. (chmn. bus. and indsl. growth com.). Clubs: Niagara Falls, St. Catharines Golf and Country, Kiwanis. Home: 4110 Glenayr Ave Niagara Falls ON Canada Office: 21 Elizabeth St St Catharines ON Canada

GRILLO, FRANK ROY, investment co. exec., educator; b. Bklyn., July 31, 1930; s. Roy and Carmela M'Panell; B.B.A., Coll. City N.Y., 1954, M.B.A., 1956; LL.B., N.Y. Law Sch., 1960, J.D., 1969, LL.M., 1964, S.J.D., 1966; m. Stella Ciraulo, Feb. 17, 1958; children—Marian, Rose, Roy, Camille. With corporate fin. depts. various investment cos., N.Y.C., 1958-67; adj. prof. econs. and law Coll. City N.Y., 1965-68; asst. prof. econs., law, fin. and income tax Bklyn. Coll., 1968-71; asst. commr. for adminstrn. and mgmt. planning N.Y.C. Taxi and Limousine Commn., 1971-72; pres. M.H. Walter & Co. Inc., N.Y.C., 1972—; adj. prof. law, econs. and mktg. Medgar Evans Coll., Bklyn., 1973—; adj. prof. fin. Pace U.; project mgr., asst. to 1st dep. commr. N.Y.C. Econ. Devel. Adminstrn., Dept. Ports and Terminals, 1974-75; dir. Astrosystems Internat. Inc., Electro-Ed Resources, Inc. Active Boy Scouts Am.; mem. parish council Holy Family Ch., Queens, N.Y.; mem. exec. com. Flushing (N.Y.) Pastoral Council, Catholic-Jewish Community Relations Assn., Flushing; fed. appeal agt. SSS, Queens. Recipient Am. Jurisprudence awards, 1963. Mem. N.Y. Soc. Fin. Analysts, N.Y. Soc. Securities Analysts, Nat. Assn. Securities Dealers, Assn. Investment Bankers, Assn. Investment Brokers. Democrat. Contbr. articles in field to profl. jours. Home: 2555 College Point Blvd College Point NY 11356

GRIMES, MARY CATHERINE, ret. naval officer, former nursing orgn. exec.; b. N.Y.C.; d. Patrick A. and Mary (Foley) Grimes; R.N., Manhattan State Hosp. Sch. Nursing, 1937; B.S., N.Y. U., 1947, M.A., 1948. Charge nurse Coney Island Hosp., Bklyn., 1938-40; teaching supr. Fordham Hosp. Sch. Nursing, Bronx, N.Y., 1941-42; commd. ensign USN, 1942, advanced through grades to comdr., 1965; charge nurse U.S. Naval Hosp., Charleston, S.C., 1942-43; instr. Hosp. Corps Sch., Bainbridge, Md., 1943-44; flight nurse Air Evacuation VRE-Squadron, Pacific, 1945, VR-1 Squadron Naval Air Sta., Patuxent River, Md., 1948-52; liaison officer Sch. Aviation Medicine, Randolph Field, Tex., Gunter AFB, Montgomery, Ala., surg. supr. St. Albans Naval Hosp., 1953; instr. Sch. Aviation Medicine, Pensacola, Fla., 1954; ednl. coordinator U.S. Naval Hosp., Bethesda, Md., asst. chief nursing service, 1955-58; chief nursing service U.S. Naval Hosp., Annapolis, Md., 1958-59; head Nurse Corps Res. liaison br. Nursing Div., Bur. Medicine and Surgery, Navy Dept., Washington, 1959-65; ret., 1965; dir. dept. practical nursing programs Nat. League Nursing, N.Y.C., 1965-68, dir. hosp. and related instnl. nursing services, 1968-70. Recipient certificate of merit for distinguished and outstanding service to Med. Dept. Navy, 1965. Mem. D.C. (past 1st v.p.) Nurses Assn., Assn. Mil. Surgeons (1st chmn. Nurse Corps sect.), Aerospace Med. Assn. (v.p. 1969), N.Y. U. Sch. Edn. Alumni, Kappa Delta Pi, Pi Lambda Theta. Address: 180 Cabrini Blvd New York City NY 10033

GRIMES, PETER JOSEPH, criminal justice specialist, educator; b. Wantagh, N.Y., Mar. 4, 1942; s. Thomas Francis and Mary (Maher) G.; B.A., Adelphi U., 1969; M.A., State U. N.Y., Stonybrook, 1972; m. Myra R. Maken, Mar. 21, 1967; children—Michael Gary, Kerry Elizabeth. Counselor, Nassau Community Coll., Garden City, N.Y., 1966-69, dir. spl. programs, 1969-71, prof., chmn., dept. criminal justice, 1971—; cons. external degree program, developer coll. proficiency exams. criminal justice and investigation, N.Y. Edn. Dept.; cons. Nassau County (N.Y) Police Dept. Mem. Internat. Assn. Chiefs Police, Am. Acad. Profl. Law Enforcement (dir.), N.Y. Criminal Justice Educators Assn. Home: 1776 Cornelius Ave Wantagh NY 11793 Office: Nassau Community Coll Stewart Ave Garden City NY 11530

GRIMM, BEN EMMET, librarian; b. Jersey City, Sept. 27, 1924; s. Benjamin Harrison and Eunice Blanche (Whitenack) G.; B.A., Washington and Lee U., 1949; M.S., Columbia U., 1950; m. Jean Kay Bohrer, Aug. 19, 1950; children—Jeffrey, Kevin, Mark, Wendy. Librarian youth services Detroit Pub. Library, 1950-52; sr. librarian Fair Lawn (N.J.) Pub. Library, 1952-54; reference and lending librarian Montclair (N.J.) Pub. Library, 1955-56, asst. dir., 1956-61; dir. Belleville (N.J.) Pub. Library, 1961-72; dir. Jersey City Pub. Library, 1973—; cons. library bldgs. services and adminstrn., 1966—; mng. editor Library Trustee Newsletter, 1978—. Chmn., Hudson County Am. Revolution Bicentennial Celebration Com., 1973-74, vice chmn., 1975-76; chmn. Hudson County Audio-Visual Aids Commn., 1975—. Served with USAAF, 1942-45. Decorated D.F.C., Air medal with oak leaf clusters; recipient Better Belleville award, 1968. Mem. Am., N.J. (pres. 1968-69) library assns. Club: Rotary. Home: 76 Sherman Ave Glen Ridge NJ 07028 Office: 472 Jersey Ave Jersey City NJ 07302

GRIMM, JAY VAUGHN, investment banker; b. Sabetha, Kans., Jan. 28, 1926; s. Benjamin W. and Emma Marie (Hunzeker) G.; B.A., Kans. U., 1949; LL.B., Yale U., 1952; m. Teresa McGarry, July 29, 1956; children—Katherine, Cordelia, Jay Vaughn. Admitted to N.Y. Bar, 1953; asso. firm Chadbourne, Parke, Whiteside, Wolff & Brophy, N.Y.C., 1952-56; pres. Grimm & Davis, Inc., N.Y.C., 1962—. Served with USN, 1944-45. Decorated Purple Heart; chartered fin. analyst. Mem. Kans. U. Alumni Assn. (regional v.p. 1973-76), Phi Beta Kappa. Democrat. Episcopalian. Clubs: Downtown, Yale (N.Y.C.). Home: 950 Park Ave New York City NY 10028 Office: 76 Beaver St New York City NY 10005

GRIMM, RALPH EMANUEL, electronics co. exec.; b. Stanley, Va., Aug. 3, 1922; s. William and Ethel N. (Kite) G.; student Capitol Radio Engring. Inst., 1939-40; m. Eugenia Kielbasa, Mar. 20, 1947; 1 son, Ralph E. Elec. engr. Md. Electronics Co., College Park, 1946-47; chief engr. Clarke Instrument Corp., Silver Spring, Md., 1947-50, Nems-Clarke Co., Silver Spring, 1950-58; dir. engring. Vitro Electronics Co., Silver Spring, 1958-60; exec. v.p., dir. Communication Electronics, Inc., Bethesda, Md., 1960-64, v.p., 1964, pres., chmn. bd., 1965-68; v.p., div. mgr. Watkins-Johnson Co., Gaithersburg, Md., 1968-74, v.p. engring., 1974-75; chmn. bd., pres. R.E. Grimm Co., Gaithersburg, 1975—. Served with USCG, 1943-46. Mem. IEEE, Soc. Photog. Scientists and Engrs., Soc. Motion Picture and TV Engrs., Assn. Old Crows, Def. Orientation Conf. Assn. Patentee. Home: 9330 W Parkhill Dr Bethesda MD 20014 Office: 16000 Industrial Dr Gaithersburg MD 20760

GRIMMETT, ROBIN, univ. adminstr.; b. Lakewood, Ohio, Jan. 21, 1947; d. Robert John and Mary Laurel (Ernstmeyer) Rudd; B.S., Kent (Ohio) State U., 1969, M.A. (grad. fellow), 1972; m. Richard Fieldon Grimmett, Aug. 9, 1969. Asst. to v.p. student affairs Kent State U., 1970-74; asst. dir. commuter affairs U. Md., College Park, 1974-75, asst. dir. campus activities, 1975—; asst. dir. Nat. Clearinghouse for Commuter Students, 1974-76. Recipient Pierce Meml. award Kent State U., 1969; named Outstanding Young Career Woman, College Park, 1975. Mem. Assn. Coll. Personnel Adminstrs., Am. Personnel and Guidance Assn., Nat. Assn. Student Personnel Adminstrs., Phi Delta Kappa. Episcopalian. Home: 1131 University Blvd W #1903 Silver Spring MD 20902 Office: 1191 Student Union U Md College Park MD 20742

GRIMSHAW, HERBERT JAMES, shopping center mgr.; b. Grand Forks, N.D., Jan. 6, 1918; s. Herbert Abbott and Alice Catherine (McCanna) G.; student St. Thomas Coll., 1935-40, U. Minn., 1937, U. Omaha, 1954, Fairleigh-Dickenson U., 1965-68, State U. N.Y. at Albany, 1969-70, Russell Sage U., 1970-71; B.S., Air Force Inst. Tech., 1959; m. Margarette Jeanette Hauk, Nov. 20, 1942; children—Karen Ann Grimshaw Berner, Herbert James II, Gary George. Commd. 2d lt. USAF, 1942, advanced through grades to col., 1965; ret., 1965; assigned hdqrs. 3d Air Div., 1949-51, 3d Air Force, 1951-52, SAC, Omaha, 1952-55, Air Materiel Forces European area (Germany), 1955-58, Air Materiel Command, Dayton, Ohio, 1958-62, Def. Electronic Supply Center, Def. Supply Agency, 1962-65, ret., 1965; mgr. systems devel. RCA, 1965; v.p. Northeastern Indsl. Park and 16 related corps., Guilderland, N.Y., 1969-72; gen. mgr. Stanford Assos., Schenectady, 1972—; lectr. Air Force Inst. Tech., 1959-65, Dept. Defense Inst., 1965, Russell Sage U., 1972—, U. Ga. Center Advanced Edn., 1974. Scout counselor Internat. Council Boy Scouting Europe, 1955-58; rep. of archbishop Cin. to Boy Scouting, 1958-65; 1st trustee St. Thomas parish Convent Sta., N.J., 1965-68; bd. dirs., chmn. from Schenectady County to Capital Dist. Consumer Relations Bur., 1972-77, gen. chmn., 1978. Mem. Reserve Officers Assn., Retired Officers Assn., Schenectady County C. of C. (dir., v.p. 1972—). Roman Catholic. Club: Wright Patterson AFB Officer's, Kountry Kousins Internat. Square Dance (Germany). Home: 12 Heldervue St Slingerlands NY 12159 Office: 440 Mohawk Mall Balltown Rd Schenectady NY 12304

GRIMSTED, PATRICIA KENNEDY, historian, educator; b. Elkins, W.Va., Oct. 31, 1935; d. John A. and Ellen Bruce (Lee) Kennedy; student U. Lausanne (Switzerland), 1952-53, Swarthmore Coll., 1953-55; B.A. with honors, U. Calif., Berkeley, 1957, M.A., 1959, Ph.D., 1964; m. David A. Grimsted, July 13, 1960 (div. 1974); children—Jennifer Sea, Rolf Davidson, Almon John. Teaching asst. dept. history U. Calif., Berkeley, 1958-60, research asst. in Slavic studies, 1960-62; lectr. dept. history Bucknell U., Lewisburg, Pa., 1965-67; research asso. Russian Research Center, Harvard U., Cambridge, Mass., 1964, 67-68, research asso. Ukrainian Research Inst. and Russian Research Center, 1974—; sr. fellow Russian Inst., Columbia U., N.Y.C., 1969-70, research asso., 1970-74; lectr. in history U. Coll., U. Md., 1968-70; asso. prof. dept. history Am. U., Washington, 1970-71, adj. prof., 1971-72; vis. exchange prof. Inst. History, Acad. Scis. USSR, summer 1970, 1973, 76, 78; vis. exchange research prof. U. Warsaw (Poland), 1977, 79; adviser U.S./USSR archival and acad. exchanges, 1969—, U.S. Nat. Archives, Dept. State, 1969—. Internat. Research and Exchanges Bd. grantee, 1970, 73, 76, 77, 78, 79; Am. Council Learned Socs. grantee, 1969, 72, Nat. Endowment for Humanities grantee, 1971-73, 74, 75-78, 78—; Radcliffe Inst. fellow, 1967-69. Mem. Am. Hist. Assn., Soc. Am. Archivists (com. on internat. archival affairs 1971—), Internat. Council Archives, Am. Assn. Advancement of Slavic Studies. Author: The Foreign Ministers of Alexander I: Political Attitudes and the Conduct of Russian Diplomacy, 1801-1825, 1969; Archives and Manuscript Repositories in the USSR: Moscow and Leningrad (Waldo G. Leland prize award 1973), 1972, supplement, 1976; Archives and Manuscript Repositories in the USSR: Estonia, Latvia, Lithuania, and Belorussia, 1979; contbr. articles and book revs. on Russian history and Soviet archives to scholarly jours.; editor microfiche reprint collection of reference materials and finding aids for Soviet archives. Home: 39 Walker St Cambridge MA 02138 Office:

Harvard Ukrainian Research Inst 1583 Massachusetts Ave Cambridge MA 02138

GRINBERG, RAUL, physician, scientist; b. Buenos Aires, Argentina, Aug. 15, 1922; s. David and Ana (Tabachnickoff) G.; M.D., U. Buenos Aires, 1946; m. Claire Cantor, Aug. 16, 1965; children—George, Ricardo, Stephen, Diego, Andrew; came to U.S., 1958, naturalized, 1967. Intern, Municipal Office Pub. Welfare, Buenos Aires, 1944-46; resident dept. exptl. tumorgenesis Roffo Inst. Exptl. Medicine, Buenos Aires, 1946-50, dept. internal medicine Rivadavia Hosp. Teaching Hosp., U. Buenos Aires, 1950-52; active staff internal medicine and endocrinology Rivadia Hosp., 1952-58; research asso. Columbia Coll. Physicians and Surgeons-Presbyn. Hosp., N.Y.C., 1958-61; sr. internist dept. breast surgery Roswell Park Meml. Inst., Buffalo, 1961-65; vis. prof. endocrinology Cornell U., Ithaca, N.Y., 1966-68; practice internal medicine, endocrinology, metabolic diseases, cancer, Binghamton, N.Y., 1966—; teaching resident Rivadavia Hosp., 1954-58, Roswell Park Meml. Inst., 1961-65, Wilson Meml. Hosp., Binghamton, 1968—. Active Am. Cancer Soc., 1965—. Fellow Am. Geriatrics Assn., Clin. Soc. N.Y. Diabetes Assn., A.C.P.; mem. Endocrine Soc., AMA, Am. Assn. Cancer Research, AAAS, Am. Soc. Clin. Oncology, N.Y. Soc. Internal Medicine, N.Y. Acad. Scis., Buffalo, Binghamton acads. medicine, Broome County Med. Soc. Contbr. articles to profl. jours. Home: 8 Brevity Ct Binghamton NY 13905 Office: 86-88 Walnut St Binghamton NY 13905

GRINDLE, ROGER LEE, historian; b. Rockland, Maine, June 10, 1936; s. Edward Webster and Marguerite Belle (Wincapaw) G.; B.S., U. Maine, Farmington, 1959; M.A., U. Maine, Orono, 1962, Ph.D., 1971; m. Anita Stewart, Aug. 23, 1959; children—Richard Stewart, Nathan Patrick. Asso. instr., Ft. Kent (Maine) State Coll., 1962-64, instr., 1965-66, asst. prof., 1967; asso. prof. history, U. Maine, Ft. Kent, 1968-70, prof., 1971—; Title VII bd. dirs. Commn. mem. Maine Mus. Commn., 1976—. Recipient award of merit Am. Assn. State and Local History, 1978. Mem. Am. Hist. Assn., Orgn. Am. Historians, AAUP, Maine Academic Historians, Maine Hist. Soc. (publs. com.), Maine League Hist. Socs. and Mus. (trustee 1972—), Maine Mus. Commn. Democrat. Baptist. Author: Quarry and Kiln: A History of the Maine Lime Industry, 1971; Tombstones and Paving Blocks: The History of the Maine Granite Industry, 1977. Home: 12 Pleasant St Fort Kent ME 04743 Office: Univ Maine Fort Kent Pleasant St Fort Kent ME 04743

GRINNELL, GARY SHAWN, recreation mgr.; b. Rochester, N.Y., Feb. 19, 1952; s. Robert Earl and Ruth Marie (Indlekofer) G.; B.A., State U. Coll., Brockport, 1974; m. Janice Bartholomay, Mar. 13, 1976. With Craig Hill Country Club, Brockport, N.Y., 1967-74, 75—, mgr., 1975—; asst. mgr. Royal Scot Steak House, Irondequoit, N.Y., 1974-75. Mem. Club Mgrs. Assn. Am. (dir. N.Y. State, v.p.). Democrat. Roman Catholic. Home: 132 Andiron Ln Rochester NY 14612 Office: 2879 Clarkson Parma Town Line Rd Brockport NY 14420

GRINOCH, PAUL, physicist-engr.; b. N.Y.C., Aug. 24, 1922; s. Naphtal and Bertha (Goren) G.; evening student Coll. City N.Y., 1938-41, Cooper Union, 1941-43; B.S., N.Y. U., 1948, postgrad., 1948-57; m. Etelle Elia, Feb. 2, 1951 (div. Apr. 1969); 1 dau., Eve-Michele. Group leader nuclear weapons effects group Materiel Lab., N.Y. Naval Shipyard, Bklyn., 1948-53; scientist theoretical sect. W. Kidde Nuclear Labs., Garden City, N.Y., 1953-56; head power reactors core physics and theoretical groups Am. Machine & Foundry Corp., Greenwich, Conn., 1956-58; staff scientist Grumman Aerospace Corp., Bethpage, N.Y., 1958-60, dir. nuclear and radiation physics research 1960-73, spl. asst. to corp. dir. research, 1973—. Served with AUS, 1943-46. Mem. Am. Phys. Soc., Am. Nuclear Soc., A.A.A.S., I.E.E.E., Tech. Group on Nuclear Sci. Home: 3 Birchwood Ct Apt 5K Mineola NY 11501 Office: Research Dept Plant 35 Grumman Aerospace Corp Bethpage NY 11714

GRIPALDI, BENEDICT VICTOR, assn. exec.; b. N.Y.C., Nov. 3, 1920; s. Victor and Julia (Cracolici) G.; student Southwestern U., 1943, Rutgers U. at Newark, 1945-47, Armed Forces Inst., India, 1944; m. Pauline Bennett, Jan. 27, 1952; 1 son, Peter Victor. Specialist Office Dependency Benefits Civil Service, Newark, 1945; with personnel dept. Edn. Tng. Sect. VA, Newark, 1946; owner, dir. adminstrn. Park Beauty Sch., Newark, 1947-70; exec. dir. Nat. Assn. Cosmetology Schs., Boonton, N.J., 1967—. Served with AUS, 1942-45; CBI. Mem. N.J. Beauty Sch. Owners Assn. (pres. 1966-68), Am., N.J., N.Y. socs. assn. execs., Am. Inst. Parliamentarians. Lion (pres. Host Club 1962, dir. 1970—; zone chmn. 1968; dep. gov. region 2 dist. 16-E 1970), Elk, K.C. (4 deg.). Editor: Assn. News Letter, monthly 1967—, Assn. Conv. Program Jour., ann. 1967—. Home: 9 Sunset Trail Indian Lake Denville NJ 07834 Office: 808 Main St Boonton NJ 07005

GRISWOLD, GEORGE, communications exec.; b. N.Y.C., Mar. 5, 1919; s. George and Isabel (Bridgman) G.; student Ecole des Beaux Arts, Fontainebleau, France, 1939; B.A., Yale U., 1941; postgrad. N.Y. U., 1947; m. Tracy Haight, May 15, 1942; children—Tracy Griswold Glass, Mariana Van Rensselaer Griswold Geer, Alice Bradford Griswold Stetson. Editor, Fairchild Publs., N.Y.C., 1945-46; pub. relations, operating positions long lines dept. AT&T, 1946-49, pub. relations exec., N.Y.C., 1962—; pres. Litchfield Distbrs., Inc. (Conn.), 1949-52; exec. Newsweek mag., N.Y.C., 1951-55; exec. dir. pub. relations and publs. div. Bell Telephone Labs., Inc., N.Y., N.J., 1955-62; tchr. Fairleigh Dickinson U. Grad. Sch., 1961. Pres. Norfolk (Conn.) Library. Served to comdr. USNR, 1941-45. Mem. Pub. Relations Soc. Am., Nat. Assn. Sci. Writers, AAAS, Am. Med. Writers Assn., Overseas Press Club Am., N.Y. C. of C., S.R., Soc. Mayflower Descs., Soc. Colonial Wars, Huguenot Soc. Am. Clubs: Yale (N.Y.C.); Litchfield Country; Doolittle Lake (Norfolk). Home: Chestnut Hill Litchfield CT 06759 also 245 E 63d St New York City NY 10021 Office: 195 Broadway New York City NY 10007

GRISWOLD, RAYMOND JAMES, computer co. exec.; b. Rochester, N.Y., Oct. 18, 1946; s. Augustus Wharton and Janice Ellen (Burns) G.; B.S., Clarkson Coll. Tech., 1968; postgrad. U. Paris, 1968-69. Editorial asst. Rochester Democrat and Chronicle, 1969-70; property mgr. Assn. for the Blind, Rochester, N.Y., 1970-72; production mgr. XCS Inc., Rochester, 1972-74, sales mgr., 1974-77, v.p. sales, 1977—. Mem. Nat. Micrographic Assn. (exec. com. West N.Y. chpt.), Assn. Record Mgrs. and Adminstrs. Roman Catholic. Home: 720 Park Ave Rochester NY 14607 Office: 65 Broad St Rochester NY 14614

GROCKI, JOHN JAMES, mgmt. cons. co. exec.; b. Chicopee, Mass., July 6, 1941; s. John Joseph and Marcella Florence (Weldon) G.; B.S., Worcester Poly. Inst., 1962; M.S., Calif. Inst. Tech., 1964; M.B.A., Stanford U., 1965; m. Judith Ann Dixon, June 20, 1964; children—Cheryl Ann, Lisa Marie, Jennifer Ellen. Mgr. market devel. chem. Penn Central Transp. Co., Phila., 1969-71, acting mgr. market devel. foods, 1970-71; gen. mgr. mktg. and indsl. devel. Central R.R. Co. N.J., Newark, 1971-73; v.p., mgr. indsl. parks I. Heller Constrn. Co., Edison, N.J., 1973-75; con. Gellman Research Assos., Inc., Jenkintown, Pa., 1973-75, v.p., 1975—; dir. Dover and Rockaway Ry. NSF fellow, 1962-63; recipient Saulsbury Chemistry award, 1962. Mem. Am. Railroad Devel. Assn., N.J. Indsl. Devel. Assn., Rail System and Mgmt. Assn., Nat. Assn. Indsl. Parks, Early Am. Soc., Sigma Xi. Contbr. articles to profl. jours. Home: 1696 Yarnall Rd Pottstown PA 19464 Office: 100 West Ave Jenkintown PA 19046

GRODBERG, MARCUS GORDON, pharm. co. exec.; b. Worcester, Mass., Jan. 27, 1923; s. Isaac and Rosalie (Hirsch) G.; A.B., Clark U., 1944; M.S., U. Ill., 1948; m. Shirley Florence Merkle, Apr. 15, 1951; children—Joel David, Kim Gordon, Jeremy Daniel. Jr. research chemist Schenley Labs., Inc., Lawrenceburg, Ind., 1944-47; research and devel. chemist Marine Products Co., Boston, 1948-50, Brewer & Co., Inc., Worcester, 1950-55; tech. dir. Gray Pharm. Co., Inc., Newton, Mass., 1955-58; dir. research and devel. Davies Rose Hoyt pharm. div. Kendall Co. (now Hoyt Labs. div. Colgate-Palmolive Co.), Needham, Mass., 1958—. Mem. Internat. Assn. for Dental Research, Am. Soc. Dentistry for Children, Orthopedic Research Soc., Am. Pharm. Assn., ADA, AAAS, Acad. Pharm. Scis. Patentee in field. Home: 111 Hyde St Newton MA 02161 Office: 633 Highland Ave Needham MA 02194

GRODEN, GERALD, psychologist; b. Cambridge, Mass., Apr. 11, 1931; s. Eugene and Ruth (Patten) G.; A.B., U. Vt., 1959; M.A., Purdue U., 1960, Ph.D., 1963; m. June Handwerger, Mar. 25, 1975; 1 son, John. Instr., then asst. prof. dept. neurology Ind. U. Med. Sch., Indpls., 1963-66, asso. faculty mem. dept. psychology, 1964-66, U. R.I. extension, Providence, 1966—, clin. asso. prof., Kingston, 1969-71; dir. psychology dept. R.I. Hosp. Child Devel. Center, Providence, 1966-78; dir. Behavioral Devel. Center, Providence, 1976—; cons. in field; bd. dirs. Sophia Little Home, R.I. Protective and Advocacy System, Providence, 1975-77. Served with USNR, 1952-54. State of R.I. grantee, 1972. Mem. AAAS, Am., Eastern, New Eng., R.I. (dir.) psychol. assns., N.Y. Acad. Scis., Am. Assn. for Advancement Behavior Therapy, Internat. Neuropsychol. Assn., Soc. Research in Child Devel., Sigma Xi. Contbr. articles in field to profl. jours. Home: 99 Fosdyke St Providence RI 02906 Office: 80 Mount Hope Ave Providence RI 02906

GRODY, DEBORAH, psychologist, educator; b. Munich, Germany, Mar. 10, 1949; d. Sol and Jenny Chinitz; came to U.S., 1951, naturalized, 1957; B.A., Queens Coll., 1970; M.S., Bklyn. Coll., 1972; postgrad. Hofstra U., 1978—; m. June 6, 1970; 1 son, Michael. Supervising testing and evaluation cons. Bur. Ednl. Research, N.Y.C., 1970-72; chief psychologist Buckingham Sch., N.Y.C., 1972-75; coordinator psychol. services Summit Sch., N.Y.C., 1973-76; psychologist N.Y.C. Bd. Edn. Bur. Evaluation and Placement, 1977—; cons. psychologist Rugby Sch., N.Y.C., 1978; tchr. early childhood edn. E. Manhattan Sch. Bright and Gifted Children, 1971; tchr. N.Y.C. Bd. Edn., 1971-72, counselor, 1974. Fellow Am. Orthopsychiat. Assn.; mem. Am. Psychol. Assn., Nat. Assn. Sch. Psychologists, Orton Soc. Home: 333 E 30th St New York City NY 10016 Office: 362 Schermerhorn St Brooklyn NY 11217

GROEGER, THEODORE OSCAR, chemist; b. Gross Kunzendorf, Czechoslovakia, Nov. 25, 1927; s. Oscar and Maria (Eder) G.; Tchrs. diploma U. Vienna, Austria, 1952; Ph.D., Univ. and Tech. U. Vienna, 1957; m. Elfriede Marie Korber, Apr. 22, 1957; children—Theodore Christian, Alexander Martin. Asst. to dean tech. U. Vienna, 1951-55; prof. Austrian Fed. Realgymnasium and Bus. Coll., Eisenstadt, Austria, 1953-59; patent asso. Ciba, Ltd., Basle, Switzerland, 1959-64; mgr. chem. patent affairs Ciba Geigy Corp., Summit, N.J., 1964—; lectr. to sci. tchrs., 1957-59. Recipient Austrian Ministry Edn. Achievement award, 1958; Austrian Sci. Edn. Sch. Book award, 1962. Mem. Am., Austrian, German chem. socs. Author books and articles in field; patentee in field. Home: 2 Collamore Circle West Orange NJ 07052 Office: 556 Morris Ave Summit NJ 07901

GROGAN, EDWARD JOSEPH, lawyer; b. Albany, N.Y., Apr. 5, 1930; s. Edward J. and Margaret (Ray) G.; J.D., Albany Law Sch., 1953; m. Elaine J. Torre; children—Edward P., Michael J., Christina M. Admitted to N.Y. bar, 1953; practiced in Albany, 1953—, Clifton Park, 1974—; mem. firm Grogan, Heggen & Steenburg; counsel N.Y. State Senate Health Com., 1970-77, Saratoga County Sewer Dist., 1976—; mem. Albany County legis. 37th dist., 1968-71. Chmn., Bethlehem Narcotics Guidance Council, 1970-71; mem. Albany County Republican Com., 1952-74; bd. dirs. Albany Home for Children, Home Aide Service. Mem. Am., N.Y. State (grievance com., lectr. legal edn. program), Albany County (pres. 1971), Saratoga County bar assns., Def. Research Inst. Clubs: Lions, K.C. Home: 18 Whispering Hills Clifton Park NY 12065 Office: Northway 10 Executive Park Ushers Rd Clifton Park NY 12065

GROGAN, JOSEPH WILLIAM, veterinarian; b. Springfield, Mass., Aug. 7, 1926; s. John Michael and Mae Elizabeth (Powers) G.; student Am. Internat. Coll., 1943-45, U. Mass., 1946-47; D.V.M., Cornell U., 1950; postgrad. U. Pa., 1974, U. Cin., 1975, U. Ga., 1975; m. Martha Ann Bliss, July 18, 1953; children—Patricia, Margaret, Martha, Susan, Katherine, Kelli. Practice veterinary medicine, Paris, Ky., 1948-49, Warrenton, Va., 1950-51, Westbury, N.Y., 1951-52, Depew, N.Y., 1953—; lectr. State U. N.Y., Buffalo; cons. Niagara Falls (N.Y.) Aquarium, Niagara Falls (Ont.) Aquarium, Aquarium Systems, Buffalo Zoo. Judge Am. Horse Show Assn. Certified veterinary acupuncturist. Mem. AVMA, Western N.Y., N.Y. State (small animal practice com. 1970-74, equine animal practice com. 1970-74) veterinary med. assns., Buffalo Acad. Veterinary Medicine, Internat. Veterinary Medicine Acupuncture Soc., Niagara Frontier Veterinary Med. Soc. Corr. cons. Modern Vet. Practice Mag., 1965-68, Morgan Horse Mag., 1963-70; contbr. articles to Jour. AVMA. Research on equine nutrition, also marine mammals. Home: 4650 Boncrest E Williamsville NY 14221 Office: 6020 Transit Rd Depew NY 14043

GROGAN, ROBERT HARRIS, lawyer; b. Bklyn., Feb. 25, 1933; s. Robert Michael and Nora Howarth (Johnson) G.; A.B., Harvard, 1955; LL.B., U. Va., 1961; m. Delia Ann Grossi, Dec. 23, 1967. Admitted to N.Y. bar, 1962, Va. bar, 1961, Ill. bar, 1977; asso. firm Milbank, Tweed, Hadley & McCloy, N.Y.C., 1961-66; counsel Anaconda Co., N.Y.C., 1966-68; asso. firm Shearman & Sterling, N.Y.C., 1968-75; v.p., gen. counsel staff Citibank, N.Y.C., 1975-76; partner firm Mayer, Brown & Platt, Chgo., 1976—; lectr. in field. Sec., bd. dirs. 3d. Equity Owners Corp., coop. housing corp., 1975—. Served with U.S. Army, 1956-58. Mem. Am., Ill., N.Y. (mem. exec. com. and bus. law com. 1975—), Va. bar assns., Phi Delta Phi. Clubs: Union League (Chgo.); Harvard N.Y.C. Contbg. author: The Local Economic Development Corporation, 1970. Home: 525 E 86th St New York City NY 10028 Office: Mayer Brown & Platt 277 Park Ave New York City NY 10017

GROGG, SAMUEL L., JR., edn. services exec.; b. Moline, Ill., Mar. 29, 1947; s. Samuel Luther and Hazel Ellen (Bedwell) G.; A.B., Western Ill. U., 1969, M.A., 1970; Ph.D., Bowling Green U., 1974; m. Linda Ann Hougan, June 1, 1968; 1 dau., Brady Ellen. Instr. popular culture dept. Bowling Green (Ohio) U., 1970-74; editor Popular Press, Bowling Green, 1970-74; dir. edn. services Am. Film Inst., Washington, 1974—, edn. editor Am. Film, 1975—, editor Am. Film Inst. Guide to Coll. Courses in Film and TV, 1976, 6th edit., 1978, project dir. UNESCO/AFI Internat. Symposium on Cinema and Society, summer 1978; vis. prof. Am. U., 1975; adj. prof. honors program and Am. studies program U. Md., College Park, 1975—; project dir. nat. survey/study film and TV in higher edn.; cons. Nat. Center Ednl. Statistics, 1975—; jury chmn. 6th Birmingham Internat. Ednl. Film Fest; spl. cons. symposium on film as acad. discipline U. So. Calif., summer 1977; dir. or coordinator various film programs and symposiums. Nat. Education Arts grantee, 1975-76; Rockefeller Found. grantee, 1978. Mem. Soc. Cinema Studies, Popular Culture Assn. (nat. ednl. programs coordinator, 1972-74), U. Film. Assn. (dir.), Am. Studies Assn., Modern Lang. Assn. Co-editor: Jour. of Popular Film, 1971—; editor: Popular Culture Methods, 1972-74; (with Browne and Landrum) Theories and Methodologies in Popular Culture, 1975; contbr. articles to profl. jours. Home: 6539 Gilder St Alexandria VA 22310 Office: American Film Inst Kennedy Center Washington DC 20566

GROMADA, THADDEUS VLADIMIR, historian; b. Passaic, N.J., July 30, 1929; s. John and Aniela (Pudzisz) G.; B.S. magna cum laude, Seton Hall U., 1951; M.A., Fordham U., 1953, Ph.D., 1966; m. Theresa Michalski, Aug. 25, 1951; children—Joseph, John, Ann. Asst. prof. history Jersey City State Coll., 1959-66, asso. prof., 1966-70, prof., 1970—, coordinator ethnic studies, 1972—; Am. Council Learned Soc. research grantee in Czechoslovakia, 1968; cons. on Multi-ethnic edn. NEA, N.J. Edn. Assn; cons. Learning Corp. Am. Mem. Heritage com. N.J. Bicentennial Commn.; cons. Jersey City Spirit Program. Served with U.S. Army, 1953-55. Mem. Polish Inst. Arts and Scis. in Am. (dir., sec. gen. 1971-75, 76—), Polish-Am. Hist. Soc. (adv. council 1978), Assn. Study of Nationalities in USSR and Eastern Europe (exec. com. 1978—), Am. Hist. Assn., Am. Assn. Advancement of Slavic Studies, NEA, N.J. Edn. Assn., N.J. Hist. Soc., N.J. Coll. Faculty Assn., Czechoslovak Soc. Arts and Scis. Roman Catholic. Clubs: Polish Tatra Highlanders Folk Dance and Musical Group, Kosciuszko Found. Contbr. articles in field to profl. jours.; mem. editorial bd. Polish Rev., 1968—; co-editor Tatra Eagle, bilingual folklore quar., 1947—. Home: 354 Steinhauser Ln Wyckoff NJ 07481 Office: Jersey City State Coll Dept History Jersey City NJ 07305

GROMADZKI, ZYGMUNT CONSTANTINE, radiol. physicist; b. Scranton, Pa., June 19, 1948; s. Zygmunt Andrew and Stella Tessie (Haberek) G.; B.S. in Physics, U. Scranton, 1970; Ph.D. in Physics, U. Va., 1976; m. Donna Marie Feeney, May 6, 1978. Mem. staff div. radiol. physics U. Va. Hosp., 1975-76; chief radiol. physicist Georgetown U. Hosp., 1976—. Mem. architecture com. Falls Manor Subdiv., Gt. Falls, Va. W.H. Humphreys fellow, 1970-71; Center for Advanced Studies fellow, 1971-72. Mem. Am. Phys. Soc., Am. Assn. Physicists in Medicine, Gt. Falls Jaycees, Gt. Falls Citizens Assn., Sigma Pi Sigma. Republican. Roman Catholic. Home: 902 Cantle Ln Great Falls VA 22066 Office: Radiation Oncology Dept Georgetown U Hosp 3800 Reservoir Rd NW Washington DC 20007

GRONER, BEVERLY ANNE (MRS. SAMUEL BRIAN GRONER), lawyer; b. Des Moines, Jan. 31, 1922; d. Benjamin L. and Annabelle B. (Miller) Zavat; student Drake U., 1939-40, Cath. U., 1954-56; J.D., Am. U., 1959; m. Samuel Brian Groner, Dec. 17, 1962; children by previous marriage—Morrilou (Mrs. Raymond Morell), Lewis Anthony Davis, Andrew G. Davis. Admitted to Md. bar, 1959, U.S. Supreme Court bar, 1963, D.C. bar, 1965; mem. firm Groner & Groner, Bethesda, Md., 1962—; lectr. wills and estates Montgomery Coll., Rockville, Md., 1972-73; mem. faculty domestic relations div. Montgomery-Prince George's Continuing Legal Edn. Inst., 1974-75; mem. Md. Gov.'s Commn. to Study Implementation of Equal Rights Amendment, 1974—; chmn. Gov.'s Commn. on Domestic Relations Laws, 1977—; participant numerous family law programs and seminars, radio and TV programs. Fellow Am. Acad. Matrimonial Lawyers; mem. D.C. Bar (steering com. family law div. 1974-75), Am., Md. (chmn. family law sect. 1975-77), Montgomery County (chmn. family law com. 1974-75) bar assns., Phi Alpha Delta. Contbr. articles to profl. jours. Home: 6710 Western Ave Chevy Chase MD 20015 Office: Suite 304 Perpetual Bldg Bethesda MD 20014

GROOBERT, GEORGE EDWARD, polit. columnist; b. Colchester, Conn., Oct. 29, 1915; s. Harry and Esther G.; m. Mildred Katzman, Aug. 25, 1940. Sports reporter, sports columnist Meriden (Conn.) Record and Meriden Jour., 1936-48, reporter, polit. columnist, 1958—, also Conn. state capitol corr.; part-owner Wallingford (Conn.) Vets. Profl. Basketball Team. Mem. scholarship com. Napier Co. Found.; bd. dirs. United Jewish Appeal, recipient award, 1968; judge Wallingford Jaycees Distinguished Awards, 1973. Jewish. Mem. Conn. Sports Writers Alliance. Home: 174 N Cherry St Wallingford CT 06492 Office: 11-19 Crown St Meriden CT 06450

GROOME, JOHN PHILLIP, JR., computer systems programmer; b. Pitts., Sept. 26, 1946; s. John Phillip and Jewel Marie (O'Neal) G.; student W.Va. U., 1964-68; A.A., W.Va. No. Community Coll., 1975; m. Marilyn Margaret Przelenski, Apr. 25, 1970; 1 dau., Michelle Marie. With Wheeling-Pitts. Steel Corp. (W.Va.), 1969-77, computer systems programmer, 1974-77; sr. systems programmer Dresser Industries Inc., Pitts., 1977—. Mem. Pitts. Large Users Group. Democrat. Roman Catholic. Home: 143 Mt View Dr Wheeling WV 26003 Office: 810 Parish St Pittsburgh PA 15220

GROSHANS, RUSSELL GLEN, communications co. exec.; b. Minot, N.D., Feb. 14, 1929; s. Louis Christian and Elizabeth Claire (Bosse) G.; B.S., U.S. Mil. Acad., 1953; M.S., Georgetown U., 1964; Ph.D., Georgetown U., 1967; m. Barbara Joan Mottley, June 27, 1953; children—Maris, Barbara, Russell Glen. Program physicist Office Aerospace Research, Washington, 1963-67; systems engr. RCA Corp., Hightstown, N.J., 1967-68, tech. adviser corp. research and engring. staff, Princeton, N.J., 1969-77; dir. market planning COMSAT Gen. Corp., Washington, 1978—; grad. physics lectr. RCA Corp., 1968-69. Mem. Monmouth County Environ. Council, 1972-78. Served with USAF, 1953-67. Mem. I.E.E.E., Am. Geophys. Union. Republican. Roman Catholic. Clubs: Golf (Spring Lake, N.J.); West Point Society, Georgetown Club (N.Y.C.). Home: 338 Club View Dr Great Falls VA 22066 Office: COMSAT Gen Corp 950 L'Enfant Plaza Washington DC 20024

GROSMAN, ALAN MARC, lawyer; b. Newark, Mar. 13, 1935; s. Charles M. and Grace (Fishman) G.; B.A., Wesleyan U., Middletown, Conn., 1956; M.A., Yale U., 1957; J.D., N.Y. Law Sch., 1965; m. Bette Bloomenthal, Dec. 27, 1966; children—Ellen Laura, Jill Anne, Carol Lisa. Reporter, New Haven Jour.-Courier, 1959-60, Newark Evening News, 1961-62; admitted to N.J. bar, 1965; practice law, Newark, 1965—; partner firm Grosman & Grosman, and predecessor, 1965—; asst. prosecutor Essex County, 1968-69; counsel N.J. World Trade Council, 1972-75, chmn., 1976-78; adj. asst. prof. internat. bus. law Fairleigh Dickinson U. Grad. Sch. Bus. Adminstrn., 1978—; lectr. World Trade Inst., N.Y.C., 1977—; mem. N.J. Dist. Export Council, U.S. Dept. Commerce, 1978—; mem. internat. adv. com. N.J. Econ. Devel. Council, 1976—. Fellow Am. Acad. Matrimonial Lawyers; mem. Am., Inter-Am. (chmn. corp. law sect. 1974-77), N.J., Essex County (chmn. internat. law com. 1974—) bar assns., N.J., Greater Newark chambers commerce, N.J. Bus. and Industry Assn., Phi Beta Kappa, Phi Delta Phi. Republican. Jewish. Clubs: Masons, Kiwanis (pres. Newark 1975-76); Wesleyan U. Alumni of Newark (pres. 1965-68); Wesleyan Alumni Council. Contbr. articles to law jours. and Jour. Commerce; editor N.Y. Law Sch. Law Rev., 1963-65; asst.

editor N.J. State Bar Jour., 1967-69, 78—. Home: 14 Birchwood Dr Short Hills NJ 07078 Office: 786 Broad St Newark NJ 07102

GROSMAN, BRIAN ALLEN, educator, lawyer; b. Toronto, Ont., Can.; grad. U. Toronto; postgrad McGill U. Pvt. practice law, Toronto; spl. prosecutor to minister justice, 1965; prof. criminal, criminology McGill U., 1966-71; prof. Coll. Law. U. Sask. Saskatoon, Can., 1971-79; partner firm Greenglass and Grosman, Barristers and Solicitors, Toronto, 1978—; vis. prof. U. Free Berlin (West Germany). Adviser to Que. Civil Liberties Assn., Law Reform Commn.; chmn. Law Reform Commn. Sask., 1974-78; mem. advisory council Canadian Human Rights Found., 1976-79. Recipient Canadian Bar Found. award for legal research, 1968; Beccaria award Que. Soc. Criminology, 1970. Russell Sage fellow, 1967. Mem. Am. (exec. 1972—, presdl. citation 1975), Que. (v.p.) socs. criminology, Am. Law Inst. Author: The Prosecutor, An Inquiry into the Exercise of Discretion, 1970; Justice in Crisis, 1971; Police Command: Decisions and Discretion, 1975. Spl. contbr. Montreal Star; contbr. articles to profl. jours. Office: Greenglass and Grosman Suite 2700 Commercial Union Tower Toronto-Dominion Centre Toronto ON M5K 1K2 Canada

GROSMAN, MICHAEL, engr.; b. Lvov, USSR, Mar. 28, 1949; s. Boris and Florence (Geker) G.; came to U.S., 1965, naturalized, 1971; B.Engring. in Mech. Engring., N.Y. U., 1972; m. Diane Kathryn Roy, Oct. 4, 1975. Engr. machinery stress analysis dept. Gibbs & Cox, Inc., N.Y.C., 1974, engring. cons., 1978; engring. cons. pressure vessels and piping Airco Engring. Co., Murray Hill, N.J., 1974-78; dir. applications Compeda Inc., Spring Lake, N.J., 1978—. Mem. Am. Mgmt. Assn. Office: 524 Brighton Ave Suite 12 Spring Lake NJ 07762

GROSS, CAROLINE LORD (MRS. MARTIN L. GROSS), state ofcl.; b. Laconia, N.H., May 5, 1940; d. William Shepard and Marion (Manns) Lord; A.B., Radcliffe Coll., 1963; M.A.T., Harvard, 1964; m. Martin L. Gross, Nov. 5, 1960. Research asst. Supr. Schs., Concord, N.H., 1965-66, N.H. Legislative com. ann. sessions, Concord, 1966, N.H. Fiscal com. 1967-68; adminstrv. asst. N.H. gov., Concord, 1969-70; coordinator N.H. fed. funds, Concord, 1971-72, supr. checklist, 1969—. Mem. N.H. Commn. Status Women, 1972-75; del. N.H. Republican Conv., 1968, 70, 74, 76, 78; legis. policy asst. N.H. Ho. of Reps., 1974—; trustee Concord Library, 1974-77. Mem. League Women Voters, N.H. Council Better Schs. Home: 15 Rumford St Concord NH 03301 Office: Office of the Speaker State House Concord NH 03301

GROSS, FELIKS, sociologist, educator, author; b. Cracow, Poland, June 17, 1906; s. Adolf and Augusta (Alexander) G.; came to U.S., 1941, naturalized, 1955; LL.M., Jagiellonian U. (Poland), 1930, LL.D., 1931; postgrad., Paris, 1931; m. Priva Baidaff, July 25, 1937; 1 dau., Eva Helena Gross Friedman. Sec., Gen. Central Eastern European Planning Board, 1941-45; editor New Europe and World Reconstrn. jour., N.Y.C., 1942-45; prof. sociology and anthropology City U. N.Y., Bklyn. Coll. and Grad. Center, N.Y.C., 1946—; vis. prof. N.Y. U., 1945-68; vis. prof., dir. Inst. Internat. Affairs, U. Wyo., Laramie, summers 1945-52; vis. prof. Woodrow Wilson Sch. Fgn. Affairs, U. Va., Charlottesville, 1951, 54-56, U. Vt., Burlington, 1957; sr. Fulbright lectr. U. Rome, 1957-58, 64-65, 74; lectr. other European, Am. univs.; mem. research council Fgn. Policy Research Inst., Phila., 1966—; vis. prof. Columbia U., N.Y.C., 1973; lectr. U. Florence, 1977, Italian Fgn. Office, Rome; cons. Nat. Com. on Causes and Prevention of Violence, 1968. Pres. Taraknath Das Found., N.Y., 1965. Carnegie scholar, Paris, 1931; Pub. Affairs Found. N.Y. U., 1962-63; Sloane Found. grantee, 1963; Fulbright grantee, 1956-57, 64-65, 74; City U. Research Found. grantee, 1971, 74; NSF grantee, 1972; Rockefeller Found. grantee, 1974; Golden Cross of Phoenix, King of Greece, 1963. Mem. Polish Inst. Arts and Sci. in Am. (v.p. 1964, dir. 1975), Internat. League of Rights of Man (dir. 1960), Am. Sociol. Assn., Acad. Polit. Sci., N.Y. Acad. Sci., Authors League, Sigma Xi. Club: Columbia U Faculty. Author: Polish Worker, 1945; Foreign Policy Analysis, 1954; Seizure of Political Power, 1957; Valori Sociali e Struttura, 1967; World Politics and Tension Areas, 1967; Violence in Politics, 1973; Il Paese, Values and Social Change in an Italian Village, 1974; The Revolutionary Party, 1974, others; contbr. numerous articles to profl. jours. Home: 310 W 85th St New York City NY 10024 Office: City U NY 33 W 42d St New York City NY 10036 also Polist Inst 59 E 66th St New York City NY 10021

GROSS, GARY LAWRENCE, gynecologist; b. N.Y.C., Feb. 15, 1940; s. Emanuel and Helen G.; B.S., Union Coll., 1961; M.D., Yale U., 1965; m. Betsy Shure, June 22, 1961; children—Elisabeth Shure, Andrew Lincoln. Intern, Beth Israel Hosp., Boston, 1965-66; resident Yale-New Haven Hosp., New Haven, 1966-70, dept. obstetrics and gynecology Sch. Medicine, Yale U., New Haven, 1969-70, Med. Sch., Harvard U., Boston, 1970—; med. dir. Boston Family Planning Project, 1975—; chmn. Mass. Family Planning Consortium, 1973-75. Mem. Am. Coll. Obstetricians and Gynecologists (chmn. Jr. Fellows Dist. I 1970-73, mem. com. on endocrinology 1974-76), Am. Fertility Soc., Boston Obstet. Soc., Am. Soc. Gynecol. Laparoscopists. Clubs: Yale of Boston, N.Y.C. Office: 77 Pond Ave Brookline MA 02146

GROSS, HELENE MARILYN BELLER, psychotherapist, counselor; b. Bklyn., Mar. 15, 1933; d. Lawrence and Davida Florence (Epstein) Beller; B.A., Richmond Coll., State U. N.Y. 1973; Ph.D., Union Grad. Sch., Antioch Coll. 1976; m. Lewis Gross, Jan. 31, 1953; children—Paul Martin, David Forrest, Nancy Sue. Founder, S.I. Counseling and Info. Center for Women, Inc., 1973, dir., 1974—; research asst. Richmond Coll., S.I., 1973-76; instr. psychology Union Grad. Sch., Bard Coll. Colliquium, N.Y. State, 1976; counselor, psychotherapist Feit Clinic, S.I., 1974—; cons. Impact, Cleve. 1975-76, NOW, S.I., 1975-76, Richmond Coll., 1973; mem. assembly com. N.Y. State Assembly, 1974; coordinator Outreach Program for Women, S.I., 1972-74; columnist S.I. Register, 1974-76, cons. 1976. Recipient Distinguished Service award S.I. Counseling and Info. Center for Women, 1977. Certified sex therapist, psychotherapist, marriage counselor, clin. counselor. Mem. Am., Humanistic psychology assns., Assn. Gen. Psychology, Psychology of Women, Assn. Community Psychology, Soc. for Psychol. Study of Social Issues, Am. Assn. Sex Edcuators, Counselors and Therapists, Am. Personnel and Guidance Assn., N.Y. Assn. Practicing Psychotherapists, Assn. for Specialists in Group Work, Am. Assn. Clin. Counselors, Kappa Delta Pi. Democrat. Contbr. articles to profl. jours., newspapers. Home: 270 Robinson Ave Staten Island NY 10312 Office: 3886 Hylan Blvd Staten Island NY 10308

GROSS, IRWIN ELLIOT, dentist; b. N.Y.C., May 25, 1930; s. Samuel and Dorothy (Fingerman) G.; A.B., N.Y. U., 1952, D.D.S., 1956; m. Sandra Lerner, Feb. 11, 1956 (div. July 1977); children—Jeffrey Keith, Clifford Wayne. Pvt. practice dentistry, Hicksville, N.Y., 1958-64, Jericho, N.Y., 1964—. Cons. to Dental Service Assn. Mem. local bd. 3 SSS. Bd. dirs. Nassau div. North Oyster Bay unit Am. Cancer Soc. Served to capt. AUS, 1956-58. Mem. Acad. Gen. Dentistry, Am. Dental Assn., N.Y. State, 10th Dist. dental socs., Alpha Omega. Rotarian (Hicksville, pres. 1970-71). Home: 23 Old Field North Hills Roslyn NY 11576 Office: 333 N Broadway Jericho NY 11753

GROSS, JEFFREY KENT, psychotherapist, educator; b. N.Y.C., Nov. 6, 1947; s. Joseph Solomon and Mildred (Kestecher) G.; B.A., Queens Coll., 1971; M.S., Coll. New Rochelle, 1977; grad. Center for Behavioral Psychotherapy; m. Eugenie Schosberg, Mar. 6, 1971; children—Jonathan Todd Harris (stepson), Jason Matthew. Tchr., N.Y.C. sch. system, 1971-73; researcher, writer throughout USSR, 1973; tchr. emotionally disturbed children Hawthorne Cedar Knolls Treatment Center, Hawthorne, N.Y., 1974—. Mem. Assn. Advancement of Behavior Therapy, Am. Assn. Advancement of Slavic Studies, Brit. Mus. Soc., Council for Exceptional Children. Jewish. Co-author: The Soviet Union: A Guide for Travellers, 1977. Home: Hessian Hills Rd Croton-on-Hudson NY 10520 Office: Hawthorne Cedar Knolls UFSD 3 226 Linda Ave Hawthorne NY 10532

GROSS, JOHN HAMMES, steel co. exec.; b. Hummelstown, Pa., Jan. 27, 1923; s. Charles Franklin and Anna Elda (Hammes) G.; B.S., Lehigh U., 1944, M.S., 1948, Ph.D., 1955; m. Phyllis Jean McKelvie, Sept. 12, 1942; 1 son, Jeffrey John. With Bethlehem Steel Corp. (Pa.), 1940-44; mem. faculty Lehigh U., Bethlehem, 1946-59; with U.S. Steel Corp., Monroeville, Pa., 1959—, asst. dir., 1967-68, mgr. steel products devel., 1968-72, dir. research, 1972—. Served with USNR, 1944-46. Am. Soc. for Metals fellow, 1972. Contbr. articles to various publs. Home: 1766 Mountainview Dr Monroeville PA 15146 Office: US Steel Research Lab Monroeville PA 15146

GROSS, LUDWIK, physician; b. Cracow, Poland, Sept. 11, 1904; s. Adolf and Augusta (Alexander) G.; M.D., Iagellon U., Cracow, 1929; Prix Chevillon, Acad. Medicine, Paris, 1937; m. Dorothy L. Nelson, Oct. 7, 1943; 1 dau., Augusta H. Came to U.S., 1940, naturalized, 1943. Intern and resident St. Lazar Gen. Hosp., Cracow, 1929-32; part time research exptl. cancer Pasteur Inst., Paris; postgrad. clin. tng. Salpetriere, U. Paris, 1932-39; cancer research Christ Hosp., Cin., 1941-43; chief cancer research VA Hosp Bronx, 1946—; research prof. dept. medicine Mount Sinai Sch. Medicine, N.Y.C., 1971--; cons. Sloan Kettering Inst., Meml. Center N.Y.C., 1955-57, asso. scientist, 1957-60. Served from capt. to maj. M.C., U.S. Army, 1943-46. Recipient Robert R. De Villiers award for research on leukemia Leukemia Soc. N.Y., 1953, Walker prize Royal Coll. Surgeons Eng., 1962, Pasteur Silver medal Pasteur Inst., 1962, Lucy Wortham James award James Ewing Soc., 1962, WHO UN prize, 1962, The Bertner Found. award, 1963, Albert Einstein Centennial medal, 1965; Albion O. Bernstein award Med. Soc. N.Y. State, 1971; Spl. Virus Cancer Program award Nat. Cancer Inst., 1972; William S. Middleton award VA, 1974; Albert Lasker Basil Med. Research award 1974; founders award for cancer immunology Cancer Research Inst., Inc., N.Y., 1975; Paul Ehrlich-Ludwig Darmstzedter prize, 1978; Prix Griffuel, Villejuif, 1978; decorated Chevalier de la Legion d'Honneur, 1978. Diplomate Am. Bd. Internal Medicine Fellow A.C.P., AAAS, Internat. Soc. of Hematology, N.Y. Acad. Scis; mem. Am. Soc. Hematology, AMA, Am. Assn. Cancer Research (dir. 1973-76), Assn. Mil. Surgeons U.S., Soc. of Exptl. Biology and Medicine, Bronx County, N.Y. State med. socs., Nat. Acad. Scis. Author: Oncogenic Viruses, 1961, 2d edit, 1970. Author numerous papers on cancer and leukemia in profl. jours. Address: 130 W Kingsbrige Rd Bronx NY 10468

GROSS, LYDIA ELIZABETH, ret. educator; b. Lock Haven, Pa.; d. Charles Edward and Susan (Ranck) Gross; student Lock Haven State Coll., 1923-25; B.S., Tchrs. Coll. Columbia, 1932, M.A., 1937; postgrad. Duke, summer 1945, Pa. State U., 1962-64. Tchr., Willimantic (Conn.) State Coll., 1935-46; faculty Lock Haven State Coll., 1946-72, prin. Campus Sch., dir. elementary edn., 1953-63, dir. elementary edn., 1963-72; prof. Alaska Meth. U., Anchorage, 1972-73, prof. emerita, 1973-74. Recipient Gold key Columbia Scholastic Press Assn., 1960. Mem. Pa. Ednl. Assn., NEA, AAUW, Nat. Soc. for Study Edn., Am. Acad. Polit. and Social Sci., AAUP, Am. Guild Organists, Assn. Childhood Edn. Internat., Delta Kappa Gamma, Phi Lambda Theta. Lutheran. Author: How a Town Grew in New England, 1964. Home: 411 Guardlock Dr Lock Haven PA 17745

GROSS, PETER ALAN, physician; b. Newark, Nov. 18, 1938; s. Meyer P. and Nathalie (Bass) G.; A.B. cum laude, Amherst Coll., 1960; M.D., Yale U., 1964; m. Regina Gittlin, May 31, 1964; children—Deborah Karen, Michael Philip, Daniel Bryan. Intern, Yale-New Haven Hosp., 1964-65, jr. resident, 1965-66, attending physician, 1971-74; sr. resident Peter Bent Brigham Hosp., Boston, 1968-69; asst. in medicine Harvard U. Med. Sch., 1968-69; virology fellow dept. epidemiology and pub. health Yale U., 1969-71, asst. prof. medicine, 1971-74; research and edn. asso. VA Hosp., West Haven, Conn., 1971-73, acting chief infectious disease, 1972-73, chief, 1973-74; dir. div. infectious diseases Hackensack (N.J.) Hosp., 1974—; asst. clin. prof. medicine Columbia U., 1974-77, asso. clin. prof., 1977—; clin. instr. U. So. Calif., 1967-69; dir. Nursing Service Inc., Ridgewood, N.J. Served with USPHS, 1966-68. NIH fellow, 1969-71; diplomate Am Bd. Internal Medicine. Fellow A.C.P.; mem. Am. Soc. Microbiology, AMA, N.J., Bergen County med. socs., Infectious Disease Soc. Am., Nu Sigma Nu. Author: Gram Stain Recognition, 1975; contbr. articles to profl. publs. Home: 807 Morningside Dr Ridgewood NJ 07450 Office: Hackensack Hosp Hackensack NJ 07601

GROSS, ROBERT ALAN, historian; b. New Haven, Feb. 17, 1945; s. Samuel and Roslyn (Chadys) G.; B.A., U. Pa., 1966; M.A. (Woodrow Wilson nat. fellow), Columbia U., 1968, Ph.D. (Univ. Pres.'s fellow), 1976; m. Ann Leslie Goldman, May 22, 1966; children—Matthew Banjamin, Stephen Alexander. Gen. sec. U.S. Student Press Assn., Washington, 1966-67; asst. editor Newsweek, N.Y.C., 1968-70; NIMH trainee in social history Columbia U., 1970-72; adj. asst. prof. Worcester (Mass.) Poly. Inst., 1973-76; asst. prof. history and Am. studies Amherst (Mass.) Coll., 1976—. Recipient Bancroft prize in Am. history Columbia U., 1977; Book award Nat. Hist. Soc., 1977. Mem. Am. Hist. Assn., Orgn. Am. Historians, Am. Studies Assn., Econ. History Assn., Phi Beta Kappa. Democrat. Jewish. Author: The Minutemen and Their World, 1976. Home: 14 Nutting Ave Amherst MA 01002 Office: Dept Am Studies Amherst Coll Amherst MA 01002

GROSS, SIDNEY, editor; b. Dusseldorf, Germany, Jan. 17, 1920; s. David and Helen (Klausner) G.; came to U.S., 1938, naturalized, 1944; B.S., Princeton U., 1942; M.A., Columbia U., 1950; m. Lillian Nee Zlotnick, Mar. 21, 1948; children—Jane Alice, Nancy Ellen. Mng. editor Boland & Boyce Pubs., Montclair, N.J., 1950-52, Breskin Pubs. Inc., N.Y.C., 1952-63; with McGraw Hill. Inc., N.Y.C., 1963—, editor in chief, 1968—, chmn. editorial bd., 1970—. Bd. dirs. Plastic Inst. Am., 1978—, pres.-elect; bd. dirs. Plastics Hall of Fame, 1975—. Served with communications system USAAF, 1942-47. Recipient Jesse Neal award, 1978. Mem. Soc. Plastics Engrs. (dir. 1972—), Soc. Plastics Industry, Soc. Bus. Paper Editors, Am. Chem. Soc., Phi Beta Kappa. Home: 65-43 181th St Flushing NY 11365 Office: 1221 Ave of Americas New York City NY 10020

GROSS, SIDNEY ESSER, apparel mfg. co. exec.; b. Trenton, N.J., Jan. 5, 1930; s. Irving and Lena (Siskowitz) G.; Asso. Sci., Rutgers U., 1960, B.S., 1964; m. Irene Lora Levin, June 27, 1954; children—Debrah Iris, Mark Barry. Methods engr. Maidenform Inc., Bayonne, N.J., 1952-62; indsl. engr. Bobbie Brooks Inc., Cleve., 1962-63, mfg. mgr., 1963-66; gen. mgr. Goulder Co. Inc., Climax Spltys. Inc., N.Y.C., 1966-72, pres., dir. 1972—. Served with AUS, 1950-52. Mem. Am. Arbitration Assn., Lehigh Valley Needle Trades Assn. (dir. 1967-73). Jewish. Home: 1230 N 36th St Allentown PA 18104 Office: 1040 Ave of Americas New York City NY 10001

GROSS, SPENCER, lawyer; b. Hartford, Conn., Dec. 22, 1906; s. Charles Welles and Hilda Frances (Welch) G.; A.B., Yale, 1928, LL.B., 1931. Admitted to Conn. bar, 1931, since practiced in Hartford; with Gross, Hyde & Williams, 1931—, partner, 1936—; asso. judge City Ct. of Hartford, 1945-47; dir. Nat. Fire Ins. Co. Hartford, Transcontinental Ins. Co., Mechanics Savs. Bank. Mem. Adv. Council Banking. Mem. Met. Dist. Commn. 1940-54; mem. Bd. Park Commrs., 1939-48, City Plan Commn., 1936-45. Mem. distbn. com. Hartford Found. Pub. Giving, 1936-68; v.p. Children's Mus. Hartford, 1948-55; sec. Wadsworth Atheneum, 1943-66; corporator Hartford Hosp., St. Francis Hosp., Am. Sch. for Deaf, Conn. Inst. for Blind; trustee Howard and Bush Found. Fellow Am. Coll. Probate Counsel, mem. Zeta Psi, Phi Delta Phi. Conglist. Clubs: University, Wampanoag Country, Twentieth Century (Hartford). Home: 229 Kenyon St Hartford CT 06105 Office: 799 Main St Hartford CT 06103

GROSSCHMID-ZSOGOD, GEZA BENJAMIN, economist; b. Budapest, Hungary, Oct. 29, 1918; s. Lajos and Jolan (de Szitanyi) de Grosschmid; came to U.S., 1947, naturalized, 1950; J.U.D., Royal Hungarian Pazmany Peter U., Budapest, 1943; m. Leonora Martha Nissler, Nov. 8, 1946; 1 dau., Pamela. Adminstrv. asst. German Mission UNRRA, 1946-47; asst. prof. econs. Duquesne U., Pitts., 1948-52, asso. prof., 1952-55, prof., 1955—, acting academic v.p., 1970-71, academic v.p., 1971-75, dir. Inst. African Affairs, 1959-70, African Lang. and Area Center, 1960-74, chmn. div. econ. scis., 1978—; expert U.S. Office Edn. Nat. Def. Fgn. Lang. Fellowship Evaluating Panel, 1965—; mem. Cambridge U. Summer Conf., 1961. Bd. visitors Coll. Arts and Scis. U. Pitts.; bd. dirs. World Affairs Council Pitts., Afuture Fund, Battle of Britain Mus. Found. Served with Hungarian Army, 1944-45. Decorated knight Order of Valor (Cameroon); knight of Obedience; comdr. Order of Merit, Hungarian Commemorative medal, all Sovereign Mil. Order Malta; knight justice Sacred Mil. Constantinian Order St. George (Two Sicilies); Familiar (Marian Cross), Teutonic Order; knight comdr. Order House of Lippe; knight grand cross Occidental Order of St. Martin (Austria); knight Order Zaire (Zaire); knight comdr. with star Order of St. Gregory the Great (Holy See); officer Order Equatorial Star (Gabon); recipient Econs.-in-Action fellowship Case Inst. Tech., 1957; Ford Found. vis. scholar Johns Hopkins U., 1958; Fulbright-Hays fellow in S. Africa, 1965. Mem. Am. Econ. Assn., Royal Econ. Soc., AAUP, Am., fgn. heraldry socs., Hungarian Mil. Order Vitez, Pi Gamma Mu, Alpha Kappa Delta, Beta Gamma Sigma. Republican. Roman Catholic. Clubs: Duquesne (Pitts.); Met., Army and Navy (Washington); Athenaeum, Middlesex County Cricket (London); Royal Forth Yacht (Edinburgh, Scotland). Author: (with P. Colombo) The Devotion of the Knights of Malta for Our Lady of Philermo, 1956; The Spiritual Heritage of the Sovereign Military Order of Malta, 1958; (with others) Principles of Economics, 1959; also articles field econs. and heraldry; contbr. Ency. Brit., New Cath. Ency. Home: 3115 Ashlyn St Pittsburgh PA 15204 Office: Duquesne U Pittsburgh PA 15219

GROSSER, GEORGE SAMUEL, psychologist, educator; b. Boston, Aug. 14, 1929; s. Sidney and Eva Risa (Shapiro) G.; A.B. cum laude, Harvard U., 1951; M.A., Boston U., 1952, Ph.D., 1957. Exptl. physiol. psychologist U.S. Army Chem. Corps, Edgewood, Md., 1957-58; asst. prof. psychology Am. Internat. Coll., Springfield, Mass., 1958-64, asso. prof., 1964—. USPHS grantee, 1959-60. Mem. Am., Eastern, New Eng. psychol. assns., AAAS, N.Y. Acad. Scis., Sigma Xi. Jewish. Clubs: Harvard (Boston); Springfield Chess. Editor: (with others) General Psychology: Selected Readings, 1967; contbr. articles to profl. jours.; author lyrics Internat. Anthem for World Peace. Home: 335 Maple Rd Longmeadow MA 01106 Office: Am Internat Coll Springfield MA 01109

GROSSMAN, ANNE RAFSKY, interior decorator; b. N.Y.C., Dec. 20, 1922; d. Henry A. and Bertha (Fischel) Rafsky; student Adelphi Coll., 1940-42; B.S., Columbia U., 1944; m. Harry Grossman, Aug. 6, 1950; children—Sandra Kay, Ilene Hope. Partner interior decorating firm Jo-Ann Designs, N.Y.C., 1957-67; owner, mgr. Anne R. Grossman Interiors, N.Y.C., 1967—. Trustee, treas. Henry A. Rafsky Research Fund, Inc.; bd. dirs. N.Y. chpt. WAIF. Mem. Am. Soc. Interior Designers, Inc., Nat. Council Jewish Women. Clubs: B'nai B'rith, Alpine Country. Address: 25 Sutton Pl S New York City NY 10022

GROSSMAN, GARY JAY, accountant; b. Bklyn., June 11, 1941; s. Sidney and Beatrice (Rappaport) G.; B.A., Brandeis U., 1962; M.B.A., Columbia U., 1964; m. Lynn Kahn, Jan. 23, 1965; children—Robert, Andrew, Michael. Accountant Anchin Block and Anchin, C.P.A.'s, 1964-68; partner firm Grossman & Tuchman C.P.A.'s, N.Y.C., 1968—. C.P.A., N.Y. State. Clubs: Middle Bay Country (bd. govs. 1975-77). Home: 7 Dell Dr East Rockaway NY 11518 Office: 370 Lexington Ave New York City NY 10017

GROSSMAN, GILBERT, cardiologist; b. Phila., Nov. 14, 1932; s. Joseph and Anne G.; B.S., Villanova U., 1953; M.D., Temple U., 1957; m. Joan Grossman, June 16, 1961; children—Jamie, Karen, Linda, Suzanne. Intern, Albert Einstein Med. Center, Phila., 1957-58, fellow in cardiology, 1962-63, now cardiology cons. No. div. sr. asst. surgeon NIH, Washington, 1959-61; resident in medicine Meml. Hosp., N.Y.C., 1961-62, Bellevue Hosp., N.Y.C., 1961-62; practice medicine specializing in internal medicine and cardiology, Jenkintown, Pa., 1963—; chmn. med. dept., pres. staff Rolling Hill Hosp., Elkins Park, Pa.; Cardiology cons. Kennedy Meml. Hosp., Oxford Hosp., Lawndale Hosp.; asst. clin. prof. medicine Temple U. Med. Center. Served with USCG, 1959-61. Fellow A.C.P., Am. Coll. Chest Physicians, Phila. Coll. Physicians, Royal Coll. Physicians (Eng.); mem. Am. Coll. Internal Medicine, Am., Phila. colls. cardiology, AMA, Pa., Philadelphia County (pres. North br.) med. socs. Republican. Jewish. Office: 1 Abington Plaza Jenkintown PA 19046

GROSSMAN, HARRY, lawyer; b. N.Y.C., Oct. 30, 1911; s. Isaac and Anna (Hoffman) G.; B.S., N.Y. U., 1933; LL.B., Columbia U., 1936; m. Barbara J. Solomon, Aug. 9, 1942 (div.); 1 dau., Patricia Joyce; m. 2d, Anne E. Rafsky, Aug. 6, 1950; children—Sandra Kay, Ilene Hope. Admitted to N.Y. bar, 1937, D.C. bar, 1948; dep. collector IRS, 1937-40; partner firm Grossman & Grossman, N.Y.C., 1950-53, Grossman, Grossman & Feigen, 1964-68, Grossman, Feigen & Rossetti, 1969-70; counsel Automobile Driving Schs. Assn., Inc., 1949-54, Eastern Dry Cleaning and Laundry Machinery Distbrs. Assn., Inc., 1960-64, Tri-State Machinery Disbrs. Council, Inc., 1964-67, Westchester Associated Stationers, Inc., 1957-68; lectr. Columbia U., Practising Law Inst., Delehanty Inst., Collegiate Inst. Pres. Atlantic Beach Property Owners Assn., 1954-55; past chmn. campaign Nat. Found. for Infantile Paralysis; trustee Harry and Jane Fischel Found. Served to maj. AUS, 1942-46; lt. col. Res. Decorated Commendation medal; recipient N.Y. Conspicuous Service award, 1946. Mem. Am. Arbitration Assn. (mem. panel, appellate div. referee for incompetants 1975—), Am., N.Y. bar assns., Assn. Bar City N.Y., N.Y. County Lawyers Assn., Fed. Bar Council, Am. Acad. Polit. and Social Sci., Res. Officers Assn., Mil. Order World Wars, Jewish War Vets., Am. Legion, Grand St. Boys' Assn., Zeta Beta Tau. Democrat. Clubs: B'nai B'rith (pres. lodge 1956-57), Elks, Alpine Country. Contbr. articles to periodicals. Home: 25 Sutton Pl S New York City NY 10022 Office: 418 Ave S New York City NY 10016

GROSSMAN, JOHN HENRY, physician; b. Rochester, N.Y., Aug. 17, 1914; s. Gustave Adolph and Mabel (Trumeter) G.; A.B., U. Rochester, 1938, M.D., 1941; m. Marya S. Fryczynski, Nov. 30, 1941; children—John Henry III, Marya Mabel. Asst. serologist Rochester (N.Y.) Health Bur., 1940-41; intern surgery New Haven Hosp., 1941-42, asst. resident obstetrics and gynecology, 1942-43, asso. resident, 1943-44, resident obstetrics and gynecology, 1944-45; asst. obstetrician and gynecologist, mem. faculty Yale U., 1941-43, instr. obstetrics and gynecology, 1943-45; asso. attending obstetrician Bridgeport (Conn.) Hosp., 1945-56, sr. attending gynecologist and obstetrician, 1957-70, sr. cons. obstetrics and gynecology, 1970—, pres. and chief attending staff, 1960-61; instr. obstetrics and gynecology U. Bridgeport and Bridgeport Hosp. Schs. of Nursing, 1945-56, asst. prof. Coll. of Nursing, U. Bridgeport, 1956—. First v.p. Nichols Village Improvement Assn. Recipient Man of Yr. award Am. Legion, Trumbull, Conn., 1969; Stanley M. Collins Meml. award, 1970; Linking Ring Feature award, 1972. Diplomate Am. Bd. Obstetrics and Gynecology. Fellow Am. Coll. Obstetricians and Gynecologists (founder), Am. Soc. Abdominal Surgeons, Royal Soc. Medicine (overseas fellow); mem. Conn., Fairfield County, Bridgeport med. socs., Magicians Guild Am., Magic Collectors Assn. (hon. life pres.), Am. Assn. Physicians and Surgeons, Pan Am. Med. Assn. (hon. life), Sigma Chi. Clubs: Univ. (Bridgeport); Magic Circle (London). Feature writer M.U.M. mag., 1958—, also research editor, monthly columnist; feature writer Magicol mag., 1959—; Am. corr. Magic Circular mag., London, 1960—; mem. Am. Magic Hall of Fame, 1977; contbr. to books. Home: 1708 Huntington Turnpike Trumbull CT 06611 Office: 144 Golden Hill St Bridgeport CT 06603

GROSSMAN, JONATHAN PHILIP, historian; b. N.Y.C., June 5, 1915; s. Jacob and Pauline (Cohen) G.; M.A., Tchrs. Coll. Columbia U., 1938; Ph.D., Columbia U., 1944; m. Rita Kurtzberg, Aug. 27, 1939 (dec.); m. 2d, Marilyn Stiles, Feb. 21, 1976. Historian, U.S. Army, 1949-54; pres. Temple Bus. Schs., Washington, 1951-68, chmn. bd., 1962-68; chief historian U.S. Dept. Labor, Washington, 1962—; sr. vis. prof. U. Md., 1974. Recipient Distinguished Career Service award Dept. Labor, 1975. Mem. Am. Hist. Assn., Orgn. Am. Historians. Jewish. Clubs: Cosmos, Nat. Press. Author: William Sylvis, Pioneer of Labor, 1945; U.S. Dept. Labor, 1974, others. Contbr. articles to profl. jours. Home: 800 25th St NW Washington DC 20037 Office: Dept Labor 200 Constitution Ave NW Washington DC 20010

GROSSMAN, JULIAN AARON, historian, educator; b. Allentown, Pa., Sept. 16, 1931; s. Joseph Samuel and Esther Badonna (Einhorn) G.; B.S., Columbia, 1953; M.L.S., Rutgers U., 1956; postgrad. Lehigh U., 1966-71; m. Carolyn Frances Judas, Aug. 28, 1969. Librarian young adults N.Y. Pub. Library, N.Y.C., 1956-57; reference, govt. documents librarian Muhlenberg Coll., Allentown, Pa., 1964-70; instr. history photography Community Coll. Phila., 1971-78; index librarian, sci. specialist COMPSET Pubs. Systems, Inc., 1978—. Muhlenberg Coll. faculty research grantee, 1969. Mem. AAAS, Valley Forge Hist. Soc. Author: Echo of a Distant Drum: Winslow Homer and the Civil War, 1974. Contbr. articles to profl. publs. Home: 211 Center Ave Norristown PA 19401

GROSSMAN, MARK IRA, communications corp. exec.; b. Newark, July 13, 1945; s. Sidney and Nettie G.; B.S. in Applied Math., Mass. Inst. Tech., 1967; M.S. in Physics, Rutgers U., 1969, M.S. in Statistics, 1974; m. Susan Helene Cohen, Nov. 22, 1969; children—Jennifer Dara, Jonathan David, Jaclyn Dyan. Ops. research analyst RCA Corp., Princeton, N.J., 1969-73; sr. analyst, 1973-74, mgr., mgmt. info. systems adminstrn., N.Y.C., 1974-75, mgr. mgmt. info. systems fin. and adminstrn., Cherry Hill, N.J., 1975-76, mgr. mgmt. info. systems RCA Am. Communications, Inc., Piscataway, N.J., 1976-78, dir. bus. systems devel. RCA corporate staff, 1978—. Exec. com. Princeton United Jewish Appeal, 1973—. Mem. Ops. Research Soc. Am., Inst. Mgmt. Scis., Am. Statis. Assn., Sigma Xi. Research presentations. Home: 12 Wallingford Dr Princeton NJ 08540 Office: RCA-David Sarnoff Research Center Princeton NJ 08540

GROSSMAN, SAMUEL, mfg. co. exec., publisher, author; b. Phila., Dec. 6, 1897; s. Mayer and Goldie (Klempner) G.; student Am. Bus. Inst., 1914-15, City Coll. N.Y., evenings 1919-20; m. Doris Boxer, Aug. 21, 1932; children—Judith, Lucille, Lawrence. Asso. editorial and accounting depts. N.Y. Times, 1915-18; founder S. Grossman Co., N.Y.C., 1921; pres. Grossman Stamp Co., Inc., N.Y.C., 1927—; founder Longacre Pub. Co., 1957. Mem. Am. Philatelic Assn., Am. Stamp Dealer's Assn. (pres. 1966-67, dir.), King County Grand Jurors Assn., Am. Numis. Assn., Assn. Stamp Exhbns., Grand Street Boys Assn., Internat. Fedn. Stamp Dealers Assns., Judaica Hist. Philatelic Soc., Royal Philatelic Soc. Can. Author: Superior World Stamp Album, 1950; Paramount World Stamp Album, 1951; Monarch World Stamp Album, 1952; Coronet DeLuxe World Stamp Album, 1954; Stamp Collector's Handbook, 1957-78; Regent World Stamp Album, 4 vols., 1957; Academy World Stamp Album, 1958; Capitol United States Stamp Album, 1959; Victory United States Stamp Album, 1959; Columbia U.S. Plate Block Album, 2 vols., 1969; Crown World Stamp Album, 3 vols., 1963; Transworld World Stamp Album, 1963; Flags and Coats of Arms of the World, 1968; Presidents and Famous Americans, 1968; Space Age Stamp Album, 1970; Philatelic Color Guide; Jefferson U.S. Stamp Album, 1972; Congress U.S. Stamp Album, 1977. Home: 10 W 16th St New York City NY 10011 Office: 860 Broadway New York City NY 10003

GROSSMAN, THOMAS, mech. and nuclear engr.; b. Michalovce, Czechoslovakia, Mar. 13, 1948; s. Henrich and Irena G.; came to U.S., 1968, naturalized, 1977; B.M.E., Coll. City N.Y., 1973, M.M.E., 1975; m. Irene I. Fischer, Dec. 26, 1974; children—Richard, Olivia. Asso. engr., designer, Paul Geringer Assos., N.Y.C., 1974; mech.-nuclear engr. Ebasco Services, N.Y.C., 1974—. Paul Elenor fellow, 1970-72. Mem. ASME. Jewish. Home: 264 Woodward Ave Staten Island NY 10314 Office: 21 West St Room 306 New York NY 10006

GROSSMANN, BERND, publishing co. exec.; b. Freiburg, Germany, Oct. 26, 1928; s. Franz Joseph and Emilia Helene (Otto) G.; came to U.S., 1957, naturalized, 1963; m. Dora Maria Polaczek, July 31, 1952; children—John Mark, Gregory Andrej. With Verlag Herder Pub. Co., Freiburg, 1944-50, Editorial Herder, Barcelona, Spain, 1950-51, Bogota, Colombia, 1951-56; mng. dir. Herder & Herder Inc., N.Y.C., 1957-62; v.p., mng. dir. Prentice-Hall Internat., London, 1962-69; mng. dir., dir. pub. Holt, Rinhart & Winston Internat., N.Y.C., 1969-70; exec. v.p., chief exec. officer Springer Verlag, N.Y.C., 1970—. Home: 14 Short Hill Rd Croton-on-Hudson NY 10520 Office: Springer-Verlag 175 Fifth Ave Suite 1900 New York City NY 10010

GROSSO, ANTHONY JOSEPH, protection services co. exec.; b. Poughkeepsie, N.Y., July 19, 1926; s. Anthony and Mary (Currieri) G.; B.E.E. cum laude, Manhattan Coll., 1950; M.E.E., N.Y.U., 1953; m. Margaret Mascarini, Oct. 31, 1953; children—Anthony, Alane. Instr. Manhattan Coll., Bronx, N.Y., 1950; with Am. Dist. Telegraph Co., N.Y.C., 1950—, sr. project engr., 1950-63, gen. mgr. diversification and expansion ops., 1963-70, chief engr., 1970, v.p. engring. and research, 1970-78, v.p. engring. and mfg., 1978—; adj. prof. math. and physics Pratt Inst., N.Y.C., 1953-70, chmn. math. dept., 1965-70. Served with AUS, 1946-47. Mem. IEEE (sr.; mem. Underwriters Lab. adv. conf. on burglar alarm systems 1970—, mem. alarm industry com. for combating crime, chmn. standards subcom. 1970-76), Central Sta. Elec. Protection Assn., Eta Kappa Nu. Patentee in field. Home: 155 Aldershot Ln Manhasset NY 11030 Office: One World Trade Center 92d Floor New York City NY 10048

GROSVENOR, GILBERT MELVILLE, mag. editor; b. Washington, May 5, 1931; s. Melville Bell and Helen (Rowland) G.; B.A., Yale U., 1954; m. Donna C. Kerkam, June 16, 1961; children—Gilbert Hovey, Alexandra Rowland. With Nat. Geog. Soc., 1954—, trustee, v.p., 1966—, asso. editor, 1967-70, editor, 1970—; dir. Am. Security and Trust Co., Peoples Life Ins. Co., Chesapeake & Potomac Telephone Co. Trustee B.F. Saul Real Estate Trust, N.Y. Zool. Soc., Internat. Center Photography, Davis Meml. Goodwill Industries; fellow Yale Corp.; dir. Found. Research into Origin of Man; trustee African Wildlife Leadership Found.; bd. overseers Sweet Briar Coll.; bd. govs. Beauvoir Sch.; ann. corporate mem. Children's Hosp. D.C. Served with AUS, 1954-56. Recipient Editor of Year award Nat. Press Photographers Assn., 1975; Distinguished Achievement award in periodical journalism U. So. Calif. Sch. Journalism and its Alumni Assn. Mem. Assn. Am. Geographers. Newcomen Soc. Clubs: Alfalfa, Overseas Writers (Washington); Explorers (N.Y.C.); Chevy Chase (Md.). Home: 1259 Crest Ln McLean VA 22101 Office: Nat Geographic Mag 17th and M Sts NW Washington DC 20036

GROTE, OTTO FREDERICK, stock broker; b. Boston, Dec. 20, 1930; s. Friedrich Franz Graf and Rachel Derby (Smith) G.; A.B. cum laude, Harvard U., 1953, M.B.A., 1957. Asso. corp. fin. dept. Hornblower & Weeks-Hemphill, Noyes, N.Y.C., 1961-67; research sales mgr. J. & W. Seligman & Co., N.Y.C., 1967-72; prin. Van Bergen & Co., Inc., N.Y.C., 1972—, chmn., 1975—. Served to 1st lt. USAF, 1954-56. Home: 72 E 86th St New York City NY Office: Van Bergen and Co Inc 1133 Ave of Americas New York City NY 10036

GROVE, DANIEL DWIGHT, anesthesiologist; b. Felton, Pa., Feb. 27, 1914; s. Daniel D. and Emma V. (Strayer) G.; B.S., Lebanon Valley Coll., Annville, Pa., 1934; M.D., Hahnemann Med. Coll., 1938; m. Kathryn Maude Mowrey, July 11, 1939; children—David, Carol. Intern, York Hosp., Pa., 1938-39; resident anesthesiology Hahnemann Med. Coll. and Hosp., 1941-43, asso. prof. anesthesiology, 1949-63, prof. surgery (anesthesiology), 1963-71, emeritus, 1971; clin. asso. prof. Woman's Med. Coll. of Pa., 1949-50; guest lectr. Grad. Sch. Medicine, U. Pa., 1949-51, vis. lectr., 1951-52; med. missionary Sierra Leone, Brit. West Africa, 1939-41. Treas. faculty Hahnemann Med. Coll., 1958-66; mem. bd. trustees Lebanon Valley Coll., Annville, Pa., 1959-68. Served to capt. AUS, 1943-46. Diplomate Nat. Bd. Med. Examiners, Am. Bd. Anesthesiology. Fellow Am. Coll. Anesthesiologists, Internat. Coll. Anesthetists; mem. AMA, Med. Soc. Pa., Phila. County Med. Soc., Am Inst. Homeopathy, Am. Soc. Anesthesiologists, Phila. Coll. Physicians, N.Y. Acad. Scis., Internat. Anesthesia Research Soc., Pa. (sec. 1949-66), Phila. socs. anesthesiologists, Homeopathic Med. Soc. Pa., Phila. Hahnemann Alumni Soc., Physiol. Soc. Phila., Assn. Am. Med. Colleges, Christian Med. Soc. Am. Mus. Natural History (asso.), Nat. Parks Assn. Methodist (trustee 1952-67). Clubs: Masons, Shriners. Author articles in field. Home and office: 5025 N Marvine St Philadelphia PA 19141

GROVE, ERNEST WILSON, economist; b. New Kensington, Pa., June 14, 1910; s. Edward Thomas and Adelaide (Wilson) G.; A.B., U. Cal. at Berkeley, 1932, Ph.D., 1948; m. Esther Elizabeth Krewson, Mar. 8, 1947; children—Kathryn Frances, Daniel Edward. Agrl. economist Bur. Agrl. Econs., U.S. Dept. Agr., 1936-41, 46-53, head farm income estimates sect. Agrl. Econs. Div., editor The Farm Income Situation, Washington, 1954-60; staff economist Agrl. Stabilization and Conservation Service, 1960-77, dep. dir. producer assns. div., 1977—. Chmn. Citizens Com. for Sch. Improvement Arlington, Va., 1961-62; mem. Arlington Pub. Utilities Commn., 1963-64; chmn., 1964. Served from 2d lt. to lt. col. Control Div., Hdqrs. Army Service Forces, U.S. Army, 1942-45. Decorated Legion of Merit. Fellow AAAS; mem. Am. Econ. Assn., Am. Agrl. Econs. Assn., Am. Statis. Assn., Conf. on Research in Income and Wealth, Internat. Conf. Agrl. Economists, Nat. Economists Club, Internat. Platform Assn., Phi Beta Kappa, Delta Sigma Rho, Omicron Delta Epsilon. Democrat. Unitarian. Author jour. articles. Home: 5429 S 5th St Arlington VA 22204 Office: Dept of Agr Washington DC 20250

GROVE, JOHN LANDIS, mfg. co. exec.; b. Shady Grove, Pa., Jan. 26, 1921; s. John F. and Almeda G. (Landis) G.; student pub. schs., Greencastle, Pa.; m. Cora I. Wagner, Apr. 24, 1943. With Landis Machine Co., Waynesboro, Pa., 1938-40, Landis Tool Co., Waynesboro, 1940-43, Westinghouse Electric Co., Lester, Pa., 1942-46; co-founder, exec. v.p., dir. Grove Mfg. Co., Shady Grove, Pa., 1946-69; founder JLG Industries, Inc., McConnelsburg, Pa., 1969—, also pres., chief exec. officer, dir.; pres., dir. Falling Spring Corp. real estate holding corp.; dir. 1st Nat. Bank Md., First Md. Bancorp., United Telephone Co. Pa. Bd. dirs. Greencastle Antrim Found. Served with AUS, 1944-45. Lutheran. Mem. Am. Legion, VFW. Clubs: Lions, Elks. Patentee hydraulic equipment. Home: 171 Apple Dr Greencastle PA 17225 Office: PO Box 695 McConnelsburg PA 17236

GROVE, KATHRYN MOWREY (MRS. D. DWIGHT GROVE), church worker; b. Harrisburg, Pa., Jan. 11, 1914; d. D. Floyd and Eva (Shearer) Mowrey; A.B. cum laude, Lebanon Valley Coll., 1934; m. D. Dwight Grove, July 11, 1939; children—David, Carol Grove Miller. Tchr. high sch., New Cumberland, Pa., 1934-39; missionary, Evang. U.B. Ch., Sierra Leone, West Africa, 1939-41; trustee Logan United Methodist Ch., 1971—; mem. bd. Christian edn. East Pa. Conf., 1957-62, children's work council, 1957-62; mem. council adminstrn. Pa. Council Chs., 1964-68, v.p., 1964-68; mem. fgn. student com., dept. united ch. women Greater Phila. Council Chs., 1960-64; pres. Women's Soc. World Service, Phila. 3d Ch., 1964-67; pres. East Pa. Conf. br. Women's Soc. World Service, 1957-62, mem. gen. program com., 1957-62, mem. com. leadership edn., 1963-67, dept. health and welfare, 1963-66, mem. nat. council, 1963-66, gen. treas., 1964-66, gen. pres., 1966-68; mem. joint commn. ch. union Evang. U.B. Ch., 1966-68; sec. jud. council United Meth. Ch., 1968-76. Founder Jr. Story League, New Cumberland, 1936; pres. Phila. Story League, 1955-57; chmn. 10th biennial conv. Nat. Story League, Phila., 1964; pres. Birney Sch. PTA, Phila., 1960-61; mem. women's planning com. Japan Internat. Christian U. Found., Inc.; trustee Lebanon Valley Coll., 1968—. Mem. AAUW, Pa. Folklore Soc., Elfreth's Assn. Republican. Club: Order Eastern Star. Contbr. articles to religious publs. Home: 5025 N Marvine St Philadelphia PA 19141

GROVE, RICHARD IRVING, computer co. exec.; b. Worcester, Mass., Dec. 19, 1926; s. Thomas Henry and Alice Marguerite (O'Brien) G.; student U. Mass., 1946-47, Clark U., 1947-50; B.B.A., Boston U., 1950; m. Helen L. Power, July 21, 1948; children—Jerome, Barry, Cheryl, Pamela, Doreen, Russell, Marena. Dist. mgr. Univac div. Sperry Rand Corp., 1954-65; nat. mgr. Gen. Electric Co., Albany and N.Y.C., 1965-68; dir. mktg. Data Products Corp., 1968-69; pres., chmn. bd. Dylaflo, Inc., Los Angeles, 1969-73; pres. Grove Assos., Worcester, Mass., 1973-76; nat. govt. mgr. Wang Labs., Inc., Lowell, Mass., 1977—; dir. Urban-Suburban, Inc., Regatta Point, Inc.; tchr. Central New Eng. Coll., Worcester, 1975—. Vol. counselor Rutland Heights Hosp., Rutland, Mass., 1976—. Served with USNR, 1943-44. Mem. Nat. Account Mktg. Assn., Am. Mgmt. Assn. Clubs: Regatta Point Sailing (pres.), Paxton Tennis. Home: 3 Robin Wood Rd Littleton MA 01460

GROVE, WILLIAM ARTHUR, JR., pub. relations exec.; b. Phila., Sept. 5, 1932; s. William Arthur and Elsie Styles (Barnett) G.; B.A., Bowdoin Coll., 1954; m. Susan Hoytense Forrest, June 23, 1956; 1 dau., Elizabeth Tyler. Mgmt. asst. Chesapeake & Potomac Telephone Co. W. Va., Wheeling, 1956-57, staff asst., Beckley, 1957-59, comml. engr., Charleston, W.Va., 1959-60, pub. relations supr., 1960-62; accounting staff supr., Chesapeake & Potomac Telephone Cos., Washington, 1962-64; dist. comml. mgr. Chesapeake & Potomac Telephone Co. W.Va., Huntington, 1964-66, pub. relations staff supr., Charleston, 1966-71; gen. pub. relations supr. Chesapeake & Potomac Telephone Cos., Washington, 1971—. Pub. relations chmn. United Fund Kanawha Valley, Charleston, 1969; mem. human relations commn., Huntington, 1966. Bd. dirs. A.R.C., Charleston, 1971. Served to lt., U.S. Army, 1954-56. Mem. Indsl. Communication Council, Pub. Relations Soc. Am., Advt. Club Charleston (pres.). Psi Upsilon. Episcopalian. Club: Bowdoin (pres. 1975-76) (Washington). Home: 1313 Capulet Ct McLean VA 22102 Office: 800 17th St NW Washington DC 20006

GROVER, SHAMSHER S., chem. co. exec.; b. Peshawar, India, Apr. 15, 1924; s. Jiwan and Har (Kaur) G.; B.Sc. in Chemistry with honors, U. Punjab (India), 1948; B.S. in Chem. Engring., Oreg. State U., 1950, M.S., 1952; M.S. in Engring., U. Mich., 1954; m. Jeanette C. Kiplinger, Feb. 5, 1953; children—Paul Jiwan, Sara Harte, Ann Margaret, Matthew James. Came to U.S., 1949, naturalized, 1957. Process engr. M.W. Kellogg Co., N.Y.C., 1954-58, mgr. computer applications div., N.Y.C., 1960-70; tech. specialist Airojet Gen. Corp., Sacramento, 1959-60; sr. asso. engr. Mobil Research and Devel. Corp., Princeton, N.J., 1970—. Named one of three top chem. engrs. U.S., Chem. Engring. Progress mag., 1969. Mem. Am. Inst. Chem. Engrs., Research Soc. Am., Sigma Xi, Phi Lambda Upsilon. Patentee in field. Contbr. to profl. jours. Home: 106 Darrow Dr Pennington NJ 08534 Office: PO Box 106 Princeton NJ 08540

GROWNEY, JAMES GERARD, assn. exec.; b. Hoboken, N.J., May 28, 1908; s. Peter and Helen (Sullivan) G.; B.S., Panzer Coll., 1933; M.A., Montclair State Coll., 1943; postgrad. Rutgers U., 1950, also N.Y. U.; m. Catherine Speer, Aug. 29, 1935 (dec.); 1 dau., Patricia Growney Ricker; m. 2d, Rosemary M. Deasy, Apr. 7, 1971. Tchr., dir. health phys. edn., athletics and safety Meml. High Sch., West New York, N.J., 1935-59; exec. sec.-treas. N.J. State Interscholastic Athletic Assn., Robbinsville, 1959—. Recipient numerous awards N.J. Interscholastic Coaches Assn., N.J. Athletic Dirs. Assn. Bd. dirs. U.S. Olympic Com., 1975—. Mem. U.S. Basketball Fedn. (bd. govs.), Nat. Football Found. Hall of Fame, Nat. Fedn. State High Sch. Athletic Assn. (exec. com. pres. 1976—), AAHPER, Am. Soc. Assn. Execs., NEA, Am. Assn. Sch. Adminstrs. Roman Catholic. Home: 36 Phillips Rd Greenbriar Section Brick Town NJ 08723 Office: Route 130 POB 487 Robbinsville NJ 08691

GRUB, PHILLIP DONALD, educator; b. Medical Lake, Wash., Aug. 8, 1936; s. Carl Dreyer and Barbara Rosalie Magdalena (Johnson) G.; B.A. in Econs., Eastern Wash. U., 1953, B.A. in Bus. Edn., 1953; M.B.A. (Scottish Rite fellow), George Washington U., 1960, D.B.A (Am. Security & Trust Co. fellow), 1964. Spl. asst. to pres. George Washington U., 1973—, Aryamehr prof. multinat. bus., 1974—; pres. Acad. Internat. Bus., 1974-77; vis. prof. internat. mktg. Helsinki Sch. Econs., 1971; spl. rep. George Washington U. to Govt. Iran; internat. cons., bd. dirs. Diplomat Nat. Bank. Bd. advisers Chung-Ang U., Helsinki Sch. Econs., Tehran Coll. Bus., Am. U. in Cairo. Served with U.S. Army, 1954-56. Recipient Distinguished Alumnus award Eastern Wash. U., 1970, High Twelve Internat. Founders award, 1978. Mem. Acad. Mgmt., U.S.-Japan Trade Soc., Am. Mgmt. Assn., Am. Econs. Assn., Soc. Internat. Devel., Alpha Kappa Psi. Clubs: Masons, Kiwanis (chmn. internat. relations com. 1974—). Author: A Guide to Personnel Development, 1966; American-East European Trade, 1968; co-author; Executive Leadership: The Art of Successfully Managing Resources, 1969; International Marketing in Perspective, 1971; The Multinational Enterprise in Transition, 1972; contbr. articles to profl. jours. Home: 3828 Cathedral Ave NW Washington DC 20016 Office: George Washington U Washington DC 20052

GRUBB, ROBERT LYNN, computer system designer; b. Knoxville, Tenn., Nov. 23, 1927; s. William Henry and DoLores Alfisi (Pierucci) Hollinshead; B.S., Central State Coll., Edmond, Okla., 1972; m. Donna Jean Chicado, May 28, 1973; children—Robert Lynn, Werner, Luke, Jubal. Air traffic controller FAA, Ft. Worth, 1955-62; engr. Philco-Ford Corp., Oklahoma City, 1962-65; service co. exec. Lear-Siegler Inc., Oklahoma City, 1965-67; computer specialist U.S. Navy, Corpus Christi, Tex., 1967-71, U.S. Army, Petersburg, Va., 1971-77, U.S. CSC, Washington, 1977—; cons. Durham Bus. Coll., Corpus Christi; cons. Corpus Christi Pub. Sch. Bd. Committeeman Boy Scouts Am., 1963-64; bd. dirs., athletic coach Southside Youth League, 1970. Served in USNR, 1945-46; PTO. Mem. Western Writers Am., Am. Hist. Soc. (charter). Author: Conversion and Implementation of CS3 Computer System, 1973; Economic Analysis of Automated System-TOPS, 1977. Contbr. articles and stories on Western history to various periodicals. Home: 11142 Saffold Way Reston VA 22090 Office: BMS Room 6410 1900 E St NW Washington DC 20415

GRUBBS, DONALD SHAW, JR., actuary; b. Bellevue, Pa., Dec. 15, 1929; s. Donald Shaw and Zora Faye (Craven) G.; A.B., Tex. A.and M. U., 1951; postgrad. Los Angeles State Coll., 1953-54, Fresno State Coll., 1954-55, Boston U., 1955-57, Princeton Theol. Sem., 1959-60, Westminster Theol. Sem., 1960-61, Georgetown U., 1975—; m. Margaret Helen Crooke, Dec. 27, 1969; children—David, Deborah, Daniel, Dawson, Dwight, Douglas. Tchr., Tulare (Cal.) Union High Sch., 1954-55; actuarial student New Eng. Mut. Life Ins. Co., Boston, 1955-58; actuarial asst. Warner-Watson, Inc., Boston, 1958-59; cons. actuary John B. St. John, Penllyn, Pa., 1959-65; cons. actuary Grubbs & Co., Phila., Balt., 1965-72; v.p., actuary Nat. Health and Welfare Retirement Assn., 1972-74; dir. actuarial div. IRS, 1974-76; chmn. Joint Bd. for Enrollment Actuaries, Washington, 1975-76; cons. actuary G.B. Buck Cons. Actuaries, Inc., Washington, 1976—; cons. to Senate Labor Subcom., 1972-74. Vice pres. Ambler N.A.A.C.P., 1961-62; chmn. Warminster Child Day Care Center, 1962-64. Served to 1st lt., AUS, 1951-53. Decorated Bronze Star medal with V. Fellow Soc. Actuaries, Conf. Actuaries in Pub. Practice; mem. Am. Acad. Actuaries, World Federalists (pres. Balt. chpt. 1971-72). Democrat. Unitarian. Author: (with G.E. Johnson) The Variable Annuity, 1967. Home: 10216 Royal Rd Silver Spring MD 20903 Office: 1629 K St NW Washington DC 20006

GRUBER, ALAN RICHARD, holding co. exec.; N.Y.C., Nov. 2, 1927; s. Abraham and Esther Lucille (Hiller) G.; S.B., Mass. Inst. Tech., 1945, S.M., 1946; M.A., Harvard U., 1948; m. Harriet C. Mandel, Nov. 7, 1948; children—James Mark, Marian Amy Gruber Montgomery, Steven Bennett. Treas., mgr. engring. Nuclear Devel. Corp. Am., White Plains, N.Y., 1948-57; div. mgr. Marquardt Corp., Van Nuys, Calif., 1958-61; exec. v.p. Capital for Tech. Industries, Inc., Santa Monica, Calif., 1961-64; dir. corporate planning Xerox Corp., Stamford, Conn., 1965-70; v.p. corporate devel. Heublein Inc., Farmington, Conn., 1970-72; pres. Triumph Am. Inc., N.Y.C., 1972-75; v.p. Internat. Basic Economy Corp., N.Y.C., 1975-76; chmn., pres. Orion Capital Corp., N.Y.C., 1976—. Trustee Am. Crafts Council. Mem. Am. Econs. Assn., N. Am. Soc. for Corporate Planning, N.Y. Soc. Security Analysts, Assn. Corporate Growth. Clubs: Harmonie (N.Y.C.); Metropolis Country (White Plains, N.Y.). Home: 876 Park Ave New York City NY 10021 Office: Orion Capital Corp 30 Rockefeller Plaza New York City NY 10020

GRUBER, JEROME MARTIN, bearings co. exec.; b. Chilton, Wis., July 21, 1919; s. John Francis and Anna Marie (Hertel) G.; B.S. in Mech. Engring., U. Wis., 1941; m. Dale Ann Perrett, Feb. 1, 1943; children—Jerome M., William J., Jeanne M., James B., Suzanne J., Judith A. Test engr. Gen. Electric Co., Schenectady, 1941, design engr., Lynn, Mass., 1946-57; chief engr. Waukesha Bearings Corp. (Wis.), 1957-65, v.p., 1965-66, v.p., Wayne, N.J., 1967—; v.p. Waukesha Industries Corp., 1966-67. Served with C.E., AUS, 1941-46. Decorated Bronze Star medal; registered profl. engr. Mass., Wis., N.J. Fellow ASME (chmn. lubrication div., Distinguished Service award 1972); mem. Soc. Naval Architects and Marine Engrs., Am. Soc. Naval Engrs., Am. Soc. Lubrication Engrs. Contbr. articles in field to profl. jours.; patentee in field. Home: 711 Cheyenne Dr Franklin Lakes NJ 07417 Office: 150 Hinchman Ave Wayne NJ 07470

GRUBER, MELVIN SAUL, dermatologist; b. Phila., Mar. 20, 1938; s. Julius Joseph and Mary (Boxman) G.; A.B., U. Pa., 1960; M.D., U. Kans., 1964; m. Beverly Satzberg, July 15, 1962; children—Frederick, Suzanne, Melissa. Intern, Madigan Gen. Hosp., Tacoma, 1964-65; resident in dermatology Temple U. Skin and Cancer Hosp., Phila., 1967-70; practice medicine specializing in dermatology, Blackwood, N.J., 1970—; v.p. Dermatology Assos., Moorestown, N.J., 1976—; clin. asst. prof. dermatology Skin and Cancer Hosp., Phila., 1978—. Served with U.S. Army, 1964-67. Diplomate Am. Bd. Dermatology. Fellow Am. Acad. Dermatology; mem. Phila. Dermatol. Soc., AMA, N.J., Camden County med. socs. Home: 21 Wagon Ln Cherry Hill NJ 08002 Office: 141 S Blackhorse Pike Blackwood NJ 08012 also W Red Bank Ave Woodbury NJ 08096

GRUBER, MURRAY PAUL, pharm. co. exec.; b. N.Y.C., Jan. 24, 1917; s. Benjamin and Sarah (Cooper) G.; Ph.B., L.I. U., 1938; m. Lila Jacobs, Aug. 21, 1952 (dec. 1970); children—Barry, Sharon, Daryl, Neil; m. 2d, Helen Molberger, Feb. 5, 1972. Pharm. salesman Almay Co., N.Y.C., 1939-42, Ayerst Labs., Inc., N.Y.C., 1945-48; pres. Dermik Labs., Inc., L.I., N.Y., 1948—, also trustee, dir.; adviser U.S. Pharmacopeia Monograph Revision Com., 1970—. Bd. dirs., trustee Lila Gruber Research Found., Syosset, N.Y. Served with AUS, 1942-45. Mem. Am. Pharm. Assn., Soc. Cosmetic Chemists, Am. Soc. Hosp. Pharmacists, Am. Acad. Dermatology (affiliate). Contbr. articles to profl. jours. Office: 150 Eileen Way Syosset NY 11791

GRUBIAK, MICHAEL ROBERT, analytical chemist; b. Yonkers, N.Y., Aug. 1, 1934; s. Michael John and Anna (Fenyo) G.; student Columbia U., Fordham U.; m. Dorothy Nyilis, May 12, 1956; 4 children. Tech. sr. Refined Syrup's & Sugars Inc., Yonkers, 1954-61; researcher Boyse Thompson Inst. Plant Research, Yonkers, 1961-78; sr. technician Philips Labs., Briarcliff, N.Y., 1978—; supr. lab. Ferroxcube Corp., Saugerties, N.Y., 1961—. Served with USNR, 1954-56. Mem. Am. Chem. Soc. Democrat. Roman Catholic. Club: Lions. Home: 44 Mountain View Ave Hurley NY 12443 Office: Ferroxcube Corp 5083 Kings Hwy Saugerties NY 12477

GRUBNER, OTTO, phys. chemist; b. Prague, Czechoslovakia, Sept. 24, 1924; s. Frantisek and Marie (Sykorova) G.; student Technol. U. Prague, 1945-47; B.S., Charles U., Prague, 1948, M.S., 1950, Ph.D. summis auspiciis, 1952; C.Sc., Technol. U. Prague, 1958, Docent, 1968; m. Hana Brabcova, Feb. 24, 1947; children—George, Martin. Asst. prof. Charles U., 1950-52; scientist Inst. Phys. Chemistry, Czech Acad. Scis., 1952-59, leading scientist, 1959-70; vis. prof. Ain Shams U., Cairo, 1965; lectr. Technol. U., Pardubice, Czechoslovakia, 1964-68, asso. prof., 1968-70; researcher Harvard U. Sch. Pub. Health, Boston, 1969—. Recipient Sci. Achievement awards Czech Acad. Scis. (5). Roman Catholic. Co-author: Molecular Sieves, 1968; Heterogeneous Catalysis, 1967; editor Jour. Chromatografia, 1959—; contbr. articles to sci. jours. Home: 23 Kladska Prague Czechoslovakia Office: 665 Huntington Ave Boston MA 02115

GRUCCIO, LILLIAN JOAN (MRS. WILLIAM TAYLOR HARRINGTON THORMAN), lawyer; b. Camden, N.J.; d. Joseph and Millie (Fornataro) Gruccio; grad. Steelman Bus. Sch., Camden, 1945; A.A., Rutgers U., 1947, LL.B., 1951, LL.D., 1968. Admitted to N.J. bar, 1952, to U.S. Supreme Ct. bar, 1960; partner of Frank C. Propert, Camden, 1952-55; asso. Lewis and Hutchinson, and successor firms, Camden, 1956-61; with legal dept. Campbell Soup Co., Camden, 1955; practiced in Pennsauken, N.J., 1961-73, Medford, N.J., 1973—; mem. Camden City Juvenile Conf. Com., 1957-62. Bd. dirs. Camden County Health and Welfare Council, 1957-61; bd. dirs. Camden and Vicinity YWCA, 1959-67, chairperson adult program com., 1957-67, fashion show com., 1967; budget com. United Fund of Camden County, 1968; mem. Burlington County Girl Scout Council, Inc., 1975—, chairperson by-laws com., 1975; chairperson legis. com. Aux. to Pennsauken United Republican Club, 1971-72. Mem. Am., N.J., Burlington County bar assns., Rutgers U. Law Sch. Alumni Assn. (chancellor South Jersey div. 1962, bd. mgrs. 1952-64), Burlington County Bus. and Profl. Women's Club (scholarship com. 1974, legis. com. 1973-74, by-laws com. 1975), LeisureTowne Civic League (rec. sec. 1974-75). Home: 63 Sheffield Pl Vincentown NJ 08088 Office: Cedarbrook Bldg Taunton Blvd Medford NJ 08055

GRUEN, PETER H., psychiatrist, educator; b. N.Y.C., June 6, 1939; s. Hans and Ilse (Marx) Wertheimer; B.A. in Psychology with honors, U. Calif. at Berkeley, 1961; M.D. (NIH summer fellow), U. Calif. at San Francisco, 1965; children—Arthur L., Kim J. Intern, Bronx Municipal Hosp. Center, 1965-66; resident in psychiatry Albert Einstein Coll. Medicine, Bronx, N.Y., 1969-72, chief resident, 1971-72; practice medicine specializing in psychiatry, N.Y.C., 1972—; asst. instr. psychiatry Albert Einstein Coll. Medicine, 1971-72, 1972-74, asst. prof. psychiatry, 1974-76; asso. prof. psychiat. inst. Columbia U. Coll. Physicians and Surgeons, 1976—; head clin. research unit dept. of psychiatry Bronx Municipal Hosp. Center, 1973-75, asso. dir. psychobiol. research, 1975-76, dir. div. clin. psychopharmacology, 1977—; asst. prof. neurosci. Albert Einstein Coll. Medicine, 1978—; attending psychiatrist Lenox Hill Hosp., N.Y.C., 1976—, Gracie Square Hosp., N.Y.C., 1975—; asst. attending psychiatrist Bronx Municipal Hosp., Center, 1972—, Presbyn. Hosp., N.Y.C., 1976-77; research psychiatrist N.Y. State Psychiat. Inst., 1976-77. Served to maj., M.C., U.S. Army, 1966-69. Recipient Anne Monika Found. prize, 1975; diplomate Am. Bd. Psychiatry and Neurology. Mem. Am. Psychiat. Assn., Am. Psychosomatic Soc., AAAS, Am. Psychopath. Assn., Alpha Omega Alpha. Contbr. articles on psychopharmacology to profl. jours. Home: 56 Spain Valley Rd Scarsdale NY 10583 Office: Albert Einstein Coll Med 1300 Morris Park Ave Bronx NY 10461 also 971 Madison Ave New York City NY 10021

GRUENBERG, ERNEST M., psychiatrist, epidemiologist, educator; b. N.Y.C., Dec. 2, 1915; s. Benjamin Charles and Sidonie (Matsner) G.; B.A., Swarthmore Coll., 1937; M.D., Johns Hopkins U., 1941; Dr.P.H., Yale U., 1955; m. Lillian Saastamoinen, 1943; children—Nicholas Benjamin, Ann Matsner, Matthew Alan; m. 2d, Judith Stainbrook, 1975. Intern, St. Elizabeth Hosp., Washington, 1941-42; resident in psychiatry Bellevue Hosp., N.Y.C., 1946-48; exec. dir. N.Y. State Mental Health Commn., 1949-54; lectr. depts. psychiatry and pub. health Yale U., 1952-72; sr. mem. tech. staff Milbank Meml. Fund, N.Y.C., 1955-61; prof. psychiatry Columbia U., 1961-75; attending psychiatrist Presbyn. Hosp., N.Y.C., 1966-75, Hudson River Psychiat. Center, Poughkeepsie, N.Y., 1967-75; dir. pyschiat. epidemiology research unit N.Y. State Dept. Mental Hygiene, 1968-75; prof., chmn. dept. mental hygiene Johns Hopkins U., 1975—; practice psychiatry, Syracuse, N.Y., 1950-55, N.Y.C., 1955-75, Poughkeepsie, 1967-75, Balt., 1975—; lectr. epidemiology Harvard Sch. Pub. Health, 1959-69, Columbia Sch. Pub. Health, 1953-72. Mem. tech. bd. Milbank Meml. Fund, N.Y.C., 1961-68, 74—; mem. tech. adv. bd. Maurice M. Falk Med. Fund, Pitts., 1963—; mem. Milbank Meml. Fund. Commn. on Higher Edn. for Pub. Health, 1972-75. Served with M.C., AUS, 1942-46. Fellow Am. Psychiat. Assn. (chmn. ad hoc com. on aging 1952-55, chmn. com. nomenclature and statistics 1965-68), Am. Pub. Health Assn. (governing council, chmn. com. mental health). Organizer, editor: (with F. G. Boudreau) Roundtable on Epidemiology of Mental Disorders, 1949; editor: Evaluating the Effectiveness of Community Mental Health Services, 1966; contbr. chpts. to books, articles to profl. jours. Home: 211 E Highfield Rd Baltimore MD 21218 Office: Dept Mental Hygiene 615 N Wolfe St Baltimore MD 21205

GRUENFELD, LEON S., computer systems cons.; b. Bklyn., Feb. 10, 1950; s. Martin and Helen (Faust) G.; B.A. cum laude in Psychology and Philosophy, 1972. Programmer, Tymshare, Inc., N.Y.C., 1973-74, systems analyst, 1974-75, systems cons., 1975-76, project leader, 1976—, mgr. systems devel. CAPS group, 1977—. Mem. Assn. Computing Machinery, Soc. Certified Data Processors. Contbr. articles to profl. jours. Home: 7 Park Ave Apt 141 New York City NY 10016 Office: Tymshare 260 Madison Ave New York City NY 10016

GRUFT, HOWARD MARTIN, microbiologist; b. N.Y.C., Nov. 19, 1935; s. Lawrence and Sylvia (Goodman) G.; B.A., N.Y. U., 1956; M.Sc., Union U., Schenectady, 1962; Ph.D., Syracuse U., 1967; m. Barbara Bender, Mar. 3, 1956; children—Richard Scott, Jill Susan, Bonnie Lynn. With div. labs. and research N.Y. State Dept. Health, Albany, 1956—, supr. Tb dept., 1961—; teaching asst. Syracuse U., 1968. Pres. Colonie Jewish Community Assn., 1962-63. Fellow Am. Acad. Microbiology; mem. Am. Soc. Microbiology, Am. Thoracic Soc., Am. Pub. Health Assn., Sigma Xi. Jewish (pres. congregation 1971-73). Contbr. articles to profl. jours. Developer media for isolation mycobacteria. Home: 42 Fairlawn Dr Latham NY 12110 Office: 120 New Scotland Ave Albany NY 12201

GRUHN, WILLIAM THEODORE, educator; b. Bridgeport, Conn., Nov. 11, 1904; s. Carl Adolph and Louisa (Vahlsing) G.; B.S., No. State Coll. Aberdeen, S.D., 1926; M.A., U. Minn., 1933; Ph.D., U. N.C., 1940; m. Myrtis May Clark, July 14, 1928; 1 dau., Myrna Kay (Mrs. Myrna K. Ginand). Tchr., prin. jr. high sch., Abderdeen, 1926-37; fellow U. N.C., 1938-39, instr., 1939-40; asst. prof. U. Conn., Storrs, 1940-43, asso. prof., 1943-47, prof. edn., 1947-73, prof. emeritus, 1973—, acting dean, 1948-49, dir. tchr. edn. 1949-58; vis. instr. U. Colo., summer 1940, N.Y.U., summer 1946, U. Tex., summer 1951. Mem. NEA, Nat. Assn. Secondary Sch. Prins., AAUP, Phi Delta Kappa, Kappa Delta Pi. Author: Modern Junior High School, 1956, 3d edit., 1971; Teaching in Secondary Schools, 1954; Practice Teaching in Elementary Schools, 1957; Principles and Practices of Secondary Education, 1962. Home: Willington Hill Rd Storrs CT 06268

GRUM, CLIFFORD J., publisher; b. Davenport, Iowa, Dec. 12, 1934; s. Allen F. and Nathalie (Cate) G.; B.A., Austin Coll., 1956; M.B.A., U. Pa., 1958; m. Dona Janelle Lewis, May 1, 1965; 1 son, Christopher J. Vice pres. Republic Nat. Bank, Dallas, 1958-65; v.p. Temple Industries, N.Y.C., 1965-68, v.p. fin., 1968-73; with Time Inc. (acquired Temple Industries 1973), N.Y.C., 1973—, treas., 1973-75, v.p., 1975—, pub. Fortune mag., 1975—. Home: 35 Deerfield Rd Chappaqua NY 10514 Office: Time Inc Time & Life Bldg Rockefeller Center New York City NY 10020

GRUNDT, LEONARD, librarian; b. Bklyn., Sept. 5, 1936; s. Louis and Augusta (Machlis) G.; B.A., Bklyn. Coll., 1958; M.S., Columbia U., 1960; Ph.D., Rutgers U., 1965; m. Barbara Joyce Schwartz, June 17, 1967; children—Adam Matthew, Amy Diahann. Acquisitions asst. Bklyn. Coll. Library, 1958-60, social sci. librarian, 1960-61; ref. librarian Free Pub. Library, Linden, N.J., 1961-62; researcher Boston Pub. Library, 1962-63; research specialist Rutgers U., New Brunswick, N.J., 1964-65; coordinator instructional services Nassau Community Coll. Library, Garden City, N.Y., 1965-66, dep. dir. library, 1966-67, dir. library, 1967-75, prof., chmn. library dept., 1975—; reference librarian Library U.S.A., N.Y. World's Fair, 1965; vis. prof. library sci. State U. Coll., Geneseo, N.Y., 1966, Queens Coll., City U. N.Y., 1973; chmn. Conf. State U. N.Y. Head Librarians, 1971-72, 78-79; pres., bd. trustees L.I. Library Resources Council, Inc., 1974. Mem. ALA, N.Y., Nassau County library assns., Assn. Ednl. Communications and Tech., ACLU, Melvil Dui Marching and Chowder Assn., Phi Beta Kappa, Beta Phi Mu. Jewish. Author: Efficient Patterns for Adequate Library Service in a Large City: A Survey of Boston, 1968; editor (with Ralph Blasingame) Research on Library Service in Metropolitan Areas 1967; contbr. articles to profl. jours. and books. Home: 12 Commander Vic Ln Nesconset NY 11767 Office: Nassau Community Coll Garden City NY 11530

GRUNDY, J(OHN) OWEN, archivist, journalist; b. Jersey City, Mar. 8, 1911; s. J. Owen and Julia E. (Salter) G.; student Cooper Union, N.Y.C. Contbg. editor Jersey Rev., Jersey City, 1928-34; exec. sec. N.J. Commn. Cleaning and Dyeing Industries, 1934-36; pub. relations asst. to U.S. senator, 1931; asst. to commr. registrations of Hudson County, N.J., 1940-43; freelance writer, 1943-46, 61-68; reporter, asso. editor The Villager, N.Y.C., 1946-59; pres., editor Greenwich Village News, 1959-61; archivist Jersey City Pub. Library, 1968—; city historian, Jersey City, 1973—, also spl. asst. to mayor; lectr. in field; adj. polit. sci. Jersey City State Coll., 1976. Founder, sec. Greenwich Village Fresh Air Fund; trustee Washington Square Outdoor Art Exhibit, N.Y.C., Lincoln Assn., Internat. Inst., Jersey City; pres. Jersey City Museum; chmn. Municipal Hist. Dists. Commn. Jersey City. Recipient various community service awards; hon. mem. Phi Alpha Theta. Author: History of Jersey City, 1976; author articles and monographs. Address: Jersey City Public Library 472 Jersey Ave Jersey City NJ 07302

GRUNER, SAUL GEORGE, career cons. exec.; b. Pittsfield, Mass., July 29, 1916; s. Harry and Augusta (Lubin) G.: B.S., U. Mass., 1938, M.S., 1939: m. Sybil B. Gale, Apr. 1, 1944; children—David Marc, Richard Gale. Mgr., Carr Hardware Co., Pittsfield, Mass., 1939-41, 45-50; v.p., gen. mgr. Luff's Hardware Inc., Little Neck, N.Y., 1950-56; pres. G and S Assos., Inc., Mfrs. Reps., N.Y.C., 1956-72, Saul G. Gruner Assos. Inc., Exec. Job Counselors, N.Y.C., 1960-69; v.p., cons. Exec. Job Counselors, Bernard Haldane Assos., N.Y.C., 1957-60; sr. v.p. profl. services Thinc Career Planning Corp., N.Y.C., 1969—, also dir. Pres. Westbury Schs. PTA, L.I., N.Y., 1956; Westbury Little League commr., 1958. Served to capt. M.C., AUS, 1941-45. Mem. Am. Soc. Tng. and Devel., Am. Personnel and Guidance Assn., Soc. Profl. Mgmt. Cons., Am. Mgmt. Assn. Coined word out-placement, developer concept, methodology for cons., author numerous tng. manuals, handbooks. Home: 25 Sutton Pl S New York City NY 10022 Office: 1345 Ave of Americas New York City NY 10019

GRUNES, ROBERT LEWIS, engring. cons. firm exec.; b. N.Y.C., Aug. 15, 1941; s. Abe and Doris (Dicker) G.; B.S. in Metall. Engring., Poly. Inst. Bklyn., 1963, M.S. in Metall. Engring., 1965, Ph.D. in Phys. Metallurgy, 1970; m. Eleonora A. Grasselli, Oct. 14, 1972; children—Natalie Margot, Daniel Arie. Engr., Pratt and Whitney div. United Tchrs. Corp., East Hartford, Conn., 1963; research fellow Poly. Inst. Bklyn., 1963-64, research asso., 1966-70; research engr. Lewis Research Center, NASA, Cleve., 1965; pres. R.L. Grunes & Assos., Inc., N.Y.C., 1970—; mem. adj. faculty N.J. Inst. Tech. Served with C.E., U.S. Army, 1964-66. Decorated Bronze Star; registered profl. engr., N.Y., N.J., Pa. Mem. Metall. Soc., AIME, ASTM, Sigma Xi, Alpha Sigma Mu. Author: An Analysis of the Pollution Control Market and Industries, 1971; contbr. articles to profl. jours.; research in induced phase transformations, 1966-70, bulk material properties, 1963-64, coatings, 1962-63, friction, wear properties of materials, 1965. Office: 505 Fifth Ave New York City NY 10017

GRUNEWALD, DONALD, coll. pres.; b. N.Y.C., Feb. 9, 1934; s. Harry A. and Tina (Gegner) G.; A.B., Union Coll., 1954; M.A., Harvard U., 1955, M.B.A., 1959, D.B.A., 1962; LL.D., Emerson Coll., 1973; Litt.D., Suffolk U., 1974. Instr., U. Kans. Sch. Bus., 1959-60; lectr. Boston U. Coll. Bus. Adminstrn., 1961-62; research agt. Harvard U. Grad. Sch. of Bus., 1962; asst. prof. Rutgers U. Grad. Sch. Bus., 1962-65; asso. prof., 1965-67; dean, prof. Suffolk U. Coll. Bus. Adminstrn., Grad. Sch. Adminstrn., Boston, 1967-69, v.p., dean, prof. Coll. Liberal Arts, 1969-72; pres., prof. Mercy Coll., Dobbs Ferry, N.Y., 1972—, also trustee; life gov. Manchester Coll., Oxford, Eng.; ednl. cons. Trustee Dobbs Ferry Hosp., Westchester Conservatory of Music. Served as lt. USAF, 1955-57. Decorated knight Order St. John of Jerusalem. Fellow Inst. Commerce (London); mem. Am. Econ. Assn., Acad. Mgmt., Westchester County Assn. (dir.), Internat. Assn. Univ. Pres.'s (exec. com.). Clubs: Harvard (N.Y.C., Boston), Proprietor, Boston Athenaeum, Ardsley Country, Rotary. Author: Cases in Business Policy, 1962; (with Moranian, Reidenbach) Business Policy and Its Environment, 1964; (with H. Bass) Public Policy and the Modern Corporation, 1966; Small Business Management, 1966; (with Fenn, Katz) Business Decision Making and Government Policy, 1966; (with S. J. Flink) Managerial Finance, 1969. Home: Hudson Rd E Ardsley-on-Hudson NY 10503

GRUNOR, JERRY ARNOLD, advt. and mgmt. cons.; b. Bklyn., Sept. 6, 1940; s. Harry Ralph and Faye (Snapper) G.; B.A., Coll. City N.Y., 1961; m. Joan Miriam Bachman, Dec. 9, 1962; children—Janice Elaine, Eric Martin. Advt. dir. Allied Stores, N.Y.C., 1962-68; v.p., advt. dir. Lane Bryant div. Town and Country, N.Y.C., 1968-77; pres. E. J. Assocs., Mgmt. Cons., Short Hills, N.J., 1977—; chief exec. officer, pres. Optical Designs, Inc. 1978—; cons. Nat. Mass. Retail Inst., 1970-76. Bd. dirs. Temple Sinai, Summit, N.J., 1978—. Served with U.S. Army, 1960-62. Mem. Discount Advt. Dirs. Assn. N.Y. (sec.-treas. 1973-76), Advt. Dirs. N.Y. (chmn. advt. council 1975-76), Nat. Mass Retail Inst., Writers Guild. Clubs: Advt., Press, B'nai B'rith. Author: Retail Advertising Approaches, 1978. Contbr. articles to profl. jours. Office: Box 282 Short Hills NJ 07078

GRUNWALD, HANS W., clin. hematologist/oncologist; b. Stuttgart, Germany, July 24, 1935; s. Walter I. and Lotte R. (Strauss) G.; came to U.S., 1968, naturalized, 1972; B.Biology, Liceo No. 1 (Chile), 1953; M.D., U. Chile, 1960; m. Doris Heine, Jan. 4, 1969; children—Michael, Judith. Intern, Mt. Sinai Hosp., Chgo., 1960-61, med. resident, 1961-63; fellow in clin. hematology Tufts New Eng. Med. Center, Boston, 1963-65; asst. instr. medicine Chgo. Med. Sch., 1962-63; asst. instr. lab. diagnosis Tufts U. Sch. Medicine, Boston, 1964-65; asst. prof. dept. pathophysiology U. Chile, 1967; clin. instr. dept. medicine State U. N.Y., Buffalo, 1968-71, clin. asso., 1971-72; asst. prof. dept. medicine State U. N.Y., Stony Brook, 1973—; hematologist Carlos van Buren Hosp., Valparaiso, Chile, 1965-68; coordinator dept. medicine Sisters of Charity Hosp., Buffalo, 1968-72; cons. in hematology Emergency Hosp., Buffalo, 1968-72; asso. hematologist Queens Hosp. Center, Jamaica, N.Y., 1972-74, asst. dir. div. hematology, 1974-76, asso. dir., 1976—; staff hematologist L.I. Jewish Hillside Med. Center, New Hyde Park, N.Y., 1972—. Diplomate Am. Bd. Internal Medicine. Mem. Colegio Medico de chile, Sociedad Medica de Valparaiso, Sociedad Chilena de Hematologia, N.Y. State Med. Soc., AMA, Internat. Soc. Exptl. Hematology, Internat., Am. socs. hematology, N.Y. Acad. Sci., N.Y. Soc. Study of Blood, Am. Fedn. Clin. Research, Tissue Culture Assn., AAAS, A.C.P., Am. Soc. Clin. Oncology. Democrat. Jewish. Contbr. articles in field to profl. jours. Home: 8 Mary Ln Greenvale NY 11548 Office: 82-68 164th St Jamaica NY 11432

GRUPPE, KARL WILLIAM, physician; b. Rochester, N.Y., May 27, 1901; s. Herman Frederick and Caroline (Emrich) G.; B.S., U. Rochester, 1927, M.D., 1930; postgrad. Lembert Sch. Ear Surgery, 1954; m. Statira Johnson, Aug. 16, 1930 (dec.); 1 dau., Jane Paula; m. 2d, Sally Edgett Sherwood, Nov. 26, 1977. Intern U. Rochester-Strong Meml. Hosp., 1930-33; practice medicine, specializing in otolaryngology, Utica, 1933—; founder, med. dir. Utica (N.Y.) Hearing and Speech Center, 1950—. Served to maj. M.C., U.S. Army, 1941-43. Diplomate Am. Bd. Otolaryngology; mem. AMA, N.Y. State Med. Soc., Sierra Club, Izaak Walton League, Audubon Soc. Republican. Presbyterian. Contbr. articles on med. instruments and tech. Office: Faxton Hosp Utica NY 13502

GRZECHOWIAK, SUSAN MARIE, city ofcl.; b. Buffalo, Oct. 31, 1952; d. Edward Anthony and Dolores Marie (Szymanski) G.; student Canisius Coll., 1970-71; B.S., SUNY, Buffalo, 1974. Housing aide Buffalo Mcpl. Housing Authority, 1973-74, asst. housing mgr. 1974-76, supr. tenant selection and placement, 1976-78, sr. dist. mgr., 1978—. Mem. Am. Fedn. State and County Mcpl. Employees (local 264 unit sec. 1978-79), Nat. Assn. Housing and Renewal Ofcls., U. Buffalo Alumni Assn., Beta Sigma Phi. Democrat. Roman Catholic.

Contbr. articles in field to profl. jours. Home: 482 Fillmore Ave Buffalo NY 14206 Office: 901 City Hall Niagara Sq Buffalo NY 14202

GRZYB, FRANK LOUIS, mfg. co. exec.; b. Webster, Mass., May 29, 1946; s. Frank Louis and Rose Mary (Mozdzierz) G.; B.B.A., Nichols Coll., 1967; M.B.A., Fairleigh Dickinson U., 1969; postgrad. Springfield Coll., 1971; m. Virginia Marie Dutra, Aug. 19, 1972; 1 son, Matthew Francis. Scheduling mgr. Providence Pile Fabric Corp., Fall River, Mass., 1971-73; materials handling mgr. Tex. Instruments, Inc., Attleboro, Mass., 1973-75; prodn. and inventory control mgr. Masoneilan Internat. Inc., Norwood, Mass., 1975—; lectr. in field. Mem. Portsmouth (R.I.) Tax Payers Assn., 1977-78. Served with U.S. Army, 1969-71. Decorated Army Commendation medal, Purple Heart, Bronze Star medal. Mem. Am. Prodn. and Inventory Control Soc. Roman Catholic. Club: Purple Heart of Am. Home: 38 Columbia Terr Portsmouth RI 02871 Office: 63 Nahatan St Norwood MA 02062

GSCHLECHT, MARIANNE PATRICIA, telephone co. adminstr.; b. Queens, N.Y., Aug. 17, 1947; d. William Vincent and Kathleen Patricia (Landers) G.; B.A., Hunter Coll., 1969; M.B.A., St. John's U., 1978. Asst. dial service supr. N.Y. Telephone Co., Queens, 1970-72, dial service supr., 1972-74, network supr., N.Y.C., 1974-76, engr., 1976, corp. planner, 1976-78, dist. staff mgr., 1978—; career guidance speaker. Mem. Omicron Delta Epsilon, Beta Gamma Sigma. Roman Catholic. Office: 1095 Ave of Americas New York City NY 10036

GUADAGNA, S. J., graphic arts exec.; b. Bklyn., Nov. 12, 1929; s. Joseph and Rose (Camera) G.; B.B.A., St. John's U., 1958; postgrad. N.Y. U., 1962; m. Dolores Therese Nagy, Sept. 18, 1954; children—Elise, Robert, Andrea, Gina, Anthony. Asst. controller James F. Newcomb Co., Inc., N.Y.C., 1956-62, controller, 1962-64, sec., treas., dir., 1964-65; dir. treas. sec. Pandick Press, Inc. N.Y.C., 1965-69, sr. v.p., sec., dir., 1969-70; founder, dir. Videographic Systems, Inc., Hauppauge, N.Y., 1966-70, pres., 1967-70; founder sr. partner Vicode Assos., Northport, N.Y., 1970-72; pres., dir. chief exec. officer Rudor Inc., N.Y.C., 1972-77; pres., dir. Automatech Graphics Corp., 1973-77, Rudor Graphics, 1977—; v.p. Sorg Printing Co., Inc., N.Y.C., 1977-78, exec. v.p., 1978—; dir. Rudor Consol. Industries, Inc., 1973-77. Speaker before profl., civic groups. Mem. Nat. Assn. Accountants, Adminstrv. Mgmt. Soc., Printing Industries Met. N.Y. (dir. 1974—). Contbr. to Handbook of Business Administration (H.B. Maynard), 1968. Contbr. articles to profl. jours. Home: 7 Tanager Ln Northport NY 11768 Office: Sorg Printing Co Inc 111 8th Ave New York City NY 10011

GUARDINO, GARY, indsl. engr.; b. Bklyn., May 10, 1946; s. James F. and Carmela E. G.; A.A.S. summa cum laude, Acad. Aeros., 1972; B.E.I.E. cum laude, N.Y. U., 1976; m. Josephine J. Scipione, July 8, 1967; 1 son, Christopher. Asso. engr. Western Electric. Co., Queens, N.Y., 1972-73; indsl. engr. Gyrotronics Inc., Bronx, N.Y., 1973-74, Alpha Metals Inc., Jersey City, 1974-75, Pirelli Cable Corp., Union, N.J., 1975—; cons. in field. Vice pres. bd. dirs. The Hills at Grasmere Condominium I, 1977, pres., 1978. Served with USAF, 1966-70. Mem. Am. Inst. Indsl. Engrs. (sr. mem.), Am. Production and Inventory Control Soc. Roman Catholic. Home: 203 Grasmere Dr Staten Island NY 10305 Office: 800 Rahway Ave Union NJ 07083

GUARINI, FRANK J., JR., congressman; b. Jersey City, Aug. 20, 1924; s. Frank J. and Caroline (Critelli) G.; B.A., Dartmouth Coll., 1947; LL.B., N.Y. U., 1950, LL.M., 1955; postgrad. The Hague (Netherlands) Acad. Internat. Law. Admitted to N.J. bar, 1951, U.S. Supreme Ct. bar, 1955; partner firm Guarini & Guarini, Jersey City, 1951-78; mem. N.J. Senate, 1966-72, chmn. air and water pollution and pub. health com., 1967-68; mem. 96th Congress from 14th Dist. N.J., Washington, 1979—. Mem. council on govt. Fairliehg Dickinson U.; mem. exec. com. Christ Hosp., Jersey City; fund chmn. Urban League Hudson County; bd. dirs. Hudson County Mental Health Assn., Hudson County Health and Tb League; mem. nat. bd. govs. ARC, also pres. Jersey City chpt.; chmn. bd. regents St. Peter's Coll., Jersey City. Served to lt. USNR, 1942-46; PTO. Recipient UNICO Man of Year award Jersey City, 1966. Mem., Am., Fed., Inter-Am., Hudson County (trustee), N.J. (gen. council) bar assns., Jersey City C. of C. (exec. com.), The Hague Acad. Internat. Law (trustee), Hudson County Bar Found. (trustee), Assn. Am. Trial Lawyers (nat. gov.), N.J. Assn. Trial Lawyers (chmn. exec. com.), Phi Delta Phi (magistrate), Alpha Delta Phi. Clubs: Rotary (dir.), N.Y. Athletic; Columbus Citizens; Bergen Carteret U. Hudson County (gov.) (Jersey City). Home: 608 Newark Ave Jersey City NJ 07306 Office: US Ho of Reps The Capitol Washington DC 20515

GUBALA, JACK J., editor; b. Franklin, N.J., Oct. 30, 1938; s. Joseph Leo and Katherine Elizabeth (Weber) G.; B.A., N.Y. U., 1962; student New Sch. Social Research, 1963-64; m. Paula Ann Kaminsky, Mar. 19, 1966; children—David D., Joan Danette. Directory editor United Bus. Publs., N.Y.C., 1962-64; asst. devel. dir. Columbia Sch. Engring. and Applied Sci., 1965-68; editor Coinamatic Trade Publs., N.Y.C., 1969-72, 74-75; exec. editor Gellert Publs. div. Ziff-Davis Pub. Co., 1964-65, 72-74; editor Reinhardt/Keymer Pub. Co., N.Y.C., 1976; directory editor Floor Covering Weekly, Bart Publs., Inc., N.Y.C., 1976-78; dir. communications Nat. Assn. Tobacco Distbrs., 1978—. Editor pub. relations and fund raising West Side YMCA, N.Y.C., 1964-68; chief pub. relations officer Henry Hudson Little League; promotional adviser Children's Arts and Sci. Workshop, N.Y.C.; mem. Riverside-Edgecombe Neighborhood Assn., Manhattan Jurors Assn.; chmn. 56-64 Ft. Washington Ave. Tenants Assn., N.Y.C., 1971—; mem. N.Y.C. Met. Council Housing, 1973—. Mem. Nat. Automatic Laundry and Cleaning Council, Internat. Fabricare Inst., Nat. Assn. Coin Laundry Equipment Operators, Nat. Carwash Council, Laundry and Cleaners Allied Trades Assn., ACLU. Democrat. Home: 56 Fort Washington Ave New York City NY 10032

GUBBINS, PAUL GORDON, lawyer, mfg. co. exec.; b. Quincy, Ill., Aug. 20, 1921; s. George H. and Edna (Wottman) G.; B.S., Northwestern U., 1942, LL.B., Harvard U., 1945; m. Corinne King, Apr. 8, 1950; children—Michael D., Paula E. Admitted to Ill. bar, 1946, Conn. bar, 1956; asso. firm Scott, MacLeish & Falk, Chgo., 1945-48; asst. gen. counsel Western claims dept. Hartford Accident and Indemnity Co., Chgo., 1948-52; v.p., gen. counsel F.H. McGraw & Co., N.Y.C., 1952-63; asst. gen. counsel Colt Industries, Inc., N.Y.C., 1963—, gen. counsel Colt Firearms, Pratt & Whitney, Elox, Chandler Evans Divs. (Conn.), Holley Carburetor (Mich.), Fairbanks Weighing (Vt.), 1963—; dir. Hartford et Cie, Paris, Pratt, Whitney & Herbert, Coventry, Eng. Mem. Am. Ordnance Assn., Am. Helicopter Soc., Am., Conn. bar assns., Am. Rifle Assn., Nat. Skeet Shooting Assn. Clubs: Wampanoag Country, Hartford, Elks. Home: 156 Westmont St West Hartford CT 06117 Office: Charter Oak Blvd West Hartford CT 06101

GUDAITIS, ALGIRD VICTOR, biochemist; b. Kaunas, Lithuania, June 6, 1924; s. Michael Otto and Maria (Pozela) G.; student U. Kaunas, 1942-43; student U. Med. Sch., Erlangen, Germany, 1946-49; M.S., U. Louisville, 1960; postgrad. Bryn Mawr Coll., 1962-64; m. Dauna Ruth Bombassaro, July 5, 1967; children—Algird Michael, Dzidra Maria, Peter Gindas. Came to U.S., 1949, naturalized, 1955. Supr. labs. Ky. Bapt. Hosp., Louisville, 1953-60; biochemist Bryn Mawr (Pa.) Hosp., 1960-65; sr. research biochemist Prudential Ins. Co. Am., Newark, 1965-71, dir. Gib Labs., Inc. subsidiary, 1971-72, pres. Aculabs, Inc., Summit, N.J., 1972—, adminstrv. and teaching supr. Sch. Med. Tech., Ky. Bapt. Hosp., 1956-60. Mem. VLIKAS, Supreme Liberation Com. of Lithuania, N.Y.C., 1963-69. Mem. Am. Assn. Clin. Chemists, Am. Assn. BioAnalysts, Am. Pub. Health Assn., Am. Assn. Clin. Pathologists. Contbr. articles to profl. jours. Home: Van Syckel Rd Clinton NJ 08809 Office: 19 Prospect St Summit NJ 07901

GUDITUS, CHARLES WILLIAM, ednl. adminstr.; b. Gilberton, Pa., Oct. 5, 1924; s. Stanley Francis and Anna (Stefero) G.; B.S., Pa. State U., 1950; M.S., Bucknell U., 1952; Ed.D., Lehigh U., 1965; m. Stella Carol Guditus, Sept. 18, 1948; children—Gregory Charles, Jean Ann, Tamara Sue. Tchr., Gilberton (Pa.) High Sch., 1950-52, Mahanoy City (Pa.) High Sch., 1952-54; adminstr. Centennial Sch. Dist., Warminster, Pa., 1954-63; supt. Frackville (Pa.) Sch. Dist., 1963-66; mem. faculty Lehigh U., Bethlehem, Pa., 1966-68, chmn. ednl. adminstrn. dept., 1968—. Team chmn. Commn. Higher Edn., Middle States Assn., 1967; cons. to sch. dists. and community colls., program evaluator to fed. and state projects, 1965—; dir. econ. edn. workshops, 1961-63; lectr. Inter-Am. U., P.R., 1971-73; v.p. Russell Williams Mfg. Co., Mahanoy City, 1970—. Chmn. Lehigh Valley chpt. World Futures Soc., Bethlehem, 1972—. Served with USNR, 1943-46. Mem. Am. Soc. Curriculum Devel., AAUP, Nat. Soc. Study Edn., Am. Assn. Sch. Adminstrs., Nat. Assn. Secondary Sch. Prins., Am. Assn. Community and Jr. Colls., Am. Ednl. Research Assn., Phi Delta Kappa. Home: 721 N 7th St Emmaus PA 18049 Office: Lehigh U Bethlehem PA 18015

GUENTHER, HARRY WILBERT, textile co. exec.; b. Cleve., Feb. 8, 1915; s. Edward and Amelia (Seitz) G.; A.B., Oberlin Coll., 1937; M.S. (Mellon Inst. fellow), U. Pitts., 1940; M.A., Princeton, 1943, Ph.D. (Monsanto fellow), 1948; m. Marilyn Scott Goodrich, July 30, 1949; children—Lynn Goodrich, Marcia Scott, Janice Amy. Indsl. research fellow Mellon Inst. Indsl. Research, Pitts., 1937-41; instr. physics, chemistry Princeton, 1941-44; research asso. Chem. Corps Research Project, 1944-46; dir. chem. research Coats & Clark, Union, N.J., 1946-68; v.p. tech. devel. Burlington Formed Fabrics, N.Y.C., 1971—; sr. tech. adviser Burlington Industries, N.Y.C., 1968-71. Mem. Am. Chem. Soc., Textile Research Inst. (research adv. council 1967-72), Assn. Research Dirs., Am. Assn. Textile Chemists and Colorists, Am. Assn. Textile Technologists, N.Y. Acad. Sci., Phi Beta Kappa, Sigma Xi, Phi Lambda Upsilon. Lutheran. Patentee in field. Home: 8 Calvert Dr Syosset NY 11791 Office: 1345 Ave of Americas New York City NY 10019

GUENTHER, KENNETH ALLEN, govt. ofc.; b. Rochester, N.Y., Dec. 1, 1935; s. Walter K. and Erna (Ahrenz) G.; B.A. cum laude, U. Rochester, 1957; postgrad. Johns Hopkins, Yale; m. Lilly Hoesli, Jan. 11, 1964; 1 dau., Christine Rose. With U.S. Dept. Commerce, 1960-65, U.S. Dept. State, 1965-69; spl. asst. to Sen. Jacob K. Javits, 1969-73; alt. exec. dir. Inter Am. Devel. Bank, 1973-74; with Office Spl. Trade Reps., Exec. Office of Pres., Washington, 1974-75; asst. to bd. govs. FRS, Washington, 1975—. Vice pres. Neighborhood Assn. Served with U.S. Army, 1961-66. Mem. Soc. Internat. Deve., Am. Fgn. Service Assn. Author various Dept. Commerce publs. Home: 4513 Dalton Rd Chevy Chase MD 20015 Office: 21st and Constitution Ave NW Washington DC 20005

GUERCIO, VINCENT JOSEPH, chem. cons. firm exec.; b. Balt., Sept. 30, 1934; s. Samuel C. and Mary Theresa (Corliss) G.; student Drexel Inst. Tech., 1952-54; B.S. in Chem. Engring., Catholic U. Am., 1960; postgrad. Princeton U., 1960-61; m. Barbara Ann Freeman, Mar. 18, 1966; children—Lisa Marie, Nina Carmela. Teaching asst. Princeton U., 1960-61; refinery engr. Mobil Oil Corp., Paulsboro, N.J., 1961-64; sr. design engr. Lummus Co., Bloomfield, N.J., 1965-68; process supr. Foster Wheeler Corp., Livingston, N.J., 1968-71; pres. Chem. Technomics Co., Montclair, N.J., 1971—; lectr. Argentina Petroleum Inst., 1970; cons. petrochems. Sonatrach, Algiers, Algeria, 1973—. Mem. Am. Inst. Chem. Engrs., Am. Petroleum Inst., Chem. Mktg. Research Assn., Common Cause, Urban League, N.Y. Chemists Club, Sigma Xi, Tau Kappa Epsilon. Office: 23 Glenridge Pkwy Montclair NJ 07042

GUERESCHI, EDWARD FRED, educator; b. Fulton, N.Y., Feb. 27, 1935; s. Angelo and Harriet (Skopanska) G.; Ph.D., U. Syracuse, 1969. Asst. prof. English, St. Johns U., Jamaica, N.Y., 1970—, chmn. Am. Studies, 1973. Mem. Modern Lang. Assn. Editor: Notes on Modern American Literature, 1976—; contbr. articles in field to scholarly jours. Office: St Johns Univ Dept English Jamaica NY 11439

GUESON, EMERITA TORRES, obstetrician, gynecologist; b. Angeles City, Philippines, Jan. 4, 1942; d. Pedro Guanzon and Lina Suarez (Torres) Gueson; A.A., U. St. Tomas, 1958; M.D., 1963. Came to U.S., 1964. Rotating intern Germantown Hosp., Phila., 1964-65; gen. practice resident Community Gen. Hosp., Reading, Pa., 1965-66; obstetrics-gynecology resident Phila. Gen. Hosp., 1966-70; gynecology research cons. U. Pa. Dental Sch., Phila., 1970; practice medicine specializing in obstetrics and gynecology, Bristol, Pa., 1971-72; mem. staff Nazareth Hosp., Phila. Fellow Am. Coll. Obstetricians and Gynecologists (jr.); mem. Am. Fertility and Sterility Soc., Blockley Obstet. Soc., Phila. County, Pa. med. socs., AMA (achievement award for continuing edn. 1970-73), Phila. Assn. Retarded Children. Home: 6305 Forge Turn Neshaminy Valley Cornwell Heights PA 19020 Office: 900 Old Orchard Ln Bristol PA 19007

GUEST, JAMES ALFRED, state ofcl.; b. Montclair, N.J., Dec. 25, 1940; s. J. Alfred and Elizabeth Laney (Montignani) G.; B.A., Amherst Coll., 1962; postgrad. M.I.T., 1963-64; LL.B., Harvard U., 1967; m. Priscilla Frances Beach, Mar. 1, 1974; children—Benjamin, Betsey. Admitted to Mass. bar, 1967; legis. asst. to Sen. Edward Kennedy of Mass., 1968-71; commr. banking and ins. State of Vt., Montpelier, 1973-76, sec. of state state, 1977—. Woodrow Wilson fellow, 1963-64. Democrat. Office: Office of Sec of State 109 State St Montpelier VT 05602

GUEST, ROBERT GERALD, physician; b. Toronto, Ont., Can., Jan. 28, 1934; s. Robert Charlton and Ida Mae (McRae) G.; M.D., U. Toronto, 1959; m. Marilyn Elizabeth Miller, Dec. 28, 1957; children—Gregory Robert, Susan Katrine, Mary Elizabeth, Paul Michael. Intern, Toronto East Gen. Hosp., 1959-60; sr. house officer Shrodells Hosp., Watford, Eng., 1960-61; practice family medicine, specializing in geriatrics, Scarborough, Ont., 1961—; physician Thompson House Home for Aged, 1969—; chmn. med. adv. bd. Extendicare North York, 1972—; med. dir. Cana Place, 1978—; pres. Corp. Indsl. Health Services Ltd., also med. dir. Fellow Acad. Medicine Toronto (chmn. history of medicine sect.), Royal Soc. Medicine, Eccles. History Soc., Canadian Geriatric Research Soc.; mem. Am. Geriatric Assn., Can., Ont. med. assns., Can. Physicians for Life, Royal Archaeol. Inst., Brit. Archeol. Inst., Soc. Medieval Archeology, Henry Bradshaw Soc., Can. Soc. Study History of Philosophy of Sci., Royal Overseas League, Phi Chi. Roman Catholic. Contbr. to hist. jours. Home: Cleeveham Hall Stouffville Rural Route 4 ON L0H 1I0 Canada Office: 1648 Victoria Park Ave Scarborough ON M1R 1P7 Canada

GUGGENHEIM, FREDERICK GIBSON, psychiatrist; b. Chgo., July 8, 1935; s. Melvin Elias and Marjorie Stone (Gibson) G.; B.A. cum laude (Chi Psi fellow 1957, Allison fellow 1956-57), Yale U., 1957; M.D. (NSF fellow), Columbia U., 1961; children—Jennifer Nicole, Hannah Carol. Intern, asst. resident in medicine Bellevue Hosp., N.Y.C., 1961-63; instr. medicine N.Y. U., 1962-63; asst. resident Presbyn. Hosp., N.Y.C., 1963-64; clin. asso. in medicine NIMH, 1964-66; asst. resident, asso. resident, resident in psychiatry Strong Meml. Hosp., 1966-69; instr. psychiatry U. Rochester, N.Y., 1968-69; instr. psychiatry Harvard U. Med. Sch., 1969-71, asst. prof., 1971—, tutor med. scis., 1974-77; asst. psychiatrist Mass. Gen. Hosp., Boston, 1970-74, asso. psychiatrist, 1974—, dir. pvt. psychiat. cons. service, 1971—, dir. med. student teaching in psychiatry, 1975—; cons. psychiatry edn. br. NIMH, 1974-75; examiner Am. Bd. Neurology and Psychiatry, 1975. Served with USPHS, 1964-66. Recipient Saybrook Fellows' prize, 1957; Walter Louis Ehrich prize, 1957. Mem. AAAS, Am. Psychiat. Assn., Am. Psychosomatic Soc., Am. Psychopathol. Assn., Assn. Acad. Psychiatry, Am. Assn. Suicidology. Co-editor: Practical Psychiatry Revs., 1976—; contbr. articles to profl. jours. Home: 4 Independence Way Marblehead MA 01945 Office: 602 Warren Bldg Mass Gen Hosp Boston MA 02114

GUGLIELMO, ROCCO MICHAEL, psychiat. social worker; b. N.Y.C., May 5, 1946; s. Michael and Rose (DiFabio) G.; B.A. in Sociology, St. Francis Coll., Bklyn., 1968; M.S.W., Yeshiva U., 1973; m. Kathleen Ann Leggett, Apr. 13, 1969. Psychiat. social worker Rockland County Mental Health, Pomona, N.Y., 1973—, sr. psychiat. social worker, 1975—; cons. to nursing homes and health related facilities in N.Y. and N.J. Recipient Rockland County Disting. Service award, 1975. Mem. Nat. Assn. Social Workers, Acad. Certified Social Workers, Nat. Assn. Clin. Social Workers. Home and office: 165 Doxbury Ln Suffern NY 10901

GUI, JAMES EDMUND, architect; b. Wooster, Ohio, Aug. 13, 1928; s. Harry Ludwig and Mabel Josephine (Olson) G.; B.Arch., Ohio State U., 1954; m. Anne Louise Outram, Oct. 15, 1955; children—Linda Anne, Jeffrey Allen. Asso. firm Charles F. McKirahan & Assos., Architects, Ft. Lauderdale, Fla., 1958-63; chief specifications Architects Collaborative, Cambridge, Mass., 1963-67; propr. James E. Gui, Archtl. Systems and Specifications Cons., Belmont, Mass., 1967—. Cons., Architects Collaborative, Benjamin Thompson & Assos., Cambridge Seven Assos., Pietro Belluschi, Harvard, Mass. Inst. Tech. Chmn. folk music com., dir. Stone Arch folk music series Belmont Music Sch. Mem. Constrn. Specifications Inst., AIA, Boston Soc. Architects, Mass. Assn. Architects. Cons. on Juilliard Sch. Music, Lincoln Center, N.Y.C.; U.S. Pavillion Expo 67, Montreal; New Eng. Aquarium; Children's Hosp. Med. Center; Harvard U. Law Sch. Complex (2d award Constrn. Specifications Inst.); Harvard Gutman Library, Harvard Obs.; Kirkland Coll.; Berkshire Community Coll.; Tufts U. Dental Health Center; U. Baghdad; Independence Nat. Hist. Park Visitors Center; Wilmington Jewish Community Center (1st award Constrn. Specifications Inst.). Address: 965 Concord Ave Belmont MA 02178

GUIDA, FRANK JOSEPH, internat. music co. exec.; b. Palermo, Italy, May 26, 1922; s. Joseph Frank and Annetta (Cannavo) G.; came to U.S., 1924, naturalized, 1928; student Am. Theatre Wing, 1947; m. Carmela Addesso, Sept. 20, 1942; children—Anne, Lydia, Joseph. With Butler Bros., N.Y.C., 1940-42; salesman Libby McNeil & Libby, N.Y.C., 1945-53; owner Frankie's Birdland Records, 1953-60; songwriter, 1959—; pres. Rockmasters, Inc., New City, N.Y., 1961—; pres. Pepe Music Co. Ltd., London, 1961—. Served with AUS, 1943-45. Recipient 14 citations of Achievement, Broadcast Music Inc. Mem. Internat. Platform Assn., Nat. Assn. Retailers and Mfrs., Harry Fox Assn., Songwriters Hall of Fame, Elect. Mech. Industries Eng., Italian-Am. Found. (charter), Sons of Italy. Republican. Roman Catholic. Club: Elk. Composer, pub. and producer songs including: High School USA, 1958; New Orleans (Gold Record award), 1959; Not Me, 1959; Quarter to Three (Gold Record award), 1960; School is Out, 1960; Dear Lady Twist, 1962; Twist Twist Senora, 1962; If You Wanna Be Happy (Gold Record award), 1963; Twistin' Matilda, 1962. Office: Rockmasters Inc 177 RTE 304 New City NY 10956

GUIDO, DENNIS FRANKLIN, cookie distbr.; b. Buffalo, July 16, 1940; s. Girard G. and Gladys G. G.; B.S. in Bus. Adminstrn., U. Buffalo, 1961; m. Barbara J. Parks, July 29, 1961; children—Ronald, Lawrence, Denise. Mgmt. trainee S.S. Kresge Co., Pitts., 1961-65; owner, operator East Aurora Auto Wash, Inc. (N.Y.), also Clark St. Auto Wash, Inc., Hamburg, N.Y., 1965-68; owner, operator Dennis Guido Cookie Distbrs., Clarence Center, N.Y., 1968—. Vice pres. Clarence Teen Center, Inc., 1977—; mem. Clarence Citizens Adv. Com. on Curriculum, 1976-78, Clarence Town Transp. Com., 1976—. Named an Outstanding Young Man Am., 1976. Mem. Clarence C. of C., Jaycees (pres. Clarence 1975, Jaycee of Yr. 1974, 76, internat. senator). Republican. Home and Office: 6038 Long St Clarence Center NY 14032

GUILD, RICHARD SAMUEL, trade assns. mgmt. co. exec.; b. Boston, Nov. 5, 1925; s. Walter Rayford and Anna (Hollander) G.; B.S., Boston U., 1949; m. Susan Jane Coughlin, July 3, 1965; children—Laura Ann, Linda Jean. With Guild Assos., Inc., Boston, 1949—, mng. dir. 1960-65, pres., 1965—; exec. dir. Mass. Nurserymens Assn., 1959—, Mass. Arborists Assn., 1973—; exec. sec. New Eng. Marine Trade Assn., 1963—; mng. dir. Mass. Automatic Merchandising Council, 1964—, Cellular Concrete Assn., 1966—, New Eng. Soc. Assn. Execs., 1974—, Shoe Pattern Mfrs. Assn., Wood Products Mfrs. Assn., Emergency Lighting Mfrs. Assn., 1977—; regional mgr. for New Eng., Nat. LP-Gas Assn., 1972—; owner, mgr. Copy PRO, 1971—. Served with USNR, 1944-45. Mem. Multiple Assn. Mgmt. Inst. (past pres.), Am. (past dir.), Boston (past pres.) socs. assn. execs., Def. Orientation Conf. Assn. Home: 5 Glengarry Rd Winchester MA 01890 Office: 715 Boylston St Boston MA 02116

GUILFOYLE, GEORGE H., bishop; b. N.Y.C., Nov. 13, 1913; s. James J. and Johanna (McGrath) G.; A.B., Georgetown U., 1935; student St. Joseph's Sem., 1939-44; J.D., Fordham U., 1939; student N.Y. Univ. School Banking, 1945; LL.M., Columbia U., 1946; LL.D., St. Francis Coll., 1958, Manhattan Coll., 1962, Iona Coll., 1966; Lit.D., St. Joseph's Coll., Phila., 1968. Ordained priest Roman Catholic Ch., 1944, named papal chamberlain, 1955, domestic prelate, 1958; admitted to N.Y. bar, 1940, asst. St. Patrick's Cathedral, 1944-45, St. Andrew's Ch., 1944-46; asst. chancellor, also asst. St. Elizabeth's Ch., N.Y.C., 1946-47; with Catholic Charities, N.Y.C., 1947-66, exec. dir., 1956-66; episcopal vicar Richmond County (S.I.), also pastor St. Peter's Ch., 1966-68; bishop of Camden, N.J., 1968—. Asso. moderator coordinating com. Cath. Lay Orgns. Archdiocese N.Y., 1954-57; archdiocesan consultor, 1960-68; nat. spiritual dir. Soc. St. Vincent de Paul, 1966—. Pres. Nat. Conf. Cath. Charities, 1959-61, bd. dirs., 1959-67; mem. N.Y.C. Adv. Bd. Pub. Welfare, 1960-66; mem. Archdiocesan Commn. for Community Planning, 1964-68. Bd. dirs. Nat. Shring Immaculate Conception; trustee Seton Hall U. Recipient John Carroll award Georgetown U., 1963; Knight grand cross Equistrian Order Holy Sepulchre Jerusalem. Home: 342 Kings Hwy West Haddonfield NJ 08033 Office: 1845 Haddon Ave PO Box 709 Camden NJ 01801

GUILLE, PETER, JR., real estate co. exec.; b. N.Y.C., Nov. 21, 1940; s. Peter and Carla (Hochstrasser) G.; B.A. in Economics, St. Lawrence U., 1963; M.B.A., U. Ariz., 1965; m. Mary R. Cifrese, Sept. 10, 1966 (div. 1976); children—Lara, Peter, Constance. Dist. rep. Esco Corp., 1965-67; sales asso. Island Realty Co., 1967-69; dir. mktg. Com-Comp Inc., Hauppauge, N.Y., 1969-70; pres. Leverage Properties Corp., Mystic, Conn., 1971—; v.p., dir. Hungars Creek Enterprises, Accomac, Va., 1971—; gen. partner Green Hills Farms, 1971—; pres. Pequot Properties, 1972—; v.p., dir. Seaside Properties, Inc., 1977; dir. Young Developers Inc., 1973-77; chmn. Gallery of Homes So. New Eng. Council. Coach LaCrosse Conn. Coll. Liscensed real estate broker, N.Y., Vt., Va., Conn., R.I. Mem. Aircraft Owners and Pilots Assn., Internat. Game Fishing Assn., Southeastern Conn. (dir.), Mystic (pres.) chambers commerce, Cousteau Soc. Republican. Episcopalian. Clubs: Wadawanuck, Nantucket Angler's. Home: Osbrook Pt Stonington CT 06378 Office: 58 Denison Ave Mystic CT 06355

GUIMOND, RICHARD PIERRE, obstetrician gynecologist; b. Chicoutimi, Que., Can., Jan. 12, 1944; s. Vincent and Therese (Cote) G.; A.B. summa cum laude, U. Laval, 1963, M.D., 1967; m. Florence Gobeil, June 8, 1967; children—Marie-Josée, Jean-David. Intern, Chicoutimi Hosp. Quebec, 1967-68; resident in obstetrics and gynecology, Royal Victoria Hosp., Montreal, 1969-72; mem. dept. obstetric and gynecology, Chicoutimi Hosp., 1972—; mem. Guimond Obstetrics Gynecology Clinic Inc., Chicoutimi, 1972—. Mem. Chicoutimi C. of C. 1973-76. Diplomate Am. Bd. Obstetrics and Gynecology. Fellow Royal Coll. Surgeons Can., Internat. Coll. Surgeons, Am. Coll. Obstetrics and Gynecology; mem. Am. Fertility Soc., Am. Assn. Gynecological Laparoscopists, Soc. Obstetricians and Gynecologists Can., Canadian Med. Assn., Association des Médecins de langue francaise du Canada. Roman Catholic. Clubs: Hunting and Fishing, Lac Francois, St. Germain. Home: 1243 Duhaime St Chicoutimi PQ G7H 3A1 Canada Office: 150 Price W Chicoutimi PQ G7J 1G8 Canada

GUINIVAN, THOMAS WAYNE, flashlight and battery mfg. co. exec.; b. Mechanicsburg, Pa., May 1, 1922; s. Thomas William and Ora Mabel (Harnish) G.; B.S., Pa. State U., 1944; m. Patricia J. Finley, Dec. 26, 1953; children—Thomas William, Stephen F. Salesman, Charles Pfizer & Co., 1950-52; asst. dir. sales tng., 1953-56; dir. sales tng. White Labs., 1956-58, asst. sales mgr., 1958-60; product sales mgr. Hoffman LaRoche, 1960-64; sr. product mgr. Colgate Palmolive Co., N.Y.C., 1964-72; gen. sales mgr. Bright Star Industries, Inc., Clifton, N.J., 1972-73, v.p., 1973—. Trustee, United Way, Summit, New Providence, 1968-73; chmn. bus. ARC, 1967-69; chmn. troop com. Watchuns Area Council Boy Scouts Am., 1966-71. Mem. Am. Supply and Machinery Mfrs. Assn., Internt. Assn. Chiefs Police. Episcopalian. Club: Loantaka Skeet, Crestview, Carlisle Fish and Game. Home: 53 Elkwood Ave New Providence NJ 07974 Office: 600 Getty Ave Clifton NJ 07015

GUISE, DAVID EARL, architect, educator; b. N.Y.C., Dec. 29, 1931; s. Jack I. and Frances (Haberman) G.; B.Arch. with honors, U. Pa., 1957; m. Gretchen Grunenfelder, Nov. 21, 1962; children—Gabrielle Ann, John George, Jacqueline Alexis, Ursula Claire. Job capt. Kahn & Jacobs, Architects, N.Y.C., 1957-60; designer-draftsman E.J. Robin, Architect, N.Y.C., 1961; architect David Guise, Architect, N.Y.C., 1962—; asst. prof. Sch. Architecture Coll. City N.Y., 1966-70, asso. prof., 1970-76, prof., 1976—. Mem. nat. panel Am. Arbitration Assn., 1967—; mem. Irvington (N.Y.) Planning Bd. Mem. AIA, Constrn. Specifications Inst., Bldg. Research Inst., Assn. Collegiate Schs. Architecture. Home: Fargo Ln Irvington NY 10533 Office: 250 W 57th St New York City NY 10019

GULAS, IVAN, clin. psychologist: b. Debrecen, Hungary, Oct. 23, 1946; s. Norman and Elisabeth (Simon) G.; came to U.S., 1959, naturalized, 1964; A.B. cum laude, Boston U., 1969; grad. Dartmouth Coll., 1969-70; Ph.D., Ohio U., 1974; m. Beth Gunsberg, Dec. 29, 1968; children—Kimberly Dara, Jordan Todd. Staff psychol. counselor Dartmouth Coll. Health Service, Hanover, N.H., 1970-71; trainee Athens (Ohio) Mental Health Center, 1971, Center for Psychol. Services, Athens, 1971-72; intern Beth Israel Hosp., Boston and clin. fellow Harvard Med. Sch., 1973-74, intake team leader, 1974-75; practice psychology, Newton, Mass., 1975—; staff psychologist Human Resource Inst., Brookline, 1974—; co-dir. Boston Neurosychology Consultation Service, Brookline, 1976—; asst. attending psychologist McLean Hosp., Belmont, Mass., 1976—; co-dir. Psychiat. Services Inst., Brookline, 1977—. Bd. advisors Mass. Sch. Profl. Psychology, 1975—. Boston U. scholar, 1966-67; Dartmouth Coll. fellow, 1969-70; Ohio U. fellow, 1971-72; NIMH fellow, 1969-70; licensed psychologist, N.Y., Mass., N.H. Mem. Am., Mass. psychol. assns. Contbr. articles in field to profl. jours. Home: 25 Old Orchard Rd Chestnut Hill MA 02167 Office: Chestnut Hill Med Center Chestnut Hill MA 02167

GULATI, SHANTI PARKASH, research found. adminstr.; b. Sargodha, India (now Pakistan), Sept. 21, 1920; s. Ram Labhaya and Bharawan Bai (Khetarpal) G.; came to U.S., 1963; B.A., Panjab U., India, 1953, postgrad., 1953-55; regional certificate in health U. Va., 1975; m. Sumitra Khetarpai, Sept. 14, 1937; children—Surinder, Narinder, Rajinder (dec.), Vinod. Served in various depts. govt., India, 1947-55; various positions fgn. service govt. India, 1955-67; adminstv. sec. research Washington Hosp. Center, Washington, D.C., 1967-68, office mgr., 1968-75, adminstrv. officer, 1975-77, dir. research adminstrn., 1977—; asst. sec. Research Found. of Washington Hosp. Center, 1972—, asst. sec. then sec. of research com. of med. staff, 1974—; pres. Gulati Catering and Restaurant Corp., 1977—. Served with recruiting orgn. Indian Army, 1940-47. Mem. Hosp. Fin. Mgmt. Assn., Am. Assn. Lab. Animal Sci. (instl. rep.), Soc. of Research Adminstrs., Nat. Soc. Med. Research, Internat. Diplonots Club. Home: 18 Barrington Fare Rockville MD 20850 Office: 110 Irving St NW Washington DC 20010

GULATI, SURESH THAKORDAS, mech. engr.; b. West Punjab, Pakistan, Nov. 13, 1936; s. Thakordas Sewaram and Vishan Devi (Kathuria) G.; came to U.S., 1958; B.S. in Mech. Engring., U. Bombay (India), 1957; M.S. in Mech. Engring., Ill. Inst. Tech., 1959; Ph.D. in Mechanics (NASA predoctoral trainee 1963-66), U. Colo., 1967; m. Teresa Davids, Aug. 19, 1961; children—Raj, Prem, Sonya. Stress analyst Continental Can Co., Chgo., 1959-62; instr. mech. engring. Ill. Inst. Tech., Chgo., 1959-61, U. Colo., Boulder, 1966-67; research scientist Corning Glass Works (N.Y.), 1967-69, sr. research scientist, 1969-74, research supr., 1974—; adj. asso. prof. Cornell U., Ithaca, N.Y., 1972—. Pres. Am. Field Service, Elmira, N.Y., 1972-73. Mem. ASME, AAAS, Am. Acad. Mechanics, Am. Soc. Engring. Edn. Club: Internat. (Corning). Contbr. articles to profl. jours. Home: 1001 W Water St Elmira NY 14905 Office: Sullivan Park Corning Glass Corning NY 14830

GULEVICH, WLADIMIR, ret. army officer, pub. health engr.; b. Brcko, Yugoslavia, Sept. 13, 1930; s. Vsevolod and Natalie (Eltchaninoff) G.; came to U.S., 1949, naturalized, 1955; B. Chem. Engring., N.Y. U., 1953, M.S. in San. Sci., 1956; Ph.D., Johns Hopkins U., 1967; m. Helena Demidoff, June 15, 1956; 1 dau., Helen. Commd. 2d lt. Med. Service Corps, U.S. Army, 1956, advanced through grades to col., 1976; ret., 1978; various assignments in Korea, Vietnam, Europe, U.S.; environ. engring. cons. U.S. Army Med. Command, Europe; pub. health engr. Va. Dept. Health, Richmond, 1978—. Mem. N.Y. Acad. Sci., Am. Acad. Social and Polit. Scis., Am. Inst. Chem. Engrs., AAAS, Sigma Xi. Home: 1126 Loxford Terr Silver Spring MD 20901 Office: 109 Governor St Richmond VA 23219

GULKER, IRA ARNOLD, dentist; b. Bronx, N.Y., Aug. 27, 1937; s. Jack Israel and Bessie (Stern) G.; student Columbia Coll., 1955-58; D.D.S., N.Y. U., 1962; m. Caryle Nicole Cohen, Apr. 4, 1965; children—Jennifer Leigh and Holly Michelle (twins), Matthew David. Instr. N.Y. U. Center for Dentistry, 1964-70, asst. prof. fixed prosthodontics, 1970-72, asso. prof., 1972—, asso. chmn. dept. fixed prosthodontics, 1976—; research fellow Murray and Leonie Guggenheim Dental Research Inst., 1962-64. Pres., New Rochelle (N.Y.) Citizens for Better Environment, 1973-76, v.p., 1976. Mem. AAUP (pres. N.Y. U. Coll. Dentistry chpt. 1968-70). Jewish. Author: (with others) Fixed Prosthodontic Procedures, 1974. Home: 580 Forest Ave New Rochelle NY 10804 Office: 1488 Metropolitan Ave Bronx NY 10462*

GULKO, HARRIS DAVID, assn. exec.; b. Toronto, Ont., Can., Oct. 30, 1927; s. Morris and Nancy (Bercovitch) G.; m. Blanche Ruth Stoll, June 12, 1949; children—Rosalind, Evelyn, Miriam, Judith, Sharon. Campaign dir. United Jewish Appeal of Toronto, 1952-53; exec. dir. Jewish Nat. Fund of Ont., Toronto, 1953-63; exec. v.p. Jewish Nat. Fund of Can., Montreal, Que., 1963—. Jewish. Clubs: Montefiore, Desola (Montreal). Home: 400 Kensington Ave Apt 103 Westmount PQ H3Y 3A2 Canada Office: 1980 Sherbrooke St Suite 250 Montreal PQ H3H 2M7 Canada

GULLER, IRVING BERNARD, psychologist, educator; b. N.Y.C., July 27, 1932; s. Hyman and Mildred (Rothman) G.; B.A., Coll. City N.Y., 1954, M.S., 1956; Ph.D., N.Y. U., 1962; m. Adele Horowitz, Apr. 5, 1955; children—Robert, Matthew. Dir. psychol. tng. and research Maine Dept. Mental Health and Corrections, Augusta, 1962-63; asst. prof. psychology, also coll. psychologist Franklin and Marshall Coll., 1963-67; asso. prof. psychology John Jay Coll., N.Y.C., 1967-71, prof. psychology, 1971—; attending psychologist, cons. St. Joseph's Hosp., Paterson, N.J., 1970—; cons. psychologist and family therapist in pvt. practice, Oakland, N.J., 1962—; founding asso. N. Jersey Mental Health Assos., Oakland. Served with AUS, 1954-56. Recipient Founder's Day award N.Y. U., 1963. Diplomate Am. Bd. Profl. Psychology. Mem. Lancaster Mental Health Assn. (dir. 1965-67), Am., Eastern psychol. assns., Am. Assn. Marriage and Family Counselors (clin.), Sex Educators Council. Author: Clinical Psychology Training Guide and Handbook, 1963; The Clinical Psychologist in Institutional Settings, 1976; contbr. articles to profl. jours. Home: 22 Stone Fence Rd Oakland NJ 07436 Office: 9 Post Rd Oakland NJ 07436 also 445 W 59th St New York City NY 10019

GULLETTE, ETHEL MAE BISHOP, pianist; b. St. Paul, Mar. 29, 1908; d. Clarence Eugene and Alma (Beckman) Bishop; Mus.B., Mac Phail Sch. Music, Mpls., 1928; B.A., U. Minn., 1931; diploma Juilliard Sch. Music, 1936; pvt. study piano with Donald N. Ferguson, James Friskin; m. William Brandon Gullette, Sept. 5, 1936; children—Ethel Mae, Charlene Ann. Concertized as pianist, accompanist, Middle West, also radio appearances, 1925-33; voice accompanist Juilliard Sch. Music, 1934-48; pvt. tchr. piano, N.Y.C., 1934-38; concert pianist Eastern U.S., 1933—; duo-pianist, accompanist, Fairfield County, Conn., 1951—; mem. New Canaan Piano Quartet, 1960-68; duo-piano concerts, N.J., Conn., N.Y.C., S.C., Ga., Mass., 1967—; Bicentennial concerts in Conn. and N.Y., 1975-76; concerts Fairfield Hills Hosp., Newtown, Conn., 1957-70; accompanist Darien Troupers, 1968, 69. Mem. New Canaan Town Players, 1952—, accompanist, 1958-63, 73; mem. accompanist Nutmeg Music Theatre 1957-61, Demi-Opera Co., Brookfield (Conn.) Summer Theatre, 1961, others. Bd. govs., rehearsal pianist Norwalk (Conn.) Symphony Orch., 1955-62; bd. dirs. New Canaan Community Concerts Assn., 1961-69, membership chmn., 1967-69; active fund drives charitable orgns. Co-pres. New Canaan High Sch. Parent's Council, 1964-65. Recipient citations for work in cancer Red Cross drives; silver tray for 23 yrs. devoted service New Canaan Community Concerts Assn., also hon. life membership, 1974. Mem. N.Y. Singing Tchrs. Assn., New Canaan Hist. Soc. (photographer Gown Exhibits 1968—), Darien Community Assn. (chmn. duo piano group; bd. dirs. 1962-64, duo piano publicity chmn. 1966-68, 70-71, 74-76, duo piano sec. 1978—), New Canaan Library, New Canaan Audubon Soc., Norwalk Symphony Women's Assn. (dir. 1976—), Am. Shakespeare Guild (fund raising chmn. New Canaan com. 1955), AAUW (New Canaan chpt. charter), Friends of N.Y. Philharmonic Orch., Fairfield County Panhellenic (New Canaan chmn. recommendation com. 1965-67), Juilliard Alumni Assn., U. Minn. Alumni Assn. (past dir. N.Y.), Mu Phi Epsilon (50 Year Mem. 1977), Delta Zeta (charter; pres. local alumnae chpt. 1961-63). Congregationalist (sec. ch. music com. 1964-67, 77—). Clubs: Schubert (St. Paul); Atlantic Beach (L.I., N.Y.); Schubert (Fairfield County, Conn.). Home: 85 West Hills Rd New Canaan CT 06840

GULLEY, RALPH GRADY, architect; b. Durham, N.C., Dec. 18, 1902; s. Samuel Robert and Ruth Ellen (Brashear) G.; B.S. in Arch., U. Va., 1927; certificate Ecole Americain Des Beaux Arts at Fontainebleau, 1928; M.Arch. (Univ. scholar), Harvard U., 1929; certificate in real estate financing N.Y. U., 1970; m. Faith Hudson, Jan. 27, 1940; children—Philip Gordon, Kenneth Hudson, Jay Bartlett, Eric Harris. Designer-draftsman Joseph Hudnut, Architect, Charlottesville, Va., 1924-27, W. Herbert Hunter, Architect, High Point, N.C., 1927; designer Bertram Goodhue Assos., Architects, N.Y.C., 1925, Bush-Brown & Gailey, Architects, Atlanta, 1927-28; prin. Ralph G. Gulley, Architect, Troy, N.Y., 1931-41; architect-partner Donald Deskey Assos., Architects, Indsl. Designers & Packaging, N.Y.C., 1943-52; cons. architect Borg Warner Corp., Chgo., St. Regis Paper Co., N.Y.C., 1952-56; project mgmt. Skidmore, Owings & Merrill, Architects and Engrs., N.Y.C., Chgo., San Francisco, Washington, 1956-73; architect, zoning and feasibility cons., N.Y.C., 1975—; instr. architecture U. Va., 1924-26, Ga. Inst. Tech., 1927-28; organizer, dean, prof. Sch. Architecture, Rensselaer Poly. Inst., Troy, 1929-41; prof. architecture U. Fla., 1941-43; asso. Rudolph Weaver, chief architect Fla. Bd. Control, 1941-43. Served with USNR, 1942-43. Recipient Boston Soc. Architects prize and Emerson prize Harvard U., 1928-29. Sheldon fellow and Julia Amory Appleton fellow Harvard U., 1929-30. Mem. AIA, N.Y. State Assn. Architects, Phi Sigma Kappa, Alpha Rho Chi. Club: Harvard (N.Y.C.). Contbr. articles to profl. jours. Home: 535 E 72d St New York City NY 10021 Office: 400 Park Ave New York City NY 10022

GUMPERT, GUSTAV, pub. relations exec.; b. Phila., Nov. 28, 1922; s. Hibbard Gustav and Lillian (Heebner) G.; A.B., Lehigh U., 1944. Reporter, Allentown (Pa.) Morning Call, 1945-46; asso. editor Mus. Digest, N.Y.C., 1946-49; health edn. dir. Dept. Pub. Health, Phila., 1950-52, health info. officer, 1952-60; writing unit head pub. relations dept. Smith Kline Corp., Phila., 1962-63, mgr. writing, editorial services, 1965-66, mgr. planning, editorial services, 1966, dir. spl. projects, 1967-78, dir. creative services, 1978—. Pres. bd. Planned Parenthood Assn. Phila., 1960-62; bd. dirs. Found. for Study Cycles, 1959-60. Mem. AAAS, Am. Med. Writers Assn., Pub. Relations Soc. Am., Phi Beta Kappa. Episcopalian. Contbr. articles to profl. jours. Home: 201 W Evergreen Ave Philadelphia PA 19118 Office: 1500 Spring Garden St Philadelphia PA 19101

GUNDERS, STEVEN OLIVER, financial cons. co. exec.; b. Manila, Oct. 1, 1943; s. Max. M. and Ruth V. (Heymann) G.; M.B.A. (Scholar), U. Chgo., 1969; m. Madelaine F. Loeb, Mar. 16, 1968; 1 dau., Deborah Anne. Partner, Touche Ross & Co., N.Y.C., 1969—; nat. treas. Odyssey Inst.; cons. fin. crisis N.Y. State and N.Y.C. C.P.A., N.Y. Mem. Am. Inst. C.P.A.'s, Nat. Assn. Accountants, Inst. Mgmt. Cons. Office: 666 Fifth Ave New York City NY 10019

GUNIA, RUSSELL BURNELL, metall. engr.; b. Springdale, Pa., Nov. 16, 1910; s. Adolph and Blanche (Durand) G.; B.S., Carnegie Mellon U., 1937; m. Gretchen J. Cullison, Dec. 20, 1941; children—Gretchen Gunia Harkness, Gertrude Gunia Phelps. Routine analyst Allegheny Steel Co., Brackenridge, Pa., 1927-28; insp. Am. Steel Foundry, Verona, Pa., 1929; routine analyst Aluminum Cooking Utensil Co., New Kensington, Pa., 1930-31; laborer coal div. Republic Iron & Steel Corp., Russellton, Pa., 1933-35; mill metallurgist Allegheny Steel Co., Brackenridge, 1937-38; product metallurgist U.S. Steel Corp., Gary Sheet & Tin Mill (Ind.), 1938-40, service metallurgist, Chgo., 1940-43, mgr. stainless steel bur., 1943-47, asst. mgr. stainless steel metallurgy, Pitts., 1947-58, mgr. stainless steel metallurgy, 1958-71, cons. metallurgist, 1971—. Mem. Planning Commn., Churchill Borough, Pa., 1950-55, councilman, 1955-72, v.p. council, 1960-72. Registered profl. engr., Ind., Pa. Fellow ASTM (vice chmn. com. A-10 1964-68, 70-71, acting chmn. 1968-70, Merit award 1961), Am. Soc. Metals (life); mem. Am. Inst. Metall. and Mining Engrs., Soc. for Advancement Material and Process Engrs., Sigma Phi Epsilon. Presbyterian. Clubs: Churchill Valley Country, Masons. Contbr. articles to profl. jours. Address: 2312 Forest Dr Pittsburgh PA 15235

GUNKEL, RALPH DANIEL, physicist; b. Rex., Oreg., Apr. 15, 1911; s. Daniel and Rosa (Softley) G.; B.S. in Physics, Wash. State U., 1933; O.D., Pa. Coll. Optometry, 1950; m. Hope Augusta Miller, Oct. 9, 1970. Practice optometry, Bethesda, Md., 1950-52; ophthalmic physicist Nat. Eye Inst., NIH, Bethesda, 1952—; pres. Visual Research Assos., Rockville, Md., 1957-60; v.p. Optics Engring. Co., Bethesda, 1964-69. Served to lt. comdr. USNR, 1942-46; PTO. Mem. Am. Optometric Assn. (hon. life mem.), Optical Soc. Am., AAAS, Assn. Research Vision and Ophthalmology, Internat. Soc. Clin. Electroretinography. Contbr. to profl. jours. Home: 120 Center Dr Bethesda MD 20014 Office: Bldg 10 9000 Wisconsin Ave Bethesda MD 20014

GUNN, HARTFORD NELSON, JR., broadcasting co. exec.; b. Port Washington, N.Y., Dec. 24, 1926; s. Hartford N. and Edith (Arnold) G.; B.S., U.S. Mcht. Marine Acad., 1948; A.B., Harvard, 1949, M.B.A., 1951; L.H.D., Northeastern U., 1967; L.H.D., Boston Coll., 1970. Dir. operations Lowell Inst. Co-op Broadcasting Council, Boston, 1951; asst. gen. mgr. WGBH-FM, Boston, 1951-55, gen. mgr. WGBH-FM and TV, 1956-70; v.p., gen. mgr. 1969-70; pres. Pub. Broadcasting Service, Washington, 1970; dir. Boston Globe; founder, chmn., pres. Eastern Ednl. Network, Cambridge, Mass., 1961-66. Past mem. nat. adv. com. Council for Pub. Schs.; past mem. corp. Ednl. Devel. Center; past vice chmn., mem. exec. com. Mass. Ednl. Communications Comm.; past mem. ednl. devel. commn. Mass. Dept. Edn.; mem. adv. council Edward R. Murrow Center Pub. Diplomacy, Tufts U.; former asso. in edn. Harvard Grad. Sch. Edn.; former trustee World Peace Found. Served with USNR, 1945-48; lt. comdr. Res. Recipient Lamp of Knowledge award New Eng. chpt. Pub. Relations Soc. Am., 1964, One of 11 Outstanding Man of Year award Boston Jr. C. of C., 1962; Ralph Lowell medal for outstanding contbns. to public TV, 1973. Fellow Am. Acad. Arts and Scis.; mem. Nat. Assn. Ednl. Broadcasters (dir., chmn. bd. ednl. TV stas. div.), Soc. Motion Picture and Television Engrs. Clubs: Harvard (Boston, N.Y.C.); Cosmos (Washington); Tavern (Boston). Home: 700 New Hampshire Ave NW Washington DC 20037 Office: 485 L'Enfant Plaza SW Washington DC 20024

GUNNING, JAMES RICHARD, accountant; b. Buffalo, May 10, 1933; s. James Taylor and Thelma Christine (Shoemaker); B.S., U. Buffalo, 1958; M.B.A., N.Y.U., 1960; children—Christopher Payson, Stephanie Page, Claire Phillips. Accountant, Burroughs Welcome (U.S.A.) Inc., Yonkers, N.Y., 1958-60; sr. accountant Price Waterhouse & Co., N.Y.C., 1960-64; controller Atlantic Gummed Paper Corp., Bklyn., 1964-67; sr. v.p., sec. Martin E. Segal Co., N.Y.C., 1967—; lectr. N.Y.U. Grad Sch. Bus., 1966. Vice pres., bd. dirs. Nat. Council on Aging; bd. dirs. Willoughby House Settlement, Inc.; pres., bd. dirs. Bklyn. Assn. Settlement Houses; bd. dirs., past pres. Forum for Corporate Responsibility; governing com. Rowe Conf. Center. C.P.A., N.Y. State. Mem. Am. Inst. C.P.A.'s, N.Y. State Soc. C.P.A.'s, Fin. Execs. Inst. Unitarian. Home: 550 3d St Brooklyn NY 11215 Office: 730 Fifth Ave New York City NY 10019

GUNTHER, GEORGE LACKMAN, state senator, natureopathic physician; b. Bridgeport, Conn., Nov. 22, 1919; s. George and Gwendolyn (Cliff) G.; grad. Nat. Coll. Drugless Physicians, Chgo., 1942; m. Priscilla A. Staples, June 5, 1941; children—Priscilla K. (Mrs. E. Cortright Phillips), Karla Gwen (Mrs. R. Mazzey), Lance Inder. Intern, Chgo. Gen. Health Service, 1940-41; practice natureopathic medicine, Bridgeport, 1943-44, Stratford, Conn., 1944—; mem. Conn. Senate, 1967—, dep. minority leader, 1971-73, dep. majority leader, 1973-74, asst. minority leader, 1975-76. Chmn., Stratford Conservation Commn., 1961-71; mem. Stratford Citizens Council on Edn., 1961—; mem. Stratford Bd. Edn., 1957-61; mem. Stratford Town Council, 1960-64, 66; mem. Conn. Bd. Natureopathic Examiners, 1946-49; mem. Stratford Drug Adv. Com., 1971—; mem. Capitol Restoration Commn.; mem. L.I. Sound Study Com. of New Eng. River Basins Commn. Bd. dirs. Stratford P.A.L., Sterling Community Center, Stratford Red Cross; bd. assos. U. Bridgeport; commr. Atlantic States Marine Fisheries Commn. Recipient Am. Motors Conservation award Am. Motors Corp., 1966; named Water Conservationist of Year for Conn., Conn. State League of Sportsmens and Conservation Clubs, Nat. Wildlife Fedn. and Sears and Roebuck Found., 1966; Nat. Water Conservationist of Year, Nat. Wildlife Fedn. and Sears and Roebuck Found., 1966; Outstanding Service award Seymour Fish and Game Club, 1966; Outstanding Civic Leader of Am., 1967; Legislative Conservationist of Year for Conn., Conn. State League Sportsmen, Nat. Wildlife Fedn. and Sears and Roebuck Found., 1969; Citizen of Year award Stratford Civitan Club, 1970; Arthur Rickerby Meml. award Ecology League Conn., 1972; Legion of Honor award Internat. Order DeMolay, 1972; Raymond J. O'Connor Meml. Community Service award Stratford Jaycees, 1974; Conservation award SHAME, Inc., 1974; AFL-CIO Citation Conn., Am. fedns. tchrs., 1974, numerous others. Mem. Stratford Antique Gun Collectors Assn. (organizer, 1st pres.), Conn. Campers Assn., Stratford YMCA, P.T.A., Central Sch. Father's Club, Milford C. of C. (hon.), Bridgeport Boat Owners Assn. (hon.), Conn. Campers Assn., Protect Your Environment, Theta Sigma, Sigma Phi Kappa. Mason (Shriner), Lion (life, past pres.). Clubs: Pootatuck Yacht (Stratford); Southern Conn. Sportsmen's (Milford). Home: 890 Judson Pl Stratford CT 06497

GUPTA, GOPAL DAS, mech. engr.; b. Meerut, India, Aug. 1, 1946; s. Chandra Bhan and Hem Devi G.; B.Tech., Indian Inst. Tech., 1967; M.S., Lehigh U., 1968, Ph.D., 1970; m. Susham Sanan, Jan. 20, 1978. Asst. prof. dept. mech. engring. and mechanics Lehigh U., Bethlehem, Pa., 1970-73; research asso. Foster Wheeler Energy Corp., Livingston, N.J., 1973-76, head systems engring. and analysis sect., 1976—. Mem. ASME (Henry Hess award), Brit. Interplanetary Soc., Jersey Soc. Parapsychology, Sigma Xi. Contbr. articles to profl. jours. Home: 86 N Belair Ave Cedar Knolls NJ 07927 Office: 12 Peach Tree Hill Rd Livingston NJ 07039

GUPTA, PREM KAMAL, cardiologist; b. Jammu, India, Sept. 22, 1941; s. Bodh R. and Kaushalaya D. G.; came to U.S., 1966; M.B.B.S., Kashmir Govt. Med. Coll., 1964; m. Neelam Mahajan, Jan. 7, 1973; 1 child, Sumita. Intern, Beekman Downtown Hosp., N.Y.C., 1966-67; resident VA Hosp., N.Y.C., 1967-68, V.A. Hosp., Bronx, N.Y., 1968-71; asso. dir. cardiology Maimonides Med. Center, Bklyn.; asst. prof. clin. medicine City U. N.Y. Mt. Sinai Sch. Medicine, 1973-76; asso. prof. medicine State U. N.Y. Downstate Med. Center, Brklyn., 1976—. Diplomate Am. Bd. Internal Medicine. Fellow Royal Coll. Physicians (Can.), A.C.P., Am. Coll. Cardiology, Am. Coll. Chest Physicians, Am. Heart Assn. Clin. Cardiology; mem. Am. Fedn. Clin. Research, N.Y. Heart Assn. Contbr. articles on cardiology to med. jours.; cons. reviewer Am. Jour. Cardiology, 1976—. Office: 4802 10th Ave Brooklyn NY 11219

GUPTA, VED PRAKASH, physician, educator; b. Gwalior, India, Jan. 21, 1944; s. Har Swaroop and Bimla (Devi) G.; M.B., B.S., Gajra Raja Med. Coll. (India), 1966; m. Chitra Lekha Umre, Nov. 20, 1969; children—Rakhi, Sonal. Intern, Crozer Chester Med. Center, Chester, Pa., 1967-68; resident medicine Bryn Mawr (Pa.) Hosp., 1968-71, chief med. resident, 1969-70; fellow in rheumatology Albert Einstein Med. Center, Phila., 1971-73, attending in rheumatology, 1972—; asst. prof. medicine Temple U., Phila., 1976—. Diplomate Am. Bd. Internal Medicine. Mem. AMA, ACP, Pa., Phila. med. socs., Am., Phila. rheumatism assns., Arthritis Found. Hindu. Club: Phila. Med. Contbr. articles to med. jours. Home: 991 Natton Ct King of Prussia PA 19406 Office: Albert Einstein Med Center York and Tabor Rds Philadelphia PA 19141 also NE Med Center Suite 15 Welsh and Roosevelt Sts Philadelphia PA 19114

GURGO, MICHAEL MATTHIAS, refining co. exec.; b. Jersey City, June 14, 1920; s. Michael and Katherine (Frank) G.; B.S., Lafayette Coll., 1942; m. Elinor Alice Birk, May 30, 1943; children—Michael Frederick, Robert Peter. Group head Exxon Research, Linden, N.J., 1942-52; engring. rep. heavy metals industry Exxon Co. U.S.A., N.Y.C. and Pitts., 1953-60, adviser world-wide sales grease, rust preventives and coke, Houston, 1961-69, SSL coordinator Bayonne, N.J., 1970—. Bd. dirs. Meml. Forest Assn. Houston, 1963-64, pres., 1966. Registered profl. engr., Tex., N.J. Fellow Am. Soc. Lubrication Engrs. (vice chmn. N.Y. sect. 1958-59, nat. pres., 1968, chmn. pres. council 1969, chmn. standards com. 1975—); mem. ASTM (tech. com. D). Home: 71 Tall Timber Rd Middletown NJ 07748 Office: Exxon Co USA E 22d St Bayonne NJ 07002

GURNARI, LARRY MATHEW, water and wastewater engr.; b. Swoyerville, Pa., Nov. 13, 1954; s. Lawrence and Helen (Varaitis) G.; B.S. in Environ. Scis., Wilkes Coll., 1976. Field service engr. Cochrane Environ. Systems div. Crane Co., King of Prussia, Pa., 1976-77, Permutit Co. Inc. div. Zurn. Industries, Paramus, N.J., 1976—. Recipient Outstanding Sr. award Environ. Sci. Dept., 1976. Research on water treatment processes. Home: 26 Pettebone St Swoyerville PA 18704 Office: E 49 Midland Ave Paramus NJ 07652

GURTIN, LEATRICE KAGAN, ednl. adminstr.; b. Bklyn., May 6, 1936; d. David and Gertrude (Goldstein) Kagan; student Russell Sage Coll., 1953-55; B.A. in English, Brown U., 1967; M.A. in English, Carnegie-Mellon U., 1975; m. Morton Edward Gurtin, June 12, 1955; children—Amy Lynn, William Robert. With customer service dept. So. Calif. Gas Co., Los Angeles, 1955-56; creative drama inst. YMCA and YMHA, Barrington and Providence, R.I., 1961-63; English and drama tchr. Winchester Thurston Sch., Pitts., 1967-74; dir. admissions and placement Sch. Urban and Pub. Affairs, Carnegie-Mellon U., Pitts., 1975-78; dir. placement and career planning Grad. Sch. Bus., U. Pitts., 1978—; actress local radio and TV commls. Sta. WPRO, Providence, 1963. Mem. personnel adv. bd. Alleghany County Health Dept. 1976—; mem. fund raising com. Am. Sch. of Florence, 1974, Brown U., 1975-78; tchr. Favela children Ambulatorio da Praia do Pinto, Rio de Janeiro, 1970, recipient Spl. Service award, 1970. Recipient Spl. Service award Liberty Sch., Pitts., 1973. Mem. Internat. City Mgmt. Assn., Middle Atlantic Placement Assn., Coll. Placement Council, Nat. Assn. Housing and Redevel. Ofcls. Clubs: Brown (Pitts.). Home: 732 College Ave Pittsburgh PA 15232 Office: U Pitts Pittsburgh PA 15260

GURVITZ, MILTON SOLOMON, psychologist; b. Buffalo, Nov. 27, 1919; s. Isidor and Rebecca (Huravitz) G.; B.S., State U. N.Y. at Buffalo, 1941; M.A., N.Y. U., 1948, Ph.D., 1950; m. Sylvia Klein, June 20, 1948; children—Lynda Irene, Robert. Psychologist, USPHS Hosp., Lewisburg, Pa., 1942-46, Center for Psychol. Services, N.Y.C., 1947-48; chief psychologist Hillside Hosp.-L.I. Jewish Med. Center, Glen Oaks, N.Y., 1949-55; clin. asso. prof. Adelphi U., Garden City, N.Y., 1950-55; cons. psychologist Jewish Community Services L.I., 1955-61; pvt. practice psychology, Great Neck, N.Y., 1950—; dir. Great Neck Consultation Center, 1960—; clin. prof. postdoctoral program in psychoanalysis Adelphi U., 1968—. Diplomate Am. Bd. Profl. Psychology. Fellow Am. Psychol. Assn., Soc. Projective Techniques; mem. Nat. Psychol. Assn. for Psychoanalysis (sr.). Democrat. Jewish. Author: Dynamics of Psychological Testing, 1950. Home: 20 Canterbury Rd 3K Great Neck NY 11021 Office: 20 Canterbury Rd The Versailles Great Neck NY 11021

GUSHIN, HAROLD, chem. and photog. products mfg. co. exec.; b. Roselle, N.J., Oct. 29, 1915; s. Hyman and Mollie (Penn) G.; B.S. in Chem. Engring., Newark Coll. Engring., 1940; postgrad. Bklyn. Poly. Inst., 1946-48; m. Lillian Bernstein, Dec. 22, 1940; children—Margo Joy, Laura Lyn. Chem. engr. GAF, N.Y.C., 1933—, successively research and devel., prodn. supr., econ. evaluation engr., supr. engr. econ. evaluation, dir. operational planning, 1933-71, dir. planning and econ. evaluation, 1971—. Mem. Bd. Edn., Roselle, N.J., 1952-64, pres., 1956-58; pres. Union County Sch. Bd. Assn., 1960-62; mem. exec. com. N.J. Federated Bds. Edn., 1960-62; mem. Cultural Affairs Com., Roselle, 1972. Served with AUS, 1941-42, to capt. USAF, 1942-46. Fellow N.Y. Acad. Sci.; mem. Am. Assn. Cost Engrs. (charter), Am. Chem. Soc., Am. Inst. Chemists, Soc. for Chem. Industry. K.P. Home: 441 W 4th Ave Roselle NJ 07203 Office: 140 W 51st St New York City NY 10020

GUSMANO, LOUIS JOSEPH, lawyer; b. N.Y.C., Oct. 23, 1917; s. Salvatore and Vita (Castiglionel) G.; LL.B. summa cum laude, St. John's U., 1940, LL.M., 1941; m. Carol-Jane Patricia Barnett, June 28, 1951; 1 son, Louis Joseph. Admitted to N.Y. State bar, 1941, U.S. Supreme Ct. bar, 1952; practice law, N.Y.C., 1842—; sr. partner firm Kirlin, Campbell & Keating, N.Y.C., 1952—; law sec. Justice Thomas D. Thacher, N.Y. Ct. Appeals, Albany, 1946-47; spl. dep. gen. State N.Y., 1948-50; spl. commr. U.S. Dist. Ct., N.Y., 1958; dir. Am. S.S. Owners Mut. Protection and Indemnity Assn., Inc., N.Y.C. Del., Comite Martime Internat., 1974—. Pres., South Strathmore Civic Assn., 1956-57, Greater Manhasset Civic Counsel, 1958-59; mem. exec. com. St. Mary's Ch. Manhasset, 1958-60. Bd. dirs. United Fund of Manhasset, 1958-60. Mem. Am., N.Y. State bar assns., N.Y. Law Inst., Am. Judicature Soc., U.S. Naval Inst., Nat. Council Juvenile Ct. Judges, Maritime Assn. Port N.Y., Assn. Bar City N.Y., Maritime Law Assn. U.S. (v.p. 1971-76, exec. com. 1969-76), N.Y. County Lawyers Assn. (chmn. admiralty com. 1972-78), St. John's Law Sch. Alumni Assn. (treas.). Clubs: Plandome (N.Y.) Country (dir. 1963-69, pres. 1969-70); India House, Bankers, World Trade Center (founder) (N.Y.C.). Home: Oak Tree Ln and Sands Point Rd Sands Point NY 11050 Office: 120 Broadway New York City NY 10005

GUSS, GORDON ROGER, real estate exec.; b. Washington, Apr. 15, 1938; s. Eli E. and Sylvia (Cornblatt) G.; B.A., Am. U., 1961; m. Ellen Ruth Dreyer, May 15, 1960; children—Joseph Allan, Gary Kevin. Pres., Major Mgmt., Inc., Bethesda, Md., 1978—. Mem. Inst. Real Estate Mgmt. Democrat. Office: 4853 Cordell Ave Bethesda MD 20014

GUSS, MAYNARD ROBERT, accountant; b. Washington, Nov. 17, 1941; s. Carl and Bella (Weaver) G.; A.B.A., Benjamin Franklin U., 1968, B.C.S., 1970. Accountant, internat. investment div., bur. econ. analysis Dept. Commerce, Washington, 1968—, owner The Plastic Sign, Silver Spring, Md. Bd. dirs., treas. Commerce Employees Recreation Assn., Carolyn Condominium Assn. C.P.A., Md. Mem. Md. Assn. C.P.A.'s, Am. Inst. C.P.A.'s, Assn. Govt. Accountants, Am. Accounting Assn., Accounting Research Assn., Oxon Hill Philatelic Soc., Soc. Philatelic Amerians, Nat. Philatelic Soc., Collectors' Club Washington. Home: 614 Sligo Ave 401 Silver Spring MD 20910 Office: Bur Econ Analysis Tower Bldg Washington DC 20230

GUSTAFSON, GEORGE VICTOR, cons. engr.; b. Pitts., Nov. 4, 1912; s. Anders George and Anna Marie (Benson) G.; B.S., Pa. State U., 1934; m. Jeanne Denison, Jan. 31, 1942; children—George D., Alice Ann, Bette Jeanne. Chmn., dir. Standard Savs. & Loan Assn., Pitts., 1957—. Served to lt. comdr. C.E., USNR, 1942-45. Registered profl. engr., Pa., W.Va. Diplomate Am. Acad. Environ. Engrs. Mem. ASCE, Am. Water Works Assn., Nat., Pa. socs. profl. engrs., Am. Soc. Planning Ofcls., Water Pollution Control Fedn., Sigma Nu. Clubs: Pitts. Press, Edgewood Country (Pitts.). Home and office: 22 Roxbury Rd Pittsburgh PA 15221

GUTHRIE, JOHN FRANCIS, JR., ins. co. exec.; b. Cambridge, Mass., Nov. 19, 1943; s. John Francis and Agnes M. (Russell) G.; B.S. cum laude, Boston Coll., 1965, M.B.A., 1967; m. Jane Peyton McCone, Aug. 16, 1969; children—Dana Peyton, Christopher Peyton. Stockbroker, Goodbody & Co., Boston, 1967-69; analyst Colonial Mgmt. Co., Boston, 1969-70; with New Eng. Life Ins. Co., Boston, 1970—, investment officer, 1974-76, sr. investment officer, 1976—. Program coordinator Medfield (Mass.) Youth Basketball program, 1973-76; active Medfield Conservation Commn. Chartered fin. analyst. Mem. Boston Soc. Securities Analysts, Pub. Utilities Analysts Boston, Petroleum Analysts Boston, Beta Gamma Sigma. Club: University (Boston). Home: 11 Arnold Dr Medfield MA 02052 Office: 501 Boylston St Boston MA 02117

GUTHRIE, MARION B., artist; b. Lansdowne, Pa., Aug. 25, 1919; d. Charles Parker and Marion Leslie (Knott) Boyd; student Washington Sch. Art, 1965, Northwestern Acad. Watercolor, 1967; m. Warrington F. Guthrie, Jr., Oct. 12, 1940; children—Robert, Thomas W., James A. Tchr. watercolors, 1965—; br. treas. Nat. League Am. Pen Women Inc., 1975—; researcher Library Brandywine River Mus., Chadds Ford, Pa., 1971—, also guide. Mem. Acad. Fine Arts Pa., Assn. Am. Matercolor Soc., Rehoboth Art League, Del. Art Mus., Chester County Art Assn. Episcopalian. Sketches: The Barns of Chester County (Bernice Ball), 1974. Home: 127 Hillendale Rd W Kennett Square PA 19348

GUTHRIE, RANDOLPH HOBSON, JR., surgeon; b. N.Y.C., Dec. 8, 1934; s. Randolph Hobson and Mabel Edith (Welton) G.; A.B., Princeton, 1957; M.D., Harvard, 1961; m. Beatrice Mills Holden, Mar. 20, 1965; children—Randolph Hobson III, Michael Phipps, Philip Holden. Intern N.Y. Hosp., N.Y.C., 1961-62, resident gen. surgery, 1962-63, resident plastic surgery 1969-71, chief resident, 1971, asst. chief plastic surgery, 1971—; resident gen. surgery St. Luke's Hosp., N.Y.C., 1963-66, chief resident, 1966; research fellow Sloan-Kettering Inst., N.Y.C., 1970-71; chief plastic and reconstructive surgery service Meml. Sloan-Kettering Cancer Center, 1971-77; asst. prof. Cornell U. Med. Coll., 1971-74, asso. prof., 1974—. Pres., East River Med. Found., N.Y.C., 1970—, Burn Center Fund; trustee Episcopal Sch., N.Y.C. Served to maj. M.C., AUS, 1966-69. Mem. A.C.S., Plastic Surgery Research Council, Am. Geriatrics Soc., Am. Soc. Plastic and Reconstructive Surgeons, Pan Am. Med. Soc., N.Y. Soc. Plastic and Reconstructive Surgery, N.Y. Med. Soc., Med. Soc. County N.Y., Herbert Conway Soc., Assn. Acad. Surgery, AMA, N.Y. Acad. Medicine N.Y. Acad. Surgery, Am. Burn Assn., N.Y. State Soc. Surgeons, Harvard Med. Soc. Clubs: Union (N.Y.C.); Doubles, Med Strollers. Contbr. articles to books and med. jours. Home: 15 E 74th St New York City NY 10021 Office: 525 E 68th St New York City NY 10021

GUTMAN, DANIEL, judge; b. N.Y.C., July 1, 1901; s. Wolf and Theresa (Brody) G.; LL.B., St. Lawrence U., 1922; LL.D., Siena Coll., 1956, N.Y. Law Sch., 1967; m. Rosamond Lease Downer, Dec. 27, 1954. Admitted to N.Y. State bar, 1923; practiced law, N.Y.C., 1923-34; asst. U.S. atty. Eastern Dist. N.Y., 1934-35; spl. asst. U.S. atty. gen., Washington, 1935-36; asst. dist. atty. Kings County (N.Y.), 1937-38; mem. N.Y. State Assembly, 1939, N.Y. State Senate, 1939-43; justice Municipal Ct., N.Y.C., 1944-54, presiding justice, 1954; chief counsel to gov. N.Y. State, 1955-58; dean N.Y. Law Sch., 1959-68, dean emeritus, 1968—; dean Acad. Judiciary, N.Y.C., 1968-72; hearing referee N.Y.C. Transit Authority, 1959—. Adminstrv. services specialist N.Y. State Bd. Regents, 1969—; mem. N.Y. State Commn. for Regulation of Lobbying, Gov.'s Com. on Pub. Disclosures, 1975—. Chmn. N.Y. State Democratic Platform Com., 1958. Decorated Grand Cross, Order EloyAlfaro (Panama), Cavallieri Order Merit (Italy). Mem. Nat. Acad. Arbitrators, Assn. Bar City N.Y., Fed., Putnam County bar assns. N.Y., N.J., Conn. (past pres.), Omega Chi, Phi Delta Phi. Clubs: Masons, K.P. Originated civil night cts. for small claims trials in N.Y.C. Home: Gypsy Trail Rd Carmel NY 10512

GUTMAN, I. CYRUS, transp. cons.; b. Perth Amboy, N.J., Mar. 28, 1912; s. Leon and Jennie (Levine) G.; B.S. in Econs., Johns Hopkins U., 1932; m. Mildred B. Largman, July 21, 1940; children—Harry L., Peggy Gutman Sheren, Richard J. S. Dist. mgr. Motor Freight Express, Inc., Phila., 1933-40; v.p., treas. gen., mgr. Modern Transfer Co., Inc., Allentown, Pa., 1940-67, dir. nat. sales, 1967-69; dir. Eastern Industries, Inc., Wescosville, Pa., 1967-76; now transp. cons.; asst. to pres. Branch Motor Express Co., N.Y.C., 1972-74; dir. Yale Express System, Inc., 1974. Pres., Lehigh County Indsl. Devel. Corp., 1959—, Lehigh's Econ. Advancement Project, Inc., 1960—; chmn. Lehigh County Indsl. Devel. Authority, 1966—; mem. nat. resources com., nat. alumni schs. com. Johns Hopkins U.; treas. Am. Hist. Truck Mus. and Library, Allentown, 1972—; mem. Lehigh-Northampton Counties Joint Planning Commn., 1962—, Lehigh and Northampton Transp. Authority, 1972-74; mem. Am. Jewish Joint Distbn. Com., Inc.; asso. Cedar Crest Coll.; chmn. adv. com. on fund raising Lehigh Valley Hosp. Planning Council, 1966—; v.p. bd. assos. Muhlenberg Coll., 1971-73, pres., 1973—; adv. bd. Lehigh Valley Center Performing Arts, 1975; exec. com. Citizens for Lehigh County Progress, 1965—; chmn. Allentown Sch. Dist. Authority, 1971—; asso. mem. Nat. Jewish Welfare Bd.; treas. Allentown Citadel Salvation Army, 1968—; mem. hon. adv. bd. Lehigh Valley Assn. Retarded Children, 1969—; mem. adv. com. Central Pa. Teamsters Pension and Health and Welfare Funds, 1969—; mem. gen. advisory council Lehigh County Vocat. Tech. Sch.; mem. advisory bd. Good Shepherd Home and Workshop, 1966—; gen. advisory com. Lehigh County Community Coll., 1977—; trustee Allentown Hosp. Assn., 1970—, Swain Sch., 1977—; bd. dirs. Lehigh Valley Jr. Achievement, United Fund, Allentown, Jewish Fedn., Allentown, 1953-70, Wiley House, 1969—; past mem. bd. trustees Internat. Assn. Machinists Local 1099 Dist. Pension Plan, Phi Sigma Delta Found. Recipient St. Patrick's Day award of Lehigh Valley, 1961, Civic Service commendation Whitehall C. of C., Service Appreciation award Central Pa. Motor Carrier's Conf., 1971, Central Pa. Joint Area Grievance Com., 1971, Congratulatory Resolutions Cities Allentown, Bethlehem, 1968, Distinguished Citizens Sales award Sales and Mktg. Execs. Internat. of Allentown and Bethlehem, 1976, Distinguished Service award Lehigh Valley Traffic Club, 1978. Mem. Asso. Traffic Clubs Am., Allentown C. of C. (past dir.), Traffic and Transp. Assn. Pitts., Met. Traffic Assn. N.Y., Johns Hopkins Alumni Assn. (past sec., past pres. Phila. area), Lehigh County Hist. Soc., Nat. Fedn. Temple Brotherhoods. Omicron Delta Kappa, Pi Delta Epsilon, Zeta Beta Tau, Delta Nu Alpha. Jewish religion (past dir. temple). Mason; mem. B'nai B'rith (founder, trustee local lodge scholarship com.). Clubs: Berkleigh Country (dir., past pres. Kutztown, Pa.); Lehigh Valley (Allentown); Locust Midcity; N.Y. Traffic (N.Y.C.); Livingston. Home: 1824 Turner St Allentown PA 18104 Office: 462 Walnut St Allentown PA 18102

GUTTERIDGE, THOMAS GEORGE, ednl. adminstr.; b. Flint, Mich., Oct. 31, 1942; s. George E. and Mary R. (Stewart) G.; B.Indsl. Engring., Gen. Motors Inst., 1965; M.S. in Indsl. Adminstrn., Purdue U., 1966, Ph.D. in Indsl. Adminstrn., 1971; m. Judith Grubbs, Aug. 28, 1965; children—Theresa, Deborah, Cynthia. Prodn. supr. Buick motors div. Gen. Motors Corp., Flint, Mich., 1962-63, labor relations investigator, 1963-64, asst. safety engr., 1964-65; asst. to mktg. v.p. Indsl. Nucleonics Corp., Columbus, Ohio, 1966-67; instr. Krannert Grad. Sch. Indsl. Adminstrn., Purdue U., W.Lafayette, Ind., 1967-69; prof. (part-time) Sch. Indsl. and Labor Relations, Cornell U., Buffalo, N.Y., 1971-72; asst. prof. human resources and indsl. relations State U. N.Y., Buffalo, 1970-76, asso. prof., 1976—, dir. Human Resources Inst., 1974—, asso. dean and exec. dir. Regional Econ. Assistance Center, Sch. Mgmt., 1978—; mediator N.Y. State Pub. Employment Relations Bd., 1972—; human resources cons., 1975—; labor arbitrator, 1977—. Mem. ho. of dels. United Way, Buffalo, 1977—; bd. dirs. Everywomen's Opportunity Center, 1977-78, v.p., 1977-78. U.S. Dept. Labor grantee, 1974-78. Mem. Am. Soc. Personnel Adminstrs., Human Resource Planning Soc., Am. Mgmt. Assn., Acad. Mgmt. (exec. bd. personnel-human resource div. 1974-77), Indsl. Relations Research Assn., Beta Gamma Sigma. Democrat. Methodist. Contbr. articles on vocat. careers and indsl. mgmt. to profl. jours. Home: 164 McNair Rd Williamsville NY 14221 Office: 328 Crosby Hall State U NY Buffalo NY 14214

GUTTMAN, SAMUEL ARNOLD, psychoanalyst; b. N.Y.C., Sept. 13, 1914; s. Morris and Ida (Goldberger) G.; A.B., Cornell U., 1934, M.A., 1935, Ph.D., 1937, M.D., 1940; m. Alice Clare Wieland, Nov. 17, 1966 (dec. June 1977); children—Elizabeth (Mrs. Bradley Sevin), Samuel Adam. Fellow Woods Hole Marine Biol. Lab., Cornell U., 1935-36; intern, Albert Einstein Med. Center, Phila., 1940-42; asst. resident neurologist Neurol. Inst. N.Y., 1942-43, chief resident neurologists, 1943-44; fellow Pa. Hosp. and Inst. Pa. Hosp., Phila., 1944-45; practice medicine specializing in psychoanalysis, Phila., 1945—, Wilkes-Barre/ Pa., 1950-55, Pennington, N.J., 1955—; asst. neurologist Presbyn. Hosp., N.Y.C., 1942-44, Pa. Hosp., Phila., 1944-46; asst. neuropsychiatrist Jewish Hosp., Phila., 1944-47; psychiat. cons. Southwark Neighborhood Center, Phila., 1946-47; psychiat. cons. Shoemaker Sch., Elkins Park, Pa., 1947-48; dir. Child Guidance Center, Lakawanna County, Pa., 1947-55; psychiat. cons. Family Service, Wilkes-Barre, Pa., 1948-52; chief div. psychiatry and neurology Wilkes-Barre Gen. Hosp., 1948-55; psychiat. cons. Family Service, Scranton, Dunmore, Pa., 1948-55; asst. attending physician Jefferson Hosp., 1963—; researcher neurophysiology Harvard Med. Sch., 1936; asst. physiology Cornell U. Med. Coll., 1934-37; asst. neurologist Coll. Phys. and Surg. Columbia, 1942-44; sr. clin. asso. Phila. Inst. Psychoanalysis, 1944-48; asso. prof. clin. psychiatry Thomas Jefferson Med. Sch., 1962-67, prof. psychiatry and psychoanalysis, 1967—; cons. dept. psychology U. Pa. Med. Sch., 1945-47, Wilkes Coll., Wilkes-Barre, Pa., 1948-55, Cleve. Psychoanalytic Inst., Cleve., 1968—. Lect. neurology Phila. Sch. Occupational Therapy, 1944-45, Phila. Assn. Psychoanalysis and Inst. Phila. Assn. Psychoanalysis, 1949-54; sr. clin. asso., lectr. Phila. Inst. Psychoanalysis, 1948-49; exec. dir., trustee Center for Advanced Psychoanalytic Studies, Princeton, N.J., 1961—, chmn., 1975—; exec. sec., pres. bd. trustees Psychoanalytic Studies at Aspen, Colo., 1968-72, pres., 1972—. Diplomate Am. Psychoanalytic Assn. (mem. bd. profl. standards 1956—). Mem. Internat. Psycho-Analytical Assn. (co-chmn. program com. internat. psycho-analytic congresses, 1969, 73), A.M.A., Am. Psychiat. Assn., Assn. for Research in Nervous and Mental Disorders, A.A.A.S., N.J. State Med. Soc., Pa., Phila. psychiat. socs., N.Y., N.J. acads. scis., Mercer County Component Med. Soc., Phila. Assn. Psychoanalysis (tng. analyst 1954—). Chief editor Bull. Phila. Assn. Psychoanalysis, 1950-59. Editorial bd. Psychoanalytic Quar., 1958-66; cons. editor Bull. Phila. Assn. Psychoanalysis, 1959—. Contbr. articles to profl. jours. Home and office: Hunter's Green Pennington NJ 08534

GUTTMANN, H(ANS) PETER, cons. engring. co. exec.; b. Berlin, Dec. 1, 1919; s. Alfonso and Gertrudis Elizabeth (Heinemann) G.; came to U.S., 1949, naturalized, 1958; B.S., King's Coll., Cambridge (U.K.) U., 1938; B.A., U. San Carlos, Guatemala, 1944; m. Margherita Gieffers, Sept. 13, 1952; 1 son, Hans Peter. Mgr. tech. dept. Leon Guttmann & Cia., Guatemala City, 1938-48; dir. internat. sales Fairbanks, Morse & Co., Chgo., 1948-61; v.p., prin. Stanley Cons.'s Inc., Washington, 1961-77; chmn. bd., chief exec. officer Amer-Asia Cons.'s, Inc., Washington, 1970-75; pres. HPG Assos., cons. engring. and constrn. industry, Washington, 1977—; lectr. in field. Spl. missions for Govt. Guatemala, 1945-54, del. to UN, 1949-51, envoy to Colombia, 1954-55. Chmn. bd. dirs. Children's Aid Internat., 1977—. Decorated Govts. Guatemala, Ecuador, Colombia, Liberia. Mem. Am. Cons. Engrs. Council, Internat. Engring. and Constrn. Industries Council of U.S., Nat. Soc. Profl. Engrs., Am. Mgmt. Assn., Washington Export Council. Clubs: Cosmos, Internat. Washington, Solomon Island Yacht. Author: The International Consultant, 1976. Contbr. articles to profl. publs. Home: 2236 46th St NW Washington DC 20007 Office: 1545 18th St NW Washington DC 20036

GUY, GORDON ROSS, writer, artist, publisher; b. Providence, R.I., Jan. 1, 1944; s. Edward Henry and Helen Dee (Ross) G.; grad. vocat. and tech. sch., 1968. Owner, publisher Gothick Gateway Publishing,

Glastonbury, Conn., Darkroom Technician, Glastonbury; Glastonbury Citizen newspaper, 19—; editor, publisher Count Dracula Soc. Quarterly, East Hartford 1968-71, Castle Dracula Quarterly, Glastonbury, 1977—; cons., co-author scripts Taylor Films Production, Dover-Foxcroft, Maine, 1977—. Clubs: County Dracula Soc., Bela Lugosi Fan Club. Office: Box 423 Glastonbury CT 06033

GWYNN, SANDRA EKMAN, comml. property exec.; b. Ft. Benning, Ga., Jan. 24, 1942; d. William Emmett and Iris Mary (Welch) Ekman; student Manatee Jr. Coll., 1962-63; children—William, Vanessa. Site mgr. Hyland Assos., Bedford, N.H., 1974-77; property mgr. Greenwich II Ltd., Manchester, N.H., 1977—; pres. Incorporated Mgmt. I, Inc., Manchester, 1978—; dir. consumer info. Capitol Super Markets, Quincy, Mass., 1974-75. Republican. Home: 130 Salmon St Manchester NH 03104 Office: 50 Bridge St Manchester NH 03101

HA, CHESTER CHIDUK, educator; b. Sanchun, Korea, Feb. 1, 1938; s. Tae Bong and Soon Dal (Moon) H.; came to U.S., 1965, naturalized, 1975; B.A., Korea U., 1960; M.S., Ill. State U., 1967; Ph.D., Ohio State U., 1974; m. Katherine K. Chang, Dec. 23, 1967; children—Sharon, Lawrence. Budget officer, Office of Budget, Korean Air Force Hdqrs., 1961-64; grad. asst. Ill. State U., Norma, 1965-67; research analyst Ill. Dept. Mental Health, Springfield, 1967-71; research asso. Faculty of Mgmt. Sci. Ohio State U., Columbus, 1972-74; asst. prof. bus. adminstrn. State U. N.Y., Brockport, 1974—, coordinator bus. adminstrn. program, 1975—, chmn. dept. econs. and bus. adminstrn., 1976—. Mem. Acad. Mgmt., Indsl. Relations Research Assn., Am. Mktg. Assn., Am. Inst. Decision Sci., AAUP. Presbyterian. Contbr. articles in field to profl. jours. Home: 75 Round Creek Dr Rochester NY 14626 Office: 291 Faculty Office Bldg Dept Business and Economics State Univ New York Brockport NY 14420

HAAN, HENDRIK MARIE, diversified mfg. co. exec.; b. Leyden, Netherlands, July 22, 1924; s. Theodorus Antonius and Theresa Catarina (Fles) H.; Baccalaureate, U. Delft, 1947; diploma in mech. engring. Gen. Motors Inst., Flint, Mich., 1949; m. Frieda Ruytenbeek, May 21, 1950; children—Henry M., Roland V., Elizabeth A. Engr. power and indsl. products Gen. Motors Continental, Antwerp, Belgium, 1949-51; tech. mgr. NAHV (Lindeteves), Elizabethville, Zaire, 1951-55; dist. mgr. Ford Motor Co., Teheran, Iran, 1956-58; liaison exec. Bendix Corp., Paris, 1959-62; merchandising mgr. Chrysler Corp., Geneva, 1963-68; chief exec. officer subs. Fuqua Industries of Atlanta, Brussels, 1968-70; project exec. ITT, Brussels, 1971-73; adviser to pres. G & W Industries, Geneva, 1973-75; dir. internat. ops. Condec Corp., Old Greenwich, Conn., 1975—. Served with RAF, 1945. Mem. Am. Mgmt. Assn., Gen. Motors Alumni Assn., Brussels C. of C., Smithsonian Assos. Club: Swissair Travel. Home: 106 Peconic Hills Dr Southampton NY 11968 Office: 1700 E Putnam Ave Old Greenwich CT 06870

HAAS, ALBERT, physician; b. Budapest, Hungary, Oct. 27, 1911; s. Francois and Jeanine (Grunfeld) H.; came to U.S., 1949, naturalized, 1957; M.D., Royal Hungarian Med. Sch., Budapest, 1937; m. Sonia Nadel, Sept. 28, 1940; 1 son, Francois. Intern, St. Janos Hosp., Budapest, 1937-38; resident in pulmonary diseases Sanatorium Mt. Blanc, Plateau D'Assi, France, 1938-40, St. Roch Hosp., Nice, France, 1940-42; fellow rehab. medicine N.Y. U. Med. Sch., 1956-57, asst. prof., 1958-65, asso. prof., 1966-73, prof. exptl. rehab. medicine, 1974—. Served with French Med. Corps, 1940. Decorated Croix de Guerre, French Legion of Honor. Mem. Am. Trudeau Soc., N.Y. Acad. Sci., Nat. French Soc. Phys. Medicine and Rehab. Democrat. Jewish. Author: (with others) Rehabilitative Application to Bronchial Asthma. Contbr. articles to profl. jours. Home: 1 Christopher St New York City NY 10014 Office: 400 E 34th St New York City NY 10016

HAAS, BERT ROBERT, investment counselor; b. Vienna, Austria, Nov. 24, 1927; s. Hugo Edward and Stella Margaret (Landesmann) H.; came to U.S., 1940, naturalized, 1945; A.B., Middlebury Coll., 1948; M.B.A., Cornell U., 1950; m. Ellen Roberta Charney, Mar. 11, 1967; children—Caroline Audrey, Paul Edward. Financial analyst S.P. Co., 1952-59; sr. editor Value Line Investment Survey, 1959-62; v.p. Paine, Webber, Jackson & Curtis, 1962-70; v.p., dir. Alliance One Instl. Services, N.Y.C., 1970-77; v.p. John Muir & Co., N.Y.C., 1977—. Served with AUS, 1950-52. Mem. N.Y. Soc. Security Analysts, Bldg. Analysts Soc. (pres.), Machinery Analysts Soc. (past pres.), Chi Psi. Club: Cornell (N.Y.C.). Home: 315 E 86th St New York City NY 10028 Office: 61 Broadway New York City NY 10006

HAAS, ELEANOR ALTER (MRS. PETER RALPH HAAS), mgmt. communications cons.; b. Jersey City, Mar. 12, 1932; d. Nicholas Mark Alter de Csanytalek and Eleanor (Cochran) Reed Alter; Alter de Csanytalek; B.A., Smith Coll., 1953; certificate N.Y. Sch. Interior Design, 1960; m. Peter Ralph Haas, Oct. 22, 1966. Exec. sec. MCA Artists, Ltd., N.Y.C., 1954-56; exec. sec. Young & Rubicam, Inc., N.Y.C., 1956-58; exec. sec. J. Walter Thompson Co., N.Y.C., 1958-59; exec. sec. Stanford Research Inst., N.Y.C., 1959, Deafness Research Found., N.Y.C., 1960, Earl Newsom & Co., N.Y.C., 1961-65; account exec. Ruder & Finn, Inc., N.Y.C., 1965-68; founder, sr. partner The Haas Group, N.Y.C., 1968—; founder, partner DeNigris, Haas & England, Inc., N.Y.C., 1978—. Bd. dirs. bus. council UN Decade for Women. Mem. Am. Mgmt. Assn., Am. Acad. Polit. and Social Scis., Pub. Relations Soc. Am., Women Execs. in Pub. Relations, Advt. Women N.Y., Am. Pub. Health Assn. Office: 59 E 54th St New York City NY 10022

HAAS, KARL ALAN, platics co. exec.; b. Englewood, N.J., June 6, 1933; s. Karl and Martha (Osterman) H.; B.Mgmt. Engring., Rensselaer Poly. Inst., 1959, M.Mgmt. Engring. (fellow), 1960, Ph.D. (Ford fellow), 1968; m. Jacqueline Crawford, Jan. 27, 1962; children—James Andrew, Susan Jennifer, David Reid, Peter Crawford. Instr. Sch. Mgmt. Rensselaer Poly. Inst., Troy, N.Y., 1960-62; asso. prof. dept. indsl. engring. and ops. research N.Y. U., N.Y.C., 1963-70; dir. mgmt. services Plymouth Rubber Co., Canton, Mass., 1970-72, v.p. adminstrn., 1972-75, group v.p., 1975—; dir. Water Guidance Systems, Inc., Canton, 1978—, pres., 1979—; cons. bus. and govt. N. and S. Am., 1961-70. Mem. Am. Inst. Indsl. Engrs., Sigma Xi, Tau Beta Pi, Epsilon Delta Sigma, Alpha Pi Mu. Presbyterian. Clubs: Indian Harbor Yacht (Greenwich, Conn.); Metropolitan (Chgo.). Home: 42 Partridge Hill Rd Weston MA 02193 Office: 104 Revere St Canton MA 02021

HAAS, LEONARD, lab. instrument co. exec.; b. N.Y.C., Jan. 13, 1933; s. Abraham and Rose (Weinberger) H.; B.S., Rider Coll., 1968; LL.B. course, LaSalle U., 1972; m. Dianne M. Popkin, June 1, 1958; children—Caryne, Debra, Richard, Robert. Salesman, A. H. Robins Co., Richmond, Va., 1959-69; sales rep. Bel-Art Products, Pequannock, N.J., 1969-70, regional mgr., sales tng. mgr., govt. accounts mgr., 1970-71; sales mgr. Manostat Corp., N.Y.C., 1971-73, dir. mktg., 1974, v.p., 1974—; cons. mktg. Pres., capt. Kendall Park Rescue Squad, 1962-69; mem. N.J. State Council Rescue Squads. Served with U.S. Army, 1953-55. Mem. Nat. Assn. Sci. Reps., Bio-Med. Mktg. Assn., Nat. Assn. Instrument Mfrs., Sci. Apparatus Makers Assn. Home: 1 Marine View Plaza Hoboken NJ 07030 Office: Manostat Corp 519 8th Ave New York City NY 10018

HAAS, MARVIN JOEL, educator, bus. cons.; b. N.Y.C., May 24, 1927; s. Julius K. and Charlotte (Feld) H.; B.S. in Indsl. Engring., U. Miami, 1950; M.S. in Engring., Stevens Inst. Tech., 1959; m. Irene Golish, Feb. 2, 1958; children—Sharon Ellen, Jeffrey. Pres. Paul-Mar Corp., 1950-53; mgr. Curtiss-Wright Corp., 1953-59, cons., 1960-63; systems, data processing exec. S. Klein Dept. Stores, 1963-65; data processing, systems cons. exec., also mgr. systems, adminstrv. service. Monroe Internat., 1965-67; prof. accounting, finance and mgmt. Pace Coll., N.Y.C., 1963-69; Fairleigh Dickinson U., 1970-74; pres. Shar-Frey Inc., Rose Realty Co. Inc., Ednl. Services; cons. to industry in data processing and adminstrn.; lectr. profl. orgns. Served with AUS, 1945-47; ETO. Mem. Am. Mgmt. Assn., Assn. Systems Mgmt. (chpt. pres. 1973). Mason. Home: 43 Burnside Pl Wayne NJ 07470

HAAS, WARD JOHN, business exec.; b. N.Y.C., Aug. 26, 1921; s. M. A. and Pauline (Ward) H.; B.S., Mass. Inst. Tech., 1943, Ph.D., 1949; m. Jane Corya, Dec. 25, 1943; children—Margaret C., Jeffrey W., Elizabeth C. Biochemist, E.I. duPont de Nemours & Co., 1949-51; fgn. service attache Am. embassy, London, 1951-54; asst. to dir. Agrl. Research and Devel. Center, Charles Pizer & Co., Inc., Terre Haute, Ind., 1954-56, asst. to pres., N.Y.C., 1957-60, dir. ops. Pfizer Labs. div., N.Y.C., 1959-64; asso. prof. mgmt., dir. Space Scis. Research Center, U. Mo., 1964-68; dir., pres. Warner-Lambert Research Inst., Morris Plains, N.J., 1968-69; v.p. research and devel. Warner-Lambert Co., 1969-72; corporate v.p. research and devel. S.C. Johnson & Son, Inc., Racine, Wis., 1972-75; v.p. research and devel. Chesebrough-Pond's, Inc., Greenwich, Conn., 1975—. Served with U.S. Army, 1943-46. Mem. Am. Inst. Chemists, N.Y. Acad. Sci., AAAS, Am. Chem. Soc., Am. Inst. Aeros. and Astronautics, Am. Aero. Soc., Dirs. Indsl. Research, Am. Mgmt. Assn. (research and devel. council), Sigma Xi. Home: 768 Sasco Hill Rd Fairfield CT 06430 Office: 40 Merritt Blvd Trumbull Indsl Park Trumbull CT 06611

HABER, DAVID L., impresario, concert mgr., theatrical producer; b. Montreal, Que., Can., July 15, 1927; s. Louis and Molly (Nahamovitch) H.; student pub. schs., Montreal, Que., Can. Prodn. stage mgr. Brae Manor Theatre, Knowlton, Que., 1947-56, Canadian Repertory Theatre, Ottawa, Ont., 1948-52; prodn. stage mgr. Nat. Ballet Can., Toronto, Ont., 1952-56, artistic dir., 1973-75; producer, dir. Nat. Film Bd., Montreal, Que., 1956-58; stage mgr., personal mgr., tour mgr. and producer for performers, 1958-61, including Sir John Gielgud, Stanley Holloway, Mahalia Jackson; agt., mgr. William Morris Agy., N.Y.C., 1961-64; producer theatre presentations World Festival Expo 67, Montreal, 1964-67; dir. programming Nat. Arts Centre, Ottawa, Ont., 1968-73; founder, prin. David Haber Artists Mgmt., Inc., Toronto, Ont., 1976—; guest. instr. York U., U. Ottawa, Banff Sch. Fine Arts, 1972—; cons. in field. Recipient Centennial medal Govt. of Can., 1967, Queen Elizabeth II Jubilee medal, 1978. Mem. Canadian Assn. Artists Mgmts. (chmn.), Canadian Conf. Arts (gov.), Internat. Soc. Performing Arts Adminstrs. (dir.), Assn. Coll., Univ. and Community Arts Adminstrn., Canadian Actors' Equity Assn., Assn. Theatrical Press Agts., Mgrs., Internat. Platform Assn., Canadian Music Council, Can.-Israel Cultural Found. (adv. bd.). Club: Celebrity. Contbr. articles to arts mags., textbooks and other profl. pubs. Home: 44 Charles St W Apt 3602 Toronto ON M4Y 1R8 Canada Office: 1235 Bay St Suite 500 Toronto ON M5R 3K4 Canada

HABER, PAUL ADRIAN LIFE, physician; b. N.Y.C., Feb. 14, 1920; s. Benjamin Walter and Gussie Esther H.; B.A., U. Tex., 1941, M.D., 1949; M.A., Columbia U., 1942; M.S., George Washington U., 1968; m. Mary Agatha Crolley, Oct. 25, 1959; children—Peter, William. Research chemist Calco Chem. Co., Bound Brook, N.J., 1942-43; intern Los Angeles County Gen. Hosp., 1949-50; resident Wadsworth VA Hosp., 1950-52; practice medicine specializing in cardiology, Los Angeles, 1952-53; with VA, 1957—, dir. extended care VA Central Office, Washington, 1970-75, asst. chief med. dir., 1976—; asst. clin. prof. medicine George Washington U. Med. Sch. Bd. dirs. Nat. Council on Aging; mem. nat. adv. council Nat. Inst. Aging. Served with M.C., USAF, 1953-55. Recipient Exceptional Service award VA, 1968. Fellow A.C.P., Am. Geriatric Soc.; mem. AAAS, Am. Dietetics Assn., Gerontol. Soc. (mem. policy com.), Phi Beta Kappa. Club: Cosmos (Washington). Author: Physicians Guidebook of Disability. Home: 7501 Honeywell Ln Bethesda MD 20014 Office: 810 Vermont Washington DC 20420

HABER, PIERRE CLAUDE, psychologist; b. Landau, Germany, June 8, 1931; s. Kurt S. and Hedwig (Kuhn) H.; came to U.S., 1943, naturalized, 1949; B.A., Bklyn. Coll., 1952; M.A., Duke U., 1953; Ph.D., U. Paris (France), 1956; Counselor, dir. adult edn. Central Sch. Dist. 2, Yorktown Heights, N.Y., 1956-59; psychologist Manpower Devel. Program, Bklyn., 1959-65; asst. prof. Queens Coll., 1965-70; exec. sec., exec. dir. Psychology Soc., N.Y.C., 1970—; cons. Student Admissions Center, N.Y.C., 1962-65; asst. prof. Jersey City State Coll., 1967—. Mem. Am. Psychol. Assn., Am., N.Y. State personnel and guidance assns., Psychology Soc., N.Y. Assn. Pub. Sch. Adult Educators (v.p. 1957-59), Pi Delta Phi. Republican. Jewish. Contbr. to Compton's Ency., also articles to profl. jours. Home: 100 Beekman St New York City NY 10038 Office: 100 Beekman St New York City NY 10038

HABER, WILLIAM BILL, psychologist; b. N.Y.C., Nov. 27, 1906; s. Aaron and Jean (Platt) H.; B.A., Coll. City N.Y., 1947; M.A., N.Y. U., 1953, Ph.D., 1954; m. Leah Sussal, July 6, 1929. Gen. practice clin. psychology, 1950—; research, writer on psychology, N.Y.C., 1950; clin. psychologist Mt. Sinai Hosp., N.Y.C., 1950-51, staff supr., 1952-56; chief psychologist Hosp for Joint Diseases N.Y., 1952-57. panel psychologist Jewish Child Care Assn., 1955-56; instr. N.Y. U., 1955-57; supr. psychologists N.Y. State Rehab. Dept. 1955-57; Hon. bd. dirs. Nat. Amputation Found. Mem. AAAS, N.Y.C. Clin. Assn., Am. Acad. Psychotherapists, Am., Eastern, N.Y. State psychol. assns., Psychologists in Pvt. Practice, N.Y. Acad. Sci., Nat. Register Health Service Providers in Psychology (council), Soc. Projective Techniques and Research Inst., Assn. Behavior Therapists, Orthopsychiatric Assn., Internat. Soc. Existential Psychiatry, Soc. Personality Assessment. Contbr. to Funk and Wagnall's New Internat. Year Book, 1954-65, also articles to profl. jours. Address: 185 E 85th St Apt 30 D-E New York City NY 10028

HABERGRITZ, GEORGE JOSEPH, artist; b. N.Y.C., June 1, 1909; s. Aaron and Jeannette (Platt) H.; student NAD, 1924-26; grad. Cooper Union, 1931; postgrad. Academie de la Grande Chaumiere, Paris, France, 1949-50; m. Maya Pollock, June 1, 1947. Artist, painter, sculptor; one-man shows Wellons Gallery N.Y.C., 1956-57, traveling show 11 maj. museums U.S., 1965-66, Gallery Klotz, Stuttgart, Germany, 1965, Artium Gallery, 1970-71, El Callejon Gallery, Bogota, Colombia, 1972, 73, 75, 76, Gallery Meindl, 1974, 76, 77; exhibited in group shows Va. Bienniel, Albright Mus., Walters Gallery, Whitney Mus., Mont. Mus., Detroit Gallery Fine Arts, Silvermine, Contemporary Arts, Heller Gallery, Hutton Gallery; represented in permanent collections Norfolk, Evansville, Purdue, Butler, Oklahoma, Wilberforce, Haifa, and others. Instr. Art Students League, N.Y.C., 1964-65; tchr. Com. Continuous Art Tng. N.Y.C., 1966—; pvt. tchr. art, N.Y.C., 1950—; workshop for profl. artists in new and advanced media, designs for jewelry as sculpture, 1966—. Served with AUS, 1942-46. Recipient painting awards N.A.D., 1940, several awards Nat. Soc. Painters in Casein and Acrylic. Mem. Cooper Union Alumni. Address: 150 Waverly Pl New York City NY 10014

HABERLAND, PETER HANS, physicist; b. Berlin, July 5, 1937; s. Hans R. and Hildegard E. (Kaiser) H.; came to U.S., 1963; Diploma Physics Technische Universitaet, Berlin, 1963; M.S., Mass. Inst. Tech., Cambridge, Mass., 1966; Dr. Eng., Technische Universitaet, Berlin, 1968; m. Anke Baronsky, Sept. 26, 1963; children—Nicole A., Corinna A., Michele A. Engr. Westinghouse Research Lab., Pitts., 1963-64, cons., 1964-65; staff engr. IBM Kingston (N.Y.) Lab., 1968-69, advanced display technology, 1969-71, sr. engr., 1974-75, program mgr. display products, 1975-78, program mgr. data security and power products, 1978—. Co-chmn. sustaining membership dr. Girl Scouts U.S.A., Ulster County, N.Y., 1974. Recipient outstanding contbr. award IBM, 1973. Mem. Am. Phys. Soc., Soc. Info. Display, Deutsche Physikalische Gesselschaft, Sigma Xi. Club: Zena Recreation Park. Contbr. articles to profl. jours. Home: 15 Oriole Dr Woodstock NY 12498 Office: Neighborhood Rd Kingston NY 12401

HABIB, MOHAMED, communications services adminstr.; b. Alexandria, Egypt, Nov. 11, 1925; B.A. in Journalism, Am. U., Cairo, 1946; postgrad. Higher Inst. for Spl. Studies, Cairo, 1947; children—Yusef, Leila. Diplomatic corr. ALAKBAR, Cairo, 1947-52; dir. fgn. press dept. Ministry of Info., Cairo, 1952-54; press attache Egyptian embassy, Washington, 1954-58, press and info. counselor, 1958-67; owner, dir. Middle East Services, Washington, 1971—; supr. prodn. Arabic edit. Forbes Mag., 1975; spokesman summit meeting Arab kings and pres., Cairo, 1964. Recipient Decoration of Merit, Pres. Abdul Nasser, 1964. Author various studies for Arab League and Egyptian govt. Home: 2508 Cliffbourne Pl NW Washington DC 20009 Office: 1321 1/2 Wisconsin Ave NW Washington DC 20036

HACKER, HAROLD SCHWORM, librarian; b. Buffalo, July 9, 1916; s. Joseph Frederick and Henrietta Catherine (Schworm) H.; A.B., Canisius Coll., 1937, L.H.D., 1976; B.L.S., U. Buffalo, 1941. Dir. pub. relations Grosvenor Library, Buffalo, 1941-44, Buffalo Pub. Library and Grosvenor Library, 1945-46; adminstrv. asst. Grosvenor Library, 1946-47, dir., 1952-53; first. dep. dir. Erie County Pub. Library, 1948-52; dir. Rochester (N.Y.) Pub. Library and Monroe County Library System, 1954-78; mem. Gov. Dewey's Com. on Library Aid, 1949, reference and research resources com. Commr. Edn., 1960-62; vice chmn. commr. of Edn. Com. on Pub. Library Service, 1956-58; chmn., commr. Edn.'s Com. Library Devel., 1967-70; mem. Gov.'s Com. on Libraries, 1965-66. Trustee St. John Fisher Coll., 1960—; bd. dirs. John F. Wegman Found., 1959—, pres., 1972-74; pres. Rochester Area Ednl. Television Assn., 1961-67, now trustee; trustee Rochester Regional Research Library Council; trustee Reynolds Library. Recipient Rochester Civic Medal award Rochester Mus. and Sci. Center, 1977. Fellow Rochester Mus. Arts and Scis.; mem. Am., N.Y. (pres. 1947) library assns. Club: Philosophers. Home and Office: 1077 East Ave Rochester NY 14607

HACKER, RAY KENNETH, librarian; b. Quakertown, Pa., Aug. 7, 1930; s. Albert Edward and Pearl Rosenberger (Keiser) H.; B.S., Kutztown State Coll., 1952; M.A. in L.S., U. Mich., 1956; postgrad. Columbia U., 1964, U. Del., 1972-74; m. Agnes Neustadter Rosenfeld, Aug. 31, 1958; children—Cheryl, Ray Scott, Douglas, Susan. Reference librarian West Chester (Pa.) State Coll., 1957-62; library dir. Mennonite Bibl. Sem., Elkhart, Ind., 1962-65; readers services librarian Rider Coll., Trenton, N.J., 1965-66; head reference dept. Millersville (Pa.) State Coll., 1966—. Vice pres. Community Historians of Lancaster County, 1972—; sec.-treas. Eastern Pa. Mennonite Hist. Library, Lansdale, Pa., 1968—; bd. dirs. Germantown Mennonite Ch. Corp., Phila., 1968—. Lilly Found. grantee, 1964. Mem. Lancaster County Library Assn. (treas. 1969-78), Area Coll. Libraries Central Pa. (chmn. ref. com. 1971-75), Pa. German Soc., Mennonite Historians Eastern Pa. (pres. 1974—), Landis Valley Mus. Assos., Pa. Library Assn. Republican. Mennonite. Author: History of the Bethel Mennonite Church, 1972; editor: Early Blacksmiths of Lancaster County (E.Z. Longenecker), 1972; Rural Lancaster County Technology of the 1850's (M.W. Shank), 1973. Home: 5323 Lake Dr East Petersburg PA 17520 Office: Gannser Library Millersville State Coll Millersville PA 17551

HACKETT, FREDERICK KEPPEL, lawyer; b. Yonkers, N.Y., Dec. 30, 1914; s. Frank Sutliff and Frances (Allen) H.; B.A., Dartmouth Coll., 1936; J.D., Columbia U., 1942; m. Olga Fiquet, Mar. 19, 1937 (div. June 19, 1959); children—Frances Jean (Mrs. William R. Jordan), Raymond A.; m. 2d, Laura Lyman, June 22, 1959. Admitted to N.Y. bar, 1942; asso. firm Simpson, Thacher & Bartlett, N.Y.C., 1942-50; founder Law Offices Frederick K. Hackett, Farmingdale, N.Y., 1950—. Dir. N.Y. Legis. Service Inc., N.Y.C., 1948-58. Mem. adv. com. on revision estates com. N.Y. 10th Jud. Dist., 1966; mem. Farmingdale Planning Bd., 1956-59. Pres., Adirondack Mountain Club Found., 1976—; trustee Suffolk County chpt. Nat. Multiple Sclerosis Soc., 1966-75. Served with 13th Armored Div., AUS, 1943-45; ETO. Mem. Suffolk County Bar Assn., N.Y. County Lawyers Assn. Clubs: Rotary; Adirondack Mountain (pres. 1972-74) (Glen Falls, N.Y.). Home: 19 Hawkins Rd Stony Brook NY 11790 Office: 375 Fulton St Box 203 Farmingdale NY 11735

HACKETT, LYNWOOD RAYMOND, SR., railroad condr., labor ofcl.; b. Waterbury, Conn., Apr. 11, 1920; s. Albert E. and Bertha Veronica (Georges) H.; ed. pub. schs.; m. Marie D. Giamarino, Nov. 29, 1944; children—Diana Louise, Lynwood Raymond, Theodore Williams. Dairy farmer's helper Wayside Farms, Orange, Conn., 1935-36; nickel plater Deep River, Conn., 1937; tire builder Armstrong Rubber Co., West Haven, Conn., 1938-48; with N.Y.-New Haven & Hartford R.R., 1951-76; part-time teller Manhattan Savs. Bank, 1968—; passenger condr. Amtrak, New Haven, 1976—; active Transp. Union AFL-CIO, 1951—, treas. Local 328, 1971—. Served with U.S. Army, 1942-43. Democrat. Roman Catholic. Clubs: K.C., Anchor. Home: 281 Richmond Ave West Haven CT 06516 Office: PO Box 111 New Haven CT 06516

HADDAD, HESKEL MARSHALL, physician; b. Baghdad, Iraq, Sept. 26, 1928; s. Moshe M. and Masuda (Cohen) H.; student (Royal) Baghdad Coll. Medicine, 1945-50; M.D., Hebrew U., Jerusalem, 1953; m. Doris I. Fatzer, July 4, 1963; children—Ava Masuda, Andreas Moshe, Albert Michael. Came to U.S., 1953, naturalized, 1962. Intern, Donolo Hosp., Jaffo-Tel Aviv, Israel, 1950-51; rotating intern Hadassah U. Hosp., Jerusalem, 1951-53; pediatric resident Children's Med. Center, Boston, 1953-56; fellow pediatric endocrinology Johns Hospkins Hosp., Balt., 1956-58; fellow clin. endocrine br. Nat. Inst. Arthritis and Metabolic Diseases, NIH, Bethesda, Md., 1958-59, pediatrician sect. clin. endocrinology, 1959-60; asst. prof. pediatrics sch. medicine Howard U., Washington, 1959-60; resident, asst. dept. ophthalmology sch. medicine Washington U., St. Louis, 1960-64 (leave of absence 1962-63); fellow pediatric ophthalmology Inst. Visual Sci., San Francisco, 1962; research fellow Hospital des Quinze-Vingts, Laboratoire de Physiologie de Vision, Ecole des Hautes Etudes, Paris, France, 1962-63; ophthalmologist Hospital Beni Messours, Algiers, Algeria, 1964; asst. attending ophthalmic surgeon, also asst. prof. ophthalmology Mt. Sinai Hosp. and Sch. Medicine, N.Y.C., 1964-67; dir. dept. ophthalmology Beth Israel Med. Center, N.Y.C., also asso. prof. ophthalmology Mt. Sinai Sch. Medicine, 1967-71; clin. prof.

ophthalmology N.Y. Med. Coll., 1971—. Pres. Am. Com. for Rescue and Resettlement of Iraqi Jews. Diplomate Am. Bd. Pediatrics, Am. Bd. Ophthalmology. Fellow A.C.S., Am. Inst. Chemists; mem. Am. Endocrine Soc., Am. Fedn. Clin. Research, Assn. Research Opthalmology and Vision, A.M.A., New York County Med. Soc., AAAS, Am. Acad. Ophthalmology, N.Y. Acad. Medicine, N.Y. Acad. Scis., N.Y. Soc. Clin. Ophthalmology, Soc. Eye Surgeons, Societe Francaise d Ophthalmologie. Author: Endocrine Exophthalmos, 1973; Metabolic Eye Diseases, 1974. Editor-in-chief Metabolic Ophthalmology, 1976. Contbr. numerous articles and revs. to profl. jours. Office: 1200 Fifth Ave New York City NY 10029

HADDAD, JAMIL RAOUF, physician; b. Mosul, Iraq, Aug. 18, 1923; s. Raouf Sulaiman and Fadhila (Shaya) H.; M.B., Ch.B., Iraqui Royal Coll. Medicine, Baghdad, Iraq, 1946; m. Mary Lou Scorsone, Aug. 1, 1959; children—Ralph J., John L., James M. Came to U.S., 1952, naturalized, 1965. Med. officer Khanaqin (Iraq) Hosp., 1946-52; asst. resident pathology Crawford W. Long Meml. Hosp., Atlanta, 1953-54; resident Bellevue Hosp., N.Y.C., 1954-56; practice medicine specializing in pathology, N.Y.C., 1963—; chmn. dept. anatomic and clin. pathology St. Clare's Hosp. and Health Center, N.Y.C., 1971—; asso. Sloan-Kettering Inst. for Cancer Research, N.Y.C., 1960-66; asst. prof. pathology N.Y. U. Coll. Medicine, 1959-65, asst. clin. prof. pathology, 1965-67, asso. clin. prof. pathology, 1967-70, clin. prof. pathology, 1970—; asst. prof. exptl. cell biology Mt. Sinai Grad. Sch. Biol. Scis., N.Y.C., 1966-70. Mem. Coll. Am. Pathologists, Am. Soc. Clin. Pathologists, AMA, N.Y. Pathol. Soc., N.Y. State, New York County med. socs. Home: 420 E 23d St New York City NY 10010 Office: 415 W 51st St New York City NY 10019

HADDAD, RAMOND A., computer and communications engr.; b. Worcester, Mass., Sept. 20, 1926; s. Abraham Isa and Nabeha Haddad; B.S., U. Mass., 1950; M.S., Clark U., Worcester, 1952; m. Elvira Pauls, June 5, 1950; children—Michael R., Barbara Marcella. Teaching fellow Clark U., 1950-52; engr., mgr. Radio Corp. Am., 1952-64; with IBM, Corp., 1964—, mgr. info. systems, advanced tech. and lab. automation, sr. engr. scientist, White Plains, N.Y. Counselor, San Fernando (Calif.) council Boy Scouts Am., 1969; area chmn. U. Mass. Alumni, 1964. Served with AUS, 1944-46. Mem. IEEE, Am. Inst. Physics, Soc. Info. Displays. Author, patentee in field. Home: Terwilliger Rd Ext Hyde Park NY 12538 Office: 1000 Westchester Ave White Plains NY 10604

HADIDIAN, DIKRAN YENOVK, librarian; b. Aintab, Turkey, June 9, 1920; s. Yenovk Haroutune and Helen (Koundakjian) H.; came to U.S., 1946, naturalized, 1956; B.A., Am. U. Beirut, 1944; B.D., Hartford Theol. Sem., 1948; M.A., Hartford Sch. Religious Edn., 1949; S.T.M., Hartford Sem. Found., 1950; M.S. in L.S., Columbia, 1960; m. Jean Root Wackerbarth, June 9, 1948; children—Eric Dikran, Andrew Dikran. Instr. Oak Grove Sch., Vassalboro, Maine, 1950-52, Sweet Briar Coll., 1952-55; librarian Hartford Sem. Found., 1957-66, Pitts. Theol. Sem., 1966—, also vis. faculty U. Pitts., 1969—. Mem. corp. bd. United Ch. World Ministries, 1971-77. Dir. Pitts. Chamber Music Soc. Mem. Studiorum Novi Testamenti, Soc. Bibl. Lit., AAUP, Am. Theol. Library Assn. Chmn. editorial bd. of Perpsective, 1967-72; editor series Bibliographia Tripotamopolitana, 1969—, Pittsburgh Theological Monograph Series, 1974—. Contbr. articles to profl. jours. Home: 4137 Timberlane Dr Allison Park PA 15101 Office: 616 N Highland Ave Pittsburgh PA 15206

HADL, HELEN, personnel co. exec.; b. N.Y.C.; d. Henry and Josephine Paula (Mohr) Litauer; B.A., Hunter Coll.; postgrad. N.Y. U.; m. William Hadl; 1 son, Robert Donald. Asst. to v.p. World Broadcasting System, N.Y.C.; tchr. Pub. Sch. 11, Pub. Sch. 125, N.Y.C.; now pres., personnel recruiter Hadle Agency, N.Y.C. Mem. Assn. Personnel Agencies N.Y., Nat. Employment Agencies, Hunter Coll. Alumnae. Office: Hadle Agency 501 Madison Ave New York City NY 10022

HADLEY, JAMES EDWARD, physician; b. Oil City, Pa., June 1, 1909; s. John L. and Gertrude (French) H.; A.B., Washington and Jefferson Coll., 1932; M.D., Hahnemann Med. Coll., 1936; m. Genevieve A. Rowley, June 3, 1939 (dec. Sept. 14, 1973); 1 son, John Bart; m. 2d, Marian A. Shreffler, Apr. 1, 1978; stepchildren—James L., Charles F., Stephen M., Robin M., Jennifer M. Intern, Shadyside Hosp., Pitts., 1937; gen. practice medicine, Oil City, 1938—; pres. med. staff Oil City Hosp., 1957, now mem. obstetrics staff. CD med. dir. Venango County; med. dir. Oil City chpt. ARC, 1949—; med. adviser Oil City Selective Service Bd., 1942-73. Fellow Am. Acad. Family Physicians (charter); mem. AMA, Pa. Med. Soc. (state com. medicine and religion 1967-69), Pa. Homeopathic Soc., Am. Inst. Homeopathy, SAR (chpt. pres. 1962, 75—), Am. Acad. Gen. Practice, Pa. Acad. Family Physicians (charter, 1st pres. 1963-64, pres. Venango chpt. 1972—), Phi Sigma, Phi Kappa Sigma. Republican. Episcopalian. Club: Elk. Home: 8 Penn Way Rayland Park Oil City PA 16301 Office: IOOF Bldg Oil City PA 16301

HADUCH, JUDITH ELLEN CONNELL, chemist; b. Jersey City, Jan. 6, 1942; d. Frank George and Ann (Garlichs) Nebel; A.B. summa cum laude, Jersey City State Coll., 1963; postgrad. (fellow 1963), Harvard U., 1963-64; M.A., Montclair Coll., 1969; m. John Connell, Apr. 6, 1963 (dec.); m. 2d. Paul Haduch, Nov. 26, 1977. Tchr. elementary sch., Ft. Wood, Mo., 1963-65; tchr. biology and chemistry, Bogota (N.J.) High Sch., 1965-67, Pompton Lakes, N.J., 1967-74; tchr. chemistry, chmn. sci. dept. Vernon (N.J.) Twp. High Sch., 1974—. Sec., Lakecrest Health Care Center; pres. Lakecrest Health Center Aux.; elder Pompton Reformed Ch. Mem. NEA, N.J. Edn. Assn., N.J. Sci. Suprs. Assn., Am. Chem. Soc., Nat. Sci. Tchrs. Assn., Cousteau Soc., Common Cause, W.Milford Masonic Aux. (bldg. fund). Author: Marine Organisms in Newark Bay, 1962; Bryozoans with Commensals and Parasites, Lake Juliet, 1968; Underwater Photography, 1975-78. Home: 5 Pilot Ave West Milford NJ 07480

HADY, EDMUND CARL, assn. exec.; b. Ashley, Pa., Mar. 3, 1923; s. Joseph and Henrietta (Kriazeki) H.; A.A. in Mechanics, Newark Coll. of Engring., N.J., 1956. Supr. Fed. Radio and Telephone Corp., Clifton, N.J., 1951-56, Elco Corp., Willow Grove, Pa., 1965-67, Am. Electronic Lab., Colmar, Pa., 1967-68; field expeditor Stone and Webster Engring. Corp., Boston, 1973—; free lance writer, 1951—. Counselor Wyoming Valley council Boy Scouts Am., 1958—; instr. first aid ARC, Paterson, N.J., 1950, Northeastern chpt., Phila., 1965, Wyoming Valley, 1976. Mem. Am. Dart Assn. (founder 1969, exec. sec., treas. 1969—), St. Conrad's Young Men's Soc. Author: American Dart Game, 1969, American and English Dart Game, 1973, Dart Game Ency., 1976. Home: 128 N Main St Ashley PA 18706 Office: 128 N Main St Ashley PA 18706

HAEFELI, ROBERT JAMES, civil engr.; b. Paterson, N.J., Sept. 7, 1926; s. Rudolph Charles and Anna Josaphine (Anderson) H.; B.C.E., U. Mich., 1948; postgrad. U. Colo., 1948-52, Va. Poly. Inst., 1945, Rutgers U., 1971—; m. Joan Hannah Mae Cochrane, Jan. 15, 1950; children—James Robert, Scott Lewis. Civil engr. U.S. Bur. Reclamation, Denver, 1948-52, Beirut, 1952-57; hydraulic engr. Ebasco Services Inc., N.Y.C., 1957-59; v.p. Hydrotechnic Corp., N.Y.C., 1960-66; asso. Hazen & Sawyer Engrs., N.Y.C., 1966-69; propr. Robert J. Haefeli, profl. engrs., Edison, N.J., 1969-72, 76-78; pres., dir. Frank & Haefeli Assos., P.A., Highland Park, N.J., 1972-77, Haefeli Engring., P.A., Highland Park, 1978—. Mem. Edison Twp. Citizens Adv. Com., 1965-69; mem. N.J. Clean Air Council, 1968—, vice chmn., 1976—; chmn. Hammond House com. YWCA, New Brunswick, N.J., 1975-77; elder Presbyterian Ch., New Brunswick, N.J. Served with inf., U.S. Army, 1944-46; with C.E., Res., 1948-62. Registered profl. engr., N.J., N.Y., Mass., Pa., Wis. Engrs. Fellow ASCE; mem. Am. Water Works Assn., Water Pollution Control Fedn., Am. Geophys. Union, AAAS, Inter-Am. Assn. San. Engrs., Air Pollution Control Assn., U.S. Com. on Irrigation Drainage and Flood Control., Am. Water Resources Assn. (pres. N.J. sect. 1972-73), Am. Acad. Environ. Engrs. (diplomate), U.S., Raritan Valley chambers of commerce, Nat. (del. bd. govs. profl. engrs. in pvt. practice div. 1974-77), N.J., Raritan Valley (pres. 1970-71) socs. profl. engrs., N.J. Water Pollution Control Assn. (pres. central N.J. sect. 1973-75), North Jersey Water Conf., Cons. Engrs. Council N.J. (mem. exec. com. 1973-77). Presbyterian. Club: Masons. Home: 407 N 8th Ave Edison NJ 08817 Office: 707 Raritan Ave Highland Park NJ 08904

HAEFNER, RICHARD CHARLES, geologist; b. Lancaster, Pa., Dec. 13, 1943; s. George P. and Ere J. (Seaber) H.; A.B., Franklin and Marshall Coll., 1965; M.S., Pa. State U., 1969, Ph.D., 1972. Asst. prof. dept. geol. scis. State U. N.Y. at New Paltz, 1973—; asst. prof. geology Coll. Charleston (S.C.), 1975; cons. to ednl. orgns., research orgns., mining cos.; lectr. coll. and hobby groups. Grantee Sigma Xi, 1967, 68; Penrose Bequest research grantee Geol. Soc. Am., 1968. Fellow Gemmological Assn. Gt. Britain; mem. Geol. Soc. Am., Mineral. Soc. Am., Pa. Acad. Sci., AAAS, Mineral. Soc. Pa., Friends of Mineralogy, Mineral Soc. Can. Research and publs. on petrology and volcanology rhyolite tuffs and lava flows in Death Valley, Calif., crystal habit of minerals, descriptive mineralogy. Home: 217 Nevin St Lancaster PA 17603 Office: Dept Geol Scis State U NY New Paltz NY 12561

HAEHNLE, ROBERT JAMES, civil engr.; b. Bethlehem, Pa., Jan. 30, 1943; s. Robert James and Lorraine Rue (Heffelfinger) H.; B.S., Lehigh U., 1964; M.S., U. Miami, 1970; m. Diane Elsie Wagner, Nov. 1, 1967; children—Jonathan Clinton, Rebecca Mae. Oceanographer, U.S. Naval Oceanographic Office, Washington, 1964-72; civil engr. Chesapeake Div., Naval Facilities Engring. Command, Washington, 1972-75; civil engr. Hdqrs Command, U.S. Air Force, Washington, 1975-76, 1185th Civil Engring. Group, Andrews AFB, Washington, 1976-78, Nuernberg Resident Engr. Office, U.S. Army Engr. Div. Europe, 1978—. Treas. Riverbend Estates Homeowners Assn., Oxon Hill, Md., 1977-78. Mem. ASCE, Nat., D.C. socs. profl. engrs., U.S. Naval Inst., Inst. Nav., Marine Tech. Soc. Office: Nuernburg Resident Engr Office US Army Engr Div Europe APO NY 09696

HAENLEIN, GEORGE FRIEDRICH WILHELM, educator; b. Mannheim, Germany, Oct. 27, 1927; s. Albrecht P. and Elizabeth (von Kameke) H.; Dipl. Eng. Agr., U. Hohenheim, 1950, Dr.Sci. Agr., 1953; M.S., U. Del., 1960; Ph.D., U. Wis., 1972; m. Elizabeth R. Zeitler, Feb. 20, 1954; children—Theodore, Elizabeth, Alice, Walter, Carl. Came to U.S., 1953, naturalized, 1957. Tchr., research asst. animal nutrition U. Hohenheim, 1948-53; asst. mgr., herdsman Zeitler Dairy Farms, Inc., Newark, Del., 1953-57; research asso. U. Del., Newark, 1957-64, supr. dairy herds, 1957—, asst. prof. animal sci. and agrl. biochemistry, 1964-69, asso. prof., 1969-74, prof., 1974—, acting chmn. dept. animal sci. and agrl. biochemistry, 1977-78, state dairy extension specialist, 1978—, residence dir. U. Del. Study Abroad, Vienna, Austria, 1977; abstractor fgn. jours. Biol. Abstracts, Phila., 1958—; dairy judge Md. Fair Bd., 1958—; chmn. com. on nutrition goats NRC, 1975— NE regional steering com. on dairy research U.S. Dept. Agr., 1976—; AID rep., Panama, 1978. Bd. dirs. New Castle County Civic League, 1973; chmn. citizen participation adv. council Del. Hwy. Dept., 1974. U.S. State Dept. exchange scholar, 1951, NSF fellow, 1965. Mem. A.A.A.S., N.Y. Acad. Scis., Am. Soc. Animal Sci., Am. Dairy Sci. Assn., German Soc. Animal Breeding, Holstein-Friesian Assn. Am., N.Y. Mus. Natural History, Nat. Mastitis Council, Nat. Geog. Soc., Am. Grasslands Council, Eastern (dir. 1964—), Del. (sec. 1954-57), Guernsey breeders assns., N.Y. Zool. Soc., Council Agrl. Sci. and Tech., Dairy Council (dir. 1978—), Am. Guernsey Cattle Club (life), Smithsonian Instn. Assos., Internat. Platform Assn., Suburban Newark Civic League (sec. 1972). Lutheran (ch. council 1974, v.p.). Contbr. articles to profl. jours. Home: 2071 S College Ave Newark DE 19702

HAENSCHEN, ROBERT WILLIAM, data processing co. exec.; b. Jersey City, Oct. 5, 1942; s. Robert William and Mildred Catherine (Greenhalgh) H.; B.S. in Elec. Engring., Newark Coll. Engring., 1963; m. Lois Eileen Davey, Mar. 8, 1974; 1 son, Robert John. Elec. engr. Broadway Maintenance Corp., L.I. City, N.Y., 1963-64, sr. data processing programmer, 1964-69; mgr. data processing Am. Bakers Coop., Teaneck, N.J., 1969-70; v.p. Execu-Data, Inc., Northvale, N.J., 1970-72; owner, operator Robert Haenschen Assos., Montvale, N.J., 1973-74; dir. mktg., data processing mgr. Cadcnce Industries Inc., Hackensack, N.J., 1974-76, Ehrhart-Babic Data Services Inc., Ft. Lee, N.J., 1976—. Republican. Roman Catholic. Club: Masons (Bergenfield, N.J.). Home: 9 Durand Pl Rochelle Park NJ 07662 Office: 120 Sylvan Ave Englewood Cliffs NJ 07632

HAESELER, WILLIAM, III, finance co. exec.; b. North Tonawanda, N.Y., Aug. 15, 1930; s. William and Mabel (Meyers) H.; B.A., Valparaiso U., 1952; M.S., Boston U., 1954; m. Gloria Ruth Barth, July 15, 1960; children—Susan Beth, Mark William, Karen Ruth, Lisa Ann. Wth Certified Finance Co., Inc., North Tonawanda, 1948—, v.p., 1957-67, treas., 1960-67, pres., 1967—, also dir.; pres. Certified Travel Tours, North Tonawanda, 1970—, also dir.; dir. Charge Account Service, Inc., North Tonawanda; owner William Haeseler III Assos., Buffalo, 1954—. Faculty, State U. N.Y. at Buffalo, 1955-66, 70—. Travel columnist Buffalo Courier Express, 1972—. Corporate mem. DeGraff Meml. Hosp., North Tonawanda, 1967—; mem. adv. bd. Niagara County Community Colls. Served with AUS, 1956-57. Mem. C. of C., N.Y. State Consumer Finance Assn. (mem. exec. com. 1965—, dir. 1965—), Luth. Laymens League, Delta Sigma Pi, Tau Mu Epsilon, Lambda Chi Alpha. Republican. Lutheran. Rotarian (past pres.). Home: 39 Bentham Pkwy Snyder NY 14226 Office: 1040 Payne Ave North Tonawanda NY 14120

HAFF, DENNIS RAYMOND, forest products co. exec.; b. Orange, N.J., Sept. 19, 1944; s. Stewart Robert and Gloria Heinisch (Smith) H.; B.S. in Chemistry, New Eng. Coll., 1969; postgrad. Newark Coll. Engring., 1971-72; m. May 13, 1972. Research chemist Eastern research div. ITT Rayonier Inc., 1968-75, tech. service rep., N.Y.C., 1975—. Vice pres. Hopatcong Gardens Community Club, 1974-76, treas., 1976-77. Mem. Am. Chem. Soc., TAPPI, Inst. Food Techs. Republican. Office: 605 Third Ave New York NY 10016

HAGAN, EILEEN, lighting co. exec.; b. Paterson, N.J., July 27, 1930; s. Thomas A. and Ruth J. (Conlon) H.; 1 son, Mark Fusco. Asst. to sales mgr. C. N. Burman Co., Paterson, 1955-61, asst. to pres., 1961-67, design coordinator, 1967-73, v.p. mktg. and design, dir., 1973—; dir. Heldak Lighting Products, Paterson Shade, Univ. Lamp, Certified Shade Co. Bd. dirs. YWCA, Paterson, 1949-53. Mem. Decorative and Fine Arts Soc. Bergen County, Nat. Assn. Variety Stores, Assn. Gen. Mdse. Chains, Paterson C. of C. Office: 781 River St Paterson NJ 07524

HAGAN, JAMES CARROLL, aerospace engr.; b. Balt., Dec. 9, 1937; s. Francis Roger and Cecelia Ann (Zeleznicki) H.; B.S., U. Md., 1960, M.S., 1968; m. Patricia Ann Rife, Apr. 16, 1966; children—Deborah Ann, Daniel Allen. Asso. engr. Applied Physics Lab., Johns Hopkins U., Laurel, Md., 1960-70, sr. engr., 1970-71, project engr., aerospace nuclear safety program, 1971—, prin. staff, 1974—; mem. Naval Aeroballistics Adv. Commn., 1974—, chmn. gas dynamics panel, 1977; mem. Interagy. Nuclear Safety Rev. Panel, 1971—. Mem. Howard County Bi-Partisan Councilman Dist. Commn., 1975-76; active Republican party campaigns. Recipient award of merit Soc. Tech. Communication, Washington, 1972. Mem. Am. Inst. Aeros. and Astronautics. Roman Catholic. Co-author handboks in field. Home: 9025 Dunloggin Rd Ellicott City MD 21043 Office: Johns Hopkins Applied Physics Lab Johns Hopkins Rd Laurel MD 20810

HAGEMAN, RICHARD PHILIP, JR., counselor; b. Derby, Conn., Dec. 21, 1941; s. Richard Philip and Jane Elizabeth (Serafinowicz) H.; B.S., Central Conn. State Coll., 1964; M.S., U. Bridgeport, 1968, 6th yr. profl. diploma, 1972; m. Mary Ethel Bowe, Apr. 15, 1967; children—Margaret Anne, Sheila Marie. House leader Camp Hillcroft, Billings, N.Y., summers 1964, 65; elementary sch. tchr. Stony Brook Sch., Stratford Bd. Edn., 1964-69, elementary sch. guidance counselor bd., 1969—; mem. adv. bd. counselor edn. Fairfield U., 1970-74, lectr. in edn., 1971—. Mem. Am., Conn. personnel and guidance assns., Nat. (life), Conn., Stratford (pres. 1978) edn. assn., Assn. Specialists in Group Work (charter), Phi Delta Kappa. Democrat. Contbr. revs., photographs to Sch. Counselor, 1972—. Home: 26 Oriole Ln Trumbull CT 06611 Office: Birdseye/Garden/Second Hill Ln Schs Stratford CT 06497

HAGER, NATHANIEL ELLMAKER, JR., physicist; b. Lancaster, Penn., June 3, 1922; s. Nathaniel Ellmaker and Ruth (Mayer) H.; B.S., Franklin and Marshall Coll., 1943; M.S., Lehigh U., 1948; Ph.D., 1953; m. Nancy Cleaver, June 26, 1948; children—Nathaniel E., Sarah Wilson. Instr. Lehigh U., Bethlehem, Pa., 1950-51; sect. head physics dept. Vitro Lab., West Orange, N.J., 1952-54; research physicist Armstrong Cork Co., Lancaster, Pa., 1954-68, research asso., 1968-76, sr. research asso., 1976—; tchr. creativity sessions for gifted Lancaster County Pub. Schs., 1967—. Mem. sch. bd. Manheim Twp., Lancaster County (Pa.), Lancaster and Lebanon Counties; dir. radiol. div. Lancaster County Civil Def., 1956—; bd. dirs. Hearing Conservation Center of Lancaster County 1957—. Served with USNR 1943-46. Mem. Internat. Inst. Refrigeration, Optical Soc. Am., Instrument Soc. Am. (sr.), AAAS, N.Y. Acad. Sci., Internat. Platform Assn., Cliosophic Soc. Lancaster. Clubs: Sphinx, Fortnightly, Hamilton. Contbr. articles in field to profl. jours.; patentee in field. Home: 1410 Clayton Rd Lancaster PA 17603

HAGER, WALTER ELLSWORTH, educator; b. Bellwood, Nebr., Mar. 29, 1896; s. Birt Ellsworth and Lona Lenora (Barnum) H.; B.Sc., U. Nebr., 1916; A.M., Columbia, 1927, Ph.D., 1931; m. Gertrude Squires, Aug. 27, 1918; children—Richard Ellsworth, Ruth (Mrs. Marion B. Petcher). Tchr. high sch., Pender, Nebr., 1916-17; instr. physics Sch. Agr., U. Nebr., 1917-18; supt. schs., Adams, Nebr., 1919-24, Cozad, Nebr., 1924-28; asst. sec. Tchrs. Coll., Columbia, 1928-36, sec., 1936-41, asso. dir. student personnel, 1938-41, asst. prof. edn., 1939-41; pres. Wilson Tchrs. Coll., Washington, 1941-55, D.C. Tchrs. Coll., 1955-58; vis. lectr. pedagogical insts., Esslingen and Heidelberg, Germany, 1958-59; vis. lectr. edn. U. Cin., 1959-61; vis. lectr., curriculum cons. Springfield (Mass.) Coll., 1961-62; exec. sec. Am. Assn. State Colls. and Univs., Washington, 1962-65, archivist and historian, 1971—. Pres. Eastern States Assn. Profl. Schs. Tchrs., 1945-46; pres. Am. Assn. Colls. Tchr. Edn., 1948-49; sec. Am. Council Edn., 1953-56; cons. workshop tchr. edn. for Wuerttemberg-Baden, Germany, 1949; mem. Nat. Commn. Accrediting, 1951-58; Am. delegation 4th Internat. Conf. Health Edn., Duesseldorf, Germany, 1959, Internat. Univs. Conf., Nice, France, 1950, world assembly Internat. Council Edn. for Teaching, Nairobi, Kenya, 1973; mem. adv. com. pub. edn. Nat. Found. Infantile Paralysis, 1948-53. Bd. dirs. Columbia Heights (D.C.) Boys Club, 1955-58, 62-73, chmn., 1956-58; chmn. Am. Found. for San Myung Women's Tchrs. Coll., Korea, 1973-78. Served as 2d lt., inf. U.S. Army, 1918-19. Recipient citation D.C. Fedn. Civic Assns., 1955, A.A.H.P.E.R., 1958. Mem. N.E.A., John Dewey Soc., Phi Beta Kappa, Kappa Delta Pi, Phi Delta Kappa; hon. mem. Am. Assn. State Colls. and Univs. (Honor award 1975). Democrat. Unitarian. Editorial bd. Ednl. Forum, 1954-67. Home. 4625 S Chelsea Ln Bethesda MD 20014 Office: Suite 700 1 Dupont Circle Washington DC 20036

HAGERTY, BETTY LEE, assn. exec.; b. Paterson, N.J., Oct. 12; John J. and Bess B. (Taylor) Benkendorf; B.S., Rutgers U., 1959; children—Clark Gregory, Kristen Dawn. Adminstr. youth services 4H Program, Rutgers U. Coop. Extension Service, Middlesex County, 1959-62; dir. youth services YWCA Central Jersey, New Brunswick, 1969-75, dir. resource devel., 1976-77; exec. dir. N.J. Soc. to Prevent Blindness, New Brunswick, 1978—; cons. Resource Devel. and Program Devel., N.E. Region, 1973—. Office: 303 George St New Brunswick NJ 08901

HAGEY, WALTER REX, banker; b. Hatfield, Pa., July 24, 1909; s. Justus T. and Martha (Mabel) H.; student U. Pa., 1931-36; LL.B., La Salle Extension U., 1938; S.T.B., Temple U., 1943; grad. Grad. Sch. Banking Rutgers U., 1951; LL.D., Muhlenberg Coll., 1963; m. Dorothy E. Rosenberger, October 17, 1931; 1 son, Donald C. With Fidelity Bank, Phila., 1929—, asst. sec., 1948—, asst. v.p., 1957-66, v.p., 1966-74. Supply pastor Lutheran Ch. Ministerium Pa., 1952-63, Eastern Pa. Synod, 1963-68; pres., dir. Phila. Luth. Social Union; treas. Evang. Lutheran Ministerium of Pa. and Adjacent States of United Luth. Ch. in Am., 1950-63; mem. bd., mem. exec. com. Luth. Council in U.S., 1962-74; treas., exec. com. Lutheran Laymen's Movement United Luth. Ch. Am., 1959-63; treas. Eastern Pa. Synod Luth. Ch. Am., 1963-68; treas. Synod S.E. Pa., Luth. Ch. Am., 1969—, acting treas. Luth. Synod, N.E. Pa., 1969-71; vice chmn. office adminstrn. and fin. Luth. Ch. Am., 1972—, v.p. bd. am. missions, 1972—; councillor Nat. Luth. Council Bd. dirs., mem. adv. bd. Muhlenberg Med. Center; treas. Bethesda House. Mem. Am. Inst. Banking, Phila. Estate Planning Council, Pa. Council Chs. (dir. 1954-70), Pa. Bible Soc. (dir., sec., treas. 1971—), Men of Mt. Airy Sem. Phila. (pres. 1976—), Hist. Soc. Lutheran Ministerium Pa., Pa. Soc. Clubs: Rotary; Split Rock, Elm (sec. 1951-65), Midday; Anglers. Home: 510 E Lawn Ave Lansdale PA 19446 Office: 6996 Germantown Ave Philadelphia PA 19119

HAGGERTY, JAMES JOSEPH, writer; b. Orange, N.J., Feb. 1, 1920; s. James Joseph and Anna (Morahan) H.; student pub. schs.; m. Marian Smith Mitten, Nov. 20, 1962; children—Karin, James Joseph, Brian (by previous marriage). Reporter Orange (N.J.) Daily Courier, 1938-40; mil. editor Am. Aviation Publs., 1948-53; aviation editor Collier's, 1953-56; free lance writer on sci. and aerospace subjects, 1956—; editor Aerospace Year Book, 1957-70; aerospace cons. Served with USAAF, 1942-48. Decorated D.F.C., Air medal with clusters. Mem. Aviation Space Writers Assn. (past pres.), AAAS, Air Force Assn. Clubs: Bethesda Country; Touchdown (Washington). Author: First of the Spacemen, 1960; Spacecraft, 1961; Flight, 1964; The U.S. Air Force: A Pictorial History in Art, 1965; Man's Conquest of Space, 1965; Food and Nutrition, 1966; Apollo Lunar Landing,

1969; Hail To The Redskins, 1973; Aviation's Mr. Sam, 1973. Address: 502 H St SW Washington DC 20024

HAGOPIAN, LOUIS THOMAS, advt. agy. exec.; b. Pontiac, Mich., June 1, 1925; s. Thomas and Sarah (Uligian) H.; student Northwestern U., 1944; B.A. in Bus. Adminstrn., Mich. State U., 1947; m. Joanne Kelly, Dec. 31, 1955; children—Susan, Thomas, Matthew. With Pontiac Motor Car Co., 1948-53, beginning as service rep., dist. sales mgr.; with Chrysler Corp., 1953-60, sales and promotion exec. Dodge div., 1953-56, dir. advt. and sales promotion Plymouth div., 1956-60; account supr. N. W. Ayer ABH Internat., 1960-62, v.p., 1962-66, Detroit mgr., 1963-66, exec. v.p., gen. mgr., N.Y.C., 1967-73, vice chmn. bd., 1973-76, chmn., chief exec. officer, 1976—, also dir. Mem. communications com. N.Y. Urban Coalition; exec. com. Hwy. Users Fedn.; vice chmn. Automotive Safety Found.; bd. dirs. N.Y. div. Am. Cancer Soc. Recipient Distinguished Alumnus award Mich. State U., 1978. Served to lt. (j.g.) USNR, World War II. Mem. Am. Assn. Advt. Agys. (dir., chmn. eastern region 1978), Adcraft Club Detroit, Internat. Radio and TV Soc. (bd. govs.), Outdoor Advt. Assn., Kappa Sigma. Clubs: Univ. (N.Y.C.); Wee Burn Country; Pine Valley Golf. Home: 5 Meadowbrook Rd Darien CT 06820 Office: 1345 Ave of Americas New York City NY 10019

HAGOPIAN, VARANT, ophthalmologist; b. Salem, N.H., Oct. 3, 1928; s. Garabed and Ovsanna Hagopian; B.S., U. N.H., 1950; M.D., Tufts U., 1954; m. Ruth E. Maranian, Dec. 20, 1953; children—Gary, Melanie, Nanine, Lisa. Intern, Cambridge (Mass.) City Hosp., 1954-55; resident in ophthalmology Kresge Eye Inst.-Wayne State U., 1957-60; practice medicine specializing in ophthalmology, Cambridge, 1960—; mem. staff Mt. Auburn Hosp., Sancta Maria Hosp., Youville Hosp.; tchr. in field; cons. Mass. Commn. for Blind. Bd. dirs. St. Stephen's Armenian Fed. Credit Union, Watertown, Mass. Served with USAF, 1955-57. Diplomate Am. Bd. Ophthalmology. Fellow A.C.S.; mem. AMA, Mass. Med. Soc., New Eng. Ophthalmol. Soc., Mass. Soc. Eye Physicians and Surgeons. Republican. Mem. Armenian Apostolic Ch. Club: Lions. Home: 3 Bryant Rd Lexington MA 02173 Office: 300 Mount Auburn St Suite 414 Cambridge MA 02138

HAHN, DO WON, pharm. co. exec.; b. Hoochang, Pyungbuck, Korea, Nov. 20, 1931; s. Sung Bum and Wanok (Cho) H.; came to U.S., 1955, naturalized, 1973; B.S., Mich. State U., 1960, M.S., 1963; Ph.D., U. Mo., 1967; m. Myungyun Kim, Aug. 31, 1963; children—Charles, Helen, Anna. Asso. scientist reproductive research div., div. pharmacology Ortho Pharm. Corp., Raritan, N.J., 1968-69, scientist, 1969-71, sr. scientist, 1971-73, group leader, 1973-75, sect. head, 1975—. Recipient Philip B. Hofman Research Scientist award Johnson & Johnson, 1973; Danforth Found. grantee, 1957-60; Ford Found. fellow, 1967-68. Mem. Korean Scientist and Engrs. Assn. N.J. (pres. 1971-72), Soc. Study of Reprodn., Endocrine Soc., Am. Fertility Soc., Am. Physiol. Soc., Am. Soc. Zoologists, Sigma Xi. Presbyterian. Contbr. articles to sci. jours. Patentee in field. Home: Shelton RD 8 Flemington NJ 08822 Office: Route 202 Raritan NJ 08869

HAHN, FRED, educator; b. Stankov, Czechoslovakia, May 28, 1906; s. Emil and Helen (Wilhelm) H.; came to U.S., 1939, naturalized, 1947; D.Law and Polit. Sci., U. Prague, 1929; M.A., Columbia U., 1951; m. Edith H. Friedman, Dec. 25, 1949; children—Susan Ann, Jeanette Emily. Atty., Prague, Czechoslovakia, 1929-39; self-employed, N.Y.C., 1941-62; lectr. Fairleigh Dickinson U., Rutherford, Madison, N.J., 1962-64; asso. prof. Trenton (N.J.) State Coll., 1964-69, prof., 1969—. Guest prof. U. Frankfurt, Germany, 1968-69, summer 1971, 73, 75. Fulbright grantee, 1968-69, summer 1973. Mem. Am. Hist. Assn., Am. Assn. for Advancement Slavic Studies, Czechoslovak Acad. Arts and Scis., History Czechoslovak Jews (dir.). Author: Marxist and Utopian Socialists, 1965; History of Russia, 1968; Stürmer, 1978. Contbr. articles to profl. jours. Home: 780 West End Ave New York City NY 10025 Office: Trenton State Coll Trenton NJ 08625

HAHN, FRED I., clin. psychologist; b. N.Y.C., Apr. 7, 1925; s. Nathan and Margaret H.; B.S.S., Coll. City N.Y., 1948, M.S., 1949; Ph.D., N.Y. U., 1965; m. Marie Kelly, Mar. 4, 1961; children—Hilary Robin, Gregory Adam. Clin. psychologist Ednl. Clinic, Coll. City N.Y., 1950-53; cons. psychologist Colonial Park Child Care Center, N.Y.C., 1953-54; staff psychotherapist Bleuler Psychotherapy Center, Jamaica, N.Y., 1953-60; pvt. practice psychology and group psychotherapy, N.Y.C., 1960—; supervising faculty Ind. Bronx Cons. Center, 1964-68; asso. in psychiatry Columbia Coll. Physicians and Surgeons, N.Y.C., 1970—; vis. lectr. N.Y. Sch. Psychiatry, N.Y.C., 1975-76. Served in Med. Dept., U.S. Army, 1943-46. Certified psychologist, N.Y. Mem. Am., Eastern, N.Y. State psychol. assns, Am., Eastern group psychotherapy assns., Am. Acad. Psychotherapists. Contbr. articles to profl. jours. Office: 1235 Park Ave New York City NY 10028

HAHN, GEORGE ALAN, obstetrician and gynecologist; b. Bklyn., Feb. 2, 1911; s. George Henry and Henrietta (Picaso) H.; A.B. (Graydon Achievement trophy), Dartmouth Coll., 1932; M.D., Yale U., 1936; m. Cynthia C. Hawkins, June 13, 1936 (dec. May 1971); children—Cynthianna, Anne Hahn Powell, Elizabeth Hahn Winslow, Doretta, George Alan; m. 2d, Anna L. Pierno, Dec. 9, 1972. Jr. intern in surgery New Haven Hosp., 1935; intern Hosp. for Women, Balt., 1936-37; asst. resident in obstetrics U. Hosp., Balt., 1937-38; fellow in malignant diseases Am. Oncologic Hosp., Phila., 1939-41, asst. gynecologist, surgeon, 1942-45, gynecologist, radiotherapist, 1945-53, chief gynecologist, oncologist, 1953—; asst. attending out-patient dept. Grad. Hosp.-U. Pa., 1940-42, asso. physician in obstetrics and gynecology, 1963—; clin. asst. in gynecology Jefferson Hosp., 1941-51, clin. asst. in radiology, 1944—, chief cancer detection clinic, 1945-57, co-dir. gynecology, dir. gynecologic malignancy, 1962—, mem. exec. staff, 1966—, attending obstetrician and gynecologist, 1963—, hon. mem., 1966—; dir. service and chief dept. obstetrics and gynecology Meth. Hosp., Phila., 1958-62, cons. in obstetrics and gynecology, 1962—; chief gynecologic sect. Phila. Gen. Hosp., 1959-60; med. dir. Supplee-Wills-Jones Milk Co., Phila., 1942-45; courtesy staff Bryn Mawr Hosp.; cons. staff Misericordia Hosp., 1968—; cons. in gynecology U.S. VA Hosp., Coatesville, Pa., 1952—; mem. staff Jefferson Med. Coll., Phila., 1941—, clin. prof. obstetrics and gynecology, 1961-63, prof. obstetrics and gynecology, 1963—, dir. pelvic malignancy service, 1963—, co-dir. gynecol. service, 1963—; vis. lectr. in obstetrics and gynecology U. Pa. Grad. Sch. Medicine, 1961—; lectr.-cons. in obstetrics and gynecology U.S. Naval Hosp., Phila., 1962—; chmn. tissue com. Jefferson Med. Coll. and Hosp., 1962—, mem. adv. com. on planning and policy, 1965; chmn. sect. obstetrics and gynecology S.S. Hope, 1966—, chmn. on research, 1966—, dir., 1968—, mem. exec. com., 1968—; co-chmn. Phila. Cancer Control Com., 1959—; chmn. Pa. Cancer Co-ordinating Com., 1956-61; sec. Phila. div. Am. Cancer Soc., 1955-57, pres., 1961, 62; adviser to com. Phila. Com. for Study Pelvic Cancer, 1961-63; pres. Wainwright Tumor Clinic Assn. Pa., 1961-62; mem. med. adv. com. Planned Parenthood Assn. Recipient Gold medal award Am. Cancer Soc., 1958; Distinguished Service award in medicine St. Matthew A.M.E. Ch., Phila., 1962; citation U. Cartagena, 1967; Gold Medal Good Citizenship award S.A.R., 1972. Diplomate Nat. Bd. Med. Examiners, Am. Bd. Obstetrics and Gynecology. Fellow Nassau Obstet. and Gynecol. Soc. (hon.); mem. Pa. (del. 1970), West Phila., Phila. County (dir. 1967—, pres. 1971) med. socs., Am. Soc. Preventive Oncology, Obstet. Soc. Phila. (pres. 1956-57), Phila. Roentgen Ray Soc., Coll. Physicians Phila., Med. Club Phila., Franklin Inst., Pa. Soc. Advancing Med. Research, AMA (Physician's Recognition award 1970), Pan Am. Med. Assn. (pres. sect. obstetrics and gynecology), Am. Radium Soc., Radiologic Soc. N.Am., Am. Soc. Study of Sterility, A.C.S. (gov. 1975—), Am. Coll. Obstetricians and Gynecologists (chmn. dist. com. on malignant disease 1962-65), Am. Assn. Obstetricians and Gynecologists (v.p. 1974), AAAS, N.Y. Acad. Scis., Am. Soc. Cytology, Am. Assn. Cancer Research, Am. Soc. Clin. Oncology, Assn. Med. Colls., Internat. Fertility Soc., Soc. Lymphology, Newcomen N.Am., N.J. Gynecol. Soc. (hon.), Blockley, Douglass obstet. and gynecol. socs., Dartmouth Coll. Alumni Assn. Phila. (pres. 1947-48), Am. Kennel Club, Am. Chesapeake Club, Owner-Handler Assn., Sigma Xi, Alpha Omega Alpha, Sigma Chi, Nu Sigma Nu. Episcopalian. Clubs: Phila. Country (chmn. tennis com. 1966-70), Sandy Run Hunting and Fishing, Physicians Motor, Roxborough Gun (Phila.); Flotsum Jetsum (N.Y.C.). Home: 110 Woodmont Rd Gladwyne PA 19035 Office: 255 S 17th St Philadelphia PA 19103

HAHN, R(OBERT) DOUGLAS, ophthalmic microsurgeon; b. Charleston, S.C., Oct. 30, 1943; s. Irving and Vilma H.; B.S., State U. N.Y., 1964, M.D., Downstate Med. Sch., 1969. Intern, Beth Israel Hosp., N.Y.C., 1969-70; resident Bklyn. Eye and Ear Hosp., 1970-73; practice medicine specializing in ophthalmology, Bklyn., 1973—; pres. Bklyn. Eye Safety Indsl. League; cons. Beekman Downtown Hosp., dir. Lions' Sight Conservation Program; pres. Bklyn. Elec. Soc., 1978. Served as 1st lt. M.C., U.S. Army, 1969-73. Mem. AMA, N.Y. State Med. Soc. Club: Montauk. Developer microcomputer approach to eye surgery, 1977; contbr. papers to newspapers and TV. Home: 430 37th St Brooklyn NY 11232

HAHN, WILLIAM JOSEPH, chem. co. exec.; b. Manasquan, N.J., July 18, 1924; s. Walter Charles and Mary (Laffey) H.; B.S. in Chemistry, Ohio U., 1949; m. Jean Carol Hyers, July 28, 1947; children—Deborah Hahn Nordstrom, William Joseph, Jack M., Timothy. Sales, mktg. regional mgr. Johnson & Johnson Co., New Brunswick, N.J., 1953-60; v.p. Harrison & Crosfield, N.Y.C., 1960-65; pres. Bofors Steels Inc., West Caldwell, N.J., 1972-74, also dir.; pres. Bofors Industries Inc., Linden, N.J., 1974—, also dir.; dir. Bofors Lakeway Chems. Inc. Muskegon, Mich. Served with USN, 1942-45; PTO. Decorated Purple Heart. Fellow Am. Inst. Chemists; mem. Chemists Club N.Y., Sociéte de Chimie Industrielle Inc., Chgo. Drug, Chem. Assn., Salesman Assn. Am. Chem. Industry (dir.), Ohio U. Alumni (pres. N.Y. chpt.). Home: 1127 Manito Rd Manasquan NJ 08736 Office: 23 Progress St Edison NJ 08816

HAIGHT, CHARLES SHERMAN, JR., fed. judge; b. N.Y.C., Sept. 23, 1930; s. Charles Sherman and Margaret (Edwards) H.; B.A., Yale U., 1952, LL.B., 1955; m. Mary Jane Peightal, June 30, 1953; children—Nina E., Susan P. Admitted to N.Y. bar, 1955; trial atty., admiralty and shipping sect. Dept. Justice, Washington, 1955-57; asso. firm Haight, Gardner, Poor & Havens, N.Y.C., 1957-68, partner, 1968-76; judge U.S. Dist. Ct. for So. Dist. N.Y., 1976—. Bd. dirs. Kennedy Child Study Center; exec. trustee Am.-Scandinavian Found., chmn., 1970-76; bd. mgrs. Havens Fund. Mem. Maritime Law Assn. U.S., N.Y. State Bar Assn., Bar Assn. City N.Y., Fed. Bar Council. Episcopalian. Office: US Courthouse Foley Sq New York City NY 10007

HAIL, BARBARA ANDREWS (MRS. EDWARD G. HAIL), mus. ofcl.; b. Phila., Nov. 2, 1930; d. James Wickersham and Elizabeth Alice (Woolridge) Kirk; student (Elisha Benjamin Andrews scholar), Brown U., 1948-50; A.B., Cornell U., 1952, A.M., 1953; postgrad. (Danforth Grad. fellow), Columbia U., 1965-67; m. Peter B. Andrews, Dec. 23, 1950 (dec. 1964); children—Clinton J., Elizabeth D., Cynthia K.; m. 2d, Edward G. Hail, May 29, 1969; stepchildren—Ted, Andrew, Peter, Elinor. Tchr. history high sch., Ithaca, N.Y., 1953-54; edn. coordinator Haffenreffer Mus. Anthropology, Brown U., Bristol, R.I., 1968-72, asst. curator, 1972-77, asso. curator, 1977—. Mem. R.I. Women's Intergroup Com. 1971-72; bd. dirs. Lüthi-Peterson Internat. Camps, 1975-78. Mem. R.I. New Democratic Coalition, 1971-72. Nat. Endowment for Arts fellow, 1976. Mem. Am. Assn. Museums, Phi Beta Kappa. Club: Lake Placid (N.Y.). Home: 220 Rumstick Point Rd Barrington RI 02806 Office: Haffenreffer Museum Mount Hope Grant Bristol RI 02809

HAINES, LARRY EUGENE, real estate broker; b. Woodbine, Md., Apr. 11, 1938; s. Arthur Levi and Evelyn Marie (Bair) B.; student Balt. City Coll., 1966; m. Jane Marie Armfield, Mar. 25, 1960; children—Garry, Kevin, Matthew K., Levi T. Owner, operator dairy farm, Woodbine, 1956-60; mgr., operator Hampstead Brown Swiss Farm, Hampstead, Md., 1960-66; gen. mgr. John D. Meyer Real Estate, Westminster, Md. 1967-72; owner, mgr. Haines Realty, Westminster, 1972—. Sec. Carroll County Republican Club. Recipient Realtor of Year award Carroll County, 1975; certificate of recognition Md. Assn. Realtors, 1975. Mem. Carroll County Bd. Realtors, Md., Nat. assns. Realtors, Carroll County Multiple Listing Bur. (pres. 1976). Clubs: Lions, Elks. Home: 300 W Main St Westminster MD 21157 Office: 147 W Main St Westminster MD 21157

HAINS, GASTON, ret. clergyman; b. Drummondville, Que., Can., Sept. 10, 1921; s. J.H. and Germaine (Gauthier) H.; B.A., U. Montreal, 1941; Lic. P.H. Rome, Italy, 1950; Dr. Sci., Social Politics, Lille, France, 1952. Ordained priest Roman Catholic Ch., 1946; bishop of Amos, Que., 1967-78, ret. Home: Rural Route 2 Harricana Ouest Abitibi PQ J0Y 1M0 Canada

HAINSWORTH, WINSTON CLARKSON, physician; b. Peterboro, Ont., Can., July 29, 1912; s. Alonzo Alfred and Edna (Reed) H.; came to U.S., 1912; B.S., Randolph Macon Coll., 1934; postgrad. William and Mary Coll., 1935-36; M.D., U. Va., 1940; m. Elizabeth Badcock, Apr. 24, 1941; children—Marie Josephine, Walter Kevin, Peter Gregory. Intern, Walter Reed Gen. Hosp., Washington, 1940-41; resident pediatrics Babies Hosp. City N.Y., Columbia Presbyn. Med. Center, 1946-47; resident Yale U., New Haven, 1948-49; practice medicine specializing in pediatrics, Willimantic, Conn., 1962—; chief of staff VA Center, Bath, N.Y., 1972—; clin. asst. prof. pediatrics Johns Hopkins U. Sch. Medicine, 1964-72. Served with U.S. Army, 1940-46. Decorated Silver Star, Bronze Star, Purple Heart. Mem. Am. Acad. Pediatrics, New Eng. Pediatric Soc., Hezekiah Beardsley Pediatric Soc. Home and Office: VA Center Bath NY 14810

HAIRSTON, ALONZO PAUL, lawyer, accountant, real estate broker; b. Columbus, Ohio, Oct. 11, 1919; s. Robert Franklin and Arizona H.; J.D., U. Balt., 1970, Eastern Coll., 1970; m. Helena Hall, July 16, 1963; children—Paul, David, Valeria, Vernita, Dorothy. Prodn. control analyst electronic div. Air Mod Corp., Balt., 1956-61; pub. accountant State of Ohio, 1961-76; pres. Nubia Inc., import-export corp., Balt., 1971—; prodn. analyst electronic div. Bendix Corp., Balt., 1966-69; admitted to Md. bar, 1972; practice in Balt., 1972—; pres. Alpha Investment Club Md. Inc., 1974—. Served with 99th Fighter Group, USAF, 1941-45. Mem. Monumental Bar Assn., Nat., Am., Md., Balt. bar assns., Alpha Phi Alpha, Mason (Shriner). Home: 4014 Loch Raven Blvd Baltimore MD 21218 Office: 222 E Baltimore St Baltimore MD 21202

HAIT, GERSHON, pediatric cardiologist; b. May 10, 1927; s. Nahum and Leah H.; came to U.S., 1952; M.D., U. Lausanne (Switzerland), 1952; m. Doris J. Coburn, Mar. 20, 1957; children—Jonathan, Yael. Intern, Michael Reese Hosp., Chgo., 1952-53; resident Cook County Hosp., Chgo., 1961-62, fellow in pediatric cardiology, 1954-56, 59-60; instr. pediatrics, NIH fellow in pediatric cardiology Albert Einstein Coll. Medicine, Bronx, N.Y., 1962-64, dir. pediatric cardiology, 1966—, asso. prof., 1972—. Mem. Am. Physiology Soc., Soc. for Pediatric Research, Am. Acad. Pediatrics, Am. Fedn. Clin. Research, Am. Heart Assn., Am. Coll. Cardiology, N.Y. Heart Assn. Jewish. Contbr. articles to profl. jours. Home: 14 Withington Rd Scarsdale NY 10583 Office: 1300 Morris Park Ave Bronx NY 10461

HAJDU, FRANCIS LESTER, elec. engr.; b. Stamford, Conn., Aug. 22, 1942; s. Frank John and Josephine Sophia (Uzwiak) H.; B.S. in Engring., U. Conn., 1967, M.S. in Elec. Engring., 1968, M.B.A., 1971; m. Henrietta Gladys Wondolowski, June 25, 1973; children—Francis Paul, Lori Ann. Project engr. Stelma Telecommunications, Data Products Corp., Stamford, 1968-69; mgr. digital equipment W.W. Gaertner Research, Inc., Stamford, 1969-70; tech. ops. mgr. NCSS, Inc., Wilton, Conn., 1970-71; pvt. practice computers and communications cons., Stamford, 1971—; head dept. electronics J.M. Wright Regional Vocat.-Tech. Sch., Stamford, 1972—; faculty Bridgeport Engring. Inst., 1978—. Dir. Stamford emergency services/Office Civil Preparedness, 1976-78; adviser Explorer Post 800, 1977—. Named Vol. of Year, Vol. Action Center, 1977; registered profl. engr., Conn. Mem. Assn. Computing Machinery, IEEE, Conn. Soc. Profl. Engrs. (pres. southwestern chpt. 1975-76). Club: Kiwanis (cert. of appreciation 1977). Office: Scalzi Park Stamford CT 06904

HAJDUCZOK, BOHDAN ZENON, mech. engr., cons.; b. Rudki, W.Ukraine, June 4, 1930; s. Peter and Irene (Sawojka) H.; arrived U.S. 1948; naturalized 1954; B.S. in M.E., N.J. Inst. Tech. 1956, M.S. 1961; m. Lydia K. Firchuk, Mar. 29, 1972. Engr. production design Curtiss Wright Corp., Caldwell, N.J., 1955-57; devel. engr. Diehl Mfg. Co., Sommerville, N.J., 1957-58; project engr. Picatinny Arsenal, Dover, N.J., 1958-63; project mgr. PMO Nike Zeus, Huntsville, Ala., 1963-64; partner Integral Design & Mfg. Co., Irvington, N.J., 1964-65; project leader, mgr. munitions program PMO Arty., U.S. Army Munitions Command, Dover, 1965-70, value engring. and system configuration mgr., 1971-72, asst. chief engr., 1970-71, asst. dir. PMO 2.75 inch rocket system, 1972-73; mgr. facilities program PMO PBM, U.S. Army Armament Research and Devel. Command, Dover, 1973—; cons. various industry and U.S. govt. agencies. Exec. dir. various Ukrainian-Am. youth devel. sports clubs and summer camps, Newark and N.Y.C., 1970—. Recipient Nat. Individual Achievement award, 1969, Economy Champion, 1970, Certificate of Merit, Spl. Act award, numerous incentive awards U.S. Govt. Mem. U.S. Army Configuration Control Bd. (chmn. 1971-73), Tech. Evaluation Com., N.J. Inst. Tech. Alumni Assn., ASME. Clubs: U.S. Volleyball Assn. Author numerous tech. brochures. Address: 16 Manger Rd W Orange NJ 07052

HAKAS, JOSEPH FRANCIS, physician; b. Pitts., Oct. 19, 1931; s. Francis Paul and Nellie (Metrosky) H.; student Allegheny Coll., 1949-51; B.S., U. Pitts., 1953, M.D., 1957; m. Edith May Holt, June 25, 1960; children—Arlene Lynn, Joseph Francis, David Roger. Intern, Columbus Hosp., Pitts., 1957-58; practice medicine specializing in family medicine, Pitts., 1958—; mem. staff South Side Hosp., Central Med. Pavilion. Diploma Am. Bd. Family Practice. Fellow Am. Acad. Family Practice (charter); mem. AMA, Pa., Allegheny County med. socs., C. of C. Mt. Washington (dir. 1975-78). Republican. Presbyterian. Club: Rotary (Mt. Washington, Pa.). Home: 1767 Helen Dr Pittsburgh PA 15216 Office: 401 Bigham St Pittsburgh PA 15211

HAKIM, TALIB RASUL, educator, composer; b. Asheville, N.C., Feb. 8, 1940; s. William Allen and Luelvert (Johnson) C.; student Manhattan Sch. Music, 1958-59, N.Y. Coll. Music, 1960-63; m. children—Lorenzo Alexander, Aisha Naima, Jamal Dawud, Khalil Rasul. Librarian, Am. Music Center, Inc., N.Y.C., 1965-68; counselor N.Y. State Narcotic Addiction Control Commn., N.Y.C., 1967-70; mem. faculty Pace Coll., 1970-71; asst. prof. dept. Afro. Am. studies Nassau Community Coll., Garden City, N.Y., 1971—. Grantee, Creative Artists Pub. Service, 1972-73, Nat. Endowment for Arts, 1973-74; commn. U. Wis., River Falls Jazz-Concert Band, 1973. Mem. ASCAP, Soc. Black Composers (pres.). Composer: Sound Gone; Visions of Ishwara; Placements. Home: 16 Lessing Pl Freeport NY 11520

HAKIM-ELAHI, ENAYAT, obstetrician, gynecologist; b. Teheran, Iran, Nov. 23, 1934; s. Mohamed-Ali and Masoomeh Rahimi; M.D., Med. Sch., Teheran, 1959; m. Renate Emsters, Nov. 15, 1967; 1 dau., Cristina; came to U.S., 1959, naturalized, 1973. Intern, Queens Hosp. Center, N.Y.C., 1960, resident in internal medicine, 1961, resident in obstetrics and gynecology, 1961-64, resident in radiotherapy of gynecologic cancer, Am. Cancer Soc. fellow Queens div., 1965; resident in gynecology Cancer Research Inst., Columbia-Presbyn. Med. Center, N.Y.C., 1964-65; practice medicine specializing in obstetrics and gynecology, N.Y.C., 1968—; mem. staff Booth Meml. Med. Center, Flushing, N.Y., N.Y. Hosp., N.Y.C., Jamaica Hosp., Jamaica, N.Y., Hillcrest Gen. Hosp., Flushing; med. dir. Margaret Sanger Center, N.Y.C., 1973—, Planned Parenthood of N.Y.C., 1977—; clin. asst. prof. obstetrics and gynecology Cornell U. Med. Coll., N.Y.C., 1973—. Served with U.S. Army, 1965-67 as civilian. Lic. physician, Maine, Conn., Vt., N.Y., N.H., Calif. Diplomate Am. Bd. Obstetrics and Gynecology. Fellow A.C.S., Am. Coll. Obstetricians and Gynecologists, Internat. Coll. Surgeons, Am. Fertility Soc.; mem. Am. Soc. Gynecol. Laparoscopists, Am. Soc. Colposcopy and ColpoMicroscopy, Am. Assn. Planned Parenthood Physicians, Royal Soc. Medicine (London), World Med. Assn., N.Y. State Med. Soc., Queens Gynecol. Soc. Contbr. articles in field to profl. jours. Office: 43-70 Kissena Blvd Flushing NY 11355

HAKOLA, JOHN WAYNE, cons. mech. engr., monument co. exec.; b. Bklyn., Feb. 18, 1932; s. Wayne E. and Esther (Lorentzen) H.; B.A.E., Poly. Inst. Bklyn., 1961, M.S., 1965; postgrad. bus. adminstrn. Adelphi U., 1977-78; m. Patricia Anne Torrington, Mar. 1, 1956; children—John W., Wayne Edward, Karen Elizabeth. Engr., sr. engr. Sperry Gyroscope Corp., Lake Success, N.Y., 1956-69; cons. engr., Dix Hills, N.Y., 1968—; pres., owner Bklyn. Monument Co. Inc., J.R. Pitbladdo Inc., Bklyn., 1969—. Mem. Nat., N.Y. State (legis. chmn. Suffolk County chpt.) socs. profl. engrs., Environ. Tech. Seminar (L.I.), Am. Def. Preparedness Assn., N.Y. Monument Builders Assn. (pres.), Asso. Granite Craftsmens Guild N.Y. (past pres.), Newcomen Soc. N.Am. Home: 1 Wright Dr Dix Hills NY 11746 Office: 242 25th St Brooklyn NY 11232

HALASI-KUN, ELISABETH CHRISTINA SZORAD (MRS. GEORGE J. HALASI-KUN), educator; b. Versec, Austria-Hungary, Oct. 18; d. Nicholaus and Mary Juliana (Honig) Szorad; came to U.S.,

1958, naturalized, 1963; B.S., Columbia U., 1966, M.A., 1968; M.Ed., U. Munich, 1967; Ph.D., N.Y. U., 1972; m. George J. Halasi-Kun, Mar. 10, 1945; children—Beatrice P. (Mrs. Ulrich A. Maniak), Georgie E. Asst. to librarian Barnard Coll., N.Y.C., 1961-66; instr. German, head German div. Marymount Manhattan Coll., N.Y.C., 1965-69; asso. Columbia U., N.Y.C., 1971—. Recipient Founders award N.Y. U., 1973. Mem. Am. Assn. U. Profs., Modern Lang. Assn., Internat. Lenau Soc., Am. Folklore Soc., Delta Phi Alpha. Author: Oral Epic Poetry of the South-Slavs, 1968; Historical, Cultural and Social Influences in the Epics of Nicholaus Lenau, 1973. Home: 31 Knowles Ave Pennington NJ 08534

HALBERG, G. PETER, ophthalmologist; b. Budapest, Hungary, Jan. 27, 1915; s. Paul and Elizabeth (Selinger) H.; M.D., Pazmany Peter U., 1942; m. Marion Emily Handschuh, Sept. 18, 1959; children—Marion Elizabeth Georgiana, G. Peter II, Paul Joseph. Came to U.S., 1949, naturalized, 1953. Intern, Royal Hungarian Pazmany Peter U., Budapest, 1937-38; asst. resident ophthalmology Szabolcs St. Hosp., Budapest, 1942-43, resident, 1943-44; Am. resident ophthalmology Newark Eye and Ear Infirmary, 1952-53; asso. Dr. Conrad Berens, N.Y.C., 1955-60; asst. dir. div. electrophysiology, dept. research N.Y. Eye and Ear Infirmary, 1957-60, asst. ophthalmic surgeon then asso. attending ophthalmologist, now attending ophthalmic surgeon, dir. glaucoma service, 1971—; attending ophthalmic surgeon, chief contact lens service and glaucoma service St. Vincent's Hosp. and Med. Center, N.Y.C., 1974—; attending physician in charge contact lens service Beekman Downtown Hosp., N.Y.C., 1974—, cons., 1976—, mem. adv. bd. Emergency Care Inst., 1976—; asso. clin. prof. ophthalmology N.Y. Med. Coll., 1966-68, also asso. attending ophthalmologist, dir. electroretinography service, dir. Glaucoma Research Lab., 1961-66, dir. div. ophthalmic physiology, 1966; dir. Inst. Visual Physiology and Optics, 1968-72; professorial lectr. dept. surgery Coll. Medicine State U. N.Y. Downstate Med. Center, 1971—; fellow Inst. Ophthalmology, Coll. Physicians and Surgeons, Columbia U., 1949-50; cons. USPHS, Washington; mem. med. tech. adv. bd. Am. Nat. Standards Inst., 1973—. Served from capt. to maj. AUS, 1953-55. Decorated Bronze Star medal. Diplomate Am. Bd. Ophthalmology. Fellow A.C.S., Am. Acad. Ophthalmology and Otolaryngology, Internat. Coll. Surgeons, N.Y. Acad. Medicine; mem. Illuminating Engring. Soc., N.Y. Acad. Scis., Internat. Contact Lens Council Ophthamology (sec. gen. 1966-1978, pres. 1978—), Contact Lens Assn. Ophthalmologists (corr. sec. 1964-74, v.p. 1975, pres.-elect 1976, pres. 1977, chmn. standards and quality control com. 1970—, pub. relations council 1974—), Ophthalmol. Soc. U.K., Med. Soc. County N.Y., Am. Soc. for Contemporary Ophthalmology (gov. 1975—), Am. Intraocular Implant Soc. (chmn. standards and quality control com. 1975-77), Assn. for Advancement Med. Instrumentation (physician chmn. ocular device standards com. 1976—), ASTM (chmn. opthalmic sub-com. F-4 com. 1977—), Am. Acad. Ophthalmology (chmn. com. standards for ophthalmic instruments and devices 1976—), A.M.A., Pan Am. Assn. Ophthalmology, Assn. for Research in Vision and Ophthalmology, IEEE (asso.), Assn. Am. Med. Colls., L.I., German, French ophthalmol. socs., Semmelweis Med. Soc., Rudolf Virchow Med. Soc., Biol. Photog. Assn. Editor-in-chief Contact Lens Med. Bull., 1967-74, Jour. Club Ophthalmology, 1974-76; bd. editors Ophthalmology Digest, 1974—; sr. cons. editor (for Am.) Contact and Intraocular Lens Med. Jour., 1975—. Office: 40 W 77th St New York City NY 10024

HALBERSTADT, ROBERT BILHEIMER, optometrist; b. Stockertown, Pa., Feb. 11, 1918; s. Joseph Victor and Lillian (Bilheimer) H.; D.O., No. Ill. Coll. Optometry, 1939; m. Mary Margaret Gassner, Nov. 9, 1940; children—Mary Diane, Victoria Milou. Optometrist, Nazareth, Pa., 1940—; cons. optometry Whitehall-Coplay Sch. Dist., 1966—, Pathway Sch., Norristown, Pa. 1966-67, Miller Clinic, Stroudsburg, Pa., 1971-74, Learning Center, Scranton (Pa.) Pub. Schs., 1971-72; staff optometrist, cons. Allentown State Hosp., 1967-68; extern Gesell Inst., New Haven, 1967-68. Active Lehigh Valley Assn. for Brain Damaged Child, 1965-68; 2d v.p. Pa. Assn. for Brain Damaged Children, 1966-68; program chmn. Lehigh Valley Assn. for Children with Learning Disabilities, 1969-74, bd. dirs., 1971-74, 1st v.p., 1973-74; mem. Council Exceptional Children; with Friendship House, Scranton, 1973-75; mem. pres.'s club Ill. Coll. Optometry, 1973—, Century Club, 1976—. Served with USNR, 1943-46. Mem. Optometric Extension Program (state dir. 1950-58, regional dir. 1958—), Pa. Optometric Assn. (treas. 1948-57), Pocono Assn. Parents of Exceptional Children, Scranton, Lehigh Valley assns. children with learning disabilities. Address: 116 S Broad St Nazareth PA 18064

HALBERT, VIRGIL ALLEN, instn. exec.; b. Jerome, Idaho, Jan. 23, 1918; s. Virgil Cyrus and Mabel Sarah (Griffith) H.; B.S. in Edn., U. Idaho, 1940; M.S. in Hosp. Adminstrn., Columbia U., 1950; m. Ruth Humphrey Craig, Nov. 14, 1942; children—William Craig, James Warren. Med. adminstrv. officer VA Center, Boise, Idaho, 1946-48; adminstrv. resident Grasslands Hosp., Valhalla, N.Y., 1949-50; adminstrv. asst. USPHS Hosp., S.I., N.Y., 1950-51; adminstrv. officer USPHS Hosp., Balt., 1951; asst. chief material mgmt. br. Bur. Med. Services, USPHS, Washington, 1951-53; exec. dir. Home for Incurables of Balt. City, 1953—. Mem. Health and Welfare Council Balt. Met. Area, 1953—; mem. Council on Med. Care of Md., 1961-66, vice chmn., 1962-63, 64-65, chmn., 1963-64; mem. Md. and Del. Govs. Com. for Indigent's Care, 1965, Md. Gov.'s Commn. To Study Problems in Nursing Homes, 1971-73; mem. bd. of Licensure-Nursing Home Adminstrn., 1976—. Committeeman, Boy Scouts Am., Balt., 1956-58. Bd. dirs. Md. chpt. Multiple Sclerosis Soc., 1956-58; trustee Community Chest Balt. Area, Inc., 1954-63, United Fund Central Md., 1976—. Served from pvt. to capt. USAAF, 1942-46; ETO. Mem. Am. Coll. Hosp. Adminstrs., Am. (council on long term care 1966-68, governing council rehab. and chronic disease hosp. sect. 1969-71), Md. (chmn. adminstrs. sect. 1958-59, chmn. personnel sect. 1959-60, treas. 1964-66, del. to Am. Hosp. Assn. ho. of dels. 1968-70, 72-73), Washington, Del. hosps. assns., S.A.R. (2d v.p. 1968-70, 1st v.p. Md. Soc. 1970-72, pres. 1972-74, nat. trustee 1974-76, Patriots medal 1970), Md. Soc. War 1812 (dir.), St. Andrews Soc. Balt., Md. Colonial Wars Soc., Am. Legion, Balt. Civil War Round Table, Sons Union Vets. of Civil War, Nat. Hist. Soc., Pershing Rifles, Kappa Delta Pi, Sigma Nu. Democrat. Episcopalian. Home: 7929 Ruxway Rd Baltimore MD 21204 Office: 700 W 40th St Baltimore MD 21211

HALE, FRANCES, former librarian; b. Brockton, Mass., June 8, 1912; d. Chester Stanley and Frances (Thomson) Hale; B.S., Simmons Coll., 1934; M.A., Hofstra Coll., 1958. Head cataloger Brockton (Mass.) Pub. Library, 1935-41; chief catalog div. Schenectady Pub. Library, 1941-45; library dir. Floral Park (N.Y.) Pub. Library, 1945-59, Garden City Pub. Library, 1959-77; professorial lectr. Pratt Inst. Library Sch., Bklyn., 1952-55. Mem. exam. com. N.Y. State Bd. Regents, 1957-59. Mem. Am., N.Y., Nassau County (pres. 1950-52) library assns., Library Pub. Relations Council, AAUW, New Eng. Historic Geneal. Soc., D.A.R., Bus. and Profl. Women's Club (pres. Nassau County 1952-54), Soc. Mayflower Descs. Republican. Clubs: Soroptimist (pres. Central Nassau 1956-58, 76-77), Woman's. Home: 70 Tulip Ave Apt 9-D Floral Park NY 11001

HALE, ROBERT DAVID, trade assn. exec.; b. Batavia, N.Y., Jan. 16, 1928; s. David William and Rea (Phillips) H.; B.A., Hamilton Coll., 1949; m. Lydia Lund, Aug. 20, 1958; children—Christina Covode, David Valentine. Mng. editor Curtiss Johnson Publs., Deep River, Conn., 1958-62; mng. dir. bookstore Conn. Coll., 1962-70; pres. Hathaway House Bookshop, Wellesley, Mass., 1970-78; asso. exec. dir. Am. Booksellers Assn., 1978—; mem. Nat. Book Awards Com.; dean Booksellers sch. of Am. Booksellers Assn./Nat. Assn. Coll. Stores; pres. Children's Books Northeast. Trustee, Sherborn Pub. Library. Mem. Sierra Club (publs. com.). Book reviewer Boston Today and Sta. WCRB. Home: 15 Apple St Sherborn MA 01770 Office: 103 Central St Wellesley MA 02181

HALEVY, SIMON, physician; b. Bucharest, Romania, June 5, 1929; s. Meyer Abraham and Rebecca (Landau) H.; M.D., U. Bucharest, 1953; m. Hilda M. Valdes, 1964; 1 son, Daniel Abraham. Came to U.S., 1963, naturalized, 1970. Intern, Univ. Hosp., Coltzea, Romania, 1952-53, resident, 1953-54; practice medicine specializing in anesthesiology, 1955—; instr. anesthesia Postgrad. Inst. Medicine, Bucharest, 1955-57, chief lab. in anesthesia, 1957-60; preparator, instr. anatomy U. Bucharest Med. Sch., 1950; attending anesthesiologist Univ. Hosp., Fundeni, Bucharest, 1960-63; intern Community Hosp., Glen Cove, N.Y., 1964-65; resident Mt. Sinai Hosp., N.Y.C., 1965-67; asst. prof. anesthesiology Mt. Sinai Sch. Medicine, 1967-68; asst. prof. anesthesiology Albert Einstein Coll. Medicine, 1969-74; asso. prof. Coll. Phys. and Surg., Columbia U., 1974-75; prof. anesthesiology State U. N.Y., 1976—; asst. attending anesthesiologist Mt. Sinai Hosp. Services and Bronx Municipal Hosp. Center, 1967-71, attending anesthesiologist, 1973-74; attending anesthesiologist, dir. obstet. anesthesiology Nassau County Med. Center, 1976—. Chmn. com. on sci. exhibits Postgrad. Assembly in Anesthesiology, N.Y.C., 1971—. Diplomate Am. Bd. Anesthesiology. Fellow Am. Coll. Anesthesiologists; mem. AMA, Am. Soc. Anesthesiologists, Assn. des Anesthésiologistes Français, Deutsche Gesellschaft für Anaesthesie und Wiederbelebung, AAAS, Am. Soc. Pharmacology and Exptl. Therapeutics. Contbr. numerous articles to sci. jours. Office: Nassau County Med Center 2201 Hempstead Turnpike East Meadow NY 11554

HALEY, BRIAN PAUL, chem. co. exec.; b. S.I., N.Y., Mar. 1, 1945; s. Francis Xavier and Marianne (Wieser) H.; B.Chem. Engring., U. Del., 1968, M.B.A., 1972; m. Beverly Teresa Leonard, Apr. 12, 1969; children—Christine Beverly, Brian Paul. With Allied Chem. Co., 1968—, asst. regional sales mgr., Valley Forge, Pa., 1977—. Mem. Am. Chem. Soc., Sigma Phi Epsilon, Beta Gamma Sigma. Republican. Roman Catholic. Home: 490 Prussian Ln Wayne PA 19087 Office: 676 Swedesford Rd Wayne PA 19087

HALEY, EDWARD EVERETT, clin. chemist; b. Pawtucket, R.I., Apr. 5, 1923; s. Clarence and Helen Jane (Smith) H.; student Brown U., 1942-43, B.S., 1949; M.S., U. Rochester, 1952, Ph.D., 1954; m. Evangeline Madge Robertson, Sept. 1, 1951; children—David Bruce, Marcia Lynne, Malcolm Glenn. Chemist, Mead Johnson Co., Evansville, Ind., 1954-56, asso. sr. chemist, 1956-57; research asso. Yale U., 1957-59; chemist VA Hosp., West Haven, Conn., 1959—; instr. Housatonic Community Coll., Quinnipiac Coll. Mem. N. Branford Scholarship Assn., 1968-74, pres. 1971-72; moderator United Ch. of Christ, New Haven, 1972-74. Served with U.S. Army, 1943-46. Fellow AAAS, Am. Inst. Chemists; mem. Am. Chem. Soc., N.Y. Acad. Scis., Am. Soc. Biol. Chemists, Am. Assn. Clin. Chemists, Sigma Xi. Contbr. research articles to jours. Home: 18 Miller Rd Northford CT 06472 Office: VA Hosp W Spring St West Haven CT 06516

HALEY, MARTIN RYAN, pub. affairs and govt. relations co. exec.; b. Hibbing, Minn., Feb. 24, 1929; s. Martin Thomas and Bertha Madeline (Ryan) H.; student Coll. of St. Thomas, St. Paul, 1946-49. Vice-pres., Walter Butler Cos., St. Paul, Miami, Washington, 1954-59; pres. Walter Butler Engring. Co., St. Paul, Washington, 1957-59; chmn. bd. Martin Haley Cos., N.Y.C., including pres. Martin Ryan Haley & Assos., Inc., N.Y.C., 1949—; chmn. Fed. State Reports, Inc., Arlington, Va., 1974—, SEIREGO, S.r.l., Rome, 1975—, World Affairs Co., N.Y.C., 1975—; dir. Pub. Affairs Analysts, Inc. Decorated knight of Malta, knight comdr. Holy Sepulchre of Jerusalem. Mem. Internat., Am. assns. polit. cons., Internat., Am. polit sci. assns., Soc. Surveyors and Engrs., Internat. Pub. Relations Assn., Pub. Relations Soc. Am. Roman Catholic. Clubs: Met. (N.Y.C.); The Capitol Hill, Nat. Capital Democratic, George Town (Washington); Algonquin of Boston; Minn., Univ., Athletic (St. Paul). Contbr. articles to profl. jours. Office: 40 Central Park S New York City NY 10019

HALEY, VINCENT PETER, lawyer; b. Phila., Oct. 6, 1931; s. Vincent Paul and Madeline R. (McCrystal) H.; B.S., Villanova U., 1953, J.D. cum laude, 1959; m. Mary Ann Harron, Apr. 14, 1956; children—Paul V., Kevin G., Maureen T., Patricia Ann M., Kathleen A., Brian M., Regina E., Christopher, Megan. Admitted to Pa. bar, 1960; accountant Arthur Young & Co., C.P.A.'s, Phila., 1955-56; asso. firm Schnader, Harrison, Segal & Lewis, Phila., 1959-67, partner, 1968—; sec. Mercy Catholic Med. Center, Darby, Pa., 1969—; lectr. law Villanova U. Law Sch., 1960-61, 63-64. Mem. bd. edn. Archdiocese of Phila., 1973—, v.p., 1975-77, pres., 1977—. Served to lt. Supply Corps, USNR, 1953-55. Mem. Am., Pa., Phila. bar assns., Villanova Law Alumni Assn. (pres. 1962-63), Order of Coif (chpt. v.p. 1962-63). Clubs: Union League (Phila.); Roosevelt Racquet (dir. 1969—, treas. 1972—) (Huntingdon Valley, Pa.). Home: 305 Madison Rd Huntingdon Valley PA 19006 Office: 1719 Packard Bldg Philadelphia PA 19102

HALF, ROBERT, personnel recruiting exec.; b. N.Y.C., Nov. 11, 1918; s. Sidney and Pauline (Kahn) H.; B.S., N.Y. U., 1940; m. Maxine Levison, June 17, 1945; children—Nancy, Peggy. Staff accountant S.D. Leidesdorf & Co., 1940-43; office and personnel mgr. Kayser-Roth Corp., 1943-48; chmn. bd. Robert Half Inc., 1948—; pres. R-H Franchises, Inc., 1964—, Accountemps Inc., 1972. Mem. bd. appeals Village of Saddle Rock, Great Neck, N.Y., 1956-62; expert witness before Senate subcoms. on accounting reforms and franchising. C.P.A., N.Y. Mem. Assn. Personnel Cons. N.Y. (pres. 1963-64, dir. 1960-65), Nat. Assn. Personnel Cons., N.Y. State Soc. C.P.A.'s, Am. Inst. C.P.A.'s, Nat. Assn. Accountants, Accountants Club Am., U.S. C. of C. Clubs: N.Y. Univ.; Fresh Meadow Country; Banyan Country. Contbr. articles to profl. jours., newspapers, mags.; pioneer in specialized personnel recruitment. Office: 522 Fifth Ave New York City NY 10036

HALFHUID, RENE HENRY, Surinamese UN counsellor; b. Paramaribo, Surinam, Jan. 30, 1926; L.L.M., U. Surinam, Paramaribo, 1974; postgrad. in Internat. Law and Internat. Relations Inst. Social Studies, The Hague, Netherlands, 1975; married; 3 children. Mem. staff Bur. for Fgn. Relations and Ministry for Gen. and Fgn. Affairs of Surinam, Paramaribo, 1967-76; counsellor Permanent Mission of Republic of Surinam to UN, N.Y.C., 1976—; mem. Surinam del. to 31st and 32d sessions UN Gen. Assembly. Office: Permanent Mission of Republic of Surinam to UN One UN Plaza 26th Floor New York City NY 10017

HALIK, EUGENE EGON, engring. cons.; b. Prague, Czechoslovakia, Aug. 26, 1912; s. Joseph Eugene and Francis Nowy (Von Wallersberg) H.; came to U.S., 1952, naturalized, 1957; student Law Sch., Charles U., Prague, 1930-32; M.S. in Mech. Engring., Inst. Tech., Prague, 1935; m. Rose-Georgia Sedlak, Feb. 26, 1946; 1 dau., Michaela-Eleonora. Mgmt. and engring. cons., Prague, 1935-48; owner, pres. Neubert & Co., Prague, 1940-48; adminstrv. mgr. Radio Free Europe, Munich, Germany, 1950-52; engring. cons., N.Y.C., 1952-58; chief engr. Asso. Univs. Inc., N.Y.C. and Greenbank, W.Va., 1958-63; mem. sci. staff, cons. Brookhaven Nat. Lab., Upton, L.I., N.Y., 1963-73; pres. EEH Cons. Assos., N.Y.C., 1965—; mem. staff, cons. Princeton U. Plasma Physics Lab., 1973-78. Mem. AAAS, N.Y. Acad. Scis. Patentee light fuel injection field. Home: 1800 Old Meadow Rd McLean VA 22102 Office: EEH Cons Assos Inc Regency McLean VA 22102

HALINA, MME. (HALINA JOZEFA LUTOMSKI, MRS. FLOYD MARTIN LUTOMSKI), dance educator, choreographer; b. Lwow, Poland, Feb. 4, 1930; d. Adam and Katarzyna (Jezierska) Dziekan; came to U.S., 1947, naturalized, 1950; student Warsaw Opera Ballet Sch., 1936-38, Wielke Theatre, Lwow, 1939-41; grad. Politechnik, Lwow, 1944; m. Floyd Martin Lutomski, Oct. 31, 1946; children—Norbert Michael, Ilona Maria, Kevin. Dancer, Warsaw Opera Ballet, 1938-39, World's Olympiade, Kiev, Russia, 1939, U.S.O., Germany, 1945-46; producer Dance Capades, 1948—; tchr. Nat. Dance Tchrs. Orgns., U.S., P.R., 1950; choreographer children's and classical ballets Kimbo Dance Records, 1954—; founder, artistic dir., choreographer Elmira-Corning Ballet, Inc., 1955—; coordinator, also dir. ednl. programs; lectr.; producer choreographer Four Seasons, 1950, Fairy Doll, 1951, Sleeping Beauty, 1953, 59, 65-67, Nutcracker, 1954, Hansel and Gretel, 1955, Cinderella, 1957, Les Ballet de Elements, 1958, Schlagobers, 1959, Gaite Parisienne, 1960-61, La Boutique Fantasque, 1961, adaptation of Les Sylphides, 1962, Swan Lake, 1952-64, Masquerade, 1962-63, Snow Maiden, 1964, Copelia, 1965, 70, Karnival Kontrasts, 1966, La Bayadere, 1966, Nutcracker, 1969, Cinderella, 1968, Aurora's Wedding, 1971; dir. choreographer ballet Nutcracker for Elmira-Corning Ballet, 1965-66, also Red-White and Blue, Comedia del Arte, Masque; directed Les Petits Riens, 1967; dir., choreographer Wooden Prince, 1971, Americana, 1972, La Fille Mal Gardee, 1972, Vignette's Classique-Comedia, 1973, Sylvia, 1974; created Chinese Ballad, 1975; dir. Witching, Am. Gaieties, 1976 Bicentennial; choreographer A to Z Ballet, 1976; produced Carnival, 1977, Peter and the Wolf, 1977, Coppelia, 1978, Snow White, 1978; speaker, guest tchr. in 5-county area, also Boston area; chairperson Roper Records, 1976—; rep. ballet dept. for Dance Educators Am. to Nat. Council Dance Tchrs' Orgns.; dir. Sch. Dance Arts, Elmira, N.Y., Corning, N.Y.; lectr. Elmira-Corning Sch. Dists., 1969-72, Schulyer County Schs., 1968-71; chmn. Performing Arts Roper Ednl. Ballet and Dance Record, N.Y.C., 1976. Recipient Steuben Crystal and Gold award Corning community. Mem. Dance Educators Am. (chmn. ballet exam. com. 1966-67, exec. bd. 1967-69, exec. dir. 1969-71). Roman Catholic. Home: 933 Fassett Rd Elmira NY 14905 Office: 410-14 W Gray St Elmira NY 14905 also 258 Dennison Pkwy E Corning NY 14830

HALL, DAVID, clergyman; b. Augusta, Ga., Dec. 22, 1938; s. Lottie E. H.; B.A. Social Work, Howard U., 1960; M.Div., Morehouse Coll., 1964; B.S. in Polit. Sci., Tex. So. U., 1967. Ordained to ministry Baptist Ch., 1965; pastor various chs., 1972-78, Grady's Chapel Rock Bapt. Ch., San Antonio, 1976—; founder Miss Black Am., Washington, 1969-70; dir. pub. relations NAACP, Washington, 1971-73; regional dir. SCLC, Washington, 1974-76; dir., founder Christian Concern for Community Action, Washington, 1970—. Chaplain CAP. Served with U.S. Army, 1959-65; Vietnam; D.C. N.G. and USAR, 1965—. Decorated Meritorious Service Medal. Mem. Nat. Black Women Polit. Leadership Caucus (nat. chaplain 1977—), Lorton Council Progressive Action (coordinator dist. adv. council 1972—). Democrat. Clubs: Acacia, Knights Kodash, Daus. Isis, Masons (32 deg.). Home and office: 1338 K St SE Washington DC 20003

HALL, EDWIN HUDDLESTON, JR., govt. ofcl.; b. Bklyn., Sept. 5, 1935; s. Edwin Huddleston and Lois (Wiley) H.; B.S., Boston U., 1957; m. Linda Robbins, July 13, 1957; children—Jeffrey, Lisa, Lesley. Account exec. Merrill Lynch, Pierce, Fenner & Smith, Inc., Rochester, N.Y., 1961-68, partner, shareholder, 1968, sales mgr., 1969, asst. v.p., 1970, asst. mgr., 1970-73, resident v.p., 1973-78; spl. asst. to pres. U.S., presdl. interchange exec. Govt. Nat. Mortgage Assn., Washington, 1978—. Div. chmn. United Community Chest, 1973-75; bd. dirs. Old Colony Red Cross, 1966-68; treas. Rochester Assn. for Blind, 1976-77; pres. bd. dirs. Opera Theatre of Rochester, 1976-77. Served with USAF, 1958-61. Named Man of Year, Boston U., 1957; recipient spl. citizenship award Gov. of Mass., 1973. Mem. Rochester Soc. Analysts, Rochester (chmn. reaccreditation implementation com. 1976, trustee), Boston (life) chambers commerce, Boston U. Alumni Club (dir. 1970-72). Republican. Episcopalian. Clubs: Fort Hill, Federal (Boston); Genesee Valley (Rochester); Daniel Webster Masons. Home: 10030 Colvin Run Rd Great Falls VA 22066 Office: Room 6100 451 7th St SW Washington DC 20414

HALL, GARY RANDALL, chemist; b. Milledgeville, Ga., Jan. 14, 1944; s. Hugh and Edna Grace (Everett) H.; B.S., U. Pitts., 1974, postgrad., 1975—; m. Cecilia Dorothy Daly, Sept. 21, 1968. Research technician Kopp Glass, Pitts., 1964-65; quality control/research technician Alcoa, Pitts., 1965-68; with Saueresen Cements Co., Pitts., 1968—, chief research chemist, 1974—. Served with USNR, 1966-68. Mem. Nat. Assn. Corrosion Engrs., Am. Inst. Chem. Engrs., Air Pollution Control Assn., Am. Chem. Soc., Am. Soc. for Metals, ASTM, Am. Ceramic Soc. TAPPI. Republican. Roman Catholic. Home: 223 Hillendale Rd Pittsburgh PA 15237 Office: 160 Gamma Dr Pittsburgh PA 15238

HALL, HOWARD ELFRETH, architect; b. Moorestown, N.J., Jan. 27, 1893; s. William Howard and Minnie (Brudon) H.; B.S., Drexel U., 1916; m. Elizabeth Butler, Dec. 16, 1923; children—Nancy, Dorothy. Architect with Lockwood Greene, 1919-20, Day & Zimmerman, William H. Boardman, Phila., 1920, Victor Talking Machine Co., 1920-25; pvt. archtl. practice, Camden, N.J., 1925—; designed 1st drive-in movie theatre, Camden, 1936. Served with U.S. Army, 1918. Mem. AIA, N.J., W. Jersey socs. architects. Mason, Elk. Home: 9 Gill Rd Haddonfield NJ 08033 Office: 840 Cooper St Camden NJ 08102

HALL, JAMES CONRAD, physiologist, educator; b. Burketon, Ont., Can., Apr. 26, 1919; s. Robert Fordsman and Edna Elisa (Biehl) H.; came to U.S., 1947; B.A., U. Toronto, 1940, Ph.D., 1946; M.A., U. Western Ont., 1942; m. Jean Elizabeth Cochrane, June 20, 1945; children—Mary Kathleen, Robert Cochrane. Asst. prof. biology U. N.B., Fredericton, 1945-47; instr. Rutgers U., Newark, 1947-48, asst. prof., 1948-56, asso. prof., 1956-60, prof. biology, 1960-62, prof. physiology, 1962—, chmn. dept. zoology and physiology, 1962-69, dir. grad. program in zoology, 1953-68, 75—, chmn. physiol. sect., 1965, 73; cons. Nat. Inst. Child Health and Devel. Trustee, Acad. Medicine N.J., 1970—. Rutgers Faculty Research fellow, 1970-71; NSF grantee, 1959-60; NIH grantee, 1960-66, 66—. Mem. Am. Physiol. Soc., Am. Soc. Cell Biology, Soc. Exptl. Biology and

Medicine, Am., Can. socs. zoologists, AAAS, N.Y., N.J. acads. sci., Sigma Xi. Presbyterian. Contbr. articles to profl. jours. Home: 7 Merklin Ave West Orange NJ 07052 Office: 195 University Ave Newark NJ 07102

HALL, JOSEPH PALTA, tech. research co. exec.; b. Somerset, Ky., Mar. 17, 1928; s. George Reddish and Ida Mae (Duncan) H.; A.A.S. in Electronics, United Electronics Lab., Louisville, 1949; m. Mary Christine Quinton, Apr. 13, 1949; children—Bernetta Ann, Brenda Kaye. With Capehart-Farnsworth Co., Ft. Wayne, Ind., 1949-62, metrology technician, 1955-62; with United Tech. Research Center, East Hartford, Conn., 1962—, unit supr. metrology, 1966-70, supr. technicians, 1970—. Served with USAAF, 1946-47, USMCR, 1952-54. Mem. Nat. Assn. Clock and Watch Collectors, VFW (life). Democrat. Home: 23 Metcalf Rd Tolland CT 06083 Office: UTRC Silver Ln MS 82 East Hartford CT 06108

HALL, MAE CRAWFORD, educator; b. Salisbury, N.C., Nov. 29, 1943; d. Walter Blease and Deyette (Jones) Crawford; B.S. in Chemistry, Livingstone Coll., 1966; M.S. in Edn. (Univ. fellow), N.C. A. and T. State U., 1971; m. George T. Hall, Dec. 30, 1972. Tchr., Mays Jr.-Sr. High Sch., Goulds, Fla., 1966-67, Charlotte-(N.C.)-Mecklenburg Schs., 1968-73, Wilmington (Del.) High Sch., 1973-77, chemistry, sci. P.S. duPont High Sch., Wilmington, 1977—; tchr. Forum to Advance Minorities in Engring., summer 1977; mem. sch. com. United Negro Coll. Fund Del. NSF grantee, 1969, 71. Deaconess, Community Presbyterian Ch., New Castle, Del. Mem. Del. Tchrs. Sci., Wilmington Fedn. Tchrs. Home: 1403 Drake Rd Wilmington DE 19803 Office: 34th and Van Buren Sts Wilmington DE 19802

HALL, PAUL, labor union ofcl.; b. Ala., Aug. 21, 1914; m. Rose Hall; 2 children. Mem. Seafarers Internat. Union N.Am., 1938—, sec.-treas. Atlantic, Gulf, Great Lakes and In Land Waters dists., 1948—, 1st v.p., 1948-57, pres., 1957—; pres. maritime trades dept. AFL-CIO, 1957—, nat. v.p., mem. exec. com., 1962—. Mem. Nat. Com. Immigration, Citizens Com. Free China; former mem. Nat. Commn. for Indsl. Peace; former mem. Pres.'s labor mgmt. adv. com. Cost of Living Council; mem. Labor Mgmt. Adv. Com. on Econ. Matters. Bd. dirs. Am. Immigration and Citizenship Conf.; a founder, mem. nat. council Eleanor Roosevelt Found.; trustee George Meany Found.; sponsor, trustee Coordinating Council Edn. to Disadvantaged; v.p. Civic Center Clinic, N.Y.C. Recipient Humanitarian award Civic Center Clinic; citation of honor Nat. Com. Rural Schs. Address: 675 4th Ave Brooklyn NY 11232

HALL, RICHARD LEWIS, engring. service co. exec.; b. Montpelier, Ohio, Aug. 18, 1920; s. Louis Grayden and Ruby Elizabeth (Wingard) H.; B.S., U. Mich., 1943, M.S., 1952; B.S., U.S. Navy Postgrad. Sch., 1952; m. Mary Wagner, Nov. 14, 1947; children—Caryn Lynn Anstine, David Richard Hall. Dir. engring. M & T Co., Phila., 1965-69; pres. M & T Co. div. CDI Corp., 1971—, sr. v.p. CDI Corp., 1976—; lectr. in field. Served with USN, 1943-63. Mem. U.S. Naval Inst., U.S. Def. Preparedness Assn., USAF Assn. Lutheran. Club: Aronimink Golf. Home: 537 Gen Learned Rd King of Prussia PA 19406 Office: 2130 Arch St Philadelphia PA 19103

HALL, SAMUEL MECHANIC, JR., vocat. counselor; b. Saginaw, Mich., Dec. 23, 1937; s. Samuel M. and Marie (Hall) H.; A.A., Ferris Inst., 1962; A.B., Western Mich. U., 1963; M.A., Mich. State U., 1965; postgrad. Rutgers U., 1968; m. Mary Josephine Fisher, Aug. 13, 1973; 1 son, John Anthony. Counseling coordinator Lansing (Mich.) pub. schs., 1965; dir., asst. prof. career devel. center Langston (Okla.) U., 1965-66; edn. program adviser Civil Rights Office, U.S. Office Edn., Washington, 1966-67; dir. career planning and placement, acad. counselor Del. State Coll., Dover, 1967-70; dir. career counseling and placement Howard U., Washington, 1970—; cons. to various groups and orgns. Mem. Am. Personnel and Guidance Assn., Nat. Vocat. Guidance Assn., Am. Coll. Personnel Assn., Middle Atlantic Placement Assn. (exec. bd.), Ferris State Coll., Mich. State U. alumni assns., Western Mich. U. Alumni (life), Alpha Phi Alpha, Alpha Phi Omega. Columnist: Equal Employment Opportunity Forum. Home: 217 Rittenhouse St NW Washington DC 20011 Office: 2400 6th St NW Washington DC 20059

HALL, STEPHEN ROBERT, JR., environ. engr., pub. utility chemist; b. New Bedford, Mass., Dec. 27, 1928; s. Stephen Robert and Ruth Anita (Pierce) H.; B.S. in Textile Chemistry, Southeastern Mass. Tech. Inst., 1950; m. Florence Arvanites, Sept. 4, 1955; children—Susan, Stephen A. Chemist, Gen. Dyestuff Corp., Providence, 1950-51, Acushnet Co., New Bedford, 1953-61; mech. engr. New Bedford Gas & Electric Light Co., 1966-67; chemist Canal Elec. Co., Sandwich, Mass., 1967-70, environ. engr., 1970—; sec. Utility/Regulatory Agy. Marine Biology Adv. Com., Cape Cod Canal; chmn. environ. subcom. Elec. Council New Eng.; dir. New Bedford Gas & Elec. Light Co. Employees Credit Union, 1966—. Civil def. radio officer Town of Sandwich, 1977—; trustee Amateur Radio Repeater Sta. WRIAEB, Sandwich, 1975—. Served with AUS, 1951-53. Mem. Air Pollution Control Assn., Cape Cod and Islands Amateur Radio Assn., Am. Radio Relay League. Mem. Ch. of Christ. Clubs: Barnstable Radio, Masons, Engrs. Blue Room of Boston. Home: 32 Kiahs Way East Sandwich MA 02537 Office: PO Box 527 Freezer Rd Sandwich MA 02563

HALL, WILBUR SHERIDAN, scientist; b. Middletown, Conn., Mar. 26, 1925; s. Joseph Sheridan and Emma (Schubert) H.; B.S. in Chem. Engring., N.Y. U., 1957; m. Jean Euston Heverling, Aug. 12, 1950. Research chemist N.Y. Times Co., 1948-52; supr. research Acheson Dispersed Pigments Co., Phila., 1952-55; scientist Amchem Products div. Union Carbide, Ambler, Pa., 1955—; lectr. Nat. Assn. Corrosion Engrs., Am. Electroplaters Soc., Houston Soc. of Fedn. of Assns. for Coatings Tech., Gordon Research Conf., other confs. in field. Served with U.S. Army, 1945-46. Mem. Am. Chem. Soc., Fedn. Socs. for Coatings Tech. (nat. 1st prize for gadgets and gimmicks 1969). Episcopalian. Contbr. articles to profl. jours.; holder numerous patents; inventor autodeposition process. Home: 126 Germantown Pike Plymouth Meeting PA 19462 Office: Amchem Products Inc Brookside Ave Ambler PA 19002

HALL, WILFRED MCGREGOR, engring. exec.; b. Denver, June 12, 1894; s. Frederick Folsom and Annie Louise (Thompson) H.; B.S., U. Colo., 1916; D.Eng., Tufts U., 1955; m. Anne Gertrude Jones, Apr. 4, 1921 (dec. Dec. 1976); children—Frederick Folson, Ann (dec.); m. 2d, Louise Hull Claire, June 23, 1978. With Chas. T. Main Co., 1916-17, engr. hydroelec. investigation and design, 1920-22, with Chas. T. Main, Inc., 1941—, dir., 1943—, v.p., 1953-57, pres., chief exec. officer, 1957-72, chmn., chief exec. officer, 1972—; asst. engr. hydroelectric constrn. Chrisfield Contracting Co., 1919; supt. constrn., engr. U.G.I. Contracting Co., 1922-28; supt. constrn. Electric Bond & Share Co., 1929-31; cons. engr., 1932-33; engr. charge constrn. TVA, 1933-37; mgr. engring. and constrn., P.R., 1937-41; partner Uhl, Hall & Rich, Boston, 1953-62, mng. partner, 1963—; chmn. bd., chief exec. officer Chas. T. Main Internat., Inc., Chas. T. Main of N.Y., Inc., Chas. T. Main of Mich., Inc., Chas. T. Main of Va., Inc., Buerkel & Co., Inc., Tech. Service Co., Inc. Mem. Dean's Club, U. Colo. Mem., past dir. U.S. Com. Large Dams, Irrigation and Drainage. Bd. dirs. Mass. Soc. for Prevention of Blindness; past bd. dirs. Mass. Heart Assn., U. Colo. Engring. Devel. Found. Fellow ASCE; mem. A.I.M. (fellow pres. council), Am. Inst. Cons. Engrs. (past pres. N.E. sect.), Newcomen Soc. (trustee, chmn. N.E. com.), Soc. Mil. Engrs., Cons. Engr. Council New Eng. (past dir.), Mass. Soc. Prof. Engrs., Boston Soc. Civil Engrs., Alpha Sigma Phi, Sigma Tau, Tau Beta Pi. Rotarian (past dir. Boston). Clubs: The Country (Brookline, Mass.); Metropolitan (N.Y.); Algonquin, Hamilton Trust (past pres.), Engineers (bd. govs.) (Boston). Home: Penthouse D The Fairfield Prudential Center Boston MA 02199 Office: Prudential Tower Boston MA 02199

HALL, WILLIAM ANTHONY, physician, educator; b. N.Y.C., Oct. 26, 1923; s. John Clarence and Therese (MacDonald) H.; A.B., Harvard U., 1950, M.D., 1956; m. Ellen Mahn, May 29, 1948; children—Britton Fathe, Jan Karen. Physician Harvard Health Services, 1961-63; dir. univ. health services, asso. prof. medicine U. Fla., Gainesville, 1963-67; physician to health services; mem. Center for Environ. Studies, Princeton, 1967-73; dir. univ. health services, prof. sci. Wesleyan U., 1973-76; physician Brockton (Mass.) VA Med. Center, 1976—; anthropologist Harvard Sch. Pub. Health, 1950-52; lectr. human physiology Boston U., 1963-67; cons. to Nat. Acad. Scis., Smithsonian Instn. and Peace Corps, also travelling fellow WHO, 1974. Served with USN, 1941-45. Recipient Maimonides award Harvard Med. Sch. NIH fellow. Fellow Am. Coll. Health Assn.; mem. Assn. Am. Vol. Physicians, Am. Pub. Health Assn., Mass., Conn. med. socs., AAAS, Assn. Computing Machinery, Fedn. Am. Scientists, Soc. Occupational and Environ. Health, Sigma Xi. Unitarian, Quaker. Contbr. articles to profl. jours. Vol. physician in Viet Nam, 1969, 71, 72. Home: Forest St Sherborn MA 01770 Office: Brockton VA Hosp Brockton MA 02401

HALL, WILLIAM STERLING, psychologist; b. Lonoke County, Ark., July 6, 1934; s. Joseph William and Mattie Ellen (Brock) H.; A.B., Roosevelt U., 1957; Ph.D., U. Chgo., 1968. Asso. research psychologist Ednl. Testing Service, Princeton, N.J., 1968-70; asst. prof. psychology Princeton (N.J.) U., 1970-73; asso. prof. psychology Vassar Coll., Poughkeepsie, N.Y., 1973-74; dir. Inst. Comparative Human Devel., Rockefeller U., N.Y.C., 1974—; adviser N.J. Civil Service Commn. Mem. council of visitors Bank Street Coll., 1976—. Served with U.S. Army, 1957-59. Fellow N.Y. Acad. Scis.; mem. Am. Psychol. Assn., AAAS, Nat. Assn. Black Psychologists, Alpha Phi Alpha. Republican. Episcopalian. Author: Culture and Language, 1975. Home: 500 E 63d St New York City NY 10021 Office: Rockefeller U 66th St and York St New York City NY 10021

HALLENBECK, NORMAN PAGE, mfg. co. exec.; b. Winsted, Conn., Feb. 23, 1928; s. Roswell J. and Esther M. (MacLelland) H.; Asso. Accounting, Morse Coll., 1951; m. Marilyn Louise Dewey, Oct. 3, 1948; children—Joan Hallenbeck Baker, Cynthia, Charles. Accountant, Arthur G. Woods, Inc., Windsor, Conn., 1949-50, office mgr., 1950-51; sales corr. U.S. Time Corp., Middlebury, Conn., 1951-52; accountant, Conn. Mech. Industries, Hartford, Conn., 1952-56, gen. mgr., 1956-58; pres., N.P. Hallenbeck Co., Inc., Andover, Conn., 1958—, now chmn. bd.; pres. Hallenbeck Sales Co., Inc., Vernon, Hallenbeck Plastic Finishing, Inc., Vernon. Served to sgt. AUS, 1946-48. Mem. Soc. Plastic Engrs., Soc. Plastics Industry, Mfrs. Assn. Conn. Patentee in field. Home: 135 Center Rd Vernon CT 06086 Office: Hillside Industrial Park PO Box 2395 Vernon CT 06066

HALLENBECK, ROBERT POTTER, JR., lawyer, pharm. co. exec.; b. Albany, N.Y., Mar. 18, 1946; s. Robert P. and Marguerite G. H.; B.A., Union Coll., 1968; J.D., Albany Law Sch., 1971; m. Dorinda S. Mitchell, Aug. 17, 1968; children—Robert Potter, III, Jessica G. Admitted to N.Y. State bar, 1973; asso. firm Hesson, Ford, Sherwood & Whalen, Albany, 1971-72; counsel ways and means com. N.Y. State Assembly, Albany, 1972-73, public health com. Conn. Legislature, Hartford, 1975-76; chief counsel joint com. on human resources and house-senate health care study Tex. State Legislature, Austin, 1973-75; dir. legis. affairs SmithKline Corp., Phila., 1977—. Bd. dirs. Pa. Health Council. Mem. Am. Acad. Pol. and Social Sci., Nat. Health Lawyers Assn., Am. Bar Assn., Am. Public Health Assn., N.Y. State Bar Assn. Republican. Contbr. articles in field to profl. jours. Home: 420 Conestoga Rd Berwyn PA 19312 Office: 1500 Spring Garden St Philadelphia PA 19101

HALLER, HENRY EDWIN, JR., mfg. co. exec.; b. Pitts., Sept. 17, 1913; s. Henry E. and Emma M. (Burns) H.; B.S., U. Pitts., 1936; m. Grace Mary Horton, Aug. 15, 1942; children—Henry E. III, Marjorie Burns. With Nat. Valve and Mfg. Co., Pitts., 1936—, pres., 1956—, also dir.; dir. Equibank N. A., Equimark Corp., Blue Cross of Western Pa. Bd. dirs. Boys Club Pitts., Pa. AAA Fedn., Animal Rescue League; trustee Thiel Coll.; adv. dir. Nat. AAA; dir. U. Pitts. A.G.F. Mem. Tristate Indsl. Assn. (dir.). Clubs: Duquesne, Pitts. Athletic Assn. (pres. 1963-64, dir. 1956-66), Rolling Rock, West Pa. Motor (dir.), Masons. Home: 516 Edgerton Pl Pittsburgh PA 15208 Office: 158 49th St Pittsburgh PA 15201

HALLIDAY, FREDERICK NICHOLAS, novelist, screenwriter; b. Watertown, N.Y., June 19, 1937; s. David Graham and Louise Lucille (Gimigliano) H.; B.A., U. Md., 1961. Newswriter, editor CBS-TV News, N.Y.C., 1961-62; freelance TV writer for Hanna-Barbera Studios, Hollywood, Calif., Warner Bros. Studios, Krantz Films, N.Y.C. and Calif., 1963-67; writer Holiday mag., 1971-72, Vintage mag., 1970-72; freelance screenwriter and novelist, 1972—. Mem. Writers Guild Am., Wine Writers Circle N.Y., Overseas Press Club Am. Author: (novels) The Chocolate Mousse Murders, 1974; The Raspberry Tart Affair, 1976; A Case of Indelicate Champagne, 1977; Sink the Grand Fleet, 1978; (screenplay) The Nine Lives of Fritz the Cat. Home: 240 Central Park S New York City NY 10019

HALLION, MARIE ELIZABETH, govt. ofcl.; b. Washington, Feb. 21, 1941; d. Richard Paul and Marie Elizabeth (Flynn) Hallion; B.A. in Govt. and Politics, U. Md., 1963, M.A., 1964, Ph.D. (fellow), 1968. Lectr. govt. and politics U. Md., 1968—, faculty rep. on acad. council Univ. Coll., 1977-78; adminstrv. asst. White House Office, Exec. Office Pres., Washington, 1971—. Mem. Am. Polit. Sci. Assn., Am. Acad. Polit. and Social Sci., Alpha Lambda Delta, Phi Alpha Theta, Pi Sigma Alpha, Phi Kappa Phi. Home: 1011 Marton St Laurel MD 20810 Office: Old Exec Office Bldg Room 62 17th St and Pennsylvania Ave Washington DC 20500

HALLION, RICHARD PAUL, JR., curator; b. Washington, May 17, 1948; s. Richard Paul and Marie Elizabeth (Flynn) H.; B.A. in History, U. Md., 1970, Ph.D., 1975. Curator, Nat. Air and Space Mus. of Smithsonian Instn., Washington, 1974—; lectr. history and aerospace engring. U. Md. Guggenheim Found. fellow, 1973-75. Mem. Am. Inst. Aeros. and Astronautics (History Manuscript award 1975), U.S. Naval Inst., Aviation/Space Writers Assn., Soc. History Tech., Air Force Hist. Found., Phi Alpha Theta, Pi Sigma Alpha, Phi Kappa Phi. Author: Supersonic Flight: Breaking the Sound Barrier and Beyond, 1972; Legacy of Flight: the Guggenheim Contribution to American Aviation, 1977; The Wright Brothers: Heirs of Prometheus, 1978; also articles in profl. jours. Home: 1003 Montrose Ave Laurel MD 20810 Office: National Air and Space Museum Smithsonian Institution Washington DC 20560

HALLORAN, KATHERINE BOSTWICK HESS, physician; b. New Haven, Aug. 14, 1929; d. Orvan Walter and Carol Maurer Hess; B.A. cum laude, Wellesley Coll., 1950; M.D., Yale U., 1954; m. Thomas Clifford Halloran, June 5, 1954; children—Charles Bostwick, Priscilla Ann, Peter Montgomery. Intern pediatrics Bellevue Hosp., 1954-55; resident pediatrics and pathology Columbia Presbyn. Med. Center, N.Y.C., 1955-58; fellow pediatric cardiology Columbia, Babies Hosp., 1958-60; N.Y. Heart Assn. trainee pediatric cardiology, 1960-61; instr. pediatric cardiology Yale U. Sch. Medicine, New Haven, 1961-67, asst. prof., 1967-72, NIH fellow in human genetics, 1972-74; asst. regional flight surgeon regional hdqrs., eastern region FAA, Jamaica, N.Y., 1974—. Meyer Berger fellow N.Y. Heart Assn., 1960-61. Fellow Am. Coll. Cardiology; mem. Am., Conn. heart assns., Am. Acad. Pediatrics, Sigma Xi. Clubs: Yale (dir., sec.), Yacht (Stamford, Conn.), Wellesley. Contbr. articles in field to profl. jours. Home: 23 Stamford Ave Stamford CT 06902 Office: JFK Airport Fed Bldg Jamaica NY 11430

HALLQUIST, CLARENCE LAMONTE, writer, pharm. co. exec.; b. Strandburg, S.D., Feb. 26, 1932; s. Walter Clarence and Edna Caroline (Anderson) H.; B.A., Temple U., 1955; m. Eleanor Thompson Borton, June 6, 1970; children by previous marriage—Lauren, Christina, Gregory, Lisa; stepchildren—Scott, Michael. With Caterpillar Tractor Co., York, Pa., 1956-60; editor, mem. public relations staff Smith Kline & French Labs., Phila., 1960-68; mgr. health info. services Merck Sharp & Dohme, West Point, Pa., 1968—; writer, lectr., film producer. Bd. dirs. Singing City, 1961-62; editor COPE Mental Health Centers, Ambler, Pa., 1977—. Recipient Distng. Public Info. Service award Am. Acad. Pediatrics, 1977, Spl. Communications award Mental Health Assn., 1977. Mem. Am. Med. Writers Assn., Am. Assn. Sci. Writers, Am. Sci. Film Assn., Public Relations Soc. Am., Nat. Communications Council for Human Resources, Internat. Union for Health Edn., Internat. Assn. for Suicide Prevention and Crisis Intervention, Am. Assn. Suicidology (dir., chmn. public relations, award 1976). Democrat. Club: Phila. Cricket. Home: 520 Spring Ln Wyndmoore PA 19118 Office: Merck Sharp & Dohme West Point PA 19118

HALLSTEAD, WILLIAM FINN, III, author; b. Scranton, Pa., Apr. 20, 1924; s. William Finn II and Winifred (Mott) H.; grad. Hill Sch., 1942; m. Jean Little, Oct. 9, 1948; children—William Finn IV, Alyssa Jean. Flight instr. Scranton Municipal Airport, 1946-50; hwy. designer Pa. Hwy. Dept., Scranton, 1950-52; hwy. and airport designer Whitman Requardt & Assos., Balt., 1952-58; free-lance writer, pres. Colony Pub. Corp., Balt., 1958-65; dir. information services Rouse Co., Balt., 1965-68; dir. devel. Md. Center for Pub. Broadcasting, Owings Mills, Md., 1968—. Served with USAAF, 1942-45. Mem. Authors Guild. Republican. Episcopalian. Author: Ev Kris, Aviation Detective, 1961; Dirigible Scout, 1967; Sky Carnival, 1969; The Missiles of Zajecar, 1969; Ghost Plane of Blackwater, 1974; How To Make Money Writing Articles for the Freelance Market, 1976; The Man Downstairs, 1979; also numerous stories in English text books, anthologies. Contbr. to popular mags., profl. and trade jours. Home: 2027 Skyline Rd Ruxton MD 21204 Office: Md Center for Public Broadcasting Owings Mills MD 21117

HALMAN, TALAT SAIT, educator, author; b. Istanbul, Turkey, July 7, 1931; came to U.S., 1952; s. Adm. Sait T. and Iclal F. (Nemlizade) H.; B.A., Robert Coll., 1951; M.A., Columbia U., 1954; m. Seniha Taskiranel, July 23, 1960; children—Hugh, Defne, Sait. Lectr. Turkish lang. and lit. Columbia U., 1953-60; v.p., gen. mgr. Record Hunter, Inc., N.Y.C., 1956-60; dir. album prodn. Atlantic Rec. Corp., N.Y.C., 1965-67; prof. Turkish lang. and lit. Princeton U., 1966-71, 72—; prof. Turkish lang. and lit. N.Y. U., 1967-71; asso. to minister culture Republic of Turkey, 1971. Served to lt. Turkish Navy, 1961-62. Decorated knight Grand Cross Queen Elizabeth II, 1971. Mem. P.E.N. (exec. bd. 1974—), Council Nat. Lits. (exec. bd.). Author (books in English) Selected Poems of Fazil Husnu Daglarca, 1969; I am Listening To Istanbul, 1971; The Humanist Poetry of Yunus Emre, 1972; On the Nomad Sea, 1974; Modern Turkish Drama, 1974; Contemporary Turkish Literature, 1974; (poetry) Shadows of Love, 1979; (in Turkish) Can Kulagi, 1968, William Faulkner, 1963, Translations Faulkner's Knight's Gambit, 1952, 62, The Poetry of Ancient Civilizations and Pre-literate Cultures, 1974; Shakespeare's Sonnets, 1964; Eskimo Poems, 1969; Selected Poems by Wallace Stevens, 1970; Selected Poems by Langston Hughes, 1971; Ancient Egyptian Poetry, 1972; Aphoristic Poems, 1976. Bd. editors: Books Abroad: International Literary Quar., 1967—, guest editor, 1973; guest editor spl. issues Lit. Rev., 1972; guest editor Rev. Nat. Lits., 1973, Lit. East-West, 1974, Contemporary Literature in Translation, 1975. Contbr. articles, poems, essays, translations to Turkish, Am., Brit. jours., encys., mags., anthologies. Columnist Istanbul Daily Milliyet, 1969-71, Istanbul Daily Aksam, 1972-73. Home: 333 E 30th St New York City NY 10016 Office: Near East Studies Dept Princeton U Princeton NJ 08540

HALO, HUGO HONA, physician; b. Casiguran, Sorsogon, Philippines, Apr. 9, 1930; s. Marcario H. and Justa C. (Hona) H.; came to U.S., 1957; naturalized, 1968; M.D., Manila Central U., 1956; m. Marie T., Jan. 30, 1964; children—Deborah, Teresita, Marisa. Intern, Union Hosp., Fallriver, Mass., 1957-58; resident in gen. practice Woonsocket (R.I.) Hosp., 1958-60; resident in psychiatry R.I. Med. Center, 1960-62, Conn. Valley Hosp., Middletown, 1962-63; chief, psychiatric service Taunton (Mass.) State Hosp., 1963-64, dir. out patient dept., day care program, 1965-66; dir. intellectual and emotional research Philippines Child Study Center, 1964-65; dir. clin. psychiatry Foxboro (Mass.) State Hosp., 1966-67; dir. neuropsychiatric dept. Charles V. Chapin Hosp. Providence, R.I., 1967-68; dir. dept. group therapy R.I. Med. Center Cranston, 1971—, clin. dir. adolescent unit, 1972, acting dir. med. edn., 1975; dir. child study and guidance clinic St. Mary's Sch., Cranston, 1970—; physician-in-charge geriatric unit R.I. Inst. Mental Health, 1978—; cons. in field including sch. psychiat. cons. Cath. Diocese, Providence, 1976. Licensed psychiatrist, N.H., R.I., 1967. Fellow Royal Soc. Health London; mem. AMA, World, Am., Can. psychiat. assns., R.I., Providence med. socs. Home: 162 E Hill Dr Cranston RI 02920 Office: 629 Budlong Rd Cranston RI 02920

HALPERIN, GEORGE BENNETT, educator, ret. naval officer; b. N.Y.C., Aug. 7, 1926; s. George and Muryal (Lesser) H.; B.S., U.S. Naval Acad., 1950; M.B.A., Stanford U., 1958; M.A. in History, U. Vt., 1976; m. Ellen Elizabeth Barber, Dec. 18, 1957; children—Gail Susan, Thomas Allyn. Commd. ensign U.S. Navy, 1950, advanced through grades to comdr., 1965; dir. systems and standards div. Naval Supply Center, Oakland, Calif., 1963-65; freight terminal officer Naval Support Activity, Danang, Vietnam, 1966-67; supply officer Naval Air Sta., Barbers Point, Hawaii, 1967-70, ret., 1970; tchr. history Stowe (Vt.) High Sch., 1972-78, asst. prin., 1975-76; chmn. social studies dept. Stowe Jr.-Sr. High Sch., 1977—. Chmn., Lamoille South Dist. Profl. Growth Com., 1977—. Decorated Navy Commendation medal. Mem. Am. Hist. Assn., Nat. Council for Social Studies, Soc. for History Edn., U.S. Naval Acad. Alumni. Clubs: Army-Navy Country (Arlington, Va.); Copley Country (Morrisville, Vt.). Home: RR 2 Box 217 Morrisville VT 05661

HALPERN, ABRAHAM LEON, psychiatrist; b. Warsaw, Poland, Feb. 2, 1925; s. Rubin M. and Helen (Perelman) H.; M.D., U. Toronto (Ont., Can.), 1952; m. Marilyn Lois Benjamin, May 10, 1947; children—Howard, Lon, Marnen, Heather, Mark, Emily, John. Came to U.S., 1957, naturalized, 1962. Intern, Toronto Western Hosp., 1952-53; resident Warren (Pa.) State Hosp., 1957-60, Eastern Pa. Psychiat. Inst., Phila., 1959; asso. research scientist Mental Health Research Unit, Syracuse, N.Y., 1961-62; commr. mental health Onondaga County, 1962-67; practice medicine specializing in psychiatry, Port Chester, N.Y., 1967—; dir. psychiatry United Hosp., Port Chester, 1967—; attending psychiatrist Beth Israel Hosp., N.Y.C., 1968-73, Westchester County Med. Center, 1971—; cons. forensic psychiatry High Point Hosp., Port Chester 1969—; clin. asst. prof. State U. N.Y., Syracuse, 1964-67; asst. clin. prof. Mt. Sinai Sch. Medicine, 1970-74; clin. asso. prof. N.Y. Med. Coll., 1973—; clin. prof. U. Bridgeport (Conn.), 1973—; mem. med. adv. com. Vis. Nurse Assn., Syracuse, 1962-67. Chmn., Syracuse chpt. Com. to Abolish Capital Punishment, 1962-65; mem. profl. adv. com. N.Y. State Assn. for Mental Health, 1964-67; mem. Westchester County Community Mental Health Bd., 1976—, chmn., 1977—; bd. visitors Harlem Valley Psychiat. Center, 1978—. Served to surgeon lt. comdr. Royal Canadian Navy, 1942-45, 53-57. Recipient Citizenship award N.Y. State Bar Assn., 1966; Liberty Bell award Onondaga County Bar Assn., 1966. Diplomate Am. Bd. Psychiatry and Neurology; certified mental hosp. adminstr. Am. Psychiat. Assn. Fellow Am. Acad. Forensic Scis., A.C.P., Am. Psychiat. Assn. (com. psychiatry and law 1973-75), Am. Pub. Health Assn.; mem. AMA, N.Y. State, Westchester County med. socs., Westchester Psychiat. Soc. (pres. 1973-74), Am. Soc. Adolescent Psychiatry, Am. Acad. Psychiatry and Law. Home: 720 The Parkway Mamaroneck NY 10543 Office: 406 Boston Post Rd Port Chester NY 10573

HALPERN, GEORGE MARTIN, educator, coll. dean; b. N.Y.C., Mar. 5, 1919; s. Isadore and Sarah (Honig) H.; B.S., N.Y.U., 1950, M.A., 1952; Ed.D., Columbia U., 1959; m. Stella Ruth Tauber, June 30, 1946; children—Ilene Sharon, Marsha Marianne, Andrea Alicia. Graphic arts instr. Jr. High Sch. 37, Bronx, 1947-48; head dept. graphic arts Fieldston Sch., Riverdale, N.Y., 1948-50; dir. Manhattan Sch. Printing, N.Y.C., 1950-52; prof., dept. chmn. N.Y.C. Community Coll., Bklyn., 1952-70, asso. dean faculty, 1970-71, dean Voorhees campus, 1971—. Pres. Nonpareil Assos., New Hyde Park, N.Y., 1964-73; cons. Bullinger's Guides, Emerson, N.J., 1952. Sec., commr. Nassau County Commn. on Vocat. and Spl. Edn., 1962-64; mem. adv. council N.Y. Joint Legis. Com. on Higher Edn., 1969-75; commr. U.S. Assay Commn., 1972, mem., 1973—. Committeeman Nassau County Republican Com., N.Y., 1954—. Served with USNR, 1942-45. Recipient gold medal award Mark Twain Soc. 1952; Craftsman of Year award Nat. Assn. Photolithographers, 1968; Gold Key award Gamma Epsilon Tau, 1973; Man of Year award Printing Tchrs. Guild N.Y., 1974. Mem. NEA, AAUP, Am. Legion, Am. Numis. Assn., N.Y. State Jr. Coll. Assn., Am. Assn. Jr. Colls., Am. Assn. Univ. Adminstrs., Tech. Assn. Graphic Arts, Internat. Graphic Arts Edn. Assn. (regional v.p., Elmer G. Voight award 1965), Faculty Assn. State U. N.Y., Internat. Assn. Printing House Craftsmen, Am. Tech. Edn. Assn., Am. Acad. Polit. Sci., Am. Mgmt. Assn., Smithsonian Assos., Phi Delta Kappa, Kappa Delta Pi. Co-author: Graphic Communications; author: Workbook for Graphic Arts; Pressman's Ink Manual. Contbr. articles to profl. jours. Home: 25 Richard Pl Massapequa NY 11762 Office: 450 W 41st St New York City NY 10036

HALPERN, NATHAN LOREN, industrialist; b. Sioux City, Iowa, Oct. 22, 1914; s. Aaron and Lena (Robin) H.; B.A., U. So. Calif., 1936; LL.B. cum laude, Harvard, 1939; m. Edith Kessel, Oct, 7, 1938; 1 son, Michael. Asst. to chmn. SEC, 1939-41; exec. asst. to dir. WPB, 1941-42, USIS, 1945; asst. to pres. CBS, 1945-49; pres. TNT Communications, Inc. 1949—; lectr. Annenberg Sch. of Communications, U. Pa., 1966. Pres., Internat. Center of Photography; benefactor, mem. corp. Met. Mus. Art, N.Y.C. Served with USNR, 1942-44. Mem. Soc. Motion Picture and TV Engrs., Phi Beta Kappa. Clubs: Harvard, Players. Home: 993 Fifth Ave New York City NY 10028 Office: 575 Madison Ave New York City NY 10022

HALPERN, SIDNEY, univ. ofcl.; b. Phila., Jan. 18, 1927; s. Bernard M. and Sophie (Swidler) H.; A.B., U. Pa., 1947, M.A., 1950, Ph.D., 1964; postgrad. Harvard, 1947-49; m. Phyllis C. Schachter, Dec. 21, 1951; children—Baruch, Nikki. Vice pres. Loyalty Life Ins. Agy., Inc., 1954-67, sec., dir., 1965-67; exec. v.p. Plymouth Mut. Life Ins. Co., 1954-57, pres., dir. 1957-67; pres. editor, pub. Mercury Books, Inc., 1961-67; asst. v.p. George Washington Life Ins. Co., 1965-67; asst. prof. history Temple U., Ambler, Pa., 1967-76, asso. prof., 1976—, dir. Ambler Campus, 1971—, dean campus, 1975—; pres. Provident Pub. Co., 1969—. Mem. Adath Zion, Zionist Orgn. Am., Jewish Def. League, Phi Beta Kappa, Sigma Rho. Author: Caesar and the Aurelii Cottae; the Passions of Caesar and Christ; Salvation is from the Jews. Contbr. articles to psychoanalytic jours. Home: 1025 Friendship St Philadelphia PA 19111 Office: Temple U Ambler PA 19002

HALPERT, BERNARD, biologist; b. Bklyn., May 26, 1920; s. Samuel and Yetta (Sacharowitz) H.; B.S., Bklyn. Coll., 1940; M.A., Hofstra U., 1954; m. Nancy Sager, Aug. 18, 1946; children—Susanna, Joan Halpert Hanson, Felicia, Jonathan. Chief chemist Puritan Dairies, Perth Amboy, N.J., 1946-47; supr. N.J. Gardner Labs., Bklyn., 1947-54; exec. dir. Hempstead (N.Y.) Gen. Hosp., 1954-57; dir. Williamsburg Labs., Bklyn., 1957-59; dir. Biometric Affiliated Research Labs., Inc., Long Island City, N.Y., 1959—; exec. dir. Biologic Cons., Glen Head, N.Y., 1966—; pres., chmn. bd. Tender Care Inc., 1973—. Bd. dirs. Nassau Civic Club. Served with AUS, 1942-46; ETO. Mem. N.Y. Diabetes Assn., AAAS, Am. Assn. Clinic Mfrs., Am. Assn. Cons. Chemists and Chem. Engrs., Am. Inst. Chemists, Am. Pub. Health Assn., Am. Soc. Pub. Adminstrn., Group Health Assn. Am., Inst. Sanitation Mgmt., N.Y. Acad. Scis., Royal Soc. Health, Smithsonian Instn., Environ. Mgmt. Assn., Am. Acad. Cons. Jewish. Clubs: Histadrut, B'nai B'rith, Masons. Home: 17 Wildwood Ln Greenvale NY 11548 Office: 3 Maple Pl Glen Head NY 11545

HALSEY, RICHARD SWEENEY, librarian, educator; b. Los Angeles, Apr. 8, 1929; s. John Calvin and Grace Thorne (Crossman) Sweeney; B.Mus., New Eng. Conservatory, 1952, M.Mus., 1954; M.L.S., Simmons Coll., 1962; Ph.D. (U.S. Office Edn. fellow), Case Western Res. U., 1972; m. Patricia Siver, July 15, 1961; children—Rachel, Gabriela. Chief audio-visual dept. Olin Library, Washington U., St. Louis, 1962-65; dir. learning resources Sch. Dist. University City (Mo.), 1965-68; info. scientist Central Midwestern Regional Ednl. Lab., St. Ann, Mo., 1968-69; asst. prof. Sch. Library Sci., U. Toronto (Ont., Can.), 1972-73; asso. prof. Sch. Library and Info. Sci., State U. N.Y., Albany, 1973—, also mem. bus. officers copyright adv. com., co-chmn. task group to develop CBTE certification program for sch. media specialists; library cons. for pub. schs. N.Y. State Edn. Dept.; mem. copyright adv. com. WMHT-TV. telephone network activator Common Cause, 28th Congl. Dist. N.Y., 1974—. Served with inf., U.S. Army, 1955-56. Mem. Am. (chmn. reference and subscription books rev. com. 1975—, Booklist editorial adv. bd. 1972—, Dartmouth medal award com. 1976—), N.Y. State (v.p., pres. elect library edn. sect.) library assns., Assn. Am. Library Schs. (chmn. conf. program com. 1974), Pi Kappa Lambda. Democrat. Author: Classical Music Recordings for Home and Library, 1976; contbr. articles to profl. jours. Home: 239 Juniper Dr Schenectady NY 12306 Office: Sch Library and Info Sci State U NY Albany NY 12222

HALVORSON, NEWMAN THORBUS, JR., lawyer; b. Detroit, Dec. 17, 1936; s. Newman Thorbus and Virginia Westbrook (Markle) H.; A.B., Princeton U., 1958; LL.B., Harvard U., 1961; m. Sally Clark Stone, May 3, 1969; children—Christina English, Charles Burgess Westbrook. Admitted to D.C. bar, 1962, Ohio bar, 1962; asso. firm Covington & Burling Washington, 1962-70, partner, 1970—. Chmn. 10th anniversary campaign Harvard Law Sch., 1971; bd. dirs., treas. Eugene and Agnes E. Meyer Found., 1972—. Bd. dirs. Lupus Found. Greater Washington, 1974—; trustee, treas. Com. of 100 of Federal City, 1976—. Served with USMC, 1961-62. Mem. Am. Bar Assn. (sec. taxation 1964—). Republican. Episcopalian. Clubs: Met., Chevy Chase. Editor: Harvard Law Rev., 1960-61. Home: 35000 Lowell St NW Washington DC 20016 Office: 888 16th St NW Washington DC 20006

HAM, JERRY DON, govt. ofcl., petroleum engr.; b. Wellington, Tex., June 29, 1935; s. Chester Meredith and Erlys Leah (Manzer) H.; B.S. in Petroleum Engring., U. Tex., 1959, M.S., 1963; Ph.D., U. Tulsa, 1972; m. Esther Ruth Clark, June 9, 1956; children—Jerri Diane, Jordan Clark, Jeffrey Craig, Elizabeth Leah. Natural gas engr. Bur. of Mines, U.S. Dept. of Interior, Bartlesville, Okla., 1964-71, asst. to asst. dir. energy, Washington, 1971-75; asst. dir. oil, gas and shale tech. ERDA/Dept. Energy, program U.S. Washington, 1975—. Registered profl. engr., Okla. Mem. D.C. Soc. Profl. Engrs. (dir.), Am. Inst. Mining and Metall. Engrs., Acacia, Pi Epsilon Tau, Sigma Gamma Epsilon Home: 5907 Lovejoy St Springfield VA 22152 Office: 20 Massachusetts Ave NW Washington DC 20545

HAM, LESLIE GILMER, beverage co. exec.; b. Winnipeg, Man., Can., Mar. 3, 1930; s. Arthur Leslie and Frances Irene (Gilmer) H.; B.A., McGill U., 1951, B.Commerce, 1953; M.B.A., U. Western Ont., 1956; m. Anne Corris Dinsmore, June 12, 1954; children—Charles Keith, Susan Lesley, Cynthia Anne. Auditor, Peat, Marwick, Mitchell, Montreal, Que., Can., 1953-55; brand mgr. Procter & Gamble Co. Can., Toronto, Ont., 1956-58; exec. v.p. Seven-Up Montreal Ltd., 1958-70; v.p. operations Pepsi Cola Can. Ltd., Toronto, 1970-74, also dir.; pres. Société Internationale de Produits Alimentaires, Paris, 1974-75; exec. v.p. sales Pepsi-Cola Met. Bottling Co. Inc., Purchase, N.Y., 1975-78; pres., chief exec. officer Pepsi-Cola Can. Ltd., Toronto, 1978—. Vice-pres. Que. Provincial council Boy Scouts Can., 1969-73. Mem. Montreal Execs. Assn. (pres. 1970), Inst. Chartered Accountants Que., McGill Grads. Soc. (dir. 1972-73), Theta Delta Chi. Anglican. Clubs: Royal Montreal Golf, Red Birds Ski (Montreal); Mississauga Golf, Granite (Toronto); Country of Darien (Conn.). Home: 43 The Kingsway Toronto ON Canada Office: 1255 Bay St Toronto ON Canada

HAMADA, GEORGE SYD, biologist, educator; b. N.Y.C., June 16, 1943; s. Morris and Miriam (Langner) H.; B.S., Bklyn. Coll., 1964; Ph.D., U. Conn., 1968; m. Marilyn Kinsberg, June 13, 1965; children—Kimberly Resa, Keith Michael. Asst. prof. Queensborough Community Coll., Bayside, N.Y., 1970-71; asst. prof. biology LaGuardia Community Coll., City U.N.Y., Long Island City, N.Y., 1971-72, asso. prof., 1973—, sci. coordinator, 1972—. Guest investigator Boyce Thompson Inst. for Plant Research, 1970-74. NIH fellow, 1966-68; NIH trainee, 1968-70. Mem. AAAS, Am. Soc. Parasitologists, Electron Microscopy Soc. Am. Contbr. articles to profl. jours. Home: 75-05 169th St Flushing NY 11366 Office: 31-10 Thomson Ave Long Island City NY 11101

HAMANN, RONALD HOWARD, hosp. adminstr.; b. N.Y.C., Oct. 23, 1927; s. Howard Sorelle and Audrey Cecil Beatrice (Twyford) H.; student Pace Coll., 1951-52; m. Patricia Helen Pollack, June 23, 1951; children—Bradford, Audrey, Trent. Clk., Grossman's Hardware & Lumber Co., Quincy, Mass., 1948-49; clk. N.Y. Hosp., N.Y.C., 1949-50, accountant, 1951-53, supr. billing sect., 1954-56, sr. accountant and asst. to chief accountant, 1957-60, adminstrv. asst. for profl. services, 1961-65, adminstrv. dir. Payne Whitney Clinic, 1965—. Served with AUS, 1945-48. Mem. Fin. Mgmt. Assn., Eastern Fin. Assn., Hosp. Fin. Mgmt. Assn., Assn. Adminstrs. Mental Health and Mental Retardation Facilities, U.S. Chess Fedn., Coalition Vol. Mental Health and Mental Retardation Agys. (v.p.). Lutheran (v.p. men's club 1959-60). Home: 435 E 70th St New York City NY 10021 Office: 525 E 68th St New York City NY 10021

HAMBLETON, GEORGE ROBERT, engr., horticulturist; b. Vineland, Ont., Can., Dec. 7, 1921; s. George S. and Evelyn E. (Butler) H.; B.A.Sc. with honors, U. Toronto, 1950; M.B.A., McMaster U., Can., 1966; m. Margaret Kathleen Collins, June 15, 1946; children—Elizabeth Ann, Margaret Catherine, Lillian M., William, Harold. Sr. equipment specialist Can Comstock Co., Ltd., St. Catharines, Ont., 1950-52; sr. design engr. Ferranti-Packard Ltd., St. Catharines, 1952-72; farmer fruit orchards, Niagara-on-the-Lake, Ont., 1974-75; mgr. tech. services Penzer Products Ltd., St. Catharines, 1976-77; design engr. Ferranti Packard, Ltd., 1978—. Bd. dirs. Niagara Falls Ch., 1971—, usher, 1975—. Served with RCAF, 1941-44. Mem. Assn. Profl. Engrs. Ont., No. Nut Growers Assn., Niagara Hort. Soc., Niagara Fruit and Vegetable Growers Assn., Soc. Ont. Nut Growers (sec., treas. 1972—), Canadian Bible Soc. (pres. Vineland br. 1963-70). Breeding and research on Carpathian walnuts. Home: Rural Route 2 Concession 6 Rd Niagara on the Lake ON L0S 1J0 Canada Office: Dieppe Rd Saint Catharines ON Canada

HAMBURG, LESTER ALBERT, wholesale trade co. exec.; b. Youngstown, Ohio, Aug. 23, 1916; s. Elmer A. and Isabel (Margolis) H.; B.A., U. Pitts., 1938. With Hamburg Bros., Pitts., 1938—, exec. v.p., 1954-60, pres., 1960-68, chmn. bd., 1969—, also chief exec. officer; dir., mem. exec. com. Pitts. Nat. Bank. Bd. dirs. Allegheny Conf. Community Devel.; trustee, chmn. fin. com. Montefiore Hosp.; treas. bd. trustees U. Pitts. Health Center; trustee United Way Allegheny County; trustee, mem. exec. com. Carnegie-Mellon U. Clubs: Concordia, Duquesne, Westmoreland County (Pitts.); Harmonie (N.Y.C.); Masons. Home: 5564 Northumberland St Pittsburgh PA 15217 Office: 40 24th St Pittsburgh PA 15222

HAMEL, BERNARD FRANKLIN, artist; b. Holyoke, Mass., May 29, 1933; s. George Francis and Mary Veronica (Fadden) H.; student Art Students League, 1951-52, Pratt Inst., 1956-59; m. Joan E. La Bare, Feb. 1, 1972. Owner, prin., artist Hamel Advt., Holyoke, until 1975; exhibited in one-man shows at Western New Eng. Coll., Springfield, Mass., 1979; exhibited in group shows at N.A.D., 1977, Nat. Arts Club, 1977, Conn. Acad. Fine Arts, 1977, Silvermine Guild of Artists, 1977, 78, Berkshire Art Assn., 1977, 78, Ellsworth Gallery, 1978, Grand Central Galleries, 1979, others; represented in collections at Phila. Mus. Art. Artist, Holyoke Bicentennial Commn. Served with USAF, 1952-56. Mem. Nat. Soc. Painters in Casein and Acrylic, Springfield Acad. Artists, Allied Artists Am., Nat. Arts Club, Springfield Art League, Berkshire Art Assn. Home and office: 144 High St Holyoke MA 01040

HAMID, MAHMUD ABDEL, educator; b. Jerusalem, June 19, 1933; s. Abdel-Hamid S. and Mouza A. Abu-Khdair; B.A., Roosevelt U., 1959; M.A., Am. U., 1963; Ph.D., Cath. U.; Dorothy M., May 27, 1969. Cultural and consular officer Embassy of Libya, Washington, 1960-66; asst. prof. social sci. Coppin State Coll., Balt., 1968-69; adminstv. asst. Iraqi interests sect. Embassy of India, Washington, 1971; substitute tchr., Washington, 1974—, also mktg. rep. Skyline Travel, 1976—. Mem. Am. Polit. Sci. Assn., Am. Soc. Internat. Law, AAUP, Middle East Inst., Internat. Polit. Sci. Assn. Contbr. to New concise Ency. of Middle East, 1973. Home: 2801 Quebec St NW Washington DC 20008

HAMILL, CHARLOTTE MARY, hosp. adminstr.; b. N.Y.C., Dec. 1, 1919; d. Andrew MacLean and Charlotte (Jung) Hamill; B.A., Coll. New Rochelle, 1940; M.A., Brown U., 1949; M.S. in Social Work, Columbia U., 1958. Field service dir. Girl Scouts U.S.A., Providence, 1940-42; instr. R.I. Hosp. Sch. Nursing, Providence, 1942-46; dir. student personnel services Hartford (Conn.) Hosp. Sch. Nursing, 1946-49; asst. exec. dir. Bayway Community Center, Exxon, Elizabeth, N.J., 1949-63; asso. dir. planning and program devel. Burke Rehab. Center, White Plains, N.Y., 1963—, co-dir. Day Hosp., 1972-78, dir., 1978—, co-dir. health careers edn. and tng. services, 1969-78; mem. faculty Rutgers U., 1958-60, Columbia U., 1960-62; mem. adv. com. human services dept. Westchester Community Coll., 1973-75; research asso. dept. pub. health Cornell U. Med. Coll., 1974—; mem. housing task force Westchester County HEW Coordinating Council, 1977—. Recipient community life award Westchester Health Facilities Assn., 1974; HEW grantee, 1969-77. Mem. Acad. Certified Social Workers, Am. Congress Rehab. Medicine, Am. Hosp. Assn., Am. Soc. Health Manpower Edn. and Tng., Am. Pub. Health Assn., Am. Soc. Allied Health Professions, Gerontol. Soc., Nat. Assn. Social Workers, Rehab. Internat., Conn. Soc. Gerontology. Home: 7 Sylvan Rd Darien CT 06820 Office: Burke Rehabilitation Center White Plains NY 10605

HAMILTON, ALICE DOWDALL, nursing adminstr.; b. Woburn, Mass., Oct. 19, 1914; d. Luther and Adina (Hall) Dowdall; grad. Faulkner Hosp. Sch. Nursing, 1936; B.S., Boston Coll., 1960; M.S., Boston U., 1965; m. Robert Appleby Hamilton, Mar. 13, 1937 (div.); 1 son, Robert Appleby. Supr., instr. maternal child health nursing Faulkner Hosp., Boston, 1951-58, head nurse maternity, 1948-51; med.-surg. supr. Lawrence Meml. Hosp., Medford, Mass., 1961-63, dir. nursing, 1963—; cons. in field. Mem. Nat. League Nursing, Faulkner Hosp. Sch. Nursing Alumnae, Cape Cod R.N.'s Assn., Sigma Theta Tau. Republican. Episcopalian. Home: PO Box 469 Ships Rudder Dr Mashpee MA 02649 Office: Lawrence Meml Hosp 170 Governors Ave Medford MA 02155

HAMILTON, CALVIN P., architect; b. Wilmington, Del., June 14, 1923; s. Harrison R. and Mattie (Jenkins) H.; B.Arch., Howard U., 1951; m. Marguerite E. Daniels, May 16, 1959. Sr. draftsman W. Ellis Preston, AIA, Wilmington, 1951-64; project dir. Richard Philips Fox, AIA, Newark, Del., 1964-67; pres. Calvin P. Hamilton, AIA, Inc., Wilmington, 1967—; chmn. Del. Com. on Bldg. Codes, 1972-74; del. of Gov. Del. to Nat. Conf. States on Bldg. Codes and Standards. Chmn. bd. Walhut St. br. YMCA, Wilmington, 1968-77; pres. United Way Del., 1976-78, chmn. planning council, 1972-76; bd. dirs. Del. chpt. ARC, 1978—; bd. dirs. Wilmington Med. Center, 1972—, mem. long range planning com., 1972-76, mem. bldg. com., 1976—; mem. community devel. com. Greater Wilmington Devel. Council, 1974—; mem. Del. Health Planning Council, 1975-77. Served with AUS, 1943-46. Recipient Design award Greater Wilmington Devel. Council-New Castle County Planning Bd., 1976, YMCA-Wilmington Community Leadership award, 1978. Mem. AIA (nat. com. on bldg. codes and standards 1975-77), Kappa Alpha Psi (Community Service award 1976). Methodist. Home: 607 W 39th St Wilmington DE 19802 Office: 218 W 9th St Wilmington DE 19801

HAMILTON, CHESTER, fin. cons.; b. Topeka, July 10, 1922; s. Clay and Ernestine Lorraine (Klein) H.; A.B., Hamilton Coll., 1944; M.B.A., Harvard U., 1948; m. Fay Aleen Wallace, June 13, 1944; children—William W., Stuart J. Staff accountant Lybrand, Ross Bros. & Montgomery, Boston, 1948-51; v.p., treas. Fidelity Group of Funds, Boston, 1951-77; fin. cons., 1977—; dir. Framingham Trust Co. Trustee Hamilton Coll. Served with USAAF, 1943-46. Mem. Am. Inst. C.P.A.'s, Mass. Soc. C.P.A.'s, Phi Beta Kappa. Republican. Episcopalian. Home and Office: 240 Morse Rd Sudbury MA 01776

HAMILTON, CLARKE THOMAS, elec. products co. exec.; b. Pitts., Aug. 24, 1929; s. Russell J.and Lois F. H.; B.A., Washington and Jefferson Coll., 1951; M.B.A., U. Pitts. 1959; m. Ann K. Hamilton, July 27, 1951; children—Mark R., Stephen C., Diane F. Personnel trainee Assos. Discount Corp., Pitts., and South Bend, Ind., 1954-56; indsl. relations rep., materials div. Westinghouse Electric Corp., Blairsville, Pa., 1956-61, mgr. employment and employee relations, advanced energy systems, Large, Pa., 1961-66, mgr. employment and reassignments, corporate hdqrs., Pitts., 1966—; mem. advisory bd. Hatchett & Cunningham Co., Charlotte, N.C.; dir. Western Pa. Christian Broadcast Co., Pitts. Served with C.E., U.S. Army, 1951-53. Mem. Am. Soc. Personnel Adminstrn. (accredited personnel diplomate), Employment Mgmt. Assn. (Human Resource award 1975), Fraternal Order Police. Presbyterian. Clubs: Masons, Shriners. Home: 163 Crescent Hills Rd Pittsburgh PA 15235 Office: Westinghouse Bldg Pittsburgh PA 15222

HAMILTON, FRANCES, educator; b. Farmington, Mo., Jan. 17, 1916; d. Roscoe Franklin and Zora (Nations) Hamilton; B.S., S.W. Mo. State Coll., 1940; M.A., Columbia U., 1948. Tchr. pub. schs., Mo., 1937-45; supr. student teaching Md. State Tchrs. Coll., Frostburg, 1945-47; tchr. Montgomery County, Md., 1947-48; supr. elementary scis. Howard County, Md., 1948-51; asso. sec. Assn. Childhood Edn. Internat., 1951-52, exec. sec., 1952-59; ednl. program specialist U.S. Office Edn., HEW, 1959—; part-time instr. edn. U. Va. Chmn. Nat. Adv. Com. Exchange of Tchrs., 1956-57; sec.-treas. Youth Conservation Clearing House, 1954—; sec. U.S. Nat. Com. on Childhood Edn., 1955-57, 59-61; mem. Office Edn. Adv. Com. of Nat. Orgns., 1955-59, co-chmn., 1958-59; chmn. Women's Joint Congl. Com., 1956-58; del. White House Conf. on Edn., 1955; tech. cons. White House Conf. on Children and Youth, 1960. Mem. Assn. Childhood Edn. Internat., World Orgn. Early Childhood Edn., D.C. Council Adminstrv. Women (exec. com., pres. 1968-69), Nat. Council Adminstrv. Women in Edn. (pres. 1971—), NEA, AAUW, Am. Vocat. Assn., Assn. Supervision and Curriculum Devel., John Dewey Soc., Am. Assn. Sch. Adminstrs., World Edn. Fellowship, Kappa Kappa Iota, Delta Kappa Gamma, P.E.O. Clubs: Internat. (Washington); Quota. Home: 4200 Cathedral Ave NW Washington DC 20016 Office: US Office Edn HEW Washington DC 20202

HAMILTON, JAMES THEODORE, univ. dean; b. Springfield, Ohio, Sept. 16, 1931; B.A. in Social Sci., Miami U., Oxford, Ohio, 1953; B.S. in Edn., Ohio State U., 1955, M.A., 1956; Ph.D. in Ednl. Adminstrn., Case Western Res. U., 1963; m. Gretchin Amlin Worley; children—Heidi, Eric, Heather. High sch. tchr., Springfield and Brooklyn, Ohio, 1956-61; asst. prof. edn. and psychology Mt. Union Coll., Alliance, Ohio, 1961-64; coordinator curriculum and research Willoughby-Eastlake Pub. Sch., Cleve., 1964-66; mem. faculty U. Bridgeport (Conn.), 1966—, dir. grad. studies, 1973-77, dean Coll. Fine Arts, 1974-77, dean grad. and internat. studies, 1977—; cons. in field. Mem. Am. Ednl. Research Assn., Am. Personnel and Guidance Assn., Am. Assn. Colls. for Tchr. Edn., Assn. World Edn., Conn.

nitrate for hypersensitive teeth. Home: 72 Overhill Rd Providence RI 02906 Office: 145 Whitmarsh St Providence RI 02907

HODSDON, ALBERT EDWARD, III, cons. engr.; b. Portland, Maine, Oct. 9, 1947; s. Albert Edward and Vivian (McPherson) H.; B.S. in M.E., U. Maine, 1969, M.E., 1975; m. Jill P. Barry, June 1, 1970. Sales engr. A.C. & S., Inc., N.Y.C., 1969-70; grad. asst. U. Maine, Orono, 1970-71; project mgr. Wright & Pierce Engrs., Topsham, Maine, 1971-74; owner, pres., dir. A.E. Hodsdon Cons. Engrs., Waterville, Maine, 1974—. Adv. com. shoreland zoning Zoning Bd. Appeals Town of Smithfield; mem. Smithfield Planning Bd., 1973. Registered profl. engr., Maine, Mass., N.H., Vt. Mem. ASCE, Am. Soc. Heating, Refrigerating and Air Conditioning Engrs., Nat. Soc. Profl. Engrs., Maine Water Utilities Assn., Main Waste Water Control Assn. Methodist. Home: RFD 2 Box 88 Oakland ME 04963 Office: 2 Silver St Waterville ME 04901

HOEHN, JAMES GURNEY, plastic surgeon; b. Detroit, Feb. 8, 1938; s. Vincent Henry and Frances Margaret (Pallai) H.; B.S., Georgetown U., 1960; M.D., Northwestern U., 1964; m. Barbara Louise Kegler, Aug. 18, 1962; children—James Gurney, Melissa Ann. Intern, Chgo. Wesley Meml. Hosp., 1964-65; resident in gen. and plastic surgery Mayo Clinic, Rochester, Minn., 1965-71, vascular surgery fellow, 1965-69; hand surgery fellow Marquette U. Med. Sch., 1969; practice medicine specializing in plastic surgery, Albany, N.Y., 1971—; mem. staff Child's, Meml., VA, Cohoes Meml., Albany Med. Center, St. Peter's hosp., Sunnyview Hosp. and Rehab. Center; clin. instr. Albany Med. Coll.; sec. Albany Plastic Surgeons Asso., P.C. Diplomate Am. Bd. Surgery, Am. Bd. Plastic Surgery. Mem. Am. Soc. Maxillofacial Surgeons, Soc. Plastic Surgeons Upstate N.Y., N.Y. State Soc. Plastic, Reconstructive and Maxillofacial Surgeons, Am. Soc. Plastic and Reconstructive Surgeons, Am. Assn. Hand Surgery, A.C.S., Am. Burn Assn., Soc. Head and Neck Surgeons, Am. Cleft Palate Assn., AMA. Roman Catholic. Club: Ft. Orange (Albany, N.Y.). Contbr. articles to med. jours. Home: Woodland Pheasant Ln Menands NY 12204 Office: 23 Hackett Blvd Albany NY 12208

HOELSCHER, ELODY M., accountant; b. New Knoxville, Ohio, Dec. 23, 1919; d. William H. and Anna M. (Bierbaum) Hoelscher; B.S., Ohio State U., 1950. Accountant, Detjen Grain Co., Wapakoneta, Ohio, 1937-47, Arthur Young & Co., N.Y.C., 1951-61; v.p., dir. corporate fin. services, asst. sec. Grey Advt. Inc., N.Y.C., 1961—. C.P.A., N.Y. State. Mem. Am. Soc. Women Accountants (past pres.), Am. Inst. C.P.A.'s, N.Y. State Soc. C.P.A.'s. Methodist. Home: 70 E 10th St New York City NY 10003 Office: 777 3d Ave New York City NY 10017

HOELTZEL, KENNETH EUGENE, educator; b. Tiffin, Ohio, Oct. 8, 1937; s. Howard Jay and Helen Dorothy (Zimmerman) H.; B.S. in Edn., Ohio State U., 1959, M.A. in Edn., 1967, Ph.D. in Edn., 1970; m. Kathleen Ann Switzer, Dec. 17, 1966; children—Kimberly Ann, Craig Ryan. Tchr. instrumental music, guidance counselor Walnut Twp. Sch., Millersport, Ohio, 1959-68; research asso. Center for Vocat. Edn., Columbus, Ohio, 1968-70; asst. prof. edn. SUNY, Plattsburgh, 1970-72, asso. prof., 1972-76, prof., 1976—; cons. in career edn. N.Y. State Dept. Edn., Albany, 1972—. Mem. Am., N.Y. State personnel and guidance assns., Assn. for Counselor Edn. and Supervision, Nat. Vocat. Guidance Assn., Phi Delta Kappa. Author: (with others) The Systems Approach: An Emerging Behavioral Model for Career Guidance, 1971. Contbr. articles in field to profl. jours. Home: 56 Champlain Dr Plattsburgh NY 12901 Office: 414 Campus School SUNY Plattsburgh NY 12901

HOENIGAN, HENRY, artist; b. Zarnovitz, Poland, Feb. 14, 1917; grad. Acad. Fine Arts, Cracow, Poland, 1938. One-man shows: Palace of Fine Arts, Cracow; Internat. Art Exhibit, Cairo, Egypt, 1944, Gallery Katz, Tel Aviv, 1947; Eglinton gallery, Toronto, Can., 1955, ACS Gallery, Buffalo, 1970, Lambton Gallery, Toronto, 1971, Walter Engel Gallery, Toronto, 1974, Soc. Canadian Artists, 1965; group shows: Four Seasons Hotel, Toronto, 1965, The Third Gallery, Toronto, 1972, Retrospective, Art Gallery Cobourg (Canada), 1975, Museum Lengyel Gallery Fine Arts, N.Y.C., 1976, 77, Polish Artists, Ont. Sci. Center, 1976-77, Art Gallery Cobourg, (Ont., Can.), 1977, Parkdale Library, Toronto, 1977; represented in permanent and pvt. collections. Grantee Ont. Arts Council, 1975; recipient hon. award for oil painting, Buffalo, 1963. Address: 36 Shelborne Ave Toronto ON M5N 1Z1 Canada

HOEST, WILLIAM PIERCE, cartoonist; b. Newark, Feb. 7, 1926; s. Earl S. and Dorothea Gamble (Whittinghill) H.; student Cooper Union, 1950; m. Madeline Mezz, Nov. 4, 1973; children—Liz, Sue, John, Chip, Sharon, Molly, Patti, Billy, Julie. Designer humorous greeting cards Norcross Greeting Card Co., 1949-51; free-lance designer humorous greeting cards, 1951-60; mag. cartoonist Sat. Eve. Post, Look, Playboy, others, 1960—; syndicated cartoonist The Lockhorns and Agatha Crumm, 1968—. Served with USN, 1944-46; PTO. Mem. Cartoonist Guild, Nat. Cartoonists Soc. (Reuben award 1976, 78), Newspaper Comics Council. Author: A Taste of Carrot, 1967; What's the Garbage Doing on the Stove?, 1975; Loretta, The Meatloaf Is Moving, 1976; Bumper Snickers, 1976; Who Made the Caesar Salad...Brutus?, 1977; Hoest Toasties, 1978; Is This the Steak or the Charcoal?, 1978; More Bumper Snickers, 1979.

HOEXTER, CORINNE ROSENFELDER KATZ, author, editor; b. Scranton, Pa., Nov. 3, 1927; d. Edward David and Aimee Helen (Rosenfelder) Katz; B.A. in English with high honors, Wellesley Coll., 1949; M.A., U. Chgo., 1950; m. Rolf Hoexter, Dec. 25, 1955; children—Vivien, Michael Frederic. Promotion asst. Expt. Internat. Living, Putney, Vt., 1950-51; editorial asst. Parents mag., 1951-53; asso. editor Mag. Mgmt., Inc., 1953-54; asso., then mng. editor Pines Pub. Inc., N.Y.C., 1954-57; picture editor J.J. Little & Ives, N.Y.C., 1957-59; mng. editor Portfolio and Art News Ann., 1959-60, Asia, mag. pub. by Asia Soc., 1978—; author: From Canton to California, The Epic of Chinese Immigration, 1976; Black Crusader: Frederick Douglas, 1970; co-author: A Nation Conceived and Dedicated, 1970; contbr. periodicals. Trustee Flat Rock Book Nature Assn., 1973-78; mem. steering com. FISH of Englewood-Tenafly, 1973-75; mem. Social Service Fedn. Englewood; mem. Asian Am. Assembly for Policy Research, 1977—. Fulbright fellow, U. Bologna (Italy), 1953. Mem. Chinese Hist. Soc. Am., Authors League, League Women Voters, N.Y. Zool. Soc., NAACP, Common Cause, Phi Beta Kappa. Clubs: Chatham (Mass.) Yacht; Wellesley of Englewood. Office: 112 E 64th St New York City NY 10021*

HOEY, EVELYN LEVINE (MRS. REID A. HOEY), librarian; b. Estill, S.C., Aug. 28, 1919; d. Hyman and Lena (Cantor) Levine; B.A., Meredith Coll., 1939; B.L.S., Simmons Coll., 1940; m. Reid A. Hoey, Apr. 14, 1960. Cataloger, Charlotte (N.C.) Pub. Library, 1941-43; br. librarian Savannah (Ga.) Pub. Library, 1943; librarian U.S. Office Postal Censorship, Chgo., 1943-44; librarian subsistence Research and Devel. Lab. U.S. Army Q.M.C., Chgo., 1944-46; librarian U.S. Army Spl. Services European Theatre, 1946-49; plant librarian Union Carbide Nuclear Co., Oak Ridge Gaseous Diffusion Plant, 1949-60; tech. librarian Rome (N.Y.) Air Devel. Center, Griffiss AFB, 1960, chief documents library, 1960-62; specialist lit. acquisition s-research Gen. Electric Co., Syracuse, N.Y., 1962-66; adminstrv. librarian State U. N.Y., Upstate Med. Center, Syracuse, 1966-69, acting dir., 1969-70, dir., 1970—. Mem. adv. com. State U. N.Y. Biomed. Communications Network, 1970-76; mem. adv. com. N.Y. and N.J. Regional Med. Library Program, 1970. Mem. Med. Library Assn. (Upstate N.Y. chpt. dir. 1969, mem. legis. com. 1970—), Profl. Womens League (sec. 1967—). Club: Stonecrest Supper (Manlius, N.Y.). Contbr. articles in field to profl. jours. Home: 215 Wedgewood Terr Dewitt NY 13214 Office: 766 Irving Ave Syracuse NY 13210

HOEY, JAMES BENEDICT, systems engr.; b. Bklyn., Apr. 15, 1931; s. John Joseph and Elizabeth Ann (McConville) H.; B.B.A., Hofstra U., 1961; postgrad. Union Coll., 1966; m. Nancy Elizabeth Boos, June 16, 1956; children—Kevin, Brian. With Servo Corp. Am., Hicksville, N.Y., 1954-59; planning supr. Mergenthaler Linotype, Plainfield, N.Y., 1959-61; materials control mgr. Lawrence Aviation, Port Jefferson, N.Y., 1961-65; system engr. IBM Corp., White Plains, N.Y., 1965—; cons. Bell Labs., 1971-76. Leader Morris council Boy Scouts Am., 1972-75. Served with U.S. Army, 1952-53. Decorated Bronze Star. Mem. Am. Prodn. and Inventory Control Assn., Am. Numis. Assn., Soc. Philatelists and Numismatists, World Proof Numis. Assn. Club: Moose. Home: 5 Mount Pleasant Rd Newtown CT 06470 Office: 75 S Broadway White Plains NY 10601

HOFER, RICHARD JOSEPH, educator, immunologist; b. Jamaica, N.Y., Dec. 3, 1942; s. Fred Jacob and Mary Anne (Barnes) H.; B.A., Hofstra U., 1965, M.A., 1969. Tchr. sci., Middleville Jr. High Sch., Northport, N.Y., 1969-70; research asst. Waldemar Med. Research Found., Inc., Woodbury, N.Y., 1966-74, research asso., 1974-77; tchr. biology Northport (L.I.) High Sch., 1970—. Mem. Am. Soc. Microbiology, Am. Mus. Natural History, AAAS, N.Y. Acad. Scis., Nat. Sci. Tchrs Assn. Home: 17 Johnson Ct Babylon NY 11702 Office: Northport High School Laurel Hill Rd Northport NY 11768

HOFF, CHARLES WORTHINGTON, III, banker; b. Balt., Mar. 1, 1934; s. Charles Worthington, Jr. and Sarah Durant (Yearley) H.; B.S. in Bus., Johns Hopkins U., 1961; postgrad. Stonier Sch. Banking, 1964-66; m. Margaret Elizabeth Ober, Sept. 7, 1967; children—Zoe Carey, Alexandra Yearley, Juliana Macgill, Margaret Frazier, Charles Worthington, IV. With First Nat. Bank Md., Balt., 1955-77, div. v.p., 1968-77; exec. v.p. Farmers & Mechanics Nat. Bank, Frederick, Md., 1977—; dir. Md. Etching Co., Yankee Engring. Co. Bd. dirs. Md. Children's Aid and Family Service Soc., Balt., 1972-77, exec. com., fin. com., 1974-76; treas. Armagh Village Improvement Assn., 1962; pres. Oriole Advocates, Inc., 1963, treas., 1964-65. Mem. Am. Inst. Banking, Republican. Episcopalian. Clubs: Elkridge, Holly Hills Country, Cap and Gown (Princeton, N.J.); Rotary; Batchelors Cotillion. Home: Route 11 Bootjack Dr Frederick MD 21701 Office: Farmers and Mechanics Nat Bank 2d and Market Sts Frederick MD 21701

HOFF, RICHARD CHARLES, machinery mfg. co. exec.; b. Akron, Ohio, July 13, 1913; s. Garfield Leo and Ida Elizabeth (DeCouvy) H.; A.B., U. Akron, 1936; m. Lillian Jean Alkire, Sept. 6, 1941; children—Richard Garfield, Mary Jo-Anne, Deborah Kathleen. With B.F. Goodrich Co., Akron, 1936-47; with Harris-Intertype Corp., Cleve., 1948-62, dir. personnel devel. and tng.- 1956-62; dir. indsl. relations Frick Co. subs. Internat. Utilities Corp., Waynesboro, Pa., 1964-72; dir. personnel JLG Industries Inc., McConnellsburg, Pa., 1973—; lectr. in field. Mem. personnel practices com. children's council Welfare Fedn. Cleve., 1955-57; chmn. arrangements com., sustaining fund campaign Marymount Hosp., Garfield Heights, Ohio, 1951; active Jr. Achievement, 1958; bd. dirs. Soc. Crippled Children, Franklin County, Pa., Waynesboro Community Chest; bd. dirs., pub. info. officer, vice chmn. Waynesboro chpt. ARC; mem. ofcl. bd. Methodist Ch.; mem. Fulton County Employment and Tng. Advisory Council; lay mem. Fulton County Coop. Edn. Com., McConnellsburg. Served to capt. USAAF, 1942-46. Mem. Cleve. Personnel Assn. (v.p.), Soc. Advancement Mgmt. (dir. chpt.), Am. Mgmt. Assn., Am. Soc. Personnel Adminstrn., Internat. Assn. Bus. Communicators, N.A.M. (mem. labor relations policy com. 1977-79), Bur. Nat. Affairs (mem. personnel policies forum 1977-79), Am. Legion. Republican. Clubs: Gt. Cove Country, Masons, Optimists, Kiwanis, Rotary. Editor Frick Fax, 1964-72, Fulton Ink, 1972-77. Home: 16 N Grant St Waynesboro PA 17268 Office: JLG Industries Inc JLG Dr McConnellsburg PA 17233

HOFF, STUART, real estate developer; b. Bklyn., Sept. 12, 1943; s. Louis and Mabel (Feinstein) H.; B.B.A., Babson Inst. Bus. Adminstrn., 1964; m. Maxine Andrea Boorstein, June 27, 1965; 1 son, Kenneth Reade. Trainee Dun & Bradstreet, N.Y.C., 1964; field accountant Textile Banking Co., N.Y.C., 1965; pres. Buddy Hoff Ins. Agy., owner Realty Mgmt. Co., West New York, N.J., 1966—; pres. Conrep, Inc., Newark, 1972—; pres. Consultants & Developers, Inc., land devel. and real estate syndication, West New York, 1972—; former owner, developer Skye Harbour on the Hudson, North Bergen, N.J.; now dir. real estate ops. Realty Assos., Englewood Cliff, N.J. Mem. Hudson County Assn. Ind. Ins. Agts. (past pres.), Container Activities Mgmt. Orgn. (pres.). Home: Duck Pond Rd Alpine NJ 07620 Office: 560 Sylvan Ave Englewood Cliff NJ 07632

HOFFBERGER, JEROLD CHARLES, brewer; b. Balt., Apr. 7, 1919; s. Samuel H. and Gertrude (Miller) H.; grad. U. Va., 1940; m. Alice Berney, June 10, 1946; children—David B., Richard J., Carol S., Charles P. Pres., dir. Nat. Brewing Co., Balt., 1947-75; chmn. bd. chief exec. officer Carling Nat. Breweries, Inc., Balt., 1975-78; chmn., pres. Divex, Inc., to 1975; dir., chmn. exec. com. Fairchild Industries; dir. BTR Realty, Inc., Real Estate Holding Co., Md. Nat. Bank; chmn. bd. Balt. Orioles. Nat. Officer United Jewish Appeal; bd. dirs. Hoffberger Found., Council Jewish Fedns., Balt. Asso. Jewish Charities and Welfare Fund; dir. Sinai Hosp.; trustee Johns Hopkins Hosp., Balt. Served to capt. U.S. Army, World War II. Mem. U. Va. Alumni Assn., Nat. Steeplechase and Hunt Assn. (past steward), Phi Epsilon Pi. Club: Suburban Country. Home; Sunset Hill Riderwood MD 21139 Office: 36 S Charles St Baltimore MD 21201

HOFFERT, PAUL WASHINGTON, surgeon; b. N.Y.C., Feb. 22, 1923; s. Charles and Rose (Isaacs) H.; B.A. with honors, Columbia, 1942; M.D. cum laude, Yale, 1945; m. Rosolyn Sheiman, Apr. 20, 1947; children—Marvin Jay, Renee Beth, Deborah Susan. Intern, New Haven Hosp., 1945-46; resident U. Pa. Hosp., Phila., 1948-49, VA Hosp., Bronx, 1949-53; practice medicine specializing in gen. and vascular surgery, Yonkers and N.Y.C., 1953—; asst. clin. prof. surgery Albert Einstein Coll. Medicine, N.Y.C., 1955—; asso. in vascular surgery Montefiore Hosp., Bronx, 1965—; attending surgeon Yonkers Gen., St. Joseph's hosps., Yonkers; chief surgery Yonkers Profl. Hosp., 1976—. Served from 1st lt. to capt. M.C., AUS, 1946-48. Recipient citation Am. Cancer Soc., 1960. Diplomate Am. Bd. Surgery. Fellow A.C.S. (pres. Westchester County chpt. 1962), Westchester Acad. Medicine (charter), N.Y. Acad. Medicine, Am. Soc. Abdominal Surgeons; mem. N.Y. Surg. Soc., N.Y. Diabetes Assn., N.Y. Soc. Cardiovascular Surgery, Am. Bd. Abdominal Surgery (founders group), Zionist Orgn. Am. (life mem., past pres. Lincoln Park region Yonkers), Phi Beta Kappa, Alpha Omega Alpha, Phi Delta Epsilon. Contbr. numerous articles to med. jours. Home: 1450 Flagler Dr Mamaroneck NY 10543 Office: 45 Ludlow St Yonkers NY 10705

HOFFMAN, BERNARD, psychiatrist; b. Bklyn., July 8, 1943; s. Simon and Estelle H.; A.B. cum laude, Bklyn. Coll., 1964; M.D., Downstate Med. Center, State U. N.Y., 1968. Intern in medicine and pediatrics Kings County Hosp., N.Y.C., 1968-69, resident in psychiatry, fellow in child psychiatry, 1969-72, fellow in child psychiatry, 1974-75, dir. male adolescent inpatient unit, 1975-76; candidate Downstate Psychoanalytic Inst., N.Y.C., 1972—; practice medicine specializing in child, adolescent, and adult psychiatry, Dix Hills, N.Y.; cons. Sagamore Children's Center, Melville, N.Y., St. Francis School for Deaf, Bklyn., 1976-78. Served as lt. comdr., M.C., USN, 1972-73. Fellow Downstate Med. Center, State U. N.Y., 1972-76. Diplomate Am. Bd. Psychiatry and Neurology with subsplty s. in adult, child and adolescent psychiatry. Mem. Am. Psychiat. Assn., Am. Psychoanalytic Assn., Bklyn. Psychiat. Soc., N.Y. Council Child Psychiatry, Council Advancement of Psychoanalytic Edn., Am. Acad. Child Psychiatry, AAAS. Home and Office: 12 Faulkner Ln Dix Hills NY 11746 also 470 Ocean Ave Brooklyn NY 11226

HOFFMAN, CARL BENTLEY, educator; b. Reading, Pa., Nov. 20, 1922; s. Carl Bentley and Marion Mildred (Snyder) H.; A.B. cum laude, Ursinus Coll., 1943; postgrad. Vanderbilt U., 1943-44; M.A., U. Pa., 1947, M.S., 1956, Ph.D., 1960; m. Doris Mildred Anderson, Dec. 27, 1950; children—Carol (Mrs. Thomas Vail), Bruce Edward. Tchr. pub. schs., Reading, 1945-47; instr. history Muhlenberg Coll., Allentown, Pa., 1947-48; asst. prof. history and govt. Beaver Coll., Glenside, Pa., 1948-51, asso. prof., 1951-53, vis. prof., summers 1961, 62; tchr. Upper Darby (Pa.) Twp. Schs., 1953-57, prin., 1957-63; dir. instrn. Tenafly (N.J.) Pub. schs., 1963-67; asst. supt. Abington (Pa.) Sch. Dist., 1967-69, supt., 1969—. Vis. prof. Rutgers U., summer 1961, Pa. State U., 1961-62, Lehigh U., 1962-63, summer 1963, Paterson State Coll., 1966-67, Evening Div., LaSalle Coll., 1967-69. Bd. dirs. Delaware County Child Guidance Clinic, 1959-63; bd. mgrs. Abington br. YMCA Phila. and Vicinity, 1970—. Served with M.I., AUS, 1943-45. Decorated Bronze Star medal. Mem. Council Ednl. Facility Planners, Am. Assn. Sch. Adminstrs., Assn. for Supervision and Curriculum Devel. (pres. chpt. 1973-74), Phi Delta Kappa. Presbyterian. Mason (32 deg.), Rotarian. Home: 407 Henley Ct Doylestown PA 18901 also 1609 N Riverside Dr Pompano Beach FL 33062 Office: 1841 Susquehanna St Abington PA 19001

HOFFMAN, CHARLES HARRY, utility co. exec.; b. Allentown, Pa., Sept. 5, 1917; s. Harry Frederick and Ruth Virginia (Peabody) H.; B.S., Lehigh U., 1938; M.S., Mass. Inst. Tech., 1939; m. Ora Louise Williams, Apr. 14, 1945; children—Christopher C., Jennifer Hoffman Lee, Emily O. With Pub. Service Electric & Gas Co., Newark, 1940—, sr. v.p. system planning and interconnections, 1977—. Served with USNR, 1942-45. Registered profl. engr., N.J. Fellow IEEE; mem. Phi Beta Kappa, Sigma Xi, Tau Beta Pi, Eta Kappa Nu. Republican. Presbyterian. Club: Essex. Contbr. articles to profl. jours. Office: 80 Park Pl Newark NJ 07101

HOFFMAN, DONALD BROOKS, former county ofcl., bus. exec.; b. Franklin, Pa., Nov. 20, 1911; s. Camilla C. and Hazel (Brooks) H.; Ph.B., Muhlenberg Coll., 1932; M.A., Lehigh U., 1963; LL.D., Otterbein Coll., 1964; m. Margaret Jane Gruber, July 27, 1935; children—Margaret J. (Mrs. Harry Adams), Donald Brooks, Edwin P., William G. Claims mgr. Liberty Mut. Ins. Co., 1934-45; bus. mgr. Phoebe Floral Co., Allentown, Pa., 1945-52; county treas. Lehigh County, Pa., 1952-55, 64-67; with firm Yarnall, Biddle & Co., Allentown, 1955-75; with Janney Montgomery Scott, Allentown, 1975—. Chmn. bd. commrs. Lehigh County, 1968-75. Trustee Muhlenberg Coll., 1963—. Mem. Orgn. Am. Historians, Am., So. hist. assns., County Treas. Assn. Pa. (sec., treas. 1954-71), Pa. Assn. Elected County Ofcls. (sec., treas. 1954-71), Assn. Coll. Honor Socs. (sec.-treas. 1965-75, pres. 1977-79), Pa. Dist. Exchange Clubs (pres. 1978-78, nat. dir.), Phi Alpha Theta (nat. sec.-treas. 1937—). Republican. Mem. United Ch. of Christ. Mason, Odd Fellow. Club: Exchange. Home: 2812 Livingston St Allentown PA 18104

HOFFMAN, ELMER, surgeon, educator; b. Balt., Sept. 5, 1921; s. Harry and Ida (Pressman) H.; A.B., Johns Hopkins U., 1941, M.D., 1944; m. Sherry Koplon, Nov. 15, 1953; children—Jo Anne, Robert Allan, Richard Allan. Intern Sinai Hosp. of Balt., 1944-45, asst. resident in gen. surgery, 1945-46, 48-51, asst. resident in pathology, 1948, resident in gen. surgery, 1951-52; practice medicine specializing in surgery, Balt., 1952—; asst. in surgery Sinai Hosp. of Balt., 1952-54, instr. surgery, 1953-63, adj. attending surgeon 1954-56, asso. attending in surgery, 1957-67, attending surgeon, 1967—, editor-in-chief Sinai Hosp. Jour., 1958-62; asst. surgeon Johns Hopkins Hosp., Balt., 1952-54, surgeon, 1954—; instr. surgery Johns Hopkins U. Sch. of Medicine, Balt., 1958-69, asst. prof. surgery, 1969—; vis. staff Greater Balt. Med. Center, Balt. County Gen. Hosp., South Balt. Gen. Hosp. Served to capt. USAAF, 1946-48. Diplomate Am. Bd. Surgery. Fellow A.C.S., Am. Geriatrics Soc., Am. Med. Writers Assn., Southeastern Surg. Congress; mem. Balt. City, Johns Hopkins med. socs., AMA, So. Med. Assn., Md. Soc. for Med. Research, Med. and Chirurg. Faculty of Md., Phi Beta Kappa. Contbr. numerous articles on surgery to med. jours. Home: 6505 Baythorne Rd Baltimore MD 21209 Office: 15 Walker Ave Baltimore MD 21208

HOFFMAN, IRWIN, cardiologist; b. N.Y.C., Apr. 30, 1925; s. Jacob and Minnie (Goldberg) H.; A.B., Harvard U., 1945; M.D., N.Y. U., 1947; m. Maya Bravy, Nov. 25, 1953; children—John Brill, Annabelle. Intern, Beth Israel Hosp., N.Y.C., 1947-48, resident in pathology, 1948-49, med. resident, 1950-51; resident Goldwater Meml. Hosp., 1949-50; practice medicine, specializing in cardiology, Cedarhurst, N.Y., 1960—; attending physician L.I. Jewish Hillside Med. Center, New Hyde Park, N.Y., 1965; asso. prof. clin. medicine State U. N.Y., Stony Brook, 1970; chief cardiology St. John's Episcopal Hosp., Far Rockaway, N.Y., 1976—. Served to capt. USMC, 1951-53. Diplomate Am. Bd. Internal Medicine. Fellow A.C.P., Am. Coll. Cardiology; mem. Am. Heart Assn., AMA. Jewish. Club: Harvard. Author: XYZ is the ABC of ECG, 1974; editor: VCG, 1965; VCG, 1970; VCG, 1975. Home: 29 Cedarhurst Ave Cedarhurst NY 11516 Office: 123 Grove Ave Cedarhurst NY 11516

HOFFMAN, JOHN ERNEST, JR., lawyer; b. N.Y.C., May 1, 1934; s. John E. and Effe K. (Dooling) H.; grad. Choate Sch., Wallingford, Conn., 1951; A.B. cum laude, Princeton U., 1955; J.D., Harvard U., 1960; m. Jean P. Wheeler, Aug. 13, 1955; children—Jean E., John Ernest, III, Katherine P., Carolyn W., Christine D. Admitted to N.Y. bar, 1961; asso. firm Shearman & Sterling, N.Y.C., 1960-68, partner, 1968—. Served to 1st lt. AUS, 1955-57. Home: 300 Millwood Rd Chappaqua NY 10514 Office: Shearman & Sterling 399 Park Ave New York City NY 10022

HOFFMAN, RALPH EMERSON, JR., researcher, antiquarian book dealer; b. McKeesport, Pa., Nov. 4, 1938; s. Ralph E. and Marie Katherine (Sherer) H.; A.A. cum laude, Robert Morris Coll., 1965; grad. certificate Am. Inst. Banking, Pitts., 1961, Palmer Writers Sch., 1968; m. Beverly J. Hanko, Sept. 4, 1961; children—Gregory Sean, Lisa Marie. Sr. staff auditor Equibank, Pitts., 1960-65; sr. cost accountant Copperweld Steel Co., Glassport, Pa., 1965-68; owner, mgr. Hoffman Research Services, Rillton, Pa., 1968—. Served with USNR, 1956-58. Contbr. articles to popular mags. Home: 7 Howell Dam Rd Rillton PA 15678 Office: PO Box 342 Rillton PA 15678

HOFFMAN, SAUL, plastic surgeon; b. Edmonton, Alta., Can., Feb. 17, 1931; s. Joseph and Gertrude H.; B.S., U. Alta., 1951, M.D., 1955; m. Alice Norma Finkelstein, June 18, 1967; children—Daniel Paul, Jeffrey Michael. Intern, Calgary (Alta., Can.) Gen. Hosp., 1955-56; resident in gen. plastic surgery Brookdale Hosp., Bklyn., 1956-59; resident in plastic surgery Bronx Municipal Hosp. Center, N.Y.C., 1959-61, Mt. Sinai Hosp., N.Y.C., 1959-62, research fellow in plastic surgery, 1962-63, asso. attending surgeon, plastic surgery, prof. surgery; attending surgeon, Beth Israel Hosp.; practice medicine specializing in plastic surgery, N.Y.C. Diplomate Am. Bd. Surgery, Am. Bd. Plastic Surgery. Fellow A.C.S.; mem. AMA, N.Y. County, N.Y. State med. socs., N.Y. Acad. Medicine, Am., N.Y. regional socs. plastic and reconstructive surgeons, Am. Cleft Palate Assn., Am. Soc. Aesthetic Plastic Surgery, Am. Assn. Plastic Surgeons. Contbr. articles in field to profl. publs. U.S., U.K.

HOFFMAN, WILLIAM ANDREW, III, chemist; b. Phila., Aug. 16, 1945; s. William Andrew and Doris May H.; B.S., Fairleigh Dickinson U., 1969; M.S., Stevens Inst. Tech., 1971, Ph.D., 1974; m. Robin-Pegg Schwartz, Dec. 21, 1970; 1 dau., Jennifer Samantha. Applications chemist Celanese Chem. Co., Summit, N.J., 1974-78; prin. chemist Dart Industries, Paramus, N.J., 1978—, group leader, 1978—; adj. asso. prof. Fairleigh Dickinson U., 1972—. Served with USAF, 1963-66. Mem. N.Y. Acad. Scis., Stevens Inst. Tech. Ph.D. Alumni Assn. (past v.p.), Sigma Xi. Conservative. Patentee polyester resins, photochem. and ionizing radiation compositions. Home: 555 Park Ave Paterson NJ 07504 Office: 115 W Century Rd Paramus NJ 07652

HOFFMANN, EVA GOTTSCHALCK, psychologist; b. Hamburg, Germany, July 6, 1913; d. Louis Martin and Anne (Peiser) Gottschalck; B.A. in Psychology, Conn. Coll., 1942; M.A., Columbia U., 1946, postgrad., 1967-69; m. Paul E. Hoffmann, Oct. 23, 1943; children—Beth Anne, Andrew Walter. Personnel clk. Calvert Distilling Co., Relay, Md., 1942-43; sec. to dir. Vocat. Adv. Service, N.Y.C., 1943-44, psychometrist, 1944-47; practice vocat. counseling, 1957-62; psychologist Vocat. Adv. Service, N.Y.C., 1948-62, supr. psychol. services, 1962-66, asst. dir., 1966-70; instr. dept. edn. Herbert H. Lehman Coll., City U. N.Y., Bronx, 1970-73; program coordinator State Project to Implement Career Edn., N.Y.C., 1973-75; mem. faculty Center for N.Y.C. affairs, New Sch. for Social Research, 1975—; career edn. coordinator dept. spl. edn. Tchrs. Coll., Columbia U., N.Y.C., 1976—. Certified psychologist, N.Y. Mem. Am., N.Y. State, N.Y.C. (pres. 1976-77) personnel and guidance assns., Nat. Vocat. Guidance Assn., Am., N.Y. State psychol. assns., Assn. Measurement and Evaluation in Guidance (chmn. ethics com. 1970-72). Author of career edn. manuals, 1975-78; contbr. book revs. on personnel guidance to profl. jours. Home: 523 W 112th St New York City NY 10025 Office: PO Box 209 525 W 120th St New York City NY 10027

HOFFMANN, JOHN J., architect; b. Tapolca, Hungary, Feb. 16, 1947; s. Zoltan and Vilma (Krausz) H.; came to U.S., 1958, naturalized, 1964; m. Susan Katz, Sept. 13, 1970; 1 dau., Alison Beth. Architect-designer Warren H. Ashley, W. Hartford, Conn., 1972, Orr deCossy, Winder & Assos., New Haven, 1972, C.W. Blakeslee and Sons Inc., New Haven, 1972-76; owner, operator John J. Hoffmann & Assos., Architects, Hamden, Conn., 1977—. Certified Nat. Council Archtl. Registration Bds.; registered architect, Conn. Mem. AIA, Conn. Soc. Architects, Constrn. Specifications Inst., Conn. Bldg. Congress, Conn. Bus. and Industry Assn. Home: 865 Mix Ave Hamden CT 06514 Office: 2781 Dixwell Ave Hamden CT 06518

HOFFMANN, KURT RUDOLF, pharm. co. exec.; b. Halle Saale Germany, May 20, 1927; s. Oskar Rudolf and Marie (Leissring) H.; M.D., U. Freiburg, 1953; m. Christine Thomas, May 20, 1953. Staff physician Dr. Karl Thomae, Biberach/Riss, Germany, 1953-57, C. H. Boehringen Sohn, Ingelheim, 1957-58; staff physician Geigy Chem. Corp., Ardsley, N.Y., 1958-63, dir. clin. research, 1963-71; v.p. med. affairs Boehringer Ingelheim Ltd., Elmsford, N.Y., 1971—, also officer. Mem. AMA, N.Y. Acad. Scis., Am. Soc. Clin. Pharmacology and Therapeutics. Author: (with Giusti and Hoffmann) The Human Heart, 1960. Home: 11 Whippoorwill Rd Armonk NY 10504 also PO Box 162 Candlewood Isle New Fairfield CT 06810 Office: 90 E Ridge Rd PO Box 368 Ridgefield CT 06877

HOFFMANN, RALF LUDWIG, chem. co. exec.; b. Berlin, Germany, Oct. 4, 1910; s. Ludwig and Marie (Weisbach) H.; grad. high sch.; m. Ingeborg Seepacher, Nov. 30, 1946; 1 son, Christopher S.L. Chmn. Canadian Hoechst, Ltd.; v.p., dir. Trans-Am. Chems., Ltd., 1958—; dir. Hoechst Industries, Ltd., Montreal, Que., Can., 1963—; dir. SKW Electro Metallurgy Can. Ltd. Mem. Can. Inst. Internat. Affairs, Soc. Chem. Industry, Can. Chem. Producers Assn., Gen. Council Industry Que. Club: Saint James. Home: 2095 Hanover Rd Mount Royal PQ H3R 2X5 Canada Office: 4045 Cote Vertu St Laurent Montreal H4R 1R6 PQ Canada

HOFFMEISTER, F. STANLEY, surgeon; b. Prague, Czechoslovakia, Nov. 8, 1914; s. Ferdinand Kamila (Steklova) H.; came to U.S. 1947, naturalized, 1954; M.D., Charles U., 1939; m. Jana Marie Pechacek, Dec. 23, 1973; children—Peter, Paul. Intern, Univ. Hosp., Prague, 1939-40, jr. asst. resident, 1942-43, sr. asst. resident, 1943-44, chief resident in surgery, 1944-45; asst. resident in surgery Hosp. St. Barnabas, Newark, 1950-51; asst. resident in plastic surgery, Nat. Cancer Inst. trainee Johns Hopkins Hosp., Balt., 1952-53, chief resident, 1953-54; asso. chief head, neck and reconstructive surgery Roswell Park Meml. Inst., Buffalo, 1954-56, chief dept. reconstructive, head and neck surgery, 1956-67; practice medicine specializing in plastic surgery, Albany, N.Y., 1967—; attending plastic surgeon Albany Med Center, St. Peters Hosp., Children's Hosp., Meml. Hosp., VA Hosp.; asso. clin. prof. plastic surgery Albany Med. Coll., 1967-76, clin. prof., 1977—. Diplomate Am. Bd. Surgery. Fellow A.C.S.; mem. AMA, Am. Assn. Plastic Surgeons, Soc. Head and Neck Surgeons, Am. Soc. Plastic and Reconstructive Surgeons, Plastic Surgery Research Council, Am. Trauma Soc., Am. Soc. Maxillofacial Surgery. Office: 1465 Western Ave Albany NY 12203

HOFFNER, HERBERT HOWARD, ophthalmologist; b. N.Y.C., Aug. 27, 1933; s. Louis and Mildred (Stein) H.; A.B. cum laude, Clark U., 1955; M.D. cum laude, Tufts U., 1959; m. Elinor Beth Caplan, July 14, 1957; children—Eileen Susan, Linda Nancy, Paul Steven. Rotating intern Montefiore Hosp., Bronx, 1959-60; resident in ophthalmology Bronx Municipal Hosp.-Einstein Med. Coll., N.Y.C., 1960-63; practice medicine specializing in ophthalmology, Far Rockaway, N.Y., 1963—; asst. attending Bronx Municipal Hosp. Center, 1963-75, clinic chief, 1971-72; asst. attending ophthalmologist S. Shore div. L.I. Jewish Hosp., 1963—; dir. ophthalmology Peninsula Hosp. Center, Far Rockaway, 1972—. Regional chmn. Tufts ann. fund, 1973-75; alumni council Clark U., 1973—, trustee, 1976—. Diplomate Am. Bd. Ophthalmology, Nat. Bd. Med. Examiners. Fellow A.C.S., Am. Acad. Ophthalmology and Otolaryngology, Royal Soc. Health; mem. Royal Coll. Medicine (affiliate), AMA, Am. Soc. Contemporary Ophthalmology, N.Y. State, Rockaway med. socs., N.Y. State, L.I. ophthalmol. socs., N.Y. Soc. Clin. Ophthalmology, Internat. Corr. Soc. Ophthalmology, Am. Assn. Ophthalmology, Clark Alumni Assn. (meritorious service award 1975), Phi Beta Kappa, Alpha Omega Alpha. Clubs: L.I. Tufts, Tufts Millenium. Home: 200 Hollywood Crossing Lawrence NY 11559 Office: 18-15 Cornaga Ave Far Rockaway NY 11691

HOFFNER, MARILYN, univ. ofcl., designer; b. N.Y.C., Nov. 16, 1927; d. Daniel and Elsie (Schulz) H.; grad. Cooper Union; m. Albert Greenberg, May 29, 1949; children—Doren Roe, Peter Cooper. Art dir. Printers' Ink mag., N.Y.C., 1953-63; art dir. Print mag., N.Y.C., 1960-62; corporate art dir. Vision, Inc., Mexico, Brazil, and London, 1963-75; dir. alumni relations Cooper Union, 1975—. Bd. dirs. N.Y. Art Dirs. Club Scholarship Fund, 1963-74, exec. treas., 1971-74. Named Alumnus of Year Cooper Union, 1968. Mem. Cooper Union Alumni Council (editor-in-chief 1971-74, 1st v.p. 1974-75), Art Dirs. Club N.Y. (exec. bd. 1973-74, exec. sec. bd., 1973-75, Gold medal 1978), Type Dirs. Club (awards). Contbg. editor Print mag., 1960-62, Art Direction, 1959-64, Graphic mag., 1959-65. Home: 51 Fifth Ave New York City NY 10003 Office: 41 Cooper Sq New York City NY 10003

HOFFSTATTER, EDWARD WILLIAM, JR., bus. exec.; b. Milw., May 18, 1931; s. Edward W. and Audry F. (Davis) H.; B.S., Rutgers U., 1954, M.B.A., 1958; m. Judy A. Danielsen, May 21, 1961; 1 son, Edward W. Mgr. by-product sales Amax, Inc., N.Y.C., 1956-70; sr. v.p. Sharps Pixley, Inc., N.Y.C., 1970—; dir. Commodity Exchange, Inc.; v.p., dir. Comex Metal Clearing Assn.; mem. Chgo. Bd. Trade, N.Y. Mercantile Exchange. Served with U.S. Army, 1954-56. Mem. Am. Inst. Mining Engrs., Kappa Sigma. Home: 123 Deer Run Rd Wilton CT 06897 Office: Sharps Pixley Inc 100 Wall St New York City NY 10005

HOFFSTEIN, HERBERT, dentist; b. N.Y.C., Jan. 24, 1928; s. Max and Flora (Lichtenstein) H.; B.A., N.Y. U., 1950; D.D.S., N.Y. U., 1955; m. Myra Jacobs, Feb. 28, 1976. Intern oral surgery Mt. Sinai Hosp., N.Y.C., 1955-56; pvt. practice dentistry, N.Y.C., 1956—; mem. staff Mt. Sinai Hosp., Park West Hosp., N.Y.C., instr. celestial nav. N.Y. Power Squadron, adminstrv. officer, 1969-71, exec. officer, 1971-73, comdr., 1973-75. Served with AUS, 1945-47. Mem. 1st Dist. Dental Soc. (lectr. oral pathology 1970—), Acad. Gen. Dentistry, Inst. Clin. Oral Pathology, Omicron Kappa Upsilon, Beta Lambda Sigma, Mu Chi Sigma. Clubs: Doctors' Gun, N, Century. Home: 74 W 68th St New York City NY 10023 Office: 74 W 68th St New York City NY 10023

HOFFSTOT, HENRY PHIPPS, JR., lawyer; b. Pitts., Nov. 13, 1917; s. Henry Phipps and Marguerite (Martin) H.; A.B., Harvard U., 1939, LL.B., 1942; m. Barbara Drew, Apr. 17, 1948; children—Thayer Drew Hoffstot Unterman, Henry Phipps, III. Admitted to Pa. bar, 1942; asso. firm Reed, Smith, Shaw & McClay, Pitts., 1946-55, partner, 1956—; pres., dir. Pennsgrove Water Supply Co. Active Commn. for Study of Common Body of Knowledge for C.P.A.'s, N.Y., 1965-67, Nat. Parks Centennial Commn., 1971-73; trustee Carnegie Library, Pitts., 1966—, v.p., 1970—; trustee Carnegie Inst., 1966—, sec., 1968—; trustee Family and Children's Service, 1962-68, 69-75, pres., 1964-66; trustee Pitts. Regional Library Center, 1967—; trustee St. Edmunds Acad., 1964-72, pres., 1968-70; bd. dirs. Community Chest of Allegheny County, 1962-68, mem. exec. com., 1968-69; bd. dirs. Mendelssohn Choir, Pitts., 1958—, treas., 1959-61; bd. dirs. Pitts. Chamber Music Soc., 1968—; bd. dirs. Vis. Nurse Assn. of Allegheny County, 1948—, pres., 1957-60, 66-67. Served with inf. AUS, 1942-46. Fellow Am. Bar Found.; mem. Am., Pa., Allegheny County bar assns., Am. Coll. Probate Counsel, Am. Law Inst. Home: 5057 5th Ave Pittsburgh PA 15232 Office: PO Box 2009 Pittsburgh PA 15230

HOFKIN, GERALD ALAN, gastroenterologist; b. Balt., July 4, 1936; s. Samuel and Sarah (Chertkof) H.; B.A., Johns Hopkins U., 1957, M.A., 1957; M.D., U. Md., 1961; m. Phyllis G. Cohen, Aug. 23, 1959; children—Leah A., Stephen L., Karen E. Intern, U. Md. Hosp., 1961-62, jr. asst. resident in medicine, 1962-63, asso. resident in medicine, 1964-65; sr. asst. resident in medicine Sinai Hosp., Balt., 1963-64, chief resident in medicine, 1965-66, mem. staff, 1969—, dir. gastrointestinal diagnostic lab., 1975—; resident in gastroenterology Letterman Gen. Hosp., San Francisco, 1966-67; practice medicine specializing in gastroenterology, Balt., 1969—; mem. staff Franklin Sq. Hosp., 1972—, chief gastroenterology, 1973—; asst. prof. medicine Sch. Medicine, U. Md., 1975—. Mem. health and instnl. services com. of bd. dirs. Asso. Jewish Charities and Welfare Fund, Balt., 1977—; trustee Har Sinai Congregation, 1978—. Served to maj. U.S. Army, 1966-69. Decorated Army Commendation medal. Diplomate Am. Bd. Internal Medicine. Macy Found. fellow, 1958, 59. Fellow A.C.P., Am. Coll. Gastroenterology; mem. Am. Soc. Internal Medicine, Am. Soc. Gastrointestinal Endoscopy (chmn. program com. 1977—), Md. Soc. Gastrointestinal Endoscopy, Med. and Chirurg. Faculty Md. (physician-patient relations com.), Balt. City Med. Soc., Am. Gastroent. Assn., Am. Radio Relay League, Balt. Amateur Radio Club, Balt. Radio Amateur TV Soc., Alpha Omega Alpha. Club: Stoneybrook Swim (dir. 1975-77, v.p. 1977). Office: 2435 W Belvedere Ave Baltimore MD 21215

HOFMANN, FREDERICK JOSEPH, civil engr.; b. Newark, Jan. 28, 1937; s. John Ludwig and Margaret Mary (Farrell) H.; B.S., Newark Coll. Engring., 1959; m. Mary Dominica Barry, May 20, 1961; children—Michael, Robert, Daniel, Kathleen Ann. Cons. engr., asso. Edwards and Kelcey Inc., Newark, 1962-64, 68-78, Mpls., 1964-67, São Paulo, Brazil, 1967-68, Livingston, N.J., 1978—. Mem. Bernards Twp. Recreation Com., 1976—; mem. troop com. Boy Scouts Am., 1977—; class coordinator St James Roman Cath. Ch. Confraternity of Christian Doctrine, 1977-78, lector, 1974—; active Little League, 1970-73; bd. dirs. Bernardsville (N.J.) YMCA, 1972. Served as meteorologist USAF, 1959-62. Registered profl. engr., N.J., Minn. Mem. ASCE, Nat. Soc. Profl. Engrs., N.J. Alliance Action, Internat. Bridge Tunnel and Turnpike Assn. Democrat. Home: Box 169B Lyons Rd Basking Ridge NJ 07920 Office: 70 S Orange Ave Livingston NJ 07039

HOFMANN, P. STEPHEN, accountant; b. Concord, N.H., Sept. 10, 1945; s. Paul L. and Martha E. (Hildreth) H.; A.A., Burdett Coll., 1966; B.S., Suffolk U., 1968; M.B.A., N.H. Coll., 1976; m. Susan L. Johnson, Aug. 26, 1967; children—Stephanie Beth, Jefferson Paul. Staff auditor, Price Waterhouse & Co., N.Y.C., 1968, sr. auditor, 1970-71; mgr. gen. accounting Northeast Electronics, Concord, 1971—. Vice pres., dir. Factory Paint & Wallpaper, Inc., Concord, 1975-76. Served with AUS, 1968-70; Vietnam. Mem. Nat. Assn. Accountants, Am. Accounting Assn., Greater Concord C. of C. (dir. 1977-78). Mem. United Ch. Christ. Club: Lamplighters. Home: Oak Hill Rd Concord NH 03301 Office: Riverside Dr Contoocook NH 03229

HOFMAR, DONALD BERNARD, advt. exec.; b. Buffalo, May 4, 1929; s. Bernard Michael and Bertha May H.; B.A., U. Buffalo, 1951; m. Joyce May Campbell, Oct. 22, 1955; children—Laura Alison, Gail Elisabeth. With Gen. Electric Co., 1954-55; pres. Bell Mar Reps., Inc., Eggertsville, N.Y., 1967—. Trustee Parkside Lutheran Ch., Calasanctius Sch.; bd. dirs. St. Johns Lutheran Home. Mem. Am. Mktg. Assn. (pres.), Assn. Indsl. Advertisers. Conservative. Clubs: Buffalo Trap and Field, Aero of Buffalo. Address: 365 Brantwood Rd Eggertsville NY 14226

HOGAN, ALICE HAMILTON, author, educator, editor; b. New Haven; d. John Joseph and Mary (Gormley) Hogan; B.S., Tchrs. Coll. Columbia U., 1932; M.A., Radcliffe Coll., 1942; spl. student Yale U. Free-lance short story writer nat. mags., anthologies, 1950—; teacher English, James E. Hillhouse High Sch., New Haven, 1938-61, chmn. dept. English, 1961-71; lectr. So. Conn. State Coll., 1971—; writer paperback intros. Airmont Pub. Co.; editor War of the Worlds. Recipient Christopher Lit. award for short story in Saturday Evening Post, 1956. Mem. Nat., Conn. edn. assns., AAUW, N.E. Assn. English Tchrs., League Women Voters, Authors Guild, Authors League Am., Internat. Platform Assn. Roman Catholic. Club: Radcliffe Coll. of New Haven. Home: 49 Osborn Ave New Haven CT 06511

HOGAN, CHARLES CARLTON, psychiatrist, psychoanalyst; b. Quincy, Ill., Oct. 5, 1921; s. Carlton Monta and Maryanne (Henry) H.; student Bradley U., 1939-41, U. Ill., 1941-42; M.D., Columbia U., 1945, D.Med.Sci., 1952; m. Nina Harriet Redman, May 23, 1959; children—Matthew Paul, Carlton Henry, Noelle Nina. Intern, Phila. Gen. Hosp., 1945-46; candidate Psychoanalytic Clinic Tng. and Research, Columbia U., 1948-52, asst. psychoanalyst, 1952-57, research asst. dept. neurology, 1948-49; resident in psychiatry N.Y. State Psychiat. Inst., N.Y.C., 1949-50; asso. in psychiatry Columbia U., N.Y.C., 1950-60; attending psychiatrist Presbyn. Hosp., N.Y.C., 1950-60; asst. vis. psychiatrist Bronx (N.Y.) Municipal Hosp., 1960—; asst. clin. prof. psychiatry Albert Einstein Coll. Medicine, Bronx, 1960—; practice medicine specializing in psychiatry and psychoanalysis, N.Y.C., 1952—. Chmn. profl. adv. com. Riverdale Mental Health Assn., 1968—. Served to capt. M.C., U.S. Army, 1946-48. Diplomate Am. Bd. Psychiatry and Neurology. Fellow Am. Psychiat. Assn., Am. Psychoanalytic Assn.; mem. AMA, Assn. Psychoanalytic Medicine, N.Y. Acad. Scis., AAAS, World Fedn. Mental Health, Pan Am. Med. Assn., Am. Psychosomatic Soc., Am. Inst. Archaeology. Clubs: Riverdale Yacht, Huguenot Yacht. Home: 6 Ploughman's Bush Riverdale NY 10471 Office: 1143 Fifth Ave New York City NY 10028

HOGAN, DANIEL EDWARD, sch. librarian; b. Brownville, Maine, Aug. 30, 1931; s. Daniel Earle and Thelma Mary (Milbery) H.; student St. Jerome's Coll., Kitchener, Ont., Can., 1949-50, Farmington (Maine) Coll., 1950-52; B.S. in Edn., Boston U., 1957; M.Ed., Bridgewater (Mass.) State Coll., 1973. Tchr. high sch., Brownville, 1956-60; librarian Morse High Sch., Bath, Maine, 1960-61; librarian, dir. sch. media services Medfield (Mass.) Pub. Sch., 1961—. Instr. library sci. Bridgewater (Mass.) State Coll., 1971-72. Served with AUS, 1952-55. Mem. N.E.A., A.L.A., Am. Assn. Sch. Librarians. Home: 4 Meade Ave Medfield MA 02052

HOGAN, JAMES CARROLL, JR., cell biologist; b. Milledgeville, Ga., Jan. 3, 1939; s. James Carroll and Leanna (Johnson) H.; student Morehouse Coll., 1955-59; B.S., Albany State Coll., 1961; M.S., Atlanta U., 1968; Ph.D., Brown U., 1972; m. Izola Stinson, Nov. 29, 1959; children—Pamela R., Gregory K., Jeffrey D. Tchr., Hancock County (Ga.) Bd. Edn., 1961-66; tchr. pub. schs., Atlanta, 1967-68; instr. Atlanta U., 1968; postdoctoral fellow in biology Yale U., 1972-73, research asso. Sch. Medicine, 1973-76; asst. prof. Howard U. Coll. Medicine, 1976-78; dir. health sci. cluster program and asst. prof. biology U. Conn., Storrs, 1978—. Chmn. R.I. Com. Sickle Cell Disease, 1971-72. Macy scholar Marine Biol. Lab., Woods Hole, Mass., summer 1978. Mem. AAAS, Am. Inst. Biol. Sci., Soc. Devel. Biology, Am. Soc. Cell Biology, Electron Microscopy Soc. Am., Soc. Protozoologists, Omega Psi Phi. Democrat. Baptist. Contbr. articles to profl. jours. Home: 51 Pool Rd North Haven CT 06473 Office: U Conn Storrs CT 06268

HOGAN, JAMES JOHN, bishop; b. Phila. Oct. 17, 1911; s. James F. and Mary E. (Molloy) H.; B.A., St. Mary's Sem., Balt., 1934; S.T.L., Gregorian U., Rome, Italy, 1938; J.C.D., Cath. U. Am., 1941. Ordained priest Roman Cath. Ch., 1937; diocesan ofcl. and consultor Diocese of Trenton, N.J., chancellor of diocese, auxiliary bishop of Trenton; pastor St. Catharine's Ch., Spring Lake, N.J.; now bishop Diocese of Altoona, Johnstown, Pa., 1966—. Home: Logan Blvd and Sylvan Hills Dr Hollidaysburg PA 16648 Office: 1406 12th Ave Altoona PA 16601

HOGAN, JOSEPH LLOYD, clergyman; b. Lima, N.Y., Mar. 11, 1916; s. Michael C. and Mary (Shaw) H.; student St. Andrew's Sem., 1934-36, St. Bernard's Sem., 1936-42; M.A., Canisius Coll., 1949; S.T.D., Pontifical U. Angelicum, Rome, 1951. Ordained priest Roman Catholic Ch.; asst. St. Mary's Ch., Elmira, 1942-45; tchr. Latin, social studies St. Andrew's Sem., 1945-49, instr. Latin, religion, 1951-53; prin. DeSales High Sch., Geneva, N.Y., 1953-55; prof. fundamental dogma, catechetics, dean studies St. Bernard's Sem., 1955-65; prof. theology St. John Fisher Coll., prof. ascetical theology Sisters St. Joseph Novitiate, 1955-65; first rector Becket Hall, 1965-67; pastor St. Margaret Mary Ch., Irondequoit, 1968; bishop Rochester, N.Y., 1969—. Named Right Reverend Monsignor, 1966. Office: 1150 Buffalo Rd Rochester NY 14624

HOGAN, ROBERT JOSEPH, state ofcl.; b. Troy, N.Y., Sept. 4, 1933; s. Frank J. and Jane M. (Barbeau) H.; A.B., N.Y. State U. at Albany, 1961; m. Joan V. Hogan, May 8, 1954; children—Carol Jane, Sean Michael, Christopher Andrew. Personnel technician N.Y. State Dept. Civil Service, 1961-65; exec. sec. N.Y. State Personnel Council, 1965-66; chief of recruitment N.Y. State Dept. Health, 1966-67; asst. exec. dir. N.Y. State Bd. Equalization and Assessment, 1967-70; dir. adminstv. adjudication N.Y. State Dept. Motor Vehicles, Albany, 1970-78, dep. commr., 1978—; exec. dir. N.Y. Gov.'s Traffic Safety Commn., 1978—; cons. various contractors. Served with USN, 1952-55. Mem. Am. Soc. Pub. Adminstr., DAV. Roman Catholic. Clubs: Elks; Ancient Order Hibernians. Home: 1059 Palazini Dr Schenectady NY 12303 Office: Empire State Plaza Albany NY 12238*

HOGAN, V(INCENT) MICHAEL, plastic surgeon; b. Newark, Sept. 3, 1930; s. Vincent Michael and Jessie H.; A.B., Princeton U., 1952; M.D., Columbia U., 1956; m. Margo McKendry, Feb. 7, 1963; children—Justin, Fiona. Surg. intern St. Luke Hosp., N.Y.C., 1956-57, resident, 1960-62; resident in surgery N.Y. Hosp., N.Y.C., 1962-63, resident in plastic surgery, 1963-65; Marks fellow in plastic surgery Queen Victoria Hosp., East Grinstead, Eng., 1965; practice medicine specializing in plastic surgery, N.Y.C., 1966—; attending surgeon Manhattan Eye, Ear & Throat Hosp., N.Y.C.; asso. attending surgeon Bellevue Hosp., N.Y.C.; asso. prof. clin. surgery, asso. attending surgeon Univ. Hosp., N.Y.C.; cons. Manhattan VA Hosp., New York Eye and Ear Infirmary; asst. clin. prof. dentistry N.Y. U. Dental Sch. Served to lt. M.C., USNR, 1957-60. Fellow A.C.S.; mem. AMA, N.Y. Acad. Medicine, New York County Med. Soc., N.Y. Regional Soc. Plastic and Reconstructive Surgery, Am. Cleft Palate Assn., Am. Maxillo-Facial Soc., Am. Soc. Aesthetic Plastic Surgery, Am. Assn. Plastic and Reconstructive Surgery. Clubs: Princeton, River (N.Y.C.). Contbr. articles to med. jours. Office: 799 Park Ave New York City NY 10021

HOGAN, WILLIAM JOSEPH, bus. exec.; b. Boston, Oct. 30, 1915; s. William Patrick and Marion Ann (Elliotte) H.; B.S.E.E., Phoenix U., 1948; B.A., George Washington U., 1953, LL.B., 1957; m. Frances

Henderson Hogan, Feb. 28, 1942; children—Marion A., William P., Cecilia A., Deborah J., Katherine A. With Bell Labs., Western Electric Co., CIA, 1945-51; served with U.S. Air Force, 1945, advanced through grades to col., 1960; ret., 1961; with Raytheon Co., Arlington, Va., 1961—, dir. internat. activities, 1970—. Mem. Republican Nat. Com., 1975—, mem. Nat. Congl. com., 1976; mem. Presdl. Council Tariffs and Trade. Served with U.S. Army, 1938-45. Decorated Air medal, Bronze Star, and others. Mem. IEEE, Inst. Elec. Electronics Engrs., Aerospace Industry Assn., Nat. Security Assn., Armed Forces Def. Preparedness Assn., Electronics Industry Assn., Am. Mgmt. Assn., N.A.M., Soc. Indsl. Realtors, Nat. Foreign Trade Council, Air Force Assn. Roman Catholic. Clubs: Elephant, Nat. Aviation, U.S. Ret. Officers. De La Brooke Foxhounds, Lions. Home: 8 S Van Dorn St Alexandria VA 22304 Office: Raytheon Co 400 Army Navy Dr Arlington VA 22202

HOGBERG, CARL GUSTAV, ret. steel co. exec.; b. Escanaba, Mich., July 19, 1913; s. Claus Emil and Anna C. (Franson) H.; B.S. in Metall. Engring., Mich. Coll. Mining and Tech., 1935; m. June Loraine Evans, June 10, 1935; children—David K., Janet H. (Mrs. Nicholas A. Matwiyoff). Blast-furnace apprentice South Chicago works, Carnegie-Ill. Steel Corp., 1935, various operating positions blast-furnace dept., 1935-39, sec. blast-furnace and coke-oven com., Pitts., 1939-41; asst. chmn. blast-furnace com. U.S. Steel Corp., Pitts., 1942-54, asst. to v.p. Mich. Limestone div., Detroit, 1955, asst. v.p., 1956, v.p., 1957-60, pres., 1960-63, v.p. raw materials service, parent co., 1964, pres. Orinoco Mining Co. subsidiary, Caracas, Venezuela, 1965-70, v.p. internat. U.S. Steel Corp., 1970-73. Mem. Am. Inst. Mining, Metall. and Petroleum Engrs. (J.E. Johnson, Jr. award 1945), Assn. Iron and Steel Engrs. (Kelly award 1950), Am. Iron and Steel Inst., Eastern Western States Blast Furnace and Coke Assns. Contbr. tech. articles trade publs. Home: 26 Captains Cove Ln North Chatham MA 02650

HOGE, WAYNE EUGENE, banker; b. West Alexander, Pa., Mar. 10, 1928; s. Morgan Tilton and Flora May (Booth) H.; B.S., Waynesburg Coll., 1952; m. Louise Ankrum, Aug. 30, 1952; children—Jeffrey Clay, Mark Lowell. Adminstrv. asst. Martin Marietta Corp., Valley Forge, Pa., 1952-65; with Am. Bank & Trust Co. Pa., Reading, 1966—, v.p., 1974—. Mem. ops. advisory bd. Nat. Bank Americard, Inc., San Francisco, 1976—. Mem. clk. of session Presbyterian Ch., East Earl, Pa., 1972—. Served with AUS, 1946-48. Mem. Berks County Credit Men's Assn., Berks County Hist. Soc. Clubs: Masons, Kiwanis (pres. 1975-76). Home: New Holland Rd Bowmansville PA 17507 Office: PO Box 478 Reading PA 19603

HOGENAUER, ALAN KRAHE, air transport economist, aviation cons.; b. N.Y.C., Sept. 17, 1941; s. Nelson Julian and Laura Mathilde (Krahe) H.; A.B., Hunter Coll., 1962; M.A., Columbia, 1968, Ph.D., 1975; m. Sarah Jane Pabst, June 26, 1965; children—Laura Margaret, William Nelson. Accounting supr. N.Y. Telephone Co., N.Y.C., 1962-64; air freight researcher Trans-Australia Airlines, Melbourne and Darwin, Australia, also Papua-New Guinea, 1965-66; airport planner R. Dixon Speas Assos., Manhasset, N.Y., 1967-68, resident mgr., Bogota, Colombia, 1968-69, airport planner, mgr. info. systems, environ. planning, Manhasset, 1969-75; air transp. researcher, East Africa, 1973-75; air transport economist, cons. UN/Internat. Civil Aviation Orgn., 1975; mgr. internat. passenger strategy planning, mgr. market research, dir. market research and planning Trans-World Airlines, N.Y.C., 1975—; chmn. IFS Task Force, Internat. Air Transport Assn., 1978; lectr. Australian Outback; founder, chmn. Darien Gap Assos. Mem.-at-large Community Chest of Port Washington, 1977—. Mem. Am. Geog. Soc., Assn. Am. Geographers. Club: Travellers' Century. Author: Around the World in 80 Ways, 1968; Air Freight Patterns and Prospects in Australia Under the Dual Airline Policy, 1968; An Aviation Firm Catalogs Its Special Collection, 1971; Air Transport Patterns and Prospects in the East African Community, 1975. Contbr. articles to profl. jours. Developer aviation mgmt. info. systems; compiler travel lists. Home: 74 Fairview Ave Port Washington NY 11050 Office: 605 3d Ave New York City NY 10016

HOGENSON, ROBERT CHARLES, composer, musical theorist; b. Kirksville, Mo., Nov. 22, 1936; s. Julius Lee and Daisy B. H.; B.S. Ed., N.E. Mo. State U., 1958; Mus. M., La. State U., 1960; Ph.D. (univ. fellow), Mich. State U., 1967; m. Evelyn Claire Utting, Nov. 24, 1962; children—Jan Ellen, Lynn Elise. Asso. prof. music S.W. Tex. State U., 1962-68; faculty U. Del., 1968—, asso. prof., 1978—, coordinator theory-composition and music lit., 1978—; compositions for band, piano and voice include: Quartal Jaunt, 1967, O.C. 309, 1968, Prelude and Fugue, 1974, Moore's Creek Bridge, 1978. U. Del. grantee, 1978. Mem. AAUP, Del. Music Tchrs. Assn. Presbyterian. Office: U Del Music Dept Newark DE 19711

HOGG, WILBUR EMORY, bishop; b. Balt., Aug. 28, 1916; s. Wilbur Emory and Ida May (Spath) H.; A.B., Brown U., 1938; Th.B., Phila. Div. Sch., 1941; D.D., Gen. Theol. Sem., 1977; m. Lota Winchell Curtiss, Sept. 5, 1948. Ordained priest Episcopal Ch., 1941, bishop, 1974; curate St. Marys Ch., Burlington, N.J., 1941-42, rector, 1943-50; priest-in-charge Ch. of the Advent, 1942-43; fellow, tutor Gen. Theol. Sem., N.Y.C., 1953-54; rector Ch. of St. Mary the Virgin, Falmouth, Maine, 1954-68; dean Cathedral of St. Luke, Portland, Maine, 1968-73; bishop of Albany, N.Y., 1974—. Served as chaplain U.S. Army, 1945-47, 51-53. Fellow Coll. of Preachers, Washington, 1964. Club: Ft. Orange (Albany). Home: 107 Menand Rd Albany NY 12204

HOGUET, DAVID DILWORTH, diversified co. exec.; b. Sharon, Conn., Aug. 16, 1951; s. Joseph Lynch and Diana (Wantz) D.; B.A., U. Pa., 1973; M.B.A., N.Y. U., 1975. With corp. fin. dept., then asst. v.p. restaurant group W.R. Grace & Co., N.Y.C., 1975-78, dep. mgr. ACD div., 1978—. Recipient Marcus Nadler key N.Y. U., 1976. Mem. Am. Mgmt. Assn., Beta Gamma Sigma. Club: Meadow (Southampton, N.Y.). Home: 47 E 64th St New York NY 10021 Office: 1114 Ave of the Americas New York NY 10036

HOHAUSER, SANFORD MORTIMER, investment adviser, indsl. designer; b. N.Y.C., Sept. 17, 1931; s. William and Diana (Arno) H.; B.Arch., Pratt Inst., 1953, postgrad., 1953; postgrad. Yale U., 1955; m. Marilyn Boos, May 2, 1959; children—William, Carol, and Sanford. Designer with William I Hohauser, Inc., 1947-52, project supr., 1952-57; pvt. architect practice, 1956-65; pres. House Mart Community Builders, 1955-56, Hohauser Asso., Inc., 1958-60; asso. Hohauser-D'Amelio, 1960-64; investment adviser, 1966—; v.p., treas. Gould's Position stock market letter, 1966; pres. Rating the Services, stock market statistical service, 1968—; v.p. Line Realty Co.; dir. Palisade Terrace Apts., Inc. Recipient 1st prize Bklyn. AIA Sch. competition, 1951; 2d prize Cowboy Hall of Fame and Nat. Mus. Competition, 1957; others; Municipal Art Soc. Profl. fellowships; Rome prize fellowship, 1958, Pratt fellowship, 1953. Mem. N.Y. Times Forum. Clubs: Nat. Arts, Nat. Realty. Author, illustrator books in field. Home: 42 E 65th St New York City NY 10021 Office: 1 Union Sq New York City NY 10003

HOHENSEE, EDWARD WILLIAM, ophthalmologist; b. Buffalo, Apr. 5, 1929; s. Edwin C. and Florence M. (Yaeger) H.; M.D., U. Buffalo, 1954; m. Elaine Ferguson, June 12, 1954; children—Helene, William Thomas, James, Jane, Teresa, Paul, Martin. Intern, Mercy Hosp., Buffalo, 1954-55; resident in ophthalmology E.J. Meyer Meml. Hosp., Buffalo, 1960-63, vol. staff rep., 1974—; practice gen. medicine, West Seneca, N.Y., 1957-60, specializing in ophthalmology, 1963—; practice medicine specializing in ophthalmology, 1963—; clin. asst. prof. ophthalmology State U. N.Y. at Buffalo, 1973—. Chmn. West Seneca br. ARC, 1961-63; bd. dirs. Better Vision Inst. Served as surgeon Div. Indian Health, USPHS, 1955-57. Mem. AMA, Am. Acad. Ophthalmology, Pan Am., Am. assns. ophthalmolgoy, N.Y. State Ophthalmol. Soc., Buffalo Ophthalmologic Club (pres. 1978-80), N.Y. State, Erie County med. socs. Conservative. Roman Catholic. Home: 43 Esther Dr East Aurora NY 14052 Office: 7531 Seneca St East Aurora NY 14052

HOHL, JEFFREY RANDOLPH, sales mgr.; b. St. Louis, Feb. 9, 1946; s. Clarence Leonard and Rebecca Rose (Leddy) H., Jr.; B.A. in Psychology, Sacred Heart U., 1968; m. Raeanne Monsky, June 15, 1968; 1 son, Timothy Shane. Guidance counselor Notre Dame Boys High Sch., Bridgeport, Conn., 1968-69; field service rep. Weatherhead Co., Milford, Conn., 1971, dist. sales mgr., 1971-77, zone mgr., 1977-78, regional mgr., 1978—. Class rep. Sacred Heart U. Alumni Council, Bridgeport, 1975—, v.p., 1976—. Served with U.S. Army, 1969-71. Decorated Army Commendation with cluster, Viet Nam Service medal; recipient Golden Saddle citation Weatherhead Co., 1975; Outstanding Sr. award Sigma Eta Upsilon, 1968. Roman Catholic. Home: 1065 Naugatuck Ave Milford CT 06460 Office: 300 E 131st St Cleveland OH 44108

HOHMANN, THOMAS CHARLES, physician; b. Pitts., Oct. 14, 1928; s. Raymond A. and Elizabeth I. (Burke) H.; B.S., U. Pitts., 1950, M.D., 1954; m. Mary Clare Wasserman, June 14, 1952; children—Natalie Clare, Thomas Charles. Intern, St. Francis Hosp., Pitts., 1954-55, resident in internal medicine, 1955-56; resident in phys. medicine and rehab. Warm Springs (Ga.) Found., 1958, Inst. of Phys. Medicine, N.Y. U. Bellevue Med. Center, N.Y.C., 1958-60; practice medicine specializing in phys. medicine and rehab., Pitts.; med. dir. dept. phys. medicine and rehab. St. Francis Gen. Hosp., Pitts., 1960-76, pres. med. staff, 1973-74; mem. active staff North Hills Passavant Hosp., 1976—, chmn. dept. phys. medicine and rehab., 1976—; mem. asso. staff Mercy Hosp., 1961-70; mem. advisory com. of John J. Kane Hosp., 1965-70; cons. in phys. medicine and rehab., Pa. Rehab. Center, Johnstown, 1960-73, Pitts. Guild for the Blind, 1961—, Children's Hosp., 1962—, St. Margaret's Hosp., 1962—; clin. asst. prof. dept. orthopedic surgery U. Pitts., 1962—, adj. prof. Grad. Sch. Edn., 1962—; guest lectr. at various hosps. and profl. assns., since 19—. Served with M.C., U.S. Army, 1955-58. Diplomate Am. Bd. Phys. Medicine and Rehab. (v.p. 1971-75, guest examiner 1965, 66); recipient Am. Legion award 19—. Fellow Am. Acad. of Phys. Medicine and Rehab. (pres. eastern sect. 1970); mem. Am. Congress of Phys. Medicine and Rehab., Pa. Acad. of Phys. Medicine and Rehab. (v.p. 1965-66), Am. Acad. of Electromyography and Electrodiagnosis, Pa., Allegheny County (chmn. restorative services com. 1963-65) med. socs., Pa. (dir. 1966-67), Am. heart assns., AMA (Physicians Recognition award 1974-77, 77-80), Vis. Nurse Assn. of Allegheny County (adv. com. 1962-68), Alpha Epsilon Delta, Phi Rho Sigma. Roman Catholic. Contbr. articles to profl. jours. Office: North Hills Passavant Hosp 9100 Babcock Blvd Pittsburgh PA 15237

HOJNACKI, JEROME LOUIS, biochemist; b. Stamford, Conn., Mar. 9, 1947; s. Louis Lawrence and Jennie Louise (Faski) H.; B.S., So. Conn. State Coll., 1969; M.S., U. Bridgeport (Conn.), 1971; Ph.D., U. N.H., 1975; m. Mary E. Riley, 1978. Instr. biology Stamford Pub. Schs., 1969-71; research asst. U. N.H., Durham, 1971-75; postdoctoral fellow Harvard U. Sch. Pub. Health, Boston, 1975-77; asst. prof. biochemistry U. Lowell (Mass.), 1977—; research cons. respiratory disease Beth Israel Hosp., Boston, 1977—; guest lectr. heart disease to community groups, N.H., 1971-75. Recipient Health Service award NIH, 1976; Am. Heart Assn. research fellow, 1975-76. Mem. Am. Heart Assn., AAAS, Sigma Xi. Democrat. Roman Catholic. Contbr. articles and abstracts to sci. jours. Home: Lakeshore Apts Worcester Rd Framingham MA 01701 Office: Univ Lowell Olsen Hall 1 Univ Ave Lowell MA 01854

HOLBROOK, GEORGE EDWARD, ret. corp. exec.; b. St. Louis, Mar. 4, 1909; s. Edward M. Holbrook and Doretta C. (Krentler) H.; B.S. in Chem. Engring., U. Mich., 1931, M.S., 1932, Ph.D., 1933, D.Sc. (hon.), 1967; m. Dorothy H. Williams, June 12, 1933; children—James E., Thomas E. Research chemist, chem. engr. Jackson Lab., E. I. duPont de Nemours & Co., Inc., 1933—, head, new products div., research and devel. new organic chems., 1933-43, asst. dir. Jackson Lab., 1943-49, gen. supt. Chambers Works, 1949, asst. dir. tech. div., organic chems. dept., 1949-1950, departmental engr., organic chems. dept., 1950, mgr. plants devel. dept. 1951, asst. dir. devel. dept., 1951-55, asst. gen. mgr. organic chems. dept., 1955-56, gen. mgr. elastomer chem. dept., 1957-58, v.p., dir., mem. exec. com., 1958-69, dir., mem. finance, bonus and salary coms., 1970-76, ret., 1976; dir. chem. div. N.P.A., 1952. Mem. devel. council U. Mich.; trustee Washington Coll. (Md.), 1970-73; trustee, vice chmn. exec. com. St. Francis Hosp., Wilmington, 1973—. Mem. Nat. Acad. Engring. (charter, exec. com. 1964-68), Am. Inst. Chem. Engrs. (pres. 1958), Am. Ordnance Assn., Am. Chem. Soc., Engrs. Joint Council (v.p., dir., exec. com. 1960-61), Soc. Chem. Industries, Am. Phys. Soc., A.A.A.S., N.Y. Acad. Scis., Franklin Inst., Sigma Xi, Tau Beta Pi, Phi Lambda Upsilon, Phi Kappa Phi, Phi Eta Sigma. Author articles on distillation, metal polishing, lubrication. Home: Box 606 Cokesbury Village Hockessin DE 19707

HOLCOMB, ROBERT CLINTON, security cons.; b. Bradford, Pa., Dec. 31, 1937; s. Robert Jay and Hilda Mae (Everitt) H.; student State U. N.Y., Buffalo, 1973, Canisius Coll., 1974; m. Theresa Rick, May 18, 1957; children—Michael, Robert, John Richard. Vice-pres. Maximum Security Centers, Inc., Buffalo, 1959—, also dir.; pres. Barco Communications, Inc., 1978—, Radio Frequency Control Corp., Inc., 1978—. Dep. sheriff sci. staff Erie County (N.Y.) Sheriff's Dept., 1978. Mem. Am. Soc. Indsl. Security (past chmn. Western N.Y. chpt.), Asso. Locksmiths Am. (past dir.), Law Enforcement Assn. Western N.Y. (past pres.), Bldg. Owners and Mgrs. Assn. (dir. chpt. 1978). Republican. Roman Catholic. Club: K.C. Home: 116 Nicholson St Buffalo NY 14214 Office: 241 S Elmwood Ave Buffalo NY 14201

HOLCOMBE, KENNETH HENRY, lawyer; b. Plattsburgh, N.Y., Feb. 22, 1927; s. Kenneth Henry and Mary (Tierney) H.; B.N.S., Coll. Holy Cross, 1946, A.B., 1948; J.D., Harvard U., 1951; m. Shirley F. Champagne, Aug. 6, 1949; children—Kenneth H., David F., Patrick J.T., Christine S. Admitted to N.Y. bar, 1951; practiced in Plattsburgh, 1951—; mem. firm Tierney and Holcombe, 1951-52, Robinson and Holcombe, 1953-67, K.H. Holcombe, 1967-69, Holcombe & Dame, 1970—. Adminstr., Clinton County Assigned Counsel Plan, 1966-74; chmn. Clinton County Draft Bd., 1966-76; mem. departmental com. ct. adminstrn. 3d Jud. Dept., 1964—. Bd. dirs. Clinton County Humane Soc. Served with USNR, 1944-47. Mem. Fedn. Bar Assns. 4th Jud. Dist. (pres. 1959-61), Am., N.Y. State (ho. of dels. 1969-76, v.p. 1974-76), Clinton County (pres. 1968-69) bar assns., Am. Legion. Clubs: K.C. Elks, Rotary (pres. 1960-61). Address: 62 Brinkerhoff St Plattsburgh NY 12901

HOLDEN, GEORGIE E. HOUGH, writer, educator; b. nr. Lucketts, Va.; d. John Wesley and Mary (Barrett) Hough; student Blue Ridge Coll.; B.A., Bridgewater Coll., 1928; postgrad. summer schs. U. Md., 1928, 45, Madison Coll.; A.A. with high honors, Prince George's Community Coll., 1973; m. John Hopkins Holden (dec. July 1961); children—Patricia H. Holden Squitieri, Mary H. Tchr. pub. schs., Montgomery County, Md.; tchr. English, Wicomico High Sch., Wicomico Church, Va.; sec. Am. Legion, Washington; clerical asst. Higher Edn. div. Dept. HEW, Washington; sec. Gallaudet Coll., Washington, 1953-56, pub. relations officer, 1956-60, dir. pub. relations, 1960-69; asst. The Stars and Stripes-The Nat. Tribune, 1972-74; free-lance poetry and prose writer; substitute tchr. Prince George's County Pub. Schs., 1975—; publicity dir. 5th Internat. Congress of Philosophy, Washington, 1957; pub. relations chmn. Workshop Identification Researchable Vocat. Rehab. Problems of Deaf, Washington, 1960, Workshop for Catholic Personnel for Deaf, Washington, 1961, Workshop for Episcopal Workers for Deaf, Washington, 1961; co-chmn. pub. relations Internat. Congress Edn. of Deaf, Washington, 1963; publicity chmn. Workshop for Lutherans on Deafness and Rehab., Washington, 1963; counselor Salvation Army Assn., 1970—; mem. study tour Communist countries Eastern Europe, 1969; mem. first Editorial Conf. on Middle East, 1974; attended Internat. Women's Year, Mexico City, 1975. Mem. Betterment for United Srs., 1976—, founder and editor Sr. Alert, pres., 1977—; co-chmn. Md. State Coalition for Generic Equivalents, 1976—; speaker on Medicaid bills and issues. Recipient plaque Gallaudet Coll., 1969. Mem. Am. Legion Aux. Police and Fire Unit 29, Nat. Capital Aux. Vets. World War I (chaplain 1966, del. conv. 1965-68, sr. v.p. 1968), Am. Coll. Pub. Relations Assn. (mem. hospitality com. nat. conv. 1960, publicity chmn. Mason-Dixon dist. conf. Washington 1961, planning com. dist. conf. Williamsburg, Va. 1964-66, registrar 1965, dist. sec. 1964-66), Am. Newspaper Women's Club (publicity com. 1966-67, ad hoc membership com. 1967-68), Ednl. Press. Assn. Am. (steering com. Washington 1962-63, 66-67, sec., publicity chmn. editor of Edpress Notes 1967-68), English-Speaking Union, Lancaster-Northumberland Edn. Assn. (chmn. pub. relations com. 1946-48), Nat. Religious Publicity Council, Ednl. Press Assn. Am., Coll. Sports Info. Dirs. Am., Prince George's County Mental Health Soc., Md. Park Improvement Area Assn. (sec. 1963), Internat. Platform Assn., World Future Soc., Nat. Assn. Deaf, Nat. Trust Historic Preservation, Smithsonian Assos., English-Speaking Union Commonwealth. Republican (sustaining mem.). Baptist (pres. adult women's class 1963-64). Clubs: Republican Congressional (charter), U.S. Senatorial (founding); Sr. Citizens (program com. 1976—) (Capitol Heights, Md.). Mem. adv. editorial bd. Newsette; editor Gallaudet Record, 1963—; adv. editorial bd. Bridgewater Alumnus, 1960-66; contbr. articles to profl. publs. Home: 5802 Athena St Maryland Park Capitol Heights MD 20027

HOLDEN, HENRY EARLE, JR., geneticist; b. Norwich, Conn., July 7, 1943; s. Henry Earle and Grace Eva (Lindell) H.; B.A., U. Conn., 1965, M.S., 1967; Ph.D. (NIH trainee), Brown U., 1970; postdoctoral fellow New Eng. Inst. Med. Research, 1970-71; m. M. Lynne Caughey, July 2, 1966; children—Todd Henry, Rebecca Lynne. Research scientist Pfizer Central Research, Groton, Conn., 1971-74, sr. research scientist dept. safety evaluation, 1974-76, project leader genetic toxicology sect., 1976—; adj. faculty W. Alton Jones Cell Sci. Center, Lake Placid, N.Y., 1977-78, course dir. continuing edn. program, 1977, 78. Mem. Environ. Mutagen Soc., AAAS, Am. Soc. Mammalogists, Tissue Culture Assn., Sigma Xi. Contbr. articles in field to profl. jours. Office: Pfizer Central Research Eastern Point Rd Groton CT 06340

HOLDEN, JAMES STUART, fed. judge; b. Bennington, Vt., Jan. 29, 1914; s. Edward Henry and Mary Anstiss (Thayer) H.; A.B., Dartmouth, 1935, LL.B. Union U., 1938; m. Helen Elizabeth Vetal, Mar. 3, 1941; children—Susan Holden Spaeth, Peter Vetal, James Stuart. Admitted to Vt. bar, 1938, practice in law, Bennington, 1938-41, 46-48; state's atty., Bennington County, 1946-48, chmn. Vt. Pub. Service Commn., 1948-49; superior judge State of Vt., 1949-56, asso. justice Supreme Ct., 1956-63, chief justice, 1963-72, U.S. dist. judge Vt. Dist., 1972—. Chmn. Vt. Statutory Revision Comm., 1957-62; chmn. Conf. Chief Justices, 1971-72. Served as maj. 43d Inf. Div., AUS, 1941-46. Mem. 43d Inf. Div. Vets. Assn. (past comdr.). Am., Vt. bar assns., Am. Judicature Soc., Am. Law Inst. Episcopalian. Home: Overlea Rd North Bennington VT 05257 Office: US Dist Ct Dist Vt Rutland VT 05701

HOLDEN, RICHARD FLETCHER, tanning chemist; b. Boston, Oct. 17, 1934; s. Robert F. and Marian Lucy (Wood) H.; B.S., U. Mass., 1956; postgrad. Northeastern U.; m. Barbara Ann Corcoran, Dec. 28, 1957; children—George Henry, Richard Fletcher. Product mgr. polyurethane chems. UBS Chem. Co., Cambridge, Mass., 1957-65; gen. mgr. Polypat Leathers Inc., Peabody, Mass., 1965-73, Mitsubishi-Fleming Joffe-Jentra Ltd., Johnstown, N.Y., 1973-76; prodn. mgr. Irving Tanning Co., Hartland, Maine, 1976—; lectr. in field. Served with U.S. Army, 1953-56, USAF, 1956-61. Mem. Am. Chem. Soc., New Eng. Tanners Club (pres. 1972-73), Am. Leather Chemists Assn. Republican. Home: RD 1 Box 299 Madison ME 04950 Office: Irving Tanning Co Main St Hartland ME 04943

HOLDER, CALVIN BERESFORD, educator; b. Barbados, W.I., Sept. 28, 1946; s. Clifford Beresford and Beryl Leotta (Smith) H.; came to U.S., 1962, naturalized, 1970; A.B., City U. N.Y., 1970; M.A., Harvard U., 1971, Ph.D., 1976; m. Idalia Phillips, Sept. 13, 1970; 1 dau., Aisha. Instr., Coll. S.I., City U. N.Y., 1975, asst. prof. history, 1976—. Woodrow Wilson fellow, 1970; Black Prize fellow, 1970-75; Coll. S.I. grantee, 1977. Mem. Orgn. Am. Historians, Am. Hist. Assn., Inst. Early Am. History and Culture, Assn. Study of Afro-Am. Life and Culture, Phi Beta Kappa. Home: 25 Eastern Pkwy Brooklyn NY 11238 Office: 130 Stuyvesant Pl Staten Island NY 10301

HOLDING, LAURA ANNE, librarian; b. Wilkinsburg, Pa., Sept. 9; d. James Clarke Carlisle and Laura May (Krepps) Holding; grad. Baldwin Sch., Bryn Mawr, Pa.; A.B., Mt. Holyoke Coll. Asst. tech. dept. Carnegie Library of Pitts.; librarian Assn. Casualty and Surety Execs., N.Y.C., Air Reduction Co., N.Y.C., Davis Polk & Wardwell, and predecessor firms, 1943-73, librarian emeritus, 1973—. Active fund drives ARC, 1949-61, Queens div. Am. Cancer Soc. 1957-64; hostess St. Nicholas Club for Servicemen, N.Y.C., 1942-44; vol. Atlantic chpt. Sierra Club, 1976. Recipient award of merit Central Queens chpt. ARC, 1954, 59. Mem. Am. Assn. Law Libraries. Law Library Assn. Greater N.Y. (v.p. 1948-49). Club: Mt. Holyoke of N.Y. Author: Subject Heading Index Guide for Opinions and Memoranda of Law, 1976. Mem. editorial bd. Manual of Private Law Library Procedure, 1960-62. Home: 69-09 108th St Forest Hills NY 11375

HOLDRIDGE, BARBARA (MRS. LAWRENCE B. HOLDRIDGE), publishing co. exec.; b. N.Y.C., July 26, 1929; d. Herbert L. and Bertha (Gold) Cohen; A.B., Hunter Coll., 1950; m. Lawrence B. Holdridge, Oct. 9, 1959; 2 children. Asst. editor Liveright Pub. Corp., N.Y.C., 1950-52; co-founder Caedmon Records, Inc., N.Y.C., 1952, partner, 1952-60, pres., 1960-62, treas., 1962-70; pres. Caedmon Records, 1970-75; founder Stemmer House Publishers, Inc., Owings Mills, Md., 1975, pres., 1975—. Co-founder v.p. Shakespeare Rec. Soc., Inc., N.Y.C., 1960—, Theatre Rec. Soc., Inc., N.Y.C., 1964—; co-founder History Rec. Soc., Inc., N.Y.C.,

1964, pres., 1964-70. Lectr. on Ammi Phillips, 1959—. Recipient Am. Shakespeare Festival award, 1962; Certificate of Appreciation, Mayor N.Y.C., 1972; named to Hunter Coll. Hall of Fame, 1972. Mem. Phi Beta Kappa Assos. Contbr. articles to Antiques, Art in Am. Office: Stemmer House 2627 Caves Rd Owings Mills MD 21117

HOLECHEK, JAMES ALBERT, pub. relations cons.; b. Williamsport, Pa., Nov. 15, 1929; s. Joseph Edward and Beatrice Geneieve (McGuire) H.; B.F.A with honors, Md. Inst. Coll. Art, 1953, M.F.A., 1969; m. Patricia Ann Phillips, Feb. 6, 1954; children—Jo Ann, Mark. Vice pres. Emery Advt. Corp., Balt., 1962-64; dir. pub. relations and advt. Md. Blue Cross & Blue Shield, 1965-68; dir. pub. relations Unitec Industries, Cockeysville, Md., 1968-70; chmn. dept. art Anne Arundel Community Coll., Annapolis, Md., 1968-69; pres. James Holechek Assos. Inc., Balt., 1970—; instr. Johns Hopkins U. Evening Grad. Sch. Served with airborne div. U.S. Army, 1953-55. Mem. Pub. Relations Soc. Am. (pres. Md. chpt. 1969, recipient 1st annual award Md. 1975), Balt. Pub. Relations Council (pres. 1970), Pub. Relations Am. Hosp. Assn., Boating Writers Internat. Republican. Roman Catholic. Clubs: Hopkins, Annapolis Yacht, Gibson Island, Gibson Island Yacht. Author: Shaping Up to Ship Out, 1977. Boating columnist Sunday Sun, Balt., 1973—. Home: Gibson Island MD 21056 Office: 204 N Liberty St Baltimore MD 21201

HOLIDAY, MARTHA JEAN, fashion adviser, show producer; b. Charleroi, Pa., Jan. 20, 1926; d. Nester L. and Mary Alice Hutch; B.A., California (Pa.) State Tchrs. Coll., 1948; postgrad. Sch. Retailing N.Y. U., 1949; m. Thomas P. Conlin, Mar. 5, 1956 (dec. Aug. 1956). Eastern sales mgr. promotions Exec., Slenderella Systems, 1952-56; asst. fashion mgr. Simplicity Pattern Co., N.Y.C., 1956-57; propr. Martha Holiday, Inc., N.Y.C., 1957—; staged Salute to N.Y.C. hist. fashion pageant Operation Sail, July 4, 1976; cons. E. Side C. of C., N.Y.C., 1978. Recipient Service awards for fundraising, PTA, hosps., polit. groups. Mem. Internat. Platform Assn., Women in Communications, Am. Women Radio and TV, N.Y. Women Bus. Owners. Author: Fashion Show Techniques, 1959. Fashion editor East, 1957; Fabulous Las Vegas, 1957-62. Address: 119 83d St E New York City NY 10028

HOLINER, LEONA, psychotherapist; b. N.Y.C., Apr. 7, 1930; d. Joseph and Pearl (Friedman) Wolkow; B.S. magna cum laude, Emerson Coll., Boston, 1973; M.Ed., Suffolk U., 1974. Therapist, Beacon Counsleing Inc., Brookline, Mass., 1974—, also dir.; out-patient therapist Human Resource Inst., Brookline, 1974; instr. womens studies Emerson Coll., 1975; instr. self assertive tng. Boston Center for Adult Edn. Mem. Am. Assn. Sex Educators and Counselors, Am. Personnel and Guidance Assn., Mass. Psychol. Assn., Soc. Family Therapy and Research, Northeastern Soc. Group Psychotherapy, Am. Assn. Marriage and Family Counselors. Home: 48 Hammond Pond Pkwy Chestnut Hill MA 02167 Office: 1166 Beacon St Brookline MA 02146

HOLLAND, NORMAN NORWOOD, lawyer; b. Princess Anne, Md., Feb. 19, 1896; s. John A. and Elizabeth (Powell) H.; B.E., Johns Hopkins U., 1920; LL.B., Fordham U., 1923; postgrad. Columbia U., 1923; m. Harriette Breder, Oct. 22, 1924; 1 son, Norman Norwood. Admitted to N.Y. bar, 1924; sr. partner Holland and Armstrong, N.Y.C., 1926-48, Holland, Armstrong & Bower, 1948-51, Holland, Armstrong, Bower & Carlson, 1951-64, Holland, Armstrong, Carlson & Wilkie, 1964-67, Holland, Armstrong, Wilkie & Previto, 1967—. Lectr., cons. to Practising Law Inst. on Patent and Trademark Law, 1950-67; pres. 880 Fifth Av. Corp., 1970-71, dir., 1966—. Mem. Am. Bar Assn. (chmn. sect. patent, trademark and copyright law 1951), Bar City N.Y. (chmn. patent com. 1959-61), Am. (bd. mgrs. 1955-58), N.Y. (pres. 1954-55) patent law assns., Internat. Patent and Trademark Assn. (exec. com. 1964-67), Johns Hopkins Alumni Assn. N.Y., N.J., Conn. (pres. 1951-53), Scabbard and Blade, Tau Beta Phi, Omicron Delta Kappa. Republican. Clubs: N.Y. Athletic, Downtown Athletic, Johns Hopkins (pres. 1942-46) (N.Y.C.). Home: 880 Fifth Ave New York City NY 10021

HOLLAND, NORMAN NORWOOD, JR., lit. critic; b. N.Y.C., Sept. 19, 1927; s. Norman Norwood and Harriette (Breder) H.; B.S., Mass. Inst. Tech., 1947; LL.B., Harvard U., 1950, Ph.D., 1956; postgrad. Boston Psychoanalytic Inst., 1960-66; m. Jane Kelley, Dec. 17, 1954; children—Katherine, John. Instr., Mass. Inst. Tech., Cambridge, 1955-56, asst. prof., 1956-62, asso. prof., 1962-66; prof. English, State U. N.Y., Buffalo, 1966—, chmn. dept., 1966-68, Faculty Research fellow, 1968-69; dir. Center for Psychol. Study of the Arts, Buffalo, 1970—; vis. prof. U. Paris, 1971-72; condr. TV programs The Film Critic, WGBH, Boston, 1957-59, The Shakespearean Imagination, 1960-61; cons. Pres.'s Commn. on Obscenity and Pornography, 1969-70, Nat. Council Tchrs. English, Ted Bates Advt. Agy., univ. and comml. pubs.; adv. bd. jour. Lit. and Psychology, 1969-75, Hartford Studies in Lit., 1969—, Gradiva, 1976—. Am. Council Learned Socs. Research fellow, 1974-75. Mem. English Inst., Modern Lang. Assn., Shakespeare Assn. Am., Soc. Cinema Studies, AAUP, Boston Psychoanalytic Soc. (spl. mem.), Western N.Y. Psychoanalytic Soc., Group for Applied Psychoanalysis (founder Boston chpt. 1963, Buffalo chpt. 1968), Am. Acad. Psychoanalysis (sci. asso.), Signet Club. Author: The First Modern Comedies, 1959; The Shakespearean Imagination, 1964; Psychoanalysis and Shakespeare, 1966; The Dynamics of Literary Response, 1968; Poems in Persons, 1973; Five Readers Reading, 1975; editor: Hamlet, 1963; Henry IV, 1965, Am. Shakespeare Festival edit., 1964; Jour. Soc. Cinematologists, 1963; contbr. articles to profl. jours., U.S. and abroad. Home: 131 High Park Blvd Amherst NY 14226 Office: State U NY Amherst NY 14260

HOLLAND, RAY GEOFFREY, psychiatrist; b. Belfast, N. Ireland, Oct. 30, 1931; s. John and Mary (Anderson) H.; B.A. cum laude, Oxford (Eng.) U., 1959, M.B., B.Chir., 1963, M.A., 1964; m. Mary Kennedy Irvine, Aug. 18, 1955; 1 son, Sean. Intern, Royal Jubilee Hosp., Victoria, B.C., Can., 1963-64; resident Buffalo State Hosp., 1969-70, E.J. Meyer Meml. Hosp., Buffalo, 1970-71; research fellow Nat. Inst. Mental Health, 1970-71; clin. instr. psychiatry State U. N.Y., Buffalo, 1969-71, 76-78, asst. prof., 1978—; practice medicine specializing in psychiatry, Port Colborne, Ont., Can., 1971-76. Served to lt. comdr. Royal Canadian Navy, 1964-69; sr. med. officer, flight surgeon. Mem. Canadian, Oxford Univ. med. assns., U.S. Naval Inst. (hon.), Aerospace Med. Assn. (hon.). Home: 57 Elgin St Port Colborne ON L3K 3J9 Canada Office: Dept Psychiatry EJ Myer Meml Hosp State Univ NY Buffalo NY

HOLLAND, SANFORD JED, anesthesiologist; b. N.Y.C., July 11, 1946; s. William Alfred and Sylvia (Schwartz) H.; B.A., State U. N.Y., Buffalo, 1968, M.D., 1972; m. Janet Miriam Seewald, Dec. 25, 1973; children—Judah, Hana Aviva. Resident in anesthesiology Brookdale Hosp. Center, Bklyn., 1972-74, chief resident, 1974-75; fellow surg. intensive care State U. N.Y., Bklyn., 1976; adj. attending anesthesiologist S.I. Hosp., 1977; asst. prof. anesthesiology Coll. Medicine and Dentistry N.J., Newark, 1978—; med. dir. respiratory therapy service, cons. intensivist Martland Med. Center, Newark, 1978—; mem. physicians adv. com. Shaare Zedek Hosp., Jerusalem, Israel. Diplomate Nat. Bd. Med. Examiners, Am. Bd. Anesthesiology. Fellow Am. Coll. Anesthesiologists; mem. AMA, Am., N.J. socs. anesthesiologists, Assn. Orthodox Jewish Scientists, Med. Soc. N.J., N.J. Soc. Critical Care Medicine. Contbr. articles to med. jours. Home: 770 Ocean Pkwy Brooklyn NY 11230 Office: Dept Anesthesiology NJ Med Sch 100 Bergen St Newark NJ 07103

HOLLANDER, ALVIN L., JR., TV program exec.; b. N.Y.C., Jan. 29, 1925; s. Alvin Lewis and Helen (Kaufman) H.; B.A., U. Va., 1948 div.; children—Alvin Lewis III, Edmund; m. 3d, Cornelia Drake Hoeffel Scott; 1 stepson, John. Mem. staff DuMont TV Network, 1948-56; set up TV ops. for 20th Century Fox Studios in Australia, 1954; mgr., radio and TV, Edward Kletter Assos. (name now changed to Parkson Advt.); 1955-56; program dir. sta. WABC-TV, N.Y.C., 1956-61; organized talent rep. firm Hollander Agy., 1961; program dir. sta. WCAU-TV, Phila., from 1962-72; with Teleprompter Corp., N.Y.C., 1972-73; TV cons. CBS, Princeton U., Children's TV Workshop, Chisanbop, N.J. Pub. Advocate, others and packager, N.Y.C., 1973—; bd. dirs. Princeton (N.J.) Cablevision. Vis. asst. adj. prof. Hahnemann Med. Coll., Phila.; cons. to subcom. air pollution and chronic respiratory diseases Philadelphia County Med. Soc.; teaching tennis profl. Princeton U. Bd. dirs. Easter Seal Soc. Served as 1st lt. inf. and parachute inf. AUS, World War II; ETO, PTO. Recipient Station Emmy award Nat. Acad. TV Arts and Scis. for prodn. Now Is The Time, 1968, also regional Emmys for prodns. Conformity, Detached Americans; Brotherhood Mass Media award NCCJ; Broadcast Media award Broadcast Industry Conf.; School Bell award, others. Mem. Franklin Inn, Wilderness Soc., Fortune Soc., Nat. Acad. TV Arts and Scis. (dir.), Phila. Lawn Tennis Assn. (chmn. publicity and publ. com.); Town Tennis (N.Y.C.); Seventh Regt. Tennis. Home: 30 Mulberry Row Princeton NJ 08540 Office: 159 W 53d St New York City NY 10019

HOLLANDER, BENTLEY AARON, physician; b. Camden, N.J., Oct. 29, 1939; s. Samuel and Matilda (Rosner) H.; B.A., Temple U., 1961, M.D., 1965; m. Clara Branzburg, June 23, 1963; children—Nadine Ann, Adrienne. Intern, Temple U. Hosp., Phila., 1965-66; resident in diagnostic radiology Columbia U., N.Y.C., 1968-71; practice medicine specializing in radiology, Millville, N.J., 1973-76, Phila., 1973—, Pennsauken, N.J., 1975—, Moorestown, N.J., 1976—; asst. radiologist Columbia-Presbyn. Med. Center, N.Y.C., 1971-72; instr. radiology Columbia U., N.Y.C., 1971-72, asst. prof. radiology, 1972-73, dir. uroradiol. procedures, 1972-73; dir. radiology Millville Hosp., 1973-76, St. Mary Hosp., Phila., 1973—, Browning Rd. Med. Center, Pennsauken, N.J., 1975—, Health Care Plan N.J., Moorestown, 1976—. Served with USPHS, 1966-68. Diplomate Am. Bd. Radiology, Am. Bd. Nuclear Medicine. Fellow Am. Coll. Angiology: mem. Am. Coll. Radiology, Radiol. Soc. N. Am., Radiol. Soc. N.J., AMA, Med. Soc. N.J., Camden County Med. Soc. Contbr. articles in field to med. jours. Home: 1017 Dell Dr Cherry Hill NJ 08003 Office: St Mary Hospital Frankford Ave Philadelphia PA 19125

HOLLANDER, GEORGE, physician; b. Phila., Apr. 17, 1914; s. Morris Fran (Krasner) H.; A.B., U. Pa., 1935; M.D., Jefferson Med. Coll., 1939; m. (dec.); children—Nina, Fredda, Debra; m. 2d, Leah Corson. Intern, Jefferson Hosp., Phila., 1939-41, resident Bklyn. Jewish Hosp., 1946-47; practice medicine specializing in internal medicine, Phila., 1947—; chief cardiology Lawndale Hosp., Phila.; asso. vascular dept. Einstein Med. Center; instr. medicine Temple U., 1950—. Served as capt. AUS, 1942-46. Diplomate Am. Bd. Internal Medicine. Fellow A.C.P., Am. Coll. Cardiology, Am. Coll. Angiology, Phila. Coll. Physicians, Phlebology Soc. Am. (founding); mem. Med. Service Assn. Pa. (dir.). Home: 1061 Susquehanna Rd Rydal PA 19046 Office: 3500 Vista St Philadelphia PA 19136

HOLLANDER, LAWRENCE JAY, elec. engr.; b. N.Y.C., Nov. 5, 1926; s. Irving Ludwig and Frances (Fensterstock) H.; B.E.E., N.Y. U., 1951, M.E.E., 1954. Cadet engr., asst. engr. Consol. Edison Co. N.Y., Inc., 1951-53; instr. elec. engring. N.Y. U. Coll. Engring., N.Y.C., 1953-59, asst. to dean, 1959-66; dir. evening div. N.Y. U. Sch. Engring. and Sci., N.Y.C., 1966-67; staff engr. Am. Gas Assn., Inc., N.Y.C., 1967-68, asst. mgr. dept. operating and engring. services, 1968-69; exec. sec. State Bd. Engring. and Land Surveying, N.Y. State Dept. Edn., 1969-77; adj. prof. engring. Cooper Union, 1978—; cons. elec. power generation, transmission and distbn.. 1954—, McCrossin & Co., N.Y.C., 1957-63; tchr. electric power courses L.I. Lighting Co., 1954-55, 57, 62; cons. Total Energy Mktg. Corp., 1964-66. Served with USNR, 1945-46. Registered engr., N.Y. Mem. IEEE (sr.), Nat., N.Y. State (dir. N.Y. County 1960-62 v.p. 1964-65), N.Y. County (pres. 1966-67) socs. profl. engrs., Am. Soc. Engring. Edn., N.Y. U. Heights Colls. Alumni Assn. (v.p. 1960-62), Alpha Phi Omega, Tau Beta Pi (councillor 1974-78, v.p. 1976-78), Eta Kappa Nu. Club: University (Albany, N.Y.). Home and Office: PO Box 8053 Albany NY 12203

HOLLANDER, LEONARD, psychiatrist; b. N.Y.C., Dec. 8, 1918; s. Herman and Tobye (Karesh) H.; B.S., City Coll. N.Y., 1940; M.A., Ohio State U., 1941; M.D., N.Y. U., 1948; m. Susan Katz, Aug. 12, 1956; children—Eric, Seth, David. Intern Lincoln Hosp., Bronx, N.Y., 1948-49; resident in psychiatry Yale U. Hosp., 1949-50; resident in psychiatry, then fellow child psychiatry U. Cin. Hosp., 1950-53; asst. prof. child psychiatry Einstein Coll. Medicine, N.Y.C., 1957-69; dir. psychiat. services Jewish Child Care Assn., N.Y.C., 1961-69; asso. prof. Emory U. Med. Sch., Atlanta, 1969-72; dir. Mercer County (N.J.) Child Guidance Center, Trenton, 1972-73; asso. prof. Coll. Medicine and Dentistry N.J.-Rutgers Med. Sch., 1973—; tchr., cons. Postgrad. Center Mental Health, Kennedy Child Study Center. Served with USPHS, 1955-57. Mem. N.J. Council Child Psychiatry, Am. Psychiat. Assn., Am. Acad. Child Psychiatry, Assn. for Academic Psychiatry. Contbr. profl. jours. Home: 104 Poe Rd Princeton NJ 08540 Office: PO Box 101 Piscataway NJ 08854

HOLLANDER, MELVYN ARNOLD, psychologist, educator; b. Newark, July 26, 1941; s. Benjamen and Beatrice Hollander; B.A., U. Mo., 1963; M.A., Bowling Green State U., 1965; Ph.D., U. Okla., 1968; m. Emily Browning, Sept. 20, 1964; children—Julie Beth, Lauren Michele. Asst. dir. residential correction centers State of N.J., 1964-65; teaching asst. psychology U. Okla., 1966-67; staff psychologist Okla. Dept. Health, Oklahoma City, 1967-68; postdoctoral fellow clin. psychology Conn. Valley Hosp. and dept. psychiatry Yale U. Med. Sch., 1968-69; dir. behavioral tng. Bronx (N.Y.) State Hosp., 1969-72; adj. asst. prof. psychology N.Y. U., 1970-72; asst. prof. psychology, mem. doctoral faculty Queens Coll., City U.N.Y., 1972—; dir. Behavior Therapy Inst., White Plains, N.Y., 1973-78; co-founder Center for Behavioral Psychotherapy, White Plains, 1978—; pvt. practice clin. psychology, White Plains, 1973—; clin. advisor Westchester Narcotics Guidance Council, 1970-75; cons. to schs., hosps., bus. Contbr. articles on psychotherapy and behavior therapy research to profl. jours.; editorial cons. to psychol. jours. Home: 95 Lakeside Dr Katonah NY 10536 Office: 23 Old Mamaroneck Rd White Plains NY 10605 also City Univ NY Queens Coll Psychology Dept Flushing NY 11367

HOLLANDER, PATRICIA ANN, lawyer, educator; b. St. Louis, Feb. 17, 1928; d. Patrick R. and Hazel A. (Schneider) Harrington; B.S., St. Louis U., 1949, J.D., 1952; postgrad. Harvard Law Sch., 1969-70; m. Edwin P. Hollander, Apr. 18, 1959; 1 son, Peter A. Admitted to Mo. bar, 1952, N.Y. bar, 1964; regional atty. Central states Internat. Ladies Garment Workers Union, St. Louis, 1952-60; pvt. practice, Buffalo, 1965-67; lectr. indsl. relations Sch. Mgmt., also asst. to dean, div. continuing edn. State U. N.Y., Buffalo, 1967-73, lectr. Law Sch., 1973—, admissions officer, 1975-76, dir. program in law and social sci. Survey Research Center, also adj. asso. prof., 1976—; gen. counsel Am. Assn. U. Adminstrs., Buffalo, 1972—; cons., lectr. in field of due process in edn. Bd. dirs. Camp Fire Girls Buffalo and Erie County, 1972-74. Recipient Adult award Camp Fire Girls Buffalo and Erie County, 1972. Mem. Nat. Assn. Coll. and U. Attys., Am. Assn. U. Adminstrs. (exec. com.), AAUP, Am., Mo., N.Y. State, Erie County, St. Louis bar assns., St. Louis U., Harvard Law Sch. alumni assns. Author: Legal Handbook for Educators, 1978. Contbr. to legal and edn. publs. Home: 30 Foxcroft Ln Williamsville NY 14221 Office: PO Box 6 Bidwell Sta Buffalo NY 14222

HOLLANDER, STANLEY JULES, ophthalmologist; b. Newark, Aug. 13, 1931; s. Irving and Beatrice (Lorber) H.; B.S. in Pharmacy, Rutgers U., 1953; M.D., U. Geneva, 1959; postgrad N.Y. U., 1964-65; m. Dorith Eva Meyer, Sept. 27, 1957; children—Margharet F., Michael D., Barbara R. Intern Beth Israel Hosp., Newark, 1959-60; resident in ophthalmology Bklyn. Eye and Ear Hosp., 1962-64; practice medicine specializing in ophthalmology; dir. dept. ophthalmology Community Hosp., Montclair, N.J., St. Vincent's Hosp., Montclair; dir. dept. ophthalmology Mountainside Hosp., Montclair, 1973-76, asso. dir. ophthalmology, 1976—. Served to capt. M.C., U.S. Army, 1960-61. Diplomate Am. Bd. Ophthalmology. Fellow Am. Acad. Ophthalmology and Otolaryngology, ACS, Internat. Coll. Surgeons; mem. AMA, N.J., Essex County (N.J.) med. socs., N.J. Acad. Ophthalmology and Otolaryngology, Am. Soc. Contemporary Ophthalmology, Am. Assn. Ophthalmology, Contact Lens Assn. Am., Am. Physicians Fellowship of Israel Med. Soc. Clubs: Temple Menorah Mens, B'nai B'rith. Home: 62 Heller Way Upper Montclair NJ 07043 Office: 63 S Fullerton Ave Montclair NJ 07042

HOLLANS, IRBY NOAH, JR., assn. exec.; b. Christiansburg, Va., Nov. 3, 1930; s. Irby Noah and Annie May (Lester) H.; B.S. in Gen. Bus. Adminstrn., Va. Poly. Inst. and State U., 1953; m. Frances Jo Cox, June 21, 1957; children—Susan Frances, Carol Leigh, Irby Neil. Mgr. promotion sta. WRVA-Radio, Richmond, Va., 1956-64, editor bus. news, 1956-64; dir. travel devel. Va. State C. of C., 1964-70, asst. exec. dir., 1970-72; exec. dir. Optical Labs. Assn., Washington, 1972—. Instr. bus. Va. Commonwealth U., Richmond, 1965-71. Appt. mem. Dulles (Va.) Internat. Airport Devel. Commn., 1958-76; appt. mem. Va. Nat. Capital Airports Acquisition Study Commn., 1971-76. Bd. dirs. Va. Thanksgiving Festival Inc., 1965-70, Keep Va. Beautiful, Inc., 1965-73, Central Va. Ednl. TV, 1970-72, Va. Travel Coordinating Com., 1964-72. Served to maj. USAF, 1953-72; Korea. Recipient Service award Va. Profl. Photographers' Assn., 1966, Nat. award Profl. Photographers' Am., 1970. Mem. Am. Soc. Assn. Execs. (certified), Va. Pub. Relations Conf., U.S. C. of C., Nat. Assn. Wholesaler-Distributors Pros-Group, Am. Nat. Standards Inst. (med. devices standards mgmt. bd. 1973—), Washington Soc. Assn. Execs., Nat. Assn. Execs. Club, Alpha Kappa Psi, Pi Delta Epsilon. Home: 2804 Albany Ct Fairfax VA 22031 Office: 6935 Wisconsin Ave Washington DC 20015

HOLLENBECK, HAROLD CAPISTRAN, congressman; b. Passaic, N.J., Dec. 29, 1938; s. Harold J. and Hazel (Howell) H.; B.A., Fairleigh Dickinson U., 1961; LL.B., U. Va., 1964; 1 son, David Maynard. Admitted to N.J. bar; city pros. atty. Carlstadt (N.J.), 1966-67; mem. E. Rutherford (N.J.) City Council, 1967—, N.J. State Assembly, 1968-72, N.J. State Senate, after 1972; mem. U.S. Ho. of Reps. from 9th N.J. Dist., 1977—. Alt. del. Republican Nat. Conv., 1968. Mem. Phi Delta Epsilon, Phi Gamma Delta. Home: 30 Boiling Springs Ave East Rutherford NJ 07073 Office: US Ho of Reps Washington DC 20515

HOLLENBERG, ROBERT DAVID, neurosurgeon; b. Winnipeg, Man., Can., Mar. 31, 1941; s. Joseph and Dorothy (Osofsky-Benaron) H.; B.A. with high honors, Swarthmore Coll., 1961; M.D., Harvard, 1965; m. Barbara Esterson, Dec. 2, 1971; 1 dau., Rachel Lara. Intern, Univ. Hosps. of Cleve., 1965-67; resident in neurosurgery Montreal (Que., Can.) Neurol. Hosp., 1967-71; practice medicine specializing in pediatric neurosurgery, Montreal, 1972—; mem. surg. staff Montreal Children's Hosp., 1972—, electroencephalographer, 1973—, mem. exec. com., 1976—, chmn. council physicians and surgeons, 1978—; asst. surgeon Montreal Gen. Hosp., 1974—; asst. prof. dept. neurology and neurosurgery McGill U. Med. Sch. Fellow Royal Coll. Physicians and Surgeons (Can.); mem. Montreal Medico-Chirurgical Soc., Montreal Clin. Soc., McGill-Osler Reporting Soc., Canadian Assn. Neurol. Surgeons, Canadian, Eastern assns. electroencephalographers, Assn. Neurosurgeons of Province of Que., Phi Beta Kappa, Sigma Xi. Home: 5685 Edgemore Ave Cote St Luc PQ H4W 1V4 Canada Office: Montreal Children's Hosp 2300 Tupper St Montreal PQ H3H 1P3 Canada

HOLLIDAY, IVAR MCDONALD, electronics co. exec.; b. Boise, Idaho, Feb. 9, 1921; s. Ivar G. and Mabel L. (Lord) H.; B.M.E., U. Idaho, 1943; postgrad. U. Pitts., U. Calif. at Los Angeles; m. Mildred J. Paul, Aug. 15, 1944; children—Donna Kathryn, Linda Joanne, David Paul; m. 2d, Donna Kathryn Hollingsworth, Sept. 7, 1967. Research engr. Westinghouse Labs., 1943-50; research physicist Hughes Aircraft, 1951-55; research physicist Space Technology Labs, Inc., 1955-58, minuteman electronics project office, 1958-61; mgr. Minuteman ops. center TRW/Space Tech. Labs., Inc., 1961-68; asst. to pres. Autonetics div. Rockwell Internat., 1968-70; dir. mgmt. devel. and tng. Raytheon Equipment div., Wayland, Mass., 1970-77; v.p. Human Resource Devel. Computervision, 1977—; lectr. U. Calif. at Los Angeles, 1961-65. Mem. IEEE, Am. Soc. Quality Control, Am. Inst. Aeros. and Astronautics, Am. Mgmt. Assn., Am. Soc. Tng. Dirs. Club: Masons. Patentee in field. Contbr. articles to profl. jours. Home: 29 Brooks Rd Wayland MA 01778 Office: Computervision 201 Burlington Rd Bedford MA 01730

HOLLINGWORTH, JOSEPH EDWIN, JR., educator, mgmt. and communications cons.; b. Lowell, Mass., June 25, 1932; s. Joseph Edwin and Blanche (Moulton) H.; B.A., Dartmouth Coll., 1955; M.A., Emerson Coll., 1968; 1 dau., Pamela Victoria. Field engr. Pratt & Forrest Co., Lowell, 1955-56, 58-62; mem. faculty Emerson Coll., 1963—, asso. prof., co-head bus. and orgnl. communication dept.; mem. staff New Eng. Inst. Law Enforcement Mgmt., 1969—; cons. in field. Bd. dirs. Family Service of Greater Lowell, 1960-63; dir. Greater Lowell Diabetes Soc., 1961-63; pres. Chemlsford Players, 1962-63. Served with U.S. Army, 1956-58. Mem. AAUP, Internat. Communication Assn., Speech Communication Assn. Am., Nat. Assn. Watch and Clock Collectors. Home: 894 West St Carlisle MA 01741 Office: 148 Beacon St Boston MA 02116

HOLLOWAY, EDWARD, JR., lawyer; b. Bklyn., Nov. 19, 1918; s. Edward and Lenora E. (Walker) H.; A.B., Princeton, 1940; J.D., Yale, 1947; m. Gail Fiske, May 17, 1974; children—Hope Lenora, Edward. Admitted to N.Y. bar, 1947; asso. firm Armitage & Holloway, 1947-49; asso. firm Bannister, Stitt, Holloway & Krause, 1949-53, partner, 1953-71; partner firm Eaton, Van Winkle and Greenspoon, 1971-76; partner firm Eaton, Van Winkle, Greenspoon & Grutman, 1976—. Served with AUS, 1942-46. Mem. Gen. Soc. Colonial Wars (sec. gen. 1966-72; gov. N.Y. 1969-71; lt. gov. gen. 1975—), Am.,

N.Y. State bar assns., Assn. Bar City N.Y., Assn. Ex-Mems. Squadron A. Mason (33 deg.). Clubs: Princeton (N.Y.C.); Princeton Elm, The Nassau (Princeton). Home: 205 W 89th St New York City NY 10024 Office: 600 3d Ave New York City NY 10016

HOLLOWELL, GLORIA NOBLE, educator; b. Chgo., Apr. 1, 1927; d. Dwight E. and Elisabeth B. Noble; B.S. in Home Econs., Purdue U., 1949; M. Equivalence in Sci. Edn., Pa. State U., 1975; M.S. in Counseling Edn., Marywood Coll., 1977; m. John Leslie Hollowell, July 25, 1953; children—Mary E., Paula J., John D. Tchr. sci. and home econs. Jackson Twp. High Sch., Valparaiso, Ind., 1950-52, St. Joseph's Protectory, Norristown, Pa., 1966-68; asst. prin., tchr. Mother of Divine Providence Sch., King of Prussia, Pa., 1968-72; tchr. sci. Upper Merion Jr. High Sch., King of Prussia, 1972—. Mem. Nat., Pa. State, Upper Merion Area edn. assns., Pa., Montgomery (county, Pa.) (adv. bd.) sci. tchrs. assns., Pa. Acad. Sci., Pa. Jr. Acad. Sci. (co-dir. Region I), Am. Personnel and Guidance Assn., Am. Sch. Counselor Assn. Roman Catholic. Home: 817 Stonybrook Dr Jeffersonville PA 19403

HOLLYWOOD, JOHN ALOYSIUS, interior designer; b. Camden, N.J., Jan. 31, 1921; s. John Francis and Mary Anselm (Slavin) H.; ed. parochial schs., art courses. Interior designer J.M. Kase, Inc., 1945-49, Allied Stores, Inc., 1949-53, John A. Hollywood Co., Reading, Pa., 1953—; cons. Albright Coll., Ursinus Coll., Berkshire Internat., Empire State Bldg. Served with USNR, 1941-45. Club: Republican of Berks County. Restored home of Judah Boone, uncle of Daniel Boone. Home and office: 424 Pine St Reading PA 19602

HOLM, ROBERT ERIC, corrugated container mfg. co. exec.; b. Worcester, Mass., Feb. 27, 1942; s. Eric Lambert and Vivian Sybil (Brunt) H.; grad. high sch.; m. Francine A. Longo, Apr. 22, 1967; children—Douglas, Gregory. With G. Fox and Co., Hartford, Conn., 1960-64, salesman, 1960-62, asst. dept. mgr., 1962-64; salesman Bosie Cascade Corp., Waterbury, Conn., 1964-67; co-founder, owner R & R Container Inc., Waterbury, 1968-73; founder, pres. Holm Corrugated Container, Inc., Southington, Conn. Home: 126 Southwest Rd Waterbury CT 06708 Office: Metals Dr Southington CT 06489*

HOLMAN, B. LEONARD, physician; b. Sheboygan, Wis., June 26, 1941; s. Max and Sophia (Penn) H.; B.S., U. Wis., 1963; M.D., Washington U., St. Louis, 1966; m. Dale Elyse Barkin, Jan. 22, 1971; children—Amy Lynn, Allison Stacy. Intern, Mt. Zion Hosp., San Francisco, 1966-67; resident in radiology Mallinckrodt Inst. Radiology, St. Louis, 1967-68, fellow in nuclear medicine, 1968-70; instr. radiology Harvard Med. Sch., Boston, 1970-73, asst. prof., 1973-76, asso. prof., 1976—; chief clin. nuclear medicine Peter Bent Brigham Hosp., Boston, 1970—; radiologist nuclear medicine Children's Hosp. Med. Center, Boston, 1970—, Sidney Farber Canncer Inst., Boston, 1970—; attending physician nuclear medicine service West Roxbury (Mass.) VA Hosp. Diplomate Am. Bd. Nuclear Medicine, Am. Bd. Radiology. Fellow Am. Coll. Cardiology; mem. Soc. Nuclear Medicine (nat. trustee 1976-77, pres. New Eng. chpt. 1978-79), AAAS, Am. Fedn. Clin. Research, Am. Heart Assn. (established investigator 1977—), Mass. Radiol. Soc., Am. Coll. Radiology, Radiol. Soc. N.Am., others. Author, contbg. author books; contbr. articles to profl. publs. Asso. editor: Cardiovascular Radiology, 1977; editorial bd. Jour. Nuclear Medicine. Office: Peter Bent Brigham Hosp 721 Huntington Ave Boston MA 02115

HOLMAN, ROBERT VOGEL, physician; b. Mason City, Iowa, Dec. 4, 1916; s. James Royal and Mae Catherine (Vogel) H.; M.D., State U. Iowa, 1940; m. Jean Ella Berry, July 4, 1942; children—Lynn Holman Russell, James B., John R., William D. Intern, U.S. Marine Hosp., S.I., N.Y.; resident in orthopedics Children's Hosp., Buffalo, Iowa City, 1946-49; practice medicine specializing in orthopedics, Bklyn., 1949-54, Pompton Plains, N.J., 1954—; mem. staff St. Joseph's Hosp. and Med. Center, Paterson, N.J.; orthopedic cons. U.S. Dept. Labor, USPHS. Serviced with USPHS, 1951-56. Diplomate Am. Bd. Orthopedic Surgery. Fellow Am. Acad. Orthopedic Surgeons, A.C.S.; mem. N.J., Passaic County med. socs., AMA, N.J., Interstate, Eastern orthopedic assns. Republican Episcopalian. Club: Upper Montclair Country. Home: 561 Cherry Tree Ln Kinnelon NJ 07405 Office: 287 Boulevard Pompton Plains NJ 07444

HOLMAN, WILLIAM GEORGE, coll. ofcl.; b. Hamilton, Mo., Apr. 28, 1903; s. Willis C. and Bertha Rose (Smith) H.; student U. Colo., 1920-22; A.B., Western State Coll., Gunnison, Colo., 1924; M.A., Columbia U., 1935; m. Ethel Simmonds, May 17, 1936; children—Susan Alice, Hazel Marie. Head comml. dept. Orlando (Fla.) High Sch., 1925-26; comml. agt. N.Y. Telephone Co., 1926-27; auditor Fairchild Aviation Corp., 1927-30; auditor, purchasing agt. Am. Airplane & Engine Corp., 1930-33; with Liberty Aircraft Products Corp., 1933-56, sec., treas., dir., 1939-56, budget adminstr. Fairchild Engine div., 1957-59; controller communications and data processing operations Raytheon Co., 1959-61; asst. to pres. and controller rep. for subsidiaries Kollsman Instrument Corp., 1962-63; chmn. dept. bus. adminstrn. U. New Haven, 1963-73, chmn. dept. accounting and fin., 1970—; vis. prof. Campbell Coll., Buies Creek, N.C., 1974-75, Alderson-Broadus Coll., Phillipi, W.Va., 1976—, Campbellsville (Ky.) Coll., 1977-78. Mem. Nat. Assn. Accountants (past pres. L.I. chpt.), Fin. Execs. Inst., N.Y., Conn. socs. C.P.A.'s, Delta Tau Delta. Republican. Episcopalian. Home: 1213 N Main St Lanesboro MA 01237

HOLMAN, WILLIAM JACOB, JR., mfg. co. exec.; b. St. Louis, Aug. 6, 1949; s. William Jacob and Ola Mae (Johnson) H.; B.S. in Bus. Adminstrn., Lincoln U. Mo., 1971, B.S. in Accounting, 1972, M.B.A., 1975; m. Gail Anita Ware, July 1, 1978. Bookkeeper, Goodwill Industries, St. Louis, 1972; resident dir. Lincoln U. Mo., Jefferson City, 1972-73; fin. specialist NCR, Dayton, Ohio, 1973; account receivable accountant Lincoln U. Mo., 1974-76; cost accountant DuPont Co., Glasgow, Del., 1976—. Vol., Cystic Fibrosis Found., Newark, Del., Leukemia Soc., Newark. Mem. Lincoln U. Mo. Alumni Assn., NAACP, Am. Mgmt. Assn., Phi Beta Lambda, Alpha Phi Alpha. Baptist. Club: Bible-A-Month. Home: 26 Winterhaven Dr 11 Newark DE 19702 Office: Route 896 Glasgow DE

HOLMAN, YERBY ROZELLE, retirement community exec.; b. Memphis, Sept. 13, 1915; s. Y. Rozelle and Elizabeth (Wills) H.; B.A., Duke U., 1936; postgrad. Union Theol. Sem., 1936-37, Harvard, 1942; M.L.A., Johns Hopkins, 1964; m. Emily Clark Brown, Dec. 31, 1941; children—Emily C., Hugh F., John S., Elizabeth W. Adminstrv. asst. Milw. Dept. Edn. and Recreation, 1937-39; supt. parks and recreation, Athens, Ga., 1939-42; asst. dir. indsl. relations Standard Brands, Inc., 1946-50; supr. tng. Continental Can Co., 1950-51; asso. partner George H. Elliott & Co., 1951-53; dir. personnel Western Md. Ry. Co., 1953-73; corp. officer equal employment opportunity Chessie System, Balt., 1973-77; exec. dir. Fairhaven Retirement Community, 1977—; guest lectr., instr. U. Ga., 1940, Coll. City N.Y., 1947-49. Pres. sch. bd., Carle Place, L.I., 1949-51. Mem. Md. Gov.'s Task Force on Crime and Correction, 1968, Operating Economy Survey, 1969. Bd. dirs. Md. council Girl Scouts U.S.A., Over 60-Employment Counseling Service, Community Chest Balt., Md. Health and Welfare Council; trustee Prisoners' Aid Assn. Md., 1957-74, pres., 1966-72. Served as maj. USAAF, 1942-46. Mem. Railroad Personnel Assn. (past chmn.). Episcopalian (vestry). Clubs: Merchants; l'Hirondelle Country; Center. Home: 7608 Club Rd Ruxton Baltimore MD 21204 Office: 105 W Monument St Baltimore MD 21201

HOLMES, CARY WILLIAM, educator; b. Newton, Mass., Sept. 5, 1941; s. Harry Hall and Elizabeth (Cox) H.; A.B. cum laude, Northeastern U., 1965, M.Ed., 1968; m. Jane Elizabeth Tromba, May 23, 1964; children—Christopher David, Stephen Alexander, Sarah Elizabeth, Susan Abigail. Tchr. social studies pub. schs., Newton, Mass.; co-dir. S. Boston Neighborhood Action Program; coordinator Mass. Mental Health Center; research asst. South Shore Mental Health Center; asst. prin. Weeks Jr. High Sch., Newton Centre, Mass. Second v.p. Weeks PTA, 1969-74. Mem. Nat. Council Social Studies, Bus. History and Econ. Life Program, U.S. Naval Inst. Episcopalian. Home: 3 Cedar St South Natick MA 01760 Office: Weeks Jr High Sch 7 Hereward Rd Newton Centre MA 02159

HOLMES, DAVID BRYAN, artist; b. Harrow, Eng., Aug. 8, 1936; s. Harold Percy and Ivy Ethel (Gregg) H.; student Twickenham Tech. Coll., Eng., 1952-57, Queen's U., Can., 1965—, Harrow Sch. Art, Eng., London Sch. Art and Design, N.Y.C. Art Students' League, 1971-72. Typography and graphic designer, St. John, N.B., Can., 1960-67; free-lance artist, Kingston, Ont., Can., 1967—; instr. graphic arts, artistic anatomy, painting, etching and silverpoint drawing St. Lawrence Coll. Applied Arts and Tech., Kingston, 1968-74; one-man shows: Galerie Gauvreau, Montreal, Que., Can., 1969, 70, Wally F. Findlay Galleries Internat., N.Y.C., 1974, 76, 78, Chgo., 1977, Beverly Hills, Calif., 1979; two man exhbn. Agnes Etherington Art Centre, Queen's U., Kingston, 1967; exhibited in group shows at Queen's U. Spring Exhbns., Kingston, 1964-72, Soc. Can. Artists Ann. Exhibition, 1968-71, Tom Thomson Gallery, Country Scenes Que., Montreal; represented in permanent collections in Europe and N. Am.; mem. Print and Drawing Council Can. Vice-Pres. Kingston Arts Council, 1971-73. Served with Royal Marines, 1957-59. Mem. Soc. Canadian Artists, N.Y. Art Students League, Internat. Soc. Artists. Address: Rural Route 3 Odessa ON K0H 2H0 Canada

HOLMES, KENNETH HOWARD, lawyer; b. St. Paul, June 13, 1936; s. John Turner and Beatrice Carolina (Johnson) H.; B.S.L., U. Minn., 1958, LL.B. magna cum laude, U. Minn., 1960; m. Karen Ruth Seeger, Aug. 6, 1960; children—John Scott, Mark Turner, Michael Bradley. Admitted to Minn. bar, 1960, N.Y. bar, 1962, U.S. Supreme Ct. bar, 1969, U.S. Dist. Ct. for So. Dist. N.Y., 1970; asso. firm Dewey, Ballantine, Bushby, Palmer & Wood, N.Y.C., 1961-69, partner, 1969—. Served to ensign USCGR, 1960-61. Mem. Am., N.Y. State bar assns., Assn. Bar City N.Y. (mem. com. on bankruptcy and corp. reorgn. 1973-75), Order of Coif. Club: Down Town Assn. (N.Y.C.). Home: 864 Hillside Ave Westfield NJ 07092 Office: 140 Broadway New York City NY 10005

HOLMES, RICHARD WILLIAM, civic worker; b. Williamsport, Pa., Mar. 16, 1909; s. George William and Mabel Mildred (Strailey) H.; student Cornell U., 1942, Fenn Coll., 1953; m. Lucille Leora Parrish, Apr. 8, 1949; children—Richard S., Dorothy E., M. Carol, Mildred E., Judith R. Chief gage br., quality control div. Cleve. Ordance Dist., 1950-53; quality control engr. to field mgr. quality control Carrier Air Conditioning Co., Syracuse, N.Y., 1953-70; mgr. quality control The Brown Corp., Syracuse, 1970—; lectr. Auburn Community Coll., Auburn, N.Y., 1965-66, Onondaga Community Coll., 1967, N. Syracuse High Sch. Adult Edn., 1968; lectr. in field. Pres., Accord, Inc. (Action Coalition to Create Opportunities for Retirement with Dignity), Syracuse, 1976-78; Rep. campaign coordinator, 1972, committeeman, 1971-77. Served with USAAF, 1926-27. Recipient Letter of Commendation, Auburn Coll., 1966. Mem. Am. Soc. Metals, Am. Inst. Indsl. Engrs., Am. Soc. Quality Control (sr.; chmn. Syracuse sect. 1957). Republican. Episcopalian. Club: Masons. Home: 8321 Lakeshore Rd RD 1 Clay NY 13041 Office: 264 E Onondaga St Syracuse NY 13202

HOLMGREN, THEODORE J., food co. exec.; b. N.Y.C., May 2, 1927; s. Oscar F. and Madeline (Thompson) H.; A.B., Brown U., 1949; M.B.A., Harvard U., 1955; m. Miriam Brady, June 3, 1950; children—Miriam Jane, Barbara Lynn, Theodore Douglas. Dir. design services Gen. Foods Corp., White Plains, N.Y., 1960-62, corp. new products mgr., 1962-65, sr. product mgr., 1965-68; sr. cons. mktg. Peat Marwick Mitchell & Co., N.Y.C., 1968; v.p. mktg., dir. Curtice-Burns, Inc., Rochester, N.Y., 1968—, also dir. Pres. Community Council Chs. Irvington, Ardsley, Dobbs Ferry, Hastings and Hartsdale, N.Y., 1961-63; trustee Orphan Asylum Soc. City N.Y., 1964-68, Curtice-Burns Charitable Found. Served to lt. (j.g.) USNR, 1951-53. Mem. Alpha Delta Phi. Club: Harvard Bus. Sch. (Rochester). Home: 16 Esternay Ln Pittsford NY 14534 Office: 1 Lincoln First Sq Rochester NY 14602

HOLMQUIST, HOWARD EMIL, chemist; b. Chgo., Mar. 21, 1927; s. Emil Constantine and Anna Gunhild (Tholander) H.; B.S., Northwestern U., 1947; Ph.D., U. Minn., 1951. Chemist, E.I. duPont de Nemours, Wilmington, Del., 1951—, central research dept., 1951-60, elastomer chems. dept., 1960—. Mem. Am. Chem. Soc., Sigma Xi. Contbr. articles to profl. jours. Patentee in field. Office: DuPont Experimental Station Wilmington DE 19898

HOLOHAN, WARREN W., JR., writer, graphic designer; b. Auburn, N.Y., Sept. 7, 1946; s. Warren William and Marion Braun H.; A.A., Mercer County Coll., 1971; 1 son, Paedrick Wolfe. Journalist, Asbury Park (N.J.) Press, 1967-69; art dir. Peterson Research Group, Princeton, N.J., 1971-72; freelance writer/graphic designer, Trenton, N.J., 1969-71, 72-76; dir. pub. relations N.J. Pub. Interest Research Group, 1971; mng. editor Spectrum and P.S. Mag., Jade Communications, Princeton, N.J.; lectr. in field. Recipient award for Investigative Reporting, Life Pub. Co., 1974; NeoGraphics Silver award for excellence of design, 1974. Mem. Am. Med. Writers Assn., Am. Heart Assn., Am. Acad. Polit. and Social Sci., Smithsonian Instn., Tau Phi Rho (founder, past pres.). Author: (poetry) Metamorphosis, 1969; Open I, 1971; Open II, 1972; (fiction) Small Town Girl, 1974; Rainy Smiles from Postcard Days, 1973; The Success of Orlo Keats Jr., 1974; (play) Merlin and Vivien, 1969. Address: 319 Prince St Bordentown NJ 08505

HOLSTEN, RICHARD DAVID, research adminstr.; b. Wilmington, Del., Jan. 26, 1937; s. John Wesley and Josephine Barbara (Berger) H.; A.B., Temple U., 1961; Ph.D. in Plant Physiology and Biochemistry Genetics, Cornell U., 1965; m. Sandra Jane Mayhew, Oct. 20, 1956; children—Amy Jo, David, Robert, Thomas. Instr. botany Cornell U., 1964-65, asst. prof. sect. genetics, devel. and physiology, 1965-66; research biologist central research dept. E.I. duPont de Nemours & Co., Inc., 1966-71, sr. research biochemist instrument products div., 1971-72, research supr., 1972-74, supr. exploratory research and devel., 1974-78, now mgr. clin. specialties instrument products div. Bd. dirs. Newark Community Aquatic Assn. Served with USAF, 1955-58. NSF fellow 1961; NIH fellow, 1962-64. Mem. AAAS, Am. Assn. Clin. Chemists, Sigma Xi. Author articles in field. Research on growth and metabolism, cell interactions, symbiotic N2-fixation, clin. chemistry. Home: 728 Fawn Rd Berkeley Farm Newark DE 19711 Office: 1007 Market St Wilmington DE 19898

HOLT, ARTHUR HENRY, JR., communications cons. co. exec.; b. Leggett, Tex., Feb. 19, 1931; s. Arthur Henry and Haddie Frances (Pinckard) H.; B.F.A., U. Tex., 1952; m. Imogene Phyllis Jones, Jan. 1, 1951; children—Gordon Arthur, Carlton Howard, Hollis Lucinda. Pres. Holt Corp. Pa., Bethlehem, offices also Dallas, Bogota, Colombia, 1969—; cons., lectr. in field. Served with 36th inf. AUS, 1948-50. Mem. Bethlehem C. of C. (dir. 1972—), Bethlehem Downtown Bus. Assn. (dir. 1973—), Nat., Pa. assns. broadcasters, Radio Advt. Bur., Inter-Am. Broadcasting Assn., Inst. Broadcast Fin. Mgmt. Episcopalian. Clubs: Livingston (Allentown, Pa.), Broadcasters. Contbr. articles to profl. publs. Home: 13 Dartford Rd Bethlehem PA 18015 Office: 2285 Schoenersville Rd Suite 205 Bethlehem PA 18017

HOLT, BARRY CLAY, govt. ofcl.; b. Washington, Oct. 25, 1931; s. Raymond Sizer and Elizabeth Vernau (Martin) H.; B.S., U. Md., 1958; postgrad. Cath. U. Am., 1958-59; m. Sally Ann Molster, May 1, 1954; children—Kyle Martin, Dwayne Clayton. Project engr. propulsion systems Navy Dept., Washington, 1958-60, project engr. simulation systems, 1960-63, supervisory engr., 1963-65, tech. dir., 1965-69, program mgr. simulation and tng. systems, 1969—; lectr. in field. Served with U.S. Army, 1953. Mem. ASME, U. Md. Alumni Assn., Nat. Contracts Mgmt. Assn. Roman Catholic. Contbr. articles in field to profl. jours. Home: 8812 Liberty Ln Potomac MD 20854 Office: Naval Air Systems Command Navy Dept Washington DC 20361

HOLT, HERBERT, psychiatrist; b. Vienna, Austria, Apr. 27, 1912; s. Leon and Cecilia (von Lempel) H.; Absolvent der Medizin, U. Vienna, 1937; Docteur en Medicine, U. Lausanne (Switzerland), 1938; m. Dolores Bolla di Osasco, July 14, 1961; children—Renata, Gerhard. Came to U.S., 1936, naturalized, 1941. Intern, Bellevue Hosp., N.Y.C., 1938-39, resident, 1939-41; practice medicine specializing in psychiatry and psychoanalysis, N.Y.C., 1951—; dean Westchester Inst., Rye, N.Y., 1970—; dir. N.Y. Inst. Existential Analysis, 1965—. Med. dir. Cathedral Counseling Service Cathedral Ch. St. John the Divine, N.Y.C., Actors Counseling Service, N.Y.C. Fellow Assn. for Applied Psychoanalysis (founding pres.), Am. Assn. for Social Psychiatry, Am. Soc. Psychoanalytic Physicians, Am. Ontoanalytic Assn., Am. Soc. Existential Psychiatry (pres. 1972—), Am. Acad. Psychoanalysis. Author: Free to Be Good or Bad, 1976; contbg. author Comprehensive Textbook of Psychiatry II, 1975. Editor: Jour. Modern Psychotherapy. Contbr. chpts. to textbooks, articles to profl. jours. Address: 185 E 85th St New York City NY 10028

HOLT, JOSEPH WILLIAM, reins. co. exec.; b. Apr. 16, 1930; s. Joseph W. and Helen G. Holt; B.A., Maryville Coll., 1950; M.A., U. Pa., 1954; m. Irina von der Launitz, July 19, 1952; children—Lise Margaret Bradley, Helen Alexandra Lizott. Mgr. Parker & Co. Internat., Phila., 1952-54; with Price Forbes, London, 1955, Interocean Agy., N.Y.C., 1956-67; co-founder, exec. v.p., dir. Duncanson & Holt, Inc., 1967; pres. R.A. Fulton & Co., Inc., 1968; exec. v.p. Reed & Brown, 1974; v.p. Aeospace Mgrs., 1974, D & H Tech. Services, Inc., 1974; exec. v.p. ERG Mgmt. Corp., 1975; exec. vp., dir. Rochdale Ins. Co., 1976—; pres., dir. United Ams. Ins. Co., 1978—. Club: World Trade. Home: 1100 Rahway Rd Plainfield NJ 07060 also 206 E 61st St New York City NY 10021 also Amen Farm Brooklin ME 04616 Office: 99 John St New York City NY 10038

HOLT, MARJORIE SEWELL (MRS. DUNCAN MCKAY HOLT), congresswoman; b. Birmingham, Ala., Sept. 17, 1920; d. Edward Roland and Alice Juanita (Felts) Sewell; J.D., U. Fla., 1949; m. Duncan McKay Holt, Dec. 26, 1946; children—Rachel (Mrs. Kenneth Hall Tschantre), Edward, Victoria (Mrs. James Stauffer). Admitted to Fla. bar, 1949, Md. bar, 1962; practiced in Severna Park, Md., 1962-66; clk., Anne Arundel Circuit Ct., Annapolis, 1966-72; mem. 93d-96th congress from 4th Md. Dist.; vice chmn. Office Tech. Assessment, 1977. Mem. housing com. Anne Arundel County (Md.) Human Relations Commn., 1964-67; supr. elections Anne Arundel County, 1963-65; del. Republican Nat. Conv., 1968, 76; counsel Md. Fedn. Rep. Women, 1972. Mem. Am., Md., Anne Arundel County bar assns., Md. Clks. Assn. (mem. exec. bd. 1967-73), Phi Kappa Phi, Phi Delta Delta. Presbyterian. (elder). Co-author, editor: The Case Against Reckless Congress, 1976; Can You Afford This House, 1978. Office: 1510 Longworth Bldg Washington DC 20515

HOLT, PHILETUS HAVENS, III, architect; b. Summit, N.J., Aug. 19, 1928; s. Robert Sherman and Alice Kathleen (Gallwey) H.; grad. Phillips Exeter Acad., 1946; A.B., with honors, Princeton, 1950, M.F.A. (A.I.A. medal), 1952; m. Nancy deFreest Brownley, June 16, 1950; children—Alexandra Foster, Robert Stephen. Designer, William F.R. Ballard, architect, N.Y.C., 1952-55; designer, asso. C.K. Agle, architect, Princeton, N.J., 1955-65; partner Holt & Morgan, architects, Princeton, 1965-72; pres. Holt & Morgan Assos. P.A., architects-planners, 1972—; guest lectr. Grad. Sch. Fine Arts, U. Pa., 1971-77; prin. works include Spring Grove reconstruction and addition, 1967, Rutgers Camden Library, 1969, Tenacre Nurses Dormitory, 1971, Classroom-Office Bldg. Douglass and Cook Colls., 1976. Mem. Princeton Mayor's Adv. Com. for Downtown, 1971-72; adv. housing subcom. Princeton Regional Planning Bd., 1971-72. Trustee Arts Council Princeton, 1970—, pres., 1972; trustee Hist. Soc. Princeton, 1977—; v.p. Architects Housing Co., Inc., 1976—. Recipient Design award N.J. Soc. Architects, 1970, 73, 75, award merit, 1971, 73. Mem. A.I.A. Club: Corinthians, New Haven Yacht. Illustrator: Gardens of Illusion, 1972. Home: 3472 Lawrenceville Rd Princeton NJ 08540 Office: 20 Nassau St Princeton NJ 08540

HOLTE, CLARENCE LEROY, publisher; b. Norfolk, Va., Feb. 19, 1909; s. Samuel and Dora (Whitted) H.; student Lincoln U., 1930-32, Am. Inst. Banking, 1932-34, New Sch. of Social Research, 1940-42; m. Audrey M. Proctor, Dec. 22, 1945; 1 dau., Helen Ruth. Teller Dunbar Nat. Bank, N.Y.C., 1932-35; race relations specialist WPA, N.Y.C., 1935-40; traffic mgr. Conlan Electric Corp., Bklyn., 1940-44; sales rep. Lever Bros. Co., 1944-52; mktg. exec. Batten, Barton, Durstine & Osborn, 1952-73; pres. Nubian Press, Inc., 1971—; editorial cons. Nat. Scene, newspaper supplement, 1975—. Mem. Nat. Assn. Mktg. Developers, Alpha Phi Alpha. Club: Masons. Editor/pub.: Nubian Baby Book; editor: Basic Afro-American Reprint Library, 57 vols., 1970-71; contbr. articles to profl. jours. Collector of Africana, with collection now housed in Clarence L. Holte Africana room at Ahmadu Bello U., Zaria, Nigeria. Home: 555 Edgecombe Ave New York City NY 10032 Office: 507 Fifth Ave New York City NY 10017

HOLTER, JOANNE CLAIRE MINARD, social worker; b. Plattsburgh, N.Y., Nov. 15, 1929; d. Dalton Arthur and Arlene R. (Antes) Minard; student U. Rochester, 1947-50; B.A., Vanderbilt U., 1955; postgrad. Sch. Social Work, Bryn Mawr Coll., 1957-58; M.S.W., Smith Coll., 1963; m. Frank Robert Holter, Sept. 9, 1950 (div. Sept. 1962); 1 son, Peter Marcus; m. 2d, Andrew J. Rector, Aug. 10, 1973. With med. social service dept. U. Rochester Med. Center, 1963-65, pediatric research social worker, asst. in pediatrics and preventive medicine, 1965-67; pediatric social worker med. social service dept. Albany (N.Y.) Med. Center Hosp., 1969-70; adminstr., therapist, children's div. York County (Pa.) Mental Health Center, York, 1970-74, 77—; instr. dept. pediatrics U. Md. Sch. Medicine, 1974-75, asst. prof., 1975-77. Mem. joint legis. com. on child care needs N.Y.

State Subcom. on Health Services and Protective Services, 1968-69; mem. regional com. protection children Pa. Dept. Pub. Welfare, 1972—, chmn. inst., 1972; chmn. York County Com. for Protection Children, 1972—; cons. to local agys. Mem. Nat. Assn. Social Workers, Acad. Certified Social Workers. Republican. Research and publs. in pediatrics. Home: 2299 Sycamore Rd York PA 17404 Office: 1001 S George St York PA 17403

HOLTHAUS, ALICE MARION FESKO, town ofcl.; b. Holyoke, Mass., Aug. 26, 1917; d. John and Barbara (Lokay) Fesko; grad. Coll. Practical Arts and Letters, Boston U., 1949; m. James Joseph Holthaus, June 14, 1952; 1 son, James Joseph. Sec., Highland Mfg. Co., Holyoke, 1936-40, Am. Bosch Corp., Springfield, Mass., 1940-41; sec. WPB, Washington, 1941-42, Springfield, 1942-43; exec. sec., auditor VA, Boston, 1945-53; asst. town clk., Rockland, Mass., 1962-67, town clk., 1967—. Served with USMCWR, 1943-45. Mem. Rockland C. of C. (dir., sec.), New Eng. Assn. City and Town Clks., Mass. Town Clks. Assn., Town and City Clks. Assn. Plymouth, Bristol and Norfolk Counties. Home: 38 Blossom St Rockland MA 02370 Office: Town Hall Rockland MA 02370

HOLTON, JOHN HILL, JR., mfg. co. exec.; b. Boston; s. John Hill and Sarah (Pierpont) H.; B.S., Yale, 1943; student Harvard Bus. Sch., 1976; m. Margaret Louise Bissett, Jan. 2, 1943; children—Linda Holton Roth, Jack, Betsy, Janice. Dist. plant supr. FMC Corp., Middleport, N.Y., 1946-53; exec. v.p., Gallow Chem. Co., Ossining, N.Y., 1954-57; exec. v.p. ops. Nat. Sugar Refining Co., N.Y.C., and Phila., 1961-68; pres., owner Bio Serv Inc., Little Silver, N.J., 1969—, also Holton Industries, Holton Foods. Mem. Sch. Bd., Medina, N.Y., 1948-52, Rumson, N.J., 1965-74. Served to lt. USNR, 1943-46. Mem. Am. Inst. Chem. Engrs., Am. Chem. Soc., Inst. Food Technologists, Am. Assn. Lab. Animal Scientists, Entomology Soc. Am. Presbyterian (elder). Clubs: Compass Point Yacht, Yale. Home: 36 E River Rd Rumson NJ 07760 Office: 466 Propsect Ave Little Silver NJ 07739

HOLTZ, GILBERT JOSEPH, steel co. exec.; b. N.Y.C., Jan. 23, 1924; s. Al S. and Carrie (Schindler) H.; student N.Y.U., 1940-42; m. Caria Kahn, July 18, 1948; children—Steven J., Robert A. Vice pres. Hanger Service Co., Yonkers, N.Y., 1946-48; owner Economy Sales Co., Yonkers, 1948-50; pres. Walnut Metal Industries, Inc., Yonkers, 1955—, Holtz Realty Corp., 1962—, 411 Walnut St. Corp., 1962—, Walnut Assn. Inc., 1961—; v.p. Belvedere Space Saving Products Inc., 1951-70; pres. Belvedere Internat. Ltd., 1970—, Belvedere Home Products, Inc., 1968—. Republican ward leader 2d ward, Yonkers. Mem. Citizens' Adv. Com., Yonkers Urban Renewal. Served with AUS, 1943-45. Mem. C. of C. Kiwanian. Patentee in field. Home: 182 Tibbetts Rd Yonkers NY 10705 Office: 1051 Saw Mill River Rd Yonkers NY 10710

HOLTZ, ITSHAK JACK, artist; b. Poland, Dec. 14, 1925; s. Leib and Lisa (Golup) H.; student Art Students League, N.Y.C., 1950-52, NAD, N.Y.C., 1952-53; m. Gertrude Ruth Beck, Feb. 25, 1950; children—Alice, Arie Oscar. One-man shows include: Bezalel Art Gallery, N.Y.C., 1978, Tyringham Gallery (Mass.), summers 1968—; group shows include: Theodor Herzel Inst., N.Y.C., 1968, Allied Artists Am., 1976, Audubon Artists, 1977, NAD, N.Y.C., 1978, others in Denver, Los Angeles, Phila. and Jerusalem; represented in permanent collections in U.S. and Israel. Mem. Art Student League (life). Home: 66 Fort Washington Ave New York City NY 10032 Studio: 118 E 28th St New York City NY 10016

HOLTZ, SIDNEY, pub. co. exec.; b. N.Y.C., Mar. 24, 1925; s. Jacob and Rose (Cholmar) H.; B.S., L.I. U., 1949; M.S., N.Y. U., 1950; B.P.A. (hon.), Brooks Inst., 1973; m. Florence Fogel, Sept. 6, 1952; children—Jeffrey, Clifford, Linda. Tchr. pub. schs., N.Y.C., 1951-53; advt. sales rep. N.Y. Herald Tribune, 1953-58; with Ziff-Davis Pub. Co., N.Y.C., 1958—, mem. sales staff Popular Photography, 1958-60, advt. dir., 1960-67, asso. pub., 1967-68, pub., 1968—, corp. v.p., 1972—. Chmn., Nonpartisan Nominating Com. for Selection of Sch. Bd. Officers; mem. Riverfront Council of Dobbs Ferry. Served with U.S. Army, 1943-46. Mem. Internat. Center Photography (dir., mem. exec. com.), Photog. Art and Sci. Found. (gov.), Photog. Mfrs. and Distbrs. Assn., Photog. Industry Internat. (chmn. pres.'s council). Clubs: Dellwood Country, Kiwanis. Office: Ziff-Davis Pub Co One Park Ave New York NY 10016

HOLTZMAN, ARNOLD HAROLD, chem. co. exec.; b. Phila., May 11, 1932; s. William and Rae (Shapiro) H.; B.S., Drexel Inst., 1954; M.S., Lehigh U., 1956, Ph.D., 1957; m. Phyllis Raskow, June 26, 1955; children—Rosalind Ann, Linda Susan, William Lewis. Asst. metallurgist J. Bishop & Co., Malvern, Pa., 1954; with duPont Co., various locations, 1957—, research mgr., dist. sales mgr. Polymer Intermediates dept., Wilmington, Del., 1973-76, mgr. new bus. programs, central research and devel. dept., Wilmington, 1976—. Recipient John Price Wetherill medal Franklin Inst., 1969. Fellow Am. Soc. Metals; mem. Sigma Xi. Patentee in processing of metals and non metals. Home: 208 Stone Crop Rd Wilmington DE 19810 Office: 1007 Market St Wilmington DE 19898

HOLTZMAN, ELIZABETH, congresswoman; b. Bklyn., Aug. 11, 1941; d. Sidney and Filia Holtzman; A.B. magna cum laude, Radcliffe Coll., 1962; J.D., Harvard, 1965. Admitted to N.Y. State bar; asso. firm Wachtell, Lipton, Rosen, Katz & Kern, N.Y.C., 1965-67; asst. to Mayor N.Y.C., 1967-70; then asso. firm Paul, Weiss, Rifkind, Wharton & Garrison, 1970-72; mem. 93d-96th Congresses from 16th N.Y. State dist. Founder Bklyn. Women's Polit. Caucus; N.Y. State Democratic committeewoman, 1970—: del.-at-large Dem. nat. conv., 1972. Mem. nat. adv. bd. Hampshire Coll. Named 1 of 10 Women of Year, Mademoiselle mag., 1972; recipient Alumnae Recognition Award Radcliffe Coll. Alumnae Assn., 1973, Myrtle Wreath award Bklyn. Hadassah, 1974; named Woman of Year, United HIAS, Service Women's div., 1974. Mem. Nat. Women's Polit. Caucus, Bar Assn. City N.Y., Hadassah. Home: Brooklyn NY 11230 Office: 1027 Longworth Office Bldg Washington DC 20515 also 1452 Flatbush Ave Brooklyn NY 11210

HOLZINGER, CECILE, artist; b. Dortmund, Germany; d. Frederic and Cecilia (Schaefer) Graeber; grad. Dortmund Coll., U. Trieste (Italy); scholarship student Art Students' League, N.Y.C., 1948-49; m. Dr. Ernest Holzinger, (dec.). Exhibited in group shows Met. Museum, Phila. Mus., Pa. Acad. Fine Arts, Library of Congress, Seattle Art Mus., Bradley U., U. So. Calif., Am. Graphic Artists, Norfolk Mus., Conn. Acad., Dallas Mus., City Center of N.Y., Nat. Assn. Women Artists, Denver Mus., Dayton Art Inst., John Herron Art Mus., New Britian Art Mus., Am. Color Print Soc., Print Club of Phila., Pratt-Contemporaries Graphic Art Center, 1959, Kuala Lumpur Brit. Council Hall, 1958, Bibliotheque Americaine Phnom-Penh, 1958, Manila, 1958, Djakarta, 1959, Japan, 1959, 67, Audubon Art Whitney Museum, Butler Art Inst., 1960, Bklyn. Mus., 1960, Nat. Acad., Albany Print Club, also India and France, 1966, Naples, Italy, Palazzo Vecchio, Florence, Italy, 1972, Germany, 1974, also S.Am.; represented in permanent collections Phila. Art Museum, Library of Congress, Jackson Gallery, Norfolk Museum of Art, Bklyn. Mus., also in pvt. collections. Traveling exhibit USIA, Far East, Europe and South Africa, 1962. Recipient 1st prize for oil City Center N.Y., 1953, purchase award Library Congress, 1956; hon. mention Henry B. Shope prize Soc. Am. Graphic Artists, 1954; Louis Comfort Tiffany Found. award, 1956; A. N. Khouri prize, 1960, Margaret Lowengrund Memorial prize, 1963. Mem. Am. Color Print Soc., Art Students League, Artists Equity, Nat. Assn. Women Artists (mem. exec. bd.), Soc. Am. Graphic Artists, Phila. Print Club. Home: 900 W 190th St New York City NY 10040

HOLZMAN, ELEANORE MARIENNE GRUSHLAW (MRS. ROBERT STUART HOLZMAN), clin. psychologist; b. N.Y.C., Nov. 22, 1912; d. Israel and Isabelle (Feinberg) Grushlaw; B.A., Barnard Coll., 1933; M.A., Columbia U., 1934; Ph.D., N.Y. U., 1950; m. Robert Stuart Holzman, May 27, 1938. Research psychologist House of Detention for Women, N.Y.C., 1935-40; co-founder, supr. psychol. clinic Exptl. Ct. for Wayward Minors, N.Y.C., 1937; staff psychologist N.Y.C. Dept. Correction, 1940-45, cons. psychologist, 1950-56, mem. med. adv. bd., 1957-61; lectr. dept. psychology Queens Coll., 1950, 51; acting asst. prof. dept. psychology Bklyn. Coll., 1952; cons. psychologist Bentley Schs., N.Y.C., 1951-76, Eisman Day Nurseries, N.Y.C., 1965-73, Headstart Program for Handicapped, Conn., 1973, 74; pvt. practice children and adolescent clin. psychology, 1951—. Registered in Nat. Register Health Service Providers. Diplomate Am. Bd. Profl. Psychology. Fellow Am. Psychol. Assn.; mem. Eastern, N.Y. State, Conn. psychol. assns., N.Y. Soc. Clin. Psychologists, N.Y. Freudian Soc. (chmn. tng. com. 1967-69, corr. sec., dir. 1966-76), Soc. Pediatric Psychologists, Phi Beta Kappa. Office: 35 Tamarack Ave Danbury CT 06810

HOLZMAN, STEVEN ELLIOTT, elec. engr.; b. Burbank, Calif., Mar. 7, 1945; s. Mark and Nadia H.; B.E.E., Calif. Poly. U., 1970; M.E.E., U. Santa Clara, 1975; m. Donnis Marie Leger, Apr. 1, 1967. Project engr. Montedoro Corp., San Luis Obispo, Calif., 1967-70; mgr. electronic countermeasures group ESL Inc., Sunnyvale, Calif., 1970-75; mgr. spl. programs Sanders Assos., Nashua, N.H., 1975—. Served with U.S. Army, 1963-67. Mem. IEEE. Home: RFD 3 Honey Brook Ln Amherst NH 03031 Office: 95 canal St Nashua NH 03061

HONAMAN, NANCY, coll. ofcl.; b. Phila., May 9, 1926; d. Ira Franklin and Clara (Baldwin) Honaman; A.B., Mt. Holyoke Coll., 1948; M. Adminstrn., Pa. State U., 1970; m George E. Rutter, June 18, 1949 (div. Apr. 1966); children—Gregory H., Geoffrey B. Instr. econs. Franklin and Marshall Coll., Lancaster, Pa., 1948-49, registrar, 1955-78, registrar and dir. spl. programs, 1978—; wage and job analyst personnel dept. Aetna Life Ins. Co., Hartford, Conn., 1949-51. Mem. edn. and research com. Lancaster Gen. Hosp.; mem. Lancaster County Crime Commn.; capt., worker United Fund drives, Hosp. Fund drives; precinct worker, mem. Lancaster Women's Republican Club; Rep. committeewoman. Mem. Pa. Soc. Mayflower Descs., Am. (editorial bd. Coll. and U. jour.; v.p. nominations and elections com.), Middle States (editor, pres., sec., exec. com.) assns. collegiate registrars and admissions officers, D.A.R. Episcopalian. Home: 465 Hawthorne Dr Lancaster PA 17603

HONAMAN, WINIFRED PINKERTON, hosp. adminstr.; b. Bklyn., Apr. 14, 1924; d. Frederick Hotchkiss and Geraldine (Crawford) Pinkerton; student Colby Jr. Coll., 1942-44; m. W. Barrett Mayer, Aug. 5, 1944; children—Susan, Lynn, Kathleen, Leirion; m. 2d, Richard K. Honaman, Jr., Nov. 25, 1970. Central service asst. Montclair (N.J.) Community Hosp., 1959-68, dir. purchasing, 1968—. Home: 168 Hawthorne Ave Glen Ridge NJ 07028 Office: 120 Harrison Ave Montclair NJ 07042

HONARVAR, ALIZA AGHDAS, pathologist: b. Tehran, Iran, July 15, 1944; d. Ezat and Iran (Zand) H.; came to U.S., 1968; M.D., Tehran Med. U., 1967; m. Zamani, Aug. 28, 1976. Intern, Pahlavi Hosp., Tehran, also St. Francis Hosp., N.Y., 1967-69; resident N.Y. Med. Coll., Flower and Fifth Ave Hosp., Met. Hosp., N.Y.C., 1969-73; chief resident, fellow Jewish Meml. Hosp., N.Y.C., 1973-74; assoc. pathologist Flushing Hosp. and Med. Center, N.Y., 1974—. Diplomate Am. Bd. Pathology, also cert. blood banking. Fellow Coll. Am. Pathologists, Am. Soc. Clin. Pathologists; mem. N.Y. State Soc. Pathologists, Am. Assn. Blood Banks, AMA. Home: 755 Plandome Rd Manhasset NY 11030

HONGO, RONALD JOSEPH, accountant; b. Lowville, N.Y., Apr. 29, 1937; s. Joseph and Eloise Evelyn (Nye) H.; B.S. in Pub. Accounting, Syracuse U., 1966; m. Joan S. Mattison, Aug. 11, 1956; children—Susan Marie, Stephen Michael, Scott Mark, Sharlene Margaret. Accountant, Haver & King, Pub. Accountants, Watertown, N.Y., 1957-61, Lybrand, Ross Bros. & Montgomery, Syracuse, N.Y., 1961-65; Charles Scrimale, Pub. Accountant, Syracuse, 1965-68; pvt. practice C.P.A., North Syracuse, N.Y., 1968—; instr. Onondaga Community Coll., Am. U. Town Comptroller, Clay, N.Y., 1970-71. C.P.A., N.Y. Mem. Am. Inst. C.P.A., Greater Syracuse C. of C., Greater N. Syracuse C. of C., Nat. Fedn. Ind. Bus., Adirondack Forty-Sixers. Presbyterian. Clubs: Republican (Clay). Mountain climber. Home: 102 Wells Ave E North Syracuse NY 13212 Office: 401 S Main St North Syracuse NY 13212

HONIG, ARNOLD, educator; b. N.Y.C., Feb. 28, 1928; s. Ralph and Margaret (Gershman) H.; B.A., Cornell U., 1948; Ph.D., Columbia U., 1953; m. Alice Sterling, Oct. 3, 1948 (div. Oct. 1977); children—Lawrence, Madeleine, Jonathan. Research asso. U. Calif. at Berkeley, 1953-54; research fellow Ecole Normale Superieure, Paris, France, 1954-56; asst. prof. physics Syracuse (N.Y.) U., 1956-59, asso. prof., 1959-61, prof., 1961—, head magnetic resonance and low temperature lab., 1956—. Cons., lectr. Research grantee Air Force Office Sci. Research, 1956-66, NSF, 1959-77; Frederick Garner Cottrell Research Corp. grantee, 1957-59; recipient Glover Meml. award Dickinson Coll., 1966. Mem. Am. Phys. Soc., Fedn. Am. Scientists, AAUP, N.Y. Acad. Scis., Sigma Xi. Contbr. articles to profl. jours. Patentee in field. Home: 4253 Oran-Delphi Rd Oran NY 13125

HONIG, HARVEY, coll. counselor; b. Bklyn., Sept. 22, 1934; s. Nathan and Sylvia (Bromstein) H.; B.S., N.Y. U., 1959, M.A., 1961; m. Mildred Glick, Mar. 17, 1974. Occupational therapist, research asst. Bellevue Hosp., N.Y.C., 1959-60; therapist St. Mary's Recreation Center, Bronx, N.Y., part-time 1961-64; vocat. rehab. counselor Jewish Guild for the Blind, N.Y.C., 1962-64; mem. teaching faculty Inst. Applied Human Dynamics, Bronx, part-time 1964-69; counselor student personnel services dept., coordinator Spl. Services for Physically Handicapped Students, N.Y.C. Community Coll., 1964—, mem. exec. bd. com. for advancement of higher edn. for disabled, 1971—, chmn. com. to advance goal of higher edn. for disabled, 1972-76, prin. investigator program devel. office, 1974-76. Vice-chmn. Soc. to Advance Travel for Handicapped, 1976—; City U. rep. to Mayor's Office for Handicapped of City N.Y., 1973—; bd. dirs. Inst. Applied Human Dynamic Center for Handicapped, Bronx, N.Y., 1976—, Guide Dog Found. for Blind Inc., Smithtown, N.Y., 1978—. Mem. Howe Soc., Am. Council of Blind, Am., N.Y. State personnel and guidance assns., Nat., N.Y.C. rehab. and counseling assns., Nat. Rehab. Assn. Home: 35 Seacoast Terr Brooklyn NY 11235 Office: 300 Jay St Brooklyn NY 11201

HONIG, MERVIN, artist; b. N.Y.C., Dec. 25, 1920; s. Joseph and Frances (Flaum) H.; student Francis Criss, Amadee Ozenfant, Hans Hofmann; B.A., Bklyn. Coll., 1973; M.A. in Humanities; m. Rhoda Sherbell, Apr. 28, 1956; 1 dau., Susan. One-man shows at Kingsworthy Art Gallery, N.Y.C., 1961, County Art Gallery, Westbury, N.Y., 1963, 65, Grace Gallery, N.Y.C. Community Coll., 1968, Westbury Meml. Pub. Library, 1969, Frank Rehn Gallery, N.Y.C., 1970, Nassau Community Coll., 1971, Nat. Art Mus. Sport, 1977; exhibited in group shows at Carnegie Inst., 1945, Met. Mus. Art, 1944, Whitney Mus. Artists Ann., 1949, Nat. Acad. Galleries, 1963, Bklyn. Mus., 1960, N.A.D., 1962, Jersey City Mus. Ann. Exhbn., 1966, Locust Valley Art Show (1st prize), 1966, Wadworth Atheneum, Conn. Acad. Fine Arts, 1965-66, Soc. 4 Arts, 1965, Am. Vets. Soc. (meml. gold medal), 1966, Purdue U., 1966, Butler Inst. Am. Art, Youngstown, Ohio, 1967, 69, Nat. Art Mus. Sport, N.Y.C., 1968, 1969, Audubon Artists Ann., 1968, 69, 70, 76-78, Allied Artists, 1975, 78, Westbury Pub. Library, 1978, Queens Mus., 1978, others. Lectr. conservation of paintings Hofstra U., 1972; represented in permanent collections Okla. Mus. Art, Oklahoma City, Colby Coll. Art Mus., Emily Love Gallery, Hofstra U. pvt. collections; conservator of paintings; lectr. conservation paintings New Sch. Social Research, 1976-78. Asso. trustee Nat. Art Mus. Sport, 1978—. Recipient bronze medal, hon. mention Am. Vets. Soc. Artists, 1968; award of excellence Grover M. Hermann Arts Center, 1970; Watson Guptil prize Knickerbocker Artists, 1978. Mem. Internat. Inst. Conversation Historic and Artistic Works, Coll. Art Assn. Am., Audubon Artists N.Y. (corr. sec. 1977-79). Address: 64 Jane Ct Westbury NY 11590

HONS, PETER WILLIAM, pharmacist; b. Greensburg, Pa., Dec. 13, 1917; s. Leonard Keck and Margaret Catherine (Hoffman) H.; B.S. in Pharmacy, U. Pitts., 1946; m. Margaret Virginia Keim, Aug. 5, 1944; 1 son, Peter Keim. Pharmacist, Kott's Pharmacy, Coraopolis, Pa., 1945-46, Sun Drug, Greensburg, 1946-48, Picking Drug Store, Somerset, Pa., 1948-52; owner Hons Drugstore, Portage, Pa., 1952-75; dir. pharamcy Miners Hosp. No. Cambria, Spangler, Pa., 1975—. Mem. bd. mgmt. Cambria County Library, 1960—; bd. dirs. Portage Pub. Library, 1955—, v.p. 1955—. Served with U.S. Army, World War II; Korea. Mem. Nat. Assn. Retail Druggists. Lutheran. Clubs: Lions, Rotary. Home: 100 Poplar St Portage PA 15946 Office: Miners Hosp No Cambria Box 58 Spangler PA 15775

HOOD, LARRY LEE, food scientist; b. Olney, Ill., Mar. 5, 1944; s. J.C. and Amy Lodema (Land) H.; B.S. in Food Sci., U. Ill., 1966; M.S. (USPHS scholar), Mich. State U., 1968, Ph.D., 1973; m. Catherine E. Harris, Aug. 31, 1968. Grad. research asst. Mich. State U., 1966-73; group leader-biochemistry Quaker Oats Co., Barrington, Ill., 1973-76; research asso.-applied research-proteins ITT-Continental Baking Co., Rye, N.Y., 1977—. Mem. Am. Chem. Soc., Inst. Food Tech., AAAS, Ill. Acad. Sci., Sigma Xi. Club: Masons. Contbr. articles to profl. jours. Patentee color stabilized product and process. Office: ITT-Continental Baking Co Box 731 Rye NY 10580

HOOD, THOMAS RICHARD, artist, graphic designer, educator; b. Phila., July 13, 1910; s. Thomas Richard and Anne Lovering (Grubb) H.; student U. Pa., 1929-30; B.F.A. in Advt. Design, Phila. Mus. Coll. Art, 1953. Design coordinator, prof. Phila. Coll. Art. Exhibited nationally, 1936—. Represented in pvt. and pub. collections including Phila. Mus., Carnegie Library, Phila. Pub. Library, N.Y. Pub. Library of Congress, Mus. Modern Art, Nat. Portrait Gallery, Smithsonian Instn. Dir. Pa. Art Program, 1940-42, Pa. War Services Program, 1943. Served with U.S. Army, 1943-45, pub. relations officer Army Med. Library, 1945-47. Recipient awards Phila. Print Club, Western Pa. Prints, 1st prize, Soldier Art; 1st prize Times Herald Exhbn., Washington; Franklin Medal, 1959, (2) 1969, 1970; Delaware Valley Graphic Arts, 1971, Silver and Bronze medals, Art Directors Gold medal, 1966, 69, 73, Silver medal, 1971, 73, Neographics Gold, Silver and Bronze medals, 1973, Nat. Graphic Arts Design Award U.S. and Can., 1968, (2) 1970; Distinguished Design award Phila. Coll. Art, 1971; Neographics Gold medal, 1976; named to Wisdom Hall of Fame, 1975. Fellow Internat. Inst. Arts and Letters; mem. Am. Color Print Soc. (pres. 1956—), Artist Decoys, Phila. Art Alliance (chmn. print com. 1977—, dir.), Mus. Modern Art, Phila. Print Club. Club: Peale. Home: 1452 E Cheltenham Ave Philadelphia PA 19124 Office: Phila Coll Art Broad and Spruce Sts Philadelphia PA

HOOF, DAVID LORNE, chemist/chem. engr.; b. Washington, Dec. 2, 1945; s. Wayne and Mary Eleanor (English) H.; A.B., Cornell U., 1969; M.S. in Inorganic Chemistry, Purdue U., 1971, Ph.D., 1974; m. Bethea Leigh Gledhill, Dec. 18, 1976; 1 dau., Laura Louise. Postdoctoral fellow Georgetown U., Washington, 1974-75, Montgomery Coll., Rockville, Md., 1974-76; program mgr. dry and pyrochem. methods reprocessing program and nat. gas-cooled reactor reprocessing program Dept. Energy, Germantown, Md., 1976-78, city energy coordinator, Rockville, Md., 1978—. Leader young people's fellowship St. Mary Magdalene Episcopal Ch., Aspen Hill, Md., 1975-77. Mem. Am., D.C. chem. socs., Sigma Xi, Phi Kappa Psi. Contbr. articles in field to profl. jours. Office: Fuel Cycle AD NPD Mail Station B-107 Dept Energy Germantown MD 20545

HOOKAILO, MELVIN FRED, photographer; b. Boston, Jan. 10, 1921; s. Fred and Rose (Moseson) H.; student Art Center Los Angeles, 1947-49; M.Photography, 1965; Photog. Craftsman, 1972; m. Marian Glenn Goldberg, Apr. 4, 1954; 1 son, Gordon David. Propr., Hookailo Studios Fine Photography, Boston, 1951-73, Needham, Mass., 1961—, Brookline Village, Mass., 1974—. Instr. photography Emmanuel Coll., Boston, 1952—, Regis Coll., Weston, Mass., 1965-71, Acadamie Modern, 1958-60, 73, Profl. Sch. Photography, Winona, Ind., 1967, 72, 77, Profl. Sch. Photography, San Angelo, Tex., 1977, also seminars, San Francisco, Los Angeles, Balt., 1977; vis. instr. photography R.I. Sch. Photography, 1975—; pvt. cons. div. occupational edn. for photog. schs. and instns. Mass. Dept. Edn., 1975—; pvt. instr., lectr., judge. Served with USAAF, World War II. Mem. Profl. Photographers Assn. Am., Profl. Photographers Assn. Mass. (pres. 1974-75), Am. Soc. Photographers, Profl. Photographers Assn. New Eng. Club: Masons. Co-author: What Price Glory, 1968. Patentee swivel bracket. Home: 80 Wayne Rd Needham Heights MA 02194 Office: 44 Washington St Brookline MA 02146

HOOKER, ARTHUR BOWLES, lawyer; b. Cleve., May 28, 1925; s. Richard and Winifred Eells (Newberry) H.; B.A. summa cum laude, Yale U., 1950, LL.B., 1953; m. Joan Kearny Fillmore, June 23, 1956; children—Samuel, Winifred Newberry, Martina Kearny. Admitted to N.Y. bar, 1954, Fed. bar, 1954; asso. Lord, Day & Lord, N.Y.C., 1953-60, partner, 1960—, supr. European office, 1962-65. Pres. Alfred T. White Community Center, Bklyn., 1966-69. Bd. govs. Brooklyn Heights Assn., 1960-62. Served with 281st Engr. Combat Bn., AUS, 1943-46. Mem. Am. Bar Assn., Assn. Bar City N.Y., Am. Arbitration Assn. (panel comml. arbitrators), Phi Beta Kappa. Democrat. Mem. Soc. of Friends. Clubs: Elizabethan, Elihu (Yale); Rembrandt (Bklyn.); Recess (N.Y.C.). Home: 33 Willow Pl Brooklyn NY 11201 Office: 25 Broadway New York City NY 10004

HOOKER, OLIVIA JULIETTE, psychologist; b. Muskogee, Okla., Feb. 12, 1915; d. Samuel D. and Anita Juliette (Stigger) Hooker; B.S., Ohio State U., 1937; M.A., Columbia U., 1947; Ph.D. (grad. fellow), U. Rochester, 1962. Intern, N.Y. State Dept. Mental Hygiene, Thiells, N.Y., 1947-48, clin. psychologist, 1948-61; dir. psychol. services Kennedy Child Study Center, N.Y.C., 1963—; asso. prof. Grad. Sch.

Arts Scis., Fordham U., N.Y.C., 1974—. Bd. dirs. White Plains-Greenburgh (N.Y.) NAACP, 1978; lay speaker Trinity United Meth. Ch., White Plains. Fellow Am. Assn. Mental Deficiency; mem. Am. Psychol. Assn. (chairperson constn. com. div. 33, 1975-78), N.Y.C. Assn. Adminstrs. in Mental Health and Mental Retardation (sec.). Co-author: Olnay Series for Retarded Children, 1955. Office: 151 E 67th St New York City NY 10021

HOOPER, ALEXANDER NELSON, pharmacologist; b. Bklyn., Dec. 26, 1939; s. Thomas Leroy and Essie Mae (Broner) H.; B.A., Shaw U., 1963, B.S., 1972; M.A., Seton Hall U., 1974; m. Adelle D. Crockett, Jan. 29, 1966; children—Darlene, Alexander, Gregory. Pharmacologist, Wilmington (N.C.) Meml. Hosp., 1963, Wyeth Labs., Radnor, Pa., 1964, Einstein Med. Coll., Bronx, N.Y., 1964-68; pharmacologist Hoffman-La Roche Inc., Nutley, N.J., 1968—, also chmn. com. substance abuse; tchr. adult edn., Newark. Mem. AAAS, N.J. Pharm. Assn., Pulmonary Research Group N.Y., N.Y. Acad. Scis., Phila. Physiol. Soc., Black Health Workers Am., Order Rosicrucians, Nu Gamma Alpha. Republican. Baptist. Club: Lions. Address: 172 E 30th St Paterson NJ 07514

HOOSHMAND, MOJTABA, physician; b. Tehran, Iran, Sept. 29, 1939; s. Abdoll and Ashraf H.; came to U.S., 1967, naturalized, 1975; M.D., Tehran U., 1965; m. Shahla Nagshi, July 27, 1970; children—Mark, Kay, Eric. Intern, St. Vincent Hosp., N.Y.C., 1968-69; resident U. Pa., Phila., 1969-72; practice medicine specializing in phys. and rehab. medicine, 1973—; dir. dept. phys. medicine and rehab. Muhlenberg Med. Center, Allentown, Pa., 1977—, pres. med. staff. Served with Iranian Army, 1965-67. Mem. AMA, Pa., Northampton County med. assns., Am. Acad. Phys. and Rehab. Medicine, Am. Congress Phys. Medicine and Rehab. Clubs: Rotary, Masons. Office: PO Box 1426 Allentown PA 18105

HOOTON, EDWARD, JR., sporting arms, ammunition co. exec.; b. Elizabeth, N.J., Oct. 7, 1923; s. Edward and Sarah Elizabeth (Murray) H.; B.S., Rutgers U., 1949; m. Ruth J. Short, Dec. 8, 1973; children—Edward J., Lorraine M. Brown, Carol L. Baker, Barbara Lombard, Irene Talley. Various assignments engring. dept. in constrn., design, bus. methods divs. E.I. Du Pont de Nemours Inc., Wilmington, Del., 1950-72; asst. dir. prodn. Remington Arms Co. Inc., Bridgeport, Conn., 1972-75, dir., 1975—, v.p., 1976—. Exec. com. Jr. Achievement Western Conn., 1974—; bd. assos. U. Bridgeport, 1975—; bd. dirs. Kennedy Center, Bridgeport. Served with USAAF, 1942-45. Decorated D.F.C., Air medal. Mem. ASME, Del. Soc. Profl. Engrs. Republican. Roman Catholic. Club: Weston Gun. Home: 32 Long Ridge Rd West Redding CT 06896 Office: Remington Arms Co Inc 939 Barnum Ave Bridgeport CT 06602

HOOVER, HERBERT CHRISTOPHER, JR., hosp. adminstr.; b. Cleve., July 18, 1929; s. Herbert C. and Margaret Test (Lingenfelter) H.; B.S.in Indsl. Engring., Lehigh U., 1951; M.S. in Bus. Adminstrn., Columbia U., 1960; m. Betty Rodes. Asst. mgr. sales research Am. Visco Corp., Phila., 1954-57; mgr. internat. bus. affairs NBC, N.Y.C., 1957-74; dir. admitting New Rochelle (N.Y.) Hosp. Med. Center, 1975—; mem. New Rochelle Citizens Advisory Com., 1963-66. Served to lt. USN, 1951-54. Mem. Nat. Assn. Hosp. Admitting Mgrs., Hosp. Admitting Officers Assn. N.Y. Republican. Episcopalian. Club: Huguenot Yacht (former rear commodore) (New Rochelle). Home: 300 Pelham Rd New Rochelle NY 10805 Office: 16 Guion Pl New Rochelle NY 10802

HOOVER, MARK EUGENE, counselor; b. Poughkeepsie, N.Y., July 4, 1950; s. Lawrence Mark and Annabel Elizabeth (lenz) H.; B.S., Juniata Coll., 1972; M.S. in Rehab. Counseling, U. Scranton, 1974; m. Karen Haning, July 29, 1972; 1 dau., Jessica Lee. Rehab. coordinator, asst. dir. Human Resource Center, Honesdale, Pa., 1974—; vocat. cons. Social Security Adminstrn. Pres., Assn. Retarded Citizens, 1977—; youth adviser St. Johns Lutheran Ch., Honesdale, 1977. Mem. Wayne County Mental Health Assn., Am. Personnel and Guidance Assn., Am. Rehab. and Counseling Assn. Home: RD 4 Honesdale PA 18431 Office: RD 4 Box 98A Honesdale PA 18431

HOOVER, RICHARD EDWIN, ophthalmologist; b. Wilkinsburg, Pa., Jan. 19, 1915; s. Charles Beaver and Dotte Edith (DeShong) H.; B.S., Pa. State U., 1936; M.D., Johns Hopkins U., 1950; m. Lydia Payne, Dec. 21, 1959; children—Brinton Huston, Stewart Payne. Intern in ophthalmology Johns Hopkins Hosp., Wilmer Inst., Balt., 1950-51, asst. resident, 1951-54, Kellogg fellow in ophthalmology, 1952-53, resident ophthalmologist, 1954-55, asst. in ophthalmology, 1951-54; instr. ophthalmology Johns Hopkins Sch. Medicine, Balt., 1954-68, asst. prof., 1969—; cons. in ophthalmology Balt. City Hosp., 1955—; active surg. staff in ophthalmology Balt. Eye, Ear, Nose, and Throat Hosp., 1960-65, Md. Gen. Hosp., 1965—; chief of ophthalmology Presbyn. Eye, Ear, Nose and Throat Charity Hosp., 1958-65; chief of ophthalmology Greater Balt. Med. Center, 1965—, vice chief staff, 1966-74; cons. in typhlo-peripatology Boston Coll., Western Mich. U.; cons. in ophthalmology Md. Sch. for the Blind, 1962—, VA, 1953-67; state supervising cons. ophthalmologist for Md., 1964—; cons. various sects. HEW, 1961-66, 1960-67, 1961-67, 1964-65, 1973; bd. dirs. Nat. Soc. for Prevention of Blindness, chmn. low vision aids com., 1960—; bd. dirs. Helen Keller Inst., 1970—, Md. Sch. for Blind, 1973—; trustee Blind Industries and Services of Md., 1973-77. Served with U.S. Army, 1943-46. Recipient Louis Braille awards Phila. Assn. for the Blind, 1962, Center for the Blind in Pa., 1970, citation for meritorious service Pres's. Com. on Employment of Handicapped, 1966, Award of merit Physician of Year, Gov.'s Com. on Employment Handicapped, 1966, Lawrence E. Blaha Meml. award Am. Assn. Workers for the Blind, 1969, Migel medal Am. Found. for the Blind, 1970, Distinguished Alumnus award Pa. State U., 1976, Alumni fellow, 1977; diplomate Am. Bd. Ophthalmology. Fellow Am. Acad. Ophthalmology and Otolaryngology (award of merit 1974), A.C.S., mem. AMA, Am. Assn. Workers for the Blind, So. Med. Assn., Med. and Chirurg. Faculty Md., Am., Md. (pres. 1962) ophthal. socs., Low Vision Clin. Soc. (hon.). Contbr. to books, articles to profl. jours. Home: 16211 Falls Rd Upperco MD 21155 Office: 14 W Mt Vernon Pl Baltimore MD 21201

HOPE, PETER BLANCHARD, physician; b. N.Y.C., Aug. 25, 1935; s. Theodore Sherwood, Jr. and Emily Louise (Blanchard) H.; A.B., Harvard U., 1957; M.D., Columbia U., 1961; m. Janet Starr Best, June 14, 1958; children—John, Anne, Catherine, Charity, Stephen, Mary. Intern, St. Vincent's Hosp., N.Y.C., 1961-62; resident in pediatrics N.Y. Hosp.-Cornell Med. Center, 1967-69; fellow in community medicine Dartmouth Coll., 1969; practice medicine, specializing in pediatrics and family practice, Center Sandwich, N.H., 1969—; partner Sandwich Health Assos., 1973—; mem. governing bd. United Health Systems; mem. Area I Health Council; mem. project review com. United Health Systems; mem. N.H. Com. on Family Practice Residency Tng.; health officer Town of Sandwich. Served to lt. col. M.C., U.S. Army, 1962-67. Diplomate Am. Bd. Pediatrics, Am. Bd. Family Practice. Mem. N.H. Med. Soc. (del., mem. sect. on med. services), Carroll County Med. Soc., Am., N.H. acads. pediatrics, Am., N.H. acads. family practice, Am. Pub. Health Assn., New Eng. Pediatric Soc., Assn. Mil. Surgeons. Democrat. Clubs: Appalachian Mountain, Harvard Mountaineering, Sierra. Home: Box 147 Center Sandwich NH 03227 Office: Sandwich Health Assos Center Sandwich NH 03227

HOPKINS, ERNEST LOYD, physician; b. Birmingham, Ala., Aug. 14, 1930; s. Clay and Ada (Fields) H.; B.S., Morehouse Coll., 1952; M.D., Howard U., 1957; L.H.D., Monrovia Coll., 1962; m. Lillie B. Blanks, Apr. 24, 1959; children—Ernest C., Loyd Byron, William E. Intern, Freedmen's Hosp., Washington, 1957-58, resident, 1958-62; resident Wester Res. U., Cleve., 1961-62, asst. prof. obstetrics, gynecology and physiology Howard U. Coll. Medicine, 1965-69, asso. prof. obstetrics and gynecology, 1969-73, prof., 1973—, now dir. maternal and fetal medicine, dept. obstetrics and gynecology, also dir. audio visual aids sect., 1967—; attending physician Providence Hosp., Cafritz Meml. Hosp., Washington Hosp. Center, Hadley Meml. Hosp., Columbia Hosp. for Woman, Freedmen's Hosp. Patron, Met. Police Boys' Clubs, 1965—, Mt. Pleasant Civic Assn. Decorated knight Humane Order of Star of African Redemption Republic of Liberia, 1962. USPHS spl. fellow, Western Res. U., Universidad de la Republica, Uruguay, 1963-65. Diplomate Am. Bd. Obstetrics and Gynecology. Mem. AMA, Nat. Med. Assn., Am. Coll. Obstetricians and Gynecologists, Am. Fertility Soc., Am. Heart Assn., AAAS, Med. Soc. D.C. (exec. com. obstetrics and gynecology sect. 1966—). Home: 9351 Mellenbrook Rd Columbia MD 21043 Office: 5501 16th St NW Washington DC 20011

HOPKINS, EVERETT PARKER, photographer; b. Bethel, Conn., Aug. 1, 1923; s. Herbert and Minnie Brady (Taylor) H.; student Boston U., 1942-43, Syracuse U., summers 1969, 70, Winnona Sch. Photography, summers 1969-70; m. Helen Marie Lesmiewski, June 4, 1945; children—Robert Parker, Cheryl Lynn. Photographer, Simpson Studio and Camera Shop, New Milford, Conn., 1946—, v.p., 1957-62, pres., 1965—. Leader, Horse Club 4H, 1963-70, mem. State Horse Adv. Bd., 1966-71. Mem. Conn. Profl. Photographers Assn. (dir. 1972-74, del. to Profl. Photographers Assn. New Eng. 1977—), profl. photographers socs. New Eng., N.Y., Profl. Photographers Assn. Am. Club: Lions. Home: Aspeturk Rd New Milford CT 06776 Office: 7 Main St New Milford CT 06776

HOPKINS, HENRY POWELL, JR., silversmith; b. N.Y.C., Aug. 29, 1917; s. Henry Powell and Constance Media (Hummel) H.; student Md. Inst. Art, 1938-40, Boston Mus. Sch. Fine Arts, 1945-50; m. Barbara Louise Wirths, Sept. 1, 1956; children—Henry Powell III, Martha McLean. Self-employed as silversmith, Balt., 1952—. Served with USNR, 1940-45. Recipient traveling fellowship Boston Mus. Sch. Fine Arts, 1950. Mem. Soc. War 1812 (dir.), Soc. Colonial Wars (mem. council 1964-66), Soc. Sons Revolution (dir. 1973), S.A.R. Democrat. Episcopalian. Home: 106 Elmwood Rd Baltimore MD 21210 Office: 1111 Lovegrove Alley Baltimore MD 21202

HOPKINS, MARY RITA, artist, educator; b. Bklyn., Aug. 28, 1928; d. John Luke and Catherine Flynn Gilbo; student Vesper George Art Sch., Boston, 1951; B.S. in Bus. Mgmt., Merrimack Coll., Andover, Mass., 1973; M.Ed. in Sch. Adminstrn., Fitchburg (Mass.) State Coll., 1976; m. Charles E. Hopkins, III; children—Charles E., Mary Katherine, John Leonard, Susan Ellen, Michael Joseph. Owner-operator comml. design studio, Lowell, Mass., 1952-54, 57-66; package designer Millen Industries, 1953-54; art dir. Comml. Offset Priting House, N.Y.C., 1954-57; package designer Lawrence (Mass.) div. Mead Packaging Co., Atlanta, 1966-67; advt. designer Addison-Wesley Pub. Co., Reading, Mass., 1967-69; instr. comml. art dept. Greater Lawrence Regional Vocat. Tech. Sch., Andover, 1969-73, chmn. dept. comml. art/graphic communications tech., 1973—; cons. in field. Mass. Dept. Edn. grantee, summer 1978. Mem. Internat. Graphic Arts Assn., Graphic Art Instrs. New Eng. (sec. 1977—), Am. Mgmt. Assn., AAUW, Mass. Assn. Vocat. Adminstrs., Mass. Assn. Occupational Edn. Dirs. Club: Art Dirs. Author articles, illustrator in field.

HOPKINS, WILLIAM EDGAR, mech. engr.; b. Balt., Nov. 29, 1903; s. Edgar Goodhand and Nellie Augusta (Price) H.; B.Engring., Johns Hopkins, 1924; m. Margarita Christiana Barba, June 7, 1940; children—Priscilla Ann, William Robert, Roger Charles, Susan Elizabeth. Mech. engr. Potomac Edison Co., Hagerstown, Md., 1924-27, Allis-Chalmers Mfg. Co., Milw., 1927-32; materials engr. Works Progress Adminstrn., N.Y.C., 1933-35; mech. engr. Stone & Webster Engring. Corp., Boston, 1936, cons. engr., 1960, v.p., 1973, mgr. projects, 1974—. Chmn. Boy Scouts Am., Newton, Mass., 1951-52; pres. Underwood PTA, 1953-54; bd. dirs. Newton YMCA, 1954-72, chmn. youth work, 1955-60; pres. Newton Improvement Assn., 1948-50; chmn. planning bd. City of Newton 1952-60, alderman-at-large, 1960-70. Served to 2d lt. C.E., U.S. Army, 1924. Registered profl. engr., N.Y., Pa., Conn., Fla., Maine, Mass. Fellow ASME (James N. Landis medal 1978); mem. Am. Nuclear Soc., Nat., Mass. (pres. met. chpt. 1947-48) socs. profl. engrs., Dynamion Soc. (organizer, 1st pres. 1946-47). Methodist. Clubs: Brae Burn Country (West Newton, Mass.); Fort Hill (Boston); Johns Hopkins (Balt.), Wiscasset (Maine) Yacht Masons. Contbr. articles to profl. jours. Home: 11 Willard St Newton MA 02158 Office: 245 Summer St Boston MA 02107

HOPSON, ANNA LEE, communications exec., social scientist; b. Richmond, Va., June 22, 1926; d. Robert Iverson and Bruce (Looney) Boswell; A.B., Vassar, 1946; Ph.D., Harvard, 1952; m. Raymond Sirine Robinson, Dec. 31, 1970. Tchr., researcher Columbia, 1955-67, Rutgers U., 1965-66; asso. research dir. J. Walter Thompson, 1967-71; research dir. Nat. Council on Alcoholism, 1972-73; research coordinator CBS, N.Y.C., 1973—. Mem. exec. com. Encampment for Citizenship, Ethical Culture Soc., 1966—. Mem. Am. Psychol. Assn., Am. Sociol. Assn., Am. Assn. Pub. Opinion Research, Alcohol and Drug Problems Assn. Clubs: Country of Va., Harvard, 7th Regiment Tennis. Author: The Effects of Rehabilitation on the Driving Behavior of Alcoholics, 1973. Contbr. articles to periodicals. Home: 8 E 96th St New York City NY 10028 Office: 51 W 52d St New York City NY 10019

HORAI, JOANN, social psychologist, assn. adminstr.; b. S.I., N.Y., Mar. 9, 1942; s. Charles J. and Stacia (Melnik) H.; B.A., U. Miami (Fla.), 1964, M.S., 1968, Ph.D., 1970. Asst. prof. psychology Hofstra U., Hempstead, N.Y., 1971-76, faculty research and devel. fund grantee, 1975-76; asso. adminstr. Am. Psychol. Assn., Washington, 1976-78, adminstrv. officer for programs and planning, 1978—. Mem. Am. Psychol. Assn., AAAS. Contbr. articles to profl. publs., papers to profl. convs. Office: Programs and Planning Am Psychol Assn 1200 17th St NW Washington DC 20036

HORAN, EDMUND MARTIN, ednl. adminstr.; b. N.Y.C., July 22, 1920; s. James Patrick and Rachel Margaret (Delaney) H.; B.A., Coll. City N.Y., 1942; M.A., Columbia, 1950, Ed.D., 1955; m. Kathryn Dolores Donohue, Feb. 8, 1945; children—Edmund, Kathleen Haydak, Patricia, Michael. Tchr. classes for children with retarded mental devel. N.Y.C. Bd. Edn., 1950-63, supr. classes, 1963-67, acting asst. dir. Bur. for Children with Retarded Mental Devel., 1967-69; dir. Center for Multiply Handicapped Children, N.Y.C., 1969—. Instr., Hunter Coll., City U. N.Y., 1966-71. Parish chmn. Catholic Charities and Edn. Appeal, 1972. Served to 1st lt. USAAF, 1942-45. Mem. Am. Assn. on Mental Deficiency, Council for Exceptional Children, Council Suprs. and Adminstrs. City N.Y. Home: 3420 Tibbett Ave Bronx NY 10463 Office: 105 E 106th St New York NY 10029

HORAN, JAMES D., author; b. N.Y.C., July 27, 1914; s. Eugene and Elizabeth (Schaub) H.; student Drake Coll., Jersey City, also Writing Center, N.Y. U.; m. Gertrude Dorrity, Sept. 4, 1938; children—Patricia, Brian, Gary, James C. Novelist, historian, newspaper editor: ret. asst. mng. editor, Sunday editor, spl. events editor N.Y. Jour. Am., N.Y.C. Recipient award Mystery Writers of Am., 1957, Westerners Buffalo award, 1960, Gold Typewriter award N.Y. Press Club, 1960, hon. mention, 1962; award N.J. Tchrs. English, 1962, Page One citation Am. Newspaper Guild, 1961. Mem. Westerners (co-founder N.Y. Corral), N.Y. Civil War Round Table (past pres.), Writers Guild Am., Am. Newspaper Guild. Club: N.Y. Press. Author: (with Gerold Frank) Out in the Boondocks, 1943, U.S. Seawolf, 1945; Action Tonight, 1945; Desperate Men, 1949; (with Howard Swiggett) The Pinkerton Story, 1951; Desperate Women, 1952; (novel) King's Rebel, 1953; Confederate Agent, 1954; (with Paul Sann) Pictorial History of the Wild West, 1954; Mathew Brady, Historian with a Camera, 1955; Across The Cimarron, 1956; The DA's Man, 1957; (novel) Seek Out and Destroy, 1958; The Mob's Man, 1959; The Great American West, 1959, rev. edit., 1978; (novel) The Shadow Catcher, 1961 (Western Heritage award); The Desperate Years, 1962; The Seat of Power, 1965 (novel of year N.J. Assn. Tchrs. English); America's Forgotten Photographer: Timothy O'Sullivan, 1966; (novel) The Right Image, 1967; The Pinkertons: The Detective Dynasty That Made History, 1968; The Life and Art of Charles Schreyvogel: Painter-Historian of the Indian Fighting Army of the American West, 1969 (Westerners Buffalo award 1970; N.J. Tchrs. English award 1970); The Blue Messiah (novel), 1971; The McKenney-Hall Portrait Gallery of American Indians, 1972; (novel) The New Vigilantes, 1975; The Authentic Wild West: The Gunfighters, 1976; The Authentic West: The Outlaws, 1977; pub. (with Mrs. Horan) Jingle Bob series; The Trial of Frank James for Murder, with Confessions of Dick Liddil and Clarence Hite; The Dalton Brothers; The Life of Tom Horn. Home: 27 Woods Rd Great Notch Little Falls NJ 07424

HORDISH, J. ARNOLD, brokerage firm exec.; b. N.Y.C., Nov. 18, 1934; s. Lester and Ann (Steiner) H.; B.B.A., Pace Coll., 1959; m. Carol Wiener, Aug. 15, 1965; children—David Lawrence, Joshua Aaron. With Dean Witter & Co., N.Y.C., 1956—, v.p., 1968—. Bd. dirs. Am. Jewish Congress, 1971-72; mem. adv. bd. Bellvue Hosp., 1971. Served with AUS, 1953-56. Recipient Man of Year award Young Israel of Fifth Ave., 1968, State of Israel Prime Minister's award, 1974; Community Service award United Jewish Appeal Fedn. Jewish Philanthropies, 1977. Mem. N.Y. (allied), Am. (mem. nominating com.) stock exchanges, N.Y. Merc. Exchange, Young Israel of Fifth Ave. N.Y. (exec. v.p. 1968-71, pres. 1971-74, chmn. bd. nursery sch. 1971—, del. nat. council 1971—, Shofar award 1972). Home: 305 E 24th St New York City NY 10010 Office: 130 Liberty St New York City NY 10006

HORDYNSKY, WALTER EUGENE, clin. chemist; b. Pidberez, Ukraine, Mar. 18, 1915; s. Jeroslav and Olena (Byrchak) H.; came to U.S., 1949, naturalized, 1954; Ph.D., Ukrainian Free U., Munich, Germany, 1955; m. Tamara Nahirniak, Apr. 15, 1944; children—Olenka Yurchuk, Ksenia Hapij, Christine Baranetsky. Clin. chemist Newark Eye and Ear Infirmary, 1952-55, St. Mary's Hosp., Orange, N.J., 1955—, Murray Bioanalytical Lab., 1955—; adj. prof. clin. chemistry Felician Coll., Lodi, N.J., 1968—; cons. clin. chemistry U.S. Army, 1965-69. Recipient citation First U.S. Army, 1968. Mem. Am. Assn. Clin. Chemistry (pres. N.J. sect. 1977), Assn. Clin. Scientists, Nat. Registry Clin. Chemistry, German Assn. Clin. Chemistry, Ukrainian Inst. Tech. Home: 28 Hillside Terr Newark NJ 07106 Office: 135 S Center St Orange NJ 07050

HORECKY, PAUL LOUIS, librarian, former govt. ofcl.; b. Trutnov, Czechoslovakia, Sept. 8, 1913; s. Bedrich and Elsa (Weinerova) H.; came to U.S., 1949, naturalized, 1952; Dr.jur., U. Prague (Czechoslovakia), 1936; M.A. (Charles Smith scholar), Harvard U., 1951; m. Emily M. Ivey, Dec. 12, 1949; 1 son, Frederick John. Admitted to Prague bar, 1936; practiced law, Czechoslovakia, 1936-37; trial atty. U.S. Office Chief of Counsel, Nuremberg, Germany, 1947-49; researcher Harvard U. Russian Research Center, 1949-51; Slavic research analyst, 1956—; Slavic and East European specialist Library of Congress, Washington, 1951-58, asst. chief Slavic and Central European div., 1958-71, chief div., 1972-77; sr. research fellow Inst. Sino-Soviet Studies, George Washington U., 1978-79; project evaluator Office Edn. and Nat. Endowment for Humanities; mem. subcom. on East-Central and S.E. European studies and Joint Com. on Eastern Europe, Am. Council Learned Socs.-Social Sci. Research Council, 1968-75; chmn. research and library resources adv. com. Am. Council Learned Socs., 1970-73. Served to capt. Brit. Armed Forces, 1944-47. Mem. Am. Polit. Sci. Assn., Am. Assn. Advancement Slavic Studies, ALA. Clubs: Cosmos, Harvard (Washington). Author: Libraries and Bibliographic Centers in Soviet Union, 1959; editor, contbg. author: Basic Russian Publications, 1962; Russia and the Soviet Union, 1965; East Central Europe, 1969; Southeastern Europe, 1969; contbr. articles to monographs, Ency. Americana, profl. jours. Home: 2207 Paul Spring Rd Alexandria VA 22307 Office: Inst Sino-Soviet Studies George Washington U Washington DC 20052

HOREL, H(ERMAN) BRUCE, community relations exec.; b. Newark, Oct. 31, 1921; s. Benjamin and Lena (Sthool) H.; B.A., Pace Coll., 1966; m. Reizel Hirschfeld, Apr. 16, 1961. Dir. news bur. Pace Coll., 1960-67, dir. pub. info., 1967-73; dir. community relations Pace U., N.Y.C., 1973-77, community relations cons., 1977—; pres. Am. Legacy, Inc., 1974—. Mem. Community Bd. 1, Burough of Manhattan, 1974—, chmn., 1975-77. Served with AUS, 1943-46. Decorated Bronze Star (3). Mem. Pub. Relations Soc. Am., N.Y., Lower Manhattan (pres., trustee) hist. socs., Council Advancement and Support of Edn., N.Y. Hist. Soc., Nat. Trust for Historic Preservation. Editor: Legacy of Manhattan Toe, 1973, rev. edit., 1975. Home: Box 982 Montauk NY 11954 Office: Pace Plaza New York City NY 10038

HORIC, ALAN, author, pub., textile distbr.; b. Kulen Vakuf, Bosnia, Croatia, Jan. 3, 1929; s. Ibrahim and Vahida (Galic) H.; M.A. in Slavic Lit. magna cum laude, U. Montreal (Que., Can.), 1957; bus. mgmt. diploma LaSalle Extension U., 1959; m. Jacqueline Rivard, Dec. 6, 1952; children—Alan, Fatima, Omer, Camil. Machine operator Citroen, Paris, France, 1950-52; buyer Dupuis, Freres, Montreal, 1952-65, A.J. Freiman, The Bay, Ottawa, Ont., Can., 1965-72, Met. Stores Can. Ltd., Montreal, 1972-75; dir. Les Editions de l'Hexagone, Montreal; adminstr. Editions Parti Pris; pres. Tissus Francais Inc. Served with French Army, 1945-50. Decorated Mil. Cross. Mem. La Societe des Ecrivains Canadiens, Union des Ecrivains Quebecois, Croatian Acad. Am. Author: (poetry) Nemir duse, Knjiznica Osvit, 1959; L'Aube assassinee, 1957; Blessure au flane du ciel, 1962; Atomises, Ecrits du Canada francais, 1965; Cela commenca par un reve et ce fut la Creation, 1969; Les coqs egorges, 1972; also poems in mags. and newspapers. Home: 2807 McWillis St Laurent PQ Canada Office: 437 Mayor Suite 3 Montreal PQ Canada

HORKA, ALFRED EDWARD, plastics co. exec.; b. Passaic, N.J., Feb. 26, 1921; s. Frank Walter and Anna (Haas) H.; B.S. in Chem. Engring., Lehigh U., 1942; m. Jean S. Lawton, Feb. 7, 1945; children—Douglas Lawton, Nancy Jean. Project engr. Bakelite Corp.,

Bound Brook, N.J., 1945-48; sales engring. various cos., N.Y.C., 1948-56; sales mgr. New Eng. Tape Co., Hudson, Mass., 1956-59; founder, pres. Plastic Extrusion & Engring. Co., Inc., Westborough, 1960—, also dir., gen. mgr.; past dir. Mut. Bldg. & Loan Assn., Garfield, N.J. Mem. adv. bd. Framingham Vocational High Sch. Served to capt. USAAF, World War II. Mem. Soc. Plastic Engrs., Lehigh U. Alumni Assn. (class agt.), U.S. Power Squadron. Presbyn. (elder, trustee). Clubs: Masons (32 ffl), Rotary (charter, dir., pres. 1970—, dist. officer); Hundred (Boston). Home: 7 Stagg Dr Natick MA 01760 Office: 170 Bartlett St Northborough MA 01532

HORN, FERDINAND RUDOLPH, JR., realtor, appraiser; b. Greenwich Village, N.Y.C., July 1, 1897; s. Ferdinand R. and Magdalena Anna (Hornung) H.; student Stuyvesant, Drakes Bus. Coll., 1916, Cornell U., 1919, Chgo. Sch. Practipedics, 1940; D.C.S. (hon.), London Inst. Applied Research, 1973; m. Hilda Louisa Knapp, Nov. 5, 1919; children—Ferdinand Rudolph III, Catherine Ann. With mfg. leather and saddlery bus., 1916-33; mem. N.Y. Legislature, 1929-33; adminstrv. exec. Home Owners Loan Corp., N.Y.C., 1935-39; adminstrv. exec., procurement agt. War Dept., 1941-45; mem. Bd. Appeals, Clarkstown Zoning Bd., 1939-50; established Rockland County Mutiple Listing Systems, Inc., Nanuet, N.Y., 1957, exec. sec., 1957—. Mem. nat. adv. bd. Am. Security Council; pres., hon. chief Nanuet Fire Engine Dept., 1919-20, vol. fireman, 1917-78; commr. comdemnation hearings Orangetown Assessment and Rev. Bd. Served in World War I. Certified real estate appraiser, real estate cons. Mem. Rockland County Bd. Realtors (past pres.), United Real Estate Brokers Rockland County (organizer, past exec. sec. and treas.), N.Y. State Appraisal Soc., N.Y. State Soc. Real Estate Bds. (past dir.), Nat. Assn. Real Estate Bds., N.Y. Vets. Police Assn., Deps. Assn. N.Y. State (hon.), Nat., N.Y. State (past dir.) assns. realtors, N.Y., Nat., Rockland County (past pres.) socs. real estate appraisers, Rockland County Vol. Firemens Assn. (life, pres. 1926), Am. Legion, Am. Societas Notariorum, Nat. Acad. Polit. Sci., Nat. Assn. Mil. Engrs. Home: 342 Holt Dr Pearl River NY 10965 Office: Horn Plaza 32-34 1st St Nanuet NY 10954 also Irving Inn Southampton NY 11968

HORN, JOHN CHISOLM, mgmt. cons.; b. N.Y.C., Jan. 16, 1915; s. William M. and Marguerite E. (Jacobs) H.; A.B., Cornell U., 1936, postgrad., 1937; LL.D., Susquehanna U., 1965; m. Solveig E. Wald, June 22, 1938; children—Phyllis Downing, John Chisolm, Stephen Lunde, Eric Laurens, Robert Gregg, Thomas Wald, Dorothy Trail, James Melchoir. With John R. Wald Co., 1937-39; sec. Prismo Safety Corp., 1939-45, sec. treas., 1945-49, v.p., 1949-62, pres., 1962-69. asst. sec. Wald Industries, Inc., 1950-51, pres., 1951-69, dir., vice chmn. Wald Found., 1949-62, chmn., 1962—; pres. Prismo Universal Corp., 1969-70. mgmt. cons. John C. Horn Assos., Huntingdon, 1970—; exec. dir. Ch. Mgmt. Service, 1971—. Asso. faculty Lancaster (Pa.) Sem., 1973—. Nat. council Boy Scouts Am., 1950—, mem. nat. profl. tng. com., 1972—, v.p. Juniata Valley council, 1951-57, pres., 1948-51, 57-58; bd. dirs. Juniata Valley Schs., 1948-63; pres. bd. dirs. Susquehanna U.; indsl. and profl. adv. council Pa. State U.; dir. bd. publ. Lutheran Ch. in Am., 1968—; pres. Juniata Valley Med. Center, 1974—. Recipient Silver Beaver award, Lamb award, Silver Antelope award, Outstanding Civic Leader award Boy Scouts Am. Mem. Inst. Traffic Engrs., Am. Road Builders Assn., Am. Ordnance Assn., Prison Industries Assn., N.A.M., C. of C. (dir. 1955), Juniata Mountains Devel. Assn. (pres. 1956), A.I.M. Lutheran (home mission bd. Central Pa. Synod 1948-56, music com. 1958-62, exec. bd. 1962-67; dir. St. James Choir). Home: Killmarnock Hall Alexandria PA 16611 Office: 301 Penn St Huntingdon PA 16652

HORN, RUSSELL EUGENE, cons. engr.; b. Yoe, Pa., May 4, 1912; s. Eugene M. and Charlotte (Snyder) H.; B.S., Pa. State U., 1933; m. Eleanor B. Baird, Jan. 12, 1934; children—Russell Eugene, Ralph Elliot, Rosalind Emily (Mrs. Lee Kunkel), Robert Errol. Foreman, Pa. Dept. Hwys., Dist. Office, York, Pa., 1933-35; draftsman, supr., designer C.S. Buchart, architect, 1935-41; exec. v.p., chief engr. Buchart Engring., 1945-59, pres., chief engr. 1959-61; pres., chief engr. Buchart-Horn, Inc., cons. engrs., 1961-72, chmn. bd., 1972—; pres., chmn. bd. PACE Resources, Inc., 1970—; pres. Yorktowne Asso. Contractors, Inc.; sec. Leaseback, Inc.; dir. W. York br. So. Pa. Bank; chmn. exec. com., dir. So. Pa. Bank. Bd. dirs. AAA White Rose Motor Club, York, chmn. bd., 1975-78; bd. dirs. York County chpt. ARC, chmn., 1978; bd. dirs. Retirement Homes Meth. Ch.; trustee Central Pa. annual conf. United Meth. Ch. Served from 1st lt. to col. AUS, 1940-45. Mem. Soc. Am. Mil. Engrs., Nat., Pa. (pres. Lincoln chpt. 1961) socs. profl. engrs., Pa. Assn. Cons. Engrs. (pres. 1965, dir. 1966), Pa. Hwy. Information Assn. (dir.), Pa. Assn. Cons. Engrs. (dir.), Am. Soc. Hwy. Engrs. (nat. pres. 1962), Tech. Socs. Council Southeastern Pa. (chmn. 1963), Engring. Soc. York, Profl. Engrs. Pvt. Practice, Am. Concrete Inst., Asso. Pa. Constructors, Assn. Hwy. Ofcls. N. Atlantic States, Assn. U.S. Army, Res. Officers Assn., ASCE, V.F.W., Cons. Engrs. Council, Am. Rd. Builders Assn., Am. Legion, Pa. State U. Alumni Club York County (pres.). Methodist (chmn. pastor-parish relations com., mem. commn. membership and evangelism). Clubs: Masons (32 deg.), Moose, University, Lake, Dutch, Exchange. Home: 1270 Brockie Dr York PA 17403 Office: 40 S Richland Ave York PA 17405

HORN, SOLVEIG WALD (MRS. JOHN CHISOLM HORN), found. exec., civic worker; b. Phila., Oct. 14, 1914; d. John Royal and Emma (Gulbrandson) Wald; A.B., Cornell U., 1936; m. John Chisolm Horn, June 22, 1938; children—Phyllis Downing, John Chisolm, Stephen Lunde (dec.), Eric Laurens, Robert Gregg (dec.), Thomas Wald, Dorothy Traill, James Melchior. Asso. Prismo Safety Corp., Huntingdon, Pa., 1943, Wald Industries, Inc., John R. Wald Co., Inc., 1952; treas., asso. John C. Horn Assos., 1970—; treas. ch. Mgmt. Service, 1970—. Active Region III, Girl Scouts Am., 1934—, camp unit leader, 1934-35, Girl Guide trainee, Waddow, Eng. 1936, leader trainer 1936-52, chmn. tng., personnel Huntington council Girl Scouts, 1938-43, chmn. lone troops com., Alexandria, Pa., 1945-48, Brownie troop leader, 1960—, dir. Hemlock council, 1963-69, field v.p. council, 1967-69; mem. Nat. Cub Scouting Com., 1970—; chmn. Pa. Area Cub Scouting, 1974—; active Boy Scouts Am., Civil Def., P.T.A. Bd. dirs. Skills of Central Pa., 1966-73, Huntingdon Developmental Workshop, 1973—, Wald Found., Huntington. Recipient Golden Eaglet award Girl Scouts U.S.A., 1932; Silver Fawn award Boy Scouts Am., 1971, Silver Antelope, 1976. Mem. J.C. Blair Meml. Hosp. Aux. (dir. 1965—), Allegheny Luth. Home Aux., Susquehanna U. Aux., Alexandria Library Aux., Audubon Soc., Delta Gamma. Republican. Lutheran (chmn. campus ministry 1965—). Clubs: Alexandria (Pa.) Garden (v.p. 1970—); Huntington (Pa.) Country. Home: Kilmarnock Hall Alexandria PA 16611 Office: 301 Penn St Huntingdon PA 16652

HORNAFIUS, WILBUR H., JR., ins. agy. exec.; b. Elizabethtown, Pa., June 2, 1927; s. Wilbur H. and Mary E. (Wolgemuth) H.; B.S. in Sci., Elizabethtown Coll., 1951; m. Patricia B. Boggs, Apr. 5, 1952; children—John Scott, Carrie Elizabeth, Holly Ann. Owner D.L. Landis Agy., Elizabethtown, 1958—; sec., mng. officer Elizabethtown Bldg. & Loan Assn. Pres., Elizabethtown Little Theatre, 1954-59, Elizabethtown Area Music Found., 1970-71; pres. Elizabethtown Pub. Library; pres. Elizabethtown Jr. C. of C., 1953-54; active Boy Scouts Am., 1949-65; trustee Community Gallery Lancaster County, 1973—; bd. dirs. Lancaster County Library, 1977—. Mem. Nat. Assn. Mut. Ins. Agts., Tri State Mut. Agts. Assn. (dir. 1973-75), Elizabethtown C. of C. (pres. 1961-62, now sec., mng. officer). Rotarian (pres. 1971-72). Clubs: Embers (pres. 1969-70), Sparks. Home: 113 Meadowbrook Ln Elizabethtown PA 17022 Office: 23 S Market St Elizabethtown PA 17022

HORNBECK, DAVID W., supt. schs.; b. Knoxville, Tenn., 1941; B.A. in History, Austin Coll., Sherman, Tex.; degree in theology Union Theol. Sem., Oxford U.; J.D. cum laude, U. Pa.; LL.D. (hon.), Austin Coll., 1976; married, 2 children. Exec. dir. Phila. Tutorial Project; adj. asso. prof. Yale Div. Sch.; admitted to Pa. bar; dep. counsel gov. Pa.; spl. asst. counsel sec. edn.; exec. dep. sec. edn. Pa., 1972-76; supt. schs. Md., 1977—; chmn. Chief State Sch. Officers Study Commn. Mem. Am. Bar Assn. Office: State Supts Office PO Box 8717 Baltimore Washington Internat Airport Baltimore MD 21240

HORNBECK, PETER LOUIS, educator; b. Southampton, N.Y., Aug. 3, 1935; s. Harold Louis and Lily Linea (Peterson) H.; B.F.A. with honors, U. Pa., 1958; M. Landscape Architecture, Harvard U., 1959. Instr. landscape architecture U. Ill., Urbana, 1959-60, asst. prof., 1960-63; asst. prof. Harvard U., 1963-67, asso. prof., 1967-73, prof., 1973—, prof. city planning, 1974—; instr. architecture Mass. Inst. Tech., Cambridge, 1963-66; prin. investigator, dir. research hwy. esthetics U.S. Dept. Transp., 1964-73; prin. Hornbeck Okerlund Assos., landscape architects, Cambridge, 1972-76; prin. Hornbeck Assos., 1976-78; v.p. Perry Dean Stahl Rogers, 1978—. Mem. Mass. Gov.'s Adv. Commn. on Open Space and Recreation, 1969-73, Gov.'s Task Force on Scenic Roads, 1971-72, design rev. commn. Boston Met. Dist. Commn., 1973-76, Garden Adv. Com., Dumbarton Oaks, Washington, 1973-75; mem. adv. com. Center for Studies in Landscape Architecture, Dumbarton Oaks, 1975—. Bd. dirs. Trustees of Reservations Mass., 1971-77, mem. adv. com., 1977—; bd. dirs. Hubbard Ednl. Trust, 1970—, North Andover (Mass.) Hist. Soc., 1971-74, New Eng. Wildflower Soc., 1977-78. Charles Eliot Travelling fellow Harvard, 1960. Mem. Am. Soc. Landscape Architects. Home: 121 Great Pond Rd North Andover MA 01845 Office: Graduate School Design Harvard Univ Cambridge MA 02138

HORNBLASS, ALBERT, ophthalmologist; b. N.Y.C., July 5, 1939; s. Maurice and Betty (Krieger) H.; B.A., Yeshiva U., 1960, B.R.E., 1960; M.D., U. Cin., 1964; m. Bernice Miriam Brooks, Dec. 23, 1973; children—David Judah, Moshe ben-Zion. Intern, Maimonides Med. Center, N.Y.C., 1964-65; resident in ophthalmology State U. N.Y. Downstate Med. Center, Bklyn., 1965-69, asst. prof., 1971-75, asso. prof., 1976—, chief ophthalmic plastic surgery, 1971—; asso. attending ophthalmologist Manhattan Eye Ear and Throat Hosp., N.Y.C., 1972—, Roosevelt Hosp., N.Y.C., 1972—, Lenox Hill Hosp., N.Y.C., 1974—; asso. chief ophthalmology Walter Reed Med. Center, 1971. Sec., Hebrew Immigrant Aid Soc., N.Y.C.; v.p. Bd. Jewish Edn., N.Y.C.; mem. nat. cabinet United Jewish Appeal Am., bd. govs. United Jewish Appeal-Fedn. N.Y. Heed Postgrad. Ophthalmic fellow, 1971; recipient Graeme Mitchel award, 1962, Warner Hoppins award, 1967, 68, Bklyn. Ophthalmol. Soc. Research award, 1966. Fellow ACS, Am. Soc. Ophthalmic Plastic and Reconstructive Surgery, Am. Acad. Ophthalmology (cons., instr.); mem. N.Y. Ophthal. Soc., Soc. Heed Fellows, N.Y. County Med. Soc. (vice chmn. legis. com.), Phi Delta Epsilon. Jewish. Contbr. articles to profl. jours. Office: 903 Lexington Ave New York City NY 10021

HORNE, MICHAEL EDWARD, advt. and pub. relations exec.; b. N.Y.C., Apr. 4, 1931; s. Alexander and Betty Horenstein; B.A., Hobart Coll., Geneva, N.Y., 1952: m. Joan Shapiro Feinberg, May 4, 1962; children—Shari, Alan, Julie. Apprentice, Robert Taplinger Assos., pub. relations, N.Y.C., 1952; publicist Max Ernest Hecht, 1953; asst. pub. relations dir. N.Y. Arthritis and Rheumatism Found., 1956; mem. advt. staff Sonotone Inc., Elmford, N.Y., 1957; partner, creative dir. Ad Agy., Inc., Detroit, 1958; creative dir. Edward Weiss Advt., N.Y.C., 1959-64; v.p., creative dir. Albert Finkle, Advt., Trenton, 1964-66; asst. dir. advt. and pub. relations Dictograph Security Systems, Florham Park, N.J., 1966-70, v.p., 1970—, charge advt. and pub. relations, 1978—; trustee, past v.p. pub. relations Nat. Found. Ileitis and Colitis. Served with AUS, 1953-55. Recipient awards Direct Mail Advt. Assn., Broadcasting mag. Mem. ASCAP, Direct Mail Advt. Assn. Author manuals, pub. service brochures, motion pictures. Home: 318 Highland Rd South Orange NJ 07079 Office: 26 Columbia Turnpike Florham Park NJ 07932

HORNER, MATINA SOURETIS (MRS. JOSEPH L. HORNER), coll. pres.; b. Roxbury, Mass., 1939; A.B. in Psychology, Bryn Mawr Coll.; Ph.D., U. Mich.; m. Joseph L. Horner; 3 children. Asso. prof. psychology and social relations Harvard U.; pres. Radcliffe Coll., 1972—; dir. TIME, Inc., 1975—; mem. council advisers Catalyst, 1976—; mem. Coll. Entrance Exam. Bd. Nat. Panel to Study Declining Test Scores, 1976-78; mem. bd. scholars Higher Edn. Research Inst., Inc., 1974—. Trustee Twentieth Century Fund, 1973—. Recipient Outstanding Service medal New Eng. Bd. Higher Edn., 1973. Mem. Nat. Inst. Social Scis., Phi Beta Kappa. Contbr. to Readings on th Psychology of Women, 1972, other publs. Address: Office of President Radcliffe College Cambridge MA 02138

HORNIK, HENRY, educator; b. Chorostkow, Poland, Jan. 5, 1927; s. Harry and Cilli (Huss) H.; came to U.S., 1939, naturalized, 1944; B.A. (Mayor's scholar), U. Pa., 1949, M.A. (G.L. Harrison scholar), 1951, Ph.D., 1955; postgrad. (Fulbright scholar) U. Sorbonne, 1952-53. Instr. Haverford (Pa.) Coll., 1953-56, Hunter Coll., City U. N.Y., 1956-57; asst. prof. Mass. Inst. Tech., Cambridge, 1957-59, Johns Hopkins, Balt., 1960-62; asso. prof. dept. Romance langs. Queens Coll., City U. N.Y., Flushing, 1964-68, prof., 1968—, founder, exec. officer Ph.D. in French, 1968-72. Served with AUS, 1945-46. Mem. AAUP, Modern Lang. Assn., Renaissance Soc. Am., Am. Assn. Tchrs. French, Phi Beta Kappa. Jewish. Home: 150-38B Union Turnpike Flushing NY 11367 Office: Dept Romance Languages Queens College Flushing NY 11367

HORNIK, JOSEPH WILLIAM, civil engr.; b. N.Y.C., May 7, 1929; s. Joseph and Josephine (Nemecek) H.; B.C.E., Cooper Union, 1952; postgrad. Columbia U., 1955-61; m. Barbara Joan Simko, Nov. 16, 1957; children—Heidi Josepha, Joseph Jared, Jason William, Heather Justine. Field engr. Stone & Webster Engring. Corp., Roanoke Rapids, N.C. and Portsmouth, Va., 1952-54; sr. engr. Howard, Needles, Tammen & Bergendorf, Jersey City, 1954-56; resident engr. Edwards & Kelcey, Bridgeport, Conn., 1956-59; project engr., project supt. The Austin Co., Bklyn. and San Juan, P.R., 1959-62; resident engr. Seelye Stevenson, Value & Knecht, Whitehall, N.Y., 1962-65; dep. county engr., dep. supt. hyws. County of Rockland, New City, N.Y., 1965-72, county engr., supt. hwys., 1972—; cons. engr., West Nyack, N.Y., 1967—; village engr. Village of Sloatsburg (N.Y.), 1972—. Mem. Rockland County Planning Bd., 1972—, Rockland County Drainage Agency, 1972—, Rockland County Soil and Water Conservation Agency, 1972—. Registered profl. engr., N.Y., Conn., Fla., P.R.; registered land surveyor, N.Y. Fellow ASCE; mem. N.Y. State County Hwy. Supts. Assn. (dir.), Nat. Soc. Profl. Engrs., N.Y. State Soc. Profl. Engrs., Nat. Assn. County Engrs., Am. Rd. and Transp. Builders Assn., Inst. Engrs., Architects and Surveyors of P.R., Soil Conservation Soc. Am., Omega Delta Phi. Clubs: West Nyack Swim and Tennis, West Rock Tennis. Home: 2 Dearborn Rd West Nyack NY 10994 Office: 23 New Hempstead Rd New City NY 10956

HOROWITZ, ALAN HERBERT, ins. and pension cons.; b. N.Y.C., Oct. 31, 1930; s. Morris and Yetta (Hibscher) H.; A.B., N.Y.U., 1951; m. Selma Steinberg, May 21, 1955; 1 son, Barry. Ins. cons. Home Life Ins. Co., N.Y.C., 1958—; mem. ethics com. Life Underwriters Assn., 1976. Founder, 1st pres. Woodlands Community Temple, Hartsdale, N.Y., 1966; chmn. Mid-Westchester Israel Affairs Com., 1975-76; chmn. United Jewish Appeal Drive, Hartsdale, 1976-78; bd. dirs. Hartsdale Civic Assn., 1970-76; chmn. transp. com. Hartsdale Sch. Dist., 1969-70, chmn. budget com., 1971; bd. dirs. Trail Blazer Camps, 1973-76. Served as lt. U.S. Army, 1951-53, C.L.U. Mem. N.Y.C., Nat. (Nat. Quality award 1961-78), assns. life underwriters, Million Dollar Round Table (life). Jewish. Contbr. articles to profl. publs. Home: 17 Carlyle Pl Hartsdale NY 10530 Office: 516 Fifth Ave New York City NY 10036

HOROWITZ, IRVING LOUIS, educator, sociologist; b. N.Y.C., Sept. 25, 1929; s. Louis and Esther (Tepper) H.; B.S.S., Coll. City N.Y., 1951; M.A., Columbia U., 1952; Ph.D., Buenos Aires (Argentina) U., 1957; postgrad. fellow Brandeis U., 1958-59; m. Ruth Lenore Horowitz, 1950 (div. 1964); children—Carl Frederick, David Dennis. Asst. prof. sociology Bard Coll., 1960; asso. prof. social theory Buenos Aires U., 1955-58; chmn. dept. sociology Hobart and William Smith Colls., 1960-63; asso. prof., then prof. sociology Washington U., St. Louis, 1963-69; chmn. dept. sociology Livingston Coll., Rutgers U., 1969—, prof. sociology grad. faculty, 1969—, Hannah Arendt prof. social and polit. theory, 1978—; vis. prof. sociology U. Caracas (Venezuela), 1957, Buenos Aires U., 1959, 61, 63, State U. N.Y. at Buffalo, 1960, Syracuse U., 1961, Rochester U., fall 1962, U. Calif. at Davis, 1966, U. Wis. at Madison, 1967, Stanford U., 1968-69; vis. lectr. London Sch. Econs. and Polit. Sci., 1962; prin. investigator numerous sci. and research projects; mem. adv. bd. Inst. Sci. Info.; mem. Presdl. Task Force Nat. Commn. Causes and Prevention of Violence, 1968-69; cons. Senate Com. Govt. Ops., 1966-67. Mem. AAAS, AAUP, Am. Philos. Assn., Am. Sociol. Assn., Authors Guild, Centre Internat. pour le Devel. (a founder), Internat. Assn. Philosophy Law and Social Thought, Internat. Studies Assn., Latin Am. Studies Assn., Midwest (chmn. com. professions 1968-69), N.Y. State sociol. socs., Soc. Internat. Devel., Soc. Study Social Problems (chmn. awards com. 1964-66). Author: Idea of War and Peace in Contemporary Philosophy, 1957; Philosophy, Science and the Sociology of Knowledge, 1960; Radicalism and the Revolt Against Reason: The Social Theories of Georges Sorel, 2d edit., 1968; The War Game: Studies of the New Civilian Militarists, 1963; Historia y Elementos de la Sociologia del Concimiento, 1963; The New Sociology: Essays in Social Science and Social Values in Honor of C. Wright Mills, 1964; Revolution in Brazil: Politics and Society in a Developing Nation, 1964; The Rise and Fall of Project Camelot, 2d edit., 1975; Three Worlds of Development: The Theory and Practice of International Stratification, 1966, 2d edit., 1972; Professing Sociology: The Life Cycle of a Social Science, 1968; Latin American Radicalism: A Documentary Report on Nationalist and Left Movements, 1969; Sociological Self-Images, 1969; The Knowledge Factory: Student Power and Academic Politics in America, 1970; Masses in Latin America, 1970; Cuban Communism, 3d edit., 1977; Ideology and Utopia in the United States; pres. Transaction; editor-in-Chief Society Mag., 1963—; founding editor Studies in Comparative Internat. Devel., 1965-79. Home: Blawenberg-Rocky Hill Rd Route 206 and Hwy 518 Princeton NJ 08540 Office: Rutgers Univ New Brunswick NJ 08903

HORSEMAN, ROY MERTZELL, fingerprint identification and security cons.; b. Queenstown, Md., June 12, 1935; s. Roy Mertzell and Anna Mary (Stuart) H.; B.Sc., Clinton U., 1957; grad. Nat. Law Enforcement Acad., 1966, Inst. Applied Sci., 1969, Ala. Sch. Fingerprinting, 1970; J.D., Blackstone Sch. Law, 1973. Owner, Horseman Pvt. Security Service, Phila., 1964-71; pres., chmn. bd. Nat. Security Systems Inc., Phila., 1971—; security cons. Brit. consulate gen., Phila., 1968-70. Named hon. citizen states of Fla., Tex., Ariz., Tenn., S.D., Minn., Okla., W.Va., and cities of Atlanta, New Orleans, Boise, Baton Rouge, Denver, Albuquerque, Cheyenne, Indpls., Sioux Falls, Topeka, and Manchester, N.H., also numerous other state awards including Ky. col. (gov. Ky.), hon. ambassador goodwill Pa. (gov. Pa.), hon. col. N.J. state militia (gov. N.J.), col. staff gov. La., internat. peace gardner (gov. N.D.), hon. recruiter U.S. Marine Corps. Mem. Internat. Assn. Criminologists (life), Internat. Assn. Universal Fingerprinting, Britannica Soc., Sunflower Soc. (hon.), Nat. Wildlife Assn., Freedom Bell Soc. Am. (life). Epsilon Delta Chi. Home: 237 S 10th St Philadelphia PA 19107 Office: POB 1311 Philadelphia PA 19105

HORSFALL, WILLIAM RHODES, JR., corp. exec.; b. Woonsocket, R.I., Nov. 21, 1929; s. William R. and Josephine (Sauner) H.; B.S. in Bus. Adminstrn., Bryant Coll., 1950; M.B.A., Northeastern U., 1960; m. Marion Eleanor Orlup, Aug. 6, 1960; children—William Rhodes III, David Willis, Deborah Josephine. Coiler operator Rice Tube & Channel Co., Inc., Pawtucket, R.I., 1953-56; cost supr. Barry Controls, Inc., Watertown, Mass., 1956-57; budget supr. Tracerlab, Inc., Waltham, Mass., 1957-62, v.p., dir. Tracerlab Employees Fed. Credit Union, 1957-60; chmn. bd. Cascade Engring. Corp., Newton, Mass., 1958-62; plant accountant Polythane Corp., subsidiary Monsanto Co., East Providence, R.I., 1962-66; asst. controller Providence Pile Fabric Corp., Pawtucket, 1966-68; treas. AA Investment Corp., Bedford, Mass., 1966-68; controller Harvard Apparatus Co., Inc., Millis, Mass., 1968-73, treas., 1969-73; controller Jayson Co., Portland, Maine, 1973—. Served with inf. AUS, 1953-55. Mem. Nat. Rifle Assn., Nat. Accountants Assn., Vet. Motor Car Club Am., Antique Car Club Am. Mason. Home: Gore Rd Alfred ME 04002 Office: 73 India St Portland ME 04112

HORST, ELEANOR, interior designer, interior architect; b. N.Y.C., Aug. 3, 1892; d. Charles and Elizabeth (Freeman) Goulding; B.A., Hunter Coll., 1912; M.A., Columbia U., 1916; student Art Students League, 1913, Parson's Sch. Interior Design, 1935-36; m. Amos Long Horst, June 20, 1920 (div. Nov. 1938); 1 dau., Nancy Horst Trowbridge. Tchr., N.Y.C. Pub. Schs., 1912-17; canteen worker World War I, France, 1918; exec. asst. to pub. Arts and Decoration Mag., 1919-20; art editor Women's Jour., 1920-23; designer interiors, N.Y.C., 1925—; mem. house and grounds com. First Ch. of Christ, Scientist, Greenwich, Conn., designer auditorium decorating and lighting. Mem. Am. Soc. Interior Designers (nat. exam. bd.), Nat. Soc. Historic Preservation, Greenwich Taxpayers Assn., Irish Georgian Soc., Conn. Conservancy, N.Y. Decorators Club (v.p. 1940-42, 67-68, mem. numerous coms., chmn. hist. com. to pub. history). Home and Office: 47 Putnam Park Greenwich CT 06830

HORST, ROBERT LEE, elec. engr.; b. Brownstown, Pa., June 5, 1930; s. Samuel G. and Elizabeth L. (Kern) H.; B.S. with honors, Pa. State U., 1958; M.S. in Elec. Engring., U. Pa., 1962; m. Ethel Mae Young, Sept. 6, 1952; children—Robert Kyle, Gayle Eileen, Eric John. Lab. technician research and devel. center Armstrong Cork Co., Lancaster, Pa., 1948-55; research engr. supr., 1958-66, sr. staff engr., 1966-75, sr. cons. engr. Central Engring., 1975—; staff engr. Pa. State U., University Park, 1955-58. Fin. sec. Salem United Meth. Ch., 1963-77, chmn. fin. com., 1968-77; dist. com. Lancaster-Lebanon council Boy Scouts Am., 1974—. Served with USN, 1951-54. Registered profl. engr., Pa.; U.S. Rubber Co. scholar, 1958. Mem. IEEE (sr.), Pa. State Alumni Assn. (life), Phi Kappa Phi, Tau Beta Pi (life), Eta Kappa Nu (life), Sigma Tau, Phi Eta Sigma. Contbr. articles to profl. publs. Patentee microwave, mfg. control fields. Office: Armstrong Cork Co Central Engring Dept 2500 Columbia Ave Lancaster PA 17604

HORTON, FRANK, congressman; b. Tex., Dec. 12, 1919; s. Frank and Mary (Hathcox) H.; B.A., La. State U., 1941; LL.B., Cornell U., 1947; m. Marjorie Mae Wilcox, Jan. 1, 1945; children—Frank Jefferson, Steven William. Admitted to N.Y. bar, 1947; asso. firm Johnson, Reif & Mullan, and predecessor, Rochester, 1947-52, partner, 1952-69; mem. 88th to 96th congresses from 34th N.Y. Dist., ranking minority mem. govt. ops. com., legis. and mil. ops. subcom.; participant Can.-U.S. Interperliamentary Group; chmn. Commn. Fed. Paperwork, 1975-77; co-chmn. N.E.-Midwest Coalition for Econ. Advancement; rep. of U.S. Ho. Reps. at dedication Israeli Knesset, 1966; guest of Ditchley Found. at Conf. Anglo-Am. Affairs, Oxfordshire, Eng., 1967. Mem. exec. com. Seneca dist. Otetiana council Boy Scouts Am., 1955—; pres. Rochester Community Baseball, Inc., 1957-62; councilman-at-large City Council of Rochester, 1955-61; bd. visitors U.S. Naval Acad. Served from 2d lt. to maj. AUS, 1941-46. Mem. Am., N.Y. (exec. com. young lawyers sect. 1952), Rochester (sec. 1953-57) bar assns., Fedn. Bar Assns. Western N.Y. (pres. 1956-57), Res. Officers Assn. (past pres.), VFW, Am. Legion, Order of Coif, Cornell Law Assn. (exec. com.), N.Y. Conservation Council, Phi Kappa Phi. Presbyterian (elder, trustee). Clubs: Masons (33 deg.), Shriners, Jesters; Capitol Hill. Co-author: How to End the Draft-The Case for an All volunteer Army, 1967; A Study of Urban Education in America, 1968; A Study of Air Safety, 1969; author: Election Reform: Remedy for an Impending Crisis, 1969. Mailing address: 9607 Hillridge Dr Kensington MD 20795

HORTON, JOHN EDWARD, dentist, immunologist, ret. mil. officer; b. Brockton, Mass., Dec. 30, 1930; s. Harold Ellsworth and Anita Helen (Samuelson) H.; B.S., Providence Coll., 1952; postgrad. U. Mass., 1952-53; D.M.D., Tufts U., 1957; M.S. in Dentistry, Baylor U., Tex., 1965; M.A. in Higher Edn., George Washington U., 1978; m. Jacqueline Alice Hansen, June 10, 1951; children—John Edward, Janet E., James E., Jeffrey E., Joseph E. Commd. 1st lt. Dental Corps, U.S. Army, 1957, advanced through grades to col., 1972, ret., 1977; staff dentist 279th Sta. Hosp., Berlin Command, West Berlin, 1957-60; chief oral diagnosis 87th Med. Detachment, Nurnberg, Germany, 1960-61; chief preventive dentistry U.S. Army Dental Detachment, Fort Hood, Tex., 1962-63, instr. preventive dentistry Ft. Hood Gen. Dentistry Residency Program, 1962-63; chief periodontic service Reynolds Army Hosp., Fort Sill, Okla., 1965-67, instr. periodontics and oral pathology for Dental Intern Tng. Program, 1965-67; chief and cons. in periodontics Nurnberg Med. Service Area U.S. Army in Europe, 1967-70; cons. in periodontics to the Surgeon, 7th Army, U.S. Army, Europe, 1967-70; instr. in microbiology and immunology U.S. Army Inst. Dental Research, Walter Reed Army Med. Center, Washington, 1972-77, chief dept. immunology, 1973-74, chief depts. immunology and microbiology, 1974-77; asst., asso., then professorial lectr. oral biology Grad. Sch. Arts and Scis., George Washington U., Washington, 1972-77; guest scientist Nat. Inst. Dental Research, NIH, Bethesda, Md., 1970-73; lectr. Sch. Hygiene and Pub. Health, Johns Hopkins U., 1975—; asso. prof., chmn. dept. periodontology Harvard Sch. Dental Medicine, 1977—; invited speaker to ann. meeting Am. Dental Soc. of Europe, Lausanne, Switzerland, 1969; invited participant to workshop on immunology of periodontal disease 2d. Internat. Congress of Immunology, Brighton, Eng., 1974. Troop councilor Transatlantic council Boy Scouts Am., 1969-70. Decorated Army Commendation medal, Meritorious Service medal, Legion of Merit. Fellow Am. Pub. Health Assn., Royal Soc. Health; mem. Am. Acad. Periodontology (Orban Prize subcom. 1975—), Am. Acad. Oral Medicine (grad. awards com. 1971-72, publicity com. 1971-74), Am. Acad. Oral Pathology, ADA, Internat. Assn. Dental Research, Am. Assn. Immunologists, AAAS, Baylor U., Tufts U., Providence Coll. alumni assns. Author: (with others) Prevention and Oral Health, 1974; co-editor: Mechanisms of Localized Bone Loss, 1978; contbr. articles on periodontics and immunological processes to profl. jours. Office: Dept Periodontology Harvard Sch Dental Medicine 188 Longwood Ave Boston MA 02115

HORVAT, JOSEPH JAMES, psychologist, educator; b. Youngstown, Ohio, Dec. 3, 1942; s. Joseph John and Sylvia Virginia (DeSalvo) H.; B.S., Youngstown State Coll., 1964; M.Ed., Westminster Coll., 1966; Ph.D., Case-Western Res. U., 1969; postgrad. Gestalt Inst. Psychotherapy, 1969, Family Inst. of Phila., 1974—. Asso. prof. psychology Millersville (Pa.) State Coll., 1969—; psychologist, therapist Lancaster (Pa.) Guidance Clinic, 1971-72; dir., therapist Psychol. Assos., Lancaster, 1972—; cons. Ohio Penal System; cons. Camp Hill project Pa. Dept. Corrections. Mem. Am., Pa. psychol. assns., Council for Exceptional Children, Family Therapy Inst., Am. Assn. Marriage and Family Therapists. Home: 49 Dogwood Ct Lancaster PA 17603 Office: 2832 Little Pike Lancaster PA 17601

HORWITZ, RUTH KAFRISSEN, ednl. adminstr.; b. Phila., Dec. 12, 1936; d. David S. and Leona L. (Snyder) Kafrissen; B.S., Temple U., 1957, M.Ed., 1961, Ed.D., 1973; m. Alan J. Horwitz, June 29, 1958; children—Abby Beth, Robert Scott. Tchr., Phila. High Sch. for Girls, 1957-62, South Phila. High Sch., N.E. High Sch., 1963, N.E. Standard Evening High Sch., Washington Adult Evening Sch., Phila., 1965-70, Olney High Sch., Phila., 1971; research asst. Temple U., 1963, instr. Community Coll., 1967-68, adj. instr. Grad. Coll. Edn., 1974; head dept. bus. edn. Gratz High Sch., Phila., 1971-77; vice prin. Alvin A. Swenson Skills Center Sch. Dist. of Phila., 1977—; ednl. cons. Temple U., 1974-75, Bethlehem Sch. Dist., 1974-76, Phila. Postal Service, 1975-76, nat. adv. bd. Scholastic Mag., 1978-79. Bd. dirs. Greater NE Congregation, 1965, 77; support campaign leader YWCA; Mem. bd. edn. Regional Hebrew High Sch., 1976—; Mem. Am. Vocat. Assn., Assn. Supervision and Curriculum Devel., Nat. Bus. Edn. Assn., Nat. Council Local Adminstrsn., Indsl. Arts and Vocat. Edn. Assn. Phila., Nat. Assn. Vocat. Edn. Spl. Needs Personnel, Pa. Congress Sch. Adminstrs., Pa. Vocat. Assn. (officer), Nat. Council Adminstrv. Women in Edn., Phila. Assn. Sch. Adminstrs., Temple U. Bus. Edn. Alumni Bd. (past pres.), Vocat. Adminstrs. Pa., Council of Orgns. in Edn., Temple U. Coll. Edn. Alumni Bd., Women's Intercollegiate Athletic Adv. Bd., Vocat. Edn. Equity Council, B'nai B'rith Women (v.p.), Women in Edn. (officer), Phi Delta Kappa (officer), Delta Pi Epsilon, Omicron Tau Theta (officer). Contbr. articles to profl. jours. Home: 9724 Portis Rd Philadelphia PA 19115 Office: Swenson Skills Center Philadelphia PA 19114

HORWITZ, SAUL, mfg. co. exec.; b. Hoboken, N.J., June 7, 1925; s. Hyman and Ida (Cherson) H.; B.M.E., Newark Coll. Engring., 1946; m. Joyce Gootman, Nov. 12, 1950; children—David Michael, Alan Steven. Pres., Central Jersey Supply Co., and Central Jersey Export Corp., Perth Amboy, N.J., 1948—. Mem. Am. Soc. Heating, Refrigeration and Air Conditioning Engrs., Newark Coll. Engring. Alumni Assn., Smithsonian Assoc., Am. Soc. Notaries. Patentee in field. Office: 201 2nd St PO Box 549 Perth Amboy NJ 08862

HOSBACH, HOWARD DANIEL, pub. co. exec.; b. North Bergen, N.J., Mar. 9, 1931; s. Howard D. and Marjorie V. (Hoffer) H.; B.S., Fairleigh Dickinson U., 1953, M.B.A., 1967; m. Eugenia Elizabeth Paracka, Apr. 10, 1954; children—Susan, Cynthia, Beth Ann, Alyssa. Advt. mgr. McGraw-Hill Book Co., N.Y.C., 1958-62, dir. mktg., 1962-66, gen. mgr. dealer and library sales, 1966-69; group v.p. Standard & Poor's Corp., N.Y.C., 1970-73, exec. v.p., 1973—, dir., 1970—; dir. Standard & Poor's Compustat Service, Inc., Denver, Standard & Poor's Securities, Inc., N.Y.C. Served with AUS, 1953-55. Mem. Holy Name Soc. Roman Catholic. Home: 175 Graham Terr Saddle Brook NJ 07662 Office: 345 Hudson St New York City NY 10014

HOSKIN, WILLIAM DICKEL, physician; b. Akron, Ohio, Jan. 24, 1920; s. Robert E. and Margaret (Dickel) H.; A.B., Hiram Coll., 1942; M.D., Western Res. U., 1947; m. Lois Black, June 1, 1951; children—Mark, Ned, David. Intern, U.S. Naval Hosp., San Diego, 1951-52; practice medicine specializing in occupational medicine, 1954—; instr. physics Hiram (Ohio) Coll., 1943; asst. supt. St. Luke's Hosp., Cleve., 1947-51; staff. physician Eastman Kodak Co., Rochester, 1954-69, asst. dir., 1969-70, med. dir. Kodak Park div., 1970—; clin. asso. preventive medicine and community health U. Rochester, 1974-75; mem. N.Y. State Senate Adv. Com. on Alcoholism, 1977—. Served as lt. USNR, 1951-54. Recipient Hiram Coll. Alumni Assn. Ann. award for Outstanding Achievement, 1972. Diplomate Am. Bd. Preventive Medicine. Fellow Am. Occupational Med. Assn., Am. Acad. Occupational Medicine, Am. Coll. Preventive Medicine, Garfield Soc.; mem. Indsl. Med. Assn. Upstate N.Y. (pres. 1969-70), Rochester Rehab. Center, Genesee Valley Heart Assn. (dir. 1965-76), N.Y. State Heart Assembly, Nat. Council Alcoholism, Health Assn. Rochester, Monroe County Learning Disabilities Assn. (vice chmn. mental health chpt. 1977—). Club: U. Rochester Faculty. Contbr. articles in field to med. jours. Home: 190 Bellehurst Dr Rochester NY 14617 Office: 1669 Lake Ave Rochester NY 14650

HOSKING, ROBERT LEROY, broadcasting exec.; b. Ramsey, N.J., Nov. 9, 1931; s. Charles E. and Luella (Barthol) H.; B.A., Gettysburg (Pa.) Coll., 1953; M.B.A., U. Mich., 1958; m. Valentina Kopach, Sept. 8, 1957; children—Gail, Janice, Elizabeth, Deborah, Patricia, Wesley. With WCBS radio, N.Y.C., 1958-69; with WCBS-TV, 1970-74, gen. sales mgr., 1963-69, v.p., gen. mgr., 1970-74; v.p., gen. mgr. WCAU-TV, Phila., 1974—; asst. to pres. CBS-TV, N.Y.C., 1970. Bd. dirs. United Fund Phila., Phila. Better Bus. Bur.; bd. fellows Gettysburg Coll. Served as lt. (j.g.) USNR, 1953-56. Mem. Pa. Broadcasters Assn. (dir.), TV Radio Advt. Club Phila. (v.p., dir.). Presbyterian. Home: 330 Thornbrook Ave Rosemont PA 19010 Office: WCAU-TV City Line and Monument Rd Philadelphia PA 19131

HOSKINS, DONALD WILLIAM, internist; b. N.Y.C., Feb. 22, 1933; s. Thomas Charles and Elise Octavia (Aichele) H.; B.S., Queens Coll., 1953; M.D., Cornell U., 1957; m. Carol Myrtice Noll, Dec. 19, 1955; children—Lauren Anne, David William, Bruce Noll. Intern, Cornell-N.Y. Hosp., 1957-58, asst. resident in medicine, 1958-60; research fellow in gastroenterology Cornell-N.Y. Hosp. Med. Center, 1960-61; practice medicine specializing in internal medicine and tropical medicine, N.Y.C., 1961—; clin. asso. prof. medicine Cornell U.; asso. attending physician N.Y. Hosp.; cons. in medicine (tropical medicine) Meml. Hosp.; attending physician Doctors Hosp. Served to lt. col. M.C., U.S. Army, 1967-69. Diplomate Am. Bd. Internal Medicine. Trustee Riverside Ch. Fellow Royal Soc. Tropical Medicine; mem. N.Y. Soc. Tropical Medicine, Am. Soc. Internal Medicine, N.Y. Acad. Scis., N.Y. State, N.Y. County med. socs. Contbr. articles on tropical medicine and gastroenterology to med. jours.; contbg. author: Drugs of Choice, 1979. Office: 311 E 79th St New York City NY 10021

HOSKINS, WALTER HUGH, biochemist; b. Indpls., Jan. 4, 1913; s. Walter Douglas and Lillian (Greist) H.; A.B., Earlham Coll., 1934; postgrad. Haverford Coll., 1934-35; Ph.D., U. Chgo., 1939; LL.B., La Salle Extension U., 1971; m. Barbara Barrett, Sept. 11, 1937; children—Steven, John, Thomas, Rebecca. Research fellow medicine Cornell Med. Sch., N.Y. Hosp., 1939-40; research chemist Maltine Co., 1940-43; asst. to research dir. Johnson & Johnson, 1943-44; med. dir. Chilcott Labs., 1944-47, research dir., 1947-52; v.p. sci. affairs Crookes Barnes Labs., 1957-64; v.p. research Chemway Corp., 1962-64; dir. clin. investigation Warner-Chilcott Labs., Morris Plains, N.J., 1952-57, dir. med. communications, 1964-70; clin. research asso. Warner Lambert Research Inst., Morris Plains, 1970-75. Fellow AAAS; mem. Am. Chem. Soc., N.Y. Acad. Sci., Assn. Med. Dirs., Endocrine Soc., N.J. Acad. Sci. Home: School House Ln Morristown NJ 07960

HOSTETLER, SHIRLEY ANN, educator; b. Meyersdale, Pa.; d. Carl E. and Florence (Shunk) H.; B.S. in Music Edn., Bob Jones U., Greenville, S.C., 1953; M.L.S., Case Western Res. U., Cleve., 1959. Instr. music Claysburg (Pa.) Greenfield-Kimmel Sch. Dist., 1953-54; supr. music Shanksville (Pa.) Stonycreek Sch. Dist., 1954-56; instr. music Shade Central City Sch. Dist., Cairnbrook, Pa., 1956-58; librarian Rockwood (Pa.) Area Sch. Dist., 1959—. Mem. NEA, Pa., Rockwood edn. assns. Mem. Brethren Ch. Home: 420 Sherman St Meyersdale PA 15552 Office: Rockwood Area High Sch Rockwood PA 15557

HOSTETTER, D(AVID) RAY, coll. pres.; b. Refton, Pa., Aug. 16, 1927; s. Christian N. and Anna B. (Lane) H.; A.B., Greenville Coll., 1950; M.A., Pa. State U., 1951; Ed.D., Columbia U., 1964; m. Audrey Faye Fisher, Sept. 16, 1950; children—David Rahn, Curtis Ray. Coach, Tabor Coll., 1951-52; coach, instr. history Messiah Coll., Grantham, Pa., 1952-55, dir. devel., 1960-61, v.p. finance and devel., 1961-64, pres., 1964—; in pvt. bus., 1955-60; bd. mem. Council for Advancement Small Colls., 1969-76, treas., 1971-76; mem. exec. com. Christian Coll. Consortium, 1970—, vice chmn., 1974-76, chmn., 1976—; chmn. steering com. Capitol Regional Planning Council, 1977—. Mem. bd. for schs. and colls. Brethren in Christ Ch., 1964—, bd. adminstrn., 1972—; mem. exec. com. Pa. Council on Alcohol Problems, pres., 1978—. Mem. Nat. Assn. Evangelicals (Higher Edn. Commn. 1964—), Pa. Commn. Ind. Colls. and Univs. (exec. com. 1974—). Republican. Club: Rotary. Author: The Challenge Grant and Higher Education, 1960. Home and Office: Grantham PA 17027

HOSTETTER, DONALD ALLEN, clergyman; b. W. Grove, Pa., July 14, 1929; s. Meyer Moyer and Rosa May (Stauffer) H.; B.A., Grove City Coll., 1950; Th.M., Princeton Sem., 1953; m. Charlotte Beatrice Mamounis, June 23, 1956; children—Mark David, Jonathan Charles. Minister edn. Webb Horton Presbyterian Ch., Middletown, N.Y., 1953-55; pastor Gilead Presbyn. Ch., Carmel, N.Y., 1956-62; asso. camps, confs., retreats Presbyn. Christian Edn. Council, N.Y.C., 1963-76, ednl. cons., 1977—; chmn. spl. task force resident outdoor edn. Community Council N.Y., 1970—; camp cons. synod units United Presbyn. Ch.; rep. Bronx Republican Com., 1965. Mem. Presbyn. Conf. Assn. (pres. 1959-62), Am. Camping Assn. (dir. N.Y. chpt.), Environ. Advisory Council N.Y.C. (past pres.), Presbyn. Camp and Conf. Assos. Home: 5700 Arlington Ave Bronx NY 10471 Office: 7 W 11th St New York City NY 10011

HOTALING, KAY CAROL, coll. adminstr.; b. Kingston, N.Y., Dec. 20, 1945; d. Kenneth LeGrand and Mary Louise (Straley) H.; B.S. in Math., State U. N.Y., 1968, M.S. in Counseling Psychology, 1970, doctoral candidate, 1970—. Adminstrv. asst. office of v.p. student affairs State U. N.Y., Albany, 1968-70, chief counselor, 1973—, asst. dean, 1973—; counselor Adirondack Community Coll., 1970-73; cons. in field. Bd. dirs. Warren Washington Mental Health, Glens Falls, N.Y., 1970-73; bd. dirs. Glens Falls Youth Center, 1970-73; bd. dirs., chmn. youth com. Voluntary Action Center Albany, 1977—; mem. Albany Council of Community Services, chmn. info. and research task force, 1973—. Recipient Nat. Mental Health Assn. Ann. citation, 1973. Mem. Am., N.Y. State personnel and guidance assns., AAUP, AAUW, Adult Edn. Assn. U.S.A., Nat. Council Tchrs. Math., Chi Sigma Theta, State U. N.Y. Alumni Assn. (dir. 1976—). Club: Jr. League of Albany (dir. 1977—). Office: State U NY at Albany Coll Gen Studies Albany NY 12222

HOTCHKISS, HENRY, petroleum geologist; b. New Haven, June 6, 1909; s. Henry Stuart and Elizabeth (Washington) H.; student Taft Sch., 1922-26, Phillips Acad., 1926-28; B.S., Yale, 1933, postgrad., 1933-35; m. Mary Bell Clark, May 19, 1936; children—Henry Washington, Anne Perrine Clark (Mrs. Robert Norton Ganz, Jr.), Frederick Hatfield Clark. Miner, Idaho, 1935-36; asst. seismic observer Phillips Petroleum Co., La., Tex., Okla., 1936-37; asst. dist. geologist Phillips Petroleum Co., Ardmore, Okla., 1937; field geologist Amiranian Oil Co., Iran, 1937-38; field geologist Iraq Petroleum Co. and asso. cos., Oman, Dhofar and Iraq, 1938-41; divisional geologist Persian Gulf, 1946-48, N. Iraq, 1948-50, asst. fields mgr. Qatar and Trucial Coast, 1950-53, fields mgr., 1953-55; regional geologist Middle East and Far East, Standard Oil Co. (N.J.), N.Y.C., 1955-64, exploration adviser Middle East and Far East, N.Y.C., 1964-69, exploration adviser Esso Middle East, 1969-70. Asso., Woods Hole (Mass.) Oceanographic Inst. Served to capt. USNR, 1941-46. Fellow Geol. Soc. London, Royal Geog. Soc. London, Am. Geog. Soc., Inst. Petroleum, London; mem. Am. Assn. Petroleum Geologists (asso. editor bull. 1956-65, East sect. pres. 1960-61), Am. Inst. Profl. Geologists, N.Y. Acad. Scis., Mass. Archaeol. Soc., Soc. Asian Affairs. Republican. Methodist. Home: The Capt Horatio Pease House 15 4th Ave Oak PO Box 1533 Bluffs MA 02557 also 80 Fort St Fairhaven MA 02719

HOTCHKISS, JEANETTE LOUISE, educator; b. New Haven, Sept. 19, 1930; d. Roy Erwin and Beulah (Westerman) H.; B.S., So. Conn. State Coll., 1953; M.S., U. Bridgeport, 1965. Tchr., Cos Cob (Conn.) Sch., 1953—. Camp dir. Greenwich Girls Day Camp, summers 1956-59; mem. selections com. Greenwich council Girl Scouts U.S.A., 1963-64; div. chmn. Greenwich Community Chest drive, 1967, 68, bd. dirs., 1974-76; mem.-at-large Greenwich Community Chest and Council, 1968-69; mem. staff adv. com. on personnel policies Greenwich Bd. Edn., 1960-64, chmn., 1962-64; mem. adv. com. tchr. evaluation Conn. Dept. Edn., 1973-74, adv. bd. state certifications tchrs., 1975-79. Recipient Outstanding Woman in Edn. award Internat. Women's Year, 1975. Mem. Assn. Childhood Edn. Internat. (br. pres. 1960, state rec. sec. 1965-66), NEA (del. nat. conv. 1969-78, mem. com. internat. relations 1975-76, life mem., sec. Conn. del.), Conn. (del. to rep. assembly 1965—, mem. inquiry team, 1970, dir. 1970-76; chmn. Tchrs. Conv. Day; v.p. 1973-74, pres. 1974-75), Greenwich (pres. 1968-70) edn. assns., Am. Assn. Colls. Tchr. Edn. (com. competency based tchr. edn. 1975-76), Northfield Sch. Alumnae Assn. (exec. council 1965-73), Delta Kappa Gamma (2d v.p. 1972-74). Home: 11 Old Wagon Rd Old Greenwich CT 06870 Office: Boston Post Rd Cos Cob CT 06807

HOU, KENNETH CHIANG, chemist; b. Kingsu, China, Apr. 22, 1929; s. Nao C. and Jean C. H.; came to U.S., 1956, naturalized, 1970; M.S. in Chem. Engring., U. Idaho, 1957; Ph.D. in Phys. Chemistry, U. Tex., 1962; m. Catherine Feng, Sept. 6, 1965; children—Howard, Selina. Postdoctoral fellow Pa. State U., 1962-64, Cornell U., 1964-66; sr. research chemist Celanese Research Co., Summit, N.J., 1966-73; sr. research engr. Cuno div. AMF, Inc., Meriden, Conn., 1973—. Recipient Outstanding Performance award AMF, Inc., 1974, Achievement award, 1976. Mem. Am. Chem. Soc., Sigma Chi, Phi Lambda Upsilon. Democrat. Contbr. chem. articles to profl. jours. Patentee in field. Home: 109 Heywood Dr Glastonbury CT 06033 Office: 400 Research Pkwy Meriden CT 06450

HOUCK, LEWIS DANIEL, JR., govt. ofcl.; b. Cleve., July 9, 1932; s. Lewis Daniel and Mary Clark (Dowds) H.; A.B., Princeton U., 1955; M.B.A. with distinction, N.Y. U., 1964, Ph.D., 1971; m. Ellen Dorothy Thayer, Sept. 8, 1962 (div. 1975); children—Marianne Jennifer, Leland Daniel. Mgr. spl. research Young & Rubicam, Inc., N.Y.C., 1957-59; mktg. mgr. Selling Research, Inc., N.Y.C., 1959-62; ednl. projects mgr. Nat. Assn. Accountants, N.Y.C., 1969-71; spl. cons. U.S. Dept. Agr., Washington, 1971-73; project leader nat. econ. analysis div. Econ. Research Service, 1973—; instr. N.Y. U. Grad. Sch. Bus. Adminstrn., 1966-69. Served as 1st lt., AUS, 1955-56. Recipient Founders Day award N.Y. U. Grad. Sch. Bus. Adminstrn., 1971. Ford Found. fellow, 1964-66. Fellow Am. Biog. Inst., Internat. Biog. Assn.; mem. Am. Accounting Assn., Am. Econ. Assn., AIM, Am. Mktg. Assn., Am. Statis. Assn., AAAS, Acad. Polit. Sci., Am. Acad. Polit. and Social Sci. Episcopalian. Club: Princeton (Washington). Home: 11111 Woodson Ave Kensington MD 20795 Office: US Dept Agr GHI Bldg 500 12th St SW Washington DC 20250

HOUGH, ELDRED WILSON, educator, petroleum engr.; b. Carrollton, Ill., Jan. 16, 1916; s. Thomas Crispin and Jennie (Eldred) H.; B.S. in Engring. Physics, U. Ill., 1939; M.S. in Physics, Calif. Inst. Tech., 1941, Ph.D., 1943; m. Jane Ruth Elder, Dec. 28, 1948; children—Christine E., Phyllis J., Roger E., Carl E. Research asst. Calif. Inst. Tech., 1941-46, sr. research fellow, 1946-49; sr. research engr. Stanolind Oil and Gas Co., 1949-52; grad. prof. petroleum engring. U. Tex., 1952-61; cons. Humble Oil and Refining Co., 1954-61; prof., head dept. petroleum engring. Miss. State U., 1961-65; asst. dean Sch. Tech., So. Ill. U. at Carbondale, 1965-69; dean U. Maine Coll. Engring. and Sci., Orono, 1969-74, prof. chem. engring., 1975-76; prof. petroleum engring., chmn. Coll. Petroleum and Minerals, Dhahran, Saudi Arabia, 1974-75; prof. petroleum engring. Miss. State U., Mississippi State, 1976—, head dept., 1976—. Research grantee Am. Petroleum Inst., 1957-60, Am. Chem. Soc., 1960-63, NSF, 1961-65, NASA, 1963-65, U.S. Army C.E., 1966-69. Registered profl. engr., Calif., Tex., Maine. Mem. Tex. Petroleum Research Commn., 1952-56. Mem. Am. Soc. Engring. Edn., Am. Chem. Soc., Am. Inst. Chem. Engrs., Am. Inst. Mining Metall. and Petroleum Engrs., Nat. Soc. Profl. Engrs., Am. Petroleum Inst. (chmn. So. dist. study com. for stimulation of oil wells with surface active agts., v.p. for Miss., So. dist. 1963-65), Sigma Xi, Tau Beta Pi, Sigma Gamma Epsilon, Phi Eta Sigma, Phi Kappa Phi. Club: Lions. Author numerous articles and reports in field. Office: Box PE Miss State U Mississippi State MS 39762

HOUGH, FREDERICK GERARD, city ofcl.; b. Susquehanna, Pa., Oct. 4, 1947; s. Frederick George and Catherine Teresa (Arnold) H.; B.A., Pa. State U., 1969. History instr. Laurel Hill Acad., Susquehanna, Pa., 1969-70; child care worker Susquehanna Valley Home, Binghamton, N.Y., 1970-71; sec.-treas. local govt. subdiv. Borough Susquehanna (Pa.) Depot, 1972—. Cons. Tri Boro Municipal

Authority, 1973; sec. Shade Tree Commn., 1972, Susquehanna Depot Council on Arts, 1974. Chmn. bd. dirs., art dir. Susquehanna Community Choral Soc., Inc., 1975-77. Mem. Pa. Local Govt. Secs. Assn., Municipal Treasurers Assn., Susquehanna County Boroughs Assn. (sec.-treas.), Northeastern, Pa. State (dir.) assns. boroughs, Pa. State U. Alumni Assn. Democrat. Roman Catholic. Home: 414 Pine St Susquehanna PA 18847 Office: 218 Exchange St Susquehanna PA 18847

HOUGH, GORDON LORD, owner pub. relations firm; b. Chgo., Sept. 18, 1918; s. Will M. and Florence E. (Lord) H.; grad. Choate Sch., 1936; A.B. with honors, Harvard, 1940; m. Barbara Kiger, Apr. 15, 1950; children—Elizabeth P., Barbara L., Gordon Lord. Asst. pub. relations mgr. Creole Petroleum Corp., N.Y.C., 1955-59; dir. internat. pub. relations Am. Machinery and Foundry Co., N.Y.C., 1959-61; suburban dir. Lincoln Center Campaign, N.Y.C., 1961-64; pvt. practice as pub. relations counsel, Darien, Conn., 1964—. Active Darien Citizens for Good Edn.; chmn. communications task force Bd. Edn., Darien, 1972-73; co-chmn. Darien chpt. Am. Field Services Internat. Scholarships, 1974-76. Trustee, sec. Nat. Art Mus. of Sport, N.Y.C. Served to comdr. USNR, 1942-46. Mem. Pub. Relations Soc. Am., Indsl. Audio-Visual Assn. Clubs: Harvard (N.Y.C.); Tokeneke (Darien, Conn.). Contbr. to consumer and trade periodicals. Home and office: 80 Christie Hill Rd Darien CT 06820

HOUGHTON, JAMES RICHARDSON, glass mfg. exec.; b. Corning, N.Y., Apr. 6, 1936; s. Amory and Laura (Richardson) H.; A.B., Harvard, 1958, M.B.A., 1962; m. May Tuckerman Kinnicutt, June 30, 1962; children—James DeKay, Nina Bayard. Investment banker Goldman, Sachs & Co., N.Y.C., 1959-61; with Corning Glass Works (N.Y.), 1962—, v.p., European area mgr. Corning Glass Internat., Zurich, Switzerland, and Brussels, Belgium, 1964-68, v.p., gen. mgr. consumer products div., 1968-71, vice chmn. bd., 1971—; mem. exec. com., 1969—, also dir.; chmn. bd., pres., dir. Corning Glass Internat. S.A., Corning Internat. Corp.; dir. Met. Life Ins. Co., N.Y.C., Sperry & Hutchinson Co., N.Y.C., Dow Corning Corp., Midland, Mich., CBS, Inc., N.Y.C.; mem. internat. council Morgan Guaranty Trust Co. N.Y. Mem. N.Y. State Council Arts. Trustee Pierpont Morgan Library, N.Y.C., Fay Sch., Southboro, Mass., Clarkson Coll. Tech., Potsdam, N.Y., Inst. Advanced Study, Princeton, N.J., Corning Glass Works Found., Corning Mus. Glass. Served with AUS, 1959-60. Mem. Bus. Com. for Arts, Council Fgn. Relations Inc., Internat. C. of C. (trustee, mem. U.S. council). Episcopalian. Clubs: Corning Country (N.Y.); Country (Brookline, Mass.); Tarratine (Dark Harbor, Maine); River, Harvard, Links, University (N.Y.C.); Rolling Rock (Ligonier, Pa.); Royal Golf (Belgium, Brussels); Augusta (Ga.) Nat. Golf; Coral Beach and Tennis. Home: Spencer Hill RD 2 Corning NY 14830 Office: Corning Glass Works Corning NY 14830

HOUGHTON, WILLIAM HENRY, book pub. co. exec.; b. Hartford, Conn., Apr. 13, 1925; s. Henry Ernest and Frances Mary (Plaunt) H.; grad. Exeter Acad., 1943; B.S. magna cum laude, Babson Coll., 1949; m. Marion Jensen, Jan. 28, 1959; children—Robert, Bradley. Comml. mgr. Asso. Program Service, Inc., N.Y.C., 1949-52; v.p. marketing Ency. Brit., Inc., Chgo., 1952-62; exec. v.p. Marketways, Inc., Chgo., 1962-63; pres. Collier Services, Inc., Riverside, N.Y., 1963-67; pres., dir. Macmillan Book Clubs, Inc., N.Y.C., 1967—. Clubs: Presidents Assn., Mt. Kisco Country. Home: 80 Annandale Dr Chappaqua NY 10514 Office: 866 3d Ave New York City NY 10022

HOULE, JOSEPH ADRIEN, orthopedic surgeon; b. Fort Saskatchewan, Alta., Can., Nov. 3, 1928; s. Adelard Joseph and Bertha Marie (Durocher) H.; Sc.B., Ottawa U., 1954; M.D., U. Laval, 1960; m. Irene Halwa, June 18, 1952; children—Valerie, Diane, Lorraine, Louis, Doreen. Intern in gen. surgery St. Vincent Gen. Hosp., Sherbrooke, Que., 1960-61; resident in gen. surgery St. Vincent's Gen. Hosp., Bridgeport, Conn., 1961-62; resident in orthopedic surgery Montreal Gen. Hosp., Montreal Children's Hosp., Queen Mary Vet.'s Hosp., Montreal, 1962-65; practice medicine specializing in orthopedic surgery, Pointe Claire, Que., 1965—; attending orthopedist Lakeshore Gen. Hosp., Pointe Claire; Queen Mary Vet.'s Hosp., Montreal, Montreal Convalescent Hosp. Served to capt. Royal Can. Army Med. Corps, 1955-65. Certified orthopedic surgeon, Que. Mem. Can., Que. med. assns., Can., Que. assns. orthopedic surgeons, U.S., Can. aircraft owners and pilots assns. Clubs: Racquet, Centaure Aero. Author ednl. film The Mechanical Knee, 1970. Home: 155 Stillview Rd Pointe Claire PQ H9R 2V1 Canada Office: 175 Stillview Rd Pointe Claire PQ H9R 4S3 Canada

HOULE, ROGER ACHILLES, ret. air traffic controller, union ofcl.; b. Manchester, N.H., Sept. 2, 1926; s. Joseph and Lucienna M. (Therrien) H.; student Marion Coll., Poughkeepsie, N.Y., 1946, N.H. Coll., 1976—; m. Pauline T. Bisson, June 5, 1954. Air technician N.H. Air Guard, Grenier Field, Manchester, 1953-56; traffic dispatcher USAF, ops. specialist, 1956-61, flight service specialist Buffalo, 1961-63, air traffic controller, Worcester, Mass., 1963-67, Manchester, 1967-76; pres. local 234 Profl. Air Traffic Controllers Orgn., Manchester, 1971-75. Served as sgt. USAF, 1951-52. Democrat. Roman Catholic. Club: East Side. Home: 608 Amherst St Manchester NH 03104

HOULE, THOMAS A., psychologist, educator; b. Ironwood, Mich., Sept. 27, 1932; s. Theodore Joseph and Carrie Mae (Britton) H.; B.A., U. Minn., 1960; M.S.W., U. Wis., 1965; Ph.D., Mich. State U., 1970; m. Mary Jane Cushwa, Nov. 10, 1966. Social worker Milw. Mental Health Center, 1965-69; psychol. cons. Devereaux Found., Washington, Conn., 1970—; mem. faculty Mattatuck Coll., 1970—; pvt. practice Southbury, Conn., 1975—; v.p. cons. Indsl. Security Consultants, 1974—. Served with U.S. Army, 1950-53. Mem. Am. Psychol. Assn. Roman Catholic. Author: Changing Your Child's Behavior: A Dr. Houle Handbook, 1975; Four Common Errors Made by Parents in Disciplining Their Children, 1976; Corrective and Creative Discipline, 1976. Home and office: Main St Southbury CT 06488

HOURDAJIAN, DAWN, guidance counselor; b. Paterson, N.J., Sept. 18, 1946; d. Andrew Hovsep and Mary (Vartanesian) Dabbakian; B.A., Douglass Coll., Rutgers U., 1968; M.Ed., Boston U., 1970; m. Ara Hourdajian, Aug. 30, 1970. Computer programmer Mut. N.Y., N.Y.C., 1968-69; bilingual tchr., originator Armenian Pvt. Day Sch., Watertown, Mass., 1970-72; guidance counselor Watertown pub. schs., 1972-74, Glen Rock (N.J.) High Sch., 1974-75, Palisades Park, (N.J.) High Sch., 1975—; leader tchr. seminars; counselor youth; bilingual tutor. Certified tchr. and guidance counselor, Mass., N.J. Mem. Am., N.J. personnel and guidance assns., Nat. Vocat. Guidance Assn., NEA, N.J. Edn. Assn., Armenian Students Assn. Mem. Armenian Apostolic Ch. Office: Palisades Park High Sch Palisades Park NJ 07650

HOUSE, STANLEY GARTENHAUS, health care cons.; b. N.Y.C., Feb. 15, 1920; s. Isidore and Jean (Pollock) Gartenhaus; m. Lillian Nathan, Apr. 11, 1943; children—Arthur, Susan, Kenneth, Richard. Mem. editorial dept. Washington Post, 1941-42; editor-in-chief Labor Relations Inst., N.Y.C., 1943-48; news editor Sta. WGMS/WQQW-FM, Washington, 1949-51; pres. Stanley G. House & Assos. Inc., Washington, 1952-78; exec. dir. Watch and Jewelry Distbrs. Assn. Am., Washington, 1953-76; cons. Research Inst., Am. Arbitration Assn., 1977—, health care program Health Facilities Assn. Md., 1977—; v.p. Community Psychiat. Clinic, Bethesda, Md., 1974, 75. Mem. Am. Med. Writers Assn., Health and Counselors sects. Pub. Relations Soc. Am. (accredited, pres. 1962), Am. Soc. Assn. Execs. Clubs: Bethesda Country, Linden Hill Racquet. Author: (with I. Ladimer and J. Solomon) Democratic Processes for Modern Health Agencies, 1978. Office: 7315 Wisconsin Ave Washington DC 20014

HOUSEHOLDER, JOHN HENRY, indsl. engr.; b. New Brighton, Pa., Apr. 9, 1917; s. Amos and Clara Esther (Flinner) H.; certificate Pitts. Acad. Sch. Bus., 1935; student in Petroleum Products, Pa. State U. Extension, 1935-40; B.S. in Indsl. Engring., Pa. State U., 1947, B.S.M.E., 1948; m. Carolyn Cook Stephens, Jan. 26, 1945; children—Nancy Ann, John Stephens, Jo Carol. Sec.-accountant Jones & Laughlin Supply Div., Bradford, Pa., 1935-40; asst. dept. mgr. Dresser Mfg. div. Dresser Industries, Inc., Bradford, summer 1941, product design and devel. engr., 1948-52; quality control mgr., proto tool div. Ingersoll-Rand Co., Jamestown, N.Y., 1952-77, indsl. engr., 1976—. Treas. Jamestown Area Mil. Ball Com., 1968—; elder 1st United Presbyn. Ch., Jamestown; mem. Republican Nat. Com., 1976—. Served with USAAF, 1942-46; MTO; lt. col. Res. ret. Recipient award Pitts. Acad., 1935; Tau Beta Pi fellow, 1947-48. Mem. Air Force Assn. (pres. local chpt. 1970—, nat. Medal of Merit 1976), Internat. Mgmt. Council (treas. local chpt. 1962-67, chmn. fin. com. 1967—), Am. Inst. Indsl. Engring. (pres. local chpt. 1976-77), United Comml. Travelers, Tau Beta Pi, Sigma Tau, Phi Kappa Phi. Circulation mgr. Pa. State Engr., 1946-48. Home: 11 Beverly Pl Jamestown NY 14701

HOUSEL, EDMUND LLEWELLYN, physician; b. Montgomery, Pa., July 1, 1910; s. Joseph Peter and Martha (Shollenberger) H.; A.B., Pa. State U., 1931; M.D., Jefferson Med. Coll., 1935; m. Marguerite Force, July 1, 1937 (dec. Mar. 1964); children—Edmund Llewellyn, Mark S.; m. 2d, Ann Weaver Lee, Nov. 28, 1964. Intern, Jefferson Med. Coll. Hosp., Phila., 1936-38, resident chemistry and pathology, 1935-36; practice medicine specializing in internal medicine, Phila., 1941—; asst. demonstrator Jefferson Med. Coll. Hosp., Phila., 1941-46, chief hypertension clinic, 1946-75, hon. asst. clin. medicine, 1964-75, hon. asst. prof., 1975—, mem. exec. com., chmn. med. revue com. Dir. Blue Shield of Pa. Chmn. med. adv. com. Selective Service Pa., 1967-75; chmn. med. coordination com. Bi-centennial Celebration Am. Revolution. Bd. dirs. United Fund Phila. Recipient honors achievement award Angiology Research Found., Purdue Frederick Co., Philadelphia County Soc. Mem. AMA (del.), Pa. (del.), Philadelphia County (pres. 1966) med. socs. Club: Union League (Phila.). Home: 1342 Youngsford Rd Gladwyne PA 19035 Office: 255 S 17th St Philadelphia PA 19103

HOUSER, JOSEPH JAY-JACKSON, pharm. rep.; b. Boston, Sept. 3, 1947; s. Jackson G. and Josephine E. (Festa) H.; student Mass. Coll. Pharmacy, 1967; B.S., U. Maine, 1976; M.B.A. candidate Thomas Coll.; m. Linda L. Brown, July 10, 1976; children—Laura Jean, John G., Jeffrey J., Andrew J. Rep. field sales Ware-Ever Aluminum Co.; research specialist animal health, dog trainer Bio-Sensor Research, Walter Reed Army Med. Center, Washington; microsurgeon Research div. Charles River Breeding Labs.; pharm. rep., legis. asst. Wyeth Labs., Augusta, Maine. Served with U.S. Army, 1968-71. Mem. AAAS. Home: 25 Gannett St Augusta ME 04330

HOUSER, MARY RUBY HILLMAN, club woman; d. Frank Herbert and Ursula F. (Handy) Hillman; student Boston U., 1918-21; m. George Crouse Houser, Oct. 8, 1925; children—George Crouse, Horace Milton. Pres. Garden Club of Brookline, 1946-48, program chmn., 1958-60; v.p. Garden Club Fedn. of Mass., 1953-55; sr. state pres. Children Am. Revolution, 1959-61, sr. nat. chaplain, 1962-64, hon. sr. nat. v.p., 1964-70, pres. sr. nat. officers' club, 1969-71, sr. nat. v.p. New Eng. region, 1972-74; state historian D.A.R., 1953-56, regent Paul Revere chpt., 1967-68, state vice regent, 1968-70, state regent, 1970-74, nat. v.p. gen., 1974-77; state corr. sec. Daus. Colonial Wars, 1959-62, state v.p., 1962-65, chaplain, 1965-68; 2d v.p., Mass. Huguenot Soc., 1962-65, 76—, 1st v.p., 1970-76; state corr. sec. Daus. Founders and Patriots Am., 1964-67, chaplain, 1967-70. Recipient citation for good citizenship Freedom, Inc., 1958, George Washington Honor medal Freedoms Found., 1960. Mem. Soc. Mayflower Descs., New Eng. Historic Geneal. Soc., Soc. Descs. Colonial Clergy, Dutch Settlers Soc. Albany, Mass. Ct. Assts., Women Descs. Ancient and Hon. Arty. Co., Daus. Am. Colonists (state corr. sec. 1967-70, 2d vice regent 1971-73, 1st vice regent 1973-76), Mass. Soc. Colonial Dames 17th Century (2d v.p. 1974—), Bostonian Soc., Dames Ct. of Honor, Soc. Preservation New Eng. Antiquities, Bunker Hill Monument Assn., Boston Browning Soc., Mass. Soc. U. Edn. Women, New Eng. Farm and Garden Assn. (dir.), English-Speaking Union. Clubs: College (Boston); China Student's (past dir.). Home: 220 Clyde St Chestnut Hill MA 02167

HOUSER, THOMAS JAMES, lawyer; b. Chgo., June 28, 1929; s. Thomas and Mayme (Mikulecky) H.; student Mich. State Mich. State U., 1947-48; A.B. in Polit. Sci., Hanover Coll., 1951; postgrad. Advanced Sch. Internat. Studies, Johns Hopkins U., 1952; J.D., Northwestern U., 1959; m. Jo Ann Ochsenhirt, Oct. 28, 1954; children—Deborah Ann, Deneen, David Gerard. Admitted to Ill. bar, 1959; commerce counsel Burlington No. R.R. Co., Chgo., 1961-65; spl. counsel to U.S. Senator Charles H. Percy of Ill., 1967-68; mem. firm Liebman, Williams, Bennett, Baird and Minow, Chgo., 1968-69; dep. dir. Peace Corps., Washington, 1969-70; commr. FCC, Washington, 1971; Ill. campaign mgr. for Pres. Nixon, 1972; partner firm Sidley & Austin, Chgo., 1972-76; dir. Office Telecommunications Policy, White House, 1976-77; individual practice law, Washington, 1977—. Legal counsel Chgo. area Boy Scouts Am., 1974-76; dir. Liberty Communications Inc. Trustee Pub. Broadcasting Sta. WTTW, Chgo., 1973-76. Served with CIC, U.S. Army, 1954-56. Recipient Service award Nat. Asthma Center, 1975, Alumni award Hanover Coll., 1951, Achievement award, 1970. Mem. Am., Fed., Chgo. bar assns. Republican. Mem. Christian Ch. Club: Union League (Chgo.). Contbr. articles to newspapers and periodicals. Home: 203 Yoakum Pkwy Alexandria VA 22304 Office: Suite 1200 1735 K St NW Washington DC 20006

HOUSER, THOMAS JUDE, computer scientist, educator; b. Plymouth, Pa., Jan. 28, 1938; s. Thomas T. and Marie A. (Surnack) H.; B.S., U. King's Coll., Wilkes-Barre, Pa., 1957; postgrad. Ohio U., 1957, N.Y. U., 1959, Ill. Inst. Tech., 1960—; m. Marilyn C. Rowe, Aug. 12, 1960; children—Linda Mary, Carol Jean, Dianne Faye. Research chemist Los Alamos Sci. Lab., 1957, Olin Mathieson Chem. Corp., New Haven, Conn., 1957-58; instr. chemistry U. Wis., GreenBay, 1958-65, Ill. Inst. Tech., 1967-68; computer applications specialist Nuclear Chgo. Corp., 1968-69; dir. computer center, asso. prof. computer sci. Millersville State Coll., 1969—; cons. in field; participant NSF summer Inst., 1961, 62, 63. NSF trainee, 1967-68; NSF Sci. Faculty fellow, 1965-66. Mem. Am. Phys. Soc., AAAS, Data Processing Mgmt. Assn., Assn. Computing Machinery, Math. Assn. Am., Soc. Indsl., Applied Mathematics. Democrat. Roman Catholic. Contbr. articles to profl. jours. Home: 428 Brookview Dr Millersville PA 17551 Office: Millersville State Coll Millersville PA 17551

HOUSLEY, NICHOLAS GEORGE, hosp. adminstr.; b. Mannheim, Germany, Sept. 14, 1925; s. Leo and Lilly (Kahn) H.; arrived U.S., 1940, naturalized, 1944; A.B., William Jewell Coll., 1947; M.S. in Indsl. Engring., Columbia U., 1949, M.S. in Adminstrv. Medicine, 1967; m. Irene Catherine Borowicz, Feb. 27, 1960; children—Ronald Lee, Pamela Irene. Jr. indsl. engr. Crucible Steel Co. of Am., Harrison, N.J., 1950-52; field staff planning mgr. Sheraton Corp. of Am., Boston, 1952-58; asst. to chief indsl. engr. UPS, N.Y.C., 1958-59; sr. auditor Curtiss-Wright Corp., Woodridge, N.J., 1959-61; adminstrv. asst. L.I. Jewish Hosp., New Hyde Park, N.Y., 1961-65; asst. adminstr. St. Johns Smithtown Hosp., N.Y., 1967-69; research coordinator Columbia U. Sch. Public Health, N.Y.C., 1969; asso. exec. dir. Morrisania Hosp., Bronx, N.Y., 1969-76; adminstr. The Animal Med. Center, N.Y.C., 1976—; cons. in field. Sec. Robin Park Taxpayers Assn., Huntington, N.Y., 1969; conv. panelist N.Y. State Assn. Med. Record Librarians, 1970; speaker 46th ann. meeting Am. Animal Hosp. Assn., 1979; mem. adv. bd. Nassau-Suffolk Hosp. Council, 1968-69. Served with U.S. Army, 1944-46. Licensed nursing home adminstr., N.Y.; recipient grant Columbia U., 1965-67. Fellow Am. Pub. Health Assn.; mem. Am. Coll. Hosp. Adminstrs., Am. Hosp. Assn., The Hosp. Execs. Club N.Y., Hosp. Mgmt. Systems Soc. Greater N.Y. (charter), Am. Inst. of Indsl. Engrs. (sr.), Am. Contract Bridge League, Am. Bowling Congress. Contbr. article in field to profl. jour. Home: 42 Brand Dr Huntington NY 11743 Office: 510 E 62d St New York City NY 10021

HOUSTON, ALFRED DEARBORN, utilities exec.; b. Quincy, Mass., Aug. 14, 1940; s. Alfred Dearborn and Merriland Curry (Westwood) H.; B.S. in Econs., Wharton Sch., U. Pa., 1962; m. Patricia Selko, Oct. 23, 1965; children—Melissa, Sherriden. With New Eng. Electric System and subs. New Eng. Power Service Co., New Eng. Power Co., Mass. Electric Co., Westborough, Mass., 1962—, asst. treas., 1973-75, v.p. corporate fin. New Eng. Energy Co. and New Eng. Power Service Co., 1975-76, v.p., dist. mgr. Narragansett Electric Co., 1976-77, v.p. and treas., 1977—. Active United Way So. New Eng., 1976. Club: U. Pa. of Boston (past pres., trustee). Office: Narragansett Electric Co 280 Melrose St Providence RI 02901*

HOUSTON, FRED WILLIAM, historian; b. Warwick, N.Y., Apr. 30, 1946; s. Frederick and Helen Adelaide Marie (O'Brien) H.; B.A. (N.Y. State Regents scholar), Syracuse U., 1968, M.A., 1974, postgrad. doctoral program, 1978—. N.Y. State Regents coll. teaching fellow Syracuse U., 1972-74, teaching asst. in history, 1977—; real estate salesman, Warwick, 1974-76. Alt. mem. Warwick (N.Y.) Republican Com., 1975-77. Served with USN, 1968-72. Mem. Warwick Hist. Soc., Am. Hist. Assn., Warwick Jaycees (sec. 1977), Phi Alpha Theta. Methodist. Author survey of published primary source materials in U.S. history at Syracuse U., 1977. Home: 401 Smith Rd Apt B5 Syracuse NY 13224 Office: Dept History Syracuse U Syracuse NY 13210

HOUSTON, RAY BERTHOLF, lawyer; b. Warwick, N.Y., June 18, 1912; s. Fred and Delia (Cooke) H.; B.S., Haverford (Pa.) Coll., 1934; J.D., Yale, 1937; m. 3d, Margaret A. Reen, July 13, 1968; children by previous marriages—Ann S., Craig B., Karen E., Brent T. Admitted to N.Y. State bar, 1938, N.J. bar, 1975, U.S. Supreme Ct. bar, 1947; practiced in N.Y.C., 1937-40, 47-54, Washington, 1940-41, 46-47, Camden, N.J., 1954-77, Cherry Hill, N.J., 1978—; asso. atty. Hines, Rearick, Dorr & Hammond, 1937-40; with litigation sect. Bituminous Coal div. U.S. Dept. Interior, Washington, 1940-41; legal adviser projects sect. U.S. Export Control Adminstrn., Washington, 1941; with Gen. Counsel's Office Lend Lease Adminstrn., Office For Emergency Mgmt., 1941; with Supreme Ct. sect. Claims div. U.S. Dept. Justice, Washington, 1946-47; atty., sr. atty. RCA, N.Y.C., 1947-54, atty., sr. atty., gen. atty. def. and indsl. electronic products, Camden, 1954-67, staff v.p., gen. atty. comml.-govt. products and staff activities, 1967-77; counsel firm Cucinotta, Sherman, Silverstein & Kohl, Cherry Hill, 1978—. Pres. Little League, Haddonfield, N.J., 1964-67; pres. Camden Housing Improvement Projects, 1974-76. Bd. dirs. Camden County YMCA, Area Council for Econ. Edn. Served to lt. comdr. USNR, 1942-45. Mem. Am., N.J., Camden County bar assns., Order of Coif, Phi Beta Kappa. Democrat. Presbyn. (elder, trustee). Clubs: University (Washington), Yale (N.Y.C.); Tavistock Country (Haddonfield, N.J.). Home: 604 Warwick Rd Haddonfield NJ 08033 Office: One Executive Campus Suite 306 Cherry Hill NJ 08002

HOUTS, EARL, educator, realtor; b. Arthur, Ill., June 29, 1912; s. D. Leaper and Emma Catherine (Ashwill) H.; B.Ed., Eastern Ill. U., 1938; M.Mus., Ill. Wesleyan U., 1942; postgrad. U. Ill., summers 1951-52; Ed.D., U. No. Colo., 1956; m. Kathryn Lydia Neumeyer, Mar. 24, 1940; children—Carol Anne Houts Purich, Jamie Lynn Houts Smith. Music supr. Georgetown, St. Elmo, Moweaqua, Ill., 1938-42, 46-57; head music dept. W.Va. Inst. Tech., Montgomery, 1957-60, dir. student personnel services, 1960-64; asso. prof. ednl. psychology Slippery Rock (Pa.) State Coll., 1964-67, Westminster Coll., New Wilmington, Pa., 1967-71, Grove City (Pa.) Coll., 1972-77; salesman, office mgr. Century 21 Thomas Real Estate, 1977—. Dir. Jennings Nature Res., Western Pa. Conservancy, 1967-70, Teatown Lake Reservation, Ossining, N.Y., 1971-72; panel participant, cons. environ. edn. Pitts. and Butler County, Pa., 1969-70; lectr. environ. edn., 1964—, psychology applied to daily living, 1970—; judge photog. contests, 1970—. Served with AUS, 1943-46. Mem. Coll. Music Educators (chmn. 1957-58), Music Educators Nat. Conf., W.Va. Coll. and Univ. Student Personnel Adminstrs. (pres. 1961-63), Nature Conservancy, Am. Museum Natural History, Photog. Soc. Am., Western Pa. Conservancy (adv. bd. 1972—). Club: Slippery Rock (Pa.) Camera. Editor Notes a Tempo, 1958-60, Newsletter, 1970-71. Home: 105 Oak St Slippery Rock PA 16057 Office: Route 19 Wexford PA 15090

HOUTS, PAUL LOUIS, editor, writer; b. Albany, N.Y., Aug. 5, 1937; s. Louis and Ethel Margaret (Keity) H.; B.A., Trinity Coll., Hartford, Conn., 1959. Editor, Prentice-Hall, Inc., Englewood Cliffs, N.J., 1961-65; asso. editor Am. Council Edn., Washington, 1965-67; asst. dir. publns. Nat. Assn. Elementary Sch. Prins., Washington, 1967-70, dir. publns., editor, 1970—. Mem. Ednl. Press Assn. Am. (regional dir. 1973—; awards 1970, 71, 72, 75), Soc. Nat. Assn. Publs. Editor Nat. Elementary Prin., 1970—; The Myth of Measurability, 1977; asso. editor Am. Jr. Colls., 1967. Home: 1612 34th St NW Washington DC 20007 Office: 1801 N Moore St Arlington VA 22209

HOVER, LOUIS JOSEPH, chemist; b. Newark, Mar. 26, 1948; s. Augustus Gordon and Angela Marie (Guida) H.; B.S. in Chemistry, Upsala Coll., 1969; postgrad. Fairleigh Dickinson U., 1977—; m. Barbara McWatters, Sept. 23, 1972; 1 son, Christopher Francis. Research chemist Witco Chem. Research Center, Oakland, N.J., 1969-73; quality investigation chemist Fisher Sci. Co., Fair Lawn, N.J., 1973—. Served with M.I., U.S. Army, 1970-72. Mem. Am. Chem. Soc., North Jersey Mktg. and Econs. Group, Am. Legion. Roman Catholic. Club: Lions. Patentee in chem. field. Home: 24 Rosemont Rd Oak Ridge NJ 07438 Office: Fisher Sci Co 1 Reagent Ln Fair Lawn NJ 07410

HOVING, THOMAS, museum cons.; s. Walter and Mary Osgood (Field) H.; grad. summa cum laude Princeton U., 1953, Ph.D. in Art History, 1959, D.Hum. (hon.), 1968; LL.D. (hon.), Pratt Inst., 1967; D.F.A. (hon.), N.Y. U., 1968; Litt.D. (hon.), Middlebury Coll., 1968; m. Nancy Melissa Bell; 1 dau., Petrea Bell. From curatorial asst. to curator The Cloisters, Met. Mus. Art, until 1966, dir. Met. Mus., 1967-77; pres. Hoving Assos. Inc., mus. cons., N.Y.C., 1977—; commr. parks and cultural affairs City of N.Y., 1966-67; dir. IBM World Trade Ams.-Far East Corp. Recipient Bronze medal Citizens Budget Commn., 1967; Cue Mag. award, 1966; Distinguished Achievement award Advt. Club Am., 1966; Creative Leadership in Edn. award N.Y. U., 1975; Woodrow Wilson award Princeton U., 1977. Office: 150 E 73d St York City NY 10021

HOWARD, BERTRAM ELLIOT, physician; b. New Bedford, Mass., Apr. 14, 1922; s. Jacob Arthur and Dora (Shill) Horvitz; M.D., Tufts U., 1947; m. Zelda Krellenstein, Sept. 5, 1948; children—Jack, Nora, Robert, Alan. Intern, Coney Island Hosp., Bklyn., 1947-48; resident New Eng. Med. Center Hosp., Boston, 1948-51; practice medicine specializing in internal medicine, New Bedford, 1956—; coordinator stroke program St. Luke's Hosp., New Bedford, 1964—, chief medicine, dir. med. services, 1972-75. Served to capt. USAF, 1951-53. Diplomate Am. Bd. Internal Medicine. Mem. Am. Heart Assn. (pres. elect 1978-80, v.p. 1976-78, exec. com. stroke council 1973-76), A.C.P., AMA, Am. Soc. Internal Medicine, Mass., Bristol S., New Bedford med. socs. Contbr. articles to med. jours. Address: 251 Hawthorn St New Bedford MA 02740

HOWARD, DAVID, ballet sch. adminstr.; b. London, Eng., June 14, 1937; s. Walter and Dorothy (Fell) Edwards; grad. Arts. Ednl. Sch., London, 1955. Came to U.S., 1966. Prin. dancer London Palladium, 1955-57; with Royal Ballet Eng., 1957-63, soloist, 1958-63; soloist Nat. Ballet Can., 1963-64; appeared in (musical) Little Me, London, 1964-66; mem. faculty Sch. Ballet, Harkness House for Ballet Arts, N.Y.C., 1966—; prin. tchr. Harkness Ballet Co., N.Y.C., 1967—; dir. Sch. Ballet Harkness House for Ballet Arts, N.Y.C., 1969—; dir. David Howard Sch. Ballet, N.Y.C., 1977—; guest faculty Hunter Coll. Mem. Nat. Assn. for Regional Ballet (dir., pres. 1977), Royal Acad. Dancing, London (Adeline Genee Silver medal for male dancers 1954), Brit. Actors Equity, Internat. Platform Assn. Choreographer: Rachmaninoff Suite, 1971; Divertissement D'Adam, 1971; Rossini Variations, 1973; Designs in Shades of Baroque, 1974, 7 German Dances, 1975. Home: 401 West End Ave New York City NY 10024 Office: 36 W 62d St New York City NY 10023

HOWARD, DORIS, psychotherapist; b. N.Y.C., June 19, 1927; d. Maurice and Dorothy Katherine (Martin) Sobel; B.A., City of U. N.Y., 1966, M.A., 1971; postgrad. L.I. U., 1971—; 1 son by previous marriage—Michael Steven Howard. Teaching asst. exptl. psychology City Coll. N.Y., 1967-69; psychologist (part-time) N.Y. State Narcotic Addiction Control Commn., Mt. Morris Park Center, N.Y.C., 1970-71; dir. aftercare program drug abuse unit Lincoln Hosp. dept. psychiatry Albert Einstein Coll. Medicine, Bronx, N.Y., 1970-72, dir. research and evaluation, 1972-73, dir. geriatrics unit, 1973-74, mem. faculty dept. psychiatry, 1966-74; pvt. practice psychotherapy, N.Y.C., 1974—; chairperson Bronx Boroughwide Geriatrics Planning Com., N.Y.C. Dept. Mental Health and Mental Retardation, 1974. Bd. dirs. Logos, Inc., N.Y.C., chairperson, 1974-77. Fellow Am. Orthopsychiat. Assn.; mem. Am., Eastern psychol. assns., Assn. for Women in Psychology, Mental Health Assn. of New York and Bronx Counties, Assn. for Advancement of Psychology, Am. Psychology-Law Soc. Address: 50 W 96th St New York City NY 10025

HOWARD, GLENN WILLARD, educator; b. Grants Pass, Oreg., Apr. 5, 1906; s. George E. and Estelle E. (Anderson) H.; A.B., U. Oreg., 1928; M.A., Columbia, 1929, Ph.D., 1937; m. Thelma E. Akey, Sept. 8, 1931; children—Glenn W., Gordon E., Katherine E. Instr. hygiene Townsend Harris Hall, Coll. City N.Y., 1929, chmn. dept. health and phys. edn. Seth Low Jr. Coll., Columbia, 1929-36, instr. hygiene, 1929-36; vis. prof. phys. edn. Purdue U., summer 1936; asst. prof., then asso. prof. phys. edn. Ohio State U., 1936-45, survey staff bur. ednl. research; vis. prof. phys. edn. U. Tex., summer 1940, U. Calif., 1946; asso. prof. Queens Coll., 1945-52, prof. health and phys. edn., 1953—, chmn. dept. health and phys. edn., 1945-56, dir. Sch. Gen. Studies, 1956—, dean of adminstrn., 1962-73, adminstrv. head, 1964-65, coordinator affirmative action program, 1970—; v.p. Queens Student Services Corp., 1967-72. Chmn. com. coll. phys. edn. and health instrn. of wartime commn. U.S. Office Edn., 1942; spl. cons. bd. examiners Bd. Edn., N.Y.C., 1947, spl. examiner, 1955-58; v.p. Met. Inter-Collegiate Soccer Conf., 1950-51, pres., 1951-52; del. Internat. Congress on Essentials of Phys. Edn. for Youth, 1954. Bd. dirs. Greater N.Y. Council for Fgn. Students, 1961—, treas., 1968—; bd. dirs. East Island Assn., 1973—, pres., 1974, 75; mem. legis. adv. com. dept. sr. citizen affairs Nassau County, 1975—, mem. housing subcom. task force on sr. citizen affairs, 1975—; vice chmn. indsl. devel. agy. City of Glen Cove, 1974—, mem. community devel. adv. com., 1975—, mem. downtown urban renewal adv. com., 1973-75, chmn. sr. citizens adv. council, 1975-76, vice chmn., 1977—; mem. Glen Cove Planning Bd., 1977—. Mem. Adminstrv. Mgmt. Soc., Nat. Coll. Phys. Edn. Assn. for Men (chmn. hist. records com. 1963), Coll. Phys. Edn. Assn. (pres. 1950), Am., N.Y. (chmn. com. on profl. preparation 1946) assns. health phys. edn. and recreation, Am. Assn. Leisure and Recreation, Am. Assn. Higher Edn., Nat. Soc. Study Edn., N.E.A., Child Service League (pres. 1962), Am. Mgmt. Assn., Assn. U. Evening Colls., Queens Coll. Retirees Assn. (v.p. 1972-74, pres. 1974-76), Phi Beta Kappa, Phi Delta Kappa. Methodist. Author: (with Edward Masonbrink) The Adminstration of Physical Education, 1963. Contbr. to profl. publs. Home: 11 Eastland Dr Glen Cove NY 11542

HOWARD, GRAEME KEITH, JR., publisher, cons., lawyer; b. Port Chester, N.Y., Sept. 29, 1932; s. Graeme Keith and Margaret (Evans) H.; B.A., Amherst Coll., 1954; LL.B., Yale U., 1960; postgrad. U. Leiden (Netherlands) (Fulbright, Torchiana awards), 1960-62; m. Carolyn Cooper Clark, Sept. 8, 1956 (div.); children—Elizabeth Lloyd, Graeme Keith III, Cooper Ann, William Reeve. Admitted to Conn. bar, 1960, Pa. bar, 1963; asso. Internat. Tax Service, Internat. Belasting Documentatie Bur., Amsterdam, Netherlands, 1961-62; asso. firm Ballard, Spahr, Andrews & Ingersoll, Phila., 1963-67; partner corp. fin. dept. Butcher & Sherrerd, Phila., 1967-72; pres. Howard & Co., Phila., 1972—; pub. Bus. Borrower, Phila., 1975—, Going Public, Phila., 1977—; lectr. in field. Mem. Com. Seventy, 1976—, also mem. fin. com. Served to capt. USAF, 1954-57. Mem. Nat. Investor Relations Inst. (v.p. Phila. chpt. 1975-77). Republican. Episcopalian. Clubs: Racquet (Phila.); Dolittle (Norfolk, Conn.). Editor European Taxation, 1961-62; sr. editor The Legal Key to Internat. Trade and Investment, 1962-67, Taxation of Patent Royalties, Dividends, Interest in Europe, 1963—; editor Internat. Bus. Law Rev., 1966, The Bus. Borrower, 1975—. Author: Going Public, 1976; Risk Capital, 1976; Bank Financing, 1977. Home: Racquet Club 215 S 16th St Philadelphia PA 19102 Office: Howard & Co 1529 Walnut St Philadelphia PA 19102

HOWARD, JACK ROHE, newspaper exec.; b. N.Y.C., Aug. 31, 1910; s. Roy Wilson and Margaret (Rohe) H.; grad. Phillips Exeter Acad., 1928; A.B., Yale U., 1932; m. Barbara Baife, Apr. 5, 1934 (dec. 1962); children—Pamela, Michael; m. 2d, Eleanor Sallee Harris, 1964. Reporter, Japan Advertiser, Tokyo, Shanghai (China) Evening Post and Mercury, 1932-33; reporter Indpsl. Times, 1933-34; asst. telegraph editor, then telegraph editor and news editor Washington Daily News, 1935; staff program dept. radio sta. WNOX, Knoxville, Tenn., also Washington and N.Y.C. offices Continental Radio Co. (now Scripps-Howard Broadcasting Co.), 1936-39; asst. exec. editor Scripps-Howard Newspapers, 1939-42, 45-48, gen. editorial mgr., from 1948; pres., dir. exec. com. Scripps-Howard Newspapers (E.W. Scripps Co.), 1953—; pres., dir. chmn. Scripps Howard Broadcasting Co., 1937-42, 45—; pres. Cleve. Press; dir. Trans World Airlines, Inc.; mem. East Side adv. bd. Chem. Bank N.Y. Bd. dirs. Boys' Clubs Am. Served with USNR, 1942-45; PTO. Mem. Am. Soc. Newspaper Editors, Am. Newspaper Pubs. Assn. (dir.), Inter-Am. Press Assn. (pres. 1965-66), Phillips Exeter Alumni Assn. (pres. 1958-60), Beta Theta Pi, Sigma Delta Chi. Clubs: Dutch Treat, Yale, River, Pilgrims (N.Y.C.); Bohemian (San Francisco); Seawanhaka Corinthian Yacht (Oyster Bay, N.Y.). Address: 200 Park Ave New York City NY 10017

HOWARD, JAMES J., congressman; b. Irvington, N.J., July 24, 1927; s. George P. and Bernice M. Howard; B.A., St. Bonaventure U., 1952; M.Ed., Rutgers U., 1958; LL.D., Monmouth Coll.; m. Marlene Vetrano, Dec. 31, 1950; children—Kathleen (Mrs. Raymond Lowther), Lenore (Mrs. Douglas Tapp), Marie. Tchr. prin. Wall Twp. (N.J.) sch. system, 1954-64; mem. 89th-94th congresses from 3d dist. N.J., chmn. Surface transp. com. Served with USNR, World War II; PTO. Mem. Nat., N.J. (del. assembly), Mommouth County (past pres.) edn. Assns. Democrat. Home: 508 G St SW Washington DC 20024 Office: House Office Bldg Washington DC 20515

HOWARD, JOHN ROBERT, coll. adminstr.; b. Boston, Jan. 24, 1933; s. John Robert and Louise (Harris) H.; A.A., Boston U., 1953; B.A., Brandeis U., 1955; postgrad. U. Calif. at Berkeley, 1955-56; M.A., N.Y. U., 1961; Ph.D., Stanford U., 1965; m. Mary Doris Adams, June 22, 1968. Asst. prof. sociology U. Oreg., 1965-68, Coll. City N.Y., 1968-69; asso. prof. sociology Rutgers U., 1969-71; prof., div. social scis. State U. N.Y. at Purchase, 1971—, dean div., 1971—; research asso. Rice U., 1966; prin. investigator, small grants research U.S. Office of Edn., 1968. Bd. dirs. Street Theater, Inc., 1976—. Brandeis fellow, 1955; Woodrow Wilson fellow, 1955-56; Russell Sage fellow, 1962-64; Falk Found. grantee for study impact of TV program Roots. Mem. Soc. for Study Social Problems (v.p. 1978-79). Author: (with W. McCord, B. Friedberg and E. Harwood) Life Styles in the Black Ghetto, 1969; The Cutting Edge: Social Movements and Social Change in America, 1974. Contbr. articles in field to profl. jours. Editor: (with S.E. Deutsch) Where It's At: Radical Perspectives in Sociology, 1970; The Awakening Minorities: American Indians, Mexican Americans, Puerto Ricans, 1970; (with R.C. Smith) Urban Black Politics, 1978. Home: 19 Marion Ave Mount Vernon NY 10552 Office: State U NY Purchase NY 10557

HOWARD, JUDITH BARBARA SCHAFFER (MRS. LEONARD HOWARD), psychologist, artist; b. Newark, Nov. 9, 1923; d. Jacob and Rose (Nussbaum) Schaffer; B.A. cum laude, Syracuse U., 1944; M.A., N.Y. U., 1964, Ph.D., 1975; m. Leonard Howard, Mar. 11, 1945; children—Charles George, Susan Ellen. Staff psychologist Child Evaluation Center, Morristown, N.J., 1965-67; sch. psychologist Livingston (N.J.) Bd. Edn., 1966, Irvington (N.J.) Bd. Edn., 1967-69; dir. spl. Services Irvington Pub. Schs., 1969—; field supr. Grad. Sch. Applied Profl. Psychology, Rutgers U., 1976—; artist, exhibited in group shows museums Jersey City, Newark, Montclair, N.J., Nat. Acad. N.Y.C., Everhart Mus., Scranton, Pa., U. Houston, U. Maine, U. Ariz., Royal Acad. Edinburgh, Scotland, Royal Acad. Galleries, Birmingham, Eng., Le Chateau de la Napoule France, Musée de Cognac France, Au Casino Municipal Cannes (France); represented in pvt. collections; cons. psychologist Title I Program, Irvington, 1968—. Chmn. exception child com., West Orange, N.J., 1955-57; chmn. exhbn. Am. art at Midcentury, Nat. Council Jewish Women, 1959, 60, overall chmn., 1961; vol. art therapist Fountain House, psychiat. rehab., Orange, N.J., 1961; mem. art com. YM and YWHA Essex County, 1967-69; mem. Essex County Roundtable on Spl. Edn., chmn., 1970-71; fellow Rutgers Grad. Sch. Applied Profl. Psychology. Alumni rep. Syracuse U., 1964-71. Mem. Am., N.J. sch. psychologists assns., N.J. Assn. Sch. Adminstrs., Irvington Adminstrs. Assn., N.J. Assn. Pupil Personnel Adminstrs., Am., N.J. psychol. assns., Assn. for Advancement of Psychology, Psi Chi, Kappa Delta Pi, Pi Lambda Theta. Contbr. articles to profl. jours. Home: 78 Winding Way West Orange NJ 07052 Office: 54 Mt Vernon Ave Irvington NJ 07111

HOWARD, KATHERINE GRAHAM (MRS. CHARLES P. HOWARD), govt. ofcl.; b. Guyton, Ga., Sept. 18??, 1898; d. Joseph Lewis and Margaret (Nowell) Graham; grad. Salem Acad., Salem Coll.; A.B. cum laude, Smith Coll., 1920; Litt.D., Calvin Coolidge Coll.; m. Charles Howard, Sept. 15, 1921; children—Margaret Howard Haskell, Herbert Graham. Corporator Warren Inst. for Savs., Boston, 1960-69. Vice pres. Women's Municipal League Boston, 1944-48. Mem. Back Bay Planning and Devel. Com., 1967-73. Mem. Reading (Mass.) Republican Town Com., 1924-42, vice chmn., 1932-42; pres. Women's Rep. Club of Mass., mem. bd. dirs., 1942-45; mem. Reading Town Meeting, 1945-51; mem. advisory council, Women's Rep. Club of N.Y.; mem. exec. com. Mass. Rep. State Com., 1945-53, adv. com., 1975—; mem. Mass. Rep. Fin. Com., organizer women's div., 1947-48, first woman vice chmn., 1950; Rep. nat. committeewoman Mass., 1945-53; sec. Rep. Nat. Com., 1948-52, also mem. exec. com.; alternate del. at large Rep. Nat. Conv., 1944, del. at large, 1948, mem. arrangements com. and resolutions com., 1948, sec. of conv., 1952, also sec. arrangements com.; mem. Eisenhower campaign policy and strategy com.; U.S. dep. commr. gen. Brussels Internat. Exposition, 1952-58; dep. adminstr. FCDA, 1953-54, spl. adviser, mem. nat. advisory council, 1954-57; nat. vice chmn. Ike Day Celebration, 1956; dep. U.S. Commr. Gen. Brussels Exhbn., 1958; vice chmn. Nixon-Lodge Vols. of Mass., 1960; chmn. civil def. Mass. Fedn. Women's Rep. Orgns.; trustee Nat. Rep. Citizens Com., 1963—; mem. Rep. Ward Five Com., 1964-70, exec. com., 1965-70. Mem. Govs. advisory com. on civil def., 1965—. Mem. advisory com. Internat. Conf. Vassar Coll.'s Centennial Celebration, 1960-61. U.S. del. to NATO com. on civil def., 1953-56, com. on evacuees and refugees, 1956; mem. rev. com. Proejct East River, 1955; U.S. mem. Interagy. Manpower Com., 1953-54; mem. U.S. Interagy. Com. Civil Emergency Planning, 1956; cons. OCDM, 1959-60. Trustee Boston State Hosp., 1945-49, Salem Coll.; vice chmn. ladies vis. com. Mass. Gen. Hosp., 1963-69; vice chmn. women's service league, Boston Lying-in-Hosp., 1963-69; chmn. Eisenhower Alumnae Reunion, 1963—; organizer, chmn. Back Bay Garden Day; organizer Reading Child Garden Kindergarten; staff asst. A.R.C., 1942; pres. Reading League of Women Voters, Marblehead Neck Club of Small Gardens; bd. dirs. Mass. Civic League, Boston Com. Met. Opera, Boston Opera Assn.; mem. exec. com. Friends of Boston Pub. Library, 1972—; mem. council of friends Boston Symphony Orch., 1971-75. Decorated comdr. Order of Leopold (Belgium), Smith medal, 1967; recipient Woman of Distinction award Salem Coll., 1972. Mem. Mass. Soc. Colonial Dames (program chmn. 1959-61, v.p., 1967-71), Needlework Guild Am. (v.p. Boston br.), English Speaking Union (dir. 1965-74, hon. mem. 1974—), Parliamentary Law Club (pres. 1966-68), Neighborhood Assn. Back Bay (v.p.). Episcopalian. Clubs: Chilton, Eastern Yacht. Author: With My Shoes Off, 1977; contbr. mags. Lectr. in field. Home: 124 Beacon St Boston MA 02116 also 299 Ocean Ave Marblehead Neck MA 01945

HOWARD, MELVIN, duplication equipment mfg. co. exec.; b. Boston, Jan. 5, 1935; s. John M. and Molly (Sagar) H.; B.A., U. Mass., 1957; M.B.A., Columbia U., 1959; m. Beverly Ruth Kahan, June 9, 1957; children—Brian David, Marjorie Lyn. Fin. exec. Ford Motor Co., Dearborn, Mich., 1959-67; v.p.-adminstrn. Shoe Corps. of Am., Columbus, Ohio, 1967-70; asst. controller Bus. Products group Xerox Corp., Rochester, N.Y., 1970-72, v.p.-fin. Bus. Devel. group, 1972-74, sr. v.p., sr. staff officer, 1974-75, corporate v.p./controller, 1975-77, corporate v.p.-fin., 1977—. Adviser Jr. Achievement, 1959-61. Treas., Boy Scouts of Pittsford (N.Y.), 1971-73; cons. N.Y. Council Arts, 1971. Served to 1st lt. U.S. Army, 1957. Mem. Fin. Execs. Inst., Planning Execs. Inst., Am. Mgmt. Assn., Beta Gamma Sigma. Club: Birchwood Country. Home: 42 Red Coat Rd Westport CT 06880 Office: High Ridge Park Stamford CT 06904*

HOWARD, NORMAN WRIGLEY, educator; b. Methuen, Mass., July 18, 1911; s. George William and Ann (Wrigley) H.; B.A. magna cum laude, Amherst Coll., 1932; postgrad. Middlebury Coll., summer 1936, Cornell U., summer 1937; m. Vesta Elizabeth Gow, June 26, 1937; children—Stephen W., Wendy L. Tutor, Brooks Sch., North Andover, Mass., 1932-33; master Stearns Sch., Mont Vernon, N.H., 1933-35; master Gow Sch., South Wales, N.Y., 1935-44, asst. headmaster, 1944-50, asso. headmaster, 1950-58, headmaster, 1958-77, headmaster emeritus, 1977—. Mem. adv. bd. Mfrs. & Traders Trust Co., East Aurora, N.Y., 1963—. Mem. Planning Bd., Aurora, 1964—, chmn., 1965—; chmn. Aurora Conservation Commn., 1973—. Trustee Buffalo Sem., 1958-64, Deveaux Sch., Niagara Falls, N.Y., 1959-75, Elmwood-Franklin Sch., Buffalo, 1977—, Gow Sch., 1977—. Mem. Orton Soc., Phi Beta Kappa, Theta Xi. Episcopalian. Kiwanian (pres. 1957). Club: East Aurora Country. Home: Emery Rd South Wales NY 14139

HOWARD, PATTIE W. (COLEMAN), nurse; b. Safford, Ala., Aug. 26, 1922; d. Willie, Jr. and Lessie (Smith) Coleman; grad. nurse Med. Center, Columbus, Ga., 1944; B.S. in Pub. Health Nursing (Lake County Tb Assn. scholar), Loyola U., Chgo., 1957; NIH grantee, St. Xavier Coll., 1966-71; M.S. in Edn., Purdue U., 1974; Advanced Edn. certificate, Howard U., 1977; m. June 19, 1944 (div.); children—Dalton, Jr., Wilfred L., Gwendolyn B. Nurse, Christian Hosp., Miami, Fla., 1944-46; caseworker Lake County Dept. Welfare, Gary, Ind., 1957-58; nurse, tchr. Gary Sch. Corp., 1958-77; nurse and counselor Sickle Cell Center, Howard U., Washington, 1975-77; nurse VA Hosp., Washington, 1977—. Mem. Friendship Council, Vermont Ave. Baptist Ch., Washington, 1975-78; mem. steering com. Lake County Tb Assn., 1956; officer, mem. Froebel Sch. PTA and Band Parents, 1952-64; mem. adv. bd. Gary Talent Search Program, 1973-75; v.p. Charles Hawkins Dr. Block Club, Gary, 1975. Recipient Outstanding Service award Lake County Fedn. Tchrs., 1970. Mem. AAUW, Am. Personnel and Guidance Assn., Am., Washington nurses assns., Am. Sch. Health Assn., Bus. and Profl. Women of Ch. Women United, Ind., Nat. ret. tchrs. assns., Mid-Town Registered Nurses Club (charter; pres. 1949-75; Gary), Sigma Theta Tau, Chi Eta Phi. Baptist. Home: 3333 University Blvd W G2 Kensington MD 20795

HOWARD, PAUL LINDSAY, cons. electrochemist; b. Hobbs, Md., Feb. 3, 1909; s. Charles and Olive Virginia (Collins) H.; A.B., Western Md. Coll., 1929; M.S., N.Y. U., 1932; postgrad. Johns Hopkins U., 1932-33, N.Y. U., 1933-34; m. Anna Elizabeth Clough, Dec. 27, 1932; children—Paul L., Carol Ann. With Bell Telephone Lab., Kearny, N.J., 1930-32, E.S.B., Inc., Phila., 1935-42; head battery devel. Navy Dept., Washington, 1942-45; div. mgr. Burgess Battery Co., Antioch, Ill., 1945-47; v.p. electrochem. research Graham Crowley & Assos., Chgo., 1947-48; engr. missile battery devel. Nat. Bur. Standards, Washington, 1948-52; tech. dir. Yardney Electric Corp., N.Y.C., 1952-56, asst. v.p., 1956-61, v.p., dir., 1961-65; pres., chmn. bd. P.L. Howard Assos. Inc., Millington, Md., 1965—. Registered profl. engr., Washington. Mem. Am. Def. Preparedness Assn. (life), Am. Inst. Aeros. and Astronautics, Electrochem. Soc. (founder Washington/Balt. sect.), Am. Chem. Soc. Clubs: Masons, Shriners, Lions. Contbr. articles to profl. jours. Patentee in field. Home and Office: Cypress St Millington MD 21651

HOWARD, REESE EVANS, corp. exec.; b. Copenhagen, Denmark, May 28, 1925 (parents Am. citizens); s. Graeme Keith and Margaret Reese (Evans) H.; student Yale, 1946-50, N.Y. U., 1956-58; m. Suzette DeMarigny Alger, Feb. 18, 1950 (div. Mar. 1973); children—Reese Evans, Suzette, Catherine; m. 2d, Ann Cave Montgomery, Sept. 16, 1974. Sr. asso. Wertheim & Co., N.Y.C., 1955-69; partner H.C. Wainwright & Co., N.Y.C., 1969-70; pres. Antaeus Distbrs., N.Y.C., 1971-72; prin. Howard & Co., financial cons., Phila. and N.Y.C., 1972—; pres. Howard Holdings Ltd., Howard Investment Co., Williams, Erben Roberts, Estates Mgmt. Co.; dir. Anchor Nat. Life of N.Y. Served to 2d lt. USAF, 1943-46. Mem. U.S. Pony Clubs (gov. 1959-68), Nat. Steeplechase and Hunts Assn. (sr.), Delta Kappa Epsilon. Republican. Episcopalian. Clubs: Brook, Anglers (N.Y.C.); White's (London, Eng.). Office: 100 Wall St New York City NY 10005

HOWARD-JASPER, JANE, coll. adminstr.; b. Rockville, Md., May 7, 1927; d. Clifard Llewellyn and Lucie Rice (Galleher) Howard; A.A., St. Mary's Sem. Jr. Coll., 1947; A.B., George Washington U., 1951; M.Ed., U. Md., 1962, Ph.D., 1978; m. June 23, 1951 (div. 1960); 1 son, James Macdonald. Field rep. pub. relations, alumni dir. St. Mary's Coll., St. Mary's City, Md., 1960-63; library technician Cleve. Pub. Library, 1952-56; counselor secondary sch. Prince Georges County, Md., 1964-68; counselor, dir. counseling, also dean student devel. Frederick (Md.) Community Coll., 1968-77; asso. exec. Am. Personnel and Guidance Assn., 1978—. Mem. Frederick County Vocat. Edn. Council, 1969-73; coprorate mem. Am. Coll. Testing Program, 1970-78; active Frederick County Scholarship and Aid Fund, 1972-74. Mem. Am. Coll. Personnel Assn., Am. Personnel and Guidance Assn., Am. Assn. Higher Edn. Democrat. Episcopalian. Home: Route 5 Box 342 Frederick MD 21701

HOWE, CARROLL VICTOR, constrn. equipment co. exec.; b. Kearny, N.J., Dec. 12, 1923; s. Wright and Ada (Hodge) H.; B.A., Princeton U., 1947; M.F.A., Yale U., 1950; m. Nancy Osborne Stivers, Nov. 24, 1951 (div.); m. 2d, Priscilla Howland Greene, Mar. 1, 1957; children—Gregory Carroll, Christopher David. Writer, producer Pemeho Prodns., N.Y.C., 1950-51, free lance actor, writer, 1952-54; salesman Atlas Rigging Supply Corp., Newark, N.J., 1954-56, office mgr., 1956-57, sales mgr., 1957-58, v.p., 1958-62, pres., 1962—; pres. Arsco Industries, Inc., Newark, 1966—; pres., dir. 15 Tenant Shareholders, Inc., N.Y.C., 1978—. Served from pvt. to 2d lt., USMCR, 1942-46; served from 1st lt. to capt., USMCR, 1951-52. Mem. West Hudson C. of C., Remsenburg Assn., Mensa, English-Speaking Union. Episcopalian. Clubs: Quandrangle; Princeton; La Ronde; Westhampton Yacht Squadron (treas. 1970-72, commodore 1974-76, dir. 1976—). Author (play): Long Fall, 1950, 1957. Home: 15 W 11th St New York City NY 10011 also Shore Rd Remsenburg NY 11960 Office: 181 Vanderpool St Newark NJ 07114

HOWE, DAVID GLEN, ceramic engr.; b. Wellsville, N.Y., Nov. 21, 1933; s. Glen Henry and Frances Annvernette (Hills) H.; B.S. in Ceramic Engring., Alfred (N.Y.) U., 1955. Ceramic engr. U.S. Gypsum Co., Oakfield, N.Y., 1955-56, U.S. Naval Research Lab., Washington, 1958—. Served with U.S. Army, 1956-58. Recipient Applied Research Pub. award Naval Research Lab. Material Scis. Div., 1977. Mem. Am. Ceramic Soc., Am. Soc. Metals, Md. Inst. Metals. Republican. Mem. Disciples of Christ Ch. Patentee in field (4). Home: 46 Ridge Rd Greenbelt MD 20770 Office: 4555 Overlook Ave SW Washington DC 20375

HOWE, STANLEY RUSSELL, museum ofcl.; b. Lewiston, Maine, Aug. 25, 1943; s. Rodney Kimball and Geraldine Alma (Stanley) H.; B.S., Gorham State Coll., 1966; M.A., U. Conn., 1967; Ph.D., U. Maine, 1977. Teaching asst. U. Maine, Orono, 1968-70, New Eng.-Atlantic Provinces fellow, Orono, 1970-71; C.D. Howe fellow, Ottawa, Can., 1971-72; research asso. C.D. Howe Found., Montreal, Que., 1972-74; dir.-curator Dr. Moses Mason House Museum-Bethel Hist. Soc., Inc., Bethel, Maine, 1974—. Trustee Citizens for Historia Preservation, Bethel Library Assn.; sec.-treas. Bethel Bicentennial Com., 1975-77; pres. East Bethel Ch. Assn., 1975—; treas. East Bethel Cemetery Assn., 1975—; mem. Bd. of Selectmen-Assessors, Town of Bethel, 1975—, chmn., 1978—; mem. Oxford County Republican Com., 1976—. Mem. Am., Canadian hist. assns., Assn. for Canadian Studies in U.S., Canadian Assn. Am. Studies, Orgn. Am. Historians, New Eng. Hist. and Geneal. Soc., Soc. for Preservation of New Eng. Antiquities, Maine League Hist. Socs. and Museums, Maine Hist. Soc., S.A.R. (v.p. Maine soc.), Grange. Club: Appalachian Mountain. Home and Office: 15 Broad St Bethel ME 04217

HOWELL, BONNIE HOWARD, hosp. adminstr.; b. Ithaca, N.Y., Dec. 7, 1948; d. Robert Leon and Helen Elizabeth (Ryerson) Howard; B.S., Cornell U., 1970, M.P.A. with honors, 1972; m. James Ward Howell, May 23, 1974. Teaching asst. Cornell U., Ithaca, 1971; planning asso. areawide and local planning for health action, Syracuse, N.Y., 1972-74; asst. hosp. adminstr. Tompkins County Hosp., Ithaca, 1974—; cons. health adminstrn. Mem. Tompkins County Comprehensive Planning Council, 1974—. USPHS scholar, 1972; HEW grantee, 1976; William H. Burns scholar, 1971. Mem. Am. Coll. Hosp. Adminstrs., Am. Hosp. Assn., Am. Pub. Health Assn., Group Practice Am., Med. Group Mgmt. Assn. Author books in field. Home: 1583 Mecklenburg Rd Ithaca NY 14850 Office: 1285 Trumansburg Rd Ithaca NY 14850

HOWELL, DAVID MCBRIER, virologist; b. Erie, Pa., July 30, 1933; s. Frank William and Cynthia Gilmore (McBrier) H.; A.B., Princeton U., 1955; M.S. (NIH fellow), Pa. State U., 1963, Ph.D. (NIH fellow), 1966. Research virologist Biol. Labs. Army Dept., Frederick, Md., 1966-71, staff scientist Nat. Cancer Inst., NIH, Bethesda, Md., 1971-73, head virus and viral reagents sect., 1974-77, dir. viral oncology cancer research emphasis grants, 1977—, spl. asst. to asso. dir. for viral oncology, 1977-78, asst. to dir. div. cancer cause and prevention, 1978—. Served with USNR, 1957-61. Mem. Am. Soc. Microbiology, AAAS, Sigma Xi. Club: Cap and Gown of Princeton. Office: National Cancer Inst Bldg 31 Bethesda MD 20014

HOWELL, JAMES BURT, III, vegetable crop seed co. exec.; b. Bridgeton, N.J., Dec. 11, 1933; s. James Burt and Catharine Stanger (Sparks) H.; B.S. with high honors, Rutgers U., 1956; postgrad. U. Del., 1976—. Agrl. sales rep. Allied Chem. Corp., Phila., 1957-59; sales specialist Asgrow Seed Co. subs. Upjohn Co., Vineland, N.J., 1960—; dir. Advance Weight Systems, Ind., Medina, Ohio. Mem. ofcl. bd. 1st Presbyterian Ch. of Cedarville (N.J.), 1960—; admissions liaison officer U.S. Mil. Acad., West Point, N.Y., 1973—. Served with U.S. Army, 1957. Recipient Burpee Hort. award Rutgers U., 1955. Mem. Am. Def. Preparedness Assn., Vegetable Growers Assn. N.J., Res. Officers Assn. U.S., Phi Beta Kappa. Home: Sayres Neck Cedarville NJ 08311 Office: 930 N Main Rd Vineland NJ 08360

HOWELL, JOHN DONALD, hosp. adminstr.; b. Canton, Ohio, June 3, 1926; s. John Donald and Evelyn May (Koontz) H.; student Ohio State U., 1946-47; postgrad. overseas extension program U. Md. 1950-53, 56-59; m. Donna Kay Hurst, Nov. 11, 1972; children—Barbara, Charles, Kenneth, Craig. Freelance cons. bus. industry N.Y.C., 1960-67; owner, operator pvt. export bus., Toronto, Ont., Can., 1967-68; cons., Harrisburg, Pa., 1969-72; adminstr. Berwick (Pa.) Hosp., 1972-77, exec. dir., 1977—; pres., owner Health Care Consultants Inc., Berwick, 1978—. Active in forming Emergency Med. Services program Susquehanna Valley, Pa., 1972-73; bd. dirs., exec. com. Central Pa. Health Systems Agency, 1976—; bd. dirs. Susquehanna Valley Health Care Consortium, 1974—; com. Susquehanna Econ. Devel. Assn., 1973-74; bd. dirs. Columbia-Montour Home Health Services, 1973-74; mem. Hosp. Assn. Pa.'s Hosp. Advisory Com. to Capital Blue Cross, 1974-75; 1st vice-chmn. Hosp. Council Central Pa., 1977, bd. dirs., 1976—. Served with USNR, 1944-46, to maj., M.I., U.S. Army, 1949-59. Fellow Am. Acad. Med. Adminstrs. Clubs: Rotary, Maria Assunta, Elks. Home: 810 Sunset Dr Berwick PA 18603 Office: 701 E 16th St Berwick PA 18603

HOWELL, ROGER, JR., educator; b. Balt., July 3, 1936; s. Roger and Katherine (Clifford) H.; A.B. summa cum laude, Bowdoin Coll., 1958, D.Litt., 1978; B.A. (Rhodes scholar 1958-60), St. John's Coll., Oxford (Eng.) U., 1960, M.A., D.Phil., 1964; LL.D., Nasson Coll., 1970, Colby Coll., 1970; L.H.D., U. Maine, 1971; children—Tracy Walker, Ian Christopher. Jr. instr. history Johns Hopkins, 1960-61; research fellow, tutor final honour sch. modern history St. John's Coll., Oxford U., 1961-64, jr. Dean Arts of coll., 1962-64; tutor history and polit. theory Oxford U. Internat. Grad. Summer Sch., 1962-63, W.E.A. lectr. delegacy extramural studies, 1963-64; mem. faculty Bowdoin Coll., 1964—, prof. history, 1968—, chmn. dept., 1967-68, acting dean coll., 1968-69, pres., 1969-78; vis. prof. U. Maine, 1968-69, mem. higher edn. planning commn., 1969-72. Fellow Royal Anthrop. Inst. Great Britain and Ireland, Royal Hist. Soc.; mem. Hist. Assn. Great Britain, Am. Hist. Assn., Past and Present Soc., Econ. History Soc., Soc. Antiquaries Newcastle, Stubbs Soc. (Oxford U.), Scottish History Soc., Soc. d'Etude du xviie siecle, Conf. Brit. Studies (exec. com. 1967-69, 78—), New Eng. Conf. Brit. Studies (exec. sec. 1967-69, hon. pres. 1969-70), Renaissance Soc. Am., Anglo-Am. Assos. (exec. com.). Author: Newcastle upon Tyne and the Puritan Revolution, 1967; Sir Philip Sidney: The Shepherd Knight, 1968; The Constitutional and Intellectual Origins of the English Revolution, 1975; Cromwell, 1977; also articles. Editor: Prescott: The Conquest of Mexico, Etc., 1966; British Studies Monitor, 1969—; co-editor: Erasmus, 1975. Home: 16 Cleaveland St Brunswick ME 04011

HOWELL, WENDELL, city ofcl.; b. St. Matthews, S.C., Sept. 14, 1942; s. Dave J. and Mary (Pickney) H.; B.S. in Polit. Sci. and Bus. Adminstrn., U. Del., 1977; m. Judith Gupton, May 23, 1975; children—Wendell Howell, Heavenly. Dir. program services Youth Pride, Washington, 1969-70; program services dir. United Neighbors for Progress, Inc., Wilmington, Del., 1970-71; dir. urban affairs, spl. asst. to mayor on drug matters, Wilmington, 1971-72; faculty Del. State Coll., Dover, 1972-73; exec. asst. to County Exec., Wilmington, 1975-76; counselor Del. Tech. and Community Coll., Wilmington, 1976-77; exec. dir., sec.-treas. Wilmington Housing Authority, 1977—. Pres., Wilmington Sch. Bd., 1974-78; mem. New Castle County Planning Bd. of Edn., 1976-78; mem. New Castle County Assessment Bd. of Review, 1977-78. Served with USAF, 1961-69. Recipient NAACP award for community leadership, 1977; 1st ann. Man of the Year award Martin Luther King Celebration Com., 1976; named Young Man of the Year, Wilmington Jr. C. of C., 1976. Mem. Jr. C. of C., Del. Assn. Pub. Adminstrs., Nat. Alliance of Black Sch. Educators, Nat. Assn. Manpower Planners, Del. Sch. Personnel Adminstrs. Contbr. articles in field to profl. jours. Home: 3410 Madison St Wilmington DE 19802 Office: PO Box 1105 Wilmington DE 19899

HOWER, ROLLAND OLIVER, scientist, govt. ofcl.; b. Fremont, Ohio, June 14, 1928; s. Oliver Nelson and Maud Isabel (Stafford) H.; student Toledo U., 1948-52; Ph.D., 1977; m. Harryette R. Bradley, Oct. 27, 1951; children—Cary, Lynn, Bradley, Nelson, Craig, Dawn. Draftsman illustrator A.O. Smith Corp., Toledo, 1951; designer exhibits Smithsonian Instn., Washington, 1951-56, chief exhibits Mus. Nat. History, 1956-64, chief research Office of Exhibits, 1964-74, chief mus. tng., 1974-75, chief freeze-dry lab., 1975—; adviser Port Tobacco Mus. Mem. Am. Assn. Museums, Port Tobacco Restoration Soc., Elysian Soc. Republican. Methodist. Author articles in field. Home: Star Route 3 Box 393 LaPlata MD 20646 Office: Smithsonian Instn 1000 Jefferson Dr SW Washington DC 20560*

HOWES, ALFRED SPENCER, business and ins. cons.; b. Troy, N.Y., Sept. 10, 1917; s. Alfred G. and Frances (Youngs) H.; student Brown U., 1934-35, U. Ala., 1935-36, Syracuse U., 1943-44; m. Elizabeth Hoffner, Oct. 10, 1942; children—Wendy Howes Decker, Mary Lee, Constance Ellen. Agt., advanced underwriting cons. for N.Y. and Vt. with Conn. Mut. Life Ins. Co.; organized own Business Cons. Co., 1946; pres. Employee Incentive Plans of Am., Inc.; chmn. bd. Utica Duxbak Corp.; pres., dir. Hyden, Inc., Wood Realty Inc.; dir. Century Planning Co., Inc., Hurd Shoe Co., Wood & Hyde Co., Bering Trading Corp., McCormick Mgmt. Cons., Inc., Mohawk Valley Oil Co., Inc., Scotsmoor Co., Inc., APMEW, Inc., Placid's Parkas, Inc., Mech. Technology Inc., Utica Bulk Terminals, Inc., Winchester Knitting Mills, Inc., Wood Realty Inc., Am. Paper Machinery, Inc., Killip Laundering & Dry Cleaning Co., Inc., Killip Services, Inc., Smiley Bros., Inc.; pub. Gray Letter. Past sec., dir. N.Y.C. Estate Planning Council. Served with Office Gen. Purchasing Agt., ETO, 1943-46. Mem. Nat. (life, pub. relations chmn. Million Dollar Round Table), N.Y. State (chmn. com. to revise laws concerning decedents and their estates, pres. 1966-67), N.Y.C. (dir., pres.) assns. life underwriters, Am. Philatelic Soc., Assn. for Advanced Life Underwriting (pres. 1970-71). Clubs: Collectors, Brown (N.Y.C.); University (Albany); Fort Schuyler (Utica). Author article on taxes. Office: 551 Fifth Ave New York City NY 10017

HOWIE, KENNETH EARLE, lawyer; b. Toronto, Ont., Can., Sept. 16, 1925; s. James Augustus and Lily Rae (Timmins) H.; B.A., U. Toronto, 1948, LL.B., 1950; LL.B., Osgoode Hall Law Sch., 1951; m. Ruth Sinclair Hurley, June 16, 1950; children—Heather, James, Carol, Robert. Admitted to Ont. bar, 1951; sr. partner firm Thomson Rogers, Toronto, 1951—; instr. bar admission Law Soc. Upper Can., 1959—. Chmn. bd. stewards First United Ch. Served with Canadian Army, 1944-46, 49-54. Fellow Internat. Acad. Trial Lawyers; mem. Am. Trial Lawyers Assn., Canadian Bar Assn. (council), County York Law Assn. (past pres. 1972), Medico Legas Soc. Toronto (pres. 1975), Advocates Soc. Toronto (past dir.). Clubs: Ontario; Mississauga Golf and Country (pres. 1977-78). Home: 1530 Pinetree Crescent Mississauga ON Canada Office: 390 Bay St Toronto ON M5H 2Y2 Canada

HOWLAND, REEVE SCOTT, obstetrician, gynecologist; b. Elmira, N.Y., Jan. 2, 1909; s. Reeve Beecher and Alice Elizabeth (Scott) H.; A.B., Cornell U., 1930, M.D., 1933; m. Louisa Broemmer, Oct. 8, 1938; 1 son, Reeve Broemmer. Intern, Lenox Hill Hosp., N.Y.C., 1933-35, resident, 1935-36; practice medicine specializing in obstetrics and gynecology, Elmira, N.Y., 1937—; mem. staff Arnot Ogden Meml., St. Joseph's hosps. (both Elmira). Trustee, chmn. bd. Elmira (N.Y.) Savs. Bank; mem. adv. bd. Marine Midland So. Bank. Trustee Elmira (N.Y.) Coll., 1961-67. Fellow A.C.S., Am. Coll. Obstetricians and Gynecologists; mem. AMA (mem. ho. of dels. 1967-73). Home: 1415 W Water St Elmira NY 14905 Office: 600 Ivy St Elmira NY 14901

HOWLETT, CHARLES FRANCIS, historian, educator; b. Bay Shore, N.Y., Nov. 11, 1946; s. John Edward and Christine Mary (Neet) H.; A.B. cum laude, Marist Coll., 1968; M.A., State U. N.Y., 1971, Ph.D., 1974; m. Patricia Marie Reichert, Jan. 22, 1977. Mem. faculty, history dept. State U. N.Y., Albany, 1968-69, 71-74; tchr. social studies West Islip (N.Y.) Pub. Schs., 1974-77, Amityville (N.Y.) Pub. Schs., 1977—; adj. prof. history Dowling Coll., 1976—. Active West Islip Civic Assn. Served with USMCR, 1969-71. State U. N.Y. research fellow, 1972-73; State U. N.Y. at Albany fellow, 1973-74. Mem. Am. Hist. Assn., Orgn. Am. Historians, Conf. on Peace Research in History, John Dewey Edn. Soc., Am. Studies Assn., Fellowship of Reconciliation, Amateur Athletic Union. Democrat. Roman Catholic. Author: Troubled Philosopher: John Dewey and The Struggle for World Peace, 1977. Contbr. articles in field to various publs. Home: 93 Gladstone Ave West Islip NY 11795 Office: Social Studies Dept Amityville Jr High Sch Amityville NY 11701

HOXIE, RALPH GORDON, educator, author; b. Waterloo, Iowa, Mar. 18, 1919; s. Charles Ray and Ada May (Little) H.; B.A., U. No. Iowa, 1940; M.A., U. Wis., 1941; Ph.D., Columbia U., 1950; LL.D., Chung-ang U., Seoul, Korea, 1965; D.Litt., D'Youville Coll., Buffalo, 1966; m. Louise Lobitz, December 23, 1953. Roberts fellow Columbia U., 1946-47, Roberts traveling fellow, 1947-48, asst. to provost, 1948-49; asst. prof. history, gen. ed. Social Sci. Found., also asst. to chancellor U. Denver, 1950-53; project asso. Columbia U. Bicentennial History, 1953-54; dean Coll. Liberal Arts and Scis., L.I. U., 1954-55, acting dean C. W. Post Coll., L.I. U., 1954-55, dean, 1955-60, 1st provost, 1960-62, pres., 1962-68; chancellor L.I. U., 1964-68, cons., 1968-69; pres. Center for Study Presidency, 1969—; cons. Franklin Nat. Bank, 1968-69; vis. lectr. Columbia, U. Tex. at El Paso, U. Calif., Irvine, Chapman Coll., U. Wis., U. Colo., Colo. State U., U. Wyo., U. No. Colo., Colo. Coll., Naval War Coll., Oglethorpe Coll., Northwestern U. Mem. adv. bd. L.I. Air Res. Center; sec. Commn. Govtl. Revision Co. Nassau; pres. Greater N.Y. Council Fgn. Students, Pub. Mems. Assn. Fgn. Service; v.p. edn. and home div., dir. Greater N.Y. Safety Council; pub. mem. fgn. service officer selection bd. U.S. Dept. State. Bd. dirs. Council Higher Ednl. Instns. N.Y.C., Downtown Bklyn. Assn., L.I. Council on Alcoholism, Bklyn. chpt. ARC; hon. trustee L.I. Theatre Soc., Tibetan Found.; bd. govs. Human Resources Center; trustee Kosciuszko Found. N.Y., United Fund L.I., Bklyn. Inst. Arts and Scis.; chmn., pres. Am. Friends Chung-Ang U. Served from pvt. to capt., USAAF, 1942-46; N. Pacific; brig. gen. Res., ret. Decorated Legion of Merit; recipient Am. Bill of Rights award, 1964; Alumni Achievement award U. No. Iowa, 1965, Korean Cultural medal, 1965; Distinguished Service medal City of N.Y., 1965; Man of Year award Paderewski Found., 1966; award Eloy Alfaro Internat. Found. Republic Panama; Cultural medal Republic of Korea; named hon. citizen Seoul (Korea). Fellow Am. Studies Assn. Met. N.Y.; mem. Internat. Assn. Univ. Pres.'s, Am. Hist. Assn., Am. Polit. Sci. Assn., Acad. Polit. Sci., L.I. Assn., Res. Officers Assn. U.S. (chpt. pres.), L.I. Assn. (dir.), Robert A. Taft Inst. Govt. (adv. council), Am. Assn. UN (chpt. adv. bd.), Nassau-Suffolk Conf. Christians and Jews (co-chmn.), Air Force Assn., Am. Legion, VFW, Am. Polar Soc., Friends N.Y. Library, Delta Sigma Pi, Kappa Delta Pi, Alpha Sigma Lambda, Pi Gamma Mu, Gamma Theta Upsilon. Episcopalian. Clubs: Met. (Washington); Mill River (hon.) (Upper Brookville, N.Y.); Old Westbury (N.Y.) Golf and Country (hon.); Bklyn., Montauk (Bklyn.); Century Assn., Adventurers, Met., Columbia Faculty (N.Y.C.). Author: John W. Burgess, American Scholar, 1950; (with others) A History of the Faculty of Political Science, 1955; Command Decision and the Presidency, 1977; editor: Frontiers for Freedom, 1952; The White House: Organizations and Operations, 1971; The Presidency of the 1970's, 1973; Presdl. Studies Quar., 1971—; contbr. to Freedom and Authority in Our Time, 1953, Coattailless Landslide, 1974; Power and the Presidency, 1976; also Ency. Britannica, World Book Ency., profl. jours. Home: 224 Laurel Cove Rd Oyster Bay Cove NY 11771 Office: 926 Fifth Ave New York City NY 10021

HOXTER, CURTIS JOSEPH, internat. pub. relations counselor, econ. adviser; b. Marburg, Germany, July 20, 1922; s. Jacob and Hannah (Katzenstein) H.; A.B., N.Y.U., 1948, M.A., 1950; m. Grace Lewis, Feb. 4, 1945; children—Ronald, Victoria Finder, Audrey. Staff contbr. AUFBAU-Reconstrn., N.Y.C., 1939-40; feature writer, reporter L.I. Daily Press, 1940-42; editor, writer OWI, 1943-45; pub. information officer Dept. State, 1945-47; info. cons. ECA, 1950-55; pub. relations cons. various cos.; dir. pub. relations U.S. Council Internat. C. of C., 1948-53; free-lance columnist N.Y. World Telegram and Sun; exec. v.p. George Peabody and Assos., Inc., 1953-56; pres. Curtis J. Hoxter, Inc., internat. pub. relations, econ. councillors, 1956—. Adviser U.S. com. UN Day; adviser internat. econ. and fin. problems to U.S. and fgn. govt. agys., Nat. Gov.'s Conf.; adv. gov. P.R.; adviser U.S. del. to Disarmament Conf., London. Served with AUS, World War II. Mem. Pub. Relations Soc. Am. Clubs: Atrium (N.Y.C.); Nat. Press, Internat. (Washington); Overseas Press; Brit. Racing; Canyon Country (Armonk, N.Y.); Bankers (San Juan, P.R.); Rotary. Author weekly column Scripps-Howard papers, The Foreign Economic Scene. Contbr. nat. mgs. Home: 34 Broadfield Rd New Rochelle NY 10804 Office: 745 Fifth Ave New York City NY 10022

HOY, JOHN WESLEY, JR., securities co. exec.; b. Waynesburg, Pa., Jan. 18, 1921; s. John Wesley and Louie (Cole) H.; B.S., W.Va. U., 1942; m. Mary Lee Ullom, Sept. 5, 1942; children—Nancy Lee. Sales exec. Parrish Securities, Pitts., 1946-77; v.p. Parrish div. Bruns, Nordsman, Rea & Co., Pitts., 1977—. Vice pres. bd. dirs. Music for Mt. Lebanon. Served as officer inf. AUS, 1942-46; ETO. Decorated Bronze Star. C.P.A., Pa. Mem. Pitts. Securities Traders Assn. (past pres.), Pitts. Bond Club, Mil. Order World Wars (life). Republican. Presbyterian. Clubs: St. Clair Country, Masons. Home: 889 Old Hickory Rd Pittsburgh PA 15243 Office: 1710 Union Bank Bldg Pittsburgh PA 15222

HOYER-ELLEFSEN, SIGURD, mfg. co. exec.; b. Oslo, Norway, July 24, 1932; s. Thomas Townshend Somerville and Inez Tenden (Michelsen) H.; B.S. in Mech. Engring., Mass. Inst. Tech., 1956, M.S., 1957, Sc.D., 1962; m. Astrid Reksten, Mar. 13, 1959; children—Thomas, Sigurd, Caroline, Anthony, Richard. Came to U.S., 1953, naturalized, 1963. With Fairchild Industries, Inc., Germantown, Md., 1964-70; v.p. research and devel. Potter Instrument Co., Inc., Plainview, N.Y., 1970-75; cons. to pres. Servo Corp. Am., 1975-76; v.p. devel. and engring. Smith-Corona group SCM Corp., N.Y.C., 1976—. Mem. IEEE. Clubs: Royal Norwegian Yacht, Oslo Golf, Seawanhaka Corinthian Yacht, N.Y. Yacht. Patentee deployable space structures, data processing. Home: PO Box 757 New Canaan CT 06840 Office: SCM Corp 65 Locust Ave New Canaan CT 06840

HRIZE, MICHAEL CHARLES, JR., mech. engr.; b. Bklyn., July 15, 1949; s. Michael Charles and Rose (Valentino) H.; B.S. in Aerospace Engring., St. Louis U., 1970; postgrad. in engring. mgmt. U. Mo., Rolla, 1971-72; m. Jean Marie Anderson, July 31, 1970; 1 son, Steven. Aerospace engr. USAAVSCOM, St. Louis, 1970-74; transportation systems engr. SEPTA, Phila., 1974-77, asst. supr. systems engring., 1977-78, supr., 1978—. Registered profl. engr., Pa., Mo., N.J. Mem. Soc. Automotive Engrs., ASME, Alpha Chi, Pi Mu Epsilon. Roman Catholic. Address: 3112 Sheffield Dr Cinnaminson NJ 08077

HRYBINSKY, BORYS OLEKSANDRIV, writer, translator, librarian; b. Ukraine; s. Oleksander Z. and Anastasia W. (Lytwakiwsky) H.; diploma Pedagogical Inst., Kiev, Ukraine, 1941; B.L.S., U. Ottawa, 1961, M.A., 1966; m. Svetlana Wakulowsky, Feb. 18, 1950; children—Boris, Oles. Editor 2 weekly newspapers, Ukraine, 1941-43; chief editor Moloda Ukraine Youth Mag., Toronto, 1950-60; chief librarian Long Br. Pub. Library, Toronto, 1962-67; dir. Vaughan Pub. Library, Vaughan, Ont., 1967—. Recipient citation Long Br. Pub. Library Bd., 1966, I. Franko Literary award, 1974. Mem. Ukrainian Writers Assn., Ont. Library Assn. Author: (poems) Moi Dni, 1946; (short stories) Svyryd Lomachka v Kanadi, 1951; (short stories) Lubov do Blyzn'oho, 1961; (poems) Tuha Za Sontsem, 1965; Kolokruh, 1972; Kaminny bereh, 1975. Contbr. articles and short stories to various jours. Home: 40 Brentwood Rd N Toronto ON M8X 2B7 Canada Office: Vaughan Public Library Maple ON LOJ 1E0 Canada

HRYCAK, PETER, mech. engr., educator; b. Przemysl, Poland, July 8, 1923; s. Eugene and Ludmyla (Dobrzanska) H.; came to U.S., 1949, naturalized, 1956; student U. Vienna, Austria, 1941-45; diploma U. Tuebingen, Germany, 1945; B.S. with high distinction, U. Minn., 1954, M.S., 1955, Ph.D., 1960; m. Rea M. Limberg, June 13, 1949; children—Maria (dec.), Michael P., Orest, Alexandra M. Adminstrv. asst. French Mil. Govt. in Germany, 1947-49; instr. mech. engring. dept. U. Minn., Mpls., 1955-60; project engr. Gen. Mills, Inc., Mpls., summers 1956-57; mem. tech. staff Bell Telephone Labs., Murray Hill, N.J., 1960-65; sr. project engr. Curtiss Wright Corp., Woodridge, N.J., 1965; asso. prof. mech. engring. N.J. Inst. Tech., Newark, 1965-68, prof., 1968—. Bd. dirs. Ukrainian Congress Com. Am., Mpls., 1956-60, Plast Camp, East Chatham, N.Y., 1963-68. Registered profl. engr., N.J. Mem. ASME, Am. Inst. Aeros. and Astronautics, Am. Soc. Engring. Edn., Am. Geophys. Union, N.Y. Acad. Scis., Ukrainian Engrs. Soc. Am. (pres. 1966-67), Ukrainian Acad. Arts and Scis. in U.S., Internat. Platform Assn. Contbr. articles to engring. jours. Home: 19 Roselle Ave Cranford NJ 07016 Office: 323 High St Newark NJ 07102

HSIA, WEI JEN, elec. engr.; b. I-Shing, Kiangsu, China, Oct. 27, 1930; s. Kan-Chun and Shih Chien H.; came to U.S., 1963, naturalized, 1971; B.Sc., Cheng-Kung U., 1956; m. Nancy Li-Hua Chu, Apr. 2, 1966; children—Henry C.H., Elizabeth C.S. Elec. engr. Taiwan Power Co., 1960-63; jr. elec. engr. N.Y.C. Transit Authority, 1964-66; elec. engr. Devel. & Resource, Inc., N.Y.C., 1967-72; sr. elec. engr. TAMS Engrs. & Architects, Inc., N.Y.C., 1972-73; sr. elec. engr. Ebasco Services, Inc., Jericho, N.Y., 1973—. Registered profl. engr., N.Y. Mem. IEEE, Nat., N.Y. State socs. profl. engrs. Home: 2717 Elliot St Merrick NY 11566 Office: 1 Jericho Plaza Jericho Turnpike Jericho NY 11753

HSIAO, MU-YUE, computer co. engr.; b. Hunan, China, July 17, 1933; s. Li-Wu and Zen-Ching H.; came to U.S., 1958, naturalized, 1969; B.S., Taiwan U., 1956; M.S., U. Ill., 1960; Ph.D., U. Fla., 1967; m. Mona Yu-chuan Shao, Sept. 1, 1962; children—Rita, Wendy, Eric. Teaching asst. Taiwan U., 1958; jr., asso. and sr. asso. engr. IBM, 1960-65; teaching asso. U. Fla., 1965-67; adv. engr. IBM, 1967, sr. engr., mgr. Poughkeepsie (N.Y.) Lab., 1969—. Served with Chinese Air Force, 1956-58. Recipient outstanding invention award IBM, 1972, Achievement award, 1977. Fellow IEEE; mem. AAAS, Eta Kappa Nu, Phi Kappa Phi. Author: Principles of Electronic Digital Computers, 1964; Error Detecting Logic for Digital Computers, 1968. Contbr. articles to research jours. Patentee in field. Home: 7 Fair Way Poughkeepsie NY 12603 Office: PO Box 390 Poughkeepsie NY 12602

HSIEH, HSIUN PHILIP, chem. engr.; b. Taipei, Taiwan, May 29, 1944; s. Chang-kung and Yin (Lee) H.; came to U.S., 1969; B.S. in Chem. Engring., Nat. Taiwan U., 1967; M.S., Clarkson Coll. Tech., 1971; Ph.D. in Chem. Engring., SUNY, Buffalo, 1975; m. Meishiang Hwang, July 5, 1970; children—Michael, Andrew. Devel. engr. alumina and chems. div. Aluminum Co. Am., East St. Louis, Ill. and Alcoa Center, Pa., 1975-78, sr. engr., Alcoa Center, 1978—; instr. faculty of engring. and applied scis. SUNY, Buffalo, 1974-75. Mem. Am. Inst. Chem. Engrs., Am. Chem. Soc., Soc. Rheology, Soc. Plastics Engrs., Sigma Xi. Contbr. articles to sci. jours. Home: 3821 Harwick Dr Murrysville PA 15668 Office: Alcoa Tech Center Alcoa Center PA 15069

HSU, BENEDICT S. (PEI-SHIUNG), journalist, author; b. Nanking, China, May 1, 1933; s. Long and Yuan-Chen (Chao) H.; came to U.S., 1967, naturalized, 1974; B.A., Chung-Hsin U., 1958; M.S., Georgetown U., 1971; m. Lena Chen Hsu, June 18, 1961; children—Johnny Y., Peter Y. Reporter, Hsin-Shen Daily News, Taipei, Taiwan, 1954-57, China Daily News, Taipei, 1957-60, China Times, Taipei, 1960-67; corr. Taiwan Hsin Wen Pao, Kao-Hsiung, Taiwan, 1967-75; U.S. corr. Newsdom Weekly, also Travelling mag., Hong Kong, 1968—; instr. Johns Hopkins U., 1971-72; lectr. Georgetown U., 1971-72. Served with Chinese Army, 1953-54, USAF, 1955-56. Recipient Best Reporting award World-Wide Overseas Chinese Assn., 1972. Asia Found. grantee, 1964. Author: Little League Baseball in China, 1969; Chi-Cheng, The Fastest Woman in the World, 1970; The Fight for China's Representation, 1971; The World As I See It, 1975. Home: 11205 Schuylkill Rd Rockville MD 20852

HSU, DONALD KUNGHSING, chem. physicist; b. Shanghai, China, Apr. 17, 1947; s. Kuo Chung and Ching Hua (Yang) H.; came to U.S., 1970; B.S., Cheng Kung U., Taiwan, 1969; M.S. (NSF predoctoral fellow), Fordham U., 1972, Ph.D., 1975; m. Salome Y. Hsiao, Mar. 18, 1972. Teaching and research asst. Fordham U., 1972; guest worker Argonne Nat. Lab., 1972; research asst. U. Tex., Dallas, also Nat. Bur. Standards, Boulder, Colo., 1973-74; research asso. Princeton (N.J.) Obs., 1975; research asso. dept. chemistry Columbia U., 1976-77; lectr. N.J. Inst. Tech., 1977—; vis. scientist Nat. Bur. Standards, 1976; cons. Princeton U., 1976-77. NSF and NASA fellow, 1975-76. Mem. IEEE, Am. Chem. Soc., Am. Phys. Soc., AAAS. Office: Div Chemistry NJ Inst Tech Newark NJ 07102

HSU, ENRICO YUN PING, mfg. co. exec.; b. Shanghai, China, Apr. 13, 1926; s. Joachim and Magdalena (Shen) H.; came to U.S., 1954, naturalized, 1972; M.S., Columbia, 1959; m. Magdalena Lee, Nov. 16, 1957; children—Joachim, Dave, Felix, Calvin. Mgr. operations research Rock Drill div. Ingersoll-Rand Co., Phillipsburg, N.J., 1968-72, mgr. phys. distbn. and information systems, 1972-73, corporate mgr. mfg. and distbn. systems, 1973—. Recipient Outstanding Achievement award Columbia, 1959. Mem. Nat. Council Phys. Distbn. Mgmt., Am. Prodn. and Inventory Control Soc. Home: 306 Westgate Rd Ridgewood NJ 07450 Office: Ingersoll-Rand Co 200 Chestnut Ridge Rd Woodcliff Lake NJ 07675

HSU, JOSEPH JEN-YUAN, biomed. physicist; b. Peking, China, Mar. 25, 1928; s. William Wang-Chih and Ping-Heng (Ling) H.; came to U.S., 1952, naturalized, 1963; B.S., Monmouth Coll., 1954; M.S., U. Mass., 1962; Ph.D., N.Y.U., 1975; m. Helen Lu-shgn Wang, Sept. 10, 1966; children—Ava, Hank, Bond. Translator, budget clk. Joint Commn. on Rural Reconstrn., Taipei, Taiwan, 1951; asst. physicist Argonne Nat. Lab., 1962-67; asso. research scientist N.Y.U. Med. Center, N.Y.C., 1967-74; v.p., dir. research and devel. Font Indsl., Inc., N.Y.C., 1975—, C.A.C. of N.Y., Inc., N.Y.C., 1975—; cons. Chinatown Manpower Porject, 1977—; authorized rep. China Pres. Line & Devel. Corp., N.Y.C., 1978—; exec. v.p. Gen. Commodities Corp.; dep. dir. Inst. Applied Biology, N.Y.C. NRC travel award, 1972. Mem. Am. Soc. Photobiology (charter), Am. Phys. Soc., AAUP. Democrat. Quaker. Contbr. articles to profl. jours. Home: 1500 Hornell Loop Brooklyn NY 11239 Office: PO Box 393 World Trade Murray Hill Station New York City NY 10016

HSU, KONRAD CHANG, microbiologist, scientist; b. Taichow, China, Aug. 28, 1901; s. George Chien and Wu (Yu) H.; B.S., St. John's U., Shanghai, China, 1921; M.A., Columbia U., 1923, Ph.D., 1924; m. Katharine D. Hawley, Jan. 31, 1951; children—Victoria Ruffner, Theodora Du, Alicia Wohl, Konrad T., Adelina, Lydia Yu, Linda Wei; came to U.S., naturalized, 1962. Mem. faculty Gt. China U., 1924-26; with Chinese Govt. Mil. and Civil Service, 1926-37; gen. mgr. Chan Hwa & Co., 1937-46; v.p. Sino-Hawaiian Corp., 1946-49; v.p. Dakon Corp., Bangkok, Thailand, Hong Kong, N.Y.C., 1949-54; mem. faculty Coll. Physicians and Surgeons, Columbia U., N.Y.C., 1954—, prof. microbiology, 1969—; vis. prof. U. Rome, U. Bonn, 1966, Ulm (Germany) U., 1969, 73; vis. scientist Inst. Gustave Roussy, Villejuif, France, 1966, Sydney U., 1967. Chmn. bd. dirs. Overseas Chinese Music and Arts Center, N.Y.C. Mem. Soc. Exptl. Biology and Medicine, Am. Assn. Immunologists, Am. Assn. Pathologists and Bacteriologists, Reticuloendothelial Soc., Harvey Soc., Am. Assn. Pathologists, Am. Assn. Immunologists, Soc. Exptl. Biol. Medicine, N.Y. Acad. Scis., Sigma Xi. Club: Masons. Author numerous publs. in field. Home: 24 Schreiber St Tappan NY 10983 Office: 630 W 168th St New York City NY 10032

HSU, ROBERT YING, educator; b. Peking, China, Oct. 10, 1926; s. Chien Tze and Ta (Feng) H.; came to U.S., 1950, naturalized, 1962; M.S., Iowa State U., 1952; M.S., Cornell U., 1955; Ph.D., U. Wis., 1961; m. Gretchen Chi Wang, Mar. 19, 1962; children—David Robert, Hanson Kelvin. Project asst. U. Wis., Madison, 1957-58, research asso., 1963-66; research scientist Armour Pharm. Co., Kankakee, Ill., 1961-62; asst. prof. Rutgers U., New Brunswick, N.J., 1966-68; asst. prof. State U. N.Y., Syracuse, 1968-70, asso. prof. biochemistry, 1970-77, prof., 1977—; vis. prof. Nat. Taiwan U., Taipei, 1962; teaching cons. Community Gen. Hosp., Syracuse, 1973—. NIH grantee, 1967—. Mem. AAAS, Am. Chem. Soc., Am. Soc. Biol. Chemists, Sigma Xi, Gamma Sigma Delta, Pi Alpha Xi. Contbr. articles to profl. jours. Home: 6329 Westerly Terr Jamesville NY 13078 Office: State U New York Upstate Medical Center 766 Irving Ave Syracuse NY 13210

HSU, SAMUEL, educator; b. Shanghai, China, June 20, 1947; s. John and Dorothy (Wong) H.; B.S., Phila. Coll. Bible, 1969, Mus.B., 1969; Ph.D., U. Calif., Santa Barbara, 1972; postgrad. with Rosina Lhevinne (Pillsbury Found. grantee) Juilliard Sch. Music, 1972-76. Instr. piano Westmont Coll., Montecito, Calif., 1971-72; instr. music history and piano Phila. Coll. Bible, 1972-74, asst. prof., 1974-76, asso. prof., 1976—, chmn. dept. piano, 1976—. instr. piano Csehy Summer Sch. Music, 1974—. Mem. Phila. Music Tchrs. Assn. (dir. 1976—), Am. Musicol. Soc., Delta Epsilon Chi, Pi Kappa Lambda. Office: 1800 Arch St Philadelphia PA 19103

HSU, YINGCHIEH, physicist; b. Changhua, Taiwan, China, Dec. 28, 1933; s. Chiulien and Chiukuei (Chiu) H.; came to U.S., 1963, naturalized, 1975; B.Sc. in Physics, Taiwan Normal U., 1961; A.M. in Physics, Clark U., 1965; Ph.D. in Physics, U. Ottawa, 1968; m. Marilyn L. Nicandro, Oct. 5, 1965; children—Gwelleh, Jesse Penn. Teaching scholar Clark U., Worcester, Mass., 1963-65; instr. U. Ottawa (Ont., Can.), 1965-68, research fellow, 1968-70; sr. scientist U. Va., Charlottesville, 1970-71; trainee Vanderbilt U. Med. Center, Nashville, 1971-72; research physicist Carnegie-Mellon U., Pitts., 1973—; med. physicist, radiation safety officer VA Hosp., Pitts., 1975—; cons. and teaching radiologic physicist McKeesport Hosp., 1976—. Mem. Am. Phys. Soc., Soc. Nuclear Medicine, Am. Assn. Physicists in Medicine, Health Physics Soc. Contbr. articles to profl. jours.

HSU, YU KAO, aerospace scientist, mathematician, educator; b. Wu Kang, Hunan, China, Apr. 24, 1922; s. Ming Yung and Zhu Ching (Liu) H.; came to U.S., 1956, naturalized, 1972; Ph.D., Rensselaer Poly. Inst., 1966; m. Martha Tih Wang, Dec. 11, 1965; children—Timothy, Melinda. Research asst. Rensselaer Poly Inst., Troy, N.Y., 1962-66; asst. prof. aerospace engring. W.Va. U., Morgantown, 1966-71; asso. prof. math. Bangor Community Coll., U. Maine, Orono, 1971—; inst. guest Mass. Inst. Tech., 1978. Faculty award W.Va. U., 1971, summer research award, 1976. Mem. Am. Math. Soc., Am. Inst. Aeros. and astronautics, Sigma Xi. Roman Catholic. Research, publs. in pressure field caused by cone rotating in non-Newtonian liquid, also supercaritating hydrofoil, also non-steady molecular beam of strong shock structure problem, laminar film condensation. Home: 121 Juniper St Bangor ME 04401

HTOO, MAUNG SHWE, chemist; b. Yenangyaung, Burma, Aug. 17, 1927; s. U Than Pe and Daw Saw Yin; came to U.S., 1949, naturalized, 1955; B.S., U. Maine, 1952, M.S., 1954; Ph.D., Rensselaer Poly. Inst., 1961; m. Ann Shraybman, Jan. 19, 1953; children—Susan, Nancy, Rhonda, Naomi. Sr. research chem. engr. Internat. Paper Co., N.Y.C., 1954-61; with IBM, Poughkeepsie, N.Y., 1961—, mgr. product tech. materials lab., 1975—; mem. faculty Dutchess Community Coll., evenings, 1967—. Fellow Am. Inst. Chemists; mem. Soc. Photog. Scientists and Engrs., Soc. Plastics Engrs., Am. Chem. Soc., Home: 10 Rabbit Trail Rd Poughkeepsie NY 12603 Office: IBM Box 309 Poughkeepsie NY 12602

HU, SHIH-EN, chemist; b. China, June 25, 1925; s. Ping Jing and Tea Pi (Chow) H.; came to U.S., 1958, naturalized, 1973; Ph.D., Wayne State U., 1962; m. Piluan Lee, Jan. 26, 1962; children—Linden, Wayne. Asso. prof. chemistry, lab. dir. Taipei Inst. Tech., 1958; research chemist Exxon Research and Engring. Co., Linden, N.J., 1963-66, sr. research chemist, 1966-69, research asso., 1969-71; asst. pres. New World Research Corp., N.Y.C., 1971—. Mem. Am. Chem. Soc. Patentee in field. Home: 229 Roger Ave Westfield NJ 07080

HUANG, JACOB CHEN-YA, physician, city ofcl.; b. Chia-Yi, Taiwan, Dec. 25, 1937; s. Chang-Chiang and Agenes Cheng-Jen H.; came to U.S., 1966, naturalized, 1974; m. Vivian Lin, Oct. 3, 1970; children—Phyllis, Albert, Edward. Intern, Taipei City Hosp., 1964-65, house officer in pediatrics, 1965-66; fellow in clin. pathology Albert Einstein Coll. Medicine-Lincoln Hosp., 1968-70; resident in family medicine Lutheran Med. Center, N.Y.C., 1970-71; clin. asso. prof. N.Y. U., 1972-76; dist. health dir. N.Y.C., Dept. Health, 1971-76; med. dir. Paterson City (N.J.) Health Dept., 1977—; bd. dirs. ambulatory care adv. bd. Beth Israel Hosp., N.Y.C., 1972-76, community adv. bd. ambulatory services St. Vincent Med. Center, N.Y.C., 1972-76. Recipient Physician's Recogniation award AMA, 1966, 69, 72. Diplomate Am. Bd. Family Practice. Fellow Am. Coll. Preventive Medicine, Am. Acad. Family Physicians; mem. Am. Pub. Health Assn. Home: 17 Waterloo Dr Morris Plains NJ 07950 Office: 4 Deerfield Pl Flanders NJ 07836

HUANG, JOSEPH CHEN-HUAN, civil engr.; b. Nanking, China, Oct. 18, 1933; came to U.S., 1962, naturalized, 1972; M.S. in Structural Engring., Va. Poly. Inst. and State U., 1964; m. Elizabeth C. Huang, Sept. 3, 1966; children—Edith, Eleanor, Evelyn, Edna. Project engr. Green Assos., Inc., Balt., 1964-68; pres. East Environ. Endeavor, Inc., Balt., 1968-76; chmn., chief exec. officer HSC Engring. Corp., Timonium, Md., 1976—. Mem. ASCE, Am. Concrete Inst., Nat. Soc. Profl. Engrs. Home: 3506 Templar Rd Randallstown MD 21133 Office: 1830 York Rd Timonium MD 21093

HUANG, SHI-SHUNG, pediatrician; b. Taiwan, Jan. 16, 1934; s. Ping and Chiang H.; came to U.S., 1962, naturalized, 1970; M.D., Nat. Taiwan U., 1961; m. Margaret Tsui-E Shi, Jan. 8, 1961; children—Peter Jun-Wun, Mark E-Wun. Intern, Norwegian-Am. Hosp., Chgo., 1962-63; asst. resident and chief resident Union Meml. Hosp., Balt., 1963-65, sr. asst. resident Johns Hopkins Hosp., Balt., 1965-66, fellow, 1965-69; practice medicine specializing in pediatrics and pediatric gastroenterology, Balt., 1969—; instr. pediatrics Johns Hopkins U., 1969-74, asst. prof., 1974—; med. dir. Greater Balt. Med. Center Community and Family Health Center, 1975—, project dir. comprehensive children and youth program, 1967—; mem. med. staff Union Meml. Hosp., Johns Hopkins Hosp. Founding mem. Balt. County Com. on Ethnic Affairs, 1977—. Recipient Certificate of Merit, Balt. City Health Dept., 1973, Greater Balt. Med. Center, 1970, 75. Diplomate Am. Bd. Pediatrics. Mem. Am. Acad. Pediatrics, So. Med. Assn., Ambulatory Pediatric Assn., Formosan Club (pres. Balt. chpt. 1971-72), Chinese Profl. Assn. (v.p. 1972-73), Orgn. Chinese-Ams. (dir. chpt. 1977—), Nat. Taiwan U. Alumni Assn. (dir. 1975-78). Republican. Buddhist. Contbr. articles to med. Jours. Home: 1221 Saint Andrews Way Baltimore MD 21239 Office: 1017 E Baltimore St Baltimore MD 21202

HUBBARD, EDWARD DERRY, physician; b. Medellin, Colombia, Mar. 12, 1926; s. Douglas Henry Cairns and Margaret Mary (Buck) H.; M.D., U. Toronto (Ont., Can.), 1950; m. Marie Nickerson, Jan. 20, 1971; children—Jeanne, John, William, Derryanne, Nancy, Derry. Intern Regina (Sask., Can.) Gen. Hosp., 1950-53; resident Weyburn (Sask.) Can., 1953-54; practice medicine specializing in family medicine, Bowmanville, Ont., 1954—; coroner, Bowmanville, 1966—. Mem. Bowmanville Municipal Council, 1970-72. Served with Army, 1944-45. Diplomate Am. Acad. Family Practice. Fellow Canadian Coll. Family Practice; mem. Ont. Coroners Assn., Am. Soc. Clin. Hypnosis. Mason. Home: 132 Wellington St Bowmanville ON L1C 1W1 Canada Office: 222 King St E Bowmanville ON L1C 1P6 Canada

HUBBARD, HERBERT HENDRIX, lawyer; b. Balt., Sept. 20, 1922; s. Amberson and Louise V. (Hendrix) H.; LL.B., Balt. City Coll., 1939; LL.B., U. Md., 1950; m. Joanne H. Nottingham, June 5, 1948; children—Melissa, Alison. Admitted to Md. bar, 1950; law clk. U.S. dist. Judge Chesnut, 1950-51; asst., and dep. U.S. atty. Md., 1952-54; asso. France, Rouzer & Harris, 1954-59; partner Weinberg & Green, Attys., 1959—; counsel Acad. Underwriters Am.; counsel, dir. Alexander & Alexander Services, Inc., Alloy Cladding Co., Inc., L.B. Smith Inc. of Va. Mem. Md. Gov.'s Com. on Ethics in State Govt., 1968-69, Gov.'s Task Force on Labor Relations in State Govt., 1968-69; mem. adv. council Sheppard and Enoch Pratt Hosp., 1977—. Served with USAAF, 1942-46. Mem. Am., Md. (chmn. com. profl. liability ins. 1976—), Balt. City bar assns., Order of Coif. Episcopalian. Home: 705 St Georges Rd Baltimore MD 21210 Office: 10 Light St Baltimore MD 21202

HUBBARD, KENNETH EDWARD, nursing home adminstr.; b. Mineola, N.Y., June 10, 1946; s. Charles Griffen and Wilma Anna Rettmer H.; B.S.E., Princeton U., 1968; M.S.E., Elec. Engring., U. Calif., Los Angeles, 1971; m. Elizabeth J. Kasin, June 21, 1969; children—Amanda, Laura. Engr., Grumman Aerospace Corp., Bethpage, N.Y., 1968-69; mem. tech. staff Hughes Aircraft Co., Fullerton, Calif., 1969-71; v.p. Robert R. Kasin Assos., Inc., Islip, N.Y., 1972-73; adminstr. Fishkill Health Related Center, Beacon, N.Y., 1973—. Bd. dirs. Dutchess County (N.Y.) Health Planning Council, 1977—. Mem. Am. Acad. Med. Adminstrs., Am. Coll. Nursing Home Adminstrs. Republican. Office: Fishkill Health Related Center Dogwood Ln Beacon NY 12508

HUBBELL, HAROLD BERRESFORD, service co. exec.; b. New Rochelle, N.Y., Apr. 10, 1924; s. Harold B. and Rose (Martin) H.; A.B., Franklin and Marshall Coll., 1948; A.M., Columbia, 1949; m. Francis Elizabeth McIntosh, Feb. 1955; children—David B., Stephen D.M.; m. 2d, Francine Adie Bradford, Dec. 1974. Mktg. and sales mgr. Texaco Inc., West and Equatorial Africa, 1952-60; v.p., dir., Liberian Services, Inc., N.Y.C., 1961-75, exec. v.p., dir., 1975—; dir. Librarian Services Ltd., London. Served with USNR, 1942-46, 50-51. Mem. Stamford Geneal. Soc. (pres. 1970-72, 76-78, v.p., 1972-73), Rowayton Hist. Soc. (pres. 1973-77), Conn. League Hist. Socs. (v.p., dir. 1969-77), Darien Hist. Soc., Conn. Hist. Soc. Editor: Conn. Ancestry, 1970-73. Home: Rowayton CT 06853 Office: New York City NY 10017

HUBER, GARY LOUIS, chest physician; b. Spokane, Wash., Jan. 30, 1939; s. Arthur J. and Frances I.; B.S., Wash. State U., 1961; M.D., U. Wash., 1966, M.S., 1970; 1 dau., Melissa. Research trainee, dept. biol. structure and dept. anesthesiology U. Wash., Seattle, 1963-64; intern Harvard Med. Service, Boston City Hosp., 1966-67, resident, 1967-68; teaching fellow in medicine Harvard Med. Sch., Boston, 1967-68, research fellow dept. physiology Sch. Pub. Health, 1968-70; clin. fellow in medicine Boston City Hosp., 1968-70; research asso. HEW, USPHS, Cin. and Durham N.C., 1968-70; practice medicine specializing in chest diseases, Boston, 1970—; instr. medicine Harvard Med. Sch., 1970-71, asst. prof., 1971-77; asst. vis. physician Boston City Hosp., 1970-71, dir. respiratory diseases clinic, 1970-73, chief div. respiratory diseases, 1970-74, asso. vis. physician, 1971-74; dir. Harvard Tobacco and Health Research Program, 1972-77; asso. Corp. for Bermuda Biol. Sta., St. Georges W., 1973-77; med. cons. Mass. Rehab. Commn., Roxbury div., Boston, 1973-77; dir. thoracic clinic Beth Israel Hosp., Boston, 1973-77, asso. physician, 1975-77, physician-in-charge pulmonary function lab., 1976-77; sr. vis. fellow Cardiothoracic Inst., Nat. Heart and Chest Hosp., Brompton Hosp., London, 1978-79; sr. editor Chest, 1973-78, Heart and Lung, 1975—; symposium editor, 1977. Served with USPHS, 1968-70. Fellow Am. Coll. Chest Physicians; mem. Nat. Heart, Lung and Blood Inst. (cons.), Am. Heart Assn. (del. Nat. assembly 1976-77, cons.), Am. Thoracic Soc., Am. Lung Assn. (trustee Boston chpt.), Aerospace Med. Assn., Air Pollution Control Assn., Am. Acad. Clin. Toxicology, Am. Assn. Lab. Animal Scis., AAAS, Am. Assn. Pathologists and Bacteriologists, Am. Assn. Respiratory Therapy, A.C.P., Am. Coll. Preventive Medicine, Am. Fedn. Clin. Research, AMA, Am. Nepal Soc., Am., New Eng. occupational med. assns., Am. Physiol. Soc., Am., Mass. pub. health assns., Am. Soc. Cell Biology, Am., Mass. socs. internal medicine, Am. Soc. Microbiology, Assn. Med. Surgeons, Bermuda Biol. Sta. for Research, Fedn. Am. Socs. Exptl. Biology, Friends of Osler Library, Handel and Haydn Soc., Internat. Anesthesia Research Soc., Mass., Suffolk Dist. med. socs., Nat. Rehab. Assn., Nat. Cystic Fibrosis Found. Asso. editor: Comprehensive Respiratory Care: A Textbook of Chest Medicine, 1978; contbr. articles in field to med. jours. Home: 34 Whitelawn Ave Milton MA 02187 Office: 330 Brookline Ave Boston MA 02215

HUBER, JOAN MACMONNIES, frozen food co. exec.; b. N.Y.C., Dec. 15, 1927; d. Wallace and Marguerite Adele (Searing) MacMonnies; B.S. in Chemistry, Northwestern U., 1949; student specialized courses; m. Don Lawrence Huber, June 23, 1951. Research chemist, then research supr. Continental Baking Co., Jamaica, N.Y., 1949-57; co-owner, asst. mgr. Sta. KALE Richland, Wash., 1957-59; with Southland Frozen Foods Co., Gt. Neck, N.Y., 1959—, mktg. mgr., 1969-72, v.p. distbn. and corporate planning, 1972—. Mem. Inst. Food Technologists, Am. Chem. Soc., Am. Mgmt. Assn., Am. Frozen Food Inst. (distbn. council, chmn. Warehousing com.). Home: 24 Rolling Dr Brookville NY 11545 Office: 1 Linden Pl Great Neck NY 11021

HUBER, RICHARD GREGORY, lawyer, coll. dean; b. Indpls., June 29, 1919; s. Hugh Joseph and Laura Marie (Becker) H.; B.S., U.S. Naval Acad., 1942; J.D., U. Iowa, 1950; LL.M., Harvard U., 1951; m. Katherine Elizabeth McDonald, June 21, 1950; children—Katherine, Richard, Mary, Elizabeth, Stephen, Mark. Asso. prof. law U. S.C., Columbia, 1952-54, Tulane U., New Orleans, 1954-57; asso. prof. law Boston Coll., 1957-59, prof., 1959—, dean, 1970—; pres. Council Legal Edn. Opportunity, 1975—; v.p. Mass. Continuing Legal Edn.-N.E. Law Inst., 1975—. Bd. dirs Newton (Mass.) Art Center, 1977—; mem. Boston Consumers Council, 1972—. Served in USN, 1941-47, 51-52. Mem. Assn. Am. Law Schs. (exec. com.), Am., Mass., Boston bar assns., Soc. Am. Law Tchrs., Citizens Housing and Planning Assn., Mass. Bar Found. Democrat. Roman Catholic. Club: Windsor. Contbr. articles to legal jours. Home: 406 Woodward St Newton MA 02168 Office: 885 Centre St Newton MA 02159

HUBER, RICHARD MILLER, ednl. adminstr.; b. Ardmore, Pa., July 27, 1922; s. John Y. and Caroline Roberts (Miller) H.; B.A., Princeton U., 1945; Ph.D., Yale U., 1953; children—Cintra, Richard M., Casilda. Mem. faculty Princeton U., 1950-54; pres. Princeton Manor Constrn. Co., Princeton, N.J., 1958-62; pub. affairs moderator WNET-TV, N.Y.C., 1967-68; dean Sch. Gen. Studies, Hunter Coll., N.Y.C., 1971-77, exec. dir. Div. Continuing Edn., 1977—. Mem. council Friends of Princeton U. Library, 1956—; mem. Gov. N.J. Com. on Arts, 1966-67. Served as 2d lt. USAAF, 1942-45; ETO. Decorated Air medal; recipient award N.J. Hist. Soc., 1965; award of merit Am. Assn. for State and Local History, 1965; Author award N.J. Assn. Tchrs. of English, 1965; Woodrow Wilson fellow, 1946-47; Danforth fellow, 1951-52. Mem. Am. Hist. Assn., Am. Studies Assn., Soc. Am. Historians. Episcopalian. Clubs: Union, Yale, Nassau, Pretty Brook Tennis. Author: The American Idea of Success, 1971; Big All the Way Through: The Life of Van Santvoord Merle-Smith, 1952. Editor: (with Wheaton J. Lane) The New Jersey Historical Series, 31 vols., 1964-65. Home: 444 E 86th St New York City NY 10028 Office: 695 Park Ave New York City NY 10021

HUBER, WILLIAM STOKES, realtor, ins. broker; b. Yonkers, N.Y., Dec. 6, 1924; s. Ira S. and Doris F. (Farmer) H.; student pub. schs., Millersville, Pa.; m. Mary Jane Eshleman, July 7, 1946; children—Anne L. Huber Heisey, William D., Frederick S. Realtor, ins. broker Huber Agy., Millersville, 1946—, owner, 1962—; pres. Old Guard Mut. Ins. Co., Lancaster, Pa.; mem. adv. bd. Commonwealth Nat. Bank. Pres. West End Ambulance Assn., 1974—. Served with USNR, 1944-46. Mem. Pa. Mut. Agents Assn., Lancaster Bd. Realtors, Lancaster County Agents Assn. Methodist. Clubs: Penn Manor Sertoma (dir.), Elks. Home: 450 N George St Millersville PA 17551 Office: 464 N George St Millersville PA 17551

HUBERMAN, BENJAMIN, govt. ofcl.; b. Havana, Cuba, Jan. 25, 1938; s. Henry and Marcella (Waisman) H.; came to U.S., 1946, naturalized, 1952; A.B., Columbia U., 1959, B.S., 1960; diploma (Fulbright scholar), Imperial Coll., U. London, 1961; m. Giselle Bialik, Oct. 13, 1963; children—Jonathan Serge, Martin Charles. Nuclear power engr. AEC, 1961-66; spl. asst. for plans ACDA, Washington, 1966-73; dep. dir. program analysis staff NSC, 1973-75; dir. Office of Policy Evaluation, Nuclear Regulatory Commn., 1975-77; asso. dir. White House Office Sci. and Tech. also sr. staff mem. NSC, 1977—; mem. U.S. dels. Disarmament Conf., Geneva, 1967, 68, Gen Assembly, UN, 1968, Strategic Arms Limitation Talks, 1970, U.S.-USSR Joint Commn. on Peaceful Uses of Atomic Energy, 1976. Served with USN, 1960-66. Mem. Am. Nuclear Soc., Internat. Inst. Strategic Studies. Club: Cosmos. Home: 9808 Conestoga Way Potomac MD 20854 Office: Office Sci and Tech White House Washington DC 20500

HUBLEY, CECIL ERNEST FRANCIS, assn. exec., criminologist; b. Halifax, N.S., Can., Jan. 24, 1920; s. George Aubrey and Mary Elizabeth (Lonar) H.; student pub. schs., St. John, N.B., Can.; grad. Inst. Applied Scis.; m. Grace Veneita Curwin, June 12, 1946; 1 son, George Aubrey. Asst. paymaster Merchant Seaman br. Dept. Transport Can., 1943-45; intelligence liaison officer Interallied Mil. Orgn. Sphinx, 1940-45; founder, dir. gen. ASI Police Internat. Inc., St. John, 1946—, spl. investigation, 1946—; founder, dir. gen. internat. criminologists div. ASI Police Internat. Chartered Investigators Assn. and Hwy. Radio Patrol Internat. Emergency Service and Community Watch; spl. asst. to dir. Gen. de Policia Y Transito, Del Dist. Fed. Republic Mexico, Div. De Investigaciones Para La Prevention De La Delincuencia; hon. capt. New Orleans Police Dept.; spl. dep. sheriff, Passaic County, N.J.; commd. col. Interallied Mil. Orgn. Sphinx, La. col., 1959, Ky. Col., 1960, col. and aide-de-camp Gov. Ky., col. and aide-de-camp Ky. Commr. Pub. Safety, 1964. Decorated Venerable Order White Eagle, medal Polish Resistance, Kapitula Order Wolnosci, Mil medal Wojska (Poland); chevalier Les Chevaliers de la Croixde Lorraine et compagnonsde la Resistance (France); Silver medal Guard of Honor (Italy); grand croix Gen. Eloy Alfaro (Panama), others. Mem. Fedn. Des Combattants Allies en Europe (life), Mil. Order Firing Squad, Assn. Nationale Des Resistants Combattants Polonais, Interallied Mil. Order Sphinx (Distinguished Service Cross 1st class 1948). Author: Homicide Investigation, 1948; Fingerprints, 1948; Insurance Investigations, 1948; Questioned Document Examining, 1948; Evidence-Statements-Confessions, 1948; Tracing & Locating Missing Persons, 1948; Theatre-Bus-Store Checking and Investigation, 1948; Canada Forever; Hail! To the Men in Scarlet; Canada's Hope for Tomorrow; Elvis Presley Has Moved Upstairs, Nos. 1 and 2; The 1977 Jail Fires; The June 21st Saint John Jail Fire; The Prisoners Last Ride; The Peanut King Becomes President; A Little Mound of Earth; Friday November 21st, 1963: Tribute to President J.F. Kennedy; M Has gone Young—P Has Gone Old; Going Home To Visit; Beneath the Weeping Willow Tree; You were Never Satisfied: I Was Just a Substitute Lover; Bing Crosby—On The Road to Heaven; Special Home Blessing; April 4th, 1968—Tribute to Dr. Martin Luther King Jr., others. Editor ASIP Newsletter; book reviewing. Home: 34 Metcalf St Saint John NB E2K 1J8 Canada Office: PO Box 434 St John NB E2L 4L9 Canada

HUBLEY, DOROTHY GRAYBILL, musician, educator; b. Lititz, Pa., Sept. 9, 1921; d. Rufus Royce and Mary Elizabeth (Fink) Graybill; student Washington U., St. Louis, 1939, St. Louis Inst. Music, 1964, Ithaca Coll., 1959; m. John A. Hubley, Jr., Aug. 6, 1943; 1 son, John A. III. Music tchr., Lititz, 1940-43, 59—. Bd. dirs. Lancaster County Youth Symphony, 1966-73. Mem. Lancaster (pres. 1971-73), Pa. (treas 1971—, Distinguished Service award 1976) music tchrs. assns., Nat. Guild Piano Tchrs. (chmn. Lancaster center), Music Tchrs. Nat. Assn., Nat. Fedn. Music Clubs. Address: 413 S Cherry St Lititz PA 17543

HUCKINS, HAROLD AARON, chem. co. exec.; b. Cambridge, Mass., Nov. 28, 1924; s. Harold A. and Julia (Nugent) H.; B.S. in Chem. Engring., Northeastern U., 1945; certificate mech. engring. Lowell Inst., 1946; m. Elizabeth L. Kearns, Nov. 15, 1952; children—Richard W., Robert M., Christopher N., Patricia A., Leslie K. Process engr. Monsanto Chem. Co., Everett, Mass., 1946-49; project mgr. Koppers Co., Pitts., 1949-52; asst. v.p. process engring., dir. project evaluation Sci. Design Co., Inc., N.Y.C., 1952-66; v.p. tech. ops. Oxirane Corp., Houston, also Princeton, N.J., 1966-73; v.p. Halcon Internat., Inc., N.Y.C., 1973—. Fellow Am. Inst. Chem. Engrs. (dir. 1967-69, nat. speaker's bur. 1977—, chmn. central Jersey sect. 1975—); mem. Materials Tech. Inst. (dir. 1977—). Author; The Chemical Plant, 1966. Patentee in energy conservation, pollution abatement, chem. processing. Home: 56 Finley Rd Princeton NJ 08540 Office: 2 Park Ave New York City NY 10016

HUCKMAN, LOUIS FILLMORE, dentist; b. Newark, Nov. 11, 1903; s. Meyer and Sarah (Fischtrom) H.; D.D.S., U. Pa., 1927; m. Mollie Lehman, June 7, 1931; children—Lenore Ruth (Mrs. Richard Turteltaub), Dr. Michael Saul. Gen. practice dentistry, Irvington, N.J., 1927—; staff dental clinic Newark Beth Israel Hosp., 1928-54; sch. dentist, Irvington, 1938. Dental examiner SSS, 1941-45. Founding mem. Hebrew U. Hadassah Dental Sch., Israel. Recipient SSS medal. Mem. Am., N.J. dental socs., Alpha Omega (pres. 1947), Omicron Kappa Upsilon. Jewish. Mason, Kiwanian. Clubs: Dental, University Pennsylvania Alumni (pres. 1952), Crestmont Country, Unity (pres. 1957) (Maplewood). Home: 26 Berkshire Rd Maplewood NJ 07040 Office: 744 Chancellor Ave Irvington NJ 07111

HUDDLESTON, ROBERT LESLIE, metallurgist; b. Covington, Va., Nov. 15, 1928; s. George Leslie and Leslie Blanche (McCaleb) H.; B.S. Metall. Engring., Va. Poly. Inst., 1950; M. Liberal Arts, Johns Hopkins U., 1971; m. Shirley Jean Reynolds, May 29, 1953; children—Rebecca, Robert Leslie, Emily. Metallurgist, Detroit Induction Heating Co., 1950-51; ordnance engr. Aberdeen Proving Ground (Md.), 1951-53, supervisory metallurgist, 1956-74, chief, phys. test br., material testing directorate, 1974—; sr. metallurgist Koppers Co., Balt., 1953-54; project leader Quadripartite Standardization Project, 1974—; mem. NATO Working Party on Standardization, 1975—. State div. dir. Izaak Walton League Am., 1974—. Registered profl. engr., Calif. Served with Ordnance Corps. U.S. Army, 1954-56. Fellow Am. Soc. Nondestructive Testing; mem. Am. Soc. Metals, ASTM, Am. Def. Preparedness Assn., Nat. Rifle Assn., Alpha Phi Omega. Republican. Mem. Christian Ch. Contbr. articles to profl. jours. Home: 301 Glenville Rd Churchville MD 21028 Office: Commander USAAPG Attention STEAP-MT-G Aberdeen Proving Ground MD 21005

HUDGENS, (LUTHER) ELMORE, religious found. exec.; b. Kansas City, Mo., Dec. 9, 1916; s. Luther Elmore and Georgia May (Mott) H.; student Baylor U., Waco, Tex., 1935-39, Episcopal Theol. Sem. of SW, Austin, Tex., 1967-69; m. Kathleen Dorothy Sherrill, Jan. 24, 1943; children—Sherrill Anne (Mrs. C. Aaron McNeece), Elmore McNair. With Met. Life Ins. Co., Waco, Tex., 1950-61; field sec. Brotherhood of St. Andrew, York, Pa., 1964-66, gen. sec., 1969—; a founder, sec. Faith Alive, 1970—; active Episcopal Charismatic Fellowship; founder Pews Action. Served to lt. comdr. USNR, 1941-46; PTO. Home: 707 Hanover Rd York PA 17404 Office: 373 W Market St PO Box 21 York PA 17405

HUDSON, EDWIN MORRIS, psychologist, human factors cons., educator; b. Perkasie, Pa., Jan. 24, 1922; s. Richard Carroll and Clara Elizabeth (Beyer) H.; B.A., Temple U., 1952, M.A., 1953; Ph.D, Columbia U., 1960; m. Caryl Ellen Johnson, Mar. 1964. Physiol. psychologist to NAVAIRDEVCEN, Johnsville, Pa., 1955-60; chief human factors Otis Elevator Co., N.Y.C., 1960-65; mgr. human factors Kollsman Instrument Co., Syosset, N.Y., 1965-69; sr. research asso. Center for Community Research, N.Y.C., 1971-76; prof. psychology William Paterson Coll., Wayne, N.J., 1975-79, chmn. dept. psychology, 1975-79; head research sect. human factors Sperry Systems Mgmt., Gt. Neck, N.Y., 1979—; cons. on nursing home care, 1974-76; cons. on human factors, 1973—. Served with U.S. Maritime Service, 1942-46. Grantee HEW, 1971-76, Noble Found., 1976-77. Author 25 sci. monographs. Patentee in field of aircraft instruments and simulators. Office: G-7 Sperry Systems Mgmt Great Neck NY 11020

HUDSON, GRACE ALBERTA POWERS, editor, writer, artist; b. Ramer, Tenn., July 9; d. James Ernest and Sallie Verdelle (Jones) Powers; student U. Tenn., 1923; diploma in Classics, Union U., 1923, A.B. in Violin, 1925; M.S., Iowa State U., 1928; student Corcoran Sch. Art, Washington, 1930-31, 59-60; m. Print Hudson, July 17. Home economist, Tenn., Iowa, 1923-31; pioneer child devel. and nursery sch., 1929-40; mem. Nat. Commn. on Edn., Athens; adviser FAO, ECA, AThens, 1947-49, Lisbon, Portugal, 1949-51, Nat. Womens Com., 1947-49, editor-writer Leaves mag., Washington, 1972—; lectr. in field. Mem. governing bd. YWCA, Washington, 1958-62; staff Sibley Hosp. Guild, Washington; founder, pres. Fgn. Friends of Creche, Athens, Am. Opera Scholarship Soc.; mem. women's com. Wolf Trap Farm Assos.; mem. benefit com. Am. Cancer Assn., bd. govs. Salvation Army Aux. Recipient Emily Gates Nat. award, 1938; citations Union U., Nat. Bd. Children's Shelter; YWCA Service award; citation for outstanding service, Salvation Army Aux., 1976-77; Distinguished Achievement citation in recognition of outstanding profl. achievement, Iowa State U., 1978, others. Mem. Nat. League Am. Pen Women (v.p. Washington 1974-76, nat. corr. sec. 1976-78, nat. v.p. 1978—, officer nat. bd. 1976—; 1st prize non-fiction award 1975, D.C. 1st prize award in watercolor paintings 1977), Am. Assn. Fgn. Service Women, Assn. Hist. Preservation, Nat. Soc. Colonial Dames, D.A.R., P.E.O., Pi Gamma Mu, Chi Omega. Clubs: Am. Newspaper Women's of Washington; Nat. Press; Capital Speakers (governing bd.), Garden, Art; Book (Spring Valley, Wesley Heights). Editor: (propectus) Research in Home Economics, 1937-40. Home: 5109 Upton St NW Washington DC 20016 Office: 4101 Sangamore St NW Washington DC 10016

HUDSON, JANE DUCLOS, mgmt. analyst; b. Great Barrington, Mass., Sept. 23, 1949; d. Edward Warren and Elaine Duclos (Connelly) H.; B.A. magna cum laude, Newton Coll. of Sacred Heart, 1971; postgrad. Syracuse U., 1971-72; M.A., George Washington U., 1975; m. Donald Lee Borod; Social sci. analyst Fed. Hwy. Adminstrn., Washington, 1972-73; mgmt. intern GSA, Washington, 1973-74, mgmt. analyst, 1974-75; mgmt. analyst Nat. Archives and Records Service, Washington, 1976-78; mgmt. analyst Nat. Archives and Records Service, N.Y.C., 1978—; lectr. pub. adminstrn. Southeastern U., Washington, 1975. Maxwell fellow Syracuse U., 1971-72, Herbert H. Lehman fellow, 1971-72. Roman Catholic. Office: 26 Federal Plaza New York NY 10007

HUDSON, NORMAN WRIGHT, forester; b. Burlington, Vt., June 9, 1929; s. James Calvert and Mary Louise (Wright) H.; B.S., U. Mass., 1956; m. Constance A. Bernardini, June 8, 1957; children—John Stephen, Sue Ann, David Scott. State lands forester Dept. Forests and Parks, State of Vt., Montpelier, 1956-57, forester Essex County, 1957-59, Washington County, 1959-70, asst. to chief, 1970-71, chief, 1971—. Chmn. Office Econ. Opportunity, Montpelier, 1968-69; commr. parks Montpelier, 1968—. Served with AUS, 1946-48. Registered land surveyor, Vt. Mem. Soc. Am. Foresters (sec.-treas. New Eng. sect. 1975-76, vice chmn. 1976-77, chmn. 1977-78), N.H.-Vt. Christmas Tree Assn. (sec. 1958, dir. 1971—), Elk. Home: 27 North St Montpelier VT 05602 Office: Dept Forests and Parks Montpelier VT 05602

HUDSON, ROBERT MCKIM, phys. chemist; b. Morristown, N.J., Oct. 1, 1926; s. Earl Austin and Florence Opal (McKim) H.; B.S., Yale, 1947, Ph.D., 1950; m. Jean Harris, Jan. 26, 1952; children—Robert Harris, Barbara Jean. Research chemist U.S. Steel Corp., Pitts., 1950-60, asso. research cons., 1960-78, research cons., 1978—. Mem. Am. Chem. Soc., Yale Alumni Assn., Sigma Xi. Republican. Presbyterian. Club: Masons. Contbr. articles to profl. jours. Patentee in field. Home: 1618 Williamsburg Pl Pittsburgh PA 15235 Office: US Steel Research Lab Monroeville PA 15146

HUEBNER, CHARLES AUGUSTUS, electric co. exec.; b. Budapest, Hungary, May 17, 1935; s. Andrew N. and Ann (Schmidlechner) H.; came to U.S., 1950, naturalized, 1955; B.S. in Mech. Engring. summa cum laude, U. Detroit, 1958; M.S. in Astronautics, Mass. Inst. Tech., 1960; Ph.D. in Mgmt., Am. U., 1967; m. Suzan Lawlor, June 13, 1959; children—Charles John, Christine M., Diane M., Andrea E. Research engr. Ford Motor Co., Dearborn, Mich., 1958; chief, earth orbital mission studies Manned Space Flight, NASA, Washington, 1962-68; dir. planning, mgr. new product devel. Am. Can Co., Greenwich, Cdnn., 1968-71; v.p., dir. planning AMF, Inc., White Plains, N.Y., 1971-75; staff exec. strategic planning Gen. Electric Co., Fairfield, Conn., 1975—; mem. U.S. Govt. sponsored trade mission to Hungary, 1974. Chmn. finance com. Diocese of Bridgeport Synod, Roman Catholic Ch., 1970-71; chmn. St. Luke Finance Com., Westport, Conn., 1974—. Served to capt. USAF, 1958-62. Recipient Thiokol award Am. Rocket Soc., 1960, Pres.'s award U. Detroit, 1958; named Engring. Grad. of Year, U. Detroit, 1958, Distinguished Mil. Grad., 1958. Tau Beta Pi fellow, 1958. Mem. Am. Soc. Aeros. and Astronautics, IEEE, N.Am. Soc. Corp. Planners, Blue Key, Sigma Xi, Tau Beta Pi, Alpha Sigma Nu. Club: Patterson (Fairfield). Home: 233 Bayberry Ln Westport CT 06880 Office: 3135 Easton Turnpike Fairfield CT 06431

HUEBNER, MILDRED HARRIET, educator; b. Buffalo, Dec. 6, 1913; d. Harrington Warner and Gertrude (Weber) Huebner; B.S., Edinboro State Tchrs. Coll., 1939; M.A., Western Res. U., 1947, Ed.D., 1955. Tchr. pub. schs., Girard Twp., Pa., 1937-41, Erie, Pa., 1941-51; asst. prin. various schs., Erie, 1951-53; asst. prof. edn. Western Res. U., Cleve., 1953-59; asso. prof. edn. So. Conn. State Coll., New Haven, 1959-61, prof. edn., 1961—; dir. Reading Center, 1959—. Mem. Internat., N.E. reading assns., NEA, Nat. Soc. for Study Edn., Conn. Assn. Reading Research, AAUP, AAUW. Author: (with Mary C. Austin and Clifford L. Bush) Reading Evaluation, 1961; (with Clifford L. Bush) Strategies for Reading, 1970. Contbr. articles to profl. jours. Home: 15 Santa Fe Ave Hamden CT 06517 Office: So Conn State Coll New Haven CT 06515

HUEBNER, STEPHEN JUDE, hosp. adminstr.; b. N.Y.C., Apr. 12, 1955; s. Gilbert Dolan and Phyllis (Glynn) H.; B.A., Coll. William and Mary, 1976; M.A., Central Mich. U., 1978; m. Diane Elizabeth Arnold, July 3, 1976. Dir. materials mgmt. Hosp. Center at Orange, N.J., 1978—. Served as 2d lt. Med. Service Corps, U.S. Army, 1976-78. Decorated Army Commendation medal. Mem. Nat. Assn. Hosp. Purchasing Mgmt., Am. Soc. Hosp. Purchasing and Materials Mgmt., Am. Pub. Health Assn., Am. Acad. Health Adminstrn., Res. Officers Assn. Home: 704A Troy Towers 40 Conger St Bloomfield NJ 07003

HUEFFMAN, ROBERT ARVID, elec. insulated wire co. exec.; b. New Haven, Mar. 4, 1933; s. Arthur George and Ellen Matilda (Hellstorm) H.; student U. New Haven, 1963; m. Delma Jane Bauer, July 2, 1955; children—Mark, Melanie, Jennifer. Mgr. data center Wallace Silversmiths Co., Wallingford, Conn., 1951-59, Am. Chain & Cable, Bridgeport, Conn., 1960-62, Cerro Wire & Cable, New Haven, 1962-69; v.p. systems, United Info. Corp., New Haven and Hartford, Conn., 1969-70; mgr. data center Rockbestos Co., New Haven, 1970—. Served with USN, 1951-55. Mem. Data Processing Mgmt. Assn. (sec. 1960). Republican. Lutheran. Club: Smithsonian Inst. Home: 48 Winding Rd Madison CT 06443 Office: 205 Nicoll St New Haven CT 06511

HUET, JAMES ARMAND, realtor; b. New Kensington, Pa., Nov. 20, 1930; s. Armand Victor and Helen (Soentgen) H.; B.S., Pa. State U., 1952; m. Carole Thomas Mosley, Sept. 10, 1954; children—Thomas, James C., John, David. Farmer, Tarentum, Pa., 1956-62; research technician Alcoa, New Kensington, Pa., 1962-66; salesman R.F. Morgan realtor, New Kensington, 1966-68; prin. James A. Huet, Realtor, Tarentum, 1970—; instr. Pa. State U., New Kensington. Served with M.C., AUS, 1954-56. Mem. Allegheny Valley C. of C. (dir., 1971—), Greater Allegheny Kiski Area Bd. Realtors (pres. 1972, 77), Pa. Assn. Realtors (v.p. 1974-75), Nat. Assn. Realtors, Ind. Fee Appraisers, Tarentum Hist. and Landmarks Soc. (sec.-treas.). Republican. Roman Catholic. Club: Optimist. Home: 1127 Park St Tarentum PA 15084 Office: 323 E 6th Ave Tarentum PA 15084

HUETTNER, RICHARD ALFRED, lawyer; b. N.Y.C., Mar. 25, 1927; s. Alfred F. and Mary (Reilly) H.; Marine Engrs. license, N.Y. State Maritime Acad., 1947; B.S., Yale Sch. Engring., 1949; J.D., U. Pa. Law Sch., 1952; m. Mary R. Harrington, 1955 (div. 1970); children—Jennifer Mary, Barbara Bryan; m. 2d, Eunice Bizzell Dowd, Aug. 22, 1971; stepchildren—Marcus B. Dowd, Elizabeth B. Dowd. Admitted to D.C. bar, 1952, N.Y. bar, 1954, U.S. Ct. Mil. Appeals bar, 1953, U.S. Ct. Claims, 1961, U.S. Supreme Ct. bar, 1969, U.S. Customs and Patent Appeals bar, 1969, also other fed. cts.; registered to practice U.S. Patent Office, 1957, Canadian Patent Office, 1968; engr. Jones & Laughlin Steel Corp., 1954-55; asso. atty. Kenyon and Kenyon, 1955-61, mem. firm, 1961-69; mem. firm Kenyon & Kenyon Reilly Carr & Chapin, N.Y.C., 1969—, specialist in patent, trademark and copyright law. Trustee N.J. Shakespeare Festival, 1972—, sec., 1977—; trustee Colonial Symphony Orch., 1972—, mem. exec. com., 1972—, v.p., 1974-76, pres., 1976—; trustee Overlook Hosp., Summit, N.J., 1978—; chmn. Yale Alumni Schs. Com. N.Y., 1972-78, mem. Yale U. Council, 1978—; chmn. bd. overseers N.J. Consortium Performing Arts, 1972-74; bd. dirs. Yale U. Communications Bd., 1978—. Served from midshipman to lt. USNR, 1945-47, 52-54; ret. 1967; certified JAG trial counsel, 1953. Asso. fellow Silliman Coll. Yale U., 1976—. Mem. Am., N.Y. State bar assns., Assn. Bar City N.Y., N.Y. Patent Law Assn. (chmn. meetings com. 1961-64, chmn. econ. matters com. 1966-69, 72-74), AAAS, N.Y. Acad. Scis., N.Y. County Lawyers Assn., Fed. Bar Council, Internat. Patent and Trademark Assn., Am. Judicature Soc., Yale Sci. Engring. Assn. (exec. bd. 1972—, v.p. 1973-75, pres. 1975-78). Clubs: Down Town Assn., Yale (N.Y.C.); Yale of Central N.J. (trustee 1973—, pres. 1975-77); Morris County Golf (Convent, N.J.); Field (Morristown, N.J.); The Grads. (New Haven). Home: 150 Green Ave Madison NJ 07940 Office: 59 Maiden Ln New York City NY 10038

HUFF, JOSEPH ANTHONY, counselor; b. Boston, Apr. 23, 1941; s. Joseph Francis and Rita Thresa (Hickey) H.; B.A., Emerson Coll., 1963; M.Ed., Boston State Coll., 1972; Ed.M., Boston U., 1976, postgrad. in counseling psychology, 1976—; m. Jenna Lucente, Aug. 23, 1975; children—Joseph Jude, Michael Lucente. Radio announcer, program cons. Sta.-WEIM, Fitchburg, Mass., 1965-66; tchr. English and econs. Columbus High Sch., Boston, 1966-68; tchr. lang. arts Cutler Jr. High Sch., Groton, Conn., 1968-75; counseling intern Center for Alt. Edn., Boston, 1975-76; teaching asst. Boston U., 1977-78; counseling intern Boston U.-Boston Public Schs. Dist. I Collaborative, 1976-78, counseling cons., 1978—. Cert. tchr. English, Mass., Conn.; cert. guidance counselor, Mass. Mem. Am. Personnel and Guidance Assn., Am. Sch. Counselor Assn., Mass. Psychol. Assn. (student affiliate), Pi Lambda Theta. Democrat. Roman Catholic. Author: Strictly Grammar, 1978. Home: 66 Sunnyside St Hyde Park MA 02136

HUG, RICHARD ERNEST, environ. co. exec.; b. Paterson, N.J., Jan. 11, 1935; s. Gustave T. and Nelly H.; B.S., Duke U., 1956, M.F., 1957; m. Lois-ann Schack, Sept. 1, 1956; children—Donald R., Cynthia A. Engr., forest products div. Koppers Co., Inc., Pitts., 1957-62; tech. rep., 1962-66, tech. sales rep., 1966-68, area sales mgr., 1968-70, mgr. product devel., 1970-72, gen. mgr. laminated products, 1972-73, v.p., gen. mgr. environ. systems div., 1973-74, corporate v.p., 1974—; pres. Environ. Elements Corp. subs. Koppers Co., Inc., Balt., 1974—. Bd. dirs. Blue Cross Md., 1974—; mem. exec. bd. Balt., Area council Boy Scouts Am., 1976—, Balt. Aquarium, 1976—, Fair Oaks Community Assn., 1978—; mem. econ. devel. council Greater Balt. Com., 1978—; asso. campaign chmn. United Way Central Md., 1977, 78. Mem. Young Presidents Orgn. (chmn. chpt. devel. 1977-78, chmn. edn. 1978), Forest Products Research Soc., Am. Wood Preservers Assn., Indsl. Gas Cleaning Inst. (forward planning com. 1976-78, govt. relations com. 1977-78). Republican. Presbyterian. Clubs: Duquesne (Pitts.); Center (Balt.). Home: 247 Oak Ct Severna Park MD 21203 Office: PO Box 1318 Baltimore MD 21203

HUGG, TERRY WAYNE, psychiatrist; b. Lake City, Ark., June 13, 1943; s. Eugene O'Neil and Imogene Lea (Martin) H.; B.S. in Chemistry, Baylor U., 1966, M.D., 1971; m. Linda Mae Wells, June 10, 1967 (div. June 1973); 1 dau., Hillery Leonore. Resident in psychiatry NIMH/St. Elizabeth's Hosp. and Columbia-Presbyn. Med. Center/N.Y. State Psychiat. Inst., 1971-77; staff psychiatrist St. Elizabeth's Hosp., Washington, 1972—; attending psychiatrist Presbyn. Hosp., N.Y.C., 1975-77; asst. dir. children's inpatient service N.Y. State Psychiat. Inst., 1977—; tchr. Columbia Coll. Physicians and Surgeons, 1974—; child psychiatrist Riverdale Mental Health Clinic, 1978—; psychiat. cons. Lexington Sch. for the Deaf. Diplomate Am. Bd. Psychiatry and Neurology. Mem. AMA, Am. Psychiat. Assn., Am. Acad. Child Psychiatry, AAAS, N.Y. Acad. Sci., A.K. Rice Inst., Inst. Applied Study of Social Systems. Author:

(poetry) Rough Edges, 1978. Home: 118 E 92 St New York City NY 10028 Office: 40 E 89 St New York City NY 10028

HUGGINS, GEORGE RICHARDSON, obstetrician, gynecologist; b. St. Louis, Oct. 18, 1937; s. George K. and Eleanor L. (Richardson) H.; A.B., DePauw U., 1959; M.D., U. Mo., 1963; m. Martha Irene Obear, Aug. 16, 1958; children—George, Eric, Jonathan, Lisa. Intern, Barnes Hosp., St. Louis, 1964; resident in obstetrics and gynecology U. Mo., 1964-67; asst. prof. obstetrics and gynecology Hosp. U. Pa., 1972-77, asso. prof., 1977—, dir. family planning program, 1972—; chmn. family planning adv. bd. Commonwealth Pa.; tng. cons. Region III HEW. Served with M.C., USN, 1967-69. Recipient C.V. Mosby award U. Mo., 1959. Mem. Am. Coll. Obstetricians and Gynecologists, Am. Fertility Soc., Assn. Planned Parenthood Physicians (sec.), Alpha Omega Alpha. Home: 3400 Spruce St Philadelphia PA 19104

HUGHES, AUDREY CLAYRE, lab. coordinator; b. Cambridge, Mass., Oct. 27, 1924; d. Arthur E. and Clara J. (Walther) H.; B.A., Coll. Notre Dame, 1945; M.A., Boston U., 1950, postgrad., 1950-55; postgrad. Tufts U., 1950-54, Rensselear Poly. Inst., 1952. Med. technologist Sacred Heart Hosp., Manchester, N.H., 1945-46; med. technologist St. John's Hosp., Lowell, Mass., 1946-48, instr. anatomy, physiology and microbiology, 1952-56, chief med. technologist, 1956-74, lab. coordinator, 1974—; instr. advanced biology Mt. St. Mary Coll., Hooksett, N.H., 1948-52; instr. anatomy and physiology Lowell (Mass.) Gen. Hosp., 1952-56; asst. prof. biology and math. Lowell State Coll., 1952-56; adj. clin. instr. U. Lowell, 1977—; mem. Mass. Gov.'s Council Adv. Com. on Clin. Labs. Mem. Mass. Assn. Med. Technology, Am. Soc. Med. Technologists, Am., Mass. assns. blood banks, Am. Assn. Clin. Chemists, New Eng. Clin. Radioassay Soc., New Eng. Med. Lab. Sci. Edn. Forum, New Eng., Catholic hosp. assns., Am. Soc. Clin. Pathologists, Tri Beta. Democrat. Roman Catholic. Office: Saint Johns Hosp Hospital Dr Lowell MA 01852

HUGHES, BLAKE, publishing co. exec.; b. N.Y.C., June 24, 1914; s. Ferdinand Holme and Ines (de Cordova) H.; A.B. summa cum laude, Dartmouth Coll., 1936; degre de civilisation Sorbonne U., Paris, 1935; postgrad. Columbia U., 1936-37; m. Betty Jean Wolf, Aug. 26, 1951; children—Diane Elizabeth, Brian Blake. Salesman, Edward B. Smith & Co., Smith, Barney & Co., investment bankers, N.Y.C., 1936-38; salesman N.Y. Life Ins. Co., N.Y.C., 1939-40; promotion mgr. Engring. News Record, Constrn. Methods McGraw-Hill Inc., N.Y.C., 1947-50; promotion mgr., dir. mktg. Archtl. Record, F.W. Dodge Corp., N.Y.C., 1951-61, asso. pub. Archtl. Record, McGraw Hill Inc., 1961-68, pub., 1968—; pub. Archtl. Record Books, 1970—. Trustee Unity (Maine) Coll., 1970—; pres. Internat. Archtl. Found., 1973—. Served to lt. USNR, 1940-45. Decorated Order of Fatherland War (Russia). Mem. Archtl. League N.Y., Sales Execs. Club (N.Y.C.), Phi Beta Kappa, Delta Sigma Rho. Episcopalian (vestryman). Home: 25 Chestnut Dr Hastings-on-Hudson NY 10706 Office: 1221 Ave of Americas New York City NY 10020*

HUGHES, HARRY ROE, lawyer, gov. Md.; b. Easton, Md., Nov. 13, 1926; s. Jonathan Longfellow and Helen (Roe) H.; B.S., U. Md., 1949; student Mt. St. Mary's Coll., 1944-45; LL.B., George Washington U., 1952; m. Patricia Ann Donoho, June 30, 1951; children—Ann Donoho, Elizabeth Roe. Admitted to Md. bar, 1952; partner firm Everngam & Hughes, Denton, Md., 1952-59; practiced in Denton, 1959-73; sec. Md. Dept. Transp., 1971-78; gov. Md., 1978—; mem. Md. Ho. of Dels., 1954-58; mem. Md. Senate, 1958-70, majority floor leader, chmn. finance com.; chmn. Md. Democratic State Com. Trustee Meml. Hosp., 1954-60. Served with USNR, 1944-45. Mem. Am., Md., Caroline County bar assns. Home: 20 Bouton Green Baltimore MD 21210 Office: Office of Gov State House Annapolis MD 21404

HUGHES, JAMES JOSEPH, pub. safety ofcl.; b. N.Y.C., Nov. 14, 1934; s. James Joseph and Mary Agnes (Walsh) H.; B.B.A., City Coll. N.Y., 1962; LL.B., U. Chgo., 1954; m. June 28, 1957; children—Anthony James, James Michael. Admitted to Ill. bar, 1955, Fla. bar, 1955; comdg. officer detective bur. Pelham (N.Y.) Police Dept., 1957-67; mgr. Burns Security Services Internat., Bridgeport, Conn., 1967-70; dir. pub. safety Maritime Coll., State U. N.Y., N.Y.C., 1970—; dir. Municipal Police Tng. Council Sch., 1973, 76; lectr. N.Y. Police Acad., 1974. Chmn. Advisory Panel for Promotional and Coll. Tng. NYC Fire Dept. with John Jay Coll. of Criminal Justice, 1976. Counsellor in law Boy Scouts Am. Served to capt. USMC, 1950-57. Decorated Silver Star; recipient commendation meritory service Bd. Trustees State Univ. N.Y., 1972-74. Mem. Internat. Chief's of Police, Am. Fed. Police, Am. Fed. Police, Police and Fire Found. (charter), Am. Legion. Clubs: Elks (Stamford, Conn.). Home: 10 Ball Ave Yonkers NY 10701 Office: State Univ NY Maritime Coll New York City NY 10465

HUGHES, JANET BLANCHE, assn. exec.; b. Buffalo, Feb. 18, 1920; d. Alpheus B. and Alice L. (Lalor) Dutro; B.A., U. Buffalo, 1965; m. G. Thomas Hughes, Oct. 23, 1948; children—Donald, Brent G. With U.S. Dept. Justice, Washington, 1943; asst. dir. pub. relations Greater Buffalo chpt. ARC, 1952-65, dir., 1965—; cons. in field. Mem. Pub. Relations Assn. Western N.Y. (pres. 1969), Pub. Relations Soc. Am. (v.p. Niagara Frontier chpt. 1976), Quota Club Buffalo (pres. 1970), Frontier Press Club, Niagara Frontier Editors Assn., Nat. Publicity Council. Republican. Home: 785 Potomac Ave Buffalo NY 14209 Office: 786 Delaware Ave Buffalo NY 14209

HUGHES, JOHN, journalist; b. Neath, South Wales, Apr. 28, 1930; s. Evan John and Dellis (Williams) H.; came to U.S., 1954, naturalized, 1965; grad. Stationers' and Newspapermakers' Sch., London, 1946; Nieman fellow Harvard U., 1961-62; LL.D., Colby Coll., 1978; m. Vera Elizabeth Pockman, Aug. 20, 1955; children—Wendy Elizabeth, Mark Evan. Mem. staffs Natal Mercury, Durban, South Africa, 1946-49, 52-54, Daily Mirror, London News Agy., Reuters, London, Eng., 1949-52; with Christian Sci. Monitor, Boston, 1954—, Africa corr., 1955-61, asst. fgn. editor, 1962-64, Far Eastern corr., 1964-70, mng. editor, 1970, editor, 1970—; dir., cons. News Jour. Co., Wilmington, Del., 1975-78. Broadcaster Westinghouse Broadcasting Co., Boston, 1962-64, from Far East, 1964-70. Recipient Pulitzer prize internat. reporting, 1967; Overseas Press Club award best daily newspaper reporting from abroad, 1970; Yankee Quill award Sigma Delta Chi, 1977. Mem. Am. Soc. Newspaper Editors (dir. 1972—, pres. 1978—, mem. Pulitzer prize adv. com. 1975—). Clubs: Overseas Press (N.Y.C.); Hong Kong Country, Fgn. Corrs. Hong Kong; Harvard (Boston). Author: The New Face of Africa, 1961; Indonesian Upheaval, 1967. Office: 1 Norway St Boston MA 02115*

HUGHES, JONAH, hosp. ofcl.; b. Eudora, Ark., May 10, 1938; s. Roosevelt and Maude (Parker) H.; Asso. Arts and Scis., Burlington County Coll., 1974, A.A., 1976; B.S., So. Ill. U., 1977; m. Margaret Willis, June 12, 1958; children—Gwendolyn, Belinda, Michael, Brian. Enlisted man U.S. Navy, 1955-75; med. technician U.S. Naval Hosp., San Diego, 1958-62; med. technician U.S. Navy Hosp., Phila., 1963-68, chief med. technician, adminstrv. asst., 1968-71; chief med. procurement and minority affairs asst. U.S. Navy, Ryukyu Islands, 1970-71; adminstrv. asst. physiol. research unit U.S. Navy, Phila., 1972-75; adminstrv. asst., dir. materials mgmt. Garden State Community Hosp., Marlton, N.J., 1975—. Mem. budget and allocations com. Burlington County United Way; committeeman 7th Dist. Democratic Com., 1976—; chmn. municipal services com. Polit. Action Coaltion, Willingboro, N.J., 1976. Mem. N.J. Purchasing Agts. Assn., Fleet Res. Assn. Baptist. Home: 59 Peppermint Ln Willingboro NJ 08046 Office: Route 73 and Brick Rd Marlton NJ 08053

HUGHES, LLOYD LYNNELL, hosp. adminstr.; b. Independence, Kans., Sept. 6, 1920; s. Lloyd Lowrey and Jess (O'Connell) H.; A.B., Washburn U., 1942, LL.B., 1947; M.H.A., U. Minn., 1951; m. Isabel Neiswanger, June 28, 1947; children—Lucinda, Nancy, Melissa, David Lloyd. Admitted to Kan. bar, 1947; asst. gen. counsel Kans. Corp. Commn., 1947-49; asst. dir. R.I. Hosp., 1951-56; supt. U. Wis. Hosp., 1957-60; dep. dir. R.I. Hosp., 1960-62, exec. dir., 1962-70, exec. v.p., 1970-73, pres., 1973—; asso. prof. hosp. adminstrn. U. Wis., 1958-60; clin. preceptor U. Minn. program hosp. adminstrn., 1958-60, 62—. Mem. R.I. Adv. Commn. on Heart Disease, Cancer and Stroke, 1969—; rep. Council of Teaching Hosps. to Am. Assn. Med. Coll., 1969-72; councillor accreditation council ambulatory health care Joint Commn. Accreditation Hosps., 1975—. Trustee, Tri-State Regional Med. Program, 1972—; bd. mgrs. Bethany Home, Providence, 1969—. Served with U.S. Army, 1943-46. Mem. Hosp. Assn. R.I. (pres. 1967-69, trustee 1969—), New Eng. Hosp. Assembly Polymer Sci-Polymer Physics, Jour. Nonmetals. Contbr. numerous research articles to sci. jours. Home: 211 Berkshire Rd Ithaca NY 14850*

HUGHES, RICHARD ELMER, thoracic surgeon; b. Orange, N.J., Aug. 15, 1923; s. Harry Elmer and Helen Garrabrandt (Wilde) H.; M.D., Harvard U., 1953; m. Doris Yvonne Stump, June 3, 1961; children—Amy Sinclair, Susan Wilde, Sarah Garrabrandt, Abigail Ruff. Intern, Phila. Gen. Hosp., 1953-54; resident York (Pa.) Hosp., 1954-58, Presbyn. Hosp., Pitts., 1958-60; asst. chief of surgery Glenn Dale (Md.) Hosp., 1959-61; attending surgeon George Washington U. Hosp. and Med. Sch., Washington, 1960-64; dir. surgery Peninsula Gen. Hosp., Salisbury, Md., 1970-73, chief div. thoracic surgery, 1970—. Pres. Eastern Shore Heart Assn., 1969-70. Served to lt. USAAF, 1942-46. Diplomate Am. Bd. Thoracic Surgeons. Mem. A.C.S., Soc. Thoracic Surgeons, So. Assn. Thoracic Surgeons, Wicomico County Med. Soc. (pres. 1968-69). Republican. Episcopalian. Clubs: Aesculapian, Harvard Varsity, Harvard of Md., Seagull (Salisbury State Coll.), Oxford Sailing Assn., Eastern Shore Sailing Assn.; Tred Avon Yacht. Performed first open-heart surgery on Eastern Shore. Home: Route 4 Snow Hill Rd Salisbury MD 21801 Office: Suite 7 Medical Center Salisbury MD 21801

HUGHES, RICHARD JOSEPH, b. Florence, N.J., Aug. 10, 1909; student St. Cahrles Coll., 1926-28, St. Joseph's Coll., 1928; LL.B., N.J. Law Sch., 1931. Admitted to N.J. bar, 1932; asst. U.S. atty. Dist. N.J., 1939-45; partner firm Lord & Hughes, Trenton, 1945-48; judge Mercer County (N.J.) Ct., 1948-52; judge Superior Ct. N.J., 1952-59, also assignment jusge Union County; gov. N.J., 1961-70; partner firm Hughes, McElroy, Connell, Foley & Geiser, Newark, after 1970; now chief justice N.J. Supreme Ct., Trenton. Mem. Am. (chmn. commn. on correctional facilities and services), N.J., Mercer County (pres. 1953-54), Essex County bar assns. Home: 90 Westcott Rd Princeton NJ 08540 Office: Supreme Ct NJ State House Annex Trenton NJ 08625*

HUGHES, RICHARD MORRELL, tenor, educator; b. Williams, Iowa, June 2, 1932; s. Thomas B. and Gladys I. (Godsell) H.; B. in Music Edn., Drake U., 1956, M.Mus., 1958; m. Gwendolyn Myrle Smyth, Nov. 24, 1955; children—Thomas Arnold, Susan Kathleen. Oratorio and opera performances Des Moines Symphony Orch., 1956-59; tenor soloist Grace Meth. Ch., Des Moines, Iowa, 1953-59, Chester Hill Meth. Ch., Mt. Vernon, N.Y., 1959-67, First Meth. Ch., Mt. Vernon, 1959, Temple Emanuel, N.Y.C., 1959-60, First Presbyn. Ch., N.Y.C., 1967-76; tenor soloist in U. Recital Series, Drake U., Des Moines, 1958-59; appeared in various recitals, Ill., 1956-59, Mich., 1956-59, Mo., 1956-59; asst. dir. adult choir Grace Meth. Ch., Des Moines, 1957-59; tchr. of music Farrar (Iowa) High Sch., 1957-59; instr. dept. music Alphonsus Coll., Woodcliff Lake, N.J., 1969-74; dir. music First Presbyn. Ch., Mt. Vernon, 1969—; pvt. tchr. voice, N.Y.C., 1964—. Mem. Nat. Assn. Tchrs. of Singing, N.Y. Singing Tchrs. Assn., Phi Mu Alpha, Phi Kappa Lambda. Democrat. Address: 27 W 96th St New York City NY 10025

HUGHES, ROBERT EMMETT, engring. and constrn. co. exec.; b. Pitts., Dec. 12, 1925; s. James H. and Mary Edna (Rice) H.; student U. Pitts.; m. Dolore T. Romanowski, Oct. 6, 1956; children—Karen, Sandra, Robert Emmett, Christopher, Janice. Buyer, Koppers Co., Pitts., 1950-54; purchasing agt. mech. products The Rust Engring. Co., Pitts., 1955-71; purchasing mgr. Far East activities Pullman-Swindell Co., Pitts., 1971—. Adv. Jr. Achievement, Pitts., 1965-69. Served with USAF, 1944-46. Republican. Home: 528 Milbeth Dr Mount Lebanon PA 15228 Office: 441 Smithfield St Pittsburgh PA 15222

HUGHES, WILLIAM JOHN, congressman; b. Salem, N.J., Oct. 17, 1932; s. William W. and Pauline Hughes; A.B., Rutgers U., 1955, J.D., 1958; m. Nancy L. Gibson; children—Nancy Lynne, Barbara Ann, Tama Beth, William John. Admitted to N.J. bar, 1959, since practiced in Ocean City; mem. firm Loveland, Hughes & Garrett; 1st asst. pros. atty., Cape May County, N.J., 1960-70; mem. 94th and 95th Congresses from 2d N.J. Dist. Bd. dirs. Cape May County Drug Abuse Council, 1968—; bd. govs. Shore Meml. Hosp., Sommers Point, N.J., 1972—. Mem. Ocean City Hist. Soc. (dir. 1972—), Ocean City C. of C. (dir. 1960—). Clubs: Masons (past master), Exchange of Ocean City (pres. 1965-66, nat. Big E award 1965). Home: 1019 Wesley Rd Ocean City NJ 08226 Office Office: 436 Cannon Office Bldg Washington DC 20515

HUHEEY, JAMES E(DWARD), chemist, herpetologist, educator; b. Cin., Aug. 2, 1935; s. Edward O'Neill and Catherine (Smythe) H.; B.S., U. Cin., 1957; M.S., U. Ill., 1959, Ph.D., 1961. Research asso. U. Mich., Ann Arbor, 1961; asst. prof. chemistry Worcester (Mass.) Poly. Inst., 1961-65; asst. prof. U. Md., College Park, 1965-68, asso. prof., 1968-75, prof., 1975—; vis. prof. So. Ill. U., Carbondale, 1974-75; dir. Chem. Assos. Md. Recipient Young Chemists award D.C. chpt. Am. Inst. Chemists, 1971; NSF grantee, 1965-67, 75-77, 78—; NSF fellow, 1959; Sigma Xi grantee, 1963; Am. Philos. Soc. grantee, 1974. Mem. Am. Chem. Soc., AAAS, Am. Soc. Icthyologists and Herpetologists, Soc. Study Amphibians and Reptiles (dir.), Herpetologists' League, Ecol. Soc. Am., Soc. Study Evolution. Author: Inorganic Chemistry: Principles of Structure and Reactivity, 1972, 78; (with Arthur Stupka) Amphibians and Reptiles of Great Smoky Mountains National Park, 1968; Diversity and Periodicity: An Inorganic Module, 1973, 78. Contbr. articles to profl. publs. Home: 6909 Carleton Terr College Park MD 20740 Office: Dept Chemistry U Md College Park MD 20742

HUK, JEROME E., psychologist; b. Lviv, Ukraine, Mar. 28, 1943; s. Wladimir and Stefanie M. (Zwir) H.; came to U.S., 1948, naturalized, 1954; B.A., Columbia U., 1969; M.A., U. Colo., 1972; Ph.D., 1973; m. Christine Luckyj, July 12, 1969; 1 son, Alexander Christopher. Teaching asst. U. Colo., Boulder, 1971-72, post doctoral spl. student clin. psychology, 1974-75; research program devel. specialist Mid Continent Regional Ednl. Lab., Kansas City, Mo., 1973-74; intern, Ill. State Psychiatric Inst., Chgo., 1975-76; clin. psychologist VA Hosp., Lyons, N.J., 1976—. NIMH grantee, 1969-73. Mem. Am., N.J. psychol. assns. Club: Center Ct. Tennis. Home: New Providence NJ 07974 Office: 60 Vose Ave South Orange NJ 07079

HUK, MICHAEL JOHN, anesthesiologist; b. Western Ukraine, Apr. 3, 1920; s. John Michael and Maria (Wiatrovicz) H.; M.D., U. Medicine Heidelberg (Germany), 1948; m. Lidia Tatiana Stefanowycz, Oct. 6, 1960; children—Camille (Mrs. Myron Smorodsky), Andrew Michael, Motria Natalie. Came to U.S., 1951, naturalized, 1956. Trainee, Krehl Clinic, Heidelberg, 1949-50; rotating intern St. Mary's Hosp., Hoboken, N.J., 1950-51; resident surgery Meml. Hosp., Morristown, N.J., 1951-52; resident anesthesiology Hahnemann Med. Coll. and Hosp., Phila., 1952-54; practice medicine specializing in anesthesiology, hypnosis, hypnoanalysis and pain-relieving therapy, Mountainside, N.J., 1958—; head dept. anesthesia St. James Hosp., Newark, 1954-59; staff anesthesiologist Muhlenberg Hosp., Plainfield, N.J., 1959—, cons. physician, respiratory care unit dept., 1968—. Fellow Acad. Medicine N.J.; mem. Internat. Assn. Anesthesiologists, Internat. Medico-Legal Soc., Internat. Anesthesia Research Soc., Am., N.J. socs. anesthesiologists, AMA, Med. Soc. N.J., Union County Med. Soc., Plainfield Med. Assn., Am. Inst. Hypnosis, Am. Acupuncture Soc. Club: Somerset (N.J.) Tennis. Address: 1513 Fox Trail Mountainside NJ 07092

HUK, STEFANIE MICHALINA (MRS. WLADIMIR HUK), physician; b. Lwiw, Poland; d. Stefan and Tekla (Kostewych) Zwir; student U. Lwiw, 1939-44, U. Graz, 1944; M.D., U. Vienna (Austria), 1946; m. Wladimir Huk, May 2, 1942 (dec. June 23, 1975); children—Jerome, Larissa; came to U.S., 1948, naturalized, 1954. Intern, East Orange (N.J.) Gen. Hosp., 1950-51, resident, 1951-54, asso. pathologist, supr. pathology lab., 1950-58; practice medicine, Newark and South Orange, 1956—; staff physician in charge pulmonary ward East Orange VA Hosp., 1966-70; attending physician Essex County Blood Bank, East Orange, 1964-71; staff physician, asst. med. dir. Seratec Biols., North Brunswick, N.J., 1969—; faculty N.J. Coll. Medicine and Dentistry, 1968-70; med. cons. Essex County Local Med. Assistance Unit, State of N.J. div. Med. Assistance and Health Services, 1970—. Mem. AMA, N.J., Essex County med. socs., Ukrainian Med. Assn. Home and Office: South Orange NJ 07079

HULACK, LAWRENCE BERNARD, pub. relations agy. exec.; b. N.Y.C.; s. Louis and Ethel (Wein) H.; B.A., U. Mich., 1956, M.A., 1958; m. Carol Ann Murphy, May 7, 1967; 1 son, Lance. Reporter Trenton (N.J.) Times, 1958-63; metals editor Fairchild Publs., N.Y.C., 1963-65; sr. account exec. Bell & Stanton, N.Y.C., 1965-68, Wolcott Carlson & Co., N.Y.C., 1968-71; sr. v.p. Lobsenz-Stevens Pub. Relations Co., N.Y.C., 1971-78; cons. Bus. Careers Inc., N.Y.C., 1978—; pres. Lanfred Properties Inc., N.Y.C., 1976—; exec. v.p. Alive Publs., Ltd., pubs. travel books, N.Y.C.; seminar speaker Am. Mgmt. Assn. Pres. W. 80th St. Neighborhood Assn., N.Y.C., 1969-77; trustee Universalist Assn. N.Y., N.Y.C., 1971-73, chmn. nominating com., 1973-74, mem. long range planning com., 1971-73. Co-author: South America on $15 a Day, 7th edit., 1978; Panama Alive, 1975; Venezuela Alive, 1975; Caracas Alive, 1977; Rio Alive, 1978; Guatemala Alive, 1977. Home: 127 W 80th St New York City NY 10024 Office: 400 Park Ave New York City NY 10022

HULL, LEWIS MADISON, ret. aircraft radio co. exec.; b. Great Bend, Kans., Feb. 27, 1898; s. Arthur Sinclair and Orlena June (Madison) H.; A.B., U. Kans., 1917; A.M., 1918; Ph.D., Harvard, 1922; m. Helen Harrison Smith, Dec. 20, 1922; 1 dau., Carolyn June. Asso. physicist U.S. Bur. Standards, Washington, 1918-20; v.p. Radio Frequency Labs., Boonton, N.J., 1922-28; v.p. Aircraft Radio Corp., Boonton, 1928-30, dir., 1928-59, pres., 1930-51, chmn. bd. dirs., 1952-59; pres. Fairway Realty Corp., 1948-51; dir. Tech-Art Plastics, 1935, Ferris Instrument Corp., 1939, LFE Corp., 1958-63, State Bank N.J., 1960-76; expert cons. sec. war, 1943-45. Pres. Boonton Found., 1945-51; chmn. land acquisiton com. Morris County (N.J.) Park Commn., 1961—. Recipient certificate of commendation U.S.A.A.F., 1946, USN, 1947. Fellow IEEE, Radio Club Am. (Armstrong medal); mem. IRE (pres. 1933, Pioneer award). Contbr. articles to profl. jours. and sporting publs.; patentee basic early devels. in radio electronics circuitry. Home: Rural Delivery 1 Powersville Rd Boonton NJ 07005

HULME, ROBERT DUBOIS, mgmt. cons. co. exec.; b. Phila., June 6, 1928; s. Norman and Elisabeth Randall (DuBois) H.; B.S., U. Va., 1950; M.B.A., Temple U., 1953; postgrad. U. Pa., 1960; m. Nancy Williams Kenyon, Sept. 11, 1954 (div.); children—Randall Kenyon, Michael Hatheway, Kimberly Dana. Tng. supr. Sun Co., Inc., Phila., 1950-60; div. personnel mgr. Ford Motor Co., Phila., 1960-64; cons. Towers, Perrin, Forster & Crosby, Inc., Phila., 1964-71, v.p., prin., N.Y.C., 1971—; lectr. bus. Temple U., 1953-61. Auditor Swarthmore (Pa.) Bd. Edn., 1958-59. Served as lt U.S. Army Res., 1951-53. Clubs: Knickerbocker (N.Y.), Racquet (Phila.); Riverton (N.J.) Country; Kennebunk River (Maine). Episcopalian. Home: 319 Nassau St Princeton NJ 08540 Office: 600 3d Ave New York City NY 10016

HULSLANDER, FRANK RAYMOND, chiropractor; b. N. Chelmsford, Mass., June 1, 1928; s. Ralph John and Edith Holt (Matley) H.; ed. Lowell Tech. Inst., 1948, Lincoln Chiropractic Coll., 1952; postgrad. Nat. Chiropractic Coll., 1974; m. Edna Estell Giffin, Sept. 7, 1948; children—Bruce Allin, Douglas Llyod, Deborah Louis, Elizabeth Sampson. Practice chiropractic, Nashua, N.H., 1953—; mem. N.H. Bd. Chiropractic Examiners. Mem. pres.'s council Daniel Webster Coll. Served with U.S. Navy, 1946-48. Named Hon. Dep. Sheriff, Middlesex County, Mass., 1964. Mem. Am., N.H. (dir.) chiropractic assns., N.H. Chiefs of Police Assn. (hon. life). Republican. Clubs: Vesper Country, Boston Gridiron, Masons, Shriners, Elks (Lowell, Mass.). Home and Office: 58 E Dunstable Rd Nashua NH 03060

HULSWIT, MARIUS JAN (MART), actor; b. Maracaibo, Venezuela, May 24, 1940; s. Marius Jan Frederik and Margaretha (deHeus) H.; brought to U.S., 1955, naturalized, 1963; student Hobart Coll., 1958-59, Am. Acad. Dramatic Arts, 1960-61; m. Maria Gellner, June 17, 1961; children—Maria Christina, Jennifer Allison. Stage appearances N.Y. Shakespeare Festival, N.Y.C., 1961-63, Romeo and Juliet, Richard II, 1961, Merchant of Venice, The Tempest, King Lear, Macbeth, 1962, Macbeth, 1963, Amazing Grace, 1967, Jeremy Troy, 1977, In Celebration, 1977; TV appearances in Naked City, 1962, The Defenders, 1963, DuPont Show, 1963, Route 66, The Nurses, The Defenders, Flipper, Hercules, Combat, 1964, Coronet Blue, Dr. Kildare, Combat, The Seaway, 1965, 12 O'Clock High, Flipper, Island of the Lost, 1966, The Desperate Hours, 1967, Directions '68, A Selective Matter, Mannix, 1968, The Guiding Light, 1969—, Primus, 1971; movie roles Come Spy With Me, 1966, A Lovely Way to Die, 1967, Loving, 1969, Doc, 1970. Trustee St. Michael's Montessori Sch., N.Y.C., Bermuda Biol. Sta. Recipient Antoinette Perry Promising Personality award, 1963; named one of top ten actors daytime TV, 1972—, Best Actor Daytime TV, 1978. Mem. Am. Malacological Union, Screen Actors Guild, Actors Equity Assn.,

AFTRA. Club: N.Y. Shell (pres. 1970-72). Home: 680 West End Ave New York City NY 10025

HUMBLE, LEON KARL, elec. mfg. co. exec.; b. Cando, N.D., June 24, 1938; s. Leonard Anthony and Hilda (Maute) H.; B.S. in E.E., Ariz. State U., 1964, M.B.A., 1968; m. Carole Ann Kowalski, June 6, 1964; children—David, Paula, Scott. Test engr. Westinghouse Corp., Muncie, Ind., 1964-66; mgr. engring. Motorola Semiconductor Inc., Phoenix, 1968-74; ops. mgr., Integrated Circuits Group, Nat. Semiconductor Inc., Danbury, Conn., 1974—. Served with U.S. Army, 1956-60. Mem. IEEE. Republican. Lutheran. Club: Cupertino Swim and Racquet. Home: 41 Flax Hill Rd Brookfield CT 06804 Office: Commerce Park Danbury CT 06810

HUME, DAVID JOHN, educator; b. Milton, Ont., Can., Aug. 7, 1940; s. William Robertson and Freida Eileen (Wallis) H.; B.S.A., Ont. Agr. Coll., 1961, M.Sc., 1963; Ph.D., Iowa State U., 1966; m. Jean Alda Fuller, Nov. 24, 1964; children—Janice Elizabeth, Brian Wallis. Asst. prof. crop sci. U. Guelph, Ont., 1966-70, asso. prof., 1970-72, 74—; asso. prof. crop sci. U. Ghana, 1972-74. Mem. Am. Soc. Agronomy, Ont. Inst. Agrologists (past pres. Guelphebr.), Crop Sci. Soc. Am., Agrl. Inst. Can. Asso. editor Agronomy Jour., 1974-77. Contbr. articles to profl. jours. Home: 75 James St W Guelph ON N1G 1E5 Canada Office: Crop Sci Dept U Guelph Guelph ON N1G 2W1 Canada

HUMES, CHARLES WARREN, II, psychologist; b. Cambridge, Mass., Mar. 5, 1924; s. Charles Warren and Alice Elizabeth (Aiksomaitis) H.; B.A., Am. Internat. Coll., 1947; M.A., N.Y. U., 1952; Ed.M., Springfield Coll., 1956; Ed.D., U. Mass., 1968; m. Marilyn Ann Harper, Aug. 7, 1965; children—Rebecca Ellyn, Malinda Maye. Fed. agt. FDA, 1948-49; tng. officer Springfield (Mass.) Armory, 1950-53; pvt. practice psychology, Springfield, 1954-55; sch. psychologist Westfield (Mass.) Pub. Schs., 1955-62, dir. guidance services, 1962-70; dir. pupil personnel services and spl. edn. Greenwich (Conn.) Pub. Schs., 1970—; asso. prof. psychology Springfield Coll., 1969-70; lectr. Westfield State Coll., 1970; sr. lectr. Western Conn. State Coll., 1975—. Bd. dirs. U.S. Civil Service Examiners, 1951-53; v.p. Westfield Area Child Guidance Clinic, 1963-65, pres., 1965-66; mem. Greenwich Hosp. Sch. Nursing Council, 1970-75; mem. Conn. Task Force Gifted, 1975—. Served with U.S. Army, 1943-46. Mem. Am. Psychol. Assn., Am. Personnel and Guidance Assn., Am. Sch. Counselors Assn., Conn. Assn. for Counselor Edn. and Supervision (pres. 1978-79), DAV, Phi Delta Kappa, Phi Kappa Phi. Contbr. articles to profl. publs. Home: 20 Lockwood Dr Old Greenwich CT 06870 Office: Greenwich Pub Schs Havemeyer Bldg Greenwich CT 06830

HUMMEL, FRANCES COPE, research librarian; b. Ann Arbor, Mich., May 13, 1911; d. Edge Taylor and Ella (Mollison) Cope; B.S. magna cum laude, U. Mich., 1930, M.S. in Chemistry, 1931; M.S. in L.S., Columbia, 1962; m. Ralph D. Hummel, Apr. 27, 1935 (dec.); 1 son, Ralph D. (dec.). Analytical chemist, nutrition research asso. Children's Fund, Mich., Detroit, 1931-40; microanalyst Parke Davis & Co., 1941-42; librarian N.Y. Pub. Library, 1961-63, Hawaiian Sugar Planters Assn., 1963-64, Allied Chem. Corp., 1965-71; lit. chemist Alcolac, Inc., Balt., 1971—. Mem. Am. Chem. Soc. (membership chmn. Md. 1975—, women chemist's com. 1976—), Spl. Libraries Assn. (past chpt. sec.), Am. Soc. Info. Sci. (treas. Chesapeake Bay chpt.), Phi Beta Kappa, Phi Kappa Phi, Iota Sigma Pi, Sigma Kappa (past chpt. pres.). Clubs: Univ. Mich., Columbia (Washington). Author papers in field. Home: 9627 Whiteacre Rd Columbia MD 21045 Office: 3440 Fairfield Rd Baltimore MD 21226

HUMPHREY, CHESTER BOWDEN, thoracic and cardiovascular surgeon; b. Marblehead, Mass., July 29, 1939; s. Leonard Graves and Mary Louise (Bowden) H.; B.S., Dickinson Coll., 1961; M.D., Temple U., 1965; m. Joyce Claire Jazwinski, Mar. 20, 1971; 1 son, Andrew Bowden. Intern, Hartford (Conn.) Hosp., 1965-66, resident in surgery, 1966-71; resident in thoracic and cardiovascular surgery USN, San Diego, 1973-75; practice medicine specializing in thoracic and cardiovascular surgery, Hartford, 1976—; asst. clin. prof. cardiovascular surgery U. Calif., San Diego, 1975-76; clin. asso. dept. surgery U. Conn., 1977—. Served with M.C., USN, 1971-76. Diplomate Am. Bd. Med. Examiners, Am. Bd. Surgery, Am. Bd. Thoracic Surgery. Fellow Am. Coll. Chest Physicians, A.C.P., Am. Coll. Cardiology. Home: 20 Owings Rd West Hartford CT 06107 Office: 85 Jefferson St Hartford CT 06106

HUMPHREY, GORDON JOHN, senator; b. Bristol, Conn., Oct. 9, 1940; s. Gordon H. and Regina H.; ed. George Washington U., U. Md., Burnside-Ott Aviation Inst.; m. Patricia Green, June 14, 1978. Civilian ferry pilot throughout U.S. and S. Am., 1964-65; pilot Universal Air Transport Co., Detroit, 1966-67, Allegheny Airlines, 1967-78; mem. U.S. Senate from N.H., 1979—. Founder, state coordinator N.H. Conservative Caucus, 1977-78. Served with USAF, 1958-62. Republican. Baptist. Home: Sunapee NH Office: US Senate Washington DC 20510*

HUMPHREY, STEVEN ROY, lawyer; b. Mineola, N.Y., June 4, 1941; s. James Roy and Adele J. (Steffens) H.; B.A., Wesleyan U., 1963; J.D., Vanderbilt Law Sch., 1966; m. Virginia Sweeney, Aug. 21, 1965; children—Kevin, Karen. Admitted to Mass. bar, 1966, Conn. bar, 1967; mem. firm Robinson, Robinson & Cole, Attys. at Law, Hartford, Conn., 1966—, partner, 1972—. Adj. prof. U. Hartford, 1970-74. Selectman, Town of West Hartford, 1972-76, corp. counsel, 1976—. Mem. Am., Mass., Conn., Hartford County bar assns. Republican. Clubs: Hartford Golf, Univ., Hartford (dir. 1972-78). Home: 30 Bainbridge Rd West Hartford CT 06117 Office: 799 Main St Hartford CT 06103

HUMPHREY, WILLIAM ROLAND, transp. exec.; b. Wilcoe, W.Va., Dec. 2, 1917; s. Church Gordon and Clarice (Booth) H.; student Harvard, 1937, Am. Mgmt. Assn., 1962-63; B.S., U. Hartford, 1968, M.B.A., 1978; student Coll. of Armed Forces, 1968-69; m. Alice E. Waters, June 30, 1956; children by previous marriage—Clarice Hilda, Margaret Helena (Mrs. Anthony P. Botticello), Stephen William. With N.Y., N.H. & H. R.R., 1937-50, traffic rep., Hartford, Conn., 1944-50; asst. traffic mgr. Billings & Spencer Co., Hartford, 1950-52; traffic mgr. Mattatuck Mfg. Co., Waterbury, Conn., 1952-56; traffic rep. Clipper Carloading Co., Chgo., 1957; traffic mgr. Kaman Corp., Bloomfield, Conn., 1957—; adj. prof. bus. and pub. adminstrn. U. Hartford, 1974—. Asst. dir. carrier agy. coordination and liaison Office Emergency Transp., 1964—; asst. dir. resource mgmt. Dept. Transp., 1971—; mem. Nat. Def. Exec. Res., 1964—; mem. Com. Strikes in Transp., Am. Security Council. Trustee East Hartford Inter-Ch. Housing Adminstrn., v.p., 1971—. Served with USCGR, 1940-44. Mem. Aerospace Industries Assn. (nat. vice chmn. traffic com. 1962-63), New Eng. Shipper-Carrier Council, New Eng. Shippers Adv. Bd., Am. Soc. Traffic and Transp., Conn. Internat. Trade Assn., Nat. Def. Transp. Assn., Nat. Assn. Purchasing Mgmt. (lifetime certified purchasing mgr.), Am. Mktg. Assn., Greater Hartford C. of C., charter Oak Shippers Assn., Jr. C. of C., Nat. Wildlife Fedn., Capitol Region Transp. Assn., Internat. Platform Assn., U.S. Naval Inst., Am. Soc. Internat. Execs., Delta Nu Alpha. Methodist (pres. ofcl. bd. 1965—, pres. bd. trustees). Kiwanian. Clubs: Transportation, Conn. Quarter-Century Traffic, City (Hartford). Home: 40 Mountain View Dr East Hartford CT 06108 Office: Old Windsor Rd Bloomfield CT 06002

HUMPHREYS, DONALD ROBERT, mktg. exec.; b. Swampscott, Mass., Mar. 20, 1923; s. Francis Henry and Ethel (Berry) H.; student pub. schs.; m. Ruth Bright Treat, July 30, 1944; children—Richard Charles, Cynthia Louise. Sr. aircraft mechanic crew chief, co-pilot Mass. Inst. Tech. Instrumentation Lab. Bedford, 1947-52; aircraft pilot Northeast Airlines, Calif. Eastern Airlines, Seabrook Farms Co., Seabrook, N.J., 1952-54; asso. engr. small aircraft engine div. Engring Testing Lab., Gen. Electric Co., Lynn, Mass., 1954-56; mgr. sales and service, gen. mgr. aircraft products div. McMillan Indsl. Corp., McMillan Lab., Inc., Ipswich, Mass., 1956-62; gen. sales mgr. E.Coast Aviation Corp., Lexington, 1962-63; mktg. mgr. United Shoe Machinery Corp., Wakefield, Mass., 1963-71; pres. Custom Radius Corp., Topsfield, Mass., 1971—, also chief operating officer, dir.; owner, operator Topsfield Airmotive. Active in civic affairs. Served with USMC, 1941-45. Mem. Am. Mktg. Assn., U.S. Power Squadron, ASME, Soc. Automotive Engrs., Quiet Birdmen. Clubs: Masons; Topsfield Rotary (pres.); Boston Yacht (fleet capt.); Topsfield Ski; New Eng. Aero. Contbr. articles to profl. jours. Home: Pequot Rd Marblehead MA 01945 Office: Custom Radius Corp Topsfield MA 01983

HUMPHREYS, JAMES PATTON, educator; b. Milw., Sept. 26, 1895; s. Otho Fairfield and Sarah Ludington (Patton) H.; student Oxford (Eng.) U., 1914-15; A.B., Williams Coll., 1919; certificate Ecole Libre des Sciences Politiques, Sorbonne, 1919; m. Frances Winchester Green, June 29, 1921; children—Mary Fisher Humphreys Staley, James Patton, Michael Fairfield; m. 2d, Caroline Mead Bartlett, Oct. 20, 1975. Tchr., Kent (Ct.) Sch., 1920-59, head dept. classics, 1935-56, tennis coach, 1921-57; head Mantoloking (N.J.) Tutoring Sch., 1924-50; tchr. Barlow Sch., Amenia, N.Y., 1961-63, Bolles Sch., Jacksonville, Fla., 1963-74; mem. borough council City of Mantoloking, 1926-45; mem. Kent Park Recreational Commn.; trustee Rectory Sch., Pomfret, Conn.; head Civil Def., Kent, 1939-54. Sr. warden St. Andrews Episcopal Ch., Kent; mem. ch. bd. St. Simons-by-the-Sea, Mantoloking. Served with U.S. Army, 1918-19; France. Mem. Classical Assn. New Eng., Conn. Classical Assn. Republican. Author: Latin Grammar, 1958; Latin Backwards, 1961; Language Backwards, 1963. Home: Box 297 South Kent CT 06785

HUMPHREYS, RAYMOND V., orgn. exec.; b. Huntington, W.Va., May 3, 1911; s. Edward and Zelda (Henson) H. Editor, pub. The Chronicle, Huntington, 1930-35; exec. sec. to mayor, Huntington, 1935-36; exec. sec. W. Va. Republican Finance Com., 1937-38; pres. Asso. Underwriters, 1938-42, Raymond V. Humphreys Assos., 1946-51; mem. W.Va. Ho. Dels., 1951-52; cons. to Congressman Will E. Neal, Washington, 1953; v.p. Trial-Craft Corp., 1955-57; exec. v.p. Nat. Sales Corp., 1955-57; field rep. Nat. Republican Congl. Com., Washington, 1957-60, dir. edn. and tng., 1960-63; dir. edn. and tng. Rep. Nat. Com., 1963-69; owner Raymond V. Humphreys Assos., polit. mgmt. consultants, 1969—; founder, dir. Nat. Center for Citizen Involvement, Hurricane, W.Va., 1974—, Raymond V. Humphreys Library of Am. Politics, Manassas, Va., 1976—; author, developer Moblzn. Rep. Enterprise program. Rep. candidate for Ho. of Reps. for 4th Dist. W. Va., 1936-38. Served from pvt. to maj., U.S. Army, 1942-46, maj. U.S. Army, 1951-52. Mem. Nat. (dir. 1950-51). W. Va. (pres. 1948-49) mut. ins. agts. assns. Baptist. Author: Republican Mobilization Training School Handbook, 1960. Contbr. articles to profl. publs. Home: Bull Run Battlefield Haymarket VA 22069 also Lonesome Cedar Farm Hurricane WV Office: 325 Pennsylvania Ave SE Washington DC 20003

HUMPHREYS, ROBERT HAROLD, assn. exec.; b. Washington, Feb. 18, 1936; s. John Harold and Dollie (McCutcheon) H.; student (scholar) George Washington U., 1954-58, postgrad., 1962-63; m. Beverly Williams Bailey, June 10, 1972; 1 stepson, Michael Jay. Congl. aide U.S. Ho. Reps., Washington, 1954-58; planning officer Asian Cultural Exchange Found., Washington, 1960-66; exec. asst. Life Underwriter Tng. Council, Washington, 1966-69; adminstrv. asst. Gen. Agts. and Mgrs. Conf., Washington, 1969-70, exec. adminstr., 1970-73, exec. dir., 1974-76, exec. v.p., 1976—. Cons. Oriental art Towson Coll., Balt., 1969—; chief exhibit curator Audubon Naturalistic Soc., 1968—; curator Turner Collection, Washington, 1960—. Bd. dirs. Asian Cultural Exchange Found., Lilliputian Found. Served with USNR, 1958-60. Hold-Fannie B. Scheffries scholar, 1962-64. Mem. Smithsonian Assos. Club: Nat. Press. Home: 29 Timber Rock Rd Gaithersburg MD 20760 Office: 1922 F St NW Washington DC 20006

HUMPHRIES, EDYTHE MARIE, marine biologist; b. Bklyn., Oct. 6, 1944; d. Howard Lawrence and Marie Ann (Sattler) Humphries; B.A. in Biology, Wittenberg U., 1966; M.S. in Biology, U. Del., 1970; Ph.D. in Zoology (NSF grantee), U. Fla., 1974. Teaching and research asst. U. Del., 1966-70, U. Fla., 1970-74; engr., scientist IV, Lawler, Matusky & Skelly Engrs., Tappan, N.Y., 1974-77, project coordinator for aquatic biol. monitoring programs on Lake Ontario; NSF trainee Friday Harbor Marine Lab., U., Wash., 1971; participant biol. surveys. Mem. Ridgewood (N.J.) Concert Singers, 1976-77. Mem. Atlantic Estuarine Research Soc. (chmn. membership), Am. Fisheries Soc., Am. Soc. Zoologists, Internat. Bryozoology Assn., Fla. Acad. Sci., N.Am. Benthological Soc., Internat. Assn. Gt. Lakes Research, Hudson River Environ. Soc., Am. Littoral Soc., Sigma Xi (hon.), Tri Beta (hon.). Contbr. articles on ultrastructure of marine invertebrates and larval fish ecology to profl. jours. Home: 1390 Milford Terr Teaneck NJ 07666

HUNGERFORD, DALE, personnel exec.; b. Le Grange, Ill., May 16, 1936; s. Jonathan Donald and Helen Blanche (Junker) H.; B.S., Bowling Green State U., 1958; postgrad. U. Md., 1963-64; m. Beverly Ann Derrick, May 6, 1961; children—Lance Byron, Rex Lee, Kimberly Derrick. Mgmt. trainee, personnel interviewer Allstate Ins. Co., White Plains, N.Y., 1961-62, personnel asst., 1967-69; mgr. salary adminstrn. Dun & Bradstreet, N.Y.C., 1969-71; dir. personnel Cooper Labs., Inc., Parsippany, N.J., 1971—, v.p., 1976—. Served to capt. Transp. Corps, AUS, 1959-61, 62-67. Mem. Am. Soc. Personnel Adminstrn. (dist. dir. 1976-77), Am. Mgmt. Assn., Westchester Personnel Mgmt. Assn. (dir. 1973-76, pres. 1975), Am. Compensation Assn., Morristown Personnel Assn., Sigma Nu. Republican. Lutheran. Home: 20 N Briarcliff Rd Mountain Lakes NJ 07046 Office: 1259 Route 46 Parsippany NJ 07054

HUNLEY, ANN BERNICE SUGGS, ednl. counselor; b. Balt.; d. Isaac and Mary Elizabeth (Jones) Suggs; A.B., Morgan State Coll., Balt., 1954; M.S., Johns Hopkins, 1975, advanced degree in theory and clin. counseling, 1977. With Balt. County Sch. Systems, 1955—, ednl. counselor Parkville Jr. High Sch., 1973—; vol. div. instructional TV, Md. Dept. Edn., 1969. Past mem. bd. Md. div. Am. Lung Assn.; incorporator, past treas. Bar Belle-Field Neighborhood Assn.; pres. Our Lady of Lourdes Roman Catholic Ch. Parish Council, 1975—; v.p. women's com. Balt., United Negro Coll. Fund, 1973—; adviser world youth affairs UN, 1966; pres. aux. Echo House, 1975—, 1st v.p. bd. dirs. found., 1978—; mem. Md. Task Force for Grad. Nursing Edn., 1975. Recipient citations for vol. work United Negro Coll. Fund, 1973, 74. Mem. NEA, Md. Tchrs. Assn., Tchrs. Assn. Balt. County, Balt. County Sch. Counselors Assn., Md. Personnel and Guidance Assn., Balt. Urban League, NAACP (life), Mental Health Assn., YWCA, Md. League Women's Clubs, Md. League Nursing, Alpha Kappa Alpha (chpt. plaque 1973), Phi Delta Gamma (1st v.p. Gamma chpt. 1976, pres. 1978—), Pi Lambda Theta. Roman Catholic.

HUNT, ANN LORETTA, dietitian; b. Pitts., Feb. 7, 1920; d. Ellis Knowles and Mary Cecelia (Johnson) H.; B.S., Carlow Coll., 1942. Pediatric dietitian Mercy Hosp. of Pitts., 1942-50, clin. dietitian, 1950-60, adminstrv. dietitian, 1960-65, exec. dietitian, 1965-78; dietary cons., 1978—; mem. dietary adv. com. Hosp. Council of Western Pa., 1978—. Mem. Am., Pa., Pitts. dietetic assns., Am. Soc. Hosp. Food Service Adminstrs., Am. Maternal and Child Health Assn., Am. Mgmt. Assn., Am. Sch. of Health Assn., Smithsonian Assos., Irish Am. Cultural Inst. Republican. Roman Catholic. Home: 922 Deely St Pittsburgh PA 15217 Office: 1400 Locust St Pittsburgh PA 15219

HUNT, DOROTHY KENDRIX, sch. counselor; b. Columbus, Ohio, May 9, 1922; d. Allen and Mabel (Boone) Johnson; A.B., Spelman Coll., 1942; M.A., George Washington U., 1964, postgrad., 1974; m. Moss H. Kendrix (div.); children—Moss H., Alan L.; m. 2d, George L. Hunt, Mar. 28, 1970. Tchr., Washington High Sch., Atlanta, 1943-44; statis. clk. Office Q.M. Gen., Fed. Govt., 1944-52; spl. instr. Walter Reed Hosp., Washington, 1952-60; tchr. D.C. Pub. Schs., Washington, 1960-64; pub. sch. counselor secondary schs., Washington, 1964—. Elder, Presbyterian Ch., 1973—; dir. Health Careers Club, 1968—; organizer Parent Tutorial Program, Sousa Jr. High Sch., 1975. Recipient Washington Post Sewing award Dept. Agr., 1954, Spl. commendation for sickle cell proposal Sch. Supt. for D.C. Pub. Schs., 1975, Jerry A. Moore award City Council, 1973, 75. Mem. Am., Nat. Capitol personnel and guidance assns., D.C. Sch. Counselors Assn., Nat. Vocat. Guidance Assn., PTA (life), Smithsonian Instn. (asso.), Nat. Urban League, Am. Fedn. Tchrs. Democrat. Club: Washington Spelman Alumnae. Editor: Home Work Questionnaire, 1976. Office: Sousa Jr High Sch 37th and Ely Pl SE Washington DC 20019

HUNT, EARL JOSEPH, optometrist; b. Johnstown, Pa., Aug. 1, 1928; s. Joseph Earl and Idella (Forsman) H.; O.D., Pa. State Coll. Optometry, 1952; postgrad. Austin Peay State Coll., 1954, Pa. State Coll. Optometry; m. Ann Douglass Salinger, Jan. 1, 1974. Practice optometry, Johnstown, 1955—; instr. anatomy and physiology Cambria-Rowe Bus. Coll., Johnstown, 1961-66. Team capt. United Fund Drive, Johnstown, 1960, 63, 64; mem. Southmont Borough Recreation Commn. 1960-66; mem. Penn's Woods council Boy Scouts Am.; bd. dirs. Council Chs. Christ Greater Johnstown, pres., 1964-66; bd. dirs. Cambria County Community Action Council, 1965-68, Cambrians for Decent Lit., 1964-76, Cambria City Mission, 1971-76, Cambria County Tb and Health Assn., 1967—, Johnstown Community Concert Assn., 1978—; bd. dirs. United Ch. Men Greater Johnstown, 1966—, pres., 1966-68; trustee 1st United Meth. Ch., Johnstown, 1976—, pres., 1977, 78; bd. dirs. Leo Clubs Pa., 1968-70, dist. chmn., 1969-72, mem. adv. council U. Pitts. at Johnstown club, 1969-74. Served with AUS, 1953-55. Recipient Distinguished Service award plaque Lions Club, Ferndale, Pa., 1967. Mem. Am. (vocat. guidance counselor 1960—), Pa. (chmn. motorists' vision and hwy. safety com. 1956-68) optometric assns., Southwestern (pres. 1964-66, dir.), Middle Tenn. (hon.), Montgomery-Christian (hon.) optometric socs., Am. Optometric Found. (life), Better Vision Inst., Vision Conservation Inst. (dir. Pa. chpt. 1955-60, certificate of merit 1957), Optometric Hist. Soc. (charter mem. 1969), Pa. Coll. Optometry Alumni Assn. (life), K.T. Eye Research Found. (life), Lincoln Fellowship Pa., Lincoln Heritage Trail Found., Johnstown C. of C., Johnstown Flood Mus. Assn. (life, dir. 1973—), Phi Theta Epsilon (outstanding mem. plaque 1952). Methodist. Clubs: Masons (32 deg.), Shriners, K.T., Lions (dir. Ferndale 1960—, pres. 1964-65, zone chmn. 1965-67). Contbr. articles to optometric publs. Home: 138 Helen St Johnstown PA 15905 Office: 226 Ohio St Johnstown PA 15902

HUNT, FLORINE ELIZABETH, librarian; b. Richmond, Va., Aug. 11, 1928; d. Alfred Carl and Elva (Blacklidge) Hunt; B.S. Richmond Profl. Inst. of Coll. William and Mary, 1949; postgrad. Western Res. U., 1949-50; M.L.S., Rutgers U., 1955. Child welfare caseworker Norfolk (Va.) Social Service Bur., 1950-52; jr. librarian Trenton (N.J.) Free Pub. Library, 1952-55; jr. asst. librarian Pub. Service Electric and Gas Co., Newark, 1955-59, sr. asst. librarian, 1959, librarian, 1959—. Mem. Spl. Libraries Assn. (treas. N.J. chpt. 1958-60, dir. 1960-62, vice chmn., chmn. pub. utilities div. 1973-74), Air Pollution Control Assn., Am. Gas. Assn. (library services com.), N.A.A.C.P., Rutgers U. Alumni Assn. (pres. 1960-61). Episcopalian. Author: Public Utilities Information Sources, 1965. Home: 56 Oak Ln Trenton NJ 08618 Office: 80 Park Pl Newark NJ 07101

HUNT, FRANCIS HOWARD, ret. navy lab. ofcl.; b. Emporia, Kans., Apr. 12, 1919; s. Frederick Raymond and Mabel (Holmes) H.; B.A., Wesleyan U., 1941; m. Kathleen McLean, June 4, 1945; children—Deborah Mary, Laurie Jane, Peter Raymond. Supr. records Columbia U. div. War Research, New London, Conn., 1941-43, tech. editor, writer, 1943-44; with U.S. Navy Underwater Sound Lab., Fort Trumbull, New London, Conn., 1945-70, successively spl. asst. to asst. tech. dir., 1945-47, staff asst. to tech. dir., head tech. information div., 1947-60, asst. tech. dir. for adminstrn., 1960-67, asso. tech. dir. for adminstrn., 1967-70; asso. dir. center operations Naval Underwater Systems Center, Newport, R.I., 1970-76; mem. E. Coast Navy interlab. com. on editing and pub., 1960-76, chmn., 1961-62. Mem. East Lyme Zoning Bd. of Appeals, 1956—, sec., 1960-78, chmn., 1978—; past mem. East Lyme Flood and Erosion Control Bd., East Lyme Jr. High Sch. Planning Com.; mem. Conn. Fedn. Planning and Zoning Agencies. Bd. dirs. Niantic Public Library, v.p., 1971—; bd. dirs. The Child Guidance Clinic of Southeastern Conn., 1959-62, East Lyme Nursing Assn., 1964-66; active Boy Scouts Am., 1968-69. Served with AUS, 1944-45. Decorated Purple Heart; recipient Outstanding mem. Town Commn. East Lyme C. of C., 1972. Mem. Soc. Tech. Communications, Fed. Profl. Assn., Am. Def. Preparedness Assn., IEEE, Am. Mgmt. Assn. New London County (mem. adv. bd. 1968-70), Columbia hist. socs., Nat. Assn. Ret. Fed. Employees. Congregationalist. Lion (past pres.). Home: 6 Clark St Niantic CT 06357

HUNT, FREDERICK TALLEY DRUM, JR., assn. exec.; b. Martinique, Sept. 19, 1947; s. Frederick Talley Drum and Eleanor (Conly) H.; B.A., Vanderbilt U., 1970; m. Acacia Lynn Graham, Dec. 4, 1976. Counselor cabinet rank staff Gov. Tenn., Nashville, 1968-71; dir. program devel. Manufactured Housing Inst., Washington, 1973-74; pres. Hunt Assos., cons.'s pub. relations, mgmt. and legis., Washington, 1974-77; dir. communications, govt. liaison Am. Acad. Actuaries, Washington, 1977—; exec. dir. Council Pres.'s Actuarial Profession, Washington, 1977—. Vice-pres. Westmoreland Citizens Assn., Washington, 1978. Served with U.S. Army, 1971-73. Mem. Newcomen Soc., Am., Washington socs. assn. execs., U.S. C. of C. Republican. Episcopalian. Clubs: Nat. Press, Met., George Washington U., Mil. Order Loyal Legion, Aztec 1847. Home: 5308 Blackstone Rd Westmoreland Hills Washington DC 20016 Office: Am Acad Actuaries 1835 K St NW Suite 515 Washington DC 20006

HUNT, HARRY DRAPER, educator; b. Boston, Jan. 25, 1935; s. Jarvis and Philomena (Blaine) H.; grad. Phillips Exeter Acad., 1953; A.B. cum laude (Coll. scholar), Harvard, 1957; M.A., Columbia, 1960, Ph.D., 1968; m. Elaine Gaza, June 20, 1958; children—Victoria, Harry Draper IV. Lectr., Hunter Coll., City U. N.Y., 1962-65; prof. history U. Maine at Portland-Gorham, 1965—. Recipient Distinguished Scholar award U. Maine, Portland-Gorham, 1976. Mem. Am. Hist. Assn., Orgn. Am. Historians, Ill., Maine (mem. standing com. 1969-78, v.p. 1977-78) hist. socs., Phi Kappa Phi. Author: Hannibal Hamlin of Maine: Lincoln's First Vice-President, 1969; The Blaine House: Home of Maine's Governors, 1974; Brother Against Brother: Understanding the Civil War Era, 1977. Home: 94 Coach Rd S Portland ME 04106

HUNT, JAMES RAMSEY, graphic arts exec.; b. Lebanon, N.J., Dec. 23, 1919; s. Arthur Whiteneck and Rose (Eick) H.; grad. Newark Sch. Fine and Indsl. Arts, 1943; m. Georgia Anna Ort, Oct. 12, 1959; children—Huldah Carolyn, Allan Howard, James Arthur. Artist, Levy Advt. Agy., Newark, 1946-47; illustrator-collaborator with Kurt Wiese, Frenchtown, N.J., 1948-65; artist Leiberman Assos., Allentown, Pa., 1966-67; art dir. Koh-I-Noor Rapidograph, Inc., Bloomsbury, N.J., 1967—; instr. adult edn. of art Hunterdon and Warren counties high schs., N.J., 1950—; aided in restoring stone mill and converting it into art gallery, Little York, N.J., 1964—. Mem. Delaware Valley Artist Assn. (pres. 1971-73), Kittatinny Arts Group (pres. 1970-73). Republican. Presbyn. (elder 1967-70). Home: Box 115 Little York NJ 08834 Office: 100 North St Bloomsbury NJ 08804

HUNT, JOHN WESLEY, coll. dean; b. Tulsa, Jan. 19, 1927; s. John Wesley and Alta Baer (Johnson) H.; student U. Minn., 1947; B.A., U. Okla., 1949; Ph.D. (Univ. fellow, Kent fellow), U. Chgo., 1961; m. Marjorie Louise Bowen, Aug. 8, 1951; children—Stuart Griggs, Susan Scott, Emily Johnson. Asst. prof. English, Earlham Coll., Richmond, Ind., 1956-62, asso. prof., 1962-66, prof., 1966-72, Bain-Swigget prof. English lang., lit., also chmn. dept., 1968-71, asso. acad. dean, 1971-72; dean Coll. Arts and Sci., prof. English, Lehigh U., Bethlehem, Pa., 1972—. Served with USNR, 1944-46. Danforth Found. Tchr. Study grantee, 1960-61; Lilly Endowment fellow, 1964-65. Recipient E. Harris Harbison Distinguished Teaching award, 1965; Ira Doan Distinguished Teaching Travel award Earlham Coll., 1970. Fellow Soc. Values in Higher Edn. (chmn. post doctoral selection com. 1968-70); mem. Nat. Council Tchrs. English, Modern Lang. Assn. Am., Ann. Conf. Modern Lit. (charter), Soc. for Study So. Lit. (charter), Am. Conf. Acad. Deans, Lawrence Henry Gipson Inst. for 18th Century Studies. Author: William Faulkner: Art in Theological Tension, 1965. Editorial bd. Quest, 1952-56, Earlham Rev., 1966-72. Home: Springtown PA 18081 Office: Lehigh U Office of Dean Coll Arts and Sci Maginnes No 9 Bethlehem PA 18015

HUNT, MARTHA ELIZABETH (MRS. ROLFE LANIER HUNT), ednl. counselor; b. Eupora, Miss., Oct. 6, 1912; d. John Luther and Theosia (Patterson) Wise; B.A., Miss State Coll. for Women, 1934; M.A. U. Chgo., 1956; M.A., Tchrs. Coll., Columbia, 1962; m. Rolfe Lanier Hunt, June 19, 1936; children—Rolfe Lanier, Susie Brunner (Mrs. Tom D. Humphreys II). Tchrs. sci. high schs., Bentonia, Miss., 1934-36, Louise, Miss., 1941-42, Magnolia, Miss., 1942-43, Arlington, Va., 1952-53, Chicago Heights, Ill., 1949-56; tchr. sci. A.B. Davis High Sch., Mt. Vernon, N.Y., 1956-62, counselor, 1962-63; counselor Mt. Vernon High Sch., 1963-70, coordinator guidance, 1971—, head counselor, 1972-74, ret. Mem. Gamma Sigma Epsilon, Delta Kappa Gamma, Pi Lambda Theta. Methodist. Author: (with Rolfe L. Hunt) High School Ahead!, 1968. Contbr. articles to profl. jours. Home: 140 Norman Rd New Rochelle NY 10804

HUNT, NORA LEE, sch. counselor; b. Seattle, Mar. 30, 1940; d. Malachy Martin and Dorothy Elizabeth (McMahon) Scanlan; B.A., Mundelein Coll., Chgo., 1963; M.Ed., Queens Coll., City U.N.Y., 1970; m. Thomas J. Hunt, June 19, 1971; children—Nathan, Matthew. Jr. high sch. English tchr., N.Y.C., 1963-69; high sch. English tchr., Mpls., 1969-70; jr. high sch. counselor, Lanham, Md., 1971-72; guidance counselor Wilde Lake High Sch., Columbia, Md., 1972—; counselor Upward Bound, U. Md., 1970, 72. Chmn. teen activities Columbia's City-wide Celebration 10th Birthday, 1977. Mem. Am. Personnel and Guidance Assn., Howard County Personnel Assn. Democrat. Home: 6551 Pennacook Ct Columbia MD 21045 Office: Wilde Lake High Sch Columbia MD 21044

HUNT, RODERICK THOMAS, Realtor; b. Bklyn., Jan. 10, 1935; s. Roderick Victor and Alice Veronica (O'Brien) H.; B.B.A., Fairfield U.; M.B.A., L.I. U. Mgr., P.J. Fitzgerald Real Estate, Bklyn., 1960-65; owner, operator R.T. Hunt Real Estate, Bklyn., 1965—; lectr. City U. N.Y., 1974-75. Licensed real estate broker, N.Y. Mem. Nat., Bklyn. bds. realtors, Soc. Real Estate Appraisers (asso.). Home: 1571 E 38th St Brooklyn NY 11234 Office: 3009 Quentin Rd Brooklyn NY 11234

HUNT, ROY ARTHUR, JR., banker; b. Pitts., Dec. 31, 1924; s. Roy Arthur and Rachel (Miller) H.; student Haverford Coll., 1943-44; B.A., Yale, 1950; M.S., U. Pitts., 1954; grad. Grad. Sch. Banking, Rutgers U., 1956; m. Sara H. Bankson, June 25, 1949 (div. 1972); children—Roy Arthur, III, Marion McMasters, John Bankson, Andrew McQuesten; m. 2d, Theresa L. Whiteside, Jan. 1976. With Mellon Nat. Bank & Trust Co., Pitts., 1953—, asst. v.p., 1959-64, v.p., 1964—; dir. Microbac Labs., Bearing Service Co., H.K. Porter Co., Nat. Union Ins. Co., Pitts. Testing Lab., Marshall Stamping Co. Bd. dirs. Salvation Army Assn. Greater Pitts.; trustee Magee-Womens Hosp., Hunt Found. Served with C.E., U.S. Army, 1943-46. Mem. C. of C. Greater Pitts., Asso. Artists Pitts. (hon.). Clubs: Pittsburgh Athletic Assn., Duquesne, Harvard-Yale-Princeton, Pittsburgh Golf, Fox Chapel Golf, Grolier, Bibliophiles (Pitts.); Rolling Rock (Ligonier, Pa.). Home: 5563 Northumberland St Pittsburgh PA 15217 Office: 514 Smithfield St Pittsburgh PA 15230

HUNT, RUTH CECELIA, writer, editor, educator; b. Chgo., Apr. 5, 1923; d. Leslie Edward and Gladys Esther (Pratt) Hunt; B.S., Loyola U., Chgo., 1943, M.A., 1969, Ph.D., 1975. Asst. editor Am. Osteo. Assn., Chgo., 1946-48; acting editor, 1948-51; advt. coordinator J.B. Roerig Co., Chgo., 1951-52; Copy editor Jordan-Sieber and Assos., Chgo., 1952-53; sci. editor Am. People's Ency., Chgo., 1953-57; mng. editor, 1957-59; editor-in-chief, 1959-63; editorial dir. LaSalle Extension U., Chgo., 1963-65; free lance writer, editor, Chgo., 1965-75; lectr. edn. Loyola U., Chgo., 1969—; cons. in psychometrics Am. Coll. Obstetricians and Gynecologists, 1972-74, adminstr. research and evaluation, 1974-75; med. evaluator Planned Parenthood-World Population, 1975—. Mem.-at-large nat. accreditation bd. for continuing edn. Am. Nurses Assn., 1975—. Mem. AAAS, Am. Statis. Assn., Am. Ednl. Reseach Assn., Nat. Council Measurement in Edn., Ill. Acad. Sci., N.Y. Acad. Scis., Phi Delta Kappa. Asso. editor Jour. Sex Edn. and Therapy, 1976—. Home: 400 E 55th St New York City NY 10022 Office: 810 7th Ave New York City NY 10019

HUNT, WILLIAM HAWARD, grain technologist; b. Phil, Ky., Aug. 26, 1910; s. Samuel Kelly and Mary Elizabeth (Spurlock) H.; B.A., Berea Coll., 1933; m. Jane Elizabeth Cowan, Apr. 14, 1937; children—Ronald Kelly, Carl Patrick, James Haward, Brian Edward. Hospitalization contracts Meth. Hosp., Pikeville, Ky., 1934; med. technologist trainee Garfield Meml. Hosp., Washington, 1935; med. technologist Children's Hosp., Washington, 1936-38; sci. aide U.S. Dept. Agr., Beltsville, Md., 1939-40, info. clk., 1940-42, transp. officer, 1942-43, chemist, 1943-67, grain technologist, 1967-78; ret., 1978; cons. moisture determination in grain, aflatoxin in corn, dwarf smut in wheat, Beltsville, 1939—. Active Boy Scouts Am.; vol. rescue squad and fire dept., Greenbelt, Md., 1950-65; 1st aid instr. A.R.C.; bd. dirs. Greenbelt Health Assn. Recipient Superior Service award, certificate of merit U.S. Dept. Agr., 1951; Silver Beaver award Boy Scouts Am., 1962. Mem. Am. Assn. Cereal Chemists, Assn. Ofcl. Analytical Chemists, Washington Acad. Sci., U. Md. Ednl. Found., Internat. Seed Testing Assn., Orgn. Internat. Legal Metrology. Republican. Researcher moisture in grain, soap analysis, oilseed analysis, aflatoxin, smut, protein. Inventor in field. Home: 11712 Roby Ave Beltsville MD 20705

HUNTER, (JAMES) GRAHAM, cartoonist, writer, advt. producer; b. LaGrange, Ill.; s. William Clarence and Rebecca (Faul) H.; student Art Inst. Chgo., Landon Sch., Cartooning, Cleve., Art Instruction Schs., Mpls.; m. Cornelia Isabel Seward. Formerly with Asso. Editors' Syndicate, Chgo., Public Ledger Syndicate, Phila., McClure Syndicate, N.Y.C.; free lance cartoonist, writer; creator Jolly Jingles strip for Chgo. Sunday Tribune, also McClure Newspaper Syndicate; Sycamore Center cartoon feature for So. Agriculturist and Farmer-Stockman; Motor Laffs, Biceps Brothers and Getting the Business for Motor mag.; Rhubarb Ridge cartoon feature for Curtis Pub. Co.; full-page bus. cartoons in Banking mag., Only Yesterday, Hometown America, The Office Cat, for Indsl. Press Service; editorial cartoons NAM newspaper service; Bessie's Barnyard Banter for Milk Marketer, Cleve.; cartoon series for Tobacco Inst., BASF Wyandotte Corp.; Hoard's Dairyman article illustrations; children's cartoon series Pizzazz mag.; also advt. copy, cartoons, mag. cover drawings, sales and bus. cartoons, light verse and prose humor; specialist in detailed busy-scene drawings, automotive cartoons and in humorous animal art. Work has appeared numerous national mags. and newspapers; represented in permanent FBI Cartoon Collection, Washington, Wayne State U. Cartoon Exhbn., Detroit, Peter Mayo Editorial Cartoon Collection, State Hist. Soc., Columbia, Mo., Freedoms Found. Cartoon Collection, Valley Forge, Pa. Recipient Distinguished Service citation U.S. Treasury Dept. for promotion nat. war savs. program; Freedoms Found. George Washington Honor Medal, for cartoon on better understanding Am. way of life, 1959, 62; Freedoms Found. Honor Certificate Editorial Cartoon award, 1960, 61, 75, 76. Presbyterian. Author: Art Instr. Schs. Lesson: Creating the Busy Scene Cartoon; Doin's in Sycamore Center. Home and Studio: Lindenshade 42 Clonavor Rd Silver Spring Park West Orange NJ 07052

HUNTER, HERBERT ERWIN, computer co. exec.; b. Washington, June 11, 1934; s. Herbert Clinton and Anna Pauline (Dieterich) H.; B.S., U. Md., 1956; M.S., Calif. Inst. Tech., 1957, Ph.D., 1960; m. Helen Louise Shelhorse, June 11, 1956; children—Erwin Lee, David Clinton, Shirley Ann, Patricia Alice, Linda Louise. With AVCO Corp., Wilmington, Mass., 1963-73; pres. ADAPT Service Corp., Reading, Mass., 1973—, chmn. bd., 1973—. Served to 1st lt. USAF, 1960-63. Mem. Am. Inst. Aeros. and Astronautics, AAAS. Contbr. articles on reentry tech. and data analysis to profl. jours. Home: 36 Main St North Reading MA 01864 Office: PO Box 58 Reading MA 01867

HUNTER, JAMES ALSTON HOPE, math. writer; b. Tigre, Argentina, Feb. 12, 1902; s. James Hope Hunter and Manuela Petrona Leopoldina de Faria y Luna; naval cadet Osborne, 1915-17, Dartmouth, 1917-18; m. Cecilia Agnes Weitzer, Mar. 31, 1939. Commd. midshipman Brit. Navy, 1918, advanced through grades to comdr., 1945; comdr. gunboat H.M.S. Nessus, 1924-26; later anti-submarine specialist; ret., 1945; controller finance German Inland Water Shipping Control Commn., 1945-51; writer Fun with Figures, syndicated math. newspaper feature, 1952—. Mem. Brit. Math. Assn. Author: Fun with Figures, 1956; Figures for Fun, 1956; More Fun with Figures, 1958; More Figures for Fun, 1959; Figures are Fun, 1959; Mathematical Diversions, 1963; Mathematical Brain-Teasers, 1965; Some Tougher Teasers, 1979; also math. problems in mags. Mem. editorial bd. Jour. Recreational Math., 1968-75; Inventor math. teasers, alphametics.

HUNTER, JEHU CALLIS, biologist; b. Washington, Mar. 11, 1922; s. Jehu Louis and Alice (Callis) H.; B.S. cum laude, Howard U., 1943; m. Frances Simons Kraft, Aug. 16, 1966; children—Joyce Alessandra (Mrs. Harry Stanton, Jr.), Maria Alice (Mrs. Tyrone Northington), Roberto Jehu (by previous marriage). Grad asst. zoology Howard U., 1947-48; research technician Nat. Cancer Inst., NIH, Bethesda, Md., 1949-51, biologist, 1953-62, research biologist, 1962-65, sci. adminstr. Nat. Inst. Child Health and Human Devel., 1965-69, asst. dir. for planning, 1969-75, asst. dir. Center for Research for Mothers and Children, 1975-78; cons. Pub. Health Assos., 1978—. Served with U.S. Army, 1943-47, 51-52. Decorated Bronze Star. Travel grantee to Attend 8th Internat. Cancer Congress, 1962. Mem. Am. Soc. for Cell Biology, AAAS, Royal Soc. Medicine, Soc. Developmental Biology. Contbr. articles to profl. jours. Research in cell physiology. Home and Office: 7822 16th St NW Washington DC 20012

HUNTER, JOHN GRAHAM, bus. services co. exec.; b. Rome, Ga., Feb. 17, 1937; s. Harold Frierson and Laura Weller (Graham) H.; student Cronell U., 1955-58; B.Indsl. Engring., Ga. Inst. Tech., 1960; M.B.A., U. Pa. Wharton Sch., 1965; m. Elizabeth Coghill Harbin, Aug. 10, 1963; children—Elizabeth Garland, Anna Graham. With Am. Stock Exchange, N.Y.C., 1965-70, asst. to pres., 1966-67, dir. market devel. div., 1968-70; finance div. mgr. Advanced Mgmt. Research Internat. Inc., N.Y.C., 1970-72, sr. v.p. ops., 1975—; lectr. fin. seminars. Pres. Woodward Sch. bd. trustees, Bklyn., 1975—. Served to lt. USNR, 1960-63. Mem. Chi Phi. Republican. Clubs: Heights Casino (gov. 1975-77), Met. Squash Racquets Assn. (exec. council 1975-77). Home: 591 2d St Brooklyn NY 11215 Office: AMR Internat Inc 1370 Ave Of Americas New York City NY 10019

HUNTER, JOSEPH VINCENT, educator; b. Bklyn., June 12, 1925; s. John Joseph and Margaret (Horstmann) H.; B.S. cum laude, St. Johns U., 1947, M.S., 1949; postgrad. Bklyn. Poly. Inst., 1950, 51; Ph.D., Rutgers, The State U., 1962; m. Ann Marie Engels, June 8, 1957; children—John, Christopher, Joseph Vincent, Margaret Ann, Suzanne Marie. Research chemist Nopco Chem. Co., 1952-55; mem. faculty Rutgers U., New Brunswick, N.J., 1955—, asso. prof. environ. sci., 1964-70, prof. environ. sci., 1970—. Cons. water pollution abatement. Fellow Am. Inst. Chemists, Royal Soc. Health; mem. Am. Chem. Soc. (nat. speakers tour 1970, 71), Am. Water Works Assn., Water Pollution Control Fedn., Am. Pub. Health Assn., Water Resources Council of Rutgers, Sigma Xi. Co-editor: Principles and Applications of Water Chemistry, 1967; Organic Compounds in Aquatic Environments, 1971; mem. editorial bd. Environ. Letters; editorial adv. bd. Environment Energy Contents Monthly. Contbr. articles to publs. Patentee in organic chemistry. Home: 13 Patton Dr East Brunswick NJ 08816 Office: Rutgers U New Brunswick NJ 08903

HUNTER, MABEL ALDEN, civic worker; b. Waterbury, Vt., Nov. 6, 1901; d. Arthur Henry and Frances (Smith) Alden; diploma Sargent Sch. for Phys. Edn., 1924; B.S., Columbia, 1929, M.A. in Edn., 1932; m. Ivor Eric Goodfrey Hunter, June 3, 1933; 1 dau., Nancy (dec.). Tchr. YWCA, Buffalo, 1924-27; instr. phys. edn. Wash. State Tchrs. Coll., Ellensburg, 1929-31; instr. Women's Christian Coll., also YWCA, Tokyo, Japan, 1932-33. Pres. League Women Voters, Groton, Conn., 1957-59, sec. state bd., 1959-63. Trustee Mitchell Coll., New London, Conn., 1952-74, sec. of bd., 1960-74. Pres. Am. Women's Club. Shanghai, China, 1937-38; chmn. joint com. Shanghai Women's Orgns., 1937-39. Mem. AAUW (Shanghai pres. 1935-37, state sec. 1952-54, 1st v.p. 1954-57, parliamentarian state bd. 1960-62, state pres. 1962-66, state nominating chmn. 1967-68), N.Y.C. Hort. Soc. Club: Town and County (Hartford). Home: Inchcliffe Dr Torrey Park Box 335 Gales Ferry CT 06335

HUNTER, MEL, artist; b. Oak Park, Ill., July 27, 1927; s. Milford Joseph and Lucille (Clarkson) H.; student Northwestern U., 1944-47; m. Nancy Sue O'Connor, Aug. 23, 1969; children—Lisa, Scott, Amy. Freelance artist-illustrator, 1952-71; work appeared in Life Mag., Colliers Mag., Nat. Geog., Ency. Americana, Time-Life Books, others; author-photographer documentary books: The Missilemen, 1960; Strategic Air Command (Aviation/Space Writers Assn. award), 1961; author-illustrator children's books: How the Earth Began, 1972; How Plants Began, 1972; How Fishes Began, 1972; How Man Began, 1972; artist-printmaker numerous edits. hand-drawn color lithographs and etchings, 1971—; pres. Gallery North Star, Grafton, Vt., 1975—; dir. Atelier North Star, Mel Hunter Graphics. Mem. Drawing Soc., Nat. Arts Club, So. Vt. Artists, Salmagundi Club. Contbr. articles to profl. jours. Home and Studio: Box 2 Townshend Rd Grafton VT 05146

HUNTER, ROBERT DOUGLAS, artist; b. Boston, Mar. 17, 1928; s. George Irvin and Hazel Francis (Costa) H.; diploma Vesper George Sch. Art, 1949; student R.H. Ives Gammell Studios, 1950-55; m. Elizabeth Ives Valsam, Oct. 12, 1968. One man shows at Shore Studio Galleries, Boston, 1956, 61, Seattle Museum Fine Arts, 1959, Tacoma Museum Fine Art, 1959, Sacramento (Wash.) Museum Fine Arts, 1959, Maryhill (Wash.) Mus. Fine Arts, 1959, Phila. Art Alliance, 1962, Grand Central Gallery, N.Y.C., 1965, Guild Boston Artists, 1963, 67, 71, 74, Andover (Mass.) Gallery, 1970, Orleans (Mass.) Art Gallery, 1967, 68; exhibited in group shows at Salmagundi Club, N.Y.C., Worcester (Mass.) Art Mus., others; represented in permanent collections at Maryhill Mus., Goldendale, Wash., Chrysler Mus., Norfolk, Va., others; instr. Vesper George Sch. Art, Boston, 1950, Worcester (Mass.) Mus. Fine Arts, 1970—, Mt. Ida Jr. Coll., 1978. Served with USMCR, 1946-47. Recipient Richard Mitton gold medal New Eng. Artists Exhbn., Boston, 1954-57, 59-61, 63-65, 67, 69-70, 74, Richard Mitton silver medal, 1969; Pierson meml. prize Ogunquit (Maine) Art Center, 1958, 63, portrait prize, 1959, 66; 1st painting award Acad. Artists, Springfield, Mass., 1961; gold medal Am. Artists Profl. League, N.Y.C., 1962, Newington prize, 1966, 67, best still life award, grant nat. exhbn., 1970; popular prize Boston Arts Festival, 1962; John Singleton Copley award Copley Soc., 1966; popular prize North Shore Art Assn., 1967, best still life award, 1968, Frederick Thompson Found. award, 1976. Mem. Guild Boston Artists (pres. 1973-78), Allied Artists Am., Hudson Valley Art Assn., Am. Artists Profl. League (dir. 1960-70), Ogunquit Art Center (dir. 1965-75), Acad. Artists, Copley Soc. (v.p. 1959-62). Episcopalian (vestry 1965). Clubs: St. Botolph (Boston); Cambrdige (Mass.) Boat. Address: 250 Beacon St Boston MA 02216

HUNTER, WILLIAM ROBERT, editor; b. Parsons, Kans., Mar. 13, 1940; s. Carl Nelson and Margaret May (McKinley) H.; B.A., So. Methodist U., 1962; M.S., Northwestern U., 1963. Editor, pub. relations rep. Ford Motor Co., Cleve. and Dallas, 1964-66; labor and polit. reporter Dallas Morning News, 1966-69; pub. relations account exec. Thomas J. Tierney & Assos., Dallas, 1969-70; editor Flagship News, Am. Airlines, N.Y.C., 1970—. Served with USAFR, 1963-64. Mem. Airline Editors Forum (chmn. 1975-76), N.Y. Bus. Communicators (bd. govs.), Pi Kappa Alpha, Sigma Delta Chi. Democrat. Methodist. Home: 360 W 22d St Apt 9C New York City NY 10011 Office: 633 3d Ave New York City NY 10017

HUNTING, MARGARET HAZEL, lawyer; b. White Plains, N.Y., Apr. 12, 1946; d. Daniel L. and Carrie Augusta (Parmele) H.; A.B., Barnard Coll., 1968; M.A., Brown U., 1969; J.D. cum laude, Dickinson Sch. Law, 1974; m. Stephen R. Jones, Dec. 29, 1971. Dir. ednl. research progress for Providence, 1969; editor, project dir. Ednl. Devel. Corp., Palo Alto, Calif., 1970-71; admitted to Pa. bar, 1974, U.S. Supreme Ct. bar, 1978; law clk. to judge Superior Ct. Pa., Carlisle, 1974-76; dep. atty. gen. Pa. Dept. Justice, Harrisburg, 1976—. Mem. Nat. Assn. Women Lawyers. Democrat. Home: 2205 Bellevue Rd Harrisburg PA 17104 Office: Pa Dept Justice Capitol Annex Harrisburg PA 17120

HUNTINGTON, EARL L., natural resources co. exec., lawyer; b. Orangeville, N.Y., Sept. 2, 1929; s. Llyod S. and Hannah Annette (Cox) H.; grad. U. Utah, 1951, J.D., 1956; LL.M., Georgetown U., 1959; m. Phyllis Ann Reed; children—Jane, Ann, Stephen. Admitted to Utah, N.Y., D.C. bars; trial atty. Dept. Justice, Washington, 1956-63; counsel Tesasgulf, Inc., N.Y.C., 1963-74, v.p., gen. counsel, 1974—, aslo dir. Tesasgulf Can. Ltd. Served with U.S. Army, 1951-53. Mem. Am., Utah, Fed. bar assns., Assn. Bar City N.Y., Order of Coif, Phi Kappa Phi, Beta Gamma Sigma. Home: 1 Maywood Ct Darien CT 06820 Office: High Ridge Park Stamford CT 06904

HUNTLEY, ROBERT ROSS, physician, educator; b. Wadesboro, N.C., Sept. 6, 1926; s. George W. and Louise (Ross) H.; B.S. in Chemistry, Davidson Coll., 1947; M.D., Bowman-Gray Sch. Medicine, 1951; m. Joan Cornoni, Apr. 10, 1976; children—Katherine, Robert, Julia, Elizabeth, Jeffress. Intern, U. Mich. Hosp., Ann Arbor, Mich., 1951-53; resident, fellow N.C. Meml. Hosp., Chapel Hill, 1959-61; pvt. practice medicine, Warrenton, N.C., 1953-58; from instr. to asso. prof. medicine and preventive medicine U. N.C. Sch. Medicine, Chapel Hill, 1959-68; asso. dir. Nat. Center for Health Services Research, HEW, 1968-70; prof., chmn. dept. community and family medicine Georgetown U. Sch. Medicine, Washington, 1970—; pres. Georgetown U. Community Health Plan, Inc., 1972—; cons. Robert Wood Johnson Found.; chmn. health care tech. study sect. HEW, 1978—. Served with USN, 1945-46. Diplomate Am. Bd. Preventive Medicine, trustee, 1974-78; diplomate Am. Bd. Family Practice. Mem. Assn. Tchrs. Preventive Medicine, Soc. Tchrs. Family Medicine, D.C. Med. Soc., Am. Public Health Assn. Democrat. Methodist. Contbr. articles to profl. jours. Office: 3900 Reservoir Rd NW Washington DC 20007

HUNTLEY, WILLIAM ROBERT, librarian; b. Spindale, N.C., Apr. 7, 1928; s. John Fredrick and Dessie Gertrude (Buff) H.; A.A., Brevard (N.C.) Coll., 1949; A.B., U. N.C., 1958; postgrad. Catholic U. Am., 1958-62; children—Teri Buff, Sheri Lynn. With Library of Congress, Washington, 1957—, supr. librarian, 1961-63, head preliminary cataloging sect., 1963-72, asst. chief descriptive cataloging div., 1972—. Mem. Allentown Civic Assn., 1975—. Served with AUS, 1952-54. Mem. Internat. Platform Assn., Spl. Libraries Assn., Library Congress Profl. Assn. Elk, Kiwanian. Home: 4215 Flam

St Oxon Hill MD 20022 Office: Library of Congress Washington DC 20540

HUNTOON, ROBERT BRIAN, chemist, food co. exec.; b. Braintree, Mass., Mar. 1, 1927; s. Benjamin Harrison and Helen Edna (Worden) H.; B.S. in Chemistry, Northeastern U., 1949, M.S., 1961; m. Joan Fairman Graham, Mar. 1, 1952; children—Brian Graham, Benjamin Robert, Elisabeth Ellen, Janet Lynne, Joelle. Analytical chemist, Mass. Dept. Pub. Health, microbiologist Met. Dist. Commn., Boston, 1950-53; research and devel. chemist Heveatex Corp., Melrose, Mass., 1953-56; with Gen. Foods Corp., 1956-70, acting quality control mgr., Woburn, Mass., 1965-67, head group research and devel., Tarrytown, N.Y., 1967-70; mgr. quality control U.S. Flavor div. Internat. Flavors & Fragrances, Teterboro, N.J., 1970—. Served with USCG, 1945-46. Com. mem. Essential Oils Assn., Flavor and Extracts Mfg. Assn.; mem. Am. Chem. Soc., Inst. Food Technologists. Republican. Lutheran. Clubs: Indsl. Mgmt. (v.p. 1967) (Woburn); Croton Yacht, Saugus River Yacht (treas. 1967-68). Contbr. articles on flavor and food quality control to profl. and co. publs.; patentee gelatin compositions and mfg. processes. Home: 7 Scotland Hill Park Spring Valley NY 10977 Office: 100 Green St Teterboro NJ 07608

HUNTSMAN, LAWRENCE DARROW, lawyer; b. Salt Lake City, Jan. 21, 1934; s. Orson Lawrence and Vera Maude (Day) H.; B.S., Pa. State U., 1956; LL.B., George Washington U., 1959; div.; children—Laura, Kathleen, Marguerite, Holbrook. Admitted to Va. bar, 1959, D.C. bar, 1959; clk. D.C. Superior Ct., 1959-60; asst. corp. counsel, D.C., 1960-61; asso. firm Welch, Mott & Morgan, 1961-64, Miller, Brown, Gildenhorn, 1964-69; partner Brown, Gildenhorn & Statland, Washington, 1969-75; pres. Pan Mediterranean Shipping Corp., 1975—. Dir. Ashley Corp., Suter's Tavern, Inc. Mem. Am., D.C., Va. bar assns. Club: Georgetown (Washington). Home: 11645 Chapel Rd Clifton VA 22024 Office: 1101 17th ST NW Washington DC 20036 also 10560 Main St Fairfax VA 22030

HUNTZINGER, THOMAS ELTON, accountant; b. Reading, Pa., Jan. 8, 1945; s. Lester Elton and Eleanore Martha H.; B.S., Albright Coll., 1966; m. Bonnie Gay Delozier, Aug. 2, 1965; children—Thomas Eric, Amy Noelle. With audit div. Arthur Andersen & Co., Phila., 1966-71, sr. accountant, 1969-71; staff Edgar Howe Co., Hanover, Pa., 1971-72; accountant, Hanover, 1973—; auditor Penn Twp. (Pa.), 1974—. Asst. treas. ch. council Lutheran Ch., Southampton, Pa., 1970-71; mem. council St. Mark's Luth. Ch., Hanover, 1977-78; chmn. Hanover Cancer Crusade, 1973; pres. PTA, 1974; active United Way, 1974; mem. com. 2d ward Hanover Republican Party, 1974—; bd. dirs., treas. Hanover Area Hotline, 1973; mem. mgmt. com. Hanoverians for Effective Govt. C.P.A. Named outstanding young man Hanover, 1976. Mem. Am., Pa. (com. of fed. taxation) insts. C.P.A.'s, Hanover C. of C. (treas. 1973, pres. 1977-78). Republican. Clubs: Rotary, Arcadian, Hanover Country. Home: 417 Clearview Rd Hanover PA 17331 Office: 637 Frederick St Hanover PA 17331

HURD, PRISCILLA PAYNE, civic worker; b. Chgo., Sept. 26, 1919; d. Frank E. and Seba. B. (Burnham) Payne; A.A., Finch Coll., 1940; B.A., Chgo. U., 1942, Th.M., 1948, D.D., 1971; m. George A. Hurd, Sept. 21, 1946; children—George A.Jr., Susan P. Bd. dirs. ladies aid soc. St. Luke's Hosp., 1954-58, Bethlehem chpt. Am. Red Cross, 1958; bd. trustees Bethlehem Rehab. Center, 1957-59; ordained minister Life Sciences Ch., 1971; state chmn. Advisory Council on Arts for Pa., 1971—; trustee Allentown Art Museum, 1969—; pres. bd. trustees Eisenhower Meml. Scholarship Found., 1970—. Am. Assn. Museums; mem. advisory bd. Am. Christian Coll., Tulsa, 1973—; State chmn. Friends of Kennedy Center of Arts, 1971—, dir. radio shows on UN sta. WGPA, 1948-52; columnist Bloomington (Ind.) Tribune, 1970—; author column Prill's Press, also travel articles for newspapers, Mem. Historic Bethlehem, Nat. Hist. Soc. (asso.), Am. Heritage Soc., Menninger Found., Smithsonian Inst. (asso.), Community Concert Assn. (bd. dirs. 1947-50); Internat. Platform Assn., Nat. Wildlife Fedn., Alpha Psi Omega, Epsilon Delta Chi, Gamma Chi Epsilon. Republican. Club: Saucon Valley Country Author: Anthology of Poetry, 1961; Chasing Culture with the Brooklyn Museum, 1969. Home: POB 398 Springtown PA 18081

HURD, YORICK GORDON, physicist; b. Santee, Nebr., June 30, 1922; s. Gordon Killiam and Ethel Grey (Pollard) H.; B.S., Tufts U., 1946, M.S., 1949; m. Luraine Fitch, Oct. 1, 1949; children—Warren W., Howard H. Instr. physics Simmons Coll., Boston, 1947-49; physicist, research dept. 20th Century Fox Films Corp., N.Y.C., 1949-61; physicist, plant supt. Design and Roller div. L.E. Cartpenter & Co., Norwalk, Conn., 1961—. Com. chmn., commr., cubmaster Boy Scouts Am.; mem. selection com. sch. bd. Served with USNR, 1943-46. Mem. Soc. Motion Picture and TV Engrs., Optical Soc. Am., Illuminating Engrs. Soc., Soc. Mfg. Engrs., Soc. Plastic Engrs., Am. Electroplaters Soc., Intersoc. Color Council, AAAS, Appalachian Mountain Club, Am. Forestry Assn., Sigma Xi, Sigma Pi Sigma. Republican. Congregationalist. Clubs: Masons, Grange. Patentee in field (3). Home: 1517 Raleigh Rd Mamaroneck NY 10543 Office: 355 Connecticut Ave Norwalk CT 06854

HURFORD, JOHN BOYCE, investment counselor; b. Bryn Mawr, Pa., Feb. 28, 1938; s. James Rayner and Helen Alice (Simon) H.; A.B., Haverford Coll., 1960; M.B.A., Harvard U., 1965. Investment mgr. Lazard Freres & Co., N.Y.C., 1967-69; dir., prin. BEA Asso. Inc., N.Y.C., 1969—. Chmn. Ann. Giving for Haverford Coll., 1974—, admissions counselor, 1975—; mem. Com. for the N.Y. Philharmonic, 1975—. Served with U.S. Army, 1961-62. John Hancock fellow, 1963, Fulbright scholar U. Delhi, 1965-67. Mem. N.Y. Soc. Security Analysts. Club: Harvard. Home: 220 E 63d St New York City NY 10021 Office: 366 Madison Ave New York City NY 10017

HURLBURT, C(HARLES) GRAHAM, mariculture food co. exec.; b. Worcester, Mass., Apr. 9, 1931; s. Charles Graham and Louise L. (Parker) H.; B.S., Cornell U., Ithaca, N.Y., 1953; grad. Advanced Mgmt. Program, Harvard Bus. Sch., 1969; m. Sarah Ellen Worley, Feb. 10, 1956; children—Sarah E., Charles Graham III, Cynthia L., Leeds D. Staff Harvard, 1956—, dir. food service systems, 1963-74, dir. adminstrn., 1974—; internat. cons. in edn. and mariculture; mem. adv. council Internat. Bus. Inst., Leysin, Switzerland; pres. Blue Gold Sea Farms, Inc., Portsmouth, R.I., 1977—. Mem. Gov. Mass. Adv. Council, 1968—, Gov's. Mgmt. Task Force, 1975. Served with AUS, 1954-56. Mem. Soc. Advancement Food Service Research (past pres., life fellow in food service research), Internat. Soc. Food Service Cons., Nat. Assn. Coll., Univ. Bus. Officers, Cornell Soc. Hotelmen (dir.), Harvard Bus. Sch. Assn. Clubs: Boston Execs., Harvard (Boston); Duxbury Yacht. Author: Blue Gold, Mariculture of The Edible Blue Mussel, 1974. Contbr. numerous articles to profl. jours., popular publs. Home: 81 Irving St Cambridge MA 02138 Office: Blue Gold Sea Farms Inc Box 504 Portsmouth RI 02871

HURLBURT, JOHN HENRY, data processing co. exec.; b. Fairfield, Conn., July 22, 1938; s. James Sturges and Winnifred Armstrong (Smith) H.; B.A. in English and Philosophy, Rice U., 1962; 1 dau., Eva Maureen. Mktg. rep. IBM, Cape Kennedy, Fla., 1966-68; nat. account mgr. RCA, Washington, 1970-72; fed. mktg. mgr. Ampex, Washington, 1972-76; gen. partner H & N Assos. Ltd., Bethesda, Md., 1975—; dir. bus. devel. Grumman Data Systems Corp., Bethpage, N.Y., 1977—. Served with USN, 1962-66, 68-70. Decorated 5 Air medals. Mem. Soc. Exptl. Test Pilots, Nat. Council Tech. Service Industries. Republican. Episcopalian. Home: 75 W Islip Rd West Islip NY 11795 Office: 20 Crossways Park N Woodbury NY 11797

HURLBUT, ROBERT HAROLD, health care service exec.; b. Rochester, N.Y., Mar. 9, 1935; s. Harold Leroy and Martha Irene (Fincher) H.; student Coll. Hotel Adminstrn. Cornell U., 1953-56; m. Barbara Cox, June 14, 1958; children—Robert W., Christine A. Adminstr. Pillars Home, Rochester, 1956—, Elmcrest Nursing Home, Churchville, N.Y., 1960—, Elm Manor Nursing Home, Canandaigua, N.Y., 1960—, Penfield Nursing Home, Rochester, 1963—, Avon (N.Y.) Nursing Home, 1964—, Newark (N.Y.) Nursing Home, 1965—, Lakeshore Nursing Home, Rochester, 1972—, others; organizer, adminstrv. dir. Rohm Services Corp., hdqrs. Rochester, 1964—, organizer, pres. Vari-Care, Inc., hdqrs. Rochester, 1969—. Mem. N.Y. State Assn. Long Term Care Adminstrs., Am. Coll. Nursing Home Adminstrs., Rochester C. of C., Lambda Chi Alpha. Clubs: Rochester, Cornell (Rochester). Home: 11 Crestview Dr Pittsford NY 14534 Office: 277 Alexander St Rochester NY 14607

HURLEY, ALFRED BENEDICT, JR., educator; b. Bayonne, N.J., May 26, 1940; s. Alfred Benedict and Rita Veronica (Sullivan) H.; B.A., Manhattan Coll., 1961; M.A., New Sch. Social Research, 1968, Ph.D., 1978. Asst. Prof. psychology Jersey City State Coll., 1968—. Served to capt. SAC, USAF, 1962-67. Mem. Am., N.J. psychol. assns. Home: 57 Brookfield Rd Dumont NJ 07628

HURLEY, FRANK EDWARD, cardiologist; b. Springfield, Mass., Feb. 14, 1917; s. John F. and Mary V. H.; B.S., Am. Internat. U., 1940; M.D., Tufts U., 1943; m. Mary Ann Barbara Leddy, Dec. 27, 1945. Intern, Mercy Hosp., Springfield, 1943-44; resident St. Vincent's Hosp., Worcester, Mass., 1946-47; sr. attending physician Mercy Hosp., Springfield, 1950—, chief dept. medicine, 1964-70, dir. medicine, med. edn., 1950—, adv. bd. sch. nursing, 1954-70, med. dir., 1973-75; practice medicine specializing in internal medicine and cardiology, Springfield, 1948—; cons. cardiologist Springfield Municipal Hosp. Served with M.C., U.S. Army, 1944-46. Decorated Legion of Merit; recipient Pynchon award AMA, 1973, Physicians Recognition award, 1969, 72, 75. Mem. A.C.P., AMA, Am. Coll. Cardiology, Mass. Med. Soc., Mass., Am. socs. internal medicine, Springfield Acad. Medicine (pres. 1962-63). Roman Catholic. Home and Office: 1090 Worthington St Springfield MA 01109

HURLEY, JEREMIAH JOSEPH, pub. accountant; b. Washington, Aug. 28, 1923; s. Jeremiah John and Annie (McInerney) H.; B.C.S., Columbus U., 1947; M.C.S., 1948, C.P.A., 1950. Asst. bookkeeper George I. Borger Real Estate, Washington, 1941-42; jr. accountant William Claybaugh & Co., Washington, 1942-43, staff accountant, 1946-50, sr. accountant 1950-52, asso. mem., 1952; prof. accountancy Columbus U., 1951-52; asso. mem. S. Frank Levy & Co., Washington, 1953-61, partner, 1962—. Served as staff sgt. Office Fiscal Dir., Finance Corps, U.S. Army, ETO, 1943-46. Mem. Am. Inst. C.P.A.'s, Assn. Practicing C.P.A.'s, Holy Name Soc., Gonzaga Alumni Assn., Columbus U. Alumni Assn., Chi Sigma Mu. Club: Rehoboth (Del.) Beach Country. Home: 5036 Weaver Terr Washington DC 20016 Office: Washington Bldg 1436 G St NW Washington DC 20005

HURLEY, JOHN PHILIP, ret. educator; b. Nanticoke, Pa., Dec. 31, 1914; s. Michael Jeremiah and Mary Alice (Mullahy) H.; B.S. in Edn., Bucknell U., 1941; grad. student Pa. State U., 1950-56. Tchr., Nanticoke (Pa.) Jr. High Sch., 1943-46; tchr., counselor physically and mentally disabled war vets. Nanticoke Vocational Sch., 1950-52, 54-56; tchr. Nanticoke High Sch., 1954-56; counselor, dir. guidance dept. Nanticoke Area Joint Sch. System, 1956-68, asst. to supt. in charge pupil services, 1968-70; coordinator guidance services Greater Nanticoke Area Sch. Dist., 1970-76, ret.; lectr., cons., test adminstr., 1965-76. Chmn. Redevel. Authority, City Nanticoke; bd. adminstrn. Urban Renewal Programs; bd. dirs. Nanticoke chpt. A.R.C.; v.p. Citizens Adv. Council. Trustee, Nanticoke State Gen. Hosp.; pres. bd. dirs. Nanticoke/Hazleton Area Mental Health and Mental Retardation, United Health and Hosp. Services Greater Wilkes-Barre Area. Mem. Nat., Pa. (pres. local br.) edn. assns., Am. Personnel and Guidance Assn., Pa. Counselors Assn., Luzerne County Guidance Assn., Nanticoke C. of C. Democrat. Roman Catholic. Kiwanian (past pres. Nanticoke). Author: Course Syllabus—Foremanship Training, 1951. Home: 394 E Green St Nanticoke PA 18634

HURST, ANDRE (BUNDY), microbiologist; b. Dej, Romania, Aug. 2, 1918; s. Francis Carol and Stephania Hurst; came to Can., 1968, naturalized, 1973; B.Sc., U. Reading (Eng.), 1943; Ph.D., 1947; M.Sc., U. London, 1964; m. Betty Anne Green, Sept. 14, 1942; children—Catherine Hurst Ja'Afar, Peter, Nicholas, Hilary Hurst Riddle, Christopher. Sr. sci. officer, Nat. Inst. Research in Dairying, Reading, U.K., 1943-52; mgr. bacteriol. lab. Unilever Research Lab., Sharnbrook, Bedford, Eng., 1952-68; research scientist Health & Welfare Dept. Can., Ottawa, Ont., 1968—; prof. U. Ottawa, 1975—. Recipient Gorini prize, 1952. Fellow Inst. Biology; mem. Can., Am. socs. microbiologists. Quaker. Contbr. to profl. jours. Editor Can. Jour. Microbiology, 1975—. Patentee in field. Author: (with G.W. Gould) the Bacterial Spore, 1969; (with J.M. Deman) Microbial Food-Borne Infections and Intoxications, 1973. Home: 684 Fraser Ave Ottawa ON K2A 2R8 Canada Office: Health Protection Bldg Tunneys Pasture Ottawa ON K1A OL2 Canada

HURT, EDWARD PAULETTE, ret. athletic adminstr. and educator; b. Brookneal, Va., Feb. 12, 1900; s. Isaac Coles and Sarah Ann (Williamson) H.; A.B. in Mathematics, Howard U., 1920; M.S. in Health and Phys. Edn., Columbia U., 1936; LL.D., Morgan State Coll., 1970; m. Beatrice Reid, Aug. 31, 1922; Tchr. math. Va. Seminary and Coll., Lynchburg, 1921-29, head coach, 1925-29; instr. math. Morgan State Coll., Balt., 1929-37, coach of basketball, 1929-47, acting head phys. edn. dept., 1937-48, prof. phys. edn., 1937-70, head coach of football, 1929-59, coach of track and field, 1929-70, dir. of athletics, 1929-70, prof. emeritus, 1970; mem. coaching staff of Pan-Am. Games, 1959, U.S. Olympic Track and Field Games Com., 1960-72; mem. coaching staff of U.S. Men's Track and Field Team in 1964 Olympics, Tokyo; referee Penn Relays, 1961, Nat. Collegiate Athletic Assn. Track and Field Championships, 1971; mem. coaching staff U.S.A.-USSR Dual Track Meet, Kiev, Russia, 1965. Mem. mayor's Com. on Aging and Edn., Balt., 1971—; bd. dirs. The Arthritis Found. Elected to Helms Found. Hall of Fame, 1972, Morgan State U. Athletic Hall of Fame, 1974, Nat. Track and Field Hall of Fame of U.S., 1975; recipient Distinguished Service award Balt. Urban League, 1953, Md. Phys. Fitness award, 1969, Morgan State Coll. Alumni award, 1954, Civic and Profl. Achievement award Central Intercollegiate Athletic Assn., 1967, Merit of Sports award Jerusalem Temple of Balt., 1965, Sports award YMCA, 1965, Howard U. Alumni Achievement award, 1965; named Track Coach of the Year, Track and Field News, 1950; selected One of the Outstanding Football Coaches of All Times, U. Tex., 1950. Mem. U.S. Track Coaches Assn., Pigskin Club of Washington, Md. League for Crippled Children and Adults. Gymnasium at Morgan State College named in his honor. Address: 2403 Montebello Terr Baltimore MD 21214

HURT, IKEY WEST, printing co. exec.; b. Mayfield, Ky., Nov. 18, 1928; s. John Bryan and Lula Belle (Harrell) H.; B.S. in Edn. cum laude, Union Coll., 1951; m. Mary Elizabeth French, Nov. 10, 1951; children—Susan, David, John. Statistician, Fawcett-Dearing Printing Co., Louisville, 1953-58, chief estimator, 1958-62, dept. head estimating and billing, 1962-65; asst. gen. mgr. Fawcett-Haynes Printing Co., Louisville, 1965-68; exec. v.p. and chief exec. officer Fawcett Printing Co., Rockville, Md., 1968—, dir., 1968—. Served with U.S. Army, 1951-53. Mem. Metropolitan Washington Bd. Trade, Am. Inst. Mgmt., U. Md. Terrapin Club, Rockville C. of C., Montgomery County C. of C., Admirals Club, Georgetown Club. Methodist. Club: Congressional Country. Home: 11310 Hounds Way Rockville MD 20852 Office: 1900 Chapman Ave Rockville MD 20852

HURT, SUSANNE MORRIS (MRS. MARSHALL HURT), artist; b. N.Y.C.; d. Harold Cecil and Cosby Meriwether (Dansby) Morris; student, Duke U., 1941-42, Corcoran Gallery Sch., 1952-53; pvt. study with Wayman Adams and A. Ginsburg; m. Marshall Hurt, Nov. 6, 1942. Exhibited one-man show at Cayuga Mus. of History and Art, Auburn, N.Y., 1971, Grist Mill Gallery, Chester, Vt., 1976; exhibited in group Shows at N.A.D., N.Y.C., N. Arts Club, N.Y.C., Lever House, N.Y.C., others; pvt. instr. art, N.Y.C., 1969—. Recipient Anna Hyatt Huntington first prize Catharine Lorillard Wolfe Art Club, 1970; first prize Composers, Authors and Artists of Am., 1972, Nat. Biennial Composers, Authors and Artists of Am. Conv., 1973; grand prize Dept. of Parks and Recreation of City of N.Y., 1978. Fellow Royal Soc. Arts; mem. Am. Artists Profl. League, Catharine Lorillard Wolfe Art Club (corr. sec. 1971-74), Hudson Valley Art Assn., Composers, Authors and Artists of Am. (nat. rec. sec. 1971-75), Acad. Artists Assn., Art Students League. Studio: 299 Riverside Dr New York City NY 10025

HURVICH, MARVIN SAMUEL, psychologist; b. Birmingham, Ala., May 7, 1930; s. Harry Arnold and Rosalia (Cohen) H.; B.S., U. Ala., 1953; M.A., U. Pa., 1955, Ph.D., 1960; postdoctoral certificate in psychoanalysis N.Y. U., 1968; m. Adrienne Marks; 1 son, Clifford. Intern, Eastern Pa. Psychiat. Inst., Phila., 1956-57; from research fellow to research asso. dept. psychiatry U. Pa., 1957-60, instr. psychology, 1959-60, staff psychologist student health service, 1959-60; staff psycholgist Camden County (N.J.) Psychiat. Hosp., 1958-60; psychologist St. Vincent's Hosp., N.Y.C., 1962-65; clin. coordinator Lincoln Inst. for Psychotherapy, N.Y.C., 1962-65; dir. clin. psychology tng. Roosevelt Hosp., N.Y.C., 1964-73; asso. research scientist N.Y. U., 1967—, clin. supr. psychology dept., 1968—, vis. prof., 1977—. Temporary asst. prof. Kans. State U., 1962; research asso. Columbia, 1965-67; adj. asso. prof. Fordham U., 1969—; prof. psychology L.I. U., 1973—, chmn. dept., 1977. Served with U.S. Army, 1960-62. Mem. Am. Psychol. Assn., Phi Beta Kappa. Co-author: Ego Functions in Schizophrenics, Neurotics and Normals, 1973. Contbr. articles to sci. jours. Home: 79 W 12th St New York City NY 10011 Office: 49 W 12th St New York City NY 10011

HURWITZ, CARLYLE HAROLD, physician; b. Fall River, Mass., Aug. 25, 1921; s. David and Augusta Lydia (Tannenbaum) H.; student Northwestern U., 1939-40; B.A., Harvard, 1946; M.D., Tufts U., 1950; m. Phyllis Ruth Ostrow, Aug. 19, 1956: children—Julie Ellen, Seth Lawrence. Intern, Cook County Hosp., Chgo., 1950-51, resident, 1951-54; practice medicine, specializing in obstetrics and gynecology, Fall River, 1954-59, Walpole, Mass., 1959—; mem. staff Truesdale Hosp., 1954-59, Union Hosp., 1954-59, Fall River Gen. Hosp., 1954-59, Norwood Hosp., 1959—, Faulkner Hosp., St. Margarets Hosp. for Women, 1975—. Served with AUS, 1942-45; ETO. Diplomate Am. Bd. Obstetrics and Gynecology. Fellow A.C.S., Am. Coll. Obstetricians and Gynecologists; mem. A.M.A., Mass. Med. Soc., Alpha Omega Alpha. Jewish. Mason. Contbr. articles to profl. jours. Home: 14 Mayfair Circle Norwood MA 02062 Office: 925 Main St Walpole MA 02081

HURWITZ, DAVID LYMAN, lawyer; b. N.Y.C., Feb. 22, 1928; s. Irving and Sophie (Ruderman) H.; A.B., Bucknell U., 1947; LL.B., Columbia, 1950; m. Betty Sperling, 1952 (div. 1966); 1 son, Peter Ethan; m. 2d, Sally L. Spencer, Sept. 30, 1967. Admitted to N.Y. bar, 1951; practiced in N.Y.C., 1954—; partner firm Hurwitz & Vail; spl. asst. atty. gen. N.Y. State, 1951-54; pres. The Algonquin Press, Inc., 1965—, Corporate Adminstrn., Inc., 1966—; lectr. Practising Law Inst. Bd. govs. NCCJ, 1972—, also nat. chmn. wills and bequests com.; bd. dirs. N.Y. NCCJ, 1958—, former co-chmn. Bus. and Profl. Mens Round Table; former mem. exec. bd., chmn. N.Y. discrimination in housing com. Am. Jewish Com.; trustee Bucknell U., 1975—; dir. N.Y. State Com. on Integrated Housing and Urban Devel., 1967—, Asso. Community Rehab. Enterprises, 1970—. Former bd. dirs. N.Y. State Com. Discrimination in Housing; former trustee Broadcasting Found. Am.; chmn. deferred giving com. Dowling Coll., 1972—, trustee, 1977—. Mem. Bucknell U. Gen. Alumni Assn. (pres. Greater N.Y.) 1967-69, v.p. nat. assn. 1972-73, pres. 1973-74), Phi Beta Kappa, Omicron Delta Kappa, Tau Kappa Alpha, Pi Sigma Alpha, Pi Delta Epsilon. Home: Hickory Kingdom Rd Bedford NY 10506 Office: 122 E 42d St New York City NY 10017

HURWITZ, RICHARD ARTHUR, radiologist; b. N.Y.C., Sept. 16, 1934; s. Philip T. and Anne (Weinberg) H.; M.D., State U. N.Y., Downstate Med. Center, 1961; m. Kathleen Hurwitz, July 27, 1975; children—Brent, Amy, Page. Intern, Walter Reed Army Hosp., 1961-62; resident in radiology Brooke Army Hosp., San Antonio, 1962-65; attending radiologist Christ Hosp., Jersey City, 1969—; clin. asst. prof. radiology N.J. Coll. Medicine and Dentistry, Newark, 1971—; individual practice medicine, specializing in radiology, Jersey City, 1969—. Served to maj., M.C., U.S. Army, 1960-69. Diplomate Am. Bd. Radiology. Mem. Am. Coll. Radiology (exec. com. N.J. chpt. 1977-78), AMA, Am. Inst. Ultrasound in Medicine, Radiol. Soc. N. Am., Med. Soc. N.J. Jewish. Club: Med. Hudson County. Home: 8200 Blvd East North Bergen NJ 07047 Office: PO Box 7100 Jersey City NJ 07307

HURWITZ, SIDNEY, pediatric dermatologist; b. New Haven, May 6, 1925; s. Max and Sophie (Levin) H.; student Trinity Coll., Hartford, Conn.; M.D., State U. N.Y., Bklyn., 1949; m. Teddy Berman, July 3, 1958; children—Wendy, Laurie, Alison. Practice medicine specializing in pediatric dermatology, New Haven, 1954-69, in dermatology, 1970—; mem. staff Yale-New Haven Med. Center, Hosp. St. Raphael; asso. clin. prof. pediatrics and dermatology Yale U. Med. Sch. Served with USNR, 1943-45, AUS, 1951-53. Decorated Bronze Star. Mem. Soc. Pediatric Dermatology (pres. 1977-79), Internal Soc. Pediatric Dermatology, AMA, Conn. Med. Soc., Soc. Investigative Dermatology, New Haven County Med. Soc., New Eng., Noah Worcester dermatol. socs. Author articles, monographs. Address: 2 Church St S New Haven CT 06519

HUSAR, EMILE, civil engr., home inspection cons.; b. N.Y.C., Aug. 21, 1915; s. Elias and Tekla (Melech) H.; B.C.E., Sch. Tech., City Coll. N.Y., 1938, M.C.E., 1940; m. Lillian Semko, 1960; 2 stepchildren, 1 dau. Jr. engineer N.Y.C. Park Dept., 1940; junior engr. def. constrn., Panama Canal, 1941; constrn. supt., designer, estimator gen. contractor, 1946-49; resident bldg. insp. N.Y.C. Bd. Edn., 1950; estimator bldgs. N.J. Turnpike 1951; dir. pub. works, boro engr. sec. planning bd. bldg. insp., Leonia, N.J., 1952-64; self-employed

1964-65; chmn. bd. Stuyvesant Catering Corp., 1960-64; dir. pub. works, twp. engr., Twp. Berkeley Heights, N.J., 1965-67; asst. city engr., East Orange, N.J., 1967-70; profl. engr., project engr. Clinton Bogert Asso. Cons. Water & Sewer Engrs., 1970-76; borough engr., dir. pub. works, Roselle, N.J., 1977; registered rep. First Investors Corp., 1967-69, Sage, 1969-76; pvt. practice as bldg. constrn. estimator and home inspection cons., 1976—. Pres., Ukrainian Nat. Home of N.Y.C., 1956-62. Served as 1st lt. C.E., U.S. Army, 1942-46. Recipient Presdl. citation for S.W. Pacific and Papuan Campaigns; licensed profl. engr., N.Y., N.J. Fellow Am. Soc. C.E.; mem. N.J. Municipal Engrs., Nat., N.J. socs. profl. engrs., Internat. Fedn. Financial Counsellors, 401 Investors Club (pres.). Home and office: 411 Charles Pl Leonia NJ 07605

HUSHARD, LINDA LEE, real estate co. exec.; b. Clinton, Mass., Nov. 25, 1936; d. Carl E. and Ethel S. Anderson; student Colby (Maine) Coll., 1956-57, Conn. Coll. Women, 1959-60; m. F. James Hushard, June 22, 1962. Asst. order librarian Conn. Coll. Women, 1960-62; chief copywriter Sta. WSUB, Groton, Conn., 1962-65; with Hushard Realty Inc. div. Century 21, Groton, 1964—, pres., 1975—, Mem. Nat., Conn. assns. realtors, New London Bd. Realtors, S.E. Conn. Homebuilders Assn., S.E. Conn. C. of C., Bus. and Profl. Women's Club. Republican. Episcopalian. Club: Elks. Home: 26 Westwood Dr Groton CT 06340 Office: 1957 Poquonnock Rd US Route 1 Groton CT 06340

HUTCHENS, WILLIAM DAVID, accounting firm exec.; b. Johnstown, N.Y., Jan. 16, 1932; s. Harold William and Genevieve (Barnes) H.; B.A., Dartmouth, 1953, M.B.A. with distinction, 1958; m. Caryl Anne Bruns, Dec. 21, 1953; children—William David, Nancy Caryl. With Price Waterhouse & Co., 1958—, mgr., N.Y.C., 1963-69, partner, Syracuse, N.Y., 1969-72, partner in charge, 1972—. Mem. adv. bd. Syracuse U. Sch. Mgmt., 1972—, Corning Community Coll., 1974—; mem. nat. exec. com. Amos Tuck Sch. Bus. Adminstrn., Dartmouth, 1969—; vestryman Trinity Ch., 1973—, chmn. fin. com., 1971-74; bd. govs. Citizen's Found., 1976; bd. dirs. Community Council on Careers, 1975—, v.p., 1975-76; finance com. United Way of Syracuse, 1974-75. Served with USN, 1953-56. C.P.A., N.Y. Mem. Am. Inst. C.P.A.'s, N.Y. State Soc. C.P.A.'s (pres. 1976-77), Greater Syracuse C. of C. (chmn. econ. devel. council 1973—, dir., exec. com., v.p. 1973—). Clubs: Century, Onondaga Golf and Country, Univ. of Syracuse, Dartmouth Alumni of Central N.Y. (enrollment com. 1969-71), Mason. Home: 417 Salt Springs Rd Fayetteville NY 13066 Office: 100 Madison Tower Syracuse NY 13202

HUTCHINS, CHRISTOPHER, energy distbg. co. exec., finance co. exec.; b. Boston, Nov. 15, 1937; s. Curtis M. and Ruth E. (Rich) H.; B.A., Washington and Lee U., 1960; postgrad. Harvard U., 1972; m. Sandra Manee, Sept. 10, 1960; children—Charles M., James B. Chmn., Maine Wood Fuel Corp., Bangor, 1976—, chief exec., 1976—; dir. Merrill Trust Co., 1964—; v.p. Dead River Co., Bangor, Maine, 1962-74, Sugarloaf Mountain Corp., 1968-74, Pepsi Cola Bottling Co., Bangor, 1968—. Mem. Citizens Adv. Com. on Housing, Maine Dept. Health and Welfare, 1969; mem. Maine Land Use Regulation Commn., 1968-74; mem. City of Bangor Zoning Bd. of Appeals, 1972-78, chmn., 1974-78; del. to Republican Nat. Conv., 1968; mem. Rep. State Com., Penobscot County, Maine, 1967-71; mem. adv. bd. Crotched Mountain Found., 1967—; bd. dirs. Dance, Inc.; trustee Husson Coll., 1966-74, Down East Projects for the Handicapped; mem. Devel. Council U. Maine, 1970—; mem. Bangor Superintending Sch. Com., 1976—, chmn., 1978—. Served to 1st lt., arty., U.S. Army, 1960-62. Mem. New Eng. Council (dir. 1972-75), Miramichi Salmon Assn. (dir. 1970-76). Congregationalist. Clubs: Bangor City; Downtown (Boston); Penobscot Valley Country (gov. 1964-75), Tarratine. Home: 49 Bruce Rd Bangor ME 04401 Office: 84 Harlow St Bangor ME 04401

HUTCHINS, THOMAS WILLIAM, transp. leasing co. exec.; b. Chester, Pa., Aug. 2, 1943; s. Thomas Morrissey and Marie T. (Bartholf) H.; student Price Sch. Journalism, 1963, LaSalle Sch. Law, U. Del.; m. Linda K. Shope, Apr. 5, 1974; children—Thomas D., Michael E. Dir. mktg. RLC Corp., Wilmington, Del., 1970-75; dir. sales and mktg. Rollins Auto Leasing, New Castle, Del., 1976; v.p. sales and mktg. Rollins Auto Leasing Corp. div. RLC Corp., Wilmington, 1976—. Served with U.S. Army, 1962. Mem. Am. Mktg. Assn., Sales and Mktg. Execs. Contbr. articles to profl. jours. Home: 18 Washington Ave Perry Park Wilmington DE 19810 Office: PO Box 622 New Castle DE 19720

HUTCHINSON, ALAN BRADFORD, clergyman; b. Fall River, Mass., Sept. 19, 1927; s. William and Doris (Hart) H.; student Bowdoin Coll., 1945; A.B., Brown U., 1948; B.D., Andover Theol. Sem., 1951; M.A., Columbia, 1959; M.S., Danbury State Coll., 1964; M.S.W., Boston Coll., 1970; Ph.D., Tenn. U., 1975; m. Jean Caryl Cobb, Feb. 14, 1953; m. 2d, Muriel S. Johnson, Sept. 22, 1972. Ordained to ministry Congl. Ch., 1951; dir. youth work Park Pl. Congl. Ch., Pawtucket, R.I., 1948-51; minister of youth United Ch., Walpole, Mass., 1951-52; pastor Congl. Ch., New Fairfield, Conn., 1952-66; dir. social services Blackstone Valley Community Action Program, Pawtucket, R.I., 1966-72; clin. psychotherapist Providence Mental Health Center, 1972-76, adminstr. outpatient services, 1976—; pastor 1st Universalist Ch., Burrillville, R.I., 1972—; instr. U. R.I., 1975—; chaplain Fed. Correctional Instn., Danbury, Conn., 1957-58. Bd. dirs. Star Island Congl. Corp. Mem. Ballou-Channing Unitarian-Universalist Ministers Assn., No. R.I. Clergy Assn., Am. Correctional Chaplains Assn., Nat. Vocational Guidance Assn., Soc. Mayflower Descs. (elder Conn.), Am. Group Psychotherapy Assn., Am. Orthopsychiat. Assn., Register Clin. Social Workers, R.I. Conf. Social Work, Nat. Assn. Social Workers, Acad. Certified Social Workers, Phi Delta Kappa. Clubs: Community (past pres.), Brown University. Home: PO Box 2351 Providence RI 02906 Office: 355 Broad St Providence RI 02907

HUTCHINSON, JOHN EDWARD, III, cardiovascular surgeon; b. Birmingham, Ala., July 7, 1932; s. John E. and Annie Laurie (Dan) H.; B.S., Morehouse Coll., 1953; M.D., Meharry Med. Coll., 1957; m. Ann H. Merritt, June 3, 1957; children—Niki Lauren, John Edward, Leigh Ann, Kerry Beth. Intern, Jewish Hosp. Assn., Cin., 1957-58; asst. resident U. Iowa Hosps., Iowa City, 1958-60, resident in surgery, 1960-61, sr. resident in surgery, 1961-62, thoracic surg. resident, 1962-63, sr. asst. cardiac and thoracic surgery, 1963-64, instr. surgery, 1962-63, asso. in surgery, 1963-64; instr. surgery Columbia U., N.Y.C., 1964-66, asst. prof. surgery, 1966—, asst. prof. clin. surgery, 1969—, asso. clin. prof. surgery, 1972-73; practice medicine, specializing in cardiovascular surgery, N.Y.C., 1964—; asst. attending surgeon Presbyn. Hosp., N.Y.C., 1964—; vis. surgeon, chief thoracic surgery Harlem Hosp. Center, N.Y.C., 1967—; asso. vis. surgeon Francis Delafield Hosp., N.Y.C., 1965—; acting asst. attending surgeon St. Luke's Hosp. Center, N.Y.C., 1966-67, asst. attending surgeon, 1967-69, asso. attending surgeon, 1969—; cons. surgeon cardiovascular surgery Sharon Hosp., Sharon, Conn., 1976—. Diplomate Am. Bd. Surgery, Am. Bd. Thoracic Surgery. Fellow A.C.S.; mem. AMA, Am. Heart Assn., N.Y. County Med. Soc., N.Y. Thoracic Soc., N.Y. Soc. Cardiovascular Surgery, Soc. Thoracic Surgeons, N.Y. Acad. Medicine, Internat. Cardiovascular Soc., N.Y. Surg. Soc., Am. Assn. Thoracic Surgery, Alpha Omega Alpha. Contbr. articles in field to profl. jours. Address: 271 S Bedford Rd Chappaqua NY 10514

HUTCHINSON, JOHN JOSEPH, credit union exec.; b. Hartford, Conn., Jan. 1, 1921; s. Frank Walker and Mary A. (Maloney) H.; m. Barbara Andrews, Mar. 17, 1966; children—John J., James M., Michael. Asst. office mgr. East Hartford Aircraft Fed. Credit Union (Conn.), 1946-52; treas. and gen. mgr. Hamilton Standard Fed. Credit Union, Windsor Locks, Conn., 1952—, dir., 1952—, sec.-treas., 1952—, mem. exec. com., 1952—. Mem. Manchester town com., 1958—; Manchester town dir., 1958-60, 61-63, 64; mem. Manchester (Conn.) Charter Revision commn., 1965—; vice chmn. Manchester citizen's adv. com. on redevel. housing commn., 1962-64; mem. planning and zoning commn. Manchester, 1972—, vice chmn., 1973-76; chmn. regional planning commn., 1973-74; mem. adv. com. Westlands, 1973—; mem. Nat. Credit Union Bd., 1971-72; chmn. adv. com. Bradley Internat. Airport Commn., 1975-76. Served to 1st lt. AUS, 1942-46; ETO. Mem. Credit Union Nat. Assn. (internat. dir. 1961-70, dir. U.S. forum 1966-70, mem. credentials com. 1969), Credit Union Exec. Soc. (dir. 1965-68), Consumers Union U.S., Center Study Democratic Socs., Nat. Parks Assn., Nat. Assn. Fed. Credit Unions (dir. 1974, legis. chmn. 1975-76, sec. 1976—), Nat. Credit Union Mgmt. Assn. (chmn. conf. 1955), Am. Forestry Assn., Nat. Travel Club, East Hartford Aircraft Fed. Credit Union, Conn. Central Fed. Credit Union, Hamilton Standard Fed. Credit Union, Manchester Land Conservation Trust, Wayfarer's Club, Conn. Credit Union League (dir. at large 1960-69, pres. 1968-69, v.p. 1966-68, chmn. finance com. 1966-68, chmn. legislative com. 1961-67, chmn. convention 1962-67). Home: 98 Irving St Manchester CT 06040 Office: Bradley Rd Box 273 Windsor Locks CT 06096

HUTCHINSON, ROBERT BAKER, author, editor; b. Hutchinson, Kans., Apr. 11, 1924; s. Orie Lowell and Lennie Ann (Baker) H.; B.A. (Summerfield scholar), U. Kans., 1947; postgrad. Union Theol. Sem., 1947-50; M.A., Middlebury Coll., 1950; M.Phil., Columbia, 1975. Instr. English, Mt. Hermon (Mass.) Sch., 1950-51; asst. prof. philosophy Ala. Coll., Montevallo, 1951-52; editor McGraw-Hill Book Co., N.Y.C., 1954-58, Dover Publs., Inc., N.Y.C., 1960-77; lectr. English, City Coll. N.Y., 1962-63. Served to 1st lt. USAAF, 1943-46. Recipient Crowell Short Story prize Prairie Schooner, 1946, Kent fellowship Nat. Soc. Religion in Higher Edn., 1952-53, Frost Poetry scholarship Bread Loaf Sch. English, 1950, Eugene F. Saxton Trust fellowship Harper and Row, 1958, DeVoto fellowship Bread Loaf Writer's Conf., 1962. Mem. Am. Acad. Religion, Phi Beta Kappa. Author: The Kitchen Dance, 1955, 75; (TV play) Drugstore Sunday Noon, 1956; Standing Still While Traffic Moved About Me, 1971. Editor: Poems of Anne Bradstreet, 1969; Poems of George Santayana, 1970. Contbr. poetry, short stories to various publs. Home: 87 Barrow St New York City NY 10014

HUTCHINSON, WILLIAM DODGE, ednl. research co. exec.; b. Boston, Oct. 11, 1941; s. Kenneth Inniss and Hazel Veda (Dodge) H.; A.S., Western Conn. State Coll., 1962, B.A., 1965; M.B.A., Adelphi U., 1974. Research coordinator nat. sales CBS-TV, N.Y.C., 1970-73; sr. research analyst Telerep, N.Y.C., 1973-74; dir. research World Radio Mission, Lancaster, N.H., 1975-77; chief exec. W.D. Hutchinson Co., ednl. research, Danbury, Conn., 1977—. Served with USN, 1965-69. Mem. Am. Personnel and Guidance Assn., Danbury C. of C. (ednl. com.). Republican. Episcopalian. Home: 11 Wheeler Dr Danbury CT 06810

HUTELMYER, CAROL M., nursing admnstr.; b. Phila., Jan. 20, 1942; d. Maurice A. and Josephine M. (Smith) H.; B.S.N. Georgetown U. Sch. Nursing 1966; M.S.N., U. Pa. 1969. Staff nurse Bon Secours Hosp., Grosse Pointe, Mich. 1966-67; clin. supr. Jefferson Hosp., Phila. 1969-72, asst. dir. med. nursing 1972-74, dir. nursing 1974—; lectr. in field of quality nursing care. Mem. Am. Nurses Assn., Am. Congress of Rehab. Medicine, Nat. League for Nursing, Sigma Theta Tau. Contbr. numerous articles to profl. jours. Office: 11th and Walnut St Jefferson U Hosp Philadelphia PA 19107

HUTNER, JOSEPH LOUIS, lawyer; b. Flushing, N.Y., May 30, 1933; s. Edward and Anne (Grapes) H.; B.A. summa cum laude, Yale, 1955; student (fellow) Heidelberg U., 1953-54; LL.B., Harvard U., 1958; m. Willa Selenfriend, Feb. 20, 1958; children—Laura, Susan, Amy. Admitted to N.Y. bar, 1959, since practiced in N.Y.C.; partner Singer, Hutner, Levine & Seeman, N.Y.C., 1966—. Lectr. Practising Law Inst., 1974—. Pres. United Fund, White Plains, N.Y., 1965; dir., ex officio dir. United Fund, Westchester, N.Y., 1963—; founder Westchester chpt. Mensa, 1962. Democratic candidate U.S. Ho. Reps. 26th Congl. Dist., Westchester, 1966. Named Young Man of Year White Plains C. of C., 1965. Mem. Assn. Bar City N.Y., N.Y. State Bar Assn., Phi Beta Kappa. Mem. B'nai B'rith (dir. N.Y. regional bd. 1969-72). Club: Yale (N.Y.C.). Home: 39 Hathaway Ln White Plains NY 10605 Office: 110 E 59th St New York City NY 10022

HUTSALIUK, LUBO, artist; b. Lvov, Ukraine, Apr. 2, 1923; s. Michael and Stephanie (Demydchuk) H.; came to U.S., 1949, naturalized, 1955; B.A., Cooper Union, 1954; m. Renata Kozicka, July 14, 1951; 1 son, Yarema. One-man shows at Galerie Volmar, Paris, 1956, Boissevain Gallery, 1957, Galerie Norval, Paris, 1959, Galleria Lorenzelli, Milan, Italy, 1959, Juster Gallery, N.Y.C., 1960, 64, W & W Gallery, Toronto, Ont., Can., 1962, Angle du Faubourg, Paris, 1963, Hilde Gerst Gallery, 1966, 68, Rolly & Michaux Gallery, Boston, 1973, Galerie Royale, Paris, 1976, Art U.S.A., N.Y.C., 1958, Salon d'Automne, Paris, 1959-63, Salon des Independents, Paris, 1959, 63, 65, Audubon Artists, N.Y.C., 1971-72; represented in permanent collections at Palm Springs Desert Museum, Palm Springs, Calif., Vt. Art Center, Manchester, Bibliotheque Nationale, Paris, also pvt. collections. Home: 260 Riverside Dr New York City NY 10025 also 103 rue de Vaugirard Paris 6 France

HUTTON, DUANE, supt. schs.; b. Batavia, N.Y., Nov. 4, 1937; s. Edward Robert and Maybelle (Nye) H.; B.S., State U. N.Y. at Brockport, 1963; M.Ed., U. Buffalo, 1967; Ph.D., Syracuse U., 1969; m. Gae Susan Phillips, Aug. 14, 1965; children—David, Jill. Adminstrv. intern to supt. schs. Syracuse, 1968-69; asst. supt. Sidney Central (N.Y.), 1969-73; supt. schs. Veronon-Verona-Sherrill Central, Verona, N.Y., 1973—. Gen. chmn. Sidney Community Chest Dr., 1972-73. Served with U.S. Army, 1955-58. Inst. Devel. Ednl. Activities fellow, 1970. Mem. Am. Assn. Sch. Adminstrs., Nat. Soc. Study Edn., N.Y. State, So. Tier (pres. 1972-73) assns. sch. bus. ofcls., Mohawk Valley Chief Sch. Officers Assn. (pres. 1976-77). Home: Indian Field Rd Clinton NY 13323 Office: School Dept Verona NY 13478

HUTTON, JACK GOSSETT, JR., psychologist, educator; b. Denver, June 20, 1931; s. Jack Gossett and Margaretta Elizabeth (Lea) H.; student Colo. Coll., 1949-51; B.A., U. Denver, 1953, M.A., 1956; Ph.D., U. Conn., 1968. Asst. dir. div. ednl. measurement and research Assn. Am. Med. Colls., Washington, 1968-71; staff psychologist, Psychol. Corp., N.Y.C., 1971-73; ednl. psychologist, asso. prof. Coll. Dentistry, Howard U., Washington, 1973—, asso. prof. Sch. Edn., 1973-77; vis. ednl. specialist Sch. Dentistry, W. Va. U., 1976—. Vis. scholar U. Mich., summer 1968; adj. asst. prof. Sch. Edn., Cath. U., 1969-71. Served with U.S. Army, 1956-58. Mem. Am. Psychol. Assn., Am. Edn. Research Assn., Nat. Council Measurement in Edn., Am. Assn. Dental Schs. (sec. sect. behavioral scis. 1975-76), AAUP, Sigma Xi, Psi Chi, Phi Sigma. Contbr. to profl. jours. Home: 1101 New Hampshire Ave NW Apt 1018 Washington DC 20037 Office: Coll Dentistry Howard Univ 600 W St NW Washington DC 20059

HUYOT, SUZANNE, mktg. and bus. cons.; b. N.Y.C., Feb. 13, 1944; d. Robert Henri and Rita (Sullivan) Huyot; B.A., Newton Coll., 1965; M.A., Harvard, 1967; student N.Y. U. Sch. Bus., 1970-78. Trainee, Esso Math. & Systems, Inc., computer subs. Exxon Corp., N.Y.C., 1967; systems analyst Franklin Computer Asso., Market Data Systems, N.Y.C., 1967-72; dancer Neubert Ballet Theatre, N.Y.C., 1972-74; sr. mgnmt. Abraham & Straus Co., N.Y.C., 1972-74; interior designer, bus. cons.; 1974—; cons. Money Market div. Citibank, N.Y.C., 1975; cons. systems and data processing ITT World Hdqrs., 1976—. Mem. Nichiren Shoshu Soka Gakkai Acad. Club: Harvard (N.Y.C.). Home: 250 1st Ave 10-D New York NY 10009 Office: ITT Corp Systems 320 Park Ave New York NY 10302

HWANG, JENNMOW, wholesale co. exec., accountant; b. Hsilo, Formosa, June 2, 1934; s. Shangju and Pongtou (Liao) H.; Tchr's. License Taipei (Formosa) Normal Sch., 1953; B.Com., Chung Hsing U., Taipei, 1960; M.B.A., Waseda U., Tokyo, 1965; LL.M., Meiji U., Tokyo, 1968; m. Tomoko Masuda, Nov. 13, 1968; 1 son, Kevin. Tchr. elementary sch., Taiwan, 1953-56; office mgr. Formosan Traders, Ltd., Taipei, 1957-63; internal auditor First Food Industries Ltd., Tokyo, 1965-66; controller Kern Stationers Ltd., Toronto, Ont., Can., 1968-71; auditor Hattin, Moses, Sugarman & Co., Toronto, 1969-70; auditor Can. Dept. Nat. Revenue-Taxation, Toronto, 1971-72; v.p. finance Scantrade Internat. Ltd., Toronto, 1972—. Recipient prize for accounting essay contest Japan C. of C. and Industry, 1965; certified gen. accountant. Mem. Certified Gen. Accountants Assn. Ont., Am. Accounting Assn. Home: 2388 Sinclair Circle Burlington ON L7P 3C3 Canada Office: 60 Horner Ave Toronto ON M8Z 4X3 Canada

HYAMS, VINCENT JOSEPH, pathologist; b. Jacksonville, Fla., Mar. 31, 1924; s. Charles Irving and Emmeline Marian (Witten) H.; B.S., Newberry Coll., 1947; M.D., Med. Coll. S.C., 1950; m. Marian Eugenia Henderson, June 2, 1949; children—Deborah, George, James, Andrew, Vincent. Intern, McLeod Infirmary, Florence, S.C., 1950-51; resident U.S. Naval Hosp., St. Albans, N.Y., 1955-59; commd. lt. U.S. Navy, 1956, advanced through grades to capt., 1958; pathologist, chief of labs. M.C., N.Y.C., Japan and Charleston S.C., 1956-63; pathologist, chmn. otolaryngic pathology dept. Armed Forces Inst. Pathology, Washington, 1963—, prof. pathology, 1976—. NIH grantee, 1963-72. Asso. fellow Am. Acad. Ophthalmology and Otolaryngology (certificate of appreciation 1977); mem. Mil. Surgeons Assn. U.S., AMA (mil. service asso.). Roman Catholic. Author: Pathology of the Ear, 1976; Tumors of the Upper Respiratory Tract and Ear, 1978; editorial bd. Annals of Otolaryngology, Rhinology and Laryngology Clin. Otolaryngology. Home: 1219 Downs Dr Silver Springs MD 20914 Office: Armed Forces Inst Pathology Washington DC 20305

HYDE, HENRY BALDWIN, lawyer; b. Paris, France, Oct. 31, 1915; s. James Hazen and Martha (Leishman) H.; came to U.S., 1936; M.A., Cambridge (Eng.) U., 1936; LL.B., Harvard, 1939; m. Marie de LaGrange, Apr. 1941; children—Lorna Hyde de Wangen, Isabel Hyde; m. 2d, Elizabeth Prokoff Piper, 1960. Admitted to N.Y. State bar, 1940, since practiced in N.Y.C.; mem. firm Goldstein, Shames & Hyde, and predecessors, 1953-78; mem. firm Wormser, Kiely, Alessandroni, Hyde & McCann, 1978—; dir. Bitter Root Stock Farm, Inc. Bd. dirs. French Inst.-Alliance Francaise; bd. mgrs. Hosp. for Spl. Surgery, N.Y.C. Served with OSS, AUS, 1942-45. Decorated Bronze Star medal with oak leaf cluster, Croix de Guerre. Mem. Vets. of OSS (exec. com.), Council Fgn. Relations. Clubs: River (N.Y.C.); Deepdale Golf (L.I., N.Y.); Travelers (Paris). Home: 565 Park Ave New York City NY 10021 Office: 100 Park Ave New York City NY 10017

HYDE, WILLIAM RAY, food and beverage co. exec.; b. Chattanooga, May 25, 1928; s. William Cornelius and Femmie Ally (Davis) H.; student Stetson U., 1950-52; m. Adelaide Emma Taylor, July 3, 1948 (div. 1975); children—William George, Kenneth Edward, Victoria Adelaide. Pub. relations editor Prudential Ins. Co., Boston, 1957-61; pub. relations account exec. Wesley Day Advt. Agy., Des Moines, 1961-64; mgr. pub. relations Sheaffer Pen Co., Ft. Madison, Iowa, 1964-67, Bell & Howell Co., Lincolnwood, Ill., 1967-69; dir. pub. relations Barton Brands, Ltd., Chgo., 1969-73; v.p. pub. relations Schieffelin & Co., N.Y.C., 1973—. Indsl. commr., Southboro, Mass., 1960-61; sec. Town Republican Com., Southboro, 1959-61; del. Mass. Rep. Conv., 1960; Rep. town committeeman, Urbandale, Iowa; del. Iowa Rep. Conv., 1964. Served with U.S. Army, 1946-49, 52-57. Mem. Pub. Relations Soc. Am., Am. Mensa. Baptist. Club: Masons. Home: 687 Lexington Ave New York City NY 10022 Office: 30 Cooper Sq New York City NY 10003

HYER, FRANK SIDNEY, instrument co. exec.; b. Madison, Wis., Dec. 29, 1933; s. Frank Perry and Lorena (Bergquist) H.; A.B., Ripon Coll., 1956; B.S., U. Del., 1958; M.S., U. Wis., 1968; m. Jane Beth Graeber, Dec. 29, 1954; children—Laura Jane, Frank S., David G. Design engr. Cutler-Hammer, Inc., Milw., 1958-60, devel. engr., 1960-63; mgr. engrng., mfg. Thayer Scale Co., Pembroke, Mass., 1963-65, gen. mgr., 1965-73; pres., chief exec. officer, dir. Hyer Industries, Inc., Pembroke, 1973—. Mem. ASME, Instrument Soc. Am. Lutheran. Club: Duxbury Yacht. Contbr. tech. articles to profl. jours.; patentee in field. Home: 152 Marshall St Duxbury MA 02332 Office: Route 139 Thayer Park Pembroke MA 02359

HYETT, MARVIN RONALD, obstetrician, gynecologist; b. Miami, Fla., Feb. 4, 1938; s. Edward and Alice (Tomsky) H.; B.S., Muhlenberg Coll., 1959; M.D., Jefferson Med. Coll., 1963; m. Joyce Karen Higgins, May 30, 1964; children—Mark, Deborah. Intern, Atlantic City Hosp., 1963-64; resident Thomas Jefferson U. Hosp., Phila., 1964-67, NIH cancer tng. grant, 1967-69, instr., 1967-69, asst. prof. obstetrics and gynecology, 1969—; practice medicine specializing in obstetrics and gynecology, Phila., 1969—; mem. staff Thomas Jefferson Univ. Hosp. Served with USAF, 1963-69. Fellow A.C.S., Am. Coll. Obstetricians and Gynecologists. Jewish. Office: 255 S 17th St Philadelphia PA 19103

HYKES, RICHARD NORMAN, med. equipment co. exec.; b. Hagerstown, Md., Mar. 1, 1939; s. Charles Melvin and Mary Louise (McCormick) H.; B.S., U. Md., 1961; M.B.A., U. Mich., 1966; m. Maria Aurora S. Isip, Apr. 27, 1967; 1 dau., Clarinda Marie. Specialist mil. sales Gen. Electric Co., Louisville, 1967-69, specialist internat. market devel., Bethesda, Md., 1970-72; v.p. mktg. Greater Washington Bus. Center, Washington, 1973-76; dir. corporate planning Acuity Systems Inc., Reston, Va., 1977—. Served with USNR, 1961-64. Mem. Am. Mktg. Assn., Am. Econ. Assn., Phi Kappa Phi, Beta Gamma Sigma. Roman Catholic. Home: 800 25th St NW Washington DC 20037

HYLAND, WILLIAM FRANCIS, lawyer, state ofcl.; b. Burlington, N.J., July 30, 1923; s. Theodore J. and Margaret M. (Gallagher) H.; B.S. in Econs. U. Pa., 1944, LL.B., 1949; m. Joan E. Sharp, Apr. 20, 1946; children—William Francis, Nancy E. Hyland Wiley, Stephen J., Emma L., Margaret M., Thomas M. Admitted to N.J. bar, 1949, U.S.

Supreme Ct. bar, 1960; mem. firm Riker, Danzig, Scherer, Debevois & Hyland, Newark, 1978—; atty. gen. N.J., 1974-78; chmn. N.J. Sports and Exposition Authority, 1978—. Mem. N.J. Gen. Assembly From Camden County, 1954-61, speaker of house, 1958; acting gov. N.J., 1958; pres. N.J. Bd. Pub. Utility Commrs., also mem. cabinet Gov. Meyner and Gov. Hughes, 1961-68; chmn. N.J. Atomic Energy Council, 1968-69; chmn. N.J. Commn. Investigation, 1969-71; co-chmn. Reapportionment Commn. Chmn. Brazilian Mission Com., 1962-65. Del.-at-large Dem. Nat. Conv., 1964, del., 1968. Asso trustee U. Pa. Served as officer USNR, 1943-46; ETO, PTO. Decoreated knight Order of St. Gregory (Pope Paul VI), 1964; recipient Outstanding Young Man in Govt. N.J. award N.J. Jaycees, 1958; Distinguished Service award Camden County Jaycees, 1954. Mem. Camden County Bar Assn. (pres. 1959), Nat. Assn. R.R. and Utilities Commrs. (exec. com. 1965-68), Phi Kappa Psi. Home: 5 Ellyn Ct Convent Station NJ 07961 Office: 744 Broad St Newark NJ 07102

HYMAN, BRUCE MALCOLM, ophthalmologist; b. N.Y.C., May 22, 1943; s. Malcolm A. and Sylvia S. H.; A.B., Columbia U., 1964; M.D., N.Y. U., 1968. Intern in surgery Albert Einstein Coll. Medicine/Bronx Mcpl. Hosp., 1968-69; resident in ophthalmology Manhattan Eye, Ear and Throat Hosp., N.Y.C., 1971-74; pvt. practice medicine specializing in ophthalmology, N.Y.C., 1974—; tchr., attending surgeon Manhattan Eye, Ear and Throat Hosp., 1974—; med. cons. U.S. Seaplane Pilots Assn., 1975—, Health Ins. Plan Greater N.Y., 1977—; ophthalmologist to Hotel Trades Council, Hotel Assn. N.Y.C., 1974—. Served with USPHS, 1969-71. Diplomate Am. Bd. Ophthalmology. Mem. N.Y. State, N.Y. County med. socs., Am. Acad. Ophthalmology and Otolaryngology. Contbr. articles to profl. jours. Office: 133 E 64 St New York NY 10021

HYMAN, IRWIN A., psychologist, educator; b. Neptune, N.J., Mar. 22, 1935; s. Henry Meltzer and Harriet (Greenitz) H.; B.A. in Sociology, U. Maine, Orono, 1957; Ed.D. in Sch. Psychology, Rutgers U., New Brunswick, N.J., 1964; children—Nadine, Debrah Nan. Sch. psychologist Lawrence Twp. schs., Trenton, N.J., 1962-66; chief clin. services Tng. Sch. at Vineland (N.J.), 1966-67; prof. Newark State Coll., Union, N.J., 1967-68; prof. dept. sch. psychology Temple U., Phila., 1968—; dir. Nat. Center Study of Corporal Punishment and Alternatives in Schs.; pvt. practice psychology, Princeton, N.J. Cons. HEW. Mem. Am. Psychol. Assn. (sec. div. sch. psychology 1974-76, pres. 1978; bd. social and ethical responsibility), AAAS, Nat. Assn. Sch. Psychologists, Am. Ednl. Research Assn., Phi Delta Kappa. Contbr. articles to profl. jours. Specialist in sch. psychology, Head Start, child advocacy studies. Home: 207 Carter Rd Princeton NJ 08540 Office: 823 Ritter Hall Temple U Philadelphia PA 19122

HYNDS, FRANCIS JOSEPH, JR., sch. counselor; b. Melrose, Mass., May 28, 1947; s. Francis Joseph and Teresa Louise (Turner) H.; B.S. in Edn., Salem (Mass.) State Coll., 1969; M.A. in Guidance and Counseling, Rider Coll., Trenton, N.J., 1973; postgrad. Bridgewater (Mass.) State Coll., 1974, Boston U., 1974, Boston State Coll., 1974. Counselor, Silver Lake Regional Jr. High Sch., Pembroke, Mass., 1973—. Mem. Plymouth Area adv. bd. Mass. Dept. Pub. Welfare, 1977—. Served with USAF, 1969-73. Decorated Air Force Commendation medal with oak leaf cluster. Mem. Am. Personnel and Guidance Assn., Am., Mass. sch. counselors assns., South Shore Guidance Assn., NEA, Mass., Silver Lake, Plymouth County tchrs. assns. Home: 18 Foster Ave Ocean Bluff MA 02065 Office: Silver Lake Regional Jr High Sch School St Pembroke MA 02359

HYNEK, WALTER JOSEPH, fabric mfg. co. exec.; b. Phila., Apr. 16, 1928; s. Joseph and Agnes (Gruca) H.; B.A., La Salle Coll., 1951; postgrad. Rutgers U., 1957-60, Columbia U., 1964; m. Gertrude Chocallo, Oct. 31, 1953; 1 dau., Stefanie. Physicist Q.M. Research Lab., Phila., 1951-54; gen. mgr. Gen. Feather Fibre Corp., Phila., 1954-55; sr. chemist Chicopee Mfg. Co., Milltown, N.J., 1955-58, supr., 1958-62, mgr. product devel., 1962-64, tech. sales cons., product dir., 1969-73, dir. affiliate sales, 1973-75, v.p., gen. mgr. affiliate div., 1975-76, v.p., gen. mgr. Converted Products div., 1976—. Served with U.S. Army, 1946-47. Fellow Am. Inst. Chemists; mem. Am. Chem. Soc., Am. Assn. Textile Tech. Patentee nonwoven fabrics. Home: 17 Inwood Dr Milltown NJ 08850 Office: Chicopee Mfg Co Ford Ave Milltown NJ 08850

HYSON, CHARLES DAVID, economist; b. Hampstead, Md., Dec. 29, 1915; s. Harry Perry and Rose (Miller) H.; A.B., St. John's Coll., Annapolis, 1937; M.S., U. Md., 1939; M.A., Harvard, 1942, Ph.D., 1943; m. Winifred Chandler Prince, Sept. 7, 1946; children—David Prince, Pamela Chandler Hyson Martin, Christopher Perry. Agri. economist FCA, 1939-40; staff Surplus Mktg. Adminstrn., Washington, 1940-41; resident tutor, then sr. tutor Harvard, 1942-49, research asso., 1943-44, resident cons. Grad. Sch. Pub. Adminstrn., 1943-49, instr. econs., 1946-48, asso. dir. mktg. research program, 1948-49; regional economist, then chief prices and cost of living br. U.S. Bur. Labor Statistics, 1944-46; indsl. economist Fed. Res. Bank Boston, 1946-48; asst. econ. commr. ECA Mission to Norway, Oslo, 1949-50; trade specialist, staff spl. rep. in Europe, Paris, 1950, spl. asst. to chief of mission ECA, Mut. Security Agy., Lisbon, Portugal, 1950-52; dep. dir. U.S. Ops. Mission to Portugal, Mut. Security Agy., FOA, ICA, 1952-55; spl. rep. to Portugal, ICA, 1955-57, chief Western Europe div., Washington 1957-59, chief European div., 1959-60; Nat. War Coll., 1960-61; counselor of embassy for econ. affairs Am. Embassy, Lisbon, 1955-57; dep. asst. dir. for exec. staffing AID, Washington, 1961-62; adviser for econ. affairs Office Material Resources, AID, 1962-63, spl. asst. for econ. and trade affairs, 1963-74, cons. economist, 1975—. Dept. nat. export expansion coordinator, dep. exec. dir. Cabinet Com. Export Expansion, 1964. Mem. Internat. secretariat and econ. adv. conf. on Human Skills in Decade Devel., San Juan, P.R., 1962; mem. trade com. for White House Conf. on Internat. Cooperation, 1965. Decorated Order of Merit (Portugal); recipient Spl. Commendation and Meritorious Service award, Superior Honor award U.S. Govt. Fellow Royal Econ. Soc.; mem. Am. Acad. Polit. and Social Sci., Am. Econ. Assn., Am. Agrl. Econs. Assn., Am. Fgn. Service Assn., Sigma Alpha Epsilon. Clubs: Harvard (Washington); Keene Valley (N.Y.) Country; Adirondack Mountain; Ausable (St. Huberts, N.Y.). Author books and monographs; contbr. articles to econ. jours. Address: 7407 Honeywell Ln Bethesda MD 20014

I, TING PO, research chemist; b. Yunnan, China, Feb. 20, 1941; s. Chia Ou and Shin Shu (Wu) I; came to U.S., 1966, naturalized, 1977; Ph.D., State U. N.Y., Buffalo, 1972; m. Ai Mei Chao, Sept. 6, 1969; children—Shiao Lan, David. Research asso. Brandeis U., Waltham, Mass., 1972-74; sr. scientist Central Research Pfizer Ind., Groton, Conn., 1974—. Mem. Am. Chem. Soc. Contbr. articles to Jour. Am. Chem. Soc., Analytical Chemistry, Jour. Inorganic Chemistry. Home: 4 Twin Lakes Dr Waterford CT 06385 Office: Eastern Point Rd Groton CT 06340

IACANGELO, PETER AUGUST, JR., actor; b. Bklyn., Aug. 13, 1948; s. Peter and Mary Rose (Bordini) I.; student Yankton Coll., 1967, Suffolk County Community Coll., 1968-69; B.A., Hofstra U., 1971; m. Melody Rose Marzola, Apr. 5, 1975; 1 son, Peter August III. Actor in off-Broadway prodns. with group 15 cents Token Presents, including A Nickel's Worth of N.Y., 1971, One Flew Over the Cuckoos Nest, 1972, Moon Children, 1972-74, Comedy of Errors, 1975; (TV prodns.) How To Survive A Marriage, 1974-75, Beacon Hill, 1975; (Broadway prodn.) Three Penny Opera, 1976-77; (film) Blood Brothers, 1978; regional theatre appearances Long Wharf Theatre, New Haven; appeared in various TV commls.; owner, operator Conflict Workshop Sch. for Actors, 1968-73; pres. Creative Media Assos., Selden, N.Y., 1968-71. Recipient certificate of appreciation City of N.Y., 1972, Upward Bound Program, Bowdoin Coll., 1968. Mem. Screen Actors Guild, Actors Equity Assn., AFTRA, Police Athletic League, Jacques Costeau Soc., Broadway Drama Guild (charter), Am. Film Inst., Internat. Fund for Animal Welfare. Roman Catholic. Editor in chief: Images Poetry Mag., 1968. Home: 24-30 21st St Astoria NY 11102

IACOVIDES, TASOS IACOVOS, nuclear engr.; b. Famagusta, Cyprus, July 3, 1941; s. Iacovos Leonidas and Elisavet; came to U.S., 1964, naturalized, 1972; student U. Athens (Greece), 1959-61; B.S. in Physics, St. John's U., 1968, postgrad., 1970-72; m. Kathleen A. Peterson, July 3, 1976; 1 son, Brian Tasos. Asst. engr. Ebasco Services Inc., N.Y.C., 1968-73, asso. engrs., 1973-74, engr., 1974-75, sr. engr., 1975—. Sec., Efoka, 1970-71. Democrat. Greek Orthodox. Home: 28 John St New York City NY 10956 Office: 19 Rector St New York City NY 10006

IAMS, WILLIAM BOWMAN, cardiovascular and thoracic surgeon; b. Pitts., Apr. 27, 1941; s. Charles William and Louise Bowman (Metzger) I.; student Dartmouth Coll., 1959-62; B. Med. Sci., Northwestern U., 1963, M.D., 1966; m. Helen Pamela Lore, July 7, 1962; children—Christine Louise, Kenneth William, Robert Lore, Kathryn Elizabeth. Resident in gen. surgery, then cardiovascular and thoracic surgery Johns Hopkins Hosp., Balt., 1966-72; registrar to Mr. Ronald Belsey in thoracic surgery, Bristol, Eng., 1970; chief surg. services Kirtland AFB, Albuquerque, 1972-74; practice medicine specializing in cardiovascular and thoracic surgery, Harrisburg, Pa., 1974—; asso. in cardiovascular and thoracic surgery Harrisburg Hosp.; asso. in broncho-esophagology, cardiovascular and thoracic surgery Polyclinic Med. Center, Harrisburg; asst. in thoracic surgery Holy Spirit Hosp., Camp Hill, Pa.; cons. Chambersburg (Pa.) Hosp.; clin. asst. prof. surgery Pa. State U., 1977—. Served with USAF, 1972-74. Licensed in medicine and surgery, Pa., Md.; diplomate Am. Bd. Thoracic Surgery. Fellow A.C.S., Am. Coll. Cardiology, Am. Coll. Chest Physicians; mem. AMA, Assn. Academic Surgeons, Soc. Thoracic Surgery, Dauphin County (Pa.) Med. Soc., Johns Hopkins Med. and Surg. Soc. Republican. Presbyterian. Contbr. articles in field to med. jours. Office: 2247 N Front St Harrisburg PA 17110

IANNELLI, JOSEPH GEORGE, state ofcl.; b. Cranston, R.I., Mar. 19, 1915; s. Pasquale and Cecelia (Gesmondi) I.; student pub. schs., Cranston; m. Lucy R. DeCristofaro, Nov. 24, 1938; children—Pat, William, Mary Lou. Dep. in charge adminstrn. R.I. Dept. Corrections, 1955-64; correctional industries bus. mgr. State of R.I., 1945-54; exec. sec. R.I. Retirement Bd. Trustees, 1964—; dir. R.I. Employees Retirement System, 1964—; dir., trustee Credit Union Nat. Assn. Ins. Pension Plan; pres. bd. dirs. Employees Credit Union; dir. R.I. Credit Union League. Served with U.S. Army, 1943. Recipient numerous service awards. Mem. Nat. Assn. State Retirement Adminstrs. (v.p.), Municipal Fin. Officers Assn. U.S. and Can., New Eng. Retirement Law Revision Council (chmn. retirement adminstrs.), Nat. Council Tchr. Retirement, Credit Union Nat. Assn., R.I. Employees Assn. Council. Roman Catholic. Clubs: Alpine County (Cranton); Elks (Providence); K.C. Home: 60 Yeoman Ave Cranston RI 02920 Office: 198 Dyer St Providence RI 02903

IBBOTSON, JEFFREY, oil co. exec.; b. Oldham, Lancashire, U.K., Aug. 12, 1937; s. Vincent and Edith Doris (Mitchell) Ibbotson; B.S., Manchester Inst. Sci. and Tech., U.K., 1960, M.S., 1962, Ph.D., 1964; M.B.A., U. Pitts., 1975; m. Patricia Irene Eccles, Mar. 30, 1963; children—Gaynor Louise, Andrew Jeffrey. Adviser project devel. Gulf Oil Co.-Middle East, Pitts., 1974-75; mgr. bus. devel. Gulf Trading & Transp. Co., Pitts., 1975-76; mgr. tech. planning Gulf Sci. & Tech., Pitts., 1976—. Bd. dirs. Town Council Town of Cardiff-by-the-Sea, Calif., 1970-72. Chartered engr., U.K.; registered profl. engr., Calif. Home: 275 Bower Dr Sewickley PA 15143

ICKEN, JOSEPH MARTIN, pharm. cons.; b. Warsaw, Poland, Dec. 12, 1911; s. Mowsza and Fajga (Angel) Ickowicz; came to U.S., 1950, naturalized, 1956; certificate sci. studies U. Paris, 1931; M. Philosophy in Chemistry, U. Warsaw, 1937; m. Felicia Pacholder, Nov. 2, 1939; 1 dau., Sylvia. Head analytical lab. Heparin, Inc., Jersey City, 1950-51; head devel. lab. Food Research Labs., Inc., Long Island City, N.Y., 1951-56; mgr. product devel. Isodine Pharmacal Co., Dover, Del., 1956-63; pres. United Sci. Supply Corp., Bklyn., 1964-65; dir. pharm. devel. and registration Warner-Lamber Internat., Morris Plains, N.J., 1965-76; pharm. cons., Livingston, N.J., 1977—. Active YMHA-YWHA of Met. N.J. Fellow Royal Soc. Health; mem. Am. Chem. Soc., Am. Pharm. Assn., Soc. Cosmetic Chemists, AMA (affiliate). Home and Office: 24 Tiffany Dr Livingston NJ 07039

IFILL, GORDON GREGORY LEO, psychiatrist; b. Barbados, West Indies, Apr. 20, 1931; s. Gordon Luther and Marcelina Antonia (Brown) I.; came to U.S., 1956, naturalized, 1966; B.S. cum laude, L.I. U., 1960; M.D., Howard U., 1964; m. Beverly Veronica Whyte, June 6, 1959; children—Michelle, Deidré, Gregory, Désirés. Intern, Monmouth Med. Center, Long Branch, N.J., 1964-65; resident in psychiatry N.J. State Hosp., Ancora, 1965-66, Kings Park (N.Y.) State Hosp., 1966-68; psychiatrist Kings Park State Hosp., 1967-68, N.E. Nassau Psychiat. Center, Kings Park, 1968-71; practice medicine specializing in psychiatry, Hempstead, N.Y., 1968—; med. dir. Roosevelt (N.Y.) Community Mental Health Center, 1973-74, Mercy Hosp. Family Counseling Service, Hempstead, 1975—; attending psychiatrist Mercy Hosp., Rockville Center, N.Y., 1970—, Nassau Hosp., Mineola, N.Y., 1975—; cons. Freeport (N.Y.) pub. schs., Hempstead pub. schs., 1970-74, Seaford (N.Y.) pub. schs., 1974—. Certified psychiatrist, N.Y.; certified acupuncturist, N.Y.; diplomate Nat. Bd. Med. Examiners, Am. Bd. Psychiatry and Neurology. Mem. Am. Psyhicat. Assn., Nat. Med. Assn., Nassau-Suffolk Clin. Soc., Acad. Orthomolecular Psychiatry, N.Y. Soc. Acupuncture Physicians and Dentists, AAAS. Club: 100 Black Men of Nassau-Suffolk. Home: 2 Susan Ln Dix Hills NY 11746 Office: 9 Centre St Hempstead NY 11550

IGLEWICZ, BORIS, statistician, educator; b. Omsk, USSR, Oct. 11, 1939; s. Solomon and Faiga (Brucker) I.; came to U.S., 1952, naturalized, 1959; B.S., Wayne State U., 1962; M.A., 1963; Ph.D., Va. Poly. Inst., 1967; m. Raja Brody, May 24, 1973; children—David, Alana. Instr. math. Mich. Tech. U., 1963-64; asst. prof. statistics Case Western Res. U., 1967-69; asso. prof. statistics Temple U., 1969-74, prof., 1974—, dir. Ph.D. program in statistics, 1970-75, dept. chmn., 1978—; v.p. Meco Metals Corp., 1974, also dir. NIH fellow, 1964-67. Mem. Am. Statis. Assn., Biometric Soc., Inst. Math. Statistics, Sigma Xi, Pi Mu Epsilon, Beta Gamma Sigma. Author: (with J. Stoyle) An Introduction to Mathematical Reasoning, 1973; contbr. articles to profl. jours. Home: 1912 Rolling Ln Cherry Hill NJ 08003 Office: Dept Statistics Temple U Philadelphia PA 19122

IGOU, RAYMOND ALVIN, JR., orthopedic surgeon; b. Estherville, Iowa, Dec. 2, 1933; s. Raymond Alvin and Pearl Mildred (Christensen) I.; B.S., N.Mex. State U., 1955; M.D., Boston U., 1965; m. Jan. 17, 1958; children—Raymond Alvin III, Yvette Sharon. Intern, Univ. Hosp., 1965-66, resident, 1971-75; intern Boston U. Med. Center, 1965-66; resident Boston U. Affiliated Hosps., 1971-75, Shriners Hosp. for Crippled Children, Springfield, Mass., 1971-75; resident Boston City Hosp., 1971-75, mem. staff, 1975—, asso. dir. dept. orthopedics, 1978—, chief dept. rehab. medicine, 1978—; practice medicine specializing in orthopedic surgery, Melrose, Mass., 1975—; lectr. orthopedic surgery of bone tumors Sch. Medicine, Boston U., 1975—, asst. prof. orthpedic surgery, 1978—; partner Grant Buie Hosp., Hillsboro, Tex., 1966-71. Pres. Hill County (Tex.) Cancer Soc., 1967-71; mem. Hillsboro City Council 1970-71. Served with arty. U.S. Army, 1955-60. Diplomate Am. Bd. Orthopedic Surgery. Mem. Mass., Middlesex East med. socs., Boston Orthopedic Soc. Republican. Baptist. Clubs: Masons, Shriners. Home: 30 Baldwin St Peabody MA 01960 Office: 721 Main St Melrose MA 02176

IH, CHARLES CHUNG SEN, educator; b. Hankow, China, May 15, 1933; s. Young H. and Moon Hua (Lee) I.; came to U.S., 1958, naturalized, 1969; B.S., Nat. Taiwan U. (China), 1956; M.S., Lehigh U., 1959; Ph.D., U. Pa., 1966; m. Donna M. Chou, Sept. 12, 1959; children—Ronald H., Bennet H. Electronic engr. Sperry Rand Univac, Blue Bell, Pa., 1959-63; mem. tech. staff RCA Labs., Princeton, N.J., 1967-71; sr. physicist, mgr. CBS Labs., Stamford, Conn., 1971-76; asso. prof. elec. engring. U. Del., Newark, 1975—; lectr. Bridgeport (Conn.) Engring. Inst., 1974-75; cons. to Perkin-Elmer Corp., 1975. Bd. dirs. Chinese Assn. of Fairfield County, Conn., 1974-75. Recipient RCA Labs. spl. award, 1969. Mem. Am. Phys. Soc., Optical Soc. Am. Author: A Focused-Image-Hologram Microfiche, 1974; Holographic Archival Color Image Storage, 1975; Two-Dimensional Holographic Laser Scanners, 1976; patentee in electro-optics and electronics. Home: 409 Valley Rd Newark DE 19711 Office: U Del Dept Elec Engring Newark DE 19711

IKENBERRY, HENRY CEPHAS, JR., lawyer; b. Cloverdale, Va., Mar. 23, 1920; s. Henry Cephas and Bessie (Peters) I.; B.A., Bridgewater Coll., 1947; J.D., U. Va., 1947; m. Margaret Sangster Henry, July 3, 1943; children—Anna Catherine (Mrs. Fawell), Mary Margaret (Mrs. Rauck). Admitted to Va. bar, 1947, W.Va. and D.C. bars, 1948, U.S. Supreme Ct. bar, 1954; asso. Steptoe & Johnson, Washington, 1947-49, 50-53, partner, 1953—; asst. counsel Gen. Aniline & Film Co., N.Y.C., 1949-50; dir. Union 1st Nat. Bank, Balt. Contractors Inc. Mem. com. on unauthorized practice D.C. Ct. Appeals, 1972-76. Served ensign to lt. comdr. USNR, 1941-46, commanded anti-submarine vessels, participated Atlantic, Philippine, Okinawa campaigns. Mem. Am., Va. bar assns., Bar Assn. D.C. (chmn. com. on corp. law 1960-61, chmn. comml. and bus. law com. 1969-72), Am. Judicature Soc., Raven Soc., Am. Legion, Newcomen Soc. in N.Am., Order of Coif, Phi Delta Phi, Tau Kappa Alpha. Presbyn. (ruling elder 1970-72). Clubs: Metropolitan (Washington); Chevy Chase (Md.); Farmington Country (Charlottesville, Va.). Home: 3725 Cardiff Rd Chevy Chase MD 20015 Office: 1250 Connecticut Ave Washington DC 20036

ILACQUA, ROSARIO S., securities analyst; b. Albany, N.Y., Aug. 12, 1927; s. Anthony and Carmela (Gerasia) I.; B.S., Siena Coll., 1950; M.S., Columbia U., 1955. With L.F. Rothschild, Unterberg, Towbin, N.Y.C., 1957—, partner, 1972—. Served with USNR, 1945-46. Chartered fin. analyst. Mem. Nat. Assn. Petroleum Investment Analysts (pres. 1977), N.Y. Soc. Security Analysts, Oil Analysts Group N.Y. (pres. 1972). Club: N.Y. Athletic. Home: 2 Horatio St New York City NY 10014 Office: 55 Water St New York City NY 10041

ILASI, ROBERT THOMAS, cemetery corp. exec.; b. Bklyn., Oct. 4, 1926; s. Joseph and Frances (Maenza) I.; B.S., N.Y. U., 1950; m. Mar. 31, 1951 (dec.); children—Robert, Susan, Steven, Annmarie; m. 2d, Natalie Contorno; stepchildren—Joseph Contorno, Thomas Contorno, Michael Contorno. Sr. accountant, various bus. and accounting firms, N.Y.C., 1950-57; auditor div. cemeteries N.Y. State, HUD, N.Y.C., 1957-67; v.p. The Evergreens Cemetery, Bklyn., 1967—. Dist. capt., 38th Democratic Club, 1960-67; pres. Cypress Hills Civic Assn., 1959-60; bd. mgrs. 12 Towns YMCA, 1977, chmn. fin. campaign, 1978. Served with USNR, 1944-46. Licensed pub. accountant, N.Y. Mem. Nat. Assn. Accountants, N.Y. State Assn. Cemeteries, Met. Cemetery Assn., Sons of Italy. Roman Catholic. Club: Kiwanis. Home: 22 Cardinal Ct Kendall Park NJ 08824 Office: Bushwick Ave and Conway St Brooklyn NY 11207

ILEM, PRISCILLA G. (MRS. LEN MADLANSACAY), physician; b. Imus, Cavite, Philippines; d. Narciso S. and Felisa (Guevarra) Ilem; M.D. benemeritus, U. Santo Tomas, 1954; postgrad. Syracuse Psychiat. Hosp., 1956-57, Yale Med. Sch., 1960, Polyclinic Med. Sch. and Hosp., 1969, N.Y. State Psychiat. Inst., 1969, Columbia U., 1969; M.P.H. (U.S. Children's Bur. fellow), U. Calif. at Berkeley, 1971; m. Len Madlansacay, Mar. 3, 1957; children—Rey Thomas, Priscilla Joy, May Ann. Rotating intern U. Santo Tomas Hosp., Manila, 1953-54, Truesdale Hosp., Fall River, Mass., 1955; resident psychiatry Marcy (N.Y.) State Hosp., 1956-59; sr. psychiatrist Monson State Hosp., Palmer, Mass. 1959-61; staff psychiatrist Twin Elms Hosp., Syracuse, N.Y., 1966-67; supervising psychiatrist Rome (N.Y.) State Sch., 1967-68, chief service, 1971—; chief of service Letchworth Village Hosp., Thiells, N.Y., 1972—, chief service, 1974—; practice medicine specializing in psychiatry and neurology, Manila, 1962-66, Rome, N.Y., 1967-68; cons. Calif. Dept. Mental Health. Diplomate Am. Bd. Psychiatry and Neurology. Recipient certificate of merit for Research in Psychiatry Northampton State Hosp. (Mass.), 1961; Physician's Recognition award in Continuing Med. Edn. AMA, 1969, 72, John F. Kennedy award in community psychiatry, 1974. Fellow Am. Assn. Mental Deficiency; mem. Am. Psychiat. Assn., Assn. N.Y. State Mental Hygiene Physicians, New Eng. Soc. Psychiatry and Neurology, Am. Assn. Med. Adminstrs., U. Calif. Alumni Assn. Contbr. articles to profl. jours. Address: Letchworth Village Thiells NY 10984

IMAN, FARUQ TAIWO NYAHUMA (GREGORY BREVARD SMART), psychologist; b. Phila., Nov. 11, 1945; s. Isaac D. and Sara Whittington (Popley) S.; B.A., Lincoln U., 1967; M.Ed. in Counseling Psychology, Antioch Grad. Sch., 1978; 1 dau., Ayanna Maanami Iman. Employment counselor Bernard Franklin Co., Phila., 1971; youth work counselor Sch. Dist. of Phila. (Neighborhood Youth Corps), 1971—; life skill educator Winthrop Adkins Life Skill Program, 1977—. Bd. dirs. Phila. Com. for Services to Youth, 1973—; mem. W. Phila. Parent's Group to Eradicate Gang Warfare, 1974-76; mem. Peoples Inst. of Polit. Edn., 1973-76. Served with U.S. Army, 1967-70. Decorated Army Commendation Medal. Recipient Neighborhood Youth Corps Service Award, Neighborhood Youth Corps, 1973; Career Opportunities Seminar award, 1975. Mem. Assn. Black Psychologists, Assn. of Non-White Concerns, Am. Personnel and Guidance Assn., Am. Psychol. Assn., NEA, Counseling Psychologist Assn., Kappa Alpha Psi. Home: 5917 Spruce St Philadelphia PA 19139 Office: 2600 N Broad St Philadelphia PA 19132

IMBERT, PATRICK LOUIS, educator; b. Paris, France, Feb. 4, 1948; s. Gerald Louis and Odette Cecile (Linsart) I.; came to Can., 1969, naturalized, 1975; M.A., U. Ottawa, 1970, Ph.D., 1974. Lectr.

U. Ottawa, 1969-74; asst. prof. McMaster U., Hamilton, Ont., 1974-75; asst. prof. semiotics and lit. U. Ottawa, 1975—. Mem. Canadian Assn. Research in Semiotics, Modern Lang. Assn., Canadian Linguistic Assn., Assn. Canadienne francaise pour l avancement des sciences. Roman Catholic. Home: 821 Eastbourne Ave Ottawa ON K1K OH8 Canada Office: University of Ottawa Ottawa ON Canada

IMBIER, EDWARD ALLEN, electronics engr., video cons.; b. Ware, Mass., July 22, 1943; s. Edward and Stella Marie (Kook) I.; B.S. in Elec. Engring., U. Mass., 1965; M.S. in Elec. Engring., Northeastern U., 1971; postgrad. in bus. Harvard U., M.I.T., 1973, 74; m. Gertraude L. Schroder, June 6, 1975; 1 dau., Tobia. Oceanographic field engr., photographer Smithsonian Instn., summers 1965, 66; mem. tech. staff video design RCA, Camden, N.J. and Burlington, Mass., 1967-72; video cons., instr., Cambridge, Mass., 1971—; elec. engr. Smithsonian Instn., Cambridge, 1972—. Recipient Crowell-Collier salesmanship award, 1960, 61; NATO advanced study grantee, 1972. Mem. Smaller Bus. Assn. of New Eng., Audio Engring. Soc., Soc. of Motion Picture and TV Engrs., Internat. TV Assn. Contbr. articles to profl. jours. Home: 59 Orchard St Belmont MA 02178 Office: Smithsonian Instn 60 Garden St Cambridge MA 02138

IMERTI, ARTHUR DANTE, author, scholar; b. N.Y.C., July 2, 1915; s. Vincent Anthony and Agata Italia (Catalani) I.; B.A., Coll. City N.Y., 1939; M.A. (scholar), Fordham U., 1945; (Am. Found. for Blind scholar), U. Mex., 1946; Ph.D. (N.Y. State Vocat. Rehab. Services scholar), Columbia U., 1969; m. Frances Prochep, Mar. 25, 1951. Dir., Imerti Modern Lang. Inst., N.Y.C., 1943-50; asst. prof. speech Yeshiva U., N.Y.C., 1950-59; prof. Romance langs. New Sch. for Social Research, N.Y.C., 1951-71, founding chmn. fgn. lang. dept., 1960-64; adj. asso. prof. Spanish, City U. N.Y., 1973-74; ednl. cons. Manhattan VA Hosp., 1966-68. Mem. exec. com. Village Ind. Democrats, 1978. Research grantee to Mexico, Italy and France, 1946, 49. Mem. Modern Lang. Assn., Am. Assn. Tchrs. Italian, Am.-Italy Soc., Renaissance Soc. Am. Editor/translator: The Expulsion of the Triumphant Beast (Giordano Bruno), 1964; Neapolitan Jacobin, Jurist, Reformer, 1976 (Vincenzo Catalani). Home: 69 Fifth Ave New York City NY 10003

IMHOF, HOWARD EMIL, ednl. cons.; b. Maspeth, N.Y., Aug. 11, 1917; s. Emil and Christine (Klein) I.; B.S., Springfield Coll., 1939; M.A., N.Y. U., 1947, Ed.D., 1954; m. Ruth C. Kessler, July 26, 1941; children—Hope Constance, Howard Emil, Faith Ruth. Cons. in sci. East Norwich (N.Y.) pub. schs., 1939-43; dir. phys. edn. Nassau County (N.Y.) Vocat. Edn. and Extension Bd., 1939-48; prin. elementary sch., Oyster Bay, N.Y., 1948-58; supt. schs. Oyster Bay, 1958-60, Oyster Bay-East Norwich Central Sch. Dist., 1960-77; ret.; ednl. cons.; instr. Brookville campus, L.I. U., 1952-53; adj. prof. edn. C.W. Post Coll., Brookville, N.Y., 1959-64, mem. adv. com., 1974—; adviser Oyster Bay-East Norwich Pub. Library, 1958—; mem. adv. council supts. N.Y. State Commr. of Edn., 1968-74; mem. adv. com. Raynham Hall Hist. Mus., Oyster Bay, 1958—. Pres. Oyster Bay Police Boys Club, 1952; asst. community dir. Civil Def., Oyster Bay, 1956; mem. Oyster Bay Community Social Action Com., 1964—; mem. Oyster Bay Twp. Am. Revolution Bicentennial Commn., 1975—; chmn. L.I. area NCCJ edn. com., 1965-69; bd. dirs. Oyster Bay-East Norwich Youth and Family Counseling Agy.; trustee Oyster Bay Rotary Student Found. Served to lt. USNR, 1943-46. Recipient Brotherhood award NCCJ, 1969; Distinguished Service award N.Y. State Council Sch. Dist. Adminstrs., 1977. Mem. Am. Assn. Sch. Adminstrs. (internat. study mission 1971), Nassau County Chief Sch. Adminstrs. Assn. (pres. 1968-69), N.Y. State Council Village and City Supts. (resolution com. 1961-62, higher edn. com. 1963-68), N.Y. State Council Chief Sch. Adminstrs. (dir. 1968-74), Am. Legion, Oyster Bay C. of C. (dir. 1965-67, v.p. 1966-67). Presbyterian (elder). Club: Rotary (pres. Oyster Bay chpt. 1953-54).

IMLER, JAMES HAROLD EUGENE, chemist; b. Altoona, Pa., Aug. 22, 1937; s. Irvin Chromer and Edna Pearl (King) I.; B.E., Shippensburg (Pa.) State Coll., 1959; postgrad. U. Del., 1959-60, Rensselaer Poly. Inst., summer 1961; MA. in Phys. Chemistry, Bowling Green (Ohio) State U., 1967; doctoral candidate in edn. Pa. State U., 1974—; m. Judith Ann Thomas, June 24, 1967; children—Stacey Ann, William Thomas. Sci. instr. Lampeter-Strasburg High Sch., Lampeter, Pa., 1959-60, Cumberland Valley Jr.-Sr. High Sch., Mechanicsburg, Pa., 1960-61, Camp Hill (Pa.) High Sch., 1961-67; research asst. Milton S. Hershey Med. Center, Hershey, Pa., 1967-68; sci. instr. Camp Hill High Sch., 1968-70; dean Pa. Jr. Coll. Med. Arts, Harrisburg, 1970-71; chemistry instr., academic dept. chmn. Dauphin County Vocat.-Tech. Sch., Harrisburg, 1971—; state dir.-at-large Pa. Jr. Acad. Sci., 1976—; cons. pvt. industry. Adviser, Explorer Post 51, Boy Scouts Am., 1962-70; mem. adv. com. Capitol Area Sci. Fair, 1963—; adminstrv. dir. Harrisburg Performing Arts Co.; active congressional campaign. NSF fellow, 1964-67; recipient certificate of appreciation local Jaycees, 1972; certificate of merit Pa. Jr. Acad. Sci., 1975; others. Mem. NEA, Pa. Edn. Assn., Dauphin County Tech. Sch. Edn. Assn., Pa. Acad. Sci., Pa., Nat. sci. tchrs. assns., Smithsonian Assos., Sigma Pi Sigma. Republican. Baptist. Home: 8 Cornell Dr Camp Hill PA 17011 Office: 6001 Locust Ln Harrisburg PA 17109

IMMASCHE, FRANCIS WILLIAM, econ. adviser, farmer; b. Saffordville, Kans., Oct. 21, 1907; s. William George and Margaret (Lyles) ImM.; B.S., Kans. State U., 1929; M.A., U. Chgo., 1933. Livestock economist Armour & Co., Chgo., 1930-31, Fed. Farm Bd., Washington, 1931-33; asst. chief, econ. and credit research div., FCA, Washington, 1933-42; dep. dir. livestock and dairy div. U.S. Dept. Agr., Washington, 1947-65, adviser on livestock and wool situation, including Australia and New Zealand, 1971—; pres. Goldpoint Mining Co. (Nev.), 1941—; farmer, Chase County, Kans. Pres. Meml. Lawn Cemeteries Assn., Emporia, Kans., 1959-70. Served from 1st lt. to col. USAF, 1942-47; now col. USAF ret. Mem. Sigma Alpha Epsilon, Alpha Zeta, Alpha Kappa Psi. Clubs: Congressional Country, Capital Hill (Washington); Indian Wells (Calif.) Country. Home: 3133 Connecticut Ave Washington DC 20008 also Strong City KS 66869

IMPASTATO, DAVID JOHN, psychiatrist; b. Sicily, Italy, Jan. 8, 1903; s. Dominick and Rosaria (Fugalli) Im; came to U.S., 1913; naturalized, 1926, A.B., Columbia, 1925; M.D., George Washington U., 1928; m. Jane D. Justin, July 31, 1937; children—Jane (Mrs. James Branaum), David, Mary. Intern Met. Hosp., N.Y.C., 1928; resident Central Neurol. Hosp., N.Y.C., 1929, Bellevue Neurol. Hosp., N.Y.C., 1929; mem. staff psychiatry Bellevue Hosp., 1930-37; asso. psychiatrist N.Y. U., N.Y.C. and Bellevue Hosp., 1930-37; asso. clin. prof. psychiatry N.Y. U., 1941-67; attending psychiatrist, Columbus Hosp., N.Y.C., 1936-43, cons. psychiatrist, 1971-74. Founding fellow Am. Coll. Psychiatrists; mem. Eastern Research Psychiat. Assn. (pres. 1953-54), Am. Assn. Med. Psychiatry (pres. 1960-61), Am. Psychiat. Assn. (mem. com. therapy 1958-59), Electroshock Research Assn. (pres. 1958). Club: Salmagundi. Asso. editor: Diseases of the Nervous System, 1947-72. Contbr. over 50 articles to profl. jours. Office: 46 Fifth Ave New York City NY 10011

IMPERATO, PASCAL JAMES, physician, health adminstr., author; b. N.Y.C., Jan. 13, 1937; s. James Anthony and Madalynne Marguerite (Insante) I.; B.S., St. John's U., 1958, D.Sc. (hon.), 1977; M.D., State U. N.Y., 1962; M.P.H. and Tropical Medicine, Tulane U., 1966; m. Eleanor Anne Maiella, June 4, 1977. Assn. Am. Med. Colls. Fgn. fellow, Kenya, Tanzania, Uganda, 1961; intern dept. internal medicine L.I. Coll. Hosp., 1962-63, resident dept. medicine, 1963-65; N.Y. Acad. Medicine fgn. research fellow Tulane Univ.-Universidad del Valle, Cali Colombia, 1965; Glorney Raisebeck fellow Tulane U., New Orleans, 1965-66; med. epidemiologist smallpox eradication-measles control program USPHS, Mali, 1966-72; dir. Bur. Infectious Disease Control, N.Y.C. Dept. Health, 1972-74, prin. epidemiologist, dir. immunization program, 1972-74, 1st dep. commr., 1974-77, dir. residency tng. program, 1974-77, chmn. N.Y.C. Swine Influenza Immunization Task Force, 1976-77; med. cons. Africa Bur., AID, 1974; commr. health N.Y.C., 1977—; chmn. N.Y.C. Bd. Health, 1977—; chmn. bd. N.Y.C. Health and Hosps. Corp., 1977—; chmn. exec. com. N.Y.C. Health Systems Agency, 1977—; acting health services adminstr. N.Y.C., 1977—; clin. instr. dept. medicine Cornell U. Med. Coll., N.Y.C., 1972-75, clin. asst. prof., 1975-77, clin. asso. prof., 1977—; asso. prof. dept. environ. medicine and community health State Univ. N.Y., Downstate Med. Center, 1974-77, lectr., 1977—; mem. staff N.Y. Hosp., L.I. Coll. Hosp.; lectr. dept. community medicine Mount Sinai Sch. Medicine, City U. N.Y., 1974—. Bd. dirs. Pub. Health Research Inst., Community Council Greater N.Y., Med. Health and Research Assn., Greater N.Y. Hosp. Assn., Milton Helpern Library Legal Medicine; trustee Martin and Osa Johnson Safari Mus. Served to lt. comdr. USPHS, 1966-69. Recipient Meritorious Honor award and medal Dept. State, 1971. Diplomate Am. Bd. Preventive Medicine, Nat. Bd. Med. Examiners. Fellow A.C.P., Royal Soc. Tropical Medicine and Hygiene, Royal African Soc., N.Y. Acad. Medicine, Am. Coll. Preventive Medicine; mem. Am. Soc. Tropical Medicine and Hygiene, Am. Pub. Health Assn., Tanzania Soc., East African Wildlife Soc., African Studies Assn., Herman Biggs Soc., Med. Execs., Delta Omega, Alpha Omega Alpha. Roman Catholic. Club: Explorers. Author: Doctor in The Land of the Lion, 1964; (with Osa Johnson) Last Adventure, 1966; The Treatment and Control of Infectious Diseases in Man, 1974; The Cultural Heritage of Africa, 1974; A Wind in Africa, 1975; What To Do About the Flu, 1976; African Folk Medicine, 1977; Historical Dictionary of Mali, 1977; The Making of a Disease Detective, 1978; (with wife) Historical Statistics of Mali, 1978. Contbr. articles in field to profl. jours. Office: 125 Worth St New York City NY 10013

IMRIE, ROBERT WOODALL, lawyer; b. Glens Falls, N.Y., Jan. 22, 1916; s. Daniel Ferguson and Lillian (Woodall) I.; B.A., Union Coll., 1938; J.D., Albany Law Sch., 1941; m. Doris Layman, Dec. 26, 1943; children—Daniel Ferguson, Jean Elizabeth, Robert Haines. Admitted to N.Y. bar, 1941; pvt. practice law, Glens Falls, 1941-61; asst. atty. gen. State of N.Y., Albany 1961—; corp. counsel, Glens Falls, 1954-57. Served with AUS, 1942-45. Mem. N.Y. State, Warren County bar assns., Delta Phi. Mason. Home: 7 Lawton Ave Glens Falls NY 12801

IMUS, ALDEN ELON, JR., civil engr.; b. Washington, Nov. 29, 1919; s. Alden Elon and Elizabeth Mabel (Kline) I.; B.C.E., U. Md., 1941; m. Lois Mae Bendshadler, Jan. 4, 1946; children—Elizabeth, Benjamin A. Design engr. Washington Suburban San. Commn., 1946-50; chief engr. Thomas G. Oyster & Assoc., Inc., Wheaton, Md., 1950-57; hydraulic engr. John Clarkson, Inc., Washington, 1957-58; exec. v.p. Oyster, Imus & Assoc., Wheaton, Md., 1958-75; pres. Oyster, Imus & Petzold, Wheaton, 1975—. Adv. com. Dept. Transp. Montgomery County, Md. on storm drains, 1975-76. Served as officer U.S. Army, 1941-46. Registered profl. engr., Md., Mem. Nat. Soc. Profl. Engrs. (nat. capital area water study com. 1977-78), ASCE, Tau Beta Pi. Organist, Christian Ch. Home: 13511 Sherwood Forest Ter Silver Spring MD 20904 Office: 2419 Reedie Dr Wheaton MD 20902

INCIARDI, JAMES A., research sociologist; b. Bklyn., Nov. 28, 1939; s. James Anthony and Marie Elizabeth (Craig) I.; B.S. in Sociology, Fordham U., 1961; M.A., N.Y. U., 1971, Ph.D., 1973; m. Carolyn Jo Kincaid, June 20, 1975; children—Craig, Brooks, Kristin. Parole officer N.Y. State Parole Div., N.Y.C., 1962-67; asso. research dir. N.Y. State Narcotic Commn., N.Y.C., 1967-71; research asso. U. Miami (Fla.) Sch. Medicine, 1971-73; v.p. Resource Planning Corp., Miami, 1973-75; dir. Nat. Center for Study of Acute Drug Reactions, Miami, 1975-76; dir. Div. Criminal Justice U. Del., Newark, 1976—; cons. to U.S. Senate and Fed., state and local criminal justice and drug abuse agencies. Recipient HEW grant to study crime among heroin users, 1976-78. Mem. Am. Soc. Criminology, Am. Sociological Assn., Eastern Sociological Soc., Smithsonian Inst. Author: Careers in Crime, 1975; Reflections On Crime, 1978; contbr. over 60 books and articles in field to profl. jours. Office: Div of Criminal Justice U of Del Newark DE 19711

INDEN, ARTHUR, lawyer; b. Phila., Jan. 8, 1941; s. I. Edward and Ruth R. (Rowling) I.; B.A., U. Del., 1962; LL.B., Dickinson Sch. Law, 1965; m. Sheila Fay Jacobs, Oct. 30, 1964; children—Lecia, William L., Matthew. Admitted to Pa. bar, 1965, Del. bar, 1966; asso. firm Freedman, Borowski & Lorry, Phila., 1965-66, Aaronson & Balick, Wilmington, Del., 1966-67; partner firm Young, Conaway, Stargatt & Taylor, Wilmington, Del., 1967—; prof. real estate law Brandywine Coll., 1969-72; lectr. in field. Chmn. gen. bus. unit United Fund and Council Del., 1973; mem. joint legal-dental and joint medico-legal screening panels malpractice cases, 1970—. Mem. Am. Bar Assn. Club: YMCA Health (com. chmn. 1973-74). Editor-in-chief Dickinson Law Rev., 1964-65. Home: 730 Taunton Rd Wilmington DE 19803 Office: 1401 Market Tower Wilmington DE 19899

INDERMAUR, FREDERICK NORMAN, trade assn. exec.; b. Lakewood, Ohio, Apr. 14, 1937; s. Herschel Graesser and Janice Christine (Berger) I.; B.A., Bowling Green State U., 1960; m. Barbara Ann Yackel, June 25, 1960; children—James Frederick, Elizabeth Ann, Douglas Norman. Export traffic mgr. Toledo Scale Co. (Ohio), 1960-65; sales rep. Elliott Bay Mill Co., Seattle, 1965-68, Am. Seating Co., Grand Rapids, 1968-74; pub. relations and sales staff Marquette Cement Co., Nashville, 1974-76; regional dir. Northeastern Retail Lumberman's Assn., Tolland, Conn., 1976—; instr. Sales and Product Devel. Inst., U. Mass., Amherst, 1978. Mem. Conn. Bus. and Industries Assn., Conn. Retail Mchts. Assn., New Eng. Bldg. Code Assn. Republican. Methodist. Clubs: Duck Island Yacht, Crystal Lake Yacht (commodore 1974-75), Lions (dir.), Hoo Hoo Internat. Home: 11 Elizabeth Ln Tolland CT 06084 Office: 339 East Ave Rochester NY 14604

INDIK, BERNARD PAUL, educator; b. Phila., Apr. 30, 1932; s. Jacob Joseph and Ida F. (Kaplan) I.; B.S., U. Pa., 1954, M.B.A., 1955; textile engring. certificate Phila. Textile Inst., 1955; A.M., U. Mich., 1959, Ph.D., 1961; m. Harriet Sandra Simberloff, June 26, 1955; children—Joyce Janet, Martin Karl, Jay Joseph, Debra Ruth, William Aaron. Asst. mgr. Textured Yarn Co., Phila., 1955; asst. study dir. Survey Research Center, U. Mich., 1957-60, study dir., 1961; asst. research specialist Rutgers U., New Brunswick, N.J., 1961-65, asso. research specialist research program psychology dept. Inst. Mgmt. and Labor Relations, 1965-68, asso. prof., asst. to dean Grad. Sch. Social Work, 1968-69, prof. social work, 1969—, Distinguished prof. social work, 1978—; cons. Pres. Commn. on Civil Disorders, 1967-68, Gov's. Commn. Report for Action, 1968, Dept. Labor and Industry State N.J., 1965, 74-76. Mem. exec. bd. South Brunswick Community Council, 1967-68, exec. sec., 1968-69; mem. exec. bd. South Brunswick Citizens for Johnson, 1964; trustee South Brunswick Twp. Library, 1965-70, treas., 1970; mem. South Brunswick Twp. Planning Bd., 1976—, chmn., 1979; mem. long range planning com. United Way of Central Jersey, 1976—, trustee, v.p., 1978; South Brunswick Twp. rep. Middlesex County Housing and Community Devel. Commn., 1976—. Served with U.S. Army, 1955-57. Recipient Community Appreciation award United Way Central Jersey, 1976, Mayor's Appreciation award South Brunswick, 1976. Fellow Am. Psychol. Assn., Soc. Psychol. Study Social Issues; mem. Council on Social Work Edn., Am. Acad. Polit. and Social Scis., Soc. Gen. Systems Research, Eastern Psychol. Assn. Democrat. Jewish. Club: Willows Swim (trustee 1976) (Kendall Park, N.J.). Author: (with G. Sternlieb) The Ecology of Welfare, 1973; (with R. Beauregard) A Human Service Labor Market: Developmental Disabilities, 1979; editor: (with F. K. Berrien) People, Groups and Organizations, 1968; contbr. numerous articles, monographs and book reviews to profl. jours., chpts. to books. Home: 32 Kendall Rd Kendall Park NJ 08824 Office: Grad Sch Social Work Rutgers U 536 George St New Brunswick NJ 08903

INEL, YAVUZ, psychiatrist; b. Istanbul, Turkey, June 9, 1929; s. Ekrem Necmi and Beria Yusufe (Zeki) I.; came to U.S., 1958; M.D., U. Istanbul, 1956; m. Gonul E. Orencik, Feb. 19, 1956; 1 son, Selim Mahmut. Intern, Aultman Hosp., Canton, Ohio, 1958-59; resident psychiatry Colo. State Hosp., Pueblo, 1959-60; resident psychiatry Crownsville (Md.) Hosp. Center, 1960-62, staff psychiatrist, 1962-63, 66-68, clin. dir. 1968-74; practice medicine specializing in psychiatry Istanbul, 1963-66, Annapolis, Md., 1971—; mem. staff North Arundel Gen. Hosp.; med. dir. Mental Hygiene Adminstrn. Md., Balt., 1974—; cons., clinician Anne Arundel County Health Dept., Parole, Md., 1967—; med. cons. Drug Abuse Adminstrn. Md., Balt., 1976—. Served to lt. M.C., Turkish Navy, 1956-57. Licensed to practice medicine Turkey, Pa., Md. Mem. Am. Psychiat. Assn., Md. Psychiat. Soc., Med. and Chirurgical Faculty Md., Anne Arundel County Med. Soc. Home: 138 Grafton St Chevy Chase MD 20015

INGAGLIO, DIEGO AUGUSTUS, dentist; b. Phila., Dec. 4, 1922; s. Salvatore and Maria Concetta (Giordano) I.; D.D.S., U. Pa., 1947; m. Geraldine Jean Capizzi, July 11, 1948; children—Marie, Francene. With Phila. Mouth Hygiene Dept., 1947-50; asst. clin. dir. Emerson R. Sausser Med. Dental Clinic, Jefferson Hosp., Phila., 1950-51; pvt. practice dentistry, Drexel Hill, Pa., 1953—. Served with AUS, 1943-45, 51-53. Mem. Am., Pa., Chester-Delaware County dental assns., Am. Internat., Philadelphia County socs. clin. hypnosis, AAAS, Phila. Physhodontonic Soc. (past pres.), Royal Soc. Hygiene, Nat. Space Inst., Ocean City Gardens Civic Assn., Upper Darby Forum, Nat. Rifle Assn., Omicron Kappa Upsilon. Clubs: Drexelbrook (Drexel Hill); Vespers (Phila.). Editor-in-chief U. Pa. Dental Jour., 1945-47. Address: 801 Roberts Ave Drexel Hill PA 19026

INGALLS, CHESTER WALLACE, accountant, educator; b. Ellsworth, Maine, Aug. 4, 1944; s. Eugene A. and Irene H. (Grindle) I.; B.S. in Bus. Edn. with honors, U. Maine, Machias, 1966; M.Ed. with honors, U. Maine, Orono, 1969; m. Shirley M. Bansmer, Nov. 24, 1965; children—Sherri, Jennifer. State coordinator C.P.A. Inst. for Husson Coll., 1974-75; sr. accountant and auditor Peat, Marwick, Mitchell & Co., Portland, Maine, 1968-70; partner Chester W. Ingalls & Co., C.P.A.'s., Waterville, Maine, 1971—; asso. prof. accounting Thomas Coll., 1971-76, U. Maine, 1974—, C.P.A., Maine. Mem. Nat. Fedn. Ind. Businessmen, Am. Inst. C.P.A.'s, Maine Soc. Pub. Accountants, Nat. Assn. Accountants, Am. Accounting Assn., Eastern Bus. Tchrs. Assn., Phi Beta Lambda (past pres.). Clubs: Lions (Winslow, Maine); Masons (Fairfield, Maine); Shriners (Lewiston, Maine). Home: Frankwood Dr Winslow ME 04902 Office: 173 Main St Waterville ME 04901

INGERMAN, PETER ZILAHY, systems cons.; b. N.Y.C., Dec. 9, 1934; s. Charles Stryker and Ernestine (Leigh) I.; A.B., U. Pa., 1958, M.S. in Elec. Engring., 1963; m. Carol Mary Pasquale, Dec. 19, 1970. Research investigator, U. Pa., Phila., 1958-63; tech. dir. programming research, Westinghouse, Balt., 1963-65; mgr. RCA, Cherry Hill, N.J., 1965-71, staff 1971-72; sr. staff cons., Equitable Life Assurance Soc. of U.S., N.Y.C., 1972-77; ind. cons., 1977—; adj. prof. computer sci. Pratt Inst. Tech., 1968-73; mem. working groups Internat. Fedn. Info. Processing, 1962—; rep. Conf. Data Systems Langs., 1967-71, Am. Nat. Standards Inst., 1960-69. Bd. dirs. Phila. Health Plan, Inc., 1975-77. C.L.U. Fellow Brit. Computer Soc.; mem. IEEE (Sr.), Assn. Computing Machinery, AAAS, N.J. Acad. Scis., Data Processing Mgmt. Assn., World Future Soc., Mensa, Am. Cryptogram Assn., Am. Guild Organists, Organ Hist. Soc., Sigma Xi, Upsilon Pi Epsilon. Author: A Syntax-Oriented Translator, 1966, Russian transl., 1969; contbr. papers to publs.; patentee electronic circuits. Office: 40 Needlepoint Ln Willingboro NJ 08046

INGERSOLL, RALPH MCALLISTER, II, publisher; b. N.Y.C., June 14, 1946; s. Ralph McAllister and Elaine Brown (Keiffer) I.; student U. Grenoble (France), 1965-66; B.S., N.Y. U., 1970; m. Ursula Elizabeth Daiber, Nov. 26, 1966; children—Colin McAllister, Mattias Macrae. Pub., gen. partner Ingersoll Publs. Co., owner, operator daily and weekly newspapers; dir. U.P.I. Mem. Am., Pa. newspaper pubs. assns., AP, N.Y. State Pubs. Assn (dir.), Ohio Newspaper Assn. Address: Lakeville CT 06039

INGHAM, JOHN FREDERICK, automobile service exec.; b. Kittanning, Pa., Apr. 11, 1927; s. Headley Vicars and Gladys (Bedell) I.; student U. Pitts., 1946-47; m. Pearl Jane Breakey, Feb. 11, 1953; children—Richard John, Barbara Jane, Ronald Frederick, Margaret Jean. Ofcl. city govt. Wilkinsburg, Pa., 1948-75, asst. city mgr., 1965-69, city mgr. 1969-72; city mgr. Punxsutawney, Pa., 1972-75; owner Ingham & Sons, imported automobile service specialists, Punxsutawney, 1975—. Served with USNR, 1944-46. Mem. Internat. City Mgmt. Assn., Pa. Municipal Mgrs. Assn. Mason, Rotarian. Home and office: 700 Myrtle St Punxsutawney PA 15767

INGIS, GAIL, interior designer; b. U.S., Nov. 1, 1935; d. Bernard and Claire Gerber; student in bus. Bklyn. Coll., 1953; grad. in interior architecture and design N.Y. Sch. Interior Design, 1973; children—Linda, Richard, Paul. Prin., Ingis Design Asso., Woodcliff Lake, N.J., 1970—; interior designer The Design Store, locations in Washington, Md., N.J., 1977—; asso. prof. Kean Coll., Union, N.J., 1977—. Troop leader Girl Scouts U.S.A., N.Y.C. and Woodcliff Lake, 1964-69. Mem. Am. Soc. Interior Designers (admissions com. N.J. chpt. 1978, edn. chmn. 1978—), U.S. Profl. Tennis Assn. (certified tennis instr.), Illuminating Engring. Soc. N. Am. Home and Office: 39 Clairmont Dr Woodcliff Lake NJ 07675

INGLISA, DOMENIC RONALD, cosmetics co. exec.; b. Reading, Pa., Dec. 8, 1931; s. Angelo and Sophie M.; student U. Del., 1952-54; B.S. in Accounting, U. Balt., 1970; certificate in Bus. Adminstrn. with honors, Goldey Beacom Sch. of Bus., 1957; m. Lois M. Mackie, Sept. 12, 1959; children—Denise Elaine, Domenic Ronald, Andrea Marie. Sales supr. Hoover Co., Wilmington, Del., 1954-61; sales rep. Revlon, Inc., N.Y.C., 1961-73, nat. sales tng. mgr., 1973—. Served in USMC, 1949-52. Licensed wastewater supt., Md. Mem. Am. Soc. Tng. and Devel., Sales Exec. Club N.Y., Nat. Rifle Assn. Republican. Home: 13 Pinehurst Dr Cranbury NJ 08512 Office: 767 Fifth Ave New York City NY 10002

INGRAHAM, HAROLD EDWARD, chem. co. exec.; b. Kingston, Pa., Jan. 17, 1913; s. Harold Otto Charles and Martha Liondean (Leonard) I.; m. Mary Louise Emmons, Dec. 5, 1936 (dec.); children—Thomas E., Joan B. Ingraham McGarry, Stephen R.; m. 2d, Helen Kamas, June 10, 1977. With Allied Chem. Corp., 1931-43; founder, pres. Heico, Inc., Delaware Water, Pa., 1943—. Mem. Def. Supply Bd., 1965-69, Am. Security Council, 1970-78, Nat. Adv. Bd., 1970-78. Mem. Am. Chem. Soc., Mfg. Chemists Assn., Found. Econ. Edn., U.S. Naval Inst., USAF Assn. Republican. Episcopalian. Patentee in field. Office: Delaware Water Gap PA 18327

INGRAM, ROBERT RUSSELL, JR., research chemist; b. Atlanta, Oct. 4, 1924; s. Robert Russell and Lillian I.; B.S., Johns Hopkins U., 1954; postgrad. U. Md., 1954-55; m. Dolores Ann Gallas, Nov. 23, 1957; children—Donna, Diane. Research biochemist U.S. Army, Edgewood Arsenal, Md., 1952-69, chief chem. and thermal studies br., 1970-71, chief wound ballistics br., 1972-74, chief biodynamics br., 1975-76, research chemist Chem. Systems Lab., 1977—. Mem. Am. Burn Assn., Sigma Xi. Home: 2608 Whitt Rd Kingsville MD 21087 Office: Chem Systems Lab Aberdeen Proving Ground MD 21010

INGRAM, WILLIAM TRUITT, san. engr., educator; b. Cleves, Ohio, June 16, 1908; s. Frank and Grace Lillian (Truitt) I.; B.A., Stanford U., 1930; M.P.H., Johns Hopkins U., 1942; m. Margaret B. Nelson, 1932; children—Beryl Ingram Nielsen, Judith Ingram Nelson, John E., Diane F.; m. 2d, Filomena T. Lioy, Apr. 19, 1958. Office engr. Pacific Gas & Electric Co., San Francisco, 1930-32; recorder U.S. Coast and Geod. Survey, 1932-33; regional surveyor, supr. Fed. and State Mosquito Control, So. Calif. region, 1933-34; asst. county dir. Calif. Relief Adminstrn., 1934; san. engr. San Joaquin Local Health Dist., 1935-41; regional water works adviser Calif. Bur. San. Engring., 1942; asst. regional san. engr. Office CD, 9th region USPHS, 1942-44; camp san. engr. War Refugee Camps Middle East, Brit. Army, USPHS, UNRRA, 1943-44; chief engr. health div. UNRRA, Jugoslav Mission, 1944-46; engring. field asso. Am. Pub. Health Assn., 1947-49; asso. prof. pub. health engring. N.Y. U. Coll. Engring., 1949-54, adj. prof., 1954-73; adj. prof. Poly. Inst. N.Y., 1973—; cons., 1947—; vis. prof. preventive med. div. Cornell Coll. Medicine, 1958-73, adj. prof., 1973-77; owner Wm. T. Ingram, cons. engr.; v.p. Newing Labs., Inc.; chmn. Engring. Found. Coordinating Com. Air Pollution Research, 1960-67; chmn. joint editorial bd. Revision Glossary Water and Wastewater Control Engring., 1962-76; mem. panel on space wastes, space sci. bd. Nat. Acad. Sci., 1966-69, mem. adv. com. on solid wastes research study, bldg. research adv. bd., 1967-75. Recipient Kenneth Allen Meml. award, 1960; award for tech. and professionalism of source sampling Engring. Found., 1974; Milton T. Hill award, 1976. Diplomate Am. Acad. Environ. Engrs. Fellow Am. Pub. Health Assn., AAAS, ASCE (chmn. research council air research engring. 1972), ASTM (2d vice chmn. com. D-22, 1972-78, award of merit 1976); mem. Am. Soc. Engring. Edn., Am. Indsl. Hygiene Assn., Air Pollution Control Assn., Inter-Am. Assn. San. Engring., Conf. Local Environ. Health Adminstrs., Am. Water Works. Assn., Water Pollution Control Fedn., San. Insps. Assn. (Eng.), Malba Assn. (vice chmn. 1964-65; chmn. 1970-72), Am. Pub. Works Assn., Sigma Xi. Author: The Proposed Sanitary Code-Part III, 1949; sect. 22 Sanitary Engineering: Standard Handbook for Civil Engineers, 2d edit., 1976; contbr. articles to tech. jours. Address: 7 North Dr Whitestone NY 11357

INNIS, WALTER DEANE, ret. naval officer, govt. ofcl.; B.S., U.S. Naval Acad., 1932; grad. Naval War Coll., 1948; m. Pauline B. Coleman, Aug. 1, 1959. Commd. ensign USN, 1932, advanced through grades to rear adm.; designated naval aviator, 1936; served in Atlantic Neutrality Patrol, 1941, Mediterranean area, 1942, Aleutians, 1942-43, S.W. Pacific, Saipan, 1944, Iwo Jima, Okinawa, Japan, 1945, Korea and Formosa Strait, 1950-51; exec. officer Naval Air Sta., Dutch Harbor, Alaska, 1943; comdg. officer U.S.S. Bering Strait, 1944-45, exec. officer U.S.S. Philippine Sea, 1950-51; comdg. officer Naval Air Sta., Corpus Christi, Tex., 1946; attended Naval War Coll., 1947-48; faculty Naval War Coll., 1948-50; mem. staff Chief of Naval Ops., Washington, 1951-53; mem. staff comdr.-in-chief Eastern Atlantic (NATO), London, 1953-54; mem. staff sec. def., Washington, 1954-56, mem. U.S. del. Austrian state treaty, Vienna, 1955, mem. staff U.S. ambassador to NATO, Paris, France, 1956-57; mem. spl. mission from Pres. Eisenhower to Marshall Tito, Yugoslavia, 1955, mem. operations coordinating bd., Washington, 1954-56; spl. asst. to chief Bur. Aeros., Navy Dept., Washington, 1957-59; mem. staff Sec. of Navy, 1959; cons. Argentine Govt., Buenos Aires, 1959-60; Washington cons. The MITRE Corp., Bedford, Mass., 1962-64; systems analyst Navy Dept., 1964—. Decorated Legion of Merit, Bronze Star. Mem. Ops. Research Soc. Am., Naval Hist. Found., Navy League U.S., Naval Acad. Found., Netherlands-Am. Found., Nat. Hist. Soc., Nat. Trust for Hist. Preservation, Halcyon Found., Nat. Soc. Lit. and Arts, Friends of Kennedy Center, VFW, English-Speaking Union, Naval Acad. Alumni Assn., Ind. Soc., Nat. Audubon Soc., Ret. Officers Assn. Republican. Presbyn. Clubs: Gibson Island (Md.) Yacht Squadron; Army-Navy, Cosmos (Washington); Explorers. Co-author: Gold in the Blue Ridge, 1973. Author spl. studies for Navy Dept. and Naval War Coll., MITRE Corp. Home: Watergate West 2700 Virginia Ave NW Washington DC 20037 also Skippers Row Gibson Island MD 21056 Office: Bldg 196 Washington Navy Yard Washington DC 20390

INNO, KARL, social scientist; b. Lustivere, Estonia, Nov. 14, 1908 (came to U.S. 1950, naturalized 1955); s. Jaan and Marie (Kass) I.; grad. Poltsamaa Gymnasium, 1927; dipl. economist (B.A.), Tartu U., 1932, mag. rer. oec., 1936; m. Erika Plado, Dec. 24, 1933; children—Urve-Hello, Ene-Mall. Pub. auditor Auditing Union of Agrl. Cooperatives, Tallinn, 1932-37; with Tartu U., 1937-44, sr. asst. Sem. Bus. Econs., 1937-38, adj. prof. banking, ins., 1938-40, 1941-44; chief accountant Adminstr. Hdqrs. Textile Industry, Tallinn, 1940-41; chief accountant Tufflite Plastics, Inc., Ballston Spa, N.Y., 1950-64; accountant (auditor) N.Y. State Pub. Service Commn., Albany, 1965-73. Mem. Estonian Assn. of Albany and Schenectady, Inc., Estonian Learned Soc. in Am., Assn. for Advancement Baltic Studies. Author: Tartu University in Estonia during the Swedish Rule 1632-1710, 1972. Author publs. on banking, accounting, edn. and coops.; contbr. articles to profl. jours. Home: Willow Ridge Apts 4-B Elm Ct Rensselaer NY 12144

INNS, HARRY DOUGLAS ELLIS, optometrist; b. Tryconnel, Ont., Can., June 4, 1922; s. Thomas Henry and Eleanor (Ellis) I.; student U. Toronto, 1946-48; grad. optometry Ont. Coll. Optometry, 1950, D.Optometry, 1958; m. Betty Ruth Hearne, Sept. 11, 1948; children—Susan Elizabeth, Douglas Michael. Practice optometry specializing in contact lenses practice and research; mem. adv. bd. for optometrical secretarial program Conestoga Coll., Waterloo, Ont. Mem. Citizens Urban Renewal Com.; mem. exec. com. Anglican Diocese Huron. Served with RCAF, 1941-45. Fellow Assn. Contact Lens Practitioners Eng., Am. Acad. Optometry, Royal Soc. Health; mem. Ont. Optometrical Assn., Canadian Assn. Optometrists, Better Vision Inst., Nat. Eye Research Found., Canadian Pub. Health Assn., Am. Optometric Assn., Brantford C. of C., Internat. Platform Assn., Can. Soc. Safety Engring., AAAS, Waterloo Alumni Assn., Monarchist League Can., Heraldry Soc. Can. Clubs: Anglican Men's, Kiwanis (Brantford, Ont.). Contbr. articles to profl. jours. Inventor Inns extension disc to facilitate corneal measurements. Home: 56 Sky Acres Dr Brantford ON Canada Office: 36 King George Rd Brantford ON N3R 5K1 Canada

INTEGLIA, BARBARA ANN, med. technologist; b. Providence; d. Michael and Ursula (Mancini) I.; A.A. cum laude, R.I. Jr. Coll., 1969; A.B., U. R.I., 1971; M.S. in Pharmacology, Northeastern U., 1977; postgrad. in Basic Med. Scis. N.Y. U. Med. technologist Miriam Hosp., Providence, 1970-72; med. technologist in clin. chemistry R.I. Hosp., Providence, 1972-74, research med. technologist in pediatric metabolism, 1974-76; supr.-dir. Chem Tox Labs., Inc., New Bedford, Mass., 1973-77; research med. technologist N.Y. Hosp-Cornell Med. Coll., N.Y.C., 1977—. Mem. Am. Soc. Clin. Pathologists (registered med. technologist; affiliate), N.Y. Acad. Scis., AAAS, Leukemia Soc. Am., Phi Beta Kappa. Home: 430 E 67th St Apt 11A New York NY 10021 Office: NY Hosp-Cornell Med Center Dept Pediatric Hematology Research Room N-819 525 E 68th St New York NY 10021

INTO, HENRY ALEXANDER, mfg. co. exec.; b. N.Y.C., Dec. 1, 1930; s. Albert Norman and Paula Theodora (Siedenburg) I.; B.S., Yale U., 1957; m. Frances Mary Harrison, May 22, 1971; 1 dau., Karen Jennifer. Designer, project engr. Winchester-Western div. Olin Corp., New Haven, 1956-65; engr. Sturm, Ruger & Co., Southport, Conn., 1965-67; project engr. Firearms div. Colt Industries, Hartford, 1967-72, engring. mgr. handguns, 1972-76; dir. product engring. Smith & Wesson, Springfield, Mass., 1976—. Served with U.S. Army, 1953-55. Mem. Sporting Arms and Ammunition Mfrs. Inst. (tech. com. 1971-76), Am. Def. Preparedness Assn., Nat. Rifle Assn. (life). Clubs: Hop Meadow Country (Simsbury, Conn.); Hartford Gun. Patentee comml. and mil. firearms. Office: 2100 Roosevelt Ave Springfield MA 01101

IORIZZO, LUCIANO JOHN, educator; b. Bklyn., Mar. 31, 1930; s. John and Adolorata (Veneziale) I.; student St. Francis Coll., 1948, Bklyn. Coll., 1948-51; B.A. magna cum laude, Syracuse U., 1957, M.A., 1958, Ph.D., 1966; m. Martha Marilee Bridges, Dec. 13, 1952; children—Luciano John, Dolores E., J. Thaddeus, F. Thomas, Joseph C. Tchr., Vernon, Verona, Sherrill Central Sch., N.Y., 1958, Syracuse (N.Y.) Pub. Schs., 1958-62; faculty State U. N.Y. at Oswego, 1962—, prof. history and pub. justice, 1975—; faculty State Coll. at S.E. Mo., Cape Girardeau, 1969-70; cons. Urban Inst., Washington, 1973-74. Mem. Bd. Edn., Oswego, 1968, 70-71; city clk. Oswego, 1976—; pres. Oswego County Hist. Soc., 1976—; treas. Oswego County Dem. Com., 1977-78; bd. dirs. Nat. Italian Am. Found., Washington, 1977-78, Cath. Charities, Oswego, 1968-75. Served with USAF, 1951-55. Fulbright awardee, 1962; N.Y. State Research Found. awardee, 1967, 68, 71; Am. Assn. State and Local History research grantee, 1967. Mem. Am. Hist. Assn., Am. Italian Hist. Assn., Criminal Justice Educators N.Y. State, Orgn. Am. Historians, N.Y. United Univ. Professions, Sons of Italy. Democrat. Roman Catholic. Club: Oswego Country. Author: (with Salvatore Mondello) The Italian Americans, 1971; editor: An Inquiry into Organized Crime, 1970; contbr. articles in field to profl. jours. Home: 134 W Seneca St Oswego NY 13126 Office: History Dept State Univ Coll Oswego NY 13126

IPPOLITO, ANDREW VINCENT, library exec.; b. N.Y.C., Mar. 6, 1930; s. Andrew Vincent and Antoinetta (Emanuele) I.; student Queens Coll., 1949-50; B.S. in Fgn. Service, Georgetown U., 1955; M.L.S., Pratt Inst., 1959; m. Constance Mary DiMitrio, May 31, 1954; children—Jenette, Andrew Paul, Paul, Michael. Dir. Lindenhurst (N.Y.) Meml. Library, 1959-60, North Babylon (N.Y.) Pub. Library, 1960-62, Merrick (N.Y.) Library, 1962-65; research and library dir. Newsday, Inc., Garden City, N.Y., 1965—; asso. pub. LDA Pubs.; library cons. Pres., Happytime Nursery Sch. Inc.; mem. bd. Bayside (N.Y.) Coop. Nursery, 1965-67, Sunnyside (N.Y.) Progressive Nursery Sch., 1962; mem. exec. bd. Pub. Sch. 130, P.T.A., Bayside, 1966-68, pres., 1968-69; co-chmn. bd. dirs. Queens Sch., 1973-74, chmn. bd., 1974—; 2 v.p. Italian Charieties Am. Pres., North Queens Ind. Democrats, 1967; del. Dem. Nat. Conv., 1968; 1st v.p. Democrats for New Politics. Served with M.C., USNR, 1950-52. Mem. Spl. (chmn. newspaper and news group N.Y.C., 1966-67, 71-73, nat. chmn. newspaper div. 1968-69, chmn. automation com. newspaper div.), Am. (chmn. membership com. Suffolk, Nassau Counties 1962-65), Nassau County (exec. com. 1962-65, exec. bd. 1972-74, chmn. directory com. 1971-75, chmn. 1979—), N.Y. library assns., Adminstrv. Mgmt. Soc., Am. Mgmt. Assn. (speaker 1972—; chmn. newspaper and news group 1971-73), Beta Phi Mu (mem. chpt. orgn. com. 1961-62). Home: 42-46 209th St Bayside NY 11361 Office: 550 Stewart Ave Garden City NY 11530

IPPOLITO, ANTHONY DAVID, metals co. exec.; b. Jersey City, Oct. 1, 1940; s. Joseph and Teresa (Petronico) I.; B. Engring., Stevens Inst. Tech., 1963, M.S., 1968; m. Mary Louise Keuttel, Feb. 12, 1966; children—James, Rose Anne. Metallurgist, NL Research and Devel., Metal div., NL Industries, 1963-70, mgr. new products devel., 1971-73, product mgr., 1974-75, nat. accounts sales mgr., 1975-78, mktg. mgr. fabricated products, 1978—. Mem. Am. Soc. Metals, Am. Inst. Metall. Engrs., Electronic Industries Assn., Lead Industries Assn. Patentee in coating composition, flux composition. Home: 19 Hopatcong Dr Lawrenceville NJ 08648 Office: Wycoff Mills Rd Hightstown NJ 08520

IPPOLITO, CARLO AMEDEO, physician; b. Italy, Nov. 15, 1917; s. Joseph and Christina (Cristiano) I.; student Coll. City N.Y., 1937-41; M.D., Middlesex U., 1944; m. Antoinette Caruba, Mar. 10, 1946; children—Carol, Joseph. Intern, Mary Immaculate Hosp., Queens, N.Y., 1944-45; resident in otolaryngology Fordham Gen. Hosp., Bronx, 1946-48; practice medicine, Rockville Centre, N.Y., 1959—; mem. staff Mercy Hosp., Lydia E. Hall Hosp. Served with USNR, 1945-46; PTO. Diplomate Am. Bd. Otolaryngology. Mem. AMA, N.Y. State Med. Soc., Nassau Otolaryngology Soc., Pan Am. Soc., Am. Acad. Ophtahlmology and Otolaryngology, Nassau Otolaryngol. Soc. (past pres.), Am. Acad. Facial Plastics and Reconstructive Surgery, AAAS. Republican. Roman Catholic. Club: Rockville Links. Home: 523 Hempstead Ave Rockville Centre NY 11570 Office: 165 North Village Ave Rockville Centre NY 11570

IPPOLITO, JOSEPH FRANK, state ofcl.; b. Trenton, Dec. 29, 1937; s. Frank Paul and Charlett Binder (Long) I.; student Rider Coll., 1964; now postgrad. New Sch. Social Research. Auditor, N.J. Office Fiscal Affairs, Trenton, 1966-68; sr. accountant N.J. Bur. Med. Facilities, Trenton, 1968-72; fin. mgr. spl. projects N.J. Dept. Transp., Trenton, 1972—; pres. Personal People Am., Trenton, 1972—. Mem. Hwy. Authorities Study State of N.J., 1974; mem. N.J. Gov.'s Task Force on Newark Bd. Edn., 1975; scoutmaster Boy Scouts Am., 1973-75; vol. Helene Fuld Hosp. Served with USCGR, 1957-59. Mem. Nat. Small Bus. Assn., Fedn. N.J. Taxpayers. Office: 104 Highgate Dr Trenton NJ 08618

IRELAND, HERBERT ALLEN, editor, pub.; b. Arlington, Mass., Nov. 28, 1924; s. Allen G. and Hazel (Walker) I.; B.A., Rutgers U., 1946; postgrad. U. Pa., Boston U., Northeastern U., 1956-62; m. Ruth I. Baird, July 24, 1946 (div. Dec. 1973); children—Robert A., Thomas H., Suzanne L.; m. 2d, Jean D. Zemann, June 21, 1974. Sales and sales promotion Vick Chem. Co., N.Y.C.; salaried job analyst Armstrong Cork Co., Lancaster, Pa.; indsl. salesman Central Soya Co., Ft. Wayne, Ind., 1946-50; sales and br. sales mgr. Howe Scale Co., Rutland, Vt., 1950-54; sales mgr. H.G. Davis, Cambridge, Mass., 1954-59; pres. Prospector Research Services, Inc., Waltham, Mass., 1959—. Mem. Sales and Marketing Execs. Internat., Boston Advt. Club, Direct Mail Mktg. Assn., Boston C. of C., Boston Publicity Club, Am. Marketing Assn., Waltham C. of C., Delta Upsilon. Home: 177 Bay Rd North Falmouth MA 02556 Office: 751 Main St Waltham MA 02154

IREY, NELSON SUMNER, pathologist; b. Lewisburg, Pa., July 18, 1911; s. Philip and Sarah Blanche (Sechler) I.; B.S., U. Pitts., 1935, M.D., 1938; m. Mary Ellen Sproat, Dec. 21, 1940; children—Ellen Jane, Janet Kathryn, Mary Sarah, Nelson Sumner. Intern, St. Francis Hosp., Pitts., 1938-39; resident Fitzsimons Gen. Hosp., Denver, 1946-47, Letterman Gen. Hosp., San Francisco, 1948 commd. 1st lt. U.S. Army, 1941, advanced through grades to col., 1965, ret., 1965; practice medicine specializing in pathology; chmn. dept. pathology Walter Reed Gen. Hosp., 1961-65; chmn. dept. environ. and drug-induced pathology Armed Forces Inst. Pathology, Washington, 1965—; clin. prof. pathology George Washington U., Washington, 1967—; Uniformed Services U. Health Scis., Bethesda, 1977—. Decorated Legion of Merit. Diplomate Am. Bd. Pathology. Fellow Am. Soc. Clin. Pathologists, Coll. Am. Pathologists, A.C.P., Am. Acad. Forensic Scis.; mem. Internat. Acad. Pathology, Washington Soc. Pathologists (pres. 1968), Soc. Pharmacol. and Environ. Pathologists (pres. 1974), Drug Info. Assn. Contbr. articles, monographs, chpts. to med. jours. and texts. Home: 2729 Daniel Rd Chevy Chase MD 20015 Office: Dept Environ and Drug-induced Pathology Armed Forces Inst Pathology Washington DC 20306

IRISH, GEORGE HENRY, JR., electronic engr.; b. Boston, May 25, 1932; s. George Henry and Jessica Ruby (Brewster) I.; B.S. in Indsl. Engring., Northeastern U., 1967; m. Dorithea Fontenote, May 28, 1955; children—Melvin Ledet, Jr., Ruby M., George Henry, III. With GTE Sylvania Co., 1966—, quality assurance engr., 1968-72, sr. components engr., Needham Heights, Mass., 1972—. Served with USAF, 1953-57. Recipient Article award GTE Sylvania Co., 1977. Mem. Am. Soc. Quality Control. Republican. Roman Catholic. Address: 302 West St Needham Heights MA 02194

IRISH, LEON EUGENE, lawyer; b. Superior, Wis., June 19, 1938; s. Edward Eugene and Phyllis Ione (Johnson) I.; B.A., Stanford, 1960; J.D., U. Mich., 1964; D.Phil., Oxford U., 1972; 1973; m. Carolyn Tanner, Aug. 6, 1960; children—Stephen, Jessica, Thomas, Emily. Admitted to Calif. bar, 1965, D.C. bar, 1969; law clk. to asso. U.S. Supreme Ct. Justice Byron R. White, 1967-68; cons. Office of Fgn. Direct Investments, 1968-69; atty. Caplin & Drysdale, Washington, 1969-72, partner, 1973—; spl. rep. of Sec. Def. to 7th session Law of Sea Conf., dir. law of sea task force Dept. Def., 1978; adj. prof. Georgetown U. Law Sch., 1977—; lectr. Presdl. Classroom for Young Ams. Sec., dir. Vols. in Tech. Assistance, 1975—. Alfred P. Sloan Nat. scholar, 1956-60; Ford Found. grantee, 1964. Mem. Am. Bar Assn. (tax sect.), Order of Coif. Contbr. articles to profl. jours.; note and comment editor U. Mich. Law Rev., 1963-64. Home: 3301 Highland Pl NW Washington DC 20008 Office: 1101 17th St NW Washington DC 20036

IRMIGER, ERNST HENRY, lawyer; b. Switzerland, Jan. 15, 1934; s. Ernst F. and Josefa (Ortner) I.; B.S., U. Zurich, L.I. U., 1971; J.D., New Eng. Sch. Law, 1976; m. Ria M., Sept. 1, 1960; 1 child, Lilian M.; Mktg. exec. Alina Corp., Plainview, N.Y., 1960-71; gen. mgr. Degen Corp., Lowell, Mass., 1971-73; counsel Ade Corp., Watertown, Mass., 1973-76; admitted to Mass. bar, 1977, individual practice law, Acton, Mass., Zurich, Switzerland, 1977—; dir. Primalux Corp.; counsel, trustee Brookrun Condominium Trust. Mem. Am. Bar Assn., Mass. Bar Assn., Boston Bar Assn., Internat. Bar Assn., Am. Trial Lawyers Assn. Home and Office: 368 Great Rd Acton MA 01720 also Bergstrasse 162 Zurich 8032 Switzerland

IRVINE, KENNETH ANDREW, banker; b. N.Y.C., Aug. 16, 1941; s. John J. and Marion N. (Nevines) I.; B.A., U. Mich., 1963; M.B.A., Harvard, 1966; m. Bettina Simpson Brown, Apr. 15, 1978. Asso. Lehman Bros., N.Y.C., 1964-65, Wertheim & Co., N.Y.C., 1966-70; v.p. Robert Fleming & Co., Ltd., N.Y.C., 1970-71; v.p. Chase Manhattan Bank, N.Y.C., 1972—. Served with USMCR, 1964. Mem. N.Y. Soc. Security Analysts. Club: Harvard (N.Y.C.). Home: 2 Sutton Pl S New York City NY 10032 Office: 1 Chase Manhattan Plaza New York City NY 10015

IRVINE, LOUVA ELIZABETH, artist, filmmaker, design cons.; b. N.Y.C., Jan. 3, 1939; d. Robert Urquhart and Louva Elizabeth (Goodrich) I.; student Arts Students League, 1960-61, Sch. Visual Arts, 1962-63; B.A., Hans Richter Film Inst., City Coll. 1967. Prodn. mgr., set and costume designer showcase and original prodns., 1965-68; cons., Exptl. Design unit Time-Life Inc., 1969-71, Community Makers Inc., N.Y.C., 1971-73; project cons. Pratt Inst., 1971-72; pres. Total Design Assos., N.Y.C., 1976—; mem. faculty Sch. Arts Inst. Film and Television, N.Y.U., 1976—; mentor Pratt Inst., 1976; designer, instr. Workshops Solomon R. Guggenheim Mus., 1971-73; artist-in-residence, Nat. Endowment for Arts grantee S.C. Arts Commn., 1975, Film Workshop of Westchester, 1975-76; cons. 2d Internat. Festival Women's Films, 1976; mem. Millenium Film Workshop, 1971—; creator over 200 exptl. film studies, 1966—, including Dig We Must, Walk, Don't Run, Citywalk, Rain, Elegy for My Sister, Waterdance, Murray Hill Morning, Blue Moment (Cine Golden Eagle award 1977), Revelation, Circus; co-author script Homeward Bound; cons. The Birth Film, 1971; co-producer, dir., prodn. mgr. Three Lives, 1970-71, asso. dir. play Halleluiah Day, 1973; set designer play Bathtub, 1969; film coordinator Women's Interart Center, 1972-73; co-founder Women's Film Collective, 1972; coordinator film festival UN Internat. Yr. of Woman, 1975; producer, dir. CJOH-TV, Ottawa, Ont., Can., 1975; script cons. No Place to be Somebody (Pulitzer prize, Obie award). Recipient Meyer Goldman award; MacDowell fellow, 1976, 77, Millay fellow, 1978. Mem. Soc. Women in Film, Tape and Television (co-founder, v.p. 1975-76), Nat. Assn. Broadcast Employees and Technicians, Assn. Ind. Video and Filmmakers (charter, chmn. exptl. film distbn. com.). Home: New York NY Office: PO Box 189 Murray Hill Sta New York NY 10016

IRVINE, R. GERALD, elec. engr.; b. N.Y.C., Mar. 31, 1937; s. Raymond Gerald and Jane Torrey (Schenck) I.; Regents Degree in Elec. Engring with honors, Norwich U., 1959; postgrad. in Elec. Engring., U. Vt., 1959-60, Ops. Research Program, Union Coll., 1971-73; m. Elizabeth Ann Williams Bazemore, Nov. 22, 1967; children—Wendy Lynn, Juanita Leigh, Terri Sue, Edward Bruce. Asso. design engr. Union Carbide Nuclear Div., Y-12 Plant, Oak Ridge, 1963-64; engr. elec. div. Stone and Webster Engring. Corp., Boston, 1964-68; elec. engr. FPC, Washington, 1968-70; staff engr. N.Y. State Dept. Pub. Service, Albany, 1970-74; project engr. Dubin-Mindell-Bloome, Inc., N.Y.C., 1974; staff engr. IBM-Sterling Forest, N.Y., 1974-78; sr. plant engr. Western Electric Co., 1978—; engring. cons. Served to 1st lt., Signal Corps, U.S. Army, 1960-63. Recipient Frederick Asher Spencer prize in Elec. Engring., 1959, Outstanding Service award N.Y. State Soc. Profl. Engrs., 1975. Mem. Am. Soc. Heating, Refrigerating and Air Conditioning Engrs., Assn. Energy Engrs., Internat. Assn. Elec. Insps., IEEE (contbr. publs.),

Illuminating Engring. Soc., Nat. Fire Protection Assn., Nat., N.Y. State (pres. chpt. 1974-75) socs. profl. engrs., Audubon Soc., Tau Beta Pi. Democrat. Clubs: Aircraft Owners and Pilots Assn., Masons. Office: 222 Broadway New York NY 10038

IRVINE, REED JOHN, journalist; b. Salt Lake City, Sept. 29, 1922; s. William J. and Edna Jessup (May) I.; B.A., U. Utah, 1942; postgrad. U. Colo., 1943-44, U. Wash., 1949; B.Litt. (Fulbright scholar), Oxford U., 1951; m. Kay Araki, Aug. 14, 1947; 1 son, Donald. With War Dept., Tokyo, Japan, 1946-48; economist; syndicated columnist. Bd. Govs. Fed. Res. System, Washington, 1951-77. Chmn. bd. dirs. Accuracy in Media, Inc., Washington, 1971—. Served with USNR, 1942-43, USMCR, 1943-46. Mem. Phi Beta Kappa. Mem. Ch. of Jesus Christ of Latter-day Saints. Club: Nat. Press (Washington). Home: 11120 Nicholas Dr Silver Spring MD 20902 Office: Accuracy in Media Inc 777 14th St NW Washington DC 20005

IRVING, LEONARD MORTON, photog. dealer; b. Bridgeport, Conn., June 8, 1924; s. Alexander Ajolo and Mollie (Feldman) I.; student Nat. Electronic Sch., 1943, Albert Sch. Photography, 1946; m. Rita A. Fernandez, Oct. 21, 1950; children—Alexander A., David R. With Lens Camera, Bridgeport, 1950—; ofcl. photographer Police Sq. Club Conn.; cons. in photography to elementary schs. and colls. Served with AUS, 1943-46. Recipient Certificate Achievement Law Enforcement Surveillance, Kodak, 1969; certified photog. counselor. Mem. Profl. Photographers Am., Conn. Profl. Photographers, Internat. Center Photography. Club: Masons. Home: 51 Donna Dr Fairfield CT 06432 Office: 307 Fairfield Ave Bridgeport CT 06604

IRVING, ROBERT AUGUSTINE, condr., pianist; b. Winchester, Eng., Aug. 28, 1913; s. Robert Graham and Oriane (Tyndale) I.; scholar Winchester (Eng.) Coll., 1926-32, Royal Coll. Music, 1934-36; B.A. (scholar), New Coll., Oxford (Eng.) U., 1935. Came to U.S., 1958. Prof. piano Winchester Coll., 1936-40; asso. condr. BBC Scottish Orch., 1945-48; mus. dir. Royal Ballet Eng., 1949-58, N.Y.C. Ballet, 1958—; vis. condr. numerous orchs., U.S. and Eng., 1951—; rec. artist for HMV, RCA Victor, EMI, Capitol, Angel, Kapp records. Served with Royal Arty., 1940-41, RAF, 1941-45. Decorated D.F.C. with bar. Composer; As You Like It (with K. Hepburn), 1949; also scores for films. Home: 160 West End Ave New York City NY 10023 Office: New York City Ballet NY State Theatre Lincoln Center New York City NY 10023*

IRVING, ROBERT CHURCHILL, mfg. co. exec.; b. Waltham, Mass., Sept. 15, 1928; s. Frederick Charles and Emily Alvina (Churchill) I.; A.S., Franklin Inst. of Boston, 1965; certificate of profl. achievement Northeastern U., 1975; children—Robert F., John W. Sr. draftsman Mason-Neilan, Boston, 1948-54; mgr. design services Kinney Vacuum Co., Gen. Signal Corp., Boston, 1955-69; mgr. engring. services Sturtevant div. Westinghouse Electric Corp., Hyde Park, Mass., 1978—. Served with U.S. Army, 1946-48. Mem. Am. Def. Preparedness Assn., Am. Soc. for Quality Control (sr.), Nat. Mgmt. Assn. Republican. Home: 11 Linda Ave Brockton MA 02401 Office: 25 Damon St Hyde Park MA 02136

IRWIN, HOWARD SAMUEL, JR., bot. garden adminstr.; b. Louisville, Mar. 28, 1928; s. Howard Samuel and Grace Harding (Cole) I.; B.A., U. Puget Sound, 1950, B.Ed., 1952; Ph.D. (So. Fellowships Fund fellow), U. Tex., 1960; D.Sc., Fordham U., 1977; m. Marian Sterne, Aug. 19, 1951; children—Elizabeth, Dorothy. Fulbright exchange tchr. Queen's Coll., Georgetown, Guyana, 1952-56; with N.Y. Bot. Garden, Bronx, 1960—, herbarium adminstr., 1966-68, head curator, 1968-71, exec. dir., 1971-72, exec. v.p., 1972-73, pres., 1973—. Adj. prof. Coll. City N.Y., 1968—; adj. prof. botany Columbia, 1971—; dir. Cary Arboretum, Millbrook, N.Y., 1971—. Bd. dirs. Bronx Council On Arts, Weis Ecology Center. Recipient Alumnus Cum Laude award U. Puget Sound, 1968. NSF grantee, 1964-76. Fellow N.Y. Acad. Scis.; mem. Bot. Soc. Am., Am. Soc. Plant Taxonomists (pres. 1973-74), Internat. Assn. For Plant Taxonomy, Sociedade Brasileira de Botânica, Internat. (v.p. 1974—), Am. assns. bot. gardens and arboreta, Am. Assn. Museums, Cultural Instns. Group, Assn. of Systematics Collections (pres. 1974-76), Assn. for Tropical Biology (sec.-treas. 1964-65), Torrey Bot. Club, Sigma Xi. Clubs: Explorers, Cosmos, University (N.Y.C.). Author: Roadside Flowers of Texas, 1961; Trees, Shrubs and Woody Vines of the Southwest, 1961; Amazon Jungle: Green Hell to Red Desert?, 1975. Home: NY Bot Garden Bronx Park Bronx NY 10458

IRWIN, MARIE EMILY, hosp. ofcl.; b. Timmins, Ont., Can., Sept. 23, 1938; d. Chesney Osborne and Reta (Kwekkeboom) Davison; R.N., Mack Sch. Nursing, 1959; m. Roy H. Irwin, Apr. 9, 1960; children—Kelley Jayne, Steven Douglas. Mem. nursing staff operating room St. Catharines (Ont.) Gen. Hosp., 1959-65; supr. operating room Hotel Dieu Hosp., St. Catharines, 1971-76, surg. coordinator, 1976—, mem. Hosp. Intensive Care Unit, Infection Control coms., Vice-pres. Briardale Pub. Sch. P.T.A., St. Catharines, 1967-68. Mem. United Ch. Christ (former Sunday sch. tchr.). Mem. Order Eastern Star (past matron). Home: 104 Village Rd Saint Catharines ON L2T 3C1 Canada Office: 155 Ontario St Saint Catharines ON Canada

IRWIN, WILLIAM JOSEPH, educator; b. Bklyn., June 20, 1941; s. William and Elizabeth Veronica (Kinsella) I.; B.A., St. John's U., Jamaica, N.Y., 1964; M.A., Columbia U., 1965, Ph.D., 1975; m. Maureen Elizabeth Sullivan, June 15, 1968; children-Sharon, Kenneth, Catherine. Instr., U. Dubuque, 1966-67; instr. Mercy Coll., Dobbs Ferry, N.Y., 1967-69, asst. prof. history, 1969-70; asst. prof. history Bowie State Coll., 1971-75, asso. prof., 1975—; mem. faculty senate State Univs. and Colls., 1973—, pres., 1976-78; mem. faculty senate Bowie State Coll., 1977-79, chmn., 1978-79; guest lectr. ednl. adminstrn. U. Md., George Washington U. Bd. dirs. FISH of Laurel (Md.), 1978—. Mem. Am. Hist. Assn., Council for European Studies, Md. Assn. Higher Edn., Md. Assn. Ednl. Uses of Computer, Soc. Spanish and Portuguese Hist. Studies. Roman Catholic. Club: West Arundel Swim (dir. 1976-79). Research in Spain, 1970-71, 77. Home: 313 Old Line Ave Laurel MD 20810 Office: History Dept Bowie State Coll Bowie MD 20715

ISAACS, HELEN COOLIDGE ADAMS (MRS. KENNETH L. ISAACS), artist; b. Flushing, N.Y., Jan. 17, 1917; d. Thomas Safford and Martha (Montgomery) Adams; student Miss Hewett's classes, N.Y.C., Miss Porter's Sch., Farmington, Conn., Fontainbleau (France) Sch. Art and Music, 1935, Art Students League, 1936; m. Kenneth L. Isaacs, Mar. 10, 1949; children—Kenneth Coolidge, Anne Carpenter Richards. One-woman show Chilton Club, Childs Gallery, Boston; exhibited in group shows Allied Artists, N.Y., Boston Arts Festival; portraits of various prominent persons; murals in various pub. bldgs., Boston, Rochester, N.Y., Pittsfield, Mass., Daytona, Fla. Mem. Colonial Dames Am. Clubs: Colony (N.Y.C.); Chilton (Boston). Home: 68 Beacon St Boston MA 02108

ISAACS, RICHARD BRUCE, author, sportsman; b. Evanston, Ill., Nov. 12, 1942; s. Harry Columbus and Natalie (Strauss) I.; B.A., N.Y. U., 1965; M.A. in Developmental Psychology, M.A. in Ednl. Tech., Columbia U., 1976. Vol., Peace Corps, Colombia, 1965-67; free lance comml. photographer, N.Y.C., 1968-75; photog. cons., N.Y.C., 1974—; v.p. Blackstone & West, Inc., Phila., 1969-70; instr. photography Sch. Visual Arts, N.Y.C., 1973—; rep. Sci. Time Sharing Corp., N.Y.C., 1976—. Mem. Am. Photography Assn., Soc. Sci. Study of Sex, Assn. Computer Machinery, Am. Soc. Photographers in Communications, Soc. Plastics Engrs., Rolls Royce Owners Club, U.S. Aikido Fedn., Aircraft Owners and Pilots Assn., Confrerie de la Chaine des Rotisseurs, Westchester County Police Revolver and Rifle League. Home: 80 N Moore St New York City NY 10013

ISAACSON, EDITH LIPSIG, civic worker; b. N.Y.C., Jan. 18, 1920; d. Irving A. and Bertha (Evans) Lipsig; student Radcliffe Coll., 1937-39; LL.B., St. Lawrence U., 1943; m. Selian Hebald, 1940 (dec. Feb. 1959); children—Anne, Selian; m. William J. Isaacson, May 19, 1975. Pres., Forest Knolls Corp., N.Y.C., 1960-76, Norman Homes Corp., N.Y.C., 1968-76; cataloguer Nat. Collection Fine Arts, Smithsonian Instn., 1969-73. Nat. sec. Women's Am. Orgn. for Rehab. through Tng., 1950; pres. Radcliffe Club of Washington, 1969; pres. Radcliffe Club N.Y., 1959, 63, bd. sponsors, 1974-77; chmn. clubs Radcliffe Alumnae Assn., 1966; mem. founders com. Am. Symphony Orch. N.Y., 1962; trustee Allergy Found. Am. Fellow Pierpont Morgan Library, N.Y. Clubs: Cosmopolitan, Harvard (N.Y.C.). Author club organizational handbooks, monographs on French artists. Home: 900 Park Ave New York City NY 10021

ISAACSON, H. HARDING, funeral dir.; b. N.Y.C., Apr. 29, 1921; s. Rousseau Mouton and Mary Regina (Harding) I.; student pub. schs.; postgrad. New Sch. Social Research; m. Mary-Ann Maschinot Flum, Apr. 29, 1957. Funeral dir., dir. pub. relations Frank E. Campbell, N.Y.C., 1956—. Mem. N.Y.C. Civil War Centennial Commn., 1960-65; bd. dirs. U.S. Flag Found., 1975—. Served with USAAF, 1942-45. Decorated Air medal with 4 oak leaf clusters; N.Y. State Conspicious Service cross; knight grand cross Order Temple Jerusalem; knight grand officer Order St. Dennis Zante; knight comdr. Order St. Sava and White Eagle (Yugoslavia); Order St. John (Knights of Malta). Mem. SAR (chmn. Colonial Ball 1958—), SCV, S.R., Assn. Ex-Mems. Squadron A, Mil. Order Stars and Bars, Soc. War 1812, Vets. Corps Arty. State N.Y., Mil. Order Fgn. Wars, Colonial Order Acorn, Am. Legion, VFW, Order Lafayette, Friendly Sons St. Patrick, St. George Soc., Centennial Legion, Air Force Assn., E. Mid Manhattan C. of C. (hon. dir.). Republican. Episcopalian. Clubs: Church, Metropolitan. 7th Regt. Officers, Soldiers, Sailors and Airmen's (dir. 1976—) (N.Y.C.). Home: 7 E 85th St New York City NY 10028 Office: 1076 Madison Ave New York City NY 10028

ISAACSON, SIDNEY, pediatrician; b. Bklyn., Mar. 1, 1928; s. Abraham and Florence (Soloff) I.; B.A., N.Y. U., 1949; M.D., Berne U., 1955; m. Hariet Kempler, Dec. 21, 1952; children—Arlene Isaacson Werner, Marsha Lois. Intern Queen's Hosp. Center, 1955-56, resident in pediatrics, 1956, sr. resident, chief pediatrics, 1957-58; practice medicine specializing in pediatrics, Wantagh, N.Y., 1958—; dir. pediatrics Brunswick Gen. Hosp., Amityville, N.Y., 1972—; clin. asst. prof. pediatrics Cornell Med. Sch., 1973—; pres. Wantagh Pediatric Assos., P.C., 1971—. Served with M.C., AUS, 1946-47. Diplomate Am. Bd. Pediatrics. Fellow Am. Acad. Pediatricis; mem. AMA, N.Y. State, Nassau County med. socs., Nassau Pediatric Soc. Home and Office: 2975 Jerusalem Ave Wantagh NY 11793

ISAAK, ELMER BRAMWELL, cons. engr.; b. N.Y.C., Sept. 6, 1912; s. Abe and Rose (Halper) I.; A.B., Cornell U., 1933, C.E., 1935; m. Ella Campbell, Sept. 1, 1968; 1 dau., Lauren Silberman. Cons. engr. Madigan-Hyland, N.Y.C., 1935-68; v.p. M-H So. Am. Corp., 1954-62, partner, pres., M-H de la Cruz y Cia, 1963-71; profl. engr., owner Elmer B. Isaak, N.Y.C., 1968-77; exec. v.p. URS/Madigan-Praeger, Inc., N.Y.C., 1977-79, pres., 1979—; pres. URS/Coverdale & Colpitts, Inc., 1979—; cons. Nat. Railroads of Colombia, N.Y. State Thruway Authority, Triborough Bridge and Tunnel Authority; guest lectr. N.Y. U., Cooper Union, Co-founder, chmn. Joint Urban Manpower Program for job tng. of disadvantaged youth in engring., 1969-71; pres. parents' assn. for high sch. music and art., 1965-67. Recipient Award for Meritorious Service Nat. Soc. Profl. Engrs., 1971. Fellow ASCE (nat. dir., 1972-75, pres. met. sect. 1970-71); mem. N.Y. State Soc. Profl. Engrs., Am. Cons. Engrs. Council, Cornell Soc. Engrs., Transp. Research Bd., Regional Plan Assn., The Moles, Beta Sigma Rho. Contbr. numerous articles to profl. jours. Home: 79 W 12th St New York City NY 10011

ISABELLE, RONALD ANDRE, computer mfg. co. exec.; b. Manchester, N.H., July 25, 1945; s. Maurice P. and Cecile M. (Jacques) I.; B.S., N.H. Coll., 1967; m. Linda Jean Johnson, Mar. 23, 1968; children—Kristine, Jeffrey, Rebecca. Placement dir., faculty, dir. tech. div. Hesser Coll., Manchester, 1967-73; indsl. relations mgr. Centronics Data Computer Corp., Hudson, N.H., 1973-76; dir. indsl. relations Data Printer Corp., Malden, Mass., 1976—. Mem. Am. Soc. Personnel Adminstrn., Am. Mgmt. Assn., Am. Arbitration Assn., Greater Boston C. of C., Computer Industries Personnel Assn. Home: 428 Cohas Ave Manchester NH 03103 Office: 99 Middlesex St Malden MA 02148

ISAKSON, LOUIS, ins. cons.; b. New Haven, Jan. 23, 1919; s. Louis and Lucie Almira (Rickard) I.; B.A., U. Conn., 1939; m. Virginia Lucy Bracken, Apr. 16, 1945; 1 dau., Lucy Elizabeth Isakson Silva. Traffic mgr. P & H Bliss Cd., Middletown, Conn., 1939-41; dept. mgr. Am. Cyanamid Co., Wallingford, Conn., 1941-45; cons. Provident Mut. Life Ins. Co., Phila., 1945—; asso. dir. Union Trust Co., Wallingford, 1961—. Pres. YMCA, Wallingford, 1957-58; assessor, Wallingford, 1947-55, 61-62; sec. Democratic town com., Wallingford, 1947-60, chmn. Wallingford Sch. Bldg. Com., 1956-59. Mem. Wallingford C. of C. (exec. sec. 1956—), Mfrs. Assn. Meriden and Wallingford (exec. sec. 1960—), Nat. Assn. Life Underwriters. Congregationalist (deacon 1970-71). Clubs: Elks, Masons (dir. Masonic Temple Corp. 1972—, pres. 1978—); Wallingford Country. Address: 55 Fair St Wallingford CT 06492

ISAY, RICHARD ALEXANDER, psychiatrist, psychoanalyst; b. Pitts., Dec. 13, 1934; s. Milton and Jeanette (Myers) I.; A.B., Haverford Coll., 1956; M.D., U. Rochester, 1961; m. Jane Franzblau, July 26, 1964; children—David Avram, Joshua Daniel. Intern, Case Western Res. Univ. Hosp., Cleve., 1961-62; resident Yale U., New Haven, 1962-65, clin. instr. psychiatry, 1966-68, asst. clin. prof., 1968-75, asso. clin. prof., 1975—; with Western New Eng. Inst. Psychoanalysis, New Haven, 1968-73, faculty, 1977—. Bd. dirs. Ezra Acad.; trustee Western New Eng. Inst. Psychoanalysis. Served to lt. comdr. USNR, 1965-67. Mem. Internat., Am. psychoanalytic assns., Am. Psychiat. Assn., Western New Eng. Psychoanalytic Soc., Center for Advanced Psychoanalytic Studies. Office: 100 York St New Haven CT 06511

ISCH, ANTHONY CLARENCE, educator; b. Little Rock, Aug. 6, 1917; s. A. Clarence and Iva (Strickland) I.; Mus.B., Hendrix Coll., 1939; M.A., Columbia U., 1950; D. Musical Arts, Combs Coll., 1972; m. Mathilde Gosson, Sept. 19, 1943 (dec. 1974); children—Judith Isch Kentrus, Anthony G.; m. 2d, Jacqueline Waron, May 15, 1976. Dir. instrumental music pub. schs., Helena, Ark., 1939-42, Palmyra, N.J., 1946-56; supt. music pub. schs., Moorestown Twp., N.J., 1956-63; asso. prof. music Trenton State Coll., 1963—, prof. conducting and orchestration, 1963—, dir. bands, 1963—, supr. student teaching, 1965—; violinist Creative Arts Workshop Symphony Orch., Trenton, N.J., 1963—; founder Trenton State Coll. Wind Ensemble, 1968, condr., 1968—; adjudicator numerous music festivals in N.J., Pa.; guest condr. numerous band, orch. and handbell festivals. Served with AC AUS, 1942-45; PTO. Recipient Outstanding Citizen award Cinnaminson, Palmyra and Riverton (all N.J.) c's. of c., 1956, Spl. award Atlantic City Press Newspaper, 1974; N.J. State grantee, 1970-71. Mem. NEA, N.J. Music Educators Assn., Music Educators Nat. Conf., Nat. Assn. Watch and Clock Collectors, Am. Guild English Handbell Ringers. Author: Chelsea Collection for Handbells, 1963; composer string orch. and choral music; lectr. on antique clocks for hist. socs. Home: 38 Beverly Dr Belle Mead NJ 08502 Office: Music Dept Trenton State Coll Trenton NJ 08625

ISENBERG, ARTHUR NEWTON, surgeon; b. Ballston Spa, N.Y., Apr. 1, 1937; s. Mayer and Fanny I.; B.S., St. Lawrence U., 1958; M.D., Albany Med. Coll., 1962; m. Carolyn J. Suarez, June 20, 1964; children—Beth Ann, Joshua, Matthew. Intern, Los Angeles County Gen. Hosp., Los Angeles, 1962-63; resident Albany (N.Y.) Med. Center, 1963-68; practice medicine specializing in gen. and vascular surgery, Saratoga Springs, N.Y., 1968—; mem. staff Saratoga Hosp., chmn. dept. surgery, 1976-78; mem. staff Benedict Meml. Hosp., Ballston Spa. Mem. alumni council Albany Med. Coll.; pres. Saratoga unit Am. Cancer Soc., 1972-73; bd. dirs. Saratoga YMCA, 1972—, v.p., 1977-78. Diplomate Am. Bd. Surgery. Fellow A.C.S.; mem. AMA, N.Y., Saratoga County (N.Y.) (pres. 1973-74) med. scos., Alpha Omega Alpha. Home: Nelson Ave Saratoga Springs NY 12866 Office: 505 Broadway Saratoga Springs NY 12866

ISENBERG, HENRY DAVID, microbiologist; b. Giessen, Ger., Mar. 9, 1922; s. Gerson and Flora (Gruenebaum) I.; came to U.S., 1937, naturalized, 1943; B.S., City Coll. N.Y., 1947; Bklyn. Coll., 1951; Ph.D., St. John's U., 1959; m. Lila S. Grossman, Feb. 15, 1948; children—Pepi Isenberg Stein, Gerald. Asst. dir. Angrist Labs. 1947-54; chief microbiology L.I. Jewish Hillside Med. Center, New Hyde Park, N.Y., 1954—; asst. clin. prof. orthopedic surgery State U. N.Y. Downstate Med. Center, Bklyn., 1963-68; asso. prof. clin. orthopedic surgery, 1968-71, prof., lectr., 1971—; prof. clin. pathology State U. N.Y. Health Scis. Center, Stony Brook, 1970—. Served with U.S. Army, 1943-45. Recipient Microbiologist of Year award LabWorld, 1978. Diplomate Am. Bd. Med. Microbiology, chmn., 1976-79. Fellow Am. Acad. of Microbiology (bd. govs.), N.Y. Acad. Scis., Am. Inst. Chemists, Assn. Clin. Scientists; asso. fellow N.Y. Acad. Medicine; mem. Am. Soc. for Microbiology, Soc. for Gen. Microbiology, AAAS, Infectious Diseases Soc. Am., Soc. for Protozoology, Orthopedic Research Soc., Am. Soc. Limnology and Oceanography, Sigma Xi. Jewish. Editor: Jour. Clin. Microbiology, 1974—; series editor Micorganisms and Disease; mem. editorial bd. Applied Microbiology, 1969-74; editor CRC Critical Reviews in Microbiology; editor-in-chief CRC Forum in Bacteriology; contbr. numerous articles to profl. jours. Patentee in field. Home: 40 Stoner Ave Great Neck NY 11021 Office: Long Island Jewish/Hillside Med Center New Hyde Park NY 11040

ISENBERG, MORRIS, psychiatrist; b. Boston, June 10, 1906; s. Max and Gertrude (Marcus) I.; M.D., U. Berlin, 1935; certificate in psychoanalysis Am. Inst. Psychoanalysis, 1954; m. Frieda Epstein, May 4, 1944; children—Edward, Elliott, Howard. Intern, E. Moline (Ill.) State Hosp., 1936; rotating intern Evang. Hosp., Chgo., 1937; resident in psychiatry E. Moline State Hosp., 1938-40; resident in psychiatry Mt. Zion Hosp., San Francisco, 1941-42; attending psychiatrist Queens Hosp. Center, N.Y.C., 1966-71; practice medicine, specializing in psychiatry, N.Y.C., 1947—; cons. psychiatrist Queens Hosp. Center, 1971—; supervising psychoanalyst Karen Horney Clinic, N.Y.C., 1969—; lectr. Am. Inst. Psychoanalysis, N.Y.C., 1954-66, 68—. Mem. profl. adv. com. Queens County Mental Health Soc., 1970—. Served to capt., M.C., AUS, 1942-46. Diplomate Am. Bd. Psychiatry and Neurology. Fellow Am. Psychiat. Assn.; mem. Queens County Psychiat. Soc. (pres. 1969-70), Assn. Advancement of Psychoanalysis (treas. 1960-61, councillor 1967-70), Am. Acad. Psychoanalysis, Assn. Advancement of Psychotherapy, Assn. Advancement of Psychoanalysis, AMA. Democrat. Jewish. Contbr. articles in field to profl. jours. Home: 108-24 Jewel Ave Forest Hills NY 11375 Office: 147 E 50 St New York City NY 10022

ISHIKAWA, AKIRA, educator; b. Odawara City, Japan, Apr. 20, 1934; s. Ryoji and Hisako I.; M.A. (Fgn. Exchange scholar), U. Wash., 1969; Ph.D. (Humble Oil Found. fellow; Gen. Electric Found. fellow), U. Tex., 1972; m. Minako Shirai, June 22, 1959; 1 child, Makoto. Cons., Safeco Ins. Cos., Seattle, 1969-70; instr., research asso. U. Tex., Austin, 1970-72; asst. prof. Grad. Sch. Bus. Adminstrn., N.Y. U., 1972-76; vis. prof. U. Hawaii, 1976-77; asso. prof. Grad. Sch. Bus. Adminstrn., Rutgers State U., Newark, 1976—; cons. Tatung Co., Taiwan; vis. prof., program dir. Japan Am. Inst. Mgmt. Sci. Mem. Soc. Mgmt. Info. Systems, Am. Soc. Cybernetics, Am. Accounting Assn., Assn. Computing Machinery, Japan Soc. Asso. editor Forum, Am. Soc. Cybernetics, 1974-79. Author: Corporate Planning and Control Model Systems, 1975. Office: 92 New St Newark NJ 07102

ISHIKAWA, HIDEHIKO, photog. co. exec.; b. Tokyo, Nov. 17, 1931; s. Ryoji and Hisako I.; came to U.S., 1976; B.S., Yokohama Nat. U. (Japan), 1954; Ph.D., U. Rochester, 1962; m. Michiko Angela Sasagawa, Feb. 27, 1963; 1 dau., Lina. With Konishiroku Photo Industry Co., Ltd., Tokyo, 1954-76, sr. research asso., 1969-76; sr. v.p. Konishiroky Photo Industry U.S.A. Inc., Englewood Cliffs, N.J., 1976, dir. rep. office, 1976—. Fulbright scholar, 1958-62. Mem. Soc. Photog. Scientists and Engrs., Am. Chem. Soc., others. Buddhist. Contbr. articles to profl. jours. Patentee in field. Home: 24 Louise Ln Tenafly NJ 07670 Office: 560 Sylvan Ave Englewood Cliffs NJ 07632

ISRAEL, ADRIAN CREMIEUX, investment banker, mcht.; b. N.Y.C., Nov. 6, 1915; s. Adolph Cremieux and Babette (Bloch) I.; grad. Phillips Acad., Andover, Mass., 1932; B.S., Yale, 1936; children by previous marriage—Ellen I. Rosen, Andrew C., Thomas C., Nancy; m. Joy Whitmore, June 25, 1971. With A.C. Israel Enterprises Co., N.Y.C., 1936—, pres., 1945-65, chmn. bd., 1965—; ltd. partner Bache & Co., N.Y.C., 1945-64, gen. partner, chmn. exec. com., 1964-65, pres., dir., 1965-66; chmn. bd. Havenfield Corp., N.Y.C., 1967-73; pres., chief exec. officer dir. ACLI Internat., Inc., 1971—, Adrian & James, Inc., Stamford, Conn., 1936—; chmn. bd., dir. Peoples Drug Stores, Washington, 1976, Lane Drug Corp., Inc., Toledo, 1956-76, A.C. Israel Woodhouse & Co., Ltd., London, Eng., 1970—. Mem. Chgo. Bd. Trade, N.Y. Coffee and Sugar Exchange, Inc., N.Y. Cocoa Exchange; bd. govs. Commodity Exchange. Cons. WPB, also War Food Adminstrn., 1942-46. Chmn. commodity div. Beekman Downtown Hosp.; pres., bd. dirs. A. Cremieux Israel Found., 1946—; bd. dirs. Yale Devel. Bd., 1964—; trustee Montefiore Hosp., N.Y.C., Beekman Downtown Hosp., N.Y.C.; bd. incorporators Stamford (Conn.) Hosp. Mem. Comex Clearing Assn. Inc., N.Y. Cocoa Clearing Assn. (dir.), Cocoa Mchts. Assn. Am., Inc., Futures Industry Assn., N.Y., African-Am. C. of C. (dir.). Clubs: Governors, Wall Street, Bond (N.Y.C.); Yale (Stamford and N.Y.C.); Century Country (Purchase, N.Y.); Landmark (Stamford); Stanwich (Greenwich, Conn.); Federal City, Metropolitan (Washington); Bermuda Dunes (Calif.) Country; Mid-Ocean (Bermuda). Home: 247 Ingleside Rd Stamford CT 06903 Office: 110 Wall St New York City NY 10005

ISRAEL, DAVID JOSEPH, furniture mfg. and import co. exec.; b. Worcester, Mass., June 3, 1925; s. Harry I. and Lillian (Gourse) I.; B.S. in Econs., Yale, 1946; m. Charlotte M. Epstein, Mar. 28, 1954; children—Nancy, Mark, Susan. Vice pres. Wood Novelities Mfg. Co., Fall River, Mass., 1947-52; gen. mgr. Harvey Probber, Inc., Fall River, 1952-55; sales mgr. Meldan Co., Inc., Boston, 1955-59; pres. Trouvailles, Inc., Watertown, Mass., 1959—; pres. Trouvailles of Can., Inc., Toronto, Ont., 1972—, Trouvailles/EUROPA, S.A., Barcelona, Spain, 1971—, Trouvailles/Italia, Florence, 1974—. Served with CIC, AUS, 1943-46. Club: Yale. Home: 14 Old Orchard Rd Chestnut Hill MA 02167 Office: Trouvailles Inc 64 Grove St Watertown MA 02172

ISRAEL, HYMAN, dentist; b. Poland, Jan. 27, 1919; s. Samuel and Bertha (Rosmarin) I.; B.S., Western Res. U., 1942, D.D.S., 1943; M.P.H., Harvard, 1949; m. Edith Oringer, Oct. 30, 1949; children—David, Cindy. Asst. chief dental service VA Hosp., Bronx, N.Y., 1949-53; pvt. practice dentistry, Belleville, N.J., 1953-74; v.p. dental services Group Health, Inc., N.Y.C., 1959—; asst. clin. prof. dentistry Columbia, 1976—; dental cons. N.Y. State Dept. Edn., Program Planners, Inc., N.Y.C. Served as capt. Dental Corps, U.S. Army, 1943-46. Fellow Am. Pub. Health Assn.; mem. Am. Dental Assn., Dental Soc. State N.Y., First Dist. Dental Soc. N.Y.C. Home: 4 Bromley Dr West Orange NJ 07052 Office: 326 42d St New York City NY 10036

ISRAELS, CHARLES HENRY, composer; b. N.Y.C., Aug. 10, 1936; s. Carlos Lindner and Irma Commanday (Bauman) I.; B.A., Brandeis U., 1959; student Lenox Sch. Jazz, 1957-58, 60; m. Margaret Hanson, May 31, 1969; children—Sarah, Jessica. Instr., Indian Hill Music Workshop, Stockbridge, Mass., 1958-74; asst. prof. jazz studies Bklyn. Coll., 1972-76; lectr. continuing program program State U., N.Y., Purchase, 1975—; vis. asso. prof. music Bard Coll., 1978—; founder, dir. Nat. Jazz Ensemble, N.Y.C., 1973—; composer: Blues for O.P., Extract I, Iridescence, Music for Trombones and Saxophones, Sarabande, Skipping Tune, Solar Complexes. Crofts fellow, 1971; Guggenheim fellow, 1978; Nat. Endowment Arts grantee, 1972, 74, 76. Address: 155 Bank St New York City NY 10014

ISRAELSON, BYRON JAMES, newspaper exec.; b. Portland, Maine, July 8, 1922; s. Philip and Rebecca (Cohen) I.; student pub. schs., Portland; m. Jayne P. Israelson, May 16, 1954; children—Palmer Peters, Matthew S. With Portland Press Herald, 1941-42, 45—, day city editor, 1967-75, promotion mgr., 1975—; mem. Am. Press Inst. at Columbia, 1968; speaker in field. Bd. dirs. Blind Children's Resource Center, Portland. Served with arty. U.S. Army, 1942-45; ETO. Mem. Maine A.P. News Execs. Assn. (past pres.), New Eng. Soc. Newspaper Editors (pres. 1973). Jewish religion. Home: Portland ME 04102 Office: 390 Congress St Portland ME 04104

ISSELBACHER, KURT JULIUS, educator, physician; b. Wirges, Germany, Sept. 12, 1925; s. Albert and Flori (Strauss) I.; came to U.S., 1936, naturalized, 1945; A.B., Harvard U., 1946, M.D. cum laude, 1950; m. Rhoda Solin, June 22, 1955; children—Lisa, Karen, Jody, Eric. Intern, then resident Mass. Gen. Hosp., Boston, 1950-53; investigator NIH, 1953-56; chief gastrointestinal unit Mass. Gen. Hosp., 1957, chmn. com. research, 1967; prof. medicine Harvard Med. Sch., 1966—, chmn. exec. com. depts. medicine, 1968—, Mallinkrodt prof. medicine, 1972—, chmn. cancer com., 1973—. Fellow Am. Acad. Arts and Scis., A.C.P., Am. Gastroenterol. Assn. (pres. 1974-75); mem. Nat. Acad. Sci., Assn. Am. Physicians (pres. 1977-78). Editor: (Harrison) Principles of Internal Medicine, 1977. Discovered cause of galactosemia as 1st definitely proven disease due to hereditary enzyme defect; elucidated mechanism of intestinal fat absorption and causes of fatty liver; described disturbance of amino acid and lipid metabolism (isovaleric acidemia); demonstrated changes in surface membranes of malignant cells. Home: 20 Nobscot Rd Newton Center MA 02159 Office: Mass Gen Hosp Boston MA 02114

ISSERSTEDT, SIEGFRIED GORDON, electronic co. exec.; b. Elberfeld, Germany, Dec. 20, 1907; s. Kurt and Maysie (Langlois) I.; naturalized Canadian citizen, 1935; Dipl. Ing., Technische Hochschule Berlin-Charlottenburg (Germany), 1929; B.A.Sc., U. Toronto (Ont., Can.), 1932; m. Mary Elizabeth McBain, Apr. 6, 1962; 1 son, Robert Kurt. Chief engr. Gen. Sound Equipment, DeForest Phonofilm and Photocell Control Co., Toronto, 1930-36; project engr. as cons. on process control Mpls. Honeywell Regulator Co., also Honeywell Brown, London, Holland, Belgium, France, Poland, Russia, Italy, Rumania, Egypt, Turkey, 1936-42; v.p., dir. Phoenix Engineered Products and Canadian Aircraft Instruments Longbranch, Can., 1942-46; pres., dir. Corex Ltd., Toronto, 1946—; dir. Andall Ltd., GEAC Computer Corp.; pres., dir. Gordis Ltd. Mem. Am. Inst. Aeros and Astronautics, Assn. for Computing Machinery, Aircraft Owners and Pilots Assn., IEEE (life), Royal Canadian Inst., AAAS Bd. of Trade. Club: Explorers. Patentee computers, flight controls and automatic controls. Home: 106 Poplar Plains Rd Toronto ON M4V 2N2 Canada Office: Corex Ltd Box 720 Station Q Toronto ON M4T 2N5 Canada

ITKIN, STANLEY LAWRENCE, librarian; b. N.Y.C., Mar. 23, 1936; s. Philip and Henrietta (Goldstein) I.; A.A.S., N.Y.C. Community Coll., 1954; B.A., Columbia, 1957; M.S. in L.S., Fla. State U., 1958; M.A., Simmons Coll., postgrad., 1974-76; m. Ann Horowitz, Dec. 1974. Librarian, N.Y. Psychoanalytic Inst., N.Y.C., 1956-58, Queens Borough Pub. Library, 1958-60; dir. East Paterson (N.J.) Pub. Library, 1961-66, Hillside Pub. Library, New Hyde Park, N.Y., 1967—. Tchr., Nassau County Prison, 1967-70. Fellow, U. Md., 1969. Mem. N.Y., Am. library assns., Freedom to Read Found., U.S. Naval Inst. Rotarian (pres. local club 1974—). Home: 215 Adams St Brooklyn NY 11201 Office: 1950 Hillside Ave Hyde Park NY 11040

IUTCOVICH, MARK, sociologist, educator; b. Braila, Romania, Sept. 17, 1929; s. Joseph and Matilda (Iutcovich) I.; came to U.S., 1965, naturalized, 1971; Licentiate U. Bucharest, 1950; M.A., U. Man. (Can.), 1962; P.D., Case Western Res. U., 1970; m. Joyce Ann Miller, Sept. 29, 1972. Teaching asst. U. Man., Winnepeg, 1961-62, hon. lectr., 1963; teaching asst. U. Toronto (Ont.), 1964-65; asst. prof. Xavier U., Cin., 1966-67; asst. prof. sociology Coll. Mount St. Joseph, Cin., 1965-67; vis. prof. U. Ala., Huntsville, 1971-72; prof. sociology Edinboro (Pa.) State Coll., 1967—; dir. research Northwest Inst. for Research, Erie, Pa., 1975—; cons. Inst. Psychiatry, Montreal, Que., Can., 1965, Inst. Research, Huntsville, 1971-72, Inst. Research, Pakistan, 1975—. Royal Commn. on Biculturalism grantee, 1964, Pa. Gov.'s Justice Commn. grantee, 1972, Edinboro State Coll. grantee, 1968-70; recipient certificate exceptional academic service Pa. Dept. Edn., 1977; citation distinguished teaching Pa. Ho. of Reps., 1977. Mem. Am. Sociol. Assn., Soc. Sci. Study of Religion, Pa. State Ednl. Assn., AAUP, Alpha Kappa Delta. Democrat. Contbr. articles on sociol. problems to profl. jours. Home: 430 Pittsburgh Ave Erie PA 16505 Office: Dept Sociology Edinboro State Coll Edinboro PA 16444 also NW Inst Research Erie PA 16502

IVANHOE, HERMAN, dentist; b. Russia, Aug. 18, 1908; s. Samuel and Rose (Kelmenson) I.; came to U.S., 1912, naturalized, 1930; B.S., Columbia, 1929, D.D.S., 1931; m. Lynn Rugof, Mar. 6, 1943; children—Eliot Richard, Cindy Beth. Practice gen. dentistry and orthodontics, Bklyn., 1931—; acting attending in charge dept. dentistry Maimonides Hosp., Bklyn., 1959; mem. staff Caledonia, Samaritan, Community hosps.; guest of Chilean Govt. to help dental profession, 1968; cons. orthodontics Edn. Alliance N.Y.; hon. dean Sch. Dentistry, Cho Sun U., Korea, 1973. Served with USAAF, 1943-46. Recipient Conspicuous Alumni Service medal Columbia U., 1974, commendation State Dept.-AID. Fellow Internat. Coll. Dentistry, Am. Coll. Dentists; mem. Am. Soc. Study Orthodontics, Am. Dentists for Fgn. Service (founder, pres. 1967—), ADA (life), Assn. Dental Alumni Columbia (pres. 1966-67, recipient meritorious award 1972). Mem. B'nai B'rith (pres. Jordan lodge). Contbr. to profl. publs. Introduced topical fluoridation program Carribbean area, 1974—. Established over 800 dental clinics in fgn. indigent countries; active promoting dental practice fgn. countries; equipped 6 fgn. dental schs., Korea, Peru, Honduras, Uruguay, Chile, Ecuador. Home: 1151 E 7th St Brooklyn NY 11230 Office: 619 Church Ave Brooklyn NY 11218

IVARSON, KARL CHRISTIAN, microbiologist; b. Champion, Alta., Can., May 7, 1924; s. Karl Gustav and Christinia (Kost) I.; B.Sc., U. Alta., Edmonton, 1953, M.Sc., 1956; Ph.D., Rutgers U., 1956. Research officer Can. Dept. Agr., Ottawa, Ont., 1956-59, research scientist Soil Research Inst. Central Exptl. Farm, Ottawa, 1959—. Served with Canadian Army, 1943-46. Mem. Am. Soc. Microbiology, Agrl. Inst. Can., Canadian Soc. Soil Sci. Contbr. articles to profl. jours. Home: 314 Athlone St Ottawa ON K1Z 5M4 Canada Office: Soil Research Inst Central Exptl Farm Ottawa ON K1A 0C6 Canada

IVASHKIV, EUGENE, chem. engr.; b. Ukraine, Mar. 21, 1923; s. Nicholas and Anastasia (Stasiuk) I.; B.S., Ukrainian Poly. Inst., Germany, 1950, Columbia U., 1957, Bklyn. Poly. Inst., 1959; M.S., Newark Coll. Engring., 1963; m. Eugenia Smolij, Aug. 8, 1953; children—Lionel, Sophia. Chemist, E.R. Squibb & Sons, Bklyn., 1957-60; research scientist Squibb Inst. Med. Research, New Brunswick, N.J., 1960-65, sr. research scientist, 1965—. Sec., Ukrainian Am. Youth Assn., 1950-55; bd. dirs. Orgn. for Def. 4 Freedoms Ukraine (dir. 1968-71, 77—); sec. bldg. com. St. George's Ukrainian Cath. Ch., 1975—; nat. council, v.p. Ukrainian Congress Com. Am., 1976—; pres. United Am. Ukrainian Orgns. N.Y.C., 1976—. Mem. Am. Inst. Chem. Engrs., N.Y. Acad. Scis., Ukrainian Engrs. Soc. Am. (sec. 1962-63, pres. 1972-74). Contbr. articles to profl. publs. Patentee separation steroids. Office: Georges Rd New Brunswick NJ 08903

IVERSON, WARREN PHILIP, microbiologist, govt. ofcl.; b. Plymouth, Wis., Sept. 23, 1923; s. Barthold Alfred and Edna Catherine (Hall) I.; B.A., U. Wis., 1944; Ph.D. (Commonwealth fellow), Rutgers U., 1949; m. Margaret Ellen Golibart, Feb. 4, 1956; children—Martin Philip, Mary Katherine. Microbiologist, Parke, Davis & Co., Detroit, 1949-52, U.S. Army Biol. Lab., Fort Detrick, Frederick, Md., 1952-67, Nat. Bur. Standards, Washington, 1967—. Lectr. bacteriology U. Md., 1957-61; U.S. del. to group on biol. corrosion OECD, 1963-66; co-chmn. Internat. Congress on Marine Corrosion, 1972. Recipient Charles Thom award, 1974, Silver medal Dept. of Commerce, 1974; Office of Naval Research grantee, 1967-71; Environmental Protection Agy. grantee, 1972-73. Mem. Nat. Assn. Corrosion Engrs., Am. Soc. for Microbiology, Soc. Indsl. Microbiology, Research Soc. Am., A.A.A.S., Biodeterioration Soc. Republican. Roman Catholic. Contbr. chpts. to books, articles to profl. jours. Home: 1208 Beechwood Dr Frederick MD 21701 Office: Nat Bur Standards Washington DC 20234

IVES, DAVID OTIS, broadcasting exec.; b. Salem, Mass., Apr. 21, 1919; s. Oscar Jackson and Elinor (Goodhue) I.; A.B., Harvard U., 1941, M.B.S., 1943; D.H.L. (hon.), Northeastern U., 1975; D.Hum. (hon.), Suffolk U.,1977; m. Cecilia Coale van Hollen, Dec. 12, 1953; children—David van Hollen, Stephen Goodhue. Reporter, Salem Evening News, 1947; reporter, desk editor, bur. chief Wall St. Jour., N.Y.C., Detroit, Washington and Boston, 1947-58; editorial writer Sta.-WBZ-TV-Radio, Boston, 1958-60; asst. gen. mgr., dir. devel., pres. WGBH Ednl. Found. for Public TV, Boston, 1960—; vice chmn. bd. mgrs. Pub. Broadcasting Service, 1974-77; trustee, mem. exec. com. Eastern Ednl. (TV) Network, 1976—. Pres. Fair Housing, Inc., Boston, 1967-71; overseer Boston Symphony Orch., 1971-77, chmn. bd. overseers, 1975-77, trustee, 1975-77; trustee Wellesley Coll., 1973—; mem. overseers com. to visit dept. visual, environ. studies Harvard U., 1974—; v.p. Boston Community-Media Council, 1977-78. Mem. Asso. Harvard Alumni (dir. 1974-77). Office: 125 Western Ave Boston MA 02134*

IVEY, JEAN EICHELBERGER, composer; b. Washington, July 3, 1923; d. Joseph S. and Elizabeth (Pfeffer) Eichelberger; A.B. magna cum laude, Trinity Coll., 1944; Mus.M. in Piano, Peabody Conservatory, 1946; Mus.M. in Composition, Eastman Sch. Music, U. Rochester, 1956; Mus.Dr., U. Toronto, 1972. Dir. electronic music studio, tchr. composition Peabody Conservatory, 1969—; performed in piano recitals, on concert tours U.S., Mexico, Europe, including own compositions. Recipient Distinguished Alumni award Peabody Conservatory, 1975; Nat. Endowment Arts grantee, 1978; subject of TV documentary A Woman Is. Mem. Am. Soc. U. Composers (editor newsletter 1968-70), A.S.C.A.P., Internat. Soc. Contemporary Music (dir. U.S. sect. 1972-75), Coll. Music Soc. (council 1971-74), Phi Beta Kappa (hon.). Compositions include: Passacaglia for chamber orch., 1954; Sonata for piano, 1957; 6 Inventions for 2 Violins, 1959; (choral anthems) O Come Bless the Lord, Lord Hear My Prayer, 1960; Sonatina for Unaccompanied Clarinet, Dinsmoor Suite (wind and percussion), 1963; Enter Three Witches (electronic piece), 1964; Pinball (electronic piece, Folkways rec.), 1965; Tribute: Martin Luther King (baritone and orch.), 1969; Terminus (mezzo and tape), 1970; 3 Songs of Night (soprano, 5 instruments, tape), 1971; Forms in Motion (symphony), 1972; Hera, Hung from the Sky, 1973; Testament of Eve, 1976; also music for art films, TV. Contbr. articles to publs., to book Electronic Music a Listener's Guide, 1972. Recs. Folkway records, 1973, Composers Recs. Inc., 1974. Home: 320 W 90th St New York NY 10024 Office: Peabody Conservatory Johns Hopkins U Baltimore MD 21202

IVIE, EVAN LEON, computer systems designer; b. American Fork, Utah, May 15, 1931; s. H. Leon and Ruth (Ashby) I.; B.S., Brigham Young U., 1956, B.E.S., 1956; M.S., Stanford U., 1957; Ph.D. (NSF fellow), Mass. Inst. Tech., 1966; m. Betty Jo Beck, Mar. 29, 1957; children—Dynette, Mark, Joseph, Robert, Ruthann, Rebecca, John, James, Mette, Emily, Peter. Dep. dir. programming sect. USAF Intelligence Agy., Washington, 1957-60; teaching, research asst. elec. engring. Mass. Inst. Tech., 1960-66; with Bell Telephone Labs., 1966—, supr., Whippany, Piscataway and Murray Hill, N.J., 1969—, process adminstr., Whippany, 1969-71; vis. sr. lectr. Stevens Inst. Tech., 1969—. Tchr. geneal. research, 1960—; active Boy Scouts Am.; founder N.J. Br. Geneal. Library, 1969; mem. Warren Twp. (N.J.) Bd. Edn., 1975—; mem. high council Bishopric Ch. of Jesus Christ of Latter-day Saints, Boston and Short Hills, N.J. Served with USAF, 1957-60. Mem. Assn. Computing Machinery, IEEE, N.J. Geneal. Soc. Contbr. articles to profl. publs.; demonstrator time-shared computers for info. retrieval, 1963; software designer, tester Safeguard anti-ballistic missile project, 1968-71; designer back-end computer concept and supr. implementation, 1973; originator programmer's workbench concept and supr. first system, 1975; designer photocomposition for producing telephone directories, 1975-77. Home: 86 Mountain Ave Warren NJ 07060 Office: Bell Telephone Labs 600 Mountain Ave Murray Hill NJ 07974

IWAMOTO, TAKEO, educator; b. Hyogo-ken, Japan, Feb. 21, 1927; s. Yoshio and Minoru (Iwamoto) I.; came to U.S., 1968; M.D., U. Tokyo, 1955, Dr.Med. Sci., 1962; m. Masako Araki, May 29, 1957; children—Satori, Mami. Asst. prof. ophthalmology Columbia U., 1968-71, asso. prof., 1971-75, asso. prof. clin. ophthalmology, 1975—. Nat. Council Fight for Sight fellow, 1962-65; NIH grantee, 1974-76. Mem. Assn. Research in Vision and Ophthalmology, Japanese Assn. Ophthalmology, Japanese Assn. Med. Doctors, Japanese Soc. N.Y., Tetsumon Club Alumni Assn. U. Tokyo Med. Faculty. Contbr. to profl. jours. Electron microscope research on normal and pathologic ocular tissues. Home: 204 W Morningside Ave Cresskill NJ 07626 Office: 630 W 168th St New York City NY 10032

IWANISZIW, NICHOLAS, cannery exec.; b. Ansbach, Ger., Nov. 24, 1947; s. John and Julianna (Kocur) I.; came to U.S., 1950, naturalized, 1966; B.S. in Chemistry, Drexel U., Phila., 1971. With Cadillac Pet Foods Co., Pennsauken, N.J., 1972—, quality control mgr., 1973-75, asst. mfg. mgr., 1976-78, mfg. mgr., 1978—. Mem. Inst. Food Technologists, Am. Prodn. and Inventory Control Soc. Democrat. Greek Catholic. Home: 729 N 3d St Philadelphia PA 19123 Office: 9130 Mohican Trail Pennsauken NJ 08110

IWATA, HARRY MASANDO, chem. engr.; b. Spokane, Oct. 18, 1920; s. Seiji and Masuko (Onbe) I.; B.S., Gonzaga U., 1942; M.S., Ohio State U., 1947; m. Margaret Yaeko Nakagawa, Feb. 16, 1944; children—Carol Ann, Brian, Mary Ellen. Supr., Dodge & Olcot, Inc., Bayonne, N.J., 1948-53, U.S. Indsl. Chem. Co., Balt., 1953-55; with indsl. chem. div. FMC Corp., Balt., 1955—, tech. supt., 1964-68, area prodn. supr., 1968-72, dir. safety and tng., 1972-76, dir. tng. and communications, 1976-77, project engr., 1977—. Chmn. 1st aid com. Balt. regional chpt. ARC, 1978-79. Served with inf. U.S. Army, 1944-46: ETO. Decorated Bronze Star. Recipient St. George's medal Boy Scouts Am., 1968, Silver Beaver award, 1973. Mem. Am. Inst. Chem. Engrs. (chmn. 1973-74), Am. Soc. Tng. and Devel., Mfg. Chemists Assn. Democrat. Roman Catholic. Patentee in insecticides. Home: 7602 Far Hills Dr Baltimore MD 21204 Office: FMC Corp POB 1616 Baltimore MD 21203

IYER, SURY, research chemist; b. Madras State, India, Dec. 15, 1938; Kaveripattinam Kalyanasundaram and Sivakami; B.Sc. with honors in Chemistry, Mysore U., Bangalore, India, 1958; Ph.D. in Chemistry, Boston U., 1968; came to U.S., 1962, naturalized, 1976; m. Padma Iyer, Feb. 9, 1970; 1 son, Shilesh. Chemist, Bhabha Atomic Research Center, Bombay, India, 1958-62; AEC research fellow chemistry dept. Brookhaven Nat. Lab., Upton, N.Y., 1966-67; research chemist Armament Research and Devel. Command, U.S. Army, Dover, N.J., 1968—; shelter mgr. for nuclear fall-out Fed. CD and Disaster Control Program, 1976-77. Mem. Am. Chem. Soc., N.Y. Acad. Scis., Sigma Xi. Contbr. numerous articles on photochemistry, radiation chemistry, time-resolved laser kinetic spectroscopy to profl. publs. Home: 7 Treaty Rd Randolph NJ 07801 Office: Bldg 3021 Armament Research and Devel Command US Army Dover NJ 07801

IZZI, JOHN DONALD, educator, author; b. Providence, Dec. 31, 1931; s. Joseph and Elizabeth (Kinney) I.; B.A., Providence Coll., 1953; M.Ed., R.I. Coll., 1965; postgrad. (NSF grantee), U. Vt., 1959, 60, 63, Seton Hall U., 1961, Yale U., 1966, Boston U., 1968-70; children—Kathleen, Donna, James, John. Tchr. various schs., R.I., 1955-62; head math. dept. Seekonk (Mass.) High Sch., 1966-67; with Mass. Dept. Edn., 1967-68; tchr. Pilgrim High Sch., Warwick, R.I., 1962-66, head math, dept., 1968-72; head math. dept. Toll Gate High Sch., Warwick, 1972—; pres. Smallstate Co., Warwick, 1975—; extension lectr. U. R.I., 1976—; dir. Prep Inst., Warwick; dir. Math. Edn. Service, Providence, 1965-66; dir. Metrication Project Toll Gate Edn. Complex, Warwick, 1972-73; advisor Am. Security Council, 1973—; metrication cons. Nat. Council Tchrs. Math., 1973—; Mem. Gov.'s Volpe's Hwy. Safety Act Com., 1967-68. Served with U.S. Army, 1953-55. Recipient Distinguished Achievement award Ednl. Press Assn. Am., 1974. Mem. NEA, Am. Fedn. Tchrs., Nat. Council Tchrs. Math., Am. Assn. Sch. Adminstrs. Metric Assn., New Eng. Regional Metric Assn. (edn. commr. 1976—), Mass. Dept. Edn. Assn. (v.p. 1967-68). Textbook reviewer AAAS, 1968—; book reviewer Phi Delta Kappan, 1974—. Author: Metrication, American Style, 1974. Contbr. articles to various publs. Office: PO Box 796 Warwick RI 02888

IZZO, JOSEPH DOMMINICK, painter; b. Mechanicville, N.Y., June 18, 1924; s. Jospeh S. and Anna Marie (Enziena) I.; A.A., N.Y.C. Community Coll., 1949; grad. Famous Artist Sch., Conn., 1969, Art Student League, Woodstock, N.Y., 1969, Phila. Acad. of Fine Arts, 1970, John Pike Sch. of Watercolor, 1969; m. Laura H. Lofrumento, June 1, 1952; children—Thomas, Nancy Jean, Theresa, Janet. Pvt. tchr. painting, Kennebunkport, Maine, 1969, Albany Inst. History and Art, 1970-74; chmn. Bi-centennial Com. on Art Exhibits, Ballston Spa, N.Y., 1976—; one-man-shows Mechanicville High Sch., 1938, 46, Art Student League, 1969, Waterford (N.Y.) Mus., 1970, Albany Art Gallery, 1972, Saratoga County Art Assn. Gallery, 1973; group shows include Phila. Acad. Fine Arts, 1970, N.Y. Art Student League, N.Y.C., 1969, N.Y.C. Community Coll., 1949, Butler Inst., Youngstown, Ohio, 1968, Albany (N.Y.) Inst. of History and Art, 1975, Schertle Gallery, Albany, 1976, Berkshire Mus., Pittsfield, Mass., 1972, Christmas Gallery, Kennebunkport, 1969, Burnt Owl Galleries, Burnt Hills, N.Y., 1976; represented in permanent collections Art Student League, Albany Inst. History and Art, N.Y.C. Community Coll., Mechanicville High Sch.; appeared on Peoples Art show radio sta. WKAJ, Saratoga, 1969, Cable TV Channel 16, 1975-76. Served with USNR, 1942-46; ETO. Recipient 1st prize in watercolor Saratoga County Art Show, 1968; 1st prize in oils Waterford Mus., 1971; 1st prize in watercolor Art Student League. Mem. Saratoga County (past pres.), Lower Adirondack Arts Council, Smithsonian Assos., Cooperstown, Berkshire art assns., So. Vt. Artists, Am. Legion. Republican. Roman Catholic. Contbr. numerous articles on art to newspapers. Home: 28 Stillwater Ave Mechanicville NY 12118 Office: PO Box 384 Mechanicville NY 12118

IZZO, LOUIS DOMINIC, psychologist; b. Rochester, N.Y., June 12, 1925; s. Joseph M. and Erminie C. (Pelusio) I.; B.S., U. Rochester, 1953; M.A., 1957; postgrad. U. Mich., 1965-78; m. Helen Theresa Baliski, June 12, 1950; children—Erminie Ann, Joseph Mario, David John, Stephen Anthony. Psychologist, Pub. Schs. Rochester, 1956—, initiator Early Detection and Prevention Program, 1957, sr. psychologist program, 1958-69, chief psychologist, program cons. city and county schs. in the Primary Mental Health Project, 1969—; sr. clin. psychologist Rochester State Hosp., 1958, 59; staff psychologist Center Community Studies, U. Rochester, 1969—; sr. clin. psychologist, asst. chief service, mental hygiene unit Albion State Tng. Sch., Western Reformatory and Prison for Women, 1963-71; practice hypnotherapy. Served with USAAF, 1945-46: PTO. Mem. Am., N.Y.

State, Genesee Valley (pres., 1966-67) psychol. assns., Sch. Psychologists Upper N.Y. State, Rochester Tchrs. Assn., N.Y. State Tchrs. Assn., NEA, Assn. Advance Ethical Hypnosis, Am. Inst. Hypnosis. Author: (with others) New Ways in School Mental Health: Early Detection and Prevention of School Maladaptation, 1975; contbr. articles to profl. jours. Home: 4479 St Paul Blvd Rochester NY 14617 Office: 13 Fitzhugh St S Rochester NY 14614

IZZO, THOMAS NICHOLAS, dentist; b. Beverly, Mass., Oct. 25, 1913; s. Joseph and Giovannina (Galluzzo) I.; B.S., Fordham U., 1941; D.D.S., Georgetown U., 1947; m. Marie Italia Miraglia, May 21, 1949; children—Joseph T., Frank P., Joanne Marie. Pvt. practice dentistry, White Plains, N.Y., 1947—. Served with U.S. Army, 1942-44, to capt. USAF, 1950-52. Recipient Fauchard medal, 1953, Silver Jubilee citation Georgetown U., 1972. Mem. Am. Dental Assn., N.Y. State, 9th Dist. dental socs. Address: 141 S Broadway White Plains NY 10605

JABLONSKI, WANDA MARY, pub. co. exec.; b. Czechoslovakia; d. Eugene and Mary Jablonski; B.A., Cornell U., 1942; postgrad. Columbia, 1943; L.H.D. (hon.), St. Lawrence U., 1978. Came to U.S., 1938, naturalized, 1945. Oil editor Jour. Commerce, N.Y.C., 1943-54; sr. editor Petroleum Week, McGraw-Hill, N.Y.C., 1954-61; founder, owner, editor, pub. Petroleum Intelligence Weekly, N.Y.C., 1961—. Mem. Council on Fgn. Relations, Middle East Inst., Fgn. Policy Assn., U.S. Arab C. of C., Nat. Press Club. Contbr. articles to Colliers, other mags. Home: Centre Island Oyster Bay NY 11771 Office: 49 W 45th St New York NY 10036

JABUSH, MARJORIE LOIS, interior designer; b. Lakewood, N.J., Nov. 10, 1931; d. Horace Voorhees and Marjorie Carolyn (Costello) Grant; grad. N.Y. Sch. Interior Design, 1963; postgrad. Newark Sch. Fine Arts, 1965; m. Milton Jabush, Apr. 30, 1963 (dec. 1974); 1 son, Jondavid; children by previous marriage—Mario, Janice, Darren. Apprentice designer to Michael Love, Shrewsbury, N.J., 1963; free-lance interior designer, Lakewood, 1964-70; interior designer Grebows, Howell, N.J., 1970-73, Huffman Koos, Freehold, N.J., 1975—; lectr. Lakewood Community Sch. Mem. Lakewood C. of C. (dir. 1970-72). Author design column Shore Builder Jour., 1964-66. Home: 671 North Lake Dr Lakewood NJ 08701 Office: Huffman Koos Route 9 Freehold NJ 07728

JACKEL, SIMON SAMUEL, food products co. exec., tech. cons.; b. N.Y.C., Nov. 11, 1917; s. Victor and Sadie (Ungar) J.; A.M., Columbia, 1947, Ph.D., 1950; B.S., Coll. City N.Y., 1938; postgrad. U. Ill., 1941-42; m. Betty Carlson, Jan. 22, 1954; children—Phyliss Marcia, Glenn Edward. Head fermentation div. Fleischmann Lab., Stamford, Conn., 1944-59; v.p. research and devel. Vico Products Co., Chgo., 1959-61; dir. lab., research and devel. Quality Bakers of Am. div. Sunbeam Baked Foods, N.Y.C., 1961—, v.p. lab. and tech. research, 1976—; dir. research and devel., mem. operating com. Bakers Research Devel. Service, N.Y.C., 1969—; pres. Plymouth Tech. Services, N.Y.C., 1951—; dir. hearing aid audiology Jewish Home and Hosp. for Aged, N.Y.C., 1951-76. Mem. sci. adv. com. Am. Inst. Baking, 1970—, mem. sanitation edn. adv. com., 1978—. Mem. industry adv. com. N.D. State U., 1971—. Recipient USAAF Exceptional Civilian Service award, 1943; Wisdom Hall of Fame award, 1974; USPHS research grantee, 1947-50. Fellow Am. Inst. Chemists, A.A.A.S.; mem. Am. Chem. Soc., Am. Assn. Cereal Chemists (chmn. milling and baking div. 1973-74, chmn. N.Y. sect. 1973-74) Am. Soc. Bakery Engrs. (chmn. engrs. info. service 1970—), ASTM, Am. Bakers Assn. (tech. food regulatory affairs com. 1971—, chmn. tech. liason com. to U.S. Dept. Agr. 1965—, alt. gov. 1978—), Assn. for Environ. Protection, Environ. Mgmt. Assn., Ind. Bakers Assn. (labeling com., tech. affairs com.), Inst. Food Technologists, Am. Mgmt. Assn., Nutrition Today Soc., Soc. Nutrition Edn., N.Y. Acad. Sci., N.Y.C. Chemists Club, Sigma Xi, Phi Lambda Upsilon. Jewish. Author tech. articles; tech. editor Bakery Prodn. and Marketing Mag., 1968—; contbr. articles to tech. jours. Patentee in field. Home: 46 Kings Hwy N Westport CT 06880 Office: 1515 Broadway New York NY 10036

JACKIEWICZ, IRENE ELIZABETH, data processing service co. exec.; b. Bridgeport, Conn., Dec. 16, 1940; d. Stephen John and Irene Erma (Samu) Fulop; m. Chester Edward Jackiewicz, Oct. 22, 1960; children—Cythia Marie, Theresa Ann. Clk., reservationist dept. traffic Norden div. United Technology, Norwalk, Conn., 1960-61; data entry operator Keypunch Services, Bridgeport, 1968-70; owner, mgr. Key Preparations, Bridgeport, 1971—. Mem. Data Processing Mgmt. Assn. (past sec.). Roman Catholic. Home: 117 Greenbrier Rd Trumbull CT 06611 Office: 180 Fairfield Ave Bridgeport CT 06604

JACKIM, HALAS LEONADUS, educator; b. Bklyn., May 30, 1925; s. Joseph and Isabelle (Stine) J.; B.A., N.Y. U., 1950, Ed.D., 1962; M.S., Columbia U., 1951; m. M. Lois Jones, Dec. 26, 1955; children—David, Richard. Tchr. Green Av. Elementary Sch., Sayville, N.Y., 1951-53; prin. Painted Post, (N.Y.) Elementary Sch., 1953-54; supervising prin. Corning (N.Y.) Area 3 Elementary Schs., 1954-60; exec. dir. ETV, Corning, 1960-64; prof. edn. State U. N.Y. at Oswego, 1964—, dir. devel. Tchr. Assessment Center for N.Y. Edn. Dept., 1976—; cons. Brazilian Ministry of Edn., 1966-68, New South Wales, Australia, 1971-72; pres. North Coast Realty Corp., Oswego, 1973—. Served with USAAF, 1942-45. Mem. Am. Ednl. Research Assn., N.E.A., One Room Schoolhouse Assn. Oswego County (pres. 1973-75), Phi Delta Kappa. Rotarian. Home: Jackim Rd RD 7 Oswego NY 13126

JACKOVICH, ANTHONY BARTHLOV, artist; b. Cummings, Ia., Dec. 6, 1923; s. Anton Matija and Matilda Jelisav (Viakovich) J.; student Art Students League, N.Y.C., 1946-47, Chgo. Art Inst., 1947-48, Ecole Superieur Nationale des Beaux Arts, Paris, France, 1948-49, Academic Julian, Paris, 1949-50, Academic Grant Chaumiere, Paris, 1950-53; m. Sheala O'Brien, Sept. 12, 1957; children—Gina, Ivan, Tonia. Ann. exhbns. include N.A.D., N.Y.C., Am. Watercolor Soc., N.Y.C., Allied Artists, N.Y.C.; various exhbns. throughout the nation including colls. and galleries; dir. Down East Artist Workshop. Mem. Assn. for Romantic Representational Art. Home: Round Pond ME 04564

JACKS, ULYSSES, lawyer; b. Coatesville, Pa., Jan. 15, 1937; s. Fred Douglas and Mable (Pruitt) J.; B.S., Va. Union U., 1959; J.D. cum laude (Teaching fellow), Howard U., 1970; m. Esterlene Gibson, Aug. 11, 1973. Admitted to Mass. bar, 1971; adminstrv. asst., univ. counsel Howard U., Washington, 1968-70; decision writer Equal Employment Opportunity Commn., Washington, 1969-70; asso. firm Csaplar & Bok, Boston, 1970-77; dep. chief counsel, agy. Mass. Dept. Pub. Works, Boston, 1977—. Asst. to scoutmaster Boy Scouts Am., South Coatesville, Pa., 1966-67. Served with AUS, 1960-62. Mem. Am., Boston bar assns. Baptist. Home: 1000 Governors Dr Apt 13 Winthrop MA 02152 Office: 100 Nashua St Boston MA 02114

JACKSON, ALEXANDER WALLACE, publisher; b. Los Angeles, Oct. 10, 1944; s. S.J. and Della Jackson; B.A., L.I. U., 1969; m. Virginia Jackson, July 1, 1970. Pub., N.J. Voice, East Orange, 1970—. Served with USMCR, 1960-64. Mem. Am. Pilot Assn. Author: Pledging My Love, 1975; Come Back to Me, 1977. Home: 25 S Munn Ave East Orange NJ 07018

JACKSON, ARTHUR GREGG, lawyer; b. Phila., June 19, 1921; s. Arthur and Anna M. (Gregg) J.; B.S., Yale, 1943; J.D., Harvard U., 1950; m. Dorothy K. Hollis, June 26, 1943; children—Gail, Laura, Nancy, Sarah. Admitted to Pa. bar, 1951; asso. firm Mancill Cooney Semans & Hedges, Phila., 1953-60; partner firm MacCoy Evans & Lewis, Phila., 1961-75, Montgomery, McCracken, Walker & Rhoads, Phila., 1976—. Pres., Merion (Pa.) Community Assn., 1974—, Merion Civic Assn., 1972-73; bd. dirs. Merion Bot. Soc.; trustee Friends Central Sch. Served with Signal Corps, U.S. Army, 1943-46, 51-52. Mem. Am., Pa., Phila. bar assns., Am. Legion (past post comdr.). Republican. Quaker. Club: Union League (Phila.). Office: 3 Parkway Philadelphia PA 19102

JACKSON, CHARLES NEASON, II, assn. exec.; b. Richmond, Va., Mar. 16, 1931; s. Miles Merrill and Thelma Eugertha (Manning) J.; B.S., Va. Union U., 1957; postgrad. Temple U., 1957-60; M.S., Southeastern U., 1976; m. Marlene Costella Mills, Jan. 31, 1959; children—Renata, Andrea, Charles. Auditor, City of Phila., 1959-61; spl. agt. IRS, Phila., 1961-67; sr. auditor AID, Nigeria, 1967-69; v.p. adminstrn. and finance Nat. Urban Coalition, Washington, 1969—; dir. Media Assos. Trustee Washington Hosp. Center; treas. Vols. in Tech. Assistance. Served with USAF, 1951-55. Mem. Nat. Assn. Accountants, Am. Accounting Assn., Nat. Soc. Pub. Accountants. Roman Catholic. Home: 13822 Turnmore Rd Silver Spring MD 20906 Office: 1201 Connecticut Ave Washington DC 20036

JACKSON, DANIEL RUDOLPH, biologist; b. Millboro, Va., Dec. 28, 1938; s. Ruby Virginia (Jackson) J.; student U. Md., 1965-68, 72-74; m. Johnetta Charmagne Daugherty, Aug. 26, 1961; children—Shelley D., Danielle J. Biologist, div. biol. standards NIH, HEW (name changed to Bur. Biologics/FDA 1972), Bethesda, Md., 19S8-62, 64—. Served with AUS, 1962-64. Recipient Award of Merit, FDA, 1975. Mem. Electron Microscopy Soc. Am. Democrat. Discover/extractor Hepatitis Virus A and B. Home: 5300 Varnum Pl Bladensburg MD 20710 Office: 8800 Rockville Pike Bethesda MD 20014

JACKSON, DONALD EDWIN, underwater communications engr.; b. Bklyn., Aug. 17, 1930; s. Howard L. and Mildred N. (Nieber) J.; B.E.E., Poly. Inst. Bklyn., 1953, M.E.E., 1956; m. Eleanor I. Pearson, Apr. 6, 1958; children—Diane, Christine, Donald, Karen. With Sperry Gyroscope Co., Great Neck, N.Y., 1952—, developer navigation plotting system, 1952-57, submarine fire control, 1957-62, sonar techs., research sect. supr. underwater communications, 1962—; instr. co. space courses; chmn. ad hoc studies Nat. Security Indsl. Assn. Tchr. Bethel Bible study, Lutheran Ch. Recipient certificate of recognition Office of Chief of Naval Ops., 1972. Mem. IEEE (sr.), Acoustical Soc. Am., Nat. Security Indsl. Assn., Sigma Pi Sigma, Tau Beta Pi, Eta Kappa Nu. Contbr. tech. papers to sci. confs.; patentee optical scanning system, photoelectric navigation plotter, underwater communication system. Home: RFD 1 Box 723 Upper Brookville Oyster Bay NY 11771 Office: Sperry Gyroscope Great Neck NY 11020

JACKSON, DONALD VOORHEES, educator; b. East Orange, N.J., Nov. 12, 1947; s. Samuel F. and Hazel T. Phillips; B.A., Hofstra U., 1971; M.A. in Am. History, Rutgers U., 1978; m. Aug. 28, 1971; 1 son, Noah. Tchr., Scotch Plains (N.J.)/Fanwood High Sch., 1974-77; tchr. history Gilford (N.H.) High Sch., 1977—, chmn. social studies dist. curriculum. Secondary teaching certificate, N.J., N.H. Mem. Nat. Council for the Social Studies, Am. Hist. Assn. Home: 7 Mark Rd Franklin NH 03235 Office: Gilford Middle High Sch Gilford NH 03246

JACKSON, FRITZ ROBERT, clothing co. exec.; b. Beaumont, Tex., Aug. 7, 1922; s. Fritz R. and Hilda Lee (Holmes) J.; student U. Md., 1942-43, Colgate U., 1943-44; B.A., U. Calif. at Berkeley, 1949; m. Naomi Louise Hauerbach, Mar. 25, 1950; children—Whitney Robert, Daniel T., Laurie L. Engaged in equipment rental bus., 1955-61; founder, pres. Vested Gentry, Inc., Norristown, Pa., 1961—. Served to maj. USMC, 1944-46, 51-54. Home: Country Club Rd Valley Forge PA 19481 Office: 102 W 7th Ave Trappe-Collegeville PA 19426

JACKSON, GERALD GREGORY, psychologist; b. N.Y.C., Feb. 15, 1944; s. Charles Henry and Ruby Arlene (Harden) J.; B.A., Howard U., 1967; M.Ed., U. Maine, 1970; postgrad. Rutgers U., 1972—; div.; children—Monique Annette, Melanie Kim. Sr. counselor Poland Spring (Maine) Job Corps Center, 1967-69; asso. dir. Yale U. Summer High Sch., 1969-70; dir. transitional Year program Yale U., 1970-71; asso. dean student affairs Essex County Coll., 1971-74, asso. prof. psychology, 1974—; psychology intern N.Y. U. Med. Center, 1977-78. Mem. Essex County (N.J.) Mental Health Bd., 1972-76; committeeman City of East Orange (N.J.) 1974—. Mem. Am. Coll. Personnel Assn., Assn. Advancement Behavior Therapy, Assn. Advancement Social Psychology, Nat. Assn. Black Psychologists, Am. Personnel and Guidance Assn., Kappa Alpha Psi. Baptist. Contbr. articles to profl. jours.; editorial bd. Jour. Black Psychology 1976—, Jour. Counseling and Values, 1977—. Home: 77 S Munn Ave East Orange NJ 07018 Office: Behavioral Sci Dept Essex County Coll 303 University Ave Newark NJ 07102

JACKSON, GERARD JAMES, ins. broker; b. N.Y.C., Feb. 27, 1934; s. Gerard Edward and Anne (Cotter) J.; ed. Holy Cross Coll., Worcester, Mass., 1956; m. Frances Loftus, Dec. 14, 1958; children—Gerard K., Robin A., Victoria M. Engaged in ins., 1963—; partner Jackson & Kelly Ins. Brokerage, Harrison, N.Y., 1963—; agt. Prudential Ins. Co. Am., 1975—. Mem. Nat., N.Y. State, Westchester County assns. life underwriters. Republican. Roman Catholic. Home: 209 Garth Rd Scarsdale NY 10583 Office: 550 Mamaroneck Ave Harrison NY 10528

JACKSON, GILBERT SERGE, chem. engr.; b. Bklyn., Apr. 4, 1941; s. Norman and Lillian (Pakula) J.; B.S., Coll City N.Y., 1963; M.S., U. Md., 1969, Ph.D. (Minta Martin fellow), 1971. Chem. engr. Pratt & Whitney Aircraft Co., East Hartford, Conn., 1963-65, U.S. Naval Ordnance Labs., White Oak, Md., 1966-67; Fed. Water Pollution Control Adminstrn. research fellow U. Md., 1965-71, mem. chancellors adv. council, 1970, faculty senate, 1969, tenure com., 1969; program mgr. EPA, Washington, 1971-74; sr. scientist Nat. Center for Resource Recovery, 1974-75; internat. cons. chem. engring. EPA, UN, pvt. corps. in Vienna, Austria and Warsaw, Poland, 1975-77; ind. cons., Washington, 1975—; program moderator Viewpoint, WGTB-FM, 1976—; prof. chemistry Montgomery Coll., Takoma Park, Md., 1970-71. Recipient three EPA Spl. Achievement awards, 1973-75. Mem. Am. Inst. Chem. Engrs., Internat. Ozone Inst. (charter), water Pollution Control Fedn., World Future Soc., Lock and Key, Sigma Xi, Tau Beta Pi, Omega Chi Epsilon, Phi Kappa Phi. Jewish. Club: Toastmasters Internat. Contbr. articles to profl. jours. Patentee high speed firing mechanism. Home and Office: 7001 Exeter Rd Bethesda MD 20014

JACKSON, JAMES EDWARD, statistician; b. Rochester, N.Y., Jan. 12, 1925; s. James Arthur and Laura (Hitchcock) J.; A.B., U. Rochester, 1947; M.A., U. N.C., 1949; Ph.D., Va. Poly. Inst., 1960; m. Suzanne Montgomery, June 24, 1947; children—James M., Janice E., Judith S. Statistics cons. Eastman Kodak Co., Rochester, 1948-57, 59—; asst. process engr. Hercules Powder Co., Radford Arsenal, Va., 1957-58; asst. prof. Va. Poly. Inst., Blacksburg, 1958-59; instr. evening sch. U. Rochester, 1963-69, dir. statistics program, 1966-68; cons. to various indsl. concerns, 1958-59. Served with U.S. Army, 1943-45. Decorated Purple Heart. Fellow Am. Statis. Assn., Am. Soc. Quality Control (cert. quality engr.; Brumbaugh award 1978), AAAS; mem. Inst. Math. Statistics, Biometrics Soc., Statis. Soc. Can., DAV, Nat. Railway Hist. Soc., Sigma Xi. Republican. Presbyterian. Book rev. editor jour. Technometrics, 1975—; contbr. articles on statis. methods, theory to tech. jours. Home: 371 Edgemere Dr Rochester NY 14612 Office: Eastman Kodak Co Mgmt Services Div Bldg 56 Kodak Park Works Rochester NY 14650

JACKSON, JAMES EDWARD, mfg. engr.; b. Oneonta, N.Y., Dec. 12, 1949; s. Robert Edward and Dorothy Lee (Tripp) J.; A.A.S. in Auto Tech., Morrisville Agrl. & Tech. Coll., 1969; B.S. in Indsl. Arts, Oswego State Tchrs. Coll., 1972; m. Brenda Irene Tooley, July 4, 1971; children—Dwayne Edward, Jennifer Louise. Weldor, Raymond Corp., Greene, N.Y., 1972, mfg. technician B, 1972-73, mfg. technician A, 1973-76, mfg. engr., 1976—. Recipient Wood Badge, Scoutmasters award Boy Scouts Am., 1975. Mem. Soc. Mfg. Engrs., Am. Soc. Metals. Republican. Baptist. Home: RD 3 New Berlin NY 13411 Office: Wheeler St Greene NY 13776

JACKSON, LLOYD PETER, research agr. scientist; b. North Sydney, N.S., Can., Dec. 26, 1914; s. Robie Moore and Sarah Mary (Nelson) J.; B.S. MacDonald Coll. McGill U., 1948; M.S., Mich. State U., 1956; m. Mary Evelyn Cochran, Sept. 16, 1950; children—Ruth Jackson Lawrence, Peter, Gordon. Self-employed farmer, North Sydney, 1932-45; research agr. scientist Can. Dept. Agr. Exptl. Farm, Nappan, N.S., 1948—. Mem. Amherst Citizens Concert Band, 8th Canadian Hussars Marching Band. Mem. Profl. Inst. of Pub. Service, N.S. Inst. of Agrologists, Canadian Soc. Soil Sci., Internat. Soc. Soil Sci., Agrl. Inst. Can. Baptist. Club: Masons. Contbr. articles to profl. jours. Home: 30 Clarence St Amherst NS Canada Office: Nappan NS BOL 1CO Canada

JACKSON, MARILYN ANN, psychologist; b. Cleve., June 18, 1936; d. Jerome B. and Myrna B. (Sachs) J.; A.B. cum laude, U. Miami, Fla., 1957; M.A. (fellow), Northwestern U., 1960, Ph.D., 1962. Clin. psychology intern VA Hosps., Chgo., Ill., 1961, Chgo., 1961; clin. staff psychologist Ill. State Psychiat. Inst., Chgo., 1961-63; psychotherapist Central Counseling Center, Chgo., 1963-65; cons. in employee selection Daniel D. Howard & Associates, Chgo., 1964-65; clin. staff psychologist VA Hosp., Hines, Ill., 1963-65, New Hope Guild Guidance Center, Bklyn., 1965-66, VA Out-Patient Clinic, Bklyn., 1966-73; practice clin. psychology, N.Y.C., 1966—. Mem. Am., N.Y. State psychol. assns., Assn. Humanist Psychologists, N.Y. Soc. Clin. Psychologists, ACLU, Sigma Xi, Psi Chi. Contbr. articles to profl. jours. Address: 250 E 63rd St New York City NY 10021

JACKSON, MARION TILLMAN, sch. guidance counselor; b. Washington, Oct. 28, 1914; d. Joseph A. and Bessie Viola (Robinson) Tillman; B.S., Miner Tchrs. Coll., Washington, 1936; M.A., N.Y.U., 1948; m. Eugene L. Jackson, June 30, 1941; 1 son, Eugene L. Elementary tchr. Randle Highlands Elementary Sch., Washington, 1940-67, guidance counselor, 1967—; cons. to grad. students U. Va., 1975-76, Cath. U. Am., 1977. Recipient career edn. grant NDEA Title II, 1975. Mem. D.C. Sch. Counselors Assn. (exec. com.), Washington Tchrs. Union (exec. com., v.p. spl. services), Am., Nat. Capital (Counselor of Yr. 1976) personnel and guidance assns., Assn. Non-White Concerns (pres.-elect). Republican. Roman Catholic. Clubs: Peter and Wendy, Spans Soc., Coll. Alumnae. Research on career edn. and counseling with black lit. Home: 5345 Blaine St NE Washington DC 20019 Office: Randle Highlands Elementary School 30th and R Sts SE Washington DC 20020

JACKSON, PATRICIA LEE (MRS. CLIFFORD L. JACKSON), psychologist, educator; b. N.Y.C.; d. Albert George and Lisbeth P. (Lee) Scharf; B.A., Barnard Coll.; M.A., Tchrs. Coll. Columbia, Ph.D., 1950; m. Clifford L. Jackson. Dir. psychol. testing R. H. Macy & Co., Inc., 1941-49; employment dir. Alexander's Dept. Stores, Inc., Bronx, 1949-52; asst. prof. Hunter Coll., 1951-60, asso. prof., coordinator Sch. Gen. Studies Counseling Services, 1960-77; treas. Murray Hill Com., N.Y.C., 1977—; pvt. practice psychology, 1962—. Trustee Alfred Adler Mental Hygiene Clinic, N.Y.C., 1976—; research dir. Klein Inst. for Aptitude Testing, Inc., N.Y.C., 1953-59. Mem. AAAS, Am. Personnel and Guidance Assn., Am. Psychol. Assn., Am. Statis. Assn., Psychometric Soc., Am. Group Psychotherapy Assn., N.Y. Soc. Clin. Psychologists. Author articles in field. Home: 129 E 35th St New York City NY 10016

JACKSON, PAZEL G., JR., bank exec.; b. Bklyn., Feb. 21, 1932; s. Pazel G. and Adalite M. (Morton) J.; B.C.E., City Coll. N.Y., 1954, M.C.E., 1959; M.S. in Bus. Adminstrn., Columbia, 1972; m. Catherine M. Faulkner, Aug. 4, 1962; children—Karen, Pazel, Peter, Allyson, Civil engr., N.Y.C., 1956-62; chief of design Worlds Fair Corp., N.Y.C., 1962-66; dep. gen. mgr., N.Y.C. Dept. Pub. Works, 1966-67, asst. commr. N.Y.C. Dept. Bldgs., 1967-69; sr. v.p. Bowery Savs. Bank, N.Y.C., 1969—; chmn. Mutual Real Estate Investment Trust, 1975—; dir. Nat. Housing Partnership Corp., N.Y. State Urban Devel. Corp., N.Y.C. Housing Devel. Corp., Bedford Stuyvesant Restoration Corp. Bd. dirs. Community Service Soc., Citizens Housing and Planning Council. Served to lt. C.E., U.S. Army, 1954-56. Named Man of Yr. Bklyn. Civic Assn., 1967; recipient spl. award for bldg. design Paragon Fed. Credit Union, 1968. Mem. N.Y. Profl. Engrs. Soc., Am. Soc. Civil Engrs., N.Y. Bldg. Congress, City Coll. Alumni Assn. Lambda Alpha. Episcopalian. Club: Columbia Business. Home: 135 Rutland Rd Brooklyn NY 11225 Office: 110 E 42d St New York City NY 10017

JACKSON, ROBERT GENE, elec. engr.; b. New Castle, Ind., May 13, 1937; s. Howard Loren and Mary Roberta (Good) J.; B.E.E., Rose Hulman Inst. Tech., 1959; M.S. in Math., John Carroll U., 1965; m. Anita Lee Walden, Mar. 5, 1960; children—Steven Robert, David Lee, Michael Rush. Design engr. Power Equipment Co., Galion, Ohio, 1959, 60, Regulus, Inc., Mt. Gilead, Ohio, 1960-61; aerospace engr. NASA Lewis Research Center, Cleve., 1961-65; engr. scientist Tracor, Inc., Washington, 1965-69, project dir., 1969-71, program mgr. 1971-73, dept. dir., 1973—. Mem. adminstrv. bd. Good Sheperd United Meth. Ch., 1966-74, trustee, 1970-73; Webelos leader Boy Scouts Am., 1973-75, cubmaster, 1974-76, scoutmaster, 1976—. Served with C.E., U.S. Army, 1959-60. Recipient Leader of Distinction award Boy Scouts Am., 1975. Mem. IEEE, Nat. Contract Mgmt. Assn., Nat. Security Indsl. Assn., Am. Def. Preparedness Assn. (chmn. spl. study com. computer softward mgmt. 1977-78, chmn. undersea systems div. sonar sect. 1977), Sigma Nu. Republican. Home: 9008 Eton Rd Silver Spring MD 20901 Office: 1601 Research Blvd Rockville MD 20850

JACKSON, ROBERT WILSON, orthopaedic surgeon; b. Toronto, Ont., Can., Aug. 6, 1932; s. Charles and Isabella Victoria Chisholm (Strachan) J.; M.D., U. Toronto, 1956, M. of Surgery (Markle Found. scholar), 1970; m. Marilyn Frederica Wade, June 14, 1961; children—Marnisan Elizabeth, Robert Wade, Julia Lynn, Johannah Isabella, Gillian Windsor. Rotating intern St. Michaels Hosp., Toronto, 1956-57; clin. research fellow dept. surgery Banting Inst., Toronto, 1957-59; asst. resident in surgery Toronto Western Hosp.,

Toronto Gen. Hosp. 1958-60; research fellow Orthopaedic Research Labs., Mass. Gen. Hosp., Boston, 1960-61; registrar in orthopaedic surgery Royal Nat. Orthopaedic Hosp., London, Eng., Bristol Royal Infirmary, 1961-63; resident in orthopaedic surgery Toronto Gen. Hosp., 1963-64; R. Samuel McLaughlin Traveling fellow Tokyo U., Mass. Gen. Hosp., 1964-65; asst. surgeon Toronto Gen. Hosp., 1965-71; dir. orthopaedic research lab. Banting Inst., 1965—; staff surgeon Toronto Gen. Hosp., 1970-75; chief orthopaedic surgery Toronto Western Hosp., 1975—; asso. prof. Inst. Med. Sci., U. Toronto, 1974—; med. staff council St. John's Convalescent Hosp., Toronto; med. staff Hillcrest Convalescent Hosp. Recipient Lister prize in surgery, U. Toronto, 1970; Civic award of merit City of Toronto, 1976. Fellow Royal Coll. Surgeons; mem. AAAS, Canadian Med. Assn., N.Y. Acad. Scis., Acad. Medicine (Toronto), Orthopaedic Research Soc., Assn. Acad. Surgeons, Clin. Research Soc. (Toronto), Canadian Wheelchair Sports Assn., Canadian Orthopaedic Assn., Continental Orthopaedic Soc., Canadian Acad. Sports Medicine, Canadian Orthopaedic Research Soc. (past chmn.), Internat. Standards Council Can., Internat. Arthroscopy Assn. (v.p.), 1976 Olympiad for the Physically Disabled (organizing chmn.), Internat. Stoke Mandeville Games Fedn. (v.p.), Societe Internationale de Chirurgie Orthopedique et de Traumatologie, Bermuda Internat. Orthopaedic Soc. (sec. Can.), Inst. Med. Sci. Author: (with D.J. Dandy) Arthroscopy of the Knee, 1976; contbr. numerous articles in field to profl. jours.; collaborator with dept. med. photography Toronto Gen. Hosp. Home: 128 Collier St Toronto ON M4W 1M3 Canada Office: 25 Leonard Ave Suite 405 Toronto ON M5T 2R2 Canada

JACKSON, RUSSELL FFOLLIOTT, physician; b. Dublin, Ireland, Jan. 23, 1922; s. Thomas and Kathleen Marion (Darling) J.; B. Medicine, B. Surgery, Trinity Coll., Dublin, 1949; Dr.P.H., U. Toronto, 1958; m. Sarah Oriel Perrott, Apr. 25, 1953; 1 son, Bryan Thomas. Intern, Lagan Valley Hosp., Lisburn, N. Ireland, 1949-50; resident S. W. London Hosp. Group., London, Eng., 1951-52; med. officer P & O Steamship Co., London, 1950-51; commd. capt. RCAF, 1952; advanced through grades to col., 1973; served with NATO Forces, Germany, 1959-63, med. liason officer Can. Embassy, Washington, 1969-73. Mem. Can. Med. Assn., Aerospace Med. Assn., Canadian Soc. Aviation Medicine. Clubs: Royal Philatelic Soc. Can., Mason. Home: 2216 Louisiana Ave Ottawa ON K1H 6T6 Canada

JACKSON, THEODORE MARSHALL, oil co. exec.; b. Beaumont, Tex., Oct. 18, 1928; s. Robert and Mary Louise (Watler) J.; A.A., Lamar U., 1947; B.B.A., U. Tex., 1951; m. Maria Pierracou-Dobrowolska, June 19, 1954; 1 son, Mark Andrew. Statistician, Mobil Oil Corp., Beaumont, Tex., 1947-49, 50; v.p., sec./treas. Purvin & Gertz, Inc., Dallas, 1955-71; v.p. treasury and strategic planning New Eng. Petroleum Corp., N.Y.C., 1971-75; v.p. fin. Crown Central Petroleum Corp., Balt., 1975—. Served to lt., USNR, 1952-55. Mem. Fin. Execs. Inst., Am. Mgmt. Assn. Republican. Presbyterian. Home: 8 Wythe Ct Glen Arm MD 21057 Office: 1 N Charles St Baltimore MD 21201

JACKSON, THOMAS HAROLD, sheet metal fabrication co. exec.; b. Danbury, Conn., Jan. 23, 1938; s. Harold Henry and Joan Marsha (Baynor) J.; m. Margaret Roberta Gillotti, June 14, 1958. With Republic Aviation Co., Farmingdale, N.Y., 1962-68; environ. supr. technician, then liaison engr. testing lab. div. Dayton T. Brown, Inc., 1968—, sales mgr. mfg. div., Bohemia, N.Y., 1968—. Served with USMC, 1957-60. Named Salesman of Year, Purchasing mag., 1977. Mem. Inst. Environ. Scis. Address: 16 Leeside Dr Great River NY 11739

JACOB, ADIR, research phys. chemist; b. Ramat Gan, Israel, Nov. 11, 1938; s. Martin and Heia (Jamszon) J.; came to U.S., 1968, naturalized, 1974; B.Sc. (fellow), Hebrew U., Jerusalem, Israel, 1963; Ph.D. (NRC Can. and Def. Research Bd. grantee), McGill U., Montreal, Que., Can., 1968; m. Rochelle Zelmanovitch, June 27, 1965; children—Andria, Daniel. Research asso., AEC grantee chem. physics dept. Mass. Inst. Tech., Cambridge, 1968, 69; prin. staff scientist, process control div. LFE Corp., Waltham, Mass., 1969, head, plasma research and devel. lab., 1969—. Served with Israeli Def. Forces, 1956-59. Mem. Am. Phys. Soc., Electrochem. Soc. Contbr. articles in field to profl. jours.; patentee in field. Home: 20 Knight Rd Framingham MA 01701

JACOB, CHARLES ELMER, educator; b. Detroit, June 5, 1931; s. Charles Henry and Thelma (Church) J.; A.B., U. Mich., 1953, M.A., 1954; Ph.D., Cornell U., 1961; m. Gale Sypher, Dec. 23, 1961; children—Charles Whitney, Andrew Wylie, John Church. Instr. polit. sci. Vassar Coll., 1960-62, asst. prof., 1962-67; asso. prof. Rutgers U., 1967-75, prof., 1975—, chmn. dept. polit. sci., 1974-77. Served with U.S. Army, 1954-56. Mem. Am. Polit. Sci. Assn., Am. Soc. Pub. Adminstrn., AAUP. Democrat. Lutheran. Author: Policy and Bureaucracy, 1966; Leadership in the New Deal, 1967; (with others) The Performance of American Government, 1972; (with others) Politics in New Jersey, 1975; (with others) The Election of 1976, 77. Home: 532 Bradford Ave Westfield NJ 07090 Office: 050 Murray Hall Rutgers U New Brunswick NJ 08903

JACOB, JAMES THECATTIL, research pharmacist; b. Ranni, Kerala, India, June 18, 1936; s. Chacko Chacko and Rachel Vettimala (Kunjummen) Thecattil; B.S., U. Rajasthan (India), 1958; M.S., U. Wash., 1963, Ph.D., 1966; m. Sally George, Aug. 30, 1964; children—Rebecca, Beena. Came to U.S., 1961, naturalized, 1972. Pharmacist, Bipha Drug Labs., Kottayam, India, 1958-60; sr. pharmacist Merck & Co., Rahway, N.J., 1967-71; sect. head pharm. formulations Cooper Labs., Inc., Cedar Knolls, N.J., 1972-75, asso. dir. product devel., 1976-78, dir. new product devel., 1978—. Postdoctoral fellow, U. Tex. at Austin, 1966-67. Recipient Wash. State Initiative award, 1963-65. Mem. Am. Pharm. Assn., Acad. Pharm. Scis., Sigma Xi. Home: 4 Valley Rd Succasunna NJ 07856 Office: 110 E Hanover Ave Cedar Knolls NJ 07927

JACOB, JONAH HYE, physicist; b. Calcutta, India, May 15, 1943; s. Nissim Rahamin and Rachel (Ekaireb) J.; came to U.S., 1964, naturalized, 1977; B.Sc., Univ. Coll. London U., 1964; Ph.D., Yale U., 1970; m. Laura Newman, Sept. 10, 1970. Research asso. Yale, 1970-71; sr. scientist Avco-Everett Research Lab., Everett, Mass., 1971—. Mem. Am. Phys. Soc. Research, publs. on plasma physics, high energy lasers, discharge physics and transport theory. Home: 3 Houston Park Cambridge MA 02140 Office: Avco-Everett Research Lab Everett MA 02149

JACOBOWITZ, WALTER ERWIN, obstetrician and gynecologist; b. Jersey City, Apr. 2, 1933; s. Morton and Helen Ruth (Weinberger) J.; B.A. cum laude, Princeton U., 1954; M.D., N.Y.U., 1958; m. Sue Cylinder, Oct. 29, 1958; children—Glenn, Dana, Karen. Intern, Phila. Gen. Hosp., 1958-59; resident in obstetrics and gynecology N.Y.U-Bellevue Med. Center, 1959-63; practice medicine, specializing in obstetrics and gynecology, Morristown, N.J., 1963—; asso. prof. obstetrics and gynecology Coll. Medicine and Dentistry N.J., Piscataway, 1975—; chmn. dept. Morristown Meml. Hosp., 1977—. Diplomate Am. Bd. Obstetrics and Gynecology. Fellow Am. Coll. Obstetrics and Gynecology. Jewish. Office: 41 Elm St Morristown NJ 07961

JACOBS, ALVIN DAVID, dentist; b. N.Y.C., Sept. 30, 1931; s. Max D. and Bertha (Heiss) J.; B.A., N.Y. U., 1952, D.D.S., 1957. Pvt. practice gen. dentistry, N.Y.C., 1959—. Attending orthodontist Abe Stark Philanthropies Dental Clinic, 1968—. Mem. Greater N.Y. Oral Health Com., 1967—, chmn., 1973-75; city-wide chmn. Children's Dental Health Week, N.Y.C. 1972, mem. Oral Health Coordinating Council, 1975—. Served to capt. Dental Corps, AUS, 1957-59. Mem. Eastern Dental Soc. (editor Bull. 1967-71, lectr. continuing edn. program 1969—, mem. exec. com. 1968—, pres. 1975, v.p. 1973, sec. 1972), Fedn. Orthodontic Assns. (dir. 1976—), First Dist. Dental Soc. (dir. 1975-76; lectr. continuing edn. program), Am. Dental Assn., Am. Soc. for Study Orthodontics (exec. bd. 1972—, treas. 1978, chmn. edn. program 1978-79), Am. Assn. Dental Editors, European Orthodontic Soc. Originator auto-counter method for reconstrn. dental occlusion. Home: 333 E 34th St New York City NY 10016 Office: 107 E 36th St New York City NY 10016

JACOBS, AVERILLE ESTHER, graphic artist, illustrator; b. Washington, Mar. 24, 1947; d. Frank Maurice and Esther (Mayle) Costley; student U. D.C., 1970-78; m. Charles W. Jacobs, Apr. 11, 1976; children—Djakarta A., Charles W. Graphic artist graphics dept. DeLeuw, Cather-Parsons, Washington, 1977—; part owner, asst. dir. Gallery Triangle, Washington; group shows include: Powell Art Gallery, Washington, 1966, Pres.'s Park, Washington, 1970, Nat. Collection Fine Arts, Washington, 1973, Kennedy Center for Performing Arts, Washington, 1977, Martin L. King Meml. Library, Washington, 1978, Foxtrappe Gallery and Pvt. Club, Washington, 1978, Washington Women's Arts Center, 1979, Mus. Temporary Art, 1978. Mem. Women's Caucus for Art, Washington Women's Arts Center, Nat. Conf. Artists, Artists Equity Assn., Internat. Soc. Artists. Democrat. Unitarian. Home: 1700 Swann St NW Washington DC 20009

JACOBS, DENHOLM MUIR, business exec.; b. Ardmore, Pa., Dec. 31, 1922; s. Reginald R. and Sophia (Yarnall) J.; B.A. Yale U., 1945; student Haverford Coll., 1946, Harvard Bus. Sch., 1947-48; m. Margaret W. Sanne, May 4, 1974; children by previous marriage—Mary Muir, Robert Bottomly, Denholm Muir, Margaret Yarnall. Real estate devel. work, Boston, 1948-49; v.p. Johnson Gun Co., Boston, 1949-50; regional sales mgr. Thomas A. Edison, Inc., Boston, 1951-52; asst. pres. Multiple Breaker Co., Boston, 1952-53; asso. dir. Mass. Eye and Eye Infirmary, Boston, 1955-58; vice chmn. devel. Retina Found., Boston 1958-62, life mem. corp.; asst. dir. Boston U. Med. Center, 1962-64; financial cons., Boston, 1964-72; v.p. Leathem, Lowell & Jacobs, Inc., financial advisers, 1973-76; v.p. Morrison-Jenkins & Co., Inc., Boston, 1977—. Acting dep. commr. Mass. Dept. Commerce, 1953-55. Trustee, v.p. Boston Bio-Med. Research Inst. Recipient Carnegie Medal. Member Society of Colonial Wars. Republican. Episcopalian Church. Clubs: Boston Yale; Norfolk Hunt; Harvard of Boston. Home: 5 West Cedar St Boston MA 02208 Office: 55 Kilby St Boston MA 02109

JACOBS, E(UGENE) GARDNER, JR., psychiatrist; b. Providence, Jan. 3, 1926; s. E. Gardner and Edna Jacobs; student Brown U., 1943-44; A.B., Yale U., 1948; M.D., U. Pa., 1952; m. Alice Louise Smith, Apr. 12, 1951; children—Susan, Nancy, John, Peter. Intern, Pa. Hosp., Phila., 1952-53; resident Neurol. Inst. N.Y., 1953-54, Columbia-Presbyn. Hosp., N.Y.C., N.Y. State Psychiat. Inst., 1955-58; practice medicine specializing in psychiatry and psychoanalysis, Phila.; staff psychiatrist Inst. Pa. Hosp., 1958-62, sr. attending psychiatrist, 1974—; chief psychiatrist Temple U. Student Health Service, 1971-77; clin. dir., dir. continuing med. edn., dept. psychiatry Naval Regional Med. Center, Phila., 1977—; clin. asst. prof. psychiatry U. Pa.; clin. asst. prof. Hahnemann Med. Coll.; research fellow Columbia U., 1954-55. Served as lt. comdr. USNR, 1977. Fellow Am. Psychiat. Assn.; mem. Am., Internat. psychoanalytic assns., Phila. Assn. Psychoanalysis, Assn. Mil. Surgeons U.S., Res. Officers Assn. U.S. Contbr. articles to profl. jours., ency. Home: Hopkinson House Washington Sq S Philadelphia PA 19106 Office: NRMC Broad and Pattison Sts Philadelphia PA also 111 N 49th St Philadelphia PA 19139

JACOBS, ELEANOR ALICE, clin. psychologist; b. Royal Oak, Mich., Dec. 25, 1923; d. Roy Dana and Alice Ann (Keaton) Jacobs; B.A., U. Buffalo, 1949, M.A., 1952, Ph.D., 1955. Clin. psychologist VA Hosp., Buffalo, 1954—, equal employment opportunity counselor, 1962—, clin. psychologist research sect. psychology service, 1967—; clin. prof. State U. N.Y. at Buffalo, 1950—. Speaker on psychology to community orgns., clubs, 1952—. Mem. adult devel. and aging com. NICHD, HEW, 1971-75. Recipient Outstanding Superior Performance award Buffalo VA Hosp., 1958, Spl. Recognition award State U. N.Y. at Buffalo, 1971, W.L. McKnight award Miami Heart Inst., 1972, Adminstrs. commendation VA, 1974, Dirs. commendation VA Med. Center, Buffalo, 1978; named Woman of Year, Bus. and Profl. Women's Clubs Buffalo, 1973. Mem. Am., Eastern, N.Y. State psychol. assns., Am. Group Psychotherapy Assn., Am. Soc. Group Psychotherapy and Psychodrama, Nat., Western N.Y. leagues nursing, Psychol. Assn. Western N.Y. (Distinguished Achievement award 1976), Group Psychotherapy Assn. Western N.Y. Research and publs. on hyperbaric medicine, hyperoxygenation effect on cognitive functions in aged. Home: Pleasant Ave Ridgeway ON Canada Office: VA Hosp 3495 Bailey Ave Buffalo NY 14215

JACOBS, EUGENE LESLIE, psychiatrist; b. Bklyn., July 18, 1933; s. Martin and Ceil (Sager) J.; B.A., Wesleyan U., Middletown, Conn., 1955; M.D., State U. N.Y., Bklyn., 1959; m. Gail Steinberg, Feb. 26, 1961; children—Hilary, Amanda. Intern, Kings County Hosp., Bklyn., 1959-60; resident in psychiatry Bronx VA Hosp., 1960-61, 62-63, N.Y. State Psychiat. Inst., 1961-62; admitting psychiatrist Bronx VA Hosp., 1963-65; asso. dir. psychiatry, then acting dir. psychiatry Jewish Meml. Hosp., N.Y., 1964-67; chief dept. adolescent psychiatry, then unit dir. spl. projects clinic Beth Israel Hosp., N.Y.C., 1967-69, 76; practice medicine specializing in psychiatry, N.Y.C., 1963—; asst. attending Beth Israel Hosp.; attending Gracie Sq. Hosp.; asst. psychiatry Mt. Sinai Sch. Medicine. Diplomate Am. Bd. Psychiatry and Neurology. Mem. Am. Psychiat. Assn., N.Y. Acad. Medicine, N.Y. County Med. Soc. Democrat. Jewish. Office: 163 E 82d St New York City NY 10028

JACOBS, GEORGE B., neurol. surgeon; b. Lodz, Poland, Jan. 9, 1934; s. Maurice and Lena Jacobs; came to U.S., 1948, naturalized, 1953; A.B., N.Y. U., 1954; M.D., State U. N.Y., Syracuse, 1958; children—Leigh, Alexander. Intern Bronx Municipal Hosp. Center, 1958-59; resident in neurol. surgery, Montefiore Hosp., Albert Einstein Med. Center, 1959-64; attending neurosurgeon Hackensack (N.J.) Hosp., 1966-76; chief neurosurgeon Holy Name Hosp., Teaneck, N.J., 1966-76, Pascack Valley Hosp., Westwood, N.J., 1966-76; clin. asst. prof. neurosurgery N.J. Coll. of Medicine, Martland Hosp., Newark, 1970-73; vis. prof. surgery U. Saigon (Viet Nam), 1965-66; clin. asst. prof. neurosurgery Albert Einstein Coll. Medicine, N.Y., 1974-75, clin. asso. prof., 1975—. Served to capt. U.S. Army, 1964-66; Viet Nam. Diplomate Am. Bd. Neurol. Surgery, 1967; certified neurosurgeon, N.J., N.Y., Calif., Fla. Fellow ACS, ICS, Internat. Coll. Angiology, Am. Coll. Angiology; mem. Bergen County Med. Soc., AMA, Congress Neurol. Surgeons, Assn. Mil. Surgeons U.S., Am. Assn. Neurol. Surgeons, Neurol. Soc., N.Y. Soc. Neurosurgery, N.J. Neurol. Soc., Western Neurosurg. Soc., Pan Pacific Surg. Assn., Acad. Medicine N.J., Internat. Soc. Pediatric Neurosurgery, N.Y. State Neurosurg. Soc. Contbr. numerous articles to profl. jours. Office: 277 Forest Ave Paramus NJ 07652

JACOBS, HAROLD MILTON, lay ch. worker, Orthodox Jewish Congregations; b. Oct. 25, 1912; s. Max and Kate (Fried) J.; B.S. in Econs., Columbia, 1934, M.S., 1936; m. Pearl Schraub, Apr. 11, 1939; children—Vivian, Joseph, Paul. Pres., Union Orthodox Jewish Congregations Am.; chmn. Jewish Bd. Higher Edn., N.Y.C., 1975-76; dir. Shaare Zedek Hosp., Dir., Am. Bank & Trust Co.-N.Y.; fin. cons. to maj. pub. cos. Chmn. adv. bd. U.S. SBA; dir. ops. U.S. Naval Yard, Bklyn. Recipient Religious award Bklyn. Hall of Fame, 1968; named Man of Year, Nat. Council Young Israel. Home: 67 Sutton Pl Lawrence NY 11559 Office: 50 Court St Brooklyn NY 11201*

JACOBS, HARRY LEWIS, psychologist, research adminstr.; b. Phila., Apr. 10, 1925; s. Sidney and Rae J. (Katz) J.; B.A., U. Del., 1950, M.A., 1951; Ph.D., Cornell U., 1955; m. Phyllis Jones, June 6, 1950; children—Steven, Laura, Emily, David. Asst. prof. psychology Bucknell U., Lewisburg, Pa., 1955-60; asso. prof. dept. psychology U. Ill., Urbana, 1961-67; asso. dir. behavioral scis. Pioneering Research Lab., U.S. Army Labs., Natick, Mass., 1966-74; chief behavioral sci. div., food scis. lab. Natick Research and Devel. Command, 1974—; vis. lectr. Nutrition Food Scis., Mass. Inst. Tech., Cambridge, 1966-67; affiliate asso. prof. physiology Clark U., Worcester, Mass., 1966-70, adj. prof. physiology, 1970-76. NIH spl. research fellow in physiology U. Rochester (N.Y.), 1958-61. Served with USAAF, 1943-46. Fellow Am. Psychol. Assn.; mem. Am. Physiol. Assn., Am. Inst. Biol. Scis., Psychonomic Soc., AAUP, AAAS, Animal Behavior Soc., Soc. Exptl. Biology and Medicine, N.Y. Acad. Scis., Sigma Xi. Contbr. articles on research in physiology, psychology and nutrition to profl. jours. Home: 63 Moore Rd Wayland MA 01778 Office: US Army Natick Research and Devel Command Natick MA 01760

JACOBS, HARVEY MICHAEL, accountant; b. Bklyn., Mar. 6, 1943; s. Alex and Jeanne (Rubin) J.; B.S., Bklyn. Coll., 1964; M.B.A., St. John's U., 1966; m. Aimee Schlosberg, Aug. 23, 1970; 1 dau., Alanna Sue. Accountant, auditor Metro-Goldwyn Mayer, N.Y.C., 1966-68, mgr. spl. projects, 1968-69; sr. accountant N.Y.C. Bd. Edn., Bklyn., 1969-73, mgr. payroll accounting, 1973—; lectr. Chaykin's C.P.A. Rev. course, adj. asso. prof. Hofstra U. Served with U.S. Army, 1967. C.P.A., N.Y. Mem. Am. Inst. C.P.A.'s, Delta Mu Delta. Home: 123 Bulson Rd Rockville Centre NY 11570

JACOBS, JEROLD LANCE, govt. ofcl.; b. N.Y.C., June 12, 1943; s. Irving and Alyce (Quain) J.; B.A., Amherst Coll., 1965; J.D., Harvard U., 1968; m. Laura Nancy Goodman, Aug. 15, 1965; children—Michael Jared, Benjamin Marc, Shira Suzane. With FCC Cable TV Bur., Washington, 1968—, chief Certificates of Compliance div., 1973-74, asst. chief Cable TV Bur., 1974-76, dep. chief, 1976—; admitted to N.Y. State bar, 1969, D.C. bar, 1972. Pres. Burke (Va.) Townhouse Homeowners Assn., 1972-73; pres. Arlington-Fairfax Jewish Congregation, 1975-77, Simpson Meml. fellow, 1965. Mem. Am., Fed. bar assns. Home: 1501 Allview Dr Rockville MD 20854 Office: 1919 M St NW Washington DC 20554*

JACOBS, JOHN FRANCIS, engring. corp. exec.; b. Golva, N.D., Feb. 22, 1923; s. Ralph and Florence (Matter) J.; B.E.E., Ill. Inst. Tech., 1950; M.E.E., Mass. Inst. Tech., 1952; m. Mary Ann George, Sept. 2, 1946; children—John Jr., Patricia, James, Richard, Constance, Joel. Instr., Am. TV Inst., 1946-50; research asst. research lab. electronics Mass. Inst. Tech., 1950-51, digital computer lab., 1951-52, tech. staff, sec. head, group leader, asso., then asst. div. head, asso. div. head, Lincoln Lab., 1952-58; asso. dir., tech. dir. systems div. MITRE Corp., Bedford, Mass., 1958-60, asst. v.p., v.p., Bedford ops., 1961-69, sr. v.p., 1969-75, sr. v.p. corporate planning and devel., 1975-77, cons., 1977—. Served with USN, 1944-46. Mem. Am. Mgmt. Assn., AAAS, Internat. Inst. Strategic Studies, Smithsonian Instn., Mass. Inst. Tech. Alumni Assn., Sigma Xi, Tau Beta Pi, Eta Kappa Nu. Clubs: Officers' Open Mess. Co-patentee digital computer with inherent shift, 1961. Home: 79 Griffin Rd Framingham MA 01701 Office: MITRE Corp Route 62 Bedford MA 01730

JACOBS, JOSEPH, pediatrician, educator; b. South Wales, U.K., Sept. 9, 1917; s. Max and Esther (Demchuck) J.; M.D., St. Bartholomew's Hosp. Med. Sch., London, 1935; m. Margaret Sylvia Gavzey, Feb. 29, 1948; children—David Paul, Sara Allison. Intern St. Bartholomew's Sector Hosps., 1940-41, resident in pediatrics 1941-42, United Cardiff (Wales) Hosps., 1946-48; asso. prof. pediatrics Welsh Nat. Sch. Medicine, Cardiff, U.K., 1948-69; prof. pediatrics McMaster U., Hamilton, Ont., Can., 1969—; vis. prof. Johns Hopkins U., 1960; prof. pediatrics Hadassah Med. Sch., Jerusalem, 1963-64; advisor child tuberculosis Govt. of Can., 1970—. Served with Royal Air Force, 1942-46. Fellow Royal Coll. Physicians (Eng.), Royal Coll. Physicians (Can.); mem. Brit., Can. (chmn. mental health com) pediatric assns., Can. Med. Assn., Assn. Genetic Counselors. Office: Dept Pediatrics McMaster U Hamilton ON Canada

JACOBS, LAWRENCE DAVID, physician; b. Buffalo, July 20, 1938; s. Louis Melvin and Genevieve Margaret (Bibby) J.; B.S. in Natural Sci. cum laude, Niagara U., 1961; M.D., St. Louis U., 1965; m. Pamela Regis Ryan, May 22, 1965; children—Christopher Louis, Luke Thomas, Lawrence David, Jessica Elizabeth. N.Y. State fellow Rosewell Park Meml. Inst., Buffalo, 1960-61; intern Kings County (N.Y.) Hosp., Bklyn., 1965-66; resident Mt. Sinai Sch. Medicine, N.Y.C., 1966-69, instr. neurology, 1970-71, asso. in neurology, 1971-72, asst. prof., 1972-73; practice medicine specializing in neurology and neuro-ophthalmology. Buffalo, 1973—; mem. staff Millard Fillmore Hosp.; asst. clin. prof. State U. N.Y. at Buffalo, 1973-76, asso. clin. prof., 1976—. Mem. Council to Select Local Candidates for Appt. to U.S. Mil. Acads.; capt. med. div. United Way campaigns; head med. div. fund raising campaigns Studio Arena Theater, Buffalo. Served to lt. USNR, 1966-73. NIH Spl. fellow, 1969-73; U. City N.Y. fellow, 1970. Diplomate Nat. Bd. Med. Examiners, Am. Bd. Psychiatry and Neurology. Mem. AMA, Am. Acad. Neurology, Am. Epilepsy Found., Assn. Research in Nervous, Mental Disease, Med. Soc. County and State N.Y., N.Y. Neurol. Assn., Am. Fedn. Clin. Research, AAUP, Assn. Psychophysiology Study of Sleep. Clubs: Montefiore, Saturn (Buffalo). Contbr. numerous articles to profl. publs. Research in vision, eye movement physiology, perception. Home: 24 Middlesex Rd Buffalo NY 14214 Office: 3 Gates Circle Buffalo NY 14209

JACOBS, LINDA JOAN (MRS. MARTIN HOWARD JACOBS), educator; b. Balt., Mar. 25, 1941; d. Bernard and Freda (Statter) White; B.A., U. Md., 1962, M.A., 1965, Ed.D., 1971; m. Martin Howard Jacobs, Aug. 3, 1963; Tchr., Baltimore County Pub. Schs., 1962-64; research teaching asst. U. Md., Balt., 1964-65, demonstration tchr., 1965, research asso., 1965-67, instr. spl. edn., 1968-71, asst. prof. 1971—, coordinator undergrad programs in spl. edn., 1971-73. Pres. Innovative Learning, Inc., Balt., 1972—; sec. Compar Chesapeake Electronics Representation, Pikesville, 1962—; coordinator spl. edn. pub. schs. Anne Arundel County, Md., 1974-76, dir. spl. edn. programs, 1976-77; asst supt. schs. State of Md., Balt., 1977—; ednl. cons. pub. sch. St. Clairsville, Ohio, Cin., Bowling Green, Ohio, Panama City, Fla., St. Mary's, Prince George's, Charles,

Calvert, Balt., Baltimore County, Howard County, Harford County, Anne Arundel County, Kent County, Md., Md. Dept. Edn.; cons. Sparta (Ill.) pub. schs., Montgomery County (Md.) pub. schs. Bd. dirs. Council for Exceptional Children, Baltimore County Gen. Hosp. Recipient Excellence in Teaching nomination Spl. Edn. Dept. U. Md., 1970. Mem. Council for Exceptional Children (state student coordinator 1966-73, v.p. Md. fedn. chpts. 1969-70, pres. Md. fedn. 1970-72, Md. rep. to Nat. Bd. Govs. 1973—, Md. del. to internat. conv. 1966, 69, 70, 71, 72, 74, chmn. nat. com. study exec. functions, 1972—). Author: Instructional TV Series for Md. Pub. TV, 1973; Approaches to Reading, 1975. Columnist learning problems Northwest Star Newspaper. Research in cognitive model for diagnosing learning characteristics. Home: 8808 Sonya Rd Randallstown MD 21133 Office: BWI Airport Baltimore MD 21240

JACOBS, NORMAN ALLAN, mfg. co. exec.; b. Providence, Aug. 17, 1937; s. Daniel and Bertha (Fain) J.; B.E., Yale, 1958; M.S. (NSF fellow), Mass. Inst. Tech., 1959; M.B.A. (Baker Scholar), Harvard, 1961; m. Elaine Marcia Kritz, Aug. 16, 1959; children—Marjorie Ilene, Alan Jeffrey. With spl. products dept. market devel., Rohm & Haas Co., Phila., 1961-62; treas., dir., v.p. Amicon Corp., Lexington, Mass., 1962-71, pres., dir., also, dir. Amicon subsidiaries in U.S., Europe, Japan, 1971—; dir. Romicon, Inc. (joint venture of Amicon and Rohm and Haas Co.), 1972—; lectr. Harvard Bus. Sch. Mem. Licensing Execs. Soc. (pres.-elect 1974-75, pres. 1975-76, treas. 1970-74), Am. Chem. Soc., Research Mgmt. Assn. (bd. govs. 1973-76), Sci. Apparatus Mfrs., Internat. Center New Eng. Contbr. articles to profl. jours. Home: 141 Worthen Rd Lexington MA 02173 Office: 25 Hartwell Ave Lexington MA 02173

JACOBS, RICHARD DAVID, orthopedic surgeon; b. N.Y.C., Oct. 4, 1939; s. Morris A. and Anna J.; A.B., Cornell U., 1961; M.D., N.Y. U., 1965; m. Sheila J. Lehrhaupt, Nov. 4, 1961; children—Marcy, Sharon. Intern in surgery, Bellevue Hosp., N.Y. U. Med. Center, N.Y.C., 1965-66, resident in gen. surgery, 1966-67, resident in orthopedic surgery, 1967-70; practice medicine specializing in orthopedic surgery, Paterson, N.J., 1970—; attending St. Joseph's Hosp.; instr. orthopedic surgery Sch. Medicine, N.Y. U.; staff St. Joseph's Hosp. and Med. Center, Greater Paterson Gen., Fair Lawn Meml., Valley, Preakness hosps. Recipient Valentine Mott award N.Y. U., 1965. Diplomate Am. Bd. Orthopedic Surgery. Fellow A.C.S., Am. Acad. Orthopedic Surgery; mem. AMA, N.J. State, Passaic County med. socs., N.J. Orthopedic Soc., N.Y. U. Orthopedic Alumni Assn. (pres. 1977-78). Contbr. articles to profl. surg. jour. Office: 2 E 40th St Paterson NJ 07514

JACOBS, STANLEY RALPH, trust funds exec.; b. N.Y.C., Sept. 10, 1898; s. Ralph J. and Adele (Ansbacher)J.; A.B., Columbia, 1918; m. Elisabeth Gombos, May 7, 1972. With Salomon Bros. & Hutzler, N.Y.C., 1921-27, mem. N.Y. Stock Exchange, 1927-71; trustee numerous trust funds, N.Y.C., 1931—; executor 10 estates, 1937—. Life trustee Fedn. Jewish Philanthropies N.Y.; hon. trustee Hillside Hosp., Ednl. Alliance; mem. council Columbia Coll.; trustee Eisenhower Coll., Seneca Falls, N.Y., 1966-78, also chmn. investment com. Served as 2d lt. inf., U.S. Army, 1918, to maj., AUS, 1942-46. Decorated Bronze Star, 4 combat stars. Mem. Soc. Security Analysts N.Y., N.Y. State C. of C. Republican. Clubs: Princeton, Harmonie, Univ. (N.Y.C.); Century Country (Purchase, N.Y.). Home: 1130 Park Ave New York City NY 10028 Office: 30 E 60th St New York City NY 10022

JACOBS, THEODORE ALAN, scientist; b. Atlanta, Oct. 19, 1927; s. Samuel M. and Fay (Williams) J.; A.B., Emory U., 1950; M.S. (Robert Shaw Fulton fellow), U. So. Cal., 1954; Ph.D. (Drake scholar, Inst. scholar), Cal. Inst. Tech., 1960; m. Joan Alicia Granit, Apr. 30, 1961; 1 stepson, Steven Douglas. Design engr. Douglas Aircraft, 1951-53; research engr. G.O. Noville Assos., 1953-55; mem. faculty, research asso. U. So. Cal., 1955-57; sr. research engr. Rocketdyne, 1957-58; cons., 1958-61; mem. faculty Cal. Inst. Tech., 1960-61; head chem. kinetics sect. Aerospace Corp., Los Angeles, Cal., 1961-67, head aerophysics dept., 1967-71; sr. scientist, dir. high energy laser tech. TRW Systems, Redondo Beach, Calif., 1971-76; Supt. Optical Services div. Naval Research Lab., Washington, 1976—. Served with AUS, 1945-47. Fellow Am. Inst. Chemists; mem. Am. Phys. Soc., Am. Chem. Soc., Am. Ordnance Assn., Nat. Rifle Assn., Sigma Xi, Sigma Pi Sigma. Contbr. to sci. jours. Home: 4915 Loose Strife Ct Annandale VA 22003

JACOBS, WALTER DARNELL, educator; b. Hobart, Okla., Mar. 11, 1922; s. John Clayton and Patience (Goodlander) J.; B.S., Columbia, 1955, M.A., certificate Russian Inst., 1956, Ph.D., 1961. Exchange specialist Library of Congress, Washington, 1957-59; research scientist Spl. Operations Research Office, 1959-61; asst. prof. U. Md., College Park, 1961-65, asso. prof., 1965-68, prof. govt. and politics, 1968—. Mem. European adv. council Dept. State. Republican del. Md. Conv., 1964. Served with AUS, 1942-53; col. Res. Mem. Am. African Affairs Assn. (chmn. 1971—), Washington Friends of Antibolshevik Bloc of Nations, World Peace Soc. (dir. 1967—), Am. Mil. Inst., Am. Polit. Sci. Assn., Def. Orientation Conf. Assn. (dir. 1971-74), Delta Kappa Epsilon, Pi Sigma Alpha. Club: Mukumburu Surf. Author: Modern Governments, 3d edit., 1966; Frunze, The Soviet Clausewitz, 1969; Terrorism in South Africa, 1973; At the Sharp Edge in Africa, 1974; Bewitched Anteater, 1976; African Turmoil and American Interests, 1976. Contbr. articles to profl. jours. Home: PO Box 450 College Park MD 20740

JACOBSEN, WILLIAM DUTTON, govt. ofcl., former army officer; b. Boston, May 31, 1936; s. Emil E. and Jean (Dutton) J.; B.A., U. Nebr., 1971; M.S. in Edn., U. So. Calif., 1974; postgrad. in higher edn. U. Pitts., 1975-79; m. Renate Wilden, Dec. 30, 1959; children—Barbara Jean, Susan Elizabeth. Enlisted in U.S. Army, 1957, advanced through grades to maj., 1976; personnel staff officer, Germany, 1967-68, 73; logistician adviser, Vietnam, 1969-70; asst. prof. mil. sci. U. Pitts., 1974-77; ret., 1977; logistics mgmt. specialist U.S. Army Logistics Evaluation Agy., New Cumberland, Pa., 1978—. Decorated Bronze Star. Mem. Am. Assn. Higher Edn., Nat. Assn. Personnel Research, Am. Def. Preparedness Assn., Soc. Logistics Engrs., Assn. Higher Edn. Suprs., DAV. Episcopalian. Club: Masons. Home: 454 Woodcrest Dr Mechanicsburg PA 17055 Office: New Cumberland Army Depot Bldg 54 New Cumberland PA 17055

JACOBSON, ALF EDGAR, educator; b. Spokane, Wash., Apr. 4, 1924; s. Carl Magnus and Emmy (Bjoresson) J.; A.A., North Park Coll., 1950; B.S., Northwestern U., 1952; M.A., Tufts U., 1954; S.T.B., Harvard, 1954, S.T.M., 1955, Ph.D., 1962; m. Sonja Ruth Torstenson, Dec. 8, 1951; children—Kurt Torsten, Brent Burgess. Prof. social studies Colby Jr. Coll., New London, N.H., 1958—, chmn. dept. social and behavioral studies, 1970-77. Mem. New London Planning Bd., 1965-71, chmn., 1969-71; moderator Kearsarge Regional Sch. Dist., 1968—, Town New London, 1970-73; mem. N.H. Senate, 1969—, pres., 1975—; mem. New London Bd. Selectmen, 1973—, chmn., 1975-76, 78-79; library trustee Town New London, 1960-63. Served with USMCR, 1943-46. Recipient Dr. Maurice Blake award, Boston Philatelic Soc.; Fulbright Found. to Sweden, summer 1968. Mem. Am. Econ. Assn., Swedish Pioneer Hist. Soc., Am. Soc. Ch. History (Brewer prize 1965), Bibliog. Soc. Am., Essex Inst., Manuscript Soc., Am. Philatelic Soc. Clubs: Rotary, State Grange. Home: Burpee Hill Rd New London NH 03257

JACOBSON, AVROHM, psychiatrist; b. Toronto, Ont., Can., July 12, 1919; s. Morris and Tillie (Gorback) J.; came to U.S., 1919, naturalized, 1944; B.A., U. Mich., 1941; M.D., Tulane U., 1944; m. Shirley S. Applebaum, Jan. 3, 1948; children—Debra Ann, Nancy Ellen, Aric Daniel. House physician Newark Beth Israel Hosp., 1944-45; resident psychiatry State Hosp., Middletown, N.Y., 1945-46; fellow psychiatry St. Elizabeths Hosp., 1948-49; trainee in psychoanalysis Washington-Balt. Psychoanalytic Inst., 1948-52; pvt. practice psychiatry and psychoanalysis, 1952—; instr. psychiatry Georgetown U. Med. Sch., 1948-52; asso. clin. prof. psychiatry N.Y. Med. Coll., 1956-64; prof. clin. psychiatry Seton Hall Coll. Medicine, 1960-63; clin. prof. psychiatry Rutgers U. Med. Sch., 1970—; cons. psychiatry Pollak Meml. Clinic, Long Branch, 1953-66, VA Hosp., Lyons, N.J., Jersey Shore Med. Center, Neptune; sr. attending psychiatrist Monmouth Med. Center, Long Branch; cons. psychiatry Trenton State Hosp. Mem. med. bd. Monmouth County Heart Assn., 1956-58, Monmouth Med. Center. Councilman, Boro of Interlaken; mem. Monmouth County Mental Health Bd. Served with U.S. Army, 1946-47, 50-52. Fellow A.C.P., Am. Psychiat. Assn., AAAS, Am. Acad. Polit. and Social Sci., Am. Acad. Psychosomatic Medicine; mem. Am. Soc. Psychoanalytic Physicians, Pan Am. Med. Assn., Eastern Psychoanalytic Assn., A.M.A., N.J. Psychiat. Assn. (treas. 1966, sec. 1967, pres. 1968-70, trustee 1963-66, del. to Am. Psychiat. Assn. 1970), Monmouth County Med. Soc. (pres. 1969-70), Phi Delta Epsilon. Mason, Kiwanian. Contbr. articles to profl. jours. Home: 701 Grassmere Ave Interlaken NJ 07712 Office: Franklin Ave at Hwy 35 Ocean NJ 07712

JACOBSON, CHESTER FREDERICK, mech. engr.; b. Worcester, Mass., Sept. 5, 1931; s. Christian and Antonia (Frederickson) J.; B.S. in Mech. Engring., Worcester Poly. Inst., 1959; postgrad. in elec. engring. Duke U., 1967-69; m. Louis Edith Johnson; children—Karen Louise, Kyle Christian and Kurt Oscar (twins). Design engr. Gen. Electric Co., various locations, 1959-69, mgr. mech. engring. outdoor power equipment dept., Schenectady, 1969-71; prin. engr. new product devel. research and devel. Gillette Co., Boston, 1971—. Instnl. rep. Boy Scouts Am., Southboro, Mass.; supt. ch. sch. Pilgrim Ch., Southboro, 1973-75, deacon, 1976-78. Served with U.S. Army, 1952-55. Mem. ASME, IEEE, Pi Tau Sigma. Registered profl. engr., N.C. Democrat. Club: Masons. Patentee in field. Home: 10 Pinecone Ln Southboro MA 01772 Office: Gillette Park Boston MA 02106

JACOBSON, HAROLD GORDON, physician; b. Cin., Oct. 12, 1912; s. Samuel and Regina (Dittman) J.; B.S. U. Cin., 1934; M.B., 1936, M.D., 1937; m. Ruth Enenstein, Aug. 10, 1941; children—Richard, Arthur. Intern Los Angeles County Gen. Hosp., 1936-38; fellow pathology Longview Hosp., Cin., 1938; resident Mt. Sinai Hosp., N.Y.C., 1939-41, Asso. Hosps. U. Tex., 1941-42; asst. radiology U. Tex., 1941-42, asso. radiol. New Haven Hosp. 1942; instr. radiology Yale, 1942; asst. chief, asso. radiologist VA Hosp., Bronx, N.Y., 1946-50, chief radiology service, 1950-53; asst. clin. prof. radiology N.Y.U., 1952-53, clin. prof., 1953-59, prof. clin. radiology, 1959—; prof. radiology Albert Einstein Coll. Medicine, 1964-71, prof., chmn. dept. radiology Albert Einstein Coll. Medicine-Montefiore Hosp. and Med. Center, 1972—, chmn. com. continuing med. edn., 1965-69; dir. dept. roentgenology Hosp. for Spl. Surgery, N.Y.C., 1953-55; chief div. diagnostic radiology, radiologist-in-charge teaching program Montefiore Hosp., N.Y.C., 1955—, Rigler lectr., 1964, 70; Crookshank lectr., London, Eng., 1974; Holmes lectr., Boston, 1974; vis. prof. radiology Inst. Orthopaedics, U. London, 1975—; cons. radiology VA Hosp., Bronx, N.Y., 1958—. Chmn. commn. on affairs of museum Am. Coll., Radiol. Found., 1969—. Served from 1st lt. to maj., M.C., AUS, 1942-46. Diplomate Am. Bd. Radiology (trustee 1971—, chmn. written exams. com. in diagnostic radiology 1973—, treas., exec. com. 1976—, mem. residency rev. com. 1976—), Nat. Bd. Med. Examiners (sr. cons. in radiology). Fellow Am. Coll. Radiology (councilor 1960—, bd. chancellors; chmn. com. radiolog coding 1965—, co-chmn. com. on diagnostic coding index and thesaurus 1973—, awarded Gold medal 1978), Royal Coll. Radiologists (hon.); mem. Am. Inst. Radiology (chmn. commn. on affairs 1971—), N.Y. Roentgen Soc. (pres. 1959-60, historian 1969—), Internat. Skeletal Soc. (co-founder, pres.-elect 1973—, chmn., exec. com. 1976—), AMA, N.Y. State, N.Y. County med. socs., Radiol. Soc. N. Am. (pres. 1966-67, dir. 1964-67, awarded Gold medal 1972), Soc. Acad. Radiology Depts. (exec. council 1972—, pres. 1973-74), Am. Roentgen Ray Soc., Royal Soc. Medicine (hon.), Alpha Omega Alpha. Author books including: (with R. O. Murray) Radiology of Diseases of the Skeleton: Exercises in Diagnosis, 2d edit., 1977; (with C. Schein and W. Stern) The Common Bile Duct; (with C. Zaino) The Pharyngoesophageal Sphincter; co-editor Bone Disease Syllabus, 2d series, 1976; Third Edition of Index for Roentgen Diagnosis, 1975; co-editor in chief Jour. Internat. Skeletal Soc., 1976—; editorial bd. Excerpta Medica, 1974—; coordinator Topics in Radiology, Jour. AMA. Contbr. numerous articles to profl. jours. Home: 3240 Henry Hudson Pkwy New York NY 10036 Office: 210th St and Bainbridge Ave New York NY 10067

JACOBSON, JACOB LEON, electronics co. exec.; b. Johannesburg, South Africa, Nov. 2, 1939; s. Simon and Gertrude (Sulski) J.; came to U.S., 1965, naturalized, 1976; B.Sc. with honors, U. Witwatersrand (South Africa), 1961; M.B.A. with distinction, Harvard, 1970; Ph.D., U. London, 1965; m. Sylvia Greta Serebro, Feb. 26, 1962; children—Russel, Andrew, Rachel. Research fellow U. Pa., Phila., 1965-66; research scientist Am. Cyanamid, Stamford, Conn., 1966-68; mgmt. cons. McKinsey & Co., N.Y.C., 1970; ops. mgr. Teradyne Inc., Boston, 1970—. Asso. chmn. Combined Jewish Philanthropies Met. Boston (Newton), 1975-78. Council for Sci. and Indsl. Research grantee, 1959, 60, 61. Mem. Am. Phys. Soc., Am. Chem. Soc. (chmn. ed. com. S.W. Conn. 1967), IEEE, Harvard Bus. Sch. Assn. Club: Harvard of Boston. Contbr. articles to profl. jours. Home: 206 Windsor Rd Newton MA 02168 Office: 183 Essex St Boston MA 02111

JACOBSON, JAMES PETER, educator; b. Hoboken, N.J., Apr. 9, 1939; married, 4 children. B.A. in Secondary Edn., Jersey City (N.J.) State U., 1962, M.A. in Reading, 1964; postgrad in Spl. Edn., Yeshiva U., N.Y.C. Reading cons. North Bergen (N.J.) Bd. Edn., 1964-74; asst. prof. edn. St. Peter's Coll., Jersey City, 1966—; ednl. cons. Tucker Found. Dartmouth Coll., Hanover, N.H., 1969-70; ednl. cons. Random House, Inc., N.Y.C., 1972-74. Contbr. articles in field to profl. jours. Certified in secondary English, social sci., spl. edn.; specialist in child psychology, reading. Home: 11 Acorn Rd Secaucus NJ 07094 Office: 51 Glenwood Ave Jersey City NJ 07306

JACOBSON, NITA JEAN GROSSMAN (MRS. IRWIN ROBERT JACOBSON), ednl. cons.; b. Boston; d. Joseph Arthur and Sadie (Feldberg) Grossman; student Syracuse U., 1948-49; B.S., Boston U., 1952; M.Ed., Northeastern U., 1965; m. Irwin Robert Jacobson, Mar. 20, 1955; children—Lisa Faye, Barry Steven. Tchr., Plympton Sch., Waltham, Mass., 1952-55; dean of women Emerson Coll., Boston, 1965-68; cons., dir. edn. research Spl. Legis. Commn. on Drug Abuse State of Mass., Boston, 1969-70; cons. personal rights and responsibilities div. NEA, 1971; Mass. commr. to Edn. Commn. States, 1970-73, also mem. coms.; pres. Nat. Ednl. Evaluation Services, Inc., 1971—; dir. employee edn., trainer in mgmt. and supervisory skills Faulkner Hosp., Boston, 1976—; cons. to CETA 112 program div. occupational edn. Mass. Dept. Edn., 1976. Dir. Northeastern area programs World U., Internat. Inst. Ams., Hato Rey, San Juan, P.R., 1968; project mgr., 3d party evaluator Project CAREER, 1973—, CEDIS, 1974-75; lectr. in field. Mem. pub. affairs com. Mass. Easter Seal Soc. Trustee Parker Hill Med. Center, 1961—, pres. women's aux., 1960, 71, rec. sec., 1963-64, asst. sec. bd. trustees, 1969-72, rec. sec. bd. trustees, 1972-77, v.p. bd., 1977—; mem. exec. bd. Womens Scholarship, 1969-70; mem. exec. bd. friends of League Sch. Boston, 1968—. Recipient Advocate Rose, Jewish Advocate, 1960. Mem. Nat., Mass. assns. women deans and counselors, NEA, Nat. Assn. Adminstrv. Women, Am. Ednl. Research Assn., AAUW, Am., Mass., Boston personnel and guidance assns., Am. Assn. Higher Edn., Nat. Vocat. Guidance Assn., Child Study Assn. Am., Am. Counselor Edn. Suprs., Brookline Mental Health Assn., Internat. Child Study Assn., Am. Soc. Tng. and Devel., Pi Lambda Theta, Kappa Delta Pi, Phi Kappa Phi. Mem. B'nai B'rith, Hadassah. Contbr. articles to profl. jours. Home: Chestnut Hill MA

JACOBSON, WILLARD JAMES, educator; b. Northfield, Wis., May 22, 1922; s. Harold Wilhelm and Julia (Thompson) J.; B.S., U. Wis., 1946; M.A., Columbia U., 1948, Ed.D., 1951; m. Carol Elizabeth Whitaker, July 21, 1946; children—Susan, Ellen, Thomas. Tchr., Palmyra (Wis.) Pub. Sch., 1946-47, Horace-Mann-Lincoln Sch., N.Y.C., 1948-49; cons. Royal Afghan Ministry Edn., Kabul, 1954-56; prof. natural scis. Columbia U., N.Y.C., 1951—. Fulbright sr. lectr. London U., 1960; vis. prof. U. Hawaii, 1962. Dir. Citizens and Sci. Edn. Project, 1975—. Served to 1st lt. USAAF, 1943-45. Decorated Air medal with seven oak leaf clusters; named Distinguished Alumnus, U. Wis. at River Falls, 1976, Distinguished Sci. Educator award, 1977. Mem. N.Y. Acad. Sci. (bd. govs. 1977—), AAAS (v.p. 1968), Nat. Assn. Research Sci. Teaching (pres. 1969-70), Assn. for Edn. Tchrs. Sci. (pres. 1962-63), Council for Elementary Sci. Internat. (pres. 1959-60), Nat. Sci. Tchrs. Assn. (Distinguished Sci. Edn. award 1977). Author: Modern Elementary School Science, 1961; Science Curriculum Improvement Study Science Sourcebook, 1968; Thinking Ahead in Science, 6 vols., 1968; Inquiry Into Science, 3 vols., 1969; The New Elementary School Science, 1970; Investigating in Science, 6 vols., 1972; Population Education: A Knowledge Base, 1978. Home: 106 Morningside Dr New York City NY 10027

JACOBUS, DAVID PENMAN, pharm. co. exec.; b. Boston, Feb. 26, 1927; s. David Dinkel and Margaret Elizabeth (Penman) J.; B.A., Harvard, 1949; M.D., U. Pa., 1953; m. Claire Robinson, Oct. 6, 1956; children—Marget H., Claire H., William P., Laura R., John L. Intern, Hosp. of U. Pa., 1953-54, resident, 1954-57; asst. chief dept. nuclear medicine Walter Reed Army Inst. of Research, D.C., 1957-59, chief dept. radiology, 1959-63, chief dept. medicinal chemistry, 1963-65, dir., 1965-69; v.p. inflammation and Arthritis Research Merck Sharp & Dohme Research Labs., div. Merck & Co., 1969-77; owner Jacobus Pharm. Co., Princeton, N.J., 1977—. Trustee Cold Spring Harbor Lab., N.Y.; cons. exptl. medicine St. Luke's Hosp. Center, N.Y.; mem. U.S. Pharmacopeial Com. on Revision. Served to capt. U.S. Army, 1957-59. Decorated Meritorious Civilian Service, 1969; recipient certificate of Achievement Walter Reed Army Inst. Research, 1969. Fellow Royal Soc. Medicine, London; mem. AAAS, Am. Soc. for Info. Sci., N.Y. Acad. Scis., Internat. Inflammation Research Soc. Episcopalian. Clubs: Harvard, N.Y. Contbr. articles to profl. jours. Patentee in field. Home: 37 Cleveland Ln Princeton NJ 08540 Office: Jacobus Pharm Co Princeton NJ 08540

JACOBY, ARTHUR WILLIAM, physician; b. Paterson, N.J., July 3, 1926; s. Simon S. and Betty (Richter) J.; B.S., Rutgers U., 1949; M.S., McGill U., 1950; M.D., Chgo. Med. Sch., 1954; m. Barbara Ann Bronston, Aug. 15, 1954; children—Andrew Martin, Nancy Lynn, David Michael. Intern, Newark Beth Israel Hosp., 1954-55; resident VA Hosp., East Orange, N.J., 1955-57, Hosp. for Joint Diseases, N.Y.C., 1956-59; practice medicine specializing in orthopaedic surgery, Westwood, N.J., 1959—; gen. active staff Pascack Valley Hosp., sec., 1976, v.p., 1977, pres., 1978—; asst. attending orthopaedic surgeon Hosp. for Joint Diseases. Mem. adv. bd. Pascack Valley Bank and Trust Co., Hillsdale, N.J., 1972-73, Citizen's 1st Nat. Bank N.J., 1973—. Mem. Bd. Edn. Old Tappan, N.J., 1962-72, v.p., 1963-68, pres., 1971-72; chmn. evaluation com. Extended Sch. Year Project, 1972—; trustee No. and Pascack Valley UJA, 1977—. Served with AUS, 1944-46. Diplomate Am. Bd. Orthopaedic Surgery. Fellow Am. Acad. Orthopaedic Surgeons; mem. A.M.A., Pan Am. Med. Assn. Club: Scarlet R (Rutgers U.). Home: 27 Greenwoods Rd Old Tappan NJ 07675 Office: 223 Old Hook Rd Westwood NJ 07675

JACOBY, ROBERT EAKIN, JR., advt. exec.; b. Union City, N.J., Mar. 26, 1928; s. Robert E. and Anna M. (Bach) J.; A.B. cum laude in Econs., Princeton U., 1951; m. Monica Ann Flynn, Oct. 23, 1954; children—Debra Jean, Cynthia Marie, Patricia Ann, Laura Jayne. Econ. analyst Shell Oil Co., N.Y.C., 1951-52; v.p., account supr. Compton Advt. Agy., N.Y.C., 1952-62; sr. v.p., dir. Needham, Harper & Steers Advt., N.Y.C., 1963-65; v.p., account group head Ted Bates & Co., N.Y.C., 1962-63, chmn., pres., chief exec. officer, 1973—; dir. George Patterson Pty. Ltd. (Australia), Spitzer Mills (Can.), Hobson Bates (U.K.), AC&R Advt., N.Y.C., Diener, Hauser, Inc., N.Y.C. Served with AUS, 1946-47; Japan. Mem. Sales Execs. Club N.Y., Assn. Am. Advt. Agys., Phi Beta Kappa. Home: 1 Saddle Ridge Rd Ho-Ho-Kus NJ 07423 Office: Ted Bates & Co 1515 Broadway New York City NY 10038

JACOLEV, LEON, research co. exec.; b. Libau, Latvia, Dec. 16, 1914; s. Sergei Akim and Sophie (Butkus) J.; came to U.S., 1932, naturalized, 1937; B.S. in Chem. Engring. with high honors, Northeastern U., 1939; M.S., U. Pitts., 1945; m. Ruth L. Leffler, June 15, 1944; children—N. Gail, Stephen Leon. Cadet chemist Eastern Gas & Fuel Assos., Everett, Mass., 1936-39; rating examiner tech. personnel Civil Service Commn., Boston, 1940-41; asst. chem. engr. high explosives U.S. Bur. Mines, Bruceton, Pa., 1941-43; chem. engr. Nat. Def. Research Com., 1943-45; chem. engr. research div. Texaco, Inc., N.Y.C., 1945-53; with Asso. Tech. Services, Inc., Glen Ridge, N.J., 1953—, pres., tech. dir., 1957—. Cons. poly. dictionaries Engrs. Joint Council, N.Y.C., 1959; mem. nat. council Northeastern U., Boston, 1965—. Bd. dirs., mem. gov. bd. Engring. Socs. Library, N.Y.C., 1964-68, also vice chmn., 1967-68. Recipient Naval Ordnance Devel. award, 1945. Registered profl engr., N.J., Ohio, Pa. Mem. Am. Inst. Chem. Engrs., Am. Chem. Soc., Spl. Libraries Assn., Geoscis. Information Soc., AAAS, Am. Soc. Information Sci., Soc. Photog. Scis. and Engrs., Am. Translators Assn., Tau Beta Pi. Episcopalian. Club: Glen Ridge Country (N.J.). Patentee in field. Translator, editor more than 20 Russian books and monographs on chemistry, chem. engring. Co-author: (with De Vries) German-English Science Dictionary, 1978. Home: 30 The Fairway Upper Montclair NJ 07043 Office: 855 Bloomfield Ave Glen Ridge NJ 07082

JACOLOW, JERALD JOSHUA, drug co. exec.; b. N.Y.C., Mar. 17, 1931; s. Henry and Eleanor (Varon) J.; B.B.A., City Coll. N.Y., 1952; m. Joan Grossman, Oct. 3, 1953 (div. Oct. 1966); children—Ellen Sue, Sanford; m. 2d, Joyce Slano, Nov. 19, 1966 (div. Oct. 1976).

Accountant, J.J. Fried & Co., C.P.A.'s N.Y.C., 1952-55; accountant, auditor A.A. Miller & Co., C.P.A.'s, 1956-58; gen. practice accounting, 1958-63; controller Ormont Drug & Chem. Co., Inc., Englewood, N.J., 1964, treas., v.p. finance, 1964-66, exec. v.p., dir., 1966-76, pres., chief operating officer, dir., 1976—; pres., dir. Gold Leaf Pharmacal Co., Inc.; pres., dir. Lawton Labs., Inc.; pres., dir. Ormont-Gotham Mfg. Co., Inc.; exec. v.p., dir. A-G Pharmaceuticals, Inc.; exec. dir. Bydand, Ltd.; dir. Burnside Air Conditioning Co., Inc., 1963-70, Natural Scis., Inc.; pres., dir. Funds for Expansion, Ltd., N.Y.C., 1963-72, N.J., 1966-73; v.p., dir. Minetta Garage, Inc., 1960-66, Bedford-Acme Surg. Instrument Co., Fed. Pharmacal Corp., Mark II Press, Inc., Pan Am. Pharm. Co., 1973-75, Amfre-Grant, Inc., Edcoa Inc., 1973-77. Mem. Mail Users Council Englewood. C.P.A., N.Y. Mem. Am. Inst. C.P.A.'s, N.Y. State Soc. C.P.A.'s, N.Y. State Assn. Professions, Am. Mgmt. Assn., N.Y. Credit and Fin. Mgmt. Assn., Nat. Assn. Pharm. Mfrs. (dir., mem. exec. council, treas., chmn. ins. com., pres. 1973-76, chmn. bd. 1976—), Tau Delta Phi. Home: 9E Sheffield Ave Englewood NJ 07631 Office: 520 S Dean St Englewood NJ 07631

JAFFE, DONALD, metall. engr.; b. N.Y.C., May 17, 1931; s. Paul and Frieda (Schall) J.; B.S., Mass. Inst. Tech., 1952, M.S., 1953; Ph.D., Carnegie Mellon U., 1963; m. Carol Jean Rodgers, Feb. 1, 1953; children—Nancy Anne, Rodger Scott, Joan Susan, Richard Glen, Robert Eric. Engr., Gen. Electric Co., Lynn, Mass., 1953—, Schenectady, N.Y., 1955-56, Lynn, Mass., 1956-58; engr. Westinghouse Electric Co., Pitts., 1958-65; mem. tech. staff Bell Telephone Labs., Allentown, Pa., 1965-68, tech. supr., 1968—; evening instr. Carnegie Mellon U., Pitts., 1963-64. Mem. E. Penn Sch. Bd., 1968-70, Emmaus (Pa.) Bd. Health, 1972—. Served to 1st lt. U.S. Army, 1953-55. Mem. IEEE, Internat. Soc. Hybrid Microelectronics. Patentee in field; contbr. articles to profl. jours. Home: 962 Donald Dr Emmaus PA 18049 Office: 555 Union Blvd Allentown PA 18103

JAFFE, FREDERICK STANLEY, health agy. exec.; b. N.Y.C., Nov. 27, 1925; s. Samuel and Clara (Cherno) J.; B.A., Queens Coll., 1947; m. Phyllis Shelley, Aug. 7, 1947; children—Paul, David, Richard. Journalist N.Y. Daily Compass, 1949-52; asso. dir. information and edn. Planned Parenthood Fedn. Am., N.Y.C., 1954-64, v.p. for program planning and devel., 1964-77, dir. Center for Family Planning Program Devel., 1968-74; pres. Alan Guttmacher Inst., 1974—. Mem. N.Y. State Health Planning Adv. Council, 1968-75; spl. cons. U.S. Commn. on Population Growth and Am. Future, 1970-72 spl. cons. review reproductive biology and contraceptive devel. Ford Found., 1975-76. Served with USAAF, 1944-46. Mem. Inst. Medicine, Nat. Acad. Scis., Population Assn. Am., Am. Pub. Health Assn., AAAS, Nat. Family Planning Forum. Author: (with Alan Guttmacher) Birth Control and Love, 1969; (with R.O. Greep and M. Koblinsky) Reproduction and Human Welfare, 1976; (with Phillips Cutright) Impact of Family Planning Programs on Fertility: the United States Experience, 1976. Contbr. articles to profl. jours. Office: 515 Madison Ave New York City NY 10022

JAFFE, HAROLD, environ, designer, antiques and fine arts appraiser, educator; b. N.Y.C., Mar. 26, 1922; s. Selig and Mary J.; student Pratt Inst., 1945-48, Parsons Coll., 1948-50; m. Giselle Haiman, June 21, 1944; 1 son, David Howard. Pres. Unlimited Design Co., Great Neck, N.Y., 1950—; founder, since pres. Inst. Environ. Studies, Gt. Neck, 1973—; pres. Solar Energy Dynamics Co., Gt. Neck, 1974—; lectr. solar engery Energy Bur., N.Y.C., 1976—; dir. appraisal studies C.W. Post Coll.; lectr. Hofstra U.; cons. in field. Served with U.S. Army, 1941-45. Fellow Assn. Environ. Designers (trustee 1975—), Inst. Profl. Designers; mem. Am. Soc. Appraisers Fine Arts (sr.) (gov. L.I. 1975—), Am. Soc. Heating and Air Conditioning Engrs. (asso.) Home: 5 Devon Rd Great Neck NY 11023 Office: PO Box 1295 Great Neck NY 11023

JAFFE, HERBERT M., electronics co. exec.; b. Berlin, Germany, Dec. 1, 1924; s. Fred F. and Rose R. (Marcy) J.; came to U.S., 1941, naturalized, 1945; B.A., Athenee Royale d'Ixelles, Belgium, 1941; Baccalaureat, U. Wis., 1947; Radio Engring. degree RCA Inst., N.Y., 1945; m. Evelyn L. Laske, Jan. 13, 1952; children—Robert M., Carole A., Charles A. Asst. to chief engr. Executone, Inc., N.Y.C., 1942; br. mgr. RCA Comml. Sound Div., Albany, N.Y., 1948-51; successively dist. mgr., Eastern regional mgr., gen. sales mgr. DuKane Corp., St. Charles, Ill., 1951-69; dir. mktg. Atlas Sound Co., Parsippany, N.J., 1969—; dir. No. Communications, Chgo.; cons. U.S. Dept. State, U.S. Dept. Commerce. Campaign mgr. candidates for Bd. Edn., Town Council. Served with USAAF, 1945-46. Mem. Audio Engring. Soc., Nat. Fire Protection Assn., Internat. Assn. Police Chiefs, Electronic V.I.P. Club. Contbr. to electronic mags. Office: 10 Pomeroy Rd Parsippany NJ 07054

JAFFE, MARK M., lawyer; b. Paterson, N.J., Sept. 18, 1941; s. Irving and Bertha (Margolis) J.; B.S., Wharton Sch. U. Pa., 1962; J.D., Columbia U., 1965; postgrad. Sch. Law N.Y. U., 1965; m. June Fisher. Admitted to N.J. bar, 1965, La. bar, 1968, N.Y. State bar, 1970; asso. Hill, Betts & Nash, N.Y.C., 1969-72, partner, 1972—. Sec. Dart Containerline, Inc., N.Y.C., 1974—; v.p., sec., dir. Tower Cranes of Am., Inc., Fairfield, N.J., 1976—. Served to lt. USCGR, 1965-68. Mem. Am., N.J., La. bar assns., Am. Judicature Soc., Maritime Law Assn., N.Y. Law Inst. Club: Downtown Athletic. Home: 50 E 89th St New York City NY 10028 Office: 1 World Trade Center Suite 5215 New York City NY 10048

JAFFE, NISSEN ASHER, engring. co. exec.; b. San Francisco, Mar. 3, 1936; s. Simon Baer and Mona (Brown) J.; B.S., U. Calif. at Berkeley, 1958, M.S., 1960, Ph.D., 1962. Sr. scientist McDonnell Douglas, Long Beach, Calif., 1962-70; gen. mgr. Gas Generation Assos., div. Acurex Corp., Reading, Pa., 1978—; lectr. UCLA, 1963-68, Ohio State U., 1974, Cranfield (Eng.) Sch. Aeros., 1967, Cambridge (Eng.) U., 1967, M.I.T., 1968, many others; mem. Brit. Adv. Com. Aeros. and Astronautics, 1967. Brit. Ministry of Aviation grantee and lectr. Oxford (Eng.) U., 1966-67; NATO grantee, Belgium, 1969. Fellow AIAA (asso.). Jewish. Contbr. articles to profl. jours., chpts. to books. Office: 485 Clyde Ave Mountain View CA 94042

JAFFE, RUBIN ISRAEL, optometrist; b. Willamantic, Conn., Apr. 10, 1923; s. Abraham Rubin and Rose (Jaffe) J.; B.S., U. Conn., 1947, M.S., 1948; Dr. Optometry, Ill. Coll. Optometry, 1950; m. Barbara Joan Weiss, Sept. 2, 1950; children—Andrew Michael, Elizabeth Fern, Anne Louise. Practice optometry Portsmouth, N.H., 1950—; lectr. New Eng. Congress Optometrists, Boston, 1959-62; pres. N.H. Bd. Examiners Optometry, 1963-64; cons. sub-normal vision State of N.H., 1962—; lectr. N.H. Sch. Bds. Assn., 1972-74. Pres. Portsmouth chpt. A.R.C., 1962-63. Mem. Portsmouth Bd. Edn., 1959-74, vice chmn., 1972-74, chmn. supervisory union No. 52, 1970-74; chmn. joint bldg. com. Portsmouth, 1967—. Treas., Youth Tennis Found., 1976; bd. dirs. SE N.H. Mental Health Clinic, Portsmouth, 1962-65. Served with USAAF, 1942-45. Fellow Am. Acad. Optometry; mem. Ill. Coll. Optometry New Eng. Alumni Assn. (pres. 1966-67, mem. coll. Pres.'s Club), Am. Optometric Assn., N.H. (pres. 1964-65), New Eng. (del. at large 1962-68, treas. 1976—), lawn tennis assns., New Eng. Council Optometrists (1st v.p. 1963-64, pres. 1965-66, lectr. Boston 1966-68, chmn. scholarship awards com. 1968-72), Phi Sigma Delta, Jewish religion. Mason (32 degrees). Club: Seacoast Indoor Tennis (1st v.p. 1969-71, 76—). Research special applications contact lenses in sub-normal vision. Contbr. to profl. jours. Capt., New Eng. Tennis Team for Internat. Friendship Cup Matches, 1969—. Home: 570 Union St Portsmouth NH 03801 Office: 7 Islington St Portsmouth NH 03801

JAFFE, STEVEN, librarian; b. N.Y.C., Sept. 7, 1928; s. Aaron and Rose (Levine) J.; A.B., Yeshiva Coll., 1952; M.A., Columbia, 1953, M.S., 1958; m. Louise Neuwirth, Aug. 26, 1962 (div. Feb. 1975); 1 son, Aaron Lawrence; m. 2d, Rae Rosenberg, Dec. 26, 1976. Reference librarian Pollack Library, Yeshiva U., N.Y.C., 1952-60; head librarian U.S. Naval Applied Sci. Lab., N.Y.C., 1960-70, Consol. Edison Co., N.Y.C., 1970—. Mem. Spl. Libraries Assn. (pres. tech. scis. group 1967, sec.-treas. pub. utilities div. 1973-74, chmn. 1977-78), U.S. Naval Inst., Edison Engring. Soc. Club: Edison Camera (pres. 1972-74). Home: 67-15 102d St Forest Hills NY 11375 Office: 4 Irving Pl New York City NY 10003

JAFRI, MOKARRAM HUSAIN, psychiatrist; b. Rewa, India, Aug. 5, 1935; s. Musharraf and Hidyat-Un Nisa (Ali) J.; came to U.S., 1966, naturalized, 1974; M.B., B.S., M.G.M. Med. Coll., Indore, India, 1959; diploma in pub. health (research fellow endocrinology), U. Toronto, 1973; diploma in psychol. medicine Royal Coll. Physicians, London, 1975; m. Antoinette M. Clarke, Sept. 23, 1962; children—Mokarran Jr., David, Monette. Sr. psychiatrist Taunton (Mass.) State Hosp., 1969-70; chief community services Binghamton (N.Y.) Psychiat. Center, 1973-75, Otsego Chenango County Unit, 1975-77, chief out of hosp. care unit Binghamton Psychiat. Center, 1977—; clin. asst. prof. psychiatry State U. N.Y., Syracuse, 1978—; pvt. practice adult and child psychiatry, Apalachin, N.Y., 1970—; asso. staff Wilson Meml. Hosp. Johnson City, N.Y., 1977—. Founder Tioga Health Planning Com., chmn. 1970-72; bd. dirs. N.Y. and Pa. Health Planning Council, Community Mental Health Services and Clinic, Tioga County, N.Y., 1970-73. Diplomate Am. Bd. Psychiatry and Neurology. Mem. Am. Psychiat. Assn., Am. Pub. Health Assn., N.Y. Med. Soc., N.Y. State Pub. Health Assn., Assn. Fgn. Med. Grads., AAAS, Am. Acad. Psychiatry and Law. Contbr. articles to profl. jours. Home and Office: Hilton Rd Apalachin NY 13732

JAGEL, KENNETH IRWIN, JR., chem. corp. exec.; b. Jamaica, N.Y., Feb. 2, 1927; s. Kenneth Irwin and Grace (Bloomfield) J.; diploma N.Y. State Maritime Coll., 1947; B.S., Columbia, 1951, M.S., 1953, D.Engring. Sci., 1961; m. Mildred Grace Noble, June 16, 1951; children—Pamela Noel, Donald Laurence. Teaching asst. Columbia, 1951-53, research asst., 1955-57; research engr. Mobil Oil Co., Paulsboro, N.J., 1957-59, sr. research engr., 1959-65, group leader, 1965-68, engring. asso., 1968-71; mfg. mgr. Engelhard Mineral & Chem. Corp., Murray Hill, N.J., 1971-72, mgr. process engring. and devel., 1972-73, dir. product assurance, 1973—. Pres., Greenfield Village Civic Assn., 1960-62, Anvil Points Recreation Assn., 1965-66. Served to lt. USNR, 1953-55. Fellow Am. Inst. Chemists; mem. Am. Inst. Chem. Engrs. (chmn. S. Jersey area 1970-71), A.A.A.S., Am. Chem. Soc., Am. Mgmt. Assn., ASTM, Sigma Xi, Theta Tau, Phi Lambda Upsilon, Tau Beta Pi. Author: The Capacity and Efficiency of Grid-Type Distillation Trays, 1961. Patentee in field. Home: Box 112 Stanton NJ 08885 Office: 70 Wood Ave S Iselin NJ 08830

JAGODZINSKI, NORBERT STEVEN, project engr.; b. Buffalo, May 8, 1929; s. Stephen and Celia (Ruszaj) J.; B.A. in Math., U. Buffalo, 1961, M.S. in Indsl. Engring. and Ops. Research, 1966; m. Sara B. Cammilleri, Apr. 16, 1955; children—Stephen, Phillip, Michael, Daniel, Andrew. Statis. aide Bell Aircraft Co., Buffalo, 1956-59; reliability engr. Sylvania Electronics Co., Buffalo, 1959-60, research engr., 1962-64; systems engr. Bell Aerosystems Corp., Buffalo, 1960-62; project engr. Eastman Kodak Co., Rochester, N.Y., 1964—; mem. adj. faculty Rochester Inst. Tech., 1975—. Pres., Rochester Christian Family Movement, 1965; pres. council St. Lawrence Parish, 1973-74, pres. communication com., 1975—; v.p. Dimensional Communication Ltd., 1969-72; pres. Fund Raising Program for Brick Factory, La Paz, Bolivia, 1968. Served with U.S. Army, 1951-54; Korea. Mem. Aircraft Owners and Pilots Assn. Republican. Roman Catholic. Contbr. articles to profl. publs. Home: 290 Berkshire Dr Rochester NY 14626 Office: 901 Elmgrove Rd Rochester NY 14650

JAGOW, CHARLES HERMAN, corporate fin. cons., lawyer; b. Winona, Minn., Jan. 23, 1910; s. Walter Paul and Anna Marie (Thode) J.; student LaCrosse State Tchrs. Coll., 1928-30; A.B. cum laude, U. Wis., 1932, LL.B. cum laude, 1934; LL.M. (fellow) Columbia, 1936; m. Alice MacFarlane, Aug. 3, 1940 (dec. 1967); children—Paul M., Richard C. Admitted to Wis. bar, 1934, N.Y. State bar, 1937; research atty. bankruptcy law Dean Lloyd K. Garrison, U. Wis. Law Sch., 1934-35; asso. firm Cravath, Swaine & Moore, N.Y.C., 1936-52; with Met. Life Ins. Co., N.Y.C., 1952-75, asso. gen. counsel, 1957-75, v.p., 1967-75; dir. corporate debt financing project Am. Bar Found., Chgo., 1975—; cons. corporate fin., N.Y.C., 1975—. Mem. Assn. Life Ins. Counsel, Am. Bar Assn., Assn. Bar City N.Y., Am. Assn. Gifted Children (counsel), Order Coif, Phi Kappa Phi, Delta Sigma Rho, Gamma Eta Gamma. Presbyn. (elder). Home: Smalley Corners Rd Carmel NY 10512 Office: 510 E 23d St New York City NY 10010

JAHIEL, DEBORAH BERG (MRS. RENE JAHIEL), virologist; b. Bklyn., Feb. 28, 1929; d. Abraham and Martha (Dubinsky) Berg; B.A. Hunter Coll., 1949; postgrad. Columbia, 1952-56; m. Rene Jahiel, May 8, 1955; children—Abigail Ruth, Richard Moses, Beth Lillian. Virologist, Walter Reed Inst. Research, Washington, 1956-57, U. Colo. Sch. Medicine, Denver, 1957-59; asst. investigator tissue culture research dept. pathology Mt. Sinai Hosp., N.Y.C., 1959-61. Contbr. articles on immunology of Dextran, tissue culture to profl. jours. Home: 100 Bleecker St Apt 22D New York City NY 10012

JAKAB, IRENE, physician, educator; b. Oradea, Rumania; d. Odon and Rosa A. (Riedl) Jakab; came to U.S., 1961, naturalized, 1966; M.D., Ferencz Jozsef U., Kolozsvar, Hungary, 1944; license in psychology, paedagogy, philosophy cum laude Hungarian U., Kolozsvar, 1947; Ph.D. summa cum laude psychology, paedagogy, gen. lit., Pazmany Peter U., Budapest, 1948. Rotating intern Ferencz Jozsef U., Kolozsvar, 1943-44; resident psychiatry Univ. Hosp., Kolozsvar, 1944-47, resident in neurology, 1947-50; resident internal medicine Univ. Hosp. of Internal Medicine, Pecs, Hungary, 1950-51; chief physician Univ. Hosp. for Neurology and Psychiatry, Pecs, 1951-59; staff neuropath. research lab. Neurol. Univ. Clinic, Zurich, Switzerland, 1959-61; sect. chief Kans. Neurol. Inst., Topeka, 1961-63, dir. research and edn., 1966; resident psychiatry Topeka State Hosp., 1963-66; asst. psychiatrist McLean Hosp., Belmont, Mass., 1966-67, asso. psychiatrist, 1967-74; with Western Psychiat. Inst. and Clinic, Pitts., 1974—; mem. faculty dept. psychiatry Med. Sch., Pécs, 1951-59; asst. Univ. Hosp. Neurology, Zurich, 1959-61; asso. in psychiatry Harvard Med. Sch., Boston, 1966-69, asst. prof. psychiatry, 1969-74, dir. grad. course in mental retardation, 1970—, dir. planning Children's Treatment and Ednl. Center, 1971-74; prof. clin. psychiatry U. Pitts., 1974-77, prof., 1977—. Fellow Menninger Sch. Psychiatry, Topeka, 1963-66. Recipient Prinzhorn prize, 1967; Ernst Kris prize, 1973. Diplomate Am. Bd. Psychiatry. Mem. Societe Medico Psychologique de Paris, Internat. Rorschach Soc., Internat. (v.p. 1959—), Am. (chmn. 1965—) socs. psychopathology of expression, Internat. Soc. Child Psychiatry and Allied Professions, Am. Psychol. Assn., Internat. Soc. Applied Psychology, Kansas City Neurol. Soc., A.M.A., Am. Psychiat. Assn., Deutschsprachige Gesellschaft für Psychopathologie des Auscrucks (hon.), Latin Am. Soc. Psychopathology of Expression (hon.). Author: Dessins et Peintures des Aliénés, 1956; Zeichnungen und Gemälde der Geistes-Kranken, 1956. Editor: Psychiatry and Art, Procs. of Fourth Internat. Colloquium of Psychopathology of Expression, 1968; Psychiatry and Art, Vol. II, 1969, Vol. III, 1971, Vol. IV, 1975. Co-editor: Dynamische Psychiatrie (Berlin), 1968; gen. editor Confinia Psychiatrica (Basel), 1968. Reviewer Annales Medico-Psychologiques, 1957—, Acta Paedo Psychiatrica, 1963—. Contbr. articles to publs. Home: 228 Parkman Ave Pittsburgh PA 15213 Office: 3811 O'Hara St Pittsburgh PA 15261

JAKES, RONALD WALTER, accountant; b. Sayre, Pa., Sept. 5, 1943; s. John Hans and Hildegard (Mahler) J.; A.B. in Econs., Brown U., 1964; M.B. A. in Accounting, Cornell U., 1966; m. Carole Sanders, Aug. 26, 1967; 1 son, Ronald, Jr. Sr. staff accountant Coopers & Lybrand (formerly Lybrand, Ross Bros. & Montgomery), Springfield, Mass., 1966-69; div. controller Passive Components, Sprague Electric Co., N. Adams, Mass., 1969—. Treas., dir. Williamstown Community Day Care Center, 1973-75; trustee, treas. Pine Cobble Sch., Williamstown, 1976—; mem. Williamstown long-range planning com., 1975-76. C.P.A., Mass. Mem. Am. Inst. C.P.A.'s, Mass. Soc. C.P.A.'s, Phi Kappa Phi, Alpha Phi Omega. Club: Rotary (dir. Williamstown 1974—, pres. 1978-79). Home: 167 Longview Terr Williamstown MA 01267 Office: 87 Marshall St North Adams MA 01247

JAKLITSCH, JOSEPH JOHN, JR., mag. editor; b. Bklyn., Mar. 28, 1919; s. Joseph John and Josefa (Stonitsch) J.; B.S., Pratt Inst., 1940; m. Eleanor Mulligan, May 29, 1948; children—Gary, Diane. With planning dept. Brewster Aero. Corp., N.Y.C., 1940-41; test engr. ordnance dept., U.S. Army, 1941-44, editor, 1944-45; tech. editor ASME, N.Y.C., 1945-50, asso. editor, 1950-55, acting editor, 1956, editor, Mech. Engring. mag., also trans. ASME, 1957—; editorial adv. com. Engrs. Joint Council; cons. editor Crowell-Collier Ednl. Corp.; spl. cons. Barnhart World Book Dictionary; cons. editor-at-large Marcel-Dekker, Inc.; contbg. editor Am. Year Book, 1946-50, Collier's Year Book, 1951-59; asso. editor Applied Mechanics Revs., 1948-56; information com. Engrs. Council Profl. Devel. Adv. council Pratt Inst. Sch. Engring. Fellow ASME (Outstanding Leadership in Engring. award 1968); mem. N.Y. Bus. Press Editors. Clubs: Tamarack Assn. (N.J.); Walkill Country (Franklin, N.J.); Overseas Press. Home: 158-14 Oak Ave Kissena Park Flushing NY 11358 Office: 345 E 47th St New York City NY 10017

JAKMAUH, EDWARD, architect; b. Boston, Sept. 9, 1942; s. Edward Bernard and Marie (Cassone) J.; B.S. in Bldg. Sci., Rensselaer Poly. Inst., 1964, B.Arch., 1965; M.Arch. in Urban Design, Harvard U., 1966; m. Joan Cannady, Dec. 12, 1976; children—Haile, Matthew, Rachel. Fulbright research fellow London U., 1967; architect Ahrends, Burton & Koralek, London, 1967-68; asso. RTKL Assoc., Balt., 1970-76; sr. design architect, planner, asst. mgr. archtl. studio Ballinger Architects, Phila., 1976—; vis. critic Columbia U., Princeton U., Tex. A&M U., Pa. State U., U. Md., and Neighborhood Design Center, Balt.; cons. Soc. for Preservation of Fells Point & Fed. Hill, Balt., 1973-76; cons. USPHS Research for Health Planning, 1970—. Served as lt. USPHS, 1968-70. Recipient AIA hon. award for Wills Eye Hosp., Phila., 1978; City Options grant Nat. Endowment for Arts, 1974; best thesis award Rensselaer Poly. Inst., 1965; design award Portland Cement Co., 1963; exchange fellow Assn. Collegiate Schs. Architecture, London, 1964; William Stoughton fellow Harvard U., 1965; registered architect, Pa., Md.; recipient certificate Nat. Council Archtl. Registration Bds. Asso. mem. Am. Inst. Planners; mem. AIA. Club: Harvard of Phila. Concept design architect, sr. planner major bldg. projects including U.S. Fed. Dist. Ct. House, Balt., Wills Eye Hosp., Johns Hopkins Hosp. redevel., Balt., St. Elizabeth's Hosp., Ky. Author: (with G. Schmitz) Relocatable Multiphasic Health Screening: Two Systems, 1969; (with R. Plunz) Manuta Primer: Towards a Program for Environmental Change, 1970; also articles in field. Office: 841 Chestnut St Philadelphia PA 19107

JAKUBOWSKI, JOHN ANTHONY, microbiologist; b. Somerville, N.J., Sept. 27, 1940; s. Bernard and Adele (Puchowski) J.; B.S., Rutgers U., 1962; m. Yolanda Skiba, Sept. 24, 1977. Chief microbiologist, Troy Chem. Corp., Newark, 1962-65; group leader indsl. biocides Merck & Co., Rahway, N.J., 1965—. Basketball coach, Our Lady of Mt. Virgin Sch., Middlesex, N.J., 1964-70; coach Pop Warner Football, Middlesex, 1968-73; pres. Little League, Middlesex, 1964, mgr., 1969-72; chmn. Middlesex Recreation Commn., 1971-74; active Boy Scouts; mem. Republican County campaign com., 1964-66, county committeeman, 1964-68; mem. Middlesex Bd. Health, 1965-68. Recipient Distinguished Service award Jr. C. of C., 1970. Mem. ASTM, Soc. Indsl. Microbiology. Roman Catholic. Club: Elks. Research in eliminating mercury from environment. Contbr. articles to profl. jours. Home: 5 Winterberry Circle Piscataway NJ 08854 Office: Lincoln Ave Rahway NJ 07065

JALETTE, RONALD JOSEPH, electronic technician; b. Woonsocket, R.I., Oct. 18, 1947; s. Joseph Adelard and Jeannette Gabriel (Boucher) J.; student Vocat. Tech. Sch. R.I., 1964-65, Brown U., 1965-66; m. Lorraine Handfield, Oct. 16, 1965; children—Lisa Simone, Lorrie Ann. Technician, Wilmington Piano Co., 1966-69, J. C. Penney's, 1969-72, Star Electronics, 1972-74, Richards TV, 1974-76; dispatcher Woonsocket (R.I.) Fire Dept., 1976—. Mem. Electronic Technicians Guild. Home: 28 Nelson St Woonsocket RI 02895 Office: PO Box 862 Woonsocket RI 02895

JALOWSKI, WALTER AUGUSTINE, state ofcl.; b. Brighton, Mass., Aug. 23, 1913; s. Waclaw George and Veronica Emily (Benkoski) J.; student Norwich (Conn.) Comml. Coll., 1951; LL.B., LaSalle Extension U., 1968; B.A., Brantridge Forest Sch., Sussex, Eng., 1973; Ph.D., Sussex Coll. Tech., 1976. Mem. editorial staff Norwich Post, 1935-38; mgr. First Nat. Stores, 1938-41; instr., then asst. prin. Norwich Comml. Coll., 1950-65, dir., 1965-75; tax examiner State of Conn., 1973—. Served with AUS, 1941-45. Decorated Bronze Star. Mem. NEA, Eastern Bus. Tchrs. Assn., Conn. Soc. Govt. Accountants, Am. Legion, VFW. Democrat. Roman Catholic. Home: 16 Germania Ave Taftville (Norwich) CT 06380 Office: 110 Broadway Norwich CT 06360

JAMES, CHARLES ROBERT, youth services adminstr.; b. Nuremberg, Germany, Apr. 4, 1947; s. Willie Martin and Dolores L. (Kern) J.; B.A., John F. Kennedy Coll., 1969; M.Ed., Springfield Coll., 1970; M.P.A., Rutgers U., 1978; m. Deborah Scafati, Aug. 24, 1974; 1 dau., Trisha. Youth counselor and adminstrv. asst. Youth Services Bur., Middletown, N.J., 1971-72, dir. youth services bur., 1972—; adj. prof. Kean Coll. of N.J. Spl. police officer Middletown Twp., 1971—; pres. First Aid Squad, Port Monmouth, 1977—; bd. dirs. Monmouth-Ocean County Pub. Employees Fed. Credit Union. Recipient Distinguished Service award Middletown Jaycees, 1976, testimonial dinner Boys Club of Middletown, 1976; N.H. State Law Enforcement Planning Agy. grantee. Mem. N.J. State Assn. for Youth Services, Monmouth County Coalition for Human Services, N.J. Personnel and Guidance Assn., Nat. Assn. Human Rights Workers,

Nat. Council on Crime and Delinquency. Home: 24 7th St Belford NJ 07718 Office: 1 Kings Hwy Middletown NJ 07748

JAMES, EDWARD MONROE, academic counselor; b. Cambridge, Md., Nov. 9, 1953; s. Edward Exodus and Eunice Vandolla (Lake) J.; B.A., U. Md., 1975; M.S., N.C. A. and T. State U., 1977; m. Constance Brooks, Dec. 31, 1977. Dep. sheriff Henry County Sheriff's Dept., Collinsville, Va., 1975; vol. crisis counselor Drug Action Council, Greensboro, N.C., 1976; bus driver Lake's Bus Service, Cambridge, Md., 1977; academic counselor U. Md., Eastern Shore, Princess Anne, Md., 1978—; adult edn. instr. Manpower, 1978—. Mem. Am. Personnel and Guidance Assn., Am. Coll. Personnel Assn., Pub. Offender Counselor Assn., Phi Beta Sigma. Methodist. Club: Rosicrucian Order. Home: 1201 Palmer Rd Apt 9 Oxon Hill MD 20022 Office: U Md Eastern Shore Princess Anne MD 21853

JAMES, JESSE, educator; b. Waycross, Ga., Aug. 8, 1915; s. Simon Peter and Mary Emma (Alderman) J.; student Ga. Tchrs. Coll., 1933-35; B.S.A., U. Ga., 1937, M.S. in Agr., 1950; m. Enid Vose, Sept. 14, 1957; children—Thomas Mark, Catherine, Lora Ann. County agr. agt. U. Ga., Atlanta, 1937-40; ednl. dir. Am. Turpentine Farmers, Valdosta, Ga., 1940-42; asst. state 4-H leader N.C. State Coll., Raleigh, 1946-49; tchr. sci. Waresboro (Ga.) High Sch., 1951-52; 4-H agt. Middlesex County, Mass., 1952-57; state leader 4-H youth devel. U. N.H., Durham, 1957-75, Merrimack Valley (N.H.) asso. prof. occupational edn., 1975—, asso. prof. occupational edn., 1976—; developer N.H. youth camps, also camp for mentally disturbed, also camp for retarded persons. Vol. leader 4-H clubs, N.H., 1957—; chmn. Madbury (N.H.) Planning Bd., 1958-70; chmn. Madbury Bicentennial Com., 1975—; deacon United Ch. Christ, Durham, 1974-76. Served with USNR, 1942-46. N.H. Hwy. Commn. grantee, 1974-75. Mem. Nat. 4-H Agts. Assn., Nat. 4-H Aerospace Devel. Com., Am. Camping Assn., Internat. 4-H Alumni Assn., Epsilon Sigma Phi, Alpha Gamma Rho. Republican. Clubs: Kiwanis, Masons. Contbr. articles to numerous 4-H publs. Home: 56 Old Stage Rd Madbury NH 03820 Office: Taylor Hall Univ of NH Durham NH 03824

JAMES, (WALTER) RAYMOND, educator; b. Russellville, Ala., Mar. 11, 1916; s. John Clark and Lily White (Johnson) J.; B.A., George Washington U., 1942, M.A., 1945; Ed.D., Columbia, 1954; m. M. Louise Howard, Aug. 25, 1938; 1 son, Mark Howard. Tchr. social scis. Cherokee (Ala.) High Sch., 1937-40; tchr. Washington Lee High Sch., Arlington, Va., 1941-44; vice consul U.S. Fgn. Service, Leopoldville, 1945; asso. prof. psychology Coll. Arts and Scis., Plattsburgh, N.Y., 1949-55, prof., 1955-62; asso. prof. psychology Ill. State U., Normal, 1962-66; prof. State U. N.Y. Coll. at Oneonta, 1966—. Mem. Am., Eastern psychol. assns., Nat. Soc. Study Edn., AAUP, NEA, Phi Delta Kappa, Kappa Delta Pi, Sigma Tau Delta. Home: 7 Suncrest Terr Oneonta NY 13820

JAMES, ROBERT HAROLD, optical physicist; b. Arlington, Mass., Jan. 2, 1943; s. Raymond Winfield and Lilla Maud (Calderwood) J.; B.S. in Engring. Physics, U. Maine, 1964, M.S. in Physics, 1966. Grad. asst. physics U. Maine, 1964-66; instr. physics Lowell Tech. Inst., 1966-67; aerosol physicist SW Radiol. Health Lab., USPHS, Las Vegas, Nev., 1967-70, optical physicist, 1970-71; optical physicist USPHS-FDA Bur. Radiol. Health, Rockville, Md., 1971—, also lectr. tng. courses; liaison officer to ASTM laser radiation measurements sect. Soc. Physics Students (formerly Sigma Pi Sigma). coordinator Nat. Conf. on Laser Emissions, 1974. Youth adviser Christ Episcopal Ch., Las Vegas, also Christ Episcopal Ch., Rockville, Md., 1968—, lay reader, 1966—. Serves with USPHS, 1967—. Recipient Commendable Service group award FDA, 1975, commendation medal USPHS, 1978. Mem. Am. Phys. Soc., Council Optical Radiation Measurements. Co-developer laser products performance standard Fed. Register, summer 1975. Home: 177 Gold Kettle Dr Gaithersburg MD 20760 Office: 5600 Fisher Ln HFX 220 Rockville MD 20857

JAMES, RONALD LEE, mktg. communications co. exec.; b. Oak Park, Ill., May 22, 1948; s. David E. and Mary A. (Bour) J.; B.S. in Chemistry (Proctor and Gamble scholar), Case Inst. Tech., 1970. Sales rep. Stauffer Chem. Co., Westport, Conn., 1970-74, product mgr., 1974-75, mktg. mgr., 1975-77; pres. Mktg. Communications, Southport, Conn., 1978—. Recipient Bausch and Lomb Sci. award, 1966. Mem. Am. Soc. Lubrication Engrs., Am. Mgmt. Assn., Fluid Power Soc., Nat. Fire Protection Assn. Republican. Baptist. Contbr. articles to profl. jours. Home: Bear Hills Rd Newtown CT 06470 Office: Mktg Communications PO Box 39 Southport CT 06490

JAMES, WILLIAM HALL, former state ofcl.; b. North Providence, R.I., July 20, 1910; s. John William and May (Hall) J.; student U. Lausanne, 1928-29; B. Phil., Brown U., 1933; M.A., Yale, 1946, Ph.D., 1953; LL.D., U. New Haven, 1976; m. Virginia Stowell, June 24, 1950; one dau., Hillery Stowell. Tchr., New Canaan (Conn.) Bd. Edn., 1933-36; teaching prin. Easton (Conn.) Bd. Edn., 1936-42, 1946-47, supervising prin., 1947-53, supt. schs., 1953-58; supt. schs. Branford (Conn.) Bd. Edn., 1958-66; staff Commn. Higher Edn., Hartford, Conn., 1966-77, dir. accreditation and scholarships, 1966-77, ret., 1977; cons. Greater New Haven State Tech. Coll., 1977—; lectr. in field. Served to maj. USAAF, 1942-46. Mem. NEA, Conn. Edn. Assn., Conn. Assn. Pub. Sch. Supts., Conn. Assn. Advancement Sch. Adminstrn., Am. Assn. Sch. Adminstrs., Yale Post-Doctoral Seminar Group (pres. 1968-69), Conn. State Employees Assn., Conn. Council Higher Edn. (treas., 1971—), Am. Assn. Higher Edn., Royal Can. Geog. Soc., Conn. Shoreline Bd. Realtors, PTA. Clubs: Rotary (sec.-treas. Schoolmaster's U.S. 1965-69), Am. Legion (post comdr. Easton 1948-49), Exchange. Home: 373 Reeds Gap Rd Northford CT 06472

JAMES, WINFIELD HENRY, newspaper exec.; b. Hampton, Va., Oct. 24, 1918; s. W. S. and Lucy (Heath) J.; B.S., Mass. Inst. Tech., 1940; m. Marian Theo Perry, June 10, 1944; children—Scott, Ellen (Mrs. Daniel Demeure), Carol, Brian. With N.Y. News, pubs. N.Y. Daily and Sunday News, N.Y.C., 1940—, acting circulation dir., 1962-63, exec. asst. to pub., 1962-65, exec. v.p., 1965-70, pres., 1970—, pub., 1973—, also dir.; v.p., dir. Tribune Co., 1968—; dir. Met. Sunday Newspapers, Inc. Mem. Planning Bd., Mammoroneck, N.Y., 1965-69; mem. com. 2d Regional Plan N.Y. Met. Region, 1968-69; mem. Bd. Police Commn., Mamaroneck, 1969-72; bd. dirs. N.Y. Conv. and Visitors Bur., 1965-74, Newspaper Advt., Bur.; trustee Outward Bound. Andover, Mass., 1972-73, Garland Jr. Coll., Boston, 1972-76; bd. govs. New Rochelle Hosp. Med. Center, 1973—. Served to capt. ordnance dept. AUS, 1942-46. Mem. Am. Newspaper Pubs. Assn. (dir. research inst. 1972). Clubs: Board Room (N.Y.C.); Larchmont Yacht; Winged Foot Golf (Mamaroneck, N.Y.). Home: 43 Eton Rd Larchmont NY 10538 Office: 220 E 42d St New York City NY 10017

JAMESON, SANFORD CHANDLER, educator; b. Toronto, Ohio, Feb. 12, 1932; s. Sanford Frank and Dorothy Lee (Robinson) J.; B.S., Miami U., Oxford, Ohio, 1954; M.A., Case Western Res. U., 1960; m. Joan Sheridan, June 29, 1963; children—Jennifer Joan, Julie Jo. Asst. dir. admission Case Western Res. U., 1957-60; asso. dir. admissions Carleton Coll. Northfield, Minn., 1960-63; asst. regional dir. Coll. Entrance Exam. Bd., Evanston, Ill., 1963-66, asst. dir. internat. edn. Central office, N.Y.C., 1966-69, asso. for internat. edn., 1969-71, dir. internat. edn., 1971—; chmn. Nat. Council Evaluation Fgn. Student Credentials, 1974—. Served as lt. USNR, 1954-57. Mem. Assn. Coll. Admission-Counselors, Nat. Assn. Fgn. Student Affairs (bd. dirs., chmn. admission sect., pres. 1976-77), Am. Assn. Collegiate Registrars and Admission Officers' Nat. Liaison Com. Fgn. Student Admissions (chmn. 1972-74, permanent sec. 1974—), Sigma Alpha Epsilon. Presbyterian (elder). Clubs: Mason (32 deg.), Shrine. Author, editor workshop reports in field. Home: 5609 Springfield Dr Bethesda MD 20016 Office: 1717 Massachusetts Ave Washington DC 20036

JAMESON, WILLIAM CHARLES, accountant; b. Washington, June 18, 1939; s. Douglas William and Gertrude Rose (Lee) J.; B.A., Howard U., 1963; postgrad. in bus. adminstrn. Am. U., 1965-67; m. Margaret Brawner, Oct. 12, 1963; children—Shawn W., Eric B. Accountant, Howard U., Washington, 1960-62; asso. accountant King-Reynolds, Washington, 1962-64; accountant Morton's Dept. Store, Washington, 1964-65; loan devel. supr. Sml. Bus. Devel. Center, Washington, 1965-66; exec. dir., asso. dir. Interracial Council for Bus. Opportunity, Washington, 1967-75; pres. Greater Washington Bus. Center, 1975—. Mem. action constrn. task force SBA, 1970; adv. council Inst. for Minority Bus. Enterprise, 1971-72; active Neighborhood Reinvestment Commn., 1977-78. Mem. D.C. C. of C., Assn. for Tech. Assistance, Upper N.W. Bus. and Profl. Assn., Nat. Assn. Market Devel., Nat. Assn. Accountants, Nat. Assn. Black Accountants, Am. Mgmt. Assn. Democrat. Roman Catholic. Address: 1705 Desales St NW Washington DC 20036

JAMIESON, JOHN ANTHONY, cons. infrared physics and engring.; b. Barnet, Eng., Mar. 16, 1929; s. John P. and Jean (Kerr) J.; B.S., Univ. Coll., London, Eng., 1953; Ph.D. (Wesix fellow), Stanford, 1957; m. Barbara Armstrong, 1956; children—John Gordon, Sara Felicity, John Douglas. Came to U.S., 1953, naturalized, 1962. With Aerojet-Gen. Corp., Azusa, Calif., 1956-59, gen. mgr. electro-optics div., 1962-70; with Aeronutronic div. Ford Motor Co., Newport Beach, Calif., 1959-62; asst. dir. U.S. Army Advanced Ballistic Missile Def. Agy., Arlington, Va., 1970-73; now cons. USAF, ARPA, various cos. Program chmn. WINCON, Los Angeles, 1970. Served with RAF, 1947-49. Mem. I.E.E.E., Am. Optical Soc., Air Pollution Control Assn. Club: Kenwood (Chevy Chase). Author: Infrared Physics and Engineering, 1963. Home: 5306 Kenwood Ave Chevy Chase MD 20015 Office: 7315 Wisconsin Ave NW Washington DC 20014

JAMISON, CHARLES NEWMAN, govt. ofcl.; b. Topeka, May 22, 1925; s. Charles Percil and Matilda Ann (Newman) J.; student Washburn U., 1946; B.S. in Constrn. Mgmt. Engring., Columbia, 1956; m. Vivian Theresa Shaw, Sept. 27, 1952; children—Charles Newman, Roxie Ann, Lois Elizabeth. Constrn. engr., contract specialist N.Y. Dist. C.E., N.Y.C., 1956-60; with FAA, 1960—, chief contract unit and material sect. Cleve., 1965-70, chief procurement br., chief contract sect. Pacific Region, Honolulu, 1970-72, chief procurement br. Eastern region, Jamaica, N.Y., 1974—. Served with U.S. Army, 1948-52. Decorated Purple Heart, Bronze Star award; recipient Order Red Carpet City of Lexington (Ky.), 1967. Mem. Kappa Alpha Psi. Democrat. Episcopalian. Club: Lit. Book (Jamaica); Freeport (Grand Bahama Island). Author, editor Small Purchase Procedures Handbook, 1974. Home: 18 Melrick Ct Westbury NY 11590 Office: FAA Fed Bldg JFK Airport Jamaica NY 11430

JAMISON, GRADY EARL, physicist; b. Charlotte, N.C., Aug. 6, 1941; s. William Gertrude and Mattie Ethel (Grier) J.; B.S., N.C. A. and T. State U., 1963; M.S. in Physics, U. Md., 1972. Physicist, Nat. Bur. Standards, Washington, 1964-65; physicist Goddard Space Flight Center, Greenbelt, Md., 1965-69; teaching asst. U. Md., College Park, 1969-72; physicist Johns Hopkins U. Applied Physics Lab., Laurel, Md., 1972—. Pres. bd. dirs. Ridgecrest Condominium, 1974-78. Burlington Industries scholar, 1961-63; recipient Hamilton Watch award, 1963. Mem. Nat. Inst. Sci., Beta Kappa Chi. Democrat. Presbyterian. Clubs: Lamond Riggs Bowling, Tuesday Night Men's Comml. Bowling. Home: 511 Oglethorpe St NE Washington DC 20011 Office: JHUIAPL Johns Hopkins Rd Laurel MD 20810

JAMISON, HOWARD MALOY, chem. engr.; b. Shinnston, W.Va., May 24, 1920; s. Jesse Wright and Bertie Pearl (Atha) J.; B.S. in Chem. Engring., W.Va. U., 1944; m. Mary Jane Wass, July 29, 1950; children—William Wright, Beth Ann. Fellowship asst. Mellon Inst., Pitts., 1944; chem. engr. dept. product Union Carbide Corp., Charleston, W.Va., 1947-49; chem. engr. dept. research J & L Steel Corp., Pitts., 1949-56; sr. chem. process staff engr. Rust Engring. Co., Pitts., 1956-71; sr. process engr., project mgr. chem. plants div. Dravo Corp., Pitts., 1971—. Served to lt. USNR, 1944-46. Registered profl. engr., Pa. Mem. Am. Inst. Chem. Engrs., Nat., Pa. socs. profl. engrs., TAPPI. Presbyterian. Home: 625 Kenilworth Dr Pittsburgh PA 15228

JAMISON, PATRICIA ANN RICHARDSON (MRS. EDGAR MERRITT JAMISON, JR.), civic worker; b. N.Y.C., May 5, 1931; d. Wilfred Lawson and Mary Jane (Coates) Richardson; B.A., Bryn Mawr Coll., 1952; m. Edgar Merritt Jamison, Jr., May 26, 1951; children—Ann Elizabeth, Mary Edith, John Lawson. Apprentice, Westchester Playhouse, Mt. Kisco, N.Y., summers 1946-48. Vol. worker N.Y. Infirmary, 1954-55; N.Y. regional scholarship com. Bryn Mawr Coll., 1956-59; mem. Bronxville League for Service, 1961—, 1st v.p., 1969-70; pres. PTA, 1968-70, publicity dir. Westchester Dist., 1971-72, rec. sec., 1972-73, asso. dir., 1973-74, dist. dir., 1974-77; edn. chmn. N.Y. State PTA, 1977—; information chmn. Westchester area Bryn Mawr Coll. Bd. dirs. Pub. Health Nursing Orgn. Eastchester, 1965-68, sec., 1967-68. Class sec. of 1952, Bryn Mawr Coll., 1966-70, class pres., 1973—. Club: Bronxville Women's (dir. 1973—). Home: 26 Birch Brook Rd Bronxville NY 10708

JAMISON, RICHARD GATES, mfg. co. exec.; b. York, Pa., Aug. 11, 1930; s. Earnest Gates and Evelyn (Pritz) J.; B.S., Drexel U., 1953; m. Mary E. von Glahn, July 12, 1952; children—Robert B., Douglas G., Karen L., Pamela L. Asst. personnel mgr. Vick Mfg. div. Richardson Merrell Inc., 1953-56, personnel mgr. Nat. Drug div., Phila., 1956-64; dir. compensation Gen. Mills, Inc., Mpls., 1964-74; dir. compensation Rockwell Internat., Pitts., 1974—. Chmn. bd. Inds. Sch. Dist. #287 Minnetonka, Minn., 1973-74; mem. Sch. Bd., 1968-74. Mem. Am. Soc. Personnel Adminstrn. (nat. v.p. 1973-75, nat. treas. 1971-73, dir. 1969—), Am. Compensation Assn., Mgmt. Compensation Assn., Pitts. Personnel Assn. (dir.). Clubs: Valleybrook Country, Lakeview Country. Home: 344 Oaklawn Dr Pittsburgh PA 15241 Office: 600 Grant St Pittsburgh PA 15219*

JAMME, SUSAN HAMLIN (MRS. LOUIS THEODORE JAMME), social worker; b. N.Y.C., Nov. 26, 1915; d. Francis B. and Clara (Danforth) Hamlin; B.A., U. N.C., 1937; M.S., Columbia, 1955; m. Louis Theodore Jamme, May 3, 1941 (dec. Mar. 1949); 1 dau., Frances (Mrs. Stephen Carlson). Caseworker, Nassau County (N.Y.) Dept. Pub. Welfare, Mineola, 1938-41, Nassau County chpt. ARC, Mineola, 1943-44, Nassau County Dept. Social Services, Mineola, 1949-66; supr., asst. dir. Childrens Services, Social Service, 1953-66; sch. social worker Bd. Coop. Ednl. Services, Dix Hills, N.Y., 1966—; instr. sociology Molloy Catholic Coll. for Women, 1964-66. Zone chmn. Garden City Community Fund, 1973. Mem. Nat. Assn. Social Workers (vice chmn. 1966-68), N.Y. State Sch. Social Workers Assn., Acad. Certified Social Workers, N.Y. State Tchrs. Assn., Nature Conservancy, Am. Fern Soc. Episcopalian. Home: 250 Harrison Ave Mineola NY 11501 Office: 507 Deer Park Rd Dix Hills NY 11746

JANCZAK, ANDREW ANTHONY, engring. products co. exec.; b. Buenos Aires, Argentina, Feb. 20, 1950; s. Zygmunt and Gertrude (Sierocki) J.; came to U.S., 1955, naturalized, 1960; B.S. in Applied Mechanics and Aerospace Engring., Poly. Inst. of Bklyn., 1972; M.S. in Mgmt., Poly. Inst. of N.Y., 1976; m. Helen Mary Gimber, Jan. 27, 1973; children—Andrew Stephen, Jeanette Mary. Marketing Dir. Tele-Sonic/Trescott div. of Empsco, Inc., Long Island City, N.Y., 1972-75; products mgr. Belzona Molecular Metalife, Inc., Garden City, N.Y., 1975—. Mem. Nat. Assn. Corrosion Engrs., Poly. Inst. of N.Y. Alumni Assn. (asso. dir. 1972—), Sigma Gamma Tau. Roman Catholic. Home: 12 Sheep Ln Levittown NY 11756 Office: 224 7th St Garden City NY 11530

JANELLI, DONALD ERNEST, surgeon; b. N.Y.C., Dec. 4, 1920; s. Ernest and Helen May (Pettengill) J.; B.A., Columbia, 1942; M.D., N.Y. Med. Coll., 1945; M.S. in Surgery, N.Y. U., 1953; m. Gloria Patricia Enge, Aug. 30, 1943; children—Jeffrey Donald, Chris Pettengill, Bruce Drury. Intern Jersey City Med. Center, 1945-46; resident Nassau Hosp., Mineola, N.Y., 1948-52; practice medicine, specializing in surgery, Williston Park, N.Y., 1952-70, Mineola 1970—; chief of surgery Nassau Hosp.; prof. clin. surgery State U. N.Y. at Stony Brook, 1973—; cons. in surgery Nassau County (N.Y.) Med. Center, East Meadow, St. Francis Hosp., Roslyn, N.Y., VA Hosp., Northport, N.Y. Served to capt. as flight surgeon M.C., USAAF, 1946-48. Diplomate Am. Bd. Surgery. Fellow A.C.S., Internat. Coll. Surgeons, Nassau Acad. Medicine (founding); mem. Nassau County, N.Y. State med. socs., Nassau Surg. Soc., AMA. Episcopalian. Club: The Creek. Contbr. numerous articles to profl. jours. Home: Brookville Ln Old Brookville Glen Head NY 11545 Office: 222 Front St Mineola NY 11501

JANESAK, CHARLES PAUL, ednl. media specialist; b. Garfield, N.J., Oct. 14, 1946; s. Anthony George and Marie Sophie (Rosza) J.; B.S., Tusculum Coll., 1969; M.L.S. (Elementary and Secondary Edn. Act fellow), Pratt Inst. Tech., 1970; m. Mary Elizabeth Kody, Apr. 4, 1970; 1 dau., Christine. Elementary sch. ednl. specialist Fort Lee (N.J.) Pub. Schs., 1970—; sr. reference librarian Passaic (N.J.) Pub. Library, 1970—. Trustee Garfield (N.J.) Pub. Library, treas., 1974, pres., 1975—. Mem. NEA, N.J. Ednl. Media Assn., ALA, N.J. Library Trustee Assn., Bergen County Sch. Librarians Assn., Beta Phi Mu, Phi Gamma Mu. Mem. Hungarian Reformed Ch. Home: 99 Hartmann Ave Garfield NJ 07026 Office: Public School 2 Jones Rd Fort Lee NJ 07024

JANESKI, WILLIAM LOUIS, realtor; b. Pittsburg, Kans.; s. William Charles and Elnora Fern (Sanders) J.; student U. Kans., 1951-52, Strayer Coll. Accountancy, 1955-56; m. June Elizabeth Cover, Feb. 19, 1955; children—David Scott, Stephen Gregory, William Andrew, Nancy Elizabeth. Co-owner, pres. Home Arts of Va., Arlington, 1957-60; owner, pres. Fashion House, Ltd., Arlington, 1960-68; v.p., gen. sales mgr. Kettle Realty Co., Vienna, Va., 1968-72; exec. v.p., regional dir. Century 21 Real Estate Corp. McLean, Va., 1973-74; pres., co-founder Realty World Corp. Washington, 1974—, also dir.; cons. in field; dir. Realty World Mass., Inc.; mem. edn. com. (chmn.) No. Va. Bd. Realtors, 1973-74. Named to Realtors Million Dollar Club, 1969-73. Served with USN, 1953-54. Mem. Nat. Assn. Realtors, Optimist Internat. (pres. 1971-72). Methodist. Contbr. articles to profl. jours. Home: 8926 Colesbury Pl Fairfax VA 22030 Office: 1001 Connecticut Ave NW Washington DC 20036

JANETTA, NICHOLAS JOHN, psychologist, educator; b. Vineland, N.J., May 27, 1933; s. Nicholas and Angelina (Zitto) J.; B.S. in Edn., Temple U., 1960, M.Ed., 1969; M.A., Glassboro State Coll., 1975; m. Barbara Kairis, Aug. 1, 1964; children—Stephen, Gregory, Keith. Tchr. pub. sch. Cumberland County (N.J.), 1960-64; clin. psychologist Vineland State Sch., 1965-67, 74—; sch. psychologist Camden County (N.J.) Sch. Systems, 1967-70, Atlantic County (N.J.) Sch. Systems, 1970-74; instr. psychology Atlantic Community Coll., 1970-75, Glassboro (N.J.) State Coll., 1970-75; interviewer N.J. Employment Security Div., Vineland, 1964-65. Served with AUS, 1953-55. Certified as tchr., sch. psychologist, clin. psychologist, N.J. Mem. Am., Eastern, N.J., Pa. psychol. assns., Phi Delta Kappa. Home: 1150 Fairmount Ave Vineland NJ 08360

JANICKE, JACK M., electronic co. exec.; b. Hawthorne, N.J., Aug. 10, 1921; s. William and Ethel (Onderdonk) J.; student Vanderbilt U., 1942-43; m. Thelma Hennion, Sept. 8, 1946; 1 son, Frederick. Service mgr. Pompton Lakes Radio Service, 1946-52; with RFL Industries, Inc., Boonton, N.J., 1952—, chief applications engr., 1957-61, v.p., 1961—, also dir.; pres., dir. Magnetic Research, Inc., Butler, N.J.; dir. RFL Internat. Mem. adv. bd. Permanent Magnet Users Assn. sect. Franklin Inst., Phila., 1969-70. Served with AUS, 1942-46. Mem. Am. Radio Relay League, Instrument Soc. Am., Am. Ordnance Assn., I.E.E.E., Radio Club Am., Royal Signals Radio Assn. Club: Elks. Author: How to Magnetize, Stabilize and Measure Permanent Magnets, 1958. Patentee in field. Home: 122 Bellevue Ave Butler NJ 07405 Office: Powerville Rd Boonton NJ 07005

JANICKI, CASIMIR A., chemist; b. Milw., Sept. 20, 1934; s. Casey J. and Helen (Bonikowski) J.; B.A., LaSalle Coll., 1956; M.S., Marquette U., 1958; Ph.D., Loyola U., Chgo., 1964; m. Antoinette Chendorain, May 2, 1959; children—Camille M., Casimir G. Analytical chemist Smith, Kline & French Labs., Phila., 1957-60; sect. head analytical pharmacy McNeil Labs., Fort Washington, Pa., 1963—. Com. chmn. Cub Scouts, 1972-74, Boy Scouts Am., 1975-78. Karr fellow, 1960-63. Mem. Am. Pharm. Assn., Acad. Pharm. Assn., Phila. Discussion Group Acad. Pharm. Sci., Am. Chem. Soc., Order Alhambra. Elk, K.C. Home: Hickory Hill Dr RD 1 Norristown PA 19401 Office: Camp Hill Rd McNeil Labs Fort Washington PA 19034

JANJIGIAN, EDWARD RUPEN, physician, author; b. Armenia, Aug. 4, 1910; s. Reupen and Rebecca (Kondazian) J.; student Dartmouth, 1929-33, U. Va., 1933; Ph.B., U. Chgo., 1934; M.D., Boston U., 1936; postgrad. U. Pa., 1947; Georgetown U., 1950; m. Hannah McEwen, Aug. 23, 1937; children—Jessie, Hannah. Physician, Danville State Hosp., 1938-40; asst. chief neuropsychiat. service Walter Reed Hosp., 1940-43; div. psychiatrist, act. div. surgeon, chief neuropsychiat. service VA regional office and VA Hosps., 1947-74, cons., 1974—; chief psychiatry, neurology service Mercy, Nesbitt hosps., Wilkes-Barre, Pa., 1947—. Served with AUS, 1940-45, ETO. Diplomate Am. Bd. Psychiatry and Neurology. Fellow A.C.P., Am. Psychiat. Assn.; mem. Acad. Neurology, Am. Electroencephalogram Soc., Luzerne County Med. Soc. (pres.), Am. Legion, V.F.W., Phi Chi. Methodist. Clubs: Masons, K.T., Shrine. Home and office: 22 Pierce St Kingston PA 18704

JANJIGIAN, HANNAH M. (MRS. EDWARD R. JANJIGIAN), broadcasting exec., civic worker; b. Edinburg, Ind., Dec. 7, 1911; d. W. Alfred and Elsie (Meier) McEwen; student (Am. Assn. U. Women scholar), Franklin Coll., 1930-31; B.S. in Home Econs. (4-H scholar 1931-34), Purdue U., 1934; postgrad. U. Chgo., 1933-34, Ohio State U., 1934-35, Coll. Misericorida, 1964, Pa. State U., 1965-66, Mansfield State Coll., 1968; m. Edward R. Janjigian, Aug. 22, 1937;

children—Jessie, Hannah, Edward R. Instn. mgmt. work U. Chgo., 1933-34, Carson, Pirie Scott & Co., Chgo., 1934, Ohio State U., 1934-35; nat. range home economist Westinghouse Electric Co., Mansfield, Ohio, 1935-36; home demonstration agt. U.S. Dept. Agr., 1936-37; owner, mfr. Feather Brand Cakes, Kingston, Pa., 1947-54; originator med. TV series sta. WILK-TV, Luzerne County Med. Soc., Kingston, 1956, co-producer Safeguard Your Health series, 1956—. Pres. Nebbitt Hosp. Aux., Kingston, 1951-53, fund raiser, 1958-68; conferee Working with Disadvantaged Youth, Dept. Health, Edn. and Welfare, 1965; publicity chmn. Luzerne County Nutrition Com. Dept. Agr., 1965-66; vol. dir. YWCA Tutorial, Wilkes-Barre, Pa., 1969—; mem. adv. com. Upward Bound Wilkes Coll., Wilkes-Barre, 1972—. Recipient Governor's award for safety Commonwealth of Pa., 1965; citation Nat. Safety Council, 1965; Benjamin Rush award Luzerne County Med. Soc., 1972. Mem. Woman's Aux. Luzerne County Med. Soc. (TV-radio-press chmn. 1959-65, pres. 1955-56, 64-65), Woman's Aux. Pa. Med. Soc. (pub. relations chmn. 1956-58, mental health chmn. 1958-59; editor newsletter 1961-63), V.F.W. Aux., Aux. Am. Acad. Neurology, D.A.R. (treas. Wyoming Valley 1956—). Methodist. Home: 22 Pierce St Kingston PA 18704

JANKOWSKI, WALTER JOSEPH, bus. exec.; b. Bayonne, N.J., Dec. 15, 1920; s. Michael J. and Cecelia M. (Ludwiecheski) J.; student N.Y.U., 1940-41, postgrad., 1967; B.B.A., Rutgers U., 1950; m. Sylvia D. Keller, May 8, 1948; children—W. Jan, Deborah A. Asst. treas. Chipman Chem. Co., Inc., Bound Brook, N.J., 1956-64; mgr. credit So. Nitrogen Co., 1964-69; v.p. Arboreal Assos., Inc., Harriman, N.Y., 1971, exec. v.p., 1971, pres., chief exec. officer, 1972-76; chmn. bd. World Wall Systems, Inc., 1973-75; chmn. bd., pres. Winslow Farms, Inc., 1973-76; chmn. bd. Arboreal Environ. Botanists, Inc., Harriman, 1976—, Engagé Fragrances Inc., Harriman, 1979—; sec. treas., dir. Humsey Chem. Co. Inc., Bklyn., 1977—. Fin. chmn. St. Francis Cabrini Ch., Savannah, Ga., 1970; charter mem. Exchange Club Met. Savannah, 1967-69; sec., committeeman Boy Scouts Am., Bayonne, 1931-41. Served with USAAF, 1941-45. Recipient Community Leader and Noteworthy Americans award, 1975-76. Fellow Internat. Biog. Soc.; mem. Alumni Assn. Grad. Sch. Credit and Fin. Mgmt. N.Y. U., DAV (life). Club: La Vida Country (Savannah). Author: Changing Patterns in Agricultural Marketing, 1967. Home: 208 Holly St Cranford NJ 07016 Office: Box 7 Main St Harriman NY 10926

JANNEY, MARY DRAPER, social and ednl. service orgn. adminstr.; b. Bklyn., May 28, 1921; d. Ernest Gallaudet and Mary White (Childs) Draper; B.A. in Sociology, Vassar Coll.; M.A. in Sociology, Yale; m. Frederick Wistar Morris Janney, Jan. 15, 1944; children—Peter Wistar, Christopher D. Tchr. Am. history Potomac Sch., McLean, Va., 1961-64, head history dept., student adviser, 1961-64; founder, pres. Wider Opportunities for Women, Inc., Washington, 1966—. Mem. Washington Commn. on the Status of Women, 1973—; bd. dirs. The Maderia Sch., Greenway, Va., 1969-72, Potomac Sch., McLean, 1966-72; trustee Vassar Coll., 1975—, Fed. Woman's Award. Named One of 1975's Washingtonians of the Year. Home: 2960 Terr Washington DC 20016 Office: 1649 K St NW Washington DC 20006

JANOWSKI, STANLEY JOSEPH, counselor, ednl. adminstr.; b. Trenton, N.J., Oct. 27, 1938; s. Stanley Walter and Bertha Madeline (Ball) J.; B.A., St. Francis Coll., Burlington, Wis., 1962; M.A., Christ the King Theol. Sem., West Chicago, Ill., 1967; M.A., Villanova (Pa.) U., 1971. Joined O. F. M., 1956; ordained priest Roman Catholic Ch., 1966; faculty Archbishop Ryan High Sch. Boys, Phila., 1967—, chmn. counseling center, 1967-75, vice-prin., 1975—; counselor, asst. chaplain Ill. Reform Sch. Boys, St. Charles, 1965—; chaplain Phila. Police Dept. Chmn. exec. bd. Archdiocese of Phila. Counselors Assn., 1967—. Certified profl. counselor, Pa. Mem. Am. Personnel and Guidance Assn., Nat. Cath. Guidance Conf. Profl. Counselors Assn., Am. Psychol. Assn., Fraternal Order Police (chaplain), Phila. Polish Police Assn. (chaplain 1976—). Address: 11051 Academy Rd Philadelphia PA 19154

JANSCHKA, FRITZ, artist; b. Vienna, Austria, Apr. 21, 1919; s. Friedrich and Josephine (Vogl) J.; student Akademie der bildenden Kuenste, Vienna, 1943-49; children—William F., Nina M.; m. 2d, Kathryn Porter Aichele, Nov. 26, 1976. Came to U.S., 1949. One man shows Schurz Found., Phila., 1953, Carlen Gallery, Phila., 1950-52, Newman Contemporary Galleries, 1959, 62, 68, 73, Torbandenda Gallery, Trieste, 1971, Grafische Sammlungen, Zurich, Switzerland, 1972, others; exhibited in group shows Art Club Vienna, 1947-50, Gramercy Park Gallery, N.Y.C., 1956, Acad. Art, Phila., Phila. Mus., others; represented in permanent collection Vienna Hist. Mus., Acad. Fine Arts, Vienna, Municipal Mus., Vienna, Phila. Watter Collection, Mus. XX Century, Vienna, Albertina, Vienna, Grafische Sammlurg, Zurich, others. Mem. faculty Bryn Mawr (Pa.) Coll., 1949—, prof. art, 1949—. Pub. Ulysses Alphabet, 26 etchings, 1973. Office: Dept Art Bryn Mawr College Bryn Mawr PA 19010

JANUZZI, RONALD EVERETT, field mineralogist; b. Danbury, Conn., June 13, 1929; s. Anthony and Ines Thelma (LaPine) J.; student pub., pvt. schs., Danbury, Conn.; pvt. studies in field mineralogy, 1950-60. Co-founder, field dir. Danbury Mineral. Soc. Inc., 1940-60; curator Trainer collection minerals Southeast Museum, Brewster, N.Y., 1966—; dir. research, curator mineral collections Januzzi Inst. for Regional Field Mineraology, Brewster, 1965—; pub. Mineral Press; tchr., lectr. in field mineralogy, Conn., N.Y. State; tchr. in mineralogy Danbury Adult Edn. Program, 1969-71. Served with U.S. Army, Korean War. Recipient Danbury War Meml. award for public service City of Danbury, 1954. Mem. Mineral. Soc. Am. Congregationalist. Author: Connecticut Minerals on Parade, 1953; New York State Minerals on Parade, 1953; A Field Mineralogy of the World Famous Tilly Foster Iron Mine in Tilly Foster, New York, 1966; The Mineral Localities of Connecticut and Southeastern New York State, 1960, rev. 2d edit., 1972; (with David M. Seaman) Pegmatite Minerals of the World, 1976; author filmstrip series: Minerals on Parade, 1958. Office: Route 6 Brewster NY 10509

JANZ, ABRAHAM ALAN, mfg. co. exec.; b. N.Y.C., Aug. 25, 1924; s. Samuel Z. and Bertha (Kooksis) J.; B.A., Rutgers U., 1954; postgrad. N.Y. U., 1954-57, Montclair State Coll., 1957-59; m. Mildred Gelfer, Feb. 25, 1950; children—Burton Howard, Stephen David, Daniel Adam. Plant mgr. Graphic Arts Center, N.Y.C., 1954-60, Bon R. Reprodns., N.Y.C., 1960-70; with Miller Wohl Co., Inc., Secaucus, N.J., 1970—, plant mgr. inplant printing and display dept., 1970—; dir. PTG House Craftsmen, Newark. Mem. Pequannock Twp. (N.J.) Planning Bd., 1962—; Republican County committeeman, 1964-65. Served with AUS, 1943-46; ETO. Decorated Purple Heart, Bronze Star. Mem. N.J. Fedn. Planning Ofcls. (dir. 1962—, pres. 1968-70), In-Plant Mgmt. Assn. N.J. Jewish. Club: Workmen's Circle. Contbr. articles to profl. jours. Home: 19 Foothills Dr Pompton Plains NJ 07444 Office: 915 Secaucus Rd Secaucus NJ 07094

JARECKI, RICHARD WILHELM, physician; b. Stettin, Ger., Dec. 1, 1931; s. Max Moritz and Gerda (Kunstmann) J.; came to U.S., 1940, naturalized, 1943; student Duke U., 1949-51; M.D., U. Heidelberg (Ger.), 1957; m. Carol Hedwig Fuhse, Jan. 10, 1964; children—Didi Merriweather, Lianna Louise, John Henry. Intern, Monmouth Med. Center, Long Branch, N.J., 1958-59; resident internal medicine Jersey Shore Med. Center, Neptune, N.J., 1959-61; mem. faculty N.J. Coll. Medicine, 1963-67; research asso. U. Heidelberg, 1967-74; v.p. Brody White & Co., N.Y.C., 1973—, Mocatta Commodities Corp., 1973—, Mocatta Corp., 1975—; asst. v.p. Mocatta Metals Corp., 1975—; dir. Mocatta Trade Corp.; gov. N.Y. Merc. Exchange. Recipient Dag Hammarskjoeld Internat. prize l'Organisation Mondiale de la Press Diplomatiques, 1968. Mem. Chgo. Bd. Trade, N.Y. Commodity Exchange, N.J. Acad. Sci. Contbr. articles to profl. jours. Home: 536 Navesink River Rd Red Bank NJ 07701 Office: 25 Broad St New York City NY 10004

JARMAN, RONALD BRIAN, ins. co. exec.; b. London, Eng., June 30, 1929; s. Ronald and Mary (Cumming) J.; 2d Officer's Certificate, The Nautical Coll., (Eng.), 1946; m. Dorothy Lucille Reafleng, Sept. 14, 1957 (dec. Feb. 1974); m. 2d, Gloria Seelandt, Sept. 17, 1976; stepchildren—James, Lisa, Susan. Came to U.S., 1954, naturalized, 1975. With British Merchant Marine, 1943-50; Lloyd's broker Alexander Howden & Co., Ltd., London, 1950-54; prodn., underwriting supt. Continental Nat. Am. Group, Chgo., 1954-65; with Am. Internat. Group, N.Y.C., 1965—, v.p. comml. casualty dept. Am. Home Assurance Co., 1970-71, sr. v.p., 1971-74, also dir.; v.p. Am. Internat. Underwriters Corp., N.Y.C., 1971—; exec. v.p., dir. Am. Home/Nat. Union Group, 1974-76. Served with Royal Nav. Res., 1943-50. Mem. St. Georges Soc. Am. Mgmt. Assn. Home: 1249 E 26th St Brooklyn NY 11210 Office: 102 Maiden Ln New York City NY 10005

JARNES, FREDERIC MYRON, dentist; b. Lynn, Mass., Sept. 4, 1932; s. Abel and Jeanette (Cohen) J.; A.B., Boston U., 1954, M.A., 1955; D.M.D., Tufts U., 1959; m. Janet Steiner, June 9, 1957; children—Amy Beth, Debra Susan. Practice dentistry, Lynn, 1961—; mem. faculty dept. oral diagnosis Sch. Dental Medicine, Tufts U., Medford, Mass., 1961—. Served to capt. U.S. Army, 1959-61. USPHS research fellow, 1956, 57, 59. Mem. Acad. Gen. Dentistry, ADA, Am. Analgesia Soc., Mass. Dental Soc. (certificate of merit 1964, 65, 67, 69). Club: Dolphin Yacht (sec. 1969, rear commodore 1970) (Marblehead, Mass.). Research in fields of peripheral vascular research, oral carcinogen research. Home: 14 Casino Rd Marblehead MA 01945 Office: 80 Broad St Lynn MA 01902

JARON, DOV, biomed. engr., educator; b. Tel Aviv, Israel, Oct. 29, 1935; s. Meir and Sara (Levit) Yarovsky; came to U.S., 1958, naturalized, 1972; B.S. magna cum laude, U. Denver, 1961; Ph.D., U. Pa., 1967; m. Linda Ann Hufnagel, Dec. 23, 1969 (div.); children—Shulamit, Tamara; m. Brooke E. Ballin, Sept. 16, 1978. Sr. research asso. Maimonides Med. Center, Bklyn., 1967-70; dir. surg. research Sinai Hosp. of Detroit, 1970-73; asso. prof. dept. elec. engring. U. R.I., Kingston, 1973-77, prof. dept. elec. engring., 1977—, coordinator biomed. engring., 1973—; vis. prof. dept. elec. engring. Rutgers U., New Brunswick, N.J., 1968-73; adj. prof. biomed. engring. Wayne State U., Detroit, 1971-73. NSF, NIH, pvt. founds. research grantee. Mem. Biomed. Engring. Soc., Assn. Advancement of Med. Instrumentation, Am. Soc. Artificial Internal Organs, N.Y. Acad. Scis., IEEE, AAAS, Sigma Xi, Tau Beta Pi, Eta Kappa Nu. Researcher in cardiac assist devices, cardiovascular modeling, biomed. instrumentation; contbr. articles to sci. jours. Home: Tomaquag Valley Rd RFD Bradford RI 02808 Office: Univ Rhode Island Kingston RI 02881

JAROSLAWICZ, ISAAC MORDECHAI, stockbroker, fin. planner; b. Bronx, N.Y., Aug. 31, 1953; s. Joseph and Mania (Reich) J.; student Yeshiva U., 1969-71, Bklyn. Coll., 1971-73, Coll. Fin. Planning, 1977-78; m. Adrian Birenbaum, Oct. 6, 1975. Account exec. D.H. Blair & Co., Inc., N.Y.C., 1973-75; with Butcher & Singer, Inc., N.Y.C., 1975-78; investment exec., fin. planner Blyth Eastman Dillon & Co., Inc., N.Y.C., 1978—; condr. seminars in field; cons., lectr.; mem. N.Y. Stock Exchange. Mem. Nat. Assn. Securities Dealers, N.Y. Stockbrokers Club, N.Y. Stockbrokers Forum. Democrat. Jewish. Author articles on personal fin. planning. Office: Blyth Eastman Dillon 1221 Ave of Americas New York City NY 10020

JARVIS, EDWARD BAXTER, psychiat. social worker; b. Benham, Ky., May 31, 1927; s. Ambrose and Olliff Marlowe (Baxter) J.; B.S., Lincoln Meml. U., 1951; M.S.W., N.Y. Sch. Social Work, 1954. Psychiat. social worker Child Guidance Inst., Yonkers, N.Y., 1954-55; social worker adoption and foster care Soc. for Seamen's Children, S.I., N.Y., 1955-59; caseworker Inwood House, N.Y.C., 1959-60; social worker, supr. casework Beekman-Downtown Hosp., N.Y.C., 1963-65; social worker Norwalk (Conn.) Bd. Edn., 1965—; supr. students N.Y. U., Fordham U., Western Conn. U. Bd. dirs. Project Friendship, 1977-79. Served with USAF, 1942-46. Decorated Bronze Star (5). Mem. Nat. Assn. Social Workers, Acad. Certified Social Workers, Conn. Assn. Sch. Social Workers, Registry Clin. Soc. Workers, Greenwich Kennel Club, Bronx County Kennel Club, Scottish Terrier Club Greater N.Y., Scottish Terrier Club Am. Research on socio-cultural factors in psychiat. clinic services for children. Home: 20 Ridgebury Rd Ridgefield CT 06877

JARVIS, LYNVILLE WALTER, broadcasting co. exec.; b. East Haverhill, N.H., Aug. 9, 1939; s. Alvin Franklin and Mona (Williams) J.; B.A., Emerson Coll., 1961; M.A., U. Ala., 1963. Stage mgr. Sta. WSFA-TV, Montgomery, Ala., 1963-64; producer, dir. broadcasting services U. Ala., Tuscaloosa, 1964-67; producer, dir. Vt. Ednl. TV, Winooski, 1967-75; TV specialist Extension Service and Agrl. Expt. Sta. of Coll. Agr., U. Vt., Burlington, 1975—. Mem. Vt. Adv. Com. for Consumer and Homemaking Edn. Bd. dirs. Essex Community Players, 1969-71, treas., 1971-73; trustee Vt. Arthritis Found., 1977-78; bd. dirs. Ask Us First; mem. pub. relations com. 4-H Clubs of Vt., 1976-78. Recipient awards of execllence So. Speech Assn., 1966; Blue Ribbon award Am. Assn. Agrl. Coll. Editors, 1968, 70, 71, 73, 76, 77. Mem. Nat. Assn. Ednl. Broadcasters, Chittenden County Hist. Soc., Calvin Coolidge Meml. Found., Vt. Archaeol. Soc., Vt. Assn. Extension Profls. (chmn. pub. relations com. 1976-78), Vt. Old Cemetary Assn., Friends of Spruce Mt., Green Mt. Folklore Soc., Vt. Council on Arts, No. Vt. Artists Assn., Am. Assn. Agrl. Coll. Editors (Vt. rep.), Postal Commemorative Soc., Nat. Audubon Soc., Green Mt. Audubon Soc. (dir. publicity 1973-76, task force for devel. 1975-76), Alpha Epsilon Rho. Clubs: 251, Gourmet. Home: 109 N Willard St Burlington VT 05401 Office: 205 Morrill Hall U Vt Burlington VT 05401

JASEN, DAVID ALAN, educator; b. N.Y.C., Dec. 16, 1937; s. Barnet and Gertrude (Cohen) J.; B.A., Am. U., 1959; M.S., L.I. U., 1972; m. Susan Alice Pomerantz, Dec. 30, 1963; 1 son, Raymond Douglas. Supr. network news videotape CBS, N.Y.C., 1959-66; adminstrv. asst. Am. Ednl. Theatre Assn., Washington, 1967; field service rep. Florists Transworld Delivery Assn., Detroit, 1968-69; asst. to pres. Reading Devel. Center, Inc., 1969-70; asso. prof. fine arts. C.W. Post Coll., Brookville, N.Y., 1971—. Mem. Pi Delta Epsilon, Alpha Psi Omega. Clubs: Ragtime Society (Weston, Can.); Maple Leaf (Los Angeles). Author: A Bibliography and Reader's Guide to the First Editions of P.G. Wodehouse, 1970; Recorded Ragtime, 1897-1958, 1973; P.G. Wodehouse: A Portrait of a Master, 1974; The Uncollected Wodehouse, 1976; Rags and Ragtime, 1978. Home: 225 E Penn St Long Beach NY 11561 Office: CW Post Center Greenvale NY 11548

JASKOLL, IRA LESLIE, coll. adminstr.; b. Bronx, Feb. 5, 1949; s. Saul Jacob and Edith Alva (Presberg) J.; B.A., Yeshiva U., 1971; M.B.A., L.I. U., 1973; m. Hannah Topel, June 24, 1974; children—Shabtai, Chaim. Asst. to dean L.I. U., Bklyn., 1973-76; fin. systems cons. Rapidata, Fairfield, N.J., 1976-77; dir. Bramson ORT Tech. Coll., N.Y.C., 1977—; adj. prof. Fairleigh Dickinson U., Rutherford, N.J., 1976—, Kean Coll. of N.J., 1975-76. Recipient Norman Palefsky award Yeshiva U., 1971. Mem. Soc. Advancement of Mgmt., Am. Mgmt. Assn., Assn. Computer Machinery, Nat. Bus. Edn. Assn., Assn. M.B.A. Execs., Am. Assn. Univ. Adminstrs., Am. Soc. Pub. Adminstrn., Am. Vocat. Assn., Pi Mu Epsilon. Jewish. Home: 616 Rutland Ave Teaneck NJ 07666 Office: 44 E 23d St New York City NY 10010

JASPEN, NATHAN, educator; b. N.Y.C., Oct. 21, 1917; s. Jacob J. and Sarah (Kantor) J.; B.S., Coll. City N.Y., 1942; M.A., George Washington U., 1944; Ph.D., Pa. State U., 1949; m. Helen G. Shulman, June 11, 1944; children—David, Robert, Sandra, Daniel, Richard. Occupational analyst USES, Washington, 1942-47; research fellow Pa. State U., 1947-49, asso. prof., 1949-52; dir. statistics, automation Nat. League Nursing, N.Y.C., 1952-59, also cons.; asso. prof. N.Y.U., N.Y.C., 1959-62, prof. ednl. statistics, 1962—, chmn. dept. ednl. statistics, 1963—; cons. Am. Pub. Health Assn., USPHS, Bd. Coop. Edn. Services, Westchester. Fellow AAAS, Am. Psychol. Assn.; mem. AAUP, Am. Ednl. Research Assn., Am. Statis. Assn., Assn. For Computing Machinery, Inst. Math. Statistics, Math. Assn. Am., Psychometric Soc., Sigma Xi, Pi Mu Epsilon. Contbr. articles to profl. jours. Home: 200 Winston Dr Cliffside Park NJ 07010 Office: NY Univ Washington Sq New York City NY 10003

JASSER, RONALD M., chem. co. exec.; b. Bklyn., Apr. 26, 1948; s. Edward S. and Muriel (Farber) J.; A.A.S., Rochester Inst. Tech., 1967, B.S., 1969; m. Paula D. Braunstein, Aug. 16, 1970; children—Evan S., Jordan P. Vice pres. Anchor Chem. Co., Inc., Hicksville, N.Y., 1971—; pres. Anchor Chem. Co. Ltd. (Can.), 1975—; v.p. A.C.P. Inc. (Internat.), 1971—; v.p. Agnate Chem. Co., 1971—; v.p. Anky Realty, 1971—. Mem. Graphic Arts Advertisers Council (pres.), N.Y. Craftsman Club (sec.), Graphic Arts Tech. Found. (ednl. com.), L.I. Graphic Arts Assn., Alpha Epsilon Pi. Club: B'nai B'rith (graphic arts lodge). Home: 4 Kristi Ln Lake Grove NY 11755 Office: 500 W John St Hicksville NY 11801

JASTAK, JOSEPH FLORIAN, psychologist, pub.; b. Gostyczyn, Poland, Mar. 19, 1901; s. Jakob and Marya (Siewert) J.; Teaching Dipl., U. Poznan (Poland), 1925; M.A., Columbia U., 1928, Ph.D., 1934; m. Sarah Rickards, Apr. 26, 1946; 1 son, Jan Theodore. Psychologist, Bklyn. Child Guidance Clinic, 1932-36; chief psychologist Del. State Hosp., Farnhurst and New Castle, 1936-51; research prof. U. Del., 1952-56; cons. psychologist, Wilmington, Del., 1951—; dir. Psychol. Services, Del. State Vocat. Rehab. Service; pres. Jastak Assos., Inc., Wilmington, 1966—; cons. schs., agencies, industry. Bd. dirs. Kosciuszko Found. Licensed psychologist, Del. Fellow Am. Bd. Profl. Psychology; mem. Am., Del. psychol. assns., Nat., Del. assns. sch. psychologists, Nat., Del. rehab. assns., Del. Mental Health Assn., Am. Assn. Mental Deficiency, Council for Exceptional Children. Clubs: Univ., Whist. Home: 4002 Springfield Ln Wilmington DE 19807 Office: 1526 Gilpin Ave Wilmington DE 19806

JASTRAB, ROBERT FRANK, counselor; b. Chgo., Apr. 4, 1938; s. Casimir Andrew and Elizabeth Mary (Oleska) J.; B.A. (athletic scholarships 1955-59), St. Mary's Coll., Winona, Minn., 1959; M.S. in Edn. (grad. asst. 1959-61), So. Ill. U., Carbondale, 1961; m. Sandra Lee Kain, Dec. 23, 1966; children—David, Ann. Elementary sch. tchr., Holt, Mich., 1963-64; tchr., guidance dir. Gabriel High Sch., Lansing, Mich., 1964-67; acting dir. counseling Mohawk Valley Community Coll., Utica, N.Y., 1969-70, counselor, 1967—. Mem. Am., Oneida County personnel and guidance assns., Nat. Vocat. Guidance Assn., Hart's Hill PTA, Mowhawk Valley Golf Assn. Home: 13 Cheriton Dr Whitesboro NY 13492 Office: Mohawk Valley Community Coll Utica NY 13501

JASZCZUN, WASYL, philologist, educator; b. Snyriv, Ukraine, Jan. 24, 1915; s. Stephan and Anna (Panasiuk) J.; Ph.D. in Slavic Philology, U. Graz (Austria), 1948; m. Maria Machovsky-Wohn, Oct. 21, 1948; children—Irene Bohdanna, Olga Martha. Tchr. secondary sch., Leshniv, USSR, 1939-41; lectr. Russian and Polish, U. Pa., Phila., 1956-59; asst. prof., head Russian dept. State U. Iowa, Iowa City, 1959-60; asst. prof., Slavic dept., U. Pitts., 1960-61, acting chmn., 1960-62, asso. prof., 1961-65, prof., 1965—, Charles E. Merril faculty fellow, 1963, research grantee, 1969. Mem. Am. Assn. Tchrs. Slavic E. European Langs. (v.p. Pa. chpt.), Am. Name Soc., Ukrainian Am. Assn. Univ. Profs., Shevchenko Sci. Soc. Author: Religious and Moral-Ethical Tenets of Taras Shevchenko, 1959; Phonetic, Morphological and Lexical Peculiarities of the Snyriv Dialect, 1964; The Term and Name Brody, 1965; (with T. Kelly, J. Mastroni) Russian Pattern Drills, 1965; A Dictionary of Russian Idioms and Colloquialisms, 1967; Ukrainian Dialect of the District of Brody in Western Ukraine, 1972. Home: 1415 N Euclid Ave Pittsburgh PA 15206 Office: 122 Loeffler Bldg Univ Pittsburgh Pittsburgh PA 15260

JAVITS, JACOB KOPPEL, U.S. senator; b. N.Y.C., May 18, 1904; s. Morris and Ida (Littman) J.; LL.B., N.Y. U., 1926; LL.D., Lincoln U. Hartwick Sem., L.I. Univ., Ithaca Coll.; D.C.L., Pace Coll.; D.H.L., Hebrew Union Coll., N.Y. Med. Coll.; hon. degrees Yeshiva U., Hartford Coll., N.Y. Med. Coll. Flower and 5th Av. Hosp., N.Y. U., Fordham U., Jewish Theol. Sem. Am., Colgate U., Pratt Inst., Council U. Niagra, Bar-Elan U., Israel, U. Louisville, Bard Coll., Hofstra U. Syracuse U., Hamilton Coll. Dartmouth Coll., U. Buffalo Law Sch., Alfred U.; m. Marion Ann Borris, Nov. 30, 1947; children—Joy, Joshua, Carla Ida. Admitted to N.Y. bar, 1927; past mem. Javits, Trubin, Sillcocks, Edelman & Purcell, N.Y.C.; spl. asst. to chief of Chem. Warfare Service, U.S. Army, Washington, 1941-42; mem. 80th to 83d Congresses, 21st N.Y. Dist.; mem. Com. on Fgn. Affairs, 1947-54; atty. gen. N.Y. State, 1954-56; U.S. senator from N.Y., 1957—, ranking Republican mem. com. human resources; ranking minority senator on joint econ. com.; mem. fgn. relations com., govt. ops.; chmn. com. of nine to study NATO, North Atlantic Assembly (formerly NATO Parliamentarian's Conf.); U.S. del. UN 25th Gen. Assembly. Commd. major U.S. Army, Mar. 1942, asst. to chief of operations C.W.S.; served in U.S., ETO, PTO, 1942-45; disch. lt. col.; col. C.W.S. Res., AUS (ret.). Decorated Legion of Merit, Commendation ribbon. Mem. Am. Legion, V.F.W., Jewish War Vets., Republican. Jewish religion. Clubs: City Athletic, Nat. Republican (N.Y.C.); Army and Navy (Washington). Author: A Proposal to Amend the Anti-Trust Laws, 1939; Discrimination U.S.A., 1960; Order of Battle, A Republican's Call to Reason, 1964; Who Makes War: Congress versus The President, 1973; series of articles on polit. philosophy for Rep. party, 1946. Lecturer on econ. and polit. subjects. Office: 110 E 45th St New York NY 10017 also Russell Senate Office Bldg Washington DC 20515

JAWOREK, TERRANCE EDWARD, podiatric surgeon; b. Erie, Pa., Jan. 3, 1946; s. Edmund Casmir and Winifred Luella (Lund) J.; B.S., Murray State U., 1968; D.P.M., Ohio Coll. Podiatric Medicine, 1972; m. Karol Anne Szepanski, June 12, 1971. Asst. prof. anatomy and surgery Ohio Coll. Podiatric Medicine, Erie, Pa., 1974—, dir.

research, 1974—; practice podiatry, Erie, 1975—. Fellow Am. Coll. Podiatric Medicine; mem. Am., Pa. Podiatry Assns., Am. Med. Writers Assn. Republican. Roman Catholic. Editor: Jour. Am. Podiatric Assn. Contbr. articles to jours. Home: North Mill Rd Paper Mill Hollow North East PA 16428 Office: 4348 Iroquois Ave Erie PA 16511

JAWORSKA, TAMARA, artist; b. Archangelsk, Russia, July 20, 1928; d. Anthony and Alexandra (Totlgin) Jankowski; B.F.A. with honors, State Acad. Fine Arts, Lodz, Poland, 1950, M.F.A., 1952. Mem. faculty State Acad. Fine Arts, Lodz, 1952-58; artistic dir. Artists Guild, Poland, 1954-59, Lab. for Design of linen Industry, Poland, 1959-63, Polish Guild for Arts and Crafts, 1963-68; free lance artist, designer, tapestry maker, 1969—; one woman shows include: Warsaw Art Gallery, 1965, Richard Demarco Art Gallery, Edinburgh, Scotland, 1968, Fine Art Mus., Plymouth, Eng., 1968, Merton Gallery, Toronto, 1970, Ont. Assn. Architects, Toronto, London (Ont.) Art Gallery, Art Gallery, Windsor, Ont., 1971, Glendon Art Gallery, Toronto, 1972; represented in permanent collections: Nat. Mus., Warsaw,Poland, Nat. Mus. History of Weaving, Lodz, Pushkin Gallery European Art, Moscow, and numerous pvt. collections. Fellow Royal Can. Acad. Arts; mem. Can. Guild Crafts. Address: 49 Don River Blvd Willowdale ON M2N 2M8 Canada

JAY, BARRY, rubber co. exec.; b. N.Y.C., Oct. 16, 1938; s. Sam and Rose Jay; B.S. in Econs., Babson Coll., Wellesley, Mass., 1961; LL.D. (hon.), London U., 1972; m. Ronnay Harrison, Apr. 11, 1965; children—Toni, Kimberly, Cindy. With Salco Rubber Co., Inc., Bronx, N.Y., 1961—, v.p., 1965-68, pres., 1968—; dir. SRC Trading Corp., S.&B. Tire Co., Holon Tire Co. Hon. dep. sheriff, Westchester County, N.Y. Office: 1150 Webster Ave Bronx NY 10456

JAY, FRANCIS, realtor; b. Syracuse, N.Y., May 13, 1919; s. Nicholas and Angeline (Lodico) J.; student pub. schs.; m. Alice M. McGowan, Sept. 9, 1946; children—Jean Ann Jay Cicaarelli, Linda Jay Robinson. Pres., United Realty, Syracuse, 1952—. Bd. dirs. Syracuse Youth Center. Republican. Roman Catholic. Moose. Home: 310 Bear St Syracuse NY 13208 Office: 238 Charles Ave Solvay NY 13209

JAY, HILDA LEASE, librarian, educator; b. Indpls., Dec. 29, 1921; d. Frank and Hilda (Whitton) Lease; B.S., Ind. U., 1945; M.S., Danbury State Coll., 1960; 6th yr. certificate U. Bridgeport, 1964; Ed.D., N.Y. U., 1970; m. John Jay, July 11, 1942; children—Sarah Louise, Margaret Ellen. With Burroughs Pub. Library, Bridgeport, Conn., 1942-44; media specialist Ridgefield (Conn.) Bd. Edn., 1958—; lectr. U. N.H., Concord, 1968, So. Conn. State Coll., New Haven, 1972-74, U. Conn., Storrs, 1977—. Pres. Bridgeport council Girl Scout U.S.A., 1955-58; mem. Norwalk Symphony, 1959-65; sec. adult adv. bd. Norwalk (Conn.) Youth Symphony; bd. dirs. Conn. Library Found., 1977—. Mem. Assn. for Ednl. Communications and Tech., Assn. for Supervision and Curriculum Devel., ALA, Am. Assn. Sch. Librarians, New Eng. Media Assn., Nat. Conn. edn. assns., Conn. Ednl. Media Assn. (dir. 1976—, pres. 1976-77), Kappa Delta Pi, Pi Lambda Theata. Episcopalian. Contbr. articles in field to profl. jours., editor Teen column, Bridgeport Post, 1947-55. Home: PO Box F Sandy Hook CT 06482 Office: Ridgefield High Sch Library 600 N Salem Rd Ridgefield CT 06877

JAY, MURRAY, houseware mfg. co. exec.; b. N.Y.C., Jan. 27, 1925; s. Harry H. and Minnie B. (Beerbohm) J.; B.S., Columbia, 1947; D.Bus. Adminstr. (hon.), London Inst., 1972; m. Vivian Gamsa, Apr. 6, 1953; children—Michael Anthony, Debra Lynn, Robert Walter. Founder, exec. v.p. Gemco-Ware, Inc., Freeport, N.Y., 1954—; pres. Gemco Internat. Sales Corp.; dir. Gemco Hausaltwaren GmbH, Germany, Gemco-Ware (U.K.) Ltd. Founder, pres. Howard Evan Schlessel Found., 1967—. Served to capt. USAF, 1943-46. Recipient design and merchandising awards Am. Merchandising Inst. and Service Merchandisers Am. Mem. Am. Mgmt. Assn., Chgo., N.Y.C. housewares clubs. Clubs: American (London, Eng.); Columbia University, Princeton, Middle Bay Country (N.Y.C.). Home: 170 Willow Rd Woodsburgh NY 11598 Office: 1 Gemco Plaza Freeport NY 11520

JAYNES, JULIAN, psychologist; b. W. Newton, Mass., Feb. 27, 1923; s. Julian Clifford and Clara Merrithew (Bullard) J.; B.A., McGill U., Montreal, 1944; M.A., Yale U., 1948. Reader in psychology Toronto U., 1944-45; instr. Yale U., 1954-60; research asso. Princeton U., 1964-66, master Wilson Coll., 1965-69, research psychologist, 1966—; NSF lectr. history of psychology U. N.H., 1968; trustee Archives Am. Psychology, Brain Bio Research Center; mem. com. brain scis. panel NRC, 1972-77. Mem. Eastern Psychol. Assn., Cheiron. Author: The Origin of Consciousness in the Breakdown of the Bicameral Mind, 1976; also articles; editor: Histrical Conceptional of Psychology, 1975; Lateralization in the Nervous System, 1977; editorial bd. Internat. Emcy. Neurology, Psychiatry, Psychoanalysis and Psychology, 1976-77; asso. editor Behavioral and Brain Scis., 1977—. Office: Dept Psychology Green Hall Princeton Univ Princeton NJ 08540

JAZWINSKI, ANDREW HONORE, research co. exec.; b. Pruszkow, Poland, Jan. 11, 1936 (mother Am. citizen); s. Stanley Teodor and Helen (Fryling) J.; brought to U.S., 1946; B.S. in Geophysics, Pa. State U., 1959; M.S., Calif. Inst. Tech. 1961; postgrad. U. Md., 1963-65; Ph.D. (hon.), Center Advanced Study, Huntsville, Ala., 1970; m. Anita Louise Sabatine, Jan. 30, 1959; children—Julie Helena, Elizabeth Lynne. Research engr. Gen. Dynamics Corp., San Diego, 1961-62; sr. research engr. Martin Co., Balt., 1962-65; sr. analyst, mgr. guidance and control Analytical Mechanics Assos., Inc., Seabrook, Md., 1965-71; pres., prin. scientist Bus. and Technol. Systems, Inc., Seabrook, 1971—, also chmn. bd.; cons. several cos., including Booz Allen Applied Research, Inc., Bethesda, Md., 1971-72, Nuclear Assos. Internat. Corp., Rockville, Md., 1970-72. Instr. McCoy Coll., Johns Hopkins, 1964, Drexel Inst. Tech., Balt., 1964. Recipient Martin honors award outstanding tech. achievement Martin Marietta Corp., 1965; citation contbns. to engring. edn. U. Wis., 1970; Am. Heritage award J.F.K. Library for Minorities, 1974. Mem. Am. Inst. Aero. and Astronautics, Soc. Indsl. and Applied Math., A.A.A.S., Phi Kappa Phi. Author: Stochastic Processes and Filtering Theory, 1970. Contbr. articles to profl. jours. Home: 12904 Cheswood Ln Bowie MD 20715 Office: Suite 440 10210 Greenbelt Rd Seabrook MD 20801

JEFFEE, SAUL, industrialist; b. Elizabeth, N.J., Mar. 30, 1918; s. Michael and Frieda (Copeland) J.; student N.Y. U., Columbia; m. Beatrice Ball Kahn, Oct. 26, 1952; 1 dau., Gail Susan. Pres., founder, chmn. bd. Movielab, Inc., 1934—; chmn. bd. Movielab-Hollywood, Inc.; chmn. bd., pres. Movielab Theatre Service, Inc. Vice chmn. Film Soc. Lincoln Center; patron Lincoln Center for Performing Arts. Chmn. Am. tech. rep. U.S.-U.S.S.R. Cultural and Sci. Exchange Agreement, Russia, 1965; mem. N.Y.C. Mayor's Adv. Council for Motion Pictures; adv. bd. Cinema lodge B'nai B'rith; nat. adv. com. on scouting for handicapped Boy Scouts Am.; trustee United Jewish Appeal, Fedn. Jewish Philanthropies, Will Rogers Hosp. and Research Center; chmn. bd. trustees Lorge Sch. Tech. Fellow Soc. Motion Picture and TV Engrs. (treas.); mem. Assn. Cinema Labs. (pres. 1963), Motion Picture Pioneers, Acad. Motion Picture Arts and Scis., Max Steiner Music Soc., Variety Clubs Internat. (life), Jewish Chatauqua Soc. Clubs: City Athletic, Friars; Fairview Country (Greenwich, Conn.), Masons (Shriner, 32 deg.). Author: Narcotics-An American Plan, 1966. Patentee motion picture equipment. Office: 619 W 54th St New York City NY 10019

JEFFERDS, CHARLES DENNIS, banker; b. Summit, N.J., Feb. 23, 1950; s. Charles Palmer and Mary (Steed) J.; B.A., Fairleigh Dickinson U., 1974; m. Lynne Marie Bruen, July 8, 1972. Adminstrv. asst. Morris County Savs. Bank, Morristown, N.J., 1974-76, asst. treas., 1976, asst. treas., br. mgr. Flanders office, 1976—. Episcopalian. Clubs: Rotary, Masons. Office: Route 206 Morris County Savings Bank Flanders NJ 07836

JEFFERSON, DAVID ROWE, educator; b. Hillsdale, Mich., June 18, 1931; s. Howard Bonar and Genevieve (Rowe) J.; B.A., Harvard, 1953; M.Div., Yale, 1956; postgrad. U. Edinburgh, Scotland, 1954-55, N.Y. U., 1958-60; m. Anne Morgan, June 22, 1957; children—David Rowe, Peter Hamilton. Asso. dir. YMCA Student Hostel, Edinburgh, 1954-55; exec. sec., chaplain Student Christian Movement of Qeens and Nassau, 1956-58; asst. prof. philosophy, sociology, dir. admissions C.W. Post Coll., 1958-63; dean admission., asst. prof. sociology Dickinson Coll., Carlisle, Pa., 1963-69; headmaster Worcester (Mass.) Acad., 1969-70; dean of students Bradford (Mass.) Coll., 1971—. Trainer, New Eng. Vol. Employment Service Team; justice of peace; notary public. Mem. Hasty Pudding Inst. 1770, Pi Gamma Mu. Episcopalian (lay reader, sr. warden). Mason (32 deg., K.T.), Rotarian. Clubs: Harvard (N.Y.C.), Iroquois (Cambridge, Mass.); Worcester. Editor: Guide to Private Two Year Colleges in New England. Home: Oak Rd Hampton Falls NY 03844

JEFFERSON, JOSEPH, coll. ofcl.; b. N.Y.C., Mar. 26, 1921; s. Edwin I. and Irma (Hilbert) J.; A.B., Columbia, 1947; m. Shirley M. Cushman, Dec. 29, 1943; children—William Charles, Jo Anne, Peter Bigelow, David Parker. Mem. staff Coll. Entrance Exam. Bd., 1954; asst. to dir. admissions Mass. Inst. Tech., Cambridge, 1954-57, asst. dir. student aid, 1954-56, placement officer, 1956-57; asst. provost Columbia, N.Y.C., 1957-60; dir. admissions and financial aid, 1957-60; exec. sec. Assn. Coll. Admissions Counselors, Evanston, Ill., 1960-66, dir. Coll. Admissions Center, 1960-66; editor jour., 1960-66; bd. mem. Am. Council for Emigres in Professions, Inc., N.Y.C., 1963-76; v.p. for devel. Bowdoin Coll., Brunswick, Maine, 1969-71, spl. asst. to pres. 1971-72; v.p. New Eng. Coll. Optometry, 1972—. Mem. nat. adv. bd. Nat. Scholarship Service and Fund for Negro Students; trustee Tougaloo (Miss.) Coll., 1970—. Served with USAAF, 1943-47. Mem. AAUP, Sachem Soc., Osiris. Home: 279 Concord Ave Lexington MA 02173 also Hurricane Ridge South Harpswell ME 04079 Office: 424 Beacon St Boston MA 02115

JEFFERY, SEYMOUR, govt. ofcl.; b. N.Y.C., Jan. 13, 1922; s. Reuben and Celia (Cohn) J.; B.S., USAF Inst. Tech., 1956; M.S., Stanford, 1961; m. Julie Randall, July 1, 1950; children—Ralph K., Douglas R., Robert D., Janine K. Commd. 2d lt. USAF, 1949, advanced through grades to maj., 1961, ret., 1965; dir. research, air devel. center USAF, Rome, N.Y., 1956-59; tech. dir. Air Force System Design Lab., Bedford, Mass., 1961-65; dir. software products TRW, Redondo Beach, Calif., 1965-72; chief, systems and software div. Nat. Bur. Standards, Washington, 1972—. Served with AAC, 1942-45. Decorated Air medal. Registered profl. engr., Ohio. Mem. IEEE (sr.). Contbr. to profl. jours. Home: 7420 Westlake Terr Bethesda MD 20034 Office: National Bureau Standards Washington DC 20234

JEFFERY, WILLIAM PRENTISS, JR., toiletries and chem. mfg. co. exec.; b. N.Y.C., Sept. 17, 1919; s. William Prentiss and Idelle (Scott) J.; B.A., Yale, 1941; m. Elizabeth Phillips Meek, Mar. 6, 1948; children—Priscilla Jane Adkins, William Jeremy, John MacKnight, Charles Robert, Patrick Gillespie. Vice-pres. Vick Products div. Richardson-Merrell Inc., N.Y.C., 1941-62; pres. Cos-Chem Corp. (formerly Parachem Corp.), Westwood, N.J., 1962—, also dir.; pres. Lanman & Kemp-Barclay & Co. Inc., Westwood, 1972—, also dir. v.p. Molecular Energy Research Co. Inc., Houston, 1974—, also dir. Served with USNR, 1942-45. Episcopalian. Club: Field Greenwich (Conn.). Author: Unless ..., 1975; Dear Jimmy, 1977. Home: 123 Park Ave Greenwich CT 06830 Office: 25 Woodland Ave Westwood NJ 07675

JEFFORDS, JAMES MERRILL, congressman; b. Rutland, Vt., May 11, 1934; s. Olin Merrill and Marion (Hausman) J.; B.S., Yale U., 1956; LL.B., Harvard U., 1962; m. Elizabeth Daley, Aug. 26, 1961; children—Leonard Olin, Laura Louise. Admitted to Vt. bar, 1962; law clk. Judge Ernest Gibson, Vt. Dist., 1962; partner firm Bishop, Crowley & Jeffords, Rutland, 1963-66, Kinney, Carbine & Jeffords, Rutland, 1967-68; atty. gen. State of Vt., 1969-73; mem. 94th Congress from Vt.; town agt. Shrewsbury, 1964-68, zoning adminstr., 1966-68; mem. Jud. Selection Bd., 1967-68; chmn. Hwy. Dept. Investigating Com., 1968; mem. Vt. Senate, 1967-68. Served with USNR, 1956-59; comdr. Res. Mem. Am., Vt., Rutland County bar assns., Am. Judicature Soc. (dir. 1973—). Republican. Congregationalist (trustee). Clubs: Lions, Elks. Home: 8 Kingsley Ave Rutland VT 05701 Office: Federal Bldg Box 676 Montpelier VT 05602

JEFFREY, ADI-KENT THOMAS (MRS. GILBERT JEFFREY), author; b. Atlantic City, Oct. 1, 1916; d. Adolph Alexander and Helen Elizabeth (Rowe) Thomas; B.A., Barnard Coll., 1938; m. Gilbert Jeffrey, Jan. 17, 1942; 1 dau., Lynda Elizabeth. Model, Vera Maxwell fashion designer, N.Y.C., 1938-39; host. Around New York overseas radio talk show NBC, N.Y.C., 1939; fashion copywriter John Wanamakers, Phila., 1959-60. Mem. Internat. Platform Assn., Am. Assn. Journalists and Authors, D.A.R., Bucks County Writers Guild (past pres.). Clubs: Overseas Press, Nat. Press. Author: They Dared Niagara, 1968; Witches and Wizards, 1971; Ghosts in the Valley, 1971; More Ghosts in the Valley, 1972; Bermuda Triangle, 1973; Triangle of Terror, 1974; Across the Land from Ghost to Ghost; They Dared the Devil's Triangle, 1975; Ghosts of the Revolution, 1976; Parallel Universe, 1977. Office: 37 N Main St New Hope PA 18938

JEFFREY, LOUIS PAUL, pharmacist, hosp. services adminstr.; b. Everett, Mass., Nov. 23, 1928; s. Samuel F. and Pauline (D'Angelo) J.; B.S., Mass. Coll. Pharmacy, 1953, M.S., 1955; children—Paul L., Anne D. Jeffrey Izzo, Michele T. Adminstrv. asst. Albany (N.Y.) Med. Center Hosp., 1954-66, dir. of pharmacy and central supply, 1954-66; dir. hosp. and pharmacy relations Roche Labs., Nutley, N.J., 1966-68; dir. of pharmacy services Emma Pendleton Bradley Hosp., Riverside, R.I., 1975—, Rhode Island Hosp., Providence, 1969—; cons. USPHS, div. of Indian affairs, from 1962; participant in revision program of Nat. Formulary, 1955-60. Bd. dirs. Northeastern N.Y. Speech Center, 1960-64. Recipient Award of Merit, Nat. Catholic Pharmacists Guild, 1974, Alumni Achievement award Mass. Coll. of Pharmacy, 1970. Mem. Am. Coll. of Apothecaries (hosp. com. 1961-62, 69-70, 72-73, 77-78), Am. Soc. of Hosp. Pharmacists, (pres. 1962-63), Am. Pharm. Assn. (trustee 1975-76, 1st prize award 1964), R.I. Pharm. Assn. (1st v.p. 1977-78, Guido L. Pettinichio award 1976), R.I. Soc. Hosp. Pharmacists (Named Outstanding Hosp. Pharmacist of the Year 1970, pres. 1970-71, editor 1968—), Am. Soc. Hosp. Pharmacists, N.Y. State Council Hosp. Pharmacists, New Eng. Council Hosp. Pharmacists (pres. 1972-73), Hosp Assn. of R.I. (chmn. pharmacy sect. 1972-73), Am. Pub. Health Assn., AMA, AAAS, Am. Inst. of History of Pharmacy (councilor 1962-63), Internat. Pharm. Fedn., Nat. Pharm. Council (chmn. com. on hosp. pharmacy relations 1967-68), Am. Cancer Soc. (dir. 1964-65), U.S. Jr. C. of C. (Segil Horluchi award 1961), Phi Delta Chi, Rho Chi. Home: 19 Old Oak Dr Warwick RI 02886 Office: Rhode Island Hosp 593 Eddy St Providence RI 02902

JEFFREYS, JOYCE ESTER, dietitian; b. Bolivia, N.C., Feb. 20, 1947; d. John Calvin and Sallie Irene (Hankins) Galloway; B.S. cum laude, A. and T. State U., 1969; M.S., Howard U., 1973; m. Harry Jeffreys, Jr., Apr. 10, 1971. Dietitian, Doctors Hosp., Washington, 1970-71, Marriott Corp., Washington, 1971-75; chief dietetic services Hadley Hosp., Washington, 1975—. Recipient Winston-Salem Dietetic Assn. award, 1965. Mem. Am., D.C. dietetic assns., Am. Soc. for Hosp. Food Service Adminstrn., Nutrition Today Soc., Soc. for Nutrition Edn. Baptist. Office: 4601 ML King Jr Ave SW Washington DC 20032

JEGHERS, HAROLD JOSEPH, physician; b. Jersey City, Sept. 26, 1904; s. Albert and Matilda (Gerckens) J.; B.S., Rensselaer Poly. Inst., 1928; M.D., Western Res. U., 1932; D.Sc. (hon.) Georgetown U., 1975, Coll. Medicine and Dentistry N.J., 1976; m. Isabel J. Wile, June 21, 1935; children—Harold, Dee, Sanderson, Theodore. Intern Boston City Hosp., 1933-34, resident, 1935-37, physician-in-chief 5th Med. Service, 1943-46, now hon. physician; instr. to asso. prof. medicine Boston U. Sch. Medicine, 1935-46; prof. and dir. dept. medicine Georgetown U. Sch. Medicine, 1946-56; prof., dir. dept. medicine N.J. Coll. Medicine and Dentistry, Jersey City, 1956-66, emeritus, 1966—; med. dir. St. Vincent Hosp., Worcester, Mass., 1966-78; prof. Tufts U., 1966-74; dir. med. ward service Jersey City Med. Center, 1958-66; dir. Tufts med. service Boston City Hosp., 1969-71; cons. med. edn. Cleve. Health Scis. Library, Cleve. Med. Library Assn.; prof. med. edn., office med. edn. research and curriculum devel. Northeastern Ohio Univs. Coll. Medicine, 1977—; cons. med. edn. St. Elizabeth Hosp. Med. Center, Youngstown, 1977—; cons. internal medicine Georgetown U. Hosp. Rep. from A.C.P. to div. med. scis. NRC, 1950-53. Recipient Laetare award Guild of St. Luke, Boston, 1958; Alumni award Case Western Res. U. Med. Alumni Assn., 1974. Fellow A.C.P., Am. Soc. Clin. Investigation; mem. AMA, Am. Fedn. Clin. Research, So. Soc. Clin. Research (v.p. 1948-49), Assn. Am. Physicians, Mass. Med. Soc., Sigma Xi. Contbr. articles and sects. in books. Home: 17 Carolina Trail Marshfield MA 02050 Office: 25 Winthrop St Worcester MA 01604

JEHU, JOHN PAUL, lawyer; b. N.Y.C., Oct. 17, 1908; s. John Milton and Pauline (Burger) J.; Dr. Roman and Canon Law, univs. Munich, Leipzig and Erlangen; LL.B., Cornell U., 1937; m. Virginia Linder Corones, May 1, 1974; children—Susan Jehu Kessler, Lynn Jehu Amadon. Admitted to N.Y. State bar, 1939; asso. firm Sherry & Picarello, 1938-40; mem. contract div. Mergenthaler Linotype Co., 1937-41; research counsel Temporary Commn. for Revision and Codification of Laws Relating to Municipal Finance, 1941-43; asst., then asso. counsel charge recodification edn. law Joint Legis. Com. on N.Y. State Edn. System, 1945-47; sr. atty., dir. law div. N.Y. State Edn. Dept., 1947-68, asso. counsel, 1968-76; practice law, Albany, N.Y., 1976—; part-time asso. prof. ednl. adminstrn. State U. N.Y. at Albany, 1960-76; spl. counsel for reorgn. sch. system V.I. Bd. Edn., 1967, Center Sq. Assn., 1977; spl. counsel St. David's Soc. State N.Y., 1978—, pres. Capitol dist. Served as officer U.S. Army, World War II. Mem. N.Y. State Bar Assn., Cornell Law Assn. Presbyterian. Clubs: Cordial Greens Country, University. Home and Office: 49 Dove St Albany NY 12210

JELINEK, JOSEF EMIL, dermatologist; b. Prague, Czechoslovakia, Feb. 12, 1928; s. Frank and Olga (Frankl) J.; came to U.S., 1958, naturalized, 1964; M.B., B.S., U. London, 1951; postgrad. U. London Postgrad. Sch., 1956, N.Y.U., 1963-78; m. Vera Adrienne Schnitzer, June 19, 1960; children—David Frank, Paul William. Intern, house surgeon in orthopedics St. Mary's Hosp., London, 1951-52; house physician in internal medicine Harold Wood Hosp., Essex, Eng., 1952, Princess Beatrice Hosp., London, 1955; registrar internal medicine Royal Victoria Hosp., Bournemouth, Eng., 1955-57, Dulwich Hosp., London, 1957-58; precepteeship in dermatology with Norman B. Kanof, N.Y.C., 1961-62; chief resident dermatology Bellevue Hosp., N.Y.C., 1962-63; chief resident Univ. Hosp., N.Y.C., 1963; cons. VA Hosp., N.Y.C., 1965-78; asst. attending physician Bellevue Hosp., N.Y.C., 1965-78; attending physician Univ. Hosp., N.Y.C., 1976-78; clin. prof. dermatology N.Y.U. Sch. Medicine, N.Y.C., 1976-78; practice medicine specializing in dermatology, N.Y.C., 1963—; cons. AMA Council on Drugs and the Dept. of Drugs, 1972. Served to lt. RAF, 1952-54. Diplomate Am. Bd. Dermatology. Fellow ACP, Am. Acad. Dermatology; mem. Atlantic Dermatologic Conf. (past chmn.), Dermatologic Soc. Greater N.Y. (pres.), N.Y. Acad. Medicine (past chmn.), Manhattan Dermatol. Soc. (past pres.). Contbr. articles in field to profl. jours., also chpts. to textbooks. Office: 15 W 12th St New York City NY 10011

JENDRAS, HENRY JOHN, exec.; b. Bklyn., July 21, 1940; s. Stanley and Mary (Czujak) J.; B.B.A., Pace Coll., 1968; postgrad. Columbia, 1970; m. Joan Hearn, Sept. 4, 1961; children—Kevin, Brian, Douglas, Jeannine, Kerri. Accountant, Home Ins. Co., N.Y.C., 1959-61; group supr. sales analysis A.C. Nielsen Co., N.Y.C., 1963-65, sr. analyst, 1962-63, jr. analyst, 1961-62; sr. sales research analyst The Nestle Co., White Plains, N.Y., 1965-66, supr. sales research, 1966-67, supr. chocolate div. research, 1967-68, mgr. coffee div. research, 1968-69, mgr. marketing research dept., 1969—. Mem. Mahopac Falls (N.Y.) Vol. Fire Dept., 1967—, treas., 1972, 74, pres., 1974, 76, mem. long range planning com., 1976—; asst. cub master Boy Scouts Am., Mahopac Falls, N.Y., 1971-74, mem. com., 1971—; baseball commr. Mahopac Sports Assn., 1971—. Mem. Am. Mktg. Assn., Assn. Nat. Advertisers, Assn. for Advancement of Pub. Opinion Research, Assn. for Consumer Research, Nat. Coffee Assn. (research adv. com. 1969—), Mktg. Research Council. Clubs: Red Mills Beach (treas. 1974-78), Secor Sports (membership chmn. 1974—, v.p. 1977—). Home: Red Mills Rd RD 3 Mahopac NY 10541 Office: 100 Bloomingdale Rd White Plains NY 10605

JENKINS, GEORGE POLLOCK, ins. co. exec.; b. Clarksburg, W.Va., Feb. 24, 1915; s. Roy N. and Gertrude S. (Pollock) J.; grad. Blair Acad., 1932; A.B., Princeton, 1936; M.B.A., Harvard, 1938; m. Marian E. O'Brien, Apr. 10, 1945; children—James P., Robert N., Richard G. With Met. Life Ins. Co., N.Y.C., 1938—, v.p., 1956-62, financial v.p., 1962-65, chmn. finance com., 1965—, vice chmn., 1969-73; chmn. bd., 1973—; dir. St. Regis Paper Co., Citibank, ABC, W.R. Grace & Co., Bethlehem Steel Corp. Trustee Blair Acad., Blairstown, N.J., U. So. Calif. Served to capt. AUS, 1942-46. Mem. Phi Beta Kappa. Clubs: Links (N.Y.C.); Baltusrol Golf (Springfield, N.J.); Laurel Valley Golf (Ligonier, Pa.). Office: 1 Madison Ave New York City NY 10010

JENKINS, HARRY ALEXANDER, food mgmt. service exec.; b. Ridgewood, N.J., May 6, 1932; s. George W. and Harriett (Bender) J.; B.S., Lehigh U., 1953; 1 son, Joseph. Sr. accountant Price Waterhouse & Co., N.Y.C., 1953-61; mgr. corp. taxes and ins.

Warnarco, Inc., Bridgeport, Conn., 1961-65; controller Sure Fit Products Co., Bethlehem, Pa., 1965-70; treas., asst. sec., Kleinert's Inc., Kutztown, Pa., 1971-77; controller M.W. Wood Enterprises, Inc., Allentown, Pa., 1978—; treas. Pyramid Food Mgmt. Services, Inc., Allentown, 1978—. Mem. Am. Inst. C.P.A.'s, Pi Kappa Alpha. Club: Bethlehem. Home: 2832 W Emans Ave Allentown PA 18103 Office: 3320 Hamilton Blvd Allentown PA 18103

JENKINS, JOHN BURR, mgmt. cons.; b. Carbondale, Pa., Dec. 15, 1911; s. Joseph Burnell and Natalie (Burr) J.; A.B., Cornell U., 1934; m. Margaret Barker Boisen, Jan. 18, 1947. In retailing Bloomingdale's, 1935-38; mem. sales staff Talon, Inc., 1939-41, Linde div. Union Carbide, 1941-44; sales mgr. Emory Thompson Machine Co., 1944-45; sales staff Tabin-Picker Co., 1945-49; mem. advt. sales staff Motor Boating mag., 1949-51; mem. advt. sales staff, Saturday Evening Post mag., 1951-54, asst. mgr. N.Y. office, 1955-57, asso. mgr., 1957-60; nat. sales mgr., Naegele Advt. Cos., 1960-61, v.p., dir., 1961-65; v.p., dir. Bolte Advt. Co., N.Y.C., 1965-67; marketing mgr. Good Housekeeping mag., 1967-70; dir. corporate relations Campusamp, Inc., N.Y.C., 1970; marketing mgr. Woman's Day mag., 1970-76; mktg. cons., 1977—. Mem. Pelhamwood Assn. (pres. 1968-69), Delta Kappa Epsilon. Clubs: N.Y. Yacht (N.Y.C.); Pelham (N.Y.) Country (gov. 1972-76); Huguenot Yacht (commodore 1955-57) (New Rochelle, N.Y.); Eastward Ho Country, Monomoy Yacht (Chatham, Mass.). Home: 41 Palmer Dr Chatman MA 02633

JENKINS, KENNETH VINCENT, educator, author; b. Elizabeth, N.J.; s. Thomas Augustus and Rebecca Meredith (Williams) J.; A.B., Columbia, 1952, A.M., 1953, postgrad., 1965; m. Elizabeth A. Hunte, Oct. 16, 1954; children—Roderick, Howard, Rebecca, Leah, Roland. Tchr., South Side Sr. High Sch., Rockville Centre, N.Y., 1953-72, chmn. dept. English, 1965-72; prof. Afro-Am. lit. Nassau Community Coll., Garden City, N.Y., 1972—, chmn. Afro-Am. studies dept., 1975—, supr. adj. faculty, 1974—. Cons. in English, N.Y. State Dept. Edn., Albany, 1965-72; mem. Regents Question Com. in English, Albany, 1966-71. Chmn. bd. dirs., founder Target Youth Centers, Inc., 1973-76; mem. nat. bd. Pacifica Found., 1973-79, chmn., 1975-76, pres., 1976-78; bd. dirs. Nassau County Youth Bd. Pennington grantee, 1953. Mem. N.Y. State United Tchrs., Afro-Am. Inst., Assn. Study of Afro-Am. Life and History, Unitarian Black Caucus, Phi Delta Kappa. Author: Last Day in Church, 1955; Teaching of African Literature, 1960. Contbr. revs., poems to profl. publs. Home: Freeport NY 11520 Office: Nassau Community College Garden City NY 11530

JENKINS, MAC DEAN, lawyer; b. Salisbury, Md., June 14, 1945; s. Mac Banks and Olevia Irene (Hastings) J.; B.A., U. Md., 1967; J.D., Georgetown U., 1970. Admitted to Md. bar, 1970; pvt. practice, 1971-73; partner firm Ayres, Jenkins & Gordy, Ocean City, Md., 1973—; sec. Madison Devel. Corp.; chmn. Com. to Study Alcoholic Beverage Laws of Worcester County, Md., 1976—. Mem. Md., Worcester County bar assns., Phi Beta Kappa. Democrat. Methodist. Club: Ocean City Golf and Yacht. Home: 9 Baltimore Ave Ocean City MD 21842 Office: 4100 Coastal Hwy Ocean City MD 21842

JENKINS, MARTIN EDWARD, personnel exec.; b. Ithaca, N.Y., Dec. 28, 1921; s. Clinton Bartram and Elizabeth Marie; B.A. in Economics and Psychology, Duke U., 1949; m. Mary Wise Rixey, Oct. 3, 1963; children—Jeffrey, Martin, Douglas, Elizabeth. With labor relations dept. Philco Corp., Phila., 1949-53; compensation specialist Johnson & Johnson New Brunswick, N.J., 1953-55; personnel specialist, Burroughs Corp., Paoli, Pa., 1956-58, Link Aviation, Binghamton, N.Y., 1958-63; dir. personnel SCOA, Columbus, Ohio, 1966-70, Delaware River Port Authority, Camden, N.J., 1970—; cons. major corps., 1963-65. Served with USAAF, 1942-45. Mem. Am. Soc. for Personnel Adminstrn., Adminstrv. Mgmt. Soc., Nat. Hist. Soc. Republican. Episcopalian. Clubs: Union League of Phila., Phila. Skating and Humane Soc. Home: 529 Spring Mill Rd Villanova PA 19085 Office: Bridge Plaza Camden NJ 08101

JENKINS, PAUL REIBER, lawyer, found. exec.; b. Pitts., Apr. 14, 1932; s. Paul Whistler and Mary Elizabeth (Reiber) J.; A.B., Princeton, 1954; LL.B., U. Mich., 1957; m. Alice Jane Davis, Sept. 8, 1956; children—Paul Davis, Edward Reiber, Walter Ford. Admitted to Pa. bar, 1957; asso. firm Campbell, Thomas & Burke, Pitts., 1958-63, partner, 1963-70; exec. v.p., treas., trustee Claude Worthington Benedum Found., Pitts., 1970—. Mem. adv. council Jr. League Pitts.; vice chmn. bd. trustees Shady Side Acad.; v.p., bd. dirs. George Hogg Med. Found.; bd. dirs. Pitts. History and Landmarks Found., Nat. Meth. Found.; pres. bd. trustees 1st United Methodist Ch. Pitts.; bd. trustees, finance com. Meth. Ch. Union Western Pa. Conf. Mem. Am., Pa., Allegheny County bar assns. Office: 1400 Benedum-Trees Bldg Pittsburgh PA 15222

JENKINS, RUTH ELIZABETH, investment counselor; b. Bethlehem, Pa.; d. Thomas and Mary (Weiser) Jenkins; A.B. cum laude, Radcliffe Coll. 1947. Vice pres., investment counselor Loomis, Sayles & Co., Inc., 1951—. Bd. dirs. Phila. Presbytery Homes; bd. pensions United Presbyn. Ch., Phila. Presbyn. Found. Mem. Financial Analysts Phila. (past sec., dir.), Nat. Soc. Colonial Dames Am., D.A.R. Clubs: Acorn; Waynesborough Country; Merion Cricket. Home: Ardglen Gardens 16 W Montgomery Ave Ardmore PA 19003 Office: United Engrs Bldg 30 S 17th St Philadelphia PA 19103

JENNINGS, ALICE THELMA, sch. prin.; b. Phila., Sept. 4, 1932; d. John and Amanda (Wilson) Upshaw; B.S., M.S., Temple U.; postgrad. U. Pa., 1967-70, Temple U., 1967-70; m. Clifton Jennings, June 28, 1953; children—Clifton, Bruce. Tchr., pub. schs., Phila., now prin. Bd. dirs. Edwin Luther Cunningham Community House. Mem. Women in Edn., Prins. Research and Info. Center, Pa. Assn. Sch. Adminstrs. Methodist. Clubs: Women's Duplicate Bridge, Central Bridge. Office: Mary Channing Wister Sch 8th and Parrish Sts Philadelphia PA 19123

JENNINGS, DONALD E., psychologist; b. Chattanooga, July 2, 1939; s. James Robert and Nell (Erb) J.; B.S., Livingston U., 1964; M.Ed., U. Tenn., 1968; postgrad. Temple U., 1968-70; D.Ed., U. Pa., 1977; m. Nancy Sue Sells, Feb. 18, 1965; children—Nicole, Beth, Susan. Psychologist, Moccasin Bend Psychiat. Hosp., 1965; psychiat. counselor Bur. Vocat. Rehab., Chattanooga, 1965-66; dir. rehab. unit Bur. Vocat. Rehab., Pa. Hosp., Phila., 1966-67; pvt. practice psychology, Phila., 1967—; v.p. Ednl. and Vocat. Guidance Cons., Inc., Phila., 19—. Pres. exec. bd. Unitarian Ch. So. N.J.; mem. exec. bd. Big Bros. Assn., Camden County, N.J. Served with USMC, 1957-60. Mem. Am., N.J., Pa., Camden County psychol. assns., Pa., Am. personnel and guidance assns., Am. Assn. Advancement Psychology, Nat., Pa. rehab. assns., Orthopsychiat. Assn. Am., AAAS. Contbr. articles to profl. jours. Home: 1803 Bergen St Philadelphia PA 19152 Office: 8001 Roosevelt Blvd Philadelphia PA 19152

JENNINGS, FRANK GOUVERNEUR, mech. engr.; b. N.Y.C., May 21, 1913; s. Frank Aloysius and Margaret (Madden) J.; M.E., Stevens Inst. Tech., 1934; M.M.E., N.Y.U., 1941; postgrad. Indsl. Coll. Armed Forces, 1969; m. Ethel Kathleen Richards, Nov. 24, 1937; children—Frank, Judith. Project engr., Hercules, Inc., Parlin, N.J., 1940-45, Ebasco Services, Inc., N.Y.C., 1946-60; plant engr. Royce Chem. Co., Carlton Hill, N.J., 1945-46; project mgr. Walter Kidde Constructors, Inc., N.Y.C., 1960-74, Processes Research, Inc., N.Y.C., 1974-76, Inmont Corp., Hawthorne, N.J., 1976—. Mem. Mantoloking (N.J.) Bd. Adjustments, 1974-77. Registered profl. engr., Ala., Calif., Conn., Del., D.C., Fla., Ga., Idaho, Ill., Ind., Ky., Maine, Md., Mass., Mich., N.H., N.J., N.Y., Ohio, Pa., R.I., S.C., Vt., Va., Wis. Roman Catholic. Home: 1530 Ocean Ave PO Box 299 Mantoloking NJ 08738 Office: care Inmont Corp 607 Lafayette Ave Hawthorne NJ 07506

JENNINGS, MARLENE HELEN LUKE, food service co. exec.; b. Bradford, Pa., Dec. 11, 1942; d. John Eugene and Helen Katherine Luke; Asso. Applied Sci., Bryant and Stratton Bus. Inst., Buffalo, 1979; student State U. N.Y., Buffalo and Am. Mgmt. Assn., 1976. Asst. to v.p. mktg. Programming and Systems Inst., Tonawanda, N.Y., 1971-73; exec. asst. to U.S. Congressman Richard Max McCarthy, Washington, 1965-71; mgr. personnel adminstrn. Service Systems Corp., Buffalo, 1973-75, Sportservice Corp., Buffalo, 1975—. Mem. Democratic Com., Town of Amherst (N.Y.), 1971-73, 73-75; co. rep. United Way, 1975—. Mem. Am. Soc. Personnel Adminstrn., Indsl. Relations Assn. Western N.Y. Roman Catholic. Home: 154 Tampa Dr Buffalo NY 14220 Office: 700 Delaware Ave Buffalo NY 14209

JENNINGS, MICHAEL GLENN, author; b. Buena Vista, Va., Apr. 17, 1931; s. Glen Edward and Vaughnye Mae (Bays) J.; student Va. and N.J. schs.; m. Susan Berger, Oct. 25, 1975; children by previous marriage—Marc Emery, Jason Glenn, Dana Michael. Advt. copywriter, 1948-51; promotion copywriter Louisville Courier-Jour., 1955-56; disc jockey Sta. WKLO, Louisville, 1955-56; house organs editor Home Life Ins. Co., N.Y.C., 1956-58; creative dir. Burke, Charles & Guignon, Ltd., Great Neck, N.Y., 1958-61; pres. Michael Jennings & Colleagues, Williston Park, N.Y., 1961-64; producer, host radio program Michael Jennings' Kaleidoscope, Sta. WLIR, L.I., 1964-65; advt. mgr. Aeolian Pianos, Inc., 1965-68; promotion mgr. G.P. Putnam Sons, pubs., 1968-69; author: (novel) There Was a Young Lady From Windmere, 1973; (children's novels) Mattie Fritts and the Flying Mushroom, 1973, Mattie Fritts and the Cuckoo Caper, 1976, The Bears Who Came to Breakfix, 1977; (young adult non-fiction) Tape Recorder Fun: Be Your Own Favorite Disc Jockey, 1978. Actor, chmn. coms., dir. Antrim Players, Suffern, N.Y., 1975—; narrator Island Lyric Opera, Garden City, N.Y., 1978—. Served with USAF, 1951-55. Mem. Authors Guild. Address: Rockland County NY

JENNINGS, ROBERT LEE, aircraft maintenance exec.; b. N.Y.C., May 6, 1946; s. Leo William and Ruth Helen (Fehrenbach) J.; grad. Teterboro (N.J.) Sch. Aeros., 1971; m. Francine Marie DiPietro, May 30, 1976. Line serviceman Atlantic Aviation Corp., Teterboro, 1970-74; instr. Teterboro Sch. Aeros., 1972-73; supr. aircraft maintenance Dart Industries Inc., Teterboro, 1974—; pres., chief exec. officer Big A Flying Club, Inc., 1974—. Served with USN, 1964-69; Vietnam. Mem. Profl. Aircraft Maintenance Assn., Nat. Bus. Aircraft Assn. Republican. Roman Catholic. Home: RD 6 Box 416 Newton NJ 07860 Office: 121A Billy Diehl Rd Teterboro NJ 07608

JENNINGS, WILLIAM MITCHELL, lawyer; b. N.Y.C., Dec. 14, 1920; s. Harry B. and Nettie I. (Mitchell) J.; A.B., Princeton U., 1941; J.D., Yale U., 1943; m. Elizabeth Hite, Oct. 16, 1943; children—William Mitchell, Jeffrey H., Eunice M., Elizabeth B., Priscilla H. Law clk. to judge U.S. Circuit Ct. Appeals for 2d Circuit, N.Y.C., 1943-44; admitted to N.Y. bar, 1945; practiced in N.Y.C., 1944—; asso. firm Simpson Thacher & Bartlett, 1944-51, partner, 1952—; pres., dir. N.Y. Rangers, Inc.; adv. dir. Madison Sq. Garden Corp.; dir. Suburban Propane Gas Corp., Lee Nat. Corp., Warnaco Inc., Warnaco Can., Ltd. Gen. chmn. Thunderbird Golf Classic, 1963-65; founder, gen. chmn. Westchester Golf Classic, 1967—; mem. nat. adv. com. Profl. Golfers Assn. Am., Inst. Sports Medicine and Athletic Trauma; bd. govs. NHL, 1962—, chmn. bd. govs., 1968-70; pres. United Hosp., Port Chester, N.Y., 1959-69, chmn., 1969-74, hon. chmn., 1974—; trustee Rye (N.Y.) Presbyterian Ch. Recipient Lester Patrick trophy NHL, 1971; Distinguished Service award Met. Golf Writers Assn., 1975, Gold Tee award, 1977; elected to Hockey Hall of Fame, Toronto, 1975, Westchester Sports Hall of Fame, 1979. Mem. N.Y. State Bar Assn., N.Y.C. Bar Assn. Clubs: Apawamis (Rye); Country of N.C. (Pinehurst); Links, Downtown Assn., Madison Sq. Garden (N.Y.C.); Blind Brook (Port Chester, N.Y.). Office: 350 Park Ave New York NY 10022

JENNISON, GEORGE L., financial cons.; b. New Glasgow, N.S., Can., June 19, 1906; s. John Leslie and Florence (Des Barres) J.; student U. Toronto, 1923-25; m. Frances McPherson Playfair, Oct. 12, 1929; children—Joan (Mrs. Robert Wright), Elizabeth (Mrs. Wilson McLean). Chmn. Wills, Bickle & Co. Ltd., until 1968, financial cons., 1968—, dir. Teck Corp., G. & J. Plantations, Inc., Tampax, Inc., Can. Permanent Mortgage Corp. Gov., Toronto Stock Exchange 1947-56, Chmn. bd. govs., 1953-55. Dir. priorities br. Dept. Munitions and Supply, 1941-45. Bd. dirs. Can. Permanent Trust Co. Mem. Toronto Bd. Trade, Delta Kappa Epsilon. Mem. Anglican Ch. Clubs: Toronto, Toronto Golf, Canadian, Rosedale Golf, York; St. Andrews (Delray Beach, Fla.). Home: 243 Warren Rd Toronto ON M4V 2S7 Canada Office: care AE Osler Wills Bickle Ltd PO Box 60 Royal Bank Plaza Toronto-Dominion Centre Toronto ON M5J 2K6 Canada

JENNY, ALBERT, ednl. researcher; b. Phila., Apr. 7, 1918; s. Benno and Viola (Jenny) J.; B.A., U. Pa., 1940, M.A. in Linguistics, 1959, postgrad., 1959-61; postgrad. Am. U., 1965—; m. Elizabeth Park, June 19, 1951; children—Albert, Elizabeth Viola, Margaret Melinda, Barbara Alice. Research analytic specialist fgn. affairs Dept. Def., Washington, 1947-51; communications officer Dept. State, Nicosia, Cyprus, 1951-54; gen. mgr., dir. Internat. Translators, Inc., Phila., 1954-56; systems analyst Remington-Rand Univac, Blue Bell, Pa., 1956-62; program designer Gen. Electric Info. Systems, Bethesda, Md., 1962-64; research scientist Human Scis. Research, Inc., McLean, Va., 1964-68; research asso. Central Atlantic Regional Ednl. Lab., Washington, 1968-69; coordinator data systems div. statis. services dept. ednl. accountability Montgomery County (Md.) Pub. Schs., 1969—. Served with AUS, 1944-46; PTO. Democrat. Unitarian. Home: 12263 St James Rd Potomac MD 20854 Office: Ednl Services Bldg 850 Hungerford Dr Rockville MD 20850

JENNY, ROBERT JAMES, civil engr.; b. Irvington, N.J., Feb. 20, 1932; s. Adam John and Nina Beatrice (Oder) J.; B.C.E., Newark Coll. Engring., 1960, M.S. in C.E., 1963; m. Marcelline Delores Acosta, Aug. 31, 1958; children—Matthew John, Barbara Rita. Land surveyor Lehlbach Bros., Newark, 1949-52, Borrie & McDonald, Newark, 1955-57, R.J. Jenny & Assos., Newark, 1957-60; field engr. P.S. Miller & Assos., West Orange, N.J., 1954-55; soils and foundations engr. F.H. Lehr Assos., Newark, 1960-61; project design and constrn. engr. Perini Corp., Framingham, Mass., 1961-65, Morrison-Knudsen Co. Inc., Boise, Idaho, 1961-65; pres. Jenny Engring. Corp., South Orange, N.J., 1965—; tunnel and underground structure engring. cons. Served with U.S. Army, 1952-54; Korea. Recipient Engring. Excellence honor award Cons. Engrs. Council N.J., 1972; licensed profl. engr., land surveyor, profl. planner, Washington, N.J., also 17 other states. Mem. ASCE, Nat. Soc. Profl. Engrs., Brit. Tunneling Soc., N.J. Inst. Tech. Alumni Assn., Am. Underground Space Assn., Moles. Author: (with Thomas Adair and Robert S. Mayo) Tunneling, The State of the Art, 1968; (with Robert S. Mayo and James E. Barrett) Tunneling, The State of the Industry, 1976. Home: 412 Vose Ave South Orange NJ 07079 Office: 318 S Orange Ave South Orange NJ 07079

JENSEN, ARTHUR S(EIGFRIED), research physicist; b. Trenton, N.J., Dec. 24, 1917; s. Emil A. and Emma A. (Lund) J.; B.S., U. Pa., 1938, M.S., 1939, Ph.D., 1941; diploma advanced engring. sci. Westinghouse Sch. Engring. Sci., 1972, diploma computer sci., 1977; m. Lillian Elizabeth Reed, Aug. 9, 1941; children—Alan F. and Deane E. (twins), Nancy Lorraine Jensen. Research fellow in physics, U. Pa., 1939-41; research physicist Naval Research Lab., Washington, 1941; research physicist David Sarnoff Research Center, RCA Labs. Div., Princeton, N.J., 1945-57; mgr. spl. electron devices of Westinghouse Electric Corp., in Electronic Tube Div., Applied Research Dept., Balt., 1957-65, sr. adv. physicist Westinghouse Def. and Electronic Systems Center, Balt., 1965—. Served as lt. comdr., USNR, 1941-45; instr. physics Naval Acad.; now capt. USNR ret.; comdg. officer USNR Research Co. 5-4, 1961-62. Recipient Westinghouse Patent award, 1965, 1977, Spl. Corporate Patent award, 1972; Outstanding Paper award Soc. Info. Display, 1975. Registered profl. engr., Md. Fellow IEEE, Washington Acad. Scis.; mem. U.S. Naval Inst., Am. Phys. Soc., Am. Assn. Physics Tchrs., Res. Officers Assn., Ret. Officers Assn. (life), AAAS (life), Md., N.Y. acads. sci., Optical Soc. Am., Engring. Soc. Balt., Sigma Xi, Pi Mu Epsilon, Kappa Phi Kappa. Home: 5602 Purlington Way Baltimore MD 21212 Office: Westinghouse Defense and Electronic Systems Center Baltimore MD 21203

JENSEN, BETTY, physicist; b. Lodz, Poland, June 20, 1949; d. Sam and Gussie (Alter) Klainminc; came to U.S., 1962, naturalized, 1968; B.S. summa cum Laude in Math., Bklyn. Coll., 1970; M.A. in Physics, Columbia U., 1972, M.Phil., 1973, Ph.D., 1976; m. Richard Alan Jensen, Dec. 19, 1971. Grad. research asst. recitation instr. Columbia U., 1970-76; sr. physicist research Pub. Service Electric and Gas Co., 1976—; adj. lectr. Richmond Coll., S.I., N.Y., 1973-76, N.Y.C. Community Coll., Bklyn., 1973-76; tutor for profl. sch. entrance exams Kaplan Tutoring Sch., Bklyn., 1970. Mem. Am. Jewish Com. Recipient Math. prize Bklyn. Coll., 1968. N.Y. State Regents scholar, 1967-70; NSF grad. asst., 1970-72. Mem. Am. Phys. Soc., Ams. for Energy Independence, Assn. Women in Sci., Am. Nuclear Soc., IEEE, Phi Beta Kappa, Sigma Xi. Jewish. Home: 630 Armstrong Ave Staten Island NY 10308 Office: Pub Service Electric and Gas Co 80 Park Pl Newark NJ 07101

JENSEN, DAVID LYNN, mathematician; b. Brigham City, Utah, Sept. 8, 1941; s. Jacob Lynn and Florence (Tanner) J.; B.S., Utah State U., 1964, M.S., 1972; m. Marva Myler, June 21, 1963. Lab. technician Thiokol Chem. Corp., Brigham City, 1961-64; computer programmer Utah State U. Computer Center, Logan, 1964-65; mathematician, computer programmer USAF Logistics Command, Hill AFB, Utah, 1965-68; instr. data processing Weber State Coll., Ogden, Utah, 1968-69; data analyst Reentry and Environ. Systems Div., Gen. Electric Co., Hill AFB, 1969-71; mathematician Advanced Tech. Center, Calspan Corp., Buffalo, 1972—; asso. vis. faculty mem. Lincoln Inst. Land Policy, Cambridge, Mass., 1977—. Program chmn. exploring com. Lake Bonneville council Boy Scouts Am., Ogden, 1969-71, program chmn. exploring com. Bird Haven Dist., 1969-71, tng. chmn. exploring com. Greater Niagara Frontier council, Buffalo, 1973-76, recipient Scouters Tng. award, 1971. Mem. Am. Statis. Assn. Mem. Ch. of Jesus Christ of Latter-day Saints. Home: 40 Nancy Ln North Tonawanda NY 14120 Office: Dept 75 Advanced Tech Center Calspan Corp 4455 Genesee St Buffalo NY 14225

JENSEN, GRADY EDMONDS, apparel mfg. co. exec.; b. Pitts., Nov. 8, 1922; s. Claude Henry and Margaret (Edmonds) J.; B.A., Hobart Coll., 1943; M.B.A., U. Pa., 1949; certificate Stonier Sch. Banking, Rutgers U., 1967; m. Mary Margaret Wilber, July 5, 1952; children—Timothy Sage, Margaret Eliza, Caroline Grosvenor. Asst. to asst. treas. U. Pa., Phila., 1949-50; staff engr. Cresap, McCormick & Paget, mgmt. consultants, N.Y.C., 1950-55; bus. mgr. Sta. WABC-TV, N.Y.C., 1955-56; asso. bus. mgr. N.Y. U., N.Y.C., 1956-61; asst. budget dir. Eastern Air Lines, Inc., N.Y.C., 1961-62; asst. to v.p. bus. and finance Columbia, N.Y.C., 1962-63; 2d v.p. internat. dept. Chase Manhattan Bank, 1963-70; dir. orgn. and mgmt. devel. Am. Express Co., N.Y.C., 1970-74; v.p. adminstrn., sec. The Harwood Cos., Inc., N.Y.C., 1974—. Mem. Scarsdale (N.Y.) Village Bd. Trustees, Scarsdale Police Commn. Served with USNR, 1943-45. Mem. Guild of Book Workers (dir.), Am. Soc. Corporate Secs., Am. Revolution Round Table of N.Y., Naval Aviation Commandery, Cross and Cockade, Westchester County, Scarsdale hist. socs., S.A.R., Soc. Mayflower Descs., Pilgrim Soc., New Eng. Hist. Geneal. Soc., N.Y. Geneal. and Biog. Soc. Clubs: Town (past pres.) (Scarsdale); Hobart (N.Y.) (past pres.); U. Pa., Grolier, Wings (N.Y.C.). Home: 16 Ridgecrest W Scarsdale NY 10583 Office: 666 Fifth Ave New York City NY 10019

JENSEN, J. MICHAEL, life ins. co. exec.; b. Phila., Apr. 6, 1948; s. Hugh Francis and Dolores Teresa (Callahan) J.; B.A., Allentown Coll., 1971; postgrad. Temple U. Tchr., Phila. Pub. Schs., 1972-73; ins. agt. Penn Mut. Life Ins. Co., 1973-77; estate planner, office mgr. Physicians Planning Service, Cherry Hill, N.J., 1977—; cons. profl. corps. Mem. alumni bd. dirs. St. Joseph's Prep. Sch., Phila., 1971—; Republican committeeman, Phila., 1971-73. Mem. Million Dollar Round Table, 1974, 78. Mem. Nat. Assn. Life Underwriters, Life Underwriters Polit. Action Com., Am. Mgmt. Assn., Lehigh Valley, Phila. estate planning councils. Roman Catholic. Home: 208 Winthrop Ave Lindenwold NJ 08021 Office: 2 Executive Campus Suite 300 Cherry Hill NJ 08002

JENSEN, RICHARD ALAN, mech. engr.; b. Hagerstown, Md., May 1, 1944; s. Jens and Pearl Betty (Weismann) J.; B.Engring., Cooper Union, 1966; M.S. (scholar), Columbia U., 1967, D.Engring. Sci., 1974; m. Betty Klainminc, Dec. 19, 1971. Research asst. Columbia U., N.Y.C., 1968-70; adj. instr. dept. pure and applied scis. Richmond Coll., S.I., N.Y., 1970-73; mech. engr. Burns & Roe, Inc., Woodbury, N.Y., 1973—. Registered profl. engr. Mem. ASME, AAAS, Am. Phys. Soc. Author: Dislocation Scattering of a Shear Wave in a Crystal Model, 1974. Home: 630 Armstrong Ave Staten Island NY 10308 Office: 185 Crossways Park Dr Woodbury NY 11797

JENSEN, ROBERT P., metals mfg. co. exec.; b. Chgo., Dec. 29, 1925; s. Louis P. and Ellen (Goede) J.; B.S. in Mech. Engring., Iowa State Coll. at Ames, 1947; postgrad. U. Mich., 1953-54; grad. advanced mgmt. program Harvard, 1965; m. Donna M. Seaberg, Nov. 1, 1950; children—Erik P., Curtis R. Salesman, br. and dist. mgr., gen. sales mgr., ops. mgr. Kaiser Aluminum & Chem. Sales, Inc., 1954-61, gen. mgr. bldg. products div., 1963-66, dir. bus. planning aluminum div., 1967; exec. v.p., gen. mgr. Olin Foil Packaging Corp. subs. Olin Mathieson Chem. Corp., 1961-63; v.p. aluminum group Howmet Corp., N.Y.C., 1967-68, exec. v.p. Howmet Corp., 1968-70, chief operating officer, dir., 1970, pres., chief exec. officer, 1971-72; pres., chief exec. officer, dir. Gen. Cable Corp., Greenwich, Conn., 1973—, chmn. bd., 1978—; chmn. Automation Industries, Inc.; dir. Charter N.Y. Corp., Phillips Cables Ltd., Mostek Corp., State Nat. Bancorp, Continental Oil Co., Sprague Electric Co. Trustee Council of Ams.,

Stamford Hosp.; mem. corp. Greenwich Hosp. Assn.; bd. dirs. Greenwich Boys Club Assn., Nat. Multiple Sclerosis Soc. Served to lt. (j.g.) USN, 1944-46. Mem. Aluminum Assn. (chmn.'s adv. council), U.S. Power Squadron. Clubs: Westchester Country (Rye, N.Y.); Union League, Economic, Board Room (N.Y.C.); Captiol Hill (Washington); Indian Harbor Yacht, Greenwich Country (Greenwich); Landmark (Stamford). Home: POB 956 Greenwich CT 06830 Office: 500 W Putnam Ave Greenwich CT 06830

JENSEN, ROY JOSEPH, JR., restaurant exec.; b. Princeton, N.J., Aug. 7, 1951; s. Roy Peter and Mary Anna (DiBiose) J.; student Jones Coll., Jacksonville, Fla., 1969-71; m. Marilyn Strong, Feb. 26, 1977; children by previous marriage—Maureen, Chuck. With Moms Drive In Inc., 1969—, mgr., Hightstown, N.J., 1972—. Mem. Am. Mgmt. Assn., N.J. Jaycees. Roman Catholic. Home: 1 Little Brook Ln Jamesburg NJ 08831 Office: Moms Drive In Route 130 Hightstown NJ 08520

JENSH, RONALD PAUL, anatomist, educator; b. N.Y.C., June 14, 1938; s. Werner G. and Dorothy (Hensle) J.; B.A., Bucknell U., 1960, M.A., 1962; Ph.D., Jefferson Med. Coll., 1966; m. Ruth Eleanor Dobson, Aug. 18, 1962; children—Victoria Lynn, Elizabeth W. Instr. in anatomy Thomas Jefferson U., Phila., 1966-68, asso. in radiology, 1966-68, asst. prof. radiology and anatomy, 1968-74, asso. prof. anatomy and radiology, 1974—, div. head of anatomy Coll. of Allied Health Scis., 1975—, co. dir. pre-postdoctoral tng. program, 1971—; cons. in reproductive biology Ortho Research Found., 1971—; staff mem. Operation Concern, Inc., Cherry Hill, N.J., 1970-72. Mem. task force com. on communications, S. Jersey Methodist Conf., 1974—; chmn. Learning Resources Center, Haddonfield (N.J.) United Methodist Ch., 1976—. Recipient Distinguished Teaching award Christian R. and Mary F. Lindback Found., 1973; NIH grantee, 1975—. Mem. Am. Soc. Zoologists, N.Y. Acad. Scis., AAAS, The Teratology Soc., Am. Assn. of Anatomists, AAUP, Inst. of Soc., Ethics and Life Scis., Sigma Xi. Contbr. articles on teratology, embryology, radiation biology and behavioral toxicology to sci. jours. Home: 230 E Park Ave Haddonfield NJ 08033 Office: 561 Jefferson Alumni Hall 1020 Locust St Philadelphia PA 19107

JENTSCH, SUELLEN, pharm. co. exec.; b. Passaic, N.J., Aug. 22, 1947; d. Rudolph and Evelyn Claire (Ainsworth) J.; A.A., Alphonsus Coll., 1968; A.B., Coll. of St. Elizabeth, 1970; M.B.A., Fairleigh Dickinson U., 1974. Bookkeeper, N.J. Bank, Passaic, 1966; technologist in endocrinology Albert Einstein Coll. Medicine, Bronx, 1970-72; analyst Hoffmann-LaRoche, Nutley, N.J., 1972-73, supr. pharm. product auditing, 1973-75, supr. product auditing services, 1975—. Mem. Am. Chem. Soc., Assn. for M.B.A. Execs. Club: Hoffmann La Roche Tennis, Roche Camera. Office: 340 Kingsland Rd Nutley NJ 07110

JEPSON, JOHN WILLISFORD, mfg. co. exec.; b. N.Y.C., Nov. 7, 1931; s. Milton Willisford and Flora Maud (Bennett) J.; B.S. in Mech. Engring., Northeastern U., 1954; M.Eng., Yale, 1955, D.Eng. (univ. fellow), 1958; m. Joan Lorraine Lavalley, Sept. 6, 1954; children—Nancy Ellen, Robert Evan. With Bell Telephone Labs., Whippany, N.J., 1958-68, supr. hydrophone and projector devel., 1963-68; dir. corp. research and devel. Acushnet Co., New Bedford, Mass., 1968-74, v.p. research and devel., 1974—. Mem. profl. adv. com. Southeastern Mass. U., 1974—. Mem. Am. Soc. M.E., Acoustical Soc. Am., Am. Chem. Soc., Sigma Xi, Tau Beta Pi, Pi Tau Sigma. Club: Kittansett (Marion, Mass.); Wamsutta (New Bedford). Contbr. articles to profl. jours. Patentee in field. Home: 56 Olde Knoll Rd Marion MA 02738 Office: Belleville Ave New Bedford MA 02742

JERNIGAN, HARRY WILLIAM, III, home accessories co. exec.; b. Augusta, Ga., Oct. 11, 1942; s. Harry William and Frances (Hundley) J.; B.B.A., U. Ga., 1960-64, postgrad. law sch., 1967-70; m. Belva Duncan, Sept. 18, 1961; children—Ashley, Lorina, Belva Ann, Harry IV. Pvt. practice pub. accounting, Augusta, 1964-66; v.p. Cornwall Industries (formerly H.O. Cornwall Co.), South Paris, Maine, 1970-73, pres., 1973—, also dir.; instr. U. Ga. Sch. Bus., 1967-70. C.P.A., Maine. Mem. Pres.'s Assn., Am. Mgmt. Assn., Nat., Maine chambers commerce, Am. Inst. C.P.A.'s, Nat. Assn. Mfrs., Ga. Soc. C.P.A.'s, Kappa Alpha. Clubs: Paris Hill Country, Cumberland, So. Furniture, Ponte Vedra, Sandy Shore Swimming. Home: Lincoln Rd Paris Hill ME 04271 Office: 10 Hill St South Paris ME 04281

JERNIGAN, THOMAS PRIESTLY, III, physician; b. Paris, Tenn., July 11, 1920; s. Thomas Priestly and Laura Swift (Mayo) J.; B.A., Vanderbilt U., Nashville, 1942, M.D., 1944. Intern, Balt. City, 1944-45, resident in internal medicine, 1945-46, 48-50; med. dir. N.Y. Life Ins. Co., N.Y.C., 1955—; physician-outpatients N.Y. Hosp., N.Y.C., 1957—; clin. instr. medicine Cornell U., N.Y.C., 1957—; individual practice medicine specializing in internal medicine, N.Y.C., 1956—. Served with M.C., U.S. Army, 1946-48, to lt. col., 1949-55. Decorated Bronze Star with cluster. Diplomate Am. Bd. Internal Medicine, Bd. Life Ins. Medicine. Mem. A.C.P., AMA, Am. Heart Assn., Assn. Life Ins. Med. Dirs. Am., Tenn. Soc. N.Y. Presbyterian. Home: 1 Lincoln Plaza New York City NY 10023 Office: 51 Madison Ave New York City NY 10010

JEROME, FREDERICK LOUIS, sci. info. exec., journalist; b. N.Y.C., Feb. 10, 1939; s. Victor Jeremy and Alice Rose (Hamburger) J.; B.A. magna cum laude, (N.Y. State scholar), Coll. City N.Y., 1960; m. Jocelyn Beatrice Boyd, May 1, 1963; children—Rebecca, Mark. Daniel. Staff writer Wilmington (N.C.) Star-News, 1961, Augusta (Ga.) Herald, 1962, AP, San Francisco, 1967-71; asso. editor Pub. Employee Press, N.Y.C., 1963; editorial asst. Newsweek Mag., N.Y.C., 1964-66; publs. dir. Center for Health Studies, San Francisco, 1972-74; pub. relations writer St. Lukes Hosp., N.Y.C., 1975; pub. info. dir. Scientists' Inst. for Pub. Info., N.Y.C., 1975—; lectr. environ. health State U. N.Y. Empire State Coll., 1975; adj. prof. grad. div. State U. N.Y., Stony Brook, 1976; adj. prof. journalism N.Y. U., 1977—; mem. adv. bd. Center for Health Studies, 1973-74; mem. adv. com. occupational safety and health project U. Calif., Berkeley, 1974; cons. Center Biomed. Edn. City U. N.Y. Mem. Pub. Relations Soc. Am., Phi Beta Kappa. Contbr. articles to Newsweek, Environment, Politicks; asso. editor Environment mag., 1976—. Home: 230 W 79th St New York City NY 10024 Office: 355 Lexington Ave New York City NY 10017

JERREHIAN, CHARLES KRIKOR, home furnishings co. exec.; b. Phila., Aug. 13, 1935; s. John K. and Arax T. J.; student Franklin and Marshall Coll., 1954, Drexel Inst. Tech., 1955-57; m. Joanne Shipley Wood, May 26, 1956; children—Carol, John, C. Gregory. Apprentice, Jerrehian Bros. Co., Phila., 1956-59; founder, pres. Charles K. Jerrehian, Inc., West Chester, Pa., 1959—; lectr. on Oriental rugs, interior designing. Trustee, adv. bd. Goshen Baptist Ch., West Chester. Recipient Outstanding Sales award Sales Devel. Inst., 1970. Mem. Nat. Inst. Rug Cleaning (dir.), Rug Cleaners Inst. Phila. (pres. 1967-70, dir. 1967—), Interior Design Soc., Nat. Home Furnishing Assn., Fellowship Christian Athletes. Republican. Clubs: N.E. River Yacht, Lions. Home: Thistlewood Line Rd RD 2 Malvern PA 19355 Office: 1528 West Chester Pike West Chester PA 19380

JERRELLS, THOMAS RAY, immunologist; b. Wickenburg, Ariz., Feb. 28, 1944; s. Wilbur Ray and Marjorie Lee; B.S. in Microbiology with distinction, U. Ariz., 1972; M.S. in Bacteriology and Pub. Health, Washington State U., 1974, Ph.D., 1976; m. Janice Merle Walter, Oct. 2, 1965; children—Michael Ray, Jennifer Merle. Med. technologist Santa Rosa Hosp., San Antonio, 1968-70, St. Joseph's Hosp., Tucson, Ariz., 1970-72; teaching asst. Wash. State U., Pullman, 1972-73, research asst., 1973-76; immunologist Litton Bionetics, Inc., Kensington, Md., 1976—. Served to staff sgt. U.S. Army, 1966-70. Certified med. technologist. Mem. AAAS, Am. Med. Technologists, Nat. Registry of Microbiologists, Am. Soc. for Microbiology, Sigma Xi, Phi Kappa Phi. Lutheran. Contbr. articles in field to profl. jours. and presentations at profl. meetings. Office: 5516 Nicholson Ln Kensington MD 20795

JESCH, PAUL DOUGLAS, gen. aviation exec.; b. Hoboken, N.J., Feb. 3, 1922; s. Paul John and Agnes Marie (Robertson) J.; B.S., Va. Poly. Inst., 1947; m. June Adriane Seelig, May 14, 1949; children—Paul Douglas, Laura Leigh, Barbara Jo. Salesman, buyer Air Assos., Inc., Teterboro, N.J., 1947-50; with Van Dusen Aircraft Supplies, Teterboro, 1950—, purchasing agent, 1952-54, asst. br. mgr., 1954-57, asst. regional mgr., 1957-64, br. mgr., 1965-66, regional mgr., 1966-73, sales support center mgr., 1974-76, gen. mgr. Eastern div., 1976—. Mem. Wayne (N.J.) Bd. Recreation, 1969—. Served with USAF, 1942-46. Mem. Nat. Pilots Assn., Aircraft Owners and Pilots Assn. Republican. Dutch Reformed. Home: 1609 Ratzer Rd Wayne NJ 07470 Office: Teterboro Airport Teterboro NJ 07608

JESSAR, JONATHAN SANDER, pub. relations exec.; b. Phila., Nov. 27, 1943; s. Joseph and Betty Lois (Salsburg) J.; student Temple U., 1962-66. Writer, editor Anchorage (Alaska) Daily Times, 1967-69; pub. relations specialist Gen. Foods Corp., White Plains, N.Y., 1969-72; asst. dir. pub. affairs Soap and Detergent Assn., N.Y.C., 1972-73; v.p. Hill & Knowlton Inc., pub. relations and pub. affairs, N.Y.C. and Washington, 1973—. Chmn. pub. relations United Fund Westchester County, 1970. Served with AUS, 1966-69. Mem. Pub. Relations Soc. Am., Chem. Pub. Relations Soc., N.Y. Assn. Indsl. Communicators, Arctic Hacks Assn., Alaska Press Club, Pi Lambda Phi (pres. 1965). Home: 4849 Connecticut Ave NW Washington DC 20008 Office: 1425 K St Washington DC 20005

JESSEN, MARTIN DANIEL, excavation co. exec.; b. Perth Amboy, N.J., Sept. 12, 1926; s. Martin and Hannah (Hughes) J.; B.S. in Civil Engring., Rutgers U., 1950; m. Barbara Jane Bruner, Dec. 16, 1950; children—Nancy Elizabeth, Martin Andrew. Field engr. Arnolt Bros., Inc., Metuchen, N.J., 1952-54, v.p., 1954-60, pres., 1960—; pres. Metuchen Savs. & Loan, 1963—, also dir. Bd. dirs. Metuchen YMCA, 1948—, nat. YMCA, 1972—; pres., Met. YMCA, 1960-61; mem. Edison (N.J.) council Boy Scouts Am., 1967—; chmn. Metuchen Hist. Commn., 1973—; vice chmn. Delaware and Raritan Canal Commn., 1975—. Served with USNR, 1944-46; to lt. (j.g.), 1951-52. Mem. Asso. Gen. Contractors N.J. (trustee 1968—, v.p. 1976—), C. of C. (sec. 1970; pres. 1972). Mem. Reformed Ch. of Am. (deacon 1958-62). Rotarian (local pres. 1962-63; dist. sec. 1971-72). Home: 191 E Chestnut Ave Metuchen NJ 08840 Office: PO Box 489 Metuchen NJ 08840

JESSUP, MICHAEL HYLE, educator; b. Washington, Oct. 25, 1937; s. Gerald E. and Doris Quigley (Skinner) J.; student Ga. State U., 1956, U. Va. extension, 1957-59; A.B., George Washington U., 1961; A.M., 1963, Ed.D., 1967; m. Joanne Lutz, Nov. 1, 1957; children—Michael Hyle, Mark Gerald. Tchr. history and govt. J.E.B. Stuart High Sch., Falls Church, Va., 1962; asst. dir. off campus div. George Washington U., 1962-63, field rep., 1963-66; asst. prof. edn. Hood Coll., Frederick, Md., 1966-67; mem. faculty Towson State U., Balt., 1967—, prof. edn., 1972—, dir. field services and ednl. research, 1967-73, chmn. dept. secondary edn., 1969-78; manuscript cons. John Wiley & Sons, 1971-72, Prentice-Hall, Inc., 1971—, Little, Brown & Co., 1974-76; prof. edn. Johns Hopkins U. Evening Coll., 1973-76; extraordinary minister Holy Communion, Archdiocese of Balt., 1976—. Mgr., coach baseball and basketball programs Towson Recreation Council, 1971—. Mem. AAUP (pres. Towson State Coll. chpt. 1969-71), Md. Tchrs. Assn., Assn. for Higher Edn. (1st v.p. 1973-74), N.E.A., Am. Ednl. Studies Assn., Phi Delta Kappa (pres. George Washington U. chpt. 1968-69). Author: (with Margaret A. Kiley) Discipline: Positive Attitudes for Learning, 1971; contbr. articles to profl. jours. Home: 7503 Rocksham Dr Towson MD 21204 Office: Dept Secondary Education Towson State U Baltimore MD 21204

JESTER, ROBERTS CHARLES, JR., engring. services co. exec.; b. Atlanta, July 12, 1917; s. Roberts Charles and Lynwood (Waters) J.; B.S., U. Ga., 1940; grad. Advance Mgmt. Program, Harvard, 1957; m. Ann Nell Padgett, Dec. 31, 1936; children—Rita (Mrs. Charles B. Jones, Jr.), Carol (Mrs. John M. Sisk, Jr.), Janell (Mrs. Michael C. Patty). Chief clk. Ga. R.R., 1936-40; project mgr. Mich. Design & Engring. Co., 1941-42; partner Allstate & Engring. Co., Dayton, Ohio, 1943-45, pres., 1945—; pres., chief exec. officer Allstates Design & Devel. Co. Inc., Trenton, N.J., 1954—; dir. N.J. Nat. Bank. Bd. dirs., vice chmn. Greater Trenton Symphony Assn.; bd. dirs. George Washington council Boy Scouts Am.; bd. govs. Hamilton Hosp.; trustee YMCA, Trenton; mem. lay adv. bd. St. Francis Hosp. Mem. Greater Trenton C. of C. (dir.), Metro 49'ers. Republican. Presbyn. Mason (Shriner, Jester). Clubs: Engineers, Trenton Country (past pres.); Key Biscayne (Fla.) Yacht; Metropolitan (N.Y.C.); Pittsburgh Athletic; Little Egg Harbor Yacht (N.J.). Home: 119 Windsor Rd Yardley PA 19067 Office: 367 Pennington Ave PO Box 1693 Trenton NJ 08607*

JETER, KATHERINE FEAGIN, enterostomal therapist; b. lLangley, Va., Oct. 25, 1938; d. John A. and Katherine D. (Terrell) Feagin; student U. Tex., 1955-58; B.S. in Sociology, State U. N.Y., 1977; M.A. in Counseling, Ball State U., 1977; cert. enterostomal therapy Emory U., Woodruff Med. Center, 1972; m. John Randolph Jeter, Jr., Apr. 5, 1958; children—Sara Ann, John Randolph III, Stephen T. Enterostomal therapist Squier Urol. Clinic, Babies and Presbyn. hosps., N.Y.C., 1968-72; practice enterostomal therapy, 1973-75; cons. Orange County (Calif.) Med. Center, U. Calif. at Irvine, 1974-75; vis. prof. Volusia Acad. of Medicine, Daytona Beach, Fla., 1972, Halifax Hosp. Med. Center, Daytona Beach, Fla., 1973, Johns Hopkins Sch. Nursing, Balt., 1975, Tucson (Ariz.) Med. Center, 1975, Handikappinstitutet, Bromma, Sweden, 1977; guest lectr. to various med. orgns. and schs., 1970—. Chmn. Pediatric Vols. for ARC, 1963-65. Named Mil. Wife of Year, Western region U.S. Army Recruiting Command, 1973. Mem. United Ostomy Assn. (hon.), Volusia Acad. Medicine (hon.), Internat. Assn. Enterostomal Therapy (pres. Calif. div. 1973), Internat. Ostomy Assn., World Council Enterostomal Therapy, Am. Cancer Soc. (service com. Orange county unit 1974), Daus. U.S. Army, Jr. League, Kappa Alpha Theta. Episcopalian. Author: Count Your Blessings, 1965; Management of the Urinary Stoma, 1970; Urinary Ostomies: A Guidebook for Patients, 1972, rev. edit., 1977; contbr. numerous articles on rehab. of ostomy patients to profl. jours. Home: 3101 S Glebe Rd Arlington VA 22202 Office: Squier Urological Clinic 620 W 168th St New York City NY 10032

JETTE, ROGER JOSEPH, univ. computing lab. dir.; b. Attleboro, Mass., Feb. 27, 1939; s. Joseph Alexis and Florence Louise (Rondeau) J.; M.A., Brown U., 1971; m. Jacquelyn Chapel Grieder; children—Barbara Ann, Karen Louise. Sr. field engr. IBM Corp., 1961-67; dir. computing lab. Brown U., 1967-75; bus. mgr. Nantucket (Mass.) pub. schs., 1975—. Cons. Processing Mgmt. Inc.; certified flight instr.; motor boat capt. Served with USN, 1956-61. Mem. Nat. Aero Club, Aircraft Owners and Pilots Assn. Home: 1 Chapel Way Nantucket MA 02554 Office: Atlantic Ave Nantucket MA 02554

JETTER, LAWRENCE KLOSSON, materials engring. cons.; b. Williamsport, Pa., Apr. 24, 1915; s. Max Willard and Helen Natalie (Johnson) J.; B.S., Carnegie-Mellon U., 1936, M.S., 1937, D. Sc., 1939; m. Rhea Mae Wagner, Dec. 15, 1938; children—Barbara Mae Jetter Cudnik, Karen Eileen Jetter Robertson. Staff metallurgist Aluminum Co. Am., New Kensington, Pa., 1939-47; prin. metallurgist Oak Ridge Nat. Lab., 1947-60; sr. research metallurgist Curtiss-Wright Corp., Quehanna, Pa., 1961-62; supr. materials devel. Allis-Chalmers Mfg. Co., Milw., 1962-64; sr. research scientist Kaiser Aluminum & Chem. Corp., Spokane, Wash., 1964-68; instr., lectr. in field; cons. materials engring. Williamsport, 1968—. Aluminum Co. Am. fellow, 1936-39; certified profl. engr. metall. engring. Mem. Am. Inst. Mining, Metall. and Petroleum Engrs., Am. Soc. Metals, AAAS, Am. Def. Preparedness Assn., Sci. Research Soc. Am., Sci. of Metals Club, Sigma Xi, Theta Tau, Tau Beta Pi, Phi Kappa Phi, Theta Xi. Home and office: 1257 Pennsylvania Ave Williamsport PA 17701

JETTER, WALTER W., physician; b. Buffalo, Sept. 4, 1905; s. George E. and Eleanor (Kleindinst) J.; M.D., U. Buffalo, 1931, M.S., 1938; m. Edna M. Watson, Feb. 4, 1933 (dec. Sept. 1970); children—Mildred Elizabeth, Margaret Ann; m. 2d, Wilma R. Wigle, June 3, 1972. Resident in pathology, Buffalo City Hosp. and U. Buffalo Med. Sch., 1934-39; asst. prof. legal medicine Harvard Med. Sch., 1941-49; prof. legal medicine and pathology Boston U. Sch. of Medicine, 1949-54, lectr. on toxicology, 1954-72; adj. prof. allied health professions Indiana U. of Pa., 1972—, dir. labs. Latrobe Hosp. (Pa.), 1954—, Frick Meml. Hosp., Mt. Pleasant, Pa., 1954—; chief investigator AEC project, 1952-53. Diplomate Am. Bd. Pathology. Mem. A.M.A., Am. Soc., Clin. Pathologists, Coll. Am. Pathologists. Clubs: Harvard (Boston); University (Pitts.). Contbr. numerous articles med. jours., also Anderson's Textbook Pathology, 5 edits. Research on different phases of alcoholism. Home: 720 Weldon St Latrobe PA 15650 Office: Latrobe Hospital Latrobe PA 15650

JEWELEWICZ, RAPHAEL, physician; b. Nowogrodek, Poland, Dec. 26, 1932; s. Chaim and Chaia (Tawricki) J.; came to U.S., 1963, naturalized, 1968; M.D., Hadassah-Hebrew U., 1960; m. Roni Oved, 1955; children—Rachel, Dov, Daniel, Dory. Intern Hadassah-Hebrew U. Hosp., 1961; resident N.Y. U. Med. Center-Bellevue Hosp., N.Y.C., 1964-68; chief Sloane Endocrine Clinic, N.Y.C., 1969—, chief sect. reproductive endocrinology, 1975—; cons. reproductive endocrinology Roosevelt, Harlem hosps.; mem. faculty Columbia Coll. Phys. and Surg., 1969—, asso. prof. obstetrics and gynecology, 1975—. Diplomate Am. Bd. Obstetrics and Gynecology (subsplty. reproductive endocrinology). Fellow A.C.S., Am. Coll. Obstetrics and Gynecology; mem. Soc. Gynecol. Investigation, Endocrine Soc., Am. Fertility Soc., Soc. Study Reprodn., N.Y. Obstet. Soc., N.Y. Gynecol. Soc., N.Y. Acad. Scis., N.Y. Acad. Medicine. Jewish. Home: 199-12 Epsom Course Holliswood NY 11423 Office: 630 W 168th St New York City NY 10032

JEWELL, MARVIN EUGENE, microbiologist; b. Terre Haute, Ind., Oct. 2, 1927; s. Charles Enoch and Dorsey Edith (Woodsmall) J.; B.S., Ind. State U., 1966; m. Leah Joyce Deer, Sept. 24, 1950; children—Sandra Lea, Randal Wayne. Research technician, Charles Pfizer & Co., Terre Haute, 1951-67; research microbiologist Merck Sharp & Dohme Research Labs., Rahway, N.J., 1967—. Served with USNR, 1945-46. Research in human and vet. vaccine. Home: 165 Rues Ln East Brunswick NJ 08816 Office: Merck Sharp & Dohme Research Labs Rahway NJ 07065

JEWETT, JOHN WILLITS, JR., educator; b. Yokosuka, Japan, Sept. 18, 1947; s. John Willits and Gretchen Joan (Whims) J.; came to U.S., 1949; B.S., Drexel U., 1969; M.S., Ohio State U., 1971, Ph.D., 1974; m. Beth Ann Wichman, Jan. 31, 1976; children by previous marriage—Andrew John, Charles Robert. Teaching asst. Ohio State U., Columbus, 1969-74, NASA trainee, 1970-72; asst. prof. physics, dept. natural sci. and math. Stockton State Coll., Pomona, N.J., 1974-75, 76—; asst. prof. physics Sinclair Community Coll., Dayton, Ohio, 1975-76. Recipient Distinguished Teaching award Ohio State U., 1973. Mem. Am. Phys. Soc., Am. Assn. Physics Tchrs., AAAS. Home: RD 2 Box 303R Absecon NJ 08201 Office: Dept Natural Sci and Math Stockton State Coll Pomona NJ 08240

JHAVERI, INDRA SARABHAI, quality assurance engr.; b. Bombay, India, July 8, 1950; s. Sarabhai C. and Kantaben C. (Sheth) J.; came to U.S., 1973, naturalized, 1976; B.S. in Mech. Engring. with honors, U. Bombay, 1973; M.S. in Mgmt. Engring., U. Bridgeport, 1978; m. Mary Talitha Jones, Aug. 2, 1975; children—Kavita Sarah, Darshan Daniel; adopted dau., Keri Lynn. Test engr. Gen. Electric Co., Bridgeport, Conn., 1974-76; prodn. supr. Beck Mfg. Co., Stamford, Conn., 1975; quality control engr. Marlin Rockwell div. TRW Inc., Plainville, Conn., 1976-78, Falconer, N.Y., 1978—. Loaned exec. United Way, Plainville, 1977. Mem. Am. Soc. Quality Control. Home: 220 Valley View Ave Jamestown NY 14701 Office: 402 Chandler St Jamestown NY 14701

JILLETTE, ARTHUR GEORGE, JR., coll. dean; b. Malden, Mass., May 1, 1937; s. Arthur George and Esther (Peachy) J.; student Plymouth (N.H.) State Coll., 1956-58; B.S., Boston U., 1960, M.R.E., 1964; postgrad. Hartford Sem. Found., 1960-61, N.Y. U., 1965-68, U. Okla., 1977; 1 son, Joseph Arthur; m. 2d, Beatrice Miriam Ellis Hopkins; stepchildren—Andrew P., Timothy N. and Grace Hopkins. Tchr. deaf Crotched Mountain Found., Greenfield, N.H., 1961-62; ednl. cons. N.Y. League for Hard of Hearing, N.Y.C., 1965-68; asso. research scientist Deafness Research and Tng. Center, N.Y. U., N.Y.C., 1965-68; cons. spl. edn. N.H. Dept. Edn., Concord, 1968-72, acting dir. spl. edn., 1972-73, dir. planning and devel., 1973-77; dean spl. services N.H. Vocat. Tech. Coll., Claremont, 1977—; instr. spl. edn. St. Anselm's Coll., Manchester, N.H., 1970—, Keene (N.H.) State Coll., 1971—; co-founder Amoskeag Center for Ednl. Services, Manchester, 1971; cons. industry, edn.; field faculty mem. Goddard Coll., Plainfield, Vt., 1971—; dir. Bancroft Products, Inc., Concord. Mem. nat. adv. com. Demographic Studies Deaf, Gallaudet Coll., Washington, 1970—. Mem. Zoning Bd. Adjustment; auditor Town of Goshen (N.H.). Office Edn. fellow, 1964-65. Mem. N.H. Ednl. Assn., Conf. Execs. of Am. Schs. for the Deaf, Assn. Children with Learning Disabilities. Mem. United Ch. Christ. Mason, Odd Fellow, Elk. Clubs: Shamus (Concord); National Association Watch and Clock Collectors (Columbia, Pa.). Editor: (with E.S. Levine) Denominational Work with the Deaf, 1968. Home: Brickyard Rd Star Route 2 Goshen NH 03752 Office: NH Vocat Tech College Hanover St Extension Claremont NH 03743

JIMENEZ, SERGIO ASTETE, physician, biochemist; b. Cuzco, Peru, Feb. 21, 1942; s. Julio Alexander and Bertha Margarite (Astete) Jimenez; came to U.S., 1966; B.S., Nat. U. San Marcos, Lima, Peru, 1959, M.D. magna cum laude, 1964; m. Jeanette A. Artway, June 30, 1966; Intern, Phila. Gen. Hosp., 1966; resident in rheumatology U. Pa. Hosp., 1972-73; fellow in internal medicine Mayo Clinic, 1967-69; practice medicine specializing in rheumatology and internal medicine, Phila.; asso. in medicine U. Pa., 1973-74, asst. prof., 1974—, attending physician rheumatology sect., 1974—; attending physician rheumatology VA Hosp., Phila., 1978—. Bd. dirs. Washington Sq. W. Project Area Com., Phila., 1978—, Bellavista Community Assn., Phila., 1974—, Spruce St. Community Assn., Phila., 1977—, Washington Sq. W. Civic Assn., 1978—. Diplomate Am. Bd. Internal Medicine. Fellow Arthritis Found., A.C.P.; mem. Peruvian Soc. Rheumatology, Mayo Alumni Assn., Am. Rheumatism Assn., Am. Fedn. Clin. Research, Phila. Biochemistry Soc. Contbr. articles to profl. jours. Home: 708 S 10th St Philadelphia PA 19147 Office: 3600 Spruce St Philadelphia PA 19174

JIMESON, ROBERT MACKAY, JR., cons.; b. Charleroi, Pa., Jan. 29, 1921; s. Robert MacKay and Marie (Heupel) J.; B.S. in Chem. Engring., Pa. State U., 1943; M.S. in Ops. Research, George Washington U., 1965; Ph.D. in Systems Analysis, Stanford U., 1967; m. Rose Marie Wolny, Aug. 16, 1945; children—Robyn, Shelley, Robert, Jeffrey. Aircraft designer Martin Co., Middle River, Md., 1942-44; organic synthesis fellow Union Carbide-Mellon Inst., Pitts., 1945-48; chief plant design and ops. synthetic fuels program Bur. Mines, Pitts., 1949-59, research coordinator, Washington, 1959-64; chief of fuel policy, program planning and evaluation Nat. Air Pollution Control Adminstrn. EPA, Washington, 1964-70; environ. adviser to chmn. FPC, Washington, 1970-75; mem. profl. staff Office Tech. Assessment U.S. Congress, 1975-76; mgr. fossil tech. overview ERDA, Washington, 1976—; mem. faculty Pa. State U., 1956-59, George Washington U., 1977—; participant Pres. Johnson's Mid-Career Ednl. Program, 1966-67; internat. del. Engrs. Joint Council, 1976—. Lay preacher, mem. ofcl. bd., tchr., vice chmn. commn. on edn. Mt. Olivet Meth. Ch., Arlington, Va. Recipient Spl. Service award Dept. Interior, 1957; registered profl. engr., Pa. Fellow Am. Inst. Chem. Engrs.; mem. Nat. Soc. Profl. Engrs., Am. Chem. Soc., Air Pollution Control Assn., Assn. Pub. Program Analysts. Author: Pollution Control and Energy Needs; contbr. numerous articles on energy and environ. matters to profl. jours.; formulated various indsl., comml. and residential chem. products; inventor chem. cleaning and coal conversion processes. Home: 1501 Gingerwood Ct Vienna VA 22180

JINDRAK, FRANK, accountant; b. N.Y.C., Feb. 9, 1914; s. George and Frances (Bower) J.; grad. Pace U., 1935; m. Lillian Grace Stermer, Jan. 3, 1933; children—Frank, Jr., Barbara Jean Jindrak Horner. Asst. office mgr. Distillers Co., Ltd., Gordon's Dry Gin, Ltd., Linden, N.J., 1934-42; internal auditor cost accountant Hyatt Bearings div. Gen. Motors Corp., Harrison, N.J., 1942-43; sr. accountant Scovell, Wellington & Co., N.Y.C., 1943-44, Price, Waterhouse & Co., N.Y.C., 1944-45, Ernst & Ernst, N.Y.C., 1945-49; pvt. practice accounting, Linden, N.J., 1949—. C.P.A., N.J., N.Y. Mem. Am. Inst. C.P.A.'s, N.Y. State Soc. C.P.A.'s. Mem. Reformed Ch. Clubs: Princeton Hills Country, Moose, Mason, Elks, U.S. Coast Guard Aux. Home: 216 Princeton Rd Linden NJ 07036 Office: 15 N Wood Ave Linden NJ 07036

JODOIN, MAURICE ALAIN, business exec.; b. Montreal, Que., Can., Mar. 30, 1939; s. Lucien and Donalda (Cormier) J.; B.A., U. Montreal, 1959, L.Sc.Com., 1962; m. Louise Marchand, June 29, 1963; children—Nathalie, Valerie. Economist, Bank of Can., 1962-65; portfolio mgr., v.p., dir. Bolton, Tremblay & Co., 1965-74; v.p., gen. mgr. Sodarcan, Montreal, 1974—, also mem. exec. com., dir.; dir. Gerard Parizeau Limitee, J.E. Poitras, Inc., La Nationale Compagnie de Reassurance du Canada, Hebert, LeHouillier & Assos., leBlanc, Eldridge, Parizeau, Inc., P.H. Plourde Inc., Canadian Internat. Reins. Brokers Ltd., Intermediaries of Am. Inc., Gestas Corp., Reins. Mgmt. Co. Can. Inc., Société de Gestion Nationale-MGFVie. Past pres., bd. dirs. Vie des Arts. Chartered fin. analyst. Mem. Montreal Soc. Fin. Analysts (past pres.). Office: 2 Complexe Desjardins 1700 PO Box 183 Montreal PQ H5B 1B3 Canada

JOENS, CLAUS JURGEN, electronic mfr.; b. Baden-Baden, Germany, Feb. 16, 1941; s. Werner Heinrich and Lily (Blum) J.; B.S., U. Minn., 1966. Apprentice, Brabender OHG, Duisburg, Germany, 1961-62; mgr. comml. devel. C.W. Brabender Instrument, Inc., South Hackensack, N.J., 1967-69; exec. v.p. Elnik Instruments, Inc., Lodi, N.J., 1969—; dir. W.H. Joens & Co. GmbH, Dusseldorf, Germany. Mem. Instrument Soc. Am. Home: 19 Oak Knoll Rd Glen Rock NJ 07452 Office: 410 Garibaldi Ave Lodi NJ 07644

JOFFE, JULIA ELIZABETH SCHUELKE (MRS. LESTER L. JOFFE), social worker; b. Denver, Feb. 7, 1926; d. Max Norman and Mary Nalle (Sheldon) Schuelke; B.A., U. Tex., 1945; diploma in social work Our Lady of Lake Sch. Social Work, 1946; M.S.W., Columbia, 1949; certificate Westchester Center Study Psychoanalysis and Psychotherapy, 1977; m. Lester L. Jeffe, Sept. 5, 1949; children—Barbara, Susan, Paul, Elizabeth. Caseworker, Charity Assn., San Antonio, 1946; pediatric caseworker U. Tex. Med. Br., Galveston, 1947-48; sr. social worker Dallas Community Guidance, 1949; program and social work cons. N.Y. State Assn. for Crippled Children, N.Y.C., 1949-53; caseworker Abbott House, Irvington N.Y., 1965-66; adminstr. dept. psychiatry. White Plains (N.Y.) Hosp. Med. Center, 1966—; pvt. practice, specializing in psychoanalysis and psychotherapy, White Plains, 1958-64. Bd. dirs. PTA, Irvington, 1958-64. Fellow Westchester Center Psychoanalytical Soc. (pres. elect), Am. Orthopsychiat. Assn.; mem. Nat. Assn. Social Workers, Am. Am. Group Psychotherapy Assn., League Women Voters (pres. Irvington 1964-65). Home: 499 Broadway White Plains NY 10603 Office: White Plains Hosp Med Center Davis Ave at Post Rd White Plains NY 10603

JOFFREY, ROBERT (ABDULLAH JAFFA BEY KHAN), ballet co. dir., choreographer, dancer; b. Seattle, Dec. 24, 1930; s. Dolha and Marie (Galetti) J.; student Mary Ann Wells Sch. Dance, Seattle, 1944-48, Cornish Sch. Music, Seattle, 1945-48, Sch. Am. Ballet, 1948; pupil Alexandra Federova, student modern dance with May O'Donnell, Gertrude Shurr, 1949-52. Mem. faculty High Sch. Performing Arts, N.Y.C., 1950-55, also Am. Ballet Theatre Sch.; founder ballet sch. Am. Ballet Center, 1953, dir. faculty, 1953-65; resident choreographer N.Y. City Center Opera, 1955-61; founder 1956, since artistic dir., choreographer City Center Joffrey Ballet (formerly Robert Joffrey Ballet Co.); co. toured Near East for State Dept., 1962-63, toured Russia 1963, performed at White House, 1963, 65, ann. U.S. tours, 1956-64; organizer dance dept. Chautauqua, N.Y., 1959; choreographer NBC-TV Opera, 1955, 57, 58; creator ballets: Persephone, Scaramouche, Umpateedle, Pas des Déesses, Bal Masque, Pierot Lunaire, Harpsichord Concerto, Gamelon, Astarte, Remembrances. Pres. Ballet Am. Found.; bd. dirs. Found. Am. Dance. Recipient ann. award Nat. Acad. Dance Masters, Chgo., 1962; Dance mag. award, 1964; Dance Masters Am. award, 1965; Ford Found. grant Robert Joffrey Ballet, 1964. Office: 434 6th Ave New York City NY 10009 also 130 W 56th St New York City NY 10019*

JOHANSON, PATRICIA MAUREEN, artist, design cons.; b. N.Y.C., Sept. 8, 1940; d. Alvar Einar and Elizabeth (Deane) J.; student Bklyn. Mus. Art Sch., 1958, Art Students League, 1961; A.B., Bennington Coll., 1962; M.A., Hunter Coll., 1964; B.S., B.Arch., City Coll. Sch. Architecture, 1977; m. E.C. Goossen; children—Alvar Deane, Gerrit Hull. Exhibited one-man shows Tibor de Nagy Gallery, N.Y.C., 1967, State U. N.Y. at Albany, 1969, Montclair (N.J.) State Coll., 1974, Rosa Esman Gallery, N.Y.C., 1978; retrospective, Bennington Coll., 1973; exhibited group shows Hudson River Mus., Yonkers, 1964, Bennington Coll., 1964, Stable Gallery, N.Y.C., 1966, Tibor de Nagy Gallery, N.Y.C., 1966, 68, Larry Aldrich Mus., Ridgefield, Conn., 1968, Mus. Modern Art, N.Y.C., 1968, Grand Palais, Paris, 1968, Kunsthaus, Zurich, 1969, Tate Gallery, London, 1969, Vassar Coll., 1969, Finch Coll. Mus., 1971, Everson Mus., Syracuse, N.Y., 1971, Detroit Inst. Arts, 1973, Mass. Inst. Tech., 1974, Casa Thomas Jefferson, Brasilia, Brazil, 1975, Pa. Acad. Fine Arts, Phila., 1975, Greenwich (Conn.) Library, 1977, Bklyn. Mus., 1977, New Gallery Contemporary Art, Cleve., 1977, Cleve. State U., 1977, Cooper-Hewitt Mus., N.Y.C., 1978; represented in permanent collections Detroit Inst. Arts, N.Y. State Council on Arts Film Collection, Syracuse, N.Y., Storm King Art Center, Mountainville, N.Y., Mus. Modern Art, N.Y.C., Crawford and Chester Sts. Park, Cleve.; films: The Art of the Real, USIA, 1968; Stephen Long, CBS-TV, 1968; Patricia Johanson: Cyrus Field, 1974; The City Project: Cleveland, 1977; vis. prof. art State U. N.Y. at Albany, 1969; vis. artist Mass. Inst. Tech., 1974, Oberlin (Ohio) Coll., 1974, Alfred U. (N.Y.), 1974; cons. Mitchell-Giurgola Assos. Architects, N.Y.C. also Phila., 1972—, N.Y. State Council on Arts, 1978; works include sculpture, landscape sculpture, street furniture, pavement designs, site planning for Consol. Edison Co., Yale U., Columbus East High Sch. (Ind.), others. Recipient 1st prize Environ. Design competition Montclair (N.J.) State Coll., 1974; Internat. Women's Yr. award, 1976. Guggenheim fellow, 1970, Nat. Endowment for Arts fellow, 1975. Mem. Women's Caucus for Art, Soc. Archtl. Historians. Home: RFD 1 Buskirk NY 12028 Office: 795 Lexington Ave New York NY 10021

JOHNPOLL, BERNARD KEITH, educator; b. N.Y.C., June 3, 1918; s. Israel Joseph and Ray (Elkin) J.; A.B. magna cum laude, Boston U., 1959; A.M., Rutgers U., 1963; Ph.D., State U. N.Y., 1966; m. Lillian Kirtzman, Feb. 14, 1944; children—Janet (Mrs. James Greenlee), Phyllis. Reporter, rewriter Post-Gazette, Pitts., 1946-51; copy editor, news editor Boston Record Am., 1951-61; asst. prof. polit. sci. Hartwick Coll., 1963-65; vis. asst. prof. U. Sask., 1965-66; prof. polit. sci. State U. N.Y., Albany, 1966—. Nat. Def. fellow, 1960-63, Nat. Council Jewish Culture fellow, 1963-65. Mem. Am. Polit. Sci. Assn., Soc. Propagation Judaism (trustee 1971—), Pi Sigma Alpha. Democrat. Jewish religion. Club: Workmen's Circle (Albany, N.Y.). Author: The Politics of Futility, 1967; Pacifist's Progress, 1970; The Impossible Dream, 1976. Editor, contbns. in Polit. Sci., 1977—. Home: 149 Holmes Dale St Albany NY 12208 Office: 1400 Washington Ave Albany NY 12222

JOHNS, ANTHONY GEORGE, automobile sales exec.; b. Washington, Pa., Jan. 27, 1915; s. Michael and Mary; student pub. schs., Washington, Pa.; student Ford merchandising schs., Pa. State Police training sch.; m. Margaret Cramer, Sept. 18, 1948; children—Catherine, Diane, Mary. Store mgr. trainee, McCrorys Co., 1932-36; Pa. State policeman, 1938-55; parts and service dept. Butler County Motor Co., 1955-57, salesman, 1956-58, gen. mgr., 1958-69, pres., 1969—, also dir. Dir., vice chmn. Pitts. dist. Ford Dealer Advt., Inc.; chmn. Zone C Pitts. dist. Ford Dealer Council; dir., treas. Superior Auto Parts, Inc. Pres., Butler County Symphony Assn., 1967-68, Butler County Traveling Library, 1972—, Butler County Safety Council, 1957-58; bd. dirs., 1st v.p. Butler Community Devel., 1972—, now sec.; bd. dirs. Pa. Assn. for Retarded Children, 1955-58, Butler County Music and Art Festival, 1963-70; active Cancer Soc., United Fund, Boy Scouts Am., YMCA; sec. City of Butler Parking Authority, Butler County Indsl. Devel. Corp. Mem. Nat. Automobile Dealers Assn., Pa. Automobile Dealers Assn. Democrat. Roman Catholic. Clubs: Butler Country, Knights of Columbus, Lions (past pres.). Home: 106 Edgewood Rd Butler PA 16001 Office: 400 S Main St Butler PA 16001

JOHNS, ELIZABETH LAMBERT, ednl. adminstr.; b. Richmond, Va., Feb. 11, 1935; d. Benjamin J. and Mary F. (Warden) Lambert; B.S., Va. State Coll., Petersburg, 1955; M.A., Case-Western Res. U., 1957; Ed.D., Va. Poly. Inst. and State U., 1977; m. John S. Johns, Aug., 1960; 1 son, John Stanley. Instr. speech pathology and audiology Hampton (Va.) Inst., 1957-60; clin. tchr. Children's Hosp. of D.C., 1960-63; hearing clinician Montgomery (Md.) Pub. Schs., 1963-67; tchr. spl. edn. Montgomery County Pub. Schs., Rockville, Md., 1968-70; supr. speech and hearing Arlington (Va.) Pub. Schs., 1970-74, program specialist, 1976-77; spl. asst. Bur. Edn. for Handicapped, HEW, Washington, 1974-76; asso. dir. for mgmt. Inst. for Ednl. Leadership, George Washington U., Washington, 1977—. Fellow Am. Speech and Hearing Assn. (edn. and tng. bd. 1977-79), Nat. Council of Negro Women, Delta Sigma Theta (exec. bd. 1974-79). Democrat. Baptist. Home: 3708 Maryland St Alexandria VA 22309 Office: 1001 Connecticut Ave NW Washington DC 20036

JOHNS, WALTER SCOTT, III, lawyer; b. Akron, Ohio, Jan. 18, 1926; s. Walter Scott and Ellen (Mercer) J.; B.S., Lehigh U., 1949; J.D., U. Pa., 1955; m. Star Colleen Johns, June 25, 1949; children—Susan Caryl, Walter Scott, IV, Peter Mercer. Student engr. Phila. Electric Co., 1948; jr. engr. Atlantic Refining Co., Phila., 1949-52; admitted to Pa. bar, 1955; since practiced in Wayne, Pa.; sr. mem. firm of W. Scott Johns III. Served as sgt., AUS, 1944-46. Mem. alumni council Mercersburg Acad., 1961-67, 71—, v.p., 1972-74, pres., 1974-76, bd. regents, 1977—. Mem. IEEE, Am. Judicature Soc., Am., Pa., Delaware County (dir. 1971-72) bar assns., Am. Arbitration Assn. (panel arbitrators), Beta Chi Assn. of Lehigh U. (trustee 1952-68), Phi Gamma Delta, Tau Beta Pi, Eta Kappa Nu. Republican. Presbyterian. Clubs: Philadelphia Curling (dir. 1958—, sec. 1958-68, v.p. 1968-70, pres. 1970-72), Waynesborough Country. Home: 573 Tory Hill Rd Devon PA 19333 Office: 130 W Lancaster Ave Wayne PA 19087

JOHNS, WILLIAM, JR., educator; b. Scranton, Pa., Feb. 9, 1947; s. William and Janet E. (O'Hora) J.; B.A., Alfred U., 1969, M.S., 1971; postgrad. U. Scranton, 1972-73, Oneonta Coll., 1974, Marywood Grad. Sch., Scranton, 1974-75, State U. N.Y., Cortland, 1977—; m. Mary E. Johns, May 22, 1971; 1 dau., Jennifer Suzanne. Guidance counselor Binghamton (N.Y.) Psychiat. Center, 1970-76, edn. supr., 1976—, Title I Elementary and Secondary Edn. Act. project mgr. for adolescent unit, 1976—. Served as capt. Mil. Intelligence, U.S. Army, 1969-77. Certified secondary sch. social studies, N.Y.; certified guidance counselor, N.Y. Mem. Am. Personnel and Guidance Assn., Assn. N.Y. State Edn. of Emotionally Disturbed, Delta Sigma Phi. Home: 7 Alice St Binghamton NY 13901 Office: 425 Robinson St Binghamton NY 13901

JOHNSON, ALFRED, clergyman; b. Tyler, Tex., Sept. 6, 1925; s. William Alfred and Pauline Pickering (Palmer) J.; student Universidad Nacional Autonimo de Mexico, 1943; J.D., U. Tex., 1949; M.Div., Episcopal Theol. Sem., 1958; postgrad. Tex. A. and M. U., 1962-66; m. Mildred Garbern, Sept. 6, 1969; children—William Alfred, Stanley Dunstan, Thomas Hampton, Bartholomew Andrew. Admitted to Tex. bar, 1949; mem. firm Hornsby, Kirk and Johnson, Austin, Tex., 1949-57; ordained priest Episcopal Ch., 1958; vicar St. Luke's Ch., Belton, Tex., Grace Ch., Georgetown, Tex., 1958-60; chaplain Tex. A. and M. U., 1960-62; vicar St. Stephen's Ch., Huntsville, Tex., 1962-68; dep. dir. ops. Houston Met. Ministries, 1968-70, interim exec. dir., 1971; dir. chaplaincy Episcopal Mission Soc., Diocese of N.Y., 1971-76; pub. affairs officer Exec. Council, Episcopal Ch. in the U.S.A., 1977—. Chmn. N.Y. State Commn. Instl. Ministries; mem. council of reps. N.Y. State Council of Chs., 1971-77; bd. dirs. Chinatown Mission Project, N.Y.C., 1975-77; bd. dirs. CEDOAS, N.Y.C., 1972-75; trustee Internat. U., Houston, 1970-72. Served with U.S. Army, 1944-46; served to maj. U.S. Army Res. Decorated Bronze Star. Mem. Interfaith Center for Corporate Responsibility, Interfaith Task Force on Criminal Justice, Tex. Bar Assn. Home: 589 Locust Ave Port Chester NY 10573

JOHNSON, ANGELA BLANCHE, educator; b. Freetown, Sierra Leone, July 23, 1926; d. Claudius Hotobah-During and Olaymi Letitia Tuboku-Metzer; came to U.S., 1948, naturalized, 1978; B.S., Allen U., 1951; M.A., Fisk U., 1953; Ed.D., Boston U., 1978; m. Kenneth A. Johnson, June 8, 1954. Instr. chemistry Fort Valley State Coll., 1953-54; instr. sci. So. U., Baton Rouge, 1954-55; asso. prof. chemistry Talladega (Ala.) Coll., 1955-56; asst. prof. sci. Jackson (Miss.) State Coll., 1956-58; sci. specialist Martin Luther King Sch., Cambridge, Mass., 1970-76, sci. tchr. Cambridge Fundamental High Sch., 1976—. Bd. dirs. Middlesex-Cambridge Lung Assn., 1972—, exec. mem., 1977. NSF fellow. Mem. Nat. Sci. Tchrs. Assn., Mass. Assn. Sci. Tchrs., New Eng. Assn. Chemistry Tchrs., Mass. Sch. Masters Club, Mass., Cambridge tchrs. assns., Zeta Phi Beta, Beta Kappa Chi, Pi Lambda Theta. Home: 162 Elliot St Newton Upper Falls MA 02164 Office: 122 Rindge Ave Cambridge MA 02138

JOHNSON, BARBARA DIGIACOMO, real estate co. exec.; b. Ossining, N.Y., July 19, 1937; d. Thomas Peter and Concetta Barbara (Arminio) DiGiacomo; diploma Squire Sch. Bus., 1955; grad. Realtor's Inst., 1977; children—Peter A., Julie Anna. With Dorothy Byington Real Estate Co., Ossining, N.Y., 1965-69; owner, pres. Barbara D. Johnson Realtors, Ossining, 1969—; dir. Multiple Listing No. Westchester. Active Boy Scouts Am., Girl Scouts U.S.A. Mem. Greater Ossining C. of C., Nat. Assn. Realtors, N.Y. State Realtors Assn., Westchester County Bd. Realtors, Realtors Nat. Mktg. Inst., Women's Council Realtors, NOW. Republican. Roman Catholic. Office: 139 Croton Ave Ossining NY 10562

JOHNSON, BENJAMIN WASHINGTON, state ofcl.; b. Hamilton, Va., July 24, 1914; s. Benjamin John and Ellen (Washington) J.; student Columbia, 1934-38; A.B., U. Md., 1963, postgrad. 1966-70; m. Hannabel Yvonne Branche, July 6, 1942 (dec. Dec. 1968); 1 son, Norbert Carl Benjamin; m. 2d, Alice Leonese Dungey, Oct. 16, 1970 (dec. Feb. 1975); 1 stepdau., Lynne Royce Ottley (Mrs. Richard S. Harris); m. Nanette Mack Palmer, June 24, 1976. Tchr. N.J. Manual Tng. High Sch., Bordentown, N.J., 1938-42; enlisted in U.S. Army, 1942, commd. 2nd lt., 1943, advanced through grades to col., 1964; comdr. arty. and transp. units; assigned Europe, Korea, Gen. Staff Dept. Army; retired, 1969; dir. Office Affirmative Action and Compliance, Pa. Dept. Pub. Welfare, Harrisburg, 1970—. Decorated Legion of Merit, Army Commendation medal; Ulchi medal (Korea). Mem. NAACP, VFW, Urban League, Assn. U.S. Army, Ret. Officers Assn., Alpha Phi Alpha. Mason. Home: 3301 N 3d St Harrisburg PA 17110 Office: Health and Welfare Bldg Harrisburg PA 17120*

JOHNSON, BONNIE LUTZKY, hotel exec.; b. Washington, June 23, 1947; d. Joseph and Jeanne (Hertz) Lutzky; B.S. in Sociology, U. Md., 1970, also postgrad.; m. Ronald Wayne Johnson, Nov. 4, 1978. Sales rep. Am. Foresight, Inc., 1965-66; asst. sales mgr. Executive House Hotel, Washington, 1970-71; sales rep. Gramercy Inn, Washington, 1970-73, sales mgr., 1973-76, sales mgr., mgr. tour and travel sales, 1976-78, dir. sales, dir. tour and travel sales, 1978—. Active Congl. Action Fund, 1971-72. Named one of Ten Outstanding Salespeople, Am. Foresight Co., 1966. Mem. Hotel Sales Mgmt. Assn., Am. Assn. Sex Educators, Counselors and Therapists, Alpha Lambda Delta. Democrat. Jewish. Clubs: German Shepherd Dog of Greater Washington, Humane Soc. Home: 311 Ladson Rd Silver Spring MD 20901 Office: Gramercy Inn 1616 Rhode Island Ave NW Washington DC 20036

JOHNSON, BRUCE, educator; b. Hawarden, Iowa, Sept. 4, 1932; s. York and Dorothy Ellen (DeBruce) J.; B.S. in Mech. Engring., Iowa State U., 1955; M.S. in Mech Engring., Purdue U., 1962, Ph.D., 1965; m. Dorothy Jane Rylander, Aug. 27, 1955; children—Sharon Lee, Kristen Kay. Instr. U.S. Naval Acad., Annapolis, 1957-59, asso. prof., 1964-70, prof., 1970—, project dir. model basin, 1968—, Naval Sea Systems Command prof. hydrodynamics, 1975—, dir. hydromechanics lab., 1976—; instr. Purdue U., 1959-64; chmn. 18th Am. Towing Tank Conf., 1977; U.S. rep. commn. on presentation and info. Internat. Towing Tank Conf., 1975—. Trustee Bauman Bible Telecasts, 1970—. Served with USN, 1955-59. Ford Found. grantee, 1962-64, recipient award for excellence in engring. teaching Western Electric Fund, 1971. Mem. ASME, Am. Soc. for Engring. Edn., Soc. Naval Architects and Marine Engrs., Am. Soc. Naval Engrs., AAAS. Methodist. Research in hydrodynamics and brain wave analysis. Home: 12600 Kilbourne Ln Bowie MD 20715 Office: Naval Systems Engring Dept US Naval Acad Annapolis MD 21402

JOHNSON, CARL HAROLD, physician; b. Williamsport, Pa., Oct. 17, 1909; s. Charles Gustav and Anna Kristina (Lindgren) J.; B.S., Gettysburg Coll., 1931; M.D., U. Pa., 1935; m. Nancy McCurdy Keith, Oct. 30, 1936; children—John Keith, Carl Harold, Nancy Lindgren. Intern, Phila. Gen. Hosp., 1935-37, resident in pathology, 1937-38, asst. chief heart clinic, 1937-38; asst. instr. pathology U. Pa. Med. Sch. and Post Grad. Med. Sch., Phila., 1937-38; practice medicine specializing in internal medicine, Gettysburg, Pa., 1938—; pathologist Annie M. Warner Hosp., Gettysburg, 1939—, chief internal medicine, 1948—, pres. staff, 1968-70; cons. cardiology and pathology Samuel G. Dixon State Hosp., South Mountain, Pa., 1947-75. Pres., Adams County Cancer Soc. Trustee Gettysburg Coll. Recipient Service award Adams County unit Am. Cancer Soc., 1958, Distinguished Alumni award Gettysburg Coll., 1977. Diplomate Am. Bd. Internal Medicine. Fellow A.C.P., Am. Coll. Chest Physicians, Am. Soc. Clin. Pathologists, Am. Soc. Internal Medicine; mem. M.A., Pa., Adams County med. socs., Am., Pa. (v.p. 1952-53), South Central Pa. (pres. elect 1966-67), Adams County (pres. 1965-66) heart assns., A.A.A.S., Assn. Clin. Scientists, Phila. Path. Soc., Harrisburg Acad. Medicine, Dwight D. Eisenhower Soc. (life), Phi Sigma Kappa, Phi Rho Sigma. Beta Beta Beta. Presbyn. (ruling elder). Rotarian (past pres. Gettysburg). Contbr. articles on hypertension and heart disease to med. jours. Home: 52 E Broadway Gettysburg PA 17325 Office: 31 S Washington St Gettysburg PA 17325

JOHNSON, CATHERINE COMMON, newspaper, radio, TV exec.; b. Watertown, N.Y., Feb. 12, 1914; d. James Allison and Minna (Anthony) Common; B.A., St. Lawrence U., 1935; M.S. in Journalism, Columbia, 1937; m. John Brayton Johnson, June 21, 1941; children—John Brayton, Ann Catherine, Deborah Jane, Harold

Bowtell. Reporter, editor Watertown Daily Times, 1937-41, editorial and spl. features writer, 1950—; v.p., sec. Johnson Newspaper Corp., owners Watertown Daily Times, WWNY-TV, Carthage-Watertown, radio sta. WWNY, Watertown, WMSA, Massena, N.Y., 1951—; dir. N.Y. Casualty Ins. Co., Watertown, Creg Systems Corp., Watertown. Vice chmn. Thousand Islands State Park Commn. Mem. Nat. League Am. Pen Women, Watertown Artists Guild (dir.), AAUW. Presbyn. Club: College Women of Jefferson County (pres. 1954-56). Home: 221 Flower Ave W Watertown NY 13601 Office: 260 Washington St Watertown NY 13601

JOHNSON, CECILE RYDEN (MRS. PHILIP JOHNSON), artist; b. Jamestown, N.Y.; d. Ernest Edwin and Agnes E. (Johnson) Ryden; A.B., Augustana Coll.; postgrad. Am. Acad. Fine Arts, Art Inst. Chgo., U. Wis., U. Colo., Pa. Acad. Fine Art, Scripps Coll.; m. Philip Arthur Johnson; children—Pamela Cecile, Stevan Philip. One-woman shows Davenport Municipal Gallery, 1954, Chgo. Galleries, 1957, J. Walter Thompson, N.Y., 1958, Hudson River Mus. 1960, N.W. Ayer, Phila., 1960, Charter Gallery, Scarsdale, N.Y., 1960, Grand Central Gallery, N.Y.C., 1965, 67, 69, 71, 73, 75, TWA Paris, 1973; exhibited with Am. Watercolor Soc., Washington Watercolor Soc., Artist Guild of Chgo., Art Dirs. Annual, Nat. Acad., N.Y.C., Soc. of Illustrators; designed and executed stainglass windows for Nursery Chapel, Augustane, Chgo., 12 paintings on Bermuda for collection Bank of Bermuda, 1964, mural for Bermuda Airport, 1966, 32 paintings for U.S. Naval Art Collection on women in naval service; traveling solo exhibit, Am. Univs., 1964, 65, 66; designed covers Ford Times, Chgo. Tribune Sunday Mag., others; designed Am. UNICEF Christmas card for 1968; illustration in Motor Boating, Ford Times, Lincoln Mercury Times; designed and executed Memorable Mountains series for Skiing mag., 1965-74, folios of ski prints for Aspen, Vail, Snowbird, Lake Tahoe, series of 16 prints for TWA on Paris, London, Rome, 1973, series of paintings and folio prints for Napa Valley Vintners, 1975, Broadmoor Hotel, Colorado Springs, 10 originals and 450 signed prints for Broadmoor West, 1976, mural for 1st Fed. Savings and Loan, St. Paul, Bicentennial painting of St. Paul's Fed. Courts Bldg., silk screen for U.S. Hockey Team, 1976 Olympics; represented in permanent collections Augustana Coll., Ford Motor Co., Nat. Safety Council, Garcia Corp., Wagner Coll., Skiing mag., Laurance Rockefeller, Davenport Municipal Art Gallery, others; affiliation Grand Central Galleries, N.Y.C. Recipient awards All Ill. Watercolor, 1953, Ill. Fedn. Music Clubs, 1955; Outstanding Achievement award Alumni Assn. Augustana Coll., 1962; Woman of Achievement award in Art Nat. League Pen Women, 1962, named 1st Woman Artist by USN and NACAL com. Salmagundi Club; Catherine Lorillard Wolffe gold medal for watercolor, 1965. Mem. Am. Watercolor Soc., Soc. Illustrators. Lutheran. Film: Creating in Watercolor. Home: 340 Riverside Dr New York NY 10025 Studio: Des Artistes One W 67 St New York NY 10023

JOHNSON, CHARLES FRANK, plastic surgeon; b. Hazleton, Pa., Apr. 23, 1938; s. Charles F. and Charlotte I. (Zearfoss) J.; A.B., Princeton U., 1960; M.D., Johns Hopkins U., 1964; m. Martha Carolyn Jarmus, June 20, 1964; children—Charles Edward, Robert Andrew, Amanda Caroline. Intern, U. Chgo. Hosps. and Clinic, 1964-65, resident in gen. surgery, 1965-66, 68-71; research asso. Nat. Cancer Inst., Roswell Park Meml. Hosp., Buffalo, 1966-68; resident in plastic surgery U. Rochester, Strong Meml. Hosp., 1971-73; practice medicine specializing in plastic surgery, Pawtucket, R.I. and Providence, R.I., 1973—; mem. staffs R.I. Hosp., Miriam Hosp., Meml. Hosp., Pawtucket, Woonsocket (R.I.) Hosp., Womens and Infants Hosp., Providence; instr. surgery Brown U., Providence, 1973—. Am. Cancer Soc. fellow, 1969. Diplomate Nat. Bd. Med. Examiners, Am. Bd. Surgery, Am. Bd. Plastic Surgery. Fellow A.C.S.; mem. Am. Soc. Plastic and Reconstructive Surgeons, New Eng. Soc. Plastic and Reconstructive Surgeons, Am. Orchid Soc., Epiphyllum Soc. Am. Contbr. articles in field to profl. jours. Home: 489 Wayland Ave Providence RI 02906 Office: 333 School St Pawtucket RI 02860

JOHNSON, CHARLES VICTOR, mgmt. cons.; b. Newark, Nov. 20, 1913; s. Charles V. and Hulda O. (Linderoth) J.; B.S., N.Y. U., 1939, M.B.A., 1940; postgrad Walden U., 1979—; m. Cynthia Foxman, May 6, 1973; children—Carl Richard, Gary Walter, Glen Victor. With Mobil Oil Corp., various locations, 1945-77, asst. mgr. employee relations Mobile Internat., N.Y.C., 1958-62, corporate employee benefits mgr. Mobil Oil Corp., 1961-64, mgr. compensation and benefits Mobil Chem. Co., N.Y.C., 1964-77; labor relations cons. Econ. Devel. Council N.Y.C., 1976-77; exec. dir., com. on retirement policy for fed. personnel Office of Pres., Washington, 1952-54; pres. VIMCO Inc., Stamford, Conn., 1977—; fire commr. City of Stamford, 1977-78. Nat. bd. dirs. Am. Heart Assn., 1957-64; mem. acad. policy bd. Walden U., 1978-79. Served to lt. comdr. USNR, 1942-45. Republican. Presbyterian (deacon). Club: Oronoque Village Golf and Country (Stratford, Conn.). Home and office: 97a Seminole Ln Stratford CT 06497

JOHNSON, CHARLES WARREN, seafood co. exec.; b. Elkhart, Ind., June 9, 1935; s. Warren E. and Kathryn (Cart) J.; A.B., DePauw U., 1957; M.B.A., Ind. U., 1959; m. Norine Carroll Goode, Aug. 23, 1958; children—Cammarie, Kathryn Carroll, Margaret Ellen. With Scott Paper Co., Shaker Heights, Ohio, 1959-68, dist. mgr. sales, 1965-68; nat. sales mgr. Brilliant Seafoods Inc., Boston, 1968-70, v.p. mktg., 1970-75, sr. v.p., 1975—; dir. CTA Corp. Bd. dirs., incorporator Center Creative Arts, Medfield, Mass., 1968—; bd. dirs., fin. chmn. Life Experience Sch., Sherborn, Mass.; v.p. Kennedy assos. Kennedy Meml. Hosp. Mem. Nat., Midwest, Eastern frozen food assns., Am. Mktg. Assn., Nat. Fisheries Inst., Delta Tau Delta. Clubs: Racquet (Miami Beach); Milton Hoosic Country. Home: 138 Central Ave Milton MA 02187 Office: 315 Northern Ave Boston MA 02210

JOHNSON, CURTISS SHERMAN, journalist; b. Meriden, Conn., Apr. 7, 1899; s. Sherman Foster and Adele (Curtiss) J.; B.S., Wesleyan U., 1921; m. Mary Lawton, Sept. 12, 1922 (dec. 1968); children—Curtiss Sherman, Dorothy L. (Mrs. Robert Pollitt); m. Barbara Burleigh, Nov. 1968. Advt. mgr. Manning Bowman & Co., Meriden, Conn., 1921-26; v.p. The Silex Co., Hartford, 1927-28; rep. Curtis Publishing Co., Phila., 1928-32; pres. Curtiss Johnson Publs., Deep River, Conn., 1946-60; dir., Deep River Nat. Bank. Mem. Conn. Flood Control and Water Policy Commn., Hartford, 1954; mem. staff Gov. of Conn., 1940-46; mem. Conn. Safety Commn. Bd. dirs. Middlesex Meml. Hosp.; trustee Henry Whitfield State Mus.; chmn. Conn. River Found., 1978. Served as lt., inf. U.S. Army, World War I; maj. Conn. State Guard, World War II. Mem. Conn, Editorial Assn. (pres. 1941-43). Author: Three Quarters of a Century, 1949; Politics and a Belly-Full, 1962; The Indomitable R. H. Macy, 1964; America's First Lady Boss, 1965; Deadline, 1969; Raymond E. Baldwin, Connecticut Statesman, 1972; History of Pratt-Read Corporation, 1976. Home: River Rd Essex CT 06426

JOHNSON, DAVID MICHAEL, psychologist, educator; b. Adams, Mass., Feb. 28, 1946; s. Richard A. and Lea H. (Desroisiers) J.; A.A. Berkshire Community Coll., 1966; B.A. in Psychology, U. Mass., 1967; M.S. in Psychology, Springfield (Mass.) Coll., 1968, certificate advanced grad. studies in psychology, 1969; postgrad. U. Miss., 1969-70. Counselor, Neighborhood Youth Corps, Northampton, Mass., 1968; psychologist Northampton State Hosp., 1969; research asst. Biocontrol Systems Lab., U. Miss., Oxford, 1969-70, adminstr. psychol. tests Child Clinic, psychology dept., 1970; vis. instr. psychol. statistics Springfield Coll., 1970; asst. dir. of program for disadvantaged students Greenfield (Mass.) Community Coll., 1971, counselor psychology dept., 1971-72, asst. prof., 1971—; cons. to Vets. Assistance Center, 1973, 74, Vets. Club, 1973, 74; vis. lectr. Bur. for Exceptional Children, Holyoke, Mass., 1971; pvt. practice psychol. therapy, Greenfield, Mass., 1972—; instr., counselor Hampshire Correctional Service, Northampton, Mass., 1973-74. Bd. dirs. Franklin County (Mass.) Hot Line, 1972-74, chmn., 1972—; bd. dirs. Hampshire Correctional Services, 1973—. Mem. Am., Mass. psychol. assns., Mass. Tchrs. Assn., Psi Chi. Contbr. articles to profl. pubis. Home: 47 Scout Rd Greenfield MA 01301 Office: Psychology Dept Greenfield Community College College Drive Greenfield MA 01301 also 16 Federal St Greenfield MA 01301

JOHNSON, EARL, assn. exec.; b. Albany, Ga., Sept. 20, 1947; s. S.J. and Bernice E. Motley; B.B.A., Albany State Coll., 1970; children—Earl, Keesha Nichol. Prodn. control specialist Gen. Electric Co., Syracuse, N.Y., 1970, 72; coordinator night program Dunbar Recreation Center, Syracuse, 1974-75; contract adminstr. Gen. Electric Co., 1973-75; exec. dir. Jr. Achievement of Central N.Y., Liverpool, 1975-78; adminstrv. mgr. Aetna Ins. Co., Syracuse, N.Y., 1978—; mem. County Manpower Youth Council. Served with U.S. Army, 1970-72. All-Star basketball player, 1971; subject TV program, Syracuse. Mem. Albany State Coll. Alumni Assn., Kappa Alpha Psi. Baptist. Clubs: Lions (pres. Syracuse Central chpt. 1978-79, environ. chmn. dist. cabinet 1978-79), Masons. Home: 30 Galloway Dr # 12 Liverpool NY 13088 Office: Aetna Regional Office Syracuse NY

JOHNSON, EDNA DECOURSEY (MRS. LAURENCE H. JOHNSON), orgn. adminstr.; b. Balt., June 1, 1922; d. Jacob Garfield and Rosa Felicia (Wilson) DeCoursey; B.S., Coppin State Coll., 1944; postgrad. Rutgers U., 1950, 56, Johns Hopkins, 1952, U. Md., 1959-63, U. Wis., 1966; m. Laurence Harry Johnson, Sept. 30, 1956. Tchr. pub. schs., Balt., 1944-63; asso. dir. Family Life Project, Balt. Urban League, 1963-65, project dir. consumer protection program Community Action Agy., 1965-68, dir. consumer services, 1968-78; exec. dir. N.W. Balt. Corp., 1978—; mem. faculty U. Dayton, 1967; cons. Sears, Roebuck and Co. Treas. Md. Council on Family Relations, 1970—; mem. Commn. on Status Women, 1968-78, Nat. Consumer Adv. Council, 1974—. Bd. dirs. Consumers Union, Balt. Area Council on Alcoholism, Balt. chpt. ARC; adv. council FRS. Named Tchr. of Week Afro-Am. Newspapers, 1947; recipient outstanding community service awards Pi Beta Sigma, 1958, Balt. Club Nat. Assn. Negro Bus. and Profl. Women's Clubs, 1968, Nat. Negro Coll. Fund, 1970, Tau Gamma Delta, 1971, Lambda Kappa Mu, 1972. Mem. Nat. Assn. Negro Bus. and Profl. Women's Clubs (Mid-Atlantic gov. 1967-70, 73-75, nat. corr. sec. 1971-73; pres. Balt. Club 1970-73), Am. Council on Consumer Interest, Md. Conf. Social Welfare, Citizens Housing and Planning Assn., Coppin State Coll. Alumni Assn., Zeta Phi Beta, Pi Beta Sigma. Mem. United Ch. of Christ. Home: 3655 Wabash Ave Baltimore MD 21215 Office: NW Balt Corp 3319 W Belvedere Ave Baltimore MD 21215

JOHNSON, ESTELLA SCOTT (MRS. RUFUS C. JOHNSON), educator; b. Harrisburg, Pa., July 17, 1910; d. John Paul and Estella (Harris) Scott; B.S., Cheyney State Coll., 1934; M.S., U. Pa., 1936, postgrad; m. Rufus C. Johnson, Aug. 7, 1945. Elementary pub. sch. tchr., Harrisburg, 1928-30; research fellow, head resident Fisk U., Nashville, 1936-39, sociology prof., adminstrv. asst. to head social sci. dept. 1939-43; adminstrv. asst. to pres. Cheyney (Pa.) State Coll., 1943-53, asso. prof. social sci. 1957-66, prof., 1966-76, prof. emeritus, 1976—, acting dean Arts and Scis., 1969-70; dir. World Cultures Center, Pub. relations, fashion coordinator Peg Connor Modiste, Phila., 1965-66. Mem. evaluation panel, ad hoc com. higher edn. act U.S. Office Edn., field reader, 1973—; mem. ad hoc black history adv. com. Pa. Hist. Commn.; bd. dirs. Opportunities Industrialization Centers Internat. Recipient fashion award Nat. Assn. Fashion and Accessory Designers, 1959; Commonwealth of Pa. Distinguished Acad. Service award, 1975; named Outstanding Educator in Am., 1970. Gen. Edn. fellow, Julius Rosenwald fellow, 1941-42. Fellow Am. Sociol. Assn.; mem. Nat., Pa. State edn. assns., Am. Sociol. Soc., Nat., Pa. (pres. 1972-73) councils for social studies, AAUP (past sec. Pa. div.), African Studies Assn., AAUW, Internat. Studies Assn., Smithsonian Assos., M.M.S. Host, coordinator television series Afro-Am. Experience. Address: RD 4 Box 156B Glen Mills PA 19342

JOHNSON, EUGENE MANFRED, educator; b. Milford, Del., Oct. 21, 1940; s. Willis M. and Elizabeth Ann (Duling) J.; B.S., U. Del., 1962, M.B.A., 1964; D.B.A., Washington U., St. Louis, 1969; m. Carolyn Ann Passwaters, July 7, 1962; children—Laura, Greta. Instr., St. Louis U., 1966-67; research fellow Mktg. Sci. Inst., Phila., 1967-68; asst. prof. bus. adminstrn. U. Del., Newark, 1968-71; asso. dean Coll. Bus. Adminstrn., prof. mktg. U. R.I., Kingston, 1971—; mktg. and ednl. cons. to various bus. firms. Daniel Bates fellow, 1963-64. Mem. Am. Mktg. Assn., Am. Inst. Decision Scis., Grad. Mgmt. Admissions Council, Methodist. Contbr. articles to profl. jours. Home: Saugatucket Rd RFD 3 Wakefield RI 02879 Office: U RI Kingston RI 02881

JOHNSON, F. EUGENE (GENE), photog. co. exec.; b. Kansas City, Mo., Feb. 27, 1922; s. Tade E. and Ruth (Sloan) J.; B.S., U. Okla., 1944; m. Elaine Helen Cole, Feb. 1971. With Eastman Kodak Co., Rochester, N.Y., 1944—, successively photographer, tchr., writer, editor, lectr., 1944-57, specialist, 1957—, supervising specialist 1969-70, sr. specialist color photography, 1970—. Mem. Soc. Motion Picture and Television Engrs., Photog. Soc. Am., Soc. Photog. Scientists and Engrs., Soc. Tech. Writers and Pubs, Internat. Platform Assn. Contbr. articles to profl. jours. Home: 3654B Monroe Ave Pittsford NY 14534 Office: 343 State St Rochester NY 14650

JOHNSON, FLORENCE GIFFIN, cons.; b. Newark, Apr. 4, 1899; d. Clarence Shepard and Elizabeth Burnside (MacDonald) Giffin; B.A., St. Lawrence U., 1919, D.H.L., 1973; postgrad. N.Y. U. Sch. Commerce, 1923-24; m. A. Pemberton Johnson, 1977. New bus. clk. Chase Manhattan Bank, 1919-21; sec. to editor Good Housekeeping mag., 1921; advt. asst. F. H. Bennett Biscuit Co., 1921-26; head new bus. dept. Bank of N.Y., 1927-30; supr. prospect and donor records Emergency Unemployment Relief Com., 1931-35; office mgr. The Don Herold Co., 1935-40, sec. of corp., 1937-40; organized prospect records N.A.M., 1940; organized prospect and donor records British War Relief Com., 1940-41; personnel specialist Johns-Manville Corp., N.Y.C., 1941-58; organizer women's fund raising activities Community Service Soc., 1958-61. Mem. adv. com. Business Tech. N.Y. State Agr. and Tech. Inst., Farmingdale, N.Y., 1953-60. Emeritus trustee St. Lawrence U. Mem. N.Y. Personnel Mgmt. Assn., Internat. Assn. Personnel Women, New Eng. Hist. Geneal. Soc., Conn. Soc. Genealogists, St. Lawrence County Hist. Assn., St. Lawrence U. Alumni Assn. (v.p. 1955-57), AAUW, Scottish Am. Heritage, Pan Hellenic, Delta Delta Delta. Presbyn. (chmn. ch. employment counseling com. 1952-55, mem. budget com. 1949-52, mem. women's assn. 1949—, Lenten sch. com. 1966-68). Compiler (as F. G. Martin): Simon Giffin & His Descendants, 1971. Home: 123 Medford Leas Medford NJ 08055

JOHNSON, GEARY JUAN, mgmt. cons.; b. Plainfield, N.J., Oct. 27, 1953; s. Robert J. and Vernell J. (Brown) J.; grad. Drew U., 1970. With G II Enterprises, Plainfield, N.J., 1974—, pres., 1977—; pres. Let's Make It Real Mgmt. Service, Plainfield, 1977—. Mem. Citizens Sch. Budget Adv. Com., Plainfield, 1978—. Address: PO Box 2661 Plainfield NJ 07060

JOHNSON, GEORGE BABCOCK, communications exec.; b. Cedar Rapids, Iowa, Aug. 27, 1921; s. George Andrew and Esther Mable (Babcock) J.; B.S. in Elec. Engring., Iowa State Coll., 1943; grad. Indsl. Coll. Armed Forces, 1974; m. Betty Ruth Spurlock, Mar. 11, 1972; children—Lindsey Spurlock, Martha Esther Owen, George Christopher, Julie Ann, David Eric. Engr. Douglas Aircraft Co., Santa Monica, Calif., 1943-44, Turner Microphone Co., Cedar Rapids, 1944, Raytheon Co., Burlington, Iowa, 1946; project engr. USAF, 1946-50, tech. adviser All-Weather br. Air Research and Devel. Command, Wright-Patterson AFB, Ohio, 1951-55, asst. chief TRACALS System Office, 1955-57, asst. dep. for electronic systems, 1957-60, chief program control, also guidance and communications br. X-20 System Program Office, 1960-63, asst. dir. Air Traffic Control Identification Friend or Foe Mil. System, System Program Office, 1964-71; program mgr. RCA govt. and comml. systems, Moorestown, N.J., 1971-74; program mgr. ITT Def. Comm. Div., Nutley, N.J. and Tehran, Iran, 1975-77, Near East area mgr. ITT Telecomm and Electronics Group, 1977—. Served with USNR, 1944-46, USAF, 1951-53. Decorated Air medal. Mem. Inst. Navigation, Armed Forces Communications and Electronics Assn., Air Force Assn., Res. Officers Assn., Ret. Officers Assn., Smithsonian Assos., Am. Philatelic Soc., Bur. Issues Assn. Home: Box 222 Masonville NJ 08054 Office: 500 Washington Ave Nutley NJ 07110

JOHNSON, GUSTAVE HILMER, JR., photographer; b. Hartford, Conn., Feb. 21, 1939; s. Gustave Hilmer and Hilda (Lessor) J.; student pub. schs. Hartford; m. Carol Christensen, May 27, 1961; children—Gustave Hilmer III, Ann Marie. Owner, photographer Gus Johnson Photographer, Windsor, Conn., 1964—. Served with AUS, 1961-63. Mem. Profl. Photographers Am., Evidence Photographers Internat. Council, Nat. Rifle Assn. (life). Photos publ., Readers Digest, 1974, Guns and Ammo, 1974, Time-Life, 1975. Home and office: 53 Bina Ave Windsor CT 06095

JOHNSON, HOWARD EUGENE, sociologist, educator; b. Orange, N.J., Jan. 30, 1915; s. Howard MacPherson and Gertrude Parker (McGinnis) J.; B.S. in Comparative Lit., Columbia, 1966; M.A. in Sociology (Martin Luther King fellow), N.Y. U., 1977; m. Martha Sherman, Apr. 2, 1941; children—Wendy Kay, Wini Lorie, Lisa Alin. Documentation specialist psychiat. epidemiol. research unit Columbia, 1966, field supr. social scis. research unit, 1966; asst. to dir. Ethical Culture Schs., N.Y.C., 1969-71; asso. prof. sociology State Univ. Coll., New Paltz, N.Y., 1971—; cons. minority affairs com. Nat. Assn. Ind. Schs., 1969-75; organizer Black History Project Mid-Hudson, 1976; resource person edn. for Black and P.R., Legis. Caucus N.Y. State, 1975-76. Served with 92d Inf. Div., AUS, 1943-46. Decorated Purple Heart with oak leaf cluster. Mem. AAUP, Black Caucus Sociologists, Am. Sociol. Assn., Nat. Assn. Black Social Workers, Assn. Study Afro-Am. Life and History, Mensa, Phi Delta Kappa. Democrat. Contbr. to profl. jours. Office: Sociology Dept State Univ Coll New Paltz NY 12561

JOHNSON, HOWARD WESLEY, univ. adminstr.; b. Chgo., July 2, 1922; s. Albert H. and Laura (Hansen) J.; B.A., Central Coll., Chgo., 1943; M.A., U. Chgo., 1947; certificate Glasgow (Scotland) U., 1946; also numerous hon. degrees; m. Elizabeth J. Weed, Feb. 18, 1950; children—Stephen Andrew, Laura Ann, Bruce Howard. Asso., R. N. McMurry, 1947-48; from asst. to asso. prof., dir. mgmt. research U. Chgo., 1948-51, 53-55; asst. to v.p. personnel adminstrn. Gen. Mills, Inc., 1952-53; asso. prof., dir. exec. programs, asso. dean Sloan Sch. Mgmt., Mass. Inst. Tech., 1955-59, prof., dean, 1959-66, pres. Mass. Inst. Tech., 1966-71, chmn., 1971—; exec. v.p. Federated Dept. Stores, 1966, dir., 1966—; vice chmn., 1971-73; chmn. Fed. Res. Bank Boston, 1968-69; dir. Hitchiner Mfg. Co., 1961-71, John Hancock Mut. Life Ins. Co., 1968—, Champion Internat. Corp., 1970—, Morgan Guaranty Trust Co., 1971—, E.I. du Pont de Nemours & Co., 1972—. Mem. sr. execs. adv. council Conf. Bd., 1970-76; chmn. Environ. Studies Bd. Nat. Acad. Scis.-Nat. Acad. Engring., 1973-75. Mem. Pres.'s Adv. Com. Labor-Mgmt. Policy, 1966-68, Nat. Manpower Adv. Com., 1967-69, Nat. Commn. on Productivity, 1970-72. Trustee Com. for Econ. Devel., 1968-71, WGBH Ednl. Found., 1966-71, Inst. Def. Analyses, Wellesley Coll., Aspen Inst. Humanistic Studies, Radcliffe Coll.; mem. corp. Woods Hole Oceanographic Instn.; mem. corp. Mus. Sci., Boston; pres. Mus. Fine Arts, Boston, 1975—; overseer Boston Symphony Orch., 1968-72; mem.-at-large Boy Scout Am.; mem. sci. adv. com. Mass. Gen. Hosp., 1968-70. Served with AUS, 1943-46. Fellow Am. Acad. Arts and Scis., AAAS; mem. Council Fgn. Relations, Phi Gamma Delta. Clubs: University, Century Assn. (N.Y.C.); Tavern, Commercial, St. Botolph, Somerset (Boston). Home: 100 Memorial Dr Cambridge MA 02142

JOHNSON, JAMES PEARCE, historian; b. Birmingham, Ala., Aug. 20, 1937; s. James Blackmer and Ella (Pearce) J.; A.B., Duke U., 1959; student Union Theol. Sem., 1959-60; M.A., Columbia U., 1962, Ph.D., 1968; m. Carolyn ApMadoc Brown, Oct. 24, 1959; children—Deborah, Katherine. Instr., Poly. Prep. Country Day Sch., Bklyn., 1960-61; instr. Pace U., 1965, 66; instr. Bklyn Coll., City U. N.Y., 1966-68, asst. prof., 1968-75, asso. prof., dep. chmn. dept. history, 1975—; cons. N.J., Bklyn. High Schs. Mem. Westfield (N.J.) Bd. Edn., 1972-75; mem. Westfield Bicentennial Com., 1976—. Danforth Grad. fellow, 1961-66; recipient Louis B. Pelzer prize, Orgn. Am. Historians, 1966; City U. N.Y. Summer Research grantee, 1969, research found. grantee, 1977. Mem. Am. Hist. Assn., Orgn. Am. Historians, Soc. Values in Higher Edn., Soc. History Edn., Social Sci. History Assn., Group for Use of Psychology in History, Internat. Psychohist. Assn., Bklyn. Coll. Group for Interdisciplinary Use of Psychology, Internat. Soc. Polit. Psychology, Phi Beta Kappa, Phi Eta Sigma. Unitarian. Club: Westfield Tennis. Author: Westfield: From Settlement to Suburb, 1977; The Politics of Soft Coal, 1978; contbr. articles to profl. jours. Home: 716 Clark St Westfield NJ 07090 Office: Dept History Brooklyn Coll Brooklyn NY 11210

JOHNSON, JANE MILLER (MRS. NAPOLEON B. JOHNSON), social worker; b. Welch, W.Va.; d. Leon P. and Mildred (Foster) Miller; A.B., Fisk U., M.S.W., Atlanta U.; m. Napoleon B. Johnson, Aug. 29, 1953; children—Napoleon B. III, Patrelle E. Asst. to dir. social service Tuskegee (Ala.) Inst., 1953-54; caseworker Traveler's Aid Soc., Atlanta, 1955, Bur. Child Welfare, Atlanta, 1955-59; caseworker, instr. sch. nursing U. Okla. Med. Center, 1959-61; supr. Milw. County Welfare Dept., 1961-63; supr. social service dept. Milw. County Hosp., 1961-64; supr. social service Columbia-Presbyn. Med. Center, N.Y.C., 1964-69; coordinator direct services Planned Parenthood N.Y., 1969-72, asso. exec. dir., 1972—. Lectr. human relations Herman Lehman Coll., Coll. City N.Y. Home: 225 Voorhees St Teaneck NJ 07666 Office: 300 Park Ave S New York City NY 10010

JOHNSON, JOHN BRAYTON, editor, pub. exec.; b. Watertown, N.Y., Dec. 14, 1916; s. Harold Bowtell and Jessie R. (Parsons) J.; grad. Phillips Exeter Acad., 1935; A.B., Princeton, 1939; m. Catherine Amelia Common, June 21, 1941; children—John Brayton, Ann, Deborah (Mrs. Fitzhugh Elder III), Harold B. Editor, pub., Watertown Daily Times, 1949—; owner radio stas., WWNY, Watertown, 1949—, WMSA, Massena, N.Y., 1949—; owner TV sta., WWNY-TV, Watertown, 1954—; dir. Nat. Bank No. N.Y., Watertown; dir. Mchts. Nat. Bank & Trust Co., Syracuse, N.Y. Trustee St. Lawrence U., Canton, N.Y.; chmn. N.Y. State Dormitory Authority; chmn. Upstate Med. Council, 1955—. Presbyn. Clubs: Black River Valley (Watertown), Princeton (N.Y.). Home: 221 Flower Ave W Watertown NY 13601 Office: Watertown Daily Times Watertown NY 13601

JOHNSON, JOHN HENRY, chemist; b. Orangeburg, S.C., Oct. 18, 1946; s. John H. and Janie Mae (Cobbs) J.; B.S., S.C. State U., 1966; postgrad. N.Y. U., 1973—. Chem. technician CBS Labs., 1966-68; supr. pilot plant Polymer Industries, 1968-70; chemist Nat. Products, Bklyn., 1970-75; chem. supr. Geosci. Instruments Corp., Stamford, Conn., 1975—. Sec., Jackie Robinson Little League, 1977-78; pres. N.Y. Police Athletic League, 1976-77. Mem. Chem. Soc. Am., Farm House, Alpha Phi Alpha. Office: 420 Fairfield Ave Stamford CT 06902

JOHNSON, JOHN ROBERT, dept. store exec.; b. Frankfort, Ky., Sept. 27, 1936; s. John and Iva Mae (Johnson) J.; B.S. (math. dept. fellow), U. Ky., 1959; m. Emma Jean Prather, May 31, 1958; children—Tracy, Lori, John Robert. Accountant, Am.-Standard Co., Louisville, 1959-60; sr. accountant Cox & Oldham, Louisville, 1961; math instr., Washington Court House, Ohio, 1961-62; accountant SCOA Industries, Boston, 1962-65, comptroller, 1965-69; v.p., controller Zayre Corp., Framingham, Mass., 1969-73; v.p. finance and adminstrn. Gen. Wholesale Supply Co., Boston, 1973-74; sr. v.p. fin. J.M. Fields Dept. Stores, Phila., 1974-78; sr. v.p. fin. and adminstrn. Commonwealth Trading Corp., Stoughton, Mass., 1978—. Active Boy Scouts Am. Mem. Controller's Council Mass. Retail Inst., New Eng. Controllers Assn., Planning Execs. Inst. (pres. 1971-72, regional dir. 1972-73), Beta Alpha Psi, Delta Sigma Pi. Clubs: U.S. Lawn Tennis Assn., Norwood Tennis (pres. 1973—). Home: 222 Eastbourne Terr Moorestown NJ 08057 Office: 100 Campanelli Way Stoughton MA 02072

JOHNSON, JOHN WILLIAM, securities analyst; b. Jersey City, May 8, 1937; s. J. Ward and Marie (Murphy) J.; B.S. in Bus. Adminstrn., Monmouth Coll., 1962; m. Karen Marie Nielson, Nov. 29, 1975; children—Phyllis, Christopher, Marie. Securities analyst Merrill Lynch, Pierce, Fenner & Smith, N.Y.C., 1961-68; portfolio mgr. Composite Fund, Spokane, Wash., 1968-69, Olympia Research and Mgmt., Spokane, 1969-74; v.p. Nomura Securities Internat., N.Y.C., 1974-77; v.p., securities analyst Lexington Mgmt., Englewood Cliffs, N.J., 19—. Served with USN, 1955-59. Chartered fin. analyst. Mem. N.Y. Soc. of Security Analysts. Republican. Episcopalian. Home: 77 Columbus Ave Harrington Park NJ 07640 Office: 476 Hudson Terr Englewood Cliffs NJ 07632

JOHNSON, KATHARYN PRICE (MRS. EDWARD F. JOHNSON), civil worker; b. Smyrna, Del., Mar. 24, 1897; d. Lewis M. and Jennie Cairl (Smithers) Price; grad. Centenary Coll., 1915; student Goucher Coll., 1915-18; m. Edward F. Johnson, Nov. 16, 1920; children—Edward A., Jane Cairl (Mrs. Warner W. Kent, Jr.). With Library Loan Com. for Md. and Liberty Loan Assn. of Balt., 1918-20; pres. Women's Guild Hitchcock Meml. Ch., 1930-32; dir. Scarsdale Woman's Club, 1933-36; dir. White Plains Thrift Shop, 1930-43, pres. 1936-43; mem. exec. com. Scarsdale Community Fund, 1934-38; active Scarsdale council Girl Scouts, 1937-53, commr., 1939-41; mem. region 2 com. Girl Scouts U.S.A., 1942-56, mem. nat. bd., exec. com., 1947-55, chmn. orgn. and mgmt. com., 1952-55, mem. nat. field com., 1943-55, mem. equipment service com., 1956-59, mem. internat. com., 1956-60, meml. gifts and adv. com. to internat. div.; mem. NGO com. on UNICEF, 1965-72, sec., 1968-70; disaster chmn. Scarsdale chpt. A.R.C. 1942-45. Rep. World Assn. Girl Guides and Girl Scouts to UN, 1957-71, attended world confs., 1960, 63, 66, 69, 72, 75, 79; hon. mem. Scarsdale-Hartsdale council Girl Scouts, 1953-69. Mem. Scarsdale Bd. Edn., 1943-46; mem. Nat. Women's Republican Club. Mem. Nat. Council Women U.S., Pi Beta Phi. Presbyn. Club: Scarsdale Woman's (life). Home: 165 Brewster Rd Scarsdale NY 10583

JOHNSON, KENNETH LEROY, program mgmt. co. exec.; b. Chgo., Jan. 24, 1922; s. Stanley C. and Nell L. (Lundberg) J.; student Kansas State Coll., 1940-42, U. So. Calif., 1956-57; B.S., U. Omaha, 1959; m. Tran Thi Phuong, July 3, 1946; children—Jeffery John, Candy Ann, James J. Commd. U.S. Air Force, 1942, advanced through grades to col., 1960; ret., 1969; contract mgr. Pacific Architects & Engrs. Co., Vietnam, 1970-74; program mgr. Bell Helicopter Internat., Tehran, Iran, 1977—. Decorated Purple Heart, Bronze Star, Air Medal with seven oak leaf clusters. Mem. Nat. Assn. Security Dealers. Republican. Club: Masons. Home: PO Box 1076 Rogers AR 72756 Office: PO Box R-BHI Pgm Mat Bell Helicopter Internat APO New York City NY 09202

JOHNSON, KENNETH THEODORE, lawyer; b. Jamestown, N.Y., May 28, 1912; s. Carl E. T. and Hilma (Olson) J.; A.B., Allegheny Coll., 1934; J.D., U. Mich., 1937; m. Marion L. Larson, Aug. 12, 1939. Admitted to N.Y. bar, 1938, U.S. Supreme Ct. bar, also U.S. Tax Ct., Interstate Commerce Commn., Ind. Pub. Service Commn.; law clk. Lombardo & Pickard, 1937-39; lawyer Clive L. Wright, 1939-40; pvt. practice Jamestown, N.Y., 1940-43, 46-52; partner Johnson & Peterson, 1952-56; partner Johnson Peterson, Tener & Anderson, 1956—. Del. N.Y. State Gubernatorial conv. 1934. Mem. Pres.'s Com. on Employment of Physically Handicapped, 1958-74; Gov.'s Com. Employ the Physically Handicapped, 1957—. Mem. adv. bd. Wesley Theol. Sem., Washington. Served from ensign to lt. USNR, 1943-46. Mem. Am., N.Y. State bar assns., Am. Legion, Motor Carrier Lawyers Assn., Assn. ICC Practitioners, Alpha Chi Rho, Delta Sigma Rho, Omicron Delta Kappa. Republican. Methodist. Clubs: Capitol Hill, Conewango, Moon Brook Country, Rotary. Home: Waldheim Jamestown NY 14701 Office: Bankers Trust Bldg Jamestown NY 14701

JOHNSON, LAURANCE DEAN, JR., realtor, insurer; b. Asbury Park, N.J., Aug. 12, 1932; s. Laurence D. and Louise B. J.; B.S. in Bus. Adminstrn., Babson Coll., 1954; m. Barbara Elizabeth Lancaster, June 20, 1959; children—Laurance Dean III, Lauran Mead. Vice pres., treas. Johnson Agency Inc., realtors and insurers, Westfield, N.J., 1955—. Pres. Westfield Bd. Realtors, 1969-71. Mem. Westfield Area C. of C. (dir. 1963-68, v.p. 1967-68), N.J. Assn. Realtor Bds. (dir. 1969-71), Somerset County, Westfield (dir. 1963-68) bds. realtors, N.J. Ind. Ins. Agts. Assn. Republican. Episcopalian. Home: 223 Sinclair Pl Westfield NJ 07090 Office: 20 Prospect St Westfield NJ 07090

JOHNSON, LAWRENCE H., lighting co. exec.; b. Philipsburg, Pa.; s. Michael and Anna V. J.; student Wayne State U., 1942, Carnegie Inst. Tech., 1946, Pa. State U., 1948; B.A. in English, U. Pitts., 1949; m. Claudia R. DePrizio, Jan. 27, 1951; children—Kenneth, Gregg, Karen, Neal. Pub. relations asst. Hill & Knowlton, Inc., N.Y.C. 1949-51; v.p., account supr. Bernard Relin Assos., 1951-58; dir. pub. relations D'Arcy Advt. Agy., N.Y.C., 1958-61; account supr. J. Walter Thompson Co., N.Y.C., 1961-70; v.p. advt. and pub. relations Duro-Test Corp., North Bergen, N.J., 1972—. Served with USAAF, 1943-46. Recipient Gold Key award Pub. Relations News, 1970, 72. Mem. Pub. Relations Soc. Am., Pi Delta Epsilon. Home: Mamaroneck NY 10543 Office: 2321 Kennedy Blvd North Bergen NJ 07047

JOHNSON, LAWRENCE WILLIAM, JR., county ofcl., urban planner; b. Chgo., Oct. 13, 1941; s. Lawrence William and Dorothy Louise (Molohan) J.; B.S. in Landscape Architecture and Urban Planning, Ia. State U., 1967; postgrad. Catholic U., 1968-70; M.A. in Urban Studies, U. No. Colo., 1972; m. Judy Kay Drewry, Aug. 8, 1964; children—Todd Anders, Brian Ford, Mikael Lawrence. Planner Ia. Devel. Commn., Des Moines, 1965-67; asso. planner Frederick County Planning Commn., Frederick, Md., 1967-70, dir., 1970—. Lectr. Frederick Community Coll., 1972—, Catholic U., 1974—; adviser Frederick Improvement Found., Inc., 1973—. Mem. Frederick Downtown Action Com., 1969-72; mem. Frederick Historic Dist. Commn., 1969-70; exec. sec. Frederick County Council of Govts., 1970—. Recipient Achievement award Nat. Assn. of Counties, 1975. Registered landscape architect. Mem. Md. Assn. County Planning Ofcls. (dir. 1972-73, pres. 1975), Am. Soc. Planning Ofcls., Am. Inst. Planners. Methodist (mem. adminstrv. bd. 1969-72). Club: Sertoma. Author: The Environmental Impact of the Mobile Home on Frederick Country; The Urbana Regional Plan. Address: Box 434 Middleton MD 21769

JOHNSON, LESTER FREDRICK, artist, educator; b. Mpls., Jan. 27, 1919; s. Edwin August and Helma Marie (Holmes) J.; student Mpls. Art Inst., 1939-41, St. Paul Art Sch., 1939-41, Art Inst. Chgo., 1943; m. Josephine Valenti, Feb. 12, 1949; children—Leslie Maria, Anthony Edwin. Exhibited art in many one-man shows, including Zabriskie Gallery, N.Y.C., Martha Jackson Gallery, N.Y.C., Gimpel & Weitzenhoffer Gallery, N.Y.C., Donald Morris, Detroit, Mpls. Art Inst., Dayton Art Inst., Ft. Worth Art Inst., Yale U. Mus.; exhibited art in numerous group shows; represented in permanent collections Albright Knox Mus., Dayton Art Inst., Mus. Modern Art, New Sch. for Social Research, Phoenix Art Mus., U. Nebr., Walker Art Mus.; prof. painting Yale, 1964—, dir. studies, 1968—. Mem. Milford Fine Arts Council, Milford, Conn., 1972-73; mem. art adv. com. Housatonic Community Coll., Stratford, Conn., 1969—. Recipient fellowship Trumbull Coll., 1966—, Yale U., Guggenheim fellowship, 1973; Brandeis U. Creative Arts award, 1978. Home: 191 Milbank Ave Greenwich CT 06830 Office: Yale Univ Sch of Art York and Chapel Sts New Haven CT 06520

JOHNSON, MALCOLM CLINTON, JR., pub. exec.; b. Jersey City, Sept. 4, 1925; s. Malcolm Clinton and Edna Menard (Freeman) Johnson; student Harvard, 1943-44; A.B., Dartmouth Coll., 1946; M.S., U. Ill., 1947; m. Jean Anne Guinane, Dec. 28, 1963 (div. 1974); children—Clinton, Brian. Editor, McGraw-Hill Book Co., N.Y.C., 1949-60, sr. editor, 1960-62, editor-in-chief engring. and sci., 1962-65; editor, pub. coll. dept. Time-Life Books, N.Y.C., 1965-67; v.p., pub. W.A. Benjamin, Inc., N.Y.C., 1967-70; v.p., editorial dir. book div. R.R. Bowker, N.Y.C., 1970-73; dir. N.Y. U. Press, N.Y.C., 1973—. Served to lt. (j.g.) USNR, 1943-45. Mem. Coll. Pubs. Group (chmn. 1968-69), Chi Phi. Clubs: Harvard, Saltaire Yacht (N.Y.C.); Potlatch (Eluthera, B.W.I.); Publishers Lunch. Home: 1 Washington Square Village New York City NY 10012 Office: NYU Press 21 W 4th St New York City NY 10012

JOHNSON, MARGARET HILL, ednl. adminstr.; b. Dundee, Scotland, June 26, 1923; d. John Barnet and Isabella Rae (Watson) Hill; came to U.S., 1946; student Edinburgh Royal Coll. Art, 1940; m. Peter Dyer Johnson, Nov. 22, 1965; children—Anne Hill Doughty, James Appleton Doughty, Joanna Elizabeth. Remedial English tchr. Harvey Sch., Hawthorne, N.Y., 1947-53; tchr. athletics Shore County Day Sch., Beverly, Mass. and Pingree Sch., Hamilton, Mass., 1954-63; asso. dir. and cons. Theodore S. Jones & Co., Inc., Milton, Mass., 1964-73; dir. career planning and placement Mass. Coll. Art, Boston, 1973—. Served with Women's Royal Naval Service of Gt. Britain, 1942-45. Mem. Coll. Art Assn., Nat. Assn. Women Deans and Counselors, Am. Assn. Higher Edn., Eastern Coll. Placement Officers, Coll. Placement Council. Author: Your Career in Art and Design, 1977. Home: PO Box 75 Off Summer St Marshfield Hills MA 02051 Office: Mass College of Art 364 Brookline Ave Boston MA 02051

JOHNSON, MARIE LOVE, speech and lang. pathologist; b. South Bend, Ind., Dec. 18, 1925; d. Eugene Thomas and Emma June (Ross) Love; B.S., Ind. U., 1951; M.Ed., Hillyer Coll., U. Hartford, 1953; Ph.D., U. Conn., 1978; m. Arthur Lyman Johnson, Aug. 23, 1950. Speech pathologist East Hartford (Conn.) Bd. Edn., 1949-60, supr. lang., speech and hearing, 1960-77; clin. dir. Shadybrook Lang. & Learning Center, Vernon, Conn., 1971—; pres. Shadybrook Corp., 1971—, exec. dir., 1977—. Vice-chmn. Vernon Democratic Town Com., 1964-70; Justice of Peace, Town of Vernon, 1964-66; mem. Vernon Bd. Finance 1963-65; chmn. bd. mgrs. East Hartford YMCA, 1978. Mem. Conn. (pres. 1971-75), Am. (v.p. profl. and govtl. affairs 1977-78) speech and hearing assns., Pilot Internat., Assn. Children with Learing Disabilities, Delta Kappa Gamma, Phi Kappa Phi, Delta Sigma Theta. Democrat. Union Baptist. Home: 78 Warren Ave PO Box 2026 Vernon CT 06066 Office: 664 Farmington Ave Hartford CT 06105

JOHNSON, OLAF ANDREAS, automatic machine design cons.; b. Brevik, Norway, Mar. 27, 1901; s. Anders Johan and Olga Gunhilde (Olsen) J.; came to U.S., 1923, naturalized, 1936; grad. Skiensfjordens Mekaniske Fagskole, Norway, 1920; m. Hilma Debora Blomberg, Aug. 26, 1924; children—Edgar Anker, Ray Clifford. Designer, Berger Mfg. Co., Canton, Ohio, 1923-26; research and devel. engr. Timken Roller Bearing Co., Canton, 1926-30, 35-37; chief engr. Tyson Roller Bearing Co., Massillon, Ohio, 1930-35; sr. design engr. Gleason Works, Rochester, N.Y., 1937-66; engring. designer Lockheed Aircraft Corp., Burbank, Calif., 1943-44; navy engr. Comml. Control Corp., Rochester, 1952-55; cons. engr. automatic machinery, Rochester, 1966—; occasional tchr. evening schs. Served with Coast Def., Norway, 1921. Republican. Author: Design of Machine Tools, 1971 (one of Outstanding Sci-Tech books for 1971 Library Jour.); Fluid Power, Pneumatics, 1975; Fluid Power, Hydraulics, 1978; contbr. articles to tech. jours. Patentee automatic machinery. Address: 1400 East Ave Apt 502 Rochester NY 14610

JOHNSON, ORVILLE HOWARD, machine developer; b. Marseilles, Ill., July 13, 1911; s. Oscar and Gertie (Hendrickson) J.; ed. high sch.; m. Priscilla E. Markut, Dec. 4, 1937; one dau., Rita D. Glasenapp. Mem. staff explosives mfg. E.I. Du Pont de Nemours & Co. Inc., Wilmington, Del., 1930-50, engring., 1950-68, explosive products tech., 1968-76; indsl. hydraulic cons., Wilmington, 1976—; instr. Del. Tech. and Community Coll., Wilmington, 1977—. Mem. ASME, Fluid Power Soc. Lutheran. Club: Dupont Country. Author: (with Steve Elonka) Industrial Hydraulics-Questions and Answers, 1967. Patentee dynamite loading and tamping machine. Home and Office: 2422 Kingman Dr Wilmington DE 19810

JOHNSON, PAUL EDWARD, health maintenance orgn. exec.; b. Boston, Jan. 2, 1942; s. Arnold Edward and Mildred Ella (Erickson) J.; B.E.E., U. Vt., 1964; M.E.E., Northeastern U., 1966; m. Brenda Kay Meredith, Nov. 26, 1965; children—Meredith Christie, Justin Barrett. Test and installation engr. High Voltage Engring. Corp., Burlington, Mass., 1964-66; with Gen. Radio Co., Concord, Mass., 1966-69; regional sales mgr. Lehigh Valley Electronics div. Tech. Service, Inc., Fogelsville, Pa., 1969-71; corporate sales mgr. Coulbourn Instruments Co., Lehigh Valley, Pa., 1972-76; dir. mktg. Eastern Pa. HMO, Allentown, Pa., 1977—. Pres. Donald Meml. Playground, Inc. Served with USAF, 1962. Mem. Am. Mgmt. Assn., Am. Mktg. Assn., Group Health Assn., Nat. Rifle Assn. (endowment mem.), Allentown-Lehigh County, Bethlehem Area, Easton Area chambers commerce. Clubs: Sertoma, Masons (Allentown). Home: 23 Parkway Ct Allentown PA 18104 Office: 1503 N Cedar Crest Blvd Allentown PA 18104

JOHNSON, PAUL NATHANIEL, JR., accountant, packaging co. exec.; b. Bklyn., Sept. 18, 1949; s. Paul N. and Lillie M. (Monroe) J.; B.A., Cornell U., 1970, M.B.A., 1972; m. Shelley L. Smith, June 12, 1971; 1 son, Kyle J. Sr. accountant Touche Ross Co., N.Y.C., 1972-75; asst. v.p. Citibank, N.Y.C., 1975-78; control adminstr. Am. Can Co., Greenwich, Conn., 1978—; vis. prof. in Black exec. exchange program for Nat. Urban League, 1977—. C.P.A., N.Y. Mem. Am. Inst. C.P.A.'s, N.Y. State Soc. C.P.A.'s. Office: American Can Co American Ln Greenwich CT 06830

JOHNSON, PAUL O., supt. schs., b. Charlestown, N.H., July 15, 1926; s. Otia M. and Georgianna (Poisson) J.; B.S., Springfield Coll., 1950; M.Ed., Rivier Coll., 1957; postgrad. U. N.H., 1964, Keene State Coll., 1966-68; Ed.D., Boston U., 1971; m. Annette F. Boucher, Aug. 21, 1954; children—David, Paula, Mark, Suzanne, Donna. Tchr., coach Alvirne High Sch., Hudson, N.H., 1950-59; prin. Somersworth (N.H.) High Sch., 1959-63, Salem (N.H.) High Sch., 1963-68; supt. schs., Salem, 1969—; faculty, U. N.H., Durham, 1972—; dir. N.H. Blue Cross Blue Shield, 1973-75. Served with USNR, 1944-46. Mem. N.H. Secondary Sch. Prins. Assn. (pres. 1962), N.H. Sch. Adminstrs. Assn. (pres. 1975), Am. Assn. Sch. Adminstrs., New Eng. Sch. Devel. Council (chmn. 1976), New Eng. Assn. Univ. and Coll. Staffing (dir. 1969-72), Phi Delta Kappa. Kiwanian (dir. 1970-73). Home: 8 Sullivan Ave Salem NH 03079 Office: Main St Salem NH 03079

JOHNSON, PHILIP EDWARD, health ins. co. exec.; b. Jersey City, Dec. 2, 1918; s. Robert J. and Katherine (Davis) J.; B.S. in Bus. Adminstrn., Duquesne U., 1941; m. Ann Marie Ely, Apr. 15, 1944; children—Kathleen Marie, Philip Edward, Richard Joseph, Edward George, Anna Marie, James Michael, David Michael. Sr. accountant Scovill Wellington & Co., Phila., 1946-48; sr. accountant Price, Waterhouse & Co., Pitts., 1948-53; with Blue Cross of Western Pa., Pitts., 1954—, now v.p., treas.; v.p., treas., dir. Standard Property Corp., Madison Realty Corp., Jacsan Inc., 1975—. Mem. accounting com. Gov.'s Hosp. Study Commn., Commonwealth of Pa., 1963-71. Bd. dirs., chmn. Central Blood Bank, Pitts., 1964—. Served to capt. Ordnance Corps., AUS, 1941-46. C.P.A. Mem. Hosp. Financial Mgmt. Assn., Am. Mgmt. Assn., Duquesne U. Alumni Assn., Financial Execs. Inst. Republican. Roman Catholic. K.C. Home: 716 Pinetree Rd Pittsburgh PA 15243 Office: 1 Smithfield St Pittsburgh PA 15222

JOHNSON, RALPH JAMES, home bldg. research co. exec.; b. Peoria, Ill., Aug. 29, 1915; s. Arthur Frank and Birdie May (Downes) J.; student Bradley U., 1934-37; B.S. in Civil Engring. cum laude, U. Ill., 1939; M.S. in Civil Engring. cum laude, Harvard, 1940; m. Flo Elizabeth Gamblin, June 12, 1943; children—Ralph James, Stephen Downes. Commd. lt. (j.g.) USPHS, 1940, advanced through grades to comdr.; stationed Washington, D.C., 1940-41; engr. Peoria, 1941-42; housing specialist USPHS, Washington, 1942-45, various locations, 1955-65; dir. constrn. dept. and research inst. Nat. Assn. Home Builders, Rockville, Md., 1965—, v.p. Nat. Assn. Home Builders Research Found., Inc., 1965—. Mem. Bldg Research Adv. Bd., 1952-57. Bd. dirs. Epping Forest Corp. Registered profl. engr., Ida. Mem. Sigma Xi, Tau Beta Pi, Chi Epsilon, Sigma Tau, Delta Omega. Home: 8200 Kenfield Ct Bethesda MD 20034 Office: NAHB Research Foundation Inc 627 Southlawn Ln Rockville MD 20850

JOHNSON, RICHARD F.Q., psychologist; b. Boston, July 11, 1943; s. Frederick and Alice H. (Kullen) J.; A.B. with honors, Northeastern U., 1966; M.A. in Psychology, Brandeis U., 1968, Ph.D. in Psychology (Woodrow Wilson fellow), 1970; m. Sharyn L. Doyle, Sept. 11, 1965; children—Wendy, Adam. Research asso. Medfield (Mass.) Found., 1968-70, sr. research psychologist, 1972-76; research psychologist U.S. Army Natick Research and Devel. Command, 1976—; pvt. practice psychotherapy, 1978—; lectr. in psychology Northeastern U., Boston, 1972-76; cons. to Jour. of Cons. and Clin. Psychology, 1973—; mem. faculty Psychiat. Residency Tng. Program, Medfield State Hosp., 1974-76. Chmn. Human Rights Com., Mass. Dept. Mental Health, 1974-77. Served to capt. Med. Service Corps, U.S. Army, 1970-72. Mem. Am., Eastern Southeastern psychol. assns., AAAS, Am. Soc. Clin. Hypnosis, Sigma Xi. Contbr. articles on suggestion psychophysiology and stress to profl. jours. Home: 15 Sahlin Circle Franklin MA 02038 Office: Human Factors CE and MEL US Army Research and Devel Command Natick MA 01760

JOHNSON, ROBERT ALAN, hosp. adminstr.; b. Brockton, Mass., May 13, 1933; s. Arthur B. and Ruth E. (McGrath) J.; B.S. in B.A., Suffolk U., 1962; student Bentley Coll., 1956-58; postgrad. Northeastern U., 1967, Columbia U., 1968; m. Lois Pierson, Mar. 10, 1954; children—Cheryl, Scott, Kevin. Auditor, Bur. Hosp. Costs and Fins., Boston, 1958-62; controller Free Hosp. for Women, Brookline, Mass., 1962-63, Goddard Meml. Hosp., Stoughton, Mass., 1963-68, Meml. Hosp., Worcester, Mass., 1968-71; v.p. Medco Inc., Springfield, Mass., 1971-72; v.p., treas. Brockton (Mass.) Hosp., 1972—; corporator Brockton Savs. Bank, 1975—. Mem. Hosp. Blue Cross Negotiating Team, 1977, mem. fin. adv. group, 1977—; chmn. Joint Com. on Adminstrn. of Blue Cross Contract, 1976—; chmn. Mgmt. Group for Systems Engring., 1975-76; mem. Health Systems Agy. #5 of Southeastern Mass, 1976—; bd. dirs. Brockton Vis. Nurses Assn., 1976—. Served with U.S. Army, 1953-55. Fellow Hosp. Fin. Mgmt. Assn. (pres. Mass. chpt. 1978—); mem. Am. Hosp. Assn. Conglist. Clubs: Brockton Country (treas. 1975—), Kiwanis, Univ. Home: 6 Priscilla Rd South Easton MA 02375 Office: 680 Centre St Brockton MA 02402

JOHNSON, ROSWELL DORR, pediatrician, univ. adminstr.; b. Ottumwa, Iowa, Mar. 14, 1913; s. Otto Axel and Moss Ina (Dorr) J.; B.A., U. Iowa, 1935, M.D., 1938; M.A. (hon.) Brown U., 1964; m. Katherine Buchtel, Dec. 30, 1939 (dec. 1973); children—Steven, Judith, Clinton; m. 2d, Sarah Stanley Frisbie, Mar. 3, 1974. Intern, Henry Ford Hosp., Detroit, 1938-39; resident Yale-New Haven Med. Center, 1939-40, 41-42, Strong Meml. Hosp., Rochester, N.Y., 1940-41; practice medicine specializing in pediatrics, 1944-63; instr. pediatrics Yale U., New Haven, 1940-44; mem. staff Bassett Hosp., Cooperstown, N.Y., 1944-47; instr. pediatrics Tulane U., New Orleans, 1947-49; chief pediatrics Found. Hosp., New Orleans, 1947-49, New Britain (Conn.) Gen. Hosp., 1951-63; asso. clin. prof. pediatrics Yale U., 1949-56; dir. health services Brown U., Providence, 1963—, clin. prof. community health, 1971—; cons.

physician R.I. Hosp.; mem. courtesy staff Butler Hosp. Fellow Am. Acad. Pediatrics, Am. Coll. Health Assn.; mem. Am., R.I. med. assns., New Eng. Coll. Health Assn., Am. Med. Soc. on Alcoholism (chmn. R.I. br.), Sigma Xi. Republican. Episcopalian. Contbr. articles, chpts. to med. jours., texts. Home: 22 Benevolent St Providence RI 02906 Office: PO Box 1928 Brown U Providence RI 02912

JOHNSON, SELINA TETZLAFF, museologist, historian; b. N.Y.C., Sept. 7, 1906; d. John Victor and Augusta Bertha (Seidel) Tetzlaff; A.B. cum laude, Hunter Coll., 1925; postgrad. Harvard, 1926, Columbia, 1927; M.S. in Edn., Coll. City N.Y., 1954; Ph.D. in Museology, N.Y. U., 1962; m. H. Herbert Johnson, June 1, 1927; (dec.); children—Jaqueline (Mrs. Donald J. Horvath), Frank Wheeler. Instr. phys. edn. and Kinesiology Hunter Coll., N.Y.C., 1925-26; instr. comparative anatomy and biology Coll. City N.Y., 1926-32, N.Y. U., 1931-32. Mem., 1st chmn. Bergen County (N.J.) Cultural and Heritage Commn., 1972—; commr. Girl Scouts Am., 1949-51; founder, pres. Conservation Council N.J., 1953-56; chmn. cultural events Bergen Mall, 1957-68; cons. Hall History County, 1968—; chmn. commn. Thomas Alva Edison Centennial Program, 1978-79. Founder, dir., trustee Youth Mus. Leonia, 1950-56; co-dir. Nantucket Island (Mass.) Nat. Sci. Mus., 1959-65; trustee Jersey Blues Armory Mus., 1959—; founding trustee North Jersey Opera Theatre, 1969—; founder, 1st pres., dir. Bergen Community Mus., 1956-70, trustee, 1970—. Mem. Nantucket Hist. Assn. (life, field archeologist 1973—, curator Greater Light 1975—), N.Y. Acad. Scis., Council Northeast Hist. Archeology, Leonia Home and Sch. Assn. (pres. 1943-47), English Neighborhood Hist. Soc. (charter trustee 1959—), Palisades Nature Assn. (life dir.), Caduceus Soc. (hon.), Maria Mitchell Assn. (bd. mgrs. 1975—), N.J. State Fedn. Women's Clubs (recipient Silver Orchid award 1951), Mus. Council N.J. (chmn. standards com. 1965-67), Leonia Woman's Club (chmn. art, garden and youth conservation depts. 1940-70), Nat. Hist. Soc. (founding asso.), China Stamp Soc., Nat. Chrysanthemum Soc., Nantucket Conservation Found., Nat. Trust Historic Preservation, Phi Beta Kappa. Illustrator: Classification of Insects; Adventures With Living Things; Angina Pectoris; Hunt for the Mastodon. Author: Creating A Community Museum, 1954; Museums for Youth in the United States: Their Origins, Development and Cultural Contributions, 1962. Editor: Greater Light On Nantucket, 1973. Home: 24 Hawthorne Terr Leonia NJ 07605

JOHNSON, SHILDES RISDON VAIL, clergyman, educator; b. Waco, Tex., Oct. 24, 1916; s. William Shildes Strong and Mary Olive (Vail) J.; B.S., Butler U., 1938; Th.M., Cal. Bapt. Theol. Sem., 1947; B.D., No. Bapt. Theol. Sem., 1948; Ph.D., U. Edinburgh, 1955; Th.D., So. Bapt. Theol. Sem., 1957; m. Ruth Sullivan, July 26, 1946; children—Sheryl Lee Anna, Shildes Colin David. Asst., Butler U., 1935-38; grad. asst. Syracuse U., 1938-39; ordained to ministry Bapt. Ch., 1942; student instr. Cal. Bapt. Theol. Sem., 1946-47; instr. No. Bapt. Theol. Sem., 1947-48; librarian, instr. Bible, Clarke Meml. Coll., 1952-53; asst. prof., chmn. dept. classical langs, Taylor U., 1954-57; asso. prof., acting chmn. div. philosophy and religion Wayland Bapt. Coll., 1957-58; head librarian, asso. prof. Bloomfield Coll., 1958-62; prof. Bibl. langs., head librarian Northeastern Collegiate Bible Inst., Essex Fells, N.J., 1962-68; prof., chmn. dept. religion and philosophy Barber-Scotia Coll., 1968-69; prof. Bible, Nyack (N.Y.) Missionary Coll., 1969-70; research dir. Inst. Contemporary Christianity, 1971—; pastor Sardina Congl. Christian Ch., Bryant, Ind., 1954-57. Book rev. editor Harvester Highlights, 1963-68; mng. editor Classical World, 1964-66. Served to 1st lt. AUS, 1941-46. Mem. Nat. Assn. Profs. Hebrew, Am. Schs. Oriental Research, Soc. Bibl. Lit., Soc. Old Testament Study, Am. Oriental Soc., Acad. Religion, Evang. Theol. Soc., Am. (former sec.-treas., Essex County chpt. reference services div.), N.J. (past chmn. reference services div., mem. coll. and univ. div.) library assns., Christian Librarians' Fellowship, Am. Sci. Affiliation, Kappa Delta Pi, Pi Mu Epsilon, Lambda Chi Alpha, Phi Kappa Phi. Co-author: Stars, Signs and Salvation, 1971; The Occult Explosion; Witches. Home: 1564 Broad St Bloomfield NJ 07003 Office: 410 Ramapo Valley Rd Oakland NJ 07436

JOHNSON, SUE STORER (MRS. DONALD C. JOHNSON), state ofcl.; b. Indpls., Feb. 2, 1935; d. Horace Elbert and Billie Mae (Kreider) Storer; B.S., Purdue U., 1956; m. John C. Jamison, June 2, 1956 (div. Dec. 1963); m. 2d, Donald C. Johnson, Jan. 1964; children—Susan Storer, Anne Lucille, Alice Anne. Research engr. Convair div. Gen. Dynamics, San Diego, 1957-59; profl. staff mem. Arthur D. Little, Inc., Cambridge, Mass., 1960-63; research sect. head Sperry Gyroscope Co., Great Neck, N.Y., 1963-64; cons. Airborne Instruments Lab., Deer Park, N.Y., 1965-66; cons. Sci. and Tech. Task Force, Pres.'s Commn. on Law Enforcement and Adminstrn. of Justice, Washington, 1966-67; cons. Franklin Inst. Research Labs., Phila., 1968—; pres. Brookville (N.Y.) Systems Co., Inc., 1969-74; dir. mgmt. and planning and govt. info. service N.Y. State Office of Ct. Adminstrn., 1974-77, asst. chief adminstr., 1977—; cons. U.S. Dept. Justice, 1969—. Mem. Ops. Research Soc. Am., Am. Judicature Soc., Am. Acad. Polit. and Social Sci., Theta Delta Phi, Kappa Kappa Gamma, Mortar Bd. Republican. Episcopalian. Patentee in field. Home: 91 McCouns Ln Old Brookville NY 11545

JOHNSON, THEODORE MARTIN, clin. psychologist, educator; b. Fresno, Calif., May 8, 1940; s. Clarence Netzler and Myrl LaVern (Martin) J.; B.A. in Psychology, Fresno State U., 1962; postgrad. San Jose State U., 1964-66; Ph.D. in Clin. Psychology, Fuller Theol. Sem., 1972, Th.M., 1975; m. Nancy Sue Smith, Aug. 8, 1964; children—Christopher Allen, Neil David. Youth minister, 1966-68; clin. psychologist Philhaven Hosp., Lebanon, Pa., 1971-74, chief psychology, 1974—; asst. prof. family relations Messiah Coll., Grantham, Pa., 1972—, Evang. Congl. Sch. Theology, Meyerstown, Pa., 1975—; clin. psychologist Lebanon Valley (Pa.) Coll., 1974—; cons. Messiah Children's Home, VA Hosp., Lebanon. Bd. dirs. Lebanon County Mental Health Assn., 1971—, pres., 1977—; bd. dirs. Pa. Mental Health Assn., Phila., 1975-77. Recipient Theodore Perkins Meml. award Calif. Psychol. Assn., 1971. Mem. Pa., Am. psychol. assns. Democrat. Contbr. articles Jour. Ednl. Research, Christian Living, Christian Assn. Psychol. Studies, United Evangel. Home: Box 385 RD 5 Lebanon PA 17042 Office: Box 345 RD 5 Lebanon PA 17042

JOHNSON, THOMAS BRADFORD, JR., cons. psychologist; b. Lewiston, Maine, May 12, 1942; s. Thomas B. and Virginia A. (Hamblin) Jr.; B.S. with honors, Ariz. State U., 1964; postgrad. (USPHS fellow) in Social Psychiatry, Brown U., 1965; Ed.M. in Counseling Psychology, Harvard, 1966; Ed.D. in Counseling Psychology (NDEA fellow), U. Calif., Berkeley, 1969; m. Mary Elizabeth Hinkle, July 12, 1969; 1 dau., Catherine Alice. Counselor trainee Suffolk U. Counseling Center, Boston, 1966; counseling psychologist Central City Hospitality House, San Francisco, 1967-68; counseling psycholgist trainee U. Calif. at Berkeley Counseling Center, 1968; cons. psychologist Peace Corps, Phila., 1971; clin. psychologist div. of psychiatry, dept. of medicine, Central Maine Med. Center, Lewiston, 1974-76, Child and Family Mental Health Center, Lewiston, 1969-72; pvt. practice family counseling, 1972-76; cons. psychologist, founder Dr. Thomas B. Johnson & Assos., clin., family and sch. psychology, Auburn, Maine, 1972—; lectr. in psychology (part-time) Bates Coll., 1970-72; vis. asst. prof. Rutgers U., 1969—; adj. prof. (part-time) U. Maine, Portland-Gorham, 1971-76. Chairperson Profl. Standards Pev. Com., State of Maine, 1974-76; sec. Sabbathday Lake Assn., 1974-75. Mem. Am., Maine psychol. assns., Am. Assn. Marriage and Family Counselors (supr. tng. 1975-78, pres. Maine div.), Am. Humanist Assn., Am. Personnel and Guidance Assn., New Gloucester Hist. Soc., Phi Delta Kappa, Alpha Kappa Delta. Contbr. articles to profl. jours. Home: PO Box 89 Poland Spring ME 04274 Office: Two Goff St Auburn ME 04210

JOHNSON, THOMAS FRANK, economist; b. Lynchburg, Va., Sept. 27, 1920; s. Thomas Frank and Inez (McDaniel) J.; student Lynchburg Coll., 1939-41; B.A., U. Va., 1943, M.A., 1947, Ph.D., 1949; m. Margaret Ann Emhardt, Dec. 29, 1951; children—Thomas Emhardt, Sarah Lee, William Harrison Johnson. Economist U.S. Dept. Agr., Washington, 1949-51, U.S. C. of C., 1951-54; asst. commr. FHA, 1954-58; dir. legislative analysis Am. Enterprise Inst. for Pub. Policy Research, Washington, 1958-59, dir. research, 1960-76, dir. econ. policy studies, 1977—. Sec.-treas. Inst. Social Sci. Research, Washington. Served to lt. USNR, 1943-45, PTO; lt. comdr. Res. Mem. Am., So., Western, Royal econ. assns., Nat. Tax Assn., Am. Finance Assn., Nat. Assn. Bus. Economists (chpt. pres. 1971). Episcopalian. Club: Cosmos. Contbr. articles to profl. jours. Home: 1113 N Gaillard St Alexandria VA 22304 Office: 1150 17th St NW Washington DC 20036

JOHNSON, VIOLA VICTORIA, hosp. admistr.; b. Monroe, La., Aug. 21, 1929; d. Garfield and Viola (Hattisburg) J.; B.S. in Foods and Nutrition, So. U., 1950. Dietetic intern Freedman's Hosp., Washington, 1951-52; staff dietitian VA Hosp., Perry Pt., Md., 1952-64; asst. chief dietitian VA Hosp., Lebanon, Pa., 1964-66, Indpls., 1966-68; chief dietitian VA Hosp., Battle Creek, Mich., 1968-72; hosp. adminstrv. officer trainee VA Hosp., Chgo., 1972; asst. hosp. dir. VA Hosp., Fayetteville, N.C., 1972-73; hosp. administrv. specialist VA Central Office, Washington, 1973-76; asst. hosp. dir. VA Hosp., Lyons, N.J., 1976—. Mem. Somerset County Mental Health Bd., 1977—. Mem. Asst. Hosp. Dirs. Assn. N.J. Office: VA Hosp Lyons NJ 07939

JOHNSON, WALTER HERBERT, engr.; b. Boston, Jan. 6, 1931; s. Helge Ernest and Mary Frances (Fleck) J.; student Wentworth Inst., 1950-52, 71, Sch. Pub. Health U. Minn., 1967, U.S. N. Atomic Warfare Sch., 1968; m. Dorothy Alban Maguire, Apr. 19, 1954; children—Steven Helge, Mark Edward, Linda Marie. Electrician ICC, 1954-62; insp., foreman, asst. gen. foreman Boston & Maine R.R., 1962-66, maintenance supr. Carney Hosp., Boston, 1966-68, dir. maintenance, 1968-71, dir. engring., 1971—. Mem. Stoughton (Mass.) Town Meeting, 1957-75; mem. Stoughton Bd. Health, 1975—, now chmn.; 1st v.p. SE Regional Bds. Health Mass. Licensed master electrician, stationary engr., master steam fitter, Mass. Mem. Am. (sr.), New Eng. assns. hosp. engrs., Mass. Elec. Contractors Assn., Am. Hosp. Assn., Amvets (past post comdr.), Nat. Rifle Assn., Am. Legion. Club: K.C. Home: 66 Elizabeth St Stoughton MA 02072 Office: 2100 Dorchester Ave Boston MA 02124

JOHNSON, WALTER J., publisher; b. July 29, 1912; ed. U. Heidelberg, U. Paris a la Sorbonne, U. Coll., London; Sc.D. (hon.), Albany Med. Coll., 1978; married. Founder, pres. Walter J. Johnson, Inc., N.Y.C. and London, 1942—; founder, pres. Academic Press, N.Y.C. and London, 1942-72; founder, pres. Johnson Reprint Corp., N.Y.C. and London, (became subsidiary Acad. Press 1967), 1946-72; merger Acad. Press and Harcourt Brace Jovanovich, N.Y.C., 1969. Trustee Albany (N.Y.) Med. Coll. Fellow Pierpont Morgan Library. Served with Nat. Guard, 1941-44. Mem. A.L.A., Am. Med. Library Assn., Friends Columbia U. Club: Grolier (N.Y.C.). Home: 19 Hewitt Ave Bronxville NY 10708 Office: 355 Chestnut St Norwood NJ 07648

JOHNSON, WILLIAM CHARLES, chem. engr.; b. Marquette, Mich., June 12, 1921; s. Frederick Appleton and Elnora Louise (King) J.; B.S., Mich. Tech. U., 1942; m. L. Elinor Greene, July 28, 1962; children—Frederick Craig, Blake Andrew, Tracy Anne. Chem. engr. Toni Co., St. Paul, 1946-48; prodn. engr. Upjohn Co., Kalamazoo, 1948-67; chief engr. Upjohn Internat., Inc., Kalamazoo, 1967-75; dir. engring. indsl. div. Bristol-Myers Co., Syracuse, N.Y., 1975-78; chief engr. Otisca Industries Ltd., 1978—. Served to capt. C.E., AUS, 1942-46. Decorated Purple Heart. Registered profl. engr., Mich. Mem. Am. Inst. Chem. Engrs. Club: Masons. Home: 4836 Carey Dr Manlius NY 13104

JOHNSTON, DON, advt. exec.; b. Elmira, N.Y., 1927; grad. Mich. State U., 1950. Pres., chief exec. officer and dir. J. Walter Thompson Co., Advt., N.Y.C. Home: 33 Woodridge Dr New Canaan CT 06840 Office: 420 Lexington Ave New York City NY 10017

JOHNSTON, JOSEPHINE R., chemist; b. Cranston, R.I., Aug. 9, 1926; d. Robert and Rose (Varca) Forte; student Carnegie Inst., 1945-47; B.S., Mich. State U., 1972, M.A., 1973; postgrad. Mass. Inst. Tech., 1973— m. Howard Robert Johnston, Mar. 7, 1949; 1 son, Kevin Howard. Med. technologist South Nassau Community Hosp., Rockville Centre, N.Y., 1947-50, Mich. State U., East Lansing, 1950-53, dept. veterinary pathology Albany (N.Y.) Med. Center, 1953-54; med. lab. supr. Bulova Watch Co., Jackson Heights, N.Y., 1954-57; sr. chemistry technologist Mid Island Hosp., Bethpage, N.Y., 1958-66; faculty specialist Mich. State U., East Lansing, 1966-76; sr. research asso. Uniformed Services Univ., Bethesda, Md., 1976-78, asst. to chmn. dept. psychology, 1978—. Mem. Analytical Chem. Soc., Data and Electronic Soc. Lutheran. Contbr. articles in field to profl. jours. Office: 4301 Jones Bridge Rd Bethesda MD 20014

JOHNSTON, KEVIN PHILIP, mem. Conn. Ho. of Reps.; b. Putnam, Conn., Oct. 11, 1950; s. Loretta Mary (St. Onge) J.; B.A., St. Michael's Coll., Vt., 1972. Mem. Town of Putnam Bd. Selectmen, 1973—, Zoning Commn., 1973—, energy com., 1974; mem. Conn. Ho. of Reps., 51st. Dist., 1974—, appropriations com.; Mem. Putnam Mayor's Youth Council, 1972-73, N.E. Conn. Alcohol Council; mem. Conn. Gov.'s finance adv. com., 1976—; v.p. Windham County Democratic Assn., 1973—, vice-chmn. Putnam town com., 1976—; bd. dir. Quinnebaug Valley Sr. Citizens Center. Mem. Council of Small Towns. Clubs: Foresters, Elks. Home: Rural Route 1 Park St Putnam CT 06260 Office: 126 Church St Putnam CT 06260

JOHNSTON, LAURA LEE, adjustment counselor; b. Sioux Falls, S.D., Nov. 4, 1953; d. Robert Dean and Lorreto Jean (Volin) J.; B.S., U. S.D., 1976, M.A., 1977; m. Steven Joel Savonen, Oct. 22, 1977. Birth control counselor U. S.D. Health Center, Vermillion, 1976; psychol. intern Central Plains Clinic, Sioux Falls, 1977; crisis counselor Medford (Mass.) High Sch., 1977-78; adjustment counselor Spl. Needs Office, Malden (Mass.) Pub. Schs., 1978—. Certificate spl. edn., Mass., S.D. Mem. Am. Psychol. Assn., Am. Assn. Sex Educators, Counselors and Therapists, Am., Greater Boston personnel and guidance assns. Democrat. Roman Catholic. Home: Apt 427 200 Swanton St Winchester MA 01890 Office: Special Needs Office Malden Pub Schs 200 Pleasant St Malden MA 02148

JOHNSTON, THOMAS MATKINS, govt. ofcl.; b. Okmulgee, Okla., Dec. 8, 1921; s. Alexander and Lillian Grace (Matkins) J.; B.S., U.S. Mil. Acad., 1943; M.E., N.Y. U., N.Y.C., 1949; postgrad. N.Y. U., 1958-60, Mass. Inst. Tech., 1960, Case Inst., 1962; m. Esther Elizabeth Logan, June 7, 1943; children—Thomas Garrett, Robert Alexander, Hugh Samuel, Ann Logan. Served to maj. C.E., U.S. Army, 1943-58; instr. math. U.S. Mil. Acad., West Point, N.Y., 1949-52, lectr., 1969-71; mgr. systems analysis group RCA, Moorestown, N.J., 1958-67; mgr. info. systems dept. Raytheon Co., Bedford, Mass., 1967-71; chief tech. programs div. FAA, DOT, Washington, 1971—; lectr. math. U. Calif., 1954-55, U. Md., 1956-59, Am. U., Washington, 1956-59. Decorated Bronze Star with oak leaf cluster. Fellow AAAS; mem. Ops. Research Soc. Am. Author tech. papers on def. electronic products. Research in field of weapons systems analysis. Registered profl. engr. Home: 3720 Carriage House Ct Alexandria VA 22309 Office: 800 Independence Ave SW Washington DC 20591

JOHNSTON, WILLIAM ANDREW, JR., engring. exec.; b. Canton, Ohio, July 25, 1927; s. William Andrew and Jane Katherine (Miller) J.; B.S. in Elec. Engring., U. Va., 1949; m. Florence Marilyn Butt, Nov. 2, 1957; children—Janet Katherine, William Andrew III. With Fairchild Industries, 1949—, engr. Fairchild Guided Missiles div., Wyandanch, N.Y., 1949-54, system mgr. Republic Missile Systems div., Mineola, N.Y., 1955-65, program dir. Fairchild Space and Electronics Co., Germantown, Md., 1966-75, v.p. engring., 1975—; chief engr., program dir. launching Applications Tech. Satellite, 1968-74. Mem. engring. adv. com. Montgomery Coll., Rockville, Md. Served with USNR, 1945-46. Asso. fellow Am. Inst. Aeronautics and Astronautics (tech. com. on space systems); sr. mem. IEEE. Republican. Presbyterian. Clubs: Lakewood Country, Nat. Space. Home: 12516 Knightsbridge Ct Rockville MD 20850 Office: Fairchild Space and Electronics Co Germantown MD 20767

JOHNSTONE, DORN KENNETH, hosp. adminstr.; b. Bellefonte, Pa., Mar. 24, 1941; s. B. Kenneth and Helene E. (Hetzel) J.; B.S., Pa. State U., 1963; M.B.A., George Washington U., 1971; m. Penelope Anne Duff, Feb. 13, 1965; children—Bryan, Timothy, Heather. Bus. mgr. Warren (Pa.) Gen. Hosp., 1963-66; asst. controller Citizen's Gen. Hosp., New Kensington, Pa., 1966; planning asst. Hosp. Planning Assn., Pitts., 1966-68; advanced fellow in health services adminstrn. Am. Hosp. Assn. and Blue Cross Assn., Chgo., 1971-72; asst. to exec. v.p. Albert Einstein Med. Center, Phila., 1972-73; exec. dir. Eastern Allegheny County Health Corp., Pitts., 1973-77; dir. hosp./community planning Western Pa. Hosp., Pitts., 1977—; mem. faculty supervisory mgmt. tng. program Hosp. Assn. Pa. Mem. Am. Coll. Hosp. Adminstrs., Am., Pa. hosp. assns., Am. Pub. Health Assn. Episcopalian. Home: 682 Presque Isle Dr Pittsburgh PA 15239 Office: Western Pa Hosp 4800 Friendship Ave Pittsburgh PA 15224

JOINER, ROBERT RUSSELL, adminstrv. chemist; b. Belleville, N.J., May 3, 1916; s. Robert and Louise C. (Gailing) J.; B.S. in Chemistry, Poly. Inst. Bklyn., 1941; m. Marie F. Mermet, Sept. 26, 1942; children—Lynne M. Joiner Malley, Robert J., Susan M. Group leader Wallace & Tiernan, Inc. (name changed to Pennwalt Corp. 1971), Belleville, N.J., 1942-54, pharm. researcher, 1942-46, researcher agrl. chems., 1948-52, researcher water waste, 1952, researcher cereal chemistry, 1952-54, asst. dir. research, 1954-58, mgr. lab., 1958-64, mgr. flour research, 1964-67, tech. dir. food agr. div., 1967—. Mem. Am. Chem. Soc., Am. Assn. Cereal Chemists, Inst. Food Technologists. Contbr. tech. articles to profl. jours.; patentee in field. Home: 136 Antietam Rd Cherry Hill NJ 08034 Office: 3 Pkwy Philadelphia PA 19102

JOISON, JULIO, surgeon; b. Cordoba, Argentina, Oct. 2, 1932; s. Moises and Sofia (Moses) J.; came to U.S., 1960, naturalized, 1971; grad. summa cum laude Dean Funes Nat. Coll., Argentina, 1949; grad. Nat. U. of Cordoba Sch. Medicine, 1959; Ph.D., U. Buenos Aires, 1970. Intern, research asst. surgery Sinai Hosp., Balt., 1960-61; resident in surgery Met. Hosp., N.Y.C., 1961-62; asso. fellow in surgery Lahey Clinic div. Lahey Clinic Found., Boston, 1962; sr. asst. resident surgery Boston City Hosp., 1962-63, sr. resident, 1963-64, chief resident, 1964-65; sr. teaching fellow in surgery Boston U., 1964-65; asso. in surgery Mt. Sinai Sch. Medicine, N.Y.C., 1967-68; research fellow in surgery Harvard U. Med. Sch., Boston, 1965-66, 68-70; clin. and research fellow Mass. Gen. Hosp., Boston, 1965-66; ednl. asst., asst. attending surgeon Mt. Sinai-Elmhurst Hosp., N.Y.C., 1966-68; research fellow in surgery Harvard Surg. Services Boston City Hosp., 1968-70; individual practice medicine specializing in gen. surgery, Brookline, Mass., 1970—; asso. staff gen. surgery St. Elizabeth's Hosp., Boston, 1976—; courtesy staff gen. surgery Hahnemann Hosp., Boston, 1976—, Brookline Hosp., 1971—, Parker Hill Med. Center, Boston, 1970—. Diplomate Am. Bd. Surgery. Fellow Am. Coll. Angiology, Am. Geriatrics Soc., Am. Coll. Gastroenterology, N.Y. Acad. Sci.; mem. AMA, Mass. Med. Soc., Am. Fedn. Clin. Research. Jewish. Contbr. over 40 abstracts and articles in field to profl. jours.; discoverer metabolic factor produced by pancreas; developer surg. technique for transplanting pancreas. Home: 216 Saint Paul St Brookline MA 02146 Office: 1180 Beacon St Brookline MA 02146

JOLINE, ROBERT MERRITT, financial co. exec.; b. Phila., June 15, 1909; s. Frederick E. and Gertrude (Paxson) J.; student U. Pa., 1933; m. Ruth E. Price, July 1, 1933. With Benjamin Franklin Fed. Savs. & Loan Assn., Phila., 1946-74, v.p., 1946-51, pres., 1951-70, chmn. bd., chief exec. officer, 1970-74. Pres. Savs. and Loan Council, Phila., 1972. Served with USNR, 1942-45. Mem. Execs. Assn. Phila. (pres. 1962), Fed. Assn. Phila. and Suburbs (pres. 1957), Franklin Inst., Chestnut St. Assn. (pres. 1972-73), U. Pa. Evening Sch. Alumni Soc. (pres. 1971). Kiwanian (gov. 1970-71). Club: Union League. Home: 3331 Ryan Ave Philadelphia PA 19136 Office: 1624 Chestnut St Philadelphia PA 19103

JOLLY, WAYNE TRAVIS, geologist, educator; b. Jacksonville, Tex., Aug. 15, 1940; s. Edward B. and Alfreda J. (Sharp) J.; B.F.A., U. Tex., 1963, M.A., State U. N.Y. at Binghamton, 1967, Ph.D. (univ. fellow), 1970. Postdoctoral fellow U. Sask., Saskatoon, 1970-71; asso. prof. Brock U., St. Catherines, Ont., Can., 1971—. NRC Can. grantee, 1971-77. Mem. Geol. Soc. Am., Am. Geophys. Union, Geol. Assn. Can. Office: Brock University Dept Geol Science St Catharines ON Canada

JON, MIN-CHUNG, metall. engr.; b. China, Feb. 14, 1945; s. Yen-Tseng and Men-Yu (Lee) J.; D.Engring. Sci., Columbia U., 1975; m. Fei-Yua Wen, Sept. 5, 1972. Mem. research staff Engring. Research Center, Western Electric Co., Princeton, N.J., 1975—. Campbell fellow, 1971, 72. Mem. Am. Inst. Metal. Engrs., Am. Soc. Nondestructive Testing. Contbr. articles to profl. jours.; patentee in field. Home: 8 Hemlock Ct East Windsor NJ 08520 Office: PO Box 900 Princeton NJ 08540

JONAS, CHARLES SAUL, orthodontist; b. Phila., Mar. 6, 1914; s. Max and Fannie (Mickelson) J.; D.D.S., U. Md., 1934; certificate in orthodontics, Columbia, 1938; m. Sara Chesler, Aug. 18, 1940; children—Carol (Mrs. Larry Gage), John A. Pvt. practice orthodontics, Atlantic City, 1940-42, 45-66, Northfield, N.J., 1966—; chief orthodontist Children's Seashore House, Atlantic City, 1950—. Asst. prof. orthodontics U. Pa. Grad. Sch. Medicine, Phila., 1949-66. Chmn. Atlantic City March of Dimes, 1958; chmn. Medico-Dental com. A.R.C. Atlantic City, 1953. Chmn. fluoridation com., Margate, N.J., 1958. Bd. dirs. Atlantic City Community Chest; trustee Hebrew

Old Age Home; mem. exec. council Fedn. Jewish Charities. Served to capt., Dental Corps, AUS, 1942-45. Diplomate Am. Bd. Orthodontists. Fellow Am. Coll. Dentists, Internat. Coll. Dentists; mem. Am. Dental Assn., Atlantic County Dental Soc. (pres. 1959), Phila. Soc. Orthodontists (pres. 1963), Middle Atlantic Soc. Orthodontists (pres. 1963), Alpha Omega. Jewish Religion (trustee temple). Rotarian. Club: Linwood (N.J.) Country. Home: 8600 Winchester Ave Margate NJ 08402 Office: Jackson Ave and Shore Rd Northfield NJ 08225

JONAS, GILBERT, pub. relations and fund raising exec.; b. Bklyn., July 22, 1930; s. Harry and Mitzi (Rosenstein) J.; B.A., Stanford, 1951; graduate certificate Chinese studies Columbia, 1953, M.A., 1955; m. Barbara L. Selby, Sept. 1953 (div. Nov. 1961); 1 dau., Susan; m. 2d, P. Joyce Theise, Dec. 27, 1964; children—Jillian, Stephanie. Exec. sec., Am. Friends of Vietnam, N.Y.C., 1956-57; v.p. Harold L. Oram Inc., N.Y.C., 1958-61; Far East cons., acting dir. Far East, Peace Corps, Washington, 1961; pres., owner Gilbert Jonas Co., Inc., N.Y.C., 1962—. Exec. sec. Am. Med. Center for Burma, N.Y.C., 1959-61. Dir. pub. information N.Y. Youth for Stevenson, 1956; mem. exec. com. N.Y. Com. for Democratic Voters, 1959-62; pres. Reform Ind. Democrats of N.Y., 1958-59; mem. civil rights staff Nat. Citizens for Kennedy-Johnson, 1960; mem. steering com. N.Y. Citizens for Humphrey-Muskie, 1968; nat. coordinator Charles Evers for Gov. Miss., 1971; co-founder N.Y.C. Reform Movement, Democratic party, 1958-63. Bd. dirs. Am. Com. on Africa, 1955-59, League Indsl. Democracy, 1972—. Served with AUS, 1953-55. Recipient Annual Freedom award Miss. NAACP, 1970. Mem. Overseas Press Club, NAACP (life), Phi Beta Kappa, Sigma Delta Chi. Home: 215 E 80th St New York City NY 10021 Office: 150 E 58th St New York City NY 10022

JONASSOHN, KURT, sociologist, educator; b. Cologne, Germany, Aug. 31, 1920; s. Richard and Frieda; came to Can., 1940, naturalized Canadian citizen, 1946; B.A., Sir George Williams Coll., 1953; M.A. (Samuel Lapitsky fellow), McGill U., 1955; postgrad. (Univ. scholar) U. Chgo., 1955-56; m. Pearl Pepper, Jan. 26, 1956; children—Frieda, Joseph David. Asst. study dir. U. Chgo., 1957-59; research sociologist, Directorate of Personnel Planning, RCAF Hdqrs., Ottawa, Can., 1959-61; asst. prof., then prof. sociology Sir George Williams U. (now called Concordia U., Sir George Williams campus), Montreal, Can., 1961—. Bd. dirs. Candian Youth Hostels Assn., 1975-77; bd. dirs. Hostelling Tours Agency Inc., pres. 1976-77. Imperial Oil grad. research fellow, 1955-58. Mem. Internat. Sociol. Assn. (dep. exec. sec. 1974-78, exec. sec. 1978—), Canadian Sociology and Anthropology Assn. (sec.-treas. 1971-74), Am. Sociology Assn. Jewish. Contbr. articles and revs. to profl. jours.; co-editor ISA Bull. Office: Dept of Sociology Concordia Univ SGW Campus 1455 de Maisonneuve Blvd W Montreal PQ H3G 1M8 Canada

JONES, ANDREW ROSS, elec. engring. adminstr.; b. Brown County, Ill., May 3, 1921; s. John William and Mary Ettie (Cooley) J.; student Western Ill. U., 1939-42; B.E.E., Clemson U., 1947; M.S.E.E., U. Pitts., 1953; m. Sara Jeannette Wiggs, Oct. 21, 1944; children—Andrew Ross, Susan Jones Harper. Tchr., Dale Sch. Dist., 1941-42; with Westinghouse Electric Corp., Pitts., 1947—, mgr. advt. devel., 1964-66, mgr. projects, 1966-71, sr. cons., 1971-73, mgr. spl. projects, 1973-76, mgr. engring. Advanced Engring. Systems div., 1976—. Served with AUS, 1942-46. Recipient Norris and Riggs medals Clemson U., 1947. Mem. IEEE, Am. Nuclear Soc., Soc. Naval Architects and Marine Engrs., Am. Inst. Aeros. and Astronautics. Home: 3167 Windgate Dr Murrysville PA 15668 Office: PO Box 10864 Pittsburgh PA 15236

JONES, BARCLAY GIBBS, educator; b. June 3, 1925, Camden, N.J.; s. Barclay and Kathryn (Prince) J.; B.A., U. Pa., 1948, B.Arch., 1951; M.R.P., U. N.C., 1955, Ph.D., 1961; m. Ann Van Syckel Tompkins, June 8, 1957; children—Barclay Gibbs, Louise Tompkins. Community planner Citizens' Council on City Planning, Phila., 1951; instr. city and regional planning U. Calif., Berkeley, 1956-57, asst. prof., 1957-61; asso. prof. city and regional planning Cornell U., Ithaca, N.Y., 1961-67, prof., 1967—, asso. dir. urban studies Center for Housing and Environ. Studies, 1962-70, acting dir. Center Urban Devel. Research, 1970-72, asso. dir., 1970-76, co-dir. program in urban and regional studies, 1976-78, dir., 1978—, chmn. dept. policy planning and regional analysis, 1971-74; adv. bd. Historic Am. Bldgs. Survey, U.S. Dept. Interior; cons. govt. agys.; Distinguished Sr. Fulbright-Hayes lectr., Yugoslavia, 1972. Served with U.S. Army, 1943-46. Decorated Purple Heart. Mem. AAAS, Am. Econ. Assn., AIA, Am. Inst. Planners, Am. Soc. Planning Ofcls., Am. Statis. Assn., N.E. Regional Sci. Assn. (pres. 1975-76), Regional Sci. Assn. (councillor 1976—), Soc. Archtl. Historians, Urban and Regional Info. Systems Assn. (pres. 1966-69). Republican. Episcopalian. Contbr. argicles to profl. jours.; author monographs. Home: 502 Turner Pl Ithaca NY 14850 Office: 109 W Sibley Hall Cornell U Ithaca NY 14853

JONES, CHARLES DAVIS, art prodn. co. exec.; b. Abraham, W.Va., Jan. 6, 1917; s. Benjamin Franklin and Mary Catherine (Smith) J.; A.B., Marshall U., 1947; M.A., N.Y. U., 1956; m. Letha Arbell Plumley (div.); children—Charles Davis, Irvin Howard; m. 2d, Margaret Lee Greene, Aug. 4, 1951. With Social Security Adminstrn., HEW, Balt., 1951-77, dir. gen. policy coordination and liaison Bur. Supplemental Security Income, Balt., 1971-75, chief eligibility policy Office Policy and Regulations, 1975-77; mem. HEW Task Force Medicaid and Related Programs, 1969, Social Security Adminstrn. Task Force Regional Orgns. and Functions, 1970; partner Jones & Jones Art Unltd., graphic arts, Balt., 1976—. Served to 1st lt. USAAF, 1942-45. Decorated Air medal (4). Mem. Nat. Rehab. Assn., Disability Examiners, VFW, Nat. Trust for Historic Preservation, Nat. Hist. Soc., Balt. Mus. Art, Roland Park Civic League. Home: 903 W University Pwky Baltimore MD 21210

JONES, CHARLES HILL, JR., banker; b. N.Y.C., July 14, 1933; s. Charles Hill and Susan Roy (Johnston) J.; B.A., U. Va., 1956; m. Hope Haskell, Jan. 28, 1961; children—Hope H., Charles Hill, Henry M.T. With Wood, Struthers & Winthrop Inc., N.Y.C., 1956-73, gen. partner, 1968-69, v.p., dir., dir. research, 1970-73; v.p., sr. trust officer, chief investment officer Midlantic Nat. Bank, Newark, 1974—; pres., treas. McBee Jones Corp., N.Y.C., 1964—. Trustee Rumson Country Day Sch.; trustee, chmn. fin. com. Monmouth Med. Center; trustee, treas. Assn. for Children N.J. Served to capt., N.Y. N.G., 1956-64. Chartered fin. analyst. Mem. Inst. Chartered Fin. Analysts, N.Y. Soc. Security Analysts, Fin. Analysts Fedn., Bond Club N.Y. Republican. Episcopalian. Clubs: Racquet and Tennis, City Midday (N.Y.C.); Essex (Newark); Rumson Country. Author: (with Joseph D. Davis) Toll Revenue Bonds, 1960. Home: 90 Ridge Rd Rumson NJ 07760 Office: 744 Broad St Newark NJ 07101

JONES, CHRISTINE CONSTANCE DI GRANDI, Realtor; b. Beverly, Mass., Mar. 13, 1949; d. George Joseph and Mary Stephanie (Clemenzi) diGrandi; A.A.S., Dutchess Community Coll., 1976; m. Mace Earl Jones, June 8, 1968; children—Trisha Marie, Mace diGrandi. Pvt. practice mgmt. cons., Poughkeepsie, N.Y., 1971—; real estate salesman Sofka Real Estate, Poughkeepsie, 1970-74; prin. Old Homestead Realty Properties, Inc., Hyde Park, N.Y., 1974—; cons. in field. Bd. dirs. Regina Coeli Sch., Hyde Park, 1976-77; mem. Dutchess County Bd. Realtors (sec., treas.), Dutchess County Multiple Listing Service, Hyde Park C. of C., Nat. Market Inst., Nat., N.Y. State Bds. realtors. Office: 5 Pinewoods Rd Hyde Park NY 12538

JONES, COMPTON SETH, advt. and pub. relations exec.; b. Mpls., July 16, 1925; s. Alexander F. and Edna (Schultz) J.; A.B. in Fgn. Affairs, George Washington U., 1949; m. Ruth Helen Barton, Jan. 10, 1953; children—Compton Seth, Caroline B. With W.R. Grace Co. and Grace Line, Inc., 1949-51, U.P.I. Nat., 1951-54, Asso. Gen. Contractors Am., 1954-55, J. Walter Thompson Co., 1955-59, Ketchum, MacLeod & Grove, Inc., 1959-61, S.G. Stackig, Inc., 1961-63; pres. Compton Jones Assos., Bethesda, Md., 1963-76; exec. v.p. S.G. House & Assos., Bethesda, 1976-77; chmn. bd., chief exec. officer Zung Internat., Ltd., McLean, Va., also Washington, 1977—. Trustee Davis Meml. Goodwill Industries; vice chmn. Potomac Conservation Found. Served to lt. (j.g.) USNR, 1943-46; PTO. Mem. Pub. Relations Soc. Am., Aerospace Writers. Assn., Assn. Indsl. Advertisers (past pres. Washington chpt.), Montgomery County C. of C., Advt. Club Met. Washington, Internat. Wine and Food Soc., Alpha Delta Sigma, Sigma Chi. Mason. Clubs: Nat. Press (Washington); Middletown (Md.) Valley Hunt. Author: A Guideline to Public Relations and Advertising Activities in Public Securities Registration. Home: 11790 Glen Rd Potomac MD 20854 Office: 6870 Elm St McLean VA 22101

JONES, CURTIS EDISON, banker; b. Bellevue, Pa., Oct. 21, 1918; s. Chester D. and Jane (Green) J.; B.S., U. Pitts., 1950; m. Margaret R. McFarland, Apr. 21, 1943; children—Craig W., R. Scott. With Union Trust Co., Pitts., 1936-46; with Mellon Bank, N.A. (merger Union Trust Co. and Mellon Bank). Pitts., 1946—, asst. cashier, 1950-53, asst. v.p., 1953-56, v.p., 1956-70, sr. v.p., 1970-73, exec. v.p. 1973-74, pres., 1974—; dir. Koppers Co., Inc., Martin Marietta Corp. Trustee Allegheny County Med. Soc. Found.; bd. dirs. Suburban Gen. Hosp. Served to lt. col. AUS, 1941-46. Mem. Assn. Res. City Bankers. Mason. Clubs: Board Room (N.Y.C.); Rolling Rock, Laurel Valley Golf (Ligonier, Pa.); Duquesne, Fox Chapel Golf (Pitts.). Office: Mellon Bank NA Mellon Sq Pittsburgh PA 15230

JONES, DAVID MILTON, economist; b. Newton, Iowa, June 22, 1938; s. Charles Raymond and Mary Evelyn (Corrough) J.; B.A., Coe Coll., 1960; M.A., U. Pa., 1961, Ph.D., 1969; m. Becky Ann Strait, Aug. 4, 1962; children—David, Jennifer, Stephen. Economist, Fed. Res. Bank N.Y., N.Y.C., 1963-68; financial economist Irving Trust Co., N.Y.C., 1968-72; v.p., economist Aubrey G. Lanston & Co., Inc., 1972—. Lectr., thesis examiner Stonier Banking Sch., Rutgers U., 1971—, others. Bd. dirs. United Ch. Bd. World Ministries, 1972—. Woodrow Wilson fellow, 1960-63. Mem. Am. Econ. Assn., Nat. Assn. Bus. Economists. Contbr. articles to profl. jours., chpt. to bus. forecasting book. Home: 168 Gates Ave Montclair NJ 07042 Office: 20 Broad St New York City NY 10005

JONES, DONALD IRVINE, dentist; b. Montclair, N.J., Oct. 20, 1936; s. Maurice Arthur and Margaret (McCord) J.; B.S. in Microbiology, U. Md., 1959; D.D.S., Fairleigh Dickinson U., 1963; m. M. Rosalind Jannuzi, July 9, 1960; children—Owen Donald, Cordell Tomasson. Practice dentistry, Wayne, N.J., 1965—; mem. staff Chilton Meml. Hosp., Pompton Plains, N.J., pres. staff, 1971-73, sec.-treas., 1967-71; mem. staff St. Joseph's Hosp., Paterson, N.J., 1967-71; v.p. Dental Assos. P.A., 1970-77, pres., 1978—; instr. Fairleigh Dickinson U. Dental Sch., Teaneck, N.J., 1969-70, clin. asst. prof., dept. continuing edn., 1974—, clin. asst. prof. dept. prosthodontics, 1977—, sect. chmn. occlusion, dir. myofascial pain dysfunction clinic. Co-chmn. Indsl. and Comml. Devel. Commn., Pequannock Twp., N.J., 1971-74. Mem. profl. adv. council Jersey City State Coll. Served to lt. USNR, 1963-65. Fellow Am. Acad. Gen. Dentistry; mem. Am. Acad. Oral Medicine, Am., N.J. (council on dental edn. 1974-77) dental assns., Passaic County Dental Soc. (chmn. postgrad. edn. program 1971-75, trustee 1970-75, fin. sec. 1975-76, treas. 1976-77, 2d v.p. 1977-78, 1st v.p. 1978—), Pompton Plains Men's Bowling League (pres. 1969-70), Omicron Kappa Upsilon, Sigma Alpha Epsilon. Home: 5 Mead Pl Pompton Plains NJ 07444 Office: 1520 Route 23 Wayne NJ 07470

JONES, DONALD LEROY, data co. exec., physicist; b. St. Joseph, Mo., Feb. 5, 1932; s. Clifton Youree and Veda Belle (Goodnight) J.; B.S., U. Colo., 1957, M.S., 1967; m. Christine A. Kircher, Aug. 28, 1965; children—Stephanie, Eric, Kit, Ashley. Physicist/mathematician, U.S. Nat. Bur. Standards, Boulder, Colo., 1955-67; physicist Gen. Electric Co., King-of-Prussia, Pa., 1967-71; pres. Commodity Info. Services, Phila. and Chgo., 1971—; dir. Commodity Mgmt. Service Corp., 1973-74. Served with USNR, 1951-53. Mem. Math. Assn. Am., Am. Geophys. Union, Am. Phys. Soc., Sigma Xi. Home: 361 Mine Run Rd Schwenksville PA 19473 Office: 33 W Ridge Pike Limerick PA 19468 also 175 W Jackson Chicago IL 60604

JONES, E. STEWART, JR., lawyer; b. Troy, N.Y., Dec. 4, 1941; s. E. Stewart and Louise (Farley) J.; B.A., Williams Coll., 1963; LL.B., J.D., Albany Law Sch., 1966; m. Constance Patricia Mack, Dec. 28, 1968; children—Christopher Fitzgerald, Brady Atkinson. Admitted to N.Y. bar, 1966, U.S. Supreme Ct. bar, 1970; trial lawyer firm E. Stewart Jones, Troy, N.Y., 1966—; asst. dist. atty. Rensselaer County, N.Y., 1968-70, spl. prosecutor, 1974. Mem. Am. (criminal law sect.), N.Y. (lectr., mem. criminal justice sect., dir. 1977—) bar assns., Assn. Trial Lawyers Am., Roscoe Pound Assn., Trial Lawyers Am. Found. (fellow), N.Y. (gov. 1973—), Capital Dist. (N.Y.) (dir. 1973-76, lectr.) trial lawyers assns. Republican. Roman Catholic. Contbr. chpt. to legal book. Home: Strawberry Hill 394 Loudonville Rd Loudonville NY 12211

JONES, EUGENE HARVEY, coal mining co. exec.; b. Akron, Ohio, May 30, 1925; s. William Thomas and Nellie Belle (Fowler) J.; B.S. in Mining Engring., U. Pitts., 1949; m. Delrose Marie Ager, Apr. 28, 1951; children—Marvin, Susan, Bonnie, Donna, Cathy. With Rochester & Pitts. Coal Co., Indiana, Pa., 1949—, asst. chief engr., 1960-69, asst. v.p. ops., 1969-76, v.p., ops., 1976—; instr. coal mining Pa. State U., 1968. Republican. Contbr. tech. papers in field. Home: 945 McKnight Rd Indiana PA 15701

JONES, FARRELL, health service exec.; b. Chgo., May 6, 1926; s. Farrell and Kathryn (Crum) J.; B.A., Lincoln U., 1950; J.D., N.Y. U., 1957; m. Audrey E. Howard, June 16, 1951; children—Joanne Kathryn and Jacqueline Elinor (twins). Social investigator N.Y.C. Dept. Social Services, 1957-58; admitted to N.Y. State bar, 1958; research asst. Gov. Harriman's Com. to Rev. N.Y. State Parole System, 1958; field rep. N.Y. State Commn. for Human Rights, 1958-60, sr. field rep., 1960-61, regional dir. L.I. region, 1961-63; exec. dir. Nassau County (N.Y.) Commn. on Human Rights, 1963-70; 2d dep. county exec. Nassau County, 1970-71; asso. dir., clin. asst. prof. div. alcoholism and drug dependence State U. N.Y. Downstate Med. Center, 1971; 1st dep. adminstr. N.Y.C. Human Resources Adminstrn., 1971-74; asst. v.p. Blue Cross and Blue Shield Greater N.Y., 1974—; cons. N.Y. State Dept. Edn. on Intergroup Relations; cons. L.I. Sch. Dists.; bd. dirs. Am. Com. on Africa. Bd. dirs. Family Service Assn. Nassau County, N.Y.C. Comprehensive Health Planning Agy., 1971-74, Cow Bay Housing, Port Washington, N.Y., 1975—; chmn., pres. Nassau County Econ. Opportunity Commn., 1971-72; pres. Nassau County Law Services Com., 1969-71; bd. dirs. Health and Welfare Council of Nassau County, Nassau County Community Econ. Devel. Corp., Nassau Community Health Services Found., 1966-69; mem. Nassau County Crime Council, 1966-71; trustee Adelphi U., mem. adv. bd. Sch. Social Work, 1964—, chmn., 1970—; asso. trustee North Shore Hosp., 1970-74; trustee Port Washington Pub. Library, 1976—, Urban League L.I., 1976—; mem. Nassau County Youth Bd., 1964-71; mem. adv. council Hofstra U., 1967-72, v.p., 1971-72; v.p. Vols. in Partnership with Srs., N.Y.C., 1976—; mem. adv. bd. New Dimensions in Comprehensive Health, 1972—. Served with AUS, 1951-53. Mem. Nat. Assn. Intergroup Relations Ofcls., Nassau County Bar Assn., NAACP (life), Alpha Phi Alpha. Unitarian. Home: 22 Driftwood Dr Port Washington NY 11050

JONES, FLORETTA JEANETTE, nurse; b. Balt.; d. Melvin Caesar and Mary Frances (Gregory) Johnson; R.N., Dixie Hosp.-Hampton Inst., Va., 1947; B.A., Antioch Coll., 1973; M.S. Ed., Johns Hopkins U., 1976; m. Hilton Jones, Sept. 10, 1947; children—Jennifer Marie, Kevin Hilton. Vis. nurse Instructive Vis. Nurse Assn., Balt., 1951-54; nursing team leader Sinai Hosp., Balt., 1961-64; instr. fundamentals of nursing, student health nurse Provident Hosp., Balt., 1964-70, student adviser, 1970, med.-surg. instr., 1970-73; staff developer, 1973-76, trustee, 1977—; coordinator inservice edn. South Balt. Gen. Hosp., 1976—; asso. prof. Catonsville Community Coll., 1976—. Active Girl Scouts U.S., 1959-66, Boy Scouts Am., 1965-67, PTA, 1967-70, Am. Heart Assn. Mem. Adult Edn. Assn., Am., Md. nurses assns., Council Continuing Edn., Health, Manpower, Edn. and Tng. Assn., Quality Assurance Interest Group, Phi Delta Gamma, Chi Eta Phi. Democrat. Baptist. Clubs: Astronettes Social, Bowling, Vol. Circle, Balt. Symphony. Author, editor tng. materials in field. Office: 3001 S Hanover St Baltimore MD 21230

JONES, FRANKLIN REED, artist; b. Needham, Mass., May 18, 1921; s. Benjamin Reed and Samantha Jane (Spavold) J.; student pub. schs., Mass.; m. Florence Marjorie Hull, June 5, 1942; children—Susan Candy, Carolyn Leslie, Sharon Reed, Deborah Virginia. Free lance artist, 1946-53; instr. art Famous Artists Schs., Westport, Conn., 1953-64, asst. to dir., 1964-74; fine arts painter, Stockbridge, Mass., 1974—; represented in permanent collections at Mus. Art, Sci. and Industry, Bridgeport, Conn. Served with USMC, 1943-46. Recipient award of excellence Ellsworth Nat. Exhibit, 1977. Mem. Am. Watercolor Soc. (Gold medal of honor 1975), Akron Soc. Art (hon.), Grand Central Galleries, Inc. Author: The Pleasure of Painting, 1975; Painting Nature, 1978. Address: RFD 1 West Stockbridge MA 01266

JONES, GEORGE GREEN, lawyer; b. Martinsville, Va., Sept. 22, 1946; s. Kate Ethel (Bow) J.; B.S. in Bus. Adminstrn., Johnson C. Smith U., 1969; M.B.A. (Martin Luther King fellow), Northeastern U., 1972; J.D., Boston Coll., 1976; m. Marian E. Howard; 1 son, Andre. Admitted to Mass. bar, 1977; accountant Polaroid Corp., Cambridge, Mass., 1969-71, fin. analyst, 1976-77, atty., tax dept., 1977—; cons. Elma Lewis Sch. Fine Arts, Boston, 1974; law clk. New Eng. Mut. Life Ins. Co., Boston, 1975; dir. World Wide Enterprises. Bd. dirs. Roxbury Defenders Com. Mem. Am., Mass., Boston bar assns., Mass. Black Lawyers Assn., Eastern Mass. Urban League, Soc. Notary Public, M.B.A. Assn., Omega Psi Phi. Home: 55 Langdon St Suite 6 Cambridge MA 02138

JONES, GEORGE RICHARD, physicist; b. Los Angeles, Aug. 16, 1930; s. George Michael and Edna Catherine (Hannibal) J.; B.S., Western Md. Coll., 1951; M.S., Cath. U. Am., 1953, Ph.D., 1963; m. Jeanne Dougherty, Nov. 22, 1952; children—Michael, George, Ralph, Susan, Karen, Thomas. Jr. engr. Davies Labs., Inc., Riverdale, Md., 1952-54; physicist Diamond Ordnance Fuze Labs., Washington, 1954-59; research physicist Harry Diamond Labs., Washington, 1959-66; research physicist, math. physicist Night Vision Lab., Ft. Belvoir, Va., 1966—; supervisory com. Twin Pines Savs. & Loan Assn., 1958-59, dir., 1959—, v.p., 1961-62, pres., 1962-73, sec., 1973—; cons. physicist Am. Machine and Foundry, Alexandria, Va., 1961-63. Mem. Cath. Interracial Council, Prince Georges County, Md., 1965; league rep. Princemont Swim League, Rockville, Md., 1968—, div. chmn., 1969—; pres. Rapidan Camps, Inc., Madison, Va., 1962, 65. Mem. Greenbelt (Md.) Fair Housing Com., 1963-67. Mem. Am. Phys. Soc., IEEE, AAAS, Sigma Xi. Roman Catholic. Home: 113 Northway Rd Greenbelt MD 20770 Office: Night Vision Lab Ft Belvoir VA 22060

JONES, GERRE LYLE, marketing and pub. relations cons.; b. Kansas City, Mo., June 22, 1926; s. Eugene Riley and Carolyn (Newell) J.; B.J., U. Mo., 1948, postgrad., 1953-54; m. Charlotte Mae Reinhold, Oct. 30, 1948; children—Beverly Anne Jones Putnam, Wendy Sue. Exec. sec. Ill. C. of C., 1948-50; field rep. Nat. Found. Infantile Paralysis, N.Y.C., 1950-57; dir. pub. relations Inst. Logopedics, Wichita, Kans., 1957-58; owner Gerre Jones & Assos., Pub. Relations, Kansas City, Mo., 1958-63; info. officer Radio Free Europe Fund, Munich, Germany, 1963-65, named spl. asst. to dir. pub. relations, 1965-66; exec. asst. pub. affairs Edward Durell Stone, architect, 1967-68; dir. mktg. and communications Vincent C. Kling & Partners, Phila., 1969-71; mktg. cons. Ellerbe Architects, Washington, 1972; v.p. Gaio Assos., Ltd., Washington, 1972-73, exec. v.p., 1973-76; exec. v.p. Bldg. Industry Devel. Services, Washington, 1973-76; owner Gerre Jones Assos., Inc., Washington, 1976—; sr. v.p. Barlow Assos., Inc., Washington, 1977-78; lectr. in field numerous colls., univs. Served with USAAF, 1944-45; ret. maj. Res. Mem. Internat. Radio and TV Soc., Nat. Assn. Sci. Writers, Pub. Relations Soc. Am., Internat. Assn. Chiefs Police, Newsletter Assn. Am., Sigma Delta Chi, Alpha Delta Sigma, Phi Delta Phi. Republican. Clubs: Masons; Kansas City Press; Overseas Press; Deadline (N.Y.C.); Phila. Press. Author: How to Market Professional Design Services, 1973; How to Prepare Professional Design Brochures, 1976; (with Stuart H. Rose) How To Find and Win New Business, 1976; contbr. articles to profl. jours.; editor/pub. Profl. Mktg. Report. Home: 2123 Tunlaw Rd NW Washington DC 20007 Office: PO Box 32387 Washington DC 20007

JONES, GUY WILSON, pub. exec.;b. White Mills, Ky., Mar. 16, 1915; s. Guy Wilson and Beth (Duncan) J.; B.A., Western Ky. U., 1937; M.A., North Tex. U., 1941; postgrad. U. Ill., 1941-43; m. Suzanne Sanders, Dec. 3, 1953; 1 dau. Pam Dorcas. Tchr. high sch., Sonora, Ky., 1937-40; mem. faculty U. Ill., 1941-43; with Charles Scribners Sons, N.Y.C., 1946-72, dir. coll. dept., 1958-60, v.p., 1960-68, sr. v.p., head edn. div., 1968-72, dir. firm, 1967-72; edn. adviser David McKay Co., 1972-73; acad. cons. Franklin Watts Inc., N.Y.C., 1973—, now v.p. co., gen. mgr. New Viewpoints div. Trustee Perrot Meml. Library, 1975-76. Served to lt. comdr. USNR, 1943-46. Mem. Assn. Am. Pubs., Modern Lang. Assn., Am. Polit. Sci. Assn. Republican. Conglist. Club: N.Y. Athletic. Home: 140 Field Point Rd Greenwich CT 06830 Office: 730 Fifth Ave New York City NY 10019

JONES, HARRY MCCOY, cons. engr., investor; b. Stillwater, N.Y., Oct. 19, 1896; s. Louis Benson and Isabelle (Gray McCoy) J.; B.S., U.S. Naval Acad., 1918; grad. work finance, N.Y. U., 1927-28; m. Caroline A. Murray-Browne, May 10, 1969. Financial work Wall St. firms, N.Y.C., 1927-28; engring. work Walker Signal Equipment Co.,

1928-30; dist. mgr. Dry-Ice Corp. of Am., 1930-34; pvt. practice cons. engring., 1934-37; partner Weaver Asso., 1937-39; sr. partner Dunn & Jones, engrs., 1940-48, sole partner, 1949-65; dir. Malmstrom Chem. Co., Linden, N.J.; pres. dir. H-H Inc., real estate and investments, 1940—. Founder, U.S. Naval Acad. Found., 1942, chmn. bd., 1946-64, trustee, 1960—; pres. trustee H. McCoy Jones Found.; trustee Textile Museum, Washington, 1967-72. Served as midshipman USN, 1915-18, ensign to lt., 1918-26, lt. to lt. comdr., USNR, 1926-43. Recipient Meritorious Pub. Service citation Dept. Navy; Scroll of Honor, Navy League U.S.; Ann. award U.S. Naval Acad. Alumni Assn. N.Y., 1961; named Hon. Adm., Brigade of Midshipmen, U.S. Naval Acad. Mem. Mil. Order of World Wars, Soc. Am. Mil. Engrs., Am. Def. Preparedness Assn., Am. Soc. Naval Engrs., Soc. Naval Architects and Marine Engrs., U.S. Naval Acad. Athletic Assn., U.S. Naval Acad. Alumni Assn., Navy League U.S. (life), U.S. Naval Inst. (life), Internat. Hajji Baba Soc. (pres.), Brit. Inst. for Persian Studies, Am. Inst. for Iranian Studies. Episcopalian. Clubs: Army and Navy Country, Cosmos (Washington); Hajji Baba, Army and Navy (N.Y.); Family, Marines' Memorial (San Francisco); Prospectors (Reno); Oriental Rug (Toronto, Ont., Can.); Las Crucas (Baja California, Mexico). Lectr., writer, collector Oriental rugs. Contbr. numerous articles to antique and collectors' mags. Home: 2280 Idlewild Dr Reno NV 89502 also: 6122 Massachusetts Ave NW Washington DC 20016

JONES, HENRY WILLIAM, JR., pianist, composer; b. Vicksburg, Miss., July 31, 1918; s. Henry William and Olivvia (Griffin) J.; grad. pub. schs.; m. Theodosia Leonora von Seele, June 21, 1958. Jazz pianist Philharmonic Orch. nat. and world tours. 1947-51; accompanist Ella Fitzgerald, 1948-52; free lance rec. artist, 1952—; staff pianist CBS, 1959—, TV shows including Andy Williams, 1958-59, Garry Moore, 1959-64, Jackie Gleason, 1962-64, Ed Sullivan, 1966—; TV spls. including Carol Burnett at Carnegie Hall, 1962, Ed Summerlin Jazz Liturgy, 1963, Benny Goodman Sounds of Benny Goodman, 1963, Carol Burnett's Once Upon A Mattress, 1964, Barbra Streisand's Color Me Barbra, 1965, Gene Kelly, 1965, Harry Bellafonte's Strolling Twenties, 1965, Benny Goodman Bell Telephone Hour, 1965, My Name is Barbara, 1966; featured show CBS, 1972-73; also appeared with Benny Goodman for concert tours; also personal concert tours. Pres. Thank Music Corp. Mem. Nat. Acad. TV Arts and Scis., Nat. Acad. Rec. Arts and Scis., ASCAP, Am. Guild Authors and Composers, Am. Fedn. Musicians. Composer: All The While, 1940; Blues For Lady Day, 1947; Rough Riding, 1950; Lets Split, 1955; Let Me Know, 1958; Ergo The Blues, 1958; Just For Today, 1959; Bag O Rags, 1964; Is This To Be Or Not To Be, 1964; A-Thats Freedom, 1965; Angel Face, Odd Number, Minor Competition, 1965, Take a Good Look, 1966, Sweet and Tender, 1970, Lullaby, 1973, Minority Anyone?, Satellite, Recapitulation, 1977, I Can't Forget, Re: Union, A Quiet Scene, Peedlum, Ah, Oui, 1978, others. Home: 39 7th St Cresskill NJ 07626

JONES, HOMER WALTER, math. statistician; b. N.Y.C., Sept. 3, 1925; s. Homer Walter and Margaret (Campbell) J.; M.E., Stevens Inst. Tech., 1947, M.S., 1950; M.B.A., Am. U., 1959; M.S., George Washington U., 1965, postgrad. in math. statistics, 1965-70, 75; m. Shirley Jean Dabbs, June 15, 1957; children—Laura Gwen, Linda Margaret. Math. statistician U.S. Treasury Dept., Internal Revenue Service, Washington, 1959—; ltd. partner Vista Lakes Estates, Alta Pres., IRS Chess Club, 1968—; certified intermediate tournament dir., 1973-78; mem. exec. com. Va. Chess Fedn., 1975—; organizer Region III Chess Championship, 1974-77; dir. U.S. Jr. Chess Championship, Memphis, 1978. Mem. and host family Am. Field Service, 1977-78. Served with USNR, 1944-45. Recipient Certificate of Award, U.S. Treasury Dept., 1978. Mem. Nat. Treasury Employees Union (exec. v.p. chpt. 1974), U.S. Chess Fedn. (regional v.p. 1973-76, voting mem. 1973—), Assn. U.S. Chess Journalists (sec.-treas. 1976—). Presbyn. (treas. 1971-72, deacon 1970-72, elder 1973-76, 78). Editor: Kings File mag., 1974. Asst. editor Va. Chess Fedn. Newsletter, 1976-77, games editor, 1978—. Home: 3400 Russell Rd Alexandria VA 22305 Office: 1201 E St NW Washington DC 20224

JONES, HOWARD LAMAR, psychologist; b. Houston, Aug. 14, 1938; s. Johnnie and Susie J.; B.S., Tex. So. U., 1962; B.S., U. Houston, 1964; M.S., Howard U., 1969; postgrad. George Washington U., 1973—; m. Mary Catherine Moore, June 4, 1965; children—Susan Renee, Jenna Katrin. Psychologist, Howard U., Washington, 1971-73; profl. lectr. Am. U., Washington, 1971-75; cons. psychologist Urban Profl. Assos., Washington, 1973—; psychologist Sharpe Health, Washington, 1976—. Block capt. Crestwood Citizens Assn., 1977-78; precinct chmn. Republican party, 1975—. Mental Health Adminstrn. grantee, 1973-78. Mem. Am. Psychol. Assn., Am., Nat. Capitol personnel and guidance assns., Group Analytic Soc. (London), Council Exceptional Children, Phi Delta Kappa. Episcopalian. Home: 1809 Shepherd St NW Washington DC 20011 Office: 4300 13th St NW Washington DC 20011

JONES, HOWARD LANGWORTHY, educator; b. Pelham, N.Y., Nov. 16, 1917; s. Dyer Tillinghast and Margaret (Langworthy) J.; A.B., Colgate U., 1939, LL.D., 1969; M.A., Syracuse U., 1949, Ed.D., 1951; m. Margaret Irene Lloyd, Apr. 27, 1940; 1 son, Dyer Lloyd. Tchr., coach Easthampton (N.Y.) High Sch., 1939-43; prof. edn. Colgate U., 1948-57, v.p., 1957-61; pres. Northfield Mt. Hermon Schs., Northfield, Mass., 1961—; dir. Pioneer Nat. Bank, Greenfield, Mass., Imagetics Inc., Elderhostel Inc. Trustee Colgate U.; vice chmn. bd. Coll. of V.I.; bd. dirs. Nat. Assn. Ind. Schs., A Better Chance Program. Served with USAAF, 1943-47. Mem. Am. Mgmt. Assn. (dir. 1965-68), Phi Delta Kappa, Phi Kappa Tau. Clubs: University, Anglers (N.Y.C.). Home: 94 Main St Northfield MA 01360 Office: Revell Hall Northfield MA 01360

JONES, IRA SNOW, ophthalmologist; b. Morganton, N.C., Mar. 31; s. Ira Franklin and Mamie Victoria (Snow) J.; A.B., Columbia U., 1940, M.D., 1943; m. Vasso Agnew, Apr. 2, 1976; children—Frances, Ira, Victoria, William. Practice medicine, specializing in ophthalmology, N.Y.C., 1951—; clin. prof. ophthalmology Columbia U., N.Y.C.; attending ophthalmologist Presbyn. Hosp., N.Y.C. Served to capt., M.C., AUS, 1944-46. Mem. Am. Ophthalmol. Soc., N.Y. Acad. Medicine, Med. Soc. County of N.Y., N.Y. State Med. Soc., AMA. Republican. Episcopalian. Clubs: Univ., Am. Yacht. Author: (with F. A. Jakobiec) Diseases of the Orbit, 1978. Office: 73 E 71 St New York City NY 10021

JONES, JAMES EDWARD, artist; b. Paducah, Ky., Jan. 27, 1937; s. Moses Scott and Cathrine Ruth J.; diploma Phila. Coll. Art, 1959, B.F.A., 1960; M.F.A., U. Pa., 1961; m. Mary L. Jackson, Oct. 8, 1960; children—Jeri Eileen, Jade Anton. Asso. prof. art edn. Morgan State U., Balt., 1962—; instr. Dundalk Community Coll., Balt., 1977—; one-man exhbns. include: Morgan State U., 1963, 77, Elizabethtown Coll., 1967, U. Md., 1972, McDonogh Sch., 1964, 77, Town House Gallery, 1968, Karamu Gallery, Cleve., 1966, Studio 13, Pa., 1960, Gallery One, Balt., 1962, Internat. Gallery Art, Md., 1965, Jerry Gilden Gallery, 1971, U. Md., 1971, U.S. Ala. Ethnic Slide Library, 1970-78; group exhbns. include: Balt. Mus. Art, 1963, 67, Corcoran Gallery Art, Washington, 1964, Wilmington (Del.) Soc. Fine Arts, 1965, Denison U., Ohio, 1965, Loyola Coll., Balt., 1968, Goucher Coll., 1977, Towson (Md.) State Coll., 1976, Smithsonian Gallery, 1978; represented in permanent collections: Dundalk Community Coll., Morgan State U., McDonogh Sch.; lectr. Recipient Stewart Art award, N.J., 1956; Creative Achievement award U. Pa., 1962; research grantee Morgan State U., 1962-67; fellow Phila. Coll. Art, 1959-60, scholar, 1958-59; fellow U. Pa., 1961-62. Mem. Artists Equity (dir.). Office: Box 427 Morgan State Univ Baltimore MD 21239

JONES, JAMES ROBERT, obstetrician, gynecologist, educator; b. Bklyn., Dec. 16, 1934; s. Harold Edward and Elenor Jean (O'Connor) J.; B.S., Manhattan Coll., 1956; M.D., State U. N.Y., Bklyn., 1960; m. Carolann Patricia Contiguglia, Aug. 1, 1972; children—Michael, Francis, Leslie, Laurie, Christopher. Intern, L.I. Coll. Hosp., Bklyn., 1960-61, resident in obstetrics and gynecology, 1961-64, cons. reproductive endocrinology, 1964-66; NIH fellow reproductive endocrinology U. Calif., San Francisco, 1964-66; practice medicine specializing in obstetrics and gynecology, San Francisco, 1964-66; asst. prof. obstetrics gynecology State U. N.Y., Bklyn., 1969-72, dir., reproductive endocrinology, 1969-77, dir. residency obstetrics and gynecology, 1970-75, asso. prof. obstetrics and gynecology, dir. gender identity service, 1972-77; prof., chmn. dept. obstetrics and gynecology Rutgers Med Sch., Piscataway, N.J., 1977—; cons. reproductive endocrinology Wycoff Heights Hosp., Bklyn.-Cumberland Hosp., L.I. Coll. Hosp., Glen Cove Hosp. Served to maj., USMCR, 1966-68; Vietnam. Decorated Bronze Star medal. Diplomate Am. Bd. Obstetrics and Gynecology. Mem. Am. Coll. Obstetrics and Gynecology, AMA, AAAS, Assn. Prof. Gynecology and Obstetrics, Endocrine Soc., Am. Fertility Soc., Bklyn. Gynecol. Soc. (sec. 1976—), N.Y. Obstet. Soc., N. Shore Sci. Mus., Am. Mus. Natural History, Democrat. Editor: Am. Cancer Soc. teaching tapes Advances in Cancer Management, 1971, Gynecologic Oncology, 1975; asso. editor N.Y. Jour. Medicine, 1970—; contbr. articles in field to profl. jours. and books. Home: Private Rd Mendham NJ 07945 Office: Dept Obstetrics Gynecology Rutgers Med Sch Piscataway NJ 08854

JONES, JOHN WILEY, chem. co. exec.; b. Emporium, Pa., Apr. 10, 1901; s. George Poole and Sarah (Wiley) J.; grad. U. Pa., 1924; LL.D., Lycoming Coll., 1978; m. Helen Lucille Kline, Sept. 5, 1924; children—Jack, Robert, David, Nancy. With Butterick Pub. Co., 1924-28, Erwin Wasey Co., 1928-30; owner, chmn. bd. Jones Chems., Inc., mfrs. and distbrs. environ. chems., Caledonia, N.Y. Pres. exec. com. Genessee council Boy Scouts Am.; trustee Eisenhower Coll., Rochester Inst. Tech.; Recipient Certificate of Achievement in World War II; Navy award; Silver Beaver award Boy Scouts Am.; Nathaniel Rochester Soc. award Rochester Inst. Tech., 1977. Named Ky. col. Mem. NAM, U.S., Rochester, Livingston (past pres.) chambers commerce, Friars Sr. Soc., Beta Theta Pi. Presbyn. (lay reader). Mason, Lion. Clubs: Admirals (N.Y.C.); Rochester; Ponte Vedra (Jacksonville, Fla.); Batavia (N.Y.); Stafford Country; Capitol Hill (Washington). Home: 3225 East Ave Caledonia NY 14423 Office: 10 Iroquois Rd Caledonia NY 14423

JONES, JOSEPH, ct. reporter; b. N.Y.C., Feb. 13, 1928; s. Joseph W. and Edith B. (Phillips) J.; m. Verneta G. Fant, Dec. 18, 1954; children—Joseph, Gregory L., Pamela L. Hearing reporter N.Y. State Dept. Placement and Unemployment Ins., N.Y.C., 1950; free-lance reporter, 1953; hearing reporter N.Y. State Workmen's Compensation Bd., N.Y.C., 1953-63; ct. reporter N.Y. State Ct. Claims, Albany, after 1963, now chief ct. reporter; owner, dir., instr. Stenotype Sch. of Albany. Active Boy Scouts Am., Guilderland Central Schs.; pres. Concerned Citizens of the Capitol Dist.; mem. com. to study student rights and responsibilities Guilderland High Sch.; v.p. N.Y. State Black Rep. Conf.; Republican committeeman, Town of Guilderland; founding mem. Children's Community Praying Band; bd. dirs. Trinity Inst., 1967—; sec.-treas., pres. Camp Opportunities, Albany, N.Y., 1969-71. Served with U.S. Army, 1951-53. Certified shorthand reporter, State N.Y. Mem. NAACP, Urban League (bd. dirs. 1969-71), Nat. Shorthand Reporters Assn., N.Y. Shorthand Reporters Assn., Northeastern Shorthand Reporters Assn., Assn. Black Shorthand Reporters. Clubs: Sojourners Travel, Lion. Home: 20 Drawbridge Dr Westmere NY 12203 Office: Justice Bldg Empire State Plaza Albany NY 12223

JONES, LEWIS POSEY, govt. ofcl.; b. Sheridan, Ind., Jan. 23, 1921; s. James Ira and Bertha (Masden) J.; student Ohio Wesleyan U., 1938-41, Ohio State U., 1941-42; B.S., Purdue U., 1943; m. Ellen Chloupek, Aug. 29, 1942; children—Donald L., Nancy E. Hart, J. Lawrence. Sr. engr. Aeroproducts div. Gen. Motors Corp., 1944; weight and balance engr. U.S. Navy Dept., 1946-49; chief engr. Thompson Trailer Corp., Alexandria, Va., 1949-50; sr. project engr. U.S. Navy Dept., 1950-54; asst. to comdr. U.S. Naval Aviation Safety Center, Norfolk, Va., 1954-60; sr. analyst NASA, 1960-65, dep. dir. program and spl. reports div., 1965-70; head program review office NSF, Washington, 1970—; dir. Organizational Media Services Corp., Ft. Worth, 1978—. Bd. dirs. Fed. and Internat. Media Communicators. Served to lt. (j.g.), USNR, 1944-46. Recipient Apolio achievement award NASA, 1969. Rear Adm. L.D. Coates award Bur. Naval Weapons, 1965. Mem. Am. Inst. Aeros. and Astronautics, AAAS, Am. Soc. for Pub. Adminstrn., Internat. Tape Assn. (producers adv. council). Home: 404 E Jefferson St Falls Church VA 22046 Office: 1800 G St NW Washington DC 20550

JONES, MAURICE BRUCE, chemist; b. Palmerton, Pa., Aug. 9, 1946; s. Maruice William and Doris Louise J.; B.S., U. Del., 1968; m. Judith Leslie Woodward, July 6, 1968; children—Mark Eric, Erin Kay. Project chemist Mannington Mills, Inc., Salem, N.J., 1971-74, plant supt., 1974-75, chief plant chemist, 1975—. Bd. mgrs. So. br. Salem County YMCA, 1978—. Served with Chem. Corps, U.S. Army, 1968-70. Mem. Am. Chem. Soc., Soc. Plastics Engrs., ASTM, Resilient Floor Covering Inst. (mem. tech. com.), Pi Kappa Alpha. Presbyterian. Home: Greenwich and Water Sts Alloway NJ 08001 Office: PO Box 30 Salem NJ 08079

JONES, PARKER TULL, court reporter; b. Chester, Pa., May 22, 1930; s. Parker and Lessie (Tull) J.; student Stenotype Inst. N.Y., 1952; m. Ruth E. Anderson, Jan. 15, 1966; children—Raymond P., Robert C. Hearing reporter N.Y. State Unemployment Ins. Referee Sect., N.Y.C., 1954-55; hearing reporter N.Y. State Workmen's Compensation Bd., N.Y.C., 1955-62; ofcl. ct. reporter N.Y. State Ct. of Claims, N.Y.C., 1962—. Chmn., Willoughby Walk Tenants Council, 1968-75; adv. com. Pratt Inst., 1971-73; Dist. Community Dist. Planning Bd. 2, Bklyn., 1971-74; bd. dirs. Citizens Com. for N.Y.C., Inc., 1975—; mem. Willoughby Walk Cooperative Council. Served with JAG, U.S. Army, 1952-54. Recipient certificate of appreciation Judge Advocate, 1954, Bklyn. Borough Pres's. Office, 1973; certified shorthand reporter, N.Y. Mem. Nat., N.Y. State shorthand reporters assns., Assn. Black Shorthand Reporters (pres.). Methodist. Home: 185 Hall St Apt 1015 Brooklyn NY 11205 Office: 84-68 Two World Trade Center New York City NY 10047

JONES, PAUL DANIEL, food co. exec.; b. Buffalo, Apr. 5, 1934; s. Harley T. and Margaret (Stone) J.; A.A.S., Erie Community Coll., Buffalo, 1952; postgrad. Cornell U., 1969, Harvard U., 1977; m. Judith Allen, July 15, 1961; children—Peggy, Penny, Jeffrey. Sales mgr. Will Poultry Co., Buffalo, 1956-66; nat. sales mgr. food service Glidden-Durkee div. SCM Corp., Cleve., 1966-75; v.p. sales Zemco Foods Inc., Buffalo, 1975—. Served with U.S. Army, 1954-56. Mem. Food Service Execs. Assn., Am. Meat Inst., Western N.Y. State Sales Execs. Assn., Am. Fedn. Musicians, Buffalo C. of C., N.Y. State Food Mchts. Assn., N.Y. State Food Industry Exec. Council. Home: 365 Willowgreen St Amherst NY 14150 Office: 665 Perry St PO Box 1065 Buffalo NY 14210

JONES, PAUL EUGENE, JR., corp. planning cons.; b. Oberlin, Ohio, Aug. 2, 1932; s. Paul Eugene and Dorothy (Landis) J.; grad. Phillips Exeter Acad., 1950; B.A., Harvard, 1954, B.S., 1959; m. Janet Fitzhugh Wright, Dec. 28, 1957; children—Peter Cunningham, David Blandford. Research asso. Harvard Computation Lab., 1958-60; mem. profl. staff Arthur D. Little, Inc., Cambridge, Mass., 1960-69, 75—; mem. exec. staff Corp.-Tech. Planning, Inc., Waltham, Mass., 1969-75, v.p., dir., 1973-75. Pres., Brooks Sch. of Concord, Inc., 1968-69, exec. com., 1966-69, mem. corp., 1965-69. Served to lt.(j.g.) USN, 1954-57. Mem. Assn. Computing Machinery, Am. Soc. Information Sci., Sigma Xi. Club: Harvard Varsity. Co-author: Automatic Language Processing, 1969; Data Base Design Methodology, 1976. Contbr. papers to profl. lit. Patentee in field. Home: 113 Jennie Dugan Rd Concord MA 01742 Office: 35 Acorn Park Cambridge MA 02140

JONES, REGINALD HAROLD, elec. mfg. co. exec.; b. Stoke-on-Trent, Staffordshire, Eng., July 11, 1917; s. Alfred John and Gertrude (Cartlidge) J.; came to U.S., 1925, naturalized, 1930; B.S. Econs., U. Pa., 1939; m. Grace Butterfield Cole, Mar. 2, 1940; children—Keith Edwin, Grace Seymour. With Gen. Electric Co., Schenectady, 1939-50, bus. trainee, asst. to comptroller, apparatus dept. assignments, 1950-56, gen. mgr. Air Conditioning div., 1956-58, gen. mgr. Gen. Electric Supply Co. div., 1958-61, v.p. parent co., 1961-70, gen. mgr. constrn. industries div., 1964-67, group exec., 1967-68, v.p. finance, 1968-70, sr. v.p., 1970-72, vice-chmn. bd., mem. corporate exec. office, 1972, pres., chmn. bd., chief exec. officer, 1972—, also dir. Office: General Electric Co 3135 Easton Turnpike Fairfield CT 06431

JONES, RICHARD DITZEL, clergyman, social worker; b. Elizabeth, N.J., Sept. 17, 1906; s. John Richard and Hannah Marie (Ditzel) J.; B.A., Wesleyan U., 1928; M.A., Boston U., 1932; LL.D., Windsor U., 1968, York U., 1976; m. Evelyn Allen, June 26, 1937; children—Richard Allan, Nancy Lamoreaux. Ordained to ministry, Methodist Ch., 1933; pastor Gladstone (N.J.) Meth. Ch., 1934-37, Grace Meth. Ch., Kearney, N.J., 1937-47; exec. dir. Canadian Council Christians and Jews, Toronto, Ont., 1948-65, pres., 1965-76, pres. emeritus, 1976—. Chaplain Met. Toronto Police Assn., 1963—. Served with U.S. Mcht. Marine, 1939-40. Decorated officer Order Can.; recipient Merit award, City of Toronto, 1967; Beth Sholem Brotherhood award, 1957; Good Servant medal Canadian Council Christians and Jews created in his honor, 1976. Mem. Canadian Council Christians and Jews. Clubs: Kiwanis, Rotary, Lions. Contbr. articles to profl. jours. Home: 2466 Shepard Ave Mississauga ON Canada Office: 49 Front St E Toronto ON Canada

JONES, ROBERT ALLAN, physicist; b. Guilford, Conn., Feb. 25, 1938; s. Richard Arthur and Margaret Helen (Wissley) J.; B.S., Union Coll. (N.Y.), 1959; M.S., Syracuse U., 1964; m. Janice Helene Manning, June 26, 1960; children—Robert A, Karen D. Physicist, Rome Air Devel. Center, Griffiss AFB, 1960-64; project mgr. Perkin-Elmer Corp., Norwalk, Conn., 1964-68, dept. mgr., 1968-72, sr. staff engr., 1972-78, mgr. computer controlled polishing ops., 1978—; paper chmn. Photo-Electronics Imaging Symposium, 1968. N.Y. Regent scholar, Union Coll. scholar, 1955-59; Air Force scholar, 1963-64; recipient Certificate of Appreciation, Soc. Photog. Scientists and Engrs., 1969. Fellow Optical Soc. Am.; mem. Soc. Photo Instrumentation Engrs., Sigma Xi. Democrat. Methodist. Contbr. articles in field to profl. jours.; sect. editor Abstracts of Photog. Sci. and Engring., 1970-72. Patentee in field. Home: 48 High Pastures Ct Ridgefield CT 06877 Office: MS 429 Perkin Elmer Corp Main Ave Norwalk CT 06856

JONES, ROBERT CHARLES, elec. engr.; b. Pottsville, Pa., Dec. 11, 1938; s. William Evan and Josephine Louise (Spitzner) J.; student Wyo. Sem., 1957; B.S. in Elec. Engring., Lehigh U., 1961; M.S. in Elec. Engring., Drexel U., 1965; postgrad. Montclair State Coll., 1971-72; m. Joan Carvell, Aug. 26, 1967; 1 son, Eric Charles. Coop. student, jr. engr., engr., sr. engr. Philco-Ford Corp., Phila., 1960, 61-70; sr. systems design engr., Univac-Sperry Rand assigned to Bell Telephone Labs., Whippany, N.J., 1970-72; devel. engr., General Electric Co., Syracuse, N.Y., 1972—; part time instr. electronics B.O.C.E.S., 1974. Lay minister United Ch. Christ. Winner award for co-authored paper, IEEE publ., 1965. Mem. Optical Soc. Am. Patentee electron gun structure; contbr. articles to profl. publs. Home: 4148 Silverado Dr Liverpool NY 13088 Office: General Electric Co EP6-222 Syracuse NY 13221

JONES, ROBERT EMMET, educator; b. N.Y.C., Sept. 16, 1928; s. Robert Emmet and Lois Kathryn (UpdeGrove) J.; A.B., Columbia, 1948, Ph.D., 1954; certificat de phonetique Sorbonne (France), 1949. Vis. instr. French, Columbia, N.Y.C., 1953-54; asst. prof. French, U. Ga., Athens, 1954-61, U. Pa., Phila., 1961-67; asso. prof. French and humanities Mass. Inst. Tech., Cambridge, 1967-71, prof. French and humanities, 1971—; tchr. French cooking, 1976—. Mem. Modern Lang. Assn., Am. Assn. Tchrs. French, French Library Boston. Episcopalian. Clubs: St. Anthony, St. Botolph. Author: The Alienated Hero in Modern French Drama, 1961; Panorama de la nouvelle critique en France, 1968; Gerard de Nerval, 1974; contbr. articles to profl. jours. Home: 452 Beacon St Boston MA 02115 Office: 14N 212 Mass Inst Tech Cambridge MA 02139

JONES, ROBERT MICHAEL, artist; b. Wilmington, Del., Feb. 25, 1951; s. Robert Henry and Lois Alice (Hoffmann) J.; B.A., U. Del., 1973. Vice pres., dir. JFO Art Ltd., Wilmington, 1973—; dir. Fifth St. Gallery, Wilmington, 1973—; tchr. filmmaking, art Middle Sch., Newark, Del., 1973-74; research artist Witco Chem. Co.; mem. Com. to Revise Art Edn. Del. One man shows Del. Art Mus., 1975, Bloomsburg State Coll., 1973, U. Del., 1972; represented in permanent collections Del. Art Mus., Haas Gallery, Bloomsburg, Pa., Reading (Pa.) Mus., U. Del., Newark. Democrat. Home and office: 1 E 5th St Wilmington DE 19801

JONES, ROBERT ST. CLAIR, mech. engr., cons. acoustics; b. Rockland, Maine, May 6, 1925; s. Ernest Payson and Dorothy Allen (Robinson) J.; grad. Franklin Tech. Inst., 1952; m. Josephine Regina Buckminster, Nov. 5, 1943; children—Christopher, Bradford, Eric. Project engr. Bueckel & Co., Boston, 1949-66; mgr. heating, ventilating and air-conditioning dept. Francis Assos., Cambridge, Mass., 1966-72; supervisory cons. Bolt Beranek and Newman, Cambridge, 1972—; guest lect. Boston Archtl. Center, Northeastern U., U. Wis. Served with U.S. Army, 1943-46; PTO. Mem. Am. Soc. Heating, Refrigerating and Air Conditioning Engrs., Engring. Soc. New Eng. Mem. Jehovah's Witnesses. Contbr. articles to profl. publs., lectr. profl. orgns. Home: 26 James St Winchester MA 01890 Office: 50 Moulton St Cambridge MA 02138

JONES, RUSSELL RICHARD, steel co. exec.; b. Lehighton, Pa., Mar. 12, 1924; s. Russell Wehr and Noelie Delores (Richard) J.; B.S., Lehigh U., 1948; m. Margery C. Currier, Oct. 6, 1951;

children—Suzan C., Nancy C. With Bethlehem Steel Co., 1948—, asst. to supt. coke plant Sparrows Point Plant, Md., 1954-57, asst. supt. coke plant, 1957-59, asst. supt. steelmaking, 1959-65, supt. steelmaking, 1965-67, asst. gen. mgr., Burns Harbor, Ind., 1967-72, asst. gen. mgr., Sparrows Point, 1972-75, gen. mgr., 1975—. Pres. exec. bd. Boy Scouts Am.; bd. dirs. Jr. Achievement Met. Balt., 1975. Served with AUS, 1943-46. Mem. Am. Iron and Steel Inst., Assn. Iron and Steel Engrs., Am. Inst. Mining and Metall. and Petroleum Engrs., Nat. Alliance Businessmen (adv. bd.), Md. C. of C. (exec. bd.). Republican. Lutheran. Clubs: Sparrows Point Country, Hillendale (Md.) Country, Md. Home: 7 Linkview Ct Phoenix MD 21131 Office: Bethlehem Steel Corp Sparrows Point MD 21219

JONES, RUTH ELLA, sch. counselor; b. Somerset, Ky., Jan. 5, 1926; d. Elmer and Nellie (Sears) J.; B.A., U. Ky., 1948; M.Ed., Coll. Idaho, 1961; M.A., Wash. State U., 1970, postgrad., 1970-71; postgrad. Duke U., 1951-52. Tchr. English, high sch., Somerset, Ky., 1948-51, Nyssa, Oreg., 1952-59, Molalla, Oreg., 1959-68; counselor elementary schs. Selah, Wash., 1971-73, Def. Dept. Schs., Goose Bay, Labrador, 1973-75, Def. Dept., Guantanamo Bay, Cuba, 1975—. Mem. Overseas Edn. Assn. (exec. com.), Orton Soc., Am. Personnel and Guidance Assn., NEA, Nat. Elementary Counselor Assn., Delta Kappa Gamma. Address: Box 84 B0Q 237 FPO New York City NY 09593

JONES, SIDNEY ALEXANDER, obstetrician, gynecologist; b. Dominica, Brit., West Indies, Sept. 25, 1934; s. Herbert Arthur and Ann Elizabeth (Frederick) J.; came to U.S., 1964; M.D., U. Coll. West Indies, 1963; m. Vuriley Maria Harris, June 24, 1966; children—Raquel Maria, Erika Andrea. Intern, Pub. Hosp., Kingston, Jamaica, 1963-64; intern Freedmens Hosp., Washington, 1964-65, resident in obstetrics, gynecology, 1965-69; practice medicine specializing in obstetrics and gynecology, Washington, 1969—; clin. instr. obstetrics, gynecology Howard U., Washington, 1969-71, asst. prof., 1971—; chief Parkside Neighborhood Health Center, Washington Dept. Pub. Health, 1969-71; med. officer, obstetrics, gynecology D.C. Gen. Hosp., 1971—, acting chief med. officer, 1976—, dir. residency tng. in obstetrics and gynecology Howard U. Service, 1977—; mem. adv. council Georgetown Univ. Midwifery Service. Vice pres. Children Handicapped in Lang. Devel., Prince Georges County, Md., 1974-76. Diplomate Am. Bd. Obstetrics and Gynecology. Fellow Am. Coll. Obstetrics and Gynecology, Internat. Coll. of Surgeons; mem. Am. Fertility Soc., D.C. Med. Soc., Royal Soc. of Medicine, Montgomery County Assn. for Hearing Impaired Children, Assn. of Former Interns and Residents Freedmens Hosp. Methodist. Contbr. articles to profl. jours. Home: 1108 Gresham Rd Silver Spring MD 20904 Office: DC Gen Hosp Washington DC 20003

JONES, THOMAS EDWARD, photographer; b. New London, Conn., Apr. 11, 1944; s. Elliott Woodbury and Helen Elizabeth (Lasky) J.; grad. high sch.; grad. Doscher Sch. Photography, 1967; m. Valentine Mélin, 1975; 1 son, Benjamin Woodbury. Self-employed photographer, mag. and comml. work, 1970—. Served with USNR, 1962-66. Named Photographer of Year, New Eng. Press Assn., 1968, 69. Mem. Profl. Photographers Am. (councilman), Me. Profl. Photographers Assn. (past dir.). Illustrator: Maine Lines, 1970. Address: Buttermilk Cove at Gurnet Brunswick ME 04011

JONES, VERNON, ednl. psychologist; b. Portsmouth, Va., Oct. 13, 1897; s. Frank A. and Pattie Ann (McLemore) J.; B.A., M.A., U. Va., 1920; M.A., Columbia, 1924, Ph.D., 1926; m. Harriet Clement Marble, Nov. 2, 1929; children—Patricia (Mrs. Hugh C. Lovell), Nancy Clement (Mrs. Roy A. Pearson, Jr.). Sch. prin., Richmond, Va., 1921; dir. research Richmond Pub. Schs., 1923; asso. prof. ednl. psychology Clark U., 1928-37, prof. ednl. psychology, chmn. dept. psychology and edn., 1937-49, organizer, chmn. dept. edn., 1949-66; personnel cons. Norton Co., Worcester, Mass., 1968—. Writer; dir. VA Guidance Center of Clark U., 1945-51; dir. guidance in Techniquest, Worcester Poly. Inst., summers 1934-66; summer lectr. various univs. Mem. planning com. Nat. Conf. on Citizenship; mem. governing bd. Worcester Jr. Coll.; mem. adv. com. Worcester Ecumenical Inst. Social Sci. Research Council grantee, 1934, 35. Recipient award for outstanding research Am. Ednl. Research Assn., 1940; award for citizenship devel. program Freedom Found., 1951. Mem. Am. Psychol. Assn., NEA, Am. Personnel and Guidance Assn., Phi Beta Kappa, Raven Hon. Soc. Author: Character Education through Cases from Biography, 1931; Character and Citizenship Training in the Public Schools, 1936; Character and Citizenship Education, 1950; Youth Decides-Group Guidance in Everyday Citizenship, 1952; Monograph: Attitudes of College Students and their Changes-A 37 Year Study, 1970. Contbr. articles to profl. jours., chpts. to books, sects. to encys. Home: 267 Salisbury St Worcester MA 01609

JONES, WALTER LEWIS, JR., mktg. exec.; b. Fairfield, Ala., June 6, 1941; s. Walter Lewis and Nannie Lenora (Stuart) J.; student U. Va., 1959-60; B.S. in Chem. Engring., U. Ala., 1964; m. Jane Frederick Jones, Aug. 11, 1962; children—Walter Lewis III, Jennifer Ruth. Process engr. Westvaco Corp., Charleston, S.C., 1964; plant mgr. chem. div. Union Camp Corp., Savannah, Ga., 1966-73, sales rep., nat. account rep., Chgo., 1973-76, mktg. specialist, Wayne, N.J., 1976—. Served with U.S. Army, 1964-66. Decorated Army Commendation Medal. Episcopalian. Club: Chatham. Home: 15 Rocky Ln Basking Ridge NJ 07920 Office: 1600 Valley Rd Wayne NJ 07470

JONG, ANTHONY, pub. health dentist; b. Hong Kong, Aug. 1, 1938; s. Goddard S. and Lily (Fung) J.; (mother Am. citizen); B.S., Coll. City N.Y., 1960; D.D.S., N.Y. U., 1964; M.P.H., Harvard, 1966, certificate Sch. Dental Medicine, 1968; D.Sc. in Dentistry, Boston U., 1976. Intern, Jewish Meml. Hosp., N.Y.C., 1964-65; resident Mass. Dept. Pub. Health, 1966-67; dental supr. Project Head Start, Boston, 1966; dir. dental services Boston Maternity and Infant Care Project, 1968-69, dir. Boston Maternity, Infant Care and Children and Youth Projects, 1969-70; asst. dean student affairs Harvard Sch. Dental Medicine, 1971-73; prof., chmn. dept. pub. health and community dentistry Boston U. Sch. Grad. Dentistry, 1973—, asst. dean postdoctoral studies, 1978—. Research fellow Harvard Sch. Dental Medicine, 1966-68, research asso., 1968-69, asst. prof. dental ecology, 1969-73; cons. Med. Found., Boston, 1968—, Boston Head Start Health Services, 1966-70; mem. dental health research and edn. adv. com. U.S. Dept. Health, Edn. and Welfare, 1971-73. Bd. dirs. N. Am. Riding for Handicapped Assn. Recipient USPHS Research Career Devel. award, 1969. Mem. Am. (mem. dental sect. council 1974-77, chmn. dental sect. 1978-79), Mass. (chmn. dental sect. 1971-72) pub. health assns., Am. Dental Assn., Internat. Assn. for Dental Research, Am. Assn. Pub. Health Dentists, Omicron Kappa Upsilon (treas.-sec. 1972-74). Contbr. articles to profl. jours. Home: 33 Pond Ave Brookline MA 02146 Office: 100 E Newton St Boston MA 02118

JORDAIN, PHILIP BERNARD, bank exec.; b. Paris, France, Feb. 2, 1919; s. John Howard and Simone Juliette (Bousquet-Deschamps) J. (parents Am. citizens); B.S., Ecole Superieure De Mecanique et d'Electricite, France, 1940; B.S., Columbia, 1951; postgrad. N.Y. U., 1952-54; m. Eleanor Elizabeth Gillespie, June 9, 1948; children—Sheila (Mrs. John Dickson), John, Philip, Patricia Ann. Asst. to distbn. mgr. Mobil Co., N.Y.C., 1951-59; mgr. advanced planning RCA, Cherry Hill, N.J., 1960-61; mgr. operations research Lybrand, Ross & Montgomery, N.Y.C., 1962-63; dir. operations research Thomas J. Lipton, Englewood Cliffs, N.J., 1964-68; with First Nat. City Bank, N.Y.C., 1969—, sr. research officer, 1970—; asso. Artronic Info. Systems, N.Y.C., 1969—, AETA Corp., Dover, Del., 1978—. Mem. AAAS, Ops. Research Soc. Am., N.J. Acad. Sci., Inst. Mgmt. Sci. Editor: Condensed Computer Encyclopedia, 1969; cons. editor, contbr. McGraw-Hill Sci. and Tech. Dictionary, 1974, 76. Home: 9 Brinkerhoff Ave Teaneck NJ 07666 Office: 399 Park Ave New York NY 10022

JORDAN, DENNIS EDWARD, ins. co. exec.; b. Davenport, Iowa, Sept. 24, 1937; s. Clifford Homer and Virginia June (Russell) J.; B.A., State U. Iowa, 1959, J.D., 1961; m. Linda Kay Hansen, Aug. 17, 1958; children—Melissa Ann, Amy Beth, Richard Christian, Carrie Hansen. Admitted to Mass. bar, 1962; mem. firm Mirick, O'Connell, DeMallie & Lougee, Worcester, Mass., 1961-68; asso. counsel, asst. sec. The Paul Revere Cos., Worcester, 1968—. Chmn. Town of Holden Planning Bd., 1965-69; mem. Holden Town Rep. Com., 1965—; mem. Wachusett Regional Sch. Com., 1976—; trustee New Eng. Spl. Olympics for Mentally Retarded Children Trust, 1969-71; bd. dirs. Mass. chpt. ARC, 1975—; chmn. bd. trustees U.S. Jaycees Found., 1972-76. Named Outstanding Young Man of Worcester County, Greater Worcester Jr. C. of C., 1967. Fellow Mass. Bar Found.; mem. Am., Mass., Worcester County bar assns., Jr. C. of C. (hon. life Mass.; pres. Mass. 1968-69, v.p. U.S. 1969-70, life senator Jr. Chamber Internat. 1967), Worcester Area C. of C. (v.p., dir. 1972-75), Phi Delta Theta, Phi Delta Phi. Home: 815 Salisbury St Holden MA 01520 Office: 18 Chestnut St Worcester MA 01608

JORDAN, HELEN SANKEY, nurse, adminstr.; b. Reedsville, Pa., Jan. 24, 1930; d. Foster J. and Sara Katherine (Kretzing) S.; diploma Sch. Nursing Hosp. U. Pa., 1950; B.S. Nursing, U. Pa., 1969, M.S. Nursing, 1975; m. 2d Edmund H. Jordan, Feb. 18, 1972; children—Patricia A., Michelle J., Steven C., Yvonne H., Dwayne S. Ramsey. Staff nurse Hosp. U. Pa., 1950-51; psychiat. nurse Eugenia Hosp., Whitemarsh, Pa., 1955-65, mental health unit Pa. Hosp., Phila., 1966; supr. Moss Rehab. Hosp., Phila., 1967, asst. dir. nursing, 1968-76, dir. nursing, 1976—. Mem. Am. Nurses Assn., Nat. League Nursing, Am. Congress Rehab., Alumna Assn. Sch. Nursing U. Pa., Hosp. Assn. Pa. Home: Route 309 and Mill Rd Hatfield PA 19440 Office: 12th St and Tabor Rd Philadelphia PA 19141

JORDAN, JAMES NICHOLAS, educator; b. Houston, Sept. 16, 1938; s. Eric Wall and Betsy Ann (Donnelly) J.; B.A., U. Tex., Austin, 1961, Ph.D., 1966; m. Cathleen Hill Gunn, Aug. 26, 1961. Asst. prof. philosophy S.W. Mo. State Coll., 1965-66; asso. prof., chmn. dept. philosophy U. S.D., 1966-70; asso. prof., chmn. dept. Queens Coll., City U. N.Y., Flushing, 1970—. Mem. Am., S.W. Philos. assns. Episcopalian. Editorial bd. Jour. Critical Analysis, 1973-76. Contbr. articles to profl. jours. Home: 51 W 69th St Apt 1A New York City NY 10023 Office: Dept Philosophy Queens Coll City U NY Flushing NY 11367

JORDAN, LAWRENCE MARCELLUS, physicist; b. Greensboro, N.C., Apr. 6, 1936; s. L. M. and Edna Mona (Thompson) J.; B.S. in Physics, Fisk U., 1957; Ph.D., Princeton, 1964; m. Carolyne Juanita Lamar, June 10, 1960; children—Lara Gayle, Samuel Lamar. Asst. prof. physics Colgate U., Hamilton, N.Y., 1962-66; staff scientist space systems div. Avco Corp., Wilmington, Mass., 1966-68, sr. scientist, 1968-70; physicist NASA, Cambridge, Mass., 1970; physicist U.S. Dept. Transp., Cambridge, 1970—; cons. in field. Mem. Lexington Citizens for Conservation. Nat. Sci. Research participation fellow, 1965. Mem. NAACP, Am. Phys. Soc., Sigma XI, Phi Beta Kappa, Alpha Phi Alpha. Contbr. articles to profl. jours. Home: 3 North St Lexington MA 02173 Office: Transportation Systems Center US DOT Kenda 1 Sq Cambridge MA 02142

JORDAN, LOUIS HAMPTON, educator; b. Owassa, Ala., Jan. 1, 1922; s. Isaac Newton and Bertha (Edeker) J.; B.S., Auburn U., 1947; M.B.A., Northwestern U., 1951; Ph.D., Columbia, 1954; m. Carolyn Maureen Carter, June 2, 1956; children—Louis Hampton, Mark Stephen. Asso. prof. Tulane U., New Orleans, 1955-60; prof. accounting Columbia, 1960-75; prof. accounting, asso. dean Grad. Sch. Bus. Adminstrn., Fordham U., N.Y.C., 1975—; cons. Westinghouse Electric Corp., Touche Ross & Price Waterhouse; vis. prof. Robert Coll., Istanbul, Turkey, 1966-67, 70-71. Served to capt., arty. U.S. Army, 1942-46. Mem. Am. Inst. C.P.A.'s, Am. Accounting Assn. Democrat. Roman Catholic. Author: (with M. Moonitz) Accounting: An Analysis of Its Problems, 2 vols., 1963, 64. Home: 20 Kingston Ave Yonkers NY 10701 Office: Fordham U 624 Lincoln Center New York City NY 10023

JORDAN, MARILYN KEYS, interior designer; b. Paterson, N.J., Sept. 5, 1946; s. Summer and Mary Elizabeth (Garnett) K.; diploma cum laude, Dover Bus. Coll., 1965; grad. Internat. Inst. Interior Design, 1974; m. Frank C. Jordan, Jr., July 27, 1968; 1 dau., Tiffany. With Warner Lamber Pharm. Co., Morris Plains, N.J., 1965; showroom asst. Decorators Walk, Washington, 1966-67; secretarial positions Fotomat Corp., Silver Spring, Md., 1968-69, Franklin Life Ins. Co., Silver Spring, 1972-73; interior designer Jumanne Design, Inc., Silver Spring, 1973—. Mem. Nat. Home Fashions League (v.p. consumer affairs). Home: 8772 Cloudleap Ct Apt 13 Columbia MD 21045 Office: 814 Thayer Ave Silver Spring MD 20910

JORDAN, PAUL, musician, educator; b. N.Y.C., Mar. 12, 1939; s. Henry P. and Irene (Brandt) J.; student Harvard, 1956-57, Columbia, 1958-60; Mus.M., Yale, 1967; State Degree in Sacred Music, State Inst. Music, Frankfurt, Germany, 1963. Dir. music United Church on the Green, New Haven, 1964-74; mem. faculty Sarah Lawrence Coll., Bronxville, N.Y., 1967-68, Yale, 1968-69, State U. N.Y. at Binghamton, 1973—. Condr., composer; organist, tour and radio appearances in U.S., Sweden, Germany, France, Cuba. Recording of J.S. Bach's Orgelbüchlein nominated for Deutscher Schallplattenpreis, 1977; pvt. grant for composition in Southern France, 1972-73. Mem. Am. Symphony Orch. League, Am. Guild Organists, Coll. Music Soc., Am. Recorder Soc. Composer, vocal/instrumental chamber music, organ works. Home: 81 Main St Binghamton NY 13905 Office: Dept Music State Univ New York Binghamton NY 13901

JORDAN, ROBERT PAUL, editor, author; b. Omaha, July 6, 1921; s. Paul Hyde and Lillian Ada (Walters) J.; B.A., George Washington U., 1947; postgrad. Am. U., 1953-54; m. Jane Carol Taylor, Sept. 8, 1956; children—Robert Paul, Meredith, Julia. Asst. Sunday editor Washington Post, 1946-61; writer, editor Nat. Geog. Mag., Washington, 1962—. Served with U.S. Army, 1942-46, USAF, 1951-53. Recipient Recognition award Higher Edn. Alumni Council Okla., 1971. Mem. White House Corrs. Assn., Overseas Writers, Washington Press Club, Sigma Delta Chi. Presbyn. Club: Congressional Country. Author: The Civil War, 1969. Cons. editor: The Mighty Mississippi (Bern Keating), 1971; As We Live and Breathe (various authors), 1971; American Cowboy (Bart McDowell), 1972; Great American Deserts (Rowe Findley), 1972; The Alps (various authors), 1973; The Incredible Incas and Their Timeless Land, 1975. Home: 9717 Brimfield Ct Potomac MD 20854 Office: 17th and M Sts NW Washington DC 20036

JORDAN, RONALD JOSEPH, accountant, educator; b. Bridgeport, Conn., Oct. 19, 1944; s. Eric and Trude G. (Metzger) J.; B.S. magna cum laude (Dana scholar), U. Bridgeport, 1966; M.B.A. (scholar), N.Y. U., 1969, Ph.D., 1971; m. Sheryl Anne Levine, Dec. 22, 1973. Teaching fellow N.Y. U., 1969-70; asst. prof. fin. and investments U. Conn., 1970-74; asso. prof. accounting U. Bridgeport, 1976—; spl. cons. SEC, 1978; author, cons. NDEA fellow, 1967-71. Recipient Founders Day award N.Y. U., 1971; C.P.A., Conn. Mem. Am. Fin. Assn., Fin. Mgmt. Assn., Am. Inst. Decision Scis., Am. Inst. C.P.A.'s, Conn. Soc. C.P.A.'s, Beta Gamma Sigma. Jewish (fin. sec. congregation). Mason. Author: (with D.E. Fischer) Security Analysis and Portfolio Management, 1974, rev. 2d edit., 1979; asso. editor Fin. Rev., 1973-75; reviewer Fin. Mgmt., 1972—. Home: 24 Pontiac Rd West Hartford CT 06117 Office: 632 Prospect Ave Hartford CT 06105 also U Bridgeport Bridgeport CT 06602

JORDAN, RUTH ANN, physician; b. nr. Richmond, Ind., Oct. 12, 1928; d. Willard T. and Esther (Fouts) Jordan; A.B., Ind. U., 1950; M.D., Columbia U., 1957; children—Diane M., Linda J. Intern, St. Luke's Hosp., N.Y.C., 1957-58, asst. resident in medicine, 1958-59; physician clinic Met. Life Ins. Co., N.Y.C., 1960-62; physician med. clinic Standard Oil Co. of N.J., N.Y.C., 1962; physician in med. dept. Mass. Inst. Tech., 1963-72; asst. med. dir. New Eng. Mut. Life Ins. Co., Boston, 1972-74, physician med. clinic, 1963-66, Northeastern U., 1976-78; asso. med. dir. New Eng. Telephone Co., Boston, 1978—; therapeutic dietitian Meth. Hosp., Indpls., 1951-53, Presbyn. Hosp., N.Y.C., part-time, 1954-57; fellow in internal medicine Mass. Gen. Hosp., Boston, 1974-75; physician Simmons Coll., Boston, 1975-78, John Hancock Ins. Co., summer 1976. Active Brownies. Mem. AMA, Mass., Norfolk County med. socs., Ind. Dietetic Assn. (past pub. relations chmn.), Alpha Chi Omega. Club: Annisquam Yacht. Home: 105 Rockwood St Brookline MA 02146 Office: 99 High St Boston MA

JORDAN, TRENHOLM DOUGLAS, viticulturist; b. Bath, N.H., Feb. 28, 1927; s. Clyde W. and Lillian (Hutchins) J.; B.S., U. N.H., 1950; M.Ed., U. Calif. at Davis, 1963; m. Mary Williams, Aug. 18, 1945; children—Nancy Jordan Schuster, Teresa, Douglas, Michael. Asst. county agrl. agt. Chatauqua County Extension Service, Jamestown, N.Y., 1951-54, asso. county agt., 1955-65, coop. extension agt., 1966-69; coop. extension specialist Gt. Lakes Grape Industry, Cornell U., Fredonia, N.Y., 1970—. Sec., N.Y. State Grape Prodn. Research Fund, Inc.; cons. viticulturist. Mem. Portland (N.Y.) Town Planning Commn., 1971-73, Portland Zoning Commn., 1974-75. Served with USNR, 1945-46. Recipient Distinguished Service award Nat. Assn. County Agrl. Agts., 1965. Mem. N.Y. State (pres. 1974), Nat. assns. county agrl. agts., N.Y. State Hort. Soc., Am. Soc. Hort. Sci., Am. Soc. Enologists. Home: 9090 Pecor St Portland NY 14769 Office: 412 E Main St Fredonia NY 14063

JORDAN, VERNON EULION, JR., assn. exec., lawyer; b. Atlanta, Aug. 15, 1935; s. Vernon Eulion and Mary Belle (Griggs) J.; B.A., DePauw U., 1957; J.D., Howard U., 1960; hon. degrees Boston U., Brandeis U., 1970, DePauw U., Mich. State U., 1972, Duke, Wilberforce U., 1971, Yale, Morris Brown U., 1971, Bloomfield Coll., 1971, Benedict Coll., Notre Dame U., Williams Coll., Tougaloo U., Tuskegee Inst.; m. Shirley M. Yarbrough, Dec. 13, 1958; 1 dau., Vickee. Admitted to Ga. bar, Ark. bar; practiced in Ga. and Ark.; field sec. for Ga., N.A.A.C.P.; dir. voter edn. project So. Regional Council, 1964-68; atty. U.S. OEO, 1969; exec. dir. United Negro Coll. Fund, 1970-71; pres. Nat. Urban League, N.Y.C., 1972—; dir. Am. Express Co., Bankers Trust Co., Bankers Trust N.Y. Corp., Celanese Corp., Xerox Corp., J.C. Penney Corp., MIT Corp. Mem. council White House Conf. To Fulfill These Rights, 1966; mem. nat. adv. com. on SSS, 1966-67; mem. Presdl. Clemency Bd., 1974. Bd. dirs. Am. Revolution Bi-Centennial Commn., Clark Coll., John Hay Whitney Found., Nat. Multiple Sclerosis Soc., Nat. Urban Coalition, Potomac Inst., Rockefeller Found., Twentieth Century Fund. Mem. Am., Nat. bar assns., Nat. Conf. Black Lawyers. Mem. A.M.E. Ch. Office: Nat Urban League 500 E 62d St New York City NY 10021

JORDAN COX, CARMEN ANTOINETTE, coll. adminstr.; B. b. Savannah, Ga., Mar. 19, 1950; d. Carl Rankin and Annie (Knight) Jordan; A.B., Ind. U., 1971; M.Ed., Pa. State U., 1972; postgrad. (Nat. Fellowships Fund fellow) Boston Coll., 1975—; m. McClellon D. Cox, III, Aug. 13, 1977. Dir. multi-media resources center Ind. U., 1972-73; dir. student programs and services Bryant Coll., 1973-77; spl. services counselor Union for Experimenting Colls. and Univs. Urban Regional Learning Center, Balt., 1977-78; counselor Anne Arundel Community Coll., Arnold, Md., 1978—; mem. adv. bd. on black programming Ednl. TV, Providence, 1974-77; originator, moderator The Black Experience, TV series, 1974. Mem. Am. Assn. Higher Edn., AAUW. Roman Catholic. Home: 1005 Marlau Dr Baltimore MD 21212 Office: Anne Arundel Community Coll Arnold MD 21012

JORDANO, JOSEPH PETER, bldg. constrn. exec.; b. Williamson, W.Va., May 12, 1927; s. Vincent Andrew and Catherine Marie (Minel) J.; B.S., Cooper Union, 1949; m. Marge Raitan, Aug. 29, 1948; children—Cathy, Stephen, Tina. Vice pres. Electronics and Missile Facilities, 1957; pres. Trans-Am. Ind. Co., 1957-64; v.p. San Juan Gen. Concentrates Corp., 1964-70; exec. v.p. Jordan-Ried Corp., Great Neck, N.Y., 1970-75; pres. Jordan Industries Corp., Great Neck, 1975—; cons. to health care industry, 1970-77. Recipient Golden Shofar award Nat. Council of Young Israel, 1976. Clubs: Exchange; Civil Engineers of P.R. Office: 425 Northern Blvd Great Neck NY 11021

JORGENSEN, ALFRED H., computer network services co. exec.; b. South Gate, Calif., May 1, 1934; s. Peter Hansen and Anna Christine (Nielsen) J.; A.A., El Camino Coll.; student U. Calif., Los Angeles, 1958; m. Carole Jean Scott, Sept. 3, 1959; children—Mark Alan, Lora Jean. Asso. engr. Litton Industries, Beverly Hills, Calif., 1957-60; engr. Daystrom, Inc., 1960-64; with control systems div. Foxboro Co., Pitts., 1964-67, dist. and regional mgr., 1967-69; with Interactive Scis., Pitts., 1969-72, v.p., 1971-72; v.p. Computeria Inc., 1972, pres., 1972-73; v.p. Interactive Scis. Corp., Braintree, Mass., 1973-77, pres., 1977—. Bd. dirs. Mass. Assn. Mental Health, 1977-78. Served with U.S. Army, 1954-56. Mem. Data Processing Mgmt. Assn., Assn. Iron and Steel Engrs., Instrument Soc. Am., IEEE. Home: 15 Richard Rd Hingham MA 03043 Office: 60 Brooks Dr Braintree MA 02184

JORGENSEN, CHARLES WILLIAM, human resources specialist; b. Newton, Mass., June 8, 1915; s. Charles William and Maude (Ellison) J.; student Am. Internat. Coll., 1932-33; B.S., Springfield Coll., 1941; postgrad. Columbia, 1957; M.P.A., Maxwell Sch., U. Syracuse, 1972; m. Dorothy Elvira Gralow, Sept. 27, 1941; children—Charles William III, Richard E., Peter E., Elizabeth E. Youth Worker Phila. YMCA, relief, rehab. work China, exec. S.I. YMCA, 1941-58; ednl. fund raising dir. United Bd. Christian Higher Edn. in Asia, Bd. Nat. Missions Presbyn. Ch., 1958-61; area sec. for colls. Central Atlantic YMCA, exec. Bergen County YMCA, Wyckoff, N.J., 1961-66; anti-poverty exec., Syracuse, N.Y., 1966-67; exec. dir. Onondago County chpt. N.Y. State Assn. for Retarded Children, Syracuse, 1968-69; dir. devel. Pa. Sch. for Deaf, Phila., 1969-71; with N.Y. State County Officers Assn., Albany, 1971-76; bus. mgr. Planned Parenthood Syracuse, 1977—. Pres. P.T.A., 1959;

mem. Human Relations Council, Englewood, 1960; pres. Bergen County Presbyn. Interracial Council, 1964; co-chmn. Bergen County Conf. Religion and Race, 1964; exec. dir. Ulster County (N.Y.) Community Action Com.; mem. city council, Englewood, 1964-67. Mem. Am. Soc. Pub. Adminstrn., Nat. Assn. Social Workers, Acad. Certified Social Workers, Nat. Assn. Community Devel. Author: Four Fronts and Other YMCA Clubs, 1955; An Unchanging Purpose in a Changing World, Part II, 1956; Leadership in Megalopolis, 1961. Career Opportunities in County Government, 1975. Home: 105 Lockwood Rd Syracuse NY 13214 Office: 1120 Genesee East Syracuse NY 13210

JORGENSEN, NORMA ANDERSON (MRS. ALBERT NELS JORGENSEN, JR.), coll. adminstr.; b. Hartford, Conn., Dec. 12, 1920; d. Carl Ernest and Anna Maria (Johnson) Anderson; B.S., U. Conn., 1943; m. Albert Nels Jorgensen, Jr., Oct. 30, 1943; children—Catherine Anne (Mrs. Richard Phillips), Albert Nels III. Mem. Bd. Higher Edn., State of Conn.; pres. Foursquare Inc.; corporator Burritt Mut. Savs. Bank, New Britain, Conn., 1973—. Trustee U. Conn., Storrs. Mem. Nat. Assn. Women Deans, Adminstrs. and Counselors, Nat. Rifle Assn., Nat. Wildlife Fedn., Nat. Audubon Soc., U. Conn. Alumni Assn. (dir. 1967-76, council 1976—), Kappa Alpha Theta (nat. pres. 1968-72, del. Nat. Panhellenic Conf.). Home: 295 E Cedar St Newington CT 06111 also 58 Mountain Shadows E Scottsdale AZ 85253

JOSE, NORMAN LORD, cons. engr.; b. Gardiner, Maine, May 16, 1924; s. Bion Fremont and Nellie Sterns (Lord) J.; B.S. in Civil Engring., U. Maine, 1949; m. Frances Lillian Pierce, July 25, 1950. Asst. bridge constrn. engr. Maine State Hwy. Dept., Augusta, 1964-68, bridge engr., 1968-70; constr. mgr., bridges, Vietnam project Ray Jorgensen Assos., Inc., Gaithersburg, Md., 1973-75; cons. engr., Randolph, Maine, 1970-73, 75—. Served with AUS, 1942-46. Decorated Purple Heart. Registered profl. engr., Maine. Mem. ASCE, Maine Soc. Engrs., Maine Good Roads Assn. Republican. Episcopalian. Home: 36 Closson St Randolph ME 04345

JOSEPH, EDNA WHITEHEAD (MRS. LAWRENCE J. JOSEPH), bank exec.; b. Everett, Mass., Feb. 4, 1924; d. Alfred Edward and Mary Kathleen (Butler) Whitehead; student Am. Inst. Banking; m. Lawrence James Joseph, May 30, 1958. With Nat. Shawmut Bank (name now Shawmut Bank of Boston, N.A.), Boston, 1941-55, 57—, asst. tax officer, 1965-69, tax officer, 1969—; income tax mgr. Sam C. Charlson, Manhattan, Kans., 1955-57. Mem. liaison com. Soc. of Jesus in New Eng., 1974-75, mem. exec. com., 1975-76. Bd. dirs. Found. of Hope, Boston. Mem. Fiduciary Tax Assos., Mass. Bankers Assn. (vice chmn. taxation com. 1971-72, chmn. 1972-73, tax cons. com. 1975—), Nat. Assn. Bank Women, Am. Inst. Banking, Nat. Early Am. Glass Club, Boston Mus. Fine Arts, Soc. for Preservation of New Eng. Antiquities, Friends of Sandwich Mus., North Shore Antique Assn., Colletors Club, Bostonian Soc., Victorian Soc., Essex Inst., Peabody Mus. Club: Women's Republican Essex County. Home: 8 Laurel Rd Lynnfield MA 01940 Office: One Federal St Boston MA 02109

JOSEPH, J. JONATHAN, interior designer; b. Gloucester, Mass., Jan. 14, 1932; s. George Stephen and Maryann (Lattof) J.; certificate Vesper George Sch. Art, Boston, 1952; student theater design Boston Conservatory Music, 1951. Asso. designer Reva Lewitt, Boston, 1952-67; owner interior design bus., Boston, 1967—. Bd. dirs. Maury A. Bromsen Assos., Inc.; also cons. in fine arts; spl. research 19th century glass in Am., also Tiffany glass; exhibited Tiffany glass collection Mus. Fine Art, Boston, 1965, Worcester (Mass.) Art Mus., 1968. Important decorating works include: restoration of Plaza Hotel, N.Y.C. Recipient award Internat. V'Soske Rug Design. Mem. Am. Inst. Interior Designers (chmn. bd. New Eng. chpt. 1965-66, chpt. v.p. 1969-71, pres. 1971-72), Nat. Early Am. Glass Club (1st v.p. 1967-69), Appraisers Assn. Am., Mus. Fine Arts Boston. Contbr. reviews and articles to profl. publs. Address: 39 Prince St Beverly Cove MA 01915

JOSEPH, LEONARD, lawyer; b. Phila., June 8, 1919; s. Harry L. and Mary (Pollock) J.; B.A., U. Pa., 1941; LL.B., Harvard, 1944; m. Norma Hamberg, 1942; children—Gilbert M., Stuart A., Janet H. Admitted to N.Y. bar, 1949; asso. firm Dewey, Ballantine, Bushby, Palmer & Wood, N.Y.C., 1948-57, partner, 1957. Served with U.S. Army, 1943-46. Fellow Am. Bar Found., Am. Coll. Trial Lawyers; mem. Am., N.Y.C., N.Y. State bar assns. Clubs: Harvard (N.Y.C.), Plandome Country. Office: 140 Broadway New York City NY 10005

JOSEPH, RONALD ANTHONY, automobile co. exec.; b. Providence, R.I., Jan. 12; s. John M. and Amelia M. (Pepin) J.; student U. R.I., U. Miami, 1957-61; certificate Gen. Motors Inst., 1964; student Dale Carnegie Inst., 1971; m. Donna Marie Grimsley, Mar. 4, 1966; children—Cheryl, Ronald, Michael. Pres., New Imports, Inc., 1965-70, New Eng. Toyota Distbr., Inc., Woburn, Mass., 1971-77; pres. New Eng. Import Distbr., Inc., Woburn, 1978—, also dir.; pres., dir. Import Auto Parts, Inc.; dir. N.E. Advt., N.E. Leasing. Co-sponsor Kahlil Gibran Meml. and dedication Gibran Sq., Boston; co-host, sponsor benefit for Alma Lewis Sch. Fine Arts. Served with Intelligence Corps, U.S. Army, 1971-73. Recipient numerous sales awards. Mem. Nat. Automobile Dealers Assn., Smithsonian Assos., Sigma Phi Epsilon. Democrat. Roman Catholic. Club: K.C. Home: 5 Lexington Burlington MA 01803 Office: 39 Olympia Ave Woburn MA 01801*

JOSEPH, STANLEY ROBERT, advt. co. exec.; b. N.Y.C., May 28, 1949; s. Julian and Matilda Joseph; B.A. in Communications, U. Wis., 1971; m. Veronica Rita Pucklis, May 19, 1974; children—Jason Christopher and Erin Lindsay (twins); children by previous marriage—Aleck W. Gilner, Adrienne Rite Gilner. Account exec. Bernard Hodes Advt. Co., N.Y.C., 1971-73, regional mgr., 1978—; account exec. Woman's Day Mag., N.Y.C., 1973-74; sales rep. Pebsco of Md., Balt., 1975-77, Mut. Life Ins. Co. N.Y., Balt., 1977-78; sales mgr. Monarch Life Ins. Co., Balt., 1978. Named Rookie of Yr., Mut. of N.Y., 1977; Mt. Sinai Hosp. Coll. scholar, 1967-68. Mem. Nat. Assn. Life Underwriters. Club: Optimists. Home: 807 Staffordshire Rd Cockeysville MD 21030 Office: 6175 Barfield Rd Suite 100 Atlanta GA 30328

JOSEPHSON, JULIAN, writer, cons., educator, engr.; b. Bklyn., Aug. 28, 1934; s. Murray K. and Rhea (Rudd) J.; B.A., N.Y. U., 1955, postgrad. 1956; diploma U. Paris (France), 1959; postgrad. Cath. U. Am., 1967-68; m. Aliza Simha, Apr. 14, 1959; children—Ron, Naomi. With U.S. Naval Oceanographic Office, Washington, 1956-59, 61-69, cartographer, 1961-65; civil engr., Washington, 1965-69; phys. scientist Bur. Mines, 1970-71; instr. chemistry and English, Sch. Marine and Environ. Sci., Fla. Inst. Tech., Jensen Beach, 1971-73; asso. editor Environ. Sci. and Tech., Am. Chem. Soc., Washington, 1973—; sec. 3d World Inst. Sec. Internat. Buoy Tech. Symposium, 1964. Recipient U.S. Govt. Superior Accomplishment award, 1958, 63; Invention award, 1966, 67, 68, 69, 70. Mem. Marine Tech. Soc. (finance chmn. 1965, treas. conf. 1966, founding patron, sec., dir. Cape Canaveral sect. 1971-72). Club: Nat. Press. Contbr. articles to sci. jours. and encys. Patentee in field. Home: 10001 Woodhill Rd Bethesda MD 20034

JOSEPHSON, MARK ERIC, cardiologist; b. N.Y.C., Jan. 27, 1943; s. Sidney B. and Miriam (Etman) J.; B.S., Trinity Coll., Hartford, Conn., 1965; M.D., Columbia U., 1969; m. Joan Eisenberg, 1967; children—Rachel Laurie, Stephanie Paige. Intern, Mt. Sinai Hosp., N.Y.C., 1969-70, resident, 1970-71; practice medicine, specializing in cardiology, Phila., 1973—; dir. clin. electrophysiology labs. U. Pa. Hosp., 1975—, co-dir. med. intensive care unit, 1975—. Served with USPHS, 1971-73. Recipient award Southeastern Pa. Heart Assn., 1974-75, Research Career Devel. award NIH, 1978—. Diplomate Am. Bd. Internal Medicine. Fellow Am. Coll. Cardiology, A.C.P.; mem. Phila. Acad. Cardiology, Am. Heart Assn., Am. Fedn. Clin. Research, Cardiac Electrophysiology Group. Contbr. articles on clin. electrophysiology to med. jours. Home: 1600 Winston Ave Gladwyne PA 19035 Office: 666 White Bldg Hosp U Pa 3400 Spruce St Philadelphia PA 19104

JOSEY, E(LONNIE) J(UNIUS), state ofcl.; b. Norfolk, Va., Jan. 20, 1924; s. Willie and Frances (Bailey) J.; A.B., Howard U., 1949; M.A. in History, Columbia, 1950; M.S. in L.S., State U. N.Y. at Albany, 1953; L.H.D., Shaw U., 1973; 1 dau. by previous marriage, Elaine Jacqueline. Librarian, Free Library of Phila., 1953-54; instr. social scis. Savannah (Ga.) State Coll., 1954-55, librarian, asso. prof., 1959-66, founder undergrad. library sci. program, 1960; librarian, asst. prof. Del. State Coll., Dover, 1955-59; asso. in acad. and research libraries N.Y. Dept. Edn., Albany, 1966-68, chief, 1968—. Cons. Tex. So. U. Library, Houston, 1967. Mem. tech. task force Econ. Opportunity Authority Savannah, 1964-66; mem. bd. mgrs. Savannah Pub. Library, 1962-66; bd. advisers Children Book Rev. Service, Bklyn., 1972—. Bd. dirs. Coretta Scott King Award, Nat. Black Bibliographic and Research Center, Newark, Del.; trustee Minority Edn. and Devel. Agy., Islip, N.Y. Served with AUS, 1943-46. Recipient Savannah State Coll. Library award, 1967; Jour. Library History award, 1970. Mem. Am. (cert. appreciation for disting. service as councillor 1978), N.Y. (John Cotton Dana award 1962, 64) library assns., Assn. for Study Afro-Am. Life and History, AAUP, Am. Acad. Polit. and Social Sci., N.Y. Library Club, N.A.A.C.P. (exec. bd. Savannah br. 1960-66, Ga. youth adviser 1962-66, exec. bd. Albany, N.Y. br. 1969—, treas. Albany br. 1970-72, Nat. Office award 1965), ACLU, Alpha Phi Omega. Author: The Black Librarian in America, 1970; What Black Librarians Are Saying, 1972; New Dimensions for Academic Library Service, 1975. Editor: Del. Library Assn. Bull., 1959; co-editor: A Century of Service, 1976; Opportunities for Minorities, 1977; Handbook of Black Librarianship, 1977; The Information Society: Issues and Answers, 1978; numerous directories. Contbr. articles to profl. jours. Home: 12C Old Hickory Dr Albany NY 12204 Office: Cultural Edn Center Room 10C47 Empire State Plaza Albany NY 12230

JOSHI, KAILASH CHANDRA, metall. engr.; b. Pauri, India, June 29, 1941; s. Bishal Mani and Lalita Devi (Thapliyal) J.; came to U.S., 1963; B.Sc., Agra U., India, 1960; B.Eng., Indian Inst. Sci., 1962; M.S., Wash. State U., 1965; Ph.D., Cornell U., 1967; m. Hem L. Kala, May 27, 1968; 1 son, Himanshu (Monty). Mem. faculty Cornell U., Ithaca, N.Y., 1967-68; staff engr. IBM Corp., Endicott, N.Y., 1968-70, adv. engr., 1970-73, sr. engr., 1973-74, mgr. adv. tech., 1974-77, program mgr. Endicott Lab, 1977—. Mem. Am. Inst. Mining, Metall. and Petroleum Engrs., Am. Soc. Metals, AAAS. Contbr. articles to tech. jours. Patentee in field. Home: 963 Southern Pines Dr Endwell NY 13760 Office: Endicott Lab IBM Corp Endicott NY 13760

JOSKOW, JULES, econ. research co. exec.; b. N.Y.C., July 19, 1922; s. Abraham and Mollie (Neuberg) J.; B.S., Coll. City N.Y., 1941; M.A., Columbia, 1942, Ph.D., 1953; m. Charlotte Epstein, June 24, 1945; children—Paul, Margaret, Andrew. Faculty, econs. dept. Coll. City N.Y., 1941-60; research dir. Boni, Watkins, Jason & Co., N.Y.C., 1952-61; v.p. Nat. Econ. Research Assos., N.Y.C., 1961-70, sr. v.p., 1970-76, exec. v.p., 1976—. Mem. nat. governing council Am. Jewish Congress, 1968-71; v.p. Temple Emanuel of Gt. Neck, 1975-77. Mem. Am. Econ. Assn., Am. Statis. Assn., Nat. Assn. Bus. Economists. Clubs: Bankers, Harborview, Glen Head Country. Home: 127 Station Rd Kings Point NY 11023 Office: 80 Broad St New York City NY 10004

JOUBERT, LUCIEN LÉON, med. adminstr., physician; b. Montreal, Que., Can., Dec. 7, 1929; s. Lionel Olivaint and Stella (Patenaude) J.; B.A., Ste-Marie Coll., 1952; M.D., U. Montreal, 1958, M.S. in Pharmacology, 1965; m. Georgette Pelletier, June 24, 1961. Intern Notre Dame and Maisonneuve Hosp., Montreal, 1957-58; resident in pediatrics and surgery St. Justine Hosp., Montreal, 1958-59; practice medicine in gen. practice Montreal, 1959-63; asst. med. dir. Smith Kline & French (Can.), Montreal, 1964-67; asst. dir. clin. pharmacology Hoffman-LaRoche Co., Nutley, N.J., 1967-70; asso. dir. clin. research Bristol-Myers Internat., N.Y.C., 1970-72; dir. clin. research Internat. Winthrop Products Inc., N.Y.C., 1972, acting med. dir., 1973, med. dir., 1974-77; dir. clin. pharmacology Merck Sharp & Dohme Research Labs., Rahway, N.J., 1977—; lectr. anatomy U. Montreal, 1960-63, pharmacology, 1963-65. Que. Health Ministry fellow, 1963-65. Mem. Assn. Médecins Langue Francaise Can., Can. Med. Assn., AAAS, Am. Soc. Clin. Pharmacology and Therapeutics (sect. chmn. 1974-77), Coll. Physicians and Surgeons Province Que., N.Y. Acad., Sci., Biometric Soc., Med. Council Can. Club: East Orange Golf. Author books. Contbr. articles to profl. publs. Home: 12 Westover Terr West Caldwell NJ 07006 Office: Merck Sharp & Dohme Research Labs PO Box 2000 Rahway NJ 07065

JOUKHADAR, MOUMTAZ, painter, gallery exec.; b. Damas, Syria, Apr. 29, 1940; s. Niazy and Zynab J.; came to U.S., 1969, naturalized, 1978; M.A. in Interior Design, Accademia di Belle Arti, Rome, 1968; student Art Students League, N.Y.C., 1969-72. Prof. fine art Public Sch. System, Homs, Syria, 1960-62; art dir. Adalia Anstalt, Rome, 1964-68, Med. Tribune, N.Y.C., 1970-73, Media Properties, N.Y.C., 1973-75, Joukhadar Gallery, N.Y.C., 1975—; one-man shows: Nader Art Gallery, N.Y.C., 1974, Joukhadar Gallery, 1976; group shows: Nat. Museum Damascus (Syria), 1961, Venice Biennial Internat. Exhibit, 1966 (award), Group Exhbn. for Fgn. Artists, Rome, 1968 (medal City of Rome). Mem. Soc. Classic Guitar. Composer: Primativity. Office: 440 E 85th St New York NY 10028

JOURNEY, DREXEL DAHLKE, lawyer; b. Westfield, Wis., Feb. 23, 1926; s. Clarence Earl and Verna L. Gilmore (Dahlke) J.; student U.S. Mcht. Marine Acad., 1944-45; B.B.A., U. Wis., 1950; LL.B., 1952; LL.M., George Washington U., 1957; m. Vergene Harriet Sandsmark, Oct. 24, 1952; 1 dau., Ann Marie. Admitted to Wis. bar, 1952, U.S. Supreme Ct. bar, 1955, D.C. bar, 1970, also other fed. ct. bars; practice utility law; with FPC, Washington, 1952-77, dep. gen. counsel, 1970-74, gen. counsel, 1974-77; partner firm Schiff Hardin & Waite, Washington, 1977—. Served with Mcht. Marine Res.-USNR, 1944-46; with U.S.N.G., 1948-50. Knapp scholar U. Wis., 1952. Mem. Am., Fed. bar assns., Phi Kappa Phi, Phi Eta Sigma, Theta Delta Chi. Mason. Contbr. articles to profl. jours. Home: 4540 Windom Pl NW Washington DC 20016 Office: 1101 Connecticut Ave NW Washington DC 20006

JOVANOVIC, MIODRAG, surgeon, educator; b. Tabonovic, Yugoslavia, May 3, 1936; s. Stevan and Zivana Jelena (Antonic) J.; B.A., Coll. of Sabac, 1954; M.D., Faculty of Medicine, Belgrade, Yugoslavia, 1963; married; 3 children. Intern in France and Can., resident in surgery in Can., 1965-72; practice surgery, Quebec City, Que., Can., 1972—; mem. staff Jeffery Halle Hosp., Notre Dame Hosp.; prof. Faculty Medicine, Laval U., 1972—. Fellow Royal Coll. Surgeons Can., Am. Coll. Chest Physicians, Med. Council Can., A.C.S., Internat. Coll. Surgeons; mem. Canadian Med. Assn., Assn. des Medecins de Langue Francaise du Canada, Royal Coll. Surgeons and Physicians Can. Home: 2219 Bourbonniere Quebec PQ Canada Office: Dept Anatomy Faculty Medicine Laval Univ Quebec PQ Canada

JOYCE, BERNITA ANNE, govt. ofcl.; b. Omaha, Aug. 11, 1927; d. Albert A. and Margaret C. (Rogers) Joyce; B.A. Duchesne Coll.; M.B.A., U. Santa Clara (Calif.), 1968, Ph.D., 1974; m. Kenneth Bradley Lucas, Aug. 2, 1975. Treas. Soc. of Sacred Heart, Seattle, also Menlo Park, Calif., 1957-71, regional treas., San Francisco, 1969-71; sr. accountant Wolfe & Co., Washington, 1971-72; fin. dir. Nat. Forest Products Assn., Washington, 1972-74; budget and fiscal officer ICC, 1974—, also fed. women's program coordinator; mem. reorgn. team Exec. Office Pres., 1977-78; adj. prof. Southeastern U., Washington. C.P.A., Wash. Mem. Am. Inst. C.P.A.'s, Am. Mgmt. Assn., Planning Execs. Inst., Assn. Govt. Accountants, AAUP, AAUW, Beta Gamma Sigma. Address: 6001 Bradley Blvd Bethesda MD 20034

JOYCE, CHARLES RAYMOND, JR., librarian; b. West Tremont, Maine, Jan. 3, 1929; s. Charles Raymond and Lessie Emeline (Bridges) J.; B.A., Tufts Coll., 1951; M.S., Simmons Coll. Sch. Library Sci., 1955; m. Ingrid Maria Thale, June 1, 1963; children—Lillian, Gareth. Librarian, Detroit Pub. Library, 1955-57, Branford (Conn.) Pub. Library, 1957-59; asst. librarian Wellesley (Mass.) Pub. Library, 1959-61, Winchester (Mass.) Pub. Library, 1961-62; dir. Norwood (Mass.) Pub. Library, 1962-68; asso. state librarian Conn., 1968-73; dir. Bur. Library Extension Mass., Boston, 1973—. Mass. adminstr. Interstate Library Compact, 1974—; chmn. New Eng. Library Bd., 1975—, New Eng. Document Conservation Center, North Andover, Mass., 1975—. Served to 2d lt. AUS, 1951-53. Mem. A.L.A., New Eng., Mass., Conn. library assns., Chief Officers of State Library Agencies. Home: 20 Poplar Rd Wellesley MA 02181 Office: 648 Beacon St Boston MA 02215

JOYCE, DAVID, city ofcl.; b. Providence, Aug. 17, 1919; s. Charles Edward and Mary Agnes (Silva) J.; Ph.B., Providence Coll., 1942; postgrad. Boston Coll., 1944, Providence Coll. Sch. Adult Edn., 1944-46, U. Notre Dame, 1943; m. Mary Agnes Costello, June 28, 1944; children—David, Michael Kevin, Paul Brian, Kevin Walsh, Anne Kathleen, Charles Christopher, Mary Elizabeth. Substitute tchr. City of Pawtucket, Providence Sch. Dept., 1943, City of Providence, R.I. Sch. Dept., 1944; probation counselor Juvenile Ct., 1944-48; sr. social worker R.I. Dept. Social Welfare, 1948-49; exec. sec. to Mayor Dennis J. Roberts, Providence, 1949; exec. dir. Family Relocation Services and Bus. Relocation Bur., 1949-67; dir., div. minimum housing standards City of Providence, 1967, chief div., code enforcement Dept. Planning and Urban Devel., 1967, chief community services, 1967-70, sec.-treas., exec. dir. Housing Authority, 1970—. Dep. dir. Providence Civil Def. Council, 1952-58; vol. tchr. R.I. Tng. Sch. for Boys, 1946-48; cons. U. Pa. on Displacement Elderly Residents Facing Relocation, 1963-65; recreational vol., youth leader R.I. State Home and Sch., 1939; relocation cons. Housing and Home Finance Agy., U.S. Govt., 1951; mem. R.I. state adv. Council Nat. Housing and Mortgage Finance Corp. Mem. Mayor Joseph A. Doorley, Jr. Adv. Council, 1968-70; adv. com. Model Cities Multi-purpose Social Service Center, 1968-70; mem. evaluating com. Providence Human Relations, 1972—; commr. Adv. Com. on Community Devel.; mem. adv. com. Narragansett council Boy Scouts Am., 1950-62; mem. U.S. Assn. Civil Def. Dirs. Assn., 1953-58; mem. health and first aid com. Providence chpt. A.R.C., 1952-58. Bd. dirs., asst. treas. Friends for People, Inc. Served with USNR, 1943. Recipient Certificate of Appreciation, City of Providence, 1970; resolution of recognition Providence City Council, commendation citation Gov. of R.I., 1977, proclamation Mayor of Providence; Providence Bd. Commrs. established David Joyce ann. outstanding award for employee of Providence Housing Authority, 1977. Ford Found. grantee, 1963-65. Mem. Nat. Assn. Housing and Redevel. Ofcls. (nat. gov. 1970-74, nat. housing prodn. com., pres. New Eng. Council 1970-72), R.I. Assn. Exec. Dirs. Housing (recognition plaque 1977), Providence Coll. Alumni Assn., Laborers Internat. Union N.Am. (hon. local 1217). Roman Catholic. Author: Elderly, 1966. Home: 28 Doane Ave Providence RI 02906 Office: 673 Academy Ave Providence RI 02908

JOYCE, JOSEPH ROBERT, personnel exec.; b. Ashland, Pa., Sept. 25, 1941; s. Marlin Joseph and Margaret E. (Patton) J.; B.A., Susquehanna U., 1963; M.Ed., Temple U., 1969; m. Carol Ann Bollinger, June 19, 1965; children—Joseph Robert, Michael Patrick, Christina Marie. Vice pres. human resources Fed. Res. Bank Phila., 1963-74; v.p. personnel Ryan Homes, Inc., Pitts., 1974-77; dir. personnel U. Md., 1977—; adj. prof. mgmt. Temple U., 1973-74, Ursinus Coll., 1967-72; guest lectr. operation enterprise Am. Mgmt. Assn., 1973-76; mem. Fels Inst. U. Pa., 1970. Served with USAR, 1964-70. Mem. Am. Soc. Personnel Adminstrs. (dir. Phila. chpt. 1972-74), Am. Soc. Tng. Dirs. Roman Catholic. Home: 452 Old Orchard Circle Millersville MD 21108 Office: South Adminstrn Bldg U Md College Park MD 20742

JOYCE, ROBERT PAUL, hosp. adminstr.; b. Boston Apr. 16, 1940; s. Martin Joseph and Bernice Marguerite (Fisher) J.; B.S., Boston Coll., 1963; m. Jane Phyllis McCarron, June 15, 1963; children—Robert Paul, James Phillip. Accountant, auditor James O. Dunn, C.P.A., Boston, 1963-65; comptroller Cardinal Cushing Gen. Hosp., Brockton, Mass., 1965-68, asst. adminstr., 1968—. Firm chmn. Old Colony United Way, Brockton, 1971-76, allocations com., 1975, 76; treas. Hanover Youth Hockey Assn., 1977—. Mem. Mass. Hosp. Assn., New Eng. Hosp. Assembly, New Eng. Conf. Cath. Hosp. Assn., Hosp. Fin. Mgmt. Assn., Health Care Mgmt. Assn. Mass. Roman Catholic. Clubs: Elks, K.C. Home: 72 Willow Rd Hanover MA 02339 Office: 235 N Pearl St Brockton MA 02401

JOYNER, CLAUDE REUBEN, JR., physician; b. Winston-Salem, N.C., Dec. 4, 1925; s. Claude R. and Lytle (Mackie) J.; B.S., U. N.C., 1947; M.D., U. Pa., 1949; m. Nina Glenn Michael, Sept. 21, 1950; children—Emily Glenn, Claude Courtney. Intern, Hosp. U. Pa., 1949-50; resident Bowman Grey Sch. Medicine, 1950; resident U. Pa., 1954-55, fellow in cardiology; Nat. Heart Inst. trainee, 1952-53, 55-56; asst. instr. medicine Hosp. U. Pa., Phila., 1951-53, instr. medicine, 1953-56, asso. medicine, 1956-59, asst. prof. medicine, 1959-64, asso. prof. medicine, 1964-72, also ward chief; attending in cardiology VA Hosp., Phila., 1962-72; prof. medicine U. Pitts., 1972—; chief medicine Allegheny Gen. Hosp., Pitts., 1972—. Served to lt. M.C., USNR, 1950-52. Fellow Am. Coll. Cardiology, A.C.P.; mem. Am. Soc. for Study Arteriosclerosis, A.A.A.S., Am. Heart Assn., Am. Clin. and Climatol. Soc. Contbr. articles to profl. jours. Home: Pulpit Rock Little Sewickley Creek Rd Sewickley PA 15143 Office: 320 North East Ave Pittsburgh PA 15212

JUAN, GERARDO AGUSTIN, psychiatrist, educator; b. Obando, Bulacan, Philippines, Oct. 3, 1941; s. Nicolas T. and Teresa A. (Agustin) J.; B.A., Ateneo de Manila (Philippines), 1961; M.D., U.

Philippines, 1966; m. Alicia V. Hembrador, Apr. 20, 1969; children—Edgardo, Jennifer. Intern, Philippine Gen. Hosp., Manila, 1965-66, resident, 1966-69; resident Buffalo Psychiat. Center, 1969-72; instr. dept. psychiatry U. Philippines, Manila, 1968-69; staff psychiatrist Buffalo Psychiat. Center, 1972-75; asst. clin. prof. psychiatry State U. N.Y., Buffalo, 1975—; practice medicine specializing in psychiatry, Buffalo, Niagara Falls and Lockport, N.Y., 1975—; cons. psychiatrist Jewish Family Service, Buffalo, 1975. Diplomate Am. Bd. Psychiatry and Neurology. Mem. AMA, Am. Psychiat. Assn., Erie County Med. Soc., Phi Kappa Mu. Roman Catholic. Home: 136 Northington St East Amherst NY 14051 Office: 231 S Transit St Lockport NY 14094 also 549 4th St Niagara Falls NY 14301

JUDD, ALVAN BRADFORD, psychiatrist, neurobiologist; b. Detroit, Sept. 9, 1929; s. Irving Howes and Abbie Elmyra (Hanlon) J.; A.B., Cornell U., 1950; M.D., Harvard, 1954; m. Eleanore Marguerite Gridley, Feb. 24, 1962. Intern, Mass. Gen. Hosp., Boston, 1954-55; resident in psychiatry and child psychiatry Mass. Mental Health Center, Boston, 1957-60, Children's Hosp., Baker, Putnam, Boston, 1960-61; pvt. practice child psychiatry, Shrewsbury, N.J., 1961—, N.Y.C., 1967—; dir. tng. Childrens Psychiat. Center, Eastontown, N.J., 1961-64, med. dir., 1964-67; asst. clin. prof., attending psychiatrist Cornell U. Med. Center, 1967-70, research neurobiologist, 1970—; pres. Brisbane Child Treatment Center, Allaire, 1967-71; mem. faculty Harvard Med. Sch., 1957-61, Rutgers U., 1962-64, Newark State Coll., 1967-71. Founder, pres. Shrewsbury Democratic Club, 1967-71. Recipient N.J. Broadcasters award for pub. services, 1965; grantee USPHS, NIMH. Fellow Am. Orthopsychiat. Assn.; mem. AMA, N.J., Monmouth County med. socs., Am. N.J., Mon-Ocean psychiat. assns., Am. Acad. Child Psychiatry, Internat. Assn. Child Psychiatry, Soc. Neruoscience, Internat. Soc. Devel. Psychobiology, AAAS, Writers Guild Am. Dem. Episcopalian. Clubs: St. Botolph (Boston); Lotos (N.Y.C.). Author: Sex Education for Young Americans, 1966. Contbr. profl. jours. Home: El Barakah Broad St Shrewsbury NJ 07701 Office: 812 Broad St Shrewsbury NJ 07701

JUDD, JOHN EDMUND, instrument mfg. co. exec.; b. New Haven, June 23, 1930; s. Thomas F. and Grace C. (Byrnes) J.; Asso. Sci. in Elec. Engring., U. New Haven, 1954; m. JoAnne Pettrelle, Oct. 4, 1954; children—Robert, Leslie, Bryant. Exptl. test project engr. M.B. Electronics div. Textron, Inc., 1956-62, sales engr., 1962-64, sales mgr. internat. div., 1964-67; gen. sales mgr., products marketing mgr., 1967-72; v.p. Vibra Sciences, Inc., East Haven, Conn., 1973-76; pres. Vibra-Metrics, Inc., East Haven, Conn., 1972-76. Chmn. indsl. adv. council Opportunities Industrialization Center, New Haven, 1970-76; treas. Hamden Figure Skating Assn., 1975-76; mem. Conn. Citizens Cons. Com. Served with USAF, 1947-50. Mem. Inst. Environ. Scis., Instrument Soc. Am. (sr.), Greater New Haven Mfrs. Assn. (exec. bd.), Vibration Inst., Conn. Bus. and Industry Assn. Roman Catholic. Club: Rotary. Home: 80 Squire Ln Hamden CT 06518 Office: 150 Bradley St East Haven CT 06512

JUDSON, ARTHUR, II, investment banker; b. Phila., Sept. 6, 1930; s. Francis Edward and Henrietta (Chapman) J.; A.B., Dartmouth, 1952; M.B.A., Harvard, 1956; m. Bright Miller, Nov. 30, 1957; children—Arthur III, Virginia Wallis, Henrietta Chapman, Christopher Bright. Asst. area sales mgr. Procter & Gamble, Phila., 1956-57; registered rep. C.C. Collings & Co., Phila., 1957-60, corporate syndicate mgr., 1960—, v.p., 1964-76, exec. v.p., 1977—, mem. exec. com., 1971—; pres., dir. Arthur Judson, Inc.; dir. Stock Clearing Corp., Phila. Chmn. bd., trustee, mem. exec. and finance coms. Phila. Stock Exchange, 1968—. Active various community drives. Bd. dirs. Arthur Judson Found., Settlement Music Sch., Phila., Armed Services br. YMCA; chmn., treas. World Service Commn. Served with USNR, 1952-54; ETO. Mem. Pa. Soc., Investment Assos. Phila. (treas. 1962), Phila. Securities Assn., Bond Club Phila. (sec.), Mil. Order Fgn. Wars (sec.), Navy League U.S. (v.p., dir.), Theta Delta Chi. Republican. Episcopalian. Clubs: Harvard Business School (treas. Phila. 1961, 66), Dartmouth (exec. com. Phila. 1962-64). Home: 149 Northwestern Ave Philadelphia PA 19118 Office: Fidelity Bldg Philadelphia PA 19109

JUDSON, JEANNETTE ALEXANDER (MRS. HENRY JUDSON), artist; b. N.Y.C., Feb. 23, 1912; d. Phillip George and Gertrude (Leichter) Alexander; student N.A.D., 1956-59, Art Student League, N.Y.C., 1959-61; m. Henry Judson, Sept. 23, 1945; children—S. Robert Weltz, Jr., Pauline (Mrs. Raiff); 1 stepson, E. William Judson. Exhibited one-man shows Fairleigh Dickinson U., 1965, Bodley Gallery, N.Y.C., 1967, 69, 71, N.Y. U., 1969, Pa. State U., 1969, Laura Musser Mus. Art, Muscatine, Iowa, 1969, Bodley Gallery, N.Y.C., 1973, Syracuse U. House, N.Y.C., 1975; exhibited in group shows including anns. Nat. Assn. Women Artists, N.Y.C., France, Italy, 1965—, Audubon Artists, N.Y.C., 1962, 64, 65-67, Allied Artists, N.Y.C., 1966-67; represented in permanent collections Joseph H. Hirshhorn, N.Y. U., Norfolk (Va.) Mus. Arts and Scis., Brandeis U., Peabody Art Mus., Mus. of N.Mex., Sheldon Swope Art Mus., Syracuse U., Evansville Mus. Arts and Scis., Rutgers U., Colby Coll., Butler Inst. Am. Art, Laura Musser Mus., Fordham U., Lehigh U., Ga. Mus. Art, U. Ga., Fairleigh Dickinson U., Lowe Mus., U. Miami, Washington County (Md.) Mus. Fine Arts, Miami Mus. Modern Art, Bruce Mus., Greenwich, Conn., Hudson River Mus., Dartmouth Coll. Mus., Mus. Modern Art, Lending Service, Bklyn. Mus., Columbia, U.S. Dept. State, also numerous pvt. collections. Mem. Nat. Assn. Women Artists, Artists Equity N.Y., Art Students League (life), League Present Day Artists, N.Y. Soc. Women Artists, Am. Soc. Contemporary Artists (Dorothy Feigin award 1976, Heyden Ryk award 1978). Home and Studio: 1130 Park Ave New York City NY 10028

JUENEMAN, ROBERT READE, communications co. exec.; b. Los Angeles, June 3, 1939; s. Frederick Reade and Rodney Whitelaw (Carmack) J.; B.S., S.D. Sch. Mines and Tech., 1963; student Mass. Inst. Tech., 1959-60; m. Marian Louise McKinney, Oct. 12, 1968; 1 dau., Tracey McKinney. With IBM Corp., Gaithersburg, Md., 1962-77; adv. programmer Satellite Bus. Systems, McLean, Va., 1977—. Mem. Sch. Bd. Boonton, Twp. (N.J.), 1972-74. Mem. Assn. of Computing Machinery. Club: Gaithersburg Camera (pres. 1977-78). Patentee in field. Home: 19355 Frenchton Pl Gaithersburg MD 20760 Office: 8003 Westpark Dr McLean VA 22102

JUHL, DANIEL LEO, friction materials mfg. co. exec.; b. Sioux City, Iowa, Aug. 18, 1935; s. Burnett A. and Margaret L. (O'Singer) J.; B.S. in Engring., U. S.D., 1958; postgrad. Calif State U. at Long Beach, 1959; m. Co-leen A. Eagan. Dec. 20, 1958; children—Gregory, Michael, Jennifer. Plant mgr. RM Friction Materials Co. div. Raybestos-Manhattan Corp., Fullerton, Calif., 1968-69, mgr. mfg., Manheim, Pa., 1969-70, plant mgr., Manheim, 1974-75, v.p.-mfg., Trumbull, Conn., 1975—; pres. R/M Can., Ltd. div. R/M, Inc., Peterborough, Ont., 1970-72, R/M Germany GmbH., Radevormwald, W.Ger., 1972-74. Active United Way. Mem. Mfrs. Assn. of Pa. and Conn. (dir.), Soc. Plastics Industry, Soc. Automotive Engrs. Club: Elks. Patent lightweight plastic material. Contbr. articles to profl. jours. Office: 100 Oakview Dr Trumbull CT 06611

JULIANO, FRANK ANTHONY, engring. co. exec.; b. New Haven, Conn., Mar. 30, 1923; s. Anthony Gonsalves and Joaquina Rosa (Cunha) J.; student Internat. Corr. Schs.; m. Laura Anastasio, June 30, 1961; children—Frank Anthony, James Philip. With L.G. Defelice & Son, New Haven, 1948-49, Mariani Constrn. Co., New Haven, 1949-63; supr., corporate prin. Leone Constrn. Co., E. Haven, 1963-66; insp., chief insp., chief constrn. adminstrn. Cahn Engrs., Wallingford, Conn., 1966-69, sr. v.p., chief constrn. adminstrn., 1970—, also dir. Bd. dirs. Conn. Constrn. Inst.; mem. adv. bd. Central Conn. State Coll. Tech. Sch.; pres. East Haven (Conn.) Aux. Police, 1957-60. Served with U.S. Navy, 1941-46. Roman Catholic. Home: 518 Summit Dr Orange CT 06477 Office: Alexander Dr Wallingford CT 06492

JULIANO, JOHN LOUIS, lawyer; b. Queens, N.Y., Oct. 21, 1944; s. John Carmine and Jeannette Helen (Ciotti) J.; B.B.A., St. John's U., 1966; J.D., Bklyn. Law Sch., 1969; m. Maryjane Groccia, July 4, 1966; children—Jennifer Kristen, Jonathan Christian. Self-employed music tchr., Commack, N.Y., 1960-66; with Hillside Van Lines, Inc., East Northport, N.Y., 1968—, pres., 1970—; admitted to N.Y. bar, 1970; practice in N.Y., 1970—; mem. firm Juliano, Karlsson & Weisberg, 1970-72. Mem. Suffolk County budget com. L.I. Assn., 1973-74. Mem. Huntington C. of C., Am., N.Y., Suffolk County bar assns., Assn. Interstate Commerce Practitioners, Trial Lawyers Assn., Columbian Lawyers Assn. (treas. 1973, pres. 1974-75), Am. Movers Conf., N.Y. State Warehousemen's Assn., N.Y. Furniture Warehousemen's Assn. Home: 129 Grissom Way Hauppauge NY 11787 Office: 39 Doyle Ct East Northport NY 11731

JUNICE, WILLIAM JOSEPH, chem. engr.; b. Passaic, N.J., Jan. 7, 1917; s. Andrew and Josephine (Basnianin) Junikiewicz; B.S. Chem. Engring., Newark Coll., Engring., 1938; M.S., N.Y. U., 1943, postgrad., 1943-46; m. Eugenia Geron. Aug. 6, 1939; children—Carolyn, William W., Paul S. Chem. engr. various chem. industry ops., 1938-48; gen. mgr., owner Junice Labs., Inc., Clifton, N.J., 1948-66; cons. Napp Chems., Inc., Clifton, 1966-70; cons. engring. appraising, real estate appraising, solar energy and energy conservation, Clifton, 1971—. Registered profl. engr., N.J. Mem. Am. Cons. Engrs. Council, Nat. Soc. Profl. Engrs., Am. Soc. Appraisers, Am. Inst. Chem. Engrs., Am. Chem. Soc. Democrat. Roman Catholic. Club: Rotary (Clifton). Inventor recovery of silver from photog. film.

JUNKERMAN, WILLIAM JOSEPH, lawyer; b. N.Y.C., May 5, 1904; s. Otto J. and Margaret Anne (McCarthy) J.; A.B., N.Y.U., 1925; LL.B., Fordham U., 1928; m. Helen Veronica Barrett, June 28, 1930. Admitted to N.Y. bar, 1929; asst. counsel L.I. State Park Commn., 1929-32; pvt. law practice N.Y.C., 1932-41, 45-47; regional atty. CAA Pacific N.W., 1947-48; with Haight, Gardner, Poor & Havens, N.Y.C., 1948—, gen. partner, 1950—, splty. aviation trial and appellate. Pilot in AC, USNR, 1925-52, comdr. ret. Decorated Naval Res. Medal, Asiatic-Pacific Area medal, World War II Victory medal. Fellow Am. Coll. Trial Lawyers; mem. Am., N.Y. State bar assns., N.Y. County Lawyers Assn., Maritime Law Assn. U.S., Nat. Pilots Assn., Inc., Am. Legion (past comdr.), Mil. Order World Wars, Naval Aviation Commandry (council), Navy League U.S., Quiet Birdmen, Internat. Assn. Ins. Counsel. Clubs: The Wings, Downtown Athletic (N.Y.C.). Contbr. articles in field law jours. Home: 311 W 245th St Fieldston NY 10471 Office: 1 State St Plaza New York City NY 10004

JUNKINS, DAVID RANDALL, environ. engr.; b. Indpls., June 25, 1945; s. William Alva and Thelma Paulene (Frederick) J.; B.S. in Civil Engring., Purdue U., 1968, M.S. in Environ. Engring., 1973; m. Vicki Sue Harroff, Sept. 2, 1967; children—David Ryan, Todd Christopher. Sr. project engr. Roy F. Weston, West Chester, Pa., 1973—; cons. water and wastewater treatment. Served as office C.E., AUS, 1969-72; Vietnam. Registered profl. engr., Pa. Mem. Soc. Am. Mil. Engrs. (past post sec.-treas.), ASCE, Water Pollution Control Fedn., Am. Acad. Environ. Engrs., Am. Water Works Assn., Eastern Pa. Water Pollution Control Operators Assn. Author papers in field. Home: RD 1 Lenora Ln Downington PA 19335 Office: 1 Weston Way West Chester PA 19380

JURKOWSKI, FRANCES FARRELL, soprano, educator; b. Port Washington, N.Y., July 17, 1947; d. William Robert and Jacklyn (Weil) Farrell; student Peabody Conservatory of Music, 1964-66; B.S., Hofstra U., 1969; m. Paul Jurkowski, Oct. 21, 1972; children—David, Jason. Soloist, L.I. Opera Showcase, 1966-72, L.I. Oratorio, 1966-72, Port Singers, 1964—, Christ Episcopal Ch., Manhasset, 1971—, Community Synagogue, Sands Point, 1963—; tchr. music Port Washington Pub. Schs., 1969—. Commr. health Village of Manorhaven, Port Washington, 1970-72. Mem. Port Washington Tchrs. Assn., L.I. Chorale Soc., Mu Psi Epsilon. Republican. Home: 59 Hickory Rd Manorhaven Port Washington NY 11050

JURMA, MALL KUUSIK, radio script writer; b. Estonia; d. Juhan and Pauline (Kaasik) Kuusik; Magister Philosophiae, U. Tartu, Estonia, 1927; m. Endel Jurma, Sept. 28, 1929 (dec. Oct. 1943). Came to U.S., 1949, naturalized, 1954. Sr. librarian Central Municipal Library, Tallinn, Estonia, 1926-42; insp. pub. libraries Ministry of Edn., Tallinn, 1942-44; radio information specialist, asst. editor Estonian Service, Voice of Am., Washington, 1951-71. Pres. Baltic Women's Council, N.Y.C., 1947—. Recipient Medal of Merits for cultural service Estonian Red Cross, 1936; cultural award Found. for Estonian Arts and Letters, 1976. Mem. Estonian Arts and Letters Found., Estonian Learned Soc., P.E.N., Estonian Ednl. Soc. Lutheran. Contbr. to Acta Baltica, Germany; also lit. essays and criticisms to Books Abroad, World Lit. Today, other lit. mags. and newspapers U.S. and abroad. Home: 24 Central Ave Ridgefield Park NJ 07660

JURSHEVSKI, HARALD WILLIAM, ins. exec.; b. Libau, Latvia, Dec. 14, 1920; s. Karl Julius and Irma Elizabeth (Pernitz) J.; B.A., Latvia, 1939; Candidatus Rerum Politicarum, State U. Poznan, 1944; B.com., Concordia U., Montreal, 1957; came to Can., 1952; m. Nina Nikolayev, Dec. 2, 1944; children—Sven Harald, Alexander Michael. Dir. info. div. internat. tracing div. UNRRA-IRO, Arolsen, Germany, 1945-52; supr. prime contracts Canadair, Montreal, 1952-54; chief internal auditor Montreal Life Ins. Co., 1954-64, mgr. accounting dept., 1964—. Certified internal auditor. Mem. Inst. Internal Auditors Montreal (pres., 1975). Home: 3185 5th St Chomedey PQ H7V 1M3 Canada Office: 630 Sherbrooke St W Montreal PQ H3A 1E4 Canada

JUSTER, BARBARA WALLACH, editor; b. N.Y.C., Apr. 12, 1927; d. David A. and Madeleine (Spiro) Wallach; B.A., Adelphi U., 1947; M.L.S., L.I. U., 1970; m. Julian J. Juster, Nov. 14, 1948; children—Nancy Juster Schiff, Valerie Jane. Tchr. elem. schs., N.Y.C., 1947-52; sch. librarian Nassau County, N.Y., 1969-75; columnist The Baldwin (N.Y.) Citizen, 1973-75, mng. editor, 1975—. Recording sec. Union Reform Temple, Freeport, 1970-73; v.p. Baldwin Harbor Jr. High Sch. PTA, 1973-74; vice chmn. ednl. trends com. Baldwin Ednl. Assembly, 1977-78. Recipient Steele Sch. PTA Service award, 1971. Contbr. articles in field to newspapers and profl. jours. Home: 816 Chess Dr Baldwin NY 11510 Office: 1998 Grand Ave Baldwin NY 11510

JUSTICE, MARGARET KELLEY, educator; b. Gumboro, Del., Nov. 29, 1934; d. William Alfred and Maggie Mae (Littleton) Kelley; B.S. in Elementary Edn., Salisbury (Md.) State Coll., 1962; M.Ed. in Reading, U. Del., Newark, 1966, postgrad. in Adminstrn., 1968; m. Clifton Sanford Justice; 1 dau., Kelley Margaret. Reading cons. Greenwood (Del.) Elementary Sch., 1966-67, prin., 1967-68; supr. reading Milford (Del.) Sch. Dist., 1969-75; asst. prin. Laurel (Del.) Central Middle Sch., 1975—. Pres., Del. Vol. Firemen's Aux. Assn., 1971-72, Lord Baltimore br. Fedn. Women's Clubs, 1974-76. Mem. Internat. (pres. local council 1974—), Del. (dir. 1972-75, sec. 1975-77) reading assns., Del. Assn. Supervision and Curriculum Devel. (sec. 1974-76), Del. Assn. Sch. Adminstrs. (treas. 1978—), NEA (life). Home: 303 E 6th St Laurel DE 19956 Office: 801 Central Ave Laurel DE 19956

JUTRAS, RENE, pediatrician; b. Victoriaville, Que., Can., Sept. 7, 1922; s. Euclide and Eva (Lafond) J.; B.A., U. Laval, 1945, M.D., 1952; m. Therese Martel, Sept. 6, 1952; children—Rene Euclide, Maryse, Michel, Annik, Vincent, Mathilde, Jerome, Catherine, Jean-Sebastien, Maite, Yseult. Intern Univ. Hosp., U. Quebec., 1951-52; resident St. Mary's Hosp., Waterbury, Conn., 1952; resident in pediatrics Children's Hosp., Detroit, 1953-55, Children's Hosp., Washington, 1955-56; chief dept. pediatrics Hôtel-Dieu, Arthabaska, Que., Can., 1958-78; asst. prof. pediatrics, faculty medicine U. Sherbrooke. Founder, pres. Regroupement Nat., 1964; founder, co-pres. Ralliement Nat., 1966; pres. Bd. Trade Victoriaville, 1973. Recipient Long Service medal Boy Scouts Assn. Can., 1963; diplomate Coll. Physicians and Surgeons Province Que., Mem. Canadian Pediatric Soc., Canadian Med. Assn., Assn. des Medecins de Langue Francaise du Can., Assn. des Pediatres de la Province de Que., Assn. des Medecins de Que. Pour le Respect de La Vie (v.p.). Roman Catholic. Author: Quebec Libre, 1965. Home: 42 Potvin St Victoriaville PQ G6P 5K1 Canada Office: 66 St Jean-Baptiste Victoriaville PQ G6P 4E6 Canada

JUVONEN, TOICO ARVI, indsl. corp. exec.; b. Terijoki, Finland, Oct. 18, 1925; s. Juho and Vilhelmiina (Paju) J.; came to U.S., 1956, naturalized, 1961; student in Merchant Marine Engring., Helsingin Teknillinen Koulu, 1952-56; certificate in mech. engring. Lowell Inst. Sch., Mass. Inst. Tech., 1962, certificate in elec. engring., 1963; m. Alma J. Sumen, June 23, 1948; children—Toivo Tapio, Aila Irmeli. Mech. insp. Northtronics, Norwood, Mass., 1960-64; engring. technician Electronic Corp. Am., Cambridge, Mass., 1964-65; process and devel. engr. Honeywell Radiation Center, Lexington, Mass., 1965-74; mgr. product engring. Princeton (N.J.) Infrared Equipment, 1974-76; v.p., mgr. product engring. Infra Red Assos. Inc., Newark, 1976—. Served with Finnish Army, 1943-45. Lutheran. Clubs: Lowell Inst. Sch. Alumni Assn., Fitchburg Sportsmans. Patentee variable temperature cooling apparatus. Home: 35C Galewood Dr Matawan NJ 07747 Office: 14A Jules Ln New Brunswick NJ 08901

JUZAITIS, JOHN DANIEL, distbn. and traffic exec.; s.; John Kasmier and Philomena (Dowder) J.; grad. Wharton Evening Sch., U. Pa., 1950; m. Genevieve V. Venskus, Oct. 10, 1943; children—John Anthony, Jeffrey Francis. Asst. forman shipping and traffic dept. Singer Mfg. Co., Elizabethport, N.J., 1936-42; traffic mgr. Renuzit Home Products Co., Phila., 1946-58, dir. traffic, 1961-63; dir. traffic and distbn. Franklin Research Co. & Purex Corp., Ind. div., Phila., 1958-61; pres. John-Jeffrey Corp., Camden, N.J., 1963—, Manoa-Cynwood Assos., Inc., Camden, N.J., 1968, City Express, Inc., Honolulu, 1972, John-Jeffrey (Balt.) Corp., 1977. Cubmaster Cub Scouts, Manoa, Pa., 1951-54. Served with USMC, 1941-46. Mem. Phila. Comml. Traffic Mgrs. (pres. 1957-58), Phila. Traffic Club (dir. 1959-60), Am. Soc. Traffic and Transp., Am. Mgmt. Assn., Pres.'s Assn., Nat. Council Phys. Distbn. Mgmt. Home: 56 Heritage Rd Haddonfield NJ 08033 Office: PO Box 1969 Camden NJ 08101

JYDSTRUP, RONALD ALBERT, govt. ofcl.; b. Mpls., Feb. 13, 1923; s. Albert E. and Ellen V. (Brandelius) J.; B.B.A., U. Minn., 1948, M.H.A., 1950; m. Lyla Lauraine Johnson, June 24, 1972; children by previous marriage—Karen, Jan, Nan, Kathleen, Mary Ellen. Instr. hosp. adminstrn. course U. Minn., also hosp. cons. James A. Hamilton & Asso., Mpls., 1950-53; sec., accounting specialist Am. Hosp. Assn., also spl. lectr. St. Louis U. and U. Minn., 1953-56; dir. N.D. Blue Cross also spl. lectr. U. Minn., 1956-61; sec. Dist. X Blue Cross Plans, 1958-61; exec. dir. Rochester (N.Y.) Hosp. Reviewing and Planning Council, 1961-67; asst. sec. Rochester Hosp. Fund, 1961-67; v.p. Block, McGibony & Assos., health and hosp. consultants, Silver Spring, Md., 1967-70; dir. planning and devel. Group Health Assn., Washington, 1970-75; financial mgr. HEW-HRA-BHM Div. Medicine, 1975-77; chief HMO qualification br. HEW, Rockville, Md., 1977—; cons. HEW, 1970—; asst. prof. George Washington U., 1968-70. Mem. Fargo United Fund Planning Com., 1959-61; mem. Montgomery County (Md.) Health Planning Adv. Council, 1973—; chmn., mem. bd. dirs. Fargo Community Council of Social Agys., 1958-61; pres., dir. Red River Valley council Camp Fire Girls, 1957-61; bd. dirs. Home Care Rochester, Monroe County; mem. N.Y. State Hosp. Rev. and Planning Council's Com.; mem. steering com. health div. Council Social Agys. Rochester, Monroe County; mem. adv. com. on study prepayment plans Columbia U. Hosps.; chmn. council mgrs. com. Hosp. Purchasing Bur., N.Y.C. Bd. dirs. Mpls. War Meml. Blood Bank, 1953, Mental Health Council Rochester and Monroe County. Recipient Silver Key, Mpls. Jr. C. of C., 1953; Sabre Hamilton award U. Minn., 1950. Fellow Royal Soc. for Health; mem. U. Minn. Alumni Assn. (pres., dir. Red River Valley chpt.), Am. Assn. Hosp. Accountants, Am. Hosp. Assn., N.Y. State Hosp. Assn., Beta Alpha Psi. Lutheran. Home: 10613 Montrose Ave Apt 102 Bethesda MD 20014 Office: HEW Bldg Room 16A-08 5600 Fishers Ln Rockville MD 20857

KABADI, BALACHANDRA N., research chemist; b. Gadag-Betgeri, India, July 15, 1933; s. Narayansa R. and Lokubai N. (Bankapur) K.; came to U.S., 1960; B.S. in Tech. Pharmacy, Bombay U., 1960; M.S., U. Wash., Seattle, 1963, Ph.D., 1965; m. Kamala Hosmani, Apr. 27, 1950; children—Mohan, Ashok, Dileep, Nirmala. Research fellow chemistry U. S.C., Columbia, 1965-66, U. Mich., 1966-67; asso. prof. Fla. A. and M. U., Tallahassee, 1967-68; research chemist E. R. Squibb and Sons, New Brunswick, N.J., 1968—. Mem. Am. Chem. Soc., Am. Pharm. Assn., Sigma Xi, Rho Chi. Club: East Brunswick Health. Contbr. articles to profl. jours. Home: 34 Colin Dr South River NJ 08882 Office: 26 Georges Rd New Brunswick NJ 08903

KABAK, DANIEL M., constrn. co. engr.; b. N.Y.C., July 28, 1924; s. William and Dorothy (Brainin) K.; B.E.E., Poly. Inst. Bklyn., 1951; M.S., N.Y. U., 1973; m. Marcia J. Polakoff, Feb. 19, 1944; 1 dau., Sharon Louise K. Schlesinger. With Standard Switchboard Co., Celanese Corp., Westinghouse Electric Corp., 1941-56; engr. M&T Co., N.Y., Conn., 1956-60; sr. engr. AMF, Pitney-Bowes, 1960-71; sr. engr. Triborough Bridge and Tunnel Authority, N.Y.C., 1971—; cons. engr. in field, 1963—; advisory com. Hofstra U., 1977—. Dir. alumni assn. Poly. Inst. N.Y., 1976—; pres. Yonkers Brotherhood, 1967-69; trustee Temple Emanu-El, Yonkers, 1967-69. Served with U.S. Army, 1943-46. Registered profl. engr., N.Y., Conn., N.J., Calif.; certified safety profl., Ill. Mem. Nat. Soc. Profl. Engrs., IEEE, Am. Soc. Safety Engrs., Tau Beta Pi, Eta Kappa Nu. Republican. Patentee in field. Home: 189 Rumsey Rd Yonkers NY 10705

KABAK, MARTIN, housewares co. exec.; b. N.Y.C., Oct. 26, 1922; s. David and Anna (Weinstein) K.; B.S., N.Y. U., 1944; m. Vivian Witkowsky, Nov. 3, 1945; children—Anne, Wayne. Asso. exec. Loring Fabrics, Inc., N.Y.C., 1945-51; sales mgr. Heller Hostess Ware, Inc., N.Y.C., 1951-56; gen. sales mgr. Salton, Inc., N.Y.C., 1956-67, v.p. sales, 1967-76, vice chmn. bd., 1976—. Republican. Home: 1 Redwood Rd White Plains NY 10605 Office: 1260 Zerega Ave Bronx NY 10462

KAC, ARTHUR WAYNE, radiologist; b. nr. Warsaw, Poland, Nov. 10, 1904; s. Joseph and Sophie (Milchman) K.; came to U.S., 1927, naturalized, 1940; B.A., U. Minn., 1931, M.D., 1934; m. Jean K. Kac, Aug. 15, 1935; 1 dau., Sandra P. Kac Emala. Practice medicine, specializing in radiology. Diplomate Am. Bd. Radiology. Mem. Am. Coll. of Radiology, Radiol. Soc. N.Am., Md., Baltimore County med. socs., Md. Radiol. Soc. Author 4 books in Bibl. lit. Home: 2419 Eastridge Rd Timonium MD 21093

KACZERA, ZYGMUNT STEFAN, microbiologist, educator; b. Krakow, Poland, Jan. 1, 1928; s. Stefan and Jozefa (Raczy) K.; came to U.S., 1971; B.S., Jagellonian U., Krakow, 1953, D.Natural Scis., 1970; M.S., Madam Curie-Sklodowska U., Lublin, Poland, 1956. Research asst. Zeromski's City Gen. Hosp., Krakow, 1956-58; head clin. lab. Dist. Children's Hosp., Swietochlowice, Poland, 1958-64; head dept. bacteriology Dist. Lab., Krakow, 1964-65; asso. research scientist Krakow Sch. Medicine Inst. Pediatrics, 1965-71; research scientist N.Y. U. Med. Center, 1971-74; research scientist Mt. Sinai Sch. Medicine, N.Y.C., 1975—. Mem. N.Y. Acad. Scis., Am. Soc. Microbiology, AAAS. Contbr. numerous articles on immunohematology to profl. jours. Home: 53-01 32d Ave Apt 6J Woodside NY 11377 Office: Mt Sinai Sch of Medicine Fifth Ave and 100th St New York City NY 10029

KADE, CHARLES FREDERICK, JR., pharm. co. exec.; b. Sheboygan, Wis., Apr. 4, 1914; s. Charles Frederick and Glenore (Baltz) K.; B.A., Carleton Coll., 1936; M.A. N.D. State U., 1938; Ph.D., U. Ill., 1941; m. Marjorie Matheson, June 15, 1946; children—Kristina Mary Kade Troost, Roslyn Glenore Kade Hollingsworth, Heidi Ann Kade Wells, Charles Frederick III, Charlotte Matheson, James Martin. Asst. chemist Carleton Coll., Northfield, Minn., 1935-36, N.D. State U., Fargo, 1936-38, U. Ill., Urbana, 1938, asst., 1939-41, fellow, 1941-43; dir. biochemistry research Frederick Stearns & Co., Detroit, 1943-47; research chemist Sterling-Winthrop Research Inst., Rensselaer, N.Y., 1947-49; dir. div. med. sci. McNeil Labs., Inc., Ft. Washington, Pa., 1949-60, v.p., dir. research, 1960-65; v.p., Johnson & Johnson Internat., New Brunswick, N.J., 1966—. Mem. AAAS, Assn. Research Dirs., Am. Pharm. Assn., Soc. Indsl. Chemists, Am. Inst. Chemistry, N.Y. Acad. of Sci., Pharm. Mfrs. Assn. (chmn. research, devel. sec. 1958-60), The Chem. Soc., Swiss Chem. Soc., Sigma Xi, Alpha Chi Sigma. Unitarian. Clubs: Chemists (N.Y.C.). Contbr. articles to profl. jours. Home: 983 Butler Pike Blue Bell PA 19422 Office: Johnson & Johnson Internat 501 George St New Brunswick NJ 08903

KADEN, WILLIAM STEPHEN, physician; b. Boston, July 4, 1935; s. George Jacob and Anne G. K.; B.A., Harvard U., 1956; M.D., Yale U., 1960; m. Elizabeth Armstrong Howe, July 25, 1970; children—Felice Aimee, Benjamin Harris, Gregory Owen. Intern, Peter Bent Brigham Hosp., Boston, 1960-61, jr. resident, 1961-62; sr. resident Beth Israel Hosp., Boston, 1964-65; sr. resident in renal metabolic disease Boston VA Hosp., 1965-66; dir. health services Harvard Bus. Sch., Boston, 1973—, physician Harvard U. Health Services, Cambridge, Mass., 1966—, instr. medicine Harvard Med. Sch., Boston, 1966—. Served to capt., M.C., U.S. Army, 1962-64. Diplomate Am. Bd. Internal Medicine. Mem. AAAS, Mass. Med. Soc., Phi Beta Kappa, Alpha Omega Alpha. Home: 75 Mount Auburn St Cambridge MA 02138 Office: Cumnock Hall Harvard Bus Sch Boston MA 02163

KADISON, HERBERT, ret. univ. pub. relations dir.; b. N.Y.C., Sept. 19, 1915; s. Louis and Dora (Parmett) K.; B.S., Ohio U., 1938; m. Mary Morton, Apr. 6, 1940; children—Deborah, Robert; m. Catherine Rita Liegey, Mar. 9, 1967. Exec. asst. Dorothy Kay Assos., N.Y.C., 1939-42; prin. Herbert Kadison pub. relations, N.Y.C., 1946-50; dir. pub. information The Lighthouse, N.Y. Assn. for the Blind, N.Y.C., 1954-58; pub. relations officer Barnert Meml. Hosp., Paterson, N.J., 1959-60; dir. pub. relations N.Y. U. Med. Center, N.Y.C., 1960-78. Mem. Community Planning Bd. 6, N.Y.C., 1972-77. Served with USNR, 1942-46, 50-54, 61-62; capt. Res. ret. Mem. Acad. Hosp. Pub. Relations (dir. 1974—, sec. 1976, pres. 1976), Am. Acad. Compensation Medicine (exec. sec.), Am. Soc. Hosp. Pub. Relations (dir. 1973-75), Hosp. Pub. Relations Soc. Greater N.Y. (pres. 1972-73), Assn. Am. Med. Colls. (group on pub. relations 1975-76, sec. 1975-76). Co-author: Diabetes Explained: A Layman's Guide, 1976. Home: 340 E 34th St New York City NY 10016

KAFKA, FRITZ, statistician, educator; b. Linz, Austria, Mar. 25, 1908; s. Richard and Ida (Adler) K.; J.D., U. Vienna, 1931, Pol.Sc.D., 1934; postgrad. Columbia, George Washington U., Grad. Sch. U.S. Dept. Agr., Washington; m. Peggy Katz, Dec. 1, 1951 (dec. Feb. 1966); 1 son, James David; m. 2d, Beatrice Levine, Aug. 29, 1969. Came to U.S., naturalized 1943. Economist statistician House Dress Inst., N.Y.C., 1946; lectr. City Coll. of N.Y., 1946-51; statistician Bur. Labor Statistics, Washington, 1951-53, 64-67, sr. statistician Chas. Pfizer & Co., N.Y.C., 1953-64; statistician Bur. Mines, Washington, 1967-73; instr. U.S. Dept. Agr. Grad. Sch., 1971—. Served with AUS, 1942-45. Mem. Am. Statis. Assn., Am. Mktg. Assn. Author: Statistics without Numbers, 1950; (co-author) Das Oesterreichische Bausparwesen, 1932; Basic Statistics, 1952, rev. edit. 1957. Home: 3201 University Blvd W Kensington MD 20795

KAFKA, ROGER, pub. relations cons.; b. N.Y.C., Aug. 30, 1912; s. Oscar and Edna (Wachtel) K.; A.B., Dartmouth, 1933; m. Theda Brouner, Apr. 5, 1941; children—Lenore Kafka Hardy, Judith Mary. Editor, Ltd. Edits. Club, Heritage Club, Readers Club, N.Y.C., 1940-42; editor Sea Power ofcl. mag. Navy League of U.S., N.Y.C., 1942-48; copy chief Geffen, Dunn & Co., pub. relations, N.Y.C., 1944-50; asst. account exec. Dudley, Anderson Yutzy, N.Y.C., 1950-53; co-founder, exec. v.p. Farley Manning Assos., pub. relations agy., N.Y.C., 1954-71; prin. Roger Kafka Pub. Relations Counsel, N.Y.C., 1971-76; exec. v.p. Samuel Krasney Assos., N.Y.C., 1976—. Author: Warships of the World, 1944, rev. edit., 1946; contbr. numerous articles to profl. jours. Home: 20 E 35th St New York City NY 10016 Office: 40 Exchange Pl New York City NY 10005

KAGAN, MICHAEL BRUCE, writer, photographer; b. Boston, Feb. 19, 1941; s. Philip Paul and Sadie (Goldman) K.; A.A.S. summa cum laude in Bus. Admnstrn., Newbury Jr. Coll., 1976; m. Shirler Ann Barber, Oct. 2, 1967 (div. Oct. 1978); 1 son, David Scott. Computer ops. cons. Gen. Dynamics Corp., Quincy, Mass., 1972-74; computer test cons. Mass. Blue Cross, Boston, 1969-72, data processing tech. writer, 1974—; author more than 30 books and jours. in data processing and related subjects. Mem. Brockton (Mass.) Community Sch. Bd., 1975—; scouting coordinator Cub Scout troop, Boy Scouts Am., Brockton, 1977—; fundraiser Cystic Fibrosis Fund, Kiddie Kamp Fund. Served with U.S. Army, 1960-63. Mem. New Eng. Data Processing Assn. (documentation com.), Data Processing Mgmt. Assn., Asso. Photographers Internat. Jewish. Clubs: Toasmasters, K.P. Home: 7 Village Way Box 63B Brockton MA 02401 Office: 100 Summer St Boston MA 02110

KAGANOV, ALAN LAWRENCE, pharm. co. exec.; b. Bklyn., Dec. 7, 1938; s. Morris and Sally (Scher) K.; B.S., Duke U., 1960; M.B.A., N.Y.U., 1966; M.S., Columbia U., 1971, Sc.D., 1974; m. Carol Marcia Kaufman, Sept. 17, 1967. Packaging engr. Amstar Co., N.Y.C., 1960-64; new products engr. Johnson & Johnson, Somerville, N.J., 1964-68; with Am. Cyanamid Co., Danbury, Conn., 1973—, dir. med. products research and devel., 1978—. Mem. Am. Chem. Soc., ASTM, Sigma Xi. Home: 150 Gary Rd Stamford CT 06903 Office: American Cyanamid Co 1 Casper St Danbury CT 06810

KAGGEN, ELIAS, physician; b. Bklyn., Dec. 27, 1915; s. Joseph and Lena (Zalbowitz) K.; student N.Y.U., 1932-34; D.O., Phila. Coll. Osteo. Medicine, 1938; M.D., Chgo. Coll. Medicine, 1947; m. Sylvia Muntner, May 15, 1941; children—Lois S., Marilyn D. Sr. attending physician Interboro Gen. Hosp.; asso. head dept. of gynecology, out patient Osteo. Hosp. and Clinic N.Y., 1951—, also mem. bd. mgmt.; adj. clin. asso. family practice N.Y. Coll. Osteo. Medicine. Diplomate Am. Osteo. Bd. Gen. Practice. Mem. Am. Coll. Osteo. Obstetricians and Gynecologists, Osteopathic Soc. City N.Y. (trustee, chmn. pub. relations, past dir., v.p. 1959-60, pres. 1961-62, chmn. bd. dirs. 1962-63; chmn. com. health and edn. 1963-64), Lambda Omicron Gamma. Jewish religion. Home: 479 Rugby Rd Brooklyn NY 11226 Office: 917 8th Ave Brooklyn NY 11215

KAHALAS, HENRY NOREN, elec. engr.; b. Boston, Aug. 27, 1932; s. James and Betty (Appel) K.; B.S. in Indsl. Engring., Boston U., 1956; M.S. in Elec. Engring., Northeastern U., 1967; postgrad. Mass. Inst. Tech., 1956-57, U. Calif. at Los Angeles, 1957-59, Syracuse U., 1959-64; m. Rheta Pearl Solomon, July 30, 1956; children—Susan Ellen, Beth Robin, Steven Haywood. Asso. engr., Douglas Aircraft Co., Santa Monica, Calif., 1956-59; systems analyst Gen. Electric Co., Syracuse, 1959-64; advanced research engr. Gen. Tel. & Electronics, Waltham, Mass., 1964-67; mgr. operations and cost analysis Raytheon Co., Bedford, Mass., 1967-75; mgr. systems support GTE Sylvania Co., Needham, Mass., 1975—; instr. math. Syracuse U., 1959-63. Served with USMC, 1950-55. Mem. Operations Research Soc. Am., Am. Ordnance Assn., Am. Statis. Assn., Am. Soc. Quality Control, Electronics Industries Assn. (chmn. design integration 1975-78, group chmn. design effectiveness group 1978—). Mason. Home: 96 Westover Pkwy Norwood MA 02062 Office: 189 B St Needham Heights MA 02194

KAHEN, HAROLD I., lawyer; b. Chgo., Aug. 14, 1918; s. Gabriel and Jennie (Weisberg) K.; A.B., U. Chgo., 1938, J.D., 1940; m. Florence Gold, Dec. 21, 1946; children—Deborah Judith (Mrs. Kayman), Daniel Seth, David Ezra. Admitted to Ill. bar, 1940, N.Y. bar, 1947; spl. asst. to fed. circuit judge Evan A. Evans, 1940; mem. legal staff SEC, 1941-46; asso. firm Poletti, Diamond, Rabin, Freidin & Mackay, 1946-50; gen. atty. Hudson & Manhattan R.R. Co., 1950-55; asso. counsel N.Y. Supt. of Ins., 1955 Welfare Fund Inquiry; mem. firm Delson & Gordon, 1956-72, Burns, Jackson, Miller, Summit & Jacoby, 1973—; spl. prof. Hofstra U. Law Sch., 1971—. Mem. N.Y. State Bar Assn. (com. corp. law), Assn. Bar City N.Y. (past spl. com. securities regulation), Order of Coif, Phi Beta Kappa. Home: 85-26 Kendrick Pl Jamaica NY 11432 Office: 445 Park Ave New York City NY 10022

KAHN, B. FRANKLIN, real estate investment exec.; b. Washington, Feb. 4, 1925; s. I. Lewis and Elizabeth L. Kahn; B.S., Wharton Sch., U. Pa., 1946; m. Joan F. Freed; children—Daryl, Laura, William. Owner, B. Franklin Kahn Real Estate Investments, Washington, 1948-60; pres. trustees Washington Real Estate Investment Trust, 1960—; vis. lectr. Wharton Sch. Finance, 1946-76. Served with USAF, 1951-52; Korea. Home: 5215 Edgemoor Ln Bethesda MD 20014 Office: 7910 Woodmont Ave Bethesda MD 20014

KAHN, EDWARD, obstetrician and gynecologist; b. N.Y.C., Sept. 16, 1913; s. Emile and Pauline (Andorn) K.; B.S., N.Y.U., 1934; M.D., L.I. Coll. Medicine, 1939; m. Faith Hope Green, May 29, 1942; children—Ellen Leora, Faith Hope, Paula Amy. Intern and resident obstetrics and gynecology, Knickerbocker Hosp., Kings County Gen. Hosp., 1939-42; chief of female sterility clinic Sydenham Hosp., N.Y.C., 1950—, asso. attending staff, 1955—, cons., 1974—; attending gynecologist Deepdale Gen. Hosp., Queens, N.Y., 1963—. Served as 1st lt., AUS, 1942-44. Fellow Am. Coll. Obstetricians and Gynecologyists (founding), Internat. Coll. Surgeons, Am. Geriatric Soc., Am. Fertility Soc., Internat. Fertility Assn.; mem. AMA, N.Y. County, Suffolk County, N.Y. State med. socs., Am. Com. Maternal Welfare, Queens Gynecol. Soc., N.Y. Acad. Scis., Pan Am. Cancer Cytology Soc., Soc. Med. Jurisprudence of N.Y., AAAS, Internat. Platform Assn. Contbg. lectr. in field. Originator numerous gynecol. instruments and techniques. Home and Office: 213-16 85th Ave Queens Village NY 11427

KAHN, GLORIA BATKIN, psychologist; b. Bklyn., July 14, 1939; d. Stanley Irving and Selma Lucille (Loinger) Batkin; student Vassar Coll., 1957-58; B.A., Sarah Lawrence Coll., 1963; M.A., Tchrs. Coll. Columbia U., 1968, Ed.D., 1975; m. Robert Wolff Kahn, June 22, 1969; children—Karin Rose, Erik Wolff, Jennifer Anne. Instr. psychology Westchester Community Coll., Valhalla, N.Y., 1972-73, Coll. New Rochelle (N.Y.) Grad. Sch., 1973-74; asst. prof. Bklyn. Coll., 1974-76; dir. Scarsdale (N.Y.) Consultation Center, 1977—; cons. psychologist Horace Mann Sch., Riverdale, N.Y., 1976—; practice psychology, Scarsdale and N.Y.C., 1977—; mem. planning evaluation com. for coop. programs in coll. skills devel. and career preparation Bd. Higher Edn. N.Y.C., 1975. Mem. Am., N.Y. State psychol. assns., Orton Soc., Nat. Reading Conf., Internat. Reading Assn., Assn. Children with Learning Disabilities. Jewish. Contbr. articles to profl. jours., confs. and yearbooks. Home: 22 Innes Rd Scarsdale NY 10583 Office: 192 Garth Rd Scarsdale NY 10583 also 104 E 40 St New York City NY

KAHN, ROBERT SAMUEL, metal co. exec.; b. Chgo., Feb. 14, 1918; s. Lee and Mildred (Arnheim) K.; B.S. in Chem. Engring., Rose Hulman Inst. Tech., 1939; m. Louise F. Schock, Apr. 5, 1942. Dist. mgr. R. Lavin & Sons, Chgo., 1945-51; v.p. Tube City Iron & Metal Co., Glassport, Pa., 1952-59; v.p. Luria Bros. & Co. Inc., Pitts., 1960-68; chmn. bd., pres. Keystone Resources Co., Pitts., 1969—; dir. Bumgardner & Co., Wheeling, W.Va. Served with USNR, 1942-45. Decorated Bronze Star. Mem. Nat. Assn. Recycling Industries (pres. 1974—), Am. Inst. Mining, Metall. and Petroleum Engrs., Alpha Tau Omega. Republican. Lutheran. Clubs: Duquesne, St. Clair Country, Rolling Hills Country, Downtown, Allegheny (Pitts.); Mining, Chemists (N.Y.C.); Ill. Athletic (Chgo.). Office: Keystone Resources Co Frick Bldg Pittsburgh PA 15219

KAHN, SAMUEL, psychiatrist, author; b. Atlanta, June 16, 1897; s. Marcus and Janice Kahn; B.S., Emory U., 1920, M.D., 1921; M.A., N.Y.U., 1923, Ph.D., 1932. Intern Met. Hosp., N.Y.C., 1921-22; resident City Hosp., 1922-23, Kings Park State Hosp., 1923-25; Kings County Hosp., 1925-29; lectr. N.Y.U., 1925-27; psychiatrist Sing Sing, 1929-31; clin. prof. neurology and psychiatry Georgetown U. and George Washington U., also chief psychiatrist Gallinger Hosp., 1929-31; asso. prof. L.I. U., 1945-54, adj. prof. psychiatry; dir. Quakerbridge Sch., 1952-66, 67; chief psychiatrist Induction Bd., II Corps Area, U.S. Army, 1939-42; now pvt. practice psychoanalysis; clin. psychiatrist Mt. Sinai, N.Y. Post Grad. hosps., N.Y. State Psychiatric Inst.; cons. psychiatrist Muhlenberg Hosp.; psychiatrist Union County Psychiatric Clinic; asso. dir. Dr. Moreno's Sanitarium. Chief psychiatrist U.S. Army Induction Bd. for N.J. and Del. World War II. Commd. col. N.Y. Militia, 1962. Med. officer Legion of Honor. Fellow Royal Soc. Health, Wisdom Soc., Am. Authors League, mem. N.Y. Med. Soc., Am. Sociol. Soc., N.Y. Dynamic Psychol. Soc. (dir.), Israel Med. Soc. U.S. Mil. Surgeons, Am. Soc. Advancement Psychotherapy, Bklyn. Psychiat. Soc., N.Y. Acad. Sci., Alpha Epsilon Pi, Phi Delta Kappa. Jewish religion. Mason (Shriner), Rotarian; mem. B'nai B'rith. Club: Optimist (Westchester, N.Y.). Author: Sing Sing Criminals, 1936; Mentality and Homosexuality, 1937; Psych-Definitions, 1938; Suggestion and Hypnosis, 1939; How to Study, 1939; Understanding Love Problems, 1946; Master Your Mind, 1951; Public Speaking, 1952; Inferiorities and Superiorities, 1954; Child Guidance and Mental Hygiene; Rorschach Rseume; TAT Resume: Statistical Dictionary; On Psychology, Psychiatry and Psychoanalysis; Parent-Teacher-Child Guidance; Parapsychology; Memory Development, 1962; Psi and ESP Phenomena; Psychodrama Explained, 1964; Psych of Love, 1968; (autobiography) Directed Nonsense; Effective Studying and Learning, 1973; Essays on Longevity, 1974; Why We Laugh, 1975; Essays on Freudian Psychology, 1976; Origins of Prejudice, 1976; Anxieties, Phobias and Fears, 1977; The Best Child Guidance for Parents, Grandparents and Teachers, 1978; Suggestion and Hypnosis Advanced, 1979. Former asso. editor Modern Psychologist, Modern Thinker, Psychol. Digest. Contbr. articles to profl. jours. Home: 410 Albany Post Rd PO Box 361 Croton NY 10520

KAHN, SIDNEY, physician; b. Paterson, N.J., Mar. 30, 1913; s. Jacob Moses and Bert. . (Orleansky) K.; B.A., N.Y. U., 1933, M.D., 1937; m. Henrietta Berger, Aug. 31, 1939; children—Barbara Kahn Pollack, Rhoda (Mrs. Samuel R. Nussbaum). Intern, Bronx Hosp., N.Y.C., 1937-39, resident in surgery, 1939-42; pvt. practice medicine specializing in surgery, N.Y.C., 1946—; attending plastic surgeon Bronx Municipal Hosp. Center, N.Y.C., 1955—; clin. prof. plastic surgery Mt. Sinai Sch. Medicine, N.Y.C., 1968—; chief plastic surg. services Beth Israel Med. Center, 1967—, Bronx-Lebanon Hosp. Center, N.Y.C., 1958—; cons. plastic surgeon N.Y. Rehab. Hosp., West Haverstraw, N.Y., 1953-66, Nyack (N.Y.) Hosp., 1953—; pres. med. bd. Bronx-Lebanon Hosp. Center, 1970. Served with M.C., AUS, 1942-46. Diplomate Am. Bd. Surgery, Am. Bd. Plastic Surgery. Fellow A.C.S.; mem. A.M.A., Am. Soc. Plastic and Reconstructive Surgery, Am. Assn. Plastic Surgeons, N.Y. Acad. Medicine, Am. Cleft Palate Assn., Am. Soc. Surgery of Hand. Author: (with A.J. Bersky and B.E. Simon) Principles and Practice of Plastic Surgery, 1964. Contbr. articles to profl. jours. Home: 361 Lewelen Circle Englewood NJ 07631 Office: 102 E 78th St New York City NY 10021

KAHN, WALTER, steel co. exec.; b. Cologne, Germany, Aug. 27, 1917; s. Nathan and Betty (Mayer) K.; student Moriya Sch., Cologne, 1922-26, Jawne Coll., Cologne, 1926-36; m. Grace Roeder, Aug. 17, 1952; children—Nathan S., Simon Mark, Vivian. Pres., Empire Steel Trading Co., Inc., 1940—. Mem. Belgian C. of C., Asso. Steel Industries, Am. Iron and Steel Inst., Wire Assn., Assn. Steel Distbrs., Nat. Assn. Secondary Material Industries Inc. Office: 80 Wall St New York City NY 10005

KAHN, WERNER DAVID, mathematician; b. Gemmingen, Baden, Germany, May 26, 1930; s. Josef and Fanny (Mannheimer) K.; B.S., U. Ill., 1952, M.S., 1955; m. Gladys Homer, Jan. 1, 1956; 1 son, Joel Sheldon. Mathematician U.S. Army Map Service, Washington, 1956-60; aerospace engr. NASA, Goddard Space Flight Center, Greenbelt, Md., 1960—. Served to 1st lt. USAF 1953-56. Home: 9310 Weaver St Silver Spring MD 20901 Office: Goddard Space Flight Center Greenbelt MD 20771

KAISER, FREDERICK MARTIN, govt. ofcl.; b. Salem, Ohio, Aug. 30, 1944; s. Frederick Martin and Victoria (Oana) K.; A.B. (scholar), Cornell U., 1966; M.A., U. Pitts., 1967; m. Agnes Marie Kolozsi, Oct. 10, 1965; children—Lisa Ann, Teresa Lynn. Teaching fellow, lectr. U. Pitts., 1969-70; asst. prof., faculty research grantee Waynesburg (Pa.) Coll., 1970-74; spl. staff cons. com. on Internat. Relations Ho. of Reps., 1974; sr. analyst in Am. nat. govt. Congl. Research Service, Library of Congress, Washington, 1975—; expert witness Democratic charter commn., 1973; cons. div. edn. affairs Am. Polit. Sci. Assn., 1974-75; cons. Pa. legislators orientation, 1972; reviewer Nat. Sci. Found., 1974; participant nat. and internat. confs. Chmn. Democratic Election Hdqrs., Greene County, Pa., 1972; chmn. Citizens for McGovern, Greene County, 1972. Mem. ACLU, AAUP, Midwest Am. (cons. 1972) polit. sci. assns., Am. Sociol. Assn., Pi Sigma Alpha, Pi Gamma Mu. Lutheran. Contbr. numerous articles in field to profl. jours. Home: 11316 Cherry Hill Rd Beltsville MD 20705 Office: Congressional Research Service Library of Congress Washington DC 20540

KAISER, HANS ELMAR, comparative pathologist; b. Prague, Czechoslovakia, Feb. 16, 1928; s. Rudolf and Charlotte (Thiel) K.; student U. Rostock (Germany), 1948-53; Dr. rer. nat., Eberhard Karls U., Tubingen, Germany, 1958; m. Charlotte Möhring, Oct. 12, 1960. Vis. investigative pathologist Hanover Veterinary Acad., 1958-60; cons., vis. investigator Sloan Kettering Inst. Cancer Research, 1961-62; spl. lectr. anatomy U. Sask. (Can.), Saskatoon, 1962-63; with biol. communications project George Washington U., 1964-65; asst. prof. George Washington U., Washington, 1965-69; research pathologist, author, cons. Forest Phys. Lab. U.S. Dept. Agr., Beltsville, Md., 1969-74; research asso. pathology U. Md., Balt., part time, 1974—; research dir. Great Lakes Area Paleontological Museum, Traverse City, Mich., 1975—. Mem. AAAS, Am. Soc. Zoology, Am. Microscope Soc., Am. Statis. Soc., Am. Assn. Cancer Research, Am. Chem. Soc., N.Y. Acad. Scis., Pan Am. Assn. Anatomy, Soc. Invertebrate Pathology, Am. Assn. Pathologists, Am. Assn. Anatomy, Washington Acad. Scis. Clubs: Bryce Mountain, Pine Mountain Lakes. Author: Atlas of the Domestic Turkey, 1968; Das Abnorme in der Evolution, 1970; Morphology of the Sirenia, 1974; Pocket Atlas of Human Anatomy, English edit. of Anatomisches Bildwörterbuch (H. Feneis), 1976. Home: 433 South West Dr Silver Spring MD 20901 Office: Dept Pathology Univ Med School Baltimore MD 21201

KAISER, KATHERINE ELIZABETH, educator; b. Albany, N.Y., May 15, 1915; d. George Andrew and Elizabeth Alexandria (Cochrane) K.; B.S. cum laude, Bob Jones U., 1954; M.A., Columbia U., 1955; postgrad. in-service tng. various univs., summer seminars Hebrew U., Nairobi U. Office worker, 1934-50; tchr. Schenectady Pub. Schs., 1955-60; AID sponsored team Columbia U., Kabul, Afghanistan, 1960-62; cons., resource tchr. Schenectady Pub. Schs., 1963-68; tchr. Central Park Middle Sch., Schenectady, 1968—; speaker community resources, world affairs; coordinating com. Tchrs. on Vol. Service in Israel, 1975—; vol. lang. tchr., Ashkelon, Israel, summer 1974-76. Program coordinator Schenectady Interfaith Community Coordinating Council, 1977-78; adv. bd. Refreshing Spring Child Day Care Center, 1974—, vol. service award, 1977. Recipient patent award Gen. Elec. Co., 1948; fellow in African studies

Northwestern U., 1967; certified in teaching English. ednl. guidance and home econs. edn., N.Y. Mem. UN Assn. (v.p., dir. Capital area), World Federalist Assn. (dir. Capital area), AAUW, Nat., N.Y., Schenectady (pres., dir.) fedns. bus. and profl. women's clubs. Republican. Presbyterian. Writer series on Asia for Schenectady Gazette, 1960-62.

KAISER, RONALD SAUL, psychologist; b. Mpls., Nov. 19, 1937; s. Lawrence I. and Sonia (Kool) K.; B.S., U. Minn., 1959, M.A., 1960; Ph.D., U. Pa., 1976; m. Louise Ruth Rubenstein, Sept. 7, 1970; children—Jeffrey David, Brian Alan. Teacher, counselor Los Angeles City Schs., 1960-65; exec. dir. Twin Cities B'nai B'rith Career and Counseling Services, Mpls. and St. Paul, 1965-67, dir. profl. field services nat. office, Washington, 1967-69, exec. dir., Phila., 1969-78; pvt. practice psychology, Phila., 1978—; adj. asso. prof. Temple U., 1978—; vocat. expert Social Security Adminstrn., Bur. Hearings & Appeals; cons. Gen. Rehab. Services. Lic. psychologist, Pa.; cert. sch. psychologist, Pa. Mem. Am., Pa. psychol. assns., Phila. Soc. Clin. Psychologists, Am., Pa. (pres. 1978-80) personnel and guidance assns., Personnel and Guidance Assn. Greater Phila (pres. 1976-77). Home and office: 298 Forrest Ave Elkins Park PA 19117

KAISER, WILLIAM TUSTIN, engr.; b. Wheeling, W.Va., Feb. 18, 1942; s. William Louis and Miriam Elisabeth (Tustin) K.; B.S., W.Va. U., 1966, M.S., 1967. Research mech. engr. Battelle Meml. Inst., Columbus, Ohio, 1967-69; sr. design engr. Essex Internat., Lancaster, Ohio, 1969-71; sr. structural engr. Westinghouse Bettis, W. Mifflin, Pa., 1971-77; sr. structural materials engr. Westinghouse NES, Pitts., 1977—. Bausch and Lomb Sci. award, 1960. Mem. ASME, Westinghouse Engrs. Soc., Nat. Soc. Profl. Engrs., ASTM, Smithsonian Assos., Phi Kappa Sigma. Lutheran. Club: Order Demolay. Home: 800 Penn Center Blvd Apt 701 Pittsburgh PA 15235 Office: Westinghouse NES Penn Center Bldg 2 PO Box 355 Pittsburgh PA 15230

KALADOW, ARTHUR ROBERT, educator; b. Cin., Jan. 5, 1930; s. Phillip and Jennie (Dauber) K.; B.S. in Edn., U. Cin., 1952; M.A., Xavier U., Cin., 1963; m. Karen Sue Williams, June 11, 1967; 1 dau., Jennifer Kristi. Tchr., asst. athletic dir., athletic coach George Washington High Sch., Agana, Guam, 1952-54; tchr., athletic coach, Mariemont High Sch., Cin., 1954-55, North Coll. Hill High Sch., Cin., 1955-68; asst. social studies supr., tchr. Tappan Zee High Sch., Orangeburg, N.Y., 1968—; recreation specialist City of Cin., 1950-51; recreation specialist, athletic coach USN Spl. Services, Apra Harbor, Guam, 1952-54. Served with U.S. Army, 1947-48. Named Coach of Yr., Hamilton County (Ohio), 1967; Coe Found. fellow Coll. Wooster, 1957; NCCJ fellow U. Cin., NDEA fellow U. Cin., 1965; Fulbright fellow, New Delhi, India, 1969. Mem. N.Y. State Tchrs. Assn., Ohio Edn. Assn., Edn. Assn. South Orangetown (N.Y.), N.Y. State Council Social Studies, Ohio Assn. Health, Phys. Edn., Recreation, Ohio High Sch. Football Coaches Assn., Rockland Counay (N.Y.) Coaches Assn., Fulbright, U. Cin., Xavier U. alumni assns., Ohio Gun Collectors Assn., Am. Ordnance Assn., Nat. Rifle Assn. Home: 21 Broome Blvd Nyack NY 10960 Office: 10 Western Hwy Orangeburg NY 10962

KALAPINSKI, ALPHONSE ANTHONY, mfg. co. exec.; b. Lynn, Mass., Nov. 30, 1935; s. Anthony Edward and Helen Mary K.; B.A., So. Ill. U., 1962, M.A., 1963; m. Marie C. Madsen, Apr. 16, 1966; 1 dau., Cristina. With Stanley Tools, New Britain, Conn., 1963—, v.p. mktg., 1977—. Served with USAF, 1954-62. Mem. Am. Mgmt. Assn., Central States Hardware Club, Hardware Industry Research and Devel. Council (dir.). Republican. Roman Catholic. Office: 600 Myrtle St New Britain CT 06050

KALEMARIS, STANLEY GEORGE, JR., aero. engr.; b. Coronado, Calif., Feb. 17, 1943; s. Stanley George and Helen Georgia (Kokinis) K.; B.S. in Engring., Princeton, 1964; M.S., N.Y.U., 1969; M.B.A., L.I. U., 1976; m. Agnes Marie Walsh, Nov. 30, 1968; 1 dau., Victoria Terhecte. With Grumman Aerospace Corp., Bethpage, N.Y., 1964—, asst. project engr., 1974-76, project engr., 1976—, adviser scholarship program, 1970—. Mem. Am. Inst. Aeros. and Astronautics (career environ. com., program chmn. council L.I. sect.), Princeton Engring. Assn., Aircraft Owners and Pilots Assn., GACE Flying Club (past activities officer), Am. Helicopter Soc. (aero. tech. com.). Home: 6 Burlington Ave Melville NY 11746 Office: Grumman Aerospace Corp Bethpage NY 11746

KALFUS, STANLEY, cons. engr.; b. Bklyn., Jan. 21, 1925; s. Samuel and Helen (Engel) K.; B.A., N.Y. U., 1948; B.S. in Mech. Engring., Purdue U., 1951; m. Hilda Scherliss, June 19, 1955; children—David Henry, Jonathan Alan, Ethan Adam. Pres., Stanley Kalfus, P.C., N.Y.C. Mem. Queens County Grand Jury Assn. Served with U.S. Army, 1943-45. Deocrated Purple Heart; registered profl. engr., N.Y., N.J., Conn., Mass., Pa., Md., D.C., Fla., Wis., Tex. Mem. Nat. Soc. Profl. Engrs., Am. Soc. Heating, Refrigerating and Air Conditioning Engrs. Jewish. Club: Masons. Home: 98-19 64th Avenue Forest Hills NY 11374 Office: 309 Fifth Ave New York City NY 10016

KALIJARVI, THORSTEN VALENTINE, polit. scientist, former ambassador, educator; b. Gardner, Mass., Dec. 22, 1897; s. Gustaf and Ida Christina (Kuniholm) K.; A.B., Clark U., 1920, A.M., 1923; postgrad. (Carnegie Endowment fellow) Harvard U., 1920-22; LL.B., LaSalle U., 1933; Ph.D., U. Berlin, 1935, A.L.M., 1935; postgrad. Hague (Netherlands) Acad. Internat. Law, 1928-29, Geneva Sch. Internat. Studies, 1929; m. Dorothy Corbett Knight, Sept. 4, 1926; 1 dau., June. Head dept. polit. sci. U. N.H., 1927, prof. govt., 1939-45, dir. inst. pub. affairs and chmn. bur. govt. research, 1939-42; exec. dir. N.H. State Planning and Devel. Commn. and mem. and sometimes officer of nat., state and local commns., 1942-47; prin. analyst European affairs Legis. Reference Service, Library of Congress, 1947; research counsel in internat. relations Legis. Reference Service, 1947-50, sr. specialist fgn. affairs, 1950-52, staff asso. and cons. U.S. Senate Fgn. Relations Com., 1947-53; asst. sec. state for econ. affairs Dept. State, Washington, 1953-57, asst. sec. state for econ. affairs, 1957, acting undersec. state econ. affairs, 1956-57; U.S. ambassador to El Salvador, 1957-61; cons. Dept. State, Washington, 1961; ret. from Dept. State, 1961; prof. internat. and pub. affairs Pa. State U., 1962-64; dean faculty Cape Cod Community Coll., 1964-68, prof. emeritus, 1968—; lectr. John Hopkins U., 1952-53; arbitrator labor disputes; lectr. in internat. affairs. Fellow Am. Acad. Scis., AAAS; mem. Am. Arbitration Assn., U.S. C. of C. (internat. com. 1977), Phi Kappa Phi, Pi Gamma Mu. Clubs: Dacor, Am. Legion, Harvard; Cosmos (Washington). Author books, including: Recent American Foreign Policy, 1952; Modern World Politics, 1953; Soviet Power and Policy, 1954; Central America, Land of Lords and Lizards, 1962; editor publs., including: Fascism in Action, 1948; Congress and Foreign Relations, 1953; contbr. articles to profl. jours. Address: Blue Blinds Barnstable MA 02630 also 1552 33d St Washington DC 20007

KALIMIAN, MANOUCHEHR MICHAEL, real estate and investment exec.; b. Kabul, Afghanistan, Apr. 30, 1936; s. Morad and Frances (Sarraf) K.; came to U.S., 1955, naturalized, 1961; B.S., N.Y. U., 1961; children by previous marriage—Bonnie Michele, Morad John. Real estate exec., N.Y.C., 1959—. Mem. Real Estate Bd. N.Y. Republican. Home: 500 E 83d St New York City NY 10028 Office: 919 3d Ave New York City NY 10022

KALINA, IVAN, pediatrician; b. Czechoslovakia, May 22, 1932; s. Geza and Helen (Fedorak) K.; came to U.S., 1965, naturalized, 1969; M.D., Charles U., Prague, 1956; m. Atlas, July 1, 1956; children—Peter, Yvette. Intern, Univ. Hosp., Czechoslovakia, 1956, Univ. Hosp., Vienna, Austria, 1965; resident Bellevue Hosp., N.Y.C., 1966-68; practice medicine, specializing in pediatrics, Rocky Point, N.Y., 1968—; mem. staffs St. Charles, Mather hosps. Diplomate Am. Bd. Pediatrics. Fellow Am. Acad. Pediatrics; mem. N.Y. State, Suffolk County med. socs., Panam. Med.-Pediatric Soc., Suffolk County Pediatric Soc. Republican. Address: 81 Broadway Rocky Point NY 11778

KALINICH, JOHN, photographer; b. Bayonne, N.J., Nov. 17, 1915; s. Michael and Mary (Serdula) K.; grad. pub. schs.; pvt. studies of art, sculpture; m. Avril H. Gore, Feb. 26, 1949; children—John, Carol Elizabeth. Mem. advtg. dept. Corning Glass Works (N.Y.), 1933-39; rep. Glass Center, N.Y. World's Fair, 1939, mgr. photo dept., chief photographer, cinephotographer, 1940-53; free lance photographer, indsl., comml., 1953-56; sr. tech. rep. Eastman Kodak Co., N.Y.C., 1956—; part-time vineyardist; instr. New Eng. Inst. Profl. Photography, U. N.H., 1968, 72. Recipient numerous Certificates of Merit, Profl. Photographers of Am., Inc., 1960-72; Achievement award, Indsl. Photographers Am., Inc., 1965; Nat. award Profl. Photographers Am. Inc., 1967, Photographic Craftsman award, 1971; Mexican, Vontury and Indsl. awards, Am. Ceramic Soc., 1950; Salon Lom U Mostu, Czskoslovensko (Czechoslovakia), 1938; Balt. Internat. Salon of Photography award, 1938; World Exhbn. of Photography, Lucerne, Switzerland, 1952. Mem. Indsl. Photographers of N.J., Inc., Profl. Photographers Am. Inc., Am. Soc. Photographers. Republican. Presbyterian. Clubs: Keuka Yacht, Masons. Home: 14 Spring Brook Rd Morristown NJ 07960 Office: 1133 Ave of Americas New York City NY 10036

KALKHOF, THOMAS CORRIGAN, physician; b. Wellsville, N.Y., Aug. 12, 1919; s. Arthur Albert and Evelyn (Corrigan) K.; B.S., Gannon Coll., 1943; M.D., Marquette U., 1946; m. Mary E. Jones, Mar. 3, 1946 (dec. 1955); children—Thomas E., Susan A., Mark A., Patricia D.; m. 2d Constance N. McCarthy, Apr. 19, 1958; children—Christopher J., Constance M., Craig Alan. Intern, resident St. Vincent's Hosp., Erie, Pa., 1946-47; pvt. practice gen. geriatrics and psychosomatic medicine, Erie, 1947—, owner, adminstr. Twinbrook Nursing and Convalescent Home, 1960—; dir. Iroquois Med. Centre, Erie; staff mem. St. Vincent's Hosp., Hamot Hosp., Erie; pres., dir. Small Hosp. Cons., Inc., Erie, 1954—. Past chmn. Pa. Bd. Accreditation Nursing Homes and Related Facilities. Served with M.C., AUS, 1943-44. Fellow Am. Geriatric Soc. (v.p.), Am. Coll. Nursing Home Adminstrs.; mem. Pa. Assn. Nursing and Convalescent Homes, Acad. Psychosomatic Medicine (past pres.), Pa. Acad. Family Physicians (past chmn. sub-com. long term care, pres. Erie chpt.), Assn. Physicians in Chronic Disease Facilities (past pres.), Am. Soc. Clin. Hypnosis, A.M.A., Pa., Erie County med. socs., Am. Acad. Family Physicians, Nat. Geriatric Soc. (1st v.p.), Internat. Platform Assn., Am. Trudeau Soc. Republican. Roman Catholic. K.C. (4 deg.). Home: 3749 E Lake Rd Erie PA 16511 Office: Iroquois Medical Centre 3815 Field St Erie PA 16511

KALKUS, STANLEY, librarian; b. Prague, Czechoslovakia, Apr. 27, 1931; s. Frank and Zdenka (Hynkova) K.; came to U.S., 1952, naturalized, 1953; arbitur Classical Gymnasium, Prague, 1950; M.A., U. Chgo., 1959; m. Marta J. Pokorna, Jan. 12, 1952; children—Michaela Z., Olen A., Hynek P. Asso. fellow U. Chgo., 1957-59; hdqrs. librarian U.S. Army, 5th Army Hdqrs., Chgo., 1959-60; librarian, audio-visual coordinator Southeast Coll., Chgo., 1960-62; base librarian Sidi Slimane AFB, Morocco, 1962-63, Hahn AFB, Germany, 1963-68; bibliographer, lectr. U. N.C., 1968-69; librarian Naval Underwater Weapons Research and Engring Sta., Newport, R.I., 1969-71, head library dept. Naval Underwater Systems Center, 1971-78; dir. library Dept. Navy, 1978—; participant Tech. Info/Panel AGARD (NATO) meetings, Brussells, Copenhagen, Oslo. Mem. core com. R.I. Gov.'s Conf. Libraries, 1976-77. Served with U.S. Army, 1952-53. Recipient Dept. Navy Underwater Systems Center Cost Reduction award, 1972, 74. Mem. ALA (pres. Armed Forces sect. 1974), Spl. Libraries Assn. (chmn. mil. libraries div. 1978-79), Am. Transls. Assn., Council Navy Sci. and Tech. Librarians (east coast pres. 1974-76) Czechoslovak Nat. Council Am. Roman Catholic. Club: Newport Ski. Editor: Navy Libraries in the 1980's, 1976; contbr. articles in field to profl. jours. Home: 9304 Lancelot Rd Oxon Hill MD 20022 Office: Bldg 220 Room 220 Washington Navy Yard Washington DC 20374

KALLER, HAROLD MILTON, dentist; b. Meriden, Conn., July 7, 1921; s. Samuel Leo and Gladys (Zempsky) K.; student U. Conn., 1938-40; D.D.S., U. Pa., 1944; m. Marsha Luchnick, June 20, 1943 (dec.); children—Marlene, Douglas Henry; m. 2d, Arline Menus Berman, Apr. 11, 1976. Pvt. practice gen. dentistry, Meriden, 1946—. Pres. Meriden Jewish Fedn., 1970-72; program chmn. Nat. Probus Club, 1968-69, chmn. ann. educator award, 1970, 76; v.p. Meriden Probus, 1972-73; bd. dirs. Curtis Home, 1973-75; bd. dirs. Temple B'nai Abraham, Meriden, Conn., 1978-79, chmn. cultural affairs, 1977-79. Served to capt. Dental Corps, AUS, 1944-46. Mem. Meriden Wallingford Dental Soc. (v.p. 1948-49, pres. 1949-50), Am., Conn. dental assns., Meriden (pres. 1951-53), Conn. Valley camera clubs, (pres. 1954-56), Photog. Soc. Am., Alpha Omega. Democrat. Jewish religion (pres. Temple Mens Club 1972-73). Mason. Exhibited monochrome photog. prints in numerous internat. exhbns., 1952-67. Home: 245 Brownstone Ridge Meriden CT 06450 Office: 130 E Main St Meriden CT 06450

KALMANOFF, MARTIN, composer; b. Bklyn., May 24, 1920; s. Joseph and Anna (Mirin) K.; B.A. cum laude, Harvard U., 1941, M.A., 1942; m. Margaret Tharaldsen, Sept. 21, 1974. Composer: (opera) Opera, Opera (libretto by Saroyan), 1956, The Insect Comedy (radio excerpts), 1966; Bald Prima Donna (libretto by Ionesco), 1963, Great Stone Face, 1968, Photograph 1920 (libretto by Gertrude Stein), 1972, (children's Bicentennial musical) Give Me Liberty; also musical theatre including The Fourposter, 1963, Victory at Masada, 1968, also choral-orchestral works including Kaddish for a Warring World, 1972; popular songs including Just Say I Love Her; pieces for radio and TV; composer, lyricist children's musicals Christopher Columbus (premier N.Y.C. 1976), Smart Aleck & The Talking Wire, toured 1977-78, Young Tom Edison, 1962-78; N.Y. State Council on Arts grantee for musical setting of Lao-Tse's The Way of Life for voice and 11 instruments (premiered by Bronx Arts Ensemble 1978); composer songs Portrait of a Bohemian: Lamento di Puccini and Aria from the Missing Act of La Boheme (in movie about Puccini). Winner Robert Merrill Best Opera contest, 1950. Richard Rodgers grantee, 1968. Mem. ASCAP, Nat. Opera Assn., Central Opera Service. Contbr. to profl. jours. Home: 392 Central Park W New York City NY 10025

KALSNER, STANLEY, educator, pharmacologist; b. N.Y.C., Aug. 21, 1936; s. William Louis and Sadie (Feldman) K.; A.B., N.Y. U., 1958; postgrad. State U. N.Y. Downstate Med. Center, 1959-62; Ph.D., U. Man., 1966; postdoctoral Cambridge (Eng.) U., 1966-67; m. Jenny Book, Aug. 4, 1963; children—Lydia, Pamela, Louisa. Asst. prof. pharmacology U. Ottawa, 1967-72, asso. prof., 1972-77, prof., 1977—, also med. research scientist; sci. referee Med. Research Council Can., Canadian Heart Found. USPHS fellow, 1960-67; Med. Research Council and Ont. Heart Found. grantee, 1970—. Mem. AAAS, Canadian Pharmacology Soc., Am. Soc. Pharmacology and Therapeutics, AAUP. Editor, contbr. chpts. to books, articles to jours.; asso. editor Canadian Jour. Physiology and Pharmacology; referee European Jour. Pharmacology, Circulation Research. Home: 115-860 Cahill Dr W Ottawa ON Canada Office: 275 Nicholas St Ottawa ON K1N 9A9 Canada

KALTER, JERALD SCOTT, physician; b. Balt., Feb. 20, 1914; s. Louis and Dorothy K.; M.D., U. Md., 1938; m. Mildred Berman, Mar. 14, 1976; children by previous marriage—James A., Valerie J., Jerald Scott. Intern, N.Y.C. Hosp., 1938-40, med. resident, 1940-41; practice medicine specializing in internal medicine and cardiology, N.Y.C., 1948—; asso. attending physician Beekman Downtown Hosp., N.Y.C. Pres., Guideposts for Children, 1956—. Served to comdr. M.C., USN, 1941-48. Fellow A.C.P.; mem. AMA, Am. Heart Assn., N.Y. Acad. Medicine, N.Y. Cardiol. Soc., Internat. Soc. Internal Medicine, N.Y. State, N.Y. County med. socs. Jewish. Club: Metropolis Country (White Plains, N.Y.) Home: 130 E 67th St New York City NY 10021 Office: 18 E 62d St New York City NY 10021

KALUGIN, DAVID, author, poet; b. Bklyn., Mar. 8, 1914; s. Isadore and Sarah (Wolchok) K.; student pub. schs., Manhattan Med. Assts. Sch.; m. Sophie Sabathie, June 25, 1954; 1 son by previous marriage, Eric. Internat. rep. Retail Wholesale Dept. Store Union, CIO, 1947-49, labor reporter, pvt. sec. to pres., 1948-49; grocery clk., 1951-56; with N.Y.C. Post Office, 1957—. D. Kalugin Manuscript Collection Syracuse U. Served with M.C., AUS, World War II. Recipient Superior Accomplishment award Post Office Dept., 1963, 67, 70, award certificate, 1964, Unusual Achievement plaque U.S. Post Office, 1968, 69, 70; Outstanding Suggester of Year award N.Y.C. Post Office, 1966-69, 70, 71; citation Nat. Assn. Suggestion Systems, 1968, 69, 70, also others. Mem. Internat. Platform Assn., Poetry Soc. Am. Author: Tomorrow is So Far From Now, 1952; Naturally, 1953; For the Loneliest of Reasons, 1955; The Leaves Still Talk, 1959; The Tintinnabulations of Boos and Applause, 1964. Contbr. to various U.S. and fgn. publs. Home: 36-19 Bowne St Flushing NY 11354

KALYNYCH, LUBOMYR EUGENE, archtl. designer; b. Peremyshl, Ukraine, Apr. 28, 1925; s. Teofil and Iwanna (Jarosevych) K.; came to U.S., 1950, naturalized, 1956; student Sch. Architecture U. Graz, Austria, 1946-49; B.Arch., U. Minn., 1956. Designer, Lang & Raugland, Architects, Mpls., 1956; designer Liebengerg & Caplain, Architects, Mpls., 1958-59, David Ludlow, Architect, Summit, N.J., 1960-61, Asso. Designers, Morristown, N.J., 1962-74; self-employed, Irvington, N.J., 1974-75; partner, asso. George N. Chuchra, Engrs. and Constructors, Rutherford, N.J., 1976—. Mem. Irvington Planning Bd., 1968—. Mem. Ukrainian Engrs. Assn. (past pres.), Ukrainian Cultural Workers Assn. (pres.), Ukrainian Jaroslaw Soc. (v.p.), Shevchenko Sci. Soc. Works include Community Bldg. SUMA, Ellenville, N.Y., 1973, gymnasium St. John's Ukrainian Catholic Sch., Newark, 1976, auditorium and cultural center Ukrainian Orthodox Ch. U.S.A., South Bound Brook, N.J., 1978; also pvt. residences, bldgs.; designer Ukrainian Nationality Room in Cathedral of Learning, U. Pitts.; author archtl. sketches; contbr. articles to profl. jours. Home: 10 Fleetwood Pl Irvington NJ 07111

KAMBACK, MARVIN C., psychologist; b. Yankton, S.D., July 15, 1939; s. Carl Melvin and Pauline Elizabeth (Albrecht) K.;B.A. in English Lit., U. S.D., 1961, M.A. in Psychology, 1962; Ph.D., in Psychology (NIMH fellow), Vanderbilt U., 1965; children—Elizabeth, Christopher. NIMH postdoctoral 1 fellow Stanford U. Sch. Medicine, 1965-67; lectr. dept. psychology U. Calif. at Santa Barbara, 1966-67, asst. prof. psychology and physiology, 1967-69; asst. prof., dir. primate lab., U. S.D., 1969-71; intern Balt. City Hosps., also sr. clin. psychologist, 1971-74; asst. prof. behavioral biology Johns Hopkins U. Sch. Medicine, 1971-74; asso. prof. Psychiat. Inst. U. Md. Sch. Medicine. Balt., 1974—; dir. Families and Children's Center U. Md. U. Sch. Medicine, 1974—. Certified psychologist, Md. Mem. Am., Md. psychol assns., Nat. Register of Health Service Providers in Psychology, Soc. Gen. Systems Research, Sigma Xi. Unitarian. Contbr. numerous articles in field to profl. jours. Home: 1510 W Mt Royal Ave Baltimore MD 21217 Office: 721 W Redwood St Baltimore MD 21201

KAMELL, MICHAEL W., educator; b. Cairo, Egypt, Oct. 3, 1918; s. Kamel and Josephine (Andrews) K.; B.A., Cairo U., 1941, diploma, 1943, M.A. in Psychology, 1947; Ph.D., Rennes U., 1953; D.Sc., Lausanne U., 1955; m. Laila Youssif, July 14, 1944; children—Wagdy, Ralph. Came to U.S., 1958, naturalized, 1964. Tchr. Mansoura Secondary Sch., Egypt, 1943-47, Cairo high schs., also tchr. edn. insts., 1948-51; prof. Tchrs. Coll., Heliopolis, Cairo, Egypt, 1952-57; asst. prof. Jersey City State Coll., 1958-60, asso. prof. social scis., 1960-63, prof., 1964—, chmn. sociology dept., 1964-73, dir. internat. studies, 1973—. Mem. Am. Psychol. Assn. Author textbooks including The Child and the Study of Literature, 1958, The Middle East; A Humanistic Approach, 1973. Contbr. articles to profl. jours. Home: 23 Barnard Pl Elizabeth NJ 07208 Office: Jersey City State Coll Jersey City NJ 07305

KAMEN, MAX LAWRENCE, physician, lawyer; b. N.Y.C., Feb. 25, 1913; s. Isidore and Dora (Stavsky) K.; B.S., N.Y. U., 1934; LL.B., Bklyn. Law Sch., 1937, LL.M., 1967, J.D., 1967; D.O., Phila. Coll. Osteo. Medicine, 1946; m. Vera Jordan, 1956; children—Laurence (Mrs. Michael Goodman), JoAnne Heidi, Leslie Patricia. Admitted to N.Y. bar, 1938; licensed in medicine and surgery, N.Y., 1947, in osteopathy, Pa., 1946, in osteopathy and surgery, Pa., 1961; pvt. practice law, 1938; pvt. practice osteo. medicine, N.Y.C., 1948; cons. med. jurisprudence and legal medicine; postdoctoral faculty mem., chmn. dept. forensic medicine Leroy Hosp.; faculty N.Y. Post Grad. Inst. Osteo. Medicine and Surgery; pres. med. bd. chmn. staff LeRoy Hosp.; adj. prof. dept. health scis. L.I. U., 1976—; head dept forensic medicine N.Y. Coll. Osteo. Medicine. Sec.-treas. Nat. Bd. Examiiners Osteo. Physicians and Surgeons, 1963—, examiner med. jurisprudence, 1961—, cons. emeritus Nat. Bd., 1968—. Mem. N.Y. State Bd. for Medicine, 1971—; dir. N.Y.C. div. Am. Cancer Soc.; hon. mem. Honor Leagion N.Y.C. Police Dept. Trustee Post Grad. Inst. Osteopathic Medicine and Surgery; mem. council regents St. Francis Coll., Bklyn. Mem. Am. Trial Lawyers Assn., Soc. Med. Jurisprudence, Am. Osteo. Assn. (1st v.p. 1965-67), N.Y. Osteo. Soc. (pres. 1963-65), N.Y.C. Soc. Osteo. Physicians and Surgeons (pres. 1962-63), Iota Theta, Lambda Omicron Gamma, Sigma Alpha Omicron. Jewish (trustee temple). Club: Unity (Bklyn.). Author: Medical Jurisprudence, 1969. Editor, contbr.: The Osteopathic Profession, 1961-68. Address: 165 W 46th St New York City NY 10036

KAMERER, DONALD BAILEY, physician; b. Pitts., Aug. 13, 1933; s. Lawrence S. and Irene E. (Bailey) K.; B.A., Washington and Jefferson Coll., 1955; M.D., Temple U., 1959; m. Carol Ann Scialabba, 1970; children—Deborah, Donald, Douglas, Alison. Intern, Allegheny Gen. Hosp., Pitts., 1959-60; resident otolaryngology Charity Hosp., New Orleans and U. Pitts. Health Center, 1962-66; clin. asst. prof. otolaryngology U. Pitts., 1977—, chief otolgy div. Falk Clinic; clin. asso. prof. otolaryngology W.Va. U., 1974; indivual practice medicine, specialzing in otology, Pitts., 1967—; med. staff Eye and Ear, Mercy, VA, St. Margaret Meml. hosps., Pitts. Mem. adv. council Pa. for Hearing Aid Sales Registration Law, 1977—; bd. dirs. DePaul Inst. for Deaf. Served to capt. U.S. Army, 1960-62. Fellow otology Baylor U. Med. Center, Houston, 1966-67. Mem. Pa. Acad. Ophthalmology and Otolaryngology (sec. 1971—), Alumni Assn. Washington and Jefferson Coll., AMA (Physicians Recognition award 1975—), Pa., Allegheny County med. socs., Am. Acad. Opthalmology and Otolaryngology, A.C.S. Home: 138 Riding Trail Ln Pittsburgh PA 15215 Office: 1501 Locust St Pittsburgh PA 15219

KAMERMAYER, ARTHUR STUART, sch. psychologist; b. N.Y.C., June 2, 1929; s. Arthur Anthony and Elizabeth Ann (Keresztury) K.; B.A., St. John's U., 1951; B.S., Columbia U., 1957, M.A., 1959, Profl. Diploma, 1963; m. Patricia Diane Flader, Aug. 24, 1957; children—Douglas Arthur, Kristin Ann. Mgr., Blackstone Legal Products Co., N.Y.C., 1952-58; tchr. emotionally disturbed Pub. Sch. 168, N.Y.C., 1958-60; coordinator psychol. services Bloomfield (N.J.) Pub. Schs., 1960—; lectr. psychology Tchrs. Coll., Columbia U., also cons. Inst. of Field Studies, also supr. Reading Clinic; cons. North Essex Child Guidance Clinic; chmn. Inter-Agy. Council of Bloomfield, 1965; vice-chmn. Bloomfield Municipal Youth Guidance Council, 1967-73. Certified as sch. psychologist, reading specialist, tchr. emotionally disturbed, N.Y. Mem. Am., N.J. psychol. assns., Internat. Reading Assn., N.J. Assn. Sch. Psychologists, Nat., N.J. edn. assns., N.J. Reading Tchrs. Assn., Essex County (N.J.) Sch. Psychologists Assn., (chmn., 1972-74), Kappa Delta Pi. Unitarian. Home: 91 Ernst Ave Bloomfield NJ 07003

KAMIKAWA, ALDEN TANEMITSU, trade assn. exec.; b. Fresno, Calif., Dec. 18, 1940; s. Thomas Taneichi and Miyeko Lorene (Kawamoto) K.; B.A., San Francisco State U., 1963, M.S., 1968. Vol., Peace Corps, Colombia, South America, 1963-65; counselor U.S. War on Poverty Program, Job Corps, 1965-66; vocat. rehab. counselor Calif. Dept. Rehab., San Jose, 1968-71; asso. dir. manpower devel. and tng. dept. Nat. Assn. Home Builders, Washington, 1971—. Mem. Am. Rehab. Counseling Assn., Nat. Assn. Trade and Indsl. Edn., Am. Vocat. Assn., Am. Personnel and Guidance Assn. Democrat. Asso. producer film: Build a Better Life, 1977. Home: 1721 P St NW Washington DC 20036 Office: National Association of Home Builders 15th and M Sts NW Washington DC 20005

KAMIL, BONNIE BETH, clin. psychologist; b. Bronx, N.Y., Sept. 3, 1946; d. Max and Rose (Globerman) K.; student City U. N.Y., 1964-69; Ph.D., San Francisco State Coll., 1967; Student analyst Columbia-Presbyterian Coll. Physicians and Surgeons, N.Y.C., 1972-75; adminstr., research asso. Riverdale Children's Assn., N.Y.C., 1975-77; asst. prof. Marymount Coll., Tarrytown, N.Y., 1978—; pvt. practice clin. psychology, 1972—; cons. Bur. Child Guidance, N.Y.C. Bd. Edn. NIMH grantee, 1970-71. Mem. Am. Psychol. Assn. Jewish. Office: 750 Kappock Bronx NY 10463

KAMIN, ARTHUR ZAVEL, publishing exec.; b. South River, N.J., Nov. 25, 1930; s. Isadore and Elsie (Kaminsky) K.; B.A., Rutgers U., 1954; m. Virginia Palew, Jan. 30, 1955; children—Blair, Brooke. Reporter, The Daily Register, Red Bank, N.J., 1956-61, copy editor, 1961-62, asso. editor, 1962-65, editor, 1965—, pres., 1971—; mem. adv. bd. Colonial First Nat. Bank; lectr. journalism Monmouth Coll. Mem. Monmouth County Transp. Coordinating Com.; mem. Monmouth County Criminal Justice Coordinating Council; former pres. N.J. AP; past chmn. Rutgers Alumni Fund Council; bd. overseers Rutgers U. Found.; past mem. N.J. Energy Crisis Study Commn.; mem. pres.'s adv. council Brookdale Coll., Monmouth Coll. Bd. dirs. Monmouth Arts Found., Children's Psychiat. Center; mem. adv. bd. Fair Haven Community Appeal; bd. dirs. Nat. Conf. Christians and Jews, Multiple Sclerosis Soc., Family and Children's Service; vice chmn. bd. trustees Rutgers U.; past pres. Monmouth County Community Services Council; active Monmouth County United Way. Served to lt. AUS, 1954-56; capt. Res. ret. Mem. Rutgers Alumni Assn., Am. Soc. Newspaper Editors, Am. Newspaper Publishers Assn., N.J. Press Assn. (dir.). Jewish (past trustee congregation). Club: Monmouth County Rutgers (past pres.). Home: 15 Grange Walk Fair Haven NJ 07701 Office: 1 Register Plaza Shrewsbury NJ 07701

KAMINSKY, JACK ALLAN, photographer, printmaker; b. New Brunswick, N.J., Sept. 8, 1949; s. Samuel and Renee Leah (Benjamin) K.; B.S. cum laude, Bklyn. Coll., 1972, M.F.A., 1975. Tchr. photography Midwood Adolescent Project, Bklyn., 1973-76; dir. dept. graphics Bklyn. Museum Art Sch., 1973—; photographer Aunt Len's Doll and Toy Mus., N.Y.C., 1974—; one-man shows: Aunt Len's Doll and Toy Mus., 1975, Third Eye Photography Gallery, 1975, Jamaica Bay Wildlife Refuge, Jamaica, N.Y., 1974; group shows: Third Eye Photography Gallery, 1976, Greenwich House, N.Y.C., 1977, Katonah (N.Y.) Gallery, 1977, Washington Sq. Art Gallery, N.Y.C., 1978, Heckscher Mus., Huntington, N.Y., 1978, Bank St. Coll., N.Y.C., 1978, Edna Carlsten Gallery, Stevens Point, Wis., 1978, Hansen Galleries, N.Y.C., 1978, Salmagundi Club, N.Y.C., 1979, others; commd. work for City Mass Transit Authority for Eastern Pkwy. Subway Sta., Bklyn., 1974; Am. the Beautiful Fund artist in residence Palisades Interstate Park, summer 1977. Club: Salmagundi (scholarship mem.). (N.Y.C.). Home: 855 E 19th St Brooklyn NY 11230 Office: 188 Eastern Pkwy Brooklyn NY 11238

KAMM, LAURENCE RICHARD, TV dir.; b. Long Branch, N.J., Oct. 10, 1939; s. Herbert and Phyllis (Silberblatt) K.; B.S., Northwestern U., 1961; m. Claire Louise Cadieux, Oct. 5, 1977. Prodn. asst. ABC-TV, N.Y.C., 1962-64; asso. dir. ABC Sports, N.Y.C., 1964-70, dir., 1970—. Recipient Emmy award for coverage 1976 Winter Olympics, 1976. Mem. Dirs. Guild Am., Nat. Acad. TV Arts and Scis., Hollywood Acad. TV Arts and Scis. Home: 420 E 51st St New York City NY 10022 Office: 1330 6th Ave New York City NY 10019

KAMM, LEWIS ROBERT, French scholar, educator; b. N.Y.C., Nov. 14, 1944; s. Herbert and Phyllis Irene (Silberblatt) K.; B.A., Rutgers, 1966; A.M., Brown U., 1967, Ph.D. (Woodrow Wilson dissertation fellow), 1971; m. Ann Marie Larrivee, May 12, 1974; children—Jeffrey, Thomas. Teaching asst. French lang. and lit. Brown U., Providence, R.I., 1968-69, 70-71; asst. prof. French lang. and lit., Southeastern Mass. U., N. Dartmouth, 1971-76, asso. prof., 1976—, pres. faculty senate, 1976—; mem. program documentation research studies on Emile Zola and naturalism, U. Toronto (Ont., Can.); mem. parents advisory council U.S. Title I Reading Program, Tiverton, R.I., R.I. Assn. Learning Disabled Children. Bd. dirs. Southeastern Mass. U. Found., 1976—. Mem. Modern Lang. Assn. Am., NE Modern Lang. Assn., Am. Assn. Tchrs. French, Council Devel. French in New Eng. Author: The Object in Zola's Rougon-Macquart, 1978; contbr. articles in field to lit. jours. Home: 38 Church St Tiverton RI 02878 Office: Southeastern Mass Univ North Dartmouth MA 02747

KAMP, GERALD WESLEY, rabbi; b. Syracuse, N.Y., Nov. 13, 1948; s. Herbert F. and Claudine Ruth (Georgia) K.; B.A., Ithaca Coll., 1970; postgrad. Cornell U., 1971-72. Salesman, Mayer's of Ithaca (N.Y.), 1967-71; corp. sec. Tobacconalia, Inc., 1971-72; corp. sec., chief buyer Hill Bookstall, Inc., Syracuse, 1972-78; asst. dir., counselor Mainline Crisis Center, Ithaca, 1971-72; elected rabbi, 1974; rabbi Kehilah Rodeph Shalom, Syracuse, 1974-78; sec.-treas. House of Ga. Since 1736, Inc., Fayetteville, N.Y., 1978—; dir. Univ. Hill Corp., Syracuse, 1974-75. Mem. Retail Tobacco Dealers Assn., Tobacco Mchts. Assn., Nat. Assn. Coll. Stores, Pipe and Tobacco Council, Gift and Decorative Accessories Assn., Nat., N.Y. Syracuse chambers commerce. Republican. Clubs: Odd Fellows, Masons. Author: Tzion and Zion; Modern Rabbinic Counseling and Victimless Crime. Office: PO Box 147 Syracuse NY 13210

KAMP, THEO, advt. agy. exec.; b. Amsterdam, Netherlands, Mar. 18, 1936; s. Theo and Margarete (Klaussner) K.; student Fordham U. and Columbia U., 1954-58; m. Adele Edelman, Dec. 17, 1967; children—Ariane Rose, Teddy Alex. Account supr., creative dir. Will Grant Advt., N.Y.C., 1961-65; mktg. and advt. cons., 1965-68; pres. Kamp, Paiste, Hammer & Beaudrot, Inc., Elmsford, N.Y., 1968—; dir. Action Advt., Inc., Hartsdale, N.Y., Westchester Prodn. Group, Hartsdale. Pres. Leukemia Soc. Am., Scarsdale, N.Y. Served with AUS, 1959-61. Mem. Dirs. Guild Am., Writers Guild Am., Bank Mktg. Assn., Pub. Relations Soc. Am., Sales and Mktg. Execs. Internat., Am. Advt. Fedn., League Advt. Agys. Club: Chappaqua Town. Office: 2 Westchester Plaza Cross Westchester Executive Park Elmsford NY 10523

KANDALAFT, SOUHEIL IBRAHIM, surgeon; b. Damascus, Syria, Nov. 16, 1932; s. Ibrahim Elian and Alice Habib (Mouacdieh) K.; came to U.S., 1960, naturalized, 1971; B.S., Am. Damascus Coll., 1952; M.D., Damascus U., 1958; m. Ruth Ann Quick, May 28, 1966; children—Fareed Alexander, Charles Firaz. Intern Mercy Hosp., Canton, Ohio, 1960-61; resident in gen. surgery St. Clare's Hosp., N.Y.C., 1962-66, spl. fellow in exptl. surgery, 1966-68; practice medicine specializing in surgery, N.Y.C., 1969—; asso. attending surgery St. Joseph's Hosp., Yonkers, N.Y., St. Clare's Hosp., N.Y.C.; asst. attending Cabrini Health Care Center, N.Y.C.; asst. clin. prof. surgery N.Y. Med. Coll. Served to 1st lt. M.C., Syrian Army, 1958-60. Diplomate Am. Bd. Surgery. Fellow A.C.S.; mem. AMA, N.Y. State (Gold medal 1969), Bronx County (N.Y.) med. socs., Soc. Surgery Alimentary Tract, Collegium Internationale Chirurgiae Digestivae. Mem. Syrian Orthodox Ch. Contbr. articles to profl. publs. Home: 29 Topland Rd Hartsdale NY 10530 Office: 408 W 57th St New York City NY 10019

KANDRAVY, JOHN, lawyer; b. Passaic, N.J., May 9, 1935; s. Frank and Anna (Chan) K.; B.A., Wesleyan U., Middletown, Conn., 1957; J.D., Columbia, 1960; m. Alice Elizabeth Sullivan, Feb. 17, 1962; children—Elizabeth Ann, Katherine Ann. Admitted to N.J. Bar, 1960; asso. firm Shanley & Fisher, Newark, 1961-67, partner, 1968—; admitted to D.C. bar, 1969, U.S. Supreme Ct. bar, 1973; sec. Linden Chems. and Plastics Inc., 1972—; dir. City Nat. Bank N.J., 1973—. Mem. Gov's Mgmt. Commn. N.J., 1970; chmn. bd. trustees Central Bergen Community Mental Health Center, Area 46, N.J., 1970-73; mem. Wesleyan Alumni Council, 1965—, chmn. continuing edn. com., 1975-76, mem. exec. com., 1977—; sec. N.J. Research Found. Mental Hygiene, 1966—, trustee, 1967—; ruling elder W. Side Presbyn. Ch., Ridgewood, N.J., 1973—, mem. session, 1973-75, chmn. exec. com., 1975; trustee Palisades Counseling Center, Rutherford, 1968—, Forum Sch. Found., 1978—; mem. Ridgewood (N.J.) Zoning Bd. Adjustment, 1976—. Served with U.S. Army, 1960-61. Edward John Noble Found. leadership grantee, 1957-60. Mem. Am., N.J., Essex County, D.C. bar assns. Republican. Presbyterian. Clubs: Essex (Newark); Ridgewood (N.J.); Indian Trail (Franklin Lakes, N.J.). Home: 56 Monte Vista Ave Ridgewood NJ 07450 Office: 550 Broad St Newark NJ 07102

KANE, DAVID SCHILLING, lawyer; b. Far Rockway, N.Y., Jan. 20, 1907; s. David and Bertha Dorothy (Schilling) K.; student N.Y. U., 1924-26, LL.B., 1930; m. Mildred Irene Thompson, Sept. 23, 1931; children—David H., T. Sheila, Kathleen. Admitted to N.Y. bar, 1931; asso. Delafield, Dunn & Anderson, N.Y.C., 1931-34; partner Duell & Kane, 1934-52; sr. partner Kane, Dalsimer, Kane, Sullivan & Kurucz, and predecessor firms, 1952—; pres. Camloc Fastener Corp., 1942-44; dir. C.F. Mueller Co. Lectr. grad. div. N.Y. U. Sch. Law, 1946-59, adj. asso. prof. law, 1960-64, adj. prof., 1964—. Mem. sch. bd., Port Washington, N.Y., 1948-50; mem. bd. appeals, Village Sands Point, N.Y., 1948-63, trustee, 1963-65; mayor, 1965-69. Bd. dirs. Vanderbilt Assos. of N.Y. U. Law Sch., 1968—; trustee N.Y. U. Law Center Found., 1967—, C.F. Mueller Scholarship Found. Recipient Certificate Meritorious Service, 1950. Mem. Nat. Council Patent Law Assn. (chmn. 1963-64), Am. (pres. 1962-63), N.Y. (pres. 1958-59) patent law assns., Am., N.Y. State, N.Y.C. bar assns., N.Y. County Lawyers Assn., Am. Judicature Soc., Fed. Bar Council, Nat. Lawyers Club, Phi Delta Phi. Mason. Clubs: Union League, Pinnacle, N.Y. University (founder mem.) (N.Y.C.); Naples Yacht; Royal Poinciana Golf. Contbg. author Annual Survey Am. Law, 1945—. Home: Millertown Rd Bedford NY 10506 also 140 2d Ave N Naples FL 33940 Office: 420 Lexington Ave New York City NY 10017

KANE, EDWARD RYNEX, chem. co. exec.; b. Schenectady, Sept. 13, 1918; s. Edward Marion and Elva (Rynex) K.; B.S. in Chemistry, Union Coll., 1940; Ph.D. in Phys. Chemistry, Mass. Inst. Tech., 1943; m. Doris Norma Peterson, Apr. 3, 1948; children—Christine, Susan. Instr. chemistry Mass. Inst. Tech., 1942-43; with E.I. duPont de Nemours & Co., Inc., Wilmington, Del., 1943—, gen. mgr. indls. and biochems. dept., 1967-69, v.p., mem. exec. com., dir., 1969-73, pres., vice chmn. exec. com., mem. fin. com., dir., 1973—; dir. J.P. Morgan & Co., Morgan Guaranty Trust Co. Past chmn. Nat. Adv. Council on Minorities in Engring.; trustee Com. for Econ. Devel., Nat. Fund for Minority Engring. Students; bd. dirs. Council Fin. Aid to Edn.; mem. corp. Mass. Inst. Tech. Mem. Nat. Acad. Engring., Am. Chem. Soc., Soc. Chem. Industry (chmn. Am. sect. 1973-74), Mfg. Chemists Assn. (chmn. bd. 1975), Am. Inst. Chem. Engrs., Sigma Xi. Episcopalian. Clubs: DuPont Country, Wilmington Country (Wilmington); Greenville (Del.) Country; Links (N.Y.C.). Home: Greenville DE 19807 Office: duPont Bldg Wilmington DE 19898

KANE, GEORGE EUGENE, educator; b. York, Pa., Sept. 7, 1925; s. Paul Edward and Grace Elizabeth (Shenberger) K.; B.S., Pa. State U., 1948; M.S., Lehigh U., 1954; m. Regina Marea Harman, July 3, 1947; children—George E., Eric D., Patrick H., Sean E. Indsl. engr. Western Electric Co., Allentown, Pa., 1948-50; instr., prof. Lehigh U., Bethlehem, Pa., 1950—; cons. U.S. Army, 1955-76, Sperry-New Holland, 1965—. Served with USN, 1942-46, to lt., 1952-53. Mem. ASME, Am. Soc. Engring. Edn., Am. Inst. Indsl. Engrs., Soc. Mfg. Engrs., Am. Soc. Indsl. Engrs., Sigma Xi, Alpha Pi Mu. Patentee; contbr. articles in field to profl. jours. Home: 3586 Browning Ln Bethlehem PA 18017 Office: Indsl Engring Dept Lehigh Univ Bethlehem PA 18015

KANE, JAMES KARL, audiologist; b. Canonsburg, Pa., Dec. 2, 1942; s. Charles and Julia Jane (Milavec) Komovic; B.S., California (Pa.) State Coll., 1970; M.S., U. Pitts., 1973, Ph.D., 1976; m. Maxine Karla Pallas, Aug. 14, 1976. Audiology fellow VA Hosp., Pitts., 1972-76; research fellow bioacoustics lab. dept. otolaryngology Eye & Ear Hosp., Pits., 1976-77; clin. research audiologist Keystone Audiological Assocs., Inc., Johnstown, Pa., 1977—, pres., 1977—; cons. Conemaugh Valley Meml. Hosp., Johnstown, 1978—. Served with USAF, 1961-65. Mem. Am. Speech and Hearing Assn, Acoustical Soc. Am., Phi Sigma Pi, Sigma Alpha Eta. Contbr. Articles in field to sci. jours. Home: 307 N Phaney St Ebensburg PA 15931 Office: 1111 Franklin St Suite 010 Johnstown PA 15905

KANE, JAY BRASSLER, banker; b. Bklyn., June 4, 1931; s. Arthur Ferris and Margaret (Brassler) K.; grad. Poly. Prep. Sch., 1949; A.B.; Columbia, 1953, postgrad. Sch. Bus., 1954; M.B.A., N.Y. U., 1961; m. Marian Albertson, Oct. 15, 1960; children—Lisa Ferris, James Brassler. With Met. Life Ins. Co,, N.Y.C., 1954-55; with Bankers Trust Co., N.Y.C., 1955—, asst. v.p., 1965-68, v.p., 1968—, also mgr. corporate pension funds, mktg. dir. trust services. Speaker Am. Bankers Assn. Mem. N.Y. Soc. Security Analysts, Financial Analysts Fedn., Am. Pension Conf. Clubs: Riverside (Conn.) Yacht. Contbr. articles to profl. jours. Home: Hilton Heath Cos Cob CT 06807 Office: 280 Park Ave New York City NY 10017

KANE, JOHN JOSEPH, city ofcl.; b. Phila., Oct. 12, 1928; s. John James and Agnes Catherine (Fleischut) K.; B.S., LaSalle Coll., 1951; postgrad. (Inst. fellow) Fels Inst. U. Pa., 1962-66; certificate in advanced mgmt. U. Chgo., 1964; certificate in water works mgmt. (Am. Water Works Assn. fellow) U. Mich., 1969; certificate of urban exec. program (Inst. fellow) Mass. Inst. Tech., 1973; certificate Fed. Exec. Inst., 1977; m. Ruth Grace Sealy, June 26, 1955. Chief investigator customer service Stetson Hat Co., Phila., 1951-55; chemist, pres. Ind. Union, Franklin Research, Phila., 1956-61; adminstrv. planner City of Phila., 1962-63; municipal mgr., Elizabethtown, Pa., 1964-65, Phoenixville, Pa., 1966-70, Somerset, Pa., 1971—; sec. Somerset Area Joint Tax Collection Com., Somerset Borough Municipal Authority; mem. Somerset County, So. Alleghenies regional manpower coms.; coordinator, project dir. Hwy. Safety and Criminal Justice projects; asst. dir. civil preparedness. Mem. Somerset Vol. Fire Dept. Recipient awards Elizabethtown C. of C., 1965, Kiwanis, 1970, Phoenixville C. of C., 1971, V.F.W., 1971. Mem. Pa. State Assn. Boroughs (exec. com., dir.), Pa. Housing, Improvement and Code Assn. (dir.), Somerset County Boroughs Assn. (sec., chmn. legis. action), Pub. Adminstrn. Acad., Internat. City Mgmt. Assn., Am. Water Works Assn. (v.p. SWPa.), Water Pollution Control Assn., Am. Soc. Planning Ofcls., Am. Soc. Pub. Adminstrn., Am. Soc. Hwy. Engrs., Am. Mgmt. Assn., Pa. Municipal Mgrs. Assn., Pa. Local Govt. Secs. Assn. Republican. Roman Catholic. Clubs: Rotary (award 1971), K.C. Home: 603 N Edgewood Ave Somerset PA 15501 Office: 340 W Union St Somerset PA 15501

KANE, JOHN MARTIN, clothing co. exec.; b. Orange, N.J., Dec. 13, 1947; s. Martin Francis and Agnes Elizabeth (Kane) K.; B.S., Villanova U., 1969; m. Mary Elizabeth Kempton, Apr. 17, 1968; 1 son, John. Accounting supr. Continental Can Co., Teterboro, N.J., 1969-71; asst. controller Silna Corp., Moonachie, N.J., 1971-75; asst. controller Lord Jeff Knitting Co., Inc., Norwood, N.J., 1975-78, ops. mgr., 1978—. Pres., Montvale Athletic League, 1978—. Mem. Nat. Assn. Accountants, Am. Arbitration Assn. Home: 49 Rutherford Pl Montvale NJ 07645 Office: 10 Maple St Norwood NJ 07648

KANE, JOHN THOMAS, san. engr.; b. York, Pa., Dec. 25, 1928; s. Paul Edward and Grace Elizabeth (Shenberger) K.; B.S., Pa. State U., 1952; m. Edna M. Grissinger, Sept. 11, 1948; children—Karen, Deborah, Joan, John Thomas. Engr., project engr., asso., partner, chief engr., now dir. Municipal Services div. Chester Engrs., Coraopolis, Pa., 1952—. Served with U.S. Army, 1946-47. Registered profl. engr., Pa. Diplomate Am. Acad. Environ. Engrs. Mem. Am. Soc. Appraisers, Pa. Water Pollution Control Assn., Water Pollution Control Fedn., Nat., Pa. socs. profl. engrs. Roman Catholic. Home: 112 Sunnyhill Dr Pittsburgh PA 15237 Office: 845 4th Ave Coraopolis PA 15108

KANE, JOSEPH HENRY, assn. exec.; b. Buffalo, June 4, 1926; s. Henry Francis and Anna Marie (Nea) K.; B.S. in Econs., Niagara U., 1950; M.S., Western Reserve U., 1954; m. Jacqueline Jacobs, June 19, 1954; children—Stephen, Michael, Karen Ann, Kevin. Dir. social services N.Y. State Tng. Sch. for Delinquents, Industry, 1954-59; sr. welfare cons. N.Y. State Dept. Social Services, Albany, 1959-63; dir. N.Y. State Tng. Sch., Goshen, 1963-66; resident dir. Graham Home for Children, 1966-71, exec. dir., 1971-77; exec. dir. Graham-Windham Services to Families and Children, N.Y.C., 1977—; adj. faculty U. Buffalo, 1957-58, Russell Sage Coll., 1961-63; cons. in field. Mem. Union Free Sch. Dist. #10 Bd., 1968—, dist. clerk, 1972—. Served in U.S. Army 1945-46. Mem. Nat. Assn. Social Workers, Acad. Certified Social Workers, N.Y. State Assn. Human Services; certified social worker, N.Y. State. Democrat. Roman Catholic. Clubs: Rotary (Hastings, Dobbs Ferry, Ardsley) (chmn. scholarship com. 1975-76). Author: An Institutional Program for the Seriously Disturbed Delinquent, 1966; Social Walfare Institutions Serving Delinquent Children, 1964. Home: 5 Jordon Rd Hastings on Hudson NY 10706 Office: One Park Ave New York City NY 10016

KANE, MARGARET BRASSLER, sculptor; b. East Orange, N.J., May 25, 1909; d. Hans and Mathilde (Trumpler) Brassler; student Packer Collegiate Inst., 1920-26, Syracuse U., 1927, Art Students League, 1927-29, N.Y. Coll. Music, 1928-29, John Hovannes Studio, 1932-34; Ph.D. (hon.), Colo. State Christian Coll., 1973; m. Arthur Ferris Kane, June 11, 1930; children—Jay Brassler, Gregory Ferris. Work has appeared at Jacques Seligmann Gallery, N.Y., Whitney Ann. Exhbns., all Sculptors Guild Mus. and Outdoor Shows, Nat. Sculpture Soc. Ann. Bas-Relief Exhbn., 1938, Whitney Mus. Sculpture Festival, 1940, Bklyn. Mus. Sculptors Guild, 1938, Bklyn. Soc. Artists, 1942, Lawrence (Mass.) Art Mus., 1938, N.Y. World's Fair, 1939, Sculptors Guild World's Fair Exhbn., 1940, Robinson Gallery, N.Y., 1939, Traveling Museums and Instns., 1938, Lyman Allyn Mus., 1939, Met. Mus., Internat. Exhbns., 1940, 1949, Roosevelt Field Art Center, N.Y.C., 1957, Phila. Mus., N.Y. Archtl. League, Nat. Acad., Penn. Acad., Chgo. Art Inst., Am. Fedn. Arts, Riverside Mus., Montclair Mus., Grand Central Art Galleries, Lever House (N.Y.C.), 1959-79, Rye (N.Y.) Library, 1962, and exhbns. of nat. scope, 1938—; solo sculpture exhbn. Friends Greenwich (Conn.) Library, 1962; executed plaque for Burro Monument, Fairplay, Colo.; exhibited N.Y. Bank for Savs., 1968, Mattatuck Mus., Con., 1967, Lamont Gallery, N.H., 1967. Head craftsman for sculpture, arts and skills unit ARC, Halloran Gen. Hosp., N.Y., 1942-43; 2d v.p. Nat. Assn. Woman Artists, Inc., 1943-45; sec. to exec. bd. Sculptors Guild, Inc., 1942-45; chmn. exhbn. com. Sculptors Guild, Inc., 1942, 44; mem. Greenwich Arts Council, 1976. Fellow Internat. Inst. Arts and Letters (life); mem. Sculptors Guild, Nat. Assn. Women Artists, Artists Council, U.S.A., Bklyn. Soc. Artists, Greenwich Soc. Artists (council mem.), Pen and Brush, Nat. Trust Historic Preservation, Silvermine Guild Artists. Recipient Anna Hyatt Huntington award, 1942; Am. Artists Profl. League and Montclair Art Assn. awards, 1943; 1st Henry O. Avery Prize, 1944; Sculpture prize Bklyn. Soc. Artists, Bklyn. Mus., 1946, John Rogers award, 1951; Lawrence Hyder Prize, 1952, 54; David H. Zell Meml. award, 1954, 63, hon. mention U.S. Maritime Commn., 1941 and A.C.A. Gallery Competition, 1944, Nat. Assn. Med. of honor for sculpture, 1951, Nat. Assn. Women Artists, Nat. Acad. Galleries, N.Y.; prize for carved sculpture, 1955, animal sculpture, 1956, 1st award for sculpture Greenwich Art Soc., 1958, 60. ann. New Eng. Exhbns., Silvermine, Conn. Jury mem. Bklyn. Mus., 1948, Am. Machine & Foundry Co., 1957; com. mem. An American Group, Inc. Contbr. articles to magazine. Reprodns. in Contemporary Stone Sculpture, 1970, Woodcarving Reproductions, 1972, Greenwich Time Publs., 1950-77. Home and studio: 30 Strickland Rd Cos Cob CT 06807

KANE, MARGARET C., nurse, materials mgr.; b. Bklyn., Oct. 4, 1938; d. James Thomas and Josephine Agnes (Plunkett) Eldridge; R.N., Lenox Hill Hosp., 1959; student St. Johns U., 1960-62, Upper Div. Coll., 1977—; m. John Charles Kane, Aug. 7, 1965; children—John M., Brian J., Darren J. Nurse operating rm. Lenox Hill Hosp., N.Y.C., 1959-65; nurse operation rm., emergency rm. Little Falls Hosp., Little Falls, N.Y., 1965-71, Mohawk Valley Gen. Hosp., Ilion, N.Y., 1971—, central supply supv., 1971-74, materials mgr., 1974—; vice-chmn. Central N.Y. Hosp. Group Purchasing Assn., 1978—. Advisory staff Explorer Scouts, Boy Scouts of Am., Herkimer, N.Y., 1977—; vol. for Cub Scouts, Ilion, N.Y., 1977—; mem. PTO Annumciation Sch., Illion; mem. Ilion Council of Catholic Women. Registered nurse, N.Y. Mem. Assn. of Operating Rm. Nurses, Am. Hosp. Assn., Assn. of Materials Mgrs. Roman Catholic. Contbr. weekly article Herkimer Telegram newspaper, 1978—. Home: 25 Frederick St Ilion NY 13357 Office: 295 W Main St Ilion NY 13357

KANE, NOLAN PAUL, surgeon; b. Regina, Can., Nov. 18, 1943; s. Lewis Allin and Patricia Vivian (Kofman) K.; M.D., U. Toronto (Ont., Can.), 1967; m. Janese Oliver, July 11, 1975; 1 dau., Carolyn Lee. Intern, Mt. Sinai Hosp., Toronto, 1968; resident Mt. Zion Hosp., San Francisco, 1969-70, U. Toronto Hosps., 1970-72; chief resident otolaryngology Toronto Gen. Hosp., 1972; practice medicine specializing in otolaryngolocial surgery, Toronto, 1972—; chief dept. Toronto Northwestern Gen. Hosp., Toronto Branson Hosp.; cons. Canadian ASE Industries, Toronto, 1975—, U. Toronto Athletic Assn.; dir. Gibson Girl Placement, Toronto, Nolise Mgmt. Corp., Toronto. Fellow Royal Coll. Surgeons Can., Am. Coll. Otolaryngologists; mem. Royal Soc. Medicine (Brit.), Can., Ont. med. assns., Am. Med. Tennis Assn., Acad. Medicine of Toronto, Pan-Am. Bronchoesophagolgical Assn. (Canadian rep.). Jewish. Clubs: Toronto Lawn Tennis, Winston Churchill Tennis, Victoria Tennis, Forest Hill Platform Tennis. Contbr. numerous articles to profl. jours.; mem. Canadian Maccabian Games Team, 1965, Canadian Nat. Basketball Team, 1966; Canadian platform tennis champion, 1977. Home: 209 Forest Hill Rd Toronto ON M5P 2N3 Canada Office: 304 St Clair Ave W Toronto ON Canada

KANE, ROBERT FRANCIS, pub. relations co. exec.; b. Topeka, Aug. 15, 1916; s. Robert Bernard and Viola Ethel (Morrison) K.; B.S., Kans. State U., 1938; m. Aileen Mitchell, Sept. 26, 1943; children—Philip D., Cameron M. Reporter, writer Radio Guide Mag., Chgo., 1938-39; reporter Life Mag., N.Y.C., 1939-41; reporter, writer Parade Mag., 1941-48; dir. pub. relations F.H. McGraw & Co., N.Y.C., 1948-60; owner Robert Francis Kane Assos., N.Y.C., 1960—. Pres., dir. Nat. Time Research Inst., N.Y.C., 1956-67. Served with USAAF, 1942-45. Mem. Aviation Writers Assn., Nat. Football Found., Kans. State Alumni Assn. (pres. 1958—), Indsl. Publicity Assn. (sec.-treas. 1959), Phi Kappa. Roman Catholic. Clubs: N.Y. Touchdown (N.Y.C.); Nat. Press (Washington). Home: 82 Barnyard Ln Roslyn Heights NY 11577 Office: 12 E 41st St New York City NY 10017

KANE, ROBERT PATRICK, atty. gen. Pa.; b. York, Pa., July 10, 1930; s. Paul Edwin and Grace Elizabeth (Shenberger) K.; B.A., Dickinson Coll., 1952, LL.B., 1955; m. Marie Celine Eck, Jan. 24, 1953; children—Timothy Eck, Kathleen Eck, Dennis Eck. Corporate taxing officer Pa. Dept. Revenue, 1956-57, asst. dir. bur. county collections, 1957-58, acting dir. bur., 1958-59; adminstrv. asst. to Congressman N. Craley, Jr., Washington, 1965-66; dep. chmn. Pa. Democratic State Com., 1959-64; sec. revenue Commonwealth of Pa., 1971-74; atty. gen. Pa., 1975—; admitted to Pa. bar, 1959; practiced in York, 1959—. Active gubernatorial campaigns. Home: 182 Highland Rd York PA 17403 Office: Office of Attorney General Harrisburg PA 17127*

KANE, SARAH TAYLOR, former ednl. adminstr.; b. Richmond, Va., Sept. 22, 1915; d. William Benjamin and Harriett Rebecca (Brooks) Taylor; B.S., Va. Union U., 1936; M.A., N.Y.U., 1956; m. Aaron C. Kane, Apr. 8, 1939; 1 son, Aaron. Elementary sch. tchr., Va., 1936-38; tchr. Bel Air High Sch., Harford County, Md., 1938-46; tchr. Pomonkey High Sch., Charles County, Md., 1946-52, vice-prin./tchr., 1952-57, vice-prin., 1957-66; vice-prin. Milton M. Somers Middle Sch., Charles County, 1966-69, 71-72, prin., 1972-77, ret., 1977; vice-prin., organizer Gen. Smallwood Middle Sch., Charles County, 1969-71; tchr. illiterates; lectr. Literacy Council; distbr. Shaklee Corp., 1974-77, supr., 1977—. Vice chmn. adminstrv. bd. Met. U. Methodist Ch. Mem. Charles County Edn. Assn., Md. State Tchr. Assn. (life), NEA, Nat., Md. assns. secondary sch. prins., League of Women Voters, Delta Pi Omega, Alpha Kappa Alpha, Delta Kappa Gamma. Clubs: Eastern Star, Dau. of Elks, Glymont Homemakers. Republican. Methodist. Home and Office: Route 1 Box 88 Indian Head MD 20640

KANE, STEVEN IRWIN, mech. engr.; b. Boston, Aug. 24, 1941; s. Samuel and Vivian (Rubin) K.; B.S. in Aero. Engring., Boston U., 1963, M.S., 1971; m. Susan May Miller, Mar. 3, 1968; children—Russell Lloyd, Allison Laura. Engr. instrumentation lab. Mass. Inst. Tech., Cambridge, 1963-68; sr. engr. Raytheon Co., Bedford, Mass., 1968-72, 74—; sr. engr. Northrop Corp., Norwood, Mass., 1972-73, Atkins & Merrill Inc., Ashland, Mass., 1973-74. Mem. Am. Inst. Aeros. and Astronautics. Mem. West End House Alumni Assn. Home: 20 Juniper Ln Newton Centre MA 02159 Office: Hartwell Rd Bedford MA 01730

KANE, SYDNEY H., pharm. co. exec.; b. Phila., Oct. 2, 1916; s. Maxwell and Reba (Heller) K.; M.D., Temple U., 1940; m. Emma Benjamin, July 25, 1958; 1 son, David. Intern, Frankford Hosp., Phila., 1940-41; practice medicine specializing in pediatrics, 1941-68; mem. hon. staff Frankford Hosp.; mem. cons. staff Northeastern Hosp.; with Ciba Geigy Corp., Summit, N.Y., 1968—, sr. dir. methodology and long term trials, 1977—. Served with M.C., U.S. Army, 1940-43. Fellow Am. Pub. Health Assn.; mem. Acad. Medicine of N.J., AAAS, AMA, Am. Statis. Assn., Assn. for Computing Machinery, Assn. Health Records, Assn. Mil. Surgeons, Biometric Soc., Coll. Physicians Phila., Drug Info. Assn., N.J., Summit, Union County med. socs., Phila. Pediatric Soc., Soc. Computer Medicine, Soc. Epidemiologic Research. Contbr. articles to profl. jours. Home: 12 Stockade Rd Warren NJ 07060 Office: Ciba Geigy Corp 556 Morris Ave Summit NJ 07901

KANE, THOMAS JOSEPH, social worker; b. Portland, Maine, June 19, 1934; s. Martin J. and Delia (Curran) K.; A.B., U. Prince Edward Island, Can., 1955; M. Social Sci., Boston Coll., 1960, M.S.W., 1961; D.S.W., Cath U. Am., 1972; m. Marlene D. Sylvester, Sept. 3, 1960; children—Rosemary, Thomas Joseph, Karen, Joseph. Caseworker Cath. Family Service, Hartford, Conn., 1961-63; asst. dir. Child and Family Service, Lewiston, Maine, 1963-66, exec. dir., 1966-70; chief Commn. Mental Health Service, State Bur. Mental Health, 1970-74; exec. dir. York County (Maine) Counseling Services, 1974—. Mem. Maine Gov.'s Advisory Com. Mental Health, 1977—, also mem. Com. on Revision of Juvenile Laws, 1976—; sec. Maine Council Community Mental Health Centers, 1977—. Recipient Distinguished Service award Gov.'s Adv. Com. on Mental Health, 1967. Mem. Nat. Conf. State Mental Health Social Workers (exec. com. 1974-75), Nat. Assn. Social Workers, Assn. Mental Health Adminstrs., Nat. Conf. Social Workers in Mental Health Programs (pres.-elect 1976-78). Roman Catholic (exec. com. diocesan convocation 1977—). K.C. Home: 39 Oceanside Dr Saco ME 04240 Office: York County Counseling Services 204 Main St Saco ME 04072

KANEV, PHILLIP SYDNEY, dentist; b. Phila., Nov. 15, 1912; s. Carl and Celia (Hochbaum) K.; D.D.S., Temple U., 1934; postgrad. (fellow) Internat. Coll. Dentists, 1969; m. Rita Jacobs, June 5, 1941; children—Arthur Carl, Donald Neal. Resident intern Lincoln Hosp., N.Y.C., 1934-35, practice dentistry, Phila., 1935—. Guest lectr. Temple U. Dental Sch., Phila., 1952-67; tchr. mouth rehab. U. Pa. Grad. Hosp., Phila., 1959-67; head temporomandibular joint sect. Albert Einstein Med. Center, Phila., 1958—; cons. dentistry Kensington Hosp., Phila., 1947-60. Mem. dental com. Gov.'s Health Task Force, Harrisburg, Pa., 1972—. Bd. dirs. Brant Beach (N.J.) Assn. Served with Dental Corps, AUS, 1942-45; ETO. Fellow Am. Coll. Dentists; mem. Am. Prosthodontic Soc., Am. Equilibration Soc., Phila. Clinic Club (pres. 1964-66), Phila. Dental Study Club (pres. 1955-57). Jewish religion (dir. congregation). Club: Sportsman (pres. Phila. 1957). Contbr. articles to profl. jours. Address: 2029 Delancey Pl Philadelphia PA 19103

KANG, HANK HAENGJUNG, anesthesiologist; b. Korea, Feb. 28, 1944; s. Keng Ho and Duck Jo (Do) K.; came to U.S., 1972, naturalized, 1978; M.D., Pusan (Korea) Nat. U., 1968; m. Hee Sook Jeon, Apr. 20, 1972; children—Caroline, Jennifer, Peter. Intern, Elmhurst sect. Mt. Sinai Hosp., N.Y.C., 1972-73; resident St. Vincent's Med. Center, N.Y.C., 1973-75, N.Y. U., Med. Center, N.Y.C., 1975-76; practice medicine specializing in anesthesiology, Vestal, N.Y., 1976—; mem. staff Wilson Meml. Hosp., Johnson City, N.Y.; instr. clin. anesthesiology Coll. Medicine, Upstate Med. Center, State U. N.Y., Syracuse, 1978—. Served with Korean Navy, 1968-71. Diplomate Am. Bd. Anesthesiology. Fellow Am. Coll. Anesthesiologists; mem. AMA, Am., N.Y. State socs. anesthesiologists, N.Y. State, Broome County (N.Y.) med. socs. Home: 621 Stonehedge Dr Vestal NY 13850 Office: 300 E Main St Vestal NY 13850

KANIA, ARTHUR JOHN, lawyer; b. Moosic, Pa., Feb. 11, 1932; s. Stanley J. and Constance (Jerry) K.; B.S., U. Scranton, 1953; LL.B., Villanova U., 1956; m. Angela Volpe, Apr. 24, 1954; children—Arthur, Sandra, Kenneth, Karen, James, Linda, Steven. Admitted to Pa. bar, 1956; accountant Peat, Marwick, Mitchell & Co., Phila., 1954-55; asso. firm Davis, Marshall & Crumlish, Phila., 1956-58, partner, 1958-61; sr. partner firm Crumlish & Kania (now Kania & Garbarino), Phila., 1961—; dir. AID Inc. and subsidiaries; sec.-treas., dir. Piasecki Aircraft Corp.; sec., dir. Indsl. Operations Corp., Jordan Chem. Co., Title Ins. Corp. of Pa., Consol. Mortgage Co., Opt-Scis. Corp.; chmn. bd., dir. Center City Assos. Inc.; dir. Continental Bank, Capitol Exchange Corp. Mem. chmn.'s adv. com. dept. health adminstrn. Temple U.; mem. Phila. Com. of 70. Bd. dirs. Piasecki Found.; bd. dirs. Delaware Valley Hosp. Council; chmn., dir. Villanova U. Devel. Council; chmn. bd. trustees Hahnemann Med. Coll. Mem. Fed., Am., Pa., Phila. bar assns. Clubs: Overbrook (Bryn Mawr, Pa.); Squires Golf (Phila.); Los Angeles; Boca Raton (Fla.). Home: 21 Righters Mill Rd Gladwyne PA 19035 Office: Two Bala Cynwyd Plaza Bala Cynwyd PA 19004

KANIGOWSKI, WALTER WOLFGANG, ednl. adminstr., health assn. exec.; b. Riverside, N.J., Oct. 7, 1924; s. Leonhard B. and Olga A. (Kitzinski) K.; B.A., LaSalle Coll., 1950; postgrad. Villanova U., 1951-54. Water safety chmn. Burlington County (N.J.) chpt. ARC, 1947—, Burlington County chpt. chmn., 1970-74, bd. dirs., 1950—, instr. trainer in water safety, 1964—; mem. faculty Am. Nat. Red Cross Aquatic Schs., Medford Lakes, N.J., 1955-56; propr., dir. Kanigowski Sch. of Swimming, Riverside, 1950—; founder, dir. Delaware Valley Safety Programs Inst., 1957-78. Pres. Riverside Bd. of Edn., 1967-68, 69-71; bd. dirs. Ednl. Improvement Center of N.J., 1970-72; trustee Burlington County United Fund, 1974, 75; mem. exec. com. Burlington County chpt. ARC, 1968—. Served with USAAF, 1943-45; ETO, NATOUSA. Decorated five Air medals; recipient Pro Mundi Beneficio medal Brazilian Acad. Humanities, 1975; Vol. Life-saving Service medal ARC, 1974, Commodore Longfellow Soc. award, 1975. Mem. N.J. Sch. Bds. Assn. (mem. finance com. 1972-73, dir. 1969-73, chmn. ann. workshop 1973), Air Force Assn. Home and office: 116 Monroe St Riverside NJ 08075

KANT, EDWARD JACOB, civil engr.; b. Pitts., July 21, 1939; s. Gustave and Gertrude Jean (Isaacson) K.; B.S. in Civil Engring., Carnegie-Mellon U., 1963; postgrad. Yale, 1963-65; m. Elizabeth Gordon, Jan. 28, 1967; children—Adrien Jean, Aaron Edward. Project engr. Cahn Engrs., cons. engrs., New Haven, 1967-68, L.G. Defelice, Inc., gen. contractors, New Haven, 1968-70; chief engr. HUB Corp., cons. engrs., Colchester, Conn., 1970-71; cons. engr., owner Edward J. Kant & Assos., Inc., Colchester, 1971-78; project mgr. Loureiro Engring. Assos., Avon, Conn., 1978—. Vis. lectr. Mohegan Community Coll., Norwich, Conn., 1971-72. Pres., Montessori Children's House, Colchester, 1973-74; mem. Colchester Ednl. Bus. Adv. Council, 1973-74; chmn. Colchester Econ. Devel. Agy., 1971-76; mem. Colchester Sewer Commn., 1971—. Mem. Colchester Republican Town Com., 1971—. Registered profl. engr., Conn., Vt., R.I. Mem. Am. Soc. C.E. (treas. Conn. sect. 1966-68), Nat., Conn. socs. profl. engrs., Conn. Engrs. in Pvt. Practice, Conn. Soc. Civil Engrs., Constrn. Specifications Inst. Home: 25 Broadway Colchester CT 06415 Office: 25 Broadway PO Box 266 Colchester CT 06415

KANTER, SPENCER I., mech. engr.; b. N.Y.C., June 21, 1918; s. Frederick and Mary (Fager) K.; student schs., N.Y.C.; m. Elizabeth Harriet Ewing, July 20, 1942. Tool engr. small tool div. Pratt & Whitney Co., W. Hartford, Conn., 1941-51; chief engr., dir. research Hanson-Whitney Co., Hartford, Conn., 1951—. Sec., dir. Wethersfield Vol. Ambulance Assn.; pres. Conn. Vol. Ambulance Assn.; mem. Governor's Adv. Com. on Emergency Med. Service; treas. Wethersfield Republican Town Com.; justice of the peace. Served with U.S. Army, 1944-46. Registered profl. engr., Conn. Mem. Soc. Mfg. Engrs. (certified), Metal Cutting Tool Inst., Am. Nat. Standards Com. Lutheran. Patentee plastic tap packages. Home: 123 Charter Rd Wethersfield CT 06109 Office: 169 Bartholomew Ave Hartford CT 06101

KANTOR, MARTIN LEONARD, chemist; b. Bklyn., June 2, 1928; s. William E. and Beatrice (Millman) K.; B.S., City Coll. N.Y., 1949; postgrad. Bklyn. Poly. Inst., 1950-52, Temple U., 1953-55, U. Del., 1957-58, N.Y. U., 1962-64; m. Eileen Ratchik, Dec. 24, 1949; children—Kenneth, Eric. Chemist, Hexagon Labs., N.Y.C., 1949-52; asst. mgr. P.D. & S., Phila., 1952-54; sr. group leader Wyeth Labs., West Chester, Pa., 1954-62; chief devel. chemist Hexagon Labs., N.Y.C., 1962-64; tech. dir. Chemurgics, Inc., N.Y.C., 1964-66; asso. dir. USV Labs., Tuckahoe, N.Y., 1966—; liaison capt. Phila. Chem. Soc., 1956-62. Committeeman, Town of Mamaroneck, N.Y., 1967. Mem. Am. Chem. Soc., AAAS, City Coll. N.Y. Chemistry Alumni Assn. Patentee in field; contbr. articles in field to profl. jours. Home: 811 Rockland Ave Mamaroneck NY 10543 Office: 1 Scarsdale Rd Tuckahoe NY 10707

KANUK, LESLIE LAZAR, govt. ofcl.; b. N.Y.C., Aug. 9, 1929; d. Charles and Sylvia (Hoffman) Lazar; B.B.A., Coll. City N.Y., 1950; M.B.A., Baruch Coll., 1964; Ph.D., City U. N.Y., 1973; m. Jack Lawrence Kanuk, Apr. 8, 1951; children—Randi Ellen, Alan Robert. Advt. mgr. Radiac Co., N.Y.C., 1950-56; acting research dir. Skill Advancement, Inc., N.Y.C., 1966-68; pres. Leslie Kanuk Assos., mgmt. consultants, 1956-78; prof., dep. chmn. mktg. dept. Baruch Coll., N.Y.C., 1967-78; adj. prof. dept. command communications U.S. Army Signal Sch., Ft. Monmouth, N.J., 1967-69; adj. prof. U.S. Mcht. Marine Acad., Kings Point, N.Y., 1970-71; mem. Fed. Maritime Commn.; cons. U.S. Maritime Adminstrn., N.Y. State Dept. Edn., Revlon, Ergonomics Inc., AT&T, N.Y.C. Human Resources Adminstrn., Merc. Dept. Stores, Curtis-Wright Corp., Skill Achievement, Inc., Universal Transistor Corp., others; mem. Maritime Transp. Research Bd., Nat. Acad. Scis., 1975-78; panelist NRC, Nat. Acad. Scis. Mem. AAAS, Acad. Mgmt., Am. Mktg. Assn., Am. Assn. for Pub. Opinion Research, Beta Gamma Sigma. Author: Upgrading the Low Wage Worker: An Ergonomic Approach, 1968; Environmental and Behavioral Study of U.S. Merchant Marine Officers, 1971; Improving the Efficiency of Maritime Personnel, 1972; Consumer Behavior, 1978; also articles. Contbg. editor Breaking the Barriers of Occupational Isolation, 1966; editor The American Seafarer monographs; Occupational Hazards in the U.S. Merchant Marine, 1972; editor Management of a Seaport, 1972; mem. editorial rev. bd. Jour. Mktg. Home: 594 Floyd St Englewood Cliffs NJ 07632 Office: 1100 L St NW Washington DC 20573

KANWISHER, WALTER CHARLES, JR., corporate exec.; b. Balt., July 21, 1930; s. Walter Charles and Elizabeth (Lambrecht) K.; B.S. in Bus. Adminstrn., Johns Hopkins, 1953; m. Mary Ann Shepherd, Mar. 6, 1966; children—William Walter, Susan Ellen, Jeffrey Lambrecht. Budget dir. Community Chest Balt., 1959-62; exec. dir. Happy Hills Hosp., Balt., 1962-65; exec. sec. Alpha Delta Phi, Pleasantville, N.Y., 1965-74, also sec. bd. govs.; owner, pres. Pleasantville Bus. Service, 1974—; pres., treas. Homeport Enterprises, Inc., 1975—. Pres. Bedford Rd. Sch. PTA, 1970-72; mem. Parks and Recreation Adv. Bd., Pleasantville, 1970-71. Mem. Pleasantville adv. bd. United Way No. Westchester; trustee Village of Pleasantville, 1971-73, dep. mayor, 1972-73, mayor, 1973-77; elder, trustee Presbyterian Ch.; bd. dirs. Westchester County Community Service Council, 1977—. Served with USNR, 1953-58, comdr. Res. ret. Mem. U.S. Naval Inst., N.Y. Naval Militia, Res. Officers Assn., Naval Res. Assn., N.Y. State Council Retail Mchts., Nat. Council Retail Mchts., Florists Transworld Delivery Assn., Teleflorists Internat., Met. Retail Florists Assn., Alpha Delta Phi. Home: 301 Bedford Rd Pleasantville NY 10570 Office: 399 Manville Rd Pleasantville NY 10570

KAPETANAKOS, CHRISTOS ANASTASIOS, physicist; b. Xirocabion, Greece, Jan. 2, 1936; s. Anastasios C. and Alexandra K. (Doukas) K.; came to U.S., 1962, naturalized, 1974; B.S., Nat. U. Greece, 1960; M.S., Mass. Inst. Tech., 1964; Ph.D., U. Md., 1970; m. Ioanna Plafoutzi, June 23, 1962; children—Tassos, Yula. Research physicist Goddard Space Flight Center, Greenbelt, Md., 1965-66; research engr. sci. asso. IV, U. Tex., Austin, 1970-71; research physicist, then supervisory research physicist Naval Research Lab., Washington, D.C., 1971—. Served to 2d lt., arty., Greek Army, 1960-62. NATO fellow, 1965-69; Greek Atomic Energy Commn. fellow, 1961-62; ERDA grantee, 1975-77; Dept. Energy grantee, 1977—; recipient Naval Research Lab. awards, 1972, 73, 76, 77. Mem. Am. Physics Soc., IEEE Nuclear and Plasma Sci. Soc., Mirror League, Sigma Xi. Contbr. numerous articles to profl. jours. Inventor (with K.R. Chu) neutral beam sustained Astron reactor, (with J. Golden) intense ion beam producing reflex triode, (with Mahaffey, Sprangle and Golden) high power microwaves. Home: 6101 Overlea Rd Bethesda MD 20016 Office: Naval Research Lab Code 6761 Washington DC 20375

KAPLAN, ALAN, mech. engr.; b. N.Y.C., Jan. 14, 1941; s. Bernard E. and Josephine (Bernhardt) K.; B.S. in Textile Engring., Lowell Technol. Inst., 1962; m. Carole Soltz, June 29, 1977; children by previous marriage—Kevin, Mark; 1 stepdau., Michelle Lebovitz. Plant engring. asst. Waldrich Co., Clifton, N.J., 1962-63; engr. Vogelbach & Baumann, Cons. Engrs., Scotch Plains, N.J., 1963-65; gen. partner Arthur L. Spaet & Assos., Cons. Engrs., N.Y.C., 1965-74; v.p. engring. Limbach Systems Co., Pitts., 1975—; cons. TWA, Bklyn. Union Gas Co., Pepsi-Cola, Equitable Life Ins. Co., others. Mem. N.Y.C. Mayor's Com. on Energy Conservation, 1973-74. Registered profl. engr., Pa., N.Y., N.J., Conn., Mich., Ohio, Mass. Mem. Am. Soc. Heating, Refrigeration and Air Conditioning Engrs., Am. Arbitration Assn. Jewish. Home: 54 Carleton Dr Pittsburgh PA 15243 Office: 4 Gateway Center Pittsburgh PA 15222

KAPLAN, GARY, exec. recruiter; b. Phila., Aug. 14, 1939; s. Morris and Minnie (Leve) K.; B.A. in Polit. Sci., Pa. State U., 1961; m. Linda Ann Wilson, May 30, 1968; children—Michael Warren, Marc Jonathan, Jeffrey Russell. Tchr. biology N.E. High Sch., Phila., 1962-63; coll. employment rep. Bell Telephone Labs., Murray Hill, N.J., 1966-67; supr. recruitment and placement Univac, Blue Bell, Pa., 1967-69; pres. Electronic Systems Personnel, Phila., 1969-70; staff selection rep. Booz, Allen & Hamilton, N.Y.C., 1970-72; mgr. exec. recruitment M&T Chems., Rahway, N.J., 1972-74; dir. exec. recruitment IU Internat. Mgmt. Corp., Phila., 1974—. Served to capt. Adj. Gen. Corps, U.S. Army, 1963-66. Mem. Am. Soc. for Personnel Adminstrn., Employment Mgmt. Assn., Am. Soc. for Tng. and Devel. Home: 18 Pelham Rd Marlton NJ 08053 Office: IU Internat Mgmt Corp 1500 Walnut St Philadelphia PA 19102

KAPLAN, HAROLD IRWIN, psychiatrist, psychoanalyst; b. Bklyn., Oct. 1, 1927; s. William and Fannie (Rose) K.; M.D., N.Y. Med. Coll., 1949, certificate in psychoanalysis, 1954; m. Helen Singer, June 20, 1953 (div. 1971); children—Phillip, Peter, Jennifer. Intern, Bklyn. Jewish Hosp., 1949-50; resident in psychiatry VA Hosp., Bronx, N.Y., 1950-53; fellow in psychiatry Mt. Sinai Hosp., N.Y.C., 1952; fellow in child psychiatry Jewish Bd. Guardians, N.Y.C., 1953; practice medicine specializing in psychiatry, practice psychoanalysis, N.Y.C., 1953—; instr. in psychiatry N.Y. Med. Coll., 1956-57, asst. clin. prof., 1957-61, asso. clin. prof., 1961-65, prof. psychiatry, 1965—; attending and vis. psychiatrist Met. Hosp. and Flower Hosp., N.Y.C., 1954—; chief psychiat. edn. and tng. N.Y. Med. Coll.-Met. Hosp. Center, N.Y.C., 1960—; mem. med. bd. Met. Hosp., 1964—; specialist in psychiat. tng.; mem. Preparatory Commn. on Psychiat. Edn., NIMH-Am. Psychiat. Assn., 1974-75. NIMH grantee, 1960-72; diplomate Am. Bd. Psychiatry and Neurology (examiner 1961—asso. examiner 1965). Fellow Am. Psychiat. Assn. (chmn. com. on med. edn. 1973-75, certificate of commendation 1976), Acad. Psychoanalysis, Acad. Psychosomatic Medicine, A.C.P. (life), Soc. Med. Psychoanalysts, N.Y. Acad. Medicine (life), Am. Acad. Compensation Medicine; mem. Am. Psychosomatic Soc., Assn. Research in Nervous and Mental Diseases, Med. Soc. County and State N.Y., AMA, Am. Geriatric Soc., World Psychiat. Assn., Assn. Advancement Psychotherapy, Am. Med. Writers Assn., Can. Psychiat. Assn., N.Y. Acad. Scis. (life), AAAS (life), Pan Am. Med. Assn. (diplomate), Royal Soc. Medicine (London), Am. Public Health Assn., Assn. Dirs. Psychiat. Residency Tng. Programs, Assn. Acad. Psychiatry, Am. Group Psychotherapy Assn., Alumni Assn. Bklyn. Jewish Hosp., Alumni Assn. N.Y. Med. Coll., Psychiat. Soc. N.Y. Med. Coll. (treas.), Soc. Sex Therapists N.Y. Med. Coll., AAUP,

Alpha Omega Alpha. Co-Author: Modern Group Therapy series; Studies in Human Behavior series, 1972; co-editor: Comprehensive Group Psychotherapy (Williams and Wilkins), 1971; Comprehensive Textbook of Psychiatry, 2d edit., 1975; Modern Synopsis of Comprehensive Textbook of Psychiatry, 2d edit., 1976; The Sexual Experience (Williams and Wilkins), 1976; contbr. numerous articles to med. publs. Office: 50 E 78th St New York NY 10021

KAPLAN, JUDITH HELENE, philatelic co. exec.; b. N.Y.C., July 20, 1938; d. Abraham and Ruth (Kiffel) Letich; B.A., Hunter Coll., 1955; postgrad. New Sch. for Social Research, 1955-56; m. Warren Kaplan, Dec. 31, 1958; children—Ronald Scott, Elissa Ann. Registered rep. Herzfeld & Stern, N.Y.C., 1963; agt. New York Life Ins. Co., N.Y.C., 1964-69; registered rep. Scheinman, Hochstin & Trotta, 1969-70; v.p. Alpha Capital Corp., N.Y.C., 1970-74; pres. Tipex, Inc., N.Y.C., 1966—; v.p. Alpha Pub. Relations, N.Y.C., 1970-73; pres. Utopia Recreations Corp., 1971-73, Howard Beach Recreation Corp., 1972-73; chmn. bd. Alpha Exec. Planning Corp., 1970-72; field underwriter N.Y. Life Ins. Co., 1974-75; creator, producer N.Y. Women's History series NOW. Named Outstanding Young Citizen, Manhattan Jaycees, 1978. Mem. NOW (ins. coordinator nat. task force on taxes, cachet dir., treas. N.Y.), Nat., Manhattan women's polit. caucuses, Women Leaders Round Table, Nat. Assn. Life Underwriters. Author: Woman Suffrage, 1977. Home: 86-55 Santiago St New York NY 11423 Office: Box 338 Hollis Sta NY 11423

KAPLAN, LEONARD MARTIN (ARYEH), writer, theologian; b. Bronx, N.Y., Oct. 23, 1934; s. Samuel and Fanny (Lackman) K.; Rabbi, Rabbinical Coll., Mir, Jerusalem, 1956; B.S. summa cum laude, U. Louisville, 1961; M.S., U. Md., 1963; m. Tobie Leah Goldstein, June 13, 1961; children—Joseph M., Ronald M., Abigail F., Deborah H., L. Micah, Rochel L., Reuben Y., Shimeon Y., Haim Simhah. Ordained rabbi, 1956; physicist, head magnetohydronamics projects Nat. Bur. Standards, Washington, 1961-63; NSF fellow U. Md., 1963-64; rabbi Adas Israel, Mason City, Iowa, 1964-66, B'nei Sholom, Blountville, Tenn., 1966-67, Adath Israel, Dover, N.J., 1967-69; chaplain State U. N.Y., Albany, 1969-71; Hunter and Baruch colls., 1971-72; asso. editor Intercom, publ. Assn. Orthodox Jewish Scientists, N.Y.C., 1972-73; editor Jewish Life, publ. Union Orthodox Jewish Congregations Am., 1973-74; dir. publs. Nat. Conf. Synagogue Youth, N.Y.C., 1974-75; freelance writer, lectr., 1975—; author: Rabbi Nachman's Wisdom, 1973; God, Man and Tefillin, 1973, Russian transl., 1976; Maimonides' Principles, 1973; Hashkafa Series, 5 vols., 1973, 74; The Real Messiah, 1974; Day of Eternity, 1974; Love Means Reaching Out, 1975; The Waters of Eden, 1976, Dutch transl., 1978, French and German transls., 1978; The Way of God, 1977; The Torah Anthology, 5 vols., 1977; The Laws of Chanukah, 1977; translator; The Bahir (Rabbi Nehuniah ben Hakanah), 1978; contbr. articles to profl. jours. founder, 1st dir. Collegiate Youth for Torah, N.Y.C., 1972-73. Mem. Am. Phys. Soc., Rabbinical Council Am. Founding editor Jewish Student, 1975—. Home: 4804 16th Ave Brooklyn NY 11204

KAPLAN, NOLAN SCOTT, mfg. co. exec.; b. Phila., June 1, 1951; s. Meyer and Etta (Kaufman) K.; B.S., Drexel U., 1973; m. Norma F. Simkins, Mar. 20, 1977. Pipe stress engr. Stone & Webster Engring. Corp., Cherry Hill, N.J., 1973-77; mech. engr. Selas Corp. Am., Dresher, Pa., 1977—. Vice pres. Drexel U. Young Alumni Assn., 1975-77. Recipient Merit certificate St. Bonaventure U., 1973. Asso. mem. ASME. Jewish. Club: B'rith Sholom. Home: 574 Pine Tree Rd Jenkintown PA 19046 Office: Limekiln Pike and Dreshertown Rd Dresher PA 19025

KAPLAN, ROBERT, govt. ofcl.; b. Boston, Nov. 20, 1912; s. Israel and Anna (Hoffman) K.; A.B. summa cum laude, Harvard U., 1934, J.D., cum laude, 1937; m. Evelyn Shirley Gordon, July 8, 1945; children—Richard A., Martin J. Admitted to Mass. bar, 1937; practiced in Boston, 1937-39; atty. civil div. Justice Dept., Washington, 1940-52, 53-62, asst. chief comml. litigation sect., 1962-77, spl. counsel appellate sect. civil div., 1977—; chief counsel consumer goods div. OPS, 1952-53. Recipient Sustained Superior Performance award Justice Dept., 1968. Mem. Fed. Bar Assn., Harvard Law Sch. Assn., Phi Beta Kappa. Jewish (past pres. temple). Mem. B'nai B'rith (past pres. met. lodge, past pres. Greater Washington Area assn. lodges). Home: 7420 Westlake Terr Bethesda MD 20034 Office: Main Justice Bldg 10th and Pennsylvania Ave NW Washington DC 20530

KAPLAN, RONALD V., investment co. exec.; b. N.Y.C., Oct. 23, 1930; s. Morris and Ethel (Glass) K.; B.B.A., N.Y. U., 1951; M.B.A. in Accounting, Columbia, City U. N.Y., 1956; m. Bette Wise, June 27, 1954; children—Bruce, Jerry, Michael. Supervising sr. accountant S. D. Leidesdorf & Co., C.P.A.'s, N.Y.C., 1954-66; treas., chief fin. officer Gen. Hose & Coupling Co., Caldwell, N.J., 1966-68; v.p., treas., chief fin. officer Midland Capital Corp., N.Y.C., 1968—; chmn. bd., pres. Flight Service, Inc.; chmn. bd. Sunstream Jet Center, Inc.; dir. 1st Fulton Corp., Nat. Nursing Home Devel. Corp. C.P.A., N.Y. Mem. Am. Inst. C.P.A.'s, N.Y. State Soc. C.P.A.'s, Beta Gamma Sigma. Club: K.P. Home: 21 Tammy Terr Wayne NJ 07470 Office: 110 William St New York City NY 10038

KAPLAN, SANFORD ALLEN, physician; b. Elizabeth, N.J., Feb. 27, 1929; s. Isadore and Rose (Fisher) K.; B.S., Ind. U., 1950; M.D., Chgo. Med. Sch., 1954; m. Maxine Jewel Kaplan, July 4, 1954; children—Lloyd Austin, Dean Ian, Keith Wayne. Intern, Kings County Hosp.. Bklyn., 1954-55; practice medicine, specializing in internal medicine and allergy, Yonkers, N.Y., 1958—; attending in medicine Mt. Vernon (N.Y.) Hosp.; asst. attending in medicine Lawrence Hosp., Bronxville, N.Y.; procter in dept. family practice St. Joseph's Hosp., 1975-77; fellow in allergy Misericordia Hosp. Allergy Clinic, 1963-68; clin. cons. N.Y. State Dept. Health; mem. exec. com. Westchester County Med. Center Hosp. Bd., 1975-76; mem. med. bd. Mt. Vernon Hosp., 1977—. Vice-pres. Big Brothers-Big Sisters of Yonkers, 1972-74, mem. adv. bd., 1974—; chmn. Yonkers Narcotics Guidance Council, 1972-75; advisor on health and drug affairs Mayor of Yonkers, 1970-74; bd. dirs. Milton Budnick Found., Inc., Taxpayers Assn. N.E. Yonkers. Diplomate Am. Bd. Family Practice, Am. Bd. Allergy and Immunology. Fellow Am. Coll. Allergy, Am. Assn. Clin. Immunology and Allergy; mem. N.Y.C., Westchester allergy socs., AMA, N.Y. State (Presdl. Citation award 1975), Westchester County (pub. relations com. 1966-68; legis. com. 1973—, vice chmn. 1974-76; hosp. and pub. health com. 1972-76; chmn. drug abuse com. 1974—; commr. community health 1975—) med. socs., Am. Geriatrics Soc., Phi Delta Epsilon (pres. Westchester chpt. 1963—). Jewish. Home: 125 Pietro Dr Yonkers NY 10710 Office: 821 Bronx River Rd Bronxville P O NY 10708

KAPLAN, WILLIAM MEYER, lawyer; b. N.Y.C., Dec. 10, 1920; s. Morris and Lena (Hammer) K.; B.S.S., Coll. City N.Y., 1940; LL.B., Fordham U., 1947; J.S.D., N.Y. U., 1951; m. Ann Auerbach, Sept. 21, 1947; children—Cathy Melissa, Darlene Melinda. Admitted to N.Y. bar, 1947; asso. atty. Linder & Mayer, N.Y.C., 1947-49; asso. firm Pindyck & Bernstein, N.Y.C., 1950, Paul, Weiss, Rifkind, Wharton & Garrison, N.Y.C., 1951; partner firm Aranow, Brodsky, Bohlinger, Benetar & Einhorn, N.Y.C., 1951—; dir. Triangle Pacific Corp. Bd. govs. N.Y. Young Republican Club, N.Y.C., 1947-48; pres. Bronx Young Rep. Club, 1946-47. Served with AUS, 1942-46. Mem. Am. Bar Assn. (mem. fee arrangements com. sect. econ. law 1975—), New York County Lawyers Assn. (sec. com. profl. ethics 1956-58, mem. com. 1976—), Phi Beta Kappa. Contbr. articles to profl. jours. Home: 4455 Douglas Ave Riverdale New York City NY 10471 Office: 469 Fifth Ave New York City NY 10017

KAPLOW, HERBERT ELIAS, news corr.; b. N.Y.C., Feb. 2, 1927; s. Solomon and Belle (Bernstein) K.; B.A., Queens Coll., 1948; M.S.J., Northwestern U., 1951; m. Betty Rae Koplow, Aug. 10, 1952; children—Steven E., Robert G., Lawrence M. News corr. NBC News, Washington, 1951-72, ABC News, Washington, 1977—; lectr. Served with U.S. Army, 1945-46. Recipient alumni award Northwestern U., 1959, Queens Coll., 1963. Mem. Sigma Delta Chi. Home: 211 Van Buren St Falls Church VA 22046 Office: 1124 Connecticut Ave NW Washington DC 20036

KAPNER, KERMIT HAROLD, pub. relations exec.; b. Bronx, N.Y., Oct. 9, 1918; s. Philip and Edna (Karasinsky) K.; B.S., Ohio State U., 1941; m. Thomasine Blankenship, Sept. 27, 1962; children—Michael Bruce, Linda Louise. Columnist, real estate editor Bergen Record, Hackensack, N.J., 1946-52; pres., owner Kaylon Pub. Relations, Paramus, N.J., 1953—; dir. Franchise Hdqrs., Paramus; sec.-treas. Haileo, Inc. Served with USAAF, 1941-45. Mem. Builders Assn. No. N.J., Nat. Assn. Real Estate Editors, Internat. Platform Assn., Advt. Club. North Jersey, Ohio State U. Varsity O Assn., Fraternal Athletic Cultural Tech. Soc. Mem. B'nai B'rith. Clubs: Englewood (N.J.) Men's (pres. 1947); North Jersey Press. Home: 472 Elbert St Ramsey NJ 07446 Office: 27 Madison Ave Paramus NJ 07652

KAPOTES, CHARLES NICHOLAS, psychologist; b. Bklyn., Mar. 25, 1927; s. Nicholas and Anna (Papatheodore) K.; B.A., St. John's U., 1950; Ph.D., N.Y. U., 1955; m. Despina Joakimides, Mar. 4, 1956; children—James C., Nicholas, Alexandra (Twins). Pvt. practice psychology, Manhasset Hills, N.Y., 1958—; clin. child psychologist St. Mary's Episcopal Hosp., Bayside, N.Y., 1959—; psychologist N. Nassau Mental Health Center, Manhasset, N.Y., 1958—, chief psychologist, 1968—; psychologist Bleuler Psychotherapy Center, Jamaica, N.Y., 1958—, chief psychologist, 1972—; cons. Family Consultation Service Episcopal Diocese L.I., Jamaica, 1976—. Served in USN, 1945-46. Grantee Asthmatic Children's Found., 1965-66; recipient Founders Day award N.Y. U., 1955. Mem. Am. Psychol. Assn., Archeol. Inst. Am., N.Y. Acad. Sci. Greek Orthodox. Address: 111 Executive Dr Manhasset Hills NY 11040

KAPP, EDWIN VICTOR, cons. engring. co. exec.; b. Balt., Feb. 4, 1918; s. Victor Randolph and Ruth (Mason) K.; Maintenance Engr., Yale U., 1944; student U. Balt., 1947-50; m. Cecilia Elizabeth Fisher, Jan. 25, 1974; children by previous marriage—Nancy L., Thomas C., Heidi A. Various cons. engr. positions with numerous cos., 1953-71; with Martin Marietta Co., Balt., 1956-62; with Bechtel Power Corp., Gaithersburg, Md., 1971-78, DCO, Washington, 1978—; owner, operator Woodfield (Md.) Country Store, 1975—, The Mustard Seed, 1974—. Served as 1st lt. USAAF, 1943-47. Registered profl. engr., Mass. Democrat. Roman Catholic. Club: Elks. Home: 23716 Woodfield Rd Woodfield MD 20760 Office: 1201 Connecticut Ave Washington DC 20036

KAPPEL, R. ROSE, artist; b. Hartford, Conn., Sept. 23, 1910; d. Morris and Anna Evlyn (Superior) Kappel; student Pratt Inst., 1930; B.S., N.Y. U., 1947, M.A., 1950, Ed.D., 1953; postgrad. Washington U., Wis. U., Yale U.; Ed.D., 1953; m. Irving Gould, Dec. 24, 1944. Art specialist Bur. Edn. Physically Handicapped Children, Bd. Edn., Bklyn., 1944—. Numerous one-man shows leading galleries, N.Y., 1935-50; exhibited Nat. Acad. Art, 1960-67, Wash. Art Assn.; represented in permanent collections Fogg Mus., Cleve. Mus., Boston Mus., Orange Mus., Met. Mus. Art, Mattatuck Mus. Art, New Britain Mus. Am. Art, Mt. Holyoke Mus.; lithographs exhibited with Am. Graphics Art Soc., Kennedy Galleries, N.Y.C., 1955-60, others; art cons. AAUW; lectr. on art. Recipient Beth Creedy Hamm prize for water color Nat. Acad., 1960, prize for water color Nat. Assn. Women Artists, 62, Nat. Acad., 1961. Mem. Council Exceptional Children, Nat. Assn. Women Artists, Print Council Am., Internat. Platform Assn., Center for Am. Living, Assn. Council Arts, AAUW (area rep. in cultural interests for N.Y. state, dir.-at-large, v.p. N.Y.C. br.), V. Gildersleeve Internat. Fund for Univ. Women, Onumastic Soc., Interstate League Orgn. for N.Y., N.J and Conn., League Women Voters (resource chmn.), Internat. Artists. Illustrator: Ships and Sails, 1947. Home: 35-36 76th St Jackson Heights NY 11372

KAPPLER, ROBERT PAUL, elec. engr.; b. Moberly, Mo., Nov. 4, 1938; s. Edward Louis and Margaret (Sump) K.; gen. edn. certificate Moberly Jr. Coll., 1958; B.S. in Elec. Engring., U. Mo., 1961, M.B.A., 1970; m. Marilyn Sue Lankford, June 20, 1964; children—Christiana Susanne, David Bradley, Carolyn Douglas. Elec. engr. Army Test and Evaluation Command, White Sands Missile Range, N.Mex., 1961-71, Office Asst. Chief Staff for Force Devel., Pentagon, Washington, 1971-74, head TEMPEST mgmt. div., Naval Electronic Systems Security Engring. Center, Washington, 1974-75, head field programs mgmt. div., Naval Electronic Systems Security Engring. Center, Washington, 1975—. Mem. IEEE, Nat. Soc. Profl. Engrs., Am. Inst. Aeros. and Astronautics (pres. Inland Missile Range chpt. 1967), Beta Gamma Sigma. Roman Catholic. Home: 11024 Stanrich Ct Fairfax VA 22030 Office: Naval Electronic Systems Security Engring Center Attn Code 201 3801 Nebraska Ave NW Washington DC 20390

KAPROW, MAURICE SHALOM, ednl. adminstr.; b. Buffalo, Nov. 15, 1944; s. Gedaliah and Geraldine (Shapiro) K.; B.A., Yeshiva U., 1966, B.H.L., 1966; M.A., Columbia, 1972; m. Sheila Irene Weinstein, June 28, 1970; children—Marc Gordon, Philip Scott. Tchr., prin. intern N.Y.C. Pub. Schs., 1967-72; supr. instrn. Howell Twp. Pub. Schs., Farmingdale, N.J., 1972-75; coordinator research and devel. Monmouth Adult Edn. Commn., Eatontown, N.J., 1975-76; asst. supt. schs. Berkeley Twp. Pub. Schs., Bayville, N.J., 1976—. Asso. nat. dir. Nat. Council Young Israel, 1964-72; mem. Freehold Boro Recreation Com.; chmn. Freehold Boro Recreation Com., 1976. Recipient Stanley W. Schlessel Service award Nat. Council Young Israel, 1972. Mem. Am., N.J. assns. sch. adminstrs., Phi Delta Kappa (pres. Columbia U. chpt.). Jewish. Club: Lions. Home: 46 Schiverea Ave Freehold NJ 07728 Office: 60 Veeder Ln Bayville NJ 08721

KAR, ANIL KRISHNA, engring. corp. exec.; b. Dacca, Bangladesh, July 9, 1941; s. Manoranjan and Nirmala (De) K.; B.S., Bangladesh U. Engring. and Tech., 1962; M.S., Pa. State U., 1969, Ph.D., 1971; came to U.S., 1967; m. Parul Chakrabarti, Dec. 12, 1977. Resident engr. Engrs. Ltd., Dacca, 1962-65; civil engr. Bhagwati & Kumbhani, Calcutta, India, 1966-67; structural engr. Bertram S. Warshaw & Assos., Miami, Fla., 1967-68; research asst. Pa. State U., 1968-71; civil engr. Burns & Roe, Inc., L.I., N.Y., 1972-74; prin. engr. Stone & Webster Engring. Corp., N.Y.C., 1974-75; sr. structural engr. Gibbs & Hill, Inc., N.Y.C., 1975-77; sr. engr. Ebasco Services, Inc., N.Y.C., 1977—; cons. civil engr., 1973—. Mem. Internat. Assn. Shell and Spatial Structures, (chmn. several coms.), Chi Epsilon. Contbr. articles in math., structural and geotech. engring. to profl. jours. Home: 118-70 80th Rd Kew Gardens NY 11415 Office: Ebasco Services Inc 2 Rector St New York City NY 10006

KARAN, VAL ELLIOT, psychologist; b. Dubuque, Iowa, Sept. 28, 1942; s. Herman and Rose Ann (Nosofsky) K.; B.A. cum laude, Yeshiva Coll., 1965; M.S., Coll. City N.Y., 1968; Ph.D., N.Y.U., 1973; m. Annette Kagan, Apr. 16, 1967; children—Suzanne Beth, Edward Solomon. Sch. psychologist, gifted programs coordinator Fort Lee (N.J.) Bd. Edn., 1968—; adj. asst. prof. edn. Hunter Coll., N.Y.C., 1970-76, Touro Coll., N.Y.C., 1976—; staff psychologist N.J. YMHA Camps; cons. psychologist Solomon Schechter and Frisch High Schs., Bergen County, N.J., 1971—. Mem. bd. edn. Salanter/Akiba/Riverdale Acad. N.Y., 1975—; trustee Riverdale Jewish Center, 1973-75. Recipient Founders' Day award N.Y.U., 1974; certified clin. psychologist, N.J. Mem. Am. Psychol Assn., Assn. Sociol. Study Jewry, Nat. Assn. Sch. Psychologists. Home: 3515 Henry Hudson Pkwy Bronx NY 10463 Office: 2024 Hoefley's Ln Fort Lee NJ 07024

KARDON, LEROY, packaging co. exec.; b. Phila., June 25, 1951; s. Robert J. and Janet Doris (Stolker) K.; B.S. in Bus. Adminstrn., Boston U., 1973; M.B.A., Temple U., 1975; m. Gail Helene Friedman, May 25, 1975. Dir. indsl. relations United Container Co., Phila., 1975-76; sales rep. Kardon Composite Can & Tube, St. Paris, Ohio, 1977-78; mgr. mfg. Kardon Industries, Inc., Phila., 1978—. Mem. Am. Soc. Personnel Adminstrn., Am. Soc. for Tng. and Devel. Home: 226 W Rittenhouse Sq Philadelphia PA 19103 Office: 1201 Chestnut St Philadelphia PA 19107

KARL, DOROTHY THERESA, ret. ednl. adminstr.; b. Allegany, N.Y., Mar. 27, 1917; d. Vincent E. and Theresa (Gallets) K.; B.S. in Math., St. Bonaventure (N.Y.) U., 1939; diploma State U. Coll. N.Y. at Geneseo, 1941. postgrad. Boston Coll., Chestnut Hill, Mass. Instr. and coordinator math. Allegany Central Sch. Dist. 1, 1941-78. NSF grantee, 1960, 61. Mem. Assn. Math. Tchrs. of N.Y. State, Nat. Council Tchrs. Math., Nat. Ret. Tchrs. Assn., Allegany Central Sch. Tchrs. Assn. Women's Golf Assn., Am. Assn. Ret. Persons, St. Bonaventure U. Alumnae Assn. Club: Bartlett Country. Home: Five Mile Rd Allegany NY 14706

KARLAN, FRANCES ROSS, dentist, ins. co. exec.; b. Boston, Apr. 15, 1921; d. Robert and Etty (Feitelberg) Ross; B.S., Mass. Inst. Tech., 1942; D.D.S., Columbia, 1949; M.B.A., Fordham U., 1972; m. Jac H. Karlan, Sept. 24, 1942; children—Debora Karlan Block, Daniel M. Programmer, Lederle Labs., Orangeburg, N.Y., 1942; research technician Babies Hosp., N.Y.C., 1942-44, Columbia U. Dental Sch., 1944-45; dentist Rockland State Hosp., Orangeburg, N.Y., 1952-53; asst. v.p. Met. Life Ins. Co., N.Y.C., 1953—; asso. prof. dept. stomatology Sch. Dental Oral Surgery Columbia. Mem. ADA, Assn. Indsl. Dentists (past pres.), Alumni Assn. Columbia U. Dental Sch. (past pres.). Home: 37A Haddon Rd Cranbury NJ 08512 Office: 1 Madison Ave New York City NY 10010

KARLIN, MURIEL SCHOENBRUN (MRS. LEONARD KARLIN), educator; b. N.Y.C.; d. Henry B. and Frieda (Berger) Schoenbrun; B.A., Bklyn. Coll., 1945; M.A., N.Y. U., 1946; m. Dr. Leonard Karlin, Sept. 5, 1945; children—Henry Edward, Lisa Yvonne. Tchr. Jr. High Sch. 51, S.I., N.Y., 1958-63; ednl. and vocational counselor Jr. High Sch. 27, S.I., 1963-66, asst. prin., 1966—; dir. Muriel S. Karlin Counseling Services, S.I. Columnist, S.I. Advance; ednl. cons. Slow Learner Workshop. Author: (with Regina Berger) Successful Methods for Teaching Slow Learner, 1969, Survival Instructions for the Teacher, 1970, Experiential Learning: An Effective Teaching Program, for the Elementary and Junior High Schools, 1971, Developing an Effective Student Activities Program, 1971, Discipline and the Disruptive Child, 1972; Individualized Instruction: A Complete Guide for Diagnosis, Planning, Teaching and Evaluation, 1974; An Administrator's Guide to a Practical Career Education Program, 1974; (with Morton Margules) Pathways to Careers, 1975; Solving Your Career Mystery, 1975; Classroom Activities Desk Book for Fun and Learning, 1975; Administering and Teaching Sex Education in the Elementary School, 1975; Teachers Handbook of Special Learning Problems and How to Handle Them, 1977. Editor: Career Education Workshop; tech. reviewer Parker Pub. Co. Contbr. articles to profl. jours. Home: 63 Haven Esplanade Staten Island NY 10301

KARLSON, JANET FALTER WEIL (MRS. CARL KARLSON), educator, writer; b. Cleve., Apr. 5, 1918; d. Francis and Clair (Falter) Weil; B.S., Western Res. U., 1937, M.A., 1938; Ph.D., Columbia, 1940; m. Carl Karlson, Apr. 24, 1943; children—Tommy, Ellen, Kathe, Danny. Organized and taught remedial reading program, 1962-68; author articles on edn. pub. in profl. jours. Nat. exec. sec. Child Care Center Parents Assn., 1945-49. Pres. P.T.A., 1958-64; chmn. Joint Schs. Com., N.Y.C., 1964—; chmn. Manhattanville Improvement Assn., 1967-69. Home: 545 W 126th St New York City NY 10027 Office: 514 W 126th St New York City NY 10027

KARNIOL, HILDA HUTTERER (MRS. FRANK KARNIOL), artist, educator; b. Vienna, Austria, Apr. 28, 1910; d. Simon and Josephine (Weisman) Hutterer; student Acad. for Women, Vienna, 1926-30, Mrs. Olga Konetzky-Maly and A.F. Seligman, Vienna, 1925-28; m. Frank Karniol, June 25, 1933; 1 son, William George. Exhibited in more than 100 one man shows including Susquehanna U., 1952-73, Pa. State Mus., Harrisburg, 1954, Neville Mus., Green Bay, Wis., 1958, Addha Artzt Gallery, N.Y.C., 1960, Cornell Library Gallery, Ithaca, N.Y., 1960, Drexel Inst. Tech., Phila., 1960, Farnsworth Mus., Rockland, Maine, 1960, Mary Buie Mus., Oxford, Miss., 1960, Columbus (Ga.) Mus., 1962, Laurel (Miss.) Rogers Mus., 1962, Rutgers U., 1965-66, La Salle Coll., Phila., 1964, Hallmark Art Gallery, Kansas City, Mo., 1967, U. Mich., Ann Arbor, 1969, U. Minn., St. Paul, 1969, U. Ill., Urbana, 1968, U. Ky., Elizabethtown, 1970, La. State U., New Orleans, 1971, Kans. State Coll., Pittsburg, 1972, Purdue U., West Lafayette, Ind., 1973, Ohio U. at St. Clairsville, 1974, Ky. State Coll., Frankfort, 1974; represented in permanent collections at St. Vincent Arch Abbey, Latrobe, Pa., Susquehanna U., Selinsgrove, Pa., Lincoln Sch., Honesdale, Pa., Del. Art Center, Wilmington, HEW, Lycoming Coll., Williamsport, Pa., Pa. State Coll. at Bloomsburg, Lewisburg (Pa.) Art Council; instr. fine arts Susquehanna U., 1959-75; lectr., artist-in-residence Fed. Govt. Cultural Enrichment Program for Clearfield, Clinton, Centre and Lycoming counties, Pa., 1967; art adviser Sunbury (Pa.) Bicentennial Com., 1972; demonstrator, exhibitor Laurel State Festival, Wellsboro, Pa., 1975. Recipient 1st prize in portraiture Berwick (Pa.) Arts Center, 1965; 1st Merit and Purchase prize Lewisburg (Pa.) Art Assn., 1975, 1st prize, 1978. Mem. Société d'Honneur Française, Mid-State Artists Pa., Nat. Forum Profl. Artists, Art Alliance Central Pa., Pi Delta Phi, Sigma Alpha Iota. Club: Soroptimist (Sunbury, Pa.). Home: 960 Race St Sunbury PA 17801

KAROL, EUGENE MICHAEL, sch. adminstr.; b. Mifflinville, Pa., Nov. 28, 1933; s. Michael F. and Catherine R. Karol; B.S., U. Md., 1955; M.Ed., Western Md. Coll., 1964; Ed.D., Nova U., 1975; Taylor, May 28, 1971; children—Paul Eugene, Eugene Michael. Tchr. biology, Baltimore County, Md., 1955-65, adminstrv. asst., 1965-68, vice prin., 1968-70; exec. asst. to state supt. Md. Dept. Edn., Balt., 1970-75; supt. schs. Bd. Edn. Somerset County, Princess Anne, Md., 1975—. part-time instr. Western Md. Coll., Westminster, Md., 1971—. Pres., TABCO Assistance, Inc., 1965—, Md. Council Urban Edn. Assns., 1965-67; chmn. Md. Polit. Action Com. of Educators,

1969-70. Recipient Golden Apple award Md. PTA, 1969. Mem. Am. Assn. Sch. Adminstrs., Md. Tchrs. Assn. (pres. 1968-69), NEA (exec. com. 1969-71), Tchrs. Assn. Baltimore County (pres. 1965-66), Phi Delta Kappa. Address: Bd Edn Prince William St Princess Anne MD 21853

KAROL, ROBERT STANLEY, allergist; b. Rockaway Beach, N.Y., Sept. 26, 1930; s. Israel and Bertha (Butow) K.; B.A. cum laude, N.Y. U., 1951; M.D., Downstate Med. Center, State U. N.Y., 1955; m. Carolyn Jacobson, Mar. 16, 1958; children—Nancy, Rhonda, Ian. Intern, Jackson Meml. Hosp., U. Miami (Fla.), 1955-56; resident in internal medicine VA Hosp., N.Y.C., 1958-60; resident in allergy Roosevelt Hosp., N.Y.C., 1960-61; dir. allergy clinic Peninsula Hosp., Queens, N.Y., 1969-78; asso. attending staff allergy clinic Roosevelt Hosp.; cons. Pkwy. Hosp., Forest Hills, N.Y.; asso. attending physician St. John's Queens Hosp., Elmhurst, N.Y.; asso. physician St. Johns' Episc. Hosp., Far Rockaway, N.Y. Served to capt. USNR and USMC, 1956-58. Diplomate Am. Bd. Internal Medicine, Am. Bd. Allergy and Immunology. Fellow A.C.P., Am. Acad. Allergy, Am. Assn. Certified Allergists; mem. Rockaway Med. Soc. (pres.), Nassau-Suffolk Allergy Soc. (exec. com.), Robert Cooke Allergy Alumni Soc., Park History Honor Soc., Phi Beta Kappa, Beta Lambda Sigma. Home: 218 Juniper Circle S Lawrence NY 11559 Office: 108 48 70th Rd Forest Hills NY 11375

KARP, HARVEY LAWRENCE, mfg. co. exec.; b. N.Y.C., Nov. 26, 1927; s. Harry and Sadie (Zimmerman) K.; B.A., Coll. City N.Y., 1949; LL.B., Yale, 1952; m. Beverly Bailis, Nov. 24, 1955; children—David, Nicholas. Admitted to N.Y. bar, 1952, Calif. bar, 1954; lawyer Chesapeake Industries, Inc., 1952-54; gen. counsel, v.p. Houston Fearless Corp., 1955-60; founder, vice-chmn. bd., pres. Mongram Industries, N.Y.C., 1960—; dir. Craig Corp. Bd. dirs. Neuroscis. Research Inst., M.I.T., 1977—. Served with USNR, 1945. Clubs: Yale; Harmonie (N.Y.C.). Home: 10 Gracie Sq New York City NY 10028 Office: 450 Park Ave New York City NY 10022

KARP, PETER SIMON, research inst. exec.; b. N.Y.C., Dec. 9, 1932; s. Joseph Bernard and Esther (Wexler) K.; B.A., Hobart Coll., 1954; M.F.A., Columbia U., 1957; m. Mona Leea Pecheux, Sept. 9, 1956; children—Matthew Henry, Mark Andrew. Mem. research dept. Bur. Advt., Am. Newspaper Publishers Assn., N.Y.C., 1956-57; dir. media and research Smith Hagel & Knudsen, Inc., N.Y.C., 1958-60; exec. v.p. Bennett-Chaikin Research Inc., N.Y.C., 1961-66; pres. MMRA Marketing & Opinion Research, N.Y.C., 1966—; dir. The Concept Testing Inst., N.Y.C., 1968—; chmn. Bus. Sci. Internat.; dir. Children's Marketing Workshop. Research project dir. Kenneth Keating Senate Campaign, 1966, William Scranton Gubernatorial Campaign, 1964. Mem. fund raising bd. Grand Central Y.M.C.A., 1964; active Boy Scouts Am. Recipient Thomas T. Semon Research Contbns. award, 1969. Mem. Am. Marketing Assn., Advt. Research Found., Spl. Libraries Assn., Phi Phi Delta. Jewish. Clubs: Upper Nyack Tennis Club, West Rock Tennis Club. Home: 4 Radcliff Dr Upper Nyack NY 10960 Office: 598 Madison Ave New York City NY 10022

KARP, WILLIAM B., civil engr.; b. Stamford, Conn., Sept. 21, 1918; s. David and Rebecca (Altman) K.; B.S. in Civil Engring., U. Ala., 1940; postgrad. George Washington U., 1941; m. Golde B. Barnowsky, Aug. 25, 1940; children—Marilynn L., Robert L., Rebecca L. With Constructing Engrs. and U.S. Dist. Engrs. on constrn. of Camp Blanding, Fla., 1941-42, Wright-Patterson Airfield, Ohio, 1942-43, Rome (N.Y.) Air Depot, 1943-45; pres. Hills of Westchester Inc., Brentwood, Md., 1948—. Served with U.S. Army, 1943. Mem. Am. Soc. Bakery Engrs., Nat. Food Distbrs. Assn., ASCE, Nat. Fancy Food and Confections Assn., others. Republican. Jewish. Clubs: Masons, Lions, K.P. Home: 7110 Wells Pkwy University Park MD 20782 Office: 3400 Windom Rd Brentwood MD 20722

KARPATI, FRANK STEPHEN, ednl. counselor; b. Budapest, Hungary, Feb. 14, 1943; s. Oszkar and Magdolna (Molnar) K.; came to U.S., 1957, naturalized, 1961; M.A., William Paterson Coll., 1971; m. Anna Futar, Oct. 13, 1976. Dir., Counseling Assos., Hackensack, N.J., 1977—. Mem. Am. Personnel and Guidance Assn., Am. Sociol. Assn., Am. Ednl. Studies Assn., Nat. Assn. Coll. Admissions Counselors, N.J. Vocat. Counselors Assn. (v.p.), Phi Delta Kappa. Asso. editor: N.J. Coll. Profiles, 1977—; contbr. articles to profl. publs. Home: 25 Grand Ave Hackensack NJ 07601

KARPEN, EDWARD WILLIAM, electronics engr.; b. Dumont, N.J., Sept. 16, 1923; s. William and Hannah (Mayer) K.; B.E.E., Pratt Inst., 1950; M.S.E.E., Poly Inst. N.Y., 1972. With AIL div. Cutler-Hammer, Inc., Deer Park, N.Y., 1950—, devel. engr., project engr., engring. mgr. automatic and manual track-while-scan systems, 1950-58, engring. mgr., sect. head electronic reconnaisssance systems, 1958-63, sect. head electromagnetic compatibility sect., 1963—. Served with U.S. Army, 1943-46. Mem. IEEE (electromagnetic compatibility group), AAAS, Tau Beta Pi. Patentee in field. Home: 419 W Main St Huntington NY 11743 Office: Comac Rd Deer Park NY 11729

KARPINSKI, JOSEPH PAUL, acctg. co. exec.; b. Erie, Pa., Nov. 6, 1948; s. Joseph Anthony and Mary (Zipperi) K.; B.S., Gannon Coll., 1970, M.B.A., 1972; m. Marsha K. Desanzo, Dec. 31, 1973; 1 son, Michael J. With Root, Spitznas & Smiley, C.P.A.'s, Erie, Pa., 1969-72; corp. internal auditor, head audit staff Am. Sterilizer Co., Erie, 1972-73, divisional controller, Harrisburg, Pa., 1973-74; mgr. corp. acctg. Equimark Co., Pitts., 1974-75; mgr. internal audit Pitts. & Lake Erie R.R., Pitts., 1975-77; coordinator internal audit Alcoa, Pitts., 1977-78; v.p. finance M. Waddell & Co., Inc., Pitts., 1977-78; partner Karpinski & Soroka, Beaver, Pa., since 1978—; lectr. in field. Certified internal auditor, financial prin. Mem. Inst. Internal Auditors, Nat. Assn. Accountants, Beaver C. of C. Democrat. Roman Catholic. Home: 116 Glenfield Dr Glenfield Estates Beaver Falls PA 15009 Office: 445 State Ave Beaver PA 15009

KARSEN, SONJA PETRA, educator; b. Berlin, Germany, Apr. 11, 1919; d. Fritz and Erna (Heidermann) K.; came to U.S., 1938, naturalized, 1945; Titulo de Bachiller, 1937; B.A., Carleton Coll., 1939; M.A. (scholar in French 1939-41), Bryn Mawr Coll., 1941; Ph.D., Columbia, 1950. Instr. Spanish, Lake Erie Coll., Painesville, Ohio, 1943-45; instr. modern langs. U. P.R., 1945-46; instr. Spanish, Syracuse U., 1947-50, Bklyn. Coll., 1950-51; asst. to dep. dir. gen. UNESCO, 1951-52, Latin Am. Desk, tech. asst. dept., 1952-53, mem. tech. assistance mission Costa Rica, 1954; asst. prof. Spanish, Sweet Briar Coll., 1955-57; asso. prof., chmn. dept. Romance langs. Skidmore Coll., Saratoga Springs, N.Y., 1957-61, prof. Spanish and chmn. dept. modern langs. and lits., 1961—; Fulbright lectr. Free U. Berlin, 1968. Decorated chevalier dans l'Ordre des Palmes Academiques, 1964; recipient Leadership award N.Y. State Assn. Fgn. Lang. Tchrs., 1973; exchange student auspices Inst. Internat. Edn. at Carleton Coll., 1938-39; Buenos Aires Conv. grantee for research in Colombia, S.A., 1946-47; faculty research grantee Skidmore Coll., summer 1959, 61, 63, 65, 67, 69, 70. Mem. AAUP, Modern Lang. Assn. (mem. del. assembly 1976-78), Am. Assn. Tchrs. Spanish and Portuguese, AAUW, Nat. Geog. Soc., Instituto Internacional De Literatura Iberoamericana, Asociacion Internacional De Hispanists, UN Assn., of U.S.A. Author: Guillermo Valencia, Colombian Poet, 1951; Educational development in Costa Rica with Unesco's Technical Assistance, 1951-54, 1954; Jaime Torres Bodet: A Poet in a Changing World, 1963; Selected Poems of Jaime Torres Bodet, 1964; Versos y prosas de Jaime Torres Bodet, 1966; Jaime Torres Bodet, 1971. Contbr. articles to profl. jours. Office: Skidmore Coll Saratoga Springs NY 12866*

KARSTETTER, ALLAN BOYD, coll. ofcl.; b. Williamson, N.Y., May 19, 1927; s. Richard Foster and Elsie Mae (Van Hall) K.; B.E., State U. N.Y. at Brockport, 1949; M.A., Northwestern U., 1953; Ph.D., Pa. State U., 1963; m. Anne Louise Nelson, Dec. 22, 1957; children—Matthew Nelson, Emily Anne. Asso. prof. speech State U. N.Y. at Brockport, 1955-64; sr. research asso. Pa. Dept. Pub. Instruction, Harrisburg, 1964-66; program dir. Eastern Regional Inst. Edn., Syracuse, N.Y., 1966-68; prof. speech Tex. Woman's U., Denton, 1968-72, dean Coll. Arts and Scis., 1971-72; pres. Unity (Maine) Coll., 1972-78; provost Deree Coll. of Am. Coll. of Greece, 1978—; mem. Maine State Council on the Humanities, 1973-74; mem. exec. com. Maine Higher Edn. Council, 1974—, pres., 1977—; mem. exec. com. Conf. Small Pvt. Colls., 1974—, v.p., 1978—; mem. Maine Post-Secondary Edn. Commn., 1975—. Bd. dirs. Tex. Non-Profit Theatres, Inc. Served with AUS, 1945-46. Mem. Speech Communication Assn., Am. Assn. Higher Edn. Democrat. Office: Deree Coll Aghia Paraskevi Attiki Greece

KASBERG, ALVIN HARVEY, metall. engr.; b. Superior, Wis., Jan. 11, 1923; s. Alvin Halford and Mabel (Hansen) K.; student Gogebic Jr. Coll. 1940-41; B.S. in Metall. Engring., U. Wis., 1949, M.S., 1950; m. Mary Jane Dignan, June 6, 1953; children—Karl, Kevin, Mary Karen, Kris, Kimberly, Keith. Supervisory engr. Bettis Atomic Power div. Westinghouse Elec. Corp., Pitts., 1950-57; mgr. metallurgy and ceramics Nuclear Materials & Equipment Corp., Apollo, Pa., 1957-72; adv. engr. Westinghouse Advanced Reactors Div., Madison, Pa., 1972—. Vice pres. Franklin Regional PTA, Murrysville, Pa., 1969-71. Served with USAAF, 1942-45. Decorated D.F.C., 4 Air medals. Recipient Nat. award Lincoln Arc Welding Found. 1949. Mem. Am. Nuclear Soc., Phi Eta Sigma, Tau Beta Pi. Holder 9 U.S. patents, 1 patent pending; contbr. editor Metallurgy of Zirconium, 1955, Metallurgy of Hafuium, 1961; contbr. numerous tech. papers in field. Home: 3437 MacArthur Dr Murrysville PA 15668 Office: PO Box 158 Madison PA 15663

KASDAN, LOUIS ROSS, natural resources co. exec.; b. N.Y.C., July 11, 1923; s. Meyer and Carrie (Rosenwasser) K.; student Swarthmore Coll., 1942; B.A., Queens Coll., 1950; postgrad. edn. N.Y. U., 1952-53; m. Marian Ruth Smith, Sept. 26, 1948; children—Jane, Steven, Laura. Editorial asst. Wave Pub. Co., N.Y.C., 1950-52; writer-editor McGraw-Hill Book Co., N.Y.C., 1952-57; account exec. pub. relations Michel-Cather Inc., N.Y.C., 1957-59, Etkes Assos., N.Y.C., 1959-60; account exec. Cunningham & Walsh, N.Y.C., 1960-61, account supr., 1961, mgr. pub. relations dept., 1961-65, asso. dir. pub. relations dept., 1965-70; mgr. group pub. relations and corporate advt. Amax Inc., Greenwich, Conn., 1970-75, asst. dir. pub. relations and advt., 1975—; cons. in field. Gov. Home Rule Party, Rockville Center, L.I., 1962-66. Served with U.S Army, 1942-46. Mem. Pub. Relations Soc. Am., Indsl. Publicity Assn. N.Y. (treas. 1963-65), Bus.-Profl. Advt. Assn. Author: Casting Aluminum, 1955; Public Relations Handbook, 1964. Contbr. U.S. edit. Oxford Ency., 1960. Home: Cider Mill Rd Stamford CT 06903 Office: Amax Center Greenwich CT 06830

KASDON, LAWRENCE W., educator; b. Los Angeles, July 26, 1918; s. David and Lillian (Collins) K.; A.B., U. Calif. at Los Angeles, 1941; M.A., Stanford, 1950, Ed.D., 1955; m. Nora Sauer, Dec. 16, 1950 (dec. Aug. 1978). Tchr., Colton, Calif., 1940-42, San Carlos, Calif., 1948-51; elementary supr., Paramount, Calif., 1952-54; dir. lang. arts State Dept. Edn., Hawaii, 1955-64; asso. prof. Case-Western Res. U., 1964-67; asso. prof. Ferkauf Grad. Sch., Yeshiva U., N.Y.C., 1967-77, prof., 1977—. Cons. Ednl. Testing Service, 1971-73, UNESCO, 1947, Pitman Found., 1969-73. Commr., Aloha council Boy Scouts Am., 1958-64; co-founder Honolulu Day Sch., 1959; mem. Statehood Celebration Commn. Hawaii, 1959-60; sec. bd. dirs. Jobs for Youth, N.Y.C. Served with AUS, World War II. Decorated Purple Heart. Recipient Key award Crossroads Sch., South Africa, 1973. Grantee, McInery Found., 1958, Calif. Test Bur., 1959, U.S. Office Edn., 1965, 67; Nat. Council Research in English fellow, 1972. Mem. Internat. (pres. Hawaii chpt. 1960-62), Coll. (pres.-elect) reading assns., Nat. Council Tchrs. English (pres. Hawaii chpt. 1961-63), Am. Ednl. Research Assn., Pacific Speech Assn. (pres. 1959). Author: (with Norris W. Potter) Hawaii-Our Island State, 1964. Contbr. articles to profl. jours. Home: 13 W 13th St New York City NY 10011

KASE, HAROLD MICHAEL, health and welfare exec.; b. N.Y.C., Dec. 2, 1912; s. Jacob L. and Anna (Grossberg) K.; B.S., St. Johns U., 1934; M.A., Columbia, 1936, M.S., 1946, Ed.D., 1959; m. Sara Lee Persky, Jan. 15, 1939; children—John L., Martin R. (dec.). Asst. exec. dir. A.R.C., N.Y.C., N.Y., 1950-60; asst. exec. dir. Altro Health & Rehab. Services, N.Y.C., 1960-69, exec. v.p., 1969—; pres. Altro Workshops Inc., N.Y.C., 1969—. Adj. asso. prof. community orgn. Fordham U. Sch. Social Service, 1961-70; adj. faculty Albert Einstein Coll. Medicine, 1973-76. Mem. adv. council Columbia Sch. Social Work, 1964-67, N.Y. State Vocational Rehab. Service, 1970; dir. Block Camps for Aged, 1969-70; chmn. bd. Assn. Bronx Community Orgns., 1967. Recipient Naomi and Howard Lehman award, 1977, Rose and Samuel Hurowitz award, 1976 (both Fedn. Jewish Philanthropies N.Y.); Ecumenical award Council Chs. N.Y.C., 1976. Fellow Am. Pub. Health Assn., Am. Orthopsychiat. Assn.; mem. Nat. Assn. Social Workers, Nat. Rehab. Assn., Royal Soc. Health, Columbia Sch. Social Work Alumni Assn. (pres. 1959-60). Club: Rotary (pres. Bronx 1976—). Home: 329 Post Rd Danbury CT 06810 Office: 225 Park Ave S New York City NY 10003

KASE, STUART, urologist; b. Bklyn., Aug. 7, 1934; s. Murray and Gertrude (Solomon) K.; A.B. cum laude, Brown U., 1955; M.D., N.Y. Med. Coll., 1959; m. Roslyn Nusblatt, June 7, 1959; children—Jodi Lynne, Daniel Jay, Jamieson Lee. Intern, Beth Israel Hosp., N.Y.C., 1959-60, resident in urology, 1960-64; practice medicine specializing in urology, Massapequa Park, N.Y., 1966—; asst. prof. urol. surgery State U. N.Y. (Stony Brook); attending urologist Nassau County Med. Center. Pres. Woodbury Civic Assn., 1972-77. Served to capt. U.S. Army, 1964-66. Decorated Army Commendation medal. Diplomate Am. Bd. Urology. Fellow A.C.S.; mem. AMA, Nassau County Med. Soc., Nassau Surg. Soc., Pan Am. Med. Assn., Soc. Univ. Urology Residents, N.Y. State Urol. Soc. Clubs: Cold Spring Country (Cold Spring Harbor, N.Y.); Boca West (Boca Raton, Fla.). Contbr. articles to med. jours. Home: 2 Northwood Ct Woodbury NY 11797 Office: 4760 Sunrise Hwy Massapequa Park NY 11762

KASEY, GARY ALEX, ednl. and counseling cons.; b. New Britain, Conn., June 7, 1941; s. Alex Joseph and Josephine Joan Kasey; B.A. in Philosophy, St. Mary's Sem. and U., 1963, M.A. in Div., 1979; M.Ed. in Psychol. Testing, U. Hartford, 1968, Sixth Yr., Counseling, 1969; postgrad. in counseling psychology, U. Conn., 1972—. Spl. tchr. New Britain Bd. Edn., 1966; tchr. Bloomfield (Conn.) Bd. Edn., 1966; tchr. emotionally distrubed Hartford (Conn.) Bd. Edn., 1967-68; psychol. cons. Town of Berlin, Conn., 1968-69; dir. testing, counseling and career devel. Post Coll., Waterbury, Conn., 1970-74, asst. dean students, 1975-77; asst. dept. research in health edn. U. Conn., 1974-75; pvt. practice cons. and counseling, Triage, Plainville, Conn., St. Joseph's Coll., West Hartford, Conn., U. Hartford, 1977—. Dir. personnel com. Southington (Conn.) Pub. Health Assn., 1973-74. Mem. New Eng. Ednl. Research Orgn. (pres. 1974-75), Am., Conn. (pres. 1978-79) personnel and guidance assns., Am. Psychol. Assn., AAUP, Phi Delta Kappa. Roman Catholic.

KASHGARIAN, MICHAEL, physician, educator; b. N.Y.C., Sept. 20, 1933; s. Toros and Arax (Almasian) K.; A.B., N.Y. U., 1954; M.D., Yale, 1958; m. Jean Gaylor Caldwell, July 2, 1960; children—Michaele, Thea. Intern Barnes Hosp., St. Louis, 1958-59; asst. in medicine Washington U., St. Louis, 1958-59; asst. resident in pathology, Yale-New Haven Med. Center, 1959-61, resident in pathology, 1962-63; research fellow in renal physiology U. Goettingen, Germany, 1961-62; practice medicine specializing in pathology, New Haven, 1962—; instr. in pathology Yale, New Haven, 1962-64, asst. prof., 1964-67, asso. prof., 1967-74, prof., 1974—, vice-chmn. dept. pathology, 1976-79; asso. pathologist Yale-New Haven Hosp., 1964-66, asst. attending pathologist, 1966-69, attending pathologist, 1969—; cons. in pathology to various hosps. in Conn., 1962—. Chmn. Ednl. Adv. Council, N. Haven Bd. Edn., 1971; chmn. Christian Edn. Com., Ch. of Christ in Yale, 1970. Served to 1st. lt., M.C. USAR, 1954-65. USPHS fellow, 1963-65; USPHS Research Career Devel. award, 1965-75. Diplomate Am. Bd. Pathology, Nat. Bd. of Med. Examiners. Fellow Am. Soc. of Clin. Pathologists; mem. AMA, Am. Assn. of Pathologists and Bacteriologists, Am. Soc. of Nephrology, Internat. Acad. of Pathology, Conn. State Med. Soc., New Haven County Med. Assn., Am. Soc. for Exptl. Pathology, Conn. Soc. of Pathologists (pres. 1975), Am. Heart Assn., AAAS, Am. Physiol. Soc., Sigma Xi, Alpha Omega Alpha, Alpha Kappa Alpha. Author: (with J.P. Hayslett, B.H. Spargo) Renal Disease, 1974; (with G.N. Burrow) The Endocrine Glands; contbr. numerous articles on research in nephrology to med. jours.; editorial bd. Nephron, 1970—. Home: 22 Old Orchard Rd North Haven CT 06473 Office: 310 Cedar St New Haven CT 06510

KASHIN, PHILIP, physiologist, educator, clin. researcher; b. N.Y.C., Oct. 27, 1930; s. Hyman and Zena (Kessler) K.; B.A., Bklyn. Coll., 1953; M.Ed., Columbia, 1958; M.S. in Biochemistry (USPHS fellow), N.Y. U., 1961; Ph.D. in Biology, Ill. Inst. Tech., 1970; m. Theda Schepps, Mar. 2, 1958; children—Peter Simon, Thomas Benjamin, Sarah Beth. Chemist, Chem. Compounding Corp., Bklyn., 1956-57; substitute tchr. chemistry N.Y.C. Bd. Edn., 1957-58; research asst. in immuno-chemistry research div. Hosp. for Spl. Surgery, N.Y.C., 1961-62, in biochemistry State U. N.Y. Downstate Med. Center, Bklyn., 1962-63; research biochemist div. life scis. Ill. Inst. Tech. Research Inst., Chgo., 1963-70; NIH Spl. postdoctoral fellow U. Oreg., 1970-71; asst. prof. biology Queens Coll., City U. N.Y., 1971-76; sr. asst. dir. clin. research USV Pharm. Corp., Tuckahoe, N.Y., 1976—. Served with U.S. Army, 1953-55. Recipient I-R 100 award Indsl. Research Mag., 1967, Biomed. Research award Queens Coll., 1971-72, 72-73, Faculty Research award City U. N.Y. Research Found., 1975-76. Mem. AAAS, Am. Inst. Biol. Sci., Am. Physiol. Soc., Am. Soc. Zoologists, Fedn. Am. Socs. Exptl. Biology, N.Y. Acad. Sci., Soc. Neurosci., Sigma Xi. Contbr. articles to profl. jours. Patentee in field. Home: 47 Glen Cove Dr Glen Head NY 11545 Office: Dept Clin Research USV Pharm Corp 1 Scarsdale Rd Tuckahoe NY 10707

KASHIWA, SHIRO, fed. judge; b. Kohala, Hawaii, Oct. 24, 1912; s. Ryuten and Yukiko (Matsubara) K.; J.D., U. Mich., 1936; m. Mildred Aiko Yamagata, July 20, 1941; children—Gregg R., Wendy Y. Admitted to Hawaii bar, 1937; atty. gen. Hawaii, 1959-63; asst. atty. gen. Land and Natural Resources div. Dept. Justice, Washington, 1969-72; judge U.S. Ct. of Claims, Washington, 1972—. Mem. Am., Fed., Hawaii bar assns., Am. Judicature Soc., Internat. Acad. Trial Lawyers, Nat. Lawyers Club, Japan-Am. Soc. Washington, Japanese Am. Citizens League (Nisei of Biennium 1970). Clubs: Internat. (Washington); River Bend Golf and Country. Home: 2510 Virginia Ave NW Washington DC 20037 Office: US Ct Claims 717 Madison Pl NW Washington DC 20005

KASICH, ANTHONY MILOSH, ret. physician; b. Dubrovnik, Yugoslavia, Mar. 15, 1898; s. Spaso and Mary (Bulatovich) K.; student Columbia, 1918-19; M.D., N.Y. U., in 1926, postgrad., 1934; postgrad. U. Pa., 1946; m. Fern Jansen, Aug. 16, 1941. Intern N.Y.C. Hosp., 1926-28; practice specializing in internal medicine, N.Y.C., 1928—; asst. physician Montefiore Hosp., Bellevue Hosp., 1946-52; asst. prof. medicine N.Y.U., 1947-52; lectr. medicine Columbia, 1947-52; chief div. gastroenterology Lenox Hill Hosp., N.Y.C., 1953-63, cons. gastroenterologist, 1963—; cons. gastroenterologist U.S. Army, Manhattan State Hosp. Served to lt. col. M.C., AUS, 1940-46. Diplomate Am. Bd. Internal Medicine and Gastroenterology. Fellow N.Y. Acad. Medicine, A.C.P.; mem. Pan Am. Med. Assn., A.M.A., Am. Gastroent. Assn., Soc. Gastrointestinal Endoscopy, Internat. Soc. Internal Medicine, Bockus Internat. Soc. Gastroenterology. Author: (J.L. Kantor) Handbook Digestive Diseases, 1949. Contbr. articles to profl. jours. Home: Cokesbury Rd Lebanon NJ 08833

KASIEWICZ, ALLEN BERNARD, tech. co. exec.; b. Darien, Conn., Feb. 22, 1941; s. Thomas Michael and Stella Edna (Gardocki) K.; A.A.E.E., Coll. San Mateo, 1964; student Bridgeport U., 1965; m. Linda Jean Kolbe, June 22, 1968; children—Simon Elliot, Christopher Allen. Process engr. semicondrs. Sperry Semicondrs., Norwalk Conn., 1964-68; area mgr. mktg. Benrus Technipower Co., Ridgefield, Conn., 1968-71; gen. products mgr. Amphenol Co., Danbury, Conn., 1971-77; product mgr. fiber optics Rank Precision Industries, West Nyack, N.Y., 1977—. Dir. water quality assessment Lake Lillinonah Authority, regional environ. protection authority, 1972-76; sec. Roxbury Republican Town Com., 1973—. Mem. Fiber Optic Communication Info. Soc. (founding mem., v.p. 1977—), Am. Optical Soc. Home: Route 67 Roxbury CT 06783 Office: 260 N Route 303 West Nyack NY 10994

KASINDORF, BLANCHE ROBINS, ednl. adminstr.; b. N.Y.C., May 18, 1925; d. Samuel David and Anna (Block) Robins; B.A., Hunter Coll., 1944; M.A., N.Y.U., 1948; postgrad. Cornell U., 1946-50; m. David Kasindorf, July 1, 1960. Tchr. pub. schs., Bklyn., 1945-56; instr. Bklyn. Coll., 1956-57; asst. in research for Puerto Rican study Ford Found. and N.Y.C. Bd. Edn., 1956-57; asst. prin. N.Y.C. Pub. Schs., 1957-59; research asso. ednl. programming and stats. N.Y.C. Bd. Edn., 1959-63, coordinator spl. edn. liaison div. child welfare for Bur. Curriculum Research, 1963-64; jr. prin., integration coordinator Bklyn. Sch. Dist. 44, 1964-65; prin. Pub. Schs. 7 and 8, Bklyn., 1965—; cons. to numerous social agys. Mem. NEA, Council Exceptional Children, N.Y.C. Elementary Sch. Prins., Council Supervisory Assns. Contbr. to profl. publs.; also editor instructional materials. Home: 50 Kenilworth Pl Brooklyn NY 11210 Office: PS 378 Hicks St Brooklyn NY 11201

KASNER, VICTOR HERBERT, periodontist; b. N.Y.C., June 22, 1931; s. Leon and Dora (Duboys) K.; B.A., Bklyn. Coll., 1953; D.D.S., N.Y. U., 1958, postgrad., 1968-72; m. Martha Goobich, June 21,

1953; children—David Neil, Lisa Joy, Robin Sue. Gen. practice dentistry, West Orange, N.J., 1960-70, specializing in periodontics, 1970—; dentist Piscataway Twp. Bd. Edn., Middlesex, N.J., 1962-65; chief dental dept. St. Barnabas Med. Center, Livingston, N.J., 1968—; lectr., clinician Essex County Dental Soc., Newark Dental Club; lectr. Montclair State Coll., Maplewood, and South Orange, N.J., adult edn. dept. Livingston Sch. System, USAF. Served to capt. USAF, 1958-60. Fellow Acad. Medicine N.J.; mem. Am., N.J. dental assns., Am. Acad. Periodontology, Northeastern Soc. Periodontology, N.J. Soc. Periodontists, Am. Acad. Oral Medicine, Essex County Dental Soc. (mem. exec. bd. 1969—, treas. 1978), Alpha Omega (lectr., clinician; pres. chpt. 1975-76). Mem. B'nai B'rith (past pres. lodge). Home: Livingston NJ 07039 Office: 97 Northfield Ave West Orange NJ 07052

KASPER, ROLF GUNTHER, research mech. engr.; b. Wilhelmshaven, W. Germany, June 11, 1942; s. Rudolf and Martha (Dirksen) K.; came to U.S., 1954, naturalized, 1960; B.M.E., Union Coll., 1966; M.S.E.M., Ga. Inst. Tech., 1968; M.Phil., Yale U., 1969, M.S., 1970, Ph.D., 1971; m. Mariana DeLeeuw, June 17, 1967; 1 son, Kent Dirksen. Exptl. engr., stress analyst Sikorsky Aircraft, United Tech., Stratford, Conn., summers 1961, 62, 65, 66, 67; lectr. Union Coll., Schenectady, 1965-66, Ga. Tech., Atlanta, 1967-68; supr. material testing lab. Yale U., New Haven, 1968-71; adj. prof. math. and mech. engring. U. New Haven, 1974—; applied scientist Office Engring. Mechanics, Naval Underwater Systems Center, New London, Conn., 1971—; reviewer, evaluator govt. and indsl. research and devel. proposals, 1975—; lectr., cons. in field. NDEA fellow, 1966-70; NASA fellow, 1970-71; recipient Superior Accomplishment award U.S. Navy, 1976, Spl. Achievement award, 1978. Mem. Assn. Engrs. and Scientists (dir. 1975-78), AAAS, ASME, Yale Engring. Assn., Sigma Xi. Congregationalist. Contbr. articles to profl. jours. Home: 35 Oakridge Dr Old Lyme CT 06371 Office: Code 401 Office of Engring Mechanics Naval Underwater Systems Center New London CT 06320

KASPERBAUER, JAMES CLEMENS, air force officer; b. Manning, Iowa, Sept. 12, 1937; s. John Sixtus and Clara Mary (Balk) K.; B.A. in Bus. Mgmt., U. Nebr., 1965; M.A. in Personnel Mgmt., Central Mich. U., 1973, M.A. in Pub. Adminstrn., 1975; m. Margaret Ruth Craig, June 5, 1971; children—Susan, Jean, Jamie. Enlisted U.S. Air Force, 1955, advanced through grades to lt. col., 1976; br. chief research and devel. contracts, Wright-Patterson AFB, Ohio, 1972-75; dep. chief space, missile and systems div. Andrews AFB, Washington, 1976—; mgmt. cons. Identity Research Corp. Decorated D.F.C. with 2 oak leaf clusters, Air medal with 12 oak leaf clusters, Meritorious Service medal, Air Force Commendation medal with 2 oak leaf clusters. Certified profl. contracts mgr. Mem. Nat. Contract Mgmt. Assn., Aero. Navigators Assn., Air Force Assn., Tech. Marketing Soc. Am., Smithsonian Assos. Roman Catholic. Clubs: Optimists, Toastmasters. Home: 4753 Fairway Dr Camp Springs MD 20335 Office: Hdqrs Air Force Systems Command Andrews Air Force Base MD 20334

KASPERSSON, EINO VICTOR, sculptor; b. Bronx, N.Y., Sept. 7, 1908; s. Frederick and Olga (White) K.; student Art Students League, NAD, 1929-32, Rand Sch. Social Sci., 1933-35, New Sch. Social Research, 1950-52; m. Mabelle Sutherland, Apr. 9, 1934; children—John Richard, Jean. With fabrication div. Aluminum Co. Am., Edgewater, N.J., 1944-66; child counselor N.Y. Sch. for the Deaf, White Plains, 1967-70; sculptor, Sterling, Conn., 1976—. Mem. steering bd. edn., bd. dirs. Northeastern Area Regional Edn. Services. Gould Found. Art scholar, 1929-32. Mem. Conf. on Methods in Sci. and Philosophy (New Sch. Social Research), UN Assn., AAAS, White Plains Suprs. Assn., Edgewater Camera Club, United Steelworkers Am. (hon.). Founder, pub., editor Houseparents Mag., 1970; contbr. articles to mag. Home and Office: Route 1 Box 72A Sterling CT 06377

KASS, BENNY LEE, lawyer; b. Chgo., Aug. 20, 1936; s. Herman and Ethel (Lome) K.; B.S., Northwestern U., 1957; LL.B., U. Mich., 1960; LL.M., George Washington U., 1967; m. Salme Lundstrom, Aug. 30, 1963; children—Gale, Brian. Admitted to D.C. bar, 1960; atty. Maritime Adminstrn., 1960-61; counsel House Information Subcommittee, 1962-65; asst. counsel Senate Adminstrv. Practice Subcom., Washington, 1965-69; pvt. practice law, Washington, 1969—; mem. firm Kass, Skalet and Frosh; prof. communication law Am. U.; pub. mem. Nat. Advt. Rev. Bd., 1971-75; commr. D.C. Conf. on Uniform State Laws. Chmn. consumer affairs subcom., Mayors Econ. Devel. Com., 1968-70; chmn. Ad Hoc Com. on Consumer Protection, 1965—. Served with USAF, 1961-62. Am. Polit. Sci. Assn. Congl. fellow, 1966. Mem. Am., Fed. bar assns., Am. Polit. Sci. Assn., Sigma Delta Chi. Contbr. articles to profl. jours. Home: 3642 Jocelyn St NW Washington DC 20015 Office: Kass Skalet and Frosh 1528 18th St NW Washington DC 20036

KASSAB, VINCENT, elec. engr., housing co. exec.; b. Beirut, Feb. 4, 1942 (parents Am. citizens); s. John and Olga K.; B.S., State U. N.Y. at Buffalo, 1964, M.S., 1968. Devel. engr., Sylvania Electronic Systems, Buffalo, 1964-68, Boston, 1968-69; tchr. physics Kensington High Sch., Buffalo, 1969-70; asst. prof. elec. tech. Erie Community Coll., Williamsville, N.Y., 1970—; pres. Belvoir Homes Inc., Williamsville, 1977—. Grantee Vocat. Edn. Adminstrn., 1974. Mem. Asso. Community Coll. Faculties, Faculty Fedn. Erie Community Coll. Home: 120 Meyer Rd Buffalo NY 14226 Office: Main and Youngs Rd Williamsville NY 14221

KASSAY, MICHAEL BELA, mech. engr.; b. Budapest, Hungary, Feb. 6, 1924; s. Bela Zsigmond and Camille Maria (Jeszenszky) K.; diploma, degree in mech. engring. Royal Hungarian U., 1950; m. Mary Consolation Cukor, Nov. 3, 1956; children—Sheila Judith, Elizabeth. Came to U.S., 1956, naturalized, 1962. Project engr. Indsl. Design Inst. Hungary, 1950-53, asst. dept. head, 1953-56; project engr. Sidney W. Barbanel Cons. Engrs., Long Island City, N.Y., 1957-65, asso., 1965—; v.p., chief computer operations Sabara, Inc., 1966—. Course dir. Indsl. Tng. Program for Blind, 1948-50. Served with Royal Hungarian Army, 1943-45, Hungarian Revolutionary Army, 1956. Decorated Cross for Distinguished Valor (2). Registered profl. engr., N.Y. Mem. Am. Soc. Heating, Refrigeration and Air Conditioning Engrs. (chmn. energy conservation com. 1973-75), Nat. Rifle Assn., Competitive Pistol Assn., Fedn. Internat. des Artilleur, Am. Contract Bridge League (life master). Republican. Lutheran. Patentee in field. Office: 29-28 41st Ave Long Island City NY 11101

KASSER, IVAN MICHAEL, cons. and investment cos. exec.; b. Budapest, Hungary, Dec. 9, 1940; s. Alexander Sandor and Elizabeth K.; came to U.S., 1950, naturalized, 1956; S.B., S.M., Mass. Inst. Tech., 1961; D.Eng., U. Grenoble (France), 1964; M.B.A., Harvard U., 1968; m. Lynn von Kersting, Feb. 2, 1974. Project engr. Technopulp de Ingeneria, Madrid, 1964-66; sr. fin. analyst W. R. Grace & Co., mfr. chems. and consumer products, N.Y.C., 1968-69, dir. mgmt. info. systems Chem. Group, 1969-70, mgr. fin. planning and evaluations Indsl. Chem. Group, 1970-71; pres. Technopulp, Inc., cons. to pulp and paper industry, Montclair, N.J., 1971—; pres. Imaco, Inc., Montclair, investment co., 1972—; chmn. bd. Booher Lumber Co., Lafayette, N.Y., Sundowner Mgmt. Co., real estate mgmt., Montclair; cons. in finance, gen. mgmt., tech. bd. dirs. Am. Hungarian Found.; trustee Actors' Studio. Registered profl. engr., N.J. Mem. TAPPI, Am. Chem. Soc., Assn. Technique de l'Industrie Papetiere, Nat. Hardwood Lumber Assn. Contbr. articles to profl. jours.; patentee in field. Home: 159 Gates Ave Montclair NJ 07042 Office: 26 Park St Montclair NJ 07042

KASSOFF, EDWIN, judge; b. Bklyn., July 15, 1924; s. Leo and Sarah (Steinberg) K.; B.B.A., Coll. City N.Y., 1947; LL.B., Bklyn. Law Sch., 1953; grad. U. Nev. Nat. Coll. State Judiciary, 1972; m. Phyllis Brafman, Nov. 6, 1949; children—Mitchell Jay, Robert Stephen. Admitted to N.Y. State bar, 1953, U.S. Supreme Ct. bar, 1963; individual practice law N.Y.C., 1953-71; judge Civil Ct. N.Y.C., Queens, 1971-73; justice Supreme Ct. State N.Y., Jamaica, 1974—. Instr. law Queens Coll., N.Y.C., 1956-63; vis. lectr. law Columbia, 1966-67; asst. prof. Pace U., N.Y.C., 1964-70, asso. prof., 1970-73, prof., 1973—; co-counsel legislature coms. N.Y. State Constl. Conv., 1967; research counsel majority party N.Y. State Assembly, 1968; asst. counsel Joint Legislative Com. Mass Transp., 1969; faculty adviser U. Nev. Nat. Coll. State Judiciary, 1973. Alternate del. Democratic Nat. Conv., 1968; sec., jud. conv. Queens County Dem. party, 1969-71; chmn. Dem. Law Com. Queens County, 1969-71. Mem. staff Temporary State Commn. to Study Causes of Campus Unrest, 1970. Served to lt., inf. AUS, 1943-46: ETO. Mem. Am. Bus. Law Assn. (pres. 1970), N.E. Regional Bus. Law Assn. (pres. 1964), Queens, Am. bar assns. Author: Business Law Text, 1964; Instructor's Manual for Business Law Text, 1964; Test Manual for Business Law Courses, 1964; Sales and Bailments Text, 1973; American Commercial Law Text, 1975. Office: Supreme Ct State of NY 88-11 Sutphin Blvd Jamaica NY 11435

KASSUM, SALEEM, personnel adminstr.; b. Dar-es-Salaam, Tanzania, May 25, 1944; s. Al-Noor and Shirin (Nazerali) K.; came to U.S., 1967; B.A. with high honors, State U. N.Y., Binghamton, 1970; M.S. in Indsl. and Labor Relations, Cornell U., 1972. Tng. officer UN Devel. Programme, N.Y.C., 1973-76, chief tng. sect. div. personnel, 1977-78, human resources devel. officer, integrated systems improvement project, 1978—; co-trainer Nat. Tng. Lab., Bethel, Maine, 1976—. Served with RAF, 1962-67. Asso. mem. Am. Psychol. Assn. Muslim. Club: RAF (London). Office: 1 United Nations Plaza New York City NY 10017

KASTNER, WILLIAM JOSEPH, brewery exec.; b. Jersey City, May 27, 1928; s. Herman J. and Julia E. (Byrnes) K.; B.M.E. cum laude, Cath. U. Am., 1951; m. Nelda I. Moore, Sept. 10, 1955; children—Joseph B., Margaret E., Ann Marie, Timothy W., David E., John R. Mech. engr. Navy dept. Bur. Ships, Washington, 1951-52; engr. George J. Meyer Mfg. div. A-T-O, Inc., Worcester, Mass., 1956, sales engr., Union, N.J., 1956-66, area mgr., 1966-67, eastern regional mgr., 1968-70; eastern mgr. machinery sales Crown Cork & Seal Co., Inc., Phila., 1970-71; v.p. new machinery Fowler Products Co., Inc., Athens, Ga., 1971-72; v.p., gen. mgr. N.J. Materials Co., Inc., Matawan, N.J., 1972; mgr. engring. Canada Dry Corp., N.Y.C., 1972-75; v.p. mktg. Metramatic Corp., Landing, N.J., 1975-77; prodn. mgr. Champale Inc., Trenton, N.J., 1977—. Trustee Colts Neck Vol. Fire Co., 1968-70, pres., 1967; pres. Colts Neck Exec. Fire Council-Fire Dept., 1967. Served with USNR, 1952-55; now capt. Res. Registered profl. engr., Vt., N.J. Mem. ASME, Am. Internat. Plant Engrs., Brewers and Beverage Packaging Assn. (v.p. 1968-71), Navy League (dir. 1971, v.p. 1972, exec. v.p. 1973, pres. 1974-76, v.p. N.J., nat. dir.), Res. Officers Assn., Naval Res. Assn., Am. Soc. Naval Engrs., Naval Inst. Roman Catholic (pres. parish council 1969-72, tchr. parish sch. 1971-75, asst. prin. 1975—). Home: RD 1 Fernwood Ct Colts Neck NJ 07722 Office: 1024 Lamberton St Trenton NJ 08611

KASUGA, BILL, electronics mfg. co. exec.; b. San Francisco, Feb. 28, 1915; s. Genshi and Toyo (Yano) K.; A.B.A., Marin Jr. Coll., 1939; B.S., U. San Francisco, 1941; m. Sadaye Nagayama, May 1, 1949; children—Albert Rikio, Joan Naomi. Accountant, The Emporium Co., San Francisco, 1941-42; chief accountant Community Enterprises, Poston, Ariz., 1942-43; lang. instr. U.S. Army Lang. Sch., Mpls., 1943-46, Monterey, Calif., 1946-58; sr. v.p. Kenwood Electronics Inc., Secaucus, N.J., 1958—. Mem. Electronics Industry Assn. of Japan, Japanese Am. Assn. of N.Y. Inc., Inst. High Fidelity (dir.). Buddhist. Office: 75 Seaview Dr Secaucus NJ 07094

KATAYAMA, DANIEL HIDEO, physicist; b. Honolulu, Sept. 26, 1939; s. Charles and Kimiko (Kajiwara) K.; B.S., U. Hawaii, 1962, M.S., 1963; Ph.D., Tufts U., 1970; m. Jane Sato, Sept. 22, 1963. Research physicist Air Force Geophys. Lab., Bedford, Mass., 1971—. Served to lt. USAF, 1963-66. NDEA Title IV fellow, 1966-69. Mem. AAAS, Am. Phys. Soc., Sigma Xi. Contbr. articles in field to profl. jours. Home: 2 Fox Run Rd Bedford MA 01730 Office: Air Force Geophys Lab Bedford MA 01731

KATAYAMA, ISAO, pathologist; b. Mishima, Japan, June 13, 1930; s. Koji and Kachi K.; came to U.S., 1963; M.D., Keio U., 1954, Ph.D., 1961; m. Yukiko Yanai, Mar. 30, 1961; children—Ken, Taul, Makoto. Intern, U.S. Army Hosp., Tokyo, 1954-55; resident E. Tenn. Baptist Hosp., 1956-58, Boston City Hosp., 1964-66; mem. staff U. Mass. Med. Center; asso. prof. pathology U. Mass. Med. Sch., Worcester, 1974—. Sheldon Hank Hyatt Hairy Cell Leukemia Fund research grantee, 1976—. Mem. Am. Assn. Pathologists, Internat. Acad. Pathologists, New Eng. Soc. Pathologists. Buddhist. Contbr. articles on leukemia to Am. Jour. Medicine. Home: 50 Devon Rd Newton MA 02159

KATAYAMA, JANE HATSUE, librarian; b. Ewa, Oahu, Hawaii, July 23, 1941; d. Kikuo and Shizue (Abe) Sato; Ed.B., U. Hawaii, 1963; M.S., Simmons Coll., 1969; m. Daniel H. Katayama, Sept. 22, 1963. Reference librarian Cary Meml. Library, Lexington, Mass., 1964; reference librarian M.I.T., Lincoln Lab., Lexington, Mass., 1965-73, asst. library mgr., 1973-74, library mgr., 1975—. Mem. Am. Mgmt. Assn., Am. Soc. Info. Sci., Spl. Libraries Assn. (chpt. sec. 1974-75). Home: 2 Fox Run St Bedford MA 01730 Office: 244 Wood St Lexington MA 02173

KATEB, GEORGE ANTHONY, polit. scientist, educator; b. Bklyn., Feb. 27, 1931; s. Anthony Francis and Victoria Anna (Mesnooh) K.; A.B., Columbia, 1952, A.M., 1953, Ph.D. (univ. fellow), 1960. Faculty Amherst (Mass.) Coll., 1957—, chmn. dept. polit. sci., 1966-67, 73-75, Kenan prof. polit. sci., 1974-78; vis. lectr. Mt. Holyoke Coll., 1958, Yale, 1973. Cons. Nat. Endowment for Humanities, 1976—. Served with AUS, 1950-54. Rockefeller Found. grantee, 1963-64; Guggenheim Found. fellow, 1971-72. Mem. New Eng. (exec. com. 1965-66, pres. 1978-79), Am. polit. sci. assns., Harvard Soc. Fellows, AAUP, Am. Soc. Polit. and Legal Philosophy (v.p. 1972-74), Conf. for Study Polit. Thought, Phi Beta Kappa. Author: Utopia and Its Enemies, 1963; Political Theory: Its Nature and Uses, 1968; Utopia, 1971. Book rev. editor Mass. Rev., 1961-63, contbr. editor, 1964-72; editorial bd. Polit. Theory, 1971—, Jour. History Ideas, 1976—, Am. Polit. Sci. Rev., 1977—, Alternative Futures, 1977—. Home: 99 Northampton Rd Amherst MA 01002

KATES, KENNETH CASPER, SR., zoologist, parasitologist, educator; b. Millville, N.J., Apr. 29, 1910; s. Harry Clarence and Martha (Volz) K.; A.B., Columbia, 1932; M.A., Duke, 1934, Ph.D., 1937; m. Marguerite Ann Urban, July 1, 1941; children—Julia Ann Kates Johnson, Kenneth Casper, Virginia Day Kates Wilis. Grad. asst., univ. fellow Duke, 1932-35; from jr. zoologist to prin. zoologist U.S. Dept. Agr., Washington, 1938-60, 66-75; veterinary parasitologist, FDA, HEW, Washington and Beltsville, Md., 1960-66; lectr. zoology George Washington U., Washington, 1946—. Vis. lectr. U. Md., 1951, 60; lectr. U. Ill., 1965. Served to capt. AUS, 1943-46. Fellow AAAS; mem. Am. Soc. Parasitologists, Helminthological Soc. Washington (pres. 1946), World Assn. Veterinary Parasitologists. Democrat. Contbr. articles to profl. jours. Home: 2601 Imperial Ct Apple Green Dunkirk MD 20754

KATIMS, HERMAN, publisher, musician; b. N.Y.C., Jan. 1; s. Harry and Caroline (Spiegel) K.; scholar Bklyn. Conservatory Music, 1914; grad. Inst. Mus. Art, N.Y.C., 1925; m. Miriam Lapin, July 7, 1929. Debut, Bechstein Hall, Berlin, 1928; appeared at N.Y. Town Hall, 1934, Carnegie Hall, 1935; coach numerous successful concert pianists, tchrs. and dirs. Mem. Conn. Music Tchrs. Assn. Author: (poems) Twenty-Four Preludes, 1934. Composer: Caprice and Fugue, 1968; transcription for piano Vitali Chaconne, 1971; Chant d'Amour, 1953; Cupid, 1951; Humoresque, 1972; Legend, 1958; Melody in D-Flat, 1962; Sonatina, 1971; Idyll for piano and violin, 1974; (songs) My Country's Flag, 1945, Knickerbocker on Parade, 1938, No Longer, 1939; Waltz in C Sharp Minor, 1978. Home and Office: 4 Belmont Pl Rowayton CT 06853

KATIS, JAMES GEORGE, physician, psychiatrist, educator; b. Westchester, N.Y., Apr. 3, 1933; s. George Demetrius and Speridola (Christos) K.; B.A., Wesleyan U., 1956; M.D., McGill U., 1960; m. Lauma D. Upelnieks, Dec. 12, 1964; children—Peter D., Thomas E., James A. Intern, Bellevue Hosp., N.Y.C., 1960-61; resident in psychiatry Inst. of Living, Hartford, Conn., 1961-64; candidate N.Y. Psychoanalytic Inst., 1965-68; mem. staffs Hartford Hosp., 1964-65, St. Luke's Hosp., N.Y.C., 1965—, Presbyn. Hosp., N.Y.C., 1967—; practice medicine specializing in psychiatry, N.Y.C., 1965—; instr. psychiatry Coll. Physicians and Surgeons, Columbia U., N.Y.C., 1967—; clin. dir. Silver Hill Found., New Cannan, Conn., 1971—. Fellow Am. Psychiat. Assn., N.Y. Acad. Medicine; mem. A.C.P., AMA, Conn. Psychiat. Soc. (councillor-at-large 1973—, mem. peer rev. com. 1973—), Conn. State, N.Y., Fairfield County (Conn.) med. socs. Greek Orthodox. Home: 162 Old West Mountain Rd Ridgefield CT 06877 Office: Silver Hill Found Box 1177 New Canaan CT 06840 also 1215 Fifth Ave New York City NY 10029

KATKIN, SYLVIA SOBEL, ednl. adminstr.; b. N.Y.C., Aug. 24, 1928; d. Julius and Ida Sobel; B.A., Bklyn. Coll., 1950; M.S. with honors, C.W. Post Coll., 1970, M.S., 1978; m. Arthur S. Katkin, Nov. 25, 1950 (dec.); children—Caryn Etta, Beth Ann. Spl. services librarian U.S. Army, 1951-53; activity worker pleasantville Cottage Sch., 1950-51; tchr. visually handicapped N.Y.C. Bd. Edn., 1971-72, guidance counselor emotionally handicapped, 1974-75, curriculum coordinator, 1975-76, unit coordinator, 1976—, chmn. com. on the handicapped, 1978—; adj. asso. prof. C.W. Post Coll., 1971-78. Founder, dir. Women's Inst. Survival and Enlightenment, L.I. Mem. Am. Personnel and Guidance Assn., NEA, Am. Fedn. Tchrs. Home: 26 Dunhill Rd New Hyde Park NY 11040 Office: 125-20 Sutphin Blvd New York NY

KATSAROS, THOMAS, educator; b. N.Y.C., Feb. 21, 1926; s. John and Helen (Drivas) K.; B.A., N.Y. U., 1953, M.A., 1956, M.A., 1958, P.h. D., , 1963, advanced prof. certificate, 1975; m. Nancy Louise Massa, June 26, 1971. With Gerdau Export-Import Co., N.Y.C., then Argos Import Co., N.Y.C., 1955-63; asst. prof. State U. N.Y., Potsdam, 1963-65; faculty U. New Haven (Conn.), 1965—, prof., chmn. dept. history, 1968—. Served with AUS, 1944-47. Decorated Bronze Star. Mem. Am. Hist. Assn., Am. Econ. Assn., Eastern Econ. Assn., Am. Mgmt. Assn., AAUP. Author: (with Nathaniel Kaplan) The Western Mystical Tradition, 1969, The Origins of American Transcendentalism, 1975; (with George J. Schiro) A Brief History of the Western World, 1978. Home: 11 Carriage Dr North Haven CT 06473 Office: University of New Haven West Haven CT 06505

KATSH, ABRAHAM I(SAAC), educator, former coll. pres.; b. Poland, Aug. 10, 1908; s. Reuben and Rachel (Maskilleison) K.; A.B., N.Y. U., 1931, A.M., 1932, J.D., 1936; postgrad. Princeton, 1941; Ph.D., Dropsie U., 1944, LL.D., 1976; D.H.L., Hebrew Union Coll.-Jewish Inst. Religion, 1964; D.Lit., Spertus Coll. Judaica, Chgo., 1968; D.D., Christian Theol. Sem., Indpls., 1968, U. Dubuque, 1971; LL.D., Lebanon Valley Coll., 1971; m. Estelle Wachtell, Feb. 20, 1943; children—Ethan, Salem, Rochelle. Came to U.S., 1925, naturalized, 1932. Instr. Hebrew, N.Y.U., 1934-37, exec. dir. Jewish Culture Found., 1937-44, exec. chmn., 1944-67, instr. edn., 1937-44, asst. prof., 1944-45, asso. prof., 1945-47, prof. edn., 1947-65, dir. Inst. Hebrew Studies, 1962-67, prof. Hebrew and Near Eastern Studies, 1934-67, chmn. dept. Hebrew and Near Eastern Studies and prof. Grad. Sch. Arts and Scis., 1966-68, distinguished prof. research, 1967-68, prof. emeritus, 1976—; pres. Dropsie U. Hebrew and Cognate Learning, Phila., 1967-76, pres. emeritus, 1976—, distinguished research prof. Hebraica, 1967—; Arabic instr., 1942-43, dir. Library Judaica and Hebraica, 1942, curator, 1952-67, chmn. dept. fgn. langs., 1953-54, chmn. dept. Hebrew culture edn., 1953-66, dir. Hebrew lang. and lit. sect. Wash. Sq. Coll., 1957—; lectr. New Sch. Social Research; dir. Am. Workshop on Israel Life and Culture, held in Israel sponsored by N.Y.U., 1949-67; asst. editor charge Hebrew, Modern Lang. Jour., 1949—; mng. editor Jour. Ednl. Sociology, 1951-56; editor Bar Mitzvah, 1955. Mem. Exec. Bd. License for Tchrs. and Prins. of Jewish Schs. N.Y.C.; chmn. Nat. Bd. of License for Tchrs. and Colls. in field of Hebrew Studies, 1957—; exec. mem. World Hebrew Congress, Hadassah Reference Bd.; mem. Com. on Internat. Exchange Persons; spl. examiner Bd. Edn., N.Y.C.; chmn. nat. screening com. Inst. Internat. Edn.; mem. conf. bd. Asso. Research Councils, Washington; cons. Hebrew, Nat. Assn. on Standard Med. Vocabulary. Lectr. World Congress for Jewish Scholarship. Jerusalem, 1947, 57, 73, Internat. Oriental Congress, Munich, 1957; Moscow, 1960 chmn. Hebraic sect. 26th congress, India, 1964. Dir. Land of the Bible Profl. Workshop with Dept. of State, 1962-67. Recipient B'nai Zion Meritorious key, 1944; Founders Citation, N.Y. U. Chair Hebrew Culture Edn., 1953; Brith Abraham Gold Medal, 1952; Tercentary citation Jewish Book Council Am., 1954; 1st prize Hebrew Acad. Am., 1956; Matz Found. prize, 1956. 1st prize Hebrew Acad. Histadruth Ivrith, 1957, Dropsie Coll. jubilee citation, 1957, Ky. Col., 1957, prof. chair named in honor, 1957, scholarship named in honor, 1965 (both N.Y. U.); Am. Assn. for Jewish Edn. award, 1959, Ernest O. Melby Award, 1962; Schneiderman prize, 1965; N.Y.U. Presdl. citation, 1965; N.Y. Mayor's citation, 1965; also numerous grants. Mem. Modern Lang. Assn. (chmn. evaluation com. modern Hebrew materials), N.Y.U. Soc. for Libraries (pres.), N.Y. State Fedn. Fgn. Lang. Tchrs. (dir.), World Congress for Hebrew Lang. and Culture (exec. com.), Jewish Book Council Am. (nat. com.), Zionist Orgn. Am. (nat. chmn. 1949-51), Nat. Council Jewish Edn. (exec. com.), Jewish Acad. Arts and Scis. (chmn. bd. govs.), Nat. Assn. Profs. Hebrew in Am. Instns. of Higher Learning (founder, pres. 1951-53, hon. pres., 1953—), Am. Assn. Jewish Edn. (nat. chmn. bd. licenses), Am. Oriental Soc. Soc. for Bibl. Lit., Acad. Religion, Phi Delta Kappa. Author: Einstein's Theory of Relativity (Hebrew), 1937; Hebrew in American Higher Education, 1941; Hebraic Contributions to American Life, 1941; Krochmal and the German Idealists, 1948; Hebrew Language,

Literature and Culture in American Institutions of Higher Learning, 1950; Education and Racial Prejudices; Democracy and Interfaith; Hebraic Backgrounds of American Democracy, 1951; Judaism in Islam, 1954; Judaic Backgrounds of Islam (Hebrew), 1957; Midrash David ha-Nagid, Vol. I, 1961; Land of the Bible, 1962; Judaism and the Koran, rev. 1962; Midrash David Hanagid, Vol. II, 1964, 67; Yiggal Hazan, 1964; A Scroll of Agony, 1965; Chomique D'une Agonie, 1966; Buchder Agonie, 1967; Megilat Yesurin, 1965; Ginze Mishna, 1971; The Diary of Ch. A. Kaplan, 1973; Ginze Talmud, 1976; Biblical Heritage of American Democracy, 1977; also many articles in leading U.S. and fgn. scholarly mags. Editor: Hebrew Abstracts, 1954, Ginze Russia, 1959, Antonin Geniza Catalogue, 1963, The Kaplan Diary of the Warsaw Ghetto, 1962, Jewish Quar. Rev., 1978—; asso. editor Universal Jewish Ency., 1958—; editorial com. Nat. Study for Jewish Edn., 1957; founder, editor-in-chief Hebrew Abstracts; contbr. to Ency. Judaica; rev. editor Hebrew sect. Modern Lang. Jour. Home: 1520 Spruce St Philadelphia PA 19102

KATSIFIS, CHRISTOS C., mech. engr.; b. Klidi Biotia, Greece, Dec. 24, 1935; s. Constantine A. and Athena C. (Nenos) K.; came to U.S., 1963, naturalized, 1975; B.S. in Mech. Engring., Ind. Inst. Tech., 1966; m. Georgia C. Kontogiannis, May 27, 1967; children—Athena, Constantine. Marine engr. S. Livanos Co., Greece, 1955-59, 61-63; design engr. Hydrotechnic Corp., Chgo., 1966-68; sr. mech. engr. Daniel, Irbuhn, Seelye and Fuller, architects and engrs., Batavia, Ill., 1968-69; engring. mgr. Aeronix Inc., Linden, N.J., 1969-71; co-founder, mgr. ops. Control Air Inc., Cranford, N.J., 1971—, also sec., treas., dir. Served with C.E., AUS, 1959-60. Registered profl. engr., N.J. Mem. N.J. Soc. Profl. Engrs. Democrat. Greek Orthodox. Address: 17 Huntington Rd East Brunswick NJ 08816

KATZ, ASCHER, lawyer, town justice; b. N.Y.C., Apr. 16, 1927; s. Morris Joseph and Tessie (Appel) K.; B.E.E., Coll. City N.Y., 1948; J.D., Harvard, 1951; m. Barbara Dorothy Novins, Aug. 17, 1957; children—Arlene Elizabeth, Beverly Ann, Rochelle Bonnie. Admitted to N.Y. bar, 1952; staff atty. civil br. Legal Aid Soc., N.Y.C., 1952-54; law asst. Office Corp. Counsel, N.Y.C., 1954-55; pvt. practice law, N.Y.C., 1955—, White Plains, N.Y., 1965—; small claims night ct. arbitrator Civil Ct. N.Y., N.Y.C., 1970-75, compulsory arbitrator, 1972-75; justice Town of Greenburgh, Westchester County, 1976—. Mem. nat. governing council Am. Jewish Congress, N.Y.C., 1962—, pres. Westchester div., 1978—; chmn. religious sch. bd. Temple Israel Center, White Plains, 1972-74, trustee, 1972—. Served with USNR, 1945-46. Mem. Am., N.Y. State, Westchester County bar assns., Assn. Bar City N.Y., Assn. Trial Lawyers Am., Am. Judicature Soc., N.Y. State, Westchester County magistrates assns., N.A.A.C.P., Urban League, White Plains C. of C., Am. Arbitration Assn. (arbitrator), Jewish War Vets. (sr. vice comdr. White Plains post 1976-78), City Coll. N.Y. Alumni Assn., Harvard Law Sch. Assn. Mason. Club: Harvard (N.Y.C.). Home: 24 Primrose Ave W White Plains NY 10607 Office: 180 E Post Rd White Plains NY 10601 also 60 E 42d St New York City NY 10017

KATZ, CAROLE SUE, sociologist, therapist; b. N.Y.C., Nov. 27, 1936; d. Henry Jonas and Mildred (Fassler) Rosenfeld; B.A., N.Y. U., 1968, M.A., 1972; children—David Jonathan, Stephen Charles. Therapist, Jewish Bd. Guardians, N.Y.C., 1964-67; researcher Dept. Community Psychiatry, Roosevelt Hosp., N.Y.C., 1967-69; dir. research and evaluation Vera Inst. Justice, N.Y.C., 1969-72; chief program analyst, health and hosp. corp. dept. mental health, N.Y.C., 1972-73; founder, dir. Found. Community Innovation Inc., N.Y.C., 1973—; dir. program planning, psychotherapist Inst. for Mental Health Edn., Englewood, N.J., 1977—; cons. in field. Mem. Assn. Humanistic Psychology (pres. women's caucus N.Y.C. 1971—), Am. Sociol. Assn., Am. Psychol. Assn. Office: Found for Community Innovation Inc 520 Fifth Ave New York City NY 10036

KATZ, FRIEDRICH JOACHIM, power tool mfg. co. exec.; b. Vienna, Austria, May 26, 1934; s. Ignaz Wilhelm and Alice Emma (Grossman) K.; B.S. in Mech. Engring., U. Ill., 1958; grad. Mackenzie U.; m. Carol Pauline Ranieri, May 9, 1956; children—Ricardo Antonio, Katryn Alice. Came to U.S., 1963, naturalized, 1967. Chief product engr. H.W. Constrn. Equipment Corp., Sao Paulo, Brazil, 1958-61; factory mgr. Hyster Corp., 1961-63; projects engr. Outboard Marine Corp., 1963-65; mgr. engring. Hahn Inc., 1965-69; corp. chief engr. Huffman Mfg., 1969-72; dir. engring. Black & Decker Mfg. Co., Towson, Md., 1973—. Tech., gen. cons. mgmt. matters; expert witness in legal affairs. Moravia grantee. Mem. Am. Soc. Agrl. Engrs., Soc. Automotive Engrs. Republican. Roman Catholic. Clubs: Engineers, Admirals. Patentee in field. Home: 661 Tewkesbury Ln Severna Park MD 21146 Office: Black & Decker Mfg Co Towson MD 21204

KATZ, GILBERT, pharm. researcher; b. Bklyn., Jan. 17, 1936; s. Samuel Hershel and Sylvia K.; B.A., N.Y. U., 1961; certificate Columbia Coll. Pharmacy, 1972; m. Micaela Karl, Aug. 7, 1966. Pharm. formulator Purdue Frederick Research Center, Yonkers, N.Y., 1962-68; asst. scientist Hoffman-LaRoche, Nutley, N.J., 1968-70; asso. scientist Ortho Research Co., Raritan, N.J., 1970-73; sr. scientist Cooper Labs. Inc., Cedar Knolls, N.J., 1973—. Mem. Acad. Pharm. Scis., Am. Chem. Soc. Patentee in field. Home: Hunter Rd RD 2 Boonton NJ 07005

KATZ, HERBERT MARVIN, educator; b. Bklyn., Apr. 4, 1926; s. Abraham and Edna (Goldstein) K.; B.Ch.E., Coll., City N.Y., 1949; M.S., U. Cin., 1949, Ph.D., 1953; m. Evelyn Greene, July 1, 1954; children—Susan, Joel. Asst. chem. engr. Argonne (Ill.) Nat. Lab., 1954-56; chem. engr. Brookhaven Nat. Lab., Upton, N.Y., 1957-66; prof. Howard U., Washington 1968—, chmn. chem. engring., 1968-74. Treas., Human Relations Com. Eastern Suffolk County, N.Y., 1964-65, Alliance for Democratic Reform, Montgomery County, Md., 1969-70. Served with U.S. Army, 1944-46. Mem. Am. Inst. Chem. Engrs., Am. Chem. Soc., Sigma Xi. Patentee in field. Home: 1602 Sherwood Rd Silver Spring MD 20902 Office: Dept Chem Engring Howard U Washington DC 20001

KATZ, HILDA (HULDA WEBER), artist, author; b. June 2, 1909; d. Max and Lina (Schwartz) K.; student NAD; scholar New Sch. Social Research, 1940-41. One woman shows: Bowdoin Coll. Art Mus., 1951, Calif. State Library, 1953, Print Club of Albany-Albany Inst., 1955, U. Maine, 1955, 58, Jewish Mus., 1956, Miami Beach (Fla.) Art Center, 1958, Richmond (Ind.) Art Assn., 1959, Old State Capitol. Mus., La., La. Art Commn.; spl. collections: U.S. Nat. Mus., 1965, U. Maine Art Mus., 1965, Library of Congress, 1965, 71, Met. Mus., 1965, Nat. Coll. Fine Arts, 1965, 71, 78, Nat. Gallery of Art, 1966, Nat. Air and Space Mus., N.Y. Pub. Library, 1971, 78, Nat. Mus. History and Tech., 1972, N.Y. Pub. Library, 1978; group shows include: Albany (N.Y.) Print Club, Albany Inst., Jewish Mus., NAD, Conn. Acad. Fine Arts, Bklyn. Mus., Delgado Mus. Art, 1959, Calif. State Library, Bowdoin U., State Tchrs. Coll. Pa., Art Assn. Richmond, Boston Pub. Library, Massillon Mus., Springfield Art Mus., N.Y. Pub. Library, Miami Beach Art Center, Hartford (Conn.) Children's Mus., Peoria (Ill.) Art Center, Pa. Acad. Fine Arts, also internat. exhbns., Europe, Asia, S.Am., Africa; represented in permanent group collections: Library of Congress, U.S. Nat. Mus., Met. Mus. Art, N.Y.C., Balt. Mus. Art, Franklin D. Roosevelt Coll., Fogg Mus., Santa Barbara (Calif.) Art Mus., Syracuse (N.Y.) U., Colorado Springs Fine Arts Center, Pennell Collection, Am. Artists Group, U. Minn., Calif. State Library, Pa. State Library, Bezalel Nat. Mus., Jerusalem, Newark Pub. Library, Addison Gallery Am. Art, Bat Yam Mcpls. Mus., Israel, U. Maine, State Tchrs. Coll. Pa., Safed Mus., Israel, Peoria Art Center, N.Y. Pub. Library, Boston Pub. Library, St. Margaret Mary Sch. Art Coll., Conn., Columbia. Recipient awards Miss. Art Assn., 1947, 51, Delgado Mus. Art, 1950, Peoria Art Center, 1950, Soc. Miniature Painters, Gravers, Sculpture, 1959; Editor's award Orphic Lute, 1963, 1st award The Explorer, 1961, Bettie Payne Wells award Am. Bard Mag., 1972, James Joyce Poetry award Poetry Soc. Am., 1975; named Daughter of Mark Twain for Outstanding Contbn. to Modern Art, 1970; named Life fellow Met. Mus. Art, 1966; life mem., recipient Plaque of Honor, Hall of Fame, 1966; hon. mem. Dell'Accademia Di Scienze, Lettere, Arti nella Classe Accademica Nobel, Milan, Italy, 1975. Mem. Am. Graphic Artists, Conn. Acad. Fine Arts, Print Club Albany, Boston Printmakers (award 1955), Am. Color Print Soc., Phila. Water Color Club, Audubon Artists (award 1944), Nat. Assn. Women Artists (award 1945), Artists Equity N.Y., Hunterdon Art Center, Internat. Platform Assn., Washington Printmakers, Poetry Soc. Am., Internat. Poets Shrine, Authors Guild, Authors League Am., Internat. Poetry Soc. Eng. (founder 1974). Contbr. poems to anthologies including: Blue River Anthology, 1959; Treasures of Parnassus, 1962; Melody of the Muse, 1964; Avolan Anthology, 1960; Golden Harvest Anthology, 1967; International Poetry Society's First Anthology, 1975; American Supplement-India, Ocarina 100 Best Poets, 1978. Contbr. children's short stories to mags. Home and Office: 915 West End Ave Apt 5D New York City NY 10025

KATZ, IRWIN ALAN, pharm. researcher; b. Malden, Mass., Feb. 13, 1940; s. Aaron and Eva (Kantrovitz) K.; A.B., Boston U., 1961; B.S. (Mass. State Pharm. Assn. scholar), Mass. Coll. Pharmacy, 1968, M.S. (Coll. fellow), 1969, Ph.D. (Coll. fellow), 1971; postgrad. Northeastern U., 1968-70; m. Gloria Miriam Kaizerman, Aug. 2, 1964; children—Gary Scott, Lisa Michelle, Jeffrey Craig, Michael Ari. Pharmacist Washington Park Pharmacy, Newtonville, Mass., 1968-71; instr. pharmacy Mass. Coll. Pharmacy, Boston, 1970-71; hosp. pharmacist Boston Hosp. for Women, 1970-71, J.F. Kennedy Med. Center, Edison, N.J., 1974-75, Raritan Valley Hosp., Green Brook, N.J., 1975—; research investigator formulation design sect. pharm. research and devel., then liquid formulation devel. E.R. Squibb Inst. for Med. Research, New Brunswick, N.J., 1971-76, process devel. mgr. U.S. mfg. E.R. Squibb & Sons, 1976-77, group leader pharm. tech., 1977—. Served to lt., USNR, 1961-65. Mem. Am. Pharm. Assn., Acad. Pharm. Scientists, Soc. Cosmetic Chemists, Rho Chi. Office: 5 Georges Rd New Brunswick NJ 08903

KATZ, IRWIN B., hosp. adminstr.; b. N.Y.C., Sept. 5, 1946; s. Ely and Lillian (Blackman) K.; B.A., Coll. City N.Y., 1973; M.P.H., Columbia U., 1975; m. Eugenia Raymond, Sept. 11, 1970. Auditor, N.Y. State Dept. Labor, 1972; mgmt. intern N.Y.C. Mayor's Intern Program, 1973; asst. adminstr. Beekman-Downtown Hosp., N.Y.C., 1975—; mem. faculty Sch. Pub. Health, Cornell U., 1978—. Bd. dirs. N.Y.C. Health Systems Agy., 1976-77. Served with U.S. Navy, 1966-70. Mem. Am. Coll. Hosp. Adminstrs., Am. Hosp. Assn., Am., N.Y. pub. health assns., Am. Mgmt. Assn., N.Y. Assn. Ambulatory Care. Contbr. articles to profl. jours. Home: 419 Rich Ave Fleetwood NY 10552 Office: Beekman-Downtown Hosp 170 William St New York City NY 10038

KATZ, JOEL RICHARD, pediatrician; b. Bklyn., Feb. 2, 1939; s. Louis and Frances (Salamone) K.; A.B. cum laude, Bklyn. Coll., 1959; M.D. with honors, N.Y. Med. Coll., 1967; m. Carol Ann Graepel, June 12, 1965; children—Lauren Beth, Andrew John, Paul Evan. Intern medicine Beth Israel Med. Center, N.Y.C., 1967-68, resident in pediatrics, 1968-70, chief resident, 1970-71; practice medicine specializing in pediatrics; mem. staffs Johns Hopkins Hosp., Balt., Howard County Gen. Hosp., Columbia, Md., St. Agnes Hosp., Balt.; asst. prof. pediatrics Johns Hopkins U., Balt., 1972—. Pres. Howard County (Md.) Sch. Health Council, 1977—. Diplomate Nat. Bd. Med. Examiners, Am. Bd. Pediatrics. Fellow Am. Acad. Pediatrics; mem. Howard County Med. Soc., Am. Sch. Health Assn., Med. and Chir. Faculty Md., Ambulatory Pediatric Assn. Democrat. Roman Catholic. Home: 3021 Fawnwood Dr Ellicott City MD 21043 Office: 5999 Harpers Farm Rd Columbia MD 21044

KATZ, JULIAN, gastroenterologist, educator; b. N.Y.C., Apr. 3, 1937; s. Abraham M. and Fay (Sher) K.; A.B., Columbia U., 1958; M.D., U. Chgo., 1962; m. Sheila Moriber, Aug. 18, 1963; children—Jonathan Peter, Sara Katherine. Intern, U. Chgo. Hosps., 1962-63; resident in medicine Duke U., Durham, N.C., 1963-65; fellow in gastroenterology Yale U., New Haven, 1965-67; practice medicine, specializing in gastroenterology, internal medicine, Phila., 1969—; prof. medicine, lectr. in physiology and biochemistry Med. Coll. Pa., Phila., 1970—; chief clin. gastroenterology Med. Coll. Pa., Phila. Served with USN, 1967-69. Diplomate Am. Bd. Internal Medicine. Fellow ACP; mem. Am. Gastroenterological Assn. Contbr. articles to profl. jours. Home: 701 Dodds Ln Gladwyne PA 19035 Office: Gastrointestinal Specialists 555 City Ave Bala Cynwyd PA 19003

KATZ, LEONARD ALLEN, physician; b. Buffalo, Aug. 7, 1935; s. Samuel and Minnie (Etkin) K.; B.A., Yale, 1957; M.D., Columbia, 1961; m. Judith Horowitz, June 26, 1958; children—Jeffrey, Linda, Andrew. Intern, Bronx (N.Y.) Municipal Hosp. Center, 1961-62; resident, 1962-64; fellow in gastroenterlogy Yale, 1964-66; asst. prof. medicine State U.N.Y. at Buffalo Sch. Medicine, 1968-72, asso. prof., 1972—, asso. dean student and curricular affairs, 1975—; attending physician E.J. Meyer Meml. Hosp; cons. gastroenterology Roswell Park Meml. Inst.; asst. phys. Buffalo Gen. Hosp.; cons. Nat. Library Medicine. Mem. nat. sci. adv. com., patient edn. com. Nat. Found. for Ileitis and Colitis. Served to capt. USAF, 1966-68. Nat. Fund for Med. Edn. grantee, 1971-73, 78-80. diplomate Am. Bd. Internal Medicine, Am. Bd. Gastroenterology. Fellow A.C.P., Am. Gastroenterol. Assn., Am. Fedn. Clin. Research, Am. Soc. Gastrointestinal Endoscopy, G-I Liver Soc. Western N.Y., Assn. Am. Med. Colls., Yale Assn. Western N.Y. (dir. 1970-76), Alpha Omega Alpha. Jewish. Mem. editorial bd. Annals of Gastroenterology. Home: 138 Carriage Circle Williamsville NY 14221 Office: Sch Medicine State UNY Buffalo NY 14214

KATZ, MORRIS, artist, entertainer; b. Poland, Mar. 5, 1932; came to U.S., 1949, naturalized, 1955; s. Marcus and Lea (Mann) Katz. Specializes in entertainment shows with instant oil paintings, U.S., Europe, Israel, India, Australia, N.Z., Singapore, 1968—; appearance on Mike Douglas show, other TV programs. Mem. Internat. Platform Assn., Artists Equity Assn., Am. Guild Variety Actors, Nat. Acad. TV Arts and Scis. Represented in permanent collections. Address: 406 6th Ave New York City NY 10011

KATZ, NORMAN, apparel mfg. co. exec.; b. Zwickau, Germany, Apr. 10, 1925; s. Paul and Dora (Ungar) K.; came to U.S., 1940, naturalized, 1944; B.A. in Econs., Columbia, 1943; children—Ira and Stephen (twins). Exec. v.p. John Weitz Jrs., Inc., N.Y.C., 1947-52; pres. Norman Katz, Inc., N.Y.C., 1952-58; pres. At Home Wear, Inc., N.Y.C., 1959-75; pres. I. Appel Corp., N.Y.C., 1976—. Instr. econs. Coll. City N.Y., 1947-51. Trade chmn. Fedn. Jewish Philanthropies, 1957-71. Served with AUS, 1943-46. Clubs: Saugatuck Harbor Yacht (Westport, Conn.); Harrow U.S.A. (N.Y.C.). Home: 10 Waterside Plaza New York City NY 10010 Office: 99 Madison Ave New York City NY 10016

KATZ, PHILIP CARLTON, economist; b. Paterson, N.J., Jan. 18, 1932; s. Carl and Charlotte Margaret (Ulrich) K.; student Seton Hall U., 1949; A.A., Bergen Jr. Coll., 1952; B.S.C., U. Pa., 1954; M.B.A., N.Y. U., 1966; m. Mary Ann Duke, June 25, 1955; children—Kathleen, John, James, Paul, Christopher, Caroline. Price analyst Schenley Industries, N.Y.C., 1956-57; statistician U.S. Brewers Assn., Washington, 1957-63, mgr. market and statis. services, 1963-64, dir. research, 1965-69, v.p. mem. services, 1969-70, v.p. research and info., 1970-75, sr. v.p. research services, 1975—; mem. com. on productivity and tech. U.S. Dept. Labor Bus. Research Adv. Council. Served with AUS, 1954-56. Mem. Am. Marketing Assn., Am. Econ. Assn., Am. Statis. Assn. Contbr. articles to trade jours. Home: 1925 Relda Ct Falls Church VA 22043 Office: 1750 K St NW Washington DC 20006

KATZ, ROBERT, truck rental co. exec.; b. Chgo, June 26, 1924; s. JAcob and Hannah (Bergida) K.; grad. Burlington County (N.J.) Tech. Sch., 1968; m. Harriet Florence Balous, Apr. 8, 1951; 1 son., Steven Richard. Dispatcher, driver Yale Transp. Corp., N.Y.C., 1946-48; route driver Hartford (Conn.) Transp. Corp., 1948-51; route salesman Rego-Forest Cleaners, Forest Hills, N.Y., 1951-59; v.p. Manhattaan Motor Rental Inc., N.Y.C., 1959—. Vol. Forest Hills Ambulance Corp, 1972-76; chmn. troop com. Boy Scouts Am., Queens, N.Y., 1961-77. Mem. Soc. Fleet Suprs., K.P. Jewish. Home: 6770 Yellowstone Blvd Forest Hills NY 11375 Office: 756 Washington St New York City NY 10014

KATZ, ROBERT NATHAN, ceramic engr.; b. Williamsport, Pa., Sept. 2, 1939; s. Louis and Rose Bernice (Golbitz) K.; S.B., Mass. Inst. Tech., 1961, Ph.D., 1969; M.S., U. Mich., 1963; m. Karen Cecily Wurmser, July 26, 1964; children—Pamela Lynn, Johathan Adam. Research asst. U. Mich., 1961-62; metallurgist Army Materials Research Agy., Watertown, Mass., 1962-65; ceramic engr. Army Materials and Mechanics Research Center, Watertown, 1965-70, chief ceramics research div., 1970—; liaison mem. various coms. Nat. Materials Adv. Bd.; cons. Dept. Def., Dept. Energy; mem. U.S. del. NATO Com. on Challenges of Modern Soc., 1974; mem. organizing com., lectr. NATO Advanced Study Inst. Nitrogen Ceramics, 1976. Fellow Am. Ceramic Soc.; mem. Nat. Inst. Ceramic Engrs., New Eng. Ceramic Soc., Am. Soc. Metals, Sigma Xi. Editor: Ceramics for High Performance Applications, 1974; Ceramics for High Performance Applications II, 1978. Contbr. articles to tech. publs. Home: 18 Oxbow Rd Natick MA 01760 Office: Army Materials and Mechanics Research Center Watertown MA 02172

KATZ, SEYMOUR, pharmacist; b. Bronx, N.Y., Oct. 19, 1936; s. Herman and Ida (Chesler) K.; B.S., Columbia U., 1959; M.S., L.I. U., 1974; m. Elizabeth Ruth Santana, Oct. 2, 1960; children—Ronald, Gail, Laura. Staff pharmacist Nyack (N.Y.) Hosp., 1963-66, Univ. Hosp., N.Y.C., 1966-67; asst. chief pharmacist Brookdale Hosp. Med. Center, Bklyn., 1967-69, dir. pharmacy, 1969—. Served with USNR, 1955-63. Mem. N.Y. Soc. Hosp. Pharmacists (pres. 1977—), N.Y. Council Hosp. Pharmacists (pres. 1978—), Greater N.Y. Hosp. Assn. Contbr. articles in field to profl. jours. Home: 134 Norman Dr East Meadow NY 11554 Office: Brookdale Hospital Medical Center Brookdale Plaza Brooklyn NY 11212

KATZ, SEYMOUR, gastroenterologist; b. N.Y.C., Dec. 1, 1938; s. Hyman and Rose (Kaplan) K.; B.S. magna cum laude (Jonas Salk Scholar), City Coll. N.Y., 1960; M.D., N.Y. U., 1964; m. Arlene E. Wachsberg, Mar. 6, 1966; children—Joshua, Ellen, Samuel. Med. intern and resident, Albert Einstein Coll. Medicine, Bronx Municipal Hosp. Center, N.Y.C., 1964-66, chief med. resident, 1968-69, asst. instr. dept. medicine, 1968-69; fellow in gastroenterology Cornell U. Med. Coll., N.Y., Hosp., Meml. Hosp., N.Y.C., 1969-71, asst. physician, gastroenterology sect., 1969-71, clin. instr. medicine, 1971-74, clin. asst. prof. medicine, 1974—; research fellow Sloan Kettering Inst. for Cancer Research, N.Y.C., 1970-71; attending physician in gastroenterology N. Shore U. Hosp., Manhasset, N.Y., and L.I. Jewish-Hillside Med. Center, New Hyde Park, N.Y., 1971—; med. advisor Nat. Digestive Disease Found., L.I. Ileostomy Soc., Nat. Found. Ileitis and Colitis. Trustee Temple Beth Sholom, Roslyn, N.Y. Served with M.C., USAF, 1966-68. Recipient Caduceus Soc. award, 1960, Maurice Freimann Award, 1960; Am. Cancer Soc. fellow, 1970-71; USPHS clin. trainee, 1970-71; diplomate Am. Bd. Internal Medicine. Fellow A.C.P., Am. Coll. Gastroenterology, N.Y. Acad. Gastroenterology; mem. Am., N.Y. Socs. Gastrointestinal Endoscopy, N.Y., L.I. gastrointestinal assns., Phi Beta Kappa, Alpha Omega Alpha. Jewish. Contbr. articles, abstracts in field to profl. pubis.; patentee cytology instrument. Office: 1300 Union Turnpike New Hyde Park NY 11040

KATZ, STEVEN EDWARD, psychiatrist, psychoanalyst; b. Phila., Pa., Aug. 10, 1937; s. Benjamin R. and Charlotte (Tomkins) K.; B.A., Cornell U., 1959; M.D., Hahnemann Med. Coll., 1963; certificate in psychoanalysis Columbia Psychoanalytic Center for Tng. and Research, 1972; m. Marjorie Ann Billstein, June 12, 1960; children—Barri Lynn, Stacey Jane. Intern in mixed medicine Montefiore Hosp., Bronx, N.Y., 1963-64; resident in psychiatry Columbia U.-N.Y. State Psychiat. Inst., 1966-69; practice medicine specializing in psychiatry, gen. practice psychoanalysis, N.Y.C., 1969—; dir. edn. Roosevelt Hosp., N.Y.C., 1971-74, mem. staff, 1971-78, asso. dir. psychiatry, 1974-78; asso. dir. Bellevue Psychiat. Center, 1978—; attending psychiatrist Psychiat. Consultation Service, Columbia-Presbyterian Med. Center, N.Y.C., 1969-71; cons. in psychiatry Manhattan VA Hosp., N.Y.C., 1978—; staff psychoanalyst Columbia Psychoanalytic Clinic for Tng. and Research, 1971—; asso. clin. prof. psychiatry Columbia, 1976-78; asso. clin. prof. psychiatry N.Y. U., 1978, asso. prof. clin. psychiatry, 1978—. Mem. N.Y. State Dept. Mental Hygiene Task Force on Admissions and Readmissions, 1975-76. Served with U.S. Army, 1964-66. Am. Psychiat. Assn. fellow, 1976—. Diplomate Am. Bd. Psychiatry and Neurology. Mem. AMA, Am. Psychoanalytic Assn., N.Y. Acad. Medicine, Assn. Psychoanalytic Medicine (councillor), Am. Psychiat. Assn. (chmn. continuing edn. com. N.Y. County dist. br., task force on sex therapy, dep. rep.), N.Y. State Med. Soc., Alpha Omega Alpha, Psi Chi. Research, publs. on cardiac surgery, addiction, sexuality, chronic psychiat. patient. Home: 58 Eastern Dr Ardsley NY 10502 Office: Dept Psychiatry NY U Med Center 550 1st Ave New York City NY 10016

KATZ, THEODORE HARRY, educator; b. Phila., July 29, 1937; s. Sidney and Mitzi (Soltroff) K.; A.B., Franklin and Marshall Coll., 1959; Ed.M., Harvard U., 1969, Ed.D., 1972. Master tchr., curriculum developer N.C. Advancement Sch., Winston-Salem, 1964-67; dir. communication program Pa. Advancement Sch., Phila., 1967-68; fellow T.T.T. Project, Harvard U., 1968-72; dir. Ford Found. Project, Dept. of Interior, Inst. Am. Indian Arts, Santa Fe, 1962-74; dir. outreach program Appalachian Regional Library, North Wilkesboro, N.C., 1965-66; chief div. edn. Phila. Mus. Art, 1977—; lectr. and cons. in field; tchr. trainer N.C. Pub. Schs., 1965-67; cons. N.Y. State Bd. Edn., 1966-67; lectr., resource person Phila. Bd. Edn., 1966-67; master trainer, curriculum developer Project PEP, Skidmore Coll., 1967; cons. Sch. Dist. Phila., 1967-68; field reader arts and humanities

HEW, Washington, 1967-71; cons., curriculum writer N.W. Regional Ednl. Lab., Portland, Oreg., 1971; dir. Workshop for Change, Inst. Am. Indian Arts, 1972, dir. Workshop in Confluent Edn., 1973; mem. dance panel N.Mex. Arts Commn., Santa Fe, 1973-74; project dir. N.W. Regional Ednl. Lab., Portland, 1974, Ford Found., Glorietta, N.Mex., 1974; adv. com. Paul Robeson Internat. Film Festival, Phila., 1977; instr. Phila. Area Cultural Consortium, 1978, adv. bd., 1978; project dir. Nat. Museum Act Program, 1977-78; lectr. Phila. Coll. Art, 1978—. Rep. Museum Showcase, 1977; mem. exec. bd. Nat. Exhibit of Art by the Blind, 1977; mem. program supporting com. Creative Growth Exhbn., Phila., 1977, philosophy and enquiry com. Please Touch Mus. for Children, Phila., 1978; chmn. panel judges Nat. Exhibits by Blind Artists, 1978. Recipient grant 3d Century Artists Program, N.C. Arts Council, Raleigh, 1976, grant in aid Pa. Council of the Arts, 1977-78. Mem. NEA, Nat. Art Edn. Assn., Am. Assn. Museums, Assn. Supervision and Curriculum Devel., Coll. Art Assn. Am., Phi Delta Kappa. Contbr. articles to profl. jours. Home: 1922 Waverly St Philadelphia PA 19147 Office: Philadelphia Museum of Art PO Box 7646 Philadelphia PA 19101

KATZ, WILLIAM DAVID, psychologist, psychoanalytic psychotherapist; b. N.Y.C., Sept. 14, 1915; s. Charles and Esther (Dann) K.; A.B., Bklyn. Coll., 1940; M.A., N.Y. U., 1942, Ph.D., 1953. Clin. intern Hillside Hosp., 1950-53; pvt. practice as cons. psychologist and psychotherapist, N.Y., 1942—; cons. psychologist Human Relations Guidance Center, 1946-56; exec. dir. Civic Center Clinic, Bklyn. Assn. for Rehab. Offenders, Inc., 1951-55, Play Research Inst., Inc., 1953-57; psychotherapist Group for Community Guidance Centers, 1955-57; psychotherapist Mental Health Inst., 1957-59, asso. dir., 1957, exec. dir., 1958; clin. asso. Psychol. Service Center, N.Y.C., 1968—; supr. psychotherapy Met. Center, for Mental Health, N.Y.C., 1969—; asst. prof. psychology L.I. U., 1958-64, asso. prof., 1964-70, prof., 1970—; prof. U.S. Army Chaplain Center and Sch., Fort Wadsworth, 1970-77; asst. chmn. psychology dept. L.I. U., 1963-72, 74-76, acting chmn., 1966, 75. Recipient Cross of Honor, La Fundacion Internacional, Eloy Alfaro, 1964. Fellow Am. Internat. Acad. (certificate and medallion 1957), Assn. Applied Psychoanalysis (exec. sec. 1963-67, 78-79, pres. 1968-69, 74-75); mem. AAAS, Am. Acad. Polit. and Social Scis., Interam. Soc. Psychology, Am. Acad. Psychotherapists, AAUP, Soc. Clin. and Exptl. Hypnosis, Council Psychoanalytic Psychotherapists, Am., N.Y. State psychol. assns., N.Y. Soc. Clin. Psychologists, Bklyn. Psychol. Assn. (pres. 1971-72), N.Y. Acad. Scis., S.I. Mental Health Soc., Bklyn. Assn. Mental Health, Richmond County Psychol. Assn. (pres. 1975), N.Y. U. Alumni Assn., Psi Chi, Alpha Phi Omega, Tau Delta Phi. Clubs: K.P., Masons, Shriners. Contbr. articles in field to profl. jours.; asso. editor Am. Imago, 1978, Am. Psychol. Assn., 1950—. Home: 85 Medford Rd Staten Island NY 10304

KATZEN, HOWARD MARVIN, biochemist; b. Balt., May 2, 1929; s. Louis Nathan and Irene (Shor) K.; B.Sc., Johns Hopkins, 1956; M.S., George Washington U., 1958; Ph.D., 1962; m. Carole Sandra Sonnenschein, Nov. 5, 1960; children—Leora, Louis, Eugene. Biochemist, NIH, Bethesda, Md., 1954-62; Am. Cancer Soc. postdoctoral fellow, Mass. Inst. Tech., Cambridge, 1962-63; asst. dir. pediatric research biochemistry Johns Hopkins U. Med. Sch. and Sinai Hosp., Balt., 1963-65; vis. scientist Nat. Inst. Arthritis and Metabolic Diseases, Bethesda, 1965; sr. research biochemist Merck Inst. Therapeutic Research, Rahway, (N.J.) 1965-68, research fellow, 1968-74, asst. dir., 1974—; sr. investigator, Columbia U.-St. Lukes Hosp. Med. Center-NIH Obesity Center, N.Y.C., 1973-77; guest vis. scientist Imperial Coll. Sci. and Technology, London, 1969; distinguished lectr. U. Rochester Med. Sch., 1974. Fellow Am. Inst. Chemists; mem. Am. Soc. Biol. Chemists, Am. Diabetes Assn., AAAS, Am. Inst. Chemists, Am. Diabetes Assn., Am. Chem. Soc., Fedn. Am. Scientists, So. Sugar Club Assn., Sigma Xi. Jewish religion. Contbr. articles to profl. jours. Chief co-editor, vol. 2 Advances in Modern Nutrition entitled Interrelationships in Diabetes, Obesity and Vascular Disease, 1978. Discoverer protein disulfide interchange enzyme, 1961, hexokinase isozymes, 1964. Home: 109 Meadowbrook Rd North Plainfield NJ 07062 Office: Merck Inst Scott Ave Rahway NJ 07065

KATZEN, LILA PELL (MRS. PHILIP KATZEN), sculptor; b. Bklyn.; d. Harry and Rose (Schultz) Pell; student Art Students League, 1946, Cooper Union Coll., 1949, Hans Hofmann Sch., 1949-51; m. Philip Katzen, June 6, 1948; children—Denize, Hal Zachary. Instr., Md. Inst. Coll. Art, Balt., 1962—; works exhibited Archtl. League, N.Y., 1968, Ga. Mus. Art, 1968, 69, Smithsonian Nat. Collections, Washington, 1968, Flint (Mich.) Art Center, 1968, Santa Barbara (Calif.) Mus., 1969, N.Y. U., Max Hutchinson Gallery, N.Y.C., 1970, Sao Paulo Biennale, 1970, Max Protecht Gallery, Washington, 1972, Sculptors Internat., N.Y.C., 1974, Everson Mus. Art, Syracuse, N.Y., 1975, Carnegie Mus., Pitts., 1975, Balt. Mus., 1975, William Benton Mus., Storrs, Conn., 1977, U. Iowa Mus. Art, 1977, others; permanent exhibits include Nat. Gallery Art, Washington, Wadsworth Atenium, Hartford, Conn., Everson Mus., Syracuse, N.Y., U. Iowa Art Mus. Lectr., Balt. Mus., Kalamazoo Art Center, Archtl. League, N.Y.C., Centro Venezolano, Caracas, Santa Barbara (Calif.) Mus., Mass. Inst. Tech., Coll. Art Conf., N.Y.C. and Washington, Art Students League State U. N.Y. at Purchase, U. Mich., Cranbrook Acad. Tiffany Found. fellow, 1964; Archtl. League N.Y. grantee, 1968; Nat. Endowment grantee, 1973; AAUW Goodyear fellow, 1974. Mem. Archtl. League N.Y., Coll. Art Assn. Works include: Light-Floors. Archtl. League, N.Y.C., 1968; Universe As Environment, N.Y.U. and State U. N.Y. at Stonybrook, 1969; Laterna Magika Facade, Expo 70, Osaka, Japan, 1970; Liquid Tunnel, Sao Paulo Exhibit, 1970; Paintings and Sculpture Today, 1970; Contemporary Am. Painting and Sculpture, Indpls. Mus. Art, 1973; Slipedge-Bis, Whitney Mus., N.Y.C., 1973; Traho II, World Trade Center, N.Y.C., 1973; Monumenta, Newport, R.I., 1974; Sculpture '76, Greenwich, Conn., 1976; Sculpture Fordham U., Lincoln Center, N.Y.C., 1978. Office: 345 W Broadway St New York NY 10013

KATZIN, DICK, ophthalmologist; b. Newark, N.J., Oct. 28, 1934; s. Eugene Maurice and Ethel (Rosa) K.; A.B., Cornell U., 1956, M.D., 1965; m. Loretta Pollick, June 9, 1959; children—Richard Joseph, James Scott, Eugene Maurice II, Darcy Fanchon. Intern, Allegheny Gen. Hosp., Pitts., 1965-66; resident ophthalmology U. Pitts. Eye and Ear Hosp., 1966-69; instr. ophthalmology U. Pitts. Sch. Medicine, 1969-70, asst. prof. ophthalmology, 1970—; practice medicine specializing in ophthalmology, Monroeville, Pa., 1975—. Bd. dirs. Medical Eye Bank Western Pa. Served with USMCR, 1958-62, later Res. Diplomate Am. Bd. Ophthalmology. Mem. Am., Pa. acads. ophthalmology and otolaryngology, AMA, Pa., Allegheny County med. socs., A.C.S. Home: 8 Elmcrest Rd Oakmont PA 15139 Office: 2545 Mosside Blvd Monroeville PA 15146

KATZIN, HERBERT MAURICE, ophthalmologist; b. Newark, Sept. 20, 1913; s. Samuel and Ada (Samuels) K.; M.D., Harvard, 1937; m. Annette Stollman, May 27, 1942; children—Richard, Mary. Intern, Mt. Sinai Hosp., N.Y.C., 1937-40, resident in ophthalmology, 1941-43; post-doctoral Presbyn. Eye Inst., N.Y.C., 1940-41; mem. staff Mt. Sinai Hosp.; staff Manhattan Eye, Ear and Throat Hosp., mem. bd. surgeon dirs., 1969—, pres. bd., 1976-77; dir. Corneal Clinic, 1965—; instr. Columbia, 1943-47; dir. Eye Bank Lab., 1946—; asso. clin. prof. ophthalmic surgery Cornell U.; cons. in ophthalmology Monmouth Med. Center; asso. clin. prof. Cornell Med. Sch., 1971—; mem. adv. council, hon. de Merito professorship Gandhi Eye Hosp. and Post Grad. Sch., Allgarh, India. Mem. bd. Eye Bank for Sight Restoration; nat. trustee, exec. com. Am. Physicians Fellowship Inc. for Israel Med. Assn. Diplomate Am. Bd. Ophthalmology, examiner, 1950-68. Fellow A.C.S.; mem. N.Y. Acad. Scis., N.Y. Acad. Medicine, Am. Acad. Ophthalmology and Otolaryngology, Pan Am. Soc. Ophthalmology. Editor: Ophthalmic Surgery, 1970-71. Contbr. numerous articles in field to med. jours. Home: 176 E 71st St New York City NY 10021 Office: 178 E 71st St New York City NY 10021

KAUFER, GERALD IRA, surgeon; b. Wilkes-Barre, Pa., Oct. 16, 1937; s. Woodrow Wilson and Esther (Lieb) K.; B.S. cum laude, U. Pitts., 1959, M.D., 1963; m. Virginia Gross, June 21, 1959; children—Michael, Jill, Jonathan, Wendy, Elizabeth, Abigail, Amy. Intern, U. Okla. Hosp., Oklahoma City, 1963-64; resident in gen. surgery Tex. Med. Center/Baylor U. Coll. Medicine, Houston, 1964-68; practice specializing in medicine and surgery, Pitts., 1970—; instr. surgery U. Pitts., 1970—. Bd. dirs. Central Med. Pavillion, 1975-76; mem. sch. bd. Beth El Religious Sch., Pitts., 1973—; bd. dirs. Sch. Advanced Jewish Studies, Pitts., 1977—. Served with M.C., USN, 1968-70; Vietnam. Diplomate Am. Bd. Surgery. Fellow Am. Coll. Angiography, A.C.S.; mem. AMA, Am. Physicians Fellowship, Pitts. Med. Forum, Pitts. Surg. Soc., Allegheny County Med. Soc., Gut Club, Phi Delta Epsilon. Republican. Jewish. Contbr. articles to profl. jours. Home: 1574 Tiffany Dr Pittsburgh PA 15241 Office: 222 S Trenton Ave Pittsburgh PA 15221

KAUFFMAN, BETTY CRAFT, nurse; b. Bremerton, Wash., Oct. 16, 1920; d. William James and Ruth Sarah (Craft) K.; B.A., Hunter Coll., 1941; B.S., N.Y. U., 1946; M.A., Columbia U., 1953. Research asst. nursing Med. Coll., N.Y. U., N.Y.C., 1940-41; insp.Pl, Signal Corps, U.S. Army, Phila., 1941-43; serologist Oreg. Bd. Health, Portland, 1943-44; staff nurse Bellevue Hosp. Center, N.Y.C., 1947-48, head nurse, 1948-58, supr., instr., 1958-62, asst. dir. nursing, 1962-64, asst. dir. nursing dept. obstetrics, 1964-65, nursing adminstr., asso. dir. nursing adminstr., 1965-67, acting dir. nursing, 1967-68, dir. nursing, 1968—. Coordinating council, adv. bd. Hunter Coll.-Bellevue Sch. Nursing, 1968—; community bd. Bellevue Hosp. Center-Greenberg Police Community and geriatric program, 1974—. Named distinguished alumnus Bellevue Obstet. and Gynecol. Soc., 1974. Mem. Am. Pub. Health Assn., Pub. Health Assn. N.Y.C., Am. Soc. Hosp. Nursing Service Adminstrs., Bellevue Alumnae Assn., N.Y. U., Tchrs. Coll. alumni assns. Republican. Home: 100B High Point Dr Hartsdale NY 10530 Office: Bellevue Hosp Center 462 E 27th St New York City NY 10016

KAUFFMAN, BRUCE WILLIAM, lawyer; b. Atlantic City, Dec. 1, 1934; s. Joseph Bernard and Lilyan (Abraham) K.; B.A., U. Pa., 1956; LL.B., Yale, 1959; m. Rita Marie Wisneski, Dec. 31, 1971; children—Bradley Leonard, Marjorie Beth, Robert Andrew, Lauri Ann. Admitted to N.J. bar, 1960, Pa. bar, 1961, U.S. Supreme Ct. bar, 1965; law clk. to judge N.J. Superior Ct., Trenton, 1959-60; asso. firm Dilworth, Paxson, Kalish & Kauffman, Phila., 1960-65, partner, 1966—, chmn. litigation dept., 1975—; mem. com. of censors U.S. Dist. Ct. Eastern Pa., 1976—. Del. Pa. Constl. Conv., 1967-68; chmn. Montgomery County Govt. Study Commn., 1973-74; mem. Police Civil Service Commn., Lower Merion Twp., 1978; pres. Merion Park Civic Assn., 1966-68. Fellow Am. Coll. Trial Lawyers; mem. Am., Pa., Phila. bar assns., Am. Judicature Soc., Juristic Soc., Lawyers' Club Phila., Yale Law Sch. Assn., Pa. Soc., USCG Aux., Pi Sigma Alpha, Phi Gamma Mu, Phi Beta Kappa, Order of Coif. Clubs: Locust, Midday, Ashbourne Country. Office: 2600 Fidelity Bldg Philadelphia PA 19109

KAUFFMAN, GEORGE ELWOOD, III, health devel. adminstr.; b. Hazleton, Pa., Mar. 14, 1943; s. George Elwood and Geraldine Annette (Knorr) K.; B.A. in Creative Writing, U. Pa., 1965; M.P.A., Cornell U., 1976; m. Margaret Catherine McKerns, July 30, 1966; children—Amanda Beth (dec.), Kaete Lynn, Molly Aileen, Brian Richard. Staff writer dept. pub. relations U. Pa., 1965-66; fund raiser Project Hope, Washington, 1969-71, program planner, 1971-73, coordinator domestic programs, 1973, cons. health planning to sec. health State of Rio Grande do Norte (Brazil), 1971-76; adminstr. community health system devel. Navajo Reservation, Ganado, Ariz., 1974; dir. plan devel. Health Systems Agy. N.E. Pa., Avoca. Chmn., Md. Orgnl. Devel. Commn., 1972-73. Served to capt. AUS, 1966-69. Mem. Am. Pub. Health Assn., Jaycees (pres. Silver Spring, Md. 1970-71, pres. Montgomery County 1971-72, external v.p. Md. 1973, internat. senator), Am. Soc. Pub. Adminstrn., Phi Kappa Sigma. Democrat. Home: RD 8 Box 426 Mountaintop PA 18707 Office: Health Systems Agy WARM Bldg Avoca PA 18641

KAUFFMAN, LEON A., physician, educator; b. Phila., July 26, 1934; s. Isadore and Clara (Kenig) K.; B.A., Temple U., 1957, M.D., 1961; m. Rita Aurora B. Young, Apr. 2, 1969; children—Christopher I., Chandler S. Intern, Einstein Med. Center, Phila., 1961-62, resident in pathology, 1962-63; resident in internal medicine Hahnemann Med. Coll. and Hosp., Phila., 1963-65, fellow in pulmonary physiology and chest diseases, 1965-66; sr. instr. medicine Hahnemann Med. Coll., 1966-70, asst. prof., 1970-77, asso. prof., 1977—, dir. pulmonary function lab., 1968-70, dir. respiratory intensive care unit, 1969-73, pulmonary cons. to shock and trauma unit, 1970—; asst. dir. div. pulmonary medicine, 1970-73; pulmonary cons. U.S. Naval Hosp., 1973-77; med. dir. respiratory therapy St. Agnes Hosp., Phila., 1973—, asso. attending in medicine; chmn. div. pulmonary medicine Met. Hosp., Phila., 1974—; attending physician W. Park Hosp., Phila.; chmn. sub com. on sterilization of respiratory therapy equipment Am. Lung Assn. of Phila., 1975—. Mem. advisory com. Sch. Respiratory Therapy, Community Coll. Phila. Diplomate Am. Bd. Internal Medicine. Fellow Am. Coll. Chest Physicians, Phila. Coll. Physicians; mem. Laennec Soc. Phila. (pres. 1975-76, exec. com. 1977—), AMA, Pa. Med. Soc., Phila. County Med. Soc. (com. chronic respiratory disease and air pollution), Am. Thoracic Soc., A.C.P., Assn. Advancement Med. Instrumentation, N.Y. Acad. Scis. Contbr. articles in field to profl. jours. Office: 1900 Spruce St Philadelphia PA 19103

KAUFFMAN, RONALD HUGH, pharmacist; b. Lancaster, Pa., Dec. 15, 1932; s. Harold Hershock and Thelma Madeline (Ruth) K.; B.S. in Pharmacy, Phila. Coll. Pharmacy and Sci., 1954; m. Olympia Lambros, Apr. 20, 1958; children—Eileen, Barbara, Michael, Constance. Pharmacist, Queen Pharmacy, Lancaster, 1954-60; asst. dir. pharmacy Lancaster Gen. Hosp., 1960-76, dir. pharmacy, 1976—; instr. pharmacy Temple U. Sec. bd. dirs. Hellenic Orthodox Ch., Lancaster, 1961-62, pres. bd. dirs., 1963-64. Served with U.S. Army, 1955-57. Mem. Am. Pa., Lancaster County (pres. 1973), pharm assns., Am., Pa., S.E. Pa. (treas. 1973-78) soc. hosp. pharmacists, Am. Hellenic Ednl. Progressive Assn. Republican. Greek Orthodox. Club: Lions. Home: 1777 Longview Dr Lancaster PA 17601 Office: 555 N Duke St Lancaster PA 17604

KAUFFMAN, STEPHEN H., hosp. adminstr.; b. Chester, Pa., Apr. 16, 1943; s. Alex and Gertrude (Rosenthal) K.; B.A. in Biology, Weidner Coll., 1965; M.P.H., U. Mass., 1967; m. Elizabeth Baumann, June 19, 1966; children—Jennifer, Rebecca, Scott. Teaching asst. U. of Mass., Amherst, 1967; resident Boston City Hosp., 1968; dir. clin. adminstrn. Mass. Gen. Hosp., Boston, from 1969, subsequently dir. adminstrv. service, instr. mgmt.; cons. hosp. unit mgmt. USPHS fellow, U. Mass., Boston, 1967. Mem. Mass. Unit Mgmt. Assn., (pres. 1976), Brandeis U. Women's Club (workshop leader 1977), Am. Coll. Hosp. Adminstrs., Am. Public Health Assn., Am., Mass. hosp. assns., Mass. Public Health Assn. Jewish. Contbr. articles in field to profl. jours.; developer close-circuit TV for patient edn. Address: Mass Gen Hosp Fruit St Boston MA 02114

KAUFFMANN, HOWARD C., oil co. exec.; b. Tulsa, Feb. 25, 1923; s. Howard C. and Polly Ethyl (Myers) K.; B.M.E., U. Okla., 1943; m. Suzanne McMurray, Nov. 5, 1944; children—Craig, Robert Lane, Kristine, Douglas, Scott. Petroleum engr., prodn. mgr. Carter Oil Co., 1946-57; ops. mgr. Internat. Petroleum Co., Ltd., Peru and Colombia, 1958-61; asst. coordinator Latin Am., Standard Oil Co. (N.J.), 1962-63; dir., v.p., then exec. v.p., pres. Internat. Petroleum Co. Ltd., Coral Gables, Fla., 1964-66, pres., dir. Esso Inter-Am., Inc., Coral Gables, 1967-68; exec. v.p., dir., then pres. Esso Europe, Inc., London, 1969-73; sr. v.p., dir. Exxon Corp., N.Y.C., 1974-75, pres., dir., 1975—; dir. The Chase Manhattan Corp., Chase Manhattan Bank N.A., United Techs. Corp.; dir. Am. Petroleum Inst. Bd. dirs. United Fund Greater N.Y., Economic Devel. Council N.Y.C. Inc.; mem. adv. com. on bus. programs Brookings Inst. Emergency Com. Am. Trade; chmn. Nat. Advisory Council on Minorities in Engring.; trustee Nat. Fund Minority Engring. Students. Served to lt. (j.g.) USNR, World War II. Mem. Nat. Planning Assn. (co vice-chmn. exec. com. changing internat. realities), N.Y. Chamber Commerce and Industry (dir.), U.S. Internat. Council, Phi Gamma Delta, Tau Beta Pi, Sigma Tau. Pi Tau Sigma, Tau Omega. Baptist. Home: Short Hills NJ 07078 Office: Exxon Corp 1251 Ave of Americas New York City NY 10020

KAUFMAN, BARRY MORTON, mfg. co. exec., engr.; b. San Francisco, Aug. 19, 1934; s. Edward and Florence Gladys (Blue) K.; B.E.E., U. Calif. at Berkeley, 1958; m. Audrey Herson, Jan. 11, 1962; children—Debra, Steven. Pres., MuWestern Electronics, San Carlos, Calif., 1963-67; dir. engring. Vega Electronics, Santa Clara, Calif., 1968-71; dir. engring. ITT Mobile Communications, Clark, N.J., 1972-73; v.p. engring., corporate dir. RFL Industries, Inc., Boonton, N.J., 1973—. Mem. IEEE (sr.), Radio Club Am., Audio Engring. Soc. Republican. Jewish. Patentee telecommunications (5); contbr. articles to tech. jours. Home: 30 Cheryl Rd Pinebrook NJ 07058 Office: Powerville Rd Boonton NJ 07005

KAUFMAN, FRANK ALBERT, fed. judge; b. Balt., Mar. 4, 1916; A.B. summa cum laude, Dartmouth Coll., 1937; LL.B. magna cum laude, Harvard U., 1940; m. Clementine Alice Lazaron, Apr. 22, 1945; children—Frank Albert, Peggy Kaufman Wolf. Admitted to Md. bar, 1940; atty. Office Gen. Counsel, Dept. Treasury, 1940-41, Office Gen. Counsel, Lend Lease Adminstrn., 1941-42; Lend Lease rep. in Turkey, 1942-43; asst. to chief Psychol. Warfare Bd., Air Force Hdqrs., 1943-44; chief leaflet div. Psychol. Warfare Div., SHAFE, 1944-45; asst. to gen. counsel Fgn. Econ. Adminstrn., Washington, 1945; asso. firm Frank, Bernstein, Conaway, Kaufman & Goldman, Balt., 1945-47, partner, 1948-66; judge U.S. Dist. Ct. for Md., 1966—; cons. Psychol. Warfare Dept., U.S. Army, Washington, 1952; lectr. adminstrv. law U. Balt., 1948-62; lectr. contracts U. Md. Law Sch., 1953-54; chmn. Md. com. Harvard Law Sch. Fund; mem. Gov.'s Commn. on Certain Aspects Mgmt. and Labor Relations, 1960, Gov.'s Commn. to Study Sentencing in Criminal Cases, 1962-66, Gov.'s Com. on Higher Legal Edn. in Md., 1975-76. Bd. mem. Balt. Hebrew Congregation, 1947-48; mem. nat. exec. bd. Am. Jewish Com., 1960-70, mem. exec. bd. Balt. chpt., 1960-66, pres. Balt. chpt., 1955-56; mem. Gov.'s Inter-Agy. Com. for Comprehensive Health Planning, 1968-69; bd. dirs. NCCJ, Asso. Jewish Charities and Welfare Fund, Balt., 1953-54, Jewish Welfare Bd., Balt., 1965-67, Md. Partners of Alliance, Inc., 1965-72, Good Samaritan Hosp., 1967-73, Goucher Coll., 1956—; bd. dirs. Md. Inst. Coll. Art, 1956—, vice chmn. bd., 1962-70; bd. dirs. Park Sch., Balt., pres., 1963-66; bd. dirs. Sinai Hosp. of Balt., 1957-75, v.p., 1967-70; bd. dirs. Balt. Jewish Council, 1954-66, pres., 1964-66; bd. dirs. Jewish Family and Children's Service, 1946-54, pres., 1953-54; bd. dirs. Suburban Club of Baltimore County, 1941-42, 53-60, pres., 1956-60. Fellow Md. Bar Found. (charter); mem. Fed., Am., Md. bar assns., Rule Day Club (past chmn.), Wranglers Law Club (past chmn.), Lawyers Round Table, Harvard Law Sch. Assn. Md. (past pres.), Jud. Conf. U.S., Am. Judicature Soc. (adv. com. criminal rules), Nat. Conf. Trial Judges, Phi Beta Kappa. Club: Hamilton. Home: 7 Clovelly Rd Pikesville MD 21208 Office: US Courthouse 101 W Lombard St Baltimore MD 21201

KAUFMAN, HAROLD ALEXANDER, chemist; b. Bklyn., Jan. 27, 1933; s. Joe and Rose (Mangel) K.; B.S., Bklyn. Coll., 1955; Ph.D. (AEC fellow, Monsanto Jr. Research fellow), U. Pitts., 1961; m. Elaine Sue Sommers, June 24, 1956; children—Michele Beth, Roy Sommers. Instr. chemistry Bklyn. Coll., 1955; research chemist John R. Evans & Co., Camden, N.J., A.M.P. Inc., Harrisburg, Pa., 1956; project mgr., mgr. crop chem. research, devel. Mobil Chem. Co., Edison, N.J., 1961-76; v.p. research and devel. J.T. Baker Chem. Co., Phillipsburg, N.J., 1976—. Committeeman, Middlesex County, N.J., 1970-74; mem. Am. Jewish Com. Mem. Am. Chem. Soc., British Chem. Soc., Entomol. Soc. Am., Weed Sci. Soc. Am., Sigma Xi, Phi Lambda Upsilon. Clubs: Anshe Emeth Meml. Temple Couples (pres.). Patentee insecticides, herbicides, synergists, plant growth regulants. Home: 142 Fountain Ave Piscataway NJ 08854 Office: J T Baker Chem Co 222 Red School Lane Phillipsburg NJ 08865

KAUFMAN, HARRY HARRIS, mfg. co. ofcl.; b. Newark, Apr. 22, 1913; s. Samuel and Miriam (Ackerman) K.; B.S., City Coll. N.Y., 1936; postgrad. Upsala Coll., 1938; M.A., Montclair State Coll., 1940; m. Ruth Baletin, Feb. 8, 1942; children—Mitchell Alan, Joel Henry. Tchr. physics and chemistry Newark High Sch., 1938-41, 49-50; with Joseph E. Seagram & Sons, Balt., Louisville, 1941-45; chief chemist Flintkote Co., East Rutherford, N.J., 1945-53, Genasco Co., Perth Amboy, N.J., 1953-57; asst. mgr. quality control Ruberoid Co. (now part of GAF Corp.), South Bound Brook, N.J., 1957-78, cons., 1978—. Mem. ASTM (coms. E-34, E-39, E-5), Am. Chem. Soc., Am. Soc. Quality Control, Am. Soc. Safety Engrs. Home: 124 Timothy Pl Bridgewater NJ 08807 Office: 114 Canal Rd South Bound Brook NJ 08880

KAUFMAN, HERMAN SAMUEL, polymer chemist, ednl. adminstr.; b. N.Y.C., Mar. 31, 1922; s. Morris and Sarah (Bronson) K.; B.S., Bklyn. Coll., 1942; M.S., Poly. Inst. Bklyn., 1945, Ph.D. (Allied Chem. fellow), 1947; m. Natalie J. Zuckerbraun, June 20, 1943; children—Linda (Mrs. George Hiltzik), Mark, Joel. Chemist, Manhattan project, Columbia U., N.Y.C., 1942-45; research leader M.W. Kellogg, Jersey City, 1949-57; asst. tech. dir. Minn. Mining & Mfg. Co., Jersey City, 1957-59; corp. dir. research planning Allied Chem., Morristown, N.J., 1959-68; dir. Sch. Sci. Ramapo Coll. N.J., Mahwah, 1970-76, exec. dir. Office Research and Devel., 1976—; adj. prof. chemistry Poly. Inst. Bklyn., 1947-67; asso. prof. chemistry Yeshiva U., N.Y.C., 1968-70; tech. cons. UN, 1968-70; cons., lectr. polymer sci. Soc. Plastic Engrs., Am. Chem. Soc., 1968—. Trustee, Teaneck (N.J.) Jewish Center; trustee Planned Parenthood, Bergen County, N.J. v.p., chmn. bd. edn. Solomon Schecter Day Sch., Bergen County, N.J. Postdoctoral fellow Am. Chem. Soc., 1947-49; named distinguished mem. Soc. Plastics Engrs., 1969. Mem. Am. Chem. Soc.,

Am. Phys. Soc., Soc. Plastic Engrs. (mem. engring. bd. 1965-67, chmn. com. 1965-68), Plastics Inst. Am. (dir. research 1962-69, chmn. bd. trustees 1970). Editor: Textbook of Polymer Science and Technology, 1977. Asso. editor Jour. Polymer Engring. and Sci., 1965-69; editor Internat. Jour. Polymeric Materials, 1970—. Contbr. articles to profl. jours. Patentee in field. Home: 152 Golf Ct Teaneck NJ 07666 Office: 505 Ramapo Valley Rd Mahwah NJ 07430

KAUFMAN, IRVING ROBERT, U.S. judge; b. N.Y.C., June 24, 1910; s. Herman and Rose (Spielberg) K.; LL.B., Fordham U., 1931; LL.D., Jewish Theol. Sem. Am., Fordham U., Oklahoma City U.; D.C.L., N.Y. U.; D.Litt., Dickinson Sch. Law; m. Helen Ruth Rosenberg, June 23, 1936; children—James Michael, Richard Kenneth. Admitted to N.Y. bar, 1932; spl. asst. to U.S. atty. So. Dist. N.Y.; asst. U.S. atty., spl. asst. to atty. gen. U.S. charge of lobbying investigation, 1947-78; established, head permanent lobbying unit for Dept. Justice; pvt. practice law, N.Y.C.; partner firm Noonan, Kaufman & Eagan; U.S. dist. judge So. Dist. N.Y., 1949-61; circuit judge U.S. Ct. Appeals, 2d circuit, 1961—, chief judge, 1973—. U.S. del. 2d UN Congress Prevention Crime and Treatment Offenders, Conf. Anglo-Am. Adminstrv. Law Exchange, Ditchley, Eng., 1969. Trustee Mt. Sinai Med. Center, Sch. Medicine and Hosp.; trustee emeritus Riverdale Country Sch. Recipient Achievement in Law award Fordham Coll. Alumni Assn., Fordham Coll. Encaenia award, medal Fordham Law Sch. Alumni; Silver Anniversary Vanderbilt award Inst. Jud. Adminstrn.; Harlan Fiske Stone award Assn. Trial Lawyers City N.Y.; 1st ann. Thomas Jefferson award Unitarian Universalist Ch.; Learned Hand medal for excellence in fed. jurisprudence Fed. Bar Council; Fellow Inst. Jud. Adminstrn. (pres. 1969-71; chmn. exec. com., chmn. juvenile justice standards project); mem. U.S. Jud. Conf. (mem. com. pretrial procedure 1955-68, chmn. com. ops. jury system 1966-73, exec. com. 1978—), Am. Law Inst., Assn. Bar City N.Y., Fed., N.Y., Am. (mem. spl. com. standards jud. conduct) bar assns., Am. Judicature Soc., Fordham Law Alumni Assn. (dir.), Tau Epsilon Phi (Man of Year citation), Phi Alpha Delta (hon.). Eleventh ann. James Madison lectr.; The Message, The Medium and the First Amendment; 3d ann. John F. Sonnett lectr. Fordham Law Sch. Prison: The Judge's Dilemma. Contbr. articles to profl. jours. Home: 1185 Park Ave New York City NY 10028 Office: U S Courthouse Foley Sq New York City NY 10007

KAUFMAN, JOHN ROBERT, advt. agy. exec.; b. New Cumberland, Pa., Dec. 13, 1931; s. Jean Coulsen and Mercedes Katherine (Beshore) K.; A.B., Pa. State U., 1953; M.B.A., U. Pa., 1955. Vice pres. N.W. Ayer ABH Internat., Phila., 1965-72, N.Y.C., 1972—; dir. Burgess and Why, 1963-64. Served with USNR, 1955-58. Mem. Advt. Data Processing Assn., Am. Mktg. Assn., Market Research Soc. Eng., Nat. Microfilm Assn., Navy League U.S., Navy Res. Assn., Navy Sea Cadets, Navy Supply Corps Sch. Alumni Assn., Phila. C. of C., Spl Libraries Assn. Republican. Presbyterian. Home: 522 Market St New Cumberland PA 17070 Office: N W Ayer 1345 Ave of Americas New York City NY 10019

KAUFMAN, KENNETH FRANKLIN, psychologist; b. N.Y.C., Dec. 8, 1945; s. Israel and Mollie (Luria) K.; B.A. (Regents scholar), Queens Coll., 1966; Ph.D. (Regents teaching fellow), State U. N.Y., Stony Brook, 1971; m. Lana Jane Barcham, Aug. 18, 1968; children—Lauren, Julie. Intern psychol. services State U. N.Y., Stony Brook, 1968-69, N.E. Nassau Psychiat. Hosp., Kings Park, N.Y., 1969-70; psychologist Sagamore Childrens Center, Melville, N.Y., 1970-73, prin. psychologist, 1973-76, chief outpatient service, 1977, dir. treatment services, 1978—; pvt. practice, Setauket, N.Y., 1973—; cons. Suffolk Child Devel. Center, Smithtown, N.Y., 1972-74, 78—; adj. prof. Tchrs. Coll. Columbia, 1972, State U. N.Y., Stony Brook, 1974-75, 77—, Adelphi U., 1976; vis. instr. State U. Coll. at Brockport, 1978. Mem. Am. Psychol. Assn., Council Exceptional Children, Nat. Soc. Autistic Children, Psi Chi. Jewish religion. Home: 2 Cedar Wood Ct Setauket NY 11733 Office: Sagamore Childrens Center Box 755 Melville NY 11746

KAUFMAN, MICHAEL DAVID, duplication machinery mfg. co. exec.; b. Bklyn., Apr. 7, 1941; s. Abraham and Shirley (Blank) K.; B.S.M.E., Poly. Inst. Bklyn., 1962, M.S. in Indsl. Mgmt., 1967; m. Susan G. Zipkis, June 30, 1962; children—Robert Jay, Craig Douglas. Mgr. advance mfg. planning Grumman Aircraft Engring. Corp., Bethpage, N.Y., 1963-67; with Xerox Corp., Stamford, Conn., 1967—, dir. corporate fin. planning, 1976-77, dir. corp. product and strategy analysis, 1977—; lectr. M.B.A. program U. Conn. Bd. dirs. Poly. Inst. N.Y. Alumni. Mem. Am. Inst. Indsl. Engrs. (sr.), ASME, Nat. Soc. Profl. Engrs. (affiliate). Home: RFD Arden Dr Amawalk NY 10501 Office: High Ridge Park Stamford CT 06904

KAUFMAN, MICO, sculptor; b. Buzeu, Rumania, Jan. 3, 1924; s. Herman and Adela (Kupferberg) K.; student Acad. Fine Arts Rome and Florence, 1947-51; m. Katherine Sanidas, 1947 (div. June 1968); children—Adele, Arthur, Emile; came to U.S., 1951, naturalized, 1956. One-man shows: Rivier Coll., Nashua, N.H., 1967, Andover (Mass.) Gallery Fine Arts, 1968, Concord (Mass.) Art Assn., 1969, Rockport Art Assn., 1969, Lawrence Acad., Groton, Mass., 1970, Arts and Sci. Center, Nashua, 1970; exhibited group shows: Nat. Sculptors Soc., 1970, 71, North Shore Art Assn., 1970-72, Rockport Artists Assn., 1967-73, Internat. Expn. Contemporary Numismatists, Crakow, Poland, 1975, many others; commd. medals include ofcl. inaugural medal Vice Pres. Gerald Ford, 1974, 200 medals in History of Am. series, Danbury Mint, 1974—, 87th issue Soc. Medalists, ofcl. inaugural obverse of Ford Presdl. Medal, 2 sets of sculpture for Am. Sculpture Soc., 1975-76; represented in permanent collections: Rivier Coll., Kiski Acad., Pa., also numerous pvt. collections; tchr. sculpture Boston Center for Adult Edn., 1959-62, New Eng. Sch. Art, Boston, 1969-70, Nashua Arts and Sci., 1970-71; also pvt. instr. Recipient 1st prize Am. Numis. Assn., 1976, Sculptor of Yr. award, 1978. Mem. Nat. Sculpture Soc., New Eng. Sculptors Assn., Rockport, North Shore artists assns. Club: Rotary. Home and Studio: 23 Marion Dr North Tewksbury MA 01876

KAUFMAN, MYRON L., real estate developer; b. N.Y.C., July 29, 1928; s. Louis and Berdie Lillien (List) K.; A.B., State U. N.Y., 1946-49; m. Joan Schwartz, Mar. 28, 1954; children—Steven, Martin, Lois. Partner Basser-Kaufman Real Estate, Lawrence, N.Y., 1963—. Commr. pub. works Hewlett Harbor, N.Y., 1968-74; trustee Hewlett Harbor, N.Y., 1975—, chmn. planning bd.; trustee Peninsula Hosp. Center. Served with AUS, 1951-52. Decorated Bronze Star medal, Purple Heart. Recipient first prize for excellence in constrn. in Borough of Queens, Borough of Queens C. of C., 1969. Mem. Internat. Council Shopping Centers, L.I. Builders Inst. (trustee 1959-61), L.I. Real Estate Bd., N.Y. State Soc. Real Estate Appraisers, Nat. Assn. Home Builders, Am. Pub. Works Assn., Inst. for Municipal Engring., Inst. for Solid Wastes. Club: B'nai B'rith, The Woodmere (N.Y.), Point Set Indoor Racquet. Home: 1325 Huckleberry Ln Hewlett Harbor NY 11557 Office: 335 Central Ave Lawrence NY 11559

KAUFMAN, ROBERT MAX, lawyer; b. Vienna, Austria, Nov. 17, 1929; s. Paul M. and Bertha (Hirsch) K.; came to U.S., 1939, naturalized, 1945; B.A. with honors, Bklyn. Coll., 1951; M.A., N.Y.U., 1954; J.D. magna cum laude, Bklyn. Law Sch., 1957; m. Sheila Seymour Kelley, Nov. 20, 1959. Admitted to N.Y. bar, 1957, U.S. Supreme Ct. bar, 1960; successively jr. economist, economist, sr. economist N.Y. State Div. Housing, 1953-57; atty. antitrust div. U.S. Dept. Justice, 1957-58; legis. asst. to U.S. Senator Jacob K. Javits, 1958-61; asso. firm Proskauer Rose Goetz & Mendelsohn, N.Y.C., 1961-69, partner, 1969—; dir. Pirelli Cable Corp., Union, N.J., Pirelli U.S. Am. Rep. Corp., N.Y.C., Pirelli Cable Systems, Inc., N.Y.C., Solari Am., Inc., N.Y.C. Mem. N.Y. State Legislature Adv. Com. on Election Law, 1973-74; chmn. adv. com. N.Y. State Bd. Elections, 1974-78. Mem. platform com. N.Y. Republican State Com., 1974; mem. jud. selection adv. coms. to Senators Javits and Moynahan; treas., mgr., counsel various polit. campaigns; bd. dirs. Lawrence M. Gelb Found., Inc.; bd. dirs., sec. Community Action for Legal Services, Inc.; bd. dirs., exec. v.p. Ernest and Mary Hayward Weir Found.; exec. com. bd. visitors U.S. Mil. Acad., 1976—. Served with AUS, 1957-58. Mem. Assn. Bar City N.Y. (exec. com., past chmn. com. profl. responsibility, past chmn. spl. com. on campaign expenditures, past chmn. com. civil rights, past vice chmn. com. grievances), New York County Lawyers Assn. (past chmn. com. on civil rights). Co-author: Congress and the Public Trust, 1970; Disorder in the Court, 1973. Home: 345 E 52d St New York City NY 10022 Office: 300 Park Ave New York City NY 10022

KAUFMAN, SEYMOUR ALVIN, radiologist; b. Boston, Apr. 5, 1926; s. Frank S. and Ida K. (Ganick) K.; M.D., Boston U., 1948; m. Charlotte F. Rothberg, Feb. 10, 1951; children—Lisa Nan, John Andrew, Peter Ross. Intern Boston City Hosp., 1948-49; resident Boston City Hosp., 1949-50, Mass. Meml. Hosp., Boston, 1952-54; practice medicine specializing in radiology, Boston, 1963—; mem. staffs Boston U. Hosp., Boston City Hosp., Northeastern U.; clin. prof. radiology Boston U. Active in fund raising United Fund, Alumni funds, Combined Jewish Philanthropies. Served to capt. M.C., USAF, 1950-52. Fellow Am. Coll. Radiology; mem. Radiol. Soc. N.Am., Am., New Eng. Roentgen ray socs., Mass. Radiologic Soc., AMA, Mass. Med. Soc. Contbr. numerous articles to profl. publs. Home: 64 Bishopsgate Rd Newton Center MA 02159 Office: 454 Brookline Ave Boston MA 02215

KAUFMAN, STEPHEN FREDERICK, financial counselor; b. Bklyn., Apr. 22, 1939; s. Jacob Joseph and Alice Dell (Shanman) K.; B.A. cum laude in Edn., Bklyn., Coll., 1976; m. Jaclyn Ann Spodek, May 4, 1963; children—Lita Bonni, Adam Seth. Free-lance sales cons., N.Y.C., 1961-75; sales exec. Dun and Bradstreet Corp., N.Y.C., 1975-76; pres. Centurion Comml. Collection Corp., N.Y.C., 1976—; lectr. on finance and credit to bus. community; mem. pres.'s. com. on planning and priorities for Bklyn. Coll., 1975-76. Karate master and self def. instr. Neighborhood Youth Groups, Bklyn., 1969—; coach Little League, Bklyn., 1973-74. Served with USAF, 1957-61. Recipient Myrtle Jacobson Small Coll. award for Humanities, Bklyn. Coll., 1976, Dean Myrtle Jacobson Scholarship award, 1976. Mem. Bklyn. Coll. Alumni Assn. (dir.), Small Coll. Alumni Assn. Bklyn. Coll. (exec. com.). Contbg. editor Bklyn. Coll. Evening Newspaper, 1974-76. Office: 114 Liberty St New York City NY 10006

KAUFMAN, STEPHEN LAWRENCE, radiologist; b. Phila., Nov. 7, 1942; s. Abraham Saul and Genevieve June (Finestone) K.; A.B., U. Pa., 1963, M.D., 1967. Intern, Presbyn. U. Pa. Med. Center, Phila., 1967-68; resident in radiology Johns Hopkins U., Balt., 1970-74, fellow in cardiovascular radiology, 1974-75; asst. prof. radiology, 1975—; cons. Balt. City hosps. Served with USPHS, 1968-70. Diplomate Am. Bd. Radiology. Mem. Am. Coll. Radiology, Radiol. Soc. N.Am., Md. Radiologic Assn. Home: 6920 Donachie Rd Baltimore MD 21239 Office: Johns Hopkins Hosp Baltimore MD 21205

KAUFMANN, AXEL, architect; b. Frankfort, Main, Germany, Nov. 19, 1924; came to U.S., 1938, naturalized, 1944; s. Hermann and Erna (Schlomann) K.; B.Arch., Mass. Inst. Tech., 1949; m. Marion Ruth Allen, Oct. 27, 1962; children—Laura Ruth, Jessica Ann. With Adden, Parker, Clinch & Crimp, Boston, 1949-50, 52-54, Stone & Webster, Boston, 1950-52, Samuel Glaser Assos., Boston, 1954-55, G.W.W. Brewster, Boston, 1955-56; asso. partner Campbell & Aldrich, Boston, 1956-65; pvt. practice architecture, Boston, 1965—. Instr., Boston Archtl. Center, 1957-58. Founder, pres. Tennis Films Internat. Inc., 1970—, Tennis/Now, Inc., 1973—. Mem. exec. com. Fund for Urban Negro Devel., 1970-71; founder Newton Youth Found.; bd. dirs. Youth Tennis Found., 1970—. Served with AUS, 1943-46. Mem. A.I.A., Mass. Assn. Architects, Boston Soc. Architects. New Eng. Lawn (1st v.p. 1973-77, sec. 1977—), U.S. (chmn. facilities com. 1973—) tennis assns. Unitarian (chmn. bd. trustees 1968-69). Clubs: Longwood Cricket (Chestnut Hill, Mass.); Badminton and Tennis (Boston). Author: Pardon Me, Your Forehand Is Showing, 1956. Exec. producer Tennis Fundamentals. Home and Office: Puritan Rd Newton Highlands MA 02161

KAUFMANN, ED, lawyer; b. Davenport, Iowa, May 17, 1938; s. Ed and Jean (Plohn) K.; B.A., Cornell U., 1960; LL.B. cum laude, Harvard U., 1966; m. Ruth V. Morgan, Mar. 9, 1968; children—Anna, Laura. Admitted to N.Y. bar, 1967; asso. firm Hughes Hubbard & Reed, N.Y.C., 1966-73, partner, 1974—. Served with USN, 1960-63. Mem. Am. Bar Assn., Phi Beta Kappa. Home: 44 Fairway Ave Rye NY 10580 Office: 1 Wall St New York City NY 10005

KAUFMANN, WALTER (ARNOLD), educator, author; b. Freiburg, Germany, July 1, 1921; s. Bruno and Edith (Seligsohn) K.; came to U.S., 1939, naturalized, 1944; B.A., Williams Coll., 1941; M.A., Harvard, 1942, Ph.D., 1947; m. Hazel Dennis, July 12, 1942; children—Dinah, David. Mem. faculty Princeton, 1947—, prof. philosophy, 1962—; vis. prof. Cornell U., 1952, Columbia, 1955, U. Wash., 1958, U. Mich., 1959, Purdue U., 1966; Fulbright research prof. Heidelberg U., 1955-56; Fulbright prof. Hebrew U. Jerusalem, 1962-63, vis. prof., 1975; Phi Beta Kappa vis. scholar, 1971-72; vis. fellow Research Sch. Social Scis., Australian Nat. U., 1974. Mem. adv. screening com. philosophy and religion Com. Internat. Exchange of Persons, 1957-61, chmn., 1959-61; co-founder, chmn. bd. InterFuture (student exchange program), 1970-71. Served with M.I., AUS, 1944-46. Recipient Internat. Leo Baeck prize, 1961. Mem. Phi Beta Kappa. Author: Nietzsche, 1950, rev., enlarged 4th edit., 1974; Critique of Religion and Philosophy, 1958; From Shakespeare to Existentialism, 1959, rev., enlarged edit., 1960; The Faith of a Heretic, 1961; Twenty German Poets, 1962; Cain and Other Poems, 1962, 3d edit., 75; Hegel, 1965; Tragedy and Philosophy, 1968; Without Guilt and Justice, 1973; Twenty-five German Poets, 1975; Religions in Four Dimensions, 1976; Existentialism, Religion, and Death, 1976; The Future of the Humanities, 1977; Man's Lot: A Trilogy, photographs and text, Life at the Limits, Time Is an Artist, What Is Man?, 1978. Translator: Leo Baeck's Judaism and Christianity, 1958; Goethe's Faust, 1961; 4 of Nietzsche's works in the Portable Nietzsche, 1954; The Will to Power (Nietzsche), 1967; 5 more works in Basic Writings of Nietzsche, 1968; I and Thou (Martin Buber), 1970; The Gay Science (Nietzsche), 1974. Editor: Existentialism from Dostoevsky to Sartre, 1956, enlarged edit., 1975; Hegel's Political Philosophy, 1970. Contbr. to encys. and anthologies. Home: 429 Prospect Ave Princeton NJ 08540

KAUFMANN, YORAM, psychologist; b. Tel-Aviv, Oct. 3, 1939; s. Zvi Herbert and Lina (Rochlin) K.; came to U.S., 1967, naturalized, 1976; Ph.D., N.Y. U., 1972; m. Rise Jacobson, Aug. 1, 1972. Staff psychologist Ministry of Health, Israel, 1963-67, Lincoln Inst. for Psychotherapy, N.Y.C., 1968-72; pvt. practice Jungian analysis, N.Y.C., 1972—; tchr., supr. C.G. Jung Tng. Center, N.Y.C., 1972—. Served as 1st lt. Israeli Armed Forces, 1962-67. Mem. Internat. Assn. Analytical Psychologists, Am., N.J. psychol. assns., Bergen County Assn. Lic. Psychologists. Club: B'nai Brith. Home: 159 Deer Trail N Ramsey NJ 07446 Office: 257 Central Park W Room 3C New York City NY 10024

KAUNITZ, RITA DAVIDSON, planner; b. N.Y.C., Apr. 18; d. David and Bessie (Golden) Davidson; B.A. magna cum laude, N.Y. U., 1942; M.A., Columbia U., 1946; Ph.D., Radcliffe Coll., 1951; m. Paul E. Kaunitz, Aug. 10, 1947; children—Victoria Moss, Jonathan Davidson, Andrew Moss. Adminstrv. analyst Office Price Adminstrn., Washington, 1943-44; columnist on planning and housing Progressive Architecture Mag., N.Y.C., 1944-46, editor Plan for Rezoning, N.Y.C., 1948-49; asso. editor Bull. Housing and Town and Country Planning UN Secretariat, N.Y.C., 1950-52, cons. Center for Housing, Bldg. and Planning 1960-66; research asso. grad. program in city planning Yale U., 1955-57; seminar asso. Columbia U., 1966-70; policy and program specialist Model Cities Program, Bridgeport, Conn., 1969; project dir. Regional Plan Assn. of N.Y.C., Conn. Issues and Answers, 1976—; vis. lectr. U. R.I., 1967-69; mem. Conn. Clean Air Commn., 1969-71; sci. adviser L.I. Sound Regional Study, New Eng. River Basins Commn., New Haven, 1972-75; chmn. Conn. Pub. Utilities Control Authority Reorgn. Task Force, 1976-77; cons. project on individual risk-taking and health care Sch. Law, N.Y. U., 1978—; co-chmn. legislation and public info. com. Council High Blood Pressure, 1978—. Bd. dirs. Woman's Place, Darien, Conn., 1976—. Recipient certificate for distng. service Nat. Screening Com., Fulbright-Hayes Fellowships in Architecture/City Planning, 1969-75; Conn. Humanities scholar Suburban Women's Program, 1978—. Mem. Am. Soc. Planning Ofcls. (dir. 1973-76), Am. Inst. Planners. Democrat. Club: Radcliffe of Lower Fairfield County (Conn.). Contbr. articles to profl. jours. Home and Office: 14 Red Coat Rd Westport CT 06880

KAUTH, BENJAMIN, podiatrist; b. N.Y.C., Oct. 20, 1914; s. Samuel and Edith (Schrier) K.; student Coll. City of N.Y., 1932-35; Dr. Podiatry, L.I. U., 1939, postgrad., 1945-46; m. Bertha Locke, Nov. 24, 1946. Intern, Foot Clinics of N.Y., 1938-39; in pvt. practice, N.Y.C., 1940—; chief podiatry staff Hosp. for Aged and Infirm Hebrews, 1942—, also Village Nursing Home; chief podiatry staff staff St. Clare's Hosp. and Health Center, French and Polyclinic Med. Sch. and Health Center; cons. on foot care to various groups. Mem. Nat. Council Am. Jewish Joint Distbn. Com., 1949—. Podiatrist of Year, Podiatry Soc. N.Y., 1957. Trustee, exec. com. N.Y. Coll. Podiatric Medicine. Mem. Am. Coll. Foot Surgeons (asso.), Podiatry Soc. State N.Y., Acad. Podiatry. Clubs: Fair Harbor Yacht (sec.), Friars. Author: Walk and Be Happy, 1960. Exec. editor Jour. Podiatry, 1954; editorial asst. N.Y. Podiatrist; contbr. articles in field. Writer weekly column for Fire Island News. Tech. dir. sound film The Walking Machine. Home: 302 W 12th St New York City NY 10014 Office: 888 8th Ave New York City NY 10019

KAVARNOS, GEORGE JAMES, clin. chemist; b. New London, Conn., Feb. 25, 1942; s. James Spiros and Mary (Pantelis) K.; B.A., Clark U., 1964; Ph.D., U. R.I., 1968. NIH research fellow Columbia, 1968-71; research fellow Albert Einstein Coll. Medicine, N.Y.C., 1971; clin. chemist, co-dir. Cyto Med. Lab. Inc., Norwich, Conn., 1971—, v.p. Bio-Analytical Labs., 1971—; adj. prof. chemistry U. R.I., 1978—. Mem. Am. Chem. Soc., Am. Assn. Clin. Chemistry, Chemists Soc. Columbia, Sigma Xi. Greek Orthodox. Researcher in clin. chemistry and photochemistry. Home: 121 Riverview Ave New London CT 06320 Office: 12 Case St Norwich CT 06360

KAVEE, ROBERT CHARLES, brokerage co. exec.; b. N.Y.C., Aug. 9, 1934; s. Julius and Kate K.; A.B. in Math., U. Rochester, 1956; M.S. in E.E., Columbia U., 1959; postgrad. U. Pa., 1974; m. Donna Helene Auld, Jan. 31, 1959; children—Andrew L., Patti M., Stacie R. Def. space electronics and systems engr. ITT Labs. and Sperry Rand Systems Group, Nutley, N.J. and Great Neck, N.Y., 1959-66; NSF sr. research fellow Poly. Inst. Bklyn., 1966-68; sr. systems specialist ITT Data Services, Paramus, N.J., 1968-70; mgr. ops. research ITT World Hdqrs., N.Y.C., 1970-75; mgr. instnl. applications devel. Merrill Lynch Pierce Fenner & Smith, N.Y.C., 1975—. Mem. Inst. Quantitative Research in Fin., Bond Quantitative Group, Am. Fin. Assn., IEEE. Club: Old Greenwich Yacht. Designer early cardiac ballisto-cardiogram, early cardiac pacemaker, 1959. Home: 51 Mary Ln Riverside CT 06878 Office: Merrill Lynch Pierce Fenner & Smith 1 Liberty Plaza New York City NY 10006

KAVIC, MICHAEL STEPHEN, surgeon; b. Oravosburgh, Pa., Mar. 24, 1941; s. Stephen and Violet (Gruber) K.; B.S. in Chemistry, U. Pitts., 1962; M.D., Meharry Med. Coll., 1966; m. Vennie Anne Yuhouse, Sept. 9, 1967; children—Suzanne Marie, Alicia Anne, Stephen Michael, Christian Eban. Intern, St. Francis Gen. Hosp., Pitts., 1966-67; resident in surgery St. Elizabeth Gen. Hosp., Youngstown, Ohio, 1967-71; gen. surgeon, chief of surgery Ohio Valley Gen. Hosp., McKees Rocks, Pa., 1974—; cons. surgeon Aliquippa (Pa.) Hosp.; rep. Allegheny County Profl. Standards Rev. Orgn., chmn. utilization rev. com.; med. lectr. Am. Cancer Soc. Mem. profl. adv. com. N.W. Allegheny Home Care Program, 1977—; bd. dirs. N.W. Allegheny Hosps. Corp. Served with USN, 1970-71. Diplomate Am. Bd. Surgery. Fellow A.C.S., Internat. Acad. Proctology; mem. AMA, Pa., Allegheny County med. socs., Pitts. Surg. Soc., Pitts. Gut Club, Am. Soc. Abdominal Surgeons, Am. Coll. Utilization Rev. Physicians. Eastern Orthodox. Home: Box 175A Aliquippa PA 15001 Office: 927 Broadhead Rd Coraopolis PA 15108

KAVNER, RICHARD STANLEY, optometrist; b. Bklyn., Feb. 12, 1936; s. Saul and Sylvia (Goodman) K.; student L.I. U., 1953-55; B.S., Mass. Coll. Optometry, 1957, Dr. Optometry, 1959; m. Carole Wolper, June 30, 1963; children—William, Theodore. Practice optometry, Bronx, N.Y., 1961-71; chief optometry dept. Assn. for Help Retarded Children, 1967; optometric cons. Liberty (N.Y.) Sch. System, 1967, St. Josephs Home for Deaf, 1968; cons. Harlem Eye and Ear Hosp., Optometric Center N.Y., Rugby Sch. Retarded Children, Home and Hosp. Daughters of Israel, N.Y.C. Bd. Edn., Dist. 11, 1976; lectr. Mass. Coll. Optometry; attending staff N.Y. Optometric Center; chief behavioral vision lab. N.Y. Coll. Optometry, 1975; asst. clin. prof. optometry State U. N.Y., 1972-73; lectr. vision and behavior Brown U., 1977; mem. profl. adv. bd. Brain Injured Childrens Assn., 1968; participant Optometric Center N.Y. Symposium on Vision Therapy in the Classroom, 1970; pres. Investors Assos., 1960-62; chmn. Kavner Found., 1962—. Served with M.C., U.S. Army, 1959-60. Diplomate in binocular vision and perception Am. Acad. Optometry. Fellow N.Y. Acad. Optometry; mem. Am., N.Y., Bronx optometric socs., Council for Exceptional Children, N.Y. Acad. Scis., Pub. Health Assn., Am. Optometric Found., Optometric Extension Program. Author: The Effect of Stress Upon Vision, 1959; Handbook on Pleoptics, 1964; co-author: Total Vision, 1978. Address: 245 E 54th St New York City NY 10022

KAWATRA, MAHENDRA P., educator; b. India, June 22, 1935; s. Behari Lal and Chanan Devi (Sachdeva) K.; came to U.S., 1963, naturalized, 1976; B.S. with honours, U. Delhi, 1955, M.S., 1957,

Ph.D., 1962; m. Ved Suri, Sept. 30, 1962; children—Anjali, Anita. Lectr. physics U. Delhi, 1957-63; vis. scholar Mass. Inst. Tech., 1963-64; asso. research scientist Courant Inst., N.Y. U., 1964-66; asso. prof. Fordham U., 1966-71; asso. prof. physics Medgar Evers Coll., City U. N.Y., 1971-74, prof., 1975—. Trustee Hindu Temple, Queens, N.Y., 1975—. Smith Mundt-Fulbright fellow, 1963-64; grantee NSF, 1967-71, Navy Dept., 1967-71. Mem. AAAS, N.Y. Acad. Scis., Am. Phys. Soc. Author: Dynamical Aspects of Critical Phenomena; also articles. Home: 10 Seagull Ln Port Washington NY 11050 Office: 1150 Carroll St Brooklyn NY 11225

KAY, STANLEY ROBERT, clin. psychologist; b. N.Y.C., June 7, 1946; s. Leslie Laszlo and Anne K.; B.A., N.Y. U., 1968; M.A. cum laude, Fairleigh Dickinson U., 1970; postgrad. New Sch. Social Research, 1971-73, State U. N.Y. at Stony Brook, 1978—; m. Theresa Maria De Monte, June 27, 1970; children—Lisa Paula, Stacy Lynn. Research psychologist, psychometrist Klein Inst. Aptitude Testing, N.Y.C., 1970; clin. research psychologist Clin. Psychopharmacology Service, Bronx (N.Y.) Psychiat. Center, 1970-76; dir. clin. program, also dir. research and evaluation, Cognitive Devel. Service, 1976—; individual practice clin. psychology, Mahopac, N.Y., 1975—; cons., lectr. in field. Mem. N.Y. U. Coat of Arms Soc., Am., Eastern psychol. assns., N.Y. Psychologists in Pub. Service. Contbr. articles to profl. publs.; lectr. profl. orgns.; research on evaluation mental disorders and treatment. Home: Kirkwood Rd RFD 2 Mahopac NY 10541 Office: Bronx Psychiat Center 1500 Waters Pl Bronx NY 10461

KAYALI, KALED MUHAMAD, polit. scientist, educator; b. Lydda, Palestine, Aug. 8, 1939; s. Muhamad Ali and Fahima (Salim) K.; B.A., Tex. Tech U., 1967, M.A., 1970; M.A., U. Md., 1975, Ph.D., 1975; m. Gay N. Beyer, Aug. 31, 1969; children—Lyela Emily, Ramzey Adam. Mgr. Fair Dept. Store, Lamesa, Tex., 1964-66; teaching asst. Tex. Tech U., Lubbock, 1967-69; grad. asst. U. Md., College Park, 1970-74, instr. polit. sci., 1974-75; asst. prof. polit. sci. Shippensburg (Pa.) State Coll., 1975—. Mem. Am., So., Western polit. sci. assns., Am. Soc. Pub. Adminstrn., Pi Sigma Alpha. Muslim. Contbr. chpts. to books. Home: 269 High St Chambersburg PA 17201 Office: Shippensburg State Coll Dept Govt Shippensburg PA 17257

KAYALOFF, JACQUES, investment counselor; b. Nakhichevan, Russia, Oct. 12, 1898; s. Jean and Elisabeth (Bagdasarian) K.; grad. Medvednikov Lyceum (Moscow, USSR), 1916; m. Anna Avakoff Avakian, Dec. 15, 1945; 1 dau., Isabelle. Came to U.S., 1924, naturalized, 1929. With Louis Dreyfus Orgn., N.Y.C., 1922-63, pres., 1955-63, cons., 1963—; dir. Radix Orgn. Inc., N.Y.C., Sidcor, Inc., N.Y.C. Mem. adv. bd. Maison Francaise of N.Y. U. Served with Armenian Army, 1918-20. Author: Afro's World, 1972; The Battle of Sardarabad, 1973; The Fall of Baku, 1976. Contbr. articles to hist. mags. Home: 40 E 78th St New York City NY 10021 Office: 230 Park Ave New York City NY 10017

KAYATT, EDITH SUTPHEN, editor; b. N.Y.C., Dec. 31, 1944; d. Jack and Linda (Sutphen) Rubinstein; A.B., Vassar U., 1962-66; postgrad. Sorbonne, 1965; m. William Kayatt, June 6, 1972. Editorial asst. Time Mag., N.Y.C., 1969-71; asst. acct. supr. Young & Rubicam, N.Y.C., 1972-74; advt. mgr. Colgate Palmolive Co., N.Y.C., 1975-76; editor Our Town News, N.Y.C., 1977—. Mem. Am. for Democratic Action, Sierra Club, Advt. Women of Am., Am. Soc. for Prevention Cruelty to Animals. Democrat. Home: 445 E 86th St New York NY 10028 Office: 500 E 82nd St New York NY 10028

KAYE, JUDITH SMITH (MRS. STEPHEN RACKOW KAYE), lawyer; b. Monticello, N.Y., Aug. 4, 1938; d. Benjamin and Lena (Cohen) Smith; B.A., Barnard Coll., 1958; LL.B. cum laude, N.Y. U., 1962; m. Stephen Rackow Kaye, Feb. 11, 1964; children—Luisa Marian, Jonathan Mackey, Gordon Bernard. Admitted to N.Y. bar, 1963; atty. firm Sullivan & Cromwell, N.Y.C., 1962-64; staff atty. IBM, N.Y.C., 1964-65; mem. firm Olwine Connelly Chase O'Donnell & Weyher, N.Y.C., 1969—; bd. dirs. Legal Aid Soc., 1977—. Mem. Am. (litigation sect.), N.Y. State (mem. internat. law com. 1962-63) bar assns., Assn. Bar City NY (mem. adminstrv. law com. 1972, ethics com. 1975—). Home: 101 Central Park W New York City NY 10023 Office: 299 Park Ave New York City NY 10017

KAYE, ROBERT EDWARD, physician; b. Port Chester, N.Y., Mar. 8, 1938; s. Abraham and Etta (Cummins) K.; B.A., Princeton U., 1959; M.D., U. Pa., 1963; m. Wendy Burnham, Feb. 1, 1964; children—Anthony Cummins, Hilary, Andrey Burnham. Intern, Jersey City Med. Center, 1963-64; resident N.Y. Hosp., N.Y.C., 1966-70; practice medicine specializing in obstetrics and gynecology, N.Y.C., 1970—; mem. staffs N.Y. Hosp.; asst. clin. prof. Cornell U., N.Y.C., 1970—. Served with AUS, 1964-66. Fellow Am. Coll. Obstetrics and Gynecology; mem. Am. Fertility Soc., Am. Soc. Planned Parenthood Physicians. Clubs: Century Country, Princeton. Home: 445 E 80 St New York NY 10021 Office: 475 E 72 St New York NY 10021

KAYE, ROBERT MARTIN, realtor; b. Long Branch, N.J., Mar. 12, 1937; s. Ivring and Jean (Weisman) K.; student U. Conn., 1954-58, Boston Coll., 1958-59; children—Jonathan Steven, Steven Andrew, Kimberly Jean. Pres., Planned Residental Communities, Inc., West Long Branch, N.J.; mem. advisory bd. N.J. Nat. Bank. Mem. N.J. Shore Builders Assn. (past dir.), Inst. Real Estate Mgmt. (dir. N.J. chpt.), Young Pres. Orgn. Office: 60 Monmouth Park Hwy West Long Branch NJ 07764

KAYE, STEPHEN RACKOW, lawyer; b. Nyack, N.Y., May 4, 1931; s. Edward and Florence (Karp) K.; B.A., Cornell U., 1952, LL.B. cum laude, 1956; m. Judith Ann Smith, Feb. 11, 1964; children—Luisa Marian, Jonathan Mackey, Gordon Bernard. Admitted to N.Y. bar, 1956; asso. firm Sullivan & Cromwell, N.Y.C., 1956-63; asso. Proskauer, Rose, Goetz & Mendelsohn, N.Y.C., 1964-68, partner, 1968—, mng. partner, 1978—. Treas., dir. 103 Central Park W. Corp., N.Y.C., 1974—. Served to 1st lt., inf. AUS, 1952-54. Korea. Mem. Am., N.Y. State bar assns., Assn. Bar City N.Y., Am. Judicature Soc., Order of Coif, Phi Kappa Phi. Jewish. Club: City Athletic (N.Y.C.). Contbr. articles to profl. jours. Home: 101 Central Park W New York City NY 10023 Office: 300 Park Ave New York City NY 10022

KAYE, WILLIAM MARK, coll. adminstr., counselor; b. N.Y.C., June 29, 1949; s. Philip Richard and Leona Harriet (Cohen) K.; B.A., Wilkes Coll., 1971; M.S., Syracuse U., 1973. Mem. housing staff Wilkes Coll., Wilkes Barre, Pa., 1970-71, Syracuse (N.Y.) U., 1971-73; tchr. K-12, Syracuse City Sch. Dist., 1971-73; dir. summer camps Syracuse Jewish Community Center, 1972—; dir. housing W.New Eng. Coll., Springfield, Mass., 1973-76; dir. housing and fin. aid Penn Coll. Podiatric Medicine, Phila., 1976—; cons. personnel counseling various firms Phila. Recipient service award W.New Eng. Coll. 1973-76. Mem. Am. Personel and Guidance Assn., Assn. Coll. Personnel Adminstrs., Assn. Coll. and Univ. Housing Officers, Nat. Assn. Student Personnel Adminstrs. Jewish. Club: Phila. YM and YMHA. Contbr. articles in field. Address: 801 Cherry St Box 712 Philadelphia PA 19107

KAYLANI, NABIL MUSTAFA, educator; b. Hama, Syria, Mar. 17, 1941; s. Mustafa Tawfiq and Shereen Mehdi (Haydar) K.; came to U.S., 1962, naturalized, 1969; B.A., Am. U. Beirut (Lebanon), 1962; M.A. (Univ. scholar), Clark U., 1964, Ph.D. (Univ. fellow), 1967; m. Edna Bergman, July 6, 1966; children—Marwan, Zane. Instr., Coll. Gen. Studies Rochester Inst. Tech., 1966-67, asst. prof. internat. relations, 1967-71, asso. prof., 1971-74, prof., 1974—, chmn. div. sci. and humanities, 1976-78. NSF grantee, summer 1974. Fellow Middle East Studies Assn. N.Am.; mem. Middle East Inst., Am. Hist. Assn., AAUP. Contbr. articles to Internat. Jour. Middle E. Studies, Internat. Rev. History and Polit. Sci. Office: 06-3303 Lomb Memorial Dr Rochester NY 14623

KAZEMI, HOMAYOUN, physician; b. Teheran, Iran, Sept. 28, 1934; s. Parviz and Irandokht K.; came to U.S., 1953, naturalized, 1970; B.A., Lafayette Coll., 1954; M.D., Columbia U., 1958; m. Katheryne, June 7, 1958; children—Paul, Laili. Intern, M.I. Bassett Hosp., Cooperstown, N.Y., 1958-59; resident Mass. Gen. Hosp., Boston, 1963, chief pulmonary unit, 1967—; asso. prof. medicine Harvard U., 1971-78, prof. medicine, 1979—; bd. dirs. Boston Tb Assn.; vis. prof. U. Ghent, 1975-76. Am. Heart Assn. spl. fellow, 1961-63. Diplomate Am. Bd. Internal Medicine. Fellow A.C.P.; mem. Am. Fedn. Clin. Research, Am. Thoracic Soc. (pres. Eastern sect. 1974-75), Am. Lung Assn. Boston (dir.), Mass. Med. Soc., Am. Physiol. Soc., Am. Heart Assn. Council Cardiopulmonary Diseases, Am. Soc. Clin. Investigation, Soc. Occupational and Environ. Health. Author: Disorders of the Respiratory System, 1976. Home: 162 Revolutionary Rd Concord MA 01742 Office: Mass Gen Hosp Boston MA 02114

KEADY, GEORGE CREGAN, JR., lawyer; b. Bklyn., June 16, 1924; s. George Cregan and Marie (Lussier) K.; student U. Kans., 1943-44; B.S., Fordham U., 1949; J.D., Columbia, 1950; m. Patricia Drake, Sept. 2, 1950; children—Margaret D., Marie E., George Cregan III, Catherine A., Kathleen V. Admitted to Mass. bar, 1950, since practiced in Springfield, Mass.; asso. firm Ganley & Crook, 1950-53, Peter D. Wilson, 1953-57; partner firm Wilson, Keady & Ratner, 1958—; spl. justice Dist. Ct. Springfield; dean Western New Eng. Coll. Law Sch., 1970-73; dir. Western Mass. Bar Rev., 1956-63; dir. Western New Eng. Coll. Bar Review, 1965-72; chmn. Mass. Continuing Legal Edn., Inc., 1977—. Corporator Ludlow Savs. Bank. Active United Fund, Springfield, 1950-72, Joint Civic Agys., Springfield; chmn. fund drive Am. Cancer Soc., Springfield, 1962. Selectman, Longmeadow, Mass., 1958-68, chmn. selectmen, 1960-61, 63-64, 66-68, moderator, 1968-73; vice chmn. Rep. Town Com., Longmeadow, 1956-60; alternate del. Rep. Nat. Conf., 1960, del., 1964. Pres. Hampden Dist. Mental Health Clinic, Inc., 1968-71; pres. Child Guidance Clinic, Springfield 1962-64; corporator, trustee, vice chmn. Baystate Med. Center; trustee Western New Eng. Coll., Bay Path Jr. Coll. Served with F.A., AUS, 1943-46. Decorated Bronze Star medal. Mem. Am., Mass., Hampden County (mem. exec. com., pres. 1965-67) bar assns., Phi Delta Phi. Roman Catholic. Clubs: Longmeadow Country, Colony. Home: 16 Meadowbrook Rd Longmeadow MA 01106 Office: 1500 Main St Springfield MA 01115

KEAN, JOHN VAUGHAN, lawyer; b. Providence, Mar. 12, 1917; s. Otho Vaughan and Mary (Duell) K.; A.B. cum laude, Harvard, 1938, J.D., 1941. Admitted to R.I. bar, 1942; with Edwards & Angell, Providence, 1941—, partner, 1954—. Chmn., Downtown Providence YMCA, 1964-67. Bd. dirs. Greater Providence YMCA, 1964-76. Served to capt. AUS, 1943-46, 50-52, brig. gen. Res. Decorated Legion of Merit. Mem. Am., R.I. bar assns., N.G. Assn., Assn. U.S. Army, R.I. Army N.G. (brig. gen. 1964-72). Episcopalian. Clubs: Harvard R.I. (pres. 1964-66), Agawam Hunt, Hope, Providence Art, Turks Head; Army and Navy (Washington); Sakonnet Golf (Little Compton, R.I.). Home: W Main Rd Little Compton RI 02837 Office: 2700 Hospital Trust Tower Providence RI 02903

KEAN, MICHAEL HENRY, ednl. adminstr.; b. Phila., Feb. 7, 1945; s. Milton Charles and Dorothy (Dash) K.; B.A., Pa. State U., 1966; M.A., Ohio State U., 1968, Ph.D., 1972; m. Constance Jane Gordon, Sept. 15, 1968; 2 children. Asst. to supt. schs., Phila., 1970-73; exec. dir. research and evaluation Sch. Dist. Phila., 1973—; guest lectr. 12 colls. and univs.; instnl. instr. Parkway Sch., Phila., 1970—. Ednl. cons. local bds. edn., univs., 1967—, U.S. Govt., 1969—, pvt. industry, 1970—; vis. scholar U. Calif., Los Angeles, 1977. Fellow community leadership seminar program Fels Inst. for Govt., U. Pa., 1972-73; mem. bd. edn. com. Akiba Acad., Merion, Pa., 1973—; bd. dirs. Pa. State U. Coll. Edn. Mem. Am. Assn. Social and Polit. Sci., Am. Soc. Curriculum Devel., Am. Ednl. Research Assn. (editor Sch. Evaluation (Div. H) Newsletter), Am. Assn. Sch. Adminstrs., Nat. Council on Measurement in Edn., Dirs. Instrnl. Research Large Cities in U.S. and Can. (chmn.), Tau Epsilon Phi (regional gov.), Phi Delta Kappa. Mem. B'nai B'rith. Mem. editorial bd. Ednl. Evaluation and Policy Analysis, Ednl. Researcher; contbr. articles to profl. jours. Home: 264 Forrest Rd Merion Station PA 19066 Office: 21st and Parkway Philadelphia PA 19103

KEAN, NORMAN, producer, theater owner, business mgr.; b. Colorado Springs, Colo., Oct. 14, 1934; s. Barney and Flora (Bienstock) K.; student U. Denver, 1952-55; m. Gwyda DonHowe, Oct. 12, 1958. Theatrical mgr. Camino Real, 1960, Laurette, 1960, The Pleasure of His Company, 1960, Bayanihan Philippine Dance Co., 1961, Gen. Seeger, 1961, The Royal Dramatic Theatre of Sweden, 1962, The Matchmaker, 1962, Tiger, Tiger Burning Bright, 1962, Phoenix Theatre and Laterna Magika from Prague, 1963; gen. mgr. APA-Phoenix, APA Repertory Co., N.Y.C., 1964-69; pres. Norman Kean Prodns., Inc., 1966—, Edison Theatre Corp., 1970-74, Edison Theatre, 1970—, Edison Enterprises, Inc., 1974—; owner East 74th St. Theater, 1966-69; gen. mgr. Oh! Calcutta!, 1969; producer Max Morath at the Turn of the Century, N.Y., U.S., Can., 1969—; gen. mgr. Happy Birthday, Wanda June, N.Y.C., 1970-71, Orlando Furioso from Rome, N.Y.C., 1970, Don't Bother Me, I Can't Cope, N.Y.C., Chgo. and Los Angeles, 1972-74; producer Hosanna, N.Y.C., 1974, Me and Bessie, 1975-78, Oh! Calcutta!, 1976—, By Strouse, 1977—; gen. mgr. Sizwe Banzi is Dead, The Island, 1974—; faculty div. liberal studies Sch. Continuing Edn., N.Y. U., 1976—; lectr. Sch. Continuing Edn., N.Y. U. Served with AUS, 1954-56. Mem. Am. Acad. Dramatic Arts (trustee), League N.Y. Theatres and Producers (dir.). Jewish. Clubs: Century (Denver); Friars (N.Y.C.). Home: 280 Riverside Dr New York NY 10025 Office: Edison Theatre 240 W 47th St New York NY 10036

KEANE, (MARY) ANTONIA, sociologist; b. Balt., Jan. 22, 1941; d. William James and Dorothy Marie (Uhl) Klima; B.S., Towson State Coll., 1964; M.S., Calif. State U., San Jose, 1967; 1 son, Christopher K. Instr. sociology Notre Dame of Md. Coll., Balt., 1967-69; instr. sociology Loyola Coll., Balt., 1969-70; asst. prof., 1970-72, chairperson, 1972—; dir. research women's project Nat. Center for Urban Ethnic Affairs, Washington, 1973-75; cons. Dept. Labor, U.S. Civil Rights Commn., Archdiocese of Balt., Md. Human Relations Inst., Urban Life Inst., Balt. Police Acad., Dept. Justice. Commr., Balt. Community Relations, 1972-75, chmn., 1976—; co-chmn. Balt. City Council Task Force on Rape, 1974-75; bd. dirs. S.E. Youth Diversion Project, 1973—; active steering com. Nat. Congress Neighborhood Women, 1974—; panleist WJZ-TV Square Off. Bd. dirs. Meals on Wheels of Central Md. HEW Pub. Service and Edn. grantee, 1970-71, Rockefeller research grantee, 1973-75, Loyola faculty research grantee, 1976-77. Mem. Am. Sociol. Assn., NOW. Democrat. Roman Catholic. Club: Polish Home. Home: 423 S Ann St Baltimore MD 21231 Office: 4501 N Charles St Baltimore MD 21210

KEARNEY, ANTHONY JOHN, accountant; b. N.Y.C., Feb. 6, 1937; s. Anthony A. and Theresa F. (Lane) K.; B.B.A., City Coll. N.Y., 1958; postgrad. Iona Coll., 1961; m. Loretta Imbimbo, Apr. 18, 1959. Jr. accountant Whiting, Bacon, Taylor & Beairsto, N.Y.C., 1959-63; sr. accountant Peat, Marwick, Mitchell & Co., N.Y.C., 1963-64; asst. treas. Coll. Entrance Examination Bd., N.Y.C., 1965-70, controller, asst. treas., 1971—. C.P.A., N.Y. State. Mem. Am. Inst. C.P.A.'s, N.Y. State Soc. C.P.A.'s, Am. Soc. Assn. Execs. Home: 14 Rocky Ridge Rd Harrison NY 10604 Office: 888 Seventh Ave New York City NY 10019

KEARNEY, KATHLEEN M., sch. adminstr.; b. Somerville, N.J., Jan. 5, 1944; d. Jerome P. and Mary M. Kearney; B.A., Dunbarton Coll. Holy Cross, Washington, 1966; M.Ed., U. Miami (Fla.), 1974. Elementary tchr. Bridgewater/Raritan (N.J.) Sch. Dist., 1966-70, Hillsborough (N.J.) Sch. Dist., 1970-72; admissions officer Coll. Mt. St. Vincent, N.Y.C., 1973-75; dir. student services Somerset County Tech. Inst., Bridgewater, 1976—. Mem. Nat. Assn. Student Personnel Adminstrs., Am. Personnel and Guidance Assn., Phi Kappa Phi. Roman Catholic. Home: 538 Andria Ave S Apt 282 Somerville NJ 08876 Office: North Bridge St and Vogt Dr Bridgewater NJ 08807

KEARNEY, THOMAS RAYMOND, psychiatrist; b. Cork, Ireland, Oct. 15, 1929; s. Joseph and Margaret Mary (Callanan) K.; came to U.S., 1958, naturalized, 1965; B. Medicine, B. Surgery, Nat. U. Ireland, 1954; m. Marilyn Johnson, Sept. 25, 1972; Intern, St. Vincent's Hosp., Dublin, 1954-55; resident Bethlem-Royal and Maudsley Hosp., London, 1957-58, Seton Inst., Balt., 1958-60; practice medicine specializing in psychiatry, 1961—; dir. psychiatry Norwalk (Conn.) Hosp., 1963-68; cons. psychiatrist Conn. Juvenile Ct., 1963-65, County Dublin, Ireland, 1972-74; chief service Mid-Hudson Psychiat. Center, New Hampton N.Y., 1974-77; sr. psychiatrist St. Francis Hosp., Hartford, Conn., 1978—; asst. clin. prof. psychiatry U. Conn., 1978—; clin. instr. psychiatry Yale U., New Haven, 1966-69. Bd. dirs. Fairfield County (Conn.) Council on Alcoholism, 1965-66, Westport-Weston (Conn.) Youth Bd., 1964-66; town chmn. Caucus Conn. Dems., Westport, 1968-69. Fellow Royal Soc. Health; mem. Royal Coll. Physicians (Edinburgh), Royal Coll. Psychiatrists, AMA, Am. Pub. Health Assn., Am. Psychiat. Assn. Roman Catholic. Club: Litchfield County (Conn.) Hunt. Contbr. articles to med. jours. Home: Laharan Farm Killingworth CT 06417 also Laharan House Kilbrittain County Cork Ireland Office: 8 Lowell Rd West Hartford CT 06119

KEARNS, KAREN WISTER, counselor; b. Phila., Jan. 12, 1949; d. William Wister and Dorothy Gabriel (Reed) Kearns; B.S. in Edn., Villanova U., 1971, M.A. in Counseling, 1975; m. Robert L. Domagalski, June 18, 1977. Tchr. Lower Merion Sch. Dist., Ardmore, Pa., 1972-73; juvenile probation officer Montgomery County (Pa.), 1975—; counselor, partner Adolescent Adjustment Service, Boyertown, Pottstown, Pa.; family therapist Perkiomen Valley Acad., Limerick, Pa., 1978—; cons., vol., counselor crisis intervention Boyertown and Pottstown Police. Certified tchr., counselor, Pa. Mem. Am. Personnel and Guidance Assn., Am. Rehab. Counseling Assn., Pub. Offender Counseling Assn., Pa. Assn. Probation, Parole & Correction, Middle Atlantic States Conf. of Correction, Juvenile Advisory Assn. Republican. Home: Colebrookdale Rd Boyertown PA 19512 Office: 1004-08 W Washington St Norristown PA 19404

KEATING, FRANK EDWARD, fishing editor; b. Bklyn., July 18, 1909; s. Thomas Frank and Ida May (Inglehart) K.; student N.Y. U., 1929; m. Helen Irene Lewand, Aug. 7, 1943. Gen. assignment reporter, police reporter Jamaica (N.Y.) L.I. Daily Press, 1935-51, outdoors editor, 1951-77; fishing editor Newsday, Garden City, N.Y., 1977—; cons. in field; radio program local L.I. stas. Mem. Met. Rod and Gun Assn. (pres. 1959), Outdoor Writers Assn. Am. Democrat. Roman Catholic. Club: N.Y. Press. Editor: Guide for Sport Fishermen, 1952-54. Contbr. articles to nat. mags., publs. outdoors topics; co-author fishing sect. Ency. Brit. Home: 100 Randall Ave Freeport NY 11520 Office: Newsday Garden City NY

KEATING, FRANK J., paper co. exec.; b. Phila., Jan. 2, 1928; s. Joseph Gerald and Alice (Quinn) K.; student Londonderry Coll., No. Ireland; children—Carolyn M., Mary E., Frank J. With Daring Paper Co. div. Kardon Industries, Inc. Phila., 1946-71, successively truck loader, shipping clk., asst. shipper, shipper, prodn. scheduler, prodn. mgr., asst. to gen. mgr. United Container Co., 1957-58, asst. to pres. Daring Paper Co., 1958-60, v.p., gen. mgr., 1960-71, exec. v.p., also v.p. parent co., exec. v.p. Morris Sales Service Corp., KFC Fibre, Inc.; now pres. Keating Fibre Inc., Keating Fibre Internat., Inc. Mem. Chester County Conservation Com. Served with USNR, 1944-46. Mem. Am. Mgmt. Assn., Downingtown C. of C., Pa. Water Pollution Control Assn., Am. Paper Inst., Fibre Box Assn., T.A.P.P.I., Nat. Council Steam Improvement, Montgomery County C. of C., Internat. Platform Assn. Clubs: Whitemarsh Valley Country; Phila. Aviation Country. Home: 614 Meadow Rd Huntingdon Valley Abington Twp PA 19006 Office: Whitemarsh Plaza 15 Ridge Pike Conshohocken PA 19428

KEATING, JAMES FRANCIS, JR., mech. engr.; b. Boston, Jan. 10, 1924; s. James Francis and Marion Anna (Flood) K.; B.M.E., Tufts U., 1947; m. Margaret Eileen Murphy, June 3, 1950; children—Corinne Marie, Sandra Patricia. Mech. jr. engr. Stone & Webster Engring. Corp., Boston, 1947-51; jr., sr. mech. engr. Jackson & Moreland Engring. Co., Boston, 1951-57, prin. mech. engr., 1957-62, project mgr., 1962-64; project mgr. United Engrs. & Constructors, Boston, 1964-67, chief mech. engr., gen. engring. div., 1967—. Served with AUS, 1943-46. Mem. ASME. Home: 96 Oakland Ave Arlington MA 02174 Office: 100 Summer St Boston MA 02110

KEATING, JUNE GERTRUDE, nursing service adminstr.; b. Balt., Mar. 14, 1921; d. Edward Owen and Isabel Anne (Taylor) K.; grad. Mercy Hosp. Sch. Nursing, 1942; B.S. in Nursing, Johns Hopkins U., 1972; 1 dau., Carole Anne Shipley. Indsl. nurse Western Elec. Co., Point Breeze, Md., 1942-46, Gen. Elec. Co., Balt., 1955-60; asst. to Dr. R.C. Kimberly, Balt., 1950-55; nursing supr. Montebello Hosp., Balt., 1960-72, acting dir., 1975-77, asst. to dir. nursing, 1977—. Active vol. various local charities. Recipient 15 yrs. service award State of Md., 1975. Mem. Johns Hopkins U. Alumni Assn., Early Am. Soc., Am. Hist. Soc. Democrat. Roman Catholic. Clubs: Nat. Geographic Soc., Green Spring Inn. Actively engaged in rehab. nursing, attendant pertinent seminars and workshops. Home and office: 2201 Argonne Dr Baltimore MD 21218

KEATING, WILLIAM FRANCIS, JR., publisher, coll. adminstr., found. and bus. exec.; b. Holyoke, Mass., Aug. 6, 1932; s. William Francis and Florence Dorothy (Bissell) K.; B.A., Trinity Coll., 1957; M.S., Loyola Coll., Balt., 1973; student Southwestern Law Sch., Los Angeles, 1960-62; m. Ruth Ann McCracken, Nov. 20, 1958; children—William Francis, Jon, Kenneth, Edwin, Marina Jane. Pres., Am. News Service, Inc., Washington, 1970—, Quality Distbrs., Inc., Washington, 1974—, Internat. Expn., Inc., Washington, 1978—; asst. to pres. Washington Tech. Inst., 1971-75; dean Muskingum (Ohio) Tech. Inst., 1970-71; editor A.M. Best Co., N.Y.C., 1968-70; exec.

v.p. Found. for Bus. Edn., N.Y.C., 1966-68; dir. mktg. services Cahnirs Pub. Co., Boston, 1965-66; pres., pub. Valley Publs., Inc., Los Angeles, 1962-65; editor, pub. Export-Import News, Inc., Los Angeles, 1960-62; dir. Found. Edn., 1974—, Internat. Safety Found., Inc., 1970—, Chesapeake Mag., Inc., 1974—. Legis. chmn. Howard County (Md.) PTA, 1975—. Served with AUS, 1953-55. Recipient indsl. mktg. gold medal; Rotary scholar, 1951-53. Mem. Am. Mktg. Assn., Am. Soc. Indsl. Security, Am. Geophys. Union, Am. Hort. Soc., So. States Coops., Sigma Nu, Nat. Press Club, Los Angeles Press Club. Club: Kiwanis. Home: 8418 W Grove Rd Ellicott City MD 21043 Office: PO Box 9837 Washington DC 20015

KEECH, ROGER LEE, bldg. mfg. co. exec.; b. Grand Rapids, Mich., Jan. 15, 1935; s. Richard E. and Ruth I. (Jamison) K.; B.B.A., Western Mich. U., 1957; m. Sandra Marlin, Nov. 24, 1956; children—Michelle, Bryan. With Kaiser Aluminum & Chem. Corp., 1957-70, br. sales mgr., Indpls., 1964-66, mktg. mgr., Oakland, Calif., 1967-70; v.p. planning and mktg. Kearney-Nat., Inc., N.Y.C., 1970-71, group v.p., gen. mgr., Evansville, Ind., 1971-72; exec. v.p. Arrow Group Industries, Inc., Pompton Plains, N.J., 1972-73, pres., 1974—; pres., dir. Chromalloy Consumer Products Co.; dir. Esterline Corp., N.Y.C., Morse Electro Prods, Bklyn. Mem. Young Pres.'s Orgn. Republican. Clubs: Masons, Kinnelon Tennis, Rolling Hills Country, Smoke Rise Gun. Home: 529 Cherry Tree Ln Smoke Rise NJ 07405 Office: 100 Alexander Ave Pompton Plains NJ 07444

KEEFE, THOMAS JOSEPH, JR., elec. engr.; b. Springfield, Mass., Apr. 7, 1942; s. Thomas Joseph and Helen Marie (Corcoran) K.; B.E.E., U. Lowell, 1963; M.E.E., U. R.I., 1965; m. Margaret Mary Johnson, Oct. 29, 1966; children—Thomas Edward, Michael Stephan. NASA fellow U. R.I., 1963-66, research asst., 1966-72, teaching asst., 1972-75; cons. elec. engring., Kingston, R.I., 1975—; lectr. R.I. Jr. Coll., 1975-76; adj. faculty Roger Williams Coll., 1976-77; resource person Univ. without Walls, Providence, 1976-77; lectr. U. R.I., 1976—; instr. physics R.I. Jr. Coll., 1976—. Mem. Tower Hill Vol. Fire Co., Wakefield, R.I., 1976—. Mem. AAAS, Am. Assn. Physics Tchrs., IEEE, Providence Engring. Soc., Soc. Photog. Scientists and Engrs., Sigma Xi, Phi Kappa Phi, Tau Beta Pi. Democrat. Roman Catholic. Club: K.C. Address: PO Box 283 Kingston RI 02881

KEEFFE, JOHN ARTHUR, lawyer; b. Bklyn., Apr. 5, 1930; s. Arthur John and Mary Catherine (Daly) K.; A.B., Cornell U., 1950; LL.B., U. Va., 1953; m. Frances Elizabeth Rippetoe, July 24, 1952; children—Virginia Frances, Cynthia Louise, Amy Marie. Admitted to Va. bar, 1953, N.Y. bar, 1956; asst. U.S. atty. So. Dist. N.Y., 1955-57; asso. Rogers Hoge & Hills, N.Y.C., 1957-63; counsel Havens Wandless Stitt & Tighe Esq., N.Y.C., 1963-65; partner firm Keeffe & Costikyan, N.Y.C. and Washington, 1965-74; partner firm Keeffe Bros., N.Y.C. and Washington, 1975-77; chmn. bd., pres. Grouse Run Co., Inc., N.Y.C., 1973—. Bd. dirs., v.p. Day Care Council of Westchester (N.Y.C.), Inc., 1968-77; bd. dirs., sec. Street Theatre, White Plains, N.Y., 1973—. Mem. N.Y., Va., Am. bars. Served to 1st lt. USAF, 1953-55. Home: 269 Madison Rd Scarsdale NY 10583

KEEGAN, MARCIA KAY, photographer, writer; b. Tulsa, May 23, 1943; d. Otis Claire and Mary Elizabeth (Collar) Keegan; B.A., U. N.Mex., 1961; m. Harmon Houghton. Editor, photographer Albuquerque Jour., 1961-65; free-lance photographer, writer, N.Y.C., 1965—. Grantee N.Y. State Council Photography, 1971. Mem. Am. Soc. Mag. Photographers. Illustrator: Only the Moon and Me, 1968; author, photographer: The Taos Indians and Their Sacred Blue Lake, 1971; Mother Earth, Father Sky, 1974; We Can Still Hear Them Clapping, 1975; Pueblo and Navajo Cookery, 1977. Address: 140 E 46th St New York City NY 10017

KEEHAN, MATTHEW JOSEPH, JR., corp. exec.; b. Tannersville, N.Y., Apr. 21, 1933; s. Matthew Joseph and Bernice Margaret (Kerr) K.; B.S.E. in Elec. Engring., Cooper Union, 1965; m. Mary Patricia Dwyer, Nov. 21, 1964; children—Colleen Anne, Matthew Joseph III, Brian Michael. Sales engr., applications engr. Gen. Electric Co., N.Y.C., 1955-67; sales engr. NRC Equipment Corp., Newton, Mass., 1967-69; eastern regional mgr. Sloan Technology Corp., Santa Barbara, Calif., 1969-72; pres. Empire Technology, Inc., Clifton Park, N.Y., 1972—; pres. Nothway Exit 8 Exec. Park, Inc., 1978—. Served with U.S. Army, 1953-55. Recipient Henri D. Dickinson Fund award, Cooper Union, 1965. Mem. Instrument Soc. Am. (pres. Eastern N.Y. Sect., 1974-75), Am. Vacuum Soc. (dir. Upstate N.Y. Chpt.), Soc. Vacuum Coaters, Am. Soc. Non-Destructive Testing, So. Saratoga C. of C. Clubs: Kiwanis (treas. Shenendehowa, 1974-76), K.C. (Grand Knight, 1977-78), Elks (Clifton Park), Am. Legion (Halfmoon-Clifton Park). Home: PO Box 104 Clifton Park NY 12065 Office: PO Box 421 Northway 8 Exec Park Clifton Park NY 12065

KEEL, ALTON GOLD, JR., aerospace engr.; b. Newport News, Va., Sept. 8, 1943; s. Alton Gold and Ella Clair (Kennedy) K.; B.S. in Aerospace Engring., U. Va., 1966, Ph.D. in Engring. Physics, 1970; postdoctoral U. Calif. at Berkeley, 1970-71; m. Patricia Ann Cooke, Dec. 13, 1974; children—Sandra Dean, Kristen Ann. Research aerospace engr./mgr. Hypervelocity Research Tunnel, Naval Surface Weapons Center, White Oak, Md., 1971-76, sci. staff of asso. tech. dir. White Oak Lab., 1976-77; Congl. sci. fellow Office of Senator Howard W. Cannon, U.S. Senate, Washington, 1978—. Mem. program com. Unitarian Universalist Ch., 1976; bd. dirs. Community Co-owners Assn., 1975. Recipient Research award NRC, 1970, Sustained Superior Performance award Navy Dept., 1973. Am. Inst. Aeronautics and Astronautics Congl. Sci. fellow, 1977, Young Engr./Scientist award, 1978. Mem. Am. Inst. Aeros. and Astronautics (ground testing and simulation tech. com.), Sigma Xi, Phi Eta Sigma, Tau Beta Pi. Research in surface roughness influence on compressible turbulent heat transfer. Home: POB 4178 Silver Spring MD 20904 Office: Navla Surface Weapons Center White Oak Silver Spring MD 20910

KEELER, MARY FREAR, historian; b. State College, Pa., Jan. 1, 1904; d. William and Julia (Reno) Frear; B.A., Pa. State U., 1924; M.A., Yale U., 1929, Ph.D., 1933; m. John B. Keeler, June 30, 1938 (dec. Dec. 1950); 1 dau., Shirley Keeler Bebout. Instr. history U. Wyo., 1929-31, N.J. Coll. for Women, 1931-32; instr., asst. prof. Pa. State U., 1933-38; lectr. Vassar Coll., 1952-53, Wellesley Coll., 1953-54; dean faculty, lectr. through prof. Hood Coll., Frederick, Md., 1954-69, prof., 1969-71; research asso. Yale U., 1974-76, exec. editor Yale Center for Parliamentary History, 1974—. AAUW fellow, 1935-36; sr. fellow Folger Library, 1971-72; Am. Philos. Soc. grantee, 1972-73; named Pa. State Woman of Year, 1959. Fellow Royal Hist. Soc.; mem. AAUW (nat. com. chmn.), Conf. Brit. Studies (council 1972-77), Am. Hist. Assn., Berkshire Conf. Women Historians, Internat. Commn. for Study of Rep. and Parliamentary Instns., Soc. History of Geog. Discovery, Kappa Kappa Gamma. Democrat. Presbyterian. Author: The Long Parliament 1644-1641, 1954; editor: Bibliography of British History, Stuart Period, 1603-1714, 2d edit., 1970; Accounts of Sir Francis Drake's West Indian Voyage, 1976; joint editor Commons Debates 1628, 1977—. Home: 302 W 12th St Frederick MD 21701

KEELER, RUSSELL M., JR., mech. engr.; b. Sellersville, Pa., July 10, 1945; s. Russell M. and Edith B. (Edge) K.; B.S. Engring., Calif. Poly. State U., 1972; m. Ann I.; 1 son, Jason R. Staff engr. Ralph E. Phillips Inc., Los Angeles, 1969-70, D. J. Ververelli, Inc., Phila., 1972-73; v.p. Walter F. Spiegel, Inc., cons. engrs., Jenkintown, Pa., 1973—. Served with U.S. Army, 1966-68. Mem. ASHRAE (mem. nat. edn. com.; bd. govs. (Phila. chpt.), Cons. Engrs. Council. Co-author: Practical Energy Management in Health Care Institutions, 1975. Developer air conditioning course Temple U. Home: 1034 Ashbourne Rd Cheltenham PA 19012 Office: 321 York Rd Jenkintown PA 19046

KEELY, ANN, marketing cons.; b. Milton, Pa.; d. Robert Russell and Mary Catherine (D'Angelo) Keely; student Dana Hall Sch., Principia Coll.; B.F.A., Chgo. Art Inst.; M.A., N.Y. U.; Designer, artist for various theatre, TV, trade shows and interiors; then interior decorator Armstrong Cork Co., Lancaster, Pa.; partner Group Interviewing Services, N.Y.C.; now pres. Ann Keely/Ideational Research, N.Y.C.; lectr. Columbia Coll., Chgo., Pa. State U., University Park. Mem. Am. Mktg. Assn., United Scenic Artists, Allied Bd. Trade, Mensa. Contbr. articles to profl. jours. Home: 140 E 81st St New York NY 10028 Office: 133 E 56th St New York NY 10022

KEEN, RAYMOND WALLACE, librarian, educator; b. Havre de Grace, Md., July 30, 1948; s. Raymond Carl and Ida Janette (Owens) K.; B.A., Washington Coll., 1970; M.A., U. Del., 1974; Order of Christian Journeyman, Dundalk Sch. Religion, 1974; m. Kathleen Thomas, June 12, 1976; 1 dau., Catherine Mary; stepchildren—Cary John Wright, Renee Nicole Wright. Lectr. philosophy Anne Arundel Community Coll., Arnold, Md., 1972-73; asst. spl. collections Univ. Library, U. Del., Newark, 1972, 73-74; instr. philosophy Cecil Community Coll., North East, Md., 1973-77, asst. to librarian, 1974—; instr. philosophy Dundalk Community Coll., Balt., 1973-74. Mem. Am. Philos. Assn., Md. State Tchrs. Assn., NEA. Episcopalian. Author numerous book reviews. Home: The Wren Box 108 W Gordon St Bel Air MD 21014 Office: Cecil Community Coll North East MD 21901

KEENAN, MICHAEL EDGAR, advt. agy. exec.; b. Columbus, Ohio, Mar. 15, 1934; s. Edgar Charles and Kathryn (Dowden) K.; A.B. in Econs., Duke U., 1955; m. E. Jane Bergeron, Sept. 13, 1958; children—Margaret, Matthew, Emily, Jennifer, Andrew, Martha. Mktg. exec. Compton Advt. Inc., N.Y.C., 1957-60, Foote, Cone & Belding Inc., N.Y.C., 1960-62, Lennen & Newell, Inc., N.Y.C., 1962-64; v.p., mktg. exec. Fuller & Smith & Ross Inc., N.Y.C., 1964-70; pres., chief exec. officer Keenan & McLaughlin Inc., N.Y.C., 1970—, also chmn. bd.; lectr. mktg. N.Y. U., N.Y.C., 1964-66, Coll. City N.Y., 1965-67, Rutgers U., Newark, 1966. Served with CIC, AUS, 1955-57. Mem. Am. Assn. Advt. Agys. Roman Catholic. Club: Thursday (N.Y.C.). Home: 350 Central Park W New York City NY 10025 Office: 919 3d Ave New York City NY 10022

KEENAN, TERRANCE, found. exec.; b. n. Phila., Feb. 1, 1924; s. Peter Joseph and Marie (Sloupova) K.; A.B., Yale, 1950; LL.D. (hon.), Alderson-Broaddus Coll., 1975. Asst. headmaster Thomas Jefferson Sch., St. Louis, 1950-55; writer Merrill Lynch, Pierce, Fenner & Smith Inc., N.Y.C., 1955-56; editor Office of Reports, Ford Found., N.Y.C., 1956-65; sr. exec. asso. Commonwealth Fund, N.Y.C., 1965-72; v.p. spl. programs Robert Wood Johnson Found., Princeton, N.J., 1972—; Trustee Solebury Sch., New Hope, Pa. Served with USNR, 1944-46; PTO. Mem. Pub. Relations Soc. Am., Am. Coll. PUb. Relations Soc. Democrat. Roman Catholic. Clubs: Yale (N.Y.C.); Nassau, Yale (Princeton). Contbr. short fiction, pub. affairs articles to popular publs. Home: 179 Hamilton Ave Princeton NJ 08540 Office: Forrestal Center PO Box 2316 Princeton NJ 08540

KEENE, PHILIP, cons. engr.; b. Newton, Mass., Oct. 31, 1902; s. Thomas Means and Edith (Shankland) K.; B.S. cum laude, Harvard, 1925, M.S., 1940; m. Virginia Thornton, Sept. 6, 1941; children—Thomas Philip, Charles Thornton, David Lacy. Asst. engr. Ralph R. Rumery, cons. engr., N.Y.C., 1925-28; field engr. Marcus Contracting Co., N.Y.C., 1928-31, office engr., 1931-33; asst. to asso. engr. Fed. Pub. Works Adminstrn., Washington, 1934-37; valuation engr. Continental Ins. Co., N.Y.C., 1937-39; head engr. soils and foundations Conn. Dept. Transp., Hartford, 1940-72; lectr. NSF-Govt. India, India, 1971, various instns. in U.S., Turkey, 1973; cons. UN-Govt. Poland, 1974. Panel mem. Am. Arbitration Assn. Mem. Hwy. Research Bd. Corporator Middlesex Meml. Hosp. Mem. Am. Soc. C.E., Conn. Soc. Profl. Engrs., Harvard Engrs. and Scientists Assn. Methodist (trustee). Club: Harvard. Author profl. articles. Home and office: 34 Home Ave Middletown CT 06457

KEENEY, JUNE MARIE, educator; b. Palmyra, Pa., June 18, 1933; d. Lloyd B. and Ruth M. (Wagner) Gibble; B.S. in Elementary Edn., Millersville State Coll., 1955; M.Ed. in Elementary Edn. Pa. State U., 1959; now postgrad. Ph.D. in Elementary Edn. U. Md.; m. Paul E. Keeney. Tchr. pub. schs., York, Pa., 1955-64; tchr. reading Dover (Pa.) Area Schs., 1964-71, reading specialist, 1972—; grad. asst. Coll. Edn. U. Md., 1971-72; adj. faculty York Coll. Pa., 1979. Mem. Coll., Internat. reading assns., Dover Area, Pa. State, Nat. edn. assns., Am. Assn. Supervision, Curriculum Devel. Editor Md. Reading Inst. Abstracts, 1972. Certifications: Reading specialist, Pa. Home: Route 8 Box 468 York PA 17403 Office: Dover Area Intermediate Sch 4500 Intermediate Ave Dover PA 17315

KEESEE, THOMAS WOODFIN, JR., financial cons., corp. dir.; b. Helena, Ark., Feb. 11, 1915; s. Thomas Woodfin and Sarah Gladys (Key) K.; B.A., Duke, 1935; LL.B., Harvard, 1938; m. Patricia Peale, Apr. 7, 1940 (div. 1951); 1 son, Allen P.; m. 2d, Patricia Hartford, June 26, 1953; children—Thomas Woodfin, III, Anne H. Admitted to N.Y. bar, 1939; asso. firm Simpson, Thacher & Bartlett, N.Y.C., 1938-42; adminstrv. asst. to pres. Sperry Gyroscope Co., Inc., Garden City, N.Y., 1942-46; with Bessemer Securities Corp., N.Y.C., 1946-76, pres., 1970-76, dir., 1968—; past pres., chmn. exec. com., dir. Bessemer Trust Co. N.A. (N.Y.), Bessemer Trust Co., N.J. and Palm Beach Trust Co., Fla.; dir. Inversiones Cremerca C.A., Caracas, Venezuela, ITT Corp., N.Y.C., United Piece Dye Works, N.Y.C., S.D. Securities Co., N.Y.C., Zurich Life Ins. Co., Chgo., Am. Guarantee & Liability Co., Chgo., Dymo Industries, Inc., San Francisco; trustee, chmn. exec. com. Phipps Houses, Inc., N.Y.C.; trustee Franklin Savs. Bank, 1957-74; mem. U.S. adv. bd. Zurich (Switzerland) Ins. Co., 1970—. Mem. investment com. Duke U. Endowment Fund; trustee Citizens Budget Commn., N.Y.C., 1955-69, Citizens Housing and Planning Council of N.Y. Inc., 1956-69, trustee Arthur W. Butler Meml. Sanctuary, Bedford, N.Y., bd. dirs. Nat. Tennis Edn. Found., N.Y.C., Nat. Health and Welfare Retirement Assn., N.Y.C., 1966-74, Mem. Harvard Law Sch. Assn., N.Y. Bar Assn., Nat. Audubon Soc. (dir., chmn. exec. com.), Pilgrims of U.S.A., Phi Beta Kappa, Sigma Chi. Episcopalian. Clubs: Harvard, Racquet and Tennis, Board Room (gov.) (N.Y.C.); Clove Valley Rod and Gun (Millbrook, N.Y.), Bedford (N.Y.) Gold and Tennis. Home: Sarles St Rural Delivery # 2 Mount Kisco NY 10549 Office: 245 Park Ave New York City NY 10017

KEGELMAN, WILLIAM, optical instrument co. exec.; b. Bridgeport, Pa., Nov. 27, 1907; s. Jacob and Bertha (Graf) K.; B.S.E.E., Drexel U., 1930; m. Lisa Ihle, Oct. 19, 1934; children (adopted)—Michael (dec.), Thomas. With AT&T, Phila., 1930-32, Philco Co., Phila., 1934-36, Pa. R.R., Phila., 1937-59; with Phila. Electric Co., 1937-59; owner, operator Kegelman Bros., Huntingdon Valley, Pa., 1959—. Registered profl. engr., Pa. Mem. IEEE, Nat. Soc. Profl. Engrs., Optical Soc. Am., Nat. Contract Mgmt. Assn., Soc. Indsl. Math., Soc. Mfg. Engrs., Phi Kappa Phi, Tau Beta Pi. Republican. Lutheran. Home and Office: 393 County Line Rd Huntingdon Valley PA 19006

KEGGI, JOHN, physician; b. Riga, Latvia, Oct. 31, 1906; s. John and Olga (Smirnova) K.; grad., U. Latvia, 1933, M.D. Surgeon, 1937; m. Ruta Berzins, June 14, 1931; children—Janis John, Kristaps J., Andrejs, Ludvigs. Came to U.S., 1949, naturalized, 1955. Postgrad. scholar Biologiska Instituet. Copenhagen, Denmark, 1935; surg. dir. Municipal Hosp., Aluksne, Latvia, 1938-44; surgeon, attending physician for aliens, Emmendingen, Germany, 1944-45; physician for displaced persons, French Zone Occupation, Emmendingen, 1945-46; surgeon Hosp. Militaire, Emmendingen, Germany, 1946-49; house physician Luth. Hosp. of Manhattan, N.Y., 1949-52; practice medicine and in surgery, N.Y.C., 1952—; surgeon Park West Hosp., N.Y.C. Served in Latvian Army, 1937-38. Mem. A.M.A., N.Y. State Med. Soc., Med. Soc. County N.Y. Latvian Acad. Tchrs. Assn., West Side C. of C., Lettonia. Lutheran. Address: 330 W 72d St New York City NY 10023

KEGL-BOGNAR, DESI, media specialist, cons.; b. Hungary, May. 5, 1928; s. Dezsö and Anna (Kegl) Bognar; came to U.S., 1957, naturalized, 1962; Dipl., Tech. Coll. Budapest (Hungary), 1949; B.S. in Communication Arts (Univ. scholar), Boston U., 1960; postgrad. Columbia Center for Mass Communications, 1960-61; m. Katalin H. Szentpaly, July 31, 1968; children—Istvan Gabor, Janina Csilla. Reporter, NBC News and UPI, Lagos, Nigeria, 1961-62; vis. prof. Sch. Dramatic Arts, U. Sao Paulo (Brazil), 1963-65; coordinator for S.Am. cultural programs Nat. Ednl. TV, N.Y.C., 1966; ind. producer, coordinator and cons. for overseas indsl. and advt. films, N.Y.C., 1967; producer, cons. AFI-Atelier Films Internat.-Atelier Films Inc., Mt. Vernon, N.Y., 1968—; vis. fellow in broadcasting and film, Fulbright-Hays grantee U. Ibadan (Nigeria), 1973-76; Internat. Writers Guild and Writers Guild Am. rep. at UNESCO-Inter-Am. Copyright Conf., Rio de Janeiro, Brazil, 1966; juror Am. Film Festival, Ednl. Film Library Assn. African travel grantee, 1961. Mem. Writers Guild Am. (East), Nat. Acad. Television Arts and Scis., Soc. Motion Picture and Television Engrs., Am. Film Inst., PEN. Editor: Hungarians in America, 1972, 77; The Language of Broadcasting and Film, 1976. Producer films, videotapes; writer intro. to The Hostage (B. Behan), 1965, Broadcasting and Film Terminology, 1976. Contbr. articles and pictures to profl. publs. Office: PO Box 8 Fleetwood Mount Vernon NY 10552

KEHL, PETER JEROME, dairy farmer; b. Sheldon, N.Y., Oct. 11, 1913; s. Peter and Anna (Pasch) K.; m. Catherine E. Fugle, June 16, 1937; children—Norman, Robert, Joan, Donald. Diary farmer, Strykersville, N.Y., 1927-77; mem. Wyoming County Farm Bur., 1936—, bd. dirs., 1956-61; mem. Wyoming County Coop. Ext. Service, 1936—; mem. Buffalo Milk Producers Coop., Buffalo, N.Y., 1938-76, pres., 1952-53, 60-76; pres. Frontier Federated Milk Coop., 1960-65; pres. Upstate Milk Coops. Buffalo and Rochester, N.Y., 1965-76; dir., treas. Regional Common Mktg. Agy., Syracuse, N.Y., 1973-76; dir. Oatka Milk Products Coop. Batavia, N.Y., 1961-76, v.p., 1976; dir. Niagara Frontier Coop. Bargaining Agy. Inc., Buffalo, 1954-76, pres., 1961-66. Mem. Sheldon Vol. Fire Co., 1931—, pres., 1947; mem., town justice Sheldon Town Bd., 1948-63; trustee Sheldon St. Cecilia's Roman Cath. Ch., 1962—. Mem. Nat. Milk Producers Fedn. Washington (dir. 197-77, mem. exec. com., 1975-77), Dairy Council Niagara Frontier Area (dir. 1955-76). Home: 1075 Route 20A Strykersville NY 14145

KEHNEMUI, AZER, structual engr.; b. Istanbul, Turkey, Feb. 22, 1939; s. Kazem and Sogra (Parsa) Kehnemuipur; came to U.S., 1962, naturalized, 1969; B.S., Robert Coll., Istanbul, 1962; M.S., U. Ill., 1963; Sc.D., George Washington U., 1971; m. Gladys S. Kehnemui, Jan. 23, 1965; children—Sharon Hale, Susan Hope. Structural engr. Smislova & Carcaterra, cons. engrs., Silver Spring, Md., 1963-65; asso. Smislova & Assos., cons. engrs., Rockville, Md., 1965-75; pres. Smislova, Kehnemui & Assos., Rockville, 1975—; asso. prof. lectr. engring. George Washington U., Washington, 1975—. N.Y. Herald Tribune fellow, 1956. Mem. Am. Cons. Engrs. Council, ASCE, Am. Concrete Inst. Registered profl. engr., Washington, Md., Va., N.C., Calif., Pa. Democrat. Home: 10109 Garden Way Potomac MD 20854

KEHOE, VINCENT JEFFRÉ-ROUX, photographer, author, cosmetic co. exec.; b. Bklyn., N.Y., Sept. 12, 1921; s. John James and Bertha Florence (Roux) K.; student Mass. Inst. Tech., 1940-41, Lowell Technol. Inst., 1941-42, Boston U., 1942; B.F.A. in Motion Picture and TV Production, Columbia U., 1957; m. Gene Irene Marino, Nov. 2, 1966. Dir. make-up dept. CBS-TV, N.Y.C., 1948-49, NBC Hallmark Hall of Fame series, 1951-53; make-up artist in charge of make-up for numerous film, TV and stage prodns., 1942—; dir. make-up Turner Hall Corp., 1959-61, Internat. Beauty Show, 1962-66; pres., dir. research Research Council of Make-up Artists, Inc., Lowell, Mass., 1963—; chief press officer at Spanish Pavilion, N.Y. World's Fair, 1965; free-lance photographer, 1956—; contbr. photographs to numerous mags. including Time, Life, Sports Illustrated, Argosy, Popular Photography. Author books including: The Technique of Film and Television Make-up for Color, 1970; The Make-up Artist in the Beauty Salon, 1969; We Were There-April 19, 1775, 1975; The Military Guide, 1975; author-photographer bullfighting books: Aficionado! (N.Y. Art Dirs. Club award 1960); Wine, Women and Toros (Both-Hastings House Publrs. award 1962). Served with inf. U.S. Army, World War II; ETO. Decorated Purple Heart, Bronze Star. Mem. Soc. for Preservation of Colonial Culture (curator), Tenth Foot Royal Lincolnshire Regimental Assn. (named hon. col. 1968). Producer documentary color film: Matador de Toros, 1959. Address: 52 New Spalding St Lowell MA 01851

KEHOE, WILLIAM VINCENT DE PAUL, schs. supt.; b. Orange, N.J., Mar. 28, 1938; s. William Thomas and Catherine Elizabeth (Dyer) K.; B.A.Ed., N.J. State Coll., Upper Montclair, 1959; postgrad. (Univ. grantee) U. Syracuse, 1960; M.Ed., U. Del., 1966; m. Mary Louis Brand, Dec. 21, 1971; children—Andrew Thomas, Melanie Beth. Prin., James Groves High Sch., Wilmington, Del., 1971-72; asst. supt. Cath. Diocese of Wilmington, 1972-75, supt. schs., 1975—, sec., 1975—, sec. dept. Christian formation, 1976—; bd. dirs. St. Mark's High Sch., Ursuline Schs.; chmn. Del advisory com. Elementary and Secondary Edn. Act, 1975-76, 76-77, 77-78; mem. advisory council Magnet Schs. Concept, Newcastle County, Del., 1977. Mem. Del. Assn. Sch. Adminstrs., Nat. Cath. Edn. Assn., Chief Adminstrs. Cath. Edn. Clubs: Kiwanis (Wilmington); K.C. Home: 102 Colorado Ave Wilmington DE 19803 Office: 1626 N Union St Wilmington DE 19806

KEHR, CLIFTON LEROY, chemist; b. Brodbeck, Pa., May 25, 1926; s. Paul Emory and Jennie Margaret (Kopp) K.; A.B., Gettysburg Coll., 1949; M.S., U. Del., 1950, Ph.D., 1952; m. Louise Walterick, May 29, 1948; children—Alan Douglas, David Dorney, Alison Jean. Research asso. Princeton U., 1952-53; research chemist du Pont Co., Wilmington, Del., 1953-59; dir. organic research W.R. Grace & Co., Columbia, Md., 1959—. Served with USAAF, 1944-45. Mem. Am. Chem. Soc., Phi Beta Kappa, Sigma Xi. Republican. Lutheran.

Author, patentee in field. Home: 1216 Ednor Rd Silver Spring MD 20904 Office: 7379 Route 32 Columbia MD 21044

KEIMEL, FRED ALBERT, adhesives and sealants cons. co. exec.; b. Newark, Aug. 3, 1922; s. William and Isabelle (Harris) K.; A.A., Union Coll., Cranford, N.J., 1958; B.A. in Econs., Rutgers U., 1961, M.B.A., 1963; m. Alice Marie Knudsen, June 22, 1947; children—Fred R., Patricia A. Lab. technician DuPont Corp., Arlington, N.J., 1941-48; tech. service technician France, Campbell & Darling, Kenilworth, N.J., 1948-49; paint chemist United Lacquer, Elizabeth, N.J., 1949-50; tech. dir. Infropake Coatings, Union, N.J., 1950-51; adhesives cons. Bell Labs., Murray Hill, N.J., 1951-77; pres. Adhesives & Sealants Cons., Berkeley Heights, N.J., 1977—. Served in U.S. Army, 1942-46. Mem. Soc. Advancement of Material and Process Engring., VFW (post comdr.). Club: Murray Hill Canoe. Pub., editor-in-chief Adhesives and Sealants Newsletter, 1977—; contbr. Ency. Chem. Tech. Home: 52 Brook St Berkeley Heights NJ 07922 Office: 425 Springfield Ave Berkeley Heights NJ 07922

KEISER, GERD EMDO, applied physicist, engr.; b. Burlington, Wis., Oct. 8, 1944; s. Hans and Hertha Louise (Klattenhoff) K.; B.A., U. Wis., 1966, M.S., 1968; Ph.D., Northeastern U., 1973; m. Helen Ching-Yun Wang, Sept. 4, 1971. Sr. research engr. Honeywell Electro-Optics Center, Lexington, Mass., 1973-74; research and devel. scientist GTE Sylvania, Needham Heights, Mass., 1974—. Mem. Am. Phys. Soc., IEEE, Greater Boston Chinese Cultural Assn., Phi Kappa Phi. Contbr. articles to profl. jours. Home: 156 Day St Newton MA 02166 Office: 77 A St Needham Heights MA 02194

KEISER, HENRY BRUCE, lawyer, publisher; b. N.Y.C., Oct. 26, 1927; s. Leo and Jessie (Liebeskind) K.; B.A., U. Mich., 1947; J.D. cum laude, Harvard, 1950; m. Jessie E. Weeks, July 12, 1953; children—Betsy Cordelia, Matthew Roderick. Admitted to N.Y. bar, 1950, D.C. bar, 1955, Fla. bar, 1956, U.S. Supreme Ct. bar, 1954; trial atty. CAB, Washington, 1950-51; head counsel alcoholic beverages sect. OPS, 1951-52; legal asst. to Judge Eugene Black, Tax Ct. U.S., 1953-56; practice in Washington, 1956—; pres., chmn. bd. Fed. Pubs., Inc., Washington, 1959—; chmn. bd. Gene Galasso Assos., Inc., Washington, 1963—, Crown Eagle Communications, Ltd., London. Mem. adv. cabinet Southeastern U., 1965—; cons. AEC, 1965-75; profl. lectr. Dept. Agr., 1960—, George Washington U., 1961—, U. San Francisco, 1965—, Air Force Inst. Tech., 1975-76, Coll. William and Mary, 1966-75, Calif. Inst. Tech., 1967-72, U. So. Calif., 1973-74, U. Denver, 1975—. Served to 1st lt. Judge Adv. Gen. Corps, USAF, 1951-52; maj. Res. (ret.). Fellow Nat. Contract Mgmt. Assn.; mem. Am. (council pub. contract law sect. 1972-75), N.Y., Fla., D.C. (dir. 1965-66, chmn. adminstrv. law sect. 1964-65) bar assns. Jewish religion. Home: 6009 Plainview Rd Bethesda MD 20034 Office: 1725 K St NW Washington DC 20006

KEISMAN, IRA B., psychologist; b. N.Y.C., Aug. 10, 1927; s. Mark Z. and Genia (Tzpich) K.; Ph.D., N.Y. U., 1958; m. Judith Tomashoff, Oct. 5, 1950; children—Jeremy, Maud, Margaret. Clin. psychologist Topeka State Hosp., Menninger Found., Topeka, Kans., 1953-54; clin. psychologist Calif. Dept. Corrections, Tracy, 1954-55; clin. psychologist VA, N.Y.C., 1955-57; psychologist Long Island Cons., N.Y.C., 1957-61; lectr., dir. intern tng. program L.I. Consultation Center, N.Y.C., 1959-62; pvt. practice psychotherapy and psychoanalysis, N.Y.C., 1958—; dir. spl. services, mem. adminstrv. and teaching faculty Washington Sq. Inst., 1974—. Served with USN, 1945-46. Certified clin. psychologist, N.Y. State, also Nat. Register Health Service Providers in Psychology; accredited psychoanalyst Nat. Accreditation Assn. for Psychoanalysis. Mem. Am. Psychol. Assn., Am. Group Therapy Assn., AAAS, N.Y. State Psychol. Assn., N.Y. Soc. Clin. Psychologists. Democrat. Jewish. Contbr. articles to profl. jours. Home: 239 Central Park West New York City NY 10024 Office: 125 E 87th St New York City NY 10028

KEITH, ALLAN REED, banker; b. Boston, July 26, 1937; s. Eldon Bradford and Vernie Lucile (Pruet) K.; B.A., Amherst Coll., 1959; M.B.A., Harvard, 1961; postgrad. Yale, 1962; m. Winifred Alling Ward, May 2, 1964; children—Lucy Ward, Lesley Pruet. With corporate finance and sales Smith Barney & Co., Inc., N.Y.C., 1963-73, 2d v.p., 1968-69, v.p., 1969-73; investment officer Brown Brothers Harriman & Co., N.Y.C., 1973-74, asst. mgr., 1974-76, 78—; with Dillon, Read & Co., Inc., 1976-78. Treas., Internat. Council for Bird Preservation, U.S. Sect., Inc., N.Y.C., 1970—; mem. Harding Twp. Bd. Edn., 1972-78, v.p., 1973-76, pres., 1977-78; trustee N.J. Conservation Found., 1970—. Served with AUS, 1961. Mem. Am. Ornithologists' Union (life), Cooper Ornithol. Soc. (life), Wilson Ornithol. Club (life), Chi Psi. Clubs: Nuttall, The Explorers (mem. environment com. 1968-75, chmn. 1969-73). Contbr. articles to profl. jours. Home: Blue Mill Rd New Vernon NJ 07976 Office: 46 William St New York City NY 10005

KEITH, LEROY, JR., state ednl. adminstr.; b. Chattanooga, Feb. 14, 1939; s. Leroy and Lula M. K.; B.S., Morehouse Coll., 1961; M.S., Ind. U., 1968, Ed.D., 1970; m. Anita Rose Halsey, Oct. 6, 1961; children—Lori, Susan, Kelli. Tchr. sci. team teaching coordinator pub. schs., Chattanooga, 1961-66; dir. Neighborhood Services Program, Chattanooga, 1966-68; asso. dean, asst. prof. Dartmouth Coll., 1970-73; asso. v.p. for policy and planning U. Mass., 1973-75; chancellor Mass. Bd. Higher Edn., 1975—; cons. E.I. duPont de Nemours & Co., Inc.; mem. policy com. Harvard U. Center Urban Studies; bd. dirs. Mass. Higher Edn. Assistance Corp.; mem. Mass. State Coll. Bd., Mass. Regional Community Coll. Bd., Mass. Bd. Edn., New Eng. Bd. Higher Edn., Lexington (Mass.) Edn. Study Com. Bd. dirs. United Way of Mass., Phoenix Investment Council Money/Market Options Fund, Boston; mem. Lexington Police Rev. Bd.; mem. adv. com. Boston Pub. Housing Tenants Policy Council. Recipient Resolution for Outstanding Achievement, Tenn. Ho. of Reps., 1976, award for exemplary service Black Educators Alliance Mass., 1976, Distinguished Alumni Service award Ind. U. Commencement, 1977; Univ. fellow, 1969-70. Mem. AAUP, Am. Assn. Higher Edn., State Higher Edn. Exec. Officers, (exec. com.), State, Nat. Center for Higher Edn. Mgmt. Systems (sub-com. edn. com.), New Eng. Morehouse Alumni Assn. (pres. 1975-76), Phi Delta Kappa. Episcopalian. Club: Rotary (Boston). Editorial bd. Jour. Afro-Am. Issues, 1972-75. Home: 11 Birch Hill Ln Lexington MA 02173 Office: 31 St James Ave Room 632 Boston MA 02116

KEITH, QUENTIN GANGEWERE, educator; b. Bethlehem, Pa., Aug. 14, 1919; s. Stanley Raymond and Estelle (Gangawer) K.; B.A., Lehigh U., 1940; postgrad. Sorbonne, U. Paris, 1945, Columbia, 1947-48; B.A., King's Coll., Cambridge U., 1947, M.A., 1952; m. Sylvia E. Phillips, Nov. 29, 1945; children—Jennifer Estelle, Vaughn Phillips Montaigne. Research writer Columbia U. Press, 1947-48; instr. humanities Rutgers U., 1948-51; lectr., dir. devel. Monmouth Coll., West Long Branch, N.J., 1954-60, asso. prof. English, 1961—; army officer res. affairs adviser to Army Comdr., Governors Island, 1963-66, chief plans and operations (logistics) Hdqrs. II U.S. Army Corps, Ft. Wadsworth, S.I., N.Y., 1966-67; dep. dir. fgn. liaison Army Gen. Staff, Washington, 1972; cons. faculty U.S. Army Command and Gen. Staff Coll. Ft. Leavenworth, Kans., 1968-73; specialist Anglo-Am. relations, 1973—; dir. James Gray, Inc., dir. The Keith Library and Gallery, rare book cons.; appraiser Lit. properties. Served from 2d lt. to capt. AUS, 1940-46, capt. to maj., 1951-54, lt. col., 1963-67, col., 1968-73. Decorated Bronze Star medal, Legion of Merit; Croix de Guerre. Mem. AAUP (chpt. pres.), Am. Acad. Polit. Sci., English-Speaking Union U.S. (chmn. Region III, br. pres., charter, dir. Monmouth), St. George's Soc. N.Y., Seventh Regiment Assn. N.Y., Ret. Officers Assn., Res. Officers Assn., Oxford and Cambridge Soc. N.Y. (dir.), Modern Lang. Assn. Episcopalian. Clubs: British Schools and Universities, Williams (N.Y.C.); Army and Navy (Washington and London). Contbr. articles to profl. jours. Home: 335 Broad St Red Bank NJ 07701 Office: Wilson Hall Annex Monmouth Coll West Long Branch NJ 07764

KEITH, WILLIAM HALE, meteorologist; b. Sioux Falls, S.D., June 14, 1931; s. Hale Gress and Evelyn Marie (Fox) K.; B.A., M.A., U. Wis., 1953; M.S., U.S. Naval Postgrad. Sch., 1966; J.D., New Eng. Sch. Law, 1960; m. Dolores Beatrice Foote, Apr. 19, 1952; 1 son, Scott William. Commd. ensign U.S. Navy, 1953, advanced through grades to comdr., 1968; meteorol. officer Naval Air Sta., Kwajalein, Marshall Islands, 1955-56, South Weymouth, Mass., 1957-60; staff meteorologist Airborne Early Warning Wing, Pacific, 1956-57; wintering over meteorologist McMurdo Sound, Antarctica, 1960-61; exec. officer Fleet Weather Facility, London, 1961-64; research officer Navy Weather Research Facility, Norfolk, Va., 1966-69; exec. and comdg. officer Fleet Weather Facility, Suitland, Md., 1969-72; chmn. environ. scis. dept. U.S. Naval Acad., Annapolis, Md., 1972-76; ret., 1976; meteorologist Air Resources Lab. Nat. Oceanic and Atmospheric Adminstrn., on assignment to EPA, Washington, 1976—. Mem. Am. Meteorol. Soc., Am. Littoral Soc., U.S. Naval Inst., Md. Acad. Scis. (environ. research guidance com.). Democrat. Roman Catholic. Editor: Navy Weather Research Facility publs., 1966-69; condr. research on Antarctic climatology and meteorology, meteorol. satellite imagery of the Antarctic. Home: 13001 Renfrew Circle Tantallon MD 20022 Office: 401 M St SW Washington DC 20460

KELEMEN, EMERY IMRE, civil engr., city ofcl.; b. Balatonboglar, Hungary, Nov. 23, 1929; s. Imre and Gizella (Body) K.; came to Can., 1957, naturalized, 1962; B.S. in Engring., Tech. U. Budapest (Hungary), 1953, M.S. in Hydraulics, 1955; postgrad. U. Montreal, 1968-70; m. Ilona Judity Kecskes, Apr. 22, 1960. Design engr. Brette, Ouellette & Blauer Assos., cons. engrs., Montreal, 1958-63; prodn. mgr. Recstone Ltd., Montreal, 1963-64; pres. Omega Bus. Assistance Ltd., engring. mgmt., Montreal, also Edmonton, Alta., London and Vienna, 1965-68; hydraulic engr. St. Lawrence Seaway Authority, Montreal, 1968-73; city engr. City of Beaconsfield (Que.), 1973—; lectr. in field. Mem. Corp. Profl. Engrs. Que., Engring. Inst. Can., Am. Pub. Works Assn. Club: Pointe Claire Yacht. Researcher wave motion in navigational channel, ship motion in navigational lock. Home: 4000 deMainsnneuve Blvd W Apt 1201 Westmount PQ H3Z 1J9 Canada Office: 303 Beaconsfield Blvd Beaconsfield PQ H9W 4A7 Canada

KELLAND, DONALD EDGAR JACKMAN, hosp. adminstr.; b. Heart's Content, Nfld., Can., July 20, 1924; s. Edgar Mark and Violet (Sinyard) K.; student Bishop Feild Jr. Coll., 1939-40, Bishop Spencer Coll., 1940-41; m. Barbara C. Bartlett, June 6, 1950; children—David Mark, Donna Lynn. Andrea Joy. Various positions Nfld. Dept. Health, 1941-64, asst. adminstr. health services, St. John's, 1965-66; asst. adminstr. St. John's Gen. Hosp., 1964-65; adminstr. Children's Hosp., St. John's, 1966—; dir. St. John's Hosp. Council, Day Care Licensing Bd. Mem. Canadian (dir.), Nfld. (dir.) hosp. assns., Canadian Pediatric Hosps. Assn., Canadian Coll. Health Service Execs., Am. Coll. Hosp. Adminstrs. Anglican. Clubs: Masons, York Cross of Honor. Home: 11 Rodney St St John's NF A1B 3B3 Canada Office: Newfoundland Dr St John's NF A1A 1R8 Canada

KELLER, DAVID MATHIAS, educator; b. N.Y.C., Sept. 12, 1936; s. Benjamin J. and Rose (Geller) K.; A.B., Bklyn. Coll., 1959; M.F.A., Yale U., 1963; Ph.D., Columbia U., 1975; m. Joan Jeffri, May 25, 1973; 1 son, Joshua Hillel. With CBS-TV, N.Y.C., 1963-64, prodn. supr., dir. Eye on N.Y. series, 1963; prof. dramatic lit. English dept. Kingsborough Community Coll., Bklyn., 1964—; fellow Pierpont Morgan Library; distinguished panelist, mem. Nat. Bd. Cons. for Nat. Endowment for Humanities; dir. major grants in higher edn. HEW; vis. prof. Cornell U., 1977-78; cons. spl. higher edn. project WNET-TV, 1976-78; research asso. Columbia U. Served with U.S. Army, 1960-66. Nat. Endowment for Humanities grantee, 1973-74, 75-76, City U. N.Y. grantee, 1974-75; HEW grantee (three), 1970-73. Mem. Am. Shakespeare Assn., Modern Lang. Assn., Am. Theatre Assn., Am. Soc. Theatre Research (treas.), Dirs. Guild Am. Author text, interviewer ednl. TV series The Dramatic Experience, 1976; author: The Meanings of Freedom, 1976; producer, lectr., 1967-68. Home: 2302 Ave O Brooklyn NY 11210 Office: Dept English Kingsborough Community Coll Brooklyn NY 11235

KELLER, DONALD MONROE, investments co. mgr.; b. Tuscaloosa, Ala., Feb. 4, 1933; s. Allen Dudley and Marion (Monroe) K.; A.B., Dartmouth Coll., 1954, M.B.A., 1955; m. Jo Ann Duval, June 4, 1955; children—Patricia Ann, Donald Monroe, Joseph Bourey. With Touche Ross & Co., 1958-68, Boston, 1958-60, 62-65, supr., 65-66, mgr., 66-68, Detroit, 1960-62; analyst Keystone Custodian Funds Inc., Boston, 1968-73, asso. portfolio mgr., 1973-76, portfolio mgr. Keystone S-4 Fund, 1976—, v.p., 1977—. Chmn. Needham Republican Town Com., 1967-69; chmn. future sch. needs com. Town of Needham, 1970-73; pres. Needham Boosters Club, 1975-76. Served with USN, 1955-58. C.P.A., Mass.; Chartered Fin. Analyst. Mem. Am. Inst. C.P.A.'s, Mass. Soc. C.P.A.'s. Boston Soc. Security Analysts (dir., chmn. accounting com.), Inst. Chartered Fin. Analysts. Clubs: Exchange, Needham Pool and Racquet (dir., v.p. ops.). Home: 55 Nichols Rd Needham MA 02192 Office: 99 High St Boston MA 02104

KELLER, GEORGE WILLIAM, orgn. exec.; b. Portsmouth, Ohio, Aug. 26, 1917; s. Reamer M. and Emma (Hosey) K.; B.A., Ohio State U., 1942; M.Ed., Loyola Coll. (Balt.), 1953; m. Virginia Marie Wagner, 1942; children—Virginia (Mrs. James Beauchamp), Stephen Charles. Placement counselor Ohio Commn. for the Blind, Columbus, 1942-44; rehab. counselor for blind div. Vocat. Rehab., Md. State Dept. Edn., Balt., 1944-46, supr. Services for Blind, 1946-68, state coordinator Services for the Blind, 1968-77; ret., 1977; exec. dir. Sight Assn. Md. Lions, Balt., 1977—; cons. Rehab. Services Adminstrn., HEW, 1953. Exec. dir. Sight Assn. of Md. Lions, 1976—. Mem. Nat. Rehab. Assn. (life), Am. Assn. Workers for the Blind, Inc. (pres. D.C. Md. chpt. 1968—). Methodist (chmn. commn. on Christian social concerns 1974—). Home: 1503 Winston Ave Baltimore MD 21239 Office: 301 W Hamilton St Baltimore MD 21201

KELLER, MARGARET GILMER (MRS. GEORGE HENRY KELLER, III), educator; b. Harrisburg, Pa., July 11, 1911; d. Charles Greenawalt and Mary Ellen (Sullivan) Gilmer; A.B., Trinity Coll., 1933; A.M., Columbia U., 1934, certificate, 1942; certificate State Tchrs. Coll., Bloomsburg, Pa., 1934; m. George Henry Keller, III, July 13, 1940; children—Mary Ellen, Margaret Marie, George Henry. Acting chmn. dept. history Trinity Coll., Washington, 1935-36; chmn. classical dept. Convent Sacred Heart, 1936-37, Steelton (Pa.) High Sch., 1937-41; adj. asst. prof. English dept. U. Coll., Rutgers U., 1946—, mem. dean's adv. com. Univ. Coll., 1968—, also advisor to women's clubs Univ. College; chmn. classical dept. Glen Rock (N.J.) High Sch., 1956-59, chmn. fgn. lang. dept., 1959—. Active Am. Cancer Soc., Community Chest, ARC, Girl Scouts U.S.A.; mem. nominating bd. Ridgewood (N.J.) Nursing Service, 1959-60; Republican county committeeman. Trustee Trinity Coll., Washington, 1963-67, 74—, chmn. 75th anniversary fund, 1974-75. Honored by Rutgers U., 1953, 61, 64, 65, 71, Newman Province of N.J., 1963, Nat. Jaycees, 1973, Middle States Assn. Commn. on Secondary Schs., 1970, 74; recipient Robert Ax citation Glen Rock High Sch., 1971, Case Inst., 1976. Mem. NEA, N.J. Edn. Assn., Am. Classical Soc., AAUW (former dir.), Archeol. Inst. Am., Modern Lang. Assn., Suprs. Assn. N.J. (sec. 1973-76), Am., N.J., Mid-Atlantic States classical socs., AAUP, Chaplain's Aid Assn., Trinity Coll. Alumnae Assn. (nat. pres.), Phi Chi Theta (hon.). Clubs: Newman (adviser Rutgers U.), Univ. Coll. Women (hon. Rutgers U.), Coll. Home: 200 Phelps Rd Ridgewood NJ 07450 Office: Rutgers U New Brunswick NJ 08901

KELLEY, FRANCIS JOSEPH, market research co. exec.; b. Brookline, Mass., Sept. 17, 1929; s. William Leo and Mary Lillian (Coughlin) K.; A.A., Boston U., 1950, B.S., 1952; m. Dorothy Marie Hefferan, Sept. 12, 1959; children—John William, Francis Joseph, Edward H., Katherine M., Mary E. With Am. Airlines, N.Y.C., 1953-55; with Frank J. Kelley Co., bldg. materials, Norwood, Mass., 1955-67; co-owner, treas. Attitude Research Assos., Inc., Norwood, Mass., 1967—. Mem. Town Meeting, Norwood, 1972—; corporator Norwood Hosp. Mem. Am. Mktg. Assn. (chpt. treas. 1972—). Clubs: Lions, Walpole Country (pres. 1976-77), K.C., 1776 (pres. 1965-66). Home: 78 Bond St Norwood MA 02062 Office: PO Box 7 Norwood MA 02062

KELLEY, MAURICE LESLIE, JR., physician; b. Indpls., June 29, 1924; s. Maurice Leslie and Martha (Daniel) K.; student U. Vt., Va. Poly. Inst., Princeton, 1943-45; M.D., U. Rochester, 1949; m. Carol J. Povec, Feb. 11, 1967; children—Elizabeth Ann, Mary Sarah. Intern, resident Strong Meml. Hosp., Rochester, N.Y., 1949-51, Bixby fellow in medicine, 1953-56; fellow gastroenterology Mayo Clinic, Rochester, Minn., 1957-59; asst. prof. medicine U. Rochester, 1959-64, asso. prof., 1964-67; practice medicine, specializing in gastroenterology, Rochester, N.Y., 1959-67; asso. prof. clin. medicine Dartmouth Med. Sch., Hanover, N.H., 1967-74, prof. clin. med., 1974—; chmn. sect. internal medicine Hitchcock Clinic, 1972-74, chmn. sect. gastroenterology, 1974-78; mem. staff Strong Meml. Hosp., Hitchcock Clinic, Mary Hitchcock Meml. Hosp.; cons. Canadaigua VA, Rochester Gen., Genesee hosps., VA Med. Center, White River Junction. Served with AUS, 1942-45, M.C., USAF, 1951-53. Fellow A.C.P. (gov. for N.H.), Am. Gastroent. Assn.; mem. A.M.A. (chmn. sect. gastroenterology 1970-71), Am. Physiol. Soc., Am. Soc. Gastrointestinal Endoscopy. Contbr. articles to profl. jours., also chpts. in books. Home: 15 Ledge Rd Hanover NH 03755 Office: 2 Maynard St Hanover NH 03755

KELLEY, MICHAEL ARMSTRONG, state ofcl.; b. Hartford, Conn., Nov. 7, 1949; s. John Armstrong and Mary Alberta (Marsden) K.; B.A., Nasson Coll., 1971; m. Gretchen Eve Schluter, Sept. 28, 1974; children—Allison Maura and Audra Maureen (twins). Asst. microbiologist Webber Hosp., Biddeford, Maine, 1971; medical technologist Goodall Hosp., Sanford, Maine, 1971-72; public safety officer Town of Sanford, 1973-74; chemist Maine Dept. Pub. Safety, Augusta, 1974—; expert witness in serology, body fluids and forensic chemistry. Mem. Internat. Narcotic Enforcement Officers Assn., Northeastern Assn. Forensic Scientists, Am. Acad. Forensic Scientists, Nat. Assn. Underwater Instrs. Home: PO Box 95 Cooper's Mills ME 04341 Office: Hospital St Augusta ME 04333

KELLEY, SHEILA SEYMOUR (MRS. ROBERT M. KAUFMAN), pub. relations co. exec., polit. media specialist; b. Bronxville, N.Y.; d. William J. and Jane (Seymour) Kelley; B.A. magna cum laude, Syracuse U., 1949; m. Robert M. Kaufman, Nov. 1959. Reporter, Yonkers (N.Y.) Herald Statesman, 1950; reporter Close-Up column N.Y. Herald Tribune and Tribune Syndicate, 1950-52; editor Close-Up, 1952; producer, dir. Tex & Jinx McCrary radio and television programs WNBC, N.Y.C. and NBC Network, 1953-54; media cons. Rep. Jacob K. Javits, 1954; spl. asst. to Alfred Gwynne Vanderbilt, pub. relations dir. World Vets. Fund, 1955; media cons. to Atty. Gen. Javits in race for U.S. Senate, 1956; asst. and press sec. to Senator Javits, Washington, 1956-60; account exec., later v.p. Harshe-Rotman & Druck, Inc., N.Y.C., 1961-76; v.p. Doremus & Co., N.Y.C., 1976—; pres. VOTES, Inc., polit. advt., 1973—; media dir. Javits campaign for re-election, 1962, 68, 74, Kenneth B. Keating for Senate, 1958 Judge Wachtler for N.Y. State Ct. Appeals, 1972; founder, pres. VOTES Inc., specializing in polit. advt., 1973-78. Mem. Pub. Relations Soc. Am. (accredited), Women Execs. in Pub. Relations (officer), Phi Beta Kappa. Office: 120 Broadway New York NY 10005

KELLNER, GEORGE ANDREW, fin. co. exec.; b. Budapest, Hungary, Nov. 28, 1942; s. Paul John and Clare Elizabeth (Balint) K.; came to U.S., 1947, naturalized, 1952; B.A., Trinity Coll., 1964; J.D., Columbia, 1967; M.B.A., N.Y.U., 1973; m. Martha Henry Bicknell, July 22, 1967; children—Peter B., Catherine S. Admitted to N.Y. bar, 1967; asso. firm Carter, Ledyard & Milburn, N.Y.C., 1967-70; v.p. Madison Fund, N.Y.C., 1970-76; partner Ivan Boesky & Co., 1976-78; sr. v.p. Donaldson, Lufkin & Jenrette, 1978—; instr. Sch. Continuing Edn., N.Y.U. Mem. N.Y. Bar Assn., N.Y. Soc. Security Analysts. Clubs: Union, Racquet and Tennis. Home: 530 E 86th St New York City NY 10028 Office: 660 Madison Ave New York City NY 10021

KELLNER, LOUIS DANIEL, lawyer; b. N.Y.C., May 24, 1927; s. Charles and Irene (Grunberger) K.; student Kans. State Coll., 1945-46, Coll. City N.Y., 1946-48; LL.B., N.Y. Law Sch., 1951; m. Carol Linzer, July 8, 1951; children—Lawrence Dean, Lynn Dee. Admitted to N.Y. State bar, 1952; since practiced in N.Y.C.; builder one and two-family houses, apt. houses N.Y.C., Westchester County, 1955-67; owner, operator L. Kellner & Co. Inc., real estate, mortgage banking, 1960—; bd. govs. Bronx Bd. Realtors, 1973-78; lectr. Bronx Community Coll., 1975-76; pres. Esperanto Gallery Fine Arts Inc., N.Y.C., 1965—. Trustee Argus Community Inc., 1972-78. Mem. N.Y.C. Home Builders Assn. (pres. 1963), Bronx County Bar Assn., Mortgage Bankers Assn. N.Y. Home: 9 Tanglewood Rd Scarsdale NY 10583 Office: 2622 & Tremont Ave New York City NY 10461

KELLOGG, RALPH MARTIN, realtor; b. Wolcott, Conn., Dec. 13, 1895; s. Henry Martin and Stella Georgette (Alton) K.; B.S., U. Pa., 1918; m. Sigrid Constance, Sept. 4, 1933; children—Janet Lois, Sandra Joy Constance. Mgr. Argentine office S. Cookman & Co., exporters-importers, 1919-21; sales supr. Aluminum Cooking Utensil Co., Boston, 1921-26; sales mgr. West Bend Aluminum Co., Boston, 1926-30; spity. sales promotion mgr. Certainteed Corp., N.Y.C., 1930-33; mgr. hardware div. Dain Lumber Co., Katonah, N.Y., 1933-39; owner Inter-City Hardware Co., also Welch's Hardware Co., Norwalk-Westport, Conn., 1939-59; owner Ralph Kellogg Agency, realtors-appraisers, Norwalk, 1959—. Pres. Norwalk Bd. Realtors, 1965—; mem. Norwalk Planning Com., 1949-59, vice-chmn., 1956; mem. Norwalk Parking Authority, 1954—. Served as ensign USNR, 1917-19. Named realtor of yr., Norwalk, 1965. Mem. Mchts. Assn. Norwalk (chmn. 1941—), Norwalk C. of C. (pres. 1945—), Nat. Assn. Ind. Fee Appraisers (pres. Fairfield, Conn., 1970-71, state dir. 1973—), Nat. Inst. Real Estate Brokers, Methodist. Clubs: Mason,

Rotary (pres. Katonah 1938-39). Home: 4 Camelot Dr Norwalk CT 06850

KELLOGG-SMITH, OGDEN, educator, sculptor; b. N.Y.C., Apr. 21, 1920; s. Jewell and Margaret (Shearer) Kellogg-Smith; A.B., St. John's Coll., 1943; postgrad. Mass. Inst. Tech., 1952; M.A., Putney Grad. Sch. Tchr. Edn., 1962; postgrad. Chesapeake Biol. Lab., Solomons, Md., 1968, Md. Inst. Coll. Art, 1975—; studied yacht design under Franz Plunder, sculpture under Etienne Desmet, Italy, also Reuben Kramer and Arthur Benson; children—(guardianship) Peter von Pein, Lee von Pein Schreitz, Ruth Bueneman Burket, Cynthia Taylor. Tchr. math and sci. Ojai (Calif.) Valley Sch., 1944-46; organizer, acting head Happy Valley Sch., Miners Oaks, Ojai, 1946-47; yacht broker, designer, Chestertown, Md. 1947-61; asst. head Gunston Sch., Centerville, Md., 1950-57; tchr. Abano (Turkey) Grapha-English, 1956; founding headmaster Key Sch., Annapolis, Md., 1958-62; founding headmaster, dir. oceanography Bay Country Sch., Arnold, Md., 1962-71; founding dir. Bay Country Inst., 1971-77; tchr. sculpture Acad. Arts, Easton, Md., 1973-76; vis. seminar leader Md. Inst. Coll. Art, 1976-77. Mem. Marine Tech. Soc., Chesapeake Bay Maritime Mus., Assn. for World Edn., World Future Soc., Internat. Oceanographic Found., Ocean Soc., Chesapeake Bay Found., Chestertown Arts League (past pres.), Md. Fedn. Arts, Acad. Arts. Democrat. Episcopalian. Club: Corsica River Yacht (Centreville, Md.). Address: 226 Haverton Rd Arnold MD 21012

KELLOW, WILLIAM FRANCIS, physician, med. coll. adminstr.; b. Geneva, N.Y., Mar. 14, 1922; s. Robert Leo and Mary Loretta (Kelley) K.; B.S., U. Notre Dame, 1943; M.D., Georgetown U., 1936; Sc.D., St. Joseph's Coll., 1967; L.H.D., Hahnemann Med. Coll., 1978; m. Stella Margaret Tozylowski, Apr. 21, 1951; children—Suzanne Kellow Portfolio, Joanne, Jennifer, Mary, Kathleen. Intern, D.C. Gen. Hosp., Washington, 1936-37, resident, 1947-51; resident Georgetown U. Hosp., also Walter Reed Hosp., 1947-51; clin. instr. surgery Georgetown U. Sch. Medicine, 1947-48, clin. instr. medicine, 1948-53; clin. instr. medicine U. Ill. Coll. Medicine, 1953-55, asst. prof. medicine, asst. dean, 1955-59, asso. prof., asso dean, 1959-61; prof. medicine, dean Hahnemann Med. Coll., Phila., 1961-67; prof. medicine, dean, v.p. Jefferson Med. Coll., Phila., 1967—; dir. Federated Med. Resources, Inc., pres., 1973-77; trustee Ednl. Commn. for Fgn. Med. Grads., treas., 1969-76. Trustee Chgo. Inst. Tb, 1958-61; bd. dirs. Greater Delaware Valley Regional Med. Program, 1966-73, chmn., 1969-73; bd. dirs. United Health Services, Phila., 1967-71; mem. Mayor's Com. on Mcpl. Health Services, Phila., 1958-71; mem. gen. research support program adv. com. NIH, 1971-74. Served to capt. M.C., USAF, 1951-53. Recipient Shaffrey award St. Josephs Coll., 1978. Fellow A.C.P. (regent 1970-76, treas. 1970-76); mem. AMA (mem. adv. com. on undergrad. med. edn. council on med. edn. 1974—, chmn. 1977—), Assn. Am. Med. Colls. (mem. liaison com. med. edn. with AMA), Am. Fedn. Clin. Research, Am. Thoracic Soc., Phila. Coll. Physicians, Pa. Med. Soc., Phila. County Med. Soc., AAAS, Sigma Xi, Alpha Omega Alpha, Kappa Beta Phi. Roman Catholic. Club: Union League (Phila.). Contbr. articles to profl. jours. Home: 457 Moreno Rd Wynnewood PA 19096 Office: 1025 Walnut St Philadelphia PA 19107*

KELLY, CLARENCE JAMES, clergyman; b. Bklyn., Nov. 23, 1941; s. Edward and Claire (Bonar) K.; B.A. in Philosophy, Catholic U. Am., 1969; student Immaculate Conception Sem., Huntington, N.Y., 1969-71, Internat. Sem. St. Piux X, Econe, Switzerland, 1971-73. Joined Soc. St. Piux, 1971; ordained priest Roman Cath. Ch., 1973; rector St. Piux V Cath. Sch., Wantagh, N.Y., 1973-76; U.S. dist. supr. Soc. St. Piux X, Oyster Bay Cove, N.Y., 1976—, editor For You and For Many newsletter, 1976—. Served with USAF, 1959-63. Author: Conspiracy Against God and Man, 1973. Home and office: 8 Pond Pl Oyster Bay Cove NY 11771

KELLY, CORNELIUS JAMES NOEL, explosives co. exec.; b. Cork City, Ireland, Dec. 16, 1932; s. Michael and Violet Mary (Sheehan) K.; came to U.S., 1966; certificate chemistry Paisley (Scotland) Inst. Tech., 1956; m. Pearl Cassellis, July 26, 1958; children—Kevin, Joan, Noel, Fiona, Declan. Lab. asst. Imperial Chem. Industries Nobel div., Scotland, 1952-56, exptl. officer, 1956-64; explosives chemist Canadian Industries Ltd., Montreal, Que., Can., 1964-66; mgr. research and devel. E-B Industries, Inc., Simsbury, Conn., 1970—. Mem. Am. Chem. Soc., Combustion Inst., Sigma Xi. Patentee in field. Home: 7 Michael Rd Simsbury CT 06070 Office: 660 Hopmeadow St Simsbury CT 06070

KELLY, DAVID AUSTIN, oil co. exec.; b. Mt. Kisco, N.Y., June 24, 1938; s. William Andrew and Katharine Elizabeth (Barrett) K.; B.A., Lafayette Coll., 1962; M.B.A., U. Chgo., 1964; m. Judith Boesel, June 18, 1966; children—Carolyn Boesel, Douglas Austin. Asst. treas. Gulf Oil Corp., Pitts., 1974—; asst. v.p. investment mgmt. group 1st. Nat. City Bank, N.Y.C., 1964-69; portfolio mgr., v.p. J.M. Hartwell & Co. Inc., N.Y.C., 1969-72; pres., dir. P/H Mgmt. Corp., Pitts., 1972-74. Mem. fin. policy com. Lafayette Coll., 1976—. Served with U.S. Army, 1957-59. Mem. N.Y. Soc. Security Analysts, Fin. Analysts Fedn., Pitts. Soc. Fin. Analysts, World Affairs Council Pitts., N.Y. Soc. Order Founders and Patriots Am. (past councilor) Inst. Chartered Fin. Analysts, Internat. Mgmt. and Devel. Inst. (corp. strategic planning council), Internat. Bus. Forum. Clubs: Duquesne Pitts., Fox Chapel Golf. Home: 40 Woodland Farms Rd Pittsburgh PA 15238 Office: PO Box 1166 Pittsburgh PA 15230

KELLY, DONALD JOHN, banker; b. N.Y.C., Oct. 2, 1932; s. J. Bertram and Genevieve (Archipoli) K.; B.A., St. Bonaventure (N.Y.) U., 1954; M.B.A., U. Colo., 1969; m. Virginia C. Lamanda, Oct. 8, 1955; children—Nancy, Diane. Dist. mgr. AT&T Co., 1957-67; v.p., gen. sales mgr. Christmas Club A Corp., Phila., 1967-74; sr. v.p., dir. mktg. Suburbia Fed. Savs. & Loan Assn., Garden City, N.Y., 1974—; dir. Gotham Life Ins. Co., N.Y.C. Served to 1st lt. AUS, 1954-57. Mem. Garden City C. of C. (dir., pres.), Am. Mktg. Assn., Savs. Instns. Soc. Am., Fin. Advt. Assn. N.Y., St. Bonaventure U. Alumni Assn. Clubs: Garden City Country, Garden City Kiwanis. Author articles in field. Home: 280 Prince Ave Freeport NY 11520 Office: 1000 Franklin Ave Garden City NY 11530

KELLY, DONALD KAEMPFER, osteo. physician, med. co. exec.; b. Kingston, N.Y., Sept. 14, 1932; s. Delmer Goff and Elwine (Kaempfer) K.; B.A., State U. N.Y. at Albany, 1951; D.D., Kansas City Coll. Osteopathic Medicine, 1955; M.D., Calif. Coll. Med., 1962; P.H.S.M., Harvard Bus. Sch., 1972; m. Suzanne Deschamps, Dec. 16, 1972. Intern, Doctor's Hosp., Columbus, Ohio, 1955-56; adminstr. Calif. Med. Group, 1960-74; pres., chmn. bd. HMO Internat., Los Angeles, 1969-74, Consol. Med. Systems, Ltd., Los Angeles, 1971—; pres. Metro Med Health Plan, Inc., N.Y.C., 1975—; dir. HMO Internat., Consol. Med. Systems, Ltd. Served to capt. USPHS, 1956-58. Mem. A.M.A., Los Angeles County, Calif. med. assns., Group Health Assn. Am., Health Maintenance Orgn., Am. (pres. 1974—), Beverly Hills Acad. Medicine, Young Presidents Orgn., Fedn. Fly Fishermen. Clubs: Palm Bay, Riviera, Marina City. Contbr. articles in field to med. jours. Home: 151 E 79th St New York City NY 10022 Office: 425 E 61st St New York City NY 10022

KELLY, DORIS LILLIAN, educator; b. Boston, Oct. 3, 1921; d. Gilbert Holmes and Lillian May (Campbell) K.; B.S., Eastern Nazarene Coll., Quincy, Mass., 1954; M.B.A., Boston U., 1959; cert. advanced grad. study in counseling U. N.H., 1978. Bookkeeper, State St. Trust Co., Boston, 1940-42; asst. bookkeeper Eastern Nazarene Coll., Quincy, Mass., 1952-56; tchr. math. and bus. Reading Meml. High Sch. (Mass.), 1956-63; instr., asst. dept. head bus. adminstrn. Champlain Coll., Burlington, Vt., 1963-67; mission bookkeeper, high sch. tchr., librarian Nazarene Mission Sta., Manzini, Swaziland, South Africa, 1967-68; prof., head bus. adminstrn. dept. N.H. Tech. Inst., Concord, 1968—. Treas., New Eng. dist. Nazarene World Missionary Soc., 1976—; missionary pres. Concord Ch. of the Nazarene, 1969—, organist, 1969—, mem. ch. bd., 1969—, auditor, 1969—; pres. faculty forum N.H. Tech. Inst., 1975-76. Served with WAC, 1942-52; ETO. Fellow Am. Biog. Inst.; mem. Am. Accounting Assn., AAUP, Am. Personnel and Guidance Assn., Smithsonian Assos., Nat. Hist. Soc., Nat. Bus. Edn. Assn. Republican. Home: 203 Loudon Rd B-6 A-16 Concord NH 03301 Office: NH Tech Inst Fan Rd Concord NH 03301

KELLY, DOROTHY LIBBY, assn. exec.; b. Newfield, Maine; d. Eugene E. and Nellie (Thompson) Libby; B.S., U. N.H., 1938, postgrad., 1939-43. Tchr., Cushing Acad., Ashburnham, Mass., 1943-45, Lyman Hall Sch., Wallingford Conn., 1945-49; legal sec., Washington, 1949-51; treas. Dairy Service Corp., Washington, 1949-51; mem. legal staff Johns Hopkins U. Applied Physics Lab., Balt., 1951-57; with Nat. Alcoholic Beverage Control Assn., 1957—, exec. v.p.-treas., 1967—. Sec.-treas. joint Com. of States to Study Alcoholic Beverage Laws, 1967—. Gen. chmn. Heart Fund dr. Montgomery County, Md., 1976; bd. dirs. Sky Ranch Found. Mem. Am. Mgmt. Assn., Nat. Assn. Execs., U.S., Montgomery County chambers commerce, Washington Bd. Trade, Am. Soc. Assn. Execs. Club: Congressional Country. Home: 5007 Battery Lane Bethesda MD 20014 Office: Nat Alcoholic Beverage Control Assn Inc 5454 Wisconsin Ave Washington DC 20015

KELLY, EDWARD ALOYSIUS, JR., physician; b. Darby, Pa., Mar. 16, 1948; s. Edward Aloysius and Adele Rosemarie (Angelucci) K.; A.B., St. Joseph's Coll., 1969; M.D., Jefferson Med. Coll., 1973; m. Sharon Colleen Quinn, May 17, 1975; 1 dau., Kristin Colleen. Intern, Wilmington, (Del.) Med. Center, 1973-74, resident in family practice, 1973-76; practice medicine, specializing in family practice, Downingtown, Pa., 1976—; staff Chester County, Coatesville hosps. Diplomate Am. Bd. Family Practice. Fellow Am. Acad. Family Physicians; mem. Pa., Chester County med. socs. Republican. Roman Catholic. Office: 36 West Lancaster Ave Downingtown PA 19335

KELLY, FRANCIS W., psychiatrist; b. Bklyn., 1913; s. William F. and Mary Anne (McMahon) K.; M.D., L.I. Coll. Medicine, Bklyn., 1939; m. Mary Rose Mackovjak, Dec. 1, 1944; children—William, Mavreen, Francis, Jr., Jonathan Richard, Margaret Anne Kelly, Kathleen Kelly. Intern, Mary Immaculate Hosp., Jamaica, N.Y., 1939-40; psych. resident Bklyn. State Hosp., 1940-41; psychiatrist Mary Immaculate Hosp., Jamaica, Weeks School, Vergennes, Vt., 1947-50, supt. Brandon (Vt.) State Sch., 1947-51; instr. psychiatry U. Vt. Med. Sch., 1947-51; physician-in-charge, Brigham Hall Hosp., 1951-56; pvt. practicing psychiatrist; staff St. Marys, Strong Memorial, Highland hosps., Rochester; cons. psychiatrist Frederick Ferris Thompson Hosp., 1951—, St. Mary's Hosp., Rochester; clin. instr. psychiatry U. Rochester Sch. Med. and Dentistry; qualified psychiatrist, N.Y. State, 1947—. Served from 1st lt. to maj. AUS, 1942-46. Diplomate Am. Bd. Psychiatry, 1946; certified mental hosp. adminstr. Fellow Am. Psychiat. Assn., Am. Geriatric Soc., A.A.A.S., Royal Soc. Health (England); mem. A.M.A., N.Y. Acad. Scis., Acad. Psychomatic Medicine, N.Y. State Med. Soc., Guild Cath. Psychiatrists (pres. 1954-55), Am. Assn. Mental Deficiency, Am. Hosp. Assn., Am. Assn. Indsl. Physicians and Surgeons, Am. Assn. for Advancement Psychotherapy, Assn. Mil. Surgeons of U.S., Assn. Am. Physicians and Surgeons, Am. Sociol. Assn., Am. Soc. Criminology, Am. Judicature Soc., Air Force Assn. K.C. Home: 7 Harwood Ln East Rochester NY 14445 Office: 1351 Mt Hope Ave Rochester NY 14620

KELLY, GERALD RAY, editor; b. Milw., Jan. 18, 1930; s. Walter William and Grace Mathilda (Gilbertson) K.; student U. Wis., 1955-56; B.A., Mexico City Coll., 1959. Editor, Mexico/This Month, Mexico City, 1960-63; lit. agt. J.F. McCrindle Co., N.Y.C., 1963-65, Kelly, Bramhall & Ford Co., Boston, 1965-67; free lance writer, 1967-71; editor Grapevine, Martha's Vineyard, West Tisbury, Mass., 1971—; dir. Felix Neck Press, West Tisbury. Served with USNR, 1951-55. Author: (with William Spratling) File on Spratling, 1968; (with Elizabeth Anderson) Miss Elizabeth, 1969. Address: PO Box 57 West Tisbury MA 02575

KELLY, JOHN WILLIAM, JR., hosp. adminstr.; b. Phila., Mar. 6, 1940; s. John William and Helen Marie (Campbell) K.; B.S. in Bus. Adminstrn., St. Joseph's Coll., 1967; M.B.A., Pa. Mil. Coll., 1970; m. Phyllis Elaine Guenther, Feb. 3, 1962; children—John William III, Helen, Phyllis, Catherine, Maria, Jenifer, Colleen. Indsl. engr. Boeing Co., Morton, Pa., 1963-70; mgr. Scott Paper Co., Chester, Pa., 1970-71; sr. mgmt. engr. Mgmt. Engring. & Cost Control Service, Princeton, N.J., 1971-72; exec. v.p. adminstrn. Children's Hosp. of Phila., 1972—. Mem. Am. Coll. Hosp. Adminstrs., Am. Inst. Indsl. Engrs. Home: 129 Wood Rose Lane Glen Mills PA 19342 Office: 1 Children's Center 34th and Civic Center Philadelphia PA 19104

KELLY, MARCUS RAY, sch. supt.; b. Webb, Ala., Nov. 10, 1925; s. Charles Marvin and Essie Vee (Gamble) K.; A.B. in English and Elem. Edn., Asbury Coll., 1952; Ed.M., U. Fla., 1954; postgrad. Columbia U. Tchrs. Coll., 1955-56; Ed.D., U. Ky., 1971; postgrad. N.Y. U., 1971; m. Bette Irwin Belle, Apr. 16, 1949; 1 dau., Melinda. Tchr., Wyoming Park Sch., Ocala, Fla., 1952-53; instr. Asbury Coll., Wilmore, Ky., 1953-57; asst. prof. Pasadena (Calif.) Coll., 1957-60, Rollins Coll., Winter Park, Fla., 1960-61; tchr. Teaneck (N.J.) pub. schs., 1961-72, curriculum coordinator, 1963-64, dir. of elem. edn., 1964-72; asst. supt. Plainfield (N.J.) pub. schs., 1972-75; supt. schs. North Penn Sch. Dist., Lansdale, Pa., 1975—; pres. Internat. Reading Found., Washington, 1971-72; pres. N.J. Curriculum Workers Council, 1973-74; dir. various workshops in edn., guest speaker various colls. and univs., 1964—. Mem. adv. bd. Salvation Army, Norristown, Pa., 1978—, United Way, 1978; Sunday sch. tchr. United Methodist Ch., Panama City, Fla., 1946-49; bd. dirs. Am. Cancer Soc., 1977—. Served with USN, 1944-46. Danforth Found. fellow, 1957-58; Kettering fellow, 1978. Mem. NEA (life), Am. Assn. Sch. Adminstrs., Nat. Council Tchrs. English, Internat. Reading Assn., Nat. Council Tchrs. Social Studies, Assn. for Supervision and Curriculum Devel., Phi Delta Kappa. Contbr. articles on teaching to profl. jours. Home: 101E Valley Stream Apts Line St Lansdale PA 19446 Office: North Penn Sch Dist 400 Penn St Lansdale PA 19446

KELLY, ROBERT LYNN, advt. agy. exec.; b. Chgo., Oct. 25, 1939; s. Carl Robert and Annabel Pauline (Lindsay) K.; B.A., Gettysburg Coll., 1961; m. Maria Graciela Gonzalez, Oct. 26, 1963; children—Albert E., Elizabeth A. Dir. pub. info. Oxnard AFB, Calif., 1961-64; with Armstrong Cork Co., Lancaster, Pa., 1964-67; owner Bob Kelly Advt., Quito, Ecuador, S. Am., 1967-70; partner, writer, account exec., mgr. Ibold & Kelly Advt., Lancaster, 1970-72; founder, pres. Kelly Advt., Inc., Lancaster, 1972—; guest lectr. F & M Coll., 1971—; lectr. Lancaster Community Gallery, 1977—. Active various civic orgns.; bd. dirs. Lancaster Community Gallery, 1978—; mem. campaign coms., Lancaster County Rep. orgns., 1973—; bd. dirs. Rockford Plantation, 1979—. Served with USAF, 1961-64. Mem. Nat. Advt. Agy. Network, N.G. Assn. U.S., Sales and Mktg. Execs. Presbyterian. Clubs: Susquehanna Yacht, Kiwanis. Contbr. articles in field to profl. jours. Home: 1112 Wheatland Ave Lancaster PA 17603 Office: 416 W Marion St Lancaster PA 17603

KELLY, ROBERT WILLIAM, govt. ofcl.; b. Washington, June 11, 1939; s. Robert Joseph and Emily Thersa (Markiewicz) K.; B.A., U. Wyo., 1963; M.A., U. Pitts., 1965; m. Lily Hsui, Dec. 28, 1966. With Dept. State, Saigon, Bangkok and Washington, 1965-72; dir. policy group food controls Cost of Living Council, Washington, 1973-74; policy adviser to dep. adminstr. Fed. Energy Adminstrn., 1974-75; dir. planning and analysis, Office Commercialization ERDA, 1975-76, dir. commercialization studies and policy adviser, 1976-77; dir. policy analysis Office Energy Resources, Dept. Energy, 1977—; mem. faculty U. Kans., 1968-69, George Mason campus U. Va., 1971-72. Served with USMCR, 1958-60. Ford fellow, 1963-64; recipient certificate of achievement Fed. Energy Adminstrn., 1974. Mem. Am. Econs. Assn., Assn. Energy Economists, Omicron Delta Kappa. Roman Catholic. Author Articles, papers. Home: 8309 Bella Vista Terr Oxon Hill MD 20022 Office: 20 Massachusetts Ave NW Washington DC 20545

KELLY, STEPHEN JOHN, criminologist; b. Waterbury, Conn., Nov. 5, 1931; s. Stephen John and Catherine Mary (Delaney) K.; B.S.S., Fairfield (Conn.) U., 1958, M.A., 1967; postgrad. Fordham. U.; m. Marilyn Irene Dunn, Sept. 5, 1955; children—Barbara, Stephen IV, Cynthia, Sherilyn, Linda, Stacy. Police officer, Waterbury, 1953-58; tchr., then counselor Conn. high schs., 1958-61, 62-73; social worker, Waterbury, 1961-62; dir. tng. Conn. Police Acad., Meriden, 1973—; mem. law enforcement evaluation team Middlesex C. of C. and Manchester C. of C., 1978-79; mem. pub. safety adv. com. Central Conn. State Coll., 1978—; cons. in field. Chmn. Wolcott (Conn.) Conservation Commn., 1972-74; mem. Town of Wolcott Park and Recreation Commn., 1968-72; mem. social action com. St. Pius X Roman Catholic Parish Council, Wolcott, 1973-77; adviser Heal Our Present Environment Com., 1972-74. Served with AUS, 1951-52. NSF grantee, 1963, 67; recipient Alumni Service award Fairfield U., 1974; Distinguished Service award Waterbury Jaycees, 1959. Life mem. NEA, Nat. Sci. Tchrs. Assn.; mem. Am. Assn. Profl. Police, Conn. Personnel and Guidance Assn., Conn. Assn. Criminal Justice Scis., Conn. Assn. Police/Community Relations Officers. Home: 44 Woodward Dr Wolcott CT 06716 Office: 285 Preston Ave Meriden CT 06450

KELLY, THOMAS CAJETAN, clergyman; b. Rochester, N.Y., July 14, 1931; s. Thomas A. and Katherine E. (Fisher) K.; A.B., Providence Coll., 1953; L.S.T., Pontifical Faculty of Immaculate Conception, Washington, 1959; D.C.L., U. St. Thomas, Rome, 1962. Joined Dominican Order, Roman Cath. Ch., 1951, ordained priest, 1958; sec. to Dominican Provincial, N.Y.C., 1962-65, to Apostolic del., 1965-71; asso. gen. sec. Nat. Conf. Cath. Bishops, Washington, 1971-77, gen. sec., 1977—; aux. bishop of Washington, 1977—. Author articles. Address: 4001 14th St NE Washington DC 20017

KELLY, WALTER JOSLYN, bus. services co. exec.; b. N.Y.C., Apr. 22, 1946; s. Richard Francis and Eileen J. K.; A.A., Pace U., N.Y.C., 1963; m. Linda Bishop, Oct. 27, 1973; 1 dau., Heather L. Founder Kelly & Haigney Advt. Co., Riverside, Conn., 1967-70, Kelly Advt., 1970—; v.p., dir. Richard F. Kelly Co. Inc., Riverside, 1972—; v.p., dir. R.F.K. Internat. Disc. Corp., Riverside, 1974—; cons. in field. Mem. Am. Mgmt. Assn., Am. Mktg. Assn., Am. Equipment Distbrs., New Eng. Export Mgmt. Cos., Profl. Horsemen's Assn. Club: World Trade (N.Y.C.). Office: Richard F Kelly Co Inc PO Box 4330 Greenwich CT 06830

KELLY, WILLIAM (EAGER), psychoanalyst; b. Nashville, Mar. 17, 1914; s. Charles Peck and Alice (Eager) K.; student Antioch Coll., 1932-34; B.S. in Edn., U. Va., 1938, M.D., 1945; m. Martha L. Parks, June 6, 1953; children—Susie Eager, Penelope Ellen, Benjamin Alexander. Intern, Kings County Hosp., Bklyn., 1945-46; resident psychiatrist U. Va. Hosp., 1946, Inst. of Pa. Hosp., Phila., 1948-50; sr. research psychiatrist VA Hosp., Coatesville, Pa., 1950-51; asst. vis. physician Phila. Gen. Hosp., 1951-59; staff psychiatrist Lakeland Mental Hosp., Camden, N.J., 1951-55; practice medicine specializing in psychiatry, Phila., 1951—; mem. staff Jefferson Hosp., 1951-71; sr. attending staff Inst. of Pa. Hosp., 1951-78, pres. staff, 1968-70, cons., 1978—; attending physician VA Hosp., Phila., 1955-66; cons. neuropsychiatrist Graterford Penitentiary, 1954-58; asst. cons. neuropsychiatrist Devereaux Schs., 1956-58; asst. neurologist Wills Eye Hosp., Phila., 1959-71; cons. psychiatry Valley Forge Gen. Hosp., 1965-74; staff psychiatrist Coatesville (Pa.) VA Hosp., 1974-77, dir. profl. edn., 1977—; instr. psychiatry U. Pa. Med. Sch., 1951-54; instr. neurology Jefferson Med. Coll., 1951-71, clin. prof. psychiatry, 1974—; asst. clin. prof. psychiatry Med. Coll. Pa., 1971-74; grad. psychoanalysis Phila. Assn. Psychoanalysis, 1964, mem., 1966—, dir., lectr. extension sch., 1967-73. Served to capt. M.C., AUS, 1946-48. Diplomate Am. Bd. Psychiatry and Neurology. Fellow Am. Psychiat. Assn., Phila. Psychiat. Soc., Phila. Coll. Physicians, A.C.P., Am. Coll. Psychiatrists, Am. Coll. Psychoanalysts; mem. Am. Psychoanalytic Assn., AMA, Union League Phila., Internat. Psychoanalytic Assn. Home: 159 Woodgate Ln Paoli PA 19301 Office: 30 S Valley Rd Paoli PA 19301

KELLY, WILLIAM GERARD, banker; b. Waltham, Mass., July 12, 1950; s. Francis Joseph and Eleanor Eileen (Hayes) K.; B.S. in Mktg., Northeastern U., Boston, 1973; m. Mary Beth Dalton, Sept. 16, 1972. Mgr. mktg. Newton Waltham Bank & Trust Co., 1974; mktg. officer, pub. relations officer N. Conway Bank (N.H.), 1974—. Treas. N. Conway Vis. Nurse Assn., Eastern N.H. Hwy. Assn.; chmn. Volvo Internat. Tennis Tournament; bd. dirs. Mt. Washington Valley Repertory Theatre; chmn. fund raising com. Home Health Agy., N. Conway Meml. Hosp. Mem. New Eng. Bank Mktg. Assn., N.H. Bankers Assn., Mt. Washington Valley Jaycees (charter). Democrat. Roman Catholic. Club: Lions. Home: Woodland Dr North Conway NH 03860 Office: 240 Main St North Conway NH 03860

KELMAN, WOLFE, rabbi; b. Vienna, Austria, Nov. 27, 1923; s. Hersh Leib and Mirl (Fish) K.; B.A., U. Toronto (Ont., Can.), 1946; M.H.L., Jewish Theol. Sem. Am., 1950, D.D. (hon.), 1973; m. Jacqueline Levy, Mar. 2, 1952; children—Levi Yehuda, Naamah Kathrine, Abigail Tobie. Came to U.S., 1946, naturalized, 1962. Rabbi various congregations; vis. rabbi West London Congregation Brit. Jews, London, Eng., 1957-58; exec. v.p. Rabbinical Assembly, 1951-; dir. joint placement commn. Rabbinical Assembly, United Synagogue Am. and Jewish Theol. Sem. Am., 1951-66; vis. prof. homiletics Jewish Theol. Sem. Am., 1966-73, adj. asst. prof. history, 1973—. Mem. governing council World Jewish Congress, 1968-, chmn. cultural commn., 1975—. Pres. Com. Neighbors Concerned for Elderly, Their Rights and Needs, 1971—; bd. dirs., exec. com. Hebrew Immigrant Aid Soc., 1974—. Served with RCAF, 1943-45. Home: 845 West End Ave New York NY 10025 Office: 3080 Broadway New York NY 10027

KELMENSON, LEO ARTHUR, advt. exec.; b. N.Y.C., Jan. 3, 1925; s. Joseph A. and Ruth (Rothberg) K.; B.S., Columbia, 1951, postgrad. Grad. Sch. Bus., 1952; div.; children—Todd-Arthur, Joel Adam; m. Barbara Dauphin, Feb. 20, 1973. From TV prodn. to sr. v.p.; asst. to pres. Lennen & Newell, 1951-65; exec. v.p., mem. exec. com. Norman Craig & Kummel, 1965-66; sr. v.p., dir. mem. exec. com. 1968—; pres., chief exec. officer, chmn. exec. com. Kenyon & Eckhardt 1967-68; pres. Kenyon & Eckhardt Advt. Inc., 1968—; pres., chief exec. officer, chmn. exec. com. Kenyon & Eckhardt Inc., C.P.V., 1970—; pres. Kelmerson Funds Ltd.; dir. Locations Unltd.; lectr. New Sch. Social Research. Adviser communications office U.S. Atty. Gen., 1960-63; spl. project officer Dept. State, 1952-64; v.p., bd. dirs. African Med. and Research Found., 1957—, Am. Soc. Prevention Cruelty to Animals, 1976—; mem. pres.'s adv. council Am. Diabetes Assn., 1976—; adv. com. Nat. Cultural Center, 1962; pres. Shoes for Little Souls, 1960, Remsenburg Assn., 1968. Served with USMCR, 1942-46. Recipient Theodore Roosevelt Man of Year award, 1955; Silver Quill Poetry award 1955; Res. Officers Assn. award, 1965; Guggenheim World Peace award, 1951. Mem. U.S. Olympic Com., N.Y. Advt. Club, Soc. Am. Businessmen Club, Sigma Phi Epsilon. Clubs: Sands Point (N.Y.) Yacht; L.I. Polo. Author: (poetry) Epilogue, 1964; aslo short stories. Office: 200 Park Ave New York City NY 10017

KELSEY, CHESTER CREED, engring. co. exec.; b. Floral Park, N.Y., Apr. 19, 1929; s. Chester W. and Dorothy (Forman) K.; B.C.E., Coll. City N.Y., 1955; m. Wilma Joan Zeiss, Feb. 15, 1953; children—Scott, Glenn, Gregg, Lynn. Draftsman, Sidney B. Bowne & Son, Mineola, N.Y., 1955-56, design engr., 1957-61, supervising engr., 1961-64, asso. mem., 1961-64, partner, 1964—. Counselor, Jr. Methodist Youth Fellowship, 1969-71; mem. parents group Boy Scouts Am., 1970-71; asso. committeeman Nassau County Republican Com., 1965—. Served with U.S. Army, 1951-53. Recipient Chpt. Distinguished Service award Nassau chpt. N.Y. State Soc. Profl. Engrs., 1977; named N.Y. State Engr. of Year, 1977; registered profl. engr. and land surveyor, N.Y. Fellow ASCE; mem. Nat. (nat. dir. 1974-78, chmn. profl. engr. com. 1976-78), N.Y. State (pres. Nassau chpt. 1969-71, state pres. 1976) socs. profl. engrs., Am. Arbitration Assn. (arbitrator 1966—), N.Y. State Assn. Professions (v.p.), Cons. Engrs. Council, N.Y. Profl. Engrs. in Pvt. Practice (chmn. 1977—). Clubs: Masons; L.I. Old Car; Arrowhead Hunting (Narrowsburg, N.Y.). Editor, gen. mgr. N.Y. Profl. Engr., 1971-76. Home: 2379 Elk Ct North Bellmore NY 11710 Office: 161 Willis Ave Mineola NY 11501

KELSEY, ROGER RAYMOND, educator; b. Northfield, Minn., May 1, 1912; s. Raymond D. and Elizabeth (Walsingham) K.; student Carleton Coll., 1930-31; B.A., St. Olaf Coll., 1934; M.A., U. Minn., 1940; Ed.D., George-Peabody Coll. for Tchrs., 1954; postgrad. Wash. State U., 1950-52; m. Berniece Cary, Mar. 23, 1940; 1 son, Richard Irving (dec.). Tchr. pub. high schs., S.D. and Minn., 1934-41; instr. St. Olaf Coll., 1941-42; registrar Deluth Jr. Coll., 1946-48, dean, 1948-50; pres. Grays Harbor Coll., 1952-53; registrar Kans. State Tchrs. Coll., 1954-60, asso. prof. psychology, 1954-57, prof. edn., 1958-60; ednl. research ICA, Korea, 1957-58; lectr. higher edn. U. Md., 1960-63, asso. prof. higher edn., 1964—. Served to lt. USNR, 1942-46. Mem. NEA, Am. Assn. Jr. Colls., Am. Ednl. Research Assn., Nat. Soc. Study Edn., Am. Assn. for Higher Edn., Phi Delta Kappa, Kappa Delta Pi. Author: A.A.H.E. Bibliography on Higher Education, 1964-72; A Bibliography On Higher Education, 1969; contbr. articles to profl. jours. Home: 700 Ludlow St Takoma Park MD 20012 Office: U Md College Park MD 20740

KELSO, TIMOTHY EDWARD, transp. regulatory cons.; b. Portland, Oreg., Feb. 1, 1947; s. Earl and Vivian Ione (Ingham) K.; B.A. in Geography, Wash. State U., 1970. Traffic and sales Pacific Far East Line, San Francisco, 1970-74; dir. pricing, dir. markets, asst. to pres. Fesco Pacific Line (U.S.A.), Inc., Moram Agencies, Clark, N.J., 1974-78; asst. v.p. Internat. Tariff Services, Inc., Washington, 1978—; practitioner Fed. Maritime Commn. Home: 2636 S West St Falls Church VA 22046 Office: 815 15th St NW Washington DC 20005

KELTING, HOWARD WILLIAM, securities co. exec.; b. Bklyn., Feb. 11, 1938; s. Howard William and Ann (Gilroy) K.; A.B., Yale, 1959; postgrad. N.Y. U., 1959-61; m. Mary Whitney Peters, Apr. 4, 1959 (div. Oct. 1972); children—Anne, Jeannette, Mary Whitney. Gen. partner Stuart Bros., N.Y.C., 1966-73; v.p. Mitchell Hutchins, N.Y.C., 1973-77; sr. v.p. Scandinavian Securities Corp., N.Y.C., 1977—. Home: 52 W 9th St New York City NY 10011 Office: 125 Broad St New York City NY 10004

KELTON, JOHN T(REMAIN), lawyer; b. Bay City, Mich., Mar. 12, 1909; s. Frank P.S. and Jessie (Eleanor Tremain) K.; student Culver (Ind.) Mil. Acad., 1925-28; S.B. in Chem. Engring., Mass. Inst. Tech., 1932; LL.B., Harvard, 1935; m. Carol E. Copeland, July 9, 1935; children—Carol E.M., Joy T. Admitted to N.Y. bar, 1935; practiced patent law as asso. and mem. firm Watson, Bristol, Johnson & Leavenworth, N.Y.C., 1935-40, 46-49; mem. firm Watson Johnson Leavenworth & Blair, 1950-53, Watson Leavenworth Kelton & Taggart, 1954—. Served from 2d lt. to lt. col. AUS, 1940-46. Mem. Assn. Bar City N.Y., N.Y. Patent Law Assn. (president 1967), Am. Patent Law Assn. (pres. 1973-74). Conglist. Clubs: Harvard, Chemists, Union League. Home: Nutmeg Ln Westport CT 06880 Office: 100 Park Ave New York City NY 10017

KEM, JAN ALAN, cons. environmental engr.; b. Richmond, Ind., Mar. 10, 1939; s. Charles Edward and Janice Allene (Beard) K.; A.B., Earlham Coll., 1962; B.C.E., Rensselaer Poly. Inst., 1962, M.S., 1963; postgrad. U. Ill., 1963-64; m. Shirley Elaine Dean, May 1, 1965; children—Elaine Sue, Burt Alan, Andrew Charles. Project engr. Stearns & Wheler, cons. engrs., Cazenovia, N.Y., 1964-67; project mgr. Roy F. Weston, Inc., environmental scientists and engrs., West Chester, Pa., 1967-71; dir. environmental engrs. Harnish & Lookup Assos., engrs. and land surveyors, Newark, N.Y., 1971-76; prin. Jan A. Kem, civil and environ. engring., Newark, N.Y., 1976—. Vice pres. Kem Realty Corp., Richmond, Ind., 1969-72. Mem. Newark Village Municipal Bd., 1978—. Mem. ASCE, N.Y. Water Pollution Control Assn., Am. Water Works Assn., Am. Acad. Environ. Engrs. (diplomate). Presbyn. (trustee). Mason. Clubs: Rotary, Newark Rod and Gun. Home: RD 3 Box 379B Newark NY 14513 Office: 203 W Miller St Newark NY 14513

KEMBLE, RICHARD, artist, sculptor, printmaker; b. Erie, Pa., Nov. 7, 1932; s. Arthur H. and Bessie Maude (Dunthorne) K.; B.A., Trenton State Coll., 1972. Instr., U. Buffalo (N.Y.), 1957-63; adj. asst. prof. Pratt Inst., Bklyn., 1965—; one-man shows include: Allentown (Pa.) Art Mus., 1976, Gallery Daberkow, Frankfurt, Germany, 1976, Pratt Inst., Bklyn., 1971, Charles and Emmas Frye Mus., Seattle, 1976, Sombol Gallery, Guatamala City, 1975, Internat. Print Soc., New Hope, Pa., 1978, Suzuki Gallery, N.Y.C., 1977, numerous libraries and univs.; represented in permanent collections N.J. State Mus., Trenton, Allentown Art Mus., Mus. Modern Art, Sao Paulo, Brazil, Free Library, Phila., Kresge Art Center, Mich. State U., Princeton U., Morris Mus. Arts and Scis., Trenton State Coll. Library, also various corp. collections including IBM, Eastern Airlines, Deutsche Bank, Frankfurt, Germany, McGraw Hill Pub. Co., artist in residence N.J. State Council Arts. Served with USAF, 1952-57. Nat. Endowment Arts Printmakers fellow, 1974-75. Mem. Artist Equity, Am. Color Print Soc., Pratt Graphic Center, Mus. Contemporary Crafts, Mus. Modern Art, DeYoung Mus. Author: The Quiet Forest, 1977. Home: Box 82 Washington Crossing PA 18977 Office: DeKalb Hall Pratt Inst Brooklyn NY 10025

KEMBLE, ROBERT PENN, psychiatrist; b. Mt. Carmel, Pa., May 31, 1905; s. William Penn and Bertha Doty (Miller) K.; A.B., Princeton, 1927; B.S., Susquehanna U., 1929; M.D., Jefferson Med. Coll., 1933; m. Luella Robinson North, Dec. 26, 1936; children—Sarah, Penn, Eugenia, Grover. Intern, Pa. Hosp., Phila., 1933-35; resident Payne Whitney Clinic N.Y. Hosp., N.Y.C., 1936-37; dir. Worcester (Mass.) Child Guidance Clinic, 1939-41; psychiatrist various guidance clinics, Pa., 1946-55; dir. York County (Pa.) Mental Health Clinic, 1956-57, Morris County (N.J.) Guidance Center, 1958-66; psychiatrist Mt. Holyoke Coll., 1966-70; child psychiatrist Holyoke Area Mental Health Center and Franklin County (Mass.) Mental Health Center, 1967-73; chief mental hygiene clinic Northampton (Mass.) VA Hosp., 1973—; exec. dir. Psychiat. Outpatient Centers Am., 1961-64, dir., 1972—. Served to maj., M.C., AUS, 1941-45. Diplomate Am. Bd. Psychiatry and Neurology. Mem. Otto Rank Assn. (dir.), N.J. Assn. Guidance Clinics (past pres.), Western Mass. (past pres.), Am. psychiat. assns., AMA, AAAS, Am. Orthopsychiat. Assn., Am. Acad. Child Psychiatrists, Alpha Omega Alpha. Methodist. Club: Masons (Mt. Carmel). Contbr. articles in field to profl. jours. Home: 24 Brock Way South Hadley MA 01075 Office: VA Hosp Northampton MA 01060

KEMELHOR, ROBERT ELIAS, mech. engr.; b. N.Y.C., May 19, 1919; s. Louis and Rebecca (Edelson) K.; B.S. in Mech. Engring., George Washington U., 1949; m. Shirley P. Tennen, June 28, 1947; children—Judith Ellen, Joel Martin, Barry Alan. Sr. engr. Navy Dept. Bur. Ships, Ordnance and Aeros., Washington, 1939-52; chief engr. McLean Devel. Labs., Copiague, N.Y., 1952-57; dir. research and devel. Pesco div. Borg Warner Corp., Cleve., 1957-58; prin. profl. staff Johns Hopkins U. Applied Physics Lab., Laurel, Md., 1958—. Cons. Thompson-Ramo-Wooldridge, Aerojet Gen., others. Served with USNR, 1943-46. Fellow Am. Inst. Aeros. and Astronautics (Asso.); mem. ASME, Sigma Tau., Tau Beta Pi. Patentee in field. Home: 6211 Redwing Ct Bethesda MD 20034 Office: APL/JHU Johns Hopkins Rd Laurel MD 20810

KEMENY, JOHN GEORGE, coll. pres.; b. Budapest, Hungary, May 31, 1926; s. Tibor and Lucy (Fried) K.; B.A., Princeton, 1947, Ph.D., 1949, LL.D., 1971; D.Sc. (hon.), Middlebury Coll., 1965; LL.D., U. N.H., 1972; m. Jean Alexander, Nov. 5, 1950; children—Jennifer M., Robert A. Came to U.S., 1940, naturalized, 1945. Asst. theoretical div. Los Alamos Project, 1945-46; asst. in teaching and research Princeton U., 1946-48, Fine instr. and Office Naval Research fellow math., 1949-51, asst. prof. philosophy, 1951-53; research asst. to Dr. Albert Einstein Inst. for Advanced Study, 1948-49; prof. math Dartmouth Coll., 1953-70, chmn. math. dept., 1955-67, Albert Bradley 3d Century prof., 1969-72, adj. prof. math. 1972—; coordinator ednl. plans and devel., 1967-70, pres., 1970—; cons. Rand Corp., Santa Monica, Calif., 1953-70. Chmn. U.S. Commn. on Math. Instrn. 1958-60; mem. NRC, 1963-66; lectr., Austria, Israel, India, Japan, 1964-65. Mem. Hanover (N.H.) Sch. Bd., 1961-64; mem. Nat. Commn. on Libraries and Information Sci., 1971—; Health, Edn. and Welfare Regional Dir.'s Adv. Com., 1971—. N.H. state chmn. United Negro Coll. Fund, 1972—. Trustee Found. Center, Carnegie Found. for Advancement of Teaching. Served with AUS, 1945-46. Mem. Assn. for Symbolic Logic. Math. Assn. Am. (chmn. New Eng. sect. 1959-60, mem. bd. govs. 1960-63, chmn. panel biol. and social scis. 1963-64), Am. Math. Soc., Am. Philos. Assn. Phi Beta Kappa, Sigma Xi (nat. lectr. 1967). Author: A Philosopher Looks at Science; Random Essays; Man and the Computer, 1972. Co-author: Introduction to Finite Mathematics; Finite Mathematical Structures; Finite Markov Chains; Mathematical Models in the Social Sciences; Finite Mathematics with Business Applications: Denumerable Markov Chains; Basic Programming, 1967; The Computer Language Basic. Cons. editor jour. Symbolic Logic, 1950-59; asso. editor Jour. Math. Analysis and Applications. Contbr. to Ency. Brit., articles to profl. jours. Home: 1 Tuck Dr Hanover NH 03755

KEMLER, RAPHAEL LEONARD, cardiovascular and thoracic surgeon; b. Hartford, Conn., Oct. 24, 1918; s. Louis Elliot and Esther (Wedeen) K.; B.A., Yale U., 1939, M.D., 1943; m. Joan Rosen, Dec. 28, 1950; children—David, Louise. Intern in surgery Barnes Hosp., St. Louis, 1943-44, resident gen. surgery, 1944-45, 47, thoracic surgery, 1947-48, fellow thoracic surgery, 1948-49; individual practice medicine, specializing in cardiovascular and thoracic surgery, Hartford, 1950—; asst. surgery Washington U., St. Louis, 1944-47, asst. thoracic surgery, 1947-49; asst. clin. prof. surgery U. Conn., Farmington, 1973—; active staff attending thoracic surgeon New Britain (Conn.) Gen. Hosp.; asso. attending thoracic and cardiovascular surgeon Hartford Hosp., attending thoracic surgeon Mt. Sinai Hosp., Hartford, 1950—, dir. cardiovascular, thoracic surgery, 1975—; cons. thoracic surgery various hosps. Pres. Emanuel Synagogue, Hartford, 1970-72, also bd. dirs.; bd. dirs. Greater Hartford Community Council, 1975-77, Greater Hartford Jewish Fedn., 1977—, Hartford chpt. Am. Heart Assn. 1958-63, Hartford County Lung Assn., 1959-65. Served as lt. (j.g.), USNR, 1945-46. Diplomate Am. Bd. Surgery, Am. Bd. Thoracic Surgery. Mem. Hartford (pres. 1970-71), Conn. med. socs., Conn. (pres. 1971-72), Am. thoracic socs., AMA, Am. Assn. Thoracic Surgery; fellow Am. Coll. Chest Physicians, Am. Coll. Cardiology, Am. Coll. Angiology. Democrat. Club: Tumble Brook Country. Home: 65 Norwood Rd West Hartford CT 06117 Office: 21 Woodland St Hartford CT 06105

KEMP, DARRYL RUSSELL, ednl. adminstr.; b. Washington, Dec. 23, 1946; s. Elmer Thomas and Louise Russell (Allen) K.; B.A. in Sociology, Va. Union U., 1969; postgrad. D.C. Tchrs. Coll., 1970-75, Am. U., 1975-76, Nat. Grad. U., 1977—; m. Sandra Rose Morris, Nov. 24, 1976. Tchr., D.C. Pub. Sch., Washington, 1969-74; instr. Opportunities Industrialization Center, Washington, 1974-75, coordinator community corrections program, 1975-76, supr. correctional edn., 1976-77, vocat. guidance specialist, 1977—; founder, pres. Effective Communications Corp., 1978—. Mem. Adult Edn. Assn., Am. Correctional Assn., Am. Personnel and Guidance Assn., Am. Vocat. Assn., Inc., Correctional Edn. Assn., Human Service Personnel Assn., Internat. Halfway House Assn., NEA, Nat. Rehab. Counseling Assn., Washington Area Council Alcoholism and Drug Abuse, Washington Halfway Home for Women (dir. 1977-78). Home: 4410 20th St NE Washington DC 20018

KEMP, JACK F., congressman; b. Los Angeles, July 13, 1935; B.A., Occidental Coll., 1957; postgrad. Long Beach State U., Calif. Western U.; m. Joanne Main; children—Jeffrey, Jennifer, Judith, James. Spl. asst. to gov. of Calif., 1969; mem. 92d-96th Congresses from 38th Dist. N.Y.; former profl. football player for 13 years; pub. relations officer Marine Midland Bank of Buffalo. Named Outstanding Young Man of Year, Buffalo Jr. C. of C.; recipient Distinguished Service award N.Y. State Jaycees; Outstanding Citizens award Buffalo Evening News. Mem. Nat. Assn. Broadcasters, Engrs. and Technicians, Buffalo Area C. of C., Sierra Club, Pres.'s Council on Phys. Fitness and Sports, Am. Football League Players Assn. (cofounder and pres. 1965-70), Nat. Football League Players Assn. (exec. com. and player pension bd.). Republican. Address: House of Reps Washington DC 20515*

KEMP, JOHN BARTLETT, III, investment banker; b. Jacksonville, Fla., Apr. 3, 1942; s. John B. and Barbara Lamb (Kammire) K.; B.A., U. Colo., 1965; m. Kathleen Rosemary Kane, Sept. 20, 1969; children—Kristin Anne, Linsey Elizabeth. Registered rep. Dean Witter, Paramus, N.J., 1967-74, asso. v.p., sales mgr. Dean Witter, 1974-77, v.p., br. mgr., N.Y.C., 1977-78, 1st v.p., nat. sales mgr. corp. bonds Dean Witter Reynolds, N.Y.C., 1978--; dir. Provident Savs. Bank, Jersey City. Served with AUS, 1965-67. Named 1975 Wall Street's Top Ten Brokers. Mem. Bond Club N.J., Phi Delta Theta. Republican. Presbyn. Clubs: The Exchange of Ridgewood, Arcola Country, Brookside Racquet. Home: 234 Phelps Rd Ridgewood NJ 07450 Office: 130 Liberty St New York City NY 10006

KEMPER, ALBERT GILBERT, univ. ofcl.; b. Balt., Aug. 21, 1927; s. Henry Theodore and Evelyn Marie K.; student Holy Cross Sch., 1933-42. With Balt. & Ohio R.R. Co., 1944-46, Bur. Transp., City of Balt., 1946-50, Oscar T. Smith Co., Balt., 1956-67, Schenuit Rubber Co., Balt., 1967-70; supply officer sci. dept. Towson (Md.) State U., 1971—. Vol. VA Hosps., 1973—. Served with U.S. Army, 1950-57. Recipient certificate of merit VFW, 1974. Mem. Mil. Order of Cootie, VFW, Am. Mgmt. Assn. Democrat. Roman Catholic. Home: 402 E Fort Ave Baltimore MD 21230 Office: Towson State U Smith Hall Receiving Baltimore MD 21204

KEMPNER, CARL LOEB, stock broker; b. Pitts., Dec. 29, 1923; s. Alan Horace and Margaret Adeline (Loeb) K.; grad. Choate Sch., Wallingford, Conn., 1941; student Harvard, 1941-42; student N.Y. Inst. Finance, also N.Y. U.; m. Doris Cecile Coleman, July 10, 1947; children—Kathryn Margaret, Margaret Adeline, Carl Loeb, Michael Coleman. Partner, Coleman & Co., 1948-59; with instl. dept. L.F. Rothschild & Co., N.Y.C., 1959-66; sr. partner Hamsershlag, Kempner & Marks, N.Y.C., 1966—. Chmn., Small Firms Adv. Com.; pres. bd. trustees Rectory Sch., Pomfret, Conn.; trustee Choate Sch., Wallingford, Conn.; treas. Choate-Rosemary Hall. Served as lt. (j.g.) USNR, 1943-46. Clubs: Century Country (Purchase, N.Y.); Bankers, N.Y. Stock Exchange, Madison Square Garden (N.Y.C.); Duchess Valley. Home: 800 North St White Plains NY 10605 Office: 140 Broadway New York City NY 10004

KEMPNER, ROBERT MAX WASILII, internat. lawyer, polit. scientist; b. Freiburg, Germany, Oct. 17, 1899; s. Walter K. and Lydia (Rabinowitsch) K.; student of law, polit. sci., pub. adminstrn., criminol., univs. of Berlin, Freiburg, Breslau (Dr. of Law and Public Adminstrn.); student U. of Pa.; m. Ruth Lydia Hahn; children—Lucian Walter and Andre Franklin. Naturalized U.S. citizen. Asst. to state atty., 1926; judge municipal ct., 1927; superior govt. counselor, Ministry of the Interior, Berlin (chief legal adviser of Prussian police system of 76,000 men; (recommended suppression of Nazi party and prosecution of Hitler for high treason and perjury, 1930, later expatriated by Hitler); lectr. German Acad. Politics, Sch. Social Work, Police Inst., Berlin, 1926-33; counselor migration problems, 1934-35. Pres. and prof. polit. sci., Fiorenza Coll., Florence, Italy, and Nice, France, 1936-39; research asso. inst. Local and State Govt., U. of Pa. (on machinery of European dictatorships under Carnegie and Carl Schurz grants), 1939-42; expert cons. to Fed. courts, Dept. of Justice, OSS and to sec. of War on legal, polit., police and intelligence techniques of European dictatorships and fgn. orgns. in U.S., 1942-45; U.S. staff prosecutor in Nuremberg trials against Goering, Frick et al, research dir. U.S. prosecution, 1945-46; dep. U.S. chief of counsel and chief prosecutor of German Reich cabinet members, state sec. and diplomats, Nuremberg, 1946-49. Research on German-Russian relations and annihilation of European Jewry. Vis. prof. law and polit. sci. Erlanger U., 1946-48; U.S. rep. at Inst. of Publ. Affairs, Frankfurt, 1949; in charge of Exchange Civil Servants for the Am. Council on Edn., 1950; cons. fgn. claims, internat. law and fgn. relations, trying internat. law cases and prosecuting Nazi war criminals in Germany, 1951—; lectr. univs. Pa., Mich., Wis., Columbia, Heidelberg, U.S. Mil. Acad., federal officials, civic assns.; also in France and Switzerland, on fgn. relations. Hitler's plans against the Cath. Ch.; secrets of World War II, internat. law in various European cities; German-Soviet relations, and Near Eastern affairs; founder first anti-Nazi German lang. radio program in U.S., 1942. Decorated Order Polonia Restituta; German Order Merit with Star; recipient medal Charles U., Prague, 1969; Carl von Ossietzky and Wilhelm Leuschner medals, 1975; fellow Jerusalem U., 1970. Mem. Am. Polit. Sci. Assn., Am. Soc. for Internat. Law, German Bar. Author (in German, pub. in Berlin); Prussian Civil Service, 1931; Police Adminstrn. Code, 1933; Twilight of Justice, 1932, 2d edit., 1963; Internal Security (with Drews), 1933; (in U.S.); Blueprint of the Nazi Underground, 1943; The German Nat. Registration System, 1943; Women in Nazi Germany (with Ruth Kempner), 1944; The Judgment in the Wilhelmstrasse Case, 1950; Police Adminstration (in Governing Post-War Germany), 1953; The Case Against Eichmann, 1961; Cross Examination of SS Elite Guards, 1964; Edith Stein and Anne Frank, Two from Hundred-thousand, 1968; The Third Reich under Cross-Examination, 1969; The Murder of 35000 Berlin Jews, 1971; How Hitler Stole the Ullstein Publishing House, 1977. Editor: (German edition) Warren Report. Contbr. Am. Jour. Internat. Law, Am. Polit. Science Review, The Sat. Eve. Post, U. of Pa. Law Rev., Readers Digest, Teaching Foreign Relations, Internat. Law. Comparative Adminstrn. and Govt., Police Techniques, Criminology, Modern European History. Home: 112 Lansdowne Ct Lansdowne PA 19050

KEMPTER, RUDOLPH HARBISON, JR., cost tech. firm exec.; b. St. Albans, Vt., Sept. 5, 1922; s. Rudolph Harbison and Marjorie (Prentiss) K.; B.S. in Engring., U. Notre Dame, 1948; postgrad. in bus. adminstrn. U. Calif. at Berkeley, 1949; m. Margaret Ann Gilkinson, Oct. 15, 1950 (dec. June 1975); children—Carlton J., Bryan C., Paul C. Apprentice engr. Gruman Aircraft Engring. Corp., Bethpage, N.Y., 1942-43; test engr. U.S. Navy Indsl. Plant, Pomona, Calif., 1958-62; rocket devel. engr. Aero-jet Gen. Corp., Azusa, Calif., 1954-57; missile system program mgr. Navy Dept., Washington, 1962-66; dep. dir. value engring. Office Sec. Def., Washington, 1966-70, staff engr. prodn. engring., 1971-73; partner Kempter-Rossman Internat., Washington, 1973—. Staff lectr. Schs. Engring., George Washington U., 1968-74, Va. Poly. Inst., 1969—, Va. Mil. Inst., 1969—, Ill. Inst. Tech., 1974, U. Calif., 1975; doctoral adviser George Washington U. Grad. Sch. Bus. Adminstrn., 1970—. Served with USNR, 1943-46; PTO; 1950-54, Korea. Recipient certificate commendation Asst. Sec. of Def., 1969; certificate of merit for cost reduction achievement U.S. Navy, 1966. Mem. Soc. Am. Value Engrs. (officer), Soc. for Performance Improvement, Am. Soc. Engring. Edn., Sigma Phi. Presbyn. Contbr. numerous articles on tech. mgmt. and value engring. to tech. jours. Home: 1616 Chain Bridge Rd McLean VA 22101 Office: 1625 E St NW Suite 906 Washington DC 20006

KEMSLEY, WILLIAM GEORGE, JR., pub. co. exec.; b. Detroit, Apr. 11, 1928; s. William G., and Verna (Smith) K.; student Columbia, 1948-49; Wayne State U., 1949-52; m. 3d, Marcella Bennis Myers, Sept. 10, 1966; children—Diane Amelia (from previous marraige), Molly O. (adopted), Katie, William George III, Andrew Dae Sung (adopted), Maggie Mi Sook (adopted). Adminstrv. dir. Archives of Am. Art, Detroit, 1958-60; free lance writer, cons., 1961-64; asst. to pres. Detroit Bolt & Nut Co., Detroit, 1960-61; exec. v.p. Corporate Ann. Reports, Inc., N.Y.C., 1964-68; propr. William Kemsley Assos., Inc., N.Y.C., 1968-72, WKA Corporate Graphics, Inc., 1972—; pub. Backpacker mag., N.Y., 1972—. Served with USNR, 1945-46. Mem. Winderness Soc., Nat. Wildlife Fedn., Friends of Earth, Explorers Club, Sierra Club, Audubon Soc., Appalachian Mountain Club, Adirondack Mountain Club, Outdoor Writers Assn., Am. Hiking Soc. (founder, chmn.). Episcopalian. Contbr. articles on travel and sports to mags. and newspapers. Home: 83 Adams St Bedford Hills NY 10507 Office: 65 Adams St Bedford Hills NY 10507

KEMSLEY, WILLIAM GEORGE, SR., edn. and tng. cons.; b. Brandon, Man., Can., May 11, 1908; s. Albert William and Florence Amy (Williams) K.; came to U.S., 1920, naturalized, 1941; student Detroit pub. schs.; m. Verna Smith, June 28, 1927; children—William George, June Lorraine, Brian; m. 2d, Ann Terech, Dec. 28, 1948; children—Michael Albert, Joan Olga. Head labor tng. sect. Productivity and Tech. Assistance div. Marshall Plan, Paris, 1951-54; dir. N.Y. office, UN rep. Internat. Confedn. of Free Trade Unions, 1954-63; propr. Parkhurst Gen. Store, Weston, Vt., 1960-70; dir. New Eng. Trade Union Leadership Tng. Program, U. Mass., 1969-73; propr. Backpacker Books, 1974-76; cons., mem. Vt. State Labor Relations Bd., 1976—; chmn. bd. Backpacker Mag.; pres. The Kemsley Corp. Dir. Vt. Office of Manpower Servies, 1975-76; chmn. Vt. advisory com. U.S. Commn. on Civil Rights. Mem. UAW, Am. Fedn. Tchrs., Vt. Labor Forum (exec. bd.), Nat. Humanities Faculty, Jewish Labor Com. (Vt. vice chmn. New Eng. region), Democratic Socialist Orgn. Com. Unitarian. Home and Office: Missing Link Rd Bellows Falls VT 05101

KENDALL, DONALD MCINTOSH, mfg. co. exec.; b. Sequim, Wash., Mar. 16, 1921; s. Carroll C. and Charlotte (McIntosh) K.; student Western Ky. State Coll.; LL.D., Stetson U., 1971; m. Baroness Sigrid Ruedt von Collenberg, Dec. 22, 1965; children—Donna L., Edward McDonnell, Donald McIntosh, Kent. Pres., chief exec. officer Pepsi-Cola Co., 1963-65 (merger with Frito-Lay 1965), PepsiCo, Inc., 1965-71, chmn. bd., chief exec. officer, 1971—, also dir.; dir. Pan Am. Airways, Atlantic Richfield, Investors Diversified Services Mut. Fund Group. Chmn., Nat. Alliance Businessmen, 1969-70, dir., 1970-78; bd. dirs. Nat. Center for Resource Recovery, Inc., 1970—, chmn., 1970-76; mem. Emergency Com. for Am. Trade, 1969—, chmn., 1969-76; U.S. co-chmn. U.S.-USSR Trade and Econ. Council. Chmn., Am. Ballet Theatre Found. Served to lt. AC, USNR, 1942-47. Mem. Internat. C. of C. (trustee council), C. of C. of U.S. (dir.), Bus. Council. Clubs: Blind Brook, Links, Lyford Cay, River, Round Hill. Home: Porchuck Rd Greenwich CT 06830 Office: PepsiCo Inc Purchase NY 10577

KENDALL, KATHERINE ANNE, social worker; b. Muir-of-Ord, Scotland, Sept. 8, 1910; d. Roderick and Annie Scott (Walker) Tuach; B.A., U. Ill., 1933; M.A., La. State U., 1939; Ph.D., U. Chgo., 1950; m. Willmoore Kendall, June 22, 1935 (div. Apr. 1950). Naturalized, 1940. Asst. prof. Richmond Sch. Social Work, 1941-42; asst. dir. home service A.R.C., 1942-44; lectr. U. Chgo. Sch. Social Service Adminstrn., 1944-45; asst. dir., tng. supr. Inter-Am. and Internat. Tng. Units, U.S. Children's Bur., 1945-47; social affairs officer UN Secretariat, 1947-50; exec. sec. Am. Assn. Schs. Social Work, 1950-52; ednl. sec. Council on Social Work Edn., 1952-58, asso. dir., 1958-63, exec. dir., 1963-66, dir. internat. edn., 1966-71; sec., mem. exec. bd. Internat. Assn. Schs. Social Work, 1954-66, sec.-gen., 1966-78, hon. pres., 1978—, ofcl. non-govtl. rep. UN, 1954—; dir. Internat. Conf. on Social Work Edn., Population and Family Planning, East-West Center Hawaii, 1970—; Carnegie vis. prof. U. Hawaii, 1960-61. Mem. UN Internat. meeting experts on Social Work Tng., Munich, 1956; faculty mem. UN Seminar, Keeru, Finland, 1952; assignment by UN, U.S. Govt. and pvt. orgns. on spl. missions social work edn., Guatemala, 1949, Brazil, 1952, Paraguay, 1954; dir. 1st Seminar for Schs. Social Work in C. Am., 1963; mem. Fulbright Adv. Com. Social Work, 1968-71. Mem. Nat. Assn. Soc. Workers, Nat. Conf. Social Welfare, Internat. Council on Social Welfare, Mortar Bd., Phi Beta Kappa, Chi Omega. Author: (UN reports) International Exchange of Social Welfare Personnel, 1949; Training for Social Work: First International Survey, 1950; Reflections on Social Work 1950-1978; also articles in field. Editor: Social Work Values in an Age of Discontent, 1970; Population Dynamics and Family Planning: A New Responsibility for Social Work Edn., 1971; co-editor: Internat. Social Work. Home: 350 1st Ave New York NY 10010

KENDALL, LEIGH WAKEFIELD, surgeon; b. Brattleboro, Vt., Mar. 8, 1937; s. Irwin Samuel and Laura Eliza (Walbridge) K.; A.B., U. Pa., 1959; M.D., U. Vt., 1963; M.S., U. Ill., 1965; m. Grace Eleanor Fullarton, July 1, 1961; children—William Leigh, Bradley Edward. Intern, U. Ill. Hosp., Chgo., 1963-64, resident in surgery, 1964-69; research fellow Am. Cancer Soc., Chgo.. 1964-65, clin. fellow, 1968-69; practice medicine specializing in gen. surgery, Lancaster, Pa., 1971—; mem. staff St. Joseph, Lancaster Gen. hosps.; instr. surgery U. Ill., Chgo., 1968-69; surg. cons. Franklin & Marshall Coll., Masonic Home, Elizabethtown, Pa. Served to lt. comdr. M.C., USN, 1969-70. Decorated Mil. Honor medal First Class Republic Viet Nam. Diplomate Am. Bd. Surgery. Mem. A.C.S., AMA, Pa. Med. Soc., Warren H. Cole Soc., Pa. Soc. Colon and Rectal Surgery, Am. Cancer Soc. (dir.), Wainwright Tumor Clinic Assn., VFW, Sigma Nu. Republican. Congregationalist. Home: 1314 Quarry Ln Lancaster PA 17603 Office: 822 Marietta Ave Lancaster PA 17603

KENDALL, TERRY LEE, ins. co. exec.; b. Springfield, Mass., Sept. 10, 1946; s. Merle T. and Marion F. Kendall; B.B.A., Western New Eng. Coll., 1968; M.B.A., U. Conn., 1976; m. Joanne Gatti, Jan. 20, 1968; children—Jennifer, Bryan. Sr. accountant Price Waterhouse & Co., Hartford, Conn., 1972-76; dir. investment accounting Conn. Gen. Life Ins. Co., Hartford, 1976, controller investment ops., 1976—. Served with U.S. Army, 1968-72; Vietnam, C.P.A. Mem. Conn. Soc. C.P.A.'s, Am. Inst. C.P.A.'s, Planning Execs. Inst., Am. Mgmt. Assn., Assn. M.B.A. Execs. Republican. Roman Catholic. Home: 10 Meadow Brook Rd Somers CT 06071 Office: Conn Gen Life Ins Co Hartford CT 06152

KENDER, DOROTHY, constrn. co. exec.; b. Bklyn., Feb. 12; d. Emil and Mary (Schenone) Perosio; B.S., Duquesne U., 1950; m. Joseph Kender, Apr. 15, 1948; children—Karen, Scott. Adminstr., Ring Engring., Pitts., 1950-53, Tom Mistick, Inc., Monroeville, Pa., 1953-57; with Bldg. Stone Inst., N.Y.C., 1958—, exec. asst., 1960-75, exec. v.p., 1975—, researcher, producer Stone Catalog, 1962—, Stone Info. Manual, 1974, editor Building Stone News, 1970—; sec. Met. Masonry Council, 1975—. Home: 65 Tappan Landing Tarrytown NY 10591 Office: 420 Lexington Ave New York NY 10017

KENDER, WALTER JOHN, pomologist, educator; b. Camden, N.J., Dec. 20, 1935; s. Walter and Martha K.; B.S., Delaware Valley Coll., 1957; M.S., Rutgers U., 1959, Ph.D., 1962; m. Carole Holm, May 26, 1957; 1 son, David. Asst. prof. horticulture U. Maine, Orono, 1962-66, asso. prof., 1966-69; asso. prof. pomology Cornell U., N.Y. State Agrl. Experiment Sta., Geneva, 1969-75, prof., 1975—, head dept. pomology and viticulture, 1972—, chmn. dept. pomology Cornell U., Ithaca, N.Y., 1975—; co-chmn. task force fruit research N.E. U.S., U.S. Dept. Agr. State Experiment Stas., 1973—. Sec. Internat. Working Group on Juvenility of Woody Plants, 1974—. Distinguished scientist Agrl. U., Wageningen, Netherlands, 1974. Mem. Am. Soc. Hort. Sci. (dir. 1975-76), N.Y. State Fruit Testing Assn. (sec.-treas. 1972—), Am. Pomological Soc., Internat. Soc. Hort. Sci., N.Y. State Hort. Soc., Am. Soc. Enologists, Council for Agrl. Sci. and Tech., Sigma Xi (pres. Geneva 1974-75). Contbg. author: Blueberry Culture, 1966. Contbr. articles to profl. publs. Office: Dept Pomology and Viticulture NY State Agrl Experiment Sta Cornell U Geneva NY 14456

KENDREE, JACK MCLEAN, urban planning cons.; b. Trenton, Mo., Mar. 28, 1926; s. Ulmont Redvers and Mary Margaret (McLean) K.; B.C.E., U. Kans. 1948; M.Arch., Columbia U., 1952; m. Gloria S. Vilaro, May 2, 1953; children—Jack M., Cynthia M., Michael K. Dir. planning and urban renewal City of Ponce (P.R.), 1952-55; cons. city planning and urban renewal, Phila., 1955-72; asst. to pres. Robino-Ladd Co., Wilmington, Del., 1972-73; planning cons., Ft. Washington, Pa., 1974—. Chmn. Bd. Suprs. Whitemarsh Twp. (Pa.), 1965-66. Mem. Am. Soc. Cons. Planners (pres. 1976-78), Nat. Council Profl. Service Firms (dir.), Am. Inst. Planners. Republican. Author publs. in planning and zoning, 1955—. Home: Wedgefield Plantation Route 4 Georgetown SC 29440 Office: PO Box 582 Fort Washington PA 19034

KENNARD, JOHN FREDERICK, pathologist; b. Clearfield, Pa., Mar. 9, 1931; s. Walter B. and Grace A. (McKenrick) K.; B.S., Grove City Coll., 1953; M.D., Jefferson Med. Coll., 1957; m. Janice Gail Matthews, Aug. 11, 1956; children—John Frederick, Paul D., James A., Daniel T. Intern and resident Altoona (Pa.) Hosp., 1957-59; resident and asso. pathologist Grisinger Med. Center, Danville, Pa., 1962-66; pathologist Punxsutawney (Pa.) Hosp., 1968-75; pathologist, dir. lab. Clearfield Hosp., 1966—; cons. pathologist area hosps.; teaching appointee Hershey Med. Sch. Bd. dirs. YMCA; mem. dist. and Eagle Scout Assn., Bucktail council Boy Scouts Am.; pres. Am. Cancer Soc., 1967-69, 75; chpt. pres. ARC, 1975. Served with M.C., USAF, 1959-61. Fellow Am. Cancer Soc., 1962-64, diplomate Am. Bd. Pathology. Mem. AMA, Pa., Clearfield County, Christian med. socs., Coll. Am. Pathologists, Am., Pa. assns. clin. pathologists, Assn. Clin. Scientists, Wainwright Tumor Clinic Assn. Republican. Baptist. Club: Kiwanis. Home: RD 4 TL Box 281 Du Bois PA 15801 Office: PO Box 1088 Clearfield PA 16830

KENNEDY, CHESTER RALPH, JR., assn. exec.; b. Middleboro, Mass., Apr. 22, 1926; s. Chester Ralph and Mary Carmen (Mello) K.; B.F.A., Mass. Coll. Art, 1951; postgrad. New Eng. Adult Edn. Inst., 1959, Boston U., 1966; m. Barbara Ann Partridge, June 27, 1953; children—Karen Brooke, Scott Douglas. Supr. pub. health edn., Mass. Dept. Pub. Health, Boston, 1953-56, coordinator health edn., 1956-74, asst. dir. health edn., 1974—; asst. art dir. Barchét Studios, Middleboro, Mass., 1949-59, art dir., co-owner, Sherborn, Mass., 1959—; cons. USPHS, Assn. State and Territorial Health Officers; lectr., instr. Harvard, Boston U., Mass. Coll.; mem. Academic Master Plan Advisory Commn., Mass. State Coll. System; exhibit chmn. 22d World Health Assembly. Pres. Reach Out, Inc., 1970-74, bd. dirs. 1974—; bd. dirs. Greater Framingham Mental Health Assn., 1974-76; elected to Bd. Health, Sherborn, Mass., 1974—; mem. Solid Waste Recovery Tech. Com., 1975—. Served with USN, 1944-46. Recipient Boy Scouts Am. Organizer award 1941, Commonwealth Mass. Distinguished Service Citation 1971, Health Edn. Citation, New Eng. Consortium fo Health Edn. Assn. 1975; Reach Out award, 1977; certified health officer Commonwealth of Mass. Mem. New Eng. Health Edn. Assn. (pres. 1971-72), New Eng. (prog. com. 1965-76, governing council 1976—), Mass. (health edn. chmn. 1974-76) pub. health assns., Mass. Health Council, New Eng. Health Promotion Council, Soc. Pub. Health Edn. New Eng. Chpt. Clubs: Mass. Audubon, Archeol. Socs., Mass. Coll. Art Alumni (pres. 1968-72), Assn. Mass. State Colls. Alumni (pres. 1973-75). Editor of Commonwealth of Mass. Secretarial Reference Manual, 1969; designer blue ribbon exhibit New Eng. Hosp. Assembly, 1969; designer five pvt. homes. Home: 178 Washington St Sherborn MA 01770 Office: Room 200 600 Washington St Boston MA 02111

KENNEDY, CORNELIUS BRYANT, lawyer; b. Evanston, Ill., Apr. 13, 1921; s. Millard Bryant and Myrna (Anderson) K.; A.B., Yale, 1943; J.D., Harvard, 1948; m. Anne Martha Reynolds, June 20, 1959; children—Anne Talbot, Lauren Asher. Admitted to Ill. bar, 1949, D.C. bar, 1965; practiced in Chgo., 1949-54, 55-59, Washington, 1965—; sr. mem. firm Kennedy & Webster, Washington, 1965—; asst. U.S. atty., Chgo., 1954-55; counsel to minority leader U.S. Senate, Washington, 1959-65. Pub. mem. Adminstrv. Conf. U.S., chmn. com. rule making and pub. info. Trustee St. Johns Child Devel. Center, Washington. Served with USAAF, 1943-46. Fellow Am. Bar Found.; mem. Am. Law Inst., Am. (chmn. adminstrv. law sect.), Fed., Chgo. bar assns. Clubs: Chevy Chase; Gibson Island (Md.); F Street, Metropolitan, Capitol Hill (Washington); Adventurers (Chgo.); Explorers (N.Y.C.). Contbr. articles in field to profl. jours. Home: 7720 Old Georgetown Pike McLean VA 22102 Office: 888 17th St NW Washington DC 20006

KENNEDY, DANIEL G., lawyer; b. Elmira, N.Y., Sept. 29, 1912; s. Daniel J. and Katharine (Landy) K.; A.B., Hamilton Coll., 1934; J.D., Harvard, 1937; m. Nancy Colgan, Sept. 5, 1942; children—Susan E., Daniel, Mary Claire, James O. Admitted to N.Y. State bar; mem. firm Nixon, Hargrave, Devans & Doyle, Rochester, 1954—. Dir. Rochester Gas and Electric Corp., Rochester Community Baseball, Inc. Mem. legal com. Edison Electric Inst.; trustee St. John Fisher Coll. Highland Hosp. Served to lt. col., AUS, 1940-45. Decorated Bronze Star medal. Mem. Am., N.Y. State (v.p. 1975-77), Monroe County, Rochester (pres. 1968) bar assns. Republican. Roman Catholic. Clubs: University (dir. 1959-62), Country. Home: 1450 Clover St Rochester NY 14610 Office: Lincoln First Tower Rochester NY 14603

KENNEDY, DONALD GERRY, ednl. adminstr.; b. Concord, Mass., Feb. 23, 1936; s. Malcolm Gerry and Dorothea Mary (Lassell) K.; A.B., Colby Coll., 1958; M.A. in Teaching, Wesleyan U., 1965; Ed.D., Harvard U., 1977; m. Jean Ann Merrill, Apr. 4, 1959; children—Kimberly Jean, Christie Elizabeth. Tchr., Guilford (Conn.) High Sch., 1964-65, Weston (Mass.) High Sch., 1965-72; asst. supt. schs., Weston, Mass., 1972—; teaching fellow Harvard U., 1972-74. Served as lt. USAF, 1959-63. Decorated Air Force Commendation medal. Mem. Am. Hist. Assn., Pilgrim John Howland Soc. Democrat. Unitarian. Home: 402 North Ave Weston MA 02193 Office: 89 Wellesley St Weston MA 02193

KENNEDY, EDWARD MOORE, U.S. senator; b. Boston, Feb. 22, 1932; s. Joseph Patrick and Rose (Fitzgerald) K.; A.B., Harvard U., 1954; LL.B., U. Va., 1959; m. Virginia Joan Bennett, Nov. 29, 1958; children—Kara Ann, Edward Moore, Patrick Joseph. Admitted to Mass. bar, 1959; asst. dist. atty., Suffolk County, Mass., 1961-62; U.S. senator from Mass., 1962—, asst. majority leader 91st congress, chmn. Com. on Judiciary, 1979—. Pres. Joseph P. Kennedy, Jr. Found. 1961—; trustee Children's Hosp. Med. Center, Boston, Mus. of Sci., Boston, John F. Kennedy Meml. Library, Boston, U., John F. Kennedy Center for Performing Arts, Boston Symphony; bd. visitors Fletcher Sch. Law and Diplomacy, Tufts; mem. corp. Mass. Gen. Hosp., Northeastern U. Served with AUS, 1951-53. Decorated Order of Merit (Italy). Mem. Mass. Trial Lawyers Assn., Am. Legion, V.F.W., Fed. Bar Assn. Club: One Hundred of Mass. Office: US Senate Washington DC 20510

KENNEDY, EVELYN SIEFERT, investment co. exec.; b. Pitts., Nov. 11, 1927; d. Carmine and Assunta (Iacobucci) Rocci; B.S. magna cum laude, U. R.I., 1969, M.S. in Textiles and Clothing, 1970; m. George J. Siefert, May 30, 1953 (div 1974); children—Paul, Carl, Ann Marie; m. 2d, Lyle H. Kennedy, Oct. 12, 1974. Tchr., Pitts. Pub. Schs., 1945-50; with Goodyear Aircraft Corp., Akron, Ohio, 1950-54; clothing instr., dept. adult edn., Groton, Conn., 1958-68; pres. Sewtique, Groton, 1970—; dir. Kennedy Capital Advisers, Groton, 1973, Kennedy Mgmt. Corp., Groton, 1974—, Kennedy Inter Vest, Inc., Groton, 1975—, mem. nat. adv. council SBA, 1976—; clothing cons. U. Conn. Extension, 1975—, instr. continuing edn. for women, 1974—; chmn. Conn. Home Economists in Bus., 1977-79. Bd. dirs. Easter Seal of Southeastern Conn., Child Guidance Clinic of S.E. Conn., League Women Voters. Named Woman of Year Bus. and Profl. Women, 1977. Mem. Conn. Home Econs. Assn. (pres.), Coll. and Univ. Bus. Instrs. Conn. (dir.), Omicron Nu, Phi Kappa Phi. Democrat. Roman Catholic. Home: 7 Mulberry Dr Gales Ferry CT 06335 Office: 1159 Poquonnock Rd Groton CT 06340

KENNEDY, HELEN MARIE, nurse; b. Jersey City, May 3, 1942; d. Paul Joseph and Helen Mary (Murray) K.; R.N. (Hudson County Med. Soc. Women's Aux. Scholar), St. Mary Hosp. Sch. Nursing, Hoboken, N.J., 1962; B.S. in Nursing, Fairleigh Dickinson U., 1971; M.A. in Nursing Service Adminstrn., Tchrs. Coll., Columbia U., 1974. Staff nurse, med.-surg. unit St. Mary Hosp., Hoboken, N.J., 1962, asst. head nurse med.-surg. unit, 1962-63, head nurse unit, 1963-65; asst. sec. Med. Assos. of Hudson County, 1972-75; adminstr. Central Med. Group, P.A., Union City, N.J., 1965-75; dir. nursing service Riverside Gen. Hosp., Secaucus, N.J., 1975-78, asst. adminstr., 1978—. Bd. dirs. Hudson Health Systems Agy., 1976—. Mem. Am., N.J. State nurses assns., Am. Soc. Hosp. Nursing Service Adminstrs. *

KENNEDY, JAMES JEROME, cons. san. engr.; b. Detroit, Aug. 31, 1922; s. James Jerome and Anna Louise (McAndrew) K.; student U. Detroit, 1940-43; B.S. in Civil Engring., U. Mich., 1944; m. Irene Francis Wajda, May 7, 1949; children—Kathleen Ann, Eileen Marie, Kristeen Mary, James Jerome, Michael John, David Joseph. Field engr. City Engrs. Office, Birmingham, Mich., 1946-47; supr. field surveys Ford Bacon & Davis Inc., N.Y.C., 1947-48; constrn. supr. S.S. Kresge Co., Detroit, 1948-52; project engr. D.L. Briegel & Assos., Inc., Birmingham, 1952-54; partner, treas. Pentad Engrs. Inc., Detroit, 1954-62; partner, treas. Alfred Crew Cons. Engrs. Inc., Ridgewood, N.J., 1962—, v.p., 1962-78, pres., 1978—, also dir. Served as ensign C.E., USNR, World War II; PTO. Registered profl. engr., Mich., N.J., N.Y. State. Mem. Nat. Soc. Profl. Engrs., Am. Water Works Assn., Water Pollution Control Fedn., Am. Arbitration Assn. Clubs: Exchange (pres. Ridgewood 1972). Home: 302 Meadowbrook Rd Wyckoff NJ 07481 Office: 75 N Maple Ave Ridgewood NJ 07450

KENNEDY, JOHN ANTHONY, physician; b. Woonsocket, R.I., July 3, 1918; s. T. Frank and Isabel (McCabe) K.; B.S., Providence Coll., 1939; M.D., Columbia U., 1943; m. Muriel Matson, Aug. 24, 1944; children—John A., Thomas L., James M., Mary C., Timothy G. Intern, Presbyn. Hosp., N.Y.C., 1943-44, resident in ophthalmology Eye Inst., 1948-51; practice medicine, specializing in ophthalmology, Watertown, N.Y. Served with USAMC, 1944-46. Decorated Bronze Star. Diplomate Am. Bd. Opthalmology. Mem. AMA, Jefferson County, N.Y. State med. socs., Jefferson County Assn. for the Blind; fellow Am. Acad. Ophthalmology and Otolaryngology, A.C.S. Republican. Roman Catholic. Club: Ives Hill Country. Contbr. articles in field to profl. jours. Home: 5391 Plank Rd Star Route Watertown NY 13601 Office: 200 Mullin St Watertown NY 13601

KENNEDY, JOHN FRANCIS, landscape architect; b. Springfield, Pa., Feb. 13, 1933; s. Francis Pennington and Florence (Cameron) K.; B.S. in Horticulture, Pa. State U., 1956; m. Charlene Houssell, June 18, 1955; children—John Scott, Susan Lynn. Landscape architect firm Wheelwright, Stevenson & Langran, Phila., 1958-62; sr. landscape architect firm Richard J. Cripps, Lambertville, N.J., 1962-65; chief landscape architect Bucks County Park Bd., Doylestown, Pa., 1965-69; partner firm Kennedy & Brown, Lambertville, N.J., 1970—. Mem. Doylestown Twp. Planning Commn., 1964-72, chmn., 1972—. Recipient design awards Pa. Nurserymen's Assn., 1971, N.J. Mfrs. Assn., 1973, Good Neighbor award Great Falls Hist. Park, Paterson, N.J., 1973. Mem. Am. Soc. Landscape Architects, Nat. Geog. Soc., Nat. Wildlife Fedn. (asso.), Nat. Rifle Assn. (life), Central Bucks C. of C., Nat. Fedn. Ind. Bus. Home: 60 Cherry Ln Doylestown PA 18901 Office: Bridge and Union Sts Lambertville NJ 08530

KENNEDY, JOYCE LAIN (MRS. WILLIAM A. KENNEDY), newspaper columnist; b. Louisiana, Mo.; d. Miller and J. Irma (Pitman) Lain; B.S. in Bus. Adminstrn., Washington U., St. Louis, 1953; m. William A. Kennedy, May 23, 1970. Air talent prodn. asst. Ed Wilson Show, Sta. KWK-TV, St. Louis, 1954-55; asst. to pub. Prom Mag., St. Louis, 1955-59; pub. relations cons. United Fund Greater St. Louis, 1959-63; creative dir. Civic Service, Inc., St. Louis, 1963; advt. and pub. relations dir. Mansion House Center, St. Louis, 1964-66; communications dir. Greater St. Louis council Girl Scouts U.S.A., 1966-68; columnist Careers, Suburban Features, Inc., Cardiff, Calif., 1968—, exec. editor Career World mag., 1972—. Mem. Youth Commn., St. Louis and St. Louis County, 1968-69. Author: Secrets of Finding Your First Job, 1970; Automotive Careers, 1972. Office: 1160 Rockville Pike Rockville MD 20852

KENNEDY, LYLE H., investment cons.; b. N.Y.C., Mar. 29, 1933; s. Michael M. and Margaret E. (Kennedy) Kuhn; student Columbia, 1949-50, Grinnell Coll., 1952-53, N.Y. U., 1953; LL.B., Blackstone Sch. Law, 1970; m. Hertha G. Baird, July 29, 1961 (div. July 1974); children—Peter W., Lyle H., Lyla H.; m. 2d, Evelyn R. Siefert, Oct. 12, 1974; children—Paul K., Carl J., Ann M. Vice pres. Devon Plans Fidelity Funds, Boston, 1960-61; cons. to pres. Investors Planning Corp. Am., N.Y.C., 1961-62; dir. Inst. Financial Independence, Seattle, 1962-63; v.p. Blue Ridge Distbrs. and Winfield Distbrs., San Francisco, 1963-65; cons. to pres. Value Line Securities, N.Y.C., 1965-66; chmn., dir. Kennedy Capital Advisors, Inc., Groton, Conn., 1966—; pres., dir. Kennedy Mgmt. Corp., Groton, Conn., 1972—; gen. partner Kennedy InterVest Fund, Ltd., 1976—; pres. Kennedy InterVest, Inc., 1976—; chmn. Kennedy Intervest Ins. Inc., 1978—, Kennedy InterVest Realty, Inc., 1978—; pres. Kennedy InterVest Securities, Inc., 1978—; adj. prof. N.Y. U., 1976. Bd. dirs. Blue Curtain Youth Found., N.Y.C., Eastern Conn. Symphony; bd. regents Internat. Coll. Financial Counselling; also pvt. trusts. Served with AUS, 1953-55. Mem. Photographers Soc. Am., Mut. Fund Council. Republican. Unitarian. Clubs: Lawyers, Lambs (N.Y.C.); Shennecossett Yacht. Asso. editor Stock Market Mag., 1969. Home: 7 Mulberry Dr Gales Ferry CT 06335 Office: 1159 Poquonnock Rd Groton CT 06340

KENNEY, ALAN JOHN, dept. store exec.; b. Medford, Mass., Apr. 4, 1950; s. William John and Anna Louise (diMilla) K.; B.S. in Bus.Adminstrn., Northeastern U., 1972. Clk., Bradlee's Inc., Somerville, Mass., 1966-68, dept. mgr., 1968-72, asst. store mgr., 1973, mgr. elec. register program, Braintree, Mass., 1973—. Mem.

Somerville Sch. Com., 1972—, vice-chmn. 1974, chmn. 1975—, del. to state conv. Mem. Am. Mktg. Assn., Nat., Mass. (2d v.p.) assns. sch. coms., Greater Boston Assn. Retarded Citizens, Holy Name Soc., Young Adults Club, Smithsonian Inst. Democrat. Roman Catholic. Home: 8 Central St Somerville MA 02143 Office: 1 Bradlee Circle Braintree MA 02184

KENNEY, DOUGLAS BLAINE, electronic funds transfer co. exec.; b. Hancock Village, N.Y., Dec. 17, 1938; s. James Jerome and Edith Margaret (Seidel) K.; student U. Md., 1961-65, Stonier Sch. Banking, 1970-71, Northeastern U., 1971-73; m. Linda Betty Baer, May 16, 1970. Mgr. computer mktg., banking industry, RCA, N.Y.C., 1963-71; regional mgr. Citicorp., N.Y.C., 1971-76; exec. dir. Thrift Transfer Services Corp., N.Y.C., 1976-77; pres. Kenney Co., cons. electronic funds transfer services bus. planning and tech., Westbury, N.Y., 1977—; speaker banking seminars. Served with USMC, 1959-63. Mem. IEEE., Assn. Computing Machinery, Gideons Internat. Home and Office: 82 5th Ave Westbury NY 11590

KENNEY, GUILEA LEHAN, business educator; b. Manchester, N.H., Dec. 30, 1917; d. Daniel Joseph and Alice Amanda (Julius) Lehan; B.S., Mt. St. Mary Coll. (N.H.), 1940; M.A., N.Y. U., 1968; m. Gerald Joseph Kenney, Oct. 25, 1941; 1 foster son, Walter R. Goddard. Office mgr. Burroughs Adding Machine Co., Manchester, N.H., 1940-44; rep. U.S. CSC, 1944-46; bus. instr. Griswold High Sch., Jewett City, Conn., 1958-78; ret., 1978; job counselor, placement asst. Mem. Griswold (pres. 1962-63), Nat., Conn. edn. assns., Eastern, Conn., New Eng. bus. edn. assns., Delta Pi Epsilon, Delta Kappa Gamma Internat., Alpha Kappa (pres. Gamma chpt. 1974-76, state sec. 1977-79). Democrat. Roman Catholic. Club: Bus. and Profl. Women's (woman of yr. 1977, parliamentarian 1978—). Home and Office: Box 211 Route 1 Voluntown CT 06384

KENNEY, RICHARD ALEC, educator; b. Coventry, Eng., Oct. 4, 1924; s. Alec and Dorothy Ada (Cooke) K.; B.Sc. with honors, U. Birmingham, Eng., 1945, Ph.D., 1947; m. Bette Gladys Green, Aug. 8, 1959; 1 son by previous marriage—Michael Alec. Came to U.S., 1967. Lectr. physiology U. Leeds, Eng., 1947-51; with Colonial Research Service, Nigeria, 1951-54; staff mem. W.H.O., S.E. Asia Region, 1955-60; chmn. physiology U. Singapore, 1960-65; reader physiology U. Melbourne, Australia, 1965-67; prof. physiology George Washington U. Med. Center, 1968—, chmn. dept., 1970—. Tutor physiology Royal Australian Coll. Surgeons, 1965-67. Mem. Physiol. Soc. (London), Am. Physiol. Soc., Renal Assn. (London), Am. Coll. Sports Medicine, Internat. Nephrological Soc. Contbr. articles to profl. jours. Home: 4424 Reservoir Rd NW Washington DC 20007 Office: 2300 I St NW Washington DC 20037

KENNY, JAMES CONNOLLY, wire and cable co. exec.; b. Bennington, Vt., July 16, 1926; s. Thomas B. and Celia (Connolly) K.; B.S. in Indsl. Engring., Purdue U., 1954; m. Lois M. Stocker, Nov. 17, 1956; children—James II, Ellen, Peter, Sara. Vice pres. Am. Super Temperature Wires Inc., Winooski, Vt., 1956-63; dir. ops. HiTemp Wires Inc., Westbury, L.I., N.Y., 1963-65; pres., co-founder Harbour Industries Inc., Shelburne, Vt., 1965—; chmn. bd., dir. Harbour Industries Ltd., Farnham, Que., Can.; v.p., dir. Shelburne Realty Corp.; partner Sheila's Uniform Shop, Burlington, Vt.; dir. Delton Harbour Industries, Ltd., New Delhi, India. Served with USAAF, 1944-46. Fellow AIM (pres.'s council); mem. Nat. Elec. Mfrs. Assn. (dir. wire and cable div.), Wire Assn., Asso. Industries Vt., New Eng. Council, Lake Champlain Regional C. of C. Elk. Club: Ethan Allen. Pioneer high temperature wire field. Home: 11 Sandalwood Rd South Burlington VT 05401 Office: PO Box 188 Shelburne VT 05482

KENNY, LISA ANN, artist, sculptor; b. Mineola, N.Y.; d. Thomas Henry and Patricia Anne (Flowers) K.; M.F.A., Ohio Christian U., 1974. One man shows include: Miami (Fla.) Mus. Art, 1974; represented in permanent collections Mus. Modern Art, Miami, Madison (Wis.) Art Center, U. Mo. Mus. Art, Columbia. Clk., Bd. of Elections, North Hills, N.Y., 1975-77. Mem. Assn. Am. Artists, Am. Fedn. Art, Inst. Contemporary Arts London, Visual Artists and Galleries Assn. Author children's books. Home and studio: Oak Ridge Ln North Hills Roslyn NY 11576

KENSIL, JAMES LEWIS, football exec.; b. Phila., Aug. 19, 1930; s. Lewis Martin and Kathryn Beatrice (Rush) K.; B.A., U. Pa., 1952; m. Catherine Tighe, Jan. 2, 1954; children—Michael, Joseph, Mary Jo, Daniel. Newsman, AP, N.Y.C., 1952, Columbus, Ohio, 1954-56, sports writer, N.Y.C., 1956-61; dir. pub. relations Nat. Football League, N.Y.C., 1961-67, exec. dir., 1968-77; pres. N.Y. Jets Football Club, Inc., 1977—. Served with U.S. Army, 1952-54. Home: 241 Riviera Dr W Massapequa NY 11758 Office: 410 Park Ave New York City NY 10022

KENT, BARRY J., accountant; b. Hartford, Conn., May 14, 1934; s. Saul Kantrowitz and Minnie Kantrowitz; B.S., U. Conn., 1956; m. Hyla Phyllis Marcus, Aug. 14, 1955; children—Craig, Robert, Robin. Individual practice as accountant, Hartford, Conn., 1956-58, 60-67; C.P.A. with Lester E. Kasin, Hartford, 1959-60; C.P.A., Kasin & Kent, Hartford, Conn., 1968-72, Kasin, Kent & Rapport, 1972-77, Barry J. Kent & Co., 1977—; prof. accounting and econs. Morse Bus. Coll., 1960-63. Consul Costa Rica to Conn., 1975—. Served with U.S. Army, 1957-58. Mem. Am. Arbitration Assn., Am. Inst. C.P.A.'s, Conn. Soc. C.P.A.'s. Home: 84 Kirkwood Rd West Hartford CT 06117 Office: 410 Asylum St Hartford CT 06103

KENT, CHARLES IMBRIE, III, coll. adminstr.; b. Phila., July 22, 1913; s. Charles Imbrie and Marguerite Brittain (Rudy) K.; B.S., West Chester (Pa.) State Coll., 1936; M.S., Case Western Res. U., 1940; certificate psychol. counseling Pa. State U., 1946; m. Martha W.S. Kent, May 15, 1937; children—Lynne, Lesley, Deborah. Dir. aquatics Harrisburg (Pa.) YMCA, 1936-38; social worker, Cleve., 1938-40; dir. guidance Hershey (Pa.) Pub. Schs., 1940-48; dir. personnel Hershey Chocolate Corp. & Estate, 1948-53; dean students F & M Coll., Lancaster, Pa., 1953-54; dir. student personnel, asst. v.p. acad. affairs Pa. State Coll., Millersville, 1954-77; pres. Lancaster Hearing Conservation Center, 1959-70, 76—, sec., 1971-75; pres. bd. dirs. YMCA Lancaster, 1976—. Bd. dirs. Student Services Inc., Lancaster, 1956-65. Served with Amphibious Forces, USNR, 1943-46, 50-51; ETO. Mem. Nat. Assn. Social Workers, Pa., Am., Keystone (organizer, 1st. chmn. 1941) personnel and guidance assns., Am. Legion. Republican. Presbyterian. Clubs: Hershey Country, Conestoga Country, Masons (past master). Home: 1407 Clayton Rd Lancaster PA 17603

KENT, DONALD SEYMOUR, internist, cardiologist; b. N.Y.C., Dec. 8, 1920; s. Samuel and Mildred (Zellermayer) K.; B.A., Cornell U., 1942, M.D., Med. Coll., N.Y.C., 1945; m. Madelaine Ring, Mar. 19, 1946; children—Alison, Stephen, Ilene, William. Intern, Mt. Sinai Hosp., N.Y.C., 1945-46, resident in medicine, 1948-50; practice medicine specializing in internal medicine and cardiology, Roslyn Heights, N.Y., 1948—; attending physician North Shore Univ. Hosp., Manhasset, N.Y., L.I. Jewish Med. Center; clin. asso. prof. medicine Cornell U. Med. Coll.-North Shore Univ. Hosp., 1972—. Served to lt. (j.g.) USN, 1946-48. Diplomate Am. Bd. Internal Medicine. Fellow A.C.P., Am. Coll. Cardiologists; mem. Nassau Soc. Internal Medicine (pres. 1975-76), Am. Trudeau Soc., Am. Soc. Internal Medicine, Alpha Omega Alpha. Office: 70 Glen Cove Rd Roslyn Heights NY 11577

KENT, SHERMAN VAN NESS, coll. dean; b. Phila., Dec. 12, 1912; s. Ralph and Ida Elizabeth (Peterson) K.; B.S., West Chester State Coll., 1936; M.S., U. Pa., 1941; Ed.D., Temple U., 1963; m. Helen Louise Clayton, June 25, 1938; 1 son, Christopher Van Ness. Instr. English, Scott High Sch., Coatesville, Pa., 1936-43; dir. civilian tng. U.S. Army Depot, New Cumberland, Pa., 1943-45; prin. high sch., Damascus, Pa., 1945-46; dir. 2d session Rider Coll., Trenton, N.J., 1946-50; asst. dean, 1950-58, dean evening sch., 1958-78; ret., 1978; cons. Pub. Broadcasting Corp. Mem. Assn. Continuing Higher Edn. (pres. region 4 1964-65, dir.), Adult Student Personnel Assn. (dir., Bernard Webster Reed Meml. award 1975), Am. Psychol. Assn., Adult Edn. Assn., Internat. Platform Assn., Phi Delta Kappa, Alpha Sigma Lambda, Sigma Iota Chi, Phi Alpha Theta. Contbr. articles to profl. jours. Home: 503 Curtis Dr Morrisville PA 19067

KENT, WILLIAM HORACE, mcht. banker; b. Phila., Sept. 7, 1935; s. Horace Leesor and Evelyn Louise (Huber) K.; B.A., Cornell U., 1958; postgrad. N.Y. U., 1964; m. Susannah Strickland Simpson, June 21, 1958; children—Elizabeth Patterson, Harlan McBriar. Sr. research analyst, mgr. corporate cons. dept. R. W. Pressprich & Co., N.Y.C., 1961-65; chmn. Berger-Kent Adv. Corp., pres., dir. Berger-Kent Spl. Fund, Wilmington, Del., 1965-72; chmn. William Kent & Co., Greenwich, Conn., 1965—; pres. Mideast Am., Inc.; dir. Internat. Fin. Advisers, Kuwait; lectr., cons. to firms doing bus. in Middle East. Trustee Internat. Coll., Beirut, Lebanon; mem. corp. Woods Hole Oceanographic Inst. Served to lt. USN, 1958-61. Mem. Middle East Inst., Arab-Am. Assn., China Inst., Newcomen Soc., Certified Fin. Analysts Fedn., N.Y. Soc. Security Analysts. Clubs: Turf (London); Round Hill (Greenwich); Verbank (Millbrook, N.Y.); Explorers (N.Y.C.). Home: 1005 Lake Ave N Greenwich CT 06830 Office: 1 Greenwich Plaza Greenwich CT 06830

KENTNER, HAROLD MILLER, educator; b. Rochester, N.Y., Mar. 14, 1917; s. Osbert Charles and Irma Delia (Miller) K.; A.B., U. Rochester, 1938, M.Ed., 1951; diploma indsl. mgmt. Rochester Inst. Tech., 1942; m. Katherine Carol Nowack, Nov. 14, 1941; children—Jeanne C. (Mrs. Joel E. Clarke), Louise A. (Mrs. Robert C. Smith, Jr.), Maryann R. (Mrs. Robert J. Newman). With N.Y. State Dept. Labor, Rochester, 1938-39; supr. tng. Rochester Products div. Gen. Motors Co., Rochester, 1939-44; with Ritter Co. div. Sybron, Rochester, 1944-49; with Hickok Co., Rochester, 1949-50; faculty Rochester Inst. Tech., 1950—, prof., asst. dean, 1971—, mem. adj. faculty, mgmt. div., 1941-50. Adj. faculty Indsl. and Labor Relations Sch. Cornell U. Extension, 1970-71, 78; chmn. continuing edn. com. occupation edn. council Rochester Schs., 1977—. Bd. dirs. Regional Council on Aging, 1973—, v.p., 1978—; program chmn. N.Y. State Mental Health Assn., 1968-70; mem. exec. com. mental health planning council Rochester Regional Health Council, 1967-68. Bd. dirs. Mental Health Assn. Rochester and Monroe County, 1965—, chpt. chmn., 1965-67; bd. dirs. Health Assn. Rochester and Monroe County, chmn. personnel com., 1970-73, v.p., 1969-70; bd. dirs. Henrietta Community Council, 1971—; bd. dirs. East House, 1976—, v.p., 1978—. Mem. Genesee Valley Psychol. Assn., Am. Soc. Tng. and Devel., Nat. Soc. for Study Edn., Internat. Congress Adult Edn., Am. Personnel and Guidance Assn. (chpt. pres. 1958), Retirement Planners Profl. Assn. Western N.Y. (pres. 1971), Nat. Univ. Extension Assn. (regional chmn. 1970-71, nat. dir. 1971-73, 77—, chmn. council on adminstrn. 1978—), Genesee Valley Sch. Devel. Assn. (trustee). Author: (with Laurence Lipsett, Frank P. Rodgers) Personnel Selection and Recruitment, 1964, rev. edit. (with Lipsett), 1972. Home: 68 Biltmore Dr Rochester NY 14617 Office: 1 Lomb Memorial Dr Rochester NY 14623

KENTON, EDGAR JACKSON, III, neurologist; b. Phila., Mar. 5, 1940; s. Edgar Jackson, Jr., and Jessie Elizabeth (Jones) K.; A.B., Rutgers U., 1961; M.D., Cornell Med. Coll., 1965; m. Sandra Kay Payne, June 21, 1969; children—Adrienne Danielle, Brian Michael. Intern, Jefferson Med. Coll. Hosp., Phila., 1965-66, resident in internal medicine, 1966-67; fellow in cerebral blood flow studies Stroke Research Center, Phila. Gen. Hosp., 1970; acting chief neurology dept. Lankenau Hosp., Phila., 1972, chief, 1973—; instr. in neurology Thomas Jefferson U. Med. Coll., 1972-74, asst. prof., 1974-78, asso. clin. prof., 1978—; cons. neurologist Bryn Mawr Coll. Child Study Inst.; mem. cardiovascular risk identification and risk reduction com. and stroke council Am. Heart Assn. Bd. dirs. Hilltop Preparatory Sch. Served to maj., M.C., USAF, 1970-72. Diplomate Am. Bd. Psychiatry and Neurology. Mem. Am. Acad. Neurology, Phila. Neurol. Soc. Episcopalian. Contbr. articles in field to profl. publs. Home: 54 Lakeside Ave Devon PA 19333

KENTON, GLENN C., state ofcl.; b. Washington, Dec. 21, 1943; s. William K. and Jean C. Kenton; A.B., Swarthmore Coll., 1965; J.D., Georgetown U., 1968. Admitted to Del. bar, 1969; with firm Brown, Shiels & Barros, Dover, Del., 1969-71; counsel Del. Ho. of Reps., Dover, 1969-71, to Congressman P.S. du Pont, 1971-76; sec. of state State of Del., Dover, 1977—. Office: Office Sec State Dept State Townsend Bldg Dover DE 19901

KENZORA, JOHN EDWARD, physician; b. Toronto, Ont., Can., Sept. 10, 1940; s. John and Margaret (Mlymarchy) K.; came to U.S., 1966; M.D., U. Toronto, 1965; m. Elizabeth J. Swirsky, June 20, 1946; children—Kristen Tracey, Kyra Leah. Intern, Toronto Gen. Hosp., 1965-66; orthopedic research fellow Mass. Gen. Hosp.-Harvard Med. Sch., Boston, 1966-68; asst. resident in orthopedic surgery Mass. Gen. Hosp., 1969-70; resident in surgery Children's Hosp. Med. Center, Boston, 1970-71, Robert Breck Brigham Hosp., Boston, 1971, Beth Israel Hosp., Boston, 1971; chief resident in orthopedic surgery Peter Bent Brigham Hosp., Boston, 1971-72; practice medicine specializing in orthopedic surgery, Boston, 1972-78, Balt., 1978—; instr. in orthopedic surgery Harvard Med. Sch., 1972-72; asst. in orthopedic surgery Children's Hosp. Med. Center, 1972-78, Peter Bent Brigham Hosp., 1972-76, asso. in orthopedic surgery, 1974—; asso. prof. surgery U. Md., 1978—. Diplomate Am. Bd. Orthopaedic Surgery. Mem. Orthopedic Research Soc., Am. Acad. Orthopedic Surgeons, Md. Orthopedic Assn. Alpha Omega Alpha. Office: U Md Hosp 22 S Green St Baltimore MD 21201

KENZY, JOHN QUINTON, clergyman; b. Morrill, Nebr., Nov. 29, 1941; s. Eugene Edward and Opal Edna (Fees) K.; B.A., Central Bible Coll., Springfield, Mo., 1964; m. Carol Ann Young, June 20, 1964; children—Renée, Rachelle, Ronda, Raelene. Ordained to ministry Assemblies of God Ch., 1967; asst. dir. Teen-Age Evangelism, Springfield, 1962-63, dir. 1963-64; asso. dir. Bklyn. Teen Challenge, 1964-65; co founder Teen Challenge Inst. Missions, Rhinebeck, N.Y., 1965—; acad. dean, dean men, registrar, 1965-68; pres. Teen Challenge Inst., Sunbury, Pa., 1968—; bd. dirs. Faith for This Day radio broadcast, 1966—, radio evangelist, 1978—. Mem. Hudson Valley Evang. Ministerial Assn. (sec.), Inter-Agy. Council Susquehanna Valley, N.Y., Pa. Assemblies of God dist. councils. Republican. Composer religious songs for youth. Home and office: RD 2 Box 33 Sunbury PA 17801

KEOHAN, EDWARD JOSEPH, electronics co. exec.; b. Somerville, Mass., Dec. 24, 1933; s. Timothy Joseph and Mary Beatrice K.; B.S. in Bus. Adminstrn., Boston Coll., 1955; M.B.A., Northeastern U., 1958; LL.B., Blackstone Sch. Law, 1968; m. Judith Mary Keohan, Aug. 6, 1955; children—Debra, Edward Joseph, Michael. Supr. contract adminstrn. Sylvania Corp., Waltham, Mass., 1961-64; contracts mgr. RCA, Burlington, Mass., 1964-67; dir. contracts and procurement Am. Sci. and Engring. Inc., Cambridge, Mass., 1967-68, corporate comptroller, 1968-75, treas., 1969, v.p. finance, treas., 1973—, dir. subs. Package House Inc., Clifton, N.J. Mem. Finance Com. Town of Acton (Mass.), 1974. Certified profl. contracts mgr., Mass. Mem. Fin. Execs. Inst., Nat. Assn. Accountants, Nat. Contract Mgmt. Assn., Am. Accounting Assn., Am. Mgmt. Assn. Clubs: Univ. Boston, Celtics Tap Off. Home: 14 Brucewood Rd Acton MA 01720 Office: Am Sci and Engring Inc 955 Massachusetts Ave Cambridge MA 02139

KEPLER, JACQUELINE COSETTE, design draftsman; b. Johnson City, N.Y., Sept. 2, 1925; d. Leroy L. and Marie M. Anderson; A.A.S. in Drafting Tech., Mercer County Community Coll., Trenton, N.J., 1976; m. Charles E. Kepler, Jr., Aug. 20, 1949. Electro-mech. draftsman Barber Coleman Co., Rockford, Ill., 1953-63; mech. draftsman Vogel Peterson Co., Elmhurst, Ill., 1963-65; electro-mech. draftsman Binks Paint Spray Co., Franklin Park, Ill., 1965-67; design draftsman Dow Jones & Co., Inc., Princeton, N.J., 1974—; speaker in field. Mem. Civil Def. Disaster Team, Wheaton, Ill., 1965. Mem. Soc. Women Engrs., Indsl. Engring. Assn., Trenton Bus. and Profl. Women. Home: Box 90 Rural Route 1 Titusville NJ 08560 Office: Box 300 Princeton NJ 08540

KEPPLER, JOHN JACOB, cons.; b. N.Y.C., Dec. 13, 1909; s. Fred Charles and Ellie Marie (Schillinger) K.; A.B., Columbia, 1934, M.S., 1947; m. Catherine Lapp, Sept. 29, 1939. Probation officer Children's Ct., Nassau County, N.Y., 1935-42; asst. area dir. N.Y. State Dept. Social Welfare, 1947-50, asst. to state commr., 1950-53, exec. officer, 1953-60; first dept. commr. N.Y.C. Dept. Social Welfare, 1960-64; exec. v.p. Fedn. Protestant Welfare Agys., N.Y.C., 1964-75; sr. cons. N.Y. Community Trust N.Y.C., 1975—; Chmn. adv. bd. N.Y.C. Dept. Social Services, adj. prof. Sch. Social Work, N.Y.U., Columbia. Bd. dirs. Greenwich House, N.Y.C., Plays for Living, N.Y.C.; vestryman St. Johns-Trinity Ch., Hewlett, N.Y. Served to maj. AUS, 1942-46; PTO. Mem. Nat. Assn. Social Workers, Am., N.Y. State pub. welfare assns., Council Social Work Edn., Nat. Council Aging, Welfare Research, Inc. Republican. Episcopalian. Clubs: Church, Univeristy, Mid-Ocean Bermuda, Rockaway Hunting. Contbr. articles to profl. jours., yachting mags. Home: Berkshire Pl Lawrence NY 11559 Office: 415 Madison Ave New York City NY 10017

KERBY, WILLIAM FREDERICK, publishing co. exec.; b. Washington, July 28, 1908; s. Frederick Monroe and Helen Frances (Hunter) K.; A.B., U. Mich., 1930; m. Frances Justina Douglass, June 8, 1935;children—Jean Frances, Judith Ann. Staff corr. United Press Assn., Washington, 1930-32, The Wall St. Jour., Washington, 1933-35, copy editor, N.Y.C., 1937-38, news editor, 1938-40, asst. mng. editor, 1941-42, mng. editor, 1943-44, exec. editor, 1945-51, v.p. Dow Jones & Co., Inc., Wall Street Jour., 1951-60, exec. v.p., 1961-66, pres., chief exec. officer, 1966-72, chmn. bd., 1972-78, dir., chmn. exec. com., 1978—, editorial dir., 1958-66, also dir.; trustee Williamsburgh Savs. Bank, Bklyn. Pres. Newspaper Fund; regent L.I. Coll. Hosp.; trustee New Coll. Found. Mem. Phi Beta Kappa, Sigma Delta Chi, Phi Kappa Tau. Episcopalian. Clubs: Union (N.Y.C.); Rock Spring (West Orange, N.J.). Office: 22 Cortlandt St New York City NY 10007

KERN, ARTHUR HOWARD, foam products mfg. exec.; b. N.Y.C., Feb. 22, 1934; s. George I. and Gladys K.; B.S., Ga. Inst. Tech., 1956; m. Sandra Riesberg, May 22, 1970; children—Daniel, Jacqueline. Pres., Nat. Foam Products Corp., Newark, 1963-73; pres., chmn. bd. Kern Foam Products Corp., Somerville, N.J., 1973—. Mem. Bd. Edn., E. Amwell Twp., N.J., 1972-78, pres., 1977-78. Served to capt., U.S. Army, 1956-58. Mem. Am. Mgmt. Assn., Soc. Plastics Industry, Mensa. Patentee in field. Home: RD 1 Ringoes NJ 08851 Office: 412 Roycefield Rd Somerville NJ 08876

KERN, FRANK NORTON, lawyer; b. Waymansville, Ind., Feb. 19, 1920; s. Frank W. and Irene (Everdon) K.; B.A., Ohio Wesleyan U., 1941; M.B.A., Harvard, 1943, LL.B. cum laude, 1948; m. Minnetta Louise Wooden, Apr. 9, 1944; children—Cynthia Jennifer, Candace. Admitted to Ohio bar, 1948, Pa. bar, 1953, N.Y. bar, 1956, D.C. bar, 1970; practiced in Cleve., 1948-51, N.Y.C., 1956—; asso. firm Squire, Sanders & Dempsey, Cleve., 1948-51; tax atty. U.S. Steel Corp., Pitts., 1951-54; partner charge tax dept. Reid & Priest, N.Y.C., 1955—. Mem. Ohio Wesleyan U. Assos. and Investment Com., 1962—. Served to lt. with USNR, 1943-46. Mem. Am., Inter-Am. bar assns., Phi Beta Kappa. Republican. Episcopalian. Clubs: Metropolitan (Washington); Apawamis (Rye, N.Y.); Recess (N.Y.C.). Contbr. articles to profl. jours. Home: Puritan Rd Rye NY 10580 Office: 40 Wall St New York City NY 10005

KERN, HERBERT LOUIS, mfg. co. exec.; b. Boston, Aug. 19, 1923; s. Harry M. and Minnie (Miles) K.; B.A., U. Mass., 1949; B.S., Northeastern U., 1950; m. Marjorie Brickman, Nov. 8, 1966; children—Russel Handler, F. John Handler, Michael Kern, Jonathan Kern. With Geigy Pharm. div. Ciba Geigy, Summit, N.J., 1953-71, dir. gen. sales, 1967-71; exec. v.p., gen. mgr. USV Pharm. Corp., Tuckahoe, N.Y., 1971-74; chief operating officer Boyd Labs., Washington, 1977—, also dir.; pres. Kenwood Labs. Inc., New Rochelle, N.Y., Internat. Biochem. Corp., Englewood Cliffs, N.J. Pres. bd. dirs. Kings Point (N.Y.) Civic Assn., 1967-74, Great Neck Community Concert Assn., 1972-74, Great Neck Sr. Citizens Found., 1968-74. Served with USAAF, 1942-45: ETO. Mem. Am. Mgmt. Assn., Sales Execs. Club N.Y.C., Pharm. Advt. Club N.Y.C., Am. Pharm. Assn. Home: 275 Kings Point Rd Kings Point NY 11024 Office: 600 Watergate Suite 720 Washington DC 20037

KERNER, FRED, publisher; b. Montreal, Que., Can., Feb. 15, 1921; s. Sam and Vera (Goldman) K.; B.A., Sir George Williams U., Montreal, 1942; m. Jean Elizabeth Somerville, July 17, 1945 (div. Apr. 1951); 1 son, Jon Fredrik; m. 2d, Sally Dee Stouten, May 18, 1959; children—David Lassen, Diane Gail. Asst. sports editor The Montreal Gazette, 1942-44; news editor The Canadian Press, Montreal, Toronto, N.Y.C., 1944-50; asst. night city editor A.P., N.Y.C. 1950-57; editor Hawthorn Books N.Y.C., 1957-58, pres., dir., editor-in-chief, 1964-67; exec. editor Fawcett Crest-Premier Books, N.Y.C., 1958-62; editor-in-chief Fawcett World Library, 1963-64; pres., editor-in-chief Centaur House, Inc., 1964—; pub. dir. book and ednl. div. Reader's Digest Assn. (Can.) Ltd., 1969-75; dir. pub. Harlequin Enterprises, Ltd., Don Mills, Ont., 1975—; pres. Paramount Security Corp., 1965-67; dir. Nat. Mint Inc., Publitex Internat. Corp., Personalized System, Inc., Pennorama Crafts, Inc., Disque Designs, Inc., Peter Kent, Inc.; pres. Athebaska House, 1975-77; mng. dir. Fred Kerner Pub. Projects. Chmn. book pubs. com., chmn. promotion committee Edward R. Morrow Memorial Fund; trustee Gibson Lit. awards, Benson & Hedges Lit. awards; judge Dr. William Henry Drummond Nat. Poetry Contest; mem. Screening Com. N.Y.C. Dist. Sch. Bd., 1968-69; chmn. Sch. Com. Westmount High Sch., 1971-72; bd. govs. Concordia U., 1975-77, Canadian

Copyright Inst., 1975—. Mem. Canadian Book Pubs. Council (dir. 1975-77), Assn. Alumni Sir George Williams U. (pres. 1971-73), Canadian Authors Assn. (nat. v.p. 1972-74, 75—, br. pres. 1974-75, trustee lit. awards), Canadian Soc. for Restoration Lost Positives (pres.), Mystery Writers Am., Canadian Soc. (N.Y.C.), Am. Mgmt. Assn., Author's League Am., Am. Acad. Polit. and Social Sci., Internat. Platform Assn., Sigma Delta Chi. Clubs: Dutch Treat, Advertising, Overseas Press, Deadline (N.Y.C.); Toronto Men's Press; Authors' (London, Eng.). Author: (with Leonid Kotkin) Eat, Think and be Slender, 1954; (with Walter M. Germain) The Magic Power of Your Mind, 1956; (with Joyce Brothers) Ten Days to a Successful Memory 1957; Stress and Your Heart 1961; (under pseudonym Frederick Kerr) Watch Your Weight Go Down, 1962; A Treasury of Lincoln Quotations, 1965; (with Walter M. Germain) Secrets of Your Supraconscious, 1965; (with Jesse B. Reid) Buy High, Sell Higher!; (with David Goodman) What's Best for Your Child--and You, 1966; (under pseudomyn M.N. Thaler) It's Fun to Fondue, 1968; (with Ion Grumeza) Nadia, 1977. Editor: Love is a Man's Affair, 1958. Contbg. author Successful Writers and How They Work, 1958, Words on Paper, 1960, Overseas Press Club Cookbook, 1964, Chamber's Encyclopedia, 1946. Office: 220 Duncan Mill Rd Don Mills ON M3B 3J5 Canada also 51 E 42d St New York City NY 10017

KERNER, JEROME, architect; b. Bklyn., Sept. 1, 1935; s. Sol and Lillian (Levinson) K.; B.Arch., Pratt Inst., 1958; children—Ariel, Jordan. Mem. firms Abbott Merkt & Co., N.Y.C., 1957-61, S. A. Seiler Co., Liberty, N.Y., 1961-64, Seiler & Kerner, Liberty, 1964-72, Nakrosis and Kerner, Liberty, 1972-74, Jerome Kerner, Architect, Phoenicia, N.Y., 1974—; mem. Design Alternatives with Nature Group, solar energy designs, Phoenicia, N.Y. and Arlington, Va., 1974—; coordinator environ. studies Alternative Community Tech. Program, N.Y. State U., 1974-75; guest lectr. Goddard Social Ecology Program. Mem. Town of Neversink Planning Bd., 1963-72. Served with U.S. Army, 1958. Mem. Nat. Council Archtl. Registration Bds., New Alchemists, Nat. Audubon Soc. (pres. county chpt. 1965-68). Co-author: Low Cost Energy Efficient Shelter, 1976. Address: Center for the Living Force Phoenicia NY 12464 also 175 W 93d St New York City NY 10025

KERNSTOCK, ELWYN NICHOLAS, educator; b. Bronx, N.Y., Dec. 24, 1917; s. Charles Henry and Irene (Paollilo) K.; B.Ed., Central Conn. State U., 1961, M.S., 1965; Ph.D., U. Conn., 1972; m. Peggy Giles, Dec. 21, 1947; children—Stephan Giles, Nicholas Charles, Christopher John, Wendy Irene. Enlisted in U.S. Army, 1942, commd. 2d lt., 1943, advanced through grades to maj., 1962; ret., 1962; instr. social studies New Britain (Conn.) Sr. High Sch., 1962-65; chmn. social studies dept. Woodstock (Conn.) Acad., 1966-70; prof. Am. politics St. Michael's Coll., 1971—. Advisor to chmn. Vt. Democratic Com., 1974-76; del. Conn. Dem. Conv., 1970, Vt. Dem. Conv., 1972, 74, 76; pres. New Britain Unitarian Universalist Soc., 1962. Mem. AAUP, Am., New Eng. polit. sci. assns. Home: 14 Kingsland Terr Burlington VT 05401

KERPCHAR, MICHAEL, astroelectronic engr., electronics co. exec.; b. Passaic, N.J., June 19, 1924; s. Peter and Veronica (Warholack) K.; student pub. schs., Clifton, N.J.; m. Jennie Hallock, Apr. 12, 1953; 1 dau., Lorraine. Sect. head of astronautics lab. Kearfott Co., Inc., Clifton, N.J., 1950-56, chief engr., 1956-62; mgr. of spacecraft systems RCA Corp., Princeton, N.J., 1962-64; research scientist astrotracker systems engring. Northrop Nortronics, Palos Verdes Peninsula, Calif., 1964-66; chief of underwater viewing systems Kollsman Instrument Corp., Elmhurst, N.Y., 1967-69; v.p. of engring. Ocean Metrics, Inc., Fairfield, N.J., 1968-73; mgr. of advanced programs Harris Corp., Syosset, N.Y., 1973-76; dir. progress devel. Dewey Electronics, Paramus, N.J., 1976—. Mem. Am. Astronautical Soc. (nat. chmn. of edn. com. 1962-67, mem. space navigation com. 1960-64, chmn. N.J. sub.sect. 1960-62, mem. guidance and control com. 1960-64), Air Force Assn., Am. Inst. Aeros. and Astronautics. Roman Catholic. Author: (with others) Air to Surface Guidance Systems, 1955; contbr. articles on underwater optics to profl. publs.; patentee in field. Office: Dewey Electronics 11 Park Pl Paramus NJ 07652

KERR, ANDREW DAVID, JR., anesthesiologist; b. Paterson, N.J., Mar. 14, 1922; s. Andrew David and Hazel Grace (Doremus) K.; student (Charles Hayden scholar), U. Newark, 1939-42; M.D., N.Y. U., 1945. Intern, Hackensack (N.J.) Hosp., 1945-46; resident in anesthesiology VA Hosp., Washington, Gallinger Mcpl. Hosp., Washington and George Washington U. Hosp., 1947-49, VA Hosp., Oteen, N.C., 1948; attending anesthesiologist Doctors Hosp., N.Y.C., 1949—, dir. dept. anesthesiology, 1968—; mem. courtesy staff Hosp. Spl. Surgery, N.Y.C., 1955—; health officer Pittsfield (N.Y.) Twp., 1973—, Morris Dist., N.Y., 1975—. Served with M.C., U.S. Army, 1946-48. Diplomate Am. Bd. Anesthesiology. Fellow Am. Coll. Anesthesiology; mem. AMA, N.Y. State Med. Assn., N.Y. County Med. Assn., Am., N.Y. State socs. anesthesiologists, Internat. Anesthesia Research Soc., Assn. Mil. Surgeons (life), Am. Profl. Practice Assn. (life), Flying Physicians Assn., Am. Legion, Aircraft Owners and Pilots Assn. Republican. Home: Box Q Edmeston NY 13335 Office: 55 East End Ave New York NY 10028

KERR, ANN THOMAS (MRS. WILLIAM ERNEST KERR), civic worker, author; b. Pitts., June 3, 1911; d. Alfred Cyrus and Lucy Eliza (Forquer) Thomas; student pub. schs.; m. William Ernest Kerr, July 14, 1944 (dec. 1974); children—William David, John Alexander. Sec. to pres. J&L Steel Corp., Pitts., 1940-44; tchr. Pitts. Acad., 1938-43. Pres., Magee Womens Hosp. Aux., Pitts., 1968-71; mem. Pitts. Opera, 1962—, now v.p.; mem. Pitts. Symphony Soc., 1960—, Civic Light Opera, 1958—, Opera Workshop, Pitts., 1954—. Mem. Nat. Soc. Arts and Letters. Clubs: Oakmont Country, St. Clair Country, Pitts. Athletic; Twentieth Century (Pitts.); Surf, Cricket, Kenilworth (Fla.). Author: My Trip to Europe, 1964; Around the World, 1968. Home: 11A Chatham Towers Pittsburgh PA 15219

KERR, FRANK JOHN, educator; b. St. Albans, Eng., Jan. 8, 1918; s. Frank Robison and Myrtle Constance (McMeekin) K.; B.Sc., U. Melbourne (Australia), 1938, M.Sc., 1940, D.Sc., 1962; M.S., Harvard, 1951; m. Maureen Parnell, Jan. 7, 1966; children—Gillian Wheeler, Ian Kerr, Robin Lowry. Research scholar U. Melbourne, 1939-40; mem. staff radiophysics lab. Commonwealth Sci. and Indsl. Research Orgn., Sydney, Australia, 1940-68; vis. prof. U. Md., 1966-68, prof., 1968—, dir. astronomy program, 1973-78, acting provost div. math., phys. scis. and engring., 1978—; vis. scientist Leiden U., 1957; vis. prof. U. Tex., 1964, U. Tokyo, 1967. Mem. NSF Adv. Panel Astronomy, 1969-72, chmn., 1971-72. Fulbright travel grantee, 1950-51; Leverhulme fellow, 1967; NSF research grantee, 1967-78; Guggenheim fellow, 1974-75. Mem. Internat. Astron. Union (pres. commn. 33, 1976—), Am. Astron. Soc. (councillor 1972-75). Club: Cosmos (Washington). Co-editor Procs. Internat. Astron. Union, 1963, 73. Contbr. numerous articles to profl. jours. Home: 12601 Davan Dr Silver Spring MD 20904 Office: Astronomy Program U Md College Park MD 20742

KERR, HAZEL MAUD SMITH, newspaper woman; b. Winchester, Mass., Aug. 8, 1901; d. Fred Warren and Alice Maud (Whitney) Smith; B.S. in Home Econs., Simmons Coll., 1924; m. John Clark Kerr, May 21, 1924; children—John Smith and Priscilla Julia (Mrs. Bernard Jackson Lee) (twins), Fred Smith. Tchr. grad. sch., Western Springs, Ill., 1922-23; tchr. adult edn. classes, South Haven, Mich., 1954-55, children's art classes, 1956; tchr. pub. schs., Otis AFB, Bourne, Mass., 1963-64, Dennis, Mass., 1964-65, Barnstable, Mass., 1965—; corr., news photographer Benton Harbor (Mich.) News Palladium, 1953—, radio and TV news and photography, 1953—; feature writers, news photographer Cape Cod Standard Times, 1961—; publicity dir. Belmont Hotel, West Harwich, Mass., 1962, mem. interviewing staff Survey Research Center, U. Mich., 1955—. Mem. community theater groups, organized and directed summer theater; pres. South Haven Art League, 1959—; chmn. blood procurement program for ann. Red. Cross dr., 1959; Red Cross Nurses's Aide, 1942—; county chmn. A.R.C. home nursing, 1945-50; Cub Scout den mother, leader Boy Scouts Am., 1940-45; vol. office Chgo. Infant Welfare Sta., 1933-35; officer Civil Air Patrol; regional chmn. fund campaign Simmons Coll. Sci. Center Program; v.p. Dennis Bicentennial Commn., 1974—. Exhibiting artist temp. exhibits in South Haven and St. Joseph, Mich. Mem. Chgo. Art Inst. (life), AAUW (organizing pres. South Haven br), Bus. and Profl. Women's Club, Internat. Reading Assn., Dennis C. of C. (sec. 1961-66, v.p. 1966, pres. 1967-69), D.A.R. (chpt. treas. 1969—), Mass. Tchrs. Assn., N.E.A. Conglist. (past pres. ch. women group.). Rebekah. Clubs: Scott (past pres.), Federated Women's (South Haven, Mich.); Cape Cod Simmons (organizing pres. 1959-63, pres. 1968—, corr. sec. 1976—). Home: 90 Pleasant St Dennis Port Cape Cod MA 02639 Office: 319 Main St Hyannis MA 02601

KERR, JAMES WILSON, engr.; b. Balt., May 21, 1921; s. James W. and Laura Virgia (Wright) K.; B.S. with honors, Davidson Coll., 1942; M.S., N.Y.U., 1948; postgrad. Freiburg U., 1957-60, Brookings Inst., 1970, 75; m. Mary Thomas Montgomery, Feb. 25, 1945 (div.); children—April (Mrs. Rodney H. Miller), Catherine (Mrs. Charles M. Wood III) (dec.), Wilson, Andrew. m. 2d, June Walker, Dec. 27, 1977. Commd. 2d lt. U.S. Army, 1942, advanced through grades to lt. col., 1964; with inf., World War II, Korea; electronic staff, Ft. Bragg, N.C., 1948-51; weapons research, N.M., 1953-57; adviser French Army, 1957-60; staff electronics, Ft. Monroe, Va., 1960-62; research mgr., div. dir. CD, Pentagon, 1962-64, as civilian, 1964—; v.p. Latherow & Co., Arlington, Va., 1965—. Advanced English instr. French Army, 1957-60; cons. Am. Nat. Red Cross Mus., 1968—, Smithsonian Instn. Dept. Postal History, 1966—, NSF, 1976—. Vol. fireman N.Y. State, 1946-48, Fairfax County, Va., 1969—; fire commr. Fairfax County, 1975—, chmn., 1977—; leader Kit Carson council Boy Scouts Am., 1938—; chmn. library bd., Orangeburg, N.Y., 1946-48. Decorated Bronze Star (4), Purple Heart; recipient Silver Beaver award Boy Scouts Am., 1956; registered profl. engr., Calif. Fellow Explorers Club; mem. Nat. Acad. Sci. (mem. com. on fire research 1970—), Internat. Assn. Fire Chiefs (chmn. fire research com. 1969—), Fed. Fire Council, Nat. Fire Protection Assn. (chmn. hosp. disaster com. 1973—), AAAS, SAR, Black Forest Mardi Gras (Germany), Nat. Broadcasters Club, Pentagon Officers Athletic Club, Phi Beta Kappa, Gamma Sigma Epsilon, Delta Phi Alpha. Presbyn. (elder 1963—). Author: Korean-English Phrase Book, 1951; 19th Century Korea Postal Handbook, 1965. Editor Korean Philately mag., 1971—. Contbr. articles to profl. jours. Office: Def Civil Preparedness Research Pentagon Washington DC 20301

KERR, MABEL DOROTHEA, physician; b. Toronto, Ont., Can. (parents Am. citizens); d. George Houston and Mabel (Wark) Kerr; B.S., Ohio State U., 1944; M.D., Columbia, 1950. Intern dept. medicine St. Luke's Hosp., N.Y.C., 1950-51, resident, 1951-52; psychiat. resident Payne Whitney Clinic, N.Y. Hosp., 1952-57; practice medicine specializing in psychiatry, N.Y.C., 1954—; asst. attending psychiatrist N.Y. Hosp.; clin. asst. prof. psychiatry Cornell U. Med. Coll., 1968—; asst. med. examiner, officer chief med. examiner City of N.Y., 1957-66, med. investigator, 1966—. Pres. Elmora Found. Fellow N.Y. Acad. Medicine; mem. A.M.A., Am. Psychiat. Assn., Am. Acad. Forensic Scis., Pan Am. Med. Assn., Women's Med. Soc. N.Y. State. Address: 20 E 68th St New York City NY 10021

KERR, ROBERT MCNAB, JR., cons., former mfg. co. exec.; b. Detroit, Sept. 12, 1908; s. Robert M. and Irene (Carrier) K.; student Dartmouth, 1926-28 children—Sharon (Mrs. Robert MacDonald), Robert Kerr III, Francis (Mrs. Peter Ness) (by previous marriage); m. Rena Glenn, June 25, 1963; 1 son, Lyndall Cook. Research, Kerr Mfg. Co., 1929-34, sales mgr., 1934-39, v.p., treas. 1939-45, pres., 1945-66; group v.p. Sybron Corp. (formerly Ritter Pfaudier), 1966-73, ret.; cons., 1973—; pres. Hi Seas Corp. Trustee Fund for Dental Edn., Found. for Prevention Oral Disease. Mem. ADA. Clubs: University, Bayview Yacht, Detroit Boat, Country of Detroit (Detroit); Rochester Yacht, Genesee Valley (Rochester); N.Y. Yacht; Grosse Pointe (Mich.) Yacht. Home: 177 Whitewood Ln Rochester NY 14618 Office: Midtown Tower Rochester NY 14604

KERR, ROSE GLADYS HALL, home economist; b. San Francisco, June 20, 1913; d. Albert John and Orabelle Ann (DesChamps) Hall; B.S., U. Idaho, 1936; m. John Harry Kerr, Mar. 1, 1941. Home econs. tchr. Blackfoot (Idaho) High Sch., 1936-37, Rupert (Idaho) High Sch., 1937-40; dir. home econs. Weiser (Idaho) Vocat. Sch., 1940-41; home economist U.S. Dept. Agr., Washington, 1943; chief Nat. Home Econs. Research Center of U.S. Dept. Interior, U.S. Dept. Commerce, College Park, Md., 1944-72. Recipient certificate appreciation meritorious service Dept. Army, 1944; performance awards Dept. Interior, 1946-65; Blue Pencil award Fed. Editors Assn., 1966; Bronze medal Superior Fed. Service Dept. Commerce, 1972. Mem. Am., D.C. home econs. Author govt. publs. Home: 4522 Roxbury Dr Bethesda MD 20014

KERR, WILLIAM EDWARD, architect; b. Pitts., July 25, 1936; s. Charles and Elizabeth (Fohl) K.; B.A., U. Va., 1959; B.Arch., Carnegie-Mellon U., 1962; m. Constance Clark Unkovic, June 26, 1962; children—Elizabeth, William Edward. Officer, dir. The Design Alliance, architects and engrs., Pitts. Mem. Edgewood (Pa.) Borough Council, 1975—. Mem. AIA, Pa. Soc. Architects. Republican. Clubs: University (Pitts.); Edgewood Community. Address: 1100 Union Trust Bldg Pittsburgh PA 15219

KERSEY, GEORGE EUCLID, lawyer; b. Pueblo, Colo., Apr. 3, 1927; s. George D. and Maria (Prignon) K.; B.S., U. Colo., 1952; postgrad. (Rotary Found. fellow) Cambridge (Eng.) U., 1952-53; M.S., Mass. Inst. Tech., 1956; LL.B., Harvard, 1959; m. Joan Harrison; children—Wendy, Catherine, William Alan, James George. Teaching staff Mass. Inst. Tech., 1953-56; admitted to N.Y. bar, 1960, N.J. bar, 1963, Mass. bar, 1966, U.S. Supreme Ct. bar; patent atty. Bell Tel. Labs., Murray Hill, N.J., 1959-66; patent atty. Dike, Thompson & Bronstein, Boston, 1966-68; patent atty. Western Elec. Co., N.Y.C., 1968-72, Woodward, Kersey, Kojima, N.Y.C., 1972-73; cons. legal aspects of indsl. property, 1973—. Served to 1st lt. with Chem. Corps, AUS, 1946-49. Mem. Am., N.Y. State, N.J. State bar assns., N.Y. County Lawyers Assn., Internat. Fedn. Indsl. Prop. Cons., Sigma Xi, Sigma Tau, Tau Beta Pi, Delta Sigma Rho, Sigma Pi Sigma, Eta Kappa Nu, Pi Mu Epsilon. Patentee in elec. field. Home and Office: Allerton Rd Annandale NJ 08801

KERSHAW, GORDON ERNEST, historian; b. Sanford, Maine, May 5, 1928; s. Clifford and Violet (Gilpin) K.; A.B., U. Maine, 1950; A.M., Boston U., 1954; A.M., U. Pa., 1964, Ph.D., 1971; m. Carolyn Agnes Groves, July 21, 1976; 1 dau., Christina Elizabeth. Prof., head dept. history Frostburg (Md.) State Coll., 1971—. Served with U.S. Army, 1951-53. Mem. Maine Hist. Soc., Am. Hist. Assn., Orgn. Am. Historians. Author: The Kennebeck Proprietors, 1975; James Bowdoin, Patriot and Man of the Enlightenment, 1976; co-author: Allegany County: A History, 1976. Home: 17 Dogwood Circle Frostburg MD 21532 Office: Frostburg State Coll Frostburg MD 21532

KERSHAW, THOMAS MARTIN, religious orgn. exec.; b. Fall River, Mass., Nov. 24, 1933; s. George Henry and Josephine Ashworth (Martin) K.; B.S. with honors, Northeastern U., 1959; M.Div. (Hobson fellow), Episcopal Theol. Sch., 1963; m. Elizabeth Mary Gallagher, Apr. 23, 1954; children—Elisabeth, Karen, Katherine. Analyst, Electronics Corp. Am., Boston, 1954-55; office bus. mgr. Northeastern U., Boston, 1955-59; asst. to comptroller Bethlehem Steel Corp., (Pa.), 1959-60; with Ch. of Meditor, Allentown, Pa., 1963-64; headmaster St. Anne's Sch., Arlington, Mass., 1965-68; exec. officer, treas. Order St. Anne, Arlington, Mass., 1968-73; exec. officer, trustee of donations to the Protestant Episcopal Ch. Diocese of Mass., Boston, 1973—. Cons. to various pvt. and non-profit orgns. Lectr. World Fedn. Mental Health, 1971. Vice chmn. Arlington Redevel. Bd., 1968-73; founder Bethany, Lincoln, Mass., 1970, chmn. bd. trustees, 1974—; chmn. adv. bd. Mass. Dept. Pub. Welfare, 1973-75; trustee United Community Planning Corp., Boston, 1975-78, Sherrill House, Boston, 1976—. Served with AUS, 1950-54. Mem. Arlington C. of C. (pres. 1969-71, dir.). Clubs: Rotary (hon.), Harvard of Boston, Union. Home: PO Box 361 Goose Pond Rd Lincoln MA 01773 Office: 1 Joy St Boston MA 02108

KERSHNER, BERNARD, real estate co. exec.; b. Burlington, Vt., Feb. 12, 1927; B.A., U. Vt.; m. Beulah Bertha, Apr. 18, 1947; children—Gary Ronald, Cynthia Sue, Brian Joseph. Mgr. Wilbar's Shoes, Inc., Boston, 1946-59; gen. mgr. Arbor Homes Inc., Milford and New Haven, Conn., 1959-67; v.p. Whitney-Kershner Co., Real Estate, New Haven, 1967-73; pres. The Kershner Co., Realtors, West Haven, Conn., The Kershner-Fiorello Co., Ins., West Haven. Chmn. West Haven Flood and Erosion Control Bd., 1966-76; chmn. 50th Anniversary celebration City of West Haven; active Blood Bank, Muscular Dystrophy, Arthritis drives; rep. city of West Haven R.T.M. Served with U.S. Army, 1944-46. Mem. West Haven C. of C. (dir. 1970, pres. 1976-78), Nat. Marketing Inst. of Real Estate Brokers, Nat. Farm and Land Inst., Nat. Assn. Realtors, Realtors of Greator New Haven (budget com. 1971-74), Conn. Assn. Realtors (state dir.). Jewish religion. Clubs: Mason (32 deg.), West Haven Fish and Game (trustee), Aimes Point, City Point Yacht, Elks, Shriners, New Haven Jewish Community Center, Hejaz Grotto. Home: 23 Templeton St West Haven CT 06516 Office: 393 Meloy Rd West Haven CT 06516

KERTZ, HAROLD ALLAN, lawyer; b. Allentown, Pa., Dec. 2, 1906; s. Christian J. and Elizabeth (Rudy) K.; J.D., Georgetown U., 1928; LL.M., Catholic U., 1932; m. Genevieve Hastings, Mary 1, 1944; 1 son, Robert Allan. Admitted to D.C. bar, 1929; practiced law, Washington, 1929-31; trust officer Nat. Met. Bank, Washington, 1931-40; partner Roberts & McInnis, 1940-54, Mercier, Kertz & Sanders, 1954-57; vice chmn. Pub. Utilities Commn. D.C., 1957-62; prof. of wills and estates, Georgetown U., Washington, 1955-65; dir. Harlowe Typography, Inc., Ehrbit Aids, Inc., Sho-Tel, Inc. O'Donnell's Sea Grill, Inc., R.E. Darling Co., James R. Dunlop, Inc. Mem. ICC Practitioners Assn., FCC Bar, Am., D.C. bar assns., Sigma Nu Phi. Episcopalian. Clubs: University, Nat. Press, Farmington County, The Counsellors. Legal contbg. editor to Trusts and Estates, 1944-74. Home: 2500 Virginia Ave NW Washington DC 20037 Office: 1906 Sunderland Pl NW Washington DC 20036

KERZMAN, NORBERTO LUIS MARIA, research mathematician, educator; b. Buenos Aires, Argentina, Feb. 1, 1943; s. Isidoro Norberto and Maria Luisa (Remussi) K.; licenciado en matematicas, U. Buenos Aires, 1966; Ph.D., N.Y. U., 1970. Came to U.S., 1967. Lectr. math. Princeton, 1970-71, asst. prof., 1971-73; asst. prof. math. Mass. Inst. Tech., 1973-76, asso. prof., 1976—; vis. prof. univs. Gottingen and Munster (West Germany), summer 1971. Courant Inst. fellow, 1967-70; Sloan fellow, 1973-75. Mem. Am. Math. Soc. Contbr. articles to profl. jours. Home: 19 Mellen St Cambridge MA 02138

KESHEN, ALBERT SIDNEY, journalist; b. Newark, Apr. 13, 1905; s. Meyer and Augusta (Wagman) K.; B.J., U. Mo., 1927; M.A. equivalent, Nat. U. Mexico-Mexico City Coll., 1949. Reporter, N.J. newspapers, 1926-28; editor, pub. Union (N.J.) Register, 1928-32, Wallkill Valley News, Franklin, N.J., 1932-35; suburban editor Hudson Dispatch, Union City, 1935-42; copyreader Fairchild Publs., N.Y.C., 1945-46, Washington Star, 1946-47, Chgo. Sun, 1947-50; editor Nat. Jeweler, N.Y.C., 1950-52; pub. relations exec. Denson-Frey & Affiliates, N.Y.C., 1952-53, Hamilton Wright Orgn., N.Y.C., 1953-55, David Resnick Assos., N.Y.C., 1955-60; editor Modern Windows, N.Y.C., 1960-65; free lance reporter, photographer, 1965—. Served with USAAF, 1942-45; Panama. Mem. Soc. Silurians, Fossils, Elbeetian Legion (Lone Scout alumni), Sigma Delta Chi. Jewish. Club: Overseas Press. Contbr. numerous articles, photographs to specialty and consumer publs. Home: 47 Bonnell St Flemington NJ 08822

KESHISHOGLOU, JOHN ELIAS, educator, coll. dean; b. Thessaloniki, Greece, June 19, 1932; s. Elias P. and Areti (Tastsoglou) K.; A.A., Anatolia Coll. (Greece), 1950; B.A., Morningside Coll., 1961; M.A., U. Iowa, 1962; Ph.D., Syracuse U., 1969;; m. Barbara Ann Steele, Apr. 20, 1963; 1 son, Elias John. Came to U.S., 1958, naturalized, 1967. Audiovisual cons. U. Iowa, Iowa City, 1962-65; asst. prof. radio and tv, films dir. instructional resources center Ithaca (N.Y.) Coll., 1965-68, asso. prof., 1968-70, prof., 1970—, chmn. dept., dir. center, 1970—, dean Sch. Communication, 1972—. Staff officer Hellenic Nat Def. Gen. Staff, NATO Registry, Athens, Greece, 1954-56. Recipient various grants awards in photography and film; NDEA fellow, 1966. Mem. Nat. Assn. Ednl. Broadcasters, Univ. Film Assn., So. Zone (pres. 1967-69), N.Y. State (dir.) audiovisual assns., European Broadcasting Union, Alpha Epsilon Rho. Author two textbooks. Contbr. articles to profl. jours. Home: 292 Nelson Rd Ithaca NY 14850

KESLER, MICHAEL GUBERMAN, engring. exec.; b. Dubno, Poland, July 6, 1925; s. Moses B. and Manya (Guberman) K.; came to U.S., 1947, naturalized, 1953; B.Sc. in Chem. Engring., Mass. Inst. Tech., 1951, M.Sc. in Biophysics, 1954, M.Sc. in Chem. Engring., 1954; Ph.D., N.Y. U., 1968; m. Regina R. Chanowicz, Dec. 22, 1952; children—Mark, May, David, Teddy. Combustion engr. Atlantic Research Corp., Arlington, Va., 1955-56; process engr. M.W. Kellogg, N.Y.C., 1956-60, mgr. computer applications, 1960-63; head sci. and engring. computer applications Esso Research & Engring., Florham Park, N.J., 1963-69; sr. asso. Mobil Engring., Princeton, N.J., 1971-74, mgr. computer methods, 1974-75, engring. cons., 1975—. Bd. dirs. Fluid Properties Research Inst. Recipient various fellowships. Mem. Am. Inst. Chem. Engrs., Am. Chem. Soc., Assn. for Computing Machinery, Sigma Xi. Mem. B'nai B'rith. Contbr. articles to profl. jours. Home: 26 University Rd East Brunswick NJ 08816 Office: POB 1026 Princeton NJ 08540

KESSLER, HERMAN EUGENE, educator; b. N.Y.C., Apr. 26, 1923; s. Herman Eugene and Anna (Noering) K.; A.B., Harvard U., 1943, M.B.A. (Baker scholar), 1950; M.A., George Washington U., 1964; m. Mary Clarkson Boykin, Feb. 1, 1949; children—Mary Brisbane Boykin, Eugene deSaussure Burroughs. Commd. 2d lt. U.S. Army, 1943, advanced through grades to col., 1967; service in Europe; dir. resource mgmt. and control studies, mem. faculty Army War Coll., 1967-70; ret., 1970; asst. dir. test devel. Ednl. Testing Service, Princeton, N.J., 1970-71; exec. dir., treas. EDUCOM, Princeton, 1971—, v.p., 1977—; cons., tchr. in field. Vestryman, lay reader Episcopal Ch., Heidelberg, W. Ger., 1964-66. Decorated Legion of Merit, Army Commendation medal. Mem. Assn. U.S. Army, Ret. Officers Assn., Nat. Assn. Uniformed Services, Phi Beta Kappa. Republican. Club: Harvard (treas. Heidelberg 1965-66; v.p. Princeton 1970-73). Author articles. Home: 6 Riverside Dr Princeton NJ 08540 Office: PO Box 364 Rosedale Rd Princeton NJ 08540

KESSLER, JACQUES ISAAC, gastroenterologist, hosp. exec., educator; b. Roussè, Bulgaria, May 23, 1929; s. Isaac Joseph and Liza Leah (Schwartz) K.; came to Can., 1963; naturalized, 1966; student Nat. U., Sofia, Bulgaria, 1947-50; M.D., Hadassah Med. Sch. Hebrew U., Jerusalem, Israel, 1955; m. Roslyn Norma Sobcov, Nov. 21, 1965; children—Liza Daphna, Linda Ruth, Audrey Joan, Joseph Isaac. Intern Beilinson Hosp., Petach Tiqva, Israel, 1954-55, resident in internal medicine, 1955-59; resident, research fellow in gastroenterology and metabolism Mount Sinai Hosp., N.Y.C., 1959-63; dir. research lab. Jewish Gen. Hosp., Montreal, Que., Can., 1963-67; sr. physician, dir. div. of gastroenterology Royal Victoria Hosp., Montreal, 1967—; prof. medicine McGill U., Montreal, 1972—; cons. Montreal Children's Hosp., Jewish Gen. Hosp., Montreal, Lakeshore Hosp., Pt. Claire. Recipient L. Doljansky Gold medal Hebrew U., Jerusalem, 1955. Med. Research Council of Can. research asso., 1968—, also grantee, 1964—; USPHS grantee, 1967-70. Certified specialist in internal medicine and gastroenterology Royal Coll. Physicians, Can. Fellow Royal Coll. Physicians of Can., Am. Coll. Gastroenterology; mem. Am. Soc. Clin. Investigation, AAAS, Am. Fedn. Clin. Research, Am. Gastroenterol. Assn., Canadian Soc. Clin. Investigation, Canadian Med. Assn., Canadian Assn. Gastroenterology. Jewish. Asso. editor Canadian Jour. of Physiology and Pharmacology, 1968-73. Contbr. numerous articles to profl. jours., also chpts. to books. Home: 624 Carleton Ave Westmount PQ H3Y 2Y2 Canada Office: Royal Victoria Hosp 687 Pine Ave W Montreal PQ H3A 1A1 Canada

KESSLER, MILTON SEYMOUR, educator; b. Newark, Aug. 12, 1913; s. Morris and Lena (Markowitz) K.; B.A., N.Y. U., 1937, M.A., 1939, Ph.D., 1952; m. Claire Kast, Oct. 19, 1941; children—Michael, Brian. Social worker Dept. Pub. Welfare, Newark, 1940-43; psychologist, registration officer VA, Newark, 1946-50; instr. sociology N.Y. U., 1951-53; tchr. Newark Pub. Schs., 1953-63; dir. B'nai B'rith Vocat. Services No. N.J., Newark, 1954-61; guidance dir. Weequahic High Sch., Newark, 1963-68; dir. Weequahic Adult Sch., 1967-68; instr. Rutgers U., Newark, Montclair State Coll., Newark State Coll., various times 1948-71; asso. prof. William Paterson Coll., Wayne, N.J., 1968—, also mem. Master Planning Council, Coll. Forum. Served with AUS, 1943-45. Mem. Am., N.J. psychol. assns., Am., N.J. personnel and guidance assns., Nat. Vocat. Guidance Assn. (chmn. credentials com. 1970-73), Am. Sch. Counselors Assn., NEA, N.J. Ednl. Assn., Alpha Kappa Delta. Jewish. Clubs: B'nai B'rith (past v.p.); Men's of Temple (past pres.). Home: 40 Cypress Ave Verona NJ 07044 Office: 300 Pompton Rd Wayne NJ 07470

KESSLER, RONALD BOREK, newspaper reporter; b. N.Y.C., Dec. 31, 1943; Ernest Borek and Minuetta K.; student Clark U., Worcester, Mass., 1962-64; children—Gregory, Rachel. Reporter, Worcester Telegram, 1964; investigative reporter, editorial writer Boston Herald Traveler, 1964-68; N.Y. bur. reporter Wall St. Jour., 1968-70; investigative reporter Washington Post, 1970—. Recipient George Polk Meml. award community service, 1972; 1st prize newswriting UPI, 1967; Sevellon Brown award AP, 1967; Front Page award Washington-Balt. Newspaper Guild, 1973; Bill Pryor award, 1973; Pub. Affairs Reporting award Am. Polit. Sci. Assn., 1973, Community Service award AAUW, 1972; named Newspaper Fund intern, 1964; Washingtonian of Yr., Washingtonian mag., 1972. Home: 4615 N Park Ave Apt 1012 Chevy Chase MD 20015 Office: 1150 15th St NW Washington DC 20071

KESSLER, STUART ALAN, architect, real estate developer; b. N.Y.C., Feb. 10, 1939; s. Melvin E. and Mildred I. (Jacobson) K.; B.A., U. Va., 1959; postgrad. N.Y. U. Sch. Law, 1959-60, Columbia Sch. Architecture, 1960-64; m. Catharina M. Aulin, Nov. 9, 1967; children—Nils Robert, Karl Tyko, Jonas Gustav. Constrn. supr. DeMatteis Orgn., Elmont, N.Y., 1959-62; pres. Claridge Co., N.Y.C., 1966-75; v.p. S.J. Kessler & Sons, N.Y.C., Boston, 1962-74; owner Stuart A. Kessler, architect, 1974—; chmn. bd. Nordic Investment Co. Ltd., 1975—; lectr. architecture and planning U. Bath, Eng., 1972, Univ. Coll., Dublin, Ireland, 1972, Archtl. Assn. Sch. Arch., London, Eng., 1973, Canterbury (Eng.) Coll. Art, 1973; instr. Zeman Profl. Inst., N.Y.C., 1975—; housing cons. City of Marsta, Sweden, 1973—. Mem. Zoning Adv. Council N.Y.C., 1963—. Recipient Service to Industry award Nat. Apt. Assn., 1969, Multi-Housing Leadership award, 1978. Mem. AIA, Royal Inst. Brit. Architects, Am. Inst. Planners, N.Y., Boston socs. architects, Urban Land Inst., Constrn. Specifications Inst., Nat. Assn. Homebuilders. Club: City Athletic (N.Y.C.). Author: Architects . . . Tomorrow's Dinosaurs?. Inventor, Phased Community Redevel. Home: 21 E 79th St New York NY 10021 Office: 654 Madison Ave New York NY 10021

KESSMAN, ALAN STUART, communications co. exec.; b. N.Y.C., Sept. 29, 1946; s. Herbert and Florence (Citron) K.; B.B.A., Lehigh U., 1968; 1 son, Marc. Staff accountant Ernst & Ernst, C.P.A.'s, N.Y.C. 1968-69, sr. accountant, 1969-70, supr., mgr., 1970-71; asst. treas. EDP Resources, Inc., White Plains, N.Y., 1971-72; treas. Tele/Resources, Inc., White Plains, N.Y., 1972-73, v.p. ops., treas., 1973-75, exec. v.p. chief operating officer, 1975—; pres. Rolm Corp. Ill., 1978—. C.P.A., N.Y. Mem. Nat. Assn. Accountants, Am. Inst. C.P.A.'s, N.Y. Soc. C.P.A.'s, N.Am. Telephone Assn., Am. Mgmt. Assn. Jewish. Home: 642 Locust St Mount Vernon NY 10552 Office: One E Wacker Dr Chicago IL 60601

KESTER, NANCY CONRAD, physician; b. Winston-Salem N.C., June 22, 1928; d. Julius Curtis and Connie (Fowler) Kester; A.B., Duke U., 1949; M.S., Bowman Gray Sch. Medicine of Wake Forest Coll., 1951, M.D., 1955. Intern in pediatrics N.C. Bapt. Hosp., Winston-Salem, N.C., 1955-56; intern, internal medicine U. Calif. Hosp. San Francisco, 1956-57; research fellowship neurosurgery Bowman Gray Sch. Medicine, Winton-Salem, N.C., 1957-58; resident physical medicine and rehab., N.Y.U. Med. Center, N.Y.C., 1958-61; acad. career tng. fellow, dept. phys. medicine and rahab., N.Y.U. Med. Center, N.Y.C., 1961-63; physiatrist on S.S. Hope in Peru, 1963; attending physician Inst. of Rehab. Medicine, 1963—; coordinator rehab. medicine Univ. Hosp., N.Y.U. Med. Center, 1963—, instr. phys. medicine and rehab., 1964-65; asst. prof. rehab. medicine N.Y.U. Sch. Medicine, 1965-69, asso. prof., 1969—. Bd. visitors Wake Forest U., 1974—. Recipient Am. Women's Med. Assn. award, 1955, Distinguished Alumnus award in medicine Wake Forest U., 1975. Mem. Am. Cong. of Rehab. Medicine, Am. Acad. Phys. Medicine and Rehab., N.Y. County, N.Y. State med. socs., A.M.A., Am. Heart Assn. (mem. council cerebrovascular disease), Alpha Omega Alpha. Contbr. articles to profl. jours. Home: 200 E 66th St New York City NY 10021 Office: 400 E 34th St New York City NY 10016

KESTIN, HOWARD H., lawyer, ednl. adminstr.; b. Passaic, N.J., July 24, 1937; s. Oscar and Annette (Moichich) K.; B.S., St. Louis U., 1959; J.D., Rutgers U., 1962; m. Joan H. Bard, Aug. 22, 1970; children—Bette Lynn, Anita Louise. Admitted to N.J. bar, 1962, U.S. Supreme Ct. bar, 1965; law sec. Hon. F.W. Hall, Asso. Justice, Supreme Court N.J., 1962-63; dep. atty. gen. N.J., 1963-65; asst. dir. Inst. Continuing Legal Edn., Newark, 1965-66, 69-70, dir., 1970—; dir. State N.J. Legal Services to the Poor Program, Trenton, 1966-68; pvt. practice law, Wayne, N.J., 1968-69. Adj. prof. law Seton Hall U. Sch. Law, Newark, 1972—; counsel N.J. Family Court Study Commn., 1972-75. Pres. Passaic City Democrats, 1970-72. Pres. bd. trustees Passaic County (N.J.) Children's Shelter, 1972-73. Recipient Media award for TV series on Bill of Rights, N.J. State Bar Assn.-Am. Bar Assn., 1971; Distinguished Alumnus award Rutgers U. Sch. Law, 1977. Mem. N.J. State (chmn. adminstrv. law sect. 1972-74, chmn. young lawyers sect. 1968-69, trustee 1969-70, chmn. com. on legal edn. and admissions to bar 1976—), Am. (membership com. 1968-73, state legis. com. 1972-73) bar assns., Assn. Continuing Legal Edn. Adminstrs. (chmn. standards and accreditation com. 1972—), Passaic County Bar Assn. Jewish Religion. Moderator-host The Blessings of Liberty, WNBC-TV 1971, The Right of the People, WNBC-TV, 1975. Home: 88 Anderson Dr Wayne NJ 07470 Office: 15 Washington St Suite 1400 Newark NJ 07102

KETCHAM, ORMAN WESTON, former judge; b. Bklyn., Oct. 1, 1918; s. Walter Seymour and Arline (Weston) K.; A.B., Princeton, 1940; LL.B., Yale, 1947; m. Anne Phelps Stokes, Dec. 22, 1947; children—Anne Weston, Helen Louisa Phelps, Elizabeth Miner, Susan Stokes. Admitted to D.C. bar, 1948; practiced in Washington, 1948-52; Washington rep. Fund for the Republic, 1953; asst. gen. counsel U.S. Fgn. Operations Agy., 1953-55; trial atty. Antitrust div. U.S. Dept. Justice, Washington, 1955-57; Judge Juvenile Ct. D.C., Washington, 1957-71; asso. judge Superior Ct. D.C., 1971-77; sr. William and Mary Law Sch., 1977—. Adj. prof. law Georgetown U. Law Center, 1963-67, U. Va. Law Sch., 1971-76; lectr. Staff atty. Nat. Center State Cts., 1977— Bd. dirs. Nat. Council Crime and Delinquency, 1973—. Served as lt. comdr., USNR, 1941-46. Recipient Princeton Club award Distinguished Community Service, 1972. Mem. Am. Bar Assn., Bar Assn. D.C., Nat. Council Juvenile Ct. Judges (pres. 1965-66), Internat. Assn. Youth Magistrates (v.p. 1966-74), Am. Law Inst. Conglist. Clubs: Cosmos (Washington); Chevy Chase. Author: (with Monrad . Paulsen) Cases and Materials Relating to Juvenile Courts, 1967. Home: 2 E Melrose St Chevy Chase MD 20015 Office: 300 Newport Ave Williamsburg VA 23185

KETCHUM, ALTON HARRINGTON, advt. exec.; b. Cleve., Oct. 8, 1904; s. Wesley H. and Velma M. (Davis) K.; B.A., Western Res. U., 1926; m. Robyna Neilson, Apr. 27, 1940; 1 dau., Deborah (Mrs. Harvey Lambert). Spl. corr. United Press, 1926-27; editorial, advt. work Penton Pub. Co., Powers-House Co., Nesbitt Service Co., 1927-33; with McCann-Erickson, Inc., 1934-63, successively copy writer, copy group head, v.p., creative supr. internat. div., 1948-63; v.p. Infoplan, 1963-64; member corporate staff Interpublic Group Cos. Inc., 1964-69; mng. dir. Harrington's (Hist. Resources), 1969—. Editor Inst. Marketing Cummunications Bull. Spl. asst. Petroleum Adminstrn. for War, 1943-44; supr. nat. campaign to explain Am. econ. system sponsored by Advt. Council, 1948-51; spl. rep. USIA, India, 1954, cons., 1956—, mem. exec. res., 1957-69; mem. exec. council Fed. World Govt., Inc., 1947-51; designed People's Capitalism exhibit for USIA, 1956, Golden Key Exhibit for Dept. of Commerce, 1956. Organizer Westchester-Fairfield (Conn.) Com. of Am. Assn. for UN, 1946; gave original designs for baton and badge of marshals of France to French people, 1953; creative dir. anti-recession campaign Advt. Council, 1958, author Key booklet. Mem. Greenwich (Conn.) Aux. Police. Recipient award of merit USIA, 1956, award Freedoms Found., 1949, Ohio Gov.'s award for achievement, 1965; named 1 of 100 top copywriters, 1954. Mem. adv. com. U.S. Civil War Centennial Commn., 1960; pres. India-Am. League, 1960-63. Mem. Assn. Am. Geographers, Nat. Planning Assn., Am. Acad. Polit. and Social Sci., Am., Greenwich hist. socs., Hist. Assn. Gt. Britain. Author: Follow the Sun, 1930; The Miracle of America, 1948; The March of Freedom, 1951; Let Freedom Ring, 1952; Our Hopes March Side By Side, 1955; Your Great Future in a Growing America 1958; Uncle Sam, the Man and the Legend, 1959. Editor: Principles and Practices of Marketing Communications, 1966; mem. internat. editorial bd. World Govt. News, 1949-52. Home: 333 Cognewaug Rd Cos Cob CT 06807

KETCHUM, WILLIAM CLARENCE, JR., lawyer, author; b. Columbia, Mo., Mar. 29, 1931; s. William C. and Mildred Ann (Roberts) K.; B.A., Union Coll., 1953; J.D., Columbia, 1956; m. Patricia M. Forbes, July 6, 1963; children—Rachel, Aaron. Admitted to N.Y. bar, 1960; atty. Kriendler & Kriendler, N.Y.C., 1956, Martin, Clearwater & Bell, N.Y.C., 1960-65, R.S. Lane, N.Y.C., 1965-69; law sec. to Judge Lane of Civil Court, New York County, N.Y.C., 1969-76. Instr. course on Am. antiques New Sch., N.Y.C., 1970—; instr. antiques course Hunter Coll., N.Y.C., 1978—; guest curator Museum Am. Folk Art, N.Y.C., 1974—; guest speaker Seminar on Early Am. Life, Pa. Farm Museum, Lancaster, 1974; guest lectr. Flemington Hist. Soc., 1975-76, antiques seminar N.Y. U., 1973-75, New Haven Hist. Soc., 1975, Shelburne (Vt.) Mus., 1976, 78, St. Mary's of the Woods Coll., Terre Haute, Ind., 1976-78; cons. antique series Time-Life, Inc., 1976-78; guest speaker Smithsonian Instn., 1976, Mercer Mus., 1977, Hancock Shaker Mus., 1977. Served to lt., USNR, 1956-60. Mem. N.Y.C. Bar Assn. (mem. com. uniform state laws 1972-76, mem. art com. 1976-78), N.Y. State Bar Assn., N.Y. State Hist. Soc. Author: Early Potters and Potteries of New York, 1970; The Pottery and Porcelain Collectors Handbook, 1971; American Basketry and Woodenware, 1974; American Bottles, 1975; American Hooked Rugs, 1976; A Catalog of American Antiques, 1977; The Family Treasury of Antiques, 1978; American Crafts, 1979. Contbr. articles to profl. jours. Home: 312 W 20th St New York City NY 10011 also Gen Delivery Harrington ME 04643

KETO, CLEMENT TSEHLOANE, historian, educator; b. Matatiele, S. Africa, Feb. 23, 1937; s. V. Lentsoe and C. Naniwe (Mazibu) Tsehloane; came to U.S., 1968; B.A., Nat. U. Lesotho, 1963; M.A., Am. U., 1967; Ph.D., Georgetown U., 1972; m. Louise Mosley, Nov. 5, 1966. Tchr., Zambia, 1966-68; instr. Lincoln U., Oxford, Pa., 1969-70; asst. prof. African studies U. Kans., Lawrence, 1970-73; asso. prof. history Temple U., Phila., 1973—; asso. editor Jour. So. African Affairs, 1976—. Am. Philos. Soc. grantee, 1973-75. Mem. Am. Hist. Soc., African Studies Assn., So. African Research Assn., African Heritage Studies Assn, Assn. Study of Afro-Am. Life and History. , Unitarian. Co-author: American-South African Relations, 1978. Home: 316 Roberts Dr Somerdale NJ 08083 Office: History Dept Temple U Broad and Montgomery sts Philadelphia PA 19122

KETTER, ROBERT LEWIS, univ. pres.; b. Welch, W. Va., Dec. 7, 1928; s. E. F. and Ella Louise (Drummn) K., B.C.E., U. Mo., 1950, M.C.E., Lehigh U., 1952, Ph.D., 1956; D.Sc., Kyungpook Nat. U., Taegu, Korea, 1973; m. Lorelei Zimmerman, Dec. 22, 1948; children—Katharyn K. Ross, Susannah K. McIsaac, Mary, Michael. From research asst. to research asst. prof. civil engring. Lehigh U., 1950-58; prof. civil engring., chmn. dept. U. Buffalo, 1958; acting dean Grad. Sch. State U. N.Y. at Buffalo, 1964-65, dean grad. sch., 1965-66, v.p. univ. 1966-69, pres., 1970—; dir. Marine Midland Bank-Western, Sierra Research Corp. Chmn. bd. trustees Western N.Y. Nuclear Research Center, Inc., 1970; chmn. bd. Comprehensive Health Planning Council of Western N.Y., Inc., 1970-71; mem. N.Y. State Com. Electric Power Research, 1973—. Mem. N.Y. Commn. on Jud. Nomination, 1978; bd. mgrs. Buffalo and Erie County Hist. Soc.; bd. visitors Roswell Park Meml. Inst., 1972—; bd. dirs. Greater Buffalo Devel. Found.; trustee Univs. Research Corp., 1977—. Recipient Adams Memorial award Am. Welding Soc., 1968; Disting. Service award U. Mo., 1971. Mem. ASCE (dir. Niagara Frontier sect., chmn. several nat. coms.), Column Research Council of Engring. Found. (chmn. tech. coms.). Internat. Inst. Welding (ofcl. expert rep. U.S. on commn. X), Internat. Assn. Bridge and Structural Engrs., Am. Welding Soc., Buffalo Fine Arts Acad., Buffalo Soc. Natural Scis., Sigma Xi, Tau Beta Pi, Phi Eta Sigma, Omicron Delta Kappa, Pi Mu Epsilon, Chi Epsilon, Beta Gamma Sigma. Author: (with S.P. Prawel, Jr.) Modern Methods of Engineering Computation, 1969; (with G.C. Lee and S.P. Prawel, Jr.) Structural Analysis and Design, 1978. also articles in field and in edn. Home: 186 LeBrun Rd Buffalo NY 14226

KETTING, JAAP, med. service co. exec.; b. Rotterdam, Netherlands, Apr. 25, 1916; s. Jaap and Margareta Cornelia (Van der Horden) K.; Ph.G., Sch. Pharmacy Rotterdam, 1937; m. Conny Van Rossen, May 4, 1950; 1 son, Jaap Jan. Came to U.S., 1946, naturalized, 1951. Pharmacist, Rathkamp & Co., Batavia, Netherlands East Indies, 1938-40, area sales rep., 1940-42, purchasing agt., N.Y.C., 1946-50; purchasing agt. Consol. Midland Corp., Brewster, N.Y., 1950-54, v.p., 1954-62, pres., 1962—. Served with Netherlands East Indies Air Force, 1941-46. Decorated D.F.C., Bronze Lion with clusters. Mem. Am. Pharm. Assn., Chemist Club. Republican. Presbyn. Lion (chpt. pres. 1962-63). Club: Netherlands of New York. Home: 25 Roosevelt Dr Bedford Hills NY 10506 Office: 195 E Main Brewster NY 10509

KETTLER, MILTON ELLSWORTH, home builder; b. Washington, May 31, 1923; s. Clifford Ellsworth and Elsie Belle (Weaver) K.; B.A., U. Mich., 1945; m. Barbara Elizabeth Walker, Oct. 4, 1947; children—Ellen Luise, Robert Charles, Peter Brookes. Real estate salesman Phillips, Canby & Fuller, Washington, 1945-49; real estate broker C.H. Hillegeist Co., Washington, 1949-52; chmn. bd., dir. Kettler Bros., Inc., Washington, Gaithersburg, Md., 1952—; dir. C & P Telephone Co. Md., Union 1st Nat. Bank, Washington. Trustee, Am. U., Washington. Served to ensign, USNR, 1945. Mem. Nat. Assn. Home Builders (Bill Molster Nat. Mktg. award, 1970; hon. life dir.), Md. Inst. Home Builders (pres. 1971-72), Met. Washington Builders Assn. (pres. 1969-70), Suburban Md. Home Builders Assn. (pres. 1974-75), Inst. Residential Mktg. (charter), Theta Chi, Lambda Alpha. Methodist (trustee). Mason. Clubs: Columbia Country; Montgomery Village Golf, Queen Anne Golf, Kent Island Yacht, Annapolis Yacht, Potomac Squash, George Towne. Home: 5510 Pollard Rd Bethesda MD 20016 Office: 19110 Montgomery Village Ave PO Box 2127 Gaithersburg MD 20760

KETVIRTIS, ANTANAS, elec. engr.; b. Lithuania, Apr. 13, 1919; s. Ignas and Emilie K.; came to Can., 1950, naturalized, 1956; E.E., Engring. Coll., Kaunas, 1943; student U. Kaunas, 1941-44; m. Antanina Gecas, July 4, 1949; 1 son, Anthony Emil. With Fenco Cons. Ltd., Toronto, Ont., 1955—, chief elec. engr., 1971—, dir. visual environment, 1972—; mem. faculty Ryerson Poly. Inst., 1974—. Recipient Engring. medal Assn. Profl. Engrs. Ont., 1977; Jubilee medal Gt. Britain, 1975. Fellow Illuminating Engring. Soc.; mem. IEEE (sr.), Assn. Profl. Engrs. Ont. Author: Highway Lighting Engineering, 1967; Lighting and Traffic Safety, 1977. Home: 32 Hopperton Dr Willowdale ON M2L 2S6 Canada Office: One Yonge St Toronto ON M5E 1E7 Canada

KETZ, LOUISE BILEBOF, editor; b. N.Y.C., Jan. 20, 1945; d. Alexander and Helen Joan (Korz) Bilebof; B.A., Hunter Coll., 1966; m. Gerard Eustis Ketz, Sept. 8, 1973. Editor, production coordinator, Collier's Ency. and Year Book, Macmillan Dictionary projects, Crowell-Collier Ednl. Corp., N.Y.C., 1966-70; adminstrv. editor, mng. editor, Dictionary Sci. Biography, Dictionary Am. Biography, Dictionary Am. History, Charles Scribners Sons, N.Y.C., 1970—, mng. editor trade editorial dept.; speaker publishing course State U. N.Y., Stony Brook. Mem. Am. Hist. Assn., Nat. Trust Hist. Preservation, Nat. Hist. Soc. Home: 301 E 79th St New York City NY 10021 Office: 597 5th Ave New York City NY 10017

KEYES, CHARLES DON, clergyman, educator; b. Wewoka, Okla., Jan. 24, 1937; s. Robert and Ruth (Brown) K.; B.A., U. Okla., 1958; B.D., Seabury-Western Theol. Sem., 1961, S.T.M., 1964; Th.D., Trinity Coll., Toronto, Ont., Can., 1966; M.A., U. Toronto, 1966; Ph.D., Duquesne U., 1968; m. Aileen May Johnston, Aug. 20, 1966. Ordained priest Episcopal Ch., 1961; vicar St. Stephen's Episc. Ch., Guymon, Okla., 1961-63; div. tutor Trinity Coll., 1964-66; instr. philosophy Duquesne U., 1966-67, asso. prof., 1969-77, prof., 1977—; asst. prof. theology Gen. Theol. Sem., 1967-69. Danford asso., 1970—; Episc. Ch. Found. fellow, 1964-67. Mem. Am. Heidegger Circle, Phi Beta Kappa. Author: Four Types of Value Destruction, 1978. Mem. editorial bd. Research in Phenomenology, 1969—. Contbr. articles to profl. jours. Home: 339 Barnes St Pittsburgh PA 15221 Office: Dept of Philosophy Duquesne U Pittsburgh PA 15219

KEYES, HENRY WILDER, lawyer, banker; b. North Haverhill, N.H., Mar. 22, 1905; s. Henry Wilder and Frances Parkinson (Wheeler) K.; A.B., Harvard, 1927, LL.B., 1930; m. Betty Louise Main, June 2, 1938; children—Margaretta Main (Mrs. Alfonso G. Orbegoso), Frances Parkinson II (Mrs. Christian L. Keidel), Sarah Louise (Mrs. John C. Rettew). Asso., Boston Legal Aid Soc., 1929; admitted to Mass. bar, 1930, N.H. bar, 1933; with Sherburne, Powers & Needham, Boston, 1930-50; with Spencer & Stone and predecessor, 1950-59, partner, 1960—; dir. Woodsville Nat. Bank (N.H.), 1938-75, v.p., 1939-58, pres., 1959-75, chmn. bd., 1974-75; with Mass. Title Ins. Co., 1953—, v.p., 1953-65, gen. mgr., 1953-72, 74—, pres., 1965—, also dir.; v.p. Lafayette Nat. Bank, 1975-77, dir. emeritus, 1977—; asst. sec. 1st Am. Title Ins. Co. N.Y., N.Y.C., 1976—. Mem. sch. com. City of Newton, 1950-57, chmn., 1954-57. Mem. Rep. City Com., Newton, Mass., 1940-68. Trustee, sec. Keyes Found., 1948—. Mem. Am. Land Title Assn., Mass. Conveyancers Assn., N.H., Mass., Boston (exec. sec. 1946, mem. council 1955-58) bar assns., New Eng. Land Title Assn. (exec. com. 1970, pres. 1972-73), New Eng. Law Inst. (exec. com. 1955-74, adv. com. 1974-77), Harvard Musical Assn., Greater Boston Legal Services, Charles River Boating Conf. (sec. 1976—), S.A.R. Episcopalian (lay reader). Mason (32 degree). Clubs: The Country (Brookline, Mass.); Harvard, Union Boat, Abstract (Boston); Cambridge Boat. Author articles profl. jours. Home: 40 Puddingstone Ln Newton Centre MA 02159 Office: 50 Beacon St Boston MA 02108

KEYES, JOSEPH PATRICK, assn. exec.; b. N.Y.C., Dec. 14, 1935; s. Edward A. and Jane M. (Manning) K.; B.S., Fordham U., 1957; m. Barbara Ann Germano; children—Kristine, Kevin, Patricia, Joseph. Asst. to picture editor Look mag., N.Y.C., 1952-55, circulation-promotion exec., 1955-61; publicity dir. TV Guide mag., N.Y.C., 1961-64; dir. pub. relations WABC-TV, N.Y.C., 1964-69; dir. U.S./internat. pub. relations Am. Mgmt. Assns., N.Y.C., 1969-77, v.p. pub. relations, 1977—. Mem. Pub. Relations Soc. Am., Am. Soc. Tng. Dirs., Internat. Radio and TV Soc., Nat. Cath. Office for Radio and TV (bd. mem. 1967-69), TV Acad., Promotion Dirs. Quorum, Publicity Club N.Y. (mem. edn. com. 1973-74), Am., N.Y. socs. assn. execs., N.Y. Bus. Press Editors, N.Y. Vet. Police Assn. Roman Catholic. Home: 22-34 Parsons Blvd Whitestone NY 11357 Office: 135 W 50th St New York City NY 10020

KEYKO, GEORGE JOHN, watch and electronics co. exec.; b. New Britain, Conn., May 6, 1924; s. John Simonovich and Nellie Ivanovna (Gretcha) K.; B.S., Yale, 1949; m. Anne Romanchuk, Jan. 31, 1948; children—David, Mark. Spl. rep. Lederle Labs., Conn. and N.Y., 1949-52; pres. Teacher Toys, Inc., Conn., 1952-56; sales mgr. Washington Forge, N.J., 1956-60; sales mgr. shaver div. Ronson Corp., Woodbridge, N.J., 1960-63; sales mgr. Caravelle and BEP div. Bulova Watch Co., N.Y.C., 1963-66; v.p. marketing Technipower div. Benrus Watch Co., Ridgefield, Conn., 1966-68; exec. v.p. Heuer Time & Electronics Corp., Springfield, N.J., 1969, pres., 1970-74; pres. George Keyko Internat. Inc., 1974—; dir. Electrodata Concepts, Inc., Conn., Angel Moped U.S.A. Co. Ltd. Field solicitor United Fund, Westfield, 1965-67, 69, 70; chief timer Internat. Ski Racers Assn., 1970—. Recipient Spl. award from INTREPID 22 - 12 Meter Yacht America's Cup, 1970. Mem. Am. Watch Mfg. Assn., Sports Car Club Am., N.Y. Sales Exec. Club. Republican. Episcopalian. Club: Echo Lake Country (Westfield, N.J.). Home: 931 Kimball Ave Westfield NJ 07090 Office: 155 US Route 22 Springfield NJ 07081

KHADEM, RAMIN, economist; b. Teheran, Iran, Jan. 21, 1944; s. Zikrullah and Javidukht (Javid) K.; B.S., U. Ill., 1967; Diplômé Spéciale, Sorbonne U., Paris, 1968; M.A., McGill U., 1970, Ph.D., 1975; m. Faraneh Vargha, Sept. 20, 1969; children—Paryssa, Varqa Kiyan. Tchr., McGill U., 1970-72; sr. statis. analyst Bell Can. Montreal, 1972-73, cons. demand studies, 1973-74; supr. mktg. planning and research Can. Overseas Telecommunication Corp., Montreal, 1974-75; mgr. mktg. planning and research Teleglobe Can., Montreal, 1975—; lectr. Internat. Telecommunications Union seminars, Hong Kong, 1976; mem. econ., mktg. and fin. panel Internat. Maritime Satelite Orgn., chmn. Internat. Working Party on Market Assessment, 1977-78. Mem. Canadian Econ. Assn., Am. Mktg. Assn., Canadian Assn. Bus. Economists, N.Am. Soc. Corporate Planning. Baha'i World Faith. Contbr. various publs. Office: 680 Sherbrooke St W Montreal PQ Canada

KHAJAVI-NOORI, FARROKH, psychiatrist; b. Tehran, Iran, Jan. 26, 1940; s. Ziaeddin and Nezhat (Maleki) K-N; came to U.S., 1967; M.D., U. Tehran, 1965. Intern Tehran U. Hosps., 1964-65, Ill. Masonic Med. Center, Chgo., 1967-68; resident in psychiatry Ill. State Psychiat. Inst., Chgo., 1968-71; fellow in community mental health Harvard Med. Sch., Boston, 1970-71; practice medicine specializing in psychiatry, Boston, 1971—; physician City of Chgo. Bd. of Health, 1969-71; staff psychiatrist Lab. of Community Psychiatry, Harvard Med. Sch., Boston, 1971-74; dir. Tri-City Mental Health Center, Commonwealth of Mass. Dept. Mental Health, 1972-75; dir. psychiat. edn. Center for Human Services, New Eng. Meml. Hosp., Stoneham, Mass., 1972-76; chief dept. psychiatry Whidden Meml. Hosp., Everett, Mass., 1976—; staff psychiatrist Choate Meml. Hosp., Glenside Hosp., Malden Hosp., Melrose-Wakefield Hosp., Newton-Wellesley Hosp.; clin. instr. Abraham Lincoln Sch. Medicine, U. Ill., Chgo., 1970-71; vis. prof. U. Mass. Sch. Nursing, N. Dartmouth, 1970-72; lectr. dept. psychiatry Harvard Med. Sch., 1971-74; cons. to WHO, 1975—, Boston Sch. Dept., 1970-73, Mass. Dept. Youth Services, 1971, Boston Model Cities Adminstrn., 1970-71. Served with Iranian Health Corps., 1965-67. Diplomate Am. Bd. Psychiatry and Neurology. Fellow A.C.P., Am. Acad. Psychosomatic Medicine, AAAS, Mass. Med. Soc., Royal Soc. of Health (London), Am. Psychiat. Assn., Am. Soc. for Adolescent Psychiatry, Mass. Psychiat. Soc., Chgo. Soc. for Adolescent Psychiatry. Moslem religion. Author: (with A. Broskowski, W. Mermis) Managing the Dynamics of Change and Stability, Annual Handbook for Group Facilitators, 1975; contbr. numerous articles on mental health care and psychiatry to profl. jours. Home: 12 Everett Ave Winchester MA 01890 Office: 5 Woodland Rd Stoneham MA 02180

KHAKEE, ABDULAZIZ GULAMALI, psychiatrist; b. Zanzibar, East Africa, Oct. 27, 1929; s. Gulamali N. Noorbanu (Peerbhoy) K.; came to U.S., 1957, naturalized, 1969; M.B., B.S., Grant Med. Coll., Bombay, India, 1954; m. Lois Lynette Bixby, Dec. 10, 1960; children—Susan Yasmin, Judith Fatima, Robert Abdul. Intern, Lynn (Mass.) Hosp., 1957-58; resident in psychiatry Medfield State Hosp., 1960-61, Danville (Ill.) State Hosp., 1961-62, Taunton (Mass.) State Hosp., 1966-67; clin. dir., sr. psychiatrist N.H. Hosp., Concord, 1968-72, mem. staff 1972—; practice medicine specializing in psychiatry, Concord, 1972—. Diplomate Am. Bd. Psychiatry and Neurology, Mem. Am. Psychiat. Assn., N.H., Merrimack County med. socs., Royal Coll. Psychiatry (London). Moslem. Club: Concord Country. Home: 36 Norwich St Concord NH 03301 Office: 7 Perley St Concord NH 03301

KHALIL, HATEM MOHAMED, computer scientist; b. Cairo, Egypt, July 2, 1935; s. Mohamed and Khedewah (Fakhrel-Deen) K.; came to U.S., 1962, naturalized, 1974; B.S. with honors, Manchester Inst. Sci. and Tech., 1962; M.S. (research fellow), Rice U., 1964; Ph.D., U. Del., 1969; m. Mary Jeanne Kalid, June 27, 1970. Analyst, Brown and Root, Inc., Houston, 1964-65; tchr., research fellow U. Del., 1965-67, asso. prof. computer sci., 1968—, chmn. dept., 1968—; cons. in field; vis. prof. Cairo U., 1973, Am. U., 1976. U. Del.; reviewer NSF proposals. Research Found. grantee, 1971, 72. Fellow British Computer Soc.; mem. Manchester Inst. Sci. Tech., AAUP, Assn. Computing Machinery, Sigma Xi. Author: General Computer Science, 1976, Concepts in Computer Science, 1976. Asst. editor Signum Newsletter, 19—. Editorial reviewer: Assn. Computing Machinery Computing Reviews; British Computer Soc. Contbr. articles in field to profl. jours. Home: PO Box 296 Newark DE 19711 Office: Dept Computer and Info Sci U Del Newark DE 19711

KHALIL, TAWFIK ABDULKARIM, physician; b. Jerusalem, May 4, 1939; s. Abdulkarim Hussein and Aisheh (Hassan) K.; came to U.S., 1967; M.B., B.Ch., Cairo U. (Egypt), 1964; m. Eva A. Marcus, Jan. 26, 1973; children—Attila, Shereef, Amir, Omar, Tawfik. Med. officer UN, Jordan, 1965-67; fellow in cardiovascular surgery St. Luke's Hosp., Houston, 1967-68; intern Nassan Hosp., Mineola, N.Y., 1968; resident Columbus Hosp., Jacksonville, Fla., 1971-73; attending surgeon St. Joseph's Hosp., Paterson, N.J., 1973—, Paterson Gen. Hosp., 1973—. Diplomate Am. Bd. Surgery. Mem. AMA, Passaic County Med. Soc. Moslem. Club: Montclair Beach. Home: 1036 Main St Patterson NJ 07503

KHAN, ABDUL JAMIL, physician; b. Allahabad, India, May 5, 1940; s. Abdul Majeed and Sarver (Begum) K.; came to U.S., 1969; B.Sc., Allahabad U., 1957; M.B. B.S., King George Med. Coll., Lucknow, India, 1962; D.C.H., Agra Med. Coll., India, 1965; M.D. (Ped.), Postgrad. Med. Inst., Chandigarh, India, 1967; m. Farida Ghani, July 6, 1968; children—Faiz, Faiza. Intern, Lucknow Med. Coll., 1962-63; resident in pediatrics Chandigarh Inst., 1966-67; registrar pediatrics Aligarh U., 1968-69; resident in pediatrics Kings County-State U.N.Y. Med. Center, Bklyn., 1969-70, attending physician, 1973—, asso. prof. clin. pediatrics, 1978—; resident in pediarrics Jewish Hosp., N.Y.C., 1971, fellow pediatric nephrology, 1971-72, attending physician, 1973—, chief pediatric nephrology, 1973—. Fellow Am. Acad. Pediatrics, Bklyn. Pediatric Soc., N.Y. Pediatric Soc.; mem. Am. Fedn. Clin. Research, Am. Soc. for Microbiology, Am. Soc. Pediatric Nephrology, AMA, N.Y. State, Kings County med. socs., Soc. Exptl. Biology and Med. Contbr. articles to profl. and sci. jours. Research in renal disease in children, newer antibiotics, white blood cell functions. Home: 192 Executive Dr Manhasset Hills NY 11040 Office: 555 Prospect Pl Brooklyn NY 11238

KHAN, AIJAZ MOHAMMAD, UN ofcl.; b. India, Jan. 2, 1929; s. Wazir Mohammad and Jannat-Un-Nisa K.; migrated to Pakistan, 1949; M.A. in Econs., Sind U., Pakistan, 1952; m. Masarrat Mahjabeen, Aug. 24, 1964; children—Virna, Reema, Ummni. Asst. to supr. devel. br. Ministry Finance Pakistan, 1949-53; tng. auditor, then supervising auditor Margolese and Assos., Montreal, Can., 1955-63; sr. auditor UN Emergency Force, Gaza, 1963-67; sr. auditor UN Hdqrs., N.Y.C., 1968-69; chief fin. officer UN Force in Cyprus, 1970-73, UN Emergency Force in Middle East, 1974-76, supervising auditor UN Polit. and Peacekeeping Missions Unit, 1977—. Sec. Pakistan Assn. Montreal, 1955-57. Mem. Can. Inst. Chartered Accountants, Order Inst. Chartered Accountants (Que.), Inst. Internal Auditors. Islam. Club: Waterside (N.Y.). Office: UN IAS Room A-3412 PO Box 20 GCPO New York NY 10017

KHANDELWAL, DEEN DAYAL, microwave semicondr. engr.; b. Ranoli, India, Dec. 25, 1940; s. Suraj Mal and Ram Pyari Devi (Bhukmaria) K.; B.E. with honors, U. Rajasthan, India, 1962, M.E., 1963; M.A. in Math., U. Mich., 1967, Ph.D. in Elec. Engring., 1969; m. Savita Devi Ghiya, May 18, 1963; children—Akshay, Anjay. Research asst., teaching fellow, research asso. U. Mich., Ann Arbor, 1965-69; mem. tech. staff Tex. Instruments Inc., Dallas, 1969-71; mgr. advanced diode devices, mgr. communication device devel. TRW Semicondrs., Lawndale, Calif., 1971-73; mem. tech. staff TRW Systems, Redondo Beach, Calif., 1973-74; tech. staff engr. G.E. Space Center, King of Prussia, Pa., 1974—. Dir., Fedn. India Student Assns., 1970-71; vol.-in-charge Ugandan Refugee program via Internat. Rescue Com., 1972-74. Recipient various prizes including 3 gold medals for scholastic achievements. Mem. IEEE, Sigma Xi, Eta Kappa Nu. Mem. India Temple Assn. Holder patent in field. Home: 696 General Scott Rd King of Prussia PA 19406 Office: PO Box 8555 Philadelphia PA 19101

KHANTZIAN, EDWARD JOHN, psychiatrist, psychoanalyst; b. Haverhill, Mass., May 26, 1935; s. John Stephen and Nuvart K.; A.B., Boston U., 1958; M.D., Albany Med. Coll., 1963; m. Carol Ann DeAndrus, May 17, 1959; children—Nancy Jo, Susan Joyce, Jane Elizabeth, John Stephen. Intern, R.I. Hosp., Providence, 1963-64; resident Mass. Mental Health Center-Boston Psychopathic Hosp., 1964-67; practice medicine specializing in adult psychiatry, 1967—, specializing in psychoanalysis, Haverhill, Mass., 1973—; chief psychiat. consultation service Cambridge (Mass.) Hosp., 1967-71, dir. drug treatment program, 1971-74, asso. dir. dept. psychiatry, 1976—; dir. drug treatment services Cambridge-Somerville Mental Health and Retardation Center, 1974-76, asso. dir. clin. services, 1976—; program dir. Drug Problems Resource Center, Cambridge, 1974-76; instr. psychiatry Harvard Med. Sch., Boston, 1967-73, asst. prof., 1973-78, asso. prof., 1978—; prin. collaborator Polydrug Treatment Program, Nat. Inst. Drug Abuse, 1974—; collaborator, cons. Nat. Drug/Alcohol collaborative Project, 1975-77; mem. Drug Rehab. Adv. Bd. Commonwealth Mass., 1973—, chmn., 1976—; mem. Gov's. Drug Abuse Prevention Planning Council, Commonwealth Mass., 1975—. Served to maj. M.C., U.S. Army, 1967-70. Diplomate Am. Bd. Psychiatry and Neurology. Fellow Am. Psychiat. Assn.; mem. Boston Psychoanalytic Soc. and Inst. (Felix and Helen Deutsch prize 1973), Am. Psychoanalytic Assn., Alcohol and Drug Problems Assn. N. Am., Mass. Psychiat. Soc., North Essex County Med. Soc., North Essex Mental Health Assn. (dir., 1st v.p. 1975-77). Clubs: Cederdale Tennis; Haverhill Monday Evening. Contbr. articles to profl. jours. Home: 55 King St Groveland MA 01834 Office: 160 Summer St Haverhill MA 01830

KHELLA, LEWIS, physician; b. Beni suef, Egypt, Mar. 24, 1922; s. Gobranious and Lucia (Makary) K.; came to U.S., 1966, naturalized, 1972; Faculty of Sci., Cairo U., 1940, M.D., M.B., Ch.B., 1946; m. Mary Ibrahim Gabriel, Feb. 3, 1957; children—Sami, Hani. Intern, Kasr el Ainy Hosp., Cairo U., 1946-47; resident internal medicine Ch. Missionary Hosp., Cairo, 1947; diploma in internal medicine Cairo U., 1948, diploma in cardiology, 1966; rotating intern Doctors Hosp., Cleveland Heights, Ohio, 1966-67; fellow in phys. medicine and rehab. Columbia Presbyn. Med. Center, N.Y.C., 1968-70; chief dept. phys. medicine and rehab. City of Phila. Nursing Home, 1975—; physician Inglis House, Phila., 1977—; attending physician Magee Meml. Hosp., 1971, Albert Einstein Med. Center, Phila., 1972-76. Mem. AMA, Philadelphia County Med. Soc., Pa., Phila. socs. phys. medicine and rehab., Am. Acad. and Congress Rehab. Medicine, Am. Assn. Electromyography and Electrodiagnosis. Coptic Orthodox Ch. Home: 15 Railroad Ave Haverford PA 19041 Office: 700 Civic Center Blvd Philadelphia PA 19104

KHOJA, MIRZA A., biomed. engr.; b. Gokak, India, Feb. 10, 1947; s. Abdulrahiman S. and Rahimatbai A. K.; came to U.S., 1971; M.S., George Washington U., 1974; doctoral candidate in Biomed. Engring., 1974—. Prodn. mgr. Titan Engring. Works, Bombay, India, 1969-70; chief engr. S.C. Bros., Bombay, 1970-71; mech. engr. Am. Instrument Co., Silver Spring, Md., 1974—. Diamond Jubilee scholar, 1963-69. Mem. ASME. Patentee blood cell separator. Home: 7005 Deepage Dr Columbia MD 21045 Office: 8030 Georgia Ave Silver Spring MD 20910

KHOURI, FRED JOHN, educator; b. Cranford, N.J., Aug. 15, 1916; s. Peter and Mary (Rizk) K.; student Union Jr. Coll., Roselle, N.J., 1934-36; B.A., Columbia, 1938, M.A., 1939, Ph.D., 1953; m. Catherine McLean, June 24, 1964. Instr., Brownsville (Tex.) Jr. Coll. and High Sch., 1939-40; instr. polit. sci. U. Tenn., 1946-47, U. Conn., 1947-50; asst. prof. Villanova (Pa.) U., 1951-61, prof., 1964—; vis. prof. Am. U. of Beirut (Lebanon), 1961-64; mem. Brookings Instn. Middle East Study Group, 1975-76; sr. fellow Middle East Center, U. Pa., 1978-79; lectr. in field. Served with U.S. Army AC, 1941-45. Decorated Order of Cedars (Lebanon). Fellow Middle East Studies Assn.; mem. Middle East Inst., Am. Polit. Sci. Assn., Am. Soc. Internat. Law, Internat. Studies Assn., Am. Acad. Polit. and Social Sci., World Affairs Council, Phi Kappa Phi. Democrat. Roman Catholic. Author: The Arab States and the UN, 1954; The Arab Israeli Dilemma, 1968, 2d edit., 1976. Asso. editor Jour. South Asian and Middle Eastern Studies. Contbr. to books and profl. jours. Home: 1209 W Wynnewood Rd Apt 310 Wynnewood PA 19096 Office: Villanova U Villanova PA 19085

KHURY, COSTANDY KHALIL, ins. co. exec.; b. Nazareth, Palestine, June 3, 1942; s. Khalil and Nour Khalil (Kourkour) K.; came to U.S., 1959, naturalized, 1968; B.A. in Math., Ohio Wesleyan U., 1962; M.Sc. in Math., Ohio State U., 1965; m. Susan Bernadine Moriarty, Sept. 17, 1966; children—Alison Bernadine, James Khalil. Sr. actuarial asst. State Farm Mutual Automobile Ins. Co., Bloomington, Ill., 1962-63; instr. math. Ohio State U., 1965-69; v.p., actuary Utica Mut. Ins. Co., 1969-72; asso. dir. Prudential Property & Casualty Ins. Co., Woodbridge, N.J., 1972-73, actuarial dir., 1973-78, v.p., 1978—; instr. math. Mohawk Valley Community Coll., 1969-71; teaching fellow Ohio State U., 1963-65. Trustee Battleground Arts Center, 1978—. Recipient 1st prize Boleslaw Monic Fund essay competition, Amsterdam, Netherlands, 1971, 74; C.L.U. Fellow Casualty Actuarial Soc. (dir. 1977—, Woodward and Fondiller prize 1973, 74); mem. Casualty Actuaries N.Y. (sec.-treas. 1974-76, v.p. 1976-77, pres. 1977-78, dir. 1974—), Soc. Ins. Research, Am. Acad. Actuaries. Home: 7 Cambridge Rd Freehold NJ 07728 Office: 23 Main St Holmdel NJ 07733

KIBBE, JAMES WILLIAM, real estate broker; b. Bound Brook, N.J., Oct. 5, 1926; s. Orlando A. and Anna Rose (Tomb) K.; B.S., U. Md., 1951; m. Bettie Brooks Dailey, June 11, 1949; children—James William Jr., Linda Jean. Real Estate salesman Eig & Mc Keever, Silver Spring, Md., 1955-57, Weaver Bros, Inc., Chevy Chase Bldg., Washington, 1957-70, asst. v.p. sales, leasing dept., 1970-72, sales mgr., 1972-73, v.p. sales mgr., 1973—; lectr, in field; chmn. Brokers and Salesmen's council, 1968-69. Served with USNR, 1944-46. Mem. Soc. Indsl. Realtors, Nat. Assn. Realtors, Washington Bd. Realtors, Washington Bd. Trade, Nat. Inst. Real Estate Brokers (state chmn. 1968-70). Republican. Methodist. Club: Sandy Spring Lions (pres. 1965-66). Home: 1000 Ashland Dr Ashton MD 20702 Office: 5530 Wisconsin Ave Washington DC 20015

KIBBEE, ROBERT JOSEPH, edni. adminstr.; b. N.Y.C., Aug. 19, 1921; A.B., Fordham U., 1943; M.A., U. Chgo., 1947, Ph.D., 1957; LL.D., Polytechnic Inst., Bklyn., 1972; m. children—Robert Joseph, Katherine, Douglas. Asst. dir. survey Ark. Com. Higher Edn., 1949-50; asst. dean So. State Coll. Ark., 1950-52, academic dean, 1952-55; dean students Drake U., Des Moines, 1955-58; adv. to Pakistan Govt., asso. prof. U. Chgo., 1958-61; asst. to pres. planning Carnegie Inst. Tech., Pitts., 1961-65, v.p. planning Carnegie-Mellon U., 1965-68, v.p. adminstrn. and planning, 1968-71; chancellor City U. N.Y., 1971—. Bd. dirs. Children's Med. Relief Internat., Mt. Sinai Sch. Medicine, Mt. Sinai Med. Center, Mt. Sinai Hosp.; trustee Inst. Internat. Edn., N.Y. Interface Devel. Projects, N.Y. State Higher Edn. Services Corp. v.p. Com. on Urban Program Univs.; hon. advisor to nat. adv. bd. Exec. High Sch. Internships Am.; bd. dirs. City U. N.Y. Urban Acad. Mgmt.; pres. exec. com. trustees Assn. Colls. and Univs. of State of N.Y.; mem. com. on urban affairs, com. on fed. legislation Nat. Assn. State Univs. and Land Colls. Contbr. articles to profl. jours. Office: City U NY 535 E 80th St New York City NY 10021

KIBRE, PEARL, historian, educator; b. Phila.; d. Kenneth and Jane (du Plone) Kibre; student U. Calif. at Los Angeles, 1920-22; A.B., U. Calif. at Berkeley, 1924, M.A., 1925; Ph.D., Columbia, 1936. Instr. history Pasadena (Calif.) Jr. Coll., 1925-28; research asst. Columbia, 1929-37; instr. history Bklyn., 1937-38; mem. faculty Hunter Coll., City U. N.Y., 1938—, prof. history, 1957-71; prof. history Grad. Center City U. N.Y., 1964-71, prof. emeritus, 1971—. Research fellow N.Y. Acad. Medicine, Nyon, Switzerland, 1938-39; Guggenheim fellow, 1950-51; recipient Haskins medal for most distinguished work in mediaeval studies, 1964. Co-chmn. Columbia U. seminar in Legal and Polit. Thought, 1972-74. Fellow Mediaeval Acad. Am. (v.p. 1964-67, pres. of fellows 1975-78, del. to Am. Council Learned Socs. 1976-77), History Sci. Soc., AAUP, Mediaeval Club N.Y.C., Am. Hist. Assn., Phi Beta Kappa, Phi Beta Kappa Alumnae (mem. council 1964-66); mem. corr. Acad. internationale d'histoire des sciences. Author: The Library of Pico della Mirandola, 1936; (with Lynn Thorndike) A Catalogue of Incipits of Mediaeval Scientific Writings in Latin, 2d edit., 1963; The Nations in the Mediaeval Universities, 1948; Scholarly Privileges in the Middle Ages, 1962; Hippocrates Latinus, Traditio, Vol. XXXI, 1975—. Co-editor: Osiris, vol. XI, 1954. Contbr. to books, profl. jours., also New Cath. Ency., Dictionary of Scientific Biography, The New Century Italian Renaissance Encyclopedia. Home: 1100 Madison Ave New York City NY 10028

KIDD, JEROME THOMAS, univ. adminstr.; b. Boalsburg, Pa., Mar. 16, 1933; s. Walter Joseph and Myrtle Bell (McMahan) K.; B.S., Pa. State U., 1955, M.Ed., 1961, postgrad., 1968-71; postgrad. U. Buffalo, 1958-59; m. Nancy Miriam Van Tries, May 23, 1970; stepchildren—Linda Ann Rowley, Joseph J. Rowley III, Bruce W. Rowley; 1 dau. by previous marriage, Lisa M. Tchr., Amherst Central Sr. High Sch., Snyder, N.Y., 1957-59; mgr. union bldg. and student activities Pa. State U., Hazleton, 1957-61; dean student affairs Pa. State U., McKeesport, 1961-62, field sec., Pa. State Alumni Assn., 1962-68, asst. dir. assn., 1968-70; part time instr. geography Pa. State U., Harrisburg, University Park, 1965-73, systems mgmt. analyst, University Park, 1970-73; dir. alumni and devel. records and research Brown U., Providence, 1973-77; spl. asst. to pres. for alumni affairs Southeastern Mass. U., North Dartmouth, 1977—. Past pres., Citizens for Edn., North Kingstown, R.I. Mem. Assn. Am. Geographers, Council Advancement and Support Edn., Assn. Records Mgrs. and Adminstrs., Assn. Computer Programmers and Analysts, Penn State Fed. (past dir.), Brown (past dir.) credit unions, Lion's Paw Alumni Assn. of Pa. State U. (dir.), Phi Delta Kappa, Omicron Delta Kappa. Home: 21 Edgar Nock Rd North Kingstown RI 02852 Office: Southeastern Mass U North Dartmouth MA 02747

KIDDE, JOHN LYON, diversified co. exec.; b. Montclair, N.J., June 5, 1934; s. John Frederick and Katherine (Lyon) K.; grad. Hotchkiss Sch., 1952; A.B., Princeton, 1956; postgrad. Columbia Law Sch., 1956-57; m. Constance Anson Jordan, Mar. 18, 1955 (div. 1966); children—Wilson Hand, Andrew Davis, Geoffrey Carter, Jonathan Lawrence, Jeremy Adam; m. 2d, Ruth Carol Mandeville, Mar. 14, 1970. Financial dir. Walter Kidde S.A. (Brazil), Rio de Janeiro, 1959-61; European mgr. Walter Kidde & Co. Inc., Paris, France, 1961-66, v.p., dir. internat. ops., 1967—; mem. regional adv. bd. N.J. Bank N.A., Paterson, 1970—; dir. Passaic (N.J.) Herald News, D.H. Baldwin Co., Cin., W.S. Kirkpatrick Co. Internat., Fairfield, N.J., Constrn. Spltys. Corp., Cranford, N.J. Trustee Pace U., Internat. Coll. Cayman Islands, Nat. Council Crime and Delinquency, Clara Maass Meml. Hosp., Belleville, N.J., Montclair (N.J.) Art Mus., Concord (Mass.) Acad. Served with AUS, 1956-58. Clubs: Fellsbrook Tennis (Essex Falls, N.J.); Princeton (N.Y.C.); Quantuck Beach (Westhampton, N.Y.); Nassau (Princeton, N.J.); Pennington (Passaic, N.J.). Home: 154 Oldchester Rd Essex Fells NJ 07021 Office: 9 Brighton Rd Clifton NJ 07012

KIDDER, NATHANIEL REMINGTON, bldg. contractor; b. Boston, Apr. 4, 1921; s. Ray N. and Louise May (Remington) K.; A.B., Harvard, 1942, A.M., 1950; certificate in Elec. Engring., Northeastern U., 1943; m. Elise Page Lee Skylstead, Sept. 12, 1953;

children—Elizabeth Page, Ray Skylstead, Nathaniel R., Charles Henry Lee. Asst. prof. anthropology, dir. lab. Syracuse (N.Y.) U., 1949-50; research asso. Johns Hopkins U., 1950-53; div. mgr. Jones & Lamson Machine Co., Springfield, Vt., 1953-55; dir. Isnt. Tech. Devel., Cambridge, Mass., 1955-60; dept. mgr. Lear Siegler, Inc., Electronic Instruments, Cleve., 1960-64; v.p., chmn. policy com. All States Freight, Inc., Akron, Ohio, 1964-65; exec. dir. Physical Distribution Inst., Hudson, Ohio, 1965-69; dir. adminstr. aviation and electronic group Am.-Standard, McLean, Va., 1969-72; div. mgr. Sears Roebuck & Co., Bethesda, Md., 1972-74; div. mgr. Pulte Home Corp., Gaithersburg, Md., 1974-75; pres., chief exec. officer Potomac Home Improvement Co., Inc., Potomac, Md., 1975—; dir. Ala. Industries, Inc., Davis-Liddle & Co., Inc. Sec. Peabody Mus., Cambridge, Expdn. to Yap Island, 1947-48. Served with AUS, 1942-44. Fellow Am. Anthrop. Assn.; mem. Am. Mktg. Assn. (dir.), IEEE, Nat. Home Improvement Council. Club: Harvard (Phila.). Author: (with E.E. Hunt, Jr., D.M. Schneider and W.D. Stevens) The Micronesians of Yap and Their Depopulation, 1949. Consulting editor Jour. Mktg., 1953-64; contbg. editor Babcox Bus. Publs., 1965-75. Home: Box 34031 Bethesda MD 20034 Office: 9213 Paddock Ln Potomac MD 20854

KIENZLE, JOHN FRED, educator; b. Allentown, Pa., Apr. 1, 1945; s. Fred John and Florence Mary K.; B.A. in History and Social Studies, SUNY, Albany, 1967; M.A. in History, N.Y. U., 1969; postgrad. Princeton (N.J.) U. Asst. Near East collection, N.Y. U. Library, N.Y.C., 1967-69, Oriental collection Firestone Library, Princeton U., 1969-70; instr. Asian, African, Middle Eastern, Soviet Union studies, chief Media Center technician Maple Hill High Sch., Schodack Central Sch. Dist., Castleton, N.Y., 1970—; lectr. in field. Officer Renssalaer County Radio Civil Emergency Service, 1974—. Mem. Nat. Audio-Visual Assn., Nat. N.Y. State, Capitol Dist. councils for social studies, N.Y. State Ednl. Communications Assn., Middle East Inst. Recipient award N.Y. State Regents' Council, 1975. Office: Maple Hill High Sch 1216 Maple Hill Rd Castleton NY 12033

KIERMAN, FRANK ALGERTON, JR., historian, educator; b. Boston, Apr. 19, 1914; s. Frank Algerton and Lily Jean (Fraser) K.; B.A., Wesleyan U., 1935; M.A., Reed Coll., 1943; Ph.D., U. Wash., 1953; m. Marilois Ditto, Feb. 20, 1941; children—Sean A., Jean Elaine Kierman Fischer. Tchr. English, George Sch., Bucks County, Pa., 1935-36, Harvey Sch., Hawthorne, N.Y., 1937-40; dir. drama Reed Coll., Portland, Oreg., 1941-43; with Fgn. Service Dept. State, Nanking, China, 1948-50, Hong Kong, 1951-53, Karachi, 1954-57, Nairobi, 1960-63; exec. sec. Chinese Linguistics Project, Princeton U., N.J., 1967-71; prof. history Rider Coll., Lawrenceville, N.J., 1971—, chmn. dept., 1973—. Served to capt., USMCR, 1944-46. Decorated Bronze Star, Air medal. Mem. Am. Hist. Assn., Assn. for Asian Studies, Am. Oriental Soc., AAUP, Phi Beta Kappa, Phi Alpha Theta. Episcopalian. Author: Four Warring States Biographies, 1961; Chinese Ways in Warfare (with John F. Fairbank), 1974; translator China in Antiquity, 1978. Home: 6 Alyce Ct Lawrenceville NJ 08648

KIERNAN, DAVID HASTINGS, pub. relations exec.; b. New Haven, Jan. 3, 1930; s. Walter and Helen (Hastings) K.; B.A., Holy Cross Coll., 1951; m. Joan Glaser, Nov. 3, 1956; children—Kathleen, Gregory, Patricia, Jeanne Anne, Kevin. Reporter, producer Sta. WNHC, New Haven, 1951-52, 54-56; newscaster Sta. WNHC-TV, New Haven, 1956-58, news dir., 1958-60; pub. relations dir. St. Raphael Hosp., New Haven, 1960-62; adminstr. spl. events ITT, N.Y.C., 1962-64, v.p World Directories div., N.Y.C., 1968-70, dir. pub. info., 1970-73, dir. pub. relations, 1973—; dir. pub. relations Puerto Rico Tel. Co., San Juan, 1964-68. Served with U.S. Army, 1952-54. Mem. Pub. Relations Soc. Am. Republican. Roman Catholic. Clubs: Cornell, Middlesex, Holy Cross. Home: 33 Georgian Ln Darien CT 06820 Office: 320 Park Ave New York City NY 10022

KIESEL, BEATRICE, nun, dietitian; b. N. Braddock, Pa., Nov. 29, 1912; d. Andrew Kelian and Clara Catherine (Berk) Kiesel; student U. Pitts., 1930, Duquesne U., 1930-39; B.S. in Home Econs., Mt. Mercy Coll., 1942. Joined Sisters of Divine Providence, Pitts., 1932; dietetic intern St. Louis U. Hosps., 1942-43; dietitian San Rosario Nursing Home, Cambridge Springs, Pa., 1943-48, 50-55, adminstrv. and therapeutic dietitian, 1956-61, dir. dietary services, 1975—; therapeutic dietitian St. Johns Hosp., Pitts., 1948-50, Divine Providence Hosp., Pitts., 1955-56; dir. dietary services Braddock (Pa.) Gen. Hosp., 1961-71, therapeutic dietitian, 1971-75; cons. dietitian Presbyn. nursing homes. Mem. Am. (registered dietitian), Northwestern Pa. (pres. 1955) dietetic assns., Am. Soc. for Hosp. Food Service Adminstrs. Author: Delightful Dining and Dietary Prescription, 1968. Home and Office: San Rosario Nursing Home 110 Canfield St Cambridge Springs PA 16403

KIESSEL, WILLIAM CARL, writer; b. Tenafly, N.J., June 19, 1917; s. William Carl and Mabel Elizabeth (Kaufmann) K.; B.A., Rutgers U., 1947; M.A., N.Y. U., 1950, also postgrad.; m. Miriam Anne Dodd, Dec. 3, 1950. Free-lance ghostwriter Neil Farber Assos., 1947-53; research asst. N.Y. State Edn. Dept., N.Y.C., 1947-50; research editor Grolier Pub. Corp., N.Y.C., 1950-58; publs. specialist U.S. Army and Air Force Exchange Service, 1958-68; freelance writer, book rev. critic, hist. researcher; compiler geneal. family histories. Served with 36th Inf. Div., U.S. Army, 1942-45. Decorated Bronze Star. Mem. Am. Hist. Assn., Assn. Am. Historians, Nat. Geneal. Soc., Am. Soc. Indexers, VFW. Republican. Lutheran. Club: Masons. Home: Box 97 Bearsville NY 12409

KIEV, ARI, psychiatrist; b. N.Y.C., Dec. 30, 1933; s. I. Edward and Mary (Nover) K.; A.B., Harvard, 1954; M.D., Cornell Med. Coll., 1958; m. Phyllis Eve Kovens, Mar. 27, 1960; children—Jonathan, Marshall. Head program social psychiatry Cornell U. Med. Coll., N.Y.C., 1967-75, clin. asso. prof., 1967—; adj. prof. psychology N.Y. U., 1975-76; lectr. Sunrise Semester Series, Sta. WCBS-TV; vis. prof. anthropology Brandeis U., Waltham, Mass., 1967-68; research asso. Columbia U. Coll. Phys. and Surg., 1964-67; med. dir. Internat. Com. Against Mental Illness, Inc., 1965-70. Pres., Psychodynamic Research Corp.; dir. Social Psychiatry Research Inst. Served to capt. with USAF, 1962-64. Recipient Outstanding Man of Yr. award N.Y.C. Jr. C. of C., 1970. Fellow Am. Psychiat. Assn.; mem. A.M.A., Royal Medico-Psychol. Assn. Author: Curanderismo, Mexican-American Folk Psychiatry, 1968; Transcultural Psychiatry, 1972; Mental Health in Latin America, 1972; (with M. Argandona) The Drug Epidemic, 1974; A Strategy for Daily Living, 1973; Handling Executive Stress, 1974; The Suicidal Patient, 1976; A Strategy for Success, 1977. Editor: Magic Faith and Healing, Studies in Primitive Psychiatry Today, 1964, Psychiatry in the Communist World, 1968; Editor: Attitude; Social Psychiatry, 1969; Somatic Aspects of Depressive Illness, 1974. TV producer Videotape Seminars in Psychiatry, Perspectives in Mental Health, Transcultural Psychiatry. Home: New York City NY 10021 Office: 150 E 69th St New York City NY 10021

KIHN, HARRY, electronics engr., mfg. co. exec.; b. Tarnow, Austria, Jan. 24, 1912; s. Morris and Sabina K.; came to U.S., 1920, naturalized 1927; B.S. in Elec. Engring., Cooper Union Inst. Tech., 1934; M.S. in Elec. Engring., U. Pa., 1952; m. Minna Schechter, Nov., 1937; children—Michael Allan, Leslie Morris. Devel. engr. Hygrade-Sylvania Co., Clifton, N.J., 1935-38, Ferris Instrument Co., Boonton, N.J., 1938; radio, TV research engr. RCA Mfg. Co., Camden, N.J., 1939-42; electronics computer and TV researcher, corp. staff engr. patents and licensing RCA Labs., Princeton, N.J., 1942-75, sr. staff tech. adviser, 1975-77; pres. Harry Kihn Assos., electronics cons., 1977—; instr. electronics Rutgers U. Extension. Vice-pres. Lawrenceville sch. bd., 1957-60; bd. dirs. Lawrenceville Adult Sch., 1960-62, George Washington Council Boy Scouts Am.; chmn. Lawrenceville Ednl. Found., 1950-74. Recipient Microminiaturization award Miniature Precision Bearings, Inc., 1958, 2 research awards RCA Corp., 1952, 56. Registered profl. engr., N.J. Fellow IEEE; mem. N.Y. Acad. Sci., AAAS, Nat. Acad. Sci. (materials adv. bd. 1961-62), Nat. Soc. Profl. Engrs., Am. Def. Preparedness Assn., Sigma Xi. Clubs: Lions, Rotary. Contbr. articles to profl. jours., tech. confs. Patentee in field. Home: 30 Green Ave Lawrenceville NJ 08648

KIKOSKI, JOHN FRANK, JR., educator; b. Greenfield, Mass., July 8, 1940; s. John Frank and Anna Joan (Bubrowski) K.; B.A., Wesleyan U., 1963; M.A., U. Mass., 1967, Ph.D., 1972; m. Catherine Kano, July 4, 1964; children—John N., Andrei B., Nicole L. Jr. high sch. tchr. Town of Montague (Mass.) Sch. System, 1966-67; spl. agt. Northwestern Mut. Life Ins. Co., Greenfield, 1967-71; instr. St. Francis Coll., Biddeford, Maine, 1971-72, asst. prof., 1972-74; asst. prof. polit. sci. Springfield (Mass.) Community Coll., 1974—, dir. pub. adminstrn. program, 1975—. Mem. Am. Polit. Sci. Assn., Pi Sigma Alpha. Roman Catholic. Home: 119 Riddell St Greenfield MA 01301 Office: Springfield Tech Community Coll Springfield MA 01105

KIKTA, EDWARD JOSEPH, JR., analytical chemist; b. Buffalo, June 11, 1948; s. Edward Joseph and Arline M. K.; B.A., State U. N.Y., Buffalo, 1970, Ph.D., 1978; M.S. Canisius Coll., 1972. Teaching asst. chemistry Canisius Coll., Buffalo, 1971-72; teaching asst. chemistry State U. N.Y. at Buffalo, 1972-75, research asst., 1975-76; analytical research chemist Agrl. Chem. Group, FMC Corp., Middleport, N.Y., also supr. analytical sect. formulations group, 1976—; chmn. exec. com. NE Regional Chromatography, 1977—. Recipient Alox Corp. award, 1974. Mem. Am. Chem. Soc., ASTM, AAAS, Am. Inst. Chemists, Air Force Assn., U. Buffalo Alumni Assn. Contbr. articles to profl. publs. Office: FMC Corp 100 Niagara St Middleport NY 14105

KILBURN, HENRY THOMAS, JR., investment banker; b. N.Y.C., Aug. 1, 1931; s. Henry Thomas and Florence (Cross) K.; A.B., Princeton, 1953; J.D., Columbia, 1959. Exec. trainee Bankers Trust N.Y.C., 1953-54; admitted to N.Y. State bar, 1959; asso. firm Kelley Drye Newhall & Maginnes, N.Y.C., 1959-66; v.p. finance, gen. counsel W.E. Parfitt & Assos. Inc., N.Y.C., 1967-71; asso. 1st v.p., sr. v.p., dir. utility finance Blyth Eastman Dillon & Co., Inc., N.Y.C., 1972-78, exec. v.p., mem. exec. com., 1978—, also dir.; pres. Wyodak Constrn. Co., 1975-77; dir. Bedco Leasing Corp. Served to 1st. lt, F.A., U.S. Army, 1954-56. Mem. Securities Industries Assn. (regulated industries com.), N.Y. Bar Assn. Republican. Episcopalian. Home: 2 E 86th St New York City NY 10028 Office: Blyth Eastman Dillon & Co Inc 1221 Ave of Americas New York City New York 10020

KILEY, EDWARD E., mfg. co. exec.; b. Chgo., Dec. 5, 1939; s. John and Ellen (Connors) K.; B.A., U. Ill., Champaign-Urbana, 1961; M.B.A., U. Mass., 1969; m. Susan O'Riley, May 16, 1962; children—Patrick, JoAnne, Barbara. Mktg. rep. Richter Mfg. Co., New Haven, Conn., 1961-63, 65-69, dir. mktg., 1969-73; v.p. mktg. Tongsten Mfg. Co., Watertown, Mass., 1973-78, pres., 1978—; instr. Watertown Community Coll., 1975—. Active New Haven chpt. ARC, 1965-69, Watertown chpt., 1973—; mem. fin. com. Watertown Public Library, 1975—, vice chmn. 1977-78. Served with U.S. Army, 1963-65. Mem. Am. Mktg. Assn., Watertown C. of C., Am. Mgmt. Assn. Democrat. Roman Catholic. Club: Watertown Country. Address: 28 Commonwealth Rd Watertown MA 02139

KILLEN, CARROLL GORDEN, marketing exec.; b. Provencal, La., Mar. 22, 1919; s. Carroll Gorden and Ella (Crowder) K.; B.S., La. Northwestern State Coll., 1938; postgrad. La. State U., 1939-40; m. Clara Butler, Aug. 15, 1941; children—Carroll Gorden, III, Karen, Lloyd, Sara. Electronics engr. Magnolia Petroleum Oil Co., Dallas, 1940-42, Watson Labs., Red Bank, N.J., 1942-45; chief application engr. Sprague Electric Co., North Adams, Mass., 1947-55, mgr. field engring., 1955-60, v.p., 1960-73, sr. v.p., 1973—; dir. Sprague-Goodman Electroncs, Inc. Cons. U.S. Dept. Def. Served to 1st lt. USAAF, 1945-47. Mem. Electronic Industries Assn. (mgmt. policy com. on reliability, indsl. marketing com., govt. liaison com. parts div.), Am. Ordnance Assn., Newcomen Soc., Nat. Security Indsl. Assn. (trustee), Am. Mgmt. Assn., IEEE (conf. bd.), Sales Execs. Club N.Y. Republican. Baptist. Mason. Home: 511 Gage St Bennington VT 05201 Office: 87 Marshall St North Adams MA 01248

KILLIAN, JOHN DORAN, lawyer; b. Woodhaven, N.Y., Nov. 5, 1928; s. John D. and Lily E. (Gulliksen) K.; B.A., Hofstra U., 1950; J.D., Cornell U., 1953, LL.M., 1954; m. Sally Gephart, July 23, 1955; children—David B., Joan E. Admitted to N.Y. State bar, 1954, Pa. bar, 1958; dep. atty. gen. Pa., 1957-64; pvt. practice, Harrisburg, 1965—. Chmn., Pub. Sch. Employees Retirement Bd., 1971—; Democratic candidate for Pa. Senate, 1964, for judge Dauphin County, 1971. Served with AUS, 1955-57. Recipient citation Pa. Dept. Pub. Instrn., 1961, Presbyn. Homes, 1972; Ecumenical Leadership citation Pa. Council Chs., 1970. Mem. Am., Pa., Dauphin County bar assns., Am., Pa. trial lawyers assns., Phi Kappa Phi, Phi Alpha Theta, Phi Delta Kappa. Presbyterian. Clubs: Rotary, Shriners. Author articles. Home: 3737 Maple St Harrisburg PA 17109 Office: 218 Pine St POB 886 Harrisburg PA 17108

KILLIAN, ROBERT KENNETH, former state ofcl.; b. Hartford, Conn., Sept. 15, 1919; s. Edward F. and Annie (Nemser) K.; B.A., Union Coll., Schenectady, 1942, LL.D., 1978; LL.B., U. Conn., 1948; LL.D., Sacred Heart U., 1976; m. Evelyn Farnan, Dec. 7, 1942; children—Robert Kenneth, Jr., Cynthia Elaine. Admitted to Conn. bar, 1948; asst. corp. counsel, Hartford, 1951-54; atty. gen., Conn., 1967-75, lt. gov., 1975-79; partner firm Gould, Killian & Wynne, Hartford. Chmn. Democratic Town Com., Hartford, 1963-67; bd. dirs. St. Francis Hosp.; trustee Nat. Jewish Hosp., Denver. Served with AUS, 1942-46. Decorated Purple Heart; recipient numerous citations from civic and pub. service orgns. Mem. Hartford County, Conn., Am. bar assns., Nat. Conf. Lt. Govs., Nat. Conf. Democratic State-Wide Elected Ofcls. (exec. com.). Clubs: Elks, K.C.'s. Home: 234 Terry Rd Hartford CT 06105 Office: 37 Lewis St Hartford CT 06103

KILMANN, RALPH HERMAN, educator; b. N.Y.C., Oct. 5, 1946; s. Martin Herbert and Lilli (Loeb) K.; B.S., Carnegie-Mellon U., M.S., 1970; Ph.D., U. Calif. at Los Angeles, 1972; m. Audrey Ann Sabol, July 7, 1977; 1 dau., Catherine Mary. Instr. grad. sch. bus. U. Pitts., 1972, asst. prof., 1972-75, asso. prof., 1975—; pres. Organizational Design Cons., Inc., Pitts., 1975—. Mem. Eastern Acad. Mgmt. (treas. 1975-76), Am. Psychol. Assn., Inst. Mgmt. Scis. (1st prize Nat. Coll. Planning competition 1976), Beta Gamma Sigma. Author: Social Systems Design: Normative Theory and the MAPS Design Technology, 1977; co-author: Methodological Approaches to Social Science: Integrating Divergent Concepts and Theories, 1978; co-editor: The Management of Organization Design: Vols. 1 and II, 1976; cons. editor Elsevier Pub., 1977—; contbr. chpts. to books, articles to profl. jours. Developed Kilmann Insight Test, Learning Climate Questionnaire, Thomas-Kilmann Conflict-Mode Instrument in Ednl. Testing Service, MAPS Design Tech. for Social Systems Design. Home: 435 Allenberry Dr Pittsburgh PA 15237 Office: Grad Sch Bus U Pitts Pittsburgh PA 15260

KILMARTIN, JOSEPH FRANCIS, JR., mgmt. communications cons.; b. New Haven, Mar. 11, 1924; s. Joseph Francis and Lauretta M. (Collins) K.; student St. Thomas Sem., 1944; B.A., Holy Cross Coll., 1947; m. Gloria M. Schaffer, June 26, 1954; children—Joanne, Diane. Prodn. mgr. A.C. Gilbert Co., New Haven, 1947-49; TV producer NBC-TV, N.Y.C., 1950-53; v.p. sales Cellomatic Corp., N.Y.C., 1953-59; sr. v.p. Transfilm Inc., N.Y.C., 1959-62, MPO Videotronics, N.Y.C., 1962-66; pres. Bus. Programs Inc., Larchmont, N.Y., 1966-75, Greenwich, Conn., 1975—; lectr. in field, cons. Mexican Dept. Agrarian Affairs and Colonization 1974—. Active fund-raising Community Chest, 1947-49, ARC, 1947-49, Boy Scouts Am., 1958-66, United Fund, 1970-73. Recipient medal of excellence Mexican Agrarian Affairs and Colonization Dept., 1976; Golden Medallion award in bus. communication Miami Internat. Film Festival, 1978. Mem. Am. Mgmt. Assn., N.Y. Sales Exec. Club, TV Execs. Soc. Republican. Roman Catholic. Clubs: Larchmont (N.Y.) Yacht; Bonnie Brair Country (bd. govs. 1970-72); Westchester Country; University (N.Y.C.) Home and office: 30 Bowman Dr S Greenwich CT 06830

KILSHEIMER, SISTER JEAN DOLORES, dietitian; b. N.Y.C., Jan. 25, 1914; d. James Breen and Florence Gertrude (Oppenheim) K.; B.S. in Home Econs., Coll. St. Elizabeth, 1935. Dietetic intern Good Samaritan Hosp., Cin., 1941-42; therapeutic and teaching dietitian St. Raphael's Hosp., New Haven, 1937-41, nutrition dir., 1942-57; chief dietitian St. Elizabeth's Hosp., Elizabeth, N.J., 1957-59, All Souls Hosp., Morristown, N.J., 1959-62; coffee shop mgr., teaching dietitian, dir. vols. St. Mary's Hosp., Passaic, N.J., 1962-71, dietary dir., 1971—; teaching dietetic asst., 1970—; state coordinator Dietetic Asst. Program, 1974—. Mem. Am., N.J. (pres. 1962-63), No. Dist. N.J. (pres. elect 1977-78), Conn. (pres. 1948-49) dietetic assns., Am. Soc. for Hosp. Food Service Adminstrs., Nutrition Edn. Soc., Nutrition Today Soc. Mem. Sisters of Charity of St. Elizabeth, 1935—. Home and office: 211 Pennington Ave Passaic NJ 07055

KIM, ANDREW BYONG-SOO, fin. analyst; b. Seoul, Korea, Sept. 12, 1936; s. Y.C. and Y.K. (Lee) K.; came to U.S., 1956, naturalized, 1977; student Seoul Nat. U., 1955, Columbia U. Grad. Sch., 1960, M.B.A., Cornell U., 1963; m. Wan-Kyun Rha, June 10, 1961; children—Gene Y., Ty Y. Asso. dir. research, instl. research dept. F. Eberstadt & Co., N.Y.C., 1972—, v.p. corp., 1972—, also dir. Mem. bus. travel adv. council United Airlines, 1971. Mem. N.Y. Soc. Security Analysts, Chartered Fin. Analysts, Soc. Airline Analysts (pres. 1973), Am. Inst. Aeros. and Astronautics, Soc. Aerospace Analysts. Home: 627 Long Hill Rd W Briarcliff Manor NY 10510 Office: 61 Broadway New York City NY 10006

KIM, CHARLES CHANG SUH, surgeon; b. Seoul, Korea, Feb. 28, 1935; s. Jong Tae and Soon Ah (Yoo) K.; M.D., Seoul Nat. U., 1960, M.S. in Pathology, 1962; m. Sunsook Ann, July 8, 1961; children—Lionel, Vivian, Lisa, Caroline, Eileen, John. Intern, Queens Hosp. Center, N.Y.C., 1962-63; resident in gen. surgery Lincoln Hosp. and Wyckoff Heights Hosp., N.Y., 1963-68; resident and fellow in cardiothoracic surgery Yale-New Haven Hosp., 1968-69, 72-74; resident in cardiothoracic surgery U. Utah Med. Center and Latter-day Saints Hosp., 1974-75; instr. surgery Yonsei U., Seoul, 1969-71; practice medicine, specializing in cardiothoracic surgery, New Haven, 1975—; mem. staff Hosp. St. Raphael, Meriden-Wallingford Hosp., World War II Meml. Hosp.; cons. Gaylord and Bradley Meml. hosps. Served in Korean Army, 1952-53. Diplomate Am. Bd. Surgery, Am. Bd. Thoracic Surgery. Fellow A.C.S., Am. Coll. Chest Physicians; mem. AMA, Conn., Korean med. socs., Korean Surg. Soc., Conn. Thoracic Soc. Presbyterian. Home: 10 Sturbridge Ln Woodbridge CT 06525 Office: 1481 Chapel St New Haven CT 06511

KIM, CHARLES WESLEY, educator; b. Nashville, Mar. 20, 1926; s. Hebert Hyungsik and Kyung Sook (Lee) K.; student U. Mich., 1944-46, U. Calif. at Berkeley, 1946-48, Los Angeles, 1948-49; A.B., U. Calif. at Berkeley, 1949; M.S. in Pub. Health, U. N.C., 1952, Ph.D., 1956; m. Soo Johung Kim, June 9, 1956; 1 son, Charles Wesley. Instr. N.Y. Med. Coll., 1956-59, asst. prof., 1959-64; asso. scientist Brookhaven Nat. Lab., 1965-68, scientist, 1968-70; asso. prof. Health Scis. Center, State U. N.Y. at Stony Brook, 1970—, asso. dean Health Scis. Center, 1972-74, asso. dean grad. sch., 1974—, also chmn. adv. council Fine Arts Center; program chmn., editor 3d Internat. Conf. on Trichinellosis, 1974, editor 4th Internat. Conf., 1978. China Med. Bd. fellow, La. State U. Sch. Medicine 1958; USPHS fellow Argonne Nat. Lab. and U. Chgo., 1964-65. Mem. AAAS, Am. Inst. Biol. Sci., Am. Assn. Immunology, Am. Soc. Microbiology, Royal, Am. socs. tropical medicine and hygiene, Am. Soc. Parasitology, N.Y. Acad. Sci., Sigma Xi. Democrat. Presbyterian. Editor, author over 20 books on microbiology and parasitology; contbr. articles to profl. jours. Home: Box 744 26 Lubber St Stony Brook NY 11790 Office: Grad Sch State U NY Stony Brook NY 11794

KIM, DAE UN, pathologist; b. Korea, June 1, 1941; s. Bong Soon and Sung Shim (Choi) K.; came to U.S., 1968, naturalized, 1975; M.D., Seoul Nat. U., 1965, M. Med. Sci., 1968; m. Ock-Nam Chung, Mar. 4, 1972; children—Peter I., Philip I. Intern, Yale-New Haven Hosp., Yale U. Sch. Medicine, Conn., 1969-70; resident in pathology Martland Hosp., Coll. Medicine and Dentistry N.J., Newark, 1970-73; career devel. fellow Merck Inst. Therapeutic Research, Rahway, N.J., 1973-74; asso. attending pathologist St. Barnabas Med. Center, Livingston, N.J., 1974—; instr. Coll. of Medicine and Dentistry N.J., 1971-73, clin. instr., 1973-74. Recipient Arthur Casilli award N.J. Soc. Pathologists, 1973. Diplomate Am. Bd. Pathology. Fellow Coll. Am. Pathologists, Am. Soc. Clin. Pathologists; mem. AMA (Physicians Recognition award 1972, 77), Med. Soc. N.J., Am. Assn. Blood Banks, Electron Microscopy Soc. Am., Am., Internat. socs. nephrology. Methodist. Home: 87 Westminster Rd Chatham NJ 07928 Office: St Barnabas Med Center Livingston NJ 07039

KIM, DAMIAN BYUNGSUK, psychiatrist, psychoanalyst; b. S. Korea, Mar. 15, 1934; s. Bong-Joo and Sang-Im (Park) K.; came to U.S., 1964, naturalized, 1976; m. Yung-Sook Lee, May 15, 1965; children—Namgi, Jeanhee, Wonki. Intern, Rochester (N.Y.) Gen. Hosp., 1964-65; resident in psychiatry Bellevue-N.Y. U. Med. Center, N.Y.C., 1965-68; chief alcohol program, attending psychiatrist Coney Island Hosp., Bklyn., 1969—; asst. psychoanalyst Karen Horney Clinic, Psychoanalytic Inst., N.Y.C., 1975—; individual practice medicine, specializing in psychiatry S.I., N.Y., 1973—. Served with M.C., Korean Air Force, 1959-64. Diplomate Am. Bd. Psychiatry and Neurology. Mem. N.Y. Acupuncture Soc. (v.p. 1975—), N.Y. State Med. Soc., Am. Psychiat. Assn., Am. Acad. Psychoanalysis, Am. Soc. Clin. Hypnosis. Home: 154 Logan Ave Staten Island NY 10301 Office: 136 Greenleaf Ave Staten Island NY 10310

KIM, GEUN-EUN BARTHOLOMEW, surgeon; b. Seoul, Korea, July 2, 1941; s. Doo-man and Ki-ok K.; came to U.S., 1965, naturalized, 1977; M.D., Seoul Nat. U., 1965; m. Eun-Kyung Choi, Oct. 14, 1967; children—Catherine Mee-A, Judy Hee-Jung. Intern, resident Albert Einstein Med. Center, Phila., 1965-70; fellow in vascular surgery N.Y. U. Med. Center, N.Y.C., 1970-72; practice medicine specializing in vascular surgery, N.Y.C.; mem. staffs VA Hosp., N.Y.C., N.Y. U. Med. Center, Drs. Hosp., N.Y. Infirmary, Bellevue Hosp., St. Clare's Hosp.; clin. asst. prof. surgery N.Y. U.; cons. surg. Health Ins. Plan Greater N.Y. Diplomate Am. Bd. Surgery. Fellow A.C.S., Internat. Coll. Angiology; mem. N.Y. Soc. Cardiovascular Surgery, Assn. Academic Surgeons, N.Y. County Med. Soc., Internat. Cardiovascular Soc., N.Y. Acad. Scis. Roman Catholic. Contbr. articles to med. jours. Home: Cross Pond Rd Pound Ridge NY 10576 Office: 333 E 30th St New York NY 10016 also 426 W 52d St New York NY 10019

KIM, IH CHIN, pediatrician; b. Seoul, Korea, Aug. 6, 1925; s. Young Whan and Young Ho (Cho) K.; came to U.S., 1953, naturalized, 1965; M.D., Seoul Nat. U., 1950; student Yon Sei U., 1944-46; postgrad. U. Pa., 1954-55; m. Helen Fern Wagner, Mar. 15, 1957; children—Catherine Joy, Stephen Thomas. Intern, Transp. Hosps., Seoul and Pusan, Korea, 1950-51; resident in pediatrics Pusan Children's Charity Hosp., 1951-53, Children's Hosp. Phila., 1953-55, fellow in pediatric gastroenterology, 1955-58, research asso., 1958-67, med. staff, 1963-67; practice medicine, specializing in pediatrics, Easton, Pa., 1965—, Phillipsburg, N.J., 1971—; staff dept. pediatrics Hahnemann Med. Coll. and Hosp., Phila., 1967—, Easton Hosp., 1965—, Warren Hosp., Phillipsburg, N.J., 1966—, chief dept. pediatrics, 1978—; clin. asst. prof. pediatrics Hahnemann Med. Coll., Phila., 1971—. Fellow Am. Acad. Pediatrics; mem. AMA. Presbyterian. Club: Country of Northampton County. Address: 6 Ivy Court Easton PA 18042 Office: 985 Belvidere Rd Phillipsburg NJ 08865

KIM, ILPYONG JOHN, educator; b. Seoul, Korea, Aug. 15, 1931; s. Suk Dae and Ui-Bong K.; came to U.S., 1954, naturalized, 1964; M.A. (NDEA fellow), Columbia, 1962, Ph.D. (Internat. Devel. fellow), 1968; m. Hyunyong Chung, June 22, 1963; children—Irene, Katherene. Asst. prof. govt. Ind. U., 1965-69; asso. prof. polit. sci. U. Conn., Storrs, 1970-75, prof., 1976—; Fulbright prof. internat. relations U. Tokyo, 1976—. Served with UN Forces, 1950-54; Korea. Decorated Bronze Star. Mem. Am. Polit. Sci. Assn., Assn. Asian Studies, Internat. Studies Assn., New Eng. Assn. Asian Studies (v.p. 1977-78, pres. 1978-79), Pi Sigma Alpha. Author: The Politics of Chinese Communism, 1973; Communist Politics in North Korea, 1975. Editorial bd. Asian Thought and Soc., 1973-75, Jour. Korean Affairs, 1971-76, Korean Jour. Internat. Studies. Home: 61 Hillyndale Rd Storrs CT 06268 Office: Dept Polit Sci U of Conn Storrs CT 06268

KIM, JE CHUL, nuclear power engr.; b. Korea, Mar. 1, 1940; s. Yong Ho and Chong Won (Wu) K.; B.S., Mass. Inst. Tech., 1964; M.S., Northeastern U., 1967; Ph.D., Purdue U., 1970; m. Chong Bok Lee, June 6, 1964; children—Janet, Clara. Vis. asst. prof. Purdue U., 1967-70; asst. to v.p. Blocked Iron Corp., N.Y.C., 1970-71; nuclear power engr. Stone & Webster Engring. Corp., Boston, 1971-73; prin. engr. nuclear safety group Ebasco Services, Inc., N.Y.C., 1973—. Mem. ASME, Sigma Xi. Presbyterian. Home: 778 Klondike Ave Staten Island NY 10314 Office: Ebasco Services Inc 19 Rector St New York City NY 10006

KIM, KYU SUNG (HUGH), librarian; b. Korea, July 6, 1937; s. Tong Sup and Kum Ye (Lee) K.; came to U.S., 1964, naturalized, 1978; B.A., Chung-ang U., Korea, 1963; M.A. (Exchange fellow), L.I. U., 1966, M.L.S., 1968; Ph.D., St. John's U., 1973; m. Yeun Sook, July 4, 1973; children—Sandra, Edward. Spl. librarian C.W. Post Coll. Library, 1966-68, librarian, 1968-72; coll. archivist, librarian S.I. Community Coll. Library, 1972-76, Coll. S.I. Library, 1976—; adj. prof. St. John's U., 1973-74; tchr. history and library services Coll. S. I. Served with Korean Army, 1959-61. Recipient summer research award Coll. S.I., 1977. Mem. ALA, Am. Hist. Assn., Library Assn. City U. N.Y., Melvil Dui Chowder and Marching Assn. Home: 533 Cumberland St Englewood NJ 07631

KIM, SEONG HWAN, plant pathologist; b. Seoul, Korea, Nov. 23, 1938; s. Dong Hwa and Shin Deuk (Chae) K.; came to U.S., 1965, naturalized, 1977; B.S., Seoul Nat. U., 1963; M.S., U. Del., 1968; Ph.D., U. Md., 1972; m. Byung Ju Min, Aug. 30, 1970; children—Glen, Donald. Research asst. U. Del., 1965-67; research and teaching asst., then jr. instr. U. Md., 1968-71; plant pathologist Pa. Dept. Agr., Harrisburg, 1972—, charge plant disease diagnostic lab., 1972—. Served with Korean Army, 1959-61. Mem. Am. Phytopathol. Soc. Presbyterian. Author articles. Home: 984 Galion St Harrisburg PA 17111 Office: 2301 N Cameron St Harrisburg PA 17120

KIM, TAI KYUNG, chemist; b. Pyungyang, Korea, June 19, 1927; s. Byung O. and Chang O. Kim; came to U.S., 1952, naturalized, 1971; B.S. in Engring., Seoul Nat. U., 1951; B.S., Adrian Coll., 1955; M.S., U. Detroit, 1959; Ph.D., Duquesne U., 1963; m. InSoon Lee, Aug. 29, 1959; children—Elizabeth, David, Lisa. Sr. engr. precision metal group Chem. and Metall. div. GTE Sylvania Inc., Towanda, Pa., 1963-66, devel. engr., 1966-68, advanced devel. engr., 1968-73, engring. specialist, 1973—. Mem. Am. Chem. Soc., Korean Engrs. and Scientists Assn. in Am. Republican. Presbyterian. Patentee in field. Home: RD 1 Hillcrest Dr Towanda PA 18848 Office: GTE Sylvania Inc Hawes St PO Box 70 Towanda PA 18848

KIM, YOON CHOO, physician; b. Hamjong, Korea, Nov. 10, 1923; s. Iksoo and Yo Ok K.; came to U.S., 1953, naturalized, 1963; M.D., Yonsei U., Seoul, Korea, 1947; 1 son, Seung K. Resident, Stanford Univ. Hosp., Palo Alto, Calif., asst. prof. U. Tenn. Sch. Medicine, Memphis, 1961-64; pathologist Bapt. Meml. Hosp., Memphis, 1964-68; dir. lab. Martin Meml. Hosp., Mt. Vernon, Ohio., 1968-71, Divine Providence Hosp., Pitts., 1971—; vis. asst. prof. W.Va. U. Sch. Medicine, 1972—. Diplomate Am. Bd. Pathology. Fellow Am. Soc. Clin. Pathologists; mem. Internat. Acad. Pathology, AMA, Pa. Med. Soc. Unitarian-Universalist. Office: 1004 Arch St Pittsburgh PA 15212

KIM, YOU SONG, utility co. exec.; b. Seoul, Korea, Sept. 1, 1929; s. Back M. and Hwa N. (Lee) K.; came to U.S., 1954, naturalized, 1968; B.S., Seoul Nat. U., 1953; B.S., N.C. State U., 1956, M.S., 1958; Ph.D., Rutgers U., 1961; m. Kyu Sun Lee, Oct. 25, 1958; children—David, John, Esther. Mem. tech. staff Bell Telephone Labs., Allentown, Pa., 1961—. Mem. Am. Ceramic Soc., IEEE, Internat. Soc. Microeletronics, Keramos. Republican. Presbyterian. Contbr. articles in field to profl. jours. Home: 923 Turner St Emmaus PA 18049 Office: 555 Union Blvd Allentown PA 18103

KIM, YOUNG HO, dentist; b. Seoul, Korea, Oct. 17, 1927; s. Woo Hyun and Doo Keum (Park) K.; D.D.S., Seoul Nat. U., 1949; M.S., U. Rochester, 1958; D.M.D., Tufts U., 1960; m. Mazie Ann Lim, May 19, 1956; children—Stuart K., Jonathan C. Came to U.S., 1952, naturalized, 1962. Specialist in orthodontics, Weston, Mass., 1964—; instr. Harvard Dental Sch., 1960-65; asso. prof. Boston U. Grad. Sch. Dentistry, 1967-70; clin. prof. Yonsei U. Coll. Dentistry, 1972; cons. VA Hosp., Roxbury, Mass. Chmn. bd. trustees Myung Hwee Won Found. Diplomate Am. Bd. Orthodontists. Mem. Am. Dental Assn., Am. Assn. Orthodontists, Mass. Dental Soc., Angle Soc. Orthodontists, Omicron Kappa Upsilon. Home: 154 Summer St Weston MA 02193 Office: 30 Colpitts Rd Weston MA 02193

KIMAN, RICHARD AARON, dentist; b. N.Y.C., Apr. 21, 1919; s. Saul and Jennie (Katz) K.; B.S., N.Y. U., 1940; D.D.S., U. Pitts., 1943, D.M.D., 1970; m. Shirley Hollander, Feb. 8, 1948; 1 dau., Susan Ilene. Practice dentistry, N.Y.C., 1946—; mem. dental staff Community Service Soc. N.Y., 1949-56; attending dentist Boys' Club of N.Y. Dental Clinic, 1948-71, chief dental surgeon, 1962-71; cons. to Mt. Sinai Hosp., 1947-49, Dental Service Assn. N.Y., 1965—; mem. dental panel Asso. Hosp. Service, 1970—, mem. group health dental panel, 1950—; mem. dental panel N.Y.C. Police Benevolent Assn., 1964—; mem. pub. health div. N.Y.C. Office Civil Def., 1946—; clin. instr. operative dentistry, instr. operative technique N.Y. U. Coll. Denistry, 1972-75, clin. asst. prof., 1975—. Chmn., Pythian Blood Bank, 1950-60. Served from 1st lt. to capt. AUS, 1943-46; ETO. Fellow N.Y. Acad. Dentistry (asso., mem. boys club com. 1958-61), N.Y. Acad. Dentistry; mem. Am., N.Y. State (mem. pub. and profl. relations com. 1955-57) dental assns., First Dist. Dental Soc., Internat. Assn. Anesthesiologists. K.P. (chancellor N.Y.C. 1950-51, Pythian of Year award 1956). Contbr. articles on dental survey, dental oral hygiene to profl. jours. Home: 45 Sutton Pl S New York City NY 10022 Office: 235 E 22d St New York City NY 10010

KIMBALL, GEORGE HARDY, music, drama critic; b. Mattoon, Ill., Feb. 4, 1912; s. George Pearl and Barbara Stacy (Hardy) K.; B.A., U. Nebr., 1946; m. Jeanne Cady Boyd, May 9, 1943; children—Boyd Cady, Robert Hugh. Reporter, music critic Lincoln (Nebr.) Star, 1936-41; reporter Rochester (N.Y.) Times-Union, 1946-73, asst. music critic, 1951-61, music critic, 1961—, asst. drama critic theatre editor, 1951-73; editor Diocese, Rochester Episc. Diocese, 1975—. Served with USAAF, 1941-45, USAF, 1951-52. Mem. Phi Mu Alpha Sinfonia, U. Neb. Alumni Club (pres. 1960-63), Sigma Delta Chi. Home: 163 Wendover Rd Rochester NY 14610 Office: 935 East Ave Rochester NY 14607

KIMBALL, MARY LEE EVANS (MRS. CHASE KIMBALL), educator; b. St. Louis, Jan. 27, 1911; d. Dwight Durkee and Elmira (Lee) Evans; A.B. cum laude, Smith Coll., 1933; M.A., Radcliffe Coll., 1935; diplome d'etudes Univ. (Am. fellow Inst. Internat. Edn., 1936-37) Universite de Paris (France), 1937; diplome Ecole du Louvre, Paris, 1962; postgrad. (predoctoral fellow) U. Conn., 1967-68; M.A., Trinity Coll., 1971, U. Conn., 1971; m. Chase Kimball, June 27, 1942; children—Elmira (Mrs. H. Thomas Byron, Jr.), Helen Chase, Mary Eliza. Tchr. French, Cambridge Sch., Kendall Green, Mass., 1937-38, Wheaton Coll., 1938-41, Greenwood Sch., Ruxton, Md., 1941-42, Montessori Sch., Calgary, Alta., Can., 1945, Milton Acad., Mass., 1948-52; instr. French, Tufts U., 1952-58; asst. prof. French, Newton Coll. Sacred Heart, 1958-59; asst. prof. French, Stonehill Coll., 1959-64; asso. prof. French, Salem (Mass.) State Coll., 1965; asst. prof. French, U. Mass., Boston, 1965—. Bd. dirs. Heart Fund, Boston, to 1970; mem. womans bd. Day-Kimball Hosp., Conn.; Milton chmn. Boston Arts Festival, 1957-60. Pres., Milton Womens Republican Club, 1958-60; sec. Milton Rep. Town Com. Bd. dirs. French Library Boston, 1972-78. Instr. French, U.S. Army, Whitehorse, Yukon, 1944. Decorated chevalier de l'ordre des Palmes Académiques (France). Mem. League Women Voters (voters' service chmn., internat. relations chmn. Milton 1948-52), Am. Assn. Tchrs. French, Modern Lang. Assn., Alliance Francaise, Am. Hist. Assn., Fragment Soc. Boston, Colonial Dames Am. Clubs: Chromatic (pres. 1977—), Smith College (dir. 1955-61, 70-75, pres. Class of 1933, 1973-78), Women's City (Boston); Milton Women's (internat. relations chmn. 1958-60, 62-64 garden and conservation chmn. 1960-61), Chromatic of Boston (pres. 1977—). Home: Pomfret Centre CT 06259 also 434 Brush Hill Rd Milton MA 02186 Office: U Mass Boston MA 02116

KIMBLE, EDWIN LOCKARD, JR., former assn. exec.; b. Princeton, N.J., Apr. 17, 1944; s. Edwin Lockard and Mary Cecilia (King) K.; B.S., Ursinus Coll., 1966; M.A., W.Va. U., 1969, Ph.D., 1972; m. Carline Ann Swanson, Aug. 5, 1972. Tchr. math and sci. Oxford Acad., Pleasantville, N.J., 1967-70; exec. dir. Westmoreland County Mental Health Assn., Greensburg, Pa., 1973-77. Mem. Am. Psychol. Assn. (asso.), Mental Health Assn. (staff council). Episcopalian. Home: 4 Hamilton Ave Princeton NJ 08540

KIMBLE, SERUCH TITUS, physician; b. Washington, Feb. 21, 1921; s. Seruch Titus and Harriet Louise (Zebley) K.; A.B., George Washington U., 1942, M.D., 1944; m. Helen Louise Matchett, Jan. 15, 1949; children—Claudia, Kathryn, Stephen, Henry, David, Richard, Robert. Intern Presbyn. Hosp., Chgo., 1944-45; med. resident Suburban Hosp., Bethesda, Md., 1945-46, VA Hosp., Los Angeles, 1950-51, Mt. Alto VA Hosp., Washington, 1951-52; practice medicine specializing in internal medicine, Washington, 1947-50, Silver Spring, Md., 1953—; attending internist Washington Adventist Hosp., Takoma Park, Md., pres. med. staff, 1972-73, trustee, 1976—; attending internist Holy Cross Hosp., Silver Spring, Suburban Hosp., Bethesda. Mem. Montgomery County Adv. Com. on Health Facilities, 1968-69. Served to capt., M.C., AUS, 1946-47, 51-52. Diplomate Am. Bd. Internal Medicine. Fellow A.C.P. (life); mem. AMA, Montgomery County Med. Soc. (past pres.), Med. and Chirurg. Faculty Md. (councillor 1968-74), N.Y. Acad. Scis., Pan Am. Med. Assn., Internat. Soc. Internal Medicine, AAAS. Republican. Methodist. Club: Civitan of Silver Spring (pres. 1960-61). Home: 3333 Emory Church Rd Olney MD 20832 Office: 9801 Georgia Ave Silver Spring MD 20902

KIMM, RICHARD MILES, aviation tng. center mgr.; b. Ft. Monroe, Va., Feb. 20, 1938; s. Virgil M. and Margaret (Furey) K.; B.S., U. Conn., 1959; postgrad. U. Va., 1962-63; m. Patricia A. Morrison, June 20, 1959; children—Michael, Susan, Melissa. Officer, U.S. Navy, 1959-69; advanced through grades to comdr.; carrier pilot, aide to adm./Sec. Navy, 1959-69; comdg. officer Naval Res. Unit, 1978—; mgr. flight ops. sales Eastern Airlines, Miami, Fla., 1969-72; nat. sales mgr. Atlantic Aviation, 1972-74; mgr. tng. center Flight Safety Internat., Wilmington, Del., 1974—; chmn. Greater Wilmington Airport Ops. Com., 1974; mem. Del. Gov.'s Transp. Task Force; mem. New Castle County Bd. Transp. Named Assn. Rookie of Year, Greater Wilmington YMCA, 1974, recipient enrollment award, 1975. Mem. Del. C. of C. (chmn. air transp. com.). Club: Wilmington Racquet (dir.). Home: 511 Andover Rd Wilmington DE 19803 Office: Box 15003 Wilmington DE 19850

KIMMEL, ROBERT IRVING, state govt. ofcl.; b. Uniontown, Pa., Jan. 28, 1922; s. Andrew Filson and Dorothy Jean (Walker) K.; student Bucknell U., Lewisburg, Pa., 1940-41, 43-44, Washington U., St. Louis, 1942, Pa. State U., 1972; divorced; children—Donna Jean, Robert Filson, LuAnna Pat, Kevin Normaine, Gregory Paul. Self-employed entertainer, 1944; mgr. Cassiday Theaters, Midland, Mich., 1945-46; engring. illustrator Dow Chem. Co., Midland, 1946-59; engring. mgr. Radio Communications Co., Bloomsburg, Pa., 1959-64; chief electronics Pa. State Police, Harrisburg, 1964-74, dir. communications div., 1974—; chmn. Pa. Law Enforcement Telecommunications Planning Com., 1976-78; cons., lectr. in field. Mem. task force Cultural Center, Harrisburg, 1975-76; head coach Lakevue Midget Baseball Assn., 1978; pres. council St. Mark's Lutheran Ch., Harrisburg, 1975-78. Served with USAAF, 1942-43. Recipient various pub. service awards, certificates merit. Mem. Asso. Pub.-Safety Communications Officers (pres. 1978-79), Pa. Chiefs Police Assn. (chmn. frequency adv. com. 1967-78), Engrs. Soc. Pa. (pres. 1978-79), Nat. Assn. Dance and Affiliated Artists (past v.p.), Radio Club Am., Greater Harrisburg Arts Council (dir.). Author papers in field. Developer vehicle location system, elec. security systems. Home: 1002A N 26th St Harrisburg PA 17102 Office: 1800 Elmerton Ave Harrisburg PA 17120

KIMMINS, WARWICK CHARLES, educator; b. Isleworth, Eng., July 20, 1941; s. Horace Charles and Eileen May (Beck) K.; B.Sc. with honors, London U., 1962, Ph.D., 1965; m. Ruth Willcock, July 28, 1964; children—Eliot, Sarah. Cons. library research dept. Ency. Britannica, 1963-65; asst. prof. biology Dalhousie U., 1965-69, asso. prof., 1969-73, prof., 1973—. Co-founder, chmn. E. Coast Community Sch.; v.p., ward council leader Cub Scouts of Can.; pres. Le Marchant Home and Sch. Assn.; bd. dirs. Canadian Cancer Soc., Halifax. NRC grantee, 1965-69, 69-72, 73-76. Mem. Assn. Applied Biologists, Soc. Exptl. Biology, Soc. Gen. Microbiology, Canadian, Am. socs. phytopathology. Unitarian. Club: Waegwoltic. Contbr. chpts. to books, articles to profl. jours. Home: 1684 Edward St Halifax NS B3H 3J3 Canada Office: Dalhousie U Halifax NS Canada

KIMPEL, BENJAMIN FRANKLIN, educator; b. Racine, Wis., May 9, 1905; s. Benjamin F. and Agnes (Beltz) K.; B.A., U. Wis., 1926; postgrad. (fellow in anthropology), U. Nebr., 1927-28; Ph.D. (Tew fellow), Yale, 1932. Ordained to ministry Am. Unitarian Assn., 1937; faculty Kans. Wesleyan U., Salina, 1933-36, prof., 1935-36; prof. philosophy Drew U., Madison, N.J., 1938-72. Mem. Am. Assn. U. Profs., Am. Philos. Assn., Beta Beta Beta, Kappa Pi, Pi Gamma Mu, Psi Chi, Phi Sigma Tau, Sigma Phi. Author: Religious Faith, Language and Knowledge, 1952; Faith and Moral Authority, 1953; Symbols of Religious Faith, 1954; Moral Principles in the Bible, 1956; Language and Religion, 1957; Principles of Moral Philosophy, 1960; Kant's Critical Philosophy, 1964; Hegel's Philosophy of History, 1964; Nietzsche's Beyond Good and Evil, 1964; Schopenhauer's Philosophy, 1965; Philosophy of Zen Buddhism, 1966. Home: North Bennington VT 05257

KIMURA, MICHIO, chem. co. exec.; b. London, Eng., July 9, 1924; s. Seizo and Chiyo (Nose) K.; came to U.S., 1959; B.A. in Econs., Keio U., Tokyo, 1949; m. Haruko Wada, Feb. 22, 1954; children—Yukiko, Kathryn Mari. With Nichimen Co., Ltd., Osaka, Japan, 1949-59; with Nichimen Co., Inc., N.Y.C., 1959-67, sec., 1966-67; with Nippon Shokubai Kagaku Kogyo Co., Ltd., Osaka, Japan, 1967-73; pres., treas. Japan Catalytic Internat., Inc. subs. Nippon Shokubai Kagaku Kogyo Co. Ltd., N.Y.C., 1973—. Served lt. j.g. Japanese Navy, 1944-45. Mem. U.S., Japanese chambers commerce, Japan Soc. Buddhist. Club: Nippon. Home: 241 Walnut Rd Glen Cove NY 11542 Office: 1221 Ave of Americas New York City NY 10020

KINARD, CHARLES DONALD, univ. adminstr.; b. Washington, May 25, 1933; s. James Henry and Mary Jane (Simms) K.; B.A., Howard U., 1956; M.A., Fed. City Coll., 1972; Ed.D., certificate advanced grad. study, Va. Poly. Inst. and State U., 1975; m. Helen Hall, Aug. 21, 1954; children—Karen Kinard Porter, Karyl Kathleen. Sr. counselor Howard U., 1964-69; dir. student activities Fed. City Coll., 1969-73; dean students D.C. Tchrs. Coll. and Fed. City Coll., 1973-77; asso. v.p. for student affairs U. D.C., 1977—; vis. instr. Fed. City Coll., 1969-76. Adviser, Hospitality House, Washington, 1971-73; pres. bd. Mission Community Concern, Washington, 1974-77. Recipient Outstanding Citizenship award D.C. Mayor, 1964, Recognition award Washington Urban League, 1966, Commr. award D.C. Govt., 1968, Citizen Salute award Sta. WOL, 1970. Mem. Assn. Coll. Unions, Internat., Nat. assns. student personnel adminstrs., Am. Personnel, Guidance Assn., Am. Assn. Polit. and Social Scis., Phi Beta Kappa, Kappa Alpha Psi. Democrat. Methodist. Editor Soul Force, 1966-68. Home: 2801 Tennyson St NW Washington DC 20015 Office: 929 E St NW Washington DC 20004

KINAS, ERNEST NICHOLAS, mech. engr.; b. Boston, Nov. 28, 1930; s. Nicholas Arthur and Evangelia (Psaras) K.; B.S. in Indsl. Engring., Northeastern U., 1953, postgrad., 1957-63; m. Nelly Christopher, Aug. 21, 1966; children—Ernest Stephen, Carol Ann. Indsl. engr. Sylvania Electric, Seneca Falls, N.Y., 1953-54; prodn. engr. Fed. Telephone and Electric div. ITT, Nutley, N.J., 1954-55; mech. engr. Picatinny Arsenal, Dover, N.J., 1955-56; mech. engr. U.S. Air Force Cambridge Research Center, Boston, 1956-57; sr. mech. engr. U.S. Army Materials and Mechanics Research Center, Watertown, Mass., 1957—; cons. hot metalworking, ammunition, ordnance material. Active Newton (Mass.) PTA. Recipient U.S. Army Invention award, 1974. Mem. Am. Soc. for Metals, Am. Def. Preparedness Assn., Am. Ordnance Assn. Greek Orthodox. Clubs: Businessmen's Athletic, Pequossette Masons, Triad. Contbr. articles to profl. jours. Office: US AMMRC Arsenal St Watertown MA 02172

KINDL, FRED HENRY, mech. engr.; b. Los Angeles, July 4, 1920; s. Fred Henry and Flora Ethel (Kellett) K.; B.S. in Mech. Engring., Carnegie Inst. Tech., 1942; m. Catherine Mary Quinlan, Sept. 4, 1943; children—Jean Marie, Rosemary, Ellen, Patrice. Mgr. electromech. engring. materials and process lab. General Electric Co., Schenectady, 1960-65, mgr. mech. and thermal engring. large steam turbine generator dept., 1965-69, mgr. engring. medium gas turbine dept., 1969-73; pres. Encotech, Inc., Schenectady, 1973—, also dir. Chmn. Ballston Spa (N.Y.) chpt. ARC, 1955-60. Served with USAAF, 1942-46. Fellow ASME; mem. Am. Soc. Metals, ASTM, Am. Petroleum Inst. Republican. Episcopalian. Clubs: Lake George, Mohawk. Patentee in field. Home: 14 N Church St Schenectady NY 12305 Office: PO Box 714 Schenectady NY 12301

KINDLE, CECIL HALDANE, ret. educator; b. Elmira, N.Y., Oct. 16, 1904; s. Edward Martin and Margaret (Ferris) K.; B.A., Queen's U., Can., 1926; Ph.D., Princeton, 1931; m. Mary Ethel Smyers, Jan. 26, 1941; children—Mary (Mrs. Roger Allan Stafford), Elizabeth (Mrs. Burke Baker III), Cecil Haldane, Millicent Robb. Mem. faculty, dept. geology Coll. City N.Y., 1931-75, prof., 1970-75. With Geol. Survey Can., summers 1927-31, Geol. Survey Nfld., summers 1939, 40, 45. Trustee Paleontol. Research Instn., Ithaca, N.Y., 1971-74. NSF grantee, 1957-59. Fellow Geol. Soc. Am., Geol. Assn. Can., Paleontol. Soc.; mem. Palaeontol. Assn. Home: 332 N Midland Ave Upper Nyack NY 10960

KINDLE, MARY ETHEL SMYERS (MRS. CECIL HALDANE KINDLE), librarian; b. Aplin, Ark., Sept. 24, 1913; d. Dan Taylor and Ruby Robb (Neale) Smyers; B.S., U. Ark., 1936; M.S. in L.S., Columbia, 1941, postgrad., Tchrs. Coll., 1941, 54-57, 69—; postgrad. Fordham U., 1962-63; m. Cecil Haldane Kindle, Jan. 26, 1941; children—Mary Anne (Mrs. Roger Alan Stafford) (dec.), Elizabeth Lee (Mrs. Burke Baker III), Cecil Haldane, Millicent Robb. Asst. children's and adult depts. Little Rock Pub. Library, 1930-34; librarian elementary schs., Fort Smith, Ark., 1936-39, Liberty St. Elementary Sch., Nyack, N.Y., 1940-41; librarian young people's dept. Bloomingdale br. N.Y. Pub. Library, 1954, Nyack High Sch., 1954-57, Hilltop Jr. High Sch., Nyack, N.Y., 1957-68, Valley Cottage

Elementary Sch., 1968-76. Cons. Bethlehem (Conn.) Pub. Library, 1958; sec., dir. Rockland Fed. Credit Union. Mem. Vols. for Internat. Tech. Assistance, 1965-68. Recipient Martha Washington medal S.A.R., 1971. Mem. N.E.A., (co-chmn. membership Rockland County, N.Y., 1967-69), Am., N.Y., library assns., Rockland County Sch. Librarians Assn. (rec. sec. 1963), N.Y. State, Rockland County (rec. sec. 1968-72), tchrs. assns., Am. Security Council, Internat. Platform Assn., Little Rock Jr. Fedn. Women's Clubs (charter), Kappa Delta Pi, Delta Kappa Gamma (chmn. publicity and publs. com. Alpha Eta chpt.). Editor: Authors of Rockland County, 1960. Home: 332 N Midland Ave Upper Nyack NY 10960

KINDRED, GEORGE CHARLES, lithographing exec.; b. Bklyn., Nov. 20, 1898; s. Robert C. and Caroline (Hoag) K.; spl. courses, Columbia and N.Y. U.; m. Dorothy Estabrook, Mar. 10, 1928; children—George Estabrook, John MacGregor. Buyer, W. R. Grace and Co., 1919-23; western sales mgr. Snyder and Black, 1923-28; pres. Kindred, MacLean and Co., 1928-59; pres. Underhill, Inv., Inc., 1959—. Served in U.S. Army World War I, USCG Aux., World War II. Mem. A.I.M., St. Andrews Soc., Point Purchase Advt. Inst. (founder, past pres.), Met. Lithographers Assn. (past pres.), Lithographic Tech. Found. (past treas., dir.), Am. Legion, U.S. Power Squadrons, Lithographers Nat. Assn. (past treas., dir.). Episcopalian (vestryman). Clubs: Lotos (1st v.p., chmn. admissions; dir.) (N.Y.C.); Country (governor), Yacht, Squadron (Westhampton); Fox Meadow Tennis; Saugatuck Harbor Yacht (Westport, Conn.); Sanderling (Siesta Key, Fla.). Home: 338 Nod Hill Rd Wilton CT 06897 also 4822 Ocean Blvd Siesta Key Sarasota FL 33581 Office: Wilton CT 06897

KING, ALICIA, mental health adminstr.; b. Washington, Feb. 2, 1948; d. George E. and Irene E. K.; B.A., Mercyhurst Coll., 1970; M.Ed., Temple U., 1975; postgrad., 1975—. Edn. specialist Erie (Pa.) Urban Coalition, 1970; asst. researcher Appalachian Regional Commn., Washington, 1971-72; gen. analyst traffic Gen. Telephone Co. Pa., Erie, 1972; counselor/instr. Opportunities Industrialization Center, Phila., 1972-74; asst. dir. drug abuse tng. N. Central Phila. Community Mental Health/Mental Retardation Center, 1974—. Mem. Am. Pub. Health Assn., Am. Psychol. Assn., Assn. Black Psychologists, Pa. Evaluation Network. Democrat. Roman Catholic. Home: 4615 Pulaski Ave Philadelphia PA 19144 Office: N Central Phila Community Mental Health/Mental Retardation Center 3701 N Broad St Philadelphia PA 19140

KING, BARBARA JEAN, pub. relations exec.; b. N.Y.C., Feb. 10, 1941; d. Philip and Antoinette (Mack) K.; B.A., Jackson Coll. Tufts U., 1963. Shareowner corr. stock and bond div. AT&T, N.Y.C., 1963-66; asst. editor Saturday Rev. mag., N.Y.C., 1966-73; mgr. classical publicity Columbia Records Co. subs. CBS, Inc., N.Y.C., 1974-77; dir. press and pub. info. Teleprompter Corp., N.Y.C., 1977—. Mem. Nat. Acad. Rec. Arts, Scis., Nat. Acad. TV Arts and Scis. Contbr. articles to Saturday Rev., Met. Opera Program, Vivian Beaumont Theater Program, 1966-73. Home: 333 E 55th St New York City NY 10022 Office: Teleprompter Corp 888 Seventh Ave New York City NY 10019

KING, CHARLES THOMAS, ret. educator; b. Coatsville, Pa., July 19, 1911; s. John Henry and Estella (Orr) K.; B.S., West Chester State Coll., 1932; Ed.M., Temple U., 1944; Ed.D., Rutgers U., 1957; m. Dorothy Eckman, Nov. 30, 1933; children—Marilyn Mae, Kenneth Alan, Donald Edwin. Tchr., West Pottsgorve Twp. Sch., Stowe, Pa., 1933-35, Haverford Twp. Sch., Havertown, Pa., 1935-38; dir. elementary health and phys. edn. Havertown Twp. Sch., 1938-42; prin. Llanerch Sch., Havertown, 1942-45; supervising prin. West Pottsgrove Twp. Sch., 1945-47; prin. Glenwood and Short Hills Schs., Milburn, N.J., 1947-51; asst. to supt., 1951-59, asst. supt., 1959-62, supt., 1962-74. Mem. state adv. council on Handicapped 1968-72; mem. state certification appeals com., 1972-74. Pres. Milburn (N.J.) Community Council, 1954-56. Dir. Milburn Pub. Library; chmn. N.J. Council on Econ. Edn., 1972-74. Mem. Essex County Supts. Roundtable (chmn. 1965-66), Phi Delta Kappa (chpt. pres. 1959-60). Conglist. (deacon). Rotarian (pres. 1957-58). Home: 115 Hobart Ave Short Hills NJ 07078

KING, CONRAD DAVID, toxicologist-pathologist, cons. co. exec.; b. Peoria, Ill., Aug. 10, 1927; s. Cuvier David and Emma Nell (Helms) K.; B.S., U. Nebr., 1949; D.V.M., Colo. State U., 1961; M.S., U. Wis., 1964, Ph.D., 1967; m. Marilyn Jean Boettger, Dec. 29, 1950; children—Joel David, Kristen Louise. Practice veterinary medicine, Rock City, Ill., 1961-63; NIH trainee in veterinary sci. U. Wis., 1963-64, NIH postdoctoral fellow, 1964-67; research pathologist The Dow Chem. Co., Midland, Mich., 1967-69; chief pathology and toxicology sect. Norwich Pharmacal Co. (N.Y.), 1969-73; dir. drug safety evaluation div. Ortho Pharm. Corp., Raritan, N.J., 1973-77; chmn. Xenos, consultation in drug safety assessment, North Branch, N.J., 1977—; cons. in toxicology to Shrewsbury (N.J.) Conf.; lectr. toxicology Med. Coll. Va., 1974—; guest lectr. in pathology and toxicology Coll. Medicine and Dentistry, Rutgers U., New Brunswick, N.J., 1977—; mem. adv. council in animal scis. Somerset County Coll., Somerville, N.J., 1976—. Served to 1st lt., arty., U.S. Army, 1950-52; Korea. Decorated Bronze Star. Mem. Soc. Pharmacol. and Environ. Pathologists (bd. editors 1975—, exec. com. 1976—), AVMA, Am. Assn. Lab. Animal Sci., Indsl. Veterinarians Assn., AAAS, Soc. Study of Reprodn., Pharm. Mfrs. Assn., Environ. Mutagen Soc. Clubs: Masons, Indoor Tennis. Contbr. articles in pathology and veterinary medicine to profl. jours. Home: 143 Howell Dr Somerville NJ 08876 Office: Xenos PO Box 5008 North Branch NJ 08876

KING, DONALD DEWOLF, electronics co. exec.; b. Rochester, N.Y., Aug. 7, 1919; s. James Percival and Edith Marianne (Seyerlen) K.; A.B., Harvard U., 1942; Ph.D., 1946; m. Mary Anne Henderson, June 21, 1944; children—Alison, Stuart, Scotty, James. Asst. prof. applied physics Harvard U., 1947-48; dir. radiation lab. Johns Hopkins U., Balt., 1948-55; v.p. research div. Electronic Communications, Inc., Timonium, Md., 1956-64; dir. electronics research lab. Aerospace Corp., Los Angeles, 1964-67; pres. Philips labs div. N. Am. Philips Corp., Briarcliff Manor, N.Y., 1967—. Fellow IEEE, AAAS, Am. Phys. Soc., Indsl. Research Inst. (dir.), Sigma Xi. Presbyterian. Club: Chemists. Author: Measurements at Centimeter Wave length, 1952. Home: 920 Hardscrabble Rd Chappaqua NY 10514

KING, EDWARD JOSEPH, gov. Mass.; b. Chelsea, Mass., May 11, 1925; s. Edward and Helen Veronica (Dawson) K.; A.B., Boston Coll., 1948; postgrad. Bentley Sch. Accounting and Fin., 1951-53; m. Josephine Teresa Hurley, Nov. 22, 1952; children—Brian Edward, Timothy D. With Buffalo Bills, All Am. Conf., 1948-49, Balt. Colts, Nat. Football League, 1950; accountant, Lybrand Ross Bros. & Montgomery (name now Coopers & Lybrand), Boston, 1953-56; asst. dir., comptroller, Mus. of Sci., Boston, 1956-58; comptroller, sec.-treas., Mass. Port Authority, Boston, 1959-63, exec. dir., 1963-74; pres., New Eng. Council Inc., Boston, after 1975; now gov. trustee, Eaton & Howard Cash Mgmt. Fund, Charlestown Savs. Bank; dir. Baird Atomic. Gen. chmn. Greater Boston Leukemia Soc. Am., 1975-76; co-chmn. Little Sisters of the Poor Bldg. Fund, 1975-76. Served with USN, 1943-44. Roman Catholic. Clubs: Boston Coll. Varsity, Elks. Home: 20 Dix St Winthrop MA 02152 Office: 1032 Statler Office Bldg Boston MA 02116

KING, FRANCIS MICHAEL, pathologist; b. Chgo., Nov. 27, 1931; s. Francis Michael and Ethel Marie (Fant) K.; B.Sc., Northwestern U., 1954, M.D., 1957. Intern, Cook County Hosp., Chgo., 1957-58; resident in pathology Northwestern-Wesley Hosp., Chgo., 1958, New Eng. Deaconess Hosp., Boston, 1961-62; cancer fellow Meml. Hosp.-Sloan Kettering Inst., N.Y.C., 1963-64, Children's Hosp. Med. Center, Boston, 1964-65; instr. pathology Harvard Med. Sch., 1964-65; asst. pathologist Armed Forces Inst. Pathology, Washington, 1965-66, chief hematology and lymphatic pathology br., 1967-74, chief div. B., 1970-75, chmn. dept. hematologic and lymphatic pathology, 1975—; clin. prof. pathology Uniformed Services U. Health Scis., 1975—. Served to lt. comdr. USNR, 1959-61. Am. Cancer Soc. fellow, 1961-62; diplomate Am. Bd. Pathology. Fellow Am. Soc. Clin. Pathologists; mem. AMA, Internat. Acad. Pathologists. Contbr. chpts. to books, articles on pathology, radiology to profl. jours. Office: Room 3025 Armed Forces Inst Pathology Washington DC 20306

KING, FRANCIS PAUL, pension fund exec.; b. Medford, Oreg., May 5, 1922; s. George Patrick and Ruth Elodie (Voruz) K.; B.S., U. Oreg., 1943; M.A., Stanford, 1948, Ph.D., 1953. Research asso. Hoover Inst. Library, 1943-46; teaching asst. polit. sci. Stanford, 1946-49; cons. Gen. Electric Co., N.Y.C., 1953; with Tchrs. Ins. & Annuity Assn., N.Y.C., 1953—, sr. research officer, 1971—. Chmn. bd. Tuition Exchange, Inc., Allentown, Pa., 1972—. Served to 1st lt. AUS, 1943-46. Fulbright research fellow Institut D'etudes Politiques, Paris, 1952-53. Mem. Am. Pension Conf., Am. Risk and Ins. Assn., Gerontol. Soc., Assn. for Instnl. Research, Phi Beta Kappa. Author: Financing the College Education of Faculty Children, 1954; Retirement and Insurance Plans in American Colleges, 1959; (with M.H. Ingraham) The Outer Fringe, 1964; (with M.H. Ingraham) The Mirror of Brass, 1968; (with W.C. Greenough) Benefit Plans in American Colleges, 1969; Benefit Plans in Junior Colleges, 1970; (with W.C. Greenough) Pension Plans and Public Policy, 1976. Home: 360 E 72d St New York City NY 10021 Office: Tchrs Ins and Annuity Assn 730 3d Ave New York City NY 10017

KING, HENRY BRAZELL, trade assn. exec.; b. Phila., Apr. 2, 1921; s. Henry Bendall and Rosetta (Brazell) K.; B.B.A., Manhattan Coll., 1942; LL.B., N.Y. Law Sch., 1949; M.B.A., Pace U., 1970; D.H.L., Mercy Coll., 1978; m. Ottilie Rosina Sandrock, Dec. 26, 1944; children—Michael Christopher, Henry Brazell, Mary Rosetta, Matthew Sandrock, John Reilly, Patrick Ambrose, Vincent de Lasalle, Anthony Gabriel, David Peter, Gregory Joseph, Ottilie Rosina, Robert Campion, Margaret Anne, Elizabeth Ann, Bibiana. Exec. sec. Coop. Food Distbrs. Am., 1954-56; mng. dir. Supermarket Inst., 1956-59; grocery mktg. dir. J. Walter Thompson, Inc., 1959; pres., gen. mgr. Quaker City Grocery Co., Phila., 1960-62; pres. U.S. Brewers Assn., Inc., Washington, 1962—. Bd. dirs. Keep Am. Beautiful, Inc., 1962-76, Nat. Council Alcoholism; founding dir. Nat. Council Adequate Alcohol Programs. Served with USNR, 1942-45. Decorated Silver Star, Purple Heart. Mem. Am. Soc. Assn. Execs., Washington Soc. Assn. Execs., Navy League, Am. Legion, Knight Malta, Knight Holy Sepulchre. Democrat. Roman Catholic. Clubs: Army Navy, Spring Lake Golf. Home: Spring Lake NJ 07762

KING, HENRY LAWRENCE, lawyer; b. N.Y.C., Apr. 29, 1928; s. H. Abraham and Henrietta (Prentky) K.; A.B., Columbia Coll., 1948; LL.B., Yale, 1951; m. Barbara Hope, 1949 (dec. May 1962); m. 2d, Alice Mary Sturges, Aug 1, 1963 (div.); children—Elizabeth Hope, Patricia Jane, Matthew Harrison, Katherine Masury, Andrew Lawrence, Eleanor Sturges. Admitted to N.Y. State bar, 1952; mem. firm Davis Polk & Wardwell, N.Y.C., 1951—, partner, 1961—. Trustee, mem. exec. com. Pres.'s Lawyers Com. Civil Rights Under Law; bd. dirs., treas. Berkshire Farm Center and Services for Youth, Yale Lawyers Assn.; pres. Assn. Alumni Columbia Coll., 1966-68; chmn. Columbia Coll. Fund, 1972-73; pres. Columbia U. Alumni Fedn., 1973-75; trustee Columbia U. Press., Purnell Sch., Yale Law Sch. Fund. Recipient Columbia Alumni medal for Conspicuous Service. Fellow Am. Coll. Trial Lawyers; mem. Am., N.Y. State (chmn. antitrust law sect. 1979—) bar assns., Bar Assn. City N.Y., N.Y. County Lawyers Assn., Am. Judicature Soc., Am. Law Inst. Clubs: Fishers Island Country (gov.); Century, River, Anglers, Wall St. (N.Y.C.); Hay Harbor (gov.). Home: 47 E 64th St New York NY 10021 also Fishers Island NY 06390 Office: 1 Chase Manhattan Plaza New York City NY 10005

KING, JENNIFER LANDRY, interior designer; b. Baton Rouge, La., Nov. 29, 1952; d. Warren Clement and Marion (Bourgeois) Landry; B.A., La. State U., 1974; m. Allan Richard King, Feb. 7, 1976. Interior designer Harvey & Callari, architects, 1974; Dameron-Pierson Co., New Orleans, 1974-76; dir. interior design KEH Design Group, interior environments, Baton Rouge, 1976-77; interior designer/space planner Perry, Dean Stahl & Rogers, Architects. Boston, 1977—; guest lectr. La. State U., 1975; mem. adv. council Interior Design Mag., 1977-78. Mem. Am. Soc. Interior Designers. Home: 39 Purdue Dr Milford MA 01757 Office: 177 Milk St Boston MA 02109

KING, JOAN HONE, art dealer, book researcher; b. N.Y.C., Nov. 27, 1929; d. John Hone and Frederica (Stevens) Auerbach; certificate studies Inst. Polit. Scis., Paris, 1950; B.A. cum laude, Bryn Mawr Coll., 1951; m. Nicholas LeRoy King, Feb. 19, 1955; children—Sarah, Bayard, Ledyard. Cons. J. Walter Thompson, Paris, 1951-52; researcher, librarian Time-Life Inc., Paris, 1952-54; mgr. Ohrbach Dept. Store, N.Y.C., 1956-57; housing locator U.S. Embassy, Paris, 1963-69; spl. asst. for book and art research to Cass Canfield, Harper & Row, N.Y.C., 1971—; art dealer, N.Y.C., 1973—; cons. in field; also free-lance writer. Active fund raising Bryn Mawr Coll., 1970-72, Sr. Citizens' Center, Newport, R.I., 1975. Me. Colonial Dames Am., Colony Club, Bryn Mawr Club N.Y.C. Republican. Episcopalian. Illustrator: The Incredible Pierpont Morgan (Cass Canfield), 1974. Home: 39 E 79th St New York City NY 10021 Office: Harper & Row Pubs Inc 10 E 53d St New York City NY 10022

KING, JOHN EDWARD, city ofcl.; b. Burlington, Vt., Nov. 26, 1954; s. Carl William and Helena Beryle (Bluto) K.; A.A. summa cum laude, Champlain Coll., 1975. Bookkeeper, Burlington Dept. Water Pollution Control, 1975-76, accountant, 1976-77, adminstrv. asst., 1977—; clk. Burlington Water Pollution Control Commn., 1976—; cons. Small Bus. Inst., 1975—. Alumni mem. devel. com. bd. trustees Champlain Coll., 1975-77; selectman Town of Milton, Vt., 1976—, clk. bd., 1976-77, chmn. bd., 1977—; mem. Milton Civil Bd. Authority, 76—, Bd. Tax Abatement, 1976—, Bd. Health, 1976—, mem. Liquor Control Commn., 1976—, chmn. commn., 1977—, chmn. CD, 1977-78; mem. local Democratic Com., 1976—, alt. Vt. Dem. Conv., 1976; high sch. religion instr. St. Anne's Roman Catholic Ch., Milton, 1975-76, mass lector, 1975—. Mem. Am. Mgmt. Assn., Green Mountain Water Pollution Control Assn., Vt. League Cities and Towns. Home: Middle Rd Milton VT 05468 Office: Maple St Burlington VT 05401

KING, JOSEPH PATRICK, mktg. authority adminstr.; b. Albion, Nebr., Sept. 25, 1910; s. John and Anna Maria (Heffron) K.; student U. Nebr.; B.S., Cornell U., 1936; m. Ethel Lillian MacConnie, Jan. 1, 1937; children—Elizabeth Anne, Mary Ellen. County agrl. agent, Canton, N.Y., 1938-42; regional dir. farm, food processing labor War Manpower Commn., N.Y.C., 1942-44; mgr. agrl. devel. Birds Eye div. Gen. Foods Corp., Rochester, N.Y., 1944-52; agrl. cons. Grocery Mfrs. Am., N.Y.C., 1952-53; exec. chmn. Fairmost Canning Co., Fairmont, Minn., 1953-58; adminstr. Genessee Valley Regional Market Authority, Rochester, 1958—; dir. Mfrs. Hanover Trust Co. Central N.Y. Trustee Cornell U., Nazareth Coll. of Rochester; hon. trustee Aquinas Inst. of Rochester; mem. exec. com. Rochester Center for Govt. Research. Mem. Rochester C. of C. (trustee 1965-74), Alpha Zeta. Roman Catholic. Clubs: Rochester Rotary (past v.p.), Oak Hill Country (past pres.). Home: 53 Country Club Dr Rochester NY 14618 Office: 900 Jefferson Rd Rochester NY 14623

KING, NORMAN CHANCIS, advt. and pub. relations exec.; b. Bklyn., Apr. 9, 1926; s. Louis and Bessie (Sacks) K.; student Cornell U., 1943; B.A., N.Y. U., 1949, postgrad. Law Sch., 1949-52; m. Barbara Joan Kavaleer, Dec. 16, 1955; 1 son, Laurence B. Conversationalist King's Corner, WAAT Radio, 1952-55; pres., chmn. King TV Prodns., 1955-60; chmn. bd. Celebrity Cons., 1960-64, Am. Resort & Recreation Resort Hotels, 1964-66, U.S. Media-Internat. Corp., 1966-71, SyndiVision Prodns., Inc.; pres. Corporate Image, Inc., N.Y.C., 1960—; dir. U.S.I. Network Ltd., Am. Marketing Complex, Robert Alda Career Schs.; chmn. bd. Male Potency Centers Am.; pres. Broadcasting for The Blind, Inc.; media counsel, adv. council U.S. Senate Com. on Vets. Affairs, 1971—; internat. lectr. Mem. Selective Service Commn. U.S. Served with AUS, 1944-46. Named among top 10 newsworthy people in Am., Advt. Age, 1968, 69, 71. Clubs: Friars, El Morocco, Atrium. Home: 330 E 33d St New York City NY 10001 Office: 375 Park Ave New York City NY 10022

KING, NORVAL WILLIAM, vet. pathologist; b. Salisbury, Md., Apr. 29, 1938; s. Norval William and Madeline Mae (Hastings) K.; student U. Md., 1956-58; D.V.M. cum laude, U. Ga., 1962; m. Carol Sue Jaite, Sept. 26, 1964; children—Carrie Sue, Heather Anne. Research fellow dept. pathology Harvard Med. Sch., Boston, 1965-67, research asso., 1968-69, asso., 1970-72, prin. asso., 1972-76; asso. prof. comparative pathology New Eng. Regional Primate Research Center, 1976—, chmn. div. pathobiology, 1974; dir. v.p. Pathobiology, Inc., Marlboro, Mass. Chmn. Bd. Health, Hudson, Mass., 1969—. Served from lt. to capt. Vet. Corps, U.S. Army, 1963-65. Certified vet. pathologist. Mem. Internat. Acad. Pathology (mem. edn. com. 1973-77, council 1977—), Am. Vet. Med. Assn., Am. Coll. Vet. Pathologists (mem. edn. com. 1972), Am. Soc. Exptl. Pathology, Comparative Pathology Colloquy, Am. Assn. Lab. Animal Sci. (Research award 1969), Electron Microscopy Soc. Am., New Eng., Mass. socs. pathologists, Phi Kappa Phi, Phi Zeta. Republican. Episcopalian. Contbr. articles to profl. jours. Home: 10 John Robinson Rd Hudson MA 01749 Office: 1 Pine Hill Dr Southborough MA 01772

KING, PAUL CLINTON, psychiatrist; b. Farmingdale, N.Y., Nov. 23, 1928; s. Carl Clinton and Agnes Madeline (Coye) K.; B.S. cum laude, City Coll. N.Y., 1953; M.D. Georgetown U., 1957; grad. N.Y. Sch. Psychiatry, 1972; m. Mary Gwendolyn Smith, June 7, 1969; children—Paul Brian, Thomas David. Intern, St. Vincents Hosp., N.Y.C., 1957-58, Kings County Hosp., Bklyn., 1958-59; resident in psychiatry Central Islip Psychiat. Center, 1968-71, staff psychiatrist, 1971—; practice medicine specializing in psychiatry, Hauppauge, N.Y., 1971—; clin. instr. Adelphi U. Served with U.S. Army Med. Corps, 1948-50. Diplomate Am. Bd. Psychiatry and Neurology. Mem. Am. Psychiat. Assn., Psychiat. Soc. N.Y. Med. Coll., Phi Beta Kappa. Roman Catholic Home: 3 Bluff Circle Hauppauge NY 11787 Office: Central Islip Psychiatric Center Central Islip NY 11722

KING, RACHEL HADLEY, educator; b. Leavenworth, Kans., Apr. 27, 1904; d. Frank Campbell and Georgianna May (Brackett) King; B.A., Smith Coll., 1926; M.A., U. Chgo., 1927, U. Colo., 1931; Ph.D., Yale, 1937, Bible tchr., then head dept. Northfield Sch. Girls, 1928-31, 35-66; tchr. English, Kobe Coll., Japan, 1937-38; adj. prof. Bibl. studies Barrington (R.I.) Coll., 1972—; vol. tchr. underprivileged children N.Y.C. Pub. Schs., summers 1969-71. Mem. Kobe Corp., 1960—; alumni council Yale Div. Sch., 1968-75. Recipient citation Council Religion in Ind. Schs., 1967. Mem. Am. Acad. Religion, Nat. Assn. Bible Instrs. (chmn. curriculum com. 1946-64), Am. Sch. Oriental Research, So. Bibl. Lit. Presbyterian. Author: George Fox and The Light Within 1650-1660; 1940; God's Boycott of Sin, 1946; Theology You Can Understand, 1956; The Omission of the Holy Spirit from Reinhold Niebuhr's Theology, 1964; The Creation of Death and Life, 1970. Home: The 60 Broadway Providence RI 02903 Office: Barrington Coll Middle Hwy Barrington RI 02806

KING, ROBERT JAMES, metallurgist; b. Rochester, N.Y., Aug. 19, 1918; s. James Thomas and Margaret (Meek) K.; B.S., U. Rochester, 1940; M.S., U. Cin., 1942; M.S., Carnegie-Mellon U., 1946; Ph.D., U. Pitts., 1967; m. Dorothy Wilma Pervin, May 28, 1949; children—David James, Richard Pervin. Research engr. Dow Chem. Co., Midland, Mich., 1942-45; instr. dept. metall. engring. U. Pitts., 1948-51, asst. prof., 1952-56; sect. supr. U.S. Steel Corp., Monroeville, Pa., 1956-75, research cons., 1976—. Mem. Am. Soc. for Metals, Am. Inst. Mining, Metall. and Petroleum Engrs. Home: 2337 Marbury Rd Pittsburgh PA 15221 Office: 125 Jamison Ln Monroeville PA 15146

KING, ROBERT OGDEN, broadcast and airline co. exec.; b. New Rochelle, N.Y., July 28, 1932; s. Fletcher and Julia (Hill) K.; grad. Choate Sch., 1951; B.A., Cornell U., 1955; m. Marie Therese Dodge, Apr. 23, 1971; children—Julia H., Robert O.H., Lloyd Wendt, Cornelia Dodge. Distbr., Cessna Aircraft Co., Honolulu and San Juan, P.R., 1958-68; pres. Montauk Caribben Airways, Inc., Montauk, N.Y. and San Juan, 1960-75, chmn. bd. dirs., 1976—; chmn. bd. dirs. Ocean Reef Airways, Inc., Key Largo, Fla., 1976—; pres. Lazarette Corp., N.Y.C., 1970—; pres. East Coast Broadcasting Corp., Sag Harbor, N.Y., 1968—, Del. LeaseBank, Inc., Wilmington, 1966—, Stolports Corp., N.Y.C., 1965—. Mem. Aircraft Owners and Pilots Assn. Hawaii (pres. 1958-61), Civilian Jet Owners Assn. (pres. 1957-58), Commuter Airline Assn. Am., Nat. Assn. Broadcasters. Episcopalian. Clubs: Wings (N.Y.C.), Larchmont Yacht, Ocean Reef Yacht, Devon Yacht, Sag Harbor Yacht, Card Sound Sailing, Model T Ford. Office: PO Box 2000 Sag Harbor NY 11963

KING, S(AMUEL) EDWARD, physician; b. N.Y.C., Nov. 9, 1900; s. Samuel and Ida K.; B.S., Columbia U., 1921, M.D., 1923, M.P.H., 1937; m. Cecilia Van Ilenberg Johnston, Mar. 13, 1923. Intern, Univ. Hosp., N.Y.C., 1923-24, resident, 1924-26, asst. attending physician Univ. and Bellevue Hosps., 1927-32, asso. attending physician, 1932-42, 48—; vis. physician, dir. metabolic service Sea View Hosp., N.Y.C., 1932-42, cons., 1950—; vis. physician Goldwater Meml. Hosp., N.Y.C., 1940-47; chief med. service Halloran VA Hosp., S.I., N.Y., 1948-50; cons. U.S. Army Surgeon Gen., 1951-63, USPHS, 1957-63, N.Y.C., Health Dept., 1958-60, Sea View Hosp., 1951—, Castle Point VA Hosp., 1948-60, Jour. AMMA, 1970-76. Served to col. M.C., AUS, 1942-47, 50-52. Decorated Bronze Star medal;

diplomate Am. Bd. Internal Medicine. Fellow Am. Coll. Physicians, N.Y. Acad. Medicine; mem. AMA, Am. Soc. Nephrology. Home and office: 67 Park Ave New York NY 10016

KING, THOMAS GORDEN, educator; b. Alma Center, Wis., Feb. 13, 1921; s. Thomas Raymond and Elva Orilla (Van Gorden) K.; B.S., U. Wis. at Stout, 1946, M.S., 1947; Ed.D., Wayne State U., 1959; m. June Dixon Birchard, Oct. 11, 1942; 1 dau., Susan King Burke. Tchr. indsl. arts Detroit Pub. Schs., 1947-59; prof., founder, 1st dept. chmn. indsl. edn. R.I. Coll., Providence, 1959—; cons. on curriculum, mem. advisory com. Hall Drafting Inst., Providence, 1968—, New Eng. Regional Commn. for Vocat. Edn., 1966-74; chmn. bd. dirs. New Eng. Resource Center for Occupational Edn., Inc., Cambridge, Mass., 1967, 70-71. Trustee First Bapt. Ch., Pawtucket, R.I., 1963-66, deacon, 1966-69, 75-78; mem. commn. edn. Am. Bapt. Chs. R.I., fin. subcom., 1976-78. Served with U.S. Army, 1942-45. Mem. NEA (life), Am. Indsl. Arts Assn., Am. Council Indsl. Tchrs. Educators (life), Am. Council Elementary Indsl. Arts, Nat. Assn. Indsl. and Tech. Tchr. Educators, Am. Vocat. Assn., R.I. Vocat. and Indsl. Arts Assn., New Eng. Indsl. Arts Tchrs. Assn., Epsilon Pi Tau (trustee Beta Sigma chpt. R.I. Coll., laureate mem.), Phi Delta Kappa (life). Contbr. articles to profl. jours. Home: 15 Arlington Dr Lincoln RI 02865 Office: Dept Indsl Edn RI College Providence RI 02908

KING, VERNE LORENE, apparel co. exec.; b. Danbury, Conn., Oct. 20, 1921; d. Vernon and Mildred M. (Roswell) Elsenboss; B.S. in Journalism, Boston U., 1943; m. Gerald G. King, Aug. 5, 1944 (dec. Feb. 1950); children—Gerald G., Susan V. Editor, Chance Vought Aircraft Co., Stratford, Conn., 1944-45, Columbia Record Co., Bridgeport, Conn., 1951-61; publs. editor Olin Co., New Haven, 1961-62; editor Warnaco Inc., Bridgeport, Conn., 1962-72, mgr. employee communication, 1972-77, mgr. communications and community relations, 1977—; trustee Mechanics & Farmers Savs. Bank, 1976—. Lectr. employee communication, 1965—. Chmn. employee publs. United Way Bridgeport, 1958-73, mem. pub. relations com. 1958-73, chmn., 1974, dir.-at-large, 1977—; mem. pub. info. com. Bridgeport Mayor's Energy Adv. Commn., 1974; bd. dirs. Bridgeport Child Care, Inner City Children's Center, Bridgeport, Jr. Achievement of Western Conn., Vis. Nurse Assn., Bridgeport. Mem. Barnum Festival Soc. (historian 1972-73, gov. 1971-73), Conn. Assn. Profl. Communicators (pres. 1966-67), Internat. Assn. Bus. Communicators (dir. chpt. affairs 1967-69), Bridgeport Area C. of C. (dir., v.p. 1976—, 1st vice chmn. 1978, chmn. 1979). Home: 1 Barrows St Stratford CT 06497 Office: 350 Lafayette St Bridgeport CT 06602

KING, WILLIAM DOUGLAS, luggage, sporting goods mfg. co. exec.; b. Balt., Nov. 21, 1941; s. James and Mary Jane (Molloy) K.; B.S., U. N.C., 1964; M.B.A., Harvard, 1969. Sr. asso. McKinsey and Co. Inc., Los Angeles, 1969-73; controller N.Am. Housing ops. Kaufman & Broad Inc., Los Angeles, 1973-74; pres. Davis Pacific Corp., Los Angeles, 1974-76; pres. Leeds Travelwear, Clayton, Del., 1976—; dir. King & Morgan, Inc., Sugar Loaf Groves Inc. Advance staff Pres. Gerald R. Ford, 1976. Served with USMCR, 1964-67; Vietnam. Mem. Young Pres.'s Orgn. Republican. Episcopalian. Clubs: Los Angeles Country, California, Harvard N.Y.C. Office: 33 Bassett St Clatyon DE 19938

KINGERY, BERNARD TROY, physicist, educator; b. Metter, Ga., July 16, 1920; s. Thomas Eddie and Ruth Alma (Trapnell) K.; diploma Freeman Bus. Coll., 1938; B.S., Ga. So. Coll. 1948; M.A., Columbia U., 1949, profl. diploma, 1951; m. Catherine Murgia, Aug. 16, 1959; children—Deborah Ann, Jacqueline. Accountant, WWNS, Statesboro, Ga., 1946-48; instr., Orange County Community Coll., Middletown, N.Y., 1950-52; asst. prof. physics N.J. Inst. Tech., Newark, 1952—. Served with USNR, 1942-46. Sci. Manpower Project fellow, 1957-59. Mem. Am. Assn. Physics Tchrs., Am. Soc. Engring. Edn., Assn. Edn. Tchrs. in Sci., Nat. Geog. Soc., Kappa Delta Pi. Republican. Home: 92 Oakridge Ave Nutley NJ 07110 Office: 323 High St Newark NJ 07102

KINGSBURY, RICHARD ALAN, surgeon; b. Taunton, Mass., Apr. 27, 1936; s. Curtis Burt and Lolita (Regnier) K.; B.S., Tufts U., 1956; M.D., Harvard, 1960; m. Joan Ann Banovic, June 28, 1958; children—Elizabeth Ann, Rebecca Lynn, Katherine Joan. Intern, Med. Sch. Hosp., U. Oreg., Portland, 1960-61, resident in surgery, 1961-65; instr. surgery U. Oreg., 1965; practice medicine specializing in gen. surgery, Winchester, Mass., 1966—; clin. instr. surgery Tufts U. Sch. Medicine, 1977—. Diplomate Am. Bd. Surgery. Fellow A.C.S.; mem. AMA, Mass., Middlesex E. Dist. med socs. Episcopalian. Home: 14 Ginn Rd Winchester MA 01890 Office: 15 Dix St Winchester MA 01890

KINGSBURY, SLOCUM, architect; b. Governor Island, N.Y., Jan. 31, 1893; s. Henry P. and Florence Rice (Slocum) K.; B.Arch., Cornell U., 1915; m. Marion Schell, June 2, 1923. Partner, Faulkner, Kingsbury & Stenhouse, Washington, 1939-65, ret., 1965; cons. on hosps. VA, U.S. Air Force, Am. Psychiat. Soc.; vis. critic Sch. Architecture Howard U.; mem. advisory com. D.C. Dept. Health. Served to capt. U.S. Army, 1918-19; France. Fellow AIA (chmn. com. hosps. and pub. health). Episcopalian. Clubs: Cosmos (Washington); Chevy Chase (Md.). Contbr. articles on architecture, hosp. design to profl. jours. Home: 3406 Reservoir Rd NW Washington DC 20007

KINGSLEY, EARL JAMES, II, assn. exec.; b. Portland, Oreg., Feb. 7, 1926; s. Earl James and Erva Belle (Burdick) K.; B.A., U. Calif. at Berkeley, 1946; M.Div., Ch. Div. Sch. Pacific, Berkeley, 1949; M.A., San Francisco State Coll., 1968; m. Margaret Marie Hitchcock, Feb. 13, 1961. Ordained to ministry Episcopal Ch., 1949; pastor Episcopal Diocese Oreg., 1949-52; dean central convocation, also vicar St. Peter's Ch., Albany, Oreg.; city missioner, adminstrv. asst., vicar St. Bartholomew's Ch., Beaverton, Oreg., 1955-61; commd. 1st lt. U.S. Air Force, 1953, advanced through grades to col., 1978; instr. USAF Chaplain Sch., 1967-71; all-Europe archdeacon, 1971-73; exec. dir. Mil. Chaplains Assn., cons. human relations, equal opportunity, drug abuse. Pres. Albany Timber Carnival, 1952. Mem. Albany City Zoning Commn., 1950-52. Bd. dirs. St. Helen's Hall, Portland, 1955-58. Decorated Air Force Commendation medal, Meritorious Service medal with oak leaf cluster; named Jr. First Citizen, Albany, 1952. Mem. Air Force Assn., Am. Legion. Elk. Clubs: Albany Exchange (pres. 1952); Multnomah Athletic (Portland). Author: Faith and Reason in Episcopal Theology, 1949; The Air Force Chaplaincy, vols. I-IV, 1968-71; The Air Force Chaplain Manager, vols. I and II, 1970, 71. Compiler: Readings of Air Force Chaplaincy. Home: 7420 Lakeview Dr Bethesda MD 20034 Office: Mil Chaplains Assn 401 Blackwell 7758 Wisconsin Ave NW Bethesda MD 20014

KINNARD, DOUGLAS, polit. scientist; b. Morristown, N.J., Sept. 13, 1921; s. Frederick Henry and Mary (Toomey) K.; B.S., U.S. Mil. Acad., 1944; M.S., Princeton U., 1948, M.A., 1972, Ph.D., 1973; grad. Army War Coll., 1961; m. Wade Tyree, July 6, 1951; 1 son, Frederick Douglas. Commd. 2d lt. U.S. Army, 1944, advanced through grades to brig. gen., 1968; service in, France, Ger., Korea and Vietnam; chief staff II Field Force, Vietnam, 1969-70; ret., 1970; asst. prof. polit. sci. U. Vt., Burlington, 1973-76, asso. prof., 1976-79, prof., 1979—, dir. area and internat. studies, 1976—; vis. asso. prof. Princeton U., 1976-77, vis. fellow Center Internat. Studies, 1976-77; cons. on nat. security affairs. Decorated D.S.M., Legion of Merit, D.F.C.; Nat. Order Vietnam with gallantry cross. Mem. Am., New Eng. polit. sci. assns., Internat. Inst. Strategic Studies, Assn. Grads. U.S. Mil. Acad., Princeton U. Alumni Assn. Clubs: Nassau (Princeton); Princeton (N.Y.); Army and Navy (Washington). Author: President Eisenhower and Strategy Management: A Study in Defense Politics, 1977; The War Managers, 1977; also articles. Address: 343 S Prospect St Burlington VT 05401

KINNE, KATHARINE (MRS. CHARLES E. SIGETY), home economist; b. Herkimer, N.Y., Nov. 23, 1921; d. Cornelius Harry and Katharine (Kinne) Snell; B.S., Cornell U., 1944; m. Charles Edward Sigety, July 17, 1948; children—Charles Birge, Katharine Kinne, Robert Griswold, Cornelius, Elizabeth. Tng. squad J.L. Hudson Co., Detroit, 1944; overseas recreation work ARC, 1945-46, nat. fund campaign speaker, 1947; publicity work Union Carbide and Carbon Corp., 1947-48; dist. sales mgr. Berger Bros., New Haven, 1948-50; European tour condr. Olson Travel Orgn., 1950; TV home economist Sally Smart's Kitchen, WOR-TV, 1951-53; on camera food editor, Home Show, NBC-TV, 1953-56; owner, dir., gen. mgr. Video Vittles, Inc., N.Y.C., 1953—. Co-chmn. nat. parents com. Bates Coll., Lewiston, Maine; bd. dirs. Parents League N.Y., Trinity Sch. Mothers Orgn., Grace Ch. Sch. Parents Orgn., 1966-67. Recipient scholarships N.Y. State Fedn. Women's Club, D.A.R. Home Econ., Women in Bus., Mortar Bd., Delta Delta Delta. Mem. Am. Home Econs. Assn., Am. Women in Radio and TV, AFTRA, Screen Actors Guild. Presbyn. Address: 175 E 96th St New York City NY 10028

KINNEY, SAMUEL MARKS, JR., corp. exec., lawyer; b. Jenkintown, Pa., July 10, 1925; s. Samuel Marks and Margaret R. (Rennie) K.; grad. Lawrenceville (N.J.) Sch., 1942; student Allegheny Coll., 1942-43; B.A., Pa. State Coll., 1946; J.D., Rutgers U., 1948; m. Kathryn Clouser, Sept. 21, 1946; children—Lee Kinney Anthony, Samuel Marks III, Brian Scott. Admitted to N.J. bar, 1949, also U.S. Supreme Ct. bar; asso. atty. Martin & Reiley, Newark, 1949-51; counsel, mgr. army contracts Daystrom Instrument div. Daystrom, Inc., 1951-54; asst. sec., counsel Daystrom, Inc., 1954-57, sec., counsel, 1957-59, asst. v.p. finance, 1959-61, v.p., gen. counsel, 1961-62; v.p. Union Camp Corp., N.Y.C., 1962-69, sec., 1962-72, sr. v.p., 1969-70, exec. v.p., 1970-72, pres., 1972-77, vice chmn. bd., 1977—, also dir., mem. exec. com.; dir. LaFarge Emballage, S.A. (France), Cartonajes Union, S.A. (Spain), Philibert Delastre S.A. (France), 1st Nat. State Bank N.J., 1st Nat. State Bancorp. Chmn. Union County (N.J.) Young Rep. Club, Inc., 1951-52. Mem. Town Council, Westfield, 1961-67, chmn. finance, laws and rules coms. Mem. bus. exec. research com. Bus. Execs. Research Center, Rutgers U., 1957-58; trustee N.J. State Safety Council; mem. alumni council Pa. State U.; trustee Overlook Hosp.; overseer Rutgers U. Found. Served with USMCR, 1943-45. Recipient Distinguished Alumnus award Pa. State U., 1977. Mem. Am. Judicature Soc., Am. Bar Assn., NAM (dir.). Episcopalian (vestryman). Clubs: Echo Lake Country (trustee, Westfield); Baltusrol Golf (Springfield, N.J.); Economic, Union League (N.Y.C.). Author papers. Home: 109 Golf Edge Westfield NJ 07090 Office: Union Camp Corp 1600 Valley Rd Wayne NJ 07470

KINSELLA, JAMES HALL, judge; b. Hartford, July 12, 1924; s. George Francis and Dorothea (Mooney) K.; B.A., Trinity Coll., 1947; LL.B., U. Nebr., 1952; m. Anne Marie Lehrman, Oct. 21, 1958. Admitted to Conn. bar, 1953; partner firm Kinsella and Krass, Hartford, 1971—; judge Hartford Probate Dist., 1960—. Pres., Hartford Urban Research Co., 1971—; pres. judge Conn. Probate Judges Assembly, 1973-75. Mem. Hartford City Council, 1953-60, dep. mayor, 1953-55, mayor, 1957-60. Served with USMC, 1942-45. Recipient Alumni of Year award Trinity Coll., 1966. Mem. Am. Bar Assn. (legal pre-pay com., probate div.), Hartford Jewish Community Center. K.C. (3 deg.). Home: 70 Elizabeth St Hartford CT 06105 Office: 550 Main St Hartford CT 06013

KINSMAN, BRADLEY QUAIF, glass co. exec.; b. Amsterdam, N.Y., June 25, 1930; s. Daniel Francis and Clara Ella (Quaif) K.; B.S., Alfred U., 1952; m. Olga Mazzella, June, 1952 (div. June 1964); children—Sharon Anne, James Bradley, Thomas Andrew; md. 2d, Elizabeth Manning, Sept. 5, 1964; children—Karen Marie, Daniel Robert. Design engr. Batch facilities Corning Glass Works (N.Y.), 1955-59, supr. engring., 1959-64, sr. project mgr. facilities design, constrn. plant facilities in Romania and Brazil, 1964-77, mgr. furnace and related constrn., 1977—; lectr. on project mgmt., contracting. Vice-chmn. operating com. Corning Area Community Concert Band, 1976—; organizer, dir. brass ensemble, Brass Works, 1976—. Served with Band, U.S. Army, 1953-55. Licensed profl. engr., N.Y. Mem. Constrn. Specifications Inst. (certified constrn. specifier), Nat., N.Y. State socs. profl. engrs., Am. Ceramic Soc. Republican. Baptist. Home: 388 Beartown Rd Painted Post NY 14870 Office: Corning Glass Works Main Plant 52-4 Corning NY 14830

KINSTLER, EVERETT RAYMOND, artist; b. N.Y.C., Aug. 5, 1926; s. Joseph E. and Essie Kinstler; student Art Students League, N.Y.C., 1943-45; m. Lea C. Nation, June 23, 1958; children—Katherine G., Dana C. Started career as illustrator, N.Y.C., 1943, began specializing in portraiture, 1955; portraits include ofcl. White House portrait Pres. Gerald R. Ford, Mrs. Irenee duPont, Jr., Sarah Mellon Scaife, N.Y. Gov. Herbert Lehman, Gen. W. Ball, Astronaut Alan B. Shepard, Jr., Astronaut Scott Carpenter, UN Sec.-Gen. Kurt Waldheim, J. Edgar Hoover, Byron Nelson, Richard K. Mellon, Sec. Agr. Earl Butz, Sec. Labor Willard Wirtz, Sec. Def. Melvin R. Laird, Gov. John Connally, Sec. Treasury William Simon, Sec. Def. Elliott Richardson, Sec. Commerce Rogers C.B. Morton, John Wayne, Roy Rogers and Dale Evans, numerous others; one man show at Grand Central Art Galleries, N.Y.C., 1960, Columbia (S.C.) Mus., 1970; rep. in permanent collections Mus. City N.Y., The Pentagon, Mystic Seaport Mus., Smithsonian Instn., U.S. Mil. Acad., Carnegie Institute, Players Club, New York Stock Exchange, Met. Museum of Art, Bklyn. Mus., also numerous colls., univs., bus. firms. Instr. Art Students League, N.Y.C., 1969-75. Recipient Gold medals Nat. Arts Club, 1956, Lotos Club, 1972, U.S. Navy Combat Art Medal, 1967. Mem. Allied Artists Am., Artists Fellowships, Inc. (president 1967-70), Art Students League (life), Portraits Inc., N.A.D., Hudson Valley Art Assn., Am. Watercolor Soc., Audubon Artists, Pastel Soc. Am., Grand Central Art Galleries. Clubs: Century Assn., Dutch Treat, Nat. Arts (vice pres.), Players, Lotos (N.Y.C.). Author: Painting Portraits, 1972. Address: National Arts Club 15 Gramercy Park New York City NY 10003

KINTER, WILLIAM LEWIS, educator; b. St. Thomas, Pa., Oct. 21, 1915; s. John Henry and M. Gertrude (Blair) K.; A.B., Lafayette (Pa.) Coll., 1938; A.M., Yale U., 1940; Ph.D., Columbia U., 1958. Master English and Latin, Westminster Sch., Simsbury, Conn., 1944-46; asst. prof. English, Muhlenberg Coll., Allentown, Pa., 1946-51, 54-62, Loyola Coll., Balt., 1962-66; asst. prof. English, chmn. dept. lang. and lit. Md. Inst. Coll. Art, Balt., 1966—. Life mem. bd. dirs. Franklin County Heritage. Mem. Nat. Trust Historic Preservation, Tri State Natural Weather Assn. (sec.), Wilderness Soc., Nat. Gay Task Force, Medieval Acad. Am., Gay Acad. Union (charter), Delta Kappa Epsilon, Omicron Delta Kappa. Episcopalian. Co-author: Prophetess and Fay: The Sibyl, 1967; author rev. notes. Home: 258 N Main St Chambersburg PA 17201 Office: Md Inst Coll Art 1300 Mt Royal Ave Baltimore MD 21217

KINTNER, ROBERT JENNINGS, electronic component mfg. co. exec.; b. Maplewood, N.J., June 19, 1939; s. Edwin K. and Florence (Livingston) K.; B.S. in Econs., U. Pa., 1961; m. Susan Pollock, Dec. 18, 1977; 1 dau., Laurie Danielle. Fin. analyst Gen. Foods Corp., White Plains, N.Y., 1961-63; v.p. mktg. Kintner Valve Co., Pitts., 1963-69; market planning mgr. Am. Standard Inc., Dearborn, Mich., 1969-72; mktg. mgr. Rotron, Inc., Woodstock, N.Y., 1972—. Mgr. pub. service div. United Way, 1978; active Little League, Bloomfield Hills, Mich., 1971. Served with USMCR, 1962-67. Mem. Soc. Mfg. Engrs. Republican. Roman Catholic. Patentee sliding plug valve. Home: 48 Allen Dr Woodstock NY 12498 Office: Rotron Inc Hasbrouck Ln Woodstock NY 12498

KIPFER, BERNICE MAY, ednl. adminstr.; b. Gridley, Kans., Mar. 29, 1929; d. George Ransom and Anna (Williams) Brown; B.S. in Edn., Kans. State Tchrs. Coll., 1957, M.S. in Psychology, 1959; Ed.D., Syracuse U., 1965; m. Robert Cecil Kipfer, Sr., Aug. 21, 1949; children—Robert Cecil, Joseph Douglas, Georgiann Iola. Tchr. pub. schs. Kan., 1946-61; tchr. Syracuse (N.Y.) City Sch. Dist., 1963-64, dir. spl. edn., 1964-75; asst. commr. edn. for handicapped N.Y. State Dept. Edn., Albany, 1975—. Vis. lectr. Syracuse U., 1962, 63, 67, 70-71; cons. N.Y. Dept. Edn., 1964—; cons. Aid to States br., U.S. Office Edn., 1969-70, dir. computer project, 1969-75. Mem. Gov.'s Adv. Com. on Mental Retardation, 1974—. U.S. Office Edn. fellow, 1961-62; U.S. Office Edn. grantee, 1964, 69—. Mem. N.Y. State Assn. Spl. Edn. Adminstrs. (past pres.), N.Y. State Fedn. Council Exceptional Children (past pres.). Club: Zonta. Home: 2725 Midland Ave Syracuse NY 13205 Office: 55 Elk St Albany NY 12234

KIPP, EGBERT MASON, mgmt. cons.; b. Angola, Nov. 27, 1914; s. Ray Bassett and Letitia Mary (Mason) K.; (parents Am. citizens); B.S., Iowa Wesleyan Coll., 1934, D.Sc. (hon.), 1961; M.S., Boston U., 1935; Ph.D., Pa. State U., 1939; m. Pauline Sylvia Lougee, Dec. 24, 1935; children—David Alden, Richard Mason, Rebecca Weldon. Chief lubricants div. Alcoa, New Kensington, Pa., 1947-59; dir. research and devel Foote Mineral Co., Exton, Pa., 1957-59; asst. to mgr. product devel., research and devel. Sun Oil Co., Marcus Hook, Pa., 1959-60, mgr. basic research, 1960-62, asso. dir. research and devel., 1962-70; mgmt. cons. in sci. and tech., tribology, Paoli, Pa., 1971—. Mem. Am. Soc. Lubrication Engrs. (pres. 1946, chmn. long range planning com. 1967-70), Pitts. Chemists Club (pres. 1952), Am. Assn. Cons. Chemists and Chem. Engrs., Am. Assn. Small Research and Devel. Cos., Am. Chem. Soc., Am. (Honor award Phila. chpt. 1965), Pa. (pres. 1974-75) insts. chemists., Research and Mgmt. Group Phila. (pres. 1975). Methodist. Author: People Aspects of Research and Development Custom Buliding Your Management Career, 1967; also tech. and mgmt. articles; patentee in field of lubricants. Address: Suite A Station Square 2 Paoli PA 19301

KIPP, MICHAEL HAROLD, restaurant exec.; b. Ann Arbor, Mich., Mar. 25, 1943; s. Edward Louis and Wilhelmina (Birk) K.; B.A. in Bus. Adminstrn., U. Richmond, 1961; m. Nadine Jane Bennett, June 7, 1969. With John Mandis Inc., Washington, 1959—, gen. mgr., 1969—. Republican, Methodist. Home: 9003 Fort Craig Dr Burke VA 22015 Office: 200 E St SW Washington DC 20024

KIRALIS, KARL, educator; b. Binghamton, N.Y., June 25, 1923; s. Joseph and Anna (Marchalonis) K.; A.B., Hamilton Coll., 1947; A.M., Brown U., 1948, Ph.D., 1954; children—Susan, Karl, Geoffrey William, Karen Damon, Nikole Hillary. Instr. Brown U., Providence, 1947-50; asst. prof. Carleton Coll., Northfield, Minn., 1950-52; asso. prof. St. Lawrence U., Canton, N.Y., 1952-67; asso. prof. U. Houston, 1967-70; prof. English, Calif. State Coll. of Pa., California, 1970—. Served as lt. (j.g.) USNR, 1943-46. Mem. Coll. English Assn., Modern Lang. Assn., English Inst. Contbg. author: The Divine Vision; Art of William Blake, 1957; Discussions of William Blake, 1961; Milton Reconsidered, 1976; contbr. articles in field to profl. jours. Home: 423 Wood St California PA 15419 Office: Dept English California State Coll of Pa California PA 15419

KIRALY, BELA KALMAN, historian; b. Kaposvar, Hungary, Apr. 14, 1912; came to U.S., 1956; s. Jozsef and Etelka (Lutz) K.; B.A., Ludovika Mil. Acad., Budapest, 1935; M.A., War Acad. Budapest, 1942; M.A., Columbia U., 1958, Ph.D., 1962. Comdr. in chief N.G. Hungary, 1956; vis. prof. history St. Johns U., 1969-71, Columbia U., 1971-73; prof. history Bklyn. Coll., 1963—, chmn. East European sect. Center for European Studies, Grad. Sch. City U. N.Y., 1970—, editor in chief Bklyn. Coll. Studies on Society in Change, 1976—. Served to maj. gen. Hungarian Army, 1935-51. Decorated Kossuth Order; Guggenheim fellow, 1976-77; Nat. Endowment Humanities grantee, 1978-81. Mem. Am. Hist. Assn., Am. Assn. Advancement Slavic Studies. Author: Hungary in the Late Eighteenth Century, 1969; Ferenc Deak, 1975; Tolerance and Movements of Religious Dissent, 1976; others. Home: PO Box 568 Highland Lakes NJ 07422 Office: Dept History Brooklyn Coll Ave H Brooklyn NY 11210

KIRBY, JOHN JOSEPH, JR., lawyer; b. Washington, Oct. 22, 1939; s. John Joseph and Rose Elizabeth (Mangan) K.; B.A., Fordham Coll., 1961; B.A. (Rhodes scholar), Oxford U., 1964; LL.B., U. Va., 1966; m. Priscilla Ann Pickens Keller Katz, Apr. 8, 1967; 1 son, John Pickens. Admitted to Va. bar, 1966, N.Y. bar, 1969; asst. prof. law U. Va., 1966-67; spl. asst. civil rights div. U.S. Dept. Justice, Washington, 1967-68; asso. Mudge, Rose, Guthrie & Alexander, N.Y.C., 1968-70, partner, 1971—; dep. dir. Pres.'s Commn. on Campus Unrest, 1970. Mem. Am. Bar Assn., Assn. Bar City N.Y., Va. State Bar, Lawyers Club. Home: 417 Park Ave New York City NY 10022 Office: 20 Broad St New York City NY 10005

KIRBY, RALPH CLOUDSBERRY, metallurgist; b. Washington, July 21, 1925; s. Charles Cloudsberry and Mildred Louise (Denton) K.; B.Chem. Engring. magna cum laude, Catholic U. Am., 1950; m. Madge Anita Barbour, Aug. 14, 1950; 1 son, Charles Edward. With U.S. Bur. Mines, Washington, 1950—, staff metallurgist Metallurgy div., 1966-70, sr. staff metallurgist, 1971, chief, 1972-76, asst. dir. metallurgy, 1976—. Served with U.S. Army, 1943-45. Decorated Purple Heart; recipient Am. Inst. Chemists Gold medal, 1950; U.S. Bur. Mines Invention award, 1962, Spl. Service awards, 1968, 75; Meritorious Service honor award U.S. Dept. Interior, 1978. Mem. Am. Inst. Mining, Metall. and Petroleum Engrs. (dir. Metall. Soc. 1976-79), Am. Inst. Chem. Engrs., AAAS, Sigma Xi., Phi Eta Sigma. Methodist. Contbr. articles in field to profl. jours. Home: 116 Southwood Ave Silver Spring MD 20901 Office: U S Bureau of Mines Washington DC 20241

KIRBY, WILLIAM KENT, clergyman, behavioral and sexuality therapist; b. Dallas, Sept. 24, 1941; s. C. Carney and Geneva (Satterfield) K.; A.B., So. Meth. U., 1964; M.Div., Perkins Sch. Theology, Dallas, 1964, ST.M., 1967; D.A., Inst. Advanced Study Human Sexuality, 1978; m. Nancy Lamb, Aug., 1964; children—Charles, Jason. Ordained to ministry United Methodist Ch., 1968; dir. vol. services So. Meth. U., Dallas, 1968; asst. dean chapel Stephens Coll., Columbia, Mo., 1968-71; dir., chaplain Wesley (Meth.)-Westminster (Presbyn.) Founds., Princeton U., 1971—; sexuality counselor, co-counselor Sexuality, Edn., Counseling and Health Service, Princeton U., 1972—, developer comprehensive religious program for students, 1971—; behavioral therapy trainee, dept. psychiatry, Temple U., Phila., 1972—; leader tng. seminars in sexuality counseling, nine cities U.S. and Can., 1975-77; founder sexuality edn. courses for adults, Boston, N.Y.C., Princeton, Phila., 1976-78; pres. Princeton Interfaith Council, fund-raiser for world hunger, 1975; participant talk shows, interviews newspapers N.Y.C., Boston, Princeton, Phila. Mem. Nat. Assn. Coll. and Univ. Chaplains, Am. Assn. Pastoral Counselors, Eastern Assn. Sex Therapists, Am. Assn. Sex Educators and Therapists, So. N.J. Conf. United Meth. Ch. Home: 405B Route 4 Kingston Terr Apts Princeton NJ 08540 Office: Murray Dodge Hall Princeton University Princeton NJ 08540

KIRCHEM, RONALD GRIGSBY, editor; b. Colorado Springs, July 19, 1945; s. Ellis John Cobb and Carolyn (Grigsby) Cobb Kirchem; B.A., magna cum laude, U. Tex. at Austin, 1966; M.A., Yale U., 1967; postgrad. N.Y. U., 1968-74. Cons. N.Y.C.-Rand Inst., 1972-73; asst. editor Gen. Ency. dept. Macmillan Ednl. Corp., N.Y.C., 1973-75, asso. editor, 1975-77; editing supr. Webster div., McGraw-Hill Book Co., N.Y.C., 1977-78, sr. editing supr., 1978, asso. editor, 1978—; freelance editor Gregg div., 1977. Woodrow Wilson Nat. fellow, 1966-67, Yale fellow, 1967, NDEA Title IV fellow, 1968-71. Mem. Phi Beta Kappa, Phi Eta Sigma, Phi Alpha Theta. Democrat. Contbg. author: The Bicentennial Almanac, 1975. Home: 60 E 8th St New York City NY 10003 Office: McGraw-Hill Book Co 1221 Ave of Americas New York City NY 10020

KIRCHER, FREDERICK JOHN, structural engr.; b. Montclair, N.J., July 16, 1924; s. Frederick Daniel and Helena Josephine (Brown) K.; B.C.E., Cornell U., 1945; m. Betty Ann Mueller, Sept. 17, 1949; children—Ruth, Barbara. Structural designer Elwyn E. Seelye & Co., N.Y.C., 1946-47, Seelye Stevenson & Value Co., N.Y.C., 1947-50; structural engr. Seelye Stevenson Value & Knecht, N.Y.C., 1950-57, asso., 1957-66, partner, 1967-71; sr. v.p. Seelye Stevenson Value & Knecht, Inc., N.Y.C., 1971-76, also dir.; mgr. structural engring. Malcolm Pirnie Inc., White Plains, N.Y., 1976-77, mgr. archtl.-engring. services, 1978—. Served with USNR, 1943-45. Registered profl. engr., N.Y., N.J., Conn., N.H., Vt., R.I., Pa., Del., Va., D.C., Mass. Mem. ASCE, Am. Concrete Inst. Home: 13 Oakland Ave West Caldwell NJ 07006 Office: 2 Corporate Park Dr White Plains NY 10602

KIRCHICK, JULIAN GILBERT, physician; b. Bklyn., Aug. 1, 1913; s. Isadore and Pauline (Safier) K.; B.A., U. Mich., 1936; M.D., U. Md., 1940; m. Jean Kostinsky, June 29, 1941; children—Calvin, Howard, William, Wendy. Intern St. Vincents Hosp., Bridgeport, Conn., 1940-41; med. officer Civil Service Commn., Washington, D.C., 1942-44; resident Bellevue Hosp., N.Y.C., 1944-46; practice medicine, specializing in otolaryngology, Washington, 1946-47, Hempstead, L.I., N.Y., 1947—; mem. staff Nassau Hosp., Meadowbrook Hosp., Central Gen. Hosp., Hempstead Gen. Hosp., Nassau County Med. Center; asst. prof. clin. surgery State U. N.Y. Med. Sch. at Stony Brook; clin. cons. otolaryngology and allergy N.Y. State Dept. Health, 1952. Diplomate Am. Bd. Otolaryngology, Pan Am. Med. Assn. Fellow Am. Coll. Allertists, Am. Soc. Ophthalmologic and Otolaryngologic Allergy, A.C.S.; mem. Am. Acad. Allergy, Nassau Otolaryngological Soc. (past pres.), A.M.A., Nassau Acad. Medicine, Pan-Am. Assn. Otorhinolaryngology, Internat. Platform Assn., Am. Counsel Otolaryngology, Nassau Surg. Soc., Phi Delta Epsilon. Republican. Clubs: Michigan (N.Y.C.); Exchange. Home: 3 Ridge Dr Old Westbury NY 11568 Office: Plainview Profl Bldg 1070 Old Country Rd Plainview NY 11803

KIRIAKOPOULOS, GEORGE CONSTANTINE, dentist; b. Derby, Conn., June 3, 1926; s. Constantine Elias and Rose (Yerontakis) K.; A.A., U. Paris (France), 1947; A.B., Bklyn. Coll., 1950; D.D.S., Columbia, 1954; m. Virginia Demos, June 3, 1956; 1 dau., Stephanie. Pvt. practice gen. dentistry, Fort Lee, N.J., 1955—; asso. dir. dept. dentistry St. Giles Hosp., Bklyn., 1955-60; attending dept. oral surgery Lenox Hill Hosp., N.Y.C., 1956-60, adj. oral surgeon, 1960-64; asso. prof. dept. pedodontics Columbia, 1956-77. Served with AUS, 1943-46. Decorated Bronze Star, Silver Star, D.S.M.; recipient Medal of Meritorious Service, Lenox Hill Hosp., 1964. Fellow Royal Soc. Health; mem. ADA, Am. Assn. Hosp. Dentists, N.Y. State Dental Soc., Columbia U. Alumni Assn., Psi Omega. Greek Orthodox (trustee, v.p. Fairview and Tenafly (N.J.) 1968-71). Author: Your Child's Teeth - the Layman's View, 1966; Who Wants to Be a Dentist?, 1968. Home: 2205 Mackay Ave Fort Lee NJ 07024 Office: 415 West St Fort Lee NJ 07024

KIRK, GEORGE VALLANCE, supt. schs.; b. Phila., May 11, 1923; s. George Everett and Christine (Vallance) K.; A.B., Temple U., 1949; M.S., U. Pa., 1952, Ed.D., 1959; m. Shirley M. Rowe, Aug. 13, 1949; children—Cheryl Elaine, George Andrew, John Robert. Tchr. pub. sch., Mohnton, Pa., 1949-52, Central Bucks Sch., Doylestown, Pa., 1952-54; adminstrv. asst. Seaford (Del.) Pub. Schs., 1954-56; supr. Smyrna (Del.) Pub. Schs., 1956-62; area dir. Montgomery County Schs., Rockville, Md., 1962-63; asst. supt. schs., Newark, Del., 1963-67, supt., 1967—. Bd. dirs. Del. Conservation Assn.; trustee Wesley Coll., Dover, Del. Served with AUS, 1942-45. Recipient Am. Educators medal Freedoms Found., 1969. Fellow A.A.A.S.; mem. Del. Chief Sch. Officers (pres. 1970), Del. Assn. Adminstrs. (pres. 1962), Assn. Supervision and Curriculum Devel. (chpt. pres. 1964-65). Methodist. Rotarian. Home: 302 Wilson Rd Newark DE 19711

KIRK, JAMES ALLEN, mech. engr., educator; b. Cleve., Nov. 3, 1944; s. Charles J. and Helen T. (Tulas) K.; B.E.E., Ohio U., 1967; M.M.E., Mass. Inst. Tech., 1969, Sc.D. in Mech. Engring., 1972; m. Cynthia L. Ambler, Feb. 13, 1977. Research engr. Ford Motor Co., Dearborn, Mich., 1967; research asso. Mass. Inst. Tech., Cambridge, 1968-72; asst. prof. mech. engring. U. Md., College Park, 1972-77, asso. prof., 1977—; owner, dir. Kirk Cons. Co., 1972—. Recipient Ralph Teetor award Soc. Automotive Engrs., 1975. Mem. ASME, Am. Soc. for Metals, Am. Soc. for Engring. Edn. (Down Outstanding Young Faculty award 1977). Contbr. articles to profl. jours. Designer emergency stopping system for U.S. Capitol-House subway system. Home: 3605 Jefferson St Hyattsville MD 20782 Office: U Md College Park MD 20742

KIRK, JAMES STANLEY, clin. psychologist, psychotherapist; b. Sisseton, S.D., May 25, 1938; s. Saxo A. and Frances (Stanley) K.; A.B., Huron Coll., 1960; B.D., McCormick Sem., 1960; Ph.D., Boston U., 1971; m. Nancy Charlene Betts, July 24, 1960; children—Jennifer Lynn, Kristin Elizabeth, Lisabeth Charlene. Dir. tng. Boston Inst. for Psychotherapies, Inc., 1970—; asst. dir. Boston U. Counseling Center, 1969-75; pvt. practice individual, group, child, marriage and family therapy, Newburyport and Haverhill, Mass., 1970; chief psychologist Hampstead (N.H.) Hosp., 1975-77; clin. dir. Baldpate Hosp., Georgetown, Mass., 1977—; asso. in pvt. practice Harris St. Assos., Newburyport, Mass., 1978—. Bd. dirs. Childrens Protective Soc., Haverhill unit Am. Cancer Soc.; pres. bd. dirs. North Charles Mental Health Found., Cambridge, Mass. Mem. Am., Mass. psychol. assns., Am. Group Psychotherapy Assn., Am. Assn. of Marriage and Family Counselors, Boston Inst. for Psychotherapies (founding). Democrat. Presbyterian. Home: 87 High St Newburyport MA 01950 Office: 4 Harris St Newburyport MA 01950 also 215 Summer St Haverhill MA 01830

KIRKLAND, BRYANT MAYS, clergyman; b. Essex, Conn., May 2, 1914; s. Henry Burnham and Helen Josephine (Mays) K.; A.B., Wheaton (Ill.) Coll., 1935; Th.B., Princeton Theol. Sem., 1938; Th.M., Eastern Baptist Theol. Sem., Phila., 1946; D.D. (hon.), Beaver Coll., 1949; Lafayette Coll., 1962; LL.D., U. Tulsa, 1962; D.D. (hon.), Dennison U., 1964; S.T.D., Parson Coll., 1966; Litt.D. (hon.), Washington and Jefferson Coll., 1968; m. Bernice Eleanor Tanis, Aug. 19, 1937; children—Nancy Tanis (Mrs. Tom L. Thompson), Elinor Ann (Mrs. Elinor Kirkland Hite), Virginia Lee (Mrs. Laird James Stuart). Ordained to ministry Presbyn. Ch., 1938; pastor in Pa., 1938-46, N.J., 1946-57, Tulsa, 1957-62, Fifth Ave. Presbyn. Ch., N.Y.C., 1962—; vis. lectr. homiletics, Princeton Theol. Sem., 1951-56, 64-78; overseas guest lectr. U.S. Armed Forces, 1965, 68, 72, 78 and U.S. Army Chaplain Sch.; Thomas Staley lectr., 1978. Mem. Commn. Ecumenical Mission and Relations, Presbyn. Ch., 1949-62, mem. Commn. on Continuing Edn., 1967; mem. council Nat. Presbyn Ch. Center, Washington, 1962-65. Mem. bd. Tulsa Community Chest, 1958-61; trustee Beaver Coll., U. Tulsa; pres. bd. trustees Princeton Theol. Sem. Named Clergyman of Year, Religious Heritage Am. Found., 1975. Mem. Bible Soc. (trustee). Clubs: Princeton; Tulsa; Rotary, University (N.Y.C.). Author: Growing in Christian Faith, 1963; Home Before Dark, 1965; Living in a Zig Zag Age, 1972; Experiencing God in Unexpected Ways, 1978. Contbr. Evang. Sermons of Our Day, 1959, Year of Evangelism in Local Church, 1960. Home: 1158 Fifth Ave New York City NY 10029 Office: 7 W 55th St New York City NY 10019

KIRKPATRICK, PHILIP R., educator; b. Nashua, N.H., Mar. 30, 1947; s. Philip and Cecile (Gagnon) K.; B.A. magna cum laude, U. N.H., 1970; M.A., U. Wis., Madison, 1972; m. Linda Pritchard, Feb. 14, 1970. Tchr., Columbus (Wis.) High Sch., 1971-72; inst. U. Wis., Madison, 1971-73; tchr. Keene (N.H.) High Sch., 1973—. Recipient S. Morris Locke prize U. N.H., 1970; Fulbright scholar, Munich, Ger., 1970. Mem. Nat. Assn. Tchrs. Fgn. Langs., Classical Assn. New Eng., N.H. Classical Assn. (pres. 1974-76), NEA, Phi Beta Kappa, Phi Kappa Phi, Pi Gamma Mu, Pi Sigma Alpha. Editor: Cantus Cunarum 1977. Home: 135 Liberty Ln Keene NH 03431 Office: Keene High School 43 Arch St Keene NH 03431

KIRKWOOD, ROBERT, assn. exec.; b. Belfast, No. Ireland, Aug. 6, 1923; s. Robert and Florence Rebecca (Cairns) K.; came to U.S., 1927, naturalized, 1946; B.A., Rutgers U., 1947; Ph.D. (fellow), U. Rochester, 1956; LL.D. (hon.), Waynesburg Coll., 1973; m. Mary Moore, Feb. 1, 1949. Instr. Clarkson Coll. Tech., 1950-52, asst. prof., 1952-56, asso. prof., 1956-59; dean of coll., prof. history Washington Coll., Chestertown, Md., 1959-66; asso. exec. sec. Commn. on Higher Edn., Middle States Assn. Colls. and Schs., Phila., 1966-72, exec. dir. Commn. on Higher Edn.; exec. dir. Fedn. Regional Accrediting Commns. of Higher Edn., 1972-75; program exec. Danforth Found., St. Louis, 1975-76; mem. edn. commn. States Task Force on Chartering Postsecondary Ednl. Instns.; mem. adv. com. Project Athena; cons. grad. fellowship program Danforth Found. Served with RCAF, 1943-45; served to 1st lt. USAAF, 1945. Mem. Am. Hist. Assn., Am. Assn. Higher Edn., Phi Beta Kappa, Omicron Delta Kappa. Contbr. to publs. in field. Home: 1810 Rittenhouse Sq Philadelphia PA 19103 Office: 3624 Market St Philadelphia PA 19104

KIRPICH, PHILLIP ZIGMUND, exec. World Bank; b. Phila., Nov. 1, 1914; s. Alexander and Fanya (Agronsky) K.; B.S., U. Pa., 1935; m. Laura Myrtho Papayannopoulou, June 15, 1952. Hydraulic engr. C.E., U.S. Army, Balt., N.Y.C., 1936-42; resident mgr., Colombia and Greece, Tippetts-Abbett-McCarthy-Stratton, N.Y.C., 1947-62; div. chief-agr. Latin Am., World Bank, Washington, 1963—; mem. exec. com. U.S. com. Internat. Congress Irrigation, Drainage and Flood Control, 1977—; chief adviser, nat. plan land-water devel., Mexico, 1971-76. Served with San. Corps, AUS, 1943-46. Mem. ASCE, Am. Geophys. Union, Internat. Assn. Hydraulic Research, Internat. Water Resources Assn. Office: 1818 H St NW Washington DC 20433

KIRSCHBAUM, ROBERT WARREN, ins. co. exec.; b. Kearny, N.J., Aug. 8, 1928; s. Richard Warren and Arla (Kaften) K.; student Seton Hall U., 1949; B.A., N.Y. U., 1951; postgrad. Columbia U., 1962-63; m. Jean Ellen Silverman, May 30, 1957; children—William, Mary Ellen, Kenneth. Reporter, Newark News, 1951-61; dir. spl. activities Ins. Info. Inst., N.Y.C., 1961-65; supr. AT & T, N.Y.C., 1965-67; asst. v.p. U.S. Life Corp., N.Y.C., 1967-69; dir. advt. and pub. relations Royal Globe Ins. Co., N.Y.C., 1969-71; with N.Y. Property Ins. Underwriting Assn., N.Y.C., 1971—, now asst. to pres. Past pres. bd. govs. Millburn (N.J.) South Mountain Estates Civic Assn.; former mem. Democratic Com., Millburn. Served with AUS, 1946-48. Mem. Pub. Relations Soc. Am. Jewish religion. Club: B'nai B'rith (past pres.). Home: 90 Whittingham Terr Millburn NJ 07041 Office: 110 William St New York City NY 10038

KIRSCHMAN, MARY MARDAS, counselor, mgmt. cons. and trainer; b. Ashland, Pa., Feb. 18, 1935; d. Milton and Edna (Christos) Mardas; diploma Lankenau Sch. Nursing, 1960; B.S. in Nursing, Villanova U., 1960; M.Ed., U. Del., 1974; certificate Gestalt Inst. Cleve., 1976; m. C. Frederick Kirschman, June 16, 1962; children—Brenda Mary, Charles Frederick. Nurse, Lankenau (Pa.) Hosp., 1953-57, nursing instr., 1957-60; nursing instr. Presbyn. Hosp., Phila., 1960-64, Meml. Hosp., Wilmington, Del., 1964-66; with Blood Bank, Lawrence, Kans., 1967-71; youth conselor Md. synod Lutheran Ch. Am., Del., 1974-77; pvt. practice counseling individuals and couples, Wilmington, 1975—; tchr. course on organizational behavior Grad. Sch., U. Del., 1977—; tchr. bus. Wilmington Coll., 1978; cons. to industry, chs., univs. Active Girl Scouts U.S., 4-H, polit. campaigns; chmn. spl. edn. com. PTA, 1975. HEW scholar, 1959. Mem. Assn. Humanistic Psychology, Am. Personnel and Guidance Assn., Gestalt Inst. Cleve., Lankenau Hosp. Nurses Villanova U., U. Del. alumni assns. Office: 3113 Limestone Rd Wilmington DE 19808

KIRSCHNER, FRANCIS, sound control mfg. co. exec.; b. Hungary, July 20, 1923; s. Morris and Cecile (Wolfsohn) K.; came to U.S., 1954, naturalized, 1959; B.S. in Physics, U. Brussels, 1950, M.S. in Physics cum laude, 1952, Solvay fellow, 1952-54; m. Liliane Zentkowski, Jan. 20, 1955; children—Eric, Michele. Research engr. Columbia U., N.Y.C., 1954; acoustical engr. Gen. Electric Co., Bloomfield, N.J., 1954-58; sr. engring. scientist Arthur D. Little, Inc., Cambridge, Mass., 1958-59; chief engr. acoustics and instruments div. Korfund Dynamics Corp., Westbury, N.Y., 1959-66; v.p., dir. engring. Soundcoat Co., Inc., Bklyn., 1966—, chmn. bd. dirs., 1978—; lectr. in field. Fellow Acoustical Soc. Am. Club: Cornell. Contbr. articles to profl. jours. Patentee acoustical panels. Office: 175 Pearl St Brooklyn NY 11201

KIRSCHNER, MICHAEL FRANK, psychologist; b. N.Y.C., Feb. 22, 1943; s. Fred and Grete (Mayer) K.; B.S., Coll. City N.Y., 1964, M.S., 1966; Ph.D., Hofstra U., 1971; m. Annette Breuer, Aug. 30, 1964; children—Eva, Hillel, Uri. Tchr., pub. schs., N.Y.C., 1964-65; intern psychologist Psychol. Service Center, Teaneck, N.J., 1965-66, Nassau County Med. Center, East Meadow, N.Y., 1968-69; sch. psychologist, Hicksville, N.Y., 1966-67, Beechwood Sch., Wantagh, N.Y., 1967-68, Bellmore Merrick Central High Sch. Dist., Merrick, N.Y., 1969—; pvt. practice psychol. counseling, Hempstead, N.Y., 1973—; coordinator psychol. services Ednl. and Developmental Learning Center, Seaford, N.Y., 1975-77; faculty asso. dept. psychology Hofstra U., 1972—; cons. psychologist Head Start, 1968-69, N.Y. State Dept. Edn. Office Vocat. Rehab., 1974—. Bd. dirs. Palisades Gardens Found., Inc., Palisades, N.Y. Mem. Am., Nassau County psychol. assns., N.Y. Soc. Clin. Psychologists, Phi Beta Kappa. Home: 570 Fort Washington Ave New York City NY 10033 Office: 33 Front St Hempstead NY 11550

KIRSCHSTEIN, RUTH LILLIAN (MRS. ALAN S. RABSON), physician; b. Bklyn., Oct. 12, 1926; d. Julius and Elizabeth (Berm) K.; B.S. magna cum laude, L.I. U. 1947; M.D., Tulane U., 1951; m. Alan S. Rabson, June 11, 1950; 1 son, Arnold. Intern, Kings County Hosp., Bklyn., 1951-52; resident in pathology VA Hosp., Atlanta, 1952, Providence Hosp., Detroit, 1952-54; Nat. Heart Inst. fellow, instr. dept. pathology Tulane U. Sch. Medicine, New Orleans, 1954-55; resident Clin. Center, NIH, Bethesda, Md., 1956, pathologist div. biologics standards, 1957-64, chief lab. pathology, 1964-72, asst. div. dir., 1971-72; dep. dir. Bur. Biologics, FDA, 1972-73, dep. asso. commr. sci., 1973-74; dir. Nat. Inst. Gen. Med. Sics., NIH, Bethesda, 1974—. Diplomate Am. Bd. Patholoty. Mem. Am. Assn. Immunologists, Am. Assn. Pathologists. Research on health sci. adminstrn., pathogenesis of viral diseases, viral oncogenesis. Home: 4 West Dr Bethesda MD 20014 Office: Nat Inst Gen Med Scis Nat Insts Health Bethesda MD 20014

KIRSHENBAUM, RICHARD IRVING, pub. health physician, city-county adminstr.; b. Bklyn., Aug. 19, 1933; s. Joseph and Anne (Hantman) K.; B.A., Temple U., 1955; D.O., Phila. Coll. Osteo. Medicine, 1959; M.P.H., Columbia U., 1971; m. Jean Shicher, Aug. 17, 1957; children—Miriam, Susan, Rachel. Rotating med.-surg. intern Met. Hosp., Phila., 1959-60; practice family medicine, Bklyn., 1960-70; resident in pub. health Columbia U., 1970-71, N.Y.C. Dept. Health, 1970-73; dist. health officer N.Y.C. Dept. Health, 1971-77, regional health dir. Queens County, 1977—; clin. asst. prof. community medicine N.Y. Coll. Osteo. Medicine-N.Y. Inst. Tech. Recipient Physician Recognition award AMA, 1973, 76. Diplomate Am. Bd. Preventive Medicine. Fellow Am. Coll. Preventive Medicine; mem. Am., N.Y.C. pub. health assns., Am., N.Y. State osteo socs., N.Y.C. Soc. Osteo. Physicians and Surgeons. Contbr. articles to med. jours. Home: 313 Whitman Dr Brooklyn NY 11234 Office: NYC Dept Health Jamaica Dist Health Center 90-37 Parsons Blvd Jamaica NY 11432

KIRSHON, STEPHEN ARNOLD, accounting exec.; b. N.Y.C., Mar. 16, 1944; s. Sidney Arthur and Jean (Ehlin) K.; B.S., Syracuse U., 1965; m. Linda Rennie Laskowski, Mar. 10, 1968; children—Sarah Jennifer, Jason Edward. Prin. Stephen A. Kirshon C.P.A., Poughkeepsie, 1970-75, pres. Stephen A. Kirshon P.C., 1975—; v.p. Delegate Enterprises, Inc., Dutchess County, N.Y., 1972-77; pres. B & S Properties Inc., Dutchess County, 1973-77; treas. Brookmeade Assos. Inc., Dutchess County, 1973—, Sodano Estates Inc., Dutchess County, 1974—; auditor, lectr. accounting financial reporting, not-for-profit orgns.; adviser to investment com. employees pension profit sharing trusts, Mid-Hudson Med. Group, P.C. Treas., Dutchess County Sci. Fair, 1965-71; trustee Mid-Hudson Hebrew Day Sch., 1978—; bd. dirs. Jack and Pauline Freeman Found., Bal Harbaur, Fla. Served with USAR, 1967. C.P.A. Mem. Am. Inst. C.P.A.'s, N.Y. Soc. C.P.A.'s. Home: 28 DeGarmo Hills Rd Wappingers Falls NY 12590 Office: 311 Mill St Poughkeepsie NY 12601

KIRSTEIN, LINCOLN, promoter Am. ballet; b. Rochester, N.Y., May 4, 1907; s. Louis E. and Rose (Stein) K.; B.S., Harvard U., 1930; m. Fidelma Cadmus, Apr. 1941. Founder, Hound and Horn Periodical, 1927, editor, 1927-34; established Sch. Am. Ballet, N.Y.C., 1933. now dir.; dir. N.Y. City Ballet Co.; dir. gen. Am. Ballet. Author: Dance: A Short History of Theatrical Dancing, 1935; Blast at Ballet, 1938; Low Ceiling (poems), 1935; Ballet Alphabet, 1939; pub. Pavel Tchelitchew Drawings, 1947; Elie Nadelman Drawings, 1949; The Classic Ballet, 1952; Ryhmes & More Rhymes of a Pfc., 1965; Movement and Metaphore: Four Centuries of Ballet, 1969; Elie Nadelman, 1973; New York City Ballet, 1973; Nijinsky Dancing, 1975. Address: Sch Am Ballet 144 W 66th St New York City NY 10023*

KISAK, EUGENE, educator; b. Mormant, France, June 5, 1939; s. Wasyl and Stephanie (Starecky) K.; came to Can., 1951, naturalized, 1957; B.Sc. (Internat. Nickel Co. scholar), Ecole Poly., Montreal, 1962; M.Sc., McGill U., 1971, Ph.D., 1976; m. Daria Nowostawsky, July 21, 1962; children—Alexander, Nadia. Research engr. Aviation Electric Ltd., Montreal, 1962-63; faculty Ecole Polytechnique, Montreal, 1963—, prof. dept. math., 1963—. Mem. Order of Engrs. Que., IEEE, Soc. Exploration Geophysicists. Byzantine (Ukrainian) Catholic. Home: 846 56th Ave Lachine PQ H8T 3C2 Canada Office: Ecole Polytechnique C P 6079 Sta A Montreal PQ H3C 3A7 Canada

KISE, JAMES NELSON, urban designer, city planner; b. Trenton, N.J., May 2, 1937; s. Charles Richard and Gladys Mae (Doll) K.; student Lafayette Coll., 1953-55; B.Arch., U. Pa., 1959, M.Arch., 1963, M. City Planning, 1964; postgrad. U. Rome, 1959-60; m. Rachel Bok, Dec. 20, 1958; children—Jefferson Bok, Charles Curtis; m. 2d, Sarah Ludlow Ogden Smith, June 15, 1974. New town planner Harvard-Mass. Inst. Tech. Joint Center of Urban Studies' Ciudad Guayana Project, Caracas, Venezuela, 1961-62; center city planner Phila. City Planning Commn., 1962-66; project dir. Wallace McHarg Roberts & Todd, Phila., 1966-67; dir. urban design center Urban, Am., Inc. and successor, Nat. Urban Coalition, Washington, 1967-70; partner David A. Crane & Partners, Phila. and Boston, 1970—; lectr. urban design U. Pa., 1962-67; adj. instr. urban design Drexel U., 1974-76; dir. Curtis Pub. Co., 1970-75. Trustee Settlement Music Sch., 1963—; trustee Washington Community Sch. Music, 1967-70, pres. bd., 1968-70; chmn. Friends of Phila. Mus. Art, 1972-75; trustee Fleischer Art Meml., 1970—, Phila. Mus. Art, 1975—. Mem. Am. Inst. Planners, Tau Sigma Delta. Democrat. Clubs: Racquet, Germantown Cricket, Phila. Cricket, Penn. Designer master plans for Schuykill River Park, Phila., 1965, downtown Harrisburg, Pa., 1975, Sadat City, Egypt, 1977. Home: 235 Delancey St Philadelphia PA 19106 Office: 1316 Arch St Philadelphia PA 19107

KISELIK, PAUL HOWARD, folding carton co. exec.; b. Newark, Nov. 29, 1937; s. Jerome W. and Rose (Ramo) K.; B.S. with honors, Lehigh U., 1960; M.S., Newark Coll. Engring., 1965; m. Teri Nimaroff, Sept. 6, 1959; children—Daniel, Jonathan. Vice-pres. Nimrow Carton Co., Elizabeth, N.J., 1961-71; pres., chief exec. officer, Sebro Packaging Corp., South Hackensack, N.J., 1971—, Rayart Folding Box Co., South Hackensack, 1971—. Served with ordnance U.S. Army, 1960-61. Registered profl. engr. N.J., Pa. Mem. TAPPI, Newtonian Soc., Tau Beta Pi, Alpha Pi Mu. Author: Equity Financing of a Small Business, 1965. Office: 262 Green St South Hackensack NJ 07606

KISER, MARIE VIVA JEAN, coll. educator; b. Balt., Feb. 18, 1929; married, 3 children. B.S. in Elementary and Spl. Edn., Millersville (Pa.) State Coll., 1965, M.Ed. in Spl. Edn., 1968; postgrad. in Spl. Edn. U. Md., College Park; m. Norman Kiser; children—Dennis, Linda, David. Substitute tchr. So. York County Sch. Dist., Glen Rock, Pa., 1953-63, classroom tchr., 1963-68; instr. dept. spl. edn.

Millersville State Coll., 1968-71, asst. prof., 1971-79, asso. prof., 1979—. Mem. Council for Exceptional Children, Council Tchrs. Educators of Children with Learning Disabilities, Assn. for Gifted, Council for Adminstrs. in Spl. Edn., Council for Ednl. Diagnostic Services, Council Child with Communication Disorders, Council Child with Mental Retardation, Council Child with Behavior Disorders, Am. Assn. Edn. Severely and Profoundly Handicapped, Am. Assn. Mental Deficiency, Pi Lambda Theta. Certified elementary tchr., tchr. mentally retarded, emotionally handicapped, Pa. Home: 1057 Church St Landisville PA 17538 Office: Gerhart Bldg Millersville State Coll Millersville PA 17551

KISH, ROBERT STEPHEN, urologist; b. Easton, Pa., Apr. 30, 1940; s. Stephen Andrew and Ione Emma K.; student Pa. State U., 1957-61; M.D., Temple U., 1965; m. Teresa Shaules, Aug. 24, 1962; children—Erica, Jessica, Susanna, Julia. Intern, Harrisburg (Pa.) Hosp., 1965-66; resident in urology SUNY Upstate Med. Sch., Syracuse, 1970; practice medicine specializing in urology State Coll., Pa., 1970—; chief surg. staff Centre Community Hosp., State College, 1975-78. Diplomate Am. Bd. Urology. Mem. Am.Urol. Assn. Inventor illuminating catheter. Office: 211 W Beaver Ave State College PA 16801

KISNER, JACOB, poet, editor, publisher; b. Chelsea, Mass., Apr. 30, 1926; s. Louis and Sarah (Kotel) K.; student Calvin Coolidge Coll., 1945-46, Burdett Coll., 1943-45, Harvard Extension, 1944-48; m. Gladys Selma Feinstein, May 29, 1947; 1 dau. Lesley Kisner Cafarelli. Sunday dept. writer Boston Globe, 1943-45; local news editor Jewish Advocate, Boston, 1945-46; founder, editor, pub. Dorchester (Mass.) Herald, 1946-47; trade reporter Fairchild News Service, Boston, 1948-49; sr. proof-reader Rec. and Statis. Corp., Boston, 1950-54; editor Crossroads, Toronto, Ont., Can., 1964-67; Am. editor View, 1967—; research dir. N.Y. bur. Moneytree Publs., N.Y.C., 1972—; free lance writer, 1943—; discussion moderator Great Books Found., Boston, 1948-51; judge of poetry contests, Rochester, N.Y., also N.Y. Poetry Forum, 1969—; N.Y.C. chmn. World Poetry Day Com., 1971—; v.p., incorporator N.Y. Poetry Forum, 1973-75; author plays: First Came Paula, 1954, Speak of the Devil, 1955, The Monkey's Tail, 1956; author TV plays: The Late Mr. Honeywell, 1957, A World Apart, 1957; author: (poetry) I Am Hephaestus, 1966; contbr. poetry to various lit. jours. and anthologies. Recipient World Peace award Ky. State Poetry Soc., 1970, Gold Medal award Internat. Poets' Shrine, 1971, Radio award sta. WEFG, 1970, Spl. Citation award Poetry Pageant, 1970. Mem. Acad. Am. Poets, Wilson MacDonald Poetry Soc. Can. (exec. com. 1967-77, v.p. 1977—), Am. Philatelic Soc., Soc. Israel Philatelists, Am. Revenue Assn., Confederate Stamp Alliance (founder, postmaster Park Ave. Local Post 1978—). Address: 750 Park Ave New York City NY 10021

KISSA, ERIK, chemist; b. Abja, Estonia, Apr. 7, 1923; s. Mats and Selma (Wilson) K.; M.S., Tech. U. Karlsruhe (Germany), 1951; Ph.D., U. Del., 1956; m. Selma Alide Tamm, Sept. 6, 1952; children—Erik Harold, Karl Martin. With E.I. duPont de Nemours, Wilmington, Del., 1951—, sr. research chemist, 1967-74, research asso., 1974—; UN tech. assistance expert, India, 1978. Fellow Am. Inst. Chemists; mem. Am. Chem. Soc., AAAS, Soc. Dyers and Colourists. Lutheran. Clubs: Del. Camera, DuPont Country. Contbr. articles to profl. jours. Patentee in field. Home: 1436 Fresno Rd Green Acres Wilmington DE 19803 Office: Jackson Lab duPont Co Wilmington DE 19898

KISSANE, THOMAS, criminologist; b. Bronx, Mar. 14, 1927; s. James M. and Elizabeth (Sheridan) K.; A.A.S., Baruch Coll., 1961; B.S., John Jay Coll., 1969; M.S. in Edn., Iona Coll., 1979; m. Marion O'Shea, Nov. 18, 1950. With N.Y.C. Police Dept., 1949-74, capt., 1965-74, cmdg. officer burglary larceny div., 1971-74; dir. cargo theft program U. Louisville, 1975-76; asst. dir. criminal justice studies Iona Coll., New Rochelle, N.Y., 1976—; cons. on criminal receiving U.S. Senate Com. Mem. Bd. Ethics, Eastchester Twp. Named Man of Yr., N.Y. State Motor Truck Assn., 1974, Nat. Assn. Former State Troopers, 1972. Mem. Capts. Endowment Assn., Nat. Assn. Former State Troopers, Ret. Detectives Assn., Am. Soc. Indsl. Security. Office: Criminal Justice Program 715 North Ave New Rochelle NY 10801

KISSEL, WILLIAM THORN, JR., sculptor; b. N.Y.C., Feb. 6, 1920; s. William Thorn and Frances A. (Dallett) K.; student Choate Sch., 1935-39; B.A., Harvard, 1944; postgrad. Pa. Acad. Fine Arts, 1951-53; grad. Barnes Found., 1953. Rinehart Grad. Sch. Sculpture, Balt., 1958; m. Barbara Eldred Case, June 17, 1943; children—William Thorn III, Michael C. Exhibited sculpture Lever House, N.Y.C., N.A.D., N.Y.C., Balt. Sculptor's Exhibit, York, Pa., Beverly, Mass., Gloucester, Woodmere Gallery, Germantown, Pa.; represented in pvt. collections, U.S.; executed large granite meml., Montclair, N.J., also many animal sculpture studies and commns. Served to lt. (j.g.) USNR, 1942-45. Recipient Mass. Sculptor's award Regional Exhibit, Beverly, Mass., 1958; Speyer award, N.A.D., 1966, 68, Am. Artists Profl. League award, 1966. Fellow Pa. Acad. Fine Arts; mem. Am. Artists Profl. League, Nat. Sculpture Soc., Municipal Art Soc. N.Y.C., Soc. of Cincinnati. Republican. Episcopalian. Home: 223 Valley Rd Owings Mills MD 21117

KISSINGER, HENRY ALFRED, former sec. of state; b. Fuerth, Germany, May 27, 1923; s. Louis and Paula (Stern) K.; A.B. summa cum laude, Harvard, 1950, M.A., 1952, Ph.D., 1954; m. Ann Fleischer, Feb. 6, 1949 (div. 1964); children—Elizabeth, David; m. 2d, Nancy Maginnes, Mar. 30, 1974. Came to U.S., 1938, naturalized, 1943. Exec. dir. Harvard Internat. Seminar, 1951-69, lectr. dept. govt., 1957-59, dir. def. studies program, 1958-69, asso. prof. govt., 1959-62, prof., 1962-69, faculty Center Internat. Affairs, Harvard, 1960-69; asst. to Pres. Nixon on nat. security affairs, 1969-74; dir. NSC, 1969-75; sec. of state, 1973-77; vis. prof. diplomacy Georgetown U., Washington, 1977—, counselor Center for Strategic and Internat. Studies, 1977—; spl. cons. world affairs NBC, 1977—; sr. fellow Aspen Inst. Study dir. nuclear weapons and fgn. policy Council Fgn. Relations, 1955-56; dir. spl. studies project Rockefeller Bros. Fund. Inc., 1956-58; cons. Ops. Research Office, 1950-61, cons. to dir. Psychol. Strategy Bd., 1952; cons. Ops. Coordinating Bd., 1955, cons. weapons systems evaluation group, 1959-60; cons. NSC, 1961-62, ACDA, 1961-68; cons. Dept. State, 1965-69. Served with AUS, 1943-46. Recipient citation Overseas Press Club, 1958; Woodrow Wilson prize for best book in fields of govt., politics, internat. affairs, 1958; Distinguished Pub. Service award Am. Inst. Pub. Service, 1973; Nobel Peace prize, 1973; Presdl. Medal of Freedom, 1977. Guggenheim fellow, 1965-66. Mem. Am. Polit Sci. Assn., Council Fgn. Relations, Am. Acad. Arts and Scis., Phi Beta Kappa. Clubs: Cosmos, Federal City, Metropolitan (Washington); Century, River (N.Y.C.). Author: Nuclear Weapons and Foreign Policy, 1957; A World Restored: Castlereagh, Metternich and the Restoration of Peace, 1812-22, 1957; The Necessity for Choice: Prospects of American Foreign Policy, 1961; The Troubled Partnership: A Reappraisal of the Atlantic Alliance, 1965. Editor: Problems of National Strategy: A Book of Readings, 1965; Confluence, An Internat. Forum, 1951-58. Contbr. articles to profl. jours. Office: Suite 520 1800 K St NW Washington DC 20006

KISSINGER, WALTER BERNHARD, automotive parts and service equipment mfg. co. exec.; b. Furth, Germany, June 21, 1924; s. Louis and Paula (Stern) K.; came to U.S., 1938, naturalized, 1939; B.E., Princeton, 1951; M.B.A., Harvard, 1953; m. Eugenie Van Drooge, July 4, 1958; children—William, Thomas, Dana Marie, John Frans. Asst. to v.p. fgn. operations Gen. Tire & Rubber Co., Akron, Ohio, 1953-56; pres. Advanced Vacuum Products Co., Stamford, Conn., 1957-62; exec. v.p. Glass-tite Industries, Providence, 1960-62; asst. to pres. Jerrold Corp., 1963-64; exec. v.p., dir., chmn. exec. com. Jervis Corp., Hicksville, N.Y., 1964-68; chmn., pres., chief exec. officer Allen Electric & Equipment Co. (name changed to Allen Group, Inc.), Melville, N.Y., 1969—; mem. adv. bd. Mfrs. Hanover Trust Co. Served to capt. AUS, 1943-46, 50. Decorated Commendation medal. Club: Princeton of New York. Home: Lower Dr Huntington Bay NY 11746 Office: 534 Broad Hollow Rd Melville NY 11746

KISSMEYER-NIELSEN, ERIK, agr. and food cons.; b. Silkeborg, Denmark, Oct. 22, 1922; s. Thorgny and Gudrun (Kissmeyer) Nielsen; came to U.S., 1948, naturalized, 1966; B.S., in Agr., Royal Vet. and Agr. Coll., Copenhagen, 1948; M.S., Cornell U., 1960; Ph.D. in Food Sci., U. Wis., 1964; m. Perla Minda S. Santos, Sept. 8, 1962; children—Paul Erik, Kirsten. Trainee food technician Am. Scandinavian Soc., 1948-50; quality control research and devel. R.T. French Co., N.Y.C., 1950-53; asst. mgr. Grimstrup Coop. Starch and Dehydration Plant, Denmark, 1953-58; asst. food scientist Cornell U., 1958-60, U. Wis., 1960-63; asst. prof. biochemistry and food sci. U. Del., 1963-66; adviser to food and agrl. industry, 1966—; regional agrl. and food industry adviser Econ. Commn. Africa, 1973-75. Fellow AAAS; mem. Inst. Food Technologists, Am. Chem. Soc., Inst. Biol. Scis., Am. Potato Assn., European Assn. Potato Research. Club: Maynard (Mass.) Gun and Rod. Author numerous papers in field. Address: 65 Crabtree Rd Concord MA 01742

KISTLER, DAVID WALTER, physician; b. Wilkes-Barre, Pa., Nov. 17, 1923; s. Walter William and Nellie Davis (Hammer) K.; B.A., Colgate U., 1944; M.D., Hahemann Med. Coll., 1947; m. June Ann Carpenter, Nov. 23, 1945; children—David W., Christopher, William Alex, John. Intern, Wyoming Valley Hosp., Wilkes-Barre, 1947-48; practice medicine specializing in family practice, Wilkes-Barre, 1948-61; sr. partner Family Physician Assos., 1961-75; lectr. in field. Served with USAF, 1950-52. Diplomate Am. Bd. Family Practice. Mem. Am. Acad. Family Physicians, Pa., Am. med. assns. Democrat. Presbyterian. Home: 52 Maffet Wilkes-Barre PA 18702 Office: 245 E South St Wilkes-Barre PA 18709

KISTLER, JONATHAN HIPPERLING, educator; b. Tamaqua, Pa., Dec. 26, 1909; s. Charles Edward and Elizabeth K.; grad. Swarthmore Coll., 1932; postgrad. (fellow) U. Mich., 1932-36; m. Patricia Tostevin, Nov. 24, 1938; children—Natasha, Thomasin, Teresa, Patricia. Grad. asst., instr. U. Mich.; instr. Iowa State U.; chmn. dept. English, Doane Coll., until 1947; prof. English, Colgate U., 1947—; cons. N.Y. State Bd. Regents, N.Y. State Edn. Dept., Mobil Oil Co. Served with USN. Ford Found. fellow in Oriental lit. Mem. Modern Lang. Assn., AAUP, Nat. Council Tchrs. English. Home: Randallsville Rd Hamilton NY 13346 Office: Colgate U Dept English Hamilton NY 13346*

KISTLER, WARREN DOUGLAS, ophthalmologist; b. Nanticoke, Pa., Jan. 26, 1934; s. Guy Agustus and Helen Conrad (Nalbach) K.; A.B., U. Pa., 1957; M.D., Temple U., 1961; m. Nancy Jean Dworsack, June 30, 1962; children—Jennifer Lynne, Amy Beth, Grant Douglas. Intern, Presbyn. Hosp., Denver, 1961-62; resident in ophthalmology, Temple U., 1962-65; practice medicine, specializing in ophthalmology, Chambersburg, Pa., 1965—; mem. staff, chmn. dept. surgery, chief of surgery Chambersburg Hosp.; pres. Chambersburg Specialty Corp. Bd. dirs. Franklin County Heritage, Presbyterian Ch. of Falling Spring. Diplomate Nat. Bd. Med. Examiners, Am. Acad. Ophthalmology and Otolaryngology. Mem. Intra Ocular Lens Implant Soc. Am., AMA, Pa. Med. Soc., Pan Am. Soc. Ophthalmology, Pa. Acad. Ophthalmology, Smithsonian Assos., Alpha Tau Omega. Republican. Club: Masons. Home: Box 140 Rural Route 10 Chambersburg PA 17201 Office: 1035 Wayne Ave Chambersburg PA 17201

KISZELY, ANDOR, pianist, educator; b. Balassagyarmat, Hungary, Nov. 17, 1922; s. Andor and Gizella (Szilard) K.; came to U.S., 1959, naturalized, 1964; diploma in piano F. Liszt Royal Acad. Music, Budapest, 1948; diploma in conducting Akademie fur Musik und Darstellende Kunst, Vienna, 1959; Ph.D., P. Pazmany U., Budapest, 1947; m. Joy Miller, Sept. 2, 1967. Piano soloist, accompanist in Hungary, Austria, Germany and U.S.A., 1945—; lectr. Bartok's Piano Music and Kodaly's Music Ednl. Concept; tchr. piano and solfege Budapest Municipal Music Schs., 1948-56; founder, dir. Main Line Conservatory Music, Ardmore, Pa., 1967—. Decorated Four Chaplains Legion of Honor. Mem. Music Tchrs. Nat. Assn., Pa. (contbr. News), Phila. (pres. 1973—) music tchrs. assns., Nat. Guild Piano Tchrs. (chmn. Ardmore unit, named to Hall of Fame), Am. Liszt Soc., Am. Fedn. Musicians, Matinee Mus. Club of Phila. Home: 925 Coopertown Rd Bryn Mawr PA 19010 Office: 27 W Lancaster Ave Ardmore PA 19003

KISZELY, JOY MILLER, educator, pianist; b. Cleve., May 16, 1941; d. Robert Karl and Betty (Andrews) Miller; student Mozarteum, Salzburg, Austria, 1961-62; B.M., Oberlin Coll., 1963; postgrad. Ind. U., 1966-67; m. Andor Kiszely, Sept. 2, 1967. Co-founder, co-dir. Main Line Conservatory of Music, Ardmore, Pa., 1967—; musical dir., condr. string orch., Wayne, Pa., 1972—. Chmn. music com. Lower Merion Vol. Resource Program, 1972—. Mem. Music Tchrs. Nat. Assn. (certified), Pa. (v.p. 1973-75, certified), Phila. music tchrs. assns., Am. Liszt Soc., Nat. Guild Piano Tchrs. (certified), Matinee Mus. Club Phila. Home: 925 Coopertown Rd Bryn Mawr PA 19010 Office: 27 W Lancaster Ave Ardmore PA 19003

KITABJIAN, HAGOP ARTIN, architect; b. Aleppo, Syria, Nov. 24, 1932; s. Artin Garabed and Nargiz (Minassian) K.; came to U.S., 1956, naturalized, 1966; B.Arch. (Gulbenkian scholar), Am. U., Beirut, Lebanon, 1956; M. Arch., U. Pa., 1958, postgrad. 1958-59; m. Pamela Joyce Zartarian, Apr. 20, 1963; children—Sona, David, Paul. Archtl. designer H.A. Kuljian & Co., Phila., 1958; project designer Samuel I. Oshiver and Assos., Phila., 1958-63, George M. Ewing Co., Phila., 1963-64; chief designer, project architect Alfred Panepinto, Architect, Phila., 1964-73; partner Alfred Panepinto Co., Inc., Phila., 1973—, v.p., sec., 1973—; lectr. on Armenian architecture, 1965—; pvt. tchr. math. and engring. mechanics, Phila., 1956—; major archtl. works include: Phys. Edn. Bldg. and Sci. Bldg., Hampton (Va.) Inst., 1968; J. Howard Pew Fine Arts Center, Grove City (Pa.) Coll., 1975; Learning Center, Widener Coll., Chester, Pa., 1971; Library for Gordon Conwell Theol. Sem., Hamilton, Mass., 1973; DuPont Research and Devel. Facility, Brevard, N.C., 1974. Chmn. Armenian Inter-Communal Com., 1963—; trustee St. Sahag and St. Mesrob Armenian Ch., Phila.; deacon, bd. dirs. Armenian Sisters Acad. Recipient award St. Sahag and St. Mesrob Armenian Ch., 1975; registered profl. architect, Pa. Mem. AIA, Pa. Soc. Architects, Armenian Students Assn., Armenian Hist. Research Assn., KNAR Armenian Choral Group, ARARAT Song and Dance Ensemble, Knights of Vartan. Mem. Armenian Apostolic Ch. Contbr. articles on architecture to profl. publs. Home: 308 Robinson Dr Broomall PA 19008

KITAHATA, LUKE MASAHIKO, physician; b. Osaka, Japan, Jan. 12, 1925; s. Chujiro and Yuki (Nishikawa) K.; B.S., Osaka Coll., 1943; M.D., Tokyo Imperial U., 1947; Ph.D. in Neuropharmacology, Kyoto (Japan) U., 1960; M.A. (hon.), Yale, 1974; m. Carolyn Vivian Massey, Sept. 3, 1955; children—Amy M., Mari M., Luther M. Came to U.S., 1949, naturalized, 1963. Intern, N.C. Bapt. Hosp., Winston-Salem, N.C., 1950-51, resident in surgery, 1949-55; chmn. dept. surgery Japan Baptist Hosp., Kyoto, 1956-60; rotating intern Kings County Hosp., Bklyn., 1961-62; resident in anesthesiology N.Y. Hosp.-Cornell Med. Coll., N.Y.C., 1962-64; mem. faculty dept. anesthesiology Med. Sch., Yale, New Haven, 1964—, asst. prof., 1966-70, asso. prof., 1970-73, prof., chmn. dept., 1973—; chief of service Yale-New Haven Hosp., 1973—. NIH grantee, 1971—. Diplomate Am. Bd. Anesthesiology. Mem. Assn. Univ. Anesthetists, Am., Conn. socs. anesthesiologists, Am. Soc. Pharmacology and Exptl. Therapeutics, N.Y. Acad. Scis., Conn., New Haven County med. socs., Soc. for Neurosci., Soc. Acad. Anesthesia Chmn., Internat. Assn. Study of Pain, Am. Assn. Neurol. Surgeons, Sigma Xi. Home: 64 Van Rose Dr Hamden CT 06517 Office: 333 Cedar St New Haven CT 06510

KITCHEN, OTIS DORSEY, educator; b. Williamsport, Md., July 5, 1931; s. Paul Dorsey and Estella Olive (Byers) K.; B.S., Bridgewater Coll., 1953; Spl. Services degree, Navy Sch. Music, 1955; Mus.M., Northwestern U., 1964; m. Alma Irene Phibbs, June 18, 1955; children—Sharon Lynne, Gary Wayne. Dir. band, tchr. music Greenville County High Sch., Emporia, Va., 1953; tchr. band, dir. music William Fleming High Sch., Roanoke, Va., 1956-65; band dir. woodwinds, jazz band asso. prof. instrumental music Elizabethtown (Pa.) Coll., 1965—. Cons. Continental Press, Elizabethtown, 1969—; asso. prof. U. Center, Harrisburg, Pa., 1966-71; adjudicator, guest condr. numerous band and orch. festivals including Invitational Festival of Mexico, 1978. Founder, Elizabethtown Coll. Community Symphony, Youth Symphony Camp Lancaster County, 1971; mus. dir. for community shows, 1970-72; dir. Lancaster County Youth Symphony, 1969—. Bd. dirs. Music Found., Elizabethtown; bd. dirs. Am. Youth Symphony and Chorus. Served with AUS, 1954-56. Summer grantee Northwestern U., 1968, Wis. State U., 1969; Morehead State U., 1971. Mem. Music Educators Conf., Nat. Band Assn. (dir. 1975-76), Nat. Fedn. Music Clubs (merit award 1970-72, 76-78), Nat., Pa. music educators assns., Internat. Soc. Promotion Wind Band Music, Nat., Pa. (v.p. 1976-77, sec.-treas. 1977-78) coll. band dirs. assns., Lancaster Mus. Art Soc. Republican. Mem. Ch. of Brethren. Rotarian. Club: Tennis (Hershey, Pa.). Contbr. articles to various publs. Home: 120 Foreman Rd Elizabethtown PA 17022 Office: Music Dept Rider Hall Elizabethtown PA 17022

KITCHIN, DAVID JACKSON, III, army officer; b. Balt., Dec. 17, 1940; s. David Jackson II and Hilda M. K.; B.S., U. Miami, Coral Gables, Fla., 1962; m. Carol Taylor, 1965; children—David Jackson IV, Kyle Howard, James Craig. Commd. 2d lt. U.S. Army, 1962, advanced through grades to maj., 1978; service with Army Med. Service Corps in Ryukyu Islands, Vietnam and P.R.; project officer Dwight David Eisenhower Army Med. Center, Ft. Gordon, Ga., 1970-76; assigned U.S. Army-Baylor U. Grad. Program Health Care Adminstrn., Ft. Sam Houston, Tex., 1976-78, U.S. Army Health Facility Planning Agy., Washington, 1978—. Decorated Army Commendation medal with 2 oak leaf clusters; Vietnamese Cross Gallantry with palm. Mem. Am. Assn. Hosp. Engrs., Am. Hosp. Assn., Nat. Assn. Power Engrs., Assn. Mil. Surgeons U.S., Assn. U.S. Army, Am. Coll. Hosp. Adminstrs., Soc. Am. Mil. Engrs. Co-author: Planning Aspects of Health Care Facilities, 1978. Address: US Army Health Facility Planning Agy Room 2C468 Pentagon Washington DC 20310

KITTRIE, NICHOLAS N., law cons., educator; b. en route Bilgoraj, Poland, Mar. 26, 1928; s. S.K. Kronenbergh and Peria F. (Ver Standig) K. (parents Brit. citizens); student U. Cairo, 1946, U. London, 1947; LL.B., U. Kans., 1950, M.A., 1951; postgrad. (Raymond fellow) U. Chgo., 1954-55; LL.M., Georgetown U., 1963, S.J.D., 1968; m. Sara Yudovic deBurak, June 1, 1962; children—R. Orde Felicien, Norda Nicole, Zachary McNair. Research asst. U. London, 1947; instr. Western civilization dept. U. Kans., 1948-50; legal analyst Kans. Govt. Research Center, 1951-54; asst. to dir. legis. service Am. Bar Assn., 1955-56; project dir. Am. Bar Found., 1956-58; legal asst. to Senator Wiley, 1959; counsel U.S. Senate Antitrust and Monopoly Subcom., 1959-62; mem. firm DeGrazia & Kittrie, Washington, 1962—; lectr. comparative law Washington Coll. Law, Am. U., Washington, 1963-64, asso. prof., 1964-66, prof., 1967—, dean, 1977—, dir. research, 1968—; dir. Center for Adminstrn. Justice, 1969-71; dir. Inst. Advanced Studies in Justice, 1970—; vis. prof. London Sch. Econs., 1973-74; lectr. U. Ottawa, 1966; research scholar U. Warsaw, U. Berlin, summer 1967, 68; research asso. U. Chgo. Center for Studies in Criminal Justice, 1967-68; dir. Law and Policy Inst., Jerusalem, summers 1970-75; vis. fellow Inst. Advanced Legal Research, U. London, 1973-74; cons. Nat. Commn. on Marijuana and Drug Abuse, 1972; Internat. Assn. Penal Law rep. to UN Social and Econ. Council, 1975—; mem. task force on role of psychology in criminal justice Am. Psychol. Assn., 1975—; vice chmn. UN Alliance for Crime Prevention and Criminal Justice, 1976—; dir. First Washington Devel. Corp., Bank of Chios; dir., gen. counsel Avoca Pub. Corp. Mem. senate Am. U., 1964—; vice chmn. sci. com. U. Messina (Italy), 1977—. Sr. fellow Nat. Endowment for Humanities, 1973-74. Served with Brit. Army, 1944-45. Mem. Am. Soc. Pub. Adminstrn., Am. Soc. Criminology (pres. 1973-74), Internat. Assn. Penal Law (v.p. 1971—), Judicature Soc., Am. Soc. Internat. Law, Internat. Inst. Space Law, Internat. Assn. Comparative Pub. Law (dir. 1976—), Kans., D.C., U.S. Supreme Ct. bar assns. Author: International Legal Responsibility for Colonial People, 1915; Survey of Administration of Criminal Justice, 1956; (with others) The Mentally Disabled and the Law, 1959; The Right to be Different: Deviance and Enforced Therapy, 1971; The Comparative Law of Israel and the Middle East, 1971; The Real Estate Settlement Process and Its Cost, 1972; Crescent and Star: Arab-Israeli Perspectives on the Middle-East Conflict, 1972; The Juvenile Drug Offender, 1972; Medicine, Law and Public Policy, 1975. Contbr. articles to profl. publs. Home: 6908 Ayr Ln Bethesda MD 20034

KITTROSS, JOHN MICHAEL, educator; b. N.Y.C., Apr. 25, 1929; s. John H. and Lucile S. (Vossen) K.; A.B., Antioch Coll., 1951; M.S., Boston U., 1952; Ph.D., U. Ill., 1960; m. Sally Sprague, Dec. 27, 1951; children—David M., Julia A. Various positions broadcasting, summer stock, motion picture prodn., 1946-52; research asst. U. Ill. Inst. Communications Research, Urbana, 1955-59; instr. to asso. prof. dept. telecommunications U. So. Calif., Los Angeles, 1959-68; prof. communications Temple U., Phila., 1968—, asst. dean Sch. Communications and Theater, 1971-73, asso. dean, 1973—. Active ACLU, 1966—. Served with AUS, 1952-54. Mem. Broadcast Edn. Assn., Assn. for Edn. in Journalism, Internat. Communications Assn., Internat. Inst. Communications, Radio-Television News Dirs. Assn., AAUP, Sigma Delta Chi. Unitarian (trustee ch. 1966-68). Contbr. articles to profl. jours. Co-author: Stay Tuned: A Concise History of American Broadcasting, 1978. Editor: Free and Fair: Courtroom

Access and the Fairness Doctrine, 1970; Jour. Broadcasting, 1960-72; Documents in American Telecommunications Policy, 1977; compiler: Bibliography of Theses and Dissertations in Broadcasting 1920-1973, 1978. Home: 2318 Fairway Rd Huntingdon Valley PA 19006 Office: Sch Communications and Theater Temple U Philadelphia PA 19122

KITZINGER, GRACE MARIAN LIVENGOOD, editor; b. Hillsdale, N.J., Dec. 15, 1927; d. William Winfred and Dorothy Grace (Edmed) Livengood; B.A. cum laude, Bucknell U., 1949; m. Stanley A. Kitzinger. Free-lance writer, 1949-50; with Am. Cyanamid Co., Wayne, N.J., 1951—, mgr. tech. info., agrl. products internat. divs., 1968—. Recipient ann. award for excellence in tech. pub. N.Y. chpt. Soc. Tech. Writers and Editor, 1960, certificate of spl. merit Printing Industries Met. N.Y., 1962, 63, award of merit N.Y. chpt. Soc. Tech. Communication, 1972, Distinguished Publ. award, 1977, Internat. Tech. Publ. Achievement award, 1978. Mem. Am. Med. Writers Assn., Nat., N.J. Audubon socs., AAAS, Soc. for Tech. Communication, Internat. Communication Assn., In-Plant Printing Assn., North Jersey Tennis Assn., Phi Beta Kappa, Phi Sigma, Alpha Lambda Delta. Clubs: Tenafly, Ahdeek Tennis (Bergenfield, N.J.). Home: 471 Haworth Ave Haworth NJ 07641 Office: Am Cyanamid Co Wayne NJ 07470

KIZALA, RUTH LILLIAN, mfg. co. exec.; b. Nashua, N.H., Feb. 7, 1927; d. Robert Harold and Alice Julia (Stepanovich) Field; student Rivier Coll., 1944-45; m. Victor P. Kizala, Apr. 23, 1949; children—Victoria Ann, Cynthia Jane, Robert Michael, Patricia Ann. With Improved Machinery Co. (now Ingersoll Rand Co.), Nashua, 1944—, cost clk., 1957-65, balance clk., 1965-67, systems programmer, 1967-72, adminstr. data coordination, 1972, mgr. cost accounting, 1972-76, mgr. advanced material and planning, 1976-77, mgr. material services, 1977-78, adminstr. mfg. systems, 1978—. Mem. Am. Prodn. Inventory Control Soc. Rpublican. Roman Catholic. Home: 22 Labine St Nashua NH 03060 Office: 150 Burke St Nashua NH 03060

KLAGES, ROBERT DEDRICK, lawyer, bus. equipment mfg. exec.; b. Mt. Kisco, N.Y., May 25, 1931; s. Frederick William and Katherine Mary K.; B.S., U.S. Mcht. Marine Acad., 1952; J.D., Georgetown U., 1957; m. Susan V. Woodward, July 14, 1962; children—Brian Geoffrey, Jeremy Stefan. Admitted to D.C. bar, 1957, Md. bar, 1962, Pa. bar, 1976, U.S. Supreme Ct. bar, 1962; atty., civil and antitrust divs. Dept. Justice, Washington, 1957-62; individual practice law, Balt. and Washington, 1962-69; licensing counsel Xerox Corp., Stamford, Conn., 1969-71; counsel Sperry Rand Corp., Washington Office, counsel worldwide mktg. and services, v.p. and gen. counsel, Sperry Univac, Blue Bell, Pa., 1971—; mem. com. office machines and computers Nat. Export Expansion Council, 1971-73; mem. Computer Systems Tech. Adv. Com. to Sec. Commerce, 1973-75; participant U.S. del. to UN Econ. Commn. for Europe Seminar, Geneva, Switzerland, 1975. Served as lt. (j.g.) USNR, 1953-55. Mem. Am., Fed. bar assns., Computer Bus. Equipment Mfrs. Assn. (chmn. fgn. trade com. 1972-74, chmn. plans and policies com. 1976-77). Roman Catholic. Home: 1764 Rock Hill Ln Valley Forge PA 19481 Office: Sperry Univac PO Box 500 Blue Bell PA 19422

KLANCKO, ROBERT JOHN, chem. engr.; b. Derby, Conn., Sept. 8, 1945; s. John Joseph and Eunice (Karlak) K.; B.S. in Engring., U. Conn., 1967; postgrad. U. New Haven, 1967, So. Conn. State Coll., 1968-72; m. Yvonne Shia, July 11, 1970; children—William, Daria, Gregory. Research chemist water pollution Anaconda Co., Brass Div., Waterbury, Conn., 1967-68, research chemist electrochemistry, 1968-69, mill metallurgist in casting, 1969-70, chmn. engr. Engineered Environment Div., 1970-73, mgr. engineered environments, 1973-77; mgr. engring. CEA Combustion, Stamford, Conn., 1977-78; pres. Klancko & Klancko, Cons., Woodbridge, Conn., 1978—; lectr. spl. programs facility Hartford Grad. Center, 1972-77. Adv. com. sci. dept. Mattatuck Community Coll., Waterbury, 1972-76; mem. adv. com. chem. tech. dept. Waterbury State Tech., 1972-78; tech. advisor Waterbury Environ. Control Com., 1973-75; mem. energy/environ. com. Conn. Bus. and Industry Assn., 1974-75; mem. Congress of Russian Ams., Tolstoy Found. Registered profl. engr., Calif., Conn., Ill., Ind., Idaho, Ky., Mass., Mich., N.Y., N.J., Ohio, Pa., R.I., Wis. Mem. Am. Inst. Chem. Engrs., Am. Inst. Chemists, Am. Soc. Metals, Am. Soc. Safety Engrs., Am. Safety Mgmt. Assn., Wire Assn. Eastern Orthodox. Club: Masons. Contbr. articles in field to profl. jours.; contbg. editor Industry-Jour. of Safety Mgmt., 1975-77; Co-author: Occupational Safety and Health, EPA, Manual for Metal Treating, 1972. Address: 59 Mill St Waterbury CT 06720

KLARFELD, JOSEPH, physicist, educator; b. Poland, Dec. 22, 1935; s. Arie and Jaffa (Strasburg) K.; B.Sc., Technion-Israel Inst. Tech., 1959, M.Sc., 1962; Ph.D. (fellow), Yeshiva U., 1969. Isntr. physics Technion-Israel Inst. Tech., Haifa, 1958-61; research asso. Soreq Nuclear Research Center AEC, Yavne, Israel, 1961-63; asst. prof. physics Queens Coll., City U.N.Y., 1969-73, asst. chmn. dept. physics, 1969-76, dep. chmn., 1976—, asso. prof., 1974—. Served with Armor Corps, Israeli Army, 1954-55. Mem. Internat. Soc. Gen. Relativity Gravitation, Am. Phys. Soc., N.Y. Acad. Scis., Assn. Math. Physics, Sigma Xi. Contbr. research articles in gen. relativity and quantum field theory to Phys. Jour. Office: Dept Physics Queens Coll Flushing NY 11367

KLASSEN, DONALD AUGUST, transp. co. exec., accountant; b. Weehawken, N.J., Oct. 31, 1934; s. August H. and Mary V. (Perkins) K.; B.A., Gettysburg Coll., 1956; postgrad. N.Y. U., 1960-61; m. Virginia A. Saxon, June 29, 1957; children—David, Carol, Nancy, Donna. Mgr., Lybrand, Ross Bros. & Montgomery, C.P.A.'s, N.Y.C., 1959-69; controller, treas. Perkins Trucking Co., Inc., Long Island City, N.Y., 1969-73; exec. v.p., chief operating officer Perkins System, Inc., Hicksville, N.Y., 1974—, dir. Served to lt. j.g., U.S. Navy, 1956-59. C.P.A., N.Y. Mem. Am. Inst. C.P.A.'s, N.Y. State Soc. C.P.A.'s, Tri-State Traffic Assn., Am. Trucking Assn. (dir. Short Haul Carrier Conf.), N.Y. State Motor Truck Assn. (dir., mem. exec. com.). Lutheran. Club: Huntington Crescent. Home: 29 Darby Dr Huntington Station NY 11746 Office: 250 Miller Pl Hicksville NY 11801

KLATSKIN, BERTRAM, oral surgeon; b. N.Y.C., Feb. 11, 1916; s. Archibald and Celia (Golubowski) K.; A.B., Cornell U., 1937; D.D.S., Columbia, 1941; m. Ruth Weiner, Nov. 20, 1941; children—Andrew, Lois (Mrs. David Kolstad), Beth. Intern in oral surgery Morrisania City Hosp., Bronx, N.Y., 1941-42; resident Sea View Hosp., S.I., N.Y., 1942-43; gen. practice dentistry, S.I., 1943-61; practice oral surgery, S.I., 1961—; mem. staff Sea View Hosp., 1943—, chief oral surgery, 1950—, dir. dental services, 1973—, also mem. exec. bd., v.p. exec. bd., 1976—; asso. attending oral surgeon S.I. Hosp., 1970-72, attending oral surgeon, 1972—, mem. exec. bd., 1974—, also mem. tumor bd.; asst. attending oral surgeon Columbia-Presbyn. Hosp., 1972-74, asso. attending oral surgeon, 1974—; oral surgery staff Columbia U. Dental Sch., 1943—; clin. prof. oral surgery Columbia, 1976—; lectr. community and profl. groups; malpractice cons. N.Y. State Supreme Ct.; dental cons. nursing homes. Mem. Sea View Community Adv. Bd.; mem. exec. bd. S.I. unit Am. Cancer Soc., vice chmn., 1974-76; mem. advisory bd. dentistry N.Y.C. Health and Hosp Corp. Served as maj. Dental Corps, AUS, 1953-55. Recipient Community Leader of Am. award, 1969; honor S.I. unit Am. Cancer Soc., 1978. Diplomate N.Y. State Bd. Oral Surgery. Fellow Am. Coll. Dentists, Internat. Assn. Oral Surgeons, Royal Soc. Health; mem. Am., N.Y. State, Second Dist. (trustee 1964), Richmond County (pres. 1963) dental socs., N.Y. State Soc. Oral Surgeons, Am. Dental Soc. Anesthesiology, Met. Conf. Hosp. Dental Chiefs, Am. Assn. Hosp. Dentists, Am. Assn. Oral and Maxillofacial Surgeons, Clin. Soc. Sea View Hosp. (pres. 1975—), Cornell Club, Columbia Dental Alumni Assn., Omicron Kappa Upsilon, Alpha Omega (pres. 1968-70). Mason. Contbr. articles to profl. jours. Home: 202 Merrill Ave Staten Island NY 10314 Office: 25 Victory Blvd Staten Island NY 10301

KLAUBER, GEORGE THOMAS, pediatric urologist; b. Subotica, Yugoslavia, Jan. 1, 1939; s. Walter and Eva Elizabeth (Strass) K.; came to U.S., 1971; M.B., B.S., Guy's Hosp. Med. Sch., U. London, 1964; children—Adam Ferrier, Blake Elizabeth, Rachel Amber. Resident, St. James Hosp. and Hosp. Sick Children, London, 1965-66; resident in urology, also transplantation fellow McGill U., Montreal, Que., Can., 1967-71; practice medicine specializing in pediatric urology, Newington and Farmington, Conn., 1972—; dir. pediatric urology, asst. prof. surgery (urology) U. Conn., Farmington, 1971-78, asso. prof., 1978—, asst. prof. pediatrics, 1974—; dir. urology Newington Childrens Hosp. 1972—. Diplomate Am. Bd. Urology. Fellow Royal Coll. Surgeons Can., Am. Acad. Pediatrics, Am. Coll. Surgeons; mem. Soc. Pediatrics Urology, Brit. Assn. Urol. Surgeons. Contbr. papers in pediatric urology to urol. jours. Home: 271 Ciderbrook St Avon CT 06001 Office: 181 E Cedar St Newington CT 06111

KLAUS, GEORGE LEONARD, corporate exec.; b. Chgo., Aug. 17, 1924; s. George Michael and Marie (Schaaf) K.; B.S. with honors, U. Ill., 1949; m. Joan Ruthy, June 6, 1949; children—Cynthia, Susan, Jill. Staff accountant W.H. Stout, 1949-50; accountant Darling & Co., 1950-52; sr. auditor Arthur Andersen & Co., Chgo., 1952-58; corporate budget mgr. Brunswick Corp., Chgo., 1958-63, dir. internal auditing, 1963-68; audit mgr. Internat. Telephone & Telegraph Co., N.Y.C., 1968-72, dir. spl. projects, 1972—. Village treas. Glen Ellyn, Ill., 1959-62; mem. police pension bd., Glen Ellyn, 1959-62. Served to 1st lt. USAAF, 1942-45. Decorated Air Medal. C.P.A., Ill.; certified internal auditor. Mem. Am. Inst. C.P.A.'s, Budget Execs. Inst., Inst. Internal Auditors, Schwaben-Verein, Assn. 4th Fighter Group USAAF-World War II, Beta Alpha Psi, Chi Gamma Iota (nat. pres. 1949). Presbyn. (deacon). Home: 33 Glenwood Rd Weston CT 06883 Office: ITT 320 Park Ave New York NY 10022

KLAVAN, ISRAEL, clergyman; b. Zaskevitch, Lithuania, June 9, 1915; s. Joshua and Fannie (Sheifer) K.; came to U.S., 1924, naturalized, 1927; B.A., Yeshiva Coll., 1937; rabbi, Rabbi Isaac Elchanan Theol. Sem., 1940; student Bernard Revel Grad. Sch., Yeshiva U., 1938-40; D.D. (honoris causa), Yeshiva U., 1970; m. Sadie Rabinowitz, Feb. 22, 1942; children—Avram Macy, Judith Rachelle. Ordained rabbi, 1940; rabbi in Fitchburg, Mass., 1940-42, Williamsport, Pa., 1942-46, Mt. Vernon, N.Y., 1946-53; exec. v.p. Rabbinical council Am., 1953—. Mem. commn. Jewish chaplaincy Nat. Jewish Welfare Bd. Recipient Bernard Revel Meml. award Yeshiva Coll. Alumni Assn., 1963; award Fedn. Jewish Philanthropies, 1967, Ann. Tzdakah award, 1974; Mordecai Ben David award Yeshiva U., 1974. Home: 108 22 64th Rd Forest Hills NY 11375 Office: 1250 Broadway New York City NY 10001

KLEE, GERALD D'ARCY, psychiatrist; b. N.Y.C., Jan. 29, 1927; s. Bertel Bernard and Eleanor (D'Arcy) K.; student Princeton U., 1944-45, McGill U., Montreal, Que., Can., 1947-48; M.D., Harvard U., 1952; m. 1950; children—Brian, Kenneth, Sheila, Susan, Louise. Intern, USPHS Hosp., N.Y.C., 1952-53, Springfield, Mo., 1953-54; resident VA Hosp., Perry Point, Md., U. Md. Hosp. and Johns Hopkins Hosp., 1954-56; asso. prof. psychiatry U. Md., 1956-67; prof. Temple U., 1967-70; practice medicine specializing in psychiatry, Balt., 1970—, Towson, Md., 1978—; lectr. Johns Hopkins U.; mem. staff Johns Hopkins, Sheppard and Enoch Pratt, Sinai and Balt. County Gen. hosps. Served with U.S. Army, 1944-46, USPHS, 1952-54. Fellow Am. Psychiat. Assn.; mem. Md. Psychiat. Soc. (pres. 1962-63). Contbr. numerous articles to med. publs. Home: 42 Theo Ln Towson MD 21204 Office: 28 Allegheny Ave Towson MD 21204

KLEEMAN, ROBERT HERBERT, dentist; b. Bklyn., Feb 4, 1931; s. Louis and Rae (Schwartz) K.; grad. Pennington Sch., 1949; B.S., L.I. U., 1952; D.D.S., Loyola U., 1956; postgrad. in oral surgery N.Y. U., 1956-57; m. Roselyn Marmolejo, Nov. 26, 1975; 1 son, Robert Joseph. Intern oral surgery Queens Gen. Hosp. Center, 1957-58, attending dentist, 1958-63; practice dentistry specializing in oral surgery, Riverdale, N.Y., 1959—; attending dentist St. Agatha Home for Children, 1958-62; guest lectr. spl. radiation procedure course Queens Gen. Hosp. Center, 1958-62. Corp. exec. Beta Internat., Inc., Interglobal Investment Ltd. Fellow Am. Endodontic Soc.; mem. ADA, Am. Dental Soc. Anesthesiology, Internat. Acad. Orthodontics, Am. Soc. Dentistry for Children, Am. Sch. Health Assn., Royal Soc. Health, Am. Orthodontic Soc., Am. Philatelic Soc., New Rochelle Art Assn. Exhibited XIII Internat. Dental Congress in Cologne, Germany, 1962, Art Exhibit Bronxville Theater, 1963, Art Exhibit YM-YWHA of Mid-Westchester, 1978. Office: 6645 Broadway Riverdale NY 10471

KLEIMAN, HOWARD, educator; b. N.Y.C., Apr. 15, 1929; s. Louis and Mollie (Blefeld) K.; B.A., N.Y. U., 1950, M.S., 1961; M.A., Columbia, 1954; Ph.D., Kings Coll., U. London, 1969; m. Edna Madge Benjamin, July 26, 1956; children—Michele, Jeffrey, Daniel. Tchr. pub. schs. N.Y.C., 1955-65; asst. prof. Queensborough Community Coll., City U. N.Y., 1967-70; asso. prof. math., 1970-78, prof., 1978—. Part-time lectr. math. S.I. Community Coll., 1960-63, Hunter Coll., 1963-69; adj. asso. prof. Queens Coll City U. N.Y., 1970—. David Diamond scholar music, 1951; Ernst Toch scholar, 1954; Berkshire Music Center scholar, Tanglewood, summer 1954. Mem. Math. Assn. Am. (mem. math. fair com. Met. N.Y. sect. 1969, vice chmn. for 2-yr. colls. 1971-73, treas. sect. 1973—, dir. speaker's bur. 1974—, mem. adv. panel com. on high sch. contests 1977—), London Math. Soc. Author: (with E. Just) A Sourcebook of Fundamental Mathematics, part II, 1971. Contbr. articles to profl. jours. Home: 188-83 85th Rd Holliswood NY 11423 Office: Math Dept Queensborough Community College Bayside NY 11364

KLEIN, ALEXANDER, pub. relations exec., author, film producer; b. Hungary, Nov. 12, 1923; s. Anton and Rose (Judowitch) K.; brought to U.S., 1924, naturalized, 1929; B.S., Coll. City N.Y., 1942; m. Virginia Copeland, July 23, 1947 (div. 1959); m. 2d, Janis S. Hadad, Mar. 1, 1977. Speech writer United Jewish Appeal, N.Y.C., 1941-42, sr. pub. relations asso., 1947-50, 57-60; writer, producer Documentary Edn. Films, Caravel Films, N.Y.C., 1942-47, 1956-58, Caravel-Transfilm Films, 1963-66; free-lance writer books, articles, also films, 1947—; v.p., account exec., dir. pub. relations and TV J.D. Tarcher Advt. Agy., N.Y.C., 1950-54; sr. asso. Personnel Inst., N.Y.C., 1954-57; v.p. Roy Blumenthal Assn., N.Y.C., 1966-70. Dir. pub. relations CARE, 1972—; cons. to film cos., advt. agys., 1947—; founder with Norman Thomas ann. Arden House convocations on fgn. policy, 1957—; tchr. creative writing City Coll. N.Y., 1950-53; adj. prof. history, polit. sci., sociology Fordham U., N.Y.C., 1970—; spl. counsel Senator Abraham Ribicoff of Conn., 1962, 68, 72; adviser to John Gardner on formation and devel. of Common Cause, 1969-72; cons. Nat. Coalition Responsible Congress, 1970, Theatre for Ideas, 1967—. Recipient Golden Reel award for film on Boys Clubs Am., 1957; Variety mag. award, 1957; Israeli Govt. prize for best theatrical film script Shalom, Baby, 1973. Author: Armies for Peace, 1950; Courage is the Key, 1953; The Empire City, 1955; Grand Deception, 1955; Counterfeit Traitor, 1958 (movie 1962); The Double Dealers, 1959; The Fabulous Rogues, 1960; The Magnificent Scoundrels, 1961; Rebels, Rogues, Rascals, 1962; That Pellet Woman, 1965; Natural Enemies, 1970; Dissent, Power and Confrontation, 1972; (screenplay) Daisyfresh, 1976. Contbr. short stories to Best Am. Short Stories, 1947, 49, 52, 62. Contbr. articles, stories, revs. to numerous nat. mags., anthologies and textbooks. Author numerous documentary, pub. relations and ednl. films. Home: 75 Bank St New York City NY 10014

KLEIN, BERNARD, publisher, author; b. N.Y.C., Sept. 20, 1921; s. Joseph J. and Anna (Wolfe) K.; B.A., Coll. City N.Y., 1942; m. Betty Stecher, Feb. 17, 1946; children—Cheryl Rona, Barry Todd, Cindy Ann. Founder, pres. U.S. List Co., N.Y.C., 1946—; founder, pres., chief editor B. Klein Publs. Rye, N.Y., Coral Springs, Fla., 1953—. Cons. on direct mail advt. and reference book pub. to pubs. and industry, 1950—. Served with AUS, 1942-45; ETO. Mem. Direct Mail Advt. Assn. Mason. Author: Guide to American Directories, Guide to American Educational Directories, Mail Order Business Directory, Directory of College Media, Reference Encyclopedia of the American Indian, all pub. biennially, 1954—. Home: 10 Rapids Rd Stamford CT 06905 Office: PO Box 535 Rye NY 10580

KLEIN, CLAUDE ALOIS, physicist; b. Strasbourg, France, Nov. 4, 1925; s. Louis Claude and Elisabeth (Diebold) K.; came to U.S., 1957, naturalized, 1964; B.Sc., U. Strasbourg, 1949; E.E., U. Paris, 1951; Ph.D., Sorbonne, 1955; m. Genevieve Steinmetz, Jan. 2, 1950; 1 dau., Carine R., Prin. research scientist Raytheon Co., Waltham, Mass., 1957—. Served with German Navy, 1943-45. Fellow Am. Phys. Soc.; mem. IEEE, U.S. Naval Inst. Contbr. 85 articles to profl. jours. Home: 9 Churchill Ln Lexington MA 02173

KLEIN, EDWIN, hosp. engr.; b. Detroit, Nov. 21, 1923; s. Louis and Esther (Liebowitz) K.; B.C.E., City Coll., N.Y., 1944; m. Sandra Blumenthal Bernstein, Sept. 7, 1974; children—Roberta, Scott, Rebecca Bernstein, Elizabeth Bernstein, Andrea Bernstein. Engr., Triborough Bridge and Tunnel Authority, 1946, 47, Poirier & McLane Corp., N.Y.C., 1948-58; sr. project mgr. Am. Airlines, N.Y.C., 1967-73; engr. Mt. Sinai Hosp., N.Y.C., 1974—; cons. Goodyear Tire & Rubber Co., others, 1958—. Pres. Oakfield Gables Civic Assn., 1962-72. Served with C.E., U.S. Army, 1944-46. Registered profl. engr. N.Y.; certified fall out shelter analyst U.S. Dept. Def. Mem. Am., N.Y. State socs. hosp. engring., Hosp. Engring. Soc. Greater N.Y. (corr. sec.), Adolph Ullman Aid Soc. Democrat. Jewish. Home: 2762 Ellen Rd Bellmore NY 11710 Office: 1 Gustave L Levy Pl New York City NY 10029

KLEIN, ESTHER (MRS. PHILIP KLEIN), author; b. Phila., Nov. 3, 1907; d. Louis and Rebecca (Feldman) Moyerman; B.S., Temple U., 1929; student U. London, 1954; m. Philip Klein, Apr. 26, 1930; children—Arthur, Karen Louise (Mrs. Paul Mannes). Reporter, Phila. Jewish Times, 1925, Atlantic City Times, 1927; feature writer Pub. Ledger Syndicate, 1928-29, Pub. Ledger, Evening Bull. Phila. Record, 1929-32; pub. relations counsellor, editor Art Alliance Bull. 1945-49; radio commentator WPEN, 1949-53; pub. Phila. Jewish Times, 1953-73; lectr. Women's Clubs, 1951—. Del. Internat. Conf. of Residential Adult Edn., Holland, 1957, Germany, 1959; participant in first workshop of Residential Adult Edn. for Adult Edn. Assn. of U.S., 1954. Chmn. Rittenhouse Sq. Women's com. for Phila. Orch., 1957; bd. dirs. Rittenhouse Found.; pres. Phila. Jewish Times Inst.; mem. exec. com. Long Beach Island Found. for Arts and Scis., N.J., 50th Anniversary Phila. Art Alliance. Recipient Gimbel award, 1975. Mem. Pa. Newspaper Pubs. Assn., Temple U. Alumni (honored at 80th Anniversary 1964), Phila. High Sch. for Girls Alumnae, Hannah Penn House, Emergency Aid of Pa., Chgo. Art Mus., Mus. Modern Art N.Y., Pan Am. Assn. Club: Print. Author: A Guidebook to Jewish Philadelphia, International House Celebrity Cookbook, Fairmount Park, History and Guidebook, 1975; Women Composers and Conductors in the American Scene, 1977. Home: 1520 Spruce St Philadelphia PA 19102

KLEIN, JOEL TIBOR, clergyman, psychotherapist; b. Megyaszo, Hungary, Jan. 1, 1923; s. Jeno and Serena (Reich) K.; Ph.D., U. Sci., Budapest, Hungary, 1947; ordained Theol. Sem. Hungary, 1949; m. Anna Berkovits, June 17, 1949; children—Leslie M., Judith Klein Golden. Came to U.S., 1957, naturalized, 1963. Rabbi, 1948; chief rabbi Central South Region, Baja, Hungary, 1948-51, North Western Hungary, Győr, 1951-56; asst. rabbi Beth El, Springfield, Mass., 1957-59; rabbi Temple Meyer David, Claremont, N.H., 1959-62, Congregation Am Echod, Waukegan, Ill., 1962-64, Temple Israel, Manchester, N.H., 1964-77; psychotherapist, clin. marriage, sex and pastoral counselor. Adviser, Parents without Partners, Manchester, 1964-75; co-founder Manchester Smile Center, 1968; mem. Task Force Gov.'s Com. on Aging, Concord, N.H., 1966-68; chmn. Citizens Adv. Com. to N.H. Services for Blind, 1974-76. Mem. Rabbinical Assembly, N.Y., Mass. (treas. 1972-74, v.p. 1974—), Chgo. bds. rabbis, N.H. Psychol. Assn., Am. Assn. Sex Educators, Counselors and Therapists, Nat. Alliance for Family Life, Am. Assn. Marriage and Family Counselors. Club: Elks. Home: 721 Chestnut St Manchester NH 03104

KLEIN, MARTIN IRA, lawyer; b. N.Y.C., Nov. 12, 1947; s. Lawrence Elliot and Bernice (Lefcourt) K.; B.A., Lehigh U., 1969; J.D., Am. U., 1972; m. Diane Rebecca Levbarg, May 23, 1974. Mem. profl. staff U.S. Senate Com. on Labor and Pub. Welfare, Office of Senator Jacob Javits, Washington, 1969-72; admitted to N.Y. bar, 1973, Fla. bar, 1978; asso. firm Levin & Weintraub, N.Y.C., 1973-75, Rosenman, Colin, Freund, Lewis & Cohen, N.Y.C., 1975-78, Kramer, Lowenstein, Nessen, Kamin & Soll, 1978—; adj. prof. law Cardozo Law Sch., Yeshiva U., N.Y.C. Bd. dirs. law com. Jewish Guild for the Blind. Apptd. del. White House Conf. on Youth, 1971. Mem. Am., N.Y. State (com. on corps. and bankruptcy), Fla. bar assns., Assn. Bar City N.Y. (com. on state legislation). Republican. Clubs: Harmonie (N.Y.C.); Fenway Golf. Contbr. articles legal jours. Home: 225 E 57th St New York City NY 10022 Office: 919 3d Ave New York City NY 10022

KLEIN, MARTIN JOHN HERMAN, electronic engr.; b. Phila., Feb. 26, 1937; s. Martin and Emma (Jans) K.; A.S., Spring Garden Inst., 1959; diploma Gen. Elec. Co. Electronics Components Center, 1961, Radio-TV Tng. of Am., 1962, Gen. Elec. Co. Valley Forge Space Tech. Center, Phila., 1963, 64, RCA Inst., Inc., 1963, Cleve. Inst. Electronics, 1965; student Computer Ednl. Inst., 1969-70. Electronic technician Spring Garden Inst., Phila., 1956-59; radio frequency technician ITE Circuit Breaker Co., Phila., 1959-60; elecronic technician Comprehensive Designers, Inc., Phila., 1960-62; instrumentation technician Gen. Elec. Co., King of Prussia, Pa., 1962-63, systems test technician Valley Forge Space Tech. Center, Phila., 1963-64, electronic specialist vehicle calibration Re-Entry Systems Dept., 1964-70; employment counselor Snelling & Snelling, Inc., Phila., 1970; lectr., cons. audio/elec/electronic engring.,

1970-73; electronic engr. Andresen Indsl. Instruments Inc., Phila., 1973—. Dep. constable Abington Twp., 1968-74. Mem. IEEE, Am. Soc. Certified Engring. Technicians, U.S. Olympic Soc., Internat. Brotherhood of Magicians. Republican. Profl. magician appearing as Martinus the Great. Home: 1247 June Rd Huntingdon Valley PA 19006 Office: 926 Fox Chase Rd Rockledge Philadelphia PA 19111

KLEIN, MARY SOLOMON, librarian; b. New Brunswick, N.J., Nov. 15, 1916; d. Harry W. and Anna (Ginden) S.; B.Sc., N.J. Coll. for Women, 1937; m. Rudolph Klein, Apr. 7, 1949. Tchr., Freehold (N.J.) High Sch., 1938-40; analytical chemist Nat. Grain Yeast, Bloomfield, N.J., 1940-42: librarian Squibb Inst. Med. Research, New Brunswick, 1942—; v.p. MEDCORE, 1978-79. Research and devel. chmn. United Way, 1972-78. Mem. Spl. Libraries Assn. (pres. Pharm. div. 1977), Med. Library Assn., Bklyn. Bot. Garden. Clubs: Squibb Quarter Century (pres. 1975-77), Raritan Yacht, Ft. Monmouth Officers. Home: 49 Patton Dr East Brunswick NJ 08816 Office: PO Box 191 New Brunswick NJ 08903

KLEIN, MELVIN JOEL, physician; b. N.Y.C., June 21, 1936; s. Julius and Regina K.; B.A., N.Y. U., 1956; M.D. cum laude, State U. N.Y., Syracuse, 1960; m. Luise Michaelson, Nov. 20, 1960; children—Stephen, Richard, Nancy. Intern, resident in medicine Beth Israel Hosp., Boston, 1960-62; resident in cardiology Mt. Sinai Hosp., N.Y.C., 1962-63; resident in medicine Kings County Hosp., Bklyn., 1963-64; practice medicine specializing in internal medicine, Manhasset, N.Y., 1966—; chief internal medicine Manhasset Med. Center Hosp. Served as capt. U.S. Army, 1964-66. Diplomate Am. Bd. Internal Medicine. Fellow Am. Coll. Chest Physicians; mem. AMA, A.C.P., Alpha Omega Alpha. Republican. Jewish. Club: Shelter Rock Tennis. Home: 58 Monterey Dr Manhasset Hills NY 11040 Office: 1554 Northern Blvd Manhasset NY 11030

KLEIN, MICHAEL DAVID, editor, illustrator; b. Pittsfield, Mass., Apr. 17, 1942; s. Edward John and Ada Sarah (Jaffe) K.; student U. Mass., 1959-61; B.F.A., Paier Sch. Art, 1964; m. Carol Ann Moote, Oct. 11, 1972. With United Aircraft Co., East Hartford, Conn., 1964; dir. Eco-Arts, New Milford, Conn., 1964-74; pub. relations mgr., editor, illustrator The Automobiler, Am. Automobile Assn., West Hartford, Conn., 1974—; instr. art Karafin Ednl. Center, Mt. Kisco, N.Y., 1964-72. Recipient Mass. Med. award for bacteriological illustration, 1959, Boston Graphics Art award, 1962, Conn. Artist of Year award So. Conn. State Coll., 1963, Darien Arts Festival award, 1964. Mem. Outdoor Photog. Soc., Advt. Club Conn., Audubon Soc., Nat. Wildlife Fedn., North Shore Animal League. Home: 949 Plesant Valley Rd South Windsor CT 06074 Office: 815 Farmington Ave West Hartford CT 06119

KLEIN, PETER MARTIN, lawyer, transp. co. exec.; b. N.Y.C., June 2, 1934; s. Saul and Esther (Goldstein) K.; A.B., Columbia U., 1956, J.D., 1962; m. Ellen Judith Matlick, June 18, 1961; children—Amy Lynn, Steven Ezra. Admitted to D.C. bar, 1964, N.Y. State bar, 1962, U.S. Supreme Ct. bar, 1966; asst. counsel mil. sea transp. service Office Gen. Counsel Dept. Navy, Washington, 1962-65; trial atty. civil div. Dept. Justice, N.Y.C., 1966-69; gen. atty. Sea-Land Service Inc., Menlo Park, N.J., 1969-76, v.p. law, gen. counsel, sec., 1976—, dir., 1976—; mem. advisory com. on pvt. and internat. law State Dept., 1974—; mem. U.S. dels. UNCTAD and UNCITRAL treaty sessions, 1975-76. Trustee, v.p. Temple B'nai Abraham of Essex County (N.J.), 1976—. Served as officer with USN, 1956-59. Mem. Am. Polar Soc., Am., Fed., N.Y. State bar assns., Maritime Law Assn. U.S., Am. Maritime (dir. 1974—, chmn. com. on law and legislation 1974—), D.C. Bar. Home: 42 Billingsley Dr Livingston NJ 07039 Office: Sea Land Service Inc PO Box 900 Edison NJ 08817

KLEIN, PHILIP, educator; b. Phila., Dec. 20, 1906; s. Sigmund and Rosa (Jacoby) K.; student U. Pa., 1924-28, U. London, 1954; Mus. D. (hon.), Coombs Coll. Music, 1961; L.H.D. (hon.), Moore College of Art, 1962, Hahnemann Coll., 1975; m. Esther Moyerman, Apr. 26, 1930; children—Arthur, Karen. Reporter, Phila. Inquirer, 1924-26; pres. Philip Klein Advt. Inc. 1930-49; pub. Phila. Jewish Times, 1946-56; pres. Harcum Jr. Coll., 1952-62, now chmn. bd. trustees; pres. The Junto, 1954—, Phila. Marina, 1959—; treas. Sta. WHYY, 1952—. Vice chmn. Phila. City Planning Commn. 1958-62; pres. U.S. CD Council, 1959-60, Phila. All Star Forum; commr. Dept. Pub. Property, Phila., 1961-62; chmn. Pathway Sch., 1968-71; pres. Walnut Street Theatre, 1967-74; del. U.S. Commn. to UNESCO, 1955; hon. chmn. Long Beach Island Found. Arts and Scis.; mem. adv. com. World Affairs Council; bd. dirs. Phila. Orch., Phila. Opera Co., Pa. Coll. Podiatric Medicine, S.E. Pa. chpt. Am. Heart Assn., Casa Fermi House, Big Bros. Am.; v.p. Buten Mus. of Wedgewood, 1957—; chmn. exec. com. United Seamen's Service. Served as staff officer U.S. Mcht. Marine, 1942-46. Decorated Officer Order So. Cross (Brazil). Benjamin Franklin fellow Royal Soc. Arts. Fellow Internat. Gerontol. Soc.; mem. Adult Edn. Assn. U.S. (pres. 1958-59); mem. Hist. Soc. Pa. (dir.), Pan Am. Soc. (dir.), also numerous other orgns. Club: Masons. Home: 1520 Spruce St Philadelphia PA 19102 Office: 1601 Walnut St Philadelphia PA 19103

KLEIN, RICHARD BARRY, educator, assn. exec.; b. Chgo., Nov. 20, 1938; s. Alfred Arnold and Lucylle Vivian (Nuss) K.; B.A., Elmhurst Coll., 1960; M.A., U. Ill., 1962, Ph.D., 1970; m. Carol Ann Ebersol, Aug. 27, 1966; children—Garrett Christian, Lauren Monika. Instr. in Romance langs. DePauw U., Greencastle, Ind., 1962-67; instr. Spanish, U. Ill., Champaign, 1968-69; asst. prof. modern langs. Holy Cross Coll., Worcester, Mass., 1969-72, asso. prof., 1972—; named rep. Spanish govt. for U.S. Bicentennial Celebration, 1976. Decorated caballero de la Orden del Mérito Civil (Spain); Batchelor Found. fellow, 1970. Mem. Am. Assn. Tchrs. Spanish and Portuguese (exec. sec. 1975—), Am. Council Teaching Fgn. Langs., Modern Lang. Assn., Nat. Com. for Langs. (chmn. 1979—), AAUP, Luth. Soc. Worship, Music and the Arts, Sociedad Honoraria Hispánica (sec.-treas. 1963-74), Sigma Delta Pi. Contbr. articles to profl. jours. Home: 121 Newton Ave N Worcester MA 01609 Office: Holy Cross Coll Worcester MA 01610

KLEIN, RICHARD HAROLD, educator; b. N.Y.C., Apr. 18, 1940; s. Theodore and Daisy Anna (Hallar) K.; B.A., City Coll., N.Y., 1960; M.B.A., Dartmouth, 1962; Ph.D., U. Tex., 1969. Asso. prof. fin. Temple U., Phila., 1968—; fin. economist U.S. Small Bus. Adminstrn., Washington, 1973-75; fin. analyst Nat. Progress Movement, Phila., 1969-70; faculty adviser Entrepreneurial Assistance Service, Phila., 1970-76. Mem. Phila. regional bd. Anti-Defamation League, 1977—. Served with U.S. Army, 1962-65. Am. Assembly Collegiate Schs. Bus. Sears Roebuck Found. fed. faculty fellow, 1973. Mem. Am. Econ. Assn., Am. Fin. Assn., Fin. Mgmt. Assn. Jewish. Contbr. articles to profl. jours. Home: 2200 Benjamin Franklin Pkwy Apt E 1103 Philadelphia PA 19130 Office: Dept Finance Sch Bus Adminstrn Temple U Philadelphia PA 19122

KLEIN, RICHARD JOSEPH, microbiologist, educator; b. Lugoj, Romania, June 11, 1926; s. Alfred Samuel and Zelma (Neumann) K.; came to U.S., 1972, naturalized, 1977; M.D., Bucharest Inst. Medicine, 1951, D.Sc., 1967; m. Elena Maciuca, Oct. 3, 1962; 1 son, Dorian. Instr. microbiology Inst. Medicine, Bucharest, Romania, 1949-52; sr. research scientist Cantacuzino Inst., Bucharest, 1951-72; asso. prof. microbiology research Sch. Medicine and Coll. Dentistry, N.Y. U., 1972—. Mem. N.Y. Acad. Sci., Am. Soc. Microbiology. Contbr. articles to profl. jours. Home: 27 Nob Ct New Rochelle NY 10804 Office: NY U Med Center Dept Microbiology 550 1st Ave New York City NY 10016

KLEIN, RICHARD STEPHEN, internist; b. N.Y.C., Nov. 20, 1938; s. Sydney G. and Rosalind (Paul) K.; B.S., Queens Coll., 1962; M.D., N.Y. Med. Coll., 1967; m. Susan Lois Teller, Dec. 29, 1963; children—Brian Seth, Elyse Lynn. Intern, N.Y. Med. Coll., 1967-68, resident, 1968-69; resident Montefiore Hosp., Bronx, 1969-70, clin. fellow infectious diseases, also Einstein Hosp., 1970-71; practice medicine specializing in internal medicine, Yorktown, N.Y., 1970—; chief infectious disease clinic N.Y. Med. Coll., 1971-72, clin. asso. prof. medicine, attending physician, 1971—; chief infectious disease dept. Fordham & Misericordia Hosp., Bronx, 1971-72; attending physician, cons. in infectious diseases No. Westchester Hosp. Center, Mt. Kisco, N.Y., 1971—, chmn. infection control com., 1973—; med. bd. dir. Tech. Exchange Corp., N.J., 1971—; cons. Peekskill Community Hosp., 1974—; faculty medicine and surgery U. Rome (Italy), 1962-65. Bd. dirs. Yorktown High Sch. Scholarship Found., 1973—, United Jewish Appeal of Greater N.Y. Area; trustee Yorktown Jewish Center, 1973—; campaign chmn. United Jewish Appeal, Yorktown and Mt. Kisco, 1974—, co-chmn. No. Westchester div., chmn. Westchester fedn., 1977—. Served with USNR, 1957-59. A.C.P. scholar, 1969-70, 70-71; recipient E. Spiegle award for distinction in allergy, 1967. Mem. Am. Soc. Microbiology, Am. Physicians Fellowship, Med. Soc. N.Y., Med. Soc. Westchester County (N.Y.), Flying Physicians Assn. Am. Clubs: Men's (Yorktown); Shorin-Ryu Karate Do-Philapine Karate Assn. Contbr. articles to profl. jours. Home: 46 Annandale Dr Chappaqua NY 10514 Office: 1940 Commerce St Yorktown Heights NY 10598

KLEIN, SEYMOUR, stock broker; b. Bklyn., Nov. 23, 1925; s. Nathan and Zina (Saslofsky) K.; B.B.A., Coll. City N.Y., 1950, M.B.A., 1957; postgrad. Columbia, 1954; diploma Biarritz Am. U., 1946; m. Libby Sebold, Mar. 24, 1951; children—Cheryl, Risa, Neil. Vice pres., stock broker Advest Inc., N.Y.C., 1949—; instr. finance and investments City U. N.Y., 1957—. Served with AUS, 1943-46; ETO. Mem. Met. Econ. Assn., Am. Statis. Assn. K.P. Contbr. to profl. jours. Home: 111 Howard Ave Tappan NY 10983 Office: 666 Fifth Ave New York City NY 10019

KLEIN, SOLOMON ALEXANDER, physician; b. N.Y.C., Jan. 16, 1908; Henry and Esther (Schwartz) K.; B.S., Coll. City N.Y., 1929; M.B., Ch.B., U. St. Andrews (Scotland), 1933; m. Norma Cohen, Sept. 4, 1929 (dec.); 1 dau., Elizabeth. Intern, Trinity Hosp., Bklyn., 1933-34; dermatologist VA Hosp., Newark, 1958—, chief psychiatry, 1976—. Diplomate Am. Bd. Dermatology. Mem. Med. Soc. N.J., AMA. Home: 152 W 58th St New York City NY 10019 Office: VA Hosp 20 Washington Pl Newark NJ 07102

KLEIN, STANLEY, Educator; b. Bklyn., Nov. 7, 1930; s. Joseph and Jennie (Rosen) K.; B.S., N.Y.U., 1952, postgrad., 1958-60; M.S., So. Conn. State Coll., 1957; profl. certificate U. Conn., 1962, postgrad. 1964; m. Leila Dibner, June 29, 1952; children—Nancy, Jamie Ann. Elementary and secondary sch. tchr., 1955-58; instr. So. Conn. State Coll., 1958-60; editor Am. Edn. Publs., Middletown, Conn., 1960-64; sr. editor Holt, Rinehart and Winston, Inc., N.Y.C., 1964-69; dir. research projects and corporate planning Gen. Learning Corp., N.Y.C., 1969-71; asso. prof. edn. Western Conn. State Coll., Danbury, 1971—; pres. Stanley Klein Assos., Inc., Stamford, Conn., 1971—; vis. lectr. U. Conn.; officer Update Pub. Corp.; cons. in field. Mem. Nat., Conn. edn. assns., AAUP, Phi Delta Kappa. Club: North Stamford Exchange (dir.). Author: A World in a Tree, 1969; A World of Differences, 1971; (juvenile) The Final Mystery (named an outstanding sci. book Am. Book Council-Am. Assn. Sci. Tchrs.), 1974; also articles. Editor: Science Update, 1977; Science Update, 1978; Home: 42 Fawn Dr Stamford CT 06905 Office: 181 White St Danbury CT 06810

KLEIN, THEODORE ULMER, pub. relations and mktg. co. exec.; b. Cleve., Dec. 15, 1926; s. Joseph Emry and Martha (Ulmer) K.; B.S., Western Res. U., 1947; M.A., Goddard Coll., 1975; m. Carole Honig, Aug. 4, 1956; children—William, Emily. Pres., Comtact Corp., N.Y.C., 1965-69; v.p. Paul Klemtner & Co., N.Y.C., 1954-69; pres. Ted Klein & Co., N.Y.C., 1969—, also Med. Mktg. Distaff, Inc., N.Y.C. Pres. West Orange (N.J.) Council for Social Action, 1965-70; leader Cub Scouts Am., West Orange, 1965-66; bd. dirs. Child Guidance and Family Service Agy., Orange, N.J., 1969-74. Mem. Nat. Assn. Sci. Writers, N.Y. Acad. Sci., AAAS, Am. Med. Writers Assn., N.Y. Acad. Sci. Author: (with Robert M. Mitchell) Nine Months to Go, 1961; The Fathers Book, 1969; (with Fred Danzig) How To Be Heard, 1974. Home: 145 Forest Hill Rd West Orange NJ 07052 Office: 118 E 61 St New York City NY 10021

KLEIN, VINCENT M., real estate mgr.; b. Auburn, N.Y., June 1, 1916; s. Herman and Jennie (Schwartz) K.; student N.Y. U.; m. Dorothy Bryant, Oct. 9, 1949; children—Heather, Beth. With Samuel Schwartz & Sons, Inc., Auburn, 1938—, pres., sec. and dir., 1976—; mgr. Schwartz Assos., 1971-76; trustee Cauga County Savs. Bank, Auburn. Bd. dirs., sec. Samuel and Bertha Schwartz Found., Inc.; campaign chmn. United Fund, 1973, treas., 1976—; pres. YMCA, 1975-76; mem. Owasco (N.Y.) Planning Bd., 1971-76; bd. dirs. Auburn Civic Theater, Cayuga County chpt. Assn. Retarded Children; chmn. bd. trustees YMCA-WEIU; trustee Cayuga County Community Coll., Ft. Hill Cemetery Assn., Auburn Meml. Hosp.; vice chmn. bd. dirs., treas., past pres. Auburn Community Non-Profit Baseball Assn. Served with USAF, 1942-45. Mem. Am. Legion. Jewish. Clubs: Elks, Owasco Country, Auburn Golf and Country (v.p.). Home: 300 Woodhollow Dr Auburn NY 13021 Office: Nat Bank Bldg Auburn NY 13021

KLEINCHESTER, JOSEPH WILLIAM, JR., educator; b. Orange, N.J., 1943; B.A. in Art Edn., Montclair (N.J.) State Coll., 1967, M.A. in Art Edn., 1971; postgrad. Rutgers U., New Brunswick, N.J., 1971—; married; 1 son, Kevin. Tchr. art Hanover Park High Sch., Hanover, N.J., 1967-68; chmn. art dept. Butler (N.J.) High Sch., 1968-69; dist. coordinator Montville (N.J.) Twp. Pub. Schs., 1969-73; supr. art instruction and printing services Edison (N.J.) Township Pub. Schs., 1973—. Coordinator Edison Township Arts Festival, 1973—. Certified tchr., supr., prin., sch. adminstr. Mem. Art Educators N.J. (pres.). Nat. Art Edn. Assn., N.J. Edn. Assn., Am. Craftsmen Council, Edison Township Suprs. Assn., Better Edn. in Huntendon County Assn. (treas. 1974-75). Home: Old Chester Rd Gladstone NJ 07934 Office: Office of Superintendant 2825 Woodbridge Ave Edison NJ 08817

KLEINKE, DAVID JOSEPH, educator, univ. adminstr.; b. Albany, N.Y., June 7, 1936; s. Willard Bert and Margaret Theresa (Gutman) K.; student Columbia, 1952-54; B.A., State U. N.Y., Albany, 1957, M.A., 1962, Ed.D., 1970; m. Christine Theresa DiNorcia, Apr. 17, 1960; children—John David, Elizabeth Ann. Tchr., Albany Pub. Schs., 1957-59; safety services rep. ARC, Alexandria, Va., 1959-60, safety services dir., Albany County chpt., 1960-62; personnel examiner N.Y. Dept. Civil Service, Albany, 1962-63; asst. and asso. in ednl. testing N.Y. Dept. Edn., Albany, 1963-68; asst. prof. edn. and psychology Syracuse (N.Y.) U., 1969-73, asso. prof., 1973—, head, measurement and statistics, 1973-78, asso. dir. test scoring and evaluation Center Instructional Devel., 1974—; cons. Psychol. Corp., Alta. Oil Sands Environ. Research Project. Served with U.S. Army, 1958-59. Dept. Def. grantee, 1970; Nat. Inst. Edn. grantee, 1971; HEW grantee, 1972-73. Mem. Am. Ednl. Research Assn., Nat. Council Measurement Edn., Northeastern Ednl. Research Assn., Psychometric Soc. Author: Syracuse Environmental Awareness Tests, 1972; Uniform National Examinations in Landscape Architecture, 1976—; Community Index, 1978; contbr. articles to tech. jours. Home: 7904 Red Fox Dr Manlius NY 13104 Office: Skytop Offices Syracuse NY 13210

KLEINMAN, IRVING, mech. engr.; b. N.Y.C., Apr. 9, 1929; s. Philip and Rebecca (Hellerstein) K.; B.Mech. Engring., Coll. City N.Y., 1949, postgrad., 1950-54; m. Gloria Poseman, Sept. 24, 1950; children—Lawrence Richard, Roni Lynn. Designer, mech. contractors and cons. engring. firms, 1949-58; self-employed as cons. engr., Massapequa, N.Y., 1958—; pres. Laron Assos., Inc., 1968-77, Irving Kleinman & Assos., P.C., 1973—. Trustee Bd. Edn., Plainedge, N.Y., 1961-67, pres. bd., 1964-65. Registered profl. engr., N.Y., N.J., Conn., Mass. Mem. Am. Soc. M.E., Am. Soc. Heating, Refrigeration and Air Conditioning Engrs., Nat. Soc. Profl. Engrs., Cons. Engrs. Council (pres. elect N.Y. State chpt. 1978-79), Illuminating Engring. Soc., Nat. Fire Protection Assn. Contbr. articles to profl. jours. Home: 18 Hastings Rd Massapequa NY 11758 Office: 90 New York Ave Massapequa NY 11758

KLEMENS, PAUL GUSTAV, physicist, educator; b. Vienna, Austria, May 24, 1925; s. Walter and Ida (Klug) K.; came to U.S., 1959, naturalized, 1968; B.Sc., U. Sydney, 1946, M.Sc., 1948; Ph.D., Oxford U., 1950; m. Ruth Hannah Wiener, July 30, 1950; children—Michael Walter, Susan Margaret. With Nat. Standards Lab., Sydney, Australia, 1950-59, research officer, 1950-52, sr. research officer, 1952-57, prin. research officer, 1957-59; physicist Westinghouse Research Lab., Pitts., 1959-64, mgr. transport properties of solids dept., 1964-67; prof. physics U. Conn., 1967—, head dept. physics, 1967-74; vis. prof. Leiden U. (Netherlands), 1963-64; mem. adv. bd. on heat Nat. Bur. Standards, 1967-70, cryogenics, 1974—; mem. governing bd. Internat. Thermal Conductivity Confs., 1973—. Fellow Am. Phys. Soc., Inst. Physics (Eng.); mem. Conn. Acad. Sci. and Engring. Club: Cosmos (Washington). Contbr. articles to sci. jours. Home: 232 Ferguson Rd Manchester CT 06040 Office: Dept Physics U Conn Storrs CT 06268

KLEMONS, JEROME, dental technician; b. Bklyn., June 13, 1927; s. Albert and Rose (Bernstein) K.; student Bklyn. Coll., 1948-49, Kerpel Sch. Dental Tech., 1950-51; m. Harriet Leder, May 24, 1952; children—Gary, Cindy. Owner, operator, pres. Jerome Klemons Inc., Bklyn., 1951—; pres. Ceramic Gold Inc., Bklyn., 1966—. Served with AUS, 1945-47. Certified dental technician. Mem. Nat. Assn. Certified Dental Technicians. Office: 1 Hanson Pl Brooklyn NY 11243

KLENK, EUGENE LESLIE, pediatrician, pediatric nephrologist; b. N.Y.C., Apr. 23, 1930; s. William George and Emma Leslie (Heckman) K.; A.B., Dartmouth Coll., 1952; M.D., Temple U., 1962; M.Pub. Health and Tropical Medicine (NIH trainee), Tulane U., 1968; m. Anne Carver Stribling, June 27, 1959; children—Rebecca Marshall, Christian William, Sarah Ambler, Melissa Stribling. Intern, Mass. Gen. Hosp., Boston, 1962-63; asst. resident Babies Hosp., Columbia-Presbyn. Med. Center, N.Y.C., 1963-65, chief resident, 1965-66; asst. in pediatrics Columbia U., 1965-66, asso. in pediatrics, 1968-69, asst. prof., 1968-74, asso. prof. clin. pediatrics, 1974, asso. clin. prof. pediatrics, 1974—; asst. vis. physician Charity Hosp. La., New Orleans, 1966-68; asst. attending pediatrician Babies Hosp. and vanderbilt Clinic, Columbia-Presbyn. Hosp., N.Y.C., 1968-74, asso. attending pediatrician, 1974; attending pediatrician Mary Imogene Bassett Hosp., Cooperstown, N.Y., 1974—; dir. pediatric kidney clinic Vanderbilt Clinic, N.Y.C., 1968-74; dir. pediatric renal clinic Harlem Hosp. Center, N.Y.C., 1968-74, also cons. in pediatrics, 1968-75. Served to lt. j.g. USN, 1952-55. Pa. State Senatorial scholar, 1958-62; Smith, Kline and French Fgn. fellow, 1961; Wyeth Pediatric Residency Fellow, 1963-65; recipient William Harvey Perkins prize, 1962. Diplomate Nat. Bd. Med. Examiners, Am. Bd. Pediatrics, Am. Bd. Pediatric Nephrology. Fellow Am. Acad. Pediatrics; mem. Am. Internat. socs. nephrology, Am. Soc. Pediatric Nephrology, Internat. Pediatric Nephrology Assn., Nat. Kidney Found., Renal Physicans Assn., Assn. Mil. Surgeons, Naval Res. Assn., Alpha Omega Alpha, Alpha Kappa Kappa, Delta Upsilon. Club: Cooperstown Country. Contbr. articles, abstract to med jours. Home: Strawberry Hill Farm RD 3 Cooperstown NY 13326 Office: Mary Imogene Bassett Hosp Cooperstown NY 13326

KLENK, WILLIAM GEORGE, II, city ofcl.; b. Phila., May 9, 1933; s. William G. and Emma Leslie (Heckman) K.; B.A., U. Pa., 1955, LL.B., 1958; m. Jane Kathryn Lennox, Jan. 4, 1964; children—Leslie K., Kimberly L. Admitted to Pa. bar, 1961; asst. city solicitor Phila., 1963; asst. dist. atty., Phila., 1965-68; asso. mem. firm Ehreinreich, Sidkoff, Edelstein & Pearl, Phila., 1968-72; partner firm Sidkoff, Pincus, Greenberg & Golden, Phila., 1972-74; asso. firm Brobyn and Forcero, 1975—; city controller, 1973—; mem. sinking fund commn., loan com. Phila. Gas Works, chmn., 1975—. Mem. Mid-Atlantic Intergovernmental Audit Forum, 1974—, chmn., 1976-78; mem. Nat. Intergovernmental Audit Forum, 1978—. Club: Racquet (bd. pensions and retirement). Home: 300 W Springfield Ave Philadelphia PA 19118 Office: 1230 Municipal Services Bldg Philadelphia PA 19107

KLEVANA, LEIGHTON QUENTIN JOSEPH, lawyer; b. Czechoslovakia, Oct. 7, 1934 (born Am. citizen); s. Joseph V. and Bellina N. (Karlovsky) Farbman; B.A., Cornell U., 1957; postgrad. U. Paris, The Sorbonne, 1958; J.D., U. Va., 1961; 1 son, Leighton Alexis Christian. Admitted to N.Y. bar, 1963, Vt. bar, 1971; asso. atty. Meyer, Kissell, Matz & Seward, N.Y.C., 1961-63, Olwine, Connelly, Chase, O'Donnell & Weyher, 1963-67; sec. Helme Products, Inc., N.Y.C., 1967, sec., gen. counsel 1967-70; asst. atty. gen. State of Vt., 1970-73; partner firm Mahady & Klevana, 1973-74; v.p., sec., dir. Transit Air Freight, Inc., 1966-76; v.p., sec. Sagatrans, Inc., 1975-76; pres. Practicing Real Estate Inst., Inc., 1974—; partner firm Klevana & Rounds, 1976—. Mem. Am., Vt. bar assns., Assn. Bar City N.Y. Home: 929 Massachusetts Ave Cambridge MA 02139 Office: 62 Main St Windsor VT 05089

KLEVESAHL, FRED CARL, chem. co. exec.; b. Milw., Oct. 26, 1924; s. Baldwin Fred and Alma (Schultz) K.; B.S., U. Md., 1961; M.B.A., Syracuse U., 1962; m. Shirley Joann Henningsgaard, Sept. 20, 1947; children—Candice Yvonne, Kathleen Joan, Roxanne. Archtl. designer Erich Gnant & Assos., Milw., 1946-48; commd. 2d lt. U.S. Army, 1948, advanced through grades to col., 1965; chief planning br. Office Chief of Staff, Pentagon, 1964-68; ret., 1968; securities analysis and mgmt. staff duPont Co., Wilmington, Del., 1968-75, ops. mgr., pension fund investment dept., 1975—. Served with AUS, 1943-46. Decorated Legion of Merit, Bronze Star (2), Combat Infantryman Badge. Mem. Ret. Officers Assn., Beta Gamma Sigma, Phi Kappa Phi. Republican. Lutheran. Home: 206 Welwyn Rd Wilmington DE 19803 Office: 10th and Shipley Sts Wilmington DE 19898

KLIGMAN, ALBERT MONTGOMERY, dermatologist; b. Phila., Mar. 17, 1916; s. Samuel and Nettie (Crisbel) K.; B.A. (John W. White fellow), Pa. State U., 1939; Ph.D., U. Pa., 1942, M.D. (Senatorial scholar), 1947; m. Lorraine Heller Lesnik, Nov. 25, 1972; children—Gail, Douglas Evan, Michael. Intern, Albert Einstein Med. Center, 1947-48; fellow USPHS, 1948; resident dermatology Hosp. U. Pa., 1948-51, asso. dermatologist, 1951-53, asso. prof. dermatology, 1953-57, prof., 1957—, attending physician, 1951—; cons. Duhring Labs., Riverview Home for Aged; pres. Ivy Research Labs., Inc. Fellow Pa. Acad. Dermatology; mem. Soc. Investigative Dermatology (dir., pres.), Phila. Dermatology Soc. (past pres.), Rockefeller Inst. Med. Research, Am. Acad. Dermatology and Syphilology (prize 1950), AAAS, AMA, Am. Acad. Dermatology, Soc. Exptl. Biology, Am. Dermatol. Assn. (prize 1954), Phi Beta Kappa, Sigma Xi, Alpha Omega Alpha, Phi Deta Sigma. Contbr. articles to profl. jours. Home: 637 Pine St Philadelphia PA 19106 Office: Suite 203 3500 Market St Philadelphia PA 19104

KLIMAN, SYLVIA MAY STERN (MRS. ALLAN KLIMAN), editor, writer, real estate broker; b. Boston, July 16, 1934; d. Edward I. and Bernice Stern; A.B., Vassar Coll., 1956; m. Allan Kliman, June 24, 1956; children—Gilbert Harrow, Douglas Hartley. Editorial asst. Harvard Law Sch. profs., Cambridge, Mass., 1956-58; editor Vassar Miscellany News, Poughkeepsie, N.Y., 1953-56; founder Park Parent, Brookline, Mass., 1968, editor, 1968-73; pres. Sylvia S. Kliman, Real Estate Brokerage, 1971—. Polit. speechwriter, 1960—. Trustee the Park Sch.; bd. dirs. Friends of Peter Bent Brigham Hosp., Friends of Mus. of Transp., Spl. Com. to Restore Ogunquit Dunes. Mem. Park Sch. Parents Assn. (pres. 1968-70), Norfolk Dist. Med. Soc. Womens Aux., Boston Mus. Fine Arts. Unitarian. Club: Vassar (dir.) (Boston). Home: 40 Newton St Brookline MA 02146 also Dunewind Ogunquit ME 03907

KLIMAS, ANTANAS, linguist, educator; b. Pelekonys, Lithuania, Apr. 17, 1924; s. Vincas and Marija (Siugzdinis) K.; student Tchrs. Tng. Coll., Kaunas, Lithuania, 1941-42; student U. Kaunas, Lithuania, 1941-43, Baltic U., Hamburg, Germany, 1946-47; M.A., U. Pa., 1950, Ph.D., 1956; m. Dana Liormanas, June 19, 1954; children—Tadas, Ruta, Paulius, Lina. Came to U.S., 1948, naturalized, 1959. Asst. instr. German, U. Pa., 1950-56, instr., 1956-57; asst. prof. U. Rochester (N.Y.), 1957-62, asso. prof., 1962-70, prof., 1970—. Mem. Linguistic Soc. Am., Assn. Advancement Baltic Studies, Am. Tchrs. German, Lithuanian Cath. Acad. Sci., Delta Phi Alpha. Author: (with William R. Schmalstieg and Leonardas Dambriunas) Introduction to Modern Lithuanian, 1966, 2d edit., 1972; Lithuanian Reader for Self-Instruction, 1967; (with William Schmalstieg) A Glossary of Lithuanian Linguistic Terminology, 1972. Editor: Lituanus. Contbr. articles on linguistics to profl. jours. Home: 533 Winton Rd S Rochester NY 14618

KLIMENT, CHARLES KAREL, polymer chemist; b. Prague, Czechoslovakia, Aug. 2, 1932; s. Karel and Marie K.; came to U.S., 1969, naturalized, 1977; D.Chemistry, Tech. U., Prague, 1956; m. Daniela Tuckova, June 29, 1957; children—Zuzana, Charles Karel. Researcher, then head press rooms Czechoslovak Gramophone Industry, 1956-60; head dept. research and devel. hydrophilic polymers, soft contact lens, med. implants Inst. Macromolecular Chemistry, Czechoslovak Acad. Sci., 1960-69; with Hydron Labs., Inc. div. Nat. Patent Devel. Corp., New Brunswick, N.J., 1969—, dir. process devel., plant mgr., 1974—. Mem. ADA, Soc. Cosmetic Chemists. Author, patentee mfg. and uses hydrophilic polymers. Home: 321 Walnut Ln Princeton NJ 08540 Office: 783 Jersey Ave New Brunswick NJ 08902

KLIMENT, ROBERT MICHAEL, architect; b. Prague, Czechoslovakia, June 9, 1933; s. Felix and Sophie (Baltinester) K.; came to U.S., 1950, naturalized, 1955; B.A., Yale U., 1954, M.Arch., 1959; m. Janet Drury McClure, Sept. 12, 1959; 1 son, Nicholas McClure; m. 2d, Frances Halsband, May 1, 1971. Architect, Mitchell/Giurgola Architects, Phila. and N.Y.C., 1961-71; partner R. M. Kliment Architect, N.Y.C., 1972-76, R.M. Kliment & Frances Halsband Architects, N.Y.C., 1977—; instr. architecture U. Pa., 1963-66, vis. critic, 1972-73; asst. prof. architecture Columbia U., 1966-70; vis. critic Mass. Inst. Tech., 1970, Yale U., 1972-74, Columbia U., 1977, N.C. State U., 1978; exhibited in group shows: Bklyn. Museum, 1977, Cooper Hewitt, N.Y.C., 1977, 78, Drawing Center, N.Y.C., 1977. Served with U.S. Army, 1955-57. Fulbright fellow, Italy, 1959-60. Mem. AIA. Club: Univ. (N.Y.C.). Contbr. articles to archtl. jours. Home: 35 W 90th St New York NY 10024 Office: 1013 Carnegie Hall 881 7th Ave New York NY 10019

KLIMENT, STEPHEN ALEXANDER, architect; b. May 24, 1930; s. Felix and Sophia (Baltinester) K.; student Ecole Speciale d'Architecture, Paris, 1948-49; B.Arch., Mass. Inst. Tech., 1953; M.F.A., Princeton, 1957; m. Felicia Drury, Dec. 24, 1957; children—Pamela Drury, Jennifer Anne. Draftsman, Jean Labatut, Princeton, N.J., 1957; designer Skidmore, Owings & Merrill, N.Y.C., 1957-59; designer Reeb-Draz Assos., Cleve., 1959-60; editor Archtl. and Engring. News, Upper Montclair, N.J., 1961-69; v.p. Caudill Rowlett Scott, N.Y.C., 1969-72; architect, cons., 1972—; lectr. U. Oreg., Tex. A. and M. U., Carnegie-Mellon U., Pa. State U., Yale, Harvard, A.I.A., Constrn. Specifications Inst. Bd. dirs. Bldg. Research Inst., 1969-71; chmn. adv. Council Princeton Sch. Architecture and Urban Planning, 1970—; mem. governing bd. Assn. Princeton Grad. Alumni, 1972-75. Served with AUS, 1953-55. Fellow A.I.A. (dir. N.Y. chpt. 1966-68, sec. 1976-78). Episcopalian. Club: Univ. (N.Y.C.). Author: Into the Mainstream: Barrier-free Design; Planning City Hall; (with R.H. McNulty) Neighborhood Conservation; Creative Communications for a Successful Design Practice; editor Advt. and Pub. News. Home: 120 E 81st St New York City NY 10028 Office: 663 Fifth Ave New York City NY 10022

KLINE, ALMA, sculptor; b. Nyack, N.Y.; d. Charles D. and Charita (Hall) Kline; A.B., Radcliffe Coll., 1929; student sculpture with Jose De Creeft, 1939-41. Exhibited one man shows Creative Gallery, 1952, Burr Gallery, 1963, Thomson Gallery, 1969, Caravan House Gallery, 1976 (all N.Y.C.); exhibited one-man shows museums throughout U.S., 1964-65; exhibited group shows U.S., 1947—, Eng., 1955—, Argentina also Mexico, 1963—; represented in permanent collections, including Cronkhite Grad. Center, Cambridge, Mass.; Norfolk Museum of Arts and Sci., Va.; St. Lawrence U. Recipient Grumbacher award Audubon Artists, 1960; Knickerbocker Artists medal honor, 1964; Nat. Arts Club award, 1969; Patrons of Art award, Painters and Sculptors of N.J., 1969. Mem. Audubon Artists Inc. (past dir.), Nat. Assn. Women Artists (dir.), Soc. Animal Artists (dir.), Knickerbocker Artists, Silvermine Guild Artists. Club: Harvard Club of N.Y.C. Home and Office: 225 E 74th St New York City NY 10021

KLINE, CHARLES RALPH, electro-optical systems mgr.; b. Centralia, Ill., Apr. 25, 1928; s. Amos G. and Laura E. (Eckhardt) K.; B.S. in E.E., U. Mo., Rolla, 1951; m. Doris J. Oldham, Nov. 23, 1952; 1 dau., Melissa A. With Westinghouse Elec. Corp., 1951—, beginning as grad. student trainee, successively mem. Def. and Electronic Systems Center, Balt., designer airborne radar fire control Systems and other radar systems and electro-optical imaging systems, mem. task force devel. mil. lasers and laser systems, 1951-71, mgr. electro-optical systems devel., Balt., 1971—. Served with AUS, 1954-56. Registered profl. engr., Md. Mem. Nat. Assn. Remotely Piloted Vehicles, U. Mo. Alumni Assn., Phi Kappa Phi. Episcopalian. Club: Forest Hills. Contbr. articles to profl. jours. Patentee in field. Home: 3926 Hawthorn Rd Ellicott City MD 21043 Office: Mail Stop 360 PO Box 746 Baltimore MD 21203

KLINE, ERNEST P., lt. gov. of Pa.; b. Allentown, Pa., June 20, 1929; s. Allen J. and Elna (Natali) K.; m. Josephine Recupero; 7 children. Former radio newsman; lt. gov. of Pa., 1971—; workman's compensation referee, 1961-63. Mem. Beaver Falls (Pa.) City Council, 1956-59; mem. Pa. Senate, 1967-70, also minority leader; del. Democratic Nat. Conv., 1968. Roman Catholic. Address: Executive House Indiantown Gap Annville PA 17003

KLINE, HARRIET (MRS. EUGENE MONROE KLINE), artist, printmaker; b. N.Y.C., Sept. 25, 1916; d. James H. and Beatrice (Kheel) Meyer; B.A., Hunter Coll., 1938; pvt. study of oil painting with Isaac Soyer, Robert Phillip, Morris Kantor, 1945-59; pvt. study Chinese watercolor Y.C. Wang; m. Eugene Monroe Kline, July 2, 1939; children—Robert Andrew, Thomas Russell. Pvt. tchr. oil painting, Scarsdale, N.Y., 1959-68; exhibited in one-woman shows at Selected Artists Gallery (now Contemporary Masters Galleries), N.Y.C., 1960, 66, 68, 73, 75, Little Gallery of Hudson Park Br. N.Y. Pub. Library, 1962; exhibited in group shows at Art U.S.A., 1958, Silvermine Nat. Exhbn., 1959, Riverside Mus. and Nat. Acad., N.Y.C., 1959—, Okla. Printmakers Soc., 1960, 61, Butler Inst. Am. Art, 1974; also Nat. Assn. Women Artists Traveling Shows, Europe, 1965, U.S.A., 1969, Europe and Can., 1969, in traveling graphics show U.S.A., 1973; Old Bergen Art Guild Traveling Graphics Shows in U.S.A., 1973; represented in permanent collections N.Y. U., State U. Coll. at Oswego, N.Y., Western New Eng. Coll., Springfield, Mass., I.B.M., and numerous pvt. collectors. Recipient numerous awards. Mem. Nat. Assn. Women Artists, Silvermine Guild of Artists, Art Students League (life), Greenwich Art Soc., Hudson River Contemporary Artists, Am. Soc. Contemporary Artists, Mamaroneck Artists Guild, Artists Equity Assn. of N.Y. Home: 390 Heathcote Rd Scarsdale NY 10583

KLINE, HENRY CHAPMAN, aerospace co. exec.; b. N.Y.C., Feb. 11, 1921; s. Walter P. and Clara M. (Haase) K.; B.E.E. Cornell U. 1950; postgrad. program for sr. execs. Mass. Inst. Tech. 1968; m. Juliet E. Gentile, Apr. 14, 1951; children—Henry Chapman, Elizabeth, Victoria, Anne, Mary. Program mgr. integrated logistics support dept. Grumman Aerospace Corp., Bethpage, N.Y. 1952-64, chief engr., chief elec. engr. 1964-73, dir. 1973-77, gen. mgr. tng. systems dept., dir. integrated logistics, 1977—. Com. chmn. Boy Scouts Am., Smithtown, N.Y., 1966-69; v.p. Dogwood Sch. PTA, Smithtown, 1963-64; treas. Smithtown Civic Assn. 1962-63. Served to 1st, lt. USAAF, 1942-46. Mem. Aerospace Industries Assn., Soc. Logistics Engrs., Am. Def. Preparedness Assn., Cornell U. Alumni Assn. Lutheran. Contbr. articles to profl. jours. Home: 7 Dogwood Dr Smithtown NY 11787 Office: S Oyster Bay Rd Bethpage NY 11714

KLINE, MICHAEL S., ret. educator; b. Ithaca, N.Y., Jan. 15, 1916; s. Samuel and Shayna (Rapson) K.; B.S., Trenton State Coll., 1936; M.A., Columbia, 1942; Ed.D., Rutgers U., 1958; m. Harriet Schwartz, Dec. 22, 1940; children—Florence Ellen, Shirley Helen. Tchr. Princeton (N.J.) Borough pub. schs., 1936-54, asst. prin. Witherspoon Sch., 1954-58; prin. Garfield (N.J.) High Sch., 1958-59; dir. student teaching and placement Trenton (N.J.) State Coll., 1959-72, dir. acad. career planning and placement, 1972-77, dir. emeritus, 1978—. Founder Cub Scouts Am., Princeton, N.J., 1937; founder, dir. Camp Tomahawk Day Camp., Princeton, 1948-59; founder N.J. Inter-Coll. Council Lab. Experience in Profl. Edn., 1963; mem. Somerville (N.J.) Recreation Commn., 1951-58; founder, dir. Somerset County Park Commn. Golf Tournaments, 1961-67, Somerville Recreation Commn. Golf Tournament, 1953—; chmn. Trenton State Coll. Centennial Homecoming, 1956. Served with AUS, 1943-46. Mem. N.E.A., N.J. Council Edn., N.J. Edn. Assn., Nat., Mid-Atlantic Assn. for Sch., Coll. and Univ. Staffing, Middle Atlantic Placement Assn., Trenton State Coll. Alumni Assn. (pres. 1940), Assn. Trenton State Coll. Adminstrs. (founder-pres. 1970-71), N.J. Assn. State Coll. Adminstrs. (founder 1970), Jewish War Vets., Am. Legion, Kappa Delta Pi, Phi Delta Kappa. Mem. B'nai B'rith. Author: How To Do Your Best as a Student Teacher, 1961; Hammett Master Series of Teacher Publications, 1965; Master Guide for Student Teaching, 1968; Guide for Career Placement, 1973; The Student Teacher's Duomaster, 1978. Home: 166 N Middaugh St Somerville NJ 08876 Office: Trenton State Coll Trenton NJ 08625

KLINE, MILTON VANCE, psychologist; b. Bklyn., Mar. 25, 1923; s. Joseph and Elizabeth (Zimmerman) K.; B.A., Pa. State U., 1944; M.A., Columbia, 1946; Ph.D., N.Y. U., 1950; m. Dorothy Weller, Feb. 25, 1952; 1 dau., Jill. Chief psychologist Westchester Health Dept., White Plains, N.Y., 1948; dir. research dept. psychology L.I. U., 1948, research project dir. grad. sch., 1953; research cons. VA, N.Y.C., 1950; pvt. practice hypnoanalysis N.Y.C., 1950—, professorial lectr. Seton Hall Med. Sch., 1960-62; pres. Inst. for Research in Hypnosis, N.Y.C., 1954—; lectr. Fairleigh Dickinson U., Rutherford, N.J., 1964—; dir. Morton Prince Clinic for Hynotherapy; pres. Morton Prince Services, N.Y.C. and Balt.; cons. NBC, Nat. Assn. Broadcasters; pres. Internat. Grad. U., Switzerland. Chmn. council sci. and profl. advisers Internat. Grad. Sch. Behavioral Scis., Fla. Inst. Tech. Served with AUS, 1942-44. Recipient award for best book in hypnosis Soc. Clin. and Exptl. Hypnosis, 1958, 67, award for Best Paper on clin. hypnosis, 1973, Roy M. Dorcus award, 1971. Fellow Am. Med. Writers Assn., Acad. Psychosomatic Medicine; mem. Soc. Clin. and Exptl. Hypnosis (pres. 1961-63), Am. Psychol. Assn. (council reps.). Author: Hypnodynamic Psychology, 1955, A Scientific Report on The Search for Bridey Murphy, 1953; Freud and Hypnosis, 1958; The Nature of Hypnosis, 1962; Clinical Correlations of Experimental Hypnosis, 1965; Psychodynamics and Hypnosis, 1967. Editor: Obesity: Etiology, Treatment and Research (C.C. Thomas), 1975. Editor emeritus Internat. Jour. Clin. and Exptl. Hypnosis. Home: 15 Kerry Ln Chappaqua NY 10514 Office: 10 W 66th St New York NY 10023

KLINE, NATHAN SCHELLENBERG, research psychiatrist, educator; b. Phila., Mar. 22, 1916; s. Ignatz and Florence (Schellenberg) K.; B.A., Swarthmore Coll., 1938; postgrad. Harvard, 1938-39; M.D., N.Y. U., 1943; postgrad. Princeton, 1946-47; M.A., Clark U., 1951; 1 dau., Marna Ellen Kline Anderson. Intern St. Elizabeth's Hosp., Washington, 1943-44; chief research projects VA, Lyons, N.J., 1946-50; dir. research Worcester (Mass.) State Hosp., 1950-52; dir. Research Center Rockland State Hosp., Orangeburg, N.Y., 1952-75, Columbia-Greystone Assn., 1947-50; dir. Rockland Research Inst., 1975—; N.Y. State Brain Research Asso., 1948-50; with dept. neurology Columbia Coll. Phys. and Surgs., 1948-55, dept. psychiatry, 1955—, asst. clin. prof., 1957-69, asso. clin. prof., 1969-73, clin. prof., 1973—; dir. psychiat. service Bergen Pines County Hosp., Paramus, N.J., 1963-74, now emeritus; attending physician Lenox Hill Hosp., 1974—. Mem. profl. adv. com. Manhattan Soc. Mental Health, Nat. Com. Against Mental Illness, Nat. Health Edn. Com.; pres. Internat. Com. Against Mental Illness; former clin. adv. NIMH; mem. expert com. on mental health WHO, 1973—. Decorated knight grand comdr. Liberian Humane Order of African Redemption (Liberia); knight gt. cross by master's grace Serenissimi Mil. Order St. Mary the Glorious; grand officeur Legion d'Honneur et Merit, commandeur Order Toussaint-Louverture (Republique d'Haiti). Recipient Page One award sci. N.Y. Newspapers Guild, 1956; Adolf Meyer award Assn. for Improvement of Mental Health, 1956; Albert Lasker award Am. Pub. Health Assn., 1957; Henry Wisner Miller award Manhattan Society of Mental Hygiene, awarded in 1963; Albert Lasker clinical research award, 1964. Diplomate in psychiatry Am. Bd. Psychiatry and Neurology. Fellow A.C.P., AAAS, Am. Psychiat. Assn., N.Y. Acad. Medicine, N.Y. Acad. Scis., Royal Soc. Medicine (Eng.), Royal Coll. Psychiatrists (hon.), Am. Coll. Neuropsycho-pharmacology (life); mem. A.M.A., Am. Philos. Assn., Am. Psychol. Assn., Am. Chem. Soc., Soc. Exptl. Biology and Medicine, Assn. Research Nervous and Mental Disease, A.I.A.A., Med. Soc. County New York, Indian Psychiat. Assn., Royal Coll. Psychiatry (Eng.), Soc. Biol. Psychiatry, Societe Moreau de Tours (France), Am. Therapeutic Soc., Sigma Xi. Author books and articles in field. Mem. med. adv. council, trustee Medico; adv. editorial bd. Psychopharmacologia, 1958—, Internat. Jour. Social Psychiatry, 1958—; internat. editor Excerpta Medica, 1955—. Office: 130 E 77th St New York NY 10021 also Rockland Research Inst Orangeburg NY 10962

KLINE, RICHARD CHARLES, educator; b. Shickshinny, Pa., Feb. 8, 1950; s. Charles and Margaret (Kobosko) K.; B.S., Pa. State U., 1972, M.Ed., 1977; married. Adminstrv. asst. continuing edn. Pa. State U., Abington, 1975-77, adj. instr. health edn., 1977—; biology tchr. Abington High Sch., 1972-78, Bloomsburg (Pa.) Area High Sch., 1978—. Mem. Polit. Action Com. for Edn., 1972—. Mem. Abington Edn. Assn. (dir.), Nat., Montgomery County sci. tchrs. assns., Nat. History Assn., Pa., Abington edn. assns., Nat. Assn. Biology Tchrs., Phi Delta Kappa. Democrat. Roman Catholic. Home: Box 11A RD 1 Stillwater PA 17878 Office: Bloomsburg Area High Sch Bloomsburg PA 17815

KLINE, ROBERT EDWARD, lawyer; b. Hazleton, Pa., Sept. 22, 1916; s. Eli and Mayme (Schless) K.; grad. Exeter, 1934; A.B., Harvard, 1938, LL.B., 1941; m. Rae R. Marks, May 30, 1957; children—Pamela Iris, Elisabeth Ingrid, Douglas Edmund. Admitted to Pa. bar, 1942; asso. firm Baker, Watts & Woods, Pitts., 1960-62, Kline & Smith, Pitts., 1963—. Served to capt. USAAF, 1941-46. Decorated Legion of Merit. Mem. UN Assn. (nat. legacies com.). Home: 1012 Gilchrest Dr Pittsburgh PA 15235 Office: Grant Bldg Pittsburgh PA 15219

KLINE, ROBERT PARKS, banker; b. Lincoln, Nebr., Nov. 17, 1923; s. Leonard Wilson and Daisy Irene (Parks) K.; B.S. in Bus. Adminstrn., U. Nebr., 1947; M.B.A., Harvard U., 1949; postgrad. Stonier Grad. Sch. Banking, 1960; m. Marcia Virginia Seely, Apr. 25, 1953; children—Stephen Parks, Karen Sue. Credit analyst No. Trust Co., Chgo., 1949-53, loan officer comml. banking dept., 1953-60, v.p., 1960-67, v.p., div. head, 1967-69; exec. v.p. Ill. Nat. Bank & Trust Co., Rockford Ill., 1969-71, pres., 1971-74, also dir.; chmn., pres., chief exec. officer, dir. Lake View Trust & Savs. Bank, Chgo., 1974-76; pres., chief exec. officer, trustee Peoples Savs. Bank, Providence, 1976—; pres., chief exec. officer, dir. Peoples Corp., 1976—, Peoples Trust Co., 1976—, 667 Corp., 1977—; dir. R.I. Pub. Expenditure Council, Bus. Devel. Co. R.I., 1977—. Div. chmn. campaign Rockford United Fund, 1971, campaign chmn., 1972; mem. exec. bd. Blackhawk Area council Boy Scouts Am., 1970-74, treas., 1971-74, exec. bd. N.W. Surburban council, 1974-76; chmn. Rockford Econ. Expansion Task Force, 1971-73; pres. Rockford Area Econ. Devel. Commn., 1973-74. Bd. dirs. Rock River Valley chpt. Jr. Achievement, 1970-73. Served to 2d lt., USAAF, 1943-45. Mem. Harvard Bus. Sch. Alumni Assn., Robert Morris Assos., Sigma Nu. Clubs: Hope, Turk's Head (Providence); Warwick (R.I.) Country. Home: 1255 Waterford Dr East Greenwich RI 02818 Office: 145 Westminster St Providence RI 02903

KLINGE, JOHN GORMAN, chewing gum mktg. exec.; b. Englewood, N.J., Jan. 19, 1939; s. John Henry and Mary Elizabeth (Gorman) K.; B.Chem. Engring., Cornell U., 1961; M.B.A., Harvard U., 1965; m. Jeanne O. Bange, Aug. 22, 1964; children—John, Courtney, Jeffrey. Product mgr. Gen. Foods, White Plains, N.Y., 1965-71; bus. group mgr. Church & Dwight, N.Y.C., 1971-72; v.p. mktg. Topps Chewing Gum, N.Y.C., 1972—; lectr. bus. mgmt. Sacred Heart Coll., 1977—. Coach youth programs. Served to lt. USN, 1961-63. Republican. Roman Catholic. Office: Topps Chewing Gum 254 36th St Brooklyn NY 11232

KLINGERMAN, ETHEL, librarian; b. Muncy, Pa., Mar. 4, 1929; d. Foster J. and Ida (Black) Klingerman; A.B., Wilson Coll., 1950; M.S., Drexel Inst. Tech., 1951. Cataloger, Lippincott Library, U. Pa., Wharton Sch. Commerce and Finance, 1951-54, James V. Brown Library, Williamsport, Pa., 1954-55; field dir. Lycoming County council Girl Scouts U.S.A., Williamsport, 1955-56; librarian Eastern Coll., St. Davids, Pa., 1956-66; library dir. Moorestown (N.J.) Library, 1966—. Mem. N.J. Library Services and Constrn. Act Adv. Council, 1972—. Mem. Am., Pa., N.J. (pres. adult services sect. 1971-72) library assns., Assn. Coll. and Research Libraries (chpt. sec.-treas. 1965-67), Libraries Unlimited (sec.-treas. 1968-69), AAUP, AAUW, League Women Voters. Club: Wilson College (v.p. 1964 Phila.). Home: 5 Andover House Moorestowne Woods Moorestown NJ 08057 Office: 2d and Church Sts Moorestown NJ 08057

KLINK, ARTHUR EDWIN, JR., chem. engr.; b. N.Y.C., June 2, 1943; s. Arthur Edwin and Martha Dolores (Murphy) K.; B.A., Columbia Coll., 1965; B.S., Columbia U., 1965, M.S., 1967, Ph.D., 1973; m. Marilyn Georgina O'Brien, June 28, 1961; children—Arthur, Kevin. Sr. research fellow Merck & Co., Rahway, N.J., 1965-77; dir. worldwide engring. and constrn. E. R. Squibb & Sons, Princeton, N.J., 1977—; chmn. faculty adv. com. Columbia Engring. Sch., 1976—. Mem. Am. Inst. Chem. Engrs. (exec. com.), Parenteral Drug Assn., Am. Mgmt. Assn. Contbr. articles in field to profl. jours. Home: RD 2 Box 76A Lebanon NJ 08833

KLINK, JAMES JOSEPH, accountant; b. Detroit, May 7, 1931; s. Anthony A. and Lila (Kenny) K.; B.S., U. Notre Dame, 1953; J.D., Wayne State U., 1960; m. Regina G. Miller, Apr. 24, 1954; children—James, Sheryl, Thomas, Larry, Michele. Accountant Price Waterhouse & Co., Detroit, 1953-69, partner, 1969-70, partner, N.Y.C., 1970—, chmn. real estate accounting com., 1971—; instr. Walsh Inst. Accounting, 1960-62. Served with U.S. Army, 1953-55. Mem. Am. Inst. C.P.A.'s (chmn. com. auditing HUD devel. costs; mem. real estate accounting com. 1971-76), Inst. Internal Auditors (bd. govs. 1966-69), Nat. Assn. Real Estate Investment Trusts (mem. accounting com. 1972—, vice chmn. 1977—, chmn. com. on reporting practices 1973—, bd. govs. 1974-77), N.Y. (chmn. com. on real estate accounting 1973-77), N.J. (chmn. practice rev. com. 1974-76, mem. auditing and accounting standards com. 1976—) socs. C.P.A.'s. Clubs: University, Downtown Athletic (N.Y.C.); Ridgewood (N.J.) Country. Home: 2 Stratford Ln Ho-Ho-Kus NJ 07423 Office: 153 E 53d St New York City NY 10022

KLINO, JAMES LOUIS, civil engr.; b. Lockport, N.Y., Mar. 21, 1953; s. Louis Charles and Margaret (Crowley) K.; student Niagara U., 1971-73; B.C.E., U. Detroit, 1976; postgrad. State U. N.Y., Buffalo; m. Eleonora K. Szostak, Aug., 1975. Civil engr. D.W. Winkleman Co. Inc., Syracuse, N.Y., 1972-75, FMC Corp., Mesch &

Assos., Lockport, N.Y., 1975-77, Dushscherer & Oberst, Buffalo, N.Y., 1977, McIntosh & McIntosh Inc., Lockport, N.Y., 1977—; project civil engr., ice coordinator Power Authority of State of N.Y., Niagara Falls, 1977—; cons. Mesch & Assos. Mem. Nat. Soc. Profl. Engrs., ASCE, Am. Concrete Inst. Republican. Roman Catholic. Clubs: K.C., Soc. for Preservation and Encouragement of Barber Shop Quartets Am. Home: 392 Walnut St Lockport NY 14094 Office: PO Box 277 Lewiston Rd Niagara Falls NY 14302

KLION, DANIEL EARL, mech. engr.; b. N.Y.C., Nov. 30, 1925; s. Harry and Jeannette Hilda (Stern) K.; B.S. in Mech. Engring., U. Ill., 1950; m. Helga Eichenwald, Sept. 19, 1954; children—Pamela Diane, Roger Jay, Douglas Alan, Andrea Beth. With Ebasco Services, Inc., N.Y.C., 1950-55, 67-73, asst. chief project engr., 1978—; with Burns & Roe, Inc., Oradell, N.J., 1956-63, Energy Corp. of Am., N.Y.C., 1963-67, Stone & Webster Engring. Corp., N.Y.C., 1973-78; mem. faculty N.Y. U., N.Y.C., 1965. Drainage commr. Town of Clarkstown (N.Y.), 1968-69. Served with U.S. Army, 1944-46. Registered profl. engr., N.Y., Pa., Fla., Tex., La., Ga., Va. Mem. ASME. Author: Handbook for Electrical Engineers, 1978; patentee for film flow over plate surface. Home: 23 Jill Dr West Nyack NY 10994 Office: Two World Trade Center New York City NY 10006

KLIOT, DAVID ALLEN, obstetrician, gynecologist; b. N.Y.C., Nov. 30, 1932; s. Nathan and Lee K.; A.B., U. Chgo., 1952; M.D., Downstate Med. Center, State U. N.Y., 1959; m. Harriet Silverstein, June 23, 1957; children—Gregory, Nancy, Benjamin. Intern, Brookdale Hosp. Med. Center, Bklyn., 1959-60, resident, 1960-64; dir. resident tng. Bklyn. Women's Hosp., 1966-70; asst. dir. dept. obstetrics and gynecology Brookdale Hosp. Med. Center, 1968-70; clin. asst. prof. obstetrics and gynecology Downstate Med. Center, State U. N.Y., Bklyn., 1970—; specialist cons. N.Y.C. Dept. Health. Served to capt. USAF, 1964-66. Diplomate Am. Bd. Obstetrics and Gynecology. Fellow A.C.S., Am. Coll. Obstetrics and Gynecology, Bklyn. Gynecol. Soc., Am. Soc. Abdominal Surgeons, Internat. Coll. Surgeons; mem. Internat. Soc. Psychosomatic Obstetrics and Gynecology, Am. Soc. Psychoprophylaxis in Obstetrics (physician chmn. N.Y.C.). Contbr. research articles in field to profl. publs. Home: 177 Westminster Rd Brooklyn NY 11218 Office: 225 Marlborough Rd Brooklyn NY 11226

KLIR, GEORGE JIRI, educator; b. Prague, Czechoslovakia, Apr. 22, 1932; s. Jan and Emilie (Pritasilova) K.; came to U.S., 1966, naturalized, 1972; M.S.E.E., Czech Inst. Tech., Prague, 1957; Ph.D., Czechoslovak Acad. Scis., Prague, 1964; m. Milena Reholova, Jan. 26, 1962; 1 dau., Jane. Research fellow Inst. Computer Research, Prague, 1960-64; lectr. U. Baghdad (Iraq), 1964-66, U. Calif. at Los Angeles, 1966-68; asso. prof. Fairleigh Dickinson U., 1968-69; asso. prof. Sch. Advanced Tech., State U. N.Y. at Binghamton, 1969-72, prof., 1972—, chmn. dept. systems sci., 1977—. IBM research fellow, 1969; Netherlands Inst. for Advanced Studies fellow, 1975-76. Mem. IEEE, AAUP, Philosophy of Sci. Assn., Assn. Computing Machinery, Am. Soc. Cybernetics, Soc. Gen. Systems Research. Author: Cybernetic Modelling, 1967; An Approach to General Systems, 1969; Methodology of Switching Circuits, 1972. Contbr. articles in field to profl. jours. Editor: Trends in General Systems Research, 1972; editor-in-chief International Jour. General Systems, Book Series on Basic and Applied General Systems Research, Book Series on Frontiers in Systems Science: Implications for the Social Sciences. Home: 916 Murray Hill Rd Binghamton NY 13903 Office: Sch Advanced Tech State U NY Binghamton NY 13901

KLITZBERG, RICHARD, investment co. exec.; b. Bklyn., Dec. 9, 1941; s. Samuel and Lillian R. (Gruber) K.; B.A., Western Md. Coll., 1963; J.D., U. Balt., 1966; m. Judith N. Callahan, Apr. 9, 1965; children—Robert, Dana, James. Admitted to Md. bar, 1967; account exec. Bache Halsey Stuart Shields, Inc., N.Y.C., 1969-74, regional coordinator asset mgmt., 1974-75, nat. mgr. investment mgmt. services, 1975—, asst. v.p., 1976-77, 2d v.p., 1977-78, v.p., 1978—. Mem. adv. bd. Metuchen (N.J.) Pool Commn.; mem. Temple Neve Shalom, Metuchen, N.J., 1976—. Served to capt. U.S. Army, 1967-69. Mem. Am., Md. bar assns., Common Cause, Sierra Club, Am. Pension Conf., Assn. Pvt. Pension and Welfare Plans, Internat. Found. Employee Benefit Plans. Club: Inman Racquet. Home: 9 Whitman Ave Metuchen NJ 08840 Office: 100 Gold St New York City NY 10038

KLITZKE, THEODORE ELMER, coll. dean; b. Chgo., Nov. 4, 1915; s. John Frederick and Edith (Bachman) K.; B.F.A., Chgo. Art Inst., 1940; B.A., U. Chgo., 1941, Ph.D., 1953; m. Margaret Bridget Gaughan, Feb. 23, 1946; children—Annetta, Margaret. Instr. art history U. Chgo., 1946-47; edn. adviser U.S. Armed Forces in Germany, Nurnberg, 1948-51; asst. prof. art history N.Y. State Coll. Ceramics, State U. N.Y. at Alfred, 1953-59; prof. art history, chmn. dept. art U. Ala., 1959-68; v.p. acad. affairs, dean Md. Inst. and Coll. Art, 1968—, acting pres., 1977—; lectr. Am. art Amerika Haus. Erlangen, Germany, Anglo-Mexican Inst. Cultural Relations, Mexico City. Bd. dirs. Nat. Assn. Schs. Art, 1971-74, mem. commn. on accreditation, 1975—; pres. Print and Drawing Soc. of Balt. Mus. Art, 1974-76. Bd. dirs. Ala. chpt. Am. Civil Liberties Union, 1965-68, v.p. Tuscaloosa chpt., 1967-68; bd. dirs. S.W. Ala. Self-Help Housing, 1966-68. Served with AUS, 1942-46. Recipient First Annual Peace and Freedom award Democratic Student Orgn., U. Ala., 1968; citation Civil Liberties Union Ala. Mem. Southeastern Coll. Art Conf. (pres. 1961-62), Soc. Archtl. Historians, Am. Studies Assn., Am. Assn. U. Profs. (chpt. pres. 1956-57), Coll. Art Assn. Author articles in field. Home: 7918 Sherwood Ave Baltimore MD 21204 Office: 1300 Mt Royal Ave Baltimore MD 21217

KLITZNER, ROBERT ARTHUR, metal mfg. co. exec.; b. Providence, Oct. 30, 1924; s. Harry and Francis Marion (Pockar) K.; grad. high sch., 1943; 1 son, Michael. Apprentice, Klitzner Industries, Providence, 1946-49, treas., 1953-60, pres., 1960—; pres. Bobill Corp., Providence, 1957—, J.H. Collingwood & Son, Ltd., Montreal, Que., Can., 1966—. Served with USNR, 1943-46. Mem. Mfg. Jewelers and Silversmiths. Mason (Shriner), Elk. Home: 222A Harrison St Providence RI 02903 Office: 44 Warren St Providence RI 02907

KLOSK, EMANUEL, physician; b. New York, N.Y., Aug. 22, 1910; s. Hyman and Fannie (Petchesky) K.; B.S., Rutgers U., 1931; M.D., N.Y. Univ., 1935; m. Norma R. Weinstein, Aug. 25, 1935. Intern, Queens Gen. Hosp., Jamaica, L.I., 1935-37; resident, Sea View Hosp., Staten Island, 1937-39; attending in medicine Newark (N.J.) Beth Israel Hosp., 1939—, also dir. medicine; clin. asso. prof. dept. medicine N.J. Coll. Medicine. Trustee Newark Beth Israel Med. Center. Diplomate Am. Bd. Internal Medicine. Fellow Am. Coll. Cardiology, Am. Coll. Chest Physicians, A.C.P.; mem. A.M.A., Trudeau Soc. Am., Phi Beta Kappa. Author articles on chest and heart disease. Home: 30 Carter Rd West Orange NJ 07052 Office: 2115 Millburn Ave Maplewood NJ 07040

KLOSKOWSKI, VINCENT JOHN, JR., educator, sch. adminstr., author; b. Sept. 30, 1934; s. Vincent and Maryk.; B.S. with honors, Seton Hall U., N.J., 1960, M.A., 1971; postgrad. Newark State Coll., 1960-62, Trenton (N.J.) State Coll., 1961-64; M.Ed. (Asian Found. scholar), Rutgers U., 1964; Ph.D., U. Western Ont., 1971; postdoctorate Harvard, 1975; Ed.D. in Ednl. Adminstrn., Nova U., Fla., 1976; m. Geraline Brinson, June 29, 1957; 1 son, Vincent John III. Substitute tchr. South River (N.J.) High Sch., 1958-60; tchr. Madison Twp. (N.J.) Pub. Schs., 1960-64; co-adj. mem. staff Rutgers U., 1961-64; remedial specialist North Brunswick (N.J.) Pub. Schs., 1964-65; vice prin. Jamesburg (N.J.) High Sch., 1965-66; asst. to supt., child study coordinator, curriculum coordinator, fed. coordinator urban funding Pub. Schs., Jamesburg, 1966—. prin. elementary, jr. high sch. and spl. edn. bldg., 1966—; cons. to para-profls. Mercer County Community Coll., Trenton, 1972; pvt. practice ednl. counseling 1973—; speaker Ann. Conf. on incoming students Seton Hall U., 1959, Jamesburg Pub. Schs. In-Service Program, 1965, Middlesex County Child Study Team, 1970, PTA Jamesburg Pub. Schs., 1970, 72, Middlesex County Curriculum Council, East Brunswick Vocat. Sch., 1971, Holy Innocence Soc., Avenel, N.J., 1971, St. Catherines PTA, Clayton, N.J., 1971; panelist child study devel. Madison Twp. Pub. Schs., 1961; participant Internat. Reading Assn., Somerville, N.J., 1964, 42d Summer Sch. Conf. on Sch. Adminstrn., Harvard, 1970, Scott Foresmen New Programs in Reading, Freehold, N.J., 1971, Ann. Reading Inst., Rutgers U., 1971, 72, McGraw-Hill-Sullivan Reading Program, Hightstown, N.J., 1972, use of para-profls. in pub. schs. N.J. State Dept.-Middlesex County Community Coll., Edison, 1972; cons. Setting Up Pvt. Spl. Edn. Facility, South Brunswick, 1969, Ednl. Cons. Service of N.J., 1971—, reading techniques for para-profl. Mercer County Community Coll., Trenton, 1971. Merit badge counselor Boy Scouts Am., 1966-70; notary pub. N.J. Mem. Am. Assn. Sch. Adminstrs., N.J. Assn. Sch. Prins., Nat. (life), N.J., Middlesex County, Jamesburg edn. assns., Nat. Ednl. Assn. Sch. Prins., N.J. Classroom Tchrs. Assn., N.J. Assn. Retarded Children, Internat., N.J. reading assns., Middlesex County Audio-Visual Assn., Am. Soc. Notaries, Phi Delta Kappa, Alpha Epsilon Mu. Author: Didacticism-Montessori and the Special Child, 1969; Amish Sch. System and Spl. Edn., 1971. Asst. editor Seton Hall U. Newspaper and Coll. Yearbook, 1959-60; book reviewer Narod Polski. Home: 41 Daily St South River NJ 08882

KLOTZ, HOWARD SANFORD, telecommunications exec.; b. N.Y.C., Dec. 4, 1939; s. Arthur Aaron and Rose Klotz; A.B., Columbia U., 1961; J.D., Harvard U., 1964; m. Jane Ellen Boller, Apr. 6, 1968. Admitted to N.Y. bar, 1964, D.C. bar, 1965; atty. SEC, Washington, 1965-67; atty. firm Willkie Farr & Gallagher, N.Y.C., 1967-68; v.p., gen. counsel Arthur Lipper Corp., N.Y.C., 1968-72; partner KC Co., N.Y.C., 1972—, atty., 1972—, pres., treas., dir. KC Corp., 1976—; cons. to U.S. Commodity Futures Trading Commn., 1977. Mem. Am., N.Y. State bar assns., Assn. Bar City of N.Y. Club: Harvard. Office: 419 E 57d St New York NY 10022

KLOTZ, LOUIS HERMAN, educator; b. Elizabeth, N.J., May 21, 1928; s. Herman Martin and Edna Theresa (Kloepfer) K.; B.S. in Civil Engring., Pa. State U., 1951; M.C.E., N.Y. U., 1956; postgrad U. Ill., 1959-61; Ph.D., Rutgers U., 1967; m. Virginia Helen Roll, Apr. 3, 1966; children—Emily Louise, Jennifer Virginia. Structural engr., various firms, N.Y.-N.J., Met. area, 1951-56; civil engr. Ebasco Internat. Corp., N.Y.C., 1956-58; constrn. project engr., RCA, Moorestown, N.J., 1958-59; research asso. U. Ill., Urbana, 1959-61; cons. engr., Roselle Park, N.J., 1961-65, Durham, N.H., 1965—; mem. faculty U. N.H., Durham, 1965—, asso. prof. civil engring., 1969—, chmn. dept., 1971-74. Ford Found. fellow, 1962-65; NASA/Am. Soc. Engring. Edn. fellow, summer 1975; GAO fellow, Washington, 1975-76. Registered profl. engr., N.J., N.H. Mem. N.Y. Acad. Scis., Am. Acad. Mechanics, ASCE, Internat. Assn. Bridge and Structural Engring., AAAS, Am. Soc. Engring. Edn., Internat. Soc. Soil Mechanics and Found. Engring. Republican. Episcopalian. Author: User's Manual for Intergrated Geometry System, 1971. Home: 55 Mainmast Circle New Castle NH 03854 Office: Dept Civil Engineering Univ NH Durham NH 03824

KLOTZ, RICHARD DAVID, ophthalmologist; b. N.Y.C., Sept. 6, 1942; s. Arthur Aaron and Rose (Cohen) K,; B.A., Grinnell Coll., 1964; M.D., State U. N.Y., Syracuse, 1968; m. Barbara Joan Caplin, Feb. 19, 1972; children—Evan Laurence, Alison Dawn. Intern, USPHS Hosp., San Francisco, 1968-69; resident in ophthalmology North Shore Univ. Hosp., Cornell U. Med. Sch., Manhasset, N.Y., 1970-73, instr., 1973—; practice medicine specializing in ophthalmology, Gt. Neck, N.Y., 1973—. Served with USPHS, 1968-70. Diplomate Am. Bd. Ophthalmology, Nat. Bd. Med. Examiners. Fellow A.C.S., Am. Acad. Ophthalmology and Otolaryngology; mem. AMA, Med. Soc. State N.Y., Nassau County Med. Soc., Am. Assn. Ophthalmology, Soc. Contemporary Ophthalmology, Am. Intraocular Implant Soc., L.I., N.Y. State ophthal. socs., Nassau Acad. Med. Home: 3038 Riverside Dr Wantagh NY 11793 Office: 15 Bond St Great Neck NY 11021

KLOTZBACH, ROBERT JAMES, chem. engr.; b. N.Y.C., Aug. 27, 1922; s. Charles James and Mary Agnes (Reilly) K.; B.S., Fordham U., 1943; certificate Army Specialized Tng. Program N.Y. U., 1944; m. Myrtle Anna Byrd, Oct. 26, 1946; 1 son, Robert Byrd. Chem. engr. Manhattan Dist., 1944-46; project engr., dir. long range planning Oak Ridge Nat. Lab., 1946-55; project mgr. Nuclear div. Union Carbide, N.Y.C., 1955-57, mgr. engring., 1957-65, mgr. engring. Mining and Metals div., Niagara Falls, N.Y., 1965-68, dir. tech., 1968-75, dir. tech. Metals div., 1975-78, dir. tech. Mineral Products, 1978—. Election commr., Oak Ridge, 1950. Served with AUS, 1943-46. Mem. Niagara Frontier Research Dirs., AAAS. Republican. Roman Catholic. Clubs: Niagara, Niagara Falls Country. Home: 5140 Dana Dr Lewiston NY 14092

KLUGE, JOHN WERNER, broadcasting and advt. exec.; b. Chemnitz, Germany, Sept. 21, 1914; s. Fritz and Gertrude (Donj) K.; student Wayne U.; B.A. (4 year honor scholar), Columbia, 1937; m. Yolanda Zucco, Apr., 28, 1969; children—Samantha, Joseph B. Vice pres., sales mgr. Otten Bros., Inc., Detroit, 1937-41; pres., dir. radio sta. WGAY, Silver Spring, Md., 1946-59, St. Louis Broadcasting Corp., Brentwood, Mo., 1953-58, Pitts. Broadcasting Co., 1954-59; pres., treas., dir. Capitol Broadcasting Co., Nashville, 1954-59; Asso. Broadcaster, Inc., Ft. Worth-Dallas, 1957-59; partner Western N.Y. Broadcasting Co., Buffalo, 1957-60; pres., dir. Washington Planagraph Co., 1956-60, Mid.-Fla. Radio Corp., Orlando, 1952-59; treas., dir. Mid.-Fla. Television Corp., 1957-60; owner Kluge Investment Co., Washington, 1956-60; partner Nashton Properties, Nashville, 1954-60, Texworth Investment Co., Ft. Worth, 1957-60; chmn. bd. Seaboard Service System, Inc., 1957-58; pres. New Eng. Fritos, Boston, 1947-55, N.Y. Inst. Dieteics, N.Y.C., 1953-60; chmn. bd., pres., dir. Metromedia, Inc., N.Y.C., including met. broadcasting div., world wide broadcasting div. and Foster & Kleiser div., outdoor advt.; chmn. bd., treas., dir. Kluge, Finkelstein & Co., food brokers, Balt.; chmn. bd., treas. Tri-Suburban Broadcasting Corp., Washington, Kluge & Co., Washington, Silver City Sales Co., Washington; dir. Mariott-Hot Shoppes, Inc., Nat. Bank Md., Waldorf Astoria Corp., Just One Bread, Inc.; mem. advt. council Mfrs. Hanover Trust Co. Mem. Washington Bd. Trade. Bd. dirs., Brand Names Found., Inc.; v.p. bd. dirs. United Cerebral Palsy Research and Ednl. Found., 1972—; turstee Strang Clinic Miliken U. Served to capt. AUS, 1941-45. Mem. Nat., Washington (pres. 1958) food brokers assns., Grocery Wheels Washington, Grocery Mfrs. Reps. Washington, Advt. Club Washington, Nat. Assn. Radio and Television Broadcasters, Advt. Council N.Y.C., Nat. Sugar Brokers Assn. Clubs: Army and Navy, University, Figure Skating, National Capital Skeet and Trap, Broadcasters (Washington); Metropolitan, Columbia Associates, University (N.Y.C.); Olympic (San Francisco); Marco Polo (N.H. gov.). Office: 485 Lexington Ave New York City NY 10017

KLUMPP, OSCAR EDWARD, gear co. exec.; b. Rochester, N.Y., Apr. 1, 1917; s. Ernest and Louisa (Greffrath) K.; grad. high sch.; m. Mary Elizabeth LaDue, Sept. 18, 1948; children—Barbara, Laraine, Stephen, Nancy, Joanne. Machinist apprentice Gleason Works, Rochester, 1934-38, machine insp., 1938-40, traveling service engr., 1940-45; founder Rochester Bevel Gear Co., Inc. (N.Y.), 1945, pres., 1945—. Mem. Soc. Mfg. Engrs., Am. Gear Mfrs. Assn. Presbyterian. Home: 857 Embury Rd Penfield NY 14526 Office: 20 Saginaw Dr Rochester NY 14623

KLUNDER, HANS KARL FRIEDRICH, urban planner; b. Erlangen, Germany, June 14, 1928; s. Werner Adolf and Marianne Margarete (Freiin von Seckendorff) K.; came to U.S., 1951, naturalized, 1964; B.S. cum laude, U. N.H., 1954; M.City and Regional Planning, Harvard U., 1957; m. Lee Booth, Sept. 1, 1955 (div. 1976); children—Hans P., Steven C., Heidi M. Dir. city planning City of Bangor (Maine), 1956-59; dir. planning div. James W. Sewall Co., Old Town, Maine, 1959-61; spl. cons. State of Maine, Augusta, 1961-62; pres., chief planner Hans Klunder Assoc., Inc., Bradford, Vt., 1962—; instr. community planning U. Maine, 1959-61; vis. critic Harvard U., 1962—, Dartmouth Coll., 1962—. N.H. rep. to White House Conf. on Communities of Tomorrow, 1972. Served in German Army, 1943-45. Recipient Am. Indsl. Devel. Council award of excellence, 1968; Fulbright scholar U. N.H., 1952. Mem. Am. Soc. Planning Ofcls., Soc. Protection of N.H. Forests, Am. Inst. Planners. Club: Lions (pres. 1974, 77). Home: Main St Bradford VT 05033 Office: PO Box 455 Main St Bradford VT 05033

KLUSS, WILFRED MARTIN, oil co. exec.; b. Waterloo, Iowa, June 19, 1921; s. Fred John and Harriet Maude K.; S.B., Harvard Coll., 1942, postgrad. Bus. Sch., 1946-47; B.A., New Coll., Oxford (Eng.) U., 1949, M.A., 1949; m. Doree H. Gongwer, Dec. 2, 1950; children—Stewart Radford, Annette Elizabeth, Suzanne Caroline. Specialist overseas devel. Econ. Cooperation Adminstrn., Paris, 1949-50; jr. statistician Morgan Stanley & Co., N.Y.C., 1950-51; asst. loan officer Internat. Bank Reconstrn. and Devel., Washington, 1951-54; in Middle East affairs, marine transp. Mobil Oil Co., N.Y.C., 1954-71; with Continental Oil Co., Stamford, Conn., v.p., 1975—; trustee Union Savs. Bank N.Y. Mem. exec. com. European Republican Com., London, 1968; bd. govs. New Rochelle Hosp. Med. Center, 1977—, treas., 1978. Served with USNR, 1943-46. Decorated Bronze Star with combat V. Harvard Coll. Nat. scholar, 1938-42; Am. Rhodes scholar, 1947-49. Mem. Soc. Naval Architects and Marine Engrs., Am. Bur. Shipping, Oil Cos. Internat. Marine Forum, Fedn. Am. Controlled Shipping (exec. com. 1977—), Am. Petroleum Inst. (vice-chmn. com. transp. water 1977—), Phi Beta Kappa. Republican. Presbyterian. Clubs: Larchmont Yacht (commodore 1973-76), Storm Trysail (gov. 1977—), Cruising Am., Royal Ocean Racing, N.Y. Yacht, Harvard N.Y.C. Home: 1061 Bay Head Rd Mamaroneck NY 10543 Office: High Ridge Park Stamford CT 06904

KNAPP, AUDENRIED WHITTEMORE, sales exec.; b. St. Louis, Feb. 6, 1933; s. George and Damaris (MacBeth) K.; B.S. in B.A., Washington U., 1958; M.B.A., Creighton U., 1970; m. Agatha Krantz, Feb. 6, 1960; children—Audenried Whittemore, Elizabeth Ravenel. With 3M Co., St. Paul, 1959-71; mktg. mgr. Am. Type Founders, Whitinsville, Mass., 1972-75; sales mgr. Keyline Corp., Clark, N.J., 1976-77; nat. sales mgr. Macbeth Corp., Newburgh, N.Y., 1977—. Served with U.S. Army, 1953-55. Address: 828 Cedar Terr Westfield NJ 07090

KNAPP, CHARLES ALBERT, cons. environ. engr.; b. N.Y.C., Aug. 25, 1916; s. Charles and Minnie (Koch) K.; B.C.E., N.Y. U., 1940; m. Violet Eggert, Aug. 6, 1939; children—Dianne (Mrs. Donald A. Semsel), Nancy (Mrs. Paul J. Wilt). Jr. engr. C.E., Army Dept. Sault Ste. Marie, Mich., 1941-42; project engr. Dorr Co., N.Y.C., 1942-44, san. engr., N.Y.C., also Stamford, Conn., 1944-54; eastern mgr. san. div. Dorr-Oliver Inc., Stamford, 1955-62, nat. mgr. san. div., mfg. equipment for water and wastewater treatment plants, 1962-63; v.p. Metcalf & Eddy Inc., cons. environmental engrs., Boston, 1963—. Diplomate Am. Acad. Environ. Engrs. Registered profl. engr., Mass., Conn., N.Y. Fellow ASCE; mem. New Eng. Water Pollution Control Assn. (pres., 1974), Am. Pub. Works Assn. (named New Eng. Man of Year 1972, sec.-treas. 1979—), Am. Water Works Assn., Water Pollution Control Fedn. (dir. 1975-78), Soc. Am. Mil. Engrs. Patentee clarifier equipment, prefabricated sewage treatment plant. Home: PO Box 478 West Chatham MA 02669 Office: Metcalf & Eddy 50 Stansford St Boston MA 02114

KNAPP, GORDON ALWYN, elec. engr.; b. Afton, N.Y., Sept. 9, 1921; s. Frank and Flora Belle (Lord) K.; A.A.S., N.Y. State U., 1952; student Utica Coll., 1952-58; m. Elizabeth Louise Badger, Sept. 20, 1958; children—James Robert, Donald Thomas, Joanne Elizabeth. Electronics testman IBM Corp., Endicott, N.Y., 1951; sales investigator Better Bus. Bur., Binghamton, N.Y., 1952; draftsman Gen. Electric Co., Syracuse, N.Y., 1952-53, designer, Utica, N.Y., 1953-61, electronics specialist, 1961-63, standards engr., documentation specialist, 1963—; cons. NASA, 1963. Active Boy Scouts Am.; mem. Planning Bd. Clayville (N.Y.), 1960-66, assessor, trustee, 1966-73. Served with USNR, 1945-47. Mem. IEEE, Am. Def. Preparedness Assn., Am. Nat. Standards Inst., Nat. Elec. Mfrs. Assn., ASME. Republican. Roman Catholic. Home: Clay Manor Clayville NY 13322 Office: Gen Electric Co French Rd Utica NY 13503

KNAPP, NANCY HAY, psychologist; b. Cleve., June 2, 1922; d. Henry Homer and Aurore Louise (LaCroix) Hay; student Bennington Coll., 1939-40; B.A., Hunter Coll., 1957; M.S.Ed., U. Pa., 1971, postgrad., 1971—; m. Richard Dominick Knapp, Sept. 11, 1955; children—Pamela. Counselor, Johnson O'Connor Research Found., N.Y.C., 1944-46; staff analyst Personnel Lab., N.Y.C., 1946-48; employment mgr., acting personnel mgr. Allied Purchasing Corp., N.Y.C., 1948-51; cons. supervising analyst Personnel Lab., 1951-55; ind. cons., Rochester, N.Y. and Chapel Hill, N.C., 1955-65; clin. and counseling dir. Resources for Women, U. Pa., Phila., 1972-78, bd. dirs. 1975—; v.p., dir. profl. services Wittreich Assos., Phila., 1978—; cons. women's career devel. to various ednl., religious, community groups, 1972-78; tchr. Main Line Sch. Night, Lower Merion, Pa., 1978—. Coordinator, steering com. Coalition for the Edn. and Placement of Women, Phila., 1976-78. Mem. Am. Personnel and Guidance Assn., Am. Psychol. Assn., Nantucket Hist. Assn., Nantucket Conservation Found., Sons and Daus. of Nantucket, Phi Delta Kappa, Pi Lambda Theta, Sigma Tau Delta. Contbr. articles to profl. jours. Home: 326 Sprague Rd Narberth PA 19072 Office: Wittreich Assos 7600 Stenton Ave Philadelphia PA 19118

KNAPPER, WILLIAM HEDRICK, surgeon; b. Hanover, Pa., Sept. 20, 1933; s. Howard Park and Jessie Marie (Hedrick) K.; student U. Fla., 1951-56; M.D., Temple U., 1962; m. Barbara Jean Biringer, June 12, 1954; children—William Park, Brenda Lee, Beverly Biringer. Intern, Reading (Pa.) Hosp., 1962-63; resident in gen. surgery Temple U. Hosp., Phila., 1963-67; sr. resident in surgery Meml. Hosp.,

N.Y.C., 1967-69; fellow in surgery Cornell U. Med. Coll., N.Y.C, 1968-69; practice medicine specializing in surgery N.Y.C., 1969—; clin. asst. surgeon Meml. Hosp., 1969-70, asst. attending surgeon, 1970-72, asso. attending surgeon, 1972—; instr. surgery Temple U. Health Scis. Center, Phila., 1966-67; instr. in surgery Cornell U. Med. Coll., 1969-72, asst. prof. surgery, 1972—; asst. clinician Sloan-Kettering Inst., N.Y.C., 1971—; cons. in surg. oncology Kingston (N.Y.) Hosp., 1973—, Nyack (N.Y.) Hosp., 1975—. Sr. clin. trainee USPHS, 1967-69. Diplomate Am. Bd. Surgery, Nat. Bd. Med. Examiners. Mem. A.C.S., N.Y. State, N.Y. County med. socs., N.Y. Cancer Soc., Pan Pacific Surg. Assn., N.Y. Acad. Scis., N.Y. Acad. Medicine, James Ewing Soc., AMA, Am. Radium Soc., Am. Soc. Clin. Oncology. Republican. Presbyterian. Club: N.Y. Athletic. Contbr. articles on surgery to profl. jours.; mem. editorial bd. Meml. Sloan-Kettering Clin. Bull., 1971—. Home: 124 Corona Ave Pelham NY 10803 Office: 1275 York Ave New York City NY 10021

KNAUF, JANINE BERNICE, educator; b. Rochester, N.Y., Apr. 10, 1945; d. William Charles and Ila May (Hauss) Knauf; S.B., Mass. Inst. Tech., 1967; M.B.A., Rutgers U., 1971; postgrad. Columbia, 1972—; 1 son, Christopher Robert Burgess. Research engr. Northrop/Norair, Hawthorne, Calif., 1965-66; sci. research engr. Rockwell Internat., Los Angeles, 1967-68; accountant Knauf and Knauf, Rochester, 1968-69, 76-78; lectr. mgmt. dept. Poly. Inst. N.Y., 1972-73; asst. prof. info. systems Rutgers U., Newark, N.J., 1973—. C.P.A., N.Y. State. Mem. N.Y. State, Am. Women's Socs. C.P.A.'s. Soc. Women Engrs., Internat. Platform Assn., Am. Inst. Aeros. and Astronautics, Am. Accounting Assn., AAUP, Aircraft Owners and Pilots Assn., Beta Gamma Sigma, Sigma Gamma Tau. Office: 92 New St Newark NJ 07102

KNEAREM, JAMES LESTER, chem. co. exec.; b. Joliet, Ill., Dec. 26, 1930; s. Claude Lester and Dorthy Louise (Mattke) K.; B.S. in Mech. Engring., U. Mo.-Mo. Sch. Mines, 1953; M.E. (hon.), U. Mo., Rolla, 1974; m. Mary Louise Perella, Aug. 2, 1953; children—Keith, Kay. Test engr. Allison div. Gen. Motors Corp., Indpls., 1953; with Hercules Inc., Wilmington, Del., 1955—, mgr. market devel. plastic products group, 1973-76, project mgr. food and fragrance devel. dept., 1976-78, product mgr. PFW Gums, 1978—. Active Boy Scouts Am., 1971-73. Served with AUS, 1953-55. Mem. ASME, Am. Inst. Aero. and Astronautical Engrs., Mo. Sch. Mines Alumni Assn., Kappa Alpha. Presbyterian. Clubs: Cumberland Country; Radley Run Country (West Chester, Pa.). Home: 1108 Independence Dr West Chester PA 19380 Office: 910 Market St Wilmington DE 19899

KNEAVEL, THOMAS CHARLES, JR., psychologist; b. Balt., Oct. 30, 1941; s. Thomas Charles and Caroline Frances (Noha) K.; B.S., Loyola Coll., Balt., 1963, M.Ed., 1968; Ph.D., U. Ottawa, 1979; m. Ann Callanan, Dec. 18, 1970; 1 child, Meredith. Tchr. Ridge Sch., Towsen, Md., 1961-65; psychologist Balt. City Schs., 1965-68; clin. psychologist D.C. Children's Center, Laurel, Md., 1969-70; psychology intern Child Study Center, U. Ottawa, 1970-71, Child Diagnostic and Devel. Clinic, Children's Hosp. of Eastern Ont., Ottawa, 1971-72; sch. psychologist Cape Henlopen Sch. Dist., Nassau, Del., 1972—; psychologist Community Mental Health Clinic, Beebe Hosp., Lewes, Del., 1973—. Mem. citizens adv. bd. Community Mental Health Clinic, Beebe Hosp., Lewes, 1974—. Mem. Am., Del. psychol. assns., Nat. Assn. Sch. Psychologists (charter), Del. Sch. Psychologists Assn. (pres. 1976-77). Roman Catholic. Home: RD 1 Box 219 Sandy Brae Lewes DE 19958 Office: Cape Henlopen Dist Office Nassau DE 19969

KNEELAND, DONALD EARL, ins. co. exec.; b. Corning, N.Y., Apr. 18, 1933; s. William Francis and Ethel Mary (Keenan) K.; A.B., Niagara U., 1955; postgrad. Sch. Journalism, Pa. State U., 1960-61; m. Judith Zammett, July 13, 1968; children—Beth Ann, Kristine. Communications supr. R.T. French Co., Rochester, N.Y., 1963-67; publs. editor Darcy Assos., Rochester, 1967-68; pub. relations/advt. dir. Blue Cross and Blue Shield, Rochester Area, 1968—. Pub. relations chmn. Genesee Valley Citizens League for Nursing, Rochester, 1973-74; chmn. pub. relations com. Monroe County Cancer and Leukemia Assn. mem. Rochester region blood program com., pub. relations com. ARC, 1975—; bd. dirs., sec. Rochester Adv. Council, 1973-75. Served with AUS, 1955-57. Recipient 1st award N.Y. State Press Assn. and Wall St. Jour., 1960. Mem. Rochester Soc. Communicating Arts (treas. 1973-74, award 1970), Pub. Relations Soc. Am. (dir. 1974-77, sec. 1975-76). Home: 14 Lowell Dr Macedon NY 14502 Office: 41 Chestnut St Rochester NY 14647

KNEIPP, SALLY ANN, educator; b. Washington, Oct. 7, 1945; d. John Albert and Janet Pierce (Rettew) K.; B.A., Roanoke Coll., 1967; M.Ed., U. N.C., 1970; Ph.D., U. Md., 1977. Vocat. rehab. counselor N.C. Div. Vocat. Rehab., Durham, 1969-71; vocat. rehab. counselor D.C. Bur. Rehab. Services, 1971-76, staff devel. specialist, 1976-78; dir. tng. Temple U. Rehab. Research and Tng. Center, Phila., 1978—, asst. prof. dept. rehab. medicine Sch. Medicine, 1978—; part-time instr. U. Md. Rehab. Counseling Program, 1975-78, Fed. City Coll., 1973-74. Recipient Superior Performance award D.C. Govt., 1976. Mem. Nat. Rehab. Assn., Nat. (Counselor of Year, Mid-Atlantic Region 1976), Am. rehab. counseling assns., Am. Personnel and Guidance Assn., Am. Soc. Tng. and Devel. Democrat. Home: 5919 Greene St Philadelphia PA 19144 Office: Moss Rehab Hosp 12th and Tabor Rd Philadelphia PA 19141

KNELLER, JOHN WILLIAM, ednl. adminstr.; b. Oldham, Eng., Oct. 15, 1916; A.B., Clark U., 1938, Litt.D., 1970; A.M., Yale, 1948, Ph.D., 1950; French govt. fellow, Fulbright fellow U. Paris (France), 1949-50; Asst. in instruction Yale, 1947-49; instr. French, Oberlin Coll., 1950-52, asst. prof., 1952-55, asso. prof., 1955-59, prof., 1959-65, chmn. romance langs. dept., 1958-65, dean. Coll. Arts and Scis., 1967-68, provost, 1965-69; pres. Bklyn Coll., City U. N.Y., from 1969, now prof. humanities and arts Hunter Coll., Grad. Sch. and Univ. Center; trustee Independence Savings Bank; mem., chmn. subcom. on enrollment goals and projections N.Y. Edn. Commr.'s Adv. Council on Higher Edn. Trustee Bklyn. Inst. Arts and Scis.; bd. dirs. Downtown Bklyn. Devel. Assn., G.F. Kneller Found.; Am. Israel Friendship League; cons. Nat. Endowment for Humanities. Decorated chevalier Ordre des Palmes Academiques. Mem. Am. Assn. Tchrs. French (exec. council 1962-68), Modern Lang. Assn. (exec. council 1965-69), Yale Grad. Sch. Assn. (exec. council 1967-71), Bklyn. C. of C. (dir.), Kappa Delta Pi, Alpha Sigma Lambda. Clubs: Brooklyn, Century, Rembrandt, University, Yale of N.Y. Co-author: Introduction a le poesie francaise, 1962; Initiation au francais, 1963; chpts. to books. Asso. editor Yale French Studies, 1947-48; mng. editor The French Review, 1962-65, editor, 1965-68. Contbr. articles to profl. jours. Office: Hunter Coll Dept Humanities 695 Park Ave New York NY 10021*

KNEPPAR, STANLEY ROBERT, data communication co. exec.; b. Bklyn., June 13, 1930; s. Joseph and Rachel (Baum) K.; B.A. in Indsl. Mgmt., Rochester Inst. Tech., 1969; student Queens Coll., 1950-61, Monroe Community Coll., 1970; m. Clara Aronson, May 6, 1950; children—Raymond J., Samuel C. Structural engr. Republic Aviation Co., Farmingdale, N.Y., 1949-59; cons., structural engr. Grumman Aircraft Co., Bethpage, N.Y., 1959-61; cons., design engr. Xerox Co., Webster, N.Y., 1964-68; sr. project engr. Friden div. Singer Co., Rochester, N.Y., 1968-70; v.p. ops., sec., dir. Techtran Industries, Inc., Rochester, 1970—; v.p. A.D. Dats subs. Techtran Industries, Inc., 1977—; active Monroe County React, Am. Cancer Soc.; v.p. Temple Sinai, 1971. Mem. Am. Buyers Assn. Republican. Club: Masons. Home: 16 Winding Brook Dr Fairport NY 14450 Office: 200 Commerce Dr Rochester NY 14623

KNIGHT, EDWARD R., lawyer, judge, educator, psychologist; b. Milw., Oct. 5, 1917; s. Harry and Lillian (Bachman) K.; A.B., U. Wis., 1940, J.D., 1941; A.M., N.Y. U., 1942, Ph.D., 1943; m. Judith A. Weidberg, July 6, 1941; 1 dau., Barbara Jane. Admitted to Wis. bar, 1941, N.J. bar, 1976; master Oxford Sch., Pleasantville, N.J., 1941, psychologist, 1942, head psychologist, 1943, asst. headmaster, 1945-47, headmaster, 1947-73, emeritus, 1973—; U.S. magistrate, 1976—; judge Municipal Ct., Margate City, N.J., 1976—. Dir. 1st Nat. Bank of South Jersey. Pres., bd. govs. Atlantic City Med. Center, 1973—; chmn. Master Planning Bd. Egg Harbor Twp., N.J., 1961-73; chmn. Atlantic County (N.J.) Charter Study Commn., 1973-74. Served from pvt. to capt., USAAF, 1943-45; personnel com., personnel div. Air Tech. Service Command, Wright Field. Diplomate Am. Bd. Profl. Psychology. Fellow Am. Psychol. Assn. (sch. psychologists div.); mem. Eastern, N.J. psychol. assns., Nat. Assn. Ind. Schs., N.J. Assn. Sch. Psychologists, Interam. Soc. Psychology, Boarding School Headmasters Assn. Middle States (pres. 1966-67), Wis. Alumni Assn., U. Wis. Mem. Union (life), Phi Delta Kappa, Kappa Delta Pi. Author: Self-Discipline and Academic Failure. Author articles edn., psychology; editorial. Parental Delinquency. Home: 7 N Thurlow Ave Margate City NJ 08402

KNIGHT, GEORGE LITCH, clergyman; b. Rockford, Ill., Jan. 2, 1925; s. Bradley Jay and Grace (King) K.; B.A., D.D., Centre Coll. of Ky., 1947; B.D., Union Theol. Sem. N.Y., 1951. Ordained Presbyn. Ch. 1951; asst. minister West Side Presbyn. Ch., Ridgewood, N.J., 1951-56, co-pastor, 1956-57; minister, Lafayette Avenue Presbyn. Ch., Bklyn., 1957-67, 68—, Old First Presbyn. Ch., Newark, N.J., 1967-68; tchr. New Brunswick (N.J.) Sem., 1957-63, Biblical Sem., N.Y.C., 1960-63, Union Sem. Sch. Sacred Music, N.Y.C., 1967-71; moderator Presbytery of N.Y.C., 1963. Fellow Hymn Soc. Am. (founder The Hymn, quar. mag.). Contbr. articles to profl. jours. Office: 85 S Oxford St Brooklyn NY 11217

KNIGHT, JAMES JOHN, dental services co. exec.; b. Mpls., May 28, 1942; s. John Louis and Grace Marion (Barton) K.; B.F.A., Mpls. Coll. Art and Design, 1965; M.B.A., U. Pa., 1970; children—Kathleen Mary, Kristeen Marie. Indsl. designer Brooks Stevens Assos., Milw., 1965-67; market devel. staff designer Rohm & Haas Co., Phila., 1967-69, asst. product mgr., 1969-72, consumer mktg. mgr., 1972-75; dir. mktg., mktg. services mgr. Codesco, Inc. subs. I.U. Internat., Phila., 1976—. Recipient Cine Golden Eagle award for Non-Theatrical Film for Industry, 1975, Silver award N.Y. Internat. Film Festival, 1975, certificate merit Chgo. Internat. Film Festival, 1975. Mem. Am. Mktg. Assn., Assn. M.B.A. Execs., Sales and Mgmt. Execs. Roman Catholic. Established self-help minority co. utilizing Rohm and Haas plastics methodology, created and directed ednl. services group nationwide jr. and sr. high sch. students in plastics tech. Home: Westgate Village Apts 115 Frazer PA 19355 Office: 460 N 6th St Philadelphia PA 19101

KNIGHT, JAMES KENNETH, chem. co. exec.; b. Norhampton, Mass., Apr. 3, 1951; s. Kenneth William and Helen (Weidhaas) K.; B.S. in Bus. Mgmt., U. Hartford (Conn.), 1974; m. Janice Mooney, June 21, 1978. With Butchers Wax Co., 1974-77, Mid-Atlantic zone sales mgr., 1976; nat. sales mgr. Bestall Chem. Corp., Maspeth, N.H., 1977-78; mktg. mgr. Hercon Products div. Health-Chem Corp., N.Y.C., 1978—; cons. Furst & Mooney. Mem. N.Y.C. and N.J. San. Supply Assn. Home: 277 W 10th St New York NY 10011 Office: 1107 Broadway New York NY 10010

KNIGHT, WILLIAM JAMES, engring. supplies co. exec.; b. Buffalo, Aug. 22, 1933; s. Herbert and Ella (Forster) K.; student Babson Inst., 1951-52, Millard Fillmore Coll., 1952-53; m. Yvonne Onalee Catlin, Apr. 5, 1953; children—Candyce Louise, James Herbert, Richard William. Br. mgr. Seneca Blue Print Co., Inc., Kenmore, N.Y., 1955-58, gen. mgr. engring. supply div., 1958-60, gen. mgr. sales and accounting offices, Cheektowaga, 1960-68, exec. v.p., Buffalo, 1968—, also dir. Lectr. audio-visual procedures at area colls. Served with AUS, 1953-55. Mem. Internat. Platform Assn. Mason (Shriner), Rotarian (pres. Cheektowaga 1965-66, dir. 1961-63, 69—). Home: 114 Exeter Rd Williamsville NY 14221 Office: 3360 Union Rd Buffalo NY 14225

KNIPE, ROBERT DANIEL, interior designer; b. Abington, Pa., Dec. 11, 1937; s. Wilmer Stanley and Mary (Smith) K.; student Phila. Mus. Coll. Art, 1955-59. Prin., Robert Daniel Knipe, Interior Designer, Phila. Mem. Inst. Contempporary Art, Phila. Mus. Art. Republican. Methodist. Address: 2031 Locust St Philadelphia PA 19103

KNISELY, RALPH FRANKLIN, microbiologist; b. Altoona, Pa., Mar. 30, 1927; s. Calvin Ross and Frieda Pauline (Neher) K.; B.S., Pa. State U., 1953, postgrad., 1953; m. Ann Martin, May 21, 1960; 1 dau. by previous marriage—Patricia Ann Knisely Durante. Bacteriologist, Altoona Hosp., 1953-56, adminstrv. asst. to pathologist, 1956-59; microbiologist Chem. Corps Dept. Army, Ft. Detrick, Frederick, Md., 1959-72; research microbiologist Edgewood Arsenal Aberdeen Proving Ground, Md., 1972—. Pres. Eastview Civic Assn., Frederick, 1968-69. Served with USN, 1945-46, 50-51; comdr. Res. Lic. dairy lab. dir., Pa. Mem. Am. Soc. Microbiology, Research Soc. Am., Assn. Mil. Surgeons U.S., Ret. Officers Assn. (v.p. chpt. 1969-70), Am. Legion. Republican. Lutheran. Clubs: Heidelberg Country, George Washington Masonic Stamp (pres. 1978—), Masons, Shriners (Altoona); Elks, Nat. Sojourners (pres. Ft. Detrick chpt. 1965-66). Contbr. articles to profl. publs. Home: Route 8 Eastview Frederick MD 21701 Office: Chem Systems Lab DRDAR-CLC-B Aberdeen Proving Ground MD 21010

KNOB, RICHARD EDWARD, corporate publs. mgr.; b. N.Y.C., July 11, 1925; s. John Christopher and Catherine Rebecca (Bruning) K.; B.S., Union Coll., 1946; postgrad. Harvard U., 1946; E.E., Bklyn. Poly. Inst., 1955; m. Helen Grace Simon, May 11, 1946; children—Randolph E., Janet V. Knob Tullo, Kevin J., Richard J., Julie E., Michael C. With Sperry Gyroscope div. Sperry-Rand Corp., Great Neck, N.Y., 1947—, publications mgr., 1967—. Mem. Am. Defense Preparedness Assn., Aerospace Industries Assn., Nat. Security Indsl. Assn., Am. Mgmt. Assn. Republican. Roman Catholic. Home: 3311 Austin Ave Wantagh NY 11793 Office: Sperry Gyroscope Great Neck NY 11020

KNOBLER, WILLIAM I., mktg. research exec.; b. Bklyn., May 10, 1933; s. Isaac and Minnie (Schneider) K.; B.B.A., Coll. City N.Y., 1953; M.S., Columbia, 1954; postgrad. N.Y. U., 1956; m. Florence Schwartz, Aug. 1, 1953; children—Caren, Sheri. Asso. research dir. Prudential Ins. Co., Newark, 1956-59, Reach, McClinton & Co., N.Y.C., 1960-63, Lennen & Newell, Inc., N.Y.C., 1963-65; v.p. Comml. Analysts Co., N.Y.C., 1965-67, Russell Mktg. Research, N.Y.C., 1967-69; mktg. research dir. Am. Bankers Assn., N.Y.C., 1969-71; founder, pres. William Knobler Co., Inc., N.Y.C., 1971—; adj. asso. prof. Grad. Sch. Bus., Pace U.; adj. adj. lectr. mktg. dept. Baruch Coll., City U. N.Y., 1971—. Served with AUS, 1954-56. Mem. Am. Mktg. Assn. (chpt. dir., 1st v.p. 1970—), Am. Assn. Pub. Opinion Research. Democrat. Publisher: Internat. Directory Mktg. Research Houses, 1970—. Home: 109 Garden St Great Neck NY 11021 Office: 420 Lexington Ave New York City NY 10017

KNORR, BETTY JEWEL BENKERT (MRS. NEIL MCLEAN KNORR), naturalist; b. Summit, N.J., Aug. 10, 1928; d. William R. and Amelia (Kreutzer) Benkert; grad. high sch.; Ph.D. (hon.), Hamilton State U., 1973, Colo. State Christian Coll., 1973; m. Neil McLean Knorr, Dec. 13, 1946. Licensed bird bander Fish and Wildlife Service, U.S. Dept. Interior, 1957—; banded over 50,000 wild birds of 175 different species; spl. ornithol. research on shorebirds, hummingbirds and blackbirds; other varied research in bird banding; established extensive wildflower preserve and rhododendron gardens at home; engaged in propagation rare native wildflowers donating same to pub. arboretums, preserves and sanctuaries; vol. tchr., cons, on conservation and nature study, 1948—; tchr. Brookdale Coll.; active many local, state, nat. conservation issues; responsible for sav. wilderness area threatened with destruction and now preserved as part of Cheesequake State Park; organizer nation-wide Project Snap to salvage threatened native plants and replant them for ednl. and civic purposes. Active Girl Scouts U.S.A., 1938—; counselor, cons. Boy Scouts Am., 1960—. Mem. Amateur Organists Assn. Internat., Monmouth, Shore organ socs., Eastern Bird Banding Assn., Nat., N.J. Audubon socs., Torrey Bot. Club. Home: 81 Hope Rd Tinton Falls NJ 07724

KNOTT, CHARLES ARTHUR, devel. co. exec.; b. Balt., May 31, 1910; s. Henry Aden and Martha M. (Doyle) K.; student Calvert Hall Coll., 1928; grad. archtl. design Md. Inst., 1935; m. Catherine W. Williams, May 15, 1940; children—Charles Arthur, William Henry, Mary Catherine, Henry Aden II. With Knott Industries, Inc., Balt., 1929—, chmn. bd., 1950—; dir. Md. Nat. Bank. Mem. exec. bd. Balt. area council Boy Scouts Am., 1954—. Pres., Charles and Martin F. Knott Found, Inc.; trustee Md. Inst. Art, Calvert Hall Coll.; pres. bd. trustees Benedictine Sch.; past pres. Bldg. Congress and Exhange Balt.; Mem. Nat. Catholic Com. for Scouts, Asso. Builders and Contractors Assn. (past pres., founder), Nat. Assn. Indsl. Parks (founder, dir. emeritus), Md. Honor Soc., Md. Hist. Soc. Clubs: Balt. Country; Seaview Country (N.J.); Center; Ponte Vedra (Fla.). Home: 19 Theo Ln Towson MD 21204 Office: 6665 Security Blvd Baltimore MD 21207

KNOWLAND, R. THOMAS, printmaker, educator; b. Boston, May 11, 1942; s. Ashton Ansley and Margaret Allison (Watson) K.; B.F.A., Mass. Coll. Art, 1964; M.F.A in Printmaking and Painting, Pratt Inst., 1966; m. Carol Jane Heath, June 7, 1964 (div.); children—Jason Ansley, Meghan Beth; m. 2d, W. Susan Lundgren, Aug. 12, 1978. Tchr. art Middle Country Central Sch. Dist. 11, Centereach, N.Y., 1966—; one-man shows 75 Rockefeller Plaza Gallery, N.Y.C., Southampton (N.Y.) Coll. exhibited in group shows N.A.D., Soc. Am. Graphic Artists, Boston Printmakers, N.W. Printmakers, Miami Graphics Biennial, Painters and Sculptors Soc. N.J., Dickinson State Coll. N.D., Western N.Mex. U., many others; commn. bronze sculpture The Phoenix, 1975. Louis Comfort Tiffany Found. grantee, 1966. Recipient numerous awards, purchase prizes. Mem. N.E.A., Boston Printmakers, Graphics Soc. N.H., Am. Fedn. Tchrs., N.Y. United Tchrs. Home: 28 Gail Dr Lake Ronkonkoma NY 11779

KNOWLES, MARY GARDNER, librarian; b. Waltham, Mass., July 10, 1910; d. William E. and Annie (Mackin) Gardner; student Bates Coll., 1930-33; m. Clive D. Knowles, Apr. 1933 (div. 1948); 1 son, Jonathan. Children's librarian Watertown (Mass.) Free Pub. Library, 1935-38; br. librarian Morrill Meml. Library, Norwood, Mass., 1949-53; librarian William Jeanes Meml. Library, Lafayette Hill, Pa., 1954—. Home: 543 Whitehall Rd Norristown PA 19401 Office: 4051 Joshua Rd Lafayette Hill PA 19444

KNOWLTON, KENNETH FRANKLIN, sanitary engr.; b. Natick, Mass., May 22, 1913; s. Samuel Edgar and Alice Boynton (Johnson) K.; B.S. in Civil Engring., Northeastern U., 1935; postgrad. Harvard, 1936; m. Isabel Lawrence Ward, June 28, 1941; children—Thomas Ward, Peter Brooks. Jr. san. engr. Mass. Dept. Pub. Health, 1935-41; resident engr. H.K. Barrows, Bristol, R.I., 1937; engr. Cabot Carbon Co., Pampa, Tex., 1938-39; supt., chemist Salem and Beverly Water Supply Bd. (Mass.), 1941—. Cons. U.S. AID, Salvador, Brazil, 1964; lectr., Northeastern U., 1960-72. Chmn., Essex County (Mass.) Mosquito Control, 1958—, Ipswich River (Mass.) Watershed Dist. Commn., 1966-71; mem. adv. com. Mass. Dept. Pub. Health, Div. Environmental Engring., 1966-72. Served with San. Corps, AUS, 1943-47. Registered profl. engr., Mass., R.I., N.H., Maine Desmond Fitzgerald scholar Boston Soc. C.E., 1935. Mem. Am. (Man of Year award New Eng. sect. 1973, chmn. New Eng. sect. 1972-73), New Eng. (Commemorative award 1954, pres. 1963-64) water works assns., Boston Soc. Civil Engrs. (dir. 1957-58). Conglist. (deacon 1958-64). Clubs: Appalachian Mountain (Boston); Manchester (Mass.) Harbor Boat; Bass Haven Yacht (Beverly). Home: 74 Conant St Beverly MA 01915 Office: 50 Arlington Ave Beverly MA 01915

KNOX, DONALD ROBERT, landscape architect; b. Somerville, Mass., Sept. 5, 1936; s. Harold Lester and Gladys Anne (Laye) K.; B.A. in Econs., Tufts U., 1958; B. Landscape Arch., U. Mass., 1960; m. Rita Doris Courcy, Aug. 22, 1964; children—Kimberley Anne, Linda Leanne, Cheryl Lynne. Landscape architect Donald R. Knox, Inc., Greenville, Del., 1967—; exec. dir. Kennett Pike Assn., Inc., Greenville, 1975—; dir. Internat. Mini Computer Applications, Inc., Los Angeles; design chmn. Del. Flower Show, 1977. Chmn., New Castle County Beautification Bd., 1970-73; mem. citizens participation adv. council Del. Dept. Hwys. and Transp.; mem. community devel. adv. com. New Castle County Dept. Community Devel. and Housing; bd. dirs. Civic League of New Castle County; trustee Wilmington (Del.) Montessori Assn., Served with USAFR, 1959-65. Mem. Del. C. of C. (exec. com. 1971-73), Am. Soc. Landscape Architects, Am. Arbitration Assn. (Phila. constrn. adv. com. 1972—), Del. C. of C. (state community redevel. exec. com.). Club: Skating (Wilmington). Home: 5 Hollingsworth Dr Centerville DE 19807 Office: PO Box 3968 Greenville DE 19807

KNOX, GAYLORD SHEARER, radiologist; b. Bangkok, Thailand, Oct. 18, 1923; s. Harry Gaylord and Lela Emogene (Shearer) K.; student Ohio State U., 1946-47; M.D., Tulane, 1951; m. Barbara Ruth Snyder, June 8, 1946; children—Laura Elizabeth, Margaret Hunanian, Robert Gaylord. Intern Charity Hosp., New Orleans, 1951-52; resident in radiology Walter Reed Gen. Hosp., Washington, 1955-58; asso. prof. U. Okla. Med. Sch., 1961-65; asso. prof. U. Md., 1965—; asst. prof. Johns Hopkins U., 1965—; chief dept. radiology Balt. City Hosp., 1965—; pres., Chesapeake Physicians P.A., 1974-78, Chesapeake Casualty Ins. Co. (Colo.), 1976—; vis. prof. Pahlavi U. Med. Sch., Shiraz, Iran, 1975. Mem. dist. com. Boy Scouts Am., adviser Order of the Arrow. Served with AUS, 1953-61. Fellow Am. Coll. Radiology; mem. Md. Radiol. Soc. (pres. 1972), Radiol. Soc. N.Am. Home: 7924-C Starwood Ct Glen Burnie MD 21061 Office: 4940 Eastern Ave Baltimore MD 21224

KNOX, SEYMOUR H., banker; b. Buffalo, Sept. 1, 1898; s. Seymour Horace and Grace (Millard) K.; B.A., Yale U., 1920; m. Helen Northrup, Nov. 20, 1923; children—Seymour Horace III, Northrup.

Banker, 1920; became v.p. Marine Trust Co., 1927, chmn. bd., 1943-70; dir. Marine Midland Bank N.Y. Trustee Aiken Prep. Sch.; pres., dir. Buffalo Fine Arts Acad.; chmn. N.Y. State Council on Arts. Mem. Scroll and Key Soc. (Yale U.), Delta Kappa Epsilon. Clubs: Buffalo, Country, Saturn, Tennis and Squash (Buffalo); Racquet and Tennis, River (N.Y.C.); Bucks (London); Travellers (Paris). Home: 57 Oakland Pl Buffalo NY 14222 Office: Marine Trust Bldg Buffalo NY 14203*

KNUDSEN, RAYMOND BARNETT, clergyman, writer; b. Denver, Nov. 11, 1919; s. Franklin Ole and Julia (Nielsen) K.; student Coll. Emporia, 1937-38. Wheaton Coll., 1938-39; B.A., U. Denver, 1941; Th.N., McCormick Theol. Sem., 1948; student U. Chgo., 1948; D.D., Burton Coll., 1955, LL.D., 1964; m. Edna Mae Nielsen, January 26, 1940; children—Raymond Barnett, Silas John, Mark Allen, Ann Delight. Pastor 8th Ave. Presbyn. Ch., Denver, 1939-40; dir. Martin M. Post Larger Parish, Logansport, Ind., 1941-44; asst. Faith Presbyn. Ch., Chgo., 1945; pastor 1st Presbyn. Ch., Warsaw, Ill., 1946-52, 5th Presbyn. Ch., Springfield, Ill., 1952-63; sr. pastor Webb Horton Meml. Presbyn. Ch., Middletown, N.Y., 1963-70; exec. dir. for fin. devel. Nat. Council of Chs. of Christ in U.S.A., 1970—, asst. gen. sec., 1972-77; pres. Nat. Consultation on Fin. Devel., 1977—; lectr. philosophy Orange County Community Coll., cons. Funding Sources Clearinghouse Inc., 1975—. Chmn. broadcasting press Synod of Ill., 1954-60, mem. gen. council, 1954-62; chmn. founding com. Ill. Presbyn. Home, Springfield, 1954; bd. dirs. Alcohol Edn. Found., 1953-63, Aid to Retarded Children, N.Y., 1963-66; chmn. Fifty Million Dollar Fund, Presbytery Hudson River; pres. Webb Horton Presbyterian Assos., Inc., bd. trustees Orange County Workshop for Disabled, N.Y., 1963; pres. The Counselor Assn., Inc.; v.p. Inst. for Activation Research, Inc.; bd. dirs. United Presbyn. Student Found.; pres. bd. dirs. Occupations, Inc., 1964-69, treas., 1969-71, pres. emeritus, 1975—; exec. bd. Orange County chpt. Aid Retarded Children, 1963-67; pres. bd. trustees Camp Townsend, 1964-70; trustee Homemaker Service of Orange County, 1963-70; pres. Middletown Council Chs., 1967-69; mem. Middletown Narcotics Guidance Council, 1969-70. Chaplain Ill. State Senate, 1953, 55, 57, 59, 60, 61. Mem. Nat. Assn. Ch. Fund Raisers (pres. 1976—), Temperance League Ill. (pres. 1953-56, dir. 1954-63), Nat. Temperance League (hon. v.p.). Mason, Rotarian (chmn. internat. contacts). Author: The Trinity, 1937; New Models for Financing the Local Church, 1974; New Models for Creative Giving, 1976; Models for Ministry, 1978; Developing Dynamic Stewardship, 1978; Administering Ministry and Mission, 1979. Mem. bd. rev. Antenna, 1963—. Contbr. religious columns and broadcasting. Home: 31 Langerfeld Rd Hillsdale NJ 07642 Office: 475 Riverside Dr New York City NY 10027

KNUEPPEL, DANIEL PAUL, sch. adminstr.; b. Olean, N.Y., Oct. 9, 1939; s. Daniel Julius and Helen Marie (Oelschlager) K.; student Concordia Jr. Coll., 1957-58; B.A. in History, Valparaiso U., 1961; postgrad. U. Buffalo, 1961-62; M.A., N.Y. U., 1965, Ed.D., 1968; m. Carol A. Petersen, Dec. 28, 1961; children—Jeffrey, Karen, Bradley. Tchr., Westfield (N.Y.) Acad. and Central Sch., 1961-63, L.I. Luth. High Sch., Brookville, N.Y., 1963-65, Walt Whitman High Sch., Huntington Station, N.Y., 1965-67; asst. prin. Pelham (N.Y.) Meml. High Sch., 1967-68, prin., 1968-70; prin. Tenafly (N.J.) High Sch., 1971—. Life mem. N.Y. State P.T.A. Recipient Founder's Day award N.Y. U., 1969; Community Service award V.F.W., 1975. Mem. Am. Assn. Sch. Adminstrs., Nat. Assn. Secondary Sch. Prins., Nat. Soc. for Study Edn., Kappa Delta Pi, Phi Delta Kappa. Lutheran. Rotarian. Home: 8 Oak Ave Tenafly NJ 07670

KO, HARVEY WAYNE, elec. engr.; b. Phila., May 21, 1944; s. Thomas and Alice K.; B.S. in Elec. Engring., Drexel Inst. Tech., 1967; Ph.D., Drexel U., 1973. Engring. asst. Bell Telephone Co. of Pa., Phila., 1964-65; engr. U. Pa.-Presbyn. Med. Center, Phila., 1966; engr. applied physics lab. Johns Hopkins U., Laurel, Md., 1973—; instr., grad. adviser Drexel U.; evening coll. adviser Johns Hopkins U.; cons. NASA trainee, 1969-70; NSF trainee, 1971-73. Mem. IEEE, Eta Kappa Nu, Tau Beta Pi. Home: 5429 Luckpenny Pl Columbia MD 21045 Office: Applied Physics Lab Johns Hopkins U Johns Hopkins Rd Laurel MD 20810

KO, JERRY JER-CHING, structural engr.; b. Taipei, Taiwan, China, Aug. 2, 1942; s. Tien-Chiu and Liu-Chiu Ko; M.S., Poly. Inst. Bklyn., 1970, postgrad.; m. Kathleen Chiang, Feb. 13, 1968; children—Jimmy, Gene. Engr., Vollmer Assos., N.Y.C., 1968, Amman & Whitney, N.Y.C., 1967-68; squad leader, structrual engr. Gibbs & Hill, Inc., N.Y.C., 1968-77; structrual engr. Ebasco Services, Inc., N.Y.C., 1977—; cons. engr. nuclear and fossil power plants. Scholar civil engring. dept., Cornell U., 1970; lic. profl. engr., N.Y. Mem. ASCE, Am. Concrete Inst. Designer, engr. Omaha Pub. Power Plant, Comanche Peak Nuclear Power Plant, China Steel Co. Power Plant, Taiwan Power Co. Hsieh Ho Power Plant, Talin Power Plant, Petersburg Generating Sta., Indpls. Power & Light Co., power plants Duquesne, Houston, Caroline, air pollution control project. Office: Ebasco Services Inc 2 Rector St New York City NY 10006

KO, ROBERT JER-CHIEN, publisher; b. Taipei, Taian, June 12, 1946; s. Tien Chiu and Liu (Chou) K.; came to U.S., 1969, naturalized, 1978; B.A., Fu Jen Catholic U., Taipei, 1958; m. Sofia Ji-Jeu Huang, Mar. 3, 1973; children—Terris, Gina. Founder, 1970, since pres. Chieng Hua Social Service Amity, Inc., N.Y.C.; pres. Chinese Robert Ko Enterprises Corp., N.Y.C., publishers Chieng Hua News, 1973—. Founder Chieng Chieng Chorus, Taipei, 1966; dir. China commn. Captive Nations Com., 1971-78. Recipient Chinese Best News Writer award, 1975; Chinese Best Overseas Youth award, 1976. Democrat. Author: Viaje en Espana, 1973. Address: PO Box 61 Flushing NY 11352

KOBLENZ, LAWRENCE WILLIAM, physician; b. Bronx, N.Y., Dec. 9, 1948; s. Stuart and Elsie (Kissel) K.; A.B. cum laude, Columbia U., 1969; M.D., Cornell U., 1973. Intern, N.Y. Hosp.-Cornell Med. Center, 1973-74, resident in medicine, 1974-76, asst. physician, 1976—, fellow in medicine Cornell U. Med. Coll., 1974-76, fellow in gastroenterology, 1976-78; clin. asst. Mt. Sinai Hosp. Services, 1976-78. Mem. A.C.P., Am. Soc. Internal Medicine, Am. Gastroenterol. Assn., Am. Soc. Gastrointestinal Endoscopy, N.Y. Acad. Gastroenterology, Am. Chem. Soc., Am. Assn. Polit. and Social Scis., Cornell U. Med. Coll. Alumni Assn., Phi Beta Kappa, Phi Lambda Upsilon. Home: 155 W 68th St New York City NY 10023 Office: 2A E 77 St New York City NY 10021

KOBLINER, RICHARD, educator; b. Bronx, N.Y., May 29, 1935; s. Meyer and Celia (Kanter) K.; B.A., Coll. City N.Y., 1959, M.A., 1962; postgrad. U. Wis., 1962, 68; m. Suzanne Moch, July 11, 1965. Tchr. jr. high sch., Bronx, 1959-64, De Witt Clinton High Sch., Bronx, 1964-71, Hillcrest High Sch., Jamaica, N.Y., 1971—; lectr., Bronx Community Coll., 1969-71; cons. Anti-Defamation League. Bd. dirs. Bay Terrace Condominium. NDEA grantee, 1967; N.Y. State Edn. grantee, 1969; NSF grantee, 1974. Mem. Assn. Tchrs. of Social Studies in N.Y.C. (pres. 1973-75), Nat., N.Y. (dir.) councils for social studies, Orgn. Am. Historians, Am. Hist. Assn., Assn. Curriculum and Supervision Devel., Am. Jewish Hist. Soc., DeWitt Clinton Alumni Assn. Author: The Teaching of Social Studies, 1971; The History of Black Americans, 1972. Home: 18-26 Corporal Kennedy St Bayside NY 11360 Office: 160-05 Highland Ave Jamaica NY 11432

KOBRINE, ARTHUR IRWIN, neurosurgeon; b. Chgo., Oct. 9, 1943; s. Maurice William and Katherine (Lovrencic) K.; B.A. in Chemistry, Northwestern U., 1964, M.D., 1968; m. Cynthia Elizabeth, Apr. 19, 1969; children—Nicole, Steven. Intern, Univ. Hosp., Ann Arbor, Mich., 1968-69; resident in neurosurgery Northwestern U., 1969-70; resident in neurosurgery Walter Reed Gen. Hosp., Washington, 1970-73, asst. chief neurosurgery service, 1973-75; prin. research investigator Armed Forces Radiobiology Research Inst., Bethesda, Md., 1973—; asso. prof. dept. neurosurgery Med. Sch., George Washington U., Washington, 1977—; mem. staffs Washington Hosp. Center, Children's Hosp. Nat. Med. Center. Served with M.C., U.S. Army, 1970-75. Recipient Raymond F. Metcalf award U.S. Army Med. Dept., 1971. Diplomate Am. Bd. Neurol. Surgery. Mem. Am. Assn. Neurol. Surgeons, Congress Neurol. Surgeons, Research Soc. Neurol. Surgery, AMA, A.C.S., Soc. Neurosci., Am. Physiol. Soc., Brit. Brain Research Assn. (hon.), Alpha Omega Alpha. Contbr. articles in field to med. and sci. jours. Office: 2150 Pennsylvania Ave NW Washington DC 20037

KOBUS, RONALD STANLEY, accountant, govt. ofcl.; b. Bklyn., Dec. 12, 1944; s. Joseph Francis and Ceslava (Bartosiewicz) K.; B.S. in Bus. Adminstrn., Seton Hall U., 1966; m. Patricia Shirley Voelkel, June 14, 1969; children—Sherry, Ronald Philip. Accountant, Ryan, Harrington & Mortenson, C.P.A.'s, Newark, N.J., 1966; auditor Def. Contract Audit Agy., N.Y., N.J., Va., 1969-73; asso. dir. fin. mgmt. tng. U.S. CSC, Washington, 1973—. Served with arty., U.S. Army, 1967-69. C.P.A., Va. Mem. Am., D.C. insts. c.p.a.'s, Inst. Internal Auditors. Roman Catholic. Home: 4001 Cool Brooke Way Alexandria VA 22306*

KOCH, EDWARD I., mayor; b. N.Y.C., Dec. 12, 1924; student Coll. City N.Y.; LL.B., N.Y. U. Admitted to N.Y. bar, 1949; Democratic dist. leader, Greenwich Village, N.Y.C., 1963-65, former mem. N.Y. City Council; former sr. partner firm Koch, Lankenau, Schwartz & Kovner; mem. 91st-95th Congresses from 18th N.Y. Dist., resigned, 1977; mayor, N.Y.C., 1978—. Mem. Village Ind. Dems. Office: Office of the Mayor City Hall New York City NY 10007

KOCH, EDWIN ERNEST, artist; b. Bronx, N.Y.C., Feb. 21, 1915; s. Henry and Elsie K. One-man shows include: Artzt Gallery, N.Y.C., 1962, 66; group shows include: Met. Mus. Art, 1952, Bklyn. Mus., 1953, Pa. Acad., 1953, NAD, 1958, Am. Watercolor Soc., 1953; represented in permanent collections: Butler Art Inst., Youngstown, Ohio. Served with AUS, 1942-46. Mem. Audubon Artists Am., Nat. Soc. Painters in Casen and Acrylic (dir. 1975-76), Painters and Sculptors Soc. N.J. (v.p. 1978), Knickerbocker Artists, Artists Equity. Address: RD 1 Box 76 Hoagberg Hill Rd Wallkill NY 12589

KOCH, ERIC, broadcasting exec., author; b. Frankfurt, Germany, Aug. 31, 1919; s. Otto and Ida (Kahn) K.; B.A., St. John's Coll. Cambridge (Eng.) U., 1940; LL.B., U. Toronto, 1943; m. Sonia Mecklenburg, May 11, 1948; children—Tony, Monica, Madeline. With Canadian Broadcasting Corp., 1944—, asso. gen. supr. policy, English Services div., Toronto. Author: The French Kiss, 1969; The Leisure Riots, 1973; The Last Thing You'd Want to Know, 1976; Good Night, Little Spy, 1979. Home: 59 Standish Ave Toronto ON M4W 3B2 Canada Office: 1255 Bay St Toronto ON Canada

KOCH, JAMES HAROLD, advt. exec., author; b. Milw., Mar. 5, 1926; s. Harold E. and Margaret (Thomas) K.; B.A., Carleton Coll., Northfield, Minn., 1949; Woodrow Wilson fellow, Princeton, 1949-50; m. Anne-Marie Beledin Sautour, Feb. 6, 1954. With Dun & Bradstreet, Inc., N.Y.C., 1952-65; sr. partner Aquarian Advt. Assos., Inc., N.Y.C., 1964-72, pres., 1972—; author: Pitfalls in Issuing Municipal Bonds, 2d edit., 1975; A Selected, Annotated Bank Marketing Bibliography, 2d edit., 1971; How Banks Can Use Direct Mail as an Effective Marketing Tool, 1972; also booklets, articles, poetry; editor monthly newsletter Country Property News 1971—. Served with USNR, 1944-46. Mem. Poetry Soc. Am., Mensa, Direct Mktg. Writers Guild, Men's Gallery, Parliament of Women. Office: 1020 Park Ave New York City NY 10028

KOCH, RUTH MARGUERITE, educator, artist; b. Hazleton, Pa., July 11, 1901; d. Henry George and Margaret (Zimmerman) Koch; grad. Bloomsburg State Tchrs. Coll., 1921; Ph.B., Muhlenberg Coll., 1931; M.A., Bucknell U., 1948; student Sch. Fine and Applied Arts, Chgo., 1923; postgrad. N.Y. U., 1925, 28, Pa. State U., 1935; visited art schs., galleries, Europe, 1952, 57, 61, 65, 71. One man shows at Penn State U. Center, 1937, Hazleton Art League, 1948; exhibited annually in group shows Lehigh Art Alliance, Lehigh U., Muhlenberg Coll., nat. shows Miniature Painters Soc., Smithsonian Inst., Corcoran Gallery, also N.Y., N.J., Pa., Kan., Washington; represented in permanent collections at Lehigh U. Art Gallery, Call Chronicle Newspaper Art Collection, Allentown, Pa., also pvt. collections in U.S., P.R., Eng. Art tchr. elementary sch., Hazleton, Pa., 1921-39, jr. high sch., 1939-40, sr. high sch., 1940-67; designed, painted children's stories on glass lantern sides, 1930-35; lectr. art and travels various religious and civic groups, clubs, schs., colls. Recipient 1st place water color, Hazleton, 1938, 3d water color award, Harrisburg, 1940, 41. Mem. Pa. Edn. Assn. (pres. art group Scranton 1947), Nat., Pa., Luzerne County ret. tchrs. assns., Community Concert Assn., Lehigh Art Alliance, Hazleton Art League (Purchase award 1968), Internat. Platform Assn., Delta Kappa Gamma. Lutheran. Contbr. art periodicals. Home and studio: 551 Lincoln St Hazleton PA 18201

KOCH, VERNON CHARLES, ednl. adminstr.; b. St. Louis, Jan. 17, 1939; married, 2 children. M.S. in Elementary Reading, Central Conn. State Coll., New Britain, 1967, certificate in grad. studies, 1975. Tchr., Immanuel Luth. Sch., Bristol, Conn., 1961-74, headmaster, 1974—. Mem. Am. Guild Organists, Luth. Edn. Assn., Internat. Reading Assn., Luth. Elementary Sch. Prins. Certified in teaching and reading cons. Home: 117 Wilcow St Bristol CT 06010 Office: 154 Meadow St Bristol CT 06010

KOCH, VIRGINIA GREENLEAF, painter; b. Chgo., Aug. 28, 1925; d. William Henry and Henrietta Irene (Moser) Greenleaf; pupil of Ivan Olinsky, 1941-42; student Yale U., 1943-45; pupil of Robert Brackman, 1946; student Am. U., Washington, postgrad. 1956-57; pupil of Gene Davis, 1968-70; m. Henry Koch, Aug. 20, 1962 (dec.); children—Deidra G., William G. One-man shows at Studio Gallery, Washington, 1970, 72, 74 Haslem Gallery, Madison, Wis., 1971, In Town Gallery, Cleve., 1973, World Bank, Washington, 1972, Art League No. Va., 1973, Studio Gallery, 1976, Main St. Gallery, 1976, 77, 78, Nantucket, 1977; group shows include Maritime Mus., Newport News, Va., 1971, 72, U. No. Va., 1973, U. Richmond (Va.), 1972, U. Md., 1975, Haller Gallery, N.Y.C., 1976, 77; represented in permanent collections at Dept. of State, Washington, also various ambassadors' residences. Active Olde Town Citizens' Com., Alexandria, Va., 1964-73, Georgetown Citizens' Assn., Washington, 1971-75, Hosp. Thrift Shop, Nantucket, Mass., 1968-71, Nat. Symphony of Washington, D.C. Com., 1970—; bd. dirs. Arts Council of Nantucket. Mem. Studio Gallery, Foundery Group Women Painters, Artists' Equity, Art League Va., Art Found. Nantucket Conservation Assn., Nantucket Hist. Found. Home: 26 Pleasant St Nantucket MA 02554 Studio: 58 Main St Nantucket MA 02554

KOCH, WAYNE ARTHUR, ins. co. exec.; b. Endicott, N.Y., Oct. 31, 1949; s. Arthur Julius and Dorothy Mary (Lewis) K.; A.A.S., Broome Community Coll., 1969; B.S., Mansfield State Coll., 1972; M.B.A., SUNY, Binghamton, 1974; m. Marie Ann Barno, July 15, 1972; 1 dau., Jennifer Michelle. Sales rep. Met. Life Ins. Co., Endicott, 1974-77, sales mgr., Binghamton, N.Y., 1977—. Mem. Nat. Assn. Life Underwriters (dir. chpt. 1974-76, Nat. Quality award 1975, 76), Assn. M.B.A. Execs. Home: 261 Riverside Dr Johnson City NY 13790 Office: Met Life Ins Co 99 Hawley St Binghamton NY 13901

KOCHANEK, STANLEY ANTHONY, educator; b. Bayonne, N.J., May 10, 1934; s. Anthony John and Wanda (Wronski) K.; B.A., Rutgers U., 1956, M.A., 1957; Ph.D., U. Pa., 1963; m. Patricia Sharpe, Jan. 29, 1959; children—Christopher, Kevin. Teaching fellow polit. sci. U. Pa., 1961-63; asst. prof. polit. sci. Pa. State U., 1963-67, asso. prof., 1967-73, prof., 1973—, grad. officer of dept., 1969-70, 1974-76, acting head dept., 1976; cons. Commn. on Orgn. Govt. for Conduct Fgn. Policy, 1974; cons. various pub. cos. Served with U.S. Army, 1957. Fulbright fellow, India 1959-61; NSF grantee, summer 1966; Am. Inst. Indian Studies fellow, 1967-68, 72-73; Fulbright-Hays sr. research fellow, Pakistan, 1976-77. Mem. Am., So. polit. sci. assns., Assn. Asian Studies. Author: The Congress Party of India: The Dynamics of One-Party Democracy, 1968; Business and Politics in India, 1974; editor Comparative Politics, Apr. 1973. Contbr. articles to profl. jours. Home: 1362 Greenwood Circle State College PA 16801 Office: Dept Polit Sci Pa State U University Park PA 16802

KOCHER, BEN LEON, newspaper editor; b. Harrisburg, Pa., July 17, 1945; s. Leon Emanuel and Margaret Marie (Hoke) K.; B.S. in Secondary Edn., Elizabethtown Coll., 1967. Reporter, Millersburg (Pa.) Sentinel, 1967-69, asso. editor, 1969-70, owner, editor, 1970—, Elizabethville (Pa.) Echo and Williamstown (Pa.) Times, 1971—, Upper Dauphin (merger of Millersburg Sentinel, Elizabethville Echo, Williamstown Times) Sentinel, Millersburg, 1972—. Republican. Clubs: Lions, Masons. Office: 510 Union St Millersburg PA 17061

KOCISKO, STEPHEN JOHN, clergyman; b. Mpls., June 11, 1915; s. John Z. and Anna (Somosz) K.; Ph.B., Propaganda Fide U., 1937. S.T.L., 1941. Ordained priest Roman Catholic Ch., 1941. consecrated bishop, 1956; chancellor Byzantine Cath. Diocese of Pitts., 1956; rector Byzantine Cath. Sem., Pitts., 1958-63; 1st bishop Byzantine Eparchy (diocese) of Passaic, 1963-69; archbishop of Pittsburgh, 1969—. Address: 50 Riverview Ave Pittsburgh PA 15214

KODROFF, JUDITH KATZ, psychologist; b. Phila., May 19, 1938; d. Philip William and Audrey Jacqueline (Greenbarg) Katz; B.S. in Edn., Temple U., 1959, M.Ed., 1971, Ph.D., 1973; children—Margo Elizabeth, Kurt Stuart. Tchr., Phila. Bd. Edn., 1959-60; teaching fellow Temple U., 1972; asso. prof. psychology and edn. Community Coll. Phila., 1973—, acting dir. div. social and behavioral scis. and human service careers, 1978, head dept. behavioral scis., 1976-78; vol. therapist N.E. Community Mental Health Center, 1977. Edn. task force Phila. Urban Coalition, 1974-77. Mem. Am. Psychol. Assn., Jean Piaget Soc., Phi Delta Kappa. Office: Community Coll Phila 34 S 11th St Philadelphia PA 19107

KOEGEL, WILLIAM FISHER, lawyer; b. Washington, Aug. 18, 1923; s. Otto Erwin and Rae (Fisher) K.; B.A., Williams Coll., 1944; LL.B., U. Va., 1949; m. Barbarb Bixler, Feb. 2, 1946; children—John Bixler, Robert Bartlett; m. 2d, Ruth Swan Boynton, June 21, 1969. Admitted to N.Y. State bar, 1950; asso. Rogers & Wells and predecessor firms, N.Y.C., 1949-58, partner, 1958—, sr. partner, 1968—. Chmn. Scarsdale Republican Town Com., 1965-71; pres. bd. trustees Hitchcock Presbyterian Ch., Scarsdale, 1970-73, 78—. Served with AUS, 1943-46; ETO. Fellow Am. Coll. Trial Lawyers; mem. Am., N.Y. State bar assns., Assn. of Bar City N.Y., Order of Coif. Clubs: The Town (pres. 1976-77) (Scarsdale); Sky (N.Y.C.); Shenorock Shore, Fox Meadow Tennis, Williams. Home: 7 Chesterfield Rd Scarsdale NY 10583 Office: 200 Park Ave New York City NY 10017

KOEHLER, ISABEL WINIFRED, writer, artist; b. Boston, Feb. 5, 1903; d. George Wallace and Mary Elizabeth (Strout) Goodwin; student art courses Harvard, Mass. Inst. Tech., others; m. Frederick Mills Koehler, Apr. 16, 1925; 1 son, Alden Goodwin Koehler. Contbr. articles to Boston Daily Post, Boston Herald-Traveler, poetry to Boston Daily Globe, Melrose Free Press, Everett Leader Herald, Albo D'Oro, Masters of Modern Poetry, others; exhibited numerous galleries, festivals, ann. exhbns. Recipient commemorative medal for art achievement Leonardo da Vinci Accademia, Rome, 1973, Silver medal Masters of Modern Poetry and Masters of Modern Art, 1975, Blue ribbon Everett Bicentennial Arts Exhibit, 1976, other awards, prizes. Mem. Mass. Poetry Soc., New Eng. Women's Press Assn., Agnes Carr Writers Club (past pres., exec. bd.), Internat. Poetry Soc., Nat. Writers Club, Internat. Platform Assn., Everett Art Assn., Old Boston Soc. Ind. Artists, Centro Studi e Scambi Internazionali, Accademia Leonardo Da Vinci (hon. rep. 1974-75), N.Y. Poetry Forum, Internat. Biography Assn. Author: Bouquets of Poems, 1974; Masters of Modern Poetry-"Versified Variety", 1978. Address: 30 Fremont Ave Everett MA 02149

KOEL, AKE ILMAR, librarian; b. Kuressaare, Estonia, May 20, 1920; s. Augustin and Karin (Haggman) K.; B.A., U. Toronto (Ont., Can.), 1961, B.L.S., 1962, M.L.S., 1969; m. Maria Ottilia Nemeth, Feb. 6, 1959. Came to U.S., 1965, naturalized, 1971. Documentalist-librarian AB BAHCO, Enkoping, Sweden, 1944-54; salesman CENCO of Can. Ltd., 1954-61; head serial div., catalogue dept. U. Toronto Library, 1962-65; head tech. services Hamilton Coll. Library, Clinton, N.Y., 1965-66; head Dutch-Scandinavian sect. Shared Catalogue Div., Library of Congress, Washington, 1966-69; asso. librarian for tech. services Yale U. Library, 1969—. Mem. ALA, Am. Soc. Info. Sci., New Haven Colony Hist. Soc. Home: 89 Charlton Hill Hamden CT 06518 Office: Yale Univ Library New Haven CT 06520

KOELBL, DOROTHY JUNE, librarian; b. Lancaster, Pa.; d. George Anthony and Florence (Walters) K.; B.S., Millersville State Coll., 1963, M.Ed. in Elementary Edn., 1972; postgrad. U. London, 1967, Temple U., 1973—. Librarian, Solanco Sch. Dist., Quarryville, Pa., 1963-64, Lancaster Sch. Dist., 1964—. Mem. Lancaster Unitarian Service Com., chmn., 1973-76; mem. Contact of Lancaster, Community Alert Plan. Life fellow Internat. Biog. Assn.; mem. Philatelic Soc. Lancaster County (pres. 1972-74), Lancaster Hiking Club (treas. 1973-75), Am., Lancaster County library assns., Nat., Lancaster, Pa. edn. assns., Lancaster Lebanon Reading Assn., Am. Topical Assn., Pi Lambda Theta (chpt. corr. sec. 1973, historian 1978). Office: James P Wickersham Sch Reservior St and Lehigh Ave Lancaster PA 17602

KOELSCH, WILLIAM ALVIN, educator; b. Morristown, N.J., May 16, 1933; s. Alvin Charles and Alice Boniface (Smith) K.; Sc.B. summa cum laude, Bucknell U., 1955; A.M. (Danforth fellow), Clark U., 1959; Ph.D. (Danforth fellow), U. Chgo., 1966. Vis. asst. prof. geography Clark U., Worcester, Mass., 1963, asst. prof. history and geography, 1967-69, asso. prof., 1969—, univ. archivist, 1972—, instr., asst. prof. history Eckerd Coll., St. Petersburg, Fla., 1963-67. Mem. Nat. Trust for Historic Preservation, 1968—; corr. mem. commn. on history of geog. thought Internat. Geog. Union, 1975—; mem. Mass. Archives Adv. Com., 1974—. Trustee Lt. Michael P. Quinn Scholarship Fund, Charlestown, 1968—. Served to 1st lt. AUS, 1955-57. Recipient Penrose Fund Research grant Am. Philos. Soc., 1971. Fellow Am. Geog. Soc. (life); mem. Soc. Religion in Higher Edn., New Eng. Archivists, Soc. Am. Archivists (com. on coll. and univ. archives 1975—), Assn. Am. Geographers (chmn. com. archives and assn. history 1974-75), Orgn. Am. Historians (life), History of Edn. Soc., Phi Beta Kappa. Author: (with Barbara Rosenkrantz) American Habitat: A Historical Perspective, 1973. Editor: Lectures on the Historical Geography of the United States (Harlan H. Barrows), 1962. Contbg. editor Ripon Forum, 1972-75. Home: 16 Carruth St Dorchester MA 02124 Office: Univ Archives Clark Univ Worcester MA 01610

KOENIG, ARTHUR HOWARD, research psychologist; b. N.Y.C., June 20, 1943; s. Simon Mortimer and Rose (Bernstein) K.; B.A., Rutgers U., 1965; M.A. in Exptl. Psychology, Bklyn. Coll., 1969. Research psychologist Squibb Inst. Med. Research New Brunswick, N.J., 1967-68, Bell Tel. Labs., Murray Hall, N.J., 1968—; environ. noise specialist, 1975—. Mem. Am. Psychol. Assn., IEEE, Acoustical Soc. Am., Sigma Xi. Home: 46 Martins Ln Berkeley Heights NJ 07922 Office: 600 Mountain Ave Murray Hall NJ 07974

KOENIG, GLORIA ELEANOR, lawyer; b. Bayonne, N.J., Oct. 8, 1926; d. Benjamin M.A. and Beatrice (Abramson) Kline; B.A., Washington Square Coll., 1946; M.S., N.Y. U., 1949, J.D., 1963, LL.M., 1967, J.S.D., 1972; m. Burton G. Koenig, June 27, 1954. Teacher math. Bayonne Tech. and Vocat. High Sch., 1946-48; research chemist Vitro Labs., West Orange, N.J., 1948-57; admitted to N.J. bar, 1963; pvt. practice law, specializing in patent law, Bayonne, 1963—; dir. Mr. Liberty Industries Inc., Bayonne. Pres. bd. dirs. Bayonne Community Mental Health Center, 1978—; pres. Sisterhood Temple Emanu-El, Bayonne, 1976-78, trustee temple, 1978. Recipient Frances Lewis Haymen award N.Y. U. Sch. Law, 1967. Mem. Am., N.J. State, Hudson County, Bayonne bar assns., N.J. Patent Law Assn., Nat. Council Jewish Women, Eclectic Honor Soc. (Washington Sq. Coll.), Hadassah, Orgn. for Rehab. Tng. Jewish. Author: Patent Invalidity: A Statistical and Substantive Analysis, 1974, supplement 1976. Contbr. articles to profl. jours. Home: 807 Ave C Bayonne NJ 07002 Office: 664 Broadway Bayonne NJ 07002

KOENIG, GOTTLIEB, educator; b. Gottschee, Yugoslavia, Apr. 14, 1940; s. Ernst and Aloisia (Kump) K.; came to U.S., 1952, naturalized, 1960; B.S. in Mech. Engring., Cooper Union, 1967; M.S., N.Y.U., 1968, Ph.D., 1976; m. Berta Poje, June 25, 1966; 1 son, Robert Gottlieb. Mem. faculty Acad. Aeros., La Guardia Airport, N.Y., 1960-67, 70—, chmn. aircraft design tech. dept., 1971-73, chmn. spl. studies dept., 1973—, chmn. techs. dept., asso. dean acad. affairs, 1976—. Recipient Alumni award Cooper Union Alumni Assn., 1967. NDEA fellow, 1967-70. Registered profl. engr., N.Y. Mem. ASME, Am. Inst. Aeros. and Astronautics, Soc. Automotive Engrs., Tau Beta Pi, Pi Tau Sigma. Roman Catholic. Contbr. articles to profl. jours. Office: 86-01 23d Ave Flushing NY 11371

KOENIG, JOHN HENRY, educator, former govt. ofcl.; b. Watertown, Wis., July 28, 1920; s. John Albert and Anna (Mathey) K.; student U. Mich., 1951; B.A., Western Mich. U., 1953, M.A., 1954; Ed.D., Fairleigh Dickinson U., 1973; m. Segri Jean Stebbins, Apr. 18, 1949. Instr. indsl. edn. Midland (Mich.) Pub. Schs., 1954-62; instr. indsl. arts edn. Western Mich. U., Kalamazoo, 1953-54; asst. prof. dept. indsl. edn., tech. Trenton (N.J.) State Coll., 1964-65, vis. prof., 1976—; asso. state dir. div. vocational edn. N.J. Dept. Edn., Trenton, 1965-75; supr. occupational edn. Perth Amboy (N.J.) Pub. Schs., 1977—; vis. prof. Central Mich. U., Mount Pleasant, 1963-64. Served with USAAF, 1940-45; PTO. Mem. Am. Assn. Sch. Adminstrs., Am. Vocat. Assn., Am. Indsl. Arts Assn., NEA, Phi Delta Kappa, Epsilon Pi Tau, Kappa Delta Pi. Mason (32 deg.). Home: 47 Van Duyn Dr Trenton NJ 08618

KOESTER, ROBERT JOSEPH, JR., ednl. adminstr.; b. Scranton, Pa., Oct. 23, 1948; s. Robert Joseph and Ann Marie (Wielebinski) K.; B.S. in mktg., Husson Coll., 1970; M.B.A. in Mktg., U. Scranton, 1977; postgrad. Temple U., Lehigh U.; m. Nancy T. Brennan, Dec. 18, 1971; 1 son, Robert Joseph III. Sales rep. McKinney Mfg. Co., Scranton, Pa., 1970-72; with mktg. dept., Lomma Enterprises Inc., Scranton, 1972-73, asst. mktg. dir., 1973-75, v.p. mktg., head platform tennis div., 1974-76; dir. coop. edn., contracted edn. and placement Lackawanna Jr. Coll., 1976-77, also, instr. in bus.; dir. coop. edn. Wilkes Coll., Wilkes-Barre, Pa., 1977—, adj. prof. mktg., 1978—; coop. edn. and mktg. cons.; lectr. mktg. and mgmt. Mem. advisory bd. Scranton Salvation Army; mem. N.E. Pa. Employers Advisory Bd., Drug and Alcohol Advisory Bd. Mem. Am. Mktg. Assn., Am. Soc. Tng. and Devel., Coop. Edn. Assn. Pa., Coop. Edn. Assn. U.S., Wilkes-Barre C. of C. (edn. com. 1977—), Am. Platform Tennis Assn. Democrat. Roman Catholic. Clubs: Scranton Kiwanis (bd. dirs. 1974-76, (pres.-elect 1979—), Elks (co-chmn. youth activities 1975-76). Home: 226 Stephen Ave Scranton PA 18505 Office: Wilkes Coll Wilkes Barre PA 18703

KOGSTAD, ROLF EGIL, mfg. co. exec.; b. Oslo, Norway, July 21, 1932; s. Ole W. and Gudrun (Sangvik) K.; B.Sc., U. Glasgow (Scotland), 1955; diploma Royal Tech. Coll. (Scotland), 1955; m. Sylvia Elizabeth Lane, Sept. 14, 1962; children—Karin, Erik, John, Kirsten. Came to U.S., 1955, naturalized, 1961. Process engr. Collier Carbon & Chems., Brea, Calif., 1956-61; sales engr. Catalysts & Chems., Louisville, 1961-63; tech. mgmt. Esso Chems., S.Am., and Far East, 1963-69, C.F. Braun & Co., Los Angeles, 1969-71; project mgr. Norsk Hydro, Oslo, Norway, 1971-73, pres., N.Y.C., 1973—. Mem. Am. Inst. Chem. Engrs., Nat. Pilots Assn. Home: 11 Long Close Rd Stamford CT 06902 Office: 800 3d Ave New York City NY 10022

KOH, HESUNG CHUN, sociologist; b. Seoul, Korea, July 3, 1929; d. Hangsup and Namson (Kim) Chun; came to U.S., 1948, U.S. citizen; B.A. in Sociology and Econs., Dickinson Coll., Carlisle, Pa., 1951; M.A. in Sociology, Boston U., 1953, Ph.D., 1959; postgrad. Chinese studies Harvard U., 1960-61, Georgetown U., 1961; m. Kwang Lim Koh, June 16, 1951; children—Carolyn Kyongshin Choo, Howard Kyongju, Edward Tongju, Harold Hongju, Jean Kyongun, Richard Jongju. Lectr. sociology Boston U., also lectr. and tng. asso. Human Relations Center, 1950-60; vis. lectr. law Yale Law Sch., 1963-66; dir. info. systems Assn. Asian Studies, Ann Arbor, Mich., part-time 1969-71; dir. E. Asian area research, dir. research, and devel., asso. sec. Human Relations Files, Yale U., 1961—, lectr. Albertus Magnus Coll., New Haven, 1973-76, Yale U., 1977—; adv. bd. Jour. Korean Affairs, 1974-76; editorial com. Behavior Sci. Research, 1974—; participant UNESCO experts meetings. Mem. nat. continuing com. on observance Internat. Women's Yr., 1978—. Fellow Boston U. Human Relations Center, 1957-59, NDEA, 1960-61; grantee NSF, 1966-72, Am. Council Learned Soc.-Social Sci. Research Council, 1968, 72, Japan Found., 1975. Mem. Am. Sociol. Assn., Am. Soc. Info. Sci., Assn. Asian Studies, Asia Soc., Nat. Acad. Sci.-NRC, No. New Eng. Sch. Religious Edn., Am. Nat. Standards Inst. Author publs. in field. Home: 310 Yale Ave New Haven CT 06515 Office: 2054 Yale Station New Haven CT 06520

KOHAN, SILVIU, obstetrician, gynecologist; b. Bucharest, Rumania, Aug. 14, 1928; came to U.S., 1971, naturalized, 1976; s. Leon and Ernestine (Lobel) K.; M.D., Faculty of Medicine, Bucharest, 1952; m. Simone Schor, Dec. 26, 1951; children—Dodis, Darius. Intern, Polizu Hosp., Bucharest, 1952-54; specialist obstetrics-gynecology Grivitza Maternity Hosp., Bucharest, 1958-70; resident in obstetrics and gynecology Bellevue Hosp., N.Y.C., 1971-73; attending in obstetrics and gynecology Univ. Hosp., N.Y.C., 1975—; asst. prof. obstetrics and gynecology N.Y. U. Med. Sch., 1976—. Fellow Am. Coll. Obstetrics and Gynecology; mem. AMA, Queens Gynecol. Soc., N.Y. Med. Soc. Contbr. articles to profl. publs.

KOHL, JOHN PRESTON, clergyman, chaplain; b. Allentown, Pa., Dec. 26, 1942; s. Claude Evan and Edna Lenior (Woodland) K.; B.A. in English, Moravian Coll., 1964; M.Div., Yale U., 1967; postgrad. U. Colo., 1967-68; M.S. in Mgmt., Am. Technol. U., 1974, M.S. in Counseling, 1976; postgrad. Pa. State U., 1978; m. Nancy Ann Christensen, Mar. 11, 1966; children—John Preston, Mark Christian. Ordained to ministry Congregational Ch., 1967; pastor Christ Congl. Ch., New Smyrna Beach, Fla., 1968-71, First Congl.-United Ch. Christ, Hutchinson, Minn., 1971-73; capt., chaplain U.S. Army, Fort Hood, Tex., 1973-75; chaplain, Herbornseelbach, Germany, 1975-78; instr. bus. mgmt. U. Md. Overseas, 1975-78; instr. personnel mgmt. Pa. State U., 1978—. Mem. Volusia County (Fla.) study commn. White House Conf. on Children and Youth, 1969-70; mem. bi-racial com. Emergency Sch. Act Program, Volusia County, 1970-71; mem. governing bd. Volusia County Chaplaincy Assn., 1969-71; instl. rep. Boy Scouts Am., New Smyrna Beach, 1970-71; mem. Child Protective Council, Ft. Hood, Tex., 1974-75; bd. dirs. Smyrna Child Devel. Center, 1969-71; bd. dirs. Hutchinson Pre-Sch. Center, 1971—, v.p., 1971-72, pres., 1972-73; recorder Human Relations Equal Opportunity Council, 557th Arty. Group, 1975-78; mem. community coordinating council, Herborn-Seelbach, 1975-78. Mem. Phi Sigma Tau. Club: Optimists (Hutchinson). Home: 773 Cricklewood Dr State College PA 16801 Office: 602 Bus Adminstrn Bldg Pa State U University Park PA 16802

KOHL, SCHUYLER GEORGE, physician, educator; b. Phila., Feb. 22, 1913; s. Max Benjamin and Ray (Levy) K.; B.S., U. Md., 1936, M.D., 1940; M.S., Columbia, 1951, Dr.P.H., 1953; m. Blossom Schultz, Mar. 7, 1943; 1 dau., Eileen Ray Kohl Kaufman. Intern, Met. Hosp., N.Y.C., 1940-42; resident in obstetrics U. Md., Balt., 1942-44, instr., 1946-50; asst. prof. obstetrics and gynecology Downstate Med. Center State U. N.Y., Bklyn., 1950-52, asso. prof., 1952-62, prof., 1962—, asso. dean Coll. Medicine, 1958-71, acting dean, 1970-71, acting chmn. dept. obstetrics and gynecology, 1976-78; cons. NIH, WHO. Served to capt. M.C., AUS, 1944-46. Commonwealth Fund fellow, 1953-54; NIH grantee, Macy Found. grantee, Sloan Found. grantee, U.S. AID grantee. Diplomate Am. Bd. Obstetrics and Gynecology. Mem. AMA, Am. Coll. Obstetrics and Gynecology, Am. Pub. Health Assn., N.Y. Obstet. Soc., N.Y. Acad. Medicine, N.Y. Acad. Scis., N.Y. State Med. Assn., Bklyn. Gynecol. Soc., others. Republican. Jewish religion. Club: Cosmos (Washington). Author: Perinatal Mortality in New York City, 1955. Contbr. articles to profl. jours. Home: 31 Whig Rd Scarsdale NY 10583 Office: Box 24 Downstate Med Center Brooklyn NY 11203

KOHLBERG, IRA, physicist; b. Bklyn., Oct. 29, 1934; s. Samuel and Helen (Schan) K.; B.E.E., Coll. City N.Y., 1956; M.S., U. Pitts, 1960; Ph.D., Boston U., 1965; m. Betty Sue Beacon, June 9, 1957; children—Curt Philip, Aileen Gale, Kenneth Ray. Project engr. Foster Wheeler Corp., N.Y.C., 1956-58; scientist Westinghouse Corp., Pitts., 1958-61; math. physicist Ion Physics Corp., Burlington, Mass., 1961-65; sr. staff physicist Tech. Ops. Inc., Burlington, 1965-66; chief, physics sect. Keystone Computer Assos., Belmont, Mass., 1966-70; v.p. research Analytical Systems Corp., Burlington, 1970-71; mem. tech. staff Mitre Corp., Bedford, Mass., 1971-76; cons., owner Energy Electromagnetics, Newton, Mass., 1976—; lectr. Northeastern U., 1966-77; part-time engring. specialist communications system div. GTE-Sylvania, Needham Heights, Mass., 1977—; asst. prof. elec. engring. U. Lowell (Mass.), 1976-78. Mem. Am. Phys. Soc., Sigma Xi. Contbr. articles to profl. jours. Home: 116 Floral St Newton MA 02161 Office: Energy Electromagnetics PO Box 193 Newton MA 02159

KOHLENBERG, STANLEY, cosmetics co. exec.; b. Bklyn., Aug. 19, 1932; s. Max and Minnie (Roth) K.; B.S., Columbia, 1953; postgrad N.Y. U., 1956-58; m. Ruth Barbara Itkin, Dec. 11, 1955; children—Robin Sue, Mark Stuart, Howard Scott. Account supr. L. W. Frohlich, N.Y.C., 1959-62; advt. mgr. Pfizer Lab., N.Y.C., 1962-63; marketing dir. Tussy Cosmetics, N.Y.C., 1964; sr. v.p., dir. client service Sudler & Hennessey, N.Y.C., 1964-66; publisher Cosmetics Fair mag., N.Y.C., 1966-68; exec. v.p. Spectrum Cosmetics, 1968-70; pres. Coty Inc., 1970-72; exec. v.p. Revlon Inc., N.Y.C., 1972-76; pres. Calvin Klein Cosmetics, Inc., 1977—. Cons., Advt. and sales promotion. Served with M.D., AUS, 1953-55. Home: 975 Park Ave New York City NY 10028 Office: 205 W 39th St New York City NY 10018

KÖHLER, ECKEHART, philosopher; b. Darmstadt, Germany, Dec. 18, 1939 (mother Am. citizen); s. Franz and Leonore (Hollander) K.; came to U.S., 1946; B.A., Lehigh U., 1962; Ph.D., U. Nebr., 1976. Research asst. U. Nebr. dept. philosophy, 1970-74; asso. editor Theory and Decision, Lincoln, Nebr., 1974—; research asso. Boston U. Center for Philosophy and History of Sci., 1978—. Mem. Am. Philos. Assn., Philosophy of Sci. Assn., AAAS. Democrat. Quaker. Editor: (with Werner Leinfellner) Developments in the Methodology of Social Science, 1974; (with others) Procs. of 3d Internat. Wittgenstein Symposium, 1979. Home: Eagle Rd New Hope PA 18938

KOHLER, SAMUEL HARRY, appliance co. exec.; b. Atlantic City, May 15, 1929; s. William Henry and Bertha (Marks) K.; B.S.M.E., Drexel U., 1953; m. M. Elizabeth Ely, Sept. 22, 1956; children—Samuel H., Paul R., John D. With Black & Decker Mfg. Co., 1953-66, dir. engring., Lancaster, Pa., 1962-65, dir. tech. services, Towson, Md., 1965-66; chief engr. Dresser Industries, Ft. Wayne, Ind., 1966-69; dir. engring. Avery Internat., Phila., 1969-71; v.p. devel. and engring. Proctor-Silex, Phila., 1971-76; v.p. research devel. and engring. Schick Inc., Lancaster, 1976—. Elder, chmn. congregation Grace Lutheran Ch., Warminster, Pa., 1969-76. Served as 1st lt. Ordnance Corp, U.S. Army, 1954-56. Recipient Master Design award Product Engring., 1965, Design in Steel award Am. Iron and Steel Inst., 1965. Mem. ASME, Alpha Pi Lambda. Republican. Club: Astra. Patentee in field. Home: 272 Old Delp Rd Lancaster PA 17601 Office: 216 Greenfield Rd Lancaster PA 17604

KOHLS, ROBERT, govt. ofcl.; b. Granger, Iowa, May 28, 1927; s. Harry F. and Hulda Marie (Seibert) K.; B.A., Drake U., 1950; M.A., Columbia, 1960; Ph.D., N.Y. U., 1963; m. Norma Glee Chappell, June 17, 1949; 1 dau., Kathy Sue. Curator of edn. Des Moines Art Center, 1956-59; prof. cultural history N.Y. U., 1960-65; prof. cultural history New Sch. Social Research, N.Y.C., 1965-68; dir. tng. Westinghouse Learning Corp., Washington, 1968-71; dir. tng. Gen. Learning Corp., Washington, 1971-74; dir. tng. and devel Internat. Communication Agy. (formerly USIA), Washington, 1974—. Served with U.S. Army, 1945-47. Lydia C. Roberts fellow, 1959-61. Mem. Soc. Intercultural Edn., Tng. and Research, Am. Soc. Tng. and Devel. Democrat. Quaker. Contbr. articles to profl. jours. Home: 537 7th St SE Washington DC 20003 Office: 1776 Pennsylvania Ave NW Washington DC 20547

KOKEN, JAMES EDWARD, educator; b. N.Y.C., May 8, 1912; s. Efstratios Demetrios and Katherine (Rizakos) Kokinakis; A.B., Columbia, 1933; M.A., N.Y. U., 1940; Ed.D., Pa. State U., 1959; m. Helen Sotiro, Apr. 20, 1947; children—Kathryn Joy, Mary Diane. Employed various industries, 1933-42; tchr. Rumson (N.J.) High Sch., 1942-46, Westfield (N.J.) High Sch., 1946-47; asso. prof. chemistry Millersville (Pa.) State Coll., 1947-55, chmn. dept. sci., 1955-64, prof. chemistry, 1964-76, prof. chemistry emeritus, 1976—. Oak Ridge Inst. Nuclear Studies grantee, summer 1956. Mem. New Eng. Assn. Chemistry Tchrs., Am. Chem. Soc., NEA, Pa. State Edn. Assn. Democrat. Greek Orthodox. Home: 1125 Richmond Rd Lancaster PA 17603

KOKOSKI, ROBERT JOHN, pharmacologist; b. Chicopee Falls, Mass., Feb. 28, 1932; s. Charles Jacob and Rosalie Vera (Kusek) K.; B.S. in Pharmacy, U. Md., 1952, M.S., 1956, Ph.D., 1962; m. Patricia Ann Bell, Feb. 3, 1962; children—Patricia, Richard, Michael, Jennifer. Asst. prof. pharmacognosy U. Md., Balt., 1962-63, research asso., 1977; research chemist Friends of Psychiatric Research, Inc., Spring Grove State Hosp., Catonsville, Md., 1963-65, lab. scientist VI, 1965-76, dir. clin. lab. research dept., 1968-70; dir. drug abuse lab. Friends Med. Sci. Research Center, Inc., Balt., 1968—, research scientist, 1977—; dir. drug abuse lab. Md. Psychiatric Research Center, Catonsville, 1972-77; pvt. practice pharmacy, Arbutus Pharmacy (Md.), 195[illegible]9, Voshell's Pharmacy, Balt., 1969—. Pres., St. Louis Sch. Home and Sch. Assn., Clarksville, Md., 1975-76, mem. bd., 1976—. Registered pharmacist, Md. Mem. Assn. Drug Detection Labs. (chmn. 1977-78), Md. Pharm. Assn., U. Md. Alumni Assn., Am. Chem. Soc., Sigma Xi, Rho Chi, Phi Kappa Phi, Phi Delta Chi. Democrat. Roman Catholic. Home: 12596 Folly Quarter Rd Ellicott City MD 21043 Office: Friends Medical Science Research Center 640 Frederick Rd Baltimore MD 21228

KOLBE, STANLEY ERNEST, JR., congl. analyst; b. Marshalltown, Iowa, Feb. 1, 1953; s. Stanley Ernest and Wanda Lee (George) K.; B.S. (Tolles scholar), Cornell U., 1976; M.S. with honors, George Washington U., 1978, now postgrad. in bus. adminstrn. Legis. asst. N.Y. State Senator Linda Winikow, Albany, N.Y., 1975-76, U.S. Senator John Culver, Washington, 1976; congl. analyst U.S. Conf. of Mayors, Washington, 1976—; congl. campaign adviser and fin. dir. 3d Congl. Dist. Iowa, 1978. Mem. D.C. Area Cornell U. Student Selection Com. Mem. Am., Washington Area polit. sci. assns., Am. Soc. Personnel Adminstrs., Cornell Alumni Assn., Phi Delta Theta, Alpha Sigma Lambda. Democrat. Presbyterian. Clubs: Cornell Country; Cornell (Washington). Author publs. in field. Home: 11 S 9th St Marshalltown IA 50158 Office: 1620 I St NW Washington DC 20006

KOLBERT, GERALD SHELDON, ophthalmologist; b. N.Y.C., Apr. 29, 1935; s. William and Rose (Feldman) K.; student N.Y. U., 1952-53; B.A., U. Wis., 1955; M.D., State U. N.Y. Downstate Med. Center, 1959; m. Marlene Adele Maass, June 29, 1958; children—Elizabeth Ruth, Daniel Maass. Intern, Kings County Hosp., Bklyn., 1959-60; resident in ophthalmology Bronx VA Hosp., 1960-63; practice medicine specializing in ophthalmology N.Y.C., 1964—; ophthalmologist Montefiore Hosp. Med. Group, N.Y.C., 1964—, adj. attending hosp. and med. center, 1967—; asst. clin. prof. ophthalmology Albert Einstein Coll. Medicine, N.Y.C., 1970—; cons. in field. Chmn. Noise Commn., Village of Larchmont, N.Y., 1974—. Served with USAF, 1963-64. Diplomate Am. Bd. Ophthalmology. Fellow A.C.S.; mem. Bronx County, N.Y. State med. socs., Am. Acad. Ophthalmology and Otolaryngology, N.Y. Soc. Clin. Ophthalmology. Contbr. articles to profl. publs. Office: 3444 Kossuth Ave New York City NY 10467

KOLBYE, ALBERT CHRISTIAN, JR., govt. ofcl.; b. Phila., Feb. 15, 1935; s. Albert Christian and Marion Fisler (Bozarth) K.; A.B., Harvard U., 1957; M.D., Temple U., 1961; M.P.H., Johns Hopkins U., 1965; J.D., U. Md., 1966; m. Lise Neergaard Ottosen, July 24, 1976. Intern, Univ. Hosps., Madison, Wis., 1961-62; resident in pub. health and preventive medicine USPHS, 1962-64; with HEW, 1965—, dep. dir. Bur. Foods, FDA, Washington, 1970-71, asso. dir. scis., 1972—; asst. surgeon gen. USPHS, 1971—; admitted to Md. bar, 1967. Recipient Meritorious Service medal USPHS, 1971, 75. Fellow Am. Pub. Health Assn., Am. Coll. Legal Medicine, Am. Coll. Preventive Medicine, Am. Acad. Clin. Toxicology; mem. AMA, Md. Bar Assn., Md. Med-Chirurgical Faculty. Home: 4802 Fort Sumner Dr Bethesda MD 20016 Office: 200 C St SW Washington DC 20204

KOLBZ, ALAN CHARLES, mgmt. cons.; b. Bklyn., Aug. 15, 1934; s. Charles Thomas and Mary Elizabeth (Mitsch) K.; B.A., Gettysburg Coll., 1956; M.B.A., Fairleigh Dickinson U., 1964, postgrad., 1965-66; postgrad. U. Md. Extension, 1957-58; children—Laura Jeanne, Linda Diane. Corporate indsl. engr. Becton Dickinson & Co., Rutherford, N.J., 1959-67, ACMI, 1967; mem. corporate staff Chromalloy Am. Corp., St. Louis, 1968-70; pres. Alan C. Kolz & Assos., mgmt. cons., Derry, N.H., 1970-75, 76—; dir. non-leather ops. Allied Leather Co., Boston, 1975-76; interim instr. N.H. Coll., Manchester, 1977; instr. Hesser Bus. Coll., Manchester, 1978. Mgr. Oakland (N.J.) Little League, 1965-68; rep. Bergen County Joint Municipal Planning Com., 1970. Served with U.S. Army, 1956-58. Named hon. citizen of Okla., 1970. Mem. Am. Inst. Indsl. Engrs., Hosp. Mgmt. Systems Soc., C. of C. Nashua, So. N.H. Assn. Commerce and Industry, Gettysburg Coll. Alumni Club N. Jersey (charter mem., 1st pres. 1973). Republican. Lutheran. Club: Elks. Home: 17 Linlew Dr Derry NH Office: 17 Linlew Dr Suite 22 Derry NH 03038

KOLIN, SACHA, artist; b. Paris, France; d. Julius and Malvina (Slobodianiuk) Kolin; B.S., Realschule (Vienna, Austria), 1929; student Wiener Kunstgewerbeschule, Acad. Fine Arts, Societaire dela Societe Nat. Des Beaux Arts (Paris, France), 1934, 35. Came to U.S., 1936, naturalized, 1943. One man shows Burliuk Gallery, 1953, Contemporary Arts, 1957, Condon Riley Gallery, 1959, 60, Easthampton Gallery, 1963-67, Easthampton Gallery, N.Y., 1965, U. Center, L.I. U., 1969, Southampton Coll. of L.I. U., 1972, Everson Mus., Syracuse, N.Y., Herbert F. Johnson Mus. Cornell U., Max Hutchinson Gallery, Pace U., others; exhibited in group shows Bklyn. Mus., Boston Mus., Whitney Mus. Am. Art, Isaac Delgado Mus., Kunst Mus., Bern, Switzerland, many others; represented in permanent collections Parrish Mus., Finch Coll. Mus., Ohio State U., Brandeis U., Phoenix Art Mus., Chrysler Art Mus., Smithsonian Instn., Fordham U., Easthampton Guildhall, Southampton Coll., Wadsworth Atheneum, Hartford, Conn., Trinity Coll. Nat. Collection Fine Arts, Washington, Everson Mus., Johnson Mus. of Cornell U., many others. Address: care Chett Stoner 751 St Marks Ave Brooklyn NY 11216

KOLLER, HAROLD PAUL, pediatric ophthalmologist; b. Phila., July 7, 1937; s. William Victor and Sadie Sylvia (Gart) K.; A.B., U. Pa., 1959; M.D., Tulane U., 1964; m. Dorris Hoffman, Aug. 25, 1973; children—Melissa, Ilana, David. Intern, Temple U. Med. Center, Phila., 1964-65; resident Tulane Services, New Orleans Eye and Ear Hosp., 1965-68; practice medicine, specializing in pediatric ophthalmology, Phila. and Cherry Hill, N.J., 1971—; sr. asst. surgeon Wills Eye Hosp., 1970; chief sect. pediatric ophthalmology dept. surgery Our Lady of Lourdes Hosp., Camden, N.J., 1972; asso. surgeon Children's Hosp. Phila., 1973; asst. prof. ophthalmology Thomas Jefferson U., 1974. Served with USPHS, 1968-70. Fellow Am. Acad. Ophthalmology and Otolaryngology (course instr.; 1st prize sci. exhibit 1975), A.C.S.; mem. Am. Assn. Pediatric Ophthalmology. Club: Lions. Contbr. articles in field to profl. jours. Home: 701 Middlesex Dr Cinnaminson NJ 08077 Office: 218 Barclay Pavilion E Route 70 Cherry Hill NJ 08034

KOLLER, HERBERT, educator; b. Vienna, Austria, Sept. 22, 1924; s. Franz and Hilde (Horak) K.; Chem.E., Universidad de Ingenieria, Lima, Peru, 1947; M.S., N.Y. U., 1965; Ph.D. in Math., Belfer G. S., Yeshiva U., 1974; m. Ellen Kraessel; children—Jonie (Mrs. Thomas Fedor), Larraine (Mrs. Brent Hood), Martin, Monique; came to U.S., 1955, naturalized, 1958. Observer Huancayo Magnetic Obs., Carnegie Inst. of Washington, Huancayo, Peru, 1948; tech. dir. Proquima S.A., Lima, 1950-53; sales engr. Corporacion Comercial Sudamericana, Lima, 1953-55; devel. engr. Am. Machine & Foundry Co., Springdale, Conn., 1955-60; process engr. Crawford & Russell, Stamford, Conn., 1960-64; asso. prof. math. U. Bridgeport (Conn.), 1964—, mem. exec. com. Univ. Senate; lectr. part-time, 1960-63; lectr. spl. programs for mgmt. Bridgeport Engring. Inst.; cons. Computer Programs for Bus. and Ops. Research, 1968—; sr. lectr. dept. computing sci. Hong Kong Poly., 1976—. Mem. Am. Math. Assn., Am. Math. Soc., Am. Assn. U. Profs. (com. acad. freedom of students), Sigma Xi. Contbr. articles in field. Home: Box 3 Bridgeport CT 06601 Office: U Bridgeport Bridgeport CT 06602

KOLLEVOLL, BARBARA RALPH, realtor; b. Syracuse, N.Y., Feb. 16, 1930; d. George John and Dora Belle (Manchester) Ralph; B.A. cum laude, St. Lawrence U., 1952; postgrad. Pa. State U., 1969-72; m. Olav Bernt Kollevoll, June 24, 1950; children—Olav Bernt, Kristan George, Eric John. Salesman, Brose Realty, Easton, Pa., 1967-72, asso. broker, mgr., 1973, broker, 1974—. Licensed real estate broker, Pa. Mem. Pa., Nat. assns. realtors, Easton Area Bd. Realtors (dir. 1973-78, sec. 1977), Homes for Living Network, Sales and Marketing Execs. Easton Area (dir. 1976-78), Easton Area C. of C. (dir. 1974-78, pres. 1977-78), Phi Beta Kappa. Presbyterian. Office: 1311 Northampton St Easton PA 18042

KOLLIAS, ANTHONY VASILEIOS, physician; b. Greece, Apr. 23, 1922; s. Vasileios D. and Georgia C. (Courtis) K.; came to U.S., 1960; M.D., U. Athens, 1957; m. Polly Papadopoulos, Dec. 30, 1959; children— Georgia, Basil. Resident in surgery Athens Municipal Hosp., 1957-59; house physician Union Hosp., Elkton, Md., 1960-61; intern Meml. Hosp., Wilmington, Del., 1961-62, resident in surgery, 1962-64; pvt. practice gen. medicine, Wilmington, 1964—; mem. dir. Union Med. Found., Wilmington, 1966-75. Served with M.C., Greek Army, 1947-49. Decorated Silver Cross of Gallantry. Diplomate Am. Bd. Family Practice. Mem. AMA, Am. Acad. Family Practice, New Castle County Med. Soc. Greek Orthodox. Clubs: Masons, Hellenic Univ. (Wilmington). Home: 807 Seville Ave Wilmington DE 19809 Office: 1507 Philadelphia Pike Wilmington DE 19809

KOLODY, JOHN THEODORE, hosp. adminstr.; b. Arnold, Pa., June 19, 1920; s. Theodore and Katherine (Krawec) K.; B.S. in Edn., Indiana (Pa.) U., 1942; M.S. in Hosp. Adminstrn., Columbia, 1947; m. Mildred Carolyn Secky, May 28, 1949; 1 son, John Theodore Jr. With St. Barnabas Hosp., N.Y.C., 1946—, exec. dir., 1967—, pres., 1978—; lectr. hosp. adminstrn. Columbia, 1949—, St. John's U., 1960—; adj. asst. prof. Bernard M. Baruch Coll. Trustee N. Side Savs. Bank; Bronx Westchester adv. bd. Mfrs. Hanover Trust Co. Mem. voluntary hosp. adv. com. Bronx Red Cross Service Center. Bd. dirs. Bronx Soc. Prevention Cruelty to Children; Bronx adv. bd. Salvation Army; adv. bd. Bronx chpt. A.R.C. bd. mgrs. Bronx YMCA; nat. bd. dirs. Richmond Fellowship; bd. dirs. N.Y. State Study Unified Data Systems. Served with USNR, 1942-46. Recipient Humanitarian award Bronx County Soc. Prevention of Cruelty to Children, 1973; Good Scout award Bronx and N.Y. councils Boy Scouts Am., 1974; Brotherhood award NCCJ, 1976; Community Achievement award ARC, 1976. Fellow Am. Coll. Hosp. Adminstrs., A.A.A.S., Am. Pub. Health Assn.; mem. Am. Hosp. Assn., Gerontological Soc., Nat. Conf. Christians and Jews, Council Hosp. Adminstrs. N.Y.C., Hosp. Assn. N.Y. State (com. on govt. relations), Greater N.Y. Hosp. Assn. (bd. govs., com. on govt. relations), Am. Protestant Hosp. Assn. (ho. dels.), Adminstrs. Conf. Group N.Y.C., Hosp. Adminstrs. Club N.Y.C. (pres.), Bronx C. of C. (bd. dirs.). Mason, Rotarian (bd. dirs.), Elk. Clubs: Pelham N.Y.) Country; Seaview Country (Absecon, N.J.). Home: St Barnabas Hosp 183d St and 3d Ave New York City NY 10457

KOLONIARIS, NICHOLAS, dental technologist; b. Litohoro, Thessalonika, Greece, May 15, 1930; s. Michael and Kondilio (Vlahopanogiotis) K.; came to U.S., 1956, naturalized, 1961; m. Maria Ferlia, Dec. 7, 1969; children—Michael, John. Dental technologist, Nassau Dental Lab., Hempsted, L.I., N.Y., 1956-57, Duradent Dental Lab., N.Y.C., 1956-63, Crown Craft Lab., L.I., 1964-72, Dr. Buchman DDS, Stamford, Conn., 1972-74; prop. Koloniaris Dental Lab., Stamford, 1974—. Served with Greek Army, 1953-55. Tech. fellow Northeastern Gnathological Soc.; mem. Am. Dental Assn. Greek Orthodox. Clubs: Lidos Farm, Bass Soc. Home: 336 Glenbrook Rd Stamford CT 06905 Office: 106 Noroton Ave Darien CT 06820

KOLSON, HARRY, physician, educator; b. N.Y.C., Mar. 26, 1915; s. Morris and Jennie (Waldman) K.; B.A., N.Y. U., 1935, D.D.S., 1938, M.D., 1950; m. Ida Burstein, Apr. 27, 1941 (dec. Aug. 1944). Practice gen. dentistry, Jamaica, N.Y., 1938-43; straight surg. intern 3d div. Bellevue Hosp., N.Y.C., 1950-51, asst. res. in surgery 3d div., 1951-52, Am. Cancer Soc. fellow dept. surgery 3d div., 1951-52; resident in ear, nose, throat, head and neck surgery VA Hosp., Bronx, N.Y., 1952-55, asst. chief otolaryngology sect., 1955-56, chief head and neck surg. sect., 1955-68, chief otolaryngology sect., 1957-68, cons. in otolaryngology, 1968-71; fellow dept. surgery N.Y. U. Coll. Medicine, N.Y.C., 1951-52; lectr. bronchoscopy N.Y. Polyclinic Hosp. and Post Grad. Med. Sch., 1955-56, adj. prof., 1956—; instr. dept. head and neck surgery Albert Einstein Coll. Medicine, Bronx, 1955-59, asst. clin. prof., 1959-65, lectr., 1965-68; asst. vis. surgeon Bronx Municipal Hosp. Center, 1955-59, asso. vis. surgeon, 1959-68; asst. clin. prof. otolaryngology Columbia Coll. Phys. and Surg., 1965-66, asso. clin. prof., 1966-68; prof. clin. otolaryngology Mt. Sinai Sch. Medicine, N.Y.C., 1967-71; attending otolaryngology Mt. Sinai Hosp., 1967-71; cons. Mt. Sinai Hosp. services City Hosp Center at Elmhurst, 1968-71; prof. otolaryngology N.Y. Med. Coll., N.Y.C., 1972—; chief otolaryngology Met. Hosp., N.Y.C., 1972—; chief of staff trainee program VA Hosp., Northport, L.I., N.Y.; chief spl. med. services Suffolk County Health Dept.; chief staff VA Med. Center, Erie, Pa., 1978—; lectr., Fairleigh Dickinson U. Sch. Dentistry, 1964—; vis. prof. Sch. Medicine, Universidad Autonoma de Guadalajara (Mexico), 1974; cons. adv. com. to chief surg. service VA Central Office, Washington, 1969-73; sr. med. cons. hearing program Bur. Handicapped Children, N.Y.C. Bd. Health. Served with AUS, 1943-46. Diplomate Am. Bd. Otolaryngology, Nat. Bd. Med. Examiners. Fellow A.C.S., Am. Acad. Otolaryngology and Ophthalmology, Am. Acad. Facial, Plastic and Reconstructive Surgery, N.Y. Acad. Medicine; mem. A.M.A., N.Y. State, Queens County med. socs., Am. Soc. Maxillofacial Surgeons (constn. and by-laws com., continuing edn. and research com., nominating com., dir., treas. 1973—), Am. Soc. for Head and Neck Surgery, Am. Laryngol., Rhinol. and Otol. Soc., Am. Broncho-Esophagological Assn., James Ewing Soc., Am. Dental Assns., N.Y. State, 1st Dist. N.Y. State dental socs., L.I. Acad. Odontology, Sigma Epsilon Delta. Republican. Contbr. articles to med. jours. Home: 44 Terrehans Ln Syosset NY 11791

KOMAR, MYRON, lawyer; b. Amsterdam, N.Y., June 26, 1930; s. Stephen and Tessie (Bazar) Komaranski; B.A., Union Coll., 1952; LL.B., Albany Law Sch., 1955; m. Maria Hawryluk, May 16, 1964; children—Mark, Michael. Admitted to N.Y. State bar, 1955; asso. firm Donohue & Bohl, 1955-60, mem., 1960-64; mem. firm Donohue, Bohl, Clayton and Komar, Albany, N.Y., 1964—. Mem. Republican Com. Montgomery County (N.Y.) 1948-67; examiner guardian accounts Montgomery County, 1965-66; dir. workmen's compensation Montgomery County, 1966-67; bd. dirs. Capital Artists Opera Co., Albany-Troy-Schenectady area. Mem. Am., N.Y. State, Albany County, Montgomery County bar assns., Ukrainian Congress Com., Ukrainian Nat. Assn., Justinian Soc., Phi Beta Kappa. Ukrainian Catholic. Home: 2 Stafford St Loudonville NY 12211 Office: 101 Columbia St Albany NY 12210

KOMISAR, SURA SCHWARTZ (SONIA), orthodontist; b. Bessarabia, Romania, Mar. 9, 1918; d. Israel and Sima (Tuba) Schwartz; came to U.S., 1948; C.D., U. Brazil, 1940; certificate pedodontics U. Brazil Coll. Dentistry, 1942; D.D.S., N.Y. U., 1962, D.D.S. in Orthodontics, 1959; m. Samuel Komisar, May 23, 1943; children—Sidney Marc, Arnold. Practice dentistry specializing in orthodontics, Woodmere, N.Y., 1963—; mem. staff Peninsula Gen. Hosp. Fellow Royal Soc. Health; mem. ADA, Am. Assn. Orthodontics, Assn. Women Dentists N.Y. (pres.), Nat. Council Jewish Women, N.Y. U. Alumni Assn. Home and Office: 66 Woodmere Blvd Woodmere NY 11598

KOMMERS, WILLIAM JESSE, naval engr.; b. Madison, Wis., Jan. 8, 1918; s. Jesse Benjamin and Meta Rosine (Maurer) K.; B.S., U. Wis., 1939; postgrad. George Washington U., 1965-67; m. Janet Elizabeth Jordan, Apr. 25, 1944; children—Richard W., Stephen J. Jr. engr. Standard Oil Co. Calif., San Francisco, 1939-41; research engr. U.S. Forest Products Lab., Madison, Wis., 1941-44, 46-50; asst. supt. bearings project, head machinery noise br. U.S. Naval Marine Engring. Lab., Annapolis, Md., 1950-67; head, planning and mgmt. dept., dir. resources David Taylor Naval Ship Research & Devel. Center, Bethesda, Md., 1967-75; cons., 1975—. Asst. treas. com. to re-elect U.S. Congresswoman Marjorie Holt, 1976. Registered profl. engr., D.C., Wis. Served with USNR, 1944-46. Mem. Am. Soc. Naval Engrs., Sigma Xi, Tau Beta Pi, Phi Kappa Phi, Am. Legion, VFW. Club: County Radio. Contbr. articles in field to profl. jours. Inventor, patentee Naval bearing wear tester, 1954. Home: 109 Riggs Ave Severna Park MD 21146

KOMONS, NICK ALEXANDER, historian; b. Leros, Greece, Feb. 3, 1929; s. Alexander Nikita and Angela (Rodini) K.; came to U.S., 1935, naturalized, 1954; B.A., Marshall U., 1951; M.A., George Washington U., 1955, Ph.D., 1961; m. Betty Christine Brown, May 20, 1959; children—Alexander, Jennifer, Benjamin. Research asst. Washington History Project, Am. U., Washington, 1955-57; historian Office Aerospace Research, Washington, 1961-66, FAA, Washington, 1966-72; agency historian FAA, 1972—. Served with U.S. Army, 1951-53. Mem. Am. Hist. Assn., Orgn. Am. Historians. Author: Science and the Air Force, 1966; The Cutting Air Crash: A Case Study in Early Federal Aviation Policy, 1973; Bonfires to Beacons: Federal Civil Aviation Policy Under the Air Commerce Act, 1978. Home: 10618 Great Arbor Dr Potomac MD 20854 Office: 800 Independence Ave SW Washington DC 20591

KONECNY, JARO(SLAV) ALOIS, accountant; b. Gracanica-Bosnia, Yugoslavia, Jan. 16, 1911; s. Alois and Frida (Taborsky) K.; M.S., Maritime Acad., Bakar, Yugoslavia, 1936; m. Barbara Kukujan, July 4, 1936 (dec.); 1 son, Boris Adolf. Naval officer Intelligence Service, Yugoslavia, 1932-42; employed various industries, 1947-58; pub. accountant, Strong, Maine, 1966—; justice of the peace, State of Maine, 1966—; translator. Naturalist, writer, lectr.; cons. for nature programs; registered Maine Guide, 1950—. Active Boy Scouts Am.; mem. Maine state advisory com. Scouting for the Handicapped. Recipient Silver Beaver award Boy Scouts Am., 1937, also St. George award. Mem. Nat., Maine assns. pub. accountants, Baden Powell Guild Internat. Democrat. Roman Catholic. Address: Salem Twp PO Strong ME 04983

KONES, RICHARD JOSEPH, physician; b. N.Y.C., Apr. 8, 1941; s. Joseph I. and Ruth Murphy (Winkler) K.; B.S. in Chem. Engring. (N.Y. State Regents scholar 1958-60, Eshborn scholar 1960), N.Y. U. Heights, 1960; M.D. (Arthritis and Rheumatism Found. scholar, Physiology Honors Program scholar), N.Y. U., 1964; m. Sandra Lee Morrissey, Dec. 28, 1969; children—Kimberly Susan, Robin Melissa (dec.), Melanie Ann, Sabrina Lee. Fellow in physiology N.Y. U., 1961-62, in surgery, 1963; intern in medicine Kings County Hosp., Bklyn., 1964-65; resident in surgery Albert Einstein Coll. Medicine/Bronx Municipal Hosp., 1965-66; resident in medicine Lenox Hill Hosp., N.Y.C., 1966-68; teaching fellow in cardiology, physician-in-charge intensive care unit Knickerbocker and Logan Meml. hosps., N.Y.C., 1968-69; fellow in cardiology, acting chief resident VA Hosp., New Orleans, 1969-70; instr. internal medicine Tulane U., 1969-71, USPHS-Nat. Heart, Lung and Blood Inst. fellow in cardiology, 1970-71, vis. physician sect. cardiology, 1972—; asst. prof. clin. cardiology N.Y. Med. Coll., 1971-77; dir. med. edn., coordinator and dir. noninvasive ECG lab. No. Westchester Hosp.-Cornell Med. Center, N.Y., 1972-75; practice medicine specializing in cardiology, N.Y.C., 1971—, Bridgeport, Conn., 1976—; mem. staff Cabrini Health Care Center-Columbus/Italian Hosp., Park East, Park West hosps., N.Y. U. Med. Center-Midtown Hosp., Logan Meml. Hosp., Albert Einstein Coll. Medicine, Madison Ave., Community, Parkchester Gen., Flatbush Gen., Westchester Sq., Lefferts Gen., Mt. Eden Gen. hosps. (all N.Y.C.), Park City Hosp., Bridgeport; cons. cardiologist to hosps. and numerous ins. cos.; cons. N.Y. and Conn. burs. disability determinations Social Security Adminstrn., HEW; medicolegal cons. Tech. Adv. Service for Attys., Phoenix; lectr. in field. Recipient Freshman Chemistry Achievement award N.Y. U. Dept. Chemistry, 1958, Continuing Edn. awards AMA, 1969, 71, 76, 78. Diplomate Am. Bd. Internal Medicine. Fellow Am. Acad. Law and Sci., Am. Coll. Chest Physicians, Am. Coll. Cardiology, Am. Coll. Legal Medicine, Am. Coll. Clin. Pharmacology, Royal Soc. Health (London), Royal Soc. Medicine, Am. Coll. Angiology, Am. Geriatrics Soc. (founding mem.), Am. Soc. Bariatric Physicians, Soc. Advanced Med. Systems, Internat. Coll. Angiology, N.Y. Cardiol. Soc., Am. Coll. Emergency Physicians (charter); mem. A.C.P., Am. Physiol. Soc. (asso., charter mem.), Soc. Gen. Physiologists, Am. Fedn. Clin. Research, Am. Soc. Exptl. Biology, Am. Acad. Clin. Toxicology, Am. Soc. Internal Medicine, Am. Cancer Soc., Am. (councils on basic sci., cardiopulmonary diseases, circulation, thrombosis, clin. cardiology), N.Y., La., Conn., Westchester heart assns., Am. Toxicology Soc., Am. Chem. Soc. (award in chemistry achievement), Am. Soc. Clin. Pharmacology and Exptl. Therapeutics, Am. Med. Writers Assn., French Soc. Advancement of Sci., AAAS, Am. Diabetes Assn., Am., La. thoracic socs., Am. Zool. Soc. (charter mem. comparative physiology group), Am. Acad. Social and Polit. Sci., Am. Statis. Assn., Am. Inst. Biol. Scis., Am. Pub. Health Assn., Am. Math. Soc., Am. Lung Assn., Laennec Soc., Biophys. Soc., Biomed. Engring. Soc., Engring. in Biology and Medicine Group, Audio Engring. Soc., Am. Assn. Advancement Med. Instrumentation, Belgian Soc. Cardiology, Soc. Critical Care Medicine Med. Electronics and Data Soc., Internat. Study Group Research Cardiac Metabolism, Microcirculatory Soc., IEEE, Internat. Soc. Thrombosis Haemostatsis, World Fedn. Nuclear Medicine and Biology, Internat. Soc. Internal Medicine, Internat. Soc. Cardiology, Internat. Soc. Heart Research, Internat. Diabetes Fedn., Internat. Union Physiol. Scis., Internat. Union Pure and Applied Biophysics, U.S. Bioenergetics Group, Société Française de Cardiologie, So. Med. Assn., N.Y. Acad. Scis., N.Y. Trudeau Soc., N.Y. Allergy Soc., N.Y. State Soc. Internal Medicine, Musser-Burch Soc., Am. Med. Tennis Assn., N.Y. U. Sch. Medicine Alumni Found., U.S. Lawn Tennis Assn., Am. Mus. Natural History, East African Wildlife Soc. (Kenya), Nat. Geog. Soc., Nat. Wildlife Fedn., Tulane U., Albert Einstein med. alumni assns. Author: The Molecular and Ionic Basis for Altered Myocardial Contractility, 1973; Cardiogenic Shock, 1974; Glucose, Insulin, Potassium And the Heart, 1975; Shock Cardiogenico (in Spanish), 1977; Coronary Care Unit Handbook, 1979; (with J. H. Phillips) Inherited Diseases and the Heart, 1979, Advanced Electrocardiology, 1979; editor: Controversies in Cardiology, vols. 1-3, 1979—; contbr. numerous articles to profl. publs.; editor: (with J. H. Phillips) Basic and Clinical Pharmacology of the Heart, 1979; contbg. editor: Chest, Am. Hosp. Formulary Service, Current Prescribing; cons. editor Futura Pub. Co. Home: 356 Horseshoe Hill Rd Pound Ridge NY 10576 Office: 133 E 73 St New York City NY 10021 also PO Box 1919 Bridgeport CT 06601 also 305 Baronne St Suite 901 New Orleans LA 70112

KONETZNI, ALBERT H(ENRY) (ALKO) (AL), artist, character licensing co. exec.; b. Bklyn., May 19, 1915; s. Anton Albert and Wilma J. (Heuer) K.; grad. Pratt Inst., 1936; m. Adeline Elizabeth Gurgle, Mar. 14, 1943; children—Albert H., Douglas W., Gary, Karen. Advt. asst. Gertz Dept. Stores, L.I., N.Y., 1935-37; art dir. Specialty Press, N.Y.C., 1937-39, Personna Blade Co./Pal Blade Co., N.Y.C., 1939-53; account exec., artist/creative idea man Walt Disney Productions, N.Y.C., 1953—; photographer; contbr. photographs to greeting cards, photography and calendar cos.; exhibited photographs at N.Y. Museum Modern Art, 1952, Acad. Notre Dame de Namur, Villanova, Pa, 1979. Served with U.S. Army, 1932-33. Recipient Poster award Am. Soc. for Prevention Cruelty to Animals, 1931; Product Design citation Aladdin Industries, 1977; numerous photography awards, including N.Y. Jour.-Am., 1947 Revere Camera, 1952. Mem. Pratt Inst. Alumni Assn. Republican. Lutheran. Club: Rocky Ledge Swim (Harrison and White Plains, N.Y.). Home: 140 Old Farm Rd Pleasantville NY 10570 Office: Walt Disney Co 477 Madison Ave New York NY 10022

KONG, BASIL WAYNE, med. researcher; b. Kingston, Jamaica, July 18, 1943; s. Chan and Violet Ursula (McKenzie) K.; came to U.S., 1959, naturalized, 1964; B.A., Simpson Coll., 1967; M.A., Am. U., 1970; A.G.S., U. Md., 1975; Ph.D., Walden U., 1977; m. Leora Jeanne Yoakum, Apr. 9, 1966; children—Jillian Nicole, Melaine Rochelle. Juvenile probation officer, Montgomery County, Md., 1967-70; asst. prof. Univ. of D.C., 1970—, chmn., 1974, dir. student life, 1975-77; research dir. Urban Cardiology Research Center, Provident Hosp., Balt., 1977—; mem. Md. Statewide Coordinating Council for Hypertension Control; bd. dirs. Inst. Community Devel., Washington Halfway House for Women, Central Md. chpt. Am. Heart Assn. Mem. Nat. Rehab. Assn., Assn. Black Psychologists, No. Assn. Black Social Workers, Am. Personnel and Guidance Assn., Am. Black Cardiologists. Democrat. Baptist. Clubs: Columbia Theatre, Black Family Life. Contbr. articles to profl. jours. Home: 6537 Allview Dr Columbia MD 21046 Office: Urban Cardiology Research Center Provident Hospital Dept Cardiology 2600 Liberty Heights Ave Baltimore MD 21215

KONG, JIN AU, educator; b. Kiangsu, China, Dec. 27, 1942; s. Chin and Shiu (Chao) K.; came to U.S., 1965, naturalized, 1975; Ph.D., Syracuse U., 1968; m. Wen Yuan Yu, June 27, 1970; 1 dau., Shing. Postdoctoral research engr. Syracuse U., 1968-69; asst. prof. (Vinton Hayes fellow) Mass. Inst. Tech., 1969-71, asst. prof., 1969-73, asso. prof., 1973—; vis. scientist Lunar Sci. Inst.; cons. N.Y. Port of Authority. Mem. Am. Soc. Engrs., Am. Phys. Soc., IEEE, Am. Geophys. Union, Internat. Union Radio Sci., Optical Soc. Am., AAUP, N.Y. Acad. Sci., Chiao Tung Alumni Assn. (v.p. 1969-70, pres. 1970-71), Phi Tau Phi (sec.-treas. 1970-74). Author: Theory of Electromagnetic Waves, 1975. Reviewer various profl. jours. Home: 8-5A 100 Memorial Dr Cambridge MA 02142 Office: 36-357 Mass Inst Tech Cambridge MA 02139

KONICK, JOHN CARL, architect; b. Phila., June 8, 1943; s. Marcus and Evelyn Konick; B.S., West Chester State Coll., 1963; postgrad. in Architecture, U. Wis., 1967-69, Temple U., 1969-74; m. Ruth Ann Early, June 6, 1966; children—Donald Roger (dec.), Robert Ian. Job capt. Haag & D'Entremont Architects, Jenkintown, Pa., 1963-66; project architect Harbeson Hough Livingston & Larson, Phila., 1966-74; asso. adminstr. archtl. and engring. services Children's Hosp. of Phila., 1974-76; pres. MKR Architects, Willow Grove, Pa., 1974—. Recipient Design and Drafting Council award, 1961, Ford Found. award, 1961, various design competitions at "T" Square Atelier; registered architect. Mem. Am. Inst. Plant Engrs., Nat. Fire Protection Assn., ASTM, "T" Square Atelier (past pres.), Constrn. Specifications Inst., C. of C. of Willow Grove. Republican. Clubs: Rotary. Co-illustrator: Six Complete World Plays, 1963. Home: 731 Forrest Ave Rydal PA 19046 Office: 210 Cedar Ave Willow Grove PA 19090

KONIKOFF, JOHN JACOB, clin. research scientist; b. Phila., May 1, 1921; s. Joseph M. and Celie (Berson) K.; B.S. in Mech. Engring., Drexel Inst. Tech., 1955; postgrad. U. Pa., 1960-62; Ph.D. in Biomed. Engring. Sci., Union Grad. Sch., 1972; m. Lillian Schechter, June 4, 1944; children—Paula Karen, Bruce Robert. Project engr. Naval Air Material Center, Phila., 1941-47; specialist chemistry Naval Air Devel. Center, Johnsville, Pa., 1948-49; chief exptl. dept. Thermal Research & Engring. Co., Conshohocken, Pa., 1951-56; mgr. phys. biology Gen. Electric Co., King of Prussia, Pa., 1956-64, cons., biomed. tech., 1965-69, cons. scientist Environmental Sci. Lab., 1969-70; cons. biomed. engring., 1971-73; research scientist Hoffmann-La Roche Inc., Nutley, N.J., 1973—. Research instr. dept. physiology Thomas Jefferson U., Phila., 1968-71, adj. asst. prof., 1972, research asst. prof. orthopedic surgery, 1972-76; cons. prof. La. State U., 1968-69; cons. Bioinstrumentation Adv. Com.; cons. on biosci. to U.S. govt. Mem. Mayor's Sci. and Tech. Adv. Com., Phila., 1973-76. Served with USAAF, 1945-46. Registered profl. engr., Pa. Fellow Aerospace Med. Assn. (program com. 1965-66, sci. and tech. com. 1969—); mem. A.A.A.S., Biomed. Engring. Soc., N.Y. Acad. Sci.,

Am. Assn. Advancement Med. Instrumentation, Sigma Xi. Patentee in field. Author: Weak Electric Fields in Medicine. Contbr. to Advances in Biomedical Engineering and Medical Physics, Biomedical Engineering Systems. Contbr. articles in field to scientific jours. Home: 32 Fenton Dr Short Hills NJ 07078 Office: Hoffmann-La Roche Inc 340 Kingsland Ave Nutley NJ 07110

KONO, TOSHIHIKO, cellist; b. Nov. 8, 1930; s. Zenshiro and Miyo K.; LL.B., Kyoto (Japan) U., 1953; student Mannes Coll. Music, Stanford U., (fellow) Berkshire Music Center; m. Edna Libby, June 20, 1968; children—Miyo, Kaori. Asst. prin. cellist Kyoto Symphony Orch.; asst. prin. cellist New Orleans Philharmonic Orch., 1967-68; cellist Am. Symphony Orch., N.Y.C., 1968—, also trustee; prin. cellist Westchester (N.Y.) Philharmonic Orch., 1971-73; resident artist Bar Harbor (Maine) Festival, 1971—; mem. faculty Sch. for Strings, N.Y.C. Fromm fellow, 1971. Mem. Associated Musicians Greater N.Y., Violoncello Soc., Smithsonian Assos., Internat. Platform Assn. Home: 400 W 43d St New York NY 10036 Office: 220 W 107th St 4D New York NY 10025

KONOWITZ, HERBERT HENRY, mfg. co. exec.; b. Brookline, Mass., Feb. 13, 1937; s. Robert Isaac and Sarah (Freedman) K.; B.S. in Bus. Adminstrn., Babson Coll., 1958; m. Linda Phyllis Swartzman, Dec. 20, 1958; children—Cindy Lee, Jeffrey Scott. Vice pres. Vita Rest Sales Co., N.Y.C., 1958-63, Lady Linda Covers Inc., N.Y.C., 1963—, Comml. Drapery Contractors, Silver Spring, Md., 1978—; pres. Milford Stitching Co. (Del.), 1968—; sec. G.L.K. Inc., Milford, Del., 1978—; dir. Greater Del. Corp., Dover, Reclamation Center, Inc., Dover, Yankeeland Assos., Wilmington. Mem. Gov. Del. Council Consumer Affairs, 1971-76; lottery commr. State of Del., 1978—. Chmn., United Jewish Appeal, 1973-74; pres. County Heart Assn., 1975. Dist. chmn. local Republican Com. 1971-76; mem. Del. Rep. Central Com., 1971—, vice chmn., 1975; mem. Del. Rep. Finance Com., 1973—. Mason, Elk. Home: 55 Beloit Ave Dover DE 19901 Office: Milford Stitching Co S Marshall St Milford DE 19963

KONRAD, JANE B., educator; b. Louisville, Nov. 7, 1927; d. James P. and Wilner (Lowdenback) Bourne; B.A., U. Louisville, 1948; M.A., State U. Iowa, 1950; m. Mark G. Konrad, Dec. 28, 1947; children—Stephen J., Robert J. Psychologist, Milw. Gen. Psycopathic Hosp., 1951; sci. coordinator Sewickley (Pa.) Acad., 1976—; plant preparator vol. Carnegie Mus. Natural History, 1974-77, research vol. herbarium, 1977—. Chmn. guide orientation Little Sewickley Nature Trail, 1978—; chmn. advisory bd. Beaver Valley Community Gardens, 1977—; mem. council Carnegie Mus. Natural History. Mem. Am., Pa. psychol. assns., Spl. Edn. Council (past pres.), Beaver County Med. Aux. (sec. 1974-78), Bot. Soc. Western Pa., Early Am. Glass Club Pitts., Embroiderers Guild Pitts., Western Pa. Conservancy, Harmonie Assos., Herb Soc. Am., Am. Rhododendron Soc. Home: 437 Maple Ln Sewickley PA 15143

KONSKI, JAMES LOUIS, civil engr.; b. N.Y.C., Nov. 4, 1917; s. Herbert D. and Ruby (Louis) K.; B.S. in Civil Engring., U. Mo., 1950, M.S. in C.E., 1951 children—Alexander, Christina, Marguerite. Engr. Bur. Yards and Docks, Washington, 1951; structural engr. Sanderson & Porter, N.Y.C., 1951-52; field engr. Ebasco Services, Inc., Owensboro, Ky., 1952-53; chief structural engr. Berger Assos., Syracuse, N.Y., 1953-54, Endman, Anthony & Hosley (formerly Berger Assos.), Syracuse, N.Y., 1954-57; sr. partner Konski Engrs., Syracuse, 1957—. U.S. cons. engr. Trade Mission to Africa, 1965, to Far East, 1970; mem. State Govt. Adv. Group for Emergency Constrn. Served with USMC, 1939-46, maj. Res. now ret. Registered profl. engr., N.Y., Ky., R.I. Fellow ASCE (dir. 1966-70, v.p. 1972-73); mem. Internat. Assn. Bridge and Structural Engrs., N.Y. Assn. Cons. Engrs. (past chpt. pres.), Nat. Soc. Profl. Engrs. (past chpt. pres.), Am. Concrete Inst., Prestressed Concrete Inst., Cons. Engrs. Council (past chpt. pres.), Am. Inst. Cons. Engrs., Am. Congress Surveying and Mapping, Am. Mil. Engrs., Am. Water Works Assn., Am. Road Builders Assn., Am. Soc. Photogrammetry, Sigma Xi, Tau Beta Pi, Chi Epsilon, Pi Mu Epsilon. Club: Onondaga Cycling (pres.). Contbr. articles to profl. jours. Home: 514 Mt View Ave Syracuse NY 13224 Office: 113 E Onondaga St Syracuse NY 13202

KONVALINKA, DANILO, mech. mus. instruments museum owner; b. Celje, Yugoslavia, Sept. 23, 1931; s. Anton Josef and Hildegard (Lang) K.; ed. Austrian pub. schs.; m. Lois Eld Ernest, Dec. 29, 1955. Came to U.S., 1956. Founder, owner Musical Wonder House, Wiscasset, Me., 1962—. Cons. Smithsonian Instn., Washington, 1962—, Boston Mus. Fine Arts, 1964—, Baud Frères, L'Auberson, Switzerland, 1964—, Ency. Brit., 1972—; pub. stereo recs. antique music boxes under label Musical Wonder House Recordings, 1967—. Mem. Mus. Box Soc., Mus. Box Soc. Gt. Britain. Home and office: 18 High St Wiscasset ME 04578 also Merry Music Box 2829 W Northwest Hwy Dallas TX 75220

KONYK, MARY, nursing adminstr.; b. Perth Amboy, N.J., May 16, 1917; d. John and Mary (Lucyk) K.; diploma Muhlenberg Hosp. Sch. Nursing, Plainfield, N.J., 1947; B.S.N., Rutgers U., 1955; M.A. in Nursing Edn., N.Y. U., 1960. Staff nurse, head nurse, instr. nursing Muhlenberg Hosp., 1947-54; instr. nursing St. Marys Hosp., Orange, N.J., 1954-56; supr. nursing Mountainside Hosp., Montclair, N.J., 1956-60; asso. dir. div. patient care Perth Amboy (N.J.) Gen. Hosp., 1960—. Vol. fund raiser Am. Heart Assn., Cancer Assn. Mem. Am., N.J. (named N.J. Nurse of Yr. 1977) nurses assns., Am. Hosp. Assn., Nursing Service Adminstrs. Soc. Mem. Ukranian Cath. Ch. Home: 1083 Truxton Dr Perth Amboy NJ 08861 Office: 530 Brunswick Ave Perth Amboy NJ 08861

KONZELMAN, LEROY MICHAEL, chemist; b. Jersey City, May 27, 1936; s. Adolph Lawrence and Mary (Demcsak) K.; B.S., St. Peter's Coll., 1958; M.S., Seton Hall U., 1964, Ph.D., 1966; m. Mercedes Franz, July 2, 1960; children—Michael Lee, Patricia Anne, Christine. Research chemist Schering Corp., Bloomfield, N.J., 1960-66, indsl. fellow, 1965-66; research chemist Am. Cyanamid Co., Bound Brook, N.J., 1966-72, group leader, 1972-74, chief chemist, 1974—. Served with AUS, 1959. Mem. Am. Chem. Soc. (chmn. Bound Brook discussion group program N.J. sect. 1974—), N.Y. Acad. Sci. Roman Catholic. Contbr. to numerous publs. in field. Patentee in field. Home: 110 W Northfield Rd Livingston NJ 07039 Office: Chimney Rock Rd Bound Brook NJ 08805

KOOCHER, RONALD LAURENCE, real estate broker; b. Boston, Sept. 27, 1934; s. Jacob and Ida (Adler) K.; B.A., Boston U., 1956; m. Barbara Ruth Davis, Jan 5, 1955; children—Bonnie Lyn, Ilisa Beth. Exec., Morton's Inc., Boston, 1958-67, Lane Bryant, N.Y.C., 1967-70; pres. Koocher Realty, Newton, Mass., 1970—; dir. Shoppers' Wrold, Framingham, Mass., South Shore Plaza, Braintree, Mass. Mem. Nat., Mass. assns. realtors, Greater Boston, Newton real estate bds., Rental Housing Assn. Author: Techniques and Applications, 1975. Home: 19 Bothfeld Rd Newton Centre MA 02159 Office: 1185 Washington St Newton MA 02165

KOONCE, SAMUEL DAVID, chem. co. exec.; b. Titusville, Fla., Nov. 26, 1915; s. Martin Egbert and Sara Elizabeth (Thompson) K.; A.B., Oberlin Coll., 1936; M.S., Ohio State U., 1940, Ph.D., 1943; m. Helen Mathews, Dec. 28, 1940; children—Kathryn, Samuel, Richard. Mgr. market devel. Jefferson Chem. Co., N.Y.C., 1952-55; mgr. market research dept. comml. devel. div. Am. Cyanamid Co., N.Y.C., 1955-61; mgr. comml. devel. Lummus Co., N.Y.C., 1961-68; mgr. marketing Ugine Industries, Inc., N.Y.C., 1968-73; dir. tech. div. Ugine Kuhlmann of Am., Englewood Cliffs, N.J., 1973-76, v.p., 1975-76; v.p. Pechiney Ugine Kuhlmann Devel., Inc., Paramus, N.J., 1976—; pres. Inter Polymer Research Corp., 1970-72. Fellow A.A.A.S.; mem. Chem. Marketing Research Assn. (pres. 1954-55), Comml. Devel. Assn., Am. Chem. Soc., Sigma Xi. Club: Chemists. Contbr. to Chemical Market Research in Practice, 1954; Chemical Marketing Research, 1967. Home: 240 Hempstead Rd Ridgewood NJ 07450 Office: 13 Sun Flower Ave Paramus NJ 07652

KOONDEL, IRA STUART, stockbroker; b. Bklyn., Jan. 5, 1942; s. Benjamin and Betty (Erdman) K.; B.A. in History, N.Y. U., 1963; LL.B., Bklyn. Law Sch., 1966; m. Lynn Dara Kronfeld, Feb. 14, 1971; 1 dau., Alison Shawn, Joanna Brooke. Admitted to N.Y. bar, 1966; atty. Coburn Corp. Am., N.Y.C., 1966-67; stockbroker Brand Grumet & Siegel, N.Y.C., 1967-78, Weis Voisin & Cannon, N.Y.C., 1968-69; ind. mem. Am. Stock Exchange, N.Y.C., 1969-72; stockbroker Pressman, Frohlich & Frost, Inc., N.Y.C., 1972-76; pres. Benjamin Koondel, Inc., Bronx, N.Y., 1976—; v.p. BKI Securities Corp., Bronx. Served with AUS, 1967. Club: Cold Spring Country (Cold Spring Harbor, N.Y.). Home: 10 Cypress Ave Great Neck NY 11024 Office: Benjamin Koondel Inc NYC Terminal Market Bronx NY 10474

KOONS, TERRY LLOYD, civil engr.; b. Hershey, Pa., Sept. 16, 1940; s. Lloyd Ellsworth and Lillian Estella (Beachell) K.; B.S.C.E., Drexel U., 1964; m. Donna Marie Wagner, Sept. 30, 1960; children—Todd Alexander, Drue Anne. Design engr. Gannett, Fleming, Corddry and Carpenter, Inc., Harrisburg, Pa., 1964-71, project engr., 1972—. Coach, South Hanover Baseball Assn., Hummelstown, Pa. Registered profl. engr., Pa., Md., Va., Fla. Mem. ASCE, Am. Ry. Engring. Assn., Am. Soc. Hwy. Engrs., Pa., Nat. socs. profl. engrs. Republican. Methodist. Clubs: Optimists (pres. local club 1969), Lions (Hummelstown); Masons. Home: 48 Grandview Rd Hummelstown PA 17036 Office: PO Box 1963 Harrisburg PA 17105

KOOPMAN, KENNETH HENRY, metall. engr.; b. Westport, Conn., Sept. 8, 1916; s. Walter and Gertrude (Maddock) K.; B.S. in Metall. Engring., Rensselaer Poly. Inst., 1938, M.S., 1958; m. Jane MacDonald, June 16, 1939; children—Jani, Kenneth. Metall. engr. Bethlehem Steel Co., (Pa.), 1938-40; research metallurgist Union Carbide Corp., Niagara Falls, N.Y., 1940-47; devel. engr. Linde Co., Newark, 1947-52, project engr., 1952-55; mgr. welding metallurgy and devel. Knolls Atomic Power Lab., Schenectady, 1955-58; asst. dir. Welding Research Council, N.Y.C., 1958-60, dir., 1960-72, exec. dir., 1972—. Registered profl. engr., N.Y. Mem. Am. Soc. Metals, Soc. Naval Architects and Marine Engrs., Am. Welding Soc., ASME, Sigma Xi, Tau Beta Pi. Republican. Presbyterian, Club: Mason. Home: 625 Kenwood Ridgewood NJ 07450 Office: Welding Research Council 345 E 47th St New York City NY 10017

KOOPMAN, NICHOLAS GEORGE, metall. engr., corp. exec.; b. Bklyn., Oct. 6, 1939; s. Klaas and Muriel (Cole) K.; B.S. in Metallurgy, Lafayette Coll., 1960; M.S., Mass. Inst. Tech., 1963, Ph.D., 1966; m. Janice Marie Napier, Apr. 5, 1961; children—Nicholas George, Penny Lee. Sr. asso. engr. IBM, E.Fishkill, N.Y., 1966-68, project engr., mgr. inter-connection metallurgy, 1968-71, devel. engr., 1971-77, mgr. bonding and inter-connections, 1972—, sr. engr., 1977—. Recipient achievement award IBM Corp. 1968, 1975, 1976, 1977; grad. fellow Mass. Inst. Tech., 1960-66; Am. Soc. Metals scholar, 1956-60. Mem. Am. Soc. Metals, Electron Probe Analysis Soc. Am., ASTM, Internat. Soc. Hybrid Microelectronics. U.S. patentee in field (4); 19 inventions; contbr. research papers and presentations to profl. orgns. Home: 9 Francis Dr Hopewell Junction NY 12533 Office: IBM-EF Rt 52 Hopewell Junction NY 12533

KOOPMANS, TJALLING CHARLES, economist; b. s'Graveland, Netherlands, Aug. 28, 1910; s. Sjoerd and Wijtske (Van der Zee) K.; M.A., U. Utrecht (Netherlands), 1933; Ph.D., U. Leiden (Netherlands), 1936; hon. doctorate econs. Netherlands Sch. Econs., 1963, Catholic U. Louvain, 1967; D.Sc. (hon.), Northwestern U., 1975; LL.D., U. Pa., 1976; m. Truus Wanningen, Oct. 1936; children—Ann W., Henry S., Helen J. Came to U.S., 1940, naturalized, 1946. Lectr., Netherlands Econ. U., Rotterdam, 1936-38; specialist fin. sect. League of Nations, 1938-40; research asso. Sch. Pub. and Internat. Affairs, Princeton, also spl. lectr., sch. bus. N.Y. U., 1940-41; economist Penn Mut. Life Ins. Co., 1941-42; statistician Combined Shipping Adjustment Bd. and Brit. Mcht. Shipping Mission, 1942-44; research asso. Cowles Commn. Research Econs., U. Chgo., 1944-55, asso. prof. econs., 1946-48, prof. econs., 1948-55, dir. research Cowles Commn., 1948-54; prof. econs. Yale U., 1955—; dir. Cowles Found. for Research in Econs., 1961-67; Frank W. Taussig prof. econs. Harvard U., 1960-61. Recipient Nobel prize in Econs., 1975. Fellow Econometric Soc. (pres. 1950); mem. Am. Econ. Assn. (pres. 1978), Am. Acad. Arts and Scis., Nat. Acad. Scis. Author: Three Essays on the State of Economic Science, 1957; editor: Statisical Inference in Dynamic Economic Models, 1950; Activity Analysis of Production and Allocation, 1951; co-editor: Studies in Econometric Method, 1953; contbr. articles to profl. jours. Address: Cowles Found for Research in Economics Yale U Box 2125 Yale Station New Haven CT 06520*

KOPEC, VLADIMIR ALADAR, pharmacist, hosp. adminstr.; b. Czechoslovakia, June 20, 1914; s. John and Annie (Pollak) Manberg; came to U.S., 1957, naturalized, 1962; M.Pharmacy, Charles U., Prague, Czechoslovakia, 1945; Sc.D. honoris causa in Economy, U. Sheffield (Eng.), 1965; M.S. in Hosp. Pharmacy Adminstrn., L.I. U., 1965; m. Magdalena Hoff, June 12, 1942; children—Patricia, Daniel. Pharmacist, Kew Gardens (N.Y.) Gen. Hsop., 1957-63; dir. pharmacy and purchasing, asst. and acting adminstr. Deepdale Gen. Hosp., N.Y.C., 1963-67; dir. material control and purchasing Wyckoff Heights Hosp., Bklyn., 1967—; adj. asst. prof. hosp. pharmacy adminstrn. Bklyn. Coll. Pharmacy, L.I. U., 1967—; cons. pharmacist Forest View Nursing Home, 1972—. Mem. Rho Chi. Author: Purchasing Management and Material Control in Hospitals, 1970. Home: 83 40 Austin St Kew Gardens NY 11415 Office: 374 Stockholm St Brooklyn NY 11237

KOPENHAVER, PATRICIA ELLSWORTH, podiatrist; b. N.Y.C., Aug. 18, 1928; A.B., George Washington U., 1954; M.A., Columbia U., 1956; Dr. Podiatric Medicine, U. State N.Y., 1963. Practice podiatry, Greenwich, Conn., 1964—; mem. staff Laurelton Convalescent Hosp., Greenwich. Mem. Greenwich Woman's Gardeners Club. Recipient Hosp. Fund award for med. research translations A.R.C. Diplomate Nat. Bd. Podiatry Examiners. Mem. Am., Conn., Fairfield, Am. Woman's (pres. 1976) podiatry assns., Am. Podiatry Women's Assn. (pres. 1970, 73), Acad. Podiatry, Am. Podiatry Council, UN Assn. N.Y., NOW, AAUW, Columbia U. Alumni Assn., George Washington U. Alumni Assn., Phi Beta Kappa, Pi Epsilon Chi. Clubs: Soroptimists, Greenwich Women's (chmn. civic and pub. affairs com. 1970). Home: 2 Sutton Pl S New York City NY 10022 also 8 Dearfield Dr Greenwich CT 06830 Office: 8 Dearfield Dr Greenwich CT 06830

KOPLIN, NORMA JEAN, artist; b. Chgo., 1936; d. Harry and Hannah Ruth (Libman) Koplin; B.F.A., Yale U., 1957; postgrad. Bank St. Coll. Edn., 1976; 1 dau., Yamina Marie-Claude Katan. Illustrator A Piece of String Ivan Obolensky, 1964; works pub. Harper's mag.; exhibited in one-woman shows at David Herbert Gallery, N.Y.C., 1962, Kasha Herman Gallery, Chgo., 1963, Graham Gallery, N.Y.C., 1968, 76, Benson Gallery, N.Y.C., 1971; exhibited in group shows at Yale U., New Haven, 1959, Art Inst. Chgo., 1963, Mus. Modern Art, N.Y.C., 1962-71, Phila. Mus. Art, 1967, Finch Coll. Mus., N.Y.C., 1974; tchr. Columbia U., 1967. Recipient Art Dirs. Club award. Mem. Women in Arts, Artist Equity. Address: 525 East 86th St New York City NY 10028

KOPPE, EDWIN FREDERICK, geol. cons., b. Chgo., Dec. 13, 1920; s. William Paul and Mary (Aram) K.; A.B. in Sci. with honors, U. Ill. at Urbana, 1949; M.S. in Botany, U. Wis., 1950; postgrad. geology Pa. State U., 1952-57; m. Betty Mae Colvin, Dec. 29, 1951; children—Albert L., Thomas F., Charlotte A., Richard A. Mem. faculty Pa. State U. at University Park, 1952-57, guest instr. acid mine drainage abatement, 1972-77; geologist Pa. Geol. Survey, Harrisburg, 1957-67; geol. cons. E.F. Koppe & Assos., Harrisburg, 1967—. Del. Internat. Commn. Coal Petrology, 1965-66; mem. Council for Surface Mining and Reclamation Research in Pa., 1976—. Council trainer Boy Scouts Am., Harrisburg, 1963—, commr., 1965-73; pres. P.T.A., 1965-67, 72-73, chmn. safety, 1973; chmn., bd. dirs. Operation Understanding Team, Episcopal Diocese of Central Pa., 1970-71. Served with AUS, 1941-45. Recipient Silver Beaver award Boy Scouts Am., Harrisburg, 1973. Fellow Geol. Soc. Am.; mem. A.A.A.S., Am. Anthracological Soc., Harrisburg Geol. Soc., Sigma Xi. Episcopalian. Research in coal mining pollution abatement, uranium in coal, nature of coal, engring. geology. Home and office: 4407 Locust Ln Harrisburg PA 17109

KOPPELMAN, LEE EDWARD, regional planning ofcl.; b. N.Y.C., May 19, 1927; s. Max and Madelyn Judith (Eisenberg) K.; B.E.E., Coll. City N.Y., 1950; M.S., Pratt Inst., 1964; D. in Pub. Adminstrn., N.Y. U., 1970; LL.D. (hon.), L.I. U., 1978; m. Constance E. Lowinger, June 18, 1948; children—Leslie, Caludia, Laurel, Keith. Pvt. practice landscape architecture and site planning, L.I., 1950-60; dir. planning Suffolk County Planning Commn., Huappauge, 1960—; exec. dir. Nassau-Suffolk Regional Planning Bd., 1965—, Nassau-Suffolk Regional Marine Resources Council, 1965—; prof. polit. sci. State U. N.Y. at Stony Brook, 1970—; adj. prof. Grad. Sch. Environ. Scis., Syracuse U. Vice pres. Suffolk County council Boy Scouts Am., 1966-72; mem. planning com. L.I. Children's Hosp., Mineola, 1972—. Mem. coastal zone mgmt. adv. com. Nat. Oceanic and Atmospheric Adminstrn., U.S. Dept. Commerce, 1973-76. Nassau-Suffolk Comprehensive Health Planning Council, 1967-76; mem. Nat. Shoreline Erosion Adv. Panel, U.S. Army C.E., 1974—. Served with USNR, 1945-46. Named Community Benefactor with gold medal Long Island Assn., 1971; recipient Environmental Protection Silver Archi award L.I. chpt. A.I.A., 1971; 1st Bronze medal for career achievement City Coll. N.Y. Engring. and Architecture Alumni, 1977. Mem. Am. Inst. Planners, N.Y. State County Planners Assn. (pres. 1967-68), Internat. Fedn. Planning and Housing, Assn. Architects and Engrs. Israel, Alpha Phi Omega. Author: (with Joseph DeChiara) Planning Design Criteria, 1970; (with others) Long Island Sound: The Urban Sea, 1976; Housing Planning and Design, 1974; A Methodology to Achieve the Integration of Coastal Zone Science and Regional Planning, 1974; Urban Planning and Design Criteria, 1975; Site Planning Standards, 1976; Long Island Comprehensive Waste Treatment Management Plan, Vols. I-II, 1978. Home: 5 Cakewalk Terr Smithtown NY 11787 Office: Nassau Suffolk County Regional Planning Bd Vets Meml Hwy Hauppauge NY 11287

KOPPLE, ROBERT, lawyer, orgn. exec.; b. N.Y.C., Nov. 26, 1910; B.S., N.Y. U., J.D., N.Y. U., 1934; m. Dorothy Stuhlbarg, July 22, 1944 (dec.); children—Ann Howard, Nancy Dunn; m. 2d, Marie M. Vandevort, Oct. 7, 1978. Admitted to N.Y. bar, 1934; since practiced in N.Y.C.; spl. adviser to Mayor N.Y.C. to develop Tercentenary Celebration. Founder, 1st exec. v.p. N.Y. World's Fair 1964-65 Corp.; exec. v.p. Midtown Realty Owners Assn., Inc., 1953-77, Owners Com. on Electric Rates, Inc., 1954—; exec. Com. for Reasonable World Trade Center, 1964-69, v.p. Com. for Adequate Supply of Energy, 1971—; pres. Quick Response Service, Inc.; cons. 32B/3d Pension Fund, 1977—. Mem. Met. N.Y. adv. com. to Joint Legis. Com. on Commerce and Econ. Devel.; mem. citizens com. on fire prevention N.Y.C. Fire Dept.; chmn. Community Planning Bd. number 5 Borough Pres. of Manhattan, 1964-71; Democratic candidate for N.Y. State Senate, Nassau County, 1950; chmn. Dem. County Re-orgn. Com., Nassau County, 1951; Dem. zone leader, Roslyn; mem. Dem. County Com. Employer trustee Bldg. Service Pension Fund, Bldg. Service Welfare Fund, 1953-77, Internat. Bldg. Service Employees Pension Fund, 1968-76; sole trustee Midtown Exec. Trust Fund, Midtown Gen. Trust Fund, 1968-77. Served to 2d lt. AUS, 1942-46. Mem. Real Estate Bd. N.Y. (pub. utilities com.), N.Y. C. of C. and Industry (traffic com., tax com., property law com., pub. health com., city zoning com.), Mutual Admiration Soc. (organizer), U.S. Power Squadron (rear comdr.), Tau Delta Phi, Sigma. Home: 17 Greenway Roslyn NY 11576 also N Parish Dr Southold NY 11971 Office: 450 7th Ave New York NY 10001 also 19 Park Ave Manhasset NY 11030

KOPSER, ARNOLD WILLIAM, cons. co. exec.; b. Poughkeepsie, N.Y., May 18, 1915; s. Oscar William and Lillian Dorothy (MacMullen) K.; student Cornell U. extension, 1946-47; m. Ella Mae Owens, Aug. 2, 1946. Tool and die maker, V & O Punch Press, Hudson, N.Y., 1940-41; with IBM Corp., Poughkeepsie, indsl. edn. supr., 1946-61, safety adminstr., 1961-75; pres. Safety Service Assos., 1975—. Dir. Eastern Seaboard Apprenticeship Council, 1953-62; tchr. Dutchess Community Coll., part-time 1964-68. Served with USNR, 1943-46: ETO. Mem. Order Ky. Cols., V.F.W., Nat. Rifle Assn. Episcopalian. Contbr. articles to Jour. Brigade of Am. Revolution. Office: 41 Yates Ave Poughkeepsie NY 12601

KORANDA, JOHN TIMOTHY, financial writer; b. Fort Wayne, Ind., July 26, 1950; s. Leroy Frederick and Jean Esther (Weil) K.; B.A., Colgate U., 1971; B.S., M.S., Mass. Inst. Tech., 1973; M.B.A., N.Y. U., 1976; m. Iris Violeta Hernandez, July 22, 1973. Staff writer N.W. Ayer & Son, N.Y.C., 1973-75; broker, investment counselor Bache & Co., N.Y.C., 1975-76; free lance finanical writer, N.Y.C., 1976—; financial relations cons. GRM Communications, Inc. div. Carly Ally, also Doremus Inc., N.Y.C., 1976-78, Citibank, N.A., 1978—. Asso. mem. Commodity Futures Trading Commn.; registered mem. Chgo. Bd. Trade; mem. Nat. Democratic Club. Recipient Saturday Rev./World Corporate Communications award, 1973, Esquire Corporate Responsibility Advt. award, 1973. Mem. Assn. for Symbolic Logic, Econ. History Assn., Phi Beta Kappa. Democrat. Clubs: Copy of N.Y., Advt. of N.Y. Home: 135-10 Grand Central Pkwy Jamaica NY 11435 Office: 399 Park Ave New York City NY 10001

KORB, LAWRENCE JOSEPH, educator; b. N.Y.C., July 9, 1939; s. Joseph Anthony and Katherine Veronica (McKenna) K.; B.A., Athenacum of Ohio, 1961; M.A., St. John's U., 1962; Ph.D., State U. N.Y., Albany, 1969; m. Ann Abella Guttmann, Aug. 20, 1966; children—Mary, Karen, Julia, Lawrence Joseph. Asst. prof. polit. sci.

U. Dayton (Ohio), 1969-71; asso. prof. govt. U.S. Coast Guard Acad., New London, Conn., 1971-75; prof. mgmt. U.S. Naval War Coll., Newport, R.I., 1975—; cons. Office Sec. Defense, Office Edn., Nat. Security Council. Served with USN, 1962-66. N.Y. State Regents fellow, 1966-69, Inter-Univ. Seminar fellow, 1970—; adj. scholar Am. Enterprise Inst. for Pub. Policy Research, 1972—. Mem. Internat. Studies Assn., Am. Polit. Sci. Assn. Author: (with David Ott) Nixon-McGovern and the Federal Budget, 1972, Public Claims on U.S. Output: Federal Budget Options in the Last Half of the Seventies, 1973; The Joint Chiefs of Staff: The First Twenty-Five Years, 1976; The Price of Preparedness: The FY 1978-82 Defense Program, 1977. Editor: The System for Educating Military Officers in the U.S., 1976; contbr. articles in field to profl. jours., chpts. to books. Home: 79 Fischer Circle Portsmouth RI 02871 Office: Dept Mgmt US Naval War Coll Newport RI 02840

KORBEN, DONALD LEE, counseling psychologist; b. Bklyn., Apr. 4, 1948; s. Abraham and Betty K.; B.A., Butler U., 1972; M.S., Ind. U., 1973, Ed.D., 1976; m. Christine Clara Cook, Dec. 15, 1973. Intern counseling and psychol. services Ind. U., 1974-76; counseling psychologist Counseling Center, St. Bonaventure U., 1976—, mem. adj. faculty Grad. Sch., 1977—; counselor, adminstr. Drinking Driver Rehab. Program, 1976—; cons. Proprietory Home Assn. Western N.Y., 1976—. Mem. Butler U. Religion Council, 1968-70; vol. Salvation Army, 1966-76, Boy Scouts Am., 1966-72, Mental Health Assn. Ind., 1967-70, Nat. Epilepsy Found., 1973-76. Named Outstanding Student of Yr., Butler U., 1970; Outstanding Young Man of Am., Jaycees, 1978; NSF grantee, 1970-71; Ind. U. grantee, 1976. Mem. Am. Psychol. Assn., Am. Personnel and Guidance Assn., Am. Coll Personnel Assn., Assn. Counselor Edn. and Supervsion, Phi Delta Kappa. Democrat. Jewish. Research on effects of hibernation, factors in assertive tng. with females. Home: 757 Main St Olean NY 14760

KORBER, FRANCIS XAVIER, scientist; b. Bklyn., June 6, 1930; s. Edward John and Anna (Norton) K.; B.S., St. John's Coll., 1952; M.S., St. John's U., 1956; postgrad. Pace Coll., 1961-62, Adelphi U., 1962-63, Hofstra Coll., 1968-69; m. Margaret A. Titus, Jan. 22, 1955; children—Kenneth, Maureen, Patricia, Thomas, Dennis. Tchr. sci. and health St. Michael's High Sch., Newark, 1952-54, 54-56; tchr. biology Westbury (N.Y.) Sr. High Sch., 1956—, supr. sci. dept., 1969—; mem. ednl. adv. com. Westbury PTSA; mem. vis. com. Middle States Assn. Secondary Schs. Served with U.S. Army, 1952-54. NSF grantee, 1968, 78-79; NASA and Nat. Sci. Tchrs. Assn. certificate award, 1972; certificate Tomorrow's Scientists and Engrs., 1971. Mem. Westbury Classroom Teachers Assn. (negotiator, 1972—), N.Y. State United Tchrs., Sci. Tchrs. Assn. N.Y. State, Nassau County Sci. Suprs. Assn. Republican. Roman Catholic. Club: Smithtown Landing Country. Home: 81 Morewood Dr Smithtown NY 11787 Office: Westbury Sr High School Post Rd Jericho Turnpike Westbury NY 11590

KORCHYNSKY, MICHAEL, metall. engr.; b. Kiev, Ukraine, Apr. 11, 1918; s. Michael and Jadwiga (Zdanowicz) K.; came to U.S., 1950, naturalized, 1956; Dipl. Ing. in Metals Tech., Tech. U. Lviv, 1942; m. Taisija Lapin, Nov. 22, 1951; children—Michael, Marina, Roksana. Lectr., Tech. U. Lviv, 1942-44; civilian engr. C.E., U.S. Army, W.Ger., 1945-50; research metallurgists Union Carbide Co., Niagara Falls, N.Y., 1951-61; research supr. Jones & Laughlin Steel Corp., Pitts., 1962-68; dir. product research, 1969-72; dir. alloy devel., metals div. Union Carbide Co., N.Y.C., 1973-77, Pitts., 1978—; lectr. Niagara U., 1957-58. Fellow Am. Soc. Metals (Andrew Carnegie lectr. 1973); mem. Am. Iron and Steel Inst. (medalist), N.Y. Acad. Scis., Brazilian Soc. Metals, Iron and Steel Inst. Japan, Metall. Soc. U.K., Am. Soc. Metals, Am. Inst. Metall. Engrs., Soc. Automotive Engrs., ASTM. Author, patentee in field. Home: 2770 Milford Dr Bethel Park PA 15102 Office: Robinson Plaza II Route 60 Pittsburgh PA 15205

KORENTAYER, SHAY, engring. contracts mgr.; b. Osh, Russia, Aug. 22, 1945; s. Naftali and Bluma(Syrkus) K.; came to U.S., 1970, naturalized, 1976; B.S.C.E., Techion Israel, 1967; M.S.C.E., Columbia U., 1971; M.B.A., Fordham U., 1977; m. Eva Schapira, May 21, 1972; children—Elisa Anne, Daniel Ethan. Design engr. R. Rosenwasser Assos., N.Y.C., 1971-76; civil project engr. Ebasco Services Inc., N.Y.C., 1976-78; contracts mgr. Heyward Robinson Co., N.Y.C., 1978—. Served to lt. Israel Army, 1967-70. Registered profl. engr., N.J., N.Y. State. Mem. Am. Concrete Inst., AMA, Assn. M.B.A. Execs. Home: 18 Camelot Dr East Brunswick NJ 08816 Office: #1 World Trade Center New York City NY 10048

KORET, SYDNEY, psychologist; b. Providence, Apr. 11, 1916; s. Hyman and Anna (Weiss) K.; B.S., U. R.I., 1937; M.S.W., Boston U., 1949, M.A. in Psychology, 1949, Ph.D. in Psychology, 1956; m. Alice Elsie Lecht, Jan. 1, 1947; children—Richard Joseph, Peter David. Psychiat. social worker R.I. State Hosp., 1949-50; chief psychiat. social worker Emma Pendleton Bradley Hosp., Riverside, R.I., 1950-58; dir. Convalescent Hosp. for Children, Rochester, N.Y., 1958—; sr. asso. psychologist Strong Meml. Hosp., 1958—; clin. asso. prof. psychology Grad. Sch., U. Rochester, 1961—, Sch. Medicine and Dentistry, Dept. Psychiatry, 1958—; cons. Dept. Def., 1976—; councillor Joint Commn. on Accreditation of Hosps., 1975—; chmn. Nat. Consortium of Child Mental Health Services, 1977—; treas. N.Y. State br. Nat. Council Community Mental Health Centers, 1975—. Bd. dirs. Community Child Care Center, 1968—, pres., 1970-73; bd. dirs. Planned Parenthood, 1975—, Mental Health Assn. Rochester and Monroe County, 1959—; mem. advisory bd. Parents Without Partners, 1969—. Served to capt. USAAF, 1942-46. Decorated Air medal with 6 oak leaf clusters, D.F.C. with 1 oak leaf cluster; Croix de Guerre (France). Certified social worker, N.Y.; certified psychologist, N.Y.; certified Assn. Child Care Workers. Fellow Am. Psychol. Assn., Am. Orthopsychiat. Assn.; mem. N.Y. State, Genesee Valley psychol. assns., Nat. Assn. Social Work, Nat. Conf. Social Welfare, Internat. Assn. Applied Hypnosis, Assn. Mental Health Adminstrs., Am. Soc. Clin. Hypnosis, World Fedn. Mental Health, Council for Exceptional Children, Nat. Mental Health Assn., Acad. Certified Social Workers, Rochester Assn. Edn. of Young Children, Assn. N.Y. State Educators of Emotionally Disturbed, Am. Assn. Children's Residential Centers (treas. 1968-70, pres. 1971-73), Am. Assn. Psychiat. Services for Children (dir. 1970-74, 75-78), World Fedn. Mental Health. Jewish. Home: 220 Hibiscus Dr Rochester NY 14618 Office: 2075 Scottsville Rd Rochester NY 14623

KORKLAN, ELLIOT SAMUEL, photographer; b. Saginaw, Mich., Dec. 16, 1918; s. Harris and Sarah (Block) K.; student Winona Sch. Photography, 1956; m. Marilyn Cohen, July 7, 1946; children—Lisa, Paula. Founder, pres. Korday Studio, Framingham, Mass., 1947—, Indsl. Color Lab., Inc., Framingham, 1956—. Served with USAF, 1942-45, ETO. Mem. Profl. Photographers New Eng. (state v.p. 1957-58), Indsl. Photographers New Eng. (pres. 1967-68), Soc. Photog. Scientists and Engrs., Assn. Profl. Color Labs., Profl. Photographers Am. (nat. award 1972), Photog. Soc. Am., Mass. Profl. Photographers Assn., Photog. Mktg. Assn. Internat., Jewish War Vets. Jewish. Club: B'nai B'rith. Home: 580 Edmands Rd Framingham MA 01701 Office: 9 Proctor St PO Box 563 Framingham MA 01701

KORMAN, MICHAEL MEYER, cost controls engr.; b. Bklyn., July 6, 1948; s. Julius and Roslyn Sylvia (Levinson) K.; student Bklyn. Coll., 1966-68; B.M.E., Coll. City N.Y., 1971, M.Engring., 1974; m. Phyllis Irene Shapiro, June 20, 1971; 1 dau., Amy Joyce. Los prevention and control rep. Royal Globe Ins. Cos., N.Y.C., 1972; engr. power Stone & Webster Engring. Corp., N.Y.C., 1972-75; asst. project engr. Gibbs and Hill, Inc., N.Y.C., 1975-77; cost controls engr. CE Lummus, Bloomfield, N.J., 1977—. Registered profl. engr., N.J., N.Y. Mem. ASME, N.Y. Soc. Profl. Engrs., Am. Nuclear Soc., Am. Assn. Cost Engrs., Mensa. Democrat. Home: 473 Apple Valley Dr Belford NJ 07718 Office: 1515 Broad St Bloomfield NJ 07003

KORMAN, MILTON DANIEL, judge; b. Washington, Oct. 22, 1904; s. Joseph William and Ida Ethel (Beneman) K.; J.D., Georgetown U., 1925; postgrad. George Washington U., 1926; grad. Nat. Jud. Coll., 1971; m. Bernice Rosensweig, Oct. 20, 1940 (dec. Feb. 1970); children—James William, Edward Neal, Sharon Hope Korman Weiss; m. 2d, Mildred Bermann Tulman, Aug. 29, 1972. Admitted to D.C. bar, 1925, U.S. Supreme Ct. bar, 1940; individual practice law, Washington, 1925-37; asst. corp. counsel D.C. Govt., 1937-66, chief criminal div., 1941-43, chief civil litigation div., 1951-56, prin. asst. corp. counsel, 1956-65, acting corp. counsel, 1965-66; judge Superior Ct. D.C., 1967—; adj. prof. law Southeastern U., Washington, 1964-67. Mem. exec. bd. former gen. counsel Nat. Capital Area council Boy Scouts Am., 1957—, Nat. council, 1960—; v.p. Nat. Children's Center, 1970—; bd. dirs. Hebrew Home of Greater Washington, 1970—. Recipient Distinguished Pub. Service award Nat. Inst. Municipal Law Officers, 1965; Alumni Achievement award Law Center Georgetown U., 1967; Silver Beaver award Boy Scouts Am., 1960; named Hon. Fire Chief of D.C., 1974. Mem. Am., D.C. (chmn. dist. ct. com. 1964-67), Fed. (nat. council 1969-74) bar assns., Am. Judicature Soc., Jud. Conf. D.C., Municipal Officers Club D.C. (pres. 1958-59), Assn. Oldest Inhabitants, Friendship Fire Assn., Jewish Hist. Soc. D.C. (dir. 1974—), Legion Honor Order DeMolay, Delta Theta Phi (hon.). Democrat. Jewish. Clubs: B'nai B'rith, Masons (32 degree, Knight Comdr. Ct. of Honor, grand master D.C., 1969), Shriners, Indian Spring Country. Home: 4201 Cathedral Ave NW Apt 215 E Washington DC 20016 Office: Superior Ct DC Room 2440 500 Indiana Ave NW Washington DC 20001

KORN, LESTER BERNARD, business exec.; b. N.Y.C., Jan. 11, 1936; s. Raymond H. and Jetta (Spieler) K.; B.S., U. Calif. at Los Angeles, 1957, M.B.A., 1959; postgrad. Harvard, 1960; m. Carolbeth Goldman, June 30, 1961; children—Jodi Lynn, Jessica Susan. With Bank of Am., Los Angeles, 1960-61; mgmt. cons. Peat, Marwick, Mitchell & Co., Los Angeles, 1961-66, partner, 1966-69; pres. Korn/Ferry Internat., N.Y.C., 1969—; dir. Daylin, Inc.; dir. Cordura Corp. Instr., Woodbury Coll., 1966-67. Bd. dirs. Nat. Conf. Christians and Jews, Reiss-Davis Child Care Center, City of Hope Med. Center, So. Calif. Bus. Research Council. Mem. Calif. Soc. C.P.A.'s, Am. Inst. C.P.A.'s, Century City C. of C. (dir.). Clubs: Harvard Business, Los Angeles Athletic, Hillcrest Country (Los Angeles). Office: 277 Park Ave New York City NY 10017

KORNBLATT, DAVID WOLFE, real estate broker; b. Balt., June 30, 1927; s. Harry and Rebecca (Pomerantz) K.; B.S., U. Md., 1950; m. Barbara Rodbell, Apr. 1, 1951; children—Rebecca, Sondra, Henry, Anne. Chmn., David W. Kornblatt Assos., Inc., Balt., 1951-58, David Kornblatt Assos., Inc., 1958—; pres. Arthur Rubloff & Co. of D.C.; v.p. Sercuity Savings & Loan Assn., Inc.; v.p. Office Network Inc., 1978—. Vice-chmn. Balt. City Econ. Devel. Com., 1961-65; treas. Commn. of Efficiency and Economy, 1965-68; mem. exec. bd. Balt. Area Council Boy Scouts Am., 1974-76; bd. dirs. Greater Balt. Com., 1978—. Served with USCG, 1945-46. Named Outstanding Dir., Balt. Jr. C. of C., 1962. Mem. Soc. Indsl. Realtors (dist. v.p. 1975-76), Greater Balt. Bd. Realtors (past dir.). Home: 3512 Old Court Rd Pikesville MD 21208 Office: 25 S Charles St Baltimore MD 21201 also 1825 K St NW Washington DC 20006

KORNEGAY, WADE MELVIN, lab. adminstr., research scientist; b. Mt. Olive, N.C., Jan. 9, 1934; s. Gilbert E. and Estelle (Williams) K.; B.S., N.C. Central U., 1956; postgrad. Bonn U., W.Ger., 1956-57; Ph.D., U. Calif. at Berkeley, 1961; Sc.D. (hon.), Lowell Tech. Inst., 1969; m. Bettie Joyce Hunter, Sept. 9, 1960; children—Melvin, Cynthia, Laura. Research asso. physics U. Calif. at Berkeley, 1961, NSF postdoctoral fellow, 1961-62; tech. staff mem. Mass. Inst. Tech., Lincoln Lab., Lexington, 1962—, tech. group leader, 1971—. Mem. Vice Pres. Humphrey's Task Force Youth Motivation, 1964-68; mem. Eastern Mass. Urban League; bd. dirs. Boston City Missionary Soc., 1977—; bd. dirs. Nat. Consortium for Black Profl. Devel., 1976—. Fulbright fellow, 1956-57; Danforth Found. grad. fellow, 1956-61. Mem. Am. Phys. Soc., Sigma Xi, Alpha Phi Alpha. Mem. United Ch. Christ. Researcher chem. kinetics of thermal ionization, 1957-62, chemistry of hypersonic wakes, 1962-70, radar signatures and re-entry physics, 1970—. Home: 35 Hickory Rd Sudbury MA 01776 Office: 244 Wood St Lexington MA 02173

KORNFELD, ALLAN, health care exec.; b. Wilkes-Barre, Pa., Dec. 3, 1918; s. Jack and Sara (Slavitz) K.; student George Washington U., 1939-41, U. N.C., 1937-38; LL.B., N.Y. U., 1949; m. Matilda Jane Reed, June 3, 1945; children—Nancy, Andrew. Admitted to N.Y. bar, 1950; asso. atty. Hahn & Golin, 1950-51; mem. firm Dunkin & Kornfeld, 1952-62; sr. dep. county atty. Nassau County (N.Y.), 1962-67; gen. counsel Health Ins. Plan Greater N.Y., N.Y.C., 1967-72, pres., 1972-78; mem. adv. bd. N.Y. New Sch. Program in Health Adminstrn., 1976-78. Bd. dirs. L.I. Environ. Council, 1964-67, Nassau County Edn. TV Council, 1964-69; mem. Nassau County Commn. Consumer Protection, 1966-68; chmn. bd. trustees LaGuardia Hosp., 1972-78; mem. state com. N.Y. State Democratic party, 1964-68. Served to capt., Ordnance Dept., U.S. Army, 1941-46. Recipient Certificate of Merit, Nassau County, 1963. Mem. Nat. Health Lawyers Assn. (dir.), Am. Pub. Health Assn., Group Health Assn. Am. (pres. 1976-78, chmn. bd. 1978), Nassau County Bar Assn. Jewish. Home: 31 Lace Ln Westbury NY 11590 Office: 150 E 58th St New York City NY 10022

KORNFELD, LEONARD ROBERT, package mfg. co. exec.; b. Bklyn., Dec. 27, 1939; s. Louis and Bertie (Fleisig) K.; student City Coll. of N.Y.; m. Marilynn S. Kaye, Dec. 17, 1966; children—Michelle Robyn, Sean Michael. Analyst, Eastern Precision Resistor Co., Bklyn., 1957-58; prodn. mgr. U.S. Box Crafts Inc., Bklyn., 1961-62, sales mgr., 1962-65, exec. v.p., dir., 1965-78; exec. v.p., dir. U.S. Box Corp., Newark, 1965-78; pres. Acorn Box Corp., Amityville, N.Y., 1978—; packing cons. to many firms. Served with U.S. Army, 1958-60. Recipient many packaging design awards. Mem. L.I. C. of C. Am. Mensa Ltd., Mfg. Jewelers and Silversmiths Am., Nat. Rare Blood Assn., DAV, Nat. Rifle Assn. (life), Am. Def. Preparedness Assn. Jewish. Club: Masons. Patentee and trademark holder for displays and package designs. Home: 457 Wolf Hill Rd Dix Hills NY 11746 Office: 21 Dixon Ave Amityville NY 11701

KORNHAUSER, STANLEY HENRY, ednl. planner and adminstr., human relations specialist, grantsman; b. Bronx, N.Y., Nov. 8, 1934; s. Max and Anna (Farrier) K.; A.B., Hunter Coll., 1956, A.M., 1958; M.A., N.Y. U., 1965; m. Janet Gloria Divak, Dec. 24, 1961; children—Stephanie Ann, David Robert. State adminstrv. cons., office of commr., div. intercultural relations in edn. N.Y. State Edn. Dept., Albany, 1968; program adminstr. State Integration Fund, N.Y.C. Bd. Edn., 1969-71, asst. to exec. dir., div. ednl. planning and support, 1973-76, asst. adminstrv. dir. Center for Library, Media and Telecommunications, 1976—; dir. office equal ednl. opportunity planning Stamford (Conn.) Bd. Edn., 1971-72, dir. office research and program evaluation 1972-73; adj. asst. prof. L.I. U. Sch. Edn., 1973—; lectr. in field City U. N.Y., York Coll., 1973—. Mem. Internat. Soc. Ednl. Planners, Nat. Assn. Intergroup Relations Ofcls., Am. Soc. Tng. and Devel., Assn. Supervision and Curriculum Devel., N.Y. Sch. Masters Club, Phi Delta Kappa. Club: Toastmasters. Author: Planning for the Achievement of Quality Integrated Education in Desegregated Schools, 1968; Intergroup Educational Implementations of Legislative Change, 1969; Program Evaluation and Review Technique for Educational Adminstrators and Supervisors, 1975; The Art of Proposal Development, 1977; also articles and papers for Bd. of Edn. publs. Home: 211-65 23d Ave Bayside NY 11360 Office: 110 Livingston St Brooklyn NY 11201

KORNREICH, LAWRENCE DAVID, indsl. hygienist; b. N.Y.C., Jan. 31, 1940; s. Mates and Lillian Rose (Silinsky) K.; A.B., Columbia U., 1960; M.S., U. Del., 1963; M.S.P.H., U. N.C., Chapel Hill, 1967, Ph.D., 1972; m. Linda Ellen Lewis, Dec. 23, 1962; children—Wendy Lynn, Jonathan Glenn, Jill Debra. Applied research chemist E.I. duPont de Nemours & Co., Wilmington, Del., Florence, S.C., 1962-66; dir. chem. labs., industry cons. TRC-Research Corp. of New Eng., Hartford, Conn., 1969-72, also bd. dirs.; exec. dir. Triangle Univs. Consortium on Air Pollution, co-dir. Indsl. Hygiene Referral Center, U. N.C., Chapel Hill, 1972-77; indsl. hygienist, field tng. dir. ITT Corp., N.Y.C., 1977—; cons. environmental edn. Active, PTA Sch. Fairs, 1972—; bd. dirs. PTA, Chapel Hill, 1972-73. Recipient awards for excellence Soc. for Tech. Communications, 1975. Diplomate Am. Bd. Indsl. Hygiene. Mem. N.Am. Simulation and Gaming Assn. (pres. 1976, dir. 1976—), Am. Indsl. Hygiene Assn., Air Pollution Control Assn., AAAS, Sigma Xi. Democrat. Jewish. Club: B'nai B'rith. Editor: Proceedings of Symposium on Statistical Aspects of Air Quality Data, 1974; Proceedings of Symposium on Chemical Aspects of Air Quality Modeling, 1974. Office: 320 Park Ave New York City NY 10022

KOROBKIN, IRVING, physicist, govt. ofcl.; b. N.Y.C., Oct. 18, 1925; s. Charles and Eva (Satt) K.; B.M.E., Coll. City N.Y., 1945; M.S., Columbia U., 1948; Ph.D., U. Md., 1960; m. Sally R. Lipser, June 22, 1947; children—Alan, Gail, Vicki, Andrew. Instr. dept. physics Coll. City N.Y., 1947-48, dept. mech. engring. Syracuse (N.Y.) U., 1948-51; with U.S. Naval Ordnance Lab., (now Naval Surface Weapons Center), 1951-61, 68—, sr. staff scientist and head nuclear program office in advanced planning staff, 1969-76, systems engring., 1976—; sr. engr. fed. systems div. IBM, 1961-68; cons. missile and space vehicle dept. Gen. Electric Corp., 1956-59; asso. profl. lectr. George Washington U., 1957-66. Served with USNR, 1945-46. Registered profl. engr., Md.; recipient Meritorious Civil Service award, 1955. Mem. Am. Phys. Soc., Am. Inst. Aeros. and Astronautics, AAAS, Philos. Soc. Washington, Sigma Xi, Sigma Pi Sigma. Republican. Jewish. Club: B'nai B'rith. Contbr. articles and tech. reports to profl. publs. Office: Naval Surface Weapon Center White Oak Lab Silver Spring MD 20910

KOROL, WOLODYMYR, veterinarian; b. Bytkiw, West Ukraina; s. Lew and Stefanida (Baczynski) K.; came to U.S. 1948, naturalized, 1963; D.V.M., U. West Ukraina, Lwiw, 1944; m. Halyna Wachnina, May 18, 1972; children—Myroslaw, Stefania, Taras. Research asst. Connaught Research Lab., U. Toronto, 1954-58; research asst. tumor biology Charles Pfizer Co., Maywood, N.J., 1959-61, sr. research asso. leukemia clusters and breast tumor, 1962-72, sr. research asso. carcinogen program, 1973-76; veterinarian, research asso. Howmedica, Inc., Maywood, 1977—. Chmn. Ukrainian Cultural Soc., Irvington-Newark, 1965-69. Mem. Ukrainian Sci. Assn., Ukrainian Choir Assn. Republican. Contbr. articles on virology, tumor biology and tissue culture to profl. jours. Research on method for elimination of mycoplasma from infected cells; established normal lymphocytic cell line. Home: 880 Chancellor Ave Irvington NJ 07111 Office: 199 Maywood Ave Maywood NJ 07607

KOROLCZUK, STEFAN RICHARD, educator; b. Wuettemberg, Germany, Aug. 15, 1945; s. Tychon and Halina (Gonstaw) K.; B.S. in Biology, St. Francis Coll., Bklyn., 1967; M.A. in Sci. Edn., N.Y. U., 1971; m. Irene Missirlian, July 12, 1969; children—Stefan Richard, Christopher. Sci. tchr., tennis coach Bishop Ford High Sch., Bklyn., 1967-72; tchr. chemistry and health UN Internat. Sch., N.Y.C., also tennis dir.; head tennis profl. Park Shore Tennis Camp, Dix Hills, N.Y., summers 1975, 76. Mem. Nat. Sci. Tchrs. Assn., Nat. Environ. Health Assn., U.S. Profl. Tennis Assn. Home: 76 Wolf Hill Rd Huntington NY 11246

KORZENIK, ARMAND ALEXANDER, lawyer; b. Hartford, Conn., Oct. 31, 1927; s. Bernard and Dorothy (Goldman) K.; A.B. magna cum laude, Harvard U., 1951, J.D., 1951; LL.M., Yale U., 1952; m. Ursula Guttmann, June 30, 1956; children—Peter B., Jeffrey D., Andrea D. Admitted to Conn. bar, 1951; individual practice law, Hartford, 1951—. Mem. Hartford Bd. Edn., 1953-59, counsel, 1968-72; mem. Zoning Bd. Appeals, 1960-66, asst. corp. counsel, 1966-72; counsel Redevel. Agy., 1966-68; justice of peace, 1960-73; vice chmn. Capital Dist. council Boy Scouts Am.; chmn. United Negro Coll. Fund; sponsor Urban League; incorporator West End Civic Assn., Blue Hills Civic Assn.; bd. dirs. Fgn. Policy Assn., Am. Youth Hostels, Jr. C. of C.; bd. mgrs. Hartford YMCA. Served with USAAF, 1945-48; to col. Conn. Air N.G., 1953-. Mem. Conn. (del., bd. editors Conn. Bar Jour., past chmn. criminal law com.), Hartford County (chmn. pubs. com., chmn. family relations com., editor Bar-Fly) bar assns., Am. Trial Lawyers Assn., Comml. Law League, Judge Adv. Assn., Am. Arbitration Assn. Contbr. articles to legal jours. Home: 120 Terry Rd Hartford CT 06105 Office: 37 Lewis St Hartford CT 06103

KOSCHE, EUGENE ROBERT, curator; b. Pittsfield, Mass., Oct. 7, 1928; s. Albert Alfred and Madeline Mary (Vogel) K.; grad. high sch., 1947; m. Ruth Elsa Schumacher, May 11, 1958; children—Stephen Edward, David Alan. With May Engring. Co., Pittsfield, 1945-50, maintenance div. Eaton Paper Co., Pittsfield, 1952-58; mgr. factory Bennington Brush Co. (Vt.), 1958-69; curator mil. and mech. arts Bennington Mus., 1969—. Mem. Republican Town Com., Shaftsbury, 1967—. Past trustee United Counseling Service; bd. dirs. A.R.C. Served with AUS, 1950-51. Mem. Shaftsbury Hist. Soc., Royal Canadian Astron. Soc. Methodist. Clubs: H.H. Franklin, Veteran Motor Car, Battenkill Coin. Home: Shaftsbury VT 05262 Office: W Main St Bennington VT 05201

KOSER, JOHN PRIESTON, mfg. exec.; b. Mt. Holly, N.J., Feb. 2, 1943; s. Clarence Lippold and Margaret Elizabeth (Prieston) K.; B.A. in Econs., Ursinus Coll., 1967; m. Naomi Ruth Becker, Jan. 5, 1975; 1 son, John. Indsl. engr. Vertol div. Boeing Co., Phila., 1967-69; mgr. mfg. services Harris Corp. Langston div., Camden, N.J., 1969-76; div. mgr. mfg. services Indsl. Truck div. Eaton Corp., Phila., mem. corp. mfg. adv. bd.; pres. World Video Inc. Dir., Explorers, 1971-72; fund raiser YMCA, 1971-73. Mem. Numerical Control Soc., Am. Prodn. Inventory Control Soc., Soc. Value Engrs., Internat. Mgmt. Club. Clubs: Jaycees, Yale Mgmt. Contbr. articles on group tech., numerical control utilization and value analysis to profl. jours. Home: 2026 Harbour Dr Palmyra NJ 08065 Office: 11000 Roosevelt Blvd Philadelphia PA 19115

KOSINSKI, JERZY NIKODEM, author; b. Lodz, Poland, June 14, 1933; s. Mieczyslaw and Elzbieta (Liniecka) K.; M.A. in Polit. Sci., U. Lodz, 1953, M.A. in History, 1955; postgrad. (Ford Found. fellow), Columbia U., 1958-65; m. Mary Weir, Jan. 11, 1962 (dec.); came to U.S., 1957, naturalized, 1965. Asst. prof. Inst. Sociology and Cultural History, Polish Acad. Scis., Warsaw, 1955-57; fellow Center for Advanced Studies, Wesleyan U., 1968-69; sr. fellow Council Humanities, vis. lectr. English, Princeton U., 1970-72; prof. English prose and criticism Sch. Drama, Yale U.; resident fellow in humanities Davenport Coll., Yale U., 1970-73. Recipient Nat. Book award in fiction for Steps, 1969; Best Fgn. Book award for The Painted Bird, Paris, 1966, award in lit. Nat. Inst. Arts and Letters and Am. Acad. Arts and Letters, 1970; Brith Shalom Humanitarian Freedom award, 1974; Guggenheim fellow, 1967. Mem. Authors Guild, P.E.N. (pres. Am. Center 1973-75), Internat. League Human Rights (dir.), AFTRA, Nat. Writers Club (exec. bd.), AAUP, ACLU. Author: (under pen name Joseph Novak) The Future is Ours, Comrade, 1960, No Third Path, 1962; The Painted Bird, 1965; Notes Of The Author, 1965; The Art of the Self, 1968; Steps, 1968; Being There, 1971; The Devil Tree, 1973; Cockpit, 1975; Blind Date, 1977. Office: Hemisphere House 60 W 57th St New York City NY 10019

KOSS, HELEN L., state legislator; b. N.Y.C., June 3, 1922; A.B., Bennington Coll., 1942; m. Mem. Md. Ho. of Dels., 1971—; mem. Montgomery County Adv. Com. on Special Youth Needs, 1962-63, Montgomery County Commn. on Youth, 1959-61, Montgomery County Health and Welfare Council, 1958-61; mem. Gov.'s Commn. on Reapportionment, Gov.'s Commn. on Crime and Delinquency; chmn. Reapportionment, Constl. Studies Com., 1959-63. Del., Constl. Conv. of Md., 1967-68; chmn. Com. on Suffrage and Elections; bd. visitors Bowie State Coll. Address: 3416 Highview Ct Wheaton MD 20802

KOSSOFF, RICHARD MORSE, chem. and plastics cons.; b. N.Y.C., Dec. 12, 1935; s. Joseph Edward and Shirley Ruth (Bookbinder) K.; B.S., Cornell U., 1957, M.B.A., 1959; m. Arlene Edith Plitt, June 14, 1964; children—Andrew, Laura. Chemist, Am. Cyanamid Co., Pearl River, N.Y., 1957-59, Allied Chem. Co., N.Y.C., 1960-63; mgr. devel. Celanese Plastics Co., Newark, 1963-65; pres. R.M. Kossoff & Assos., Inc., internat. consultants, N.Y.C., 1965—; dir. Precision Polymer Co.; cons. UN Indsl. Devel. Orgn., 1969—; lectr. Poly. Inst. N.Y.; speaker in numerous countries, 1965—. Served with U.S. Army, 1959-60. Mem. Am. Chem. Soc., Comml. Devel. Assn., Licensing Execs. Soc., Japan Soc. Clubs: Chemists, Cornell, Masons. Author: Studies in Plastics Fabrication and Application, 1970; Guidelines for Acrylic Sheet Production in Developing Countries, 1971. Home: 375 West End Ave New York City NY 10024 Office: 680 Fifth Ave New York City NY 10019

KOSSUTH, DONALD ANDREW, chem. engr.; b. Batavia, N.Y., June 25, 1933; s. Andrew Alfred and Elizabeth (Curtis) K.; B.Chem. Engring., Rensselaer Poly. Inst., 1955; m. Helen Emelie Murphy, Aug. 29, 1959. Research engr. research and devel. center Nat. Gypsum Co., Buffalo, 1955-56, sr. research engr., 1958-67, group leader gypsum products and paper, 1967-77, group leader spl. assignment, 1977-78, group mgr. spl. projects, 1978—. Voting mem. instl. rev. com. Kenmore Mercy Hosp., 1978—. Served with Chem. Corps, U.S. Army, 1956-58. Registered profl. engr., N.Y. Mem. Engring. Soc. Buffalo (pres. 1969-70, trustee Endowment Fund 1970—), Tonawanda C. of C. (dir. 1972-73, 74). Democrat. Roman Catholic. Clubs: Gold Bond Men's Bowling League, Town of Tonawanda Twilight Golf League, Elks, Lions (dir. 1967-75, 78, pres. 1976-77). Patentee in field. Home: 381 Hartford Ave Buffalo NY 14223 Office: 1650 Military Rd Buffalo NY 14217

KOST, GEORGE JOHN, mgmt. cons.; b. Dover, N.H.; s. John P. and Mary Elpino (Adraktis) K.; B.A., U. Ill., 1940; m. Melba Ruth Schilling, July 13, 1940; children—Tara, Kim, Scanlan. Commd. ensign U.S. Navy, 1943, advanced through grades to comdr., 1959; officer charge data processing dept. Supply Depot, San Diego, 1950-53, data processing insp., insp. Gen. Supply Corps, Washington, 1955-58, planning officer Naval Supply Depot, Yokosuka, Japan, 1958-61, officer charge Data Processing Dept., Phila., 1961-65; mgr. data processing U. Pa., 1965-67; mgr. data processing TWA, N.Y.C., 1967-69; sr. planning analyst data processing long range planning, dir. Eastern data center Kennecott Copper Corp., N.Y.C., 1969-72, dir. adminstrv. and fin. systems, 1972-75, dir. mgmt. controls and info. tech., 1975-78; mgmt. cons., 1978—. Mem. Assn. Computing Machinery, Data Processing Mgmt. Assn., Am. Prodn. and Inventory Control Soc., Soc. Mgmt. Info. Systems, Assn. Systems Mgmt., Am. Mgmt. Assn. Republican. Home: 426 Barby Ln Cherry Hill NJ 08003

KOST, PAUL FREDERICK, psychiatrist; b. Sharpsburg, Pa., June 5, 1911; s. August and Antoinette Fredericka (Fehrmann) K.; B.Sc., Pa. State U., 1933, M.S., 1934; Ph.D., U. Pitts., 1941, M.D., 1952; m. Irma Lina Ickert, Aug. 4, 1936; 1 son, Richard F. Tchr. biology Aspinwall (Pa.) High Sch., 1934-42; instr. Med. Sch. U. Pitts., 1946-52; pathologist VA Leech Farm Hosp., Pitts., 1953-54, resident in psychiatry, 1954-57, asso. chief of staff, 1957-63; chief psychiat. service, dir. drug dependence treatment service VA Univ. Dr. Hosp., Pitts., 1965-73, ret., 1973; psychiatrist Woodville State Hosp., Pitts., 1965-76; practice medicine specializing in psychiatry, Allison Park, Pa., 1957—; mem. staffs Western Pa. Inst. and Clinic, Woodville State Hosp., Carnegie Pa., to 1976; med. dir. U. Pitts. Methadone Maintenance Program, 1974—; mem. adv. bd. Transitional Services, Inc., Pitts. Candidate Pa. State Legislature, 1976, 78. Served to col. M.C. USAR, 1942-72. Diplomate Am. Bd. Clin. Hypnosis (pres. bd. 1978—). Fellow Soc. Clin. and Exptl. Hypnosis, Am. Soc. Clin. Hypnosis; mem. Pa., Allegheny County med. socs., AMA, Pa. Psychiat. Soc., Am. Psychiat. Assn. Republican. Lutheran. Club: Kiwanis (past pres. chpt.). Contbr. articles on pathology and psychiatry to profl. jours. Home and office: 3241 McCully Rd Allison Park PA 15101

KOSTELANETZ, BORIS, lawyer; b. Leningrad, Russia, June 16, 1911; s. Nachman and Rosalia (Dimshetz) K.; brought to U.S. 1920, naturalized 1925; B.C.S., N.Y. U., 1933 B.S., 1936; J.D. magna cum laude, St. John's U., 1936; m. Ethel Cory, Dec. 18, 1938; children—Richard Cory, Lucy Cory. Admitted to N.Y. bar, 1936; C.P.A., Price, Waterhouse & Co., 1934-37; asst. U.S. atty. for S. Dist. N.Y., and confidential asst. to U.S. atty. S. Dist. N.Y., 1937-45; instr. accounting, N.Y. U., 1937-47, adj. prof., 1947-69; spl. asst. to Atty. Gen. U.S., 1943-46; chief war frauds, Dept. Justice, 1945-46; gen. practice law, Kostelanetz & Ritholz, and predecessors. Spl. counsel for U.S. Senate Com. Investigate Crime in Interstate Commerce, 1950-51; mem. com. on character and fitness appellate div. 1st dept. N.Y. State Supreme Ct., 1974—. Chmn. Kefauver for President Com. N.Y. State, 1952. Recipient N.Y. U. Meritorious Service award, 1954, Madden Meml. medal, 1969; St. John's U. Pietas medal, 1961. C.P.A., N.Y. State. Fellow Am. Coll. Trial Lawyers, Am. Bar Found.; mem. Internat., Fed., Am. (chmn. spl. com. on standards tax practice 1964-66; com. on appointments to tax ct. 1959—; spl. com. adminstrn. criminal justice 1957—, council sect. taxation 1978—), N.Y. State bar assns., N.Y. U. Finance Club (pres. 1953-54), N.Y. Co. Lawyers Assn. (dir. 1958-64, 71-74, v.p. 1966-69, pres. 1969-71, chmn. com. on judiciary 1965-69), Assn. Bar City N.Y., N.Y. State Soc. C.P.A.'s, N.Y. U. Sch. Commerce Alumni Assn. (pres. 1951-52), St. John's Law Sch. Alumni Assn. (pres. 1955-57). Democrat. Clubs: Nat. Lawyers (Washington); N.Y. U. Faculty. Author: (with Louis Bender) Criminal Aspects of Tax Fraud Cases, 1957, 68. Contbr. articles to legal, accounting and tax jours. Home: 37 Washington Sq W New York NY 10011 Office: 80 Pine St W New York NY 10005

KOSTMAYER, PETER HOUSTON, congressman; b. N.Y.C., Sept. 27, 1946; s. John Houston and Julia Clairborne (Carson) K.; B.A. in Am. History, Columbia, 1971. Mem. 95th-96th Congresses from 8th Dist. Pa. Democrat. Episcopalian. Home: 291 Windy Bush Rd Solebury PA 18963 Office: 125 Cannon House Office Bldg Washington DC 20515

KOSTOULAKOS, PETER, artist; b. Lowell, Mass., May 2, 1949; s. Constantine and Georgia (Vroubas) K.; diploma in advt. design Art Inst. Boston, 1970; B.S. in Fine Art, Northeastern U., 1977; M.A., Goddard Coll.; m. Anne Dupree Gates, Sept. 17, 1972. With Sears, Roebuck & Co., 1971-76; instr. painting U. Lowell (Mass.) Continuing Edn., 19—; tchr. comml. art Lowell Vocat. Sch., 1978—; cons., technician, conservation of art. Mem. Internat., Am. insts. conservation historic and artistic works, Internat. Soc. Artists, Boston Visual Artists Union, Lowell Art Assn., Chelmsford Art Soc., Sigma Epsilon Rho. Home and Office: 9 Sayles St Lowell MA 01851

KOTCH, PETER PAUL, engr.; b. Jersey City, Feb. 7, 1939; s. Paul and Mary (Kostura) K.; B.S.M.E., N.J. Inst. Tech., 1961, M.S.M.E., 1964, M.S.E.E., 1974. Equipment engr. Western Electric Co., Newark, 1961-68, cons. engr., 1968-72, sr. engring. cons. power and bldg. planning, 1972—. Mem. Citizens Advisory Com. Bayonne, 1967-72. Registered profl. engr., N.J. Mem. ASME. Home: 32 W 27th St Bayonne NJ 07002

KOTIN, ALBERT, artist, educator; b. Russia, Aug. 7, 1907; s. Joseph and Ida (Helfman) K.; brought to U.S., 1908, naturalized, 1923; student NAD, Art Students League, 1924-29, Academie de la Grande Chaumière, Acad. Julian, and Atelier de Fresque, 1929-31; pupil Hans Hofmann, 1947-51; m. Evangelyn Kuggas, May 30, 1937 (dec. Aug. 1967). Instr. Coll. City N.Y., 1947-51, Poly. Inst. Bklyn., 1952-61; vis. prof. art So. Ill. U., Carbondale, 1961; artist in residence Stout State U., Menominie, Wis., 1964-66; artist in residence Bklyn. Center, L.I. U., 1966, asso. prof. art, 1970-75; exhibited one-man shows: Hacker Gallery, 1951, Grand Central Moderns, 1958, Tanager Gallery, 1959, Byron Gallery, retrospective L.I. U., 1968, Museo Universitario, Mexico City, 1974-75; travelling show Mus. Modern Art, 1963, 64; group shows: Syracuse Mus. Fine Arts, Kalamazoo Art Inst., Pa. Acad. Fine Arts, Assn. Am. Artists, Wichita Mus. Art, Hacker Gallery; executed murals: sociology dept. N.Y. U., 1937, Arlington (N.J.) Post Office, Ada (Ohio) Post Office, 1939; represented in permanent collections Mus. Fine Arts, Syracuse, N.Y., Kalamazoo Inst. Art, Bklyn. Pub. Library, Hampton (Va.) Inst., L.I. U.; also pvt. collections; cons. to cultural com. Mexican Olympic Orgn., 1968. Served with C.E., AUS, 1943-45. Recipient awards including Purchase award Longview Found., 1962. Home: 42 E 12th St New York City NY 10003

KOTVAL, PESHOTAN SOHRAB, metallurgist; b. Nagpur, India, Aug. 31, 1942; s. Sohrab and Shirin (Kamdin) K.; came to U.S., 1966, naturalized, 1976; B.Sc., Nagpur (India) U., 1960; M.Met., Sheffield (Eng.) U., 1962, Ph.D., 1965; M.B.A., Pace U., 1977; m. Daulat Nariman, Oct. 16, 1965; children—Xerxes, Anahaita. Postdoctoral research fellow U.K. Sci. Research Council, 1965-66; staff scientist, mgr. product research Stellite div. Union Carbide Corp., Kokomo, Ind., 1966-70, sr. group leader, metals and ceramics, corporate research lab., Tarrytown, N.Y., 1971-76, mgr. materials sci. research and devel., 1977—; vis. scientist Research Inst. for Advanced Studies, Balt., 1970-71; lectr. physics Ind. U., 1968-69; asso. prof. mgmt. sci. Pace U., 1977—. Fellow Am. Soc. Metals; mem. Instn. Metallurgists (London), Am. Inst. Metall. Engrs. Contbr. articles to profl. jours. Patentee in field (5). Home: 8 Verne Pl Hartsdale NY 10530 Office: Union Carbide Corp Tarrytown NY 10591

KOULIAS, ELIZABETH MERCIA, nurse, radiologic technologist, librarian; b. Lowell, Mass.; d. Nicholas George and Helen Maria (Dragataris) Koulias; grad. nursing course Georgetown U., 1961; student U. Lowell, 1967—. Technologist trainee St. Josephs Hosp., Lowell, Lowell Gen. Hosp. for Deep Therapy, 1953-57; head med. records librarian Groton (Mass.) Community Hosp., St. Josephs Hosp., Nashua, N.H., 1957—, Mass. Hosp. Sch., Canton, 1965—; chief radiologic technologist St. Joseph's Hosp., Lowell, VA Clinic, Lowell, 1959—, Sancta Maria Hosp., Cambridge, Mass., 1963—, Lowell Gen. Hosp., 1963—, Indsl. Med. Clinic, Boston, Dr. A. Branca's Clinic, Boston; now librarian Govt. Documents and Publs. sect., state security campus police woman U. Lowell. Registered nuclear medicine technologist. Mem. Greek Orthodox Youth Assn., Am. Soc. Radiologic Technologists, Am. Soc. Med. Technologists, Am. Registry Radiologic Technologists, Med. Records Librarian Assn., Cousteau Soc., Internat. Platform Assn., Am. Security Council, Smithsonian Assn. (nat. mem.), Daus. of Penelope. Playwright: The Mosquitoes of the Soul, 1955: The Orion Hill, 1960. Home: 56 Gilmore St Corner Taunton Ct Lowell MA 01854 Office: U Lowell Textile Ave Lowell MA 01854

KOUSSA, HAROLD ALAN, nuclear engr.; b. Central Falls, R.I., June 20, 1947; s. Harold Albert and June Joann (John) K.; B.S., U. R.I., 1969; M.B.A., U. Hartford, 1975; M.S. in Engring. Sci., Rensselaer Poly. Inst., 1977; m. Marsha Lynn Heidenis, Dec. 1, 1973. Reactor engr. Conn. Yankee Atomic Power Co., Haddam Neck, 1969-77; nuclear engr. Am. Nuclear Insurers, Farmington, Conn., 1977—. Mem. Am. Nuclear Soc., Assn. M.B.A. Execs. Congregationalist. Clubs: DeMolay, U. R.I. Fast Break. Home: 73 Childs Rd East Hampton CT 06424 Office: American Nuclear Insurers 270 Farmington Ave Farmington CT 06032

KOUTSELAS, KOSMAS PHILLIP, printing plate mfg. co. exec.; b. Piraeus, Greece, Mar. 25, 1941; s. Phillip and Andriani (Katakouzinou) K.; came to U.S., 1953, naturalized, 1960; A.A. and Sci., City U. N.Y., 1962; B.S. in Chemistry, U. Denver, 1964; m. Anna Christopoulos, Dec. 27, 1967; children—Andrew, Emily Ann. Chemist, research and devel. Corning Glass Works (N.Y.), 1967-70, process engr., graphic media dept., 1970, supr. mfg. engring., graphic media dept., Newton, N.J., 1970-73; v.p., sec. Graphinetics Corp., Newton, 1973—. Mem. Am. Chem. Soc. Office: 1 Olympian Plaza Newton NJ 07860

KOUTSOUTIS, SOCRATES PETER, process control co. exec.; b. Steubenville, Ohio, June 10, 1936; s. Peter John and Martha (Tripoulas) K.; A.A., Montgomery Jr. Coll., 1956; postgrad. Garfield Meml. Hosp. Sch. Med. Tech., 1957; B.S., Am. U., 1962; J.D., U. Balt., 1969; m. Anne Stratiges, Oct. 25, 1964. Head chemistry lab. Children's Hosp., Washington, 1957-59; mem. sales staff Fisher Sci. Co., Silver Spring, Md., 1959-61, Arthur H. Thomas Co., Phila., 1962-66; Eastern regional mgr. Varian Assos., Cheverly, Md., 1966-72; pres. SOC Assos. Inc., Silver Spring, Md., 1972—. Mem. parish council Annunciation Greek Orthodox Cathedral. Served with U.S. Army, 1959. Mem. Am. Soc. Med. Technologists, Instrument Soc. Am., Am. Indsl. Hygiene Assn., Am. Chem. Soc., Am. Soc. Clin. Pathologists, Mfrs. and Agts. Nat. Assn., Am. Hellenic Ednl. and Progressive Assn. (pres. chpt. 1968, Ahepan of yr., 1970). Home: PO Box 277 Laurel MD 20810 Office: 1717 Elton Rd Suite 206 Silver Spring MD 20903

KOVATCH, JAK GENE, artist, educator; b. Los Angeles, Jan. 17, 1929; s. Jack and La Vinia Blanche (Abernathy) K.; student UCLA, 1946, Chouinard Art Inst., 1947-49; student Calif. Sch. Art, Los Angeles, 1949-50, U. So. Calif., 1951, Los Angeles City Coll., 1955-56; Art Students League, N.Y.C., 1972, 75; m. Carol Jean Wilhelm, Dec. 24, 1967; 1 son by previous marriage, Jason. Student asst. Lynton Kistler Studio, Los Angeles, 1952-53; mem. staff animation dept. Walt Disney Prodns., Inc., Burbank, Calif., 1953; stage designer for Benjamin Zemach, Los Angeles, 1953-54; free-lance illustrator, N.Y.C., 1957-58; instr. drawing and anatomy Famous Artists Schs., Inc., Westport, Conn., 1957-59; tchr. Roger Ludlowe High Sch., Fairfield, Conn., 1959-60; art instr. N.Y.C. Coll. Extension Div., 1959-60; instr. sculpture Fairfield U., 1967; lectr. U. Bridgeport, 1962-67, asst. prof., 1967-78, asso. prof. indsl. design, 1978—; group shows include: Los Angeles County Mus., 1949, 54, 55, Boston Mus. Fine Arts, 1954, Smithsonian Instn., 1954, Butler Inst. Am. Art, Youngstown, Ohio, 1954, M.H. DeYoung Meml. Mus., San Francisco, 1954, Mus. Modern Art, N.Y.C., 1956, Museo de Bellas Artes de Caracas (Venezuela), 1960, Boston Center for Arts, 1976, Honolulu Acad. Arts, 1977, Berkeley Center, Yale U., 1978, Laguna Gloria Art Mus., Austin, Tex., 1978, Ann. New Eng. Exhibit Silvermine Guild Artists, New Canaan, Conn., 1959 (award), Oak Room Exhibit Fairfield U., 1973 (award), 1977 (award), others; represented in permanent collections: Fogg Mus. Art, Cambridge, Mass., Library of Congress, Washington, Joseph Hirshhorn Collection, Greenwich, Fairfield Art Collection, John Slade Ely House Collection, New Haven, Bicentennial Art Collection Westport Town Hall, Albert Dorne Collection, N.Y.C., also numerous pvt. collections; guest lectr. anatomy and figure drawing, 1953—. Recipient award Boston Mus. Fine Arts, 1954, Wadsworth Atheneum, Hartford, Conn., 1958, Mus. Art Sci. and Industry, Bridgeport, Conn., 1962, 63, 65, 66, 75, 77, Hudson River Mus., Yonkers, N.Y., 1960, New Haven Paint and Clay Club, 1976. Mem. Albany Inst. History and Art, Artists Equity Assn. N.Y., Audubon Artists, Conn. Acad. Fine Arts, Graphics Soc., Greenwich Art Soc., Hudson River Contemporary Artists, Los Angeles Printmaking Soc., Pratt Graphics Center, Phila. Print Club, Silvermine Guild Artists, Westport-Weston Arts Council, Am. Registry Radiologic Technologists. Home: 34 Sasco Creek Rd Westport CT 06880 Office: U Bridgeport Bridgeport CT 06602

KOVEN, BERNARD J., physician, educator; b. N.Y.C., Feb. 17, 1927; s. Nathan S. and Helen (Greenberg) K.; A.B. magna cum laude, Syracuse U., 1949; M.D. cum laude, State U. N.Y., 1953; m. Martha R. Shapiro, Dec. 20, 1959; children—Joanne Lynne, Carolyn. Intern, Johns Hopkins Hosp., 1953-54; med. resident Upstate Med. Center, Syracuse, N.Y., 1954-55, Downstate Med. Center, Bklyn., 1955-57; research fellow cancer chemotherapy Meml. Sloan-Kettering Center, 1957-58; coordinator cancer teaching Seton Hall Coll. Medicine, 1959; asst. prof. medicine N.J. Coll. Medicine, 1960-71, asso. prof. medicine, 1971—; attending med. staff Meml. Hosp. N.Y., 1958—, Hackensack, 1962—, Martland Hosp., Newark, Englewood (N.J.) Hosp., 1973—; cons. neoplastic diseases Englewood (N.J.) Hosp., 1961-73, St. Mary's Hosp., Passaic, 1962-76, East Orange VA Hosp., 1966—, Holy Name Hosp., Teaneck, N.J.; chief oncology sect. Hackensack (N.J.) Hosp., 1974—; mem. N.J. Commn. on Hosp. Cost Containment. Mem. med. adv. bd. Bergen County Planned Parenthood Assn. Recipient Honors citation Am. Cancer Soc. Served with USAAF, 1945-46. Diplomate in med. oncology Am. Bd. Internal Medicine. Fellow A.C.P.; mem. N.J. Acad. Medicine, Am. Fedn. Clin. Research, Johns Hopkins Med. and Surg. Assn., Am. Soc. Clin. Oncology, Bergen County Med. Soc. (chmn. cancer com. 1962—), Am. (chpt. bd. mgrs. 1964—, div. profl. edn. com. 1962—, chmn. com. cancer promotions N.J. div.), N.Y. cancer socs., Med. Soc. N.J. (cancer control com.), Oncology Sec. N.J. (dir., pres.), Am. Assn. Cancer Edn., Pan Am. Med. Assn. Editor: Computer Van. Contbr. sci. articles to med. jours. Address: 200 Engle St Englewood NJ 07631

KOVEN, IRVING HERCHEL, surgeon; b. Grand Falls, N.B., Can., July 29, 1928; s. Herbert Ted and Annie Louise (Isaacson) K.; B.A., Mt. Allison U., 1949; M.D., Dalhousie Med. Sch., 1954; m. Florence Epstein, June 1, 1954; children—Robert Mark, Laurie Gay, Jeffrey Joel, Stephen, Allen. Asst. resident in surg. research Beth Israel Hosp., Harvard, 1954-56; asst. resident dept. pathology Mt. Sinai Hosp., Toronto, Ont., Can., 1956-57, resident in gen. surgery, 1957-58, sr. staff surgeon, 1958, chief div. gen. surgery, 1973, acting surgeon-in-chief, 1975; clin. tchr. U. Toronto Med. Sch., 1964, asst. prof. in surgery, 1972; asso. prof., 1974, dir. research div. gen. surgery, 1976, mem. Inst. Med. Scis. grad. faculty, 1976—, chmn. admissions com., continuing edn. com., Faculty of Medicine, U. bd. surg. examiners Royal Coll. Surgeons; vis. prof. U. Munich (W. Ger.). Served with RCAF, 1960-62. Fellow Royal Coll. Physicians and Surgeons Can., Am. Assn. for Surgery of Trauma, A.C.S., mem. Am. Fedn. for Clin. Research, Assn. of Acad. Surgeons, Ont., Can. Israel med. socs., Acad. Medcine, N.Y. Acad. Scis., Clin. Research Soc. Toronto, Data Processing Soc. Can., Soc. Nuclear Medcine, Medico-Legal Soc. Toronto, Defence Med. Assn. Can, Can. Socs. for Clin. Investigation and Microcirculation, European Soc. Exptl. Surgery, Central Surg. Assn., Can. Assn. Clin. Surgeons, Can. Assn. Gastroenterology, Traffic Injury Research Found. Clubs: Royal Canadian Mil. Inst., Mason. Contbr. numerous articles to profl. jours. Home: 63 Rollscourt Dr Willowdale ON M2L 1Y1 Canada Office: Room 449 600 University Ave Toronto ON M5G 1X5 Canada

KOVNER, ABRAHAM, steel constrn. consulting co. exec.; b. N.Y.C., Jan. 13, 1919; s. Benjamin and Anna (Chalkin) K.; student N.Y. Naval Shipyard Apprentice Sch., 1940-43, Pratt Inst., 1941-43, N.Y. U., 1946-47, Pace U., 1966-67; m. Sarah Lederman, Nov. 19, 1938; children—Mark, Nancy. Planner, estimator N.Y. Naval Shipyard, Bklyn., 1940-50; sr. steel inspector N.Y.C. Dept. Pub. Works, 1950-61; chief engr. Classon Welding, Bklyn., 1961-62; pres., chief engr. M.K.B. Industries, Bklyn., 1962-66; marine designer M. Rosenblatt & Son., N.Y.C., 1966-67; pres. A. Kovner Assos., N.Y.C., 1967—; lectr. in field. Maj. N.Y.C. Aux. Police, 1950-66. Recipient N.Y. State Conservation Dept. Certificate of Merit, 1955; State of N.Y. Certificate of Pub. Service, 1958; Office of CD Award of Merit, 1960; N.Y. State Certificate of Merit, 1963. Certified constrn. estimator. Mem. Am. Soc. Profl. Estimators (Eastern gov., nat. bd. trustees), Am. Soc. of Naval Engrs., Am. Defense Preparedness Assn., Am. Welding Soc., ASTM, Soc. Naval Architects and Marine Engrs., U.S. Naval Inst. Club: Nat. Rifle Assn. Contbr. articles to profl. jours. Home: 535 E 14th St New York City NY 10009 Office: PO Box 576 New York City NY 10009

KOWAL, DENNIS JOSEPH, sculptor; b. Chgo., Sept. 9, 1937; s. Dennis Joseph and Marie (Frank) K.; student U. Ill. at Chgo., 1956-57, 59-61, Art Inst. Chgo., 1958-59; B.F.A., So. Ill. U., 1961, M.F.A., 1962; m. Carole Ann Holm, Nov. 1, 1959 (div. 1975); children—Christie Ann, Jolie Renee, Denise Carol. One-man shows:

Bryson Gallery, Columbus, Ohio, 1963, Devorah Sherman Gallery, Chgo., 1964, 66, Bradley U., Peoria, Ill., 1968, Ill. Arts Council Gallery, Chgo., 1969, Haystack-Hinckley Sch. Arts and Crafts (Maine), 1971, Jaffe-Freide Gallery, Hopkins Center, Dartmouth Coll., Hanover, N.H., 1971, Boston City Hall Galleries, 1973, Cape Cod Art Assn. Gallery, Mass., 1973, Dorsky Galleries, Ltd., N.Y.C., 1974, Portland (Maine) Sch. Art, 1974, Boston Archtl. Center, 1974, Inst. Contemporary Art, Boston, 1975, Brockton (Mass.) Art Center, 1975, Concourse Gallery, Boston, 1976, Lake Forest (Ill.) Coll., 1976, Robert Freidus Gallery, N.Y.C., 1977, Worthington Gallery, Chgo., 1977, 78, Mead Art Mus., Amherst (Mass.) Coll., 1978, N.C. Mus. Art, 1978, Milton (Mass.) Acad.; exhibited in over 200 group shows; represented in more than 45 pvt. collections; pioneer work in carved acrylics and indsl. flame-cut-solid steel; instr. Columbus Coll. Art and Design, 1963-64, Frostburg (Md.) State Coll., 1964-65; asst. prof. U. Ill. at Champaign-Urbana, 1966-70, Mass. Coll. Art, Boston, 1971-72; vis. lectr. U. Ga., Athens, 1973; artist in residence Coolfont, Inc., W.Va., 1967, Yaddo, Sarasota Spring, N.Y., 1970, Dartmouth Coll., Inc., 1970-71, Haystack-Hinckley Sch. Arts and Crafts, 1971, Inst. Contemporary Art, Boston, 1975, DeCordova Mus., Lincoln, Mass., 1977, Amherst Coll., 1977-78, Oxbow Workshop '78, Mich., 1978. Fellow Edward MacDowell Colony, Peterborough, N.J., 1965, 72; U. Ill. Faculty fellow, 1967; research grantee U. Ill., 1967, 68, 69; recipient Izzac H. Meml. award Md. Mus. Fine Arts, 1965, Materials Research award Dow Chem. Co., 1969. Mem. Boston Visual Artists Union, New Eng. Sculptors Assn., Art Inst. Chgo. Author: (with Dona Mielach) Sculpture Casting, 1972; contbg. author: New Media for Sculpture; contbr. articles to art jours. Subject of numerous articles. Studio: 602 Jerusalem Rd Cohasset MA 02025

KOWALCZYK, DAVID KENNETH, hosp. adminstr.; b. Lockport, N.Y., June 11, 1945; s. Stanley Frank and Josephine Rose (Solarski) K.; B.B.A. cum laude, St. Bonaventure U., 1972; postgrad. U. Buffalo Grad. Sch. Econs.; m. Barbara Elizabeth Jones, Dec. 28, 1968; children—Wendy, Kristin. Asst. to controller St. Bonaventure U., 1968-72; chief accountant Bros. of Mercy Health Care Facility, Clarence, N.Y., 1972-73; sr. cost accountant Blue Cross Western N.Y. Inc., Buffalo, 1973-75; controller Tri-County Meml. Hosp., Gowanda, N.Y., 1975-78, dir. fin., 1978—. Team mgr. Amherst (N.Y.) Men's Softball League, 1975-77. Served with USNR, 1963-66. Mem. Hosp. Fin. Mgmt. Assn., Am. Guild Patient Account Mgrs., Chautauqua Regional Fin. Mgrs. Group. Democrat. Roman Catholic. Home: 143 Highland Dr Williamsville NY 14221 Office: 100 Memorial Dr Gowanda NY 14070

KOWALSKI, JOHN JOSEPH, educator; b. Worcester, Mass., Oct. 8, 1928; s. John Joseph and Marion Caroline (Mozevech) K.; A.B., Emerson Coll., 1955; Ed.M., Worcester State Coll., 1959; degree in adminstrn.-supervision So. Conn. State Coll., New Haven, 1975; m. Fayne Marion McMaster, Apr. 18, 1959; children—Patricia, Kathryn, Joan. High sch. English tchr., Southbridge, Mass., 1955-60, Wallingford, Conn., 1960—. Rep. ednl. council Town of Wallingford, 1973—. Served with AUS, 1947-49. Fellow Internat. Poetry Soc.; mem. Acad. Am. Poets, Conn. Edn. Assn. (legis. commn. 1976-78), Southbridge Tchrs. Assn. (v.p. 1957-59). K.C. Club: Wilsonian Professional Men's (New Haven). Contbr. articles to profl. jours. Home: 118 Algonquin Dr Wallingford CT 06492

KOWALSKI, RONALD S., co. exec.; b. Phila., Dec. 24, 1937; s. Henry John and Stella Mary (Kruszewska) K.; B.S. in Accounting, Temple U., 1958; m. Linda Ann Fricke, Aug. 4, 1961; children—Lorraine, Donna, Michael. Controller, Rentex Services Corp., 1965-69; treas. staff H. Daroff & Sons, 1969; v.p. fin. Gen. Energy Resources Inc., Willingboro, N.J., 1969-77; pres. Craig Capital Corp., Mt. Laurel, N.J., 1977—; dir. Thermo-Mold Med. Products, Inc., Phoenix Contractors, Inc. Served with USAR, 1960-66. C.P.A., Pa. Mem. Am. Inst. C.P.A.'s, N.Y. State, Pa., N.J. socs. C.P.A.'s, Young Presidents Orgn. Home: 9 Circle Ln Cherry Hill NJ 08003 Office: 131 Gaither Dr Mount Laurel NJ 08054

KOWARSKI, CHANA ROSE (MRS. AVINOAM KOWARSKI), educator; b. Kounas, Lithuania; d. Abraham and Esther (Glaser) Zass; student Hebrew U., Jerusalem, Israel, 1947-50, Ph.D., 1962; diploma Sch. Pharmacy U. Lausanne (Switzerland), 1953; m. Avinoam Kowarski, Mar. 24, 1950; children—David, Ruth. Came to U.S., 1967, naturalized, 1973. Dir. dept. pharmacy RAFA Pharm. Lab., Jerusalem, 1956-59; cons. ABIC, Tel Aviv, Israel, 1959-62; asst. prof. pharmacy Temple U., Phila., 1963-69, asso. prof., 1969-75, prof., 1975—. Served with Israeli Def. Army, 1947-49. Decorated OT-Hakomemiut; recipient Lunsford Richardson Pharmacy award Rho Chi, 1972. Mem. Am. Pharm. Assn., Sigma Xi, Lambda Kappa Sigma. Author: Pharmacy Math I, 1970; Pharmacy Math II, 1972. Contbr. articles to profl. jours. Patentee pharmaceuticals. Home: 2405 Sugarcone Rd Baltimore MD 21209 Office: School Pharmacy Temple Univ Philadelphia PA 19140

KOZIEL, WILLIAM TOM, aircraft, automotive and plastics co. exec.; b. Nowy Targ, Poland, Aug. 18, 1928; s. Walter Frank and Mary (Bryja) K.; came to Can., 1930, naturalized, 1938; Purchasing certificate Ryerson Poly. Inst. (Can.), 1958; m. Joyce Norma Tanney, Nov. 27, 1948. With Aunor Gold Mines, Timmins, Ont., Can., 1946-51; with Can. Carbon & Ribbon Co. Ltd., Toronto, Ont., 1951-64, mgr. prodn. control and planning, 1963-64; mgr. purchasing, traffic and customs G.H. Wood & Co. Ltd., Toronto, 1965-70, nat. distbn. mgr., 1970-73, operations mgr., 1973-77; ops. mgr. Anthony Foster & Sons, Ltd., Toronto, 1978—. Mem. Canadian Indsl. Traffic League, Purchasing Agts. Assn., Canadian Mfrs. Assn., Indsl. Accident Prevention Assn., AMA. Home: 13 Westacres Dr Toronto 15 ON Canada Office: 297 Carlingview Dr Toronto ON M9W 5G4 Canada

KOZLIK, THEODORE, JR., ednl. adminstr.; b. Irvington, N.J., Nov. 12, 1944; s. Theodore and Lucy Olga (Gibber) K.; B.A., Glassboro State Coll., 1966, M.A., 1968; M.A. Newark State Coll., 1972; M.Ed., Rutgers U., 1974; m. Ethel W. Weimer, Dec. 10, 1976; children—Thomas, Jon. Tchr. mentally retarded pub. schs. Madison Twp., N.J., 1966-69; learning disability specialist N.J. Dept. Edn., coordinator spl. services, Marlboro Twp. Schs., 1969-70; learning disability specialist Milltown (N.J.) Schs., 1970-71, spl. services coordinator, 1971-73, dir. spl. services, Spotswood, N.J., 1973-74; dir. pupil personnel services Franklin Twp. Schs., Somerset, N.J., 1974—. Adj. prof. Somerset County Coll., 1974—. N.J. Dept. Edn. summer fellow, 1970. Fellow Am. Assn. Mental Deficiency; mem. Assn. Learning Disability, Tchrs. Cons., Council Adminstrs. and Suprs. Spl. Edn., Council Exceptional Children, Internat. Assn. Approved Basketball Ofcls., Nat., N.J. (pres.) assns. pupil personnel adminstrs., Phi Delta Kappa. Home: Box 267G RD 1 Matawan NJ 07747 Office: 761 Hamilton St Somerset NJ 08873

KRACH, MITCHELL PETER, lumber exec.; b. Westfield, Mass., Nov. 2, 1924; s. John Joseph and Sophie Mary (Swiatlowski) K.; certificate Mass. Extension U., 1944, Harvard U. Grad. Sch. Bus. Admnstrn., 1966; m. Theresa Florence Sanczuk, May 29, 1957; children—Susan, Gregory, Mitchell, Jonathan, Matthew. Auditor, H.F. Lynch Lumber Co., W. Springfield, Mass., 1946-51, dir., 1951—, sec. bd. dirs., 1951—, mgr. purchasing, 1951-61, central mgr. purchasing, 1961-71, v.p. purchasing, 1971-76, v.p. purchasing and fin., 1976—, treas. bd. dirs. 1976—; treas., chmn. bd. dirs. Nat. Res. Corp., Longmeadow, Mass., 1957—; legal arbitrator bldg. materials. Exec. mem. bd. govs. Shriners Hosp. for Crippled Children, Springfield, 1978. Certified purchasing mgr.; notary public; registered and bonded real estate broker, Mass. Mem. Nat. Fedn. Ind. Bus. (nat. adv. council 1978), Nat. Assn. Purchasing Mgmt. (dir. nat. affairs 1965, nat. lumber chmn. 1970-78), Am. Soc. Notaries, Purchasing Mgmt. Assn. W. New Eng. (pres. 1963-64), Purchasing Mgmt. Assn. Worcester, Mfrs. Agts. Nat. Assn., Am. Def. Preparedness Assn. Democrat. Roman Catholic. Clubs: Valley Press, 100 of Mass., Am. Turners, Elks, Melha Temple, Masons, Shriners, K.T. Contbr. numerous articles to profl. jours. Home: 33 Forest Glen Rd Longmeadow MA 01106 Office: 202 Day St West Springfield MA 01089

KRACZKOWSKI, PHILIP, sculptor; b. Chelsea, Mass., Nov. 28, 1916; s. Witalis Adam and Mary (Groner) K.; student R.I. Sch. Design, 1936-38. Dairy farmer with father, Attleboro, Mass., 1927-49; commd. life size busts of Lowell Thomas, Exploreres Club, 1969, J. Edgar Hoover, Washington, 1964, Curtis E. LeMay, SAC and Air Force Acad., Colorado Springs, 1966, Cardinal Cushing medal, 1964, Pope Paul VI medallion, 1966, Dag Hammarskjold medallion, Ofcl. Lincoln's Emancipation Proclamation medal to Pres. U.S., 1963, Kennedy-Johnson gold madallion presented to Vice Pres., 1961, Kennedy-Day gold medallion, 1962, Johnson Humphrey Inaugural charm, 1965, Ofcl. Centennial Civil War series in silver and bronze, Gettysburg, Pa., 1963, Bronze statue N.W. Mounted Police, Ottawa, Ont., Can., 1960, porcelain sculpture series, Hummelwerk, Ger., 1980 Winter Olympics Commemorative Sculpture Series, others. Mem. Attleboro Mus. Mem. Am. Artists Profl. League. Home: 537 Lindsey St Attleboro MA 02703

KRAFCHUK, JOHN DAMION, dermatologist; b. N.Y.C., Dec. 13, 1922; s. David and Katherine (Nikolyn) K.; student N.Y. U., 1938-41; M.D., L.I. Coll. Medicine, 1944. Intern, U.S. Naval Hosp., Bklyn., 1944-45; fellow in bacteriology and pathology U. Rochester (N.Y.), 1946-47; instr. bacteriology La. State U. Sch. Medicine, 1947-48, asst. prof. dermatology, 1955-56; postdoctorate research fellow in mycology NIH, Bethesda, Md., 1948-49; fellow in dermatology U. Minn., 1950-53, instr., 1950-54; asst. prof. dermatology Tulane U., 1956-58; practice medicine specializing in dermatology, Hempstead, Plainview and Massapequa, N.Y., 1958—; pres. Dermcraft Ltd., Hempstead and Hialeah, Fla., 1977—; pres., dir. Kappa Labs., Inc., 1958—. Served with USMC, 1945-46; PTO. Diplomate Am. Bd. Dermatology, Am. Bd. Pathology. Mem. Am. Acad. Dermatology, Am. Acad. Allergists, Internat. Soc. Tropical Dermatology, Am. Acad. Allergy, Am. Soc. Dermatologic Surgery, Assn. Mil. Dermatologists, Am. Assn. Clin. Research, Am. Soc. Microbiology, Am. Soc. Dermatopathology, N.Y. State Soc. Dermatology, AAUP, N.Y. Acad. Scis., Royal Soc. Medicine, Am. Fedn. Clin. Research, Pan Am. Med. Assn., Sigma Xi. Republican. Clubs: Mpls., N. Hills Country (Manhasset, N.Y.). Contbr. articles in field to profl. jours. Home and Office: 158 Hilton Ave Hempstead NY 11550

KRAFT, ALAN JAY, lawyer, business exec.; b. N.Y.C., May 24, 1927; s. Max and Evelyn (Pettigoff) K.; student U. Vt., 1944-47; J.D., Boston U., 1950; m. Dorothy E. Schwartz, Dec. 4, 1954; children—Karen Leslie, Michael, Lori Meredith. Treas., Allied Indsl. Research Cons., Inc., 1950-54; admitted to N.Y. bar, 1951, D.C. bar, 1952; mem. profl. staff U.S. Senate Appropriations Com., 1954-55; asst. personnel dir. USIA, 1955-56; v.p., dir. Allied Pub. Relations, Inc., 1956-62, Highway Trailer Industries, Inc., 1957-67, Clinton Engines Corp., 1960-63; adminstrv. v.p., dir. Four Star Internat., Inc. and subsidiaries, N.Y.C., 1967-71; dir. corporate finance R.A. Wolk & Co., Inc., N.Y.C., 1971—. Served from apprentice seaman to pharmacist mate 3d class, USNR, 1945-46. Mem. Am., N.Y. Criminal and Civil Cts. (dir.) bar assns., Am. Judges Assn., Nat. Acad. TV Arts and Scis., Assn. Arbitrators of Civil Ct. of N.Y., Am. Arbitration Assn. (comml. panel), N.Y. County Lawyers Assn., Nat. Alumni Council Boston U. Club: Friars. Home: 18 Randolph Dr Dix Hills NY 11746 Office: 401 Broadway New York City NY 10013

KRAFT, C. WILLIAM, JR., fed. judge; b. Phila., Dec. 14, 1903; s. C. William and Wilhelmina J. (Doerr) K.; B.A., U. Pa., 1924, J.D., 1927; m. Frances V. McDevitt, June 27, 1942; 1 son, C. William. Admitted to Pa. bar, 1928; asso. firm Robert W. Beatty, Media, Pa., 1927-37; asst. dist. atty. County of Delaware (Pa.), 1928-37, dist. atty., 1944-52; sr. partner firm Kraft, Lippincott & Donaldson, Media, Pa., 1944-55; judge U.S. Dist. Ct. for Eastern Dist. Pa., 1955—, sr. judge, 1970—. Mem. Delaware County, Phila. lawyers clubs, Delaware County, Am., Pa. bar assns., Am. Judicature Soc., Socialegal Club, Jr. Legal Club. Address: Brickhouse Farm Box 239 Middletown Rd RD Glen Mills PA 19342

KRAFT, JOHN WILLIAM, coll. adminstr.; b. Pitts., July 10, 1933; s. John P. and Ellen G. K.; B.A., Pa. State U., 1957; M.S. in Edn., Temple U., 1966; Ph.D., Cath. U. Am., 1975; m. Elva Mary Martin, July 7, 1962; children—John William, Laura Louise. Dep. dir. continuing edn. Pa. State U., 1960-67; dir. continuing edn. Community Coll. Beaver County, Monaca, Pa., 1967-69; state dir. community colls. Commwealth Pa., Harrisburg, 1969-72; coll. v.p., exec. dean Coll. Center N., Pitts., 1972—; mem. 1202 Commn., Commwealth Pa., 1976—; cons. commn. on higher edn. Middle States Assn. Colls. and Schs., 1976-77, mem. accreditation teams, 1970—. Served with USN, 1957-59. Recipient Edn. award Pa. Assn. Retarded Citizens, 1976, Meritorius Service award Pi Kappa Alpha, 1961; William C. Arthur meml. scholar, 1952-53. Mem. Am. Assn. Higher Edn., Community Devel. Soc., Job Adv. Service (dir., chmn. fin. com.), Southwestern Pa. Higher Edn. Council (past pres.), Pitts. Council Higher Edn. (deans and continuing edn. coms.), Nat. Assn. State Dirs. Community Colls. (past com. chmn.), Nat. Council Community Service and Continuing Edn., Pi Kappa Alpha. Office: 1130 Perry Hwy Pittsburgh PA 15237

KRAFT, VIRGINIA, writer; b. N.Y.C., Feb. 19, 1932; d. George John and Jean (Gillis) Kraft; A.B., Barnard Coll., 1951; m. Robert Dean Grimm, Dec. 31, 1955 (div. 1973); children—Tana Aurland, Tara Kraft, Robert Dean, Jill Chisholm; m. 2d, Charles Shipman Payson, Dec. 28, 1977. Research editor Columbiana Archives, Columbia U., N.Y., 1951-52; outdoor writer Field & Stream mag., N.Y.C., 1952-53; writer, big game hunter; asso. editor Sports Illus. mag., 1954—. Bd. dirs. Game Conservation Internat. Recipient Headliner's award, 1967. Nobel fellow, 1951. Mem. Shikar-Safari Soc., Internat. Womens' Fishing Assn., N.Y. Zool. Soc., Alaska Sled-dog Racing Assn. (hon. life), Hunting Hall of Fame (trustee), Internat. Wilderness Leadership Found. (dir.), Safari Clubs Internat., Safari Clubs Internat. Conservation Fund (dir.), World Wildlife Safari (dir.), Nat. Rifle Assn., Mzuri Safari Found. Republican. Roman Catholic. Clubs: Key Largo (Fla.) Anglers, Ocean Reef (Fla.), Portland (Maine) Country, Jupiter Island (Fla.), Hobe Sound (Fla.) Yacht, Gipsy Trail, Pine Pond Yacht, African Safari of N.Y. (dir., v.p.), Headhunters Soc. Author: The Book of Dog Training, 1960; The Book of Shotgun Shooting, 1966; The Book of Shotgun Sports, 1966; co-author: Better Boating, 1962; The Middle-aged, Non-Athletic, Uncoordinated Sportsmen's Guide to Tennis, 1974. Home: Stonecroft 143 Foreside Rd Falmouth Foreside ME 04105

KRAIG, ABE, psychoanalyst; b. Bklyn., Nov. 5, 1912; s. Herman and Sophia (Pulitzer) Krochmalnikoff; B.A., U. Chgo., 1943, M.A., 1945, Ph.D., 1947; Ph.D., Western U., 1951; pvt. studies, Curtis Inst. Music, 1934-36, Met. Opera Co., 1936-37, Cooper Union, 1934-36; m. Zaira Astafiewa, 1955; children of previous marriage—Bruce, Karen, Frank, Dennis. Tenor Met. Opera Co., 1936-37; allied arts tchr. N.Y.C. Bd. Edn., Ednl. Alliance, Henry St. Settlement House, Hull House, 1937-40; staff Jewish Bd. Guardians, Hawthorne Cedar Knolls Sch., 1940-44; exec. dir., pres. Pinehaven Sanitarium; exec. dir. Geriatric Ambulatory Care Clinic, Group Health Care Clinics; dir. Cytotest Corp. Dir. research Center for Study Paraphenomena, Internat. Soc. for Psychic Research, Inst. for Hypnologic Studies; cons. Cancer Cytology Found.; pres. advisor, 1969-74. Bd. dirs. Kraig House, 1946-50, N.J. Welfare Council, Cardio-Vascular Studies, Ocean County Rehab. Center, City of Pines Found., N.J. Heart Assn., Muscular Dystrophy Assn., Am. Geriatric Assn., Mexico Gen. Hosp., Parapsychology Found., Med. Assos. Clinic, Bd. Sr. Services; mem. Berkeley Psychodiagnostic Therapeutic and Research Center, Berkeley Home Health Agy., Berkeley Press, Berkeley Found., Berkeley Found. Center. Spiritual Frontiers fellow Princeton Inst. Metaphysical Studies, Cancer Detection Found. Recipient award of honor Wisdom Soc., certificate of merit in achievement in psychology award. Served with USN, 1930-33, as lt. (s.g.) USNR, 1934-46; comdr. Res. ret. Fellow Am. Schizophrenic Found., N.J. Acad. Scis., Brit. Coll. Psychic Research, Am. Soc. Psychic Research, Centro Studi E. Scambi Internazionali, mem. Brit. Assn. Advancement Sci., AAAS, Nat. Geriatric Soc., Am., N.J. hosp. assns., Adult Edn. Assn., Am. Acad. Polit. and Social Sci., Soc. Social Responsibility, Gt. Britain Spiritualist Assn., Soc. for Social Responsibility, Assn. for Research and Enlightenment, Inst. for Gero-Psychiat. and Psychologic Studies, Inst. for Cardiovascular Studies, Inst. for Cytologic Studies, Inst. for Studies in Phys. Medicine and Rehab., Inst. for Bio-Engring. Studies, Am. Acad. Med. Adminstrs., Smithsonian Instn. (charter nat. asso.), Internat. Platform Assn., U.S. Naval Inst. (bd. govs.). K.P., Lion. Author: Psychometric Testing and Mental Hygiene in Care of Aged, 1947. Home: Forest Hills Pkwy Bayville NJ 07821

KRAININ, JULIAN ARTHUR, film producer, film dir., cinematographer; b. N.Y.C., Jan. 24, 1941; s. David A. and Anne N. (Wineblatt) K.; B.S., Allegheny Coll., 1962; M.F.A., Columbia, 1965; m. Martha Wineblatt, June 17, 1967; 1 son, Todd Philip. Producer spl. projects Westinghouse Broadcasting Co., N.Y.C., 1967-69, also dir., writer, 1967—; v.p., exec. producer Krainin/Sage Prodns., Inc., N.Y.C., 1969—, also dir., writer, 1969—; pres. Krainin Prodns., Inc., N.Y.C., 1976—; nat. lectr. motion pictures at various univs. and colls., 1967—; cons. on films U. Mass., 1973; juror Mid-West Film Makers and Graphic Arts Festival, 1971-72, Nat. Emmy Awards, 1975, 76, 77, 78. Recipient numerous awards and citations including Acad. award, 1973, Emmy award, 1969, Chgo. Internat. Film Festival award, 1969, 77, 78, Florence Internat. Film Festival award, 1969, Cine Golden Eagle awards, 1969, 72, 73, 74, 76, 78, Photog. Soc. of Am. award, 1968, Venice Film Festival award, 1970, Moscow Internat. Film Festival award, 1970, Cindy award Producers Assn. Am., 1971, 76, San Francisco Internat. Film Festival award, 1972, Am. Film Festival award, 1974, 76, 78, Tel Aviv Internat. Film Festival award, 1970, Atlanta Internat. Film Festival award, 1969, 72, Festival of Ams. award, 1976, N.Y. Internat. Film and TV Festival award, 1969, 72, Gabriel award, 1968-70, Oberhausen Internat. Film Festival award, 1969, Columbus Film Festival award, 1973, Mannheim Internat. Film Festival award, 1969, U.S. Indsl. Film Festival award, 1973, Ohio State award, 1967, N.Y. Film Festival at Lincoln Center award, 1970. Mem. Writers Guild Am., Am. Acad. Motion Picture Arts and Scis., Photog. Soc. Am., Dirs. Guild Am. (award 1973). Major films include The Reluctant Revolution, 1968; Exit to Nowhere, 1967; Promises to Keep, 1967; The March, 1965; Nowhere Fast, 1968; Hide and Seek, 1966; (with Jacques Cousteau) Oceans: The Silent Crisis, 1972; Art Is (Acad. award nomination 1972, hon. film screenings White House, 1972, Mus. Modern Art, N.Y.C., 1972), 1972; The Other Americans (TV Emmy award 1969), 1969; Princeton: A Search for Answers (Acad. award 1973), 1973; The American Experiment, 1974; Going Metric, 1975; To America, 1976; The Broken Silence, 1976; The World of James Michener—Hawaii Revisited, 1977; The World of James Michener—The South Pacific; End of Eden?, 1978 (hon. screening Mus. Modern Art, N.Y.C. 1978). Home: 67-38 Fleet St Forest Hills NY 11375 Office: 39 W 55th St New York City NY 10019

KRAJSA, JOSEPH CHARLES, newspaper editor; b. Allentown, Pa., Sept. 14, 1917; s. Joseph Frank and Agnes Anna (Baranek) K.; B.S. in Phys. Edn., East Stroudsburg State Coll., 1939; postgrad. Lehigh U., 1942-43; m. Romanza M. Fairman, Feb. 16, 1946; children—Joseph J., Michael J., Maryagnes A., George J. Athletic dir., tchr. Central Cath. High Sch., Allentown, Pa., 1939-50; mgr. Allentown Finance Co., 1950-64; pres. Investment Co., 1958-64; editor, mgr. printery Jednota bilingual weekly, Middletown, Pa., 1964—, also editor kalendar and annual furdek, 1964—; dir. Port Royal Hills, Inc., Middletown, Commonwealth Nat. Bank, Middletown. Mem. Slovak League Am., Slovak Cath. Fedn. Am., Slovak World Congress, 1949—; treas. Anton Bernolak Cultural Found., 1966—. Bd. dirs. 1st Cath. Slovak Union, 1958—. Served with USNR, 1942-46. Mem. Middletown (treas. 1969-72), Greater Harrisburg (bd. dirs. 1969-74, mem. exec. com. 1970-74, pres. 1973-74) chambers commerce, Am. Legion, Cath. Press Assn., Internat. Religious Press, Slovak Newspaperman's Assn. (chmn. scholarship com. 1970—, chmn. lit. com. 1970—). Democrat. Roman Catholic. Elk, Rotarian. Club: Tuesday. Home: 1001 Rosedale Ave Middletown PA 17057 Office: Jednota and Rosedale Aves Middletown PA 17057

KRAL, MICHAEL, steel co. exec.; b. Prague, Czechoslovakia, July 26, 1920; s. Dominic and Marie (Triner) K.; came to U.S., 1946, naturalized, 1948; B.S., U. Prague, 1937, M.S., 1939; m. Audrey Howland, Nov. 8, 1973. Vice pres. Overseas Raw Materials Corp., N.Y.C., 1950-54; pres. U.S. Ore Corp., N.Y.C., 1954-70, Michael Kral Co., N.Y.C., 1960—, Mihcael Kral Industries, N.Y.C., 1970—; chmn. bd. Electralloy Corp., Oil City, Pa., 1967—; dir. Venango Metall. Products, 1970—, Kokomo (Ind.) Tube Co., 1975—. Mem. Am. Iron and Steel Inst. (dir. 1975—), Assn. Iron and Steel Engrs., Am. Soc. for Metals, ASTM, Am. Def. Preparedness Assn. Clubs: Cornell U., Wanango County, Rand, RSA. Contbr. articles in field to profl. jours. Home: 200 Central Park S New York City NY 10019 Office: 1290 Ave of Americas New York City NY 10019

KRALL, GEORGE FERGUSON, JR., mgmt. services co. exec.; b. Phila., May 1, 1936; s. George Ferguson and Edna Mae (Young) K.; B.S. in Mech. Engring., Drexel U., 1958; M.B.A., U. Pa., 1962; m. Lois Jane Williamson, Dec. 31, 1959; children—George W., Cynthia L., Elizabeth O. Account exec. IBM, Phila., 1962-68; pres. Krall Mgmt. Inc., Radnor, Pa., 1969—; instr. Drexel U., 1967-69; lectr. in field. Pres. Main Line Young Republicans, 1968; accounting warden St. David's Ch. vestry, 1973—; bd. dirs. Main Line chpt. A.R.C., 1969-71. Served to 1st lt. Ordnance Corp, U.S. Army, 1959-61. Mem. Assn. Cons. Mgmt. Engrs. (dir.). Episcopalian. Clubs: Union League Phila.; Merion Cricket. Home: Tunbridge Rd Haverford PA 19041 Office: Two Radnor Corp Center Radnor PA 19087

KRAM, HARVEY I., mfg. co. exec.; b. N.Y.C., Aug. 16, 1921; s. Abraham Bernard and Gertrude (Freedman) K.; B.S., Mass. Inst. Tech., 1942; Ph.D. (hon.), Sunshine U., 1967; m. Eleanor Levine, June 4, 1942; children—Leonard, Kathy. Group v.p. Leviton Mfg. Co., Little Neck, N.Y.; pres. So. Devices Inc., Morganton, N.C., 1965—. Served with USNR, World War II. Registered profl. engr., N.Y., Mass., Fla. Mem. Mass. Inst. Tech. Alumni Assn., Am. Soc. M.E., Nat. Soc. Profl. Engrs., Chemists Club, Am. Soc. Personnel Adminstrn., Soc. Automotive Engrs. Elk. Clubs: City Athletic (N.Y.C.); Woodcrest Country (Syossett, N.Y.); Clubs of Inverrary. Home: PO Box 398 Roslyn Heights NY 11577 Office: 59-25 Little Neck Pkwy Melville NY 11362

KRAMER, AARON, educator; b. Bklyn., Dec. 13, 1921; s. Hyman and Mary (Click) K.; B.A., Bklyn. Coll., 1941, M.A., 1951; Ph.D., N.Y. U., 1966; m. Katherine Kolodny, Mar. 10, 1942; children—Carol, Laura (Mrs. William Michael Gordon). Instr. English, Adelphi U., Long Island, N.Y., 1961-63, asst. prof., 1963-66; lectr. Queens Coll., Flushing, N.Y., 1966-68; asso. prof. English, Dowling Coll., Oakdale, N.Y., 1966-70, prof., 1970—. Recipient N.Y. State Poetry award N.Y. State Poetry Day Com., 1954; Reynolds Lyric award Lyric mag., 1961, Virginia, 1969; William Oliver Song award William E. Oliver Award Com., Los Angeles, 1968; Hart Crane Meml. award Hart Crane and Alice Crane Williams Meml. Fund, 1969; 3 awards All Nations Poetry Contest, Triton Coll., 1975, award, 1976, 77, 78; various awards A.S.C.A.P.; prize Los Altos Film maker's Festival, 1965, text for Young Composers award, 1976; 2d prize, David B. Marshall award profl. theatre program U. Mich., 1978; Meml. Found. for Jewish Culture fellow, 1978-79. Mem. Assn. for Poetry Therapy (exec. bd. 1969—), ASCAP, Modern Lang. Assn., AAUP, Internat. Acad. Poets, P.E.N. Author or translator: The Glass Mountain, 1946; Poetry and Prose of Heine, 1948; Denmark Vesey, 1954; The Tinderbox, 1957; Serenade, 1957; Tune of the Calliope, 1958; Moses, 1962; Rumshinsky's Hat, 1964; (with S. Mandel) Rilke: Visions of Christ, 1967; The Prophetic Tradition in American Poetry, 1968; Melville's Poetry, 1972; On the Way to Palermo, 1973; O Golden Land!, 1976; The Emperor of Atlantis, 1977; Death Takes a Holiday, 1978; co-author Poetry Therapy, 1969; Poetry the Healer, 1973. Editor: On Freedom's Side, 1972. Home: 96 Van Bomel Blvd Oakdale NY 11769

KRAMER, ALICE MARIE POULSEN, clin. psychologist; b. N.Y.C., Jan. 10, 1937; d. Carl M. and Ellen M. (Juliussen) Poulsen; B.A., Queens Coll., 1958; M.S. cum laude, L.I. U., 1961; Ph.D., St. John's U., 1973; m. Milton Kramer Jan. 9, 1960 (div. Nov. 1971); 1 dau., Karen; m. Nathan Horwitz, May 4, 1975. Lectr. psychology L.I. U., Bklyn., 1961-64; clin. psychologist St. Vincent's Hosp., N.Y.C., 1970-75, Logan Meml. Hosp., N.Y.C., 1974-75; cons. Catholic Schs. Drug Prevention Program, 1975—; pvt. practice psychology, 1975—; adj. asso. prof. Fordham U. Grad. Sch. Social Service, N.Y.C., 1977-78. Mem. Am. Psychol. Assn. (presented paper conv. 1972), N.Y. Soc. Clin. Psychologists. Home: 140 Cadman Plaza W Brooklyn NY 11201 Office: 25 W 13th St New York City NY 10011

KRAMER, CHARLES MAURICE, dentist; b. Bklyn., Sept. 1, 1918; s. Hyman and Lena (Brodsky) K.; student U. Ala.; D.D.S., Balt. Coll. Dental Surgery, 1945; m. Gilda Fisher, Aug. 25, 1943; children—Sanford, Steven. Practice dentistry, specializing in crown and bridge and removable prothodontics, Owings Mills, Md. Served in U.S. Army, 1955-57. Mem. ADA, Md., Balt. City dental socs., Am. Equilibration Soc., Fed. Prosthodontic Orgns. Home: 19 Stone Henge Circle Pikesville MD 21208 Office: 9135 Reisterstown Rd Owings Mills MD 21117

KRAMER, DANIEL, photographer, film dir.; b. Bklyn., May 19, 1932; s. Irving and Ethel (Berland) K.; student Bklyn. Coll., 1950-54; m. Arline Cunningham, Aug. 3, 1968. Photog. asst. to Allan and Diane Arbus, N.Y.C., 1957-59, Philippe Halsman, 1959-63; photographer, N.Y.C., 1964—; instr. photography Sch. Visual Arts, N.Y.C., 1967; dir. films Effective Communications Arts, Inc., N.Y.C., 1969—. Served with AUS, 1954-56. Recipient Gold medal Art Dirs. Club Washington, 1966; Bronze medal award Atlanta Internat. Film Festival, 1972; Creativity Photography awards, 1973, 74, 75, 77; Silver award Soc. Publ. Designers, 1974; Merit award Art Dirs. Club N.Y., 1977. Mem. Am. Soc. Mag. Photographers (dir. 1977—), Soc. Photographers in Communication (trustee 1971-73), Dirs.' Guild Am. Author: Bob Dylan, 1967. Cinematographer, writer, dir. films for CBS-TV including But Not Alone, 1970, A Family from Czernowitz, 1974; producer, dir. film Born of the Sea, commd. U.S. Navy. Address: New York NY 10024

KRAMER, HERBERT WILLIAM, JR., designer; b. Phila., Oct. 12, 1930; s. Herbert William and Mary Adelaide (Campbell) K.; student U. Pa., 1950; B.F.A., Phila. Coll. Art, 1960; postgrad. Pratt Inst., 1962. Designer, Food Fair Stores Inc., Phila., 1960-61; asso. Harbeson, Houfgh, Livingston and Larson, Architects, Phila., 1961-71; v.p. corp. devel. Interspace Inc., Phila., 1971-76; pres. Herbert Kramer and Assos., Inc., Phila., 1976—; mem. faculty design dept. Drexel U.; mem. City of Cape May (N.J.) Hist. Dist. Commn. Recipient Design award Adminstrv. Mgmt. Mag., 1975, Am. Soc. Interior Designers, 1975; Edwin Guth Meml. award for lighting design, 1978. Mem. AIA (asso.), Interior Design Council (corp. and charter), Am. Soc. Interior Designers, Soc. Archtl. Historians, Victorian Soc. Am., Nat. Trust Hist. Preservation, Action for Preservation in Phila. (corp.). Episcopalian. Clubs: Phila. Raquette, Phila. Art Alliance. Designer: Haverford (Pa.) Dining Center, (Spl. Distinction award), 1969; Atlantic Richfield Co. office, Phila. (Corp. Office of Year Instns. Mag.), 1974; Atlantic Richfield Co. Centre Sq., Phila. (Inst. Bus. Designers award, 1974; Fed. Energy Adminstrn. award 1975); Herbert Bayer's Arco Garden and Mural (Phila. Golden Pretzel award), 1977; contbr. articles to profl. publs., Phila. Inquirer. Home: 248 S Third St Philadelphia PA 19106 Office: 273 S 4th St Philadelphia PA 19106

KRAMER, NORA, author, sculptor; b. Pendleton, Eng.; d. Harris and Rachel (Wolf) Atkins; student Beaux Arts Inst., N.Y. 1920-21, Sch. of Mus. of Fine Arts, Boston, 1929-30, City Coll. N.Y., 1939-43; m. Sidney David Kramer, Oct. 27, 1917; (dec. June 1955); children—Karl Robert, Virginia K. (Mrs. Jerome David Stein, Jr.), Joan (Mrs. Arthur Philip Stoliar). Cons. (under name of Eleanor Brent) The Little Bookshop, Macy's, N.Y., 1943-53; creator The Bookplan, 1944, dir., 1944—; editorial cons. Scholastic's Arrow Book Club, 1958-75; leader juvenile writing workshop Colo. U., 1955; sculptor portraits, figures in the round; works include Young Dreamer (award Caroline Lorillard Wolfe Art Club 1975), Nature Study, 1976, Home Sculptor, 1978; mem. children's book coms. Child Study Assn. of Am., 1934—, NCCJ, 1947—, English-Speaking Union Books-Across-the-Sea, 1953—, Catherine Lorillard Wolfe Art Club, 1976—. Judge for Herald Tribune spring book festival, 1947, 53, Thomas Edison awards com., 1950, Boys Clubs Am., 1952, 54, 57, Scholastic's ann. jr. writing award, 1958—. Mem. Woman's Nat. Book Assn. (past 1st v.p., bd. dirs.), Author's Guild, English-Speaking Union, Child Study Assn. Am. (children's book com.), Composers, Artists and Authors of Am., Nat. Soc. Lit. and the Arts. Author: Nora Kramer's Storybook for Threes and Fours, 1955; Nora Kramer's Storybook for Fives and Sixes, 1956; The Cozy Hour Storybook, 1960; The Arrow Book of Ghost Stories, 1960; The Grandma Moses Storybook, 1961; Princess Tales, 1971; Tricky Tales, 1970; The Ghostly Hand and Other Haunting Stories, 1972. Co-author: (with K.R. Kramer) Coppercraft and Silver Made at Home, 1958, paperback edit., 1972. Editor-in-chief The Bookwoman, 1954-56. Editor: Grimms' Fairy Tales, 1962; (abridged editions) Swiss Family Robinson, 1960, Hans Brinker, 1967, Dracula, 1971, Ramona, 1972, Journey To The Center of The Earth, 1973. Address: 46 Jane St New York City NY 10014

KRAMER, RUTH, accountant; b. N.Y.C., June 20, 1925; d. Isidore and Sarah (Heller) Kleiner; B.A., Bklyn. Coll., 1946; m. Paul Kramer, Oct. 27, 1946; children—Stephen David, Lynne Adair. Tchr. elementary sch. N.Y.C. Bd. Edn., 1946-50; accountant Lichtenstein & Kramer, N.Y.C., Lynbrook, N.Y., 1954; jr. partner Paul Kramer & Co., Lynbrook, 1954-56, partner, 1956-65, mng. partner, 1965—; cons. Nassau County (N.Y.) Dist Atty. Office, expert witness accounting matters Nassau County Grand Juries; mem. IRS liaison com. Bklyn. Dist.; dir. Huntington Laundry, Inc., Flinch & Bruns Funeral Home, Inc. Troop leader Girl Scouts U.S.A., 1947-48; chmn. Tri Town sect. Anti Defamation League, 1952-53; active Heart Fund; pres. Lynbrook Womens Republican Club, 1956-58; treas. Assembly Candidates Campaign Com., 1964; mem. Nassau County Fedn. Rep. Women, Syosset Woodbury Rep. Club. Named Women in Accounting, local TV channel, 1974. Registered pub. accountant, N.Y. Mem. Nat. Soc. Pub. Accountants (del.). Empire State Assn. Pub. Accountants (Meritorious Service award, 1st v.p. 1977-78, pres. 1978—; pres. Nassau County chpt. 1962, 63, 76, 76—), Tax Inst. C.W. Post Coll., Accounting Inst. C.W. Post Coll. Jewish. Clubs: Sisterhood North Shore Synagogue; Am. Jewish Congress, Lynbrook Pythian Sisters. (past chief). Home: 23 Hilltop Dr Syosset NY 11791 Office: 393 Sunrise Hwy Lynbrook NY 11563

KRAMER, WALTER WILLIAM, mech. engr.; b. Allentown, Pa., Feb. 6, 1918; s. William S. and Katherine (Chylyk) K.; B.S. in Mech. Engring., Pa. State U., 1940; s. Jennie K. Kowalczk, July 12, 1942; children—Cheryl L., William W., Christine Ann, Brenda Jean. Inspctr. Am. Armament Corp., N.Y.C., 1942-45; asst. mgr. John Hancock Life Ins. Co., Allentown, 1945-51; pvt. practice engring. cons., Allentown, 1951-55; chief engr. Fuller Co., Catasauqua, Pa., 1955—; cons. in field. Served with U.S. Army, 1940-42. Recipient John Vaaler award Chem. Processing Mag., 1972—. Club: Masons. Patentee numerous items; contbr. articles to profl. jours. Home: 35 S 17th St Allentown PA 18104 Office: PO Box 29 Catasauqua PA 19032

KRANEPOOL, HARRY ANTHONY, educator, union ofcl.; b. Bklyn., July 26, 1941; s. Harry M. and Marie Rose (Sorrentino) K.; B.S. in Chemistry, St. Francis Coll., Bklyn., 1962; M.A., Bklyn. Coll., 1967; M.S., City Coll. N.Y., 1969. Tchr., Bishop Loughlin Meml. High Sch., Bklyn., 1963—, chmn. dept. sci., 1971—, asst. prin. summer sch., 1975—, also dir. adult edn.; pres. Catholic Sci. Council Bklyn. Diocese, 1970-76, pres. Lay Faculty Assn., Local 1261 Am. Fedn. Tchrs. AFL-CIO. 1972-74. Recipient N.Y.C. Chemistry Tchrs. Club award, 1967; Mendalian award in Sci., Cath. Schs. Office, 1976; Franciscan Spirit award St. Francis Coll., 1962; St. John's U. scholar, 1963. Certified tchr., N.Y. State. Mem. Cath. Sci. Council of Bklyn. and Queens, Nat. Sci. Tchrs. Assn., Sci. Tchrs. N.Y. State. Democrat. Clubs: Chemistry, Biology Tchrs. (N.Y.C.). Author 4 books: contbr. articles to profl. publs. Home: 31-31 138th St 4D Flushing NY 11354 Office: 357 Clermont Ave Brooklyn NY 11238

KRASNER, LOUIS, concert violinist; b. Cherkassy, Russia, June 21, 1903; s. Harry and Sara (Lechovetzky) K.; diploma, New Eng. Conservatory Music, 1922; postgrad. study Berlin, Paris, Vienna; hon. prof. Accademia Filarmonica of Bologna, Italy; m. Adrienne Galimir, Oct. 10, 1936; children—Elsa, Vivien, Naomi. Came to U.S., 1908, naturalized, 1914. Concert appearances Europe and U.S.; soloist with orchs., of Vienna, Rome, Berlin, Paris, London, B.B.C.; appeared with Boston Symphony, N.Y. Philharmonic, others; concertmaster Mpls. Symphony, 1944; prof. violin and chamber music Syracuse U., 1949-, condr. U. Symphony Orch., 1955—; faculty mem. Internat. String Congress, 1960-64; Regents lectr. U. Calif. at San Diego, 1971; faculty Inst. for Advanced Music, Sion, Switzerland, 1973; mus. dir. Syracuse Friends Chamber Music; participant ann. series chamber music concerts pub. schs., Syracuse; 1st performances of Alban Berg Schoenberg, other violin concertos; chmn., editor 1964 string symposium Berkshire Music Center, Tanglewood, 1963-64. Music cons. WCNY-FM, Syracuse. Mem. music panel Nat. Endowment for the Arts, 1966-. Recipient Gov.'s award for excellence in arts, R.I., 1968. Mem. Am. String Tchrs. Assn. (founder, past pres. N.Y. chpt.), Coll. Music Soc. (council 1969—). Editor: String Problems, Players and Paucity, 1965. Recs. for Columbia. Home: 521 Scott Ave Syracuse NY 13224

KRASNOFF, SIDNEY OURIN, cardiologist; b. Phila., July 11, 1918; s. Abraham Max and Sophia (Ourin) K.; B.A., U. Pa., 1938, M.D., 1942; m. Ruth Buchsbaum Bernstein, June 11, 1946; children—Stuart B., Robert M. (dec.), Jonathan R. Intern, Jewish Hosp., Phila., 1942-43, resident in internal medicine, 1946-47; practice medicine specializing in cardiology, Phila., Elkins Park, Pa., since 1947; sr. attending physician Einstein Med. Center, since 1965, pres. staff, 1969-70; clin. prof. Temple U. Med. Sch.; cons. pharm. firms; bd. dirs. Care-Medico, Phila., Heart Assn. S.E. Pa., Overseas Service Medico. Judge elections Cheltenham Twp., 1977. Served to capt. M.C., U.S. Army, World War II. Fellow A.C.P., Am. Coll. Cardiology, Phila. Coll. Physicians; mem. AMA, Am. Heart Assn., Phila. County Med. Soc. (v.p. 1978), Pa. Med. Care Found. (pres. 1976-78), Pa. Profl. Standards Rev. Council (pres. 1977-78), Phila. Profl. Standards Rev. Orgn. (chmn. 1974-75), Pa. Soc. Internal Medicine (pres. 1960). Republican. Jewish. Author: Computers in Medicine, 1967; also articles. Home: 1511 Thornberry Rd Wyncote PA 19095 Office: Suite 114B Elkins Park House 7900 Old York Rd Elkins PA 19117

KRASNOW, FRANCES (MRS. MARCUS THAU), cons. biochemist, educator; b. N.Y.C., Oct. 16, 1894; d. Raphael and Sara Rifka (Lubarsky) Krasnow; B.S. magna cum laude, Barnard Coll., 1917; A.M., Columbia, 1917, Ph.D., 1922; Litt.D. (hon.), Jewish Theol. Sem. Am., 1974; m. Marcus Thau, Dec. 25, 1930; 1 dau., Hudelle K. Mem. research and teaching staff dept. biochemistry Columbia U. Coll. Phys. and Surg., 1917-32; asst. dir. Guggenheim Dental Clinic, Sch. Dental Hygiene, N.Y.C., 1932-44, head dept. research, 1944-52; research dir. Universal Coatings, Inc., Newark, 1952-72; research cons., N.Y.C., 1972—. Cons. biochemistry, 1952—. Active P.T.A., also various community drives; area chmn. A.R.C., 1943-44. Recipient various awards civic and profl. orgns. Mem. Am. Chem. Soc., Ret. Chemists Assn. (sec.-treas. N.Y. sect. 1975-76, program chmn. and pres.-elect 1976-77, pres. 1977-78), Soc. Exptl. Biology and Medicine, Am. Bd. Clin. Chemistry, A.A.A.S., N.Y. Acad. Medicine, A.M.A., Am. Assn. Clin. Chemists, Am. Soc. Microbiology, N.Y. Acad. Scis., Internat. Assn. Dental Research (pres. 1947-49, editor 1949-60), Am. Inst. Chemists, Am. Assn. Dental Editors, Alumni Assn. Tchrs. Inst.-Sem. Coll. (dir., pres. 1947-53, hon. pres. 1968—, Distinguished Alumni 60 Yr. Service award 1977), N.Y. State (hon.) N.Y.C. (hon.) dental hygiene assns., Phi Beta Kappa, Sigma Xi. Home: and Office: 405 E 72d St New York City NY 10021

KRASSNER, MICHAEL BERNARD, psychiatrist; b. Bklyn., Apr. 1, 1935; s. Nathan P. and Lillian (Fedler) K.; A.B., Columbia, 1956; postgrad. in geology U. Chgo., 1956-58, Ph.D. in Paleontology, 1958; M.D., Chgo. Med. Sch., 1962; postgrad. N.Y. Sch. Psychiatry, 1963; m. Barbara Anne Herms, Sept. 20, 1975; 1 dau., Elizabeth Anne; children by previous marriage—Katherine, Kenneth, Keith; stepchildren—Gregory, Mary, Matthew. Intern, New Rochelle (N.Y.) Hosp., 1962-63; resident in psychiatry Kings Park (N.Y.) State Hosp., 1963-65, 68-69; pvt. practice medicine specializing in psychiatry and psychosomatic medicine, Smithtown, N.Y., 1965-66, 68-76; psychiatrist adolescent unit NE Nassau Psychiat. Hosp., Kings Park 1968—; med. treatment dir. Suffolk County Mental Health Bds., Narcotic Clinic, Hauppauge, N.Y., 1968-69; asst. dir. med. service dept. Sandoz Pharms., East Hanover, N.J., 1976—; grad. gemologist Gemological Inst. Am., 1978; curator Oriental art Suffolk Mus., Stony Brook, N.Y., 1972-74; owner, operator Oriental Antiques Centereach, Suffolk County, N.Y., 1976-78; guest lectr. Oriental art State U. N.Y. at Stony Brook. Served with cav. U.S. Army, 1967-68; Viet Nam. Decorated Bronze Star, Purple Heart, Air medal. Fellow Essex County Med. Soc., Essex County Mental Health Assn.; mem. AMA, Am. Psychiat. Assn., N.J. State, N.J., S.C., Vt., N.Mex. med. socs., Gemological Inst. Am., China Soc., Oriental Art Soc. (pres. 1969-72), Japan Soc., Archaeol. Inst. of Am. (chmn. Far Eastern study grp. 1970-72), Archaeol. Study Group N.J., Asia Soc., Am. Assn. Museums, N.Y. Shell Club, Mensa. Contbr. articles on medicine, psychiatry, microscopy, antique glass, jade, oriental art, Egyptology, malacology, archaeology and gemology to various jours. Home: 16 Rossmore Terr Livingston NJ 07039 Office: Med Service Dept Sandoz Pharms East Hanover NJ 07936

KRATZ, ELIZABETH ORR (MRS. DAVID L. KRATZ), church exec.; b. Belfast, Ireland, Jan. 6, 1902; d. Robert and Ellen (Gordon) Orr; student Reed Coll., 1919-21, Oreg. Coll., 1922-23; m. David L. Kratz, Mar. 24, 1927 (dec. Nov. 1960); children—Phyllis E. (Mrs. Leon M. Hall), David G., Charles R., James S. Office sec. Meier & Frank Co., Portland, Oreg., 1920-21; tchr. pub. schs., Condon, Oreg., 1923-25, Portland, 1925-27; art supr. pub. schs. The Dalles, Oreg., 1927-28; supr. Released Time Religious Edn., Vallejo, Calif., 1945-48; minister edn. 1st Christian Ch., Lincoln, Nebr., 1960; v.p. Christian Chs., No. Calif. and Nev., Berkeley, Calif., 1962-70, acting pres.-bishop, 1970-72, asst. to pres., 1972—, exec. sec. Christian Womens Fellowship, 1962-71, interim exec. sec., 1978; Ordained to ministry Disciples Christ, 1965. Acting exec. dir. No. Calif. Ecumenical Council, 1972—; del. Ch. Leaders Consultation to Paris Peace Talks, 1971. Dir. Eskaton, Sacramento, Faith and Life Corp., Berkeley, Center for Environ. Action, Salem Oreg.; mem. adminstrv. com. Office Women's Affairs, Grad. Theol. Union, Berkeley; bd. dirs. No. Calif. Ecumenical Peace Inst., 1965-75, Western Acad. for Church Life and Mission, Oakland, Calif., Northeastern Assn. Christian Chs., 1976—. Mem. Ch. Women United (nat. bd. mgrs. 1963-65; state chmn. citizen action 1972-75), North Caif. Council Chs. (dir. 1963-75), Calif. Ch. Council, Calif. Migrant Ministry (pres. 1968-71), Common Cause, P.E.O., Democrat. Mem. Disciples of Christ (dir. disciples peace fellowship, fellowship of reconciliation, steering com. Disciples for Mission and Renewal 1969-72). Home: 78A Waterside Ln Clinton CT 06413

KRATZER, GUY LIVINGSTON, intestinal surgeon; b. Gratz, Pa., Apr. 24, 1911; s. Clarence U. and Carrie E. (Schwalm) K.; student Muhlenberg Coll., 1928-31; M.D., Temple U., 1935; M.S., U. Minn., 1945; m. Kathryn H. Miller, Jan. 27, 1940; 1 son, Guy Miller. Intern Harrisburg Hosp., Pa., 1935-36; fellow proctology, surgery, Mayo Clinic, 1942-46, fellow surgery, 1949-50; asso. surgeon Pottsville Hosp., 1936-41; asso. proctologist Allentown (Pa.) Hosp., 1946—, mem. tumor clinic, 1955—; mem. courtesy staff Sacred Heart Hosp., 1946—, chief dept. colon and rectal surgery, dir. residency tng., 1974—; cons. proctologist Quakertown Community and the Good Samaritan hosps.; chief dept. proctology, dir. residency tng. Allentown Hosp., 1958—; clin. prof. surgery, cons. Pa. State U. Coll. Medicine M.S. Hershey Med. Center. Bd. dirs. Am. Cancer Soc., v.p. Lehigh County chpt., 1963-64. Diplomate Am. Bd. Colon and Rectal Surgery. Fellow A.C.S. (pres. S.E. Pa. chpt. 1966—), Am. Proctologic Soc., Internat. Coll. Surgeons; mem. Am. Cancer Soc. (pres. Lehigh County 1966), Brazilian Proctologic Soc., A.A.A.S., Am. Med. Writers Assn., Pa. Soc. Colon and Rectal Surgery (pres. 1962-63), Pa. Med. Soc. (cancer commn.), Am. Med. Authors, Lehigh County (v.p. 1963-64), Lehigh County (pres. 1966—) med. socs. Allentown C. of C. (gov. 1963-65). Club: Lions. Asso. editor-in-chief Am. Jour. Clin. Research, 1971—. Address: 1447 Hamilton St Allentown PA 18102

KRAUNZ, ROBERT FRANK, cardiologist; b. Rome, N.Y., July 2, 1936; s. George J. and Sally (Silverman) K.; B.A., Hamilton Coll., 1957; M.D., U. Rochester, 1961; m. Phyllis Jane Hinkel, Aug. 9, 1969; children—Amy Elizabeth, Jeffrey Thomas, Stephen Gregory. Intern, U. Wis., Madison, 1961-62, resident in internal medicine, 1962-63; resident in internal medicine VA Hosp., Washington, 1965-67; cardiology fellow dept. medicine U. Wash., Seattle, 1967-68, St. Elizabeth's Hosp., Boston, 1968-69; research asso. W. Roxbury (Mass.) VA Hosp., and clin. instr. medicine Harvard Med. Sch., Boston, 1969-70; cardiologist Central Maine Med. Center, Lewiston, 1970—, chief cardiologist, 1971—; vis. physician Maine Med. Center, Portland, 1970—; courtesy staff St. Mary's Gen. Hosp., Lewiston, 1970—, Stephen's Meml. Hosp., Norway, Maine, 1970—. Bd. dirs. Emergency Care, Inc., 1972—; active Lewiston-Auburn Little Theatre, 1972—; bd. dirs. Maine Heart Assn., 1974-77. Am. Heart Assn. fellow, 1974; diplomate Nat. Bd. Med. Examiners, Am. Bd. Internal Medicine. Fellow Am. Coll. Cardiology; mem. Androscoggin County Med. Assn., Maine Med. Assn. Democrat. Unitarian. Contbr. articles in field to med. jours. Home: 79 Shepley St Auburn ME 04240 Office: 300 Main St Lewiston ME 04240

KRAUS, MOZELLE DEWITTE BIGELOW (MRS. RUSSELL WARREN KRAUS), psychologist; b. Vicksburg, Miss., Sept. 29, 1929; d. Raymond Demar and Henrietta (DeWitte) Bigelow; B.S., D.C. Tchrs. Coll., 1952; M.A., George Washington U., 1954; Ed.D., Am. U., 1965; m. Russell Warren Kraus, Sept. 30, 1961. Instr., Dept. Def., Washington, 1952-54; tchr. Wheaton (Md.) High Sch., 1954-55; grad. asst. Am. U., 1955-56; research psychologist to Dr. Leonard Carmichael sec. Smithsonian Instn., Washington, also v.p. Nat. Geog. Mag., 1956-72; pvt. practice psychotherapy, Washington, 1972—; asso. prof. psychology George Washington U., 1965—; vis. prof. U.S. Naval Sch. Hosp. Adminstrn., Bethesda, Md., 1968; lectr. psychology U.S. Dept. Agr. Grad. Sch., 1964—. Mem. AAAS, Am., D.C. psychol. assns., Nat. Health Providers in Psychology, Am. Orthopsychiat. Assn., Am. Assn. Outpatient Psychiat. Clinics, Internat. Assn. Counseling Services, D.A.R., Salvation Army Aux., Phi Delta Gamma, Sigma Xi, Psi Chi, Kappa Delta Epsilon, Sigma Kappa. Episcopalian. Contbr. articles to profl. jours. Home: 4710 Bethesda Ave Bethesda MD 20014 Office: Suite 818 1028 Connecticut Ave NW Washington DC 20036

KRAUSE, HELEN FOX (MRS. MARVIN KRAUSE), physician; b. Boston, Mar. 20, 1932; d. Nathan and Frances Lena (Rich) Fox; B.A., U. Maine, 1954; M.D., Tufts U., 1958; m. Marvin Krause, Aug. 26, 1956; children—Merrick Eli, Beth Riva, Kim Debra. Intern, Health Center Hosps. U. Pitts., 1958-59; resident Eye and Ear Hosp., Pitts., Childrens Hosp., VA Hosp., Pitts., 1959-62; practice medicine specializing in otorhinolaryngology and allergy, Pitts., 1962—; mem. staff North Hills Passavant Hosp., Eye and Ear Hosp., Suburban Gen. Hosp.; clin. instr. U. Pitts. Sch. Medicine; lectr. Allegheny Community Coll. Mem. corporate bd Western Pa. Montessori Sch., 1967-71; mem. adminstrv. bd. North Hills Jewish Community Center, 1968-75, pres., 1973-74. Diplomate Am. Bd. Ophthalmology and Otolaryngology. Fellow A.C.S, Am. Soc. Ophthalmologic and Otolarynolic Allergy; mem. A.M.A., Pa., Allegheny County med. assns., North Hills Med. Soc., Pa. Acad. Ophthalmology and Otolaryngology (dir. 1974-77, mem. governing council 1977—), Am. Council Otolaryngology (ho. dels. 1973-76, Western Pa. membership chmn.), Western Pa. Soc. Clin. Hypnosis, Pitts. Otol. Soc. (program chmn. 1973-77, sec.-treas. 1977—), Pan Am. Soc. Otorhinolaryngology and Brochoesophagology, Am. Acad. Ophthalmology and Otolaryngology. Jewish. Home: 1016 Covington Pl Allison Park PA 15101 Office: 9102 Babcock Blvd Pittsburgh PA 15237

KRAUSE, RICHARD MICHAEL, educator, immunologist; b. Marietta, Ohio, Jan. 4, 1925; s. Ellis L. and Jennie (Waterman) K.; B.A., Marietta Coll., 1947, D.Sc., 1978; M.D., Case Western Res. U., 1952. Fellow preventive medicine dept. Case Western Res. U. 1951-52; intern, asst. resident medicine Barnes Hosp., St. Louis, 1952-54; asst. Rockefeller U., 1954-57, asst. prof., 1957-61, asso. prof., 1961-62; prof. epidemiology Wash. U., 1962-66, asso. prof. medicine, 1962-65, prof. medicine, 1965-66; asso. prof., physician to hosp. Rockefeller U., 1966-68, prof., sr. physician, 1968-75; dir. Nat. Inst. Allergy and Infectious Diseases NIH, HEW, 1975—. Chmn. allergy and immunology study sect. NIH, 1966-70, mem. infectious diseases adv. com. 1970-74; mem. adv. council on research N.Y. Heart Assn., 1969-71, bd. dirs., 1967-73; mem. research com. Am. Heart Assn., 1963-66; mem. commn. streptococal and staphylococcal diseases Armed Forces Epidemiol. Bd., 1963-72, dep. dir., 1968-72; chmn. exec. com. Biomed. Sci. Working Group, WHO, 1978. Bd. dirs. Royal Soc. Medicine Found., 1971-75. Served with U.S. Army, 1944-46. Mem. Assn. Am. Physicians, Am. Soc. Clin. Investigation, Am. Assn. Immunologists, Am. Soc. Microbiology, Am. Soc. Biol. Chemists, Harvey Soc., Practitioners Soc. N.Y. Clubs: Cosmos, Century Assn. Editor Jour. Exptl. Medicine, 1973-75. Research on pathogenesis and epidemiology of streptococcal diseases; immunochem. studies on streptococcal antigens; immunogenetics; recognition of rabbit antibodies with molecular uniformity, genetics of the immune response. Home: 8 West Dr Bethesda MD 20014 Office: NIH Bethesda MD 20014*

KRAUSS, LEO, urologist; b. N.Y.C., Nov. 5, 1928; s. Moe and Marie K.; student Coll. City N.Y., 1945-46; B.A. summa cum laude, Syracuse U., 1948, postgrad., 1948-49; M.D., N.Y. U., 1953; m. Harriet Enid Powell, Dec. 4, 1955; children—Robert, Jenny. Intern, Phila. Gen. Hosp., 1953-54; resident in urology St. Luke's Hosp., N.Y.C., 1956, Mahattan VA Hosp., 1957-59; practice medicine specializing in urology, Plainview, N.Y., 1963—; chief urology Syosset (N.Y.) Hosp., 1963—; attending urologist Central Gen. Hosp., Plainview, Nassau County Med. Center, East Meadow, N.Y.; asso. prof. urology State U. Coll. Medicine, Stony Brook, 1976—; cons. urologist N.Y. State Psychiat. Hosps. Bd. dirs. L.I. Cancer Council. Served to capt. M.C., USAF, 1954-56. Diplomate Am. Bd. Urology. Fellow A.C.S.; mem. N.Y. State, Nassau County med. socs., AMA, Am. Urol. Assn., Am. Fedn. Clin. Research, Am. Soc. Nephrology, Nassau Surg. Soc., Phi Beta Kappa, Alpha Omega Alpha. Republican. Jewish. Contbr. articles to med. jours. Office: 1181 Old Country Rd Plainview NY 11803

KRAUSS, WILLIAM, engr.; b. N.Y.C., Apr. 5, 1935; s. Max and Clara K.; B. Chem. Engring., Coll. City N.Y., 1957; M. Mgmt. and Chem. Engring., City U. N.Y., 1962; m. Alice Wilner, June 29, 1958; children—Seth, Glenn, Theodore. Asso. engr. Gen. Foods Co., Tarrytown, N.Y., 1957-61; mgr. process engring. Johnson & Johnson, New Brunswick, N.J., 1961-68; engring. dir. Jelco labs. Johnson & Johnson Co., Raritan, N.J., 1968-70; v.p. mfg. and engring. Marine Colloids div. FMC Corp., Rockland, Maine, 1971—. Dir. sci. evaluation com. Camden (Maine) Schs., 1974; dir. Buddy Werner Ski Race, 1975-77; dir. fitness program Camden YMCA, 1976—. MMem. Am. Inst. Chem. Engrs., Am. Mgmt. Assn., Comml. Devel. Assn., Tau Beta Pi. Club: Penobscot Wheelmen Bike (pres. 1976). Office: PO Box 308 Rockland ME 04841

KRAUT, JOEL ARTHUR, ophthalmologist; b. Jersey City, N.J., July 21, 1937; s. Alan and Lillian Betty (Kravitz) K.; A.B. cum laude (Cane scholar), Princeton U., 1958; M.D. (St. John-Princeton scholar), Columbia U., 1962; m. Cathy Jane Kleven, June 30, 1963; children—David Terence, Amy Melissa. Intern, Boston U. Med. Center, 1962-63; resident in ophthalmology N.Y. U.-Bellevue Med. Center, N.Y.C., 1963-66; chief of ophthalmology USAF Hosp., Tachikawa, Japan, 1966-68; practice medicine specializing in ophthalmology, Brookline, Mass., 1968—; clin. asso., clin. instr. ophthalmology Harvard Med. Sch.; clin. instr. ophthalmology Tufts Sch. Medicine, 1968—; asst. surgeon in ophthalmology, dir. Low Vision Center, Mass. Eye and Ear Infirmary, 1968—, chmn. United Way campaign, 1973; dir. physiol. optics dept. ophthalmology Tufts-New Eng. Medical Center, 1968-73; cons. U.S. 5th Air Force, Japan, 1966-68. U. Calif. research fellow, 1960. Diplomate Am. Acad. Ophthalmology and Otoloryngology, Am. Bd. Ophthalmology. Fellow A.C.S.; mem. New Eng., Mass. ophthal. socs., Soc. Geriatric Ophthalmology, Intraocular Lens Soc., Greater Boston Med. Soc., Phi Beta Kappa, Sigma Xi. Club: Hazel Hotchkiss Wightman Tennis. Contbr. articles in field to med., profl. jours. Office: 209 Harvard St Brookline MA 02146

KRAUTER, CHARLES FREDERICK, diversified industries exec.; b. Hackensack, N.J., June 26, 1929; s. Charles Frederick and Helen Marie (Faughnan) K.; student Lafayette Coll., 1947-48, Rutgers U., 1948-49, Coll. of Ins., 1954-57; m. Suzanne Clark Grove, Jan. 26, 1952; children—Neil C., Lynn G. Ins. supr. Arabian Am. Oil Co., N.Y.C., 1949-57; asst. ins. mgr. St. Regis Paper Co., N.Y.C., 1957-60; asst. treas. W.R. Grace & Co., N.Y.C., 1960—. Lectr. Coll. of Ins. Trustee, Rumson Improvement Assn. Served with USCGR, 1950-53. Mem. Am. Soc. Ins. Mgmt. (asst. treas., chmn. financial operations com.), Assn. Ex-Mems. Squadron A, Delta Kappa Epsilon. Roman Catholic. Clubs: N.Y. Yacht; Seabright Beach (bd. govs.) (Seabright, N.J.); Shrewsbury Sailing and Yacht (Oceanport, N.J.). Home: Orchard Ln Rumson NJ 07760 Office: 1114 Ave of Americas New York City NY 10036

KRAVATH, RICHARD ELLIOT, pediatrician; b. N.Y.C., May 25, 1935; s. Reuben and Fannie (Tannenbaum) K.; A.B., Columbia U., 1956; M.D., State U. N.Y., 1960; m. Pauline Hauser, Aug. 27, 1960; children—Robert, Peter, Caroline. Intern, Montefiore Hosp. and Med. Center, N.Y.C., 1960-61, resident pediatrics, 1964-65, chief resident, 1965-66, adj. attending pediatrician, 1968-73, asso. attending pediatrician, 1973—; research asst. State U. N.Y., 1961; fellow human devel. biology Albert Einstein Coll. Medicine, N.Y.C., 1966-68, asst. prof. pediatrics, 1968-75, asso. prof., 1975—; asso. vis. pediatrician Morrisania City Hosp., Bronx, 1968-73, attending pediatrician, 1973-76; adj. attending pediatrician Bronx Lebanon Hosp., 1977; attending pediatrician North Central Bronx Hosp., 1977. Served to capt., M.C., USAF, 1961-64. Diplomate Am. Bd. Pediatrics. Mem. Am. Acad. Pediatrics, AAAS, Am. Thoracic Soc., Am. Fedn. Clin. Research, N.Y. Acad. Scis., N.Y. Trudeau Soc., Bronx Pediatric Soc. Democrat. Jewish. Contbr. articles in field to profl. jours. Home: 6 Scott St Dobbs Ferry NY 10522 Office: 111 E 210th St Bronx NY 10467

KRAVCHENKO, NICHOLAS, civil engr.; b. Rymki, Russia, Mar. 31, 1929; s. Nicholas G. and Vera (Pilichovski) K.; came to U.S., 1948, naturalized, 1953; B.C.E., Coll. City N.Y., 1955; postgrad. N.Y. U., 1958-60; m. Larissa Konovalov, June 8, 1958; children—Vladimir, Alexander, Elena. Project engr. Chas. H. Sells., N.Y.C., 1955-61; engring. cons. Lockwood, Kessler & Bartlett, N.Y.C., and Boston, 1961-63, 65-69; chief transp. engr. Hardesty & Hanover, N.Y.C., 1963-65; pres. Kravchenko & Assocs., N.Y.C., 1969—; v.p. Eco Viz, Inc., Glen Cove, N.Y., 1970-73. Recipient award for Best Housing Devel., 1977. Mem. ASCE, Soc. Am. Mil. Engrs., Nat. Acad. Scis. Club: Huntington Table Tennis (sec.). Republican. Russian Orthodox. Office: 8 Teresa Ln East Northport NY 11731

KRAVITZ, BERNARD JOSEPH, physician; b. Nanticoke, Pa., Jan. 17, 1931; s. Frank L. and Josephine M. K.; A.B., U. Pa., 1952, M.S., 1953, M.D., 1961; postgrad. Columbia U., 1956; m. Emily Parmaly Peltier, June 18, 1960; children—Christopher, Thomas, Andrew, Steven. Intern, Abington (Pa.) Meml. Hosp., 1961-62, resident 1962-65; practice medicine specializing in internal medicine, Abington, 1965—; sr. attending physician Abington Hosp., 1973—, pres. staff, 1978-79; co-dir. Abington Diagnostic Clinic, 1976—; asst. clin. prof. medicine Temple U. Med. Sch., Phila., 1975—; med. dir., plant physician Rohm & Haas Research Labs., Springhouse, Pa., 1971—. Trustee, Abington Hosp., 1977-79; mem. health activities com. Abington YMCA, 1968-70. Served to lt. comdr. USN, 1953-56. Mem. A.C.P., Am. Soc. Internal Medicine, Pa., Montgomery County med. socs., Phila. Med. Club. Republican. Roman Catholic. Clubs: Country (Hungtingdon Valley, Pa.); Rotary (dir. 1975-76) (Jenkintown, Pa.). Home: 1985 Country Club Dr Huntingdon Valley PA 19006 Office: 1245 Highland Ave Abington PA 19001

KRAVITZ, HENRY, psychiatrist; b. Zawiercie, Poland, Oct. 18, 1918; s. Julius and Erna (Hops) K.; B.A., McGill U., 1946, M.D., 1949, Dyp. Psych., 1954; 1 dau., Susan; m. 2d, Mona Brenda Samuels, July 10, 1946. Intern, Montreal (Que., Can.) Gen. Hosp., 1949-50; resident Weyburn Sask. Hosp., 1950-51, Queen Mary Hosp., 1951-52, Montreal Gen. Hosp., 1952-54; practice medicine specializing in psychiatry, Montreal, 1954, psychoanalysis, 1959—; tng. analyst Canadian Psychiat. Inst., Montreal, 1964—; psychiatrist-in-chief Jewish Gen. Hosp., Montreal, 1967—; prof. med. faculty McGill U., 1971—. Chmn., Youth Commn., 1969—. Served with RCAF, 1940-46. Fellow Am. Psychiat. Assn., Am. Acad. Psychoanalysis, Am. Coll. Psychoanalysts, Am. Coll. Psychiatrists; mem. Canadian Psychoanalytic Soc. (pres. 1967-71), Canadian Inst. Psychoanalysis (dir. 1969). Contbr. articles to profl. jours. Home: 4994 Circle Rd Montreal PQ Canada Office: 4333 Cole St Catherine Rd Montreal PQ Canada

KRAVITZ, JOSEPH HENRY, govt. ofcl.; b. Nanticoke, Pa., Aug. 14, 1935; s. Joseph Henry and Julia Gertrude (Zimniski) K.; B.S. in Geology, Syracuse U., 1957; M.S. in Geology, George Washington U., 1975, M.Phil. in Geology, 1977; m. Prudence Ann Bullock, Nov. 27, 1965; 1 son, Joseph Henry III. Research asst. dept. geology Yale, New Haven, 1961-64; research geologist Lamont Geol. Obs. of Columbia U., Palisades, N.Y., 1964-65; oceanographer Naval Oceanographic Office, Washington, 1965-71, head geol. lab., 1971-77, head oceanographic labs., 1977-78; sr. geologist Outer Continental Shelf Environ. Assessment Program, NOAA, Boulder, Colo., 1978—; mem. sedimentation com. Water Resources Council, U.S., 1968-69; mem. Am. Oceanographic expedition Kara Sea, 1965; organizer Comprehensive Ocean Bottom Survey, Kane Basin, 1969. Served as 1st lt., USAF, 1957-60. Fellow Arctic Inst. N.Am., mem. Geol. Soc. Am., Assn. Profl. Geol. Scientists, Research Soc. Am. (chmn. Kaminski award com. Washington chpt. 1972), Soc. Econ. Paleontologists and Mineralogists, Delta Kappa Epsilon. Republican. Roman Catholic. Club: Explorers. Contbr. numerous articles to profl. jours. Pioneer in ocean bottom photography No. Barents Sea, 1966. Home: 8019 Inverness Ridge Rd Potomac MD 20854 Office: NOAA Boulder CO 80303

KRAVITZ, RUBIN, chemist; b. Framingham, Mass., Mar. 22, 1928; s. Abe and Lillian (Cohen) K.; B.S., Northeastern U., 1952; m. Geraldine Pudaim, Aug. 20, 1950 (dec.); children—Richard Alan, Steven Jay, Stuart Paul; m. 2d, Annabelle S. Durieux, July 16, 1978. Analytical chemist FDA, U.S. Dept. HEW, Boston, 1956-61, Alcohol and Tobacco Tax div. U.S. Treasury Dept., Boston, 1961-65; supr. phys. testing lab. Plastic div. Am. Hoechst Corp., Leominster, Mass., 1967-78, research chemist Plastic div., 1978—. Cubmaster, Boy Scouts Am., Worcester, Mass., 1967-68. Served with USAAF, 1946-48. Mem. Soc. Plastic Engrs. (newsletter editor 1969-71, treas. Pioneer Valley sect. 1972-73, v.p. 1973-74, chmn. tech. com. 1973, pres. Pioneer Valley sect. 1975-76), ASTM (chmn. compression molding 1969-70, vice chmn. publicity and papers com. D-20 on plastics 1972-76, chmn. subcom. specimen preparation, chmn. sect. plastic furniture, chmn. specimen preparation 1976, chmn. task group Kravitz impact test method 1976), Assn. Analytical Chemists. K.P. (chancellor comdr. 1963-64). Home: 141 Beaconsfield Rd Worcester MA 01602 Office: 289 N Main St Leominster MA 01453

KRAYBILL, HERMAN FINK, biochemist; b. Marietta, Pa., June 27, 1914; s. Herman Berto and Charlotte Mae (Fink) K.; B.S., Franklin and Marshall Coll., 1936; M.S., U. Md., 1938, Ph.D., 1941; m. Dorothy Ramsey, Aug. 30, 1941; children—Linda (Mrs. David Asper), Cynthia (Mrs. James Huber), David R. With Swift & Co., Chgo., 1941-43; research chemist Dept. Agr., Beltsville, Md., 1948-53; research biochemist Nat. Dairy Research Lab., Balt., 1946-48, Med. Research Lab. U.S. Army, Denver, 1953-59; sr. scientist Curtiss Wright Co., Princeton, N.J., 1959-60; chief pesticide program, sci. coordinator USPHS, Washington, 1963-66; sci. coordinator FDA, 1966-72; environmental cancer coordinator; Nat. Cancer Inst.-NIH, 1972—. Instr. chemistry U. Md., 1936-38; prof. nutrition U. Denver, 1954-58; prof. biochemistry U. Colo., Boulder, 1956-59. Pres., Glenview Citizens Assn., Silver Spring, Md., 1950-51, chmn. health and sanitation, Allied Civic Group, 1950-52. Served as capt. San. Corps, U.S. Army, 1943-46. Recipient U.S. Army Med. Dept. commendation, 1954; Mexican Acad. Gerontology award, 1956; USPHS commendation, 1966; award Area Assn. Sanitarians, 1965; Distinguished Alumni award Franklin and Marshall Coll., 1976. Fellow N.Y. Acad. Scis., AAAS; mem. Am. Chem. Soc., Am. Inst. Nutrition, Soc. Toxicology, Alpha Chi Sigma. Presbyn. Club: Gaslight (Chgo.-Washington). Editor: Biological Effects of Pesticides in Mammalian Systems, 1969. Home: 14112 Chelmsford Rd Rockville MD 20853 Office: 7910 Woodmont Ave Bethesda MD 20014

KRAYBILL, RICHARD REIST, chem. engr.; b. Dover, N.H., July 31, 1920; s. Henry Reist and Mary Ruth (Grove) K.; B.Chem. Engring., Purdue U., 1942; M.S., U. Mich., 1943, Ph.D. (Am. Cyanamid fellow, Horace Rackham fellow), 1953; m. Jean Carolyn Gilbert, Aug. 8, 1945; children—Mary, Virginia, Anne, Elizabeth. Lab. asst. Am. Viscose Corp., Parkersburg, W. Va., 1941; asst. research engr. Cal. Research Corp., El Segundo, 1944-46; asst. prof. chem. engring. U. Rochester (N.Y.), 1950-55, asso. prof., 1955-67; tech. asso. Eastman Kodak Co., Rochester, 1967—; sr. lectr. Univ. Coll. Liberal and Applied Studies, U. Rochester, 1978—; cons. in field. Fellow Am. Inst. Chem. Engrs.; AAAS, Am. Soc. for Engring. Edn., Soc. of Rheology, Soc. Plastics Engrs. (tech. vols. com. 1971—; award for best paper 1964), Rochester Engring. Soc., Sigma Xi, Triangle Frat., Alpha Phi Omega, Phi Kappa Phi, Phi Lambda Gamma. Clubs: Canandaigua (N.Y.) Yacht; Brighton-Henrietta Tennis (Rochester); Bass Lake Sailing (Pentwater, Mich.). Contbr. articles to profl. jours. Home: 1289 Calkins Rd Pittsford NY 14534 Office: Kodak Park Bldg 35 Rochester NY 14650

KREBS, MARGARET ELOISE, pub. co. exec.; b. Clearfield, Pa., Apr. 20, 1927; d. Henry Louis and Delia Louise (Beahan) Krebs; Grad High sch. With Progressive Pub. Co., Inc., Clearfield, 1945—, bus. office mgr., 1956-60, bus. mgr., 1960-63, asst. to pub., 1963-69, dir., exec. v.p., 1969-77, pres., 1977—. Dir., asst. sec. Radio Sta. WDAD-AM and WQMU-FM, Indiana, Pa., 1967-78, sec., 1978—; sec., dir. Clearfield Broadcasters, Inc., 1965—; dir., exec. v.p. Danville (Pa.) News, 1969—; asst. sec. Collier Broadcasting Co., Marco Island and Naples, Fla., 1975-78, sec., 1978—; sec. Centre Broadcasters, Inc., State College, Pa. Mem. Clearfield Bus. and Profl. Women's Club (pres. 1952-53, dist. membership chmn. 1952-53). Club: Lake Glendale Sailing (sec.-treas. 1967—). Home: 526 Ogden Ave Clearfield PA 16830 Office: 206 E Locust St Clearfield PA 16830

KREBS, RICHARD LEWIS, psychologist, clergyman; b. Balt., Aug. 10, 1939; s. Hall Brillhart and Mary Louise (Schulze) K.; A.B. cum laude, Gettysburg Coll., 1961; postgrad. (Univ. fellow 1961-62, Rockefeller Bros. fellow 1961-62) Div. Sch., U. Chgo., 1961-62, Ph.D. in Clin. Psychology, 1967; postgrad. Luth. Theol. Sem. at Gettysburg, 1972-73; m. Barbara Lucille Upperco, Dec. 16, 1961; children—Carol, Randal, Laurie. USPHS trainee in clin. psychology U. Chgo., 1963-65, USPHS trainee in child devel. and child psychology, 1965-66; prin. psychologist, acting dir. Chgo. Bd. Health Div. Mental Health-S.W. Community Mental Health Center, 1966-67; staff psychologist Sinai Hosp. of Balt., 1967-68, acting asso. chief dept. psychiatry, 1969, co-dir. lay counselor tng. program, 1969-72, asso. chief and dir. outpatient services, 1969-72, staff psychologist, 1973-74; intern Ascension Evangelical Lutheran Ch., Towson, Md., 1972-73, asst. to pastor in tent making ministry, 1974—; ordained to ministry Md. Synod Luth. Ch. of Am., 1974; pvt. practice psychotherapy, Westminster, Md., 1974—; instr. Lay Sch. Theology at Gettysburg, 1974—; cons. in field. Certified psychologist, Md. Fellow Md. Psychol. Assn. (chmn. com. on liasion with other professions 1968-69). Democrat. Author: You Don't Have to Be Crazy, But It May Help; Alone Again, 1978; contbr. articles to profl. publs. Home: 8 Ridge Rd Westminster MD 21157 Office: 19 Ridge Rd Westminster MD 21157

KREEK, LOUIS FRANCIS, JR., patent lawyer; b. Washington, Aug. 24, 1928; s. Louis Francis and Esperance (Agee) K.; S.B., Mass. Inst. Tech., 1948; J.D., George Washington U., 1952; m. Gwendolyn Schoepfle, Sept. 12, 1970. Patent examiner U.S. Patent Office, Washington, 1948-53; admitted to D.C. bar, 1952, Ohio bar, 1955, N.Y. State bar, 1964, N.J. bar, 1972; patent attorney Pitts. Plate Glass Co., 1953-54, Battelle Meml. Inst., Columbus, O., 1954-56, Merck & Co., Inc., Rahway, N.J., 1956-60; div. patent counsel Air Reduction Co., Murray Hill, N.J., 1960-63; asso. firm Kenyon & Kenyon, 1963-66; patent atty. Johns-Manville Corp., 1967-68; sr. patent atty. Esso Research Engring. Co., 1968-73; patent atty. ICI Americas Inc., 1973—. Mem. Am. Bar Assn., Am., Phila. patent law assns. Episcopalian. Home: 805 Greenwood Rd Wilmington DE 19807 Office: ICI Americas Inc Wilmington DE 19897

KREEK, MARY JEANNE, physician; b. Washington; d. Louis Francis and Esperance (Agee) Kreek; B.A., Wellesley Coll., 1958; M.D., Columbia, 1962; m. Dr. Robert A. Schaefer, Jan. 24, 1970; children—Robert A., Esperance Anne. Med. research NIH, Bethesda, Md., 1957-62; intern, resident Cornell N.Y. Hosp. Med. Center, N.Y.C., 1962-65, fellow, 1965-67; instr. medicine Cornell Med. Coll., 1966-67; acad. medicine specializing in internal medicine, endocrinology, gastroenterology and clin. pharmacology, N.Y.C., 1966—; mem. staff N.Y. Hosp.-Cornell U., adj. asso. prof., affiliate physician; asst. prof. Rockefeller U., 1967-72, sr. research asso., 1972—; physician Rockefeller Hosp., 1972—. Recipient Borden Research award, 1962; Career Scientist award Health Research Council N.Y.C., 1974; Research Scientist award HEW, 1978. Mem. Am. Fedn. for Clin. research, Shakespeare Soc. of Wellesley, Am. Gastroent. Assn., Am. Assn. Study Disease of Liver, Endocrine Soc., N.Y. Acad. Scis., Internat. Narcotic Research Club, Research Soc. Alcoholism, Phi Beta Kappa, Sigma Xi. Home: 1161 York Ave New York NY 10021 Office: Rockefeller U New York NY 10021

KREIN, CATHERINE MITCHELL, broadcasting exec.; b. N.Y.C.; d. Timothy Thomas and Catherine Agnes (Lavery) Mitchell; B.S., Fordham U., 1960; student Hunter Coll. Grad. Sch. Polit. Sci., 1961-62; film certificate N.Y. U., 1974; m. Robert Edward Krein, Apr. 18, 1970. With CBS, 1963—, polit. research, writer CBS News election unit, 1969-73, editorial dir., asso. producer spl. events unit, 1973—, polit. editor, 1976—. Mem. Writers Guild Am. (shop steward 1971-73), Nat. Acad. TV Arts and Scis., Am. Acad. Polit. and Social Scis., Center Study Democratic Instns., Center Study Presidency. Catholic. Co-author: Campaign '76, 1977; author bi-monthly CBS News polit. report, 1972, CBS News, polit. newsletters, 1974, editor newsletter, 1976—, also contbr. handbooks. Home: 151-31 88th St Howard Beach NY 11414 Office: CBS News Spl Events 518 W 57th St New York City NY 10019

KREINDLER, RUTH BILGREI, interior designer; b. N.Y.C., Jan. 5, 1932; d. Sam and Hannah (Opal) Bilgrei; B.A., N.Y. U., 1952; postgrad. Columbia U. Sch. Arch., 1962-64; m. Lee Stanley Kreindler, Sept. 1, 1952; children—James Paul, Laurie Jane. Interior designer, Chappaqua, N.Y., 1958—. Chmn. coms. LWV, 1957-74; pres. Women's Guild, Temple Beth El, Chappaqua, 1974-75, mem. community archtl. selection and bldg. com.; mem. hospitality com. UN. Mem. Allied Bd. Trade. Club: Garden of Am. Home: McKesson Hill Rd Chappaqua NY 10514 Office: 99 Park Ave New York City NY 10016

KRELL, ROBERT DONALD, pharmacologist; b. Toledo, Dec. 2, 1943; s. Robert William and Helen Margaret (Zink) K.; B.S., U. Toledo, 1966; Ph.D., Ohio State U., 1972; m. Rebecca Marie Larkins, May 14, 1966; children—Melanie Lynn, Matthew Robert. Postdoctoral fellow Johns Hopkins Sch. Hygiene and Pub. Health, 1972-73; asso. sr. investigator Smith Kline and French Labs., Phila., 1973-76, sr. investigator, 1976—. Mem. Ohio Acad. Sci., AAAS, Soc. for Neurosci., Phila. Physiol. Soc., Fedn. Am. Scientists, Am. Acad. Allergy, Am. Soc. Pharmacology and Exptl. Therapeutics, Rho Chi. Republican. Contbr. articles to profl. jours. Home: 38 Thunderhead Dr Medford NJ 08055 Office: 1500 Spring Garden St Philadelphia PA 19101

KRELLEN, FRED R., san. engr.; b. N.Y.C., Oct. 7, 1924; s. Arthur L. and Anna (Rosenblum) K.; B.C.E., 1950, M.C.E., 1954; m. Rose Kfare, June 8, 1946; children—Caryn Sandra, Joshua Neil. With cons. engring. firms Malcolm Pirnie Engrs., N.Y.C., Praeger Engrs., N.Y.C.,

Alexander Potter Assos., N.Y.C., 1950-56; with N.Y.C. Dept. Sanitation, 1956—, dep. dir. engring., 1974-77, acting chief engr., 1977—. Mem. refuse compactor standards com. Nat. Sanitation Found., mem. container standards subcom. Chmn. house and catering com. Ocean Harbor Jewish Center; mem. Ocean Harbor Civic Assn. Served with Signal Corps U.S. Army, 1943-46. Mem. Am. Pub. Works Assn., Inst. Solid Wastes (chmn. research and devel. com.), U.S. Power Squadron, Nat. Rifle Assn., 8th Regt. Vets. Gun Club, Island Rifle and Pistol Club, Tau Beta Pi, Chi Epsilon. Home: 3441 Westminster Rd Oceanside NY 11572 Office: 125 Worth St New York City NY 10013

KREMER, LEWIS NORMAN, architect; b. N.Y.C., Oct. 9, 1934; s. Charles Haim and Malvina (Weinstock) K.; B.A., Marietta Coll., 1956; B.Arch., U. Pa., 1961; m. Carole M. Joscelyn, Nov. 24, 1976; children—Leona, Dardi, Mary. Draftsman, Bellante, Clauss, Miller & Nolan, Phila., 1961-63; designer firm Harbeson, Hough, Livingston & Larson, Phila., 1963-64; project designer firm Abraham Levy, Phila., 1964-65; project architect firm Leon Clemmer & Assos., Wyncote, Pa., 1965-66; head dept. architecture, mem. fine arts com. Phila. Redevel. Authority, 1966-74; pvt. practice architecture, Old Chatham, N.Y., 1974—. Vis. design critic architecture Temple U., Phila., 1968-69; adj. asst. prof. archtl. graphics and design Columbia-Greene Community Coll., 1975—. Original vol. architect Phila. Vest Pocket Park Program, 1963-66; v.p. Spruce Hill Civic Assn., 1968-69; mem. archtl. com. Phila. Hist. Commn., 1972-74; mem. Columbia County Mental Health Task Force; bd. dirs. University City Swim Club, Phila., 1965-68, So. Christian Leadership Conf., 1968-69. Mem. A.I.A., N.Y. State Assn. Architects, Nat. Assn. Housing and Redevel. Ofcls. (dir.), Soc. Archtl. Historians (book reviewer 1972—, founder, pres. Turpin Bannister chpt. 1975-78), Columbia County Hist. Soc., Rotary Internat. Home: Cotter Rd Old Chatham NY 12136 Office: Old Chatham NY 12136

KREPS, JUANITA MORRIS (MRS. CLIFTON H. KREPS, JR.), sec. commerce; b. Lynch, Ky., Jan. 11, 1921; d. Elmer M. and Cenia (Blair) Morris; A.B., Berea Coll., 1942; M.A., Duke, 1944, Ph.D., 1948; hon. degrees, Bryant Coll., 1972, U. N.C. at Chapel Hill, 1973, Denison U., 1973, Cornell Coll., 1973, U. Ky., 1975, Queens Coll., 1975; m. Clifton H. Kreps, Jr., Aug. 11, 1944; children—Sarah, Laura, Clifton. Instr. econs. Denison U., 1945-46, asst. prof., 1948-50; mem. faculty Duke, 1955-77, asso. prof., 1962-68, prof. econs., 1968-77, James B. Duke prof., 1972-77, asst. provost, 1969-72, v.p., 1973-77; U.S. sec. commerce, Washington, 1977—. Bd. dirs. N.Y. Stock Exchange. Trustee Berea Coll., Tchrs. Ins. and Annuity Assn., 1968-72, Coll. Retirement Equities Fund, 1972-77; bd. dirs. Nat. Merit Scholarship Corp., Ednl. Testing Service; mem. Nat. Commn. Manpower Policy, Nat. Manpower Policy Task Force; mem. N.C. Manpower Commn., vice chmn. bd., 1972-74. Fellow Gerontol. Soc. (v.p. 1971-72), mem. Am., So. (pres. elect) econ. assns., Am. Assn. Higher Edn. (dir. 1973-77), AAUP, AAUW, Indsl. Relations Research Assn. (exec. com.). Author: (with C.E. Ferguson) Principles of Economics, 2d rev. edit., 1965; Lifetime Allocation of Work and Income, 1971; Sex in the Marketplace: American Women at Work, 1971; co-author: Contemporary Labor Economics, 1973. Editor: Employment, Income and Retirement Problems of the Aged, 1963; Technology, Manpower and Retirement Policy, 1966. Editor, contbr: Women and the American Economy, A Look to the 1980's, 1976. Office: Dept Commerce Commerce Bldg 14th St between Constitution Ave and E St Washington DC 20230

KREPS, ROBERT WILSON, research chemist; b. Denver, Feb. 27, 1946; s. Forrest Wilson and Margaret Rose K.; student U. Denver, 1964-67; B.S., Iowa State U., 1968; m. Janet Suzanne Graves, May 16, 1968. Staff chemist Cook Paint & Varnish Co., Kansas City, Mo., 1969-70; mgr. battery tech. Farmland Industries, Inc., Kansas City, 1970-72; mgr. quality control Celotex Corp., Charleston, Ill., 1972-73; research chemist Ball Corp., Muncie, Ind., 1973-75; research chemist pigments group SCM Corp., Balt., 1976-78; materials engr. engring. materials lab. dept. Oceanic div. Westinghouse Electric Co., Annapolis, Md., 1979—. Mem. Am. Chem. Soc. (chmn. membership com. Md. sect. 1979—), Instrument Soc. Am. Home: 412-B Hidden Brook Dr Glen Burnie MD 21061 Office: Oceanic Div Westinghouse Electric Co PO Box 1488 Annapolis MD 21404

KRESGE, WHARTON RONALD, state ofcl.; b. Allentown, Pa., June 16, 1934; s. Wharton Webster and Miriam (Markley) F.; B.A., Swarthmore Coll., 1956. Chief statistics div. Bur. Statistics, Research and Planning Dept. Commerce, Commonwealth of Pa., Harrisburg, 1957—. Asst. exec. dir. Intercollegiate Conf. on Govt.; past pres., bd. govs. Players Club, Harrisburg Community Theater. Mem. Am. Statis. Assn. (chpt. treas. 1965, exec. v.p. 1966-67, pres. 1967-68), Am. Econ. Assn., Acad. Polit. Sci., Smithsonian Assos., Am. Acad. Polit. and Social Sci., Nat. Hist. Soc. Home: 5258 River Rd Harrisburg PA 17110 Office: Bur Statistics Research and Planning Room 630 B Health and Welfare Bldg Harrisburg PA 17120

KRESKY, EDWARD MORDECAI, investment banker; b. N.Y.C., Aug. 15, 1924; s. Henry and Celia (Oltarsh) K.; B.A., Cornell U., 1948; M.P.A., N.Y. U., 1950, Ph.D., 1960; m. Mary J. McAniff; children by previous marriage—Ann Cecilia, Susan Elizabeth. Pub. adminstrn. intern State N.Y., 1950-51; personnel dir. N.Y. State Rent Commn., 1951-54; asst. personnel dir. City N.Y., 1954-57; asso. dir. N.Y. State Constl. Revision Commn., 1957-61; program asso. Office of Gov. Nelson A. Rockefeller, N.Y., 1961-65; sec. Met. Transp. Authority, N.Y.C., 1965-71; gen. partner Wertheim & Co., N.Y.C., 1971—; bd. rep. Municipal Assistance Corp., N.Y.C., 1975—; dir. Security Mut. Life Ins. Co. N.Y. Mem. N.Y. State Council on Arts, 1971—; mem. Regents Commn. on Doctoral Edn. in N.Y. State, 1971-73; mem. Gov.'s Task Force on Financing Higher Edn., 1972-73; bd. dirs. N.Y. City Ballet, 1976—; chmn. adv. council Grad. Sch. Pub. Adminstrn., N.Y. U., 1977—. Served with AUS, 1943-46. Mem. Am. Polit. Sci. Assn., Regional Plan Assn., Nat. Municipal League (council mem. 1973—). Club: Wall Street (N.Y.C.). Home: 10 W 66th St New York City NY 10023 also Brushy Hill Rd Newton CT 06470 Office: Wertheim & Co 200 Park Ave New York City NY 10017

KRESS, BERNADETTE MARIE, pub. relations exec.; b. Hoboken, N.J., Sept. 18, 1953; d. George Lewis and Gertrude Katherine (Ratigan) K.; B.A., Seton Hall U., 1975; m. James Spatz, Mar. 6, 1976. Pub. relations asst. ARC, East Orange, N.J., 1974-75; creative service dir. RKO Gen. Radio, N.Y.C., 1975-76; dir. pub. relations UA-Columbia Cablevision, Oakland, N.J., 1976-78; partner, dir. pub. relations and creative services SpatzKress, Inc., Englewood, N.J., 1978—, also dir. Editor, UA-Columbia Cablevision Monthly Guide, 1977-78.

KRESS, JAMES MORRISON, govt. ofcl.; b. Mobile, Ala., July 30, 1935; s. Maurice James and Katherine Wilson (Trawick) K.; B.S. in Forestry, Auburn U., 1958; M.S. in Watershed Mgmt., U. Ariz., 1968, M.Pub. Adminstrn., 1978. Forester, U.S. Forest Service, Springerville, Ariz., 1962-65, Tucson, 1965-66, forester, hydrologist, Tempe, Ariz., 1968-69, hydrologist, Berkeley, Calif., 1969-73, Morgantown, W. Va., 1973-76; fellowship Intergovtl. Affairs Program, Harrisburg, Pa., 1976; hydrologist, conservation, research, edn. U.S. Forest Service, Dept. Agr., Broomall, Pa., 1976—. Served with U.S. Army, 1958-60. Mem. Am. Soc. Pub. Adminstrn., Soc. Am. Foresters, Am. Geophys. Union., Am. Water Resources Assn. Episcopalian. Home: 641 W Saint Andrews Dr Media PA 19063 Office: 370 Reed Rd Broomall PA 19008

KRESS, LEE BRUCE, historian; b. Balt., June 19, 1941; s. William and Rosalyn Louise (Kahn) K.; student Balt. City Coll., 1955-58; B.A., Johns Hopkins U., 1962; M.A., Columbia U., 1967, certificate in Latin Am. studies, 1967, Ph.D., 1972; m. Leslie Diane Hirshon, Dec. 22, 1968; 1 dau., Debra Lynn. Instr., Balt. Coll. Commerce, 1969-71; asst. prof. history Glassboro (N.J.) State Coll., 1973—, asst. chmn. dept., 1973—, dir. world studies, 1973-75; asst. prof. Univ. Coll., U. Md., 1970-73; adj. instr. Community Coll. Balt., 1972-74, No. Va. Community Coll., 1973; cons., adj. prof. PACE program Old Dominion U., 1975—. Columbia U. grantee, 1970-71; N.J., Com. for Humanities grantee, 1975; Glassboro State Coll. grantee, 1977-79. Mem. Am. Hist. Assn., Conf. Latin Am. History, Am. Heritage Soc., Latin Am. Studies Assn., Inter-Am. Council. Editor: (with others) International Terrorism in the Contemporary World, 1978; contbr. articles to scholarly jours. Home: 417 Barby Ln Cherry Hill NJ 08003 Office: Dept History Glassboro State Coll Glassboro NJ 08028

KRETCHMER, NORMAN, pediatrician, govt. ofcl.; b. N.Y.C., Jan. 20, 1923; s. Emanuel and Sue (Gross) K.; B.S., Cornell U., 1944; M.S., U. Minn., 1945, Ph.D., 1947; M.D., SUNY, N.Y.C., 1952; m. Muriel Reiter, Sept. 10, 1942; children—Pamela Sue, Paul Jay, Steven David. Teaching asst. U. Minn., 1944-47; asst. prof. pathology and biochemistry U. Vt., 1947-48; fellow, research asso. pathology L.I. Coll. Medicine, 1947-52; lectr. biology Bklyn. Coll., 1950-55, intern Montefiore Hosp., N.Y.C., 1952-53; faculty Cornell U. Med. Sch., N.Y.C., 1953-59, asso. prof. pediatrics, 1958-59; faculty Stanford U., Palo Alto, Calif., 1959-74, prof. pediatrics, 1959-74, exec. head dept., 1959-69, chief div. exptl. biology, 1969-72, chmn. program human biology, 1969-72, chief sect. devel. medicine, 1972, clin. prof. pediatrics, 1974; acting dir. Nat. Inst. Aging, NIH, HEW, Bethesda, Md., 1974-75, dir. Nat. Inst. Child Health and Human Devel., 1974—; mem. sci. council Inst. de la Vie, Paris, 1974—; mem. bd. U.S.A. Israel Sci. Found., 1974—; cons. in field, mem. numerous adv., sci. coms. Served with USAAF, 1942-43. Recipient Superior Service award HEW, 1977; Commonwealth Fund fellow, 1952-54, 57, 65-66; Guggenheim fellow, 1973-74; diplomate Am. Bd. Pediatrics. Fellow Am. Acad. Pediatrics (E. Mead Johnson award 1958, Borden award 1969), AAAS; mem. AAUP, Am. Chem. Soc., Am. Pediatrics Soc. (v.p.), Am. Soc. Biol. Chemists, Am. Soc. Human Genetics, Am. Soc. Clin. Investigation (council 1964-67), Assn. Am. Med. Colls., Harvey Soc., Soc. Growth and Devel., Soc. Pediatric Research (pres. 1967-68), Western Soc. Pediatric Research (pres. 1966-67), Internat. Orgn. for Study Human Devel. (pres. 1970-76), Am. Inst. Biol. Scis., Am. Soc. Clin. Investigation, Perinatal Research Soc., Internat. Pediatric Assn. (exec. com. 1974-77), Sigma Xi, Alpha Omega Alpha; hon. mem. numerous fgn. med. socs. Author, editor publs. in field. Office: NIH Bldg 31 Room 2A03 Nat Inst Child Health and Human Devel Bethesda MD 20014*

KRETKOWSKI, RONALD CHARLES, urologist; b. Bayonne, N.J., June 13, 1942; s. Charles and Mary Kretkowski; A.B., St. Peter's Coll., 1964; M.D., N.J. Coll. Medicine, 1968; m. Victoria Rucinski, Aug. 27, 1966; children—Krista, Ronald Charles, Keith, Renee. Straight surg. intern George Washington U. Hosp., Washington, 1968-69, resident in surgery, 1969-70, resident in urology, 1970-73; practice medicine specializing in urology, Riverdale, Md., 1973—; chief urology Eugene Leland Meml. Hosp., Roverdale, 1974—. Fellow A.C.S.; mem. AMA, Am. Urol. Assn., Am. Urol. Assn.-Mid Atlantic Sect., Am. Assn. Clin. Urologist. Office: 4400 Queensbury Rd Riverdale MD 20840

KREUZER, DONALD WILLIAM, dentist; b. Jacksonville, Fla., Dec. 1, 1945; s. William Joseph and Carolyn (Wallace) K.; D.M.D., U. Pa., 1970, postgrad. in periodontics, 1970-71, in periodontal prosthesis, 1970-72; staff Albert Einstein Med. Center, 1971-72, Med. Coll. Pa., 1972—; asst. prof., dir. fixed prosthetics U. Pa., Phila., 1972-75; practice dentistry, specializing in periodontics and full mouth reconstruction, Washington, 1973—; pres. Donald W. Kreuzer, D.M.D., Profl. Corp.; partner Minker Dental Lab.; asst. prof. postdoctoral periodontics, peridontal prosthesis, U. Pa. Recipient Tchr. of Yr. award U. Pa. Sch. Dental Medicine, 1972. Mem. ADA, Pa., Phila. County, D.C. dental socs., Am. Acad. Periodontology, Pa., Phila. Socs. Periodontics, Eastern Acad. Health Scis., Maimonides Dental Soc. Republican. Roman Catholic. Clubs: President's (George Washington U.). Office: Watergate Hotel 2650 Virginia Ave NW Washington DC 20037

KREVOLIN, NATHAN, educator; b. New Haven, Nov. 21, 1927; s. Abraham and Rebecca (Rich) K.; Asso. Sci., Quinnipiac Coll., 1948; B.S., Central Conn. State Coll., 1950; M.A., So. Conn. State Coll., 1952; Profl. diploma, U. Conn., 1956, Ph.D., 1960; m. Lois Ann Silverman, July 3, 1955; children—Clay, Adam. Instr., U. Conn. Sch. Bus., Storrs, 1950-51; tchr. bus. dept. Troup Jr. High Sch., New Haven, 1951-54, Hillhouse High Sch., New Haven, 1954-55; chmn. bus. dept. King Philip Jr. High Sch., West Hartford, Conn., 1955-66; asso. prof. bus. edn. dept. Central Conn. State Coll., New Britain, 1966-73, prof., 1973—. Adviser pub. schs., West Hartford, Hartford, Meriden, Waterbury, New Britain, Bloomfield, Newington, Plainville, 1966—; lectr. bus. edn. Voice of Am. Broadcasts, 1967, other stas., 1967-68. Served with AUS, 1946-47. Mem. N.E.A., Conn. Edn. Assn., Nat., Eastern, Conn. bus. edn. assns., Am. Assn. U. Profs., Phi Delta Kappa, Delta Pi Epsilon, Kappa Delta Pi. Author: Art Typing, 1962; (with Louis C. Nanassy) Junior High Timed Writings, 1963; Timed Writings for Teen-agers, 1963; (with Alan C. Lloyd) You Learn to Type!, 1966; (with others) Personal Typing, 1970, (with others) Webster's Secretarial Handbook, 1976; Gregg Office Job Training Program—Typist Training Manual and Resource Materials, 1972. Contbr. articles to profl. jours., books. Home: 40 Osage Rd West Hartford CT 06117 Office: Business Education Dept Central Conn State Coll New Britain CT 06050

KREVSKY, SEYMOUR, electronics engr.; b. Elizabeth, N.J., July 2, 1920; s. Louis J. and Rose Z.; B.S.E.E., N.J. Inst. Tech., 1942, M.S.E.E., 1950; m. Gladys Sara Welt, Jan. 9, 1944; children—Ell Miocene, Joan Cambria. Asso. engr. Coles Signal Lab., 1946-52; chief antenna and direction finding sect. Counter-measures br. Evans Signal Lab., Ft. Monmouth, N.J., 1952-59; sr. project mem. tech. staff RCA, N.Y.C., 1959-68; asst. dep. project mgr. Def. Communications Systems, Army for Research and Devel., Ft. Monmouth, 1968—. Served with Air Tech. Service, U.S. Army, 1944-46; ATO. Recipient Dr. Harold A. Zahl meml. achievement award Armed Forces Communications Electronics Assn., 1977; registered profl. engr., N.J. Fellow AAAS; mem. IEEE (sr.)(chmn. N.J. coast sect. 1972-73), Armed Forces Communications and Electronics Assn. (pres. Ft. Monmouth chpt. 1977-78), Am. Radio Relay League (Life), Quarter Century Wireless Assn. (life). Jewish War Vets. Am. (comdr. post 515 1975-76). Club: B'nai B'rith. Contbr. articles on antennas, propagation, other topics to profl. publs. Home: 69 Judith Rd Little Silver NJ 07739 Office: US Army Communications Systems Agy Squier Hall Fort Monmouth NJ 07703

KRIDER, JAMES WHITNEY, JR., social services adminstr., counselor; Johnstown, Pa., Dec. 5, 1936; s. James Whitney and Dorothy Louise (Schnabel) K.; B.S. cum laude, U. Pitts., 1960, M.S.W., 1963; m. Carol Ann Majcher, Dec. 28, 1960. Caseworker, Family Service and Children's Aid Soc. of Warren County (Pa.), 1963-66, exec. dir., 1966—; faculty field instr. Sch. Social Welfare, State U. N.Y. at Buffalo, 1968-69; lectr. in field. Chmn., Warren County Health and Welfare Council, 1967-68; pres. Warren County Hot Line, Inc., 1971-72, 73-74. NIMH grantee, 1962-63. Mem. Family Service Assn. Am., Warren Acad. Scis. (past chmn.), Acad. Certified Social Workers, Nat. Assn. Social Workers, Phi Theta Kappa. Republican. Mem. Christian Ch. Club: Town (Jamestown, N.Y.). Contbr. articles to profl. jours. Home: 36 Glade Ave Warren PA 16365 Office: 8 Pennsylvania Ave W Warren PA 16365

KRIEBEL, CHARLES HOSEY, educator; b. Tarrytown, N.Y., Nov. 6, 1933; s. Nelson Sterly and Elizabeth Grace (Hosey) K.; B.S. in Econs., U. Pa., 1959, M.A. in Statistics, 1961; Ph.D. in Indsl. Mgmt. (Ford found. fellow), Mass. Inst. Tech., 1964; m. Jan Lilly McAuley, June 7, 1961; children—Paul Charles, Susan, James McAuley, Carl Nelson. Instr. Wharton Sch. Finance U. Pa., Phila., 1959-61; asst. prof. Sloan Sch. Mass. Inst. Tech., Cambridge, 1963-64; asst. prof. grad. sch. Indsl. Adminstrn. Carnegie-Mellon U., Pitts., 1964-67, asso. prof., 1967-70, prof., 1970—. Cons. McKinsey & Co., Inc., N.Y.C., 1964—, Rand Corp., Santa Monica, Cal., Gulf Oil Corp., Pitts., Imperial Tobacco, Montreal, Que., Can., Mellon Bank, N.A., Pitts., Jones and Laughlin Steel Co., Inc., Pitts., Weyerhauser, Tacoma, IBM, N.Y.C., Western Elec., Princeton, N.J., Gen. Reins. Corp., N.Y.C., Industrikonsulent I.K.O., Copenhagen, Denmark; rep. Nat. Acad. Scis. Fulbright-Hays adviser, 1965—. Served to sgt. Signal Corps. U.S. Army, 1954-56. Fellow AAAS (mem. nominating com. 1973-75); mem. Assn. Computing Machinery (nat. lectr.), Inst. Mgmt. Scis. (dept. editor Management Science), Econometric Soc., Operations Research Soc. Am., Am. Econ. Assn., Am. Statis. Assn., Delta Kappa Epsilon. Editorial bd. Internat. Fedn. Information Processing, 1971—, editorial cons. Prentice-Hall, Inc., 1967—. Contbr. numerous articles to profl. jours. Home: 108 Silent Run Rd Fox Chapel Pittsburgh PA 15238 Office: Graduate Sch Indsl Adminstrn Carnegie-Mellon University Pittsburgh PA 15213

KRIEG, ADRIAN HENRY, mfg., wholesale co. exec., internat. real estate exec.; b. St. Gallen, Switzerland, Oct. 23, 1938; s. Victor J. and Gertrude (Altheer) K.; student U. Mexico at San Miguel de Allende, 1957-58, Elmhurst Coll., 1959-60; m. Audrey Ann Jones, Oct. 23, 1968; children—Ivan Victor, Alastair William. Came to U.S., 1952, naturalized 1957. From sec. to exec. v.p. V.J. Kreig Inc., N.Y.C., 1960-62; founder Widder Corp., Mamaroneck, N.Y., merged with Victor J. Krieg, Inc., 1962, then pres., chief exec. officer; sec., treas., Rovic Mfg. Co., Inc., Mamaroneck, 1976—; sec., treas., mgr. Depot Plaza Corp., Mamaroneck, 1965—; sec., gen. mgr. Nugget Realty Co. of Conn., Inc., 1977—. Served with AUS, 1960-62; Germany. Recipient Advt. Efficiency award Thomas Pub. Co., 1975, Sci. in Engring. award Soc. Mfg. Engrs., 1976. Mem. Soc. Mfg. Engrs. (founder, chpt. 216, vice-chmn. 1976), Am. Welding Soc., Am. Importers Assn. (internat. fin. advisory council 1976), Am. Supply & Machine Mfg. Assns., Mfg. Jewelers and Silversmiths of Am. Mason (32 deg., K.T.). Contbr. articles to profl. jours. Patentee in field. Notary public. Home: 119 Maple Vale Dr Woodbridge CT 06525 Office: Great Hill Rd Naugatuck CT 06770

KRIEG, RICHARD EDWARD, JR., bacteriologist; b. N.Y.C., Oct. 16, 1942; s. Richard Edward and Ruth Elizabeth (Klein) K.; B.S., Rutgers U., 1964; M.S., Iowa State U., 1966, Ph.D., 1968; m. Monica Clair Musgrove, June 25, 1966; children—Anne Marie, Michael Edward, Eric Robin. Research microbiologist Sch. Aerospace Medicine, Brooks AFB, Tex., 1968-70, biomed. analyst, aerospace med. div., 1970-73; research microbiologist Armed Forces Inst. Pathology, Washington, 1973-74, chief bacteriology br., 1974—; faculty U. Md., 1973—. Fellow Am. Acad. Microbiology; mem. Am. Soc. Microbiology, AAAS, Soc. Armed Forces Med. Lab. Scientists (sec.), Nat. Registry Microbiologist (specialist, editor LOOP), AAU, Sigma Xi. Roman Catholic. Clubs: Road Runners, Walter Reed Army Med. Center Running (v.p.) (Washington). Contbr. articles in field to profl. jours. Home: 13014 Turkey Branch Pkwy Rockville MD 20853 Office: AFIP-CPF-M Armed Forces Inst Pathology Washington DC 20306

KRIEG, SAUL, pub. relations exec.; b. Chgo., Sept. 15, 1917; s. Abraham and Beatrice (Beichman) K.; student Coll. City N.Y., 1939; m. Helen Cohen, Jan. 25, 1941; children—Bonnie Feldman, Andrew G., Robin Nevins. Publicist, Twentieth Century Fox Films, 1939-41, Paramount Pictures, 1942-44; publicity dir. Phillips H. Lord Prodns., 1943-46; established Saul Krieg Assos., Inc., N.Y.C., 1946. Recipient award Am. Cancer Soc., 1948; award, Conf. Christians and Jews, 1949. Mem. Navy League U.S. Club: Friars. Author: (cookbooks) The Spirit of Grand Cuisine, 1969; The New Spirit of Grand Cuisine, 1971; W.C. Fields Guide for the Drinking Man, 1972; The Alpha and Omega of Greek Cooking, 1973; What's Cooking in Portugal, 1974; The Spirited Taste of Italy, 1975. Columnist on Wine N.Y. Post, 1974—. Home: 875 Park Ave New York City NY 10021

KRIEGER, ABBOTT JOEL, neurosurgeon; b. N.Y.C., Apr. 29, 1939; B.A., Bklyn. Coll., 1959; M.D., N.Y. Med. Coll., 1963; D.M.S. in Pharmacology, Columbia U., 1970; m. Marsha Tomback; children—Lloyd, Lara, Dana. Intern in surgery Montefiore Hosp., N.Y.C., 1963-64; resident in surgery, then in neuropathology Montefiore Hosp. and Med. Center, 1964-65; resident in neurol. surgery Albert Einstein Coll. Medicine, 1966-67, 70-71, in neurology, 1968; chief neurosurgery VA Hosp., Pitts., 1971-73; asst. prof. neurosurgery U. Pitts. Sch. Medicine, 1971-73; chief neurosurgery VA Hosp., E. Orange, N.J., 1974—; prof., dir. neurosurgery N.J. Med. Sch., Coll. Medicine and Dentistry, Newark, 1974—; cons. United Hosps. Newark, Beth Israel, St. Michael's hosps. (all Newark), 1975—. Served with USMCR, 1956-62. Diplomate Am. Bd. Neurol. Surgery. Fellow A.C.S.; mem. Congress Neurol. Surgeons, Research Soc. Neurol. Surgeons, Am. Assn. Neurol. Surgeons, N.J. Neurosurg. Soc. Contbr. articles to med. jours. Home: 49 Nottingham Rd Short Hills NJ 07078 Office: 100 Bergen St Newark NJ 07103

KRIEGER, CARL, mfg. co. exec.; b. N.Y.C., Mar. 16, 1928; s. Harry and Sally (Kuhlman) K.; B.Mech. Engring., Coll. City N.Y., 1950; m. Iris Berlin, July 11, 1948; children—Howard, Sandra. Mech. designer Munston Mfg. Corp., N.Y.C., 1948-50; asst. project engr. Presto Recordings Corp., Paramus, N.J., 1951-54; with CanRad-Hanovia, Inc., Newark, 1954—, exec. v.p., 1972—, pres., 1974—. Club: Masons. Home: 153 Kennedy Ct Paramus NJ 07652 Office: 100 Chestnut St Newark NJ 07104

KRIEGER, PAUL DAVID, physician; b. N.Y.C., Oct. 10, 1942; s. Jerome and Ruth K.; B.S., State U. N.Y., Binghamton, 1964; M.D., State U. N.Y., Downstate Med. Center, 1968; children—Allyson, Daniel. Intern, resident in obstetrics and gynecology Mt. Sinai Hosp., N.Y.C., 1968-73; practice medicine specializing in obstetrics and gynecology, Greenwich, Conn., from 1975, now New Milford, Conn.; mem. staff Greenwich Hosp. Served with M.C., U.S. Army, 1973-75. Mem. Am. Coll. Obstetricians and Gynecologists, Am. Fertility Soc., Am. Assn. Gynecol. Laparoscopists, Greenwich Hosp. Assn., Greenwich Health Assn. Office: 56 Danbury Rd New Milford CT 06776

KRIHAK, MARY KATHLEEN LESKANIC, freelance writer; b. Jersey City, May 7, 1948; d. Michael Bernard and Clemaline Catherine (Donnelly) Leskanic; B.A., Kean Coll. N.J., 1974; m. William Krihak, Oct. 13, 1968; children—Michael, Jonathan. Substitute tchr. Cranford (N.J.) Pub. Schs., 1977—; polit. speech writer, Kenilworth, N.J., 1976—. Mem. Am. Hist. Assn. Democrat. Roman Catholic. Home: 366 Boulevard Kenilworth NJ 07033

KRING, JAMES BURTON, entomologist; b. Monett, Mo., May 25, 1921; s. Jesse Burton and Mildred Theresa (Schofield) K.; B.S., Rockhurst Coll., 1947; M.S.; Kans. State U., 1948, Ph.D., 1952; m. Louise Maltby McNellis, May 31, 1947; children—Marilyn, Stephen J., Michael D., Anne M., Timothy J. With Kans. State U., 1950-51; entomologist Conn. Agrl. Expt. Sta., New Haven, 1951-77; mem. grad. faculty U. Conn., Storrs, 1956—, also prof., head dept. entomology U. Mass., Amherst, 1977—. Mem. Wallingford (Conn.) Conservation Commn., 1970-77. Served to ensign USNR, 1940-45; PTO. Mem. Intersoc. Consortium for Plant Protection (exec. com. 1978—), Entomol. Soc. Am. (pres. 1978-79), Entomol. Soc. Can., AAAS, Royal Entomol. Soc. London. Contbr. articles to profl. jours. and popular publs. Home: 21 Maplewood Dr Amherst MA 01002 Office: Fernald Hall Dept of Entomology University of Massachusetts Amherst MA 01003

KRISTAL, MARK BENNETT, educator; b. N.Y.C., Apr. 19, 1944; s. Emanuel and Helen B. (Goldin) K.; B.A., Rutgers U., 1965; M.S., Kan. State U., 1970, Ph.D., 1971; m. Tova Iskovits, Oct. 8, 1967; 1 dau., Morgan. Probation officer, Newark, N.J., 1967; postdoctoral fellow Jackson Lab., Bar Harbor, Maine, 1971-73; asst. prof. psychology State U. N.Y., Buffalo, 1973-78, asso. prof., 1978—. Sci. adviser to bd. dirs. Buffalo Zoo. NIMH grantee, 1974-75; NSF grantee, 1976-79. Mem. Eastern Psychol. Assn. (program com. 1978—), Soc. Neurosci., Behavior Genetics Assn., Animal Behavior Soc., AAAS, N.Y. Acad. Scis., AAUP. Contbr. articles to profl. jours. Home: 122 Old Farm Circle Williamsville NY 14221 Office: Dept Psychology State U NY Buffalo NY 14226

KRISTENSEN, ALFRED EMERY, orthopedic surgeon; b. Bklyn., Sept. 18, 1942; s. Alfred Thorvald and Emma Sofie (Eilertsen) K.; B.S., St. John's U., 1964; M.D., N.Y. Med. Coll., 1968; m. Mary Ellen Spiegel, June 6, 1964; children—Sandra, Daniel, Deborah, Erik. Intern, Gen. Rose Meml. Hosp., Denver, 1968-69; resident in surgery L.I. Jewish Med. Center, New Hyde Park, N.Y., 1969-70; resident in orthopedics Ind. U. Med. Center, Indpls., 1972-75; practice medicine specializing in orthopedic surgery, Glens Falls, N.Y., 1975—; mem. staff Glens Falls Hosp. Served with M.C., USN, 1970-72. Fellow A.C.S., Am. Coll. Orthopedic Surgeons; mem. Am. Fracture Assn. (Henry W. Meyerding Meml. Essay contest prize 1975). Office: 81 Park St Glens Falls NY 12801

KRISTIC, NORMAN, air force officer; b. Detroit, Apr. 29, 1933; s. George W. and Milka W. K.; B.S., Wayne State U., 1956; postgrad. Indsl. Coll. Armed Forces, 1976, Air War Coll., 1977; M.S. in Counseling and Guidance, Troy State U., 1977; m. Marilyn Kay Bos, July 31, 1959; children—Norman, Stephan James. Commd. 2d lt. U.S. Air Force, 1956, advanced through grades to col., 1978; ops. officer 4671st Ground Observer Corps, Grand Rapids, Mich., 1958-59; aircraft comdr. McCoy AFB, Fla., 1960-63; air ops. officer, Vietnam, 1963-64; flight examiner McGuire AFB, N.J., 1964-67; wing chief Airlift Control Element, Frankfurt, W. Ger., 1967-72; flight examiner, chief pilot C5A, Dover AFB, Del., 1972-76, squadron comdr., 1977-. Vice pres., Little League, Felton, Del., 1977—; troop com. chmn. Boy Scouts Am., Felton, 1977—. Decorated Meritorious Service medal, Commendation medal, Air medal, Vietnam Valor medal. Mem. Am. Personnel and Guidance Assn., Am. Rehab. Counseling Assn., Air Force Assn., Comml. Pilots Assn., Nat. Rifle Assn., U.S. Coast Guard Aux. Mem. Eastern Orthodox Ch. Club: Mil. Officers. Home: RD 3 Box 543 Felton DE 19943 Office: Comdr 436 TRNSS Dover AFB DE 19901

KRIVKA, HERBERT ANTHONY, naval systems engr., b. N.Y.C., Feb. 27, 1925; s. Anton F. and Anni (Sypta) K.; student Coll. City N.Y., 1942-43; B.M.E., Yale U., 1947; postgrad. exec. devel. program Cornell U., 1967; m. Naomi Louise Nunnally, Nov. 14, 1953; children—Patrice D., Michael A. With sci. dept. Cox and Stevens, Naval Architects, N.Y.C., 1942-43; instrumentation process control engr. Am. Cyanamid, N.Y.C., 1947-48, Kellex Corp., N.Y.C. and Hanford, Wash., 1948-54, head inst. engring. div., Oak Ridge, 1952-55; with Vitro Labs. div. Automation Industries, Inc., Silver Spring, Md., 1955—, head Polaris FBM test dept., 1962-66, head Polaris Logistics support dept., 1966-70, head Polaris Systems coordination dept., 1970-74, mgr. ship systems engring. br., dir. support programs Naval Ship Engring. Center, mgr. anti-submarine warfare programs, 1974-77, v.p. ship systems br., 1977—; mem. nat. advisory bd. Am. Security Council. Served with USNR, 1943-51. Recipient Commemorative Apollo 8 medallion award NASA, 1969; Apollo Achievement award 1st Moon Landing, 1969. Mem. Am. Def. Preparedness Assn., Am. Soc. Naval Engrs., Instrument Soc. Am. Democrat. Roman Catholic. Clubs: Elks, White Sands Yacht and Country (Patuxent River, Md.); Yale (Washington). Contbr. tech. articles to profl. jours. Office: Automation Industries Vitro Labs Div 14000 Georgia Ave Silver Spring MD 20910

KRIZEK, THOMAS JOSEPH, physician, educator; b. Milw., Dec. 1, 1932; s. Chester Francis and Elizabeth Ann (Flynn) K.; B.S., Marquette U., 1954, M.D., 1957; M.A. (hon.), Yale U., 1974; certificate in health systems mgmt. Harvard, 1975; m. Claudette Reid; children—Thomas Joseph, Kelly Ann, Mary Ellen. Intern, Univ. Hosps. of Cleve., 1957-58, resident in gen. surgery, 1958-59, 61-64, research fellow in plastic surgery, 1964, resident in plastic surgery, 1964-66; asst. prof. plastic surgery Johns Hopkins, 1966-68, U. Md., 1966-68; chief div. plastic surgery Balt. City Hosps., 1966-68; asso. prof. Yale, 1968-73, prof., 1973-78, dir. trauma program, 1974-77, asso. dean for grad. and continuing med. edn., 1975-77; chief sect. plastic and reconstructive surgery Yale-New Haven Med. Center, 1968-78, asso. chief staff for grad. and continuing med. edn., 1975-77; prof., chief plastic surgery Columbia-Presbyn. Med. Center, 1978—; cons. VA Hosp., West Haven, Conn., 1968-78. Served to lt. M.C., USNR, 1959-68. Diplomate Am. Bd. Surgery, Am. Bd. Plastic Surgery. Fellow A.C.S. (pres. Conn. chpt.); mem. Assn. Acad. Surgery, Am. Assn. Plastic Surgery (treas.), Am. (sec. plastic surgery program dirs. group 1975-77, pres. 1977-79), New Eng. (exec. com., pres. 1976-77) socs. plastic and reconstructive surgeons, Plastic Surgery Research Council (chmn. 1974-75), Am. Soc. Aesthetic Plastic Surgery, Am. Soc. Maxillofacial Surgeons (mem. sci. program com.), Assn. Am. Med. Colls., Am. Burn Assn., Internat. Soc. Burn Injuries, Soc. Head and Neck Surgeons, Am. Assn. Surgery Trauma, Am. Assn. Automotive Medicine, Am. Geriatrics Soc., AAAS, New Haven County, Am. med. assns., Conn. State Med. Soc., N.Y. Acad. Scis., Am. Soc. Microbiology, Am. Trauma Soc., So. New Eng. Hand Soc., Am. Assn. Hand Surgery, Sigma Xi, Alpha Omega Alpha. Republican. Roman Catholic. Clubs: Pine Orchard Yacht and Country, Harvard, K.C. Author: (with R. Touloukian) Diagnosis and Early Management of Trauma Emergencies: A Manual for the Emergency Service, 1974; editor: Basic Science in Plastic Surgery, 1976; contbr. articles to profl. jours. Office: Columbia-Presbyterian Med Center 161 Fort Washington Ave New York NY 10032

KRIZINOFSKI, RONALD JOSEPH, assn. exec.; b. N.Y.C., Oct. 2, 1936; s. Anthony Roger and Edna (Gurska) K.; student U. Buffalo, 1958-60; B.A., Harper Coll., State U. N.Y. at Binghamton, 1967; m. Marian Theresa Lesko, Sept. 2, 1961. Office mgr., Spaulding Bakeries, Binghamton, 1962-69; asst. to v.p., treas., sec. Broome Delaware & Otsego County Med. Soc., Binghamton, 1968-69, exec. dir., 1969—; adj. lectr. State U. N.Y. at Binghamton, 1975. Sec., treas., exec. dir. Broome County Med. Bur., 1969—. Bd. dirs. Broome County Heart Assn., 1969—, Cancer Soc., 1969—; exec. dir. Broome Found. for Med. Care, 1972—, Found. of Broome County Med. Soc., 1969—; bd. dirs. Empire Med. Polit. Action Com., 1975—, Sch. Mgmt.-Mgmt. Game, State U. N.Y. at Binghamton, 1975—. Served with USAF, 1954-58. Fellow, Off-Campus Coll., State U. N.Y. at Binghamton, 1976. Mem. A.M.A. (asso.), Am. Assn. Med. Soc. Execs. Home: 4149 Cheryl Dr Binghamton NY 13903 Office: 4500 Old Vestal Rd Box 897 Binghamton NY 13902

KROCHMAL, CHARLES FRANCIS, mgmt. analyst; b. Dansville, N.Y., Aug. 7, 1952; s. Casimer Herman and Eleanor (Kucmierz) K.; B.S., Rensselaer Poly. Inst., 1974, M.B.A., 1975; m. Kristine Louise Sandholdt, June 14, 1975. Student mgmt. engr. Samaritan Hosp., Troy, N.Y., 1974-75; mgmt. analyst trainee VA Hosp., East Orange, N.J., 1975-76; mgmt. engr., 1976-78; mgmt. analyst, computer assisted systems staff VA Central Office, Washington, 1978—. Recipient Eagle Scout award Boy Scouts Am., 1966, William T. Hornaday Conservation award, 1969. Mem. Health Mgmt. Systems Soc., IEEE Computer Soc., Fed. ADP Users Group, Rensselaer Poly. Inst. Alumni Assn., Nat. Eagle Scout Assn., Alpha Phi Omega. Club: Dansville Area Coin, Am. Contract Bridge League. Home: 11202 Dewey Rd Kensington MD 20795 Office: 810 Vermont Ave NW Washington DC 20420

KROEBER, C. KENT, personnel exec.; b. Pelham, N.Y., Oct. 14, 1939; s. Clement Ausbury and Helen M. (Roche) K.; B.S., N.Y. U., 1962; m. Sharon Lee, June 8, 1963; children—Jennifer Lynne, Jonathan Kent, Suzanne Lee, Timothy Beyer. With F. Miller Asso., N.Y.C., 1961-62, McCall Corp., N.Y.C., 1963-66; with The Interpublic Group of Cos., Inc., 1966—, compensation mgr., 1966-67, personnel mgr., 1968, v.p., dir. personnel McCann-Erickson Internat., 1968-71, dir. personnel Interpublic Internat., 1972, v.p., dir. personnel McCann-Erickson Worldwide, also v.p. personnel devel. Interpublic, 1973-75, staff v.p. personnel Interpublic, 1975-78, v.p. human resources, 1978—. Mem. Internat. Platform Assn. Home: 52 Malcolm Rd Mahwah NJ 07430 Office: 1271 Ave of the Americas New York City NY 10020

KROL, JOHN CARDINAL, archbishop; b. Cleve., Oct. 26, 1910; s. John and Anna (Pietruszka) K.; grad. St. Mary's Sem., Cleve., 1937; J.C.B., Gregorian U., Rome, 1939, J.C.L., 1940; J.C.D., Cath. U. Am., 1942; LL.D., John Carroll U., 1955; Ph.D., La Salle Coll., 1961; LL.D., St. Joseph Coll., 1961, St. John U., N.Y., 1964, Coll. Steubenville, 1967, Lycoming Meth. Coll., 1966, Temple U., 1964, Bellarmine-Ursuline Coll., 1968, Drexel U., 1970; D.S.T., Villanova U., 1961; L.H.D., Alliance Coll., 1967, Chestnut Hill Coll., Phila., 1975, Holy Family Coll., Phila., 1977, Thomas More Coll., Ft. Mitchell, Ky., 1978; D.Theol., U. Lublin (Poland), 1977; D.D., Susquehanna U., 1970. Ordained priest Roman Catholic Ch., 1937, pvt. chamberlain, 1945, domestic prelate, 1951; parish asst., 1937-38; prof. Diocesan Sem., also chaplain Jennings Home for Aged, 1942-43; vice chancellor Cleve. Diocese, 1943-51, chancellor of diocese, 1951-53, promoter of justice, 1951-53; consecrated bishop, 1953; auxiliary bishop to bishop of Cleve., also vicar gen. Diocese of Cleve.. 1953-61; archbishop of Phila., 1961—; elevated to Sacred Coll. for Cardinals, 1967; undersec. II Vatican Council, 1962-65; mem. Pontifical Commn. Communications Media, 1964-69; chmn. Nat. Cath. Office for Radio and TV, 1963-64, Nat. Cath. Office for Motion Pictures, Cath. Communications Found., 1965-70; chmn. Pa. Cath. Conf., 1961—; v.p. Nat. Conf. Cath. Bishops, 1966-71, pres., 1972-74; mem. Pontifical Commn. for Mass Media Communications, 1966-70; mem. Sacred Congregation for Evangelization of Nations, 1967-72, Sacred Congregation for Oriental Ch., 1967—, Sacred Congregation for Doctrine of Faith, 1973-78; mem. President's Nat. Citizens Com. Community Relations. Trustee Cath. U. Am., Washington, 1961-71, Nat. Shrine of Immaculate Conception, Washington, Cath. League for Religious Assistance to Poland; pres. Center for Applied Research in Apostolate, 1967-70. Decorated comdr. of cross Order of Merit (Italy), Nat. Order Republic of Chad; recipient gold medal Paderewski Found., 1961; Nat. Human Relations award NCCJ, 1968; Father Sourin award Cath. Philopatrian Inst., 1967; John Wesley Ecumenical award Old St George's Meth. Ch., 1967; Phila. Freedom medal, 1978. Mem. Canon Law Soc. Am. (pres. 1948-49). Home: 5700 City Ave Philadelphia PA 19131 Office: 222 N 17th St Philadelphia PA 19103

KROLL, ARNOLD HOWARD, investment banker; b. N.Y.C., Jan. 20, 1935; s. Henry and Jean (Brecker) K.; B.A., Dartmouth, 1956; LL.B., Harvard, 1959; m. Lois Ann Montana, Aug. 11, 1965; children—Alison Cordelia, Luisa Clayton, Heather Todd. Admitted to N.Y. bar, 1959; asso. Lehman Bros., N.Y.C., 1960-70; 1st v.p. Dean Witter & Co., Inc., N.Y.C., 1970-72; partner C.E. Unterberg, Towbin Co., N.Y.C., 1972-77, L.F. Rothschild, Unterberg, Towbin, 1977—. Trustee Lexington Sch. for Deaf, N.Y.C., 1972—. Served to 1st lt., arty. U.S. Army, 1959-60. Clubs: Century Country (Purchase, N.Y.); India House, University (N.Y.C.). Home: 4 E 72d St New York City NY 10021 Office: 55 Water St New York City NY 10041

KROLL, JOHN LEON, athletic equipment co. exec.; b. Buffalo, Sept. 5, 1925; s. Hammond and Sylvia (Heinberger) K.; B.S. in Phys. Edn. and Recreation, N.Y. U., 1948, M.A. in Health Edn., 1948; postgrad. U. Conn., 1953-55; m. Evelyn Maher, Dec. 29, 1966; 1 dau., Sharon Ann Kroll; stepchildren—John Brennan, James Brennan. Tchr. phys. edn. N.Y.C. Bd. Edn., 1948-49; dir. phys. edn. Waterford (Conn.) Pub. Schs., 1949-51; founder Jayfro Corp., mfr. athletic equipment, Waterford, 1953, now pres., chmn. bd.; co-founder Nat. Athletic Mfrs. Catalog Distbg. Service Corp., Harbor City, Calif., 1973, owner, 1975—; pub. Jayfro Periscope, 1973—; dir. N. Am. Recreation Convertibles, Westport, Conn., Snitz Mfg. Corp., East Troy, Wis., Arrow Systems, Inc., Lawrence, Mass.; cons., bd. advisers Gymnastic Supply Co., Inc., San Pedro, Calif., 1975—. Chmn. promotional programs com. U.S. Com. Sports for Israel, Inc., N.Y.C., 1975—; bd. dirs. Tennis Found. N.Am., 1973—, Athletic Inst. Chgo., 1975—; hon. bd. dirs. Flatbush Boys Club, Bklyn., 1975—. Served with USN, 1943-46, U.S. Army, 1951-53. Mem. Nat. Sch. Supply and Equipment Assn. (dir., exec. com., chmn. conv. and exhibits com. 1974, mem. legis. com.), Edn. Industries Assn. (dir., co-editor monthly newsletter, co-chmn. pub. relations com. 1973-75), Exhibitors Assn. of AAHPER (dir.), Nat. Intramural-Recreational Sports Assn. (hon. life), Nat. Sporting Goods Assn. (sustaining mem.), Sporting Goods Mfrs. Assn. (chmn. membership com. 1975), So. New Eng. C. of C. Clubs: Jockey (Las Vegas); Lambs (N.Y.C.); La Coquille (Palm Beach, Fla.); Mystic (Conn.) Seaport; Racquet, Rotary (Waterford). Patentee in field. Contbr. articles to profl. and trade jours. Home: 535 Pequot Ave New London CT 06320 Office: PO Box 400 Waterford CT 06385

KROLL, MARTIN NEIL, lawyer; b. N.Y.C., Nov. 30, 1937; s. Jacob and Ruth (Strassman) K.; A.B., Cornell U., 1959; postgrad. Columbia, 1960; J.D., U. Pa., 1963; m. Rita Evangeline Grossman, Aug. 14, 1964; children—Spencer Daniel, Jonathan Emanuel, Evan Michael. Admitted to N.Y. bar, 1963; with firm Phillips, Nizer, Benjamin, Krim & Ballon, N.Y.C., 1963, Kroll, Baron & Postmantur, N.Y.C., 1964—; pres. Can-Am Chem. Ltd., N.Y.C., exec. v.p., dir. Jahn's Since 1897, Inc., N.Y.C. Pres., Solomon Schechter Day Sch. Nassau County, 1972-74. Recipient Jewish Edn. award United Synagogue Am., 1973. Mem. Am., N.Y. State, Nassau County bar assns., Fed. Bar Council, Jewish Lawyers Assn. Nassau County (pres.), Tau Epsilon Phi. Jewish religion (trustee temple). Clubs: Glen Head Golf and Country, Manhattan. Home: 15 Fir Dr Roslyn NY 11576 Office: 600 Fifth Ave New York City NY 10020

KROLL, NATHAN, radio, TV producer, dir.; b. N.Y.C., Nov. 5, 1911; s. Samuel Louis and Sarah (Silverstein) K.; student (fellow) Juillard Sch. Music, 1929; m. Lucy Rosengardt, Nov. 5, 1939 (div. 1974); 1 son, Stephen. Concert violinist, 1925-32; condr., composer; producer, dir. various radio-TV films including Casals Master Class Series, 1961, Heifetz and Segovia Master Class Series, films, 1966, Helen Hayes-Portrait of an Am. Actress, Guns of August, Martha Graham films; producer Lillian Gish and the Movies, tour U.S. and Can., 1971-72, film Third Internat. Choral Festival Lincoln Center Performing Arts, 1973; creator, producer Who's Afraid of Opera?, 1973-74; producer, dir. film for Nat. Endowment for the Humanities (with John Hope Franklin) Racial Equality in America, 1976. Lectr. film prodn. for TV, 1968-73. Address: 201 E 77th St New York City NY 10021

KROLL, PAUL FRANCIS, ednl. adminstr.; b. Worcester, Mass., Aug. 25, 1931; B.S. in Social Sci., Suffolk U., Boston, 1957; M.Ed. in Elementary Adminstrn., State Coll., Worcester, 1962; m. Mary Ellen Kroll; children—Kathleen M., Sue Ellen M. Tchr., prin., coordinator, adminstrv. asst. West Boylston (Mass.) pub. schs., 1957—. Mem. Mass. Elementary Prins. Assn., Mass. Assn. for Supervision and Curriculum Devel. (dir, corr. sec.), Mass. Assn. Sch. Supr. Club: Rotary (pres. 1976). Home: Box 31 Sterling Junction MA 01565 Office: Edwards Sch West Boylston MA 01583

KRON, WILLIAM GODSHALL, ednl. adminstr.; b. N.Y.C., Jan. 29, 1942; s. William Laudan and Marion (Godshall) K.; B.S., Coll. William and Mary, 1963; M.S. in Secondary Edn., Hofstra U., 1964; certificate of advanced studies Wesleyan U., Middletown, Conn., 1972; m. Gail Frances Weisenburger, Sept. 4, 1965; children—Kari Marie, Robert Woellner. Tchr. chemistry and physics The Forum Sch., Southbury, Conn., 1964-66; chmn. dept. sci. Avon (Conn.) Old Farms Sch., 1966—, on summer sabbatical, 1974, 76, diving coach; prodn. and tech. adviser to WAOF Radio Sta.; pres. CVISSTA, sci. tchr's. orgn., 1974. NSF grantee, 1969-73. Mem. Nat. Sci. Tchrs. Assn., Assn. Am. Physics Tchrs. Episcopalian. Home and Office: Avon Old Farms Sch Avon CT 06001

KRONENTHAL, RICHARD LEONARD, chemist; b. N.Y.C., Oct. 6, 1928; s. Robert and Florence (Sichel) K.; B.S., Bklyn. Coll., 1951; Ph.D., Poly. Inst. Bklyn., 1955; m. Beverly Rose Greenberg, Dec. 18, 1949; children—David Roy, Susan Harriet. Sr. project chemist Colgate Palmolive Co., Jersey City, 1954-57; sr. scientist Ethicon, Inc., Somerville, N.J., 1957-60, sect. head, 1960-63, mgr. organic and polymer chemistry dept., 1963-67, asso. dir. research, 1967-71, dir. research, 1972—; instr. Poly. Inst. Bklyn., 1958-64. Mem. Am. Chem. Soc., Chem. Soc. London, AAAS, Am. Inst. Chemists, N.Y. Acad. Scis., Assn. Advancement Med. Instrumentation, Am. Soc. for Artificial Internal Organs, Am. Soc. for Testing and Materials, Sigma Xi. Research in field. Home: 33 Garwood Rd Fair Lawn NJ 07410 Office: Ethicon Inc Route 22 Somerville NJ 08876

KRONFELD, ARTHUR ISIAH, veterinarian; b. Bklyn., Feb. 9, 1934; s. Max and Edith (Feiner) K.; student Rutgers U., 1952-55; D.V.M., Cornell U., Ithaca, N.Y., 1959; m. Mona Arlene Ross, June 29, 1958; children—Sheryl Leslie, Lauren Gail. Veterinarian, Animal Med. Center, Hempstead, N.Y., 1959-60, Great Neck (N.Y.) Animal Hosp., 1960-63; veterinarian, owner, dir. Port Washington (N.Y.) Animal Hosp., 1963—; cons., veterinarian North Shore Animal League, 1963—, dir., 1964-67; cons., veterinarian Town of North Hempstead (N.Y.) Animal Shelter, 1973—. Mem. Am., N.Y. State (exec. bd.), L.I. (N.Y.) (pres. 1972-73) vet. med. assns., Am. Animal Hosp. Assn. Jewish. Club: Glen Head (N.Y.) Country. Contbr. articles to Jour. Vet. Medicine, Small Animal Clinician. Home: 7 Brook Ln Manhasset NY 11030 Office: 16 Willowdale Ave Port Washington NY 11050

KRONFELD, FRED NORMAN, mfg. co. exec.; b. N.Y.C., June 20, 1929; s. Max and Edith (Feiner) K.; B.S. in Econs., U. Pa., 1951; M.B.A., U. Fla., 1952; m. Zelda Barbara Bernstein, Feb. 8, 1953; children—Gary Harris, Andrew Steven. Accountant, Pan Am. World Airways, Long Island City, N.Y., 1952-53; with Spirite Industries Inc. (formerly Spirite Mfg. Co. Inc.), N.Y.C., 1955—, partner, 1958—, also exec. v.p., treas.; dir. Syl-Bee Mfg. Co. Inc.; N.Y. adv. bd. Banco Popular. Mem. N.Y.C. men's spl. gifts com. Am. Cancer Soc. Served to 2d lt. USAF, 1952-53, with U.S. Army, 1953-55. Mem. Corset and Brassiere Mfrs. Assn. (dir.), Beta Alpha Psi, Tau Epsilon Phi. Address: 84 Buckingham Rd Tenafly NJ 07670 Office: 150 S Dean St Englewood NJ 07631

KRONSTADT, NANCY ALICE, coll. ofcl.; b. Washington, Dec. 8, 1951; d. Nathan and Marion (Howorth) K.; B.A. in Sociology, U. Md., 1973; M.Ed. in Coll. Counseling and Student Personnel Adminstrn., U. Del., 1975. Hall dir. U. Del., 1973-74, counselor, summers 1974, 75, asst. to coordinator, 1974-75; area coordinator Ithaca Coll., 1975-78, asst. dir. for housing ops., 1978—, instr. in helping relationships, 1974—; campus liaison Alcohol Info. Center, 1973-74. Recipient Gold award Job Corps, 1971. Mem. Am. Coll. Personnel Assn., Am. Personnel, Guidance Assn., Nat. Assn. Student Personnel Adminstrs., Student Personnel Assn. N.Y. State. Office: Office Residential Life Ithaca Coll Ithaca NY 14850

KROPCZYNSKI, THADDEUS JOHN, educator; b. Plainfield, N.J., July 7, 1913; s. Joseph and Julia (Kowalski) K.; B.S., N.Y. U., 1938, M.A., 1948, postgrad., 1964-65; postgrad. Rutgers U., 1946; m. Marion Catherine Jefferies, Apr. 28, 1945; children—Pamela Julia, Kim Ann Jefferies. Dir. music, pub. schs., Bound Brook, N.J., 1940-42, Englewood, N.J., 1946-71; dir. music and art, pub. schs., Bayonne, N.J., 1971—. Dir. choral music Englewood Cliffs (N.J.) Coll., 1969-71; dir. nursing choruses Englewood Hosp., 1952-77, Holy Name Hosp., Teaneck, N.J., 1954-75; dir. Englewood Cliffs Youth Orch., 1963-65, Jewish Community Club Chorus, Englewood, 1951-62. Served to capt. USAAF, 1942-46. Decorated Bronze Star medal; Order Brit. Empire; recipient Distinguished Service award UN, 1965. Mem. Music Educators Nat. Conf., Nat. Bandmasters Assn., Nat. Sch. Orch. Assn., N.J. Music Edn. Assn., Hudson County Music Educators Assn., Internat. Platform Assn., Nat. Art Edn. Assn., Assn. Secondary Sch. Suprs. and Dept. Heads of N.J., Phi Mu Alpha, Sinfonia. Republican. Roman Catholic. Rotarian (pres. 1969). Club: Englewood. Composer, arranger choral and instrumental selections. Home: 25 Whitewood Rd Tenafly NJ 07670 Office: Adminstrn Bldg Av A and 29th St Bayonne Public Schs Bayonne NJ 07002

KROSNICK, ARTHUR, physician; b. Trenton, N.J., Mar. 11, 1923; s. Samuel and Rose (Cohen) K.; A.B., Temple U., 1944, M.D., 1950; m. Evelyn Rieber, Dec. 31, 1945; children—Jon A., Jody A. Intern, Mercer Med. Center, Trenton, 1950-51; resident in internal medicine Presbyn. Hosp., Phila., 1951-52, Grad. Hosp. of U. Pa., Phila., 1952-54; practice medicine specializing in diabetes, Trenton, 1954—; sr. pub. health physician N.J. State Dept. Health, 1954-77; chmn. dept. medicine Mercer Med. Center, Trenton, 1977—; cons. diabetes and arthritis program USPHS, 1962-70; med. cons. Diabetes in the News, Ames Co., 1976—; clin. asso. prof. dept. community medicine Rutgers Med. Sch., Piscataway, N.J., 1977—; cons. to subcom. edn. Nat. Commn. on Diabetes, 1975-76. Served to lt. (j.g.), M.C., USN, 1941-45. Diplomate Am. Bd. Internal Medicine. Fellow Coll. Physicians Phila.; mem. Med. Soc. N.J. (dir. 1975—, editor Jour. 1973—), A.C.P., Am. Diabetes Assn. (chmn. com. on publs. 1977—), Am. Soc. Internal Medicine, Acad. Medicine N.J. (dir. 1975—), AMA, Mercer County Component Med. Soc. Republican. Jewish. Contbr. articles on diabetes to med. jours. and chpts. on internal medicine to med. books; contbr. numerous editorials on medicine and health edn. to profl. jours.; producer ednl. films on medicine. Home: Warwick Rd Morrisville PA 19067 Office: 416 Bellevue Ave Suite 406 Trenton NJ 08618

KROUSE, JOHN HOBART, psychologist; b. Pitts., June 29, 1954; s. John Frederick and Phyllis Jean (Rhey) K.; B.F.A., Carnegie-Mellon U., 1975; M.A., U. Pitts., 1976. Rehab. counselor Goodwill Industries of Pitts., 1975-76; rehab. specialist Turtle Creek Valley Mental Health/Mental Retardation, Inc., Braddock, Pa., 1976-77; NIMH fellow in clin. psychology U. Rochester, N.Y., 1977—. Regional coordinator McGovern for Pres., 1972. Mem. Am. Assn. Mental Deficiency, Am. Personnel and Guidance Assn., Am., Pa. psychol. assns., Am. Rehab. Counseling Assn. Democrat. Lutheran. Clubs: Masons (32 deg.), Shriners. Home: 466-D Clay Rd Rochester NY 14623 Office: Psychology Dept U Rochester Rochester NY 14627

KRUEGER, RICHARD GUSTAVE, sci. instrument co. exec.; b. Phila., June 24, 1928; s. Fred Emil and Edna Elizabeth (Effinger) K.; student Drexel U., 1947, B.S. in Chem. Engring., 1956; student Temple U., 1947-50; children by previous marriage—David Allen, Paul Stewart, Mark James, Ruth Ann. Profl. musician, 1947-65; indsl. hygienist Electric Storage Battery, Phila., 1951-54; sales engr. Foxboro Co., Bala Cynwyd, Pa., 1954-58; sales engr. Am. Instrument Co., Phila., 1958-65, regional sales mgr., Collingswood, N.J., 1971-75; market mgr. chem. process industries Leeds & Northrup Co., North Wales, Pa., 1965-69; market mgr. process control Barber Colman Co., Rockford, Ill., 1969-71; mktg. mgr. Flexitallic Gasket Co., Inc., Camden, N.J., 1975—. Publicity mgr. Lansdale (Pa.) Pop Warner Midget Football, 1966-70; active Boy Scouts Am., 1966-71; mem. Ambler Symphony Orch., 1952-60, Willow Grove Am. Legion Concert Band, 1952-60. Mem. Am. Chem. Soc. (sr.), Instrument Soc. Am. (sr., v.p. Phila. sect. 1971), Am. Inst. Chem. Engrs. (sr.), Am. Petroleum Inst. (subcom. on instrumentation 1967-72). Lutheran (asst. supt. Sunday Sch. 1956-60, asst. chmn. Christian edn. 1963-65). Asso. editor Analysis Instrument Div.-ISA Ann. Procs., 1968-69. Address: Apt 8-C Chapel Ave and Bellows Lane Cherry Hill NJ 08034 Office: 5 Linden St Camden NJ

KRUG, HARRY EVERISTUS PETER, JR., nuclear engr.; b. Kearny, N.J., Aug. 1, 1932; s. Harry E. and Helen (Miliski) K.; B.S., U.S. Merchant Marine Acad., 1955; M.S. in Nuclear Engring., N.Y. U., 1961; m. Madonna Eileen Krug, Nov. 23, 1977; children by previous marriage—Kirk Stanley, Karen Helen, Lynn Allison. Officer-in-charge of vessel, United Fruit Co., 1955-56; nuclear engr. George G. Sharp, Inc., N.Y.C., 1958-60; nuclear engr. systems evaluation sect. United Nuclear Corp., White Plains, N.Y., 1961; nuclear engr. reactor analysis sect. of Westinghouse Astro-Nuclear Lab., Pitts., 1961-63, fellow engr. physics and mathematics group Comml. Atomic Power Devel., Pitts., 1963-69; v.p. and gen. mgr. Nuclear Computations, Inc., Pitts., 1969-70; prin. nuclear engr. Jersey Nuclear Co., Richland, Wash., 1970-71; industry mgr. Atomic/Nuclear Industries, Control Data Corp., Mpls., 1971-73; supr. of nuclear engring. group Ill. Power Co., Decatur, 1973-74; project mgr. U.S. Nuclear Regulatory Commn., NRC, Bethesda, Md., 1974-76, nuclear engr., 1977—; comml. pilot. Served with USN, 1956-58. Registered profl. engr., Calif. Mem. Am. Nuclear Soc. (pres. upper mid-west chpt. 1972-73), Am. Soc. of Naval Engrs., Am. Defense Preparedness Assn., Aircraft Owners and Pilots Assn. Roman Catholic. Contbr. articles on nuclear reactor design to profl. jours. Home: 12203 Braxfield Ct Rockville MD 20852 Office: 7920 Norfolk St Bethesda MD 20014

KRUGER, JEFFREY SONNY, concert impressario, music pub., record mfg. co. exec.; b. London, Eng., Apr. 19, 1931; s. Samuel and Thela (Shafron) K.; B.Sc., London U., 1949; m. René Fifer, Oct. 12, 1958; children—Howard, Loraine. Came to U.S., 1957. Sales exec. Columbia Pictures, London, 1948-50; south coast sales mgr. Eros Films, London, 1950-52; owner music leisure co., 1952; pres. Ember Records Internat. Ltd.; pres. Ember Enterprises, Inc.; dir. Sparta Florida Music, Flamingo Film Products, Kenwood Music Inc., Hillbrow Music Inc., Ember Concert Promotions, Ltd., Ember Film Distbrs., Ember Mgmt. Agy. Ltd. Club: Masons. Composer: Jingle Bell Rock; No Tears; Riviera Carnival, numerous others. Home: Flamingo Hill Brow Hove Sussex BN3 6QG England Office: Carlton Tower Pl Sloane St London England also 747 3d Ave 27th Floor New York NY 10017

KRUGER, SELDON MARTIN, educator; b. N.Y.C., June 30, 1930; s. Irving Martin and Sara (Rosenberg) K.; A.B., Rutgers U., 1952, postgrad., 1953-56; postgrad. U. Lancaster, 1967-68; m. Ruth Silvera, June 17, 1956; children—Helen, Nancy. Research asst. in polit. sci. Rutgers U., New Brunswick, N.J., 1954-55, World Peace fellow in polit. sci., 1955-56, instr. history and polit sci., 1956-58, asst. instr. Douglas Coll., 1957-58; asso. prof. social sci. State U.N.Y. Agrl. and Tech. Coll., Delhi, 1958-61, asst. prof., head dept., 1961-65, prof., chmn. div. arts and sci., 1965-72, prof., dean acad. affairs, 1972-76, v.p. acad. affairs, 1976-78, acting pres., 1978—. Mem. youth adv. council Mid-Century White House Conf. on Children and Youth, 1949-50; accredited observer UN, 1952-54; v.p. Catskill Center for Conservation and Devel., 1969; mem. exec. com. Erpf Catskill Cultural Center, 1975—, pres., 1977-78. Mem. Am. Polit. Sci. Assn. Am., Assn. Jr. and Community Colls., Am. Assn. for Higher Edn., Am. Field Service, Pi Sigma Alpha. Home: 14 Clinton St Delhi NY 13753 Office: Bush Hall State UNY Agrl and Tech Coll Delhi NY 13753

KRUGMAN, ABRAHAM ARTHUR, orthodontist; b. Bialystok, Poland, Aug. 23, 1913 (parents Am. citizens); s. Sam and Bertha (Trachimovski) K.; student Bklyn. Coll., 1931-34; D.D.S., N.Y.U., 1938; certificate Dewey Sch. Orthodontia, 1948; student Orthodontic Workshop-S.J. Lewis, 1955, Northwestern U., 1956, Columbia, 1961, Tweed Found. Orthodontic Research, 1961, U. Pa., 1962, orthodontics Loyola U., 1962, St. Barnabas Med. Center, 1972; m. Estelle Rockower, Dec. 26, 1948; children—Carole Ann, Michele Pam. Practice dentistry, Bklyn., 1938-42, 1946-48, practice orthodontics, 1948—. Served to maj., Dental Corps. U.S. Army, 1942-46. Decorated Bronze Star. Diplomate Am. Bd. Orthodontics. Mem. Am. Dental Assn., Am. Assn. Orthodontists. Jewish. Home: 68 Cedar Dr Great Neck NY 11021 Office: 1845 Ocean Ave Brooklyn NY 11230

KRUPER, JOHN GERALD, sales and mktg. exec.; b. Carbondale, Pa., Feb. 10, 1949; s. John Joseph and Evelyn (Bernosky) K.; B.S. in Bus. Adminstrn. and Accounting, U. Scranton, 1970; postgrad. State U. N.Y., 1974; m. Renee Jane Shugg, Aug. 4, 1973; 1 son, Kevin John. Store mgr. Endicott Johnson Corp., Schenectady, 1970-71, retail mdse. distbr., Endicott, N.Y., 1971-72, asst. mdse. buyer, 1972-74, full line mdse. buyer, 1974-76, dir. advt. and sales, 1976—. Served with U.S. Army, 1970. Home: 3601 Matthews Dr Endwell NY 13760 Office: 1100 E Main St Endicott NY 13760

KRUPPA, J(OHN) RUSSELL, educator; b. Leetsdale, Pa., Mar. 29, 1929; s. George Richard and Catherine S. (Shafer) K.; B.S. in Indsl. Arts Edn., California (Pa.) State Coll., 1951; M.Ed., Pa. State U., 1956, Ed.D., 1968; m. Maryagnes Gardner, June 26, 1954; children—Richard Ross, Diane Louise. Head tchr. indsl. arts Bald Eagle Nittany Sch. Dist., Mill Hall, Pa., 1953-61; asst. prof. State U. N.Y., Oswego, 1961-64; prof., chmn. indsl. arts dept., Trenton (N.J.) State Coll., 1964—. Ednl. cons. to comml. and ednl. instns.; field center dir. Hamilton Twp., Trenton, New Brunswick Indsl. Arts Curriculum Project, 1968-71; dir. Curriculum Devel. Grant, Bur. Handicapped, State of N.J., 1972-73. Trustee, v.p. Mercer Christian Acad., 1974—. Served with U.S. Army, 1951-53. Mem. Am., N.J., Mercer County (v.p. 1969) indsl. arts assns., Nat. Assn. for Indsl. Tchr. Educators, Nat., N.J. edn. assns., Am. Council for Indsl. Arts Tchr. Edn., N.J. Vocat. Edn. Assn., Indsl. Arts Edn. Assn. N.J., Phi Delta Kappa, Iota Lambda Sigma, Epsilon Phi Tau, Phi Sigma Pi. Conservative Baptist (deacon, elder, trustee, Bible sch. tchr., chmn. bd. Christian edn., presently deacon, usher). Contbr. articles on indsl. arts to profl. publs. Home: 25 Delaware Ave Trenton NJ 08628 Office: Armstrong Hall Trenton State College Trenton NJ 08625

KRUSOS, DENIS ANGELO, communications co. exec.; b. N.Y.C., Oct. 27, 1927; s. Angelo and Mary (Razzi) K.; B.S., City Coll. N.Y., 1949; M.S., Newark Coll. Engring., 1951; J.D., St. Johns U., 1968; m. Catherine Bezas, July 30, 1955; children—Peri Denise, Denis Zachary. Sr. engr. Arma div. Am. Bosch Arma Corp., 1956-60; devel. engr. missile div. Republic Aviation & Fairchild Engring. Corp., 1952-56; founder, officer, dir. Automation Labs., Inc., Mineola, N.Y., 1955-65; founder, chmn. bd., dir. Integrated Electronics Corp., Huntington Sta., N.Y., 1966—; pres., dir. Panafax Corp., 1977—; dir. Visual Scis., Inc., Data Services Corp. Served with U.S. Army, 1946-47. Mem. Am., New York, Suffolk County bar assns., IEEE. Home: Middle Hollow Rd Lloyd Harbor NY 11743 Office: 900 Walt Whitman Rd Huntington Station NY 11746

KRYSZAK, WAYNE DOUGLAS, business librarian; b. Canton, Ohio, Nov. 9, 1936; s. Peter John and Grace (Vogt) K.; B.S. in Bus. Adminstrn., Kent State U., 1958, M.L.S., 1965; m. Sarah Jane Bauer, Nov. 22, 1958; children—Peter John, Douglas Michael. Reader's adviser D.C. Pub. Library, 1961-64, 65-68, chief bus. div., 1968—; asst. br. librarian, bus. and tech. divs. Akron (Ohio) Pub. Library, 1964-65. Bd. commrs. Town of Cottage City, Md., 1967—, sec., police commr., 1967—. Served with U.S. Army, 1960-61. Mem. Am., D.C. library assns., Md., Prince George's County municipal leagues, Municipal Police Assn. Prince George's County. Author: The Small Business Index, 1978. Contbr. to Not of One Mind, 1976; also articles to profl. jours. Book reviewer for Library Jour. Home: 3308 Mill Br Pl Mitchelleville MD 20716 Office: 901 G St NW Washington DC 20001

KRZYS, RICHARD ANDREW, educator; b. Cleve.; s. Michael and Helen Krzys; B.S.S. cum laude, John Carroll U., Cleve., 1956; M.A., U. Denver, 1958, N.Mex. State U., 1958; Ph.D., Case Western Res. U., 1965. Asst. prof. Fla. State U., 1965-67; vis. asso. prof. State U. N.Y., Geneseo, summer 1967; asso. prof. L.I. U., 1967-69, asso. prof., asst. dir. Sch. Library Service Dalhousie U., Halifax, N.S., Can., 1969-70; prof. library sci., dir. Internat. Library Info. Center, U. Pitts., 1971—. Fulbright scholar, Bogota, Colombia, 1960-61. Mem. ALA, Fla., Canadian library assns. Co-author: A History of Education for Librarianship in Colombia, 1969. Contbr. articles to profl. jours. Home: 5619 Kentucky Ave Pittsburgh PA 15232 Office: 410 LIS Bldg 135 N Bellefield St Pittsburgh PA 15260

KSZEPKA, JOSEPH ANTHONY, ins. and real estate broker; b. Three Rivers, Mass., Oct. 6, 1931; s. Joseph and Helena (Sakowski) K.; student Alliance Coll., 1951, U. Mass., 1952; m. Frances H. Dragon, May 11, 1957; children—Louise, Paul, Jane, Joan, Irene. Owner ins. and real estate agy., broker, Three Rivers, 1956—; trustee Palmer Savs. Bank. Clk. Three Rivers Fire Dist., 1965—. Notary pub., 1960—; justice of peace, 1973—; mem. Palmer Bd. Health, 1957-62; trustee Wing Meml. Hosp.; mem. Kosciuszko Found. Served with U.S. Army, 1953-55. Named man of year, Three Rivers C. of C., 1972. Licensed pub. accountant. Mem. Mass. Ins. Agts. and Brokers Assn., New Eng. Mut. Ins. Agts. Assn., Three Rivers C. of C. (treas. 1960—, sec.-treas. 1966—), Amvets, Polish Nat. Alliance, Polish Roman Cath. Union, St. Stanislaus Polish Lyceum (past pres.). Club: Rotarian. Address: 398 Main St Three Rivers MA 01080

KU, ROBERT TIEN-HUNG, physicist; b. Shanghai, China, Jan. 19, 1947; s. Charles Chia-Kuan and Ko-Fang H. (Hsieh) K.; came to U.S., 1962; B.S., U. Ill., 1967, M.S., 1968, Ph.D., 1973; m. Janet Jen-I Lee, Aug. 21, 1971; children—Roger, Brian. Mem. tech. staff Lincoln Lab., Mass. Inst. Tech., Lexington, 1973—. Served with Signal Corps, U.S. Army, 1973. Mem. IEEE, Optical Soc. Am., Am. Phys. Soc. Contbr. articles in field to sci. jours. Home: 132 Wright Rd Concord MA 01742

KU, Y.H., educator; b. Wusih, Kiangsu, China, Dec. 24, 1902; s. Ken Ming Ku and Ching-Su Wang; S.B., Mass. Inst. Tech., 1925, S.M., 1926, Sc.D., 1928; M.A., LL.D., U. Pa.; m. Wei-Zing Wang, Apr. 1, 1929; children—Wei-Lien, Wei-Ching, Wei-Wen (Mrs. Chi-Liang Hsieh), Walter, Wei-Chung, Victor, Anna (Mrs. Y. Kai Lau). Came to U.S., 1950. Prof. elec. engring., head dept. Chekiang U., China, 1929-30; dean engring. Central U., China, 1931-32, pres., 1944-45; dean engring. Tsing Hua U., China, 1932-37; vice minister Ministry Edn., Republic of China, 1938-44; edn. commr., Shanghai, 1945-47; vis. prof. Mass. Inst. Tech., 1950-52, prof. U. Pa., 1952-71, emeritus prof., 1972—; cons. Gen. Electric Co., RCA. Recipient gold medal Ministry Edn., Rep. of China; Pro Mundi Beneficio medal Brazilian Acad. Humanities, 1975. Fellow Academia Sinica, Inst. I.E.E.E. (recipient Lamme Gold Medal award 1972). Instn. Elec. Engrs. (London); mem. Am. Soc. Engring. Edn., Internat. Union Theoretical and Applied Mechanics (mem. gen. assembly), Chinese Inst. Elec. Engrs. (recipient Gold Medal award 1972, past pres.), Sigma Xi, Eta Kappa Nu, Phi Tau Phi. Author: Analysis and Control of Nonlinear Systems, 1958; Electric Energy Conversion, 1959; Transient Circuit Analysis, 1961; Analysis and Control of Linear Systems, 1962; Collected Scientific Papers, 1972; also Collected Works (poems, plays, novels, essays in Chinese), 1961; Woodcutter's Song, 1963; Pine Wind, 1964; Lotus Song, 1966; Lofty Mountains, 1968; The Liang River, 1970; The Hui Spring, 1971; The Si-Shan Mountain, 1972; The Great Lake, 1973; 500 Irregular Poems, 1972; 1000 Regular Poems, 1973; 360 Recent Poems, 1976; History of Chinese Chan (Zen) Masters, 1976; History of Japanese Zen Masters, 1977; History of Zen (In English), 1978. Home: Apt 22G 1420 Locust St Philadelphia PA 19102 Office: 200 S 33d St Philadelphia PA 19104

KUBIC, WILLIAM LOUIS, engring. co. exec.; b. Jacobs Creek, Pa., Jan. 19, 1924; s. Louis Joseph and Susan Anne (Kestella) K.; B.S.C.E., U. Pitts.; m. Roberta Mologne, Dec. 28, 1949; children—Charles, Mary, William, Rebecca, Roban, Michael. Engr., Dravo Corp., Neville Island, Pa., 1945-47, Eichleay Corp., Pitts., 1947-49, Moore Metal Mfg. Co., Greensburg, Pa., 1949-59; pres. Kubic Engring. Co., Greensburg, 1959—. Served to capt. USAAF, 1942-45. Licensed profl. engr., Pa., Ohio, Md., W.Va.; licensed landscape architect, Pa. Mem. Nat., Pa. socs. profl. engrs., Soc. Am. Mil. Engrs., Am. Arbitration Soc., Nat. Fedn. Ind. Bus. Club: Elks. Home: 1114 Mount Pleasant Rd Greensburg PA 15601 Office: 450 S Main St Greensburg PA 15601

KUBIK, EDWARD STANISLAUS, chemist; b. Wilbraham, Mass., Oct. 18, 1934; s. Sebastian J. and Blanche (Kwiecinzka) K.; B.S., Holy Cross Coll., 1955, M.S., 1956; postgrad. U. Mass., 1970; m. Jeanne R. Duquette, Nov. 15, 1958; children—E. Stanley, Sharon, Gregory, Geralynn, Rosalie. Research chemist John H. Breck, Inc., Springfield, Mass., 1956-65, analytical chemist, 1960-65; asst. research dir. Tampax Corp., Palmer, Mass., 1965-67; analytical group leader DeBell & Richardson, Inc., Hazardville, Conn., 1967-75; analytical sect. mgr. Loctite Corp., Newington, Conn., 1975—; cons. in field. Mem. fin. com. Town of Wilbraham, 1972-77, mem. personnel bd., 1976-77. Served with U.S. Army, 1957. Mem. Am. Chem. Soc., Soc. Applied Spectroscopy. Democrat. Roman Catholic. Club: Polish Am. Veterans (Mass. state comdr. 1976). Home: 12 Glenn Dr Wilbraham MA 01095 Office: 705 N Mountain Rd Newington CT 06111

KUBOTA, JOE, soil scientist; b. Stockton, Calif.; s. Kiichi and Yae (Ametani) K.; B.S., U. Calif., Berkeley, 1942; M.S., U. Nebr., 1944; Ph.D., U. Wis., 1948; m. Mildred Elizabeth Phares, Feb. 18, 1950; children—Robert Joe, John Stuart, Randall Keith, Carolyn June. Soil scientist, U.S. Soil Conservation Service, Cornell U., Ithaca, N.Y., 1954—, asso. prof., 1966-78, prof., 1978—. dirs. Ithaca Youth Hockey Assns., 1969-72. Served with AUS, 1944-46. Fellow AAAS, Japan Soc. Promotion Sci. (sr.); mem. Soc. Environ. Geochemistry and Health (councilor 1973-76), AAAS, Soil Sci. Soc. Am., Am. Soc. Agronomy, Internat., Brit. soil sci. socs., Sigma Xi. Club: Rotary. Home: 203 Texas Ln Ithaca NY 14850 Office: US Plant Soil and Nutrition Lab Cornell Univ Ithaca NY 14853

KUCHTA, RONALD ANDREW, mus. ofcl.; b. Lackawanna, N.Y., June 23, 1935; s. Andrew and Clara May (Barnes) K.; B.A., Kenyon Coll., 1958; M.A., Western Res. U., 1961; m. Sique Stoll, Nov. 3, 1969. Apprentice, Cleve. Mus. Art, 1961; curator Chrysler Art Mus., Provincetown, Mass., 1962-68, Santa Barbara (Calif.) Mus. Art, 1968-74; dir. Everson Mus., Syracuse, N.Y., 1974—; adj. prof. museology Syracuse U., 1974—; cons. Instituto de Antropologia Historia y Arte, Guatemala. Served with 18th Inf., AUS, 1959-60. Author exhbn. catologs: Modern Mexican Painting, 1970; Tantra, 1970; Drawings from the Collection of Santa Barbara Museum of Art, 1970; Interior Vision, European Abstract Expressionism, 1945-60, 1972; 15 Abstract Artists—Los Angeles, 1973; Animals in African Art, 1973; Lila Katzen, Sculpture & Site, 1975; Polish Constructivists, 1975; Marcia Marcus Paintings, 1975; The Art Deco Environment, 1976; New Works in Clay, 1976; Francisco Zuñiga-Sculpture and Drawings, 1977; Provincetown Painters, 1977. Home: 109 Euclid Terr Syracuse NY 13210 Office: 401 Harrison St Syracuse NY 13202

KUCZALA, ZDZISLAW JERRY WALTER, hosp. adminstr.; b. Hahn, Germany, Sept. 24, 1948; s. Walter Jacob and Kathryna Ann (Mahinich) K.; came to U.S., 1949, naturalized, 1964; B.S., So. Conn. State Coll., 1970; postgrad. State U. N.Y., 1976—; m. Paulette Ann Arsenault, Nov. 21, 1970. Asso. in research Lab. of Internal Medicine, Yale Med. Sch., 1971-74; supr. chemistry and radioimmunoassay labs. dept. lab. medicine Binghamton (N.Y.) Gen. Hosp., 1974—, instr. lab. med. technology, 1974—. Mem. AAAS, Am. Assn. Clin. Chemistry, Clin. Radioassay Soc. Republican. Roman Catholic. Contbr. articles in field to profl. jours. Office: Mitchell Ave Binghamton NY 13903

KUDON, HERMAN ZVEE, optometrist; b. Plattsburg, N.Y., Apr. 11, 1915; s. Benjamin and Dorothy (Goldblatt) K.; student Union Coll., 1932-34; B.S., Columbia U., 1936; O.D., Mass. Coll. Optometry, 1960; m. Frances Drooz, Oct. 13, 1942; children—Henry Kenneth, Sandra Lynn (Mrs. Howard Newell). Pvt. practice optometry, Albany, N.Y., 1938—. Mem. Albany Jewish Community Council. Fellow Am. Acad. Optometry (diplomate contact lens sect.); mem. Eastern N.Y. Optometric Soc. (pres. 1958-60), N.Y. State Optometric Assn. (dir. 1958-60), Multi State Vision Conservation Inst. (pres. 1961-62), Am. Optometric Assn., Am. Optometric Found., Masonic Trustees Assn. (pres. 1955), Alpha Mu Sigma. Mason (master 1954, trustee 1971). Mem. Zionist Orgn. Am. Mem. B'nai B'rith. Club: Shaker Ridge Country (bd. govs. 1973). Home and Office: 24 Rosemont St Albany NY 12203

KUEBLER, BERNARD DONALD, med. device co. exec.; b. S.I., N.Y., Sept. 23, 1934; s. Charles Gottlieb and Margaret Mary (Freeland) K.; B.S., Wagner Coll., 1962; m. Joan Elizabeth Forsyth, Dec. 24, 1953; children—Mary Beth, Caroline Joan, Charles Donald, Bernard Donald. Instr. S.I. Community Coll., 1958-62, instr. mech. engring., 1962-65; with C.R. Bard Inc., Murray Hill, N.J., 1965—, dir. tech. services, 1973—; dir. thermoplastics Sci., Stirling, N.J. Served with USMC, 1953-56. Mem. ASTM, Am. Soc. Chem. Engrs., Am. Assn. Textile Chemists and Colorists. Roman Catholic. Home: 20 Lurline Dr West Millington NJ 07946 Office: C R Bard Inc 111 Spring St Murray Hill NJ 07974

KUECHLE, JAMES EDWARD, health adminstr.; b. Buffalo, Apr. 19, 1927; s. Julius Otto and Gertrude Anna (Schwab) K.; B.A., U. Buffalo, 1951; diploma hosp. adminstrn. U. Toronto, 1966; m. Carolyn Elnora Snyder, Oct. 6, 1956; children—Robert, Karen, Peggy, Joan, Cathy. Planning cons. Hosp. Rev. and Planning Council, Buffalo, 1967-69; hosp. adminstrn. cons. Erie County Health Dept., Buffalo, 1969-73; exec. dir. Mt. View Hosp., Lockport, N.Y., 1973-76; dep. commr. social services, adminstr. Erie County Home and Infirmary, Alden, N.Y., 1976—; lectr. telelecture series Regional Med. Program, 1971-72; mem. instl. care com. Comprehensive Planning Council, 1973-74; adv. council nursing dept. Niagara Community Coll., Buffalo, 1974-76. Asst. scoutmaster, Merit badge counselor local Boy Scouts Am., 1970-74, asst. dist. commr. Amherst dist., 1976—. Served with USNR, 1945-46. Mem. Am. Coll. Hosp. Adminstrs., Am., Western N.Y. (chmn. long term care com. 1973—) hosp. assns., Western N.Y. Assn. Homes for Aging (sec., dir.). Club: Tonawanda Sportsman's. Home: 195 Heim Rd Williamsville NY 14221 Office: 11580 Walden Ave Alden NY 14004

KUEHN, PAUL GERHARD, surgeon; b. West Hartford, Conn., Dec. 15, 1922; s. Edward Ray and Marie (Ross) K.; B.S., Trinity Coll., 1948; M.D., U. Rochester, 1952; m. Barbara Strider Kuehn, Apr. 19, 1952; children—Katherine, Stephen, Suzanne, Carolyn. Surg. fellow Genesee Hosp., Rochester, N.Y., 1951; intern Hartford (Conn.) Hosp., 1952, asst. med. resident, 1952-53, surg. resident, chief resident, 1953-58; Nat. Cancer Inst. fellow Meml. Hosp., N.Y.C.,

1958-61, sr. resident surgery, 1958-61; research fellow in exptl. surgery Sloan-Kettering, 1961-62; sr. surgeon Hartford Hosp.; cons. surgeon McCook Hosp., Hartford; mem. courtesy surgery staff St. Francis Hosp., Hartford; cons. surgeon Rocky Hill (Conn.) Vets. Hosp.; mem. cons. staff Manchester (Conn.) Meml. Hosp., Newington (Conn.) Children's Hosp., Inst. Living, Hartford; mem. courtesy surg. staff Mt. Sinai Hosp., Hartford; mem. cons. staff Backus Hosp., Norwich, Conn.; clin. asso. dept. surgery U. Conn. Health Center Sch. Medicine. Served to lt. (sr. grade) USN, 1942-46; PTO. Vocat. Rehab. Adminstrn. grantee, 1969. Diplomate Am. Bd. Surgery. Fellow A.C.S. (chmn. New Eng. cancer commn. 1971-74); mem. Internat. Acad. Proctology (state rep.), AMA, Soc. Head and Neck Surgeons (membership com.), James Ewing Soc. (chmn. audit com.), Am. (1st v.p. Conn. div.), Conn. State (dir., mem. exec. com.), New Eng. (treas. 1973-77, sec., mem. exec. com.) cancer socs., Conn. State Med. Soc. (cancer com.), Greater Hartford Hosp. Council, New Eng. Surg. Soc., Hartford County Med. Soc. (program com.). Contbr. articles in field to profl. jours. Office: 85 Jefferson St Hartford CT 06106

KUEHN, WALTER, JR., mech. engr.; b. Pitts., Sept. 4, 1931; s. Walter and Flora (Behrndt) K.; B.S., Carnegie Mellon U., 1953; M.S., Rensselaer Poly. Inst., 1970; m. Lois M. Marks, July 3, 1954; children—Walter III, Arthur G. Fuel engr. U.S. Steel Edgar Thomson Works, Braddock, Pa., 1953-62; sr. test. engr. Hamilton Standard div. United Tech. Corp., Windsor Locks, Conn., 1962-64; research and devel. engr. Combustion Engring. Inc., Windsor, Conn., 1964-74, supr. engring. computer services devel. and data analysis. Fossil Power Systems, 1974—. Sec./treas. Conn. Fedn. Aid Assn. Lutherans, 1975-77; bd. dirs. Windsor YMCA, 1964-67, recipient Distinguished service award, 1967. Served to 1st lt. C.E., AUS, 1954-56. Registered Profl. engr., Pa. Mem. ASME, Assn. Computing Machinery. Patentee in field. Home: 3A Heritage Dr Windsor CT 06095 Office: Dept 8115-2301 1000 Prospect Hill Rd Windsor CT 06095

KUEHNI, NORMAN ARNOLD, govt. ofcl.; b. Green County, Wis., July 17, 1928; s. Arnold Samuel and Amelia (Mani) K.; student U. Wis., 1946-49; m. Joanne Beth Voeck, Sept. 4, 1948; children—Kathleen Ann Porta, Barbara Dawn Kuehni Rector, Pamela Jo Kuehni. With Dane County (Wis.) Traffic Dept., 1954-63; criminal investigator Bur. Alcohol, Tobacco and Firearms, Treasury Dept., Chgo., 1963-66, area supr., 1966-70, organized crime dr. coordinator, 1970-72, spl. agt. in charge, Falls Church, Va., 1972-73, regional insp., Washington, 1973-75, dept. asst. dir., 1975—. Served with AUS, 1947-48. Mem. Internat. Assn. Chiefs of Police, Mensa, Fraternal Order Police. Lutheran. Clubs: Westwood Country (Vienna, Va.); Masons, Order Eastern Star. Home: 1920 Contralto Ct Vienna VA 22180 Office: PO Box 6199 Washington DC 20044

KUETHER, CARL ALBERT, biochemist; b. Ripon, Wis., Oct. 15, 1915; s. Frederick C. and Anna Elizabeth (Volberg) K.; A.B., Miami U., 1936; M.S., Wayne U., 1940; Ph.D., George Washington U., 1943; m. Edith Fiske Lyman, June 16, 1939; children—Christian L., Elizabeth J. Kuether. Instr., George Washington U., 1942-43, Western Res. U., 1943-46; asst. prof. biochemistry U. Wash., 1946-51; research biochemist Eli Lilly & Co., 1951-60; asso. prof. chemistry Youngstown (Ohio) U., 1960-62; asso. program dir. NSF, Washington, 1962-65; program adminstr. Nat. Inst. Gen. Med. Sci., NIH, Bethesda, Md., 1965—; professorial lectr. George Washington U., 1962-65. Mem. Am. Chem. Soc., AAAS, Sigma Xi, Phi Eta Sigma. Home: 3708 Stewart Dr Chevy Chase MD 20015 Office: Pharmacology Toxicology Program Nat Inst Gen Med Sci NIH Bethesda MD 20014

KUGEL, ROBERT BENJAMIN, educator; b. Chgo., May 2, 1923; s. H. Kenneth and Rebecca (von Kaas) K.; student Dartmouth, 1941-42; B.A., U. Mich., 1945, M.D., 1946; M.A., Brown U., 1964; m. Dorothy Annetta Bowdle, Jan. 31, 1950; children—Rebecca Anne, Gretchen Lucinda, Jennie Louisa. Intern U. Mich. Hosp., Ann Arbor, 1947-48, resident, 1948-50, instr. pediatrics, 1952-53; instr. pediatrics Yale, 1951-52; asst. prof., research asso. maternal and child health Johns Hopkins, 1955-56; asst. prof. State U. Iowa, dir. Child devel. clinic Univ. Hosp., 1956-63; prof. med. sci. Brown U., Providence, 1963-65, prof. child health, 1965-66; prof., chmn. dept. pediatrics U. Nebr. at Omaha, 1966-68, dean Coll. Medicine, 1969-74, chmn. dep. med. and ednl. adminstrn. Coll. Medicine, 1973-74, spl. asst. to chancellor, interim dean UN Med. Center, 1974; v.p. health sers. U. N.Mex., 1974-76, prof. pediatrics, 1976—; chief adminstrv. officer Bernalillo County Med. Center, Albuquerque, 1974-76; exec. vice chancellor U. Kans. Coll. Health Scis. and Hosp., 1976-77; v.p. med. affairs Georgetown U. Community Health Plan, Washington, 1977—; practice medicine, specialziing in pediatrics, Omaha, 1966-74. Mem. Pres.'s Commn. on Mental Retardation, 1966-69. Pres., Josephine E. Kugel Found., 1968—. Past bd. dirs. Greater Omaha Assn. for Retarded Children, John E. Fogarty Found.; bd. dirs. research and tng. Meyer Therapy Center, Omaha. Mem. Am. Acad. Pediatrics, AMA, Am. Pediatrics Soc., Midwest Soc. Pediatric Research, Am. Assn. Mental Deficiency. Democrat. Presbyn. Contbr. articles to profl. jours. Home: 6016 Claiborne Dr McLean VA 22101 Office: Georgetown U Community Health Plan Suite 300 4200 Wisconsin Ave NW Washington DC 20016

KUGELMAN, LAWRENCE RICHARD, assn. exec.; b. Montreal, Nov. 1, 1936; s. Lawrence J. and Hilda (Blockman) K.; A.B., Dartmouth Coll., 1959; M.B.A., Northwestern U., 1961; Inst. for Not-For-Profit Mgmt., 1977; m. Lynn C. Wilson, June 20, 1959; children—Lawrence Richard, Kristen Greeley. Mem. staff spl. devel. program Chase Manhattan Bank, 1961-64; budget coordinator CBS, N.Y.C., 1964-66; mgr. spl. studies internat. group Singer Co., N.Y.C., 1966-69; dir. fin. and adminstrn. Reeves Telecom Corp., 1969-70; v.p., treas. Camp Affiliates, Inc., 1970-74; exec. dir. Planned Parenthood of N.Y.C., Inc., 1974—; spl. cons. Family Planning Advs., 1977-78. Episcopalian. Home: 60 Cowdin Circle Chappaqua NY 10514 Office: 300 Park Ave S New York City NY 10010

KUGLER, GARY SYD, polit. scientist, assn. exec.; b. Bklyn., June 28, 1935; s. Hyman and Ethel (Straus) K.; B.A., Hofstra U., 1967; M.A. (scholar), Temple U., 1968; Ph.D., Pacific State U., 1976; m. Carole Ann Wagner, Jan. 12, 1957; children—Craig, Mitchel, Susan. Mem. faculty, chmn. polit. sci. dept. Southampton Coll. of L.I. U., 1969-72, spl. asst. dean, 1970-72, dir. personnel relations, 1972-75, chief labor negotiator, 1972-75, asst. to pres., 1973-74; adminstr. labor relations, asst. vice chancellor L.I. U., Bklyn., 1974-75, dir. Grad. Bus. Sch., 1975—; exec. v.p. Asso. Fur Mfrs., N.Y.C., 1975—; dir. Am. Fur Industry, 1975—, Fur Info. and Fashion Council, 1975—; labor relations cons., 1971—; dir. Bonaker Ins. Assos. Mem. Sachem Youth Bd., 1969-74, Suffolk County Econ. Opportunity Council, 1970-74. Served with U.S. Army, 1954-56. Recipient teaching awards Southampton Coll., 1971, 72. Am. Leadership Inst. for UN scholar, 1967. Mem. Acad. Polit. Sci., AAUP, Am. Judicature Soc., Am. Polit. Sci. Assn., Coll. and Univ. Personnel Assn., Acad. Acad. Personnel Adminstrn. (pres. 1975), Nat. Center for Study Collective Bargaining in Higher Edn., Am. Soc. Assn. Execs., Stony Brook C. of C. Jewish. Contbr. to The Presidency of the 1970's, 1971. Home: 15 Mystic Way Stony Brook NY 11790 Office: 101 W 30th St New York City NY 10001

KUHN, BRENDA, art historian; b. N.Y.C., June 13, 1911; d. Walt and Vera (Spier) Kuhn; student Friends Sem., N.Y.C., 1918-29. Co-mgr. Kuhn Estate, 1949-56, mgr., 1956-66; mgr. Estate of Brenda Kuhn, 1967-75; founder Cape Neddick Park, 1965, Kuhnhouse, 1967; pres. Kuhn Meml. Corp., 1968-75, 3d v.p., 1975—. Mem. State of Maine Art Commn., 1967-71; a founder Assn. To Control Epilepsy (merged with Nat. Epilepsy League and Nat. Epilepsy Found.), 1942; mem. York County Democratic Com., 1974—; trustee Nordica Meml. Assn. Mem. Am. Fedn. Arts, Archives Am. Art, Nat. Audubon Soc., Met. Mus. Art, Copley Soc. of Boston, also numerous museums, art, hist. and nat. hist. socs., Smithsonian Assos., Old York Improvement Soc. Quaker, Am. Assn. Ret. Persons. Clubs: Womens League (York, Maine), Yorksters. Home: Kuhnhouse Cape Neddick ME 03902

KUHN, DOUGLAS ELTON, govt. ofcl.; b. Albany, N.Y., June 26, 1940; s. John George and Dorothy Mae (Wells) K.; student Calif. State U., Sacramento, 1974, Mich. State U., 1978, Hudson Valley Community Coll., 1977; m. Barbara Jean Pittz, July 15, 1961; children—Douglas Elton Jr., Deborah Ellen, Edward John. Salesman, supr. Tri State Indsl. Laundries and Indsl. Uniform Co., Albany and Schenectady, 1959-65; plant operator Bethlehem Sewer Dist., Delmar, N.Y., 1966-74, chief operator, 1974—; chief operator, supr. K.E. Drautz cons. chemist, Glenmont, N.Y., 1976—; chief operator Camp Woodstock, 1976—. Asst. chief, treas. Slingerlands Vol. Fire Dept.; treas. Hudson Mohawk Vol. Firemens Assn.; mem. Republican Com. 15th Dist. Bethlehem. Mem. N.Y. State Water Pollution Control Assn. (recipient Safety award 1977; vice chmn. Capitol dist. com.) Water Pollution Control Fedn. Lutheran. Club: Elks. Home: RD 2 Box 287 South Albany Rd Selkirk NY 12158 Office: 393 Delaware Ave Delmar NY 12054

KUHN, LOUIS, apparel co. exec.; b. Bklyn., May 18, 1912; s. Jacob and Malvina (Futtersack) K.; student Bklyn. Coll. evenings 1929-33; m. Lee Kahn, Dec. 15, 1940; children—Robert L., Karen J. Salesman, Neptune Raincoat Co., N.Y.C., 1936-43, 45-46; founder Lou Kuhn, Inc., 1947 (name changed to Chief Apparel, Inc. 1947), N.Y.C., chmn., 1956—. Mem. adv. bd. Marine Midland Bank-N.Y., N.Y.C. Mem. Philanthropic 50, N.Y., 1949—, Fedn. Jewish Charities N.Y., 1949—; vice chmn. United Jewish Appeal, 1970; founder Albert Einstein Sch. Medicine, 1967; pres. Lee and Lou Kuhn Found., 1965—. Served with AUS, 1943-45. Decorated Combat Inf. badge. Address: 136 Sutton Pl S Lawrence NY 11559

KUHN, MARY DRAPER, interior designer; b. Tulsa, Sept. 2, 1930; d. Norbert Charles Edward and Louise Barbara (Jeffers) Draper; student U. Okla., 1948-50, U. Houston, 1950-52, Fordham U., 1952, Queens Coll., 1976; m. Adrian Andrew Kuhn, June 27, 1966; 1 dau., Kelly Michele; children by previous marriage—Linda Anne Richburg, Jack Lawrence Richburg, John Michael Richburg. Mgr., Pascoes of Houston, 1953-60; designer Joskes of Houston, 1961; head interior design Flint and Horner, Garden City, N.Y., 1961-69; asst. prof. interior design Queens Coll., 1968-78, coordinator Inst. Design, 1972—; head interior design W & J Slodnes, Garden City, 1970; coordinator Inst. Design Hunter Coll., 1978—; pres. Mary Draper Interiors; tchr. design courses, 1968—; mem. advisory panel Interior Design Mag. Republican. Lutheran. Feature writer Bklyn. Today Mag., 1972. Home and Office: 161 Willow St Garden City NY 11530

KUHN, THOMAS RICHARD, trade assn. exec.; b. Atlantic City, May 31, 1946; s. Thomas Herman and Audrey (Kostenbader) K.; B.A., Yale U., 1968; M.B.A., George Washington U., 1972; m. Virginia Elaine Rote, Jan. 31, 1970; 1 dau., Melissa Elaine. White House liaison officer Office of Sec. Navy, Washington, 1970-72; investment analyst Alex Brown & Sons, Balt., 1972-75; v.p. govt. affairs Am. Nuclear Energy Council, Washington, 1975—. Served to lt. USN, 1968-72. Mem. Am. Nuclear Soc. Club: Jaycees (Falls Church, Va.). Home: 6351 Crosswoods Dr Falls Church VA 22044 Office: Am Nuclear Energy Council 1750 K St NW Washington DC 20006

KUJAWSKI, WALTER RICHARD, accountant; b. Warwick, N.Y., Mar. 28, 1947; s. Walter M. and Anna (Prochneski) K.; B.S. in Accounting, U. Ky., 1968; M.B.A., Pace U., 1975. Accountant, Haskins & Sells, N.Y.C., 1969-74; pvt. practice accounting, Florida, N.Y., 1974—. Treas., chief fiscal officer Village of Florida; capt. Florida Vol. Fire Dept.; mem. Florida Vol. Ambulance Corp. C.P.A., N.Y. Mem. Am. Inst. C.P.A.'s, N.Y. State Soc. C.P.A.'s, N.Y. State Soc. Municipal Fin. Officers, The Florida Fire Dept. Vol. Exempt Firemens Benevolent Assn. (treas.), Orange County Fire Chiefs Assn., N.Y. State Assn. Fire Chiefs, Pace U., Orange County Community Coll., U. Ky. alumni assns., Delta Mu Delta, Beta Alpha Psi. Republican. Roman Catholic. Club: Elks. Home: 69 N Main St Florida NY 10921 Office: 62 N Main St Florida NY 10921

KUKLA, GEORGE JIRI, paleoclimatologist; b. Prague, Czechoslovakia, Mar. 14, 1930; s. Milos and Jindra (Duskova) K.; D.Natural Scis., Charles U., Prague, 1953; m. Helena Kupka, May 19, 1955; children—Susan, Michael. Chief geologist Non-metallic Prospection Nat. Enterprise, Prague, 1953-58, Ceylon, Argentina and Caribbean, 1956-66; sr. research scientist Archeol. and Geol. insts. Czechoslovak Acad. Scis., Prague, 1958-70; sr. research asso. Lamont-Doherty Geol. Obs., Columbia U., 1971—; vis. prof. paleoclimatology Brown U., Providence, 1972-73; vis. prof. paleoclimatology and stratigraphy U. Wash., Seattle, 1975; project leader Internat. Geol. Correlation Programme; cons. paleoclimatology and magnetostratigraphy. Recipient Sr. Fgn. Scientist Fellowship award NSF, 1970; NSF research grantee, 1972—. Mem. Internat. Union Geol. Scis. (commns.), Internat. Union Quaternary Research, AAAS, Geol. Soc. Am., Am. Geophys. Union, Nat. Weather Assn. Am., Am. Assn. Quarternary Geology, Deutsche Quartärvereinigung (W. Ger.). Club: Explorers. Editor: Periglazialzone, Loess und Paleolithikum der Tschechoslowakei, 1969; The Present Interglacial: How and When Will It End, 1972; World Food Supply in Changing Climate, 1975; editor Catena (W. Ger.), 1974—. Contbr. articles to profl. jours. Office: Lamont Doherty Geological Observatory Palisades NY 10964

KUKUIA, FAUSTINUS KOFI, fin. exec.; b. Blekusu, Keta, Ghana, W. Africa, Oct. 4, 1940; s. Abusah Kodzo and Afiwor (Flogbo) K.; came to U.S., 1970; B.S., St. Joseph's U., 1975; m. Margaret M. Torker, Sept. 1967; children—Gordon, Katherine. Asst. pool accountant Ghana Airways Corp., 1965-70; circulation mgr. N.Am. Pub. Co., Phila., 1972-74; fin. mgmt. accountant Phila. Bd. Edn., 1975-76; fin. and property accountant Kewanee Oil Co., Bryn Mawr, Pa., 1976-77; bus. devel. specialist EDTC, Phila., 1977—; pres., exec. dir. FMDC Ltd., internat. mktg. devel. co.; bus. cons.; fgn. trade rep. Nat. coordinator United African Ednl. Found., 1971-72. Mem. Nat. Assn. Accountants, Am. Inst. Mgmt. (exec. council 1978), Acad. Internat. Bus., Soc. Internat. Devel. Club: Masons (32 deg.). Home: 34-11 Revere Rd Drexel Hill PA 19026 Office: 1501 N Broad St Philadelphia PA 19122

KULKA, KURT, research chemist; b. Hranice, Czechoslovakia, Aug. 5, 1904; s. Maximilian and Malvine (Friedmann) K.; Ph.D., U. Vienna, 1927; m. Margit Czoyagy-Fenyves, Feb. 5, 1943. With State Serotherapeutic Inst., Vienna, 1927-35; asst. to pres. Internat. Serum Union, Vaduz, Liechtenstein, 1935-38; cons. chem., pharm. industries Paris, from 1938, London, until 1940; research chemist, mgr. research Dodge & Olcott Inc., N.Y.C., 1941-52; dir. research lab. Fritzsche Dodge & Olcott Inc., N.Y.C., 1952-75, chief research chemist, 1952-75, cons., 1976—; lectr. N.Y. U., 1950-53. Symposium chmn. nat. meeting Am. Chem. Soc., Los Angeles, 1971; U.S. Area chmn. VI Internat. Congress Essential Oils, San Francisco, 1974. Fellow Am. Inst. Chemists, AAAS, Royal Soc. Health (London); mem. Am. Chem. Soc., N.Y. Acad. Scis., Am. Inst. Food Technologists, European Chemoreception Research Orgn. Paris, London. Mason. Contbr. numerous articles to chem. publs. Patentee in field. Home: 175 W 73d St Apt 15-G New York City NY 10023

KULKARNI, AVINASH DATTATRAYA, metall. engr.; b. Gwalior, India, Jan. 26, 1942; s. Dattatraya Vishnu and Sudha Dattatraya (Potdar) K.; came to U.S., 1965; B. Tech., Indian Inst. Tech., Bombay, 1963; Ph.D., U. Pa., 1968; M.B.A., Fairleigh Dickinson U., 1975; m. Veena Karkarey, Jan. 10, 1970; children—Anjali, Vikram. Metall. cons. M.N. Dastur & Co. Ltd., Calcutta, 1963-65; staff scientist casting lab. Chase Brass & Copper Co., Cleve., 1968-71; sr. research engr. lamp div. Westinghouse Electric Corp., Bloomfield, N.J., 1971—. Mem. Am. Soc. Metals, Am. Inst. Metall. Engrs., Indian Inst. Metals, Illuminating Engrs. Soc. Democrat. Hindu. Club: India Assn. Cleve. (pres. 1970-71). Contbr. articles to profl. jours. Patentee in field. Home: 6 Auburn Ct Monsey NY 10952 Office: Lamp Div Westinghouse Corp 1 Westinghouse Plaza Bloomfield NJ 07003

KULP, AIMEE KATHERINE, librarian; b. Mercersburg, Pa., Oct. 28, 1924; d. Benjamin Frank and Aimee (Fry) Kulp; A.B., Wilson Coll., 1946; B.S. in L.S., Drexel U., 1948. Clerical asst. Sterling Meml. Library, Yale, New Haven, 1946-47; serials librarian H. Firestone Meml. Library, Princeton, 1948-49; library dir. Mercersburg (Pa.) Acad., 1949—, instr. driver tng., 1972—. Mem. Chambersburg (Pa.) Hosp. Aux., 1973—. Recipient Best-of-Show award, also 1st prize Cumberland Valley Photog. Exhibit, 1960. Mem. Cumberland Valley (v.p. 1971-72), Pa., Am. library assns., Am., Pa. sch. librarians assns., Nat. Assn. Ind. Schs. Clubs: Order Eastern Star; Avon Literary (sec. 1953-54, 60-61); Faculty Women's (pres. 1954). Home: 304 Johnston's Ln Mercersburg PA 17236 Office: Mercersburg Acad Mercersburg PA 17236

KULP, ARTHUR CLAUDE, librarian; b. Ithaca, N.Y., Apr. 4, 1921; s. Claude Livingston and Mabel Deltha (Ross) K.; B.A., Cornell U., 1942; B.S. in L.S., Columbia, 1947; M.S., U. Ill., 1954; m. Helen Lois Reddout, June 14, 1947; children—William Arthur, Margaret Ann (Mrs. Edward Schoneman), Deborah Helen (Mrs. Miles Munson). Mem. staff Cornell U. Libraries, 1947—, circulation librarian, 1950-75, coordinator space planning, 1975—, also asso. personnel officer; mem. access com. Five Asso. Univ. Libraries, 1968-69, chmn., 1969; mem. access com. S. Central Research Library Council, 1973-74, interim dir., part-time 1976. Co-chmn. Cornell div. Tompkins County United Fund, 1962-63; former mem. advancement com. Louis Agassiz Fuertes council Boy Scouts Am., also asst. scoutmaster, 1965-70. Served with AUS, 1942-45. Mem. Am., N.Y. State library assns., Acacia, Beta Phi Mu. Methodist. Mason, Rotarian. Home: 116 Irving Pl Ithaca NY 14850

KULPA, ROBERT HAROLD, educator, realtor; b. Middletown, Conn., Sept. 27, 1923; s. George J. and Mary (Kowalski) K.; student U. Conn., U. Hartford, Chilcothe Bus. Coll., 1943; m. Ruth Goff, May 14, 1949; 1 dau., Roberta. Real estate broker, pres. R. Kulpa & Co., Moodus, Conn., 1950—; pres. Heraldic Symbols Co. Instr. real estate appraisal U. Conn., 1967—. Served with USAAF, 1942-45. Mem. Soc. Real Estate Appraisers (sr. residential appraiser 1963—), Am. Right of Way Assn., Am. Real Estate and Urban Econs. Assn., Fin. Mgmt. Assn. Home and office: Falls Rd Moodus CT 06469

KUMAI, MOTOI, physicist; b. Nagano, Japan, Mar. 22, 1920; s. Matsunosuke and Chika (Kinebuchi) K.; came to U.S., 1958; B.S., Science U. Tokyo, 1941; Ph.D. in Physics, Hokkaido U., 1957; m. Mutsuko Yamanouchi, Oct. 8, 1948; children—Keiko (Mrs. Satoru Ihara), Etsuko. Research asso. physics Hokkaido U., 1942-55, lectr. physics, 1955-58; research asso. cloud physics U. Chgo., 1958-61; research physicist U.S. Army Cold Regions Research and Engring. Lab., Hanover, N.H., 1961—. Mem. Am. Meteorol. Soc., Internat. Glaciol. Soc., Phys. Soc. Japan, Meteorol. Soc. Japan, Sigma Xi. Contbr. articles sci. jours. Research on snow crystal nuclei, radioactive materials in snow crystals from nuclear weapon tests, process of scavenging aerosols by snow crystals, cloud physics, ice physics, soil minerals. Home: 12 Reservoir Rd Hanover NH 03755 Office: USACRREL PO Box 282 Hanover NH 03755

KUMAR, SURIENDER, educator; b. Panjab, India, Dec. 1, 1938; s. Chhaju Ram and Devki Devi (Bhardwaj) Sharma; came to U.S., 1962, naturalized, 1976; Ph.D. in Chemistry, Boston U., 1967; m. Lavinia Anne Connell, Nov. 4, 1965; children—Jay, Neena. Lectr. chemistry Deshbandhu Coll., Delhi U., 1960-62; postdoctoral asso. Cornell U., 1966-68; research asso. and biochemist U. Wis., 1968-70; asst. prof. biochemistry Coll. Medicine and Dentistry of N.J., Newark, 1970-75, asso. prof., 1975—. NIH grantee, 1976—; Am. Heart Assn. grantee, 1976—. Fellow Am. Inst. Chemists; mem. AAAS, Am. Soc. Biol. Chemists, N.Y. Acad. Sci., Am. Chem. Soc., Sigma Xi. Contbr. articles to profl. jours. Home: 5 Park Rd Maplewood NJ 07040 Office: 100 Bergen St Newark NJ 07103

KUMM, WILLIAM HOWARD, energy and ocean systems co. exec.; b. Bahia, Brazil, Feb. 6, 1931; s. Henry William and A. Joyce (Beale) K.; brought to U.S., 1938, naturalized, 1949; B.A., Amherst Coll., 1952; certificate bus. adminstrn., McCoy Coll., Johns Hopkins, 1959; m. Anne K. Gibson, July 11, 1953; children—John H., Elizabeth A., Katharine L. With Westinghouse Electric Corp., 1952-78, with AirArm div., Balt., 1952-60, Westinghouse Surface div., Balt., 1961-62, supervisory engr. systems ops. div., 1962-65, mgr. Westinghouse Ocean Research & Engring. Center, Annapolis, Md., 1965-71; presdl. interchange exec. Pres.'s Commn. on Personnel Interchange, assigned NOAA, 1971-72; staff Nat. Adv. Com. on Oceans and Atmosphere, Washington, 1972; program mgr. submarine transp. project U.S. Maritime Adminstrn., 1972-73; mgr. marine programs Westinghouse Oceanic Div., 1973-78; pres. Arctic Enterprises Inc., Annapolis, Md., 1978—; Participant joint Nat. Acad. Scis.-Nat. Acad. Engring. planning effort on Internat. Decade Ocean Exploration for Nat. Council on Marine Resources and Engring., 1968-69. Mem. Rural Area Devel. Bd., Carroll County, N.H., 1964-65; mem. Citizens Adv. Council on Edn., 1970-72; del. County Council P.T.A.'s, 1970, 71. treas. Cub Scout pack 332, Boy Scouts Am., Catonsville, Md., 1963-65. Registered profl. engr., Md. Mem. U.S. Naval Inst., Marine Tech. Soc., Presdl. Interchange Exec. Assn., Am. Oceanic Orgn., Nat. Security Indsl. Assn. (research and engr. adv. com.). Patentee in field. Contbr. chpt. to Man Beneath the Sea, 1972. Home: 511 Heavitree Ln Severna Park MD 21146 Office: Arctic Enterprises Inc 1220L Gemini Dr Annapolis MD 21403

KUNDIN, ROBERT HERBERT, chem. co. ofcl.; b. Newark, June 24, 1933; s. Samuel E. and Sara S. (Hudson) K.; A.B., in Psychology, Rutgers U., 1963; profl. certificate in indsl. and labor relations Cornell U., 1976; student law, Pace U., 1976—; m. Sheila Carol Peck, July 6, 1954; children—Cynthia, Karen. Personnel supr. Nat. Gypsum Co.,

Dover, N.J., 1960-63; indsl. relations rep. Union Carbide Corp., Newark, 1963-64; personnel dir. PKI Foods, Inc., Englewood Cliffs, N.J., 1964-67; mgr. personnel and pub. relations Nepera Chem. Co., Inc., Harriman, N.Y., 1967—. Bd. dirs. Hudson Valley Philharmonic Orch., 1974-76, McQuade Home for Children, 1974-76, Newburgh Community Action Com., 1973—. Served with AUS, 1953-55. Recipient award for legal scholarship West Pub. Co., 1977. Mem. Am. Soc. Personnel Mgmt., Indsl. Relations Research Assn., Am. Compensation Assn., Personnel Mgmt. Council, Bur. Nat. Affairs. Home: 3 Stoneledge Ln New Windsor NY 12550 Office: Route 17 Harriman NY 10926

KUNG, FRANKLIN HSIEN-CHEUK, pharm. and toiletries mfg. co. exec.; b. China, June 14, 1942; s. William C. and Norma S. K.; Came to U.S., 1963, naturalized, 1973; B.B.A., Nat. Taiwan U., 1963; M.B.A., St. Louis U., 1966; postgrad. in Bus., Ind. U., 1967; m. Betty E. Chen, Aug. 3, 1965; children—Sylvia C., Douglas C. Sr. ops. research analyst, then sr. mktg. research analyst Miles Labs., Inc., Elkhart, Ind., 1965-70; mgr. creative and advt. research Toiletries div. Gillette Co., Boston, 1972-74; asso. mktg. research mgr. Gen. Foods Co., White Plains, N.Y., 1974-75; asst. dir. market research, then group dir. market research Carter Products div. Carter-Wallace Inc., N.Y.C., 1975—; dir. King's Internat. Corp; gen. partner K & W Enterprise; cons. Vol. Urban Cons. Group, Inc. Mem. bd. Yorktown Chinese Sch. Mem. Am. Mktg. Assn. Address: RFD Watergate Dr Amawalk NY 10501

KUNIN, MADELEINE MAY, state legislator Vt.; b. Zurich, Switzerland, Sept. 28, 1933; d. Ferdinand and Renée (Bloch) May; came to U.S., 1940, naturalized, 1947; B.A., U. Mass., 1956; M.S. in Journalism, Columbia U., 1957; M.A., U. Vt., 1967; m. Arthur S. Kunin, June 21, 1959; children—Julia, Peter, Adam, Daniel. Reporter, Burlington (Vt.) Free Press, 1957-58; writer Sta. WCAX-TV, Burlington, 1959-60; instr. English, Trinity Coll., Burlington, 1969-70; mem. Vt. Ho. of Reps. from Chittenden Dist., 1972—, house majority whip, chmn. appropriations com. Mem. Vt. Gov.'s Commn. on Status of Women, 1965-67, Gov.'s Commn. Adminstrn. Justice, 1975—, Gov.'s Commn. Children and Youth, 1973—; mem. Chittenden Country Democratic Com., 1973—; del. Dem. Nat. Conv., 1976. Address: 122 Dunder Rd Burlington VT 05401

KUNSTADT, HERBERT, cons. engr.; b. Austria, July 28, 1931; s. Lipman and Rosalie (Merling) K.; came to U.S., 1962, naturalized, 1967; M.S. in Mech. Enging., U. Bucharest, 1954; Ph.D., Tech. U. Vienna, 1972; m. Dorothy Rubinstein, Oct. 20, 1967. Project engr. Sulzer Bros., Vienna, Austria, 1955-61; project mgr. Cosentini, N.Y.C., 1961-67; asso. Syska and Hennessy, N.Y.C., 1967-73; chmn. bd., chief exec. officer Falotico Inc., N.Y.C., 1973-75; pres. Kunstadt Assos., N.Y.C., 1975—; asso. prof. life support systems Pratt Inst. Sch. Architecture, Bklyn. Served with res. Rumania C.E., 1951-53. Registered profl. engr., N.Y., N.J., Conn., D.C., Tex., Calif., Fla. Mem. Nat. Soc. Profl. Engrs., Am. Soc. Heating, Refrigeration and Air Conditioning Engrs., Assn. Energy Engrs. Club: Harvard of N.Y. Contbr. articles in field to profl. publs. Home: 870 Fifth Ave New York NY 10021 Office: 415 Lexington Ave New York NY 10017

KUNZMAN, MITCHE, art co. exec.; b. N.Y.C., Oct. 10, 1950; s. Murray and Ada (Katz) K.; B.F.A., City U. N.Y., 1973; m. Helen A. Adamcio, Apr. 16, 1977. Salesman, Lenem Arts Inc., N.Y.C., 1974-75, East coast rep., 1975, prin. sales rep. U.S. and Can., 1975—. Mem. Art and Antique Dealers League Am. Office: Lenem Arts Inc 321 E 45th St New York City NY 10017

KUPERSMITH, AARON HARRY, lawyer, real estate, bus. exec.; b. Newark, June 13, 1925; s. David and Bessie (Rubinstein) K.; student Drury Coll., 1943; B.S. cum laude, N.Y. U., 1948; LL.B., Bklyn. Law Sch., 1954, J.S.D., 1956, J.D., 1968; m. Cynthia Skolnick, Dec. 24, 1947; children—Farrell Preston, Mark Jeffrey, Linda Ellen. A. H. Kupersmith & Co. Fin., Real Estate, Tax and Investment Cons., N.Y.C., 1948—; admitted to N.Y. bar, 1954; practice as atty., accountant, tax, bus. and fin. cons., N.Y.C., 1954—; partner Ramapo Manor Nursing Center, Suffern, N.Y., 1957-75; pres., chmn. Verson Prodns., Inc., N.Y.C., 1962-67, Exec. Fin. Planning Corp., N.Y.C., 1956-75; exec. v.p., sec.-treas., dir., mem. exec. com. DEL Labs., Inc., and subs., N.Y.C., 1962-65; pres., chmn. Am. Inst. for Econ. Growth, N.Y.C., 1965—, Medispas, Inc., 1968-72; chmn. Computer Systems for Edn. and Medicine, Inc. and subsidiaries, 1969-71; gen. counsel Council Jewish Orgns., Civil Service Orgns. Ind. Party, 1971—; partner Patchogue Nursing Homes, 1968-71, McQuire Holiday Hotel, N.J., 1962-70; dir. RAM Group, Inc.; spl. counsel, cons. to various assns.; lectr., instr. various groups on law, taxes, corporate fin., real estate, mergers, acquisitions, housing, tax shelters, 1958—; financial, legal, tax and bus. cons. to various pub. and pvt. corps., legal and accounting firms. Mem. N.Y. State Nursing Home Adv. Com. on Reimbursement, 1966-69; mem. Columbia U. adv. com. rates for nursing home care, 1966-69; mem. pres.'s club Union Central Life Ins. Co. Trustee Martin Revson trusts, also various pvt., charitable founds. Served with USAAF, 1943-45. Recipient Wisdom Honor award 1969. Mem. N.Y. County Lawyers Assn., Am. Mgmt. Assn., Am. Bar Assn., Bar Assn. City N.Y., Internat. Platform Assn., Alpha Epsilon Pi, Psi Chi Omega, Beta Gamma Sigma. Author: An Economic Study of the American System, 1956; Tax Havens, 1959; Corporate Finance and Taxes, 1959; Tax Treaties of United States, 1960; United States Industry and Executives Abroad, 1960; Executive Compensation Constructive Receipt, 1961; Corporate Finance and Taxes Defined, 1963; Considerations in Mergers and Acquisitions, 1965; Break Even Techniques, 1965; Men and Their Money, 1966; Is Nursing Home Business for You?, 1968; Major Health Crisis, 1968; Nursing Home Industry Review, 1968. Financial editor, columnist Drug Trade News, N.Y.C., 1965-68; Equity and Venture Capital, 1970; Tax and Investment Shelters, 1971; Capital Growth, 1971; Investments-Rental Housing vs. Condominium, 1972; Purchase and Sale of Business Checklist, 1972; Real Estate, Partnerships, Government and the Private Investor, 1973; Tax Shelter Investments, 1973. Home and office: 45 Woodland Ave West Orange NJ 07052 Office: 275 Madison Ave New York City NY 10017 also 4130 NW 88th Ave Coral Springs FL 33065

KUPERSTEIN, IRA S(TANLEY), civil engr.; b. N.Y.C., Dec. 3, 1941; s. Paul and Jeanette (Sheiner) K.; B.C.E., Coll. City N.Y., 1963, M.C.E., 1966; Ph.D., N.Y. U., 1973; m. Judith Eve Sazer, Mar. 20, 1972; children—Alana, Emily. Asst., jr. engr. City of N.Y., 1963-65; supr. Shell Oil Co., N.Y.C., 1965-67; staff engr. Bklyn. Union Gas Co., 1968; instr. Cooper Union, 1969-70; asst. prof. N.J. Inst. Tech., Newark, 1971—; cons. engr. and planner, 1970—. Commr., chmn. Newark Parking Authority, 1971—. Registered profl. engr., N.Y., N.J. Mem. ASCE, Inst. Transp. Engrs., Am. Soc. Engring. Edn., Transp. Research Bd. Contbr. tech. articles to profl. jours. Home: 72 Saint John's Ave Mount Tabor NJ 07878 Office: NJ Inst Tech 323 High St Newark NJ 07102

KUPFER, CARL, ophthalmologist; b. N.Y.C., Feb. 9, 1928; s. James and Hannah (Goldwasser) K.; A.B., Yale U., 1948; M.D., Johns Hopkins U., 1952; m. Muriel Kaiser, Dec. 10, 1969; children—Charles David, Sarah Delia. Intern, asst. resident Wilmer Eye Inst., Johns Hopkins Hosp., 1952-54, lab. asst. biostatistics Sch. Medicine, 1953-54, Inst. research fellow in ophthalmology, 1957-58; research fellow in ophthalmology Harvard Med. Sch., 1958-60, instr., 1960-62, asst. prof. ophthalmology, 1962-66; prof., chmn. dept. ophthalmology U. Wash. Sch. Medicine, 1966-70; dir. Nat. Eye Inst., NIH, HEW, Bethesda, Md., 1970—. Bd. dirs. Am. Found. for Overseas Blind. Served with USAAF, 1954-56. Diplomate Am. Bd. Ophthalmology. Mem. Am. Physiol. Soc., Assn. Research in Ophthalmology, Am. Acad. Ophthalmology and Otolaryngology, Am. Ophthalmology Soc., Pan Am. Ophthalmal. Soc. Mem. editorial bd. Investigative Ophthalmology, 1969—, Am. Jour. Ophthalmology, 1971—; contbr. articles to med. jours. Office: Nat Eye Inst NIH HEW Bethesda MD 20014*

KUPKOWSKI, GERALD STEVEN, chem. mktg. co. exec.; b. Buffalo, Mar. 29, 1930; s. Steven Joseph and Charlotte Mary (Kupkowski-Modzelewski) K.; student Canisius Coll., 1952; B.S., U. Buffalo, 1957; m. Patricia Alice Mentel, June 23, 1956; children—Sharon, David. Chemist, Trico Corp., Buffalo, 1956-58; cancer research scientist Roswell Park Meml. Inst., Buffalo, 1958-68; chemist Grand Island Biol. Co., Buffalo, 1976—, biochem. products mgr., 1976—; pres. Omicron Cons.'s, Grand Island, N.Y., 1978—; v.p. Rokore Concepts, Grand Island, 1976—; profl. adv. panelist, med. lab. observer. Asso. baseball commr. Town of Cheektowaga; team mgr., equipment mgr. U-Crest Little League. Served with U.S. Army, 1952-54. Mem. Am. Soc. Safety Engrs., U.S. Fedn. Culture Collection. Republican. Roman Catholic. Contbr. articles in field to publs. Home: 4 Joseph St Cheektowaga NY 14225

KURIYAMA, MASAO, physicist; b. Tokyo, Japan, Oct. 29, 1931; s. Zennosuke and Miyo (Suzuki) K.; S.D., Tokyo Met. U., 1953; M.S., U. Tokyo, 1955, Ph.D., 1958; m. Tomi Iwano, Oct. 12, 1958; 1 son, William Akio. Came to U.S., 1962, naturalized, 1972. Research asso. Tokyo Met. U., 1958-59; research asso., inst. solid state physics U. Tokyo, 1959-62, asso. prof., 1966-67; sr. scientist Westinghouse Electric Corp., Pitts., 1962-66; physicist Nat. Bur. Standards, Washington, 1967—. Mem. Am. Phys. Soc., Am. Crystallographic Assn., N.Y. Acad. Sci., Phys. Soc. Japan. Contbr. papers to sci. jours. Home: 19208 Racine Ct Gaithersburg MD 20760 Office: Nat Bur Standards Washington DC 20234

KURJAKOVIC, MIRA BOGUNOVIC, chem. engr.; b. Glina, Yugoslavia, Sept. 20, 1924; d. Ilija and Katica (Davidovic) Bogunovic; came to U.S., 1970, naturalized, 1975; B.S., U. Zagreb (Yugoslavia), 1954; m. Zorislav Kurjakovic, Apr. 8, 1950; children—Vel, Nevenka. Food analyst Food and Drug Adminstrn., City of Osijek (Yugoslavia), 1954-56; research engr. Metall. Inst., Sisak, Yugoslavia, 1956-69; chem. analyst Energy Research, Analytical Research Lab., Dept. Energy, Pitts., 1976—. Mem. Am. Chem. Soc. Office: 4800 Forbes St Pittsburgh PA 15213

KURLAND, NORMAN EDWARD, restaurant chain exec.; b. Bklyn., July 10, 1944; s. Irving Ira and Mildred Carol (Bendheim) K.; A.B. in Econs., Upsala Coll., East Orange, N.J., 1966; M.B.A. in Personnel Mgmt., Pace U., 1968. Dir. personnel King George Ltd., N.Y. and Fla., 1967-72; dir. personnel adminstrn. Merco Enterprises, Inc. div. Capitol Records, 1972-73; dir. personnel Essex Personnel Agencies, Inc., N.Y.C., 1973-74; with Ky. Fried Chicken Corp., 1973—, dir. field human resources, 1978—. Served with AUS, 1966-67. Mem. Fast Food Labor Relations Assn., Nat. Restaurant Assn., Alpha Kappa Psi (life), Sigma Gamma Phi (past pres.). Republican. Jewish. Home: 4 Pine Hill Ave East Norwalk CT 06855 Office: PO Box 32070 Louisville KY 40232

KURLANDER, HONEY W. WACHTEL (MRS. NEALE KURLANDER), artist; b. Bklyn., Oct. 17, 1927; d. Charles B. and Sara (Alexander) Wachtel; certificate Pratt Inst., 1948; m. Neale Kurlander, June 25, 1949; children—Harold Michael, Susan Laurie. One man shows Gallerie Marcel Bernheim, Paris, Gallery, Hempstead, N.Y., Adelphi U., Garden City, N.Y., Kaigado, Tokyo, Verzyl, Northport, N.Y., Country Art Gallery, Westbury, N.Y., Garden City Galleries, Ltd.; exhibited in group shows Nat. Acad. Galleries (N.Y.), Smithsonian Instn., Heckscher Mus., Contemporary Arts Gallery, N.Y.C., N.Y. Internat. Art Show, 1970, Robley Gallery, Roslyn, N.Y., L.I. U., Bklyn., others; represented in permanent collections C.W. Post Coll. Art Center, Greenvale, N.Y., Nassau Community Coll., Garden City, N.Y., Grumbacher, N.Y.C., Gregory Mus., Hicksville, N.Y., L.I. U. Tchr. painting East Meadow, N.Y., East Meadow High Sch., 1959—; mem. art adv. bd. East Meadow (N.Y.) Pub. Library; exhbn. chmn. United Cerebral Palsy Art Exhbn. Recipient 1st prize awards Country Art Gallery, 1961, others. Mem. Nassau County Art League, Nat. League Am. Penwomen (1st prizes 1961, 65, 67-77), Prof. Artists Guild, Artists Equity, Salmagundi Club. Home: 6 Kings Dr Old Westbury NY 11568

KURLANS, ALICE JOAN, research specialist; b. Phila., May 4, 1940; d. John Joseph and Tivia Marie (Scalella) Kateiva; B.A. in Microbiology, U. Pa., 1962; postgrad. Hahnemann Med. Coll., 1965; M.S. in Info. Sci., Drexel U., 1971; m. William H. Kurlans, June 22, 1968. Microbiologist, Campbell Soup Co., Camden, N.J., 1963, Hahnemann Med. Coll., 1963-65, 66-70, Med. Coll. Pa., 1966; chemist Inst. Sci. Info., Phila., 1966; research specialist U. Pa., 1975—; info. analyst sci. research documents Franklin Inst.; cons. USPHS fellow, 1965. Mem. Am. Soc. Microbiology, Am. Inst. Biol. Scis., Am. Soc. Info. Sci., NOW, Beta Phi Mu. Contbr. articles to sci. jours. Home: 1324 Locust St Philadelphia PA 19107 Office: Connective Tissue Research Inst U Pa Sci Center 3624 Market St Philadelphia PA 19104

KURNIK, BARRY ARNOLD, microbiologist; b. LaBelle, Pa., June 7, 1936; s. Joseph Robert and Violet Gloria (Lucas) K.; B.S., Purdue U., 1958; Asst. microbiologist St. Mary's Hosp., Rhinelander, Wis., 1959-60; head microbiologist St. Mary's Hosp., Racine, Wis., 1960-74, chmn. hosp. personel com., mem. environ. control com. with quality control dept. Lake State Yeast Co.; microbiologist Butler County Meml. Hosp., Butler, Pa., 1977—. Registered microbiologist Am. Soc. Clin. Pathologists. Mem. Am. Soc. Microbiologists. Home: 107 Pittsburgh Rd Bentleyville PA 15314 Office: 317 S Monroe St Butler PA 16001

KURODA, KOSON, radiologist; b. Long Beach, Calif., July 18, 1929; s. Mumekichi and Tokuyo (Yoshihara) K.; B.A., U. Calif. at Berkeley, 1954; M.D., Northwestern U., 1960; m. Karen Lee White, Dec. 23, 1966; children—Greg Koson, Alexandra Mariko. Intern, Phila. Gen. Hosp., 1961, resident in radiology, 1961-64; fellow in cardiovascular radiology Grad. Hosp., Phila., 1964-65; asst. inst. grad. Sch. Medicine U. Pa., 1964-65, instr. radiology, 1965-67, asso. radiology, 1967-68; asst. prof. radiology Thomas Jefferson U. Hosp. Med. Coll., Phila., 1968-70, asso. prof., 1970-77, clin. prof., 1977—; asst. radiologist Grad. Hosp. U. Pa., 1965-68, Presbyn. Hosp., 1966-68; asst. radiologist Thomas Jefferson U. Hosp., Phila., 1968-70, attending radiologist, 1970—, chief cardiovascular radiology, 1968-77; cons. radiology Pa. Hosp., Phila., 1970—, Mercer Med. Center, Trenton, N.J., 1970—; chmn. diagnostic radiology Cooper Med. Center, 1977—. Pres., Phila. chpt. Japanese-Am. Citizens League, 1976, bd. mem., 1974-78. Served with U.S. Army, 1954-56. Mem. Am. Coll. Radiology, Assn. Univ. Radiologists, Council Am. Heart Assn., Pan Am., Pa., Philadelphia County med. socs., Pa. Radiol. Soc., Phila. Roentgen Ray Soc. Contbr. articles in field to profl. jours.

KUROSAKA, GEORGE, JR., cons. engr.; b. Lake George, N.Y., July 29, 1928; s. George Y. and Sato Ann (Tago) K.; B.C.E., Rensselaer Poly. Inst., 1954; m. Mikiko Kashiwabara, Feb. 1, 1958; children—Jan Sueko, Kimiko Lynn. Employed with various contractors and cons., 1954-56; chief civil engr. A.J. Macchi, engrs., Hartford, Conn., 1956-57; office engr. Seelye, Stevenson, Value & Knecht, cons. engrs., N.Y.C., 1957-58; sr. civil engr. Rist-Frost Assos., cons. engrs., Glens Falls, N.Y., 1958-61; project engr. BCH Constrn. Corp., Buffalo, 1961; project engr. Barker & Henry, architect-engr., Glens Falls, 1962-64; partner Bright, Kurosaka & McAndrews, cons. engrs. and architects, Glens Falls, 1964-68; partner in charge engring. Kurosaka & McAndrews, Glens Falls, 1968-71; self-employed as cons. engr., Glens Falls, 1971—. Mem. drafting tech. adv. com. Adirondack Community Coll., Glens Falls, 1972—; asst. commr. Mohican council Boy Scouts Am., 1969—, Silver Beaver award, 1970; mem. Town of Queensbury Zoning Bd. Appeals, 1967—, sec., 1975-78; exec. bd. Adirondack council Girl Scouts U.S.A., 1967-72, 75-78. Served with USN, 1946-49. Mem. N.Y. State Soc. Profl. Engrs., V.F.W. Republican. Episcopalian. Mason, Kiwanian. Home: 13 Arbutus Dr Queensbury NY 12801 Office: 206 Glen St Glens Falls NY 12801

KUROWSKI, ZBIGNIEW THOMAS, child psychiatrist; b. Poznan, Poland, Jan. 18, 1921; s. Alexander and Leokadia (Lewik) K.; came to Can., 1969, naturalized, 1974; Ph.B., U. Nancy (France), 1938; M.D., Acad. of Medicine, Poznan, 1950; Specialist in Pediatrics, Acad. of Medicine, Warsaw, Poland, 1954, Specialist in Child Psychiatry, 1963; m. Zofia Sobieszczanska, Sept. 2, 1956; children—Alexandra, Thomas. Asst. prof. Pediatric Clinic, U. Poznan, 1950-51; head pediatric dept. Mil. Hosp., Przemysl (Poland), 1951-57; dir. Pediatric Clinic, Kielce, Poland, 1957-60; head dept. child psychiatry State Hosp., Morawica/Kielce, Poland, 1963-69; mem. med. staff Provincial Hosp., Campbellton, N.B., Can., 1969-70; acting clin. dir. Mental Health Clinic, Bathurst, N.B., Can., 1970-74; cons. in child psychiatry for the North of N.B., 1974—. Served as lt. Polish Underground Army, 1940-45, maj. Polish Armed Forces, 1951-57. Mem. Am. Acad. Child Psychiatry, N.B. Psychiat. Assn. Roman Catholic. Contbr. articles to profl. jours. Home: 1280 Johnson Ave Bathurst NB E2A 3T5 Canada Office:Mental Health Clinic Bathurst NB E2A 4A4 Canada

KURPIEWSKI, ELIZABETH ANN, nurse; b. New Haven, Apr. 23, 1950; d. Vincent Henry and Elizabeth Carol (Fuchs) Kurpiewski; R.N., Hosp. St. Raphael Sch. Nursing, New Haven, 1971; student So. Conn. State Coll., 1968-69; B.S. in Nursing summa cum laude, U. Bridgeport, 1975. Staff nurse Hosp. St. Raphael, 1971-72, head nurse. 1975-77, clin. supr. surg. nursing, 1977—. Mem. Conn. Nurses Assn. Office: Hospital of St Raphael 1450 Chapel St New Haven CT 06511

KURRELMEYER, LOUIS HAYNER, lawyer; b. Troy, N.Y., July 26, 1928; s. Bernhard and Lucy Julia (Hayner) K.; A.B., Columbia, 1949, LL.B., 1953; M.A., U. N.Mex., 1950; m. Phyllis A. Damon 1952 (div. 1973); children—Ellen Laura, Louis Hayner, Nancy Snow; m. 2d, Martina S. Kluis, 1975. Admitted to N.Y. bar, 1953, D.C. bar, 1968; practiced in N.Y.C., 1953—; asso. atty. Debevoise, Plimpton, Lyons & Gates, N.Y.C., 1953-66; partner firm Hale Russell Gray Seaman & Birkett, N.Y.C., 1967-75, counsel, 1976—. Vice pres. Emerson Sch. Bd., N.Y.C., 1960-64, chmn. 1964-69; asst. transp. adminstr. City of N.Y., 1966-67; chmn. prudential com. Fire Dist. 1, Shelburne, Vt., 1977—. Mem. Am. Bar Assn. Club: Wings. Author: The Potash Industry, 1951. Home: RD 2 Box 462 Shelburne VT 05482 Office: Hale Russell Gray Seaman & Birkett 122 E 42d St New York City NY 10017

KURTH, WALTER RICHARD, assn. exec.; b. Normal, Ill., Jan. 21, 1932; s. Walter H. and Irene (Freitag) K.; B.S., U. Ill., 1954; m. Mary Elisabeth Taylor, Aug. 23, 1958; children—Mary Helen, Sarah Jane, Elisabeth Irene. Publ. dir. Asso. Credit Burs. of Am., Inc., St. Louis, 1954-57, marketing dir., 1957-62, asst. gen. mgr., 1962-66, asst. gen. mgr., treas., Houston, 1966-68, adminstrv. v.p., treas., 1968-69, exec. v.p., treas., 1969-75; vice chmn. bd. ACB Services, Inc., 1974-75; sec.-treas. Credit Bur. Automation, Inc., Houston, 1966-75; vice chmn. bd. Credit Services Internat., 1974-75; sr. v.p. Nat. Consumer Finance Assn., Washington, 1976-77, exec. v.p., 1977—; mem. Credit Research Center Advisory Council, 1977—; mem. bd. Economic Edn. Found. for Clergy, 1976—. Bd. mgrs. Thompson Retreat Center, St. Louis, 1963-64. Mem. Houston dist. SBA, 1971-75. Republican precinct chmn., 1969-75, chmn. dist. 15 fund drive, 1970-72. Mem. Am. Mgmt. Assn., Am. (ins. bd. govs. 1977—), St. Louis (pres. 1962), Tex., Houston (pres. 1974), Washington socs. assn. execs., Star and Scroll (pres. 1953), C. of C. of U.S. (assn. com. 1977—), Alpha Kappa Lambda (pres. 1953). Presbyn. (elder). Mason (32 deg., Shriner). Home: 9205 White Chimney Ln Great Falls VA 22066 Office: 1000 16th St Suite 601 Washington DC 20036

KURTZ, NORMAN RUDOLPH, educator; b. Delmont, S.D., Sept. 11, 1931; s. Rudolph and Erna Bertha (Weisz) K.; B.A., Wartburg Coll., 1953; B.D., Wartburg Sem., 1957; Ph.D., U. Colo., 1966; m. Loretta May Boe, May 28, 1955; children—Richard Leigh, Jeannie Lynn. NIMH fellow U. Colo., 1962-63, teaching asso., 1963-64, research asst., 1963-65; dir. devel. social sci. research Boston City Hosp., 1966-67, lectr. Sch. Nursing, 1967-68, prin. investigator, 1967-68; research dir. Brandeis U. and Mich. Health and Social Security Research Inst., Inc., Detroit, 1968; cons. Downeast WICS, Inc., U.S. Dept. Labor, Portland, Maine, 1967-69, Welfare Revision Study, Model Cities, Boston, 1969-71, Boston City Hosp. Sch. Nursing, 1970-71; adviser Coop. Met. Ministries, 1970-73; cons. Subcom. on Alcoholism, Greater Lynn Mental Health Area, 1971-73; cons., lectr. Gen. Command and Staff Tng. Inst., New Eng. Police Chief Assn., Babson U., Wellesley, Mass., 1967—; adviser Upward Bound program Brandeis U., also asso. prof. Florence Heller Grad. Sch. Advanced Studies in Social Welfare, 1973—; cons. Evaluation of Kidney Transplant Patients; 1963-71, 1972—, Nat. Center Health Service Research; dir. Alcoholism Tng. Grant, 1972—; prin. investigator Cambridge (Mass.) Dist. Ct., 1972—, Mass. Parole Bd., 1973—, Harvard U. Sch. Pub. Health postdoctoral fellow, 1975-76. Mem. Nat. Inst. Alcohol Abuse and Alcoholism (chmn. tng. rev. com.), AAUP, Am., Eastern, Midwestern sociol. assns., Alpha Kappa Delta. Lutheran. Author: Gatekeepers in the Process of Acculturation, 1966; America's Troubles: A Casebook on Social Conflict, 1969; Coming Home; co-author study deinstitutionalized mentally retarded people, 1978; contbr. articles in field to profl. jours. Home: 32 Miller Hill Dr Dover MA 02030 Office: Florence Heller Grad Sch Advanced Studies in Social Welfare Brandeis U Waltham MA 02154

KURTZ, PAUL, educator; b. Newark, Dec. 21, 1925; s. Martin and Sara (Lasser) K.; B.A., N.Y. U., 1948; M.A., Columbia U., 1949, Ph.D., 1952; m. Claudine C. Vial, Oct. 6, 1960; children—Valerie L.; Patricia A., Jonathan. Instr., Queens Coll., 1950-52; instr. philosophy Trinity Coll., Hartford, Conn., 1952-55, asst. prof. 1955-58, asso. prof. 1958-59; asso. prof. Vassar Coll., Poughkeepsie, N.Y., 1960-61; vis. prof. New Sch. Social Research, N.Y.C., 1960-65; asso. prof. Union Coll., Schenectady, 1961-64, prof., 1964-65; vis. prof. U. Besancon (France), 1965; prof. State U. N.Y., Buffalo, 1965—; chmn. Com. for

Sci. Investigation of Claims of Paranormal. Pres. greater capitol dist. N.Y. State United World Federalists, 1965; chmn. Council on Internat. Studies and World Affairs, 1966-69. Trustee Behavioral Research Council, Great Barrington, Mass.; bd. dirs. U.S. Bibliography of Philosophy, 1958-71, Internat. Humanist and Ethical Union, University Center for Rational Alternatives. Served with AUS, 1944-46. Behavioral Research Council fellow, 1962-63; French Govt. fellow, 1965. Mem. Am. Philos. Assn., Am. Ethical Union, Am. Humanist Assn. (dir.). Author: (with Rollo Handy) A Current Appraisal of the Behavioral Sciences, 1964; Decision and the Condition of Man, 1965; The Fullness of Life, 1974; Exuberance, 1977. Editor: Sidney Hook and the Contemporary World, 1968; Moral Problems in Contemporary Society, 1969; Language and Human Nature, 1970. Editor: American Thought Before 1900, 1966; American Philosophy in the Twentieth Century, 1966; co-editor: International Directory of Philosophy and Philosophers, 1965, 72; (with S. Stojanovic) Tolerance and Revolution, 1971; (with A. Dondeyne) A Catholic Humanist Dialogue, 1972; The Humanist Alternative, 1973; The Idea of a Modern University, 1974; The Philosophy of the Curriculum, 1975; The Ethics of Teaching and Scientific Research, 1977; University and State, 1978. Editorial bd. The Humanist, 1964—, editor, 1967—; editorial bd. Philosophers' Index, Question (Gt. Britain), The Skeptical Inquirer; moderator TV series The Humanist Alternative. Home: 660 LeBrun Rd Amherst NY 14226

KURTZ, STEWART KENDALL, physicist; b. Bryn Mawr, Pa., June 9, 1931; s. Stewart Sylvanus and Ellen (Chase) K.; B.S., Ohio State U., 1956, M.S., 1957, Ph.D. (ITT fellow, NSF fellow), 1960; m. Dora Grandinetti, July 1, 1951; children—Philip, David, Timothy, John. Mem. tech. staff Bell Tel. Labs., Murray Hill, N.Y., 1960-69; group dir. exploratory research Philips Labs., Briarcliff, N.Y., 1969—; sabatical Eindhoven, Holland, 1976-77; lectr. Am. Phys. Soc. Sec. Riverbend Civic Assn., 1963-69. Served with USN, 1951-55; Korea. Mem. IEEE (chmn. fermoelectrics com.), Am. Phys. So., Am. Crystalgraphic Assn., Electrochem. Soc., N.Y. Acad. Scis., Phi Beta Kappa. Clubs: Yorktowners Square Dancing. Patentee in field; editorial bd. Internat. Jour., 1969; contbr. articles to profl. jours. Home: Blossom Ct Yorktown Heights NY 10598 Office: 345 Scarborough Rd Briarcliff Manor NY 10510

KURTZ, THEODORE STEPHEN, psychoanalyst, educator; b. N.Y.C., Apr. 25, 1944; s. Maxwell Arthur and Evelyn R. (Rosenberg) K.; A.B., Boston U., 1964; M.A., N.Y. U., 1965; postgrad. N.Y. Soc. Freudian Psychologists, 1968-74; m. Maritza J. Zurita, Sept. 12, 1975. Caseworker, N.Y.C. Dept. Social Services, 1965-66; tchr., coordinator classes for emotionally disturbed Northport (N.Y.) Pub. Schs., 1966-70; pvt. practice psychoanalytic psychotherapy, 1968—; prin. Luther E. Woodward Sch. for Emotionally Disturbed Children, Freeport, N.Y., 1970-74; asst. prof. edn. C.W. Post Coll., L.I. U., Greenvale, N.Y., 1974—; psychol. cons. to pvt. industry, 1971—. Fellow Am. Orthopsychiat. Assn.; mem. Am. Assn. Marriage and Family Counselors (clin. mem.), Am. Acad. Psychotherapists, Am. Group Psychotherapy Assn., Am. (asso.), Nassau County (exec. bd. 1977-78, chmn. com. on acad. psychology 1977-78) psychol. assns., N.Y. Soc. Clin. Psychologists (asso.), Council Advancement of Psychol. Professions and Scis. Jewish. Contbr. articles to profl. jours. Home: Willow Brook Rd Cold Spring Harbor NY 11724 Office: CW Post College LI U Greenvale NY 11548

KURTZKE, JOHN FRANCIS, neurologist, epidemiologist; b. Bklyn., Sept. 14, 1926; s. John Ambrose and Teresa Rosa (Knipper) K.; B.S. summa cum laude, St. John's U., 1948; M.D., Cornell U., 1952; m. Margaret Mary Nevin, June 30, 1950; children—John Francis, Catherine Kurtzke Brown, Elizabeth Kurtzke Siebert, Joan, Robert, James, Christine. Intern, Kings County Hosp., Bklyn., 1952-53; resident in neurology VA Hosp., Bronx, N.Y., 1953-56; chief neurology service VA hosps., Coatesville, Pa., 1956-63, Washington, 1963—; faculty Jefferson Med. Coll., Phila., 1958-63, asst. prof. clin. neurology, 1963; faculty Georgetown Med. Coll., 1963—, prof. neurology, 1968—, prof. community medicine, 1970—; cons. neurology Nat. Naval Med. Center, Bethesda, Md., 1966—, Surgeon Gen. Navy, 1970—; cons. epidemiology spinal cord injury Nat. Inst. Nervous Diseases, 1973-76; mem. NIH Epilepsy Adv. Com., chmn. subcom. on epidemiology of epilepsy, 1974-77; mem. task force on neurol. services Joint Commn. on Neurology, 1971-75; mem. working group on epidemiology Nat. Adv. Commn. on Multiple Sclerosis, 1973; mem. med. adv. bd. Nat. Multiple Sclerosis Soc., 1966—, Internat. Fedn. Multiple Sclerosis Socs., 1972—; chmn. work group on epidemiolgoy, biostatistics, population genetics NIH Commn. for Control Huntington's Disease, 1976-78; med. research program specialist for neurology and neurobiology VA Research Service, 1977—. Served with USNR, 1944-46; capt. M.C. Res. Recipient Navy Commendation medal, 1974, Certificate of Merit, Surgeon Gen. Navy, 1969. Diplomate Am. Bd. Neurology. Fellow A.C.P., Am. Acad. Neurology (chmn. sect. on neuro-epidemiology 1971-75), AAAS, N.Y. Acad. Sci., Pan. Am., So. med. assns.; mem. Assn. Mil. Surgeons, Am. Neurol. Assn., AMA, AAUP, Am., Internat. epidemiol. assns., Assn. Research in Nervous and Mental Disease, Am. Pub. Health Assn., Soc. Epidemiol. Research, Am. Epilepsy Soc. Author, co-author: Epidemiology of Multiple Sclerosis, 1968, Epidemiology of Cerebrovascular Disease, 1969, Epidemiology of Neurologic and Sense Organ Disorders, 1973; contbr. chpts. to textbooks, articles to profl. jours. Home: 7509 Salem Rd Falls Church VA 22043 Office: VA Hosp Washington DC 20422

KURTZMAN, LEWIS, profl. devel. ofcl.; b. Quincy, Mass., July 3, 1943; s. Benjamin and Irene (Collin) K.; B.A., in Biology, U. Mass., 1965; postgrad. Boston U., 1966-67; m. Marjorie Ann Zetlen, May 6, 1970; children—Amy, Edward, Karen. Group leader Gen. Foods Corp., Woburn, Mass., 1967-68; applications biologist Damon Corp., Needham, Mass. 1968-70; dist. mgr. Waters Assos., Milford, Mass., 1970-77, dir. profl. devel., Ashland, Mass., 1977—. Mem. Western New Eng. Liquid Chromatography Discussion Group (founder). Jewish. Home: 15 Garry Rd Medfield MA 02052 Office: Cherry St Ashland MA 01721

KURUCZ, JOHN, lawyer; b. Yonkers, N.Y., Sept. 19, 1930; s. John J. and Anna (Timan) K.; B.C.E., Rensselaer Poly. Inst., 1952; J.D., Georgetown U., 1957; postgrad. U. Conn., 1965-66; m. Mary K. Semon, May 26, 1973; children—Mary Anne, John Joseph; children by previous marriage—Debra Jeanne, Jonna Stiles. Patent searcher Pennie, Edmonds, Morton, Barrows & Taylor, 1954; patent examiner U.S. Patent Office, 1955-56; patent adviser Dept. Army, 1956-57; admitted to Va. bar, 1957, N.Y. bar, 1959; practiced in N.Y.C., 1957—; asso. Kane, Dalsimer, Kane & Smith, 1957-69; partner Kane, Dalsimer, Kane, Sullivan & Kurucz, N.Y.C., 1969—. Dir. Diversified Investors Planning Corp., N.Y.C., Cartafax Corp., N.Y.C., Hydrostack Corp., Huntington, N.Y.; sec., dir. Impetus Industries, N.Y.C.; v.p., dir. Breed Corp., Spraysol, Inc., Ft. Lee, N.J., Spraysol GmbH, W.Ger. Served to 1st lt. C.E., AUS, 1952-54. Mem. Fed., Am., Va., N.Y. State, Westchester County, N.Y. County, N.Y.C. bar assns., Am., N.Y. patent law assns., Am., N.Y. State, Westchester County profl. engrs. socs., Chi Epsilon, Alpha Tau Omega. Club: University (N.Y.C.); Scarsdale (N.Y.) Golf; Ponte Vedra (Fla.) Golf. Home: 604 Colony Hartsdale NY 10530 Office: 420 Lexington Ave New York City NY 10017

KURZEL, RICHARD BERNARD, physician, chemist; b. Buffalo, Nov. 21, 1944; s. Bernard Maximillian and Martha (Bartczak) K.; B.A. cum laude, State U. N.Y., Buffalo, 1966; Ph.D., Mass. Inst. Tech., 1971; M.D., U. Chgo., 1975; m. Kathleen M. Bunker, 1976. Staff research scientist, dept. ophthalmology Duke, 1971-72; intern Peter Bent Brigham Hosp., Boston, Boston Hosp. for Women, 1975-76; clin. fellow Harvard, 1975-76; clin. fellow, resident physician, dept. obstetrics and gynecology State U. N.Y., Buffalo, 1977—. Mem. Am. Chem. Soc. (Chemistry Student of Year award 1966), Am. Inst. Physics, Optical Soc. Am., Sigma Chi. Republican. Roman Catholic. Contbr. articles to profl. jours. Home: 35 Williamstowne Ct Apt 5 Cheektowaga NY 14227

KURZHALS, PETER RALPH, aero. engr.; b. Berlin, Aug. 20, 1937; s. Rudolf and Ruth Elfriede (Steinhaus) K.; B.S. with honors, Va. Poly. Inst., 1960, M.S., 1962, Ph.D., 1966; grad. Exec. Leadership and Mgmt. Program, Fed. Exec. Inst., 1976; m. Dorothea Maria Frijters, Nov. 20, 1965; 1 son, Eric Peter. Aerospace engr. NASA Langley Research Center, 1960-66, head stability and control sect., 1966-70, head stability and control br., Hampton, Va., 1970-71; chief guidance and control Office Aero. and Space Tech. NASAS Hdqrs., 1971-73, dir. guidance control and info. systems, 1974-76, dir. electronics, 1976-78, dir. space systems, 1978—; instr. undergrad. aerodynamics courses Va. Poly. Inst., 1961. Recipient Langley Inventions and Contbns. awards. 1965, 67; Langley Research Center Spl. Service award, 1967, Langley Group Achievement awards, 1975, NASA Exceptional Service medal, 1976; Harvard Program for Mgmt. Devel. fellow, 1973; registered profl. engr., Va. Asso. fellow Am. Inst. Aeros. and Astronautics (chmn. computer systems tech. com. 1978—, community action com. Nat. Capital sect. 1975—); mem. Soc. Aero. Engrs. (chmn. missiles and space vehicle subcom. aerospace control and guidance systems com. 1963—), Aerospace Group Advanced Research and Devel. (guidance and control panel 1974—), Radio Tech. Commn. for Aeros. (exec. com. 1975—, tech. cons.), Sigma Xi, Tau Beta Pi, Phi Kappa Phi, Sigma Gamma Tau, Kappa Theta Epsilon. Clubs: Langley Yacht (Hampton, Va.); Waynewood Recreation. Contbr. numerous articles, reports to profl. pubis. Home: 1202 S Washington St Alexandria VA 22314 Office: 600 Independence Ave Washington DC 20546

KURZINSKI, EDWARD FRANCIS, instrument co. exec.; b. N.Y.C., Mar. 31, 1920; s. Frank and Sophie (Nowak) K.; B.M.E., Rutgers U., 1942; postgrad. Bklyn. Poly. Inst., Mass. Inst. Tech.; m. Cissie Tabor, Dec. 5, 1942; children—Edward, Cass, Donn, Alan, Brad, Farel. Head lab. div. Union Carbide Corp., N.Y.C., 1942-55; mgr. applied research and devel. Air Products & Chems., Allentown, Pa., 1955-60; staff engr. to v.p. engring. and ops. Youngstown Sheet & Tube Co., 1960-65; industry specialist Selas Corp., Dresher, Pa., 1965-68; mgr. process devel. Dravo Corp., Pitts., 1968-71; mgr. mktg. Fischer & Porter Co., Warminster, Pa., 1971—. Cubmaster, Boy Scouts Am., 1946-48, scoutmaster, 1947-49. Served to lt. USNR, 1943-46. Mem. Assn. Iron and Steel Engrs., Instrument Soc. Am., Am. Inst. Mining, Metall. and Petroleum Engrs. Roman Catholic. Contbr. articles to tech. jours. Patentee in metallurgy, food tech., process activities. Home: RD 4 Yorkshire Rd Doylestown PA 18901 Office: E County Line Rd Warminster PA 18974

KUSHNER, JACK, neurosurgeon; b. Montgomery, Ala., Dec. 5, 1939; s. Louis Harry and Rose (Feldman) K.; student Sheffield U., Eng., 1959-60; A.B., Tulane U., 1960; M.D., U. Ala., 1964; m. Annetta Horwitz, June 21, 1964; children—Reyna, Eve. Intern, George Washington U. Hosp., Washington, 1964-65; resident in surgery U. Mich. Hosp., Ann Arbor, 1965-66; resident in neurosurgery Bowman Gray Sch. Medicine, Winston-Salem, N.C., 1968-72; practice medicine specializing in neurosurgery, Annapolis, Md., 1972—; neurosurgeon Anne Arundel Gen. Hosp., Annapolis, 1972—; jr. attending neurosurgeon Washington Hosp. Center, 1972—; clin. asst. prof. neurosurgery George Washington U., 1972—; instr. neurosurgery Johns Hopkins U., Balt., 1972—. Founder, Chesapeake Soc. for Physically Handicapped, Annapolis, 1972. Served with U.S. Army, 1966-68; Vietnam. Decorated Bronze Star; diplomate Am. Bd. Neurosurgery. Fellow A.C.S.; mem. Am. Assn. Neurol. Surgeons, So. Neurosurg. Soc., Washington Acad. Neurosurgeons, Congress Neurol. Surgeons. Republican. Jewish. Contbr. articles on neurosurgery to med. jours. Home: Ferry Farms Annapolis MD 21402 Office: 20 Ridgely Ave Annapolis MD 21401

KUSSMAUL, ERNEST ARTHUR, elec. engr.; b. N.Y.C., Aug. 16, 1929; s. Karl and Ida (Heilmann) K.; B.E.E., N.Y. U., 1959; M.E.E., 1963; m. Marilyn Cejka, July 30, 1960; 1 dau., Annette Emily. Product engr. Kollsman Instruments, Elmhurst, N.Y., 1956-59; systems engr. Fairchild Stratos Co., Bay Shore, N.Y., 1959-60; engr., sect. mgr. Dorne & Margolin, Bohemia, N.Y., 1960-67; pres. Kussmaul Electronics, Sayville, N.Y., 1967—; instr. undergrad. math. Dowling Coll., Oakdale, N.Y., 1959-74. Served with AUS, 1951-53. Registered profl. engr., N.Y. Mem. IEEE, Eta Kappa Nu, Tau Beta Pi. Home: 146 Sunset Dr Sayville NY 11782 Office: 186 W Main St Sayville NY 11782

KUTANOVSKI, MILAN S., orthopedic surgeon; b. Struga, Macedonia, Yugoslavia, Mar. 6, 1929; s. Simon and Frosa S. (Pejova) K.; came to U.S., 1969, naturalized, 1973; M.D., U. Skopje, 1955; m. Voyka Kalicanin, Aug. 31, 1969; 1 son, Alek. Intern, Univ. Hosp., Skopje, 1956-57; gen. practitioner Struga Med. Center, 1957-59; resident in orthopedic surgery Univ. Hosp. for Orthopedic Surgery and Traumatology, Belgrade, Yugoslavia, 1959-63, attending orthopedic surgeon, 1963-69; resident in orthopedic surgery Catholic Med. Center Bklyn. and Queens, Inc., N.Y.C., 1970-74; orthopedic surgeon USPHS Hosp., S.I., 1974—, med. dir., asst. chief orthopedics, 1976—. Fellow Am. Bd. Orthopedic Surgery; mem. Am. Yugoslav Med. Assn., Commd. Officers Assn., Assn. Mil. Surgeons. Eastern Orthodox. Home: 68 Radcliff Rd Staten Island NY 10305 Office: USPHS Hospital Bay and Vanderbilt Sts Staten Island NY 10304

KUTASH, SAMUEL BENJAMIN, psychotherapist; b. Bklyn., May 12, 1912; s. Isadore and Jennie (Kaplan) K.; B.S., City U. N.Y., 1932, M.Sc., 1936; postgrad. Columbia, 1936-37; Ph.D., N.Y. U., 1944; m. Lee Proschansky, Dec. 24, 1936; children—Emilie (Mrs. Martin Sobel), Irwin Lawrence. Psychologist, N.Y.C. Bd. Edn., 1936-41; chief psychologist Woodbourne (N.Y.) Instn., 1941-43, Harlem Valley State Hosp. (N.Y.), 1943-46; pvt. practice psychotherapy, Maplewood, N.J., 1947—. Adj. prof. N.Y. U., 1942-52; adj. prof. Rutgers U., New Brunswick, N.J., 1952-65, vis. prof. Grad. Sch. Profl. and Applied Psychology, 1974—; adj. prof. Jersey City State Coll., 1967-76; prof. Kean Coll. N.J., 1973—; chief psychology service VA Hosp., East Orange, N.J., 1952-60; partner, v.p. Human Resources Devel. & Conservation Corp., N.Y.C., 1972; chmn. N.J. Bd. Psychol. Examiners, 1967-74; dir. N.J. div. N.Y. Center for Psychoanalytic Tng., 1970—. Bd. govs. Am. Friends Hebrew U., 1965. Recipient Distinguished Service award N.J. Psychol. Assn., 1970; Mt. Scopus citation Am. Friends Hebrew U., 1971. Diplomate Am. Bd. Profl. Psychology. Fellow Am. Psychol. Assn., Am. Orthopsychiat. Assn., Am. Group Psychotherapy Assn., AAAS. Author: Perceptual Changes in Psychopathology, 1961; Ency. of Criminology, 1944; Perspectives on Violence, 1978; also articles in field. Asso. editor Jour. Group Psychoanalysis and Process, 1965-72, Group Process, 1972—, Jour. Clin. Psychopathology, 1942-52. Home: 3 Park Rd Maplewood NJ 07040 Office: 1 Cypress St Maplewood NJ 07040

KUTEMEYER, PETER MARTIN, indsl. engring. exec.; b. Freiburg, W. Germany, Nov. 19, 1938; s. Martin Henry and Gertrude Barbara (Buechel) K.; came to U.S., 1954, naturalized, 1956; B.M.E. with distinction, Ariz. State U., 1968, M.S. in Engring. Mechanics, 1969; M.B.A., U. Utah, 1977; m. Fresquez, June 25, 1961; children—Michael, Kristina. Enlisted USAF, 1958, commd. 2d. lt. 1967, advanced through grades to capt., 1970; aero. engr., 1969-71, systems devel. engr., 1971-74, tech. liaison officer to W. German Fed. Govt., 1974-78; ret., 1978; indsl. mgr. Mining Progress, Inc., Highland Mills, N.Y., 1978—. Mem. ASME, Am. Inst. Aeros. and Astronautics, Smithsonian Nat. Assos., U.S. Naval Inst. (asso.). Home: care Reiniger PO Box 168 Edgemont PA 19028 Office: Mining Progress Inc PO Box 3 Highland Mills NY 10930

KUTILEK, RICHARD JOHN, hosp. adminstr.; b. N.Y.C., Nov. 12, 1946; s. John Joseph and Helen K.; B.A. in Sociology, St. Francis Coll., Loretto, Pa., 1968; M.P.S. in Health Care Adminstrn., C.W. Post Coll., 1977. Epidemiologist, USPHS, N.Y.C., 1968-70; logistic mgr. N.Y. U. Med. Center 1977; asso. exec. dir. Bronx Municipal Hosp. Center, 1978—. Served with U.S. Army, 1973-77. Mem. Am. Hosp. Assn., Met. Health Adminstrs. Assn. Home: 1874 Pelham Pkwy Bronx NY 10461

KUTRZEBA, JOSEPH STANISLAW, theatrical dir., and film producer; b. Lodz, Poland, Oct. 11, 1927; s. Israel and Malka (Hackman) Fajwiszys; B.A., U. Munich (Germany), 1950; M.F.A., Yale, 1956; Ph.D., N.Y. U., 1974; 1 dau., Karen Janina. Came to U.S., 1950, naturalized, 1953. Researcher, prodn. coordinator, dir., stage mgr. CBS-TV, N.Y.C., 1956-73; producer, dir., writer, narrator UN Radio, N.Y.C., 1959-69; dir.-mem. Actors Studio, 1960-62; founder, producer, artistic dir. Queens Playhouse, Flushing Meadows, N.Y., 1972-74, also mem. bd. dirs., pres.; mem. faculty New Sch. for Social Research, N.Y.C., 1975-77; producer-dir. documentary film The Lost Generation, 1978. Mem. citizens com. Study of N.Y. Theater, 1971-72. Aux. mounted officer N.Y.C. Police Dept., 1974-77. Served with AUS, 1950-52. MacDowell Colony fellow, 1973—. Mem. Dirs. Guild Am., Yale Alumni Assn. Home: 125 E 71st St New York NY 10021

KUTTNER, BERNARD A., lawyer, judge; b. Berlin, Germany, Jan. 13, 1934; s. Frank B. and Vera (Knopfmacher) K.; A.B. cum laude, Dartmouth, 1955; postgrad. U. Va. Law Sch., 1956; J.D., Seton Hall U., 1959; m. Cathy A. Ledner, Mar. 11, 1961; children—Karen Margaret, Robert Douglas, Stacey Meredith. Admitted to N.J. bar, 1960, U.S. Supreme Ct. bar 1964; clk. firm McGlynn, Stein & McGlynn, Newark, 1958-59; asso. Toner, Crowley, Woelper & Vanderbilt, Newark, 1959-62; individual practice law, Newark, 1962-75; partner firm Kuttner and Toner, Newark and Livingston, N.J., 1975—; judge N.J. Div. Tax Appeals, Livingston, 1977—. Chmn. N.J. Anti-Defamation League B'nai B'rith, 1971-77, chmn. nat. discriminations com. 1974-76; mem., pres. Essex County Park Commn., 1973—; corp. counsel Irvington, N.J., 1963-66. Democratic candidate for N.J. Legislature, 1967. Served as lt. comdr. USNR. Recipient Humanitarian award HOPE, 1973; named Outstanding Young Man N.J., 1967; Outstanding Civic Leader of Am., 1968. Mem. Am., N.J. (gen. council 1973—, chmn. conflict of interests com. 1973-75, mem. jud. selection com. 1975—), Irvington (pres., 1968), Essex County (chmn. trial and appellate litigation com. 1973, 74, treas. 1975—) bar assns., Naval Res. Assn., Zool. Soc. N.J., Zeta Psi. Lion (past pres.). Author: Code of Ethics for Municipal Officials, 1963. Home: 321 Wyoming Ave Maplewood NJ 07040 also Gregory Town Eleuthera Bahamas Office: 11 Commerce St Newark NJ 07102 also 554 S Livingston Ave Livingston NJ 07039

KUTZEN, JEROME JEFFERIES, merger specialist; b. Detroit, Jan. 21, 1923; s. Samuel P. and Ann (Stolarsky) K.; student U. Ill., 1940-43, 46-47, Oberlin Coll., 1943-44; m. Carol J. Tedoff, Dec. 9, 1945; children—Peggy Duke, Thomas T. Pres., Glenmore Corp., mortgages, N.Y.C., 1947-63; pres. Kutzen & Co., merger specialists, 1963-67, Purchase, N.Y., 1969—; dir. corp. devel. Transitron Electronic Corp., N.Y.C., 1967-69; partner Purchase Co. (N.Y.). Served to 1st lt. USMCR, 1941-45; PTO. Clubs: Squadron A (N.Y.C.); Cavalry (London). Address: Kutzen & Co Inc Purchase St Purchase NY 10577

KUZMAK, LUBOMYR IHOR, surgeon; b. Balyhorod, Ukraine, Aug. 2, 1931; s. Wolodymyr and Lidia (Litynsky) K.; came to U.S., 1965, naturalized, 1968; M.D., Med. Acad., Lodz, Poland, 1953; D.Sc., Silesian Acad. Medicine, Katowice, Poland, 1965; m. Roxanne A. Smishkewych, Jan. 22, 1966; 1 dau., Roxolana. Resident, chief resident in gen. surgery Silesian Acad. Medicine, III Surg. Clinic, Bytom, Poland, 1954-61, gen. surgeon head div., asso. prof., 1961-65; resident, chief resident in gen. surgery St. Barnabas Med. Center, Livingston, N.J., 1966-71; practice medicine specializing in gen. and vascular surgery, Newark, 1971—. Diplomate Polish Bd. Gen. Surgery. Mem. AMA (Physicians Recognition award 1970-73, 76—), Ukranian Med. Assn. N.Am., N.J., Essex County med. assns. Ukranian Catholic. Contbr. articles to profl. jours. Office: 657 Irvington Ave Newark NJ 07106

KUZMOWYCZ, NICHOLAS, physician; b. Stryj, Ukraine, Aug. 9, 1914; s. Wolodymyr and Irena (Selezinka) K.; came to U.S., 1949, naturalized, 1955; M.D., Jan Kazimir U., 1938; m. Olga Szeparowycz, Dec. 26, 1939; children—Christine Marie, George Andrew. Intern, City Hosp., Krakow, Poland, 1940-41, All Souls Hosp., Morristown, N.J., 1949-50; resident 3d City Hosp., Lviv, Ukraine, 1941-45, Gen. Hosp., Bad Ischl, Austria, 1945-46; practice medicine specializing in family practice, Babylon, N.Y., 1950—; mem. staff Good Samaritan Hosp., West Islip, N.Y., Southside Hosp., Bay Shore, N.Y. Served to 2d lt., M.C., Polish Army, 1938-39. Mem. Ukrainian Acad. Arts Scis., AMA. Am. Acad. Family Practice, Ukrainian Med. Soc. U.S.A., Assn. Ukrainian Artists N.Y., N.Y. State Med. Soc. Ukrainian Catholic. Contbr. articles on history of art to profl. jours. Home: 221 Fire Island Ave Babylon NY 11702 Office: 173 Fire Island Ave Babylon NY 11702

KUZNETS, SIMON SMITH, economist; b. Kharkov, Russia, Apr. 30, 1901; s. Abraham and Pauline (Friedman) K.; B.S., Columbia 1923, M.A., 1924, Ph.D., 1926, D.H.L., (hon.), 1954; D.Sc. (hon.), U. Pa., 1956, LL.D., 1976; D.Sc., Harvard, 1959, Princeton; Ph.D. (hon.), Hebrew U. Jerusalem, 1965; LL.D., U. N.H., 1972; D.H.L., Brandeis U., 1975; m. Edith H. Handler, June 5, 1929; children—Paul, Judith. Social Sci. Research Council Fellow, 1925-27; mem. staff Nat. Bur. Econ. Research, 1927-61; asst. prof. econ. statistics U. Pa., 1930-34, asso. prof., 1934-35, prof., 1936-54; prof. polit. economy Johns Hopkins, 1954-60; Frank W. Taussig research prof. econs. Harvard, 1958-59, prof. econs., 1960-71. Asso. dir. Bur. Planning and Statistics, WPB, 1942-44. Recipient Nobel prize in econs., 1971. Fellow Royal Statis. Soc., Am. Statis. Assn. (pres. 1949), AAAS, Econometric Soc., Brit. Acad. (corr.); mem. Am. Econ. Assn. (pres. 1954), Royal Acad. Scis. Sweden, Am. Philos. Soc., Internat. Statis. Inst., U.S. Acad. Scis. Jewish. Author: Cyclical Flucatuations, 1926; Secular Movements in Production and Prices, 1930; Seasonal Variations in Industry and Trade, 1933; National Income and Capital

Formation, 1938; Commodity Flow and Capital Formation, 1938; National Income, 1941; National Product in Wartime, 1945; National Income; A Summary of Findings, 1946; National Product since 1869, 1946; Shares of Upper Income Groups in Income and Savings, 1953; Six Lectures on the Economic Growth, 1959; Capital in the American Economy, 1961; Postwar Economic Growth, 1964; Economic Growth and Structure: Selected Essays, 1965; Modern Economic Growth, 1966; Economic Growth of Nations, 1971; Population, Capital, and Growth, 1973. Contbr. to econ. jours. Home: 67 Francis Ave Cambridge MA 02138

KUZNICKI, SISTER ELLEN MARIE, educator; b. Dunkirk, N.Y., Oct. 23, 1917; d. Dominic and Bernice (Sek) K.; B.S., Canisius Coll., 1950; M.S., Medaille Coll., 1961; Ph.D., Kans. State U., 1973. Tchr., Bishop Colton High Sch., Buffalo, 1957-61, Villa Maria Acad., Buffalo, 1961-66; prof. Villa Maria Coll., 1970—. Mem. Polish Am. (asso. editor newsletter 1973—, pres. 1977), Am. hist. assns., Polish Arts Club, Nat. Ethnic Assembly, The Kosciuszko Found., Am. Assn. Tchrs. df French. Democrat. Roman Catholic. Author: Bibliography of Sources: The Polish American Community in the Greater Buffalo, New York Area, 1976; article series Poles in Buffalo, AM-Pol Eagle, 1973-74. Home: 600 Doat St Buffalo NY 14211 Office: 240 Pine Ridge Rd Buffalo NY 14225

KWAH, HENRY HONG, surgeon; b. Seoul, Korea, Feb. 22, 1927; s. Taek and Chungyoo (Kim) K.; M.D., Seoul Nat. U., Korea, 1951; came to U.S., 1953, naturalized, 1969; m. Micha Kim, Mar. 8, 1958; children—Wesley, Marjorie. Resident in surgery and thoracic cardiovascular surgery Md. Gen. Hosp., U. Md. Hosp., 1955-61; fellow dept. cardiovascular surgery U. Toronto, 1962-64; practice medicine specializing in thoracic and cardiovascular surgery, Havre de Grace, Md., 1965; mem. staff Harford Meml., Fallston Gen., Md. Gen. hosps. Bd. dirs. Am. Heart Assn., Md. affiliate, 1972—, Md. Blood Bank, 1973—, Am. Lung Assn., Md., 1972-75; pres. Am. Heart Assn., Central Md., 1973. Diplomate Am. Bd. Surgery, Am. Bd. Thoracic Surgery. Fellow A.C.S., Am. Coll. Chest Physicians; mem. Med. and Chirugical Faculty Md.., AMA, Korean Med. Assn. Am. (chmn. sci. and ednl. com.), Am. Thoracic Soc., Am. Heart Assn., So. Thoracic Surg. Assn., Harford County Med. Soc. (pres. 1974), Seoul Nat. U. Coll. Medicine Alumni Assn. Am. (pres. 1977). Methodist. Home: 1005 Leslie Rd Havre de Grace MD 21078 Office: 601 S Union Ave Havre de Grace MD 21078

KWALICK, DONALD SIMON, physician; b. Newark, Jan. 12, 1939; s. Irwin and Esther (Silverstein) K.; B.A., Rutgers U., 1960; M.D., N.Y. U., 1964; M.P.H., Columbia U., 1969; m. Joan Herschenhorn, Dec. 27, 1958; children—Cheryl Ann, Steven Benjamin. Intern, Tripler Gen. Hosp., Honolulu, 1964-65; resident N.J. State Dept. Health, Trenton, 1967-70, dir. pesticide project, 1969-71, med. dir., health services adminstr. Trenton Neighborhood Family Health Center, 1971-73, asst. commr. community health services, Trenton, 1973—, dir. public health residency program, 1975—; asso. clin. prof. community medicine Rutgers U., New Brunswick, N.J., 1976—; chmn. N.J. Pub. Health Licensing Bd., 1976—; mem. exec. com. N.J. Developmental Disabilities Council, 1975—; trustee Newark Comprehensive Health Services Plan, 1976—. Served with USAR, 1964-67. Rutgers U. Trustee scholar, 1956-60; Robert Wood Johnson Found. grantee, 1960-64; recipient Sci. Exhbt. award Med. Soc. N.J., 1970; Physicians Recognition award AMA, 1967, 70, 73, 76. Diplomate Am. Bd. Preventive Medicine. Fellow Am. Coll. Preventive Medicine; mem. Mercer County Heart Assn. (trustee 1973-74), Trenton Vis. Nurse Assn. (trustee 1973-76), N.J., Mercer County med. socs., N.J. Pub. Health Assn. (exec. com. 1978), N.J. Health Officers Assn. Contbr. articles in field to med. jours.; mem. manuscript rev. bd. Jour. Med. Soc. N.J., 1978. Home: 6 Seven Oaks Ln Trenton NJ 08628 Office: PO Box 1540 Trenton NJ 08625

KWARTLER, CHARLES EDWARD, chemist, chem. mfg. co. exec.; b. Stanislau, Austria, Oct. 5, 1911; s. Hyman and Anna (Hager) K.; came to U.S., 1914, naturalized, 1921; B.S., N.Y. U., 1932, Ph.D., 1936; m. Ruth B. Auerbach, Apr. 6, 1941; children—Alice R., Jeanne C., David E. Asst. instr., dept. chemistry N.Y. U., N.Y.C., 1936-38; research chemist Winthrop Chem. Co., Rensselaer, N.Y., 1939-45, dir. process devel., 1946-51; dir. research Gamma Chem. Corp., Great Meadows, N.J., 1951-55, v.p., 1955-65, exec. v.p., 1965-68; exec. asst. Ashland Chem. Co., Great Meadows, 1968-69, mgr. process research and engring., 1969-70, asst. to pres., 1971—, cons., 1976—; tech. co-ordinator for research and devel. Ashland Oil, Inc., Columbus, Ohio, 1970-71; cons. Southland Corp., 1978—. Pres. Jewish Center of NW N.J., 1955-71; chmn. Hackettstown Community Hosp., 1968-72, pres. citizens adv. com., 1972-74; pres. Hackettstown Bd. Edn., 1956-67; pres. Warren County (N.J.) Tech. Sch., 1976—; trustee Warren County Guidance Center, 1969—, Hackettstown Community Hosp., 1974—; chmn. Warren County Community Coll. Com., 1976. Recipient certificate of Commendation U.S. Office of Sci. Research and Devel., 1946. Mem. Am. Chem. Soc., N.Y. Acad. Scis., Sigma Xi, Phi Lambda Upsilon. Author: (with R.I. Towse, R.M. Wehnau) A Manual for Safe Handling of Chemicals, 1947; (with R.L. Kenyon, J.A. Weisner) Modern Chemical Processes, 1950; contbr. articles on synthetic organic and medicinal chemistry to profl. jours. Home: RD 2 PO Box 322 Hackettstown NJ 07840 Office: Ashland Chemical Co Alphano Rd Great Meadows NJ 07838

KWO, CHIN CHARLES, physician; b. Loyang, Honan, China, Oct. 28, 1926; s. Fo-Shou and Mary (Han) K.; came to Can., 1962, naturalized 1969; M.S., McGill U., 1969; M.D., Nat. Def. Med. Center, Taipei, Taiwan, 1952; m. Dorothy Chen, July 8, 1962; children—Jean, Jennie, John. Intern Nat. Def. Med. Center Hosp., Taipei Taiwan, 1951-52, Reddy Meml. Hosp., Montreal (Que., Can.), 1964-65; resident in surgery Nat. Def. Med. Center Hsop., Taipei, 1952-58, Hosp. du Sacre Coeur, Montreal, Hosp. St Justine, Montreal, Lakeshore Gen. Hosp., Que., St. John Gen. Hosp., N.B., Can., 1965-72; surgeon Nat. Def. Med. Center Med. Sch. Hosp., 1961-62; surg., orthopedic research in exptl. surgery, Montreal, 1968-73; asso. in research Royal Victoria Hosp., Montreal, 1973—; med. staff Reddy Meml. Hosp., Montreal, 1970—, Acupuncture Clinic, Montreal. 1972—. Bd. dirs. Canadian Inst. Chinese Med. Sci. and Acupuncture #210, Montreal PQ H3G 1W1 Canada Mem. Med. Council Can., Gen. Med. Council London, Vt. Med. Bd., Profl. Corp. Physicians Que., Can. Med. Assn., Assn. Medècins Langue Francaise Can. Pioneer Can. use acupuncture anesthesia for surgery, dental surgery, 1973. Office: 1414 Drummond St Montreal PQ H3H 1W1 Canada

KWOLEK, JOHN PETER, biomed. engr.; b. Meriden, Conn., June 7, 1948; s. Joseph John and Helen Agnes (Bedus) K.; B.E.E., U. Conn., 1971-74. Carpenters' helper, Conn., 1966; project support engr. Digital Equip. Corp., Maynard, Mass. Served with USAF, 1967-71. Decorated Air medal with 2 oak leaf clusters; NIH fellow. Mem. IEEE. Democrat. Roman Catholic. Office: 129 Parker St Maynard MA 01754

KWON, IK HYUN, physician; b. Korea, Aug. 22, 1937; s. Soo Myong and Jin Joo (Rhim) K.; M.D., Seoul Nat. U., 1962; Ph.D., Rugers U., 1974; m. Bok Hee Suh, Oct. 4, 1969; children—Esther, James. Intern, Martland Med. Center, Newark, 1966-67; resident in internal medicine Bklyn.-Cumberland Med. Center, 1967-70; practice medicine specializing in internal medicine, South Plainfeild, N.J., 1976—; mem. staff John F. Kennedy Med. Center, Edison, N.J. Served with Korean Army, 1963-66. Mem. A.C.P., AAAS, AMA, N.Y. Acad. Scis. Home and Office: 1526 New Durham Rd South Plainfield NJ 07080

KWON-CHUNG, KYUNG JOO, research microbiologist; b. Seoul, S. Korea, Oct. 5, 1933; d. Choong Ton and Sung Ie (Cho) Kwon; B.S., Ewha Women's U., 1956; M.S., 1958; M.S., U. Wis., 1963, Ph.D., 1965; m. Young Muk Chung, Apr. 7, 1957; children—Jay, John, Mia. Asst. prof. biology Ewha Women's U., Seoul, 1959-61; research asso. bacteriology U. Wis., Madison, 1961-65; vis. asso. med. mycology Nat. Inst. Allergy and Infectious Diseases, NIH, Bethesda, Md., 1966-68, research microbiologist, 1969-73, clin. mycology, 1973—; cons. in field. Fulbright Exchange scholar, 1961-62; NSF grantee, 1962-63; U. Wis. Alumni Research fellow, 1963-65; Forgaty Internat. vis. fellow, 1966-68. Mem. Found. Edn. Scis., Am. Soc. Microbiology, Mycological Soc. Am., Med. Mycological Soc. Ams., Internat. Soc. Human and Animal Mycoloby, Sibma Xi, Sigma Delta Epsilon. Author: Medical Mycology, 1977. Contbr. articles to profl. publs. Home: 8618 Ewing Dr Bethesda MD 20034 Office: Bldg 10 11N104 NIH Bethesda MD 20014

KYANKA, GEORGE HARRY, educator; b. Syracuse, N.Y., July 17, 1941; s. George G. and Helen M. (Roscoe) K.; B.S., Syracuse U., 1962, M.S., 1965, Ph.D., 1975; postgrad. U. Ill., 1963, McGill U., 1964; m. Mary M. Keefer, Apr. 30, 1967; children—Michelle Ann, Eric Charles. Research engr. Caterpillar Tractor Co., 1962-64; instr. Syracuse U., 1964-66; asst. prof. mech. tech. Onondaga Community Coll, Syracuse, N.Y., 1966-67; asst. prof. wood products Coll. Environmental Sci. and Forestry, State U. N.Y., Syracuse, 1968-73, asso. prof., 1974—; cons. forest products, product liability. Scoutmaster Boy Scouts Am., 1976—. Recipient Chancellor's award State U. N.Y., 1973; NSF fellow, 1967. Mem. ASME, Soc. Exptl. Stress Analysis, Am. Acad. Mechanics, ASTM, Forest Products Research Soc., Amateur Athletic Assn., Sigma Xi. Club: K.C. Home: 134 Park Way Camillus NY 13031 Office: State U NY Coll Environ Sci and Forestry Syracuse NY 13210

KYRIANNIS, CHRISTOPHER NICHOLAS, clin. social worker; b. N.Y.C., Oct. 24, 1942; s. Nicholas Emanual and Aglaia (Coroneos) K.; B.A., Calif. State U., Northridge, 1965; M.S.W., Fordham U., 1974; postgrad. Fla. Inst. Tech., 1978—; m. Komissa Nicholis, July 5, 1969; 1 son, Nicholas. With Soc. for Seamen's Children, Staten Island, N.Y., 1971-72; clin. social worker Creedmore Psychiat. Center, Queens Village, N.Y., 1974—, Howard Beach (N.Y.) Child Guidance and Family Counseling Center, 1977—. Served with U.S. Army, 1966-68. Mem. Nat. Assn. Social Workers, Acad. Certified Social Workers. Republican. Greek Orthodox. Home: 23-08 144th St Whitestone NY 11357 Office: 80-45 Winchester Blvd Queens Village NY 11457

LAANO, ARCHIE BIENVENIDO MAAÑO, physician; b. Tayabas, Quezon, Philippines, Aug. 10, 1939; s. Francisco M. and Illuminada (Maaño) L.; naturalized U.S. citizen; A.A., U. Philippines, 1958, B.S., 1959, M.D., 1963; m. Maria Eleazar, May 2, 1964; 1 dau., Sylvia Marie. Rotating intern Hosp. St. Raphael, New Haven, 1963-64; resident internal medicine, 1964-65; rotating resident pulmonary diseases Laurel Heights Hosp., Shelton, Conn., 1965; affiliated rotating resident Yale-New Haven Med. Center, 1965; resident internal medicine Westchester County Med. Center, Valhalla, N.Y., 1965-66, resident cardiology, 1966-67; resident fellow cardiology Maimonides Med. Center, Bklyn., 1967-68; rotating sr. resident cardiology Coney Island Hosp., Bklyn., 1967-68; fellow internal medicine Mercy Hosp., Rockville Centre, N.Y., 1968-70; med. dir. 54 Main St. Med. Center, Hempstead, N.Y., 1971-76, Bloomingdale's, Garden City, N.Y., 1972—, Oxford Pendaflex Corp., Garden City, 1976—; attending staff Nassau County (N.Y.) Med. Center, Hempstead Gen. Hosp.; practice medicine specializing in cardiology, internal medicine, Nassau County, 1971—; med. dir. Cities Service Oil Co. (CITGO), L.I. div., 1972—. Mem. adv. bd. Vanguard Nat. Bank, Hempstead; cons. physician ICC, Citgo, Liberty Mut. Ins. Co. Boston, 1972—. Certified in acupuncture medicine, N.Y. State. Fellow Internat., Am. colls. angiology, Am. Coll. Internat. Physicians; mem. Am. Coll. Cardiology, AMA, N.Y. State, Nassau County med. socs., Am. Heart Assn., N.Y. Cardiol. Soc., World Med. Assn., Nassau Acad. Medicine, Am., N.Y. State, Nassau socs. internal medicine, N.Y. Soc. Acupuncture for Physicians, Am. Geriatrics Soc., Nassau Physicians Guild, Knights of Rizal. Club: Garden City Lions (program chmn. 1975—, chmn. bd. dirs. 1978—). Home: 80 Stratford Ave Garden City NY 11530 Office: 230 Hilton Ave Suite 111 Hempstead Med Center Hempstead NY 11550

LABALME, GEORGE, JR., library adminstr.; b. Paris, Nov. 17, 1927; s. George and Ethel (Ehrman) L.; A.B., Kenyon Coll., 1950; postgrad. Sch. Architecture, Princeton U., 1951, Art Center Sch., 1953; m. Patricia Hochschild, June 6, 1958; children—Jennifer Rose, Henry George, Lisa Gertrude, Victoria Ann. Apprentice architect, designer Gio Ponti, architect, Milan, Italy, 1952; asst. office mgr. Raymond Loewy, indsl. designer, Paris, 1953-56, account exec. Raymond Loewy-William Snaith Inc., N.Y.C., 1956-58; founder Labalme Assos., Inc., N.Y.C., chmn., 1958-71; v.p. N.Y. Pub. Library, N.Y.C., 1972—. Trustee Adirondack Hist. Assn., Jacob & Valeria Langeloth Found., Hochschild Fund, Renaissance Soc. Am.; bd. govs. Hotchkiss Sch. Served with AUS, 1946-47. Clubs: Century (N.Y.C.); Polo (Paris); Hollenbeck Fishing (Falls Village, Conn.). Home: 25 East End Ave New York City NY 10028 Office: NY Pub Library 42nd St and Fifth Ave New York City NY 10018

LABENSKYJ, IHOR NICHOLAS, telephone co. exec.; b. Bavaria, Germany, Apr. 23, 1946; s. Stefan and Olga (Seginowycz) L.; came to U.S., 1961, naturalized, 1967; B.S. in Elec. Engring., Monmouth Coll., 1971; certificate in Electronic Tech., RCA Inst., 1966; m. Irena Donetz, June 5, 1971. Tech. aide Bell Labs., Holmdel, N.J., 1966-72; systems analyst N.Y. Telephone Co., N.Y.C., 1972-75, mktg. supr., 1975—. Pres. New Salem Civic Assn., Port Washington, N.Y., 1977-79. Named Exec. Adviser of the Year, Jr. Achievement of N.Y., 1975. Mem. Ukrainian Engrs. Soc. U.S. Home: 31 Lowell Rd Port Washington NY 11050 Office: NY Telephone Co Room 3035 1095 Ave of Americas New York City NY 10036

LABIANCA, FRANK MICHAEL, elec. engr.; b. Bklyn., Aug. 17, 1939; s. Dominick Leonard and Maria (Saulle) L.; B.E.E., Poly. Inst. Bklyn., 1961, M.S., 1963, Ph.D., 1967; m. Grace Ann Piscitelli, June 6, 1970; children—Carla Marie, Elena Ann. Instr. elec. engring. Poly. Inst. Bklyn., 1961-67; tech. staff Bell Telephone Labs., Whippany, N.J., 1967—; lectr. in field; prin. investigator research contract Office Naval Research, 1975—. Mem. Acoustical Soc. Am., IEEE, Info. Theory Group IEEE, Sigma Xi, Eta Kappa Nu, Tau Beta Pi. Research in electromagnetic, acoustic propagation, scattering and signal processing. Office: Bell Telephone Labs Whippany Rd Whippany NJ 07981

LABOON, LAWRENCE JOSEPH, personnel cons.; b. St. Louis, Aug. 4, 1938; s. Joseph Warren and Ruth (Aab) LaB.; B.S. magna cum laude, Tex. Wesleyan Coll., 1962; m. Anne McAllister, Aug. 30, 1969. Operating mgr. Firestone Tire & Rubber Co., Akron, Ohio, 1962-66; pres. Met. Personnel, Inc., Phila., 1966—. Spl. com. for placement of disabled Magee Meml. Hosp., Phila., 1970-78; chmn. pvt. employment agy. adv. council Pa. Dept. Labor and Industry, 1973—; guest lectr. Drexel U., 1976—. Bd. govs. Am. Diabetes Assn., 1975-78. Served with USAF, 1954-60. Certified Employment Cons., 1968. Mem. Nat. Employment Assn. (state certification bd. chmn. 1969-71, dir. 1972-74, chmn. bd. regents 1973), Greater Phila., Valley Forge and Main Line C. of C., Better Bus. Bur., Pa. Assn. Personnel Services (pres. 1971-72, Blanchet Meml. award 1973), Nat. Assn. Personnel Cons., Alpha Chi. Republican. Presbyterian. Club: Union League of Phila. Home: 235 Walnut Ave Wayne PA 19087 Office: 1 Belmont Ave Bala Cynwyd PA 19004

LABRECQUE, THEODORE JOSEPH, lawyer; b. Portland, Oreg., Mar. 8, 1903; s. Herman F. and Clara (Thibault) L.; ed. Manhattan Coll., 1920-21; LL.B., Fordham U., 1924; m. Marjorie Uprichard, Jan. 31, 1931; children—Theodore J., Katherine (Mrs. Elmer J. Skiba), Thomas G., Jeanne M. (Mrs. S. Thomas Gagliano), Robert S., David F., Susan (Mrs. Howard H. Woolley Jr.), Barbara Ann (Mrs. William C. Danowitz). Admitted to N.J. bar, 1925, U.S. Supreme Ct. bar, ICC bar, 1936; gen. practice law, Red Bank, N.J., 1925-60, 73—; mem. firm Quinn, Parsons & Doremus, 1929-37, Parsons, Labrecque, Canzona & Blair and predecessor firms, 1937-60; judge N.J. Superior Ct., 1960-73, assigned to appellate div., 1964-73, presiding judge, part D, 1972-73; of counsel Labrecque, Parsons and Bassler, 1973—; spl. counsel to N.J. gov., 1942; mem. div. tax appeals N.J. Dept. Taxation, 1946-60, pres., 1956-60. Chmn. Monmouth County Transp. Coordinating Com., 1973—. Fellow Am. Coll. Trial Lawyers, Am. Bar Found.; mem. Am., N.J. (pres. 1960), Essex County, Monmouth bar assns., Am. Judicature Soc., Phi Delta Phi (hon.). Democrat. Roman Catholic. Clubs: Elks, Lions (past pres.). Home: 410 Rumson Rd Little Silver NJ 07739 Office: 188 E Bergen Pl Red Bank NJ 07701

LACAVA, JAMES SALVATORE, city ofcl.; b. Paterson, N.J., July 27, 1939; s. James Guy and Filomena (Ippolito) L.; grad. Seton Hall, 1956; B.S., U. Pa., 1960; m. Beatrice Lynn McCauley, June 2, 1962; children—James Guy, Lynn Maurie, Beth Ann. Jr. accountant Robert Freifeld & Co., C.P.A.'s, Pompton Lakes, N.J., 1960-62; sr. accountant Edwin T. Boyle, C.P.A. C.P.A., Hackensack, N.J., 1962-64; self-employed pub. accountant, Paterson, 1964-69; auditor-comptroller, tax collector, treas. Dept. Finance, Hackensack, 1969—. Instr. accounting Fairleigh Dickinson U. Evening Sch., 1964. Custodian of Sch. monies Hackensack Bd. Edn.; bd. dirs. Family Life Bur. Served with N.J. N.G., 1961-66. C.P.A., N.J. Mem. Am. Inst. C.P.A.'s, Finance Officers Assn. N.J. (sec., dir.), Italian Circle of Paterson (sec. 1967-76, v.p. 1977—), N.J., Tri County (pres. 1975-76) football ofcls. assns. Lion (pres.). Home: 41 Lenox Rd Wayne NJ 07470 Office: 65 Central Ave Hackensack NJ 07620

LACCETTI, SILVIO RICHARD, educator; b. Teaneck, N.J., Jan. 14, 1941; s. Silvio and Stella Philomena (Nappi) L.; A.B., Columbia, 1962; M.A., 1963, Ph.D., 1967. Instr. dept. humanities Stevens Inst. Tech., Hoboken, N.J., 1965-67, asst. prof., 1967-73, asso. prof., 1973—. Spl. adviser Hudson County prosecutor, 1968-70; ednl. cons. N.J. Regional Drug Abuse Agy., 1970; research and devel. cons. North Hudson Mayor's Council, 1971; intern supr. N.J. Dept. Community Affairs, 1969-74. Forum dir. N.J. Com. Humanities, 1973-74; chmn. Hudson County Bi-Centennial Congress, 1974; spl. adviser Hudson County Charter Study Commn., 1974; chmn. exec. bd. Italian Am. Liaison Orgn., 1975-77. Bd. dirs. No. Bergen Drug Program, 1969-72. Fulbright fellow, Italy, 1964-65; Internship grantee N.J. Dept. Community Affairs, 1969-74; Danforth Found. teaching asso., 1978—. Mem. Sigma Nu. Author: (with H. Druks) Cities in Civilization, vol I, The City in Western Civilization, 1971; Dialogue on Drugs, 1974; New Jersey Colleges and Vocational Schools, 1977; Focus on New Jersey: A Casebook for New Jersey Studies, 1978. Home: 117 Shaler Ave Fairview NJ 07022 Office: Castle Point Station Hoboken NJ 07030

LACHANCE, PAUL ALBERT, educator, clergyman; b. St. Johnsbury, Vt., June 5, 1933; s. Raymond John and Lucienne (Landry) L.; B.S., St. Michael's Coll., 1955; postgrad. U. Vt., 1955-57; Ph.D., U. Ottawa, 1960; m. Therese Cecile Cote, Aug. 6, 1955; children—Michael P., Peter A., M.-Andre, Susan A. Lectr. dept. biology U. Dayton (Ohio), 1963; flight food and nutrition coordinator NASA Manned Spacecraft Center, Houston, 1963-67; asso. prof. dept. food sci. Rutgers U., 1967-72, prof., 1972—, dir. Sch. Feeding Effectiveness Research Project, 1969-72; cons. nutritional aspects of food processing, food service nutrition; vitamin adv. bd. Roche Chem. div. Hoffman LaRoche Co.; ordained deacon Roman Catholic Ch., 1977. Served to capt. USAF, 1960-63. Mem. Am. Assn. Cereal Chemists, AAAS, Inst. Food Tech., Am. Inst. Nutrition, N.Y. Inst. Food Technologists (chmn. 1977-78), Am. Soc. Clin. Nutrition, N.Y. Acad. Sci., Am. Dietetic Assn., Soc. Nutrition Edn., Am. Pub. Health Assn., Sigma Xi. Soc. for Advancement Food Service Research, Assn. Cath. Chaplains, Sociedad Latino Americano de Nutricion, Delta Epsilon Sigma. Editorial adv. bd. Sch. Food Service Research Rev., AVI Pub. Co. Inc., Nutrition Reports Internat., Profl. Nutritionist; contbr. articles to profl. jours. Home: 34 Taylor Rd RFD 4 Princeton NJ 08540 Office: Rutgers U PO Box 231 New Brunswick NJ 08903

LACHE, MARVIN CHARLES, dentist, biochemist; b. N.Y.C., Mar. 18, 1939; s. Alex and Jeane (Morgenstern) L.; B.S., Coll. City N.Y., 1960; Ph.D., Iowa State U., 1966; D.D.S., N.Y.U., 1975; m. Shani Nudel, Feb. 2, 1969; children—Nimrod, Dina. Asso. dept. biochemistry and biophysics Iowa State U., Ames, 1962-66; sci. researcher U. Liege (Belgium), 1966-68; asso. research scientist dept. microbiology N.Y.U., 1968-71; pvt. practice dentistry, Wayne, N.J., 1975—. Mem. Am. Chem. Soc., Am. Dental Soc., Phi Lambda Upsilon. Contbr. articles to profl. jours. Home: 63 Benson Dr Wayne NJ 07470 Office: 150 Hinchman Ave Wayne NJ 07470

LACKAS, JOHN CHRISTOPHER, educator; b. N.Y.C., Oct. 15, 1904; s. John William and Caroline (Mildenberger) L.; B.S., N.Y. U., 1930, M.A., 1931, Ph.D., 1938; J.S.D., St. John's U., 1938; LL.B., Rutgers U., 1929, LL.M., 1935; M.S.S., New Sch. Social Research, 1936; m. Genevieve Mary Meekins, June 29, 1935. Dir. Sch. Bus., Seton Hall U., 1938-42; commd. 1st lt. U.S. Army, 1942, advanced through grades to col., 1950; from asst. comdt. to comdt. U.S. Army Finance Sch., 1948-52; asst. comptroller for internat. affairs Army Gen. Staff, 1952-56; mem. faculty Indsl. Coll. Armed Forces, 1956-60; ret., 1960; prof. bus. Queensborough Community Coll., 1960-74, prof. emeritus, 1974—, dean adminstrn., 1960-68, acting pres., 1961-63. Pres. bd. dirs. Queensboro Council Social Welfare Agys.; trustee L.I. Ednl. TV Council. Decorated Legion of Merit; recipient Excellence in Teaching award Bd. Higher Edn., U. City N.Y., 1974. Mem. Acad. Polit. Sci., AAAS, Mil. Order World Wars, AAUP (pres. City U. N.Y. council 1972), Ret. Officers. Assn., Am. Econs. Assn. Author: (with Col. Seeds) Military Supply Management, 1957; also articles. Home: 41 Hicks Ave Syosset NY 11791 Office: Queensborough Community Coll Bayside NY 11364

LACOSTE, PAUL, univ. rector; b. Montreal, Que., Can., Apr. 24, 1923; s. Emile and Juliette (Boucher) L.; B.A., U. Montreal, 1943, M.A., 1944, L.Ph., 1946, LL.L., 1960; fellow U. Chgo., 1946-47; Doctorate, U. Paris, 1948; LL.D. (hon.) McGill U., 1975, U. Toronto, 1978; m. Louise Marcil, Aug. 31, 1973; 1 dau. by previous marriage,

Helene. Prof. philosophy and law U. Montreal, 1946—, vice rector, 1966-68, exec. vice rector, 1968-75; called to bar, Que., 1960, since practiced in Montreal; mem. Que. Edn. Council, 1964-68, Royal Commn. on Bilinguism and Biculturalism, 1965-71, Que. Univs. Council, 1969-77. Bd. dirs. Ecole Polytechnique de Montreal, Institut de Recherches cliniques de Montreal; co-chmn. Can. Studies Found. Mem. Conf. Rectors and Prins. Que. Univs. (pres. 1977—), Canadian Assn. U. Tchrs., Assn. Univs. and Colls. Can. (pres. 1978—), Canadian Assn. Philosophy, Assn. des Universités Partiellement ou Entièrement de Langue Française (pres. 1978—), Montreal Bar Assn., Montreal Mus. Fine Arts. Club: St. Denis. Author: (with others) Justice et Paix scolaire, 1962, A Place of Liberty, 1964, Le Canada au seuil du siecle de l'abondance, 1969, Principes de gestion universitaire, 1970. Office: U Montreal PO Box 6128 Montreal PQ Canada

LACY, LLOYD HAMILTON, univ. security supr.; b. Warms Springs, Va., Sept. 3, 1931; s. Everett Hamilton and Berlyn Marcella (Morris) L.; student Howard U., 1972-73, 75-76; m. Barbara Jean Lee (div.); 1 dau., Kimberly. Campus security guard Howard U., Washington, 1961-65, supr., 1965-71, dep. dir., chief security officer Office of Security and Safety Services, 1971—; counselor univ. students, staff in area of personal safety and security. Served with U.S. Army, 1948-60. Recipient award for Outstanding Service, Howard U. student body, 1973-74, 75. Mem. Internat. Assn. Chiefs of Police, Internat. Assn. Coll. and Univ. Security Dirs., Nat. Sheriffs Assn., Assn. Fed. Investigators, Am. Judicature Soc. Democrat. Home: 1462 Ogden St NW Washington DC 20010 Office: 2400 6th St NW Washington DC 20059

LACZ, STANLEY JOHN, architect, engr., planner; b. Paterson, N.J., Mar. 8, 1938; s. John Stanley and Harriet (Strezeski) L.; B.Arch., U. Notre Dame, 1960; children—Darria, Kimberly, Scott, Kristin; m. Peggy Dujets, June 23, 1974. Prin., Stanley John Lacz, Architecture, Engring., Planning, Hawthorne, N.J., 1965—. Mem. Nat. Soc. Profl. Engrs., N.J. Soc. Profl. Engrs. (trustee 1972), Passaic County Soc. Profl. Engrs. (pres. 1971), Am. Inst. Planners (chpt. sec. 1972), AIA, Architect League No. N.J., Constrn. Specifications Inst., Passaic County Interprofl. Council (pres. 1973). Office: 662 Goffle Rd Hawthorne NJ 07506

LADD, EVERETT CARLL, JR., data center dir., educator; b. Saco, Maine, Sept. 24, 1937; s. Everett Carll and Agnes Mary (MacMillan) L.; A.B. magna cum laude, Bates Coll., 1959; Ph.D. (Woodrow Wilson fellow, Social Sci. Research Council fellow), Cornell U., 1964; m. Cynthia Louise Northway, June 13, 1959; children—Everett Carll, III, Corina Ruth, Melissa Ann, Benjamin Elliot. Asst. dean students for pub. affairs Cornell U., 1963-64; asst. prof. U. Conn., Storrs, 1964-67, asso. prof., 1967-69, prof., 1969—, dir. Social Sci. Data Center, 1968-77, co-exec. dir. Roper Center, 1977—, also trustee; research fellow Center for Internat. Studies, Harvard, 1969-75; mem. exec. council Inter-Univ. Consortium for Polit. and Social Research, 1975-77; spl. cons. editorial adv. in social sci. to Carnegie Commn. on Higher Edn., 1969-73; W.W. Norton Co., 1977—. Ford Found. fellow, 1969-70; Guggenheim fellow, 1971-72; Rockefeller Found. fellow, 1976-77; fellow Hoover Instn., 1976-77. Mem. AAAS, Am. Polit. Sci. Assn., Am. Sociol. Assn., Am. Assn. for Pub. Opinion Research, Acad. Polit. Sci., Phi Beta Kappa, Delta Sigma Rho. Author: Negro Political Leadership in the South, 1966, 69; Ideology in America: Charge and Response in a City, a Suburb, and a Small Town, 1969, 70; Where Have All the Voters Gone: The Fracturing of America's Political Parties, 1978; (with S.M. Lipset) Professors, Unions, and American Education, 1973, Academics, Politics, and the 1972 Election, 1973, The Divided Academy: Professors and Politics, 1975, 76; (with C.D. Hadley) Political Parties and Political Issues: Patterns in Differentiation Since the New Deal, 1973, Transformations of the American Party System: Political Coalitions from the New Deal to the 1970's, 1975, 78. Mem. editorial bd. Pub. Opinion Quar., 1976—, Polit. Behavior, 1978—; cons. editor, mem. editorial bd. Pub. Opinion, 1977—. Home: 86 Ball Hill Rd Storrs CT 06268 Office: Roper Center U Conn Box U-164 Storrs CT 06268

LADD, SAMUEL APPLETON, JR., educator; b. Newton, Mass., Oct. 17, 1906; s. Samuel Appleton and Katherine (Mills) L.; B.S., Bowdoin Coll., 1929; m. Estelle Hamilton, Aug. 15, 1932; 1 son, Samuel Appleton III. Research analyst Jordan-Lyman Co., investment bankers, Boston, 1929-32; account exec. Dickie-Raymon Advt. Agy., Boston, 1933-37; sales rep. Milton, Bradley Co., Springfield, Mass., 1937-40, J.L. Hammett Co., Cambridge, 1940-44; placement dir., adminstrv. officer Bowdoin Coll., Brunswick, Maine, 1944-72, tennis coach, 1950-56; corporator Brunswick Savs. Instn., 1956-78. Adv. bd. Coll. Guidance Service, 1956-60; mem. adminstrv. bd. Coll. Placement Publs. Council, 1957-60. Mem. Brunswick Planning Bd., 1950-55; mem. Maine, Brunswick coms. ARC, 1940-60, YMCA, 1950-66, Manpower Commn., 1944-46; mem. Maine Natural Resources Council, 1966-72. Pres. bd. trustees Brunswick Community Hosp., 1955-60; trustee Regional Meml. Hosp., Brunswick, 1961—, also v.p.; bd. dirs. Youth Tennis Found., 1960-70. Recipient Alumni Achievement award Bowdoin Coll., 1976; Citizen of Yr. award Brunswick C. of C., 1978. Mem. Soc. Colonial Wars, New Eng. Lawn Tennis Assn. (dir., mem. exec. com. 1958-70), U.S. Assn., Ipswich (Mass.) Hist. Soc., Pejepscot Hist. Soc. (pres. 1975-77, dir.), Maine Hist. Soc., N.H. Piscataqua Pioneers, Maine Soc. Order Founders and Patriots Am. (charter, sec., gov., councillor gen.), Zeta Psi (mem. ednl. found., pres. Lambda chpt. house corp. 1950-72). Republican. Conglist. Rotarian (pres. Brunswick 1943-44), Mason. Clubs: Town and College (Brunswick, Me.); Cumberland (Portland, Me.). Author: The Ladd Family History; Placement and Counseling; Zeta Psi at Bowdoin—100 Years; Names and Places; the Secret of Paul Revere; Appleton Papers; Sir William Phipps, One of Twenty Seven; Bullfinch's Boston; Brahmin Bailiwick; Yankee Obelisk; Old Customs and Traditions in New England. Contbr. articles to profl. publs. Home: 7 Longfellow Ave Brunswick ME 04011

LADEN, STEVEN, investment banking co. exec.; b. Chgo., Apr. 28, 1935; s. Harold S. and Florence R. L.; B.S. in Mech. Engring., Cornell U., 1958; m. Lee Voigt, Jan. 27, 1963; children—Scott, Drew. Account exec. Paine Webber Jackson & Curtis, Phila., 1966-69; br. mgr. Blair & Co., Phila., 1969-70; resident br. mgr. and v.p. instl. sales Drexel Burnham Lambert, Inc., Phila., 1970-77, 1st v.p., 1977—. Mem. council bd. trustees Cornell U. Served with USAF, 1958-59. Mem. Phila. Securities Assn., Jr. C. of C. (v.p., dir. 1961-64; Outstanding Bd. Mem. 1964). Clubs: Tower of Cornell, Phila. Racquet, Cornell of Phila. (dir. 1964-68). Home: 108 Windsor Ave Philadelphia PA 19126

LADENHEIM, JULES CALVIN, neurosurgeon; b. Union Hill, N.J., Apr. 21, 1923; s. Solomon and Mina (Preminger) L.; A.B., Harvard U., 1944; M.D., N.Y. Med. Coll., 1947; m. Janet Bloom, Feb. 15, 1958; children—Eric, Frederick, Karen. Intern, Queens Gen. Hosp., 1947-48; resident surgery Flower Fifth Ave. Hosp., N.Y.C., 1948-50, Pitts. Med. Center, 1952-53, Mt. Sinai Hosp., Cleve., 1953-54; resident neurosurgery Sarafimer Hosp., Stockholm, 1954-56, Med. Coll. Va., Richmond, 1957, Neurol. Inst. N.Y., N.Y.C., 1958, Dartmouth Med. Center, Hanover, N.H., 1958-60; practice medicine specializing in neurosurgery, Hackensack, N.J., 1960—; mem. staffs Hackensack Hosp., Holy Name Hosp., Bergen Pines Hosp.; asst. prof. N.J. Med. Coll., Newark, 1970—. Served with USNR, 1950-52. Diplomate Am. Bd. Surgery, Am. Bd. Neurosurgery. Fellow A.C.S., Internat. Coll. Surgeons; mem. Am Assn. Neurol. Surgeons, Am. Congress Neurosurgery, Scandanavian Neurosurg. Soc. Author: Congenital Aneurysms, 1957; Meningiomas of the Choroid Plexus, 1962. Office: 401 Hackensack Ave Hackensack NJ 07601

LADERMAN, JACK, mathematician; b. N.Y.C., Jan. 6, 1914; s. Joseph and Fannie (Freeman) L.; B.S., Coll. City N.Y., 1934; M.A., Columbia, 1935, Ph.D., 1953; m. Marion Frances Shupnik, June 8, 1947; 1 son, Julian David. Statistician FCC, N.Y.C., 1937; analyst State Dept. of Labor, N.Y.C., 1938; mathematician Nat. Bur. of Standards, 1939-40, 46-49; statistician Chem. Corps, War Dept., 1940-46; research scientist Columbia, N.Y.C., 1949-51; mathematician Office of Naval Research, Washington, 1951-54, N.Y.C., 1954-62, 63-74, dep. chief scientist, 1966-74, ret., 1974; tech. dir. Service Bur. Corp., N.Y.C., 1962-63; adj. asso. prof. math. N.Y. U., 1957-64; cons. to corps. on application math. to indsl. problems. Recipient Superior Civilian Service award Navy Dept., 1974. Fellow AAAS; mem. Inst. Mgmt. Scis., Am. Math. Soc., Inst. Math. Statistics, Am. Statis. Assn., Biometric Soc., Ops. Research Soc. Am., Soc. Indsl. Applications Math., N.Y. Acad. Scis., Math. Programming Soc., Sigma Xi. Author articles in field. Mng. editor Naval Research Logistics Quar., 1954, 1961-62. Home: 2630 Kingsbridge Terr Bronx NY 10463

LADUE, THOMAS SHELDON, cons. sanitary engr.; b. Plattsburgh, N.Y., Nov. 15, 1940; s. Robert Hagar and Virginia (Thomas) L.; B.S.C.E., Clarkson Coll. Tech., 1964; postgrad. Syracuse U., 1970-71; children by previous marriage—Michael, Thomas; m. Georgia Ann Kinney, Dec. 24, 1971; 1 dau., Toma; stepchildren—Raymond, Terry, Pamela, George. With Barton, Brown, Clyde & Loguidice, North Syracuse, N.Y., 1964-70, designer, 1966-68, project engr., 1968-70; chief environ. services Capital Engring. Corp., Dillsburg, Pa., 1971-77, v.p. environ. services, 1977—, also dir.; cons. on water, sewerage service to municipal groups. Registered profl. engr., N.Y., Pa., Ohio. Mem. ASCE, Am. Water Works Assn. Nat. Soc. Profl. Engrs., Water Pollution Control Fedn. Home: RD 1 York Springs PA 17372 Office: 124 W Church St Dillsburg PA 17019

LADY, ROY ANDREW, coll. adminstr.; b. Reading, Pa., Dec. 24, 1924; s. Harold R. and Clara E. (Hohl) L.; A.A. magna cum laude, Williamsport Dickinson Jr. Coll., 1948; A.B. cum laude, Lycoming Coll. 1949; M.S., Pa. State U., 1951, D.Ed., 1967; m. Nancy Jean Haney, June 9, 1951; children—Paul Allen, Linda Lee, Carol Ann, Scott Andrew. Jr. psychologist Danville (Pa.) State Hosp., 1951-53; personnel evaluation specialist Buick-Oldsmobile-Pontiac div. Gen. Motors Corp., Kansas City, Kans., 1953-57; asst. to pres. Lycoming Coll., Williamsport, Pa., 1957-74, dir. instl. relations, 1974—. Vice pres., dir. Central Pa. United Meth. Fed. Credit Union, 1970-72, asst. treas., 1970—, security officer, 1971-75; sec. northeastern jurisdictional conf. United Meth. Ch., 1973—; bd. dirs. Lycoming County Child Day Care Center, chmn. fin. com., 1974-76, v.p., 1974-75, pres., 1975-76; bd. dirs. Internat. Student Coordinating Assn. Lycoming County, 1973-76, chmn. fin. com., 1974-76, v.p., 1974-75. Served with USNR, 1943-46. Mem. Am., Pa. assns. higher edn., Pa. Edn. Drs. Soc., Williamsport-Lycoming C. of C. (dir. 1975-78), Tau Kappa Epsilon, Phi Delta Kappa, Psi Chi. Methodist (trustee). Clubs: Masons (32 deg.), Rotary (dir. 1973-74, 2d v.p. 1974-75, 1st v.p. 1975-76, pres. 1976-77). Home: 123 Upland Rd Williamsport PA 17701

LA FALCE, JOHN JOSEPH, congressman; b. Buffalo, Oct. 6, 1939; s. Dominic E. and Catherine M. (Stasio) LaF.; B.S., Canisius Coll., 1961; J.D., Villanova U., 1964. Admitted to N.Y. bar, 1964; practiced in Buffalo, 1967-74; mem. 94th-95th Congresses from 36th N.Y. Dist.; chmn. Small Bus. Subcom. Small Bus., Devel., Investment and Commodities; legal counsel N.Y. State Jr. C. of C., 1970-71. Pres., Catholic Lawyers Guild, Diocese of Buffalo, 1971-72; chmn. legis. com. Community Welfare Council of Buffalo and Erie County, 1969-71; hon. chmn. Assn. for Research Childhood Cancer; mem. N.Y. State Senate, 1971-72, N.Y. State Assembly, 1973-74; bd. dirs. United Irish-Am. Assn. of Erie County, Inc. Served to capt. U.S. Army, 1965-67. Decorated Army Commendation medal; recipient All Am. Columbus award Fedn. Italian-Am. Democratic Orgns., 1974, N.Y. Cath. War Vets. award, 1976, award Niagara Frontier chpt. Nat. Assn. Homebuilders, 1976, Man of Year awards N.Y. State chpt. Asso. Gen. Contractors Am., 1975, Tonawanda Labor Council, 1975, Niagara-Orleans Labor Council, 1975, Western N.Y. chpt. Cystic Fibrosis Found., 1975, Fedn. Italian-Am. Socs., 1976. Mem. Erie County Bar Assn., Justinian Legal Soc., Am. Judicature Soc., Italian-Am. Legislators Club, Kenmore C. of C., Am. Legion. Clubs: K.C.; Mercy Hosp. Mens Sustaining Soc.; Tonawanda Sportsman; Lewiston 3-F; Marshall. Home: 800 Starin Ave Buffalo NY 14223 Office: 230 Cannon House Office Bldg Washington DC 20515

LAFALCE, RAYMOND PETER, hosp. adminstr.; b. Bklyn.; s. Thomas and Teresa Rita (Muzzio) LaF.; B.S. in Pharmacy, Fordham U., 1951; M.S. in Hosp. Adminstrn., Columbia, 1967; m. Dolores Maloney, Apr. 19, 1952. Sec.-treas. LaFalce Chemists, Inc., Levittown, N.Y., 1953-65; asst. adminstr. Methodist Hosp., Bklyn., 1967-68, asso. adminstr., 1970-72; adminstr. Carson C. Peck Meml. Hosp., Bklyn., 1968-70, Astoria Gen. Hosp., L.I. City, N.Y., 1972-74, Florence Nightingale Nursing Home, N.Y.C., 1974-75, Interboro Gen. Hosp., Bklyn., 1975-77; exec. dir. Corning (N.Y.) Hosp., 1977—. Served with USNR, 1943-44. Mem. N.Y. State Bd. Pharmacy, Am. Coll. Hosp. Adminstrs., Nat. Assn. Bds. Pharmacy, Am. Hosp. Asso. Home: 34 Tall Meadow Painted Post NY 14870 Office: 176 Denison Pkwy E Corning NY 14830

LAFAYE, WILBUR PAUL, aerospace and electronics engr.; b. New Orleans, May 14, 1921; s. Sidney Paul and Geraldine Josephine (Lovretich) L.; student Tulane U., 1937-41; B.S. in Engring., U. Mich., 1942; postgrad. George Washington U., 1948-49; m. Adele Mary Wells, Dec. 24, 1953; 1 dau., Barbara Anne. Aero. engr. Dow Chem. Co., Bay City, Mich., 1942-44; engr. aero. engine lab. Phila. Navy Yard, 1946-48; with Navy Bur. Aeros., Washington, 1948-54, devel. engr., 1950-53, sr. turbojet engine devel. engr., 1953-54; with Redstone Arsenal, Ala., 1954-61, ballistic missile prodn. engr., 1956-60, asso. dir. system design lab., 1960-61; with U.S. Army Satellite Communications Agency, Ft. Monmouth, N.J., 1961-76, chief product assurance, 1970-73, chief system simulation and control, 1973-76; engr.-cons. Kentron Internat., Inc., Tinton Falls, N.J., 1976-78, Analytics, Inc., Tinton Falls, 1977—; v.p. for programs Log-Tech Services, Inc., Tinton Falls, 1978—; mem. combustion subcom. Nat. Adv. Com. Aeros., 1950; coop. observer Nat. Weather Service at Long Br., N.J., 1965-76; dir., owner East Pass Motel-Apts., Destin, Fla., 1970—. Served with USN, 1944-46. Recipient various performance awards and commendations. Mem. Am. Meteorol. Soc., Internat. Platform Assn., Aircraft Owners and Pilots Assn., U.S. Seaplane Pilots Assn., Internat. Arrow Iceyacht Assn. Roman Catholic. Club: Drexelbrook (Drexel Hill, Pa.). Contbr. articles to profl. publs. Home: PO Box 884 Wrightstown NJ 08562 Office: 980 Shrewsbury Ave Tinton Falls NJ 07724

LAFFERTY, CHARLES DOUGLAS JOSEPH, advt. sales co. exec.; b. Rochester, Pa., Mar. 27, 1930; s. William Charles and Kathryn (Devine) L.; B.A., U. Pitts., 1956; m. Inger A. Sorum, Nov. 20, 1967. Vice pres., sales devel. mgr. Moloney, Regan & Schmitt, N.Y.C., 1956-69; dir. mktg., exec. v.p., corp. treas. Branham Corp., N.Y.C., 1969—; lectr. Am. Press Inst., Reston, Va. Served with USMC, 1948-52. Mem. Internat. Newspaper Advt. Execs., Am. Mktg. Assn., Am. Mgmt. Assn., Internat. Newspaper Promotion Assn. (dir.), Newspaper Research Council (dir.), So. Newspaper Pubs. Assn. Republican. Clubs: Cedar Point Yacht (Westport, Conn.); Marco Polo (N.Y.C.). Home: 58 Redcoat Rd Westport CT 06880 Office: 733 3d Ave New York City NY 10017

LAFLAMME, DIANE LUCILLE, counselor; b. New Bedford, Mass., Dec. 22, 1945; d. Alphee Napoleon and Simone Bertha L.; A.B. in English, Emmanuel Coll., 1967; M.A. in Counseling Psychology, Assumption Coll., 1971. Tchr., Foxboro (Mass.) Intermediate Sch., 1968-70; counselor, Foxboro High Sch., 1971—; instr. evening div. Bryant Coll., Smithfield, R.I., 1975-76; counseling intern, Interfaith Counseling Center, Foxboro, 1976-77. Mem. Am. Personnel and Guidance Assn., Mass. Sch. Counselors Assn. Clubs: Appalachian Mountain, U.S. Ski and Sports. Office: Foxboro High School Foxboro MA 02035

LAFOND, JAMES FREDERICK, accountant; b. Springfield, Mass., Oct. 13, 1942; s. Frederick H. and Mildred E. (O'Conner) L.; B.S., Am. Internat. Coll., 1964, M.B.A., 1975; m. Sandra J. Ianello, June 27, 1964; children—Christopher, Matthew, Carrie, Mark. With Coopers & Lybrand, Springfield, 1964—, partner, 1974—, in charge emerging bus. services Western New Eng. area, 1974—. Recipient Elijah Watts Sells award, 1965; CPA. Mem. Springfield. C. of C., Am. Inst. C.P.A.'s, Mass. Soc. C.P.A.'s, Nat. Assn. Accountants (dir. Springfield chpt. 1971-74). Roman Catholic. Club: Rotary. Home: 156 Randall Dr Suffield CT 06078 Office: 2300 Valley Bank Tower Springfield MA 01101

LAFORCE, WILLIAM LEONARD, JR., editor; b. Albemarle County, Va., Aug. 24, 1940; s. William Leonard and Florence Alberta (Sandridge) L.; student U. Va., 1958-60; B.S., Johns Hopkins U., 1967, M. Liberal Arts, 1972; m. Dorothy Lee Kesler, June 8, 1963; children—William Parry, Glenn Edward. Dir. Photography Balt. Sun papers, 1962-73; chief photographer N.J. edit. N.Y. Daily News, N.Y.C., 1974—; lectr. to various press and photography orgns. Pres. Rumsey Island Residents Assn., Joppa, Md., 1969-72, Rumsey House Restoration Found., 1968-70, Mountain Lakes (N.J.) Fire Dept., 1977—; Democratic committeeman, Mountain Lakes, 1976-78; chmn. Wildwood Sch. Bd., 1976-77; bd. dirs. Joppatowne Civic Assn., 1969-71. Recipient Distinguished Service award Jr. C. of C., 1971; award for distinguished community service Rumsey Island Residents Assn., 1972. Mem. Nat. Press Photographers Assn. (exec. bd. 1972-73, pres. Mid-Atlantic region 1977-80), Picture Adminstrs. N.Y., N.Y. Press Photographers Club, N.J. Press Photographers Club. Home: 7 Center Dr Mountain Lakes NJ 07046 Office: New York Daily News 220 E 42nd St New York City NY 10017

LAFORD, RICHARD JOHN, quality engr.; b. Winchendon, Mass., Sept. 4, 1942; s. Tuffield Andrew and Elizabeth Altana (Hebert) L.; B.S., U. Hartford, 1971, M.B.A., 1976; m. Alice Rawson, Nov. 18, 1961; children—Timothy, John, Reta, Lisa. Devel. sheetmetal worker Hamilton Standard div. United Aircraft Corp., Windsor Locks, Conn., 1966-67; quality control rep. and source insp. Kaman Aerospace Corp., Bloomfield, Conn., 1967-68; tchr. shop and drafting Enfield High Sch., Conn., 1968-70; sr. materials control analyst Turbo-Power and Marine Systems, Inc., Farmington, Conn., 1970-71; sr. insp. Ensign Bickford Co., Simsbury, Conn., 1972-73; field process control engr. Gen. Electric Co., Lynn, Mass., 1973-74, product quality engr., 1974-76; sr. quality engr. Digital Equipment Corp., Maynard, Mass., 1977—; prof. adj. faculty N.H. Vocat. Coll., Nashua, 1977—. Swimming instr. ARC, Hartford, 1961-71; Mem. Am. Soc. Quality Control (certified; award 1974, 75, 76). Instrumental in establishing quality control degree program in schs. of eastern U.S. Home: 16 Klondike St Nashua NH 03060 Office: 97 Piper Rd Acton MA 01720

LAGARENNE, LAWRENCE EDWARD, lawyer; b. Bklyn., Jan. 18, 1921; s. John Lawrence and Elizabeth Anna (Vath) L.; B.A., Ohio Wesleyan U., 1941; LL.B., Cornell U., 1947; m. Grace Aileen Rogers, Dec. 19, 1943; children—Edward John, Cecile Ann. Admitted to N.Y. State bar, 1947; mem. firm Hinman, Howard & Kattell, Binghamton, N.Y., 1947-49; mem. firm Wiess & Costa, Monticello, N.Y., partner, 1963-78; partner firm Wiess, Ingber & Lagarenne, Monticello, 1979—. Pres. Legal Aid Soc. Sullivan County, Inc. Served with USNR, 1942-45. Mem. Am., N.Y. State (ho. of dels., exec. com., com. profl. discipline), Sullivan County (past pres.) bar assns., Am. Arbitration Assn., Am. Judicature Soc. Republican. Methodist. Clubs: Kiwanis, Masons. Home: 7 Alva Ln Monticello NY 12701 Office: 230 Broadway PO Box 111 Monticello NY 12701

LAHEY, ROBERT WILLIAM, mech. engr.; b. East Orange, N.J., May 20, 1946; s. Edward William and Mary (Dykes) L.; B.Engring., Stevens Inst. Tech., 1969. With Am. Smelting & Refining Co., Perth Amboy, N.J., 1965-68; devel. engr. N.J. Dept. Environ. Protection, Trenton, 1969-72; sr. environ. engr., mgr. tech. services dept. Amerada Hess Corp., Woodbridge, N.J., 1972—. Served with USAF, 1965-67. Mem. Soc. Automotive Engrs., Assn. Energy Engrs. (founder N.J. chpt.), Air Pollution Control Assn., Am. Inst. Plant Engrs., Chi Phi. Home: 180 Statesir Pl Red Bank NJ 07701 Office: 1 Hess Plaza Woodbridge NJ 07095

LAI, RALPH WEI-MEEN, mineral scientist, engr.; b. Tou-Lu, Taiwan, Dec. 17, 1936; s. Chung-Teng and Kaku; came to U.S., 1962, naturalized, 1975; B.S., Cheng-Kung U., 1959; M.S., S.D. Sch. Mines and Tech., 1964; Ph.D. in Material Sci. and Engring., U. Calif., Berkeley, 1969; m. Cindy Shing-Tze Chen, Aug. 16, 1966; children—Naline LeRue, Melisa Wenna. Research scientist Cyprus Mines Corp., Trenton, N.J., 1969-72; mineral processing scientist Anglo-Am. Clays Corp., Sandersville, Ga., 1973-74; sr. project engr. Ledgemont Lab., Kennecott Copper Corp., Lexington, Mass., 1974. Recipient Dorr Metall. Engring. prize S.D. Sch. Mines and Tech., 1963. Mem. Am. Inst. Mining, Metall. and Petroleum Engrs., Clay Minerals Soc., Mining and Metall. Inst. Japan. Democrat. Buddhist. Contbr. articles on surface chemistry, minerals beneficiation, and liquid-liquid extraction to profl. jours. Home: 3 Graham Rd Lexington MA 02173 Office: 128 Spring St Lexington MA 02173

LAIKIND, JEFFREY, fin. co. exec.; b. Tel-Aviv, Israel, Oct. 15, 1935; s. Leonard and Lili Rudin (Tairstein) Braitman; came to U.S., 1940, naturalized, 1969; B.A., Cornell U., 1957; B.A., N.Y. U., 1958-62; m. Donna Ressler, June 29, 1969; children—Rachel Kate, Daniel Aaron. Asst. treas. Marine Midland Trust Co., N.Y.C., 1958-62; analyst David J. Green & Co., N.Y.C., 1962-67; asst. v.p. A.G. Becker & Co., N.Y.C., 1967-71; v.p. Wertheim & Co., N.Y.C., 1971—. Chmn. com. on audience devel. N.Y.C. Opera Guild, 1974—; bd. dirs., chmn. fin. com. N.Y.C. Opera. Chartered fin. analyst, N.Y. Mem. N.Y. Soc. Security Analysts, Fin. Analysts Fedn., Chartered Fin. Analysts Soc. Clubs: Harmonie, Fairview Country. Home: 165 E 66th St New York City NY 10021 Office: 200 Park Ave New York City NY 10017

LAINE, MATTHEW THOMAS, mktg. cons.; b. Bklyn., Jan. 21, 1932; s. Thomas J. and Mildred Theresa (Marcelle) L.; B.M.E., Poly. Inst. Bklyn., 1960; m. Rose Riconda, Sept. 13, 1959; children—Christine, Andrea, Laura. With Meyer, Strong & Jones, cons., N.Y.C., 1960; partner Richman Assos., Bayside, N.Y., 1960-65; mktg. mgr. Alcan Aluminum Corp., N.Y.C., 1965-68; owner, operator MTL Assos., mktg. cons., Dix Hills, N.Y., 1968—; dir. Mr. Brush, Inc., Primus Group, Ltd., Hungry Hero Systems, Inc. Served with U.S. Army, 1954-56. Mem. Am. Mktg. Assn. Roman Catholic. Club: Kiwanis. Home and Office: 4 S Hollow Rd Dix Hills NY 11746

LAIRD, ANTONIA BISSELL, poet; b. Phila., Nov. 8, 1932; d. Alfred Elliott and Julia duPont (Andrews) Bissell; student Bennett Jr. Coll., 1952; m. Walter Jones Laird, Jr., Nov. 24, 1951; children—David Elliott, William Ian, Philip Lee, Walter Jones, III, Emily Bissell, Stephen Packard. Author: A Quite Voice, 1969; A Parasol of Leaves (Nat. League Am. Penwomen 1st prize), 1973; A Melody of Words, 1978; poems pub. in numerous mags.; poet laureate of Del., 1969-71. Trustee Holderness Sch., Plymouth, N.H.; bd. mgrs. Wilmington (Del.) Library; mem. U. Del. Library Assn. Recipient 1st prize Katherine King Johnson Meml. Poetry contest, 1967, Del. Scene contest, 1966, St. David's Writers Conf., 1971; 2d prize Major Poets contest, 1971. Mem. Nat. League Am. Pen Women. Republican. Episcopalian. Address: 1103 Barley Mill Rd Wilmington DE 19807

LAIRD, ARCHIBALD, ophthalmologist; b. Cecil, Pa., Sept. 30, 1902; s. Thomas and Elizabeth (Hyslop) L.; student Slippery Rock State Normal Sch., 1924; B.S., U. Pitts., 1926, M.D., 1929; postgrad. U. Pa., 1932, U. Glasgow, 1936, U.S. Army Air Corps Sch. Aviation Medicine, 1935; m. Ruth Washburn, May 16, 1936; children—Winthrop Washburn, Robert Hyslop, Elizabeth Louise, Archibald. Telegraph office clk. Peoples Natural Gas Co., Pitts., 1918-19; dir. summer playground, Pitts., 1925, 26; instr. phys. edn. U. Pitts., 1924-29; intern Western Pa. Hosp., Pitts., 1929-30; resident Children's Hosp., Pitts., 1930-31, Polk (Pa.) State Sch., 1931-36; pvt. practice ophthalmology, Wellsboro, Pa., 1936—; med. lectr. in psychology U. Pitts. Grad. Sch., 1933-35; lectr. in neurology C.H. Buhl Hosp., Sharon, Pa., 1934-35; instr. Pa. N.G. Acad., 1960-61; selective service med. staff officer, 1959-62; aviation med. examiner FAA, 1965—. Dist. chmn. Gen. Sullivan council Boy Scouts Am., 1946-51. Served from 1st lt. to maj. U.S. Army Med. Res. Corps, 1929-37, to lt. col. AUS, 1942-46, to brig. gen. NG, 1962—. Recipient 25 year service medal Pa. N.G., 1962, 50 year Masonic service emblem, 1974, Physicians, Recognition award AMA, 1972, 1973-76, 1976-79. Diplomate Nat. Bd. Med. Examiners 1932, Am. Bd. Ophthalmology 1939. Fellow A.C.S. (life), Am. Acad. Ophthalmology and Otolaryngology (life), Assn. Mil. Surgeons U.S.; mem. AMA, Pa. (sr.), Tioga County (pres. 1947) med. socs., Am. Acad. Ophthalmology (life), Aerospace Med. Assn., Co. Mil. Historians, N.G. Assn. (life), Pa. N.G. Vets. Assn. (life), Am. Legion, Democrat. Presbyterian. Clubs: Wellsboro Rotary (pres. 1940), Masons. Designer treatment frame for infants, 1930; author: Twentieth Century Wildcats, 1966; Monuments Marking the Graves of the Presidents, 1971; editor Tioga County Med. Soc. Bull., 1947-55, Wellsboro Rotary Club News Letter, 1967-72; contbr. articles to med. jours. Home: Route 1 Box 1 Meade St Wellsboro PA 16901 Office: 12 Main St Wellsboro PA 16901

LAKAYTIS, GEORGIA O'BRIEN, assn. exec.; b. Dallas, July 2, 1945; d. Jack Dallas and Jane Childs O'Brien; B.J., U. Mo., Columbia, 1967, postgrad., 1970-71. Reporter, editor Wichita Falls (Tex.) Record News, 1965-67; tech. writer Regional Med. Programs, Columbia, Mo., 1967-70; program asso. and media center dir. U. Mo., Columbia, 1970-76; dir. pub. relations Am. Home Econs. Assn., Washington, 1976—. Founder, U. Mo. Women in Athletics, 1975; bd. dirs. Unitarian-Universalist Ch., Columbia, Mo., 1974-76. Mem. Pub. Relations Soc. Am., Am. Soc. Assn. Execs., Nat. Press Club. Democrat. Home: 2727 29th St NW Washington DC 20008 Office: 2010 Massachusetts Ave NW Washington DC 20036

LAL, SAMARTHJI, psychiatrist; b. London, Mar. 23, 1938; s. Yadu Nandan and Om Kumari (Ram) L.; came to Can., 1962, naturalized, 1970; M.B./B.S., Guy's Hosp. Med. Sch., 1962; m. Maureen Elizabeth Kiely, Apr. 27, 1974; 1 son, Sikander Samarth. Diploma in psychiatry with distinction, McGill U., 1967; intern Victoria Hosp., London, Ont., Can., 1962-63; resident Conn. Valley Hosp., Middletown, Conn., 1965-67, Queen Mary Vets. Hosp., Montreal, Que., Can., 1965-67; chief psychiat. consultation service Montreal Gen. Hosp., 1971-75, staff, 1971—, sr. psychiatrist, 1978—, dir. clin. and basic research in psychiatry, 1975—; asso. prof. psychiatry McGill U., 1976—; mem. staff Douglas Hosp., 1976—. Med. Research Council Can. Fellow, 1967-71. Fellow Royal Coll. Physicians, Am. Psychiat. Assn.; mem. Brit. Med. Assn., Canadian Psychiat. Assn., Indian Psychiat. Assn. (life), Soc. Biol. Psychiatry. Contbr. articles to profl. jours. Home: 4858 Cote des Neiges Montreal H3V 1G8 Canada Office: Montreal Gen Hosp Dept Psychiatry Montreal PQ H3G 1A4 Canada

LALLEY, RICHARD ANDREW, ednl. admnstr.; b. Bridgeport, Conn., Jan. 7, 1945; s. Broderick Andrew and Rita Louise (Des Jardins) L.; B.S. in Agrl. Economics, U. of Conn. 1966, M.A. in Vocat. Edn. 1968; Ph.D. in Endl. Admnstrn., Cornell U. 1972; m. Ann Marie La Plante, June 24, 1967; children—Sean, Jeffrey, Marc, Matthew. Adminstrv. aide Office Instl. Studies Cornell U., 1969-70, instr. Reading and Study Skills Center, 1969-70; tchr., cons., curriculum coordinator Concord (N.H.) Union Sch. Dist., 1970-75; asst. supt. Sch. Supervisory Union #32, Lebanon, N.H. 1975—; adj. prof. edn. N.H. State Coll. and U. System, Durham 1972-76. Dir. for Town of Canaan UpperValley-Lake Sunapee Regional Planning Council, 1976—; mem. citizens' advisory com. W.Central Div., N.H. Community Mental Health Services, Hanover, N.H., 1976—; bd. dirs. Pine Haven Boys Center, Allenstown, N.H., 1972-75. Cert. supt. of schs., asst. supt. of schs., tchr. cons., prin. elementary and secondary levels, N.H. Mem. Assn. for Supervision and Curriculum Development, Am. Assn. of Sch. Admnstrs., N.H. Assn. for Supervision and Curriculum Devel. (pres. 1975-76), N.H. State Profl. Standards Bd. Phi Kappa Phi, Gamma Sigma Delta, Phi Delta Kappa, Alpha Zeta, Alpha Gamma Rho. Roman Catholic. Club: Granite State Sailing Assn. Author: Management by Objectives and Results Manual, 1976; Evaluation Standards Set for K-12 Tchrs., 1977; Staff Development Master Plan, 1978; editor N.H. Assn. for Supervision and Curriculum Devel. newsletter 1973-76; organizer pre-sch. Home Edn. Project, 1970; co-dir. Schs.-within-a-Sch. Project, 1973-75. Office: 84 Hanover St Lebanon NH 03766

LAMB, MATTHEW JOSEPH, mech. engr.; b. Phila., Nov. 1, 1943; s. Joseph Matthew and Mary Catherine (Schneider) L.; B.M.E., Villanova U., 1969, M.M.E., 1973; postgrad. USAF Air War Coll., 1976-77, Indsl. Coll. Armed Forces, 1977-78; m. Carol Ann Connor, Jan. 22, 1966; children—Mark J., John D., Christopher M. Design engr. Phila. Gear Corp., King of Prussia, Pa., 1970-71; sr. project engr., aircraft and crew systems tech. dept. Naval Air Devel. Center, Warminster, Pa., 1971—. Asst. scoutmaster Boy Scouts Am., 1977—. Recipient Govt. Outstanding Performance awards, 1972-76; registered profl. engr., Pa. Mem. Aerospace Med. Assn., Am. Inst. Aeros. and Astronautics, Survival and Flight Equipment Assn., Nat., Bucks County socs. profl. engrs. Democrat. Roman Catholic. Club: Atglen Sportsmans. Patentee in field. Home: 116 Bucks Meadow Ln Newtown PA 18940 Office: Code 60336 Naval Air Devel Center Warminster PA 18974

LAMBERSON, DANE GEORGE, engr.; b. Salonika, Greece, Sept. 23, 1929; s. George Pandelis and Kassandra (Anagnostou) Lambropoulos; came to U.S., 1948, naturalized, 1955; B.S. in Aeros., 1951; m. Rita Papastergiou, Feb. 24, 1952; children—Maria-Sandra, George Lee. Propulsion/aerodynamics engr. Vertol Aircraft, Morton, Pa., 1956-58; aerodynamics engr. Bell Aircraft, Buffalo, 1958-59; aerodynamic, flight test engr. Grumman Aerospace Corp., Bethpage, N.Y., 1959—. Sec. Port Jefferson, N.Y. Greek Orthodox Church, 1961-64, v.p., 1965, pres., 1966, recognition award, 1969; trustee Civic Assn. Setaukets, 1964-70. Served with U.S. Army, 1951. Mem. Am. Inst. Aeros. and Astronautics, Soc. Flight Test Engrs., Smithsonian Instn. Club: Am. Hellenic Ednl. Progressive Assn. (chpt. sec. 1965, v.p. 1966, pres. 1967-69; named Ahepan of Yr. 1969). Home: 106 Glenwood Ln Port Jefferson NY 11777 Office: Grumman Aerospace Corp Bethpage NY 11714

LAMBERT, ABBOTT LAWRENCE, accountant; b. N.Y.C., Mar. 19, 1919; s. Woolf W. and Estelle (Wittcover) L.; B.A., Columbia U., 1940, M.S. in Accounting, 1946; m. Lois H. Ribman, Oct. 9, 1958; children—Nancy, Jane. Accountant, N.Y.C., 1940-42, 46-48, 71—; v.p. Chopak Mills, Inc., N.Y.C., 1948-71; pres. Carthage Fabrics Corp. (N.C.), 1964-71; pres., dir. 1025 Fifth Ave. Corp., N.Y.C., 1965-71, dir., 1975—; mem. nat. panel arbitrators Am. Arbitration Assn., 1967—. Trustee Fedn. Jewish Philanthropies N.Y., 1958—, life trustee, 1975—; trustee Asso. YM-YWHA Greater N.Y., 1970—; trustee Assn. Jewish Sponsored Camps, 1964—, pres., 1964-67, 76—. Served to capt. AUS, 1942-46. Decorated Bronze Star. C.P.A., N.Y. State. Mem. N.Y. State Soc. C.P.A.'s, Zeta Beta Tau. Clubs: Fairview Country (Greenwich, Conn.); Harmonie, City Athletic (N.Y.C.). Home: 1025 Fifth Ave New York City NY 10028 Office: 535 Fifth Ave New York City NY 10017

LAMBERT, ARTHUR GORMAN, lawyer; b. Washington, Feb. 10, 1899; s. Wilton J. and Elizabeth (Gorman) L.; grad. The Hill Sch., 1918; A.B., Princeton U., 1922; LL.B., Harvard U., 1925; m. Mary Lemon Sipple, Sept. 4, 1926; children—William S., Arthur Gorman. Admitted to D.C. bar, 1926; partner firm Lambert & Hart, Washington, 1930; asst. U.S. dist. atty., Washington, 1929-33; partner firm Lambert, Furlow, Elmore & Heidenberger and predecessor firms, Washington and Rockville, Md., 1933—; v.p., dir., mem. exec. com. Madison Nat. Bank, Washington. Chmn. bd. mgrs. Village of Chevy Chase (Md.), 1955-64, atty., 1964—. Atty., trustee Suburban Hosp. Assn., Inc., Bethesda, Md.; chmn. bd. trustees Landon Sch. Served with U.S. Army, World War I. Clubs: Metropolitan (Washington); Chevy Chase; Hillsboro (Pompano Beach, Fla.); Wianno (Cape Cod, Mass.); Harvard; Burning Tree; Princeton of Washington. Home: 17 Grafton St Chevy Chase MD 20015 Office: 1629 K St NW Washington DC 20006 also 22 W Jefferson St Rockville MD 20850

LAMBERT, HENRY AUGUST, realtor; b. N.Y.C., July 20, 1935; s. Henry L. and Marion Frances (Lisberger) L.; A.B., Bucknell U., 1957; postgrad. New Sch. Social Research, 1959. With Webb & Knapp, 1958-60; with Canal-Randolph Corp., N.Y.C., 1960-76, exec. v.p., 1964-76, also dir.; sr. v.p. Reliance Group and pres. Continental Cities Co., Inc. subs., N.Y.C., 1977—. Dir. Theatre Now, 1975—. Underwriting mem. Loyd's Fgn. Nationals. Home: 131 E 69th St New York City NY 10021 Office: 919 Third Ave New York City NY 10022

LAMBERT, JEREMIAH DANIEL, lawyer; b. N.Y.C., Sept. 11, 1934; s. Noah D. and Clara (Ravage) L.; A.B., Princeton U., 1955; postgrad. (Fulbright scholar) U. Copenhagen, 1955-56; LL.B., Yale U., 1959; m. Vicki Anne Asher, July 25, 1959; children—Nicole Stirling, Alix Stewart, Leigh Asher. Admitted to D.C. bar, N.Y. State bar, 1960; asso. firm Cravath, Swaine & Moore, N.Y.C., 1959-63; pvt. practice law, Washington, 1963-66; partner firm Drew & Lambert, Washington, 1966-69; sr. partner firm Peabody, Rivlin, Lambert & Meyers, Washington, 1969—; adj. prof. law Georgetown U., Washington, 1978—. Treas., Gas Employees Polit. Action Com., 1978—. Served to 1st lt. JAGC, U.S. Army Res., 1963-65. Mem. Am., Fed., N.Y.C., D.C. bar assns., Am. Soc. Internat. Law. Clubs: Univ., Yale (Washington); Princeton (N.Y.C. and Washington); Cleve. Park. Contbr. articles to legal publs. Home: 3400 Newark St NW Washington DC 20016 Office: Peabody Rivlin Lambert & Meyers 1150 Connecticut Ave NW Washington DC 20036

LAMBERT, RICHARD BOWLES, JR., oceanographer; b. Clinton, Mass., Apr. 20, 1939; s. Richard B. and Dorothy Elizabeth (Peck) L.; A.B. cum laude, Lehigh U., 1961; M.S., Brown U., 1964, Ph.D., 1966; postdoctoral studies (Fulbright fellow), Technische Hochschule Munich, Germany, 1966-68; m. Sherrill Faye Smith, July 4, 1964; 1 dau., Lisa-Beth Lauren. Asst. prof. phys. oceanography U. R.I., Kingston, 1968-74, asso. prof., 1974-77, adj. prof., 1977—; program dir. for phys. oceanography NSF, Washington, 1975-77; research oceanographer Sci. Applications, Inc., McLean, Va., 1977—. NSF grantee, 1968-75. Mem. Am. Phys. Soc., AAAS, Am. Geophys. Union, Phi Beta Kappa, Sigma Xi. Presbyterian. Contbr. numerous articles on geophys. research to profl. jours.

LAMMERT, THOMAS KING, anesthesiologist; b. Bklyn., Dec. 14, 1925; s. Charles Roy and Margaret Alice (King) L.; student Fordham U., 1942-44; M.D., St. Louis U., 1948, M.S., 1950; m. Jean Evon Turcott, Jan. 26, 1957; children—Thomas, J. Kevin, Karl, Margaret, Lois Jean, Kathryn. Intern St. Louis U., 1948-49; resident in anesthesiology St. Louis U., 1949-51, Hartford (Conn.) Hosp., 1951-52; clin. asst. anesthesiology Hartford Hosp., 1952-57; attending anesthesiologist St. Vincent's Hosp., N.Y.C., 1957—, trustee, pres. med. staff and med. bd., 1972-74. Served to capt. USAF, 1952-54. Diplomate Am. Bd. Anesthesiology. Mem. AMA, N.Y. State (chmn. sect. anesthesiology), N.Y. County med. socs., Am. Coll. Anesthesiology, Am. (ho. of dels. 1966—), N.Y. State (dir. 1969—, contbg. editor 1964—, pres. 1977—) socs. anesthesiologists. Club: Edgemont EE (bd. govs. 1973). Address: 37 Andrea Ln Scarsdale NY 10583

LAMOND, GAYLORD MARVIN, retail co. exec.; b. Chgo., Feb. 16, 1923; s. Herbert M. and Lotti (Glouser) LaM.; student Colo. State U., 1942-44, Wayne State U., 1947-50; m. Jean Elizabeth Carl, Sept. 20, 1947; children—Michele, Gary. Retail salesman Campbell Sales Co., Detroit, 1947-48, salesman food service, 1950-51, instl. supr. Western div., Los Angeles, 1951-53, asst. mgr. instl. sales, 1953-57, mgr. 1957-59, sales mgr. S.W. div., Dallas, 1959-62, mng. dir. mktg., Geneva, Switzerland, 1962-63, asst. to gen. sales mgr., Camden, N.J., 1963-66, sales mgr. food service div., Camden, 1963-66, dir., v.p. Campbell Sales Co., dir. mktg., sales mgr. food service div. Campbell Soup Co., 1966, pres., dir. Chock Full O'Nuts Corp. div., N.Y.C., 1966-68; pres. New Dimensions Food Service div. Federated Dept. Stores, Inc., 1968-72; chmn. bd., pres. Isaly Co., Pitts., 1972—; dir. Clabin Corp., Greenwich, Conn. Home: 121 Pheasant Dr Pittsburgh PA 15238 Office: 3380 Blvd of Allies Pittsburgh PA 15213

LAMONSOFF, NORMAN CHARLES, psychiatrist; b. Bklyn., Sept. 16, 1936; s. Isidore and Kate L.; B.A., Cornell U., 1954-58; M.D., State U. N.Y. Downstate Med. Center, 1958-62; m. Sheila Kaplan, Aug. 27, 1961; children—Karen Mary, Jacob David. Intern, Bklyn. Jewish Hosp., 1962-63; resident in psychiatry Kings County Hosp., Bklyn., 1963-66; sr. supervising psychiatrist St. Vincent Med. Center, S.I., 1968-70; dir. psychiat. services N.Y.C. Dept. Mental Health, 1970-74; program dir. addiction services unit Jersey City Med. Center, 1975-76; med. dir. Somerset County Community Mental Health Center, Somerville, N.J., 1976—; individual practice medicine, specializing in psychiatry, Somerville, 1977—. Served to capt., M.C., U.S. Army, 1966-68. Diplomate Am. Bd. Psychiatry. Mem. AMA, N.J., Am. psychiat. assns. Home: 644 Glen Ridge Dr Bridgewater NJ 08807 Office: 88B Grove St Somerville NJ 08876

LAMONT, EDWARD MINER, banker; b. N.Y.C., Dec. 10, 1926; s. Thomas Stilwell and Elinor B. (Miner) L.; B.A., Harvard U., 1948, M.B.A., 1951; m. Camille Haines Buzby, June 23, 1951; children—Edward Miner, Helen B., Camille H. Staff ECA, Washington, 1951-52; economist secretariat NATO, Paris, 1952-53; loan officer IBRD, Washington, 1953-56; investment officer Internat. Finance Corp., Washington, 1956-61; v.p. Morgan Guaranty Trust Co. N.Y., N.Y.C., 1961-71, 74—; dep. adminstr. New Communities Adminstrn., Washington, 1971-74; pres. Morgan Community Devel. Corp. subs. J.P. Morgan & Co., Inc., 1974—. Vice pres. Children's Aid Soc.; bd. dirs. N.Y.C. Community Preservation Corp., 1974-78, Adv. Service for Better Housing, Regional Plan Assn., 1978—; trustee Phillips Exeter Acad., 1962-71; vestryman St. John's Ch., Cold Spring Harbor, N.Y. Served with USNR, 1945-46. Home: Moores Hill Rd Syosset NY 11791 Office: 23 Wall St New York City NY 10015

LAMONT, EDWIN BURGESS, II, car rental co. exec.; b. Lynbrook, N.Y., Apr. 25, 1942; s. Edwin Burgess and Helen Matilda (Sinnigen) L.; B.A., Colgate U., 1964; M.B.A., Wharton Sch., U. Pa., 1969; m. Elinor Rosalyn Hausner, Aug. 6, 1967; children—Bradley Howard, Jeffrey David, Liana Barbara. Mktg./fin. analyst Am. Airlines, Inc., N.Y.C., 1969-71; mktg. mgr. Avis Rent A Car System, Inc., Garden City, N.Y., 1971-76, dir. mktg., 1977—; dir. mktg. AAMCO Industries, Bridgeport, Pa., 1976-77; adj. prof. mktg. N.Y. Inst. Tech., Old Westbury, N.Y., 1975—. Served to capt. USMCR, 1964-67; Vietnam. Mem. Travel Research Assn. Club: Racquet at Old Field. Address: 7 Haig Dr Dix Hills NY 11746

LAMONT, FREDERICK FRANCIS, JR., pub. relations and mkgt. cons.; b. Trenton, N.J., May 7, 1927; s. Frederick Francis and Helen Elizabeth (Westenburger) L.; A.B., Harvard U., 1948, M.B.A., 1951; Asso. in Econs., London Sch. Econs., 1966; m. Mary Louise Kingsbury, Oct. 3, 1959; children—Catherine Ann Lamont McDonald, Frederick Francis III, Sarah Kingsbury. Research editor New Yorker mag., N.Y.C., 1949-51; producer dir. ABC-TV, N.Y.C., 1951-55; radio-TV account exec. Compton Advt., Inc., N.Y.C., 1955-63; mktg. dir. So. Ariz. Bank & Trust Co., Tucson, 1963-67; v.p., mgr. Bozell & Jacobs, Advt., Phoenix, 1967-69; v.p., dir. fin. relations Aztec Mining Corp., Denver, 1969-71; v.p. N.W. Ayer & Son, Inc., 1971-73; cons., 1973—; cons. N.J. Div. Youth and Family Services, Trans World Internat., Cleve. Dir. radio-TV, Nat. Assn. Retarded Children, N.Y.C., 1961-63; v.p., chmn. Ariz. Civic Theatre, 1965-67; trustee Triangle Properties, Chesterfield, N.H. Served in AC, USNR, 1944-46. Diplomate Fin. Pub. Relations Soc. Am. Fellow Pub. Relations Soc. Am. Clubs: Harvard, Players (N.Y.C.); Garrick (London); Old Pueblo (Tucson); Denver Athletic; Houston. Home: 1703 Lawrenceville Rd Lawrenceville NJ 08648

LAMPERT, DORRIE ELINORE, artist; b. Hartford, Conn., June 26; d. Abraham and Marian Leikind; student Hartford Art Sch., Yale U. Sch. Fine Arts, Art Students League, Nat. Acad., N.Y.C.; pupil of Countess Zichy, Herbert Fouts, Zita Davisson; protegé Jacques Marroger; m. June 4, 1939; children—David, Tish. One-woman exhbns. include: Caravan Gallery, N.Y.C., 1973, Grist Mill Gallery, Chester Depot, Vt., 1974, 75, Advt. Club, N.Y.C., 1975; group exhbns. include: Met. Mus., N.Y.C., Mus. Modern Art, Paris, N.C. Mus., Lever Bros. Bldg.; designer charity balls, commd. for pvt. collections. Mem. Nat. Arts Club, Burr Artists. Democrat. Club: Old Oakes Country. Address: 2 Beeckman Pl New York City NY 10022

LAMPERT, S. HENRY, dentist; b. Bklyn., Mar. 10, 1929; s. Joseph and Sadie (Bass) L.; B.A., U. Ill., 1950; D.D.S., N.Y. U., 1954; m. Jacqueline Adler, Mar. 27, 1955; children—Karen Ann, Beth Robin, Judith Ellen. Intern in dentistry Mt. Sinai Hosp., N.Y.C., 1954-55; gen. practice dentistry, Essex Junction, Vt., 1957—; dir. Temporo Mandibular Joint Program, Med. Center Hosp. Vt., Burlington, 1970-76, attending staff 1957-76, peer rev. com., 1978—; mem. staff Fanny Allen Hosp., Winooski, Vt., 1961—; asso. prof. Sch. Allied Health Scis., U. Vt., Burlington, 1963-73, clin. instr. Coll. Medicine, 1974-75. Sec., Vt. Bd. Dental Examiners, 1973-76, pres., 1976-77; mem. NE Regional Bd. Dental Examiners, 1973—. Served to capt. AUS, 1955-57. Mem. ADA (standard setting com. of council on nat. bd. exams. 1978—), Vt., Champlain Valley (pres. 1961-62) dental socs., Am. Assn. Dental Examiners, Alpha Omega. Jewish (bd. govs. synagogue 1967-70, 72-73, chmn. bd. edn.). Club: Masons. Contbr. articles to profl. jours. Home: 22 Forest Rd Essex Junction VT 05452 Office: 48 Main St Essex Junction VT 05452

LAMPRON, EDWARD JOHN, state justice; b. Nashua, N.H., Aug. 23, 1909; s. John P. and Helene (Deschenes) L.; A.B., Assumption Coll., 1931, LL.D., 1954; LL.B., Harvard U., 1934; m. Laurette L. Loiselle, Sept. 22, 1938; children—Norman E., J. Gerard. Admitted to N.H. bar, 1935; practice law, Nashua, 1935-47; justice Superior Ct. N.H., 1947-49; justice Supreme Ct. N.H., Concord, 1949—, chief justice, 1979—; city solicitor, Nashua, 1936-46. Mem. adv. bd. St. Joseph's Hosp., Nashua. Trustee, Nashua Pub. Library. Mem. Am., N.H., Nashua (past pres.) bar assns., Nashua C. of C. (past pres.), Assn. Canado-Americaine (v.p., dir.). Club: Exchange (hon.). Home: 27 Wood St Nashua NH 03060 Office: Supreme Ct NH Concord NH 03301 also 115 Main St Nashua NH 03060

LAMY, PETER PAUL, educator; b. Breslau, Germany, Dec. 14, 1925; s. Rudolf and Luise (Bettinger) L.; B.S. in Pharmacy, Phila. Coll. Pharmacy and Sci., 1956, M.S., 1958, Ph.D. in Biopharmaceutics, 1964; m. Angela Pogorilich, Nov. 27, 1952; children—Rudolf, Margaret, Carl. Instr. pharmacy Phila. Coll. Pharmacy and Sci., 1956-63; instr. pharmacology Woman's Hosp., Phila., 1960-62; asst. prof. pharmacy U. Md., 1963-67, asso. prof., 1967-72, prof., 1972—, dir. instl. pharmacy programs, 1968—, co-dir. profl. experience program, 1970—, faculty Med. Sch., 1974—; dir. dept. instl. pharmacy practice U. Md. Hosp., Balt., 1970—; cons. Yager Drug Co., Balt., 1966—, USPHS Hosp., Balt., 1966-71, Provident Hosp., Balt., 1972-73, Levindale Hebrew Geriatric Center and Hosp., Balt., 1972—, Sound Mgmt., Phoenix, 1972, VA Hosp., Balt., 1973—, pharmacy dept. Clin. Center, NIH, 1974, John L. Deaton Med. Center, 1974—, VA Hosp., Washington, 1975—; lectr. psychopharmacology Sch. Nursing, Catholic U. Am., 1973. Vice pres. Catonsville (Md.) Elementary PTA, then pres. Served with AUS, 1948-51. Fellow AAAS, Am. Coll. Apothecaries, Am. Coll. Clin. Pharmacology; mem. Am. Geriatrics Soc., Am. Soc. Hosp. Pharmacy, Acad. Pharm. Sci., Am. Pharm. Assn., Sigma Xi, Rho Chi. Reviewer Jour. Pharm. Scis., 1968—, Jour. Am. Pharm. Assn., 1968—, Am.

Jour. Hosp. Pharmacy, 1972; instl. pharmacy editor Md. Pharmacist, 1974-76; editorial bd. Hosp. Pharmacy, 1968—, Drug Intelligence and Clin. Pharmacy, 1978—, Hosp. Formulary, 1978—; editor Contemporary Pharmacy Practice, 1978; contbr. articles to sci. jours. Home: 110 Glenwood Ave Baltimore MD 21228 Office: 636 W Lombard St Baltimore MD 21201

LAN, DONALD, state ofcl.; b. Newark, Dec. 19, 1930; s. Samuel and Mary (Kufferman) L.; student Seton Hall U., 1948-51; m. Hannah Resnik, July 15, 1951; children—Donald Paul, Richard Alan, Barbara Susan. With Dell Products Corp., Hillside, N.J., 1952-74, pres., 1975-76; exec. sec. to Gov. Brendan Byrne, Trenton, 1974-75; sec. of state State of N.J., Trenton, 1977—; mem. Employee Relations Policy Council; mem. N.J. Bicentennial Commn.; trustee Support Free Public Schs.; mem. N.J. Bd. Canvassers and Electoral Coll. Mem. Union County (N.J.) Democratic Com., 1968-71, exec. dir., 1972-73; mem. N.J. Dem. Com., 1972-75, Dem. Nat. Com., 1974-76; municipal chmn. Springfield Dem. Party, 1968-71; chmn. Union County Dem. Party, 1975-77; v.p. Temple Sharey Shalom, Springfield; asst. campaign mgr. Gov. Brendan Byrne, 1973; co-founder Springfield Instructional Football League; co-dir., coach Springfield Youth Baseball, League. Served with USAF, 1951-52, also Air N.G. Clubs: B'nai B'rith (chmn. civic affairs) (Springfield). Home: 34 Cypress St Springfield NJ 07081 Office: Box 1330 State House Trenton NJ 08625

LANCASTER, LESLIE EUGENE, math. statistician, ops. research analyst; b. Elma, Wash., Jan. 15, 1932; s. Fred H. and Anna (Hliboki) L., B.S. in Math., U. Wash., 1960; M.S., U. Nebr., 1965; postgrad. George Washington U., 1966—; m. Margaret Gutierrez, Feb. 12, 1966. Reliability engr. Aerojet-Gen. Corp., Azusa, Calif., 1961, Space Gen. Corp., El Monte, Calif., 1963-64; asst. tchr. computing center, U. Neb., 1961-63, 64-65; programmer Roland F. Beers, Alexandria, Va., 1965-66; sr. programmer Center for Naval Analysis, Arlington, Va., 1966-68; sr. analyst Wolf Research and Devel., Riverdale, Md., 1968-70, Computer Scis. Corp., Silver Spring, Md., 1970-73, Braddock, Dunn and McDonald, Inc., Vienna, Va., 1973-75; ops. research analyst Operational Test and Evaluation Agy., Falls Church, Va., 1975—. Served with USAF, 1952-56. Mem. Am. Statis. Assn., Assn. Computing Machinery, Inst. Math. Statistics. Home: 5812 Lamont Dr New Carrollton MD 20784 Office: 5600 Columbia Pike Falls Church VA 22401

LANCASTER, MARGARET GUTIERREZ, mathematician; b. Chapel Hill, N.C., July 27, 1938; d. Andrew and Margaret (Nesbitt) Gutierrez; B.S., U. N.C.; m. Leslie Eugene Lancaster, Feb. 12, 1966. Mathematician ops. evaluation group Mass. Inst. Tech., Pentagon, Washington, 1957-59; mathematician Analytic Services, Inc., Baileys Crossroads, Va., 1959-63, Roland F. Beers, Alexandria, Va., 1963-65, Environ. Research Corp., Alexandria, 1965—. Active local chpts. Cancer Soc., Heart Assn., Diabetes Assn. Mem. Sigma Alpha Iota. Methodist. Home: 5812 Lamont Dr New Carrollton MD 20784

LAND, EDWIN HERBERT, physicist, corp. exec., inventor; b. Bridgeport, Conn., May 7, 1909; s. Harry M. and Martha G. (Land) L.; prep. edn., Norwich Acad.; student Harvard U., Sc.D. (hon.), Tufts Coll., 1947, Poly. Inst. Bklyn., 1952, Colby Coll., 1955, Harvard U., 1957, Yale U., 1957; Northeastern U., 1959, Carnegie Inst. Tech., 1964, Columbia U., 1967, Loyola U., 1970, N.Y. U., 1973; LL.D., Bates Coll., 1953, Washington U., 1966, U. Mass., 1967; L.H.D., Williams Coll., 1968; m. Helen Maislen, 1929; children—Jennifer, Valerie. During coll. yrs. began devel. of means for polarization of light as an applied sci.; invented polarizer used as camera filter; organized Polaroid Corp., Cambridge, Mass., 1937, becoming pres., chmn. bd., dir. research; invented camera that delivers finished photograph immediately after exposure is made, 1947; early research include automobile headlight system and three-dimensional pictures. During World War II conducted research leading to devel. of plastic optical lenses for devices for seeing at night, filters for pre-adapting eyes of personnel for night duty, new types of lightweight stereoscopic rangefinders and an infinity optical ring sight used on anti-aircraft guns and bazookas. Fellow Sch. for Advance Study, Mass. Inst. Technology, 1956, also vis. prof., 1956—; mem. Pres.' Fgn. Intelligance Adv. Bd. Nat. Commn. on Tech., Automation and Econ Progress, 1965-66, Carnegie Commn. on Ednl. TV, 1966-67; William James lectr. on psychology Harvard, 1966-67. Trustee, Ford Found., 1967—; bd. overseers for physics astron. chem., biol. and Bessey Inst., Harvard, Recipient Hood medal Royal Photog. Soc.; Cresson medal, also Howard N. Potts medal Franklin Inst. Phila.; Scott medal Phila. City Trusts; Rumford medal Am. Acad. Arts and Scis., 1945; Holley medal ASME, 1948; Duddell medal Brit. Phys. Soc., 1949; Progress medal Soc. Photog. Engrs., 1955; Progress medal Royal Photog. Soc. Gt. Britian, 1957; Presdl. medal of Freedom, 1963, Nat. Medal of Sci., 1967. Fellow Photog. Soc. Am., Am. Acad. Arts and Scis. (pres.), Royal Photog. Soc. Gt. Britain, Royal Micros. Soc.; mem. Am. Philos. Soc., Nat. Acad. Scis., Optical Soc. Am. (dir.), Nat. Acad. Engrs., Nat. Modern Pioneers, Nat. Mfg. Assn., Sigma Xi. Clubs: Harvard (N.Y., Boston); St. Botolph, Harvard Faculty (Boston); Cosmos (Washington); Century Assn. Inventor first light-polarizer in form of extensive synthetic sheet; developer sequence subsequent polarizers. Home: 163 Brattle St Cambridge MA 02138 Office: 730 Main St Cambridge MA 02139

LAND, EMMETT MATTHEW, JR., pharmacist; b. Phila., Sept. 19, 1942; s. Emmett Matthew and Lillian (Chesko) L.; B.S., Phila. Coll. Pharmacy and Sci., 1966; m. Louise M. Murray, July 8, 1967; children—Jennifer, David. Resident in hosp. pharmacy Hosp. U. Pa., Phila., 1966-67, pediatric specialist, 1967-69; dir. pharmacy Appalachian Regional Hosp., Inc., Hazard, Ky., 1969-71, asst. dir. central pharm. services, 1972-74; pharmacy dir. Crozer-Chester Med. Center, Chester, Pa., 1974—; clin. affiliate Phila. Coll. Pharmacy and Sci., Temple U. Coll. Pharmacy, Delaware County Community Coll. Mem. Am., Pa., Del. Valley socs. hosp. pharmacists, Am. Pharm. Assn. Republican. Roman Catholic. Editorial bd. Hosp. Formulary, 1974—. Home: 477 McGregor Dr West Chester PA 19380 Office: Crozer-Chester Medical Center 15th St and Upland Ave Chester PA 19013

LAND, HENRY BRUCE, III, instrument engr.; b. Newton, N.C., June 10, 1946; s. Henry Bruce and Evelyn Janette (Adams) L.; student (DuPont scholar) U. Va., 1964-65; A.A., Catonsville Community Coll., 1979; m. Sharon Lee Headley, June 5, 1971; children—Cynthia Dawn, Janette Elizabeth. Electronics technician Sperry Rand Co., Charlottesville, Va., 1966-67; launch controller Goddard Space Flight Center, Greenbelt, Md., 1967; contract chem. cons. Applied Physics Lab., Johns Hopkins U., Laurel, Md., 1967-69, instrument engr., 1969—. Chmn. Republican Precinct 74-9, Anne Arundel County, Md., 1971-74; mem. data processing vocat. edn. adv. com. Balt. City Pub. Schs., 1978—; dir. Sunday sch. Elkridge (Md.) Baptist Ch., 1976-77, chmn. bd. trustees, 1978—. Contbr. articles on gas sampling and analysis to profl. jours. Home: 6916 Park Pl Baltimore MD 21227 Office: Applied Physics Lab Johns Hopkins Rd Laurel MD 20810

LANDALE, THOMAS DAVID, mfg. and constrn. exec.; b. Omaha, Nebr., Jan. 2, 1927; s. Edwin Munderich and Olive Margaret (Williams) L.; B.C.E., Cornell U., 1948; S.M. in C.E., Mass. Inst. Tech., 1954; m. Suzanne Therese Chevalier, Dec. 23, 1950; children—Edwin Thomas, David Paul, Carol Jeanne, Nora Margaret, Raymond Daniel, Louis Arthur, James Benjamin, Marjorie Suzanne, Katherine Lucille, Stephen Andrew. Project engr. Brown-Roberts & Assos., Marion, Ohio, 1955-56; v.p., treas., chmn. Nalews, Inc., Meredith, N.H., 1960-62; with Pullman Kellogg div. Pullman, Inc. and predecessor and affiliated cos., 1954-77, office and field poistions, 1954-55, 56-60, dir. constrn. Kellogg Internat. Corp., London, Eng., 1962-68, gen. mgr. Chimney div., Williamsport, 1968-72, v.p., gen. mgr. Power Piping and Chimney, Williamsport, 1972-77, with Pullman Power Products div., 1977—, pres., Williamsport, 1977—; dir. K.U.B. Co. Can., Ltd., Montreal, Schweizer-Dipple, Inc., Cleve., Williamsport Nat. Bank. Bd. dirs. Lycoming County United Way, 1973—. Served with USNR, 1945-46. Registered profl. engr., Ohio, N.Y., N.H. Mem. Nat. Soc. Profl. Engrs., Cornell Soc. Engrs., Sigma Xi. Club: Williamsport Country. Home: 90 Selkirk Rd Williamsport PA 17701 Office: PO Box 3308 Williamsport PA 17701

LANDAU, SIEGFRIED, musical dir., condr.; b. Berlin, Sept. 4, 1921; s. Ezekiel and Helen (Grynberg) L.; came to U.S., 1940, naturalized, 1946; student Stern Conservatory, Berlin, 1932-38, Klindworth-Scharwenka Conservatory, Berlin, 1938-39, Guildhall Sch. Music and Drama, London, 1939-40, Mannes Coll., N.Y.C., 1941-43; m. Irene Gabriel, May 2, 1954; children—Robert, Peter. Faculty, N.Y. Coll. Music, 1944-60, Cantors Inst., Jewish Theol. Sem., N.Y.C., 1949-69; music dir. Bklyn. Philharmonic, 1954-71, Chattanooga Opera Assn., 1960-73, Westphalian Symphony Orch., W.Germany, 1973-76, Music for Westchester Symphony Orch., 1961—. Recipient award N.Y. Music Tchrs., 1963, Arts award Westchester Arts Council, 1976. Fellow Jewish Acad. Arts and Sci., 1971. Mem. Am. Musicol. Soc., Jewish Music Council, ASCAP, Societa Amli Della Musica, Jesi, Italy. Composer: (opera) The Sons of Aaron, 1959; (symphonic poem) 3 Ballets, 1960; also music for chorus, piano and chamber music. Office: Box 35 Gedney Sta White Plains NY 10605

LANDAU, SYBIL HARRIET, lawyer, educator; b. N.Y.C., Nov. 26, 1937; d. Sidney and Janice (Katz) Landau; B.A. cum laude, Hunter Coll., 1958; LL.B., Columbia U., 1961; B.C.L., Oxford (Eng.) U., 1963. Asst. prof. law Bristol (Eng.) U. Faculty Law, 1963-65; asst. dist. atty. New York County, 1965-72; asso. prof. law Hofstra U. Sch. Law, Hempstead, N.Y., 1972-74; cons. reporter N.Y. State Family Ct. Adv. and Rules Com., 1974-75; asso. prof. Benjamin N. Cardozo Sch. Law, N.Y.C., 1975—, asst. dean, 1975-77; vis. adj. prof. law Bklyn. Law Sch., 1975. Mem. N.Y.C. Mayor's Task Force on Rape, 1974-77; lectr. on rape Nat. Confs. Women and the Law, 1973, 74, 76, Western Regional Conf. on Women and Law, 1975; mem. adv. bd., subcom. on juvenile delinquency Temp. N.Y. State Commn. on Child Welfare, 1977-78. Harlan Fiske Stone scholar, 1961; Brookdale fellow Hunter Coll., 1977-78; barrister-at-law Honourable Soc. Middle Temple. Mem. Am. Law Inst., Am., N.Y. State, N.Y.C. (family ct. com. 1972-76, 77—, spl. com. on children's rights 1977—) bar assns., Hunter Coll. Alumni Assn. (dir. 1976-79), Phi Beta Kappa, Alpha Phi Theta, Alpha Chi Alpha. Office: 55 Fifth Ave New York City NY 10003

LANDAUER, JAMES DITTMAN, real estate cons.; b. N.Y.C., Dec. 27, 1902; s. Ian N. and Bella (Fackenthal) L.; B.S., Dartmouth Coll., 1923; student Harvard Law Sch., 1923-24; m. Ruth Yarbrough, June 25, 1925; children—Beverly Foy, Barbara Rutherford Landauer Widdoes, Barrie Waters Landauer Estes. Vice pres., dir. Douglas L. Elliman & Co., Inc., 1924-36, Webb & Knapp, Inc., 1936-46; partner Cross & Co., 1939-46; chmn., dir. James D. Landauer Assos., Inc., N.Y.C., 1946—, now hon. chmn. bd.; dir. Dartmouth Real Estate Corp., Home Title div. Chgo. Title Ins. Co., C. Oliver Tyrone Corp.; trustee East River Savs. Bank. Asst. dir. Office Decentralization Service, Washington, 1941-42; dir. N.Y. City Pub. Devel. Corp.; bd. overseers Dartmouth Coll.; pres. Dartmouth Alumni Council; v.p., trustee Meml. Sloan-Kettering Cancer Center; treas., trustee Fifth Ave. Presbyn. Ch. Served as lt. col. USAAF, 1942-45. Awarded Legion of Merit, Order of Sun (Brazil). Mem. Mil. Order World Wars, Air Force Assn., Am. Legion, Nat. Assn. Real Estate Bds., Real Estate Bd. N.Y. (gov.), Internat. Real Estate Fedn. (dir. 1957-59), Inst. Polit. Sci., French Inst., N.Y. Hist. Soc. (trustee), Soc. Real Estate Counselors. Clubs: Univs., West Side Tennis, Dartmouth, Blind Brook, Wings, The Links, Lyford Cay, Century Assn., Anglers, U.S. Sr. Golf Assn., Army and Navy (Washington); Moisie Salmon (Can.); Woodstock Country (Vt.). Home: 510 Park Ave New York City NY 10022 Office: 1221 Ave of Americas New York City NY 10022

LANDAUER, ROBERT NEIL, accountant; b. N.Y.C., Apr. 15, 1939; s. Sol and Charlotte Frost (Schlossberg) L.; student W.Va. U., 1956-59; B.B.A., Adelphi U., 1961; M.B.A., N.Y. U., 1969; m. Ruth Marilyn Zwick, Dec. 24, 1961; children—Caryn Sue, Kenneth Ross. Accountant, Peat, Marwick, Mitchell & Co., N.Y.C., 1962-71, partner, 1971—; guest lectr. Am. Mgmt. Assn., Hosp. Fin. Mgmt. Assn., Sundry State Soc. C.P.A.'s. Treas., trustee Temple Sinai, Stamford, Conn.; treas., bd. dirs. Greenwich (Conn.) Tennis Assn., 1975—; bd. dirs. Westbury Community Tennis Assn., 1968-73, Sherwood Civic Assn., Westbury, N.Y., 1967-70; bd. dirs. Vis. Nurse Service N.Y., 1976—, mem. fin. and audit coms.; trustee Westbury Community Nursery Sch. and Kindergarten, 1967-73. Served with U.S. Army Res., 1961-67. Testified at Congressional House Ways and Means Com. on nat. health ins., 1974. C.P.A., N.Y. Mem. Am. Inst. C.P.A.'s, N.Y., La., N.C. socs. C.P.A.'s, Hosp. Fin. Mgmt. Assn. (William G. Follmer merit award 1976), Nat. Assn. Accountants. Club: Innis Arden Golf (Old Greenwich, Conn.). Home: 15 Wesskum Wood Rd Riverside CT 06878 Office: Peat Marwick Mitchell & Co 810 7th Ave New York City NY 10019

LANDE, LAWRENCE MONTAGUE, author, bibliophile; b. Ottawa, Ont., Can., Nov. 11, 1906; s. Nathan and Rachel (Freiman) L.; B.A., McGill U., 1928, D.Litt., 1967; diploma U. Grenoble (France), 1928; LL.B., U. Montreal, 1931; m. Helen Vera Prentis, June 14, 1939 (dec.); children—Denise Lande Farber, Nelson Prentis; m. 2d, Helen Ackerman. Bibliog. research in Canadiana; founder Lawrence Lande Found. for Canadian Hist. Research, McGill U.; also composer works for piano; author poems. Past pres. Montreal Friends of Hebrew U. Gov. Montreal Children's Hosp. Decorated officer Order of Canada; recipient Centennial medal, 1968. Fellow Intercontinental Biog. Assn. (life); mem. Canadian Writer's Found. (dir.), P.E.N. (past pres. Can.), Royal Soc. Arts (London) (hon. corr. Que.), Sigma Alpha Mu. Liberal. Jewish. Clubs: Montefiore, Palm Beach Country, Elm Ridge Country, Beaver, Grolier, Univ. Author: Psalms Intimate and Familiar, 1945; Towards the Quiet Mind, 1954; The Third Duke of Richmond, 1956; Old Lamps Aglow, 1957; Experience, 1963; Lande Bibliography of Canadiana, 1965, Supplement, 1971; Adventures in Collecting Books, 1975; also recs. Home: 4870 Cedar Crescent Montreal PQ H3W 2H9 Canada Office: Lande Room McLennan Library McGill U Montreal PQ Canada also 147 Dunbar Rd Palm Beach FL

LANDEAU, RALPH, chem. engr.; b. Phila., May 19, 1916; s. Stanley and Deanna L.; B.S., U. Pa., 1937; Sc.D., Mass. Inst. Tech., 1941; m. Claire, July 14, 1940; 1 dau. Research asst. in chem. engring. Mass. Inst. Tech., 1939-41; devel. engr. M.W. Kellogg Co., 1939, 1941-43, 1946; head chems. dept. Kellex Corp., 1943-45; exec. v.p., dir. Sci. Design Co., Inc., N.Y.C., 1946-63; pres. Halcon Internat., Inc., 1963-75, chmn., 1975—. Life mem. corp. Mass. Inst. Tech. Recipient Chem. Industry medal. Mem. Nat. Acad. Engring., Sigma Xi, Tau Beta Pi. Clubs: Sky, Princeton, Chemists (N.Y.C.); Tryall (Jamaica). Author papers, chpts.; patentee in field. Office: 2 Park Ave New York City NY 10016

LANDERS, PATRICIA ANN, sch. counselor; b. Bangor, Maine, Feb. 21, 1934; d. John T. and Isael E. (Barry) L.: B.A., Seton Hill Coll., Pa., 1955; M.Ed., U. Maine, 1959, certificate advanced grad. study, 1969. Tng. supr. Jordan Marsh Co., Boston, 1955-58; asst. dir. guidance Farmington (Maine) Schs., 1959-62; dir. guidance Newington (Conn.) High Sch., 1962—. Mem. Newington Tchrs. Assn., Conn. Edn. Assn., Conn. (sec. 1972-73), Am. personnel and guidance assns., Nat., Am., Conn. schs. counselors assns., Conn. Assn. Women Deans and Counselors (treas. 1972—), NEA. Roman Catholic. Home: 23 Brightwood Ln West Hartford CT 06110 Office: 605 Willard Ave Newington CT 06111

LANDIS, FREDERICK, fed. judge; b. Logansport, Ind., Jan. 17, 1912; s. Frederick and Bessie (Baker) L.; student Wabash Coll., 1928-29; A.B., Ind. U., 1932, LL.B., 1934; m. E. Joyce Stevenson, July 4, 1945; children—Diana, Frederick, Susan, Gillian, Kenesaw Mountain. Admitted to Ind. bar, 1934; asso. firm Long & Yarlott, 1935-38; mem. firm Landis & Hanna, 1938-46, Landis & Landis, 1946-54, Landis & Michael, 1954-55; pros. atty. 29th Jud. Circuit, 1938-40; justice Supreme Ct. Ind., 1955-65; judge U.S. Customs Ct., N.Y.C., 1965—; mem. Ind. Ho. of Reps., 1950-52; mem. Ind. Senate from Cass and Fulton counties, 1952-55. Served to lt. USNR, 1942-46. Mem. Ind., Cass County (pres. 1948-51) bar assns., Am. Judicature Soc., Am. Legion, Phi Delta Phi, Delta Tau Delta. Clubs: Elks; Columbia, Scarsdale Golf; Press (Indpls.). Office: US Customs Ct One Fed Plaza New York City NY 10007

LANDIS, WILLIAM RUTTER, research chemist; b. Lancaster, Pa., May 27, 1938; s. Charles Andrew and Dorothy Eby (Rutter) L.; A.B., Ohio Wesleyan U., 1960; postgrad. U. Colo., 1960-62, Johns Hopkins U., 1967-68; m. Dorothy Mae Dildine, May 28, 1966; 1 dau., Margaret Eby. Research chemist sect. microanalytical services and instrumentation Nat. Inst. Arthritis and Metabolic and Digestive Diseases, NIH, Bethesda, Md., 1963—; participant NIH Grad. Sch. Teaching Program, 1964-68; sci. cons. Montgomery County Pub. Schs., Rockville, Md., 1965, Adams-Morgan Community Sch., Washington, 1973. Recipient award USPHS, 1973. Mem. Am. Chem. Soc., Am. Soc. for Mass Spectrometry, AAAS, Phi Mu Alpha Sinfonia, Phi Delta Theta. Republican. Lutheran. Contbr. articles to sci. jours. Home: 1661 Crescent Pl NW Washington DC 20009 Office: NIH Bldg 4 Room B2-35 Bethesda MD 20014

LANDMAN, LOUIS, psychoanalyst; b. N.Y.C., Dec. 23, 1910; s. Joseph Michael and Francis (Kinberg) L.; student N.Y. U., 1927-30; M.D., Royal Coll. Surgeons Edinburgh, 1935; m. Joan Neill, June 11, 1937; children—James, Steven, Eric. Intern Beth-El Hosp., Bklyn., 1936-37; pvt. practice specializing in psychiatry and psychoanalysis, Englewood, N.J.; tng. and supervising analyst Am. Inst. Psychoanalysis. Served with M.C., AUS, 1941-46. Fellow Am. Psychiat. Assn., Acad. Psychoanalysis; mem. N.J. Psychiat. Soc. Contbr. articles to Psychoanalysis, Group Psychoanalysis. Home: 31 Royden Rd Tenafly NJ 07670 Office: 200 Engle St Englewood NJ 07631

LANDON, JOHN HENRY, econ. cons.; b. Lansing, Mich., Apr. 19, 1942; s. John Henry and Helen Jean (Landon) Butts; B.A. with highest honors, Mich. State U., 1964; M.A., Cornell U., 1966, Ph.D., 1968; m. Valerie Ann Johnson, June 20, 1964; children—John Patrick, David Matthew. Asst. prof., then asso. prof. Case Western Res. U., 1968-73; asso. prof. econs. U. Del., Newark, 1973—, dir. Center Policy Studies, 1975-77; mem. Gov. Del. Econ. Adv. Com., 1973-77; sr. cons. Nat. Econ. Research Assos., 1977—. Grantee HEW, Unidel Found., U. Del. Research Found. Mem. Am., Western, So. econs. assns., Inst. Mgmt. Sci. Roman Catholic. Author articles, chpts. in books. Home: RD 2 Little Egypt Rd Newark DE 19711 Office: Nat Econ Research Assos 1800 M St NW Washington DC 20036

LANDON, SEALAND WHITNEY, IV, banker; b. Springfield, Vt., Jan. 31, 1955; s. Sealand Whitney, III, and Joan (Johnson); B.A. cum laude (McConnell fellow), Princeton U., 1976. Pres., Found. for Student Communication, Princeton, N.J., 1975; editor Bus. Today mag., Princeton, 1975; officer's asst. Chem. Bank, N.Y.C., 1976—. Club: Princeton. Home: 13-15 Laight St New York City NY 10013 Office: 20 Pine St New York City NY 10005

LANDRUM, FRANCES ANN, dancer, educator; b. N.Y.C., Apr. 5, 1918; d. Edmund Charles and Mary Elizabeth (Lannon) Lourie; student Vestoff-Serova Sch. Dance, 1927-35, Tarasoff Sch. Dance, 1929-31, Martha Graham Sch. Dance, 1935-36; m. Robert Bascom Landrum, June 30, 1938; children—Elizabeth Ann Landrum, Robert Bascom II. Ballet dancer Russian Opera Co., 1930, Lee Schubert Prodns., 1931; mem. corps de ballet, soloist Radio City Music Hall, N.Y.C., 1933-42; founder, owner, dir. Landrum Sch. Dance, N.Y.C., 1948—; founder Young Peoples Dance Group L.I., 1964—; artistic dir. Ballet Repertory L.I., 1964—; produced, directed and choreographed dance recitals RKO Keiths Flushing Theatre, 1955—, Andre Eglevsky Co., 1960-61. Artistic dir. Bicentennial Com. College Point, N.Y., 1975—; active nat. council auxs. Am. Med. Center at Denver. Recipient Merit certificate N.Y. State Com. on World's Fair, 1964. Charter mem. Assn. Am. Dance Companies, Concerned Citizens for the Arts in N.Y. State, N.Y. Dance Alliance. Presbyterian. Home: 13-43 Parsons Blvd Whitestone NY 11357 Office: 14-34 150th St New York City NY 11357

LANDRY, FERNAND RAYMOND, dental technician; b. Lewiston, Maine, Apr. 5, 1921; s. Pierre Joseph and Marie Ann (Lebel) L.; grad. high sch.; m. Lucette M. Lamontagne, July 17, 1948; children—Patricia, Diane, Jeanne. Shipfitter, South Portland, Maine, 1940-41; dental lab. technician, Portland, Maine, 1946-48, Lewiston, 1948-53; partner Twin City Dental Lab., Lewiston, 1953—; trustee Peoples Savs. Bank, Lewiston. Served with M.C., AUS, 1942-45. Mem. Nat. Assn. Dental Labs., United Comml. Travelers. Democrat. Roman Catholic. Clubs: Musical Lit., Elks, Exchange (Maine Exchangeite of Year 1971) (Lewiston). Home: 91 Charles St Lewiston ME 04240 Office: 171 Lisbon St Lewiston ME 04240

LANDSBERG, JERRY, mgmt. and investment cons.; b. Dallas, June 30, 1933; s. Max and Rose (Hechtman) L.; grad. So. Meth. U., 1954; m. Gloria Zale, Sept. 2, 1956; children—Steven Jay, Jeffrey Paul, Karen Beth, Ruth Ellen. Salesman, Remington Rand div. Sperry Rand, 1955-57; salesman Zale Corp., 1957-59, asst. mgr., 1959-60, mgr., 1960-63, merchandiser, 1963-67; registered rep., security analyst Silberberg & Co., 1967-69; owner Jerry Landsberg & Assos., 1969-72; v.p. Ross Watch Case Corp., gen. mgr. Kenfield jewelry div., Long Island City, N.Y., 1971-75; pres., chief operating officer King Optical Corp., Dallas, 1974-75; pres. Jerry Landsberg Assos., Great Neck, N.Y., 1975—. Trustee, Village of Kensington, 1967-75, commr. police, 1967-69, commr. pub. works, 1969-75, dep. mayor, 1969-75, mayor, 1973; fin. v.p. Temple Emanuel, Great Neck, 1964-66, trustee, 1964-74; bd. dirs. Great Neck Symphony Soc., 1974—, pres., 1978—; bd. dirs. Great Neck Community Fund; v.p. Zale Found.; Great Neck chmn. Fedn. Jewish Philanthropies; active various community drives. Mem. So. Meth. U. Alumni Assn. (dir. nat. bd., pres. N.Y. club). Clubs: U.S. Power Squadron, Masons, Shriners. Office: 375 Great Neck Rd Great Neck NY 11021

LANDSMAN, BOBBIE, educator; b. N.Y.C.; d. Nathan and Lillian Pauline (Kaplan) Lipow; B.B.A., Coll. City N.Y., 1943; M.S., Queens Coll., 1960; postgrad. NDEA Inst., Columbia U., 1965; m. George D. Landsman, June 17, 1945; children—Nikki D., Sherry G., Dean F. Sec., J. Early Wood & Co., Inc., N.Y.C., 1943-44; guidance counselor Livingston Sch., N.Y.C., 1960-74, Bellevue Psychiat. Hosp. Sch., N.Y.C., 1974-76; tchr. secondary schs. N.Y.C. Bd. Edn., 1944-60, chmn. com. on handicapped, 1976—. Troop leader Girl Scouts U.S.A., 1955-57, interviewer, 1957-58. Mem. Assn. N.Y. State Educators of Emotionally Disturbed, N.Y. Assn. for Brain Injured Children, Am., N.Y. State personnel and guidance assns., Am., N.Y.C. sch. counselors assns., Nat. Vocat. Guidance Assn., N.Y. State Assn., Specialists in Group Work. Contbr. articles to profl. jours. Home: 135 E 54th St New York City NY 10022 Office: 281 9th Ave New York City NY 10001

LANE, BARBARA G., educator; b. Phila., May 31, 1941; d. Leon H. and Ethel S. Greenhouse; A.B., Barnard Coll., 1963; Ph.D., U. Pa., 1970; m. Joseph M. Lane, June 23, 1963; children—Debra, Jennifer. Instr. art history U. Md., 1968-69; asst. prof. Rutgers U., Camden, N.J., 1970-76, asso. prof., Douglass Coll., 1976—. Mem. Coll. Art Assn., Medieval Assn. Am., AAUP. Contbr. articles to profl. jours. Home: 180 East End Ave Apt 5H New York City NY 10028 Office: Dept Art Douglass Coll Rutgers U New Brunswick NJ 08903

LANE, BEN CLARENCE, optometrist; b. Jersey City, June 6, 1932; s. Morris J. and Celia (Goldstein) L.; A.B., Princeton, 1954; Dr. Optometry, Pa. State Coll. Optometry, 1958; M.S., State U. N.Y., 1973. Designer, gen. mgr. Princeton Ski Bowl, 1953-58, pres., 1955—; practice optometry Jersey City, 1958-76, Lake Hiawatha, N.J., 1961—; vis. staff clinician Pa. Coll. Optometry, 1967-73, vis. lectr., 1972-74; optometric cons. Ohio State U. Research Found., 1963-68; clin. investigator Dura Soft contact lenses, 1975—. Chmn. Morris and Hudson Counties Optometric Extension Program Study Groups, 1963-75; regional dir. N.J. Optometric Extension Program Found., 1968-74, asso. state dir., 1974—; cons. Jersey City Child Devel. Center, 1967-69. Named Optometrist of Yr., Hudson County Optometric Soc., 1969; recipient Sci. Lit. award N.J. Optometric Assn., 1971, Sci. Achievement award, 1978; Am. Optometric Found. fellow, 1972-73. Diplomate Nat. Bd. Examiners in Optometry, Gesell Inst. Child Devel. Fellow Am. Acad. Optometry, AAAS, N.J. Acad. Sci., Internat. Coll. Applied Nutrition, N.J., N.Y. (exec. council 1976—, editor newsletter 1976—, distinguished service award 1978) acads. optometry, Coll. Optometrists in Vision Devel. (nat. chmn. membership devel. 1972-77, N.J. state dir. 1973—); mem. Am., N.J. (trustee 1969-72) optometric assns., Hudson County (pres. 1967, 70), Tri-County (sec. 1966-68, 70-71, pres. 1976—) optometric socs., Assn. Research in Vision and Ophthalmology, Eastern States Optometric Congress, Nat. Eye Research Found., Am. Optometric Found., Internat. Myopia Prevention Assn., Internat. Acad. Preventive Medicine, Optical Soc. Am., Assn. for Children with Learning Disabilities, Am. Acad. Nutritional Cons. (adv. panelist 1978. Tech. editor N.J. Jour. Optometry, 1969-73. Contbr. articles to profl. jours. Research in functional photo phobia, intraocular pressure, vision deterioration asso. with reading, stereopsis, nutrition, other. Nationally syndicated TV panelist on vision and nutrition. Address: 16 N Beverwyck Rd Lake Hiawatha NJ 07034

LANE, CAROL HARMON FEIT, career counselor; b. N.Y.C., Feb. 4, 1934; d. Bert S. and Belle G. (Kirschner) Harmon; B.A., Smith Coll., 1955; M.A., Columbia U., 1967; m. Stuart Feit, June 25, 1955; children—Wendy, Laurie; m. 2d, Frederick M. Lane, Apr. 2, 1978. Career counselor N.Y. State Guidance Center Women, Suffern, 1967-69; acting dir. career counseling Sarah Lawrence Coll., Bronxville, N.Y., 1969-70; dir. Life Planning Workshops for Women, Scarsdale (N.Y.) Family Counseling Agy., 1970-74; asso. dir. Career Services, Barnard Coll., N.Y.C., 1974-78, acting dir., 1978—; faculty Womanschool, N.Y.C., 1977—, New Sch. Social Research, 1979. Mem. Am. Personnel and Guidance Assn., Eastern Coll. Placement Assn., NOW (mem. speakers bur.), Democrat. Jewish. Address: 115 E 87 St New York City NY 10028

LANE, CAROLYN BLOCKER (MRS. M. DONALD LANE, JR.), author, playwright; b. Providence, June 4, 1926; d. Harry Theodore and Margaret (Breitenfeld) Blocker; B.A., Conn. Coll., New London, 1948; m. M. Donald Lane, Jr., Apr. 28, 1951; 1 son, Jay Donald. Author: Uncle Max and the Sea Lion, 1970; Turnabout Night at the Zoo, 1971; The Voices of Greenwillow Pond, 1972; The Winnemah Spirit, 1975; (plays) Turnabout Night at the Zoo (12th Ann. Merit award Community Children's Theatre, Kansas City, Mo.), 1967; The Wayward Clocks (Merit award Pioneer Drama Service), 1969; The Last Grad (1st prize Theatre Guild Webster Groves, Mo.), 1970; Child of Air, 1972; The Runaway Merry-Go-Round, 1978; Tales of Hans Christian Andersen, 1978. Mem. Authors Guild, Soc. Children's Book Writers. Home: Ward Rd Salt Point NY 12578

LANE, MARTIN DONALD, JR., architect; b. Wilmington, Del., June 1, 1920; s. Martin Donald and Caroline (Angerstein) L.; B.Arch., Cornell U., 1946; m. Carolyn Elsie Blocker, Apr. 28, 1951; 1 son, Jay Donald. Prin., M.D. Lane, architects and interior designers, Poughkeepsie, N.Y., 1958—; prin. works include Sheehan Hall, Marist Coll., Poughkeepsie, N.Y., 1960, Poughkeepsie Savs. Bank, 1964, Ulster Savs. Bank, Poughkeepsie, 1971, Tappan House (restorations), Kingston, N.Y., 1976, Ellenville Savs. Bank, Monticello, N.Y., 1971, Bankers Trust Co., Monticello, 1969, Poughkeepsie Parking Garage, 1970, Newburgh Savs. Bank, 1971, also branches in West Haverstraw, N.Y., 1973, Vail's Gate, N.Y., 1968, also Heritage Savs. Bank branches in Fishkill, 1973, Pleasant Valley, 1976 and Middletown, 1977. Mem. bus. search com. Dutchess County; bd. dirs. Dutchess County Econ. Devel. Corp. Served to maj. as pilot, USMCR, 1942-45, 50-51. Decorated D.F.C., Air medal with 4 oak leaf cluster; recipient Charles Goodwin Sands Meml. award Cornell U., 1946; 1st prize nat. lighting contest Lighting mag., 1957. Mem. AIA. Clubs: Amrita (past dir.), Poughkeepsie Tennis, Kiwanis (past dir.). Home and Office: Ward Rd Salt Point NY 12578

LANG, EVERETT FRANCIS, JR., ins. co. exec.; b. Providence, Sept. 27, 1942; s. Everett Francis and Catherine Mary (Cuddigan) L.; B.S., Boston U., 1965; M.Ed., U. Va., 1969, Ed.D., 1976; m. Margaret Letitia McKenna, June 21, 1970; 1 son, Joseph Peter. Elementary sch. tchr. Henrico County Sch. System, Highland Springs, Va., 1970-71, middle sch. tchr., 1971-72; asst. regional dir. Sch. Continuing Edn., U. Va., Charlottesville, 1972-76; asso. dir. human resources Met. Property & Liability Ins. Co., Warwick, R.I., 1976—; mem. faculty U. Va., 1972-76. Mem. Va. State Volunteerism Task Force on Substance Abuse, 1976. Served with USAF, 1965-68. Decorated Army Commendation medal, Bronze Star; licensed profl. counselor, Va.; certified ednl. cons. Mem. Am. Soc. Tng. and Devel., Am. Personnel and Guidance Assn., Ins. Co. Edn. Dirs. Soc., Phi Delta Kappa, Kappa Delta Pi.

LANG, VICTOR JOHN, JR., bus. exec.; b. Galveston, Tex., June 28, 1936; s. Victor John and Katherine Loretta (Burkett) L.; B.A., U. Tex., 1960, postgrad. Sch. Law, 1960-61, Grad. Sch. Bus., 1961-62. Asst. exec. sec. to Gov. Price Daniel, Austin, Tex., 1957-61; adminstrv. asst. state Sen. Aaron R. Schwartz, Austin and Galveston, 1961-63; adminstrv. asst. Congressman Clark W. Thompson, Washington, 1963-66; congressional liaison officer HUD, 1966-67; prof. staff mem. Subcom. on Intergovtl. Relations, U.S. Senate, 1967; v.p. govt. affairs IU Internat. Corp., Phila., 1968—; mem. Pa. State Planning Bd.; lectr. contemporary politics New Studies Center, Phila. Coll. Performing Arts. Bd. dirs. Athenaeum of Phila., 1977—, Phila. Opera Co., 1978. Served with U.S. Army, 1960-62. Mem. Nat. Water Co. Conf. (govt. relations com.). Clubs: Confrerie des Chevaliers du Tastevin; Galveston Arty.; George Town; Penn; Racquet, Union League (Phila.); Savile (London). Home: Apt 2602 Hopkinson House Washington Sq S Philadelphia PA 19106 Office: 1500 Walnut St Philadelphia PA 19102

LANGBEIN, LELAND HENRY, ret. army officer, educator; b. New Brunswick, N.J., Aug. 2, 1915; s. Henry August and Maude (Tucker) L.; B.S., Rutgers U., 1936; M.S., U. Pitts., 1949, M.Litt., 1950, Ph.D., 1960; m. Maxine Gallatin, Jan. 16, 1950; children—Barbara L. Franklin, George L., Fred H., William D. Commd. 2d lt., U.S. Army, 1940, advanced through grades to lt. col., 1952, ret., 1961; engr. Gibbs & Hill, Inc., N.Y.C., 1936-37, Jersey Central Power & Light Co., Lakewood, N.J., 1937-40; asso. prof. Muskingum Coll., 1961-63; asso. prof. Monmouth Coll., West Long Branch, N.J., 1963-65, prof., 1965—; lectr. grad. sch. bus. adminstrn. U. Pitts., 1960-61. Mem. Am. Econ. Assn., U.S. Coast Guard Aux. (flotilla comdr. 1974-75), Ret. Officers Assn., Transp. Research Forum. Republican. Methodist. Author: International Movement of Petroleum and Petroleum Products, 1960. Home: 501 Windermere Ave Interlaken NJ 07712 Office: Cedar Ave West Long Branch NJ 07764

LANGBERG, MARTHA DIANE, psychologist; b. Riverside, Calif., Dec. 2, 1948; d. William Frederick and Martha (Riddel) Mandt; B.A., Taylor U., Ind., 1970; M.A., Temple U., Phila., 1972, Ph.D., 1976; m. Langberg, May 13, 1973. Dir. counseling Harcum Jr. Coll., Bryn Mawr. Pa., 1972-73; psychologist Profl. Counseling Center, Ft. Washington, Pa., 1972-77; practice psychology, North Wales, Pa., 1977—. Mem. Am. Psychol. Assn., Christian Assn. Psychol. Studies. Home: Buckingham Valley Farm RD 2 New Hope PA 18938 Office: English Village Profl Center Suite 105 North Wales PA 19454

LANGDON, JERVIS, JR., r.r. ofcl.; b. Elmira, N.Y., Jan. 28, 1905; s. Jervis and Eleanor (Sayles) L.; A.B., Cornell U., 1927, LL.B., 1930; student Dijon (France) U., 1926; m. Irene Fortner, Aug. 26, 1949. Law clk., asst. gen. solicitor Lehigh Valley R.R. Co., 1930-33; commerce counsel N.Y.C. R.R. Co., 1934-36; asst. gen. atty. C.&O. Ry. Co., 1936-37, gen. atty., 1937-41, asst. v.p. traffic, 1941-42; spl. counsel Assn. Southeastern R.R.'s, Washington, 1947-53, chmn., 1958-61, pres., 1961-64; chmn. bd., pres. C.R.I. & P.R.R., 1965-70; trustee Penn Central Transp. Co., 1970-74, pres., 1974-76, spl. counsel, 1977—. Served from capt. to col. USAAF, 1942-46; asst. chief Staff Indian-China div. Air Transp. Command, chief staff S.W. Pacific Wing. Decorated Legion of Merit with 2 oak leaf clusters, Distinguished Combat Unit award. Home: Quarry Farm Elmira NY 14902 Office: 3200 IVB Bldg 1700 Market St Philadelphia PA 19104

LANGE, BERTRAM JEREMY, fine arts dealer; b. Phila., July 7, 1912; s. Charles Frederick and Rose (Falk) L.; student Phila. pub. schs.; m. Jean Hatfield, Black, Mar. 4, 1939; children—Patricia Falk, Peter Van Strycker. Promotion dir. Carpet Inst., N.Y.C., 1945-48, Mdse. Mart, Chgo., 1948-50; advt. dir. Swank Jewelry, Attleboro, Mass., 1950-54; account exec. Bryan Houston Advt. Agy., N.Y.C., 1954-59; merchandising mgr. LIFE, 1959-62; v.p., gen. mgr. Pictorial Maps, Inc., N.Y.C., 1962-66; founder, pres. Pinchpenny Galleries, Ltd., Mt. Kisco, N.Y. and Boothbay Harbor, Me., 1966—; cons. to Ford Motor Co., Cott Beverages, Time-Life, Cazenave Galerie (Paris), pvt. art collections, Tulane U. Founder, actor, dir. Chappaqua (N.Y.) Community Theatre. Served to capt., USAAF, 1942-45. Decorated Air Medal, Bronze Star (U.S.), Croix de Guerre (France). Liberal Democrat. Clubs: Lotos (N.Y.C.), Down East Yacht. Editor, pub. N.Y.C. Bird's Eye View Map, ofcl. map of N.Y. World's Fair; suburban newspaper columnist How to Buy Art; radio commentator Westchester Art Forum. Home: Park Rd Wild Oaks Village Goldens Bridge NY 10526 Office: 564 Lexington Ave Mount Kisco NY 10549

LANGE, KURT, physician; b. Berlin, Germany, Oct. 31, 1906; s. Georg and Pauline (Neumann) L.; M.D., U. Berlin, 1930; m. Helen Marcus, June 14, 1936; children—Peter, Monica. Came to U.S., 1939, naturalized, 1944. Intern University of Berlin (Charite); resident in pathology 2d Med. U. Hosp., Berlin, Germany; instr. internal medicine U. Berlin, 1931-34; practice medicine specializing in internal medicine, Berlin, 1934-38, N.Y.C., 1939—; instr. medicine N.Y. Med. Coll., N.Y.C., 1939-44, asso. prof. medicine, 1945-62, prof. clin. pediatrics, 1962-71, prof. pediatrics, 1971—, prof. medicine, 1962—; attending physician Flower and Fifth Av hosps.; cons. physician Chenango Meml. Hosp., Norwich, N.Y., Horton Meml. Hosp., Middletown, N.Y., Lenox Hill Hosp., N.Y.C.; vis. physician Met. Hosp., Bird S. Coler Hosp.; dir. renal service N.Y. Med. Coll., 1952-78, Met. Med. Center, 1952-78. Chief renal service and lab. OSRD, U.S. Army, 1941-48. Recipient 2d award N.Y. State Med. Soc., 1946, hon. mention A.M.A., 1944-63, bronze medal, 1946, certificate of merit, 1961, also Hectoen Gold medal AMA, 1966; First award N.Y. State Med. Soc., 1967; Franz Volhard medal German Nephrology Soc., 1976. Fellow A.C.P., Am. College Cardiology; mem. Harvey Soc., Soc. Exptl. Biology and Medicine, Soc. Exptl. Pathology, Alpha Omega Alpha. Club: Explorers. Home: 519 E 86th St New York City NY 10028 Office: 11 E 68th St New York City NY 10021

LANGE, RICHARD LOUIS, ednl. psychologist; b. Buenos Aires, Argentina, June 24, 1940; s. Richard Gustav and Haydee (Kaul) L.; came to U.S., 1971; B.Sc. in Psychology, U. Buenos Aires, 1969; M.Ed., Temple U., 1973, postgrad., 1974; m. Myrta Elisa Micheluzzi, Jan. 24, 1969. Ednl. psychologist Avellanedz High Sch., Buenos Aires, 1954-58, U. Buenos Aires, 1970-71, Olivetti Corp., Buenos Aires; designer tng. programs Dominion Psychiat. Center, Washington, 1976-77, Human Service Group, 1975-76, Am. Health Services, 1974-76; cons. ednl. and community orgns., Washington Met. Area, 1977—; psychologist YMCA Buenos Aires, 1966-71. Served with Argentine Army, 1963-64. Fulbright fellow, 1971. Mem. Australian Psychol. Soc., Am. Personnel and Guidance Assn., D.C. Mental Health Assn. (dir.), Soc. Internat. Devel., Adult Edn. Assn. U.S., Temple U. Alumni (pres. Washington chpt.). Home: 8811 Colesville Rd #1120 Silver Spring MD 20910

LANGENBERG, FREDERICK CHARLES, steel assn. exec.; b. N.Y.C., July 1, 1927; s. Frederick Charles and Margaret (McLaughlin) L.; B.S., Lehigh U., 1950, M.S., 1951; Ph.D., Pa. State U., 1955; postdoctoral Mass. Inst. Tech., 1955-56; m. Jane Bartholomew, May 16, 1953; children—Frederick C., Susan Jane. Technologist, U.S. Steel Corp., Pitts., 1951-53; supr., pyrometallurgy Crucible Steel Co., Pitts., 1956-58, material and process engr., 1958-59, chief devel. metallurgist, 1959, mgr. process research, asst. dir. process research and devel., 1959-64, dir. process research and devel., 1964-65, dir. technology, 1965-67, v.p. research and engring., 1967-68, also mem. exec. policy, operating and appropriations coms.; pres. Trent Tube Co. subs. Colt Industries, 1968-70; exec. v.p. Jessop Steel Co., Washington, Pa., 1970, pres., 1970-75; pres., dir. Am. Iron and Steel Inst., 1975-79; pres., chief operating officer Interlake, Inc., Oak Brook, Ill., 1979—; dir. Millcraft Industries, Inc. Served with USNR, 1945-46. Mem. Am. Inst. Mining, Metall. and Petroleum Engrs. (chmn. phys. chemistry of steelmaking com. iron and steel div.), Am. Soc. Metals, Am. Chem. Soc., Am. Ordnance Assn. (dir., pres. Pitts. chpt. 1971), Internat., Am. (dir. 1971—), Brit. iron and steel insts., Am. Iron and Steel Engrs., U.S. C. of C. (mem. edn. and manpower devel. com. 1973-75), Phi Beta Kappa, Tau Beta Pi, Sigma Xi, Phi Lambda Upsilon, Phi Kappa Phi. Clubs: Congressional, Cosmos, Nat. Democratic, Duquesne, University, St. Clair, Oakmont Country, Carlton; Burning Tree, University (Washington). Contbr. articles in field to profl. jours. Patentee in field. Office: Interlake Inc 2015 Spring Rd Oak Brook IL 60521

LANGFORD, SIDNEY, church assn. adminstr., missionary; b. Phila., May 1, 1912; s. Chris and Alice Muriel (Burns) L.; diploma Phila. Bible Coll., 1931-33, Shelton Coll., 1933-34; m. Jennie Catherine Long, Jan. 22, 1938; children—Lois Langford Wing, Virginia Langford Stonehouse, David, Ronald. Ordained to ministry Conservative Baptist Assn., 1934; missionary Republic of Zaire, 1935-52, supt. Aba Sta., 1939-52; field dir. Africa Inland Mission, So. Sudan, 1953-56, mem. internat. council, 1955—; home dir. Africa Inland Mission in U.S., Pearl River, N.Y., 1956-77, home dir. emeritus, minister at large, 1977—; chmn. U.S. coordinating com. Africa Com. for Rehab. of So. Sudan, 1972—. Recipient Alumnus of Year award Phila. Bible Coll., 1970. Mem. Interdenoml. Fgn. Mission Assn. (past v.p., past mem. ofcl. bd.). Editor Inland Africa, 1956-77. Home: 21 Roxbury Pl Glen Rock NJ 07452 Office: PO Box 178 Pearl River NY 10965

LANGHAM, NORMA, educator; b. California, Pa.; d. Alfred Scrivener and Edith (Carter) Langham; B.S., Ohio State U., 1942; B.Theatre Arts, Pasadena Playhouse Coll. Theatre Arts, 1944; M.A., Stanford, 1956, postgrad. Summer Radio-TV Inst., 1960; student Pasadena Inst. Radio, 1944-45. Tchr. sci. California High Sch., 1942-43; asst. office pub. info. Denison U., Granville, Ohio, 1955; instr. speech dept. Westminster Coll., New Wilmington, Pa., 1957-58; instr. theatre dept. California (Pa.) State Coll., 1959, asst. prof., 1960-62, asso. prof., 1962—, co-founder, dir. Children's Theatre, 1962—. Recipient Freedoms Found. award for play John Dough, 1968, certificate for exceptional acad. service Pa. Dept. Edn., 1974-75, appreciation award Pa. Bicentennial Commn., 1977. Mem. AAUP, Am. Theatre Assn., Theatre Assn. Pa., Internat. Children's Theatre Assn., Internat. Speakers Platform, Assn. Pa. State Colls. and U. Faculty, AAUW (co-founder California br., pres. 1972), California State Coll. Assn. Women Faculty (founder, pres. 1972-73), Alpha Psi Omega, Omicron Nu. Presbyn. Author: (play) Magic in the Sky, 1963; Public Speaking: The Science of The Art, 1966; (play) John Dough, 1968; (play) Dutch Painting, 1968. Home: Box 455 California PA 15419

LANGHANS, LESTER FRANK, JR., constrn. co. exec.; b. Salamanca, N.Y., July 13, 1924; s. Lester Frank and Mildred Irene (Chamberlain) L.; student Salamanca pub. schs.; m. Lois Jane Keeler, July 25, 1946; children—Lester Frank III, Jeanne Lynn Langhans Cole, Kenneth N., Kim Ann. Asst. mgr. constrn. dept. Corning Bldg. Co., Inc. (N.Y.), 1946-52; v.p. Smith, Langhans & McLaughlin Constrn. Corp., 1952-69; pres., 1969-70; pres. Cape Assos., Inc., Cape Cod, Mass., 1971—. Pres. A.I.M. Med. Center of Cape Cod Hosp. Served with USAAF, 1943-46. Decorated Air medal with oak leaf clusters. Mem. Chemung Valley Builders Assn. (past pres.), Cape Cod Contractors and Builders Assn. Republican. Methodist. Home: Drawer D North Sunken Meadow Rd North Eastham MA 02651 Office: Massasoit Rd North Eastham MA 02651

LANGLEY, STEPHEN GOULD, educator, author, performing arts adminstr.; b. Gardner, Mass., Dec. 25, 1938; s. Delma N. and Marjorie (Gould) L.; B.A., Emerson Coll., 1960, M.A., 1961; diploma Central Sch. Speech and Drama, London, 1959; Ph.D., U. Ill., 1966. Owner, mgr. Marionette Touring Co., Athol, Mass., 1949-56; tchr. Boston YMCA Adult Edn. program, 1960-61; mng. dir. Falmouth (Mass.) Playhouse, 1958-78; prof. theatre Bklyn. Coll., City U. N.Y., N.Y.C., 1963—, also gen. mgr. performing arts office and center, 1967-76, dir. performing arts mgmt. div., 1976—, dep. chmn. grad. studies, 1977—. Mem. Dramatists Guild, U.S. Inst. for Theatre Tech., Am. Theatre Assn., Asso. Arts Adminstrn. Educators, Am. Dance Guild (dir.). Author: Theatre Management in America, 1974; Producers on Producing, 1976; contbr. numerous articles to profl. publs. Home: Box 1527 GPO Brooklyn NY 11202 also Performing Arts Center Bklyn Coll Brooklyn NY 11210

LANGLITZ, HAROLD NATHAN, public adminstr.; b. Oshkosh, Wis., Apr. 30, 1925; s. David and Mary (Benner) L.; B.S., Fredonia State Coll., 1950; M.S., U. Rochester, 1954; Ph.D. Syracuse U., 1958; grad. Advanced Mgmt. Program, Harvard U., 1975; m. Ann Langlitz; children—David, Mark, Susan H. Steven. Tchr., Fairport (N.Y.) Central Schs., 1950-54; grad. asst. Syracuse U., 1954-56; prin. Williamson (N.Y.) Central Schs., 1956-60, Westhill (N.Y.) High Sch., 1960-64; supr. schs. Westhill Central Schs., 1964-67; exec. dir. N.Y. State Tchrs. Retirement Bd., 1967—. Bd. dirs. Child's Hosp., Albany, 1970—; mem. Northeastern N.Y. Community Trust Com., Albany, 1971—. Served with AUS, 1943-46; ETO. Recipient Outstanding Alumnus of Yr. award Fredonia State Coll., 1970. Mem. Am. Pension Com., Municipal Fin. Officers Asn., Nat. Council Tchr. Retirement (pres. 1977-78), Am. Soc. Assn. Execs. (certified assn. exec.). Office: 143 Washington Ave Albany NY 12210

LANGLOIS, ETHEL GALAGAN, pub. co. exec.; b. Milw., Sept. 22, 1919; d. James Edward and Emma Mary (Schroeder) Galagan; B.S., U. Wis. at Milw., 1941; m. Joseph Edward Langlois, Oct. 15, 1954; children—Edward, James, Michael, John. Tchr. Latin, Random Lake (Wis.) High Sch., 1941-42; local advt. sales Milw. Jour., 1942-43; mem. planning and prodn. staff U.S. Printing Office, Washington, 1944-46; publs. officer UN, N.Y.C., 1946-59; dir. prodn. and mfg. Elsevier-North Holland Pub. Co., Inc., N.Y.C., 1969—. Mem. Typophiles, Soc. Scholarly Pub., N.Y. Book Guild, Coalition of Pubs. for Employment (adv. panel). Democrat. Roman Catholic. Home: 472 Freeman Ave Oceanside NY 11572 Office: Elsevier-North Holland Pub. Co Inc 52 Vanderbilt Ave New York City NY 10017

LANGLYKKE, ASGER FUNDER, cons.; b. Pleasant Prairie, Wis., July 17, 1909; s. Peter Iversen and Anna (Funder) L.; B.S., U. Wis., 1931, M.S., 1934, Ph.D., 1936; Sc.D., Trinity Coll., 1965; m. Margaret Hays Page, Dec. 16, 1939; children—Peter Page, Kristin Margaret, Gerald Page, Cynthia Jane. Research chemist Hiram Walker & Sons, Inc., Peoria, Ill., 1937-40; supt. Butyl Alcohol Plant, Asociacion Azucarera Coop. Lafayette, Arroyo, P.R., 1940-43; sect. head, acting div. head U.S. Dept. Agr., Peoria, 1943, div. head, 1945-47; chief pilot plants, also chief tech. officer CWS, 1943-45; successively dir. microbiol. devel., dir. research and devel. labs., v.p. E.R. Squibb & Sons, New Brunswick, N.J., also N.Y.C., 1947-67; exec. dir. Am. Soc. Microbiology, Washington, 1968-74; project mgr. Frederick Cancer Research Center (Md.), 1974-77; cons., 1977—; cons. U.S. Army,

1945-66, Office Def. Research and Engring. Adv. Panel Biol. and Chem. Def., 1960-63; adj. prof. Rutgers U., 1968-76. Recipient Unit award for superior service U.S. Dept. Agr., 1956. Fellow Am. Acad. Microbiology, AAAS, N.Y. Acad. Scis., Am. Inst. Chemists; fgn. mem. Societas Biochemica, Biophysica et Microbiologica Fenniae (Finland); mem. Am. Soc. Microbiology (Barnett Cohen award Md. sect. 1978), Am. Chem. Soc. (div. chmn., councilor 1951-54), Am. Inst. Chem. Engrs., Assn. Research Dirs., Biochem. Soc. London (emeritus), Internat. Union Pure and Applied Chemistry (vice chmn., chmn. fermentation commn. 1965-73, v.p. applied chemistry div. 1977—), Sigma Xi, Tau Beta Pi, Phi Lambda Upsilon, Phi Sigma, Gamma Alpha. Research, publs., patents in field. Home: 240 Dill Ave Frederick MD 21701 Office: Frederick Cancer Research Center PO Box B Frederick MD 21701

LANGMEAD, JOSEPH MICHAEL, public accountant; b. Balt., Nov. 5, 1944; s. Richard James and Dorothy Kathleen (DeCarlo) L.; B.S. in Accounting magna cum laude, Loyola Coll. Balt., 1968, M.B.A. with honors, 1973; m. Judy Kay Kearney, June 26, 1969; children—Maureen Evelyn, Gregory Charles. Staff accountant Kushnick and Waldman, Balt., 1965-68; accountant Peat, Marwick, Mitchell & Co., Balt., 1968—, partner, 1976—; lectr. fin. Loyola Coll. Balt., 1975—; speaker profl. orgns. Bd. dirs., chmn. fin. com. Center Stage, regional theater, 1975—; parish accountant St. William of Work Ch. Served with U.S. Army, 1968-75. C.P.A. Mem. Md. Assn. C.P.A.'s (chmn. accounting standards com. 1976—, chmn. govtl. accounting com. 1977—), Am. Inst. C.P.A.'s (mem. subcom. relations with ednl. instns.), Bank Adminstrn. Inst., Md. Pub., Municipal fin. officers assns., Columbia Assn., Loyola Coll. Alumni Assn. (treas. 1976—, dir.). Democrat. Roman Catholic. Home: 706 Dryden Dr Baltimore MD 21229 Office: Peat Marwick Mitchell & Co 25 S Charles St Baltimore MD 21201

LANGRALL, CLARKE, ins. broker; b. Balt., Dec. 1, 1924; s. H. Morton and Hazel (Clarke) L.; B.S., U.S. Mcht. Marine Acad., 1945; postgrad. Johns Hopkins U., 1947-49; m. Bettie Carolyn Davis, May 2, 1964. Sales engr. The Pilbrico Co., Balt., 1946-50; ins. broker, solicitor Thompson & Jones, Balt., 1950-55; pvt. ins. broker, Balt., 1955—; pres. Clarke Langrall, Inc., 1962—. Pres., Loch Raven Sch. PTA, 1956, Loch Raven Inter-Community Council, 1958; chmn. fin. com. Agnew for Gov. Com., 1966; chmn. Gov.'s Inaugural Ball Com., 1967; chmn. Vice Presdl. Ball Com., 1969, also Md. coordinator inaugural activities for v.p. and press. Served with USNR, 1943-46; MTO, PTO. C.L.U. Mem. Soc. St. George, Eastern Shore Soc. Md., Am. Soc. C.L.U.'s, Advt. Club Balt., Nat. Assn. Ins. Agts., Nat. Assn. Life Underwriters, Alumni Assn. U.S. Mcht. Marine Acad. Mem. Baha'I Faith. Club: Kiwanis (pres. Loch Raven 1957). Contbr. articles to ins. trade jours. Lectr. sales, religious topics; moderator radio talk show Religion Today, 1970-72. Office: 204 E Joppa Rd Towson MD 21204

LANIGAN, JOHN PATRICK, editorial cartoonist; b. Chgo., Oct. 8, 1922; s. Thomas Patrick and Bertha Marie (Gundersen) L.; student Art Inst. Chgo., 1946-49, Art Students League N.Y., 1949-50; m. Carmela Emily Caltabinano, Apr. 9, 1961. Editorial cartoonist, New Bedford (Mass.) Standard Times, 1964—. One man shows Town Hall, Chgo., 1948, Rockford (Ill.) Club, 1960, Saratoga Centenial, 1962; exhibited in group shows including Mt. Sinai Hosp. Show, Chgo., Millicent Library, Fairhaven, Mass.; executed murals St. Bonaventure Novitiate, Lake Forest, Ill.; represented in permanent collection Syracuse. Bd. dirs. Animal Rescue League New Bedford, 1967. Served with USNR, 1941-45, 52-55. Recipient Meritorious Achievement award AEC, 1952, Prima Prezienzia, 22d Internat. Exhibit of Humor, Bordighera, Italy, 1969; hon. asso. Syracuse U. Library. Fellow Internat. Inst. Community Studies. Home: 105 Summer St New Bedford MA 02740 Office: 555 Pleasant St New Bedford MA 02742

LANING, ROBERT COMEGYS, surgeon; b. Cape Haitian, Haiti, Sept. 20, 1922 (parents Am. citizens); s. Richard Henry and Marguerite (Boyer) L.; student U. Pa., 1941-43; M.D., Jefferson Med.Coll., 1948; m. Alice T. Lech, Sept. 9, 1961; 1 dau., Maria Alice. Intern, Jefferson Hosp., Phila., 1948-50; resident Naval Hosp., Portsmouth, Va., 1953-56; practice medicine specializing in surgery, 1956—; commd. lt. j.g. USN, 1950, advanced through grades to rear adm., 1972, ret., 1977; chief surgery U.S. Naval Hosps., Chelsea, Mass., 1966-67, Portsmouth, N.H., 1963-66, San Diego, 1967-71; asst. chief bur. medicine and surgery, Washington, 1975-77; dept. dir. surgery service VA, Washington, 1977—. Decorated Legion of Merit. Diplomate Am. Bd. Surgery, Nat. Bd. Med. Examiners. Fellow A.C.S.; mem. AMA, Am. Mil. Surgeons U.S., Soc. Med. Cons.'s to Armed Forces, U.S. Naval Inst., Ret. Officers Assn., Mil. Order of World Wars. Roman Catholic. Office: Surgery Service (112) 810 Vermont St NW Washington DC 20420

LANKFORD, WILLIAM THOMAS, JR., steel co. research exec.; b. Rockwood, Tenn., Nov. 1, 1919; s. William Thomas and Pearl (Chastain) L.; B.S. in Metall. Engring., Carnegie-Mellon U., 1941, D.Sc. in Metall. Engring., 1945; m. Gretchen Goldsmith, July 29, 1944; children—William Thomas, Andrew James, John Robert, Kathleen. Devel. engr. Carnegie-Ill. Steel Corp., 1945; chief research engr. splty. products U.S. Steel Corp., Monroeville, Pa., 1953-60, div. chief sheet products, 1960-63, asst. dir. steel products devel., 1963-67, mgr. steel processing, 1967-75, asso. dir., mgr. basic research, 1975—; Howe Meml. lectr. AIME. Registered profl. engr., Pa. Fellow Metall. Soc. of AIME, Am. Soc. Metals, ASME; mem. ASTM (Charles B. Dudley medal, Richard L. Templin award), Am. Iron and Steel Inst., AAAS. Club: Univ. Contbr. articles on mech. behavior of metals, steelmaking and continuous casting to tech. jours. Home: 200 Mayfair Dr Pittsburgh PA 15228 Office: US Steel Corp Research Lab 125 Jamison Ln Monroeville PA 15146

LANNING, FRANKLIN VAN LIER, orch. music dir.; b. Phila., Nov. 30, 1912; s. Milton Batten and Leona (Van Lier) L.; student N.J. State Tchrs. Coll., 1930-32; B.S. in Music Edn., Ithaca Coll., 1934; postgrad. Curtis Inst. Music, 1934-37; m. Birta Eileen Cooke, Oct. 15, 1939; children—Elaine (Mrs. David L. DeLones), Dwight Van Lier, Bette (Mrs. Joseph J. DeCourcelle III). Music dir. Washington Sinfonietta, 1939-45, Arlington (Va.) Symphony, 1945-50, Jacksonville (Fla.) Symphony, 1950-52, Atlantic City Symphony, 1952-55, Wilmington (Del.) Symphony (name changed to Del. Symphony 1970), 1955—. Dir. music div. WPA, Washington, 1940-42; employee relations officer WPB, Washington, 1942-44; supr. music Arlington Pub. Schs., 1945-49; pres. Lanning Music Co. Inc., Wilmington, 1962-72, chmn. bd., 1972—; chmn. bd. Lanco Realty Corp., 1975—, Music Service & Investment Co., 1975—. Mem. Wilmington Music Commn., 1957-67; minister music Aldersgate Methodist Ch., Wilmington, 1959—; mem. nat. adv. council Nat. Fedn. Ind. Bus., 1972—. Mem. Am. Fedn. Musicians, Am. Symphony Orch. League, Nat. Assn. Composers and Condrs. Home: 1400 Fresno Rd Wilmington DE 19803 Office: 2302 Concord Pike Wilmington DE 19803

LANSBURGH, THERESE WEIL (MRS. RICHARD M. LANSBURGH), social worker; b. New Orleans, Oct. 29, 1919; d. Harold S. and Rosetta (Hirsch) Weil; B.A., Smith Coll., 1940; M.S.W., Tulane Sch. Social Work, 1943; m. Frankel Wolff, May 22, 1943 (dec.); children—Randolph, Deborah; m. 2d, Richard Lansburgh, Jan. 10, 1959. Founder, pres. Rebelles, AWVS USO, New Orleans, 1941-43; case worker ARC, Boston, 1943-45; vis. tchr. Columbus, Miss., 1947-49; social worker Children's Guild, 1959-61; pres., PTA, Franklin Sch., Columbus, 1953-55; bd. mem. Nat. Assn. Jr. Auxs., 1956-58, Miss. State PTA, 1955-57; pres. Md. Com. for Day Care Children, 1965-68, 72-76, hon. pres., 1968-72, 76—, bd. mem. nat. com., 1963-68, pres., 1967-68; pres. Day Care and Child Devel. Council Am., 1968-71, hon. pres., 1971-73; mem. Md. Com. on White House Conf., 1968-71; vice chmn. Developmental Child Care Forum, White House Conf. on Children, 1970; bd. dirs. Balt. County Dept. Social Services, 1967-76; sec. Md. Assn. Mental Health, 1976-78; bd. dirs. Richmond Fellowship Md., Md. Com. Day Care of Children, Md. Community Coordinated Child Care, Balt. Symphony; speaker in field. Mem. Nat. Assn. Social Workers, Nat. Conf. Social Work, Nat. Assn. for Edn. Young Children, Am. Orthopsychiat. Assn., Soc. Research in Child Devel., Delta Kappa Gamma (hon.). Contbr. chpts. Ency. Social Work, 1971, 76; also articles. Established 1st classroom for retarded children in Miss., 1951; leader nat. day care movement. Home: 3503 Midfield Rd Baltimore MD 21208

LANT, JEFFREY LADD, univ. adminstr.; b. Maywood, Ill., Feb. 16, 1947; s. Donald Marshall and Shirley Mae (Lauing) L.; B.A. summa cum laude, U. Calif., Santa Barbara (at U. St. Andrews, Scotland 1967-68), 1969; M.A., Harvard U., 1970, Ph.D. (Woodrow Wilson fellow), 1975; certificate advanced grad. studies in higher edn. adminstrn. Northeastern U., 1976. Teaching fellow in history Harvard Coll., 1971-72, 73-74, in expository writing, 1974-75, asst. to master and resident tutor Dudley House, 1974-75; coordinator student services Boston Coll. Evening Coll., 1976-78; asst. to pres. Radcliffe Coll., Cambridge, Mass., 1978—; active in radio, TV. Recipient Sir Henry Taylor prize in moral philosophy U. St. Andrews, 1968; Master's award Harvard Coll., 1975; ofcl. citation Mass. Ho. of Reps., 1977, Boston City Council, 1978, Gov. Mass., 1978; Harvard traveling fellow, 1972-73, prize fellow, 1969-75. Mem. Am. Hist. Assn., Adult Edn. Assn., Assn. Continuing Higher Edn., AAUP, NEA, New Eng. Research Orgn., Phi Delta Kappa, Kappa Delta Pi, Phi Alpha Theta. Democrat. Clubs: Hasty Pudding, Signet, Harvard Faculty (Cambridge). Contbr. numerous articles in history, edn. and politics to profl. jours., newspapers and mags. Office: Byerly Hall Radcliffe Coll Cambridge MA 02138

LANTAY, GEORGE CHARLES, sch. psychologist, psychotherapist, ednl. cons.; b. N.Y.C., Aug. 1, 1942; s. George Sylvester and Geraldine LeMae (Ogline) L.; B.A., Hope (Mich.) Coll., 1965; M.A., U. Ill., 1968; m. Marilynn Schreur, June 1, 1962; children—Scott Christopher, Christina, Susan Kimberly; m. 2d, Patricia Marx, June 14, 1968. Asst. prof. psychology Westminster Coll., Princeton, N.J., 1969-70; mgmt. tng. asso. Western Elec. Co., N.Y.C., 1970; behavioral scientist, dir. Wagner Assos., Princeton, 1969—; certified sch. psychologist St. Agnes Cathedral High Sch., Rockville Centre, 1976—; ednl. cons. Test Preparation Centers, Riverdale, N.Y., 1975—; intern psychologist N.Y. State Dept. Mental Hygiene, 1973-75; psychologist Odyssey House Parents Program, Wards Island, N.Y., 1973; adj. prof. behavioral scis. N.Y. Inst. Tech., Old Westbury, L.I., 1974-75; dir. div. field services N.Y. Testing and Guidance Center, Flushing, 1976—; dir. Shangri-La Day Camps, N.Y.C., 1976—; contbr. Pres.'s Commn. Mental Health, 1977-78; cons. Eastern Regional Inst. Edn., N.Y. U. Med. Sch. Dept. Psychiatry, Newark Council Social Agencies, N.Y.C. Bd. Edn., Astor Program Intellectually Gifted Children, 1977-78, Camp Northwood for Learning Disabilities, summer 1977. Named an outstanding young man of Am., 1975; certified sch. psychologist, N.Y. State. Mem. Am. Psychol. Assn., AAUP, Am. Ednl. Research Assn., Am. Assn. Sex Educators, Counselors and Therapists. Clubs: St. Bartholomew's Community, Downtown Glee (N.Y.C.). Author: Activities for Learning Disabled Children, 1979; contbr. articles to Ch. Herald mag.; research on underachievement and masculine identification. Home: 23 Lantern Rd Hicksville NY 11801 Office: 28 Greenwich Ave New York City NY 10011

LANZANO, RALPH EUGENE, civil and san. engr.; b. N.Y.C., Dec. 26, 1926; s. Ralph and Frances (Giuliano) L.; B.C.E., N.Y. U., 1959. Engring. aide Seelye, Stevenson, Value, Knecht, N.Y.C., 1957-58; jr. civil engr. N.Y.C. Dept. Pub. Works (now Dept. Water Resources), div. plant design Bur. Water Pollution Control, 1960-63, asst. civil engr., 1963-68; civil engr., 1968-71; sr. san. engr. Parsons, Brinckerhoff, Quade & Douglas, N.Y.C., 1971-72; civil engr. N.Y.C. Dept. Water Resources, 1972-77, N.Y.C. Dept. Environ. Protection, 1978—. Registered profl. engr., N.Y. Mem. ASCE, ASTM, Nat., N.Y. socs. profl. engrs., Soc. Plastic Engrs., Water Pollution Control Fedn., Am. Water Works Assn., Am. Pub. Health Assn., Am. Fedn. Arts (sustaining), Met. Mus. Art (sustaining), Am. Mgmt. Assn., U.S. Inst. Theatre Tech., Royal Soc. Promotion Health, N.Y. U. Alumni Assn., Am. Nat. Theatre and Acad., Lincoln Center Performing Arts (ann. asso.), Am. Theatre Assn., Am. Film Inst., Nat. Rifle Assn. (life), U.S. Lawn Tennis Assn. (life), Nat., Internat. wildlife fedns., Nat. Parks and Conservation Assn., Nat. Geog. Soc., Nat. Audubon Soc., Am. Automobile Assn., Bklyn. Bot. Garden, Am. Mus. Natural History, Chi Epsilon. Republican. Conglist. Home: 17 Cottage Ct Huntington Station NY 11746 Office: 40 Worth St New York City NY 10013

LANZISERA, A.D., civil engr.; b. Valley Stream, N.Y., July 30, 1930; s. Giuseppe and Angela Maria (Masiello) L.; B.C.E., Tri-State U., 1955; m. Elizabeth M. Duggan, Jan. 1953 (div. 1964); children—Kathleen, Elizabeth, Eileen, Mary. Asst. post engr., chief bldgs. and grounds C.E., Bklyn. and Germany, 1964-66; asso. Teas & Barrett, Malverne, N.Y., 1966-74, partner, 1976—; prin. engr. A.D. Lanzisera, Profl. Engr., Valley Stream, 1974-76; village engr. Malverne & Laurel Hollow (N.Y.), 1976—; asst. city engr. Hamilton (Ohio), 1956-64; dir. engring. CD program, Butler County, Ohio, 1960-64. First lt. search and rescue ops. CAP, Hamilton, Ohio, 1961-65. Served with U.S. Army, 1948-52. Registered profl. engr., Ohio, N.Y.; land surveyor, Ohio; certified aircraft pilot. Diplomate Am. Acad. Environ. Engrs. Mem. Soc. Am. Mil. Engrs., Nat. Soc. Profl. Engrs., Am. Congress Surveying and Mapping, Smithsonian Inst. Republican. Roman Catholic. Home: 87 S Corona Ave Valley Stream NY 11580 Office: 125 Church St Malverne NY 11565

LANZKOWSKY, PHILIP, physician; b. Cape Town, S. Africa, Mar. 17, 1932; s. Abe and Lily (Goldberg) L.; came to U.S., 1965, naturalized, 1974; M.B., Ch.B., U. Cape Town, 1954, M.D., 1959; m. Rhona Chiat, Dec. 4, 1955; children—Shelley, David Roy, Leora, Jonathan, Marc. Intern Groote Schuur Hosp., U. Cape Town, 1955-56; resident Red Cross Children's Hosp., U. Cape Town, 1957-60; fellow in pediatric hematology Duke, 1961-62, U. Utah, Salt Lake City, 1962-63; dir. pediatric hematology N.Y. Hosp.-Cornell U. Med. Center, 1965-70; asst. prof., then asso. prof. pediatrics Cornell U. Med. Sch., 1965-70; chmn. pediatrics L.I. Jewish-Hillside Med. Center, New Hyde Park, N.Y., 1970—; prof. pediatrics State U. N.Y. Med. Sch., Stony Brook, 1970—; cons. pediatrics Nassau County Med. Center, East Meadows, N.Y., 1970—, Cath. Med. Center, Queens, N.Y., Peninsula Hosp. Center, Far Rockaway, N.Y., Jamaica Hosp., Queens, St. John's Episcopal Hosp., Far Rockaway, Hillcrest Hosp., Queens, Health Ins. Plan of N.Y.; mem. med. adv. bd. L.I. chpt. Leukemia Soc. Am., Met. chpt. Hemophilia Soc. Am., St. Mary's Hosp. Children, Bayside, N.Y., L.I. chpt. Nat. Found. Sudden Infant Death. Cecil John Adams Meml. traveling fellow, 1960; Hill-Pattison-Sruthers burser, 1960; grantee Nutrition Found., 1968. Diplomate Child Health Eng. Fellow Royal Coll. Physicians Edinburgh, Am. Acad. Pediatrics; mem. Soc. Pediatric Research, Am. Pediatric Soc., Harvey Soc., Am. Hematology Soc., Am. Soc. Clin. Oncology, Am. Assn. Cancer Research, Am. Council Emigrés in the Professions. Contbr. to med. jours. Home: 159 W Shore Rd Great Neck NY 11024 Office: LI Jewish-Hillside Med Center New Hyde Park NY 11040

LANZKRON, ROLF WOLFGANG, mfg. co. exec.; b. Hamburg, Germany, Dec. 9, 1929; s. Aron Artur and Hanna (Farbstein) L.; came to U.S., 1951, naturalized, 1961; B.S., Milw. Sch. Engring., 1953; M.S., U. Wis., 1955, Ph.D., 1956; m. Amy Virginia Yarri, Mar. 5, 1961; children—Paul Joshua, Sophie Miriam, Lisa Rachel. Computer designer Univac Sperry Rand, St. Paul, 1956-58; guidance and control systems integrations staff Martin Marietta, Orlando, Fla., 1958-61, systems engr., Balt., 1961-63; became chief command and service module flight project div. NASA Manned Spacecraft Center, Apollo Program, Houston, 1963; now gringle ops. mgr. Raytheon Co., Sudbury, Mass. Served with Israeli Army, 1948-51. Recipient NASA Outstanding Achievement award, 1964, Spl. Service award, 1966; registered profl. engr., Calif. Mem. Am. Inst. Aeronautics and Astronautics, Am. Math. Soc., IEEE, Am. Mgmt. Assn., Sigma Xi. Home: 35 Gardner Rd Brookline MA 02146 Office: Raytheon Co Equipment Div Sudbury MA 01776

LA PAGLIA, JOSEPH ROCCO, III, fin. analyst; b. Washington, Mar. 21, 1953; s. Joseph R. and Sally A. (Melchior) LaP.; B.A., Williams Coll., 1975; M.B.A., Columbia U., 1977; m. Lisa Evelyn Jonassen, July 29, 1978. Staff accountant Price Waterhouse & Co., N.Y.C., 1975-76; sr. fin. analyst Lever Bros. Co., N.Y.C., 1977-78; fin. analyst Service Bur. Co., Greenwich, Conn., 1978—. Roman Catholic. Office: Service Bur Co 500 W Putnam Ave Greenwich CT 06830

LAPERRIERE, PAUL JOSEPH, ins. co. exec.; b. Waterbury, Conn., June 7, 1950; s. Jean Jacques and Ethel Ledwina (Empoliti) LaP.; B.A. in Econs., U. N.H., 1972; m. Patricia Ann Mariano, Nov. 16, 1973. Tchr., Naugatuck (Conn.) Bd. Edn., 1972-73; adminstrv. asst. Allstate Ins. Co., Farmington, Conn., 1973-74, ops. supr., 1974, div. supr., 1975, sales rep., 1975-76, controllers asst., 1976, asst. dist. sales mgr., 1976, dist. sales mgr., 1977—. Mem. Nat. Assn. Life Underwriters. Club: Elks. Home: 57 Evan Rd Southington CT 06489 Office: 70 Batterson Park Rd Farmington CT 06032

LAPIDUS, ARNOLD, mathematician; b. Bklyn., Nov. 6, 1933; s. Morris and Mollie (Portnoy) L.; B.S., Bklyn. Coll., 1956; M.S., Ph.D. (Univ. scholar), N.Y. U., 1967; m. Nancy Beatrice Latner, Aug. 9, 1952. Research scientist Courant Inst., N.Y.C., 1956-68; computer application math. analyst Goddard Inst. for Space Studies, N.Y.C., 1968-70, math. analyst programming methods, 1970-71, sr. mem. tech. staff computer scis., 1971-73; asso. prof. quantitative analysis Fairleigh Dickinson U., Teaneck, N.J., 1973—. Mem. AAAS, Math. Assn. Am., Am. Math. Soc., Soc. Indsl. and Applied Math. Contbr. articles to profl. publs. Home: 160 Rockwood Pl Englewood NJ 07631 Office: 1000 River Rd Teaneck NJ 07666

LAPIDUS, HERBERT, pharm. co. exec.; b. N.Y.C., Aug. 10, 1931; s. Harry and Fanny (Bagdenofsky) L.; B.S., Columbia, 1953, M.S., 1955; Ph.D., Rutgers U., 1967; m. Iris Belle Felber, Dec, 21, 1952; children—Helane, William. Project dir., Julius Schmid Co., pharm., N.Y.C., 1957-60; dept. head Bristol Myers Co. pharms., Hillside, N.J., 1960-71; tech. dir. Combe Inc. pharm. and cosmetics, White Plains, N.Y., 1971-77, v.p. new product devel., 1977—; instr. Columbia, N.Y.C., 1955-57. Served with M.C., AUS, 1956-57. Mem. N.Y. Acad. Scis., Am. Pharm. Assn., Am. Chem. Soc., Soc. Cosmetic Chemists, Proprietary Assn., Sigma Xi, Rho Chi. Patentee in field. Home: 46 Nutmeg Ridge Ridgefield CT 06877 Office: 1101 Westchester Ave White Plains NY 10604

LAPLACA, PETER JOHN, educator; b. N.Y.C., Dec. 9, 1946; s. Damiano John and Lillian Mary (Celauro) LaP.; B.S., Rensselaer Poly. Inst., 1968, M.S., 1969, Ph.D., 1972; m. Sherry Cutler, Sept. 2, 1967; children—Michelle, Matthew. Faculty Rensselaer Poly. Inst., Troy, N.Y., 1969-70; instr. State U. N.Y., Albany, 1970-72; asso. cons. Impetus, Latham, N.Y., 1970-72; asst. prof. U. Hartford, (Conn.), 1972-74; chief cons. Unity Contractors Assn., Hartford, 1972-76; asso. prof. U. Conn., Storrs, 1974—; prin. LaPlaca Assos., Bloomfield, Conn., 1968—. Recipient hon. mention research design competition Am. Mktg. Assn., 1971-72. Mem. Am. Mktg. Assn. (dir. 1977-79), Am. Inst. Decision Scis. (v.p. fin. 1975-78), Assn. Consumer Research, Am. Council Consumer Intrests, Acad. Mgmt., Acad. Mktg. Sci. (v.p. for fin. 1978-79), World Future Soc., Epsilon Delta Sigma, Alpha Iota Delta, Alpha Chi Rho. Roman Catholic. Editorial staff mktg. abstracts sect. jour. Mktg., 1974-77; book rev. editor Indsl. Mktg. Mgmt., 1977—; editorial rev. bd. Jour. Acad. Mktg. Sci., 1977—; editor The New Role of the Marketing Professional, 1977. Contbr. articles to profl. jours. Home: 24 Quarry Dr Vernon CT 06066 Office: Dept Marketing U Conn Storrs CT 06268

LAPLANTE, LOUIS ELMER, physician; b. Verdun, Que., Can., July 17, 1943; s. Elmer Clement Gilbert and Rita Berthe (Benoit) L.; B.A., Coll. Jean Jacques Olier, 1963; M.D., U. Montreal, 1967; m. Louise Montpetit, June 27, 1970; children—Benoit, Francois. Intern Verdun Gen. Hosp., 1967-69; resident in nephrology Maisonneuve-Rosemont Hosp., Montreal, 1969-72, acting physician, 1972-76; cons. physician Vardun Gen. Hosp., 1972-76, Montreal Inst. Cardiology, 1974-76; asso. prof. medicine U. Montreal, 1972—; practice medicine specializing in nephrology, Montreal, 1972—. Fellow Royal Coll. Physicians and Surgeons Can.; mem. Coll. Physicians and Surgeons (Que.), Royal Coll. Surgeons and Physicians (Eng.) (asso.). Liberal. Roman Catholic. Contbr. articles to profl. jours. Home: 1272 Beatty St Verdun PQ H4H 1Y1 Canada Office: 5415 L'Assomption St Montreal PQ H1T 2M4 Canada

LA PORTE, JAMES ARTHUR, investment counselor; b. Kankakee, Ill., Nov. 11, 1928; s. Edmund J. and Pearl (Tammen) L.; B.A., Eastern Ill. U., 1950; J.D., Chgo. Kent Coll. of Law, 1954; postgrad. N.Y. U. Grad. Sch. Bus., 1960-62; m. Margaret Lawlor, Mar. 9, 1950 (div. 1956); 1 dau., Denise. Admitted to Ill. bar, 1954, U.S. Dist. Ct., 1955; asst. state's atty., Kankakee, 1955-58; v.p. Nat. Utility Co., internat. rate cons., N.Y.C., 1958-63; with Lionel D. Edie & Co., N.Y.C., 1963—, v.p., 1967-69, v.p. Edie Internat., Ltd., 1970-72, sales mgr., N.Y.C., 1972-76, v.p. nat. accounts, N.Y.C., 1976-78, sr. v.p. Edie Asset Mgmt. div., 1978—. Mem. Ill. State Bar Assn., Phi Delta Phi. Clubs: Explorers, N.Y. U., N.Y. Athletic. Expdn. to Surinam to study tribal customs, 1968. Home: 2 Tudor City Pl New York City NY 10017 Office: 530 Fifth Ave New York City NY 10036

LAPP, WARREN ANTHONY, obstetrician, gynecologist; b. Chicago Heights, Ill., Apr. 5, 1915; s. Reuben Roy and Gertrude Caroline (Hacker) L.; A.B., Ohio State U., 1939, M.D., 1939; m. Emma Katherine Beard, Jan. 25, 1941; children—Charles Warren, Robert Lewis. Rotating intern Kings County Hosp., Bklyn., 1939-41, resident obstetrics-gynecology, 1941-44; practice medicine specializing in obstetrics/gynecology, Bklyn., 1947-70; dir. obstetrics-gynecology St. Johns Episcopal Hosp., Bklyn., 1970—; asso. clin. prof. obstetrics-gynecology Downstate Med. Center, State U. N.Y., Bklyn., 1955—; attending physician obstetrics-gynecology Kings County Hosp., Bklyn., 1947—. Cons. adviser Flatbush YMCA, 1967—. Served from 1st lt. to maj. M.C., AUS, 1944-46. Decorated Bronze Star. Diplomate Am. Bd. Obstetrics/Gynecology. Fellow A.C.S. (gov. 1974—), Am. Coll. Obstetricians and Gynecologists, N.Y. Obstet. Soc., Bklyn. Gynecol. Soc. (pres. 1960); mem. AMA (N.Y. State del. 1964—, com. on pvt. practice 1968-70), Assn. Mil. Surgeons U.S., Med. Soc. State N.Y. (councillor 1968-74, asst. treas. 1974-76, treas. 1976—), Pan Am. Med. Soc., Med. Soc. County of Kings (pres. 1959), Marshall County Farm Bur., Early Am. Coppers, Nat. Geneal. Assn., Am. Numis. Assn., L.I. Hist. Soc., Chi Phi, Nu Sigma Nu. Club: Rotary. Editor, pub. Penny-Wise, 1967—. Home: 731 E 22d St Brooklyn NY 11210 Office: 480 Herkimer St Brooklyn NY 11213

LAPPIN, W. ROBERT, soft drink co. exec., communications exec.; b. Boston, Feb. 23, 1935; s. Albert A. and Emma G. L.; B.F.A., Ithaca Coll., 1957; m. Dorothy M. Liftig, June 2, 1967; children—Lawrence B., James H., Jennifer, Lisa A., Jonathan E. Exec. v.p. Goodyear Rubber Co., Middletown, Conn., 1959-62; pres., chmn. bd. Pepsi-Cola Bottling Co. of Hartford-Springfield, Inc., Windsor, Conn. and Pepsi-Cola Bottling Co. of New Haven, Inc., Branford, Conn., 1962—; chmn. bd. Lappin Communications, Inc., Springfield, Mass., 1977—, Bubble Up Internat., Ltd. and Bubble Up Inc., Los Angeles, 1972; past dir. Pepsi-Cola Bottling Co. of Washington, Inc. Vice chmn. United Fund, Middletown, 1961; trustee Wilbraham and Monson Acads., 1970-72, vice chmn. bd. trustees Monson Acad., 1968-69; vice chmn. fund drive Greater Hartford Arts Council, 1977. Named as Outstanding Young Man in Am., U.S. Jr. C. of C., 1970. Mem. Young Pres.'s Orgn., Nat. Soft Drink Assn., Conn. Mfrs. Carbonated Beverages (past v.p., dir.), New Eng., Conn. Pepsi-Cola bottlers assns., Nat. Broadcasters Assn., Hartford, Windsor, Springfield (Mass.) chambers commerce. Clubs: 100 of Conn. (dir. 1963—, v.p. 1977—), Masons. Office: 1050 Kennedy Rd Windsor CT 06095

LAPRADE, EDWARD THEODORE, city park ofcl.; b. N.Y.C., Feb. 14, 1944; s. Edward Alexander and Bernadette Jeanne (Senville) L.; student Tex. Christian U., Ft. Worth, also U. Md., Ramstein, Germany, 1964-65; A.B., Watertown (N.Y.) Sch. Commerce, 1969; A.A., Jefferson Community Coll., Watertown, 1972; B.S., State U. N.Y., Brockport, 1974; m. Joanne Ruth Lucas, Dec. 20, 1969; children—Steven Edward, Christopher Paul. Mgr., dept., div. merchandiser Westons Shoppers City, Watertown, N.Y., 1969-70; youth dir., recreation supr. Salvation Army Center, Watertown, 1970-72; dir. Salvation Army Recreation and Service Center, Rochester, N.Y., 1972-74, dir. Camp Troutburg, Hamlin, N.Y., 1973; exec. dir. Newark and Arcadia Recreation and Parks Dept., Newark, N.Y., 1974—. Pres., Methodist Youth Fellowship Council, Dexter, N.Y., 1959-62, Catholic Youth Orgn., Dexter, 1961, N.Y. State Youth Temperence Council, Watertown, 1961-62; adult chpt. chmn. Cath. Youth Orgn., Ramstein, Germany, 1965-66; pres. exec. bd. Watertown YMCA, 1971; chmn. pub. relations com. Newark Recreation and Parks Commn., 1974-78; dir. Arcadia Sr. Citizens Adv. Council, 1974-75; founder, dir. Newark-Arcadia Youth Adv. Council, 1975—; founder, co-chmn. Wayne County (N.Y.) Boys Basketball League, 1975—. Served as sgt. USAF, 1962-66. Recipient Cath. Youth Orgn. Outstanding Service award, 1965; USAF Sgt. of Quarter award Ramstein AFB, Ger., 1966; YMCA Youth Service Vol. award, 1968; Salvation Army Distinguished Youth Service award, 1971; awards for excellence in areas basketball, tennis, badminton and volleyball Pres.'s Council on Phys. Fitness, 1973-76; Nat. Gold Medal Finalist award Nat. Sports Found., 1975. Mem. Wayne County Recreation Service Council (treas. 1974-77), Nat. Recreation and Parks Assn., Am., N.Y. State recreation and parks socs., Smithsonian Assos., Internat. Entrepreneur Assn., Am. Mgmt. Assn., Phi Theta Kappa, Kappa Delta Pi. Clubs: Rotary, Writers Book, Old World Health, Elks, Ancient and Mystical Order of Rosicrucians.*

LAPROVA, MARIO, certified pub. accountant; b. Teano, Italy, June 29, 1932; s. Angelo and Elvira (Paolino) LaP.; came to U.S., 1961, naturalized, 1966; B.S. in Bus. Adminstrn., Bryant Coll., 1972, M.B.A., 1974; m. Viola LaProva, Aug. 12, 1974. Accounting clk. Grinnel Corp., Providence, 1966-67; accountant Puritan Life Ins. Co., Providence, 1967-68; staff accountant Newton Cohn, Providence, 1971—; C.P.A. in charge Blackway, Millman & Co., 1971-78; prin. Mario LaProva, Inc., C.P.A., N. Providence, 1978—; part time instr. accounting Bryant Coll. Served with U.S. Army, 1963-66. Mem. Am. Inst. C.P.A.'s, R.I. Soc. C.P.A.'s (mem. bd., mem. coms. auditing, continuing edn., ethics, mng. accounting practice, speakers bur., long range planning), Assn. M.B.A. Execs., Accountants for the Pub. Interest R.I. (mem. bd.), Blackstone Valley C. of C. (bus. procedures com.). Roman Catholic. Home: 77 Carriage Dr Lincoln RI 02865 Office: 1024 Charles St North Provicence RI 02904

LARABY, LARRY L., social service adminstr.; b. Escanaba, Mich., Dec. 1, 1932; s. Sherman L. and Gertrude E. Laraby; B.C.L., Northwestern U., 1957; B.S. in Human Services, Edison Coll., 1978; m. Mary Lee Ehrhardt, Nov. 22, 1978. Traffic survey coordinator State of Wis., Dept. of Hwys., 1961-63; personnel mgr. Salvation Army, Balt., 1965-70; quality control engr. Misty Harbor, Ltd., Balt., 1971-73; gen. mgr. Gen. Equipment Sales and Service, Balt., 1971-73; adminstr. Pilot House, Inc., Mount Wilson, Md., 1976—. Served with USAF, 1949-53; U.S. Army, 1958-61. Decorated Air Medal, Bronze Star, Purple Heart, Legion of lferit; cert. alcoholism counselor. Mem. Md. Addiction Counselors Assn. (v.p. 1977-78, dir. 1975-78), Alcoholism Assn. of Md. (dir. 1976—), Cert. Alcoholism Counselors of Md. (sec. 1977), Nat. Psychiat. Assn., Am. Legion, VFW, Am. Mgmt. Assn., Am. Philatelic Soc., Am. Numis. Assn. Republican. Lutheran. Home: 12006 Tarragon Rd Reisterstown MD 21136 Office: Pilot House Inc Bldg 50 Mount Wilson MD 21112

LARBERG, JOHN FREDERICK, social work adminstr.; b. Kansas City, Mo., Jan. 21, 1930; s. Herman Alvin and Ann (Sabrowsky) L.; A.A., Kansas City Jr. Coll., 1948; A.B. cum laude, U. Mo., 1950, postgrad., 1955-56; M. Social Service, Bryn Mawr Coll., 1961. With Westinghouse Electric Corp., 1953-56; dir. House of Industry Settlement House, Phila., 1957-61; asst. to exec. dir. Health and Welfare Council, Inc., Phila., 1961-66; sr. staff cons. Nat. Assembly for Social Policy and Devel., Inc., N.Y.C., 1966-73; nat. dir. community and patient services Nat. Multiple Sclerosis Soc., N.Y.C., 1974—; nat. adv. com. advocacy project Nat. Council Homemakers-Home Health Aides, 1977—; cons. to exec. com. Commn. on Vol. Service and Action, 1967-76; cons. Met. N.Y. Project Equality, 1968-73, Encampment for Citizenship, 1973-74, Symphony for UN, 1974-77. Bd. dirs. FACTS, Inc., N.Y.C., 1961-66, v.p., 1963, treas., 1964-66. Served with AUS, 1951-53. Mem. Acad. Certified Social Workers, Nat. Assn. Social Workers (chpt. legis. com. 1968-70, nat. publs. com. 1968-71), Internat. Council Social Welfare, Internat. Fedn. Multiple Sclerosis Socs. (vice chmn. patient services com. 1976—, rep. to Rehab. Internat. Med. Commn. 1976—), Nat. Conf. Social Welfare (program com. 1966-73, chmn. combined asso. groups 1969-70, nat. dir. 1971-73), Am. Acad. Polit. and Social Sci., AAAS, Nat. Urban League (nat. trustee-at-large 1968), Hawk Mountain Sanctuary Assn., Bryn Mawr Social Work Alumni Assn. (pres. 1963-65), Mo. Soc. N.Y., Am. Mus. Natural History, Nat. Audubon Soc., Nat. Wildlife Found., NAACP, Phi Beta Kappa Assn. N.Y. (v.p. 1973-75), Omicron Delta Kappa, QEBH, Alpha Phi Omega, Alpha Pi Zeta, Pi Sigma Alpha, Alpha Kappa Psi. Home: 400 E 58th St New York City NY 10022 Office: 205 E 42d St New York City NY 10017

LAREN, KUNO, investment banker; b. Tallinn, Estonia, Sept. 29, 1924; s. Alexander and Jenny (Ozolit) L.; came to U.S., 1946, naturalized, 1953; student U. Stockholm, 1944-46; B.A., Park Coll., 1948; M.A., N.Y. U., 1950; m. Mary Boondas, Nov. 18, 1950; children—Inga, Guy, Philip, Anders. Securities analyst Shearson, Hammill & Co., N.Y.C., 1953-59; mgr. investment research Jesup & Lamont, N.Y.C., 1959-62; v.p. investment banking and research McDonnell & Co., N.Y.C., 1962-70; pres. U.S. Securities Corp., N.Y.C., 1970—; chmn. Kilton's Inc., Manchester, N.H., 1974—; dir., mem. exec. council Servicemaster Industries, Inc., Downers Grove, 1963—; dir. Victor Kellering, Inc., N.Y.C. Mem. Chartered Fin. Analysts, N.Y. Soc. Security Analysts. Home: 30 Olive Pl Forest Hills NY 11375 Office: 17 Cedar St Manchester NH 03105

LARGESS, GEORGE JOSEPH, educator; b. Malden, Mass., Oct. 20, 1917; s. James Edmund and Ellen (Hyland) L.; B.S., U.S. Naval Acad., 1939; postgrad. U.S. Naval Postgrad. Sch., 1945; M.S.T., Am. U., 1972; m. Zoe McCombs, Feb. 2, 1942; children—George Joseph, Robert P., Dennis N., Mary Jude, William M. Commd. ensign USN, 1939, advanced through grades to comdr., 1949; comdr. U.S.S. Altair, 1952-53, U.S.S. Keppler, 1957-58; ret., 1961; project engr. Booz-Allen Applied Research, Inc., 1961-68; instr. math. St. Cecilia's Acad., Washington, 1968-69, D.C. Pub. Schs., 1968, 73—, Bullis Sch., Silver Spring, Md., 1969-70, Anne Arundel (Md.) Pub. Schs., 1970-72; mem. adv. group on electronic warfare U.S. Dept. Def., 1959-61. Pres., Crestwood Citizens Assn., 1960-61, del. D.C. Fedn., 1961-62; pres. Holy Name Soc., 1962-64, treas., 1974-75, del. Archdiocesan Union, 1961-68; pres. Cath. Youth Orgn., 1958-61; leader Capital council Boy Scouts Am., 1953-56; sec. Archdiocesan Union Holy Name Socs., 1968-71; mem. St. Matthew's Cathedral Council, 1968—, Holy Year com., 1974-75; mem. Calvert Sch. bd., 1968-70; mem. Am. Irish Bicentennial com. U.S.S. Yorktown Assn. Recipient Holy Name Soc. Appreciation award, 1964. Mem. Nat. Council Cath. Men, IEEE, Mil. Order World Wars, Armed Forces Communication-Electronics Assn., Washington Ops. Research Council, Internat. Platform Assn., Math. Assn. Am., Nat. Council Tchrs. Math., Assn. Tchrs. Math., Am. Security Council, John Carroll Soc., Phi Delta Kappa. Club: Serra of Washington (trustee). Home: 1908 Quincy St NW Washington DC 20011 Office: DC Pub Schs 415 12th St NW Washington DC 20004

LARKIN, JAMES THOMAS, mfg. engr.; b. Carbondale, Pa., Dec. 30, 1936; s. Thomas Ambrose and Ivy Ann (Owen) L.; diploma in ferrous metallurgy Newark Coll. Engring. and Metals Engring. Inst., 1966. Engr., Driver Harris Co., Harrison, N.J., 1957-60, prodn. supr., 1960-63; mfg. engr. Alfred Heller Heat Treating Co., Clifton, N.J., 1963—. Foreman, Passaic County Grand Jury, 1972. Registered profl. engr., Calif.; certified mfg. engr., U.S., Can.; certified rifle and pistol instr. Mem. Soc. Mfg. Engrs., Am. Soc. Metals, Grand Jury Assn., Nat. Rifle Assn. (life), African Wildlife Leadership Found., Associated N.J. Rifle and Pistol Clubs. Roman Catholic. Home: 313 South Pkwy Clifton NJ 07014 Office: 5 Wellington St Clifton NJ 07015

LA ROCHE, ROBERT WILLIAM, mfg. co. exec.; b. Cleve., Jan. 11, 1951; s. William Edward and Lillian B. LaRoche; student George Peabody Coll., Nashville, 1969-70; m. Frieda C. Sharp, Feb. 18, 1972; 1 son, Robert Edward. Sales rep. Mar/Search, Inc., Huntsville, Ala., 1970-72; with A.B. Dick Co., 1972—, spl. markets mgr. S.E. region, Atlanta, 1976-77, br. mgr. Providence br., Warwick, R.I., 1977—. Roman Catholic. Office: 1 Braemore Way Warwick RI 02886

LAROCHELLE, DONALD RAYMOND, engr., engring. co. exec.; b. Lewiston, Maine, Nov. 26, 1930; s. Philip Joseph and Dora Alexena (Poisson) LaR.; B.S., U. Me., 1953; m. Anne Marie Albert, Oct. 31, 1953; children—Paul, Gary, Theresa, Jane, Stephan, Patti. Asst. city engr. Lewiston, 1953-55; v.p., treas. Aliberti, LaRochelle & Hodson Engring. Corp., Lewiston, 1955—; pres. Comtech, Inc., Lewiston, 1969—; v.p. ALH/Quinlan Assos., architects and engrs.; chmn. bd. AL & H Constrn. Mgmt. trustee Androscoggin County Savs. Bank, 1975—. Adv. bd. St. Mary's Gen. Hosp., Central Maine Vocat. Tech. Inst.; corporator, Central Maine Gen. Hosp., Lewiston, 1969—. Registered profl. engr., Maine, N.H., Vt., Mass., R.I., Conn. Fellow Am. Cons. Engrs. Council; mem. ASCE, Nat. Soc. Profl. Engrs., Cons. Engrs. of Maine (pres. 1971-72), Auburn-Lewiston C. of C. (dir., pres. 1976-77), Phi Kappa Sigma. Republican. Roman Catholic. K.C. (3 deg.). Home: 21 Bristol Rd Lewiston ME 04240 Office: 436 Main St Lewiston ME 04240

LA ROCQUE, EUGENE PHILIPPE, bishop; b. Windsor, Ont., Can., Mar. 27, 1927; s. Eugene Joseph and Angeline Marie (Monforton) LaR.; B.A., U. Western Ont., 1948; M.A., Laval U., 1956. Ordained priest Roman Catholic Ch., 1952, consecrated bishop, 1974; asst. parish priest Ste. Therese Ch., Windsor, 1952-54; registrar Christ the King Coll., U. Western Ont., 1956-64, dean of men, lectr., 1962-64, asst. spiritual dir. St. Peter's Sem., 1964-65, prin., dean King's Coll., 1965-68; pastor St. Joseph's Ch., Rivière-aux-Canards, Ont., 1968-70, Ste. Anne's Ch., Tecumseh, 1970-74; bishop of Alexandria-Cornwall, 1974—; dean Essex County, 1970-73; trustee Essex County Roman Cath. Separate Sch. Bd., 1972-74; 1st chmn. liaison com. between Can. Jewish Congress, Can. Council Chs. and Can. Cath. Conf. Bishops, 1977—; pres. Senate Priests Can., 1973-74. Mem. Can. Cath. Conf. Bishops. Club: K.C. Address: 200 Montreal Rd PO Box 1388 Cornwall ON K6H 5V4 Canada

LAROSE, WILLIAM ROBINSON, civil engr.; b. Tonawanda, N.Y., Oct. 22, 1922; s. Howard W. and Nellie (Robinson) LaR.; B.C.E., Rensselaer Poly. Inst., 1951; m. Marjorie Coonley, Jan. 29, 1949; children—Barbara, Ann, Virginia. Engr.-in-tng. Electro Metall. Co., Niagara Falls, N.Y., 1951-52; asst. engr. Buck and Buck Engrs., Hartford, Conn., 1952-57; asso. Stearns and Wheler, Civil and San. Engrs., Cazenovia, N.Y., 1957—; lectr. on specifications, sch. for insps. Am. Pub. Works Assn., specifications com. Cons. Engrs., Assn. Pipeline Contractors. Area capt. United Community Fund Cazenovia, 1960; pres. bd. trustees First Presbyn. Ch. Cazenovia, 1963-64. Served with U.S. Army, 1942-45. Recipient Distinguished Service award Jaycees, E. Windsor, Conn., 1955; lic. profl. engr., N.Y. Mem. Nat. Soc. Profl. Engrs., Water Pollution Control Fedn. Clubs: Cazenovia Golf, Willow Bank Yacht.

LAROW, EDWARD JOSEPH, educator; b. Albany, N.Y., Dec. 22, 1937; s. William Corrigan and Alice Julia (Reil) L.; B.S., Siena Coll., 1960; M.S., Kans. State U., 1965; Ph.D., Rutgers U., 1968; m. Nancy Louise Jarvis, Aug. 24, 1963; children—Mary Anne, Edward Jr., John, Catherine. Asst. prof. biology Siena Coll., Loudonville, N.Y., 1968-71, asso. prof., 1971-75, prof., chmn. dept., 1971—; vis. lectr. biology State U. of N.Y. Recipient Distinguished Service award Albany Jr. C. of C. NSF research grantee, 1970-74. Mem. Siena Coll. Alumni Assn. (dir.), AAAS, Am. Inst. of Biol. Scis., Am. Soc. of Limnology and Oceanography, Ecol. Soc. of Am., Societas Internationalis Limnologiae, Sigma Xi. Roman Catholic. Contbr. numerous articles on aquatic biology to sci. publs. Home: 25 Sparrowbush Rd S Latham NY 12110 Office: Dept Biology Siena Coll Loudonville NY 12211

LARSEN, JOHN WALTER, JR., obstetrician, gynecologist; b. Englewood, N.J., Jan. 27, 1943; s. John Walter and Eleanor Viola (Waterhouse) L.; B.A., Dartmouth Coll., 1964; M.D., Cornell U., 1968; m. Janet Gladys Witschieben, July 3, 1965; children—Christine Carol, John Walter 3d. Intern, Presbyn.-St. Luke's Hosp., Chgo., 1968-69; resident Yale-New Haven Hosp., 1969-73; instr. dept. obstetrics and gynecology Yale U. Sch. Medicine, New Haven, 1972-73; asst. prof. obstetrics and gynecology George Washington U., Washington, 1975—, faculty fellow in maternal-fetal medicine, 1975—; guest research worker Nat. Inst. for Neurol. and Communicative Disorder and Stroke, NIH, 1975—. Served to maj., M.C., U.S. Army, 1973-75. Decorated Army Commendation medal. Fellow Am. Coll. Obstetricians and Gynecologists; mem. AMA, Med. Soc. D.C., Infectious Disease Soc. for Obstetrics and Gynecology, Teratology Soc., So. Perinatal Assn. Presbyterian. Contbr. articles on maternal-fetal medicine, perinatal infections to med. jours. Office: 2150 Pennsylvania Ave NW Washington DC 20037

LARSEN, PHILLIP DARWIN, govt. ofcl.; b. Lincoln, Nebr., July 13, 1942; s. Gerald Wilfred and Mildred Bernice (Erickson) L.; B.A., Nebr. Wesleyan U., 1964; postgrad. U. Nebr., 1964-66; m. Donna Mae Dimpsey, June 9, 1973. Spl. asst. to dir. Nebr. Dept. Agr. and Econ. Devel., Lincoln, 1966; mgmt. intern and personnel mgmt. analyst AEC, Washington, 1967-70; asst. budget and mgmt. officer Office of Mgmt. and Budget, 1970-73, budget mgmt. officer, 1973-78; adminstrv. officer White House, 1978—. Mem. Theta Chi. Home: 4509 N 20th St Arlington VA 22207 Office: White House Washington DC 20500

LARSON, CHARLES FRED, JR., indsl. assn. exec.; b. Gary, Ind., Nov. 27, 1936; s. Charles F. and Margaret Jane (Taylor) L.; B.M.E., Purdue U., 1958; M.B.A., Fairleigh Dickinson U., 1973; m. Joan Ruth Grupe, Aug. 22, 1959; children—Gregory Paul, Laura Ann. Project engr. Combustion Engring., Inc., East Chicago, 1958-60; sec. Welding Research Council, N.Y.C., 1960-70, asst. dir., 1970-75; exec. dir. Indsl. Research Inst., Inc., N.Y.C., 1975—; sec.-treas. Indsl. Research Inst. Research Corp., N.Y.C., 1975—. Mem. Wyckoff (N.J.) Bd. Edn., 1973—, v.p., 1975-76, pres., 1976-77. Registered profl. engr., N.J. Mem. ASME, AAAS, N.Y.C. Chemists Club, Pi Tau Sigma. Clubs: Masons, High Mountain Golf. Asso. editor Jour. Pressure Vessel Tech., 1973-75; contbr. articles in field to profl. jours.; editor mech. engring. articles; editorial adv. com. Am. Men and Women of Sci. Office: Industrial Research Insitute 100 Park Ave New York City NY 10017*

LARSON, JAN ALEXANDRA, counselor; b. Guam, July 8, 1950; d. John Mayne and Ruth (Alexander) L.; B.A., West Chester State Coll., 1973; M.A., M.Ed., Tchrs. Coll. Columbia U., 1977. Vocat. counselor, Psychol. Consultation Center, Columbia U., 1975-76; supr. Halfway House, Media (Pa.) Mental Health Clinic, 1978—. Rehab. Services Adminstrn. scholar, 1975-77. Mem. Am. Personnel and Guidance Assn., Am. Rehab. Counseling Assn. Home: 812 Plum St N Media PA 19063 Office: 600 Olive St N Media PA 19063

LARSON, ROLAND E., hosp. adminstr.; b. Chgo., Jan. 21, 1939; s. Elmer G. and Anna A. L.; B.A., Augustana Coll., Rock Island, Ill., 1961; M.A., State U. Iowa, 1963; m. Noel K. Brennan, June 28, 1969; children—Eric, Jennifer. Adminstrv. asst. Mary Fletcher Hosp., Burlington, Vt., 1962-64; asso. dir. Roger Williams Gen. Hosp., Providence, 1964-73; v.p. adminstrn. Norwalk (Conn.) Hosp., 1973—. Bd. dirs. Am. Cancer Soc., 1974—, Nat. Arthritis Found., N.Y.C., 1967-71, Met. Dist. Nursing Assn. R.I., 1970-75; pres. R.I. Arthritis FoundFound., 1967-71, recipient Distinguished Service award, 1971; bd. dirs. Greater Norwalk Community Council, 1975—, Coalition on Child Abuse, 1977—. Fellow Am. Coll. Hosp. Adminstrs.; mem. Am. Hosp. Assn. Home: 23 Glenwood Rd Weston CT 06880 Office: 24 Stevens St Norwalk CT 06856

LARSON, VIOLA INGEBORG SWANSON, nurse; b. Bridgeport, Conn., Jan. 19, 1931; d. Carl August and Gerda (Johanson) Swanson; B.S., U. Bridgeport, 1952; M.S., Boston U., 1977; m. Paul David Larson, Oct. 24, 1953; children—David Nathaniel, Carl Paul, Seth Leslie. With New Britain Gen. Hosp., 1952-54, 62-63, dir. nursing service, 1973—; staff nurse Bradley Meml. Hosp., Southington, Conn., 1957-62. Mem. Am., Conn. nurses assns., Am. Soc. Nursing Service Adminstrs. (vice chmn. council assos. 1978, chmn. 1978-79), U. Bridgeport Alumni Assn., Boston U. Alumni Assn., Sigma Theta Tau. Home: 300 Queen St Southington CT 06489 Office: 100 Grand St New Britain CT 06050

LASALA, VINCENT JOSEPH, sch. adminstr.; b. Bklyn., Feb. 9, 1934; s. Joseph and Mary (Modica) LaS.; B.A., St. John's U., 1955; M.S., Hofstra U., 1959; postgrad. Post Coll., 1969-72; m. Carol Ann Tricomi, June 30, 1956; children—Carol, Vanessa, Linda, Lauretta. Pharm. salesman various cos., Ohio and N.J., 1957-62; tchr., guidance counselor Mineola (N.Y.) Pub. Schs., 1962-72, adminstr. personnel and pupil services, 1972—. Mem. Herricks (N.Y.) Pub. Sch. Bd., 1969-75, pres., 1975-79. Mem. Am. Personnel and Guidance Assn., Am. Vocat. Edn. Assn., Am. Sch. Bds. Assn., Sons of Italy in Am. Club: K.C. Author: First Steps to Success, 1974; contbr. articles to profl. jours. Home: 611 Concord Ave Williston Park NY 11596 Office: 1196 Prospect Ave Westbury NY 11501

LA SARDO, CAMILLE GABRIELLA, personnel mgr.; b. Jersey City, Aug. 5, 1945; d. James F. and Ida A. (Gagliano) LaS.; student Montclair State Coll. Personnel adminstr. Luft-Tangee, Inc., Carlstadt, N.J., 1972-75; personnel mgr. Channel Cos., Inc., Whippany, N.J., 1975-76, J.L. Prescott Co., Passaic, N.J., 1976—. Mem. Am. Soc. Personnel Adminstrn., Meadowlands C. of C., Personnel Mgrs. Assn. Home: 483 Liberty Ave Jersey City NJ 07307 Office: 27 Eight St Passaic NJ 07055

LASCH, KLAUS BERNHARD, electronic engr.; b. Chemnitz, Germany, May 29, 1938; s. Erich Bernhard and Helene Martha (Seifert) L.; came to U.S., 1959, naturalized, 1968; B.Sc. in Physics, London U., 1959; M.S., Northeastern U., 1975; M.E.E., Lowell U., 1977; m. Nina Rosa Bellia, Apr. 4, 1964; children—Heidi, Tracy. Process engr. Transitron Electronic Corp., Wakefield, Mass., 1959-63; prodn. engr. ITT Semicondr., West Palm Beach, Fla., 1963-65; dept. mgr. Transitron Electronic Corp., 1965-68; project mgr. Olivetti & Co. SpA, Aprilia, Italy, 1968-71; mgr. evaluation lab., missile systems div. Raytheon Co., Bedford, Mass., 1972—; tchr. advanced math. Fitchburg (Mass.) State Coll., 1975—. Mem. IEEE, Internat. Soc. Hybrid Mfrs. Contbr. articles to profl. jours. Home: 18 Blueberry Hill Rd Andover MA 01810 Office: Hartwell Rd Bedford MA 01730

LASCHEID, WILLIAM PETER, physician; b. Cleve., June 16, 1926; s. Vincent Charles and Marie Catherine (Hinger) L.; B.S., Franklin and Marshall Coll., 1946; M.D., U. Pitts., 1950; m. Nancy Catherine Buckley, Dec. 4, 1976; children—William Frederick, Leslie Ann, Peter Joseph, Suann, Mary Ann. Intern, St. Joseph's Hosp., Pitts., 1950-51; resident in dermatology Univ. Hosp. Cleve., 1955-58;

gen. practice medicine, Pitts., 1953-55; practice medicine specializing in dermatology, Pitts., 1958—; cons. St. Clair Meml., John J. Kane hosps.; asst. clin. prof. U. Pitts. Med. Sch., 1976—. Bd. dirs. South Hills YMCA, 1968-70; pres. alumni council exec. bd. Franklin and Marshall Coll., 1978-79. Served with USNR, 1944-46, 51-53. Diplomate Am. Bd. Dermatology. Fellow Am. Acad. Dermatology; mem. AMA, Pa., Allegheny County med. socs., Pitts. (past pres.), Pa. acads. dermatology, N.Am. Clin. Dermatol. Soc. Republican. Club: St. Clair Country. Home: 74 Youngwood Rd Pittsburgh PA 15228 Office: 20 Cedar Blvd Pittsburgh PA 15228

LASHMET, PETER KERNS, educator; b. Ann Arbor, Mich., Aug. 28, 1929; s. Floyd Heaton and Irene (Spangenberg) L.; B.S.Engring. in Chem. Engring., U. Mich., 1951, M.S. Engring., 1952; Ph.D. (Union Carbide fellow), U. Del., 1962; m. Edna Pabon, June 9, 1956; children—Stephanie, Pamela, Linda, Michael, Paul. Research fellow U. Del., Newark, 1955-58; mgr. cryostat engring. Air Products & Chems. Co., Allentown, Pa., 1958-65; asso. prof., exec. officer dept. chem. engring. Rensselaer Poly. Inst., Troy, N.Y., 1965—. Cons. in field. Served with Chem. Corps, AUS, 1953-55. Mem. Am. Chem. Soc. (past chmn. div. indsl. engring. chemistry), Am. Inst. Chem. Engrs. Patentee in field. Home: 15 Center View Dr Troy NY 12180

LASKER, SIGMUND E., educator; b. N.Y.C., Sept. 5, 1923; s. Hermann Benjamin and Johanna Pauline (Fine) L.; B.S., Bklyn. Coll., 1949; M.S., N.Y. U., 1951; Ph.D., Stevens Inst. Tech., 1965; m. Lorraine Myrna Rettig, Mar. 6, 1966; 1 dau., Johanna Alexandra. Research asso. dept. chemistry and chem. engring. Stevens Inst. Tech., 1961-65; research asso. dept. surgery N.Y. Med. Coll., 1951-61, asst. prof. pharmacology, 1966-76, research asso. prof. dept. medicine, 1976—; adj. asst. prof. Rockefeller U., 1968-75, adj. asso. prof., 1975—; prin. investigator USPHS; v.p., dir. Network Film Corp., N.Y.C., Empire Studios Corp., Fla. Mem. Mayors Commn. on Phys. Fitness, 1965. Recipient 1st Research award Am. Inst. of City of N.Y. Served with U.S. Maritime Service, 1942-47. Fellow Am. Inst. Chemists, N.Y. Acad. Scis. (chmn. biophysics), N.Y. Acad. Medicine (asso.); mem. Biophys. Soc., Harvey Soc., Am. Chem. Soc., Am. Assn. Clin. Chemists Am. Heart Assn., Internat. Soc. Thrombosis and Haemostasis, Sigma Xi, Phi Lambda Upsilon. Editor: Magnetic Resonance in Biological Systems. Producer feature film documentary Holiday in Brussels, Brussels World Fair, 1958. Contbr. articles in field to profl. jours. Patentee in field. Home: Rivercross Roosevelt Island New York City NY 10044 Office: 1249 Fifth Ave New York City NY 10029

LASKEY, RICHARD ANTHONY, organic chemist, med. research co. exec.; b. N.Y.C., Oct. 24, 1936; s. Charles Lewis and Gertrude Ann (Stolzenthaler) L.; student City Coll. N.Y., B.S. in Chemistry, Ohio City Coll., 1958, M.S. in Organic Chemistry, 1959; Ph.D. in Organic Chemistry, Sussex (Eng.) U., 1970; LL.B., U. Chgo., 1972; M.D. (hon.) Med. Coll. S.A., 1975, fellow, 1976; m. Frances M. Pollack, June 29, 1975; children—Victoria Ann, Deborah Lea. Head sec. med. products, lab. mgr. Hydron Labs., North Brunswick, N.J., 1967-73; v.p. biomed. research Datascope Corp., Paramus, N.J. 1973—; cons. in field. Mem. N.Y.C. Aux. Police, 1963-65. Recipient Doctor's award, Chgo. Med. Coll., 1975; fellow Am. Acad. Behavioral Sci., 1976; diplomate Am. Bd. Examiners in Psychotherapy. Mem. Md. State Med. Soc., Med. Soc. State of Idaho, Internat. Coll. Physicians and Surgeons, Am. Psychotherapy Assn., Nat. Psychol. Assn., AAAS, Assn. Advancement Med. Instrumentation, Soc. Research Adminstrs., Nat. Rifle Assn. Biomed. inventor, patentee. Home: PO Box 133 Washington NJ 07882 Office: 580 Winters Ave Paramus NJ 07652

LASKIN, RICHARD SHELDON, orthopedic surgeon; b. Bklyn., July 13, 1940; s. Herman Myron and Gertrude (Klein) L.; A.B., Hofstra U., 1960; M.D., N.Y. U., 1964; m. Joyce Novis, June 1, 1963; children—Jonathan, Andrew. Intern and resident in gen. surgery Albert Einstein Coll. Medicine Affiliated Hosps., N.Y.C., 1964-66, resident in orthopedic surgery, 1968-70; resident in orthopedic surgery Nassau County Med. Center, 1970-71, now mem. staff; pvt. practice medicine, specializing in orthopedic surgery and total joint replacement, Long Beach, N.Y., 1971—; vis. asso. prof. Albert Einstein Coll., Medicine, 1972—; asst. clin. prof. State U. N.Y. at Stony Brook, 1974—; mem. profl. rev. com. Blue Cross and Blue Shield of Greater N.Y., 1975—; mem. staffs Long Beach Meml. Hosp., Bronx Municipal Hosp., S. Nassau Community Hosp. Served with M.C., AUS, 1966-68. Decorated Bronze Star, Air medal, Combat Med. Badge. Diplomate Am. Bd. Orthopedic Surgery. Mem. Am. Acad. Orthopedic Surgeons (com. audiovisual edn.), A.C.S., Inter. Coll. Surgeons, Internat. Arthroscopy Assn., N.Y. Acad. Medicine, Eastern Orthopedic Soc., AMA, N.Y. State Orthopedic Surgeons N.Y. State Med. Soc. Contbr. clin. research articles on orthopedic surgery to profl. jours., also papers to socs. in Amsterdam, Milan, Jerusalem, Athens, U.S. Office: 340 W Park Ave Long Beach NY 11561

LASKOWSKI, EDWARD STANLEY, social worker; b. Bridgeport, Conn., Dec. 24, 1931; s. Vincent G. and Sophie M. (Samorajczyk) L.; B.S.S., Fairfield U., 1953; postgrad. U. Conn., 1955-56; M.S.S., Fordham U., 1958; m. Marlene Guard, July 3, 1954; children—Deborah, Donna. Social worker Jewish Community Center, Bridgeport, 1955-56; social worker Cath. Charities, Diocese of Bridgeport, 1956—, dir., 1973—. Mem. Danbury Mayor's Task Force, 1968-69; mem. Gov.'s White House Conf., 1971; pres. Community Services for Greater Bridgeport, 1960; chmn. New Eng. area region A, Nat. Conf. Cath. Charities, 1976-77. Served with U.S. Army, 1953-55. Recipient Alumni award Fairfield U., 1974; Community Action Achievementa award, 1970. Mem. Nat. Assn. Housing and Redevel. Ofcls., Nat. Assn. Social Workers, Nat. Conf. Cath. Charities. Roman Catholic. Home: 15 Sharon Rd Trumbull CT 06611 Office: 238 Jewett Ave Bridgeport CT 06606

LASKY, RICHARD DONALD, psychoanalyst; b. N.Y.C., Jan. 22, 1943; s. Sidney and Alice (Presser) L.; B.A., L.I. U., 1968; Ph.D., N.Y. U., 1971; splty. certificate N.Y. U. Postdoctoral Psychoanalytic Inst., 1974; m. Judith Faye Sherman, Sept. 8, 1968. Jr. research scientist Research Found. State of N.Y., Downstate Med. Sch., State U. N.Y., 1964-68; guest lectr. dept. psychology Pratt Inst., 1969-70, Rutgers U., 1970-71; asst. prof. Post Coll., Greenvale, N.Y., 1972-74; faculty L.I. Inst. Psychoanalysis, Forest Hills, 1974-75, Inst. Mental Health Edn., Englewood, N.J., 1975-76, Am. Inst. Psychoanalysis and Psychotherapy, N.Y.C., 1976-77, N.Y. Center Psychoanalytic Tng., 1976-77, Postgrad. Center Mental Health, N.Y.C., 1976—; clin. asso. prof. and supr. psychotherapy, doctoral program in clin. psychology City U. N.Y., 1976—. Served in U.S. Army, 1961-64. NIMH fellow, 1968-69; NIH fellow, 1970-71; Vet. Rehab. Adminstrn. fellow, 1969-70. Mem. Am. Psychol. Assn., N.Y. U. Postdoctoral Psychoanalytic Soc. (dir.), N.Y. Soc. Clin. Psychoanalysts, N.Y. State Psychol. Assn., Internat. Forum Psychoanalysis. Contbr. articles to profl. jours., chpts. to books in field. Home and Office: 257 Central Park W New York City NY 10024

LASRY, JEAN-CLAUDE MAURICE, psychologist, family therapist; b. Casablanca, Morocco, July 21, 1937; s. Marcel Mordechai and Violette (Leon) L.; came to Can., 1957, naturalized, 1962; Baccalauréat, Lycée Lyautey, Morocco, 1957; B.A., U. Montreal, 1965, M.A., 1966, Ph.D., 1968; m. Gaby Benbaruk, Oct. 12, 1969; children—Eytan, Arielle. Lectr., U. Montreal, 1966-68; asst. prof., 1968-75, asso. prof., 1975—; research asso. Inst. Psychiatry, Jewish Gen. Hosp., Montreal, 1969—, family therapist, 1971—. Founding pres. Ecole Maimonide, 1969-72, pres., 1976—; exec. Allied Jewish Community Services, 1972-75, officer, 1975—; exec. Can. Jewish Congress, 1968—; dep. pres. E. region Canadian Zionist Fedn., 1970-71; pres. Assn. Sépharade Francophone, 1972-74. Recipient Barkoff Leadership award, 1972; Can. NRC scholar, 1964-68. Mem. Am., Can. psychol. assns., Internat. Assn. Applied Psychology, Que. Corp. Psychologists, Internat. Assn. Cross-Cultural Psychology. Jewish. Contbr. articles in field to profl. jours. Home: 8225 Atherton St Montreal PQ H4P 1Z2 Canada Office: Jewish Gen Hosp 3755 Côte Sainte Catherine Montreal PQ Canada

LASSIG, KENNETH H., communications co. exec.; b. Jamaica, N.Y., Nov. 20, 1934; s. Herman and Luise (Guldi) L.; B.B.A. cum laude, Hofstra U., 1956; m. Ann Errett, June 17, 1956; children—Richard K., Robert A., Virginia A. Accountant, Arthur Young & Co., N.Y.C., 1956-60; controller Dorne & Margolin Inc. Mfg., Westbury, N.Y., 1960-65; fin. analyst Celanese Corp., N.Y.C., 1966; with Western Union, various locations, 1967-77, asst. comptroller, Mahwah, N.J., 1972-73, comptroller, 1973-77; v.p. Ox Bow Constrn. Corp., Port Washington, N.Y., 1977—; dir. Distronics Corp., Cherry Hill, N.J. Served to 1st lt. AUS, 1967. C.P.A., N.Y. Mem. Am. Inst. C.P.A.'s, N.Y. State Soc. C.P.A.'s, Fin. Execs. Inst. Club: Masons. Home: 212 Wayfair Ln Franklin Lakes NJ 07417 Office: One Lake St Upper Saddle River NJ 07458

LASUCHIN, MICHAEL, educator, artist; b. Kramatorsk, USSR, July 24, 1923; s. Sergei and Agafia (Okolelow) L.; came to U.S., 1951, naturalized, 1958; B.F.A., Phila. Coll. Art, 1970; M.F.A., Temple U., 1972. Designer Mel Richman, Inc., 1954; designer Container Corp. Am., Phila., 1954-71; asst. prof. printmaking Phila. Coll. Art, 1972—; instr. Tyler Sch. Art Temple U., 1971-72, Long Beach Island Found. Arts and Scis., 1975-76; one-man exhbns. include: Print Club, Phila., 1973, U. Pa., 1974, Mc Cleaf Gallery, Phila., 1974, Venable Neslage Galleries, Washington, 1976, Rosenfeld Gallery, Phila., 1977. Mem. Nat. Watercolor Soc., Am. Color Print Soc., Print Club, Boston Printmakers, Audubon Artists, Los Angeles Printmaking Soc., Graphics Soc. Home: 120 E Cliveden St Philadelphia PA 19119 Office: Phila Coll Art Broad and Spruce Sts Philadelphia PA 19102

LATCHUM, JAMES LEVIN, judge; b. Milford, Del., Dec. 23, 1918; s. James H. and Ida Mae (Robbins) L.; A.B. cum laude, Princeton U., 1940; J.D., U. Va., 1946; m. Elizabeth Murray McArthur, June 16, 1943; children—Su-Allan, Elizabeth M. Admitted to Del. bar, 1947; asso. Berl, Potter & Anderson, Wilmington, 1946-53, partner, 1953-68; judge U.S. Dist. Ct. Del., Wilmington, 1968—, now chief judge; New Castle County atty. Del. Hwy. Dept., 1948-50; asst. U.S. atty., 1950-53; atty. Del. Interstate Hwy. Div., 1955-62, Delaware River and Bay Authority, 1962-68. Chmn. New Castle County Democratic Com., 1953-56, Wilmington City Com., 1959-63. Served to maj. Insp. Gen. Corps, U.S. Army, 1942-46; PTO. Mem. Am., Del., Va., N.Y.C. bar assns., Order of Coif, Sigma Nu Phi. Presbyterian. Club: Wilmington Country. Home: 2209 Baynard Blvd Wilmington DE 19899 Office: US Dist Ct Wilmington DE 19899

LATENDRESSE, JAMES JOSEPH, pharm. co. exec.; b. St. Paul, Aug. 17, 1927; s. James Joseph and Vina Marie (Maranda) L.; B.S., Ind. U., 1955; M.B.A., Rutgers U., 1962; m. Irene Clara Goodspeed, May 5, 1951; children—James Joseph III, Candace Ann, Mark Jeffery, Lisa Marie. With indsl. relations P.R. Mallory Co., Indpls., 1955-57; dir. personnel Haag Drug Co., Indpls., 1957-58; with research div. personnel and adminstrn. with Merck & Co., Inc., Rahway, N.J., 1958-73, corporate dir. orgn. devel., 1966-73; v.p. ops. in Far East and Middle East, Warner-Lambert Co., 1974, pres. Warner-Lambert Europe, 1974; v.p. internat. pharms., diagnostics, chems. and capsules, Morris Plains, N.J., 1976-77; pres. internat. div. William H. Rorer, Inc., Fort Washington, Pa., 1977—. Served to capt. USAF, 1949-53. Mem. Am. Mgmt. Assn., Soc. for Advancement Mgmt., Ind. U., Rutgers U. alumni assns., Beta Gamma Sigma. Republican. Roman Catholic. Club: Am. (Sydney, Tokyo and London); K.C. Home: 32 Oak Knoll Rd Mendham NJ 07945 Office: 500 W Virginia Dr Fort Washington PA 19034

LATHAM, EUNICE STUNKARD (MRS. JOHN R. LATHAM), ednl. adminstr.; b. N.Y.C., Sept. 4, 1923; d. Horace Wesley and Frances Grace (Klank) Stunkard; B.A., Wellesley Coll., 1945; m. John Ralph Latham, June 9, 1962. Acting dir. div. reports and analysis UNRRA, Washington, Germany and France, 1945-47; editor Unitarian Service Com., N.Y.C., 1947-49; copywriter J. Walter Thompson Co., N.Y.C., 1949-56, Lambert & Feasley, Inc., N.Y.C., 1956-62, Fuller & Smith & Ross, N.Y.C., 1962-65; v.p., creative supr. Lennen & Newell, Inc., 1965-70; headmistress Barnard Sch. for Girls, N.Y.C., 1970—. Election dist. capt. Bronx County, 1948-54; committeewoman Bronx County, 1950-62; trustee Barnard Sch. for Girls, Antoinette Fischer Williams Fund, Barnard Sch. for Girls Money Purchase Pension Plan, Baldwin Sch., Bryn Mawr, Pa. Mem. Nat. Assn. Prins. Schs. for Girls (councilor), Head Mistresses of East (pres.), Guild Ind. Schs. N.Y.C. (v.p.), Shakespeare Soc., Soc. Mayflower Descs. Home: PO Box 103 White Creek NY 12057 Office: 554 Fort Washington Ave New York City NY 10033

LATIMER, TED, life ins. agt.; b. Bronx, N.Y., Dec. 5, 1915; s. Hyman and Jennie (Stollarczik) Wladimer; student N.Y. U.; m. Martha Goldberg, Feb. 14, 1937; children—Stephen Mark, Leslie Dianne, Phyllis Beth. Designer, stylist mannequins and retail displays, N.Y.C., 1934-57; life ins. agt., 1958—; mgr. Am. Progressive Health Ins. Agy., Hempstead, N.Y., 1957—; mem. adv. council Bankers Security Life Ins. Soc., 1973-74, 78—. Mem. Profl. Ins. Agts. Assn. Democrat. Jewish. Clubs: K.P., Lions (chpt. pres. 1973-74, named Lio of Yr. 1978). Home: 92 Gauguin Ct Middle Island NY 11953 Office: 134 Nassau Blvd West Hempstead NY 11552

LATON, DEXTER WOOD, optometrist; b. Lowell, Mass., Oct. 17, 1925; s. Fred Dighton and Natalie (Wilson) L.; O.D., Mass. Coll. Optometry, 1950; m. Lois M. Sturmy, Apr. 11, 1953; children—David Fred, Janet Lois. Pvt. practice optometry, Chelmsford, Mass., 1953—; operator yearly presch. vision clinic, 1969—. Served with USNR, 1943-46, 50-53. Mem. Am. Optometric Assn., Mass. Soc. Optometrists, N.E. Council Optometrists, Mass. Coll. Optometry Alumni (contbg. editor). Republican. Clubs: Masons, Elks, Rotary. Home: 42 Bridge St Chelmsford MA 01824 Office: 34 Chelmsford St Chelmsford MA 01824

LATOURNERIE, GERARD JÉAN CLOVIS, internat. banker, cons.; b. N.Y.C., June 21, 1950; s. Jean Clovis and Helen L. Bastier (Dempsey) LaT.; B.A. in Economics/Govt., Austin Coll., 1972; M.P.A. in Internat. Mgmt., N.Y. U., 1974; Research grantee, intern N.Y.C. Commn. for UN and Consular Corps, N.Y.C., 1974; asst. dir. Univ. Yr. for Action, Mayor's Office N.Y.C., 1974; with Polytechnique Systems, Dix Hills, N.Y., 1974-76; internal mgmt. cons. Mfrs. Hanover Trust Co., N.Y.C., 1976-78; asst. to v.p. in charge internat. ops. group Chem. Bank-Internat., N.Y.C., 1978—. Mem. Assn. Pub. Adminstrs., Assn. M.B.A. Execs., N.Y. U. Alumni Assn., Austin Coll. Alumni Assn. Roman Catholic. Home: 342 E 53 St Apt L-A New York NY 10022 Office: 20 Pine St Room 700 New York NY 10007

LATTERNER, CHARLES GEORGE, cons. co. exec.; b. Syracuse. N.Y., Dec. 31, 1916; s. Charles Augustus and Irene Marion (Hoffman) L.; student Syracuse U., 1936-39, 46; B.A., Gettysburg Coll., 1947; M.A., Columbia U., 1949; Ph.D., Southeastern U., 1978; m. Mary Eleanor Eschbach, Aug. 18, 1948 (dec.); children—Samuel C., Gretchen I., Charles George; m. 2d. Gwen Day Pratt, June 25, 1977. Personnel specialist Nat. Biscuit Co., N.Y.C., 1951-55; classification analyst Nat. Council Chs., N.Y.C., 1955-56; mgr. tng. br. and DEWline tng. ITT/Fed. Electric Co., Paramus, N.J., 1956-64; mgr. personnel resources and devel. ITT/World Communications, N.Y.C., 1964-67; dir. tng. Envelope Mfrs. Assn., N.Y.C., 1967-69; dir. mgmt. devel. Coopers & Lybrand, N.Y.C., 1969—; pres., dir. Inter Mountain Mgmt. Inst., 1977. Served to capt. USAAF, 1941-46. Mem. Am. Soc. Personnel Adminstrn. (accredited personnel diplomate in tng. and devel.), Am. Soc. Tng. and Devel., Soc. Applied Learning Techniques, C.G. Jung Found. Analytical Psychology. Republican. Lutheran. Author books including: Transistors-A Self-Instructional Programmed Manual, 1962; How to Write Effective Reports, 1964; Mathematics for Electronics, 1965. Home: 25-203 Barker St Mount Kisco NY 10549 Office: Coopers & Lybrand 1251 Ave of Americas New York City NY 10020 also Inter Mountain Mgmt Inst PO Box 2521 Park City UT 84060

LAUB, GEORGE COOLEY, lawyer; b. Easton, Pa., Jan. 16, 1912; s. Herbert F. and Hannah A. (Cooley) L.; A.B., Lafayette Coll., 1933; LL.B., U. Pa., 1936; m. Elizabeth Traill Green, Jan. 19, 1939. Admitted to Pa. bar, 1936, since practiced in Easton; legal adviser Easton Home for Aged Women; dir. City of Easton Authority, 1950-76. Dir. Easton Nat. Bank & Trust Co., 1966—. Dir. Community Chest, 1943-45, 49-52, drive chmn., 1949, pres., 1951. Life trustee Lafayette Coll., 1958—, sec. bd., 1959—, counsel, 1965—. Served to 1st lt., Judge Adv. Gen.'s Dept., AUS, 1945-47. Mem. Am., Pa. (exec. com. 1952-54), Northampton County (pres. 1954-55) bar assns., SAR, Northampton County Hist. Soc., Am. Judicature Soc., Nat. Assn. Coll. and U. Attys., Trout Unlimited, Nat. Skeet Shooting Assn., Phi Delta Theta. Presbyn. (pres. bd. trustees 1957-59). Clubs: Country Northampton County: Pomfret; Skytop (Pa.); Easton Anglers. Home: 117 W Wayne Ave Easton PA 18042 Office: 340 Spring Garden St Easton PA 18042

LAUB, LEONARD, dentist; b. N.Y.C., July 29, 1918; s. Max and Malie Rose (Moriber) L.; B.S., N.Y.U., 1938, D.D.S., 1942 Intern. Bronx (N.Y.C.) Hosp., 1942; pvt. practice dentistry, N.Y.C., 1946—; now asso. attending in oral surgery Jewish Meml. Hosp., N.Y.C., jr. med. staff, dental staff. Midchester Jewish Center, N.Y. Served from 1st lt. to capt. USAAF, 1943-46. Mem. ADA, First Dist. Dental Soc., Zionist Orgn. Am., Sigma Epsilon Delta, Phi Beta Kappa. K.P. (chancellor comdr. 1977-78). Home: 9 Dimsdale Dr Scarsdale NY 10583 Office: 1825 Riverside Dr New York City NY 10034

LAUB, RAYMOND JOSEPH, athlete; b. Jersey City, May 23, 1941; s. Edwin and Rachel (Cutro) L.; student Queens Coll., 1959-62. Coach figure skating Skateland Ice Rink, Queens, N.Y., 1962-64; host Farm Resort Hotel, Lancaster, Pa., 1965-75, also owner, coach skating and skiing areas; dir. winter sports Concord Hotel, Kiamesha Lake, N.Y., 1975-77; dir. ice skating, head coach Grossingers Hotel (N.Y.), 1977—. Mem. Profl. Skaters Guild Am., U.S. Ski Assn. Home: 175A Strasburg Pike Lancaster PA 17602 Office: Grossingers Hotel Grossinger NY 12734

LAUBACH, ERIC GORDON, mfg. co. exec.; b. Bethlehem, Pa., Feb. 16, 1946; s. Edwin Carlton and Anna Geneva (Hendricks) L.; B.A., U. Del., 1969; m. Mary Susan Hastings, Aug. 31, 1968; 1 son, Aaron Andrew. Probation counselor Wilmington (Del.) Family Ct., 1968-69; employment rep. RCA Service Co., Cherry Hill, N.J., 1973-74; personnel mgr. Domestic Pump div. ITT, Shippensburg, Pa., 1974—. Bd. dirs. Shippensburg Community Services Inc., 1974—, v.p., 1976—; bd. dirs. Shippensburg Area Devel. Corp., 1978. Served with USN, 1969-73. Mem. Shippensburg C. of C., Am. Soc. Personnel Adminstrn. (past pres. local chpt.). Profl. pianist, guitarist, singer, songwriter. Home: RD 6 Box 296 Shippensburg PA 17257 Office: ITT Domestic Pump Box 250 Shippensburg PA 17257

LAUBACH, ROGER ALVIN, food co. exec.; b. Riegelsville, N.J., July 3, 1922; s. Harry and Daisy (Cyphers) L.; diploma in bus. adminstrn. Churchman Bus. Coll., Easton, Pa., 1941; B.S. cum laude in Accounting, Rider Coll., 1949. C.P.A., Lybrand, Ross Bros. & Montgomery, C.P.A.'s, N.Y.C., 1949-60; asst. to treas. Coca-Cola Bottling Co. N.Y., N.Y.C., 1960-63; mgr. audits and systems Atlantic Research Corp., Alexandria, Va., 1964-65; controller Ely-Cruikshank Co., Inc., realtors (formerly Horace S. Ely & Co.), N.Y.C., 1965-71, asst. treas., 1966-67, treas., dir., 1967-71; dir. Phila. Accounting Center, Ogden Food Service Corp., 1971-72, treas., 1972-77; dir. corp. auditing Ogden Corp., N.Y.C., 1977—. Served with U.S. Army, 1942-46; ETO. Decorated Bronze Star; C.P.A., N.Y., N.J. Mem. Am. Inst. C.P.A.'s, Inst. Internal Auditors, N.Y. State, N.J. socs. C.P.A.'s, Real Estate Bd. N.Y., Delta Sigma Pi (pres. 1948). Lutheran (treas., mem. council). Home: 2223 Laurel Dr Cinnaminson NJ 08077 Office: 277 Park Ave New York City NY 10017

LAUD, MARILYN, interior designer; b. N.Y.C., Apr. 14, 1936; d. Harry and Edith Weiner; student Syracuse U., 1953-55; B.A., Adelphi U., 1957; m. John Laud, June 16, 1957; 1 dau., Liz. Pres., Marilyn Laud Interiors, N.Y.C., 1958—; salesperson Apt. Locating, Inc., N.Y.C., 1977—. Mem. Real Estate Bd. N.Y., Allied Bd. Trade. Home: 45 East End Ave New York City NY 10028 Office: 26 E 82nd St New York City NY 10028

LAUDATO, GAETANO JOSEPH, JR., locomotive engr.; b. Wilmington, Mass., Nov. 21, 1917; s. Gaetano and Anna (Terragrossa) L.; m. Margaret Jeanne Cove, Nov. 23, 1941. Fireman, New Haven R.R., 1942-60, engr., 1960—; vol. guide on locomotive at Mus. Sci., Boston. Mem. Brotherhood Locomotive Engrs., United Inventors and Scientists of Am. Roman Catholic. Clubs: Footlight, K.C. Invented Self-powered signal buoy, sanitary and antiseptic drinking water cooler, r.r. swimming pool car. Home: 2 Lamartine Pl Jamaica Plain MA 02130

LAUDICINA, ROBERT ANTHONY, univ. dean; b. New Haven, Mar. 26, 1941; s. Vito and Mary (Sette) L.; B.A., Rutgers U., 1963, M.A., 1965; Ph.D., Columbia, 1968; m. Eleanor Marie Veglia, June 18, 1966; children—Laurence, Lea. Asst. dean Columbia, 1968-70; dean of students Fairleigh Dickinson U., 1970—; v.p., gen. mgr. Automatique, Inc., instnl. food mgmt. and cons., Long Island City, N.Y., 1977—. Chmn. Columbia U. Seminar on Higher Edn., 1970-72. Mem. Nat. Assn. Student Personnel Adminstrs., Eastern Assn. Deans and Advisors to Students (pres. 1972), Phi Beta Kappa, Pi Sigma Alpha. Author: (with others) A Legal Perspective for Student Personnel Administrators, 1974; A Legal Overview of the New Student, 1976; Guidebook For Student Rights, 1975. Contbr. articles to profl. jours. Home: 12 Green Knolls Rd Convent Station NJ 07961 Office: 36-09 34th St Long Island City NY

LAUER, JAMES LOTHAR, physicist; b. Vienna, Austria, Aug. 2, 1920; s. Max and Friederieke (Rappaport) L.; came to U.S., 1938, naturalized, 1943; A.B., Temple U., 1942, M.A., 1944; Ph.D., U. Pa., 1948; postgrad. U. Calif. at San Diego, 1964-65; m. Stefanie Dorothea Blank, Sept. 5, 1955; children—Michael, Ruth. Scientist, Sun Oil Co., Marcus Hook, Pa., 1944-52, spectroscopist, 1952-64; asst. prof. U. Pa., 1952-55; lectr. U. Del., 1952-58; research fellow mech. engring. U. Calif., San Diego, 1964-65; research prof. mech. engring. Rensselaer Poly. Inst., Troy, N.Y., 1978—; cons. Sun Oil Co. Pa., 1978—, Aluminum Co. Can. Ltd., 1976—, Active Penn Wynne Civic Assn., 1959-77. Sun Oil Co. postdoctoral fellow, 1964-65; Air Force Office Sci. Research grantee, 1974-78, NASA Lewis Research Center grantee, 1974-78. Mem. Am. Chem. Soc., Am. Phys. Soc., Soc. Applied Spectroscopy, Spectroscopy Soc. Can., Sigma Xi. Jewish. Author: Infrared Fourier Spectroscopy-Chemical Applications, 1978; patentee in field. Home: 7 Northeast Ln Ballston Lake NY 12019 Office: Dept Mech Engring Rensselaer Poly Inst Troy NY 12181

LAUER, THEODORE, historian; b. Bklyn., Sept. 5, 1946; s. Sidney and Betty (Levy) L.; B.A., Bklyn. Coll., 1968; rabbi, Rabbi Jacob Joseph Theol. Sem., 1971; postgrad. City U. N.Y., 1970—, M.Phil., 1979, doctoral candidate; m. Linda Barbara Kaminetsky, May 16, 1968; children—Elisheva Malka, Natanel. Adj. lectr. history Bklyn. Coll., 1970—; instr. history Queensborough Community Coll., N.Y.C., 1970-75; adj. lectr. history York Coll., Jamaica, N.Y. 1973; co-adj. instr. history Rutgers U., Newark, 1976—; asst. program dir. confs. change soc. Bklyn. Coll., 1976—. Vice pres. Young Israel Vanderveer Park, 1973-75; ritual chmn. Hillel Minyan and B'nai Israel Jewish Center, 1975—. N.Y. Regents scholar, 1964-68; City U. N.Y. fellow, 1975-76. Mem. Am. Hist. Assn., AAUP, Am. Com. History 2d World War, Historians Film Com. Home: 2422 Ave L Brooklyn NY 11210 Office: History Dept Brooklyn Coll Brooklyn NY 11210

LAUFER, IRA JEROME, physician; b. N.Y.C., Mar. 29, 1928; s. Irving and Evelyn (Weisman) L.; B.A., N.Y. U., 1948, M.D., 1953; m. Barbara Alfandari, July 10, 1955; children—Tina, David. Intern, resident in medicine Bellevue Hosp., N.Y.C., 1953-55; research fellow in medicine N.Y. U. Med. Sch., 1957-58, chief med. resident N.Y. U. Hosp., 1958-59; practice medicine specializing in internal medicine and diabetes, N.Y.C., 1959—; asst. prof. clin. medicine N.Y. U. Med. Sch., 1971—; dir. diabetes service Cabrini Health Care Center, N.Y.C., pres. med. bd., 1975—; dir. medicine N.Y. Eye and Ear Infirmary, 1978—. Served to capt. USAF, 1955-57. Diplomate Am. Bd. Internal Medicine. Mem. A.C.P., Am. Coll. Clin. Pharmacology, Am. Coll. Nutrition, Am., N.Y. (pres. 1978) diabetes assns., N.Y. U. Med. Sch. Alumni Assn. (pres.). Author: (with Herbert Kadison) Diabetes Explained: A Layman's Guide, 1976. Office: 45 Gramercy Park N New York City NY 10010

LAUFFER, ANDRE MARC, electronics mfg. co. exec.; b. Antwerp, Belgium, Apr. 10, 1933; s. Jacques and Freda (Spira) L.; came to U.S., 1939, naturalized, 1945; B.S., N.Y. U., 1953, M.B.A., 1956, J.D., 1960; m. Marcia Tobin, Nov. 13, 1954; children—Jason, Robin. Admitted to N.Y. State bar, 1961; supr. Stern Porter Kingston and Coleman, N.Y.C., 1955-58; mgr. accounting policy CBS, N.Y.C., 1959-61; individual practice law, N.Y.C., 1961-63; gen. counsel Profit Research, Inc., Mineola, N.Y., 1963-66; dir. corp. devel., tax counsel Walworth Co., Inc., N.Y.C., 1966-68; chmn. of office of pres., chief fin. officer, Central Foundry Co., N.Y.C. and Tuscaloosa, Ala., 1968-72; v.p., controller Servo Corp. Am., Hicksville, N.Y., 1972-74; exec. v.p. finance Marine Electric Corp., Bklyn., 1974—; dir. Marine Electric Ry. Products Div., Inc., Strauss Stores Corp., Microcom Internat.; chmn. bd. Wayne Transformer Corp.; instr. Bell and Howell Schs. Regular Republican candidate City Council, City of N.Y., 1968; Rep. county committeeman, 1968-72; bd. dirs. 39th A.D. Rep. Club, 1968-73, Mill Island Civic Assn., 1964-70; mayor mem. State Community Mayors, 1975—; Cub Scout pack chmn. Bklyn. council Boy Scouts Am., 1969-71. Served with U.S. Army, 1953-55. C.P.A., N.Y. Mem. N.Y. State Bar Assn., N.Y. State Soc. C.P.A.'s, Police Conf. N.Y., Stuyvesant High Sch. Alumni Assn. (v.p., counsel 1974-77, pres. 1977—). Clubs: Forsgate Country, Downtown Athletic, Masons. Author Bell and Howell Schs. fed. income tax textbook, 1975. Home: 2226 National Dr Brooklyn NY 11234 Office: 600 4th Ave Brooklyn NY 11215

LAUFMAN, HAROLD, surgeon; b. Milw., Jan. 6, 1912; s. Jacob and Sophia (Peters) L.; B.S., U. Chgo., 1932; M.D., 1937; M.S. in Surgery, Northwestern U., 1946, Ph.D., 1948; children—Dionne Laufman Weigert, Laurien. Intern Michael Reese Hosp., Chgo., 1936-39; resident in gen. surgery St. Marks Hosp., London, Eng., Northwestern U. Med. Sch., Cook County Hosp., Hine VA Hosp., 1939-46; faculty Northwestern U., Chgo., 1941-65, from clin. asst. to prof., attending surgeon Passavant Meml. Hosp., Chgo., 1953-65; prof. surgery, history medicine Albert Einstein Coll. Medicine, N.Y.C., 1965—; dir. inst. surg. studies Montefiore Hosp. and Med. Center, Bronx, N.Y., 1965—; practice medicine specializing in gen. surgery Chgo., 1941-65, N.Y.C., 1965—; James IV vis. prof. Israel, 1962; cons., lectr. in field. Served to maj., AUS, 1942-46. Named Ky. Col. Diolomate Am. Bd. Surgery. Fellow A.C.S., mem. Assn. Advancement Med. Instrumentation (pres. 1974-75, chmn. bd. 1976—), Am. Med. Writers Assn. (pres. 1968-69), Am. Surg. Assn., Societe Internationale de Chirurgie, Western, Central surg. assns., N.Y. Surg. Soc., Soc. Vascular Surgery, Internat. Cardiovascular Soc., Soc. Surgery Alimentary Tract, Sigma Xi, Alpha Omega Alpha, Phi Sigma Delta. Jewish religion. Clubs: Standard (Chgo.); Tammy Brook Country (Cresskill, N.J.). Author: (with S.W. Banks) Surgical Exposures of the Extremities, 1953; (with R.B. Erichson) Hematologic Problems in Surgery, 1970. Chmn. editorial bd. Diagnostica, 1974—; editorial bds. Surgery, Gynecology and Obstetrics, 1974—, Med. Instrumentation, 1972—, Med. Research Engring., 1972—. Contbg. author, contbr. articles to sci. publs. Home: 31 E 72d St New York City NY 10021 Office: 111 E 210th St New York City NY 10467

LAUG, MAURICE CHARLES, food co. exec.; b. Coopersville, Mich., Feb. 15, 1922; s. Harold George and Lottie Irene (Lillie) L.; A.B., Hope Coll., 1945; M.S., Mich. State Coll., 1950; grad. environ. sanitation program U. Ill., 1974; m. Virginia C. Hemmes, Aug. 6, 1948; children—Deborah A., Maurice Charles, Nancy H., Lise L. Sanitarian, Mich. State Coll., East Lansing, 1950-51; bacteriologist Swift & Co., Chgo., 1954-59; head chemist Holiday Food Co. div. Swift, Union, Mo., 1959-64; zone sanitarian Swift & Co., Chgo., 1964-67; mgr. sanitation Beech Nut Life Savers, Canajoharie, N.Y., 1967-68; corp. sanitarian Beech Nut Inc., Canajoharie, 1968-71; mgr. sanitation Beech Nut Foods Corp., Canajoharie, 1971—. Served to lt. comdr. USNR, 1943-46, 51-54; World War II, Korea. Kellog San. fellow, 1948. Certified pesticide applicator. Mem. Environ. Mgmt. Assn., Nat. Environ. Health Assn., Nat. Pest Control Assn., Empire State Pest Control Assn., Ret. Officers Assn., Nat. Rifle Assn. Mem. Ref. Ch. Am. (elder). Lion (past pres., sec.). Home: 66 Cliff St Canajoharie NY 13317 Office: Church St Canajohaire NY 13317

LAUGHLIN, ANITA CURRAN, marine pub. co. exec.; b. Providence, Dec. 6, 1937; d. John Thomas and Loretta (Kelley) Curran; B.F.A., U. Houston, 1969; m. Lochlin Gates Syme, Feb. 3, 1978; children by previous marriage—Lauren Laughlin, Kirk Laughlin. Layout artist Soundings Publs., Essex, Conn., 1969-71, prodn. mgr., 1971-76, advt. mgr., 1976—; instr. art appreciation Holy Apostles Sem. Coll., intro. to advt. Middlesex Community Coll. Adtive Greater Hartford Com. for Media Reform; mem. Goodspeed Opera House Found.; sponsor Capella Cantorum. Mem. Women in Communications, Inc., Nat. Assn. Engine and Boat Mfrs. (industry promotion com. 1979—), Writers League Conn. (founding mem., past pres.), Middlesex County Music Assn., ACLU. Unitarian. Office: Soundings Publs Essex CT 06426

LAUGHLIN, CYRIL JAMES, veterinarian; b. Crittenden, N.Y., Jan. 20, 1916; s. Vincent Joseph and Ellen (Casey) L.; student Canisius Coll., Buffalo, 1933, Cornell Agrl. Sch., 1934-35; D.V.M., N.Y. State Vet. Coll., Cornell U., 1935-40; m. Naomi Pearl Myers, Feb. 19, 1955. Owner, operator Laughlin Farms, Silver Spring, Md., 1940—; gen. practice vet. medicine, Washington, 1944-46. Mem. Am. Vet. Med. Assn., Am. Angus Assn. (life), Omega Tau Sigma, Chi Delta. Democrat. Roman Catholic. Clubs: Manor Country (Rockville), K.C. Cons. and researcher in field. Home and Office: 13716 New Hampshire Ave Silver Spring MD 20904

LAULICHT, MURRAY JACK, lawyer; b. Bklyn., May 12, 1940; s. Abraham and Esther (Greenfield) Goldwasser; B.A., Yeshiva Coll., 1961; LL.B. summa cum laude, Columbia, 1964; m. Linda Kushner, Apr. 4, 1965; children—Laurie, Pamela, Shellie, Abigail. Admitted to N.Y. bar, 1965, N.J. bar, 1968, U.S. Supreme Ct. bar, 1976; mem. staff Warren Commn., Washington, 1964; law clk. to Judge Harold Medina, 1964-65; asso. firm Kaye, Scholer, Fierman, Hays & Handler, N.Y.C., 1965-68, Lowenstein, Sandler, Brochin, Kohl & Fisher, Newark, 1968—; spl. counsel for State of N.J. on Port Authority bond covenant litigation, 1974-77. Mem. Am., N.J., Essex County bar assns. Home: 18 Crestwood Dr West Orange NJ 07052 Office: 744 Broad St Newark NJ 07102

LAUNER, MARTIN WILLIAM, dental supply co. exec.; b. Catskill, N.Y., Oct. 16, 1945; s. Wilbur Albert and Marian Lucille (Eckardt) L.; A.A.S., Dutchess Community Coll., 1965; B.M.E., Rochester Inst. Tech., 1970, M.B.A., 1975; m. Lauren Edith Michael, Dec. 20, 1969; 1 son, Geoffrey William. Asst. quality control engr. Xerox Co., Rochester, N.Y., 1969-70; mfg. engr. Castle Co., Rochester, 1971; vocat. evaluator Graflex Co., Rochester, 1972-73; quality control engr. Ritter Co., Rochester, 1973-74, inspection mgr., 1974-75, staff asst. to v.p. research and devel., 1975-76, mgr. quality control and govtl. regulations, 1976—. Am. Soc. Tool and Mfg. Engrs. scholar, 1963-65. Mem. Am., Rochester socs. quality control, Am. Soc. Tool and Mfg. Engrs. Home: 2187 E Whitney Rd Fairport NY 14450 Office: 400 West Ave Rochester NY 14603

LAURENDI, NAT, criminal investigator; b. Sant'Eufemia d'Aspromonte, Reggio Calabria, Italy, Aug. 7, 1923; s. Domenick and Grace (Crea) L.; grad. RCA Insts., 1951; A.A.S., Coll. City N.Y., 1969; m. Laura Autelitanto, Mar. 28, 1946; children—Domenick, Susan (dec.), Adrienne, Loretta, Diana, Robert. With N.Y. Police Dept., 1951-75, N.Y. Dist. Atty's Office, 1952-75, criminal investigator, 1951-75, polygraph expert, 1962-75; pres. Certified Lie Detection, N.Y.C., 1975—, Nat. Laurendi, 1975—; author, lectr. on polygraph. Served with CIC, AUS, 1943-46. Decorated Bronze Star medal; recipient Excellent Police Duty award N.Y. Police Dept., 1954, 62, also Meritorious Police Duty awards. Licensed pvt. investigator N.Y., N.J. Fellow Acad. Certified Polygraphists; mem. N.Y.C. CIC Assn. (pres. 1956), N.Y. State Polygraphists (chmn. membership com., 1964—), Am. Polygraph Assn., Detectives Endowment Assn., N.Y. Police Dept. Patrolmens Benevolent Assn., N.Y. Police Dept. Ret. Detectives, Ret. Patrolmen N.Y. Police Dept., Am. Soc. for Indsl. Security, Nat. Law Enforcement Assos., N.Y. Vet. Police Assn., N.Y.C. Ret. Employees Assn., Soc. Profl. Investigators. Roman Catholic. Home: 108 Village Rd S Brooklyn NY 11223 Office: Certified Lie Detection 299 Broadway New York City NY 10007

LAURIA, ROBERT JOSEPH, petroleum co. exec.; b. Jersey City, N.J., Oct. 8, 1933; s. Carmine and Eleanor Lauria; B.S., St. Peters Coll., 1956. Auditor, Peat Marwick Mitchell & Co., N.Y.C., 1959-64, audit mgr., Milan, Italy, 1964-66; dep. controller Internat. Life Ins. Co., London, 1966-71; controller New Eng. Petroleum Corp., N.Y.C., 1971—. Served with U.S. Army, 1956-58. C.P.A. Mem. N.J. State Soc. C.P.A.'s, Am. Inst. C.P.A.'s. Home: 568 Sylvan Rd Rivervale NJ 07675 Office: 825 3d Ave New York City NY 10022

LAURITSEN, JOHN PHILLIP, writer, market research co. exec.; b. Grand Island, Nebr., Mar. 5, 1939; s. Walter Perry and Sarah Marie (Grosshans) L.; B.A., Harvard U., 1963. Project dir. Marketscope Research Co., 1966-69, AHF Mktg. Research Co., N.Y.C., 1977-78; analyst, dir. ops. SDA Info. Scis. Co., N.Y.C., 1970-73. Mem. Gay Acad. Union (nat. dir.). Author: (with David Thorstad) The Early Homosexual Rights Movement 1864-1935, 1974 (also Italian and Spanish edits.); also author pamphlets; contbr. articles to The Freethinker, London, Gay News, London, Gay Liberator, Civil Liberties Rev. Home: 26 St Mark's Pl New York City NY 10003

LAURSEN, JOHANNES, newspaper publisher; b. Orum, Denmark, Oct. 17, 1915; s. Laurs Kristian and Ingeborg Elisabeth (Jensen) L.; came to U.S., 1950; grad. in Econs., U. Copenhagen, 1940; m. Faith Brewer, July 29, 1950; children—Linda, John Christian, Paul. With Ministry of Social Affairs, Copenhagen, 1940-45; with daily newspaper Nationaltidende, Copenhagen, 1945-48; press sec. Ministry of Commerce, Copenhagen, 1948-50; press officer Danish Info. Office, N.Y.C., 1950-58, 60-63; pub. Merrick (N.Y.) Life, 1958-60, 63—; Bellmore (N.Y.) Life, 1964—, Wantagh-Seaford (N.Y.) Citizen, 1976—; rep. N.Y. Press Assn. at N.Y. Fair Trial Free Press Conf., 1968—. Recipient Media award N.Y. State Bar Assn., 1968. Mem. N.Y. Press Assn. (dir. 1965-68, 73-76, officer 1968-69, pres. 1970), Nat. Newspaper Assn., Sigma Delta Chi. Author, co-author books in Danish. Home: 401 Morris Ave Rockville Centre NY 11570 Office: 1840 Merrick Ave Merrick NY 11566

LAUZON, ALINE AGNES, mfg. co. exec.; b. Palisades Park, N.J., June 22, 1934; d. Adolph John and Martha Josephine (Rolencik) Lauder; ed. pub. schs., Katherine Gibbs Sch.; m. Neil F. Lauzon, May 15, 1955; children—Thomas Andrew, Nadine Ellen, Peter Alexius. In inquiry and placement depts. Katherine Gibbs Sch., 1953-55; office mgr. Cresskill/Stillman Rubber Co., 1963-69; sec. Chem. Group, Dart Industries, Inc., Paramus, N.J., 1969-70, salary adminstrn. clk., 1970, mgr. wage and salary adminstrn., 1970-73, personnel mgr., 1973—. Recipient YWCA Tribute to Women and Industry, 1975, Am. Legion award, 1949. Mem. Am. Soc. Personnel Adminstrn. Republican. Roman Catholic. Club: Jr. Women's of Leonia (pres. 1964-66, named Clubwoman of Year 1964). Office: W 115 Century Rd Paramus NJ 07652

LAVENDER, WANDA KINZEL, nursing adminstr.; b. Wellsville, Ohio, Dec. 25, 1923; d. Leonard John and Rebecca Cecile (Thomas) Kinzel; R.N., Youngstown Hosp. Assn., 1945; postgrad. in obstetrics Margaret Hague Maternity Hosp., 1946; A.B. cum laude, Jersey City State Coll., 1970, M.A., 1974; m. James Lavender, Aug. 30, 1946; children—Nancy, Mark, Scott, Amy. Head nurse Youngstown (Ohio) Hosp., 1945; supr. Bayonne (N.J.) Hosp., 1946-47, Greenville (N.J.) Hosp., 1948, Salvation Army Door of Hope, Jersey City, 1949-52; head nurse, asst. instr., asst. supr., asst. dir. nursing Margaret Hague Maternity Hosp., Jersey City, 1958-75; inservice instr., supr., asst. dir. nursing Jersey City Med. Center, 1975—; mem. Hudson County Council on Inservice Edn., Am. Cancer Soc. Nursing Edn. Com. Mem. N.J. Civil Service Assn. Hudson Council #2. Certified sch. nurse and tchr. health edn. secondary level. Mem. Am., N.J. nurses assns., Youngstown Hosp. Nurses Alumni Assn., Kappa Delta Pi. Mem. Church of Christ (Chatham, N.J.). Clubs: DeMolay Mdthers' (pres.), Order Eastern Star (grand rep. N.J.), Past Matrons and Past Patrons Assn. N.J. (gov. 3rd. dist.), 21 Club. Office: Jersey City Medical Center 50 Baldwin Ave Jersey City NJ 07304

LAVENE, BERNARD, electronic co. exec.; b. N.Y.C., Aug. 25, 1935; s. Abram Frank and Betty (Lurie) L.; B.S. in Elec. Engring., Rutgers U., 1957; m. Lorraine J. Throckmorton, Aug. 7, 1966 (div.); children—Denise, Michele. Sales mgr., product mgr. Electronic Assos., Long Branch, N.J., 1960-67; div. mgr. Del Electronic Co., Mt. Vernon, N.Y., 1967-69; pres. Electronics Concepts Inc., Eatontown, N.J., 1969—. Served with USAF, 1958-60. Home: 13 Conaskonk Dr Ocean NJ 07712 Office: Indsl Way Eatontown NJ 07724

LAVENTHOL, HENRY LEE, artist; b. Phila., Dec. 22, 1927; s. Lewis Jacob and Sadye (Horowitz) L.; B.A., Yale U., 1947; postgrad. Columbia U., 1948-51, New Sch. for Social Research, 1952-53; m. Josephine P. Weitjens, Mar. 26, 1965. Sr. accountant Laventhol, Krekstein, Horwath, N.Y.C., 1948-51; v.p. Wings Shirt Co., N.Y.C., 1951-61; one-man shows: Bodley Gallery, N.Y.C., 1968-71, John Whibley Gallery, London, 1962, Die Brücke, Düsseldorf, Germany, 1964, Mickelson Gallery, Washington, 1972; exhibited in group shows: Phila. Mus. Art, 1969, Print Club Phila., 1969-73, Asso. Am. Artists, 1969-74, Nat. Arts Club, N.Y.C., Galerie Mati, Zurich, 1973, Athenaeum Phila., 1973, Bibliothèque Nationale, Paris, 1973-78; represented in permanent collections: Yale U., Pepsico Corp., Evansville (Ind.) U., Nat. Gallery Art, Washington, N.Y. Pub. Library Print Collection, Forbes Collection, Free Library Phila., Lowe Mus. Art, Duke U. Mus. Art, Bibliothèque Nat., Paris; guest lectr. N.Y. U., 1955, Pratt Graphic Center, N.Y.C., 1974. Mem. Artists Equity Assn. N.Y., Circulo de Bellas Artes. Book: Le Miroir Aux Alouettes', 1973. Home: RD 1 Hanover St Yorktown Heights NY 10598

LAVERTY, CHARLES RAYMOND, JR., city ofcl.; b. Somerville, Mass., Nov. 8, 1934; s. Charles Raymond and Lillian Theresa (Patterson) L.; B.S. in Bus. Adminstrn., Boston Coll., 1956; grad. Urban Exec. Sch., Sloan Sch. Mgmt., Mass. Inst. Tech., 1970; m. Judith C. Morrissey, May 11, 1964; children—Kelly, Kara, Kristin, Charles. Mem. City Cambridge Bd. Zoning Appeals, 1967; mem. City Cambridge Bd. Assessors, 1967—, chmn. bd., 1968, 70, 73, 75, 77; asso. dean Assn. Mass. Assessors Sch., U. Mass., Amherst, 1972-74. Dir. Charlesbank Trust Co., Cambridge. Pres. Cambridge Jr. C. of C., 1963. Mem. town meeting, Arlington, Mass., 1956-57. Served with U.S. Army, 1958-60. Certified Mass. assessor, certified assessor evaluator. Mem. Internat. Assn. Assessing Officers, N.E. Regional Assessors Assn., Nat. Assn. Tax Consultants, Assn. Mass. Assessors (exec. bd. 1972-76, pres. 1977-78), N.E. Regional, Middlesex (pres. 1976) assessors assns., Cambridge C. of C. (v.p. 1976-78), Cambridge Economy Club (pres. 1977-78). Contbr. to profl. jours. Home: 10 Cedar Rd Belmont MA 20178 Office: Cambridge City Hall 795 Massachusetts Ave Cambridge MA 02139

LAVEY, FREDERICK ADOLPH, lawyer, pub. co. exec.; b. Manchester, Conn., Sept. 15, 1916; s. Frederick Henry and Hilma (Anderson) L.; B.S., Harvard U., 1938, postgrad. bus. adminstrn., 1938-39; postgrad. U. Va. Law Sch., 1940-42, J.D., 1946; m. Evelyn Heatwole, Jan. 16, 1943; 1 son, Frederick Painter. Admitted to Conn. bar, 1946, D.C. bar, 1947; asso. firm Hewes and Await, Hartford, Conn., 1946-47, Awalt Clark and Sparks, Washington, 1947-51; with Pub. Utilities Reports, Inc., Washington, 1951—, exec. v.p., 1956-61, gen. mgr., 1959-61, pres., gen. mgr., 1961—, dir., 1968—; exec. sec. Utilities Publ. Com., Washington, 1961—; dir. Lebhar-Friedman, Inc., N.Y.C., 1976—; mem. pub. mgmt. com. Am. Bus. Press, Inc., 1963-68, dir., 1968-70. Pres., chmn. bd. dirs. Shenandoah Retreat Civic Assn., 1958-62, 69-71; mem. Postmaster Gen.'s Tech. Adv. Com., 1966-68, 70-73; pres. 2d Class Mail Publs., Inc., N.Y.C., 1966-70, dir., 1966—; chmn. local troop com. Boy Scouts Am., 1961-63; bd. dirs. Shenandoah Retreat Land Corp., 1965-68. Served to USNR, 1942-46. Mem. Am. (chmn. publ. com. pub. utility law sect. 1974—, council 1978—), D.C. bar assns., Raven Soc., Delta Theta Phi. Lutheran. Clubs: Retreat Golf and Country, Harvard, Harvard Bus. Sch., U. Va., Internat. (Washington); Farmington Country (Va.). Home: 4204 Thornapple St Chevy Chase MD 20115 Office: 1828 L St NW Washington DC 20036

LAVIN, CLAIRE MARIE, educator; B.A. in Early Childhood Edn., St. Joseph's Coll., Bklyn., 1962; M.S. in Spl. Edn., Fordham U., N.Y.C., 1965, Ph.D. in Ednl. Psychology, 1971. Early childhood coordinator Pub. Sch. 177, Bklyn., 1969-70, asst. prin., 1970-71; asst. prof., dir. grad. programs in spl. edn. Coll. of New Rochelle (N.Y.), 1972—. Mem. Council for Exceptional Children, Am. Ednl. Research Assn., Assn. for Retarded Children, Assn. for Supervision and Curriculum Devel. Certified psychologist, elementary prin., elementary supr., tchr. early childhood, tchr. mentally retarded, N.Y. State; specialist in learning disabilities, spl. edn., early childhood edn. Office: Coll of New Rochelle New Rochelle NY 10801

LAVINE, DAVID, author, state legislator; b. N.Y.C., Nov. 11, 1928; s. Abraham Lincoln and Joan (Bragman) L.; B.A., DePauw U., 1950; student N.Y. U., 1950-51; m. Gladys Bozyan, Apr. 28, 1963; children—Rachel, Adam, Rebecca. Adminstrv. intern N.Y. State CSC, 1953-54; with N.Y. State Dept. Welfare, 1953-54; tchr. N.Y.C. Pub. Schs., 1954-61; author: What Does a Peace Corps Volunteer Do?, 1964; What Does a Congressman Do?, 1965?; What Does a Senator Do?, 1967; The Mayor and the Changing City, 1966; Outposts of Adventure: The Story of the Foreign Service, 1966; Under the City-the Wondrous World Beneath the Streets, 1967; Evaluation of Inland Wetland and Watercourse Functions, 1974; ednl. cons. Community Participation in Education Program, N.Y.C., 1966-71; mem. Conn. Gen. Assembly, 1971-73, 76—, mem. fin. com., regulated activities com.; dir. Conn. Inland Wetlands Project, 1973-75. Adv. bd. Conn. Valley Hosp., 1975—; citizens edv. group Conn. river basins program New Eng. River Basins Commn., 1975—; exec. dir. Temporary Nuclear Power Evaluation Council, 1976. Recipient numerous awards for conservation. Home and Office: Dead Hill Rd Durham CT 06422

LAVOIE, ELAINE FRANCES, C. of C. exec.; b. Boston; d. Theodore Thomas and F. Irene (McCarthy) Stopyre; B.S. in Govt. and Journalism summa cum laude, Suffolk U. Regional coordinator McGovern for Pres. Campaign, 1971-72; dir. communications Dunfey Family's Hotels, Boston, 1973-77, Greater Boston C. of C., 1977—. Bd. dirs., mem. exec. com. Mass. Salvation Army; mem. Friends of Eunice Kennedy Shriver Spl. Olympics Com.; apptd. to Mayor's Parkman Center for Urban Affairs; mem. Boston Coll. Citizens Seminars; mem. Marblehead Democratic Town Com., 1976; del. Dem. Mid-Term Conv., Kansas City, Mo., 1974, Dem. Nat. Conv., N.Y.C., 1976; mem. affirmative action council Dem. State Com., 1973. Mem. Am. Chambers of Commerce Execs. (Nat. Communications award 1977-78), Pub. Relations Soc. Am., Pub.

Relations Soc. Boston, New Eng. Circle. Clubs: Publicity of Boston, Boston Press. Office: 125 High St Boston MA 02110

LAVOIE, JOSEPH JEAN-GUY, health service adminstr.; b. Papineauville, Que., Can., May 24, 1930; s. Paul E. and Simonne L. (Boyer) L.; diploma in hosp. orgn. U. Montreal (Que.), 1972; m. Denyse Perron, Sept. 22, 1956; children—Yves, Danielle, Jocelyne, Josee. Clk., Canadian Nat. Bank, Amos, Que., 1947-51; payroll clk. and cost accountant Simard & Freres Cie. Ltd., Amos, 1951-56; asst. accountant Que. Lithium Corp., Barraute, Que., 1956-65; dir. fin. Saint-Sauveur Hosp., Val d'Or, Que., 1965-70, dir. gen., 1970-71; adminstr. Extendicare (Que.) Ltd., Cote St. Luc, Que., 1971-72; dir. gen. Hopital de Gagnon (Que.), 1972-73, Hotel-Dieu de Hauterive (Que.), 1973-77. Mem. Canadian Coll. Health Execs., Assn. Dirs. Gen. Que. Roman Catholic. Home: 268 Rouleau St Hauterive PQ G5C 1T5 Canada Office: 635 Joliet St Hauterive PQ G5C 1P1 Canada

LAVOIE, JOSEPH NORMAN, accountant; b. London, Ont., Can., Apr. 18, 1946; s. Joseph Gerrard and Jean Emily (Arnold) L.; student Windsor (Can.) Inst. Tech., 1965-66, Queens U., 1966-67; m. Norma J. Martyn, Sept. 24, 1966. Internal auditor, accountant Holiday Inns, London, Toronto, 1962-67; assesor County of Middlesex (Can.), 1967-69; chief internal auditor Supertest Ltd., London, 1969-72; sr. internal auditor, plant accountant Emco Ltd., London, 1972; chief accountant Univ. Hosp., London, 1972—. Certified internal auditor, Can. Mem. Inst. Internal Auditors (gov. Forest City 1977-78), Certified Gen. Accountants Ont. Baptist. Home: Rural Route 2 Inderton ON N0M 2A0 Canada Office: 339 Winderemere Re London ON N6G 2K3 Canada

LAVOIE, PAUL LEO, antiquarian horologist; b. Haverhill, Mass., June 7, 1932; s. Napoleon and Lillian Jeanette (Duquette) L.; came to Can., 1964, naturalized, 1972; student Catholic U. Am., 1953-55, Sacred Heart Coll., Balt., 1955-56, Suffolk U., Boston, 1959-61. Statis. clk. AVCO Research and Advanced Devel., Wilmington, Mass., 1957, 59-64; payroll supr., personnel mgr. John Forsyth Co., Ltd., Kitchener, Ont., Can., 1965-77; antiquarian horologist, 1977—. Served with AUS, 1957-59. Fellow Nat. Assn. Watch and Clock Collectors (sec.-treas. Ont. chpt.); mem. Antiquarian Horol. Soc. Eng., Commemorative Collectors Soc. Eng., Antiquarian Horol. Soc. (research mem. Am. br.), Assn. Nat. des Collectionneurs et Amateurs d'Horlogerie Ancienne (France). Publisher, compiler: Clocks Made in Canada by the Arthur Pequegnat Clock Co., 1973. Home: 63 Wilsonview Ave Guelph ON N1G 2W5 Canada

LAW, JOHN RANDOLPH, orthodontist; b. Morgantown, W.Va., Dec. 16, 1927; s. Harry Randolph and Gail (Davis) L.; A.B., W.Va. U., 1949, M.S. in Zoology, 1951; D.D.S., Georgetown U., 1955; M.S.D. (USPHS, NIH fellow), U. Wash., 1969; m. Frances A. Mc Manis, Jan. 14, 1978; children—John, Carolyn, Christopher, Andrew. Instr. microbiol. technique lab. W.Va. U., 1949-51, instr. ornithology lab. course, 1949-51; asst. curator W.Va. U. Zool. Mus., 1949-51; asso. prof. orthodontics Georgetown U. Sch. Dentistry, 1960-62, asst. clin. prof. orthodintics, 1962-64, guest lectr. dept. anatomy Med. Sch., 1966-68; guest lectr. orthodontics Montgomery Jr. Coll., 1968-70; asst. prof. orthodontics Howard U. Dental Sch. Grad. Orthodontic Program, 1969; practice orthodontics, Washington, 1962—; partner Potomac Real Estate Assos. Mem. Alumni Senate, Georgetown U.; bd. dirs. D.C. Pilot. Action Com. Served to lt. USN, 1955-58. Mem. D.C. Dental Soc., Am. Assn. Orthodontics (chmn. council on ethics and discipline), Middle Atlantic (dir.), Balt. Washington socs. orthodontists, Eastern Strang Tweed, Greater Washington (past pres.) orthodontic study clubs, Am. Soc. Dentistry for Children, AAAS, Am. Soc. Preventive Dentistry, Georgetown U. Dental Sch. Alumni Assn., Phi Kappa Psi, Psi Omega, Kiwanian (past pres., dist. lt. gov.). Club: Potomac Swimming and Tennis (Potomac, Md.). Home: 104 W Jefferson St Rockville MD 20850 Office: 4633 41st St NW Washington DC 20016

LAW, NORMAN CRAIG, biochemist; b. Chgo., Sept. 21, 1917; s. William Duple and Marion A. (Craig) L.; B.A., U. Toronto, 1949; m. Sylvia Mae Ross, Sept. 12, 1953; 1 son, Ross Craig. Technician, Ont. Research Found., Toronto, 1937-42, U. Toronto, Ont., 1945-49; med. asso. Inst. Aviation Medicine RCAF, Toronto, 1949-54, RCAF Hosp., Rockeliff, 1954-62; asso. biochemist Nat. Def. Med. Centre, Ottawa, Ont., 1962-64; biochemist Suburban Hosp., Bethesda, Md., 1964—. NIMH grantee, 1971-74. Mem. Am. Assn. Clin. Chemists (chmn. Capital sect. 1972-73, Joseph H. Roe award 1970, registered clin. chemist), Can. Soc. Clin. Chemists (founding, certified clin. chemist), Mid Atlantic Assn. Forensic Scientists (charter, sec.-treas. 1974-76), Am. Chem. Soc., Assn. Clin. Scientists. Contbr. articles to profl. jours. Home: 6503 Stoneham Rd Bethesda MD 20034 Office: Suburban Hosp Assn 8600 Old Georgetown Rd Bethesda MD 20014

LAW, STEPHEN LEROY, chemist; b. Cheyenne Wells, Colo., Apr. 21, 1939; s. Edgar LeRoy and Lucy Ellen (Ault) L.; Asso. Sci., Ft. Lewis Jr. Coll., 1959; B.S., 1964; M.S., U. Hawaii, 1967; Ph.D., U. Md., 1976; m. Donna Lee Harris, Apr. 24, 1964; children—Eric LeRoy, Michael Dodd, Christina LeeAnn, Vincent Perry, Teresa LuEllen, Daniel Harris, Brian David. Phys. sci. aide USPHS, HEW, Salt Lake City, 1963; tchr. chemistry and math. Bayfield (Colo.) High Sch., 1964-65; teaching and research asso. U. Hawaii, Honolulu, 1965-67; research chemist College Park (Md.) Metallurgy Research Center, Bur. Mines, U.S. Dept. Interior, 1967—, coordinator for elemental analysis, particulate mineralogy unit, project leader Avondale (Md.) Metallurgy Research Center, 1973—; radiation protection officer Bur. Mines, 1968—, OD radiol. monitor 1972—, equal employment opportunity counselor, 1971—. Bishop, Ch. Jesus Christ of Latter-day Saints, 1977—. Mem. Am. Chem. Soc., Soc. Applied Spectroscopy (chmn. Balt.-Washington sect. 1978-79), Am. Inst. Mining, Metall. and Petroleum Engrs., Water Pollution Control Fedn., Prince Georges County Geneal. Soc. Home: 4905 Blackfoot Rd College Park MD 20740 Office: Avondale Metallurgy Research Center Bur Mines Avondale MD 20782

LAWLIS, JOHN FRANK, pharm. co. exec.; b. Indlps., Oct. 23, 1923; s. John Frank and Mabel Marie (Updike) L.; B.S., Butler U., 1949, M.S., 1951; Ph.D., Ind. U., 1958; m. Patricia Jean Palmer, Aug. 28, 1946; children—Johnette Lawlis Tollin, John Frank, Janene M. Dir. biol. quality control Lederle Labs., Pearl River, N.Y., 1960-61; mgr. quality control Merck, Sharp & Dohme, West Point, Pa., 1961-70; v.p. ops. Merrell Nat. Labs., Swiftwater, Pa., 1970—. Chmn. Worcester Twp. Zoning Bd., 1970-76; trustee Perkiomen Sch. Served with USAAF, 1943-45. Nat. Cancer Inst. fellow, 1955-58; Raymond Rice scholar, 1954-55. Mem. Pharm. Mfrs. Assn., Am. Assn. Microbiology, Sigma Xi. Republican. Home: 2690 Shady Ln Lansdale PA 19446 Office: Merrell Nat Labs Swiftwater PA 18370

LAWRENCE, ALONZO WILLIAM, envrion. engr., educator; b. Rahway, N.J., Apr. 11, 1937; s. Alonzo Welchman and Marjorie Jeanette (Hollings) L.; B.S., Rutgers U., 1959; M.S., Mass. Inst. Tech., 1960; Ph.D., Stanford U., 1967; m. Louedda Lillian Etzel, June 18, 1960; children—Lynelle Thatcher, Brooks Hollings, Alden Warren. Asst. prof. environ. engring. Drexel U., Phila., 1965-67; asso. prof. environ. engring. Cornell U., Ithaca, N.Y., 1967-76; v.p. environ. resources Koppers Co., Inc., Pitts., 1976—; cons. in water pollution to numerous industries, 1970-76. Served to lt. U.S. Amry, 1960-62. Registered profl. engr., N.Y. Mem. ASCE, Pa. Water Pollution Control Assn., Am. Water Works Assn., Am. Chem. Soc., Assn. Envrion. Engring. Profs., Sigma Xi, Tau Beta Pi. Contbr. articles to profl. jours. Office: Koppers Bldg Pittsburgh PA 15219

LAWRENCE, GEORGE HUBBARD CLAPP, investment co. exec.; b. Bronxville, N.Y., Aug. 9, 1937; s. Christopher and George-Anne (Collin) L.; student Columbia Coll., N.Y.C., 1956-58; B.Profl. Studies, Pace U., 1975; m. Suzanne Spear, June 4, 1966; children—Christopher C., Arthur W. Asso., R.W. Pressprich & Co., N.Y.C., 1964-67, G.H. Walker & Co., N.Y.C., 1967-70; pres., chief exec. officer Lawrence Investing Co., real estate, Inc., Bronxville, 1970—; v.p., dir. Davis & Lawrence Co., Bronxville; dir. Cotton Petroleum Corp. subs. United Energy Resources; mem. adv. bd. Manhattan Savs. Bank, Bankers Trust Co. Pres., Charles Edison Meml. Youth Fund, 1971-75; exec. bd. Westchester Putnam council Boy Scouts Am.; chmn. Westchester Heart Fund, 1977-78; mem. nat. adv. council SBA, 1971-77; bd. dirs. Westchester Heart Assn., Kensico Cemetery, Legal Aid Soc. Westchester; mem. Republican State Com.; mem. staff Richard M. Nixon, 1968-69; dir., officer Westchester County Assn., 1973—. Mem. Nat., N.Y. State assns. realtors, Westchester County Real Estate Bd. Episcopalian. Clubs: Mill Reef Ltd., Adirondack League, Bedford Golf and Tennis, Links. Home: Charles Rd RFD 2 Mount Kisco NY 10549 Office: 4 Valley Rd Bronxville NY 10708

LAWRENCE, GEORGE ROBERT, elec. engr.; b. Phila., May 15, 1942; s. Robert Hart and Anne Louise (Gibson) L.; B.S., Pa. Mil. Coll., 1964; M.S., George Washington U., 1973, Profl. Degree in Engring., 1978; m. Judith Millicent Anderson, Mar. 20, 1965; children—Heidi, Eric, Sharon. Instrumentation engr. Gulf Research and Devel. Co., Pitts., 1964-66; fed. systems engr. IBM, Gaithersburg, Md., 1966-69, staff engr., 1969—. Indian Guides nation chief YMCA, 1977-78. Mem. Smithsonian Assocs., IEEE. Republican. Methodist. Clubs: Midget Ocean Racing, Potomac River Sailing (exec. bd. 1972), Cougar Catamarans (fleet capt. 1971-72), Montgomery Village Sports Assn. Home: 9841 Meadowcroft Ln Gaithersburg MD 20760 Office: 9500 Godwin Dr Manassas VA 22110

LAWRENCE, JAMES, III, otolaryngologist; b. Boston, Aug. 9, 1936; s. James and Martina Louise (Brandegee) L.; B.A., Harvard U., 1958; M.D., Boston U., 1962; m. Jane Skudder Burgin, Apr. 20, 1963; children—Langdon Swain, James. Intern straight medicine Barnes Hosp., St. Louis, 1962-63; resident in otolaryngology Johns Hopkins U., Balt., 1967-71; individual practice medicine, specializing in otolaryngology, Balt.; asst. prof. otolaryngology Johns Hopkins Hosp. Served with USAF, 1964-66. Teaching fellow Armed Forces Inst. Pathology, 1971-73. Diplomate Am. Bd. Otolaryngology. Mem. Am. Acad. Ophthalmology and Otolaryngology, Med. and Chirurg. Faculty Md., AMA, Baltimore County Med. Soc. Episcopalian. Home: 6137 Barroll Rd Baltimore MD 21209 Office: 6901 Dunmanway St Baltimore MD 21222

LAWRENCE, JUSTUS BALDWIN, pub. relations exec.; b. Cleve., Dec. 16, 1903; s. L. N. and Dorothy (Lyman) L.; Ph.B., Yale U., 1927; m. Mary Peace (dec.); m. 2d, Carlene Roberts Teetor. Newspaperman and mag. writer, 1928-33; advt. and publicity dir., asst. to Samuel Goldwyn, motion pictures, 1933-39; pub. relations dir. Assn. Motion Picture Producers, Hollywood, Calif., 1939-41; exec. v.p. J. Arthur Rank Orgn., Inc., N.Y.C., 1945-51; now pres. J.B. Lawrence, Inc., pub. relations and research, N.Y.C. Dep. chief pub. info. SHAPE, Paris, 1951-52, U.S. del. Tenth UNESCO Conf., 1958; presdl. mem. USO Corp., 1960-62. Served as pub. relations aide to Lord Mountbatten, Commandos, attached to Brit. Army, 1942-43; col., gen. staff U.S. Army, chief pub. relations officer ETO, 1943-45. Decorated Legion of Merit, Bronze Star (U.S.); Legion of Honor (France); Order Brit. Empire. Clubs: Yale, Overseas Press, Sky (N.Y.C.); Army and Navy, Nat. Press (Washington); The Travellers (Paris); Bucks (London); Pilgrims U.S.; Univ. (Mexico City). Contbr. articles to popular mags. Home: 580 Park Ave New York City NY 10021 Office: 280 Madison Ave New York City NY 10016

LAWRENCE, MARGERY H(ULINGS), utilities Harmarville, Pa., June 17, 1934; d. Richard Nuttall and Alva (Burns) Hulings; student Bethany Coll., 1951-52; B.S. in Home Econs., Carnegie-Mellon U., 1955. Asst. mdse. buyer Joseph Horne Co., Pitts., 1955-57; home econs. editor Pitts. Group Cos. Columbia Gas System, Pitts., 1957-64, dir. home econs., 1962-72; home economist Columbia Gas Pa., Jeannette, 1964-68, dist. mktg. mgr., 1972-74, dist. gas utilization mgr., 1974—. Mem. Am. (Home Service Achievement award 1964), Pa. (residential com.) gas assns., Internat., Pitts. sales and mktg. execs., Assn. Iron and Steel Engrs. (asso.). Episcopalian. Republican. Office: Columbia Gas Pa Inc 1405 McFarland Rd Pittsburgh PA 15216

LAWRENCE, RENA MAE, nurse, educator; b. Lebanon, Pa., Sept. 2, 1933; d. John Henry and Mildred Bertha (Wagner); diploma Harrisburg Hosp. Sch. Nursing, 1954; B.S. in Nursing, Lebanon Valley Coll., 1961; M.S. in Nursing, U. Md., 1964, Ph.D., 1970. Nurse jr. grade VA Hosp., Lebanon, Pa., 1955-57; instr. Harrisburg (Pa.) Hosp. Sch. Nursing, 1957-62; guest lectr. U. Md., Balt., 1962; staff nurse (part-time) Good Samaritan Hosp., Lebanon, Pa., 1963; dir. nursing edn. Lancaster (Pa.) Gen. Hosp. Sch. Nursing, 1963-66; staff nurse Mercy Hosp., Balt., 1967, evening supr., 1967, night nurse, 1967-69; prof., chmn. dept. nursing Albright Coll., Reading, Pa., 1969—; cons. for various ednl. programs, 1969—. Mem. Nat. League for Nursing, Am. Nurses Assn., Am. Heart Assn., U. Md. Alumni Assn., Delta Kappa Gamma, Sigma Theta Tau. Author: (with S.A. Lawrence) Student Laboratory Manual, 1973. Home: 48 Pilgram Dr Lancaster PA 17603 Office: Albright College 13th and Exeter St Reading PA 19604*

LAWRENCE, ROBERT SCOTT, educator; b. Bklyn., Mar. 11, 1947; s. Arthur and Libbie (Lusthaus) L.; B.A. in History, State U. N.Y., Stony Brook, 1969; M.S. in Guidance and Counseling, L.I. U., 1972; M.S., profl. diploma ednl. adminstrn. and supervision with distinction, Pace U., 1975; m. Marlyn Lopoten, Mar. 26, 1978. Tchr., guidance counselor, asst. prin. N.Y.C. Pub. Schs., 1969—; tchr. phys. edn. Pub. Sch. 56, Bklyn., 1974—. Recipient Silver Bowl award for outstanding phys. edn. program, N.Y.C., 1978. Mem. Am. Personnel and Guidance Assn., Internat. Reading Assn., AAHPER, Phi Delta Kappa. Home: 67-71 Yellowstone Blvd Forest Hills NY 11375 Office: Public Sch 56 170 Gates Ave Brooklyn NY 11238

LAWRENCE, STELLA HERTCHIKOFF, educator; b. Montreal, Que., Can., Feb. 2, 1918; d. M. and Fannie (Broide) Hertchikoff; came to U.S., 1924, naturalized, 1943; B.A. magna cum laude, N.Y. U., 1938, M.S., 1941; B.E.E., Poly. Inst. Bklyn., 1949, M.E.E., 1952. Devel. engr. Control Instrument Co., 1943-47; instr. elec. engring. Pratt Inst., 1958-60; lectr. physics City Coll. N.Y., 1958-70; mem. switching systems devel. dept. Bell Telephone Labs., 1947-60; asst. prof. Bronx Community Coll., 1960-65, asso. prof. elec. engring. tech., 1966—; AEC research fellow Argonne Nat. Lab., summer 1974; cons. advanced tech. dept. Ampex Corp., summer 1975; NASA-Am. Soc. Engring. Edn. fellow Langley Research Center, summer 1976, Marshall Space Center, summer 1977; NSF fellow Aerospace Corp., summer 1978. Mem. Community Planning Bd. 7, Bronx, N.Y.C., 1970—. Fellow Bklyn. Engrs. Club; mem. IEEE (sr., exec. com. N.Y. sect. 1956, exec. com. region I, 1975—), Soc. Women Engrs. (sr., charter), Am. Soc. for Engring. Edn., Sigma Xi, Phi Beta Kappa, Pi Mu Epsilon, Sigma Pi Sigma. Home: 3288 Reservoir Oval E Bronx NY 10467 Office: 181st and University Ave Bronx NY 10453

LAWRY, ELEANOR MCCHESNEY, musicologist, pianist, educator; b. Pitcairn, Pa., June 17, 1908; d. Enoch Davies and Mary Alice (Ferguson) L.; student Pitts. Music Inst., 1925-28; pupil Wynne Pyle, N.Y.C., 1929-41, Harold Bauer, 1931-32; A.B., N.Y. U., 1943, M.A., 1947, Ph.D. in Musicology, 1954. Pvt. tchr. piano, N.Y.C., 1938—; recitals include Lake Minnewaska Mountain Houses, 1932, Capitol Theatre, Newark, 1940, Am. Women's Assn., N.Y.C., 1937, 40, AAUW, N.Y.C., 1960, 61; soloist Riverside Symphony Orch., N.Y.C., 1957, lectr. Am. Guild Organists, East Orange, N.J., 1949, N.Y. chpt. Am. Musicological Soc., 1955. Mem. Internat., Am. musicological socs., Music Library Assn., Renaissance Soc., Music Tchrs. Nat. Assn., N.Y. State Music Tchrs. Assn., N.Y. Fedn. Music Clubs, Nat. Guild Piano Tchrs. (faculty), AAUW. Republican. Compiler: Historical Chart of Composers, 1937; contbr. to chpt. Reese, Music in the Renaissance, 1954; The Psalm Motets of Claude Goudimel, 1954; Claude Goudimel Oeuvres Completes, vols. II, IV, VI, VIII, 1967-73. Home and Studio: 186 Pinehurst Ave New York City NY 10033

LAWRY, JOHN DANIELS, psychologist, educator; b. Pitts., May 26, 1938; s. John E. and Ruth (Daniels) L.; B.A., St. Charles Borromeo Coll., 1960; M.A., Duquesne U., 1965; Ph.D., Fordham U., 1972; 1 dau., Liliana. Psychol. asst. Psychol. Services of Pitts., 1962-65; head-start psychologist Day Care Center Nyack (N.Y.), 1966; research asst., emotional health of children in a family setting, NIMH, Westchester County, N.Y., 1968-69; asso. prof. and chmn. psychology Marymount Coll., Tarrytown, N.Y., 1965—; research asso. and instr. Women in Mgmt. Seminars, 1974—. Mem. Am. Psychol. Assn., AAUP. Office: Marymount Coll Tarrytown NY 10591

LAWSON, ALICE MARIE, librarian; b. Rye, N.Y., Dec. 31, 1934; d. Francis Joseph and Mary Ann (McKeon) Webb; B.A., City U. N.Y., 1971; m. William B. Lawson, June 1, 1957 (dec.); children—Patricia Anne, Rosemary, Alice Elizabeth. Keypunch operator Met. Life Ins. Co., 1952-57; bibliog. asst. Am. Mus. Natural History, N.Y.C., 1973-74; adminstrv. asst. and bibliographer Ecol. Sci. div. NUS Corp., Pitts., 1974-75, head library, info. retrieval specialist, 1975—. Mary Neil White scholar, 1971. Mem. ALA, Soc. for Bibliography of Natural History, Spl. Libraries Assn. Office: 1910 Cochran Rd Pittsburgh PA 15220

LAWSON, ANN MARIE MCDONALD, librarian; b. Jersey City; d. William and Mary Agnes (Dolan) McDonald; student Columbia U., 1947, N.Y. U., 1949, City Coll. N.Y., 1959, Pratt Inst., 1963; m. Philip James Lawson, Apr. 26, 1952. Methods analyst Reuben H. Donnelley Corp., N.Y.C., 1953-57; librarian chems. div. Union Carbide Corp., N.Y.C., 1957-65, Tatham Laird & Kudner, N.Y.C., 1965-67, Met. Transp. Authority, N.Y.C., 1967—. Active library tng. program Ballard Sch. (YWCA), 1949—; cons. WHO, Geneva, Switzerland, 1950; lectr. Pratt Inst. Grad. Library Sch., 1967, Mem. Assn. Assn. Records Mgrs. and Adminstrs. (pres. 1948-50); Spl. Libraries Assn. Republican. Contbr. articles to mags. Home: 119 Washington Pl New York City NY 10014 Office: 1700 Broadway New York City NY 10019

LAWSON, ASHFORD LEE, curator; b. Balt., Mar. 6, 1929; s. Harvey Linston and Effie Lee (Payton) L.; grad. high sch.; m. Alice Louise Walker, Nov. 21, 1970. Curator dept. anatomy Balt. Coll. Dental Surgery, Dental Sch., U. Md., Balt., 1971—. Served in U.S. Army, 1943-44, 45-46. Mem. Smithsonian Assos. Democrat. Lutheran. Home: 8029-C Woodgate Ct Baltimore MD 21207 Office: 666 W Baltimore St Baltimore MD 21201

LAWSON, DAVID, educator, writer; b. London, Oct. 11, 1927; s. Albert and Marjorie (Turner) L.; B.S., City U. N.Y., 1950; M.A., Columbia U., 1952, Ed.D., 1959; m. Sondra Ewing, Nov. 1954 (div. 1958). Asst. prof. edn. U. B.C., Vancouver, 1960-63, City U. N.Y., 1964-65; asso. prof. edn. Western Wash. State Coll., Bellingham, 1966-68, McGill U., Montreal, Que., 1968-70; vis. prof. edn. Boston U., 1971-72; curator Quaker House, Montreal, 1976—. Discussion leader Freedom Agenda and World Politics adult edn. programs, 1955-57; active mental health com. Beacon Hill Civic Assn., Boston, 1971-72; active Eugene McCarthy campaign, Portland, Oreg., 1968. Served with U.S. Army, 1946. Mem. History of Edn. Soc., Philosophy of Edn. Soc., Am. Ontoanalytic Assn., B.C. Tchrs. Fedn., Am. Ednl. Studies Assn., AAUP. Author: Alcestis: A Narrative Poem, 1967; The Teaching of Values, 1970; Peregrines: Poems, 1970; Patches: A Novel, 1975; contbr. articles to profl. jours. and poetry to various publs. Home and office: 2196 Blvd de Maisonneuve W Montreal PQ H3H 1L1 Canada

LAWSON, GUSTAF RUDOLPH, elec. components mfg. co. exec.; b. Abington, Mass., June 4, 1918; s. Franz Oscar and Ellen Aurelia (Anderson) L.; student pub. schs., Abington; m. Rose De Costa, Sept. 9, 1950; children—Eric Warren, Diane Roberta. Design engr., mgr. switch and control engring. Gen. Electric Co., Providence, 1948-62; chief engr. Leviton Mfg. Co., Bklyn., 1962-63, Thomas & Betts Co., Elizabeth, N.J., 1963-65; dir. research Circle F Industries, Trenton, 1965-69; staff. engr. AMP Spl. Industries Co. div. Amp, Inc., Paoli, Pa., 1969—. Served with Signal Corps U.S. Army, 1937-40, 43-45. Fellow Coll. Relay Engrs. Contbr. articles on product design, engring. mgmt. to profl. jours. U.S., fgn. patentee; discovered arcing phenomena in elec. contacts, 1960. Home: 205 Eastbrook Ln Willingboro NJ 08046 Office: PO Box 1776 Paoli PA 19301

LAWSON, J. SCOTT, architect, educator; b. Jamestown, N.Y., May 12, 1940; s. Donald Andrew and Dorothy (Husband) L.; B.Arch., Rensselaer Poly. Inst., 1963; m. Edith Blakeslee, Apr. 23, 1977. Asso., Todd & Giroux, Architects, Rochester, N.Y., 1963-72; prin. J. Scott Lawson, Architect, Rochester, 1972-77, Lawson, Knapp & Pulver, Architects, Rochester, 1977—; asst. prof., coll. architect Nat. Tech. Inst. for the Deaf at Rochester Inst. Tech., 1973—; works include Bellinger Hall, Dormitory/Conf. Center. Mem. Rochester Bd. of Election Examiners, 1973—; founder, bd. dirs. Soc. for Environ. Edn. Corp., 1975—, Schumann Meml., 1977—; mem. Rochester Com. for Sci. Info., 1976—. Licensed architect, N.Y. Mem. AIA, N.Y. State Assn. Architects/AIA (architects tng. and edn. com.), Rochester chpt. AIA (dir., sec., commr. edn. and research). Republican. Unitarian. Clubs: Univ. of Rochester, Chautauqua Yacht. Patentee exhibit systems; research on alternate energy sources. Home: 204 Wilshire Rd Rochester NY 14618 Office: Rochester Inst Tech Nat Tech Inst for the Deaf 1 Lomb Memorial Dr Rochester NY 14623

LAWSON, MARGARET MOTT (MRS. RALPH E. LAWSON), home economist; b. Blairstown, N.J.; d. Lewis Aaron and Leola May (Bird) Mott; B.S. in Home Econs., Cedar Crest Coll., 1946; M.Ed. in Adult Edn., Rutgers U., 1968; m. Ralph Elmer Lawson, Sept. 3, 1960. Asst. to dir. Needlework Design Studio, McCall Corp., N.Y.C., 1946-51; home economist Bell Sewing Machine Corp., N.Y.C., 1951-54; extension home economist Mercer County Extension

Service, Trenton, N.J., 1954—; needlework design cons. Flax Processing & Linen Co., N.Y.C., 1948-50. Mem. Mercer County Council on Aging, 1970—. Recipient Distinguished Service award Nat. Assn. Home Economists, 1966, Florence Hall award, 1970. Mem. Nat. (alt. regional dir. 1965-67, 2d v.p. 1978—), N.J. (pres. 1965-67) assns. extension home economists, Am., N.J. (pres. Mercer unit 1978-79) home econs. assns., Adult Edn. Assn., Zonta Internat. (1st v.p. Trenton Club 1962-64). Club: Hopewell (N.J.) Valley Golf. Home: 143 W Farrell Ave Trenton NJ 08618 Office: 930 Spruce St Trenton NJ 08648

LAWSON, RAY NEWTON, surgeon; b. London, Ont., Can., Apr. 17, 1914; s. Ray Frank and Helen Agnes (Newton) L.; B.A., U. Western Ont., 1936, M.D., 1937; M.S., McGill U., 1963; children by previous marriage—Mary, Ray, Wendy; m. Anne Richardson, Oct. 8, 1960; children—Joseph, Peter. Intern, St. Joseph's Hosp., London, Ont., 1936-37, Univ. Coll., London, Eng., 1938; resident Royal Victoria Hosp., Montreal, Que., Can., 1944-46, Montreal Gen. Hosp., 1947; practice medicine specializing in breast cancer Royal Victoria Hosp., 1948—; pres. Westmount Breast Centre, Montreal, 1969—; faculty McGill U., Montreal, 1948—, asso. prof. surgery, 1966—; mem. staff Pine Ave. Hosp., Montreal. Dir. Internat. Tuna Cup Match, N.S.; propr. oyster farm, Baddeck, Cape Breton, N.S. Served with RCAF, 1939-44. Fellow Royal Coll. Surgeons. Club: Skeet (Montreal). Inventor med. thermography; patentee in field. Home: Rural Route 2 Big Harbour Baddeck NS BOE 1BO Canada

LAWTON, HENRY WILLIAM, social worker, psychohistorian; b. Trenton, N.J., July 1, 1941; s. William Joseph and Bettina (Bowers) L.; B.A., Trenton State Coll., 1968; M.A., Fairleigh Dickinson U., 1971; M.L.S., Rutgers U., 1977; m. Helen Claire Sieswerda, June 22, 1968; children—Jennifer, Jason. Social caseworker N.Y.C. Dept. Social Services, 1968-71, Passaic County Welfare Bd., Passaic, N.J., 1971; social worker N.J. Div. Youth and Family Services, Hackensack, 1971—; research asso. Inst. for Psychohistory, N.Y.C., 1976—. Served with USAF, 1959-63. Mem. Internat. Psychohist. Assn., (sec., librarian), Mid-Atlantic Radical Historians Orgn., Am. Hist. Assn. Democrat. Contributing editor Jour. of Psychohistory, 1977—; contbr. articles in field to profl. jours. Address: 266 Monroe Ave Wyckoff NJ 07481

LAWTON, JAMES NORBERT, librarian; b. Chgo., Aug. 6, 1939; s. James Norbert and Madeline Elizabeth (McGoorty) L.; B.A., St. Procopius Coll., 1961; M.A., U. Mich., 1966, M.A., 1967; m. Bonnie Joy Banca, Nov. 28, 1961; children—Elizabeth Ann, Melissa Clare. Rare book asst. U. Mich. Library, 1963-67; rare book bibliographer Syracuse (N.Y.) U. Library, 1967-68; curator manuscripts Boston Pub. Library, 1968-73, curator manuscripts and archives, asst. keeper rare books, 1974—. Recipient Intercultural award Office Religious Affairs, U. Mich., 1966. Mem. Bibliog. Soc. Am., Soc. Am. Archivists, Am. Assn. State and Local History. Contbr. articles to profl. jours. Home: 16 Linden Pl Brookline MA 02146 Office: Boston Pub Library Copley Sq Boston MA 02117

LAWTON, SUSAN WALLIS, med. technologist; b. Alton, Ill., Nov. 29, 1941; d. William Francis and Florence Elanore (Lauck) Wallis; student Rollins Coll., 1960-61; B.S., Purdue U., 1963; M.A., Central Mich. U., 1978; children—William, Jennifer, Gef. Trainee Med. Tech. Sch., Meth. Hosp., Memphis, Tenn., 1970-71, technologist spl. chemistry, 1971-73, head spl. chemistry, 1974; chemistry supr. Altoona (Pa.) Hosp., 1975, edn. coordinator med. tech. program 1976-78; dir. med. tech. program St. Vincent Health Center, Erie, Pa., 1978—. Mem. Am., Pa. (treas. S. Central chpt.) socs. med. technologists. Republican. Methodist. Home: 2023 Devon Ln Erie PA 16509 Office: 232 W 25th St Erie PA 16512

LAWYER, VIVIAN MOORE, coll. adminstr.; b. Cleve., Jan. 6, 1946; d. Walter Frank and Everine (Stanton) Moore; B.S., Bowling Green State U., 1967, M.Ed., 1968, m. Cyrus Jefferson Lawyer III, June 8, 1968; children—Lenaye Lynne, Sonya Alyse. Asst. dean students Bowling Green (Ohio) State U., 1968-72, dir. office equal opportunity, 1972-73, coordinator human resources, 1973-75; dir. affirmative action Montgomery Coll., Rockville, Md., 1975—. Mem. Lucas County health service com. Health Planning Assn. NW Ohio, 1972-73. Toledo Neighborhood Health Assn., 1972-73; trustee Toledo YWCA; mem. Montgomery County Martin Luther King Commemorative Com.; mem. com. on edn. for handicapped students Md. Bd. for Community Colls. Recipient distinguished service to univ. award Bowling Green State U., 1967, Midwest region adviser's award Delta Sigma Theta, 1972. Mem. Nat. Council Negro Women (comm. on higher edn.), Nat. Assn. Women Deans and Counselors, Montgomery County Internat. Personnel Mgmt. Assn. Ohio Assn. Women Deans, Adminstrs. and Counselors, Am., Md., Ohio affirmative action officers. Home: 717 Somerset Pl Hyattsville MD 20783 Office: Adminstrv Center Montgomery Coll Rockville MD 20850

LAX, PHILIP, interior design co. exec.; b. Newark, Apr. 22, 1920; s. Nathan and Beckie (Hirschhorn) L.; B.S., N.Y. U., 1940, postgrad., 1941-42; m. Mildred Baras, Feb. 15, 1948; children—Corinne Lax Gehr, Barbara Lax Rogal. With Lax & Co., Newark, 1942-77, v.p., 1950-77; pres. Chathill Mgmt., Inc., 1977—. Pres. B'nai B'rith Center, Rochester, Minn., 1965-70, now hon. pres.; pres. Rutgers U. Hillel Found., 1969—, Ellis Island Restoration Commn., 1978; chmn. United Jewish Appeal, Maplewood, N.J., 1966; mem. Gov.'s Conf. on Edn., N.J., 1966, Mayor's Budget Com., Maplewood, N.J., 1958-59; co-chmn. N.J. Opera Ball, 1977; trustee B'nai B'rith Found., Washington, 1967—, Henry Monsky Found., Washington, 1968—, Leo N. Levi Hosp., Hot Springs, Ark., 1968-71, Nat. Arthritis Hosp., 1976—; mem. steering com. to Restore Ellis Island, 1977—; chmn. United Jewish Appeal, Maplewood, 1976. Recipient Found. award B'nai B'rith, 1968, Humanitarian award, 1969, Pres.'s Gold medal, 1975; Pro Mundi Beneficio medal Brazilian Acad. Humanities, 1976; chapel named for him B'nai B'rith Found., Washington, 1975. Mem. Nat. Soc. Interior Designers (trustee 1970-73), Am. Arbitration Assn., Phi Alpha Kappa. Clubs: Masons (32 deg.), Shriners, B'nai B'rith (v.p. Supreme Lodge 1968-71, internat. bd. govs. 1971—, internat. council 1978), N.Y. U. (founder N.Y.C. 1956). Home: 35 Claremont Dr Maplewood NJ 07040 Office: 830 Morris Turnpike Short Hills NJ 07078

LAY, RICHARD VICTOR, dentist; b. Buffalo, Dec. 20, 1924; s. Victor Weller and Mae C. (Ernst) L.; student U. Rochester, 1943-44, Northwestern U., 1944-45; D.D.S., U. Buffalo, 1951; m. Mary Elizabeth Goodman, June 22, 1948; children—Ronald A. (dec.), Craig T., Mark S., Laura A. Pres., Niagara Abrasive Corp., Lockport, N.Y., 1953-54; gen. practice dentistry, Buffalo, 1951—; active in oil exploration U.S. and Can., 1969-78. Mem. Republican Nat. Com. Served with USN, 1943-46. Fellow Royal Soc. Health; mem. Internat. Platform Assn., ADA, N.Y. State, 8th Dist. dental socs., Smithsonian Assos. Republican. Episcopalian. Home: 403 Rosedale Blvd Eggertsville NY 14226 Office: 422 Niagara Falls Blvd Buffalo NY 14223

LAYFIELD, VIRGINIA BANES, hosp. adminstr.; b. Carney, Md., Nov. 18, 1918; s. Clark Ross and Mary Ellen (Harvey) Banes; student U. Md. Sch. Nursing, 1934-37, U. Md., 1949-62; B.S., Johns Hopkins U., 1964; m. Samuel B. Layfield, Jan. 22, 1938; 1 son, Philip B. Asst. supr. outpatient dept. Univ. Hosp., Balt., 1937-40; field nurse Atlantic Seaboard Agrl. Workers Health Assn., 1945-47; successively head nurse, instr. nursing, asst. dir. nursing service and sch. nursing, asst. adminstr. Peninsula Gen. Hosp., Salisbury, Md., 1948-72, asso. adminstr. med. center, 1972—. Mem. advisory bd. Eastern Shore Council Alcoholism, 1968—; chmn. med. advisory bd. hosp. licensing Md. Dept. Health and Mental Hygiene, 1972—; mem. Somerset-Wicomico County Mental Health Bd., 1973—. Named man of yr. Salisbury Area C. of C., 1972. Mem. Am. (alt. del. Md.), Md. (vice-chmn. adminstrv. mgmt. and functions com. 1970—) hosp. assns., Md. Heart Assn. (sec. 1973-74), Am. Coll. Hosp. Adminstrs., Am. Nurses Assn., Nat. League Nursing, U. Md., Johns Hopkins U. alumni assns. Democrat. Methodist. Clubs: Soroptimists, Green Hill Country, Order Eastern Star. Home: 410 S Somerset St Princess Anne MD 21853 Office: 100 E Carroll St Salisbury MD 21801

LAYMAN, WILLIAM ARTHUR, psychiatrist; b. West New York, N.J., Feb. 8, 1929; s. Frank Kyle and Lucy Geraldine (Rooney) L.; student N.Y. U., 1946, 48; B.S. cum laude, St. Peter's Coll., 1951; M.D., Georgetown U., 1955; 1 son, William Kraft. Intern Hackensack (N.J.) Hosp., 1955-56; resident in psychiatry Lyons (N.J.) VA Hosp., 1956-57, Fairfield Hosp., Newtown Conn., 1957-58; clin. fellow Yale, 1958-59; instr. psychiatry Seton Hall Coll. Medicine, 1959-61, asst. prof., 1961-65; asso. prof. psychiatry N.J. Med. Sch., Newark, 1965-74, clin. prof., 1974-77, prof., 1977—; pvt. practice medicine specializing in psychiatry, Newark, 1959—; dep. chmn. ednl. services dept. psychiatry and mental health sci. N.J. Med. Sch., 1976—; cons. VA Hosp., East Orange, N.J., 1963-69, Greystone Park State Hosp., 1974—; attending Martland Hosp., 1970—. Served with U.S. Army, 1946-48. Diplomate Am. Bd. Psychiatry and Neurology. Fellow Am. Psychiat. Assn.; mem. N.J., Bergen County med. socs., AAUP. Contbr. articles profl. jours. Home: 208 Anderson St Hackensack NJ 07601 Office: 100 Bergen St Newark NJ 07103

LAZAR, ALLAN WILLIAM, physician; b. Bklyn., June 11, 1931; s. Benjamin Barney and Sylvia (Berkowitz) L.; B.S. cum laude, U. Scranton, 1953; M.D., Jefferson Med. Coll. Phila., 1957; m. Peggy Waite, May 22, 1955 (dec. 1961); children—Jennifer, Julie, Deena, David; m. 2d, Diane Childress, Jan. 13, 1962; children—Michael, Matthew, Benjamin. Intern, Detroit Receiving Hosp., 1957-58; resident pathology U. Chgo., 1958-62, chief resident, 1961-62, instr., 1961-62; asso. pathology Columbia U., Coll. Phys. and Surg., 1964-65; dir. Met. Cytology Services, Teaneck, N.J., 1965-70; pres., chmn. bd. Gyn., Cytology & Pathology Assos., Teaneck and Englewood, 1970—; practice medicine specializing in pathology, Washington, 1964, N.Y.C., 1965, Englewood, Teaneck, Leonia, 1965—; asso. prof. pathology Farleigh Dickinson U. Served to capt., M.C., USAF, 1962-63. Diplomate Am. Bd. Pathology. Mem. Coll. Am. Pathologists, N.Y. Acad. Scis., AAAS, AMA, Sigma Xi. Research and numerous publs. on biol. relationships in interaction of tumor and host in various lab. animals. Address: 740 Carroll Pl Teaneck NJ 07666

LAZAR, IRVING, educator; b. N.Y.C., Feb. 20, 1926; s. Charles and Sylvia (Hoffman) L.; B.S., Coll. City N.Y., 1948; M.A., Columbia U., 1950, Ph.D., 1954; m. B. Jeanne Mueller, Jan. 13, 1976; children by previous marriage—Kathryn Scott, James Bradford, Richard Alan. Intern, Menninger Clinic, Topeka, 1946-47; instr. psychology U. Pitts., 1947-48, U. Rochester, 1948-49, U. Ill., 1950-54; asso. chief Nev. Dept. Mental Health, Las Vegas, 1954-60; instr. sociology, dir. Peterson-Guedel Family Center, U. So. Calif., 1960-63; dir. Neumeyer Found., Beverly Hills, Calif., 1963-70; asso. dir. Appalachian Regional Commn., Washington, 1970-72; prof., chmn. community services edn. Coll. Human Ecology, Cornell U., 1972—; chmn. developmental continuity task force Edn. Commn. of the States, 1975—; mem. adv. com. on juvenile problems NIMH, 1970-75; cons. HEW, govs. various states. Served with USAAF, 1943-46. Decorated Bronze Star. Fellow Am. Psychol. Assn., Am. Orthopsychiat. Assn., Sigma Xi; mem. Am. Home Econs. Assn. Designed prototype community mental health and comprehensive human service programs. Home: 319 Wait Ave Ithaca NY 14850 Office: Coll Human Ecology Cornell U Ithaca NY 14853

LAZAR, MAX SEYMOUR, pharm. co. ofcl.; b. N.Y.C., Dec. 6, 1943; s. Harry and Bessie L.; A.B. in Chemistry, Bklyn. Coll., 1966; postgrad. Baruch Sch. Bus., City U. N.Y., 1967-68; m. Sherry Dorf, Sept. 5, 1965; children—Lawrence, Lisa. With Hoffmann-LaRoche, Inc., Nutley, N.J., 1966-68, analyst quality control, 1966, asst. chemist, 1967, supr., 1968, head quality control, Belvidere, N.J., 1969-73, mgr. quality control, 1973-78, dir. quality control, 1978—. Mem. Am. Chem. Soc., AAAS, N.J. Pharm. Quality Control Assn., ASTM (chmn. D-19.05.04), Pharm. Mfrs. Assn. (chmn. environ. quality assurance com.), Sigma Xi. Office: PO Box 238 Belvidere NJ 07823

LAZARCIK, GREGOR, educator, financial research co. exec., economist; b. Horna Streda, Slovakia, Mar. 10, 1923; s. Gaspar and Maria (Rehak) L.; B.S., State Coll. (Slovakia), 1945; M.S., Coll. Agr. (Brno, Czechoslovakia), 1948; certificate Swiss Inst. Tech. (Zurich), 1949; A.M., U. Strasbourg (France), 1952; LL.M., LL.D. (fellow), U. Paris, 1953; Ph.D. (fellow), Columbia, 1960; m. Theresa M. Good, Aug. 14, 1971. Came to U.S., 1953, naturalized, 1958. Asst. to mgr. Central Butter Dairy, Lucerne, Switzerland, 1948-49; controller dairy products Agrl. syndicate, Hazebruck, France, 1949-50, with Research Project on Nat. Income, Columbia U., N.Y.C., 1956—, sr. research economist, 1961—; with L.W. Internat. Financial Research, Inc., N.Y.C., 1961—, dir. research, pres., 1962—, chmn. exec. com., 1961—, chmn. bd.; teaching fellow in econs. Tech. U., Brno, Czechoslovakia, 1947-48; lectr. econs. Hunter Coll., City U., N.Y.C., 1963-64, econs., Columbia U., 1964-68; prof. econs. State U. N.Y., 1968—. Mem. Am. Econ. Assn., Am. Regional Sci. Assn., Assn. for Study Soviet-Type Economies. Roman Catholic. Author: Le Commerce en Matiere Agricole Entre l'Europe de l'Ouest et l'Europe de L'Est, 1959; Czechoslovak National Income and Product, 1947-56, 1962 (co-author); The Performance of Socialist Agriculture, 1963; Scientific Research and its Relation to Earnings and Stock Prices, 1965; Comparison of Agricultural and Nonagricultural Income, 1937, 48-65, 1968; Agricultural Output and Productivity in Eastern Europe and Some Comparisons with the USSR and USA, 1977; Defense, Education and Health Expenditures and Their Relation to GNP in Eastern Europe, 1978; Economic Growth in Eastern Europe, 1965-78, 1978; contbr. to East European Economics Post-Helsinki, 1977. Address: 633 W 115th St New York City NY 10025

LAZARUS, BERNARD, fin. and adminstrv. exec.; b. N.Y.C., July 29, 1930; s. Harry H. and Etta (Mann) L.; B.B.A., Coll. City N.Y., 1952; m. Wilma Fradin, Sept. 4, 1960; children—Richard, Kenneth, Jeanne. Sr. accountant Alexander Grant & Co., N.Y.C., 1956-59; exec. v.p. Lear Siegler, Inc., Bogen Div., Paramus, N.J., 1959-69; exec. v.p. Spiral Metal Co., Inc., N.Y.C., 1971-74; dir. adminstrn. and fin. law firm Fried, Frank, Harris, Shriver & Jacobson, N.Y.C., 1974—. Served with U.S. Army, 1952-54. C.P.A., N.Y. Mem. Fin. Execs. Inst., Am. Inst. C.P.A.'s, N.Y. State Soc. C.P.A.'s, Assn. Legal Adminstrs. (v.p. N.Y. chpt.). Home: 12 Fieldstone Ct Woodcliff Lake NJ 07675 Office: 120 Broadway New York City NY 10005

LAZELL, JAMES DRAPER, JR., biologist; b. N.Y.C., Sept. 5, 1939; s. James Draper and Katee Augusta (Quin) L.; B.A., U. of South, Sewanee, 1961; M.S., U. Ill., 1963; M.A., Harvard U., 1966; Ph.D., U. R.I., 1970. Head sci. dept. Palfrey St. Sch., Watertown, Mass., 1966-74; field rep. Nature Conservancy, Miss. Natural Heritage Program, 1974-75; mem. sci. staff Mass. Audubon Soc., Lincoln, 1967-75, wildlife biologist, 1975—; adj. field biologist Tufts U.; asso. Mus. Comparative Zoology; officer Harvard U. Nat. Geog. Soc. grantee, 1972, Edward John Noble Found. grantee, 1974, Center for Field Research grantee, 1973, 75—. Mem. AAAS, Am. Soc. Zoologists, Am. Soc. Mammalogists, Am. Soc. Ichthyologists and Herpetologists, Soc. Study Amphibians and Reptiles, The Nature Conservancy, Zero Population Growth, Nat. Rifle Assn. Author: The Anoles of the Lesser Antilles, 1972; Reptiles and Amphibians in Massachusetts, 2d edit. rev., 1974; This Broken Archipelago, Quadrangle, 1976; contbr. articles to profl. jours. and mags. Home: 346 Grapevine Rd Wenham MA 01984 Office: S Great Rd Lincoln MA 01773

LAZENBY, WILLIAM JOSEPH, accountant; b. Elmira, N.Y., Dec. 1, 1922; s. James Dewitt and Alice Florence (Hughes) L.; B.S. in Accounting, L.I. U., 1949; m. Marian Leonard, July 24, 1971; children—Leonard, James, Marilyn, Nida, William, Helene, Thomas, Lewis. Tax and ins. accountant Thatcher Glass Mfg. Co., Elmira, 1949-57; dir. cost accounting Am. LaFrance, Inc., Elmira, 1957-69; asst. treas., controller, dir. Capabilities Inc., Elmira, 1969—. Active Cub Scouts Am., 1967-69; pres. Civ-Ex Club, 1975-79. Served with U.S. Army, 1943-46. Mem. Nat. Assn. Accountants, Am. Assn. Corp. Controllers. Republican. Presbyterian. Clubs: Shepard Hills Country, L.I. U. Varsity, Elks. Home: Beckwith Rd RD 2 Pine City NY 14871 Office: 1149 Sullivan St Elmira NY 14902

LAZET, FRANK JOHN, chem. engr.; b. Smithtown, N.Y., Mar. 2, 1921; s. Teunis John and Florence May (Bowers) L.; B.S. in Chem. Engring., Clarkson Coll. Tech., 1945; m. Hilda Strauss, Oct. 20, 1945; children—Thomas, Bruce, John, Steven. Process engr. Phila. Quartz Co., Valley Forge, Pa., 1945-55, project engr., 1956-64, mgr. design engring., 1965-69, sr. devel. engr., 1970—. Councilman, Borough of Ridley Park (Pa.), 1963-64; trustee Presbyterian Ch., Ridley Park. Mem. Am. Inst. Chem. Engrs., Phila. Ship Model Soc. (treas.). Republican. Patentee in field. Home: 397 Highland Ave Media PA 19063 Office: PO Box 840 Valley Forge PA 19482

LAZICH, GILBERT STEVAN, ednl. adminstr.; b. Detroit, July 20, 1926; s. Steven P. and Anna (Mamula) L.; B.A. in History and Slavic Area Studies, U. Mich., Ann Arbor, 1952. M.Ed. in Ednl. Adminstrn. and Supervision, Wayne State U., Detroit, 1968, Ed.D., 1974; m. Lis Hellgren Jørgensen; children—Nils H., S. Peter, Lis Anne, Julia. Tchr., prin. Cromie Elementary Sch., Warren, Mich., 1957-68; instr.-coordinator student teaching Wayne State U., 1968-69; asst. supt. curriculum and instrn. Niles (Mich.) Community Schs., 1970-74; asst. supt., instrn. Interboro Sch. Dist., Lester, Pa., 1974—; Charles S. Mott fellow, Flint, Mich., 1969-70. Bd. dirs. Lansdowne Symphony; adv. council Nationalities Service Center. Mem. Mich. Assn. Elementary Sch. Prins. (dir., exec. council 1965-69), Pa. Assn. Supervision and Curriculum Devel. (exec. council Delaware Valley region 1975), Am. Ednl. Research Assn., Nat. Community Edn. Assn. Certified in elementary and secondary edn., Mich.; asst. supt., supt., Pa. Home: 202 Garnet Lane Wallingford PA 19086 Office: 9th and Washington Aves Prospect Park PA 19076

LAZZARO, E. CLIFFORD, ophthalmologist; b. Bklyn., Dec. 5, 1939; s. Emanuel and Olga (Andreozzi) L.; A.B. in English Lit., N.Y. U., 1961; M.D., State U. N.Y. Downstate Med. Center, 1965; m. Nicoletta Giametta, Jan. 31, 1958; children—Clifford, Douglas, Lance, Richard, Randall. Intern, USPHS Hosp., S.I., N.Y., 1965-66; resident in ophthalmology Bklyn. Eye and Ear Hosp., 1968-71; resident in basic scis. in ophthalmology N.Y. U. Postgrad. Med. center, 1969-70; attending ophthalmologist, chief of glaucoma clinic Bklyn.-Cumberland Med. Center, Bklyn., 1971—; instr. ophthalmology Downstate Med. Center, Bklyn., 1971-77, clin. asst. prof., 1977—; attending ophthalmologist Holy Family Hosp., Lutheran Med. Center, Victory Meml. Hosp.; dir. residency tng. Bklyn. Eye and Ear Hosp., 1973-76. Del. to Bay Ridge Community Council, 1975-76, mem. Com. on Health and Safety, 1975-76. Served with USPHS, 1965-68. Diplomate Am. Bd. Ophthalmology. Fellow A.C.S., Am. Coll. Ophthalmology and Otolaryngology; mem. N.Y., Kings County (mediation com. 1977—), Bay Ridge (pres. 1977-78) med. socs. Roman Catholic. Clubs: N.Y. Athletic, Allenhurst Beach. Contbr. articles in field to ophthal. jours. Home and Office: 83 83d St Brooklyn NY 11209

LEA, LOLA STENDIG, lawyer; b. N.Y.C., Sept. 20, 1934; d. Hershel and Sophie (Golub) Stendig; B.A. cum laude, N.Y. U., 1954; LL.B., Yale U., 1957; m. Robert M. Lea, Sept. 12, 1953 (div. Apr. 1976); 1 dau., Jennie. Admitted to N.Y. bar, 1958; law clk. to U.S. dist. judge So. Dist. N.Y., 1957-59; asst. U.S. atty. So. Dist. N.Y., 1959-61, asso. C.C. Davis, N.Y.C., 1961-67; mem. firm Davis & Cox, N.Y.C., 1967-71, Lea, Goldberg & Spellun, P.C., N.Y.C., 1971-77, Trubin, Sillcocks, Edelman & Knapp, N.Y.C., 1977—; spl. counsel to N.Y. 1st dept. joint interprofl. com. Drs. and Lawyers, 1972—; lectr. Practicing Law Inst., N.Y.C., 1969-70, 74; spl. mediator Med. Malpractice Mediation part Supreme Ct. N.Y., 1971—. Fellow Am. Bar Found.; mem. Am. Bar Assn., N.Y. Bar Assn. (del. 1972-77, exec. com. 1976-77), Assn. Bar City N.Y. (chmn. grievance com. 1978—, medicine and law com. 1969-71, new members com. 1973, mem. judiciary com. 1971-74, grievance com. 1974—, audit com. 1977—), N.Y. County Lawyers Assn. (dir. 1978—). Home: 24 Garden Pl Brooklyn NY 11201 Office: 375 Park Ave New York City NY 10022

LEAB, DANIEL JOSEF, educator; b. Berlin, Aug. 29, 1936; s. Leo and Herta (Marcus) L.; came to U.S., 1938, naturalized, 1944; B.A., Columbia U., 1957, M.A., 1961, Ph.D., 1969; m. Katharine Kyes, Aug. 16, 1964; children—Abigail Elizabeth, Constance Martha, Marcus Rogers. Instr., asst. prof. history Columbia U., 1966-73, asso. dean coll., 1969-70, asst. dean univ. faculties, 1971, spl. asst. exec. v.p., 1973-74; asso. prof. Seton Hall, 1974—; pub., co-editor Am. Book Prices Current; mng. editor Labor History; dir. Bancroft-Parkman; cons. AEC, 1972-73; lectr. USIS, summers 1970, 72, 75; sr. Fulbright lectr., 1977. Fellow Met. Mus. Art. Am. Council Learned Socs. grantee, 1972; Chamberlain fellow, 1972. Mem. Am. Hist. Assn., AAUP, Orgn. Am. Historians. Club: Grolier. Author: A Union of Individuals, 1970; From Sambo to Superspade: the Black and Film, 1975. Home: PO Box 216 Washington CT 06793

LEACH, ERNEST ROY, coll. dean; b. Sunnyside, Wash., Dec. 8, 1935; s. Roy Fay and Helen Marie (Wilson) L.; B.A., Seattle Pacific Coll., 1958; M.Ed., U. Wash., 1967, PH.D., 1972; m. Romayne Rachel Renberg, Dec. 21, 1957; children—Kathryn Rae Lawrence Roy, Karyn Rene. Dir. admissions Seattle Pacific Coll., 1959-61; asst. dir. admissions U. Wash., Seattle, 1962, asst. dean students, 1963-65; dean student personnel services Edmonds Community Coll., Lynnwood, Wash., 1969-71; dean student affairs Prince George's Community Coll., Largo, Md., 1972—; cons. to numerous colls. Bd. dirs. Univ. YMCA, Seattle, 1963-65, Ft. Washington Area Recreation Council, 1975-76. NDEA fellow, U. Wash., 1966-69. Mem. Nat. Council Student Devel. (nat. chmn. 1977), Am. Coll. Personnel Assn. (nat.

chmn. commn. XI, 1975-76), Nat. Assn. Student Personnel Adminstrs., Phi Delta Kaapa. Democrat. Contbr. articles in field to profl. jours.; author: (with Nelson, Deller, McCarty & Norman) A Manual for Student Services for Community Colleges in the State of Washington, 1971. Home: 13518 Reid Circle Fort Washington MD 20022 Office: 301 Largo Rd Largo MD 20870

LEACH, KEVIN THOMAS, real estate exec.; b. St. Louis, Aug. 22, 1945; s. Kenneth Fredrick and Katherine Estelle (McNiff) L.; B.S. in Civil Engring., Lehigh U., 1967; m. Linda Stewart, June 8, 1968; children—Catherine Elizabeth, Thomas George. Civil engr. George A. Fuller Co., N.Y.C., 1963-69; project mgr. George B. H. Macomber Co., New Haven, 1969-71; v.p. F.I.P. Corp., Farmington, Conn., 1971-78; pres. Devel. Cons., Inc., Farmington, 1978—. Bd. mgrs. Metro. br. YMCA, Farmington Valley, 1977—. Registered profl. engr., Conn., N.Y. Mem. ASCE, Conn. Soc. Profl. Engrs., Nat. Soc. Profl. Engrs. Episcopalian. Home: 52 Wheeler Rd Simsbury CT 06070 Office: 196 Trumbull St Hartford CT 06103

LEACH, RALPH F., banker; b. Elgin, Ill., June 24, 1917; s. Harry A. and Edith (Sanders) L. A.B., U. Chgo., 1938; m. Harriet C. Scheuerman, Nov. 18, 1944; children—C. David, H. Randall, Barbara E. Investment analyst Harris Trust & Savs. Bank, Chgo., 1940-48, Valley Nat. Bank, Phoenix, 1948-50; chief govt. fin. sect. Fed. Res. Bd., Washington, 1950-53; treas. Guaranty Trust Co., N.Y.C., 1953-59, v.p., 1958-59; v.p., treas. Morgan Guaranty Trust Co., N.Y.C., 1959-62, sr. v.p., treas., 1962-64, exec. v.p., treas., 1964-68, vice chmn. bd. dirs., 1968-71, chmn. exec. com., 1971-77; dir. Bowery Savs. Bank, Merrill Lynch & Co., So. R.R. Co., Urban Nat. Corp., Energy Conversion Devices, Inc., Continental Corp., Mem. fin. adv. com. U.S. Postal Service. Trustee Presbyn. Hosp., Juilliard Sch. Served to capt. USMC, 1940-45. Mem. Phi Kappa Psi. Clubs: Bronxville Field; Siwanoy Country. Home: 60 Hampshire Rd Bronxville NY 10708 Office: 23 Wall St New York City NY 10015*

LEAHY, EDWARD VINCENT, city ofcl.; b. Medford, Mass., Feb. 16, 1930; s. Joseph John and Mildred Sarah (Donlin) L.; B.S., Northeastern U., 1958; postgrad., 1959-61; m. Martha Elizabeth Donnelly, Apr. 30, 1966; children—Carolee Suzanne, Edward Joseph. Engr., Franchi Constrn. Inc., Newton, Mass., 1958-59, C.J. Maney Co., Inc., Lexington, Mass., 1959-60, Welbilt Constrn., Inc., Newton, 1960-61; supt., engr. Henry Wile Co., Newton, 1962-63; project engr. Bond Bros. Inc., Everett, Mass., 1964-68; pub. works adminstr., engr. Town of Billerica (Mass.), 1968—. Mem. Mass. Municipal Engrs. Assn., New Eng. Water Works Assn., Am. Pub. Works Assn., Norfolk-Bristol-Middlesex, Mass. hwy. assns. Home: 39 Lockeland Rd Winchester MA 01890 Office: 250 Boston Rd Billerica MA 01862

LEAHY, MIRIAM KRAMER, civic worker; b. Maryland Line, Md., Nov. 6; d. Thomas Best and Luanna (Crook) Kramer; student George Washington U., 1912-13; LL.D., Georgetown U., 1975; m. William E. Leahy, Nov. 26, 1913 (dec. June 1956). Asst. vol. tchr. ARC, Washington, 1917-20, 39-41, chmn. Motor Corps, 1942-45, Grey Lady, Walter Reed Hosp., 1945-56; chmn. blood donor service, 1956-59, chmn. nursing services, 1959-69; pres. ladies bd. Georgetown U. Hosp., 1950-52; now active ARC, Georgetown Hosp., Nat. Captial Law League. Episcopalian. Clubs: Twentieth Century. Columbia Country (ltd. mem.) Cosmos (asso.). The Washington (v.p. 1958-59) (Washington); Am. Newspaper Women's, Rotary. Home: 3325 Garfield St NW Washington DC 20008

LEAHY, PATRICK JOSEPH, U.S. senator; b. Montpelier, Vt., Mar. 31, 1940; s. Howard and Alba (Zambon) L.; B.A., St. Michael's Coll., Vt., 1961; J.D., Georgetown U., 1964; m. Marcelle Pomerleau, Aug. 25, 1962; children—Kevin, Alica, Mark. Admitted to Vt. bar, 1964; U.S. Supreme Ct. bar; state's atty., Chittenden County Burlington, 1966-75; U.S. senator from Vt., 1975—. Mem. Vt. Bar Assn. Office: 232 Russell Senate Office Bldg Washington DC 20510

LEAHY, THOMAS FRANCIS, broadcasting exec.; b. N.Y.C., June 30, 1937; s. Thomas Donald and Mary Ann (McCarthy) L.; B.E.E., Manhattan Coll., 1959; m. Patricia B. Flanagan, May 5, 1962; children—Patricia Ann, Allison, Thomas Francis, Kirstin Elizabeth. Sales service ABC-TV, N.Y.C., 1960-61; account exec. WGN, N.Y.C., 1961-62; account exec. WCBS-TV, N.Y.C., 1962-64, v.p., gen. mgr., 1973-77; pres. CBS TV Stas., 1977—; account exec. CBS TV Network Sales, Chgo., 1964-66, N.Y.C., 1966-69, dir. daytime sales, 1969-71; v.p. sales CBS TV Stas., N.Y.C., 1971-73. Mem. pres.'s council Fordham U., 1978—; mem. TV Advt. Bur.; past bd. dirs. Red Cross of Greater N.Y.; trustee Big Bros. of N.Y. Served with U.S. Army, 1959-65. Mem. Internat. Soc. Radio and TV, Nat. Acad. TV Arts and Scis. Clubs: Friars; Siwanoy Country. Home: 25 Studio Lane Bronxville NY 10708 Office: 51 W 52 St New York City NY 10019

LEAHY, WILLIAM F., lawyer, ret. ins. co. exec.; b. N.Y.C., July 28, 1913; s. William F. and Anna (Murphy) L.; pre-law certificate Coll. City N.Y., 1936; LL.B. cum laude, Bklyn. Law Sch., 1939, LL.M., 1940; m. Catherine Patricia Carlin, Oct. 19, 1940; children—William C., Michael J. Admitted to N.Y. bar, 1940; with Met. Life Ins. Co., N.Y.C., 1932-78, asso. gen. counsel, 1962-65, v.p. real estate financing, 1965-76, sr. v.p., 1976-78; dir. City Title Ins. Co., Dollar Fed. Savs. & Loan Assn., Malverne, N.Y., Bd. govs. N.Y. Real Estate Bd. Served to lt. col. USAAF, 1941-46. Mem. Am. Bar Assn., N.Y. State Title Assn. Home: 34 Roosevelt Ave Lynbrook NY 11563 Office: 1 Madison Ave New York City NY 10010

LEAHY, WILLIAM HAROLD, assn. exec.; b. Hopkinton, Mass., Oct. 9, 1897; s. John Henry and Mary (Harrall) L.; student Boston U., 1918-19; LL.B., Suffolk U., 1924; J.D., 1968; m. Anna Mary Healy, Sept. 26, 1928. Admitted to Mass. bar, 1926; with Dennison Mfg. Co., Framingham, Mass., 1917-20, 22-65, mgr. advt., 1930-38, corp. gen. counsel, 1938-65. Mem. Framingham Fin. Com., 1939-50; dir. Framingham Civil Def. Unit, 1953-56; chmn. Framingham Hist. Commn., 1973—; pres. Framingham Hist., Natural History Soc., 1969—. Corporator, Framingham Union Hosp., Framingham Civic League. Served with U.S. Army, 1918. Legion. Author: How to Put the Win in Windows, 1933; How to Protect Business Ideas, 1936; Analysis of Robinson-Patman Decisions, 1946. Home: 25 Swift Rd Framingham MA 01701

LEAL, JOSEPH ROGERS, chemist; b. New Bedford, Mass., Sept. 14, 1918; s. Joaquim S. and Mary C. (Rogers) L.; diploma Southeastern Mass. U., 1940; B.S. summa cum laude, U. Mass., 1949; Ph.D. (Frederick Gardner Cottrell fellow, Corn Industries Research fellow), Ind. U., 1953; m. Mary Desmond, Apr. 25, 1944; children—Joseph E., Michael J., Patricia M., Victoria A. Asst. chemist CPC Internat., Edgewater, N.J., 1940-42; asst. chemist Revere Copper & Brass Co., New Bedford, Mass., 1942-43, 45-46; chemist Am. Cyanamid Co., Bound Brook, N.J., 1952-57, tech. rep., Washington, 1957-63, mgr. contract relations, Stamford, Conn., 1963-67; sr. staff asso. Celanese Research Co., Summit, N.J., 1967—. Served with U.S. Army, 1943-45. Mem. Am. Chem. Soc., AAAS, Am. Inst. Chemists, Soc. Advancement Materials and Process Engring., N.Y. Acad. Scis., Am. Def. Preparedness Assn., Sigma Xi. Home: 10 S Crescent Maplewood NJ 07040 Office: Box 1000 Summit NJ 07901

LEAMAN, DAVID MARTIN, cardiologist; b. Lancaster, Pa., Apr. 24, 1935; s. Benjamin Denlinger and Elsie Mae (Martin) L.; student Franklin and Marshall Coll., 1956-58; B.A., Eastern Mennonite Coll., 1960; M.D., Temple U., 1964; m. Jean Heisey, Aug. 20, 1960; children—Gretchen Jane, Heidi Jean, Erika Ingrid. Intern, Mary Hitchcock Meml. Hosp., Hanover, N.H., 1964-65, resident, 1965-66; resident cardiology U. Vt. Hosp., Burlington, 1968-71; faculty Pa. State U., Hershey Med. Center, 1971—, asso. prof. medicine, 1977—; academic practice medicine specializing in cardiology, Hershey, 1971—. Mem. Lower Dauphin (Pa.) Sch. Bd., 1977—; vice chmn. Conewago Twp. Planning Commn., 1973-77. Served with USPHS, 1966-68. Research grantee NIH, 1968-71. Fellow Am. Coll. Cardiology, Am. Heart Assn., ACP, Am. Coll. Chest Physicians; mem. Heart Assn., ACP, Am. Coll. Chest Physicians, Am. Coll. Angiology; mem. Alpha Omega Alpha. Republican. Mennonite. Contbr. articles to profl. publs. Home: 53 Woodbine Dr Hershey PA 17033 Office: Dept Cardiology Hershey Med Center Pa State U Hershey PA 17033

LEAR, ERWIN, anesthesiologist; b. Bridgeport, Conn., Jan. 1, 1924; s. Samuel Joseph and Ida (Ruth) L.; M.D., State U. N.Y. Downstate Med. Center, 1952; m. Arlene Joyce Alexander, Feb. 15, 1953; children—Stephanie, Samuel. Intern, L.I. Coll. Hosp., Bklyn., 1952-53; asst. resident anesthesiology Jewish Hosp., Bklyn., 1953-54, sr. resident, 1955, asst., 1955-56, adj., 1956-58, asso. anesthesiologist, 1958-64; attending anesthesiologist Bklyn. VA Hosp., 1958-64, cons., 1977—; asso. vis. anesthesiologist Kings County Hosp. Center, Bklyn., 1957—; vis. anesthesiologist Queens Gen. Hosp. Center, 1955-67; dir. anesthesiology Queens Hosp. Center Jamaica, 1964-67, cons., 1968—; chmn. dept. anesthesiology Catholic Med. Center Queens and Bklyn., 1968—; clin. instr. State U. N.Y. Coll. Medicine, Bklyn., 1955-58, clin. asst. prof., 1958-64, clin. asso. prof., 1964—. Served with USNR, 1942-45. Diplomate Am. Bd. Anesthesiology, Nat. Bd. Med. Examiners. Fellow Am. Coll. Anesthesiologists; mem. AMA, Am. (chmn. com. on communications 1968-69, ho. of dels. 1973—), N.Y. State (chmn. pub. relations 1963-73, chmn. com. on local arrangements 1968-73, dist. dir. 1972-73, v.p. 1974-75, pres. 1976—, chmn. jud. com. 1977—, asso. editor Bull. 1963—) socs. anesthesiologists, N.Y. State (chmn. sect. on anesthesiology 1966-67, sec. sect. 1977—), Queens County med. socs. Author: Chemistry Applied Pharmacology of Tranquilizers; contbr. articles in field to profl. jours. Address: 18 Holiday Park Dr Williston Park NY 11596

LEARNARD, WILLIAM EWING, bus. exec.; b. Joliet, Ill., July 21, 1935; s. Roy Stevens and Clara Daphne (Ewing) L.; B.A., Trinity Coll., 1957; m. Susan Diane Douglas-Willan, Oct. 1, 1960; children—Matthew Douglas-Willan, Roger Ewing, Vanessa Baldwin. Trainee, pub. relations Smith, Kline & French Labs., Phila., 1957-58, exec. pub. relations, govt. relations, 1961-78, v.p. corporate affairs Smith Kline Corp., Phila., 1978—. Mem. Pa. Gov.'s Sci. Adv. Panel, Shafer, 1971-72, Gov.'s Mgmt. Task Force, Shapp, 1972-73, Pa. Pub. Welfare Adv. Com., 1973-74. Bd. dirs. Allergy Found. Am. Served to capt. USAF, 1958-61. Club: Phila. Cricket. Home: 48 Hillcrest Ave Philadelphia PA 19118 Office: 1500 Spring Garden St Philadelphia PA 19101

LEARY, DANIEL FRANCIS, architect; b. Syracuse, N.Y., Sept. 4, 1939; s. Gerald Richard and Erna L. (Fischer) L.; B.Arch. (Alumni scholar), Rensselaer Poly. Inst., 1961; m. Gretchen Baker, June 17, 1961; children—Daniel Lawrence, Shawn Gerard, Christopher Joseph, Kelly Ann. Instr., Hudson Valley Community Coll., 1960-62; draftsman, project capt., designer J.A. Cappuccilli, architect, Syracuse, 1962-65; project capt. N.L. Caruso, architect, Syracuse, 1965-66; pvt. practice as architect, Syracuse, 1966—; v.p. Asso. Architects (P.C.), Syracuse, N.Y., 1971—; supr. Town of Onondaga (N.Y.), 1976-77. Cub Scout committeeman Hiawatha council Boy Scouts Am., 1970-72; constrn. div. chmn. United Fund, Onondaga County, N.Y., 1972-73; mem. local bd. SSS, 1972-76; mem. Syracuse Landmarks Preservation Bd., 1976—; Dem. chmn. Town of Onondaga, 1978—. Bd. dirs. Onondaga County Planning Fedn., Onondaga Free Library, 1978—. Recipient Beatrice Fishbach Meml. Found. award in architecture, 1960-61. Mem. AIA (dir. central N.Y. chpt. 1972-73, v.p. 1974), Nat. Council Archtl. Registration Bds., N.Y. State Assn. Architects. Roman Catholic. Clubs: Onondaga Cycling (Syracuse); League Am. Wheelmen (nat.). Home: 5100 Harris Rd Camillus NY 13031 Office: 528 Oak St Syracuse NY 13203

LEARY, HERBERT JOSEPH, surgeon; b. Syracuse, N.Y., Aug. 18, 1924; s. Herbert Benedict and Ellen Agnes (McGraw) L.; B.Chem.E., Syracuse U., 1944; M.D., Upstate Med. Center, Syracuse, 1948; m. Mary Teresa Maher, May 24, 1952; children—Ellen Marie, Brian Joseph, John Patrick, James, Paul, Dennis Michael. Intern, Upstate Med. Center, Syracuse, 1948-49, resident in surgery, 1949-50; teaching fellow pathology Syracuse Med. Coll., 1950, cancer fellow, 1951; instr. surgery Upstate Med. Center, 1952, asst. clin. prof. surgery, 1952-55; pvt. practice specializing in gen. surgery, Dutchess County, N.Y., 1958—; dir. surgery Mid-Hudson Med. Group; attending surgeon Vassar Bros., St. Francis hosps. (Poughkeepsie, N.Y.); cons. surgery VA Hosp., Syracuse, 1952-55; attending surgeon Syracuse U., Meml. hosps., 1952-55. Liaison fellow Cancer Commn., State of N.Y. A.C.S., 1968—. Served to capt. M.C., USAF, 1955-57. Diplomate Am. Bd. Surgery, Nat. Bd. Med. Examiners. Fellow A.C.S.; mem. N.Y. State, Dutchess County (dir. 1976—, bd. censors 1977-78) med. socs., AMA, Mid-Hudson Surgery Soc. (council 1975—, pres. 1978—). Roman Catholic. Club: Dutchess Golf and Country. Contbr. articles to profl. jours. Home: 38 Slate Hill Dr Poughkeepsie NY 12603 Office: Mid Hudson Medical Group Main and Jackson Sts Fishkill NY 12524

LEASK, JOHN MCPHERSON, accountant; b. Bridgeport, Conn., Oct. 21, 1942; s. Haldane Burgess and Laura (Manchester) L.; student U. Mich., 1961-67; A.Sci. in Accounting, Bryant Coll., 1972, B.S. in Accounting, 1973. Salesman, Winthrop Labs. div. Sterling Drugs, Hartford, Conn., Providence, 1968-73; partner Leask & Leask, C.P.A.'s, P.C., Fairfield, Conn., 1973—; instr. Fairfield (Conn.) U., 1976—. Mem. Town of Fairfield Library Bldg. Com., 1977—; v.p. fin. Child Care of Greater Bridgeport (Conn.), 1976—, Daycare and Neighbor Facilities Devel. Corp., 1977—; co-chmn. budget and fin. com. Greater Bridgeport Regional Narcotics, Inc., 1978—. Mem. Am. Inst. C.P.A.'s, Conn Soc. C.P.A.'s. Republican. Baptist. Club: Rotary. Home: PO Box 1468 Fairfield CT 06430 Office: Leask & Leask CPAs 1177 Post Rd Fairfield CT 06430

LEATHAM, JOHN TONKIN, ins. exec.; b. Chgo., July 4, 1936; s. Chester and Betty (Collins) L.; B.A., Lawrence U., 1958; m. Sheila K. Andersen, Sept. 13, 1958; children—Lisa M., John A., Bronwen Gay, Douglas Q. Asst. cashier, lending officer Continental Ill. Nat. Bank & Trust Co., Chgo., 1962-68; with Reliance Group, Inc. (formerly Leasco Corp.), N.Y.C., 1968—, treas., 1968-69, v.p., 1969-71, sr. v.p., 1971-72, chief fin. officer, 1971—, exec. v.p., chief operating officer, 1972—, also dir., mem. exec. com.; dir. ORI, Inc., Reliance Ins. Co. Nat. bd. dirs. Reading is Fundamental, Inc. Served to 1st lt. USAF, 1958-62. Mem. Lawrence U. Alumni Assn. (dir. 1965-71, 2d v.p. 1966-68, v.p. 1968-70). Clubs: Union League (Chgo.); Country (Darien, Conn.). Home: 6 Hummingbird Ln Darien CT 06820 Office: 919 Third Ave New York City NY 10022

LEATON, EDWARD K., actuarial and cons. co. exec.; b. Mt. Vernon, N.Y., Oct. 2, 1928; s. Lionel M. and Henrietta (Kline) L.; B.S. in Mech. Engring., Lehigh U., 1949; M.B.A., Yale U., 1950; m. Janet Kemp; children—Edward M., Kenneth (dec.), William (dec.), Robert, Thomas, James, Richard. Grad. instr. Yale U., 1949-50; from trainee to asst. supt. Gen. Motors Corp., 1950-54; asst. to exec. v.p. Rowe Mfg. Corp., Whippany, N.J., 1955-56, v.p., dir. mfg., 1956-57; cons. Lambert M. Huppeler Co., Inc., N.Y.C., 1957-69, exec. v.p., 1969-74, pres., chief exec. officer, 1974-78, chmn. bd., pres., chief exec. officer, 1978—, also dir.; pres. Leaton & Huppeler Co., Inc., N.Y.C., 1967—, also dir.; gen. agt. Leaton Agy., N.Y.C. Mem. leadership com. Community Fund; sr. warden, lay reader St. Paul's Ch. Trustee Barrington (R.I.) Coll. Mem. Am. Ordnance Assn. (pres. Lehigh Valley post 1948-49), Life Mgrs. Assn. N.Y. (pres., dir.), Life Underwriters Assn. N.Y.C. (chmn. bd.), Am. Soc. Pension Actuaries (v.p., dir.), Nat. Assn. Pension Cons. and Adminstrs. (v.p., dir.), Assn. Advanced Life Underwriters, Am. Soc. C.L.U.'s, Am. Mgmt. Assn., Am. Pension Conf. Clubs: Union League, Yale (N.Y.C.); Country of Darien (gov., trustee), Nutmeg Curling (Darien, Conn.); Mid-Ocean (Tucker's Town, Bermuda). Contbr. articles to profl. jours.; speaker before numerous nat. and regional orgns. Office: 430 Park Ave New York City NY 10022

LEAVITT, DAVID HARRIS, govt. ofcl.; b. Bklyn., N.Y., Oct. 4, 1932; s. Philip and Rhoda (Levine) L.; A.S., Miami-Dade Coll., 1963; m. Benece Goldfarb, Mar. 6, 1965; children—Craig Steven, Renee Philece. Mgr., Housing and Home Finance Agy., Washington, 1963-67; mgmt. analyst Civil Service Commn., Washington, 1967-68; paperwork mgr. Nat. Archives and Records Service, Washington, 1969-70; mgmt. analyst Nat. Hwy. Traffic Safety Adminstrn., Washington, 1971-74; mgr. Agr. Mktg. Service, U.S. Dept. Agr., Washington, 1974—. Mem. Fed. Paperwork Commn. Task Force, 1976. Served with USAF, 1953-56. Recipient Nat. Jr. Achievement award, 1949, Jaycee Spoke award, 1961, High Quality Performance award Nat. Hwy. Traffic Safety Adminstrn., 1973, 11th Ann. Fed. Paperwork Mgmt. award of Spl. Merit, U.S. Dept. Agr., 1975. Mem. Assn. Rcords Mgrs. and Adminstrs., Internat. Word Processing Assn., Nat. Microfilm Assn. Contbr. articles in field to profl. jours. Home: 409 Dorchester Rd Falls Church VA 22046 Office: Room 1094 South Bldg United States Dept Agriculture Washington DC 20250

LEAVITT, FREDERIC PERLEY, JR., civil engr.; b. Peabody, Mass., Apr. 25, 1931; s. Frederic Perley and Cora Louis (Currier) L.; diploma N.W. Schs. Jet Engine Tech., 1958; grad. Inst. for Cert. Engring. Technicians, 1974; m. Vera May Bowers, July 23, 1954; children—Frederic Thomas, Jeffrey Scott, Laura Ann. Final assembly foreman Cannon Elec. Co., 1963-64; dept. foreman Webster Industries, Salem, Mass., 1964-65; with Mass. Air N.G., 1965—, br. chief base civil engring., ops. and maintenance, 1973—. Sec. Plymouth (Mass.) Sch. Bldg. Com., 1965-68. Served with USNR, 1949-53, USAF, 1959-63. Recipient Air Force Meritorious Service award; cert. asso. engring. technician. Mem. Mass. Air N.G. Hist. Assn., Air Civil Engring. Assn. Club: Monument Beach Sportsman's. Research on pollution equipment. Home: PO Box 775 30 Spinnaker Ln Pocasset MA 02559 Office: Base Civil Engineering Bldg 971 Otis Air Force Base MA 02542

LEAVITT, URBAN JAMES DESROSIER, supt. schs.; b. Orlando, Fla., July 10, 1924; married, 3 children. B.S. in Elementary Edn. and English, U. Tex., Austin, 1954, M.Ed. in Ednl. Adminstrn., 1956, Ed.D. in Ednl. Adminstrn., 1960. Supt. schs., Bay Village, Ohio, 1961-64, Roslyn, N.Y., 1964-70, Aurora, Colo., 1970-74; supt. schs. Somerville (Mass.) pub. schs., 1974—. Mem. steering com. Cambridge and Somerville Program for Alcoholism Rehab., 1974—, Somerville Bicentennial Commn., 1974—; bd. corporators Somerville Hosp.; mem. Mayor's Task Force on Drug Abuse, Citizen's Health Adv. Com. Mem. Mass. Assn. Sch. Supts., Am., New Eng. assns. sch. adminstrs., New Eng. Sch. Devel. Council, Mass. Reading Assn., Assn. for Supervision and Curriculum Devel., Assn. for Children with Learning Disabilities, Phi Delta Kappa. Recipient numerous awards. Certified supt., Ohio, N.Y., Pa., Colo., Mass. Office: 81 Highland Ave Somerville MA 02143

LEAVY, LYNNE R., social worker; b. Bklyn., Mar. 8, 1931; d. George and Perle G. (Goldman) Zuckerman; B.S. in Edn. and Sociology, L.I. U., 1953; M.S. in Counseling, Hofstra U., 1973; M.S.W., N.Y. U., 1977; m. Jack M. Leavy, Oct. 4, 1953; children—Jeffrey Alan, Roger Scott. Tchr. elementary schs. Plainedge Pub. Sch. System, Massepequa, N.Y., 1953-55, pub. schs., Woodmere, Hewlett, N.Y., 1960-65; faculty lectr. social sci. div. Laguardia Community Coll., City U. N.Y., 1973—; social worker Little People Am., NCCJ, Downs Syndrome Assn. Nassau County; group leader Johns Hopkins Hosp. Moore Clinic, Balt.; cons. social work; mem. N.Y.C. Mayor's Com. for Handicapped; tchr. adult edn. Recipient Pub. Service award Little People Am., 1976. Mem. Nat. Assn. Social Workers, Am., N.Y., personnel, guidance assns., Mental Health Assn. Nassau County, NCCJ, Nat. Council Jewish Women, Panel Ams. Jewish. Club: B'nai B'rith. Research on psychosocial aspects of dwarfism. Home: 184 Bay Dr Woodmere NY 11598 Office: North Shore Univ Hosp Child Devel Center 300 Community Dr Manhasset NY 11030

LEBEAU, BERNARD ADOLPH, educator, writing center specialist; b. Adams, Mass., Apr. 10, 1925; s. Joseph D. and Georgiana E. (Genereux) LeB.; A.B., Bowdoin Coll., 1949; A.M., Harvard, 1950; M.L.A., Johns Hopkins, 1973. Tchr. English, Emerson Inst., Washington, 1951-66; asso. prof. English, Montgomery Coll., Rockville, Md., 1966—. Trustee, Washington Hall Jr. Coll., Washington. Served with AUS, 1945-46. Mem. AAUP, Modern Lang. Assn. Am., Nat. Council Tchr. English. Office: Dept English Montgomery Coll Rockvlle MD 20850

LEBEDOFF, VICTOR RICHARD, historian; b. Cando, Sask., Can., Sept. 14, 1915; s. Elia and Matrona (Klushnichenko) L.; B.A., Columbia Union Coll., 1947; M.A., Andrews U., 1958; Ph.D., U. Md., 1965; m. Catherine May Zalinko, July 23, 1939. Profl. photographer, Sask., Can., 1934-43; ministerial intern, Can., 1943-45; supt. schs., French W.I. and Haiti, 1947-61; asst. prof. history So. Miss. Coll., 1965-66; asst. prof. history D.C. Tech. Coll. (now U. D.C.), Washington, 1966-69, asso. prof., 1969-74, prof., 1974—; dir. Voix de l'Esperance radio broadcasts, Haiti, 1958-61. Elder, Seventh-day Adventist Ch., Haiti, 1947-61, Sligo, Wash., 1961-65, Tenn., 1965-66, Washington, 1970—. Mem. Nat. Geog. Soc., Am. Acad. Polit. and Social Sci., Am. Hist. Assn., Nat. Council Social Studies, NEA. Contbr. articles to profl. jours. Home: 2116 Charleston Pl Hyattsville MD 20783 Office: 425 2d St NW Washington DC 20009

LEBEGERN, CHARLES HOWARD, JR., govt. ofcl.; b. Wilmington, Del., Aug. 12, 1927; s. Charles Howard and Helen Geneva (Burrows) L.; B.A., U. Del., 1950; m. Esther Ellen Rowley, Nov. 1, 1952; children—Janet, Carla. With firing tables br. Ballistics Research Lab., Dept. Army, Dept. Def., Aberdeen Proving Ground, Md., 1950—, supervisory mathematician, 1959-64, chief br., 1964—; U.S. del arty. panel NATO, 1960—, chmn. ballistics panel, 1976—; chmn. Joint Munitions Effectiveness Manuals for Surface to Surface Arty., 1967—; mem. Study Adv. Group Arty. Accuracy Analysis, 1974. Chmn. nominating com. Rolling Green (Md.) Community Assn., 1971; bd. dirs. Churchville (Md.) Day Care Center. Served with

USNR, 1945-46. Recipient Sustained Superior Performance award Dept. Army, 1960, Meritorious Civilian Service award, 1972. Mem. Am. Def. Preparedness Assn. Presbyterian (ruling elder 1973—, supt. Sunday sch. 1970-74, chmn. stewardship, music coms. 1973—). Home: 200 Finney Ave Churchville MD 21028 Office: Ballistic Research Lab Aberdeen Proving Ground MD 21005*

LEBEL, GIRARD RICHARD, banker; b. Salem, Mass., Mar. 13, 1929; s. Alfred P. and Marie (Gagnon) L.; B.B.A., Northeastern U., 1958; grad. U. Wis. Banking Sch., 1970; m. Jean B. Mitchell, May 16, 1953; children—Christine A., Fredric C., Suzanne M. Instr., Burdett Coll., Lynn, Mass., 1958-68; mgr. accounting Essex County Bank & Trust Co., Lynn, 1953-66; v.p. Bay Bank & Trust Co., Beverly, Mass., 1966—. Instr. Am. Inst. Banking, Salem, Mass., 1971-78. Served with AUS, 1951-53. Mem. Mass. Assn. Pub. Accountants, Beverly C. of C., North Shore Clearing House Assn. (sec.-treas. 1972-73), Bank Adminstrn. Inst. (dir.). Home: 14 Cherry St Wenham MA 01984 Office: 165 Cabot St Beverly MA 01915

LEBEL, ROBERT, bishop; b. Trois-Pistoles, Que., Can., Aug. 11, 1924; s. Wilfrid and Alexina (Belanger) L.; B.A., U. Laval, 1946; Lic. Theology, U. St. Paul, Ottawa, Ont., 1950; Th.D., Angelicum U., Rome, 1951. Ordained priest, 1950; consecrated bishop, 1974; bishop of Valleyfield, Que., 1976—. Bd. dirs. Canadian Cath. Conf. Bishops; pres. theology com. Assemblee des Eveques du Que. Home and office: 31 Fabrique St Valleyfield PQ J6T 4G9 Canada*

LEBHERZ, RICHARD THOMAS, columnist, drama critic; b. Frederick, Md., Nov. 3, 1921; s. Harry J. and Mary (Hershberger) L.; student St. Johns Lit. Inst., Frederick, Md., 1927-39, Columbia U., 1947-48, Inst. Contemporary Arts, Washington, 1950-51. Copyboy, Time mag., N.Y.C., 1946-47; advt. mgr. William S. Hood, Frederick, 1960-62; columnist Frederick News Post, 1965-75; freelance writer Washington Post, Washington Star News, Queen mag., London; contbg. editor Memo Mag., Washington, 1973-74. Bd. dirs. Frederick County Landmarks Found., 1972. Served with USAF, 1942-45: ETO. Mem. Am. Theatre Critics Assn., Nat. Press Club. Author: The Altars of the Heart, 1957; The Nazi Overcoat, 1967; The Man in the White Raincoat, 1965; Conversations With Practically Everybody, 1977. Home: Rt 6 Box 182 Parkview Apts Frederick MD 21701

LEBLANC, ALDOR JOSEPH OLIVIER, health care adminstr.; b. College Bridge, N.B., Can., July 12, 1927; s. Antoine O. and Ella M. LeBlanc; student St. Joseph U., 1941-45; C.P.H.I., Canadian Pub. Health Assn., 1953; E.Co.M., Canadian Hosp. Assn., 1976; m. Colombe Leger, July 27, 1949; children—Janice, Muriel, Conrad, Gilles, Monette, Gaetan. Pub. health insp. Municipality, Westmoreland County, Moncton, N.B., 1951-55, chief health insp. Westmorland County Bd. Health, 1955-65; regional supr. N.B. Provincial Dept. Health, 1965-67; provincial dir. div. environ. health, 1967-70; dir., adminstr. Villa Providence, Shediac, N.B., 1970—. Mem. Greater Moncton Town Planning Com., 1960-70; chmn. Shediac Town Planning Commn., 1973—. Registered sanitarian, Can. Fellow Royal Soc. Health; mem. Canadian Inst. Pub. Health Insps., Canadian Pub. Health Assn. (certified pub. health insp.), Canadian Coll. Health Execs., Canadian Hosp. Assn., Am. Coll. Nursing Homes. Liberal. Roman Catholic. Club: Beausejour Curling. Home: 24 Smith Ave Shediac NB E0A 3G0 Canada Office: 215 Main St Shediac NB E0A 3G0 Canada

LE BLANC, JOHN ROGER, chemist; b. Montreal, Que., Can., Feb. 7, 1927; s. Ubald Donat and Alice Amanda (Le Clerc) Le B.; came to U.S., 1934, derivative citizenship, 1944; B.S. in Chemistry, Boston Coll., 1950; M.S. in Chemistry (Monsanto scholar), Ohio State U., 1960; m. Dorothy J. Sweeney, Dec. 27, 1948; children—John, Lawrence, Paul, Suzanne, Stephen, James, Michele. Supr. mfg.-control lab. Monsanto Co., East St. Louis, Ill., 1950-52, supr. mfg., 1952-53; research chemist central research, Dayton, Ohio, 1953-60, plastics research, Springfield, Mass., 1961-64, research group leader, 1964—. Mem. Wilbraham (Mass.) Democratic Town Com., 1965-67. Served with USN, 1945-46. Mem. Am. Chem. Soc. (editor Val Chemist 1963-65). Roman Catholic. Contbr. articles to profl. publs.; patentee in field. Home: 34 Decorie Dr Wilbraham MA 01095 Office: 190 Grochral Ave Indian Orchard MA 01051

LEBOVITZ, SOL, coll. dean; b. Brockton, Mass., Apr. 23, 1915; s. Meyer and Rose (Jankleson) L.; B.S., Boston U., 1942; A.M. (Thayer fellow), Harvard U., 1943, Ph.D., 1949; m. Carmen Henriette Bary, Apr. 23, 1945; children—Francoise Sara Lebovitz Puniello, Michelle Annick Berthe Lebovitz Lamar. Exec. asst. Dictaphone Corp., N.Y.C., 1957-62; mem. faculty Bryant Coll., Smithfield, R.I., 1962—, prof. polit. sci., 1965—, chmn. dept. social scis., 1963-69, dean Grad. Sch., 1969—. Served with AUS, 1944-46; ETO. Mem. Am. Polit. Sci. Assn., Internat. Studies Assn., Am. Soc. Pub. Adminstrn., Acad. Mgmt., Am. Mgmt. Assn., R.I. World Affairs Council (exec. bd.), Providence Com. on Fgn. Relations. Clubs: Rotary, Turks Head. Home: 15 Governor Bradford Dr Barrington RI 02806 Office: Grad Sch Bryant College Smithfield RI 02917

LEBOWITZ, MARSHALL, pub. co. exec.; b. Boston, Mar. 4, 1923; s. Max Nathan and Rissah (Zangwill) L.; A.B., Harvard, 1942; m. Charlotte Lily Meyersohn, Aug. 7, 1949; children—Wendy Ann, Marian Kay, Mark Louis. Statis. analyst U.S. WPB, Washington, 1942-43; periodicals mgr. J.S. Canner & Co., Boston, 1946-68, gen. mgr., 1968—. Mem. Natick (Mass.) Planning Bd., 1964-69, chmn., 1968-69; mem. Natick Town Meeting, 1954—, chmn. town by-laws revision com., 1965-67; pres. Greater Framingham Mental Health Assn., 1963-64, dir. 1954-63; mem. Greater Framingham Mental Health Area Bd., 1972-78, v.p., 1974-75, pres., 1975-77; mem. Regional Drug Rev. Bd., 1973; chmn. Natick Regional Vocat. Sch. Planning Com., 1974-77; mem. Natick Sch. Com., 1978—; mem. trustees adv. council Leonard Morse Hosp., 1973—, vice chmn., 1974—, mem. mental health adv. com., 1972—. Served with AUS, 1943-46. Jewish religion (financial sec. temple 1954-46, treas. 1952-54, vice-chmn. bd. 1958-59). Home: 2 Abbott Rd Natick MA 01760 Office: 49-65 Lansdowne St Boston MA 02215

LEBOWITZ, SHELDON HOWARD, electronic engr.; b. Bklyn., Nov. 14, 1941; s. Joseph and Margaret (Gersch) L.; A.A.S., S.I. Community Coll., 1961; B.E.E. Coll. City N.Y., 1964; m. Sheila Shein, Aug. 21, 1965; children—Michael Paul, Todd Jeffrey, Julie Beth. Engr., Electromagnetic Compatibility Analysis Center, Annapolis, Md., 1965-67, Norden div. United Aircraft, Norwalk, Conn., 1967-69; mem. tech. staff Computer Sci. Corp., Falls Church, Va., 1969-74, Comsat Labs., Clarksburg, Md., 1974—; pres. Computer Analysts Ltd.; instr. math. Strayer Coll. Recipient service award S.I. Community Coll., 1961; honorable mention award Computer Sci. Corp., 1973. Mem. Smithsonian Inst. (asso). Democrat. Jewish. Patentee light entertainment device. Contbr. articles in field to Comsat Tech. Review, Nat. Tele-Communication Conf. Home: 12904 Buccaneer Rd Silver Spring MD 20904 Office: PO Box 115 Clarksburg MD 20734

LEBRO, THEODORE PETER, property tax service exec.; b. Fulton, N.Y., Feb. 12, 1910; s. Peter and Mary (Karpala) L.; B.S., Syracuse U., 1954; m. Wanda Saffranski, Oct. 16, 1932; Farmer nr. Fulton, 1935-76; various positions restaurants, grocery, Fulton 1929-54; owner, operator Lebro Real Estate and Ins. Agency, Fulton 1951—, dir. Real Estate Property Tax Service Agy., Fulton, 1972—. Mem. Fulton Parking Authority, 1960—; bd. dirs. Lee Meml. Hosp.; pres. Catholic Youth Orgn. Fulton, 1976—. Served with 35th inf. U.S. Army, 1942-46; PTO. Certified property mgr. Mem. Soc. Real Estate Appraisers, Oswego County Bd. Realtors, N.Y. State Soc. Appraisers, Assn. County Dirs., VFW, Am. Legion, St. Michael's Soc. (pres. 1960—). Republican. Roman Catholic. Clubs: Beaver Meadow, K.C., Elks, Pathfinders Game and Fish (life). Home: RFD 2 Box 111 Rt 48S Phoenix NY 13135 Office: 316 W 1st St Fulton NY 13069

LECCA, PEDRO JUAN, health care adminstr.; b. N.Y.C., Mar. 28, 1936; s. Pedro and Angela R. (Melendez) L.; B.S., in Pharmacy, Fordham U., 1962; M.S., L.I. U., 1967; Ph.D. in Health Care, U. Miss., 1970; postgrad. (HEW fellow) U. City N.Y., Mt. Sinai Med. Sch., 1972; m. Gina Puma, July 6, 1963; children—Peter, Vincent, Anthony. Adminstr., Apothecary in Bronx, N.Y., 1963-66; research scientist Vick Research & Devel., Mt. Vernon, N.Y., 1966-68; asst. prof. pharmacy and health adminstrn. dept. U. Ill., Chgo., 1970-72, acting chmn. dept. health care adminstrn., 1970-72; spl. prin. health planner N.Y.C. Mental Health, 1973-74; asst. commr. of interagy. affairs N.Y.C. Dept. of Mental Health, 1974—; adj. prof. Grad. Sch. Pub. Adminstrn., N.Y. U., 1975—; adj. asso. prof. St. John's U., 1977—; adj. prof. pub. health York Coll., City U. N.Y., 1977—; lectr. Coll. Podiatric Medicine, N.Y.C., 1977; cons. health care Nat. Center for Health Services Research, HEW, Rockville, Md., 1976—, other govt. agys., also Human Services Mgmt. Assos., N.Y., N.C., 1975—, Coalition Spanish Speaking Mental Health Orgns., 1975—, Health Research and Analysis, Los Angeles, 1976—. Mem. adv. com. 9th Pan-Am. Congress, Panama, 1972. Served with USAF, 1954-58. Named Airman of the Month, 1955, 56. Mem. Am. (standing com. on constn. and by-laws 1975-78, program planning com. 1974—, pres. Latino caucus 1976-77), N.Y.C. (officer program com. 1975-76) pub. health assns., Am. Pharm. Assn., Hispanic Assn. of Health Services Execs. (v.p. 1975-76), Am. Social Health Assn., Puerto Rican Assn. Health Affairs, Lamar Assn. of Internat. Law, Rho Chi, Kappa Psi. Roman Catholic. Club: N.Y. Borinquen Lions. Author: (with Patrick Tharp) Principles of Management for Students and Practitioners, 1974, Health Care and Institutional Systems, 1977; chpt. in Organizations in Health Care Settings, 1977; contbr. articles on health services to profl. publs. Home: 34 Young Ave Pelham NY 10803 Office: NYC Dept Mental Health 93 Worth St New York City NY 10013

LECHENE, CLAUDE PIERRE, physiologist; b. Paris, Mar. 16, 1933; s. Leon Robert and Rose L.; Baccalaureat Latin Scis., Lycee Janson de Sailly, 1949, Math., Lycee St. Louis, 1950, 51, Spec. Math., Lycee Louis le Grand, 1952; cert. advanced studies, U. Paris, 1963, M.D., 1965; 1 dau., Valerie Lechene. Externe, Hosps. Paris, 1955-59, intern, 1960; research asso. Nat. Center Sci. Research, Paris, 1962-70; investigator Atomic Energy Commn. Center Nuclear Studies, Saclay, France, 1962-68; prof. physiology U. Sherbrooke (Can.), 1968-72, asso. dir. div. basic scis., 1971-72; asso. prof. medicine U. Paris, 1970-73; dir. nat. biotech. resource in electron probe microanalysis Harvard U. Med. Sch., Boston, 1972—, vis. prof. physiology, 1972—. Served with French Navy, 1960-62. NIH grantee, 1972. Mem. Am. Soc. Nephrology, Am. Fedn. Clin. Research, Internat. Soc. Nephrology, Fedn. Am. Scientists for Exptl. Biology, Am. Physiol. Soc., Microbeam Analysis Soc. Club: Salt and Water, Red Blood Cells. Home: 26 Whittemore St West Roxbury MA 02132 Office: Harvard Med Sch 45 Shattuck St Boston MA 02115

LECHNER, HERBERT DEAN, mfg. co. exec.; b. Salina, Kans., Nov. 8, 1932; B.A., U. Kans., 1953, postgrad., 1954; m. Barbara Jo Lechner, June 8, 1954; children—Alecia, Lynnette, Janine. Dir. IBM activities U.S. Navy, IBM, Washington, 1954-69; v.p. Computer Usage Co., Washington, 1969-70; v.p. Fireman's Fund Am. Ins. Co., San Francisco, 1970-73; sr. v.p. Am. Express Co., N.Y.C., 1973-76; v.p. Singer Co., 1976—. Served with U.S. Army. 1955-57. Mem. Am. Mgmt. Assn., Am. Math. Assn., Inst. Mgmt. Scis., Alpha Kappa Lambda. Home: 75 Colt Rd Summit NJ 07901 Office: 30 Rockefeller Plaza New York City NY 10020

LECHTRECKER, GEORGE EDWARD, lawyer; b. Bklyn., Aug. 22, 1916; s. George and Henrietta (Windecker) L.; student Coll. City N.Y., 1933-35, Alfred U., 1935-36; J.D., N.Y. U., 1939; children—Eric (dec.), Joan, Zoe, John; m. 2d, Francesca DiNaro, Aug. 28, 1972. Admitted to N.Y. bar, 1941; practiced in Patchogue, Center Moriches; sr. partner firm Dranitzke, Lechtrecker and Lechtrecker, N.Y., 1946—; atty. Town of Brookhaven (N.Y.), 1960-62; pres., gen. mgr. Island Indsl. Park of Patchogue, Inc., 1963—. Counsel, Middle Island Central Sch. Dist., 1958—; mem. med. malpractice panel Suffolk County Supreme Ct., 1977—. Mayor, Patchogue, 1952-60; chmn. Town of Brookhaven Indsl. Agy., 1979. Served with USAAF, 1942-46. Mem. N.Y. State, Suffolk County bar assns., Am. Trial Lawyers Assn., C. of C. (pres. 1964-68), Am. Arbitration Assn. (nat. panel 1964—), Suffolk County Village Ofcl. Assn. (pres. 1952-54). Democrat. Conglist. Home: 39 Bellport Ln Bellport NY 11713 Office: 73 N Ocean Ave Patchogue NY 11772

LECKBAND, GARWOOD EMERSON, physician; b. Chgo., June 25, 1935; s. Norbert Frederick and Meta (Schrader) L.; B.S., Carleton Coll., 1957; M.D., Cornell U., 1962; m. Kathleen Whalen; children—Megan, Maura. Intern, Mt. Sinai Hosp., N.Y.C., 1962-63; resident in medicine Meml. Hosp., N.Y.C., 1963-64; instr. Cornell U. Med. Coll., 1963-64; resident in medicine Lenox Hill Hosp., N.Y.C., 1966-68, fellow in cardiology, 1968-69; practice medicine specializing in internal medicine, cardiology, N.Y.C., 1969—; adj. physician Lenox Hill Hosp. Served to capt. M.C., U.S. Army, 1964-66. Diplomate Am. Bd. Internal Medicine, Am. Bd. Cardiology Mem. N.Y. Heart Assn., Med. Soc. County N.Y. Home: New York NY Office: 20 E 68th St New York NY 10021

LECLAIR, ROBERT PAUL, gymnastics coach; b. New Bedford, Mass., Mar. 28, 1946; s. Maurice Donat and Florence Clara (Morin) L.; B.S., U. Mass., Amherst, 1971; M.S. in Edn. State U. N.Y., Cortland, 1974; postgrad. Springfield Coll., 1976—; m. Ann Szafran, July 24, 1971; 1 dau., Larissa. Tchr. phys. edn. Chicopee (Mass.) Schs., 1969-70; classroom tchr. New Bedford (Mass.) Sch. Dept., 1971; instr. phys. edn., vol. Peace Corps, Morocco, 1972-73; tchr., coach Century Sch. Gymanastics, Pomona, N.Y., 1974-75, Joanne Giguere Sch. Gymnastics, Cherry Valley, Mass., 1975-76; owner, coach New Eng. Gymnastics, West Springfield, Mass., 1975—; instr., gymnastics coach Westfield (Mass.) State Coll., 1976—. Mem. U.S. Gymnastics Fedn., U.S. Gymnastics Safety Assn., U.S. Assn. Ind. Gymnastics Clubs, AAHPER, Mass. Assn. Ind. Gymnatic Clubs (v.p.), Am. Athletic Union, U.S. Tumbling and Trampoline Assn., U.S. Sports Acrobatics Assn., Nat. Gymnastics Judges Assn.-Men, Mass. Girls Gymnastics Coaches Assn. Home: 74 Althea St West Springfield MA 01089 Office: 37 Capital Dr West Springfield MA 01089

LECLERC, PAUL-ANDRE, educator; b. Pont-Rouge, Que., Can., Sept. 16, 1925; s. Eugene and Rosanna (Sanschagrin) L.; B.A., Coll. Ste. Anne at LaPocatiere, 1946; licence in theologie, Laval U., Que., 1951, licence es-lettres, 1956; D. es-lettres, Cath. Inst. Paris (France), 1966. Ordained priest Roman Cath. Ch., 1950; prof. French lit., Latin, history Coll. Ste. Anne at LaPocatiere, 1951-54, 56-64, 66-69; prof. French lit. Coll. d'Enseignement Gen. et Profl., La Pocatiere, 1969—. Mem. Hist. Soc. Cote-du-Sud (pres. 1967-74), Fedn. Hist. Socs. Que. (dir. 1969-74), Hist. Inst. French Am., Musée François-Pilote (pres.), Alumni Assn. Laval U. Address: 100 Painchaud La Pocatiere PQ G0R 1Z0 Canada

LECO, ARMAND PETER, health ins. co. exec.; b. Providence, Feb. 6, 1927; s. Armand and Susie (Virginia (Catanio) L.; B.S., Providence Coll., 1947; postgrad. U. R.I., 1948-49, Boston Sch. Law, 1949-50, Purdue U., 1974; m. Janice Louise Bostrom, Sept. 3, 1950; children—Andrea Cutler, Karen Clark, Darlene, Donna. Legal rep. Prentice-Hall, Inc., 1951-53; chem. sales rep. Dubois Chem. Co., Providence, 1953-54; zone mgr. Investors Diversified Services, Inc., Providence and southeastern Mass., 1954-57; account exec. Merrill, Lynch, Pierce, Fenner and Smith, Providence, 1957-63; dir. hosp. relations Blue Cross, Providence, 1964, asst. exec. dir., 1966-71, v.p. Blue Cross/Blue Shield, 1971-74; sr. asst. exec. dir. Delta Dental of R.I., 1974—; sr. v.p. Blue Cross/Blue Shield of R.I., 1974—; adj. prof. health care adminstrn. U. R.I., 1978. Pres. R.I. Assn. for the Blind, 1973-78, bd. dirs., 1968—; trustee R.I. Health Services Research, Inc., 1970-74; bd. dirs. Kent County Vis. Nurse Assn., 1965-72, Nat. Accreditation Council Agys. Serving Blind and Visually Handicapped, 1977—; exec. com. Cancer Control Bd. R.I.; chmn. provider relations adv. com. Blue Cross Assn.; incorporator Notre Dame Hosp., 1969, Kent County Meml. Hosp., 1968, Women and Infants Hosp. R.I., 1974, R.I. Hosp., 1976; bd. mgmt. Kent County YMCA, 1965-71; mem. Warwick Sch. Com., 1962-66, chmn., 1963-64. Mem. Am. Hosp. Assn., Hosp. Assn. R.I., New Eng. Hosp. Assembly, New Eng. Kidney Council Med. Care and Edn. Found., Med. Econs. Council of R.I., Am. Arbitration Assn. (arbitrator), Providence Preservation Soc., Providence C. of C. Execs. Roman Catholic. Clubs: Univ., Turks Head. Contbr. articles to profl. jours. Home: 4267 Post Rd East Greenwich RI 02818 Office: 444 Westminster Mall Providence RI 02901

LECO, DOMENIC EUGENE, dentist; b. East Greenwich, R.I., Aug. 27, 1922; s. Armand and Sue (Catanio) L.; student R.I. State Coll., 1940-41, R.I. Coll. Pharmacy, 1941-42, Providence Coll., 1942-43; D.M.D., Tufts U., 1947; m. Victoria Ann Petrarca, Sept. 4, 1943 (dec. Dec. 3, 1973); children—Ann Marie (Mrs. Jay Damon Hobson), Eugene Victor, Richard Armand; m. 2d, Lynne Ann Crawley, Aug. 8, 1974. Tchr. pharmacology, toxicology, R.I. Coll. Pharmacy, 1947-55; pvt. practice dentistry, Attleboro, Mass., 1947—; asso. chief dental staff Sturdy Meml. Hosp. Part-time instr. Tufts U. Sch. Dental Medicine, 1960—; spl. cons. drug research Purdue Fredericks Co., Wampole Labs.; pres. Stone Realty Co., 1970—. Mem. North Attleboro Sch. Com., 1962-65, North Attleboro Town Govt. Study Com., 1970. Served with USNR, 1942-46. Fellow Internat. Coll. Dentists; mem. ADA, Am. Acad. Oral Medicine, Nat. Assn. Real Estate Bds., Delta Sigma Delta, Kappa Psi. Rotarian. Author: (juvenile) Suedes, 1969. Contbr. articles to profl. jours. Home: 380 S Washington St North Attleboro MA 02760 Office: 20 Orne St North Attleboro MA 02760

LECROY, BARBARA LOIS PEASE, govt. ofcl.; b. Boston, Apr. 27, 1923; d. Edmund Morris and Clara Hanson (Luscombe) Pease; B.S.Ed., Mass. Coll. Art, 1944; M.A., George Washington U., 1974; postgrad. Ark. State U., 1957-59; m. William Cecil LeCroy, Jan. 19, 1946; 1 son, Edmund Deckard. Tchr., Portsmouth (N.H.) Schs., 1944-46; typist U.S. Navy, Corpus Christi, Tex., Camp LeJeune, N.C., Parris Island, S.C., 1946-49; tchr. Marine Corps Dependent Sch., Camp Lejeune, 1949-50; adminstrv. clk. U.S. Army, Boston, 1950-54; tchr. Lake City and Cash (Ark.) high schs., 1956-58; stenographer U.S. Army ROTC, Ark. State U., 1958-59; with Social Security Adminstrn., various locations, 1959—, supervisory employee devel. specialist, chief quality assurance staff tng. ops. br., Balt., 1976—. Md. convener Women's Equity Action League, 1976; mem. lay adv. council curriculum Linganore High Sch., Frederick County, 1970-71. Recipient Superior Performance award U.S. Army ROTC, 1959; Social Security Adminstrn. Commr.'s Individual citation, 1967. Mem. Am. Soc. Tng. and Devel., Am. Soc. Pub. Adminstrs., Am. Mgmt. Assn., Am. Personnel and Guidance Assn., Vocat. Guidance Assn., Assn. Non White Concerns, Assn. Counselor Edn. and Supervision, AAUW, Am. Horse Council, Am., Va., Md. quarter horse assns., Nat. Women's Polit. Caucus, Capitol Hill Women's Polit. Caucus, Federally Employed Women (nat. legis. chmn. 1976), NOW, Sullivan Sorrento Maine Hist. Soc., Garland County (Ark.) Hist. Soc., Pi Gamma Mu. Mem. Women's Nat. Party. Home: PO Box 55 Mount Airy MD 21771 Office: 6401 Security Blvd Social Security Adminstrn Hdqrs Baltimore MD 21235

LE CROY, JAMES FRANKLIN, govt. ofcl.; b. Chattanooga, Mar. 16, 1928; s. John Prior and Ruby Isabella Matilda (Duncan) L.; student George Washington U., 1946-49, 51-52, U. Va., 1962-69; B.Pub. Adminstrn., Upper Iowa U., 1978; m. Jackie Blount, Feb. 27, 1955; children—James Lynn, Judy Gail, Jackie Marie, Jenny. Cartographic aid Aero. Chart Bur., USAF, Washington, 1948; phys. scientist aide U.S. Navy, David Taylor Model Basin, Washington, 1948-49, aero. engring. aide, 1950-53; with Metall. Research Lab., Combustion Engring. Co., Chattanooga, 1953-55; project adminstr. fixed wing and convertiplane devel. U.S. Army Chief of Transp., Washington, 1955-56; multiple line ins. agt. State Farm Ins. Co., Alexandria, Va., 1956; devel. engr. Captial Airlines, Washington, 1956-60; aero. engr. United Airlines, Washington, 1960-66; supervisory aerospace engr., asst. project mgr. logistics Naval Air Systems Command Hdqrs., Washington, 1966-69, supervisory aerospace engr., supr. targets, drones, ground electronics and range instrumentation, 1969-75, supervisory aerospace engr., supr. air-to-air missiles, 1975-76, head plans and policy, 1976—. Mem. West Springfield (Va.) Civic Assn., 1965—. Served with USNR, 1949-50. Registered profl. engr., Vt. Recipient Sustained Superior Performance award U.S. Navy, 1973, 74, Outstanding Performance award, 1976, Award for Invention Disclosure, 1973, 76. Mem. Nat., Va. (dir. Fairfax chpt. 1971-72, membership com. 1973-74) socs. profl. engr., Assn. of Naval Weapon's Scientists and Engrs. (award 1969, 74), Tau Kappa Epsilon, Theta Tau. Methodist (mem. adminstrn. bd. 1958-78, chmn. adminstrv. bd. 1978, chmn. builders club 1972-78; corp. mem. Va. bd. missions). Inventor Laser Firing Error Indicator Vector Scoring System; patentee in field. Home: 6406 Charnwood St Springfield VA 22152 Office: Naval Air Systems Command Hdqrs Code Air-6101 Navy Dept Washington DC 20360

LEDEEN, ROBERT WAGNER, neurochemist, educator; b. Denver, Aug. 19, 1928; s. Hyman and Olga (Wagner) L.; B.S., U. Calif., at Berkeley, 1949; Ph.D., Oreg. State U., 1953. Postdoctoral fellow in chemistry U. Chgo., 1953-54; research asso. in chemistry Mt. Sinai Hosp., N.Y.C., 1956-59; research fellow Albert Einstein Coll. Medicine, 1959, asst. prof., 1962-69, asso. prof., 1969-75, prof., 1975—. Mem. neurol. scis. study sect. NIH. Served with AUS, 1954-56. NIH grantee, 1963-79; Nat. Multiple Sclerosis Soc. grantee, 1967-74. Mem. Internat., Am. socs. neurochemistry, Am. Chem. Soc., Am. Soc. Biol. Chemists, N.Y. Acad. Sci., Am. Oil Chemists Soc. Jewish. Contbr. articles to profl. jours.; editorial bd. Jour. Lipid Research, Jour. Neurochemistry. Home: 111 Wadsworth Ave New York City NY 10033 Office: 1300 Morris Park Ave Bronx NY 10461

LEDER, BURTON A., educator; b. Bayonne, N.J., Mar. 17, 1928; s. George and Jeanette (Shilling) L.; B.S., Trenton State Coll., 1949; M.A. in Adminstrn. and Supervision, Steton Hall, 1956, also reading specialist certificate; postgrad. in learning disabilities Temple U.; m. Sheila Leder; children—Merrille, Jeffrey, Scott. Tchr., Roselle (N.J.) Bd. Edn., 1953-65; dir. pupil services, learning cons. Deal Rumson-Fair Haven (N.J.) High Sch. Fair Haven Bd. Edn., 1965—; adj. prof. Farleigh Dickinson U.; learning cons. Jersey Shore Med. Center Evaluation Center, Neptune, N.J., 1970—. Mem. NEA, N.J. Edn. Assn. Internat. Reading Assn., Assn. Learning Cons. (pres. 1972-73), Assn. Children and Learning Disabilities, Piaget Soc., Orton Soc. Home: 6 Spring Valley Dr Holmdel NJ 07733 Office: Fair Haven Bd Edn Fair Haven NJ 07701

LEDER, LAWRENCE H., historian; b. N.Y.C., Feb. 23, 1927; s. George and Rose (Marks) L.; A.B. cum laude, L.I. U., 1949; A.M., N.Y. U., 1950, Ph.D., 1960; m. Bernice E. Kadish, Mar. 16, 1958; children—Robert H., Irene J., Evelyn N. Research asso. Sleepy Hollow Restorations, Tarrytown, N.Y., 1956-59; asst. prof. Brandeis U., Waltham, Mass., 1959-62; asso. prof. La. State U., New Orleans, 1962-65, prof., chmn. dept. history, 1965-68; prof., chmn. dept. history Lehigh U., Bethlehem, Pa., 1968—, coordinator Gipson Inst. for 18th Century Studies, 1972—. Mem. fellowship selection com. Am. Council Learned Socs., 1968-69; bd. dirs. Historic Bethlehem, Inc., 1973-79; mem. Bethlehem City Center Authority, 1974—. Served with U.S. Army, 1945-46. Recipient award of Merit, Am. Assn. State and Local History, 1957; Ann. Manuscript award Inst. Early Am. History and Culture, 1958; Distinguished Alumni award L.I. U. Alumni Assn., 1976; Folger Shakespeare Library fellow, 1972. Mem. Am. Hist. Assn., Orgn. Am. Historians, N.Y. Hist. Soc. Author: Robert Livingston, 1654-1728, 1961; Liberty and Authority, 1968; America, 1603-1789, 1972, rev., 1978; Dimensions of Change, 1972; The Colonial Legacy, 4 vols., 1971-73. Home: 222 E Market St Bethlehem PA 18018 Office: 346 Maginnes Lehigh U Bethlehem PA 18015

LEDER, SHEILA DIANE, educator; b. Newark, Feb. 10, 1928; B.S. in Edn., Math. and Sci., Trenton (N.J.) State Coll., 1949; M.L.S., Drexel U., Phila., 1972; m. Burton A. Leder; children—Merrille, Jeffrey, Scott. Tchr., Hazlet (N.J.) Pub. Schs., 1961-65; media coordinator Fair Haven (N.J.) Pub. Schs., 1965—. Bluebird leader Campfire Girls, 1958-61; exec. bd. Middle Rd. Sch. Parent Tchrs. Orgn., 1959-61; rep. Monmouth County Area Library Council. Certified tchr., librarian, media specialist. Mem. Nat., N.J. edn. assns., N.J. Sch. Media Specialists. Author: The Bookworm, programmed text of library skills. Home: 6 Spring Valley Dr Holmdel NJ 07733 Office: Knollwood Sch Media Center Fair Haven NJ 07701

LEDERBERG, JOSHUA, univ. pres.; b. Montclair, N.J., May 23, 1925; s. Zwi Hirsch and Esther (Goldenbaum) L.; B.A., Columbia U., 1944, Sc.D. (hon.), 1967; Ph.D., Yale U., 1947, Sc.D. (hon.), 1960; Sc.D. (hon.), U. Wis., 1967, Yeshiva U., 1970; M.D. (hon.), U. Turin (Italy), 1969; m. Marguerite Stein Kirsch, Apr. 5, 1968; children—David Kirsch, Anne. Prof. genetics U. Wis., 1947-59, chmn. dept. med. genetics, 1957-59; prof., chmn. dept. genetics Stanford U., 1959-78; pres. Rockefeller U., 1978—; cons. Cetus Corp.; chmn. Ann. Revs. Inc. Bd. dirs. Center Advanced Studies in Behavioral Scis., Stanford, Calif., Inst. Sci. Info., Phila. Recipient Nobel prize in physiology or medicine, 1958. Office: Rockefeller U New York City NY 10021

LEDERER, ANNE TRACY (MRS. H. AUSTIN LEDERER), educator; b. Chgo., Nov. 4, 1917; d. Howard Van S. and Ruth Alexander Tracy; A.B. with honors, Swarthmore Coll., 1938; A.M., Radcliffe Coll., 1940; m. William Rossmoore, June 24, 1938 (div.); 1 dau., Susan Tracy; m. 2d, H. Austin Lederer, Feb. 21, 1959; stepchildren—Meredith, Louise. Substitute tchr., Essex County, N.J., 1958-69. Organizer, first chmn. N.J. chpt. Parents Without Partners, Inc., 1958. Swarthmore Coll. rep. to Barnard Forum, 1955-57; pres. North Jersey Swarthmore Coll. Alumni Assn., 1957, 69; sec. class of 1938 at Swarthmore, 1958—. Mem. LWV (Verona bd. 1971-74), Alliance Francaise. Clubs: Swarthmore, Radcliffe (dir. N.J. 1966-69, 75-76). Contbr. articles to mags. Home: 32 Otsego Rd Verona NJ 07044

LEDERER, IVO JOHN, educator, internat. cons.; b. Yugoslavia, Dec. 11, 1929; s. Otto and Ruza (Oppenheim) L.; came to U.S., 1944, naturalized, 1952; student Coll. City N.Y., 1947-49; B.A., U. Colo., 1951; postgrad. Woodrow Wilson Sch. Fgn. Affairs, U. Va., 1951-52; M.A., Princeton U., 1954, Ph.D. in History, 1957; postgrad. Sch. Slavonic and E. European Studies, U. London, 1954-55; children—Michael Alexander, Philip Marquardt. Instr. to asso. prof. history Yale U., 1957-65; program officer European and internat. affairs Ford Found., 1972-76; prof. Stanford U., 1965-72, 76-77, chmn. provost's com. on future of internat. studies, 1971-72, chmn. Center for Russian and E. European studies, 1966-72; v.p. Bus. Internat. S.A., 1977-78; sr. cons. corp. relations Internat. Research and Exchanges Bd., 1978—; chmn. U.S. Nat. Com. on Future of Exchanges with U.S.S.R. and Eastern Europe, 1967-68; asso. Lehrman Inst., 1973—; trustee World Affairs Council No. Calif., 1971-72. Mem. Council on Fgn. Relations, Am. Hist. Assn., Internat. Studies Assn., Am. Assn. Advancement of Slavic Studies, Conf. Group Central European History. Author: Yugoslavia at the Paris Peace Conference: A Study in Frontiermaking (George Louis Beer prize), 1963; contbr. chpts. to books, articles to profl. jours.; editor: (with W.S. Vucinich) The Soviet Union and the Middle East: The Post World War II Era, 1974; (with P.F. Sugar) Nationalism in Eastern Europe, 1969; Russian Foreign Policy: Essays in Historical Perspective, 1962; The Versailles Settlement, 1960. Home: 210 E 58 St New York City NY 10022

LEDERER, RAYMOND FRANCIS, congressman; b. Phila., May 19, 1938; s. Miles and Susan (Scullin) L.; student St. Joseph's Coll., Phila. Community Coll., Pa. State U.; m. Eileen Coyle; children—Miles W., Mary Beth, Joseph P., Patricia, Diane, Claire. Dir., Phila. Probation Dept., to 1974; mem. Pa. Ho. of Reps., 1974-76; mem. 95th Congress from 3d Pa. Dist., mem. ways and means com. Head football coach St. Michaels Sch., Phila.; CYO football commr., Phila.; asst. scoutmaster, explorer adviser, merit badge counselor Boy Scouts Am.; Democratic committeeman; leader 18th Ward Dem. Exec. Com.; bd. dirs. Lower Kensington Environ. Center, Hahnemann Hosp. Mental Health Center, Frankford Hosp., Northeast Hosp., Centro Loyola, Pa. Com. on Probation Self-Help Treatment; trustee Roman Catholic High Sch. Recipient Gold Star Mothers award. Mem. Police Athletic League, Sports Hall of Fame (Phila.). Club: Optimist. Home: 1231 Shackamaxon St Philadelphia PA 19125 Office: 516 Cannon House Office Bldg Washington DC 20515

LEDERFEIND, ALAN, fin. co. exec.; b. N.Y.C., Mar. 22, 1943; s. Dean and Mirrie (Yoffe) L.; student U. Toledo, 1960-62; B.S., N.Y. U., 1967; m. Marsha L. Shapiro, Apr. 17, 1966; children—Dean, Lonni. Mktg. mgr. Goodbody & Co., N.Y.C., 1968-70; v.p. Butcher & Singer, N.Y.C., 1971-74; mgr. quantitative services Am. Capital Partners, N.Y.C., 1974-76; v.p., dir. Drysdale Securities Corp., N.Y.C., 1976-77; pres. The Wall Street Discount Corp., N.Y.C., 1978—. Home: Chappaqua NY Office: 100 Wall St New York City NY 10005

LEDERMAN, PETER BERND, indsl. exec.; b. Weimar, Germany, Nov. 16, 1931; s. Ernst M. and Irmgard (Heilbrunn) L.; came to U.S., 1939, naturalized, 1945; B.S. in Chem. Engring., U. Mich., 1953, M.S. in Engring., 1957, Ph.D., 1961; m. Susan Sturc, Aug. 25, 1957; children—Stuart Michael, Ellen Louise. Instr., U. Mich., Ann Arbor, 1959-61; research engr. Esso Research Lab., Baton Rouge, 1961-63; sr. engr. Esso Research & Engring. Co., Florham Park, N.J., 1963-66; asso. prof., adminstrv. officer dept. chem. engring. Poly. Inst. Bklyn., 1966-72, adj. prof., 1972—; dir. Edison Water Quality Research Lab., U.S. EPA, Edison, N.J., 1972-73, dir. Indsl. Waste Treatment Research Lab., 1973-75, dir. indsl. and extractive processes div. EPA, Washington, 1975-76; mgr. tech. devel. Research Cottrell, Bound Brook, N.J., 1976-78, v.p., gen. mgr. Cottrell Environ., 1978—; adj. lectr. Columbia U., N.Y.C., 1965-67. Mem. Environ. Control Com., New Providence, N.J., 1970-71. Served with AUS, 1953-55. Mem. Am. Inst. Chem. Engrs. (chmn. profl. devel. com.; chmn. N.J. sect. 1971-72), Am. Chem. Soc., AAAS, Am. Soc. Engring. Edn., Sigma Xi, Phi Kappa Phi, Phi Lambda Upsilon, Omega Chi Epsilon, Tau Beta Pi. Editorial bd. Chem. Engring. mag., 1968-72. Home: 17 Pittsford Way New Providence NJ 07974

LEDNEY, GEORGE, mining co. exec.; b. Jerome, Pa., Apr. 26, 1922; s. Charles and Susan (Stredney) L.; extension student Pa. State U.; m. Margaret Mihalacki, July 15, 1950; children—Gerald G., George M., Douglas A. With Berwind-White Coal Mining Co., Windber, Pa., 1941-62, supt., 1961-62; mgr. Sta. WWBR, Windber, 1964-65; ins. agt., 1962-64; supt. Reitz Coal Co., Windber, 1965-69; pres., dir. Longwall Mining Co., Windber, 1969—, C.C.&L. Trucking, Inc., 1976—; v.p., dir. Lunar Mining, Inc., 1975—; partner Colech Enterprises, 1975—. Pres. Windber Pub. Library, 1974-75, 78—, 1st v.p., 1976, bd. dirs., 1972—; mem. Somerset County Library Bd., 1978—; bd. dirs. Windber Redevel. Assn., 1970-76, Windber Recreation Assn., 1967-70; mem. adv. bd. Admiral Peary Vocat. Tech. Sch., 1975—; v.p. Windber Borough Council, 1974-78; mem. Somerset County Devel. Council, 1977—; bd. dirs. Windber Area Recreation and Park Bd., 1978—. Served with USNR, 1943-45. Mem. Am. Legion, VFW. Republican. Byzantine Catholic. Clubs: Windber Country, Windber Rotary (past dir.). Home: 1705 Hillside Ave Windber PA 15963 Office: 900 Mine 42 Windber PA 15963

LEDUC, GILLES GERMAIN, cardiologist; b. Montreal, Que., Can., Oct. 14, 1923; s. Octave Joseph and Elisabeth Marie (Lussier) L.; B.A., U. Ottawa (Ont., Can.), 1944; M.D., U. Montreal, 1950; m. Francine Mercier, Sept. 12, 1959; children—Bertrand, Martin. Intern, Hôtel-Dieu de Montreal, 1950, resident, 1951-52, attending physician, 1955; resident in cardiology St. Luke's Hosp., N.Y.C., 1952-54, Hopital Boucicaut, Paris, 1954-55; practice medicine, specializing in internal medicine and cardiology, Montreal, 1955—; cons. physician St. Justine Hosp., 1956—; prof. medicine U. Montreal, 1956—; sr. mem. Inst. Research, Montreal. Fellow Am. Heart Assn., Am. Coll. Cardiology; mem. Montreal Cardiac Soc. (past pres.), Acad. Religion Mental Health (adv. council). Roman Catholic. Contbr. sci. papers to profl. jours. Home: 82 Lockhart St Mont Royal PQ Canada Office: 110 Pine Ave Montreal PQ Canada

LEE, ALBERT KON-YING, mathematician, educator; b. Canton, China, Oct. 15, 1949; s. William Wing-You and Ching-Un (Lam) L.; came to U.S., 1966, naturalized, 1966; B.Sc., McGill U., 1969, M.Sc., 1970, Ph.D. in Math., 1977. Prof. math. N.Y. Inst. Tech., N.Y.C., 1976—, Pace Coll., N.Y.C., 1976—, N.Y.C. Community Coll., 1974—. Mem. Am., Canadian math. socs., N.Y. Acad. Sci., Pi Mu Epsilon. Home: 75 Montgomery St Apt 11C New York City NY 10002 Office: Pace U New York City NY 10038

LEE, ALFRED MATTHEW, educator; b. Louisville, July 1, 1938; s. Charles Prue and Thelma (Lewis) L.; B.A., Yale, 1960; M.F.A., U. Ia., 1963; m. Johanna Karen Tobias, Mar. 26, 1970; 1 son, Alexander Prue Tobias. Secondary sch. tchr. U.S. Peace Corps, Ghana, 1962-64; welfare caseworker Dept. Social Services, City N.Y., 1965-67; instr. English, N.J. Inst. Tech., 1967-71, asst. prof., 1971—. Del. exec. bd. Social Service Employees Union, 1966-67. Mem. Am. Assn. Higher Edn., Modern Lang. Assn., Chi Psi, Chi Delta Theta. Author: Time, 1974. Editor: The Major Young Poets, 1971. Contbr. poetry to profl. jours. Home: 57 Kendall Ave Maplewood NJ 07040 Office: 323 High St Newark NJ 07102

LEE, ARTHUR TERENCE, human resource cons.; b. Newport, R.I., Dec. 20, 1939; s. Arthur Theodore and Anne May (Brownell) L.; A.B. in History and Govt., Colby Coll., 1961; M.Ed. in Career Counseling, Northeastern U., 1975; m. Catherine Jean Walsh, Sept. 21, 1968; children—Tracy Catherine, Shannon Elizabeth. With engring. and mfg. adminstrn. Raytheon Co., Portsmouth, R.I., 1965-70; research and devel. planning Gillette Co., Boston, 1970-73; tng. dir. Kennedy's Inc., Boston, 1973-74; asso. dir. Project Pyramid, Mass. Dept. Edn., Medford, 1974-77; sr. asso. Troy Assos., Boston, 1977—; lectr. counselor edn. Grad. Sch. Edn., Northeastern U., Boston. Served to capt. USMC, 1961-64. Certified social studies tchr., dir. guidance, guidance counselor, vocat. counselor, Mass. Mem. Am. Soc. Tng. and Devel., Am., Mass. (govt. liaison), Greater Boston (trustee, 1977—, legis. chmn.; pres.-elect) personnel and guidance assns., Nat. Vocat. Guidance Assn. Roman Catholic. Condr. research on career edn., employment experiences. Home: 14 Bannister Rd Andover MA 01810 Office: 4310 Prudential Tower Boston MA 02199

LEE, ARTHUR VIRGIL, III, coll. adminstr.; b. Detroit, Nov. 24, 1920; s. Arthur Virgil and Emily S. (Burry) L.; B.A., Williams Coll., 1942; grad. in Indsl. Adminstrn., Harvard, 1943; m. Elizabeth Hoppin Chafee, Dec. 8, 1945; children—Arthur C., Sherrill Ann, William J., Henry C.; m. 2d, Jean Austin LaMothe, Dec. 30, 1967. With McKesson & Robbins, Inc., 1946-63, ops. mgr., Providence div., 1947-54, v.p., div. mgr. Providence div., 1954-59, Boston div. 1959-63, Pitts. div., 1963; asst. dean Harvard Bus. Sch., 1964-65, dir. corporate relations, 1965-72, dir. resources, 1972-73; v.p. Lesley Coll., Cambridge, 1973-77; dir. corp. relations Tufts U., Medford, Mass., 1977—; dir. Atlee Corp., L.D.C., Inc., Tech Ven Assn., Inc. Dir. New Eng. Drug Exchange, 1956-63. Mem. Weston Town Finance Com., 1961-66. Adv. bd. Coll. of Pharmacy U. R.I., 1957-58. Served from ensign to lt., USNR, 1942-46. Mem. Alpha Delta Phi. Conglist. (trustee 1962-72). Club: Weston (Mass.) Golf (dir. 1970-72). Home: 10 Cartpath Rd Weston MA 02193 Office: Packard Hall Tufts U Medford MA 02155

LEE, AUBREY MCDANIEL, ret. vet. research scientist; b. Conroe, Tex., June 12, 1899; s. Will Thomas and Lilla May (Gibbs) L.; D.V.M., Kans. State U., 1922; M.Sc., Ohio State U., 1930; m. Eugenia May Harris, Dec. 1, 1921; 1 dau., Dorothy Lee Sawyer. Instr. bacteriology U. Wyo., Laramie, 1922-29, asst. prof., 1922-29, prof. veterinary sci., 1930-48, research pathologist, 1935-48; asst. in pathology Ohio State U., Columbus, 1929-30; pathology asst. veterinarian pathology div. Bur. Animal Industry, U.S. Dept. Agr., Washington, 1948-54, research pathologist (vet.) Agr. Research Service, 1954-65, asst. to dir. animal disease parasite research div., 1959-65; head veterinary sci. bacteriology Wyo. Agrl. Expt. Sta., 1931-47; nat. coordinator research field investigations Bovine Hyperkeratosis, 1949-53; mem. Wyo. Bd. Health, 1947-48. Served with M.C., U.S. Army, 1917-19. Decorated Purple Heart; recipient Superior Service award Dept. Agr., 1954; Distinguished Service award Vet. Medicine, Kans. State U., 1960. Mem. AVMA, U.S. Livestock San. Assn., Conf. Research Workers Animal Diseases, Am. Coll. Veterinary Toxicologists, Sigma Xi. Contbr. articles in field to profl. jours. and yearbooks. Home: 12715 Brunswick Ln Bowie MD 20715

LEE, BOB, business exec.; b. Canton, China, Nov. 25, 1931; s. Yeung Po and Ngan Foon (Leung) L.; came to U.S., 1948, naturalized, 1951; B.S., N.Y. U., 1959; m. Joyce Chin, Apr. 11, 1954; 1 dau., Patricia A. Sr. accountant Peat, Marwick, Mitchell & Co., N.Y.C., 1959-66; dir. accounting United Service Orgn., Inc., N.Y.C., 1966-67; partner, controller Fahnestock & Co., N.Y.C., 1967—; dir. Dynamic Info. Corp., Eatontown, N.J., 1968-69. Asst. treas. Travelers Aid Assn. Am., 1968-71. Served with USAF, 1951-55. C.P.A., N.Y. Mem. Am. Inst. C.P.A.'s, N.Y. State Soc. C.P.A.'s, Securities Industry Assn. (dir. fin. mgmt. div. 1975—), Beta Alpha Psi, Beta Gamma Sigma. Home: 20 Avondale Rd White Plains NY 10605 Office: 110 Wall St New York City NY 10005

LEE, CHE FU, sociologist, demographer, educator; b. Taiwan, Taipei, Dec. 5, 1941; s. Lien Teng and Ying Seng (Chen) L.; came to U.S., 1965, naturalized, 1975; Ph.D., U. N.C. at Chapel Hill, 1971; m. Ling Wong, June 4, 1966; children—Conn, Tien. Asst. prof. sociology Catholic U., Washington, 1970-74, asst. dir. Inst. Social and Behavioral Research, 1972-74, asso. prof., dir. inst., 1974—; UN sr. population adviser Iran, 1975-76. N.C. Population fellow, 1967-70; research grantee USPHS, Nat. Inst. Child Health Devel., SE Asia Devel. Adv. Group Asia Soc., U.S. Bur. Census. Mem. Am. Sociol. Assn., Population Assn. Am., So. Sociol. Soc., Am. Acad. Polit. and Social Sci. Contbr. articles to profl. publs. Home: 11522 Colt Terr Silver Spring MD 20902 Office: Dept Sociology Catholic U Washington DC 20064

LEE, CHONG-JIN, mfg. co. exec.; b. Dae-Gu, Korea, Apr. 14, 1937; s. Kyoo-Won and Sun-In (Kim) L.; Sc.D., Mass. Inst. Tech., 1965; m. Yu-Ja Chang, Apr. 3, 1965; children—Hans Han-Woo, Michelle Eun Joo, Jennifer Hai-Joo. Asst. prof. mech. engring. Tufts U., Medford, Mass., 1964-68; sr. research engr. Westvaco, Charleston, S.C., 1968-69; project leader Am. Can Co., Greenwich, Conn., 1969-71; staff v.p. planning AMF, Inc., White Plains, N.Y., 1971—. Recipient Gold medal Engring. Coll., Seoul Nat. U., 1959, Achievement award AMF, Inc., 1975. Mem. Nat. Assn. Bus. Economists, N.Am. Soc. Corp. Planning, Inst. Mgmt. Scis., Sigma Xi, Tau Beta Pi. Home: 830 Swed Circle Yorktown NY 10508 Office: 777 Westchester Ave White Plains NY 10604

LEE, CLEMENT WILLIAM KHAN, church assn. adminstr.; b. N.Y.C., Feb. 7, 1938; s. William P. and Helen M. L.; B.Th., Concordia Coll., 1958; M. Div., Concordia Theol. Sem., Springfield, Ill., 1962; M.A., New Sch. for Social Research, 1976. Asst. exec. dir. Greater Detroit Lutheran Council, 1962; editor Detroit, Suburban Lutheran Newspaper, 1963; asso. communications dir. Met. Detroit Council of Churches, 1964; dir. media ops. Am. Bible Soc., N.Y.C., 1967; dir. film, broadcast relations Luth. Council U.S.A., N.Y.C., 1971-77, asst. exec. dir. communication and interpretation, 1977—; media cons. Luth. Ch.-Mo. Synod, Spaulding for Children, Metro News of Metro N.Y. Synod of Luth. Ch. Am., archtl. newsletter Window. Chmn. N.AM. Broadcast sect. World Assn. Christian Communication, 1975, broadcast ops. com. Nat. Council Chs. of Christ U.S.A., 1976—; vice chmn. bd. mgrs. Communication Commn., 1977—. Recipient Detroit Press Club Found. award, 1963; silver medallion Internat. Film and TV Festival, 1975. Mem. Assn. Edn. Communication Tech., Internat. Radio and TV Soc., Nat. Acad. TV Arts and Scis., Religious Pub. Relations Council (chmn. 42d Nat. Conv.), Radio TV News Dirs. Assn., World Assn. Christian Communication (chmn. communication edn. com.). Creator children's TV program Storyline; producer films Mission on Six Continents, 1975, A New Start, 1978. Office: 360 Park Ave S New York City NY 10010

LEE, EDMUND WOODHAM, lawyer; b. Bayshore, L.I., N.Y., Aug. 11, 1912; s. Lyndon Edmund and Bertha (Cottrell); B.A., Princeton, 1934, LL.D., Yale, 1937; m. Sylvia Sanford Lee, Dec. 30, 1939; children—Dorinne Lee (Mrs. Nicholas Bayard Mason), Sanford Edmund. Admitted to Conn. bar, 1938, N.Y. State bar, 1938, Va. bar, 1967; asso. firm Brush & Hannon, Greenwich, Conn., 1937-38, Loew's, Inc., N.Y.C., 1938-41, Donovan, Leisure, Newton, Lumbard & Irvine, N.Y.C., 1941-43, 46-47; asso. Paul V. McNutt, N.Y.C., 1947-50, partner, 1950-51; asst. gen. counsel Ethyl Corp., Richmond, Va., 1951-74; mem. firm Hubert L. Brown, profl. corp., Norwich, N.Y., 1974—; mem. Richmond Corporate Lawyers Assn., 1967-74, sec., 1971-72, v.p., 1972-73, pres., 1973—. Active charitable activities and youth orgns.; officer, legal counsel neighborhood homeowners assns., Bronxville, N.Y., 1947-63, Mamaroneck, N.Y., 1963-66, Richmond, 1966-74, Sherburne, N.Y., 1974—; vestryman Christ Episcopal Ch., Sherburne, N.Y., 1975, jr. warden, 1976, sr. warden, 1978—; bd. dirs. Team of Progress, citizens good govt. com., Richmond, 1970-74, mem. exec. com., 1972-74. Served with USAAF, 1943-45. Decorated Air medal. Recipient excellence in sports award Westchester Rugby Football Club, 1960. Mem. Va. Power Boat Assn. (atty. 1970-74, sec. 1971-74), Eastern Rugby Union Am., Inc. (officer 1934—, dir. 1954—, atty. 1954—), Richmond Rugby Football Club (dir. 1966-74, pres. 1968-70), Rugby Football Union Centennary (del. 1970), N.Y. Rugby Football Club (officer 1938-66), U.S.A. Rugby Football Union (gov., sec. 1975—) Clubs: Orienta Beach (dir. 1958-63, pres. 1960-61, sec. 1962-63 Mamaroneck, N.Y.), Rotary (v.p. Sherburne 1975, pres. 1976-77, sec. 1977-78). Office: 27 E State St Sherburne NY 13460

LEE, EDWIN BORDEN, JR., historian, educator; b. Goldsboro, N.C., Nov. 24, 1924; s. Edwin Borden and Loula Simpson (Powell) L.; A.B., Duke U., 1945; M.A., Columbia U., 1950, Ph.D., 1960. Lang. specialist U.S. Occupation Forces, Japan, 1946-47; lectr. Columbia U., N.Y.C., 1954-56, 57-58; instr. Hamilton Coll., 1958-60, asst. prof. history, 1960-65, asso. prof., 1965-70, prof., 1970—, chmn. dept., 1978—. Served to lt. USNR, 1943-46, 52-54. Fulbright scholar Waseda U., Tokyo, 1956-57, U. Tokyo, 1963-64; Hamilton Coll. faculty fellow, 1971. Mem. Am. Hist. Assn., Assn. Asian Studies, AAUP. Contbr. articles to profl. jours. Home: 113 Campus Rd Clinton NY 13323 Office: Dept History Hamilton Coll Clinton NY 13323

LEE, FRANCES HELEN, editor; b. N.Y.C. Jan. 6, 1936; d. Murray and Rose (Rothman) Lee; B.A., Queens Coll., 1957; M.A., N.Y. U., 1962. Editorial asst. Christian Herald Family Bookshelf, N.Y.C., 1957-62; rights and permissions Gordon and Breach Science Pubs., Inc., 1964-66; editorial asst. research dept. Group Health Ins., 1966-67; editorial asst. Am. Electric Power Service Corp., AEP Operating IDEAS, 1967-69, Indsl. Water Engring. mag., 1969-71; editor Media Horizons, Inc., 1971—, Indsl. Photography's Gold Book, Audio-Visual Communications, Equipment and Prodn. Buying Guide, Profl. Studio Gold Book. Supr. Bronx div. N.Y. State Civil Def., 1953-59; mem. com. on Charter Revision Citizens Union, 1975, com. on city personnel system, 1976; mem. com. Charter Revision Implementation and Com. for Reviving N.Y.C., 1976-77; mem. Com. on City Planning and Budget, 1977; mem. Com. on City Mgmt., 1977, bd. dirs., 1978-79. Mem. Women's Nat. Book Assn., 1960-61. Mem.

Women in Communication, Soc. Tech. Communication. Club: N.Y. U. Alumnae (dir., rec. sec. 1978-79). Home: 170 2d Ave New York City NY 10003

LEE, GARY A., congressman; b. Buffalo, 1933; B.A., M.A., Colgate U., 1960; postgrad. Cornell U., 1963; m. Kathleen Ann O'Brian, 1958; children—Karen, Brian, Jeffrey, Diane. Tchr., Corning (N.Y.) City Sch. Dist., 1960-63; dir. scholarships and fin. aid Cornell U., 1963-75; mem. staff, v.p. pub. affairs, 1975—; mem. N.Y. Ho. of Reps. from 128th Dist., 1974-78; mem. 96th Congress from 33d Dist. N.Y., Washington, 1979—; mem. adv. com. univ. fin. N.Y. State Regents, 1970-72. Alderman, Corning Common Council, 1961-63; councilman Town of Dryden, N.Y., 1965-67, supr., 1968-69; mem. Tompkins County Bd. Suprs., 1968-69, 70-74, chmn., 1974; chmn. Tompkins County Republican Party, 1969-74; mem. N.Y. State Rep. Com., 1972. Served with USN, 1952-56; Korea. Mem. Am. Legion, Tompkins County C. of C., Finger Lakes Assn., Varna Community Assn. Office: US Ho of Reps The Capitol Washington DC 20515*

LEE, I-CHIE, physician; b. Medan, Indonesia, May 5, 1934; s. Ka-Poat and Peh (Kho) L.; B.M., Nat. Taiwan U., 1965, M.D., 1966; m. Fay Anzelone, Oct. 26, 1968; children—Charles, Mark, Eric, Rebecca. Came to U.S., 1967, naturalized, 1974. Rotating intern Nat. Taiwan U. Hosp., 1965-66, resident urology, 1966-67; rotating intern Yonkers Gen. Hosp., 1967-68; resident obstetrics and gynecology Margaret Hauge Maternity Hosp., 1969; resident anesthesiology Albert Einstein Coll. Medicine, 1969-72; fellow medicine Montefiore Hosp. and Med. Center, 1972; anesthesiologist St. Joseph Hosp., Towson, Md., 1973—. Mem. Am. Assn. Fgn. Med. Grads., Am., N.Y. State socs. anesthesiologists, AMA, Baltimore County Med. Assn. Home: 1009 Westwind Ct Ruxton MD 21204 Office: 7620 York Rd Towson MD 21204

LEE, ILBOK, biostatistician; b. Seoul, Korea, Dec. 19, 1929; s. Chungkoo and Soobong (Han) L.; B.S., Iowa State U., 1956, M.S., 1959, Ph.D. (NIH fellow), 1962; m. Sung Jin, Sept. 10, 1967; 1 son, Morris. Dir., prin. cons. Biostatistical Services, Inc., Madison, N.J., 1970-73; prin. biostatistician Ives Labs., Inc., 1973—; adj. lectr. in statistics, Rutgers U., N.J., 1969—. Mem. Statis. Assn., Biometric Soc., Sigma Xi. Congregationalist. Contbr. articles in field to profl. jours. Home: 29 Lee Terr Short Hills NJ 07078 Office: 685 3d Ave New York City NY 10017

LEE, JAI SUNG, physician; b. Seoul, Korea, Aug. 11, 1938; s. Dai Hee and Myung Hee (Park) L.; came to U.S., 1965, naturalized, 1975; M.D., Seoul Nat. U., 1961; m. Julie S. Cho, Sept. 7, 1963; children—Jane, Gregory, Gerald. Intern, Altoona (Pa.) Hosp., 1965-66; resident in anesthesiology Balt. City Hosp., 1966-69, asst. chief-in-anesthesiology, 1969-70; sr. attending anesthesiologist St. Agnes Hosp., Balt., 1970—; instr. Johns Hopkins U., Balt., 1969-70. Served to 1st lt. M.C., Korean Army, 1962-65. Diplomate Am. Bd. Anesthesiology. Fellow Am. Coll. Anesthesiology; mem. AMA, Med. and Chirurg. Faculty State of Md., Balt. City Med. Soc., Am. Soc. Anesthesiologists, Internat. Anesthesia Research Soc., Am. Soc. Regional Anesthesia.

LEE, JAMES EDWARD, oil co. exec.; b. Kiln, Miss., Dec. 13, 1921; s. Fitzhugh and Bonnie Mae (Lenior) L.; B.S., La. Tech. U., 1942; m. Kathleen Ruth Edwards, Apr. 18, 1943; children—Kay (Mrs. Robert M. Strickland), Janet (Mrs. Gary Havens), Douglas B., James Stephen. With Gulf Oil, Corp., 1941-59, area rep. and coordinator, Manila, Philippines. 1959-63, Tokyo, 1963-66; with Petroleum Adminstrn. for Def., 1952-53; mng. dir. Kuwait Oil Co., Ltd., 1966-69; pres. Gulf Oil Co.-Eastern Hemisphere, London, 1969-72; exec. v.p. Gulf Oil Co., Pitts., 1972-73, pres., dir., 1973—; dir. Pitts. Nat. Bank. Bd. dirs. Carnegie-Mellon U., Hwy. Users Fedn., La. Tech. Engring. Found., Pitts. Theol. Sem., Shady Side Acad., West Penn Hosp., Pitts. Mem. Am. Petroleum Inst. (dir.), Greater C. of C. Pitts., Interant. Petroleum Exposition and Congress. Clubs: Pitts. Field, Rolling Rock, Duquesne (Pitts). Office: 439 7th Ave Pittsburgh PA 15219

LEE, JAMES MCCARCUM, orthopedic surgeon; b. Lexington, Tenn., Apr. 22, 1940; s. Willie Nelson and Willie (Brooks) L.; M.D., N.Y. Med. Coll., 1965. Teaching asst. dept. biol. scis. and research asst. dept. microbiology U. Pitts., 1959-61; jr. chemist Met. Hosp., N.Y.C., 1962-65; intern USPHS Hosp., San Francisco, 1965-66; resident USPHS Hosp., S.I., N.Y.; sr. asst. surgeon USPHS Hosp., San Francisco, 1965-66; surgeon S.I. USPHS Hosp., 1966-71; attending, dept. orthopedic surgery So. Permanente Med. Group, Fontana, Calif., 1971-73; instr. dept. orthopedic surgery Loma Linda (Calif.) U., 1971-73; practice medicine, specializing in orthopedic surgery, Newark and E. Orange, N.J., 1973—; asso. chief staff United Hosp. Newark, 1975-76; acting chief pediatric unit Presbyn. Hosp. Unit of United Hosp. Newark, 1976—, asso. chief dept. orthopedics, 1975-76; asst. attending, cons. Newark Beth Israel Med. Center, 1973-76, St. James Hosp., Newark, 1973-76, E. Orange Gen. Hosp., 1976—. Served to lt. comdr. USPHS, 1965-71. Diplomate Am. Bd. Orthopedic Surgery. Fellow Am. Acad. Orthopedic Surgery, A.C.S., Internat. Coll. Surgeons; mem. AMA, N.J., N. Jersey and Essex County med. socs. Office: 185 Central Ave East Orange NJ 07018

LEE, JAMES WIDEMANN, II, former innkeeper and town ofcl., ret. pub. relations counsel; b. Bklyn., Oct. 4, 1906; s. Ivy L. and Cornelia B. (Bigelow) L.; A.B., Princeton, 1929; m. Elizabeth L. Buechner, Oct. 20, 1941; children—Penelope Lee Ludwin, Patricia Lee McCormack, Elizabeth Louise Lee Sanstead. Mem. firm Ivy Lee & T. J. Ross, 1930, S. Am. rep., Santiago, Chile, 1930-31, rep. internat. sugar conf., Europe, 1931, rep. N.Y.C., 1932-33, overseas rep. Eng., France, Belgium, Germany, 1933-35, partner, 1934-61, N.Y.C., 1935-38, 59-61, Detroit, 1938-59; owner, operator Barrows House, Dorset, Vt., 1961-72. Mem. Dorset Bd. Selectmen, 1969-75, chmn., 1971-75; mem. Dorset Bd. Civil Authority, 1967-75, chmn., 1971-75; moderator United Ch. of Dorset, 1971-74, treas., 1975—; trustee, mem. grad. council Princeton, chmn. gen. giving Met. N.Y. Princeton 53 Million Dollar Campaign, 1959-61; mem. Detroit-Tomorrow Com. Mem. Am. Hotel and Motel Assn., Vt. Hotel-Motel Assn. (dir., pres.), New Eng. Innkeepers Assn., 3-Area Assn. (chmn.), Am. Ordnance Assn., Newcomen Soc., Detroit Bd. Commerce, Pub. Relations Soc. Am. (past pres. Detroit chpt.). Pilgrims U.S. Republican. Conglist. (treas.). Clubs: Princeton of Michigan, Economic, Adcraft, Press (Detroit); Otsego Ski (Gaylord, Mich.); Elm (Princeton, N.J.); Ekwanok (Manchester, Vt.); Dorset Field (gov.). Home: Dorset VT 05251

LEE, JOHN CHEE-MOU, physician; b. China, July 21, 1937; s. Ching-Ming and Hau-Ling (Koo) L.; M.D., Chekiang (China) Med. Coll., 1960; certificate in pharmacology U. Calif. at Los Angeles, 1968, certificate in psychiatry (NIMH fellow), 1970; certificate in behavioral scis. and psychobiology (NIH fellow) Duke, 1972; M.B.A., Fairleigh Dickinson U., 1977; m. Theresa T. Lau, Mar. 5, 1966; children—Jack Hong, Terry May. Practice medicine specializing in internal medicine, Hang Chow, China, 1960-61; hon. physician Hong Kong Free Clinic, 1962-63; med. rep. Beecham Research Labs., Hong Kong, 1963-64, Upjohn Internat. Co., Hong Kong, 1964-67; research pharmacologist U. Calif. at Los Angeles, 1967-68, fellow in psychiatry, 1968-70; fellow in aging Duke U., 1971-72; asst. dir. clin. research Schering Corp., Bloomfield, N.J., 1973-76; group dir. central nervous system clin. pharmacology Lederle Labs., Pearl River, N.Y., 1976—. Mem. Am. EEG Soc., N.Y. Acad. Scis., Soc. Biol. Psychiatry, Acad. Psychosomatic Medicine, Am. Med. EEG Assn., Am. Soc. for Clin. Pharmacology and Therapeutics. Contbr. articles on clin. neurophysiology and EEG'S to profl. jours. Office: Lederle Labs North Middletown Rd Pearl River NY 10965

LEE, JOHN H., JR., humanist, educator; b. Bremerton, Wash., Jan. 1, 1944; s. John H. and Lillian (Maynard) L.; B.A., U. Maine, 1967; M.S., Western Conn. State Coll., 1974; certificate ednl. adminstrn. U. Bridgeport, 1975; m. Patricia Ann Dow, Mar. 27, 1967; 1 dau., Sean Bianca. Tchr. English, Thomaston (Conn.) High Sch., 1967-69; team leader English, Brien McMahon High Sch., Norwalk, Conn., 1969-74; chmn. English dept. New Milford (Conn.) High Sch., 1974—; pres. Lee Cons. Services, New Milford, 1975—; instr. adult edn. Mem. Nat., Conn., New Milford edn. assns., Nat., Conn. councils English tchrs., New Eng. Assn. Tchrs. English, Phi Delta Kappa. Republican. Club: Housatonic. Home: 1 Fleetwood Ln Brookfield CT 06805 Office: 25 Sunny Valley Rd New Milford CT 06776

LEE, JONG-WON CECILIA, pediatrician; b. Seoul, Korea, May 31, 1937; s. Hun-Jae and Kyung-Ja (Suh) L.; came to U.S., 1964, naturalized, 1973; M.D., Soodo Med. Coll., Seoul, 1962; children—Robert Limb, Lawrence Limb. Intern, St. Joseph Hosp., Pitts., 1964-65; resident Coney Island Hosp., Bklyn., 1965-68, Meml. Cancer Center, N.Y.C., 1968-69; clin. instr. Downstate Med. Center, Bklyn., 1969-70; asst. attending Mt. Sinai Hosp. Services City Hosp. Center, Elmhurst, N.Y., 1971-73; mem. pediatric staff Central Flushing Upper Queens Med. Group, Flushing, N.Y., 1971—; asst. attending Flushing Hosp. and Med. Center, Booth Meml. Med. Center. Fellow Am. Acad. Pediatrics; mem. Queens Pediatric Soc., N.Y. State, Queens County med. socs. Home: 85-05 213th St Hollis Hills NY 11427 Office: 135-40 39th Ave Flushing NY 11354

LEE, JOSEPH YUEN-CHOR, chemist; b. Hong Kong, Nov. 3, 1933; s. Yook-Kan and Weng (Chang) L.; came to U.S., 1959, naturalized, 1969; B.A., Japan Internat. Christian U., 1958; M.S., Bklyn. Poly. Inst., 1965; Ph.D., City U. N.Y., 1970; m. Nelly D. Wang, June 17, 1961; 1 dau., May E. Analytical chemist Ungerer & Co., N.Y., 1960-62; research chemist Universal Petrochem. Inc., N.J., 1962-63; with RAI Research Corp., Hauppauge, N.Y., 1963—, dir. research and devel., 1970—. City U. N.Y. teaching fellow, 1968-70. Mem. Am. Chem. Soc., Electrochem. Soc., AAAS, Sigma Xi, Phi Lambda Upsilon. Contbg. author Zinc Silver Oxide Battery, 1971. Patentee in field. Home: 911 Hawkins Ave Lake Grove NY 11755 Office: 225 Marcus Blvd Hauppauge NY 11787

LEE, KEAT-JIN, otolaryngologist, plastic surgeon; b. Malaysia, Sept. 7, 1940; s. Cheng-Tin and Chooi-Sean (Saw) L.; came to U.S., 1958, naturalized, 1971; B.A. with honors, Harvard U., 1962; M.D., Columbia U., 1965; children—Kenneth, Lloyd. Intern, St. Luke's Hosp. Center, N.Y.C., 1965-66, resident, 1966-67; resident Mass. Eye and Ear Infirmary, Boston, 1967-70; practice medicine specializing in ear, nose, throat and facial plastic surgery, 1970—; mem. staff Hosp. St. Raphael, Yale-New Haven Hosp.; teaching fellow Harvard Med. Sch., Cambridge, Mass., 1969-70; clin. instr. U. Wash., Seattle, 1970-72; clin. instr. Yale U., 1972-76, asst. clin. prof., 1976—. Diplomate Am. Bd. Otolaryngology. Fellow A.C.S., Am. Acad. Facial Plastic and Reconstructive Surgery, Am. Assn. Cosmetic Surgery, Am. Acad. Ophthalmology and Otolaryngology, Am. Soc. Head and Neck Surgery; mem. Deafness Research Found. (life mem. Centurion Club, state co-chmn.), Assn. Harvard Chemists, Conn., New Haven County med. socs., New Eng. Otolaryng. Soc., Triological Soc. Author: The Otolaryngology Bds., 1973; Essential Otolaryngology, 1977; Differential Diagnosis in Otolaryngology, 1978; contbr. articles to profl. jours. Patentee surg. instruments for hypophysectomy, ear-mastoid air drill. Office: 98 York St New Haven CT 06511

LEE, KERMIT JAMES, JR., architect, educator; b. Springfield, Mass., Mar. 27, 1934; s. Kermit J. and Lillian (Jackson) L.; B.Arch. magna cum laude, Syracuse U., 1957; postgrad. Technische Hochschule, Braunschweig, Germany, 1958-59; m. Lore Leipelt, Oct. 19, 1963; children—Karin, Jason Anthony. With Coletti Bros., Boston, 1957-58; draftsman C.H. Erickson, architect, Lexington, Mass., 1958; chief archtl. br. Air Forces Europe Exchange, Wiesbaden, Germany, 1961-63; chief designer Pierre Zoelly, architect, Zurich, Switzerland, 1963-66; prof. architecture Syracuse (N.Y.) U., 1968—, dir. summer 76 program in Amsterdam, Netherlands, also dir. grad. programs in architecture, chmn. dean search com.; partner Lee, Scarbrough, Skoler, architecture engr., Syracuse, 1968-70; partner Architects' Partnership, 1970—; lectr. Boston Archtl. Center, 1957-58; adj. asso. prof. Columbia Grad. Sch. Architecture; profl. cons. Swiss Overseas Architects and Cons. Engrs., 1976; mem. faculty Inst. Energy Research, Syracuse U.; liaison to Inst. for Architecture and Urban Studies, N.Y.C. Mem. Syracuse Bldg. Code Bd. Appeals, Commn. to Revise City Charter; mem. nat. awards jury Reynolds design competition, 1976. Mem. Urban Am. Inc., Citizens Housing Council. Recipient Honor diploma Swiss Nat. Exhbn., 1964, 2d prize Moleson-Gruyere Design Competition, 1965. Fulbright fellow, Germany, 1958-59; Medary fellow AIA, 1960. Registered architect, N.Y., Mass. Mem. Soc. Archtl. Historians, AIA (del. conv. 1976, nat. design com. 1974-76), Everson Mus. Art, Syracuse Soc. Architects (dir.) Asso. Council Arts, AAUP, Am. Inst. Planners (asso.), N.Y. Coalition Black Architects, Nat. Orgn. Minority Architects, Assn. Collegiate Schs. Architecture, Munson-Williams Proctor Inst. Home: 104 Berkeley Dr Syracuse NY 13210

LEE, KOTIK KAI, scientist; b. Chungking, China, May 30, 1941; s. Shi Shien and Wen Ru (Hsia) L.; came to U.S., 1967, naturalized, 1975; B.S., Chung Yuan Coll., 1964; M.S., U. Ottawa, 1967; Ph.D., Syracuse U., 1972; m. Lydia Shu-Mei Ruo, Sept. 8, 1967; children—Jennifer Ming, Peter Hung. Research asso., instr. Syracuse U., 1972-73; asst. prof. Rio Grande Coll., 1973-74; vis. prof. U. Ottawa, 1974-76; research scientist Lab. for Laser Energetics, U. Rochester (N.Y.), 1977—. NRC Can. fellow, 1966-67; NRC Can. Research grantee, 1975-78. Mem. Am. Math. Soc., Am. Phys. Soc., Can. Assn. Physicists, Soc. Indsl. and Applied Math., Internat. Soc. Gen. Relativity and Gravitation. Contbr. articles to profl. jours.; reviewer sci. jours. Office: Lab for Laser Energetics U Rochester Rochester NY 14627

LEE, KWANG IN, pharm. co. exec.; b. Seoul, Korea, Jan. 4, 1941; s. Kyoung Kee and Sung Ann (Key) L.; came to U.S., 1963, naturalized, 1977; B.A., Seoul Nat. U., 1962; M.A. (fellow), So. Ill. U., 1969, postgrad., 1965-69; m. Grace Kyoung Yeun Park, Feb. 26, 1972; children—Elizabeth, David. Instr. econs. U. Mo.-Rolla, 1969-73; mktg. research analyst Hoffmann-LaRoche Inc., Nutley, N.J., 1973-74, sr. analyst, 1975, health econs. planner, 1975-76, health econs. planning mgr., 1977—. Mem. Am., Midwest econs. assns., Health Econs. Research Orgn., Am. Mktg. Assn., Omicron Delta Epsilon. Presbyterian. Home: 5 Ogden Pl Parsippany NJ 07054

LEE, MARJORIE ELLEN, chemist; b. Springfield, Ill., Mar. 8, 1934; d. Thomas Edgar and Dora Pearl (Ervin) Clayton; B.A., Millikin U., 1956; m. James Edward Lee, July 26, 1957; children—James Edgar Clayton, John Franklin, Georgette Ellen, Dora Marie. Lab. aide FBI, 1956-57; chemist U.S. Naval Engring. Experiment Sta., 1957-58; tchr. Anne Arundel County Edn. Dept., Severna Park, Md., 1962; chemist McCormick & Co., Balt., 1968-76, sr. chemist, 1976—. Mem. Inst. Food Technologists, Alpha Chi Omega. Democrat. Episcopalian. Home: 709 Arundel Pl Annapolis MD 21401

LEE, MILDRED ELSIE KIMBLE, educator; b. N.Y.C., Jan. 2, 1919; d. Ural and Ernestine Mildred (Scott) Kimble; B.A. cum laude, Hunter Coll., 1938; M.B.A., Baruch Coll., 1943; Ed.D., Fordham U., 1977; m. Granville Wheeler Lee, Nov. 9, 1940; 1 son, Granville Wheeler. Tchr., Morris High Sch., Bronx, 1949-54, guidance counselor, 1954-64, acting adminstrv. asst., 1964-66; dist. 8 supr. guidance N.Y.C. Bd. Edn., 1966-77; asst. prof. div. adminstrn., policy and urban edn. Fordham U., Lincoln Center, N.Y.C., 1977—; asso. dir., supr. practicum NDEA Inst. Guidance and Counseling, City U. N.Y., 1967-69; adj. faculty Adelphi U., Tchrs. Coll., Columbia U., 1976-77; co-dir. Humanistic Edn. Growth Center, 1975—. Mem. N.Y.C., Am. personnel and guidance assns., Ret. Sch. Suprs. and Adminstrs., Hunter Coll. Alumni Assn., City Coll., Fordham U. Sch. Edn. alumni assns., Am. Bridge Assn., Am. Contract Bridge Assn. Democrat. Baptist. Contbr. articles to profl. jours. Home: 3222 Fish Ave Bronx NY 10469 Office: 113 W 60th St Fordham U Sch Edn New York City NY 10023

LEE, MIN SHIU, research scientist; b. Taipei, Taiwan, June 30, 1940; s. T.C. and P.S. (Chen) L.; came to U.S., 1964, naturalized, 1972; Ph.D., Case Western Res. U., 1969; m. Amy Y. Su, Apr. 16, 1966; children—Terri S., David M. Teaching asst. N.Mex. Highlands U., Las Vegas, 1964-66; research asst. Case Western Res. U., Cleve., 1966-69; sr. research chemist FMC Corp./Avicon, Inc., Princeton, N.J., 1969-76; sr. research scientist Jelco Labs. div. Johnson & Johnson, Raritan, N.J., 1976—. Past chmn. steering com. Taiwan Christian Fellowship in Central Jersey, 1973—; treas. Univ. Chinese Sch. of Princeton, 1977—. Nat. Def. Ministry grantee, 1963-64; Inst. Sci. Research fellow, 1965-66. Mem. Am. Chem. Soc., AAAS, N.Y. Acad. Sci., Sigma Xi. Presbyterian. Patentee in field. Home: 14 Berkshire Dr Princeton Junction NJ 08550 Office: Johnson Dr Raritan NJ 08869

LEE, NELLIE UY, physician; b. Daet, Philippines, Oct. 7, 1943; d. Thomas and Rosita (Uy) L.; came to U.S., 1967; A.A. with high honors, Far Eastern U. (Philippines), 1961, M.D., 1966; m. Marshall Tan, Oct. 26, 1973; children—Emily Joyce, Eileen Jane. Intern, St. Vincent Hosp., Toledo, 1967-68; resident Mt. Sinai Hosp., Cleve., 1968-70, D.C. VA Hosp., 1971, St. Luke's Hosp., N.Y.C., 1971-73; internist, cardiologist Neighborhood Health Service Program, N.Y.C., 1973-78; cardiologist Am. Health Found., N.Y.C., 1973—; asst. clin. attending St. Luke's Hosp., St. Francis Hosp., Jersey City, St. Michael Hosp., Newark, Holy Name Hosp., Teaneck, N.J. Diplomate Am. Bd. Internal Medicine. Mem. AMA, Am. Heart Assn., Med. Soc. State N.J. Roman Catholic. Home and Office: 175 Hobart St Ridgefield Park NJ 07660 Office: 2675 Kennedy Blvd Jersey City NY 07306

LEE, PATRICIA KWAN-LUEN, obstetrician-gynecologist; b. Hong Kong, Nov. 17, 1924; d. Hung Chan and Yuen Heung (Wong) Li; came to U.S., 1949, naturalized, 1955; M.D., Nat. Med. Coll., Shanghai, China, 1950; postgrad. U. Minn., 1950, N.Y. U., 1954-55, Columbia U., 1965; m. Paul Che-Shen Chao, Sept. 22, 1950; children—Pauline Yuen-Wha, Philip Wan-Lan. Intern, Northwestern Hosp., Mpls., 1949-50, resident in obstetics-gynecology, 1950-52; asst. resident in obstetrics-gynecology Cumberland Hosp., Bklyn., 1953-54; practice medicine specializing in obstetrics-gynecology, Forest Hills, N.Y., 1956—; asst. vis. obstetrician-gynecologist Greenpoint (N.Y.) Hosp., 1957-62; staff N.Y. Infirmary, 1962-66, asso. attending physician, 1966-68; asst. attending physician St. John's Hosp., Queens, N.Y., 1962—. Diplomate Am. Bd. Obstetrics and Gynecology. Mem. AMA, Am.-Chinese, N.Y. State, Queens County med. socs. Home: 105-17 63 Rd Forest Hills NY 11375

LEE, PAUL TSEN-SHIONG, thoracic and cardiovascular surgeon; b. Taipei, Taiwan, Nov. 17, 1940; s. Chuen Chung and Chiu (Ping) L.; came to U.S., 1967, naturalized, 1976; M.D., Nat. Taiwan U., 1966; m. Irene A. Yeh, June 22, 1972; children—John, Stephen. Intern, Deaconess Hosp., Buffalo, 1967-68, resident in surgery, 1968-72, asst. surgeon, 1973—; resident in cardiothoracic surgery State U. N.Y., Buffalo, 1974-76; practice medicine specializing in thoracic and cardiovascular surgery, Buffalo, 1976—; asst. surgeon Erie County Med. Center, Buffalo, Kenmore Mercy Hosp., Buffalo, Buffalo Gen. Hosp. Diplomate Am. Bd. Surgery, Am. Bd. Thoracic Surgery. Roman Catholic. Home: 25 Ravensbrook Ct Getzville NY 14068 Office: 3435 Bailey Ave Buffalo NY 14215

LEE, RICHARD EDGAR, hosp. adminstr.; b. Lynn, Mass., Oct. 1, 1926; s. Oscar Bragdon and Susan (Buzzell) L.; B.S. in Bus. Adminstrn., Am. Internat. Coll., 1951; m. Joan Miller, Sept. 2, 1950; 1 son, Roger Miller. Accountant, Webster McCann, C.P.A., Boston, 1951-57; exec. dir. New Eng. Deaconess Assn., Concord, Mass., 1957-59; controller New Eng. Deaconess Hosp., Boston, 1959-63, asst. exec. dir., controller, 1963-66, asso. dir., 1966-67, dir., 1967—; dir. Joint Center for Radiation Therapy, 1968—, Med. Area Service Corp., 1974—; treas., dir. Down East, Inc., Bridgton, Maine, 1975—. Treas., trustee Carriage House Condominium Trust, Brookline, Mass., 1973—; bd. dirs. Kidney Found. Mass., 1976—. Served with USN, 1944-46. C.P.A., Mass. Mem. Nat., Mass. socs. C.P.A.'s, Mass. (treas. 1973-76, chmn. 1977-78), Am. hosp. assns., Hosp. Fin. Mgmt. Assn. (pres. Mass. chpt. 1963-64), Am. Coll. Hosp. Adminstrs., Conf. Boston Teaching Hosps., Met. Boston Hosp. Council (dir. 1975—), Greater Boston C. of C. (task force on nat. health ins. 1974), New Eng. Hosp. Assembly. Episcopalian. Clubs: Harvard of Boston, Mt. Auburn Tennis, Masons, Shriners. Home: 216 Saint Paul St Brookline MA 02146 Office: 185 Pilgrim Rd Boston MA 02215

LEE, RICHARD VAILLE, physician; b. Islip, N.Y., May 26, 1937; s. Louis Emerson and Erma Natalie (Little) L.; B.S., Yale U., 1960, M.D. cum laude, 1964; m. Susan Bradley, June 25, 1961; children—Matthew, Benjamin. Intern, Grace-New Haven Hosp., 1964-65, asst. resident in internal medicine, 1965-66, 69-70; fellow in inflammatory disease Yale U., New Haven, 1970-71; practice medicine specializing in internal medicine, New Haven, 1969-76, Buffalo, 1976—, in family practice, Poplar, Mont., 1966-68, Chester, Mont., 1968-69; asst. prof. medicine Yale U., 1971-74, asso. prof. clin. medicine, 1974-76; prof. medicine State U. of N.Y., Buffalo, 1976—; dir. primary care center Yale-New Haven Hosp., 1975-76, dir. of med. clinics, 1971-75; chief med. service Buffalo VA Hosp., 1976—; cons. in internal medicine N.Y. Zool. Soc., 1973—. Served with USPHS, 1966-68. Diplomate Am. Bd. Internal Medicine, Am. Bd. Family Practice. Fellow Am. Acad. Family Practice, ACP; mem. N.Y. Acad. Sci., Am. Fedn. Clin. Research, AMA, Flying Physicians Assn., Infectious Diseases Soc. Am., Alpha Omega Alpha. Contbr. articles on gen. medicine and infectious diseases to med. jours., also articles on health problems of isolated S. Am. Indian tribes. contbr. chpts. to books on obstetrics. Home: 7664 E Quaker Rd Orchard Park NY 14127 Office: 3495 Bailey Ave Buffalo NY 14215

LEE, (JOHN) ROBERT, JR., physician; b. N.Y.C., July 22, 1921; s. John Robert and Julia (Watts) L.; A.B., Columbia U., 1943; M.D., Cornell U., 1946. Intern, Gallinger Hosp., Washington, Meadowbrook Hosp., Hempstead, N.Y., 1946-48; resident in pathology Meadowbrook Hosp., 1948-49; resident in pediatrics, fellow in pediatric neurology, psychology and mental retardation N.Y. Med. Coll., 1954-57, from instr. to asst. prof. pediatrics, 1956—, also dir. profl. tng., asso. dir. pediatrics Mental Retardation Center, 1965-70; fellow endocrinology Johns Hopkins Hosp., 1957-58; practice medicine specializing in indsl. and pub. health medicine, N.Y.C., 1958-61, in pediatrics and mental retardation, adolescent drug addiction, N.Y.C. and Flushing, N.Y., 1961—; attending pediatrician Flower, Met. hosps.; cons. mental retardation, cerebral palsy, child and sch. health N.Y.C. Dept. Health, 1963—; med. rep. to coms. on handicapped for sch. dists. in Queens, N.Y.C., 1974—; dir. tng. Mental Retardation Center, N.Y. Med. Coll., 1965-70; med. cons., fed. monitor Head Start; med. cons. Assn. Help Retarded Children; med. examiner FAA, 1963—; med. dir. Assn. Children with Retarded Mental Devel., 1970-74, Addiction Research Treatment Corp., 1973-76. Bd. dirs. Jill Famm Found., N.Y.C., Greater Flushing Community Council. Served to lt. USNR, 1949-53. Diplomate Am. Bd. Pediatrics, Nat. Bd. Med. Examiners. Fellow A.C.P., Am. Soc. Human Genetics, Royal Soc. Medicine, Am. Acad. Pediatrics, Am. Acad. Cerebral Palsy, Am. Assn. Mental Deficiency; mem. N.Y. Acad. Sci., AMA, Am. Acad. on Mental Retardation, Mil. Order of World Wars, Navy League, Phi Chi. Address: 162-16 35th Ave Flushing NY 11358 also NY Medical College Dept Pediatrics 1249 Fifth Ave New York City NY 10029

LEE, SAMUEL CHING HSIN, pathologist; b. Kaifeng, Honan, China, Apr. 20, 1935; s. Peter H. and Ruth (Niu) L.; came to U.S., 1953, naturalized, 1958; B.S. magna cum laude, Belmont Coll., 1957; M.D., Vanderbilt U., 1961; m. Rosie Ann Lee, June 24, 1961; children—Mark S., Deanna R. Intern, Johns Hopkins Hosp., Balt., 1961-62, resident, 1962-64; resident, Am. Cancer Soc. fellow Meml. Hosp. for Cancer and Allied Diseases, N.Y.C., 1964-65, Upstate Med. Center, Syracuse, N.Y., 1965-66; asst. chief, acting dep. chief and acting dir. labs. USPHS Hosp., Balt., 1966-68; asso. pathologist, dir. blood bank St. Joseph Hosp., Balt., 1968—; vis. instr. med. tech. Towson (Md.) State U., 1972—. Served with USPHS, 1966-68. Recipient Physicians Recognition award AMA, 1974—. Diplomate Am. Bd. Pathology. Fellow Coll. Am. Pathologists, Am. Soc. Clin. Pathologists; mem. Am. Assn. Blood Banks, Internat. Acad. Pathology, Am. Assn. Tissue Banks, Johns Hopkins Med. and Surg. Assn., Md. Soc. Pathologists, AAAS, Nat.Assn. Residents and Interns, Nat. Soc. Histotechnology. Republican. Home: 14 Forest Ridge Ct Timonium MD 21093 Office: 7620 York Rd Baltimore MD 21204

LEE, SANG IK, multinational co. exec.; b. Mokpo, Korea, Apr. 10, 1930; s. Young Woo and Hyun Shim (Kim) L.; came to U.S., 1953, naturalized, 1961; student Seoul Nat. U., 1950-53; B.S. in Bus. Adminstrn., Bradley U., 1956; M.B.A., U. Pa., 1958; m. Frances Lee Ingels, June 7, 1956; children—Mark Key Nam, Andrea Mee Ryung. Accountant, U.S. Rubber Co., N.Y.C., 1958-60; systems mgr. Honeywell Electronic Data Processing, Wellesley Hills, Mass., 1960-66; advance application mgr. Western Union, Mahwah, N.J., 1966-67; v.p. Tech. Internat., Ridgewood, N.J., 1967-71; cons. Booz, Allen and Hamilton, N.Y.C., 1971-72; exec. ITT Hdqrs., N.Y.C., 1972—. Research grantee Urban League, 1957-58. Mem. Am. Mgmt. Assn., Data Processing Mgmt. Assn., Wharton Bus. Sch. Club. Presbyterian. Home: 133 Kenilworth Rd Ridgewood NJ 07450 Office: 320 Park Ave New York City NY 10022

LEE, SHEW KUHN, optometrist; b. Balt., Apr. 24, 1923; s. Mong Har and Gum Tuey (Wong) L.; Dr. Optometry, Ill. Coll. Optometry, 1949; postgrad. Catholic U. Am., 1957, Md. U., 1959; m. Florence Gin Toy, Oct. 29, 1949; children—Wayson Perry, Davin Jeffrey. Pvt. practice optometry, Washington, 1949—. Lectr. D.C. Traffic Safety Sch.; v.p. D.C. Bd. Optometry, 1959-65; mem. D.C. Bd. Examiners in Optometry, 1973—, sec., 1974; mem. Eye Bank Council; vision research cons. HEW, 1973. Bd. dirs. Eye Bank and Research Found., Washington Hosp. Center. Served with U.S. Army, 1942-45. Decorated Purple Heart, Bronze Star medal with oak leaf cluster. Mem. Am. Optometric Assn. (pres. joggers 1968—, distinguished service award 1974), Am. Legion (post comdr. D.C. 1960), D.C. Optometric Soc. (sec. 1956-57), Lees Assn. (trustee), Chinese Consol. Benevolent Assn., Flying Optometrist Assn. Am. (dir. 1974—), Beta Sigma Kappa. Lion (charter pres. Chi-Am. 1960, zone chmn. 1961, dep. dist. gov. 1963, hon. mem. Capital Hill; Extension award 1960, 75, Presdl. Banner award 1975). Research, publs. in field. Home: 2939 McKinley St NW Washington DC 20015 Office: 813 7th St NW Washington DC 20001

LEE, SIU LAM, entomologist, educator; b. Macao, China, Oct. 3, 1941; s. Ying Lam and Stella Yat-Koon (Tsang) L.; came to U.S., 1962, naturalized, 1975; M.A., Oberlin Coll., 1963; Ph.D., Cornell U., 1967; m. Evelyn Yee-Wai Miu, July 6, 1968. Teaching asst. dept. entomology Cornell U., Ithaca, N.Y., 1963-64, research asst., 1964-67; instr. biology Lowell (Mass.) State Coll., 1967-68, asst. prof., 1968-75; asst. prof. U. Lowell, 1975—; sci. cons. Town of Chelmsford (Mass.); cons. Champlain Valley Seed Growers' Corp., Westport, N.Y.; translator Chinese U. Hong Kong, 1972-75. NSF grantee, 1969-72. Mem. Internat. Bee Research Assn., Entomol. Soc. Am., AAAS, Animal Behavior Soc., Nat. Geog. Soc., Table Tennis Club (pres., faculty advisor), Sigma Xi. Research in new leaf-cutter bees, 1965, survival of introduced leaf-cutter bees, biology of leaf-cutter bees in N.Y. State, 1968. Home: 70 Acton Rd Chelmsford MA 01824 Office: Dept of Biology South Campus U of Lowell Lowell MA 10854

LEE, TAY BONG, otolaryngologist; b. Korea, Feb. 28, 1939; s. Moon Han and Soo Duck (Yoon) L.; came to U.S., 1965, naturalized, 1978; M.D., Seoul Nat. U., 1962. Rotating intern Springfield (Mass.) Hosp. Med. Center, 1965-66, resident in surgery, 1966-70; resident in surgery Meml. Hosp. for Cancer and Allied Diseases, N.Y.C., 1970-71; resident in otolaryngology Roosevelt Hosp., N.Y.C., 1971-74; asso. attending otolaryngologist St. Clare's Hosp., N.Y.C., 1975—. Diplomate Am. Bd. Surgery, Am. Bd. Otolaryngology. Fellow A.C.S.; mem. Am. Acad. Ophthalmology and Otolaryngology, AMA. Home: 100 Northwood Ave Demarest NJ 07627 Office: 30 Central Park S New York City NY 10019

LEE, THOMAS H., elec. mfg. co. exec.; b. Shanghai, China, May 11, 1923; s. Yin Chin and Nan (Hu) L.; B.M.E., Nat. Chiao Tung U. (China), 1946; M.E.E., Union Coll., 1950; Ph.D., Rensselaer Poly. Inst., 1954; m. Kin Ping Lee, June 12, 1948; children—William F., Thomas H., Richard T. Came to U.S., 1948, naturalized, 1953. With Gen. Electric Co., 1948—, sr. physicist, Phila., 1955-67, mgr. engring. research, 1967-71, mgr. lab. ops., 1971, mgr. group tech. resources operation, 1971-74, mgr. strategic planning operation power generation bus. group, Fairfield, Conn., 1974-77, staff exec. strategic planning and devel. ops., power systems, 1974-78, staff exec. power systems tech. operation, 1978—; adj. prof. Rensselaer Poly. Inst., 1954-55; lectr. U. Pa., 1959-61. Pres., Nether Providence Exec. PTO, 1963-64; vice chmn. Community Adult Edn. Classes, Media, Pa., 1963-66. Fellow IEEE (chmn. awards com. 1967-69, adminstrv. com. 1969, treas. 1972-73, v.p. 1973-74); mem. Nat. Acad. Engring., Power Engring. Soc. (pres. 1974). Patentee switching devices. Home: 1402 Melville Ave Fairfield CT 06430 Office: Gen Electric Co Fairfield CT 06431

LEE, TONG-NYONG, physicist; b. Seoul, Korea, July 22, 1927; s. Peng-Do Lee (Yi); B.S. in Physics, Seoul Nat. U., 1950; Ph.D. in Nuclear Physics, U. London, 1959; m. Mee-Hoy Lee, Aug. 15, 1959; children—Eun-Kyu, Myung-Moo, Jin-Moo. Asst. prof. physics Seoul Nat. U., 1960-63; asso. prof. space sci. Cath. U. Am., Washington, 1964-70; research physicist Naval Research Lab., Washington, 1970—. Recipient Sam-Il Cultural prize Republic of Korea, 1961; NASA research grantee, 1966-70. Mem. Am. Phys. Soc., Am. Astron. Soc. Researcher plasma physics, atomic spectroscopy, short wave length lasers, and numerous others. Home: 3301 Stonesboro Rd Oxon Hill MD 20022

LEE, TSUNG-DAO, educator; b. Shanghai, China, Nov. 25, 1926; s. Tsing-Kong Lee and Ming-Chang Chang; student Nat. Chekiang U., Kweichow, China, 1943-44, Nat. S.W. Asso. U., Kunming, China, 1945-46; Ph.D., U. Chgo., 1950; m. Jeannette Chin, June 3, 1950; children—James, Stephen. Research asso. astronomy U. Chgo., 1950; research asso., lectr. physics U. Calif., 1950-51; mem. Inst. Advanced Study, Princeton, 1951-53, prof. physics, 1960-63; asst. prof. physics Columbia, 1953-55, asso. prof., 1955-56, prof., 1956-60, 63—, Enrico Fermi prof. physics, 1964, adj. prof., 1960-62; Loeb lectr. Harvard, 1957, 64. Recipient Albert Einstein award in sci. Yeshiva U., 1957; (with Chen Ning Yang) Nobel Prize in physics, 1957. Mem. Nat. Acad. Sci. Address: Dept Physics Columbia U New York City NY 10027

LEE, WILLIAM GEORGE, clin. psychologist; b. Allentown, Pa., Apr. 14, 1948; s. Harry F. and Bette E.; B.S., Pa. State U., 1970; M.S., U. Scranton, 1974; postgrad. Temple U., 1977—; m. Jean Ann Rutt, Jan. 17, 1970; children—William, Melissa, Gregory. Activity therapist Hamburg (Pa.) State Sch. and Hosp., 1970-71; vocat. evaluator and counselor Allentown (Pa.) State Hosp., 1972-75; clin. psychologist Allentown State Hosp. and Lehigh County Crisis Intervention Unit, 1975—. Bd. dirs. Lehigh Valley Drug Abuse Services, 1975-76, Mental Health Assn. Lehigh Valley, 1975—, sec., 1976-77, v.p., 1977-78, pres.-elect, 1978-79. Certified marriage and family counselor, licensed psychologist. Mem. Am., Pa., Lehigh Valley (sec. 1977-79) psychol. assns., Am. Assn. Marriage and Family Counselors. Contbr. articles in field to profl. jours. Home: 1196 Granite Dr Bethlehem PA 18017 Office: Psychology Dept Allentown State Hosp Allentown PA 18103

LEE, WON JAY, radiologist, educator; b. Seoul, Korea, Feb. 2, 1938; s. Kang Sei and Choon Ja. (Park) L.; came to U.S., 1965, naturalized, 1976; M.D., Yonsei U., Korea, 1962; m. Moon Jung Lee, Feb. 24, 1968; children—Julie, Lisa, Jennifer. Rotating intern Wyckoff Heights Hosp., Bklyn., 1965-66; resident in radiology N.Y. U. Med. Center, N.Y.C., 1966-69; fellow, asst. radiologist in diagnostic radiology L.I. Jewish Med. Center (N.Y.), 1969-71, staff radiologist, 1975—, sect. head uroradiology, 1976—; staff diagnostic radiology and nuclear medicine Binghamton (N.Y.) Gen. Hosp., 1971-75; asst. prof. State U. N.Y. Sch. Medicine, Stony Brook, 1975—. Served to 1st lt., med. officer Korean Army, 1962-65. Diplomate Am. Bd. Radiology, Am. Bd. Nuclear Medicine. Contbr. articles to med. jours. Home: 15 Lucille Ln Dix Hills NY 11746 Office: 270 05 76th Ave New Hyde Park NY 11040

LEE, WON-KYU, cardiologist; b. Seoul, Korea, Feb. 9, 1945; s. Kun-Young and Yong-Ja (Park) L.; came to U.S., 1972; M.D., Yonsei U., Korea, 1969, M. Med. Sci., 1972; m. Hwain C., May, 1970; children—John, Charles, Julie. Intern, Daejun Base Hosp., Korea, 1969-70; med. officer Aeromed. Center, Grad. Sch., Yonsei U., 1970-72; intern L.I. Coll. Hosp., N.Y., 1972-73; resident in internal medicine Martland Hosp. unit Coll. Medicine and Dentistry N.J., Newark, 1973-75, fellow in cardiology, 1975-77; clin. asst. prof. dept. medicine, 1977—. Diplomate Am. Bd. Internal Medicine. Recipient Young Investigator's award Deborah Heart and Lung Assn., 1977; Am. Heart Assn. grantee, 1976. Fellow A.C.P., Am. Coll. Cardiology, Council Clin. Cardiology of AMA; mem. Essex County Med. Soc. of N.J. Contbr. articles to profl. jours. Home: 27 Ackerson Ave Pequannock NJ 07440

LEE, YING KAO, chemist; b. Shanghai, China, Dec. 14, 1932; s. Ding Ton and Shun Ying (Lin) L.; came to U.S., 1957, naturalized, 1970; Bs.C., Tan Tung U., Shanghai, China; Ph.D., U. Cin., 1961; m. Theresa Tai, Sept. 9, 1961; children—Arthur Carlson, Annette, Angela. Sr. research chemist Tex. U.S. Chem. Co., Parsippany, N.J., 1961-63, group leader, 1963-65; research chemist E. I. du Pont de Nemours Inc., Phila., 1965-69, staff chemist, 1969-71, research asso., 1971-76, research fellow, 1976—; partner Lee's Art Studio. NSF fellow, 1958-60. Mem. Am. Chem. Soc., Sigma Xi. Inventor lucite dispersion lacquer paint. Home: 423 Jamaica Dr Cherry Hill NJ 08034 Office: 3500 Graysferry Ave Philadelphia PA 19146

LEE, YOUNG IL, physician; b. Hamman-do, Korea, Jan. 13, 1942; s. Soon Won and Chung Hee (Choi) L.; M.D., Seoul Nat. U., 1966; m. Hyun K. Rhee, Dec. 1, 1970; children—Eugene Lee, E. John Lee, Sandra Lee. Intern, Nazareth Hosp., Phila., 1971; resident in medicine Coll. Medicine and Dentistry N.J., Martland Hosp., Newark, 1972-75, fellow in cardiology, 1975-77; practice medicine specializing in cardiology, Clark, N.J., 1977—; mem. staff Rahway (N.J.) Hosp., 1977—, St. Elizabeth Hosp., Elizabeth, N.J. Diplomate Am. Bd. Internal Medicine. Mem. Union County Med. Soc. Presbyterian. Home: 1991 Winding Brook Way Scotch Plains NJ 07076 Office: 53-59 Westfield Ave Clark NJ 07066

LEECH, ALMA DAVENPORT CASE, assn. exec.; b. Mercer County, Ky., June 26, 1922; d. John Victor and Georgia Powell (Davenport) Case; ed. Northwestern U.; m. Stephen Kenneth Leech, Dec. 27, 1952; children—S. Kenneth, Darryl C. Adminstrv. asst., conv. mgr. A.C.S., Chgo., 1945-50; exec. sec. Internat. Coll. Surgeons, Chgo., 1950-52; mng. editor Fifth Dist. Dental Bull. N.Y., Dewitt, 1955—, exec. dir Fifth Dist. Dental Soc., 1956—. Bd. dirs. Hall of Health, N.Y. State Fair. Recipient Dental Editors award Ohio State U.-Am. Dental Assn., 1969. Mem. Am. Soc. Assn. Execs., Dental Editors Assn., Component Soc. Execs. (pres. 1974-75). Episcopalian. Home: 201 Lansdowne Rd Dewitt NY 13214 Office: Box 135 Dewitt NY 13214*

LEECH, JAMES WILLIAM, clergyman; b. Providence, Oct. 12, 1940; s. James Rogers and Helen (Walker) L.; B.A., Hobart Coll., 1962; S.T.B., Gen. Theol. Sem., 1965. Ordained deacon Protestant Episcopal Ch., 1965, priest, 1966; curate Grace Ch., Bath, Maine, 1965-66; rector All Saints' Ch. in Pontiac, Warwick, R.I., 1966-72, Ch. of the Epiphany, Providence, 1972—; canon Cathedral of St. John, Providence, 1978—; asso. chaplain R.I. State Hosp., 1966-72; mem. R.I. Commn. on Christian Healing, Providence. Mem. R.I. Civic Chorale, Narcotics Guidance Council of Warwick City Council; dir. P.I.T., teen-age crisis center; bd. dirs. R.I. Tb and Respiratory Disease Assn., Providence Central YMCA, R.I. chpt. Cystic Fibrosis, R.I. chpt. Big Bros., St. Elizabeth's Home for Aged Women, Diocesean Council R.I., House of Hope; mem. health steering com. Council of Community Services; chmn. Christian Social Relations R.I. Mem. Soc. Holy Cross. Home and Office: 542 Potters Ave Providence RI 02907

LEECH, JOHN WARNER, govt. ofcl.; b. Jamaica, N.Y., Feb. 2, 1933; s. John Holdridge Dewey and Flora Teressa (Warner) L.; B.A., Williams Coll., 1955; M.S., Mass. Inst. Tech., 1958, Ph.D., 1967; m. Arlene L. Normandie, Oct. 14, 1967; children—John D., Teresina W., Katharine T., Harriet D. Research engr. Aeroelastic and Structures Research Lab., Mass. Inst. Tech., 1956-74; asso. prof. aerospace engring., asst. dean engring. Boston U., 1970-74; program mgr. NSF, Washington, 1973-75; program mgr. ERDA, 1975-77, solar energy program specialist, 1977—; ofcl. Dept. Energy, 1977—; bd. advisers So. Calif. Solar Energy Assos. Registered profl. engr., Mass. Asso. fellow Am. Inst. Aeros. and Astronautics; mem. Sigma Xi, Sigma Gamma Tau, Phi Sigma Kappa. Clubs: Stateman's, Mass. Inst. Tech. Faculty, Admirals. Home: 5216 Pooks Hill Rd Bethesda MD 20014 Office: 20 Massachusetts Ave NW Washington DC 20545

LEEDHAM, CHARLES LAURN, med. ednl. adminstr.; b. Clinton, Iowa, Feb. 11, 1904; s. Charles H. and Elizabeth (Schriener) L.; B.S., State U. Iowa, 1926, M.D., 1928; m. Esther Edith Gearhart, July 31, 1925; children—Charles Gearhart, Robin Kirkwood William, Judith Leedham Fike. Intern, Marine Hosp. S.I., 1928-29; commd. 1st lt., M.C., U.S. Army, 1929, advanced through grades to col., 1943, ret., 1955; resident internal medicine Walter Reed Gen. Hosp., Washington, 1931-33; surgeon CBI, 1942-44; chief med. services Kans., Ga., T.H., 1946-51; prof. clin. medicine U. Ga., 1948-50; chief med. cons. U.S. Forces, Far East Command, 1951-53; chief edn., tng. div. Army Med. Service, 1953-55; dir. Frank E. Bunts Ednl. Inst., 1955-62; dir. Bur. Ednl. Activities, Pa. State Dept. Health, 1962-75; dir. med. edn. Cleve. Clinic Found., 1955-62; vis. lectr. U. Pitts. Grad. Sch. Pub. Health; past vis. lectr. in preventive medicine Jefferson Med. Coll., vis. prof. preventive medicine, 1969—. Bd. dirs. Nat. Assn. Practical Nurse Edn., 1956-66, v.p., 1958-62; bd. dirs. Tb and Health Soc. Dauphin and Perry Counties, 1968—; mem. adv. bd. Harrisburg Hosp., 1973—, mem. edn. com., 1963—. Decorated Legion of Merit, Bronze Star. Diplomate Am. Bd. Internal Medicine. Licensed physician, Iowa, Tex., Ohio, Pa. Fellow A.C.P.; mem. AMA (ho. of dels. 1956-63, 72—, council on nat. security 1960-69, council on health manpower 1968-70, mem. nursing com. 1962-71, chmn. 1968-70), Am. Heart Assn. (pres. S. Central Pa. chpt. 1975-76), Soc. Med. Cons. to Armed Forces (chmn. emergency med. services com. 1965-71, mem. council 1971-75, sec.-treas. 1976-78, v.p. 1978-79), Am. Therapeutic Soc. (council 1956-69, pres. 1959-60), Cleve. Acad. Medicine (chmn. disaster relief com. 1957-59), Pa. Med. Soc. (disaster medicine commn., 1963-67, mem. com. on allied health professions 1968-73, mem. council edn. and sci. 1976—, commn. on edn. and manpower). Mason; pres. Nat. Sojourners, 1960-61. Author textbook, articles in field; editor Pennsylvania's Health, 1966-75; editorial bd. Jour. Student Am. Med. Assn., 1957-67; Resident Physician, 1955-70. Home: 2409 Midland Rd Harrisburg PA 17104 Office: PO Box 4033 Harrisburg PA 17111

LEEDS, BARRY HOWARD, educator, lit. critic; b. N.Y.C., Dec. 6, 1940; s. Andrew and Paula (Stark) L.; B.A., Columbia, 1962, M.A., 1963; Ph.D., Ohio U., 1967; m. Robin Cornwell, Apr. 20, 1968; children—Brett Ashley, Leslie Robin. Lectr. English, U. City N.Y., 1963-64; instr. English, U. Tex., El Paso, 1964-65; asst. prof. English, Central Conn. State Coll., 1968-71, asso. prof., 1971-76, prof., 1976—. Cons. Am. lit. Choice mag.; drama critic El Paso Herald-Post, 1965; lit. critic Sat. Rev., Modern Fiction Studies, other mags., jours. Mem. Am. Assn. U. Profs. Author: The Structured Vision of Norman Mailer, 1969. Home: Jerome Ave RFD 3 Burlington CT 06013 Office: Central Conn State Coll New Britain CT 06050

LEEDS, DONALD SEARCUS, educator; b. Bklyn., Feb. 5, 1926; s. Jack A. and Beatrice (Searcus) L.; A.B., N.Y. U., 1950, A.M., 1951; Ed.D., Boston U., 1969; m. Joan Boyer, Sept. 1, 1970; children—Holly, Shari. Instr. reading inst. N.Y. U., N.Y.C., 1954-62; reading coordinator pub. schs., Niagara Falls, N.Y., 1962-64; asst. prof. Northeastern U., Boston, 1965-69; asso. prof. U. Wis. at Superior, 1969-71; asso. prof. communication scis. Kean Coll., Union, N.J., 1971-74; asso. prof. reading edn. Wagner Coll., S.I., N.Y., 1974—, dir. Reading Center, 1974—. Cons. in field of reading. Bd. dirs. Harbor Day Sch., Red Bank, N.J. Served with 374th Inf. Div., AUS, 1944-45. Decorated Bronze Star, Purple Heart. Recipient Lavine research award U. Wis.-Superior, 1969. Mem. Internat. Reading Assn., Am., N.J. psychol. assns., Nat. Soc. for Study Edn., NEA, N.J. Assn. Learning Consultants, Am. Ednl. Research Assn., Council for Exceptional Children, Nat. Council Research English. Club: Masons. Home: 9 Ferland Ln Aberdeen NJ 07747 Office: Wagner Coll Staten Island NY 10301

LEEDS, KENNETH WARREN, lawyer, chem. co. exec.; b. N.Y.C., Apr. 30, 1940; s. Mark K. and Claire S. (Gursky) L.; B.A., Queens Coll. City U. N.Y., 1961, LL.B., 1964, J.D., 1968; m. Pamela Fern Jasser, Aug. 18, 1962; children—Claire Sharon, William Jason. Closing atty. Security Title & Guaranty Co., Mineola, N.Y., 1964-66; admitted to N.Y. State bar, 1966; house counsel Anchor Chem. Co., Inc., Hicksville, N.Y., 1966-71; exec. v.p., sec.-treas., counsel Anchor Chem. Co. Inc., Hicksville, N.Y., 1971—; v.p. Orlans Equipment & Machinery Corp., Great Neck, N.Y., 1975—, also dir.; pres. L.I. Graphic Arts Assn. N.Y., 1974-76; pres. Agnate Chems Inc., Los Angeles, 1971—. Mem. L.I. Graphic Arts Assn., Am., N.Y. State bar assns., N.Y. Printing House Craftsmen, Phi Alpha Delta. Club: B'nai B'rith (pres. lodge 1977—). Patentee in field. Home: 2719 Elm Dr North Bellmore NY 11710 Office: 500 W John St Hicksville NY 11801

LEEMING, BRIAN WILLIAM, radiologist; b. Christchurch, N.Z., Feb. 14, 1924; came to U.S., 1970; s. Charles Patrick and Agnes Mary (Cunningham) L.; M.B., Ch.B., Otago U., 1951; m. June Elizabeth Hayes, Jan. 3, 1953; children—Simon, Nicola, Nigel, Rupert, Gregory. Registrar radiology Guys Hosp., London, 1957-58; charge radiologist Hutt Hosp., N.Z., 1959-64; sr. radiologist Auckland Hosp., N.Z., 1965-69; lectr. radiology Harvard Med. Sch., 1970, asst. prof., 1971—; sr. radiologist Beth Israel Hosp., Boston, 1970—. Served to capt. N.Z. Army, 1954-68. Diplomate Am. Bd. Radiology. Fellow Royal Australasian Coll. Radiologists, Royal Coll. Radiologists U.K., Royal Australasian Coll. Physicians; mem. Mass. Med. Soc., Mass. Radiol. Soc., New Eng. Roentgen Ray Soc. Roman Catholic. Office: 330 Brookline Ave Boston MA 02215

LEEN, ALBERT, elec. engr.; b. Bronx, N.Y., Aug. 7, 1913; s. Benjamin and Mary (Dobkin) L.; B.E.E., Coll. City N.Y., 1939; M.S., Columbia U., 1948; M.S., N.J. Inst. Tech., 1969; m. Miriam Proskauer, Oct. 16, 1949; children—Russell Ian, Todd Kevin. Electronic engr. United Transformer Corp., N.Y.C., 1940-41, Freed Radio Corp., N.Y.C., 1941-43, Standard Electronic Research Corp., N.Y.C., 1943-50; sr. engr. McGraw-Edison Co., Manchester, N.H., 1950—. Registered profl. engr., N.H. Mem. IEEE (sr.), Am. Vacuum Soc. Home: RFD 5 Seton Dr Bedford NH 03102

LEEPER, JOHN HOPKINS, mgmt. cons. co. exec.; b. Garden City, Kans., Dec. 7, 1937; s. John Wesley and Ruth Geneva (Hopkins) L.; B.S., U. Colo., 1960; M.B.A., U. Am., Washington, 1967; m. Margaret Elizabeth Connolly, June 23, 1963; children—John Douglas,

Matthew Teal. Civilian analyst Def. Intelligence Agy., Arlington, Va., 1964-67; sr. project mgr. Maritime Transp. Research Bd., NRC, Nat. Acad. Scis., Washington, 1967-75; v.p., Simat Helliesen & Eichner, Washington, 1975—; lectr. in field. Mem. Arlington County (Va.) Republican Com., 1971; adv. mem. bd. trustees Nat. Orthopaedic and Rehab. Hosp., 1972—. Served to lt. USNR, 1960-64. Recipient Nat. Safety Council Gen. Chmn.'s award, 1977. Mem. Am. Soc. Traffic and Transp. (award 1967), Soc. Naval Architects and Marine Engrs., Permanent Internat. Assn. Nav. Congresses, Mont. State Soc. Congregationalist. Club: Propeller (pres. Washington 1976-77). Home: 6213 Nethercombe Ct McLean VA 22101 Office: 1019 19th St PH1 Washington DC 20036

LEEPER, ROBERT DWIGHT, physician; b. Lewiston, Idaho, Nov. 9, 1924; s. Robert Dwight and Grace Anne (Hanly) L.; B.S., U. Idaho, 1949; M.D., Columbia U., 1953; m. Virginia Frances Knapp, Aug. 2, 1952; children—Dwight, Paul, James, Thomas. Intern, Bklyn. Hosp., 1953-54, resident, 1954-56, chief resident, 1956-57; fellow Sloan-Kettering Inst., N.Y.C., 1957-60, asso., 1960-66, asso. mem., 1966—; mem. faculty Cornell U. Med. Sch., 1962—, asso. prof. medicine, 1974—; mem. staff Mem. Hosp. Cancer Research, 1962—, attending physician, asst. chmn. dept. medicine, 1976—; cons. Nat. Cancer Inst. Mem. sch. bd., Eastchester, N.Y., 1963-64. Served with AUS, 1943-46. Am. Cancer Soc. scholar, 1961-66; fellow N.Y. Heart Assn., 1958-60. Mem. Am. Thyroid Assn., Endocrine Soc., AAAS, N.Y. Acad. Scis., Soc. Internal Medicine, Phi Gamma Delta. Clubs: Fox Meadow Tennis; Meguntícook Golf. Author research papers, chpts. in books. Home: 28 Walworth Ave Scarsdale NY 10583 Office: 1275 York Ave New York City NY 10021

LEER, JOHN ADDISON, JR., physician, med. research adminstr.; b. Penn Twp., Pa., Dec. 8, 1922; s. John A. and Mary Ann (Cockley) L.; student Shippensburg State Coll., 1940-43; M.D., Temple U., 1946, M.S. in Pediatrics, 1952; m. Kathryn Captola Kise, Mar. 16, 1946; children—Barbara Jo, Mary Anne. Intern, Temple U. Hosp., Phila., 1946-47, resident in pediatrics, 1949-52; pracitce medicine specializing in pediatrics, York, Pa., 1952-63; mem. staff York Hosp., 1954-63, med. research div. Schering Corp., Bloomfield, N.J., 1963-65, asso. dir. med. research, 1965-68, dir. clin. investigation, 1968-73, sr. fellow med. research div., 1973-76, sr. dir. dermatology research, 1976—; clin. asst. prof. dept. pediatrics N.J. Coll. Medicine, Jersey City, 1967-72; mem. vol. teaching staff dept. pediatrics Martland Hosp., United Hosps., Newark, 1970-72. Served with USPHS, 1947-49. Diplomate Am. Bd. Pediatrics. Fellow Am. Acad. Pediatrics (chmn. sect. clin. pharmacology and therapeutics 1976-78); mem. Am. Acad. Dermatology, AMA, Am. Soc. Pharmacology and Therapeutics, N.Y. Acad. Scis., Essex County Med. Soc., Pan-Am. Med. Assn., Am. Soc. Pediatric Dermatology (charter). Presbyterian. Home: 24 Springbrook Morristown NJ 07960 Office: 60 Orange St Bloomfield NJ 07003

LEERS, WOLF-DIETRICH, physician, microbiologist; b. Halle Germany, Aug. 9, 1927; s. Walter R. and Liselotte (Guelland) L.; came to Can., 1958, naturalized, 1966; student U. Goettingen, 1949-51, U. Freiburg Med. Sch., 1951-52; M.D., U. Wuerzburg, 1955; Diploma in Bacteriology, U. Toronto, 1963, Ph.D. in Microbiology (Fitzgerald Meml. fellow), 1967; fellow Royal Coll. Physicians and Surgeons (Can.); m. Mar. 28, 1956; children—Ulrika G., Dirk R., Karen P., Heiko D. Intern, Univ. Clinic, Hamburg-Eppendorf, Germany, 1955-56; resident in otolaryngology and surgery Stadt Krankenhaus, Verden, Germany, 1956-58; intern Victoria Hosp., London, Ont., Can., 1958-59, resident in clin. bacteriology, 1960-61; resident St. Joseph's Hosp., London, 1959-60; fellow in pathology and microbiology dept. Pub. Health Labs., Toronto, 1961-62; microbiologist-in-chief Wellesley Hosp., Toronto, 1967—; cons. Princess Margaret Hosp., Toronto, 1967—; cons. Ont. Cancer Inst., 1967—; asso. prof. dept. med. microbiology U. Toronto, 1977—, asst. prof. dept. microbiology and parasitology, 1967—; civil aviation med. examiner Ministry of Transport. Served with German Navy, 1943-45. Mem. Canadian Med. Assn., Canadian, Am. socs. microbiologists, Canadian Soc. Med. Microbiologists, Canadian Pub. Health Assn., Canadian Soc. Aviation Medicine, Am. Acad. Microbiologists, N.Y. Acad. Scis., Royal Canadian Flying Club Assn., So. Ont. Soaring Assn. Clubs: Schlaraffia, Masons. Contbr. articles to med. and sci. jours. Home: 15 Plumbstead Ct Islington ON M9A 1V4 Canada Office: Wellesley Hospital 160 Wellesley St E Toronto ON M4Y 1J3 Canada

LEES, AVON, JR., sch adminstr.; b. Mpls., Sept. 13, 1915; s. Avon and Ethel (Peterson) L.; student Mpls. Coll. Art, 1934-37, U. Minn., 1946, U. Chgo., 1956; m. Mary Shattuck, Aug. 17, 1946; 1 dau., Deborah (dec.). With Dayton's Dept. Store, Mpls., 1938-40, 46-63, merchandising v.p., 1960-61, corporate v.p., 1961-63; v.p., asso. dir. Tobe-Coburn Sch., N.Y.C., 1963-68, pres., dir., 1968—. Served with USAAF and U.S. Army, 1940-45. Decorated Croix de Guerre (France), Dutch-Orange Lanyard, Belgian Fourraget. Mem. English-Speaking Union. Republican. Episcopalian. Clubs: Amateur Comedy, Regency. Home: 118 E 60th St New York City NY 10022 Office: 851 Madison Ave New York City NY 10021

LEES, CARLTON BROWN, horticulturist; b. Windsor, Conn., Feb. 16, 1924; s. Carlton Brown and Dorothy (St. John) L.; B.S., U. Conn., 1950; M.S., Cornell U., 1952; m. Marian Louise Wicks, Apr. 13, 1946; children—Peter St. John, Stephen Wicks, Barbara Ellen, James Carlton. Asst. horticulturist Bklyn. Bot. Garden, 1950-51; teaching asst. Cornell U., 1951-52; instr. W.Va. U., Morgantown, 1952-54; horticulturist Kingwood Center, Mansfield, Ohio, 1954-59; dir. Pa. Hort. Soc., Phila., 1959-63; exec. dir. Mass. Hort. Soc., Boston, 1963-73; pub., dir. Horticulture mag., 1963-73; v.p. N.Y. Bot. Garden, Bronx, 1973-77, sr. v.p., 1977—. Served with USNR, 1943-46. Recipient Helen Hull Certificate of Merit for Hort. Lit., Nat. Council State Garden Clubs, 1972. Mem. Am. Hort. Soc., Garden Writers Am. (pres. 1971-75), Pi Alpha Xi, Alpha Zeta. Author: Budget Landscaping, 1960, Gardens, Plants and Man, 1970. Home: Enoch Crosby Rd RD 1 Brewster NY 10509 Office: NY Bot Garden Bronx NY 10458

LEESE, BERNARD MCKENZIE, botanist; b. Keyser, W.Va., Jan. 17, 1925; s. Bernard McKenzie and Viola (Whitacre) L.; A.A., Potomac State Coll., 1948; B.S. in Botany, George Washington U., 1951, M.S. in Plant Physiology, 1961; postgrad. U. Md., 1961-62; m. Mary Anne Minnich, Oct. 30, 1950; children—Barry, Jeffrey M., April A. Seed and plant taxonomist U.S. Dept. Agr., Beltsville, Md., 1951-56, plant explorer, 1956-60, plant variety specialist, 1960-62, head Fed. Seed Labs., 1962-70, chief examiner Plant Variety Protection Office, 1970-78, commr. office, 1978—, exec. sec. Plant Variety Protection Bd.; Rockefeller Found. plant explorer for World Sorghum Germplasm Collection in Ethiopia, 1967-68. Mem. adv. bd. edn. St. John Baptist Sch., Silver Spring, Md. Research in identification Asiatic beans by seed characteristics, 1956. Home: 210 Kimblewick Dr Silver Spring MD 20904 Office: care US Dept Agr Beltsville MD 20705

LE FANTE, JOSEPH ANTHONY, congressman; b. Bayonne, N.J., Sept. 8, 1928; student St. Peters Inst. Indsl. Relations, 1953-55, Real Estate Inst. N.J., 1957; m. Florence Beym, Nov. 27, 1948; children—Janice, Diane, Thomas. Pres. employees assn. Corn Products Best Foods Corp., Bayonne, to 1959; pres. Pub. Service Furniture Co., Bayonne, 1959—; mem. N.J. Gen. Assembly, 1969-77, chmn. appropriations com., 1972, majority leader, 1974-75, speaker, 1976; mem. 95th Congress from 14th N.J. Dist.; mem. N.J. Law, Revision, and Legis. Commn., 1974-76, Legis. Drug Commn., 1972, Legis. Pedestrian Safety Commn., 1972, Law and Pub. Safety Com., 1970-72, N.J. Law Enforcement Planning Agency, 1976. Mem. Hudson Higher Edn. Consortium, 1973-76, Bayonne Municipal Council, 1962-70, Bayonne Bd. Sch. Estimate, 1964-67, Bayonne Charter Commn., 1960-61, Bayonne Mayor's Commn. on Drug Abuse, 1967-74; chmn. Hudson County Hosp. Planning Commn., 1972-74; chmn. Code Enforcement Agency. Recipient awards St. John's U., 1975, Columbia Coll., 1976, New Jersey Chiropratic Soc., 1972; named Man of Year, Jaycees; Layman of Year, Am. Chiropractic Assn., 1976. Mem. Bayonne Democratic Club, Greater Bayonne League, New Frontier Democratic Club, N.J. Furniture Assn. (bd. dirs. 1975—), Assumption Holy Name Soc. Internat. Narcotic Enforcement Officers Assn. Clubs: Elks, K.C. Home: 66 W 36th St Bayonne NJ 07002 Office: 507 Cannon House Office Bldg Washington DC 20515*

LEFER, JAY, psychoanalyst; b. N.Y.C., June 4, 1930; s. Ben-Zion and Gertrude L.; A.B., Columbia U., 1950; M.D., U. Lausanne, Switzerland, 1955; student Oxford U., Eng., 1953-54; m. Elizabeth Anne Griffin, July 28, 1968; children—David Gerard, Theodore Benedict. Intern, French Hosp., N.Y.C., 1956; chief resident in psychiatry Yale U., New Haven, 1960-62; chief of unit Hillside Hosp., N.Y.C., 1963-64; asst. clin. prof. Tremont Crisis Center, Albert Einstein Coll. Medicine, 1969—; asst. clin. prof. N.Y. Med. Coll., 1974—, tng. and supervisory analyst psychoanalytic div., 1978—. Recipient Gralnick Found. award in psychoanalysis, 1971. Mem. Soc. for Liaison Psychiatry (pres. 1978-79), Am. Psychosomatic Soc., Am. Acad. Psychoanalysis, Am. Psychiat. Assn., Schilder Soc. Editor: Forum of Soc. Med. Psychoanalysis, 1978—. Contbr. articles to profl. jours. and periodicals. Office: 200 East End Ave New York City NY 10028

LEFEROVICH, JOHN, JR., lawyer; b. Garfield, N.J., Nov. 6, 1931; s. John and Anna (Capko) L.; B.S., U. Pa., 1953; LL.B., Columbia, 1958; m. Kathleen Mary Gulbenkian, July 27, 1968; children—John III, Douglas. Admitted to N.Y. bar, 1958; practiced in N.Y.C., 1958—; atty. Dorsey, Burke & Keber, 1958-62; asst. gen. counsel Nat. Assn. Mut. Savs. Banks, 1962-65; counsel, sec. govt. relations N.Y. State Bankers Assn., 1965-76, gen. counsel, sec. governing council, dir., 1976—. Thesis examiner Stonier Grad. Sch. Banking Rutgers U., New Brunswick, N.J., 1973-77. Chmn. bd. govs. N.Y. Young Republican Club, 1966. Served with Finance Corps, AUS, 1953-55. Mem. Am., N.Y. State (banking law com. 1967—, mem. exec. com. banking, bus. and corp. law sect.) bar assns., Assn. Bar City N.Y. (com. on state legislation 1976—), Alpha Chi Rho. Episcopalian. Club: Larchmont (N.Y.) Shore. Home: 134 Siwanoy Blvd Eastchester NY 10709 Office: 485 Lexington Ave New York City NY 10017

LEFEVRE, EUGENE STEPHEN, corrections ofcl.; b. Rand Hill, N.Y., Dec. 4, 1931; s. Eugene Joseph and Anna Mae (Lavarnway) LeF.; student Auburn Community Coll., 1963-65, Moran Inst. Crime and Delinquency, St. Lawrence U., 1966, 67, 69; m. Margaret Frances Oros, June 20, 1959; children—Denise, Renee, Michael. Psychiat. aid Rockland (N.Y.) State Hosp., 1952; corrections officer Greenhaven and Clinton Correctional Facilities, N.Y., 1953-55; corrections camp counselor Camp Pharsalia (N.Y.), 1956-61; corrections sgt. Auburn and Clinton Correction Facilities, 1962; asst. camp supr. Pharsalia and Monterey camps, N.Y., 1963-66; corrections lt. Clinton Correctional Facility, Dannemora, N.Y., 1967-69, capt., 1969-70, asst. dep. supt., 1970-71; dep. supt. Bedford Hills (N.Y.) Correctional Facility, 1971; acting dir. program planning and devel. N.Y. State Dept. Corrections, Albany, 1972; supt. Adirondack Correctional Treatment and Evaluation Center, Dannemora, N.Y., 1973-75; supt. Green Haven Correctional Facility, 1975; mem. N.Y. State Commn. of Correction, chmn., 1975-76; supt. Clinton Correctional Facility, 1976—. Founder ACTEC Community Resource Council, Plattsburgh (N.Y.) and Clinton County, 1973—; mem. criminal justice adv. com. State U. Coll. at Plattsburgh, 1973—, Clinton Community Coll., 1972—; regional continuing ednl. adv. council State U. N.Y. Coll. at Plattsburgh, 1973—. Mem. Am. Correctional Assn., Am. Assn. Wardens and Supts. Clubs: Elks, K.C., Siberian Rod and Gun. Home: Box 706 Clinton Correctional Facility Dannemora NY 12929

LEFF, ALVIN ISAAC, mfg. co. exec.; b. Phila., Feb. 25, 1937; s. Murray A. and Elsie M. Leff; B.S. in Chem. Engring., Drexel U., 1959; postgrad. Temple U., 1962-66; m. Harriet Karr, June 21, 1958; children—Michele, Lori, David. Quality control and prodn. mgr. vinyl and silicone products thermoid div. H.K. Porter Co., Phila., 1962-68; mgr. quality control and standards, process engr. CertainTeed Corp., Valley Forge, Pa., 1968-70, tech. services mgr., 1970-74, mktg. mgr. sewer systems, 1974—; owner, operator Lion Enterprises, Inc., Phila. Pres. Parents for Neighborhood Schs., 1968-74; bd. dirs. Northeast Council for Community Progress, 1969-76; Republican committeeman, 1973-74. Served with C.E., U.S. Army, 1959-60. Mayer I. Blum Scholar, 1954-55. Mem. Am. Soc. Chem. Engrs., Am. Soc. Quality Control, ASTM, Uni-Bell Plastic Pipe Assn., Assn. Asbestos-Cement Pipe, Am. Mktg. Assn. Republican. Home: 6140 Brockton Rd Hatboro PA 19040 Office: PO Box 860 Valley Forge PA 19482

LEFF, DAVID, finance co. exec.; b. Bklyn., Dec. 19, 1933; s. Solomon and Anna (Hahn) L.; B.A. with honors, Rutgers U., 1955, J.D., 1958; m. Barbara S. Kantrowitz, Dec. 23, 1954; children—Abbey, Jody. With Mechanics Finance Co., Jersey City, 1958—, sec.-treas., 1965—; sr. partner Eichenbaum, Kantrowitz & Leff, 1964—; pres. Garden State Credit Bur., Clifton, N.J., 1966-67, now dir.; v.p. Consumer Credit Debt Counseling Service No. N.J., 1967—. Acting judge City of Jersey City Municipal Ct.; mem. N.J. Supreme Ct. Com. on Practice and Procedure in Dist. Ct. Pres., bd. dirs. United Community Fund, 1968-70, now bd. dirs.; v.p., bd. dirs. Hudson-Hamilton Boy Scouts Am., 1969—; bd. dirs., mem. exec. com. Goodwill Industries N.J., Jewish Home and Hosp. Hudson and Bergen Counties; bd. dirs., mem. exec. bd. No. Pascack Valley United Jewish Appeal. Mem. Am., N.J., Hudson County (sec. 1972, 1st v.p. 1974, pres. 1976) bar assns., Jersey City C. of C. (mem. exec. bd.). Rotarian (pres. 1974). Editor: Rutgers Law Rev. Home: 147 Beechwood Rd Oradell NJ 07649 Office: 586 Newark Ave Jersey City NJ 07306

LEFKOVITS, ALBERT MEYER, dermatologist; b. N.Y.C., June 30, 1937; s. Aaron Melchoir and Muriel (Mark) L.; A.B., Cornell U., 1958; M.D. (Lederle research fellow), N.Y. Med. Coll., 1962; m. Cheryl Beth Kornberg, Apr. 25, 1971; children—Ari Nathan, Lauren B. Intern, Newark Beth Israel Hosp., 1962-63; resident dermatology Kings County Hosp. Center, State U. N.Y., Downstate Med. Center, Bklyn., 1963-65; chief resident dermatology Mt. Sinai Hosp., N.Y.C., 1965-66, research fellow dermatology, 1966-67, asst. attending physician, 1966—; practice medicine specializing in dermatology, N.Y.C., 1966—; asst. attending physician Beekman-Downtown Hosp., N.Y.C., 1968—. Instr. dermatology Mt. Sinai Sch. Medicine, 1966-68, clin. asso. dermatology, 1968-73, asst. prof., 1974, acad. council, 1973—; instr. dermatology N.Y. Med. Coll., 1966-69. Alumni fund-raising chmn. Horace Mann Sch., 1976-78. Served to maj. M.C., AUS, 1969-71. Recipient Fredrick Wise award in dermatology N.Y. Acad. Medicine, 1965. Mem. Harvey Soc., Soc. Investigative Dermatology, Dermatology Found., Soc. Tropical Dermatology, Am. Acad. Dermatology, A.M.A., Jewish Chautaugua Soc. (life), Dermatology Soc. Greater N.Y., N.Y. State Med. Soc., Cornell Alumni Assn. N.Y. (bd. govs. 1974-76). Jewish (dir. congregation Emanu-El men's club). Clubs: Town, Cornell (N.Y.C.). Address: 1040 Park Ave New York City NY 10028

LEFKOWITZ, LEONARD ROBERT, textile scientist; b. N.Y.C., Jan. 11, 1931; s. Samuel and Flora (Kline) L.; B.S., N.C. State Coll., 1957, M.S., 1958; m. Jacqueline Alyce Feldman, Sept. 3, 1961; children—Wayne, Tara, Jeri. Textile research technologist Wool and Mohair Lab., U.S. Dept. Agr. Agrl. Research, Albany, Calif., 1958-60; spl. research project mgr. Huyck Corp., Rensselaer, N.Y., 1960-65, chief process engr. Felt div., 1965-67, group leader fabric devel., 1967-74, research asso. new products, 1974—. Served with U.S. Army, 1953-55. Mem. Air Pollution Control Assn., Vols. in Tech. Assistance, Filtration Soc. Jewish. Patentee in field of fabrics. Home: 14 Alpine Dr Latham NY 12110 Office: Huyck Research Center Washington St Rensselaer NY 12144

LEFKOWITZ, LOUIS HIRSCH, obstetrician, gynecologist; b. Bklyn., Oct. 20, 1937; s. Paul Howard and Bertha (Schulman) L.; B.A., U. N.C., 1959; M.D., N.Y. Med. Coll., 1964; 1 son, Andrew. Intern, Beth Israel Hosp., N.Y.C., 1964-65; resident N.Y. Med. Coll.-Flower Fifth Avenue and Met. Hosp. Center, N.Y.C., 1965-69; practice medicine specializing in obstetrics and gynecology, Spring Valley, N.Y., 1969—; attending obstetrician and gynecologist Good Samaritan Hosp., Suffern, N.Y.; asst. attending obstetrician and gynecologist Nyack (N.Y.) Hosp., Community Gen. Hosp. of Rockland County, Spring Valley, Westchester County Med. Center, Valhalla, N.Y. Diplomate Am. Bd. Obstetrics and Gynecology. Mem. Am. Coll. Obstetricians and Gynecologists, A.C.S., Am. Assn. Gynecological Laparoscopists, Am. Fertility Soc., N.Y. State Med. Soc. Jewish. Contbr. articles to med. jour. Home: 211 Parkside Dr Suffern NY 10901 Office: 23 Lawrence St Spring Valley NY 10977

LEFKOWITZ, LOUIS J., lawyer, former state ofcl.; b. N.Y.C., July 3, 1904; s. Samuel and Mollie (Isaacs) L.; LL.B. cum laude, Fordham U., 1925; m. Helen Schwimmer, June 14, 1931; children—Joan Lefkowitz Feinbloom, Stephen Allan. Admitted to N.Y. bar, 1926; pvt. practice law, N.Y.C.; justice Municipal Ct., N.Y.C., 1935, City Ct., 1954; atty. gen. N.Y., Albany, 1957-78. Mem. N.Y. Assembly, 1928-30; del. Republican Nat. Conv., 1944, 48, alt. del. 1956. Active numerous civic activities. Bd. dirs. Florence Crittenton League. Mem. Assn. Bar City N.Y., N.Y. County Lawyers Assn., Fed., Am. bar assns., Nat. Assn. Attys. Gen. (pres.), Assn. Lawyers Criminal Cts. Manhattan, Grand St. Boys Assn., Am. Jewish Congress. Jewish. Clubs: K.P., B'nai B'rith. Home: 575 Park Ave New York City NY 10021 Office: 80 Centre St New York City NY 10013

LEFKOWITZ, STANLEY A., metals co. exec.; b. Phila., Aug. 5, 1943; s. Henry and Ida (Jacobs) L.; B.A., Temple U., 1965; Ph.D., Princeton, 1970; m. Mary Randall. Staff dir. Citizens' Commn. on Future of City U. N.Y., N.Y.C., 1970-72; exec. asst. to vice-chancellor for urban affairs City U. N.Y., 1971-75; asst. dir. instructional devel. Queens Coll., Flushing, N.Y. 1973-75; exec. asst. to chmn. bd. Mocatta Metals Corp., N.Y.C., 1975—; instr. chemistry Hunter Coll., 1970-73; cons. N.Y. State Temporary Commn. on Powers of Local Govt., 1973, Greenville (N.C.) Govt. Study Commn., 1972; mem. Citizens' Union Com. on State Legis., 1974-75. AEC research asst., 1968-70; McKay fellow, 1967-68. Mem. Am. Phys. Soc., Fedn. Am. Scientists, Assn. Princeton Grad. Alumni (treas. 1976—). Club: Princeton (N.Y.C.). Home: 60 E 8th St New York City NY 10003 Office: 25 Broad St New York City NY 10004

LEGALOS, CHARLES NORMAN, clin. psychologist; b. Springfield, Mass., Jan. 25, 1943; s. Charles Nicholas and Jennie Constance (Cresta) L.; B.A., magna cum laude, U. Mass., 1971; M.A., York U., Toronto, 1972; m. Nina Ashurst Walsh, Aug. 14, 1968; 1 son, Jonathan Kipp. Psychotherapist Boston Area Assos. for Learning Therapies, Inc., 1971-75; staff psychologist Mass. Dept. Mental Health, Wrentham, 1976—. Mem. Internat. Assn. Study of Pain, Am. Pain Soc., Assn. Advancement Psychology. Office: 1171 Washington St Newton MA

LEGAZPI, EMIL VINCENT, accountant; b. Madrid, May 28, 1924; s. Vicente Legazpi-Arce and Maria Uttrilla-Crosa; came to U.S., 1966, naturalized, 1970; B.S., U. Dist. Santiago (Spain), 1949; m. Gloria Priscilla Christ, Aug. 30 1966. Accountant, Mt. Sinai Med. Center, N.Y.C., 1967-68; controller Leroy Hosp., N.Y.C., 1968-69; auditor Harris, Kerr, Forster & Co., C.P.A.'s, N.Y.C., 1969-70; internal auditor L.I. Coll Hosp., N.Y.C., 1970-73; controller Lefferts Gen. Hosp., N.Y.C., 1973-74; auditor Bklyn. Hosp., 1974—. Served with Spanish Army, 1947-49. Notary public. Mem. Inst. Internal Auditors, Nat. Muzzleloading Rifle Assn. Republican. Roman Catholic. Home: 142 10 Booth Meml Ave Flushing NY 11355 Office: 121 De Kalb Ave Brooklyn NY 11201

LEGER, JULES, former gov. gen. Can.; b. Saint-Anicet, Que., Can., Apr. 4, 1913; s. Ernest and Alda (Beauvais) L.; B.A., Coll. Valleyfield (Que.), 1933; postgrad. U. Montreal (Que.) Sch. Law, 1933-36; D. Litt., U. Paris (France), 1938; m. Gabrielle Carmel, Aug. 13, 1938; 1 dau., Helen. Asso. editor Le Droit, Ottawa, Ont., Can., 1938-39; prof. diplomatic history and current affairs U. Ottawa, 1939-42; 3d sec. Canadian Dept. External Affairs, 1940-43, 3d sec., Santiago, Chile, 1943, 2d sec., 1944, 1st sec., 1946; del. UN, 1948-49; on loan Canadian Prime Minister's Office, 1949-50; asst. under sec. state external affairs, 1951-53, under sec., 1954-58; ambassador to Mexico, 1953-54; permanent rep. NATO council, 1958-62; ambassador to Italy, 1962-64, to France, 1964-68; under sec. state Can., 1968-73; ambassador to Belgium and Luxembourg, 1973-74; gov. gen. Can., 1974-79; del. numerous internat. confs. Decorated chancellor, prin. companion Order Can., Order Mil. Merit. Roman Catholic. Address: Govt House Sussex Dr Ottawa ON K1A 0A1 Canada

LEGERE, MARTIN JOSEPH, bus. ofcl.; b. Caraquet, N.B., Can., Nov. 17, 1916; s. Jean B. and Beatrice (Godin) L.; student Laval U., 1945-46; M.C.S. (hon.), Moncton U., 1950, D.Sc.A. (hon.), 1971; D.S.S., Sacred Heart U., 1953; LL.D., (hon.), St. Francis Xavier U., 1974; m. Anita Godin, June 4, 1950; children—Louise, Louis, Rene, Claude. Fieldman, St. Francis Xavier U., 1938-40; insp. Credit Unions, Caraquet, N.B., Can., 1940-46; gen. mgr. Fedn. des Caisses Populaires Acadiennes, N.B., 1946—, La Société d'Assurance des Caisses Poulaires Acadiennes, 1948—; pres. Le Conseil Canadien de la Coop., 1956—; v.p. L'Evangeline newspaper, Moncton, N.B., 1958-64; pres. La Coop. de Caraquet, 1948-64, 71—; dir. La Société des Artisans-Montreal, Co-op. Ins. Services, Co-op. Life Ins., Co-op. Fire and Casualty Co., La Compagnie de Gestion Atantique Ltee., Moncton, C.I. Mgmt. Group Ltd., Co-operators Ins. Assn., Co-operators Life Ins. Assn., Co-operators Ins. Assn., Co-operators Life Ins., C.I. Mgmt. Group Ltd. Municipal councillor, Caraquet, N.B., 1946-50; chmn. Caraquet, Improvement Dist., 1950-55; dir. Maritime Provinces Bd. Trades, 1956-64; chmn. N.B. Indsl. Fin. Bd., 1960-76; adv. bd. Caraquet Hosp., 1964-74; treas. Gloucester County

Children's Aid Soc., 1945-67; bd. dirs. Conseil de la Vie Francaise en Amérique, 1970—. Decorated officer Order of Can. Mem. Internat. Coop. Alliance (central com.), Co-operators Ins. Assn. (dir.). Roman Catholic. Club: Richelieu (Caraquet). Office: Caraquet NB Canada

LEGNOS, JOHN PETER, mech. engr.; b. Hartford, Conn., Dec. 12, 1919; s. Peter John and Paraskeve (Papavasiliou) L.; B.S. in Mech. Engring., Purdue U., 1949; m. Nellie M. Masonis, June 13, 1942; children—Deitra (Mrs. John Bardon), Peter, John Peter. Design engr. firm Arthur T. Flynn, Meriden, Conn., 1950, firm Fred S. Dubin, Hartford, 1951; prin. firm John P. Legnos, Hartford, 1951-71; pres. firm Legnos and Cramer, Inc., Hartford, 1972—. Chmn., Planning Com. Groton Long Point, Conn., 1968-70; sec. Hartford Bd. Appeals, 1967-77; mem. citizens adv. com. Conn. Dept. Pub. Works, 1962-72. Served with USNR, 1942-45. Mem. Pi Tau Sigma. Home: 56 Bloomfield Ave Hartford CT 06105 Office: 30 Gillett St Hartford CT 06105

LEGUM, JEFFREY ALFRED, automobile co. exec.; b. Balt. Dec. 16, 1941; s. Leslie and Naomi (Hendler) L.; B.S. in Econs., U. Pa., 1963; student Chevrolet Sch. Merchandising and Mgmt., 1966; m. Harriet Cohn, Nov. 10, 1968; children—Laurie Hope, Michael Neil. With Park Circle Motor Co., Legum Chevrolet, Balt., 1963—, exec. v.p., 1966-77, pres., 1977—, also dir.; partner Pkwy. Indsl. Center, Dorsey, Md., 1965—; v.p. Westminster Motor Co. (Md.), 1967-72, pres., 1972—, also dir.; dir., mem. exec. com. United Consol. Industries, 1970-73; pres. One Forty Corp., Westminster, Md., 1972—; v.p., treas. P.C. Parts Co., Balt., 1967—. Mem. Naval Acad. Rev. Bd., 1975-77; chmn. auto div. Asso. Jewish Charities, Balt., 1966—. Bd. dirs. Asso. Placement Bur., Balt., v.p., 1972—. Recipient Award of Merit, Asso. Jewish Charities of Balt., 1968. Mem. Md. Auto Trade Assn., Chevrolet Dealer Council (dist. chmn. 1975-77), Greater Balt. Com., Young Pres.'s Orgn. Clubs: Suburban (Baltimore County); Univ. Pa. (Balt.). Home: 10 Stone Hollow Ct Baltimore MD 21208 Office: 7900 Eastern Ave Baltimore MD 21224

LEHANE, DEREK PATRICK, biochemist; b. Cork, Ireland, Mar. 15, 1945; s. Patrick William and Mary Margaret (Jenkins) L.; came to U.S., 1970; B.Sc., Nat. U. Ireland, 1966; Ph.D., U. Dublin, 1970. Clin. asst. biochemist St. Vincent's Hosp. and Med. Center, N.Y.C., 1973-75, asst. attending biochemist, 1975-77, asso. attending biochemist, 1977-78; clin. biochemist instrument products div. E.I. du Pont de Nemours & Co., Inc., 1978—. Cert. clin. chemist Nat. Registry in Clin. Chemistry, 1975; diplomate Am. Bd. Clin. Chemistry. Mem. Am. Assn. for Clin. Chemistry, Assn. Clin. Scientists, Nat. Acad. Clin. Biochemistry (chmn. com. on profl. ethics and standards 1977—). Roman Catholic. Contbr. articles in field to sci. jours. Home: 290 W 12th St New York City NY 10014 Office: Quillem Bldg Concord Plaza Wilmington DE 18989

LEHMAN, DENNIS GEORGE, computer sales co. exec.; b. Erie, Pa., July 24, 1948; s. Fred A. and Jeanne M. (Goodill) L.; A.S.B., Erie Bus. Center, 1969. Systems analyst Hamot Med. Center, Erie, 1969-77; mgr. data processing Erie Bus. Center, 1977-78; pres. Logical Minicomputers of Erie, Inc., 1978—. Mem. Lake City C. of C., Data Process Mgmt. Assn. Republican. Presbyterian. Clubs: Erie Maennerchor, Mason, Shriner. Home: 1006 W 8th St Erie PA 16502 Office: 359 W 8th St Erie PA 16502

LEHMAN. LAWRENCE HERBERT, cons. engr.; b. N.Y.C., Apr. 30, 1929; s. Samuel and Shirley (Freiberg) L.; B.C.E., N.Y. U., 1949; M.B.A., Iona Coll., 1978; m. Susan E. Green, June 29, 1957; children—Scott Jeffrey, Christopher Adam. Project engr. Andrews & Clark, Cons. Engrs., N.Y.C., 1951-57; project mgr. Barstow, Mulligan & Vollmer, Cons. Engrs., N.Y.C., 1957-59; chief engr., partner Vollmer Assos., Cons. Engrs., N.Y.C., 1959-67; partner Berger, Lehman Assos., Cons. Engrs., Harrison, N.Y., 1967—; chief exec. officer, dir. Berger, Lehman Assos., P.C., Harrison, 1967—. Registered profl. engr., N.Y., N.J., Ky., Ill., Mass., Conn., Ind.; recipient Third award U.S. Steel, 1966, Bridge award Pre-stressed Concrete Inst., 1975, Engring. Excellence award N.Y. Assn. Cons. Engrs., 1975. Fellow ASCE; mem. Am. Cons. Engrs. Council, Soc. Am. Mil. Engrs., Hwy. Research Bd., Nat. Soc. Profl. Engrs., N.Y. Assn. Cons. Engrs. (v.p.), Nat. Panel Am. Arbitration Assn. Home: 10 Chester Dr Rye NY 10580 Office: 550 Mamaroneck Ave Harrison NY 10528

LEHMAN, MARGARET, calligrapher, artist, educator; b. Balt.; d. John Henry and Ellen (Roddy) Lehman; B.S., Coll. Notre Dame of Md., 1940; M.A., U. Notre Dame, 1960. Instr., Coll. Notre Dame of Md., Balt., 1945-60, asst. prof., 1950-55, asso. prof. art, 1955-60; vis. prof. dept. art Mt. Mary Coll., Milw., 1961-64; in charge tchr. tng. program in art Sch. Sisters of Notre Dame Motherhouse, Balt., 1964-69; staff artist Barton-Cotton, Inc., Balt., 1969—, Monarch Services, also Avalon Hill Game Co., Balt., 1975—; designed and executed calligraphic murals for chs., schs.; heraldic designs for cathedral, hosp., high sch.; wall hangings for chs., auditoriums; group shows in Balt., Milw. Mem. Delta Phi Delta. Address: 3925 Beech Ave Baltimore MD 21211

LEHMANN, AARON, sr. investment analyst; b. Newark, Oct. 17, 1939; s. Max and Hertha (Stern) L.; B.A. cum laude, Rutgers U., 1961; M.A. (NSF grantee), Yeshiva U., 1963; postgrad. Mass. Inst. Tech., 1966-68; M.S., N.Y. U., 1967; M.B.A. with highest honors, U. Conn., 1977; m. Esther B. Strauss, Feb. 27, 1966; children—Shanna B., Shira J., Marc E., David M. Sr. engr. various corps., 1962-69; sr. securities analyst Bank of Am., San Francisco, 1969-71; sr. securities analyst Goldman Sachs, N.Y.C., 1971-73; sr. investment analyst Hartford (Conn.) Ins. Group, 1973—; cons. pvt. corps. Mem. Hartford Soc. Fin. Analysts, Diversified Cos. Analysts, Sigma Xi, Beta Gamma Sigma. Home: 4 Fairway West Hartford CT 06117 Office: 690 Asylum Ave Hartford Ct 06115

LEHMANN, MANFRED RAPHAEL, cons. and supplier to overseas govts., co. exec.; b. Stockholm, Sweden, Aug. 28, 1922; s. Hans and Fanny (Taub) L.; brought to U.S., 1940; M.A., Johns Hopkins, 1946; postgrad. Harvard, 1943, Columbia, 1946-47, U. Chgo., 1945; postgrad. Yeshiva U.; m. Sara Anne Moskovits, Apr. 3, 1949; children—James Harald, Barbara Lee, Karen Esther. Founder-chmn. Inter-Govtl. Philatelic Corp., N.Y.C., 1957-72; pres. Lehmann Trading Corp., N.Y.C., 1951—, Greater Devel. & Services Corp., N.Y.C., 1972—, Telecom Devel. Corp., 1975—; dir. Bank Adanim Mortgages Ltd., Tel Aviv, Israel. Lectr. on books and manuscripts Harvard, other instns. Hon. pres. Young Israel of Lawrence-Cedarhurst (N.Y.), 1963—. Founder Manfred R. and S. Anne Lehmann Fund for Jewish musicology, also hon. pres. Bd. dirs. Yeshiva Univ. High Schs., N.Y.C., Friends Harvard Judaica Library. Mem. Jewish Bibliophile Soc. Author several monographs Bibl. archaeology, 1954—. Home: 79 Cedarhurst Ave Lawrence NY 11516 Office: 9 W 57th St New York City NY 10019

LEHNE, WILLIAM GEORGE, cons., san. engr.; b. L.I., N.Y., June 21, 1931; s. William G. and Margaret T. (De Odene) L.; B.C.E., Manhattan Coll., 1953; m. Marsha Willene Vineyard, Aug. 8, 1959; children—William, Jr., Christopher, Stacey. Engr., Pitometer Assos., N.Y.C., 1953-58; water distbn. studies civil engr. Lock Joint Pipe Co., East Orange, N.J., 1958-59; pipe designer, asso. Lee T. Purcell, Paterson, N.J., 1959—, mgr. No. br. office, Franklin, N.J.; san. cons. to municipalities and sewerage authorities, municipal utilities, N.J. Served with Signal Corps AUS, 1953-55. Registered profl. engr., N.Y., Pa., N.J. Mem. N.J. Soc. Profl. Engrs., Am. Soc. C.E., Am. Water Works Assn., N.J. Water Pollution Control Assn., Cons. Engrs. Council. Home: 474 Herrick Dr Dover NJ 07801 Office: 35 Main St Franklin NJ 07416

LEHNKERING, MICHAEL STEPHAN, landscape architect; b. Oberstdorf, Germany, Feb. 6, 1944; s. Carl Heinz and Rosemarie (Belling) L.; came to U.S., 1957; naturalized, 1957; B. Landscape Arch., Syracuse U., 1965; m. Patricia Wilklyn Zuidema, June 22, 1972. Project architect Cornell, Bridgers & Troller, Landscape Architects, Los Angeles, 1965-66; landscape architect Port Authority of N.Y., N.Y.C., 1968-71; pvt. practice landscape architecture, planning and constrn. mgmt., Phila., 1971—; pres., prin. MSL Assos., Ltd., Landscape Architects & Planners, Malvern, Pa., planning, design cons. numerous developers on East Coast, also gen. contractors. Served to capt. U.S. Army, 1966-68; Vietnam. Decorated Bronze Star. Mem. Am. Inst. Planners. Republican. Lutheran. Project landscape architect Newark Internat. Airport, 1971. Home and Office: 279 Lapp Rd Malvern PA 19355

LEHR, FRANK HENRY, civil engr.; b. Easton, Pa., Apr. 2, 1925; s. Francis H. and Sadie (Fulse) L.; B.S., Pa. State U., 1950; M.S., Newark Coll. Engring., 1956; m. Veronica Shevock, June 24, 1950; children—Diane C., Frank F., Janice. Field engr. Central R.R. N.J., Jersey City, 1950-51; structural designer Arthur G. McKee & Co., Union, N.J., 1951-54; constrn. engr. Jersey Testing Labs., Newark, 1954-57; pres., cons. engr. Frank H. Lehr Assos., East Orange, N.J., 1957—. Mem. regional adv. panel on archtl. services Gen. Services Adminstrn., 1971-73. Mem. Bd. Appeals, Summit, N.J., 1958—; councilman, Summit, 1962—, pres. city council, 1970-75, mayor, 1976—; mem. Essex and Union Counties Joint Meeting Sewer Commn., 1966—, vice chmn., 1967—, chmn., 1970-75. Served to maj. USMCR, 1943-47, 51-53; lt. col. Res. (ret.). Registered profl. engr., N.J., N.Y. Mass., Conn., Pa., Ohio. Fellow ASCE, Cons. Engrs. Council; mem. Union County Soc. Profl. Engrs. (past pres.), Am. Soc. Testing Materials, Marine Corps Res. Officers Assn., Bldg. Ofcls. Assn. Kiwanian (dir. East Orange, N.J.). Home: 16 Myrtle Ave Summit NJ 07901 Office: 15 Freeman Ave East Orange NJ 07018

LEHRICH, JAMES RICHARD, neurologist, virologist; b. N.Y.C., Mar. 10, 1937; s. Moses Zachary and Betty Pearl (Wolfson) L.; A.B. summa cum laude (Jacob Wendell scholar), Harvard, 1958, M.D. cum laude (Nat. scholar), 1962; m. Christina Bagley, Sept. 4, 1966; children—Mark Jonathan, Christopher Ian. Intern, Mass. Gen. Hosp., Boston, 1962-63, asst. resident medicine, 1963-64, asst. neurologist, 1971-77, asso. neurologist, 1977—; clin. asso. Nat. Inst. Allergy and Infectious Diseases, Bethesda, Md., 1964-66; asst. resident neurology Neurol. Inst. N.Y., Presbyn. Hosp., N.Y.C., 1966-67; clin., research fellow neurology and neuropathology Mass. Gen. Hosp., Harvard Med. Sch., 1967-69; asso. neurology U. Pa. Sch. Medicine, Phila., 1969, asst. prof., 1970; vis. scientist, NIH Spl. fellow Wistar Inst., Phila., 1969-70; asst. prof. neurology Harvard Med. Sch., Boston, 1971—. Trustee Barrett Wendell Meml. Fund, Boston; vice chmn. bd. trustees, chmn. med. adv. bd. Mass. chpt. Nat. Multiple Sclerosis Soc. Served to lt. comdr. USPHS, 1962-64. Spl. fellow Nat. Inst. Neurol. Diseases and Stroke, 1967-69. Diplomate in neurology Am. Bd. Psychiatry and Neurology. Mem. Am. Acad. Neurology, Am. Assn. Neuropathologists, Am. Assn. Immunologists, Boston Soc. Psychiatry and Neurology, Mass. Med. Soc., Am. Neurol. Assn., Phi Beta Kappa, Sigma Xi, Alpha Omega Alpha. Home: 96 Wolcott Rd Chestnut Hill MA 02167 Office: Neurology Dept Mass Gen Hosp Boston MA 02114

LEIBNER, IRA WALLACE, pediatrician; b. N.Y.C., Aug. 23, 1918; s. Joseph Morris and Lillian (Greyer) L.; A.B. in Chemistry, U. Wis., Madison, 1939; M.D., Washington U., St. Louis, 1943; m. Dorothy Jane Goldberg, Oct. 22, 1950; children—Helen Ann, Donald Neil. Intern, Jewish Hosp. Bklyn., 1943-44, resident, 1947-48; resident Sydenham Hosp., Balt., 1947; practice medicine specializing in pediatrics, Bklyn., 1949—; mem. staffs Jewish Hosp. Bklyn., State U. Hosp., Bklyn.; clin. asso. prof. pediatrics Downstate Med. Center, State U. N.Y., Bklyn. Served as capt., M.C., U.S. Army, 1944-46. Mem. AMA, Am., Bklyn. acads. pediatrics, N.Y. Acad. Scis., N.Y. State, Kings County (past pres. pediatric sect.) med. socs., Alpha Omega Alpha. Office: 1360 Ocean Pkwy Brooklyn NY 11230

LEIBOWITT, SOL DAVID, lawyer; b. Bklyn., Feb. 18, 1912; s. Morris and Bella (Small) L.; B.A., Lehigh U., 1933; LL.B., Harvard U., 1936; m. Ethel Leibowitt, June 18, 1950. Admitted to N.Y. bar, 1937, Conn. bar, 1970; pvt. practice, N.Y.C., 1937—, Stamford, Conn., 1970-78, Milford, Conn., 1978—; gen. counsel New Haven Clock and Watch Co., 1955-59, pres., 1958-59; pres. Apco Capitol Corp., 1975—; dir., sec. Behavioral Research Labs., Inc., 1976; dir. Data Card Internat. Corp., Hevant, Eng., 1977—. Trustee Jewish Center, N.Y.C.; treas. N.Y. Adult Edn. Council; pres. Ethel and David Leibowitt Found. Recipient Human Relations award, 1969, Meml. award Anti-Defamation League, 1971. Mem. Assn. Bar N.Y.C., Am., N.Y. State bar assns., Anti-Defamation League (commr.), Am. Soc. for Technion U. (mem. bd., v.p., Conn. pres.). Clubs: Masons; Lotos, Harvard (N.Y.C.); Lotus, Rolling Hills Country. Home: Fanton Hill Rd Weston CT 06880 Office: 63 Broad St Milford CT 06460

LEIBY, CLARE C., JR., physicist; b. Ashland, Ohio, May 4, 1924; s. Clare C. and Blanche Preston (Peabody) L.; B.S., Mass. Inst. Tech., 1954; M.S., U. Ill., 1958; m. Patricia Ruth Newsome, 1952; children—Nibya Teresa, Clare C. III, Paul Newsome, Jonathan Peabody, Benjamin Taplin. Flight radio officer Pan Am. Airways, Miami, Fla., 1942-43, Rio de Janeiro, Brazil, 1946-50; physicist Air Force Cambridge (Mass.) Research Center, 1954-56; mem. research staff gaseous electronics lab. U. Ill., 1956-61, Sperry-Rand Research Center, Sudbury, Mass., 1961-64; research physicist Air Force Cambridge Research Labs., Bedford, Mass., 1964-75, Electronic Tech. Lab., 1976—; cons. Leghorn Labs., Bedford, 1965—. Served with USAAF, 1943-45. Mem. Sigma Xi. Patentee in field. Home: 229 Old Billerica Rd Bedford MA 01730 Office: Rome Air Devel Center Hanscom AFB MA 01731

LEICH, HAROLD HERBERT, water pollution control researcher; b. Evansville, Ind., Feb. 16, 1909; s. Herbert and Marcella (Jacobi) L.; A.B., Dartmouth Coll., 1929; M.A., Am. U., 1955; m. Cora McIver, Nov. 19, 1941 (dec. 1971); children—Harold, Jeffrey. With U.S. CSC, 1935-72, chief policy devel. div., Washington, 1958-72, ret., 1972; lectr., writer, condr. research on waterless methods for disposing of body wastes, 1972—; treas. Environment Forum, 1975—; chmn. recreation and wildlife com. Interstate Commn. on Potomac River Basin, 1950-55; mem. office of mgmt. and budget Task Force to Establish EPA, 1970; chmn. com. on clean water Non-Govt. Orgns., UN Conf., Stockholm, 1972. Mem. Council Washington Reps. on UN. Served to lt. comdr. USNR, 1942-46. Recipient award for distinguished service U.S. CSC, 1963. Mem. Internat. Assn. Water Pollution Research, Am. Water Resources Assn., Am. Polit. Sci. Assn., Phi Beta Kappa. Republican. Episcopalian. Clubs: City Tavern, Canoe Cruisers Assn. (chmn. 1970-71), Ski of Washington (pres. 1937-38), Potomac Appalachian Trail (v.p. 1939-40), Dartmouth of Washington (pres. 1949-50). Home: 5606 Vernon Pl Bethesda MD 20034

LEICHTENTRITT, KURT GEORGE, physician; b. Germany, June 18, 1912; s. George and Hedwig (Kant) L.; came to U.S., 1939, naturalized, 1942: B.S., Bonn (Ger.) U., 1936; M.D., State U. N.Y., Bklyn., 1943; m. Mildred Vaccarino, Sept. 15, 1947; children—Walter, Hedwig. Intern, Lenox Hill Hosp., N.Y.C., 1943-44; resident in phys. medicine and rehab. Bronx Municipal Hosp. and Albert Einstein Coll. Medicine, 1961-63; asso. attending physician Montefiore Hosp. and Med. Center, Bronx Hosp.; asst. clin. prof. Albert Einstein Coll. Medicine; dir. rehab. Pelham Bay Gen. Hosp.; med. dir. Astor Gardens Nursing Home; cons. St. Barnabas, Westchester Sq. hosps.; courtesy staff Misericordia Hosp. and Med. Center. Recipient 20-year service awards Montefiore Hosp. and Med. Center, Arthritis Found. Diplomate Am. Bd. Phys. Medicine and Rehab., Internat. Bd. Proctology. Mem. Bronx County, N.Y. State, Pan Am. med. socs., AMA, N.Y. Soc. Phys. Medicine and Rehab. (treas.), N.Y. Rheumatism Soc., Am. Rheumatism Assn., Internat. Acad. Proctology, N. Am. Acad. Manipulative Medicine, N.Y. Acad. Medicine, Am. Congress Rehab. Medicine. Republican. Roman Catholic. Contbr. articles profl. jours. Home and office: 1284 Pelham Pkwy S Bronx NY 10461

LEIDHEISER, HENRY, JR., educator, chemist; b. Union City, N.J., Apr. 18, 1920; s. Henry and Margaret Marie (Steinel) L.; B.S., U. Va., 1941, M.S., 1944, Ph.D., 1946; m. Virginia M. Townsend, Feb. 21, 1944; children—Margaret F. (Mrs. Charles S. LeBaron), Henry III. Research asso. U. Va., 1946-49; dir., chief exec. officer Va. Inst. Sch. Research, Richmond, 1949-68; prof. chemistry, dir. Center Surface and Coatings Research, Lehigh U., Bethlehem, Pa., 1968—; cons. to govt. and industry. Chmn. Gordon Conf. Corrosion, 1963. Recipient J. Shelton Horsley prize Va. Acad. Sci., 1949; Research award Oak Ridge Inst. Nuclear Studies, 1949; Westinghouse Signal and Brake award Inst. Metal Finishing, 1952. Mem. Electrochem. Soc. (chmn. corrosion div. 1964-66; Young Authors prize 1948), Am. Chem. Soc., Nat. Assn. Corrosion Engrs., Sigma Xi (chpt. pres. 1973-74). Author: Corrosion of Copper and Tin and Their Alloys, 1971. Contbr. articles to profl. jours. Editor: Virginia's Human Resources, 1962; Properties of Electrodeposits, 1975. Home: RD 7 Pleasant Dr Bethlehem PA 18015

LEIDNER, NELSON J., banker; b. Phila., Apr. 6, 1912; s. Harry and Bella (Seligman) L.; B.S. in Econs., U. Pa., 1933, LL.B., 1936; LL.M., U. New Zealand, 1943; m. Bobette J. Rosenau, June 9, 1946; children—Nelson J., Victoria D., Cynthia A., Bobette R. Admitted to Pa. bar, 1936; partner firm Leidner & Leidner, Phila., 1936-41, 46-47; v.p. Rosenau Bros., Inc., Phila., 1953-59, exec. v.p., 1959-67; v.p. First Pa. Bank N.A., Phila., 1967-78; cons. trust dept. Fidelity Bank, Phila., 1978—. Chmn. womens and childrens apparel div. United Fund of Phila., 1952-54; city del. Community Chest, 1956-58; chmn. deferred gift and bequest program U. Pa., 1968—; treas., bd. dirs. Prisoners Family Welfare Assn.; trustee United Campaign Fund, 1963-66, Phila. Orch. Assn.; trustee Acad. Music; mem. mens fund raising com. Abington Meml. Hosp.; cons. United Way of Southeastern Pa., 1976-77. Served to lt. comdr. USNR, 1941-46. Decorated Navy Commendation medal, Order Brit. Empire. Mem. Am., Pa., Phila. bar assns. Clubs: Union League, Racquet, Phila. Cricket, Brit. Officers, Lawyers, Midday (Phila.). Home: 1425 Grasshopper Rd Huntingdon Valley PA 19006 Office: Fidelity Bank Broad and Walnut Sts Philadelphia PA 19109

LEIFER, CALVIN, oral and exptl. pathologist; b. N.Y.C., Mar. 4, 1929; s. Julius Kalman and Esther (Gisser) L.; B.A., N.Y.U., 1950, D.D.S., 1954; Ph.D. (Nat. Inst. Dental Research fellow), State U. N.Y., Buffalo, 1971; m. Judith Loeb, Sept. 11, 1963; children—Dory Ethan, Amira Karin. Gen. practice dentistry, New Haven, 1957-65; asso. prof. oral pathology, Temple U., Phila., 1970-78, prof., 1978—; practice dentistry specializing in periodontics, Abington, Pa., 1974—. Mem. Chelthenham Sch. Bd. 4 yr. high sch. study com. Served to capt. USAF, 1954-56. Nat. Inst. Dental Research, grantee, 1972-75; Am. Cancer Soc. grantee, 1976. Mem. Internat. Assn. Dental Research, Am. Assn. for Dental Research, AAAS, Am. Acad. of Oral Pathology, Phila. Cancer Club. Jewish. Contbr. articles to profl. jours. Home: 103 Waverly Rd Wyncote PA 19095 Office: 3223 N Broad St Philadelphia PA 19140

LEIGH, GILBERT MERLIN, research exec.; b. Asbury Park, N.J., Mar. 29, 1917; s. Gilbert C. and Ethel Frances (Applegate) L.; A.B., Columbia, 1939, B.S. Sch. Engring, 1940, M.S. in Chem. Engring., 1944; m. Alice Florence Ussery, May 14, 1939; children—Gilbert M., Susan Amanda, Thomas Harold, William Robert. Engr., Metal & Thermit Corp., Jersey City, 1941-49; with Colgate-Palmolive Co., Inc., Piscataway, N.J., 1949—, asst. dir., 1954-59, mgr. research, 1959—. Pres. bd. trustees Summit (N.J.) Library; mem. exec. bd. N.J. Library Trustee Assn. Recipient award in Engring. Am. Inst. Chem. Engrs., 1940. Vanderpoel scholar, 1940-41. Mem. N.Y. Acad. Scis., Soc. Cosmetic Chemists, Am. Soc. Quality Control, Grand Jury Assn., Sigma Xi, Tau Beta Pi. Club: Chemists (N.Y.C.). Home: 9 Montview Rd Summit NJ 07901 Office: 909 River Rd Piscataway NJ 08854

LEIGH, HOYLE, psychiatrist, educator; b. Seoul, Korea, Mar. 25, 1942; s. Joongshin and Ok-Hi (Ahn) Leigh; came to U.S., 1965, naturalized, 1973; M.D. summa cum laude, Yonsei U. Med. Sch., 1965; m. Vincenta Masciandaro, Sept. 16, 1967. Intern, L.I. Coll. Hosp., Bklyn., 1965-66; resident in psychiatry U. Kans. Med. Center, Kansas City, 1966-67; resident in psychiatry Montefiore Hosp. and Med. Center, Bronx, N.Y., 1967-69, NIMH fellow in research and psychosomatic medicine, 1969-71; asst. prof. psychiatry Yale Sch. Medicine, 1971-76, asso. prof. psychiatry, 1976—, chief psychosomatic service, 1971—; dir. psychiat. consultation-liaison services Yale-New Haven Hosp., 1971—, asst. chief psychiatry, 1978—; cons. to State of Conn., Va, others. NIMH fellow, 1969-71; NIMH grantee, 1975. Diplomate Am. Bd. Psychiatry and Neurology. Mem. Am. Psychiat. Assn, AMA, Am. Psychosomatic Soc., Internat. Coll. Psychosomatic Medicine (exec. sec. 1975—), AAAS, Internat. Soc. for Clin. and Exptl. Hypnosis, Am. Biofeedback Research Soc., Soc. for Psychophysiol. Research. Clubs: Yale, Yale Faculty. Contbr. articles to profl. jours. Home: 51 Russet Dr Guilford CT 06437 Office: Dept Psychiatry Yale Sch Medicine 333 Cedar St New Haven CT 06510

LEIGH, MONROE, lawyer; b. Halifax County, Va., July 15, 1919; B.A. magna cum laude, Hampden-Sydney (Va.) Coll., 1940; LL.B. (editor law rev. 1946-47), U. Va., 1947. Admitted to Va. bar, 1947, D.C. bar, 1948, U.S. Supreme Ct. bar, 1950; Asso. firm Covington, Burling, Rublee, Acheson & Shorb, and successors, Washington, 1947-51; mem. U.S. mission to NATO, 1951-53; dep. asst. gen. counsel internat. affairs Office Sec. Def., 1953-55, asst. gen. counsel internat. affairs, 1955-59; counsel St. Lawrence Seaway Devel. Corp., 1954-56; with firm Steptoe & Johnson, Washington, 1959-75, 77—, partner, 1961-75, 77—; legal adviser Dept. of State, 1975-77; mem. U.S. nat. group Permanent Ct. Arbitration, The Hague, Netherlands, 1975—; lectr. U. Va. Law Sch., 1964-75, 78—; adv. com. Parker Sch. Fgn. Law at Columbia U.; adv. com. procedural aspects Internat. Law

Inst.; adv. bd. Internat. and Comparative Law Center, Southwestern Legal Found.; Served to capt. USAAF, 1943-46. Mem. Am. Bar Assn., Am. Law Inst., Am. Soc. Internat. Law (hon. v.p.), Internat. Law Assn., Council Fgn. Relations, Washington Inst. Fgn. Affairs. Contbr. to legal jours., mem. adv. bds. Address: 1250 Connecticut Ave NW Washington DC 20036

LEIGH, RUTH R. SOKOLSKI (MRS. MURRAY STUART LEIGH), realtor; b. N.Y.C., Feb. 19; d. A. Lawrence and Anne (Frieder) Sokolski; student Hunter Coll., 1934-36, U. Pa. Wharton Sch., 1942; m. Murray Stuart Leigh, June 13, 1943; 1 dau., Leslie Susan. Sales dept. mgr., buyer Saks 34th St., N.Y.C., 1935-37; radio commls. WMCA, N.Y.C., 1936-39; interior decorator Roxberg, Inc., N.Y.C., 1937-40; broker Harold N. Sloane Co., ins. brokers, N.Y.C., 1940-43; br. mgr. Manpower Inc., N.Y.C., 1952-53; interior designer Storr & Co., N.Y.C., 1949—; builder-broker Ruth S. Leigh, N.Y.C., 1965—; mem. Real Estate Bd. of N.Y. Dist. dir. Girl Scouts U.S.A., 1952-54; fund raiser N.Y. Heart Assn., 1955—, Salvation Army, 1960—; bd. dirs. Interfaith Neighbors, 1964-66; dist. liaison officer Black & White Assos. supporting Oddyssey House Drug Addicts, 1969-70; trustee Bloomingdale Ho. of Music, N.Y.C., 1971—. Mem. Unitarian-Universalist Womens Fedn. (dist. pres. 1966-70), Women's Nat. Republican Club, Am. Unitarian Assn. (asst. non-govtl. orgn. rep. UN, nat. chmn. UN seminars 1958-62). Republican. Unitarian (v.p. bd. trustees, deacon 1974—, chmn. commn. on ch. community 1977—). Home: 1010 Fifth Ave New York City NY 10028 Office: 1220 Lexington Ave New York City NY 10028

LEIGH, SAMUEL FREDERICK, mgmt. cons.; b. Bloomington, Ill., May 13, 1911; s. Fred and Mary Gertrude (Walsh) L.; B.A., Northwestern U., 1933; m. Patricia Mary Lamb, Dec. 27, 1969; children—Lynda Leigh Hahn, Lora Leigh Dauk. Sales mgr. Interstate Folding Box Co., Middleton, Ohio, 1936-42, Container Corp. Am., Chgo., 1942-55, N.Y.C., 1955-65; mgr. mktg. Fed. Paper Bd. Co., Montvale, N.J., 1965-67, sales mgr., 1967-69; gen. mgr. sales Berles Carton Co., Paterson, N.J., 1969-74; pres. Samuel F. Leigh Assos., mgmt. cons., Darien, Conn., 1974—. Rep., Town Meeting; chmn. com. pub. safety, 1974—, mem. com. selectmans' disaster, 1975—. Mem. Soc. Profl. Mgmt. Cons., Paper Packaging Council. Roman Catholic. Clubs: Princeton, Woodway Country, Seaview Country. Home and Office: 322 Noroton Ave Darien CT 06820

LEIGH, WILLIAM COLSTON, lecture and entertainment mgr.; b. N.Y.C., Aug. 7, 1901; s. William Robinson and Anna (Seng) L.; student Columbia U. Extension; m. Ardis Neff, Aug. 20, 1946; 1 son, William Colston. Pres. W. Colston Leigh, Inc., 1929—; clients managed include Eleanor Roosevelt, Mrs. Indira Gandhi, Madame Pandit, Clement Attlee, Grace Moore, Lawrence Tibbett, Alec Templeton, Art Buchwald, Abba Eban, Vincent Price, David Niven, Anthony Burgess, Celeste Holm, Betty Furness, Alvin Toffler, Justice Goldberg, Moshe Dayan, others in concert, theatre and entertainment field. Collector and authority on Am. and English antiques. Episcopalian. Home: 26 Edgerstoune Rd Princeton NJ 08540 Office: 6 E 45 St New York City NY 10017

LEIGHTON, ALBERT CHESTER, historian, educator; b. Chester, N.H., Sept. 6, 1919; s. Arthur Edmund and Sarah Elizabeth (Edwards) L.; A.B. in History, U. Calif., Berkeley, 1960, M.A. in Medieval History, 1961, Ph.D. in Medieval History, 1964; m. Estella Ruth Dietel, Jan. 17, 1958; 1 son, Cedric Edmund George. Served as enlisted man U.S. Army, 1937-46, commd. 2nd lt., 1946, advanced through grades to capt., 1953; ops. officer Army Security Agency, Germany, 1947-50, staff officer hdqrs., Washington, 1950-53, 55-57, ops. officer, Korea, Japan, Taiwan, 1954-55; ret., 1957; asso. prof. history State U. N.Y., Oswego, 1964-69, prof., 1969—, coordinator medieval studies, 1975—, coordinator internat. research in hist. crypt-analysis, 1969—, research fellow, 1967-68; Fulbright prof. U. Munich (Germany), 1978-79; mem. Am. Acad. Rome, summer 1978; fellow Southeastern Inst. for Medieval and Renaissance Studies Duke U., 1976. Decorated Commendation medal with oak leaf cluster. Mem. Am. Hist. Assn., Mediaeval Acad. Am., Soc. History Tech., Nat. Geog. Soc., MENSA, Am. Cryptogram Assn., Ancient and Hon. Arty. Co. Mass., Ret. Officers Assn. Author: Transport and Communication in Early Medieval Europe, 1972; contbr. articles to Ency. Americana and profl. publs. Home: RD 5 Dumas Rd Box 268 Oswego NY 13126 Office: History Dept State U NY Oswego NY 13126

LEIGHTON, CHARLES M(ILTON), diversified co. exec.; b. Portland, Maine, June 4, 1935; s. Wilbur F. and Elizabeth (Loveland) L.; A.B., Bowdoin Coll., 1957; M.B.A., Harvard U., 1960; m. Deborah Throop Smith, Aug. 30, 1958; children—Julia Loveland, Anne Throop. Product line mgr. Mine Safety Appliances Co., Pitts., 1960-64; instr. Harvard Bus. Sch., Boston, 1964-65; group v.p. Bangor Punta Corp., Boston, 1965-69; chmn. bd., chief exec. officer CML Group, Inc., Boston, 1969—; dir. Independence Fund, Boston, 1968—, Freedom Fund, Boston, 1968—, Mass. Income Fund, 1973—, New Eng. Life Ins. Co. Mut. Funds, 1977—. Dir., Mass. Gov.'s Pub. Service Fellowship Program, 1974—; area finance chmn., campaign Sen. Edward Brooke, 1966; trustee Concord (Mass.) Acad., 1977—, pres. bd. trustees, 1978. Served with AUS, 1957-58. Recipient Col. William Owen premium Bowdoin Coll., 1957. Clubs: Chatham Yacht (vice commodore 1955-57); N.Y. Yacht; Harvard (N.Y.C., Boston); Somerset. Contbr. articles to profl. jours. Home: 33 Liberty St Concord MA 01742 Office: 80 Thoreau St Concord MA 01742

LEIGHTON, DAVID KELLER, SR., clergyman; b. Edgewood, Pa., June 22, 1922; s. Frank Kingsley and Irene (Keller) L.; B.S., Northwestern U., 1947; D.D., Va. Theol. Sem., 1969; m. Carolyn Ruth Smith, Jan. 18, 1945; children—Charlotte, David Keller, Nancy Elizabeth (Mrs. Harold Otto Koenig). Personnel interviewer Ohio Rubber Co., Willoughby, 1947-50; asst. supr. employment Fisher Body div. Gen. Motors Corp., Pitts. plant, 1950-54; priest Episcopal Ch., 1955; curate Calvary Episcopal Ch., Pitts., 1955-56; rector St. Andrews Eipscopal Ch., Pitts., 1956-59; rector Ch. of Holy Nativity, Balt., 1959-63; tchr. sacred studies St. Paul Schs., Brooklandville, Md., 1960-63; archdeacon Episcopal Diocese Md., Balt., 1964-68, bishop coadjutor, 1968-72, bishop, 1972—. Vice pres. Diocesan Council Md., 1964-72, pres., 1972—; v.p. Cathedral chpt. Md., 1968—. Chmn. bd. Hannah More Acad., Reistertown, Md., 1968-74; bd. dirs. Md. Council Chs., Heart House, Pitts., Ch. Mission of Help, Balt.; bd. dirs. Ch. Home and Hosp., Balt., v.p., 1972—; bd. mem. U. Balt. Served with USAAF, 1942-45; ETO. Mem. Engring. Soc. Balt., Cum Laude Soc. Balt., St. Andrews Soc. Clubs: Center, University (Balt.). Home: 3601 N Charles St Baltimore MD 21218 Office: 105 W Monument St Baltimore MD 21201

LEIGHTON, THOMAS GIBBONS, pub. relations exec.; b. Mpls., Mar. 13, 1925; s. William Henry and Anna Maria (Jensen) L.; B.A. cum laude, U. Minn., 1948; grad. study, U. Wis.; m. Mary Miller, July 20, 1963; children—Pamela Ann, Thomas Jensen. Reporter, columnist Mpls. Daily Times, 1942-48; officer savs. bonds div. U.S. Treasury Dept., Washington, 1948-50; dir. info. U.S. Displaced Persons Commn., Washington, 1951-52; advisor to majority policy com. U.S. Senate Washington, 1953-56; dir. pub. relations Nat. Cultural Center for Performing Arts, Washington, 1956-60; sr. v.p., dir., dir. mgmt. counseling div. Dudley-Anderson-Yutzy Pub. Relations and Pub. Affairs, Inc., N.Y.C., 1960-77. Mgmt. cons. to W. K. Kellogg Co., 1977—. Mem. Pub. Relations Soc. Am. (counselors sect., recipient Silver Anvil award 1975). Democrat. Unitarian. Home: 91 Lee St Winchester VA 22601 Office: 440 West End Ave New York City NY 10024

LEIMKUHLER, GERARD JOSEPH, JR., fin. holding co. exec.; b. Phila., June 13, 1948; s. Gerard Joseph and Dorothy Joan (Gaffney) L.; B.B.A., Temple U., 1970; m. Karen Roberta Hall, Oct. 13, 1973. Mem. Phila. Stock Exchange, 1968-75; v.p., Oxford 1st Corp., Phila., 1975—; v.p., Hilton Head Co., Phila., 1975—; pres. Gen. Acquisitions Corp., Phila., 1977—, also dir. Mem. Newtown Twp. (Delaware County, Pa.) Planning Commn., 1976-77. Served with U.S. Army, 1970-71. Registered investment adviser SEC. Mem. Nat. Assn. Securities Dealers, Am. Mgmt. Assn. Republican. Roman Catholic. Clubs: Vesper Boat, Temple U. Varsity. Home: 535 Weadley Rd Wayne PA 19087 Office: Oxford 1st Corp 6701 N Broad St Philadelphia PA 19126

LEINWEBER, BRUCE KORNBLATT, obstetrician, gynecologist; b. Phila., Sept. 11, 1935; s. Arthur Richter and Florence (Kornblatt) L.; B.A., Lafayette Coll., 1955; D.D.S., Temple U., 1959; M.D., Jefferson Med. Coll., 1963; m. Joan Halperin, Feb. 4, 1976; children by previous marriage—Cynthia Beth, Melanie Joy; stepchildren—Suzanne, Jenifer, Adam Glick. Intern, Albert Einstein Med. Center, Phila., 1963-64, resident in obstetrics and gynecology, 1964-67; individual practice medicine, specializing in obstetrics, gynecology, Phila., 1967—; attending obstetrician and gynecologist Albert Einstein Med. Center, No. div., Phila., Frankford Hosp., Phila., Rolling Hill Hosp., Elkins Park, Pa., Jeanes Hosp., Phila.; asso. staff Moss Rehab. Hosp., 1976—, Willowcrest-Bamberger Extended Care Facility, 1976— (both Phila.); clin. asst. prof. obstetrics-gynecology Med. Coll. Pa., Phila., 1976—; clin. asst. prof. obstetrics and gynecology Temple U., Phila., 1974—. Recipient Legion of Honor, Chapel of 4 Chaplains, Phila., 1978. Diplomate Am. Bd. Obstetrics and Gynecology, Nat. Bd. Med. Examiners. Fellow Am. Coll. Obstetrics and Gynecology; mem. AMA (physician recognition award 1972, 75, 78), Philadelphia County, Pa. med. socs., Am. Fertility Soc., AAAS, Royal Soc. Medicine (London), Obstet. Soc. Phila., Am. Assn. Sex Educators, Counselors and Therapists. Republican. Jewish. Mason. Office: 3237 Bristol Rd Cornwells Heights PA 19020

LEIR, HENRY J(OHN), ore co. exec.; b. Rossberg, Germany, Jan. 28, 1900; student high schs., Beuthen, Germany; m. Erna D. Schloss, Jan. 27, 1929. Came to U.S., 1938, naturalized, 1944, Mgr. ore and pig iron dept. Wolf Netter, Ludwigshafen/Rhein, Germany, 1919-31, Magnesit GmbH, Bonn/Rhein, Germany, 1931-33, S.A. des Minerais, Luxembourg, 1933-38; became pres., dir. Continental Ore Corp., N.Y.C., 1939; now chmn. bd. Continental Metals Corp., N.Y.C. Decorated grand officer Couronne de Chêne Grande-Croix de l'Ordre de Mérite (Luxembourg); chevalier de la Légion d'Honneur (France). Office: 245 Park Ave New York City NY 10017

LEIS, HENRY PATRICK, JR., surgeon, educator; b. Saranac Lake, N.Y., Aug. 12, 1914; s. Henry P. and Mary A. (Disco) L.; B.S. cum laude, Fordham U., 1936; M.D., N.Y. Med. Coll., 1941; m. Winogene Barnette, Jan. 8, 1944; children—Henry Patrick, Thomas Frederick. Intern, Flower and Fifth Ave. Hosps., N.Y.C., 1941-42, resident, 1943-44, 46-49, attending surgeon, chief breast service, 1960—; resident in surgery Kanawa Valley Hosp., Charleston, W.Va., 1942-43; attending surgeon, chief breast service Met. Hosp., N.Y.C., 1960—, Coler Meml. Hosp., N.Y.C., 1960-76, Cabrini Hosp. Med. Center; hon. surg. staff Drs. Hosp., N.Y.C.; attending surgeon Beekman Downtown, Westchester County Med. Center, 1977—; cons. in breast surgery Bay Ridge Hosp., Bklyn., Nassau Hosp., Mineola, N.Y.; clin. prof. surgery, co-dir. Inst. Breast Diseases, 1978, chief breast surgery service N.Y. Med. Coll., 1960—; cons. in breast surgery State U. N.Y. Div. Rehab., 1965—, Med. and Surg. Specialists Plan N.Y.; mem. Am. Joint Com. on Breast Cancer Staging and End Results; v.p. N.Y. Met. Breast Cancer Group, 1975-76, pres., 1977—; cons. Med. Advisers Selective Service System, N.Y.C. Alumni trustee N.Y. Med. Coll., 1971—; adv. council Fordham U. Coll. Pharmacy, 1968—; bd. dirs. Hall Fame and Mus. Surg. History and Related Scis., 1966—. Served as capt., M.C., AUS, 1944-46; PTO. Decorated knight comdr. Equestrian Order Holy Sepulchre Jerusalem; knight Mil. and Hospitaler Order St. Lazaurs Jerusalem; knight of Malta; recipient award of Merit Am. Cancer Soc., 1969; certificate and award for outstanding and devoted services to indigent sick City N.Y., 1965; Dr. George Hohman Meml. medal, 1936; N.Y. Apothecaries medal, 1936; Internat. certificate merit for distinguished service to surgery, 1970; award of merit N.Y. Met. Breast Cancer Group, 1976; medal of Ambrogino (Italy) 1977; Service award of Honor N.Y. Med. Coll., 1969; medaille d' Honneur (France). Diplomate Am. Bd. Surgery. Fellow A.C.S., Am. Acad. Compensation Medicine, Am. Soc. Clin. Oncology, Am. Assn. Cancer Research, Am. Geriatrics Soc., Indsl. Med. Assn., Internat. Coll. Surgeons (1st v.p. 1973-74, pres. 1977, v.p., chmn. council examiners U.S. sect. 1962-68, pres. 1971, Service award of Honor 1971), Internat. Paleopathology Assn. (founder), N.Y. Acad. Medicine, N.Y. Council Surgeons, Royal Soc. Health (Eng.); mem. AAAS, AAUP, Am. Cancer Soc. (com. breast cancer), Am. Med. Writers Assn., AMA, Am. Profl. Practice Assn., Assn. Am. Med. Colls., Am. Coll. Radiology (com. mammography and breast cancer), Assn. Mil. Surgeons U.S., Cath. Physicians Guild (pres. N.Y. 1970-78), Gerontol. Soc., Internat. Platform Assn., N.Y. Acad. Sci., N.Y. Cancer Soc., N.Y. County Med. Soc., N.Y. Medico-Surg. Soc., N.Y. Soc. Med. Research, N.Y. Med. Soc., N.Y. Surg. Soc., Pan Am. Med. Assn. (v.p. N.Am. sect. on cancer 1967—), Pan Pacific Surg. Assn., Res. Officers Assn. U.S., Soc. Acad. Achievement (editorial bd. 1969—), Soc. Med. Jurisprudence, Soc. Nuclear Medicine, Surg. Soc. N.Y. Med. Coll., WHO, World Med. Assn., Alumni Assn. N.Y. Med. Coll. (gov. 1960—, pres. 1971), Assn. Mil. Surgeons U.S., Cath. War Vets. Assn., VFW, Peruvian Acad. Surgery (hon.), Hollywood Acad. Medicine (hon.), Alpha Omega Alpha, Phi Chi; hon. mem. Argentine Soc. Mammary Pathology, Argentina Cardiac and Thoracic Surg. Soc., Ecuador Med. Assn., Mo. Surg. Soc., Venezuela Surg. Soc., Italian Surg. Soc. Clubs: K.C. (4th deg.); Cresthaven Country (Whitestone, N.Y.); 400, Meissen Unanimous (N.Y.C.). Author: Diagnosis and Treatment of Breast Lesions; The Breast, Management of Breast Lesions; asso. editor: Breast; cons. editor Internat. Surgery Jour.; contbr. numerous articles to med. jours. Home: 147-03 Fifth Ave Whitestone NY 11357 Office: 55 E 87th St New York City NY 10028

LEIS, WINOGENE B., nurse assn. exec.; b. Clay, W.Va., Feb. 27, 1919; d. Gruder L. and Daisy M. (Young) Barnette; R.N. cum laude, Kanawha Valley Hosp., 1939; m. Henry Patrick Leis, Jr., Jan. 8, 1944; children—Henry Patrick, Thomas Federick. Nurse, Kanawha Valley Hosp., 1939-43. Mem. Woman's Aux. Internat. Coll. Surgeons (corr. sec. N.Y. State surg. div. 1955-57, v.p. 1961-63, pres. 1963-67; pres. U.S. sect. 1970, 77, dir. 1970-74), Flower Fifth Ave. Hosp. Woman's Aux. (dir. 1956-59, 69—), Woman's Aux. N.Y. Acad. Scis., Woman's Aux. N.Y. State Med. Soc., Woman's Aux. Internat. Coll. Surgeons (corr. sec. 1972-74, pres. 1976-78). Republican. Roman Catholic. Home: 147-03 5th Ave Whitestone NY 11357

LEISEY, ALVIN LEWIS, JR., photographic and office equipment co. exec.; b. Birdsboro, Pa., May 10, 1923; s. Alvin Lewis and E. Marie (Leidenberger) L.; B.A., Pa. State U., 1948; m. Mary Helen Abbott, Feb. 24, 1945; children—Laloni, Randall, Mary Ellen, Ronald, Kimberly, Kathryn. Systems analyst Lukens Steel Co., Coatesville, Pa., 1948-51; with New Holland Machine Co. (Pa.), 1951-56; asst. controller Internat. Latex Corp., Dover, Del., 1956-63; v.p. adminstrn., controller Morse Twist Drill & Machine Co., New Bedford, Mass., 1963-67; mgr. adminstrn. Xerox Mfg. div., Webster, N.Y., 1967-68; v.p. adminstrn. and control ITEK Bus. Products Co., 1968-73; corporate controller, chief financial officer Minolta Corp., Ramsey, N.J., 1973—; corporator Fairhaven Instn. for Savs. Cons., speaker for mgmts. on systems and work simplification. Twp. supr. West Whiteland, Pa., 1953-56; mem. Dover Bd. Edn., 1961-63; mem. Commn. on Efficiency and Economy in State Govt., State of N.J., 1976—; bd. dirs. YMCA, United Fund, New Bedford; mem. session Ringwood Community Presbyn. Ch.; mem. bd. edn. Lakeland Regional High Sch., 1977—. Served with USMCR, 1941-45. Decorated Purple Heart; named Systems Man of Year, Delaware Valley, 1962. Mem. Financial Execs. Inst., Am. Mgmt. Assn., Adminstrv. Systems Mgmt. Assn. (past pres. Keystone chpt., past pres. R.I. chpt.), Planning Execs. Inst., Adminstrv. Mgmt. Soc. (past pres. Lancaster), Internat. Systems and Procedures Assn. (dir.), No. N.J. Chamber of Commerce and Industry (dir. 1974—, treas. 1977—), Bergen County C. of C. (dir.). Republican. Mason (Shriner), Lion (past pres. Ringwood, N.J.). Clubs: National Holiday Rambler Travel Trailer (past pres.); AFS (pres.). Contbr. articles to profl. jours. Home: 5 Birch Pl Ringwood NJ 07456 Office: 101 Williams Dr Ramsey NJ 07446

LEISINGER, LEWIS MARTIN, civil engr.; b. N.Y.C., May 22, 1908; s. Albert Hess and Sarah (Distillator) L.; student N.Y. U., 1926-27; C.E., Cornell U., Ithaca, N.Y., 1931, Columbia U., 1932; m. Marjorie Charlotte Hughes, Sept. 12, 1942; children—Lynne Margaret Leisinger Chubb, Barbara Ann Leisinger Milks. With Shell Oil Co., 1938-67, ops. mgr. Mich., 1953-60, div., regional engr. N.Y., 1960-67, cons. engr., 1967—; project mgr. Teetor-Dobbins, cons. engrs., Bohemia, N.Y., 1967-68; town engr. Town of Islip (N.Y.), 1968-72; cons. engr., Islip, 1972—; prin. L.M. Leisinger and Assos., Huntington, N.Y., 1972—. Mem. Mayor's Com. on Zoning, Grosse Pointe, Mich., 1957-60; trustee Knoll Found., Ithaca, N.Y. Lt. col. C.E., U.S. Army ret. Registered profl. engr., N.Y., Mich. Fellow ASCE (life); mem. Cornell Soc. Engrs., Water Pollution Control Fedn., N.Y. State Soc. Profl. Engrs. (dir.), Phi Kappa Tau. Presbyterian (elder, trustee). Clubs: Masons, Shriners, Jesters, Rotary; Players (Detroit); Centerport Yacht. Home: 70 Old Field Rd Huntington NY 11743

LEITER-ARNOLD, BARBARA ANN, hosp. adminstr.; b. Hagerstown, Md., Mar. 25, 1946; d. Lester Ellsworth and Josephine Elizabeth (Doub) Leiter; diploma Alexandria (Va.) Hosp. Sch. Nursing, 1967; B.S., Edn., Wilkes Coll., 1969; M.Ed., Va. Commonwealth U., 1976; m. Robert Webb Arnold, June 4, 1977. Pediatric instr. Bryn Mawr (Pa.) Hosp. Sch. Nursing, 1969-72; gen. nurse instr. dept. staff devel. Med. Coll. Va., Richmond, 1972-75; dir. edn. and tng. Providence Hosp., Washington, 1976—. Recipient Gold medal Va. affiliate Am. Heart Assn., 1977. Mem. Am. Soc. Health Manpower Edn. and Tng., Wilkes Alumnae Assn., Am. Heart Assn. Office: Providence Hosp 1150 Varnum St NE Washington DC 20017

LEITMAN, NORMAN JACK, art dealer; b. N.Y.C., June 24, 1933; s. Samuel and Annabelle (Kushner) L.; B.A., Cornell U., 1954; postgrad. N.Y. U. Inst. Fine Arts, 1954-57. Asst. to dir. Paul Drey Gallery, N.Y.C., 1956-64; art dealer, 1964-65; dir. Shickman Gallery, N.Y.C., 1965—. Mem. Art Dealers Assn. Am., Rolls-Royce Enthusiasts Club (U.K.), Bentley Drivers Club (U.K.). Jewish. Author exhbn. catalogues, the most recent being: The Neglected 19th Century, part I, 1970, part II, 1971. Home: 240 E 79th St New York City NY 10021 Office: 929 Park Ave New York City NY 10028

LE KASHMAN, CAROL ANN, banker; b. Long Branch, N.J., Mar. 29, 1952; d. Raymond and Beatrice (Burke) LeK.; B.A. in English Lit., Wellesley Coll., 1973; M.B.A. in Mktg., Wharton Sch., U. Pa., 1975. With Citibank, N.Y.C., 1976—, staff internat. ops., 1977-78, mgr. internat. ops., 1979—. Democrat. Episcopalian. Club: Wellesley (N.Y.C.). Home: 201 E 17th St Apt 30E New York City NY 10003 Office: 111 Wall St New York City NY 10043

LEKUCH, ILYA, mktg. co. exec.; b. Riga, USSR, June 19, 1947; s. Lester and Leya Lekuch; came to U.S., 1967, naturalized, 1974; grad. Leningrad Poly. Inst., 1976, Rensselear Poly. Inst., Troy, N.Y., 1978; m. Aviva Taitz, Aug. 31, 1968; 1 son, David S. Dept. mgr. Logos Devel. Corp., N.Y.C., 1972; sales engr. equipment and tech. dept. Philipp Overseas Inc., N.Y.C., 1973-75; export mgr. USSR div. WJS Inc., Washington, 1975, v.p. div., 1977—. Home: 4004 N Tazewell St Arlington VA 22207 Office: 1150 Connecticut Ave NW Washington DC 20036

LELAND, GEORGE HAVENS, cons. engr.; b. Warwick, R.I., June 7, 1926; s. Richard Cutler and Katherine (Havens) L.; B.S., Harvard Coll., 1946, M.S., 1947; m. Virginia Saxe Kelcey, June 30, 1951; children—David Kelcey, Ann Louise, Suzanne. Asst. engr. to project engr. Edwards and Kelcey, Engrs. and Cons., Newark, 1947-51, asso., 1953-58, partner, 1958—; pres. Edwards and Kelcey, Inc., 1963—, chmn. bd., 1973—. Mem. Chatham (N.J.) Borough Bd. Edn., 1969-75; mem. Nat. Def. Exec. Res-U.S. Dept. Transp., 1970—. Mem. adv. com. N.J. Inst. Tech., 1966-73; adv. council Princeton Transp. Program, 1976—, dept. civil and urban engring. U. Pa., 1977—. Served to ensign with USNR, 1945-46; served to lt. comdr. C.E., USNR, 1951-53. Fellow ASCE; mem. Nat. Soc. Profl. Engrs., Soc. Am. Mil. Engrs., N.Y.C. C. of C. (transp. com. 1971-76), Am. Cons. Engrs. Council (v.p. 1973-75, chmn. com. fellows 1974-75, pres. 1979), Internat. Road Fedn. (dir.), Inst. Traffic Engrs., N.J. Cons. Engrs. Council (past pres.), Hwy. Users Fedn. (dir.), Soc. Harvard Engrs. and Scientists (mem. council 1966-68), Chi Epsilon (hon.). Clubs: Minisink (Chatham, N.J.) (trustee 1966-69; past pres.); Essex (Newark); Harvard (N.Y.C.) (N.J.). Home: Pleasantville Rd New Vernon NJ 07976 Office: 75 S Orange Ave Livingston NJ 07039 also One World Trade Center Suite 5075 New York City NY 10048

LELAND, LORRAINE ABEL (MRS. FRANK HERBERT LEE), psychologist; b. Jersey City, Aug. 23, 1911; d. Carl and Lillian (Zahn) Abel; A.B., Barnard Coll., 1930; M.A., Columbia, 1931, Ph.D., 1936, postgrad., 1943; m. Frank Leland (died June 1943); m. 2d, Frank Herbert Lee, Apr. 6, 1958. Psychologist, Bur. Juvenile Research, Columbus, Ohio, 1939-41; dir. Ohio U. Guidance Clinic, Athens, 1942-43; dir. Women's Personnel and Nursery Schs. Grumman Aircraft Engring. Corp., Bethpage, N.Y., 1943-46; cons. psychologist various sch. systems, L.I., 1947-56; rehab. co-ordinator Triboro Hosp., N.Y.C., 1947-55; pvt. practice psychotherapy, Flower Hill, Roslyn, N.Y., 1948—; cons. psychologist Meadow Brook Hosp., Hempstead, L.I., 1950-65, South Oaks Hosp., Amityville, L.I., 1973—. Mem. Internat. Psychoanalytical Congress, 1965, 67, 69, 71. Diplomate Am. Bd. Examiners in Profl. Psychology. Fellow Am. Psychol. Assn.; mem. N.Y. State Psychol. Assn., Nassau County, N.Y. Soc. Clin. Psychologists, Internat. Council Women Psychologists. Address: 2 Bayberry Ridge Flower Hill Roslyn NY 11576

LELE, PADMAKAR PRATAP, physician; b. Chanda, India, Nov. 9, 1927; s. Pratap V. and Indira (Prabhudesai) L.; came to U.S., 1958; M.D., Seth G.S. Med. Coll., Bombay, 1950; D.Phil., Oxford (Eng.) U., 1955; m. Carla Maria Tophoff, Jan. 23, 1959; children—Martin, Malcolm. Intern, Municipal Gen. Hosp., Bombay, 1950-51; resident in neurology King Edward Meml. Hosp., Bombay, 1951-52; practice medicine specializing in neurology, India and Eng., 1952-57; vis. scientist NIH, Bethesda, Md., 1958-59; asso. neurophysiologist Mass. Gen. Hosp.-Harvard U. Med. Sch., Boston, 1959-69; asso. prof. exptl. medicine Mass. Inst. Tech., 1969-74, prof., 1971—; cons. NSF, FDA, NIH. Fellow Acoustical Soc. Am.; mem. IEE, Am. Physiol. Soc., Am. Assn. Anatomists, Physiol. Soc. Gt. Britain, Sigma Xi. Club: Winchester (Mass.) Boat. Contbr. articles to profl. jours. Home: 21 Squire Rd Winchester MA 01890 Office: 26-023 Mass Inst Tech Cambridge MA 02139

LEMAN, PAUL HENRI, aluminum co. exec.; b. Montreal, Que., Can., Aug. 6, 1915; s. Beaudry J.B. and Caroline (Beique) L.; B.A., St. Mary's Coll., Montreal, 1934; LL.L., U. Montreal, 1937; postgrad. bus. adminstrn. Harvard U., 1937-38; m. Jeannine Prud'homme, May 19, 1939; children—Denise, Jacques, Nicole, Marc, Claire. Admitted to Que. bar, 1937; staff Aluminum Co. of Can., Ltd., 1938-43, asst. sec., 1943-45, treas., 1949-63, v.p., 1952-64, exec. v.p., 1964-69, pres., 1969-75, chmn. bd., 1975—; exec. v.p. smelting Alcan Aluminium Ltd., 1969-72, pres., 1972-77, vice-chmn., 1977—; dir. Bell Can., Can. Internat. Paper Co., Crédit Foncier Franco-Canadien; mem. Canadian Royal Commn. Banking and Finance, 1962-64. Gov. La Jeune Chambre de Montreal; pres. Université de Montreal Assos. Mem. Conf. Bd. Home: 445 Saint Joseph Blvd W Outremont Montreal PQ H2V 2P8 Canada Office: 1 Place Ville Marie Montreal PQ H3C 3H2 Canada

LEMAY, PAULETTE MARIE, lawyer; b. Paterson, N.J., Sept. 17, 1940; d. Albert Thomas and Yvonne Marie (Bergeron) L.; A.B., Vassar Coll., 1962; LL.B., U. Pa., 1965. Admitted to N.J. bar, 1965; practiced in Paterson, 1966-73; law clk. to judge Superior Ct., New Brunswick, N.J., 1965-66; asso. firm Cole, Berman and Belsky, 1966-69; individual practice law, Paterson, 1969; sr. editor Prentice-Hall, Inc., Englewood Cliffs, N.J., 1969-73; asso. gen. counsel Unishops, Inc., Jersey City, 1973—. Mem. Mayor's Charter Study Commn., Paterson, 1969, sec., 1969. Fellow The Hague, Netherlands, 1964. Mem. Am., N.J. bar assns. Office: 21 Caven Point Ave Jersey City NJ 07305

LEMBO, JOHN MARIO, psychologist, educator; b. Vineland, N.J., May 24, 1937; s. Joseph Anthony and Antoinette Palma (Paolino) L.; B.A., LaSalle Coll., Phila., 1961; M.Ed., Xavier U., Cin., 1964; Ed.D., Case Western Res. U., 1966; children—Anthony Michael, Daniel Vincent. Instr. psychology St. John's Coll., Cleve., 1964-66; asst. prof. St. Bonaventure U., Olean, N.Y., 1966-67; asst. prof. psychology, chmn. dept. St. John's Coll., Rochester, N.Y., 1967-68; prof. psychology Millersville (Pa.) State Coll., 1968—, chmn. dept., 1970; practice psychology, counseling and psychotherapy, 1964—. Fellow Inst. Advanced Study Rational Psychotherapy; mem. Am. Psychol. Assn. Roman Catholic. Author: The Psychology of Effective Classroom Instruction, 1969; Why Teachers Fail, 1971; When Learning Happens, 1972; Help Yourself, 1974; The Counseling Process: A Cognitive Behavioral Approach, 1976; How to Cope with Your Fears and Frustrations, 1977. Home: 1497-D Manor House Ln Lancaster PA 17603 Office: Millersville State Coll Millersville PA 17551

LEMCHEN, MARC STUART, orthodontist; b. Jersey City, July 22, 1945; s. Leo and Eleanor (Goldberg) L.; B.A., Lafayette Coll., 1966; D.M.D., Tufts U., 1970; certificate orthodontics Columbia U., 1974; m. Deborah Lynn Schneider, June 11, 1971. Practice orthodontics, N.Y.C., 1970—; mem. staffs Lenox Hill and St. Luke's hosps., N.Y.C., N.Y. Hosp. Cornell U. Med. Center; asst. clin. prof. dentistry N.Y. U., 1976-78. Licensed dentist, Mass., N.J., Conn., N.Y. Mem. Am. Assn. Orthodontists, ADA, Midtown Dental Assn. Home: 219 E 81st St New York City NY 10028 Office: 800 A Fifth Ave New York City NY 10021

LEMCKE, NORMAN ROHDE, lawyer; b. N.Y.C., Dec. 3, 1894; s. Albert William and Dora (Rohde) L.; B.S., Amherst Coll., 1917; LL.B., N.Y. Law Sch., 1924; m. Elizabeth Bouteiller, Sept. 3, 1918 (dec. Jan. 15, 1968); 1 son, Norman Rohde. Admitted to N.J. bar, 1924; practiced with Smith & Slingerland, Newark, 1924-27; joined Prudential Ins. Co. of Am., 1927, branch office atty., Montreal, 1927-28, regional appraiser, supr., Newark, home office, 1928-34, mgr. regional office, Phila., 1934-35, N.Y.C., 1935-37, supr. West Coast, 1937-44, East Coast, 1944, asst. sec., Newark, 194 46, gen. mgr., 1946-47, 2d v.p., 1947-61, v.p., 1961-63; mem. law firm Eisner & Lemcke, until 1968; individual practice, Maplewood, N.J., 1968-77. Dir. govt. sponsored Housing Enterprises of Can., 1945-47. Past v.p. Essex County Youth House. Ensign, USN, 1917-19, serving in U.S.S. Pittsburgh. Mem. Am., N.J. bar assns., Phi Beta Kappa, Alpha Delta Phi, Delta Theta Phi. Methodist. Club: Essex County Country (West Orange, N.J.). Intercollegiate 50 yd. swimming champion, 1916. Home and office: 5 W Main St Brookside NJ 07926

LEMIEN, HENRY LESTER, JR., lab. adminstr.; b. Norwalk, Conn., Dec. 26, 1934; d. Henry Lester and Helen Elizabeth (Allison) LeM.; B.Sc., U. Ala., 1959; postgrad. USAF Air War Coll., 1972-74, McGill U., 1974-75; m. Betty Jean Fendley, Nov. 28, 1953; children—Deborah Ann, Henry Lester III. Rep., Ayerst Labs., Birmingham, Ala., 1959-65, clin. research asso., Chgo., 1965-71, clin. pharmacology coordinator, Montreal, Que., Can., 1971-76, clin. research monitor, N.Y.C., 1976-77, asst. to med. dir., 1977—. Chmn. disaster ARC, Chgo., 1967-71, vice-chmn. No. Cook County, 1970-71; dir. rescue squad Bluff Park Fire Dept., Birmingham, 1961-65, asst. chief, 1961-65; lt. col. CAP, West Redding (Conn.) Fire Dept. Served with USNR, 1953-60. Recipient awards Civil Air Patrol, 1965, A.R.C., 1958, 65, 71. Mem. Am. Soc. Microbiology, AAAS, Drug Info. Assn., Am., Ill., Conn. socs. anesthesiologists, Ill. Soc. Med. Research, N.Y. Acad. Sci., Conn. Fire Dept. Instrs. Assn. Home: 19 Fire Hill Ln West Redding CT 06896 Office: 685 3d Ave New York City NY 10017

LEMIRE, ANDRE, investment co. exec.; b. Quebec City, Can., Mar. 15, 1943; s. Adrien and Gabrielle (Martel) L.; B.Sc., U. Ottawa, 1967; m. Ann C. Chisholm, Sept. 6, 1969. Tax analyst Bell Can., Montreal, 1968-69; investment analyst Jones Heward Co., Ltd., Montreal, 1969-72; asst. dir. research Levesque, Beaubien Inc., Montreal, 1972-74, dir. investment research, 1974-78, v.p. investment research, 1978—; mem. Montreal Stock Exchange Listing Com., 1976—, asst. program chmn. Mem. Montreal Soc. Fin. Analysts Montreal Mus. Arts. Roman Catholic. Club: Montreal Badmington and Squash. Home: 500 Laird Blvd Town of Mount Royal PQ H3R 244 Canada Office: 360 St James St Monreal PQ H2Y 1P7 Canada

LEMKE, HARU HIRAMA, occupational therapist, educator; b. Las Animas, Colo., Apr. 20, 1928; d. Soju and Kiyoshi (Ogasawara) Hirama; B.S. in Home Econs., Colo. State U., 1949, B.S. in Occupational Therapy, 1950; M.Ed. Lehigh U., 1974, certificate in elementary sch. counseling, 1974; children—Monica Ann, John Timothy, Christopher Mark, Susan Elaine. Dir. dept. occupational therapy Nat. Jewish Hosp., Denver, 1954-58, Allentown (Pa.) State Hosp., 1960-61, Hamburg (Pa.) State Sch. and Hosp., 1965-75; prof. occupational therapy, coordinator occupational therapy assisting program Lehigh County Community Coll., 1975—; lectr. Lehigh U., 1975—; instr. Marywood Coll., Scranton, Pa., 1976. Served to 1st lt., Med. Specialists Corps, U.S. Army, 1950-54. Registered occupational therapist. Mem. Am., Pa. occupational therapy assns., Am. Assn. on Mental Deficiency, Am. Assn. for Edn. of Severely/Profoundly Handicapped. Home: RD 1 Box 77 Auburn PA 17922 Office: Lehigh County Community Coll 2370 Main St Schnecksville PA 18078

LEMMERMAN, CHARLES HENRY, sales exec.; b. Ridgewood, N.Y.C., Sept. 13, 1920; s. Charles H. and Elizabeth Estelle (Schramm) L.; student Bucknell U., 1939-42; m. Gloralie Lores Collier, Mar. 16, 1946; children—Carl Henry, Gloralie Lores. Tool designer Glenn L. Martin Co., Balt., 1945; salesman, broker Real Estate & Bus. Brokerage, N.Y.C., 1946-48; salesman Wood-Metal Industries, Inc., Kreamer, Pa., 1948—, nat. sales mgr., 1959—, v.p., dir. mktg., 1964—. Served USAAF and OWI, 1942-44. Mem. Am. Legion (comdr. 1957-58), Kreamer Snyder County Sportsman's Assn., Forest Products Research Soc., AIM (fellow pres.'s council 1970—), Am. Mgmt. Assn., Sales and Mktg. Execs. Internat., Nat. Assn. Home Builders, Mfrs. Agts. Nat. Assn., Am. Inst. Kitchen Designers (certified), Am. Inst. Kitchen Dealers (certified), Sigma Alpha Epsilon (chpt. pres. 1942). Clubs: Elks, Moose, Susquehanna Valley Country (Sunburg, Pa.). Lutheran. Home: RD 1 Lewisburg PA 17837 Office: Wood-Metal Industries Inc Kreamer PA 17833

LEMOLE, GERALD MICHAEL, surgeon; b. S.I., N.Y., Dec. 17, 1936; s. Joseph Michael and Mary (Boylan) L.; B.S. in Biology, Villanova U., 1958; M.D., Temple U., 1962; m. Emily Jane Asplundh, Dec. 8, 1962; children—Lisa Jane, Laura Leigh, Emily Anne, Gerald Michael, Samantha, Christopher. Intern, S.I. Hosp., 1962-63; resident in gen. surgery Temple U., Phila., 1963-67; resident in thoracic surgery Baylor Affiliated Hosps., Houston, 1967-69; practice medicine specializing in thoracic surgery, Phila., 1969—, Browns Mills, N.J., 1973—; chief sect. cardiac and thoracic surgery Temple U. Hosp., Phila., 1970—; prof. surgery Temple U. Health Scis. Center, 1975-77; chmn. dept. surgery Deborah Heart and Lung Center, Phila., 1972—; vis. prof. cardiac surgery U. Dublin (Ireland), 1974; clin. prof. surgery U. Pa., 1978. Diplomate Am. Bd. Surgery, Am. Bd. Thoracic Surgery. Fellow A.C.S., Am. Coll. Cardiology, Am. Coll. Chest Physicians (cardiovascular com. 1974—); mem. Phila. Coll. Physicians, Am. Assn. Thoracic Surgery, Am. Fedn. Clin. Research, Am., Pan Am. thoracic socs., Internat., Denton A. Cooley cardiovascular socs., Am. Coll. Angiology, Pa., Phila. County med. socs., Phila. Acad. Surgery, Phila. Acad. Cardiology (pres. 1976—), Assn. Acad. Surgeons, Soc. Vascular Surgery, Pa. Assn. Thoracic Surgeons, AMA, Am. Heart Assn., Pa. Thoracic Assn. (program chmn. 1975—). Contbr. numerous articles on cardiovascular surgery and disease to med. jours.; research in cardiovascular physiology. Home: 404 Tomlinson Rd Huntington Valley PA 19006 Office: Dept Surgery Presbyn Hosp 3910 Powelton Ave Philadelphia PA 19140

LENAHAN, EDWARD PATRICK, publishing co. exec., b. Evanston, Ill., June 25, 1925; s. Edward Patrick and Emma Catherine (O'Shea) L.; A.B., Harvard, 1950; LL.D., Seattle U., 1975; m. Lois Elaine Alm, Sept. 6, 1952; children—Kathryn Crowley, Elizabeth O'Shea, Timothy Egan, Nancy Carpenter. Trainee, Asso. Mdsg. Corp., N.Y.C., 1950-51; mortgage banker J. Halperin & Co., N.Y.C., 1951-55; with Fortune mag., N.Y.C., 1955-70, 73—, advt. dir., 1969-70, publisher, 1973—; gen. mgr. Life mag., 1971-73; v.p. Time Inc., N.Y.C., 1973—, treas., 1976—. Served with USNR, 1943-46. Clubs: Harvard, Players (N.Y.C.); Creek. Home: 10 The Knolls Locust Valley NY 11560 Office: Time and Life Bldg Rockefeller Center New York City NY 10020

LENCHNER, NATHANIEL HERBERT, dentist, educator; b. N.Y.C., Aug. 28, 1923; s. Edward and Jennie (Reizes) L.; B.A., N.Y. U., 1943; D.D.S., 1950; m. Florence Smith, Jan. 25, 1959; children—Jonathan, Michael, Debra. Pvt. practice dentistry, Bklyn., 1950-60, Forest Hills, N.Y., 1960—; v.p. Whaledent, Inc., dental mfr., N.Y.C., 1955-60, dental service cons., 1977—. Instr. N.Y. U. Coll. Dentistry, 1950-55; asst. prof. Sch. Dental and Oral Surgery, Columbia, 1974—. Park commr. Village of Lake Success (N.Y.), 1971—. Served with AUS, 1944-46. Fellow Acad. Gen. Dentistry, Northeastern Gnathological Soc. (pres. 1966-70, exec. com. 1970—, editor 1974—, fellowship examiner 1972—); mem. Study Group for the Advancement of Dental Diagnosis and Treatment Planning (pres. 1968-69), ADA, Am. Prosthodontic Soc., Internat. (prosthodontic research group), Am. assns. dental research, Am. Soc. for Preventive Dentistry, 11th Dist. Dental Soc. (charter mem. Inst. for Continuing Edn.), Omicron Kappa Upsilon, Kappa Nu, Sigma Epsilon Delta. Clubs: Lake Success Golf, Lake Success Tennis Assn. Asso. editor Jour. Prosthetic Dentistry, 1974—. Contbr. articles to profl. jours. Lectr. in field. Home: 6 Bridle Path Ln Lake Success NY 11020 also 4459 Luxembourg Ct The Fountains of Palm Beach Lake Worth FL 33463 Office: 104-20 Queens Blvd Forest Hills NY 11375

LENEY, GEORGE WILLARD, exploration geologist; b. Wausau, Wis., Nov. 13, 1927; s. Bert and Iva Irene (Skoog) L.; B.S., U. Mich., 1950, M.S., 1952, M.A., 1955; m. Arax G. Tefankjian, June 25, 1955; children—Sara Ann, Janet Ellen, John Alan, Ruth Alison. Teaching fellow U. Mich., 1951-53, 53-55; geophysicist Gulf Oil Co. Research Lab., Harmarville, Pa., 1955-56; chief geophysicist Hanna Mining Co., Cleve., 1956-64; staff geophysicist Shell Oil Co., Houston, 1964-66; chief geologist H.K. Porter Co., Inc., Pitts., 1966-76, cons., 1976-77; regional geologist N.E. Nat. Uranium Evaluation Program, Dept. Energy, 1977—; v.p., dir. Pacific Asbestos Corp., 1970-75. Trustee Hamilton Presbyn. Ch., 1974-77. Served with USN, 1946-48. Mem. Soc. Econ. Geologists, Am. Inst. Mining Engrs., Soc. Exploration Geophysicists, Geologic Soc. Am. Clubs: Whitehall Country, Armenian-Am. (sec. 1978—) (Pitts.). Home: 5335 Tomfran Dr Pittsburgh PA 15236 Office: 243 Whitehall Center 4140 Brownsville Rd Pittsburgh PA 15227

LENGYEL, EDWARD GEZA, town ofcl.; b. Bridgeport, Conn., Apr. 14, 1926; s. Geza and Mary (Kapostas) L.; B.S., U. Bridgeport, 1953; postgrad. Yale U., 1961-63. Baseball player Am. League, N.Y.C., 1947-49; master Cheshire (Conn.) Acad., 1962-64; mgr. safety engring. New Eng. div. Safeco Ins. Co., 1965-73; risk mgr. Town of Fairfield (Conn.), 1974—; cons. in field. Served with USAAF, 1945-46. Mem. Am. Soc. Safety Engrs., Risk and Ins. Mgmt. Soc., U.S. Chess Fedn., Fairfield Chess Club (v.p.). Republican. Author: Risk Management for Government, 1975. Contbr. articles to profl. publs. Home: 15 Brookfield Ave Fairfield CT 06432 Office: 611 Old Post Rd Fairfield CT 06430

LENHART, KATHARINE BRADLEY (MRS. JOHN JACOBS LENHART), civic worker; b. Nyack, N.Y., Apr. 25; B.A., Vassar Coll., 1925; certificate Miss Conklin's Secretarial Sch., 1931; student Art Students' League, 1925-26, 33-34, Bank St. Coll. Edn., 1942-43, N.Y. U.; Ph.D. (hon.), U. Ariz., 1973; m. John Jacobs Lenhart, Nov. 28, 1927 (killed in action Mar. 1928). Asso. decorator with Adeline deVoo, 1928-29; exec. sec. Spence Sch., 1931-33; chmn. staff asst. service N.Y. chpt. ARC, 1939-42; exec. sec. pediatric service Bellevue Hosp., N.Y.C., 1944-45; dir. Masters Nursery, 1944-54, pres. bd., 1950-52; chmn. day care com. Welfare and Health Council of N.Y.C., 1950-53; mem. bd. Play Schs. Assn., v.p. bd., 1960-68, chmn. 1960 biennial conf.; chmn. com. on Parent Conducted Activities on Coop. Housing, 1964-68; mem. regional planning bd. Community Council Greater N.Y.; bd. dirs. Goddard Riverside Community Centers, 1961-64, G-R Housing Corp. Bd., 1962-64, Settlement Housing Fund, 1975—, Pueblo of Mayaguez Town Council, Bronx, N.Y., 1976—; bd. mem. Assn. Neighborhood Councils, 1964-67; chmn. self study com. div. Youth and Community Services, mem. coms. on legis. and nominating; bd. dirs. Fedn. Protestant Welfare Agys.; mem. steering com., bd. dirs. Center for Housing Partnerships N.Y.C.; founding bd. dirs. West Farms Land Trust, Waterford, Conn.; trustee Eugene O'Neill Theatre Center, Waterford, Conn., 1973—. Mem. LWV New London, Tappan Zee Hist. Soc., Hudson River Conservation Soc. Episcopalian. Clubs: Garden Am.; Skating N.Y., Cosmopolitan (N.Y.C.); Republican (Waterford); Pequot Point Beach; Old Lyme Country; New London Garden. Home: 2 Jordan Cove Circle Waterford CT 06385 Office: 1075 Park Ave New York City NY 10028

LENHERR, FREDERICK KEITH, neurophysiologist, computer scientist; b. N.Y.C., Feb. 4, 1943; s. Frederick Joseph and Thelma Frances (DeFrehn) L.; A.B., Harvard, 1965; M.S., U. Mass., 1973, Ph.D., 1975. Instr. biology and physics Taft Sch., Watertown, Conn., 1965-66; research and devel. engr. No. Research & Engring., Cambridge, Mass., 1966-69; turbine engr. Gen. Electric Co., Lynn, Mass., 1969-70; neurophysiologist, computer scientist Center for Systems Neurosci., U. Mass., Amherst, 1974—. Mem. AAAS, Assn. Computing Machinery, IEEE, Assn. Research in Vision and Ophthalmology, Soc. Neurosci. Democrat. Lutheran. Founding editor Brain Theory Newsletter, 1975-77. Home: W Main St New Salem MA 01355 Office: Center for Systems Neurosci U Mass Amherst MA 01003

LENIO, DONALD PETER, hosp. adminstr.; b. Wilkes-Barre, Pa., July 12, 1943; s. Peter and Helen Elizabeth L.; student Wilkes Coll., 1961-63; Asso. Mech. Engring., Pa. State U., 1965; m. Louise Elaine Vegnoli, July 2, 1966. Devel. technician Ross Engring. Div., Highland Park, N.J., 1965-68; project engr. Bellante, Clauss, Miller & Partners, Scranton, Pa., 1968-76; dir. engring. services Moses Taylor Hosp., Scranton, Pa., 1976—; mem. maintenance group purchasing com. Hosp. Central Services, Inc., 1977—. Mem. Am. Soc. Hosp. Engring., Nat. Fire Protection Assn., Am. Soc. Heating Refrigeration and Air Conditioning Engrs., Am. Inst. Plant Engrs., Pa. Soc. Profl. Engrs. Clubs: Downtown Athletic (Scranton); K.C. Home: 701 Connell St Scranton PA 18505 Office: 700 Quincy Ave Scranton PA 18510

LENNEY, ANNIE, artist, educator; b. Potsdam, N.Y.; d. Edward and Annie (Kennedy) Lenney; B.A., Coll. St. Elizabeth, Convent, N.J., 1932; postgrad. St. Lawrence U., N.Y. U., Syracuse U., Fordham U., Art Students League; pvt. study art; m. William Shannon, Oct. 6, 1935; children—Ann, Dennis, Gerald. Supr. art Main St. Sch., Tuckahoe, N.Y., 1932-35, Brookside and Montclair Acad., Montclair, N.J., 1951-53, St. Vincents Acad., Newark, 1953-55; instr. art Upsala Coll., East Orange, N.J., 1954-55; head tchr. Saturday Jr. Art Sch., Newark, 1953-55; art tchr. South Maplewood Adult Sch., 1952-62, Montclair Mus. Art Sch., 1955-56, Newton (N.J.) pub. sch. system, 1963-71, also Sch. Fine and Indsl. Arts, Newark, 1946-63. Exhibited Newark Mus., Montclair Mus., Trenton (N.J.) Mus., Oakland Art Gallery, Lehigh Art Gallery, Mus. N.Mex., Nat. Acad. Galleries, Argent Galleries, Eggleston Galleries N.Y.C., Montclair Mus., 1966, Everhart Mus., 1966, World's Fair, 1965, many others; also exhibited in Paris, Lisbon, Naples, Athens, Tokyo, Japan; numerous one man shows including Allentown Coll. St. Frances de Sales, George Washington Carver Mus., Tuskegee Inst. Ala., St. Scholastica Edn. Center, Ft. Worth, Ark., Ga. Coll., Albany (Ga.) Mus., Central Mo. State Coll., Winona State Coll., U. Wyo., Wyo. and Colo. Coll., U. Portland (Oreg.), Seton Hall U., 1966, Borzansky Galleries, N.Y.C., 1968, Centenary Coll., Hachettstown, Hardin County Mus., Kenton, Ohio, Wassenburg Art Center, Van Wert, Ohio Upper Iowa Coll., Fayette, Mayville (N.D.) State Coll., Potsdam (N.Y.) Mus., LaSalle Coll., Phila., Hoyt Inst. Art, New Castle, Pa., 1971, Calif. State Poly. Coll., 1972, Bodly Gallery, N.Y.C., 1973, Marathon Mus., Wausau, Wis., 1973, Spring Arbor (Mich.) Coll., 1973, Georgian Ct. Coll., Lakewood, N.J., 1973, Robbins Art Gallery, South Orange, N.J., 1976, Caldwell (N.J.) Coll., 1976, Bluffton (Ohio) Coll., 1977, Purdue U., W. Lafayette, Ind., 1978; represented permanent collections at Brooks Meml. Art Gallery, Everhart Mus., Norfolk Mus., Munson William Proctor Mus., Massilon Mus., Farnsworth Mus., Oklahoma City Art Center, Buie Mus., Oxford, Miss., Montclair (N.J.) Mus., Newark Mus., Paterson (N.J.) Mus., S.I. Inst. Arts and Sci., Butler Inst. Am. Art, Youngstown, Ohio, Andrew Dickson White Mus. of Cornell U., Fairleigh Dickinson U., Seton Hall U., Notre Dame U., Mpls. Inst. Art, Morris Mus., Morristown, N.J., N.J. State Mus., Trenton, Pottsdam Pub. Mus., others, also pvt. collections. Recipient Eugenie Marron award, oil, 10th Ann. Spring Lake Exhbn., 1946; 1st award water color, 15th Ann. Art Exhbn., Irvington, N.J., 1948, 12th Spring Lake Exhbn., 1948; Beth Creevy Ham award Nat. Assn. Women Artists, 1948; Samuel Karasick Meml.; 1st award, oil, 23d Ann. State Exhbn., Montclair (N.J.) Mus.; prize 62d Ann. Exhbn., Nat. Assn. Women Artists, 1954, others. Mem. Painters and Sculptors Soc. N.J., Nat. Assn. Women Artists, N.J. Water Color Club, N.Y.C. Pen and Brush Club, Asso. Artists of N.J., Audubon Artists Soc., Allied Artists, Inc. Club: Salmagundi (N.Y.C.) Author articles. Address: Gaisler Rd RD 2 Blairstown NJ 07825

LENOX, RITA CATHERINE, journalist; b. Hawthorne, N.J.; d. Paul and Katherine (Sadoski) Korzinski; A.A., Green Mountain Coll., 1943; B.S., Rider Coll., 1945; postgrad. Columbia U., 1945-47; m. Henry Joseph Lenox, Apr. 22, 1958. Reporter, columnist Paterson (N.J.) Evening News, 1948-58; editor house organ, sales mag. editor Mut. Benefit Life Ins. Co., Newark, 1958-59; social editor, asst. women's editor, drama critic Daily Jour., Elizabeth, N.J., 1959—; pres. Lenox Assos., pub. relations, Cranford, N.J., 1975—; sec.-treas. Lenox-Fugle Electronics Co., South Plainfield, N.J., 1964—; also dir. Coordinator pub. relations Hawthorne CD, 1950-58. Recipient Best Column Writing award N.J. Press Assn., 1966. Mem. N.J. Newspaper Women's Assn.

LENT, GARRY E., mfg. co. exec.; b. Cornwall, N.Y., Aug. 26, 1931; s. Elmer and Mildred Katherine (Garrison) L.; B.S., Fla. So. Coll., 1953; m. Doris Ann Borthwick, Nov. 28, 1958; children—Laura Ann, Todd Garrison. Indsl. relations clk. Ford Motor Co., Mahwah, N.J., 1955-57; personnel mgr. GAF Corp., Vails Gate, N.Y., 1957—. Pres., Fort Montgomery Fire Dept., 1966-68; vice chmn. Town Highlands Planning and Zoning Bd., 1971-72; justice Highlands, 1972-73, 75—. Served with AUS, 1953-55. Mem. SAR, Empire State Soc., Orange County, N.Y. State assns. magistrates. Club: Masons. Home: PO Box 123 Montgomery Rd Fort Montgomery NY 10922 Office: Route 94 Vails Gate NY 12584

LENT, NORMAN F., congressman; b. East Rockaway, N.Y., 1931; grad. Hofstra Coll., 1952; LL.B., Cornell U., 1957; m. children—Norman III, Barbara Anne, Thomas Benjamin. Admitted to N.Y. bar, 1957; partner firm Hill, Lent & Troescher, 1957—; asso. police justice Village of East Rockaway, 1959-62; confdl. law sec. to Supreme Ct. Justice Farley, 1961-62; mem. N.Y. Senate, 1963-70;

mem. 92d congress from 5th N.Y. Dist., 93d-95th congresses from 4th N.Y. Dist.; mem. East Rockaway Bd. Trade. Past chmn. Am. Cancer Crusade, East Rockaway Crusade; mem.-at-large S. Central Dist. Nassau County council Boy Scouts Am.; pres. Lynbrook chpt. Nassau County Republican Recruits, 1960. Served with USNR, Korean War. Mem. N.Y. State, Nassau County magistrates assns., Am., Fla., Nassau County bar assns., Hofstra Coll., Cornell Law Sch. alumni assns., Am. Legion. Club: Elks. Home: 48 Plymouth Rd East Rockaway NY 11518 Office: 2228 Rayburn House Office Bldg Washington DC 20515

LENZ, MATTHEW, JR., educator; b. N.Y.C., Aug. 30, 1922; s. Matthew and Frances Emmaline (Walker) L.; B.B.A., City Coll. N.Y., 1967; M.B.A., Baruch Coll., 1970; postgrad. City U. N.Y., 1970—; m. Winifred Mary Gentry, Jan. 19, 1946; children—Linda Louise, George Francis. With Mchts. Fire Assurance Corp. N.Y., 1940-51; account exec. Alfred Berman & Co., ins. broker, N.Y.C., 1951-54; partner Janice & Lenz, ins. agts., Mineola, N.Y., 1954-64; asso. prof., chmn. property-liability ins. div. Coll. of Ins., N.Y.C., 1964—, asst. to pres., 1976—. Cons., FTC, N.Y. State Dept. Edn., N.Y. State Bd. Regents, also pvt. industry, pub. sch. dists. Troop committeeman Boy Scouts Am. Served with USNR, 1943-45. Mem. Risk and Ins. Mgmt. Soc., Am. Risk and Ins. Assn., Ins. Co. Edn. Dirs. Soc., Ins. Soc. N.Y., Soc. Chartered Property and Casualty Underwriters (past pres. L.I. chpt.), Am. Assn. Higher Edn., Tau Kappa Epsilon. Presbyn. (exec. com., gen. council N.Y.C. Presbytery 1974). Clubs: Ins. Sq. of N.Y. (dir.), Masons. Author: Risk Management Manual, 1971; also articles in ins. trade jours. Home: 20-62 33d St Astoria NY 11105 Office: 123 William St New York City NY 10038

LEONARD, EDWIN DEANE, lawyer; b. Oakland, Calif., Apr. 22, 1929; s. Edwin Stanley and Gladys Eugenia (Lee) L.; B.A., Principia Coll., 1950; LL.B., Harvard U., 1953; LL.M., George Washington U., 1954; m. Judith Swatland, July 10, 1954; children—Garrick Hillman, Susanna, Rebecca, Ethan. Admitted to Ill. bar, 1953, D.C. bar, 1953, N.Y. bar, 1957; asso. Davis, Polk & Wardwell, N.Y.C., 1956-61, partner, 1961—. Served with AUS, 1953-56. Mem. Am., N.Y. State bar assns., Assn. Bar City N.Y. Christian Scientist. Home: 1148 Fifth Ave New York City NY 10028 Office: 1 Chase Manhattan Plaza New York City NY 10005

LEONARD, GENE FRANCIS, computer software co. exec.; b. Easton, Md., May 3, 1935; s. William J. and Marjorie (Frampton) L.; B.S. in Elec. Engring. with honors, Princeton, 1957; m. Ann M. Howard, Apr. 6, 1956; children—Lynn A., William H.; m. 2d, Theda M. Jack, Oct. 1, 1960; children—Melissa S., Matthew H.; m. 3d, Patricia I.W. Turner, Mar. 17, 1973. Computing analyst Douglas Aircraft Co., Inc., Santa Monica, Cal., 1957-58; mathematician Tech. Operations, Inc., Washington, 1958-60, Burlington, Mass., 1960-61; dir., sr. staff mem. Mass. Computer Assos., Inc., Wakefield, 1961-62, dir., v.p., treas., 1962-66, dir., exec. v.p., 1966-67, trustee profit sharing plan and trust 1962-67; dir. new products ITT Data Services div. Internat. Tel. & Tel., Paramus, N.J., 1967-68, gen. mgr., 1968, v.p., gen. mgr. Computer Services, 1968-70; v.p. Citicorp Leasing Internat., London, Eng., 1970-72; v.p. First Nat. City Bank, also gen. mgr.-Europe, Internat. Computer Services, 1972-73; chmn. Computer Projects Ltd., London, Eng., 1972-73; mng. dir. Citicorp Data Services, Geneva, Switzerland, 1971-73; v.p., gen. mgr. Softech, Inc., Waltham, Mass., 1973-74; pres. Gene F. Leonard and Assos., San Francisco, 1974-76; mgr. computer and software systems Space div. Gen. Electric Co., Phila., 1976—. Reviewer, Computing Revs. 1965-70. Mem. Assn. for Computing Machinery, AAAS, Sigma Xi. Contbr. articles to profl. jours. Researcher in programming system design, 1961-70. Home: 179 Midfield Rd Ardmore PA 19003 Office: PO Box 8555 Philadelphia PA 19101

LEONARD, JACKSON DAY, chem. co. exec.; b. Sunbury, Pa., Sept. 2, 1915; s. Walter John and Clara Adeline (Day) L.; B.S., Pa. State U., 1937; m. Virginia Cattell, Dec. 1, 1939; children—Patricia Ann, Michael John; m. 2d, Anne Taft, July 4, 1969; children—Jessica Taft, Melinda Day. With Gen. Chem. Co., 1937-40; prod. supr., plant engr. B. & A. div., 1938-39; product supr., plant tech., sr. engr. E.I. du Pont de Nemours & Co., Inc., Wilmington, Del., 1940-50; sr. engr. Merck & Co., Rahway, N.J., 1950-51; cons. chem. engr., Metuchen, N.J., 1951-54; partner Brown Blauvelt & Leonard, N.Y.C., 1954-57; pres., owner Leonard Process Co., Inc., N.Y.C., 1957—; chmn. First Republic Corp. Am., 1969—; dir. Laporte Amines Australia, Pty., Chinook Chem. Co. Ltd., Can. Chmn. various fund raising drives for charities; trustee, founder Leonard Found. Mem. Am. Chem. Soc., Am. Inst. Chem. Engrs., Nat., Ruritan Valley socs. profl. engrs. Club: Masons. Patentee chem. field. Contbr. articles to tech. publs. Home: 7002 Blvd East Guttenberg NJ 07093 Office: 560 Sylvan Ave Englewood Cliffs NJ 07632

LEONARD, JACQUELINE ARMINTA, sch. counselor; b. Washington, Feb. 22, 1937; d. Milton Eugene and Louise Consuella (Griffin) Harris; B.S., Elizabethtown (Pa.) Coll., 1958; postgrad. Howard U., 1958-59, Temple U., 1966; M.A., Rider Coll., Trenton, N.J., 1972; m. Curtis Allen Leonard, June 20, 1964; 1 son, Laurent Christopher. Histopath. technician FDA, Washington, 1958-59, NIH, Bethesda, Md., 1959-61; math. tchr., Washington, 1961-64; sci. and math. tchr. Pennsbury Sch. Dist., Fallsington, Pa., 1964-70, counselor intern, 1970-72, sch. counselor Charles Boehm High Sch., 1972—, mem. equal ednl. opportunities com., 1977—; dir. learning center of equal opportunity funding program, evening div. Rutgers U., Camden, 1976—. NSF scholar Temple U., 1965-66. Mem. NEA, Am. Personnel and Guidance Assn., Nat. Assn. Sch. Counselors, Assn. Non-White Concerns, Assn. Sch. Counselors, Pa., Pennsbury (chmn. intergroup relations com.) edn. assns., Pa. Guidance Assn., Bucks County Sch. Counselors. Democrat. Episcopalian. Home: 1115 Custis Pl Philadelphia PA 19122

LEONARD, JAMES KEVIN, communications engr.; b. Bklyn., Oct. 7, 1950; s. James Joseph and Virginia Isabel L.; student Marquette U., 1969-73, Fordham U., 1976—. Vice-pres., co-founder Lencon Communications Cons. Firm, Rockaway Beach, N.Y., 1973—. Mem. L.I. Hist. Soc., Alpha Delta Gamma. Republican. Roman Catholic. Home: 230 73d St Brooklyn NY 11209

LEONARD, VINCENT M., bishop; b. Pa., Dec. 11, 1908; student Duquesne U., St. Vincent Sem. Ordained priest Roman Catholic Ch., 1935; Cath. chaplain Allegheny County Home and Woodville State Mental Hosp.; vicar gen. Diocese of Pitts., 1959; consecrated titular bishop of Arsacal and aux. bishop of Pitts., 1964, bishop, 1969—. Address: 5078 Warwick Terr Pittsburgh PA 15213*

LEONE, RICHARD JOSEPH, hosp. adminstr.; b. Jersey City, Mar. 30, 1940; s. John F. and Marie T. (Campanile) L.; B.S., Seton Hall U., 1962. Sr. accountant Haskins & Sells, N.Y.C., 1962-67; asst. to fin. v.p. Columbia-Presbyn. Med. Center, N.Y.C., 1967-68; asst. dir., controller Point Pleasant (N.J.) Hosp., 1968-70, dir., 1970—. Chmn. Ocean County Cancer Crusade, 1975; mem. advisory council for nursing Ocean County Coll., 1972-78; bd. dirs. Central N.J. Comprehensive Health Planning Council, 1973-76; vice chmn. bd. trustees N.J. Hosp. Service Corp. Served to 1st lt. AUS, 1963-65. C.P.A., N.Y., N.J. Mem. Am. Coll. Hosp. Adminstrs., Am. Inst. C.P.A.'s, N.J. Soc. C.P.A.'s, N.J. Hosp. Assn. (mem. council on govt. relations 1974-76). Club: Manasquan River Golf. Home: 33 Locust Way Spring Lake Heights NJ 07762 Office: Point Pleasant Hospital Point Pleasant NJ 08742

LEONHART, WILLIAM HAROLD, corp. exec.; b. Parkersburg, W.Va., May 2, 1906; s. William Henry and Dorah Catherine (Chancellor) L.; student Marshall Coll. Model Sch., Huntington, W.Va., 1917-18, Balt. City Coll. night sch., 1921-26; m. Martha Elizabeth Curtis, 1935; children—William Harold, James Chancellor, John Lawrence, Martha Jean, Mery Curtis, Valerie Ann. Pres., Leonhart & Co., Inc., ins., reins., brokers, Balt., 1933—; owner Redwood House, Inc. Chmn. adv. bd. Frederick Acad. Visitation. Mem. SAR. Democrat. Roman Catholic. Clubs: Eaglehead Golf and Country, Holly Hills Country. Home: 215 E Church St Frederick MD 21701 also 550 4th Ave S Naples FL 33940 Office: 330 N Charles St Baltimore MD 21201

LEONTIEF, WASSILY, economist; b. Leningrad, Russia, Aug. 5, 1906; s. Wassily and Eugenia (Bekker) L.; M.A., U. Leningrad, 1925; Ph.D., U. Berlin, 1925-28; Ph.D. honoris causa, U. Bruxelles (Belgium), 1962, U. York (Eng.), 1967, U. Louvan, 1971, U. Paris, 1972, U. Lancaster (Eng.), 1976, U. Pa., 1976; m. Estelle Helena Marks, Dec. 25, 1932; 1 dau., Svetlana Alpers. Research economist Institut Fûr Weltwirtschaft, U. Kiel (Germany), 1927-28, 30; econ. adviser to Chinese govt., Nanking, 1929; with Nat. Bur. Econ. Research, N.Y.C., 1931; instr. econs. Harvard U., 1931, asst. prof., 1933-38, asso. prof., 1939-45, prof., 1946-75, dir. econ. project, 1948-72, Henry Lee prof. econs., 1953-75; prof. econs., dir. Inst. Econ. Analysis, N.Y. U., 1975—; cons. Dept. Labor, 1941-47, OSS, 1943-45, UN, 1961-62, Dept. Commerce, 1966—. Decorated officer Order Cherubim (U. Pisa), Legion of Honor (France); recipient Bernhard-Harms prize in econs., W.G., 1970, Nobel prize in econs., 1973; Guggenheim fellow, 1940, 50. Fellow Soc. Fellows Harvard (sr. fellow, chmn. 1964-75), Econometric Soc., Royal Statis. Assn. (hon.), Inst. de France (corr.); mem. Am. Philos. Soc., Am. Acad. Arts and Scis., Internat. Statis. Inst., Am. Econ. Assn., Am. Statis. Assn., Royal Econ. Soc., Japan Econ. Research Center (hon.), Brit. Acad. (corr.), French Acad. Scis. (corr.), Nat. Acad. Scis., Royal Irish Acad. (hon.), Brit. Assn. for Advancement Sci. (pres. sect. F 1976). Greek Orthodox. Author: The Structure of the American Economy, 1919-29, 2d edit., 1953; Studies in the Structure of the American Economy, 1953; Input-Output Economics, 1966; Collected Essays, Vol. I, 1966, Vol. II, 1978; The Future of the World Economy, 1977; contbr. articles to sci. jours. and periodicals in U.S. and abroad. Home: New York City NY 10011 summer Lake West Burke VT 05871 Office: Inst Econ Analysis 251 Mercer St NY U Washington Sq New York City NY 10012

LEOPOLD, REUVEN, mech. engr., ship designer; b. Arad, Rumania, May 5, 1938; s. Edward and Blanka (Abraham) L.; came to U.S., 1959, naturalized, 1968; B.Sc., Mass. Inst. Tech., 1961, M.Sc., 1963, Marine Mech. Engr., 1965, Ph.D., 1977; M.B.A., George Washington U., 1977; m. Dora Rejman, Jan. 30, 1962; children—Brigitte R., Edward R. Asst. research scientist Hydronautics, Inc., 1961-62; research engr. Mass. Inst. Tech., Cambridge, 1962-65; staff mem. Arthur D. Little, Inc., Cambridge, 1965-66; with Litton Industries, Inc., Culver City, Calif., dir. ship engring. and design, 1966-71; tech. dir. Ship Design div. Naval Ship Engring. Center, U.S. Navy, Hyattsville, Md., 1971-78; v.p. Pratt & Whitney Aircraft, W. Palm Beach, Fla., 1978—; asso. mem. Def. Sci. Bd.; mem. MIT Corp.; vis. com., author sect. ship design McGraw Hill Ency. Sci. and Tech. Fellow Soc. Naval Architects and Marine Engrs. (chmn. Chesapeake sect. 1977, editor-in-chief book Naval Surface Ship Design 1977); mem. Am. Soc. Naval Engrs. (Jimmy Hamilton award 1972, moderator ann. meeting 1973), Am. Def. Preparedness Assn. (life), Assn. Sr. Engrs. (chmn. profl. devel. 1973-74), Sigma Xi (asso.). Contbr. articles to profl. jours. Home: 6709 Kenhill Rd Bethesda MD 20034 Office: NAVSEC Dept Navy Washington DC 20362

LEPESCHKIN, JULIE ANNE WILSON (MRS. EUGENE LEPESCHKIN), educator; b. Ann Arbor, Mich., Sept. 2, 1915; d. Frank Norman and Juel A. (Mahoney) Wilson; B.A., U. Mich., 1936; M.A., U. Wis., 1941; m. Eugene Lepeschkin, May 30, 1949; children—Tamara Julianne, Ludmilla Francesca Eugenia, Nina Olga Grace. Grad. asst. U. Pitts., 1941, U. Mich., 1942-43; tchr. U. Mich. Lab. Elementary Sch., 1943-47; instr. Newcomb Coll. Sch. Art, also Tulane U., New Orleans, 1947-49; resource tchr. dance and dramatics Metairie Park Country Day Sch., New Orleans, 1947-49; supt. Lower Ch. Sch. Unitarian, 1958-62; asst. prof. dept. home econs. U. Vt., Burlington, 1962-72. Tchr. creative movement classes for children Fleming Mus., U. Vt., 1950-60; chmn. Community Puppeteers, 1958-60; cons. Burlington Day Care Center, 1966—; mem. U.S. Nat. Com. on Early Childhood Edn., 1967—; state presch. chmn. PTA Bd., 1963-67; chmn. subcom. on day care Gov.'s Com. on Children and Youth, 1963-66, chmn. subcom. early childhood services, 1967-69; mem. State Community Coordinated Child Care, 1969-72; chmn. adv. com. on day care Vt. Dept. Welfare, 1966-69; regional cons. Head Start, 1967-69; mem. Gov.'s Com. Children and Youth, 1968-71, White House Conf. on Children, 1970; v.p. Unitarian Universalist Ch., Burlington, 1974-76, tchr. dance and religion course, 1976-77; mem. extension com. N.H.-Vt. dist. Unitarian-Universalist Ch., 1977—; bd. clk. Vt. Religious Edn. Found., 1974, clk., 1975-78; chmn. emergency housing com. United Community Service of Chittendon County. Recipient Distinguished Service award State of Vt., 1972, citations Am. Dance Guild, 1974, Headstart, 1971. Mem. World Ednl. Fellowship, Orgn. Mundial Educacion Prescolaire (U.S.), Internat. Playground Assn., Assn. Childhood Edn. Internat. (chmn. study study conf. 1971), Ch. Women United (dir. Burlington 1976—), Pi Lambda Theta. Author: My Daddy is in Prison; Three Cardiologists From a Mural; Ecology and Early Childhood. Editor: (with Gerold Greenmore) Procs. Vt. Internat. Conf. and Follow-up Conf.; contbr. articles to profl. jours. Home: 75 Bilodeau St Burlington VT 05401

LEPORE, JOHN ANTHONY, educator; b. Phila., Feb. 19, 1935; s. Anthony Donald and Louise Elizabeth (DiSipio) L.; B.S. in Civil Engring., Drexel U., 1957; M.S. in Mech. Engring., U. Pa., 1965, Ph.D., 1967; m. Patricia Ann Luning, June 25, 1959; children—William, Thomas, Jacqueline, John. Nuclear engr. N.Y. Shipbldg. Corp., Camden, N.J., 1957-61; subsystem engr. Gen. Electric Corp., Phila., 1961-68; mem. faculty U. Pa., 1968—, asso. prof. civil engring., 1978—, chmn. dept., 1973—, curriculum chmn., 1973—, Wintertein prof. engring., 1970—; asso. Structural Mechanics Assos., 1968; mem. Mayor Phila. Adv. Com. on Urban Housing. U. Ill. fellow, 1957; NSF fellow, 1965-67, grantee, 1969; registered profl. engr., Pa. Mem. ASCE, ASME, Am. Inst. Aeros. and Astronautics, Am. Soc. Engring. Edn., AAUP, Am. Soc. Safety Engrs., Am. Acad. Mechanics, Earthquake Research Inst., Sigma Xi. Roman Catholic. Author articles, chpts. in books. Home: 731 Timber Trail Ln Springfield PA 19064 Office: 113 Towne Bldg Univ Pa Philadelphia PA 19174

LEPORE, MICHAEL JOSEPH, physician; b. N.Y.C., May 8, 1910; s. Joseph and Florence (Melucci) L.; B.S., N.Y. U., 1929; M.S., U. Rochester, 1931, M.D., 1934; m. Ardean Clough Everett, Sept. 18, 1937; 1 son, Frederick Everett. Intern, Duke Hosp., asst. resident in medicine, 1934-37; fellow in medicine Yale U., 1935-36; asst. in medicine Columbia U., 1937-46, instr., 1946-52, asso. medicine, 1952-56, asst. clin. prof. medicine, 1956-63; practice medicine, specializing in internal medicine and gastroenterology, 1937—; dir. Upjohn Gastrointestinal Service and Clinic, attending physician Roosevelt Hosp., N.Y.C., 1962-66; cons. gastroenterology Englewood (N.J.) Hosp., 1960—, St. John's Riverside Hosp., Yonkers, N.Y., 1976—; attending physician dept. medicine St. Vincent's Hosp. and Med. Center, N.Y.C., 1966—, dir. gastrointestinal sect., 1966-75, dir. emeritus, 1975—; asso. prof. clin. medicine N.Y. U. Sch. Medicine, 1968-70, prof., 1971—; asso. attending in medicine U. Hosp., 1968-71, attending, 1971—; vis. physician Bellevue Hosp. Center, 1968—. Bd. dirs. Upjohn Gastrointestinal Found.; mem. pres.'s leadership council U. Rochester. Served as lt. col. AUS, 1942-46. Decorated ribbons. Diplomate Am. Board Internal Medicine. Fellow A.C.P., N.Y. Acad. Scis., N.Y. Acad. Medicine; mem. AMA, Am., N.Y. gastroenterol. assns., Physiol. Soc. Phila., AAAS, Royal Soc. Medicine, Alpha Omega Alpha, Sigma Xi. Contbr. articles to med. jours. Home: 80 N Woodland St Englewood NJ 07631 Office: 550 Park Ave New York City NY 10021

LEPORIERE, GENE PAUL, tool mfg. co. exec.; b. Elizabeth, N.J., Jan. 18, 1938; s. Maximo and Christina Rose (Lello) L.; student Lafayette Coll., Easton, Pa., 1956-57, 58-59; B.S. in Accounting, Rutgers U., 1962, M.B.A. in Fin. Econs., 1966; m. Elaine Marie Allegrini, June 8, 1968; 1 son, Paul. Sr. accountant Peat, Marwick, Mitchell & Co., Newark, 1962-66; sr. corporate auditor Englehard Minerals & Chems. Corp., N.Y.C., 1966-71, asst. to div. controller, N.Y.C., 1972-73; mgr. corporate accounting Chgo. Pneumatic Tool Co., N.Y.C., 1973-76, mgr. fin. analysis overseas equipment, 1976-77; corp. controller Kolmar Labs., Inc., Port Jervis, N.Y., 1977—; speaker Internat. Accounting World Trade Inst., N.Y.C., 1976. Mem. Mayor's Citizens Adv. Com. Linden (N.J.), 1966-69. C.P.A. Mem. Nat. Assn. Accountants, N.J. Soc. C.P.A.'s, N.J. Jaycees (senate). Roman Catholic. Editor, contbr. Fin. Digest, Rutgers U. Sch. Bus., 1962. Home: 23 Sharon Dr Sparta NJ 07871 Office: Kolmar Labs Inc Skyline Dr Port Jervis NY 12710

LEPPARD, DALE LEROY, airline pilot; b. Fulton, Mo., Jan. 9, 1937; s. Henry Thurston and Nellie Amelia (McClatchey) L.; student Pasadena Coll., 1955-58; B.S. in Physics summa cum laude, Fairleigh Dickinson U., 1978; m. Carolyn Newell Steppe, May 27, 1971; children—Cynthia Diane, April Dawn. Pilot, Eastern Air Lines, N.Y.C., 1962—. Mem. Air Line Pilots Assn. (dir. 1966-69, accident investigation bd. 1966—, chmn. supersonic transport eval. com.), Internat. Fedn. Air Lines Pilots Assns. (accident investigation bd. 1966—), Am. Phys. Soc. Republican. Contbr. articles to profl. jours. Home: 17 Wilson Ave E Riverdale NJ 07457

LE QUAY, EDWIN GORDON, chem. co. exec.; b. Clarendon, Va., Sept. 29, 1930; s. Harold W. and Doris M. (Rumsey) La Q.; B.A., Jacksonville State U., 1954; B.L.S., U. Pitts., 1968; m. Thursia N. Daugherty, Nov. 17, 1951; children—Anthony, James, Alan, Dana. Adminstrv. coordinator phosphate div. research Monsanto Chem. Co., Anniston, Ala., 1951-52; with Mobay Chem. Co., Anniston, Ala., 1954-55, librarian, New Martinsville, W.Va., 1955-62, info. mgr., Pitts., 1962—. Mem. adv. bd. Parkway West Tech. Sch.; vol. mem. ARC, 1970—. Served with C.E., U.S. Army, 1948-51. Mem. Spl. Libraries Assn., Internat. Rescue and First Aid Assn. Republican. Baptist. Home: 29 Richmond St Pittsburgh PA 15205 Office: Penn Lincoln Pkwy W Pittsburgh PA 15205

LERCH, JAMES STANLEY, educator; b. Cin., Feb. 26, 1942; s. Stanley Carl and Gertrude (Eberhart) L.; B.S. in Chem. Engring., U. Cin., 1964; postgrad U. Akron, 1964-67; U. Del., 1968-70; children—Peter, Damian. Process engr. PPG Industries, Barberton, Ohio, 1964-67, Atlas Chem. Co., Wilmington, Del., 1967-68; with Del. Opportunities Industrialization Center, Wilmington, 1968—, co-exec. dir., 1976—; instr. Goldey Beacom Coll., 1973—; cons. in field. Mem. adv. bd. Delmar Nat. Alliance Bus.; chmn. Del. EEO Adv. Com. Mem. Assn. Continuing Edn. Adults (v.p., dir.). Roman Catholic. Home: 16 E 44th St Wilmington DE 19802 Office: 813 West St Wilmington DE 19801

LERMAN, STEVEN IRA, chemist; b. N.Y.C., Nov. 14, 1944; s. Cyrus and Pauline (Rauchwarger) L.; B.A. in Chemistry, Queens Coll., City U. N.Y., 1965; M.S., Adelphi U., 1971; m. R. Judy Mandle, June 17, 1965; children—Craig, Tracy, Erica. Sr. analytical chemist, dir. spl. projects Consol. Edison Co. N.Y., Astoria, 1965—; indsl. cons. Mem. exec. bd. Local Election Com., N.Y.C. Jr./Sr. High Sch. Sci. Fair. Recipient 1st prize Short Story Contest, 1976. Mem. Am. Chem. Soc., ASTM, Am. Inst. Sci. and Tech. N.Y.C., Am. Mus. Natural History, Nat. Rifle Assn., Mensa. Republican. Jewish. Clubs: K.P.; Workmens Circle. Home: 21 Clark St Plainview NY 11803 Office: 21st St and 20th Ave Astoria NY 11105

LERNER, ABRAM, museum dir., artist; b. N.Y.C., Apr. 11, 1913; s. Hyman and Sarah (Becker) L.; B.A., N.Y. U., 1935; student Ednl. Alliance, Art Students League, Bklyn. Mus.; m. Pauline Hanenberg, Oct. 7, 1940; 1 dau., Aline. Asso. dir. A.C.A. Gallery and Artist's Gallery, N.Y.C., 1945-57; curator Joseph H. Hirshhorn Collection, N.Y.C., 1957-66; dir. Joseph H. Hirshhorn Mus. and Sculpture Garden, Smithsonian Instn., Washington, 1967—; one-man show: Davis Gallery, 1958; group shows include: A.C.A. Gallery, Peridot Gallery, Bklyn. Mus., Pa. Acad., Davis Gallery, N.Y.C.; represented in pvt. collections; mem. adv. bd. Archives of Am. Art, 1970—. Contbr. to mags. and mus. catalogues. Office: Hirshhorn Museum and Sculpture Garden Smithsonian Instn Washington DC 20560

LERNER, LAURENCE M., orgn. exec.; b. N.Y.C., Aug. 21, 1939; s. Myer Philip and Rose (Goss) L.; B.A., N.Y. U., 1961; M.A., U. Wis., Madison, 1963, Ph.D., 1970; m. Susan Goodstein, Sept. 8, 1963; children—Elisabeth Audrey, Marc Harold. Asst. Am. history U. Wis., 1964-66; instr. Hofstra U., Hempstead, N.Y., 1967-68; sr. asso. Drummond Assos., Inc., N.Y.C., 1968-71; lectr. Am. history Barnard Coll., N.Y.C., 1971; asst. editor Bus. Internat. Inc., N.Y.C., 1972-73; dir. research United Jewish Appeal, N.Y.C., 1973—; asso., co-chmn. seminar Am. civilization Columbia U., 1971—. Bd. advisers Council Municipal Performance, 1977—; bd. dirs. U.S. Com. Sports for Israel, 1978—. Mem. Am. Hist. Assn., Nat. Assn. Bus. Economists. Jewish. Home: 45 E 85th St New York City NY 10028 Office: 1290 Ave Americas Suite 2900 New York City NY 10019

LERNER, LAWRENCE, service co. exec.; b. N.Y.C., Sept. 21, 1923; s. Abraham and May (Epstein) L.; B.A., Bklyn. Coll., 1948; m. Leslie Karpen, June 1, 1950; 1 son, Erik. Vice pres. Saphier, Lerner, Schindler (name now SLS Environetics), N.Y.C., 1951-58, exec. v.p., 1958, pres., 1958—, chmn., 1977—; vis. prof. Sch. Architecture, Design and Planning, Ohio U., Athens, 1972; vis. critic Parsons Sch. Design, N.Y.C., 1966-68. Mem. dean's council Grad. Sch. Mgmt., U. Calif. at Los Angeles, 1971—. Served to 2d lt. AUS, 1942-46. Mem. Chief Execs. Forum. Co-author: Contract Design, 1972; contbg. editor Contract Mag., 1961—; book reviewer Progressive Architecture, 1971—. Patentee in field. Home: 200 E 62d St New York City NY 10021 Office: 600 Madison Ave New York City NY 10022

LERNER, LEONARD, pharm. co. exec.; b. N.Y.C., Feb. 16, 1933; s. Samuel and Rose L.; B.A., City Coll. N.Y., 1954; m. Diana Zames, Nov. 20, 1954; children—Brad Scott, Randy Glenn, Shea Zames. Sales rep., Upjohn Co., N.Y.C., 1957-65, rep. hosp. sales, 1965-70, Lab. procedures subs., King of Prussia, Pa., 1970-72, dist. mgr., N.Y.C., 1972-76, regional sales mgr. Eastern region, King of Prussia, 1976, mgr. sales and service, 1976—. Vice-pres. Plainview (N.Y.) Civic Assn., 1970-71. Served as 1st lt. inf. U.S. Army, 1955-57. Mem. Am. Mgmt. Assn. Republican. Jewish. Home: 70 Country Dr Plainview NY 11803 Office: 1075 1st Ave King of Prussia PA 19406

LERNER, MILDRED SHERWOOD, clin. psychologist; b. N.Y.C., Mar. 29, 1929; B.A. with honors, Coll. City N.Y., 1951, M.A., 1952; Ph.D., N.Y. U., 1957. Pvt. practice, N.Y.C., Pvt. practice, N.Y.C., 1952—; supr. N.Y. Clinic Mental Health, N.Y.C.; instr. adult edn., Coll. City N.Y., 1952-54; chief psychologist High Point Hosp., Port Chester, N.Y., 1954-61; dean student tng. Nat. Psychol. Assn. for Psychoanalysis, N.Y.C., 1968-73, pres., 1972-74, bd. dirs.; cons. Children's Aid Soc., N.Y.C., 1961-65; faculty Nat. Psychol. Assn. for Psychoanalysis, Woman sch.; chmn. dept. psychoanalysis Internat. Grad. U. Switzerland. Alvin Johnson scholar, 1951; Psychology fellow Coll. City N.Y., 1952-54. Fellow Am. Psychol. Assn.; mem. N.Y. State Psychol. Assn., N.Y. Soc. Clin. Psychologists, Am. Assn. Psychotherapy, Psychotherapists in Pvt. Practice, Am. Humannistic Psychol. Assn., Am. Group Psychol. Assn., Psi Chi. Club: Westport (Conn.) Country. Contbr. articles to profl. jours. Home: 23 Old Mill Rd Westport CT Office: 2 Fifth Ave 19A New York City NY 10011

LERNER, THEODORE RAPHAEL, dentist; b. Bklyn., Sept. 28, 1932; s. Meyer and Tillie (Brimberg) L.; student Washington and Jefferson Coll., 1950-53; D.D.S., U. Pa., 1957; m. Barbara Ellen Bernstein, June 29, 1974; children by previous marriage—Andrea Holly, Evan Andrew. Practice dentistry, specializing in endodontics, Bklyn., 1957—, Forest Hills, N.Y., 1968—. Pres., Bruton Corp., Bklyn., 1967—. Diplomate Am. Bd. Endodontics. Fellow Internat., Am. colls. dentists, Am. Assn. Endodontists; mem. ADA, 2d Dist. Dental Soc. (pres. 1971), Dental Soc. State of N.Y. (gov.). Home: 70-31 108th St Forest Hills NY 11375 Office: 1 Hanson Pl Brooklyn NY 11243

LERNER, WILLIAM lawyer; b. Phila., July 17, 1933; s. Al and Tillie (Goodman) L.; B.A., Cornell U., 1955; LL.B., N.Y. U., 1960; m. G. Billie Campbell, Aug. 15, 1957; children—Bonnie, Edwina. Admitted to N.Y. bar, 1961; atty. SEC, 1960-64; asst. v.p. Am. Stock Exchange, 1965-68; sr. v.p., sec. Cogan, Berlind, Weill & Levitt, Inc. (name now Shearson Hayden Stone, Inc.), N.Y.C., 1968-70, Berg & Cornell, Buffalo, 1970-71, Kavinoky, Cook, Hepp, Sandler, Gardner & Wisbaum, Buffalo, 1971-72; v.p., counsel Utilities and Industries Corp., 1973, Saperston, Day & Radler, P.C., Buffalo, 1973-78; sr. v.p. law Sportsystems Corp., Buffalo, 1978—; dir. The Unimax Group, Inc., N.Y.C. Chmn. Erle County Pub. Utilities Task Force, 1974-75; mem. arts coll. council Cornell U., 1977—. Served to 1st lt. Q.M.C., U.S. Army, 1955-57. Mem. Am., N.Y. State (regulation of securities com. 1968—) bar assns. Club: Buffalo. Contbg. editor The Stock Market Handbook, 1969. Home: 150 Rollingwood Williamsville NY 14221 Office: 700 Delaware Ave Buffalo NY 14209

LE ROUX, JOHN J., supt. schs.; b. Saratoga Springs, Oct. 1, 1926; B.S. in Edn., Oswego State Coll., 1949, M.S. in Edn., 1951; married; 5 children. Tchr. Guildford (N.Y.) Central Sch., 1949-52; tchr., supt. bldgs. and grounds Saratoga Springs. (N.Y.) City Sch. Dist., 1952-55, asst. supt., 1955-78, supt., 1978—. Treas. Saratoga County Econ. Opportunity Council, 1972-74; bd. visitors Capitol Dist. Psychiat. Center. Certified in sch. bus. adminstrn., N.Y. Mem. Am. Assn. Sch. Adminstrs., N.Y. State Sch. Bus. Ofcls., Assn. Sch. Bus. Ofcls. U.S. and Can., Assn. Systems Mgmt. Home: Loughberry Rd Saratoga Springs NY 12866 Office: 5 Wells St Saratoga Springs NY 12866

LEROY, GEORGE ERWIN, ednl. adminstr.; b. Barre, Vt., Mar. 5, 1928; s. Glendon J. and Elizabeth (MacDonald) LeRoy; B.S. in Edn., Am. Internat. Coll., 1952, M.A. in Edn., 1955; m. Barbara C. LeRoy, children—James, Elizabeth, Richard. Elementary tchr. Springfield (Mass.) Pub. Schs., 1952-61; elementary prin. pub. schs., East Longmeadow, Mass., 1961-67; cons., author Milton Bradley Co., Springfield, 1967-69; dir. elementary edn. Windsor (Conn.) Pub. Schs., 1970—; chmn. Greater Hartford Council Economic Edn.; cons. objective-based instrn. Vice Pres. East Longmeadow PTA, Mem. Nat. Assn. Individual Guided Edn., Conn. Assn. Sch. Adminstrs., Am. Assn. Supervision and Curriculum Devel., Phi Delta Kappa. Home: 43 Hanward Hill East Longmeadow MA 01028 Office: PO Box 10 Windsor CT 06095

LEROY, HAROLD MYRON, artist; b. N.Y.C., Dec. 12, 1905; s. Charles J. and Miriam (Raphael) Levy; student Columbia U., 1924-26, Bklyn. Mus. Art Sch., 1959-65, Art Students League, 1961-62 summers, Hans Hofmann, 1958; m. Irene F. Bloom, Oct. 30, 1927; children—Zelda LeRoy Scholnick, Albert Raphael Levy. One-man shows: Matawan (N.J.) Art Gallery, 1966, Ella Lerner Galleries, N.Y.C., 1968, Gallery Royel, Bklyn., 1970, 72, Plainview (N.Y.) Pub. Library, 1972, Lexington Art Gallery, N.Y.C., 1976, Randall Galleries, N.Y.C., 1979; exhibited in group shows Audubon Artists Nat. Acad., 1970, 71, 72, 73, 77, Les Artistes de l'Ecole Francaise, Paris, 1969, 70, Donnell Art Library, N.Y.C., 1968, Va. State Coll. at Petersburg, 1969, U. Mich. at Ann Arbor, 1969, L.I. U., 1971, State U. N.Y., Alfred, 1976, Cayuga Mus. History and Art, Auburn, N.Y., 1976, George Washington Carver Mus., Tuskegee, Ala., 1976, Artists Equity Show, N.Y.C., 1977, Contemporary Circle at Lincoln Center, 1977, others; represented in permanent collections: Butler Inst. Am. Art, Mint Mus., Chrysler Mus., Miami Mus. Modern Art, Mus. Modern Art, London, Ont., Safed (Israel) Mus., Slater Meml. Mus., Norwich, Conn.; designer Charles J. Levy Co., 1927-28, also costumes for Ziegfeld Follies, 1929; writer, illustrator Hollywood Filmograph, 1931-32, Hollywood Screen World, 1932-33; contbr. Illustrated Milliner, 1929-32. Reporter, editor Midwood Manor News civic assn., Bklyn., 1922-24. Recipient Gold medal Accademia Internazionale, 1973, award Nat. Arts Club, 1976; Heydenryk award for graphic art, 1977. Mem. Am. Soc. Contemporary Artists (1st v.p.), Artists Equity Assn. N.Y. (dir., 1967-76), Am. Vets. Soc. Artists, Met. Painters and Sculptors (v.p. 1973-74). Pioneer in metaltone painting. Subject of LeRoy and the World of Art (Barbara Consolas), 1972; The Anatomy of the Mind of LeRoy (Robert S. Orlove), 1973. Author: The Role of the American Artist in the Bicentennial Year, 1976. Works and papers in Archives Am. Art, Smithsonian Instn. Home and studio: 1916 Ave K Brooklyn NY 11230

LE SCHACK, LEONARD ALBERT, research and devel. co. exec.; b. N.Y.C., Mar. 6, 1935; s. David B. and Selma (Kaminsky) Le S.; B.S., Rensselaer Poly. Inst., 1957; diploma in oceanography U.S. Dept. Agr. Grad. Sch., 1962; postgrad. Ecole Pratique, Alliance Francaise, Paris, 1963, U. Wis., 1963-64; m. Lorraine Marlene Levy, Mar. 3, 1962; children—Christopher Erik, Adam Alexander. Geophys. trainee Shell Oil Co., Houston, 1957; asst. seismologist U.S. IGY, Antarctic Expdn., 1957-59, Polar regions project officer, EXPO-67, Montreal, Que., Can., 1965-66; pres., chmn. bd. Devel. and Resources Transp. Co. (name changed LeSchack Assos., Ltd. 1978), Silver Spring, Md. and San Ramon, Calif., 1966—, Trident Exploration, Ltd., Silver Spring, 1978—. U.S. ofcl. rep. Argentine Antarctic Expn., 1962-63; del. 2d Internat. Permafrost Conf., USSR, 1973. Served to lt. (j.g.) USNR, 1959-63. Decorated Legion of Merit, 1962; recipient Antarctic Service medal Nat. Acad. Scis., NRC, 1966; grantee for study Expeditions Polaires Francaises, Paris, 1963. Mem. Soc. Exploration Geophysicists, Am. Geophys. Union, Am. Soc. Photogrammetry, AAAS, Arctic Inst. N.Am., Internat. Soc. Terrain-Vehicle Systems. Oceanographic and geophys. research in Polar Regions; environ. research expdns. S.Am. jungles. Contbr. articles to profl. jours. Address: 1111 University Blvd W Silver Spring MD 20902

LESINSKI, JOHN SILVESTER, obstetrician, gynecologist; b. Phila., Mar. 29, 1913; s. Thomas Francis and Sophia Agata (Przybylo) L.; M.D., Jagellonian U., Cracow, Poland, 1939; M.P.H., Johns Hopkins, 1967; m. Maria Oglaszka Zdzislawa, Jan. 9, 1959; children—Jolanta (Mrs. Jan Horodnicki), Jan, Krzyszysztof, Patricia. Intern dept. medicine U. Hosp., Cracow, 1939, surgery Municipal Hosp., 1939, dept. communicable diseases, surgery, obstetrics and gynecology Community Hosp., Dabrowa Tarnowska, 1939-44; pub. health officer Dabrowa Tarnowska, 1939-45; resident obstetrics and gynecology Jagellonian U., 1946-52; asso. prof. obstetrics and gynecology Nat. Inst. Mother and Child Health, Warsaw, Poland, 1952-57, dep. dir., 1952-65; prof. obstetrics and gynecology U. Warsaw, 1959-65; asso. prof. obstetrics and gynecology, asso. prof. maternal and child health Johns Hopkins, 1967—; practice medicine specializing in obstetrics and gynecology Cracow, 1947, Lublin, 1947-49, Szczecin, 1949-52, Warsaw, 1952-65; mem. staffs univ. hosps., Cracow, Lublin, Szczecin, Warsaw. Cons., temporary adviser WHO, 1961—. Fellow Royal Soc. Promotion Health, Internat. Biog. Assn., Am. Acad. Reproductive Medicine, Am. Pub. Health Assn., Am. Coll. Obstetrics and Gynecology, Am. Coll. Preventive Medicine; mem. Soc. Obstetrics and Gynecology Yugoslavia, Soc. Obstetrics and Gynecology Bulgaria, Internat. Fedn. Obstetrics and Gynecology, Internat. Planned Parenthood Fedn., Polish Acad. Scis. Author: Psychoprophylaxis, 1958; Contraception, 1960; The Injuries of the Urinary Tract During Gynecological and Obstetrical Operations, 1963. Contbr. numerous articles to profl. jours. Home: 4310 Penn Ave Baltimore MD 21236 Office: 615 N Wolfe St Baltimore MD 21205

LESKO, MATTHEW JOHN, JR., research co. exec.; b. Wilkes Barre, Pa., May 11, 1943; s. Matthew John and Anne (Balberchak) L.; B.S., Marquette U., 1965; M.B.A., Am. U., 1973; m. Leila Killen Kight, May 6, 1973. Prof. computer sci. mgmt Sch. Bus. Adminstrn. Fed. City Coll., Washington, 1970-73; dir. corporate info. systems Pierbusseti Internat. Inc., Washington, 1973-74; founder, pres. Washington Researchers Co., 1974—; info. systems cons. U.S. Navy and U.S. Army. Served to lt. U.S. Navy, 1965-70. Mem. Am. Mktg. Assn. (bd. dirs. Washington chpt.), N.Am. Soc. Corporate Planning (dir., pres. Washington chpt.). Editor: The Information Report, 1974—. Contbr. articles to profl. publs. Home: 900 24th St NW Washington DC 20037 Office: 910 17th St NW Washington DC 20006

LESKO, WILLIAM STEPHEN, ophthalmologist; b. Passaic, N.J., Jan. 16, 1937; s. William Stephen William and Cecil Imelda (Simpson) L.: B.S., Fordham U., 1958; M.D., N.J. Coll. Medicine, 1962; m. Joan Capizzano, June 13, 1959; children—William, Cecily, Gregory, Glenn, Timothy. Intern, Boston U. Med. Center, 1962-63; asst. resident in surgery Mt. Sinai Hosp., N.Y.C., 1963-64, asst. resident dept. ophthalmology, 1965-67, clin. instr., 1967-68, asst. attending ophthalmic surgeon, 1971—, asst. clin. prof., 1971—, clin. instr., 1968-71; practice medicine, specializing in ophthalmology, Clifton, N.J., 1968—; asst. attending Beth Israel Med. Center, N.Y.C., 1968-74, courtesy staff, 1968-74; sr. attending ophthalmologist St. Mary's Hosp., Passaic, N.J., 1972-73, active staff, 1974, dir. dept. ophthalmology, 1976—; asso. attending staff Passaic (N.J.) Gen. Hosp., 1972-74, dir. dept. ophthalmology, 1976—. Served with USAR, 1963-69. Recipient Mosby Student award Seton Hall Coll. Medicine, 1962; Berry Research Soc. award, 1962; NIH fellow, 1964-65. Mem. N.J. Acad. Ophthalmology and Otolaryngology (sec. 1976—). Roman Catholic. Contbr. articles in field to med. jours. Address: 1005 Clifton Ave Clifton NJ 07013

LESLEY, ALLEN, r.r. co. exec.; b. Phila., Aug. 7, 1905; s. Allen and Hermine Wilhelmina (Spamer) L.; certificate in finance, U. Pa., 1931, A.B., 1936; LL.B., Temple U., 1940; m. Bertha Hiller Kiehl, Dec. 19, 1931. Admitted to Pa. bar, 1941; practiced in Phila. until 1970; prin. legal asst. Pa. Pub. Utility Commn., 1942-44; atty. Reading R.R. Co., 1944-54, asst. gen. atty., 1954-58, asst. gen. counsel, 1958-62, gen. atty., 1962-70; exec. v.p. Phila. Belt Line R.R. Co., 1971-74, now dir., mem. exec. com. Lectr. hist. subjects. Mem. Phila., Pa. bar assns., ICC Practitioner's Assn., St. Andrew's Soc. Phila. (counsel 1950-74, dir. found.), Swedish Colonial Soc. (gov. 1968-70, hon. gov. 1971—), Pa. Soc. S.R., German Soc. Pa., Phi Delta Phi. Republican. Lutheran (mem. council 1962-75). Clubs: Masons, Downtown. Home: 502 W Mt Airy Ave Philadelphia PA 19119 Office: 323 Bourse Bldg Philadelphia PA 19106

LESLIE, JOHN, paper co. exec.; b. Coral Gables, Fla., Nov. 10, 1933; s. John C. and Marion Jean (Savage) L.; grad. Phillips Exeter Acad., 1952; B.S., Princeton, 1956; M.B.A., Columbia, 1961; m. Susan Lee Wallin, July 20, 1963; children—Michael, John, William. With Hercules Corp., 1956-60, Standard Oil Co. (N.J.), 1961-69; chmn. bd., pres. Penntech Papers, Inc., N.Y.C., 1969—. Served to capt. AUS, 1957-58. Mem. Young Pres. Orgn., Beta Gamma Sigma. Office: 600 3d Ave New York City NY 10016

LESLIE, JOHN ETHELBERT, investment banker; b. Vienna, Austria, Oct. 13, 1910; s. Julius and Valerie (Lawetzky) L.; Dr. Jur., U. Vienna, 1932; diploma Consular Acad. Polit. Sci. and Econs., Vienna, 1934; M.S., Columbia U., 1942; m. Evelyn Ottinger Goetz, Mar. 28, 1940. Came to U.S., 1938, naturalized, 1944. Sec. to judges Fed. Law Cts. Austria, 1934-36; pvt. practice, Vienna, 1936-38; sr. auditor Arthur Andersen & Co., C.P.A.'s, N.Y.C., 1941-46; prin. R.G. Rankin & Co., tax cons., N.Y.C., 1946-55; with Bache & Co., Inc. (name now Bache Halsey Stuart Shields Inc.), N.Y.C., 1955—, chmn. bd., 1969—, chmn. exec. com., 1968-69, chief exec. officer, 1970-77; chmn. bd. Bache Group Inc., 1969-78, chmn. policy com., 1978—; dir. Banom Corp.; pres., dir. 920 Fifth Ave. Corp.; mem. adv. com. on internat. capital markets N.Y. Stock Exchange, chmn., 1973-75, also mem. com. on access; chmn. Nat. Market Adv. Bd., 1975-76. Hon. consul gen. Austria in N.Y.C., 1965—. trustee Inst. Internat. Edn.; pres., dir. Bache Corp. Found.; bd. dirs. H.L. Bache Found., Beekman Downtown Hosp. Decorated Cruz Vermelha de Dedicacao (Portugal); comdr. 1st class Order Merit, Great Badge Merit, Great Gold Cross of Honor with Star (Austria), officer Nat. Order Merit (France); officer's cross Order of Merit of Fed. Republic of Germany; Golden Order of Merit (Vienna); recipient certificate appreciation City N.Y. Mem. Securities Industry Assn. (dir., bd. govs.), Soc. Fgn. Consuls in N.Y.C., chambers commerce in N.Y.C. of Austria, Belgium, France, Germany, Gt. Britain, Italy, The Netherlands, Spain, N.Y. Chamber Commerce and Industry (dir.), France-Am. Soc. (dir.), Alumni Assn. Sch. Bus. Columbia, Am. Fgn. Service Assn., Fedn. French Alliances in U.S. (dir.), Am. Soc. Internat. Law, Fgn. Policy Assn. (dir.), UN Assn. (vice chmn., bd. govs.), U.S. Austrian C. of C. (pres., dir.), Econ. Devel. Council N.Y. (dir.), Council Fgn. Relations, Pilgrims U.S. Clubs: Bond, Econ., Paris-Am., Union, 25 Limited Luncheon, Wall St. (N.Y.C.); Piping Rock. Home: 920 Fifth Ave New York City NY 10021 Office: Bache Plaza 100 Gold St New York City NY 10038

LESLIE, PHILIP, govt. ofcl.; b. Easton, Pa., July 20, 1920; s. Edward and Margaret (Phillips) L.; A.B., Lafayette Coll., 1941; M.S., U. Ill., 1952; m. Olga Mae Holden, Oct. 19, 1953; children—Sharon, Gene, Dana. Librarian, Phys. Sci. Library, Brown U., 1946-50; head librarian Sandia Corp., Albuquerque, 1952-54; head librarian Good Year Atomic Corp., Portsmouth, Ohio, 1955-57; chief tech. info. service Ryan Aeronaut. Co., San Diego, 1957-64; asst. dir. STI faculty NASA, College Park, Md., 1964-68; mgr. info. processing Leasco, Bethesda, Md., 1968-70; ops. mgr. Informatics, Rockville, Md., 1970-72; asst. dir. libraries Smithsonian Instn., Washington, 1972-75, registrar, 1975—. Served with U.S. Army, 1942-44. Mem. Am. Assn. Museums, Am. Soc. Info. Sci., Am. Assn. State and Local History. Contbr. articles to profl. jours. Home: Manor Dr Route 3 Mt Airy MD 21771 Office: Registrar Smithsonian Instn Washington DC 20560

LESLIE, RICHARD THOMAS, architect; b. N.Y.C., Aug. 17, 1901; s. Richard Henry and Jessie (Erichson) L.; ed. Mechanics Inst. Design, Atelier Hirons, Beaux Arts Inst. Design, Columbia U., U. Mich.; m. Elizabeth Carson, Mar. 22, 1929; children—Marian Carson Leslie Horan, Richard Erichson. Archtl. draftsman Dwight P. Robinson Co., N.Y.C., 1920-21, Dennison & Hirons, N.Y.C., 1923-24, Schwartz & Gross, N.Y.C., 1924-25; job capt. Holland Tunnel Commn., N.Y.C., 1925-29, Shreve, Lamb & Harmon, N.Y.C., 1929-30; with Port of N.Y. Authority, N.Y.C., 1935-56, dep. architect, 1951-56. Chief Garden City (N.Y.) Vol. Fire Dept. 1953-54. Registered architect, N.Y., N.J.; registered Nat. Council Archtl. Registration Bds. Mem. Internat., Eastern assns. fire chiefs. Episcopalian. Clubs: Masons; Cherry Valley (Garden City); Roslyn (N.Y.) Rifle. Home: 110 Huntington Rd Garden City NY 11530

LESNIAK, JAMES JOSEPH, computer co. exec.; b. Chgo., Mar. 20, 1931; s. Henry George and Margaret Mary (Bork) L.; B.S. in Social Scis., 1953; s. Mechtilde Wehner, June 18, 1955; children—James II, Ann, Daniel. Salesman Honeywell Inc. Detroit, 1955-56, account exec., Cleve., 1966-69, br. sales mgr., Westfield, N.J., 1969-73, Syracuse, N.Y., 1973—. Served with U.S. Army, 1953-55. Mem. Am. Soc. Gas Engrs. Roman Catholic. Home: 38 Stonecrest Dr Manlius NY 13104 Office: 7485 Henry Clay Blvd Liverpool NY 13088

LESNIAK, ROBERT JOHN, educator; b. Herkimer, N.Y., Sept. 10, 1936; s. John and Mary (Hinotsky) L.; B.A., Hope Coll., 1958; M.A., Syracuse U., 1964, Ph.D., 1969; m. Mary Anne Quinn, Sept. 4, 1965; children—John Francis, Kristin Ann, Nicole Marie. Head tchr. pub. schs., Herkimer, 1962-63; intern supr. Syracuse U., 1964-65, asso. dir. instrn., urban tchr. preparation program, 1965-69; asst. prof. edn. Pa. State U., Middletown, 1969-72, asso. prof., 1972—. Cons. urban teaching Ohio State U., U. Mich., 1968, Harrisburg (Pa.) Pub. Schs., 1970, Los Angeles Pub. Schs., 1972; sch. dir. Lower Dauphin Pub. Schs. Founder, pres. bd. dirs. Happiness St. Nursery Playsch., Palmyra, Pa., 1972-73; bd. dirs. Capitol Campus Child Devel. Center. Served with USNR, 1959-62. Mem. Am. Soc. Curriculum Devel., Assn. Tchr. Educators, Am. Ednl. Research Assn., Nat. Soc. for Study Edn., Phi Delta Kappa. Developer Classroom Behavior Task as prediction instrument for inner-city tchrs. Home: RD 2 Box 171B Snaveley Rd Elizabethtown PA 17022 Office: Dept Edn Pa State U Capital Campus Middletown PA 17057

LESNICK, GERSON JONAS, surgeon; b. N.Y.C., Mar. 29, 1912; s. William and Rebecca (Ginzburg) L.; B.S. cum laude, Harvard Coll., 1933, M.D., 1937; m. Norma Vernon, Oct. 10, 1937; children—David, Richard. Intern, then house surgeon Mt. Sinai Hosp., N.Y.C., 1938-40, admitting physician, surgeon in charge of emergency ward, 1940-41, asst. attending surgeon, 1947-57, asso. attending surgeon, 1957-69, chief of breast clinic, 1957-70, attending surgeon, 1969—, chief of breast service, 1970—; asso. vis. surgeon Bronx Municipal Hosp. Center, 1954-57; dir. surgery Jewish Home and Hosp. for the Aged, N.Y., 1960—; asst. clin. prof. of surgery Albert Einstein Coll. of Medicine, 1954-57; asso. clin. prof. of surgery Mt. Sinai Med. Sch., City U. N.Y., 1967-69, clin. prof. surgery, 1969—. Served to capt. AUS, 1942-46. Diplomate Am. Bd. Surgery. Fellow A.C.S., N.Y. Acad. Medicine, N.Y. Acad. Scis.; mem. N.Y. Surg. Soc., Am. Soc. Clin. Oncology, Am. Soc. Surg. Oncology, N.Y. Cancer Soc. Clubs: Harvard of N.Y. Contbr. articles to profl. jours. Home: 4515 Waldo Ave Riverdale NY 10471 Office: 3 E 76th St New York City NY 10021

LESNICK, ROBERT NATHAN, elec. engr.; b. Bklyn., Oct. 2, 1918; s. Henry Samuel and Hilda (Ginzburg) L.; B.S. in Physics, Rensselaer Poly. Inst., 1939; m. Dolores Ewing, June 24, 1956; children—Joan, Helen. Elec. engr. RCA, Camden, N.J., 1942-47; pres. Roberts Mfg. Co., Ellwood City, Pa., 1947-56; mgr. comml. engring. Stewart Warner Electronics Co., Chgo., 1958-60; mgr. space support engring. Philco Corp., Palo Alto, Calif., 1960-64; gen. mgr. Diehl div. Singer Co., Somerville, N.J., 1964-68, pres. indsl. products div., 1968-75, v.p. parent co., 1968-75; pres. Alpha Metals, Inc., Jersey City, 1975—. Mem. IEEE, Accoustical Soc. Am., Sigma Xi. Author: (with H. Lauer and L.E. Matson) Servomechanism Fundamentals, 1947. Home: 665 Donald Dr N Bridgewater NJ 08807 Office: Alpha Metals Inc 600 Route 440 Jersey City NJ 07304

L'ESPERANCE, FRANCIS ANTHONY, JR., ophthalmologist; b. N.Y.C., May 9, 1932; s. Francis Anthony and Josephine L'E.; A.B. magna cum laude, Dartmouth Coll., 1953; M.D., Harvard U., 1956; m. Ellen Victoria Saxon, Aug. 17, 1963; children—Francis Anthony III, Linda, Laura. Surg. intern Presbyterian Hosp., N.Y.C., 1956-57; resident in ophthalmology Mass. Eye and Ear Hosp., Boston, 1957-60; instr. ophthalmology Columbia U., N.Y.C., 1960-65, asso., 1965-72, asst. prof. clin. ophthalmology, 1972-77, asso. prof., 1977—; practice medicine specializing in ophthalmology, N.Y.C., 1960—; asst. attending ophthalmologist Columbia-Presbyn. Med. Center, N.Y.C., 1960-77, asso. attending, 1977—; courtesy, cons. staff hosps.; pres. Ophthalmic Research Found. Inc., N.Y.C., 1976—. Bd. dirs. Nat. Soc. Prevention of Blindness, 1969—, N.Y. Assn. for Blind, 1973—, Project Orbis, 1973—. Diplomate Am. Bd. Ophthalmology. Mem. Nat. Health Resources Advisory Com., 1978—. Fellow A.C.S. (gov. 1973—), Am. Acad. Ophthalmology and Otolaryngology, N.Y. Acad. Medicine; Am., Oxford (Eng.), N.Y. State, N.Y.C. ophthalmol. socs., Pan-Am. Assn. Ophthalmology, Am. Eye Study Club, Am. Diabetes Assn., Juvenile Diabetes Found., N.Y. Acad. Sci., N.Y. State, N.Y. County, Harvard med. socs., Am. Retina Soc., Am. Soc. Contemporary Ophthalmology Jules Gonin Club, AMA (dir. sect. ophthalmology 1968-70), Phi Beta Kappa. Author: Ocular Photocoagulation: A Stereoscopic Atlas, 1975; editor: Current Diagnosis and Management of Chorioretinal Diseases, 1976; contbr. articles to med. jours., books. Office: 1 E 71st St New York City NY 10021

LESSE, S. MICHAEL, physician; b. Phila., Aug. 13, 1910; s. Samuel and Clara (Friedman) L.; B.A., U. Pa., 1931; M.D., Jefferson Med. Coll., 1935; m. Etta Gordon, Sept. 12, 1937; children—Toni and Cathy (twins). Intern Jefferson Med. Coll. Hosp., 1935-37; psychiat.

resident Norristown State Hosp., 1937-42; neurol. resident Montefiore Hosp., N.Y.C., 1942; tng. in child psychiatry Child Guidance Clinic, Temple U. Med. Sch., Phila., 1938-42; tng. psychoanalysis Inst. Phila. Assn. for Psychoanalysis, 1950-55; pvt. practice neurology, psychiatry and psychoanalysis, 1946—; chief neuropsychiatry Easton Hosp., 1951—; attending neuro-psychiatrist Warren Hosp., Phillipsburg, N.J.; attending psychiatrist Fairmount Farm Hosp., Phila. Cons. Family Service of Northampton County, Children's Aid Soc. Northampton County; psychiatric cons. Lafayette Coll., 1965—. Mem. planning com. for seminars in psychiatry and religion in Eastern Pa., 1963-64; mem. Gov.'s Commn. on Community Mental Health Program. Served from lt. (j.g.) to lt. comdr. M.C., USNR, 1942-46. Fellow Am. Psychiat. Assn., Am. Orthopsychiat. Assn.; mem. A.M.A., Am. Acad. Neurology, Pa. Psychiat. Soc. (council), Pa., Northampton County med. socs., Am. Acad. Psychosomatic Medicine, Am. Assn. Study Headache, Phila. Assn. Psychoanalysis, Am. Psychoanalytic Assn., Lehigh Valley Neuropsychiat. Soc. (past pres.). Home: 2768 Stephens St Easton PA 18042 Office: 1230 Walnut St Allentown PA 18102

LESSENCO, GILBERT BARRY, lawyer; b. Balt., June 19, 1929; s. Jacob David and Sarah (Bank) L.; B.S., Johns Hopkins U., 1950; LL.B., Harvard U., 1953; m. Elaine Beitler, Sept. 3, 1952; children—Susan Donna, Amy Gail, Robert Howard. Admitted to D.C. bar, 1953; since practiced in Washington; mem. firm Wilner and Bergson, 1953-55; partner Wilner & Scheiner, 1955—. Mem. Democratic Central Com., Montgomery County, Md., 1970-74; bd. dirs. Thanks to Scandinavia, Inc. Found; trustee Meridian House Found. Served to lt. USAF, 1953-55. Mem. D.C. Jr. Bar (exec. council 1962-64, named Outstanding Young Lawyer of Year 1965), Phi Sigma Delta. Home: 7928 Robinson Rd Bethesda MD 20034 Office: 2021 L St NW Washington DC 20036

LESSER, JOHN DAVID, glass co. exec.; b. Warren, Pa., Sept. 2, 1927; s. Byron Virgil and Beatrice (Bradley) L.; B.S., U.S. Naval Acad., 1950; m. Eleanor Peters, July 8, 1950; children—Katherine Louis, John David, Thomas P., Frederick R., James M., Mary. Mng. partner The Lesser Ins. Agy., Warren, Pa., 1954-62; engring. and project mgr. Corning Glass Works, Bradford, Pa., 1962-73, mgr. corporate adminstrv. services, Corning, N.Y., 1973—; cons. in adminstrv. orgn. and operations; v.p., dir. Harris Hill Soaring Corp., 1975-76, 77—. Served with USN, 1946-50, USAF, 1950-54. Mem. Adminstrv. Mgmt. Soc., Finger Lakes Health Services Agency. Republican. Home: 47 Downing St Big Flats NY 14814 Office: Corning Glass Works Pulteney St Houghton Park A-1 Corning NY 14830

LESSER, STANLEY CHARLES, lawyer; b. Bklyn., Dec. 15, 1929; s. Morris and Estelle Ruth (Markowitz) L.; A.B., N.Y. U., 1950, LL.B., 1953; m. Elaine Bernice Karpf, Nov. 23, 1958; children—Karen Beth, Susan Gail, David Harris. Admitted to N.Y. bar, 1953, Fla. bar, 1978; clk. firm Nathan Goldrich, N.Y.C., 1953-54; asso. atty. Jaffe & Zabronsky, N.Y.C., 1954-58; partner Helfand & Lesser, N.Y.C., 1958—. Vice-chmn. bd. trustees UN Internat. Sch., 1974-78; class agt. N.Y. U. Law Sch., 1973-74. Recipient N.Y. U. Alumni Meritorious Service award, 1974. Mem. Am., N.Y. State bar assns., Assn. Bar City N.Y., Am. Arbitration Assn. (panel arbitrators), N.Y. U. Alumni Fedn. (dir., honor certificate 1973), N.Y. U. Law Alumni Assn. (dir. 1976—). Jewish (v.p., trustee synagogue). Clubs: N.Y. U. (gov. 1969—, sec. 1975-77, pres. 1977—, chmn. house com. 1971-72, chmn. legal com. 1973-76), N.Y. U. Varsity (pres. 1968-71). Editor-in-chief: Certiorari, law yearbook, 1953. Home: 505 La Guardia Pl New York City NY 10012 Office: 2 W 45th St New York City NY 10036

LESSNER, GARY STEVEN, advt. co. exec.; b. Bridgeport, Conn., July 8, 1943; s. David and Bernice C. (Newman) L.; B.A., Guilford Coll., 1965; m. Kathleen E. Kohl, Feb. 3, 1968. Staff, Marketing/Communications mag., N.Y.C., 1969-70; copy chief Shaw Elliott Inc., N.Y.C., 1970-71; v.p. Advt. Workshop Inc., N.Y.C., 1971-73; sr. v.p., gen. mgr. Provandie & Chirurg Inc., Boston and Hartford, Conn., 1973—. Trustee E. Conn. chpt. Multiple Sclerosis Soc., 1977—. Mem. Bus./Profl. Advt. Assn., Greater Hartford C. of C., Greater Hartford Advertisers Club, Conn. Art Dirs. Club. Jewish. Club: Hartford. Home: 727 Lovely St Avon CT 06001 Office: 111 Founders Plaza East Hartford CT 06108

LESTER, ALLEN HENRY, ret. fgn. service officer; b. Marshfield, Mass., Oct. 2, 1905; s. Samuel Allen and Josephine Turner L.; A.B. in Econs. magna cum laude, Tufts U., 1927; postgrad. Am. U., 1937-41; m. Eleanor Hovey Patterson, June 21, 1929. With investment house, Boston, 1927-29, Jones & Laughlin Steel Corp., Boston, 1929-32; tchr. pub. schs., Barre and Arlington, Mass., 1933-36; instr. econs. Middlesex U., Waltham, Mass., also research asst. Am. Inst. Econ. Research, Cambridge, Mass., 1936-37; with U.S. Dept. Commerce, Washington, 1937-41, bus. analyst N.Y. Field Office, 1958-60; econ. analyst, agrl. economist various def. agys. U.S. Govt., 1941-45; with Fgn. Service, U.S. Dept. State, 1945-65, econ. analyst Am. consulate gen., Sao Paulo, Brazil, 1945-47, Am. embassy, Rio de Janeiro, Brazil, 1947-49, asst. consular attache Am. consulate gen., Guayaquil, 1949-52, econ. officer Am. embassy, Ciudad Trujillo, 1952-54, econ. and comml. officer, consul Am. embassy, Guatemala City, 1954-57, internat. economist Fgn. Reporting Staff Washington, 1960-62, comml. officer, consul, Am. consulate gen., Barcelona, Spain, 1962-65; owner Allen H. Lester Assos., cons., Scituate, Mass., 1965-75; lectr. econs. Curry Coll., Milton, Mass., 1966-67. Trustee James Library, Norwell, Mass.; adminstr. Taunton (Mass.) Camp Scholarship Fund. Mem. Scituate, Norwell hist. socs., AAAS, Am. Fgn. Service Assn., Diplomatic and Consular Officers Ret., Pan Am. Soc. New Eng., World Affairs Council Boston, Phi Beta Kappa, Alpha Tau Omega. Unitarian. Clubs: Rotary (coordinator internat. student exchange) (Scituate, Mass.); South Shore Tufts (pres. 1976-77). Co-author: Inflation's Timing, 1936; contbr. articles to profl. jours. Home and Office: 281 Old Oaken Bucket Rd Scituate MA 02066

LESTER, BARNETT BENJAMIN, editor, govt. ofcl.; b. Toronto, Ont., Can., Aug. 7, 1912; s. Louis and Lena (Rubenstein) L.; came to U.S., 1917; student Cleveland Coll., Western Res. U., 1933; B.A. (scholar). Oberlin Coll., 1934; postgrad. (scholar) Nat. Inst. Pub. Affairs, Washington, 1935-36, Syracuse U., Acad. Internat. Law, The Hague, 1936; fellow Fletcher Sch. Law and Diplomacy. 1935-36; student Fgn. Service Inst., Dept. of State, 1952, 56; m. Rita Constance Hatcher, May 31, 1943 (dec. Nov. 1960); m. 2d, Claudette Yvonne Gionet, Apr. 19, 1970. Editorial staff Cleve. Plain Dealer, 1928-30; corr. various newspapers, 1930-38; staff reporter and feature writer Cleve. News, 1931-32; with Cleve. bur. A.P., 1933; featrue writer Boston Sunday Post, 1935-38; asso. editor The Writer Mag., 1936-38; mng. editor, later editor Exclusive Features Syndicate, Boston, 1936-38; with U.S. Dept. Justice, 1938-41; assigned to Office of Atty. Gen., Washington, 1938-40, editorial and informational asst., 1940-41, info. officer, 1941; with Office of Coordinator of Inter-Am. Affairs, 1941-45, asst. dir. feature div., 1941-45; With U.S. Dept. of State, Washington, as asst. dir. feature div., Interim Internat. Information Service (OIAA), 1945; pub. relations exec. Al Paul Lefton Co., Inc., Phila., 1945-46; info. specialist, chief motion picture unit, acting chief audio-visual sect. Office of Health Info., USPHS, Office Surgeon Gen., Washington, 1947-48; info., specialist Office Publs. and Reports, FSA, 1948-49; chief editorial and prodn. sect. Nat. Heart Inst., 1949-52; pub. information chief, 1950, information specialist, sci. reports br. NIH, 1949-52; rev. officer Dept. State, 1952-61, supervisory publs. editor, 1961-63; editor-writer, 1963-73, pub. information officer, 1973—, asso. editor Dept. State Newsletter, 1977—, U.S. Fgn. Service Res. officer, 1965-73, assigned to policy and pub. information affairs program, 1962-67, Newsletter and Information office Office Dir. Gen. of Fgn. Service, 1967—. Career counselor Oberlin Coll., 1940—. Rep. Office Surg. Gen., USPHS, on Interdepartmental com. med. tng. aids, 1947-48; invited participant U.S. Commr. Edn. Conf. Audio-Visual Aids to Edn., 1948; mem. information staff Pres.'s Midcentury White House Conf. on Children and Youth, 1950; mem. spl. survey audio-visual teaching and tng. aids Nat. Heart Inst., USPHS and Assn. Am. Med. Colls., 1951. Recipient award for services World War II Coordinator Inter-Am. Affairs, 1945, Meritorious Honor Group award Dept. State, 1967, Blue Pencil award Fed. Editors Assn., 1975, Thirty five year service award U.S. Dept. State, 1975, Bicentennial award Am. Revolution Bicentennial Adminstrn., 1977. Hon. mem. Internat. Rho Pi Phi; fellow Am. Geog. Soc.; mem. Oberlin Coll. Alumni Assn., Alumni Assn. Fletcher Sch. Law and Diplomacy, Tufts U. Alumni Assn., Diplomatic and Consular Officers Ret., Am. Polit. Sci. Assn., Am. Fgn. Service Assn., Acad. Polit. Sci., Am. Acad. Polit. and Social Sci., Fed. Editors Assn., Nat. Assn. Govt. Communicators, Soc. Tech. Communications, Internat. Platform Assn. Clubs: Oberlin, Nat. Press, Am. Foregin Service, Internat. (Washington). Author: (with others) The Writer's Handbook, 1936. Writer of articles in mags. and profl. jours., radio and motion picture scripts, and biographies. Home: 2507 N Lincoln St Arlington VA 22207 Office: US Dept State Washington DC 20520

LESTER, ROBIN D., sch. adminstr.; b. Holdrege, Nebr., Mar. 1, 1939; s. Earl L. and Evelyn Grace (Robinson) L.; student St. Andrews U., Scotland, 1959-61; B.A., Pepperdine U., 1962, M.A., 1963; M.A.T., U. Chgo., 1966, Ph.D., 1971; m. Helen Sargent Doughty, Aug. 26, 1967; children—Robin Debevoise, James Robinson. Resident head, dean students office U. Chgo., 1964-72, Ferdinand Schevill fellow dept. history, 1966-68; asst. prof. history Columbia Coll., Chgo., 1966-70, chmn. social scis. dept., 1970-72; chmn. history dept. Collegiate Sch., N.Y.C., 1972-75; headmaster Trinity Sch., N.Y.C., 1975—. Mem. Manhattan Borough Democratic Com., N.Y.C., 1977—. Mem. Am. Hist. Assn., Am. Studies Assn., Headmasters Assn., Orgn. Am. Historians. Democrat. Presbyterian. Club: Univ. (N.Y.C.). Contbr. to Dictionary of Am. Biography, 1974. Home: 147 W 91st St New York City NY 10024 Office: 139 W 91st St New York City NY 10024

LESZKIEWICZ, JOHN, JR., hosp. adminstr.; b. N.Y.C., May 13, 1947; s. John and Olga L.; B.A., Coll. City N.Y., 1969; M.Ed., Temple U., 1971; M.B.A., Bernard Baruch Coll., 1974; m. Naomi Diner, June 6, 1969; children—Daniel, Jennie. Personnel rep. Queens Hosp. Center, N.Y.C., 1971-72; asso. dir. City Hosp. Center at Elmhurst, N.Y.C., 1973-77, asso. exec. dir., 1977—; provider mem. Bd. A., Health Systems Agy., N.Y.C., 1977—. Mem. Am. Hosp. Assn., Am. Mgmt. Assn., Met. Health Adminstrs. N.Y.C. Home: 13 Kellogg St Brookfield CT 06804 Office: 79-01 Broadway Elmhurst NY 11373

LETICA, HELEN, co. exec.; b. Belgrade, Yugoslavia, July 21, 1923; d. Charles and Renee Santich; came to U.S., 1941, naturalized, 1945; B.A., N.Y. U., 1945, postgrad., 1945-47; postgrad. New Sch., Columbia U., 1947-48; m. Jack W. Fine, Aug. 3, 1968; children—Gregory, Nicholas Letica. Exec. v.p. Zeller & Letica Inc., mailing list compilers, N.Y.C., 1954-71, pres., 1971—; lectr. in field. Mem. Women's Direct Response Group, Direct Mail Mktg. Assn., Mail Advt. Service Assn. Club: Mill River Country (Brookville, N.Y.). Office: Zeller & Letica Inc 15 E 26th St New York City NY 10010

LETT, MARVIN RUSSELL, transp. engr.; b. Detroit; s. Russell Guy and Helen Christella (Dawley) L.; A.B., Fisk U., 1963; M. City Planning, Howard U., 1973. Tchr. sci. Highland Park (Mich.) Pub. Schs., 1963-68, Washington (D.C.) Pub. Schs., 1968-71; instr. anatomy and physiology Washington Inst. Tech., 1971-72; transp. engr. Sverdrup & Parcel & Assos., Inc., Washington, 1974—. Ford Found. fellow, 1971-72; John Volpe fellow, 1972-73. Mem. Am. Soc. Planning Ofcls., Am. Inst. Planners, NEA, Blacks in Transp. Engring., Experiment in Internat. Living, Smithsonian Assos., Nat. Council Transp. Disadvantaged (Recognition award 1978), Urban League, Alpha Phi Alpha. Democrat. Episcopalian. Clubs: Fisk; Howard U. Home: 1336 Missouri Ave NW Washington DC 20011 Office: 8720 Georgia Ave Room 801 Silver Spring MD 20910

LETTIERI, DAN JOHN, psychologist; b. Bklyn., May 23, 1942; s. Sesty and Rose (Gulino) L.; student N.Y. U., 1960-62; B.A., U. Calif. at Berkeley, 1964; M.A., U. Kans., 1966, Ph.D., 1970; postgrad. Johns Hopkins U., 1969-70. Psychologist, Suicide Prevention Center, Los Angeles, 1970-71; dir. research NIMH, Center for Studies of Suicide and Suicide Prevention, Rockville, Md., 1971-72, research psychologist Center for Studies Narcotic and Drug Abuse, 1972-73; research psychologist Nat. Inst. Drug Abuse, Div. Research, Psychosocial Br., Rockville, Md., 1973—; asst. med. investigator Md. Dept. Post Mortem Examiners, 1970; behavioral sci. cons., dep. coroner, Los Angeles, 1968-69. Vocat. Rehab. Adminstrn. trainee, 1966, USPHS trainee in social psychology, 1964-67. Mem. Internat. Assn. Suicide Prevention, Am. Assn. Suicidology (treas. 1975-77), Am. Psychol. Assn., Johns Hopkins Med. and Surg. Assn., Phi Beta Kappa, Psi Chi. Cons. editor Jour. Life Treatening Behavior, 1975-76; contbr. articles in field to profl. jours. Home: Box 34721 Washington DC 20034 Office: 5600 Fishers Ln Room 9-31 Rockville MD 20857

LEUBERT, ALFRED OTTO PAUL, internat. business cons.; b. N.Y.C., Dec. 7, 1922; s. Paul T. and Josephine (Haaga) L.; B.S., Fordham U., 1946; student Dartmouth, 1943; M.B.A., N.Y. U., 1950; m. Celestine Capka, July 22, 1944 (div. 1977); children—Eloise Ann (Mrs. Kevin B. Cronin), Susan Beth (Mrs. Stephen E. Melvin); m. 2d, Hope Sherman Drapkin, June 1978. Account mgr. J. K. Lasser & Co., N.Y.C., 1948-52; controller Vision, Inc., N.Y.C., 1952-53; with Old Town Corp., 1953-56, controller, 1953-54, sec., controller, 1954-56, sec., treas., 1956-57, v.p., treas., dir., 1957-58; v.p., controller Willcox & Gibbs, Inc., N.Y.C., 1958-59, v.p., treas., 1959-65, pres., dir., chief exec. officer, 1966-76; dir. Lane Office Equipment Co., 1963-76, Chyron Corp., Willcox & Gibbs Ltd., 1965-76, S.R.C. Labs., Tectra Industries Inc.; instr. accountancy Pace Coll., 1955-57. Bd. dirs. United Fund Manhasset, 1963-66; adv. bd. St. Anthony's Guidance Clinic, 1965-69. Served from pvt. to 1st lt., inf. platoon leader, USMCR, 1943-46; now capt. Res. Decorated Bronze Star; recipient Humanitarian award Hebrew Acad., Bayside, N.Y., 1971. Mem. Am. Inst. C.P.A.'s, N.Y. State Soc. C.P.A.'s, Financial Execs. Inst., Newcomen Soc. N. Am., Cath. Accountants Guild. Roman Catholic. Clubs: New York University, N.Y. Athletic (N.Y.C.). Home: 180 Central Park S New York City NY 10019 also 10390 Wilshire Blvd Los Angeles CA 90024 Office: 10390 Wilshire Blvd Los Angeles CA 90024

LEUCHTER, FRED ARTHUR, JR., navigational systems engr.; b. Malden, Mass., Feb. 7, 1943; s. Fred Arthur and Mary Elizabeth (Herrick) L.; A.B., Boston U., 1961, C.L.A., 1964. Aerial photographer, tech. dir., chief navigator NE Aerial Photos Inc., Boston, 1965-67; pub. Contemporary Products Corp., Boston, 1967-71; pres. Navigational Systems Engr., Cele-Nav Industries Inc., Boston, 1971—; lectr. in field; tchr. piano. Bd. dirs. Gunowners Action League, 1977—. Mem. Inst. Navigation, New Eng. Indsl. Photographers Assn., Mystic Valley (pres.), Melrose rod gun clubs, Nat. Rifle Assn. Patentee in field. Home: 22 Greenwood St Melrose MA 02176 Office: Cele-Nav Industries Inc Box 237 Malden MA 02148

LEUSCHNER, FREDERICK EDWARD, assn. exec.; b. Homestead, Pa., Nov. 25, 1928; s. Frederick Herman and Rosalind (Ball) L.; B.A., Pa. State U., 1950, M.A., 1951; m. Nancy Graham, Nov. 27, 1954; children—Suzanne, Megan, Frederick. Instr., Pa. State U., 1953; dir. news and prodn. sta. WTPA-TV, Harrisburg, Pa., 1953-56; dir. pub. relations Pa. Edn. Assn., 1957-70, asst. exec. dir. for pub. relations, 1970—. Mem. Pub. Relations Soc. Am. (past pres. Central Pa. chpt.), Pa. Pub. Relations Soc. (past pres.), Pa. State Edn. Assn. (life), NEA (life), Phi Sigma Sigma, Phi Kappa Psi. Republican. Clubs: Masons, Shriners. Home: 129 Oak Park Circle Harrisburg PA 17109 Office: 400 N 3d St Harrisburg PA 17105*

LE VALLEY, GUY GLENN, educator; b. Phila., Oct. 21, 1942; s. Glenn Henry and Mary Jane (Henderson) LeV.; B.A., Glassboro State Coll., 1964; M.A., U. Iowa, 1967; m. E. Raye Gerlack, June 17, 1967; 1 son, Ian G. Designer, tech. dir. Glassboro (N.J.) Summer Theatre, 1963-67, Monticello Coll., Godfrey, Ill., 1967-68; asst. tech. dir. N.Y. Shakespeare Festival Mobile Theatre Unit, N.Y.C., 1967; asst. prof. theatre Prince George's Coll., Largo, Md., 1968-73, asso. prof. speech communication, designer, tech. dir. theatre, 1974—; lighting designer Murray Spalding Movemet Arts Inc., 1975—, City Dance '77; bdlg. cons. Church St. Theatre. Mem. Am. Theatre Assn., U.S. Inst. Theatre Tech., Eastern Communication Assn. Democrat. Quaker. Reviewer, cons. Choice mag., 1974—. Author: Annotated Bibliography of Stage Lighting for the Dance, 1974, 77. Home: 9524 Hemlockhill Ave College Park MD 20740 Office: 301 Largo Rd Largo MD 20870

LE VAN, DANIEL HAYDEN, business exec.; b. Savannah, Ga., Mar. 29, 1924; s. Daniel Hayden and Ruth (Harner) LeV; grad. Middlesex Sch., 1943; B.A., Harvard, 1950; student Babson Inst., 1950-51. With underwriter's dept. Zurich Ins. Co., N.Y.C., 1951-52; liquified petroleum sales and engring. Gas, Inc., Lowell, Mass., 1952-54; customer relations Lowell Gas Co., 1954-56, in charge LP gas sales and promotion, 1956-58; co-owner, dir. Rentals Abroad, Ltd., Overseas Properties Ltd., N.Y.C., 1970—; trustee Colonial Gas Energy System, Boston, 1973—. Dir. Lowell Gas Co., Cape Cod Gas Co., Gas, Inc., Lowell Factors, Mass. Assos., Lowell Appliances, Gas Rentals, Inc. Served with AUS, 1943-46. Club: Harvard (N.Y.C., Boston). Home: Box 158 DeLeon Springs FL 32028 Office: care Colonial Gas Energy System 50 Congress St Boston MA 02109

LEVANT, RONALD FRED, psychologist; b. Los Angeles, Oct. 26, 1942; s. Harry G. and Wilma I. (Adler) L.; A.B., U. Calif. at Berkeley, 1964, A.B. in Psychology with honors and gt. distinction, 1969; postgrad. Med. Sch., U. Calif. at San Francisco, 1965-67; Ed.D. in Clin. Psychology, Harvard U., 1973; div.; 1 dau., Caren Elizabeth. Staff mem. Robert W. White Sch., Boston, 1972, asst. dir., 1972-73, dir., 1973-74; asso. prof. dept. psychology Boston State Coll., 1974-75; asso. in edn. Harvard U., 1974-75; treatment team leader inpatient unit Human Resource Inst. Boston, 1974-75, cons. clin. psychologist outpatient dept., 1974—; asst. prof. dept. counselor edn. Boston U., 1975—. Trustee Open Harbor, Inc., Boston, 1972-75. Mem. Am., Eastern, New Eng., Mass. (chmn. bd. profl. affairs) psychol. assns., Soc. for Psychotherapy Research, Am. Orthopsychiat. Assn., Acad. Psychologists in Marital and Family Therapy, Soc. Family Therapy and Research, Am., Mass., Greater Boston personnel and guidance assns., Assn. Counselor Edn. and Supervision, Phi Delta Kappa. Contbr. articles to profl. jours. Home: 55 Griswold St Cambridge MA 02138 Office: Dept Counselor Edn Boston U 232 Bay State Rd Boston MA 02215

LEVAVY, ZVI, accountant; b. Jerusalem, Oct. 1, 1910; s. Zeev and Esther (Shapiro) Leibowitz; B.C.S., N.Y. U., 1934; m. Berenice Bardin, Nov. 27, 1935; 1 son, Bardin; came to U.S., 1929, naturalized, 1944. Sec., Palestine Trust Co., Tel Aviv, 1934-36; sec., chief accountant Palestine Brewery Richon LeZion, 1936-38; comptroller Zionist Orgn. Am., 1940-43; now prin. partner Zvi Levavy & Co., C.P.A.'s. Pres. Perth Amboy Zionist Orgn., 1949-50; mem.-at-large Jewish Community Council, Perth Amboy, pres., 1963-66; mem. Internat. Council Joint Distbn. Com., Internat. Affairs Nat. Community Relations Council, 1969-74; mem. Perth Amboy Bd. Edn., 1966-74, v.p., 1972-74; mem. Perth Amboy Bd. Sch. Estimate, 1966-74; mem. Middlesex County Coll. Found.; pres. Morris J. and Betty Kaplun Found.; trustee Hillel Acad., 1966-77; bd. govs. Dropsie U., v.p., 1976—. Served as sgt. AUS, World War II, ETO. Mem. Am. Inst. C.P.A.'s, N.Y., N.J. socs. C.P.A.'s, Am. Friends Hebrew U. (trustee), Am. Assn. Jewish Edn. (trustee). Home: 148 Kearny Ave Perth Amboy NJ 08861 Office: 21 E 40th St New York City NY 10016

LEVEN, ANN RUTH, art adminstr.; b. Canton, Ohio, Nov. 1, 1940; d. Joseph J. and Bessie (Scharff) Leven; A.B., Pembroke Coll., 1962; certificate with distinction Harvard-Radcliffe Program in Bus. Adminstrn., 1963; M.B.A., Harvard U., 1964. Asst. product mgr. household products div. Colgate-Palmolive, N.Y.C., 1964-66; asst. account exec. Grey Advt., N.Y.C., 1966-67; fin. asst. Met. Mus. Art, N.Y.C., 1967-69, asst. treas., 1970-72, treas., 1972—; artist, awarded prizes for painting and graphic arts; adj. asst. prof. Grad. Sch. Bus., Columbia U., 1975-77, adj. asso. prof., 1977—; exec.-in-residence Amos Tuck Sch., Dartmouth Coll., winter 1976; dir. Alliance Capital Res., Inc., 1978—. Mem. exec. bd. new leadership div. Fedn. Jewish Philanthropies, 1968-70; mem. council N.Y. Pub. Library, mem. exec. com., 1976—; mem. museum adv. panel N.Y. State Council on Arts, 1977—; bd. dirs. Camp Rainbow, 1970—, v.p., 1976—; bd. overseers Amos Tuck Sch., 1978—; trustee Brown U., 1976—, also mem. fin. and budget com., student life com., adv. and exec. coms. Recipient Young Leadership award Council Jewish Fedns. and Welfare Funds, 1968; named N.Y. State's Outstanding Young Woman, 1976. Mem. Am. Assn. Mus., Harvard Bus. Sch. Alumni Assn. (exec. council 1976—, v.p. 1978—), Women's Fin. Assn. Clubs: Women's City, Harvard Bus. Sch. (dir.), Radcliffe, Brown. Home: 1160 3d Ave New York City NY 10021 Office: Fifth Ave and 82d St New York City NY 10028

LEVENBROOK, BRUCE EDWARD, hosp. adminstr.; b. Passaic, N.J., Mar. 31, 1950; s. Seymour Harold and Sophie (Berman) L.; B.A. in Econs., Rutgers U., 1972; M.B.A., City U. N.Y., 1975. Adminstrv. asst. St. Claire's Hosp., Denville, N.J., 1973-74; adminstrv. asst. Beth Israel Hosp., Passaic, 1974-76, asst. adminstr., 1976—. Apptd. to steering com. rehab. services Bergen Passaic Health Systems Agy.; bd. dirs. Vis. Health Services Passaic Valley. Foster G. McGraw scholar, 1972. Mem. Am. Coll. Hosp. Adminstrs., Am. Hosp. Assn., Nat. Fire Protection Agy., N.J. Soc. Personnel Dirs., Bergen-Passaic County Personnel Adminstrs., Passaic C. of C. Home: 181 Longhill Rd Little Falls NJ 07424 Office: 70 Parker Ave Passaic NJ 07055

LEVENSON, NATHAN S., architect; b. Pitts., Apr. 22, 1916; s. Max and Anne (Ashinsky) L.; B.Arch., Carnegie Inst. Tech., 1941; m. Bernice K. Klein, Aug. 31, 1947; children—David, Laura. Sr.

draftsman various cos., Pitts., 1939-41; practice architecture, Pitts., 1948—; tchr. Coll. of Phillipines, 1945-46; substitute prof. Carnegie Tech., 1959; instr. U. Pitts., 1978; pres. Bldg. Inspection Cons. Inc. Active YMHA. Served to 1st lt. C.E., AUS, 1943-46; ETO, PTO. Registered architect, Pa., Ohio, N.J., Ark., Mich., Md., W.Va. Certified fallout shelter analyst, 1970; recipient 1st pl. award Illuminating Engring. Soc., Pitts., 1965. Mem. AIA (regional rep. housing commn. 1972-77), Pa. Soc. Architects, Nat. Council Archtl. Registration Bds., Am. Arbitration Assn., Pitts. Architecture Club (dir. 1979), Clan-Carnegie-Mellon U. (v.p. 1970-72). Democrat. Jewish. Clubs: Pitts. Archtl. Patentee terr. town house, multi-housing (U.S. and Israel). Home: 1160 Bower Hill Rd Apt 704-A Pittsburgh PA 15243 Office: 421 Seventh Ave Pittsburgh PA 15219

LEVENTHAL, A. LINDA, lawyer; b. Albany, N.Y., June 10, 1943; d. David H. and Shirley R. (Asofsky) L.; B.A., State U. N.Y. at Buffalo, 1965; J.D., Union Coll., 1968. Admitted to N.Y. bar, 1968; law clk. Sanford Rosenblum, atty., Albany, 1966-68; partner Rosenblum, Leventhal & Kietzman, Albany, 1969-78, Taub & Leventhal, 1978—; gen. counsel Penquin Products, Ltd., Caribbean Contel Corp., Internat. Condominium Corp., Lazy-Days Travel, Inc., Rinewood Constrn. Corp., Daro Chartours, Inc., Lockwood Constrn. Co. Pres., v.p. bd. mgrs., bd. dirs. The Commons of East Greenbush (N.Y.) Condominium; bd. dirs. Legal Aid Soc. Albany. Mem. Am., N.Y. State bar assns., N.Y. State Trial Lawyers Assn., Nat. Assn. Women Lawyers, Capital Dist. Women Lawyers Assn., Capital Dist. Trial Lawyers Assn. Club: Zonta. Home: 26 Donna Lynn Dr East Greenbush NY 12061 Office: 90 State St Suite 1536 Albany NY 12207 also 162 Lafayette St Schenectady NY

LEVENTHAL, ALAN, physiotherapist; b. Bklyn., Mar. 3, 1930; s. Harry Gabriel and Lillian (Brodsky) L.; student N.Y. U., 1947-49; B.S. magna cum laude, Ithaca Coll., 1952, M.S. in Physiotherapy, 1954; m. Joan Lois Eckstein, Mar. 31, 1957; 1 son, David Adam. Staff Physiotherapist Jewish Chronic Disease Hosp., Bklyn., 1952-57; chief physiotherapist Maimonides Hosp. Bklyn., 1957-67; co-chmn. physiotherapy dept. Victory Meml. Hosp., Bklyn., 1967—; pvt. practice physiotherapy, Bklyn., 1952—; guest lectr. N.Y. U., 1974, 78, SUNY Downstate Med. Center, 1975-78; pres. physiotherapy grievance com. N.Y. State Edn. Dept., 1965-67; mem. regional adv. group N.Y. Met. Regional Med. Plan; mem. doctoral program com. L.I. U. Mem. Council Lic. Physiotherapists N.Y. State (chmn.), United Socs. Physiotherapists (nat. dir.), N.Y. Soc. Continuing Edn. in Phys. Therapy (v.p.), Am. Phys. Therapy Assn., N.Y. State Soc. Physiotherapists (editor-in-chief jour. 1960-63, pres. 1968-73, Meritorious Service award 1971). Jewish. Club: Masons. Home: 125 Girard St Brooklyn NY 11235 Office: 1818 Newkirk Ave Brooklyn NY 11226

LEVENTHAL, HAROLD, judge; b. N.Y.C., Jan. 5, 1915; s. Jules Joseph and Sadie (Wolcher) L.; A.B., Columbia U. (Green prize), 1934, LL.B. (Toppan and Ordronaux prizes), 1936; m. Kathryn Kumler, Sept. 18, 1948; children—Philip Henry J., Anne K. Admitted to N.Y. bar, 1936, D.C. bar, 1946; law sec. to Justice Harlan F. Stone, Supreme Ct. U.S., 1936-37, to Justice Stanley Reed, 1938; staff Office of Solicitor Gen., 1938-39; chief of litigation, bituminous coal div. U.S. Dept. Interior, 1939-40; asst. gen. counsel OPA, 1940-43; staff Justice Jackson, Nuernberg Trials, 1945-46; exec. officer, task force on ind. regulatory commns. Hoover Commn., 1948; chief counsel OPS, 1951-52; mem. firm Ginsburg & Leventhal and successor firms, 1946-65; gen. counsel Dem. Nat. Com., 1952-65; judge U.S. Ct. of Appeals, D.C. Circuit, 1965—; vis. lectr. Yale Law Sch., 1957-62. Served to lt. comdr. USCG, 1943-46. Mem. Fed. (past mem. nat. council), Am., D.C. bar assns., Nat. Lawyers Club, Phi Beta Kappa. Author articles in legal jours. Contbr. to history OPA. Home: 2406 44th St Washington DC 20007 Office: US Ct of Appeals Washington DC 20001*

LEVERETT, DENNIS HUGH, dental educator; b. Cleve., June 22, 1931; s. Everett Thomas and Mary Beatrice (Snow) L.; student Ohio Wesleyan U., 1949-52; D.D.S., Ohio State U., 1956; M.P.H. (Univ. research fellow), Harvard, 1968; children—David, Lise, Teresa, Stephen, Christopher; m. 2d, Joyce Elizabeth Hazard; children—Timothy, Amanda. Pvt. practice dentistry, New Orleans, 1960-66; with N.Mex. Dept. Pub. Health, 1966-67; exec. dir. Center for Community Dental Health, Portland, Maine, 1969-73; chmn. dept. community dentistry Eastman Dental Center, 1973—; clin. asso. prof. Sch. Medicine and Dentistry, U. Rochester, 1973—; adj. prof. Monroe Community Coll., 1973—, bd. advisers dept. dental hygiene, 1973—; dental dir. Monroe County (N.Y.) Health Dept. Faculty, Harvard, 1967-73, Tufts U., 1970-73; cons. Maine Dept. Health and Welfare, Mass. Dept. Pub. Health; profl. adv. com. Portland City Health Dept., 1970-73; chmn. Portland Model Cities Health Task Force, 1970-72; cons. Genessee Valley Group Health Assn., 1973—. Bd. dirs. Smilemobile Monroe County (N.Y.), 1973—; Westside Health Services, Rochester. Served with USPHS, 1956-60. Diplomate Am. Bd. Dental Pub. Health. Mem. Am. Pub. Health Assn., Internat. Assn. Dental Research, Am. Assn. Pub. Health Dentists, So. Me. Comprehensive Health Assn. (profl. adv. com. 1969-73), Delta Sigma Delta, Sigma Alpha Epsilon. Contbr. articles to profl. pubs. Home: 51 Bellevue Dr Rochester NY 14620 Office: Eastman Dental Center 625 Elmwood Ave Rochester NY 14620

LEVESQUE, CHARLES-HENRI, bishop, Roman Cath. Ch.; b. St. André de Kamouraska, Que., Can., Dec. 29, 1921; s. Alexis and Atala (Garneau) L.; B.A., Coll. Ste-Anne-de-la-Pocatière 1944; B.Ph., U. Laval, Que., 1945, L.Th., 1949; D.D.C., Angelicum U., Rome, 1955. Ordained priest, 1948; consecrated bishop, 1965; préfet de discipline et professeur d'histoire et de lettres Coll. de Ste-Anne-de-la-Pocatière (Que., Can.), 1949-51; sec. maître de cérémonies l'Evêché de Ste-Anne, 1951, 55; chancelier Diocese Ste-Anne, 1956; chanoine honoraire, 1956; chanoine titulaire, 1957; camerier secret, 1960; aux. bishop S. Exc. Mgr Bruno Desrochers de Ste-Anne-de-la-Pocatière, 1965-68; bishop of Ste-Anne-de-la-Pocatière, 1968—. Mem. Comité épiscopal l'Office Catéchèse du Québec, Comité Nature et Fonctionnement; pres. Com. de diffusion des célébrations liturgices; co-pres. Commn. épiscopale de Liturgie; mem. Commn. internationale francophone pour les traductions liturgiques. Mem. Chevelier de Colomb, Chevalier de L'Ordre équestre du St. Sépulcre. Home and office: 1200 4e Ave La Pocatière PQ G0R 1Z0 Canada*

LEVESQUE, GERARD D., Canadian govt. ofcl.; b. Port Daniel, Que., Can., 1926; LL.B., McGill U.; m. Denise Lefort; children—Robert, Andre, Bertrand, Suzanne, Marie. Called to Que. bar, 1949; partner firm Sheehan & Levesque, New Carlisle, Que., until 1960; mem. Que. Legislature for Bonaventure, 1956-60; minister game and fisheries Province of Que., Quebec City, 1960-62, minister industry and commerce, 1962-66, 70-72, mem. Que. Parliament, 1966-70; minister intergovtl. affairs, 1970-71, 72-75, vice prime minister, 1972-76, minister of justice, 1975-76, leader of opposition, 1976—, leader by interim Que. Liberal Party, 1977-78; partner firm Levesque & Arsenault 1966-73, Levesque & Landry, 1973-75. Mem. Quebec Assn. Automobile Dealers, Gaspe Peninsula C. of C. Mem. Liberal Party. Roman Catholic. Clubs: K.C. (4 deg.); Cercle Universitaire, Garrison (Quebec City); Reform (Quebec City). Home: 2550 de la Falaise Sillery PQ Canada Office: Parliament Bldgs Quebec PQ Canada

LEVESQUE, PASCAL, mfg. exec.; b. St. Pascal, Que., Can., May 16, 1923; s. P. Wilfrid and Rose (Marier) L.; B.A. cum laude, Ste. Ann Coll., 1943; M.A., Laval U., 1947, B.Applied Sci., 1947; postgrad. Ohio State U., 1947, U. Wis., 1947-48; Ph.D., Ill. Inst. Tech., 1953; M.B.A., Northeastern U., 1961; m. Cecile Dube, Sept. 6, 1947; children—Claude, Louise. Came to U.S. 1947, naturalized, 1954. Chemist, Nat. Aluminate Corp., Chgo., 1948-50; engr. Sylvania Electric Products, Boston, 1952-53; mem. research staff Raytheon Co., Waltham, Mass., 1953-58; mgr. materials, mfg. engring. Raytheon Co., Newton, Mass., 1959-60; pres. Electronics Metals and Alloys, Inc., Attleboro, Mass., 1960-64; gen. mgr. Electronized Chems. Corp., 1965, exec. v.p., 1966-67, pres., 1967-73, dir., 1967—; pres., dir. High Voltage Corp., 1970—. Home: Elm St Medfield MA 02052 Office: South Bedford St Burlington MA 01803

LEVEY, ALLAN CHARLES, dentist; b. Detroit, Feb. 4, 1935; s. Jerome and Elsie (Klein) L.; student Wayne State U., 1953, 56, U. Calif., Los Angeles, 1955-56; D.D.S., U. Mich., 1961; M.Oral Surgery, Georgetown U., 1965; m. Marcia Ellen Schofer, Aug. 8, 1966; children—Stephen Keith, Marc Kevin. Intern, Phila. Gen. Hosp., 1961-62; resident Georgetown and D.C. Gen. Hosp., 1962-65; asst. prof. oral surgery U. Md., 1965-66; practice dentistry specializing in oral surgery, Hillcrest Heights, Md., 1966-71, Oxon Hill, 1971—; chmn. dept. oral surgery Cafritz Hosp., Washington, 1969—; adv. bd. Peoples Nat. Bank of Md., Suitland, Md., 1971—. Pres., Prince George County (Md.) chpt. Am. Cancer Soc., 1971-73; vice chmn. Cancer Crusade, 1971; bd. dirs. Md. div. Am. Cancer Soc., state service chmn., 1971-72, chmn. bd., 1974-75. Served with AUS, 1953-55. Diplomate Am. Bd. Oral Surgeons. Mem. ADA, Am., Middle Atlanta, Greater Washington (v.p. 1971-72, pres. 1974—, coordinator health services campaign for election Pres. Ford 1976) socs. oral surgeons, U. Mich. Alumni Assn. (chpt. pres. 1970-72, dir. 2d dist. 1974—), Alpha Omega. Home: 10612 Crossing Creek Rd Potomac MD 20854 Office: 5418 Oxon Hill Rd Oxon Hill MD 20021

LEVI, HENRY THOMAS, gemologist; b. Nanticoke, Pa., May 5, 1941; s. Henry Louis and Elinor Levi; student Shenandoah Coll., 1960-62; B.S., Franklin Pierce Coll., 1966; grad. Canadian Jewellers Inst., 1976; diploma Gemnol. Assn. Gt. Britain, 1977, Gemological Inst.Am. Asst. store mgr. McCrory Corp., N.Y.C., 1966-68; supr. hardgoods Spartan Store, N.Y.C., 1968-70; mgr. Caldors, Peekskill, N.Y., 1970-73; sales mgr. Pomeroys Co., Wilkes-Barre, Pa., 1973-75; owner, gemologist Levi Jewelers, Nanticoke, 1977—; mgr. Musselmans Jewelers, Stroudsburg, Pa. Mem. Gemological Assn. Gt. Britain, Canadian Gemological Assn., Gemological Assn. Australia, Rhodesian Gem and Mineral Soc., Jewelers Vigilance Com., Retail Jewelers Am. Jewish. Editor, Lapidary Jour., 1977, Canadian Gemologist, 1977, Jewellery World, 1977. Home: 103 Prospect St Nanticoke PA 18634 Office: Stroud Mall Stroudsburg PA 18360

LEVI, JOSEPH ABRAHAM, med. center exec.; b. Sarajevo, Yugoslavia, Mar. 9, 1915; s. Abraham and Lenka (Danon) L.; LL.B., U. Belgrade, 1937; M.B.A., N.Y. U., 1953; m. Anita Danon, Apr. 30, 1941 (dec. Aug. 1972); children—Lea, Ruth, Ida, Abigail; m. Frieda Mash, Sept. 23, 1976. Came to U.S., 1950, naturalized, 1956. With bank Drzavna Hipotekarna, Yugoslavia, 1937-41; dir. adminstrn., fin. bur. Am. Joint Distbn. Com., Rome, Italy, 1943-50; mem. payroll dept. United Jewish Appeal, N.Y.C., 1950-52; asst. controller Beth Israel Hosp., N.Y.C., 1952-54; dir. fin. planning L.I. Jewish-Hillside Med. Center, New Hyde Park, N.Y., 1954—. Cons. Mercy Cath. Med. Center, Phila., 1967-73, others; faculty United Hosp. Fund, 1958-65; lectr. staff Columbia Sch. Pub. Health and Adminstrv. Medicine, 1969-75; spl. cons. Greater N.Y. Hosp. Assn., 1973—. Pres., Assn. Yugoslav Jews in U.S., 1958-60; chmn. hosp. controllers advisory com. Blue Cross, 1968—; chmn. hosp. controllers com. Fedn. Jewish Philathropies, 1962-75; chmn. Hosp. League Pension Fund, 1970-75; mem. working group on reimbursement methodologies N.Y. State Council on Health Care Financing, 1978—; mem. tech. advisory com. on health accounting and reporting manual N.Y. State Dept. Health, 1976—. Bd. dirs. Union Orthodox Jewish Congregations in Am., 1967—. Recipient Yeshiva U. award for service to Am. Jewish community, 1966. Fellow Hosp. Financial Mgmt. Assn. (life, Founders award 1961, 68, 72, Spl. award 1972, pres. 1958, 61-62, editor newsletter 1969-70, Frederick C. Morgan Individual Achievement award 1978); mem. Accountants 52 Club, Am., Greater N.Y. hosp. assns., Nat. Assn. Accountants, Internat. Hosp. Fedn. Jewish (pres. congregation 1966-67, 75-77). Mem. B'nai B'rith, B'rith Abraham. Contbr. articles to profl. jours. Home: 611 Lafayette Blvd Long Beach NY 11561 Office: LI Jewish Hillside Med Center New Hyde Park NY 11042

LEVI, MICHAEL MENAHEM, physician; b. Sarajevo, Yugoslavia, Feb. 19, 1929; s. Moric and Lenka (El Azar) Levi; B.A., Gymnasium Sarajevo, 1942; M.S., U. La., 1953; M.D., U. Geneva (Switzerland), 1957, Ph.D., 1958; m. Sharon McAdam, July 16, 1977. Came to U.S., 1958, naturalized, 1960. Intern, Beth Israel Hosp., Newark, 1958-59; resident Beth Israel Hosp., Boston, Malden (Mass.) Hosp., New Eng. Med. Center, Boston, 1959-62; practice medicine specializing in obstetrics and gynecology, Roosevelt Hosp., N.Y.C., 1970-71; clin. dir. O.B.G.Y.N. Assos., N.Y.C., 1971—; asst. dir. dept. obstetrics and gynecology Harlem Hosp., 1965-70, now mem. staff; staff Francis Delafield Hosp., N.Y.C.; asst. clin. prof. Columbia, 1968—; clin. asst. prof. State U. N.Y., 1977—. Cons. Addiction and Research Treatment Center, N.Y.C., 1970—, Harper Row Pubs., N.Y.C., 1971—. Served with Israeli Army, 1948-50. Josiah Macy, Jr. research fellow, 1962-65. Recipient WHO award, 1958; Pan Am. Cancer Cytology Congress award, 1967; Found. prize for thesis Am. Assn. Obstetritians and Gynecologists. Fellow Internat. Coll. Surgery, Am. Coll. Obstetrics and Gynecology, Am. Inst. Chemists, Internat. Coll. Surgery; mem. N.Y. Gynecology Soc. Contbr. articles to profl. jours. Home: 30 Waterside Plaza New York City NY 10010 Office: 999 3d Ave Brooklyn NY 11232

LEVIEN, MAURICE BERYL, civil and archtl. engr.; b. N.Y.C., May 27, 1918; s. Max and Ruth (Kooperstein) L.; B.C.E., N.Y. U., 1938; m. Gloria Anita Siff, June 18, 1946; children—David Harold, Philip Alan. Constrn. engr., 1938-41; archtl. and engring. designer Pub. Works Dept., 15th Naval Dist., C.Z., 1941-43; with constrn. and archtl. engring. firms, N.Y.C., 1946-49; pres., Maurice B. Levien & Co., N.Y.C., 1949—; tchr. archtl. engring. N.Y. U., N.Y.C., 1939; engring. cons. City of N.Y., 1949—, Arlen Realty & Devel. Corp., 1960—, others. Served with AUS, 1944-46. Recipient Queens C. of C. awards of archtl. design, 1964, 65, 66; S.I. C. of C. award, 1964; registered profl. engr. 20 states; certified Nat. Council Engring. Examiners. Fellow ASCE; mem. Nat. Soc. Profl. Engrs., Am. Soc. Mil. Engrs., Am. Legion. Home: 45 Sutton Pl S New York City NY 10022 Office: 305 E 46th St New York City NY 10017

LEVIN, DOUGLAS CLIFTON, psycholanalyst; b. London, Jan. 20, 1921; s. Henry Bartholemew and Martha McPhee (Davis) L.; M.B. B.S., U. London, Eng., 1951; diploma in psychiatry McGill U., 1958; m. Gillian Suzanne Higgs, Dec. 21, 1946; children—Charles Douglas, Henry John; m. 2d, Jacqueline Anne Collis, Jan. 14, 1967. Intern, Gen. Hosp. Bishop Auckland, U.K., 1951-52; resident Montreal Gen. Hosp., 1952-56, Montreal Children's Hosp., 1955-56, Montreal Gen. Hosp., 1955-56; asst. prof. McGill U., Montreal, 1964; psychanalyst Canadian Psychoanalytic Soc., Montreal, 1967; cons. physician Jewish Gen. Hosp., Montreal, 1976. Served to capt. Royal Arty., 1939-45. Mem. Canadian Psychoanalytic Soc., Canadian Psychoanalytic Inst., Royal Soc. Medicine. Home and Office: 176 Bedbrook Ave Montreal West PQ H4X 1R9 Canada

LEVIN, EDGAR WILLIAM, diversified industries co. exec.; b. Bronx, N.Y., Mar. 19, 1932; s. Herman and Frances (Kurland) L., B.S., N.Y. U., 1953; M.B.A., L.I. U., 1968; m. Carole Cynthia Citron, Apr. 3, 1955; children—Randi, Gregg. Market analyst Nat. Elec. Mfrs. Assn., N.Y.C., 1959-61; market research mgr. Metco Inc., Westbury, N.Y., 1961-66; marketing mgr. Inter-Royal Corp., N.Y.C., 1966-69; v.p. market planning Gulf & Western Industries, N.Y.C., 1969—; instr. marketing Hunter Coll., 1970-75, Fordham U., 1976—; dir. Kayser-Roth Co., Sega Enterprises. Active Little League, Basketball League. Served with U.S. Army, 1953-55. Mem. Am. Marketing Assn., Automotive Market Research Council, Am. Mgmt. Assn., Sugar Club, Internat. Exec. Assn. Home: 2123 Beverly Way Merrick NY 11566 Office: 1 Gulf & Western Plaza New York City NY 10023

LEVIN, FELICE MICHAELS (MRS. HARRY C. LEVIN), pub. affairs cons.; b. Chgo., Mar. 21, 1928; d. Harry and Fannie (Litz) Michaels; B.A. in Journalism, U. Wis., 1949, M.A. in Mass Communication and Polit. Sociology, 1967; m. Harry C. Levin, Feb. 25, 1968. Continuity writer sta. WISC, Madison, Wis., 1950-51; asst. for pub. contacts State Hist. Soc. Wis., Madison, 1951-53; dir. publs. U. Wis. Extension Div., Madison, 1953-57; staff writer Wis. State Jour., Madison, 1957-65; cons. Ford Found., N.Y.C., 1968—, WNET, 1970, Vera Inst. Justice and Community Action for Legal Services, N.Y.C. Pres., Wis. Women's Legislative Council, 1960-64, Temple Beth El, Madison, 1963-64. Mem. N.Y.C. Women in Communications, Madison Art Assn., Madison LWV, Phi Kappa Phi, Theta Sigma Phi, Sigma Epsilon Sigma. Jewish. Club: Overseas Press. Address: 360 E 72d St New York City NY 10021

LEVIN, HARRY MATTHEW, food processing exec.; b. Phila., July 5, 1903; s. Benjamin and Mollie (Schmit) L.; student U. Del., 1920-21; A.B., Temple U., 1924; spl. courses Phila. Coll. Pharmacy and Sci., 1927-28; m. Freda Harris, May 4, 1929; 1 son, Stephen Leslie. Tchr. comml. subjects night schs., food distrbr. Gelfand Foods Co., before 1932; founder, pres. Golden Brand Food Products Co., 1932-47, pres. successor corp. Cream Wipt Foods, Inc., 1947-60, sold patent and trademark to Gen. Foods Corp., adopted new name Lamaze Foods, Inc., 1960, merged with Recipe Foods, Inc. (became HCA Food Corp. subsidiary Hotel Corp. Am., now Doxee Food Corp.), became v.p., 1964-74; acquired Vogeler Mayonnaise Co., 1956, now pres.; acquired Trim Foods, Inc., 1956—, pres., 1956—. Mem. Inst. Food Technologists U.S., Am. Hist. Assn. Patentee on cream dressings, mayonnaise, also dairy salad dressing in aerosol container. Home and Office: 128 W Phil Ellena St Philadelphia PA 19119

LEVIN, JAMES BENESCH, educator; b. Balt., Mar. 9, 1940; s. Albert A. and Gertrude (Benesch) L.; B.A., U. Md., 1961; J.D., Columbia U., 1964, M.A., 1965; Ph.D., City U. N.Y., 1970. Tchr., Fieldston Sch., Riverdale, N.Y., 1964-67; faculty Coll. City N.Y., N.Y.C., 1967—, prof. history, 1972—. Mem. state bd. dirs. Am. for Democratic Action, 1976—, N.Y. del. to nat. bd. dirs., 1976—. Mem. Am. Hist. Assn., Orgn. Am. Historians, Common Cause (N.Y. gov. bd.). Home: 59 W 82d St New York City NY 10024 Office: College City of New York 311 Mott Hall New York City NY 10031

LEVIN, JOSEPH DAVID, microbiologist; b. N.Y.C., Feb. 7, 1918; s. Irving and Anna (Brener) L.; B.S., Queens Coll., 1941; m. Carol S. Silverman, Aug. 31, 1947; children—Jonathan, Susanna. With E.R. Squibb & Sons, New Brunswick, N.J., 1947—, sr. scientist, 1964-69, lab. supr., 1969—. Served with AUS, 1942-45; ETO. Recipient Man of Yr. award Nat. Fedn. Jewish Men's Clubs, 1977. Mem. Am. Assn. Microbiology, N.Y. Acad. Scis., Jewish War Vets. (comdr., 1960-61). Contbr. articles to profl. jours. Patentee in field. Home: 244 Benner St Highland Park NJ 08904 Office: Georges Rd New Brunswick NJ 08903

LEVIN, MICHAEL N., assn. exec.; b. Israel, Mar, 21, 1945; s. Itzhak and Suzann (Ashkenazi) L.; came to U.S., 1970, naturalized, 1973; B.A. in Archtl. Engring., Haifa (Israel) Technion, 1969; postgrad. Wharton Sch. Bus., U. Pa.; m. Hannah Zepkowitz, Mar. 25, 1972; 1 dau., Suzanne Leigh. Engr., Esso (Exxon), Denmark, 1969; archtl. engr. Israeli Govt., 1969-72; engr. Service Master, Inc., Valley Forge, Pa. and Chgo., 1976; archtl. engr. Pine Run Community, Doylestown, Pa., 1977; v.p. Life Care Soc. Am., Doylestown, 1977—; pres. Overseas Connections, Inc., investment mgmt., Phila., 1978—; cons. health care facilities, constrn. sites, housing devel.; realtor, notary pub. Served with Israeli Army, 1963-65. Mem. Am. Soc. Hosp. Engrs., Am. Hosp. Assn., Am. Mgmt. Assn., Nat. Fire Protection Assn., Youth Orgn. Israel. Home: 7625 Horrocks St Philadelphia PA 19152

LEVIN, MORTON LOEB, physician, educator; b. Tbilisi, Russia, Aug. 25, 1903; s. Isaac and Esther (Pogorelskin) L.; student Johns Hopkins, 1920-22, M.P.H., 1934, D.P.H., 1935; Ph.D., U. Md., 1924, M.D. summa cum laude, 1930; m. Helen Alpert, June 15, 1927; children—Brett Levin Bernstein, Hilary Levin Mindlin. Intern Sinai Hosp., Balt., 1930-31, resident asst. resident in medicine, 1931-32; practice medicine specializing in internal medicine, Balt., 1932-33; vis. prof. epidemiology Sch. Hygiene and Pub. Health Johns Hopkins, 1967—; mem. staffs Johns Hopkins Hosp., Balt., 1932-34, Roswell Park Meml. Hosp., Buffalo, 1936-40; asso. dir. N.Y. State Legis. Cancer Commn., 1938-39; asso. dir. div. cancer control N.Y. State Dept. Health, 1939-46, dir., 1946-47, asst. commr. dept. health, 1947-59; med. dir. N.Y. State Legis. Commn. to Formulate Health Program, 1947; dir. Nat. Commn. on Chronic Illness, 1950-51. Recipient Herman Biggs award N.Y. State, 1959; Haven Emerson award N.Y. State Acad. Preventive Medicine, 1962; John Snow award Am. Pub. Health Assn., 1978; Am. Cancer Soc. Research fellow, 1959-67. Mem. Am. Epidemiol. Soc., AAAS (council 1955), Am. Assn. Cancer Research. Jewish. Co-author 3 books on cancer and pub. health; contbr. numerous articles to profl. publs. Home: 349 Homeland South Way Baltimore MD 21212 Office: 615 N Wolfe St Baltimore MD 21205

LEVIN, MURRAY NEWMAN, surgeon; b. Burlington, Vt., Jan. 14, 1918; s. Charles and Sophie (Newman) L.; B.S., U. Vt., 1939, M.D., 1943; m. Patricia E. deYoung, June 6, 1948; children—Susan E. Levin Davis, C. Betsy Levin Adelman. Intern, New Rochelle Hosp., 1943-44; resident Mt. Sinai Hosp., N.Y.C., 1947-48; ward surgeon VA Hosp., Hampton, Va., 1948-50; ward surgeon VA Hosp., Manchester, N.H., 1950-56, asst. chief surg. service, 1956-58, chief surg. service, 1958-62; acting chief VA Hosp., Dayton, Ohio, 1963; chief surg. service VA Hosp., Rutland, Mass., 1963-65; mem. active staff Holden (Mass.) Dist. Hosp., 1965—, chief surg. service, 1976-78, chief of staff, 1976-78, emergency room physician, 1978—; mem. courtesy staff Hahnemann Hosp., Worcester, Mass., 1965—; cons. surgery Rutland Heights State Hosp., 1966—; asst. clin. prof. surgery Boston U. Sch. Medicine, 1959-61. Served to capt. M.C., U.S. Army, World War II. Diplomate Am. Bd. Surgery. Fellow A.C.S.; mem. Worcester Dist. Med. Soc., AMA, Mass. Med. Soc. Jewish. Home: 55 Appletree Ln Holden MA 01520 Office: Holden Hosp Holden MA 01520

LEVIN, ROBERT, engring. exec.; b. Bklyn., Feb. 12, 1942; s. Maurice and Goldie (Golub) L.; B.E.E., City U. N.Y., 1964; M.E.E., Poly. Inst. N.Y., 1968; M.B.A., L.I. U., 1977; m. Renee Sandra Homler, May 31, 1964; 1 son, Gary Brian. Sr. engr. Digital Electronics Inc., Westbury, N.Y., 1964-66; group leader div. Control Data Corp., Melville, N.Y., 1966-68; dep. dir. microwave products Comtech Telecommunications Corp., Smithtown, N.Y., 1968—; instr. elec. engring. N.Y. Inst. Tech., 1967-69, specialized engring. subjects, profl. groups. Recipient Charles Marlies Award for community service, 1964. Mem. Electronic Industries Assn. (com. small earth stas.), IEEE (bus. mgr. L.I. sect.), Tau Beta Pi, Eta Kappa Nu, Delta Mu Delta. Jewish. Contbr. articles in field to profl. publs. Home: 36 Westcliff Dr Mount Sinai NY 11766 Office: 135 Engineers Rd Smithtown NY 11787

LEVIN, ROGER M., C.P.A.; b. Easton, Pa., June 14, 1925; s. Louis M. and Dora (Novick) L.; B.A. in Econs., Pa. State U., 1948; postgrad. Columbia U., Lehigh U. Grad. Sch. Bus.; m. Patricia Wolf, July 6, 1962; children—Cathy, Jonathan, Nancy, Andrew. Owner, Chief Levin's Men's Store, Easton, 1960-68, Hen House Stores, Pa., N.J., Conn., 1965-76; acct. C.P.A. firm, Bethlehem, Pa., 1976-78; individual practice pub. accounting, Bethlehem and Easton, 1978—; lectr. acctg. Lehigh U., 1978, Northampton County Community Coll., Bethlehem, 1977, Allentown Coll., Center Valley, Pa., 1977. Bd. dirs. Easton Sch. Dist., 1960-65, Easton United Fund, 1960; founder, dir. Downtown Improvement Group, Easton, 1960. Served with AUS, 1943-45 C.P.A., Pa. Mem. Am. Inst. C.P.A.'s, Pa. Inst. C.P.A.'s, Nat. Assn. Accountants, Easton C. of C. (past dir.). Clubs: Northampton County Country. Home: 104 Pine Top Trail Bethlehem PA 18017 Office: 215 E Broad St Bethlehem PA 18018

LEVIN, RUBEN, editor; b. Warsaw, Poland, Aug. 2, 1902; s. Benjamin D. and Ida (Gochlik) L.; brought to U.S., 1904, naturalized, 1917; B.A., U. Wis., 1930; m. Bertha G. Greenberg, June 7, 1931; children—Hilda Levin Tanenholtz, David A., Jonathan H. Reporter, copyreader on various dailies, 1924-38; with Labor Newspaper, 1938—, editor, mgr., 1953—. Recipient award for distinguished service to journalism U. Wis., 1965, also awards Sidney Hillman Found.; named Dean of U.S. Labor Editors, Internat. Labor Press Assn. and Eugene V. Debs Found. Mem. Am. Newspaper Guild, Assn. R.R. Editors (pres.). Democrat. Jewish. Contbr. articles to profl. jours.; contbr. Grolier-Americana Ency. Yearbook. Home: 2712 Blaine Dr Chevy Chase MD 20015 Office: 400 1st St NW Washington DC 20001

LEVIN, S. BENEDICT, geologist, engr.; b. New Orleans, July 9, 1910; s. Israel Herman and Rose (Oppenheim) L.; A.B., Columbia, 1931, B.S., 1932, E.M., 1933, Ph.D., 1948; m. Helen Kleinberg, June 16, 1936; children—David, Roger. Mining geologist, U.S. and C.Am., 1933-37; instr. geology Hunter Coll., 1937-42; mining geologist U.S. Bur. Mines, northeastern U.S., 1942-45; research scientist Army Electronics Command, Ft. Monmouth, N.J., 1945-60; research dir. Inst. Exploratory Research, Ft. Monmouth, 1960-68; asst. dir. research Office Def. Research and Engring., Office Sec. Def., Pentagon, 1968-70; exec. v.p. Earth Satellite Corp., Washington, 1970-76; research prof. engring. and applied sci. George Washington U., 1976—; dir. Earth Satellite Corp., Eureka Resource Assos., Inc.; cons. remote sensing for resource devel. Registered profl. engr., D.C. Fellow Geol. Soc. Am., Mineral. Soc. Am., Am. Geophys. Union, AAAS; mem. Am. Inst. Mining Engrs., Am. Soc. Photogrammetry, Phi Beta Kappa, Sigma Xi, Tau Beta Pi. Club: Cosmos (Washington). Contbr. articles on geology, mineral deposits, mineralogy and geophys. research to profl. jours. Home: 4301 Massachusetts Ave NW Washington DC 20016 Office: George Washington U Washington DC 20052

LEVIN, SIMON, psychologist; b. Bklyn., July 20, 1922; s. Aaron and Sonia Yoshelofsky; B.S., Rutgers U., 1948; M.S. magna cum laude, U. Paris (France), 1950. Sr. radiation technician Frances Delafield Hosp., N.Y.C., 1951-52; research asst. Lenox Hill Hosp., N.Y.C., 1953-56; research scientist Coll. Engring. Research div. N.Y. U., 1956-58; research asso. Courtney & Co., Inc., Phila., 1958-59; human factors sr. engr. Martin Co., Denver 1959-64; sr. engring. specialist Brown Engring. Co., Huntsville, Ala., 1964-65; engring. scientist, specialist Douglas Aircraft Co., Long Beach, Calif., 1965-71; self-employed as human resources cons., Bklyn., 1971; ops. analyst Office of Mayor, N.Y.C. Model City Adminstrn., 1971-72, N.Y.C. Dept. Mental Health, 1972-75; dir. program evaluation Rockland Psychiat. Center, Orangeburg, N.Y., 1975-77, Kingsboro Psychiat. Center, Bklyn., 1977—; guest lectr. psychology Sch. for Restorative Art, N.Y.C.; vol. visitor psychometrician, lectr. psychology of handicapped Handicapped Childrens Home Service, N.Y.C.; interpreter U. Paris Conf. on Animal Socs.; cons. Operation PEP, 1967; human resources analyst Opportunities Industrialization Center, also mem. bd. dirs. Long Beach div., 1967—. Served with USAAF, 1942-45. Mem. N.Y. Acad. Scis., AAAS, Human Factors Soc., Soc. for Gen. Systems Research. Contbr. articles to profl. jours. Home: 1229 Ave Y 2F Brooklyn NY 11235 Office: Kingsboro Psychiat Center Brooklyn NY 11203

LEVIN, TOM, psychologist; b. N.Y.C., June 23, 1924; s. Charles and Rheta Levin; B.A., L.I. U., 1949; M.A., N.Y. U., 1950, Ph.D., 1961; certificate Nat. Psychol. Assn. for Psychoanalysis Inst., 1957; m. Ronny Diamond, Apr. 21, 1977; children—Erica, Jed, Kate, Clement, Natasha, Jason. Individual practice psychology, N.Y.C., 1950—; supr. Theodore Reik Clinic, 1956-58; research, staff psychologist Baldwin Sch., N.Y.C., 1959-60; dir. group therapy N.Y. Clinic for Mental Health, 1962-65, sr. clin. dir., 1963-65; asst. prof. psychiatry Albert Einstein Coll. Medicine, 1966-73, asst. prof. community health, 1967-73; pvt. practice psychoanalysis, psychotherapy, supervision, 1973—; faculty Nat. Psychol. Assn. for Psychoanalysis Inst., 1962-75, New Sch. for Social Research, 1973-76, Columbia U., 1976-77; founder, coordinator Child Devel. Group Miss., 1963-65, dir., 1965. Founder, coordinator com. of conscience Med. Com. for Human Rights, 1964-65; mem. Manhattan Borough Pres.'s Adv. Com. on Health Manpower, 1967. Served with USNR, 1942-46. Commonwealth Found. grantee, 1968-71; Citizens Crusade Against Poverty grantee, 1965. Fellow Am. Group Psychotherapy Assn. (Inst. award 1970), Am. Orthopsychiat. Assn.; mem. Am. Psychol. Assn., Nat. Psychol. Assn. for Psychoanalysis. Contbr. articles in field to profl. jours. Home: 159 W 88th St New York NY 10024

LEVIN, WILLIAM HAROLD, librarian, educator; b. Bentleyville, Pa., Sept. 30, 1926; s. Morris and Elizabeth (Amdur) L.; A.B., U. Pitts., 1949, M.Litt., 1950, M.L.S., 1965. Tchr. Latin and English, Wisner (Nebr.) High Sch., 1950-51, Latin, French, history Springdale (Pa.) High Sch., 1951-53, Latin, English social studies Prospect Jr. High Sch., Pitts., 1953-55; tchr. Latin, English, French, Spanish, Taylor Allderdice High Sch., Pitts., 1955-61, chmn. dept. fgn. langs., 1961-62; tchr. Latin, French, English, Schenley High Sch., Pitts., 1962-66; librarian Conroy Jr. High Sch., Pitts., 1966-67, Peabody High Sch., Pitts., 1967-70, 71—; librarian Pitts. Bd. Edn. Profl. Library, 1970-71. Lectr. French, Spanish, Point Park Coll., Pitts., 1962-68. Librarian, Rodef Shalom Temple, Pitts., 1957-59, 67-68. Served with AUS, 1955. Mem. Modern Lang. Assn. Pitts. (corr. sec. 1960-61, pres. 1961-62), ALA, Pa. Sch. Library Assn., Am., Pa., Pitts. fedn. tchrs., Pitts. Council Suburban Libraries, Met. Opera Guild, Buffalo Fine Arts Acad., Pitts. Symphony Soc., Carnegie Inst., Pitts. Hist. and Landmarks Found., Beta Phi Mu. Democrat. Jewish. Contbr. to Spanish lang. sect. Modern Lang. Methodology Manual, Pitts. Pub. Schs., 1961. Home: Univ Sq Apts 708 4625 5th Ave Pittsburgh PA 15213 Office: Peabody High Sch Library 515 N Highland Ave Pittsburgh PA 15206

LEVINE, ARTHUR J., accountant; b. Bklyn., July 2, 1916; s. Louis L. and Esther (Goodman) L.; B.S., N.Y. U., 1939; student New Sch. Social Research, 1949-62; m. Rosalind E. Kopman, June 22, 1941; children—Nancy Deborah, Helen Susan, Betty Ann. Chief tech. and review br. U.S. Army Audit Agy., N.Y.C., 1949-52; pvt. practice as C.P.A., N.Y.C., 1952—; cons. Exec. bd. United Synagogues Am., 1962—, pres. N.Y. met. region, 1964-66, v.p., 1961-64, nat. treas., 1967-69, nat. v.p., 1967, nat. pres., 1973-77; pres. Merrick Jewish Center, 1952-54; pres. Jewish Community Relations Council N.Y., 1967-69; mem. exec. com. Synagogue Council Am., 1971—; v.p. Nat. Conf. on Soviet Jewry, 1976—; mem. nat. Jewish com. on scouting Boy Scouts Am., 1973—. Served with Signal Corps, AUS, 1942-49. Mem. Am. Inst. C.P.A.'s, World Zionist Orgn. (exec.), Conf. of Presidents of Major Jewish Orgns., Phi Alpha. Club: 101. Author articles. Home: 27 Wooleys Ln E Great Neck NY 11021 Office: 192 Lexington Ave New York City NY 10016

LEVINE, ARTHUR LOUIS, educator; b. Cleve., Nov. 23, 1929; s. Robert and Mollie (Bremson) L.; A.B., Western Res U., 1950, M.A., 1952, Ph.D., Columbia U., 1963; m. Israela Efros, June 12, 1949; children—David Lloyd, Karen Susan. Asst. civil service examiner CSC Cleve., 1952-53; research asst. Am. Fedn. State, County and Municipal Employees, N.Y.C., 1954-55; supr. tech. recruitment Lewis Flight Propulsion Lab., NASA, Cleve., 1955-58, mgr. research staffing Lewis Research Center, 1958-61, exec. officer Goddard Inst. Space Studies, N.Y.C., 1961-73; asso. prof. pub. adminstrn. Baruch Coll., City U. N.Y., 1973—, lectr. polit. sci., pub. adminstrn., 1965-70, adj. asso. prof. dept. polit. sci., 1970-72; lectr. polit. sci., pub. adminstrn. Western Res. U., 1952, 56-61, Coll. City N.Y., 1954-55, Adelphi U., 1964, Hunter Coll., 1964-65, N.Y. U., 1968. Co-chmn. task force on employee edn. and tng. N.Y. Fed. Exec. Bd., 1966-72. Mem. Am. Soc. Pub. Adminstrn. (chpt. pres. 1973-74, editor chpt. Monograph Series 1970-73, co-chmn. sect. sci. and tech. in govt. 1976—, nat. council 1977—), AAAS, Am. Polit. Sci. Assn. Author: The Future of the U.S. Space Program, 1975; supervising editor: Educational Opportunities in Public Administration: A Directory for the New York City Area, 2d edit., 1971; editorial bd. Pub. Adminstrn. Rev., 1978—. Home: 463 Dunster Ct West Hempstead NY 11552 Office: 17 Lexington Ave New York City NY 10010

LEVINE, BERNARD, safety engr.; b. Bklyn., Oct. 5, 1918; s. David and Lena (Pinsky) L.; student Queens Coll., 1962-63; certificate Center for Safety Edn., N.Y. U., 1968; student Delehanty Inst., 1950-58; m. Yetta Zbar, June 13, 1954; children—Gary Michael, Martin Douglas. Safety officer and fireman N.Y.C. Fire Dept., 1943-57, lt., 1957-64; asst. ground safety officer Suffolk County AFB, N.Y., 1965; loss control engr. Gen. Fire & Casualty Co., N.Y.C., 1965-68, Kemper Ins. Co., N.Y.C., 1969-74; safety officer Mil. Ocean Terminal, Bayonne, N.J., 1974-75; dir. safety and fire prevention Brookdale Hosp. Med. Center, Bklyn., 1975—. Safety coordinator Jr. Achievement, N.Y.C., 1960-63. Served in U.S. Army, 1942-46. Certified safety profl. Mem. Am. Soc. Safety Engrs. Club: K.P. Contbr. articles to profl. publs. Home: 2280 E 22 St Brooklyn NY 11229 Office: Brookdale Hosp Med Center Brooklyn NY 11212

LE VINE, DAVID ELIOT, assn. exec.; b. N.Y.C., June 22, 1933; s. Harry L. and Esther (Hartman) LeV.; B.A., Harvard U., 1955; LL.B., Columbia U., 1960; m. Barbara Ann Grande, Mar. 1, 1974. Legal asst. Dramatists Guild, Inc., N.Y.C., 1960-61, asst. exec. sec., 1961-66, exec. sec., 1966—; dir. Internat. Theatre Inst.-Am. Center; founder, bd. dirs. Theatre Script Center for Hearing Impaired, Inc. Served as ensign USNR, 1955-57. Club: Harvard of N.Y.C. Home: 315 E 68th St New York City NY 10021 Office: 234 W 44th St New York City NY 10036

LEVINE, EDNA SIMON, coll. educator. M.A. in Spl. Edn., Columbia, 1942; M.A. in Clin. Psychology, N.Y. U., 1939, Ph.D. in Clin. Psychology, 1948; Litt.D., Gallaudet Coll., 1969. Prof., N.Y. U., 1960-65, prof. emeritus, 1975—. Bd. dirs. Interbranch Library Assn. Manhattan. Recipient Internat. Merit award 1st class World Fedn. Deaf; diplomate clin. psychology Am. Bd. Profl. Psychology; certified in clin. psychology, N.Y. State, Fellow Am. Psychol. Assn.; mem. Conv. Am. Instrs. of the Deaf, Profl. Rehab. Workers with the Deaf, Alexander Graham Bell Assn. for the Deaf, Phi Beta Kappa. Author: Youth in a Soundless World; Psychology of Deafness; (with James F. Garrett) Psychological Aspects of Physical Disability; (with Garrett) Rehabilitation Practices with the Physically Disabled; Lisa and Her Soundless World; mem. editorial/editorial adv. bds. American Annals of Deaf, The Volta Review in Mental Health Deafness. Specialist in the psychol. aspects of deafness. Home: 170 E 78th St New York NY 10021

LEVINE, GEORGE, lawyer; b. Hartford, Conn., May 12, 1938; s. I. Oscar and Selma R. (Katz) L.; B.A., Yale, 1960; LL.B., Columbia, 1963; m. Suzanne S. Miller, Jan. 17, 1975; children by previous marriage—Elizabeth, Andrew, Anne, John. Admitted to Conn. bar, 1963; asso. firm Levine & Katz, Hartford, 1963-68; partner, counsel firm Levine, Katz, Cohn & Goldstein, Hartford, 1968-75; partner firm Sandler & Levine P.C., Hartford, 1975—. Dir. Greater Hartford Housing Devel. Fund, Inc., Capitol Region Devel. Corp. Mem. Hartford City Council, 1968-75; commr. Conn. Transp. Authority, 1975; mem. Conn. Gov.'s Transitional Task Force on Transp., 1975; mem., sec. Pub. Utilities Control Authority Reorganization Task Force, Hartford, 1975—; counsel Hartford Democratic Town Com., 1971—; chmn. Hartford Inland Wetlands Agy., 1973-75, Hartford Community Devel. Action Plan Agy., 1971-75; mem. Hartford Model Cities Agy., 1968-74; chmn. young bus. and profl. div. Hartford Jewish Fedn., 1968-69; bd. dirs. Greater Hartford Transit Dist., 1971—, Capitol Region Council Govts., 1972-75, Community Renewal Team of Greater Hartford, 1968-75; corporator Mt. Sinai Hosp., 1974—. Mem. Conn., Hartford County bar assns. Democrat. Jewish. Home: 60 Elizabeth St Hartford CT 06106 Office: 799 Main St Hartford CT 06103

LEVINE, HAROLD A(BRAHAM), clin. psychologist; b. N.Y.C., Apr. 15, 1923; s. Herman and Rose (Eisner) L.; B.A., Bklyn. Coll., 1946; student Oxford U., 1945; M.A., Columbia U., 1949, Ph.D., 1952; postdoctoral certificate in Psychotherapy and Psychoanalysis, N.Y. U., 1967; m. Joan Sarah Price, Apr. 3, 1946; children—Henry, Flora. Instr. med. psychology N.Y. U., 1952-53; staff psychologist Northport (N.Y.) VA Hosp., 1953-56; chief psychologist, dir. dept. psychology Meadowbrook Hosp., East Meadow, N.Y., 1956-76; psychologist-in-chief, asst. chmn. dept. psychiatry and psychology Nassau County Med. Center, East Meadow, 1976—; asst. to full clin. prof. Inst. Advanced Psychol. Studies, Adelphi Univ., 1956-78; asso. clin. prof. dept. psychiatry and behavioral scis. State U. N.Y. at Stonybrook, 1978—. Served with U.S. Army, 1944-46. Diplomate Am. Bd. Profl. Psychology. Mem. Am., Eastern, N.Y. State, Nassau County psychol. assns., Soc. Personality Assessment, Nassau Psychol. Services Inst. (sec.-treas. 1977). Home: 42 Deepdale Pkwy Roslyn Heights NY 11577

LEVINE, HYMAN JOSEPH, chem. co. exec.; b. Bklyn., Aug. 11, 1909; s. Joseph and Dora (Alpert) L.; student Columbia U. Sch. Pharmacy, 1931; m. Gertrude Sendrowitz, Mar. 25, 1944; 1 son, Theodore. Owner, mgr. Adams & Nassau Pharmacy, Bklyn., 1931-46, Chelsea Pharmacy, N.Y.C., 1946-49; pres., founder Ruger Chem. Co. Inc., N.Y.C., 1949—; pres. Amend Drug & Chem. Co. Inc., Irvington, N.J., 1965—, GLS Realty Co., 1971—, A & R Sales Corp., 1974—, 500 Chancellor Ave., 1976—. Served with USAAF, 1941. Mem. Drug, Chem., Allied Trades. Jewish. Club: B'nai B'rith. Home: 300 Winston Dr Apt 3009 Cliffside Park NJ 07010 Office: 83 Cordier St Irvington NJ 07111

LEVINE, JOEL PHILIP, engring. mktg. adminstr.; b. Bklyn., Jan. 11, 1948; s. Isidore and Shirley (Tugender) L.; B.M.E., Hofstra U., 1969; M.S. in Metall. Engring., N.Y. U., 1972; M.B.A., Roth Sch. Grad. Bus. Adminstrn., 1974; m. Roberta Atlas, July 12, 1970; 1 dau., Faith Erin. Sr. engr. Nordon div. UAC, Norwalk, Conn., 1969-70; sr. engr. Instrument Systems Corp., Huntington, N.Y., 1970-72; div. mgr. F & S Central, Bklyn., 1972-76; mgr. mktg. and product devel. NPS Industries, Secaucus, N.J., Tex. N.J., 1976—; dir. BSI, Inc. Registered profl. engr., N.Y., N.J. Tex. Mem. ASME, Am. Soc. Metals, Nat. Soc. Profl. Engrs., Am. Soc. Quality Control, Am. Inst. Metall. Engrs., Am. Weld Soc., Am. Nuclear Soc. Home: 337 Blue Hill Terr Wyckoff NJ 07481 Office: NPS Industries One Harmon Plaza Secaucus NJ 07094

LEVINE, NAOMI BRONHEIM, univ. adminstr.; b. N.Y.C., Apr. 15, 1923; d. Nathan and Malvina (Mermelstein) Bronheim; B.A., Hunter Coll., 1941; LL.B., Columbia, 1946, J.D., 1970; m. Leonard Levine, Apr. 11, 1948; 1 dau., Joan. Admitted to N.Y. bar, 1946; with firm Scaadrett, Tuttle & Chalaire, N.Y.C., 1946-48, Charles Gottleib, Esquire, N.Y.C., 1948-50; with Am. Jewish Congress, 1950—, exec. dir., 1972-78; asst. prof. law and police sci. John Jay Coll., N.Y.C., 1969-73. L.I.U., 1965-69; v.p. N.Y. U., 1978—. Bd. dirs. Interracial Council Bus. Opportunities. Recipient Constl. Law prize Hunter Coll., 1944, named to Hall of Fame, 1972. Author: Ocean Hill Brownsville, Schools in Crisis, 1969; The Jewish Poor-an American Awakening, 1974. Mem. staff Columbia Law Rev., 1945-46. Home: 1036 Park Ave New York City NY 10028

LEVINE, RICHARD ALAN, mgmt. cons.; b. Boston, Nov. 17, 1939; s. Bernard and Anne Lillian (Bogg) L.; B.S., Tufts U., 1961; M.S., M.I.T., 1963; m. Elaine Cohen, June 14, 1964; children—Steven, Alissa. Bus. analyst Honeywell, Inc., 1963-65; mgmt. cons. Touche Ross & Co., N.Y.C., from 1965, now partner. Mem. Am. Public Welfare Assn. (mem. health policy com.), Inst. Mgmt. Cons., Soc. Mgmt. Info. Systems. Jewish. Clubs: Atrium, City, Orienta. Home: 285 Rockingstone Ave Larchmont NY 10538 Office: 1633 Broadway New York NY 10019

LEVINE, RICHARD STEVEN, corrosion control co. exec.; b. Pitts., Jan. 14, 1947; s. Ishmael and Rosalind (Freeman) L.; B.S. in Chemistry, Carnegie Inst. Tech., 1968; M.S., U. Ill., Champaign-Urbana, 1971; m. Susan Ellen Abramson, May 4, 1969; 1 dau., Alisa Diane. Chemist, U. Ill., Urbana, 1968-73, Drew Chem. Corp., Boonton, N.J., 1973-74; pres. Indsl. Corrosion Mgmt., Inc., Randolph Twp., N.J., 1974—. Mem. Greater Dover-West Morris C. of C., Am. Chem. Soc., Nat. Assn. Corrosion Engrs. Contbr. chem. articles to profl. jours. Office: 1152 Route 10 Randolph Township NJ 07801

LEVINE, ROBERT JOHN, ednl. co. exec.; b. N.Y.C., Aug. 30, 1921; s. Sol and Beatrice (Langendorfer) L.; M.S., Columbia U., 1948; m. Virginia Arnold, Nov. 27, 1948; children—John R., Margaret Helen. Chief engr. Avien Co., N.Y.C., 1950-55, Edin Co., Worcester, Mass., 1955-57; pres. Magnetic Instruments, Thornwood, N.Y., 1957-64, Nassau Instruments, Princeton, N.J., 1964-69; exec. v.p. Center for Profl. Advancement, East Brunswick, N.J., 1969—. Served with Signal Corps, U.S. Army, 1943-46. Mem. IEEE, Am. Soc. Engring. Educators, Instrument Soc. Am., Soc. Wine Educators (founder, pres. 1977—). Unitarian. Contbr. articles to profl. jours. Patentee aircraft fuel gages. Office: Center for Professional Advancement PO Box H East Brunswick NJ 08816

LEVINE, SOLOMON, clin. psychologist; b. Bklyn., June 7, 1913; s. Isaac and Molly L.; B.A., Bklyn. Coll., 1933; M.S., Coll. City N.Y., 1935; Ph.D., N.Y. U., 1951; m. Beatrice Stern, Nov. 23, 1941; children—Robert Ira, Ronnie Lee. Asst. chief clin. psychologist VA Hosp., Bklyn., 1950-58; chief psychologist Kingsbrook Jewish Med. Center, Bklyn., 1954-71; exec. dir. Nassau-Suffolk Cons. Service, Massapequa, N.Y., 1957-74; exec. dir. psychol. Inst. Counseling and Psychotherapy, Woodmere, N.Y., 1970—; practice psychotherapy, Woodmere, N.Y., 1950—; adj. clin. prof. psychology Grad. Sch., Adelphi U., 1958-61, Inst. Advanced Psychol. Studies, 1971-72. Served with USAAF, 1943-45. Diplomate Am. Bd. Profl. Psychology, Am. Bd. Psychol. Hypnosis. Fellow Am. Psychol. Assn.; mem. Am. Acad. Psychotherapy, N.Y. Acad. Scis., Bklyn. Psychol. Assn. (past pres.). Home: 874 Cherry Ln North Woodmere NY 11581

LEVINE, STEPHEN JAY, dentist; b. N.Y.C., Sept. 25, 1939; s. Harold Jay and Sylvia (Moskowitz) L.; B.S., Alfred U., 1961; D.D.S., Fairleigh Dickinson U., 1964; postgrad. N.Y. U., 1968-71; m. Michiko Suzuki, Nov. 8, 1970; children—Jonathan Yoh, Michael Gen. Individual practice dentistry, River Edge, N.J.; asst. prof. clin. dentistry Fairleigh Dickinson U. Sch. Dentistry, Hackensack, N.J., 1971—; vis. lectr. Tokyo Med. and Dental U. Grad. Sch. Prosthodontics, 1970. Served with Dental Corps, USNR, 1964-67. Mem. Fairleigh Dickinson Dental Sch. Alumni Assn. (pres. 1972-73), Am. Assn. Dental Schs., Am., N.J., Bergen County dental assns., Japan Soc., Omicron Kappa Upsilon. Contbr. articles to profl. jours. Address: 427 Kinderkamack Rd River Edge NJ 07661

LEVINSON, GWEN, psychotherapist; b. N.Y.C., June 6, 1929; d. Harry and Sarah Messer; B.A., Queens Coll., 1961; M.S. in Psychology, City U. N.Y., 1965, Ph.D. in Psychology, 1978; m. Marvin Levinson, Mar. 12, 1949; children—Brad, Randy. In-take St. Vincent's Hosp., N.Y.C., 1961-65; psychotherapist individuals and groups Interboro Psychiat. Center, 1967-70; individual practice psychotherapy, 1968—; supr. New Gestalt Inst. Mem. Am. Psychol. Assn., Am. Group Psychologists Assn., Eastern Group Soc. Democrat. Jewish. Author: The Good Guy Syndrome. Home: 75-35 193d St Flushing NY 11365 Office: 305 E 72d St New York NY 10021

LEVITCH, JOEL ALLEN, owner film prodn. co.; b. Kansas City, Mo., Oct. 5, 1942; s. David and Frances (Brand) L.; B.A. (Ranking scholar 1961-63), Yale, 1964, M.A. in Internat. Relations, 1966; m. Judith Lynn Rabicoff, June 16, 1963; children—Mark, Timothy. News writer CBS, N.Y.C., 1966-67; owner Jason Films, Riverdale, N.Y., 1967—. Recipient Blue Ribbon N.Y. Film Festival, 1970, Silver Hugo Chgo. Film Festival, 1969; Spl. Jury Gold medal Atlanta Film Festival, 1971, CINE Golden Eagle, 1974. Mem. Writers Guild Am. Author: Contraband of War, 1969; The Diary of Eddie Jacobson, 1973. Writer syndicated feature stories Washington Post, Parade mag., Newsday, others. Address: 2621 Palisade Ave Riverdale NY 10463

LEVITT, MORTON HILL, pathologist; b. N.Y.C., May 28, 1946; s. Benjamin and Lillian (Bernard) L.; B.S.E., Princeton U., 1968; M.D. (C.V. Mosby award), Duke U., 1972; m. Roxanne Lois Kogan, June 21, 1970; 1 dau., Lisa Michelle. Intern, Duke U. Med. Center, 1972-73, resident in pathology, 1973-74; research asso. NIH, Bethesda, Md., 1974-76, research pathologist, 1976-78, med. pathologist, 1978—, also acting dir. gastrointestinal tract prostate cancer program, acting mgr. tumor pathology br., 1977—; spl. govt. employee Bur. Foods, FDA, 1978—. Served with USPHS, 1974—. Diplomate Am. Bd. Pathology. Fellow Am. Soc. Clin. Pathologists, Coll. Am. Pathologists; mem. AAAS, AMA (physicians recognition award 1975), Durham Orange County, N.C. med. socs., Assn. Mil. Surgeons U.S., Commd. Officers Assn., Internat. Acad. Pathology, Md., Washington socs. pathologists, Mid-Atlantic Comparative Pathology Colloquy, Soc. Pharmacol. and Environ. Pathologists (councillor, exec. com. 1978—), Washington Soc. History Medicine, Sigma Xi. Clubs: Princeton N.Y. and Washington. Contbr. articles in field to profl. jours. Home: Suite A-24-S 5225 Pooks Hill Rd Bethesda MD 20014 Office: Landow Bldg Bethesda MD 20014

LEVITZ, ETHEL BELLE, guidance counselor; b. N.Y.C., Mar. 21, 1923; d. Harry and Bertha (Vagen) Aaron; B.A., Bklyn. Coll., 1944, M.S. in Guidance and Counseling, 1972; m. Meyer B. Levitz, June 27, 1948; children—Celia, Robert. Mem. staff N.Y.C. Bd. Edn., counselor Vocat. High Sch., Bklyn. Mem. Bklyn. Bur. Community Services. Grantee NSF. Mem. Am. Personnel and Guidance Assn., Student Assn. Advanced Degree (exec. bd.), Biology Tchrs. Assn., Am. Bacteriology Assn., Kappa Delta Pi (past chpt. pres.). Democrat. Jewish. Clubs: Tennis, Ski, Music. Address: 1818 E 21st St Brooklyn NY 11229

LEVKULIC, JOHN JOSEPH, engring. and archtl. co. exec.; b. Hazleton, Pa., Nov. 9, 1932; s. John and Catherine (Quinn) L.; B.S. in Engring., Pa. State U., 1954; m. Isolina Lopez, Feb. 15, 1958; children—John E., Robert S., Karen L., Thomas M., Dawn S. Chief engr. Amporico Constrn. Co., P.R., 1957-62; pres. Penneast Corp., cons. engrs., Pottsville, Pa., 1962—; mng. partner Levkulic Assos., architects and engrs., Tamaqua, Pa., 1970—. Mem. exec. bd. Hawk Mountain council Boy Scouts Am., 1966—. Served with USN, 1955-57. Registered profl. engr., Pa., P.R. Mem. Nat., Pa. (exec. bd. 1970—, also officer) socs. profl. engrs., Pa. Profl. Engrs. in Pvt. Practice (v.p. 1973-76). Club: K.C. Home: Hillside RD 1 Pottsville PA 17901 Office: 541 W Bacon St Pottsville PA 17901

LEVOKOVE, LINDA ANN, interior designer; b. Bklyn., Aug. 8, 1939; d. Irving and Rose (Winick) Gruber; grad. Wilsey Inst. Art and Interior Design, 1967; student in psychology Marymount Coll., 1977—; children—Shari, Jodi, Scott. Free lance interior designer, tchr. interior design, 1967—; owner Linda Levokove Interiors, Stamford, Conn., 1967—; leader dream appreciation workshops, 1978—; counselor women in transition, 1978—. Mem. Women's Place, Darien, Conn., 1977-78; mem. Allied Bd. Trade, N.Y.C., 1967—; mem. Sacia, Stamford, 1977—. Home: 174 Butternut Ln Stamford CT 06903

LEVOW, BARRY, bus. developer; b. New Bedford, Mass., Jan. 17, 1931; s. George Abbott and Amy (Kaplan) L.; B.A., Colby Coll., 1954; postgrad. Northeastern U., 1967-69; m. Judith Lee Holtz, Feb. 22, 1955; children—Faye Elizabeth, Lawrence Nathan. Pres., G.A. Levow, Inc., 1954—; owner, treas. Met. Centers for Speech and Hearing Therapy, Inc., West Newton, Mass., 1970—; treas., co-founder Little People's Sch., Inc., 1970—; treas., gen. mgr. Mobile Acoustic Systems Corp., 1971-75; treas., founder Centers for Human Devel., 1971-73; pres., treas. Levow/Nichols Co., 1975-77. Mem. Mass. Dept. Pub. Health Task Force Team on Guidelines for Speech and Hearing Centers, 1970, mem. task force team on nursing home homebound patient care for speech and hearing centers, 1972. Certified Coll. Hearing and Speech Adminstrs. Mem. Mass. Hearing Aid Soc. (pres.), Mass. Assn. Sch. Bus. Ofcls., Acoustical Soc. Am., Am. Audiology Soc., Nat. Hearing Aid Soc., Am. Inst. Physics. Home: 380 Winter St Weston MA 02193 Office: 1507 Washington St PO Box 182 West Newton MA 02165

LEVY, ADRIAN, vocat. rehab. adminstr., state ofcl.; b. N.Y.C., Apr. 4, 1915; s. Samuel Harry and Libbie (Margolius) L.; B.S., Coll. City N.Y., 1938; M.A., N.Y. U., 1950; m. Dorothy Rosenfield, June 16, 1940; 1 son, Kenneth Daniel. Research worker, vocat. guidance counselor Fed. Employment Service, 1940-43; asst. chief spl. rehab. advisement unit N.Y. regional office VA., 1946-51; asst. regional rep. N.Y. regional office Vocat. Rehab. Adminstrn., HEW, N.Y.C., 1951-53, regional rep., 1953-56; asst. commr. vocat. rehab. N.Y. State Edn. Dept., Albany, 1956-70, asso. commr., 1970—; cons. in field; profl. adv. com. Assn. Crippled Children and Adults N.Y. State, 1959-75; rehab. adv. panel Vocat. Rehab. Adminstrn., HEW, 1962-66; adv. com. N.Y. State Workmen's Compensation Bd., 1961-72, 77—; com. study rehab. facilities U.S. Surgeon Gen.'s Office, 1961-63; N.Y. State adv. council mental retardation facilities, 1965-70; N.Y. State developmental disabilities adv. council, 1970—. Served with USAAF, 1943-46. Certified psychologist, N.Y. State. Mem. Nat. Rehab. Assn., Am. Psychol. Assn., Am., N.Y. personnel and guidance assns., Am., Nat. rehab. counselors assns., Nat. Vocat. Guidance Assn., Rehab. Internat., N.Y. State Pub. Health Assn., Council State Adminstrs. Vocat. Rehab. (pres. 1972-73). Home: 76 Jordan Blvd Delmar NY 12054 Office: 99 Washington Ave Albany NY 12230

LEVY, ALAN JOSEPH, author; b. N.Y.C., Feb. 10, 1932; s. Meyer and Frances (Shield) L.; A.B., Brown U., 1952; M.S., Columbia, 1953; m. Valerie Wladaver, Aug. 7, 1956; children—Monica, Erika. Reporter, Louisville Courier-Jour., 1953-60; free lance contbr. to Life, Saturday Evening Post, N.Y. Times Mag., Harper's, Reader's Digest, Art News, Good Housekeeping, and others, 1960—; investigator for Carnegie Commn. on ednl. TV, 1966-67; corr., Czechoslovakia, 1967-71; expelled, 1971; free lance writer, Vienna, 1971—; dramaturg (script and program cons.) Vienna's English Theatre, 1977—; trustee Thomas Nast Found., Landau, W. Ger., 1978. Served with AUS, 1953-55. Recipient New Republic Younger Writer award, 1958, Sigma Delta Chi award, 1959; Bernard DeVoto fellow Bread Loaf Writers' Conf., Middlebury Coll., Vt., 1963. Mem. Fgn. Press Assn. Vienna, Overseas Press Club, Authors Guild, P.E.N., Am. Soc. Journalists and Authors. Author: Draftee's Confidential Guide, 1957; Operation Elvis, 1960; The Elizabeth Taylor Story, 1961; Wanted: Nazi Criminals at Large, 1962; Interpret Your Dreams, 1962; Kind-Hearted Tiger, 1964; The Culture Vultures, 1968; God Bless You Real Good, 1969; Rowboat to Prague, 1972; Good Men Still Live, 1974; The Bluebird of Happiness, 1976; Forever, Sophia, 1979; contbr. author: American Colloquy, 1963; Casebook On Waiting for Godot, 1967; College Reading and Writing, 1968; Marilyn Monroe-A Composite View, 1969. Home: Bennogasse 8/7 1080 Vienna 8 Austria Office: care Alexandria Hatcher Lit Agy 150 W 55th St New York City NY 10019

LEVY, BENJAMIN, artist; b. Tel-Aviv, Israel, Feb. 28, 1940; s. Ovadia and Bat-Sheva (Mizrachi) Mahum-Levy; student Meirovitch and Yaskil Art Sch., Haifa, Israel, 1957-58, Ecole DeMont Parnass, Paris, France, 1959, Pratt Graphic Art Center, 1966-67; m. Hanna Vroman, Oct. 10, 1962; children—Ofer, Bat-Sheva, Amnon. Came to U.S., 1965, naturalized, 1970. Exhibited one man shows Dugit Gallery, Tel-Aviv, 1961, Tchermerinsky Gallery, Tel-Aviv, 1964, Israeli Art Gallery, N.Y.C., 1966, Morris Gallery, Woodstock, N.Y., 1966, Everyman Gallery, N.Y.C., 1968, 71, Morris Gallery, N.Y.C., 1969, New Haven Jewish Center, 1970, Aleph Gallery, Mexico City, Mexico, 1971, Miami Mus. Modern Art, 1971, Graphic Art Gallery, Tel-Aviv, 1971, Galerias Del Centro Depurtivo, Mexico City, 1972, Nat. Mus. Panama, 1973, Carol Halsband Gallery, N.Y.C., 1973, Israel Art Gallery, N.Y.C., 1973, Gallery T, Amsterdam, 1975, 76, Tel-Aviv Mus., 1976, Delson Richter Galleries, Jaffa and Jerusalem, 1976, La Cadre Gallery, Toronto, Ont., Can., 1976, Mus. Modern Art, Utrecht, Holland, 1978, Galerij 565, Aalst, Belgium, 1978, Wetering Gallery, Amsterdam, Holland, 1978, Palm Springs (Calif.) Mus., 1978; exhibited group shows Georgetown Gallery, Washington, 1969, Mus. Modern Art, Utrecht, Holland, 1972, Mus. Tel-Aviv, 1973, Cabinet, Sao Paula, Brazil, 1977, and numerous others; represented in permanent collections Haifa Mus. Modern Art, Pub. Library N.Y.C., Mus. Detroit, Miami Mus. Modern Art, Utrecht Mus. Modern Art, Nat. Mus. Panama, Joseph Hirshhorn Mus., Stedelejke Mus., Amsterdam, Skirball Mus., Calif., several other pvt., pub. collections. Illustrator children's books Bobbs Merrill Co.; illustrator yearly UN envelope, also lithographs, 1976. Recipient prizes Young Israeli Artists, 1965; Helena Rubenstein Norman Fund, 1966; Audubon Artists, 1969. Address: 317 W 89th St New York City NY 10024

LEVY, BEVERLEE JAYNE, secretarial sch. adminstr.; b. Balt., Sept. 19, 1946; d. Herman and Ruth Roslyn (Goldshine) Chasnow; B.A., U. Rochester, 1968; m. Jean Claude Levy, Oct. 27, 1968; children—David E., Edward M., Catherine F. Tchr. French, Weequahic High Sch., Newark, 1968; tchr. English, Berlitz Sch., Paris, 1969; exec. dir. First Sch. Secretarial and Paralegal Studies, E. Orange, N.J., 1971—; exec. dir. Lafayette Lang. Inst., E. Orange. Vol., Am. Arthritis Assn., 1977, United Way, Am. Cancer Soc. Mem. Pvt. Career Schs. Assn., Assn. Ind. Colls. and Schs., W. Essex C. of C., Nat. Council Jewish Women. Office: 516 Main St East Orange NJ 07018

LEVY, HAROLD, food co. exec.; b. Perth Amboy, N.J., Jan. 1, 1917; s. Abraham and Ella (Goldstein) L.; B.S., N.Y. U., 1937; postgrad., 1938; m. Diana Greenspan, Apr. 27, 1941; children—Linda Levy Hamelsky, Charles L., Amy. Exec. v.p. Flagstaff Foods, Perth Amboy, 1955—; chmn. bd. Compra, Ltd., Aruba, Netherlands Antilles; dir. V-W. Elmicke Assos. Inc., Bronxville, N.Y.; bd. mgrs. Perth Amboy Savs. Instn. Chmn. bd. adjustment, Perth Amboy, 1966-74. Trustee, Rutgers Prep. Sch. Clubs: N.Y. U., Kiwanis. Home: 203 E 72 St New York City NY 10021 also 117 Smith Blvd Aruba Netherlands Antilles Office: 536 Fayette St Perth Amboy NJ 08861

LEVY, HAROLD SHELDON, telephone co. exec.; b. N.Y.C., Jan. 25, 1933; s. George Gerson and Sarah (Levinson) L.; B.A., Harvard U., 1954; J.D. (editor Law Jour., Israel Perez prize 1957), Yale U., 1957; m. Helen Rose Romanoff, July 4, 1958; children—Peter Adam, Stacey Ann. Admitted to N.Y. State bar, 1958; asso. firm Rosenman, Colin, Petschek & Freund, N.Y.C., 1957-65; with AT&T, 1965—, v.p., gen. atty. longlines dept., N.Y.C., 1973-74, gen. atty. gen. depts., 1975-78, gen. solicitor gen. depts., 1978—. Mem. Am., FCC bar assns., Phi Beta Kappa, Order of Coif. Jewish. Club: Harvard of N.J. (exec. com. 1970-73). Home: 26 Canterbury Rd Livingston NJ 07039 Office: 195 Broadway New York City NY 10007

LEVY, HERBERT MONTE, lawyer; b. N.Y.C., Jan. 14, 1923; s. Samuel M. and Hetty (Weinberger) L.; A.B., Columbia, 1943, LL.B., 1946; m. Marilyn Wohl, Aug. 30, 1953; children—Harlan A., Matthew D., Alison J. Admitted to N.Y. bar, 1946; since practiced in N.Y.C.; mem. staff Rosenman, Goldmark, Colin & Kaye, 1946-47, Javits and Javits, 1947-48; partner Hofheimer Gartlir Hofheimer Gottlieb & Gross, 1965-69; pvt. practice N.Y.C., 1956-64, 69—; staff counsel Am. Civil Liberties Union, N.Y.C., 1949-56; lectr. Practising Law Inst. Mem. Am. for Democratic Action (N.Y. dir. 1956-72, vice chmn., 1961-65); mem. exec. com. Commn. on Law and Social Action of Am. Jewish Congress, 1961-66; former dir. Amsterdam Democratic Club. Mem. Fed. Bar Council (past trustee, chmn. Bill of Rights com. 1956-65, mem. com. on fed law and practice 1968—), Bar Assn. of City N.Y. (mem. Bill of Rights com., 1961-64, mem. com. medicine and law 1966-69), N.Y. County Lawyers Assn. (mem. spl. com. practical legal edn. 1973—, mem. com. on legal edn. and admission to bar 1975—), First Amendment Lawyers Assn., Tau Epsilon Phi. Author: Justice After Trial, How To Handle An Appeal, 1968. Home: 285 Central Park W New York City NY 10024 Office: 9 E 40th St New York City NY 10016

LEVY, JEROME HENRY, ophthalmic surgeon; b. N.Y.C., Sept. 12, 1942; s. Louis and Lee (Boockvar) L.; B.A. magna cum laude, Syracuse U., 1963; M.D., State U. N.Y. at Bklyn., 1966; m. Carol Ruth Freisinger, June 20, 1964; children—Linda, David. Intern, Kings County Hosp., Bklyn., 1966-67; resident in ophthalmology Manhattan Eye, Ear and Throat Hosp., N.Y.C., 1968-70, chief resident, 1970-71, mem. staff, 1971—, coordinator phacoemulsification tng., 1971—; practice medicine specializing in ophthalmic surgery, Bronx, N.Y., 1971—. Diplomate Am. Bd. Ophthalmology. Fellow Am. Acad. Ophthalmology and Otolaryngology, Am., Internat. colls. surgeons; mem. AMA, Am. Intraocular Lens Soc., N.Y. Intraocular Lens Club (co-dir.), Contact Lens Soc. Ophthalmologists, N.Y. State, Bronx County med. socs., Phi Beta Kappa, Phi Kappa Phi. Contbr. articles to profl. pubs. Home: 23 Kennedy Rd Cresskill NJ 07626 Office: 1940 Grand Concourse Bronx NY 10457

LEVY, JOHN DANA, librarian; b. Washington, Mar. 25, 1947; s. John Reed and Doris Dana (Estep) L.; B.A., Western Md. Coll., 1969; M.L.S., U. Md., 1970. Librarian, Nat. Library Medicine, Bethesda, Md., 1970-74; librarian Library of Congress, Washington, 1975—, head NSF sci. serials project, 1975-76, head editing and input sect. serial record div., 1976—, acting head nat. serials data program, 1976. Mem. ALA (com. to study serial records 1977-78), Spl. Libraries Assn., Archaeol. Inst. Am., Beta Phi Mu. Democrat. Home: 2601 Park Center Dr C1405 Alexandria VA 22302 Office: Serial Record Div Library of Congress Washington DC 20540

LEVY, JULIUS, lawyer; b. Bklyn., Feb. 15, 1913; s. Samuel H. and Esther (Pashman) L.; B.A., U. Mo., 1934; LL.B., Columbia, 1936; m. Jane Frederick, Nov. 8, 1940; children—Fredrick J., Douglas J. Admitted to N.Y. bar, 1937; practiced in N.Y.C., 1936—; mem. firm Pomerantz, Levy, Haudek & Block. Bd. dirs. Univ. Settlement House. Served to lt. (j.g.) USNR, 1943-46. Mem. Assn. Bar City N.Y., N.Y. County Lawyers Assn., Zeta Beta Tau. Office: 295 Madison Ave New York City NY 10017

LEVY, MICHAEL HENRY, bus. exec.; b. N.Y.C., Sept. 16, 1913; s. Milton and Hannah (Gans) L.; m. Helen Green; children—Miles Donn, Lora B. Levy Weisman, Michele Carla. Chmn. bd., chief exec. officer, founder Standard Security Life Ins. Co. of N.Y., N.Y.C., 1958-77, The Federated Brokerage Group, Inc. and 7 subs.'s, 1934-58; pres. Standard Security Holding Corp. and v.p. Standard Security Investors Corp., to 1977; pres. Mktg. Innovations, Inc., Tenafly, N.J., 1978—. Trustee, sec. Inst. Study of Drug Misuse, Inc., 1970—; chmn. Nat Council on Problems of Drug Misuse, 1972—, Nat. Interagy. Publs. Coordinating Com., 1971-76; mem. Pres.'s Bus. Exec. Adv. Bd. for Drug Abuse, 1971-76; chmn. exec. com. Nat. Coordinating Council on Drug Edn., 1971—; vis. lectr. problems of drug misuse and alcoholism Harvard Med. Sch., Pace U., Yale Med. Sch., Northwestern U., U. Calif. at Los Angeles, U. Pa., others; spl. adviser, cons. state and city govts.; sponsor N.Y.C. pub. service awards for profl. achievement Coll. Ins., 1975; bd. govs. Nat. Democratic Club, N.Y.C., 1938-40, 45-65; hon. dep. commr. borough works Borough of Manhattan, N.Y.C., 1958-61; v.p. parents assn. Hobart and Wm. Smith Colls., 1976—. Served as 2d lt., inf., U.S. Army, 1934, 1st lt., 1940, capt., 1942; ETO. Decorated D.S.C., D.S.M., Bronze Star, Silver Star, Croix de Guerre. C.L.U.; recipient Internat. Pub. Service award to fight against drug abuse, 1977; spl. award for devel. family cancer care ins. and creation of polio ins. Pan Am. Med. Assn.; Ins. Man of Year award Nat. Ins. Fedn., 1951, 53, 56, 57; Ins. Mem. Nat. Ins. Brokers Assn. (pres. 1955-57), Ins. Soc. N.Y., Life Underwriters Assn. N.Y., Am. Soc. C.L.U.'s (N.Y. chpt.), Life Cos. of N.Y., Inc. (pres. 1973), Am. Council Life Ins., Nat., N.Y. ins. fedns., Vet. Assn. 12th Inf., 77th Div. Assn., 12th Regt. Vet. Officers Assn., Soc. of Purple Heart, Am. Vets. Com., N.Y. C. of C., AIM (pres.'s council), Nat. Sales Execs. Club, U.S. Flag Assn. (life), SCV, Citizens Union City N.Y., N.Y. Soc. Mil. and Naval Officers World Wars, Res. Officers Assn. U.S., Office Execs. Assn., Nat. Office Mgmt. Assn., Health Ins. Assn. Am., Nat. Assn. Life Underwriters, Ins. Econs. Soc. Am., Life Ins. Advertisers Assn., Life Office Mgmt. Assn., Assn. N.Y. State Life Ins. Cos., Nat. Indsl. Conf. Bd., Drug Problems Assn. N.Am., Nat. Orgn. Reform Marijuana Laws, Assn. Prevention of Addiction Ltd. (Eng.), Soc. Study of Addiction to Alcohol and Other Drugs (both Gt. Britain), Assn. Labor-Mgmt. Adminstrs. and Cons.'s on Alcoholism, Assn. Halfway House Alcoholism Programs N.Am., Inc., Alcohol and Drug Problems Assn. N.Am., Inst. Study of Drug Misuse, Inst. Study of Drug Dependence (Eng.), Nat. Coordinating Council on Drug Edn., Nat. Council Alcoholism, Internat. Council on Alcohol and Addictions (WHO), Nat. Council Problems of Drug Misuse, Internat. Narcotic Enforcement Officers Assn., N.Y. Vet. Police Assn., Nat. Narcotics and Dangerous Drugs Enforcement Assn., Friends of City Center, Student Assn. for Study of Hallucinogens, Nat. Com. Citizens Edn., Inst. Responsive Edn., Council Basic Edn., Met. Mus. Art, Mus. Modern Art, Am. Mus. Natural History, Am. Forestry Assn., Am. Hort. Soc., Am. Peony Soc., Garden State Rose Club (N.J.), Am., N. Jersey, Royal Nat. (Eng.) rose socs., N.Y. Bot. Garden, U.S. Chess Fedn., Am. Symphony Orch. Guild, Young Pres.'s Orgn. (sec. 1957-58). Clubs: K.P., B'nai B'rith. Author: Your Insurance and How to Profit by It, 1955; A Handbook of Personal Insurance Terminology, 1968; A Primer of Basic Selling Techniques, 1969; The Family vs. Drink & Drugs, 1974; Curriculum Planning: Drugs, Alcohol & Tobacco, 1976; Drug Misuse...Human Abuse!!!, 1976; The Consumer Guide to Life Insurance, 1978; The Consumer Guide to Business Life Insurance, 1978; The Consumer Guide to Estate Planning, 1978; articles pub. in Instns. mag., Dun's Rev., U.S. News and World report, Sch. Mgmt., Mgmt. Methods, Modern Industry, Med. Econs., Rough Notes, The Local Agt., AMA Supervisory Mgmt., Ophthalmic Econs., Ins. Advocate, Weekly Underwriter, Ins., Ins. Salesman, Ins. Selling, Ins. Index, Life Assn. News, Best's Rev., Pension and Welfare News, Spectator, others; exec. editor Internat. Jour. of the Addictions, 1973—; editor Caveat, monthly drug misuse newsletter, 1972-77. Home: 76 Oxford Dr Tenafly NJ 07670 Office: 111 Fifth Ave New York City NY 10003

LEVY, MILTON ROBERT, plastics, chem. and graphics cos. exec.; b. Bklyn., June 28, 1936; s. Nathan and Ruth (Goldstein) L.; B.S., Sch. Commerce, N.Y. U., 1958; m. Corinne Sackman, Aug. 28, 1958; children—Pamela, Norman, Michael. Gen. mgr. Direct Reprodn. Corp., Bklyn., 1959-62; pres. Nation-Wide Plastics Co., Inc., Long Island City, N.Y., 1962—, Non Tox Chem. Corp., Mamaroneck, N.Y., 1969—, Graphics One, Inc., Atlanta, 1971—; treas. Plastics of Calif., 1974—; dir. Cortes Ward Co. Bd. dirs. Hebrew Acad. High Sch., Yonkers, N.Y., 1975-76, Center Spl. Edn., Bklyn., 1978; pres. Young Israel Scarsdale (N.Y.), 1974-75, 76-77, bd. dirs., 1977-78; mem. Mayor's Com. on Welfare Reform, 1977. Served with U.S. Army, 1958-59. Mem. Nat. Assn. Photo Lithographers. Jewish Alliance Businessmen (pres. 1977-78). Home: 42 Stratton Rd New Rochelle NY 10804 Office: 43 72 11th St Long Island City NY 11101

LEVY, PAUL FRANK, dentist; b. Beverly, Mass., May 4, 1943; s. Allen Simon and Evelyn (Rosengard) L.; B.A., U. Mass., Amherst, 1964; D.D.S., N.Y. U., 1969; postgrad. Tufts U., 1973-75; m. Susan Berliner, June 28, 1969; children—Deborah Jill, Beth Joy. Pvt. practice dentistry, Waltham, Mass., 1971-73; practice periodontology, Medford, Mass, 1975—; clin. instr. Tufts U. Coll. Dental Medicine, 1975—. Served as capt. Dental Corps, USAF, 1969-71. Decorated Commendation medal USAF; recipient Am. Acad. Oral Medicine award, 1969. Mem. ADA, Mass. Dental Soc., Am. Acad. Oral Medicine, Am. Acad. Periodontology. Oral Medicine, Am. Acad. Periodontology. Office: 16 Bradlee Rd Medford MA 02155

LEVY, ROBERT ALAN, energy economist; b. Washington, Apr. 18, 1946; s. Walter James and Augusta (Soandheimer) L.; B.A., U. Pa., 1968; M.B.A., Columbia U., 1972. Tchr. elementary sch., N.Y.C., 1968; personnel asst. Beth Israel Hosp., N.Y.C., 1973-76; energy economist W.J. Levy Consultants Corp., N.Y.C., 1976—. Mem. Internat. Assn. Energy Economists, Am. Econ. Assn., Indsl. Relations Research Assn. Home: 201 W 77th St Apt 4C New York City NY 10024 Office: 30 Rockefeller Plaza Room 3232 New York NY 10020

LEVY, ROBERT ISAAC, physician, govt. ofcl.; b. Bronx, N.Y., May 3, 1937; s. George Gerson and Sarah (Levinson) L.; B.A. with high honors and distinction, Cornell U., 1957; M.D. cum laude, Yale U., 1961; m. Ellen Marie Feis, 1958; children—Andrew, Joanne, Karen, Patricia. Intern, then asst. resident in medicine Yale-New Haven Med. Center, 1961-63; clin. asso. molecular diseases Nat. Heart and Lung Inst., NIH, HEW, Bethesda, Md., 1963-66, chief resident Nat. Heart, Lung and Blood Inst., 1965-66, attending physician molecular disease br., 1965—, head sect. lipoproteins, 1966—, dep. clin. dir. inst., 1968-69, chief clin. services molecular diseases br., 1969-73, chief lipid metabolism br., 1970-74, dir. div. heart and vascular diseases, 1973-75, dir. inst., 1975—; attending physician Georgetown U. med. div. D.C. Gen. Hosp., 1966-68; spl. cons. anti-lipid drugs FDA, 1973—. Served as surgeon USPHS, 1963-66. Recipient Kees Thesis prize Yale U., 1961; Arthur S. Flemming award, 1975; Superior Service award HEW, 1975. Mem. Am. Inst. Nutrition, Am. Heart Assn. (mem.-at-large exec. com. council basic sci. 1974-76), Am. Fedn. Clin. Research, N.Y. Acad. Scis., Am. Soc. Clin. Nutrition, Am. Soc. Clin. Investigation, Am. Coll. Cardiology, Am. Soc. Clin. Pharmacology and Therapeutics, Phi Beta Kappa, Sigma Xi, Alpha Omega Alpha, Alpha Epsilon Delta, Phi Kappa Phi. Contbr. articles in field to profl. jours. Editor: Jour. Lipid Research, 1972—, Circulation, 1974-76. Office: Bldg 31 Room 5A52 Nat Heart Lung and Blood Inst Bethesda MD 20014

LEVY, STEPHEN RAYMOND, research and devel. co.; b. Everett, Mass., May 4, 1940; s. Robert George and Lillian (Berfield) L.; B.B.A., U. Mass., 1962; m. Sandra Helen Rosen, Aug. 26, 1961;

children—Phillip, Susan. Pres., chief exec. officer, dir. Bolt Beranek & Newman, Inc., Cambridge, Mass., 1976—; chmn. bd., chief exec. officer, treas. Delos Internat. Group, Inc., Waltham, Mass., 1972-75; chmn. bd. Timesharing Ltd., London, Eng., 1972-75; dir. Telenet Corp., Washington. Served with AUS, 1963-66. Decorated Army Commendation medal. Mem. Assn. for Computing Machinery, Financial Execs. Inst., Nat. Contract Mgrs. Assn. Home: 39 Lafayette Dr Sudbury MA 01776 Office: 50 Moulton St Cambridge MA 02138

LEVY, TIBBIE (MRS. ELI BENNETT LEVY), lawyer, painter; b. N.Y.C., Oct. 29, 1908; d. David and Minnie (Hoffman) Goldstein; A.B., Cornell U., 1929, postgrad., 1929-30; J.D., N.Y. U., 1931; studied with Arshile Gorky, Art Students League, Andre L'Hote, Academic de la Grande Chaumiere, Cornell U., also Vincenzo; m. Eli Bennett Levy, Nov. 19, 1931; children—Lynn (Mrs. Leland S. Zaubler), John Hoffman (dec.). Admitted to N.Y. bar, 1932; pvt. practice of law, N.Y.C., 1932—. Profl. painter under name of Lysan and Tibbie Levy; exhibited one-man shows in N.Y.C., Pa., Paris, Madrid, London, Tokyo; represented numerous permanent museum collections, Phoenix Mus. Art, Witte Mus., San Antonio, Jewish Mus. Hebrew Union Coll., Cin., Evansville (Ind.) Mus. Art and Sci., Boston U., Brandeis U., Cornell U., Ga. Mus., Jewish Mus., Cin., Mus. Modern Art, Miami, Witte Meml. Mus., Tex., George Peabody Mus., Tenn., Princeton U., Palm Springs Mus., Barnard Coll., Fairleigh Dickinson U., N.J., Syracuse U., Colgate U., Rutgers U., N.Y. U., U. Notre Dame, Fashion Inst. Tech., Horace Mann Sch.; also pvt. and indsl. collections. Pres. patrons council Barnard Sch. for Boys; mem. Speakers Bur., Anti-Defamation League; pres. Freedom chpt., mem. Speakers Bur., B'nai B'rith; pres. Parents Assn. Calhoun Sch.; bd. dirs. Hebrew Kindergarten and Infants Home, Pace U., NCCJ. Home: 2 Sutton Pl S New York City NY 10022

LEVY, WALTER, pediatrician; b. N.Y.C., Nov. 23, 1899; s. Jacob and Annie (Freeman) L.; B.S., N.Y. U., 1922, M.D., 1924; m. Gertrude Finkelstein, July 28, 1939; 1 son, James Lewis. Intern, Kingston Ave. Hosp., 1924, Lebanon Hosp., 1925-26; lectr. pediatrics Poly clinic Hosp., 1927-35; practice medicine specializing in pediatrics, N.Y.C., 1926—; asso. attending pediatrician Riverside Hosp., 1931-42 v.p. med. bd., 1958-61, pres., 1961-63; attending pediatrician Jewish Meml. Hosp., 1951-64, dir. pediatrics, 1964-69, dir. emeritus, 1969-75, dir. pediatrics, 1975—, cons. pediatrician, 1969—; cons. pediatrician Morrisania City Hosp., 1963-76, dir. dept. pediatrics, 1962-63, chmn. outpatient dept., 1952-63; attending pediatrician St. Elizabeth's Hosp., 1963-72, cons., 1972—; cons. pediatrician Misericordia Hosp., 1963—, St. Clare's Hosp. and Health Center, 1972—, Union Hosp. Bronx, 1978—; asso. clin. prof. pediatrics N.Y. Med. Coll., 1952-61; mem. vis. com. U. Coll., N.Y. U., 1951-57, chmn. alumni devel. fund. Sch. Medicine, 1962—; mem. U.S. Com. for Care European Children, 1946-54; mem. exec. com. N.Y. U. Med. Center Campaign, 1943-52; founder Morrisania Found., Med. Research Inc., 1954, pres., 1954-76; mem. adv. bd. Wood Johnson Found., Western and Upper Manhattan Regional Perinatal Network, 1976—; mem. nat. adv. council Am. Com. for Weizmann Inst. Sci., 1978—. Chmn. physicians div. United Jewish Appeal Greater N.Y., 1971—, bd. dirs., 1973—. Recipient Meritorious Service award N.Y. U. Alumni Assn., 1950, Presdl. citation N.Y. U., 1962. Diplomate Am. Bd. Pediatrics. Fellow Am. Acad. Pediatrics, N.Y. Acad. Medicine, Royal Soc. Health (U.K.); mem. Alumni Fedn. N.Y. U. (dir. emeritus 1973—), Jewish Acad. Arts and Scis., Bronx Pediatric Soc. (past pres.), N.Y. County Med. Soc., AMA (award of merit, original sci. investigation 1942), Sigma Lambda Pi (past pres.), Phi Epsilon Pi, Alpha Omega Alpha, Perstare et Praestare. Founder N.Y. U. Bellevue Hosp. Med. Center, 1943. Designer Infa-Rule. Democrat. Jewish. Clubs: Medallion, Faculty (N.Y. U.). Asso. editor Jewish Meml. Hosp. Bull., 1955-76; contbr. articles to pediatric mags. Home: 130 E 75th St New York City NY 10021 Office: 12 E 88th St New York City NY 10028

LEVY, WILBERT J., ednl. cons.; b. Bklyn., Mar. 20, 1917; s. Benjamin and Minnie (Wolfe) L.; B.S., City Coll. of N.Y., 1936; M.A., Columbia, 1938; postgrad. N.Y. U., Bklyn. Coll.; m. Jeanne I. Hassberg, Mar. 20, 1941; children—Nora Elizabeth Levy Johnston, Jonathan Ben. Examiner, N.Y.C. Civil Service Commn., 1942-45; English tchr. Midwood High Sch., Bklyn., 1945-54; chmn. dept. English, Newtown High Sch., Queens, N.Y., 1954-74; cons., author Amsco Sch. Pubs., Inc., N.Y.C., 1968—. Mem. East Norwich-Oyster Bay Bd. Edn., 1962-66. Served with USN, 1945. Mem. Nat. Council Tchrs. English. Author: Patterns of Meaning: A Program Towards More Powerful Reading, 1969; (with Samuel F. Zimbal) Reading Comprehension, 1972; Man Studies Himself, 1973; Man Studies His Past, 1973, Man Studies The World Around Him, 1973; Reading and Growing, 1975; Sense of Sentences, 1975; Paragraph Power, 1977; Poems: American Themes, 1979; gen. editor: AMSCO Lit. Program series, 1971-75.

LEWAN, ROLAND, JR., savs. and loan exec.; b. Newark, Mar. 7, 1930; s. Roland L. and Dorothy (McCance) L.; B.S. in Bus. Adminstrn., Upsala Coll., 1951; postgrad. Am. Savs. and Loan Inst., 1960, Ind. U. Grad. Sch. Savs. and Loan, 1964; m. Lois Edwards, Aug. 17, 1957; children—Roland III, Lori Ann. Asst. v.p. Yorke Savs. and Loan Assn., Newark, 1955-59; v.p. Investors Savs. and Loan Assn., Millburn, N.J., 1959-64, sr. v.p., 1964-72, pres., 1972—. Instr., Am. Savs. and Loan Inst., 1961—. Mem. council Short Hills Assn., 1971—; pres. Millburn-Short Hills Scholastic Boosters, Inc., 1971-73; bd. dirs. N.J. Coll. Fund Assn., Summit, N.J. Served with AUS, 1951-53. Mem. Soc. Real Estate Appraisers (asso.), Central Corp. Savs. and Loan Assns. (dir.), N.J. (bd. govs.), Essex County (dir.) savs. and loan leagues, U.S. Savs. and Loan League, Sales Exec. Club Northern N.J. Clubs: Masons (32 deg., Mason), Rotary; Baltusrol Golf (Springfield, N.J.). Home: Young's Rd New Vernon NJ 07976 Office: 249 Millburn Ave Millburn NJ 07041

LEWEY, MERLE CREIGHTON, govt. ofcl., ret. army officer; b. Coffeen, Ill., Apr. 30, 1921; s. Merle Walter and Flos (Roberts) L.; A.B., James Millikin U., 1948; A.M., U. So. Calif., 1959. Announcer, Sta. WSOY, Decatur, Ill., 1941-42; instr. James Millikin U., 1947-48; announcer Sta. WCRA, Effingham, Ill., 1950-51; commd. 2d lt. U.S. Army, 1942, advanced through grades to lt. col., 1962; chief audio-visual br. Office Chief Info., Dept. Army, Washington, 1964-66; ret., 1966; audio-visual support officer Office Asst. Chief Staff Communications-Electronics, Dept. Army, 1967-72, audio-visual programs officer Office Dep. Chief Staff Personnel, 1972-78, audio-visual instructional materials officer Office Dep. Chief Staff Ops. and Plans, 1978—. Decorated Bronze Star, Legion of Merit. Mem. Soc. Motion Picture and TV Engrs., Acad. TV Arts and Scis., Tau Kappa Epsilon, Alpha Phi Omega, Alpha Epsilon Rho. Home: Hyde Pk Apt 710 4141 N Henderson Rd Arlington VA 22203 Office: Office Dep Chief Staff for Ops and Plans Army Washington DC 20310

LEWINN, EDWARD BERNARD, physician; b. Hartford, Conn., July 25, 1904; s. Louis Elias and Anna (Manus) LeW.; B.S., Trinity Coll., Hartford, 1925; M.D., Jefferson Med. Coll., 1929; Sc.D. in Human Devel. (hon.), U. Plano (Tex.), 1974; m. Pearl Elsie Freedman, May 16, 1930; children—Deborah Helen LeWinn London, Margery Elizabeth LeWinn Doroshow. Intern, Beth Israel Hosp., Newark, 1929; resident Frankford Hosp., Phila., 1930; asst. in medicine Albert Einstein Med. Center, 1930-34, asso., 1934-54, dir. edn., intern and resident staff, 1954-64, sr. attending physician, 1954-66; dir. Inst. for Clin. Investigation, Inst. Achievement Human Potential, Phila., 1963—. Decorated Gold medal of Honor (Brazil); Star of Hope (Eng.); recipient statuette with pedestal Internat. Forum Neurol. Orgn., 1971; diplomate Am. Bd. Internal Medicine. Fellow A.C.P., Coll. Physicians Phila., Royal Soc. Health; mem. AAAS, World Med. Assn. (founder), Am. Heart Assn., World Orgn. Human Potential (pres. 1976—). Author: (with Erich Urbach) Skin Diseases, Nutrition and Metabolism, 1946; Human Neurological Organization, 1969; contbr. articles on metabolism, med. diagnosis, human devel. and brain injury to profl. jours.; recognized digitalis as probable endocrine agt. Home: Box 439 Upper Black Eddy Bucks County PA 18972 Office: 8801 Stenton Ave Philadelphia PA 19118

LEWINS, STEVEN, securities analyst; b. N.Y.C., Jan. 22, 1943; s. Bruno and Kaethe L.; B.A., Queens Coll., City U. N.Y., 1964, M.A., 1966; postgrad. City U. N.Y., 1969-72; postgrad. certificate pub. adminstrn. State U. N.Y., 1967; m. Rayna Lee Kornreich, July 4, 1968; children—Shani Nicole, Scott Asher. Park ranger-historian Nat. Park Service, Statue of Liberty, N.Y.C., 1964-66; traffic asst. AT&T, White Plains, N.Y., 1966; adminstrv. intern N.Y. State, Albany, 1966-67; adminstrv. asst. to commr. N.Y. State Narcotics Addiction Control Commn., N.Y.C., 1967-69; analyst A.B. & Co., Value Line Investment Survey, Value Line Data Services, N.Y.C., 1969-71, asso. research dir., 1971-74, research dir., 1974; research dir., directing editor Value Line Investment Survey, 1974—; v.p. Value Line Data Services, 1975—; v.p. Arnold Bernhard & Co., 1975—, dir., 1976—, mem. exec. com., 1977—; partner Ray-Lux Products, 1978—; dir. Value Line Mut. Funds; adviser corp. disclosure SEC; lectr. econs., securities, computer applications. Mem. Croton-on-Hudson Narcotics Guidance Council, Cortlandt Indsl. Com.; co-chmn. Democratic Pub. Affairs Com., Cortland. Fellow Fin. Analyst Fedn.; mem. N.Y. Soc. Security Analysts (sr. security analyst, mem. Membership com., computer applications symposium), Assn. Time Sharing Users, Tau Delta Phi. Democrat. Club: Shattemuc Yacht. Home: 2 Charles W Briggs Rd Croton-on-Hudson NY 10520 Office: 711 Third Ave New York City NY 10017

LEWIS, ARMAND FRANCIS, material scientist; b. Fairhaven, Mass., May 22, 1932; s. Antone Dutra and Lucienne (Martin) L.; B.S. in Textile Chemistry, Southeastern Mass. U., 1953; M.S. in Chemistry, Okla. State U., 1955; Ph.D. in Phys. Chemistry, Lehigh U., 1958; m. Joan Marie Doyle, Aug. 2, 1958; children—Jeffrey Doyle, Kent Anthony. Teaching asst. in chemistry Okla. State U., 1954-55; research fellow Lehigh U., 1955-58, postdoctoral teaching and research fellow, 1959; with Am. Cyanamid Co., Stamford, Conn., 1959-71, group leader div. plastics, 1965-70, project leader div. indsl. chems. and plastics research dept. 1971; sr. research asso. corp. devel. Lord Corp., Erie, Pa., 1971-72, sr. materials scientist, 1972—; adj. prof. metall. and materials engring. U. Pitts., 1976—; cons. USN, USAF, Nat. Acad. Sci.; mem. adv. bd. Lake Erie Marine Sci. Center. Mem. Am. Chem. Soc. (Union Carbide award 1963), Soc. Rheology (treas. 1965-67), Materials Research Soc., Soc. Advancement Materials, Processing Engrs., Plastic and Rubber Inst. (London), Soc. Plastics Engrs., World Future Soc., Sigma Xi, Phi Lambda Upsilon. Democrat. Roman Catholic. Contbr. articles on adhesion sci. and functional materials to profl. publs.; patentee in field.

LEWIS, CLAUDE, JR., shoe co. exec.; b. Jefferson City, Mo., Aug. 21, 1924; s. Claude and Opal Mae (Fowler) L.; A.B., Central Meth. Coll., 1949; postgrad. U. Mo., 1949-50; m. Aletha Avonell Harrison, Oct. 16, 1943; 1 son, Gregory Lee. Office mgr. Brown Shoe Co., Moberly, Mo., 1950, dept. supr., St. Louis, 1954-58; asst. gen. supt. Kinney Shoe Corp., Carlisle, Pa., 1959-62, gen. supt., 1962-65, dir. purchasing, 1965-68, v.p. mfg. div., 1968, pres. mfg. div., 1969-74, corp. exec. v.p., 1974—, also dir., mem. exec. com.; dir. Farmers Trust Co., Kinney Shoe Corp., Can., Ltd., Maxine Footwear (all Can.). Served with AUS, 1942-46, 50-52. Mem. Am. Footwear Industries Assn. (dir., mem. exec. com.). Republican. Methodist. Clubs: Masons (32 deg.); N.Y. Athletic; Carlisle Country, Officers of Army War Coll. (Carlisle, Pa.). Home: 627 Belvedere St Carlisle PA 17013 Office: 1275 Ritner Hwy Carlisle PA 17013

LEWIS, CLIFFORD, III, fin. analyst; b. Utica, N.Y., Sept. 8, 1904; s. Clifford and Isabel Marriner (Kernan) L., Jr.; B.A., U. Pa., 1928; m. Mary Butler, Jan. 21, 1942 (dec.); children—Eleanor Reed Lewis Koppe, Clifford Butler; m. 2d, Virginia Gray Gibson Bullitt. Researcher, asst. surveyor Mut. Assurance Co., Phila., 1930-49; stock broker, fin. analyst Battles & Co. (now Janney Montgomery Scott), Phila., 1949—. Sec. bd. Atwater Kent Mus., 1937—. Am. Philos. Soc. grantee, 1972, 73; chartered fin. analyst. Mem. Phila. Fin. Analysts, SR, Soc. War of 1812, Colonial Soc. Pa. (gov. 1973-74), Pa. Soc. of Cincinnati (chmn. Am. hist. com. 1972—, pres. 1978—), Upper Providence Twp. Citizens Assn. (pres. 1965-66). Republican. Club: Rittenhouse (Phila.). Author: Nicholas Devereux, 1791-1855, 1974; contbr. articles to hist. jours. Home: 550 Kirk Ln Media PA 19063

LEWIS, CRAIG GRAHAM DAVID, pub. relations exec.; b. Dearborn, Mich., Jan. 25, 1930; s. Floyd Berchard and Elizabeth Ann (Hickey) L.; A.B. in English, U. Calif., Los Angeles, 1951; m. Karen Elizabeth Kerns, Oct. 23, 1954; children—Mark, Kern, Arden, Robin. Corr., McGraw-Hill, Inc., Washington, 1952-56; bur. mgr. Aviation Week mag., Dallas, 1957-59, Washington news editor, 1959-61; dep. dir. pub. affairs FAA, Washington, 1961-63; v.p. pub. relations Air Transport Assn., Washington, 1963-64; dir. pub. relations Martin Marietta Corp., N.Y.C.,1964-67; asso. Earl Newson & Co. Inc., N.Y.C., 1967—, dir., 1968—, pres., 1975—. Mem. Pub. Relations Soc. Am., Am. Inst. Aeros. and Astronautics, Nat. Press Club, Aviation and Space Writers Assn. Club: Univ. (N.Y.C.) Home: 6 Avon Rd New Rochelle NY 10804 Office: 10 E 53d St New York City NY 10022

LEWIS, DAVID CHARLES, reproducing co. exec.; b. Endicott, N.Y., June 1, 1947; s. Richard Charles and Thelma Beatrice (Tilley) L.; A.A.S. in Accounting, Monroe (N.Y.) Community Coll., 1970; B.S. in Bus. Adminstrn., Rochester (N.Y.) Inst. Tech., 1976; m. Margaret L. Lantz, Mar. 4, 1967; children—Lisa Michelle, David Scott. With Xerox Corp., Webster, N.Y., 1965-66, 68—, materials analyst, 1977-78, supr. prodn. control, 1978—. Served with U.S. Army, 1966-68. Decorated Bronze Star, Purple Heart. Mem. Nat. Rifle Assn., Nat. Skeet Shooters Assn., DAV, VFW. Methodist. Club: Canandaigua Sportsman. Home: 2411 Cornwall Dr Macedon NY 14502 Office: 800 Phillips Rd (W-200E) Webster NY 14580

LEWIS, EDWARD MICHAEL, hosp. adminstr.; b. Newark; s. Harry Joseph and Eileen Veronica (Phelan) L.; B.S. in Indsl. Mgmt., Fairleigh Dickinson U., 1968, M.B.A. cum laude, 1972; m. Carole A. Lewis, May 29, 1964; children—Brian E., Daren K. Constrn. engr. Pub. Service Electric & Gas Co., Newark, 1968-70; indsl. engr. Emerson TV & Radio Corp., Jersey City, 1970-73; dir. indsl. engring. Lightolier Inc., Jersey City, 1973-77; mgmt. cons. N.J. Hosp. Assn., Princeton, 1977; asst. exec. dir. Bergen Pines County Hosp., Paramus, N.J., 1977—. Served with U.S. Army, 1960-62. Mem. Am. Hosp. Assn., Am. Inst. Indsl. Engrs., Hosp. Mgmt. Systems Soc., Am. Coll. Hosp. Adminstrs., Am. Coll. Long Term Care Adminstrs. Office: Bergen Pines County Hosp E Ridgewood Ave Paramus NJ 07652

LEWIS, EDWARD TURNER, veterinarian; b. Boston, Feb. 1, 1941; s. Edward William Werner and Judith (Andress) Lewis; B.A. with honors, Kalamazoo (Mich.) Coll., 1963; B.S., Mich. State U., 1965, D.V.M. with honors, 1968; m. Katherine Louise Seaman, Aug. 27, 1965; children—Elizabeth Dee, Aaron Matthew. Veterinarian, Stoneham (Mass.) Animal Hosp., 1968-71, Chelsea (Mass.) Animal Hosp., 1971—; lectr. in field. Corporator, Atlantic Bank. Mem. Am., Mass., State Line vet. med. assns., Am. Animal Hosp. Assn., Mich. State U. Alumni Assn. Clubs: Rotary, Masons, Star of Bethlehem. Home: 114 Main St Wakefield MA 01880 Office: 138 Washington Ave Chelsea MA 02150

LEWIS, FRANK MOHR, lawyer; b. Cambridge, Mass., Sept. 24, 1919; s. Heber and Gertrude (Sparks) L.; student Boston U., 1937-39; J.D., Northeastern U., 1948; m. Louise Elizabeth Swallow, Sept. 13, 1947; children—Frank M., Susan J., Charles E. Admitted to Mass. bar, 1949; mem. firm Cryan and Way, Boston, 1949-68; individual practice law, Belmont, Mass., 1969—. Mem. Belmont Town Meeting. Served from pvt. to capt. AUS, 1941-45. Mem. Mass. Trial Lawyers Assn., Am., Mass. bar assns.; fellow Mass. Bar Found. (life). Clubs: Masons, Shriners. Home: 563 School St Belmont MA 02178 Office: 497 Common St Belmont MA 02178

LEWIS, HARRY, educator, author; b. Newark, Apr. 4, 1917; s. Morris and Rose (Fein) Rubinstein; B.A., Montclair State Coll., 1937, M.A., 1942; Ph.D., N.Y. U., 1950; m. Beatrice Jewell Speer, Oct. 9, 1942. Tchr. math., Newark, 1939-63, chmn. dept. East Side High Sch., 1951-63; prin. Arts High Sch., Newark, 1963-70; prof. math. edn. Jersey City State Coll., 1970-77, cons., 1977—. Instr., N.Y. Actuaries Club, 1959-63, N.Y. U., 1950-52; cons. gen. bus. text Gregg Pub. Co.; compiler High Sch. Bus. Math. Library of Am. Bus. Edn. Mag., 1960. Mem. math. textbook evaluation com., Newark, 1962; mem. bd. examiners for selection of math. tchrs., 1968. Mem. Newark Council Tchrs. Math. (pres.). Author: Essentials of Business Mathematics, 1964; Business Mathematics, 1975; Mathematics for Daily Living, 1975; Introduction to Geometry, 1974; College Business Mathematics, 1976; Geometry, A Contemporary Course, 1978; Elementary Algebra for College, 1978; Arithmetic and Algebra for College, 1979; Intermediate Algebra for College, 1979. Home: 48 Brookside Terrace North Caldwell NJ 07006 Office: 2039 Kennedy Blvd Jersey City NJ 07305

LEWIS, HOWARD WILSON, JR., computer systems analyst; b. Carlisle, Pa., July 7, 1932; s. Howard Wilson and Florence Venita (Young) L.; B.S., Pa. State U., 1958; m. Mary Frances Jackson, Apr. 6, 1963; children—Venita Ann, Howard III. Civilian inventory mgmt. specialist Navy Ships Parts Control Center, Mechanicsburg, Pa., 1960-64, computer programmer, 1964-66, computer systems analyst, 1966—; chmn. joint conventional ammunition program mgmt. info. systems task group. Mem. ad hoc com. race relations to Carlisle (Pa.) Area Sch. Dist., 1969-72; exec. bd. Carlisle chpt. NAACP. Served with USN, 1951-53. Home: RD 1 Creamery Dr Boiling Springs PA 17007

LEWIS, HYLAN GARNET, sociologist, educator; b. Washington, Apr. 4, 1911; s. Harry Wythe and Ella (Wells) L.; A.B., Va. Union U., 1932; A.M. (Social Sci. Research Council fellow 1932, Rosenwald Found. fellow 1939-41), U. Chgo., 1936, Ph.D., 1951; m. Leighla Whipper, Oct. 4, 1935 (div. May 1945); children—Carole Ione (Mrs. Bovoso), Guy Edward; m. 2d, Audrey Carter, Nov. 2, 1946. Instr. sociology Howard U., Washington, 1934-41, prof. sociology, 1964-67; prof. social sci. Talladega (Ala.) Coll., 1941-42; information specialist OWI, 1942-45; asso. prof. Hampton Inst., 1945-48; asso. prof. sociology Atlanta U., 1945-48, prof., 1955-57; asso. dir. community services Unitarian Service Com., Inc., Boston, 1957-59; dir. child rearing study Health and Welfare Council, Washington, 1959-64; mem. delinquency grants rev. com. Nat. Inst. Mental Health, 1963-67, mem. social problems research rev. com., 1969-73; prof. sociology Bklyn. Coll. 1967-77, prof. emeritus, 1977—; prof. Grad. Center, City U. N.Y., 1977—; sr. v.p. Met. Applied Research Center, Inc., 1967-75; vis. scholar Russell Sage Found., 1974-75. Research asso. Inst. for Research in Social Sci., U. N.C., 1947-48; cons. Volta River Project Preparatory Commn., Gold Coast, 1954; Ashmore project Fund for Advancement Edn., 1953, So. Regional Council, 1954-58, Commn. on Race and Housing, 1956-57; cons. disaster study com. NRC, 1955-56; mem. adv. com. grants program U.S. Children's Bur., 1962-66; mem. adv. panel small grants program U.S. Dept. Labor, 1963—; chief cons. family panel White House Conf. Civil Rights Planning, 1965; mem. rev. panel U.S. Office Edn., 1965-67; mem. Head Start research adv. com. Office Econ. Opportunity, 1965-67; mem. grants adv. com. Nat. Endowment for the Humanities, Nat. Found. Arts and Humanities, 1967-68, others. Fund for Advancement Edn. fellow, 1955-56. Fellow AAAS; mem. Am. Sociol. Assn. (DuBois-Johnson-Frazier award 1976), African Studies Assn., Soc. Applied Anthropology, Alpha Phi Alpha. Author: Blackways of Kent, 1955. Home: 372 Central Park W New York City NY 10025

LEWIS, JAMES HISTED, ret. fgn. service officer; b. Carbondale, Pa., Dec. 18, 1912; s. Edward Butts and Laura (Histed) L.; A.B., George Washington U., 1935, A.M., 1939; m. Betty Prater, Dec. 12, 1942; children—Jane, Marie, David, Jon. Asst. polit. sci. George Washington U., 1934-36; mem. staff div. trade agreements Dept. State, Washington, 1936-42, fgn. service aux. officer, 1942-44, commd. fgn. service officer, 1954; assigned to Am. Embassy, London, 1942-44; economist div. comml. policy Dept. State, 1944-45, sec. Sec. State's Staff Com., 1945-46; econ. adviser U.S. del. Paris Peace Conf. and Council Fgn. Ministers, 1946; chief Brit. Commonwealth br. div. comml. policy, 1947-49; with office Brit. Commn. and No. European Affairs, Dept. State, 1949-54; mem. U.S. del. Gen. Agreement on Tariff and Trade trade negotiations, Annecy, France, 1949, head negotiator, Torquay, Eng., 1950-51, Geneva, 1956, 61; 1st sec. Embassy and Consul, London, 1954-57; counselor econ. affairs U.S. Embassy, Copenhagen, 1957-61; chief div. trade agreements State Dept., 1961-62, chief div. comml. policy and treaties, 1962-63, dep. dir. office internat. trade, 1963-65; minister-counselor for econ. affairs U.S. Mission to Geneva, dep. head U.S. del. Kennedy Round trade negotiations, Geneva, 1965-67; asst. dir.-gen. GATT Secretariat, Geneva, 1967-69; counselor U.S. Embassy, Bonn, Germany, 1969-70; dep. chief of mission U.S. Embassy, Helsinki, Finland, 1970-73; ret., 1973. Address: 8800 Clifford Ave Chevy Chase MD 20015

LEWIS, JOHN HARTLEY, distbg. co. exec.; b. Newton, Mass., July 5, 1918; s. Arthur Leon and Eva Carolyn (Hilton) L.; A.B., Harvard U., 1940; m. Joan Harding, Mar. 28, 1967; children by previous marriages—Florence H., Duncan H., Fay E., Ann L., Arthur L. Grad engr. Chrysler Corp., Detroit, 1940-41; prin. Lewis Shepard Co., Watertown, Mass., 1946-70, pres., 1965-70; treas., partner Lewis/Boyle, Inc., Waltham, Mass., 1971—; pres. Acme Walnut, Inc., Fidifisa, Inc.; treas L/B Leasing Inc., New Eng. Engines, Inc.; trustee Wartertown Savs. Bank. Served from 2d lt. to capt. Ordnance Corps, U.S. Army, 1941-46. Mem. ASME. Congregationalist. Clubs: Dedham Country and Polo, Norfolk Hunt. Home: 314 North St Medfield MA 02052 Office: 213 2d Ave Waltham MA 02154

LEWIS, JOHN LEEMAN, JR., obstetrician, gynecologist; b. San Antonio, June 5, 1929; s. John Leeman and Lois Black (Perry) L.; student U. Tex. at Austin, spring 1948; B.A., Harvard, 1952, M.D.

(Frederick Sheldon Traveling fellow 1952-53, Nat. scholar 1953-57), 1957; m. Jane Darling Davis, July 30, 1955 (div. 1976); children—Anne Darling, Elizabeth Perry, Katherine Folsom; m. 2d, Susan Vere Paris, Oct. 16, 1976. Intern Mass. Gen. Hosp., Boston, 1957-58, resident, 1958-59, 61-62; clin. asso. endocrinology Nat. Cancer Inst., Bethesda, Md., 1959-61; resident Boston Lying-in Hosp., 1962-65, Free Hosp. for Women, Brookline, 1962-65; asso. attending obstetrician and gynecologist Presbyn. Hosp., N.Y.C., July-Dec. 1967, also asso. prof. obstetrics and gynecology Coll. Phys. and Surgs. Columbia; pvt. practice medicine, specializing in obstetrics and gynecology, N.Y.C., 1967—; chief gynecology service Meml. Hosp. for Cancer and Allied Diseases, N.Y.C., 1968—. Asso. prof. Cornell U. Med. Coll. at N.Y.C., 1968-71, prof., 1971—; asso. attending obstetrician and gynecology N.Y. Lying-in Hosp., N.Y.C., 1968-71, attending obstetrician and gynecologist, 1971—. Served with USPHS, 1959-67. Recipient Alumni award Harvard Med. Sch., 1957. Diplomate Am. Bd. Obstetrics and Gynecology (dir. 1971—). Mem. Harvard Med. Alumni Assn. (councilor 1969-70). Democrat. Episcopalian. Clubs: Field (Englewood, N.J.); Griffis Faculty (N.Y.C.); Harvard (N.J. and N.Y.C.). Asso. editor Obstetrical and Gynecological Survey. Editorial bd. Gynecologic Oncology, Contemporary Ob/Gyn. Contbr. articles to profl. jours. Home: 450 E 63d St New York City NY 10021 Office: 1275 York Ave New York City NY 10021

LEWIS, PAUL LEROY, physician; b. Tamaqua, Pa., Aug. 30, 1925; s. Harry Earl and Rose Estella (Brobst) L.; A.B. magna cum laude, Syracuse U., 1950; M.D., State U. N.Y., 1953; m. Betty Jane Bixby, June 2, 1953; 1 son, Robert Harry. Intern Temple U. Hosp., Phila., 1953-54; resident in pathology Hosp. Univ. Pa., 1954-58; asst. pathologist Thomas Jefferson Univ. Hosp., Phila., 1958—, asst. dir. clin. labs., 1958-61; attending pathologist Methodist Hosp., Phila., 1961—, chmn. dept. pathology, dir. clin. labs., 1976—; cons. pathologist VA Hosp., Coatesville, Pa., 1967—, Biomed. Resources, Inc., 1969-74; pres. Penndell Labs., Inc., 1974—; asst. instr. pathology U. Pa. Med. Coll., 1957-58; instr. pathology Thomas Jefferson U. Coll. Medicine, 1958-62, asst. prof., 1962-65, asso. prof., 1965-75, prof., 1975—. Served with AUS, 1943-46. Fellow Am. Soc. Clin. Pathologists, Coll. Am. Pathologists; mem. Phila. County, Pa. State med. socs., AMA, Pathology Soc. Phila., Am. Med. Writers Assn., Internat. Acad. Pathologists, Am. Soc. Cytology, Phi Beta Kappa, Alpha Omega Alpha, Nu Sigma Nu. Club: Masons. Contbr. articles to profl. jours. Home: 521 Baird Rd Merion PA 19066 Office: 1020 Locust St Philadelphia PA 19107 also 2301 S Broad St Philadelphia PA 19148

LEWIS, RICHARD CYRUS, artist; b. Jackson, Mo., Jan. 16, 1934; s. Richard and Mary Elizabeth (Kneibert) L.; student (sch. scholar), Ringling Sch. Art, 1952-53, Parsons Sch. Design, 1956-57; m. Kathleen Helen Lucia, Sept. 8, 1959; children—Lucia, Antony, Garth, Brigid. Freelance fashion artist, N.Y.C., 1957; artist John G. Myers, Inc., Albany, N.Y., 1958-59; scenic, prodn. designer Albany Civic Theatre, 1957-59; artist fashion and layout for newspaper advt. Burdine's, Miami, Fla., 1960-62; fashion and layout chief Sears, Roebuck & Co., N.Y.C., 1963—; one man shows at Sanaa Gallery, Nyack, N.Y., 1975, Ward/Nasse Gallery, N.Y.C., 1975, Portobello, New Canaan (Conn.) Gallery, 1974-78, Del Valentino Gallery, N.Y.C., 1978, others; exhibited in group shows at Waikiki Outdoor Exhibit, 1954-55, Miami Beach, Fla., 1960-62, Lever House, N.Y.C., others; represented in permanent collections at Nyack Hosp., Rockland State Hosp., numerous pvt. collections, quick sketch portraits for ch., co. bazaars, boutiques, parties, others; freelance fashion artist for N.Y. Times, Clothes Mag.; tchr. oil painting, drawing/adult edn., Pearl River, N.Y., 1971-78; pvt. tchr. Roman Catholic. Home: 232 Centre St Pearl River NY 10965 Office: 1633 Broadway New York City NY 10019

LEWIS, RICHARD WARRINGTON BALDWIN, educator; b. Chgo., Nov. 1, 1917; s. Leicester Crosby and Beatrix Elizabeth (Baldwin) L.; grad. Phillips Exeter Acad., 1935; A.B., Harvard, 1939; M.A., U. Chgo., 1941, Ph.D., 1953; Litt.D., Wesleyan U., Middletown, Conn., 1961; m. Nancy Lindau, June 28, 1950; children—Nathaniel Lindau, Sophia Baldwin. Engaged as tchr. at Bennington Coll., 1948-50; dean Salzburg Seminar Am. Studies, 1950-51; vis. lectr. English, Smith Coll., 1951-52; asso. prof., then prof. English, Newark Coll., Rutgers U., 1954-59; vis. lectr. English, Yale, 1959-60, prof. English and Am. studies, 1960—; Fulbright lectr. Am. lit. U. Munich, 1957-58. Lit. cons. Universal Pictures, 1966—. Served to maj. AUS, 1942-46. Decorated Legion Merit; recipient award Nat. Inst. Arts and Letters, 1958; Pulitzer Prize for biography, 1976 Hodder fellow humanities Princeton, 1952-53, resident fellow creative writing, 1953-54; Kenyon Rev. fellow criticism, 1954-55; Am. Council Learned Socs. fellow, 1962-63; fellow Sch. Letters Ind. U., 1957—, sr. fellow, 1964—, chmn. English Inst., 1965; fellow Calhoun Coll. Author: The American Adam, 1955; The Picaresque Saint, 1959; Trials of the World, 1965; Edith Wharton: A Biography, 1975. Editor: Herman Melville (A Reader), 1962, The Presence of Walt Whitman, 1962; Malraux; A Collection of Critical Essays, 1964; Short Stories of Edith Wharton, 1910-1937; contbg. editor: Major Writers of America, 1962. Home: Litchfield Turnpike Bethany CT 06759 Office: Dept English Yale U New Haven CT 06520

LEWIS, ROBERT HALLAM, ret. clergyman; b. Hingham, Mass., Feb. 7, 1909; s. George Hallam and May (Kinney) L.; A.B., Tufts Coll., 1930, S.T.B., 1932; M.A., Boston U., 1970; m. Carolyn Ella Dodge, Feb. 9, 1942; 1 son, William Meriwether. Ordained to ministry Christian Ch., 1936; pastor Universalist Ch., Oldtown, Maine, 1934-36, Universalist Ch., Livermore Falls, Md., 1936-41; alien central officer U.S. Dept. Justice, Detroit, 1941-46; prof. philosophy New Eng. Coll., Henniker, N.H., 1947-51; pastor Conglist. Ch., Henniker, 1946-66; pastor Community Ch., Epping, N.H., 1966-74. Dir. Spiritual Life Rockingham County Home and Hosp., 1969-74; chaplain Rockingham County Jail, 1970-73; chmn. Fulbright Scholarship com. for N.H., 1961-63. Mason (Shriner). Home: Exeter Rd Epping NH 03042

LEWIS, STEVEN, systems cons.; b. Washington, Jan. 18, 1944; s. Melvin Earl and Beatrice (Fleischman) L.; B.S. in Indsl. Engring., Cornell U., 1965, M.Engring. in Indsl. Engring. and Ops. Research, 1967; Ph.D. in Ops. Research, Wharton Sch., U. Pa., 1978; m. Carol E. Weiss, June 26, 1966; children—Faye, Jaime. Systems engr. IBM, Princeton, N.J., Phila., 1966-73; sr. analyst Transaction Tech. Inc. subs. Citibank, 1973-74; dir. criminal justice systems Data Architects Inc., Waltham, Mass., 1974-76; sr. cons. Touche, Ross & Co., Wellesley, Mass., 1976-77; systems cons. Incoterm Corp., Wellesley, Mass., 1977—. Mem. Am. Inst. Indsl. Engrs., Inst. Mgmt. Sci., EDP Auditors Assn., Product Devel. and Mgmt. Assn. Home: 67 Chester St Newton MA 02161 Office: 65 Walnut St Wellesley MA 02181

LEWIS, STUART MILEY, lawyer; b. McLean, Va., Sept. 17, 1945; s. Guy Harold, Jr., and Helen Copp (Miley) L.; B.A., U. Va., 1967, J.D., 1970; m. Bronwen Elizabeth Begenau, Aug. 10, 1968; children—Ethan Gatewood, Cary Stuart. Admitted to Va. and D.C. bars, 1970; partner firm Silverstein & Mullens, Washington, Ivins, Phillips & Barker, Washington, 1970-73; adj. prof. law Georgetown U. Dir. Guy H. Lewis & Son, Inc. Vice pres. Va. Amateur Field Trail Assn., 1967-77; dir. Nat. Shooting Dog Championship, 1967-76. Mem. Am., Va., D.C. bar assns., Order of Coif, Phi Delta Phi, Phi Delta Epsilon, Kappa Sigma. Exec. editor Exec. Compensation Jour., 1973—; asso. editor Tax Mgmt., Inc., 1975—, Va. Law Weekly, 1969-70; editor Report of Interfaith Research Com., 1974-75; contbr. articles to profl. jours. Home: 6516 Topeka Rd McLean VA 22101 Office: 1776 K St Washington DC 20006

LEWIS, THOMAS HOWARD, psychiatrist, educator; b. Red Lodge, Mont., July 28, 1919; s. William Michel and Charlotte Amanda (Johnson) L.; B.S., U. Wash., 1943; M.D., Duke, 1946; m. Ruth Danielson, May 5, 1944; children—William Richard, Daniel John, Thomas Morgan, Linda Ruth, David Gryffdd. Lt., M.C., U.S. Navy, 1946, advanced through grades to capt., 1962; intern U.S. Naval Hosp., Houston, 1946-47; resident Nat. Naval Med. Center, Bethesda, Md., 1951-53, NIMH, 1960; dir. resident tng. in psychiatry Nat. Naval Med. Center, 1963-68, chief neurology and psychiatry, 1969-73; ret., 1973; prof. psychiatry Georgetown U. Sch. Medicine, 1975—. Diplomate Am. Bd. Neurology and Psychiatry. Fellow A.C.P., Am. Psychiat. Assn. Mem. AMA, Washington Psychoanalytic Soc., Washington Psychiat. Soc., N.Y. Acad. Sci., AAAS, Sigma Xi, Phi Sigma. Democrat. Clubs: Cosmos, St. David's Soc. (Washington). Author papers, books revs. Asso. editor Am. Indian Quar., 1975—. Home: 8503 Burning Tree Rd Bethesda MD 20034 Office: 5413 Cedar Ln 202C Bethesda MD 20014

LEWIS, WARREN REMER, photog. co. exec.; b. Rochester, N.Y., Nov. 16, 1920; s. Lawrence Remer and Elsa Caroline (Root) L.; B.A., Bucknell U., 1942; m. Gladys Eloise Rowland, Oct. 30, 1943; children—Michael Remer, Peter Rowland, Nancy Elizabeth, Paul Warren. With Eastman Kodak Co., Rochester, N.Y., 1942—, supr. apprentice tng., 1954-57, supr. personnel and tng., 1957-64, mgr. experience profl. recruitment, 1964-73, sec., 1973—, mem. fin. aid com. Trustee Nat. Council on Philanthropy; mem. nat. adv. com. Council Better Bus. Burs.; mem. sch. bd., Brighton, N.Y., 1962-67; chmn. various fund drives, 1955-73; mem. com. mgmt. YMCA, 1960-73; v.p. Rochester Bus. Com. for Arts, 1975—, Sister Cities Internat. of Rochester, 1975—; bd. dirs. Better Bus. Bur., Rochester, 1974—, Jr. Achievement, Rochester, 1976—. Served with Signal Corps, U.S. Army, 1943-46. Recipient citation Bur. Apprenticeship, U.S. Dept. Labor, 1963. Mem. Rochester C. of C., Conf. Bd., Grantmakers' Forum. Republican. Presbyterian. Clubs: Locust Hill Country, Masons, Shriners. Home: 394 Edgewood Ave Rochester NY 14618 Office: 343 State St Rochester NY 14650

LEWIS, WILLARD DEMING, univ. pres.; b. Augusta, Ga., Jan. 6, 1915; s. Willard and Constance (Deming) L.; A.B., Harvard, 1935, A.M., 1939, Ph.D., 1941; B.A., Oxford (Eng.) U., 1938, M.A., 1945; L.H.D., Moravian Coll.; LL.D., Lafayette Coll., Rutgers U., Hahnemann Med. Coll., Muhlenberg Coll., 1968; D.Sc., Med. Coll. Pa., 1972; D.Eng., Lehigh U., 1974; m. Marian Carter Chapman, Nov. 1, 1941 (dec. July 1965); children—Caroline Carter (Mrs. Ross Canterbury), Constance Carter (Mrs. Edward LaMonte), Linda Deming, Catherine Doten (Mrs. Owen Floody), Marian Chapman; m. 2d, Emmeline Ungurian Hoffman, Oct. 22, 1966; stepchildren—Cheryl Hoffman (Mrs. James Corsa), Thomas Hoffman. With Bell Telephone Labs., Inc., 1941-62, exec. dir. research communications systems, 1958-62; a founder, mng. dir. systems study center Bellcomm, Inc., 1962-64; pres. Lehigh U., 1964—. Dir. Bethlehem Steel, Pa. Power & Light Co., Fairchild Industries, Fischer-Porter Co. Mem. Polaris Communications Com., 1958-63, Def. Industry Adv. Com., 1962-63; mem. Naval Research Adv. Com., 1964-70, vice chmn., 1966, chmn., 1967-69; mem. Def. Sci. Bd., 1967-69; chmn. Space Applications Summer Study Nat. Acad. Scis., 1967-68; chmn. com. power plant siting Nat. Acad. Engring., 1970-72; chmn. Assn. Ind. Engring. Colls., 1968-70. Mem. sch. bd., Little Silver, N.J., 1949-50; chmn. Pa. State Bd. Edn., 1968-73. Mem. overseers com. to visit div. engring. and applied sci., Harvard, 1954-65; mem. council Harvard Found. Advanced Study and Research, 1959-64, chmn., 1961-62. Fellow I.E.E.E., AAAS; mem. Am. Phys. Soc., Am. Assn. Rhodes Scholars, Nat. Acad. Engring. (council 1972—, exec. com. 1973-75, 77-78), Harvard Engring. Soc., Delta Upsilon. Clubs: University (N.Y.C.); Cosmos (Washington); Saucon Valley Country (Bethlehem). Patentee in field. Home: President's House Lehigh Univ Campus Bethlehem PA 18015

LEWIS, WILLIAM C., JR., lawyer, ret. gen. air force; b. Wilburton, Okla.; B.A., U. Okla., 1934, LL.B., 1935, J.D., 1970; M.B.A., Harvard U., 1937; M. Air Law, Southeastern U., 1939; postgrad. Stanford U., 1934, U. Md., 1938, Am. U., 1939, U.S. Mil. Acad., 1931; grad. Indsl. Coll. Armed Forces, Air War Coll., Naval War Coll., Nat. War Coll. Enlisted U.S. Army, 1929, advanced through grades to lt. col., 1947; on staff comdr.-in-chief Pacific and Undersec. Navy, World War II; served from lt. (j.g.) to comdr. USN, 1942-47; from lt. col. to maj. gen. USAF, 1947-74; ret., 1974; admitted to Okla. bar, 1935, also D.C. bar, U.S. Supreme Ct. bar; individual practice law, Okla., 1935038; sr. trial atty. SEC, Washington, N.Y., N.J., other states, 1938-42; partner firm Lewis & Lewis, Washington, 1947-49; vis. prof., sr. fellow Woodrow Wilson Nat. Fellowship Found., 1973-76; gen. counsel Com. on Naval Affairs, U.S. Ho. of Reps., 1945-47; exec. asst. Senator Margaret Chase Smith, 1949-73; vis. lectr. law U. Ala. Chmn. exec. com. Margaret Chase Smith Library, 1973; trustee Freedom House, 1975. Decorated D.S.M., Legion of Merit, Meritorious Service medal, Jt. Service Commendation medal. Editor, author: (with Margaret Chase Smith) Declaration of Conscience, 1972. Mem. Air Res. Assn. (editor monthly mag. 1947-49), Res. Officers Assn., Alpha Tau Omega, Theta Nu Epsilon, Phi Lambda Epsilon. Home and Office: 807 Milestone Dr Silver Spring MD 20904

LEWIS, WILLIAM FREDERICK, physicist, r.r. exec.; b. N.Y.C., Aug. 11, 1949; s. Frederick A. and Ruth (Miller) L.; A.B., Princeton, 1971; M.S., U. Rochester, 1973; D.Engring. Sci., Columbia, 1976. Research asso. U. Rochester (N.Y.), 1971-73, Columbia, N.Y.C., 1973-76; research fellow U. London (Eng.), 1976-78; asst. mgr. strategic planning Conrail, 1978—; adj. lectr. dept. physics Coll. City N.Y., 1973; cons. physics of solids, U.S., Europe. Chmn., Princeton Schs. Com., Bklyn., 1974-76, London, 1976-78; bd. govs. Princeton Class of 1971, 1975-76. NSF grantee, 1966. Mem. Am. Phys. Soc., Inst. of Physics (U.K.), Sigma Xi. Clubs: Princeton of N.Y.; Caledonian (London); Princeton, Racquet (Phila.); Princeton of Gt. Britain (sec., gov. 1976-78). Contbr. articles in field to profl. jours. Home: Society Hill Towers W Apt 28C Philadelphia PA 19106 Office: Strategic Planning Conrail Six Penn Center Plaza Philadelphia PA 19104

LEWIS, WILSON D., banker; b. Indiana, Pa., July 17, 1908; s. I. Earl and Mary Belle (Shields) L.; A.B., Pa. State U., 1930; m. Anna B. Davis, Sept. 13, 1930; 1 dau., Elizabeth Lewis Wengert. Examiner, Pa. State Banking Dept., 1930-35; with Dauphin Deposit Trust Co., Harrisburg, Pa., 1935—, v.p., 1954-66, sr. v.p., 1966-70, pres., 1970—, chief exec. officer, 1972—, chmn. bd., chmn. exec. com., 1974—; pres., chmn. bd., chmn. exec. com., chief exec. officer Dauphin Deposit Corp.; partner Donald & Co., Campco; dir., chmn. fin. com. Millers Mut. Ins. Co.; v.p., dir. Munster Summerhill Coal Co.; dir. Union Quarries, Inc., Eastern Industries, Inc., AMP Inc., Pamcor, Inc., Stabler Cos., Inc. Bd. dirs. Harrisburg Area Indsl. Devel. Corp.; bd. dirs., v.p., chmn. fin. com. Polyclinic Med. Center; bd. dirs. Presbyn. Homes, James T. Hambay Found., Univ. Center at Harrisburg; trustee Found. for Ind. Colls., Inc. of Pa. Mem. Am. Inst. Banking (past pres. Harrisburg chpt.), C. of C. Greater Harrisburg Area (pres. 1966), Lancaster, York Area, Greater West Shore Area chambers commerce, Pa. State Alumni Assn., Kappa Sigma. Clubs: Masons (32 deg.), Shriners, Jesters; Country of Harrisburg, Blue Mountain Golf; Lafayette (York); Hamilton (Lancaster); Tuesday (Harrisburg); Surf (Miami Beach). Home: 3794 Dawn Mar St Lenker Manor Harrisburg PA 17111 Office: 213 Market St Harrisburg PA 17105

LEWISON, EDWARD FREDERICK, surgeon; b. Chgo., Feb. 11, 1913; s. Maurice and Julia (Trockey) L.; B.S., U. Chgo., 1932; M.D., Johns Hopkins, 1936; m. Elizabeth Oppenheim, June 1939 (dec. Jan. 1947); 1 son, John Edward; m. 2d, Betty Strauss Fleischmann, Mar. 21, 1948; children—Edward M., Robert S., Richard J. Intern surgery Johns Hopkins Hosp., Balt., 1936-37, asst. pathology, 1937-38, now surgeon, chief breast clinic, asso. prof. surgery, practice medicine specializing in breast surgery; resident surgery Passavant Meml. Hosp., Chgo., 1938-39; fellow surgery Beth Israel Hosp., N.Y.C., 1939-40. Pres., Md. div. Am. Cancer Soc., 1965-67, nat. med. dir. at large; vice-chmn. Internat. Reference Center, on evaluation of methods of diagnosis and treatment breast cancer WHO; mem. U.S.A.-USSR Med. Exchange Mission in Oncology, 1976. Served to lt. col. M.C., AUS, 1941-45; ETO. Recipient certificate of merit Am. Cancer Soc. Diplomate Am. Bd. Surgery. Fellow A.C.S., Royal Soc. Medicine; mem. Pan Am. Med. Assn., Brazilian Congress Surgeons. Club: Tryall (Jamaica, W.I.). Author: Breast Cancer and Its Diagnosis and Treatment, 1955. Contbr. numerous articles to profl. jours. Inventor rayable gauze used in surgery. Home: 4100 N Charles St Baltimore MD 21218 Office: 550 N Broadway St Baltimore MD 21205

LEWITUS, RICARDO, med. center admnstr.; b. Lima, Peru, Nov. 2, 1949; s. Hans and Eva (Heller) L.; came to U.S. 1977; M.D. Cayetano Heredia U. 1975. Dir., mgr. Jose E. Heller, Peru, S. Am. 1974-77; house staff mem. Maimonides Med. Center, Bklyn. 1977—. Recipient first prize for photography Municipalidad de Lima 1974. Contbr. reviews of 280 diphtheria cases, Children's Hosp., Lima, 1976. Address: 4706 Beach 47th St Brooklyn NY 11224

LEWONSKI, RICHARD FRANCIS, accountant; b. Waterbury, Conn., Oct. 12, 1934; s. Edward Walter and Sophie (Wodkiewicz) L.; B.S. in Accounting, Quinnipiac Coll., 1956; m. Leona B. Bissonnette, Apr. 25, 1959; children—Ronald, James, Sheila, Sharon, Linda, Allen. Cost estimator Gen. Electric Co., Burlington, Vt., 1958-62; internal revenue agt. IRS, Burlington, 1962-68; comptroller No. Oil Co. Inc., Burlington, 1968-70; pub. accountant Wesley A. Cilley, Registered Pub. Accountant, South Burlington, 1970—; pvt. practice, preparation of income tax returns, Winooski, Vt., 1968—. Chmn. sch. bd. St. Francis Xavier Roman Catholic Ch., Winooski. Mem. Am. Accounting Assn., Nat. Soc. Pub. Accountants, Vt. Assn. Pub. Accountants (v.p.), Assn. Enrolled Agts. Home: 33 Manseau St Winooski VT 05404

LEWY, ROBERT MAX, physician; b. N.Y.C., Oct. 18, 1945; s. Martin and Ellen L.; M.D., N.J. Coll. Medicine, 1971; M.P.H., Columbia U., 1976; m. Jocelyn Stuart Trueblood, Sept. 6, 1970; children—Jennifer Rachel, Sarah Melissa. Intern, Mary Hitchcock Meml. Hosp., Hanover, N.H., 1971-72; resident in family medicine Central Maine Family Medicine Residency, Augusta, 1974-75; Robert Wood Johnson clin. scholar Columbia U., 1975-77; asst. attending physician dept. medicine Columbia Presbyn. Med. Center, 1975-77, dir. employee health service, 1978—; asst. prof. pub. health Columbia U., 1978—; v.p. health services N.J. Health Services Corp., Newark, 1977-78. Served with USPHS, 1972-74. Mem. Am. Acad. Family Physicians, Am. Pub. Health Assn. Home: 864 Bradley Pkwy Blauvelt NY 10913

LEWY, STEPHAN HEINZ, hotel chain exec.; b. Berlin, Mar. 11, 1925; B.B.A., Northeastern U., 1952; came to U.S., 1942, naturalized, 1944; m. Frances Ina Silver, Sept. 3, 1949; children—Arthur L., Ellen G. Sr. auditor Harris, Kerr, Forster & Co., Boston, 1955-60; asst. controller Sheraton Corp. Am., Boston, 1960-71; v.p., treas. Dunfey Family Corp., Hampton, N.H., 1971—. Served with M.I., U.S. Army, 1943-45. Decorated Bronze Star. C.P.A. Mem. Mass., Am. insts. C.P.A.'s, Sigma Epilon Rho. Jewish. Home: 570 Kearney Circle Manchester NH 03104 Office: 490 Lafayette Rd Hampton NH 03842

LEYTON, ROBERT ALAN, health sci. adminstr., govt. ofcl.; b. Boston, Feb. 7, 1934; s. William Myer and Leah (Kaplan) L.; A.B. in Biology, Boston U., 1955, A.M. in Biology, 1956, Ph.D. in Med. Scis., 1968; m. Shirley Eve Segal, July 1, 1967. Research fellow in physiology Boston U. Sch. Medicine, 1966-67, teaching fellow in physiology, 1967-68; asso. in medicine Harvard Med. Sch., Peter Bent Brigham Hosp., Boston, 1968-70; Paul Dudley White fellow Mass. Heart Assn., 1968, grantee, 1969; Muscular Dystrophy Assn. fellow, 1969, grants asso. div. research grants NIH, Bethesda, Md., 1970-71, asst. for planning to asso. dir. for clin. applications and prevention Nat. Heart and Lung Inst., NIH, Bethesda, 1971-72, asst. to dir. office of program planning and evaluation, 1972-76, interagy. programs officer, office of dir., 1972-76; chief field ops. div. med. research service VA, Washington, 1976-76, dir. devel. and mgmt. service Office of Extended Care, 1978—. Mem. Electron Microscopy Soc. Am., Am. Soc. Cell Biology, Royal Microscopy Soc., Am., European microcirculatory socs., New Eng. Electron Microscopic Soc., Aerospace Med. Assn., Air Force Assn., Sigma Xi. Clubs: Harvard (D.C.), Indian Springs Country, Masons. Home: 11428 Beechgrove Ln Potomac MD 20854 Office: 810 Vermont Ave Washington DC 20420

LI, CHANG-YANG, nuclear engr.; b. Hunan, China, June 23, 1946; s. Pin-Hua and Tso-May (Liao) L.; B.S. (fellow), Tsinghua U., 1968; M.S. (univ. scholar), Catholic U. Am., 1971, Ph.D., 1978; m. Yueh-Li, July 31, 1971; children—Renee, Grace. Lead engr. Singer Simulation Products Co., Silver Spring, Md., 1973-75; sr. research asst. Martin-Marietta Lab., Balt., 1975-76; sr. engr. Bechtel Power Co., Gaithersburg, Md., 1976-78; staff engr. NUS Corp., Rockville, Md., 1978—. Pres., Chinese Assn. Cath. U. Am., 1972-73. Registered profl. engr., Md. Mem. ASME, Am. Meteorology Soc., Tsinghua U. Alumni Assn. of Washington Area (pres. 1977-78). Contbr. articles in nuclear engring. to profl. jours. Home: 16452 Tomahawk Dr Gaithersburg MD 20760 Office: 4 Research Pl Rockville MD 20850

LI, EMANUEL YUN-SUN, thoracic surgeon, physician; b. Hong Kong, Sept. 4, 1920; s. Tat-Yan and Tsui-Ying (Leung) L.; came to U.S., 1948, naturalized, 1961; M.D., Aurora U. and Med. Sch., Shanghai, China, 1945; m. Patricia Welch, Oct. 20, 1956; children—Mary F., Peter E., Margaret, Catherine, Patricia, Thomas, John, Elizabeth, Patrick M. (dec.). Intern, St. John Episcopal Hosp., Bklyn., 1948-49; resident St. Luke's Hosp., Newburgh, N.Y., 1949-50; resident gen. surgery Grace Hosp., Detroit, 1950-51, Grad. Sch. Medicine, U. Pa., 1951-52, Clifton Springs (N.Y.) Hosp., 1952-55, Meml. Hosp. Cancer, N.Y.C., 1955-56; resident St. Luke's Hosp., Newburgh, N.Y., 1949-50; chest physician Homer Falls Hosp., Oneonta, N.Y., 1956-57; asst. attending thoracic surgery Albany (N.Y.) Med. Coll. Hosp., 1959-68; resident thoracic surgery Albany Med. Center Hosp., 1957-59; attending surgeon, physician Taylor

Brown Meml. Hosp., Waterloo, N.Y., 1968—; individual practice medicine, specializing in thoracic surgery and family practice, Waterloo, 1968—. Bd. dirs. Seneca County Chest Clinic, Seneca County Health Dept., Finger Lakes (N.Y.) chpt. Am. Heart Assn. Diplomate Am. Bd. Family Practice. Fellow Am. Acad. Family Practice; mem. Y.Y. State, Seneca County med. assns., AMA, Am. Heart Assn., Am. Coll. Chest Physicians. Republican. Roman Catholic. Clubs: Seneca Country, Red Jacket Yacht (Seneca Falls, N.Y.). Author: (with others) Traumatic Aortic Aneurysm-Excision and Anastomosis without a Graft, 1961; Diseases of the Chest, 1963. Home: 100 State St Seneca Falls NY 13148 Office: Taylor Brown Med Center Waterloo NY 13165

LI, NORMAN CHUNG, chemist; b. Foochow, China, Jan. 13, 1913; s. Pei Ting and Chin Tuan (Lin) L.; came to U.S., 1930, naturalized, 1954; B.S., Kenyon Coll., 1933; M.S., U. Mich., 1934; Ph.D., U. Wis., 1936; m. Hazel Chou, Mar. 30, 1937; children—Peter, Paul, John, Mary, Eunice. Prof., Anhwei U., Anking, China, 1936-38; lectr. chemistry Yenching U., Peiping, China, 1938-40; prof. FuJen U., Peiping, 1940-46; asso. prof. St. Louis U., 1946-52; prof. Duquesne U., 1952—; cons. Argonne Nat. Lab.; adviser Nat. Sci. Council Republic of China, Chemistry Research Inst., Taiwan, Nuclear Magnetic Resonance Biomed. Facilities, Pitts. Recipient Distinguished Service Prof. award Duquesne U., 1978; NSF, NIH and ERDA grantee. Fellow AAAS, Am. Inst. Chemists; mem. Am. Chem. Soc., Soc. Applied Spectroscopy, Sigma Xi. Democrat. Roman Catholic. Club: Univ. Chinese of Pitts. Research, numerous publs. in field. Home: 5563 Beacon St Pittsburgh PA 15217 Office: Duquesne U Pittsburgh PA 15219

LI, TIEN-SHUN, physician; b. Taiwan, China, Nov. 13, 1932; s. Chao-Lieh and Chen (Wang) L.; came to U.S., 1968, naturalized, 1977; M.D., Nat. Taiwan U., 1960; Ph.D., Osaka U. Med. Sch., Japan, 1967; m. Shue-Lee Cheng, Nov. 27, 1964; children—Thomas, Robert, Henry. Research fellow U. Mich., N.Y. Med. Coll., Cornell U. Med. Coll., 1968-71; resident in obstetrics and gynecology St. Barnabas Med. Center, Livingston, N.J., 1971-73; asst. prof. obstetrics and gynecology Cornell U. Med. Coll., N.Y.C., 1973-74; asst. prof. obstetrics and gynecology N.J. Med. Sch., Newark, 1974—. Diplomate Am. Bd. Obstetrics and Gynecology. Fellow Am. Coll. Obstetricians and Gynecologists; mem. Am. Fertility Soc., Med. Soc. N.J., Bergen County Med. Soc. Contbr. articles to med. jours. Office: 2231 Lemoine Ave Fort Lee NJ 07024

LI, TINA YU HENG, art co. exec.; b. Nanking, China, Nov. 22, 1939; d. Chieh and C.H. (Tai) Teng; M.S.W., N.Y. U., 1961. Supr. psychiat. social work dept. Meyer Psychiat. Hosp., N.Y.C., 1961-71; pres. Yu Heng Art Co., N.Y.C., 1971—; exhibited one-person shows: China Art Atelier, N.Y.C., 1969, The Way Gallery, N.Y.C., 1970, Jordan Marsh, Miami, 1971. Mem. Nat. Assn. Social Workers, Acad. Certified Social Workers. Home: 303 E 57th St New York NY 10022 Office: 880 3d Ave New York NY 10022

LIANG, YU-JEAN, oceanographer; b. Fuchou, Fukien, China, Dec. 2, 1942; s. Shun-Yao and Sue-Hwei (Lee) L.; B.Sc., Chung-Hsing U., Taiwan, 1966; M.Sc., State U. N.Y. at Stony Brook, 1971; doctoral candidate U. R.I., 1973—; m. Lily Chang, Dec. 30, 1971. Research asso. soil organic chemistry Taiwan Sugar Exptl. Sta., 1966-68; research tech. specialist in marine sci. State U. N.Y. at Stony Brook, 1969-73; research asst. in oceanography U. R.I., Kingston, 1973-77, research scientist in oceanography, 1977-78; marine scientist in oceanography U. Del., Newark, 1978—. Mem. Am. Assn. Limnology and Oceanography, Am. Geophys. Union. Contbr. articles to sci. jours. Home: 906-L Peachtree Rd Claymont DE 19703 Office: U Del Newark DE 19711

LIAO, SUNG JUI, physician; b. Changsha, China, Nov. 15, 1917; s. Shu Fan and Sophie (Chou) L.; came to U.S., 1947, naturalized, 1958; M.D., Yale-in-China, 1942; M.P.H., Nat. Central U., China, 1944; acad. diploma Pub. Health U. London, 1946, acad. diploma bacteriology, 1947; postgrad. (Brit. Council scholar) London Sch. Hygiene and Tropical Medicine, 1945-47, (Milbank Meml. fellow) Yale Sch. Medicine, 1947-49; m. Karin Agren, Apr. 18, 1953; children—Thomas, Elizabeth, Margaret, John. Intern. Nat. Center Hosp., Kweiyang, China, 1941-42; clin. fellow phys. medicine Mass. Gen. Hosp., Boston, 1955-57; practice medicine specializing in phys. medicine and rehab., Waterbury and Middlebury, Conn., 1957—, Danbury, Conn., 1957-69; attending physiatrist, 1957—, dir. phys. medicine and rehab. Waterbury Hosp., 1957-73; attending physiatrist St. Mary's Hosp., Waterbury, Conn., 1957-65, Danbury Hosp., 1957-69. Asst. dir. phys. medicine and rehab. Conn. commn. chronically ill, aged and infirm Rocky Hill Hosp., 1957; med. dir. Easter Seal Rehab. Center, Waterbury, 1957-62; cons. physiatrist Middlesex Meml. Hosp., Middletown, 1957-60, New Milford Hosp., 1957—, Sharon Hosp., 1965—, St. Raphael Hosp., 1971—; dist. med. cons. Div. Vocat. Rehab., Conn. Dept. Edn., Danbury, 1963-69, Waterbury, 1966-72, adminstrv. med. cons., Hartford, 1969-72; asst. prof. preventive medicine Yale U. Med. Sch., New Haven, 1950-54; asso. research prof. bacteriology U. Utah Med. Coll., Salt Lake City, 1949-50; asso. clin. prof. rehab. medicine Boston U. Sch. Medicine, 1967-73; lectr., 1973—; hon. cons. in biomechanics Inst. Rehab. Medicine N.Y. U., N.Y., 1969—, clin. asso. prof., 1972—, clin. prof. oral surgery, 1978—. Diplomate Am. Bd. Phys. Medicine and Rehab. Fellow A.C.P., Royal Soc. Medicine Eng., Am. Pub. Health Assn., Royal Soc. Health Eng., Am. Acad. Phys. Medicine and Rehab., mem. Conn. Soc. Phys. Medicine (pres. 1961-62, 70-71), Am. Congress Phys. Medicine and Rehab., Conn. State Med. Soc. (chmn. ad hoc com. acupunctúre 1973-76), N. Am. Acad. Manipulative Medicine (councilor 1969-72, sec.-treas. 1972-74), Am. Assn. Immunologists, Am. Fedn. Clin. Research (sr.), Internat. Soc. Electromyographic Kinesiology (charter), L'Union Scientifique Mondiale des Médecins Acupuncteur et des Sociétés d'Acupuncture (sec. N.Am. 1973—), Research Inst. of Acupuncture and Chinese Medicine (pres. 1972—), Acupuncture Soc. Conn. (pres. 1975—), Am. Acad. Acupuncture (sec. 1975—), Sigma Xi. Contbr. articles to profl. publs. Home: 66 Skyline Dr Middlebury CT 06762 Office: Route 188 and North Benson Rd Middlebury CT 06762

LIAS, NICHOLAS CONSTANTINE, communications co. exec.; b. Lowell, Mass., Aug. 11, 1929; s. Constantine Petros and Katherine (Rallis) Liacopoulos; B.S., U. Lowell, 1952; M.B.A., Northeastern U., 1959; m. Anne Panagiotopoulos, Sept. 30, 1956; children—Cathy Anne, Deborah Arete. Mech. design engr. Portsmouth (N.H.) Naval Shipyard, 1952-53; devel. engr. H & V. Splts. Co., W. Groton, Mass., 1953-60; sr. engr. Western Electric Co., Inc., N. Andover, Mass., 1960-73; gen. mgr. Motorola, Inc., Carlisle, Pa., 1973—; instr. U. Lowell, 1969-73; cons. in field. Bd. dirs. United Way, Carlisle, 1976. Served with USAF, 1953. Registered profl. engr., Mass.; recipient Engring Excellence award Western Electric. Co., 1971; United Way Vol. award, 1975, 76; Dan Noble fellow Motorola, Inc., 1977. Mem. Am. Assn. Crystal Growth, ASME, Materials Research Soc., Internat. Mgmt. Council, Carlisle C. of C., Am. Hellenic Ednl. Progressive Assn., U. Lowell Alumni Assn. Greek Orthodox. Patentee high pressure quartz growth; contbr. articles to profl. jours. Office: PO Box 279 Route 11 SW Carlisle PA 17013

LIAUW, HUI-LIAN TAN, immunologist; b. Indonesia, Sept. 2, 1935; d. Chong-Teng and Siew-Bauw (Ong) Tan; came to U.S., 1960, naturalized, 1973; B.Sc., Nanyang U., Singapore, 1959; B.A., Coll. of Holy Names, Oakland, Calif., 1963; M.A., U. Calif., Berkeley, 1964; m. Koei-Liang Liauw, June 30, 1961; 1 dau., Julita M. Lab. Instr. Coll. of Holy Names, summers 1962-64; immunologist research div. CIBA-Geigy Pharm., CIBA-Geigy Corp., Ardsley, N.Y., 1965—. Mem. Am. Soc. Microbiology, N.Y. Acad. Scis., Sigma Xi. Contbr. articles to profl. jours. Home: 285 W Stevens St Wyckoff NJ 07481 Office: CIBA-Geigy Corp Research Div Saw Mill River Rd Ardsley NY 10502

LIBA, GERALD RONALD, banker; b. Bridgeport, Conn., May 3, 1944; s. Steven and Helen Elizabeth (Phillips) L.; B.S., U. Conn., 1967; M.B.A., U. Bridgeport, 1970. Project adminstr. Perkin Elmer Corp., Norwalk, Conn., 1967-68; market research analyst, field sales rep. Remington Arms Co., Bridgeport, 1968-73; asst. treas., mgr. market research Peoples Savs. Bank, Bridgeport, 1973—; lectr. U. Bridgeport, 1970-72. Active planning, budgeting and allocation task force Greater Bridgeport Area United Way. Mem. Am. Mktg. Assn. (treas. S. Conn. chpt. 1971-72, pres. 1975-76), U. Bridgeport M.B.A. Assn. (by-laws com.). Roman Catholic. Home: 41D Greenhouse Rd Bridgeport CT 06606 Office: 855 Main St Bridgeport CT 06604

LIBBY, ELLEN WEBER, counselor, educator; b. Bridgeport, Conn., July 11, 1946; d. Melvin and Shirley (Gross) Weber; B.A., George Washington U., 1967, M.A., 1970; Ph.D., U. Md., 1977; m. Henry N. Libby, Aug. 27, 1967. Sr. rehab. therapist Psychiat. Inst., Washington, 1970-72, supervisory rehab. therapist, 1972-75, asso. dir. Personal Resource Center, 1975-76; clin. dir. Tri-County Youth Services Bur., Hughsville, Md., 1977-78; asst. prof. Counseling and Personnel Services, U. Md., 1978—; clin. asso. Washington Center for Psychol. Services, specializing in concerns of women; mem. faculty No. Va. Community Coll., 1975, U. Md., 1976-77; cons. Men's Awareness Network, 1975, Md. Dept. Vocat. Rehab., 1976, referral panel Group Health Assn., 1976—. HEW research fellow, 1976-77. Mem. Am. Personnel and Guidance Assn., Assn. for Specialists in Group Work, Am. Rehab. Counseling Assn. Home: 5510 Montgomery St Chevy Chase MD 20015 Office: Counseling and Personnel Services U Md College Park MD 20742

LIBERMAN, NORMAN JACOB, psychologist; b. Paterson, N.J., Mar. 16, 1921; s. Philip and Rose (Bernstein) L.; B.Sc., N.Y. U., 1960, M.A., 1961; m. Sylvia Hittner, Nov. 24, 1944; children—Dana, Garth. Treas., Philip Liberman, Inc., N.Y.C., 1948-54; pres. Queensberry Fabrics Corp., N.Y.C., 1950-55; with First Investors Corp., N.Y.C., 1955-56, Boy Scouts Am., 1957-60; mem. faculty State U. N.Y., Bklyn., 1962-64; therapist Plainfield Cons. Center, N.J., 1963-70; faculty mem. City U. N.Y., 1970-73, Fordham U., 1971-73, Free U. Berlin, 1972, 76, Workshop Inst. Living-Learning, N.Y.C. and Zurich, Switzerland, 1966—; co-founder. Served with M.C., field arty., U.S. Army, 1941-42. New Sch. for Social Research fellow, 1961-62. Mem. Assn. Humanistic Psychology, Deutsche Gesellschaft fur Humanistische Psychologie, AAUP, Am. Personnel and Guidance Assn., Am. Soc. Group Psychotherapy and Psychodrama, N.Y. Soc. Gen. Semantics. Republican. Roman Catholic. Clubs: Califanians, Tuesday Talkers, Wm. James. Co-author: Theme-Centered Interaction, 1972; co-editor: Lines and Letters, 1959-60; asst. editor Ednl. Synopsis, 1960-61.

LICCINI, STEPHEN L., contracts adminstr.; b. Washington, May 12, 1945; s. John L. and Mary Rose (Lizzi) L.; B.S. in Mech. Engring., U. Md., 1967; M.S., Frostburg State Coll., 1972; m. Lonna Louise Schwenninger, Aug. 24, 1968; children—Kelli Marie, Mark Stephen. Engr., Celanese Fibres Co., Cumberland, Md., 1967-71, tech. services supr., 1971-73, tech. supt., 1973-75, Rock Hill, S.C., 1975-77; asst. to chief engr. Westvaco Corp., Luke, Md., 1977-78; contracts adminstr. Exxon Corp., Florham Park, N.J., 1978—; mem. faculty W.Va. U., Potomac Coll. campus, 1977—; mem. Allegany Assos., 1977-78. Gen. chmn. Westvaco Charity Campaign, 1977-78; youth basketball coach YMCA, 1971—; trustee, mem. adminstrv. bd. Davis Meml. Methodist Ch., 1977—. Mem. Am. Inst. Chem. Engrs., ASME, Am. Mgmt. Assn. Republican. Methodist. Club: Tennis. Home: 7 Kings Ridge Rd Long Valley NJ 07853 Office: Exxon Corp Florham Park NJ 07932

LICHELLO, ROBERT, author; b. Parkersburg, W.Va., Sept. 12, 1926; s. Anthony and Stella (Camorota) L.; B.A. in English, W.Va. U., 1951; m. Helen Rowe, Jan, 1957. Feature writer N.Y. Enquirer, 1957-59: editor Volitant Pub. Co., N.Y.C., 1959-64, Nat. Graphic Co., N.Y.C., 1964-67; pres. New Style News Pub. Co., Stamford, N.Y., 1970. Reader Recording for the Blind, N.Y.C., 1960. Sec. Town Planning Bd., Summit, N.Y., 1975. Served to sgt., AUS, 1945-47. Recipient Audio Devices Internat. Sound Recording prize, 1953. Author: Ju-Jitsu Self-Defense for Teen-Agers, 1961; Has Dr. Max Gerson a True Cancer Cure?. 1962; Sin Paradise, 1963; The Trouble with Marilyn's Pants, 1966; How to Build Your Fortune with Mutual Funds, 1967; Pioneer in Blood Plasma: Dr Charles R. Drew, 1968; Dag Hammarskjold, A Giant in Diplomacy, 1971; Enrico Fermi, Father of the Atomic Bomb, 1971; Edward R. Murrow, Broadcaster of Courage, 1971; Superpower Investing, 1974; How To Make $1,000,000 in the Stock Market-Automatically, 1977. Author column Mr. Investor. Inventor synchrovest investment system, 1972, automatic investment mgmt. system, 1975. Address: POB 101 Summit NY 12175

LICHTENSTADTER, ILSE, educator; b. Hamburg, Germany; d. Jacob and Flora (Levi) Lichtenstadter; Ph.D., U. Frankfort am Main (Germany), 1931; D.Phil., U. Oxford (Eng.), 1937; came to U.S., 1938, naturalized, 1944. Librarian, Queen's Coll., Cambridge, Eng., 1933-35; specialist in Oriental langs. Oxford U. Press, 1935-38; cataloguer library Jewish Theol. Sem., N.Y.C., 1938-45; asst. prof. Arabic and Islamic culture The Asia Inst., N.Y.C., 1942, prof., 1946-52; lectr. Islamic culture N.Y. U., 1952-60, Rutgers U., 1959-60; lectr. on Arabic, Harvard U., 1960-74, emerita, 1974. Cons. Arabic, The Bollingen Found., 1954—. Notgemeinschaft der Deutschen Wissenschaft fellow, 1932-33; Social Sci. Research Council fellow, 1950, 55; Fulbright travel grantee, 1963. Mem. Am. Oriental Soc. Clubs: N.Y. Oriental; Harvard Faculty (life mem.). Author: Women in the Aiyam al-'Arab, 1935; The Kitab al-Muhabbar by Muhammad ibn Habib, 1942; Islam and the Modern Age, 1958; Introduction to Classical Arabic Literature, 1974. Gen. editor: Library of Classical Arabic Literature: Vol. I Ibn Tufayl's Hayy Ibn Yaqzan, 1972, II: The Tales of the Prophets, by al-Kisa'i, 1978, Vol. III: The Case of the Animals vs. Man before the King of the Jinn, 1978. Contbr. articles to profl. jours. Home: 14 Concord Ave Cambridge MA 02138

LICHTENSTEIN, ROSALIE, gerontologist; b. N.Y.C., d. Harry and Anna Young; B.S., Coll. City N.Y., 1956; M.S., Fordham U., 1972, profl. diploma, 1973, M.S.W., 1979; Ph.D. in Gerontol. Counseling, Internat. Open U., Clayton, Mo., 1979; m. Bernard Litchenstein. Biomed. researcher; psychiat. social worker, 1974; community coordinator Harlem Valley Psychiat. Center, Wing, 1976—, team leader geratric outpatient service, 1977—; bd. dirs. Westchester Community Mental Health Bd., Westchester Community Service Council, Mental Health After Care Com.; adv. com. gerontology Fordham U. Mem. Am. Personnel and Guidance Assn., Nat. Council Aging, Gerontol. Soc., N.Y. State Sr. Action Council, Nat. Assn. Social Workers, Preretirement Council, Nat. Rehab. Assn., Newspaper Inst. Am. Contbr. to profl. publs. Address: 97 F Chestnut Hill Bethel CT 06801

LICOPOLI, FRANCIS LOUIS, psychologist; b. Floral Park, N.Y., June 5, 1933; s. Carl and Adele L.; B.S. in Engring., Villanova U., 1955; M.A. in Edn., St. Joseph's Coll., 1965; certificate in counseling psychology Lehigh U., 1973; m. Patricia June Lyon, Aug. 6, 1966; children—Charles Christopher, Robert Francis, William Joseph. Civil engr. Hendrickson Bros. Contractors, Valley Stream, N.Y., 1959-61; commd. 1st lt. U.S. Marine Corps, 1955, advanced through grades to maj., 1970; adminstrv. asst. to combat engr. schs. for all marine units, 1956-58; adj. Marine Air Control Squadron, 1965-70, ret., 1973; counselor Bucks County Community Coll., 1969-74; pvt. practice psychology, Quakertown, Pa., 1974—; instr. psychology Bucks County Community Coll., Newtown, Pa., 1974—. Chmn. Quakertown Planning Commn., 1973; pres. bd. dirs. Independence Place Community Assn., 1974; chmn. Quakertown Zoning Hearing Bd., 1976-78; psychiat. emergency del. Bucks County Mental Health/Mental Retardation Bd. Lic. counseling psychologist, Pa. Mem. Am. Psychol. Assn. Democrat. Roman Catholic. Home: 325 E Broad St Quakertown PA 18951 Office: Upper Trumbauersville Rd Quakertown PA 18951

LIDDLE, HOWARD ARTHUR, counseling psychologist; b. Hoboken, N.J., Oct. 11, 1948; s. Howard C. and Martha M. L.; B.A. in Psychology, St. Leo Coll., 1970; M.S. in Community Mental Health (NIMH fellow), No. Ill. U., 1972, Ed.D. in Counseling Psychology, 1974. Grad. teaching asst. dept. psychology No. Ill. U., 1970-71, intern, 1971-72, staff asst. office of dean Coll. Liberal Arts, 1972-73, faculty asst. div. counselor edn., div. marriage and family relations, 1973-74, asst. prof. counselor edn., summer 1974; asst. prof. counseling psychology Temple U., 1974—, also dir. Community Counseling Clinic, 1975-77; predoctoral intern Ben Gordon Community Mental Health Center, DeKalb, Ill., 1973-74; postdoctoral extern Phila. Child Guidance Clinic, 1975-77; pvt. practice psychology, marital and family therapy. Lic. psychologist, Pa.; registered psychometrist, Fla. Fellow Am. Orthopsychiat. Assn.; mem. Am. Acad. Psychologists Marital and Family Therapy, Am. Assn. Marriage and Family Therapy (approved supr.), Am. Personnel and Guidance Assn., Am. Psychol. Assn., Assn. Counselor Edn., Supervision, Family Inst. Phila., Nat. Council Family Relations, Pa. Psychol. Assn., Pa. Assn. Marriage and Family Counselors, Phila. Soc. Clin. Psychologists. Contbr. articles on tng. and supervision in family therapy to profl. jours. Developer videotape tng. materials in family therapy; survey research on nature and scope of coursework and tng. in marital and family therapy, outcome research supervision. Home: Society Hill Towers 200 Locust St Apt 26D Philadelphia PA 19106 Office: Counseling Psychology Dept Temple U Philadelphia PA 19122

LIDDY, RICHARD ANGIER, securities exec.; b. Fairfield, Ia., Sept. 3, 1935; s. Lucius B. and Ruth A. (Angier) L.; B.S., Ia. State U., 1957; postgrad. U. Conn., 1958-59; m. Joanne Sjostrom, July 3, 1957; children—Jeanne, Robert, James. With Conn. Gen. Ins. Corp., Bloomfield, Conn., 1957—, pension cons., 1957-65, reins. sales mgr., 1965-71, pres. broker/dealer securities, 1971-74, regional v.p., 1974-77, v.p. in charge brokerage, 1977—; dir. CG Equity Sales Co., Investment Co. Inst., Washington. Corporator, Hartford Sem. Found. Served with AUS, 1958. C.L.U. Mem. Life Ins. Mgmt. and Research Assn. (chmn. equity products com. 1972, 73). Republican. Universalist (trustee ch.). Club: Hartford Golf. Home: 423 Mountain Rd West Hartford CT 06107 Office: Conn Gen Ins Corp Hartford CT 06152

LIEB, ROBERT LEONARD, urologist, educator; b. Newark, Nov. 5, 1915; s. Joseph and Annie (Brownstein) L.; A.B., U. Mich., 1936; M.D., U. Western Ont., Can., 1943; m. Leatrice Chester, Sept. 18, 1948 (dec.); children—Beth, Melanie; m. 2d, Mollie A. Lieberman, Dec. 1978. Cellist, N.J. Symphony Orch., 1928-32; intern Newark City Hosp., 1943-44; resident urology Boston City Hosp., 1944, Bayonne City Hosp., N.J., 1944-46; practice medicine specializing in urology, Newark, 1947-62, South Orange, N.J., 1962-73, West Orange, N.J., 1973—; asst. clin. prof. urology N.J. Coll. Medicine, Newark, 1966—; sr. cons. VA, Lyons, N.J., 1958—. Bd. dirs. dept. urology Martland Med. Center, Newark, N.J., 1964-65. Pres., Mountain Top Civic Assn., Short Hills, N.J., 1968. Diplomate Am. Bd. Urology. Fellow A.C.S., Internat. Coll. Surgeons, N.J. Soc. Surgeons; mem. Am. Urol. Assn., A.M.A., N.J. State Med. Soc. (del. Essex county 1968-73). Mem. B'nai B'rith. Club: Crestmont Country. Editorial bd. Newark Beth Israel Med. Center, 1960-64. Home: 27 Joanna Way Short Hills NJ 07078 Office: 100 Northfield Ave West Orange NJ 07052

LIEBENSTEIN, RICHARD, computer parts mfr.; b. Guetzingen, Germany, May 4, 1922; s. Joseph and Barbara (Rudelgass) L.; Master Mechanic, Meisterschule-Handwerks Kammer Wuerzburg, 1947; m. Elfrieda Bronner, Feb. 11, 1956; children—Richard Joseph, Claire, Margaret. Came to U.S., 1953, naturalized, 1958. Apprentice, Anton Fuchs-Goldbach, Germany, 1936-40; owner machine shop, Guetzingen, 1948-51; service engr. mech. computer Casa Pratt, Rio de Janiero, 1952-53; toolmaker Steck Co., Mt. Vernon, N.Y., 1953-56, Kearfott, Clifton, N.J., 1959-63; owner Magnetic Dielectrics Corp., Hawthorne, N.J., 1963-67; pres. Magnetic Dielectrics Corp., West Milford, N.J., 1967—. Mem. West Milford Indsl. Commn. Served with German Army, 1943-45. Mem. Am. Ceramic Soc., West Milford C. of C. Lion (pres.). Home: 939 Westbrook Rd West Milford NJ 07480 Office: Industrial Dr West Milford NJ 07480

LIEBERMAN, LOUIS, architect; b. N.Y.C., Mar. 24, 1915; s. Harry and Dora (Soberman) L.; B.Arch., Pratt Inst. Sch. Arch., 1934; m. Ellie Miller, June 28, 1947; 1 son, Harvey Michael. Pvt. practice architecture, Bklyn., 1938—. Mem. N.Y.C. Mayor's Panel Architects; v.p. Bklyn. Architects Scholarship Fund. Fellow Am. Registered Architects; mem. Bklyn. Soc. Architects (pres. 1971-78), AIA (dir. Bklyn. chpt. 1969-72, sec. 1972-74, v.p. 1975-77), Nat. Council Archtl. Registration Bd., Architects Council N.Y. (pres. 1977-78). Clubs: Masons, B'nai B'rith. Home: 65 Hungry Harbor Rd North Woodmere NY 11598 Office: 82 Livingston St Brooklyn NY 11201

LIEBERMAN, MORRIS BARUCH, psychologist, educator; b. Warsaw, Poland, Nov. 8, 1925; s. Aaron and Pearl D. (Orlinsky) L.; came to U.S., 1959, naturalized, 1964; diploma bus. adminstrn. I.C.S., 1961; B.A., Connolly Coll., 1965; M.S., L.I. U., 1968, Ph.D., 1973; postgrad. (N.Y. Dept. Mental Hygiene fellow) Advanced Inst. Analytic Psychotherapy, 1969-72; m. Bilha Reichberg, Jan. 26, 1948; children—Aaron, Shiloh, Pnina. Psychiat. nurse Gena Hosp., Kupat Holim, Israel, 1944-50; dist. dir. med. servces Holon, Israel, 1952-59; research asso., neuro-psychol. lab. Einstein Coll. Medicine, Bronx, N.Y., 1965-66, sr. clin. psychologist, chief neuropsychiatry Bronx Psychiat. Center, 1968-72; psychologist Kingsbrook Med. Center, Bklyn., 1966-68; prof. psychology U. City N.Y., 1972—; cons. Nat. Council Jewish Women, Bklyn., 1974-77; prin. psychologist, dir. Heights-Hill inpatient service South Beach Psychiat. Center of N.Y. State Dept. Mental Hygiene, Richmond, 1975; chief psychologist, coordinator psychiat. service Workman Circle Med. Dept., 1975—;

pvt. practice clin. psychology, Bklyn., 1973—; adj. prof. psychology L.I. U.-Bklyn. Coll. Pharmacy, 1970—; tng. analyst Internat. Sch. for Mental Health Practitioners, 1978—, Am. Inst. for Creative Living, 1978—. Served to sgt. maj., M.C., Israeli Army, 1950-59. Cert. psychologist, N.Y. State; lic. sch. psychologist, N.Y.C.; permanent cert. in sch. psychology, New York State; cert. Council for Nat. Registry Health Providers in Psychology. Mem. Am. Psychol. Assn., Am. Orthopsychiat. Assn., N.Y. Soc. Clin. Psychologists, Internat. Orgn. for Study Group Tensions, Assn. Israeli Students and Academicians in N.Am. (past pres.), Psi Chi. Contbr. articles to profl. jours. Developer scale for assessment of cognitive and perceptual functioning in geriatrics. Home and office: 114 Ave N Brooklyn NY 11230

LIEBERMAN, THEODORE WILLIAM, ophthalmologist; b. Bklyn., Apr. 26, 1933; s. Hyman and Jean (Herships) L.; B.A., Princeton U., 1954; M.D., Yale U., 1958; m. Dora Esther Bransky, Aug. 20, 1957; children—Richard Salomon, Juanita. Intern, Mt. Sinai Hosp., N.Y.C., 1958-59; resident in ophthalmology Barnes Hosp., St. Louis, 1962-65; research asso. Mt. Sinai Hosp., 1966-72, asso. attending surgeon, 1972—, asso. clin. prof. ophthalmology Med. Sch., 1972—. Served with USAF, 1960-62. NIH grantee, 1966—; fellow Mt. Sinai Hosp., 1959-60. Diplomate Am. Bd. Ophthalmology (asso. examiner). Mem. AAAS, AMA, Am. Acad. Ophthalmology and Otolaryngology, N.Y. State Med. Soc., Med. Soc. N.Y. County. Club: White's Point Yacht (Waterford, Conn.). Contbr. articles to profl. jours. Home: 1165 Park Ave New York City NY 10028 Office: 70 E 96th St New York City NY 10028

LIEBLEIN, EDWARD, computer scientist; b. N.Y.C., Sept. 6, 1934; s. Harry J. and Mary (Walkow) L.; B.S., N.Y. U., 1955, M.S., 1963; postgrad. (Army Electronics Command fellow) U. Pa., 1964-66, Ph.D., 1968; m. Virginia Lucy Beam, June 7, 1964; children—Sheryl Ann, Susan Debra. Electronics engr. U.S. Army Communications Research and Devel. Command, Ft. Monmouth, N.J., 1955-57, sect. chief, 1957-61, leader computer orgn. group, 1961-64, computer research scientist, 1966-72, chief computer software team, 1972-74, chief computer software div., 1974—; affiliate asso. prof. Stevens Inst. Tech., 1969—; lectr. Monmouth Coll., 1969—; adj. asso. prof. U. Pa., 1977—. Recipient citation for tech. achievement and leadership U.S. Army, 1963. Mem. Assn. Computing Machinery, IEEE, Profl. Group Electronic Computers. Contbr. articles on computers and computer software to profl. jours. Home: 684 Westwood Ave West End NJ 07740 Office: US Army Communications Research and Devel Command Ft Monmouth NJ 07703

LIEBLING, BARRY A., psychologist, mgmt. cons.; b. Chgo., Mar. 16, 1949; s. Bernard Mayer and Cherry Florence (Rest) L.; B.A. in Psychology magna cum laude, U. Calif., Los Angeles, 1970; M.A. in Psychology, Columbia U., 1972, Ph.D., 1974. Fellow, Faculty Pure Sci., Columbia U., N.Y.C., 1970-74; study dir. Booz, Allen & Hamilton, Phila., 1974-76, sr. study dir., 1976; sr. cons. orgn. and personnel cons. group Arthur Young & Co., N.Y.C., 1976-78, mgr. orgn. and personnel cons. group, 1978—. NSF research fellow, 1969; NIH predoctoral fellow, 1970-74. Accredited personnel diplomate Am. Soc. Personnel Adminstrn. Mem. Am. Psychol. Assn., AAAS, Met. N.Y. Assn. Applied Psychology, Sigma Xi, Phi Beta Kappa, Psi Chi. Contbr. articles to profl. jours. Home: 225 E 57th St New York NY 10022 Office: Arthur Young & Co 277 Park Ave New York NY 10017

LIEBMAN, EMMANUEL, lawyer; b. Phila., Mar. 26, 1925; s. Morris and Pearl (Zucker) L.; B.S. in Econs., U. Pa., 1950; J.D., Rutgers U., 1954; m. Anita Forman, Dec. 24, 1953; children—Judith H. Liebman Winslow, Lawrence H. Admitted to N.J. bar, 1954, also U.S. Supreme Ct.; practice law specializing in fed. taxation, Cherry Hill, N.J., 1954—; mem. firm Liebman & Flaster, P.A.; lectr. Inst. Continuing Legal Edn. Pres. Kiwanis Club Cherry Hill Found., 1964-73; trustee N.J. State Bar Found. Served with USNR, 1943-46. Mem. Camden County C. of C., Am. Arbitration Assn., Am., N.J. (exec. council taxation sect.; chmn. com. bus. taxes 1967-69, 71-73, chmn. state capitol com.; chmn. ad hoc com. financing legal fees), Camden County (chmn. com. fed. taxation 1964, 68-70) bar assns. Club: Penn Alumni of Southern N.J. (pres. 1959). Home: 46 Dublin Ln Cherry Hill NJ 08003 Office: 409 E Marlton Pike Cherry Hill NJ 08034

LIEBMAN, LEON HERSCHEL, information services co. exec.; b. Hartford, Conn., Oct. 21, 1940; s. George H. and Florence (Brownstein) L.; B.S., U. Pa., 1962; M.S., Mass. Inst. Tech., 1967; m. Karin Hennie, June 19, 1966; 1 dau., Stina Ann. Tchr., Mass. Inst. Tech., 1967-69, U. Pa., 1969-72; chmn. Interactive Market Systems, Inc., N.Y.C., 1969—, Interactive Planning Systems, Inc., N.Y.C., 1972—, Interactive Arbitrage Systems, Inc., N.Y.C., 1974—, Software Supermarket, Inc., Lambertville, N.J., 1977—, also dir.; mng. dir. Interactive Market Systems (U.K.) Ltd., London, 1977—. Mem. Am. Accountants Assn., Nat. Assn. Accountants, Am. Marketing Assn., Inst. Mgmt. Sci., Assn. for Computing Machinery, Sigma Xi, Alpha Kappa Psi, Pi Mu Alpha, Beta Alpha Psi. Home: Mill Rd RD 2 Lambertville NJ 08530 Office: 19 W 44th St New York City NY 10036

LIEBMAN, MILTON, med. publisher, journalist; b. Bklyn., Oct. 23, 1928; s. Abraham and Zelda (Shapiro) L.; student City U. N.Y., 1946-51; m. Mary Jane Isabel Ladin, Feb. 20, 1964; children—Jessica Zoe, Katherine M. Pub. relations exec. Med. and Pharm. Info. Bur. and William Douglas McAdams, N.Y.C., 1953-59; dept. editor Med. News, N.Y.C., 1959-61; mng. editor Med. World News, N.Y.C., 1961-66; co-pub. Hosp. Practice, N.Y.C., 1966—; corp. v.p., dir. HP Pub. Co., Inc. Served with U.S. Army, 1951-53. Mem. Assn. Ind. Clin. Pubs. (pres.), Nat. Assn. Sci. Writers, Am. Med. Writers Assn., Midwest Pharm. Advt. Club, Pharm. Advt. Club, Am. Pub. Health Assn. Home: 280 Riverside Dr New York City NY 10025 Office: 575 Lexington Ave New York City NY 10022

LIEBMAN, WILLIAM NORMAN, mktg. research exec.; b. Callicoon, N.Y., Sept. 24, 1942; s. Louis and Mary (Levine) L.; B.B.A., U. Bridgeport, 1965; M.B.A., Pace U., 1968; m. Barbara Kwartler, Aug. 29, 1965; children—Gayle, Gregg. With Audits & Surveys, Inc., N.Y.C., 1965—, v.p., 1969—; instr. mktg. research Columbia U. Grad. Sch., Queens Coll. Mem. Am. Mktg. Assn., Am. Mgmt. Assn., Am. Statis. Assn. Home: 2853 Bayview Ave Wantagh NY 11793 Office: 1 Park Ave New York City NY 10016

LIEBMANN, FELIX G., lawyer; b. Braunfels, Germany, Dec. 25, 1923; B.S. cum laude, Coll. City N.Y., 1948; J.D. with distinction, Cornell U., 1951; m. Betty Virginia Osterholm, Sept. 9, 1950; children—Joanne, Karen, Susan, Geoffrey Edward. Admitted to N.Y. bar, 1951, U.S. Supreme Ct., 1960; financial investigator U.S. Treasury Dept., 1945-46; asso. Davis Polk Wardwell Sunderland & Kiendl, N.Y.C., 1951-56; tax supr. Arabian Am. Oil Co., N.Y.C., 1956-58; tax counsel Carrier Corp., Syracuse, N.Y., 1958-61; with Harris, Beach & Wilcox, Rochester, N.Y., 1961—, partner, 1963—. Dir., mem. exec. com. Superba Cravats, Inc., Rochester, N.Y.; dir. Caldwell Mfg. Co., Rochester, N.Y.; bd. dirs., pres. Hillside Children's Center, Rochester. Served with AUS, 1943-45. Mem. N.Y. State, Monroe County (chmn. sect. banking, corps. and bus. law 1974) bar assns., Acad. Polit. Sci., Am. Acad. Polit. and Social Scis., Am. Judicature Soc., Nat. Hist. Soc., N.Y. Conservation Council, Nat. Wildlife Fedn., Smithsonian Assos., Rochester Com. Fgn. Relations, Phi Beta Kappa, Order of Coif, Phi Kappa Phi. Lutheran. Editor-in-chief Cornell Law Quar., 1950-51. Office: Harris Beach and Wilcox 2 State St Rochester NY 14614

LIEBOLT, FREDERICK LEE, orthopedic surgeon; b. Fayetteville, Ark.; s. Joseph Lee and Katherine Ann (Swigert) L.; A.B., U. Ark., 1925; postgrad. U. Kans., 1926, Kans. State Tchrs. Coll., summer 1926; M.D., Washington U., St. Louis, 1930; Sc.D., Columbia U., 1937; LL.D., U. Ark., 1948; children—Frederick Lee, Karen Lee, Jerry Lee. Med. intern St. Luke's Hosp., Kansas City, Mo., 1930-31; surg. intern Barnes Hosp., St. Louis, 1931-32; orthopedic intern N.Y. Orthopedic Hosp., 1932-34, fellow, 1934-38; asst. anatomy Columbia U., 1934-38, research in anatomy, 1935-37, instr. orthopedic surgery, 1938-47; instr. surgery Cornell U., 1938-43, asst. prof. orthopedic surgery, 1943-46, asso. prof., 1946—; attending orthopedic surgeon N.Y. Hosp., N.Y.C., 1946—, Hosp. Spl. Surgery, N.Y.C., 1951—; orthopedic cons. U.S. Mil. Acad., 1956-68, Southampton (L.I.) Hosp., 1959—; clin. cons. N.Y. State Dept. Health, 1957—. Mem. devel. council and found. U. Ark. Served from maj. to lt. col., M.C., USAAF, 1943-46, col., 1957. Recipient Army commendation medal; Legion of Honor, Order of De Molay, 1957; Distinguished Alumnus citation U. Ark., 1973. Diplomate Am. Bd. Orthopedic Surgery, Nat. Bd. Med. Examiners. Fellow A.C.S.; mem. Am. Orthopedic Assn., Internat. Sec. Orthopedic Surgery and Trauma, Am. Therapeutic Soc. (3d v.p.), AMA (Physician's Recognition award 1973, 76), N.Y. State (sec. orthopedic sect. 1952-53, chmn. 1953-54, del. 1955-75), N.Y. County med. assns., Am. Med. Writers Assn., Am. Acad. Orthopedic Surgeons (gold medal for exhbn. knee 1952), N.Y. Acad. Medicine, Am. Geriatrics Soc., Indsl. Medicine Assn. (chmn. surg. sect. 1951-52), Am. Acad. Compensation Medicine, Am. Assn. Hand Surgery, Latin Am. Soc. Orthopedics and Traumatology (certificate of honor 1968), World Med. Assn., Royal Soc. Health, Am. Trauma Soc., Academia Internationali Rex et Scientia, Pan Am. Med. Assn. (pres. orthopedic sect., trustee), N.Y. Bd. Trade (hon. mem. med. sect.), W. Side Clin. Soc., Med. Strollers, Ark. Soc. N.Y. (v.p. 1941-43), Phi Beta Kappa, Sigma Xi, Phi Beta Pi (pres. 1963-67, Man of Yr. 1968, chmn. bd. trustees 1968—), Theta Nu Epsilon. Presbyterian. Club: Univ. Author sci. publs. in field; abstractor Excerpta Medica, 1948-58. Address: 150 E 69th St New York City NY 10021

LIEF, HAROLD ISAIAH, educator, psychiatrist; b. N.Y.C., Dec. 29, 1917; s. Jacob F. and Mollie (Filler) L.; B.A., U. Mich., 1938; M.D., N.Y. U., 1942; certificate in Psychoanalysis Columbia Coll. Physicians and Surgeons, 1950; M.A. (hon.), U. Pa., 1971; m. Myrtis A. Brumfield, Mar. 3, 1961; children—Polly Lief Goldberg, Jonathan F., Caleb B., Frederick V., Oliver F. Intern, Queens Gen. Hosp., Jamaica, N.Y., 1942-43; resident L.I. Coll. Medicine, Bklyn., 1946-48; asst. physician Presbyn. Hosp., N.Y.C., 1949-51; dir. Marriage Council Phila., Center for Study Sex Edn. in Medicine, U. Pa., 1968—; mem. staff Hosp. U. Pa., Phila., 1967—; asst. prof. Tulane U. Sch. Medicine, New Orleans, 1951-54, asso. prof., 1954-60, prof. psychiatry, 1960-67; prof. psychiatry, dir. div. family study U. Pa. Sch. Medicine, Phila., 1967—. Mem. La. State Commn. Civil Rights, 1958-67. Served to maj. M.C., AUS, 1943-46. Commonwealth Fund fellow, 1963-64. Fellow Phila. Coll. Physicians, Am. Psychiat. Assn. (life), Am. Acad. Psychoanalysis (pres. 1967-68), Am. Coll. Psychiatry (founding), Am. Coll. Psychoanalysis (charter), Am. Assn. Marriage and Family Counselors; mem. Sex Info. and Edn. Council U.S. (pres. 1969-71, dir.), Sigma Xi, Alpha Omega Alpha, Phi Eta Sigma, Phi Kappa Phi. Club: Germantown Cricket (Phila.). Author: (with Daniel Thompson, William Thompson) The Eighth Generation, 1960. Editor: (with Victor and Nina Lief) Psychological Basis of Medical Practice 1963; Medical Aspects of Human Sexuality, 1975; (with Arno Karlen) Sex Education in Medicine, 1976. Contbr. numerous articles to various publs. Home: 101 S Buck Ln Haverford PA 19041 Office: Div Family Study 4025 Chestnut St Philadelphia PA 19104

LIEGGI, EDWARD VINCENT, SR., mfg. co. exec.; b. Phila., July 21, 1951; s. Vincent and Mildred (Dallas) L.; B.B.A. cum laude in Indsl. Mgmt., U. Pa., 1975; m. Madeline Theresa Jochum, Aug. 8, 1971; children—Edward, Mellisa Marie. Inventory control mgr. BW Coating Co., Pennsauken, N.J., 1972-73; inventory control mgr., purchaser Mitchell Love Co., Phila., 1974-75; production and inventory control mgr. Plymouth Inc., Bellmawr, N.J., 1975—. Mem. Am. Production and Inventory Control Soc. Democrat. Roman Catholic. Designer inventory control systems. Office: Plymouth Inc Benigno Blvd Bellmawr NJ 08031

LIEGNER, FRANK FERDINAND, physician; b. Breslau, Germany, May 17, 1925; s. Benno and Lilli Liegner; came to U.S., 1936, naturalized, 1942; student U. Wis., 1942-43, U. Kans., 1944; M.D., Creighton U., 1949; m. Rosemary A. Ryan, Nov. 8, 1952; children—Joanne E., Robert M., Jeffrey T., Jonathan A. Intern, Morrisania City Hosp., N.Y.C., 1949-50; resident Margaret Hague Maternity Hosp., Jersey City, 1953-55, Hosp. for Joint Diseases, N.Y.C., 1955-56; practice medicine specializing in obstetrics and gynecology, Newton, N.J., 1956—; chief obstet. and gynecol. dept. Newton Meml. Hosp.; cons. Hackettstown (N.J.) Community Hosp. Served with U.S. Army, 1943-46, 51-52. Diplomate Am. Bd. Obstetrics and Gynecology. Mem. AMA, N.J., Sussex County med. socs., Am. Coll. Obstetrics and Gynecology, Internat. Fertility Assn., N.Y. Acad. Scis. Home and Office: 179 High St Newton NJ 07860

LIEU, HOU-SHUN, economist; b. Peiping, China, May 13, 1921; s. D. K. and Helen Yungtsing (King) L.; student Nat. S. W. Asso. U., Kunming, China, 1939-42; B.A., Nat. Chungking U., 1944; M.B.A., N.Y. U., 1948; m. Lucy Yueh-Hua Hsu, Feb. 14, 1947; children—Diane Te-Lan Lieu Dobbs, Vincent Te-Feng, Helena Te-Yun. Naturalized U.S. citizen, 1965. With Bank of China, 1946-67, econ. analyst, 1954-57, asst. chief, then chief bus. div., head office fgn. dept., Taipei, Taiwan, 1957-59, asst. chief trust div. N.Y. br., 1959-67; econ. cons. Muller & Co., N.Y.C., 1968; asso. prof. econs. Taiwan Provincial Coll. Law and Commerce, 1956-57; asso. prof. econs. Soochow U. Law Sch., Taipei, 1956, prof., 1957-59; asst. prof. econs. State U. N.Y., 1967-70, asso. prof., area chmn. econs., 1970-75, prof., 1975—; guest lectr. Summer Tng. Seminar for staff mems. Taiwan Cement Corp., 1958-59; Nat. Sci. Council vis. prof. econs. Grad. Sch. Bus. Adminstrn., Nat. Chengchih U., Taipei, 1973-74; vis. prof. econs. Soochow U., Taipei, 1973-74. Mem. adv. com. Summer Youth Tng. Corps, China, 1957; sec. com. A, Econ. Stblzn. Bd., Exec. Yuan, Republic of China, 1956-57, alt. mem. allotment com. Council for U.S. Aid, 1956-57; mem. Suffolk County (N.Y.) Pub. Employment Relations Bd., 1968—. Served from capt. to maj., interpreting officer Fgn. Affairs Bur., Nat. Mil. Council of China, 1944-45; civilian expert U.S. Dept. War, 1945-46. Recipient U.S. Presdl. medal of Freedom; medal of merit Linguistics Soc. China. Fellow Royal Econ. Soc. (London); mem. Am. Econ. Assn., Sinology Soc. (Taiwan), N.Y. Soc. Security Analysts, AAAS, Econometric Soc., Omicron Delta Epsilon. Club: Lions (1st v.p. 1968-69, sec.-treas. 1969-70, pres. 1970-71). Author: A Draft Plan for an Asian Payments Union and an Asian Development Bank, 1959; International and Inter-Regional Economics, 1960; Notes from Ipanchu, 1972; Essays on Linguistics, 1974; A General Study of the Multinational Enterprise, 1975; Learning Languages by Playing Games, 1978; The Pleasure of Reading and Writing, 1978; editor Econ. Rev. (Bank of China), 1954-56; Bi-Monthly Econ. Rev., 1956-59; The Comml. Bull. (Taipei), 1957; contbg. editor The China Economist, 1955—, The China Yearbook, 1958-59, Foreign Exchange and Trade Handbook, 1959, The World Forum, 1961-63; editorial bd. The Foreign Trade Monthly, Taipei, 1956-60; editorial adviser Jour. Lit. and Social Studies, 1971—; contbr. numerous articles to profl. jours. Home: 28 Marshmallow Dr Commack Long Island NY 11725 Office: State U NY Farmingdale NY 11735

LIFF, ZANVEL A., psychologist, clin. dir.; b. N.Y.C., Oct. 31, 1927; s. Samuel and Lena (Hoffman) L.; B.S., City Coll. N.Y., 1948, M.S., 1949; Ph.D., N.Y. U., 1955; certificate individual and group psychotherapy Postgrad. Center Mental Health, N.Y.C., 1959; m. Sylvia Barchenko, June 30, 1957; children—Sharon Ruth, Janet Susan. Pvt. practice individual and group psychotherapy, N.Y.C., 1956—; dir. psychology, sr. supr., Postgrad. Center Mental Health, 1969—; vis. prof. psychology Grad. Faculty, New Sch. Social Research, N.Y.C., 1974-77. Mem. nat. bd. govs. Am. Jewish Com., 1970—. Recipient Distinguished Service award Eastern Group Psychotherapy Soc., 1971. Fellow Am. Group Psychotherapy Assn. (sec. bd. govs. 1976—), Am. Orthopsychiat. Assn.; mem. Am., N.Y. psychol. assns., N.Y. Soc. Clin. Psychologists, Internat. Council Psychologists. Author: The Leader in the Group, 1975; contbr. articles in field to profl. jours. Home and Office: 55 E 86th St New York City NY 10028

LIFFMANN, KENNETH EMIL, surgeon; b. Dusseldorf, Ger., Apr. 14, 1929; came to U.S., 1940, naturalized, 1946; s. Max and Alice (Gabriel) L. A.B. cum laude, Brown U., 1951; D.M.D., Harvard U., 1955; M.D., Tufts U., 1958; m. Deena Brodsky, Aug. 11, 1957; children—Karen, Joel, Steven. Intern, R.I. Hosp., Providence, 1958-59, resident, 1959-60, 62-65, surgeon, 1965—; surgeon Women and Infants' Hosp., Providence, 1965—; practice medicine specializing in surgery, Providence, 1965—, asst. clin. prof. surgery Brown U., 1975—, surgeon in charge univ. health service, 1974—; vice chmn., dir. Med. Malpractice Joint Underwriting Assn. R.I., 1976—. Bd. dirs. Blue Shield of R.I. Served to capt. USAF, 1960-62. Diplomate Am. Bd. Surgery. Mem. A.C.S., Providence, R.I. med. socs., Phi Beta Kappa, Sigma Xi. Home: 189 Summit Dr Cranston RI 02920 Office: 110 Lockwood St Providence RI 02903

LIFSON, BETTY ANN GLASSER, social worker; b. Cambridge, Mass., Oct. 29, 1920; d. Myer and Rose (Cohen) Sugarman; B.A., U. Pa., 1941; M.S., Simmons Coll., 1947; children—Rona-Lee, Joyce Enid. Research psychiat. social worker demonstration and research projects Mass. Mental Health Center, Nat. Inst. Mental Health, Boston, 1958-60, 60-64; research social worker in charge orgn. of adolescent unit Boston State Hosp., 1963-66, chmn. exec. com. for VISTAS, 1968; supr., case aide coll. student vols. Phillips Brooks House, mental hosps. com. Harvard, 1963-64; supr. coll. student group work Tufts and Boston Coll., 1965-66; dir. social service Dept. Mental Health, Mass., 1968-69; unit supr. Rockland State Hosp., 1969-71; dir. Social Rehab. Center Rockland County Mental Health Center, 1971-73; social worker region VI Dept. Mental Health, Boston, 1974-76. Vice pres. Orgn. for Rehab. Through Tng., 1950; pres. suburban region Am. Jewish Congress, 1963; bd. dirs. Newton (Mass.) Mental Health Assn., 1976—. Served with WAVES, 1942-45. Recipient Maida H. Solomon award Simmons Coll. Sch. Social Work Alumni, 1965, 1st Ogilby award Simmons Coll., 1971. Mem. Nat. Assn. Social Workers, Simmons Coll. Alumnae Assn., Nat. Alumnae Assn. U. Pa. (bd. dirs. 1965-66). Author: (with others) The Prevention of Hospitalization, 1963, Adolescents in a Mental Hospital, 1968; contbr. chpt. to Rehabilitation Medicine and Psychiatry, 1976. Contbr. articles to profl. jours. Home: 18 Nancy Rd Chestnut Hill MA 02167

LIFTON, LESTER JAY, physician; b. N.Y.C., Dec. 4, 1946; s. Benjamin J. and Harriet (Zasuly) L.; B.A., U. Rochester, 1968; M.D., U. Buffalo, 1972; m. Judith Kahan, Dec. 25, 1969; children—Stacey Hope, Ilyse Danielle. Intern E. J. Meyer Meml. Hosp., Buffalo, 1972, resident in medicine, 1972-74; fellow in gastroenterology U. Conn. Med. Center, Hartford, 1975-76; pvt. practice medicine specializing in gastroenterology, Harrisburg, Pa., 1977—; mem. staff Polyclinic Med. Center, Harrisburg Hosp.; coordinator endoscopy services Holy Spirit Hosp.; pres. Jayco Pharms. Mem. ACP, Am. Soc. Gastrointestinal Endoscopy, AMA, Am. Gastrointestinal Assn., Harrisburg Model R.R Assn. (pres.). Office: 890 Poplar Church Rd Camp Hill PA 17011

LIFTON, WALTER M., educator; b. Bklyn., Nov. 2, 1918; s. Samuel S. and Sarah G. (Berman) L.; B.A., Bklyn. Coll., 1942; M.A., N.Y. U., 1947, Ph.D., 1950; m. Ruth S. Knoppow, Oct. 1, 1940; children—Hazel Miriam (Mrs. F.W. Kroesser), Robert William. Sr. vocational appraiser Vets. Guidance Center of Hunter Coll., 1946-48; psychologist research div. N.Y. U., 1948-50; asso. prof. edn., guidance and counseling U. Ill., 1950-59; dir. guidance publs. and services Sci. Research Assos., Chgo., 1959-63; coordinator pupil personnel services Rochester (N.Y.) City Sch. Dist., 1964-70; prof. edn. guidance and counseling program State U. N.Y., Albany, 1970—. Vis. prof., lectr. guidance and counseling 30 colls., univs.; cons. in field. Mem. White House Conf. on Children and Youth, 1969-70. Edn., 1965; cons. Title III E.S.E.A. project Knox County, Tenn., 1967. Dir. Action for a Better Community, 1964-65, Center for Coop. Action in Urban Edn., 1966. Served with AUS, 1942-46. Mem. Nat. Assn. Pupil Personnel Adminstrs. (pres. 1970), Nat. Vocational Guidance Assn., Assn. for Specialists in Group Work (sec. 1976—). Author: Keys to Vocational Decisions, 1964; Working With Groups, 2d edit., 1966; Educating for Tomorrow-The Role of Media, Career Development and Society, 1970; Groups-Facilitating Individual Growth and Societal Change, 1972. Contbr. articles to profl. jours. Home: 106 Greenleaf Dr Newtonville NY 12128 Office: 1400 Washington Ave Albany NY 12203

LIGHT, EDWIN STANLEY, clergyman; b. Skipton, Sask., Can., Mar. 19, 1914; s. Christopher R. and Gertrude (Bonnallo) L.; B.A., U. Sask., 1947; L.Th., Emmanuel Coll., Saskatoon, Sask., 1938, D.D. (hon.), 1964; m. Evelyn A. Leask, Mar. 16, 1943; children—G.S., Edwin M., Gregory J., Brian R. Ordained to ministry Anglican Ch. of Can., 1938; clergyman, 1938-41, 46-48; chaplain, chaplain gen. Canadian Armed Forces, 1966-68, brig. gen., 1966-68; gen. sec. Anglican Ch. of Can., Toronto, 1968—. Nat. chaplain RCAF Assn., 1969-71; exec. sec. Anglican Found. Can., 1968—. Served as chaplain RCAF, 1941-46. Decorated Canadian Decoration, Centennial Medal (Can.). Home: 15 Vicora Linkway Don Mills ON Canada Office: 600 Jarvis St Toronto ON M4Y 2J6 Canada

LIGHTBODY, FORREST EARSHAM HAY, physician; b. Haifa, Brit. Mandated, Palestine, May 28, 1924; s. William Patterson Hay and Dorothy Mildred (Cooke) L.; came to U.S., 1940, naturalized, 1967; M.B. Ch. B., U. Edinburgh (Scotland), 1951. Intern, St. Catherine's Hosp., Birkenhead, Eng., 1951-52, Broadgreen Hosp., Liverpool, Eng., 1952; resident Royal Liverpool Children's Hosp., 1952-53, David Lewis N. Hosp., Liverpool, 1952-53, N.Y. U. Inst. Rehab. Medicine, 1962-64; asso. med. dir. Inst. for the Crippled and

Disabled, N.Y.C., 1964-67; physiatrist Pa. State Rehab. Center, Johnstown, 1967-68; med. dir. Easter Seal Rehab. Center, Stamford, Conn., 1968-71; asso. dir. div. phys. medicine and rehab. Grassland Hosp., Valhalla, N.Y., 1968-71; dir. phys. medicine and rehab. Greenwich (Conn.) Hosp., 1968—; asst. clin. prof. rehab. medicine N.Y. Med. Coll., 1971—; vol. attending physician Westchester County (N.Y.) Med. Center, Valahalla, 1972—. Bd. mgmt. Nathaniel Witherell Hosp., Greenwich, 1975—. Served with RAF, 1941-46. Decorated D.F.C. Diplomate Am. Bd. Phys. Medicine and Rehab. Mem. AMA, Am. Acad. Phys. Medicine and Rehab., Congress Rehab. Medicine, Flying Physicians Assn., Conn., Fairfield County med. socs. Home: 12 Coachlamp Ln Greenwich CT 06820 Office: Greenwich Hosp Greenwich CT 06830

LIGHTCAP, KENNETH REED, pub. relations exec.; b. Pitts., Mar. 27, 1938; s. Milton William and Grace Lillian (Reed) L.; B.A., Hobart Coll., 1960; m. Priscilla Alden Bliss, July 10, 1965; children—Pamela Alden, Nina Abigail. Staff writer Hartford (Conn.) Times, 1961-63; writer, researcher Wallach Assos., Inc., N.Y.C., 1963-65; account exec. Donemus & Co., N.Y.C., 1965-67; exec. v.p. Bozell & Jacobs Pub. Relations, Inc., N.Y.C., 1967-75; dir. pub. relations Avon Products Inc., N.Y.C., 1975-77; dir. pub. relations Chesebrough-Pond's, Inc., N.Y.C., 1977—; instr. Am. and world history Carle Place Sch. System, Carle Place, N.Y., 1960-61. Bd. dirs. Louis Braille Found. of Blind Musicians, Inc., 1971-72, Friends of the Garden City Pub. Library, 1972—. Served with USCGR, 1960-68. Mem. Pub. Relations Soc. Am. (mem. counselors sect. 1968—), Nat. Investor Relations Inst., Sigma Phi. Presbyterian (bd. deacons 1966-67). Home: 42 Kensington Rd Garden City NY 11530 Office: 9 W 57th St New York City NY 10019

LIGHTFOOT, BELINDA HARRIS, univ. adminstr.; b. Richmond, Va., Aug. 29, 1949; d. William McKinnsey and Reba (Harris) Alexander; B.A., Va. State Coll., Petersburg, 1970; M.Ed., Va. Commonwealth U., 1975. Tchr., Richmond Pub. Schs., 1970-72; counselor spl. services Va. Commonwealth U., 1972-75; counselor CETA program Prince George's Community Coll., Largo, Md., 1975-76; adminstr. student activities Howard U., Washington, 1976—, asst. dir., 1976—. Chairperson D.C. chpt. Nat. Com. Overturn Bakke Decision, 1977-78; asst. rec. sec. Prince George's County br. NAACP, 1977—; exec. v.p. Md. Assn. Non-White Concerns, 1976-77. Mem. Md., Am. personnel and guidance assns., Largo Civic Assn., Nat. Council Negro Women, League Women Voters, Delta Sigma Theta. Democrat. Baptist. Home: 409 Pritchard Ln Largo MD 20870 Office: Office Student Life Howard U Washington DC 20059

LIGHTSTONE, ALAN CLIFFORD, dermatologist; b. N.Y.C., Apr. 17, 1927; s. Elias Julius and Renee (Levi) L.; B.A., Rutgers U., 1950; M.D., N.Y. Med. Coll., 1957; postgrad. N.Y. U., 1959-61; m. Renee Goldschmidt, Sept. 1, 1951; children—Judith Karen, Raymond Paul. Research chemist Am. Cyanimid Corp., N.Y.C., 1950-53; intern Lenox Hill Hosp., N.Y.C., 1957-58; resident Bellevue Hosp., N.Y.C., 1958-61; faculty N.Y. U. Med. and Postgrad. Med. Sch., N.Y.C., 1961-71; staff N.Y. Skin and Cancer Clinic, N.Y.C., 1961-71; practice medicine, specializing in dermatology, Flushing, N.Y., 1962—; staff Booth Meml. Hosp., L.I. Jewish Hillside Med. Center, New Hyde Park, N.Y.; med. research cons. Upjohn Co., N.Y.C., 1978. Served with USNR, 1945-46. Fellow Am. Acad. Dermatology; mem. Soc. Investigative Dermatology, Internat. Soc. Tropical Dermatology, A.C.P., AMA, N.Y. State, Queens County med. socs. Contbr. articles in field to med. jours. Home: 217-15 Peck Ave Queens Village NY 11427 Office: 217-10 Union Turnpike Flushing NY 11364

LIGOR, O. JUDITH DAVID, hosp. food adminstr.; b. Newton, Mass., Aug. 7, 1937; d. Lambi and Marguerite (Zicko) David; student Bridgewater State Coll., 1955-57; certificate in food Mgmt. Pa. State U., 1962; 1 son, David. Asst. to dietition Leonard Morse Hosp., Natick, Mass., 1957-58; patient service dietitian Newton (Mass.) Wellesley Hosp., 1958-60; mgr. womens aux. coffee shop and snack bar Mt. Auburn Hosp., Cambridge, Mass., 1960; asst. food mgr. Muhlenberg Med. Center, Bethlehem, Pa., 1960-63; mgr. snack bar and cafeteria Bethlehem YWCA, 1963-65; food mgr. Lum's, Falmouth, Mass., 1973; food mgr. Canteen Corp., Waltham, Mass., 1973-74; food service dir. The Jordan Hosp., Plymouth, Mass., 1975-78; food service dir. Morrison's Food Services, Inc. at Rush Found. Hosp., Meridian, Miss., 1979—. Mem. Y-Teen Adv. Bd., Bethlehem, 1963-65; advisor Y-Teen, Lawrence, Mass., 1968-69; dir. arts and crafts for handicapped and mentally retarded children Natick Recreation Dept., 1970-71; coach Bourne (Mass.) Youth Base- ball, 1977—. Mem. Mass. Hosp. Food Service Adminstrs. (bd. govs. 1978—), Am. Soc. Hosp. Food Service Adminstrs. (certified 1976). Mem. Albanian Orthodox Ch. Home: 339 Sea St Hyannis MA 02601 Office: 3222 Northview Dr Meridian MS 39301

LIJEWSKI, RONALD MATHEW, hosp. exec.; b. Milw., Mar. 10, 1940; s. Alexander Roman and Valentina Agnes (Urban) L.; B.B.A., U. Wis., Milw., 1963; m. Anita Marie Rios, Dec. 28, 1963; children—Todd, Jeffrey, Lisa, Scott (dec.), Tanya. Sr. auditor Arthur Andersen & Co., Milw., 1963-70; auditor MSL Industries, Racine, Wis., 1970-71; accounting mgr. St. Joseph Hosp., Milw., 1971-73; financial mgr. Mt. Sinai Med. Center, Milw., 1973-75; controller St. Joseph Hosp., Towson, Md., 1975—. Served with USAR, 1963. Mem. Md. Hosp. Assn. (chmn. hosp. uniform accounting and reporting task force), Hosp. Financial Mgmt. Assn., Smithsonian Assos., Am. Mus. Natural History. Republican. Roman Catholic. Home: 2422 Stanwick Rd Phoenix MD 21131 Office: 7620 York Rd Towson MD 21204

LIKER, JACK, ceramic co. exec.; b. N.Y.C., June 10, 1926; s. Boris and Lucy (Zerulnikova) L.; B.S. in Mech. Engring., Bridgeport U., 1958; m. Henriette Handel, Jan. 11, 1948; children—Karin, Jeffrey, Stephen. Floorman, Sloves Book Bindery, 1946-51; design engr. Burndy Corp., 1951-59; sales mgr. Molecular Dielectrics, 1959-65; sales mgr. Basic Ceramics, Hawthorne, N.J., 1965-71; v.p. sales Mykroy Ceramics, Ledgewood, N.J., 1971-72, v.p., gen. mgr., 1972—; dir. Ceramic Fabricators Inc.; partner Liker Travel Agy. Cons. ceramic material dept. chem. engring. Columbia; cons. Karl Roesch Inc. Served with AUS, 1944-46. Mem. Am., Canadian, N.J. ceramic socs., Internat. Hybrid Microelectronics Soc., Soc. Aerospace Materials and Process Engrs., ASTM, Elec. Insulation Conf., Soc. Plastic Engrs. Rotarian. Patentee in field. Address: RD 1 Box 434 A Lake Hopatcong NJ 07849

LILES, RAEFORD BAILEY, artist; b. Birmingham, Ala., July 20, 1923; s. Paul Wilson and Bessie (Inez von Santen) L.; student Birmingham So. Coll., 1941-42; B.S. in E.E., Auburn U., 1949; student Atelier F. Leger, Paris, 1949-51; m. Elsa Ruth Allgood, Mar. 19, 1949 (div. June 1959); children—Barbara, Janet. Engr., Def. Dept., Paris, 1952-57, SAC, USAF, Ardmore (Kan.) AFB, 1958-61; one man shows Gallery 8, Paris, 1951, Chateau Bel-Air Orleans, France, 1955, Galerie Breteau, Paris, 1955, East Hampton Gallery, N.Y.C., 1965-69, Expn. Internat., France, 1967, Monaco, 1968, Art for Peace, 1971, Stratford Coll., 1973, numerous others; exhibited in group shows Birmingham-So. Coll., 1946-47, Birmingham Art Assn., 1948, Ala. Water Color Show, 1948, Students Leger, 1950, Salon Art Inds., 1950, Salon des Art Libre, 1951; represented in permanent collection numerous museums, univs. Mem. rehearsal com. N.Y.C. Ballet, 1970. Served with USNR, 1941-46. Registered profl. engr., Kan. Mem. German Friendly Soc., Ala. Water Color Soc., Birmingham Art Assn., Friends Lincoln Center, Alpha Tau Omega. Democrat. Author: (with Moira Hodgson) Chinese Cooking with American Meals, 1970; (with Moira Hodgson) The Campus Cook Book, 1973. Home: 446 W 38th St New York City NY 10018 Office: GPO Box 509 New York City NY 10001

LILIEN, ELLIOT STEPHEN, educator; b. Newark, Jan. 1, 1939; s. Bernard B. and Judith Batson (Mullally) L.; B.A., U. Chgo., 1961; J.D., Columbia, 1964; M.A.T., Harvard, 1965. Tchr., fencing coach Concord (Mass.) High Sch., 1965-69; chmn. social studies dept. Concord-Carlisle High Sch., 1969—. Tchr. social studies edn. Wellesley (Mass.) Coll., 1971-78; lectr. Harvard, Brandeis U., Middlesex Tchrs. Conv. Chmn., U. Chgo. Schs. Com. for Mass., 1969-72; mem. nat. cabinet U. Chgo.; sponsor Masterworks Choral, Cantata Singers. New Eng. sabre champion, 1965-66. Mem. NEA, Mass., Concord-Carlisle (pres. 1971-78) tchrs. assns., U.S. Lawn Tennis Assn., Am. Fencers League Am. Home: 5 Colonial Village Dr 10 Arlington MA 02174 Office: Concord High Sch Concord MA 01742

LILIEN, GARY LOUIS, educator; b. N.Y.C., Sept. 25, 1946; s. Morris and Florence Esther (Brook) L.; B.S., Columbia U., 1967, M.S., 1968, D.E.S., 1973; m. Dorothy Hope Edelman, June 8, 1967; 1 dau., Amy Jo. Mgmt. scientist, computer systems and mgmt. scis. dept. Mobil Oil Corp., N.Y.C., 1968-73; asso. prof. mgmt. sci. Sloan Sch. Mgmt., Mass. Inst. Tech., Cambridge, 1973—; dir. Harvard Coop. Soc.; v.p. OR/MS Dialogue Inc. NDEA fellow. Mem. Inst. Mgmt. Scis., Ops. Research Soc. Am., Am. Mktg. Assn., Am. Statis. Assn., Tau Beta Pi, Alpha Pi Mu. Asso. editor Mgmt. Scis. Office: E53 353 50 Memorial Dr Mass Inst Tech Cambridge MA 02139

LILLEY, DAVID FRANK, hosp. adminstr.; b. Worcester, Mass., May 28, 1935; s. Frank Samuel and Iva Etta (Felton) L.; B.A., Boston U., 1970. With 1st Nat. Bank of Boston, 1955-60, 1st Nat. Bank, N.Y.C., 1960-61; with New Eng. Deaconess Hosp., Boston, 1961—, asst. dir., 1976—. Bd. govs. Handel and Haydn Soc., 1974-76, treas., 1975-76. Served with USN, 1957-59. Recipient certificate of appreciation United Way, 1975, 76. Mem. Am., Mass. hosp. assns., Am. Coll. Hosp. Adminstrs., Am. Mgmt. Assn. Clubs: Harvard (Boston); Mt. Auburn Tennis. Home: 770 Boylston St Apt21H Boston MA 02199 Office: 185 Pilgrim Rd Boston MA 02215

LILLIENSTEIN, MAXWELL JULIUS, lawyer; b. Bklyn., Dec. 18, 1927; s. Benjamin and Lillian (Camporeale) L.; B.Social Scis. cum laude, Coll. City N.Y., 1949; LL.B., Columbia, 1952; m. Janet Newman, June 23, 1951; children—Steven, Robert, Carol. Admitted to N.Y. bar, 1952; partner Friedberg, Blue & Rich, N.Y.C., 1958-63, Rich, Krinsly, Poses, Katz, Lillienstein, N.Y.C., 1963—; gen. counsel Am. Booksellers Assn. Pres. Maxwell Fund, 1967-72; dir. numerous corps.; investment adviser. Pres. Ardsley Democratic Club, Westchester County, 1966-67, mem. exec. bd., 1966-70; Westchester County Dem. committeeman; trustee Village of Ardsley, 1968-71, village atty., 1971—. Chmn. Ardsley (N.Y.) Library Com., 1967-68; mem. Ardsley Narcotics Guidance Council, 1971—. Served with AC, AUS, 1946-47. Contbr. numerous articles to mags. Home: 7 Rest Ave Ardsley NY 10502 Office: 99 Park Ave New York City NY 10016

LILLING, MAX IRVING, obstetrician, gynecologist; b. N.Y.C., May 2, 1938; s. Abraham and Ruth (Turk) L.; B.A. cum laude, Alfred U., 1960; M.D., State U. N.Y., Bklyn., 1966; m. Frances Podonsky, Aug. 25, 1962; children—Caryn Leslie, Adam Douglas. Intern, Maimonides Hosp., Bklyn., 1966-67; resident Brookdale Hosp., Bklyn., 1969-73, dir. high risk pregnancy unit, 1973—; practice medicine specializing in obstetrics and gynecology, Bklyn., 1973—; clin. instr. State U. N.Y. Downstate Med. Center, Bklyn., 1973—; guest lectr. N.Y. Hosp., Nassau Hosp., Hillcrest Hosp. Served to capt. M.C., USAF, 1967-69. Diplomate Am. Bd. Obstetrics and Gynecology, Nat. Bd. Med. Examiners. Mem. AMA, Kings County Med. Soc., Assn. Psychoprophylaxis in Obstetrics. Jewish. Club: Muttontown Country. Research on induction labor for prosteglandin, family centered childbirth. Home: One The Hollows Muttontown NY 11732 Office: 225 Marlborough Rd Brooklyn NY 11226

LIM, ESTHER P., physician; b. China, Oct. 21, 1921; d. Tiong-Kong and Chua-Szi (Huang) L.; M.D., Nat. Central U., Nanking, China, 1946; m. Frank H. Lee, Sept. 24, 1955; children—Grace E., Sylvia B. Intern, Univ. Hosp., Nanking, 1945-46; resident in Ob-Gyn, Luth. Hosp. of Md., 1951-53; resident in anesthesiology Fordham Hosp., N.Y.C., 1953-55, St. Luke's Hosp., N.Y.C., 1955-58; attending anesthesiologist French Hosp., N.Y.C., 1959-62; attending physician St. Barnabas Hosp., Bronx-Lebanon Hosp., 1962—; co-chief Manhasset Med. Center Hosp., Great Neck, N.Y., 1962—. Deacon, North Shore Presbyterian Ch., 1972-75, elder, 1977—. Diplomate Am. Bd. Anesthesiology. Fellow Am. Coll. Anesthesiologists; mem. AMA, Am. Soc. Anesthesiologists, N.Y. State Med. Soc., N.Y. State Soc. Anesthesiologists. Office: 2 Jeffrey Ln Great Neck NY 11020

LIM, GEORGE, physician; b. Bklyn., Oct. 26, 1925; s. NG Ying and Hom Shiee L.; B.S., Mass. Inst. Tech., 1948, M.S., 1949; M.D., State U. N.Y., N.Y.C., 1953; m. Beverly C. Lee, Sept. 21, 1952; children—Diana, Barbara, Andrew, Carolyn, Edward. Intern, Meadowbrook Hosp., E. Meadow, N.Y., 1953-54, resident, 1955-59; resident VA Hosp., Long Beach, Calif., 1954-55; practice medicine specializing in orthopedic surgery, Rome, N.Y.; clin. asso. prof. orthopedic surgery Upstate Med. Center, Syracuse, N.Y.; cons. and lectr. in field. Served to lt. USNR, 1944-47. Diplomate Nat. Bd. Med. Examiners. Fellow A.C.S., Internat. Coll. Surgeons, Am. Coll. Emergency Physicians; mem. Oneida County, N.Y. State med. socs., Rome Acad. Scis. Republican. Presbyterian. Home: 6484 Pillmore Dr Rome NY 13440 Office: 617 N James St Rome NY 13440

LIM, JONG JIN, biophysicist; b. Korea, Sept. 5, 1931; s. Jae Ung and Hyun Ie (Lee) L.; B.S., Ohio, U. 1962; M.S., N.Y. U., 1968, Ph.D., 1970; m. Bong Soon Yun, Nov. 21, 1962; children—Grace, Kay. Research asso. Columbia, 1972—; asst. research scientist in biophysics N.Y.U., 1970-71, asso. research scientist, 1971-72, instr. physics, 1967-71; instr. physics City U.N.Y., Fairleigh Dickinson U. Fight for Sight fellow, 1972-74; NIH grantee, 1975-81. Mem. Biophys. Soc., Am. Phys. Soc., N.Y. Acad. Sci. Contbr. articles to profl. jours. Home: 807 Holly St New Milford NJ 07646 Office: 630 W 168th St New York City NY 10032

LIM, PETER GANPIN, biochemical engr.; b. Manila, Philippines, July 5, 1935; s. Hee Pek and Siok Oan (Ng) L.; came to U.S., naturalized; 1972. B.S. in Chem. Engring. cum laude, U. Philippines, 1958; M.S. in Chem. Engring., Mass. Inst. Tech., 1959, Sc.D., 1963; m. Nancy Bee Gim Ngo, June 26, 1965; children—Nathan Lemuel, Bithia Jennifer. Research bioengr., Hercules, Inc., Wilmington, Del., 1963-66; sr. prodn. supr. Pfizer Inc., Groton, Conn., 1966—. Mem. Am. Chem. Soc., Am. Soc. Microbiology, AAAS, KEM Engrs. Mem. Groton Bible Chapel (pres. corp.). Patentee in field. Contbr. articles to profl. jours. Home: 25 Patricia Ct Gales Ferry CT 06335 Office: Pfizer Inc Eastern Point Rd Groton CT 06340

LIMA, BEATRICE VAN DUZER, real estate exec.; b. Sheshequin, Pa., July 27, 1912; d. Benjamin Franklin and Edith Marguerite (Shepard) Van Duzer; student U. Rochester, 1959; m. Thomas Joseph Lima, Mar. 17, 1934; 1 son, Thomas Joseph. Saleswoman, Beacon Rochester Inc., Alexander St., Rochester, N.Y., 1959—; realtor Fairport, N.Y., 1967-73, Dalton, N.Y., 1973—. Mem. Rochester Real Estate Bd., Genesee Valley Bd. N.Y., N.Y. State, Nat. assns. realtors. Club: Order Eastern Star. Home and Office: Eisaman Rd Dalton NY 14836

LIMBERAKIS, JOHN ANTHONY, clergyman; b. Boston, Oct. 7, 1925; s. Anthony John and Evangeline (Karademetriou) L.; diploma theology Greek Orthodox Sch. Theology, 1948; student Fresno U., 1950-53; B.A., Hellenic Coll., 1956, B.D., 1959; postgrad. R.I. Coll., 1964, Brown U., 1964; m. Elizabeth Constantine, Sept. 1, 1949; children—Cary J., Anthony J., Catherine J. Ordained priest Greek Orthodox Ch., 1949; pastor Greek Orthodox Ch. St. George, Fresno, Cal., 1949-55, Greek Orthodox Ch. Greater Providence, Cranston, R.I., 1955-70; vicar of So. New Eng., 1968-70; pastor, archpriest Ch. Annunciation, Greek Orthodox Community Phila., Elkins Park, Pa., 1970—; protopresbyter of Ecumenical Patriarchate of Constantinople (Istanbul), 1978; Mem. R.I. Gov.'s Ecumenical Adv. Commn., 1968-70; mem. Archdiocesan Council of Presbyters, 1970-72, 74-76; judicatory exec. Met. Christian Council Phila., 1973—; mem. Interfaith Council Correctional Justice, 1972-76. Mem. New Eng. Clergy Council (pres. 1957-58), Mixed Council Archdiocese (exec. mem. 1958-60), Eastern Montgomery County Ministerium, Lower York Ecumenical Dialogue, Holy Cross Alumni Assn. (pres. 1958-60). Initiator legislation in R.I. and Maine to recognize Greek Orthodox Ch. as major religion. Home: 1078 Kipling Rd Jenkintown PA 19117 Office: 7921 Old York Rd Elkins Park Philadelphia PA 19117

LIMING, ROBERT WARREN, radiologist; b. Boston, May, 29, 1921; s. Melville and Marjorie (Odlin) L.; B.A., Dartmouth Coll., 1944; M.D., L.I. Coll. Medicine, 1945; m. Barbara Jean Curry, May 29, 1947; children—Ann, John, Stephen, Nancy, Cynthia, Scott. Intern, King's County Hosp., Bklyn., 1945-46; resident in radiology Yale-New Haven Hosp., 1949-52; practice medicine specializing in radiology, Salem, Mass., 1952—; chief dept. radiology Salem Hosp.; staff radiologyst Mary Alley Hosp., Marblehead, Mass., 1952—, North Shore Children's Hosp., Salem, 1956—, J.B. Thomas Hosp., Peabody, Mass., 1960—. Trustee Salem Hosp., Boston U. Sch. Medicine. Served with M.C., U.S. Army, 1946-49. Diplomate Am. Bd. Radiology. Fellow Am. Coll. Radiology; mem. AMA, New Eng. Roentgen Ray Soc., New Eng. Cancer Soc., New Eng. Soc. Ultra Sound in Medicine, North Am., North Shore radiol. socs., Mass., Essex South med. socs. Episcopalian. Clubs: Eastern Yacht (Marblehead); North Shore Tennis (Salem). Home: 10 W Orchard St Marblehead MA 01945 Office: Salem Hosp 81 Highland Ave Salem MA 01970

LIMONGELLI, WILLIAM ALFONSO, oral surgeon; b. N.Y.C., Dec. 27, 1943; s. Alfonso William and Helen Rita (Gillen) L.; A.A., Westchester Community Coll., 1964; B.A., Hunter Coll., 1967; D.D.S., Howard U., 1971; certificate oral surgery Newark (N.J.) Beth Israel Med. Center, 1972. Intern in oral surgery Harlem Hosp. Center, N.Y.C., 1972-73, resident in oral surgery, 1973-74, chief resident in oral surgery, 1974-75; practice oral surgery, Newark, 1975—; clin. instr. dept. oral surgery Coll. Dentists, Columbia U., N.Y.C., 1973-75; asst. attending oral surgeon, dept. oral surgery Harlem Hosp. Center, N.Y.C., 1975—. Licensed dentist, N.Y., N.J., Md.; certified instr. basic and advanced life support Am. Heart Assn. Diplomate Am. Bd. Oral Maxillofacial Surgery. Fellow Am. Dental Soc. Anesthesiology, Acad. Medicine N.J., Internat. Assn. Oral Surgeons; mem. ADA, N.J., Essex County dental socs., Assn. Mil. Surgeons U.S., N.Y. State Soc. Oral Surgeons (affiliate), Am. Assn. Oral Maxillofacial Surgeons, N.J. Soc. Oral Surgeons, Omicron Kappa Upsilon. Contbr. articles to dental jours. and texts. Home: 63 Cypress St Yonkers NY 10704 Office: 490 Clinton Ave Newark NJ 07108 also 325 Central Ave Orange NJ 07050

LIMPE, ANTHONY TEH, mfg. co. exec.; b. Pasay, Philippines, July 18, 1934; came to U.S., 1952, naturalized, 1972; s. James V. and Juana (Teh) L.; B.M.E., Purdue U., 1956; M.M.E., Bklyn. Poly. Inst., 1964; m. Emily Ting, June 15, 1957; 1 son, Stephen. With Petro Chem. Devel. Co., Inc., N.Y.C., 1962—, pres., chief exec. officer, 1970—, chmn., chief exec. officer, 1976—; pres., chief exec. officer PC Inc., N.Y.C., 1976—; chmn. chmn., chief exec. officer Mich. Oven Co., Romulus, 1977—, Am. Econo-Therm Heater Corp., Houston, 1977—; dir. above cos. and Heurtey Petrochem, Heurtey Fours et Thermique, Petrochem Isoflow Furnaces Can., Ltd., Petro-Chem. Furnaces Inc. Mem. ASME, Pres.'s Orgn., Nat. Soc. Profl. Engrs., Am. Inst. Chem. Engrs., Am. Petroleum Inst. Roman Catholic. Contbr. articles to profl. jours. Home: 11 Rockridge Rd Ardsley NY 10502 Office: 122 E 42d St New York City NY 10017

LIN, ADA WEN-SHUNG MA, research chemist; b. Canton, China May 19, 1937; d. Yuen Cheung and Shu Ming (Wang) Ma; came to U.S., 1961, naturalized, 1972; B.S., Nat. Taiwan U., 1960; M.A., Columbia, 1963, Ph.D., 1966; m. Otto Chui Chau Lin, Sept. 7, 1963; children—Ann, Gene. Postdoctoral research asso. Columbia, 1966-67, U. Pa., Phila., 1967-68; research asso. Inst. for Cancer Research, Phila., 1969-70; research chemist Naval Regional Hosp., Phila., 1971—. NIH postdoctoral fellow. Mem. Am. Chem. Soc., AAAS, Am. Indsl. Hygiene Assn., Sigma Xi, Iota Sigma Pi. Roman Catholic. Discovered isoenzyme of human plasma monoamine oxidase, direct activity scanning method for MAO on polyacrylamide gel. Office: Broad and Pattison Ave Philadelphia PA 19145

LIN, CHANG LU, hydrogeologist; b. Miaoli, Taiwan, China, Dec. 24, 1938; s. Long En and Chao Mei Kao L.; came to Can., 1970, naturalized, 1976; B.S., Nat. Taiwan U., 1962; M.S., Wash. State U., 1967; Ph.D., U. Ill., 1970; m. Judy Chun-Yin Ho, July 28, 1967; children—David Yin-Peng, Edward Yin-Shiang. Research asst. Wash. Water Resources Center, Pullman, 1965-67; research asst. Ill. Geol. Survey, Urbana, 1967-68; engring. and ground water geologist N.S. Dept. Mines, Halifax, Can., 1970-73; ground water hydrologist N.S. Dept. Environment, Halifax, 1974-75, chief, water mgmt. sect., 1975-78, chief water resources planning sect., 1978—; grad. teaching asst. U. Ill., Urbana, 1968-70. Mem. Assn. Profl. Engrs. N.S. (mem. editorial bd. jour. 1975—), Am. Geophys. Union, Nat. Water Well Assn., Internat. Assn. Hydrogeologists (Germany). Contbr. articles to profl. jours. Home: 69 Beechcrest Dr Waverley NS Canada Office: PO Box 2107 Halifax NS Canada

LIN, FANG-JEN, physician; b. Taichung, Taiwan, Dec. 9, 1937; s. Kuo-Chin and Vivian Ben (Lee) L.; came to U.S., 1964, naturalized, 1977; M.D., Nat. Taiwan U., 1963; Ph.D. in Biochemistry, Tulane U., 1970; m. Kobkul Ariyaprakai, Dec. 27, 1970; children—Serena Pok-Hui, Patrick Pok-Tih. Intern, Roosevelt Hosp., N.Y.C., 1972-73; resident in radiation therapy Sloan-Kettering Meml. Cancer Center, N.Y.C., 1973-76; dir. radiation oncology St. Elizabeth Hosp., Elizabeth, N.J., 1976—; asso. clin. prof. Coll. Medicine and Dentistry N.J., Newark, 1976—. Diplomate Am. Bd. Radiology. Mem. Am. Coll. Radiology, Am. Soc. Therapeutic Radiologists, Radiol. Soc. N.Am., AMA, Am. Assn. Physicists in Medicine, Formosan Med.

Assn. Contbr. articles to profl. jours. Home: 82 Portland Ave Fanwood NJ 07023 Office: 225 Williamson St Elizabeth NJ 07207

LIN, JAMES FANG-MING, food technologist; b. Taiwan, Formosa, Nov. 6, 1936; s. Kuo-Chin and Bheng (Lee) L.; came to U.S., 1962, naturalized, 1972; B.S., Chung Yuang Coll., 1960; M.S., Kans. State U., 1964, Ph.D., 1968; postgrad. U. Chgo., 1972-73, George Washington U., 1978; m. Clara Shing-Ling Wang, June 11, 1966; children—Dwight J., Abraham J. Asst. chemist engring. research div. Wash. State U., Pullman, 1967-68; postdoctoral research asso. dept. food sci. and tech. Cornell U., Geneva, N.Y., 1968-70; research and devel. groupleader Quaker Oats Co., Research Lab., Barrington, Ill., 1970-75; food technologist FDA, Washington, 1975—; mem. advisory com. food sci. and tech. Republic China, 1977-79; vis. lectr. food tech. Ill. Inst. Tech., Chgo., 1972. Mem. Inst. Food Technologists (membership chmn. Washington sect. 1977-78), Am. Chem. Soc., Am. Assn. Cereal Chemists, AAAS, Sigma Xi. Contbr. articles in field to profl. jours. Home: 2002 Labrador Ln Vienna VA 22180 Office: 200 C St SW Washington DC 20204

LIN, JOSEPH PEN-TZE, neuroradiologist, clin. adminstr., educator; b. Foochow, China, Nov. 25, 1932; s. Tai Shiu and Chin Sien L.; came to U.S., 1959, naturalized, 1974; M.D., Nat. Taiwan, U., 1957; m. Lillian Y. Hsu, Dec. 23, 1959; children—James S., Carol W., Julia W. Rotating intern Robert B. Green Meml. Hosp., San Antonio, 1959-60; resident in radiology Santa Rosa Med. Center, San Antonio, 1960-61, Bellevue Hosp. Center, N.Y.C., 1961-63; fellow in neuroradiology N.Y. U. Med. Center, N.Y.C., 1963-65, instr. radiology, 1965-69, asst. prof., 1969-71, asso. prof., 1971-74, prof., 1974—; dir. neuroradiology sect. Univ. Hosp., N.Y.C., 1974—. Diplomate Am. Bd. Radiology. Fellow Am. Coll. Radiology; mem. Am. Chinese Med. Soc. (pres. 1978). Contbr. articles in neuroradiology to med. jours. Home: 15 Oxford Rd New Rochelle NY 10804 Office: New York Univ Medical Center 550 1st Ave New York City NY 10016

LIN, PO-AN, mgmt. accountant; b. Fukien, China, Nov. 12, 1927; s. Jung-Chi Lin and Kwei-Cheng Huang; came to U.S., 1961, naturalized, 1972; B.C.S., Soochow U., China, 1957; M.B.A., N.Y. U., 1963, advanced profl. certificate, certificate in mgmt. accounting, 1976; m. Helen Chang-Wan Lee, Apr. 13, 1958. Asst. to fin. sec. of Chinese Maritime Customs, Taipei, Taiwan, 1948-61; controller Internat. Ore & Fertilizer Corp. (div. Occidental Petroleum Corp.), N.Y.C., 1965—. Mem. Nat. Assn. Accountants, Am. Accounting Assn., Inst. Mgmt. Accounting. Office: 1230 Ave of Americas New York City NY 10020

LIN, RUEY YUAN, chemist; b. Amoy, China, Jan. 16, 1931; s. Chin Seng and Shou Cheng (Sheng) L.; B.S., Nat. Taiwan U., 1955; Ph.D., W.Va. U., 1962; m. Tip Kan Chan, June 6, 1964; children—Raymond, Edmund. Postdoctoral research fellow U. Buffalo, 1962-63; sr. chemist, sr. devel. asso. research and devel. div. Carborundum Co., Niagara Falls, N.Y., 1963-77; research asso. Eastern Research Center, Stauffer Chem. Co., Dobbs Ferry, N.Y., 1977—. Recipient Indsl. Research-100 awards, 1971, 72, 73, 75. Mem. Am. Chem. Soc., Sigma Xi. Contbr. papers and contract reports in field of fibrous materials devel.; patentee in field. Home: 15 Dolphin Rd New City NY 10956 Office: Eastern Research Center Stauffer Chem Co Dobbs Ferry NY 10522

LINARDUCCI, ROBERT PASQUALE, stock broker; b. Newark, Jan. 6, 1948; s. Pasquale and Evelyn (Pennacchio) L.; B.A., Seton Hall U., 1970; M.A., Abilene Christian U., 1972; postgrad. Catholic U. Am., 1972-73; m. Eileen T. Leahy, June 17, 1978. Social worker Essex County Treatment Center, Newark, 1972; program asst. HUD, Washington, 1973; staff psychologist Community Drug Program of Hudson County, Jersey City, 1974-75; stock broker Advest Co., Livingston, N.J., 1976-77, Loeb Rhoades Hornblower, Morristown, N.J., 1977—. Certified sch. psychologist, certified rehab. counselor. Mem. N.W. N.J. Estate Planning Council, Assn. Humanistic Psychology, Am. (asso.), N.J. psychol. assns., Pi Kappa Alpha. Home: 306 Tichenor Ave South Orange NJ 07079 Office: Loeb Rhoades Hornblower 90 South St Morristown NJ 07960

LINCOLN, ELIZABETH KITCHEL (MRS. ALEXANDER LINCOLN, JR.), social worker, educator; b. Englewood, N.J.; d. Cornelius Porter and Edith (Ray) Kitchel; B.A., Vassar Coll., 1933; M.A., Radcliffe Coll., 1938; M.S.W. with honors, U. Pitts., 1964; m. Alexander Lincoln, Jr., May 17, 1937; children—Eleanor (Mrs. William H. Buchanan, Jr.), Alexander III, Robert Kitchel, Margaret (Mrs. David A. Somerton). Coordinator mental health planning study Vt. Dept. Mental Health, Montpelier, 1964-65, field cons., 1965-68; field cons. N.H. Com. for Older Ams. Act, Concord, N.H., 1968-69; dir. services for aging N.H. State Council on Aging, Concord, 1969-73; regional dir. Northeast Assn. State Units on Aging, 1965-68; cons. N.H. State Council Aging, 1973-75; faculty White Pines Coll., Chester, N.H., 1973—; research asso., dept. psychiatry U. Vt. Med. Sch.; mem. adv. com. on older Americans, HEW, 1970-73. Mem. N.H. Commn. on Alcoholism, 1956-62, N.H. Commn. on Status of Women, 1971-74; sec. Govs. Mental Health Survey Com., 1957-59, Govs. Task Force on Mental Health Reorgn., 1960-61; bd. dirs. N.H. Social Welfare Council, 1957-62, 64-75, clk., 1975-77, pres., 1977—. Trustee Meredith (N.H.) Pub. Library, 1946-62; bd. dirs. White Mountain Community Services, Littleton, N.H., 1964-73, Lakes Region Mental Health Assn., Laconia, N.H., 1968-71, N.H. Swiftwater Girl Scout council, 1973—, N.H. Assn. for Mental Health, 1976—, Lakes Region Mental Health Center, 1977—; incorporator Lakes Region Gen. Hosp., Laconia, 1960—, N.H. Charitable Trust, 1971—; trustee Washingtonian Center, Boston, 1955—, Spaulding Youth Center, 1971—; governing bd. N.H. Assn. Elderly, 1973—. Mem. Nat. Assn. Social Workers, Acad. Certified Social Workers, Am. Sociol. Assn., Am. Pub. Health Assn., Boston Soc. for Gerontologic Psychiatry, Nat. Soc. Colonial Dames, Jr. League Boston, AAUW, Mayflower Soc., DAR, Am. Assn. Ret. Persons. Clubs: Womens City (Boston); Vt.-N.H. Vassar (pres. 1976—). Home: Meredith Bay Farm RFD 1 Meredith NH 03253 Office: White Pines Coll Box 278 Chester NH 03036

LINCOLN, EMMA ETHEL, ednl. adminstr.; b. East Lyme, Conn., Jan. 20, 1914; d. Daniel Higgins and Mary Emma (Holmes) Higgins Lincoln; grad. Williams Meml. Inst., 1934. Owner, Lincoln Auto Service, New London, Conn., 1940-76; pres. Lincoln Center, Inc., New London, 1963-77; ops. coordinator Waterford Country Sch., Inc., 1976—. Republican State Central Committeewoman 20th dist., Conn., 1972—; Rep. town chmn. New London Rep. Com., 1966-72; bd. dirs., past pres. YMCA New London; treas. bd. trustees Waterford Country Sch., 1976—. Mem. Bus. and Profl. Women's Club (past pres.). Home: 16 Glenwood Pl New London CT 06320

LIND, ARTHUR, physician; b. N.Y.C., Apr. 13, 1928; s. David and Bertha (Levin) L.; A.B., N.Y. U., 1946, M.D., 1950; m. Mary Eveline Dansereau, Nov. 26, 1953; children—Deborah Celia, David Esmond. Intern, Morrisania City Hosp., N.Y.C., 1950-51; asst. resident Bellevue Hosp., N.Y.C., 1951-53; instr. internal medicine Postgrad. Med. Sch., N.Y. U., 1953—; instr. clin. medicine, N.Y. U., Sch. Medicine, 1961—; practice medicine specializing in internal medicine, N.Y.C., 1956—; courtesy staff N.Y. Infirmary; attending physician Doctors Hosp.; attending internal medicine N.Y. Eye and Ear Infirmary; asst. clin. vis. physician Bellevue Hosp.; asst. in medicine Univ. Hosp. N.Y.C.; cons. internal medicine UN Health Service, Gracie Sq. Hosp. Served to capt. AUS, 1954-56. Diplomate Am. Bd. Internal Medicine. Fellow A.C.P.; mem. AMA, Am. Geriatric Soc., N.Y. State, N.Y. County (com. against discrimination, com. for hosps, com. on legis., com. on membership) med. socs., Am., N.Y. State, N.Y. County socs. internal medicine. Met. Mus. Art, Am. Mus. Natural History, N.Y. Zool. Soc., Westchester Mens Garden Club (dir., v.p., gardener of yr.), Westchester Rose Soc., N.Y. Cactus and Succulent Soc. Club: Town (Scarsdale). Contbr. articles to profl. pubIs. Home: 6 Eastwoods Ln Scarsdale NY 10583 Office: 285 West End Ave New York City NY 10023

LIND, DOUGLASS THEODORE, clergyman, marriage and family counselor; b. St. Paul, Dec. 27, 1939; s. Olaf Milton and Jennie Teresa (Skoglund) L.; A.B. cum laude, Harvard, 1961; M.Div., Union Theol. Sem., 1964; certificate Westchester Inst. Tng. in Counseling and Psychotherapy, 1971; m. Penelope Dougall, July 31, 1965. Dir. library fund Pingry Sch., Hillside, N.J., 1964; ordained to ministry United Presbyterian Ch., U.S.A., 1967; area counselor Fifty Million Fund of United Presbyn. Ch., N.Y.C., 1964-67; pastor North Ave. Presbyn. Ch. New Rochelle, N.Y., 1967-73; nat. tng. dir. Reed and Di Salvo Assos. Inc., Mgmt. Cons., N.Y.C., 1973—, pres. bd. trustees Hudson River Counseling Service, 1973—; asst. minister Wilton (Conn.) Presbyn. Ch., 1973—; trustee Westchester Inst. Tng. in Counseling and Psychotherapy, Johnson C. Smith Sem.; bd. ch. visitors Warren Wilson Coll. Vice pres. Charter League of New Rochelle, 1969-73. Fellow Am. Assn. Pastoral Counselors; mem. Am. Assn. Marriage and Family Counselors (clin.), Acad. Parish Clergy (dir.). Home: 17 Edgewater Hillside St Westport CT 06880

LINDA, DENNIS JOSEPH, educator; b. Buffalo, Apr. 11, 1943; s. Joseph W. and Charlotte K. (Klaus) L.; A.B., Canisius Coll., 1966, M.S., 1973. Instr. chemistry and physics Bishop Ryan High Sch., Buffalo, 1966-71; chemistry instr. Bishop Turner High Sch., Buffalo, 1971—, chmn. sci. dept., 1974—; sci. coordinator Buffalo Diocesan High Schs., 1977—. Judge, Nat. Scholastic Press Assn., 1978—. Named Bishop Edward D. Head Tchr. of Year, 1978; NSF grantee, 1967, 68. Mem. Am. Philatelic Soc., Am. First Day Cover Soc., Philatelic Soc. Egypt, AAAS, Secondary Lay Tchrs. Buffalo, Nat. Sci. Tchrs. Assn. Moderator, The Crozier, 1974-78. Office: 185 Lang Ave Buffalo NY 14215

LINDAHL, IVAN LEROY, govt. researcher; b. Bayard, Nebr., May 8, 1919; s. Carl J. and Dolly (Speer) L.; B.S., Nebr. Central Coll., 1941; postgrad. George Washington U., part-time 1943-50, U. Md., part-time, 1950-58; m. Angie Rhodes, June 28, 1943; 1 dau., Janice L. With U.S. Dept. Agr., Beltsville, Md., 1943—, chemist, 1943-48, biochemist, 1948-51, 54-57, 57-59, animal nutritionist, 1951-54, leader sheep nutrition, also research chemist, 1959-72, research chemist ruminant nutrition lab. Nutrition Inst., 1972—. Adminstrv. bd. Methodist Ch.; active ARC. Recipient Outstanding Performance ratings U.S. Dept. Agr., 1952, 53, 57, 59, 66, 72; Mary Farley award Am. Dairy Goat Assn., 1968. Fellow Am. Inst. Chemists, Am. Soc. Animal Sci. (Distinguished Service award NE sect. 1976); mem. Am. Dairy Sci. Assn., N.Y. Acad. Sci., Am. Inst. B'ol. Sci., Smithsonian Assos., Mass. Hort. Soc., Mental Health Asso. Prince George's County, A.A.A.S., Capitol Dairy Goat Coop. (v.p. 1967-69, dir. 1967-71), Wilderness Soc., Nat. Parks and Conservation Assn., Am. Forestry Assn., Am. Soc. Range Mgmt., Am. Dairy Goat Assn., Nat., Prince George's (dir., chmn. conservation com. 1972-73) Audubon Socs., Gideons Internat., Alpha Chi Sigma. Clubs: Lions (pres. club); Meth. Men. Research in field. Home: 12508 Sir Walter Dr Glenn Dale MD 20769 Office: Agri Research Center Beltsville MD 20705

LINDAUER, LOIS LYONS, dietary orgn. adminstr.; b. N.Y.C., Feb. 6, 1933; d. Ken and Rose (Schneidman) Lyons; A.B., Brandeis U., 1953; m. William Seltz, Nov. 12, 1972; children by previous marriage—Karen Lyons, Amy Hope. Copywriter, Herbert Frank Advt. Agy., Boston, 1956-57; pres. Paisley workshop, handmade plaques and wall decor, N.Y.C., 1962-65; nat. dir. Diet Workshop, Inc., East Meadow, N.Y., 1965—. Diet cons. Alba Non-Fat Skim Milk. Pub. relations dir. Internat. Franchise Assn. Author: It's In to Be Thin, 1971; The Diet Workshop Restaurant Manual, 1972; The Fast and Easy Teenage Diet, 1973; diet columnist Ladies Home Jour. Home: 1 Longfellow Pl Boston MA 02114 Office: 111 Washington St Brookline MA 02146

LINDE, WALTER, engring. and constrn. co. exec.; b. Wiesbaden, Germany, Apr. 28, 1928; s. Selmar Friedrich and Hildegard Frieda (Wucherer) L.; came to U.S., 1962; diploma elec. engring. Karlsruhe Technische Hochschule, 1951; m. Virginia Guest, June 14, 1958; children—Lucinda, Carl Walter, Alexandra, Annetta, Peter Guest. Maintenance electrician Barkers Biscuit Ltd., Toronto, Ont., Can., 1951-52; elec. engr. Rogers Majestic Co., Toronto, 1952-55; N.Am. rep. Linde A.G., Toronto, 1955-62, sec.-treas. Lotepro Corp. subs., N.Y.C., 1962-63, dir. cost accounting and budgets Linde A.G., Munich, W.Ger., 1963-65, v.p., dir. Lotepro Corp., N.Y.C., 1965-72, pres., dir., 1972—; pres., dir. Lotepro Engring. & Cons. Co., Calgary, Alta., 1974—. Served with anti-aircraft German Air Force, 1944-45. Mem. ASME (Outstanding Leadership award 1978), Assn. Profl. Engrs. Ont., Assn. Profl. Engrs., Geologists and Geophysicists Alta. Am. Gas Assn. (liquified natural gas com.), Am. Mgmt. Assn., Internat. Oxygen Mfrs. Assn., Compressed Gas Assn. Lutheran. Club: Ardsley Country. Patentee in field. Office: Lotepro Corp subs Linde AG 1140 Ave of Americas New York City NY 10036

LINDELL, RANDOLPH DICKINSON, III, filter products co. mgr.; b. Newark, Del., Sept. 16, 1938; s. Randolph Dickinson and Marie Elizabeth (Carson) L.; student U. Del., 1956-57; B.S. in Bus. Adminstrn., Widener Coll., 1972; m. Kay Golt; 1 dau., Deborah Kay. Product mgr., launch systems Elkton (Md.) div. Thiokol Corp., 1959-67; mktg. rep. HRB-Singer Inc., State College, Pa., 1967-69; mgr. Eastern mil. market Test Instrument div. Honeywell Inc., Denver and Annapolis, Md., 1969-71; regional mgr. filter products div. Facet Enterprises Inc., Madison Heights, Mich., 1971—. Mem. bd. edn., Newark, Del. Mem. Del. Sch. Bds. Assn., Am. Petroleum Inst., Am. Mgmt. Assn. Methodist. Home: 104 Chapel Hill Dr Newark DE 19711 Office: Commonwealth Bldg 205A University Plaza Newark DE 19702

LINDEN, KATHRYN, communications cons.; b. N.Y.C., Jan. 24, 1905; d. Robert Berthold and Anna (Jaehns) Linden; B.S. with honors, Columbia, 1953, M.A., 1956; Ph.D., N.Y. U., 1972. Asst. dept. edn. Met. Mus. Art, N.Y.C., 1937-44; dir. audio-visual edn. East and West Assn., 1944-45, chmn. film com., 1945-48; cons. audio-visual program Am. Nurses Assn., 1948-53, dir. Am. Nurses Assn.-Nat. League Nursing Film Service (now Am. Jour. Nursing Co.), N.Y.C., 1953-70, cons. ednl. services div., 1970. Tech. cons. White House Conf. Children and Youth, 1960; chmn. Audio-Visual Conf. Med. and Allied Scis., Chgo., 1960-62, program chmn., 1963-67, vice chmn., 1959; corr. sec. N.Y. Film Council, 1959-67; chmn. film forum sessions, jury screenings in health film category Am. Film Assemblies, 1957-69, juror, active workshops, 1954-56; mem. conv. film com. Nat. Social Welfare Assemblies, 1953-58. Dir. Taraknath Das Found., N.Y.C., 1972-77, v.p., dir., 1978—, trustee 1959—. Recipient Founders Day certificate N.Y. U., 1972; plaque Audiovisual Conf. of Med. and Allied Scis., 1974; Alumni medal Columbia, 1976. Mem. Alumni Assn. Sch. Gen. Studies Columbia U. (sec. 1960-63, corr. sec. 1969-70, sec. 1971-77, v.p. 1977-78), Am. Acad. Polit. and Social Scis., N.Y. U. Alumni Assn. Presbyn. Contbr. articles to profl. jours. Co-producer, prodn. coordinator filmstrips, films in field. Home: 504 W 110th St New York City NY 10025

LINDENBLAD, IRVING WERNER, astronomer; b. Port Jefferson, N.Y., July 31, 1929; s. Nils Erik and Elsie Christine (Lawson) L.; A.B., Wesleyan U., 1950; M.Div., Colgate Rochester Div. Sch., 1956; postgrad. Harvard, 1956; M.A., George Washington U., 1963; m. Ann Bolling Terry, Dec. 21, 1958; children—Irving Werner, Nils Bolling. Ordained to ministry Baptist Ch., 1956; minister Savannah (N.Y.) Congregational Ch., 1954-55, Market St. Bapt. Ch., Harrisburg, Pa., 1957, Montowese Bapt. Ch., North Haven, Conn., 1961-62; astronomer U.S. Naval Obs., Washington, 1953, 58-60, 63—. Pres. Local 1461, Nat. Fedn. Fed. Employees Union, 1967-69. Served with AUS, 1951-53. Fellow Royal Astron. Soc.; mem. Am. Astron. Soc., Am. Geophys. Union. Contbr. articles to profl. jours. Home: 4735 Arlington Blvd Arlington VA 22203 Office: US Naval Observatory Washington DC 20390

LINDER, EDWARD FREDRICK, JR., univ. dean; b. Phila., Nov. 23, 1935; s. Edward Fredrick and Helen Cecil (McCafferty) L.; B.S., West Chester State Coll., 1962; M.Ed., Ohio U., 1963; postgrad. Pa. State U., 1963-67. Dean men's staff, asst. athletic coordinator West Chester State Coll., 1959-62; research and teaching asst. Ohio U., Athens, 1962-63; dean men's staff Pa. State U., University Park, 1963-67, dean student affairs, 1967—; faculty dept. social relations Montgomery County Community Coll., 1969—. Del., U.S. Peace Corps Constl. Del., 1962; bd. dirs. Vis. Nurses of Chester, Pa., 1968—, adv. profl. com., 1970—. Served with USMC, 1954-57. Mem. Am. Psychol. Assn., Nat. Assn. Student Personnel Adminstrs., Am., Pa. personnel and guidance assns., Nat. Vocat. Guidance Assn., Am. Coll. Personnel Assn., Friar Soc., Iota Alpha Delta, Phi Delta Kappa. Republican. Roman Catholic. Clubs: Rotary (pres. 1976), K.C. (4 deg.). Home: 109 E Seven Stars Rd Phoenixville PA 19460 Office: 25 Yearsley Mill Rd Media PA 19063

LINDER, MORTON HOWARD, internist; b. Bklyn., Feb. 17, 1929; s. William B. and Claire L.; B.A., N.Y. U., 1950; M.D., U. Utrecht (Netherlands), 1957; m. Lee D'Andrea, Mar. 2, 1955. Intern, Queens Hosp. Center, Jamaica, N.Y., 1957-58; resident in internal medicine Westchester County Med. Center, Valhalla, N.Y., 1958-60, research fellow in diabetes and metabolism, 1960-61; practice medicine specializing in internal medicine and diabetes, Mt. Kisco, N.Y., 1961—; chief sect. on diabetes and dir. diabetes clinic Westchester County Med. Center; asst. prof. clin. medicine N.Y. Med. Coll.; attending physician internal medicine No. Westchester Hosp. Center. Diplomate Am. Bd. Internal Medicine. Fellow A.C.P.; mem. Am., N.Y. (past pres. Westchester chpt.) diabetes assns., Am. Fedn. Clin. Research, Am. Med. Writers Assn., AMA, N.Y. State Med. Soc., Am. Soc. Internal Medicine, Clin. Soc. N.Y. Diabetes Assn. Contbr. articles on diabetes mellitus to med. jours. Co-developer first clinically successful method of continuous measurement of blood sugar in human patients. Office: 21 Saint Marks Pl Mount Kisco NY 10549

LINDER, THOMAS EDWARD, JR., chem. engr.; b. Baton Rouge, La., Dec. 5, 1949; s. Thomas E. and Mona Elizabeth (Roberts) L.; B.S. in Chemistry and Biology, U. Maine, 1972; grad. Va. State Water Control Bd. Sch. Waste Treatment, 1975; postgrad. U. Va., 1974-76; m. Dorothy Harvey Bryant, Dec. 7, 1975. Paper quality control technician Internat. Paper Co., Chisholm, Maine, summer 1969, 70, 71; instr. biology Liberty Baptist Coll., Lynchburg, Va., 1973-74; mem. emergency nursing staff Va. Bapt. Hosp., Lynchburg, 1973-74; process engr. Va. Fibre Corp., Amherst, 1975-76; dist. rep. with indsl. sales div. Betz Labs. Inc., Trevose, Pa., 1976-77; asst. tech. dir. pulp mill Ga.-Pacific Corp., Plattsburgh, N.Y., 1977-78; mgr. environ. engring. Riegel Products Corp., Milford, N.J., 1978—. Served to ensign USN, 1972-73. Mem. TAPPI (exec. council Va. sect. 1974-76), Va. Water Pollution Control Fedn., Nat. Council Air and Stream Improvement, Va. Engring. Soc., Am. Forestry Assn., AAAS, Nat. Mammalogical Soc., Soc. Preservation for Barbershop Quartet Singing in Am., Beta Beta Beta (pres. 1970-72). Baptist. Home: 1141 E Lafayette St Easton PA 18042 Office: Riegel Products Corp Milford NJ 08848

LINDHOLM, DALE DAVID, internist, nephrologist; b. Duluth, Minn., Dec. 4, 1931; s. David and Jenny Lillian (Lind) L.; B.A., U. Minn., 1953, B.S. (James Wright Hunt fellow), 1954, M.D., 1957; m. Dolores C. Hennings, June 20, 1953; children—Ronald Dale, Cynthia Sue. Med. intern St. Luke's Hosp., Duluth, 1957-58; resident in internal medicine USPHS Hosp., Seattle, 1959-62; Am. Heart Inst. fellow in nephrology U. Wash., Seattle, 1962-64; chief of research Seamen's Meml. Research Lab. and USPHS Hosp., New Orleans, 1964-66; prof., head sect. kidney diseases Tulane U. Sch. Medicine, New Orleans, 1965-74; prof., chmn. nephrology div. U. W.Va. Med. Center, Morgantown, 1974-78; staff Moses Taylor Kidney and Hypertension Inst., Scranton, Pa., 1978—. Served with USPHS, 1958-66. Mem. AMA, Internat. Soc. Nephrology, Am. Soc. Nephrology, Am. Soc. Artificial Internal Organs, Nat. Kidney Found., Renal Physicians Assn. Baptist. Research in nephrology. Home: 107 Northern Spy Rd Clarks Summit PA 18411 Office: Taylor Kidney and Hypertension Inst 741 Quincy Ave Scranton PA 18510

LINDNER, EDMUND FREDERICK, communications and advt. exec.; b. Vienna, Austria, May 11, 1918; s. P. Theodore and Josephine (Sternfeld) L.; came to U.S., 1945, naturalized, 1948; B.S., U. Vienna, 1936; M.D., U. Algiers (Algeria), 1941; D.Sc., London Inst. Applied Research, 1974; m. Gladys Austen, Apr. 11, 1958. Intern, Kenadsa (Algeria) Hosp. and Infirmary, 1940-41; gen. practice medicine and surgery, Kenadsa, 1941-43; mgr. med. advt. Mac Millan Co., N.Y.C., 1946-56; writer, dir. Med. Film Guild, N.Y.C., 1956; asso. creative group head Ted Bates & Co., N.Y.C., 1957-59; writer Med. Horizons, TV program, 1958; writer, med. cons. Benton & Bowles, advt. co., N.Y.C., 1959-62; producer, dir. RAM Prodns., N.Y.C., 1962—; cons. med. communications and advt., 1962—; asso. dir. Inst. Newark Beth Israel Med. Center, 1967-69; exec. v.p., vice chmn. bd. Stuart Williams Assos., advt. agy., Stamford, Conn., 1968—; Pres. Scicom, Inc. Publs., 1975—; lectr. med. mktg., advt. Mem. Com. for Humane Legis., Washington; bd. dirs. Lawyers Med. Bur., Westport, Conn. Served with French Fgn. Legion, 1940, Brit. Army Pioneer Corps, 1942, OSS, 1943-45. Decorated medal of Freedom with bronze palm (U.S.); Africa Star, Italy Star (Britain); recipient Med. Writers' award Am. Med. Writers Assn., 1953. Fellow Am. Med. Writers Assn. (pres. N.Y.C. chpt. 1969-70); mem. Am. Med. Soc. Vienna (life), N.Y. Acad. Scis., Drug Info. Assn., Am. Guild Authors, Composers, Humane Soc., Broadcast Music Inc., Common Cause. Author: Lecithin in Health and Disease, 1955; Medical Advertising, 1964; Dynamics of Motivation, 1966; Taking Care of Your Arteries, 1972; Peripheral Vascular Stimulation by Physical Means, 1972; What Makes Old Folks Cranky, 1972; editor-in-chief Clin. Rev., 1972—, Burn Treatment Newsletter, 1975—; patentee in field of microfilms; producer, writer and dir. Films: Congestive Heart Failure, 1956; The 18th Day, 1957; musical compositions: Adorable, 1958; In a Little

While, 1959. Home: 2 Hazelnut Rd Westport CT 06880 Office: 40 Signal Rd Stamford CT 06902

LINDSAY, ALEXANDER DAVID, chemist; b. Passaic, N.J., May 4, 1943; s. Alexander Young and Charlotte L.; B.A., Rutgers U., 1965; M.S., Clarkson Coll. Tech., 1973, Ph.D., 1973; m. Lauren Garde Smith, Jan. 29, 1966. Research chemist Am. Cyanamid Co., Princeton, N.J., 1970-72, group leader, 1972-76; sr. research chemist Mobil Chem. Co., Edison, N.J., 1976—. Mem. Am. Chem. Soc., ASTM. Home: 3 Kirklin Pl East Brunswick NJ 08816 Office: PO Box 240 Edison NJ 08817

LINDSAY, REGINALD CARL, lawyer; b. Birmingham, Ala., Mar. 19, 1945; s. Richard and Louise (Crosier) L.; A.B., Morehouse Coll., 1967; certificate U. Valencia (Spain), 1966; J.D., Harvard, 1970; m. Cheryl E. Hartgrove, Aug. 15, 1970. Admitted to Mass. bar, 1970; asso. firm Hill & Barlow, 1970-75, 78—; commr. Mass. Dept. Pub. Utilities, Boston, 1975-77; corporator Suffolk Franklin Savs. Bank. Pres. adv. bd. Mus. of Nat. Center of Afro-Am. Artists; trustee Thompson Islands Edn. Center, Boston; bd. dirs. Casa del Sol, Adult Learning Center, Boston. Mem. Am., Nat., Mass., Boston (council 1977—) bar assns., Pi Sigma Alpha. Democrat. Office: 225 Franklin St Boston MA 02110

LINDSAY, ROBERT HENRY, trust co. exec.; b. Rossburn, Man., Can., Nov. 21, 1924; s. John Andrew and Alice Mae (Carson) L.; grad. high sch.; children by previous marriage—Robert John Thomas, Marie Elaine; m. Mary Alice Sharpe, Dec. 22, 1973; children—Allan Joseph, Laura Elizabeth. With Toronto-Dominion Bank, 1945-62, br. mgr., 1960-62; credit mgr. Acklands, Ltd., Winnipeg, Man., 1963-64; with Fidelity Trust Co., Winnipeg, Man., 1964—, sec.-treas., 1965-77, comptroller, 1965—, sec.-treas., 1977—. Served with R.C.A.F., 1943-45. Mem. Canadian Legion. Club: Masons. Home: 565 Walkers Line Burlington ON Canada Office: 350 Bay St Toronto ON Canada

LINDSEY, FRED, educator; b. Detroit, Oct. 29, 1948; B.A., Shaw Coll., Detroit, 1971; M.A., U. Detroit, 1972; M.P.A., Wayne State U., 1975; Ph.D., Howard U., 1979. Mem. staff Office of Senator Edward Kennedy, Washington, 1976-77; adminstrv. asst. State Senator Basil W. Brown, Lansing, Mich., 1973-75; adminstrv. asst. City Council Detroit, 1972-73; asst. prof. polit. sci. Stockton State Coll., Pomona, N.J., 1978—. Mem. adv. bd. Alcohol Recovery Program, Atlantic City, N.J., 1978—. Mem. Am. Soc. Pub. Adminstrn., AAUP, Internat. City Mgmt. Assn. Home: 99 Brattle St Box 133 Cambridge MA 02138 Office: Stockton State Coll Pomona NJ 08240

LINEBAUGH, JOHN HARVEY MOORE, real estate mgmt. cons.; b. Lock Haven, Pa., Oct. 15, 1917; s. Earl A. and Frances C. (Dunkle) L.; B.S. in Math., Lock Haven State Coll., 1939; m. Mary A. Kress, Apr. 4, 1942; children—Sandra Linebaugh Stewart, Susan Linebaugh Whitmore. Commd. 2d lt. USAAF, 1941, advanced through grades to col., 1962, ret., 1970; mgmt. cons. on operation of shopping centers, 1976—. Decorated Legion of Merit, D.F.C. with two clusters, Air medal with four clusters, Distinguished Air Force award with two clusters; recipient Distinguished Service award Dade County, Fla., 1968. Mem. Am. Security Council (adv. bd.), Ret. Officers Assn. Lutheran. Clubs: Air Force Officers; Shriner. Address: 21 Mary Lyon Dr South Hadley MA 01075

LINENBERG, WILLIAM BERNARD, oral surgeon; b. Phila., Apr. 12, 1931; s. Max and Rose (Schlichtmann) L.; D.D.S., Temple U., 1955; M.S.D., U. Pa., 1961; m. Geraldine Redzinak, Dec. 28, 1957; children—David Peter, Karen Ann, Michael John, Mark Thomas, Eric Matthew. Intern, resident oral surgery Grady Meml. Hosp., Atlanta, 1958-60; pvt. practice dentistry specializing in oral surgery, Westfield, N.J., 1963—; asst. instr. Emory U. Sch. Dentistry, 1958-60. Served with Dental Corps, U.S. Army, 1955-57, 60-63. Diplomate Am. Bd. Oral Surgery. Mem. Internat., Am. (1st prize research award 1962), N.J. socs. oral surgeons, ADA, Am. Acad. Oral Medicine, N.J. Dental Soc., Omicron Kappa Upsilon. Roman Catholic. Contbr. articles to profl. jours. Home: 304 E Dudley Ave Westfield NJ 07090 Office: 316 E Broad St Westfield NJ 07090

LINES, MALCOLM ELLIS, physicist; b. Banbury, Eng., Apr. 26, 1936; s. Herbert Ellis and Florence May (Wise) L.; came to U.S., 1966; B.A. with 1st class honors, Magdalen Coll., Oxford U., 1959, M.A. (Prize fellow), 1961, D.Phil., 1962; m. Kathleen Mary Morse, Dec. 22, 1962; children—Richard Maxwell, Stephen Patrick. Fellow in physics Magdalen Coll., 1961-66; theoretical physicist Bell Telephone Labs., Murray Hill, N.J., 1966—; cons. Atomic Energy Research Establishment, Harwell, Eng., 1973. Served with RAF, 1954-56. Recipient Jex Blake prize Magdalen Coll., 1958. Fellow Phys. Soc., Brit. Inst. Physics; mem. N.Y. Acad. Scis., Am. Ceramic Soc. Author: Principles and Applications of Ferroelectrics and Related Materials, 1977; also articles on magnetism, ferroelectricity and semicondr. physics in profl. jours. Home: 10 E Rayburn Rd Millington NJ 07946 Office: Bell Labs Murray Hill NJ 07974

LIN-FU, JANE SYCIP (MRS. CHING MARK FU), pediatrician; b. Singapore, Nov. 21, 1928 (came to U.S. 1955, naturalized 1963); d. Yu Y. and Unchong Y. (Sycip) Lin; M.D. cum laude, U. Santo Tomas, Manila, Philippines, 1955; m. Ching Mark Fu, May 30, 1958; children—Emanuel, Jeanette, Stephenie. Intern Bklyn. Jewish Hosp. and Med. Center, 1955-56; resident, 1956-58, fellow pediatric neurology, 1958-60; cons. children's bur. HEW 1963-69, maternal and child health service USPHS, 1969-73, White House Conf. on Children, 1970, Bur Community Health Services, Health Services Adminstrn, HEW, 1973—. Recipient award to work in lead poisoning Nat. Decorating Products Assn., 1972, Superior Service award Dept. Health, Edn. and Welfare, 1973. Diplomate Am. Bd. Pediatrics. Fellow Am. Acad. Pediatrics; mem. Washington Med. Soc. (asso.). Research and publs. on lead poisoning in children. Home: 6420 Hollins Dr Bethesda MD 20034 Office: 5600 Fishers Ln Rockville MD 20852

LING, SUILIN, mgmt. cons.; b. Shanghai, China, Oct. 13, 1930; s. Chunchen and Maisan (Dunn) L.; came to U.S., 1949, naturalized, 1963; B.S., U. Mich., 1952; Ph.D., Columbia U., 1961; m. Avril Marjorie Kathleen Button, Apr. 4, 1964; children—Christopher Charles, Charmian Avril. Mech. engr. Ebasco Services, Inc., 1953-54; with research div. Foster Wheeler Corp., 1954-64; mgmt. cons. The Emerson Cons., Inc., 1964-65; sr. economist Communications Satellite Corp., 1965-67; asst. dir. econ. and mgmt. planning Northrop-Page Communications Engrs., Inc., 1967-69, chief economist, 1967-70; founder-dir., chief economist Teleconsult Inc., Washington, 1970—; lectr. econs. Bernard M. Baruch Sch. Bus. and Pub. Adminstrn., City Coll. N.Y. Mem. Am. Mgmt. Assn., Am. Econ. Assn., ASME, Am. Acad. Polit. and Social Sci. Author: Economies of Scale in the Steam-Electric Power Generating Industry, 1964. Home: 2735 Unicorn Ln NW Washington DC 20015 Office: 2555 M St NW Washington DC 20037

LING, WILLIAM THEODORE, optometrist; b. Lake Placid, N.Y., July 23, 1929; s. Loren A. and Coraline B. (Potter) L.; student Siena Coll., 1949-51; B.S., Columbia, 1953, M.S., 1954; O.D., Mass. Coll. Optometry, 1967; m. Marilyn B. Stewart, Sept. 15, 1949; children—William T., John Thomas, Daniel James, Marilyn Ann. Pvt. practice optometry, Sanatoga Springs, N.Y., 1955—; cons. optometrist Wesley Nursing Home. Pres. Saratoga Springs Bd. Edn., 1964-66, mem. 1960-67; candidate for mayor of Saratoga Springs, 1970; dir. Health Service Agy., Region 5, 1976—; organizer Saratoga County Comprehensive Health Planning Council, 1974. Served with U.S. Army, 1946-48. Named Eastern N.Y. Optometric Soc. Optometrist of Year, 1976. Fellow Am. Acad. Optometry; mem. Am., N.Y. State (state chmn. Keyman Program 1969-75, v.p. 1978) optometric assns., Eastern N.Y. Optometric Soc. (past pres.), Omega Ipsilon Phi. Republican. Methodist. Club: Elks. Home: 168 East Ave Saratoga Springs NY 12866 Office: 205 Lake Ave Saratoga Springs NY 12866

LINGELBACH, ALBERT LANE, lawyer; b. N.Y.C., July 19, 1940; s. Robert Lane and Sarah Hodges (Lewis) L.; B.S., Wharton Sch. U. Pa., 1962, LL.B., 1965; m. Ann Norton, July 31, 1965; children—Albert Lane, Charity Ann. Admitted to N.Y. bar, 1967; asso. Jackson, Nash, Brophy, Barringer & Brooks, N.Y.C., 1965-72, mem. firm, 1972—. Co-chmn. drive Community Chest, Port Washington, N.Y., 1972-73, bd. dirs., 1973-74, sec., 1974-75, v.p., 1975-76, exec. v.p., 1976-78, pres., 1978—. Mem. Estate Planning Council N.Y., Am., N.Y. State bar assns., Assn. Bar City N.Y. Presbyterian. (elder). Clubs: University (N.Y.C.); Southport (Maine) Yacht. Home: 8 Stratford Rd Port Washington NY 11050 Office: 330 Madison Ave New York City NY 10017

LINGENFELTER, ROBERT BRIAN, banker; b. New Kensington, Pa., Aug. 29, 1944; s. Samuel Stanley and Elizabeth Avanell (Bussard) L.; B.S., Wagner Coll., 1966; M.B.A., Am. U., 1968. With Am. Security Bank, Washington, 1968—, asst. trust investment officer, 1970, trust investment officer, 1971, asst. v.p., trust investment officer, 1973—, head personal trust investment div., 1973—. Trustee, mem. fin. com. Family and Child Services of Washington, 1975—. Mem. Fin. Analysts Fedn., Washington Soc. Investment Analysts. Club: Pisces. Home: 2508 I St NW Washington DC 20037 Office: 15th St and Pennsylvania Ave NW Washington DC 20013

LINK, STEPHEN JOSEPH, electronics co. exec.; b. Albany, N.Y., June 29, 1919; s. Thomas Stephen and Amy (Saxton) L.; E.E., Rensselaer Poly. Inst., 1941; m. Mary K. Johnson, Sept. 6, 1941. Mech. designer Gen. Electric Co., Syracuse, N.Y., 1941-52, product design engr., 1952-61, mgr. design and documentation heavy mil. equipment dept., 1961-67, mgr. engring. data control, 1967-78; pres., gen. mgr. Craftsman plus 1, Inc., Oswego, N.Y., 1978—. Mem. Am. Def. Preparedness Assn., Rensselaer Poly. Inst. Alumni Assn. (pres. Syracuse chpt.), Gen. Electric Engrs. Assn. Home: 8 Dominic St Oswego NY 13126 Office: Oswego NY

LINN, HARRY, JR., constrn. co. exec.; b. Upper Darby, Pa., May 7, 1921; s. Harry and Louise Eva (Weber) L.; B.S. in Elec. Engring., Drexel U., 1956; m. Rhea Faith Hibbs, Aug. 11, 1951; children—Robert, Diane. Marine electrician Sun Shipbldg. and Dry Dock Co., 1940-42; marine electrician, engr. U.S. Maritime Service, 1942-46; v.p., gen. mgr. William Long Co., Media, Pa., 1950-65; mgr. indsl. div. Henkels & McCoy, Inc., Blue Bell, Pa., 1965—. Mem. Illuminating Engring. Soc., Engrs. Soc. Pa., Am. Theatre Organ Soc., Cross Keys, Alpha Sigma Lambda. Home: 723 Beechwood Rd Pine Ridge Media PA 19063 Office: Jolly Rd Blue Bell PA 19422

LINN, JAY GEORGE, JR., ophthalmologist, educator; b. Pitts., Aug. 15, 1916; s. Jay George and Leila Louise (Craven) L.; A.B., Allegheny Coll., 1937; M.D., Temple U., 1940; m. Barbara Eleanor Keebler, June 19, 1951; children—Jay George III, Laura Bryan, Charles Barton. Intern, Med. Center Hosps., U. Pitts., 1940-41; resident in ophthalmology N.Y. Eye and Ear Infirmary, N.Y.C., 1941-43, 46; practice medicine specializing in ophthalmology, Pitts., 1946—; mem. staffs Eye and Ear Hosp. of Pitts., 1947—; instr. ophthalmology U. Pitts., 1947, asst. prof., 1949-63, asso. prof., 1963-76, clin. prof., 1976—. Served with MC, USAAF, 1943-46. Diplomate Nat. Bd. Med. Examiners, Am. Bd. Ophthalmology. Mem. Allegheny County (Pa.), Pa. med. socs., Am., World med. assns., Pitts., Pan Am. ophthal. socs., Am., Pa. assns. ophthalmology and otolaryngology, Ophthal. Soc. U.K., AAAS. Presbyterian. Clubs: Univ., Masons. Home: 135 Martin Rd Pittsburgh PA 15222 Office: 780 Centre City Tower Pittsburgh PA 15222

LINNA, TIMO JUHANI, immunologist, researcher, educator; b. Tavastkyro, Finland, Mar. 16, 1937; foster s. Gustaf Lennart and Anne-Marie (Forsstrom) Ackell; came to U.S., 1968, naturalized, 1973; M.B., U. Uppsala (Sweden), 1959, M.D., 1965, Ph.D., 1967; m. Rhoda Margareta Popova, May, 20, 1961; children—Alexander, Fredrik, Maria. Intern, resident hosps. in Sweden; practice medicine hosps. and clinics in Sweden; asst. prof. histology U. Uppsala, 1967-71; asst. prof. microbiology, immunology Temple U., Phila., 1970-71, dir. lab. clin. immunology hosps., 1970-72, adviser clin. immunology, 1972—, asso. prof. microbiology, immunology Temple U., 1971-78, prof., 1978—; immunology cons. UNDP/World Bank/Who Spl. Program for Research and Tng. in Tropical Diseases, WHO, Geneva, 1978-79; mem. sci. adv. council Internat. Inst. Immunology Tng. and Research, Amsterdam, Netherlands. USPHS Internat. postdoctoral research fellow, 1968-70; spl. research fellow U. Minn., 1970; Eleanor Roosevelt Am. Cancer Soc. fellow, 1976; grantee Swedish Med. Research Council, 1969-71, NIH, 1972—. Mem. Am. Assn. Cancer Research, Am. Assn. Immunologists (chmn. edn. com.), Am. Assn. Pathologists, Am. Soc. Microbiology, Internat. Soc. Exptl. Hematology, Internat. Soc. Lymphology, N.Y. Acad. Scis., Reticuloendothelial Soc. (vice chmn. com. internat. relations), Royal Lymphatic Soc. Uppsala, Scandinavian Soc. Immunology, Soc. Swedish Physicians, Swedish Med. Assn. Lutheran. Author books, contbr. articles to profl. publs. exptl. pathology, immunobiology, tumor immunology. Home: 1927 Birchwood Ct Cherry Hill NJ 08003 Office: 3400 N Broad St Philadelphia PA 19140

LINNENBERG, CLEM CHARLES, JR., economist; b. Houston, May 20, 1912; s. Clem Charles and Maggie (White) L.; student So. Meth. U., 1930; B.A., M.A., U. Tex., 1933; Ph.D., Yale U., 1941; postgrad. Am. U., 1954; m. Marianne Sakmann, Aug. 15, 1942. Economist, Dept. Labor, 1934-35, Social Secuirty Bd., 1936, antitrust div. Dept. Justice, 1938-39, Bur. Budget, 1939-51; program planning officer Office Sec. Commerce, 1951-53; chief econ. analysis sect. Office Internat. Trade, Dept. Commerce, 1953; transp. economist Gen. Services Adminstrn., 1953-54, Dept. Agr., 1954-59; chief div. statistics and studies Office Vocational Rehab., Dept. Health Edn. and Welfare, 1959-62; economist USPHS, 1962-69; ind. cons. in econs. and statistics, 1969—. Lectr. in transp. Georgetown U., 1956-57. Mem. Am. Pub. Health Assn., Phi Beta Kappa, Pi Sigma Alpha, Sigma Delta Pi. Democrat. Methodist. Author: Twixt Chaos and Conformism, 1950; The Agricultural Exemptions in Interstate Trucking: Mend Them or End Them?, 1960; Economics in Program Planning for Health, 1966; Organizing and Staffing for the Program Planning Function, 1967; other monographs. Home and office: 3812 Benton St NW Washington DC 20007

LINNENKOHL, SUSAN CAROL, dietitian; b. Albuquerque, Feb. 8, 1954; d. Henry Carl and Julia Regina Linnenkohl; B.S., Eastern Ky. U., 1975. Red Cross vol. in diet therapy Wright Patterson AFB, Dayton, Ohio, 1973; dietitian ARA Services, Pineville (Ky.) Community Hosp., 1974; student nutritionist Pike County Health Dept., Pikeville, Ky., 1975; dietetic trainee Good Samaritan Hosp., Lexington, Ky., 1975-76; dietitian ARA, Pitts., 1976-77; dir. dietary St. John's Hosp., Pitts., 1977—. Registered dietitian. Mem. Am., Pa., Pitts. dietetic assns. Home: 111 Mt Lebanon Blvd Pittsburgh PA 15228 Office: 3339 McClure St Pittsburgh PA 15212

LINOWES, DAVID FRANCIS, bus. exec., educator; b. N.J., Mar. 16, 1917; B.S., U. Ill., 1941; m. Dorothy Lee Wolf, Mar. 24, 1946; children—Joanne Gail, Richard Gary, Susan Joyce, Jonathan Scott. Partner Leopold & Linowes, C.P.A.'s, Washington, 1946-62, cons. partner, 1963—; partner S.D. Leidesdorf & Co., C.P.A.'s, 1963-65, Laventhol & Horwath, 1965—; chmn. Privacy Protection Commn. of U.S., 1975—; cons. DATA Internat. Assistance Corps.; chmn. bd. Perpetual Investment Co.; dir. Baldwin-Montrose Chem. Co., Inc., Saturday Rev./World Mag., Inc., Met. Investments, Inc., Horn & Hardart Co., Inc., Chris Craft Industries, Inc.; chmn. audit com., dir. Piper Aircraft Corp.; adj. prof. Southeastern U., 1948-53; adj. prof. mgmt. N.Y. U., 1965-72; Distinguished Arthur Young prof. U. Ill., 1973-74, Harold Boeschenstein prof. polit. economy and pub. policy, 1976—. Mem. Nat. Exec. Com. Am. Thrift Assembly, 1960-62; cons. to sec. Dept. HEW; cons. U.S. Dept. State Mission to Turkey, 1967, India, 1970, Greece, 1971; del. 9th Internat. Congress, Paris, 1967, 10th Internat. Congress, Sydney; cons. UN, Mission to Pakistan, Iran and Turkey, 1968; chmn. nat. council U.S. Peoples Orgn. for UN. Chmn. profl. adv. bd. U. Ill.; chmn. internat. adv. council Tel Aviv U.; vice chmn. Charities Adv. Com. of D.C., 1958-63; chmn. nat. men's com. Religion in Am. Life. Bd. dirs. U. Ill. Found.; trustee Boys Club of Greater Washington, Inc, Asso. YM-YWHA's; mem. Greater NY bd. dirs. Nat. Conf. Christians and Jews, Adv. Services for Better Housing; trustee, treas. Am. Inst. Benevolent Fund. Recipient Human Relations award Am. Jewish Com., 1970. C.P.A., N.Y., N.C., N.J., Md., D.C., La. Mem. Am. Inst. C.P.A.'s (council 1957-69, trial bd. 1958-64, v.p. 1962-63, treas. 1964-67, vice chmn. trial bd. 1968-72, chmn. 1973—, chmn. com. fed. assisted programs 1974-75), U.S. C. of C. (del. 1960-62), D.C. Inst. C.P.A.'s, (pres. 1956), N.Y., N.J. socs. C.P.A.'s, N.Y. C. of C. (com. econ. devel.), Conf. Bd., Acad. Polit. Sci., Inst. Mgmt. Sci., UN Assn. (adv. com.), Commerce and Industry Assn. (council mem.), N.Y. C. of C. (chmn. city affairs com., mem. exec. com.), Phi Alpha Phi, Beta Gamma Sigma (dir.), Beta Alpha Psi (hon.), Phi Kappa Phi. Clubs: Woodmont Country, Federal City (Washington); Harmonie, Army-Navy, Pinnacle (N.Y.C.); Scarsdale Golf, Town (Scarsdale, N.Y.); Nat. Capital Democratic; University. Author: Managing Growth Through Acquisition, 1968; Strategies for Survival, 1973; The Corporate Conscience, 1974; Personal Privacy in an Information Society, 1977. Contbr. articles to profl. jours. Home: 9 Wayside Ln Scarsdale NY 10583 Office: 919 3d Ave New York City NY 10022 also 308 Lincoln Hall U Ill Urbana IL 61801

LINSCOTT, MORTIMER LEE, mortician; b. Hamlin, N.Y., Sept. 17, 1919; s. Earl Parish and Leora (Lee) L.; student Rochester Inst. Tech., 1938-41; m. Elizabeth Roberts, June 22, 1944; children—Diana Linscott Cooney, Roger Edward. Apprentice, Fowler Funeral Home Inc., Brockport, N.Y., 1945, mgr., 1962—, pres., 1974—. Served with U.S. Army, 1940-45. Mem. 11th Dist. Funeral Dirs. Assn., Am. Def. Assn., Nat. Wildlife Assn., Nat. Rifle Assn. Republican. Presbyterian. Club: Brockport Lions (pres. 1971-72). Home: 6984 Benedict Beach Hamlin NY 14464

LINSKY, ELIZABETH STEWART, social worker; b. Quincy, Mass., Mar. 9, 1934; d. John and Elizabeth Stewart (McWilliam) Bacon; B.A., Radcliffe Coll., 1955; M.S.W. (VA scholar), U. Wash., 1962; m. Arnold Stanley Linsky, Feb. 2, 1955; children—Nicholas, Isabella. Social worker Div. Welfare, Seattle, 1959-60, 62-63, Child and Family Services N.H., Exeter, 1968-73; child and family supr. Div. Welfare, Portsmouth, N.H., 1974-76; sch. cons., 1976—; social worker cons. Family Planning Program, N.H. Dept. Health and Welfare, 1978—. Mem. Acad. Certified Social Workers, Nat. Action for Foster Children, Nat. Assn. Social Workers. Jewish. Address: 10 Old Landing Rd Durham NH 03824

LINSTONE, ROBERT THEODORE, ednl. adminstr., ednl. cons.; b. N.Y.C., Jan. 22, 1924; s. Edward and Mae (Nielsen) L.; B.A., U. Hartford, 1953, M.Ed., 1956; certificate in Child Psychology, U. Copenhagen, 1952; postgrad. U. Conn., 1955-58; Ph.D., U. Mass., 1969; m. Gloria Ruth Arena, 1954; children—Deborah Kay, Rondi Sue, Jeffrey Dean. Ednl. cons. with bldg. com. Town of Avon (Conn.), 1962-69; supervising prin. Roaring Brook Sch., Avon, 1963; asst. prof. dept. psychology Central Conn. State Coll., New Britain, 1962-68, asso. prof. evening div., 1969—; vis. prof. U. N.C., Greensboro, summer 1966-67; workshop dir. U. Hartford, W. Hartford, Conn., 1966-68; course coordinator for continuing edn. for women U. Conn., 1966-68; adj. faculty mem. Manchester (Conn.) Community Coll., 1971, Am. Internat. Coll., Springfield, Mass., 1973-74; asst. supt. curriculum and instruction Vernon Pub. Schs., Rockville, Conn., 1969—; cons. and lectr. in edn., 1962—; guest speaker various profl. assns. and confs., 1963—; host radio show Focus on Edn., 1978-79. Trustee Edn. World Jour., 1969-74. Served with inf. U.S. Army, 1943-46; PTO. Decorated Purple Heart; recipient Outstanding Alumnus award U. Hartford, 1967, Concern for Safety award Conn. Safety Commn., 1974, Merit award Greater Hartford Council Econ. Edn., 1974. Mem. NEA, Assn. Supervision and Curriculum Devel., Am. Assn. Sch. Adminstrs., Nat. Assn. Gifted Children. Contbr. articles on edn. to profl. jours. Home: 20 Terrace Rd West Hartford CT 06107 Office: Vernon Pub Schs Rockville CT

LINTHICUM, ROGER HENRY, behavioral sci. specialist; b. Oklahoma City, Mar. 24, 1942; s. Roger Howard and Lucy Mae (Dolliver) L.; student Midwest Christian Coll., Oklahoma City, 1960-61, Johnson Bible Coll., Knoxville, 1961-62; A.B., Atlanta Christian Coll., 1973; M.A., Webster Coll., St. Louis, 1975; m. Barbara Jane Ellis, Aug. 25, 1963; children—Roger Edward, Thomas Wayne. Child care worker So. Christian Home for Children, Atlanta, 1970, Christian City Home for Children, Atlanta, 1970-71; enlisted as pvt. U.S. Army, 1974, advanced through grades to staff sgt., 1977; social worker Spl. Tng. Co., Ft. Leonard Wood, Mo., 1974-75, behavioral sci. specialist, drug and alcohol counselor Community Drug and Alcohol Assistance Center, 7th Army Tng. Command, W. Ger., 1975-78; behavioral sci. specialist Walter Reed Army Hosp., Washington, 1978—. Bd. govs. Dependent Youth Activities, 1976—. Mem. Am. Personnel and Guidance Assn., Am. Rehab. Counseling Assn., Mensa. Mem. Christian Ch. Clubs: Kiwanis, Toastmasters. Home: Route 7 Box 242 Newport TN 37821 Office: Walter Reed Army Med Center Washington DC 20012

LINTON, CALVIN DARLINGTON, educator, coll. dean; b. Kensington, Md., June 11, 1914; s. Irwin Helfenstein and Helen Pauline (Grier) L.; student Erskine Coll., S.C., 1931-32; A.B., George Washington U., 1935; A.M., Johns Hopkins, 1939, Ph.D., 1940; m. Jeanne Etling LeFevre, Aug. 1, 1951. Lecture reporter, instr. stenotyping Temple Bus. Sch., Washington, 1935-36; instr. English Wheaton (Ill.) Coll. summer 1938, Johns Hopkins U., 1939-40; asso. prof., chmn. English dept. Queens Coll., N.C., 1940-41; asst. prof. English, George Washington U., 1945-46, asso. prof., 1946-48, prof. English lit., 1948—, asst. dean Columbian Coll., 1949-56, asso. dean 1956-57, dean, 1957—; lectr. lit. subjects WGMS, Washington, 1953-54, Folger Inst. Renaissance and 18th Century Studies, Cons.

various govt. agys. in report writing. Vice chmn. Commn. Instns. Higher Edn., Middle States Assn. Served as lt. (j.g.), Office Sec. of Navy, 1941-43; lt. comdr. Minecraft Tng. Center, Norfolk, Va., 1943-45. Mem. Modern Lang. Assn. (program com.); Coll. English Assn., Modern Humanities Research Assn. (Am. chmn., sec., 1963—), Lit. Soc. Washington (pres. 1973-75), Eastern Assn. Deans (pres. 1965-66), Conf. Christianity and Lit. (pres. 1965-66). Presbyn. Clubs: Tudor and Stuart (Johns Hopkins); Cosmos (pres. 1973) (Washington). Author: Report Construction and Analysis (U.S. Map Service), 1953; How to Write Reports, 1954; Effective Writing, 1958; The Bicentennial Almanac, 1975. Contbr. articles to profl. jours. Home: 5216 Farrington Rd Washington DC 20016

LINVILLE, THOMAS MERRIAM, engr.; b. Washington, Mar. 3, 1904; s. Thomas and Clara (Merriam) L.; E.E., U. Va., 1926; grad. advanced mgmt. program, Harvard, 1950, mod. engring. program U. Calif., Los Angeles, 1960; m. Eleanor Priest, Nov. 25, 1939; children—Eleanor, Thomas Priest, Edward Dwight. Various govt. positions, 1918-26; with Gen. Electric Co., 1926-66, beginning with Advanced Engring. Program to 1931, successively in engring. dept., chmn. rotating machines product com., chmn. rotating machines development com., staff asst. to mgr. engring., mgr. engring. edn., mgmt. consultation div., mgr. exec. devel. dept., 1926-53, mgr. research operation dept., 1953-64, mgr. research application dept., research services, 1964-66; nat. pres. Tau Beta Pi Assn., Inc., 1974—. Mem. USN tech. missions Pearl Harbor, 1942, Europe, 1945, Middle East, 1964. Chmn. city planning commn., Schenectady, 1951; pres. N.Y. State Citizens Com. for Pub. Schs., 1952-53; mem. Gov.'s Council Advancement Research and Devel. N.Y. State, 1966—. Pres. Schenectady Mus., 1964-70; chmn. Community Chest, 1964. Chmn. Devel. Council for Sci. Rensselaer Poly. Inst., 1960-69; vis. com. Clarkson Inst. Tech., 1956-65, Norwich U., 1970—; pres. Mohawk-Hudson council ETV-WMHT Channel 17, 1966-69; pres. Schenectady Indsl. Devel. Council, 1967-69. Bd. dirs. Sunnyview Hosp., Schenectady Indsl. Devel. Corp. Recipient Charles A. Coffin award, USN Certificate of Commendation for outstanding submarine service; Schenectady Profl. Engrs. soc. Engr.-of-Year award, 1960. Fellow IEEE (dir. 1953-57), ASME, AAAS; mem. Nat. (v.p., dir. 1962-64, pres. 1966-67), N.Y. State (pres. 1954-55, trustee) socs. profl. engrs., Am. Soc. Engring. Edn., Am. Acad. Polit. and Social Sci., N.Y. Acad. Scis., Schenectady C. of C. (dir., v.p. 1949-58), Raven Soc., Theta Tau, Delta Upsilon. Unitarian (pres. 1940-45). Rotarian (pres. 1972-73). Clubs: Mohawk, Mohawk Golf. Contbr. articles on elec. engring. to publs.; author books on mgmt., genealogy, biography, radio communications and elec. machinery. Home: 1147 Wendell Ave Schenectady NY 12308

LIOLIN, JOHN EVANS, sales exec.; b. N.Y.C., May 4, 1925; s. Evans John and Aphrodite (Cotta) L.; A.A., Jr. Coll. Conn., 1948; B.S., U. Bridgeport, 1950; m. Helene M. Nasse, Dec. 19, 1948; children—Carole, Susan, Janet. Store mgr. New Eng. states Union Nat. Sales, 1950-52; salesman Lees Mfg., Westport, Conn., 1953-54; v.p. Jones Industries, Inc., Westport, 1954-55; sales mgr. Oneko Mfg. Co., N.Y.C., 1955-59; v.p. sales Trimtex Co., N.Y.C., 1959—; indsl. mktg. dir. William E. Wright Co., N.Y.C., 1959—. Served with USN, 1943-46; PTO. Mem. Elastic Fabric Mfrs. Inst., No. Textile Assn., Eastern Orthodox. Club: St George's Men's League. Home: 318 Putting Green Rd Fairfield CT 06432 Office: 1 Penn Plaza New York City NY 10001

LIPARI, NUNZIO OTTAVIO, physicist; b. Ali'Terme, Italy, Jan. 1, 1945; s. Eugenio and Agata (Lipari) L.; came to U.S., 1967, naturalized, 1972; Dottore in Fisica, U. Messina, 1967; Ph.D. in Physics, Lehigh U., 1970. Research asst. Lehigh U., Bethlehem, Pa., 1967-70; research asso. U. Ill., Champaign, 1970-72; asso. scientist Xerox Corp., Rochester, N.Y., 1972-73, scientist, 1973-75, sr. scientist, 1975-77; with IBM, Yorktown Heights, N.Y., 1977—; invited scientist Polytech. Lausanne (Switzerland) and Max Planck Inst., Germany, 1976. Mem. Am. Phys. Soc. Contbr. articles to profl. jours. Home: 209 Cordial Rd Yorktown Heights NY 10598 Office: IBM Yorktown Heights NY 10598

LIPKE, KENNETH EMIL, financial cons.; b. Buffalo, Feb. 14, 1929; s. Emil Edwin and Ruth Gertrude (Randle) L.; B.A., U. Buffalo, 1950; Ph.D., Palmer Coll., 1952; postgrad. N.Y. Inst. Finance, 1966-67; m. Patricia June Keane, Feb. 18, 1950; children—Brian Jeffrey, Curtis Wesley, Neil Elliott, Eric Randle, Meredith Ann. Stockbroker, R.A. Manley & Co., Buffalo, 1961-62, S.C. Parker & Co., Buffalo, 1962-65; pres. Lipke Assos., Inc., Clarence, N.Y., 1967—; chmn. bd. Manley-Lipke, Inc., Buffalo, 1965-67, COM-CIR-TEK, Inc., Buffalo, 1969—; exec. v.p., dir. United Horse Transporters Am. Inc., Batavia, N.Y., 1969—; pres., dist. dir. Am. Horse Transporters, Inc., N.Y.C., 1970—; exec. cons. to pres. Internat. Life Ins. Co., Buffalo, 1968—; pres. Am. Corporate Cons., Inc., 1971—, Gibraltar Steel Corp., 1972—, Seneca Steel Service, Inc., 1975—, Beals, McCarthy & Rogers, Inc., 1975—, Follansbee Steel, Inc., 1975—, Gibraltar Group of Cos., Inc., 1975—, Am. Corporate Industries, Inc., 1975—; mem. exec. com. Mader Corp., 1973—. Exec. dir. Operation Good Govt., Erie County, N.Y., 1961—; bd. govs. Jr. Achievement, Buffalo 1969—; pres. Gibraltar Inst., 1974—. Mem. Nat. Assn. Securities Dealers, C. of C. Clubs: Lions, Rotary, Bond (Buffalo). Office: 2545 Walden Ave Buffalo NY 14225

LIPKIN, MARTIN, physician; b. N.Y.C., Apr. 30, 1926; s. Samuel S. and Celia (Greenfield) L.; A.B., N.Y. U., 1946, M.D., 1950; m. Joan Schulein, Feb. 16, 1958; children—Richard, Steve. Fellow Cornell U. Med. Coll., 1952; practice medicine specializing in internal medicine, gastroenterology, neoplastic diseases, N.Y.C.; mem. staff N.Y. Hosp., Meml. Hosp. Asso. prof. medicine Cornell Med. Coll., N.Y.C., 1963-78, prof. medicine, 1978—, prof. Grad. Sch. Med. Scis., 1978—; asso. mem. Meml. Sloan Kettering Cancer Center, 1973—; mem. exec. com. Nat. Large Bowel Cancer Project, 1974-76. Served with USNR, 1953-55. Recipient NIH career devel. award, 1962-71, Albert F.R. Andresen lectureship, N.Y. State Med. Soc., 1971—. Diplomate Nat. Bd. Med. Examiners. Fellow A.C.P.; mem. Med. Soc. State of N.Y. (chmn. sect. gastroenterology and colon and rectal surgery 1974-75, asso. chmn. sci. program com. 1977—), Digestive Diseases Soc. (founding), Internat. Soc. Investigative Gastroenterology (founding), Am. Soc. Clin. Investigation, Am. Physiol. Soc., Am. Assn. Cancer Research, Am. Gastroenterol. Assn., Soc. for Exptl. Biology and Medicine, Am. Soc. Exptl. Pathology, Harvey Soc. Clubs: Fairview, Griffis, Cornell (N.Y.) Mem. editorial bd. Bioscis. Communications, Cell and Tissue Kinetics, others; editor Gastrointestinal Tract Cancer, 1978. Contbr. articles to profl. jours. Home: 445 E 86th St New York City NY 10028 Office: 425 E 67th St New York City NY 10021

LIPKIND, MARVIN LEE, plastics mfg. co. exec.; b. N.Y.C., Apr. 21, 1926; s. Abraham and Esther (Abramson) L.; B.S., Ind. U., 1949; m. Tania Machbitz, May 9, 1959; children—Lisa, Alec. Asst. to pres. Atlas Screw and Bolt Co., N.Y.C., 1949-50; sales trainee Comark Plastics div. United Mchts. & Mfrs. Co., N.Y.C., 1950-52, Midwest mgr., 1952-55, asst. v.p., 1965, v.p., 1970, mgr. mktg. wholesale trades, 1955-72, sr. v.p., 1972-74, exec. v.p., 1974-77, pres. div., 1977—. Served with U.S. Army, 1944-46; ETO. Decorated Combat Infantryman's Badge; Croix de Guerre (France). Mem. N.Y. Housewares Club. Office: 3601 Hempstead Turnpike Levittown NY 11756

LIPMAN, DANIEL GORDON, psychiatrist, educator; b. London, Eng., July 22, 1912; s. Jacob Meyer and Gitel (Halbmillion) L.; came to U.S., 1921, naturalized, 1928; M.D., Middlesex Med. Sch., Mass., 1940; postgrad. Harvard, 1947; m. Ida Wolfson, Dec. 19, 1934; children—Ralph I., Frances J. Lipman Yellin, Philip W., Leta P., Gail R. Lipman Mandel. Intern Harbor Hosp., Bklyn., 1940-41; resident Wadsworth Hosp., N.Y.C., 1941-42; resident in psychiatry VA Hosp., Perry Point, Md., 1959-62; gen. practice medicine, Lynn, Mass., 1942-43, 46-49, internal medicine, Lynn, 1949-55, psychiatry, Washington, 1966—, Silver Spring, Md., 1973—; dir. Stress and Hypertension Clinic, Dispensary, U.S. Naval Weapons Plant, Washington, 1955-59; chief outpatient dept. VA Hosp., Brecksville, Ohio, 1962-64; tng. officer for NIMH at St. Elizabeths Hosp., Washington, 1966-70, coordinator psychiat. tng. externs and interns. 1968-69; asst. prof. clin. psychiatry Howard U. Med. Sch., Washington, 1968—, George Washington U., Washington, 1967—; med. officer neuropsychiatry, med. adv. staff Bur. of Hearings and Appeals, Social Security Adminstrn., HEW, Washington, 1971-73, cons. in neuropsychiatry, 1973—; Vice pres. North Shore Civic Music Assn., Lynn, 1952-54; pres. Creative Research Institutes, Inc., 1975—. Served to 1st lt. U.S. Army, 1943-46. Recipient Suggestion award VA, 1963, Physician Recognition awards AMA, 1969, 77. Mem. Am. Psychiat. Assn., D.C., Mass. med. socs., Washington Psychiat. Soc., St. Elizabeth's Hosp. Med. Soc., Am. Geriatric Soc., AAAS, Assn. of Orthodox Jewish Scientists. Contbr. numerous articles on stress and hypertension to profl. publs.; inventor three dimensional stethoscope. Home: 20104 Hob Hill Way Gaithersburg MD 20760

LIPMAN, EVERETT S., dentist; b. Scranton, Pa., Feb. 18, 1918; s. Samuel and Elizabeth (Heller) L.; B.S., N.Y. U., 1939; D.D.S., Temple U., 1943; m. Helen E. Bikales, July 17, 1943; children—Lawrence W., Donald A., Judith A. Gen. practice dentistry, Newburgh, N.Y., 1947—; chmn. bd. Garnerville Holding Co, Inc. (N.Y.); v.p., sec. W. Haverstraw Improvement Corp., Garnerville; prin. partner Garnerville Improvement Assos. Mem. planning bd. Town of Newburgh; treas., dir. Jewish Community Center, Newburgh. Served to capt., Dental Corps, U.S. Army, 1943-46. Mem. ADA, Newburgh (pres. 1967-68), 9th Dist., N.Y. State dental socs. Home: 36 Commonwealth Ave Newburgh NY 12550 Office: 229 Liberty St Newburgh NY 12550

LIPMAN, IRA ACKERMAN, security service co. exec.; b. Little Rock, Nov. 15, 1940; s. Mark and Belle (Ackerman) L.; student Ohio Wesleyan U., 1958-60; LL.D. (hon.), John Marshall U., 1970; m. Barbara Ellen Kelly Couch, July 5, 1970; children—Gustave K., Joshua S., M. Benjamin. Various positions with Mark Lipman Service, Inc., 1960-63; pres. Guardsmark, Inc., Memphis, 1963—, chief exec. officer, 1966—. Met. chmn. Nat. Alliance Businessmen; mem. young leadership cabinet United Jewish Appeal; pres.'s council Memphis State U.; bd. dirs. Nat. Council Crime and Delinquency, exec. com., 1976, treas., 1978—; bd. dirs. Tenn. Ind. Coll. Fund, 1977—, exec. com., 1978—; trustee Memphis Acad. Arts, 1977—; Shelby County chmn. U.S. Savings Bonds, 1976; exec. bd. Chickasaw council Boy Scouts Am., 1978—. Entrepreneurial fellow Memphis State U., 1976. Mem. Internat. Assn. Chiefs of Police, Am. Soc. Indsl. Security (certified protection profl.). Republican. Clubs: Ridgeway Country, Economic, Racquet, Summit, Delta, Petroleum, B'nai B'rith. Author: How to Protect Yourself from Crime, 1975. Contbr. articles to numerous mags. Home: 4490 Park Ave Memphis TN 38117 also 58 W 58th St New York City NY 10019 Office: 22 S 2d St Memphis TN 38103 also 40 W 57th St New York City NY 10019

LIPMAN, RICHARD PAUL, pediatrician; b. Cambridge, Mass., Aug. 1, 1935; s. Hyman Zelig and Betty (Likovsky) L.; A.B. magna cum laude, Harvard, 1957; M.D. cum laude, Tufts U., 1961; m. Mary Alice Wilcox, Aug. 25, 1963; children—Gregory, Susan. Intern Boston Floating Hosp., 1961-62, jr. resident, 1962-63, sr. resident, 1963-64, chief resident, 1964; research fellow infectious disease Med. Sch. U. N.C. at Chapel Hill, 1967-69; practice pediatrics, West Peabody, Mass., 1969—; mem. staff North Shore Childrens Hosp., Salem, Mass., asso. chief of staff, 1974-76, pres., chief of staff, 1976—; mem. staff Tufts-New Eng. Med. Center, Boston, Boston Children's Hosp. Med. Center, Lynn (Mass.) Hosp., Salem Hosp. Clin. instr. pediatrics Tufts U. Sch. Medicine, Boston, 1969-74, asst. clin. prof., 1974-78, asso. clin. prof., 1978—. Served to capt. M.C., AUS, 1964-66. Diplomate Am. Bd. Pediatrics. Fellow Am. Acad. Pediatrics; mem. Am. Soc. Microbiology, New Eng. Pediatric Soc., Mass. Med. Soc., A.M.A., Tufts Alumni Assn. Club: Nat. Assn. Watch and Clock Collectors. Contbr. articles to profl. jours. Office: 1 Roosevelt Ave West Peabody MA 01960 also 225 Boston St Lynn MA 01904

LIPMANN, FRITZ (ALBERT), biochemist; b. Koenigsberg, Germany, June 12, 1899; s. Leopold and Gertrud (Lachmanski) L.; student U. Koenigsberg, 1917-22, U. Munich, 1919; M.D., U. Berlin, 1924, Ph.D., 1928; M.D. (hon.), U. Marseilles, 1947, U. Copenhagen, 1972; M.A. (hon.), Harvard, 1949; D.Sc. (hon.), U. Chgo., 1953, U. Paris, 1966, Harvard, 1967. Rockefeller U., 1971; L.H.D., Brandeis U., 1959, Yeshiva U., 1964; m. Elfreda M. Hall, June 23, 1931; 1 son, Stephen. Came to U.S., 1939, naturalized, 1944. Research asst. Prof. Meyerhof's Lab., Kaiser Wilhelm Inst., Berlin and Heidelberg, 1927-30; Dr. A. Fischer's Lab., Berlin, 1930-31; Rockefeller fellow Rockefeller Inst. Med. Research, N.Y.C., 1931-32; research asso. Biol. Inst. Carlsberg Found., Copenhagen, Denmark, 1932-39, dept. biochemsitry Med. Sch. Cornell U., 1939-41; research chemist, head biochem. research lab. Mass. Gen. Hosp., Boston, 1941-57; prof. biol. chemistry Med. Sch. Harvard, 1949-57; prof. Rockefeller U., 1957. Recipient Carl Neuberg medal, 1948; Mead Johnson & Co. award for outstanding work on Vitamin B-complex, 1948; Nobel prize for medicine and physiology, 1953; Nat. Medal Sci., 1966. Fellow N.Y. Acad. Sci., Danish Royal Acad. Scis.; fgn. mem. Royal Soc.; mem. Nat. Acad. Scis., Am. Chem. Soc., Am. Soc. Microbiology, Biochem. Soc., AAAS, Am. Soc. Biol. Chemists, Harvey Soc., Am. Pilos. Soc. Author: Wanderings of a Biochemist, 1971. Author sci. papers. Home: 201 E 17th St New York City NY 10003 also Rural Delivery 2 Box 347 Rhinebeck NY 12572 Office: Rockefeller University New York City NY 10021

LIPPEK, KARL TORMA, civil engr.; b. N.Y.C., Nov. 19, 1942; B.C.E., Manhattan Coll.; M.S.C.E. in Environ. Engring., N.Y. U.; m. Nancy Ellen Grix, June 1, 1968. Project mgr. Quirk, Lawler & Matusky Engrs., N.Y.C., 1965-74; v.p. engring. and constrn. Okuraya Davos Internat., Inc., N.Y.C., 1974-75; prin. K.T. Lippek Assos., engrs., planners, architects, Chappaqua, N.Y., 1975—; mem. Archtl. Bd. Rev. Scoutmaster, Greater N.Y. council Boy Scouts Am. Licensed profl. engr., N.Y., N.J., Conn., Mass., Vt., Pa., Fla. Mem. ASCE, N.Y. Water Pollution Control Assn., Water Pollution Control Fedn., Nat., N.Y. State socs. profl. engrs. Planning, designing, mgmt. wastewater treatment facilities, collection systems, water supply, treatment, storage and distbn. systems; design and devel. fourseason recreational communities. Office: Two Attitash Chappaqua NY 10514

LIPPINCOTT, BRUCE LESTER, tech. sci. co. exec.; b. Riegelsville, Pa., Feb. 2, 1942; s. Carl W. and Grace E. (Frey) L.; B.A., Colby Coll., 1964; M.S., Lehigh U., 1972, Ph.D., 1975. Instr. biology Hinckley (Maine) Sch., 1964-68, Cedar Crest Coll., Allentown, Pa., 1972-73, 75, Pa. State U., Allentown, 1975; dir. quality assurance Lawler Matusky & Skelly Engring., Pearl River, N.Y., 1975—; chmn. air and noise quality adv. bd. Bucks County, Pa., 1974—, cons. dir. water quality monitoring program, 1975. Mem. Riegelsville (Pa.) Borough Council, 1974-78, pres., 1976-78. Mem. AAAS, Pa. Acad. Scis., Am. Soc. Quality Control, Am. Fish Soc. (N.Y. Chpt.), Am. Geophys. Union, Sigma Xi. Republican. Lutheran. Home: 749 Edgewood Rd Riegelsville PA 18077 Office: One Blue Hill Plaza Pearl River NY 10965

LIPPMAN, ALFRED JULIAN, waste disposal co. exec.; b. Newark, May 7, 1900; s. Lewis Isaac and Henrietta (Meyer) L.; student pub. schs., Newark; Doctorate, Mexican Acad. Internat. Law, 1964; m. Doris Samuel, Mar. 16, 1927 (div. 1931); m. 2d, Muriel Milnes, Mar. 16, 1932 (dec. Mar. 1951). With L. Bamberger & Co., dept. store, Newark, 1912-22; buyer Symons Dry Goods Co., Butte, Mont., 1922-26; asst. mdse. mgr. Stix, Baer & Fuller Co., St. Louis, 1926-28; mdse. mgr. Union Co., Columbus, Ohio, 1928; supr. N.J. br. offices Eisele & King, mems. N.Y. Stock Exchange, 1928-38; also owner real estate bus., 1928-38; salesman, broker Feist & Feist, Newark, 1938-41; partner real estate firm John E. Sloane & Co., Newark, 1941-45, owner, pres. successor firm Alfred J. Lippman, Inc., 1945—; pres. Roselle-Lippman Co., Inc. subs. SCA Services, Inc.; pres. Lion Travel Agy. Inc., 1973—; exec. dir. Latin Am. Devel. & Ops. Co.; v.p. Aerovias Latino Americanos, S.A. of Mexico, 1951-52; chmn. bd. Mexican C. of C. of U.S., 1974—; rep. to 6 presdl. inaugurations in Mexico; hon. Mexican consul gen. in N.J., 1957—; mem. N.J. Internat. Adv. Com., 1973—. Mem. N.J. Planning Bd., 1936-43; chmn. Sea Bright State Park Commn. (N.J.), 1938; mem. Municipal Sanitation Commn., 1952; dir. extension course on solid wastes disposal Rutgers U., 1961-69. Trustee Monmouth Mus. Served with USN, World War I; with USCGR, World War II. Decorated Order of Aztec Eagle (Mexico); ofcl. Mexican Order Law and Culture, comdr. l'Ordre Internat. du Bien Public; named Outstanding Citizen of N.J., K.P., 1955, Man of Year Friends of Acapulco (Mex.)., 1971; Distinguished Achievement award Advt. Club N.Y., 1964; diploma and gold medal for extraordinary contbn. Mexican Nat. Tourist Council, 1967; medal and citation Port Authority of N.Y. and N.J., 1975. Mem. Am. Legion, Soc. Solid Waste Technicians (life mem., pres.), Circus Saints and Sinners (nat. v.p.), Nat. Sweepstakes Regatta of Red Bank, N.J. (past rear commodore), Consular Corps, Mexican Acad. Internat. Law. Republican. Jewish. Clubs: Masons, Shriners, Elks, Lions; Capitol Hill (Washington); Old Red Bank (N.J.) Yacht (past commodore); Rio Chumpan Yacht (commodore) (Mexico); Bankers of Mexico; Boca Raton. Home: 50 West End Ave Shrewsbury NJ 07701 also 3099 Spanish River Rd Boca Raton FL 33432 Office: 323 N Broad St Elizabeth NJ 07208 also Isabel la Catolica 516 Mexico City Mexico

LIPPMANN, GORHAM JAMES, assn. exec.; b. Bklyn., July 23, 1927; s. Maurice Livingston and Lillian Gorham (Kelly) L.; B.S. in Naval Architecture and Marine Engring., Webb Inst. Naval Architecture, 1951; m. Barbara Anne Drayton, Nov. 14, 1953; 1 son, Scott Lane. Pres. Jim's Boatyard Inc., Amityville, N.Y., 1952-64; propr.-owner Sailboat Equipment Co., also The Yachtsman's Shop, Amityville, 1964-68; project engr. Yacht Safety Bur., Westwood, N.J., 1968-70; asst. sec., gen. mgr. Am. Boat and Yacht Council, Amityville, N.Y., 1970-73, exec. dir., 1973—; v.p., sec. Tropical Marine Testers, Inc., North Palm Beach, Fla., Corporate mem. Underwriters Labs., Inc., Chgo.; mem. rules of road advisory com. USCG. Mem. Amityville Fire Dept., 1955—. Bd. adivsers NAEBM/Westlawn Sch. Yacht Design. Served with AUS, 1945-46. Mem. Soc. Naval Architects and Marine Engrs., Soc. Small Craft Designers, UL-Marine Engring. Council, Webb Alumni Assn. (life), Internat. Standards Orgn. (sub-com. on small craft), Nat. Fire Protection Assn., Marine Trades Assn. N.Y., Soc. Automotive Engrs. (marine tech. com.), ASTM. Clubs: Narrasketuck Yacht (life, past commodore), Unqua Corinthian Yacht (gov.). Editor, publisher: Safety Standards for Small Craft, 1971—. Home: 314 Ocean Ave Amityville NY 11701 Office: PO Box 806 Amityville NY 11701

LIPPNER, LEWIS ALAN, hosp. adminstr.; b. N.Y.C., Mar. 10, 1948; s. Sidney and Ruth L.; B.A. cum laude, Pitts., 1969; certificate internat. relations U. Oslo, 1968; M.A., George Washington U., 1972; m. Linda Beth Dorner, July 7, 1976. Adminstrv. resident Kings County Hosp., Bklyn., 1971-72; asso. Block, McGibony & Assos., Inc., Silver Spring, Md., 1972-73; asst. dir., planner Bklyn. Hosp., 1973-75; asst. hosp. adminstr. John E. Runnells Hosp. of Union County, Berkeley Heights, N.J., 1975—. Mem. Am. Coll. Hosp. Adminstrs., Am. Hosp. Assn., N.J. Asst. Hosp. Dirs. Assn., Met. Health Adminstrs. Assn. Home: 131 Paterson Rd Fanwood NJ 07023

LIPSCOMB, WILLIAM NUNN, JR., phys. chemist, educator; b. Cleve., Dec. 9, 1919; s. William Nunn and Edna Patterson (Porter) L.; B.S., U. Ky., 1941, D.Sc. (hon.), 1963; Ph.D., Calif. Inst. Tech., 1946; Dr. honoris causa, U. Munich, 1976; D.Sc. (hon.), L.I. U., 1977; m. Mary Adele Sargent, May 20, 1944; children—Dorothy Jean, James Sargent. Phys. chemist OSRD, 1942-46; with U. Minn., 1946-59, successively asst. prof., asso. prof. and acting chief phys. chemistry div., prof. and chief phys. chemistry div., 1954-59; prof. chemistry, Harvard, 1959-71, Abbott and James Lawrence prof., 1971—, chmn. dept. chemistry, 1962-65. Mem. U.S.A. Nat. Com. for Crystallography, 1954-59, 60-63, 65-67; chmn. program com. Fourth Internat. Congress of Crystallography, Montreal, 1957. Guggenheim fellow Oxford U., Eng., 1954-55, Cambridge U., Eng., 1973; NSF sr. postdoctoral fellow, 1965-66; Overseas fellow Churchill Coll., Cambridge, Eng., 1966; Baker lectr., Cornell U., 1969; Robert Welch Found. lectr., 1966, 71, Howard U. distinguished lecture series, 1966; centenary lectr. Chem. Soc. (London), 1972; lectr. Weizmann Inst., Rehoveth, Israel, 1974; plenary lectr. 100th birthday commemoration of Alfred Stock, Munich, 1976. Recipient Harrison Howe award in Chemistry, 1958; Distinguished Alumni Centennial award U. Ky., 1965; Distinguished Service in advancement inorganic chemistry Am. Chem. Soc., 1968; George Ledlie prize Harvard, 1971; Nobel prize, 1976; Distinguished Alumni award Calif. Inst. Tech., 1977. Fellow Am. Acad. Arts and Scis., Am. Phys. Soc., Nat. Acad. Scis.; mem. Am. Chem. Soc. (Peter Debye award phys. chemistry 1973, chmn. Minn. sect. 1949-50), Am. Crystallographic Assn. (pres. 1955), Royal Netherlands Acad. and Scis. (hon.), Nat. Acad. Sci., Phi Beta Kappa, Sigma Xi, Alpha Chi Sigma, Phi Lambda Upsilon, Sigma Pi Sigma, Phi Mu Epsilon. Author: The Boron Hydrides, 1963; (with G.R. Eaton) NMR Studies of Boron Hydrides and Related Compounds, 1969. Contbr. articles to profl. jours. Asso. editor: Jour. Chemical Physics, 1955-57. Clarinetist, mem. Amateur Chamber Music Players. Home: 26 Woodfall Rd Belmont MA 02178 Office: Dept of Chemistry Harvard U Cambridge MA 02138

LIPSHUTZ, ROBERT JEROME, lawyer, govt. ofcl.; b. Atlanta, Dec. 27, 1921; s. Allen A. and Edith (Gavron) L.; J.D., U. Ga., 1943; m. Barbara Levin, Apr. 16, 1950 (dec.); children—Randall M., Judith A., Wendy J., Debbie S.; m. 2d, Betty Beck Rosenberg, Feb. 10, 1973; step-children—Bobby R., Nancy R. Admitted to Ga. bar, 1943; practiced in Atlanta, 1947-77; partner Lipshutz, Macey, Zusmann &

Sikes, 1947-77; counsel to Pres. U.S., Washington, 1977—; formerly dir., chmn. exec. com. Bank of Forest Park; formerly vice chmn. Ga. Bd. Human Resources. Past pres. Roxboro Valley Assn.; treas. Jimmy Carter Presdl. Campaign Com.; formerly bd. dirs. Asso. Credit Union; formerly exec. trustee Met. Atlanta Real Estate Investment Trust. Served to capt. AUS, 1943-46. Mem. Am., Ga., Atlanta bar assns., Atlanta Lawyers Club, Atlanta, Clayton County chambers commerce. Jewish (pres. temple). Clubs: B'nai B'rith (past pres.), Commerce (Atlanta). Office: Exec Office Pres 1600 Pennsylvania Ave Washington DC 20500

LIPTON, CHARLES, pub. relations exec.; b. N.Y.C., May 11, 1928; s. Jack B. and Bertha (Lesser) L.; A.B., Harvard, 1948; m. Audrey Williams, Nov. 11, 1951; children—Susan, Jack. Market researcher Cecil & Presbury, Inc., advt., N.Y.C., 1948-49; spl. events dir. 20th Century Fox Film Corp., N.Y.C., 1949-52; with Ruder & Finn, Inc., N.Y.C., 1953—, account exec., 1953-58, v.p., 1958-63, sr. v.p., 1963-69, chmn. bd., 1969—. Guest lectr. Boston U., 1967-68. Mem. adv. council Center for Vocat. Arts, Norwalk, Conn., 1966-74; treas., mem. exec. com. Norwalk Symphony Soc., 1972—; trustee Nat. Emphysema Soc., 1972—, Norwalk Jewish Center, 1966-70, Temple Shalom, Norwalk, 1970—; chmn. parents council Washington U., St. Louis, 1976-77, trustee, 1977—. Mem. Am. Mgmt. Assn., UN Assn., Common Cause. Clubs: Harvard, Midday (N.Y.C.); Harvard Varsity. Home: 18 Douglas Dr Norwalk CT 06850 Office: 110 E 59th St New York City NY 10022

LIPTON, SIMON MORRIS, psychiatrist; b. Latrobe, Pa., Sept. 23, 1913; s. Isadore and Ida (Barash) L.; B.S. in Pharmacy, U. Fla., 1935; M.D., Brandeis U., 1940; postgrad. U. Pa., 1960; m. Betty Steingen, Nov. 23, 1963; children—Isabel, Jeffery Evan, Keith Jonathan. Intern, Harbor Hosp., Bklyn., 1943-44; resident in pediatrics Seaview Hosp., S.I., N.Y., 1945-47, Willard Parker Hosp., N.Y.C., 1948-49; resident in psychiatry VA Hosp., Coatesville, Pa., 1961-64; practice medicine, specializing in pediatrics, Miami, Fla., 1950-61; practiced psychiatry in VA hosps., 1961—; mem. attending staff Mt. Sinai Hosp., Miami Beach, Fla., 1953-59, pediatric dept. Variety Children's Hosp., Miami, Fla., 1953-59; clin. asso., clin. instr. dept. pediatrics Jackson Meml. Hosp.-U. Miami, 1954-59; mem. staff Hialeah (Fla.) Hosp., 1959-61; staff psychiatrist, asst. chief neuropsychiat. service VA Hosp., Bklyn., 1968-71; staff psychiatrist VA Hosp., Lebanon, Pa., VA Hosp., Washington, 1971—; clin. instr. psychiat. dept. Howard U., Washington, 1971-72; instr. psychiat. dept. George Washington U., Washington, 1975. Fellow Royal Soc. Health; mem. AMA (Physicians Recognition awards 1969, 72, 76), Am. Psychiat. Assn., D.C. Med. Soc., Washington Psychiat. Soc. (continuing med. edn. com. 1975—) Clubs: Elks, Lions. Contbr. articles med. jours. Home: 14315 Myer Terrace Rockville MD 20853 Office: Veterans Adminstration Hospital 50 Irving St NW Washington DC 20422

LISANTE, JOSEPH MICHAEL, banker; b. Bklyn., Feb. 21, 1943; s. Theodore Richard and Frances Josephine (Fiorenza) L.; B.B.A., Coll. City N.Y., 1965; postgrad. Baruch Coll., City U. N.Y., 1969-74; m. Peggy Cantrell Soliman, Sept. 3, 1971; stepchildren—David, Robert, Ariston. With Chase Manhattan Bank, N.Y.C., 1969—, asst. treas., ops. mgr., 1974—. Active local Boy Scouts Am., Youth Hockey. Served with USMCR, 1965-68. Decorated Vietnamese Cross Gallantry. Mem. Marine Corps Res. Officers Assn. (chpt. treas.), Res. Officers Assn. (life), Interallied Confedn. Res. Officers. Roman Catholic. Home: 42WW Pennywood Ave Roosevelt NY 11575 Office: 1211 Ave Americas Lower Level New York City NY 10036

LISLE-CANNON, RICHMOND, financial cons., art dealer and collector; b. N.Y.C., Feb. 18, 1914; s. Edward William and Edith Lisle (McCurley) Cannon; student Lincoln Meml. U., 1934-37; m. Cherry Pinckard Clark, Aug. 4, 1961; stepchildren—Anthony Eastburn Clark, Galen Pinckard Clark. Engr., Atlantic Metal Products Co., Reliance Bronze & Steel Co. to 1939; gen. mgr. Comolite Corp., Long Island City, N.Y., 1939-47; asst. to pres. Bijur Lubricating Corp., Rochelle Park, N.J., 1947-53; pres. L.H. Wright Co., Inc., N.Y.C., La Jolla, Calif., 1953-63; founder, dir. Hydrofoil Transit Corp., Tobbaccoles Smokers Corp., Auglo-Am. Stamp Corp.; founder Sovereign Am. Arts Corp.; partner A.L. Williamson Corp., stockbrokers, N.Y. and N.J.; dir. Arab-Am. Enterprises Corp. Mem. Order First Families Va., Soc. Colonial Wars, U.S. Mil. Order Loyal Legion, S.R., Magna Charta Barons, N.Y. Colonial Order Acorn, SAR, St. George Soc., English Speaking Union. Republican. Mason. Clubs: Meadow (Southampton, N.Y.); American, Curson, Clarmont, Chelsea Arts (London, Eng.); Nat. Steeplechase and Hunt, British Luncheon, Church, Tuxedo, St. Anthony (N.Y.C.); Schloss Mittersill (Salzburg, Austria); Newport Reading Room, Sprouting Rock Bathing Assn., Newport Country (Newport, R.I.); Guards (Windsor, Eng.). Pub. Yachting Monthly, 1957-60. Home: 130 E 62d St New York City NY 10021 Office: 130 E 62d St New York City NY 10021 also 27 Eaton Sq London SW 1 England

LISOWITZ, GERALD MYRON, psychiatrist; b. Johnstown, Pa., May 28, 1930; s. Charles Gerson and Tillie (Cohen) L.; B.S., U. Pitts., 1953, M.D., 1955; m. Amelia Josephine Razzando, Mar. 1, 1976; children—Mara Debra, Carlyn Gene, Scott, Laurie, Linda. Intern, Montefiore Hosp., Pitts., 1955-56; resident in psychiatry Western Psychiat. Inst., 1956-59; pvt. practice psychiatry, Pitts., 1961-69; partner Psychiat. Assos., Pitts., 1969—; mem. staff Montefiore Hosp., Western Psychiat. Inst.; instr. U. Pitts. Med. Sch., 1961—; cons. Woodville State, Westmoreland hosps., Med. Center Hosps., U. Pitts. Sch. Medicine. Served to capt. U.S. Army, 1959-61. Diplomate Am. Bd. Psychiatry and Neurology. Mem. AMA, Pa., Allegheny med. assns., Am., Pa., Pitts. psychiat. assns., Pitts. Med. Forum, Phi Beta Kappa. Home: 3212 Attleboro Rd Greensburg PA 15601 Office: 230 N Craig St Pittsburgh PA 15213

LISS, LOUIS RICHARD, real estate investor; b. N.Y.C., Sept. 6, 1911; s. Nathan and Fanny (Siegel) L.; student New Bedford Textile Inst., 1928, U. Pa., 1929-30, Wharton Sch. Finance and Commerce, 1929-31, Mitchell Sch. Design, 1932; m. Rosalyn Lucille Goldfarb, Dec. 24, 1939; children—Stuart Frederic, Ayan Judith (Mrs. Michael H. Rubin). Owner, mgr. Lewis Mfg. Co., 1947-52; pres. Schneider Tanning & Finishing Corp., New Bedford, Mass., 1952-62; v.p. Winfield Mfg. Co., New Bedford, 1956-62; pres. Logan Leather Products Co., New Bedford, 1958-62; owner-mgr. Rockdale Home Builders, New Bedford, 1963-67; trustee, dir. Liss Realty Trust & Affiliates, New Bedford. Chmn. real estate div. United Fund, New Bedford, Mass., 1969-70; mem. New Bedford Historic Dist. Study Com., 1969-71; vice chmn. New Bedford Historic Dist. Commn., 1972-74, chmn., 1974—; chmn. multiple listing services, v.p. New Bedford Bd. Realtors, 1967-68, pres., 1969-71, 74-75, recipient Realtor of Year award, 1974; clk., mem. New Bedford Bldg. Bd. Appeals, 1974—, New Bedford Growth Policy Com., 1976-77; treas. Pub. Arts Council, 1976-77; organizer, coordinator New Bedford econ. del. to La. oil industry, 1976—; bd. dirs. Friends of Touro Synagogue, Newport, R.I., 1972—; mem. Greater New Bedford Forum, 1978—. Served with AUS, 1943-46; ETO, MTO. Mem. Mass. Assn. Realtors (regional v.p. 1972-73, dir. 1974-76), Mass. Home Builders Assn. (dir. 1967-68), Home Builders Assn. South Eastern Mass., Old Dartmouth Hist. Soc., Nat. Assn. Realtors, Real Estate Polit. Edn. Com. (Mass. trustee 1969-70), New Bedford Taxpayers Assn. (dir. 1971—, v.p. 1972-74, pres. 1975-78), Greater New Bedford Area C. of C. (dir. 1974—, v.p. 1976-78, pres. 1979—), Waterfront Historic Area League New Bedford, Soc. Archtl. Historians (New Eng. chpt.), Am. Inst. Historic Preservationists, Nat. Trust for Historic Preservation, 65th Div. Assn., Phi Alpha, Phi Sigma Delta, Zeta Beta Tau. Jewish religion (treas. Tifereth Israel Synagogue 1953-56, dir. 1940-42, 47-60). Club: Wamsutta (New Bedford). Address: 49 Burns St New Bedford MA 02740

LISSENDEN, CAROL KAY, physician; b. Newark, Aug. 22, 1937; d. George Cyrus and Irene Elizabeth (Hempel) L.; B.A., U. Pa., 1959; M.D., Woman's Med. Coll. Pa., 1964; m. Bart Albert Barre, June 13, 1964; children—Lisa Kim, Bart Christopher. Intern pediatrics St. Luke's Hosp., N.Y.C., 1964-65; resident pediatrics Babies Hosp., Columbia Presbyn. Med. Center, N.Y.C., 1965-67; asst. clin. prof. pediatrics Columbia U., N.Y.C., 1975—; practice medicine specializing in pediatrics, Mountainside, N.J., 1967—; mem. staffs Presbyn. Hosp., Overlook Hosp. Diplomate Am. Bd. Pediatrics. Mem. N.J., Union County med. socs., AMA. Home: 135 Wild Hedge Ln Mountainside NJ 07092

LISSER, MORTON SAMUEL, furniture co. exec.; b. N.Y.C., Feb. 6, 1922; s. Jacob David and Bella (Newman) L.; B.B.A., Coll. City N.Y., 1942; LL.B., N.Y. U., 1957; m. Martha Schultz, Dec. 24, 1946; children—Justine, Amy. Staff, Herman J. Dobkin & Co., C.P.A.'s, N.Y.C., 1947-54; pvt. practice as C.P.A., N.Y.C., 1954-56; v.p., treas. John Stuart Inc., N.Y.C., 1956—, also dir.; asso. Columbia U. Seminar on Orgn. and Mgmt., 1975—. Chmn. bd. trustees Encampment for Citizenship, N.Y.C., 1974-77. Served with U.S. Maritime Service, 1942-46. Admitted to N.Y. State bar, 1973. C.P.A. Mem. N.Y. State Soc. C.P.A.'s, Am. Inst. C.P.A.'s. Home: 4601 Henry Hudson Pkwy New York City NY 10471 Office: John Stuart Inc 979 3d Ave New York City NY 10022

LISSIM, SIMON, painter, designer; b. Kiev, Russia, Oct. 24, 1900; s. Michel and Anna Maria (Schorr) L.; student Art Sch. of Alexander Monko; grad. Naoumenko Sch., 1919; student Sorbonne, Ecole du Louvre; m. Irene Zalchoupine, 1925 (dec. 1945); m. 2d, Dorothea Howson Waples, Jan. 25, 1946. Came to U.S., 1941, naturalized, 1946. Stage designer Theatre de l'Ouvre, 1923, Theatre de L'Atelier, Theatre National de l'Opera Comique, Theatre des Nouveautes, Paris, 1931, Theatre Michel. Theatre Antoine, 1932; head art edn. project N.Y. Pub. Library, N.Y.C., 1942-66, mem. faculty French Lycee, N.Y.C., 1943-49, Horace Mann-Lincoln High Sch., Columbia; mem. faculty The City Coll. of N.Y., 1944, art supr. adult edn. program, 1945-47, asst. prof. art, 1947-54, asso. prof., 1954-59, prof. art, 1960-71, emeritus, 1971; asst. dir. evening session charge adult edn. program, 1948-50; asst. dir. sch. gen. studies extension div., 1950-64; mem. faculty French Summer Sch., McGill U., 1949; works include painting, stage designs, window designs, ceramics, gouaches, china and silver designs; works permanently exhibited at the New York Pub. Library, Bklyn. Mus. Art, Columbus (Ohio) Gallery Fine Arts, Hyde Park Library, Met. Mus. Art, Phila. Mus. Art, Boston Mus. Fine Arts, Fogg Mus. Art, Cleve. Mus. Fine Arts, Santa Barbara Mus. Art, Cooper-Hewitt Mus., Fla. So. Coll., Victoria and Albert Mus., London, Shakespeare Meml. Mus., Stratford-on-Avon, Eng., Nat. Gallery Can. at Ottawa, Musee Nat. du Jeu de Paume, France, other museums in U.S., France, Prague, Holland, Austria, Can., Italy, Portugal, Spain, Belgium, Latvia; illustrator several books; has given over 80 one-man shows in various countries. Chmn. nat. selections com. Fulbright awards in painting, sculpture, graphic arts, 1956. Served as vol., French Army, World War II. Recipient Silver Medal, Internat. Exhbn., Paris, 1925, Gold Medal, Barcelona, 1929, 2 grand Diplome d'honheur, Paris, 1937; 1st Am. Fellows award Royal Soc., Art, 1961. Hon fellow Am.-Scandinavian Found. U.S.A.; mem. Royal Soc. Arts London (hon. corr.; v.p. of council), Societe du Salon d'Automme, Societe des Artistes Decorateurs (Paris), AAUP, Coll. Art Assn. Am., Theatre Library Assn. Am., Royal Soc. Miniature Painters (hon.), Audubon Artists. Club: Century. Subject of several monographs. Contbr. articles books, periodicals. Home: 55 Magnolia Dr Dobbs Ferry NY 10522

LISSNER, WILL, journalist; b. N.Y.C., Nov. 11, 1908; s. Ferdinand and Christina (Sayer) L.; student New Sch. for Social Research, N.Y.C., 1927-31, student grad. faculty, 1934-36; licentiate Lloyd Sem., Bklyn., 1934;; m. Dorothy L. Burnham. With Yorkville Spirit, N.Y.C., 1921-23, Harlem Press, 1923; news dept. clk. N.Y. Times, 1923-26, police reporter, 1926-30, reporter on gen. assignments, 1930, rewrite man, 1930-45, reporter specializing in econs., 1945-76; founder, 1941, since editor-in-chief Am. Jour. Econs. and Sociology (quar.); editorial com. Am. Statistician, 1947-53; pub. relations com. Am. Statis. Assn., 1950-56; dir. Robert Schalkenbach Fedn.; lectr. bus. econs. New Sch. Social Research, 1953-59; editorial bd. Social Research, 1955-70. Developed work-time statis. method for internat. price comparisons, 1947, reviewed and adopted U.S. Bur. Labor Statistics, 1948, since adopted by leading governments and internat. agencies; disclosed revision of Soviet econ. theory, 1944, Soviet fgn. policy, 1948; developed basis for linking nat. wage policy to productivity, 1949, adopted by U.S. govt., 1961; made econ. devel. survey C.A., 1950; worldwide surveys tech. assistance, econ. devel., 1952, 54, 55; lectr. Lafayette, Dartmouth, Hofstra colls., also Columbia. Pres. Suffolk Realty Corp., 1929-31; editor The Freeman (monthly), 1937-38; editorial bd. Slavonic Ency., 1945-59. Mem. Econometric Soc., Am. Econ. Assn., Am. Sociol. Soc., Am. Statis. Assn., Delta Tau Kappa (hon.). Club: Overseas Press. Author: Collective Bargaining Attitudes of Newspaper Editorial Workers, 1934; American Exploitation of Fuels and Minerals, 1939; Land Socialization in Soviet Agriculture, 1917-1949. Contbr. numerous articles to mags. Editor: Am. edits. works of Franz Oppenheimer, sociol., 1941-51; Advertising Production, 1946; others. Home: 3610 38th Ave S St Petersburg FL 33711 Office: 50 E 69th St New York City NY 10021

LIST, DE GRAFFENRIED (MRS. DANIEL CLARENCE LIST), artist; b. Winchester, Va., Dec. 12, 1902; d. Robert Wickliffe and Marguerite (Trenholm) Woolley; student George Washington U., 1921-22, N.A.D., 1924-27, Pa. Acad. Fine Arts, 1927-30; m. Daniel Clarence List, July 23, 1949. Designer walking, dancing marionettes, 1932-39; vol. instr. marionettes Washington Jr. League, Eastern Area Red Cross, 1940-43; drafting, illustrations TWA, Washington, 1943-45; illustration N.E.A., Washington, 1945-56; free lance portrait and mural painter, restorer paintings, photographer, illustrator and designer brochures, sculptor, 1956—; exhibited Nat. Press Club, 1959—; numerous pvt. collections. Cresson Traveling European Art scholar Pa. Acad. Fine Arts, 1929. Mem. Colonial Dames Am. Christian Scientist. Address: 3613 Chevy Chase Lake Dr Chevy Chase MD 20015

LISTER, MERLE, choreographer, theatre, arts dir., educator; b. Toronto, Ont., Can., Apr. 22, 1938; d. Harry and Eva (Dorfman) Lister; student Royal Conservatory Music, Toronto, 1942-55, Toronto Tchrs. Coll., 1955-57; Nat. Ballet Sch. Can., Toronto, 1955-62, Biange Rogge Sch. Modern Dance, Toronto, 1955-62, Conn. Coll. Sch. Dance, 1959-60, Mannhardt Theatre Centre, N.Y.C., 1969-72; pupil Martha Graham, Merce Cunningham; Odin Theatre Sch., Holstebro, Denmark, 1968; m. Leonard Levine, Sept. 15, 1963. Choreographer, performer Studio Six Co., Toronto, 1955-62, also tchr. dance Toronto Parks and Recreation, and Scarborough YWCA; tchr. dance edn. Guelph (Ont.) Coll., summer 1962; dancer Charles Weidman Co., N.Y.C., 1963; founder, dir. Studio of Creative Movement, N.Y.C., 1964—, dir. Poets and Writers series, 1974—; dir., choreographer Merle Lister Dance Co., N.Y.C., 1964—; guest tchr. movement, voice LaMama Plexus Theatre Troupe, N.Y.C., 1968; founder, dir. Lister Complex Theatre, N.Y.C., 1973—; arts cons., co-ordinator, program developer YWCA Greater N.Y., 1966-71, Bd. Edn. N.Y.C., 1973—. Mem. arts cons. Bicentennial Com. Chelsea Community N.Y.C., 1974—, dir. creator multi-media theatre project, 1974—. Mem. Assn. Am. Dance Companies, Am. Dance Guild, Episcopal Actors Guild. Address: 60 W 25th St New York City NY 10010

LISTERNICK, JEROME MELVIN, physician; b. Everett, Mass., Sept. 29, 1932; s. Abraham Harry and Isabel Tillie (Lister) L.; A.B. cum laude, Harvard, 1954; M.D., Tufts U., 1958; m. Judith Zonis, Mar. 26, 1960; 1 dau., Joan Isabel. Rotating intern Maine Med. Center, Portland, 1958-59; resident in pediatrics Boston City Hosp., 1962-63; practice medicine specializing in allergy, Chestnut Hill and Randolph, Mass., 1965—; asst. in allergy Children's Hosp. Med. Center, Boston, 1965-73, mem. staff, 1965—; asst. physician employee health Boston City Hosp., 1965-72; med. staff New Eng. Med. Center Hosp., Boston, Cardinal Cushing Gen. Hosp., Brockton, Mass., Newton, Wellesley and Whidden hosps.; clin. instr. medicine Tufts U. Med. Sch., 1965—; allergist adult outpatient clinic New Eng. Med. Center Hosp., 1964—. Class agt. Tufts U. Med. Sch. Alumni Fund. Served to capt. M.C., AUS, 1959-61. Allergy Pulmonary fellow New Eng. Med. Center Hosp., 1964. Diplomate Am. Bd. Med. Examiners, Am. Bd. Pediatrics, Am. Bd. Allergy and Immunology. Fellow Am. Acad. Allergy, Am. Acad. Pediatrics, Am. Coll. Allergy, Mass. Med. Soc. (councillor sect. allergy 1975-77), Am. Assn. Certified Allergists; asso. fellow Am. Coll. Chest Physicians; mem. AMA, Brookline Med. Soc. (pres. 1975-78), New Eng. Soc. Allergy, Phi Delta Epsilon (dist. gov. 1978—, pres. Boston grad. club 1974-76). Republican. Jewish. Clubs: Harvard of Boston, Chestnut Hill Rotary, Tufts Med. M. Grad. Home: 38 Kendall Rd Newton MA 02159 Office: 25 Boylston St Chestnut Hill MA 02167 also 44 Diauto Dr Randolph MA 02368 also 1319 N Main St Randolph MA 02368

LISTON, LAURENCE LOUIS, economist; b. Clarksburg, W.Va., Aug. 16, 1919; s. John Allen and Anna Virginia (Sterling) L.; B.S., W.Va. U., 1940; m. Ruth DeBaun Eckerson, Nov. 1, 1942; children—Susan Kay, John William, Robert Louis. Fin. analyst W.Va. Hwy. Dept., Charleston, 1940-42; transp. economist U.S. Bur. Rds., Washington, 1946-55; chief vehicles, drivers and fuels U.S. Dept. Transp., Washington, 1955-76; cons. transp. econs., Bethesda, Md., 1976—. Chmn. dist. leader tng. Boy Scouts Am., 1968-72, chmn. awards for achievement, 1973—. Served to maj., USAAF, 1942-46; ATO. Mem. Am. Assn. State Hwy. and Transp. Ofcls., Am. Assn. Motor Vehicle Adminstrs. Mason. Home and Office: 6021 Walhonding Rd Bethesda MD 20016

LITMAN, RAYMOND STEPHEN, banker; b. Kingston, Pa., Nov. 2, 1936; s. Stephen Vincent and Mary Helen (Wisnewski) L.; B.S. in Commerce, Wilkes Coll., 1961; m. Ann Mae Kosik, Nov. 24, 1960; children—Raymond Stephen, A. Christine. Credit mgr. Sears Roebuck & Co., eastern div., 1961-66; banking officer Phila. Nat. Bank, 1966-69; dir. Decision Dynamics Corp.,Marlton, N.J., 1969-71; asst. v.p. Bankers Trust Co., N.Y.C., 1971-75; sr. banking officer Girard Bank, Phila., 1975-78; pres. World Wide Cons. Services, Plymouth Meeting, Pa., 1977-78; asst. dir. bank card div. Am. Bankers Assn., 1978—. Mem. Citizens Adv. com. of Montgomery County (Pa.) Planning Commn., 1975—. Served with USNR, 1954-57; ETO. Mem. Internat. Assn. Credit Card Investigators (pres. Del. Valley chpt. 1976-77, dir. nat. chpt. 1976-77, life mem.), Nat. Police Res. Officers Assn., Montgomery County Police Chiefs Assn., Police Chiefs Assn. S.E. Pa., Am. Soc. Indsl. Security, Plymouth Meeting Hist. Soc., VFW, Frat. Order of Police. Republican. Roman Catholic. Home: 2057 Sierra Rd Plymouth Meeting PA 19462 Office: 1120 Connecticut Ave NW Washington DC 20036

LITMAN, ROBERT BARRY, physician, surgeon; b. Phila., Nov. 17, 1947; s. Benjamin Norman and Bette Etta (Saunders) L.; B.S., Yale U., 1967, M.D., 1970, M.S. in Chemistry, 1972, M.Phil. in Anatomy, 1972, postgrad. in Anatomy (Life Ins. Med. Research Fund fellow) Yale U. Coll. Hosp., U. London (Eng.), 1969-70; Am. Cancer Soc. postdoctoral research fellow Yale U., 1970-73; resident in gen. surgery Bryn Mawr (Pa.) Hosp., 1973-74; USPHS fellow Yale Sch. Medicine, 1974-75; practice medicine and surgery, New Haven, 1970—; chmn. dept. family practice A. Barton Hepburn Hosp.; pub. health officer and sch. physician, Waddington and Morristown, N.Y.; commentator monthly radio program Dr. Litman Speaks, Sta. WSLB, Ogdensburg. Bd. dirs. St. Lawrence County Health Assn. Diplomate Am. Bd. Family Practice. Fellow Am. Coll. Allergists (asso.), Am. Acad. Family Physicians; mem. Fedn. Am. Scientists, AMA (Physicians Recognition award 1970-73, 73-76), Conn., New Haven County, New Haven med. assns., Am. Coll. Emergency Physicians (charter), Am. Soc. Bariatric Physicians, Am. Soc. Cell Biology, AAAS, Am. Geriatrics Soc., Am. Chem. Soc., Am. Inst. Biol. Scis., Nat. Assn. Residents and Interns, Book and Snake Soc., Gibbs Soc. of Yale (founder), Am. Soc. Clin. Investigation, Am. Soc. Contemporary Medicine and Surgery, New Haven C. of C., Sigma Xi, Nu Sigma Nu, Alpha Chi Sigma. Contbr. to numerous sci. publs. Home: 124 King St Ogdensburg NY 13669 Office: 235 Bishop St New Haven CT 06511

LITMAN, ROSLYN MARGOLIS, lawyer; b. N.Y.C., Sept. 30, 1928; d. Harry and Dorothy (Perlow) Margolis; B.A., U. Pitts., 1949, J.D., 1952; m. S. David Litman, Nov. 22, 1950; children—Jessica, Hannah, Harry. Admitted to Pa. bar, 1952, since practiced in Pitts.; partner firm Litman, Litman, Harris & Specter, 1952—; adj. prof. U. Pitts. Sch. Law, 1958—; permanent del. to Conf. U.S. Circuit Ct. Appeals for 3d Circuit. Chmn. Pitts. Pub. Parking Authority, 1970-74. Mem. Pa. (bd. govs. 1976—), Allegheny County (pres. 1975) bar assns., Allegheny County Acad. Trial Lawyers (charter). Home: 1047 S Negley Ave Pittsburgh PA 15217 Office: 1701 Grant Bldg Pittsburgh PA 15219

LITOFF, JUDY BARRETT, historian; b. Atlanta, Dec. 23, 1944; d. John and Dorothy May (Wooddall) Barrett; B.A., Emory U., 1967, M.A., 1968; Ph.D., U. Maine, 1975; m. Harold Lawrence Litoff, Sept. 30, 1966; children—Nadja Barrett, Alyssa Barrett. Teaching asst. U. Maine, Orono, 1971-75; asst. prof. history Bryant Coll., Smithfield, R.I., 1975—. Mem. R.I. area com. Am. Friends Service Com., 1977—. Mem. AAUW, Am. Hist. Assn., Orgn. Am. Historians, So. Assn. Women Historians, Women Educators R.I., R.I. Fedn. Tchrs. Early Childhood Edn. Com., ACLU, R.I. Black Heritage Soc. Mem. Soc. Friends. Author: Recognition: A Source Book on Working Women in Maine, 1974; American Midwives, 1860 to the Present, 1978. Home: 248 Morris Ave Providence RI 02906 Office: Social Sci Dept Bryant Coll Smithfield RI 02917

LITSKY, BERTHA YANIS, microbiologist; b. Chester, Pa., Jan. 2, 1920; d. Edward Bernard and Harriett Hunter (Howell) Meade; B.S., Phila. Coll. Pharmacy and Sci., 1942; M. Pub. Adminstrn., N.Y. U., 1964; Ph.D., Walden U., 1974; m. Warren Litsky, Aug. 27, 1965; children—Libby Yanis Nesvold, Rosalind. Supr. biol. prodn. and quality control Nat. Drug Co., Swiftwater, Pa., 1942-45; researcher tissue culture U. Pa., Phila., 1945-50; owner, operator clin. lab. Phila., 1950-56; head microbiology lab. S.I. Hosp. (N.Y.), 1956-63; cons. to industry, govt., assns., research asso. U. Mass., Amherst, 1963—. Mem. Sharon Civic Orch., 1950-54, S.I. Civic Orch., 1954-60; active Girl Scouts U.S.; bd. dirs. Am. Home Health Care. N.Y. U. scholar, 1962-64; recipient Hosp. Mgmt. editorial award, 1964, 65, 68. Fellow Royal Health Soc.; mem. Walden Alumnae Assn. (pres. 1974), Assn. Advancement Med. Instrumentation (co-chairperson subcom. steam sterilization since 1976), Am. Pub. Health Assn., Sigma Xi (pres. Mass. 1976-77). Clubs: Central Sterilization (Eng.), Athenae Stock, Amherst Swim, Rockport Painting, Order of Eastern Star. Author books, contbr. articles to profl. publs. tissue culture, disinfection, sterilization, bacterial shedding, operating room asepsis and infection control. Home: 9 Kettle Pond Rd Amherst MA 01002

LITTERICK, WILLIAM SPENCER, clergyman; b. Pawtucket, R.I., Dec. 1, 1907; s. William Henry and Nellie (Kilburn) L.; Sc.B., Brown U., 1928, M.Sc., 1930; postgrad. Princeton U., 1931-34; Ed.D., Rutgers U., 1939; LL.D., (hon.), Ricker Coll., 1971; M.Div., Andover Newton Theol. Sem., 1975; m. Diana Doubleday, July 31, 1965; children—Jennifer Kilburn, Hilary Snowdon; children by previous marriage—William Spencer, Elizabeth Litterick Martin, Louise Litterick Shaw, David John. Instr. math. Brown U., Providence, 1928-30; asst. headmaster, dir. studies and guidance, chmn. math. dept., coach boxing and tennis, dir. instrumental music Peddie Sch., Hightstown, N.J., 1930-49, acting headmaster, 1949-50; dir. research, asst. to pres. Stephens Coll., Columbia, Mo., 1950-52; dir. Armed Forces Project of Ford Found. under Dept. Def., 1952-54; headmaster Harley Sch., Rochester, N.Y., 1954-59; cons. tchrs. tng. for elementary and secondary sch. math. N.S. Dept. Edn., 1955-63; pres. Keuka Coll., Keuka Park, N.Y., 1959-65; cons. Internat. Schs. Assn., Geneva and Internat. Sch. Services, N.Y.C., 1965-70; pres. Ednl. Records Bur.; spl. cons. Mead Sch., Greenwich, Conn. and Manhasset (L.I.) Pub. Schs., 1965-71; curriculum cons. Fleming Sch., N.Y.C., 1968-72; cons. N.Y. Child Devel., Inc., 1969-72; fin. and adminstrv. cons. Ricker Coll., Houlton, Maine, 1969-72; ordained to ministry Baptist Ch., 1975; pastor Newton Junction (N.H.) Bapt. Ch., 1972-75, Central Bapt. Ch., Jamestown, R.I., 1975—; Bd. Examiners Coll. Entrance cons. Ednl. Records Bur.; mem. div. higher edn. R.I. Council Chs.; mem. N.J. Commn. on Articulation between Secondary Schs. and Colls., Commn. on Evaluation, Gen. Higher Edn. in Am.; chmn. research com. Council on Edn.; pres. Assn. Sch. and Coll. Adminstrs., mem. Commn. on Ministry, Am. Bapt. Conv.; mem. Commn. Higher Edn., Nat. Council Chs.; bd. dirs. Rochester Council Chs., 1955-58, N.Y. State Council Chs., 1960-63. Mem. Vol. Ednl. Council, Rochester; v.p., chmn. edn. com. Rochester Assn. for UN, 1954-59; cons. Houlton Regional Devel. Corp., 1970-72; bd. dirs. Empire State Found.; trustee Rochester Inst. Mental Health, Rochester Area Ednl. TV, Inc., Coll. Center of Finger Lakes, Flemming Sch., N.Y.C. Recipient Keuka Coll. awards, 1965, 67; Newell scholar Brown U., 1924-28. Mem. N.Y. Ind. Sch. Assn., Ednl. Records Bur., Assn. Sch. and Coll. Adminstrs., Middle States Assn. Secondary Schs. and Colls., Nat. Council Tchrs. Math., Math. Soc. Am., Am. Math. Assn., Am. Personnel and Guidance Assn., Am. Ednl. Research Assn., Nat. Council Ednl. Measurement, Phi Delta Kappa. Republican. Clubs: Masons; Rotary; Torch. Author: Philosophy and Principals of General Education, 1955; Aims and Goals in General Education, 1952. Home: 32 Grinnell St Jamestown RI 02835 Office: Central Baptist Ch Narragansett Ave Jamestown RI 02835

LITTIG, LAWRENCE WILLIAM, educator; b. Madison, Wis., June 30, 1927; s. Lawrence Victor and Elsie Louise (Rosanski) L.; B.S., U. Wis., 1950, M.S., 1955; Ph.D., U. Mich., 1959; m. Iris Mark, June 15, 1957; children—Eve Alexandra, Amy Victoria, Sharon Elizabeth. Asst. prof. psychology U. Buffalo, 1959-62; asst. program dir. instl. programs NSF, Washington, 1962-63; social psychologist W. E. Upjohn Inst. Employment Research, Washington, 1963-65; prof. social psychology Howard U., Washington, 1965—; Fulbright prof. U. Nottingham, 1961-62; vis. scholar U. London, 1971-72; cons. Brookings Instn., 1968-70, U.S. Dept. Labor, 1968-70; vis. prof. U. Wis., 1970. NIMH research grantee, 1968-69, NSF research grantee, 1961-62, Nat. Inst. Child Health and Human Devel. grantee, 1971-73, U.S. Office Edn. grantee, 1965-70. Fellow Am. Psychol. Assn., Soc. Psychol. Study Social Issues; mem. AAAS, Am. Sociol. Assn., British Psychol. Soc., Sigma Xi. Cons. editor Jour. Cross Cultural Psychology, 1969-74. Club: Cosmos (Washington). Home: 7011 Meadow Ln Chevy Chase MD 20015 Office: Dept Psychology Howard U Washington DC 20059

LITTLE, GRETCHEN D(OHM), cons.; b. High Bridge, N.J., Nov. 7, 1913; d. James L. and Gretchen B. (Dohm) Little; A.B., Duke, 1934; B.S. in L.S., Drexel Inst. Tech., 1949. Asst. librarian devel. dept. Uni-Royal, 1936-37; tech. librarian Mead Corp., 1937-43, ICI Ams. Inc. (formerly Atlas Chem. Industries, Inc.), from 1943, now ret.; now cons. Mem. A.A.A.S., Am. Chem. Soc., Spl. Libraries Assn. (pres. 1954-55, chmn. sci.-tech. div.; chmn. 50th ann. conv.), Am. Soc. Information Scientists, Am. Water Works Assn., TAPPI. Club: Zonta (local pres. 1969-71). Home: 1600 Sunset Ln Wilmington DE 19810

LITTLE, JAMES KELLY, JR., publisher, editor; b. Memphis, Feb. 23, 1925; s. James K. and Lillian R. (Fuller) L.; student Hampton Inst., 1943, Northwestern U., 1946, Roosevelt U., 1947, Ill. Inst., 1947. Founder, dir. Met. Boys Clubs Chgo., 1944-55; policeman, juvenile officer, Chgo., 1947-56; dir. pub. relations Fuller Products Co., Chgo., 1956-60; pub., editor N.Y. Courier, 1960-66; mem. adv. council N.Y. Urban League, Harlem Hosp. Center, 1966-72; cons. in field; former unit supr. OTC, Merrill Lynch, Pierce, Fenner & Smith, Inc.; mgmt. devel. instr. Merrill Lynch and supr. commodity operations; confidential asst. to asst. sec. for equal opportunity U.S. Dept. Housing and Urban Devel., Washington, 1974; cons., specialist in sr. citizen affairs N.Y.C. Dept. for the Aging, 1974—. Bd. dirs. Vocational Guidance and Workshop Center, N.Y.C. Recipient Distinguished Community Service award Alpha Kappa Alpha, Outstanding Citizen award F. & M. Schaefer Brewing Co., 1967. Mem. N.Y. Urban League, Nat. Council Negro Women (hon.). Home: 45 W 132d St New York City NY 10037 Office: 250 Broadway New York City NY 10007

LITTLE, JEFFREY BERK, author, pub., securities analyst; b. Teaneck, N.J., Aug. 2, 1942; s. Anthony J. and Martia (Edds) L.; B.S. in Fin., N.Y. U., 1964; m. Judith A. Johnston, Sept. 26, 1963; children—David Christopher, Suzanne Kirsten. Securities analyst Dean Witter & Co., N.Y.C., 1964-69, F.S. Smithers & Co., N.Y.C., 1969-71; securities analyst, portfolio mgr., v.p. T.Rowe Price Assos., Balt., 1971-77; founder, pres. Liberty Pub. Co., Inc., 1977—. Mem. N.Y. Soc. Security Analysts. Lutheran. Author The Wall Street Library, ednl. series on stock market, 1977; Understanding Wall Street, 1978. Home: 615 Cranbrook Rd Cockeysville MD 21030 Office: 50 Scott Adam Rd Cockeysville MD 21030

LITTLE, OSBORNE MORGAN, JR., biostatistician; b. Mercedes, Tex., Jan. 11, 1942; s. Osborne Morgan and Gwendolyn Jeannette (Anderson) L.; B.S., U. Ariz., 1964, M.S., 1966; M.B.A., Rider Coll., 1978; m. Mary Katherine Elkins, Dec. 22, 1970. Research asst. U. Ariz., Tucson, 1966-67; asso. sci. information Pitman-Moore, Inc., Washington Crossing, N.J., 1971-75; biostatistician, pharm. div. CIBA-GEIGY Corp., Summit, N.J., 1975—. Served to lt. (j.g.) USNR, 1967-71. Recipient Twice a Citizen award 4th dist. Naval Res. Assn., 1978. Mem. Am. Soc. Animal Sci., Am. Registry of Certified Animal Scientists, Biometric Soc., Am. Statis. Assn., Naval Res. Assn. Phi Gamma Delta. Contbr. articles to profl. jours. Home: 1 Mall Dr Belle Mead NJ 08502 Office: 556 Morris Ave Summit NJ 07901

LITTLE, RALPH DONALD, med. technologist; b. Gastonia, N.C., Mar. 18, 1937; s. Coy Marshall and Stella May (Pruett) L.; B.A., U. Md., 1972; postgrad. Catholic U. Am., 1973—; m. Jacqueline Beatrice Mandel, June 10, 1967. Blood bank and med. technologist Dr. Oscar B. Hunter Meml. Lab., Washington, 1961-66; biol. lab. technologist Navl. Med. Research Inst., Bethesda, Md., 1966-68; blood bank and med. technologist Doctor's Hosp., Washington, 1959—. Served with USN, 1956-61. Mem. Am. Assn. Blood Banks, Am. Soc. Med. Technologists. Home: 6722 Raydale Rd West Hyattsville MD 20783 Office: Central Lab 1815 I St NW Washington DC 20006

LITTLEDALE, HAROLD AYLMER, pub. info. exec.; b. East Orange, N.J., Aug. 21, 1927; s. Harold Aylmer and Clara (Savage) L.; B.A., New Sch. Social Research, 1952; m. Freya Lota Brown, July 7, 1964; children—Krishna, Glenn. Editor, Dupuis Sons & Co., 1952-53, Simon & Schuster, 1953-54, Skira Art Books, 1954-55, Curtis Circulation Co., 1955-56, Parents' Mag. Enterprises, 1957-59; dir. information Goddard Coll., Plainfield, Vt., 1959-61; mem. pub. relations dept. Crowell, Collier & Macmillan, 1964-66; asso. editor Sch. Mgmt. mag., Greenwich, Conn., 1966-67; mng. editor Grade Tchr. mag. (name now Tchr. mag.), Greenwich, 1967-68, editor, 1968-74; editor Tng. in Bus. and Industry mag. (name now Tng. mag.), N.Y.C., 1974-75; editor Bus. Screen mag., N.Y.C., 1976-77; coordinator pub. info. Save the Children Inc., Westport, Conn., 1977—. Served with AUS, 1946-47. Author: The Golden Spike, 1960; Alexander, 1961; (with Freya Littledale) Timothy's Forest, 1969. Home: 125 Sturges Ridge Rd Wilton CT 06897

LITTLETON, LOUIS ANDREW, textile co. exec.; b. Fall River, Mass., Nov. 9, 1923; s. Louis O. and Edith (Repetto) L.; student Renselaer Poly. Inst., 1941-43; Lehigh U., 1944; m. Ruth Charles Williams, Mar. 6, 1970; children—Louis Andrew, Marc E., Kathleen, Theresa. Treas. Massasoit Co., N.Y., 1948-56; v.p., sales mgr., Massasoit Co., Brick Town, N.J., 1956-64; pres., gen. mgr. W. Sherman Lees Co., Brick Town, 1964—; pres. Tamaqua Corp., Point Pleasant, N.J., 1974—; cons. William E. Hooper & Sons, Balt., 1964—, Tropicolor Mfg. Co., San Juan, P.R., 1974—. Served with AUS, 1944-46; ETO. Mem. Renselaer Soc. Engrs., Am. Legion, V.F.W. Elk. Patentee in field. Home: Trenton and Davis Aves Point Pleasant NJ 08742 Office: W Sherman Lees Co Point Pleasant NJ 08742

LITTMAN, CHARLES ARTHUR, ednl. adminstr.; b. Wilmington, Del., Aug. 10, 1932; s. Arthur William and Madalyn Virginia (Brown) L.; B.S., Widener Coll., 1960; M.B.A., U. Del., 1965; m. Wendy Sue Pangborn, June 9, 1976; 1 son, Karl Arthur; children by previous marriage-Heidi Anne, Arthur William III, Heather Jane. Classroom tchr. Swarthmore (Pa.) High Sch., 1960-61; asst. dir. admissions Pa. Mil. Coll., Chester, 1961-64, alumni dir., 1964-67; asso. headmaster devel. and adminstrn. Montclair (N.J.) Acad., 1967-72; pres., chief adminstrv. officer Lankenau Sch., Phila., 1972-75, also dir.; v.p. instl. resources Bloomfield (N.J.) Coll., 1975—; spl. projects cons. Acad. Ednl. Devel., N.Y.C., 1975. Mem. alumni bd. Widener Coll., 1973-76, bd. mgrs., 1977—. Pub. relations dir. polit. campaign to elect mayor, Montclair, 1967-68; mem. Wilmington Operation Firecracker, 1958-67. Served to lt. comdr. USNR, ret. Recipient Publs. award, named Hon. alumnus Montclair Acad., 1972. Mem. Nat. Soc. Fund Raisers, Council Advancement and Support Edn., Nat. Assn. Ind. Schs., Naval Res. Assn., Union League Phila., Alpha Sigma Phi, Phi Mu Alpha. Episcopalian (lay reader 1970—). Mason. Address: 1 Mendl Terr Montclair NJ 07042

LITTMAN, EDWARD, physician; b. Bklyn., Mar. 4, 1935; s. Morris and Gertrude (Goldberg) L.; B.A., Cornell U., 1957; M.D., Chgo. Med.Sch., 1961; m.Elaine Becker, Aug. 10, 1961; children—Jay Robert, Karen Larissa. Med. intern Michael Reese Hosp., Chgo., 1961-62; resident in internal medicine Jersey City Med. Center, 1962-63, Montefiore Hosp., Bronx, 1965-66; postdoctoral fellow in renal diseases Mt. Sinai Hosp., N.Y.C., 1963-65; staff Norwalk Med. Group, 1968—; staff Norwalk Hosp., 1968—, chief sect. nephrology, 1970—; asst. clin. prof. medicine Yale U., New Haven, 1977—. Mem. med. adv.bd. Kidney Found. Conn., 1969—. Served with U.S. Army, 1966-68. Diplomate Am. Bd. Internal Medicine with subsplty. in nephrology. Fellow A.C.P.; mem. Am., Internat. socs. nephrology, Am. Soc. Artificial Internal Organs. Jewish. Contbr.articles on nephrology, hypertension and medicine to profl. jours., 1964-77. Home: 41 William St Norwalk CT 06851 Office: 83 East Ave Norwalk CT 06851

LITTMAN, EUGENE, lighting fixture mfg. co. exec.; b. N.Y.C., Apr. 23, 1928; s. William and Helen (Linsenberg) L.; B.A., Cornell U., 1948; m. Elfriede Zieger, Jan. 14, 1951; children—Robert, Sandra, Bonnie, David. Asst. mgr. Cornwall Fixture Corp., Cornwall on Hudson, N.Y., 1950-52, mgr. 1952-54; v.p. Lightron of Cornwall, Inc., Cornwall on Hudson, 1954-67, pres., 1968—; dir. Columbus Trust Co., Newburgh, N.Y., Ballite Corp., N.Y.C. Pres. United Jewish Charities, Newburgh, N.Y., 1968; v.p. Newburgh Jewish Community Center, 1966-68. Bd. dirs. Cornwall (N.Y.) Hosp.; trustee Union Am. Hebrew Congregations. Served to lt. AUS, 1948-49. Mem. Illuminating Engring. Soc. Jewish religion (pres. temple 1968-70). Club: Otterkill Golf and Country (pres. 1970-71, Campbell Hall, N.Y.). Home: 67 Susan Dr Newburgh NY 12550 Office: 195 Hudson St Cornwall on Hudson NY 12520

LITTMAN, HENRY, dentist, educator; b. Bklyn., July 17, 1920; s. Julius and Jeanette (Lamberg) L.; D.D.S., N.Y. U., 1946; M.B.A., Fordham U., 1976; m. Lillian Small, Mar. 2, 1967; children—Jeffrey Jay, Jon Eric. Gen. practice dentistry, N.Y.C., 1948-73; clin. asst. prof. Coll. Dentistry N.Y. U., N.Y.C., 1966-72; asst. prof. N.J. Coll. Medicine and Dentistry, Newark, 1973—; vis. prof. Art Restoration Tech. Inst., N.Y.C., 1976. Vice-chmn. Pioneer dist. Nassau County council Boy Scouts Am., 1960-61. Served to capt. USAF, 1950-52. Licensed dentist, N.Y. Fellow Am. Acad. Oral Medicine; mem. Dental Soc. N.Y., ADA, Am. Acad. Dental Medicine, N.Y. Acad. Scis., Am. Assn. Dental Schs., Am. Acad. Operative Dentistry, AAUP, Am. Legion. Club: Masons. Author: Introduction to Preclinical Dentistry, 1976. Contbr. to operative dentistry handbook, manual Coll. Medicine and Dentistry. Home: 10 W 76th St New York City NY 10023 Office: 100 Bergen St Newark NJ 07103

LITTMAN, SOLOMON I., psychiatrist; b. Rumania, May 1, 1923; s. Josef and Speranta (Goldenberg) L.; came to U.S., 1963, naturalized, 1968; M.D., U. Bucharest, 1948; m. Rosette Tenenbaum, Apr. 22, 1948; children—Dan, Mario. Gen. practice medicine, 1949-50; specialist in contagious diseases Colentina Hosp., Bucharest, 1950-59; chief researcher Inst. Virology, Bucharest, 1955-61; resident in psychiatry and child psychiatry Phila. Gen. Hosp., 1964-68; clin. asst. prof. Hahnemann Med. Sch., Phila., 1970—; supervising child psychiatrist Phila. Psychiat. Center, 1968—. Mem. AMA (Physician Recognition award 1969, 73, 76), Am. Psychiat. Assn., Nat. Assn. Residents and Interns, Regional Council Child Psychiatry. Author numerous articles on virology and psychiatry. Address: 527 Wynlyn Rd Wynnewood PA 19096

LITZ, MILTON BENJAMIN, mfg. co. exec.; b. N.Y.C., Apr. 4, 1917; s. Benjamin and Sophie (Madrick) L.; student N.Y. U., 1937-39, Washington U., St. Louis, 1945-46; Chem. Engr., 1940; m. Sydnee Cohen, Oct. 14, 1950; children—Gar Bradford, Terri Dee, Todd Stewart, Jamie, Brett Taylor. Pres., Litz & White, St. Louis, 1940-42, Bennat Corp., St. Louis, 1945-49, Dusty Drake Inc., St. Louis, 1949-52, Polyurethane Products Co., Inc., St. Louis and East St. Louis, Ill., 1952-58; pres., chmn. bd. Chemplastics Ind., Inc., St. Louis, 1969-70; mgr. plastics group, dir. internat. sales F & S Central div. Buildex Inc., Bklyn., 1970—; cons. pvt. corps. Served as metrologist officer USAAF, 1942-45. Decorated Bronze Ssar (2). Mem. Soc. Plastics Industry, Soc. Plastics Engrs., Cryogenic Soc. Am. Patentee in field. Home: 38 Prospect St Sea Cliff NY 11579 Office: 15 Huron St Brooklyn NY 11222

LITZENBERGER, LEONARD NELSON, physicist; b. East Macungie, Pa., Oct. 15, 1945; s. Nelson George and Cora Maggie (Hausman) L.; B.S. with highest honors, Lehigh U., 1967; S.M., Mass. Inst. Tech., 1969, Ph.D., 1971; m. Anne Fabiola Ward, Oct. 19, 1974. Research staff scientist AVCO Everett Research Lab., Inc., Everett, Mass., 1971—. Mem. Am. Phys. Soc., Phi Beta Kappa, Sigma Xi, Tau Beta Pi. Contbr. articles to profl. jours.; patentee in field of isotope separation. Office: AVCO Everett Research Lab Inc 2385 Revere Beach Pkwy Everett MA 02149

LITZKY, GERALD MAX, urologist; b. Plattsburgh, N.Y., June 16, 1931; s. Isaac and Sarah (Krinowitz) L.; B.Sc., McGill U. (Can.), 1952; M.D., Columbia U., 1956; m. Joan Altman, Mar. 4, 1956; children—Leslie, Janet, Eric. Intern, U. Chgo. Clinics, 1956-57; resident in surgery Buffalo Gen. Hosp., 1957-58; urology fellow U. Minn. Hosp., Mpls., 1958-61; instr. State U. N.Y., Downstate Med. Center, Bklyn., 1961-62, N.Y. Med. Coll., N.Y.C., 1962-64; pvt. practice medicine specializing in urology, Englewood, N.J., 1964—; attending urologist Englewood Hosp., 1966—. Diplomate Am. Bd. Urology. Fellow ACS; mem. Am. Urol. Assn., N.J. Acad. Medicine, Alpha Omega Alpha. Jewish. Club: Rotary. Contrb. articles in field to med. jours. Home: 5 Leonard Ave Tenafly NJ 07670 Office: 180 Engle St Englewood NJ 07631

LIU, SI-KWANG, veterinary pathologist, educator; b. Kwangsi, China, Dec. 1, 1925; s. Yeeshao and Sinmei (Yeh) L.; came to U.S., 1959, naturalized, 1974; D.V.M., Veterinary Coll. Chinese Army, 1949; Ph.D., U. Calif., Davis, 1964; m. Sin-Ping Chueh, Dec. 20, 1960; children—David, Ernest, Diana, Phillip. Jr. veterinarian Taiwan Provincial Agr. Improvement Sta., Taitung, 1950-52, sr. veterinarian, 1952-56, chief, 1951-56; lectr., head, pathology lab., Veterinary Teaching Hosp. Coll. Agr. Nat. Taiwan U., Taipei, 1956-59, vis. prof. veterinary pathology, 1976-77; research asst., asst. specialist, Sch. Veterinary Medicine U. Calif., Davis, 1959-64; research asso. pathologist Animal Med. Center, N.Y.C., 1964-69, sr. staff pathologist, asst. head pathology, 1969—; clin. asst. prof. comparative pathology N.Y. Med. Coll., N.Y.C., 1970—; vis. expert Chinese Nat. Sci. Council, 1976-77. Mem. AVMA, World Assn. Advancement Veterinary Parasitology, N.Y. Acad. Sci., N.Y. Heart Assn., Am. Acadm Veterinary Cardiology, AAAS, Sigma Xi. Presbyterian. Contbr. articles in field to profl. jours. and books. Home: 182-49 80th Rd Jamaica Estates NY 11432 Office: Animal Medical Center 510 E 62d St New York NY 10021

LIU, WILLIAM CHANG, chem. engr.; b. China, Nov. 25, 1936; naturalized, July 1972. Ph.D., N.Y. U., 1973; m. Ju-Yu Yang, Aug. 18, 1965; children—Stephen C., Wendy C. Chemist, Dow Chem. Co., Midland, Mich., 1965-69; asst. research scientist N.Y. U., 1969-73; tech. asso. Brunswick Corp., Skokie, Ill., 1973—. Mem. Am. Chem. Soc., Plastics Engring. Soc., Am. Inst. Chem. Engrs. Patentee in polymer process and mech. design. Office: 2033 Greenspring Dr Timonium MD 21093

LIU, YUNG SHENG, physicist; b. Anhwei, China, Sept. 23, 1944; s. Hsing C. and Li W. (Wang) L.; came to U.S., 1967; B.S. in Physics, Nat. Taiwan U., 1966; Ph.D., Cornell U., 1973; m. Ming Lee, Nov. 12, 1969; children—Alan, Jane. Research asst. Cornell U., Ithaca, N.Y., 1968-72; vis. scientist U. Calif. at Los Angeles, summer 1969; tech. staff mem. Gen. Electric Research and Devel. Center, Schenectady, 1972—. Chmn., First Nat. Youth Conf., Taiwan, 1963. Recipient Outstanding Achievement award Gen. Electric, 1977; Cornell fellow, 1969; Avco fellow, 1970. Mem. Am. Phys. Soc., Optical Soc. Am. (sect. pres.-elect 1978—), Sigma Xi. Club: Cornell Men's (sec.-treas. 1975-77). Editor-in-chief New Hope mag., 1963-65; contbr. articles to profl. jours.; patentee in field. Home: 101 Woodhaven Dr Scotia NY 12302 Office: PO Box 8 Schenectady NY 12301

LIVA, EDWARD LOUIS, eye surgeon; b. Lyndhurst, N.J., Aug. 30, 1925; s. Paul Francis and Lucy Agnes (Andreozzi) L.; B.S. cum laude, Harvard U., 1947, M.D., 1950; m. Dorothea Lucille Carter, Aug. 29, 1946; children—Edward Louis, Bradford, Douglas, Jeffrey, Elaine. Intern, Med. Coll. Va., Richmond, 1950-51; resident opthhalmology Bklyn. Eye and Ear Hosp., 1951-53; individual practice medicine, specializing in ophthalmology, Ridgewood, N.J., 1957—; attending surgeon Cornell Med. Center, N.Y., Valley Hosp., Ridgewood, Hackensack (N.J.) Hosp., Manhattan Eye, Ear and Throat Hosp., N.Y.C., N.Y. Hosp., N.Y.C.; lectr. in field. Served to capt. M.C., USAF, 1955-57. Fellow Internat. Coll. Surgeons; mem. Bergen County, N.J. med. socs., N.J., Am. acads. ophthalmology, Am. Soc. Ophthalmic Plastic and Reconstructive Surgery. Republican. Roman Catholic. Club: Rotary. Home: 225 Sollas Ct Ridgewood NJ 07450 Office: 385 S Maple Ave Ridgewood NJ 07450

LIVANIS, CONSTANTINE, metal fabrication co. exec.; b. N.Y.C., Nov. 6, 1934; s. Limberios and Elefteria (Hanos) L.; B.S., N.Y. U., 1958; m. Katherine Pattakos, Oct. 5, 1963; children—Terri, Jason. Mfg. engr. Polarad Electronics Corp., Long Island City, N.Y., 1960-61, asst. prodn. mgr., 1961-62; sr. systems and procedure analyst ITT Fed. Labs., Nutley, N.J., 1962-66; systems and procedure analyst Metal Flo Corp., Stamford, Conn., 1966; corp. supr.-systems Amerace Corp., N.Y.C., 1966-67, div. materials mgr. Swan Hose div., Bucyrus, Ohio, 1967-72, plant gen. mgr., 1972-73, corp. mgr. material resources, N.Y.C., 1974, v.p. materials and systems, elastimold div., Hackettstown, N.J., 1974-76; dir. materials Aircraft Radio and Controls div. Cessna Corp., Boonton, N.J., 1976; v.p. ops. F&S Central Mfg. Corp., Bklyn., 1977—. Chmn. indsl. com. Bucyrus United Fund, 1973; bd. dirs. JOBS, Ohio, 1973. Served with AUS, 1958-59. Mem. Purchasing Mgmt. Assn., Soc. Mfg. Engrs., Am. Prodn. and Inventory Control Soc. Greek Orthodox. Club: Elks. Home: 52 Alpine Dr Closter NJ 07624 Office: F&S Central Mfg Corp Brooklyn NY

LIVINGSTON, FREDERICK MONTGOMERY, JR., constrn. co. exec.; b. Greenwich, Conn., Apr. 8, 1915; s. Frederick Montgomery and Luretta Sadie (DeKraft) L.; C.E., Cornell U., 1939; m. Anne Elizabeth Drinkwater, July 2, 1942; children—Frederick, Barbara. Engring. analysis Sherol Corp., 1939-42; with Turner Constrn. Co., N.Y.C., 1942—, chief safety engr., 1946-51, safety dir., 1951—; mem.

constrn. safety and health adv. com. to Sec. Labor, 1972—; mem. constrn. sect. exec. com. Nat. Safety Council; chmn. A10 constrn. safety standards Am. Nat. Standards Inst., also mem. safety tech. adv. bd.; cons. in field. Dist. chmn. local Boy Scouts Am., 1954-70; bd. dirs. Nat. Safety Council. Recipient Distinguished Service award Joint Safety Com. N.Y. Bldg. and Constrn. Industry, 1970. Mem. Soc. Safety Engrs. Club: Westchester Country (Harrison, N.Y.). Home: 3 Putnam Hill Greenwich CT 06830 Office: 150 E 42d St New York City NY 10017

LIVINGSTON, FREDERICK RICHARD, lawyer; b. Newark, Nov. 26, 1912; s. Charles L. and Lillian (Gika) L.; student Rutgers U., 1929-31, LL.B., 1936; student Montclair State Tchrs. Coll., 1932-33; m. Gertrude B. Sonn, Jan. 1, 1938; 1 dau., Lucie. Admitted to N.J. bar, 1937, N.Y. State bar, 1949; atty., trial examiner NLRB, 1939-43; spl. rep. to U.S. sec. of labor, 1945-47; sr. partner firm Kaye, Scholer, Fierman, Hays & Handler, N.Y.C.; adj. prof. Columbia U. Grad. Sch. of Bus. Mem. Armour Automation Com.; gen. counsel Indsl. Relations Research Assn.; chmn. Presdl. Emergency Bd. under Ry. Labor Act; spl. mediator for U.S. sec. of labor in nat. ry. dispute; mem. Presdl. Adv. Com. on Fed. Pay. Trustee, Com. for Young Audiences; bd. dirs., v.p. Work in Am. Inst. Recipient award of merit Dept. Labor, 1972. Mem. Am., Fed., N.Y. State bar assns., Assn. Bar City N.Y., Am. Arbitration Assn. (exec. com.), Am. Arbitration Assn. (dir.), Nat. Acad. Arbitrators. Home: 1016 Fifth Ave New York City NY 10028 Office: 425 Park Ave New York City NY 10022

LIVINGSTON, GIDEON ELEAZAR, food scientist, educator; b. Rotterdam, Netherlands, Feb. 1, 1927; s. Morris S. and Rachel (Gruenfeld) L.; came to U.S., 1940, naturalized, 1945; B.A. (William H. Inman prize chemistry 1948), N.Y. U., 1948; M.S. U. Mass., 1951, Ph.D. (Sigma Xi Research award 1957), 1952; m. Cilla Mahr, Sept. 19, 1948; children—David J., Gary M., Nina J. Asst. prof., then asso. prof. food tech. U. Mass., 1951-59; pres. Food Sci. Assos., Inc., Dobbs Ferry, N.Y., 1956—; dir. food sci. program, prof. pub. health nutrition Columbia, 1966-72; adj. prof. food sci. Pratt Inst., N.Y.C., 1973—, N.Y. U., 1978—; chmn. food and nutrition com. Am. Health Found., 1970—; past chmn. bd. govs. food update Food and Drug Law Inst.; participant White House Conf. Food, Health and Nutrition, 1969; chmn. panel tng. and edn. Nat. Conf. Food Protection, 1970; cons. U.S. Army Natick Research and Devel. Com., 1970—. Served with AUS, 1945-47. Fellow AAAS; mem. Inst. Food Technologists (pres. N.Y. 1969-70), AAAS, Am. Chem. Soc., Am. Pub. Health Assn., N.Y. Acad. Scis., Assn. Food and Drug Ofcls., Am. Assn. Cereal Chemists, Research and Devel. Assos., Royal Soc. Health, European Food Law Assn., Soc. Nutrition Edn., Assn. des Chimistes, Ingenieurs et Cadres des Industries Agricoles et Alimentaires, Sigma Xi, Phi Tau Sigma (pres. 1953-55). Author: Food Service Systems; 1978; co-author: Protein Foods, 1976. Contbr. to profl. publns. Office: 145 Palisade St Dobbs Ferry NY 10522

LLEWELLYN, LYNN GRESHAM, social psychologist; b. Washington, Aug. 20, 1935; s. Haskell V. and Mae Glenn (Griffin) L.; B.S., Coll. William and Mary, 1957; M.A., George Washington U., 1959, Ph.D., 1969; m. Barbara Ann Best, June 29, 1963. Research asst. NIMH, Bethesda, Md., 1958-59, social sci. analyst, 1959-60; research psychologist, 1964-68; community organizer D.C. Commr.'s Youth Council, 1960-61; research asso. Spl. Ops. Research Office, Washington, 1961-62; social psychologist Ops. Research Inc., Silver Spring, Md., 1968-71; research psychologist Nat. Bur. Standards, 1971-75; social psychologist U.S. Fish and Wildlife Service, 1975—; cons. NSF, 1969; vis. prof. U.S. Army War Coll., 1970-71. Trustee Greater Washington Ednl. TV Assn., 1973—. Served to capt. AUS, 1959. Recipient Psi Chi Grad. award George Washington U., 1959. Mem. Am. Psychol. Assn., AAAS, AIA (cons. mem. regional devel. and natural resources com. 1973—, chmn. endangered species subcom. 1974), ASCE (com. planning environ. quality), Environ. Design Research Assn., Nature Conservancy, Nat. Audubon Soc., Sigma Xi, Pi Kappa Alpha. Editor: Studies in Environment, 1973. Home: 4209 Aspen Hill Rd Rockville MD 20853 Office: Div Program Plans US Fish and Wildlife Service Dept Interior Washington DC 20240

LLOYD, DOROTHY DAVIS, assn. editor; b. Enfield, N.C., Oct. 11, 1918; d. Donald M. and Anna Elizabeth (Davis) Burgess; B.A., Duke U., 1937; m. Thomas Jones Price Murray, Nov. 19, 1937 (div. Nov. 1961); 1 son, James Thomas; m. 2d, Robert Crawford Lloyd, Jan. 20, 1962. Mem. advt. dept. Raleigh (N.C.) Times, 1939-42; copywriter Wise Advt. Agy., Balt., 1950-52; adminstrv. sec. Tchrs. Assn. Baltimore County, Balt., 1952-56; asso. editor Md. State Tchrs. Assn., 1956-62, mng. editor, 1962-68, dir. publs., 1968—. Cons. sch. law revision publ. Md. Dept. Edn., 1967, Md. Council Edn. publs., 1967. Mem. Women's Advt. Club Balt. (pres. 1961-63; dir. 1963-64), Mid-Atlantic Assn. Indsl. Editors (dir. 1956-58), Nat. Assn. State Edn. Editors, Nat. Sch. Pub. Relations Assn., Edpress Assn., N.E.A. (life), Adminstrv. Women in Edn., Phi Beta Kappa, Kappa Kappa Gamma, Delta Kappa Gamma. Republican. Methodist. Home: 3000 W Strathmore Ave Baltimore MD 21209 Office: 344 N Charles St Baltimore MD 21201

LLOYD, GERALD DWIGHT, plastics co. exec.; b. Ft. Meade, S.D., Apr. 14, 1936; s. Harry Allen and Dellamae J. (Teabault) L.; student metall. engring. S.D. Sch. Mines and Tech., 1958; m. Jeannette Marie Trader, Feb. 7, 1959; children—Michelle R., Stuart A. Mgr. safety, fire protection and security Firestone Synthetic Fibers Co., Hopewell, Va., 1964-68; plant safety engr. Firestone Plastics Co., Perryville, Md., 1968-72, divisional sr. engr. safety and training, Pottstown, Pa., 1972—. Mem. exec. com. rubber and plastics sect. Nat. Safety Council, 1977—. Served with U.S. Army, 1961-64. Certified safety profl. Mem. C. of C., Am. Soc. Safety Engrs. (profl. mem.). Democrat. Lutheran. Contbr. articles in field to profl. jours. Home: 1619 Cortland Ave Kenhorst Reading PA 19607 Office: PO Box 699 Pottstown PA 19464

LLOYD, JOHN WILLIAM, educator; b. Westfield, N.Y., Aug. 6, 1926; s. George E. and Eva H. (Hendry) L.; B.S., Cornell U., 1949, postgrad., 1956-60; M.S., U. Rochester, 1974; St. Bonaventure Coll., 1951—, State U. N.Y., 1974-76; m. Clara Ann Newell Lloyd, June 25, 1949; children—Priscilla A., John William, Peter F., Mark A. Tchr., Downsville and Allegany (N.Y.) central schs., 1949-53; personnel mgr. Agway, Inc., Syracuse, N.Y., 1953-66; personnel dir. Sibley, Lindsay & Curr Co., Rochester, N.Y., 1966-70; asso. prof. Monroe Community Coll., Rochester, 1970—; founding partner Asso. Profl. Cons., Fairport, N.Y., 1975—. Active Monroe County Probation Employment Guidance program, 1973-76; bd. dirs. Rochester Blue Shield, 1968-76; mem. exec. com., bd. dirs. Genesee Valley Group Health Assn., 1975-76. Served with USAAF, 1945. Recipient State U.N.Y. Chancellor's award, 1976. Mem. C. of C., Assn., Mktg. Educators (v.p. 1976-78), Am. Mktg. Assn., N.Y. State Assn. Jr. Colls. Episcopalian. Author: Use of Business Simulations and Games in Higher Edn., 1973; Basic Marketing Study Guide, 1976. Home: 77 Miles Circle Fairport NY 14450 Office 1000 E Henrietta Rd Rochester NY 14623

LLOYD, RICHMOND MORGAN, educator; b. Chgo., Jan. 10, 1942; s. Richmond Morgan and Natalie Agnes (Migala) L.; B.S. (Samuel B. Havens scholar), U. Rochester, 1963, Ph.D., 1971; M.B.A. (Grad. Sch. Bus. fellow), U. Chgo., 1965; m. Barbara Ellen Morrison, June 12, 1965; 1 son, Christopher Morgan. Dir. logistics div. Center for Naval Analyses, Arlington, Va., 1968-73; prof. mgmt. Naval War Coll., Newport, R.I., 1973—; tchr. Bryant Coll., U. R.I., Salve Regina Coll. Chmn. bd. trustees New Sch., Newport. Center for Naval Analyses fellow, Mass. Inst. Tech. Center for advanced engring. fellow. Mem. Am. Econs. Assn., Inst. Mgmt. Sci., AAAS, Ops. Research Soc. Am., Tau Beta Pi, Beta Gamma Sigma. Home: Ivy Cottage Ledge Rd Newport RI 02840 Office: Mgmt Dept Naval War Coll Newport RI 02840

LLOYD, ROBERT ALBERT, notary public; b. Pitts., Apr. 21, 1930; s. Robert Morgan and Martha Elizabeth (Sauter) L.; student Carnegie Mellon U., 1948, 50, 51. Adminstrv. supr. Pitts. Inf. Sch., U.S. Army Reserve, 1951-71; asst. mgr. meml. dept. Sears Roebuck & Co., Pitts., 1960-71, notary public, 1971—. Chmn. Boro of Dormont (Pa.) Republican Com., 1974-76, committeeman 7th Dist., Allegheny County, 1970-76. Recipient Good Citizenship medal SAR, 1943; decorated Army Commendation medal. Mem. Hist. Soc. Western Pa., Assn. U.S. Army, Pa. Assn. Notaries, Am. Legion, Sons. of Union Vets. of Civil War. Republican. Presbyterian. Clubs: Masons, Knights Templar, Knights of Malta, Elks, Shrine. Home: 3089 Pinehurst Ave Dormont PA 15216

LLOYD, THOMAS GRANT, archtl. cons.; b. St. Louis, Jan. 16, 1933; s. Robert E. and Virginia A. (Battles) L.; B. Arch., Washington U., St. Louis, 1956; m. Marilyn M. Worseldine, June 12, 1971; children—Mark, Matthew, Maude, Michael, Megan. Vice pres. Winkler Thompson & Lloyd, Inc., St. Louis, 1958-69; exec. v.p. Barrier Industries, Ltd., St. Louis, 1969-76; pres., dir. Grant & Asso., Inc., St. Louis, 1973—; sr. policy analyst Arthur D. Little, Inc., Washington, 1975—; dir. Worseldine Graphic Design. Served with AUS, 1956-58. Mem. AIA, Am. Mgmt. Assn., Am. Mktg. Assn., Am. Soc. Pub. Adminstrn., AAAS, Acad. Polit. Sci., World Future Soc. Home: 1231 30th St NW Washington DC 20007 Office: Arthur D Little Inc 1735 Eye St NW Washington DC 20006

LLOYD, W. MASON, mktg. exec.; b. Buffalo, Feb. 16, 1930; s. William Mason and Bertha Marie (Taylor) L.; B.M., Boston U., 1953; MM.E., Fitchburg State Coll., 1962; children—Stephen M., Wendy M., Rebecca J., Jeffrey J., Gregory A. Supr. music Oakland (Maine) Pub. Schs., 1953-55; dir. choir Colby Coll., Waterville, Maine, 1953-55; supr. supply Records, Inc., Boston, 1955-56; dir. music Gardner (Mass.) Pub. Schs., 1956-66; tchr. band and orch. Prince Georges County (Md.) Pub. Schs., 1966-70, vice prin., 1970-78; owner, mktg. exec. Lloyd Assos., Upper Marlboro, Md., 1978—; lectr. in personal motivation; co-founder jazz workshop Franklin Pierce Coll.; played with various name bands. Served with U.S. Army, 1948-50. lMem. Citizen's Choice Assn., Upper Marlboro C. of C., Am. Legion, Kappa Gamma Psi. Republican. Unitarian. Address: 5601 Temple Hills Rd Temple Hills MD 20031

LLOYD, WILLIAM HOWARD, bank exec.; b. Cumberland, Md., July 29, 1932; s. John Leon and Julia Melissa (Copenhaver) L.; B.A., U. Pitts., 1959, M.S. in Communications, 1976; m. Alma June Dickson, Jan. 24, 1957; children—Kathleen Gay, William Howard, Richard Llewellyn. Sr. English tchr. Bellevue High Sch., 1959-60; asso. editor Constructioneer mag., South Orange, N.J., 1960-64; account mgr. Lando, Inc., 1964; product info. specialist pub. relations U.S. Steel Co., 1964-69; pub. relations mgr. Pitts. Nat. Bank, 1969—; free lance in pub. relations and photography, 1960-69; instr. indsl. communications Robert Morris Coll., 1975—. Pub. relations chmn. Churchill Area Friends of Library, 1969-72; mem. publicity com. Allegheny Trails council Boy Scouts Am., 1970-73; elder, trustee, past pres. bd. deacons Presbyterian Ch. Served with AUS, 1953-55. Recipient Merit award Financial Mag., 1969; Golden Quill for outstanding journalism and employee communications Sigma Delta Chi, 1971, 72, 73; Achievement award Nat. Publs. Assn., 1975; Circle C Appreciation award Young Life Internat. Mem. Pub. Relations Soc. Am. (profl. communicator), Pitts. Indsl. Communicators Assn., Nat. Publs. Assn., Internat. Assn. Bus. Communicators, Internat. Soc. Gen. Semantics, Pitts. C. of C., Pitts. Press Club. Home: 2407 Greensburg Pike Pittsburgh PA 15221 Office: Pittsburgh Nat Bldg Pittsburgh PA 15222

LO, HANG HSIN, consumer products co. exec.; b. China, Feb. 22, 1937; s. Chu Tsai and Jane Chiao (Wang) L.; came to U.S., 1961, naturalized, 1974; B.S. in Chem. Engring., Nat. Taiwan U., 1959; M.S. in Chemistry, Case Inst. Tech., 1965, Ph.D. in Phys. Chemistry, 1967; m. Pallas May-Jon Sun, Sept. 9, 1967; children—Serena Charlotte, Elliot Hugo. Sr. research chemist, analytical chemistry Diamond Shamrock Corp., Painesville, Ohio, 1967-68; research asso. Mass. Inst. Tech., 1968-71; asst. tech. dir. McKesson Lab., Fairfield, Conn., 1971-72; group leader, analytical instrument lab. Chesebrough-Ponds, Inc., Trumbull, Conn., 1972-77, mgr. specifications, formula control and computer applications, 1978—. Mass. Inst. Tech. research fellow, 1968-71. Mem. Am. Chem. Soc., Soc. for Applied Spectroscopy, AAAS, Am. Mgmt. Assn., Phi Lambda Upsilon. Club: Mass. Inst. Tech. Faculty (Cambridge). Home: 15 Moose Hill Rd Oxford CT 06483 Office: Trumbull Indsl Park Trumbull CT 06611

LO, TEH CHENG, chem. engr.; b. Lungyen, Fukien, China, Mar. 17, 1928; s. T.K. and K.L. (Chaing) L.; came to U.S., 1956, naturalized, 1972; B.S., Kiangsi Inst. Tech., 1947; M.S., Stevens Inst. Tech., 1960; postgrad. Poly. Inst. Bklyn., 1960-64; m. Shu Yen Kuo, Apr. 24, 1949; children—Gen, Larry. Teaching asst. Kiangsi Inst. Tech., 1947-48; asst. engr., asso. engr. research and devel. dept. Taiwan Camphor Refinery, 1949-54; asst. chief engr. charge prodn. First Wine Brewery, Taiwan, 1954-56; sr. scientist, tech. fellow Hoffmann-LaRoche, Inc., Nutley, N.J., 1958—. Invited participant, speaker, session chmn. Gordon Conf. on Mixing Research, Andover, N.H., 1971, Berwick Acad., Maine, 1973, Rindge, N.H., 1975, Internat. Solvent Extraction Confs., The Hague, Netherlands, 1971, Lyon, France, 1974, Toronto, Ont., Can., 1977; participant 4th and 5th Internat. Congress Chem. Engrs., Marianske Lane, Czechoslovakia, 1972, 75; cons. various cos. and acad. instns.; invited lectr. colls. and acad. instns., including The Netherlands, 1971, France, 1974, China, 1976, Can., 1977. Recipient Mgmt. award Taiwan Provincial Govt., 1956. Mem. Am. Inst. Chem. Engrs., AAAS. Contbg. author: Handbook of Separation Techniques for Chemical Engineers; Ency. Chem. Tech. Contbr. articles to profl. jours. Patentee in field. A pioneer in reciprocating-plate extraction columns. Home: 21 Miller Rd Wayne NJ 07470 Office: Hoffmann-La Roche Inc Kingsland St Nutley NJ 07110

LOBDELL, DAVID HILL, pathologist; b. Erie, Pa., July 9, 1930; s. Webster Alexander and Christine (Kern) L.; A.B., Kenyon Coll., 1952; M.D., U. Mich., 1956. Asso pathologist St. Vincent's Hosp., Bridgeport, Conn., 1960-63, dir. labs. St. Vincent's Med. Center, 1963—; instr. pathology N.Y. U., N.Y.C., 1959-61, asst. clin. prof., 1961-69; lectr. biology Fairfield (Conn.) U. 1964-72; adj. asso. prof. biology U. Bridgeport (Conn). 1971—. Diplomate Am. Bd. Pathology. Fellow Coll. Am. Pathologists, Am. Soc. Clin. Pathologists; mem. AMA, Am. Assn. Blood Banks, Am. Soc. Microbiology, Phi Beta Kappa, Alpah Omega Alpha. Episcopalian. Editor St. Vincent's-Park City hosps. med. bull., 1965-74. Home: 13C Algonquin Ln Stratford CT 06497 Office: 2800 Main St Bridgeport CT 06606

LOBEL, IRVING, clothing mfg. co. exec.; b. Bklyn., Jan. 18, 1917; s. Benjamin and Jennie (Gross) L.; B.S. in Econs., U. Pa., 1937; m. Selma Agar, Jan. 23, 1943; children—Bonnie, Douglas, Robert. Partner, Lo-Bel Co., N.Y.C., 1937—. Bd. dirs. Cannon Point S. Coop., 1975-78; mem. U. Pa. Ann. Giving Com. Served with U.S. Army, 1942-46. Mem. Infants and Childrens Wear Assn. (dir.), Mu Sigma, Sigma Alpha Mu. Democrat. Jewish. Club: Inwood Country. Home: 45 Sutton Pl S New York City NY 10022 Office: 390 Fifth Ave New York City NY 10018

LOBRON, BARBARA L., writer, editor; b. Phila., Mar. 19, 1944; d. Martin A. and Elizabeth (Gots); B.A. cum laude, Temple U., 1966; study photography with Harold Feinstein, N.Y.C., 1970. Reporter, writer Camden Courier-Post newspaper, Cherry Hill, N.J., 1966-68; editorial asst. Med. Insight, mag., N.Y.C., 1970-71; mng. editor Camera 35 mag., Am. Express Corp., N.Y.C., 1971-75; free-lance writer and editor, N.Y.C., 1975-77; account exec. Bozell & Jacobs, Inc., N.Y.C., 1977-79. Recipient 1st pl. award in external newsletter category Internat. Assn. Bus. Communicators Dist. One Ann. Contest, 1977. Mem. Sigma Delta Chi. A founder, contbg. editor Photograph mag., 1976; contbr. articles to photography mags. Photographs exhibited in group shows, N.Y.C., 1975, 76; photographs in permanent collection Library of Calif. Inst. Arts, Valencia. Home and Office: 85 Hicks St Brooklyn NY 11201

LOBSENZ, AMELIA, pub. relations exec.; b. Greensboro, N.C.; d. Leo and Florence (Scheer) Freitag; B.A., Agnes Scott Coll., 1944; m. Harry Abrahams, Aug. 17, 1957; children—Michael, Kay. Dir. mag. dept. Edward Gottlieb & Assos., N.Y.C., 1952-56; pres. Lobsenz Pub. Relations Co., Inc., N.Y.C., 1956-75; chmn. bd., chief exec. officer Lobsenz-Stevens Inc., N.Y.C., 1975—; condr. seminars, lectr. in field. Mem. citizens council Hofstra U., Hempstead, N.Y. Recipient article award Mag. Writers Am., 1974. Mem. Pub. Relations Soc. Am. (chpt. dir. 1977-79, President's award 1975), Am. Soc. Journalists and Authors, Am. Med. Writers Assn., Am. Women Radio and TV, L.I. Pub. Relations Soc., Nat. Assn. Sci. Writers, Publicity Club N.Y.C., Publicity Club Chgo. Clubs: Racquet (Old Westbury, N.Y.); Windham Mountain. Author: Kay Everett Calls (Jr. Lit. Guild selection), 1951; Kay Everett Works, 1952; also articles, chpts. in books. Address: 2 Park Ave New York NY 10016

LOCHANKO, ADAM, electronics engr.; b. Gorwal, Russia Mar. 9, 1916; s. Andre W. and Ksenia (Pinchuck) L.; diploma Engineering, Communications, 1941; m. Alexandra Zabuha, May 29, 1953; children—Lillian Suzanna, Elizabeth Alexandra. Came to U.S., 1960, naturalized, 1965. With I.G. Farben, Haydebreck, Germany, 1942-45, Am. Army Broadcast, Bayreuth, Germany, 1945-47; engr. Phillips, Caracas, Venezuela, 1948-50; service engr., Ministry Communications, Caracas, 1950-53; engr. Gen. Electric, Toronto, Ont., Can., 1953-60; design engr., electronics engr. RCA, Camden, N.J., 1960-69; sr. project engr. Jerrold Electronics Corp., Phila., 1969-74; sr. engr. Vector-Aydin Co., Newtown, Pa., 1974-75; sr. project engr., project mgr. AEL Corp., Colmar, Pa., 1975—. Registered profl. engr., Can. Mem. IEEE. Patentee in field. Address: 1827 Terrace Dr Maple Glen PA 19002

LOCHNER, H. ALLEN, lawyer; b. Louisville, Aug. 14, 1912; s. Herman F. and Nellie (Estes) L.; B.A., Temple U., 1936; LL.B., U. Pa., 1939; m. Winifred Beal, Aug. 5, 1940; children—Wendy Kay, Stephen Allen. Admitted to N.Y. bar, 1943; asso. atty. law office Arthur T. Vanderbilt, Newark, 1939-42; asso. atty. in predecessors of Rogers & Wells, N.Y.C., 1942-53, partner firm, 1953—. Active various philanthropic activities; trustee Marble Men's League Found., 1964—; bd. dirs. Found. Religion and Health; mem., deacon Marble Collegiate Ch. Mem. U. Pa. Law Sch. N.Y. Alumni Soc. (pres. 1967-68), Am., N.Y. State bar assns., Order Coif. Republican. Editorial bd. U. Pa. Law Review, 1938-39. Home: 123 Waverly Pl New York City NY 10011 Office: 200 Park Ave New York City NY 10017

LOCKARD, JAMES REEDER, govt. ofcl.; b. Salem, W.Va., Oct. 1, 1932; s. James Aldrich and Laura (Reeder) L.; student Salem Coll., 1950; B.S. with honors, Southeastern U., 1961; m. Janice Lee Seager, Mar. 9, 1952; 1 dau., Jeri Lockard Walke. Supr., FBI, Washington, 1951-62; br. chief U.S. Bur. Pub. Rds., Washington, 1962-65; mgmt. analyst Nat. Archives and Records Service, Washington, 1965-68; asst. chief Nat. Driver Register, U.S. Dept. Transportation, Washington, 1968--. Deacon, trustee Congress Heights Presbyterian Ch., 1958—. 4-H Charting Pin grantee, 1949. lfem. Lake Anna Recreation Assn. Club: Salem Hunting. Home: 1713 N Jefferson St Arlington VA 22205 Office: 2100 2d St S W Washington DC 20590

LOCKE, EDWIN ALLEN, III, educator; b. N.Y.C., May 15, 1938; s. Edwin Allen and Dorothy (Clark) L.; B.A., Harvard, 1960; M.A., Cornell U., 1962, Ph.D., 1964; m. Anne Hassard, June 13, 1968. Asso. research scientist Am. Inst. Research, 1964-66, research scientist, 1966-70; asst. prof. psychology U. Md., College Park, 1967-69, asso. prof., 1969-70, asso. prof. bus. adminstrn. and psychology, 1970-73, prof. bus. adminstrn. and psychology, 1973—. Grantee, Office Naval Research, 1964, Nat. Inst. Mental Health, 1967. Fellow Am. Psychol. Assn.; mem. Acad. Mgmt., Md. Psychol. Assn., N.Y. Acad. Scis. Author: A Guide to Effective Study, 1975. Cons. editor Jour. Applied Psychology, 1972—. Contbr. articles to profl. jours. Home: 2659 Carrollton Rd Annapolis MD 21403 Office: Coll Bus and Mgmt U Md College Park MD 20742

LOCKE, HOWARD PALMER, ret. lawyer; b. Charleston, S.C., July 11, 1899; s. Howard Palmer and Annie Hurst (Smith) L.; student Piedmont Coll., Demorest, Ga., 1916-18; B.C.S., Southeastern U., Washington, 1923; J.D., George Washington U., 1927; m. Margaret S. Danhaki, June 17, 1926; children—Henry Preston, John Howard. Admitted to D.C. bar, 1927, N.C. bar, 1927, S.C. bar, 1954; asst. adminstrv. officer Am. Agy. German Claims Commn., 1922-23, atty., adminstrv. officer Mexican Claims Commn., 1924-31; with Dept. Justice, 1931-54, exec. atty. tax div., 1934-54; pvt. practice, Charleston, S.C., 1954-55; clk. Tax Ct. U.S., 1955-66; with law firm Hudson & Creyke, 1967-71; lectr. tax matters U. Ga. Inst. Accountants, La. Poly Inst.; past instr. tax law Nat. U., Washington. Served with U.S. Army, World War I. Mem. Kappa Alpha (past nat. pres.), Delta Theta Phi. Episcopalian. Contbr. articles on taxes to profl. jours. Home: 3901 Connecticut Ave NW Washington DC 20008

LOCKE, RICHARD VAN DE SANDE, investment banker; b. Flushing, N.Y., Apr. 17, 1937; s. Homer F. and Ruth E. (Rosenlund) L.; B.S. in Commerce and Finance, Bucknell U., 1958; m. Kathleen Bernard Newell, Apr. 22, 1961; children—Elizabeth Denmead, Richard van de Sande III. With Kidder, Peabody & Co. investment bankers, N.Y.C., 1959-64; 1st v.p., gen. partner Eastman Dillon, Union Securities & Co. investment bankers, N.Y.C., 1964-72; exec. v.p., dir. Blyth Eastman Dillon & Co., Inc.; now exec. v.p., dir. E.F. Hutton & Co. Inc. Allied mem. N.Y., Am. stock exchanges. Served to 1st lt. AUS, 1958-59, 61-62. Mem. N.Y. C. of C., Municipal Forum N.Y. and Washington, Municipal Finance Officers Assn. Internat. Bridge, Tunnel and Turnpike Assn., Am. Pub. Power Assn., Airport Operators Council Internat., Antique Automobile Club Am., Soc. Am. Magicians, Internat. Brotherhood Magicians, Lambda Chi Alpha, Theta Alpha Pi. Clubs: India House, City Midday, Municipal

Bond (N.Y.C.); Beacon Hill (Summit, N.J.), Lake Naomi (Pocono Pines, Pa.). Home: 234 W 10th St New York NY 10014 Office: One Battery Park Plaza New York NY 10004

LOCKE, STANLEY, mathematician; b. N.Y.C., June 18, 1934; s. Emanuel and Ida (Pollak) L.; B.M.E., N.Y. U., 1955, M.S., 1957, Ph.D., 1960; m. Jane Laura Hershkowitz, Dec. 20, 1958; children—Cathy-Lynn, Peter Stuart, Ilene Jill. With Republican Corp., Farmingdale, N.Y., 1959-60; with Schlumberger Doll Research Center, Ridgefield, Conn., 1960—, mem. sci. staff, 1965—. Mem. Am. Phys. Soc., Sigma Xi. Patentee in field. Contbr. articles to profl. jours. Home: 17 Deerwood Ct Norwalk CT 06851 Office: Old Quarry Rd Ridgefield CT 06877

LOCKHART, G(LENN) ROBERT, food co. exec.; b. Glenwood, Minn., June 9, 1926; s. Glenn R. and Mattie (Gapen) L.; B.S., Northwestern U., 1948; m. Ramona Taylor, Sept. 8, 1951; children—Rebecca, Jeffrey, Sally, Greg. Dir., Club Aluminum Products, 1958-65; gen. mgr. splty. foods div. Fairmont Foods, 1965-68; v.p. mktg. and sales Roman Products, 1968-70; exec. v.p., dir. Fromageries Bel Inc., Hoboken, N.J., 1970—. Mem. Ridgewood (N.J.) Park and Recreation Bd., 1974-77; trustee Grace Ch., Ridgewood, 1973—, pres. bd., 1978; pres. Basketball Assn. Ridgewood, 1967-74; active YMCA, 1970-73, recipient Youth Service award, 1974. Served with Air Corps, USNR, 1944-46. Recipient Service to French Cheese Industry award Guilde des Fromages, 1976. Mem. Nat. Assn. Food Distbrs. (dir.), Fellowship Christian Athletes, Sigma Chi. Republican. Club: Rotary. Home: 84 Wildwood Rd Ridgewood NJ 07450 Office: Fromageries Bel Inc 1 Newark St Hoboken NJ 07030

LOCKHART, PHILIP NORTH, educator; b. Smicksburg, Pa., May 3, 1928; s. John Donald and Margaret (North) L.; B.A., U. Pa., 1950; M.A., U. N.C., 1951; Ph.D., Yale, 1959; m. Elizabeth McFarland Ayer, Aug. 8, 1959; children—Bruce McFarland, Elizabeth Barclay. Tchr., Ezel (Ky.) Mission Sch., 1951-52; instr. classical langs. U. Mo., 1954-56; asst. prof. classical studies U. Pa., 1957-63; asso. prof. classical langs. Dickinson Coll., 1963-68, prof., 1968-70, Clarke prof. Latin, 1970—; vis. prof. Ohio State U., 1969-70. Sec. for scholarships Am. Classical League, 1963-65. Mem. Phila., Pa. Classical Assns. (past pres.), Am. Philological Assn., Archeol. Inst. Am., Classical Assn. Atlantic States, Vergilian Soc. Am. (trustee 1970-76), Phi Beta Kappa. Republican. Presbyn. (elder). Contbr. articles to prof. jours. Home: 804 Stratford Dr Carlisle PA 17013

LOCKSHIN, FLORENCE LEVIN (MRS. SAMUEL D. LOCKSHIN), composer, pianist; b. Columbus, Ohio, Mar. 24, 1910; d. Samuel M. and Jennie (Klein) Levin; B.S., Ohio State U., 1931; M.A., Smith Coll., 1953; m. Samuel D. Lockshin, June 4, 1933; children—Richard A., Michael D. Pianist concerts and radio programs, 1920-53. Represented State of Ohio as composer-performer 1951 Biennial Nat. Fedn. Music Clubs. Mem. Am. Fedn. Musicians (hon., life). Composer works for full orch. performed by maj. orchs. U.S. and abroad, including The Cycle, 1956, Song Form, 1961, Paean, 1962, Aural, 1964, Introduction, Lament & Protest, 1967, Fantasy on a Negro Folk Tune, 1969, Scavarr, 1970, Do Not Go Gentle Into That Good Night, 1973; also solo piano, 4 pianos, chamber music, ballet with orch., men's chorus, women's chorus. Home: Baker Hill Northampton MA 01060

LOCKSHIN, SAMUEL D., mgmt. cons. exec.; b. Youngstown, Ohio, Mar. 10, 1908; s. Abraham A. and Anna (Lockshin) L.; B.Indsl. Engring., Ohio State U., 1930; m. Florence H. Levin, June 4, 1933; children—Richard A. and Michael D. (twins). Mgmt. cons. M.P. Pfeil Co., Dayton, Ohio, 1933-38; v.p. mfg. Dominion Electric Corp., Mansfield, Ohio, 1938-52, Hampden Splty. Products Co., Easthampton, Mass., 1952-67; pres. S.D. Lockshin Mgmt. Cons., Northampton, Mass., 1967—, Prest-Wheel of Ariz., Parker, 1968-71, Prest-Wheel, Inc., South Grafton, Mass., 1969-71. Chmn. industry integration com. bombs and pyrotechnics Ordnance Dept., Washington, 1941-45; vol. exec. Internat. Exec. Service Corps, Barranquilla, Colombia, 1972, Caracas, Venezuela, Panama, 1974. Registered profl. engr., Ohio, Mass. Address: Baker Hill Northampton MA 01060

LOCKWOOD, KENNETH RICHARD, audio engr., communications exec.; b. Oswego, N.Y., Jan. 24, 1939; s. C. Clayton and D. Arlene (Shutts) L.; grad. Buffalo Radio Inst., 1957, Cleve. Inst. Electronics, 1959, N.Y. U., 1977; m. Joyce Kathleen Seaver, Aug. 2, 1958; children—John Kenneth, Kristine Renee. Sales engr. Rochester Radio Supply, Inc. (N.Y.), 1963-65; corp. sec. treas., gen. mgr. Tel-Com/Ronco C&E, Inc., Rochester, 1965-74; prin. Lockwood Assocs., Rochester, 1974-78; br. mgr. Compuguard Corp., N.Y.C., 1977—. Scoutmaster Boy Scouts Am., Knowlesville, N.Y., 1958, adult leader, Rochester, 1976; communications chmn. Rochester Jaycees, 1966-73; mem. Rochester Republican Chairmens Club, 1971-75. Served with N.Y. Army N.G., 1956-62. Named Jaycee of month, Rochester Jaycees, 1969, recipient Project of Yr. award, 1968, Outstanding Project award, 1968; Distinguished Salesman award Rochester Sales Execs. Club, 1964; holder 2nd class FCC license. Mem. Am. Mgmt. Assn., Audio Engring. Assn., Constrn. Specifications Inst. Republican. Presbyterian. Contbr. articles to profl. jours.; designer sound template set of instrn. materials, 1975, audio-visual control system for Equibank of Pitts. and Bank of Montreal, Can., 7 bldg. communication, sound, fire and security system for Kodak Rochester, 36 bldg. computer based sound, TV, fire and security system for N.Y. State Dept. Corrections. Address: 37 Northgate Park Ringwood NJ 07456

LOCKWOOD, MOLLY A., communications co. exec.; b. London, Sept. 19, 1936; d. Warren Sewell and Ann Frances (Gleason) L.; B.S., Pa. State U., 1958. Mem. exec. tng. program Lord & Taylor, N.Y.C., 1958-60; asso. merchandising editor House and Garden, N.Y.C., 1960-65; advt. dir. Status mag., N.Y.C., 1965-70; merchandising dir. Holiday Mag., N.Y.C., 1970; account mgr. Ladies Home Jour., N.Y.C., 1970-72; advt. dir. Girl Talk mag., N.Y.C., 1972-74; mktg. dir., asso. pub. East/West Network, N.Y.C, 1974-77; v.p., treas., partner Catalyst Communications, Inc., N.Y.C., 1977—. Mem. Advt. Women N.Y., Am. Soc. Travel Agts., Kappa Kappa Gamma. Home: 1133 Park Ave New York City NY 10028 Office: Catalyst 274 Madison Ave New York City NY 10016

LOCKWOOD, WILLIAM WIRT, JR., performing arts adminstr.; b. N.Y.C., July 4, 1937; s. William Wirt and Virginia (Chapman) L.; A.B., Princeton U., 1959. Partner, Dana Attractions, San Francisco, 1960-63; gen. mgr. Civic Arts Assn. No. Calif., San Francisco, 1961-63; asso. producer, booking dir. McCarter Theatre, Princeton U., 1963-65; asst. dir. programming Lincoln Center for Performing Arts, N.Y.C., 1965-70, dir., 1970—; program dir. McCarter Theatre of Princeton U., 1965—; artistic dir. Bermuda Festival of Arts, 1975—; cons. performing arts program Asia Soc., 1968-69; cons. San Francisco Symphony, 1979—; cons. program Performing Arts Center, Princeton U., 1971-72; dir. Mostly Mozart Festival, 1966—. Served with AUS, 1959-60. Mem. Internat. Assn. Concert and Festival Mgrs., Internat. Soc. Performing Arts Adminstrs. Club: Princeton Triangle (trustee 1966—, treas. 1968—). Home: 110 Jefferson Rd Princeton NJ 08540 Office: 140 W 65 St New York City NY 10023

LODER, MARTHA KATHERINE, former educator; b. Bridgeton, N.J., July 12, 1914; d. LeRoy Ward and Maude (Woodruff) Loder; A.B., Dickinson Coll., 1934; A.M., U. Pa., 1937, Ph.D., 1943. Tchr., Bridgeton High Sch., 1935-38, 39-41, head dept. English, fgn. langs., 1943-57; tchr. Springfield Twp. High Sch., Chestnut Hill, Pa., 1941-43; supr. secondary instrn. Bridgeton pub. schs., 1957-71. Bd. dirs. Bridgeton chpt. NCCJ, Bridgeton chpt. ARC; trustee Bridgeton Free Pub. Library. Recipient Am. Legion award for meritorious community service, 1950. Mem. D.A.R., Alliance Francaise, AAUW, Nat., N.J. ret. educators assns., Phi Beta Kappa. Author: The Life and Novels of Leon Gozlan, 1943. Home: 8 South Dr Bridgeton NJ 08302

LODER, PETER CAMERON, educator, pub. policy analyst; b. Salem, Oreg., Jan. 5, 1935; s. Wayne P. and Arline L. (Cameron) L.; B.A., Columbia, 1957, M.A., 1961; Ph.D. (polit. sci. fellow), U. Pa., 1972; m. Nancy F. Cavanaugh, Aug. 15, 1964; children—Nancy Elizabeth, Amy Suzanne. Instr. in govt. Trenton (N.J.) Jr. Coll., 1961-63; instr. polit. sci. Bucknell U., Lewisburg, Pa., 1966-68; asst. prof. polit. sci., 1968-70; research asso. Community Research Assos., Waldwick, N.J., 1970-77; asst. prof. M.P.A. program Rutgers U., Newark, 1977—; cons. econs., govt., bus. exams. Am. Inst. for Property and Liability Underwriters, Malvern, Pa., 1965—. Vice chmn. citizens adv. com. Waldwick Sch. Bd., 1972-74; legis. chmn. Waldwick PTA, 1971-73. Mem. Am. Soc. Pub. Adminstrn., Assn. Mgmt. Analysts in State and Local Govt., Govtl. Research Assn., Regional Plan Assn. (N.Y.C. area), Urban and Regional Info. Systems Assn. Episcopalian. Developer state, fed. programs for environ., econ. and social problems; developer analytical framework to assist govt. ofcls. to formulate measurable organizational goals, assess program effectiveness; contbr. articles on regional info. systems to profl. jours. Home and office: PO Box 159 Waldwick NJ 07463

LODGE, HENRY CABOT, former govt. ofcl.; b. Nahant, Mass., July 5, 1902; s. George Cabot and Elizabeth Frelinghuysen (Davis) L.; A.B. cum laude, Harvard U., 1924, LL.D., 1954; hon. degree Northeastern U., 1938, Clark U., 1951, Norwich U., 1951, Laval U., Que., Can., 1952, Bishop's U., Lennoxville, Que., 1952, Franklin-Marshall U., 1953, Hamilton U., 1953, Boston U., 1953, N.Y. U., 1955, Fordham U., 1955, Rensselaer U., 1955, Lehigh U., 1956, U. Pa., 1956, Williams U., 1957, Union U., 1957, Boston Coll., 1961, U. N.H., 1959, Columbia U., 1960, Princeton U., 1961, Adelphi U., 1961, U. Notre Dame, 1962, Mass. U., 1962, Am. U., 1967, Salem State U., 1977; m. Emily Sears, July 1, 1926; children—George Cabot, Henry Sears. Mem. U.S. Senate from Mass., 1937-43, 47-53; mem. Presdl. Cabinet, Washington, 1953-60; U.S. rep. UN, N.Y.C., 1953-60; ambassador to Republic of Vietnam, 1963-64, 65-67, Germany, 1968-69, at-large, 1967-68; spl. U.S. envoy to Vatican, 1970-77; prof. U.S. fgn. policy Gordon Coll., 1978—; bd. overseers Harvard U., 1924-32, also Fletcher Sch. Diplomacy; head Atlantic Inst., Paris, 1961-63; cons. Time Inc., 1961-63; dir. John Hancock Life Ins. Co., 1961-65; chmn. Presdl. Commn. for Observance 25th Anniversary UN, 1970-71; lectr. Republican nominee for v.p. U.S., 1960; mem. nat. council Salvation Army, 1976; trustee George C. Marshall Research Found., Va. Served with U.S. Army, 1941-45; ETO, Middle East. Decorated Bronze Star, Legion of Merit (U.S.); Legion of Honor, Croix de Guerre (France); Humane Order African Redemption (Liberia); Grand Cross of Merit, Sovereign Order Malta; Grand Cross Nat. Order (Republic Vietnam); recipient Gold medal Pres. Eisenhower, 1961, Thayer medal West Point, 1960, Marshall medal Assn. U.S. Army, 1967, Distinguished Honor award State Dept., 1967. Clubs: Somerset, Tavern, Myopia (Boston); Met., Alfalfa (Washington). Author: The Storm Has Many Eyes, 1973; As It Was, 1976; first Senator since Civil War to resign from Senate for Army service; commended for Vietnam service by U.S. Senate, 1967. Home: 275 Hale St Beverly MA 01915

LODMELL, DEAN STRUTHERS, civil engr.; b. Walla Walla, Washington, May 24, 1934; s. Anton Merriam and Selma Violet (Struthers) L.; A.B. in Math. and Physics, Whitman Coll., 1956; B.S. in Civil Engring., Columbia U., 1958, M.S. in Civil Engring., 1960; m. Marilyn Maria Maki, Jan. 25, 1958; children—Dean Walter, Kimberly Ann, Richard Anton. Design and field engr. Dodger Stadium, Kavanaugh Engrs., Los Angeles, 1960-67; office and project engr. Vinnell Corp., Walla Walla, 1962-67, Mt. Shasta, Calif., 1967-69, Dacca, East Pakistan, 1969-71; sr. v.p., gen. mgr. CRS Design of N.Y., Inc., S.I., 1971—, also dir., sr. v.p., gen. mgr. A.A. Mathews div., N.Y.C., 1971—, also dir.; nat. def. exec. reservist Fed. Preparedness Agy., 1967—. Pres., Dacca Am. Sch. Bd., 1970-71; mgr. Little League Baseball, Oakland, N.J., Little League Basketball, Oakland. Mem. ASCE (nat. com. on contract adminstrn., nat. com. on tunneling and underground constrn., Robert Ridgeway award 1958), N.Y. State Water Pollution Control Assn., Municipal Engrs. N.Y.C. Republican. Congregationalist. Clubs: Masons; Elks (Walla Walla). Office: 24 Lindenwood Rd Staten Island NY 10308

LOEB, FRANCES LEHMAN (MRS. JOHN L. LOEB), civic leader; b. N.Y.C., Sept. 25, 1906; d. Arthur and Adele (Lewisohn) Lehman; student Vassar Coll., 1924-26; L.H.D., N.Y. U., 1977; m. John Langeloth, Loeb, Nov. 18, 1926; children—Judy Loeb Chiara, John Langeloth, Ann Loeb Bronfman, Arthur Lehman, Deborah Loeb Brice. N.Y.C. commr. for UN and Consular Corps., N.Y.C., 1966-78; mem. bd. Internat. Play Group, Inc.; mem. exec. com. Population Crisis Com., Washington; mem. UN Devel. Corp.; bd. dirs. N.Y. Conv. and Visitors Bur.; life mem. bd. Children of Bellevue, Inc.; trustee-at-large, mem. exec. com. Fedn. Jewish Philanthropies of N.Y.; life trustee Collegiate Sch. for Boys, N.Y.C.; trustee Inst. Internat. Edn., 1977—; chmn. bd. dirs. East Side Internat. Community Center, Inc.; mem. bd. UN Internat. Sch., N.Y. Landmarks Conservancy, Inc., UN Assn.; mem. president's council Mus. of City of N.Y.; hon. mem. Nat. Commn. on Internat. Yr. of Child, 1979. Recipient Medaille de Reconnaissance, Consul Gen. of France, 1972; La Guardia award Center N.Y.C. Affairs, New Sch. for Social Research, 1974; tribute of appreciation Dept. State, 1974; Leadership award Greater N.Y. council Girl Scouts U.S.A., 1977; Bicentennial medal King of Sweden, 1977; Woman of Conscience award Nat. Council of Women of U.S.A., Inc., 1978. Mem. Council Fgn. Relations. Clubs: Cosmopolitan, Vassar, Women's City (honoree 1969) (N.Y.C.). Home: 730 Park Ave New York City NY 10021 also Anderson Hill Rd Purchase NY 10577

LOEB, JOHN LANGELOTH, JR., investment banker; b. N.Y.C., May 2, 1930; s. John Langeloth and Frances (Lehman) L.; grad. Hotchkiss Sch., 1948; A.B. cum laude, Harvard, 1952, M.B.A., 1954; children—Nicholas, Alexandra. With Loeb, Rhoades & Co., N.Y.C., 1956—, gen. partner, mem. mgmt. com., 1959-73, mng. partner, pres., 1971-73, ltd. partner, 1973—; chmn. bd. Holly Sugar Co., Colo., 1969-71; past dir. Denver & Rio Grande Western R.R., Metro-Goldwyn-Mayer, John Morrell & Co. Spl. adviser environ. matters Gov. Nelson A. Rockefeller, 1967-73; chmn. Gov. N.Y. Council Environ. Advisers, 1970-75. Trustee Montefiore Hosp. and Med. Center, Museum City, N.Y., Winston Churchill Found., John and Frances L. Loeb Found.; mem. vis. com. of bd. overseers to visit Grad. Sch. Bus. Adminstrn. and dept. govt. Harvard. Served as 1st lt. USAF, 1954-56. Clubs: Recess, City Midday, St. Nicholas Soc. (N.Y.C.); Century, Sleepy Hollow (Westchester, N.Y.); Brooks, Buck's (London, Eng.); Royal Swedish Yacht (Stockholm); Lyford Cay (Nassau). Home: Ridgeleigh Anderson Hill Rd Purchase NY 10577 Office: Loeb Rhoades & Co 375 Park Ave New York City NY 10022

LOEFFLER, JUDITH RAE, counselor; b. Waverly, Iowa, May 23, 1942; d. Edwin Henry and Rachel Viola (Miller) Kohlmann; B.A., Colo. Woman's Coll., 1964; postgrad. U. No. Iowa, 1965-66, Boston Coll., 1972—; M.A., U. R.I., 1972; m. Henry Kenneth Loeffler, Aug. 4, 1962; 1 son, Michael. Tchr. elementary pub. sch., Oceanside, Calif., 1966-68; tchr. mathematics Middletown (R.I.) Middle Sch., 1969-73; counselor Pastoral Counseling Clinic, Inc., Newport, R.I., 1972-74; child devel. specialist, partner Counseling Clinic, Inc., Middletown, 1974—; cons. local schs., Naval Hosp. Recipient award for Service to Community Rotary, 1976. Mem. Am. Personnel Guidance Assn., Nat. Alliance Family Life (clin. mem. and supr.; guest lectr. 1977 nat. conv.), Mass., Nat., Aquidneck Island (v.p. 1975-76) assns. children with learning disabilities, Nat. Assn. Sch. Counselors, Am. Assn. Pastoral Counselors, Delta Kappa Gamma (research chmn.). Republican. Lutheran. Home: 99 Emmanuel Dr Portsmouth RI 02871

LOENING, SARAH LARKIN, author; b. Nutley, N.J., Dec. 9, 1896; d. Adrian H. and Katherine (Satterthwaite) Larkin; student Miss Chapin's Sch., Madame Marty's Sch., Paris, 1913; m. Albert P. Loening, Nov. 28, 1922; 1 son, Albert Palmer. Author: Three Rivers, 1934; The Trevals, a Tale of Quebec, 1936; Radisson, 1938; Dimo, 1940; Joan of Arc, 1951; The Old Master, 1958; Zulli, 1954; The Old Master and other Tails, 1968; Mountain in the Field, 1972; The Gift of Life, 1978. Chmn. arts and skill corp. A.R.C., Camp Upton, 1945, chmn. Hampton chpt., 1946; past pres. Cathedral guild, St. John the Divine, past chmn. of Gardeners St. John's, now chmn. Bibl. garden. Mem. Pen and Brush, Nat. Soc. Colonial Dames, Huguenot Soc. Am., Order St. John of Jerusalem (asso. dame). Clubs: Colony, Hroswitha, Southampton Garden (past pres.). Home: Lallinden 119 First Neck Ln Southampton NY 11968

LOENING, WERNER, mgmt. cons.; b. Berlin, Aug. 27, 1928; s. Alfons and Alma (Hollern) L.; came to U.S., 1955, naturalized, 1960; B.S. in Physics, Tech. U. Berlin, 1950, M.S. in Mech. Engring., 1952, M.B.A., 1952; m. Brigitte Schnase, Apr. 17, 1954; children—Peter, Cynthia. Engr., Fritz Werner A.G., Berlin, 1950-53, Vereinigte Aluminum Werke A.G., Bonn, W.Ger., 1953-55; sr. engr. Raytheon Mfg. Co., Wayland, Mass., 1955-58; dept. mgr. Perkin-Elmer Corp., Norwalk, Conn., 1958-70; v.p. automatic signal div. LFE Corp., Norwalk, 1970-73; v.p. engring. Gen. Telephone & Electronics, Stamford, Conn., 1973-76; mgmt. cons., 1976—. Registered profl. engr., Conn., Mem. Nat. Soc. Profl. Engrs., ASME, Armed Forces Communications and Electronics Assn., Am. Arbitration Assn. Republican. Mem. adv. bd. Jour. Research and Devel., 1974. Home and Office: 65 Ryders Ln Wilton CT 06897

LOEVINGER, LEE, lawyer; b. St. Paul, Apr. 24, 1913; s. Gustavus and Millie (Strouse) L.; B.A. summa cum laude, U. Minn., 1933, J.D., 1936; m. Ruth E. Howe, Mar. 4, 1950; children—Barbara Lee, Eric Howe, Peter Howe. Admitted to Minn. bar, 1936, Mo. bar, 1937, U.S. Supreme Ct. bar, 1941, D.C. bar, 1966; asso. firm Watson, Ess, Groner, Barnett & Whittaker, Kansas City, Mo., 1936-37; trial atty., regional atty. NLRB, Mpls., 1937-41; atty. antitrust div. U.S. Dept. Justice, Washington and N.Y.C., 1941-46, asst. atty. gen. charge antitrust div., 1961-63, spl. asst. to atty. gen., 1963-64; partner firm Larson, Loevinger, Lindquist, Freeman & Fraser, Mpls., 1946-60; asso. justice Minn. Supreme Ct., 1960-61; commr. FCC, 1963-68; partner firm Hogan & Hartson, Washington, 1968—; gen. counsel Craig-Hallum, Inc., investment banking, Mpls., 1950-60, v.p., dir., 1968-73; v.p., dir. Craig-Hallum Corp., Mpls., 1968-73; gen. counsel Gen. Securities, Inc., 1951-60; lectr. hosp. and nursing law U. Minn. Med. Sch., 1953-60, vis. prof. jurisprudence Law Sch., 1961; gen. counsel Minn. Nurses Assn., 1950-60; spl. counsel to subcom. on small bus. U.S. Senate, 1951-52; U.S. del. to com. experts on restrictive bus. practices OECD, 1961-64, vice chmn. com., 1963-64; U.S. del., vice chmn. extraordinary admisntrv. radio conf. Internat. Telecommunications Union, Geneva, 1964, 66; lectr. Am. U., 1968-70; mem. Adminstrv. Conf. U.S., 1972-74; U.S. del. UNESCO Conf. on Mass Media, 1975; del. White House Conf. on Inflation, 1974; dir. Petrolite Corp., St. Louis. Served to lt. comdr. USNR, 1942-46; ETO. Recipient Outstanding Achievement award U. Minn. Regents, 1968; Freedoms Found. award, 1977. Mem. Am. (law and tech. com. 1969-74, del. sci. and tech. sect. Ho. of Dels. 1974—, rep. to joint conf. with AAAS 1974-76), D.C., Minn., Hennepin County, Fed. Communications bar assns., AAAS, Broadcast Pioneers, Phi Beta Kappa, Sigma Xi, Phi Delta Gamma, Delta Sigma Rho, Sigma Delta Chi, Tau Kappa Alpha, Alpha Epsilon Rho. Author: The Law of Free Enterprise, 1949; Jurimetrics, 1949; An Introduction to Legal Logic, 1952; Defending Antitrust Lawsuits, 1977; editor, contbr. Basic Data on Atomic Development Problems in Minnesota, 1958; editorial adviser Jurimetrics Jour.; adv. bd. Antitrust Bull., Performing Arts Rev.; contbr. articles to profl. jours. Home: 5669 Bent Branch Rd Washington DC 20016 Office: 815 Connecticut Ave Washington DC 20006

LOEWER, ALVIN CONRAD, JR., structural engr.; b. Balt., Apr. 21, 1921; s. Alvin Conrad and Louise Fawcett (Siebert) L.; B.S., Engring., Johns Hopkins U., 1942, Ph.D., Engring., 1948; m. Irene Sullivan Albert, July 5, 1975; children—Douglas George, Lynne Miree. Orchestra leader Al Loewer's Serenaders, Balt., 1937-42; instr. civil engring. dept. McCoy Coll., Johns Hopkins U., 1946-48; asso. prof. dept. civil engring. and mechanics Lehigh U., Bethlehem, Pa., 1949-52; research leader Ops. Research Office, Bethesda, Md., 1952-55; partner, cons. engr. A.C. Loewer & Assos., Bethlehem, and Bethesda, 1948-55, Keller, Loewer & Assos., Silver Spring, Md., 1955-61; partner Loewer, Sargent & Assos., Kensington, Md., 1961-67; pres. Loewer & Assos., Kensington, 1968-71; pres. Md. office Dalton, Dalton, Little, Newport, Engrs., Bethesda, 1971-75; gen. partner 5-L Ltd. Partnership Comml. Devel., Berlin, Md., 1974-78, Douglynne Woods Enterprises Ltd. Partnership and Farms, 1977-78; pres. Loewer & Assos., Inc., Berlin, 1976-78. Served to capt. C.E., AUS, 1942-46. Registered profl. engr. Pa., Md., D.C., Va., Ill., N.C., Fla., Tex., Calif., W.Va., Del., Ga., Ohio, N.Y. and N.J. Mem. AMLE, Am. Concrete Inst., Soc. Am. Mil. Engrs., ASTM, Ops. Research Soc., Am. Nat. socs. profl. engrs., Ocean City C. of C. (dir.), Sigma Xi. Club: Rotary. Contbr. articles in field to profl. jours. Home: 84th St #7 Ocean City MD 21842 Office: RFD 4 Box 383-A Berlin MD 21811 also Estero Bay Ln Naples FL 33940

LOFFREDO, RONALD DANIEL, sch. psychologist, counselor; b. Newark, June 24, 1945; s. Louis S. and Dorathea (Casalino) L.; B.A. in Elementary Edn., Kean Coll., 1967, M.A. in Behavioral Scis., 1967; M.A. in Ednl. Psychology, Jersey City State Coll., 1973, profl. diploma in sch. psychology, 1973; m. Kathleen Jane Farkas, May 26, 1974. Dir psychology D.A.R.E. Residential Treatment Center, Orange, N.J., 1973-74; psychologist Mine Hill (N.J.) Schs., 1973-74, Willowbrook Ministries Counseling Service, Wayne, N.J., 1973—, Allen House, Branchville, N.J., 1975-77; dir. Center for Profl. Counseling, Belleville, N.J., 1977—; pvt. practice counseling, Belleville, 1973—; cons. psychologist Newark Boys Chorus Sch. Certified sch. psychologist, sex therapist, counselor, elementary educator (all N.J.); licensed psychologist, Pa. Mem. Am., N.J. personnel and guidance assns., Am. Group Psychotherapy Assn., Am. Assn. Sex Educators, Counselors and Therapists, N.J. Psychol. Assn.,

Nat. Alliance Family Life, N.J. Sch. Psychologists Assn., N.J. Assn. Profl. Psychologists, Feingold Assn., Am. Rehab. Counselors Assn. Home: 171 Branch Brook Dr Belleville NJ 07109 Office: 180 Washington Ave Belleville NJ 07109

LOFGREN, RICHARD H., accountant, fin. cons.; b. N.Y.C., Mar. 14, 1943; s. Harold J. and Anne Cecilia (Hultquist) L.; student Upsala Coll., 1961-63; B.S. in Accounting and Econs., Wagner Coll., 1967; m. Ruth J. Wiseman, July 19, 1970; 1 dau., Kimberly Dale. Sr. accountant Haskins & Sells, C.P.A.'s N.Y.C., 1967-74; dir. internal audit Penn-Dixie Industries, N.Y.C., 1974-76; pvt. cons., pub. accounting and mgmt. adv. services, N.Y.C., 1971—; dir. internal audit Canada Dry Corp., N.Y.C., 1976-77, asst. corporate controller 1977—. C.P.A., N.Y. Mem. Am. Inst. C.P.A.'s, N.Y. State Soc. C.P.A.'s, Am. Mgmt. Assn., Nat. Assn. Accountants. Home: Brook Farm Rd E Pound Ridge NY 10576

LOFVING, IVER, architect, educator; b. N.Y.C., July 12, 1931; s. Per August and Wilma Anna-Christina (Christianson) L.; B.Arch., U. Pa., 1956; m. Sara K.B. Middendorf, Dec. 21, 1957; children—Per, Iver, Camilla, Tore. With Philip Johnson, Architect, N.Y.C., 1957-59, Edward Larrabee Barnes, Architect, N.Y.C., 1959-61; pvt. practice architecture, N.Y.C., 1966—; asst. prof. architecture N.Y. Inst. Tech., 1969—. Registered architect, N.Y., Conn. Mem. AIA (chmn. com. on continuing edn. 1972-74), Am. Arbitration Assn. (arbitrator), Soc. Archtl. Historians, Assn. for Preservation Tech., AAUP. Works include: Katonah (N.Y.) Gallery, Bowery Savs. Bank, numerous residences. Home: Mt Holly Rd Katonah NY 10536 Office: 330 E 59th St New York City NY 10022

LOGAN, ROBERT LEE, ins. co. exec.; b. Newton, Kans., Aug. 16, 1930; s. Ferdinand Lee and Pauline Elizabeth (Boyd) L.; A.B., Ottawa U., 1952, A.M., Boston U., 1955; postgrad. Harvard, 1955-56; m. Mercedes Donelda Clark, Dec. 26, 1950; children—Audrey Diane, Laura Gay; m. 2d, Gloria Cristina Ortiz, May 22, 1974. Asst. prof. Tex. Christian U., Ft. Worth, 1956-59; sr. research engr. Gen. Dynamics Corp., Ft. Worth, 1959-67; dir. sci. computing Argonne Nat. Labs., Lemont, Ill., 1967-71; exec. v.p. Uni-Coll Corp., Phila., 1971-73; v.p. mgmt. info. systems Allendale Mut. Ins. Co., Johnston, R.I., 1973—. Pvt. cons. data processing. Served with AUS, 1951-53. Mem. AAAS, Am. Acad. Arts and Sci., Assn. for Computing Machinery, Assn. for Symbolic Logic, Assn. Atomic Scientists. Home: 26 Armington St Wickford RI 02852 Office: Allendale Park Johnston RI 02919

LO GERFO, JOHN JOSEPH, educator; b. N.Y.C., Feb. 12, 1918; s. John and Grace (Mazzinobile) LoG.; B.A., N.Y. U., 1942; M.A., Columbia, 1952, profl. diploma, 1954, Ed.D., 1961; m. Diana Grace Alagna, Apr. 30, 1955. Lab. supr. Lenox Hill Hosp., N.Y.C., 1941-57; cons. biochemist St. Claire's Hosp., N.Y.C., 1955-58; chief biochemist Clin. Lab. S. Shore, Islip, N.Y., 1957-58; asso. prof. C.W. Post Coll., L.I. U., Greenvale, 1958-69, prof., 1969—, dir. med. biology program C.W. Post Center, 1961—, chmn. pre-med. com., 1965—, chmn. health scis. dept., 1972—. Research asso. Community Hosp., Glen Cove, N.Y., 1958—; biology program dir. allied health traineeship and improvement grants Dept. Health Edn. and Welfare, USPHS, 1967-73. Mem. Nassau County (N.Y.) Tb Assn., 1967—. Served with AUS, 1943-46. Recipient Outstanding Faculty Mem. of Year award Aesculapius Soc., 1966, 69; USPHS research grantee, 1962-64. Mem. Am. Soc. Med. Technologists, Am. Soc. for Microbiology, Assn. Schs. Allied Health Professions, Blood Bank Assn. N.Y. State, AAUP, AAAS, N.Y. Acad. Scis., Royal Soc. Health, Phi Delta Kappa, K.C. Home: 45 Roxton Rd Plainview NY 11803 Office: CW Post Coll Greenvale NY 11548

LOGUE, JOHN JOSEPH, psychologist; b. Phila., Nov. 16, 1929; s. Edwin J. and Ellen V. (Mallon) L.; B.S., Temple U., 1954, M.Ed., 1958, Ed. D., 1966; m. Evelyn Bortnick, Apr. 24, 1954; 1 dau., Eileen (Mrs. David Handel). Partner, sr. cons. Rohrer, Hibler & Replogle, Phila., 1966—. Active Phila. Zool. Soc. Served with U.S. Army, 1954-56. Licensed psychologist, Pa., N.J., Md., Del. Fellow Royal Soc. of Health; mem. Am. Psychol. Assn. (indsl., orgn., cons. counseling divs.), Internat. Personnel Mgmt. Assn., Am. Soc. Personnel Mgmt., Am. Personnel and Guidance Assn., Am. Acad. Polit. and Social Sci., Newcomen Soc. N. Am. Clubs: Peale. Home: 710 Kenilworth Ave Philadelphia PA 19126 Office: #2 Penn Center Plaza Philadelphia PA 19102

LOGUE, JOSEPH CARL, electronics engr.; b. Phila., Dec. 20, 1920; s. Percival J. and Mathilda (Moser) L.; B.E.E., Cornell U., 1944, M.E.E., 1949; m. Jeanne M. Neubecker, Mar. 28, 1943; children—Raymond, Marilyn, Paul. Instr., then asst. prof. elec. engring. Cornell U., 1944-51; spl. assignment Brookhaven Nat. Lab., 1949-51; with IBM Corp., 1951—, fellow, 1971—. Recipient 5th Level Invention Achievement award IBM Corp., 1975, Outstanding Invention award, 1964. Fellow IEEE (honor roll Computer Soc.); mem. Research Soc. Am., AAAS, Sigma Nu, Eta Kappa Nu, Phi Kappa Phi. Author papers, chpt. in book. Address: 52 Boardman Rd Poughkeepsie NY 12603

LOGUSCH, GEORGE CHRISTOPHER, bus. inst. dir., educator; b. Kaufbueren, Ger., Mar. 22, 1945; s. Omelyan and Kateryna (Meshko) L.; came to U.S., 1949, naturalized, 1955; B.A., Coll. City N.Y., 1968; M.A., N.Y. U., 1971, Ph.D., 1973; m. Diane Byron, Aug. 23, 1969. Asst. prof. L.I. U., 1971-73; asst. prof. Seton Hall U., S. Orange, N.J., 1973-75; asso. prof. Grad. Sch. Bus. Adminstrn. Fordham U., N.Y.C., 1975—, chmn. dept. quantitative methods, 1975—, chmn. dept. bus. econs., 1975—, acting asst. dean, 1976-77, dir. Inst. Internat. Bus., 1975—; dir. internat. confs. on mgmt., 1977, 78; vis. prof. U. Warsaw (Poland), 1976, 77, 78; cons. to dir. N.J. Medicaid Program, 1974—; cons. to dep. com. Human Services, N.J., 1977—; cons. Teletext Corp., N.Y.C., 1977—. Recipient Founders Day award N.Y. U., 1973; recipient numerous grants and fellowships. Mem. Am. Econ. Assn., Acad. Internat. Bus., Ops. Research Soc. Am., Am. Inst. Decision Scis., Inst. Mgmt. Sci., Shevchenko Sci. Soc., Mensa. Co-author: Restructuring the State Mental Hospital System in New Jersey, 1974; co-editor: Comparative Management of Large Scale Organizations, vol. 1, 1978, vol. 2, 1979; translator: Hrushevsky, History of Ukraine, vol. 2, 1978. Home: 340 Flora Ave RD 1 Stanhope NJ 07874

LOH, HSUE-PENG, process engr.; b. Taiwan, Oct. 24, 1937; s. C.B. and F.R. L.; came to U.S., 1965, naturalized, 1975; B.S., Cheng Kong U., Taiwan, 1961; Ph.D., U. R.I., 1973; m. Jenny Sing-Mei Tsai, June 5, 1971; children—Nancy, Sandra. Prodn. supr. Taiwan Fertilizer Co., Taipei, 1962-65; chem. engring. asst. U. R.I., Kingston, 1965-73; project. engr. Exxon Chem. Co., Baton Rouge, 1974-76; sr. process engr. Stauffer Chem. Co., Dobbs Ferry, N.Y., 1976—; vis. asst. prof. chem. engring. Pratt Inst., Bklyn., 1977—. Served with Chinese Army, 1961-62. Registered profl. engr., R.I.; recipient Distinguished Service award Chinese Army, 1962. Mem. Am. Inst. Chem. Engrs., Sigma Xi. Home: 2 Villa Ct Norwood NJ 07648 Office: Livingston Ave Dobbs Ferry NY 10522

LOH, YOKE PENG, neurochemist; b. Singapore, July 27, 1947; s. Poon Lip and Sue Heng (Low) L.; came to U.S., 1970, naturalized, 1977; B.Sc. with honors, U. Coll. (Ireland), 1969; Ph.D., U. Pa., 1973. Vis. scientist NIH, Bethesda, Md., 1973-76, sr. staff scientist, 1977—. NIH fellow, 1971-73. Mem. Brit. Biochem. Soc., Am. Soc. Neurochemistry, Soc. Neurosci., AAAS. Contbr. numerous articles in field to profl. jours. Home: 10500 Grosvenor Pl Apt 705 Rockville MD 20852 Office: NIH Bldg 36 Room 2A 21 Bethesda MD 20014

LOHMAN, KENNETH ELMO, geologist; b. Los Angeles, Sept. 11, 1897; s. Herman F. and Elizabeth Mary (Young) L.; B.S., Calif. Inst. Tech., 1929, M.S., 1931, Ph.D., 1957; m. Mary Kathryn McGee, June 17, 1931. Chemist, Certified Lab. Products, Inc., Glendale, Calif., 1924-31; asst. Calif. Inst. Tech., Pasadena, 1929-30; geologist U.S. Geol. Survey, Washington, 1931-67; research asso. Smithsonian Instn., Washington, 1967—; commr. Am. Com. Stratigraphic Nomenclature, 1955-67, chmn., 1959-61. Recipient Distinguished Service medal U.S. Dept. Interior, 1967. Fellow Geol. Soc. Am., Royal Microscopical Soc., AAAS; mem. Soc. Econ. Paleontologists and Mineralogists (hon.), Am. Geophys. Union, Am. Assn. Petroleum Geologists. Club: Cosmos (Washington). Contbr. articles in field to profl. jours. Home: 3215 Old Dominion Blvd Alexandria VA 22305 Office: Nat Mus Natural History Smithsonian Instn Washington DC 20560

LOHRER, MARGUERITE, former social worker; b. Unionville, Mich.; d. William and Elizabeth (Wills) L.; B.S., Northwestern U., 1940; A.M., U. Chgo. Sch. Social Service Adminstrn., 1954. Med. social worker Am. Nat. Red Cross, Mil. and Naval Welfare-Gardiner Gen. Hosp., Chgo., 1943-46, VA Regional Office, Chgo., 1946, VA Center, Los Angeles, 1946-53, VA Research Hosp., Chgo., 1954-56, Chgo. chpt. Muscular Dystrophy Assn., 1956-58; social service dir. Muscular Dystrophy Assns. Am., N.Y.C., 1958-62; social work cons. N.Y.C. Dept. Health, 1962-64; dir. social service Manhattan Eye, Ear and Throat Hosp., N.Y.C., 1964-78, ret., 1978. Mem. Nat. Assn. Social Workers, Acad. Certified Social Workers, Internat. Soc. Rehab. Disabled, Nat. Conf. Social Welfare, English-Speaking Union, AAUW. Episcopalian. Home: 11 Fifth Ave New York City NY 10003

LOIGMAN, HAROLD, cons. engr.; b. Phila., Jan. 25, 1930; s. Victor and Florence (Paul) L.; B.C.E., U. Pitts., 1951; M.S. in Engring., U. Pa., 1963; m. Harriett Pearl Feldman, Nov. 24, 1951; children—Terry Lyn, Vicki Ann. Supervisory engr. U.S. C.E., Phila., 1955-67; v.p. Valley Forge Labs., Inc., Devon, Pa., 1967-72, Site Engrs., Inc., Cherry Hill, N.J., 1972—; faculty engring. Villanova U., 1967-68, Temple U., Phila., 1977-78. Served with USN, 1951-55, USNR to capt., 1975—. Mem. Nat. Soc. Profl. Engrs., ASCE, Marine Tech. Soc., Soc. Am. Mil. Engrs., Naval Res. Assn., Engrs. Club Phila., Aircraft Owners and Pilots Assn. Republican. Jewish. Home: 150 Lantern Ln King of Prussia PA 19406 Office: 22 Olney Ave Cherry Hill NJ 08003

LOIZES, JAMES, ret. police adminstr., county orgn. adminstr.; b. Nov. 2, 1912; s. Nicholas J. and Catherine (Jarnos) L.; student pub. schs., McKeesport, Pa.; m. Ann Bournos, May 18, 1944; children—James N., Estella Kaye Loizes Lindberg. Profl. boxer, 1928-34; mem. Jimmy Loizes Club, McKeesport, 1933-36; boxing coach YMCA, McKeesport, 1938; with McKeesport Police Dept., 1941-66, chief of police, 1953-66; coordinator of Disaster Preparedness of Allegheny County, Pa., 1969—: Served as 1st sgt., C.E., U.S. Army, World War II; ETO, PTO. Decorated Bronze Star, Silver Star; recipient Outstanding Achievement award Pan Icarian Brotherhood, 1965, Outstanding Contbr. in Boxing award Amvets 1955. Mem. Internat. Assn. Chiefs of Police, Pa. (pres. 1965-66) Western Pa. (pres. 1959-60) chiefs of police assns., Am. Legion, Fraternal Order of Police. Mem. Greek Orthodox Ch. Clubs: Elks, Moose, Eagles. Address: 1305 Meadow St McKeesport PA 15132

LOKES, JOHN, JR., engring. co. exec.; b. Chgo., Mar. 17, 1926; s. John and Mary (Hopak) L.; B.S., Chgo. Tech. Coll., 1953; m. July 6, 1950; children—Richard, Marylu, Georgianna, David. Sales, estimating, engring. cons., field and shop supervision McKeown Bros. Co., Chgo. and Denver, 1949-58; task force discipline leader Stearns-Roger, Pitts., 1958-64; discipline leader Rust Engring. Co., Pitts., 1964-67; asst. civil/structural dept. mgr. Holley, Kenney, Shott, Pitts., 1967-70; mgr. civil/structural dept. Salvucci Engrs. Inc., Pitts., 1970—. Trustee Village of Hickory Hills (Ill.) Village Bd., 1954-58, pres. pro tempore, 1954-58. Served with USNR, 1944-46; PTO. Registered profl. engr., Colo., Pa. Mem. Am. Inst. Steel Constrn., Assn. Iron and Steel, Assn. Bridge Constrn. and Design. Russian Orthodox. Clubs: Am. Legion, V.F.W. Home: 1600 Knights Dr Apt 352 Library PA 15129 Office: Salvucci Engrs Inc 327 5th Ave Pittsburgh PA 15222

LOLIS, KATHLEEN, psychologist; b. Bklyn., Mar. 11, 1923; d. Michael John and Esther (Burdett) Lolis; student St. Lawrence U., 1942, U. Conn., 1943; B.S., Columbia U., 1944, M.A., 1945; Ph.D., N.Y. U., 1962. Extern in psychology Neurol. Inst., Columbia-Presbyn. Med. Center, N.Y.C., 1945-46; sch. psychologist N.Y.C. Bd. Edn., 1946-65, research psychologist, 1965—; attending staff psychologist Bklyn. Hosp., 1949-62; pvt. practice clin. psychology, Bklyn., 1950—; instr. U. Bridgeport (Conn.), 1947, N.Y.C. Community Coll., 1964; adj. asso. prof. L.I. U., 1965; vis. prof. Coll. City N.Y., summer 1966; lectr. in psychology Grad. Sch. Edn., N.Y.U., summer 1967, Grad. Sch., Bklyn. Coll., 1968-71; adj. asso. prof. Queens Coll., 1967-76. Dir. Fed. Project to Evaluate Method Sch.-to-Home Telephone Instrn. Physically Handicapped, Homebound Adolescents, 1965-68. Founder, mng. dir. Clinton Hill Symphony Orch., 1951-54; acting dir. Emmanuel Christian Center, summer 1955. Fullbright fellow, 1955-56. Fellow Am. Orthopsychiat. Assn. (hon.); mem. Am. Psychol. Assn., N.Y. Assn. Clin. Psychologists, Assn. Psychologists in N.Y.C. Pub. Schs. (corr. sec. 1950-55), Am. English Cocker Spaniel Club, London (England) Cocker Spaniel Soc. Republican. Congregationalist. Contbr. articles to profl. jours. Home: 75 Henry St Brooklyn NY 11201 Office: 65 Court St 8th Floor Brooklyn NY 11201

LOMBARD, DAVID BISHOP, physicist; b. Lexington, Mass., June 10, 1930; s. Harold Freeman and Helen Elizabeth (Fowler) L.; B.S., Northeastern U., 1953; M.S., Pa. State U., 1955, Ph.D., 1959; m. Josephine Brown Cooper, June 14, 1952; children—Suzanne M., Jonathan D., Robin J., Patricia D., Katherine A. Sr. physicist Lawrence Livermore (Calif.) Lab., 1959-70; div. mgr. Atcor, Inc., Arvada, Colo., 1970-71; pres. Geo-Resource Assos., Arvada, Colo., 1971-72; v.p. Subcom Inc., Arlington, Va., 1972-74; program mgr. NSF, Washington, 1974; br. chief ERDA, Washington, 1975-77, Dept. Energy, 1977—. Bd. dirs. Twin Valley Assn. Retarded Citizens, Livermore, 1959-70, pres., 1961-63, 65-67. Mem. Am. Phys. Soc., Am. Nuclear Soc., Soc. Petroleum Engrs., Calif. Congress Parents and Tchrs. (hon. life), Sigma Xi. Republican. Episcopalian. Contbr. articles to profl. publs.; patentee in field. Home: 6640 Hazel Ln McLean VA 22101 Office: 20 Massachusetts Ave Washington DC 20545

LOMBARD, DONALD RICHARD, psychiatrist; b. Caribou, Maine, Feb. 3, 1932; s. Graydon Earl and Ada Margaret (Phillips) L.; B.A., U. Maine, 1953; M.D., Boston U., 1958; m. Anne Leighton Sanborn, Sept. 1, 1958; children—Karen, Pamela. Intern, Highland Hosp., Rochester, N.Y., 1958-59; resident in psychiatry U. Rochester-Strong Meml. Hosp., 1962-65; chmn. Conn. Regional Mental Health Council, Danbury, 1965-70; individual practice medicine specializing in psychiatry, Danbury, 1965-70; dir. Diamond Head Mental Health Center, Honolulu, 1970-75; chmn. exec. bd. Hawaii Mental Health Div., Honolulu, 1972-74; dir. psychiat. out-patient dept. Bay State Med. Center, Springfield, Mass., 1975—; faculty U. Rochester, 1962-65, U. Hawaii, 1970-75, U. Mass., also Tufts U., 1975—; cons. in field. Served to capt., M.C., USAF, 1960-62; Germany. USPHS fellow psychiatry 1962-65. Diplomate Am. Bd. Psychiatry and Neurology. Mem. Am. Psychiat. Assn., Mass. Psychiat. Soc. (treas.), Biofeedback Soc. Am., Soc. Psychol. Study Social Issues, Physicians for Social Responsibility. Home: 85 Woodlawn Ave Northampton MA 01060 Office: Bay State Med Center 759 Chestnut St Springfield MA 01107

LOMBARDI, ANTHONY MICHAEL, JR., hosp. exec.; b. Newark, May 27, 1938; s. Anthony Michael and Florence (Pecoraro) L.; B.S. (Victor Jacoby scholar), Fairleigh Dickinson U., 1960; M.B.A., George Washington U., 1963; m. Barbara Eileen Sarra, Oct. 14, 1967; 1 dau., Rebecca Jane. Dir. food services Columbus Hosp., Newark, 1960-61; adminstrv. resident Chgo. Wesley Meml. Hosp., 1962-63; mem. adminstrv. staff Charleroi-Monessen Hosp., North Charleroi, Pa., 1963-72, adminstr., 1967-70, exec. dir., 1970-72; exec. dir. Meml. Hosp. of Monongahela (Pa.), 1970-72; exec. dir. Monongahela Valley Hosp., North Charleroi, 1972—. Bd. dirs. Monongahela Valley Hosp. Inc., Hosp. Utilization Project, Pa. League Nurses, Washington County (Pa.) Tb and Respiratory Disease Assn., Monongahela Valley Health and Welfare Council. Served with U.S. Army NG, 1960-63, USAR, 1963-66. Recipient Outstanding Achievement award for Men, Washington County unit Am. Cancer Soc., 1974. Fellow Am., Pa. pub. health assns.; mem. Am. Coll. Hosp. Adminstrs., Am. Hosp. Assn., Hosp. Assn. Pa. (dir.), Hosp. Council Western Pa. (chmn. human resources com. 1976-77, dir.) Roman Catholic. Club: Lions. Guest author: Hosp. Vol. Handbook, 1971. Home: 78 Crestline Dr Craven Hill Charleroi PA 15022 Office: 7th St and Lincoln Ave North Charleroi PA 15022

LOMBARDI, ARTHUR VINCENT, dentist; b. New Castle, Pa., Nov. 23, 1938; s. Domenic and Anna (Matteo) L.; D.M.D. cum laude, U. Pitts., 1962; A.M., Harvard U., 1968, Ph.D., 1973; orthodontic fellow Forsyth Dental Center, Boston, 1965-67; m. Reiko Uehara, Mar. 6, 1965. Teaching fellow Harvard U., 1968; asso. prof. orthodontics U. Pacific, San Francisco, 1969-70; mem. Harvard U. Biomed. Expedition to Bougainville, 1970; clin. scholar oral biology Harvard, 1971; pvt. practice dentistry specializing in orthodontics, New Castle, 1972—; lectr. U. Oreg., 1972; U. Pa., 1975; Westminster Coll., 1976. Licensed dentist, Pa., Calif., Mass. Mem. Am. Assn. Orthodontists, Am. Assn. Physical Anthropologists, ADA, Soc. Med. Anthopologists. Contbr. articles in fields to profl. jours. Office: 2602 Wilmington Rd New Castle PA 16105

LOMBARDO, DAVID DOMENIC, govt. ofcl.; b. Reading, Pa., Nov. 20, 1939; s. Anthony D. and Mary A. (Piscitello) L.; B.A., Albright Coll., 1961; M.A., N.Y. U., 1964, Ph.D., 1978; m. Maryann Widnick, July 12, 1969; children—Michelle Ann, David Anthony. Adminstrv. officer Library of Congress, Washington, 1966-67; mgmt. intern AEC, N.Y.C., 1967-68, personnel asst., 1968, indsl. relations specialist, 1968-71; chief, employee relations sect. Social Security Adminstrn. U.S. Dept. Health, Edn., Welfare, N.Y.C., 1971-73, chief personnel br., 1973-77; chief recruitment and placement office Library of Congress, Washington, 1977—. Served with U.S. Army, 1963-65. Mem. Am. Soc. for Pub. Adminstrn., Indsl. Relations Research Assn., Internat. Personnel Mgmt. Assn., Soc. Fed. Labor Relations Profls. Home: 1741 Tarrytown Ave Crofton MD 21114 Office: Library of Congress Washington DC 20540

LOMBARDO, PIO STEPHEN, environ. engring. co. exec.; b. Winthrop, Mass., Aug. 22, 1947; s. Salvatore and Anna Marie (DiGregorio) L.; B.S., Chem. Engring., U. Mass., 1969; M.S., Civil Engring., U. Wash., 1971. Water quality analyst Hydrocomp Inc., Palo Alto, Calif., 1971-73; lead scientist water resources Environ. Research & Tech. Co., Concord, Mass., 1973-74; supv. environ. engr. R.W. Beck & Assocs., Wellesley, Mass., 1974-75; project mgr. Anderson-Nichols Co., Boston, 1975-77; pres. Pio Lombardo & Assocs., Boston, 1977—. Mem. Claremont Park Assn., 1976. Recipient Am. Inst. Chem. Engrs. Profl. Devel. award, 1968; EPA traineeship, 1969-71. Mem. Water Pollution Control Fedn., Am. Soc. Civil Engrs., Charles River Watershed Assn., Tau Beta Pi. Home: 24 Greenwich Pk Boston MA 02118 Office: 90 Canal St Boston MA 02114

LOMNITZ, ESTEBAN RAFAEL LOMNITZ, cardiologist; b. Santiago, Chile, Aug. 4, 1938; s. Kurt J. and Helene (Davies) L.; came to U.S., 1970; M.D., U. Chile, 1962; m. Eliana Suttmann, Jan. 4, 1964; children—Karen, David. Intern, Hosp. del Salvadore, U. Chile, Santiago, 1962, resident in internal medicine, 1963-68; fellow cardiology Case Western Res. U., 1970-71; fellow cardiology N.Y. Med. Coll., 1971-73, asst. prof. medicine, 1973—; clin. asso. prof. medicine Rutgers U., 1977—; chief sect. cardiology B.S. Coles Hosp., N.Y.C., 1973-74; asso. dir. cardiac labs. Muhlenberg Hosp., Plainfield, N.J., 1974—; pvt. practice cons. in cardiovascular diseases, Plainfield, 1974—. Served with Chilean Navy Reserve, 1958. Diplomate Am. Bd. Internal Medicine, Am. Bd. Cardiovascular Disease. Fellow ACP, Am. Coll. Cardiology; mem. Chilean Med. Soc., Chilean Cardiology Soc., N.J. Heart Assn. N.J., Union County med. socs. Jewish. Home: 125 Lansdowne Ave Westfield NJ 07090 Office: 157 E 7th St Plainfield NJ 07060

LONDON, ALLEN JAY, advt. agy. exec.; b. Orange, N.J., May 19, 1927; s. Nathan and Ethel Ameilia (Goldsmith) L.; student Upsala Coll., 1947-48; B.S. in Marketing, N.Y. U., 1949; m. Elaine Rose, June 17, 1950; children—Charles, Sally, David. Mgr. prodn., traffic London Advt. Agy., East Orange, N.J., 1949-70, account exec., 1949-70, office mgr., 1965-70; pres. Allen London Advt., East Orange, 1970-73, West Caldwell, N.J., 1973—; owner C.S.D. Printing Co., 1975—. Mem. adv. bd. Yorkwood Savs. and Loan Assn., West Caldwell, 1973-74. Pres. Camp Wyanokie Commn., West Caldwell, 1973, Air Force Acad. Parents Assn. N.J., 1973-74; scoutmaster Grover Cleveland dist. Boy Scouts Am., 1952-54, cub master, 1963-65, mem. dist. com., 1970—. City councilman, West Caldwell, 1967-75, council pres., 1971-75; mem. Planning Bd., West Caldwell, 1963-66, 1974-75; mem. Bd. Health, West Caldwell, 1967-70; mem. West Essex First Aid Squad, 1976—, sec., 1978—. Served with USAAF, 1945-46. Jewish religion (trustee Congregation Agudath Israel 1952-54). Mason. Home: 1 Knoll Terr West Caldwell NJ 07006 Office: 1088 Bloomfield Ave West Caldwell NJ 07006

LONDON, GENE, TV show host; b. Cleve., June 9, 1931; s. Isadore and Minna (Scott) Yulish; student U. Miami, 1950-51. Radio actor soap operas and Let's Pretend, 1951-52, Johnny Jupiter, ABC-TV, 1953-54; host Tinker's Workshop, WABC-TV, 1955-56, Gene London Shows, WCAU-TV, CBS, Phila., 1957—; instr. New Sch. Social Research, N.Y.C.; cons. Phila. Bd. Edn.; lectr. Disney films, Mus. Modern Art, others. Bd. dirs. Goodwill Industries. Recipient Emmy award, 1956, citation White House, 1967, Freedoms Found. award, 1960, award Clin. Psychologists Assn., 1968, award State of Ohio, 1962. Mem. AFTRA. Host of longest running local children's TV show in the world. Home: 815 Hillton Ln Elkins Park PA 19117 Office: Gene London Inc 10 Gramercy Park S New York City NY 10003

LONDON, MARK STANLEY, TV exec.; b. Paterson, N.J., Jan. 9, 1939; s. Ben and Lillian Rose (Lebkes) L.; M.A., Seton Hall U., 1968; m. Marcia Resnick, Dec. 20, 1959; children—Brian, Michael. Radio and TV announcer, disc jockey, various stas., 1957-73; dir. broadcasting Hanover Park Regional High Sch. Dist., Hanover, N.J., 1967-73; asst. gen. mgr. UA-Columbia Cablevision, Oakland, N.J., 1973-74; dir. devel. and pub. info. N.J. Pub. TV Network, Trenton, 1975—. Chmn., Pompton Lakes Recreation Commn., 1976—; founder, pres. Pompton Lakes Soccer Assn., 1976—. Home: 86 Albany Ave Pompton Lakes NJ 07442 Office: 1573 Parkside Ave Trenton NJ 08638

LONDON, S(OL) J., physician; b. N.Y.C., Oct. 15, 1917; s. Morris and Ida (Cantor) L.; B.A., U. Louisville, 1937, M.D., 1941; m. Estelle Steinfeld, Feb. 19, 1943; children—Nancy London Stein, Robert K. Rotating intern Coney Island Hosp., Bklyn., 1941-43; resident Sea View Hosp., S.I., N.Y., 1946-47, Halloran VA Hosp., S.I., 1947-48; practice medicine specializing in metabolic diseases, Bklyn. and Detroit, 1949-58; med. dir., v.p. Purdue Frederick Co., N.Y.C., 1958-62, M.R. Thompson, Inc., N.Y.C., 1962-64; med. dir. Vick Divs. Research, Mt. Vernon, N.Y., 1964—. Lectr. gastroenterology N.Y. Polyclinic Hosp. and Med. Sch., 1958-63. Served to capt. M.C., AUS, 1943-46; ETO. Diplomate Am. Bd. Internal Medicine. Mem. Am. Soc. for Clin. Pharmacology and Therapeutics, Am. Med. Writers Assn., Am. Acad. Clin. Toxicology, Am. Musicol. Soc., Am. Thoracic Soc., Am. Inst. Verdi Studies, Am. Inst. Archeology. Democrat. Jewish. Contbr. articles on medicine and music to profl. jours., music mags. Research in diabetes, atherosclerosis, peptic ulcer, physiology and pharmacology of cough, music therapy. Home: 85-28 215th St Hollis Hills NY 11427 Office: 1 Bradford Rd Mount Vernon NY 10853

LONDON-PERSON, SHARON DONNA, psychologist, clin. adminstr.; b. Bklyn., Apr. 22, 1939; d. Harry Morris and Edythe Bander (Pollack) London; B.A., cum laude, Bklyn. Coll., 1960; M.A., City U. N.Y., 1962, Ph.D., 1969; m. Alexander D. Person, July 3, 1977. Jr. research psychologist psychopharmacology research unit Downstate Med. Center State U. N.Y., 1961-65; psychologist N.Y.C. Dept. Social Services, 1966-72; staff psychotherapist Mental Health Consultation Center, N.Y.C., 1968-75; pvt. practice psychotherapy, N.Y.C., 1970—; supr. Met. Center Mental Health, N.Y.C., 1976—. Mem. Am. Psychol. Assn., Assn. Practicing Psychotherapists (co-dir. 1973—). Home and Office: 204 W 17th St New York City NY 10011 also 30 Stillwater Dr Pocono Summit PA 18346

LONEY, CAROLYN PATRICIA, bank ofcl.; b. N.Y.C., June 16, 1944; d. Daniel and Edna Louise (Williams) L.; B.S., Morgan (Md.) State Coll., 1969; M.B.A., Columbia, 1971. Research worker N.Y. Senate, N.Y.C., 1967; field auditor Human Resources Adminstrn., 1966, 67; rater and coder auto policies Royal Globe Ins. Co., N.Y.C., 1962-65; br. mgr. NAACP, N.Y.C., 1965; corporate lending officer Citibank, N.A., N.Y.C., 1971-77, asst. v.p., 1978—; spl. asst. bank supervision and regulations function Fed. Res. Bank of N.Y., 1977-78; cons. Interracial Council Bus. Opportunities; instr. cons. Nat. Puerto Rican Forum; lectr. adult bus. edn. N.Y. Community Coll. Named Outstanding Instr. of Year, Interracial Council Bus. Opportunities, 1974. Mem. Nat. Bankers Assn., Nat. Assn. Accountants, Urban Bankers Coalition, Nat. Credit and Fin. Women's Orgn., Harlem YWCA. Democrat. Baptist. Home: 122 Belmont St Englewood NJ 07631

LONG, ANTON VANDERFORD, educator; b. Pitts., June 11, 1914; s. Haniel Clark and Alice Lavinia (Knoblauch) L.; B.A., U. N.Mex., 1947, M.A., 1949; B.Litt., Oxford U., 1952; m. Leslie V. Murphey, Apr. 12, 1946 (dec. Sept. 1959); 1 son, Franklin Hunt; m. 2d, Helen A. C. Long, June 4, 1960. With U.S.P.O. Santa Fe, 1936-37; clk., asst. mgr. Camfield Hotel, Mpls., 1937-40; instr. N.Mex. Inst. Mining and Tech., 1947-49; tchr., bursar Priory Sch., Halfway Tree, Jamaica, W.I., 1952-59; lectr. U. Coll. W.I., 1954-57; self-employed Naples, N.Y., 1960—. Mem., Village Naples Pub. Relations Commn., 1961-63. Chmn. bd. trustees Naples Pub. Library, 1962-74; trustee Ont. Coop. Library System, 1962-70. Pres. Rose Ridge Cemetery Corp., 1965-73; bd. dirs. Naples Council Chs., 1967—. Served with AUS, 1942-45. Named Citizen of Yr., City of Naples, 1977. Mem. Phi Kappa Phi. Methodist. Rotarian. Author: Jamaica and The New Order 1827-1847, 1956; compiler Legacy from Haniel Long, 1977; editor: Poems of Alice Lavinia Long, 1967. Donor West Hill Preserve to Nature Conservancy, 1975. Home: RFD 1 Box 203 Naples NY 14512

LONG, CHARLES ROBERT MARK, librarian; b. Long Beach, Calif., Sept. 20, 1936; s. Charles Henry and Virginia Clare (Black) L.; B.A., U. Toronto, 1959; M.A., U. Mass., 1961; S.M. in L.S., Simmons Coll., 1968; m. Marie Frances Giacoppe, Jan. 28, 1962; children—Katherine S.F., Nathaniel R.M., Matthew D.J. Asst. dir. Nashua (N.H.) Pub. Library, 1968-69; librarian Gray Herbarium and Arnold Arboretum of Harvard, 1969-72; adminstrv. librarian Library N.Y. Bot. Garden, 1972—, dir. library and plant info. services, 1978—; collection cons. Lyon Arboretum, Hawaii, 1975, 77, Boyce Thompson Inst., Yonkers, N.Y., 1978. Library bldg. cons. Framingham (Mass.) Pub. Library, 1971-72. Club: Grolier. Home: 43 Dutch St Montrose NY 10548 Office: NY Bot Garden 200th St and Southern Blvd Bronx NY 10458

LONG, CLARENCE D(ICKINSON), JR., congressman; b. South Bend, Ind., Dec. 11, 1908; s. Clarence Dickinson and Gertrude (Cooper) L.; A.B., Washington and Jefferson Coll., Washington, Pa., 1932, A.M., 1933; A.M., Princeton, 1935, Ph.D., 1938; m. Susanna Larter, Dec. 20, 1937; children—Clarence Dickinson III, Susanna Elizabeth (Mrs. Philip Moore). Fellow Washington and Jefferson Coll., 1932-33; Sanxay fellow, Princeton, 1935-36; fellow John Simon Guggenheim Meml. Found., 1941-43; instr. Wesleyan U., Conn., 1936-39, asst. prof., 1940-41, asso. prof., 1941-45; asso. prof. Johns Hopkins, 1946, prof., 1947-64. Sr. labor specialist W.P.B., 1942; mem. research staff Nat. Bur. Econ. Research, 1946-56; mem. Sr. staff Pres. Eisenhower's Council Econ. Advisers, 1953-54, cons., 1954-57; mem. 88th-96th Congresses from 2d dist. Md. Mem. Inst. for Advanced Study, Princeton, 1941-46, 48; trustee Washington and Jefferson Coll. Served as lt. USNR, 1943-46. Fellow AAAS; mem. Am. Econ. Assn., Am. Statis. Assn., Econometric Soc., Acad. Polit. Sci., Phi Beta Kappa, Alpha Tau Omega. Presbyterian. Clubs: L'Hirondelle, 14 West Hamilton Street (Balt.). Author: Building Cycles and the Theory of Investment, 1940; The Labor Force in Wartime America, 1944. Co-author (with Frederick C. Mills) Task Force Report on Statistical Agencies, Appendix D. (Commn. on Orgn. of Exec. Branch of the Govt.); The Statistical Agencies of the Federal Government (Nat. Bur. Econ. Research), 1949; The Labor Force in War and Transition, 1952; The Labor Force Under Changing Income and Employment, 1958; Wages and Earnings in the United States, 1860-1960, 1960. Contbr. articles to bus. and econ. publs. Home: 1015 Boyce Ave Ruxton MD 21204 Office: House Office Bldg Washington DC 20515

LONG, HARRY (ENG ON-YUEN), rubber co. exec.; b. Passaic, N.J., June 22, 1932; s. Eng Yick and Yue York (Ng) L.; B.S., N.J. Inst. Tech., 1959; m. Linda Lai-king Yu, Sept. 18, 1960; 1 son, Steven (Eng Park-ning). With Uniroyal Inc., Passaic, 1959-71, asst. devel. engr., belts and splty. products, 1959-62, devel. engr., 1962-67, sr. process engr. hose and expansion joints, 1967-71; chief devel. engr. hose products Raybestos/Manhattan Inc., Passaic, 1971-72; chief chemist Goodall Rubber Co., Trenton, N.J., 1972-76, tech. mgr., 1976—. Mem. Am. Chem. Soc., Phila. Rubber Group, ASTM, AAAS. Office: 572 Whitehead Rd Trenton NJ 08650

LONG, LARRY HOWARD, demographer; b. Lockhart, Tex., Oct. 15, 1943; s. G. A. and Olive Grace (DeViney) L.; B.A. U., Tex., 1966, M.A., 1968, Ph.D., 1969. Postdoctoral fellow U. Pa., 1969-70; chief Population Analysis Staff, U.S. Bur. Census, Washington, 1970—. Mem. Am. Internat. sociol. assns., Am. Statis. Assn., Population Assn. Am., Internat. Union for Sci. Study of Population, AAAS. Home: 258 G St SW Washington DC 20024 Office: Population Div US Bur Census Washington DC 20233

LONG, LESLIE BRUCE, mfg. co. exec.; b. Louisville, Mar. 26, 1929; s. Leslie and Rebecca Cornell (Jones) L.; B.S.E.E., U. Louisville, 1952; postgrad. Northeastern U., 1952-54, Pace U., 1977; m. Mary Louise Rompf, June 5, 1952; children—Ellen Lynne, L. Bruce, Holly Haydon. Program mgr. Bendix Corp., Towson, Md., 1952-58, program mgr. Raytheon Co., Wayland, Mass., 1958-67; dir. research Emerson Electric Co., St. Louis, 1967-68; dir. engring., asst. div. gen. mgr. Sanders Assos., Bedford, Mass., 1968-71; asst. tech. dir. mil. electronics ITT World Hdqrs., N.Y.C., 1971—; Pres. bd. dirs. Lincoln (Mass.) Community Chest, 1960-67; bd. dirs. Middlesex Mental Health Assn., Concord, Mass., 1964-67. Mem. Assn. U.S. Army, Am. Def. Preparedness Assn., Assn. Old Crows, IEEE. Republican. Episcopalian. Patentee 3D radar. Home: 48 Greenlea Ln Weston CT 06883 Office: 320 Park Ave New York City NY 10022

LONG, PAUL, news broadcaster; b. Winnsboro, Tex., Jan. 28, 1916; s. Lucian P. and Nannie E. (Morris) L.; student N. Tex. State Tchrs. Coll., 1932-34; m. Elaine Kinder, Aug. 21, 1974; children—Holly Long Shefler, Christopher Warren. Free lance radio actor, Dallas, 1936-37; various positions, N.Y.C., 1938-40; news and sports broadcaster radio stas., KFRO, Longview, Tex., 1940, KELD, El Dorado, Ark., 1941, KWKH, Shreveport, La., 1946; news broadcaster radio sta. KDKA, Pitts., 1946-68; news anchor man sta. WTAE-TV, Pitts., 1968—. Campaign chmn. Western Pa. Heart Assn., 1971-73, now pres.; mem. zoning bd. Greater Pitts. Internat. Airport, 1972-76; bd. dirs. Big Bros. and Sisters of Allegheny County, Pitts. chpt. Am. Cancer Soc. Served to capt. USAAF, 1942-46. Recipient Sigma Delta Chi Public award, 1963, Outstanding TV News Broadcaster award 1967, 70, 71, Printers Devil award Theta Sigma Phi, 1971; named Man of Yr. in Communications, Pitts. Jaycees, 1970. Clubs: Pittsburgh Press; Aero; Fellows; Chartiers Country. Home: 223 Tech Rd Pittsburgh PA 15205 Office: 400 Ardmore Blvd Pittsburgh PA 15230

LONG, ROBERT EDWARD, x-ray sales engr.; b. Cin., Apr. 8, 1918; s. Lawrence F. and Bessie M. (Marksberry) L.; ed. high sch.; m. Jean Salicandro, Dec. 18, 1946; children—Lawrence A., Jennifer M., Andria R. Enlisted USN, 1940, advanced to chief petty officer, 1945, served in S. Am., Europe, Africa, Asia, ret. 1959; service-sales engr. Gen. Electric Med. Systems, Phila., 1959-66; sr. adviser to minister of health Govt. S. Vietnam, 1966-70; fgn. service officer U.S. Dept. State, S. Vietnam, 1966-70; sr. sales engr. Gen. Electric Med. Systems, Phila., 1970—; x-ray cons., 1978—. Certified sr. elec. engring. technologist Inst. Certification Engring. Technologists, Nat. Soc. Profl. Engrs. Mem. ASCE, Fleet Res. Assn., Am., So. Jersey (asso.) socs. hosp. engrs., Am. Soc. Planning Ofcls., Assn. Advancement Med. Instrumentation, 1st Marine Div. Assn. Clubs: Rotary, Masons. Home and Office: 21-23 Union St Medford NJ 08055

LONGAKER, RICHARD PANCOAST, coll. provost, educator; b. Phila., July 1, 1924; s. Edwin P. and Emily (Downs) L.; B.A. in Polit. Sci., Swarthmore Coll., 1949; M.A. in Am. History, U. Wis., 1950; Ph.D. in Govt., Cornell U., 1953; m. Mollie M. Katz, Jan. 25, 1964; children—Richard Pancoast, Stephen Edwin, Sarah Ellen, Rachel Elise. Teaching asst. Cornell U., 1950-53, vis. asso. prof., 1960-61; asst. prof. Kenyon Coll., 1953-54, asso. prof., 1955-60; asst. prof. U. Calif. at Riverside, 1954-55; mem. faculty U. Calif. at Los Angeles, 1961-78, chmn. dept. polit. sci., 1963-67, prof., 1965-78; provost Johns Hopkins U., Balt., 1978—; cons. U.S. Office Edn., 1965—, Calif. Bd. Edn., 1966—. Exec. com. Law in a Free Soc., State Bar Calif. Served with AUS, 1943-45. Mem. Am. Polit. Sci. Assn. Author: Presidency and Individual Liberties, 1961; also articles, revs. Office: Office of Provost Johns Hopkins U Garland Hill Baltimore MD 21218

LONGBRAKE, WILLIAM ARTHUR, govt. economist; b. Hershey, Pa., Mar. 15, 1943; s. William Van Fleet and Margaret Jane (Barr) L.; B.A., Coll. Wooster, 1965; M.A., U. Wis., 1968, M.B.A., 1969; D.B.A., U. Md., 1976; m. Martha Ann Curtis, Aug. 23, 1970; children—Derek Curtis, Mark William. Jr. asst. planner Northeastern Ill. Planning Commn., Chgo., 1966; instr. Coll. Bus. and Mgmt., U. Md., 1969-71, lectr., 1976; financial economist Fed. Deposit Ins. Corp., Washington, 1971-75, sr. planning specialist Office Corp. Planning, 1975-76; asso. dir. div. banking research Office Comptroller of Currency, Treasury Dept., Washington, 1976, dep. dir. econ. research and analysis div., 1976-77; spl. asst. to chmn., acting controller FDIC, Washington, 1977-78; dep. comptroller for research and econ. programs Office Comptroller of Currency, Washington, 1978—; small bus. cons. Mem. College Park (Md.) Citizen's Adv. Com. on Code Enforcement, 1973-74, cons., 1975. Recipient Kenneth E. Trefftz prize Western Finance Assn., 1971, certificate of recognition William A. Jump Meml. Found., 1978. Mem. Am., So. econ. assns., Am., Eastern finance assns., Financial Mgmt. Assn. (dir.), Coll. of Wooster Alumni Assn. (pres. Washington chpt. 1976). Presbyn. (trustee 1973-75, chmn. 1975, elder). Asso. editor Financial Mgmt. Contbr. articles to profl. jours.; mem. editorial adv. bd. Issues in Bank Regulation. Home: 5901 Bryn Mawr Rd College Park MD 20740 Office: 490 L'enfant Plaza E Washington DC 20429

LONGLEY, JAMES WILDON, economist, mathematician; b. San Saba, Tex., Oct. 29, 1913; s. Leon and Emily Arementi (Patton) L.; B.A., Tex. Agrl. and Mech. U., 1936, M.S., 1937; M.A., Harvard U., 1946, Ph.D., 1947; m. Letitia Jane Robinson, Jan. 19, 1961; 1 son, Roger Wayne. Economists, numerical analyst Bur. Labor Statistics, U.S. Dept. Labor, Washington, 1955—. Mem. Econometric Soc., Am. Statis. Assn., Am. Math. Assn., Am. Soc. Quality Control, Soc. Indsl. and Applied Math. Home: 8200 Cedar St Silver Spring MD 20910 Office: Dept Labor 441 G St NW Washington DC 20212

LONGMAN, RICHARD WINSTON, mech. engr., educator; b. Iowa City, Iowa, Sept. 2, 1943; s. Lester Duncan and Florence (Brown) L.; B.A., U. Calif. at Riverside, 1965, M.S., San Diego, 1967, M.A. in Math., Ph.D. in Aerospace Engring., 1969. Cons., Rand Corp., Santa Monica, Calif., 1966-69; mem. tech. staff Bell Telephone Labs., Whippany, N.J., 1969-70; asst. prof. mech. engring. Columbia, 1970-74, asso. prof., 1974—; vis. asso. prof. mech. engring. M.I.T., 1978; aerospace engr. Space Systems div. Naval Research Lab., 1978; Alexander von Humboldt fellow, W. Ger., 1977; cons. Xerox Corp., 1975. NASA-Am. Soc. Engring. Edn. summer faculty fellow NASA Goddard Space Flight Center, 1973-74; NSF Faculty research participant Martin Marietta Corp., 1975. NDEA fellow, 1966-69. Fellow Brit. Interplanetary Soc., Am. Inst. Aeros. and Astronautics (asso.); mem. Instrument Soc. Am. (sr.), ASME, Am. Astronautical Soc. (v.p. publs. 1978—), Sigma Xi, Tau Beta Pi, Pi Mu Epsilon, Pi Tau Sigma. Contbr. articles to profl. publs.; mng. editor Jour. Astronautical Scis. Home: 560 Riverside Dr Apt 2E New York City NY 10027 Office: Dept Mech Engring Columbia New York City NY 10027

LONGO, FRANK WALTER, urologist; b. Stamford, Conn., Jan. 17, 1929; s. Walter S. and Alma T. (Doran) L.; B.S., U. Md., 1951, M.D., 1955; m. Mary Lou Smiek, Mar. 11, 1955; children—Walter E., Frank P., Peter J., Christine M. Intern, New Rochelle (N.Y.) Hosp., 1955-56, resident in surg. and clin. pathology, 1956-57; asst. resident in surgery. Bellevue Med. Center, Beekman Hosp., N.Y.C., 1957-58; resident in urology Presbyn. Hosp., Babies Hosp., Vanderbilt Clinic, N.Y.C., 1958-60, asso. attending urologist 1969; practice medicine specializing in urology, N.Y.C., 1960—; asso. clin. prof. Columbia U., 1969—; chief Vanderbilt Clinic, Columbia Presbyn. Med. Center, 1971—; dir. Charles R. Lachman Cancer Research Lab., Columbia U., 1974—. Mem. Am. Urol. Assn., Internat. Soc. Urology, N.Y. Cancer Soc., N.Y. Acad. Medicine, N.Y. Acad. Sci., Am. Nat. Standards Inst. Roman Catholic. Club: Westchester Country. Contbr. articles to med. jours. Home: 40 Beech Tree Ln Pelham Manor NY 10803 Office: 161 Fort Washington Ave New York City NY 10032

LONGO, LOUIS PAUL, milk mktg. coop. exec.; b. Glastonbury, Conn., Jan. 13, 1922; s. John B. and Josephine R. (Patrucco) L.; student pub. schs., Glastonbury; m. Ruth E. Rodgers, Aug. 24, 1976; children by previous marriage, Louis Paul, Beatrice, Michael, Paul, Margaret, Joan. Dairy farmer, Glastonbury, 1943-79; owner, operator Longo Gravel Sand and Gravel Co., Glastonbury, 1945-60, Minnechaug Farms, Glastonbury, 1946-79; pres., treas. Fairway Landscapers, Inc., Glastonbury, 1949-68; treas. Fargo Corp., magnet mfg. and sales co., Glastonbury, 1957-67; pres. Consol. Milk Producers Assn., Newington, Conn., 1966-71, Yankee Milk, Inc., North Andover, Mass., 1971-79; chmn. Nat. Dairy Council, 1973-75, mem. exec. com., 1975-79; pres. Regional Common Mktg. Agy., 1973-79; mem. farm adv. com. DeLaval Corp.; dir. Glastonbury Bank & Trust Co.; 2d v.p. Vt. Liquers, Inc., Montpelier, Vt.; lectr. on agr., U.S., Can. Mem. Glastonbury Town Planning and Zoning Commn., 1959-68; trustee Manchester (Conn.) Meml. Hosp., 1961-71. Recipient Conn. Top Farm Youth award State of Conn., 1940; Outstanding Young Farmer award Nat. Jaycees, 1957; Distinguished Farm Service award U. Conn., 1968; World Man of Yr. award World Dairy Expn., Madison, Wis., 1972; named Conn. Outstanding Dairyman of Yr., U. Conn., 1966. Mem. United Dairy Industries (dir.), Nat. Milk Producers Fedn. (dir. 1969-79, exec. com. 1974-79), Farm Bur., Nat. Council Farm Coops. Republican. Author: The Pursuit of Profit, 1979; columnist Hoard's Dairyman, 1966-68; inventor Magnetrol Magnet, for prevention hardware disease, 1957. Home: 2760 Hebron Ave Glastonbury CT 06033 Office: 200 Sutton St North Andover MA 01845

LONGO, VIVIAN VITA, banker; b. Bklyn., June 19, 1952; s. Salvatore Jerome and Paula Teresa (DiBitose) L.; B.A. summa cum laude, Fordham U., 1974, M.B.A., 1977. Adminstrv. coordinator student facilities Cornell U. Med. Coll., 1974-76; fin. analyst, then project mgr. Citibank, N.Y.C., 1976, bldg. mgr. Citicorp Center, 1976—; speaker in field. Vol. ct. observer Alliance for Safer N.Y., 1974-74. Mem. AAUP, Assn. Energy Engrs., Assn. M.B.A. Execs., Gen. Fedn. Women's Clubs, Soc. Real Property Adminstrs., Kappa Delta Pi. Club: Women's Press (N.Y.C.). Office: 153 E 53d St New York City NY 10022

LONGOBARDI, ANTHONY PAUL, govt. ofcl.; b. Franklin, Mass., Nov. 1, 1918; s. Domenick and Mary (Palladeno) L.; B.S. in Comml. Edn., Bryant Coll., Providence, 1934; J.D., Suffolk U., Boston, 1952; m. Dorothy Hagerman, Oct. 1, 1961; children—Mark, Mary Ann. With Social Security Adminstrn., 1950—; dist. mgr., Nashua, N.H., 1963-. Pres. Nashua Fedn. Social Agys., 1974; v.p. Nashua Child Care Centers, 1974; chmn. religious formation com., mem. Christian doctrine com., dir. sch. religion, also lector St. Joseph's Roman Catholic Ch., Nashua, 1973; chmn. So. N.H. Legal Services, 1973; dir., sec. Hillsborough (N.H.) Community Action Com., 1967-71; sec.-treas. Franklin (Mass.) Victory Meml. Fund, 1945-75; adv. bd. St. Joseph's Hosp., Nashua, 1975-78; pres. Greater Nashua Human Services Council, 1977-78; chmn. adv. bd. Nashua Salvation Army, 1975; bd. dirs. Gore group Christian Life Center, Nashua, 1972-75, Nashua Boys' Club, 1975. Served with AUS, World War II. Mem. Am. Legion, Nashua Indsl. Mgmt. Club, Grange (past master). Clubs: K.C., Lions (past officer), Antique (Nashua). Home: 57 Lawndale Ave Nashua NH 03060 Office: 6 W Hollis St Nashua NH 03061

LONGOBARDO, ANNA KAZANJIAN, aerospace engr., mil. systems equipment co. exec.; b. N.Y.C., Jan. 8, 1928; d. Aram Michael and Zarouhy (Yazejian) Kazanjian; student Barnard Coll., 1945-47; B.S. in Mech. Engring., Columbia U., 1949, M.S., 1952; m. Guy Longobardo, July 12, 1952; children—Guy, Alicia. Sr. systems engr. Am. Bosch Arma Corp., Garden City, N.Y., 1950-65; research sect. head computer devel. dept. Sperry Rand Corp., Great Neck, N.Y., 1965-68, project mgr. air force nuclear radiation resistant equipment, 1966-68, project mgr. devel. studies of computer equipment, 1968-73, research sect. head traffic safety sect., 1970-73, mgr. engring. personnel utilization, 1973-77, mgr. program planning, 1977—; cons. on consumer protection to N.Y. State Legislature, 1966-70. Mem. N.Y. State Revenue Sharing Com., 1971-75, N.Y. State Women's Council, 1963-75. Named Woman of Yr., Salute to Women in Industry and Professions, 1964. Mem. ASME (profl. com. met. sect. 1966-69), Soc. Wbmen Engrs. (chmn. N.Y. sect. 1965-66), Am. Inst. Aeros. and Astronautics, Tech. Socs. Council of N.Y. (dir. 1966-70), Columbia Engring. Sch. Alumni Assn. (pres. 1977—). Club: Zonta. Author: (with others) Marks Mechanical Engineering Handbook, 1978; contbr. articles on systems engring. to profl. publs. Home: 15 Crows Nest Rd Bronxville NY 10708 Office: Sperry Rand Corp Great Neck NY 11020

LONGSTRETH, H(OWARD) PAUL, physician; b. Pitts., June 30, 1920; s. Willis L. and Ethel O. (Aid) L.; M.D., U. Buffalo, 1945; m. Nancy Ferguson, June 23, 1945; children—Paul Scott, Allen Lee. Intern, Allegheny Gen. Hosp., Pitts., 1945-46; resident E.J. Meyer Meml. Hosp., Buffalo, 1946-50; practice medicine, specializing in internal medicine and chest diseases, Buffalo, 1950—; asst. clin. prof. medicine U. Buffalo Med. Sch., 1957-71, clin. asso. prof., 1971—, asst. dean, 1957-59. Served to maj. M.C., AUS, 1954-56. Diplomate Am. Bd. Internal Medicine. Fellow A.C.P., Am. Coll. Chest Physicians; mem. U. Buffalo Sch. Medicine Alumni Assn (pres.), Buffalo Acad. Medicine (pres.). Home: 684 LeBrun Rd Eggertsville NY 14226 Office: 2900 Main St Buffalo NY 14214

LONKY, MARTIN LEONARD, elec. mfg. co. mgr.; b. N.Y.C., Jan. 5, 1944; s. Hyman and Irene (Feldman) L.; B.S. in Physics, Rensselaer Poly. Inst., 1964; M.S., U. Del., 1967, Ph.D., 1972; m. Merle Roberta Greenberg, Dec. 18, 1966. Teaching fellow U. Del., Newark, 1970-72; presdl. intern Land Warfare Lab., Aberdeen, Md., 1972, ops. research analyst, 1973; fellow engr. Westinghouse Electric Corp., Balt., 1975-78, supervisory engr., 1978—. Mem. Electrochem. Soc., IEEE, Am. Phys. Soc. Clubs: Mt. Scopus Lodge, Masons. Contbr. articles to profl. jours. Patentee in field. Home: 3762 Twin Lakes Ct Baltimore MD 21207 Office: Westinghouse Electric Corp PO Box 1521 Baltimore MD 21203

LONTO, BENJAMIN PHILIP, hosp. adminstr.; b. Vernon, B.C., Can., Sept. 14, 1941; s. Francis P. and Freda M. (Getty) L.; came to U.S., 1963; B.A. in Bus. Adminstrn., Walla Walla Coll., 1965; m. Jacquelyn M. Adams, Aug. 13, 1961; children—Robert, D. James, Randall, Richard. Bus. mgr., tchr. Rogue River Jr. Acad., Medford, Oreg., 1965-66; prin., bus. mgr. Greater Phila. Jr. Acad., Hatboro, Pa., 1966-68; bus. mgr. Hadley Meml. Hosp., Washington, 1968-70, personnel adminstrn., 1970-76, asst. adminstr., 1976—; instr. Sch. Bus., Strayer Coll., Washington. Mem. sch. bd. J.N. Andrews Elementary Sch., 1977—; active Citizens Choice, Inc., 1978. Accredited personnel mgr. Am. Soc. Personnel Adminstrn. Mem. Am. Hosp. Assn., Am. Soc. Hosp. Engrs., Nat. Fire Protection Assn., Am. Mgmt. Assn., Hosp. Council Nat. Capital Area (past pres. personnel dirs. div.). Home: 8113 Chester St Takoma Park MD 20012 Office: 4601 Martin Luther King Jr Ave SW Washington DC 20032

LOOKSTEIN, JOSEPH HYMAN, rabbi; b. Russia, Dec. 25, 1902; s. Jacob S. and Anna (Shapiro) L.; B.A., Coll. City N.Y., 1928; M.A., Columbia U., 1929; Rabbi, Isaac Elchannan Theol. Sem., 1926; D.D. (hon.), Yeshiva U., 1948; m. Gertrude Schlang, June 6, 1926; children—Nathalie, Haskel. Came to U.S., 1910, naturalized, 1914. Rabbi, Kings-Highway Jewish Center, 1922-23; asst. rabbi Congregation Kehilath Jeshurun, 1923-26, rabbi, 1926—; prof. sociology Yeshiva U., 1931—; prof. homiletics and practical rabbinics Rabbi Elchanan Theol. Sem., 1931—. Pres. N.Y. Bd. Jewish Ministers, Rabbinical Council Am., 1941-43, hon. pres., 1943—; chmn. acad. council Bar-Ilan U. in Israel, acting pres., 1958-66, chancellor, 1966—. Founder Hebrew Tchrs. Tng. Sch. for Girls, 1930; founder Ramaz Sch., 1937, prin., 1937—; Mizrachi Orgn. of Am.; del. to World Zionist Congress, Geneva, 1939, 1951; mem. exec. World Orgn. Religious Zionists, 1962; co-ordinator World Council on Jewish Edn. Pres. Synagogue Council Am., 1974—; mem. Jewish Welfare Bd. Mem. adminstrn. com. and chmn. Latin-Am. com. Am. Jewish Joint Distbn. Com. Visted ETO and MTO on behalf of War Dept. in connection with work of Jewish chaplains in those areas, 1945. Rep. Am. Jewish Conf. as cons. to U.S. Dept. of State, UN Conf., San Francisco. 1945. Mem. Jewish Chaplaincy Commn., 1941—, chmn., 1954-57; mem. Nat. Hillel Commn., 1947—; vice chmn. World Mizrachi. Hon. trustee Yeshiva U. Recipient Certificate of Merit and Selective Service medal for war work; Tri-State Region award Union of Orthodox Jewish Congregations Am., 1953; Franklin L. Weil award, 1957. Fellow Am. Sociol. Assn.; mem. Religious Edn. Assn. (v.p.). Author: Judaism in Theory and Practice, 1931; What is Orthodox Judaism, 1949; Sources of Courage, 1943; Faith and Destiny of Man, 1967. Contbr. to mags. Home: 1160 Park Ave New York City NY 10028 Office: 125 E 85th St New York City NY 10028*

LOOMIS, J. PAUL, automobile radiator mfg. co. exec.; b. Butler, Ind., June 1, 1924; s. Jasper and Mary Elizabeth (Duffy) L.; B.A., U. Calif. at Los Angeles, 1945; m. Apr. 12, 1947 (div.); children—Catherine S., Timothy P., Julia A., William J., David A. Employment mgr. Central Soya Co., Decatur, Ind., 1947-52; personnel dir. Electric Autolite Co., Owosso, Mich., 1952-64; plant mgr. ESB Inc., Fairfield, Conn., 1964-70; mgr. indsl. relations G & O Mfg. Co., New Haven, 1971—. Mem. employment adv. com. Urban League New Haven; chmn. Shiawassee County (Mich.), chpt. ARC, 1963-64. Served with USNR, 1943-46. Mem. Greater New Haven Personnel Assn. (pres. 1978-79), Am. Soc. Personnel Adminstrs., Conn. Personnel Assn. Home: 43 Monticello Dr Branford CT 06405 Office: 138 Winchester Ave New Haven CT 06508

LOOMIS, JOHN NORMAN, psychiatrist; b. Dallas, Aug. 9, 1933; s. Glenn LaVerne and Maria Jeanette (Doyle) L.; B.A., Rice U., 1954; M.D., Cornell U., 1958. Intern Methodist Hosp., Bklyn., 1958-59; resident Westchester div. N.Y. Hosp., White Plains, N.Y., 1959-62; practice medicine specializing in psychiatry, N.Y.C., 1962—; asst. attending staff N.Y. Hosp., 1972—; asst. prof. Cornell U. Med. Coll., 1972—; dir. Loomis Internat. Inc., oil field service co., Houston, 1964—, v.p., 1970-75, chmn. bd., 1975—. Bd. dirs. Madison Square Boys' Club, N.Y.C., 1965—. Mem. Am. Psychiat. Assn., N.Y. Acad. Scis., Phi Beta Kappa. Clubs: Knickerbocker (N.Y.C.); St. Anthony (San Antonio). Office: 521 Park Ave New York City NY 10021

LOONAN, HOWARD MARC, health care mfg. co. exec.; b. Bklyn., Sept. 16, 1945; s. Matthew and Beatrice (Gottlieb) L.; B.S., N.Y. U., 1967, M.B.A., 1971; m. Ellen Carol Cohen, Jan. 1, 1977; children—Robbin Dawn, Lisa Michelle. Sr. accountant Ernst & Ernst, N.Y.C., 1970-72; group controller Welsbach Corp., Greenwich, Conn., 1972-75; chief fin. officer Biophysics Systems, Inc. subs. Johnson & Johnson, Mahopac, N.Y., 1975-76, asst. treas. Ortho Instruments div. Johnson & Johnson, Westwood, Mass., 1976-77; budget mgr. Ethicon, Inc. subs. Johnson & Johnson, Somerville, N.J., 1977-78, mgr. cost analysis, 1978—. Bd. dirs. Vocat. Industries Somerset Area, 1977—, Bridgewater Community Pool, 1978—. Served with USN, 1967-70. C.P.A., N.Y., N.J. Mem. Am. Mgmt. Assn., Nat. Assn. Accountants, Am. Inst. C.P.A.'s, N.Y. State, N.J. socs. C.P.A.'s. Republican. Jewish. Home: PO Box 6737 Bridgewater NJ 08807 Office: Ethicon Inc Somerville NJ 08876

LOONEY, FRANCIS BENEDICT, assn. exec.; b. Bethpage, N.Y., Sept. 28, 1916; s. Patrick J. and Mary Jane (Butler) L.; B.S., St. John's U., 1937, LL.B., 1940; m. Mary K. Ahern, June 15, 1946; children—Jean M., Thomas F., Daniel G., Jane M. With Nassau County (N.Y.) Police Dept., 1939-71, commr., 1966-71; asst. to police commr. N.Y.C. Police Dept., 1971-73, dep. commr., 1973-78; counsel N.Y. State Assn. Chiefs of Police, Albany, 1978—. Pres. Nassau County council Boy Scouts Am., 1971-74; mem. N.Y. State Crime Control Planning Bd., 1969-73; chmn. police adv. commn. N.Y. Civil Service, 1971—; mem. criminal justice adv. councils State U. N.Y., Farmingdale, 1966—, N.Y. Inst. Tech., Westbury, 1971—, St. John's U., Queens, N.Y., 1973—; chmn. criminal justice adv. bd. Niagara U., Niagara Falls, N.Y., 1973—. Served to 1st lt. AUS, 1942-46; ETO. Recipient Ann. award NCCJ, 1968; Adelphi U. fellow, 1967—; State U. N.Y. fellow, 1971—. Mem. Internat. Assn. Chiefs of Police (pres. 1973-74), Police Chief Exec. Com., Am. Nassau County bar assns., N.Y. State Assn. Chiefs of Police (pres. 1969-71), Patrolmen's Benevolent Assn. Roman Catholic. Contbr. articles in field to profl. jours. Home: 4 Quaker Meeting House Rd Farmingdale NY 11735 Office: 112 State St Albany NY 12207

LOONEY, JOHN MICHAEL, structural engr.; b. Winchester, Mass., June 25, 1941; s. John Timothy and Mary Christine (Donnelly) L.; Asso. in Engring., Wentworth Inst., 1961; B.S. in Civil Engring., Tufts U., 1964; M.S. in Structural Engring., Northeastern U., 1967; m. Catherine Marie Oliver, June 24, 1967; children—Christine, Timothy. Staff engr. Souza & True, Cambridge, Mass., 1965-70; sr. engr. Thomas Rona, Boston, 1970-72; project engr. Richard J. Donovan Engr., Winchester, Mass., 1972-75; chief engr. CBT/Childs Bertram Tseckares & Casendino Inc., Boston, 1975—. Mem. Town Meeting, Winchester, 1973—, conservation commr., 1977—. Mem. ASCE, Nat. Soc. Profl. Engrs., Am. Concrete Inst., Am. Post-Tension Inst. Club: Appalachian Mountain. Home: 20 Winthrop St Winchester MA 01890 Office: 306 Dartmouth St Boston MA 02116

LOOS, AUGUST WALTER, JR., cable and chain co. exec.; b. Pomfret, Conn., Mar. 14, 1928; s. August Walter and Edith (Peterson) L.; B.A., Brown U., 1954; m. Joan C. Timmons, Sept. 14, 1961; children—William T., John P. Sales engr. Danielson Mfg. Co. (Conn.), 1954-58; v.p. sales Sanlo Mfg. Co., Michigan City, Ind., 1958-59; sales mgr. W.S. Shamban Co., Inc., Fort Wayne, Ind., 1959-61; pres. Loos & Co., Inc., Loos Realty & Leasing, Inc.; chmn. bd. Superwinch, Inc., Pomfret, Fiberoptics Tech., Inc., Pomfret; dir. William Prym, Inc., Dayville, Conn. Served with USAAF, 1945-48. Mem. Soc. Plastic Engrs. Mason, Lion. Patentee plastic coated chain, mech. cables. Home: Elsinore Pomfret CT 06258 Office: Cable Rd Pomfret CT 06258

LOOS, WILLIAM HENRY, librarian; b. North Tonawanda, N.Y., Feb. 26, 1937; s. William A. and Hildegarde I. (Nickel) L.; B.A. in History, State U. N.Y., Buffalo, 1965; M.S. in Library Sci., Syracuse U., 1968. Librarian, Tonawanda (N.Y.) Pub. Library, 1965-67; with Buffalo and Erie County Pub. Library, Buffalo, 1968—, curator rare book room, 1972—; cons. Western N.Y. Library Resources Council, 1969-70. Mem. ALA, Bibliog. Soc. Am., N.Y. Library Assn., Manuscript Soc., Librarians Assn. Buffalo and Erie County Pub. Library, Beta Phi Mu. Mem. United Ch. of Christ. Club: Salisbury (pres.). Co-editor: Western N.Y. Union List Serials. Home: 295 Grove St Tonawanda NY 14150 Office: Buffalo and Erie County Public Library Lafayette Sq Buffalo NY 14203

LOPEZ, FELIX EDWARD, psychologist; b. Bklyn., May 22, 1947; s. Felix Manual and Regina Elizabeth (Powell) L.; A.B. in Psychology, Holy Cross Coll., 1969; M.A. in Personnel Psychology, Columbia U., 1974, M.Phil. in Personnel Psychology, 1976, Ph.D. in Personnel Psychology, 1977; m. Magdalene T. Plominski, July 10, 1971; children—Felix James, Sarah Graham. Research asst. Drake-Beam Assos., N.Y.C., 1968-69; sr. asso. Felix M. Lopez & Assos., Port Washington, N.Y., 1972-76; v.p. Lopez Assessment Services, Inc., Port Washington, 1976—; adj. asso. prof. Postgrad. Sch. Bus. Adminstrn., L.I. U. Served in USNR, 1969-72. Certified psychologist, N.Y. State. Mem. Am. Psychol. Assn., Am. Soc. Personnel Adminstrs., N.Y. Personnel Mgmt. Assn., Met. Area Assn. Applied Psychologists, Sigma Xi. Home: 1-3 Vista Way Port Washington NY 11050 Office: 14 Vanderventer Ave Port Washington NY 11050

LORANGER, ARMAND WALTER, psychologist, educator; b. Lowell, Mass., Sept. 3, 1930; s. Armand Joseph and Sarah Laura (Melanson) L.; B. A., St. Mary's Coll., 1952; M. A., Fordham U., 1955, Ph.D., 195B; m. Margaret L. Martens, July 5, 1958; children—Douglas Andrew, Jane Andrea, Robert Rivard. Intern, Westchester div. N.Y. Hosp.-Cornell Med. Center, White Plains 1956-58, psychologist, 1958-60, head div. psychology, 1960-75; asst. prof. psychiatry/psychology Cornell U. Med. Coll., 1965—; cons. med. dept. N.Y. Telephone Co., 1962-70; White Plains Police Dept., 1967—. Diplomate Am. Bd. Examiners in Profl. Psychology. Mem. Am. Psychol. Assn., AAAS, Behavior Genetics Assn., Sigma Xi. Contbr. articles to profl. publs. Home: Route 2 Box 216 Pound Ridge NY 10576 Office: 21 Bloomingdale Rd White Plains NY 10605

LORD, BARBARA CHASE, coll. adminstr.; b. New Haven, Mar. 24, 1934; d. William Henry and Gladys Marion (Durlach) Balke; Asso. Sci., Vt. Coll., 1955; student Hartford Hosp. Sch. Med. Tech., 1955-56; B.S., Springfield Coll., 1975, M.S., 1977; m. Donald Richard Lord, May 9, 1959; children—Donald Richard, Kimberly Chase. Med. technologist, Hartford Hosp., 1956-59; head technologist Springfield (Mass.) Med. Group, 1965-69; chem. technologist Mt. Sinai Hosp., Hartford, 1970-74; bus. office Springfield Sch. Dept., 1974-76; dir. placement Western New Eng. Sch. Law, Springfield, Mass., 1976—; group counselor. Mem. Enfield Town Com. Republican party, 1970—; mem. Enfield Com. Health Planning, 1977—. Certified med. technologist Am. Soc. Clin. Practitioners. Mem. Mass. Bar Assn., Nat. Assn. Law Placement, Am. Soc. Med. Technologists, Am. Personnel and Guidance Assn., Psi Chi. Presbyterian. Home: 15 St James Ave Enfield CT 06082 Office: 1215 Wilbraham Rd Springfield MA 01119

LORD, EARL ROBERT, music educator; b. Farmington, Maine, Oct. 23, 1946; s. Ephraim Maitland and Ethel (Crockett) L.; grad. Wilton Acad., 1965; B.S. Edn., U. Maine at Machias, 1965-69; postgrad. U. Maine at Orono, Machias and Farmington, Brandy Wine Coll. Instrumental instr. Washington Acad., 1966-71, music supr., 1971-77. Editor, Maine Music Educators Bull., 1969-76; pres. Lord, Inc., Lord's Music. Bd. dirs. Take Five Scholarship Fund, Lorenco Music Funshop. Named Unsung Hero of Music Edn. for Maine, Nat. Sch. Orch. Assn. Orch. News, 1973. Mem. Eastern Maine (dir., past pres.), Maine (dist. V chmn. solo and ensemble festival), Kennebec Valley music educators assns., Music Educators Nat. Conf. Maine chmn. 1972). Home and office: Box 149 Unity ME 04986

LORD, JOSEPH SIMON, III, judge; b. Phila. May 21, 1912; s. Joseph Simon and Irene (Hicks) L.; A.B. with honors, U. Pa., 1933, LL.B. with honors, 1936, LL.D., Suffolk U., 1975; m. Maureen E. McCrudden, Feb. 14, 1971; 1 dau., Mary Frances Lord Halton. Admitted to Pa. bar, 1937; law clk. Phila. Ct. Common Pleas, 1936-37; with Schnader & Lewis, 1937-42, Schnader, Kenworthy, Segal & Lewis, 1945-46; partner firm Richter, Lord & Farage and successor, Richter, Lord & Levy, Phila., 1946-61; U.S. atty. Eastern Dist. Pa., 1961; judge U.S. Dist. Ct., Eastern Dist. Pa., 1961—, chief judge, 1971; mem. Judicial Panel Multidist. Litigation, 1968—; lectr. Am. Law Inst. Fellow Internat. Acad. Trial Lawyers. Commr. Delaware River Port Authority, 1961. Served from lt. (j.g.) to lt. comdr., USNR, 1942-45. Recipient Commendation ribbon, unit citation with bronze star and seven battle stars. Mem. Law Alumni Assn. U. Pa. (sec. 1939-42), Am. Law Inst. (advisory com. dir. jurisdiction between state and fed. courts), Am., Fed., Phila., Pa. bar assns. Asso. editor The Shingle, 1946-54, editor-in-chief, 1954; editorial bd. The Practical Lawyer, 1954—. Home: 3011 Foxx Ln Philadelphia PA 19144 Office: US Court House Philadelphia PA 19106

LORD, MARION E. MANNS, educator; b. Ft. Huachuca, Ariz., Dec. 17, 1914; d. George Wiley and Annie Pellett) Manns; student R.I. State Coll., 1932; B.S., Northwestern U., 1936; postgrad. Breadloaf Coll., summer 1936; M.Ed., Harvard, 1962; M.A., Ph.D. (E. B. Fred fellow), U. Wis., 1968; m. William Shepard Lord, Apr. 29, 1938 (div. May 1965); children—Caroline B. (Mrs. Martin L. Gross), Marion F. (Mrs. Fred W. Steadman), Jane B. Chapin. N.H. State rep. Gen. Ct., Concord, N.H., 1957-62; dean of women, dir. guidance New Eng. Coll., Henniker, N.H., 1962-64; asst. to div. dir. Bur. Higher Edn. U.S. Office Edn., then dir. women's project Nat. Center Ednl. Statistics, program specialist, 1968-75; dean faculty Borough of Manhattan Community Coll., City U. N.Y., 1975—. Vice pres., dir. N.H. Council for Better Schs., 1957-64; county co-chmn. Nat. Found. Infantile Paralysis-March of Dimes, Laconia, N.H., 1958; dir. N.H. Council on World Affairs, 1957-63, Laconia Hosp. Mem. Am. Psychol. Assn., Am. Polit. Sci. Assn., D.C. Sociol. Soc. (treas., mem. com. on status of women), Nat. Council Adminstrv. Women in Edn., Federally Employed Women, Order Women Legislators, N.H. State Soc. in Washington, Am. Personnel and Guidance Assn., Nat. Assn. Women Deans and Counselors, League Women Voters, AAUW, Bus. and Profl. Womens Club. Republican. Home: 307 Henry St New York City NY 11201

LORD, PRISCILLA SAWYER (MRS. PHILIP HOSMER LORD), author; b. Woburn, Mass.; d. Frank Hayward and Emelyn (Strang) Sawyer; A.B., Boston U., 1933; m. Philip Hosmer Lord, Feb. 10, 1938; children—Beverly, Roberta (Mrs. William H. Moore, Jr.). Readers' adviser Woburn Pub. Library, 1933-38; story teller Book Reviewer, 1933—. Bd. dirs. Mass. Soc. U. Edn. for Women, 1965—; active Girl Scouts U.S.A.; vol. chmn. scholarship com., past v.p. Marblehead Hosp. Aid Assn. Mem. Herb Soc. Am. (nat. bd., chmn. New Eng. Unit), Mass. Descs. of Mayflower, Nat. Soc. Colonial Dames Am., Alpha Gamma Delta. Clubs: Marblehead Garden (past pres.), Winter Garden (past pres.). Author: (with Daniel J. Foley) Easter Garland, 1963, The Folk Arts and Crafts of New England, 1965, The Eagle, 1968, Easter The World Over, 1970; (with Virginia Clegg Gamage) Marblehead: The Spirit of '76 Lives Here, 1971, The Lure of Marblehead, 1973. Contbr. articles to periodicals. Home: Dennett Rd Marblehead Neck MA 01945

LORD, RAY, economist; b. Baku, USSR, Mar. 21, 1923; s. Missagh and Ziba (Baba-zadah) Missaghi; came to U.S., 1954, naturalized, 1960; M.A. in Econs., New Sch. for Social Research, N.Y.C., 1962. Spl. cons. to dir. Iran Motor Co., Tehran, 1948-52; spl. adviser to chief U.S. Tech. Coop. Adminstrn. for Iran, 1952-54; asst. controller Import-Export Co., N.Y.C., 1962-67; dir. Middle East Info. Agy., N.Y.C., 1968—. Mem. N.Y. Commerce and Industry Assn., Am. Mktg. Assn. Address: Middle East Info Agy PO Box 1588 New York City NY 10017

LORD, VICTOR ALEXANDER, JR., lawyer; b. Schenectady, July 11, 1924; s. Victor A. and Sara M. (Bradshaw) L.; B.A., Cornell U., 1948; LL.B., Yale U., 1951; m. Athena Vavruras, Oct. 3, 1954; children—Sara M., Christopher J., Victoria M., Alexandra M. Admitted to N.Y. bar, 1951; asso. Whalen, McNamee, Creble & Nichols, Albany, 1951-58, partner, 1959-70; partner McNamee, Nichols, Lochner & Titus, Albany, 1970-73; v.p., dir. McNamee, Nichols Lochner & Titus, 1973—; dir. Broadvia Corp., Albany. Counsel, Citizens Party Suprs., Albany County Bd., 1964-72; mem. state law com. N.Y. State Liberal Party, 1967—, vice chmn. party, 1971—; spl. investigating counsel Cohoes Commn. Council, 1973; mem. Albany Diocesan Marriage Tribunal, 1963; mem. bequest com. Cornell U., 1965—; pres. exec. com. Friends Albany Pub. Library, 1975—; adv. com. work release Albany County Sheriff, 1974—; bd. dirs. Albany Interracial Council, 1957-64, v.p., 1960-64; bd. dirs. Citizens United Reform Effort, Albany, 1961-62, vice chmn., 1961; bd. dirs. Capital Dist. Resident Opera Co., 1970—, pres. 1971-75; bd. dirs. Albany Legal Aid Soc., 1972—, v.p., 1973—; mem. Empire State Plaza Council, 1978—. Served with AUS, 1943-46; lt. col. Res. Decorated Purple Heart; recipient Samuel E. Aronowitz award Albany Urban League, 1974. Mem. Am., N.Y. State (banking law com.), Albany County bar assns., Phi Beta Kappa, Theta Xi, Phi Alpha Delta. Episcopalian. Club: Univ. (Albany). Home: 21 Homestead Ave Albany NY 12203 Office: 75 State St Albany NY 12201

LORE, JOHN MARION, JR., otolaryngologist, surgeon, educator; b. N.Y.C., July 26, 1921; s. John Marion and Lillian (Langel) L.: B.S. in Biology, Holy Cross Coll., 1942; M.D., N.Y. U., 1945; m. Chalis Wanamaker, Apr. 21, 1949; children—John Marion III, Peter, Margaret, Joan. Rotating intern St. Vincent's Hosp., N.Y.C., 1945-46, resident in otolaryngology and head and neck surgery, 1948-50; asst. resident in gen. surgery St. Clare's Hosp., N.Y.C., 1950-52, sr. resident, 1954-55, fellow in exptl. surgery, 1953-54; asst. resident in surgery and radiation Meml. Cancer Center, N.Y.C., 1952-53; practice medicine specializing in gen., maxillofacial and plastic surgery of head and neck, N.Y.C., 1955-66, Buffalo, 1966—; asst. vis. surgeon Met. Hosp., N.Y.C., 1964-66; dir. su rgery Good Samaritan Hosp., Suffern, N.Y., 1965-66; head dept. otolaryngology Buffalo Gen. Hosp., 1966—, Buffalo Children's Hosp., 1966-77; head dept. otolaryngology E.J. Meyer Meml. Hosp., Buffalo, 1967-73, head dept. otolaryngology, 1972, also chief combined head and neck service Buffalo Gen., Buffalo Children's, E.J. Meyer Meml. hosps.; dir. dept. otolaryngology and head and neck surgery Buffalo Sisters Hosp.; cons. in otolaryngology Buffalo VA Hosp.; cons. dept. head and neck surgery and reconstructive surgery Roswell Park Meml. Inst.; cons. dept. otolaryngology Deaconess Hosp.; asst. clin. prof. surgery N.Y. Med. Coll., 1964-66; prof. surgery, head div. otolaryngology State U. N.Y., Buffalo, 1966-72, prof., chmn. dept. otolaryngology, 1972—; vis. prof. Baylor U., 1967, U. Denver Med. Center, 1969, U.S. Naval Med. Center, 1971-76, U. Tenn., 1972, Ohio State U., 1973; prin. investigator prototype comprehensive network demonstration project for head and neck cancer, 1975, 76, NIH grant on hyperalimemtation, 1976; chmn. Joint Council Approval Advanced Tng. in Head and Neck Oncologic Surgery, 1978. Bd. dirs. N.Y. State div. Am. Cancer Soc., 1965-67, Southtown Gen. Hosp., Inc. Served with M.C., USNR, 1946-48. Diplomate Am. Bd. Otolaryngology, Am. Bd. Surgery. Fellow A.C.S., Am. Acad. Ophthalmology and Otolaryngology (award of merit 1970), Am. Coll. Chest Physicians; mem. AMA (Hektoen gold medal 1952, Physicians Recognition award in continuing med. edn. 1969, 74—), N.Y. State (chmn. sect. otolaryngology 1971-72), Erie County med. socs., Pan Am. Med. Assn., Soc. Head and Neck Surgeons (mem.-at-large exec. council 1971-74, v.p. 1978), Am. Soc. for Head and Neck Surgery (chmn. audit com. 1970-71), Soc. Surg. Oncology, Am. Radium Soc., Soc. Univ. Otolaryngologist, John L. Madden Surg. Soc., Am. Council Otolaryngology, Soc. Acad. Chairmen Otolaryngology, Pan Pacific Surg. Assn., Pan Am. Assn. Oto-Rhino-Laryngology and Bronchoesophagology, Am. Soc. Contempory Men in Medicine and Surgery, N.Y. Cancer Soc., Am., N.Y. laryngol. socs., Buffalo Otolaryngol. Soc., Buffalo Surg. Soc., Am. Acad. Facial, Plastic and Reconstructive Surgery. Mem. Conservative Party. Roman Catholic. Club: Tamarack Ridge Ski. Author: An Atlas of Head and Neck Surgery, 1962, 2d edit., 1973. Mem. editorial bd. O.R.L. Digest, 1971—. Contbr. numerous articles to med. jours. Home: Lower East Hill Rd Colden NY 14033 Office: Seton Profl Bldg 2121 Main St Suite 208 Buffalo NY 14214

LORENTZ, GERALD TALMAGE, radiologist; b. Keene, N.Y., Apr. 2, 1916; s. Daniel Emerson and Bessie Mae (Talmage) L.; B.A., Drew U., 1940; M.D., Hahnemann Med. Coll., 1943; m. Lois Elizabeth Sitterly, July 12, 1941; children—David Gerald, Christopher Charles, Erica. Intern, Roger Williams Meml. Hosp., Providence, 1944; preceptorship radiology, Waynesboro, Pa., 1948-51; practice family medicine, McConnellsburg, Pa., 1947—; radiologist Fulton County Med. Center, McConnellsburg, 1950—, chief of staff, 1951—, med. dir. long term care units, 1976—; pres. bd. dirs. B.L.S., Inc., Fayetteville, Pa., 1969, B.L.S. of Hanover, Inc., 1973—. Chm., McConnellsburg Sewer Authority, 1963-71; bd. dirs. Fulton County unit Am. Cancer Soc., 1951—, pres., 1960-70. Served to capt., M.C., U.S. Army, 1944-47. Named Man of Year, Fulton County C. of C., 1970. Diplomate Am. Bd. Family Practice. Mem. Franklin County Med. Soc. (bd. officers 1962-65, pres. 1965), Pa. Med. Soc., AMA, Pa. Radiol. Soc., Pa., Am. acads. family practice, Am. Guild Organists, Fulton County C. of C. Republican. Presbyterian. Clubs: Lions, Great Cove Golf and Recreation. Home: 401 S First St McConnellsburg PA 17233 Office: 412 Lincoln Way E McConnellsburg PA 17233

LORENTZ, PARE, critic, film dir.; b. Clarksburg, W.Va., Dec. 11, 1905; s. to Pare Hanson and Alma (Ruttencutter) L.; student W.Va. Wesleyan Coll., 1923, D. Letters (hon.), 1972; D.Hum. (hon.), W.Va.

U., 1978; m. Elizabeth Meyer, June 27, 1943; children by previous marriage—Pare MacTaggart, Florence Matilda. Chief U.S. Film Service, Washington, 1938-40; nat. defense editor McCall's Mag., N.Y.C., 1940-41; chief films, theatre, and music Civil Affairs Div. U.S. War Dept., Washington, 1946-47; pres., treas. Pare Lorentz Assos., Inc., N.Y.C., 1947—; hon. prof. speech U. Wis., Oshkosh, 1971 spl. corr. The Washington Post, 1st UN Conf. on Peaceful Uses of the Atom, Geneva, 1955; motion picture critic Judge Mag., 1926-34, N.Y. Evening Jour., 1931-32, Vanity Fair, 1932-33, Town & Country, 1933, McCall's, 1935-40; author: (with Morris L. Ernst) Censored—The Private Life of the Movies, 1930; The Roosevelt Year, 1934; The River, 1938; to Lorentz on Film, 1975; author screenplay, dir. the Plow that Broke the Plains, The River, The Fight for Life. Served to lt. col. USAAF, 1942-46. Decorated Air medal, Legion of Merit. Mem. Beta Theta Pi. Clubs: Edgartown Yacht, Players, Century Assn. Home: 19 Whippoorwill Rd Armonk NY 10504

LORIAN, VICTOR, microbiologist; b. Bucharest, Romania, Oct. 30, 1925; s. Henry and Elvira (Mariano) L.; B.S., St. Andre High Sch., Bucharest, 1944; M.D., U. Bucharest, 1950; postgrad. Cantacuzino Microbiology Inst., Bucharest, 1950-51; married. Came to U.S., 1964, naturalized, 1972. Chief lab., Bucharest Med. Sch., 1951-59; asst. physician, Haddasah Med. Sch., Jerusalem, 1959-60; prof. microbiology Tb Inst., Rio de Janeiro, Brazil, 1960-64; dir. labs. Boston City Hosp., 1964-68, also research asso. Harvard Sch. Pub. Health, 1965-69; chmn. div. microbiology and epidemiology Bronx Lebanon Hosp. Center, 1968—; clin. asso. prof. microbiology Mt. Sinai Sch. Medicine, N.Y.C., 1969-76; prof. lab. Medicine Albert Einstein Coll. Medicine, N.Y.C., 1976—. Diplomate Am. Bd. Microbiology. Fellow Am. Acad. Microbiology; mem. Infectious Diseases Soc. Am., Am. Soc. Microbiology, Am. Thoracic Soc. Author: Antibiotics in Clinical and Laboratory Practice, 1966; Significance of Microbiology in the Care of Patients, 1977. Contbr. numerous articles to profl. jours. Home: 315 E 65th St New York City NY 10021 Office: 1276 Fulton Ave Bronx NY 10456

LORIMER, GRAEME, author, editor; b. Wyncote, Pa., Feb. 9, 1903; s. George Horace and Alma Viola (Ennis) L.; grad. William Penn Charter Sch., Phila., 1919; B.A., U. Pa., 1923; m. Sarah Moss, Oct. 2, 1926; children—Sarah Lee, Belle Burford, George Horace II, Anna Hunter Moss. Asst. editor Country Gentleman, 1926; asso. editor Ladies' Home Jour., 1930-31; asso. editor Sat. Eve. Post, 1932-38; article and fiction editor Ladies' Home Jour., 1939-44. Dir. Girard Bank, Phila., 1938-72. Pres. Pa. Soc. to Protect Children, 1953-55; mem. distbn. com. Phila. Found., 1958-70, chmn., 1961-66. Trustee Phila. Award, 1940-70; hon. trustee Phila. Museum of Art. Mem. Psi Upsilon. Episcopalian. Clubs: Franklin Inn, Merion Cricket. Author: (with wife) Men Are Like Street Cars, 1932; Stag Line, 1934; Heart Specialist, 1935; Acquittal, 1938; First Love, Farewell, 1940. Home: Magnet Stone Farm Paoli PA 19301

LORINCZ, ROBERT STEPHEN, electronic engr.; b. South Plainfield, N.J., Sept. 29, 1945; s. Stephen Joseph and Helen Mary L.; B.S. in Electronic Engring., Monmouth Coll., 1969; M.S.E.E., George Wash. U., 1973; m. Rachel Savoca, Jan. 18, 1975; 1 son, Stephen Brian. Electronic engr. Vitro Labs., Silver Spring, Md., 1969-74, EMR Photo Electric Co., Princeton, N.J., 1974-77; electronic engr., dir. soft ware devel. New Brunswick Scientific Co., Edison, N.J., 1977—. Served with U.S. Army, 1970-72. Mem. IEEE. Roman Catholic. Co-inventor in field. Home: 13 Brook Dr Milltown NJ 08850 Office: New Brunswick Scientific PO Box 986 Edison NJ 08817

LORING, CALEB, JR., lawyer; b. Boston, Feb. 5, 1921; s. Caleb and Suzanne (Bailey) L.; A.B., Harvard, 1943, LL.B., 1948; m. Rosemary Merrill, Feb. 12, 1943; children—Caleb, David, Rosemary, Keith. Admitted to Mass. bar, 1948; asso. firm Gaston, Snow, Motley & Holt, Boston, 1948-54, partner, 1954-70; dir., trustee Loring, Wolcott and Coolidge Office-Fiduciary Services, Boston, 1948—; dir. Fidelity Mgmt. & Research Co., Boston, 1959—, sec., v.p., gen. counsel, 1964-74, exec. v.p., 1974-77, treas., 1977—. Served with USNR, 1943-46. Mem. Am., Mass., Boston bar assns. Home: Paine Ave Prides Crossing MA 01965 Office: Fidelity Mgmt & Research Co 82 Devonshire St Boston MA 02109

LORING, MARVIN F., cancer researcher; b. N.J., Feb. 5, 1923; s. Benjamin and Lena Levy; B.A., U. Pa., 1944; M.D., Chgo. Med. Sch., 1947; postgrad. U. London, U. Paris, U. Stockholm; divorced; 1 son, Brook Robert. Intern, Sydenham Hosp., N.Y.C.; resident Hosp. St. Raphael, New Haven; radiation oncologist N.Y. Hosp.-Cornell U. Med. Center, 1958-68, Meml. Sloan-Kettering Hosp., N.Y.C., 1966-68, North Shore Univ. Hosp., Manhasset, N.Y., 1969—; asst. prof. Cornell U. Med. Sch., 1958—; med. research collaborator Brookhaven Nat. Lab., Upton, N.Y., 1961; vis. research scientist U. Jerusalem, 1968-69. Served to lt. comdr., M.C., USNR, 1954-56. Brit.-Am. exchange fellow cancer research, London, 1952-53; Am. Cancer Soc. travelling fellow, Paris and Stockholm, 1953-54. Fellow A.C.P., N.Y. Acad. Medicine; mem. Am. Coll. Radiology, Am. Radium Soc., Am. Soc. Therapeutic Radiology, N.Y. Acad. Scis., Am. Roentgen Ray Soc., Radiol. Soc. N.Am., Am. Tissue Culture Assn., Assn. Univ. Radiologists. Research in T-lymphocytes in cancer immunology. Address: 66 E 83d St New York City NY 10028

LORING, RICHARD WILLIAM, psychotherapist; b. Bronx, N.Y., May 26, 1928; s. William Maurice and Jeannette Edith (Bass) L.; B.A., DePauw U., 1952; M.A., Ind. U., 1954; m. Janet Teetor, Aug. 22, 1953; children—Steven, David, Lynne. Psychiat. social worker Richmond (Ind.) State Hosp., 1954-56; asst. dir. Tippecanoe County Mental Health Center, Lafayette, Ind., 1956-62; exec. dir. Venango County Mental Health Center, Oil City, Pa., 1962-71; adminstr. Mental Health/Mental Retardation Authorities, Oil City, 1970-71; dir. Venango Human Services Center, Franklin, Pa., 1971-75; clin. program dir., dir. consultation and edn. Erie County Mental Health Dept., 1975-76; pvt. practice psychotherapy, Oil City, 1976—; mem. staff dept. psychiatry Oil City Hosp.; part-time prof. sociology DePauw U., 1956-62; part-time prof. psychology Pa. State U., 1968-69; field prof. U. Pitts., 1969—; prof. sociology Clarion State Coll., part-time, 1972—; part-time prof. mental health counseling Gannon Coll., 1975; spl. cons. Corps Chaplains, U.S. Army, 1971—. Mem. profl. adv. com. Crippled Children and Adults Com., 1971-75; bd. dirs. Pa. Mental Health Assn., 1969-77, mem. exec. com., 1973; del., mem. task force on aging White House Conf. Aging, 1971; del. Nat. Conf. Mental Health, 1975; bd. dirs. Franklin Light Opera Co., 1970-74; chmn. project rev. com. Venango Regional Comprehensive Health Planning, 1973-75; chmn. Great Lakes Forum on Primary Prevention in Mental Health, 1976; chmn. N.W. Pa. Family Planning Council, 1974; mem. N.W. region steering com. Pub. Com. for Humanities in Pa., 1971-74. Served with AUS, World War II. Named Boss of the Year, Ft. Venango chpt. Nat. Secs. Assn., 1972. Mem. Psychiat. Outpatient Centers Am. (exec. sec. 1966—), Am. Pub. Health Assn., Am. Coll. Clinic Adminstrs., Oil City C. of C. Editor: Selected Papers of Psychiatric Outpatient Centers, 1967; Psychiatric Outpatient Centers and Low Income Populations, 1968. Home: 406 W 7th St Oil City PA 16301 Office: Glenview Profl Bldg 9 Glenview Ave Oil City PA 16301

LORING, STANTON DUNSTER, investment co. exec.; b. Providence, Oct. 29, 1918; s. William Cushing and Katherine Margaret (Nicol) L.; A.B., Harvard, 1941; m. Jessica Ann Stevens, Jan. 14, 1942; 1 dau., Jessica. Fin. analyst Tucker, Anthony & Co., N.Y.C., 1946-50; partner DeWitt Conklin Orgn., N.Y.C., 1952-55; pres. S.D. Loring Co., Inc., N.Y.C. and Los Angeles, 1955-72, Loring Corporate Services, Inc., 1973—; dir. Muskegon Boiler Works, Inc. (Mich.). Served with USNR, 1942-45, 50-52. Fellow Fin. Analysts Fedn.; mem. N.Y. Soc. Security Analysts (sr.), Nat. Investor Relations Inst., Pub. Relations Soc. Am. Clubs: Racquet and Tennis, Down Town Assn., Harvard (N.Y.C.). Home: 143 Park Ave Greenwich CT 06830 Office: 611 W 6th St Los Angeles CA also 74 Trinity Pl New York City NY 10006

LOSEE, THOMAS PENNY, JR., publisher; b. Mineola, N.Y., Dec. 9, 1940; s. Thomas Penny and Jeanne Hubbell (Grandeman) L.; A.B., Duke, 1963; m. Muriel Frances Hahn, Apr. 25, 1964; children—Thomas Penny III, Kendall Louise. Advt. salesman Look mag., 1964-71; advt. dir. House Beautiful, 1971-72, pub., 1976—; pub. Harper's Bazaar, N.Y.C., 1972—. Served with USAR, 1963-69. Mem. Beta Theta Pi. Republican. Episcopalian. Clubs: University; Huntington Country; Cold Spring Harbor Beach. Home: 16 Polly Dr Huntington NY 11743 Office: 717 Fifth Ave New York City NY 10022

LOSI, MAXIM JOHN, med. writer; b. Jersey City, N.J., Dec. 27, 1939; s. Maxim Fortune and Carrie (Rivoli) L.; A.B., Princeton U., 1960; postgrad. Albert Einstein Coll. Medicine N.Y. Med. Coll., 1960-62; Ph.D., N.Y. U., 1972; m. Mary Ann De Grandis, May 30, 1968; 1 son, Christopher. Lectr. English, C.W. Post Coll., Greenvale, N.Y., 1965-67; instr. English, Centenary Coll. for Women, Hackettstown, N.J., 1967-71, chmn. dept., 1970-71; med. writer Council for Tobacco Research, N.Y.C., 1972-73; free lance med. writer, 1973-74; sr. clin. info. scientist Squibb Inst. Med. Research, Princeton, N.J., 1974-77, project team leader, 1975-77; med. writer ICI Americas, Wilmington, Del., 1977—, coordinator med. communications, 1978—; FDA cons. Microbiol. Assos., Bethesda, Md., 1973; mgmt. cons. Robert S. First Assos., N.Y.C., 1974; vis. lectr. med. writing techniques St. George U. Med. Sch., Granada, W.I., 1977. Mem. Am. Med. Writers Assn., Soc. Tech. Communication, Sigma Xi. Roman Catholic. Contbr. articles to med. publs. Home: 1194 Parkside Ave Trenton NJ 08618 Office: ICI Americas Clin Research Dept Wilmington DE 19897

LOSS, DAVID EDWARD, educator, accountant; b. Malden, Mass., Mar. 13, 1938; s. Saul and Rebecca (Wiseman) L.; B.S. cum laude, Northeastern U., 1961, M.B.A., 1963; m. Rosalyn Ann Blacker; children—Adam Bradley, Ryan Michael. Instr. accounting, Univ. fellow Northeastern U., 1961-63; evening div. coordinator undergrad. bus. students U. Bridgeport, 1964-67, asst. prof., 1963-70; asso. prof. bus. Central Conn. State Coll., New Britain, 1970-77, prof., 1977—, chmn. dept. bus. adminstrn., 1972, chmn. dept. accounting, 1973—, acting dean Sch. Bus., 1973, asso. dean, 1973—. Lectr. accounting Greater Hartford Community Coll., 1971, Tunxis Community Coll., 1974, St. Joseph Coll., 1975—, C.P.A., Conn. Active Boy Scouts Am. Mem. Fin. Execs. Inst., Conn. Soc. C.P.A.'s (editorial bd.), Nat. Assn. Accountants (dir. local br.), Am. Inst. C.P.A.'s, Am. Accounting Assn., New Eng., Conn. bus. educators assns., AAUP, Coll. and Univ. Bus. Instrs. in Conn. Contbr. articles to profl. jours. Nationally syndicated radio show Tax Tips. Home: 41 Iroquois Rd West Hartford CT 06117 Office: Central Conn State Coll New Britain CT 06053

LO SURDO, ANTONIO, chemist; b. Spadafora, Italy, Jan. 1, 1943; s. Salvatore Giuseppe and Marianna (LaMacchia) Lo S.; came to U.S., 1955, naturalized, 1961; B.A., Syracuse U., 1965, Ph.D., 1970. Postdoctoral fellow, instr. chemistry Rutgers U., 1969-71; vis. faculty mem. Syracuse U., 1971-72; research asso. U. Conn., 1972; vis. research asso., lectr. chemistry Ohio State U., 1972-74; research asso. chemistry dept. Clark U., 1974-75; chief chemist Cambridge Instrument Co., Inc., Ossining, N.Y., 1975-76; research asst. prof. Rosenstiel Sch. Marine and Atmospheric Sci., U. Miami (Fla.), 1977-79, research asso. prof. Rosenstiel Sch. Marine and Atmospheric Sci., 1979—; NSF fellow, 1965-66, 74-75; NIH fellow, 1969-70; Syracuse U. Research Inst. grantee, 1966-69. Mem. AAAS, Am. Chem. Soc., N.Y. Acad. Scis., Sigma Xi, Phi Lambda Upsilon. Contbr. articles to profl. jours. Home: 312 Swansea Ave Syracuse NY 13206 Office: Rosenstiel Sch Marine and Atmospheric Sci U Miami 4600 Rickenbacker Causeway Miami FL 33149

LOTH, JOHN, research analyst; b. Edinburg, Pa., July 29, 1916; s. Julius and Augusta (Troche) L.; M.A., U. So. Calif., 1949; m. Joann Hildreth, June 15, 1951; children—Melissa, Elaine, John. Instr., Youngstown (Ohio) State U., 1961-68; with A. J. Baltes, Norwalk, Ohio, 1971; research engr. Furnco Constrn. Co., Lancaster, N.Y., 1973-77, practice research analyst, Edinburg, 1978—. Auditor, Edinburg Bd. Edn., 1937-41. Served with U.S. Army, 1941-46, 50-52. Mem. Tau Kappa Alpha. Republican. Black Muslim. Clubs: Sojourners, K.T. Author: California Missions, 1961; composer. Home: Edinburg PA 16116 Office: Old Duberry Rd Edinburg PA 16116

LOTHROP, WARREN CRAIG, mgmt. cons.; b. Brookline, Mass., Mar. 7, 1912; s. Theodore Aubrey and Fannie May (Craig) L.; A.B., Harvard U., 1933, M.A., 1935, Ph.D., 1937; m. Margaret Sevier Lotspeich, Sept. 2, 1941; children—Mark Avery, Sarah Sevier, Susan Dudley. Nat. TB fellow Yale U., 1937-38; instr. chemistry Trinity Coll., Hartford, Conn., 1938-42; tech. aide Office Sci. Research and Devel., Washington, 1942-45; asst. prof. Williams Coll., Williamstown, Mass., 1945-46; mem. staff Arthur D. Little, Inc., Cambridge, Mass., 1946-53, v.p., 1954-60, sr. v.p., 1960-63; v.p. corp. devel. Armour and Co., Chgo., 1963-70; sci. adviser Greyhound Corp., Phoenix, 1970-72; pres. Tavistock, Inc., Kennebunkport, Maine, 1970—. Mem. Am. Chem. Soc., Am. Inst. Chemists, Indsl. Research Inst., Calabash Soc. Democrat. Clubs: Chemists (N.Y.C.), Harvard of Maine. Author: Management Uses of Research and Development, 1964; Investigacion Technologica En El Comercio Y La Industria, 1966. Asst. editor Jour. Am. Chem. Soc., 1947. Contbr. articles to chem. jours. Office: Portview Route 35 Kennebunkport ME 04046

LOTITO, ERNEST ARTHUR, govt. ofcl.; b. Lyndhurst, N.J., Feb. 19, 1936; s. Ernest Anthony and Edna Mae (Amrein) L.; B.A. (Henry Rutgers scholar), Rutgers U., 1958; M.S., Columbia U., 1962; m. Margaret V. Cuthbertson, Mar. 26, 1977; children—Ernest Charles, Lisa Renee. Reporter, Washington Post, 1962-66; reporter-editor UPI, Rome, 1966-68; pres. sec. to Senator Joseph D. Tydings, Washington, 1968-70; spl. asst. to Senator Walter F. Mondale, Washington, 1971-76; staff counsel Burson-Marseteller, Washington, 1976; dir. communications Corp. Pub. Broadcasting Washington, 1977; dir. pub. affairs Dept. Commerce, Washington, 1977—; instr. journalism U. Md., 1970-76. Served to 2d lt. U.S. Army, 1960. Fulbright grantee, 1958-59; Italian Govt. grantee 1958-59; Seymour Berkson Fgn. Assignment grantee, 1966. Democrat. Mem. Washington Press Club. Author: The Political Image Merchants, 1971; Strategies in the New Politics, 1971. Home: 5120 Kenwood Dr Annandale VA 22003 Office: Dept of Commerce Pub Affairs 14th and Constitution Ave Washington DC 20230

LOTITO, THOMAS, chem. mfg. co. exec.; b. Bklyn., Oct. 10, 1934; s. Charles and Angie L.; B.S., Cornell U., 1956; M.B.A., N.Y. U., 1961; m. Helen P. Roche, Sept. 16, 1961; children—Catherine Ann, Richard Thomas. Indsl. engr. U.S. Steel Corp., 1956-57; indsl. relations asst. Western Electric Co., N.Y.C., 1957-62; tng. adminstr. Nat. Starch & Chem. Co., N.Y.C., 1962-69; dir. personnel Givaudan Corp., Clifton, N.J., 1969—; instr. Fairleigh Dickinson U., 1966-69. Bd. dirs. Plainfield (N.J.) Adult Edn. Sch., 1968-69. Served with U.S. Army, 1957. Mem. Am. Soc. Personnel Adminstrs., N.J. Pharm. Personnel Assn., North Jersey Compensation Group, Am. Compensation Group, Employment Mgmt. Group, Cornell Alumni Assn., Phi Sigma Kappa. Republican. Roman Catholic. Contbr. chpt. to The Flavor and Fragrance Industry. Home: 63 Lehmann St Mahwah NJ 07430 Office: 100 Delawanna Ave Clifton NJ 07014

LOTZ, GEORGE MICHAEL, art dir., graphic designer, indsl. graphics exec.; b. Balt., Aug. 28, 1928; s. Michael Henry and Mina Catherine (Fleck) L.; student Md. Inst. of Art, 1956-58, Johns Hopkins U., 1957-58, Catonsville Community Coll., 1975, Essex Community Coll., 1976-78; m. Anna Mae Carlson, July 21, 1950; 1 dau., Georgeanna. Mech. draftsman and designer Sinclair Scott Canning House Machinery Co., Balt., 1948-50; illustrator, designer Communications div. of Bendix Corp., Towson, Md., 1950-69, supr. graphic arts, photography, 1969-73, art dir., 1974-78, mgr. computer graphics dept., 1978—; art dir., pres. Glen Arm Graphic, 1963-74; adviser to Md. State Dept. of Art Edn. 1973-78; participant Fed. Design Assembly, 1973-78; mem. panel Nat. Endowment for Arts, 1977-78; judge for poster competition Md. State Dept. Edn., 1974-78; conf. chmn. Indsl. Graphics Internat. U. Md., 1974; guest speaker various local colls., 1973, 77, profl. groups, 1967-78. Judge, Jr. Miss Pagent, Reisterstown, Md., 1971, 72. Served with USNR, 1947-48. Recipient 27 nat. awards for art direction, graphics design including 1st pl. newsletter design Nat. Assn. Indsl. Artists, 1970, 1st pl. award Asso. Printing Industries Am., 1976, 1st pl. award Soc. Tech. Communications, 1977. Mem. Indsl. Graphics Internat. (pres. 1975-77), Council of Communication Soc. (dir. 1976-78), Advt. Assn. of Balt. (dir. 1971-78). Democrat. Clubs: Bendix Emblem, Bendix Mgmt.; Balt. Camera. Contbr. articles on graphic art and edn. to profl. publs. Home: 11212 Old Carriage Rd Glen Arm MD 21057 Office: Bendix Corp 1300 E Joppa Rd Baltimore MD 21204

LOTZ, HENRY THOMAS, ednl. cons.; b. Rockville Centre, N.Y., Sept. 2, 1926; s. Otto Huber and Lydia Annie (Dill) L.; B.A., L.I. U., 1960; M.S. in Edn., City U. N.Y., 1967; Ed.D., U. Sarasota, 1972; m. Joyce Charlotte Vincent, June 5, 1948; children—Linda Joyce, Thomas Henry. Asst. office mgr. Norton, Lilly & Co., Inc., N.Y.C., 1946-59; tchr. Hewlett-Woodmere pub. schs., Hewlett, N.Y., 1960-61, supr. sch. attendance services, 1961-78, coordinator adult basic edn. program, 1962-78, chmn. com. on handicapped, 1977-78; ednl. cons. in pvt. practice, Lynbrook, N.Y., 1974—; asst. examiner Bd. Examiners, N.Y.C. Bd. Edn., 1974-75. Chmn. Hewlett Service unit Salvation Army, 1970-77. Served with U.S. Army, 1944-46. Mem. N.Y. State Council Pupil Service Orgns. (founding pres. 1972-74), Am. Personnel and Guidance Assn., Assn. Measurement and Evaluation in Guidance, Internat. Assn. Pupil Personnel Workers (former dir.), N.Y. State (pres. 1972-74), L.I. (pres. 1966-68) attendance tchrs. assn., L.I. Assn. Spl. Edn. Adminstrs., Council Suprs. and Adminstrs., DAV. Author: Attendance Teaching, 1973; New York Laws Relating to Minors, 1979; editor Children's Champion Jour., 1965-77; Attendance Tchr. newsletter, 1965-78; columnist Dr. Lotz on Edn., 1975; contbr. articles in field to profl. jours. Home: 389 Scranton Ave Lynbrook NY 11563 Office: 389 Scranton Ave Lynbrook NY 11563

LOTZ, ROY JAMES, JR., mgmt. cons.; b. Birdsboro, Pa., Aug. 11, 1923; s. Roy J. and Viola S. Lotz; B.S. in Psychology, Pa. State U., 1948, M.S., 1949; m. Constance Klages, Apr. 26, 1975; children by previous marriage—Brenda, Roy James. Employment mgr. ESB/Stokes Co., Trenton, N.J., 1949-51; dir. personnel Wyeth Labs., Inc., West Chester, Pa., 1951-55; gen. mgr. indsl. relations Downingtown Paper Co. (Pa.), 1955-61; mgr. internat. personnel Richardson-Merrell, 1961-63; mgr. Labor relations Sperry Rand/Univac, N.Y.C., 1963-65; pres. Battalia, Lotz & Asso., Inc., N.Y.C., 1965-75; chmn., pres. Internat. Mgmt. Advisors, Inc., N.Y.C., 1975—. Pres. Massapequa Civic Assn., 1972-74. Served as capt. U.S. Air Force, 1943-46. Mem. Am. Soc. Personnel Adminstrs., Newcomen Soc. Am., N.Y. Power Squadron, SAR. Republican. Presbyterian. Clubs: Union League, Unqua Corinthean Yacht, Masons. Home: 20 Sutton Pl S New York City NY 10022

LOUCKS, WILLIAM DEWEY, JR., lawyer, investments, fiduciary; b. N.Y.C., June 16, 1918; s. William Dewey and Jane (Myers) L; grad. Hotchkiss Sch., 1935; B.A., Yale, 1939; legal edn. Harvard, 1939-41; LL.B., N.Y. U., 1947; m. Carolyn Bade, Sept. 19, 1944; children—Thomas A., Karen B. Admitted to N.Y. bar, 1947, U.S. Dist. Cts., 1957, U.S. Supreme Ct. bar, 1960; practiced in N.Y.C., 1947-73, Bronxville, N.Y., 1973—; pvt. practice, 1947—; asst. to pres. Barnsdall Oil Co., 1947-50; partner Caldarko Gas Co., Fresno, Cal., 1959—. Gov. Lawrence Hosp., Bronxville, 1964-65. Served from 2d lt. to maj., USAAF, 1941-45; lt. col. Res., 1945-50. Mem. Bar Assn. City of New York. Clubs: Am. Yacht (Rye, N.Y.); The Bronxville Field (gov., treas. 1966-68); Siwanoy Country (Bronxville). Home: 32 Sturgis Rd Bronxville NY 10708 also Londonderry VT 05148 Office: 32 Sturgis Rd Bronxville NY 10708

LOUGHERY, KEVIN MICHAEL, profl. basketball coach; b. Bronx, N.Y., Mar. 28, 1940; s. John and Mary (Moroney) L.; student pub. schs., Bronx; m. Sheila T. Quinland, Aug. 25, 1962; children—Kevin, Steven. Profl. basketball player Detroit Pistons, 1962-63, Balt. Bullets, 1963-71, Phila. 76ers, 1971-73; coach N.J. Nets, 1973—. Republican. Roman Catholic. Office: care New Jersey Nets 100 Ring Rd W Roosevelt Field Garden City NJ 11530*

LOUGHERY, RICHARD MILLER, hosp. adminstr.; b. Edinburg, Ind., Aug. 7, 1920; s. Roger S. and Margaret (Miller) L.; B.A., Ind. U., 1941, postgrad., 1941-42; m. Miriam B. McGuire, Aug. 31, 1943; children—Suzanne, Cynthia, Richard, Michelle. Adminstrv. asst. Meth. Hosp., Indpls., 1946-53; asst. adminstr. Garfield Meml. Hosp., Washington, 1953-55, adminstr., 1955-58; dep. adminstr. Washington Hosp. Center, 1956-59, adminstr., 1959—; guest faculty, preceptor grad. program hosp. adminstrn. George Washington U., 1961—; mem. Hosp. Research and Devel. Bd. Inst., 1962—; cons. surgeon gen. USAF, 1959-68; lectr. U.S. Naval Sch. Hosp. Adminstrn., 1961—. Mem. Washington Bd. Trade. Mem. adv. coms. Washington Tech. Inst.; chmn. hosp. adv. com. Health Facilities Planning Council, 1965-72; 1st v.p. adv. group Washington Med. Program, 1969-73; mem. Langley Forest (Va.) Citizens Assn., 1956—. Bd. dirs., mem. exec. com. Hosp. Council Nat. Capital Area, 1956-70, 73-74, adminstrv. dir. bd. dirs., 1971-72; bd. dirs. Found. Med. Mgmt. Research, 1973. Indsl. Health Services, 1973; adv. bd. Hospitality Nursing Homes, 1964-65. Served to capt. USMC, 1942-46. Fellow Am. Coll. Hosp. Adminstrs. (chmn. book award com. 1965, chmn. com. publs. and pub. info. 1967-70, regent 1968-71, gov. 1971—, other coms. 1971—); mem. Am. Hosp. Assn. (council adminstrn. 1964-66, vice chmn. council on legislation 1972-73, ho. dels. 1960-62, 72—), Assn. Am. Med. Colls., Md.-D.C.-Del. (trustee 1956-70, pres. 1961, sec. 1965, other councils and coms.), D.C. (pres. 1956-57),

Fairfax County hosp. assns., George Washington U. Alumni Assn. Health Care Adminstrn. (hon.). Contbr. articles to profl. jours. Home: 6901 Benjamin St McLean VA 22101 Office: 110 Irving St NW Washington DC 20010*

LOUGHRAN, WILLIAM CYRIL, mfg. co. exec., pub. relations cons.; b. Phila., Mar. 14, 1929; s. Cyril Joseph and Elizabeth (Lautenbacker) L.; A.B., Nichols Coll., 1950; m. Elena Henrietta Baran, Sept. 10, 1960; children—William Cyril, James Peter, Suzanne Elena. Owner, pres. Shore Mfg. Co., Spring Lake, N.J., 1951—; pres. Loughran Gardens Inc., real estate holding, Spring Lake, 1960—; partner Loughran & Loughran, pub. relations counsel, Spring Lake, 1970—. Treas., Cub Scout exec. com. Monmouth council Boy Scouts Am., 1969-72, chmn. Sea Girt (N.J.) Scout fund drive, 1970-72; chmn. Carnation Ball, Sea Girt, N.J., 1965-72; judge Fifty States Bicentennial Coin Collection, Franklin Mint; mem. Republican finance com. Cahill for Gov. N.J., 1969, exec. dir. Gov.'s Inaugural Ball, 1970; chmn. Gov.'s ball N.J. Rep. party, 1969, 70. Served with USNR. Roman Catholic (ch. trustee). Patentee christening bottle. Home: 637 Oceanfront St Sea Girt NJ 08750 also 2200 S Ocean Ln Fort Lauderdale FL Office: PO Box 214 Manasquan NJ 08736

LOUIS, GEORGE ARYA, semicondr. mfg. co. exec.; b. N.Y.C., Feb. 20, 1929; s. Albert Richard and Della (Rose) L.; B.S., U. Nev., 1951, M.S., 1955; m. Barbara Lucile Grosshans, Sept. 3, 1950; children—Mark Arya, Richard Lawrence. Research chemist Stauffer Chem. Co., Richmond, Calif., 1955-59; chief product engr. Semcor, Phoenix, 1959-63; product mgr. semicondr. products div. Motorola Co., Phoenix, 1963—; cons. A.I. Buehler Co., Chgo., 1962-65. Served with Chem. Corps, AUS, 1952-54. Teaching fellow U. Nev., 1954-55. Fellow Am. Inst. Chemists; mem. Am. Chem. Soc., Sierra Club, Nat. Rifle Assn. Patentee in field. Home: 145 Greenhill Dr Butler PA 16001 Office: 5005 E McDowell Rd Phoenix AZ 85008

LOUISON, MELVIN SANFORD, attorney; b. New Bedford, Mass., July 14, 1928; s. Israel and Bessie L. (Levovsky) L.; J.D., Suffolk U., 1950; m. Naomi A. Shuchatowitz, Aug. 3, 1952; children—Judith Gail, Audrey Cheryl, Debra Susan, David Jon. Admitted to Mass. Bar, 1951, U.S. Dist. Ct. Mass., 1952, U.S. Dist. Ct. Vt., U.S. Supreme Ct., 1959, U.S. Ct. Appeals, 1st Dist., 1958, U.S. Tax Ct., 1975; mem. firms Louison & Louison, Taunton, Mass., 1951-75, Louison & Cohen, Brockton, Mass., 1975—; dir. Mass. Bank & Trust Co.; instr. Massasoit Community Coll.; adv. bd. Massasoit Community Coll.; mem. Mass. Bench Bar Com. Chmn. Better Brockton Com., 1960-61; chmn. Brockton Planning Bd., 1961-73; mem. Brockton Zoning Bd. of Appeals, 1962-66; mem. pres.'s adv. com. Suffolk Law Sch. Served with U. S. Army, 1954-56. Recipient Law Day award Eagles, 1973. Mem. Am., Mass., Plymouth County bar assns., Am. Trial Lawyers Assn., Natl. Assn. of Def. Lawyers in Criminal Cases, Mass. Assn. Criminal Def. Lawyers (steering com. 1976—), Brockton Hist. Soc., Brockton Art Mus., Am. Legion. Democrat. Jewish religion. Clubs: D.A.V., Hundred (Mass.), Mason, Eagle. Home: 103 Candy Ln Brockton MA 02401 Office: 495 Westgate Dr Brockton MA 02401

LOUTHOOD, LEWIS ALEXANDER, publishing co. exec.; b. Montreal, Que., Can., Apr. 22, 1917; s. Reginald William and Alice (Sweezey) L.; student McGill U., 1935-36; m. Anne Guyon, Sept. 20, 1941; children—Donna, Laura, Katherine, Teresa (Mrs. Brent Arnett), Margaret (Mrs. Leslie Fox). Stenographer, Beauharnois Power Corp. (Que.), 1934-35; dist. circulation mgr. Curtis Pub. Co., Montreal, 1936-37; paymaster Lake Sulphite Pulp Co., Nipigon, Ont., Can., 1937-38; copywriter T. Eaton Co., Montreal, 1938-41; promotion mgr. Montreal Standard Ltd., Montreal, 1941-50, dir. promotion and circulation, 1950-51, dir. newspaper relations, 1951-67, v.p. newspaper relations, 1967-76, v.p. publishing, 1976—; dir. Magna Media Ltd., 1969—. Mem. Am. Marketing Assn. (pres. Montreal chpt. 1953-54), Internat. Newspaper Promotion Assn. (dir. 1947-48), Internat. Newspaper Advt. Execs., Internat. Circulation Mgrs. Assn., Advt. Sales and Execs. Club (dir. Montreal chpt. 1948-50), Trout Unlimited Can. (pres. 1976), Cercle de la Place d'Armes, Theta Delta Chi. Home: 225 Olivier Ave Apt PH 9 Westmount PQ H3Z 2C7 Canada Office: 231 St James St W Montreal PQ H2Y 1M6 Canada

LOUTSCH, ENRIQUE HECTOR, psychoanalyst; b. Buenos Aires, Argentina, Dec. 5, 1932; s. Luciano H. and Lucrecia D. L.; came to U.S., 1961, naturalized, 1966; M.D., Buenos Aires U., 1960; m. Erica Kimelman, Sept. 5, 1950; children—Johannes, Karen. Intern, Hosp. Buenos Aires U., 1959-60; resident Embreeville (Pa.) State Hosp., 1961-63, Central Islip (N.Y.) State Hosp., 1963-65; practice medicine specializing in psychoanalysis, N.Y.C., 1964—; asst. dir. Drug Addiction Research Inst., N.Y.C., 1968-69; dir. edn. Meyer Psychiat. Hosp., N.Y.C., 1970-73; lectr., supr. analyst postgrad. center Mental Health Clinic, N.Y.C., 1970—. Recipient Alekander Gralnick award, 1971. Diplomate Am. Bd. Psychiatry and Neurology. Fellow Am. Acad. Psychoanalysis; mem. AMA, Am. Psychiat. Assn., Am. Ontoanalytic Assn. Roman Catholic. Co-author: International Encyclopedia of Psychiatry, Psychology and Psychoanalysis, 1977. Home and Office: 1245 Park Ave New York City NY 10028

LOVE, GARY CORCORAN, coll. adminstr.; b. Rochester, N.Y., Dec. 8, 1950; s. Raymond R. and Helen A. (Lane) L.; B.A. cum laude in Edn., Siena Coll., 1973; M.S. in Counseling and Personnel Services, State U. N.Y., Albany, 1974; m. Susan Corcoran, June 14, 1975; 1 dau., Shannon C. Residence hall dir. State U. N.Y. Ag.-Tech., Alfred, 1973-76; asso. dean of students Mt. St. Mary's Coll., Emmitsburg, Md., 1976—. Mem. Am. Personnel and Guidance Assn., Am. Coll. Personnel Assn. Christian. Home: RD 2 Box 168 Emmitsburg MD 21727 Office: Mt St Mary's Coll Emmitsburg MD 21727

LOVE, JOHN ALBERT, engring. assn. exec.; b. Altoona, Pa., Aug. 26, 1926; s. Nathaniel Phillip and Alice Mary (Burkhardt) L.; B.S. in Indsl. Engring., Pa. State U., 1949; grad. Advanced Mgmt. Program, Harvard U., 1977; m. Rosemary A. Kruse, Aug. 11, 1951; children—John, Nancy, James, Kathy, Mary, Gregory. Surveyor, Factory Mut. Engring. Assn., Boston, 1949-50, inspector, Cleve., 1950-53, engr., Pitts., 1953-54, loss adjuster, Pitts., 1954-59, loss adjustor, Charlotte, N.C., 1959-63, loss adjuster, N.Y.C., 1963-65, v.p., dir. of adjustments, Norwood, Mass., 1965-75; exec. v.p. Factory Mut. Engring. Corp., Norwood, 1975-76, pres., dir., 1976—; dir. Factory Mut. Research Corp. Served with USNR, 1944-46. Mem. N.Y. Loss Execs. Assn., Norwood C. of C., Am. Legion. Clubs: Lion. Home: 68 Strasser Ave Westwood MA 02091 Office: 1151 Boston Providence Turnpike Norwood MA

LOVE, JOHN CLYDE, lawyer; b. Detroit, Feb. 12, 1940; s. John Patterson and Laurine (McLaughlin) L.; B.A., Johns Hopkins U., 1962; J.D., U. Md., 1968. Admitted to Md. bar, 1968; asso. firm Cameron & Reed, Bel Air, Md., 1969-71, partner, 1971—. Mem. peace edn. com., exec. com. Mid Atlantic region Am. Friends Service Com.; bd. dirs. ACLU, Md., v.p., 1977—. Mem. Am., Md. bar assns., Bentley Drivers Club, Rolls Royce Enthusiasts Club, Rolls Royce Owners Club (sec. 1969—). Home: Green Oak Farm Kingsville MD 21087 Office: 30 Office St Bel Air MD 21014

LOVE, RICHARD HARVEY, lawyer; b. Washington, Aug. 31, 1915; s. Leo Young and Grace Marie (Jett) L.; A.B., U. Md., 1936, LL.B., 1938; m. Betty Zane Schofield, Nov. 14, 1942 (dec. 1967); children—Richard, Robert, Edward, William, Elizabeth. Admitted to Md. and D.C. bars, 1939; legal research asst. to Hon. W. Calvin Chesnut, U.S. dist. judge, Md., 1938-40; pvt. practice law, 1940-41, 46—; counsel Bd. Zoning Appeals, Prince Georges County, Md., 1953-55. Served in enlisted grades AUS, 1941-42; commd. 2d lt. C.A.C., 1942, advanced through grades to maj., 1946; ETO; col. JAGC Res. Decorated Legion of Merit. Mem. Am., Md., D.C. bar assns., Judge Advs. Assn. (exec. sec.), Mil. Order Fgn. Wars (nat. comdr. gen.), Ft. Washington Hist. Soc., Assn. U.S. Army, Mil. Law Inst., Order of Coif, Phi Kappa Phi. Republican. Roman Catholic. Club: Army-Navy (Washington). Editor Judge Adv. Jour. Home: 6905 Carleton Terr College Park MD 20740 Office: 1010 Vermont Ave Washington DC 20005

LOVE, ROBERT ALEXANDER, physician; b. Bklyn., Apr. 4, 1913; s. Cornelius Ruxton and Grace Anderson (Smith) L.; B.A., Brown U., 1937; M.D., Cornell U., 1942; m. Josephine O'Connell, Sept. 2, 1967; children—Robert, Linda Reil, Pamela Terwilliger. Rotating intern, Kings County Hosp., Bklyn., 1942-43, resident internal medicine, 1946-47; staff Brookhaven Nat. Lab., Upton, N.Y., 1947—; asso. prof. State U.N.Y. at Stony Brook, 1968-78; cons. in field. Served with USN, 1943-46. Fellow Am. Occupational Med. Assn.; mem. N.Y. State, Suffolk County med. socs., Suffolk Acad. Medicine. Contbr. articles to profl. jours. Office: Brookhaven Nat Lab Upton NY 11975

LOVE, ROBERT LYMAN, coll. dean; b. Oswego, N.Y., July 28, 1925; s. Robert Barnum and Marion Alberta (Peavy) L.; student U. Rochester, 1943-44; A.B., Syracuse U., 1945, postgrad. in medicine, 1946-48, M.Ed., 1949; postgrad. Cornell U., 1963-64; m. Janet May Fuller, June 26, 1948; children—Robert H., Andrew L., Charles D., Cynthia S. Sci. tchr. Middlesex Valley Central Sch., Rushville, N.Y., 1949-53; mem. faculty Agrl. and Tech. Coll., SUNY, Alfred, 1953—, prof., dean Sch. Allied Health Techs.; adv. com. Nat. Tech. Inst. Deaf; health scis. adv. council SUNY; task force allied health City U. N.Y.; program evaluation steering com. AMA; allied health reviewer HEW; chmn. health sub-com. 39th Congl. Dist. Bd. dirs. Allegany County Comprehensive Health Planning Com.; adminstrv. bd. Alfred United Methodist Ch. Served with USNR, 1943-45. Fellow Sci. Tchrs. Assn. N.Y. State; mem. Am. Soc. Allied Health Professions, Am. Med. Record Assn., Am. Soc. Med. Technologists, Am. Assn. Clin. Chemists, N.Y. State Med. Record Assn., Empire State Assn. Med. Technologists, Rural Mgmt. Assn. Allegany County (pres.). Republican. Clubs: Lions, Masons, Order Eastern Star. Author: He and She, An Introduction to Human Sexuality and Birth Control, 1970. Editor: Upward Mobility for Lab Personnel, 1970. Home: Jericho Hill Alfred NY 14802 Office: SUNY Agrl and Tech Coll Alfred NY 14802

LOVE, SIDNEY IRWIN, psychologist; b. N.Y.C., Feb. 12, 1922; s. Irving Daniel and Dora (Sokol) L.; B.S.S., CUNY, 1946; M.S.S.W., Columbia U., 1948; Ph.D., Heed U., 1978; m. Shirley Belle Greenstein, May 10, 1948; children—Carolyn Beth Love Bersak, Jeanine Deborah. Asso. therapist Jewish Bd. Guardians, 1948-61; asst. prof. dept. edn. SUNY, Stonybrook, 1961-64; asst. prof. L.I. U., 1969-70, adj. asst. prof. dept. guidance and counseling, 1970—; founder, mem. faculty, tng. analyst Center for Modern Psychoanalytic Studies, N.Y.C., 1971—; mem. faculty, tng. analyst Phila. Sch. Psychoanalysis, 1974—; pres. Sidney I. Love, P.C.; mem. faculty Heed U., 1978—. Served with U.S. Army, 1943-45. Decorated Bronze Star, Purple Heart. Mem. Nat. Psych. Assn. for Psychoanalysis, Am. Orthopsychiat. Assn., Nat. Assn. Social Workers, Acad. Cert. Social Workers, Nat. Accreditation Assn. Psychoanalysis. Home: 2727 Riverdale Ave New York NY 10463 Office: 30 E 60th St New York NY 10022

LOVEJOY, LEE HAROLD, investment co. exec.; b. Aurora, Mo., July 19, 1936; s. Harold B. and Lorene E. (Spangler) L.; B.S., Drake U., 1958; m. Carol L. Nellis, Feb. 14, 1976; children by previous marriage—Steven Lee, Kristin Ann. With Paine Webber Jackson & Curtis, St. Paul, 1965-68, mgr. Twin Cities instl. dept., Mpls., 1968-72, v.p./mgr. New Eng., Boston, 1972-74, sr. v.p./mgr. nat. instl. equity dept. 1974-77; chief adminstrv. officer Paine Webber Mitchell Hutchins, N.Y.C., 1977—. St. Paul Mayor's Legal and Fin. Adv. Com. Bd. dirs. Presbyn. Homes Found.; trustee Drake U. Served to capt. USAF, 1958-65. Mem. Internat. Golf Sponsors Assn., Security Industry Assn., Boston Security Traders, Boston Investment Club, Security Traders N.Y., Sigma Alpha Epsilon. Omicron Delta Kappa, Arnold Air Soc. Republican. Presbyterian. Home: 238 W Oak St Ramsey NJ 07446 Office: 140 Broadway New York City NY 10004

LOVELACE, LINDA LEE, mfg. co. exec.; b. Milw., May 20, 1949; d. William Henry and Dorothy Caroline (Willer) Lewis; B.S. B.A., U. Denver, 1971; m. Donald Shriver Lovelace, Feb. 10, 1973. Asst. product group mgr. Lever Bros., N.Y.C., 1974, asso., 1975, group product mgr., 1976-79; dir. new products Norcliff Thayer div. Revlon, Tuckahoe, N.Y., 1979—. Office: One Scarsdale Rd Tuckahoe NY 10707

LOVELACE, RICHARD VAN EVERA, physicist; b. St. Louis, Oct. 16, 1941; s. Eldridge Hirst and Marjorie (Van Evera) L.; B.S., Washington U., St. Louis, 1964; Ph.D., Cornell U., 1970; m. Virginia Utermohlen, Dec. 22, 1972; children—Joya, Evera. Research asso. lab. plasma studies Cornell U., Ithaca, N.Y., 1970-71; research asso. Naval Research Lab., Washington, 1971-72; asst. prof. Sch. Applied and Engring. Physics Cornell U., 1972-78, asso. prof., 1978—; cons., Lawrence Livermore (Calif.) Lab., 1971-72; vis. research asso., plasma physics lab. Princeton, 1973-74. NSF fellow, 1966-69, grantee, 1973-74. Mem. Am. Astron. Soc., Am. Phys. Soc., Am. Geophys. Union, Optical Soc. Am., Tau Beta Pi, Phi Kappa Phi. Contbr. articles to profl. jours. Home: Ithaca NY 14850 Office: Dept Applied Physics Cornell Univ Ithaca NY 14850

LOVELL, RALPH MARSTON, pharmacist, state senator; b. Waldoboro, Maine, Dec. 19, 1910; s. John Harvey and Lottie E. (Magune) L.; Ph.G., Mass. Coll. Pharmacy, 1933; m. Rita Margarite Ferron, Oct. 30, 1930; children—Marilyn Lovell Burke, Maxine C., Susan Lovell Norris, Marston D., Ross Bulfinch, Dean Ralph, Barbara Ann. Pharmacist, Lovell's Pharmacy, Sanford, Maine, 1933-73; owner Lovell's Wholesale Ice Creams, 1936-70, Medicare mail order nation-wide drug bus.; mgr. Rexair Co., 1946-52; indsl. devel. cons., 1954-75; tourist and indsl. devel. specialist in Central Africa, U.S. Dept. Commerce, 1960; mem. Maine Senate, 1960-66, 76—, chmn. com. on liquor control, com. on human resources, mem. com. for vets. and retirement mem. Maine Com. on Aging; Maine senate mem. Nat. Commn. Sci. and Tech.; pres., dir. York County Bus. Devel. Corp., 1963—; mem. Maine Ho. Reps., 1974-76; owner Lovell's Ambulance Service, 1950-70. Pres. United Fund, Sanford, 1953, campaign chmn., 1955, sec., 1956-60, dir., 1950-70; field adviser Small Bus. Adminstrn., 1953-61, mem. adv. council, 1975—; dir. Pine Tree council Boy Scouts Am.; asst. dir. Civil Def., 1956-59; mem. Gov.'s Com. for Nat. Legis. Conf., 1965-66; founder Maine Sight Conservation Assn., 1955, treas., 1955-60, dir., 1955-62. Chmn. Republican City Commn., 1952-62; candidate from 1st dist. for Congress, 1966; past mem. Pa. Ho. of Reps. Recipient Presdl. medal, plaque as outstanding pharmacist Me.; citations as outstanding citizen by V.F.W., Lions, Rotary and Kiwanis. Mem. Maine (dir., exec. com. 1958—), York County pharm. assns., Newcomen Soc., Sanford C. of C. (pres. 1959, dir. 1954-62), Sanford Fish and Game Assn., Red Men, Grange. Congregationalist. Mason (Shriner), Lion (pres. 1952, dir. 1950—, dist. gov. 1955, internat. counsellor 1956—, pres.'s medal). Home: 83 Main St Sanford ME 04073 Office: 28 Winter St Sanford ME 04073

LOVELL, RICHARD HALLETT, lawyer; b. Brockton, Mass., Dec. 6, 1919; s. Stanley Platt and Mabel Lea (Bigney) L.; A.B. summa cum laude, Williams Coll., 1941; J.D. cum laude, Yale, 1948; m. Beverley Warren Smith, Feb. 28, 1942; children—Pamela L. Parker, Jonathan H., Alison L. Eisenman, Benjamin C., Christopher W. Admitted to Mass. bar, 1948; asso. firm Hill, Barlow, Goodale & Adams, Boston, 1948-53, partner, 1953-58; partner firm Rackemann, Sawyer & Brewster, Boston, 1958—; trustee W. Newton (Mass.) Savs. Bank, 1952-55; trustee, bd. investment Suffolk Franklin Savs. Bank, Boston, 1956—; dir. Gerrity Co., Inc., Mt. Waldo Ops., Inc., The Morgenthau Corp., Lovell Chem. Co. Alderman City of Newton (Mass.), 1952-55, mem. planning bd., 1950-52, chmn., 1952; treas. Newton Housing Authority, 1960-64, chmn., 1968; moderator Eliot Ch. of Newton, 1959-69, trustee, 1973—; trustee, v.p. Rebecca Pomroy Found., Newton, 1967—; trustee Newton Cemetery Corp., 1959—; trustee Newton-Wellesley Hosp., 1957—, pres., 1970-72, chmn., 1972-74; bd. dirs. Newton Community Devel. Found., 1970-72; trustee Boston Mus. Sci., 1960—, Charles A. King Trust, 1969—; bd. dirs. White Mountains (N.H.) Center for the Arts, 1975—. Served to lt. USNR, 1942-46. Mem. Am., Mass., Boston bar assns. Clubs: The Country, Union of Boston, Longwood Cricket, City. Home: 234 Park St Newton MA 02158 also Cottage Rd Jefferson NH 03583 Office: 28 State St Boston MA 02109

LOVELY, PETER MICHAEL, realtor, ins. broker; b. Brockton, Mass., Jan. 26, 1939; s. Cleveland Joseph and Marjorie Christina (Robinson) L.; A.S., Dean Jr. Coll., 1959; B.S., Babson Inst., 1962; J.D., New Eng. Sch. Law, 1972; m. Ann Elizabeth Platt, Sept. 3, 1960; children—John Michael, Jeffrey Michael, Susan Ann. Propr., The Lovely Agy., Foxboro, Mass., 1962—; trustee Hearth and Home Realty Trust, Foxboro, Mass., 1970—. Bd. dirs. Hockomock YMCA, 1974-76. Served with USMCR, 1957-65. Mem. Ind. Ins. Agts. Assn., New Eng. Mut. Ins. Brokers, Nat. Assn. Realtors. Roman Catholic. Clubs: K.C., Foxboro Community (dir. 1975-76). Home: 2 Ridge Rd Foxboro MA 02035 Office: 41 Main St Foxboro MA 02035

LOW, CHOW-ENG, chemist; b. Perak, Malaysia, May 31, 1938; s. Ah-Chow and Tiew-Tiah (Ng) L.; came to U.S., 1964, naturalized, 1977; B.S., Chinese U. Hong Kong, 1962; M.S., Tex. So. U., 1966; Ph.D., U. Tex., Austin, 1970; m. Teresa Lingchun Kao, June 26, 1966; children—Huan-Cheh, Cecilia Chia-Cheh, Jasmine I-Ming. Vis. asst. prof. La. State U., Baton Rouge, 1970-71; postdoctoral research fellow Ind. U., Bloomington, 1972-75; research asso. bio-chemistry U. Tex. Med. Branch, Galveston, 1976-78; asst. prof. biochemistry George Washington U. Med. Center, 1978—. Jr. C. of C. Overseas scholar, Hong Kong, 1958-62; Robert A. Welch Found. fellow, 1967-70. Fellow Chem. Soc. London; mem. Am. Chem. Soc., AAAS, Sigma Xi. Asso. editor Chemistry mag., 1960-61. Contbr. articles to profl. jours. Home: 9105 Bramble Pl Annandale VA 22003 Office: Dept Biochemistry George Washington U Med Center 2300 Eye St NW Washington DC 20037

LOW, DOUGLAS JOHN, accounting exec.; b. Toronto, Ont., Can., Feb. 10, 1934; s. Douglas Andrew and Florence Elizabeth (King) L.; B. Commerce U. Toronto, 1955; m. Jeanette Lynn MacDonald, Sept. 10, 1960; children—Douglas, Jacqueline. With Deloitte, Haskins & Sells, Chartered Accountants, 1955—, audit mgr., Montreal, 1962-66, partner, Toronto, 1966-71, Montreal, 1971-74, mng. partner, Montreal, 1974—, mem. mgmt. com., 1975—. Past pres. Tudor Singers of Montreal. Chartered accountant, Ont., 1955. Mem. Can. Inst. Chartered Accountants (mem. accounting research com. 1971-77, chmn. com. 1976-77), Inst. Chartered Accountants Ont., Order Chartered Accountants Que. (edn. com. 1973-77, profl. inspection com. 1978—, mem. bur. 1978—), Soc. Mgmt. Accountants. Baptist. Home: 280 Beverley Ave Mount Royal PQ H3P 1K9 Canada Office: Suite 3210 1 Place Ville Marie Montreal PQ H3B 2W3 Canada

LOWE, ETHEL BLACK, ret. educator, artist; b. Klowa County, Okla., Jan. 30, 1904; d. Benjamin Alonzo and Harriet Ann (Heaton) Black; B.A., Central State U., Edmond, Okla., 1926; M.A., U. Tulsa, 1937; student U. Okla., U. Colo., Columbia; student U. Hawaii, summer 1958; m. William Glenn Lowe, June 5, 1939 (dec. 1942). Tchr. pub. schs., Okla., 1922-39, N.Y. 1942-49, 50-68; teaching prin. Dragon Sch., Sasebo, Kyushu, Japan, 1949-50; works exhibited since 1945—; exhibitions include Nat. Assn. Women Artists, 1953, 55, 60, 62, 71-73, 76, 77, 78, Terry Nat. Art Exhibit, 1952, Provincetown Art Assn., 1952-53, Nassau Community Coll., 1971, 86th annual exhbn. Nat. Assn. Women Artists, N.Y.C., 1975. Reprodns. of works in newspapers and mags. Fellow Internat. Inst. Arts and Letters; mem. N.Y. State Ret. Tchrs. Assn., Nat. Assn. Women Artists, Am. Watercolor Soc., Delta Kappa Gamma. Home: 48-50 44th St Woodside NY 11377

LOWE, GEORGE JOHN, audio visual specialist; b. Flushing, N.Y., July 19, 1951; s. George Edward and Florence Dorothy (Kinney) L.; student N.Y. Inst. Photography, 1970. Free-lance photographer, Flushing, 1970—; with Honeywell Photo Products div., 1970-77. Recipient certificate of participation Queens Coll. Bicentennial Com. of Coll. City N.Y., 1975, certificate of recognition Fine Art Color Lab., 1976. Notary pub. State of N.Y. Mem. Profl. Photographers Am., Smithsonian Assos., Nat. Rifle Assn. Am. (certified marksmanship instr.), Queens County Sportsman's Fedn. (pub. relations ofcl. 1974—, award 1976), Flushing Sportsman's Club, Internat. Indsl. TV Assn., IEEE, N.Y. State Conservation Council. Home: 55-09 137th St Flushing NY 11355

LOWE, JAMES LEWIS, minister, educator; b. Chattanooga, Nov. 8, 1929; s. Frank Alvertus and Virginia (Bowers) L.; B.A., Tenn. Temple U., 1957; B.D., Crozer Theol. Sem., 1960, M.Div., 1970; D.D., Pioneer Theol. Sem., 1960; M.A., West Chester State Coll., 1972; D.Min., Lancaster Theol. Sem., 1978; Th.D., Clarksville Sch. Theology, 1978; m. Virginia Joann Stancliff, June 11, 1952; children—James, Jonathan, Jeffrey, Jerrold. Pastor Bethel Baptist Chapel, Chattanooga, 1955, Sholar Ave. Bapt. Chapel, 1956, Jobstown (N.J.) Bapt. Ch., 1957-61, Immanuel Bapt. Ch., Quincy, Ill., 1961-62, Third Bapt. Ch., Phila., 1962-68, Spruce St. Bapt. Ch., Newtown Square, Pa., 1973—; tchr. English Ridley Sr. High Sch., Folsom, Pa., 1968-72; lectr. English Pa. State U., 1972—. Served with USAF, 1950-54; served as chaplain USNR, 1967—. Mem. Deltiologists of Am. (founder, pres.), Nat. Assn. Tchrs. English. Republican. Club: Rotary (chaplain, Newtown Square). Author: Lincoln Postcard Catalog, 1967, 72, Standard Postcard Catalog, 1968, Washington Postcard Catalog, 1973, Bibliography of Postcard Literature, 1970, Detroit Pub. Co. Collector's Guide, 1975. Home: 3709 Gradyville Rd Newtown Square PA 19073 Office: 3701 Gradyville Rd Newtown Square PA 19073

LOWE, JOSEPH THEODORE, JR., gear co. exec.; b. Gettysburg, Pa., Dec. 5, 1941; s. Joseph T. and Hazel (Eiker) L.; B.S. in Aerospace Engring., Pa. State U., 1963; m. Judith Ann Pierce, July 25, 1964; children—Christine, Craig. Asst. project engr. Phila. Naval Shipyard, 1963-64; with Phila. Gear Corp., King of Prussia, Pa., 1964—, assembly supt., 1975-77, dir. customer service, 1977-79, gen. mgr., 1979—; mem. faculty Pa. Inst. Tech., 1964-69. Chmn. Upper Merion Community Fair Assn., 1978-79. Mem. Am. Iron and Steel Inst., Pa. (v.p. 1977-78; Outstanding Elected State Officer award 1978, regional dir. 1977, dist. dir. 1975-76), Upper Merion (pres. 1974-75) Jaycees. Republican. Presbyterian. Address: 508 Elliott Dr King of Prussia PA 19406

LOWE, MERVIN RAY, educator; b. York County, Pa., Apr. 11, 1920; s. Clark Amos and Beatrice Ray (Norris) L.; B.A., Pa. State U., 1940; M.A., U. Pa., 1948, Ph.D., 1951; certificate Biarritz-Am. U., France, 1945, Middlebury Coll., 1949. English tchr. McRae-Helena High Sch., McRae, Ga., 1940-41; asst. instr. English, U. Pa., Phila., 1946-50; editorial layout asst. Time mag., 1948-49; instr. English Pa. State U., University Park, 1950-54, asst. prof. English, 1954-62; asso. prof. Widener Coll., Chester, Pa., 1962-66, prof. English, 1966—; vis. prof. U. Dijon (France), 1953-54, U. Saigon (Vietnam), 1958-59; editorial cons. J.B. Lippincott, 1962; writer USIS, U.S. Dept. State, 1962; lectr. in field. Served with U.S. Army, 1942-46. Reader's Digest Found. teaching grantee, 1953-54; Smith-Mundt grantee, U.S. Dept. State, 1958-59. Mem. AAUP, Modern Lang. Assn., Am. Studies Assn., Nat. Council Tchrs. English, ACLU, Common Cause, Nat. Trust for Historic Preservation, Smithsonian Instn., Phila. Mus. Art, Kappa Phi Kappa. Republican. Lutheran. Asso. bibliographer Modern Lang. Assn., 1961-63. Home: 206 A W Elkinton Ave Chester PA 19013 Office: Widener Coll Chester PA 19013

LOWELL, CHAPIN MCKINNEY, mech. engr.; b. Buffalo, June 15, 1911; B.M.E., U. Mich., 1934, M.S.E. in Engring. Mechs., 1939; m. Helen Persons, May 24, 1941; children—James C., David J. Mech. engr. Worthington Pump & Machinery Corp., Buffalo, 1934-38, supr. applied mechs., 1946-73; mech. engr. Timken Roller Bearing Co., Canton, Ohio, 1939-40; cons. mech. engring., East Aurora, N.Y., 1973—. Served with Ordnance Corps, U.S. Army, 1940-46. Registered profl. engr., N.Y. Fellow ASME (life); mem. Soc. Exptl. Stress Analysis (life). Republican. Presbyterian. Author: The Crankshaft, 1975; contbr. articles to ASME, 1955-74. Home: 272 Elmwood Ave East Aurora NY 14052

LOWELL, STANLEY EDGAR, accountant; b. N.Y.C., Oct. 12, 1923; s. Benjamin and Valerie (Steinberg) L.; student Tchrs. Coll., Columbia, 1945; B.B.A. cum laude, Coll. City N.Y., 1948. Staff accountant S.D. Leidesdorf & Co., Chgo., 1952-54; chief accountant Polyplastex United Inc., Union, N.J., 1955-57; chief auditor, chief accountant Hudson Pulp & Paper, Inc., N.Y.C., 1957-64; internal audit mgr. Screen Gems div. Columbia Pictures Industries, N.Y.C. 1966-74; internal audit mgr. Alpha Metals, Inc., Jersey City, 1974-76; asst. dir. internal audit City U. N.Y., 1977—. Served with USAAF, 1943-44. Mem. Inst. Internal Auditors (certified), Am. Inst. C.P.A.'s, N.Y. State Soc. C.P.A.'s, EDP Auditors Assn. Home: 302 W 12th St New York City NY 10014

LOWELL, STANLEY HERBERT, lawyer; b. N.Y.C., Apr. 13, 1919; s. Isidore and Mildred (Cohen) Lowenbraun; B.S., Coll. City N.Y., 1939; LL.B., Harvard, 1942; m. Vivian Abrams, Mar. 29, 1947 (div. 1973); children—Jeffrey, Darcy, Lauri; m. 2d, Leona Schaevitz, June 20, 1974. Admitted to N.Y. bar, 1942; asst. U.S. atty., N.Y., 1943-47; partner law firm Lowenbraun & Lowell, N.Y.C., 1947-58, Lowell & Karassik and predecessors, N.Y.C., 1966-78, Fink, Weinberger, Fredman, Berman & Lowell, 1978—; former lectr. Coll. City N.Y., New Sch. Social Research; adj. prof. Fordham U. Sch. Social Services. Asst. to borough pres., Manhattan, 1950-53; exec. asst. to mayor, N.Y.C., 1954-58, dep. mayor, 1958; chmn. N.Y.C. Commn. Human Rights, 1960-65. Chmn., N.Y.C. com. Am. Jewish Tercentenary; past chmn. lawyers com., bd. govs. United Jewish Appeal; chmn. Nat. Conf. on Soviet Jewry, 1974-76; past chmn. Greater N.Y. Conf. on Soviet Jewry; mem. praesidium Brussels World Conf. on Soviet Jewry; chmn. Com. for Pub. Higher Edn.; past pres. Citizens Com. for Children of N.Y.; past vice chmn. Nat. Jewish Community Relations Adv. Council. Del. Democratic Nat. Conv., 1960, 64, 68; exec. com. Dem. State Com., 1960-68. Recipient medal City N.Y., 1965; John F. Kennedy Peace award Jewish Nat. Fund, 1966; Judge Joseph Proskauer award Lawyers United Jewish Appeal Fedn. Mem. N.Y. State Bar Assn., Assn. Bar City N.Y., Harvard Law Sch. Assn. N.Y. (past trustee), Coll. City N.Y. Alumni Assn. (past pres.). Home: 15 Paxford Ln Scarsdale NY 10583 Office: 551 Fifth Ave New York City NY 10017

LOWEN, WILLIAM OSCAR, educator; b. Bronx, N.Y., Dec. 19, 1937; s. Henry and Sophie (Sorenson) Lowenberg; B.S., Wagner Coll., 1958; M.S., Syracuse U., 1963; m. Dorothy May Chanin, June 8, 1958; children—Mark Shawn, Jeffrey Bruce. Sr. lab. technician Westchester County Div. Labs. and Research, Valhalla, N.Y., 1958-59; tchr., high sch., Bridgehampton, N.Y., 1963-65, Kings Park, N.Y., 1965-66; mem. faculty Suffolk County Community Coll., Selden, N.Y., 1966—, asso. prof. biology, 1969-74, prof. biology, 1974—, head dept., 1968—. Partner, Moraine Stamp & Coin, Kings Park, N.Y., 1974—. Asso. chmn. edn. com. Greentree Civic Assn., Kings Park, 1966-68; active Boy Scouts Am. Mem. AAAS, Am. Soc. Microbiology, Am. Mus. Natural History, AAUP, Nat. Audubon Soc., Sigma Xi. Jewish. Democrat. Author: Laboratory Manual for Introductory Microbiology, 1975. Home: 31 Landview Dr Kings Park NY 11754 Office: 533 College Rd Selden NY 11784

LOWENSTEIN, JOYCE SANDRA, psychologist; b. Queens, N.Y., Feb. 7, 1941; d. Louis and Ruth (Ostrover) Gorelick; student (N.J. State scholar) Douglass Coll., 1958-60; B.A. in Psychology (Univ. scholar), Hofstra U., 1962, M.A., 1964; Ph.D. in Human Devel., U. Md., 1977; 1 son, Adam. Research asst. Human Resources Found., Albertson, N.Y., 1961-63; psychology intern St. Elizabeth's Hosp., Washington, 1964-65; psychologist Prince Georges County Sch. System, Landover, Md., 1965—; cons. Systems Devel. Corp., Santa Monica, Calif., 1975. Mem. Am., Md. psychol. assns., Prince Georges County Sch. Psychology Assn. (pres. 1977-79), Psi Chi, Pi Gamma Mu, Phi Delta Kappa. Contbr. articles in field to profl. jours. Home: 1412 Post Ln Bowie MD 20716 Office: 6501 Lowland Dr Landover MD 20786

LOWERY, PEARL VIRGINIA, civic worker; b. Parkersburg, W.Va., Dec. 9, 1897; d. Artley Elmer and Ella V. (Howard) Caskey; grad. Savage Sch. Phys. Edn., 1918; B.S., Columbia U., 1923, B.S., 1943, M.A., 1947; postgrad. fellow N.Y. U., 1948; m. Thomas J. Lowery, June 22, 1921. Tchr., Mt. Vernon High Sch., N.Y., 1918-68; editor N.Y. State Bus. and Profl. Woman; free-lance writer and pub. speaker. Mem. Layman's Nat. Traffic Com., 1959; disaster chmn. local chpt. ARC, 1938-41, first aid chmn. 1941-52, br. chmn., Mt. Vernon, bd. dirs., mem. exec. com., Westchester County; mem. N.Y. State Women's Council, Dept. Commerce, 1960-65; mem. narcotics addiction com. Mt. Vernon Council Community Services, 1968—; zone chmn. N.Y. State Ret. Tchrs. Assn. Bicentennial Com., 1976; chmn. com. to lobby N.Y. legislature to restore N.Y. tchrs. pensions; active Girl Scouts U.S.A., also Nat. PTA, Nat. YWCA. Recipient Nat. Pub. Affairs award Bus. and Profl. Women's Clubs, 1950; named Bus. Woman of Year, C. of C., 1968; Mem. award Bus. and Profl. Women's Clubs, 1950. Mem. AAUW (charter mem. West County), Am. Acad. Polit. and Social Sci., Fedn. Bus. and Profl. Women's Clubs (N.Y. pres. 1958-60, mem. nat. bd. 1958-60), LWV, Nat. Council Women U.S., Internat. Platform Assn., AAUW, Falls Village-Canaan Hist. Soc., Nat. Woman's Party. Republican. Clubs: Area Ret. Teachers (pres.); Bronxville Women's. Home: 300 Hayward Ave Mount Vernon NY 10552 also 34 and 58 Pine Grove Falls Village CT 06031

LOWERY, WILLIAM HERBERT, lawyer; b. Toledo, June 8, 1925; s. Kenneth Alden and Drusilla (Pfanner) L.; Ph.B., U. Chgo., 1947; J.D., U. Mich., 1950; m. Carolyn Dodge Broadwell, June 27, 1947; children—Kenneth Latham, Marcia Mitchell. Admitted to Pa. bar, 1950; asso. Dechert, Price & Rhoads, Phila., 1950-58, partner, 1958—, mng. partner, 1970-72. Counsel, S.S. Huebner Found. for Ins. Edn., 1970—; permanent mem. Jud. Conf. of 3d Circuit Ct. Appeals. Chmn. zoning hearing bd. Tredyffrin Twp., Chester County, Pa., 1959-75. Regional chmn. Mich. Law Sch. Fund, 1966-68; bd. dirs. Paoli Meml. Hosp., 1964—, pres., 1972-75; mem. task force S.E. Pa. Regional Comprehensive Health Planning, 1970-75; mem. trustees adv. com. Hosp. Assn. Pa., 1973-76. Trustee Clin. Biochemistry and Behavioral Research Inst. Served to lt. USAAF, 1943-46. Mem. Am. (ins. law sect., vice chmn. life ins law com.), Pa., Phila. bar assns., Juristic Soc., Am., Pa. socs. hosp. attys., Am. Judicature Soc., Phi Gamma Delta, Phi Delta Phi. Republican. Presbyn. (elder 1968-72). Clubs: Urban (Phila.); Waynesborough Country (Paoli, Pa.). Home: 542 Tory Hill Rd Devon PA 19333 Office: 3400 Centre Sq W 1500 Market St Philadelphia PA 19102

LOWMAN, ROBERT MORRIS, radiologist; b. Balt., Dec. 31, 1912; s. Hyam David and Fannie (Wolfson) L.; student Johns Hopkins U., 1928-29, Harvard U., 1929-32; M.D., U. Md., 1936; m. Olga Soroka, June 27, 1937; children—Gail Stephanie, George Sumner. Intern, Balt. City Hosp., 1936-37; resident and fellow Mass. Meml. Hosp., Boston, 1937-40; practice medicine, specializing in radiology, New Haven, 1940—; instr. U. Pa. Grad. Sch. Medicine, 1940-42; dir. meml. unit, radiology dept. Yale New Haven Hosp., 1952—; prof. radiology Yale U. Sch. Medicine, 1962—, acting chmn. dept., 1972. NIH grantee, 1960-65, Conn. Heart Assn. grantee, 1965-66, James Hudson Brown Fund grantee, 1966-67, Am. Cancer Soc. grantee, 1974-75; fellow Davenport Coll., Yale U., 1974—. Mem. New Haven Med. Soc. (pres. 1962-63), Am., New Eng. (pres. 1970) roentgen ray socs., Assn. Univ. Radiologists, N.Am., Conn. radiol. socs. Contbr. articles to med. jours. Home: 26 Marlborough Rd North Haven CT 06473 Office: 789 Howard Ave New Haven CT 06504

LOWRY, BETTY, writer; b. Hollywood, Calif., July 24, 1927; d. Hans and Emily Paula (Doerges) Trishman; A.B., U. Calif. at Berkeley, 1948; M.A., Boston Coll., 1977; m. Ritchie P. Lowry, Sept. 5, 1948; children—Peter Ritchie, Robin Emily. Copy chief account exec. Abbott Kimball Co., San Francisco, 1948-50; dir. young homemaker div. Jackson's Furniture Co., Oakland, Calif., 1950-52; columnist Family Travel, N.Y.C., 1968-73; free lance writer, 1946—. Pres. Family Service League, Chico, Calif., 1963; mem. Calif. Home Soc., Chico, 1957-64; mem. steering com. Hospitality and Info. Service, Washington, 1964-66; chmn. Joint Ednl. Policies Com., Wayland, Mass., 1970-71. Bd. dir. Jr. Mus., 1962-64. Recipient award Chico C. of C., 1961; 1st pl. nat. poetry award AAUW, 1964. Mem. Nat. League Am. Pen Women (chpt. pres. 1970-72), New Eng. Poetry Club (treas.), Women In Communications, Poetry Soc. Am. Democrat. Home: 79 Moore Rd Wayland MA 01778

LOWRY, EMMERT MILLER, JR., computer co. exec.; b. Hagerstown, Md., Nov. 17, 1924; s. Emmert Miller and Eva Bell (Wellinger) L.; S.B., Mass. Inst. Tech., 1949, S.M., 1951; M.B.A., Harvard, 1956; postgrad. Dartmouth, 1963; m. Alice Martha Bell, Apr. 22, 1946; children—Emmert Miller III, Cynthia Bell (Mrs. Michael P. D'Angelo), Johnne Eve (Mrs. Kenneth Bate). Research asst., Mass. Inst. Tech., Cambridge, 1949-51; engr. in charge hydraulic testing lab. S. Morgan Smith Co., York, Pa., 1951-54; with IBM, various locations, 1956—, dir. distbn., Endicott, N.Y., 1969-70, area procurement mgr., 1970-75, mgr. mgmt. devel. and personnel research, 1975—. Instr. Pa. State Tech. Inst., York, part time, 1951-52. Pres., Morewood Home Owners Assn., Port Washington, N.Y., 1961-62; treas. York council Boy Scouts Am., 1952-54. Served with USAAF, 1943-46. Registered profl. engr., Pa. Mem. Tioga County Hist. Soc., Broome County C. of C., Tiawagha Players Assn., Sigma Xi, Phi Kappa Sigma, Tau Beta Pi, Chi Epsilon. Episcopalian. Mason. Club: Binghamton Country (Endwell, N.Y.). Home: RD 3 Box 24 Lisle Rd Owego NY 13827 Office: 1701 North St Endicott NY 13760

LOWRY, LOUIS DALE, physician; b. Ft. Scott, Kans., Mar. 1, 1937; s. Benjamin Louis and Kathryn Ruth (Tapp) L.; A.B., U. Mo., 1958, M.D., 1962; m. Judith Gene McCormick, Aug. 29, 1959; children—Bradley Alan, James Neal, Benjamin Russel, Troy William, Juliana. Commd. lt. comdr., U.S. Navy, 1961; ret., 1967; resident in otolaryngology U. Chgo., 1967-71; asst. prof. dept. otorhinolaryngology and human communication U. Okla., 1971-73; asst. prof. U. Pa., Phila., 1973—; mem. staff Pa. Hosp., VA Hosp., Phila.; attending staff Children's Hosp., Phila. Fellow ACS; mem. Pa., Phila. County med. socs., Phila. Soc. Facial Plastic Surgeons (v.p.), Phila. Laryngological Soc. (mem. exec. com.), Soc. Univ. Otolaryngologists, Assn. Research in otolaryngology, Am. Soc. Head and Neck Surgery, Am. Acad. Facial and Plastic Reconstructive Surgery. Republican. Presbyn. Club: Masons. Author: Otorhinolaryngology in Family Practice, 2d edit., 1978. Office: 3400 Spruce St Philadelphia PA 19104

LOWRY, RICHARD WURSTER, bldg. materials corp. exec.; b. Upper Darby, Pa., Apr. 22, 1936; s. Cardeen C. and Edna (Wurster) L.; A.B., Dartmouth, 1958, M.B.A., 1959; m. Carol Edwards, Apr. 7, 1962; children—Kimberly A., Jennifer B., Leslie W. Fin. analyst Champion Papers, Inc., Knightsbridge, Ohio, 1960-64, dir. planning, 1964-65, mgr., 1965-68; v.p., gen. mgr. Fed. Office Products div. U.S. Plywood-Champion Papers, Inc., Chgo., 1968-69, pres., 1969, pres. distbn. div., Chgo., 1969-74; v.p., gen. mgr. Trend Carpet div. Champion Internat. Corp., Rome, Ga., 1974-76; v.p., spl. asst. to pres., Champion Internat. Corp., Stamford, 1976—. Served to lt. USAR. Presbyterian. Home: 627 Laurel Rd New Canaan CT 06840 Office: Champion International 1 Landmark Sq Stamford CT 06921

LOWRY, ROBERT BEATTIE, banker; b. Phila., Sept. 12, 1926; s. Robert and Emily Elizabeth (Beattie) L.; student Va. Mil. Inst., 1944-45; B.S., Drexel U., 1948; postgrad. Temple U., 1951-52; m. Elizabeth V. Steele, Sept. 15, 1951; children—Robert Beattie, Debra Lowry Town. With First Nat. Bank of Phila., 1948-55, First Pa. Bank & Trust Co., 1955-57; asst. cashier mktg. and advt. div. Phila. Nat. Bank, 1958-65; v.p. mktg. div. First Nat. Bank of S. Jersey, Atlantic City, 1965—; dir. Mgmt. Inst., Glassboro State Coll., 1972-74. Treas., Upper Merion (Pa.) Sch. Bd. Dirs., 1957-66; v.p. Ocean City Bd. Edn., 1970-74; chmn. U.S. Savs. Bonds for Atlantic County, 1970—, Atlantic County chpt. Cystic Fibrosis, 1966-75; bd. dirs. Jr. Achievement, 1966-71, Atlantic City Boys Club, 1970-76; active S. Jersey Devel. Council, 1966—, Atlantic City Improvement Assn., 1966—, Atlantic City All Sports Assn., 1970—, Greater Atlantic City Pub. Interest Coalition, 1975-77. Served with USAAF, 1944-45. Recipient Young Man of Year award Valley Forge Jaycees, 1962, Achievement award Nat. Cystic Fibrosis Research Fund.. 1969; hon. treas. Jewish Nat. Fund of S. Jersey, 1971. Mem. Ams. for Competitive Enterprise System, Am. Inst. Banking, Atlantic City Hotel and Motel Assn., Nat. Bank Mktg. Assn. (N.Y. Met. chpt., Pen-Jer-Del chpt.), Greater Atlantic City (dir. 1966—), S. Jersey chambers commerce, N.J. Bankers Assn., N.J. Travel and Resort Assn., S. Jersey Pub. Relations Assn., Drexel U. Alumni Assn., Morris Guards, Newcomen Soc., So. Jersey Mfg. Assn. (dir. 1976—), N.J. Taxpayers Assn. (dir. 1970—), Internat. Assn. Approved Basketball Ofcls. (Atlantic bd. 195 1967—). Club: Centerton Golf. Home: 300 E 19th St Ocean City NJ 08226 Office: South Carolina and Atlantic Aves Atlantic City NJ 08401

LOWRY, TED HARVIE EDMUND, film producer; b. Richmond, Va., Aug. 11, 1929; s. Harvie Edmund and Mavin (Stephenson) L.; student Sch. of Art Inst. Chgo., 1948-52; m. Marianne Carter, Apr. 20, 1955; children—Stephenson, Tedde Louise, Pricilla Ann, Adam Jonas, Samantha Beth. Designer, Wilding Pictures, Chgo., 1953-54; designer, dir. Dekko Films, Boston, 1954-55; designer, dir., producer Pelican Films, N.Y.C., 1956-68; designer, dir., writer, producer Ted Lowry Prodns., Westport, Conn., 1968—. Served with USNR, 1952-53. Recipient Blue Ribbon award Ednl. Film Library Assn.; Golden Eagle award Council on Internat. Nontheatrical Events; Silver award Chgo. Internat. Film Festival; Bronze award Atlanta Film Festival; Silver award San Francisco Film Festival; Gold medal U.S. Indsl. Film Festival, numerous others. Mem. Dirs. Guild Am. Home: 30 Hillandale Rd Westport CT 06880 Office: Box 492 Westport CT 06880

LOWRY, WARREN KENNETH, info. systems dir.; b. Waynesburg, Pa., May 17, 1914; s. William John and Alice Carol (Gilliland) L.; B.A., Pa. State U., 1938; B.S., Columbia, 1939; m. R. Jane Kern, May 15, 1952; 1 son, Kevin Kern. Reference librarian Bowdoin Coll., Brunswick, Me., 1939-43; aerial navigator Northeast Airlines, Presque Isle, Me., 1943-44; chief, reference services U.S. Dept. Commerce, Washington, 1946-47; chief Navy Research sect. Library of Congress, 1948-49; dir. Army Library, Washington, 1949-52; dir. tech. info. and intelligence USAF, 1952-56; dir. libraries and info. systems Bell Telephone Labs., Murray Hill, N.J., 1956—. Cons. U.S. Govt., Univs., Founds. Pres., Internat. Fedn. Documentation, The Hague, 1965-68; trustee Engring. Index Inc., N.Y., 1962—, N.Y.C. Metro, 1974—. Mem. Sci. Info. Council, 1966-69, chmn., 1969. Vis. com. U. Pitts. Grad. Sch., 1968-72, Mass. Inst. Tech., 1973—; vis. com. Rutgers U. Grad. Sch., 1973—, chmn., 1975-76; adv. com. Nat. Commn. on Libraries and Info. Sci., 1973-75; systems planning coordinator Pahlavi Nat. Library, Iran, 1975-76; chmn. adv. bd. Clarkson Coll. Tech., 1977—; chmn. task group on tech. info. Indsl. Research Inst., 1977—. Served to lt. USNR, 1944-46. Recipient USAF Superior Performance awards, 1954-55, NATO Distinguished Service citation, 1957, Pope Paul VI Silver medal, 1968. Fellow Inst. Info. Scientists; mem. Am. Soc. Info. Sci., Sigma Pi. Club: Bell Laboratories (pres. 1971-72). Contbr. articles to profl. jours. Home: 21 Joanna Way Summit NJ 07901 Office: Bell Telephone Labs Murray Hill NJ 07974

LOWTHER, FRANK EUGENE, research physicist; b. Orrville, Ohio, Feb. 3, 1929; s. John Finger and Mary Elizabeth (Mackey) L.; grad. Ohio State U., 1952; m. Elizabeth E. Koons, Apr. 21, 1951; children—Cynthia E., Victoria J., James A., Frank Eugene. Scientist missile systems div. Raytheon, Boston, 1952-57, Gen. Electric, Syracuse, also Daytona Beach, Fla., 1957-62; pvt. cons., 1962-67; dir. Purification Sci. Inc., 1967-72; mgr. ozone research and devel. W.R. Grace Co., Curtis Bay, Md., 1972-75; sr. engring. asso. Linde div. Union Carbide Corp., Tonawanda, N.Y., 1975—. Recipient Inventor of Year award Patent Law Assn. and Tech. Socs. Council, 1976. Asso. fellow Am. Inst. Aeros. and Astronautics; sr. mem. I.E.E.E. Mason. Patentee in field of ozone tech. Home: 373 Woodbridge Ave Buffalo NY 14214 Office: Linde Div Union Carbide Corp Tonawanda NY 14150

LOWY, LOUIS, educator, gerontologist, social worker; b. Prague, Czechoslovakia, June 14, 1920; s. Max and Anna (Bolz) L.; came to U.S., 1946; B.S., Boston U., 1949, M.S., 1951; Ph.D., Harvard U., 1966; m. Ditta Jedlinsky, Dec. 2, 1946; children—Susan, Peter. Asst. exec. dir. Bridgeport (Conn.) Community Center, 1951-55; asst. prof. Boston U., 1955-62, asso. prof., 1962-66, prof., 1966—, asso. dean, 1977—; cons., asso. Center for Gerontology, 1974-77, edn. coordinator, 1977—; cons. in field U.S. and abroad. Mem. Mass. Gov.'s Commn. Aging, 1970-71; chmn. profl. adv. com. to Mass. Dept. Elder Affairs, 1972-74, 77—. Recipient distinguished alumni award Boston U., 1966, distinguished award Mass. chpt. Nat. Assn. Social Workers, 1963, 73. Fellow Gerontology Soc.; mem. Nat. Assn. Social Workers (pres. Mass. chpt. 1961-63), Council on Social Work Edn., Am. Sociol. Assn., Internat. Council Social Welfare, Internat. Assn. Schs. Social Work. Author: (with others) Integrative Teaching and Learning, 1971; Adult Education and Group Work, 1955; Function of Social Work in Changing Society, 1974; Lehrplanentwicklung, 1974; Social Work with the Aging, 1978. Contbr. articles to profl. jours. U.S. and abroad. Home: 203 Lincoln St Newton Highlands MA 02161 Office: 264 Bay State Rd Boston MA 02115

LOYND, JACK SHAPLEIGH, mfg. exec.; b. Brackenridge, Pa., June 3, 1918; s. William Richard and Annabel Irene (Crawford) L.; B.S., Washington and Jefferson Coll., 1940; J.D., U. Pitts., 1945; m. Eva Marie Rasch, Oct. 13, 1951; children—Jennifer Ann, Scott R., Geoffrey C. Admitted to Pa. bar, 1945; practiced in Pitts., 1945-55; indsl. relations counsel Allegheny Ludlum Industries, Inc., and predessor, Pitts., 1955-74, v.p. labor relations, 1974—; dir. Gen. Press Corp., Tarentum, Pa., 1966—, Shawnee Highlands, Inc., Tarentum, 1968—, Loynd & Lindquist, Inc., Tarentum, 1974—, CPIA Inc., Tarentum, 1977—, New-Ken Health Care Systems, Inc., New Kensington, 1978—. Bd. dirs. Legal Aid Soc. Pitts., 1967-76, United Mental Health, Inc., Pitts., 1975-78; alumni trustee Washington and Jefferson Coll., 1970-75. Mem. Am., Pa., Allegheny County bar assns., Am. Iron and Steel Inst. Internat. Soc. Labor Law and Social Legislation, Am. Arbitration Assn. Republican. Episcopalian. Clubs: Duquesne, University Edgewood Country, Mason (Pitts.). Contbr. law review articles to profl. jours. Home: 40 Holland Rd Pittsburgh PA 15235 Office: 2000 Oliver Bldg Pittsburgh PA 15222

LU, MILTON MING-DEH, plastic surgeon; b. Chengtu, China, Nov. 12, 1919; s. Yow-Cheng and Su-Cheng (Cheng) L.; D.D.S., W. China Union U., 1943, M.D., 1946; M.S., U. Rochester (N.Y.), 1951; m. Hiltrud Marie M. Reineke, Dec. 27, 1963; children—Barbara Ann, Winfred, Rita Doreen, Oliver. Came to U.S., 1946, naturalized, 1955. Intern, U. Hospital W. China Union U., Chengtu, 1946-50; resident Strong Meml. Hosp., Rochester, N.Y.; specializing in plastic surgery, St. Louis, 1952-56; asst., instr. Strong Meml. Hosp.-Sch. Medicine and Dentistry U. Rochester, 1946-50; asst. plastic surgeon Barnes Hosp.-Washington U., 1952-56; surgeon VA Hosp., Lebanon, Pa., 1956-58; plastic surgeon St. Joseph's Hosp., Lancaster, Pa., Lancaster Gen. Hosp., cons. Good Samaritan Hosp., Lebanon Valley Gen. Hosp. (all Lebanon). Served to maj. Med. Unit, Chinese Army, 1945. Fellow Internat. Coll. Dentists, Royal Coll. Health, A.C.S; mem. Robert Ivy

Soc. Plastic Surgeons AMA, Pa., Lancaster County med. socs. Mem. Soc. of Friends. Contbr. articles to profl. jours. Home: 2114 Oregon Pike Lancaster PA 17601 Office: 614 N Duke St Lancaster PA 17602

LUBAN, AUDREY MAE, educator; b. N.Y.C., Oct. 26, 1941; d. Milton H. and Mary Fischer; B.A. in English, Mich. State U., 1963; M.A. in English Edn., Columbia, 1964; M.A.Ed., Austin Peay U., 1968; M.S.Ed. in Spl. Edn., Hunter Coll., 1973. Tchr. spl. edn. Reading and Study Skills Center, N.Y.C., 1963-65, Iroquois High Sch., Louisville, 1968-69; tchr. spl. edn.; remedial and spl. edn. specialist Rumson (N.J.)-Fairhaven Regional High Sch., 1969—. Lol. Reading to Aged and Infirmed, Red Bank, N.J. Certified tchr. handicapped, secondary supr., prin. Mem. Nat., N.J., Monmouth County (N.J.) edn. assns., AAUW, Am. Assn. Sch. Adminstrs., Council Exceptional Children, Kappa Delta Pi, Pi Lambda Theta. Recipient Merle E. Frampton Spl. Edn. award Hunter Coll., 1973. Home: 28 Riverside Ave Apt 8-D Red Bank NJ 07701 Office: Rumson-Fairhaven Regional High Sch Ridge Rd Rumson NJ 07760

LUBETKIN, SEYMOUR ARTHUR, engr.; b. Newark, Mar. 25, 1923; s. William and Dorothy (Kimmel) L.; B.S.M.E., Newark Coll. Engring., 1947, M.E.E., 1950; M.C.E., N.Y. U., 1957; m. Shirley Lowenstein, Dec. 30, 1950; children—Sanford, Richard, Roy. Asst. chief engr. Passaic Valley Sewerage Commrs., 1950-54, chief engr., 1954-78; pres. Environ. Tech., Inc.; prin. project mgr. Roy F. Weston, Inc., adviser N.J. Dept. Environ. Protection, U.S. EPA, Water Resources Research Council of Rutgers U., Interstate San. Commn. Bd. mgrs. N.J. Y Camps, 1955-60, 70-73; bd. dirs. NJ. YM&YWHA, 1961-63. Served with U.S. Army, 1943-46. Registered profl. engr., N.J., Pa., N.Y. Diplomate Am. Acad. Environ. Engrs. Mem. Water Pollution Control Fedn. (bd. of control 1975-78), N.J. Water Pollution Control Assn. (exec. bd. 1975—, Dr. Heukelikian award 1973), Am. Contract Bridge League (life master), Tau Beta Pi. Republican. Jewish. Club: Masons. Mem. editorial adv. staff Pollution Engring. mag., 1978—; contbr. articles to engring. jours. Home: 29 Greenwood Dr Millburn NJ 07041

LUBIN, ANDREW MICHAEL, investment counselor; b. Leominster, Mass., Aug. 26, 1946; s. David Albert and Felice (Forgelman) L.; B.A., Syracuse U., 1968, M.B.A., 1970; m. Peggy Rosin, Dec. 29, 1968; children—Laura Elizabeth, Kimberly Dawn. Office mgr., property mgr. Leon N. Weiner & Assos., Wilmington, Del., 1969-72; salesman comml. and indsl. real estate Stoltz Realty Co., Wilmington, 1972-75; v.p., investment counselor Commonwealth Trust Co., Newark, Del., 1975—; pres. Del. Securities & Investments, Inc.; cons., lectr. in field. Mem. Com. 100 (dir. 1978—), Nat. Assn. Rev. Appraisers (sr.), Am. Right of Way Assn., Nat. Assn. Realtors, Jewish Fedn. Del., New Castle County Bd. Realtors. Home: 109 Chatham Pl Wilmington DE 19810 Office: Suite 201 Commonwealth Bldg Newark DE 19702

LUBOW, NATHAN MYRON, accountant; b. N.Y.C., Aug. 4, 1929; s. Cornelius William and Blanche (Igstaedter) L.; B.S. in Econs. with honors, Wharton Sch., U. Pa., 1950; Ph.B., U. Chgo., 1948; m. Joyce S. Litt, Dec. 17, 1955; children—Susan M., Andrew M. Acct., Aronson & Oresman, C.P.A.'s, N.Y.C., 1950-61, 63-69, partner, 1969-73; treas. Arlans Dept. Stores, Inc., N.Y.C., 1961-63; partner Clarence Rainess & Co., N.Y.C., 1973-78; partner Main, LaFrentz & Co., N.Y.C., 1978—. Treas., bd. dirs. B'nai B'rith Banking & Fin. Lodge, N.Y.C., 1973-78. Served with CIC, U.S. Army, 1951-53. Mem. Am. Inst. C.P.A.'s, N.Y. State Soc. of C.P.A.'s, N.Y. Credit and Fin. Mgmt. Assn., Am. Arbitration Assn., Beta Gamma Sigma, Beta Alpha Psi. Democrat. Home: 465 West End Ave New York NY 10024 Office: 280 Park Ave New York NY 10017

LUCA, WILLIAM ARTHUR, JR., silver mfg. co. exec.; b. Meriden, Conn., Sept. 22, 1943; s. William Arthur and Mary Ann (Revay) L.; grad. Hartford Inst. Accounting, 1963; student bus. adminstrn., Quinnipiac Coll., 1963—; m. Pamela J. Rudine, May 7, 1966; children—Michael, Andrew, Scott. Sr. corporate auditor Insilco Corp., Meriden, 1963-66, asst. treas., 1971-72, treas., 1972-73; controller MRM Industries, 1967-69; controller Eyelet Specialty Co., 1969-70, v.p., controller, 1970-71; v.p. finance Internat. Silver Co., Meriden, 1973-76, sr. v.p. fin. and adminstrn., 1976-78, exec. v.p., 1978—, also dir. Bd. dirs. Meriden-Wallingford Hosp. Mem. Meriden C. of C. (dir.), Nat. Assn. Accountants. Club: Elks. Office: 500 S Broad St Meriden CT 06450

LUCAS, CAROL, gerontologist; b. Hewlett, L.I., N.Y., July 11, 1929; d. Irving William and Julia (Cutler) L.; B.S., Coll. William and Mary, 1949; M.A., Columbia U., 1951, Ed.D., 1953. Field dir. Greater N.Y. council Girl Scouts U.S.A., N.Y.C., 1949-51; recreation dir. Neponsit (N.Y.) Beach Hosp., 1951-53; cons. Nat. Council Jewish Women, N.Y.C., 1954-55; area coordinator Los Angeles County Heart Assn., Los Angeles, 1955-56; rehab. cons. City of Hope, Duarte, Calif., 1955-56, Los Angeles Tb and Health Assn., 1957-58; recreation cons. Fedn. Protestant Welfare Agys., N.Y.C., 1958-60; instr. Columbia, 1959—; dir. spl. pilot study in gerontology, N.Y.C., 1958-64; exec. dir. Five Towns Senior Center; supr. adminstrn. on aging project Sr. Center of Nassau County, Uniondale, N.Y.; dir. Hempstead Office of Services for Aging, 1968; commr. Hempstead Dept. of Services for Aging, 1978. Mem. Am. Recreation Soc., Nat. Assn. Social Workers, Nat. Recreation Assn., Acad. Certified Social Workers, Royal Soc. Health (London), Kappa Delta Pi, Delta Psi Omega. Author: (with Josephine Rathbone) Recreation in Total Rehabilitation, 1958; Recreation Activity Development in Nursing Home, Homes for the Aging and Hospitals, 1962; Recreation in Gerontology, 1963; also articles profl. jours. Home: 141 Wyckoff Pl Woodmere NY 11598 Office: 393 Front St Hempstead NY 11550

LUCAS, G. BRINTON, ins. exec.; b. Phila., Sept. 9, 1889; s. Samuel and Anna Hickman (Arnold) L.; student, Episcopal Acad., 1907; m. Adelaide L. Loughead, Nov. 2, 1912 (dec.); children—Nancy B. (Mrs. Charles M. Kirkland), G. Brinton Lucas (dec.), Barbara Brooke (Mrs. W. Burling Cocks), Joan (Mrs. John Dixon). Vice pres. Ins. Co. N. Am., Phila., 1909, asst. sec., 1924, marine sec., 1937, v.p., 1943-54; v.p. Phila. Fire & Marine Ins. Co., ret., 1954. Chmn. exec. com. Inland Marine Underwriters Assn., Inland Marine Ins. Bur., 1945-46; Am. Com., Lloyd's Register of Shipping, 1939-54. Mem. United Hunts Racing Assn. Republican. Episcopalian. Home: Cape Neddick ME 03902

LUCAS, JOSEPH, biologist, author; b. Carshalton, Surrey, Eng., Dec. 13, 1928; s. Joseph and Dorothy Mary (Collier) L.; B.Sc. with honours in Zoology, U. London, 1953; m. Esther Elfreda Baker, Aug. 11, 1950; children—Caroline Mary, Esther Jane, Joseph. Fisheries officer East Africa High Commn., Lake Victoria Fisheries Service, Mwanza, Tanganyika, also hon. game ranger Serengeti Nat. Park, 1953-56; elementary and secondary sch. sci. tchr., Matlock, Derbyshire, Eng., 1957-58; asst. pathologist Children's Hosp., Sheffield, Eng., 1958-59; sci. editor Butterworth & Co., pubs., London, 1960-62, med. editor, 1962-63; life scis. editor Sci. Jour., London, 1963-67; editor Internat. Zoo Yearbook, Zool. Soc., London, 1967-71; sci. editor Internat. Union for Conservation of Nature and Natural Resources, Morges, Switzerland, 1971-73; free-lance writer, 1973-74; supt. edn. and research Met. Toronto Zoo, West Hill, Ont., 1974-77; biol. cons., 1974—; publs. officer Ont. Ministry of Environment, 1978—; mem. survival service commn. Internat. Union for Conservation of Nature and Natural Resources, 1966—, sec.-treas. Can. com., 1976—; chmn. Internat. Zoo Liaison Group, 1972-75; mem. Conservation Council of Ont., 1976—. Served with Brit. Army M.C., 1947-49. Fellow Royal Geog. Soc., Zool. Soc. (London); mem. Inst. Biology, Brit. Ornithologists Union, Assn. Brit. Sci. Writers, Fedn. Ont. Naturalists. Author: A Source Book of Animals, 1971; Encyclopedia of the Animal World, 1972; A Book of Animals, 1973; (with Pamela Jane Critch) Life in the Oceans, 1974; (with Susan Jane Hayes) Polar Life, 1976, Biological Aspects of Conservation, 1978; contbr. articles to mags. and newspapers. Home: 422 Finch Ave Pickering ON L1V 1H8 Canada

LUCCA, THOMAS GEORGE, banker; b. Bklyn., May 17, 1938; s. James Alfred and Mary (Cooper) L.; B.S., St. John's U., 1960, M.S., 1965; m. Carole Ann Celiberti, Dec. 15, 1962; children—Carolynn, Thomas George, James. Loan officer Nat. Bank of N.Am., Hempstead, N.Y., 1965-68; asst. v.p. State Bank of L.I., New Hyde Park, N.Y., 1968-72; asst. v.p. L.I. Trust Co., N.Y.C., 1972-75; v.p. Anchor Savs. Bank, N.Y.C., 1975—. Mem. Savs. Bank Assn. N.Y. (dir. 1967), Robert Morris Assos. Republican. Roman Catholic. Clubs: Lions, Elks. Office: Anchor Savings Bank 5323 Fifth Ave New York City NY 11220

LUCE, ELEANOR MARJORIE, publishing co. exec.; b. Worcester, Mass., Jan. 28, 1943; d. Francis Pope and Marjorie Evelyn (Bourgault) L.; student Clark U., 1961-62, Pace U., 1964-78; P.M.D. certificate Harvard Grad. Sch. Bus., 1975, m. John Ballantine Smith, July 11, 1976. Sales engr. RCA, N.Y.C., 1967-68; sr. system analyst/programmer Reader's Digest, Pleasantville, N.Y., 1968-75, auditor internat. ops., 1976-77, mgr. customer service, 1977—. Pres., Eastgate Condominium Assn., 1978—. Club: Harvard Bus. Sch. (N.Y.C.). Home: 84 Hoyt St New Canaan CT 06840 Office: Reader's Digest Pleasantville NY 10570

LUCE, MELVIN GEOFFREY, ins. co. exec., lawyer; b. N.Y.C., Jan. 25, 1924; s. Arthur and Freda (Corey) L.; B.A., Washington Sq. Coll., 1948; M.A., N.Y. U., 1951, J.D., 1957; m. Dorothy Strasheim, Sept. 4, 1955. Admitted to N.Y. bar, 1961, U.S. Supreme Ct. bar, 1970; asst. firm T.J. Flood, N.Y.C., 1960-68; Gillies & Mahoney, N.Y.C., 1969; asst. sec. Excess & Treaty Mgmt. N.Y.C., 1970-72; v.p. claims, dir. Agency Mgrs., Inc., N.Y.C. and v.p. claims Dominion Ins. Co. Am., N.Y.C., 1972-75; v.p. claims Gerling Global Offices, Inc., 1975—; dir. Seamens & Internat. House, N.Y.C., 1976—, v.p., 1978. Served with USAF, 1943-46. Mem. Am., N.Y. State bar assns., N.Y. State Trial Lawyers Assn., N.Y. County Lawyers Assn., Internat. Assn. Ins. Counsel, Fedn. Ins. Counsel, Reins. Assn. Am., Excess and Surplus Lines Assn., Phi Delta Phi. Lutheran. Club: Drug and Chem. (N.Y.C.). Home: 170 Emerson Ave North Babylon NY 11703 Office: 717 Fifth Ave New York City NY 10022

LUCEY, GORDON MACAULAY, lawyer; b. N.Y.C., Apr. 14, 1932; s. Gordon Acheson and Elizabeth (Macaulay) L.; B.A., Hampden Sydney Coll., 1954; J.D., Harvard U., 1957; m. Suzanne Linn; children—David Peter, Katherine Macaulay, William Gordon, Sarah Linn. Admitted to N.Y. bar, 1958, Fed. bar, 1962, Conn. bar, 1968; asso. law firm Dunnington, Bartholow & Miller, N.Y.C., 1960-63; atty.-adviser Office of Gen. Counsel, AID, U.S. Dept. State, Washington, 1963-66; group counsel, asso. div. counsel Litton Industries, Inc., Stamford, Conn. and White Plains, N.Y., 1966-69; sec., gen. counsel Gen. Interiors Corp., N.Y.C., 1970; pvt. practice law, Stamford, Conn. and N.Y.C., 1970—; partner firm Eaton, Van Winkle & Greenspoon, N.Y.C., 1972-73. Served to lt. USN, 1957-60; Germany. Mem. Am. (chmn. com. on export control and promotion, sect. internat. law 1971-76), Conn. bar assns., Assn. Bar City N.Y. Home: 73 Hillbrook Rd Wilton CT 06897 Office: 485 Madison Ave New York City NY 10022 also 441 Summer St Stamford CT 06901

LUCHSINGER, JOHN FRANCIS, dept. store exec.; b. Solvay, N.Y., Dec. 22, 1920; s. Frederick J. and Agusta D. (Suska) L.; B.A., Syracuse U., 1942; m. Marion Madeline Bex, May 29, 1943; children—John, David M. Advt. mgr. L.I. Advance, 1945-47; with Swezey & Newins Dept. Store, Patchogue, N.Y., 1947—, v.p., gen. mgr., 1958—; prof. retailing Suffolk Community Coll., 1964—. Mem. Brookhaven Planning Bd., Patchogue, 1953—, chmn., 1964—; mem. Suffolk County Planning Commn., Hauppague, N.Y., 1964—, Brookhaven Indsl. Commn., 1956—; vice chmn. Suffolk County Econ. Devel. Commn., 1977—. Bd. dirs. N.Y. Citizen Pub. Expenditure Com., 1972—. Served to lt. (s.g.) USNR, 1942-45. Mem. Nat. Retail Mchts. Assn. (bd. dirs. smaller stores div. 1974—, bd. dirs. ind. stores 1975—), N.Y. State Council Retail Mchts. (pres. 1972-74), Patchogue C. of C. (pres. 1954), Phi Kappa Alpha. Conglist (v.p. bd. trustees 1968-70). Rotarian (pres. 1963-64), Mason. Home: Whippoorwill Ln Patchogue NY 11772 Office: 1 W Main St Patchogue NY 11772

LUCHTERHAND, ELMER GUSTAV, sociologist, educator; b. Unity, Wis., May 20, 1911; s. Edwin and Bertha (Ewert) L; B.A., U. Wis., 1948, M.A., 1949, Ph.D., 1953; m. Helen Patricia Gormley, June 20, 1942; children—Dennis (dec.), Erika. Farm editor Waukegan (Ill.) Post, 1940-41; teaching asst. U. Wis., 1948-51; instr. U. Conn., 1951-53; research asso. Aluminum Co. Can., 1953-57; asst. prof. McGill U., 1957-58; mem. social sci. faculty Sarah Lawrence Coll., 1958-62; research asso. Yale, research dir. Community Progress, Inc., New Haven, 1962-67; asso. prof. sociology Bklyn. Coll., City U. N.Y., 1967-70, prof., 1971—; cons. tng. Corp. Am., 1968-70; cons. project to develop curriculae on Nazi holocaust for U.S. colls. and univs. Spertus Coll. of Judaica, 1976-77. Bd. dirs. St. George's Sch., Montreal (Que., Can.), Inc., 1957-58. Served with AUS, 1943-46; ETO. Decorated Bronze Star. Mem. Soc. for Study of Social Problems, Am., Eastern sociol. assns., AAAS, Internat., Am. assns. social psychiatry, Sigma Xi, Alpha Kappa Delta. Author: (with Daniel Sydiaha) Choice in Human Affairs: An Application to Aging-Accident-Illness Problems, 1966. Home: 46 Overton Rd Scarsdale NY 10583 Office: Dept Sociology Bklyn Coll Brooklyn NY 11210

LUCHTERHAND, PAUL FREDRICK, former union ofcl.; b. Oneida, N.Y., Aug. 22, 1943; s. Fred Edward and Betty Lou (Newcombe) L.; student pub. schs., Camden, N.Y. Painter, constrn. projects, Rome (N.Y.) area, 1967-76 with Colgate U., Hamilton, N.Y., 1969-76; fin. sec. local union, Rome, from 1970. Served with USAF, 1961-65. Mem. Am. Legion (color guard), DAV (color guard). Inventor. Home: PO Box 40 North Bay NY 13123

LUCK, ANTHONY, editor; b. Ukraine; s. Peter and Anna (Kashchuk) Luckiw; came to U.S., 1949, naturalized, 1954; B.A., Pedagogical Technicum, Kremenchuk, Ukraine, 1930; M.A., Pedagogical Inst., Voroshilovgrad, Ukraine, 1938; postgrad. Innsbruck (Austria) U., 1945-46; Ph.D., Ukrainian Free U., Munich, Germany, 1955; m. Olga Redchuk, Oct. 24, 1954; children—Alice Virginia, Andrew Peter. Instr. Russian lang. and lit., USSR, 1930-37; pedagogue, journalist, Russia and Ukraine, 1938-41; journalist, student, Innsbruck and Munich, 1945-49; free lance journalist USIA, Washington, 1957—. Served with Soviet Army, 1941-43. Mem. Internat. Platform Assn., Shenandoah Farms, Smithsonian Instn. Orthodox. Contbr. articles to mags. and newspapers. Home: 1202 Holton Ln Takoma Park MD 20012

LUCKEY, E. HUGH, physician and educator; b. Jackson, Tenn., Jan. 1, 1920; s. David William and Ethel May (Freeman) L.; B.S., Union U., Jackson, 1941, Sc.D., 1954; M.D., Vanderbilt U., 1944; Dr. honoris causa, U. Bahia (Brazil), 1961; m. Betty Ann Black, Dec. 25, 1942; children—Linda Ann, John William, James Hugh, Robert Powers; m. 2d, Veronica Kusmin, Dec. 10, 1970. Intern, asst. resident N.Y. Hosp., 1944-45, 45-46, 48; vis. physician 2d Cornell med. div. Bellevue Hosp., N.Y.C., 1949-54, dir., 1950-54; asso. prof. medicine Cornell U. Med. Sch., 1953-57, prof. medicine, chmn. dept., 1957-66, v.p. med. affairs, 1966-77, dean Med. Coll., 1954-57, asso. dean Grad. Sch., 1954-57; attending physician N.Y. Hosp., 1955—, physician-in-chief, 1957-66; v.p. Soc. N.Y. Hosp., 1966-77; pres. N.Y. Hosp.-Cornell Med. Center, 1966-77; chmn. bd. mgrs. Vincent Astor Diagnostic Service 1957-60; med. dir., sec.-treas. Russell Sage Inst. Pathology, 1958-67, now bd. trustees. Cons. to surgeon gen. U.S. Army, 1959-67; mem. com. metabolism, cons. to USPHS, mem. cardiovascular study sect., 1960-63; mem. heart spl. projects com. NIH, 1963-67; mem. President's Science Advisory Committee Ad hoc Panel Latin American Health, 1961; mem. com. medicine W. K. Kellogg Found., 1955-61. Dir., mem. exec. com. Josiah Macy Found.; trustee Cornell U., 1957-62, 66-77; mem. bd. trust Vanderbilt U., 1962—, com. visitors Med. Center, 1961—. Served from lt. to capt. USAAF, 1946-48. Named hon. prof. Nat. U. Chile, Faculty Medicine, U. Bahia. Diplomate, ofcl. examiner Am. Bd. Internal Medicine. Fellow A.C.P. (gov. 1959-63, regent 1965-68, master); mem. Assn. Am. Physicians, Am. Fedn. for Clin. Research (chmn. sect. internal medicine 1963-64), N.Y. State, N.Y. County med. socs., Practitioners Soc., Harvey Soc., Chilean Soc. Cardiology, Med. Soc. of Santiago (Chile), Council Fgn. Relations. Home: Box 468 Ocean Rd Bridgehampton NY 11932 Office: NY Hospital-Cornell Med Center 525 E 68th St New York City NY 10021

LUCKS, JOEL KENNETH, univ. adminstr.; b. Rockville Center, N.Y., Jan. 27, 1949; s. Matthew Harris and Lillian (Krutel) L.; A.Applied Sci., State U. N.Y., 1969; B.S., U. Ariz., 1973; M.S., L.I. U., 1976; m. Terri Joan Goodman, Jan. 15, 1977. Admissions counselor State U. N.Y., Farmingdale, N.Y., 1977—, prof. grad. sch., 1977—; teaching asst. L.I. U., 1975-76. Mem. Am. Personnel and Guidance Assn., Nat. Humanistic Edn. Center, Am. Assn. for Sex Educators and Counselors and Therapists, N.Y. State Assn. Coll. Admissions Counselors. Editor: Human Sexuality: A Book of Selected Readings, 1976. Home: 7543 67th Dr Middle Village NY 11379 Office: State Univ of NY Farmingdale NY 11735

LUCOW, WILLIAM HARRISON, psychologist, ednl. research statistician; b. Winnipeg, Man., Can., Oct. 11, 1916; s. Harry and Rebecca (Fishman) L.; B.A., U. Man., 1946, B.Ed., 1948, M.Ed., 1951; M.A., U. Ottawa, 1950; Ph.D., U. Minn., 1953; m. Ida Carol Abramson, Apr. 26, 1940; children—Ruth Harriet, Wendy Lois. Tchr., prin., Man., 1936-56; asso. prof. ednl. psychology U. Man., 1956-64; chief research edn. div. Dominion Bur. Statistics, Ottawa, Ont., Can., 1964-70; dir. N.J. Dept. Edn., Trenton, 1970-78; pres. Lucow Ind. Bur. Research in Edn., Willingboro, N.J. Registered psychologist, N.J. Fellow AAAS; mem. Am. Ednl. Research Assn., Am. Statis. Assn., Am. Psychol. Assn. Contbr. articles to profl. jours. Office: 12 New Coach Ln Willingboro NJ 08046

LUCZUN, ROBERT, artist; b. Passaic, N.J., Apr. 6, 1946; s. Stanley and Helen Dorothy (Chechowski) L.; student Newark Coll. Engring., 1965-68, Ridgewood Art Coll., 1968-69; B.A., William Paterson Coll., 1972; art certification Montclair State Coll., 1973-75; M.F.A., Bklyn. Coll., 1975; m. Madeline Christine Altobella, Aug. 16, 1969; 1 son, Robert Stanley Ralph. One-man shows: Gregoire Galleries, N.Y.C., 1973; group shows include: Espace Cardin, Paris, 1973, Nat. Acad. Galleries, N.Y.C., 1975, 76, 77, 78, Sunset Center of Art, Carmel, Calif., 1978, Lakes Art Center, Spirit Lake, Iowa; represented in permanent collections: City of Clifton (N.J.), City of Passaic (N.J.); contbr. works for mag. covers: N.J. Music & Arts, 1972, Traffic Engring., 1973, New Engr., 1972. Mem. Audubon Artists N.Y., Nat. Soc. Painters in Casein and Acrylic, Nat. Soc. Painters and Sculptors, Salmagundi Art Club. Address: 838 Paulison Ave Clifton NJ 07011

LUDDY, JOSEPH MICHAEL, clergyman; b. Altoona, Pa., Sept. 20, 1928; s. Michael Aloysius and Kunigunda (Greiner) L.; B.A., Pontifical Coll. Josephinum, 1950, M.Div., 1975; M.S.W., Catholic U. Am., 1959. Asst. pastor St. Mark's Parish, Altoona, 1954-57; asst. dir. Cath. Charities, Inc., Diocese of Altoona-Johnstown, 1959-73, diocesan dir., 1973—; residences Cathedral Blessed Sacrament, 1959-60; adminstr. St. Edward's Parish, Barnesboro, 1960-61; supt. St. Mary-John Homes, Cresson, Pa., 1961-64; chaplain Cath. Child Care Center and Garvey Manor Home for Aged, 1964—. Bd. dirs. Big Bros. Blair County. Mem. Nat. Conf. Cath. Charities, Pa. Cath. Conf., Nat. Assn. Social Workers, Acad. Certified Social Workers. Democrat. Roman Catholic. Home: Box 124 Logan Blvd MR Hollidaysburg PA 16648 Office: 1300 Twelfth Ave Altoona PA 16601

LUDDY, WILLIAM JOSEPH, JR., educator, mgmt. cons., lawyer; b. New Britain, Conn., Jan. 14, 1947; s. William Joseph and Mildred Frances (Rand) L.; B.S., Fairfield U., 1969; M.S., Rensselaer Poly. Inst., 1974; J.D., U. Conn., 1978; m. Sheila Mary Pearson, May 12, 1973; 1 son, Kevin Pearson. Mktg. analyst The Travelers Corp., Hartford, Conn., 1970-75; lectr. mgmt. Rensselaer Poly. Inst., Hartford (Conn.) Grad. Center, 1974-75, asst. prof. mgmt., 1975-78, asso. prof. mgmt., 1978—; v.p., sec. The Concord Group, Inc., Hartford, 1976—, dir., officer, 1976—. Loman Research fellow, 1975-76. Mem. Am. Bar Assn., Acad. Mgmt. (program com. 1976-77, chmn. health care symposium 1978), Am. Assn. Bus. Law Profs. Contbr. articles to profl. jours. Home: 192 Brookside Rd Newington CT 06111 Office: 275 Windsor St Hartford CT 06120

LUDLUM, ROBERT PHILLIPS, emeritus coll. pres.; b. Bklyn., Jan. 13, 1909; s. Walter Denton and Irene (Daniell) L.; A.B., Cornell U., 1930, M.A., 1932, Ph.D., 1935; L.H.D., Lincoln Coll., 1963; m. Ruth Althea Smith, Sept. 20, 1930 (dec. Dec. 1975); children—Susan, Margaret (Mrs. Masanori Hashimoto); m. 2d, Joyce Hall, Nov. 27, 1976. Mng. editor, LeRoy (N.Y.) Gazette-News, 1930-31; instr. hist., polit. sci., Tex. A & M, 1935-37, asst. prof., 1937-39; research asso., Gen. Edn. Bd., Cornell, 1939-40; asst. prof. history, polit. sci. Hofstra Coll., 1940-42; asso. social sci. analyst, O.W.I., 1942; asso. sec. Am. Assn. U. Profs., 1942-47; vice pres. Antioch Coll., 1947-49; pres. Blackburn Coll., 1949-65; dean Coll. Arts and Scis., Adelphi U., 1965-68, pres. Anne Arundel Community Coll., 1968-76, pres. emeritus, 1976—. Mem. Ill. Tchr. Certification Bd., 1952-62. Bd. Christian edn., United Presbyn. Ch. in U.S.A., 1959-62. Hon. fellow Consular Law Soc., 1953. Mem. Fedn. Ill. Colls. (mem. exec. com. 1956-58, pres. 1960-62), Asso. Colls. Ill. (sec.-treas., v.p., pres., chmn. bd.), Presbyn. Coll. Union (pres. 1957-58), Zeta Psi. Author: This Is America's Story (with Howard B. Wilder and Harriett M. Brown); (with others) American Government, 1964; also articles. Home: 901 Randell Rd Severna Park MD 21146

LUDMAN, JACQUES ERNEST, physicist; b. Chgo., Nov. 26, 1934; s. Oscar H. and Jennie (Hiller) L.; B.A., Middlebury Coll., 1956; Ph.D., Northeastern U., 1973; m. Doreen Tyler, June 20, 1970; children—Nicole Ruth, Jacques James Henri. Research physicist Air Force Cambridge Research Labs (name changed to Dep. for Electronic Tech., 1976), 1959—; vis. scientist Centre Nat. d'Etudes

Telecommunications, Lannion, France, 1977-78; pres., Ludman Interferometer Co. Mem. ASTM (chmn. subcom. on injection lasers, 1969-72). Contbr. tech. articles in field to profl. jours.; patentee on laser optical system; patentee interferometer optical system. Home: 98 Old Lowell Rd Westford MA 01886 Office: United States Air Force Deputy for Electronic Technology Bedford MA 01730

LUDWIG, RICHARD, precision metal mfg. co. exec.; b. Phila., Oct. 11, 1930; s. Leon Harry and Sophia (Reese) L.; B.S., Drexel Evening Coll., 1956, M.B.A., 1960; m. Sandra E. Rabinowitz, June 7, 1953; children—Carol Ellen, Sherri Ann, Donna Eileen, Michele Gail. Draftsman, Piasecki Helicopter Co., Morton, Pa., 1949-50; designer Kaiser Metal Products Co., Bristol, Pa., 1951-53; design engr. Gen. Electric Co., Phila., 1956-64; engring. mgr. Emerson Electric Co., St. Louis, 1964-65; mgr. design engring. Gen. Electric Co., Phila., 1965-70, mgr. materials, Erie, Pa., 1970-74, subcontract mgr., King Prussia, Pa., 1975-76; pres. Lavelle Aircraft Co., Newtown, Pa., 1976—. Rotarian. Home: 602 Overbrook Ln Oreland PA 19075 Office: Lavelle Aircraft Co State and Sterling Sts Newtown PA 18940

LUEBS, HAROLD WILLIAM, hosp. adminstr.; b. Milw., May 18, 1921; s. Henry Ernst and Hilda (Tamms) L.; B.Mus., U. Wis., 1947; m. Margaret L. Christenson, Feb. 9, 1951; children—Judy Ann, David Harold, John Robert. With Gen. Electric X-Ray Corp., Milw., 1947-49, Capital Airlines, Milw., 1949-50, Milw. Sanitarium, Wauwatosa, Wis., 1950-53; bus. mgr. St. Clair Hosp., Mt. Lebanon, Pa., 1953-56; asst. exec. dir. Children's Hosp., Pitts., 1956-68, adminstr., 1968—; treas. Hosp. Utilization Project; adj. asso. prof. U. Pitts.; mem. bd. Nat. Health and Welfare Retirement Assn. Pres., Bethel Park Civic Assn., 1962-63; chmn. adv. com. Child Welfare Service, 1975—. Served with AUS, 1943-46. Recipient Earl K. Shuey award, 1965-66. Fellow Am. Coll. Hosp. Adminstrs.; mem. Hosp. Fin. Mgmt. Assn., Am. Hosp. Assn. Republican. Presbyterian. Home: 509 Robinhood Ln McMurray PA 15317 Office: 125 DeSoto St Pittsburgh PA 15213

LUECKE, WALTER LOUIS, ins. agent; b. Clifton, N.J., Dec. 8, 1920; s. A.G. Louis and Emily (Schneider) L.; student Rutgers U., 1937-39, Western Reserve U., Cleve., 1959-60; C.L.U., Coll. Life Underwriters, 1968; m. Frieda E. Luecke, Sept. 12, 1943; children—Robert W. (dec.), Richard W., Randall W. Bookkeeper, N.J. Gas & Electric Co., 1937-40; owner, operator retail food store, 1946-54; agent Lutheran Brotherhood, Clifton, N.J., 1954-57, gen. agent, Cleve., 1957-72, Lehigh Valley, Pa., 1975—; agy. v.p. Luth. Life Ins. Soc. Can., Waterloo, Ont., 1972-75. Bd. dirs. Luth. High Sch. Assn., Cleve., 1960-72; bd. dirs., pres. Cleve. Big Bros., 1965-70; bd. dirs. Kitchener/Waterloo (Can.) Big Bros., 1974-75; bd. dirs. Good Shepherd Home, Allentown, Pa. Served with USAF, 1941-45. Mem. Lehigh Valley Gen. Agents and Mgrs. Assn., Lehigh Valley Life Underwriters Assn., Lehigh Valley C.L.U.'s, Pa. Assn. Life Underwriters Polit. Action Commn. Republican. Lutheran. Clubs: Brookside Country, Lions. Home and office: 114 Fairview St Macungie PA 18062

LUEK-KEEN, SUSAN PENELOPE, educator; b. Lancaster, Pa., Sept. 20, 1946; d. Otto William and Mary Sue (Pierce) Luek; A.B. magna cum laude, U. Del., 1968, M.A. (NDEA Title IV fellow 1968-71), 1970, Ph.D., 1973; m. Arthur H. Keen, June 19, 1971. Asst. prof. psychology Millersville (Pa.) State Coll., 1972-75, asso. prof., 1975—. Bd. dirs. Planned Parenthood, Lancaster, Pa., 1978—. Mem. AAUP, Am., Eastern, Pa. psychol. assns., Phi Beta Kappa, Sigma Xi, Phi Kappa Phi, Psi Chi, Pi Lambda Theta. Home: 1416D Manor House Ln Lancaster PA 17603 Office: Millersville State College Millersville PA 17551

LUFT, HERBERT ARTHUR, book store mgr.; b. Breslau, Germany, May 19, 1908; s. Arthur and Elise (Laqueur) L.; grad. high sch.; m. Hilde Dreyfuss, May 17, 1949; 1 dau., Lillian Eve. Came to U.S., 1946, naturalized, 1950. Bank clk., Germany, 1924-30; jr. bus. exec., Germany, 1931-39; bus. exec., Brazil, 1940-46; import-export asst. to customs house broker J.E. Bernard & Co., Inc., N.Y.C., 1950-65; owner Mail Order Sci. Books Sale, Oakland Gardens, N.Y., 1952-73. Reporting astron. observations to Swiss Fed. Obs., Zurich, 1925—; cons. Royal Greenwich Obs., U.S. Naval Obs. Mem. Am. Assn. Variable Star Observers, Amateur Astronomers Assn. (Silver medal 1977). Mason. Contbr. articles to astron. jours. Home: 69-11 229th St Oakland Gardens NY 11364 Office: PO Box 91 Oakland Gardens NY 11364

LUFT, RENE WILFRED, civil engr.; b. Santiago, Chile, Sept. 21, 1943; s. David and Malwina (Kelmy) L.; came to U.S., 1968; C.E., U. Chile, 1967; M.Sc., M.I.T., 1969, Sc.D., 1971; m. Monica Acevedo, Aug. 24, 1970; children—Deborah Elaine, Daniel Eduardo. Asst. prof. U. Chile, 1967-68; research asst. M.I.T., Cambridge, 1969-71; staff engr. Simpson Gumpertz & Heger, Inc., Cambridge, 1971-74, sr. staff engr., 1975-78, asso., 1978—; sec. seismic adv. com. Mass. Bldg. Code Commn., 1978—. Registered profl. engr., Alaska, Calif., Mass., R.I. Mem. ASCE, Am. Concrete Inst., Mass. Soc. Profl. Engrs. (Young Engr. of Yr. 1978), Assn. Computing lMachinery, Sigma Xi, Chi Epsilon. Jewish. Contbr. to profl. jours. Home: 1 Overlook Dr Bedford MA 01730 Office: 1696 Massachusetts Ave Cambridge MA 02138

LUGINBYHL, THOMAS TERENCE, govt. ofcl.; b. Stinnett, Tex., Feb. 20, 1923; s. Oliver Wesley and Cleo Zell (Ingram) L.; B.A., William Jewell Coll., 1946; M.B.A., U. Chgo., 1963; M.S., George Washington U., 1966; postgrad. Air War Coll., 1965-66; m. Frankie Anne White, Nov. 21, 1945; children—Cynthia Anne, Terri Lynn, Alan Kurt, Karen Sue. Aviation cadet USAF, 1943, advanced through grades to lt. col., 1970; chief engring. and testing electronics countermeasures research USAF, 1954-58, chief phys. scis. missile guidance and trajectory calculation, 1958-62; chief scis. and resources div. def. intelligence Dept. Def., 1963-65; dep. dir. sci. and tech. info. USAF, 1967-69, dir. sci. and tech. info., 1969-70; chief tech. info. Nat. Inst. Occupational Safety and Health, HEW, Rockville, Md., 1970-76; dir. Tech. Data Center, Occupational Safety and Health Adminstrn., Dept. Labor, Washington, 1976—. Guest lectr. USAF Inst. Tech., 1966-70; mem. mgmt. panel Com. Sci. and Tech. Info., Office Pres. Sci. Adviser, Exec. Office Pres., 1967-70; chmn. Internat. Conf. on Tech. Info., Geneva, 1973. Decorated Distinguished Service medal, Air medal with five cluster, Air Force Commendation medal. Mem. Am. Soc. Info. Scis., Am. Indsl. Hygienists Assn., Am. Conf. Govt. Indsl. Hygienists, Sigma Pi Sigma. Methodist (mem. adminstrv. bd. 1972-76). Masons. Editor Occupational Safety and Health Thesaurus, 1973. Editor Registry of Toxic Effects of Chem. Substances, 1972, 73, 74, 75. Home: 8425 Porter Lane Alexandria VA 22308 Office: 200 Constitution Ave NW Washington DC 20210

LUHRS, HENRY RIC, toy mfg. co. exec.; b. Chambersburg, Pa., Mar. 22, 1931; s. Henry E. and Pearl (Beistle) L.; B.A., Gettysburg Coll., 1953; m. Grace Barnhart, June 12, 1973; children by previous marriage—Stephen Frederick, Christine Michelle, Terri Ann, Patricia Denise. With The Beistle Co., Shippensburg, Pa., 1948—, pres., 1962—; dir. First Nat. Bank, 1969—; gemologist, 1977—; owner Luhrs Gem Testing Lab., 1977—, Luhrs & Son Jewelry, 1977—. Pres. Shippensburg Pub. Library, 1964-66, 70-72, 76—, bd. dirs., 1963—; pres. Community Chest, 1965, dir., 1963-72; pres. Shippensburg Area Devel. Corp., 1966-72; bd. dirs., trustee Carlisle (Pa.) Hosp., 1967-71, Chambersburg (Pa.) Hosp., 1969-75; mem. consumer advisor council Capital Blue Cross, 1976-78. Served to capt. USAF, 1953-59. Mem. Shippensburg Hist. Soc. (dir. 1968), Nat. Sojourners, SAR (life), C. of C. (pres. 1965, dir. 1964-65), Toy Mfrs. Assn. (dir. 1968-71), Nat. Small Businessmen's Assn., Nat. Rifle Assn. Am., Shippensburg Fish and Game Assn. (pres. 1963), Am. Legion. Lutheran. Mason (32 deg., K.T., Shriner), Elk. Clubs: Industrial Management, York of Printing House Craftsmen. Home: Box B Shippensburg PA 17257 Office: 14-18 E Orange St Shippensburg PA 17257

LUING, LARRY LEE, business schs. adminstr.; b. Rhodes, Iowa, Apr. 24, 1930; s. Donald Arthur and Ethel Imogene (Dodd) L.; B.S. with honors, U. Iowa, 1951; m. Mildred Joan Bona, Sept. 19, 1959; children—Kevin, Randy, Timothy, Brian. Asst. buyer Denver Dry Goods Co., 1953-55; mgr. collegiate bus. edn. dept. McGraw-Hill Book Co., 1955-65; adminstrv. v.p. Berkeley Schs., Little Falls, N.J., 1966-68, pres., 1968—; dir. Joboul Pub. Co., Evanston, Ill., 1964-77. Mem. Accrediting Commn. for Bus. Schs., 1969-74; chmn. Bus. Sch. Council, 1971, Coll. Council, 1972; participant Gov. N.J. 1st Conf. Vocat. Edn., 1970; bd. dirs. Assn. Ind. Colls. and Schs., 1973, 76—, mem. exec. com., 1973-74, 76-79, chmn. accrediting commn., 1973, pres. 1977-78; mem. exec. bd. Westchester (N.Y.) Better Bus. Bur., 1968-69. Served with AUS, 1951-53. Mem. United (exec. bd. 1972; Distinguished Service award 1964), N.J. (pres. 1968-69) bus. schs. assns., N.Y. State Assn. Registered Pvt. Bus. Schs. (dir. 1974-77), N.J. Bus. Edn. Assn. (exec. bd. 1970-71), Oakland (N.J.) Jr. C. of C. (charter dir. 1960, sec. 1961), Eastern Bus. Tchrs. Assn. (exec. bd. 1970-72), V.F.W. Republican. Author: Study Guide for Executive Profile, 1967; also articles. Home: 616 Mountain Rd Smoke Rise Kinnelon NJ 07405 Office: 44 Rifle Camp Rd Little Falls NJ

LUK, SHING CHARK, pathologist; b. Shanghai, China, Sept. 24, 1934; s. Him Sau Luk and Suk Ching Ng; came to Can., 1968; naturalized, 1973; M.B., B.S., U. Hong Kong., 1959; m. Wai-Han Li, Oct. 1, 1963; children—Men-Ching, Men-Chong, Wah-Ping. Intern, Queen Mary Hosp., Hong Kong, 1959-60; med. officer Hong Kong Govt. with tng. in dermatology and pediatrics, 1960-63, pathology, 1963-68; resident in pathology U. Toronto (Ont., Can.), 1968-70; research fellow pathology Banting Inst., U. Toronto, 1970-73; pathologist Mt. Sinai Hosp., Toronto, 1973—; asst. prof. U. Toronto, 1976—. Med. Research Council Can. grantee, 1973-76. Diplomate Am. Bd. Pathology. Fellow Royal Coll. Physicians (Can.); mem. Internat., Can. assns. pathologists, Brit., Can., Hong Kong med. assns., Microscopic Soc. Can. Contbr. to publs. on lymphoid tissues and bone. Home: 38 Foxwarren Dr Willowdale ON M2K 1L3 Canada Office: 600 University Ave Toronto ON M5G 1X5 Canada

LUKENS, DAVID LEE, marketing cons.; b. Phila., July 18, 1913; s. Maurice and Frances Karen (Schlemowit) L.; B.S., Pa. Mil. Coll., 1936; postgrad. U. Pa., 1947; m. Dorothy Leibowitz, June 14, 1940 (dec.); children—Jeffrey, Ira, Steven. Successively sports writer, feature writer, fin. columnist, advt. promotion dir. Phila. Inquirer, 1938-43; pub. relations dir. Pa. Dept. Commerce, 1943-46; pres. D.L. Lukens Co., South Orange, N.J., 1948-68; mktg. cons. new products and processes; cons. to Am. Newspaper Pubs. Assn., 1950-52. Founder, pres. Nat. Youth Sci. Found., 1956—. Capt. C.A.P., 1942. Recipient Poor Richard Gold medal as advt. man of yr., 1950. Mem. Am. Soc. Assn. Execs., Marine Tech. Soc., Am. Littoral Soc., thoroughbred Breeders Assn. N.J. Jewish religion. Author: Careers in Oceanography. Editor, pub. Advt. News Letter, 1947-51. Home: 227 Conway Ct South Orange NJ 07079 Office: PO Box 370 South Orange NJ 07079

LUKIN, JON DEHN, med. center exec.; b. Bronx, Aug. 19, 1951; s. La and Phyllis (Galowin) L.; B.A., Hofstra U., 1975; postgrad. bus. Hofstra U., 1976—. With Coca Cola Bottling Co. N.Y., various locations, 1969-72, office mgr., Greenpoint br., 1973-75, Bronx br., 1975-77; mgr. computer ops. L.I. Jewish Hillside Med. Center, Glen Oaks, N.Y., 1977—; instr. Hofstra U., 1978—. Vol. emergency med. technician Nassau County (N.Y.) Police. Mem. Nat. Police and Fire Fighter Assn., Assn. Computing Machinery, Nat. Users Group MSIS, Nat. Assn. Watch and Clock Collectors, N.Y. Users Group MSIS. Home: 317 Lucille Ave Elmont NY 11003 Office: 265th St and 76th Ave Glen Oaks NY 11004

LUKITSCH, ROBERT ALBERT, coll. adminstr.; b. Pitts., Jan. 24, 1928; s. Joseph J. and Anna M. (Sulics) L.; B.B.A., Hofstra U., 1971; M.B.A., N.Y. Inst. Tech., 1974; m. Mary Margaret Rooney, Oct. 3, 1953; children—Joanne, Nancy, Carol. Various positions Allis-Chalmers Co., Pitts., 1945-62; dir. records and operational service U. Pitts., 1962-66; with Nassau Community Coll., Garden City, N.Y., 1966—, dir. research and evaluation, 1966-70, dean adminstrn., 1970-73, v.p. adminstrn., 1973—, adj. faculty, 1971—. Trustee Nassau Higher Edn. Consortium, 1970—, vice-chmn., 1970-72. Mem. Data Processing Mgmt. Assn., Am. Inst. Research, N.Y. State Assn. Jr. Colls., AAUP. Republican. Roman Catholic. Home: 362 Rice Circle Garden City NY 11530

LUKS, ALLAN BARRY, social service agy. adminstr.; b. N.Y.C., June 27, 1941; s. Joseph and Evelyn L.; B.A., U. N.C., 1963; J.D., Georgetown U., 1966; m. Karen Greenbaum, Feb. 12, 1969; children—Rachel, David. Vol., U.S. Peace Corps, 1966-68; admitted to N.Y. State bar, 1966; legal dir. Children's Aid Soc., N.Y.C., 1968-70; asst. dir. $2 Billion Urban Investment Fund Inst., N.Y.C., 1970-72; sec.-treas. N.Y.C.-Rand Inst., 1972-74; exec. dir. Nat. Council Alcoholism, N.Y.C., 1974—. Bd. dirs. N.Y.C. Community Sch. Bd., 1975-77; pres. N.Y.C. Housing Project, 1973-78. Author: Rights of Alcoholics, 1976; Preventing Child Maltreatment, 1978; editor: Having Benn There, 1979; contbr. articles in field to jours., mags. Home: 101 Clark St Brooklyn NY 11201 Office: 133 E 62d St New York NY 10021

LULICK, MARY A., osteo. physician; b. Niagara Falls, N.Y., Mar. 7, 1911; d. Michael and Anna (Skrlin) Lulick; student U. Buffalo, 1929-31; D.O., Phila. Coll. Osteopathy, 1937; B.A. in Chemistry, U. Pa., 1958. Pediatrics fellow Phila. Coll. Osteopathy, 1937-38; practice osteo. medicine, Phila. and Media, Pa., 1937-51; sch. physician med. div., Phila. Sch. Dist., 1955-57, med. supr., 1957-76; med. cons. Pa. Com. on Adapted Phys. Edn., 1963-64. Fellow Am. Sch. Health Assn.; mem. Pa., Philadelphia County osteo. assns., Suprs. Assn. Phila. Bd. Edn., Am. Pub. Health Assn., AAUW, Pi Delta Nu, Democrat. Roman Catholic. Home: 2594 Cranston Rd Philadelphia PA 19131 Office: Med Div Sch Dist Phila 21st and Pkwy Philadelphia PA 19103

LUMADUE, DONALD DEAN, hobby and crafts exec.; b. El Reno, Okla., Sept. 30, 1938; s. Harry Basil and Muriel Ellen (Craven) L.; student U.S. Coast Guard Acad., 1956-57; m. Joyce Anne Hayes, June 28, 1958; children—Dawnia, Donald, Robert, Ronald. Lab. technician Charles Pfizer & Co., Groton, Conn., 1957-60; indsl. engr. Sonoco Products, Mystic, Conn., 1960-67; partner Joydon's, New London, Conn., 1958—, House of Leisure, New London, 1965—; Hobby Crafts, New London, 1968—; pres. NEI, Inc., New London, 1968—. Mem. New Eng. (pres. 1973-74), Am. (dir. wholesaler div. 1974—, chmn. bd. wholesale div. 1976—, chmn. bd. nat. wholesalers 1977-78) hobby industry assns., Indsl. Mgmt. Club S.E. Conn. (v.p. 1976-77, pres. 1977-78), Nat. Assn. Wholesalers (nat. trustee 1976-79). Office: 12-18 Masonic St New London CT 06320

LUMLEY, JOHN MORRIS, educator; b. Vineland, N.J., Feb. 10, 1906; s. John and Flossie (Zaner) L.; B.A., Muhlenberg Coll., 1928; M.Ed., Pa. State U., 1945; D.Ed., Waynesburg Coll., 1955; m. Kathryn Wentzel; 1 son, Joseph Ernest. Tchr.-prin. Eagles Mere (Pa.) Sch., 1928-30; prin. Dushore (Pa.) High Sch., 1930-32; supervising prin. Dushore Borough schs., 1932-38; supt. schs. Sullivan County (Pa.), 1938-52; dep. supt. pub. instruction Pa., 1952-55; supt. city schs. Wilkes Barre (Pa.), 1955-57; exec. asst., dir. div. fed. relations NEA, Washington, 1957-67, asst. exec. sec. for legis. and fed. relations, 1967-71, also mem. nat. legis. commn., now nat. legis. cons., lectr., 1971—; pres. Pa. Edn. Assn., 1951. Chmn. Sullivan County Tb Soc., 1940-51, Sullivan County Tb and Heart Assn., 1950-51, Sullivan County council Boy Scouts Am., 1950; trustee Mansfield (Pa.) Tchrs. Coll.; bd. dirs. Multiple Sclerosis Soc. Washington, 1949-53. Recipient Alumni Achievement award Muhlenberg Coll., 1955. Mem. NEA, Am. Assn. Sch. Adminstrs., Phi Delta Kappa. Lutheran. Club: Masons. Home: Rauchtown RD 2 Jersey Shore PA 17740 Office: 1201 16th St NW Washington DC 20036

LUMPKIN, LEE ROY, dermatologist; b. Oklahoma City, Sept. 6, 1925; s. Lee R. and Martha M. (Lockard) L.; B.A., U. Okla., 1949, M.D., 1963; m. Mona F. Long, Jan. 28, 1953; children—Lee Roy III, Patricia J., Meggin E., Julie A., William S. Intern, Tripler Gen. Hosp., Honolulu, 1953-54; gen. practice medicine, San Francisco, 1955-57; commd. capt. U.S. Air Force, 1957, advanced through grades to col., 1968; resident in dermatology Walter Reed Gen. Hosp., Washington, 1958-61; chief of dermatology, Madrid, Spain, 1961-64; fellow in dermatopathology Armed Forces Inst. Pathology, Washington, 1964-65; chief USAF Regional Center, Carswell AFB, Tex., 1964-67; chief dermatology USAF Med. Center, Lackland AFB, San Antonio, 1967-72; asso. clin. prof. dermatology U. Tex. Sch. Medicine, San Antonio, 1969-72, ret., 1972; prof., head div. dermatology Albany (N.Y.) Med. Center, 1972—. Decorated Bronze Star medal, Air Force Commendation medal (2), Meritorious Service medal. Fellow Am. Acad. Dermatology, Am. Soc. Dermatopathology, A.C.P.; mem. Assn. Profs. Dermatology, Dermatology Found., Soc. Air Force Physicians (pres.-elect), Noah Worcester, New Eng., Central N.Y. dermatol. socs. Episcopalian. Editor: Bull. Assn. Mil. Dermatologists, 1968-71; mem. editorial bd. Mil. Medicine, 1968-76; contbr. articles to med. jours. Home: 2696 Troy-Schenectady Rd Schenectady NY 12309 Office: Albany Med Coll 47 New Scotland Ave Albany NY 12208

LUND, ROBERT E., metall. engr.; b. Roswell, N.Mex., June 6, 1920; s. Robert Ranous and Eunice Margaret (Brown) L.; B.S. in Chem. Engring., U. Colo., 1942; postgrad. Carnegie Inst. Tech., 1952-61; m. Mildred June Anderson, Nov. 28, 1947; children—Amy (Mrs. Donald P. Storer), Michael Robert, Susan (Mrs. James B. Boyd), Stephen Douglas. Research engr. St. Joe Minerals Corp. (name formerly St. Joseph Lead Co.), Monaca, Pa., 1942-47, asst. supt. sinter and leach plants, 1947-57, research supt., 1957-67, research mgr., 1967-73, asso. dir. research, 1973-74, dir. research, 1974—. Active Boy Scouts Am., 1953—. Served with USNR, 1944-46. Registered profl. engr., Pa.; named Engr. of Year, Beaver County chpt. Pa. Soc. Profl. Engrs., 1977. Fellow Am. Soc. Metals; mem. Am. Inst. Mining, Metall. and Petroleum Engrs. (v.p. 1974, 78), Am. Inst. Chem. Engrs., Canadian, Australian insts. mining and metallurgy, Instn. Mining and Metallurgy. Contbr. articles to profl. jours. Home: 375 Barclay Hill Rd Beaver PA 15009 Office: Box A Monaca PA 15061

LUNDE, ASBJORN RUDOLPH, lawyer; b. S.I., N.Y., July 17, 1927; s. Karl and Elisa (Andenes) L.; A.B., Columbia U., 1947, LL.B., 1949. Admitted to N.Y. bar, 1949, since practiced in N.Y.C.; with firm Kramer, Marx, Greenlee & Backus, and predecessors, 1950-68, mem., 1958-68; individual practice law, 1968—; dir. numerous cos. Bd. dirs., v.p. Orchestra da Camera, Inc., 1964—; bd. dirs. Sara Roby Found., 1971—, The Drawing Soc., 1977—. Mem. Am., N.Y. State bar assns., Assn. Bar City N.Y., Met. Opera Club. Home: 1120 Park Ave New York City NY 10028 also RD 1 Hillsdale NY 12529 Office: 230 Park Ave New York City NY 10017

LUNDELL, FREDERICK WALDEMAR, psychiatrist, educator; b. Revelstoke, B.C., Can., Jan. 31, 1924; s. Arvid Waldemar and Isabel Catherine (Dunlop) L.; B.A. with honors in Zoology and Psychology, U. B.C., 1947; M.D., C.M., McGill U., Que., Can., 1951, diploma in psychiatry; m. Helen Alicia Hoult, Dec. 27, 1950; children—Heather Lundell Milliken, Catherine, Cynthia, Christine, Stacie. Intern in psychiatry Queen Mary Vets. Hosp., Montreal, Que., Can., 1952-53; asst. resident in psychiatry Montreal Gen. Hosp., Que., 1953-54, resident in psychiatry, 1954-55; asst. resident in psychiatry Montreal Children's Hosp., 1955-56; practice medicine specializing in psychiatry, Montreal, 1956—; asst. psychiatrist Montreal Children's Hosp., 1957-65, asso. psychiatrist, 1965-72, cons. psychiatrist, 1972—; dir. psychiat. research unit Queen Mary Vets. Hosp., 1960-67, coordinator psychiat. research unit, 1967—, chief of service, 1970—; asst. psychiatrist Montreal Gen. Hosp., 1963-65, dir. psychiat. research, 1963-64, asso. psychiatrist, 1965—; lectr. psychiatry McGill U., 1959-64, asst. prof., 1964-67, asso. prof. 1967—. Served with RCAF, 1942-45. Fellow Royal Coll. Physicians and Surgeons Can., Am. Psychiat. Assn., AAAS, Royal Soc. Health, Am. Geriatric Soc., Am. Acad. Polit. and Social Sci., Am. Acad. Arts and Scis.; mem. Am. (pres. Que. dist. br. 1960-61), Canadian, Que. psychiat. assns., Canadian Med. Assn., Algonquin Home and Sch. Assn. (v.p. 1961-62), Canadian Gerontol. Soc., Montreal Medico-Chirurg. Soc. (pres. div. in psychiatry 1957-58), Canadian R.R. Hist. Assn., Amateur Athletic Assn., Que. Heritabe Assn., McGill Osler Reporting Soc., N.Y. Acad. Sci., Canadian Psychiat. Assn. Clubs: Summerlea Golf and Country, Masons, Faculty. Contbr. chpts. to books, articles on mental retardation, drug studies, conjoint marital therapy to profl. jours. Home: 389 Devon Mount Royal PQ Canada Office: 1538 Sherbrooke St W Montreal PQ Canada

LUNDGREN, CARL WILLIAM, JR., physicist; b. Columbus, Sept. 17, 1933; s. Carl William and Anne Katherine (Kuntz) L.; B.E.E., U. Cin., 1957, M.S., 1959, Ph.D., 1961; m. Virginia Anne Cullis, Dec. 7, 1963; children—David John, Janet Marie. Coop. undergrad. engr. Govt. Products div. Avco Corp., Cin. and Evendale, Ohio, 1953-56; asst. supr., research fellow Basic Sci. Research Lab., U. Cin., 1959-61; mem. tech. staff Bell Telephone Labs., Murray Hill, N.J., 1961-66, Holmdel, N.J., 1966—. Served to capt., Signal Corps., U.S. Army, 1961-63. Mem. AAAS, N.Y. Acad. Sci., Am. Inst. Aeros. and Astronautics, IEEE, Engring. Soc. Cin., Delta Tau Delta, Tau Beta Pi, Eta Kappa Nu, Phi Eta Sigma, Omicron Delta Kappa. Republican. Episcopalian. Contbr. articles to profl. jours.; patentee in field. Home: Woodhollow Rd RD 3 Colts Neck NJ 07722 Office: Bell Labs Crawfords Corner Rd Holmdel NJ 07733

LUNDGREN, RICHARD JOHN, city planner; b. N.Y.C., Dec. 13, 1940; s. John H. and Helen C. (Vetter) L.; B.S., Rensselaer Poly. Inst., 1964; M.S., Pratt Inst., 1968; m. Nancy Whitin Truslow, Apr. 1, 1972; 1 son, Andrew Auchincloss. Sr. planner Herr Assos., Boston, 1968-69; project dir. Boston Redevel. Authority, 1969-72; dir. planning Charles G. Hilgenhurst & Assos., Boston, 1972-77; v.p. Hunneman and Co., Inc., Boston, 1977—. Bd. dirs., treas. Vis. Nurse Assn. Boston,

1972—; propr. Boston Athenaeum, 1974—; mem. neighborhood com. United Way of Mass. Bay, 1974-76; sec. Dover Protective Agys. Com., 1975—; rep. Met. Area Planning Council, 1976—. Served with USCGR, 1968-72. Mem. Am. Inst. Planners, Inst. Real Estate Mgmt., Citizens Housing and Planning Assn. Boston, Greater Boston Real Estate Bd., Building Owners and Mgrs. Assn., Rental Housing Assn. (dir.). Republican. Episcopalian. Club: Dedham Country and Polo. Home: 48 Center St Dover MA 02030 Office: One Winthrop Sq Boston MA 02110

LUNDGREN, RUTH (MRS. W.F. WILLIAMSON), writer, pub. relations exec.; b. Bklyn.; d. John William and Hanna (Carlson) Lundgren; student Bklyn. Coll., 1936-41, Columbia, 1942; m. W.F. Williamson, Dec. 17, 1949; children—John Ross, Mark Ward. Asso. editor Everywoman's mag., 1940-42; pub. relations staff exec. J.M. Mathes Advt. Agy., 1942-45; dir. pub. relations Pan-Am. Coffee Bur., 1945-48; pres. Ruth Lundgren, Ltd., N.Y., 1948—; pub. Ruth Lundgren Newsletter, 1950-58; writer daily column St. Petersburg Times, 1956-60; contbg. editor, writer monthly column Motor Boating & Sailing mag., 1962-75. Contbr. popular, profl. publs. Home: 3311 Bay Front Dr Baldwin Harbor NY 11510 Office: Box 184 Baldwin NY 11510

LUNDINE, STANLEY NELSON, congressman; b. Jamestown, N.Y., Feb. 4, 1939; A.B., Duke U., 1961; LL.B., N.Y. U., 1964; m. Karol Anne Ludwig, 1962; children—John Ludwig, Mark Andrew. Admitted to N.Y. bar, 1965; partner firm Ford & Lundine, Jamestown, 1965-70; mayor City of Jamestown, 1969-76, chmn. planning commn., 1968-70; mem. 94th-96th Congresses from 39th N.Y. Dist.; mem. Banking, Fin. and Urban Affairs Com. Mem. N.Y. State Conf. Mayors, U.S. Conf. Mayors. Democrat. Clubs: Kiwanis, Elks. Home: 232 Huxley St Jamestown NY 14701 Office: 430 Cannon House Office Bldg Washington DC 20515

LUNN, GAIL ILIA, interior designer; b. Bristol, Conn., Nov. 2, 1949; d. Alphebade Joseph and Patricia Jean (Hill) Castonguay; grad. Paier Sch. Art, 1970; postgrad. Porter Sch. Design, 1972; m. David John Lunn, Oct. 13, 1973. Office design specialist Conn. Mut. Life Ins., Hartford, 1973-78; sr. office design cons. Aetna Life and Casualty Co., Hartford, 1978—; prin. Interior Designs, Terryville, Conn., 1978—. Cons. Sexual Assault Center YWCA, Hartford, 1977—. Mem. Inst. Bus. Designers. Home: 32 Crestview Rd Terryville CT 06786 Office: Farmington Ave Hartford CT 06115

LUNN, RICHARD HARRY, research exec.; b. Heilwood, Pa., Dec. 15, 1929; s. Wilbert Raymond and Helen Elizabeth (Byers) L.; B.S. in Chem. Engring., U. Pitts., 1951, postgrad. in bus. adminstrn., 1952-55; m. Margaret Ann Cogley, July 3, 1955; children—Richard, Jon, Kelly. With Micarta div. Westinghouse Electric Corp., Pitts., 1951-55, Hampton, S.C., 1955-63, Astronuclear Lab., Pitts., 1963-68, Research and Devel. Center, 1968—; lectr. U. Pitts., Carnegie Mellon U. Instl. rep. Boy Scouts Am., 1968-71. City councilman, Hampton, 1960-63; sch. dir., Plum Borough Sch. Dist., 1968—, Allegheny Intermediate Unit, 1973-76. Recipient award for outstanding service to the community Westinghouse Electric Corp., 1975. Mem. Nat. Alliance Businessmen (past team capt.), Am. Inst. Chem. Engrs., Am. Mgmt. Assn. Methodist (past supt. Sunday sch.). Mason. Contbr. articles to tech. jours. Patentee light weight body armor, materials and fabrications techniques for re-entry heat shield Titan intercontinental ballistic missile. Home: 4051 Cape Cod Dr Pittsburgh PA 15239 Office: Westinghouse Research and Devel Center Pittsburgh PA 15235

LUNT, SAMUEL DORR, JR., investment banker; b. Buffalo, Mar. 13, 1936; s. Samuel Dorr and Gertrude Clinton (Wright) L.; B.S., Colgate U., 1958; M.B.A., N.Y. U., 1966; m. Shirley Ann Hawk, Dec. 13, 1958; children—Cynthia Ann, Sandra Marie, Melissa Elizebeth. Gen. partner S. D. Lunt & Co., N.Y.C., 1961; v.p. Robert B. Anderson & Co., Ltd., N.Y.C., 1977—; pres. Robert B. Anderson Securities Corp., N.Y.C., 1978—; pres., dir. Slurrytech, Inc., S.D. Lunt Jr. of Fla., Inc.; dir. Met. Maintenance Co., Robert B. Anderson Securities Corp., Conway Diet Inst., PMS Group, Nat. Recreation Industries Corp., Santek, Inc. Trustee Alfred U. Served with USMC, 1958-61. Mem. Phi Kappa Psi. Republican. Episcopalian. Clubs: Miami Lakes Country, Optimists. Home: 7520 Loch Ness Dr Miami Lakes FL 33014 Office: 630 Fifth Ave New York City NY 10020

LUPA, JOSEPH MICHAEL, mech. engr.; b. Oswego, N.Y., Jan. 8, 1946; s. Joseph Victor and Helen Irene (Koleczek) L.; B.S. in Mech. Engring., U. Detroit, 1968; A.S. in Elec. Tech., Cleve. Inst. Electronics, 1973; hon. grad. U.S. Army Missile and Munitions Center and Sch., 1970; m. Zofia Bronislawa Tobiasz, June 29, 1974; children—Michal Miroslaw, Jacek Andrew. Enlisted U.S. Army 1968, advanced through ranks to capt. 1970; guided missile maintenance officer Ordnance Corps., platoon officer, mgr. all missile, radar, computer, guidance and support equipment repair Hawk Air Defense Missile Battalion, Germany, Crete, Korea, U.S., 1968-75; capt. Res., missile material officer, 1975—; field engr. Raytheon Middle East Systems Co., Jeddah, Saudi Arabia, 1975-77; instr. Saudi Arabian Army officers, Royal Air Defense Sch., Jeddah 1976-77; factory mechan. engr. Sealright Co., Fulton, N.Y., 1978—; mem. Gilcrease Inst., Tulsa, 1971—. Mem. Met. Mus. Art, N.Y.C., 1972—. Decorated Korea Expeditionary medal, Nat. Def. service medal; licensed 2d class radio-telephone operator FCC; certified electronics warfare specialist U.S. Army Command and Gen. Staff Coll. Mem. Am. Inst. Astronautics and Aeros., ASME, Soc. Am. Mil. Engrs., Am. Def. Preparedness Assn., U.S. Naval Inst., Air Force Assn. Roman Catholic. Clubs: K.C., Polish of Am. Address: Box 157 Nestle Dr RD 5 Oswego NY 13126

LUPIANI, DONALD ANTHONY, psychologist; b. N.Y.C., June 7, 1946; s. Louis and Josephine L.; B.A., Iona Coll., 1968; M.A., Columbia U., 1971, Ph.D., 1973; certificate Am. Projective Drawing Inst., N.Y.C., 1975, Behavior Therapy Inst., White Plains, N.Y., 1976; m. Linda Moyik, June 20, 1970; 1 dau., Jennifer Lynne. Psychology intern Spence Sch., N.Y.C., 1972-73; dir. pscyhol. and spl. ednl. services Riverdale Country Sch., N.Y.C., 1973—; clin. psychology intern Psychiat. Services Center, White Plains, N.Y., 1974-76; adj. asst. prof. psychology Iona Coll., 1972—; clin. asso. dept. psychology Tchrs. Coll., Columbia U., 1975—; clin. asso. sch. psychology Fordham U., 1977; evaluator Nat. Council Accreditation Tchr. Edn.; cons. in field. NIMH fellow, 1968-73. Certified psychologist, sch. psychology, N.Y. State. Mem. Am. Soc. Psychologists in Pvt. Practice, Am., N.Y. State, Westchester County psychol. assns., Am. Assn. Psychoednl. Therapists, Nat. Assn. Sch. Psychologists, Am. Sch. Health Assn., AAAS, Assn. Advancement Behavior Therapy, Orton Soc., Am. Ednl. Research Assn., Sigma Xi, Psi Chi. Contbg. editor Sch. Psychology Newsletter, 1976—; contbr. articles to profl. jours. Home: 120 Florence St Yonkers NY 10704

LUPTON, ELMER CORNELIUS, JR., plastics engr.; b. Balt., Aug. 8, 1945; s. Elmer Cornelius and Leoni (Potucek) L.; S.B., Mass. Inst. Tech., 1965; M.Phil., Yale U., 1967, Ph.D., 1969; m. Claire Turner Cook, June 8, 1968; 1 dau., Katherine Lent. Mgr. applications research, engring. plastics Allied Chem. Co., Morristown, N.J., 1973-76, industry mgr. packaging and govt. sales, 1977—; cons. in field. Mem. nat. scout program devel. com. Northeast regional scouting com. Boy Scouts Am. Served with capt. USAF, 1969-73. Mem. Am. Chem. Soc., Soc. Plastics Engrs., Sigma Xi, Phi Lambda Upsilon. Roman Catholic. Contbr. to profl. jours. Home: 15 Cobb Rd Mountain Lakes NJ 07046 Office: Allied Chem Co Box 1057R Morristown NJ 07960

LUPTON, JOHN ANTHONY, hosp. adminstr.; b. London, Eng., Nov. 14, 1930; s. Gilbert and Hilda Artiss (Cruikshank) L.; came to Can., 1957, naturalized, 1968; student pub. schs., Eng.; m. Jean Evelyn Edwards, Apr. 25, 1964; children—Geoffrey D., Paul Gilbert. Trainee adminstr. Royal Sussex County Hosp., Brighton, Eng., 1950-52; asst. sec. Royal Alexandra Hosp. for Sick Children, Brighton, Eng., 1952-54; with King's Coll. Hosp., London, 1954-58; asst. adminstr. Royal Victoria Hosp., Montreal, Que., Can., 1965-70; adminstr. Trenton (Ont.) Meml. Hosp., 1971—. Sec.-treas. Quinte Dist. Health Planning Council, Belleville, Ont., 1971—; commr. affidavits, Ont., 1976—. Mem. Ont. Hosp. Assn. (chmn. region 8, 1976—), Royal Soc. Health, Inst. Health Service Adminstrs. G.B., Canadian Coll. Health Service Execs. Home: 25 Fairview Crescent Trenton ON Canada Office: Trenton Meml Hosp Trenton ON K8V 5S6 Canada

LURIA, SALVADOR EDWARD, biologist; b. Turin, Italy, Aug. 13, 1912; s. David and Ester (Sacerdote) L.; M.D., U. Turin (Italy), 1935; m. Zella Hurwitz, Apr. 18, 1945; 1 son, Daniel. Came to U.S., 1940, naturalized, 1947. Research fellow Curie Lab., Inst. of Radium, Paris, France, 1938-40; research asst. surg. bacteriology Columbia, 1940-42; successively instr., asst. prof., asso. prof. bacteriology Ind. U., 1943-50; prof. bacteriology U. Ill., 1950-59; prof. microbiology Mass. Inst. Tech., 1959-64, Sedgwick prof. biology, 1964—, Inst. prof., 1970—, dir. center cancer research, 1972—; non-resident fellow Salk Inst. Biol. Studies, 1965—; lectr. biophysics U. Colo., 1950; Jesup lectr. zoology Columbia, 1950; Nieuwland lectr. biology U. Notre Dame, 1959; Dyer lectr. NIH, 1963; with OSRD, Carnegie Instn., Washington, 1945-46. Guggenheim fellow Vanderbilt U. and Princeton, 1942-43, Pasteur Inst., Paris, 1963-64. Co-recipient Nobel prize for medicine, 1969. Mem. Am. Philos. Soc., Am. Soc. Microbiology (pres. 1967-68), Nat. Acad. Scis., Am. Acad. Arts and Scis., AAAS, Soc. Gen. Microbiology, Genetics Soc. Am., AAUP, Sigma Xi. Asso. editor Jour. Bacteriology, 1950-55; editor Virology, 1955—; sect. editor Biol. Abstracts, 1958-62; editorial bd. Exptl. Cell Research Jour., 1948—; adv. bd. Jour. Molecular Biology, 1958-64; hon. editorial adv. bd. Jour. Molecular Biology, 1958-64; hon. editorial adv. bd. Jour. Photochemistry and Photobiology, 1961—. Home: 48 Peacock Farm Rd Lexington MA 02173 Office: Dept Inst Tech Cambridge MA 02139

LURKIS, ALEXANDER, cons. elec. engr.; b. N.Y.C., Oct. 1, 1908; s. Louis and Rebecca (Friedman) L.; B.E.E., N.Y. U., 1934, Cooper Union, 1930; tech. tchr. certificate State U. N.Y., 1936; m. Carin S. Tendler, Nov. 8, 1930; 1 son, Jeffry L. Asst. engr. 8th & 9th Aves. Ry. Co., N.Y.C., 1925-28; elec. draftsman N.Y.C. Bd. Edn., 1928-30; asst. elec. engr. N.Y.C. Transit Authority, 1930-40, sr. elec. engr., 1942-58; elec. engr. F. R. Harris Inc., N.Y.C., 1940-41; chief engr. N.Y.C. Bur. Gas and Electricity, 1959-64, acting commr. N.Y.C. Dept. Water Supply, Gas and Electricity, 1961; partner Alexander Lurkis Assos., Floral Park, N.Y., 1964—; pres. Alexander urkis, P.C., 1971—; v.p. Peak Tech. Assn. Inc., 1951-59; sec.-treas. Glimmer Security Systems, Inc., 1976—; v.p., trustee dist. council 37 State County Municipal Employees-AFL-CIO, 1956-63; pres. Civil Service Tech. Guild, 1956-58. Pres. 10th Assembly Dist. Democratic Club of Queens, N.Y.C., 1959-62; 1st v.p. Holliswood (N.Y.) Civic Assn. Inc., 1974-76. Recipient award for Cin. streetscape Am. Iron and Steel Inst., 1971, HUD, 1972; registered profl. engr., N.Y., Fla. Fellow Illuminating Engring. Soc. (chmn. com. energy mgmt. 1974-77), N.Y. Acad. Sci; mem. IEEE (sr.), AAAS, Am. Arbitration Assn. (labor panelist), Nat. Geog. Soc., Queens Museum Friends, Cooper Union Alumni Assn. (gov. 1960-66). Jewish. Contbr. articles to profl. jours.; U.S., fgn. patentee in field (II); environ. expert FPC, Pub. Service Commn. Home: 193-12 Nero Ave Holliswood NY 11423 Office: 199 Jericho Turnpike Floral Park NY 11001

LUSCH, CHARLES JACK, hematologist; b. Lehighton, Pa., Feb. 15, 1936; s. Charles Norman and Loretta Marguerite (Gaumer) L.; A.B. in Biology, Lafayette Coll., 1957; M.D., Temple U., 1961; m. Carole Faye Eckhart, Aug. 17, 1957; children—Marjorie Sue, Susan Diane, Stephen Edward, Robert Christopher. Intern, Reading (Pa.) Hosp. and Med. Center, 1961-62, resident in medicine, 1962-65; fellow in hematology Hahnemann Med. Coll., Phila., 1967-68; pvt. practice medicine specializing in hematology, West Reading, Pa., 1968—; mem. staff Reading Hosp. and Med. Center, 1968—, chief sect. hematology and oncology, 1972—, dir. blood bank, 1968—; mem. staffs Pottstown (Pa.) Meml. Med. Center, Good Samaritan Hosp., Pottsville, Pa.: asst. prof. medicine Hershey Med. Center; dir. State Hemophilia Center, Reading. Bd. dirs. Keystone Community Blood Bank, Reading, Berks County chpt. Am. Cancer Soc. Served with USPHS, 1965-67. Mem. AMA, A.C.P., Pa., Berks County med. socs., Am. Fedn. Clin. Research, Am. Soc. Hematology, Am. Soc. Clin. Oncology, Sports Car Club Am., Internat. Motorsports Assn., U.S. Auto Club (race ofcl., med. div.), Phi Kappa Tau, Phi Beta Kappa, Alpha Omega Alpha. Republican. Lutheran. Office: 301 S 7th Ave West Reading PA 19611

LUSINS, JOHN O., physician; b. Latvia, Dec. 15, 1939; s. Janis and Elza (Berzins) L.; came to U.S., 1952, naturalized, 1958; B.A., Columbia, 1963; M.D., Albany Med. Coll., 1967; m. Anna Marie Dahlgard, June 16, 1963; children—Gillian, Noelle, Carl, John Mathew. Intern, St. Luke Hosp., N.Y.C., 1967-68, resident medicine, 1968; resident Mt. Sinai Hosp., N.Y.C., 1969-71, chief resident, 1971-72, attending neurologist, 1972—; chief attending neurologist Hosp. Joint Disease, N.Y.C., 1972—; attending neurologist Jewish Meml. Hosp., N.Y.C., 1972—; clin. asso. neurology Mt. Sinai Sch. Medicine, 1972—; co-dir. nuclear medicine Blvd. Hosp., Queens, N.Y.; cons. Vets. Hosp., Bronx, N.Y., 1973-76. Served with USAF, 1962-63. Clin. fellow Nat. Heart Assn., 1969. Diplomate Am. Bd. Nuclear Medicine, Am. Bd. Neurology and Psychiatry. Fellow A.C.P.; mem. Soc. Nuclear Medicine, N.Y. Soc. Neurology. Contbg. editor Mt. Sinai Jour. Medicine, 1974-76; contbr. articles to profl. jours. Home: 159 White Plains Rd Bronxville NY 10708 Office: 65 E 79th St New York City NY 10029

LUSK, BEN EARL, trade assn. exec.; b. McKeesport, Pa., Apr. 21, 1945; s. James Paul and Rosella Elaine (Benack) L.; student Nat. U. Argentina, 1962; B.A. (Benedum Found. scholar 1963-67), Bethany (W.Va.) Coll., 1967; postgrad. W.Va. U., 1967-69; m. Yvonne Phalen, Aug. 23, 1975; children—Casey, Kristen. Asst. to athletic dir. in charge pub. relations and promotions W.Va. U., 1967-71; pres. W.Va. Surface Mining and Reclamation Assn., 1971-77; dir. W.Va. Applied Research Inst., 1973-77; pres. Mining and Reclamation Council Am., Washington, 1977—; mem. W.Va. Bd. Miner Tng., Edn. and Certification, W.Va. Black Lung Adv. Com., W.Va. Coal Adv. Bd.; exec. com. W.Va. Research Steering Com., Council Surface Mining and Reclamation Research in Appalachia; chmn. Internat. Mining and Reclamation Conf., 1974-78. Office: Suite 700 1000 6th St NW Washington DC 20036

LUSK, JACK EDWARD, motion picture distbn. co. exec.; b. Alton, Ill., Nov. 24, 1935; s. Bruce H. and Dorothy H. (McKay) L.; B.S. in Mktg., U. Ill., 1958; m. Patricia A. Kendall, Aug. 19, 1959; children—Catherine, Robert. With Modern Talking Picture Service, N.Y.C., 1961—, v.p., 1970—. Office: Modern Talking Picture Service 45 Rockefeller Plaza New York City NY 10020

LUSKEY, J. BERNARD, food processing co. exec.; b. Brockport, N.Y., May 25, 1914; s. Francis Maria and Ida Johanna (Ryan) L.; Tchrs. Certificate, Brockport Normal Sch., 1934; m. Eleanor Ann Prince, Mar. 8, 1941; children—Peter B., Patrick F., Bettina M. With Duffy-Mott Co., N.Y.C., 1934—. mgr., 1950-64, asst. v.p., 1964-72, v.p. 1972—. Mem. Asso. N.Y. State Food Processors (pres. 1973-74), N.Y. State Apple Mktg. Bd. Democrat. Clubs: Stafford (N.Y.) Country; Ponte Vedra (Fla.). Home: Redman Rd Brockport NY 14420 Office: Lake Rd Hamlin NY 14464

LUSSI, CAROLINE FRANCES DRAPER, motel mgr.; b. Glen Falls, N.Y., Apr. 5, 1939; d. Arthur Gibb and Lili Caroline (Geadeke) Draper; student U. Colo., 1957-58; A.A.S., Paul Smith's Coll., 1960; grad. Holiday Inn U., 1969; m. Serge Gail Lussi, Feb. 7, 1960; children—Arthur, Cristina, Katrina. Profl. ski instr., 1960—; mgr. Holiday Motor Motel, Wilmington, N.Y., 1961-62, owner, 1962-69; owner, innkeeper Holiday Inn, Lake Placid, N.Y., 1969—; sec. Lake Placid Vacation Corp., 1969—. Mem. adv. bd. Alpine 1980 Olympics; bd. dirs. Lake Placid Meml. Hosp., 1975—, also mem. aux. Named Top 10% Innkeeper Holiday Inns, 1972-75. Mem. Lake Placid C. of C., Profl. Ski Instrs. Am. (certified). Episcopalian. Club: Lake Placid. Home and Office: Holiday Inn Lake Placid NY 12946

LUST, PETER, journalist; b. Nuernberg, Germany, Jan. 15, 1911; s. Arthur and Luise (Bloch) L.; M.History, U. Geneva, Switzerland, 1930; m. Evelyn Heymannsohn, June 23, 1953; children—Patricia, Arthur, Peter. Journalist, Montreal (Que., Can.), Herald, 1946-53; broadcaster Canadian Broadcasting Co., 1964—; Canadian corr. West German news mag. Der Spiegel, Hamburg, Germany, 1968-76; columnist Der Stern, 1970—, Burda Publs., Offenburg, Germany, 1976—, Suburban, Montreal, 1976—; commentator weekly TV-show, Montreal, 1970—. Served with AUS, World War II. Recipient award Govt. Province Que., 1967. Mem. Canadian Press Club. Author: Two Germanies, Mirror of an Age, 1966; The Last Seal Pup, 1967; Cuba, Time Bomb at our Door, 1970. Home: 13 Thompson Point Beaconsfield PQ Canada Office: Box 2 Dorval Airport Dorval PQ H4Y 1A2 Canada

LUSTIG, ROBERT T., profl. football team exec. Mem. mgmt. staff Buffalo Bills, formerly recruiter, now v.p., gen. mgr., dir. Office: care Buffalo Bills One Bills Dr Orchard Park NY 14127*

LUTZ, JOHN HOWARD, research physician; b. Balt., Feb. 21, 1938; s. John William and Anna Agnes L.; A.B., Johns Hopkins U., 1960; M.D., U. Md., 1964; m. Sandra Susan VanHoose, Aug. 14, 1977; children—James Alexander, Elizabeth Juliet-Lyle, Sharon Patricia. Physiologist, NIH, 1965-71; resident in endocrinology and metabolism U. Mich., 1965-70, instr. medicine, 1969-70; instr. medicine Johns Hopkins U., 1970-75; med. dir. Herner Analitics, Rockville, Md., 1974—; dir. Inst. Preventive Medicine, Washington, 1977—. Served with USPHS, 1965-71. Mem. Am. Diabetes Assn., Am. Thyroid Assn., Am. Acad. Med. Preventics, Orthomolecular Soc., Internat. Acad. Preventive Medicine, Huxley Inst. Biosocial Research, Internat. Platform Assn. Quaker. Research on fever and thyroid, vitamin deficiency states and adrenal-pituitary biochem. and orthomolecular therapy, high blood pressure, and electrical detection of ovulation. Office: 2139 Wisconsin Ave NW Washington DC 20007

LUUS, REIN, chem. engr., educator; b. Tartu, Estonia, Mar. 8, 1939; s. Edgar and Aili (Poldre) L.; came to Can., 1949, naturalized, 1955; B.Applied Sci., U. Toronto, 1961, M.Applied Sci., 1962; A.M., Princeton, 1963, Ph.D., 1964; m. Taina Hilkka Inkeri Jaakola, June 17, 1973. Postdoctoral fellow Princeton, 1964-65; asst. prof. chem. engring. U. Toronto, 1965-68, asso. prof., 1968-74, prof., 1974—; cons. in field; dir. Chem. Engring. Research Cons.'s Ltd., Toronto, 1966—. Nat. Research Council Can. Sr. Indsl. fellow, 1972-73. Fellow Chem. Inst. Can.; mem. Assn. Profl. Engrs. Ont., Can. Soc. Chem. Engring., Sigma Xi. Lutheran. Club: Royal Can. Yacht. Home: 3 Terrington Ct Don Mills ON M3B 2J9 Canada Office: Dept Chem Engring U Toronto Toronto ON M5S 1A4 Canada

LYBARGER, ADRIENNE REYNOLDS (MRS. LEE FRANCIS LYBARGER, JR.), coll. adminstr.; b. Boston, Mar. 8, 1926; d. Joseph Anthony and Albertine Mouton (Drevet) Reynolds; B.S., Mills Coll., 1947; certificate Katharine Gibbs Sch., 1948; m. Lee Francis Lybarger, Jr., Sept. 15, 1955; children—Linda, Lauretta, James (dec.), Lisa, Leslie (dec.), Jeffrey (dec.), Lucia, Lana. Asst. to dir. Mid-Century convocations Mass. Inst. Tech., Cambridge, 1949, asst. to dir. West Coast regional office Mid-Century devel. program, 1949-50, asst. dir. So. regional office, 1950-51; asst. to dir. convocation program Ithaca (N.Y.) Coll., 1951; asst. to dir., devel. program U. Buffalo (N.Y.), 1951-52; asst. to dir. Diamond Jubilee program Case Inst. Tech., Cleve., 1952-54; asst. dir., expansion and improvement program John D. Archbold Hosp., Thomasville, Ga., 1955-61; partner Lybarger Prodns., comml. films, N.Y.C.; asst. dir., then dir. regional campaigns, Ohio, Boston, Mass., N.Y.C., also supr. all other nat. regional campaigns Mt. Holyoke Coll. Fund for Future, South Hadley, Mass., 1961-63; fund-raising cons. to capital programs, Vocation Service Center and Bronx-Westchester YMCA, YMCA Greater N.Y., 1963-65; dir. devel. and pub. relations Bank St. Coll. Edn., N.Y.C., 1965—; cons. S. Bronx Overall Econ. Devel. Corp. Pres., Birch Island (Maine) Corp.; mem. Deferred Giving Group, N.Y.C. Mem. Council for Advancement and Support Edn. Author: (with L.F. Lybarger) Proven Guides to Effective Soliciting (slide film), 1950, rev., 1960. Home: Kings Manor Pittstown NJ 08867 Office: 610 W 112th St New York City NY 10025

LYDDY, GREGORY JOSEPH, oral surgeon; b. Bridgeport, Conn., Jan. 18, 1931; s. John A. and Lauretta (Naedele) L.; A.B., Holy Cross Coll., 1952; D.D.S., Georgetown Dental Coll., 1956; m. Barbara Hurlbut, Dec. 28, 1958; children—Christopher, Brian, Sarah, Catherine. Intern, Jackson Meml. Hosp., Miami, Fla., 1956-57, resident, 1960-61; practice oral surgery, Bridgeport, 1961—; chief oral surgery St. Vincent's Hosp., Bridgeport; mem. staff Bridgeport, Park City hosps. Prof. oral surgery U. Bridgeport. Served to capt. AUS, 1957-59. Diplomate Am. Bd. Oral Surgery. Mem. Am. Soc. Oral Surgery, Bridgeport Dental Assn. (pres. 1974-75). Home: 55 Elm St Fairfield CT 06430 Office: 2660 Main St Bridgeport CT 06606

LYDECKER, ROBERT CARPENTER, utilities exec.; b. Madison, N.J., June 29, 1914; s. Frederick Ackerman and Mary Catherine (Carpenter) L.; A.B., Princeton, 1935; m. Laurie Bell Kerr, Apr. 19, 1941; children—Laurie, Elizabeth, Barbara, John. Comml. asst., comml. dept. Pub. Service Electric Gas Co., Newark, 1937-49, asst. exec. asst., 1949-68, exec., asst., 1968-71, asst. to pres., 1971—, v.p., 1974—. Chmn. Millburn Short Hills Community Fund, 1972-73; v.p. Essex council Boy Scouts Am., 1976. Served with USNR, 1942-46; capt. Res. ret. Mem. Am. Gas Assn., Short Hills Assn. (v.p. 1976). Republican. Episcopalian. Home: 44 Browning Rd Short Hills NJ 07078 Office: 80 Park Pl Newark NJ 07101

LYDEN, EDWARD FRANCIS XAVIER, geologist, educator; b. Bklyn., Aug. 8, 1920; s. Daniel Francis and Anna Margaret (Putz) L.; B.S., Columbia, 1954; postgrad. Rutgers U., 1964, U. Maine, 1972; m. Marie Worsley Barber, Oct. 14, 1944; children—Daniel W., Gerald W., Timothy W. Research technician dept. geology Columbia U., 1948-53; chemist Material Testing Lab., Wright Aero. Corp., Wood-Ridge, N.J., 1953-55; geo-chemist Princeton U., 1956-58, research geologist, 1958-66; asso. mem. tech. staff Bell Telephone Labs., Murray Hill, N.J., 1966-71; tchr. sci. Van Buren (Maine) Dist. High Sch., 1971-73; lectr. geology U. Maine, Ft. Kent, 1972-73; adult edn. tchr., Presque Isle, Maine, 1977—; pvt. cons. geologist, Ft. Fairfield, Maine, 1974—; lectr. mineralogy to mineral clubs in N.J. and Pa., cons. to indsl. firms in x-ray diffraction and fluorescence. Commr. Boy Scouts Am., N.J., Maine, 1958-71, 72, recipient Scouter's Key, 1967, Arrowhead award, 1967; mem. Rep. County com., Aroostook County, Maine, 1976—. Served with AUS, 1942-46. Certified geologist, Maine. Republican. Roman Catholic. Author: scientific papers. Home: Forest Ave Fort Fairfield ME 04742

LYLES, CHARLES FRANK, univ. adminstr.; b. Atlanta, May 25, 1939; s. Frank Usher and Irene (Lyles) L.; B.A., Morehouse Coll., 1961; M.A., N.Y. U., 1971; m. Jessamine Turner, Feb. 15, 1969; 1 child, Ayodele. Adminstr., N.Y.C. Human Resources Adminstrn., 1965-70; adminstr. Bklyn. Coll., 1970-74, Essex County Coll. of Newark, 1974-76; dir. counseling and career devel. Adelphi U., Garden City, N.Y., 1976—. Bd. dirs. Harlem Youth Fedn., 1969-78. Served with U.S. Army, 1960-65. So. Edn. fellow, 1961; Woodrow Wilson fellow, 1961-62. Mem. Am. Psychol. Assn., Am. Personnel and Guidance Assn. Club: New Amsterdam Polit. Home: 209 Clinton Ave Brooklyn NY 11205 Office: 113 Levermore Hill Garden City NY 11530

LYMAN, MELVILLE HENRY, naval officer; b. Glen Ridge, N.J., Apr. 4, 1942; s. Melville Henry and Frances Fridley (Needham) L.; B.S., U.S. Naval Acad., 1964; M.A. in Mgmt. and Human Relations, Webster Coll., 1979; m. Elizabeth Ann MacIan Farquharson, May 10, 1969; 1 son., Christopher. Commd. ensign U.S. Navy, 1964, advanced through grades to comdr., 1979, supply and ops. officer U.S.S. Nautilus, 1966-69, weapons officer U.S.S. George Bancroft, 1969-73; weapons systems officer, staff comdr. submarine squadron 14, Holy Loch, Scotland, 1973-75; asst. to dep. chief of staff strategic warfare Comdr. Submarine Force Atlantic Fleet, 1975-76; exec. officer U.S.S. James Monroe, 1976—. Mem. U.S. Naval Inst., Am. Def. Preparedness Assn., U.S. Naval Acad. Alumni Assn., U.S. Naval Acad. Athletic Assn. Otranto Civic Club. Presbyterian. Contbr. articles in field to profl. jours. Home: 103 Monte Sano Dr Hanahan SC 29405 Office: USS James Monroe SSBN622 Blue FPO New York NY 09501

LYMAN, PAUL LAWRENCE, mech. engr.; b. Burrton, Kans., July 19, 1926; s. Raymond Seymour and Alice Ruth (Osborne) L.; B.S., Kans. State U., 1949, M.S., 1952; m. Josephine Ann Stroup, Oct. 2, 1949; children—Diane Ruth, Debra Kay, Joyce Elaine. Research engr. in rural electrification Kans. State U., Manhattan, 1949-52; engring. supt. Del Monte Corp., Hawaii and Philippines, 1952-56; with Boeing Co., 1956—, mgr. equipment ops., Phila. 1974—. Served with USAAC, 1944-45. Registered profl. engr., Kans. Mem. ASME, Sigma Tau, Kappa Sigma. Republican. Methodist. Clubs: Broomall Swim, Broomall Bridge. Home: 9 Sharpless Ln Wallingford PA 19086 Office: Boeing Vertol PO Box 16858 Philadelphia PA 19142

LYNCH, BROCK, surgeon; b. Boston, June 23, 1924; s. Clement F. and Eleanor (Brooks) L.; B.S., U. Notre Dame, 1945; M.D., Yale U., 1947. Intern Western Res. U. Hosp., Cleve., 1947-48; chief resident surgeon St. Elizabeth's Hosp., Boston, 1953-54; surg. resident fellowship Meml. Cancer Center, N.Y.C., 1954-58; instr. surgery Tumor Clinic, Tufts-New Eng. Med. Center, Boston, 1958-74; with VA, Springfield, Mass., 1974—. Served to capt. USAF, 1951-53. Mem. Am. Assn. Clin. Counselors (chmn. med. adv. bd.). Author articles in field. Office: VA 1200 Main St Springfield MA 01103

LYNCH, JOHN FRANCIS, psychotherapist; b. Cresson, Pa., Aug. 1, 1936; s. Joseph Francis and Jane Sophia L.; student U. Pitts., 1957; B.A., Antioch Coll., 1974; M.A., Goddard Coll., 1976; m. Donna Sue Arthur, Feb. 17, 1964; children—John, Jennifer. Human and tech. relations N.C.R. Corp., Dayton, Ohio, 1960—; exec. stress edn. tng. cons.; ordained deacon Roman Catholic Ch., 1971. Served with USAF, 1957-60. Recipient Am. Legion Pub. Service award. Mem. Am. Personnel and Guidance Assn., Nat. Vocat. Guidance Assn. Democrat. Research in mgmt. tng., exec. stress. Home: 9238 Spring Valley Rd Ellicott City MD 21043

LYNCH, JOHN PETER, mfg. co. exec.; b. Hartford, Conn., Nov. 25, 1943; s. George F. and Anne B. Lynch; B.A., Parsons Coll., 1965; m. Ruth A. Steele, Aug. 21, 1965; children—Lisa, Steven. Mktg. specialist Am. Can Co., Neenah, Wis., 1965-66, sales rep., 1967-72; sr. tech. sales rep. ICI Americas Inc., Wilmington, Del., 1973-76, nat. sales and mktg. mgr., 1977—. Chmn. external affairs Republican Town Com. Served with U.S. Army, 1966-72. Mem. Wallcoverings Mfrs. Assn., Nat. Decorating Products Assn. Home: Heather Valley Hockessin DE 19707 Office: New Murphy Rd Wilmington DE 19897

LYNCH, JOSEPH P., mgmt. and newspaper cons.; b. Grand Rapids, Mich., May 27, 1919; s. Joseph Patrick and Ellen Joan (Lynch) L.; student Northwestern U., 1939-41, Harvard Grad. Sch. Bus., 1968; m. Patsy Elizabeth Ashbolt, Apr. 29, 1944; children—Joseph P. III, Michael L., David, Pamela E., Anthony J. Mdse. mgr. asst. to advt. mgr., promotion mgr. Grand Rapids Press, 1946-54; promotion mgr. Washington Post, 1954-61, classified advt. mgr., 1961-67, advt. mgr., 1967-68, v.p. advt., 1969-74; pvt. practice mgmt. cons., 1974—. Dir. Advt. Council. Active Boy Scouts Am. Bd. dirs. Cath. Youth Orgn., Met. Boys Club. Served to 1st lt. U.S. Army, 1941-43. Mem. Internat. Newspaper Promotion Assn. (past pres.), Am. Newspaper Pubs. Assn. (plans bd. bur. advt.), Assn. Newspaper Classified Advt. Mgrs. (past v.p.), Internat. Newspaper Advt. Execs. (dir.). Clubs: University (Washington); Burning Tree; Talbot Country. Home: 5215 Portsmouth Washington DC 20016 Office: New Scotland Farm Route 2 Box 88 Trappe MD

LYNCH, KATHLEEN ALETHA, psychologist; b. Kansas City, Mo., Dec. 16, 1943; d. James and Luella Mae (Dowdy) L.; B.A., U. Mo. at Kansas City, 1964, M.A., 1969, Ph.D., 1974. Research asst. Kans. U. Med. Center, Kansas City, 1964-66; vocat. rehab. counselor Mo. Dept. Edn., Kansas City, 1966-69; supervisory psychologist Hdqrs. U.S. Army Aviation Systems Command, St. Louis, 1974-75; chief psychology service VA Hosp., West Roxbury, Mass., 1976—; instr. psychology dept. psychiatry Harvard Med. Sch., Boston, 1976—; nat. cons. Nat. Inst. Alcohol Abuse and Alcohol, 1974-76; regional cons. Alcohol, Drug Abuse and Mental Health Adminstrn., 1976-77. Mem. Am., Mass. psychol. assns., Am. Labor-Mgmt. Adminstrs. and Cons. on Alcoholism, Am. Personnel and Guidance Assn., AAAS, Sigma Xi. Home: 49 Richards St Dedham MA 02026 Office: 1400 Vets of Fgn Wars Pkwy West Roxbury MA 02132

LYNCH, PATRICK HUGH, army officer; b. Miles City, Mont., Apr. 16, 1929; s. Hugh and Agnes (Grady) L.; B.S., U.S. Mil. Acad., 1951; M.S., U. So. Calif., 1960; M.E. cum laude, Indsl. Coll. Armed Forces, 1972; m. Lois Sanford Helwig, Aug. 11, 1962; children—Erin Yvette, Shannon Marie, Patrick Hugh. Commd. 2d lt. U.S. Army, 1951, advanced through grades to col., 1971; nuclear weapons project engr. Lawrence Radiation Lab., Livermore, Calif., 1960-63; armor cavalry advisor to Imperial Iranian Army, 1963-64; project mgr. Vehicle Rapid Fire Weapons Systems, Rock Island, Ill., 1965-69; comdg. officer Ft. Lewis, Wash., 1969-70; regimental advisor to Vietnamese Army, 1970-71; dir. armaments div. U.S. Mission to NATO, Brussels, 1972-76; U.S. dir. prodn. and logistics orgn. bd. dirs. NATO-HAWK, 1972-76; staff Office of Dep. Chief of Staff for Research, Devel. and Acquisition, Dept. Army, Washington, 1976-77; army mem. Armaments/Munitions Requirements and Devel. com. Office Sec. Def., 1977—. Decorated Silver Star, Bronze Star with oak leaf cluster, Purple Heart, Legion of Merit with oak leaf cluster, Joint Service Commendation medal. Mem. Am. Inst. Aeros. and Astronautics, Am. Def. Preparedness Assn., Assn. of U.S. Army, U.S. Army Armor Assn., Am. Mgmt. Assn. Republican. Roman Catholic. Home: 11614 Helmont Dr Oakton VA 22124 Office: Office of Sec Defense (AMRAD) Washington DC 20301

LYNCH, THOMAS JAMES, JR., hosp. adminstr.; b. Boston, June 24, 1949; s. Thomas James and Mary Ellen (Kelley) L.; B.S. in Mktg. cum laude, Boston Coll., 1971; M.H.A., U. Minn., 1975; m. Lois Gay Dandreta, Aug. 27, 1972; children—Colleen, Randal. Asst. adminstr. Lawrence Meml. Hosp., Medford, Mass., 1975—. Bd. dirs. Eastern Middlesex Opportunity Council. Mem. Am., Mass. hosp. assns., Am. Coll. Hosp. Adminstrs., Health Care Mgmt. Assn. Mass., Jr. C. of C. Roman Catholic. Home: 201 Governors Ave Medford MA 02155 Office: 170 Governor Ave Medford MA 02155

LYNCH, THOMAS JOHN, lawyer; b. Syracuse, N.Y., Apr. 17, 1946; s. James Francis and Georgianna (Chrisfield) L.; B.S., Canisius Coll., 1968; J.D., U. Buffalo, 1972; m. Barbara Ann Hanley, Nov. 29, 1969; children—Bryan Chrisfield, Meegan Patricia. Admitted to N.Y. bar, 1973; asso. firm Coulter, Fraser, Carr, Ames & Bolton, Syracuse, N.Y., 1973—; acting village justice Village of Solvay (N.Y.), 1974-75, village atty., 1975—. Mem. Am., N.Y. State, Onondaga County bar assns., N.Y. State Assn. Magistrates. Home: 403 Barclay St Solvay NY 13209 Office: 700 Midtown Plaza Syracuse NY 13210

LYNHAM, JOHN MARMADUKE, banker, lawyer; b. Washington, Feb. 19, 1908; s. Edgar Hardwicke and Mera Elsie (Marmaduke) L.; B.S. in Govt., Am. U., 1935; J.D., George Washington U., 1931, LL.M., 1932; m. Adele Randolph Pugh, May 22, 1947; children—Adele Cameron, John, Mary Hardwicke Lynham Anderson, Gale Randolph. Admitted to D.C. bar, 1931, Md. bar, 1953; mem. firm Drury, Lynham & Powell (formerly Minor, Gatley & Drury), Washington, 1939-69; v.p., trust officer Nat. Savs. & Trust Co., Washington, 1969—. Bd. mgrs. Chevy Chase Village, 1963-73, vice chmn., 1969-72; trustee Nat. U., 1947-54; trustee Landon Sch., 1966-74, chmn. bd., 1967-74; dir. Gunston Hall Sch., 1941-46; trustee Ophthalmic Research Found., 1973—, Nat. Ballet Soc., 1969-72. Served from lt. (j.g.) to comdr., USNR, 1941-45. Fellow Am. Bar Found.; mem. Am., D.C., Md. bar assns., Bar Assn. D.C., Am. Judicature Soc., Inst. Jud. Adminstrn., Lawyers Club Washington, The Barristers (pres. 1960). Clubs: Chevy Chase (gov. 1949-55, 59-65, pres. 1954-55); Met. (gov. 1968-73, pres. 1972-73), Nat. Lawyers (Washington). Author: The Chevy Chase Club-A History, 1958. Home: 14 Oxford St Chevy Chase Village MD 20015 Office: Nat Savs and Trust Co 15th and New York Ave NW Washington DC 20005

LYNK, DORIS SHEAFE, vocat. and ednl. guidance counselor; b. Washington; d. Louis Charles and Lucy (Parker) Sheafe; B.A., Hunter Coll., 1935; M.A., Columbia U., 1939; postgrad. (NSF fellow) N.Y. U., 1961; m. Myles V. Lynk, II, Oct. 12, 1940 (dec. 1955); children—Patria Lucy, Myles V., Marguerite. Tchr. remedial reading, N.Y.C., 1936-39; office mgr. Community Service Soc., Family Service, N.Y.C., 1940-42; tchr. biology, Greensboro, N.C., 1942-44; tchr. jr. high sch. gen. sci., N.Y.C., 1944-61, ednl. and vocat. guidance counselor Stowe Jr. High Sch., 1961-63, 65-67, acting asst. prin., 1963-65, acting supr. guidance, 1967-68, ednl. and vocat. counselor E. Roosevelt Jr. High Sch., 1970—, producer, broadcaster WNYE-TV series Guidance for the 70's, 1970-71. Mem. Am. Personnel and Guidance Assn., N.Y. State Personnel and Guidance Assn., Am. Sch. Counselors Assn., Delta Sigma Theta (pres. chpt.). Lutheran. Home: 175 Adams St Brooklyn NY 11201 Office: 515 W 182d St New York City NY 10003

LYNN, ENID (ENID LYNN ROSENTHAL), dance co. dir.; b. Hartford, Conn., Oct. 30, 1947; d. Morton Sidney and Harriet (Schloss) Rosenthal; A.A., Hartford Coll. Women; student Hartford Ballet Co., 1960—, Martha Graham Sch., N.Y.C., 1966-67, Sigurd Leeder Sch. Dance, Switzerland, 1970. Mem. faculty, performer Hartford Ballet Co., 1964—, chmn. modern dance dept., 1969, dir. Modern Dance Theatre, 1970, exec. dir. co., 1971—, dir. sch., 1975—, dir. chamber ensemble, 1975—; mem. dance faculty Hartt Coll. Music, U. Hartford, 1967-75. Mem Creative Arts Com., 1969—; mem. dance com. Greater Hartford Civic and Arts Festival, 1970-71. Choreographer numerous works including Dover Beach, 1970, Grandstand, 1972, also works commd. Inst. Contemporary Am. Music, Hartford Symphony. Address: Hartford Ballet Co 308 Farmington Ave Hartford CT 06067

LYNN, KARYL V., JR., mfg. exec.; b. Bklyn., Mar. 20, 1922; s. Karyl V. and Hazel M. (Wendell) L.; B.B.A. with distinction, U. Mich., 1948, M.B.A. with distinction, 1949; m. Lorraine M. Mullen, July 21, 1946; children—Kevin V., Keith J., Kathleen A. Personnel dir. Dairypak, Inc., Cleve., 1949-54; personnel mgr. Gen. Mills. Corp., Mpls., 1954-56; plant mgr. Dairypak, Inc., Toledo, 1956-63, Mercury Packaging Co., Toledo, 1963-66; group dir. indsl. relations Hoover Ball Bearing Co., Ann Arbor, Mich., 1966-67, Crucible Steel Corp., Pitts., 1967-68; dir. personnel adminstrn. Colt Industries, Inc., N.Y.C., 1968—; lectr. indsl. relations John Carroll U., Cleve., 1949-54; mem. steering com. Mgmt. Compensation Services, Scottsdale, Ariz., 1975—; mem. adv. com. T.P.F.&C. Compensation Data Bank, N.Y.C., 1977—. Served with USAF, 1943-46. U. Mich. Club scholar, 1947-48, 49. Mem. Northwestern Ohio Tennis Assn. (chmn. jr. devel. 1965-66), Am. Soc. Personnel Adminstrn., Am. Compensation Assn., Internat. Assn. for Edn. Students with Tech. Experience (chmn. bd. dirs. 1970—), Am. Mgmt. Assn., Beta Gamma Sigma, Phi Kappa Phi. Republican. Unitarian. Club: Kiwanis of Downtown Toledo (dir. 1963-64). Contbr. articles to profl. jours. Home: 203 Forest Dr Hillsdale NJ 07642 Office: 430 Park Ave New York City NY 10022

LYNN, PETER CHARLES, psychologist; b. Vienna, Austria, Feb. 15, 1919; s. Arthur Anthony and Cornelia Francisca (Grunhut) Low; came to U.S., 1940, naturalized, 1943; B.S., Columbia U., 1949; Ph.D., U. Zurich (Switzerland), 1953; analyst diploma C.G. Jung Inst. Zurich, 1959; m. Hildegarde Agnes Maas, Nov. 15, 1947; 1 dau., Roxane Joy. Individual practice psychoanalysis, N.Y.C., 1953—; tng. analyst C.G. Jung Tng. Center, 1962—, dir. studies, 1968—, also bd. dirs. Served with AUS, 1943-47. Mem. Am. Psychol. Assn., N.Y. Assn. Analytical Psychology (past pres.). Office: 185 E 85th St New York City NY 10028

LYNN, YEN-MOW, educator; b. Shanghai, China, Jan. 17, 1935; s. Thuinli and Pao-Chiung (Tcheng) L.; came to U.S., 1956, naturalized, 1969; B.S., Nat. Taiwan U., 1955; M.S., Calif. Inst. Tech., 1957, Ph.D., 1961; m. Helen Han, Sept. 5, 1964; children—Edward, Kirk, Genevieve. Asst., then asso. research scientist Courant Inst. Math. Scis., N.Y.U., 1960-64; asso. prof. Ill. Inst. Tech., 1964-67; asso. prof., then prof. math. U. Md. Baltimore County, 1967—, chmn. dept. math., 1976—; sr. resident research asso. Nat. Acad. Scis.-NRC, NASA Ames Research Center, summers 1966, 67; cons. NASA Ames Research Center, 1966, U.S. Army Ballistic Research Lab., 1969-75. Mem. Am. Math. Soc., Soc. Indsl. and Applied Math., Math. Assn. Am., Am. Phys. Soc., Am. Geophys. Union, AAAS. Contbr. profl. jours. Home: 10733 Evening Wind Ct Columbia MD 21044 Office: 5401 Wilkens Ave Baltimore MD 21228

LYNNE, ARLEEN S., chemist; b. N.Y.C., May 15, 1941; d. Walter John and Helen (Porcelli) Schlamp; B.S., Cabrini Coll., 1961; m. Leo Duane Lynne, Oct. 10, 1964; 1 son, Leo Duane. Analyst, Hoffmann LaRoche, Nutley, N.J., 1961-67, asst. supr. finished products, 1968-70, supr. intermediates, quality control, 1971-74, supr. raw materials, pantene and intermediates in quality control, 1975—. Woodrow Wilson fellow, 1961. Mem. Cabrini Coll. Alumnae Assn., Concerned Women of Roche. Republican. Roman Catholic. Clubs: Atlantis Country, Ocean Acres Country. Home: White Terr E Nutley NJ 07110 Office: Roche Park Kingsland Rd Nutley NJ 07110

LYNSKEY, JOHN ANDREW, social worker; b. Newark, Oct. 7, 1940; s. Wallace Alton and Veronica Mary (Dolan) L.; A.B., St. Peter's Coll., 1963; M.S.W., Fordham U., 1966; postgrad. Columbia U., 1977—. Social worker Family Service-Asso. Cath. Charities, Newark, 1962-74; social worker Newark Bd. Edn., 1974—. Vol. big brother N.J. Div. Youth and Family Services, 1976-77; mem. juvenile conf. com. North Ward, Newark, 1976—; dir. Inner City Vol. Counseling Program, Newark, 1967-68; dir. clin. services N.J. Boystown, 1970-72. NIMH grantee, 1978—. Mem. Acad. Certified Social Workers, Nat. Assn. Social Workers, Am. Assn. Marriage and Family Counselors. Roman Catholic. Home: 25 Clifton Ave Newark NJ 07104 Office: 1 Upper Mountain Ave Montclair NJ 07043

LYON, EDWARD BRUCE AVRAM, orgn. exec.; b. Takoma Park, Md., Sept. 21, 1942; s. Daniel Irvin and Tessie Marian (Feldman) L.; B.A., U. Md., 1972; M.Edn. Adminstrn., Harvard U., 1977; Dir. student affairs English desk, youth dept. Jewish Agy. for Israel, Jerusalem, 1968-70; mem. exec. com. United Jewish Appeal Greater Washington, 1970-71; mem. youth adv. com. Jewish Community Council Greater Washington, 1970-72; exec. dir. N.Am. Jewish Student Appeal, N.Y.C., 1972-74; exec. dir. Jewish Assn. Coll. Youth, N.Y.C., 1974-76; cons. various higher edn. instns., community planning and policy orgns., 1966—; cons. various Jewish planning, policy bodies on student affairs, 1966—. Mem. Assn. Am. Geographers. Jewish religion. Home: 74 Craigie St Somerville MA 02143

LYON, HAROLD CLIFFORD, JR., psychologist, educator; b. New Brunswick, N.J., Apr. 26, 1935; s. Harold Clifford and Myrtle Marie (Briggs) L.; B.S., U.S. Mil. Acad., 1958; M.A., George Washington U., 1965; Ed.D., U. Mass., 1970; m. Edith Ann Webb, Mar. 17, 1971; children—Eric Lyon, Gregg Lyon; 1 stepson, John Gosnell. Asst. to pres. Ohio U., Athens, 1965-67; asst. dep. commr. edn. U.S. Office Edn., Washington, 1967-69; dep. asso. commr. edn., 1970-72, dir. edn. for gifted and talented, 1972-76; Horace Mann lectr. U. Mass., 1969-70; Abraham Maslow prof. psychology Antioch Coll., Columbia, Md., 1976—; distinguished vis. scholar Georgetown U., Washington, 1976—; chmn. bd. trustees Am. Excellence, Columbia, 1977—; U.S. del. World Council for Gifted and Talented Children. Served to capt. inf. U.S. Army, 1958-65. Recipient Horace Mann leadership award, 1969; lic. psychologist, Washington. Author: Learning to Feel—Feeling to Learn, 1971; It's Me and I'm Here, 1974; Tenderness Is Strength, 1978. Home: 4217 Van Ness St NW Washington DC 20016 Office: American Excellence Antioch Coll Columbia MD 21044

LYON, JAMES BURROUGHS, lawyer; b. N.Y.C., May 11, 1930; s. Francis Murray and Edith (Strong) L.; B.A. magna cum laude, Amherst Coll., 1952; LL.B., Yale, 1955. Admitted to Conn. bar, 1955; asso. lawyer, then partner Murtha, Cullina, Richter & Pinney (and predecessor firm), Hartford, 1956—. Mem. Amherst Alumni Assn. Conn., 1956—, sec., 1956-66; Conn. chmn. capital program Amherst Coll., 1962-65, mem. exec. com. Alumni Council, 1963-69, chmn., 1968-69, chmn. com. deferred gifts and bequests, 1977—; pres. Yale Law Sch. Assn. Hartford and Eastern Conn., 1966, dir. Fund, 1973—. Mem. adv. com. N.Y. U. Inst. on Fed. Taxation, 1975—. Mem. West Hartford Bicentennial Steering Com., 1973-76. Bd. dirs. Fidelco Found., Bloomfield, Conn., 1971—; mem. adv. com. Walks Found., Hartford, 1977—; bd. dirs. Kingswood-Oxford Sch., Inc., 1963—, chmn., 1976-78; bd. dirs. Noah Webster Found. and Hist. Soc. West Hartford, Old Sturbridge (Mass.) Village, 1967—; bd. dirs. Wadsworth Atheneum, v.p., 1972—; bd. dirs. Conn. Bar Found., 1974—; pres. No. Conn. chpt. Nat. Football Found. and Hall of Fame, 1966-69; nat. chmn. Friends of Trinity Coll., Hartford, 1977-78; corporator Mt. Sinai Hosp., Hartford, 1971—, Hartford Hosp., 1975—, St. Francis Hosp., Hartford, 1976—. Recipient Amherst Coll. medal, 1967; award for contbn. to athletics Amherst Alumni, 1976. Mem. Am., Conn., Hartford County bar assns., Assn. Bar City N.Y., Newcomen Soc., Greater Hartford C. of C. (chmn. sports and recreation com. 1978—), Phi Beta Kappa, Phi Delta Phi, Theta Delta Chi. Clubs: Yale (v.p. 1965), Hartford, University (pres. 1976-78), Tennis (dir. 1971-74), Hartford Golf (dir. 1972-75), Twentieth Century (Hartford); Yale, Union (N.Y.C.); Dauntless (Essex, Conn.); Yale Golf (New Haven); Limestone Trout (East Canaan Conn.). Home: 25 Bishop Rd West Hartford CT 06119 Office: 101 Pearl St Hartford CT 06103

LYON, ROSSMORE DENMAN, minister, chiropractor; b. Poughkeepsie, N.Y., Jan. 29, 1937; s. LeRoy Faust and Grace Victoria (Stone) L.; student Centre Coll. of Ky., Danville, 1955-57; B.A., Columbia Bible Coll., 1959; B.D., Covenant Theol. Sem., 1963; student Can. Meml. Chiropractic Coll., 1969-70; B.S., D.C., Nat. Coll. of Chiropractic, 1973; m. Carolyn Joy Bass, Apr. 1, 1961; children—Victoria Louise, Cathy Joy, Elizabeth Jane, David Thomas. Ordained to ministry, 1963; staff mem. Inter-Varsity Christian Fellowship, Chgo., 1959-60; pastor Evangelical Presbyterian Ch. of Trenton, N.J., 1963-65, Kenmuir Baptist Ch., Toronto, Can., 1965-70; pvt. practice chiropractic, Pottstown, Pa., 1973-74; pastor Trinity Baptist Ch., Allentown, Pa., 1974—; instr. Central Baptist Sem., 1966-68; chmn. Ref. Bapt. Assn., 1978-79. Diplomate Nat. Bd. Chiropractic Examiners. Mem. Am. Chiropractic Assn., Pa. Chiropractic Soc. Republican. Home: RD 1 Box 146 Allentown PA 18104 Office: 689 S Hillview Rd Allentown PA 18103

LYONS, EDWARD, architect; b. Cambridge, Mass., Mar. 1, 1943; s. Harry and Rose (Medoff) L.; B.S., U. Mass., 1964; certificate architecture Boston Archtl. Center, 1969; m. Linda P. Ladinsky, June 14, 1964; children—Jodi Lynn, Shari Michelle. Designer, Haldeman & Goransson Assos., Inc., architects, Boston, 1964—, project mgr., also v.p., 1969—. Mem. Hist. Commn., Sharon, Mass., 1972—; mem. Planning Bd., Sharon, 1973—, chmn., 1976-77. Mem. A.I.A., Am.

Soc. Landscape Architects, Boston Soc. Architects, Alpha Zeta, Phi Sigma Delta. Prin. archtl. works include Research Bldg., Southeastern Mass. U., Curley Sch., Boston; Student Union, State Coll. North Adams; Coll. 010, U. Mass., Boston; Salem High Sch., Elementary Schs., Brockton, New Bedford, Mass., New Breed Jr. High Sch., Lynn, Mass.; renovation to Malden Schs., Mass. Home: 5 Falcon Rd Sharon MA 02067 Office: 77 N Washington St Boston MA 02114

LYONS, ELAINE TURNER (MRS. JOHN EDWARD LYONS), state legislator; b. Boston, Sept. 27, 1928; d. Maurice Steele and Edna (Grace) Turner; B.S., Sargent Coll., Boston U., 1949, postgrad., 1950-51; m. John Edward Lyons, June 14, 1952; children—Judith Ann, Stephen Turner. Supr. phys. edn. Manchester (N.H.) Sch. Dept. 1949-57; swimming instr. Manchester YWCA, 1966, 67, 70; substitute tchr. Merrimack (N.H.) Sch. Dept., 1966-70; mem. N.H. Ho. of Reps., 1971—, mem. legislative transp. com., asst. majority leader, 1975—. Charter mem. Merrimack Federated Republican Woman's Club, v.p., 1970-71; co-chmn. Peterson for Gov. campaign, Merrimack, 1968, 70. Bd. dirs. Merrimack Med. Center. Mem. AAHPER (N.H. membership chmn. 1955-57), Nat. Council State Legislatures, Manchester Coll. Women's Club. Episcopalian. Author: (with others) Curriculum Guide to Physical Education in New Hampshire, 1954. Home: Shore Dr Merrimack NH 03054 Office: State House Concord NH 03301

LYONS, GRACE BECKER, nursing adminstr.; b. N.Y.C., June 24, 1930; d. Casper John and Grace Elizabeth (Blake) Becker; A.A.S.N.S., Queens Coll., 1958; B.S., Adelphi U., 1970; M.A., N.Y. U., 1977; m. John Joseph Lyons, 1950; 1 dau., Margaret Ellen. Staff nurse Hillside Hosp., 1958-60; asst. dir. nursing Rockville Gen. Hosp., Rockville Centre, N.Y., 1960-64, Syosset (N.Y.) Hosp., 1964-66; inservice edn. instr. S. Nassau Communities Hosp., Oceanside, N.Y., 1966-73, staff devel. coordinator, 1973—. Active Bellerose Commonwealth Civic Assn. Recipient Faculty award, Queens Coll., 1958. Mem. Am., N.Y. State nurses assns., Nassau-Suffolk Coordinating Council of Nursing Practice and Edn. (v.p. 1974-78), Intercounty Soc. Inservice Educators, Am. Soc. Tng. and Devel. (sec. L.I. chpt. 1967), Sigma Theta Tau. Home: 86-30 251 St Bellerose NY 11426 Office: South Nassau Communities Hosp 2445 Oceanside Rd Oceanside NY 11572

LYONS, HAROLD ALOYSIUS, physician, educator; b. Bklyn., Sept. 14, 1913; s. Harry A. and Louise (de Tourreil) L.; B.S. cum laude, St. John's U., 1935; M.D., L.I. Coll. Medicine, 1940; m. Rita M. Wood, Mar. 9, 1940; children—Harold Aloysius, Frances Louise, Gail Jean, Robert Louis, Margaret Alida Marie, George Christopher, J. Lawrence, Anne Marie. Intern L.I. Coll. Hosp., 1939-40, Bklyn. Hosp., 1940-41; resident U.S. Naval Hosp., St. Albans, 1945-48; instr. internal medicine, Downstate Med. Center, State U. N.Y.; dir. pulmonary disease div. King County Hosp. Center, and Downstate Med. Center, Univ. Hosp., Bklyn., 1953—; instr. L.I. Coll. Medicine, 1948-49, asst. prof. 1949-50; asst. prof. Georgetown U. Coll. Medicine, 1950-51; asso. prof. State U. N.Y. Coll. Medicine, 1953-59, prof., 1959—; vis. prof. Cath. U. Chile, Santiago, 1967, Nat. Def. Center and Nat. U. Sch. Medicine, Taipei, Taiwan, 1965, U.S. Army Hosp., El Paso, Tex., 1971, Brown U. Sch. Medicine, 1974; cons. Bklyn. Hosp., 1953—, U.S. Naval Hosp., St. Albans, N.Y., 1958-73, Mercy Hosp., Rockville Center, L.I., N.Y., 1957—, VA Hosp., Bklyn., and Brookdale Med. Center; sr. cons. USPHS Hosp., Staten Island, N.Y.; med. examiner Federal Aviation Agency; med. adv. cons. U.S. Pub. Health Social Welfare, 1964—; ofcl. examiner Am. Bd. Internal Medicine. Former chmn. com. pulmonary diseases regional med. program Naussau and Suffolk counties; mem. com. pulmonary disease regional med. program Met. N.Y.; mem. internat. adv. com. Aspen Lung Conf. Served from lt. (j.g.) to comdr. M.C., USNR, 1941-53. Decorated Air medal (Navy); recipient Achievements award Am. Acad. Angiology, 1966. Diplomate Am. Bd. Internal Medicine, Pan Am. Med. Assn. Fellow Am. Coll. Chest Physicians (mem. gov.'s com., com. postgrad. courses), A.C.P., N.Y. Acad. Medicine, N.Y. Acad. Scis., Chilean Tb Soc. (hon.); mem. Med. Research Soc. (Gt. Britain), Harvey Soc., Am. Nuclear Soc., AMA, N.Y., Kings County med. socs., N.Y., Am. heart assns., Am., N.Y. (past pres) thoracic socs., Internat. Soc. Cardiovascular Diseases, Am. Fedn. Clin. Research, Am. Assn. Med. Colls., Bklyn. Soc. Internal Medicine (past pres.), Bklyn. Thoracic Soc. (past pres.), Bklyn. Lung Assn. (v.p.), Am. Heart Assn. (del., mem. exec. com. council cardiopulmonary), Am. Physiol. Soc., AAAS, Aerospace Med. Assn., IEEE, Soc. Biomed. Engrng. (charter mem.), Sigma Xi, Alpha Omega Alpha. Editor: Vascular Diseases of Lung. Research in field. Home: Harbor Rd Sands Point NY 11050 Office: 450 Clarkson Ave Brooklyn NY 11203

LYONS, JOHN PATRICK, guidance counselor; b. Scranton, Pa., Aug. 23, 1950; s. William Francis and Catherine Winifred (Kelly) L.; B.S., Mansfield State Coll., 1972; M.S. in Counselor Edn., U. Scranton, 1977; m. Kathleen Patrice Mooty, Oct. 4, 1975; 1 son, John Patrick. Athletic dir., head basketball coach, instr. social studies West Cath. High Sch., Scranton, 1972-74; asst. basketball and baseball coach, instr. sociology, psychology and world history Scranton Prep. High Sch., 1974-77, guidance counselor, 1977-78, head baseball coach, 1978—; head basketball coach Lackawanna Jr. Coll., 1977—, Bishop O'Hara High Sch., 1978—. Mem. Am. Personnel and Guidance Assn., Pa. Guidance Assn., Am. Sch. Counselors Assn., Nat. Assn. Basketball Coaches, Sigma Tau Gamma. Democrat. Roman Catholic. Home: 737 N Main Ave Scranton PA 18504 Office: 1000 Wyoming Ave Scranton PA 18505

LYONS, JOHN THOMAS, journalist; b. Bklyn., Oct. 21, 1943; s. Austin James and Helene J. (Brennan) L.; student U. Notre Dame, 1961-65; m. Christine Floyd, Apr. 3, 1965; children—John Thomas, Bridget, Brendan. Reporter, Sta. WNDU-TV, South Bend, Ind., 1965-66, WYTV-TV, Youngstown, Ohio, 1966-67; writer, editor ABC Radio News, N.Y.C., 1967-70; sci. editor, reporter WNEW Radio Sta., N.Y.C., 1970-76; freelance journalist, 1976—; broadcast news instr. Adelphi U., Garden City, N.Y., 1975-76. Recipient Billboard award, 1974; Silurians award, 1975; Ohio State award, 1975; Scripps-Howard Found. award, 1975; Columbia U. DuPont citation, 1975; Sigma Delta Chi Deadline Club award, 1975; Radio-TV News Dir. Assn. award, 1975; Aviation Space Writers award 1974, 75, 76; N.Y. State AP Broadcasters award, 1973, 74, 75. Mem. Aviation Space Writers Assn., Air Force Assn., Am. Inst. Aeros and Astronautics. Roman Catholic. Clubs: Wings, Aerocats Flying. Contbr. articles to profl. jours. Home: 1244 E 28 St Brooklyn NY 11210

LYONS, M. DON, mgmt. cons.; b. Trenton, N.J., Dec. 29, 1919; s. Michael David and Margaret (Lowery) L.; B.S., U. Pa., 1942; m. Grace Hannah Barker, Dec. 17, 1943; children—David Joseph, Susan Grace, Mark Donald. Div. gen. mgr. Sun Chem. Corp., 1956-62; v.p. Walter F. Norton Co., Inc., N.Y.C., 1950-56; sec. Frederich H. Rahr, Inc., N.Y.C., 1948-54; mng. dir. Nat. Inst. Indsl. Research, 1954-71; exec. v.p. No. Chem. Corp., Cream Ridge, N.J., 1967-70; pres. Mgmt. Systems and Control Corp., N.Y.C., 1969-71; sr. v.p., dir. Nat. Inst. Indsl. Research, Inc., Princeton, N.J., 1971-77; sr. asso. LOR Assos., 1973—; dir. Princeton Phytochems., Inc., Walter F. Norton Co.; cons. in field. Served with USCGR, 1942-46. Mem. Internat. Materials Mgmt. Soc. (past dir., v.p.). Democrat. Roman Catholic. Club: Forsgate Country. Home: 121 Coleman Rd Hamilton Square NJ 08690 Office: 1101 State Rd Princeton NJ 08540

LYONS, PATRICIA JANE, physician, renal transplant nephrologist; b. Norwich, N.Y., Oct. 7, 1941; d. John Francis and Katherine Pearl (Scott) Lyons; B.S. in Biology, Nazareth Coll. of Rochester, 1963; M.D., Hahnemann Med. Coll., Phila., 1968. Intern, Phila. Gen. Hosp., 1968-69; resident nephrology Hahnemann Hosp., 1969-71, fellow nephrology, 1971-73, sr. instr. nephrology, 1973-74, asst. prof., 1974—, asst. dir. renal transplant program, 1973-75, asst. dir. hemodialysis unit, 1974-76, 77—, med. dir. renal transp. program, 1976—, dir. hemodialysis unit, 1976—; practice medicine specializing in nephrology, Phila., 1973—. Officer at large ESRD Network 24, 1976—. Diplomate Am. Bd. Internal Medicine, Am. Bd. Nephrology, Renal Physicians Assn. Home: Oak Hill Estates 14G Penn Valley PA 19020 Office: 230 N Broad St Philadelphia PA 19102

LYONS, RICHARD DANIEL, journalist; b. N.Y.C., May 31, 1928; s. John Michael and Mary Louise (Francis) L.; A.B., Brown U., 1950; M.S., Columbia U., 1955; m. Margaret McKenna, Sept. 2, 1961 (div. 1969); children—David, Abigail. Reporter, Plainfield (N.J.) Courier-News, 1953-54, Memphis Comml. Appeal, 1955-57; corr. Reuters, London, 1957-58; rewriteman, reporter, sci. editor N.Y. Daily News, 1958-67; sci. writer Washington Bur., N.Y. Times, 1967—. Served with USAF, 1951-53. Recipient Empire State Med. Journalism award, 1966, Albert Deutsch award, 1972. Mem. Nat. Assn. Sci. Writers. Home: South Shores Dr Port Republic MD 20676 Office: 1000 Connecticut Ave Washington DC 20036

LYSLO, ARNOLD LYNNER, social Worker; b. Fargo, N. D., Nov. 21, 1919; s. Andrew R. and Alice (Lynner) L; B.S., U. Minn., 1947; M.S.W., Columbia U., 1952. Caseworker to supr. Oreg. State Pub. Welfare Commn., Portland, 1947-53; child welfare cons. U.S. Bur. Indian Affairs, Portland, 1953-57; research asso. nat. poster care study Maas-Engler, Children in Need of Parents, Child Welfare League Am., Inc., N.Y.C., 1957-58, dir. Indian adoption project, 1958-67, asso. dir. adoption resource exchange of N.Am., 1967-68; exec. dir. Talbot Perkins Children's Services, N.Y.C., 1968—. Asso. vestry St. Bartholomew's Episcopal Ch., N.Y.C., sec., 1969-74. Served with AUS, 1942-43. Oreg. State Pub. Welfare Commn. fellow, 1951; USPHS Mental Health fellow, 1952; certified social worker, N.Y. State. Mem. Nat. Assn. Social Workers, Acad. Certified Social Workers. Home: 301 E 78th St New York City NY 10021 Office: 342 Madison Ave New York City NY 10017

LYTLE, JAMES EVANS, insulator co. exec.; b. Madison, Wis., Oct. 26, 1939; s. William Harold and Edna Agusta (Evans) L.; student Rochester Inst. Tech., 1970-73; m. Margaret H. Wirsing, June 4, 1960; children—Leslie Ann, Marcy Lynne, Holly Kim, Jamie Elizabeth, James Evans II. With Lapp Insulator Co., LeRoy, N.Y., 1963—, loss control supr., 1972—. Mem. Assessment Bd. of Rev., Town of LeRoy, 1973-76, zoning enforcement officer, 1976—; officer Jr. Achievement, 1975-76; trustee Presbyterian Ch., 1978. Mem. Am. Soc. Quality Control. Republican. Home: 23 Elm St LeRoy NY 14482 Office: Lapp Insulator Co Gilbert St LeRoy NY 14482

MA, EDWARD SHIHJEN, psychotherapist; b. Tsingtao City, China, Dec. 25, 1932; s. Ku Li and Rey Yuen (Wang) M.; came to U.S., 1963, naturalized, 1975; B.S., U. Conn., 1965, M.S.W., 1968; Certificate in Group Psychotherapy, N.Y. Med. Coll., 1974; m. Lily Shen, Dec. 26, 1969. Med. social worker N.Y. U. Med. Center, N.Y.C., 1968-69; psychiat. social worker, vol. program supr. Coney Island Hosp., Bklyn., 1969—. Bd. dirs. Chinatown Planning Council, N.Y.C., chmn. program com., 1977—. Cert. social worker, N.Y. State. Mem. Nat. Assn. Social Workers, Acad. Cert. Social Workers. Contbr. articles to Chinese behavior to profl. jours. Office: 2601 Ocean Pkwy Brooklyn NY 11235

MA, PEARL PIK CHUN, microbiologist; b. Hong Kong; d. Chiu Ki and Yee Mui (Lum) Ma; B.A., Rosemont Coll., 1950; M.A., U. Pa., 1955; Ph.D., Jefferson Med. Coll., 1961; numerous certificates advanced tng. Chief mycology, asst. bacteriologist Jefferson U. Hosp., Phila., 1954-59, cons. mycology, clin. microbiology, 1959-61, instr. nurses microbiology, 1961; research asso. in pub. health, infectious diseases Hahnemann Med. Coll., Phila., 1961-62; chief microbiology Women's Hosp., Phila., 1961-62; adj. research asso. Hahnemann Med. Coll. and Hosp., 1961-62, asso. in medicine, 1963-64; research asso. dept. pathology Med. Coll. Va., Richmond, 1964-65; chief of microbiology and cytogenetics Akron City Hosp., 1965-69; chief microbiology St. Vincent's Hosp. and Med. Center N.Y., 1970—; asst. prof. dept. pathology N.Y. U. Coll. Medicine, 1970—; lectr. virology dept. pub. health and bacteriology Wagner Coll., S.I., 1972-73; cons. in microbiology, 1961—; lectr. virology Wagner Coll., 1972-73. Guest speaker Critic Club, Haffkine Inst., Bombay, India, Hong Kong St. Stephen's Girl's Coll. Social chmn. Internat. House, Phila., 1953. Research grantee Nat. Inst. Allergy and Infectious Diseases, Bethesda, Md., 1965-68. Registered specialist pub. health and med. lab. microbiology. Fellow N.Y. Acad. Scis.; mem. Am. Soc. Clin. Sci., Am. Soc. for Microbiology, AAAS, Midwest Soc. Electronmicroscopists, Am. Soc. Clin. Pathologists, Am. Med. Woman's Assn., Med. Mycology Soc. N.Y., N.Y. Acad. Scis. (adv. com. microbiology sect.). Clubs: Art, Glee, Science. Contbr. numerous articles to profl. jours. Office: St Vincent's Hosp 153 W 11th St New York City NY 10011

MAAS, JAMES BERYL, educator; b. Detroit, Aug. 9, 1938; s. Royal Shelton and Mary (Wiener) M.; B.A., Williams Coll., 1960; M.A., Cornell U., 1963, Ph.D., 1966. Asst. dean students Cornell U., Ithaca, N.Y., 1964-65, asst. prof. psychology, 1965-70, asso. prof., 1970—, dir. Center for Improvement Undergrad. Edn., 1971-75, dir. Cornell Candid Camera Collection; cons. Eastman Kodak Co., Exxon Edn. Found.; Fulbright lectr. Uppsala (Sweden) U., 1970. Recipient Clark award distinguished teaching; 1st prize Internat. Psyche Film Festival, 1976, 1st prize Indsl. Photo Film Festival, 1978, Silver Rush medal Am. Psychiat. Assn., 1978. Fellow Am. Psychol. Assn. (Distinguished Teaching award 1973, pres. div. 1974-75); mem. Sigma Xi, Beta Theta Pi. Author: Slide Group for General Psychology, 1968; Series of Psychology Films, 1970. Home: 6 Sunset West Rd 7 Ithaca NY 14850

MAASLAND, MARINUS, cons. agrl. engr.; b. Sliedrecht, Netherlands, Dec. 7, 1924; s. Arie and Johanna (Giltay) M.; came to Can., 1968, naturalized, 1974; B.Sc. in Agrl. Engring., Wageningen U. (Netherlands), 1950, M.Sc., 1952; M.Sc. in Soil Physics (Fulbright scholar) Iowa State U., 1953; m. Mildred N. Moss, Aug. 26, 1953; children—Paul Arie, Lisa Joan, Anne Louise. Research officer Water Conservation and Irrigation Commn. of New South Wales, Australia, 1954-55, Commonwealth Sci. and Indsl. Research Orgn. of Australia, Merbein, Victoria, 1955-56; hydraulic engr. Bur. of Reclamation, U.S. Govt., McCook, Nebr., 1957-59; engr. Tippetts-Abbett-McCarthy-Stratton Co., Adana, Turkey, 1959-61; chief reclamation div. Harza Engring. Co., Lahore, Pakistan, 1961-66; adviser on water and power devel. to. Govt. of Bangladesh in Dacca for Devel. Advisory Service of Harvard, Cambridge, Mass., 1966-68; staff cons. and project dir. of Bangladesh Gen. Consultancy, 1968-72; v.p. Acres Internat. Ltd. subs. Acres Cons. Services, Toronto, 1971-72; pres. Maasland Devel. Services, Inc., Toronto, 1972—; cons. to World Bank, UN, Govts. of Mex. and Bangladesh, Canadian Internat. Devel. Agy. Recipient Spl. Service award U.S. Bur. Reclamation, 1960; registered profl. engr., Ont., Alta. Mem. Am. Geophys. Union, ASCE, Internat. Water Resources Assn., AAAS, Am. Geol. Inst., Soc. Exploration Geophysicists, Netherlands Soc. Agrl. Engrs., Am. Soc. Photogrammetry, Internat. Assn. Sci. Hydrology. Contbr. articles on water resources devel. and irrigation to profl. publs. Address: 146 Eastbourne Ave Toronto ON M5P 2G6 Canada

MAASS, JOHN, writer, city ofcl.; b. Vienna, Austria, Dec. 10, 1918; s. Julius and Edith (Landesmann) M.; came to U.S., 1941, naturalized, 1943; student Central Sch. Arts Crafts, London, 1939-40, Art Center Coll., Los Angeles, 1941-43; m. Patricia Watt, 1963 (div.); children—Valerie, Andrew. Graphic designer, Los Angeles, 1942-43, 46-48, N.Y.C., 1948-49, Phila., 1951-57; visual presentation dir. City of Phila., 1958-67, info. officer, 1967—; author: The Gingerbread Age, 1957, The Victorian Home in America, 1972, The Glorious Enterprise, 1973; contbr. to numerous other books, numerous articles, revs. to nat. mags., scholarly jours.; lectr. colls., museums, hist. socs. Served with USAAF, 1943-45. Recipient Book award Athenaeum, 1973. Mem. Am. Hist. Assn., Soc. Archtl. Historians, Fellow in Am. Studies, Victorian Soc. Am. Club: Phila. Athenaeum. Home: 439 E Mount Airy Ave Philadelphia PA 19119 Office: 1660 Municipal Services Bldg Philadelphia PA 19107

MABEN, JERROLD WILLIAM, educator; b. Detroit, Feb. 17, 1929; s. Gerald Clarence and Ina Frances (Daball) M.; B.A., Wayne State U., 1950, B.S., 1951, M.Ed., 1954; Ph.D., Ohio State U., 1971; m. Dorothy Irene Higbee, Oct. 6, 1956; children—Karen Elizabeth, Jerrold Bryce, Mark William. Coordinator, Sci. and Math. Teaching Center, Mich. State U., E. Lansing, 1956-69; asso. prof., dir. Sci. Edn. Center, U. Akron (Ohio), 1963-71; research asso. Ednl. Resources Info. Center, Center for Sci., Math. and Environ. Edn., Ohio State U., Columbus, 1969-71; prof. sci. edn. Herbert H. Lehman Coll., City U. N.Y. and dir. Bur. Ednl. Grants, Bronx, 1971-75, exec. officer Sch. Gen. Studies, 1975-76; prin. Julian Curtiss Sch. and Milbank Sch. for Trainable Mentally Handicapped, 1976—; dir. NSF Insts. for Secondary and Coll. Tchrs. of Phys. Sci., 1956-58, Earth Sci., 1968-70, Traveling Sci. Tchr. Program, 1958-61, Implementation Insts., 1956-76; dir. NASA and U.S. Office Edn. programs, 1956—; sci. edn. cons.; vis. prof. U. Nebr., 1963, U. Mich., Ann Arbor, 1956-58, Fla. State U., 1970-75, U. So. Conn., New Haven, 1975—, No. Colo. State U., 1977—; dir. Exxon, Tomorrows Scientist and Engrs. scholarship program, 1969-73; regional dir. NASA Viking Mission to Mars student recognition program, 1974-76, Skylab student project, 1973-75. Lay reader Christ Ch., Greenwich, Conn., 1971—, head usher, 1973—; coordinator pub. defender ct. intern program, Stamford, Conn., 1975. Served to 2d lt., inf. Mich. NG, 1948-63. NSF grantee, 1956-75; U.S. Office Edn. grantee, 1967-76; Burns Found. grantee, 1956-58; Mich. Soc. Mental Health grantee, 1956-58; Nat. Bd. Regents Higher Edn. fellow, 1969-71; NSF Leadership Inst. fellow, 1959-71; U.S. Office Edn., Ednl. Profl. Devel. Inst. fellow, 1971-76; recipient Presdl. Service to Edn. citation Air Force Assn., 1969. Fellow AAAS, Ohio Acad. Sci.; mem. N.Y. Acad. Sci., Council for Elementary Sci. Internat., Nat. Acad. Sch. Execs., Assn. for Edn. Tchrs. of Sci., Nat. Assn. Elementary Sch. Prins., Nat. Sci. Tchrs. Assn., Ohio Council for Elementary Sch. Sci., N.Y. Elementary Sci. Assn., Am. Ednl. Research Assn., Nat. Assn. for Research in Sci. Teaching, Assn. for Edn. Tchrs. Sci., Phi Delta Kappa, Kappa Delta Pi. Republican. Episcopalian. Editorial cons. What Is Science Series, 1976-78, Discovering Science Series, 1969-71; editorial advisory bd. Sci. and Children, 1976—; sci. edn. advisory bd. Science Screen Report, 1971—; contbr. articles in field to profl. jours. Home: 33 Midbrook Ln Old Greenwich CT 06870 Office: 180 E Elm St Greenwich CT 06830

MABRY, PAUL DAVIS, JR., educator, physiol. psychologist; b. Meridian, Miss., Sept. 28, 1943; s. Paul Davis and Frances Elizabeth (Thigpen) M.; B.S., Millsaps Coll., 1965; M.S., U. Miss., 1967, Ph.D., 1970. Undergrad. lab. asst. Lab. Exptl. Behavior, U. Miss. Med. Center, Jackson, 1964-65; grad. asst., 1966-69, research asst., trainee, 1966, research asst., 1967-69, NIMH fellow U. Miss., 1969, NINDS fellow U. Miss. Med. Center, 1969-70, instr., 1969-70; adj. prof. Trenton (N.J.) State Coll., 1970-74; research asso. Neurosci. and Behavior Program, Princeton (N.J.) U., 1970—. Mem. Soc. Neurosci., Internat. Soc. Developmental Psychobiology, AAAS, Am., Eastern psychol. assns., Sigma Xi. Contbr. articles to profl. jours. Home: 172 Nassau St Apt 10 Princeton NJ 08540 Office: Dept Psychology Princeton U Princeton NJ 08540

MACARTNEY, NORMAN SCARBOROUGH, geologist, artist; b. Port Washington, N.Y., Oct. 29, 1938; s. Horace Bramwell and Jean Sheila (MacPhail) M.; B.A., Colby Coll., 1961; postgrad. No. Ill. U., 1963, Hofstra U., 1963-64, U. Tex., Arlington, 1971, LaSalle U. Art Sch., 1975; m. Armena Virginia Dolloff, June 15, 1968; children—Lisa Kimberly, Jennifer Lynn, David Cameron. Geophysicist, Atlantic Richfield Co., Dallas, 1965; field geologist Ruberoid Co., Vt., 1961, Core Labs. S.A., Bogota, Colombia, 1964; tchr. sci. Cardigan Mountain Sch., Canaan, N.H., 1966-68, Selwyn Sch., Denton, Tex., 1968-69, Cistercian Prep. Sch., Irving, Tex., 1969-71; head upper sch. sci. Rippowamn Cisqua Sch., Bedford, N.Y., 1971—. Deacon, South Salem Presbyn. Ch., 1978; scout master, troop founder Boy Scouts Am. Served with USNR, 1961-63. Mem. Nat. Sci. Tchrs. Assn. Three one man art shows, 1973—. Home: 109 Allison Rd Katonah NY 10536 Office: Box 488 Bedford NY 10506

MACAULAY, DAVID ALEXANDER, author, illustrator; b. Burton on Trent, Eng., Dec. 2, 1946; s. James and Joan Adelaide (Lowe) M.; came to U.S., 1957; B.Arch., R.I. Sch. Design, 1969; m. Ruth Marris, Aug. 18, 1978; 1 dau., Elizabeth Alexandra. Interior designer, free lance illustrator, 1969-74; art tchr. Central Falls (R.I.) Jr. High Sch., 1969-70, Newton (Mass.) South High Sch., 1973-74; instr. Freshman Found., R.I. Sch. Design, Providence, 1974-76, instr. illustration dept., 1976-77, head dept., 1977—. Recipient Caldecott Honor medal ALA, 1974, 78. Hon. asso. mem. AIA (medal 1978). Author, illustrator: Cathedral, The Story of Its Construction, 1973; City, A Story of Roman Planning and Construction, 1974; Pyramid, 1975; Underground, 1976; Castle, 1977; Great Moments in Architecture, 1978. Office: RI Sch Design 2 College St Providence RI 02903

MACAULEY, BARBARA CART, religious assn. exec.; b. Trenton, N.J., July 6, 1927; d. Theodore Simons and Dorothy Jones (Wilson) Cart; B.A., Bennington Coll., 1949; student Katharine Gibbs Sch., 1950; m. Michael Macauley, July 12, 1951; 1 son—John Chapman Wilson. Song plugger Leo Feist Inc., music pubs., N.Y.C., 1946-47; sec. to Paulette Goddard, 1950-51, Arthur Koestler, 1951-52, Budd Schulberg, 1952-56; bd. mgrs. Am. Bible Soc., N.Y.C., 1972—, Scripture Union, Phila., 1975-77; ordained deacon United Presbyn. Ch., 1973. Mem. exec. com. Bucks County Com. Republican party, 1962, bd. dirs. county council Rep. Women, 1962-63; mem. United Presbyn. Women's Assn., 1970-75. Episcopalian. Home: Meetinghouse Rd New Hope PA 18938

MAC BRIDE, DEXTER DUPONT, assn. exec.; b. Elizabeth, N.J., Aug. 18, 1917; s. Charles Munnerlyn and Flora T. (Jerome) MacB.; student Coll. William and Mary, 1936-37; LL.B., Cumberland U., 1938; J.D., Samford U., 1970; m. Grace Anderson, Dec. 23, 1963; 1

son, Charles Dexter. Admitted to Va. bar, 1939; practiced in Norfolk, 1939-41; sr. right of way agt. City of Los Angeles, 1946-47; supervising right of way agt. State of Calif., Sacramento, 1948-63, asst. chief right of way agt., 1963-70; exec. v.p. Am. Soc. Appraisers, Washington, 1970—; dir. Nat. Valutape Program ASA. Fellow Am. Soc. Appraisers, Soc. Valuers and Auctioneers (London); mem. Am. Right of Way Assn. (nat. sec., exec. com., sr. mem.), Am. Arbitration Assn. (nat. panel arbitrators), Audubon Soc., Am. Soc. Assn. Execs. (certified), Lambda Alpha. Author: Power and Process; Freedom-USA; editor: Valuation Quar.; The Bibliography of Appraisal Literature, 1974. Home: 11457 Washington Plaza W Reston VA 22090 Office: Dulles Internat Airport PO Box 17265 Washington DC 20041

MACCAGNANO, SALVATORE JOSEPH, automobile dealer; b. Boston, Nov. 8, 1923; s. Rosario and Rosaria (Natoli) M.; B.S., B.A., Boston U., 1945; postgrad. Northeastern U., Boston, Am. Inst. Ins.; m. Florence Carilli, July 4, 1952 (dec.); 1 son, Richard. With actuary dept. Mass. Ins. Div., 1945-48; office mgr. Coombs and McBeth, Boston, 1948-51; v.p. Regan & Stapleton, Wellesley, Mass., 1961-64; chief accountant Mr. Boston Distillers, Inc., Boston, 1964-69; comptroller, treas. Goode Ford Sales Inc., Dedham, Mass., 1969—; fin. and tax cons. Served with AUS, 1942-46. Hayden scholar, 1940, 41; recipient Franklin medal Boston English High Sch., 1940. Mem. Soc. Mng. Accountants, VFW. Club: Lions. Address: 945 Providence Hwy Dedham MA 02026

MACCALLUM, DONALD CHARLES, profl. engr.; b. Chgo., Oct. 12, 1916; s. Howard MacFarlane and Jean (Duncan) MacC.; student Lower Can. Coll., 1929-32; B. Engring., McGill U., 1938; m. Marion Fenwick Wilkinson, Mar. 7, 1947. Mech. design engr. Canadian Ingersoll-Rand Co., Ltd., 1938-40; engr. charge rehab. Engring. Inst. Can., Montreal, 1945-46; adminstrv. engr. Canadair, Ltd., Montreal, 1946-48; mng. dir. Charles Warnock & Co., Ltd., Montreal, 1949-52; project engr. Defence Constrn. Ltd., 1951-52; chmn. bd. Racey, MacCallum and Assos., Ltd., Montreal, 1952—. Past pres. Montreal Port Council; past chmn. bd. govs. Lower Can. Coll.; past Pres. Montreal Citizens Com.; mem. Montreal Bd. Trade. Mayor, City of Westmount. Served from lt. to maj. Royal Canadian Armoured Corps, 1940-44, ETO. Decorated 1939-45 Star, Italy Star, U.K. Def. medal, Victory medal, Canadian Vol. Service medal. Mem. Assn. Profl. Engrs. Ont., Engring. Inst. Can. (past councilor), Am. Soc. for Metals, Am. Soc. for Testing Materials, Order Engrs. Que. (past councilor). Home: 4300 De Maisonneauve Blvd Westmount PQ H3Z 1K8 Canada Office: 8205 Montreal-Toronto Blvd Montreal West PQ Canada

MACCHI, EUGENE EDWARD, package co. exec.; b. Kearney, N.J., July 20, 1926; s. Louis Robert and Teresa D. (Maher) M.; student Army spl. tng. program, Carnegie Inst. Tech., 1943-44; student Swarthmore Coll., 1945-47; B.A., Kalamazoo Coll., 1948; m. Josephine M. Towle, May 5, 1951; children—Eugene E., Michael S., Mary Jo, Karen M., Robert C., Thomas J., Charles J. Mgr. Eastern div., Hankins Container div. MacMillan Bloedell, Union, N.J., 1954-62; pres., chmn. bd. Continental Packaging Corp., Kenilworth, N.J., New Castle, Pa., Macon, Ga., 1962-75, also dir.; pres., chmn. bd. Ind. Corrugated Container Corp. Am., Paterson, N.J., 1975—. Commr. N.W. Bergen County Sewer Authority, 1966-69, 75—, chmn., 1967-69, 76—. Mem. exec. com. Ho-Ho-Kus Democratic Club, 1964—. Served with USAAF, World War II. Mem. Assn. Eastern Corrugated Box Mfrs. (pres. 1973-75), Fibre Box Assn., Assn. Ind. Corrugated Converters (pres. 1975-77), C. of C., Nat. Honor Soc., Young Pres.'s Orgn., Phi Sigma Kappa. Contbr. articles to trade mags. Home: 63 Arbor Dr Ho Ho Kus NJ 07423 Office: 55 Jersey St Paterson NJ 07501

MAC CORKLE, DOUGLAS BEALS, coll. chancellor; b. Boston, Dec. 15, 1915; s. John and Laura (Beals) MacC.; A.B., Gordon Coll., 1944; Th.M., Dallas Theol. Sem., 1947, Th.D., 1961; m. Jeanette Astle, Nov. 28, 1939; children—David Lee, Judith Anne. Ordained to ministry Baptist Ch., 1947; pastor, Goffstown, N.H., 1942-44, Paris, Tex., 1944-47, Newton, Mass., 1947-54, Reinhardt Bible Ch., Dallas, 1955-57; acad. dean Washington (D.C.) Bible Ch., 1957-63; pres., also prof. N.T. lit. and Greek, Phila. Coll. Bible, 1963-77, chancellor, 1977—. Bd. dirs. Council on Postsecondary Accreditation, 1975—. Mem. Am. Assn. Bible Colls. (pres.), Evang. Theol. Soc., Assn. Higher Edn. Author: Prophetic Peaks, 1961; (with Charles L. Feinberg) Focus on Prophecy, 1964; (with N.A. Woychuk) Beside the Still Waters, 1959; co-author: America in Bible Prophecy, 1976. Home: PO Box 301 Wynnewood PA 19096 Office: 1800 Arch St Philadelphia PA 19103

MAC CRACKEN, CALVIN DODD, inventor, energy products mfg. co. exec.; b. Poughkeepsie, N.Y., Nov. 25, 1919; s. Henry Noble and Marjorie (Dodd) MacC.; A.B., Princeton U., 1940; B.S., Mass. Inst. Tech., 1941; m. Mary Burnham, June 25, 1969; children by previous marriage—Michael, Joan, Karen, Mark; stepchildren—Susan, Nan, Stephen Thistle. Jet engine engr., edn. supr. Gen. Electric Co., Schenectady, 1941-45; founder and pres. Calmac Mfg. Corp., Englewood, N.J., 1945—; contractor solar energy and storage U.S. Dept. Energy. Mem. planning and zoning bd., Tenafly, N.J., 1953-68, council pres., 1965-68; chmn. No. Valley Planning Assn., 1959; lectr., energy cons. Mem. Am. Soc. Heating, Refrigerating and Air Conditioning Engrs. (chmn. com. ice rinks and ice machinery), ASME, Ice Skating Inst. Am., Nat. Oil Fuel Inst., Solar Energy Industries Assn., U.S. Lawn Tennis Assn., U.S. Squash Racquets Assn. Presbyterian. Clubs: Princeton (N.Y.C.); Field (pres. 1953-55) (Englewood, N.J.); Cream Hill (West Cornwall, Conn.). Holder 80 patents in field. Home: 325 Morrow Rd Englewood NJ 07631 Office: 150 S Van Brunt St Englewood NJ 07631

MAC CRACKEN, CONSTABLE, lawyer; b. N.Y.C., May 4, 1913; s. John Henry and Edith (Constable) MacC.; grad. Hotchkiss Sch., 1931; A.B., Harvard U., 1935; LL.B., Columbia U., 1939; m. Eleanor Gregg Dickson, June 15, 1949 (div. 1974); children—Thomas Gregg, Linda Paige; m. 2d, Harriet Lyons Van Deren, July 12, 1975. Admitted to N.Y. bar, 1939, since practiced in N.Y.C.; asso. firm Curtis, Mallet-Provost, Colt & Mosle, 1939-58, partner, 1958-73, ret., 1973. Cons., U.S. Conf. for World Council Chs., 1971-77; bd. mgrs. World Council Christian Edn., 1964-71, Am. Bible Soc. Served to capt. AUS, 1942-46. Mem. Am. (com. on taxation), N.Y. State, New York County bar assns., Assn. Bar City N.Y. Clubs: University, Harvard, Down Town Assn.; Country of New Canaan; Round Hill (Greenwich, Conn.). Home: 630 Oenoke Ridge New Canaan CT 06840

MAC DONALD, ANGUS CARLETON, surgeon; b. St. Ann's, N.S., Can., Sept. 20, 1935; s. Neil and Mabel Christine (Carmichael) MacD.; B.Sc., Acadia U., 1958; M.D., Dalhousie U., 1963; m. Shirley Wilma MacDonald, Aug. 19, 1960; children—Michael, Ian. Intern Victoria Gen. Hosp., Halifax, N.S., 1962-63, resident in surgery, 1966-71; gen. practice medicine, North Sydney, N.S., 1963-66; registrar, research fellow in gastroenterology Glasgow (Scotland) U., 1971-73; practice surgery, Halifax, 1973—; asso. surgeon Victoria Gen. Hosp.; asst. prof. Dalhousie U., Halifax. John Stewart Meml. scholar, 1958-59; Dennis fellow, 1972-73; Samuel McLaughlin travelling fellow, 1971-72; Izaak Walton Killam fellow, 1969-71. Mem. N.S. Med. Soc., Can., N.S. med. assns., Can., Assn. Clin. Surgeons, Can. Assn. Gastroenterologists, Phi Rho Sigma. Home: 6057 Fraser St Halifax NS B3H 1R8 Canada Office: 5849 University Ave Halifax NS Canada

MAC DONALD, DAVID EGGERS, architect; b. Yonkers, N.Y., July 11, 1924; s. William Angus and Margaretta Marie (Eggers) MacD.; grad. Riverdale Country Sch., 1942; student Oxford U., Exeter Coll., Eng., 1945-46; B.A., Columbia, 1948, M.Arch., 1952; m. Betsy Daniels, June 30, 1954 (div. Sept. 1966); 1 son, Stuart Alexander. Designer, Gehron & Seltzer, Architects, N.Y.C., 1954-64; asso. partner William M. Barnum & Asso. Architects, N.Y.C., 1964-67; chief architect Walter Kidde Constructors, Inc., N.Y.C., 1967-73, Gibbs & Hill, Inc., N.Y.C., 1973—. Vis. prof. Bard Coll., 1949. Served with AUS, 1942-45. Decorated Bronze Star. Mem. A.I.A., Am. Arbitration Assn., N.Y. Assn. Architects, Nat. Council Archtl. Registration Bds. Prin. works in field of edn., indsl. office bldgs., power industry, residential and interiors. Home: 399 E 72d St New York City NY 10021 Office: 393 7th Ave New York City NY 10001

MAC DONALD, DUNCAN DONALD, physician; b. Dublin, Ireland, Sept. 24, 1922; s. Robert Howard and Ellen Jane (Fisher) M.; came to Can., 1964, naturalized, 1972; M.A., M.B., B.Ch., B.A.O., Trinity Coll., Dublin, 1950, L.M., 1963; M.P.S. (Hon.), Egypt, 1954; m. Rita Margaret Ball, July 20, 1965; children—Avril Ann, Duncan Donald Howard, David Robert Howard, Stephen James Howard. Med. officer, 2d sec., Brit. Legation, Bucharest, Rumania, 1955-56; head, med. info. div. May & Baker, Essex, Eng., 1957-63; gen. practice medicine, Deer Lake, Nfld., Can., 1964—; surgeon lt. Royal Can. Sea Cadet Corps, Deer Lake; pres. Deer Lake br. Red Cross Soc., 1973. Mem. Humber Valley Devel. Assn. Mem. Can., Nfld. med. assns., Brit. Assn. Allergists, Deer Lake C. of C. (pres. 1968, 74). Anglican. Home: Fairview House Deer Lake NF A0K 2E0 Canada Office: Health Centre Deer Lake NF A0K 2E0 Canada

MACDONALD, JAN PENDEXTER, II, investment banker; b. Chgo., Oct. 19, 1942; s. Jack and Anna Jeanne (Pendexter) M.; A.B., Harvard U., 1967. Analyst, John Hancock Ins. Co., 1967-69; portfolio mgr. Strand & Co., 1969-70; mgr. multi-industry group Salomon Bros., N.Y.C., 1970-71, 72—, v.p., 1977—; analyst Dean Witter & Co., San Francisco, 1971-72. Mem. pres.'s council Wayland Acad. Served with U.S. Army, 1961-64. Mem. Assn. Computing Machinery, Fin. Analysts Fedn. (mem. program com.), N.Y. Soc. Securities Analysts (chmn. program com. diversified cos. analysts group), Nat. Assn. Securities Dealers (prin.). Episcopalian. Clubs: D.U. (Cambridge, Mass.); Tennis and Racquet (Boston). Home: 345 E 81st St New York City NY 10028 Office: 1 New York Plaza New York City NY 10004

MAC DONALD, JAY DELBERT, ednl. adminstr.; b. Toronto, Ont., Can., Jan. 4, 1916; s. Clarence and Julia Elizabeth (Chalmers) MacD.; student Hamilton Tchrs. Coll., 1934-35, U. Western Ont., 1936, Royal Conservatory Music, 1937-41; B.A., U. Toronto, 1961; M.A., Cornell U., 1966. Tchr., dir. music and speech jr. high sch. Port Credit Schs., Ont., 1937-45; asst. head English, dir. theatre Upper Can. Coll., Toronto, 1945-75. Mem. Actors' Equity Assn., Stratford, Shaw festival founds., Am. Theatre Assn., Can. Speech Assn., Ont. Ednl. Assn., ACTRA. Editor, producer Sound and Image. Contbr. articles to profl. jours. Home: 111 Lawton Blvd Toronto ON M4V 1Z9 Canada

MACDONALD, JEROME EDWARD, sch. psychologist; b. Newark, Aug. 16, 1925; s. Jerome A. and Olvinia Regina (McKenna) MacD.; B.S., Niagara U., 1947, M.A. (grad. fellow), 1950; M.A. in Ednl. Psychology (experienced tchr. fellow), also profl. diploma in sch. psychology Jersey City State Coll., 1970; postgrad. Fordham U., 1950-55; m. Nan Elizabeth Kennington, June 2, 1951; children—Jerome C., Mary Jane, Charles, Blanche (Mrs. Carroll Koehler), Ruth, Gregory, Paul, Robert, Carol. Asst. prof. philosophy Seton Hall U., South Orange, N.J., 1948-55, lectr. in philosophy, edn. 1955-61; tchr. English, Newark pub. schs., 1955-60, guidance counselor, 1960-62, chmn. dept., 1963-69, psychologist, 1969-71; psychologist Metuchen (N.J.) pub. schs., 1971—. Vis. tchr. NDEA Reading Inst., Bowling Green (Ohio) U., 1966-67; extern psychologist N.J. Diagnostic Center, Menlo Park, 1969. Troop treas. Boy Scouts Am., 1967-69. Served with inf., AUS, 1943-46. Decorated Bronze Star medal. Mem. Nat. Assn. Sch. Psychologists, Internat. Reading Assn., NEA, Am., N.J. psychol. assns., N.J. Assn. Sch. Psychologists, Middlesex County Sch. Psychologists Assn. (pres. 1976-77), N.J. Catholic Tchrs. Guild (pres. 1966), VFW, Am. Legion, DAV, Holy Name Soc., Phi Delta Kappa. Roman Catholic. Clubs: Elks, Lions. Editor: (with Eli Levinson) The English Curriculum in Secondary Schools: Ninth Grade, 1964. Home: 9 Ethel St PO Box 57 Metuchen NJ 08840 Office: Metuchen Bd Edn 596 Middlesex Ave Metuchen NJ 08840

MACDONALD, JOANN MARIE KINDERMANN, sales rep.; b. Chgo., Jan. 19, 1938; d. Joseph Aloysius and MaryAnn (Reiss) Kindermann; student Harford Community Coll., 1969-71; B.S. in Biology, Towson State Coll., 1973; m. Bruce Edward Macdonald, Aug. 3, 1957 (dec.); children—Scott William, Jan Marie, Gregg Joseph, Brent Bruce. Clk., Ill. Bell Telephone Co., Chgo., 1955-56; teller Equitable Trust Co., Joppa, Md., 1966-68; tchr. Harford County Bd. Edn., Joppa, 1973-77; sales rep. Union Central Life Ins. Co., Timonium, Md., 1977-78, Office Services, Balt., 1978—. Bd. dirs. Joppatowne Civic Assn., 1978; del. Harford County Women's Coalition to form a Harford County Women's Commn.; mem. budget com. Joppatowne PTA. Standard teaching certificate, Md. Mem. AAUW, Am. Def. Preparedness Assn., Parents Without Partners, Phi Theta Kappa. Democrat. Methodist. Home: 730 Falconer Rd Joppa MD 21085 Office: 6000 Radecke Ave Baltimore MD 21206

MACDONALD, KIRKPATRICK, investment co. exec.; b. San Francisco, Oct. 21, 1940; s. Graeme Kirkpatrick and Phyllis Welch (Heinle) M.; B.Sc., Yale U., 1962; M.A., Oxford (Eng.) U., 1964; postgrad. U. Geneva, 1964-67; m. Beatrice Clèment, July 4, 1964; children—Cybille Alicia, Bryce Eduard Alan. Asso., Lehman Bros., N.Y.C., 1969-71, Blyth & Co., Inc., N.Y.C., 1971; treas.-sec. Conpar Inc. (affiliate Loeb Rhoades & Co.), N.Y.C., 1971-73; asst. v.p. Morgan Guaranty Internat. Fin. Corp., N.Y.C., 1974-76; mng. partner MacDonald & Cie., N.Y.C., 1976—. Bd. dirs. N.Y.C. Citizens Com., W. Side C. of C. Mem. Confrerie des Chevaliers du Tastevin, Leonardo Acad. Arts and Sci. (sec.-treas.). Clubs: Univ., Down Town, Paris-Am. (N.Y.C.); Bohemian (San Francisco). Home: 114 W 78th St New York City NY 10024

MACDONELL, JAMES JOHNSON, govt. ofcl.; b. Calgary, Alta., Can., Sept. 13, 1915; s. Archibald Joseph and Lillian Catherine (Johnson) M.; C.A., Inst. Chartered Accountants, Quebec, 1937, F.C.A. (hon.), Ont., 1956; m. Audrey Mary Grafton, May 15, 1941; 1 dau., Audrey Anne. Partner-in-charge mgmt. cons. services Price Waterhouse & Co. Can., Montreal, Que., 1945-68; sr. partner Price Waterhouse Assos. (Can.), Montreal, 1968-73; auditor gen. Can., Ottawa, 1973—. Bd. dirs. and hon. treas. St. Mary's Hosp., Montreal, 1966-73. Founding mem. Can. Assn. Mgmt. Cons. (pres. 1965-66). Clubs: Mount Royal (Montreal); Rideau (Ottawa). Home: 195 Clearview Ave Ottawa ON K1Z 6S1 Canada Office: 240 Sparks St Ottawa ON K1A 0G6 Canada

MACEY, DAVID ANTHONY JAMES, historian; b. Ferring, Eng., Sept. 11, 1942; s. Walter James and Eira Jane (Moon) M.; came to U.S., 1964, naturalized, 1968; A.B. summa cum laude with honors in History (Arthur C. Cole scholar 1968), Bklyn. Coll., 1968; certificate Russian Inst., Columbia U., 1970, M.A., 1971, M.Phil., 1974, Ph.D. with distinction, 1976; m. Phyllis Ann Topkins, Feb. 11, 1965; children—Peter Topkins, Robert Topkins. Engr. pupil apprentice Vickers-Armstrongs Ltd., Crayford, Eng., 1958-59; clk. P & O Steam Nav. Co., London, 1959-61, asst. purser, London, 1961-64; trainee mgr. Hertz Rent-a-Car, London, 1964; programmer-trainee Lone Star Cement Corp., N.Y.C., 1965; preceptor in history Columbia U., N.Y.C., 1974-76, Mellon fellow Soc. Fellows in Humanities, sr. fellow Russian Inst., 1976-78; asst. prof. history Middlebury (Vt.) Coll., 1978—; vis. asst. prof. U. Vt., Burlington, spring 1979. Herbert H. Lehman fellow, N.Y. State Regents grad. fellow, 1968; Gerold T. Robinson Meml. award Columbia U., 1971; NDEA Title IV Fellow, 1968-70, 71-72; Nat. Def. Fgn. Lang. fellow, 1972-73; Fulbright-Hays fellow, Finland, USSR, 1973; Whiting Dissertation fellow, 1973-74. Mem. Am. Hist. Assn., Am. Assn. Advancement Slavic Studies, AAUP, Phi Beta Kappa. Office: Dept History Middlebury Coll Middlebury VT 05753

MAC FARLANE, GLORIA MARIE, dietitian; b. Brownsville, Pa., Mar. 13, 1926; d. George and Mary Belle (Ferguson) MacF.; grad. Indiana (Pa.) U., 1948, Shadyside Hosp., Pitts., 1949. Chief dietitian Brownsville (Pa.) Gen. Hosp., 1949-52; chief dietitian Charleroi div. Monongahela Valley Hosp., Inc., North Charerloi, Pa., 1952-78; adminstrv. dietitian Monongahela Valley Hosp., Inc., Monongahela, Pa., 1978—; cons. dietitian Waddington Nursing Home. Mem. Am., Pa., Pitts. dietetic assns., Am. Soc. Hosp. Food Service Assn., Am. Hosp. Assn., Tri State, Pa., Nat. ceramic assns. Clubs: Order Eastern Star, Order Amaranth, White Shrine Jerusalem, Charleroi Area Womens (pres. 1965), Quota (pres. 1971). Home: 431 Isabella Ave North Charleroi PA 15022 Office: Charleroi Div Center Ave North Charleroi PA 15022

MAC GREGOR, CHARLES WINTERS, cons. engr.; b. Dayton, Ohio, May 25, 1908; s. Charles and Florence H. (Isenberg) M.; B.S. in Elec. Engring., U. Mich., 1929, B.S. in Math., 1929; M.S. in Mech. Engring., U. Pitts., 1932, Ph.D. in Math. and Mech. Engring., with highest honor, 1934; m. Marie Elizabeth Graham, Apr. 5, 1951; 1 son, Charles Winters. Research engr. Westinghouse Electric and Mfg. Co., Pitts., 1929-34; instr. Mass. Inst. Tech., Cambridge, 1934-37, asst. prof. applied mechanics, 1937-38, asso. prof., 1938-42, prof., 1942-52, head gun design group, 1942-52; v.p. engring. U. Pa., Phila., 1952-54; cons. engr., Phila., 1954-60; engring. cons., mgr. advanced tech. IBM, Endicott, N.Y., 1960-71; cons. engr., Boston, 1971—; mem. profl. adv. council Pa. State U., 1963-68; mem. sci. adv. com. to chief of ordnance U.S. Army, 1951-63. Trustee Brookhaven Nat. Lab., 1952-54. Recipient Ordnance Devel. award U.S. Navy, 1945. Registered profl. engr., Mass., Ohio, N.Y., Pa., N.J. Fellow Franklin Inst. (Louis Edward Levy medal 1941), Am. Acad. Arts and Scis.; mem. ASME (chmn. Boston sect. 1946-47), Am. Inst. Mining and Metall. Engrs., Nat., Mass. socs. profl. engrs., Am. Soc. for Metals, ASTM (Charles B. Dudley medal 1941), N.Y. Acad. Scis., Sigma Xi, Delta Chi. Editor: Handbook of Analytical Design for Wear, 1964; editorial bd. IBM Jour. Research and Devel., 1960-71. Contbr. numerous articles on applied mechanics, materials and stress analysis to profl. jours. and handbooks. Address: 112 Jerusalem Rd Cohasset MA 02025

MACHANIC, HARMON JACK, radiologist; b. Burlington, Vt., Feb. 2, 1923; s. Morris Robert and Rose (Levin) M.; B.S., U. Vt., 1944, M.D., 1946; m. Betty Hetler, Sept. 13, 1965; children—Mindy R., Scott L. Intern, Jewish Hosp. Bklyn., 1946, resident in radiology, 1950-53; resident in pulmonary diseases Montefiore Hosp., Bronx, N.Y., 1950-53; chief radiologist Divine Providence Hosp., Williamsport, Pa., 1953—; radiologist Troy (Pa.) Community Hosp., 1972—; cons. radiologist Eastern Fed. Penitentiary, Lewisburg, Pa., 1965-68; radiologist Muncy (Pa.) Valley Hosp., 1963-72; dir. radiologic tech. program Williamsport Area Community Coll., 1971—. Pres., Lycoming County unit Am. Cancer Soc. Served with U.S. Army, 1942-46. Diplomate Am. Bd. Radiology. Fellow Am., Internat. colls. radiology, Am. Geriatrics Soc.; mem. AMA, N.Am., Pa. radiol. socs., Lycoming Radiology Assn. (pres. 1974—), Pa. (ho. of dels. 1973—), Lycoming County (bd. censors 1979) med. socs. Republican. Club: Rotary. Home: RD 2 PO Box 77 Linden PA 17744 Office: 1100 Grampian Blvd Williamsport PA 17701

MACHAVER, HARVEY, hosp. adminstr.; b. N.Y.C., June 30, 1925; s. Samuel and Rose (Shkolnick) M.; M.S. in Indsl. Labor Relations, Cornell U., 1949; B.S. in Bus. Adminstrn., U. Calif. at Berkeley, 1948; m. Claire Newman, Oct. 23, 1949; 1 dau., Wendy Jane. Personnel dir. Jewish Hosp. of Bklyn., 1949-54; asst. dir. Montefiore Hosp., N.Y.C., 1954-59; adminstr. Trafalgar Hosp., N.Y.C., 1959-66; asso. dir. Jewish Hosp. and Med. Center, Bklyn., 1966-68; adminstr. Hosp. for Joint Diseases and Med. Center, 1968-70, exec. dir., 1970—; asst. prof. clin. adminstrv. medicine Mt. Sinai Sch. Medicine, 1970—. Bd. dirs. Comprehensive Health Planning Agy. Served as lt. (j.g.), U.S. Maritime Service, USNR, 1943-46. Fellow Am. Pub. Health Assn., Royal Soc. Health (Eng.), N.Y. Acad. Medicine (asso.); mem. Am. Coll. Hosp. Adminstrs., Am., Greater N.Y. (bd. govs.) hosp. assns., League Vol. Hosps. (trustee 1975-77), Beta Gamma Sigma. Home: 311 E 71st St New York City NY 10021 Office: 1919 Madison Ave New York City NY 10035

MACHEN, ARTHUR WEBSTER, JR., lawyer; b. Balt., Dec. 16, 1920; s. Arthur Webster and Helen Chase (Woods) M.; A.B., Princeton, 1942; LL.B., Harvard, 1948; m. Rose Bradley Purves, Jan. 24, 1948; children—Arthur Webster III (dec.), John Purves, Henry Lewis. Admitted to Md. bar, 1948; practice law, Balt., 1948—; asso. Armstrong, Machen & Eney, 1948-51; asso. Venable, Baetjer & Howard, 1951-57, partner, 1957—; dir. Waverly Press, Inc. Reporter, Charter Bd., Baltimore County, 1954; legislative draftsman Home Rule Charter, 1955; chmn. Gov.'s Com. to Study Adminstrn. of Blue Sky Law Md., 1961; chmn. Md. Blue Sky Adv. Com., 1962-68; mem. Commn. on Revision Corp. Laws Md., 1966. Bd. mgrs. Family and Childrens Soc., 1958-70, pres., 1967-69; trustee Gilman Sch., 1959-61. Served to lt. USNR, 1941-46. Mem. Am., Md., Balt. bar assns., Am. Judicature Soc., Phi Beta Kappa. Democrat. Episcopalian (chancellor diocese of Md. 1972—). Clubs: Hamilton St., Elkridge, Center (Balt.). Contbr. articles to profl. jours. Home: 1400 Malvern Ave Ruxton MD 21204 Office: Mercantile Bank & Trust Bldg Baltimore MD 21201

MACHT, LEE BRAND, psychiatrist, educator; b. N.Y.C., June 8, 1937; s. Maurice Leon and Natalie Estelle (Bernstein) M.; A.B., Princeton U., 1957; 1957; M.D., Harvard U., 1961; m. Lois Ellen Missle, Sept. 2, 1962; children—Melinda, Alisa, Joshua. Intern, Beth Israel Hosp., Boston, 1961-62; resident in psychiatry Mass. Mental Health Center, Boston, 1962-66, 68-69; dep. med. dir., prin. psychiatrist Nat. Job Corps, Washington, 1966-68; practice medicine specializing in psychiatry and child psychiatry, Cambridge and Wellesley, Mass., 1968—; asso. dir. psychiatry Cambridge Hosp., 1970-75, dir. clin. services, dept. psychiatry Cambridge Hosp. and

Cambridge-Somerville Mental Health and Retardation Center, 1976-78; asso. prof. psychiatry Harvard Med. Sch., 1974-78; commr. mental health State of Mass., Boston, 1975—; chief of psychiatry Cambridge Hosp., 1978—; prof., head dept. psychiatry Harvard Med. Sch. at Cambridge Hosp., 1978—; mem. Mass. Statewide Health Coordinating Council, 1977; cons. Pres.'s Commn. on Mental Health, 1977; pres. North Charles Mental Health Tng. Research Found.; cons. mental health Job Corps; sr. psychiat. cons. OEO. Fellow Am. Psychiat. Assn.; mem. Mass. Psychiat. Soc. (pres. 1977), Am. Pub. Health Assn., Group for Advancement of Psychiatry. Democrat. Jewish. Home: 39 Chatham Circle Wellesley MA 02181 Office: Dept Psychiatry Cambridge Hosp 1493 Cambridge St Cambridge MA 02139

MACHT, STANLEY HOWARD, radiologist; b. Crewe, Va., Sept. 3, 1914; s. Harry Elias and Jeanette Fanny (Rubin) M.; B.S., U. Va., 1934, M.D., 1939; m. Naomi Newman, July 1, 1941; children—Jay (dec.), Harold, Maury, Jon. Editor, Crewe Chronicle, 1935-36; intern U.S. Marine Hosp., Norfolk, Va., 1939-40; gen. practice medicine, Crewe, 1940-42; fellow radiology Peter Bent Brigham Hosp.-Harvard, Boston, 1942-43; resident radiology Jefferson Hosp., Phila., 1943-44, asst. radiologist, 1944-46; chief dept. radiology Balt. City Hosps. and asst. prof. roentgenology U. Md. Med. Sch., 1946-50; dir. dept. radiology Washington County Hosp., Hagerstown, Md., 1950-78. Cons. Brooklane San. and Western Md. Chronic Disease Hosp., Hagerstown, 1965—, Morgan County War Meml. Hosp., Berkely, W.Va., Fulton County Hosp., McConnellsburg, Pa.; sr. aviation med. examiner FAA, 1960—; pres. Macht, Williams & Lazo Asso. Radiologists, 1967-78, Specialists, P.A., 1978—; prof. Hagerstown Jr. Coll., 1973-78, Med. and Chirugical Faculty of Md. Vice chmn. Mason Dixon council Boy Scouts Am., 1956. Bd. dirs. Am. Cancer Soc., Washington County, 1965. Served with USPHS, 1939-40. Diplomate Am. Bd. Radiology. Fellow Am. Coll. Radiology; mem. AMA (Physicians Recognition award 1971, 75), Am. Philatelic Soc., Aircraft Owners and Pilots Assn., Hagerstown Stamp Club, Am. Philatelic Writers Club, Quiet Birdmen, Radiol. Soc. N.Am., Am. Roentgen Ray Soc., Pan. Am., So. med. assns., Interam. Coll. Radiology, Md. Radiol. Soc., Washington County Med. Soc., Zeta Beta Tau. Democrat. Jewish. Clubs: Northwood Swim and Tennis, Torch; Beaver Creek Golf; Fountain Head Country; B'nai B'rith. Author novelette. Contbr. articles to profl. jours. Home: 826 Rolling Rd Hagerstown MD 21740 Office: 215 W Washington St Hagerstown MD 21740

MACIAG, ROBERT JOHN, univ. adminstr.; b. Lewiston, Maine, Apr. 1, 1940; s. John L. and Irene (Czachorowski) M.; B.Metall. Engring., Poly. Inst. Bklyn., 1961, M.S., 1964; children—James, Nancy. Instr. metall. engring. Poly. Inst. Bklyn. Poly. Inst. N.Y.), 1961-64, asst. prof., 1964-69, asso. prof., 1969-72, dir. continuing edn., 1973-74, asst. to provost, 1972-74, exec. asst. to provost, 1974-76, asso. provost for planning, 1976—; mem. adj. faculty Queensborough Community Coll.; cons. Bklyn. Union Gas Co., Consol. Edison, N.Y., Englehard Industries, Republic Aviation, N.Y. Telephone Co., N.Y.C. Fire Dept., N.Y.C. Bldg. Dept. Naval Ships Research Center research grantee. Mem. Am. Soc. Metals (edn. award N.Y. chpt. 1971, chmn. N.Y. chpt. 1973-74, mem. exec. com. 1968—), Am. Assn. Higher Edn., Soc. Coll. and Univ. Planning, Metal Sci. Club N.Y., Sigma Xi. Republican. Home: 40 Clinton St Brooklyn NY 11201 Office: 333 Jay St Brooklyn NY 11201

MACIEJKO, ROMAIN, physicist; b. Schweinfurt, Germany, Jan. 22, 1946; came to Can., 1951, naturalized, 1957; B.A., Laval U., 1966, B.S., 1970; M.A., State U. N.Y., Stony Brook, 1971, Ph.D., 1975. Tchr., research asst. State U. N.Y., Stony Brook, 1970-75; research asso. Technische Hochschule, Aachen, W. Ger., 1975-78; staff Bell No. Research, Ottawa, Ont., Can., 1978—. Recipient Lt. Gov. Can. medal, 1966, Can. Math. Soc. Prize, 1965, Pfizer Prize, Assn. Canadienne-Francaise pour L'Avancement des Sciences, 1966. Mem. Am. Phys. Soc. Roman Catholic. Contbr. articles to sci. jours. Home: 26 Ave Juchereau Quebec PQ G1E 2L7 Canada Office: Bell-No Research PO Box 3511 Sta C Ottawa ON K1Y 4H7 Canada

MAC INTOSH, CHARLES ARCHIBALD, hosp. adminstr.; b. Haverford, Pa., Aug. 15, 1933; s. Archibald and Margaret (Taylor) MacI.; A.B., Washington and Lee U., 1956; M.P.H., Yale U., 1962; m. Elizabeth Cabell Dugdale, Aug. 20, 1960; children—William Archibald, Elizabeth Cabell, Andrew Taylor. Adminstrv. asst. Hosp. of U. Pa., 1959-60; adminstrv. resident, adminstrv. asst. Lankenau Hosp., Phila., 1961-63; asst. dir. Genesee Hosp., Rochester, N.Y., 1963-67; asst. dir. Greater Balt. Med. Center, 1967-70; asso. adminstr. Temple U. Hosp., Phila., 1970-76; dir. All Saint's Hosp. and Springfield Retirement Residence, Wyndmoor, Pa., 1976—. Served with F.A., U.S. Army, 1956-58. Mead Johnson trainee, 1962. Fellow Am. Coll. Hosp. Adminstrs., Royal Soc. Health; mem. Am. Hosp. Assn., Hosp. Assn. Pa., Del. Valley Hosp. Council Forum. Episcopalian. Home: 115 Llanfair Rd Ardmore PA 19003

MACINTYRE, LESLIE DONALD, educator; b. Rochester, Ind., August 7, 1897; s. Martin and Maud Ethel (Lewis) MacI.; student pub. schs. Rochester, Washington; m. Alice Sonnenschein, June 1, 1929; children—Carol Ann MacIntyre Purcell, Donald Martin, Martin Lewis. With Cost Accounting div. Dept. War, Washington, 1917-20; mem. staff ARC, Washington, 1920-27, 1961-62, St. Louis, 1927-45, Alexandria, Va., 1945-61; pres. Clara Barton Fed. Credit Union, 1959-61; partner The MacIntyres, pubs. Pres., Washington Ethical Soc., 1947-51, 1966-67, historian, 1962-69; sec. Am. Ethical Union, N.Y.C., 1947-51, pres., 1951-59, bd. dirs. (life), 1959—. Mem. Common Cause, Pub. Citizen, World Federalists U.S.A., Internat. Humanist and Ethical Union, ADA, Nat. Com. for Effective Congress, Comunn Chloinn an-t-Saoir (Clan MacIntyre Assn.) (founder, pres. 1978—). Author: Washington Ethical Society—1943-64, 1964, Clan MacIntyre—A Journey to the Past, 1977. Home and Office: 15301 Pine Orchard Dr Apt 3H Silver Spring MD 20906

MACISAAC, DAVID, air force officer; b. Boston, June 22, 1935; s. John Lawrence and Mary Teresa (Mullen) MacI.; B.A., Trinity Coll., 1957; M.A. (Woodrow Wilson fellow), Yale U., 1958; Ph.D., Duke U., 1970; m. Charlotte Wade, July 19, 1959; children—Donna lMarie, Paul David, Pamela Diane, Patrick Roger. Commd. 2d lt. USAF, 1957; advanced through grades to lt. col., 1974; personnel officer SAC, Tex. and Spain, 1959-64; adv. to dep. chief staff for tng. Vietnamese Air Force, 1971; instr. history USAF Acad. (Colo.), 1964-66, asst. prof., 1968-69, asso. prof., 1970-72, dep. for mil. history, 1972-75, tenure prof., 1976-78; fellow Woodrow Wilson Internat. Center for Scholars, Smithsonian Instn., Washington, 1978—; vis. prof. strategy Naval War Coll., Newport, R.I., 1975-76. Decorated Bronze Star. Mem. Air Force Assn., U.S. Naval Inst., Inter-univ. Seminar on Armed Forces and Soc., Phi Beta Kappa. Author: Strategic Bombing in World War II, 1976; Editor: The Military and Soc., 1975; Reports of the U.S. Strategic Bombing Survey, 10 vols., 1976. Office: The Wilson Center Smithsonian Inst Bldg Washington DC 20560

MAC IVER, PEGGE FARMER (MRS. DONALD GORDON MACIVER), monodramatist, educator; b. Colon, C.Z.; d. Alfred Gibson and Minnie (Cuckler) Farmer; B.A., Ohio U., 1935; B.L.L., Cin. Conservatory Music, 1938; M.A., George Washington U., 1964; m. Donald Gordon MacIver, June 7, 1957; 1 stepson, Neil. Monodramatist, lectr., writer touring U.S., Can. writing, performing own plays for one woman theatre presentations, 1938-59; speech therapist D.C. Pub. Schs., 1959-67, tchr. in-service tng. programs, program coordinator Ednl. Resources Center, 1967-70, asst. dir. dept. spl. edn., 1970-72, supervising dir. for staff devel. dept. spl. edn., 1972—; tchr. in-service tng. programs D.C. Tchrs. Coll. TV moderator, panelist Its Your World and World Headliner programs; mem. speakers burs. Dayton (Ohio) Council World Affairs, League Women Voters, 1950-57. Mem. Nat. League Am. Pen Women, Am. (certificate of clin. competence in speech pathology), D.C. speech and hearing assns., Assn. Supervision and Curriculum Devel., Internat. Platform Assn., Phi Beta Kappa, Pi Beta Phi, Alpha Delta Kappa, Delta Kappa Gamma. Contbr. articles to profl. publs. Home: 8500 New Hampshire Ave Silver Spring MD 20903 Office: DC Pub Schs Washington DC 20004

MACK, GERHARD THEODOR, internist; b. Kuenzelsau, Germany, May 22, 1928; s. Eugen and Alma (Dauch) M.; came to U.S., 1954, naturalized, 1960; M.D., U. Wuerzburg (Germany), 1953; m. Mary M. Miller, July 14, 1956; children—Stephen, Kathryn. Intern, St. Barnabas Hosp., Mpls., 1954-55; fellow U. Minn. Hosp., 1955-58; practice medicine, specializing in internal medicine, Cheshire, Conn., 1958—; chief medicine Meriden (Conn.) - Wallingford Hosp., 1975-76. Diplomate Am. Bd. Internal Medicine. Mem. AMA, Conn. Meriden Wallingford (pres. 1971-72) med. socs. Club: Rotary (pres. 1971-72). Home: 644 Mountain Rd Cheshire CT 06410 Office: 577 S Main St Cheshire CT 06410

MACK, JAY ORD, JR., metallurgist; b. Wilkinsburg, Pa., May 2, 1922; s. Jay Ord and June (Shupe) M.; B.S. in Metall. Engring., Carnegie Inst. Tech., 1942, M.S. in Metall. Engring., 1950; postgrad. Pa. State U., 1945-47, U. Pitts., 1950-51; m. Nyla McCrory, May 22, 1943; children—Nyla Jane, Debra Lee. Metall. laborer, observer Edgar Thomson works U.S. Steel Corp., Braddock, Pa., 1941-42, supervising technologist applied research labs., Monroeville, Pa., 1947-51, chief control and development metallurgist Fairless works, Fairless Hills, Pa., 1951-59, chief steel prodn. metallurgist, 1959-64, asst. chief metallurgist, inspector, 1964-71, chief metallurgist, 1971-77, mgr. process metallurgy, Pitts., 1977—. Welding engr. Naval Research Lab., Washington, 1943-45; research asst. Pa. State U., 1945-47. Mem. Am. Soc. Metals (John A. Roebling award lectr. 1976), Am. Inst. Metall. Engrs., Am. Iron and Steel Engrs. Contbr. articles to profl. jours. Home: 2331 Berkshire Dr Pittsburgh PA 15241 Office: US Steel Bldg 600 Grant St Pittsburgh PA

MACK, JEREMY ROGER, physician; b. Hackensack, N.J., Mar. 11, 1938; s. Howard and Fanne M.; B.A. with honors, Ripon Coll., 1961; M.D., Temple U., 1965; m. Aug. 28, 1970; children—Avram, David. Intern, Presbyn.-U. Pa. Med. Center, 1965-66; resident in psychiatry Temple U. Hosp., Phila., 1966-67; resident in psychiatry Mt. Sinai Hosp., N.Y.C., 1967-69, fellow in child psychiatry, 1969-71, clin asst. psychiatry, 1969-71; clin. asso., Mt. Sinai Sch. Medicine City U. N.Y., 1971-76, sr. clin. asso., 1976—, dir. therapeutic nursery, hosp.'s div. child psychiatry, 1971—; pvt. practice medicine specializing in psychiatry, N.Y.C., 1971—; staff psychiatrist Henry Ittleson Center Child Research, Bronx, N.Y., 1971—. Bd. dirs. N.Y. Council Child Psychiatry; mem. advisory bd. N.Y.C. Dept. Mental Health and Mental Retardation Services. Editorial bd. Bull. of Council N.Y. State dist. brs. Am. Psychiat. Assn., 1975—. Address: 952 Fifth Ave New York NY 10021

MACK, JOHN EDWARD, psychiatrist; b. N.Y.C., Oct. 4, 1929; s. Edward Clarence and Ruth (Prince) M.; B.A., Oberlin Coll., 1951; M.D., Harvard U., 1955; m. Sally Ann Stahl, July 12, 1959; children—Daniel, Kenneth, David Anthony. Intern, Mass. Gen. Hosp., Boston, 1955-56; resident in psychiatry Mass. Mental Health Center, Boston, 1956-59, chief resident day and night hosps., 1957-59; teaching fellow then research fellow Harvard U. Med. Sch., 1956-59; cons. Mass. Div. Legal Medicine, 1958, VA day hosps., 1959; practice medicine specializing in psychiatry, Cambridge and Brookline, Mass., 1961; candidate in tng. Boston Psychoanalytic Soc. and Inst., 1961-67; sr. physician Mass. Mental Health Center, 1961, fellow child psychiatry children's unit, 1961-63, staff psychiatrist, 1963—, staff visitor Service I, 1963-65, prin. psychiatrist, 1965, asso. dir. psychiatry, 1965-67, dir. research children's unit, 1967-70, coordinator Harvard U. Med. Sch. teaching children's unit, 1968-70; mem. staff div. legal medicine Roxbury (Mass.) Ct. Clinic, 1962-63; asst. in psychiatry Harvard Med. Sch., 1963-64, mem. faculty, 1964—, prof. psychiatry, 1972—, head dept., 1973-77; jr. vis. physicians Cambridge City Hosp., 1967, sr. vis. physician, 1968-69, chief dept. psychiatry, 1969-76; cons. Harvard U. Health Services, 1972-75, also lectr. psychology and social relations; dir. edn. Cambridge-Somerville Mental Health and Retardation Center, 1975—; mem. faculty Boston Psychoanalytic Soc. and Inst., 1969—, mem. edn. com., 1975—. Served to capt. USAF, 1959-61. Felix and Helene Deutsch Sci. prize Boston Psychoanalytic Inst., 1964; Recipient Harry S. Solomon award Mass. Mental Health Center, 1967; diplomate Am. Bd. Psychiatry. Fellow Am. Psychiat. Assn.; mem. Mass., Norfolk County med. socs., Am. Group Psychotherapy Assn., New Eng. Council Child Psychiatry, Assn. for Psychophysiol. Study Sleep, Group for Advancement Psychiatry, Am. Acad. Child Psychiatry, Boylston Soc., Alpha Omega Alpha. Author: Nightmares and Human Conflict, 1970; A Prince of Our Disorder: The Life of T.E. Lawrence (Pulitzer prize for biography 1977), 1976. Editor: Borderline States in Psychiatry, 1975. Contbr. articles in field to profl. jours. Office: care Little Brown and Co 34 Beacon St Boston MA 02106*

MACK, PHYLLIS FRIEDMAN (MRS. DAVID MACK), interior designer, civic worker; b. N.Y.C., Apr. 15, 1941; d. Maurice and Anne (Price) Friedman; grad. Brearley Sch., 1958; student Vassar Coll., 1958-60, Sorbonne, 1960; B.S., Columbia U., 1963; grad. N.Y. Sch. Interior Design; m. David Mack, Oct. 8, 1961; children—Alexander H., Nicholas R. Interior designer domestic interiors, N.Y.C., 1963—. Dir. Stanley Isaacs Community Center, 1965-67; dance chmn. George Jr. Republic, also mem. jr. bd. 1966-69; bd. dirs., mem. fund-raising com. Yorkville Youth Council; mem. pub. relations com. Asso. YM-YWHA, N.Y.C.; bd. dirs. Children's Blood Found., 1978—. Mem. Allied Bd. Trade, Brearley Alumnae Assn. Club: Fairview Country (Greenwich, Conn.). Home: 100 Bedford Rd Greenwich CT 06830 also 800 Park Ave New York City NY 10021

MAC KAY, JAMES ROBERT, psychiat. social worker; b. Medford, Mass., May 8, 1930; s. James Alexander and Julia (MacNaught) Mac K.; B.A., Tufts U., 1952, M.A., 1954; M.S. in Social Work, Boston U., 1958. Social worker Peter Bent Brigham Hosp., Boston, 1958-60; dir. alcoholism N.H. Dept. Health and Welfare, Concord, 1960-63; dir. community mental health State of N.H., Concord, 1963-64; pvt. practice psychotherapy, Concord, 1964—; sr. lectr. psychotherapy Franklin Pierce Law Center, Concord, 1978; chmn. N.H. Council Aging, 1969—; pres. N.H. Social Welfare Council; chmn. N.H. del. to White House Conf. Aging, 1974; chmn. N.H. Com. Older Am. Act, 1968-69. Recipient Ann. award N.H. Social Welfare Council, 1970; Vaughan award Activities in Aging, N.H., 1974. Contbr. articles on alcoholism, addiction and juvenile delinquency to profl. jours. Office: 139 N State St Concord NH 03301

MAC KAY, MELVILLE GORDON, food co. exec.; b. Rochester, N.Y., Sept. 10, 1933; s. Melville Gordon and Helen Marion (Stein) MacK.; A.B., Harvard U., 1955; m. Barbara Baylor Norton, Aug. 14, 1954; children—Melville Gordon, John Norton. Trust officer Lincoln Rochester Trust Co., Rochester, 1957-68, New Eng. Mchts. Nat. Bank, Boston, 1968-72; v.p., trust officer Martha's Vineyard Nat. Bank (Mass.), 1972-76; pres. Deerfield Groves Co., Wabasso, Fla., 1974—, also dir., mem. exec. com.; pres., dir. Deerfield of St. Lucie, Inc., Fort Pierce, Fla., 1974-75; corporator Dukes County Savs. Bank, Edgartown. Co-chmn. Martha's Vineyard Hosp. Drive, 1972-74; mem. council Dukes County Hist. Assn.; Democratic city councilman at large, Corning, N.Y., 1965-66; commr. Corning Fire Dept., 1965-66. Mem. Estate Planning Council Cape Cod. Club: Harvard (Boston). Home: Sengekontacket Oak Bluffs MA 02557 Office: Deerfield Groves Co Wabasso FL 32970 also PO Box 862 Vineyard Haven MA 02568

MAC KENZIE, IAN MURDOCH, chem. co. exec.; b. Bklyn., Apr. 2, 1916; s. John Murdoch and Edith Mary (Lintott) MacK.; B.S., Mass. Inst. Tech., 1939; postgrad. Adelphia U., 1950-53; m. H. Joan Plimpton, Nov. 1, 1938 (1958): children—Leslie Jane O'Donnell, Nancy Anne Hullender, Richard B. Myrick, Barbara Reid Keane; m. 2d, W. Anne Jack, July 28, 1962. Tech. dir. Am. Colloid div. E.f. Drew. 1939-43; chem. engr. Am. Cyanamid, 1946-48; pres., chief exec. officer MacKenzie Chem. Works, Inc., Central Islip, N.Y., 1946—; chmn. bd. MacKenzie Chem. Works La.; dir. Devtronix East. Served with USNR, 1943-46. Mem. Am. Chem. Soc., AAAS, Am. Def. Preparedness Assn., Am. Theatre Organ Soc., Am. Organists Assn., Internat., Nat. assns. appreciation music. Patentee processes for mfg. synthetic organic intermdiates. Office: 1 Cordello Ave Central Islip NY 11722

MACKENZIE, MALCOLM LEWIS, mktg. services co. exec.; b. El Paso, Tex., Jan. 19, [illegible]6; s. William Forbes and Grace Meldon (Lewis) M.; student Phillips Acad., Andover, Mass., 1942-44, Maine Maritime Acad., 1944-46; B.A., R.I. Sch. Design and Brown U., 1951; m. Barbara Lee Webb, Apr. 24, 1952; children—David Webb, Ellen Lee. With N.W. Ayer & Son, Phila., 1951-62, planning dept. account exec., 1960-62; head mktg. dept. Grey & Rogers, Phila., 1962-63; v.p. Daily Service, Inc., 1963-65; founder Malcolm L. Mackenzie & Assos., Wilmington, Del., 1966, mgr. market penetration research div., 1968-70, pres., 1971—; dir. Fed. Union, Inc., Washington. Mem. adv. council Brown U., 1958-60, 66—; chmn. Citizens Com. for Mt. Pleasant Sch. Bd., 1966-70; mem. Interreligious Com. on Welfare, 1966-68; chmn. Council Civic Orgns. New Castle County, 1972; scoutmaster Del-Mar-Va council Boy Scouts Am., 1969—; pres. Council Civic Orgns. Brandywine Hundred, 1972-74; chmn. advt. com. United Fund Del., 1972. Pres., Active Young Republicans Brandywine Hundred, 1964-65, state Rep. pub. relations chmn., 1965-67. Bd. dirs., pres. Am. Prestige Arts, Wilmington Del.; v.p., bd. dirs. Composite Structures; cons. adv. bd. New Castle County Community Devel. Authority; pres. Delmarva Safe Sailing Assn., 1978—; bd. dirs. Del. Safety Council, New Castle County Contract Rev. Served with U.S. Mcht. Marines, 1946-48. Named Man of Year, Brandywine Active Young Republicans, 1965; recipient Order of Arrow, Boy Scouts Am., 1971, Wood badge, Order of Merit, 1977. Mem. Delta Upsilon. Methodist (dir. Wilmington Inner-city Action Program 1968-70). Kiwanian. Clubs: Brown (pres. Phila. 1966-68, Wilmington 1966—); Windybush Swim (dir. Wilmington). Home: 108 Southwick Dr Wilmington DE 19810 Office: 200 W 10th St Wilmington DE 19801

MAC KENZIE, NORMAN HUGH, educator; b. Salisbury, Rhodesia, Mar. 8, 1915; s. Thomas Hugh and Ruth Blanche (Huskisson) MacK.; B.A., Rhodes U., South Africa, 1934, M.A., 1935, Diploma Edn., 1936; Ph.D. (Union scholar), U. London, 1940; m. Rita Mavis Hofmann, Aug. 14, 1948; children—Catherine, Ronald. Lectr. in English, Rhodes U., South Africa, 1937, U. Hong Kong, 1940-41, U. Melbourne (Australia), 1946-48; sr. lectr.in-charge U. Natal (Durban), 1949-55; prof., head English dept. U. Coll. Rhodesia, 1955-65, dean Faculty Arts and Edn., 1957-60, 63-64; prof., head English dept. Laurentian U., Ont., Can., 1965-66; prof. English, Queen's U., Kingston, Ont., 1966—, dir. grad. studies in English, 1967-73, chmn. council grad. studies, 1971-73, chmn. editorial bd. Yeats Studies, 1972-74. Exec. Central Africa Drama League, 1959-65; mem. exec. com. Can. Irish Studies, 1968-73. Served with Hong Kong Vol. Def. Corps, 1940-45 (P.O.W. China and Japan 1941-45). Brit. Council scholar, 1954. Mem. English Assn. Rhodesia (pres. 1957-65), Rhodesia Drama Assn. (vice chmn. 1957-65), Hopkins Soc. (pres. 1972—), Yeats Soc. (life), Internat. Assn. U. Profs. English, Modern Lang. Assn., Internat. Assn. for Study Anglo-Irish Lits. Author: South African Travel Literature in the 17th Century, 1955; The Outlook for English in Central Africa, 1960; Hopkins, 1968. Editor (with late W.H. Gardner) The Poems of Gerard Manley Hopkins, 1967, 70, Folio Soc. edit., 1974; U. Natal Gazette, 1954-55. Contbr. chpts. to Testing the English Proficiency of Foreign Students, 1961, English Studies Today-Third Series, 1964, Sphere History of English Literature, Vol. VI, 1970, Readings of the Wreck of the Deutschland, 1976, Festschrift for E.R. Seary, 1975, British and American Literature 1880-1920, 1976, Myth and Reality in Irish Literature, 1977. Contbr. articles to Internat. Rev. Edn., Bull. Inst. Hist. Research, Times Lit. Supplement, The Month, Modern Lang. Quar., Queen's Quar., others. Home: 416 Windward Pl Kingston ON K7M 4E4 Canada

MAC KENZIE, ROBERT PECK, investment co. exec.; b. Boston, May 9, 1945; s. Donald Hershey and Hope Martha (Peck) MacK.; student Bentley Coll., 1962-63, Am. Inst. Banking, 1968-71; m. Veronica Margaret Allan, Dec. 22, 1964; children—Andrew Donald, Sandra Hope. Investment officer govt. bond dept. Shawmut Bank, Boston, 1968-74, Hartford Nat. Bank, 1974-75; institutional salesman Blyth, Eastman, Dillon Captial Mkts Co., Hartford, 1975—; advisor South Shore Investors, Inc., 1969-74. Served with USAF, 1963-67. Mem. New Eng. Govt. Bond Club, Conn. Investment Bankers Assn., Investment Soc. Northeastern N.Y., Appalachian Trail Conf. Clubs: We Flew, Rand Class, Masons. Home: 30 Ralph Rd Manchester CT 06040 Office: 799 Main St Hartford CT 06103

MACKEY, HELEN THERESA (MRS. EDWARD G. HART), educator; b. Boston, Oct. 6, 1918; d. Mark John and Mary Elizabeth (McLaughlin) Mackey; B.S., Boston U., 1940, M.Ed., 1948, Ed.D., 1954; m. Edward G. Hart. Elementary tchr. phys. edn., Andover, Mass., 1940-41; health and phys. edn. tchr. Athol (Mass.) Jr. High Sch., also Athol High Sch., 1941-43, supr. phys. edn., 1943-45; tchr. health and phys. edn. West Jr. High Sch., Watertown, Mass., 1945-50; tchr. phys. edn. Watertown High Sch., 1950-52; prof. health and phys. edn. Salem (Mass.) State Coll., 1952—, head health and phys. edn. dept. for women, 1961-71, asst. dean women, 1959-69. Coordinator TV series WGBH, Boston, 1958; cons. New Eng. Dairy and Food Council, 1962; mem. Mass. Outdoor Edn. Com., 1959; mem. Mass. White House Conf., 1961, Regional White House Conf., N.Y.C., 1961. Fellow Am. Sch. Health Assn., AAHPER (life fellow, nat. dir. for student services 1959-62, rep. to rep. assembly 1962-63, chmn. team sports sect. 1963); mem. Mass. Assn. Health, Phys. Edn. and Recreation (v.p. health sect. 1958, Honor award 1966), Eastern Dist. Assn. for Health, Phys. Edn. and Recreation (treas. 1962-63, mem. nominating com. 1963), U.S. (umpiring chmn. 1962-63), N.E.

(selection chmn. 1961), Boston (past pres.) field hockey assns., Nat., Eastern (mem. planning com. 1962-63) assns. phys. edn. for coll. women, Mass. State Coll. Assn., Mass. Assn. for Deans and Counselors, Internat. Conf. for Phys. Edn. Coll. Women (mem. embassy com. 1961—), New Eng. Health Edn. Assn., Internat. Platform Assn., Pi Lambda Theta. Clubs: Boston University Women's Faculty (life), Boston Sargent. Author: Field Hockey: an Internation Team Sport, 1963; (with Mackey) Women's Team Sports Officiating, 1964; also articles. Home: Bible Hill Rd Warner NH 03278

MACKIE, JAMES WATSON, electronic systems exec.; b. Nanticoke, Pa., Oct. 31, 1930; s. James William and Mary Josephine (Davenport) M.; A.B., Dickinson Coll., 1953; postgrad. U. Pa., 1955, 59, Temple U., 1959-60; m. Nellie Ray Banfield, Dec. 11, 1954; children—Mary deVera, James Jeffrey, Thomas Garrison, Blythe Anne. Creditman, Hercules, Inc., Wilmington, Del., 1955-59; asst. sec.-treas. Delmarva Power & Light Co., Wilmington, 1959-67; trust officer Wilmington Trust Co., 1967-74; pres., chief exec. officer, dir. Security Electronics Systems, Inc., Wilmington, 1974—; dir. Security Communications, Ltd., Mackie Assos.; instr. Del. State Police Acad. Asst. treas., trustee Children's Home, Inc., 1960—; pres. Brookmeade Civic Assn., 1963-67. Served with USNR, 1953-55; ETO. Mem. Am. Soc. Indsl. Security, Del. Assn. Police, Del. Assn. Alarm Cos. (dir.). Co-writer Del. alarm legislation. Home: 2626 Tanager Dr Brookmeade Wilmington DE 19808 Office: 2807 Market St Wilmington DE 19802

MAC KINNON, GEORGE E., U.S. judge; b. St. Paul, Apr. 22, 1906; s. James Alexander Wiley and Cora Blanche (Asselstine) MacK.; student U. Colo., 1923-24; LL.B., U. Minn., 1929; m. Elizabeth Valentine Davis, Aug. 20, 1938; children—Catharine Alice, James Davis, Leonard Davis. Admitted to Minn. bar, 1929, U.S. Supreme Ct. bar; asst. gen. counsel Investors Syndicate, Mpls., 1929-42; engaged pvt. practice law, 1949-53, 58-61; elected mem. Minn. Ho. of Reps. from 29th dist., 1935, 36, 38, 40; mem. 80th Congress from 3d Minn. Dist., 1947-49; U.S. dist. atty. for Minn., 1953-58; spl. asst. to U.S. atty. gen., 1960; gen. counsel, v.p. Investors Mut. Funds, Mpls., 1961-69; judge U.S. Ct. Appeals for D.C. Circuit, 1969—. Republican nominee for Gov. of Minn., 1958. Served to comdr. U.S. Navy Air Force, 1942-46. Cited for meritorious service by comdr. Air Force U.S. Atlantic Fleet. Mem. Am., Minn., Hennepin County bar assns., Delta Tau Delta, Phi Delta Phi. Republican. Episcopalian. Clubs: Masons; Mpls.; Lawyers (Washington). Author: Minn. State Reorganization Act, 1939; State Civil Service Law, 1939; Old Age Assitance Act, 1936. Home: 11333 Willowbrook Dr Potomac MD 20854 Office: US Court House Washington DC 20001

MAC KINNON, WALTER ALLAN, cons. exec.; b. Pitts., Dec. 16, 1929; s. Allan D. and Elizabeth A. (Bernkopf) MacK.; B.S., Lehigh U., 1951; C.L.U., Rutgers U., 1958; m. Diane Alington, Mar. 3, 1967; children—Kathryn Dale, Patricia Lee. Spl. agt. Prudential Ins. Co., Newark, 1951-55; pres. Aero Marine Corp., Chatham, N.J., 1955-60; partner Robert Heller & Assos., Cleve., 1960-65; sr. cons. Booz, Allen, Hamilton Co., Cleve., 1965-67; cons., dir. MacKinnon Assos., Cleve., 1967-69; pres. MacKinnon Co., Inc., Wayne, N.J., 1969—, also dir.; chmn., dir. Matrix Research Inc., Wayne, N.J. and N.Y.C.; instr. Centenary Coll., Hackettstown, N.J.; dir. MacKinnon & Gomperz Inc., Beta Delta Bldg. Bd. dirs. Lehigh U. Served with USAF, 1951-53. Mem. Am. Soc. C.L.U.'s, Newcomen Soc., U.S. C. of C., Chi Psi. Club: Univ. Home: 106 Buffalo Hollow Rd Lebanon Twp NJ 08826 Office: 1459 Route 23 Wayne NJ 07470

MACKLES, LEONARD, chem. research adminstr.; b. N.Y.C., Jan. 17, 1929; s. Joseph and Eva (Doroshkin) M.; B.S. in Chemistry, L.I. U., 1951; m. Dorothy Leibovich, Nov. 28, 1954; children—Joshua, Marion. Tech. dir. Chemclean Corp., N.Y.C., 1956-61; asst. dir. research Schenley Research Inst., N.Y.C., 1961-65; prin. research investigator Bristol-Myers Co., N.Y.C., 1965—. Served with U.S. Army, 1951-53. Fellow Am. Inst. Chemists, AAAS; mem. N.Y. Acad. Scis., Am. Chem. Soc., Soc. Cosmetic Chemists. Patentee in field. Home: 311 E 23d St New York City NY 10010

MAC KOUSE, EDWARD MARVIN, physicist, educator; b. Camden, N.J., Sept. 17, 1943; s. Herman Abraham and Anne (Segal) M.; B.S., Drexel U., 1966; M.A., U. Tex., 1970; m. Luba Mackouse, Nov. 19, 1972; 1 son, Jason Aron. Physics trainee U.S. Army Electronic Labs., Ft. Monmouth-N.J., 1962-66; asso. engr. Boeing Aircraft Co., Seattle, 1966-67; teaching asst., research asst. U. Tex., Austin, 1967-70; research asst. City U. N.Y., 1970-71; chief scientist ind. research, 1971—. Mem. Am. Phys. Soc. Discoverer elementary particle hyperon wave equation, and hyperon Mass formula. Office: PO Box 123 Brooklyn NY 11236

MACKOWIAK, ROBERT, physician, educator; b. Hazleton, Pa., May 13, 1938; s. Stanley John and Helen (Chuckra) M.; A.B. cum laude, U. Pa., 1960; M.D., Jefferson Med. Coll., 1964; m. Elaine DeCusatis, Sept. 5, 1964; children—Jeffrey, Lisa. Intern Meth. Hosp., Phila., 1964-65; resident in internal medicine Mercy Cath. Med. Center, Phila., 1968-71; instr. in physiology Jefferson Med. Coll., Phila., 1965-66, asso. prof. physiology, 1971—, asst. prof. medicine, 1972-76, asso. prof., 1976—, asst. dean, 1972-74, asso. dean, 1974—; vis. prof. biol. scis. Phila. Coll. Pharmacy and Sci., 1972—; cons. cardiovascular disease Mercy Cath. Med. Center of S.E. Pa., 1972—. Co-chmn. United Fund campaign, Phila., 1976, 77. Recipient Christian R. and Mary F. Lindbach Found. award for distinguished teaching Jefferson Med. Coll., 1968. Diplomate Am. Bd. Internal Medicine. Mem. AMA, Am. Assn. Higher Edn., Am. Fedn. Clin. Research, Pa., Phila. County med. socs., Biomed. Engring. Soc. (charter), Am. Physiol. Soc., Am. Heart Assn., Assn. Am. Med. Colls., Am. Ednl. Research Assn., Nat. Council Measurement in Edn., ACP, Am. Coll. Cardiology, Phila. Acad. Cardiology (founding), Phi Beta Kappa, Sigma Xi, Alpha Omega Alpha. Contbr. articles to profl. jours. Home: 189 Hillcrest Ave Philadelphia PA 19128 Office: 1025 Walnut St Philadelphia PA 19107

MACLEAN, JAMES PARLANE, III, lawyer; b. Bridgeton, N.J., Sept. 24, 1935; s. James Parlane and Mary (Newcomb) MacL.; A.B., Wheaton Coll., 1956; LL.B., U. Pa., 1960; m. Kathleen Elaine Peterson, Sept. 29, 1956; children—Susan, Carolyn. Admitted to N.J. bar, 1960; practiced in Haddonfield, N.J., 1960—; mem. firm Archer, Greiner & Read, 1965—; govt. appeal agt. Local Bd. 8, SSS, N.J., 1966-72; mng. partner MacLean Properties; dir. Eastern Data Industries, Inc., Spectron, Inc.; v.p., dir. Ocean Services Corp. Bd. dirs. Jr. Achievement Camden County, 1965—; trustee, chmn. exec. com., chmn. bd. Phila. Coll. Bible; trustee, v.p. Am. Scripture Gift Mission; trustee Am. Bd. Missions to Negro; trustee, chmn. exec. com. Morning Cheer, Inc.; trustee, v.p. D.M. Stearns Missionary Fund. Served as 2d lt. AUS, 1956-57. Mem. Am., N.J., Camden County bar assns., South Jersey C. of C. (chmn. bd.). Clubs: Union League (Phila.); Tavistock Country. Home: 630 Clinton Ave Haddonfield NJ 08033 also 2717 Wesley Ave Ocean City NJ 08226 Office: 1 Centennial Sq E Euclid Ave Haddonfield NJ 08033

MACLEOD, ROBERT ANGUS, educator; b. Athabasca, Alta., Can., July 13, 1921; s. Norman John and Eleanora Pauline (Westerhoff) M.; B.A., U. B.C., 1943, M.A., 1945; Ph.D., U. Wis., 1949; m. Patricia Rosemarie Robertson, Sept. 1, 1949; children—Douglas, Alexander, Kathleen, David, Michael, Susan. Asst. prof. biochemistry Queen's U., 1949-52; sr. biochemist Fisheries Research Bd. Can., Vancouver, B.C., 1953-60; asso. prof. microbiology Macdonald campus McGill U., 1960-64, prof., 1964—, chmn. microbiology dept., 1974—. Recipient Can. Soc. Microbiologists award, 1973. Fellow Royal Soc. Can.; mem. Am. Soc. Biol. Chemists, Am., Can. socs. microbiologists. Contbr. numerous articles to profl. jours. Home: 448 Greenwood Dr Beaconsfield PQ Canada Office: Macdonald Campus McGill U Ste Anne de Bellevue PQ Canada

MAC MILLAN, FRANCIS PHILIP, internist, gastroenterologist; b. Everett, Mass., June 19, 1937; s. Edward Joseph and Katherine H. (Hogan) MacM.: B.S., Boston Coll., Chestnut Hill, Mass., 1959; M.D., N.Y. Med. Coll., 1964; m. Nancy Marie Mirabello, May 18, 1963: children—Frank, Edward, Paul, John and Kerry (twins). Intern in internal medicine Boston City Hosp., 1964-65, resident in internal medicine, 1965-66; resident Boston VA Hosp., Jamaica Plain, Mass., 1966-67, in gastroenterology, 1967-68; practice medicine specializing in internal medicine and gastroenterology, Haverhill, Mass., 1968—; mem. staff Hale Hosp., 1968—, pres. med. staff, 1977-78; mem. staffs Lawrence Gen., Bon Secours, Anna Jacque, Amesbury hosps.; exec. dir. N.E. chpt. Am. Heart Assn. Served with USAR, 1968-75. Diplomate Am. Bd. Internal Medicine. Fellow A.C.P.; mem. AMA, Mass. Med. Assn., Am. Soc. Internal Medicine, Am. Soc. Gastrointestinal Endoscopy. Roman Catholic. Club: Exchange. Home: 75 Woodcrest Dr North Andover MA 01845 Office: 116 Summer St Haverhill MA 01830

MACMILLAN, LEONARD JOSEPH, bibliographer; b. Boston, Aug. 10, 1914; s. Leonard and Lillian Jeanette (Hantz) M.; m. Mary Elizabeth Sammon, Sept. 20, 1936. Book purchasing asst. Boston Pub. Library, 1932-43; asst., acquisition of newspapers and periodicals, 1947-62; spl. library asst., acquisition fgn. books and spl. library materials, 1963-66, asst. serials librarian, 1967-69; coding supr. F.W. Faxon Co., Westwood, Mass., 1969-73, supr. bibliog. reference dept., 1973—. Served with U.S. Army, 1943-46. Mem. Spl. Libraries Assn. (pres. Boston chpt. 1958-59, chmn. bus. and fin. div. 1962-63), New Eng. Library Assn. (treas. 1960-61), DAV (life mem.; chpt. adjutant). Democrat. Roman Catholic. Editor bus. fin. div. Spl. Libraries Assn. Bull., 1961-62; editor births deaths meg. notes Bull. Bibliography, 1973—; compiler Serials in Transition, 1977, 78; editor bibliog. manuals; contbr. articles to profl. jours. Home: 183 Belgrade Ave Roslindale MA 02131

MAC NEAL, EDWARD ARTHUR, econ. cons.; b. Winona Lake, Ind., Apr. 19, 1925; s. Kenneth Forsyth and Marguerite Josephine (Giroud) MacN.; student Harvard, 1943; B.A., U. Chgo., 1948, M.A., 1951; m. Priscilla Creed Perry, Dec. 27, 1952; children—Catherine Wright, Madeleine Creed. Exec. sec., Internat. Soc. Gen. Semantics, Chgo., 1947-51; staff cons. James C. Buckley, Inc., N.Y.C., 1951-55; market researcher Socony Mobil Oil Co., N.Y.C., 1955-58; research dir. O.E. McIntyre, Inc., N.Y.C., 1958-61; econ. cons., N.Y., 1956-66, Wayne, Pa., 1966—; adviser local govt. agys. Served with AUS, 1943-46; ETO. Mem. Am. Statis. Assn., Am. Sociol. Assn., Am. Assn. Airport Execs., Travel Research Assn., Travel Research Forum, Nat. Aviation Club. Club: Harvard (Phila.); Wings. Home: 348 Louella Ave Wayne PA 19087 Office: 175 Strafford Ave Wayne PA 19087

MACNEILL, JOHN SEARS, civil engring. co. exec.; b. Weehawken, N.J., Jan. 24, 1927; s. John Sears and Margaret (Stalee) MacN.; B.C.E., Cornell U., 1950; m. Elizabeth Frances Hazzard, July 15, 1950; children—Allen Donald, Billie Jean (Mrs. Frederic DeHart), Claudia Lynn (Mrs. Jerome Caretti). Field engr. John Kinner & Assos., Corning, N.Y., 1950-55; chief design engr. Alleghany Homes Corp., Homer, N.Y., 1955-57; pvt. practice cons. engr., Homer, 1957-75; pres. John S. MacNeill, Jr. Engring. Corp., Homer, 1975—. Mem. tech. adv. com. Tompkins-Cortland Community Coll., 1970—; v.p. Baden Powell council Boy Scouts Am.; drum maj. Caledonia Soc. Central N.Y. Served with USNR, 1944-46. Registered profl. engr., N.Y., Maine, N.H., Vt., Pa., Mont., W.Va.; registered land surveyor, N.Y., Maine, N.H. Mem. Nat. Soc. Profl. Engrs. (dir., chm. ethical practice com. N.Y. chpt. 1974—, pres. Central N.Y. chpt. 1972-74), ASCE, Soc. Am. Mil. Engrs., Cornell Soc. Engrs., Am. Cons. Engrs. Council (pres. Central N.Y. chpt. 1974-76), Water Pollution Control Fedn., Cortland County C. of C. (v.p.), Cortland County Licensed Land Surveyors (pres.). Republican. Congregationalist. Clubs: YMCA, Rotary, Wilderness Soc., Clan MacNeill Assn., Am. Scottish Found., N.Y. State Conservation Council. Home: 10 Balmoral Way Homer NY 13077 Office: 74 N West St Homer NY 13077

MACOVSKY, MORRIS SAUL, elec. co. exec., hydrodynamics physicist; b. Paterson, N.J., Jan. 21, 1920; s. John and Sussel (Rosenkrantz) M.; A.B. in Physics, Drew U., 1941; M.S. in Physics (Univ. fellow), Cath. U. Am., 1948, postgrad., 1955-56; postgrad. U. Md., 1948-55; m. Ruth Cohen, Sept. 5, 1943; children—Susan Judith, Louis Martin. Mathematician, geophysicist Coast & Geodetic Survey, Cheltenham, Md., 1942-44; physicist David Taylor Model Basin, Washington, 1946-57; cons. specialist, mgr. advanced systems engring. Westinghouse Co., Sunnyvale, Md., 1957-65, mgr. deep submergence programs, Balt., 1965-67, mgr. dept. ocean research and engring., Annapolis, Md., 1967-71, gen. mgr. oceanic div., v.p. def. and electronic systems center, 1971—. Bd. dirs. Balt. chpt. ARC, 1973—; sec. Anne Arundel Trade Council, 1974-75, v.p., 1975, pres., 1976—. Served with USN, 1944-46. Recipient Civilian Meritorious award David Taylor Model Basin, 1955, Order of Merit Westinghouse Co., 1972. Mem. Am. Phys. Soc., Annapolis C. of C. (dir. 1967-70), Sigma Xi, Sigma Phi. Jewish. Home: 764 Fairview Ave Annapolis MD 21403 Office: Westinghouse Oceanic Div POB 1488 Annapolis MD 21404

MAC PHAIL, LELAND STANFORD, JR., baseball exec.; b. Nashville, Oct. 25, 1917; s. Leland Stanford and Inez (Thompson) MacP.; B.A., Swarthmore Coll., 1939; m. Jane Hamilton, Nov. 18, 1939; children—Leland Stanford III, Alen H., Bruce T., Andrew B. With Kennett-Murray Co., Florence, S.C., 1939-40, Reading (Pa.) Baseball Club, 1941-42, Toronto (Ont.) Baseball Club, 1942-43; tchr. math. Deerfield (Mass.) Acad., 1943; gen. mgr. Kansas City (Mo.) Baseball Club, 1946-48; dir. player personnel N.Y. Yankees Baseball Club, 1949-58; gen. mgr. Balt. Orioles Baseball Club, 1959-66; pres. Balt. Baseball Club, Inc., 1960; exec. v.p., gen. mgr. N.Y. Yankees, 1966—. Served to lt. (j.g.) USN, 1944-46. Mem. Delta Upsilon. Office: Yankee Stadium Bronx NY 10451*

MAC PHERSON, JENNIFER BAILEY, sch. psychologist: b. Scranton, Pa., Apr. 22, 1943; d. Judson Edward and Muriel (Craft) Bailey; B.A., Elmira Coll., 1964; M.S., Syracuse U., 1967; m. Edward Alan MacPherson, Sept. 18, 1968. Psychologist, Cortland County (N.Y.) Bd. Coop. Ednl. Services, 1966-68; sch. psychologist Oswego (N.Y.) Pub. Schs., 1968-74, sr. sch. psychologist, 1974—; prin. asso. A/M Assos., Syracuse, N.Y., 1975—. Mem. Nat. Assn. Sch. Psychologists (charter), Oswego County Psychologists Assn. (sec.-treas. 1972-73), Common Cause, ACLU, Syracuse Symphony Guild, Friends of WONO. Republican. Roman Catholic. Poems included in anthologies, including New Dimensions, 1967, New Voices in the Wind, 1969, Moon Age Poets, 1970, Yearbook of Modern Poetry, 1971. Home: 907 Comstock Ave Syracuse NY 13210 Office: Edn Center Utica St Oswego NY 13126*

MACQUARRIE, HEATH NELSON, Canadian govt. ofcl.; b. Victoria, P.E.I., Can., Sept. 18, 1919; s. Wilfred and Mary (Mallard) M.; B.A., U. Man., 1947; M.A., U. N.B. 1949; postgrad. McGill U., 1951-53; hon. degree U. P.E.I., 1977; m. Jean Isabel Stewart, Dec. 27, 1949; children—Heather Jean, Flora Mary, Iain Heath. Tchr. pub. and high schs., P.E.I., 1936-43; asst. boys work sec. YMCA, Winnipeg, 1943-47; asst. prof. econs. and polit. sci. U. New Brunswick, 1947-49; lectr. polit. sci. McGill U., 1949-51, prof. polit. sci. and internat. relations, 1952; faculty Brandon Coll., 1951-55; lectr. Carleton U., 1963-64; vis. lectr. Mt. Allison U. (summer), 1948, 56, asso. prof. dept. polit. sci., 1978—; vis. lectr. Acadia U. (summer) 1949, 52, U. Man. (summer) 1954; Rockefeller research asso. U. Toronto, 1955-56; instr. internat. relations Carleton U., 1963-64. Weekly news analyst sta. CKX (radio), 1952-55; analyst and commentator pub. affairs programs Canadian Broadcasting Corp. Third v.p. Progressive Conservative Party of Can., 1953-55; elected constituency of Queens, 1957, 58, 62, 63, 65; parliamentary sec. external affairs, 1963, 72, 74; elected constituency of Hillsborough, Parliament of Can., 1968—. Del., gen. assembly UN, 1957-59, 63, 71. Recipient various research awards from Canadian Social Sci. Research Council John S. Ewart Found. and Research Associateship U. Toronto, State of Israel medal, 1977. Mem. P.E.I. Hist. Soc., Inter-Parliamentary Union, Canadian Commonwealth Parliamentary Assn. (chmn.), Commonwealth Parliamentary Assn. (del. gen. assembly Bahamas 1969), Canadian Inst. Internat. Affairs, Canadian Polit. Sci. Assn., Charlottetown C. of C., Confedn. Art Gallery and Mus. Conservative. Presbyterian. Mason. Author: The Conservative Party; (with others) Canada and the Third World. Editor: Memoirs of Sir Robert L. Borden. Contbr. numerous articles to various publs. Home: 100A Queen St Box 1894 Charlottetown PE Canada Office: House of Commons Ottawa ON Canada

MAC QUEEN, VIRGINIA, realtor; b. Portland, Maine, Jan. 16, 1916; d. William Godfred and Kathleen Elizabeth (Apt) Brodine; student Cornell U., 1956; m. Charles Everal MacQueen, Jan. 16, 1933 (dec.); 1 dau., Virginia Lee MacQueen Ford. Real estate saleswoman, 1937-45; founder, prin. MacQueen Realty Co., Rochester, N.Y., 1945—; motel assignee AID, Morocco, 1964. Recipient Best Advt. award N.Y. Times, 4 yrs. Mem. Motel Brokers Assn. Am., Real Estate Bd. Rochester (dir. 1952-55), Nat. Real Estate Womans Council (v.p., editor: The Woman Realtor, 1953-54), N.Y. State, Nat. assns. Realtors, Internat. Fedn. Realtors U.S.A.-Spain, N.Y. State Soc. Real Estate Appraisers. Club: Altrusa (v.p.). Home: 233 Overbrook Rd Rochester NY 14618 Office: 1551 Monroe Ave Rochester NY 14618

MACRI, GREGORY JOSEPH, JR., chem. co. exec.; b. Brockton, Mass., June 2, 1928; s. Gregorio Joseph and Adelaide Tyler (Brown) M.; ed. high sch.; m. Betty-Ann, July 23, 1950; children—Lynn-Diana, Cheryl-Ann, Gregory Joseph, Glen James, Garrison Tyler. Truck driver Boston Sand & Gravel Co., 1948-52; salesman Magnus Chem. Co., Garwood, N.J., 1952-66; pres. Keene Products Co. (N.H.), 1966—; incorporator, trustee Walpole Savs. Bank (N.H.), 1974—. Asso. gen. chmn. Shrine Maple Sugar Bowl Game Inc., 1973—; pres. Dollars for Scholars, 1977; incorporator Cheshire Hosp., Keene, 1976—; bd. dirs. Fall Mountain YMCA, Bellows Falls, Vt., 1976—; mem. Walpole Bicentennial Fund raising Com., 1976; mem. governing bd. trustees Citizens Scholarship Found. Am., 1978—. Mem. TAPPI, Paper Indsl. Mgmt. Assn., Antique Auto Club Am. Republican. Clubs: Lions, Elks, Masons, Shriners. Home: Box 474 Old Keene Rd Walpole NH 03608 Office: 47 Victoria St Keene NH 03431

MAC RURY, KING, mgmt. counselor; b. Manchester, N.H., Oct. 14, 1915; s. Colin H. and Lauretta C. (Shea) MacR.; A.B., Rollins Coll., 1938; postgrad. St. Anselms Coll., L.I. Coll. of Medicine, Princeton U.; 1 son, Colin C. Asst. personnel dir. Lily-Tulip Cup Corp., 1939; asst. dir. market research Ward Baking Co., 1940-41; staff mem. Nat. Indsl. Conf. Bd., 1941-43; cons. indsl. relations and orgn. planning McKinsey & Co., 1946-48; internal cons. Oxford Paper Co., 1949-50; installed and directed indsl. relations Champion Internation Co., 1950-51; pvt. practice mgmt. counselor, 1951—; lectr. Indsl. Edn. Inst., 1962-68, Mgmt. Center Cambridge, 1968-71, extension div. U. N.H., 1968—, also U. Bridgeport, U. Maine, extension program U. Conn.; coordinator mgmt. edn. extension div. U. Conn., 1964-68, Philippine Council Mgmt., 1969—, Econ. Devel. Found. Philippines, 1969—, Am. Metal Stamping Assn., 1969—; condr. mgmt. seminars for Asian Assn. Mgmt. Orgns. C.I.O.S., 1972. Mem. Indsl. Devel. Commn. Andover, 1957-58; manpower com. U.S. Dept. Labor Bus. Adv. Council, 1958-61. Served to lt. USNR, 1943-46. Mem. N.H. Dental Soc. (hon.). Author: Developing Your People Potential, Key to Success in Supervisory Management. Contbr. numerous articles in field to jours. Office: PO Box 215 Rye NH 03870

MACVANE, WILLIAM LESLIE, JR., surgeon, hosp. adminstr.; b. Portland, Maine, June 12, 1915; s. William Leslie and Bertha May (Achorn) MacV.; B.A., Williams Coll., 1937; M.D., Johns Hopkins U., 1941; m. Margaret Elizabeth Owen, June 4, 1949; children—Lesley MacVane Abbott, Margaret MacVane Murray, Forbes Owen. Intern, Union Meml. Hosp., Balt., 1941-42, resident in surgery, 1942-43; resident in surgery Maine Gen. Hosp., Portland, 1946-48; surgeon VA Hosp., Togus, Maine, 1948-49, resident in thoracic surgery VA Hosp., Oteen, N.C., 1953-55; practice medicine specializing in surgery, Portland, 1949-53, in gen. and thoracic surgery, 1955—; asst. city physician City of Portland, 1949-53; fellow thoracic surgery George Washington U. Hosp., Washington, 1953-54; dir. med. edn. Mercy Hosp., Portland, from 1965, pres. staff, 1962-65, trustee, from 1973; pres. staff Portland City Hosp., 1957-58, trustee, from 1967; cons. Maine Med. Center; now field rep. Hosp. Accreditation Program, Joint Commn. on Accreditation of Hosps., Chgo. Mem. city council, Portland, from 1967, mayor, 1971-72; trustee Greater Portland Transit Dist., from 1968; chmn. Portland Bicentennial Com. and Library Bldg. Com., from 1975; trustee Hebron Acad. Served from lt. to maj. M.C., U.S. Army, 1943-46. Decorated Bronze Star; licensed physician, Maine, Md., Fla.; diplomate Am. Bd. Surgery, Am. Bd. Thoracic Surgery. Fellow ACS; mem. Maine, Cumberland County (Maine) med. assns., Am. Coll. Chest Physicians, New Eng. Surg. Soc., Assn. Hosp. Med. Edn., Assn. Am. Med. Colls., Johns Hopkins Med. Surg. Soc., Pithotomy Club, Sigma Phi. Republican. Mem. United Ch. of Christ. Contbr. med. articles and editorials to profl. jours. Home: 25 Storer St Portland ME 04102 Office: 875 N Michigan Ave Chicago IL 60611

MACWILLIAMS, ROBERT WILSON, tool mfg. co. exec.; b. Norfolk, Va., Dec. 29, 1920; s. Walter Hixon and Birdella (Rothfus) MacW.; B.S. in Elec. Engring., U. Wash., Seattle, 1946, B.S. in Indsl. Engring., 1946, M.S. in Elec. Engring., 1950; m. Elizabeth Dawson; 1 son, Charles A. Plant engr. Allis Chalmers Co., 1947-49, Gen. Alloys Co., Boston, 1950-52; supr. mgmt. services Ernst & Ernst, C.P.A.'s, Boston, 1953-60; v.p. Great Falls Bleachery & Dye Works, Somersworth, N.H., 1961-63; pres., treas. Samuel Ward Mfg. Co., Boston, 1964-68; pres. Kingston Tool Co., Inc. (Mass.), 1969—, Worcester Pressed Aluminum Co. (Mass.), 1978—; treas. H&W Mold Inc., 1971—, Dan Wesson Arms, Inc., 1973—, D.W.A. Assos., Inc., 1975—. Treas., exec. com. Morgan Meml. Goodwill Industries; pres. Internat. Goodwill Found., 1967-69. Served with USN, 1942-45. Recipient Distng. Service award Morgan Meml. Goodwill Industries; registered profl. engr., Mass., Conn.; C.P.A., Mass. Mem. Nat. Soc.

Profl. Engrs. Republican. Unitarian. Club: Fort Hill (Boston). Home: 19-4 Eaglehead Terr Shrewsbury MA 01545 Office: 15 Hope Ave Worcester MA 01603

MADDEN, DONALD EDWIN, chiropractor; b. Ledgedale, Pa., Feb. 11, 1928; s. Joseph Edward and Regina Ruth (Reidy) M.; student Rutgers U., 1958-63; D. Chiropractic, Chiropractic Inst. N.Y., 1966; m. Rita Regina Tomasso, Jan. 29, 1967; stepchildren—Richard Albert Schiessl, Arnold Edward Schiessl. Chiropractic practice with George H. Lachnicht, Elizabeth N.J., 1966-71; pvt. chiropractic practice, Roselle Park, N.J., 1971—. Served with U.S. Army, 1946-47. Mem. N.J. Chiropractic Soc. (charter, fin. sec. 1972—), Chiropractic Soc. Union Middlesex Somerset Counties (pres. 1973-74), Am. Chiropractic Assn., Sacro Occipital Technique Soc. Roman Catholic. Club: K.C. Home and office: 449 Madison Ave Roselle Park NJ 07204

MADDEN, KENNETH CROMWELL, state supt. edn.; b. Orbisonia, Pa., Sept. 20, 1917; s. Charles A. and Elsie (Cromwell) M.; B.S., Shippensburg (Pa.) Coll., 1939; M.A., U. N.C., 1946; Ed.D., Pa. State U., 1950; m. Mabel Alice Failes, Apr. 26, 1942; children—Margaret Adele, Kay Eileen, Kenneth Cromwell, Judith Marie. From tchr. to supervising prin. Orbisonia pub. schs., 1939-49; exec. asst. citizenship edn. project Columbia Tchrs. Coll., 1952; supt. Seaford (Del.) Spl. Sch. Dist., 1952-67; supt. pub. instrn., Del., 1967—; prof. U. Del. extension, 1964—. Chmn. Del. Bd. Edn. Sch. Bldg. Survey, 1955; pres. Delmarva Ednl. TV, 1960-62; regional dir. Asso. Pub. Sch. Systems (N.J., Pa., Del., Md.), 1962-64; chmn. Del. Bd. Edn. Staffing Plan for Del. Schs., 1962-64; rep. of Del. to Tri-State Instructional Broadcasting Council, 1963; pres. Del. Sch. Study Council, 1965-67. Served to maj. U.S. Army, 1941-46; brig. gen. Del. N.G., 1969—. Decorated Bronze Star; recipient Conspicuous Service medal Del., 1958; 1st winner Sussex County Distinguished Educator award, 1964; Pub. Service award VFW, 1956. Mem. Nat., Del. (dir. 1956-60) edn. assns., Del. Chief Sch. Officers Assn. (pres. 1958), Am. Legion (past post vice comdr.). Club: Kiwanis (pres. Seaford 1961). Author articles in field. Home: 1 Beaver Dam Rd Seaford DE 19973 Office: PO Box 697 Dover DE 19901

MADDEN, SISTER MARY CAROLYN, counselor; b. Saranac Lake, N.Y., Oct. 28, 1928; d. Francis Thomas and Lillian Mary (Colburn) Madden; B.S., Fordham U., 1964; M.S., State U. N.Y., Plattsburgh, 1969, postgrad. in adminstrn. and supervision, 1976—. Entered Religious Sisters of Mercy, 1945; tchr. parochial schs., N.Y., 1949-61; prin. Comdr. J.J. Shea Sch., N.Y.C., 1961-63, St. John's Sch., Plattsburgh, 1963-66, St. Agnes Sch., Lake Placid, N.Y., 1975-77; counselor St. Margaret Mary's Sch., Bronx, N.Y., O.L.V. Acad., Dobbs Ferry, N.Y., and St. Agnes Sch., Lake Placid, 1966-75; substitute St. Bernard's Sch., Saranac Lake, and Saranac Lake Middle Sch., 1977; arts in edn. coordinator Center for Music, Drama and Art, Lake Placid, 1977—; asst. to chaplain Drug Center, Raybrook, N.Y., 1972-76; individual counselor. Mem. prins. adv. council Diocese of Ogdensburg, 1976-77, mem. bishop's fund com., 1978—; mem. vis. com. Middle States Assn. Commn. on Secondary Schs., 1971. Recipient service certificate Center Advancement of Developmentally Disabled, 1977. Mem. Am. (del. conv. 1975), N.Y. State personnel and guidance assns., Cath. Sch. Adminstrs. Assn. N.Y. State, Nat. Cath. Edn. Assn., Cath. Daus. of Am. Home: RFD 1 Box 351 Saranac Lake NY 12983 Office: Center for Music Drama and Art Lake Placid NY 12946

MADDOX, GENE, JR., theatre exec.; b. Oran, Algeria, Dec. 26, 1944 (parents Am. citizens); s. Gene and Incarnation (Hernandez) M.; came to Can., 1969; student U. Colo. 1964-66, York U., 1970-73; m. Susan Talsa Ross, Jan. 23, 1969; 1 son, David Jonathan Gregory. Mgmt. trainee Travelers of Can., Toronto, 1969-71; mng. dir. Metro Internat. Caravan, Toronto, 1971-73; exec. dir. Theatre Ont., Toronto, 1974—. Pres. Circus 1976, 1975-76. Served with USAF, 1966-68. Mem. Canadian Conf. of the Arts. Roman Catholic. Home: 35 Four Winds Dr Downsview ON M3J 1K7 Canada Office: 8 York St Toronto ON M5J 1R2 Canada

MADEHEIM, HUXIEY, cons. engr., coll. prof.; b. N.Y.C., Nov. 11, 1905; s. Rudolph F. Madeheim and Anna (Dennison) M.; ed. M.E., Stevens Inst. Tech., 1926; M.B.A., N.Y. U., 1931; m. Leila Higginson, Jan. 18, 1930; children—Sandra Jane, James Frederick, Huxley Thomas; m. 2d, Rhoda Barrows, 1955. Cons. engr., 1931—; specialties include air conditioning, pvt. power plants and all mech. layout problems, work simplification projects, indsl. advt. consultation, tech. reports for ins. cos., attys.; mem. dept. bus. adminstrn. Coll. City N.Y., 1931-66, dept. mgmt. Baruch Coll., U. City N.Y., 1966-71; now prof. emeritus mgmt. Baruch Coll. City U. N.Y.; course in air conditioning Stevens Grad. Sch.; sr. manpower utilization cons., W.M.C.; cons. on layout and material handling. Registered profl. engr., N.Y., Conn., Pa.; registered safety engr., Calif.; certified safety profl. Mem. Am. Soc. M.E., Soc. Advancement Mgmt., Nat. Assn. Profl. Engrs., Am. Soc. Safety Engrs., N.Y. State Soc. Professions, Acad. Mgmt., Soc. Automotive Engrs., Nat. Fire Protection Assn., ASTM. Author: Organization and Management in Industry and Business; Plant Layout and Materials Handling; Industrial Marketing, also numerous articles; Printers' Ink monthly article on Industrial Advertising; Modern Warehouse Methods. Co-editor: Readings in Organization and Management; International Business Articles and Essays; Basic Management Series. Home: 321 E 18th St New York City NY 10003

MADEIRA, SHELDON SPENCER ROTHERMEL, former state edn. ofcl.; b. Manheim, Pa., June 6; s. Charles Calvin and Laura (Rothermel) M.; A.B., Elizabethtown Coll.; M.S., Pa. State U.; Ph.D., U. Pa.; m. T. Pauline Green, July 26, 1939. Dir. developmental reading program, state testing program, Pa., 1957-58. State Bur. of Grad. and Profl. Edn., 1957-62; adviser State Curriculum Commn., State Med. Bd., State dental, pharmacy bds. Active Salvation Army, Overseas Blind, Care, Project Hope. Served to maj. USAAF, 1942-45. Mem. NEA, Pa. Edn. Assn., Am. Soc. Curriculum Devel., Phi Delta Kappa. Republican. Contbr. articles to profl. jours. Home: 417 Arlington Rd Camp Hill PA 17011

MADGEY, JAMES JOSEPH, guidance counselor; b. Phila., Mar. 26, 1949; s. Julia C. M.; B.S., Millersville State Coll., 1969, M.Ed., 1973; postgrad. Temple U., Pa. State U. Math. tchr. pub. schs., Lititz, Pa., 1969-73, Phila., 1973-75, guidance counselor, 1975—. Bd. dirs. Paul Matthews Washington High Sch. for Emotionally Disturbed Adolescents. Mem. Am., Pa., Greater Phila. (treas.) personnel and guidance assns., Am., Pa. (membership chmn.) sch. counselor assns., Am., Pa., Phila. fedn. tchrs. Home: 1527 Rodman St Philadelphia PA 19146

MADHYASTHA, VISWESWARA LAXMINARAYANA, physicist; b. Mysore State, India, Feb. 18, 1932; s. Neelawara L. and Laxmi Gauri (Shastri) M.; came to U.S., 1956, naturalized, 1969; B.Sc. with honors (Univ. scholar 1950-56), U. Bombay, 1954, M.Sc., 1956; Ph.D., N.Y. U., 1973; m. Rosemarie Adelheid Schulze, June 6, 1964; children—Tara Maja, Mythili Lakshmi, Maitreya Visweswara. Grad. asst. physics Western Res. U., 1956-58; teaching fellow U. Alta. (Can.), 1958-60; research asst. U. Toronto, 1960-61; instr. Concord Coll. (W.Va.), 1961-62; asst. prof. St. Peter's Coll., Jersey City, 1962-64; mem. faculty Fairleigh Dickinson U., Teaneck, N.J., 1965—, asso. prof. physics, 1976—, asst. chmn. dept., 1957-59. Recipient Founder's Day certificate N.Y. U., 1974. Mem. Am. Phys. Soc., Am. Astron. Soc., Nat. Geog. Soc. Democrat. Hindu. Contbr. articles to profl. jours. Home: 759 Orangeburgh Rd River Vale NJ 07675 Office: 1000 River Rd Fairleigh Dickinson Univ Teaneck NJ 07666

MADIGAN, MARTIN JOSEPH, statistician; b. Rochester, N.Y., June 13, 1933; s. Martin and Agnes Margaret (Shoniker) M.; B.S., Rochester Inst. Tech., 1965, M.S., 1968; m. Elizabeth Jane Lindsay, Jan. 20, 1954; children—James, Cynthia, Jonathan, Martin. Quality assurance engr. Stromberg Carlson Corp., Rochester, 1963-67; mgr. local facilities Xerox Corp., Rochester, 1967-69, sr. mktg. analyst, Webster, N.Y., 1969-71, sr. quality control engr., statistician, 1971—; faculty Rochester Inst. Tech. Grad. Statistics Program, 1968—. Democratic Party aide, chmn. Town Ethics Com., 1974-76. Served with USAF, 1951-55. Registered profl. engr., Calif. Mem. Am., Rochester socs. quality control. Roman Catholic. Club: Holy Name Men's. Author: A Collation of Modern Acceptance Sampling Plans, 1973; Larson's Binomial-A Nomographic Approach to Common Acceptance Sampling Problems, 1977. Home: 198 Fox Chapel Rd Henrietta NY 14467 Office: 800 Phillips Rd Webster NY 14580

MADIGAN, RITA DUFFY, counselor; b. N.Y.C., Jan. 22, 1919; d. Anthony Edward and Mary Margaret (Feichter) Duffy; A.B., Good Counsel Coll., 1940; M.S., U. Bridgeport, 1963, postgrad. guidance, 1971; postgrad. (Nat. Assn. Social Studies scholar), Hawaii U., 1965; m. John Callanan Madigan, May 1, 1943; children—John, James, Paul. Tchr. English. Bridgeport (Conn.) Sch. System, 1960-63, 69-71, career edn. coordinator, 1971-74, guidance counselor, 1974—; tchr. English, social studies, team leader humanities Project pub. schs., Birmingham, Mich., 1963-69; bd. dirs. Mental Health Clinic, Painesville, Ohio, 1955-59; cond. career edn. workshops for tchrs., 1972-74; cons. career edn., New Haven, 1973-74; dir. Project Reentry Counseling Center, 1973-78; mem. Bridgeport C. of C. Com. for Career Edn., 1976-78; counselor Birth Right, 1976-78. Instr. cardiopulmonary resuscitation Am. Heart Assn., ARC, Fairfield County, Conn., 1973-78. Licensed real estate broker, Conn. Mem. Alumna Assn. Coll. White Plains U. Bridgeport, AAUW, Bridgeport, Conn., Nat. edn. assns., Am., Conn. personnel and guidance assns., Am. Sch. Counselors Assn. Republican. Roman Catholic. Clubs: Westport (Conn.) Cotillion, Tashua Ladies Golf League. Author career edn. curricula, kindergarten to 8th grade, 1972-74. Home: 44 Chatham Dr Trumbull CT 06611

MADISON, DANA EUGENE, computer specialist, res. army officer; b. S.I., Oct. 29, 1949; s. William Dean and Betty June (Crabtree) M.; B.S., State U. N.Y. at Brockport, 1972, M.A., 1975; m. Donna Ruth Small, Oct. 8, 1970. Served as enlisted man U.S. Army, 1972-75, commd. 2d lt., 1975, advanced through grades to capt., 1977; computer specialist, Ft. Sam Houston, Tex., 1975-76, chief automatic data processing team, 1976-77, cons./spl. projects officer, 1977—; plans and policies officer, Ft. Detrick, Md., 1977-78; asst. v.p. MIS, Inc., Bradford, Pa., 1978. Decorated Army Commendation medal; certified secondary math. tchr., N.Y. Mem. Math. Assn. Am., Brockport State Math. Club (pres. 1969-70), Brockport State Computer Sci. Club. Democrat. Episcopalian. Home: PO Box 181 Derrick City PA 16727 Office: MIS Inc 387 East Main St Bradford PA 16701

MADJID, ABDUL HAMID, physicist, educator; b. Tashkent, USSR, Aug. 16, 1922; s. Abdul and Emilia (Rauf) M.; came to U.S., 1966; B.A., Cornell U., 1945; Dr.sc.nat., Swiss Fed. Inst. Tech., Zurich, 1966; m. Anna Neukomm, Dec. 31, 1958; children—Torai, Hamid. With Afghan Nat. Bank, 1948-62, dir. purchasing and tech. planning, 1952-62; with Swiss Fed. Inst. Tech., 1962-66, sr. research asso., 1962-68; mem. faculty Pa. State U., 1966—, asso. prof. physics, 1969—, dir. Thermionic Emission Lab., 1966—; treas. Ann. Conf. Phys. Electronics, 1975-77. Mem. Am., Swiss phys. socs., Am. Assn. Physics Tchrs., Internat. Platform Assn., Gamma Alpha. Author, patentee in field. Home: 326 Harris Dr State College PA 16801 Office: Pa State Univ 104 Davey Lab University Park PA 16802

MADLE, ROBERT ALBERT, program mgr.; b. Phila., June 2, 1920; s. Vincent Robert and Mary Virginia (Kidwell) M.; B.S., Drexel U., 1951, M.B.A., 1953; m. Billie Franklin Lindsay, Nov. 7, 1943; children—Robert, Richard, Jane, Mary Anne. Asst. to sales mgr. Masland Duraleather, Phila., 1951-53; asst. to dir. indsl. relations Chadbourne Hosiery, Charlotte, N.C., 1953-54; personnel and credit mgr. Shaw Mfg. Co., Charlotte, 1954-56; personnel research specialist U.S. Army, Washington, D.C., 1956-59, research psychologist, program mgr. U.S. Navy, Washington, 1959—. Served with U.S. Army, 1942-46. Guest of honor World Sci. Fiction Conv., Miami, 1977. Mem. Sci. Fiction Writers Am., Washington Sci. Fiction Assn., First Fandom (pres.). Contbr. articles to Sci. Fiction and sports mags. Home: 4406 Bestor Dr Rockville MD 20853 Office: Naval Sea Systems Command (ATN:047C) Washington DC 20362

MADOLE, DONALD WILSON, lawyer; b. Elkhart, Kans., July 14, 1932; student Kans. State Tchrs. Coll., 1950-52; B.S., U. Denver, 1959, J.D., 1959; m. 2d, Juanita Marie Weisbach, July 12, 1975. Vice pres. Mountain Aviation Corp., Denver, 1958-59; admitted to Colo. bar, 1960, D.C. bar, 1971; trial atty. FAA, Washington, 1960-62; sr. warranty adminstr. Am. Airlines, Tulsa, 1962-63; chief hearing and reports div., atty. adviser CAB, Washington, 1963-66; partner firm Speiser, Krause & Madole, N.Y.C. and Washington, 1966—. Pres., Aerial Application Corp., Burlingame, Cal., 1968-69; v.p. Environmental Power Ltd., Pitts., 1972—; dir. Phazar Inc., San Francisco, 1969-73, Mills Estate Realty, San Francisco, 1958-72, Unitrade Ltd., Washington, Bus. Ins. Mgmt. Inc., Bethesda, Md., Environmental Power Ltd., Pitts., Pa. Pocahontas Coal Co., Pitts., Entertainment Capitol Corp., N.Y.C. Adviser, U.S. Govt. delegation Internat. Civil Aviation Orgn., 1965; U.S. Govt. rep. Aircraft Inquiry, Montreal, Que., Can., 1964. Mem. alumni com. U. Denver, 1973—. Served to comdr. USNR, 1953-57. Recipient Outstanding Performance award FAA, 1961; Meritorious Achievement award Am. Airlines, 1962; Outstanding Performance awards CAB, 1963-65; Fed. Govt. Outstanding Pub. Service award, Jump-Meml. Found., 1966. Mem. D.C., Fed., Am., Colo. bar assns., Am. Trial Lawyers Assn., Lawyer-Pilots Assn., Nat. Aviation Club, Nat. Press Club, Phi Delta Phi, Phi Mu Alpha. Author: Textbook of Aviation Statues and Regulations, 1963; International Aspects of Aircraft Accidents, 1963; CAB, Aircraft Accident Investigation, 1964. Office: 1216 16th St NW Washington DC 20036

MADORA, ALBERT WILLIAM, mech. engr., county ofcl., pub. works adminstr.; b. Wilmington, Del., July 14, 1921; s. Frank J. and Julia (Denest) M.; B.M.E., Drexel U., 1952; m. Violet Rose Glezman, June 5, 1945; children—William, A.J., Christine Madora Mercante, Michele Ann, Thomas, Paul. Engring. asst. to engr. in charge Diesel Engine Research Lab., Baldwin-Lima-Hamilton Corp., Eddystone, Pa., 1944-45, engring. asst. to engr. head of hydraulic research, 1945-52, project engr., 1952-56, sr. engr. Hydraulic Research Lab., 1956-72, rep. of co. at field tests and installations in Europe, 1956-72, dir. hydraulic lab. tests and research, 1956-72; engring. asst. to pres. and gen. mgr. James Leffel & Co., Springfield, Ohio, 1972; dir. New Castle County (Del.) Dept. Pub. Works, 1973—. Pres. Community Civic Assn., New Castle, 1951-67; commr. to Delaware River and Bay Pilot Assn., 1964-68; instl. rep. St. Peter's council Boy Scouts Am., 1954-59. Recipient County Achievement award, 1974. Mem. Am. Pub. Works Assn., ASME. Democrat. Roman Catholic. Club: Cavaliers Country. Home: 139 Woodshade Dr Newark DE 19702 Office: 2701 Capitol Trail Newark DE 19711

MADOW, PAULINE REICHBERG (MRS. SEYMOUR STEPHEN MADOW), editor, writer; b. Irvington, N.J.; d. Jacob and Sonja (Goldin) Reichberg; A.B., Rutgers U., A.M., 1963; m. Seymour Stephen Madow, June 28, 1953; 1 dau., Patricia Leslie. Asso. editor Current Biography, H.W. Wilson Co., N.Y.C., 1959-61; chief copy editor Ency. Internat. Grolier, N.Y.C., 1961-63; historian Oral History Research office, Columbia U., 1968—. Author: The Peace Corps, 1964; Recreation in America, 1965. Contbr. articles to The Nation, Current Biography, Ency. Internat., Book Week, Modern Age, and others.

MADSEN, JOHN EDWARD, JR., physician; b. Plainfield, N.J., Apr. 14, 1942; s. John Edward and Evelyn Louise (Wilson) M.; B.A., U. N.C., 1964; M.D., Cornell U., 1968; m. Louise A. Belssner, Apr. 24, 1971; children—Carrie Koss, Kelly Armstrong. Intern, Northwestern U. Med. Center, Chgo., 1969, resident in internal medicine, 1974; postdoctoral fellow in gastroenterology Yale U. Med. Sch., 1976; practice medicine, specializing in gastroenterology, New London, Conn., 1976—; staff Lawrence and Meml. Hosp., New London, mem. physicians quality rev. com. Served to lt. comdr. USN, 1970-72. Diplomate Am. Bd. Internal Medicine, Am. Bd. Gastroenterology. Mem. A.C.P., Am. Soc. Gastrointestinal Endoscopy, Conn., New London County med. socs. Club: Rotary. Contbr. articles to med. jours. Office: 342 Montauk Ave New London CT 06320

MAELAND, ARNULF JULIUS, phys. chemist; b. Akrehamn, Norway, Apr. 21, 1933; s. Erling Magnus and Dagny Marie (Nielsen) M.; arrived U.S., 1952; naturalized, 1957; B.A., Augsburg Coll., 1955; M.S., Tufts U., 1959; Ph.D., U. Vt., 1965; m. Gunhild Helgesen, June 18, 1955; children—Lynn, David, Kerry. Research asso. Tufts U., Medford, Mass., 1959-62; prof. chemistry Worcester (Mass.) Poly. Inst., 1968-75; sr. research chemist Allied Chem. Corp., Morristown, N.J., 1975—; sr. vis. fellow Inst. for Atomic Energy, Kjeller, Norway, 1974-75. Recipient NATO post-doctoral fellowship, Kjeller, Norway, 1965-66; NAS-NRC postdoctoral fellowship, Watertown, Mass., 1966-68. Mem. Am. Chem. Soc., Am. Phys. Soc., Internat. Assn. for Hydrogen Energy, Sigma Xi. Lutheran. Contbr. over 40 articles to profl. jours., textbooks. Home: 8 Cornell Dr Succasunna NJ 07876 Office: Allied Chem Corp Columbia Rd & Park Ave Morristown NJ 07960

MAESTRONE, GIANPAOLO, veterinary research adminstr.; b. Urgnano, Italy, Jan. 31, 1930; s. Frank and Elizabeth (Bresciani) M.; came to U.S., 1956, naturalized, 1960; D.V.M., U. Milan (Italy), 1951; m. Sophia Esposito, Sept. 30, 1956; children—Elizabeth, Elena, Frank. Asso. prof. infectious diseases U. Milan, 1952-56; Fulbright exchange prof. vet. hygiene Iowa State U., Ames, 1953-54; research asso. Animal Med. Center, N.Y.C., 1957-61; sr. microbiologist Squibb Inst. Med. Research, New Brunswick, N.J., 1961-66; sr. scientist, animal health research Hoffmann-LaRoche, Nutley, N.J., 1966-75, asst. group chief, 1976—. Diplomate Am. Coll. Veterinary Microbiologists. Fellow N.Y. Acad. Medicine (asso.); mem. AVMA, Am. Coll. Veterinary Microbiology, Am. Soc. Microbiology, Indsl. Veterinary Assn. Contbr. articles in veterinary microbiology to profl. jours. Home: 7 Roderick Ave Staten Island NY 10305 Office: Hoffmann LaRoche Kingsland St Nutley NJ 07110

MAFFET, VERE, waste handling co. exec.; b. Millstone, W.Va., Jan. 27, 1928; s. Ralph D. and Arvella E. M.; B.A. with honors, Marietta Coll., 1952; M.S. in Inorganic Chemistry, Purdue U., 1954; m. Lucille Bradley, Aug. 17, 1973; children—Vere, Mark. Research chemist duPont Co., Parlin, N.J., 1954-65; tech. dir. Peerless Photo Products, Shoreham, N.Y., 1965-71; pvt. practice consulting, St. Louis, 1971-75; v.p. Organic Recycling, Inc., West Chester, Pa., 1975—; lectr. in field. Served with U.S. Navy, 1946-47. Mem. Am. Chem. Soc., AAAS, Ind. Acad. Sci., Sigma Xi, Phi Beta Kappa. Patentee in field. Home: 691 E Boot Rd West Chester PA 19380 Office: 967 S Matlack St West Chester PA 19380

MAFFONGELLI, JOSEPH ANTHONY, physician; b. Paterson, N.J., Apr. 4, 1910; s. Ralph and Joan (D'arco) M.; B.S., Georgetown U., 1930, M.D., 1932; m. Joy P. Viviano, Dec. 6, 1939; children—Joan, Joseph Anthony, Ralph. Intern, Georgetown U. Hosp., Washington, 1932-33; resident St. Joseph's Hosp., Reading, Pa., 1933-34; clin. asst. dermatology Paterson (N.J.) Gen. Hosp., 1934-36, asst. attending, 1936-38, asso. attending, 1938-48, attending 1948-70, cons. dermatologist Greater Paterson Gen. Hosp., Wayne, N.J., 1970-77, emeritus, 1977—; cons. dermatology Valley View Sanatorium, Preakness, N.J., 1950-70, St. Vincent's Hosp., Montclair, N.J., 1973-77. Served to 1st lt. M.C., AUS, 1942-43. Diplomate Am. Bd. Dermatology. Mem. Am. Acad. Dermatology, N.J. State, Passaic County med. socs. Roman Catholic. Club: Hamilton (Paterson, N.J.). Home: 20 Glenwood Rd Upper Montclair NJ 07043 Office: 543 Valley Rd Upper Montclair NJ 07043

MAGARGAL, LARRY ELLIOT, ophthalmologist; b. Bethel, Conn., June 14, 1941; s. Rodney N. and Caroline (Von Bieren) M.; B.A. with honors, Temple U., 1965, M.D. (Eli Lilly awardee), 1969; m. Helga Louise Olsen, Apr. 22, 1967; children—Lauren Elizabeth, Larry Elliot, Goeffrey Robb. Intern Thomas Jefferson U. Hosp., Phila., 1969-70, resident in ophthalmology, 1970-73, clin. instr. ophthalmology, 1973—; clin. instr. ophthalmology, Temple U., Phila., 1975-76, asst. prof., 1976-78, med. dir., co-dir. retinal service, 1976-78; clin. asst. ophthalmology Wills Eye Hosp., Phila., 1974-76, asst. surgeon, co-dir. retinal vascular service, 1976—; dir. dept. ophthalmology St. Luke's and Children's Med. Center, Phila.; practice medicine, specializing in ophthalmology, Phila., 1973—. Research fellow Temple U., 1967; Pharm. Mfrs. Assn. fellow, 1968; Phila. County Med. Soc. scholar, 1967-69; retinal diseases fellow Wills Eye Hosp., 1975-76. Diplomate Am. Bd. Ophthalmology, Nat. Bd. Med. Examiners. Fellow Am. Acad. Opthalmology and Otolaryngology, A.C.S.; mem. AMA, Pa., Phila. County med. socs., Assn. Physicians and Surgeons, Research to Prevent Blindness, Am. Soc. Contemporary Ophthalmology, Coll. Physicians Phila., Ophthalmic Club Phila., Am. Intra-ocular Lens Soc. Contbr. articles to profl. publs. Home: 9601 Milnor St Philadelphia PA 19114 Office: Retinal Service Wills Eye Hosp 1601 Spring Garden St Philadelphia PA 19130

MAGARIAN, ROBERT JOHN, elastomers and plastics cons.; b. Worcester, Mass., Aug. 23, 1947; s. Robert and Nellie Therasa (Klimarski) M.; B.S. in Chem. Engring., Worcester Poly. Inst., 1969; m. Suzanne Sharigian, June 30, 1974. Prodn. supr. E.I. DuPont de Nemours & Co., Inc., 1969-71; process engr. Globe Mfg. Co., 1972-74; sales engr. Minn. Mining & Mfg. Co., W. Caldwell, N.J., 1976-78; sales mgr. Fluorocarbon Co., Pine Brook, N.J., 1978—; owner Freespan Cons., Rockaway, N.J., 1974—; cons. to various elastomer cos. Mem. Democratic Adv. Bd., Westport, Mass., 1974-76. Mem. Am. Inst. Chem. Engrs., Am. Chem. Soc. Home: 3 Monroe Pl Rockaway NJ 07866 Office: 337 Change Bridge Rd Pine Brook NJ 07058

MAGDOFF, SAMUEL, ednl. adminstr.; b. N.Y.C., Aug. 9, 1915; s. Max and Leah (Rubinstein) M.; student U. Mich., 1932-35; m. Laura J. Silver, Dec. 23, 1963; 1 dau., JoAnn M. With Elektra Film Prodns. Inc. (now Mag. Film Form Inc.), N.Y.C., 1947-50, 53-74, pres., 1962-74; film editor Bllko Show, 1951-52; lectr. Columbia U., 1960, Sch. Visual Arts, 1962-63, Pa. State U., 1964, Pratt Inst., 1964-66, Ohio U.; exec. dir., trustee N.Y. Phoenix Schs. Design, 1972-74; asso. dean Parsons Sch. Design New Sch., N.Y.C., 1974—. Trustee Screen Cartoonist Guild; bd. dirs. Save-A-Marriage, Yueh Lung Shadow Theatre; pres. Inst. for Human Devel. and Research. Served with U.S. Army, 1942-45. Decorated Bronze Star with four oak leaf clusters. Recipient numerous internat., nat. film awards. Mem. Film Producers Assn. (exec. bd., pres.), Soc. Motion Picture and TV Engrs., Art Dirs. Club N.Y., Am. Film Inst. Contbr. chpt. to book. Home: 41 Central Park W New York City NY 10023 Office: 66 Fifth Ave New York City NY 10011

MAGEE, ALBERT JAMES, financial cons.; b. Phila., May 26, 1920; s. Albert J. and Kathryn (Harley) M.; B.S. in Mech. Engring., U. Pa., 1942; M.B.A., Rutgers U., 1954; m. Stella Note, July 16, 1948; children—William, Samuel. With Curtiss-Wright Corp., Woodridge, N.J., 1942-67, asst. dir. finance, 1966-67; v.p. adminstrn. Airco Industrial Gases div. Airco, Inc., Murray Hill, N.J., 1967-74; v.p. finance Universal Tech. Inc., Clifton, N.J., 1974-75; pres. UTEC Internat. Corp., Clifton, 1975-77; cons., Fair Lawn, N.J., 1977—. Served with USNR, World War II. Mem. Fin. Execs. Inst., Nat. Assn. Accountants, Beta Gamma Sigma. Club: Ridgewood Country. Home: 11 Ramapo Terr Fair Lawn NJ 07410 Office: PO Box 252 Fair Lawn NJ 07410

MAGEE, JOHN, investment counsellor; b. Malden, Mass., Nov. 24, 1901; s. John and Louise (Church) M.; student Mass. Inst. Tech., 1920-23; m. Alice Eleanor Alderson, Oct. 20, 1928 (div. December 1933); 1 son, Alderson; m. 2d, Elinor Averre Trafford, July 2, 1936; children—John IV, Louise Cynthia, Abigail Anne. Asst. to sales mgr. vacuum cleaner dept. B.F. Sturtevant Co., Hyde Park, Mass., 1924-25; cost estimating, spl. prodn. dept. Stanley Works, New Britain, Conn., 1925-27; advt. mgr. Maxim Silencer Co., Hartford, Conn., 1927-28; account exec. William B. Remington Advt. Agy., Springfield, Mass., J.D. Bates Advt. Agy., Springfield, 1928-30; pres. Lewis & Magee, Inc., Springfield, 1930-35; owner Trafford Co., Springfield, 1935-42; investment counsellor, market research, Springfield, 1942—; sr. technician Stock Trend Service, Springfield, 1953-56; pres., treas. John Magee, Inc., 1960—; mdse. and design cons. Brooks Bank Note Co., Springfield; editor-in-chief Our Home Town; dir. radio program The Voice of Springfield; staff mem., tech. adv. Future Springfield, Inc. Mem. Republican City Com., 1944-48; pub. relations com. Town of Springfield, 1944-45; dir. East Forest Park Civic Assn., 1942-49. Author, illustrator: The General Semantics of Wall Street, 1958; author (with Robert D. Edwards) Technical Analysis of Stock Trends, 1948; Wall Street-Main Street-and You, 1972. Home: 96 Maplewood Terr Springfield MA 01108

MAGGI, VICTOR OSCAR, power engring. cons.; b. Buenos Aires, Argentina, Feb. 24, 1925; s. Jose Victor and Maria Antonia (Cruz) M.; came to U.S., 1960, naturalized, 1968; Marine Engr., Argentine Nat. Nautical Acad., 1948; Naval Architect, Argentine Superior Sch. War and Engring., 1951; Nuclear Engr., Argentine Nat. Atomic Commn., 1958; m. Raimonda Jesse, Apr. 9, 1969. Design engr. Foster Wheeler Corp., Livingston, N.J., 1964-66; sr. start up engr. Gen. Electric Corp., N.Y.C., 1966-67; sr. start up engr. Combustion Engring. Inc., Windsor, Conn., 1967-74, spl. cons., 1974—. Served to capt. Argentine Navy, 1960—. Registered profl. engr., N.J. Mem. Argentine Astronomy Soc., Liga Naval Argentina, ASME, Soc. Naval Architects and Marine Engrs., Nat. Soc. Profl. Engrs. Patentee marine cycloidal propeller, 1950. Home: 169 Mt Pleasant Ave West Orange NJ 07052 Office: Combustion Engring Inc Windsor CT 06095

MAGLIO, JOHN FRANCIS, info. processing adminstr.; b. Boston, June 30, 1949; s. John and Madeline (Spinetto) M.; B.S., Northeastern U., 1972, M.S., 1975; M.S., Mass. Inst. Tech., 1975; m. Joann Cafarella, Apr. 10, 1976. Airport design Howard Needles Tammen & Bergendoff, Boston, 1969-70; engring. asst. H.W. Lochner, Inc., Boston, 1971-72; U.S. Dept. Transp. fellow Northeastern U., 1973-74; research asst. data need study Mass. Inst. Tech., Cambridge, 1973-74, ops. mgr. New Eng. Energy Mgmt. Info. System, 1975-78, dir. East Campus Computing Facility, sr. programming analyst Info. Processing Services, 1978—; cons. Am. Energy Services, RAND Corp., Mass. Energy Policy Office, Conn. Energy Dept., Maine Office Energy Resources. Vol., New Eng. Consortium on Environ. Protection. Mem. Assn. Computing Machinery, Math. Assn. Am., ASCE, Boston Audio Soc., MIT Microprocessor Users Group. Roman Catholic. Club: MIT Faculty. Contbr. articles to profl. jours. Home: 30 Dolphin Ave Revere MA 02151 Office: MIT Bldg E52 Room 025 Cambridge MA 02139

MAGNUSON, JOHN ANDREW, wine co. exec.; b. N.Y.C., May 2, 1942; s. Gosta R. and Amy Louise M.; A.B., Wittenberg U., 1964; postgrad. N.Y. U., 1964-66; m. Louise Van Natta Jackson, Mar. 4, 1967. Pres., owner Summer Sch. Transp. Service Inc., 1958-65; sales mgr. Standard Brands Inc., N.Y.C., 1967-69, Premier Wine Distbrs. Inc., N.Y.C., 1969-72; state sales mgr. Taylor Wine Co., N.Y.C., 1972-77, asst. to nat. sales mgr., 1977—; lectr. mktg., wine appreciation St. John's U., U. Akron, Towson State Coll., 1970—; lectr. in field. Served with U.S. Army, 1966-67. Presbyterian. Home: 187 Stamford Ave Stamford CT 06902 Office: Taylor Wine Co 425 Park Ave New York NY 10022

MAGNUSON, PAUL ANDREW, educator; b. Newton, Mass., Apr. 10, 1939; s. Harold Einer and Fannie Irwin (Campbell) M.; B.A., Brown U., 1961; Ph.D., U. Minn., 1969; m. Elizabeth Hatt Campbell, Sept. 4, 1965; children—Elise, Katherine. Asst. prof. English, U. Pa., Phila., 1969-74; asso. prof. N.Y. U., N.Y.C., 1976—, dir. grad. studies, 1974-78. Served to lt. (j.g.) USN, 1961-63. Mem. Modern Lang. Assn. Am., Wordsworth-Coleridge Assn. Author: Coleridge's Nightmare Poetry, 1974; rev. editor The Wordsworth Circle, 1972—. Home: 19 Franklin Pl Maplewood NJ 07040 Office: Dept English New York Univ New York City NY 10003

MAGNUSON, PETER ALFRED, veterinarian; b. Bklyn., Oct. 26, 1945; s. Emil Lauritz and Ann Christina (Olson) M.; D.V.M. (David K. Johnston scholar, N.Y. Regents scholar), Cornell U., 1969. Asso., Sunrise Animal Hosp., Rockville Center, N.Y., 1969-74, Roosevelt Raceway, Westbury, N.Y., 1973—; chief veterinarian Bide-A-Wee Home Assn., N.Y.C., 1975; asso. White Plains (N.Y.) Animal Hosp., 1975-76; staff veterinarian Kent Animal Shelter, Calverton, N.Y., 1974-75; asso. Rego Park (N.Y.) Animal Hosp., 1975-76. Mem. AVMA, N.Y., L.I. veterinary med. assns., Am. Animal Hosp. assn. Democrat. Lutheran. Home: 2835 Natta Blvd Bellmore NY 11710 Office: Lake Animal Hosp 278 Portion Rd Lake Ronkonkoma NY 11779

MAGUIRE, ANDREW, congressman; b. Columbus, Ohio, Mar. 11, 1939; s. Bruce and Ruth Maguire; B.A., Oberlin Coll., 1961; Ph.D., Harvard, 1966; m. Margaret Lydia Green, June 29, 1968; 1 son, James Bruce (Jay). Adviser polit. and security affairs State Dept., also mem. U.S. delegation to UN Gen. Assembly, 1966-69; dir. Jamaica devel. program (N.Y.C.), 1969-72; cons. nat. affairs div. Ford Found.; mem. 94th-96th Congresses from 7th N.J. Dist. Mem. nat. campaign staff Kennedy for Pres., 1960, mem. staff Citizens for Goldberg Paterson, 1970, campaign dir. Bergen County for Gov. Brendan Byrne, 1973; dir. Washington Citizenship seminar sponsored by Nat. YMCA and YWCA, summer 1966, active Soc. for Religion in Higher Edn., 1966—, New Mems. Caucus, 1975—, Common Cause, 1970—. Mem. Phi Beta Kappa, Danforth fellow, Woodrow Wilson fellow, Fgn. Area Tng. fellow. Recipient Achievement award Jamaica C. of C., 1970; named Outstanding Young Man of Am., 1971. Democrat. Author: Toward 'Uhuru' in Tanzania: The Politics of Participation, 1969. Contbr. to Protest and Power in Black Africa, 1970. Home: 112 S Irving St Ridgewood NJ 07450 Office: 1314 Longworth House Office Bldg Washington DC 20515

MAGUIRE, JAMES PETER, interior and indsl. designer; b. Teaneck, N.J., Mar. 14, 1938; s. James Bernard and Alice Muriel (Thorsen) M.; student in Math., U. South, 1956-58, in pub. speaking Am. Acad. Dramatic Arts, N.Y.C., 1959-60, in interior design Parsons Sch. Design, 1961-64; children—Deidre Gabrielle, Brownyn Alexandre. Designer, Michel Harmouch, Beirut, 1964; sr. designer Arthur Lawrence, Assos., Cleve., 1965-67; v.p., head N.Y.C. office Ford and Earl Design Assos., 1967-75; partner Dwork/Maguire, Inc., N.Y.C., 1977—; mem. faculty Parsons Sch. Design, 1977-78; lectr. in field. Recipient Hexter award S.M. Hexter Corp., 1969, Indsl. Design Mag. award, 1973. Designer interiors Jet Star Airplane, included in Mus. Modern Art permanent design collection, N.Y.C., 1972; organizer RCA corp. art collection. Home: 230 Central Park S New York City NY 10019 Office: 425 E 51st St New York City NY 10022

MAGUIRE, JOHN JOSEPH, archbishop; b. N.Y.C., Dec. 11, 1904; s. James and Ellen (Shea) M.; student Cathedral Coll., St. Joseph's Sem., Dunwoodie, Yonkers, N.Y.; LL.D., Fordham U., Manhattan Coll., 1961. Ordained priest Roman Catholic Ch., 1928; asst. St. Patrick's Ch., Manhattan; asst. chancellor Archdiocese of N.Y., 1940-45, vice chancellor, 1945-47, chancellor of Archdiocese, 1947-53, vicar gen., 1953-59; consecrated bishop, 1959; aux. bishop of N.Y., 1959-65; co-adjutor archbishop of N.Y., 1965—; titular bishop of Tabalta. Private chamberlain to Pope Pius XII, 1945, domestic prelate, 1948. Office: 1011 First Ave New York City NY 10022

MAGUIRE, ROBERT ALAN, educator; b. Canton, Mass., June 21, 1930; s. Frederick William and Ruth Spalding (Plunkett) M.; A.B., Dartmouth Coll., 1951; M.A., certificate Russian Inst., Columbia U., 1953, Ph.D., 1961. Instr. in Russian, Duke U., 1958-60; asst. prof. Russian, Dartmouth Coll., 1960-62; asst. prof. Russian lang. and lit. Columbia U., 1962-66, asso. prof., 1966-70, prof., 1970—, chmn. dept. Slavic langs., 1977—; vis. lectr. Ind. U., 1961, 66, 69; mem. adv. bd. Nat. Endowment for the Humanities. Served with U.S. Army, 1953-55. Guggenheim fellow, 1969-70; Am. Council Learned Socs. fellow, 1967. Mem. Am. Assn. Advancement of Slavic Studies (dir. 1977—), Am. Assn. Tchrs. Slavic and East European Langs., AAUP, Modern Lang. Assn. Am., Polish Inst. Arts and Scis., PEN Club, Kosciuszko Found. Author: Red Virgin Soil: Soviet Literature in the 1920's, 1968; Gogol from the Twentieth Century; Eleven Essays, 1974, and others; co-translator: Petersburg (Andrei Bely), 1978; The Survivor and Other Poems (Tadeusz Rozewicz), 1976. Mem. editorial bd. Teaching Lang. through Lit., 1972-77, mng. editor, 1978—; mem. editorial bd. Slavic Review, 1966-69; mem. editorial adv. bd. Princeton Essays in Literature, 1972-77. Contbr. articles to profl. jours. Home: 560 Riverside Dr Apt 20-H New York City NY 10027 Office: Dept Slavic Langs Columbia U New York City NY 10027

MAHAFFY, PERRY ROGER, nursing adminstr.; b. Warren, Pa., Aug. 28, 1938; s. Perry Roger and Kathleen (Jenkins) M.; R.N., Edward J. Meyer Meml. Hosp., 1960; B.S.N., U. Buffalo, 1962; M.S.N., Yale U., 1964; Ph.D., Rochdale Coll., 1972; m. Veronica Lois Holmer, Aug. 11, 1962; children—Kimberly Autumn, Kelly Allison, Perry R., Michael Sullivan. Staff nurse, head nurse E.J. Meyer Meml. Hosp., Buffalo, 1960-62; research asso. Yale Child Study Center, New Haven, 1963-64; asst. prof. State U. N.Y., Buffalo, 1964-66; supr. U.S. Naval Hosp., Boston, 1966-68; dir. nursing Warren (Pa.) State Hosp., 1968-70; dir. nursing affairs Hamot Med. Center, Erie, Pa., 1970—. Mem. exec. com. Erie County Emergency Med. Services, 1977-78; chmn. personnel tng.; mem. exec. com. Regional Adult Learning Skills Center, Erie, 1972—; bd. dirs., exec. com. Lake Area Health Edn. Center, 1975-76. Served to lt. USNR. Mem. Nat. League Nursing, Am., Pa. hosp. assns., Am. Soc. Nursing Service Adminstrs., Am. Coll. Hosp. Adminstrs. Home: 23 Constitution Dr Chadds Ford PA 19317

MAHAFFY, REID ALEXANDER, mfg. co. exec.; b. Argyle, N.Y., Aug. 30, 1914; s. David Alexander and Susan Ester (Williams) M.; B.S., Northeastern U., 1938; postgrad. Bklyn. Poly. Inst., 1946-47; m. Margaret E. Fardelmann, Dec. 30, 1944 (div.); children—Evann Sue, Anne, Margaret, Reid Alexander, Susan; m. 2d, Josephine B. Ives, Oct. 16, 1971. Asst. mgr. packaging machinery dept. Union Camp, N.Y.C., 1946-49; dir. engring. Standard Packaging Corp., N.Y.C., 1949-56; pres. Mahaffy & Harder Engring. Co., Totowa, N.J., 1956-75, chmn. bd., 1975—; tech. guest speaker Am. Mgmt. Assn., 1971. Served to lt. (j.g.) USNR, 1943-46. Mem. Am. Soc. M.E. Clubs: Montclair (N.J.) Golf; Orient (N.Y.) Yacht. Patentee in field. Home: 52 Warren Pl Montclair NJ 07042 Office: Furler St Totowa NJ 07512

MAHAJAN, SUBHASH, materials scientist; b. Gurdaspur, India, Oct. 4, 1939; s. Ram Chand and Kunti Devi M.; came to U.S., 1961, naturalized, 1967; B.Sc. (Merit scholar), Panjab U., Chandigarh, India, 1959; B.E. (Merit scholar), Indian Inst. Sci., Bangalore, 1961; Ph.D., U. Calif., Berkeley, 1965; m. Sushma Sondhi, Sept. 3, 1965; children—Sanjoy, Sunit, Ashish. Research asst. Lawrence Radiation Lab., Berkeley, 1961-65; research metallurgist U. Denver, 1965-68; research fellow Atomic Energy Research Establishment, Harwell, Eng., 1968-71; mem. tech. staff Bell Labs., Murray Hill, N.J., 1971—. Deutscher Akademischer Austauschdienst fellow Inst. für Metallphysik, U. Göttingen (W. Germany), 1976. Mem. Am. Inst. Metall. Engrs., Sigma Xi. Home: 310 River Rd Chatham Twp NJ 07928 Office: Bell Laboratories Murray Hill NJ 07974

MAHANAND, DERSH, biochemist; b. Guyana, S. Am., Jan. 6, 1931; s. Noday and Tulsia (Bhodoo) M.; came to U.S., 1954; naturalized, 1964; student Cambridge (Eng.) U., 1948-50, Oxford (Eng.) U., 1950-53, U. Tex., 1954-55; A.B., Carthage Coll., 1957; M.A., Howard U., 1959; m. Marilyn Fleming, Aug. 10, 1963. Research asst. Georgetown U. Med. Sch., 1959-62; chief biochemist neurology Children's Hosp., Washington, 1963-72; chief biochemist No. Va. Tng. Center for Mentally Retarded, Fairfax, 1972-74; asso. pediatrics Georgetown U. Hosp., 1974—; cons. Children Brain Research Found. Fellow Am. Inst. Chemists; mem. Am. Chem. Soc., AAAS, Am. Assn. Mental Deficiency, Am. Assn. Clin. Chemists. Author: Serotonin in Down's Syndrome, 1973; The Autistic Syndromes, 1976. Home: 513 Bonifant Rd Silver Spring MD 29094 Office: 3800 Reservoir Rd NW Washington DC 20007

MAHDI, ALLAH EROS, sci. co. exec.; b. Washington, Dec. 7, 1941; s. Odin Peace and Ocea (Allat) M.; B.S., Howard U., 1963, M.S., 1965; Ph.D., Cath. U., 1968. Pres., chief energy research specialist Cosmic-Master Sci. Corp., Washington, 1974—; lectr. in field. Recipient Superior Service medal HEW, 1973. Mem. Nat. Small Bus. Assn., Nat. Rifle Assn., Am. Security Council, Kappa Alpha Psi. Democrat. Club: Playboy Internat. Address: Cosmic-Master Sci Corp 907 6th St SW Washington DC 20024

MAHER, ALLAN E., city ofcl.; b. Newcastle, N.B., Can., Feb. 16, 1938; s. Holt A. and Dorothea S. (Ferguson) M.; grad. New Eng. Inst., 1958; m. Helen K. Payne, June 13, 1959; children—Dawne Lynne, Michael, Heather, John, Alana, Derek. Sec.-treas. Maher's Funeral Homes Ltd., Dalhousie, N.B., 1960—; mayor Town of Dalhousie, 1971-77; pres. Campbellton-Dalhousie Municipal Airport Ltd., 1971—. Mem. N.B. Funeral Dirs. and Embalmers Assn. (past pres.). Mem. Liberal party. Roman Catholic. Club: Rotary (past pres.). Address: PO Box 338 Dalhousie NB E0K 1B0 Canada

MAHER, EDWARD WILLIAM, state ofcl.; b. New Haven, Conn., Dec. 21, 1927; s. Edward Andrew and Evelyn Mildred (Fitzgerald) M.; B.A., U. Conn., 1949; M.P.A. (Grad. fellow), Syracuse U., 1952; m. Marie Therese Kane, July 14, 1951; children—Brian, Jeffrey, Gary. Mgmt. analyst Conn. Dept. Fin. Control, Hartford, 1952-54, chief budget examiner, 1956-60, chief of budget, 1960-64; planning cons. N.Y. Devel. Budget, Albany, 1964-66; asst. v.p. U. Conn., Storrs, 1966-71, vis. lectr., 1966-71; exec. dept. commr. N.Y. Dept. Social Services, Albany, 1971-75; commr. Conn. Dept. Social Services, 1975—; cons. N.Y. Civil Service Commn. Served to 1st lt. USAF, 1954-56. Mem. Am. Soc. Pub. Adminstrn. (pres. Conn. chpt.), Am. Pub. Welfare Assn., Conn. Council Pub. Welfare Adminstrs., Council State Govts. (Eastern conf.). Democrat. Roman Catholic. Home: 7 Chestnut Circle Old Saybrook CT 06475 Office: 110 Bartholomew Ave Hartford CT 06115

MAHER, JOHN FRANCIS, personnel exec.; b. Sea Cliff, N.Y., Jan. 23, 1932; s. John Francis and Anna Elizabeth (Flannery) M.; B.S. in Indsl. Relations, Syracuse U., 1958, M.A. in Communications, 1968; m. Jane Esther LesVeaux, Feb. 7, 1958; children—Kathleen, Lynn, Tracy, Joann, John. Employee relations specialist Gen. Electric Co., Syracuse, N.Y., 1960-65; dir. job devel. employment Urban League Syracuse, 1965-67; indsl. relations specialist Singer Co., Auburn, N.Y., 1967-68; dir. human resources and govtl. affairs, corp. staff Garlock Inc., Rochester, 1968—, mgr. orgnl. devel., corp. staff, 1968-72, v.p. personnel, mech. rubber div., Palmyra, N.Y., 1972-75; dir. orgnl. devel. corporate staff, Rochester, 1975-78; mgr. indsl. relations Graham Mfg. Co., Batavia, N.Y., 1978—; adj. prof. bus. and mgmt. Rochester Inst. Tech., 1969—; adj. prof. mgmt. Genesee Community Coll., 1977—; clin. lectr. State U. N.Y., Buffalo, 1975—; pres. J.F.M. Assos., mgmt. cons. Mem. planning bd. Town of Perinton (N.Y.), 1973-74, chmn., pres. Perinton Residents Orgn., 1971-75. Served with USAF, 1950-54. Mem. Am. Soc. Tng. Dirs., Center Orgnl. Devel. Author: Self Appraisals, 1974. Home: 14 Crow Hill Dr Fairport NY 14450 Office: 1250 Midtown Tower Rochester NY 14604

MAHONEY, DAVID JOSEPH, JR., corp. exec.; b. N.Y.C., May 17, 1923; s. David J. and Laurette (Cahill) M.; grad. LaSalle Mil. Acad., 1941; B.S., U. Pa., 1945; student Columbia, 1946-47; m. Barbara A. Moore, May 12, 1951 (dec.); children—David Joseph III, Barbara Ann; m. 2d, Hildegarde Ercklentz Merrill, June 24, 1978. Advt. v.p. Ruthrauff & Ryan, Inc., N.Y.C., 1949-51; founder, pres. David J. Mahoney, Inc., N.Y.C., 1951-56, also dir.; pres., dir. Good Humor Corp., Bklyn., 1956-61; exec. v.p., dir. Colgate-Palmolive Co., 1961-66; pres., chief exec. officer Canada Dry Corp., 1966-68; pres. Norton Simon, Inc., 1968—, chief exec. officer, 1969—, chmn. bd., 1970—; mem. adv. bd. Continental Airlines; dir. N.Y. Telephone Co., Chris Craft. Bd. dirs. United Negro Coll. Fund; chmn. bd. Phoenix House, Charles A. Dana Found.; chmn. bd. trustees Am. Health Found.; trustee, U. Pa., N.Y. U. Recipient Patriot's award, Torch of Liberty, Horatio Alger award, Col. I. Robert Kriendler Leatherneck award, Corporate Leadership award, 1976. Mem. Boys' Club of N.Y. Alumni Assn. (hon. life). Home: 740 Park Ave New York City NY 10021 Office: 277 Park Ave New York City NY 10017

MAHONEY, PATRICK EDWARD, hosp. adminstr.; b. Syracuse, N.Y., Sept. 20, 1934; s. Peter Christopher and Bernice Ellen (Delosh) M.; A.B., Niagara U., 1956; M.P.A. in Health Services Adminstrn., N.Y. U., 1977. Asst. then asso. adminstr. affiliation adminstr. Maimonides Med. Center-Coney Island Hosp. Affiliation, 1971-77; asso. hosp. dir. State Univ. Hosp., Downstate Med. Center, Bklyn., 1977-78; asso. exec. dir. Coney Island Hosp., Bklyn., 1978—. Served with Med. Service Corps, U.S. Army, 1956-63. Decorated Army Commendation medal. Mem. Am. Coll. Hosp. Adminstrn., Am., Catholic hosp. assns., Am. Acad. Health Adminstrs., Am. Pub. Health Assn., N.Y. Assn. Ambulatory Care (dir.). Roman Catholic. Office: Ocean and Shore Pkwys Coney Island Hosp Brooklyn NY 11235

MAHONEY, THOMAS ANTHONY, accountant, fin. exec.; b. Yonkers, N.Y., June 23, 1935; s. Thomas Joseph and Irene (Lennon) M.; B.S., Fordham U., 1961; m. Celia Holovach, Sept. 1, 1974. Audit mem. Arthur Young & Co., N.Y.C., 1961-65; fin. v.p. John P. Maguire & Co., N.Y.C., 1965-69; mng. partner Mahoney, Cohen & Co., N.Y.C., 1969—. Lectr. accounting Manhattan Coll; cons. Eastern band of Cherokee Indians, Cherokee, N.C., 1973—. Served with USMC, 1954-57, C.P.A., N.Y. Mem. Am. Inst. C.P.A.'s, N.Y. Soc. C.P.A.'s (mem. fin. planning and control com.), Nat. Assn. Accountants. Republican. Roman Catholic. Club: N.Y. Athletic. Home: 301 E 78th New York City NY 10021 Office: 330 Madison Ave New York City NY 10017

MAILIS, JOHN MICHAEL, passenger service co. exec.; b. Athens, Greece, Aug. 21, 1944; s. Michael N. and Themis N. (Gatou) M.; student various schs. in Athens, Paris; diploma in Bus. Adminstrn., LaSalle Extension U.; m. Dec. 21, 1977; children—Mary Petris, Michael. Catering mgr. Nassau (Bahamas) Airport Caterers Ltd., 1962-63; mgmt. trainee Brit. Overseas Airways Corp., London, 1963-65; mgr. catering U.S. and Can., Olympic Airways, N.Y.C., 1965-69; dir. dining, commissary and inflight services Overseas Nat. Airways, Inc., Jamaica, N.Y., 1969-78, asst. v.p. passenger service, 1978; asst. v.p. passenger service United Air Carriers, Inc., Jamaica, 1978—. Mem. Am. Mgmt. Assn., Inflight Food Service Assn. Greek Orthodox. Home: 7 Cornell Ct South Smithtown NY 11787 Office: 147-27 175th St Jamaica NY 11430

MAINERO, FRANK ARTHUR, advt. agency exec.; b. Boston, Aug. 21, 1940; s. Arthur and Ann Doris (Cigna) M.; A.B., Colby Coll., 1962; M.S., Boston U. Grad. Sch. Pub. Communications, 1965; m. Catherine Veronica McCoy, Jan. 30, 1966; children—Kimberly Ann, Kristen Elyce, Stephen Arthur, Kathryn Leigh. Mktg. trainee Procter & Gamble, Boston, 1965-66; account exec. B.B.D.O. Advt. Agy., N.Y.C., 1966-68; v.p. Hill & Knowlton, Inc., N.Y.C., 1968-73; sr. v.p. Prel Corp., Saddle Brook, N.J., 1973-76; v.p., dir. pub. affairs J. Walter Thompson Co., N.Y.C., 1976—. Mem. Wyckoff (N.J.) Twp. Recreation Commn., 1970-71; deacon Roman Catholic Ch.; bd. dirs. Western Hills YMCA, 1971-73. Mem. Pub. Relations Soc. Am. Clubs: Wyckoff Jaycees (pres. 1970-71, Outstanding Jaycee of Year 1970), Indian Trails (Franklin Lakes, N.J.). Home: 210 Wayfair Circle Wyckoff NJ 07481 Office: J Walter Thompson Co 420 Lexington Ave New York City NY 10017

MAIORIELLO, RICHARD PATRICK, otolaryngologist; b. Phila., Mar. 17, 1936; s. Gesumino Theodore and Angelina (Del Rossi) M.; A.B., U. Pa., 1960; M.D., Jefferson Med. Coll., 1964; M.S., Thomas Jefferson U., 1972; children—Gabriel, Angela, Richard. Served as col. U.S. Air Force, 1963-78; intern Keesler Hosp., 1965-67; chief flight medicine USAF Base, Bitburg, Germany, 1965-68; resident in otolaryngology Thomas Jefferson Hosp., Phila., 1968-71, 72-73; fellow in physiology Thomas Jefferson U., 1971-72; dir. med. edn. Andrews AFB, 1974-78; asso. prof. uniformed services Univ. Health Scis., 1978—; cons. otolaryngology to Suregon Gen., 1977—. Served with USN, 1954-58. Decorated Air Force Commendation medal. Diplomate Nat. Bd. Med. Examiners, Am. Bd. Otolaryngology. Mem. Am. Acad. Otolaryngology, Am. Acad. Facial Plastic and Reconstructive Surgery, Am. Assn. Cosmetic Surgery, Vail Cosmetic Surg. Soc., A.C.S. Democrat. Roman Catholic. Club: Centurion. Home: 1320-1 Vanderberg Dr Andrews AFB MD 20335 Office: Dept Otolaryngology MGMC Andrews AFB MD 20331

MAITLEN, DEAN JEROLD, pub. opinion research orgn. exec.; b. Jenera, Ohio, Apr. 14, 1933; s. Edward H. and Elizabeth (Arras) M.; B.S., Ball State U., 1955; M.B.A., U. Fla., 1957; postgrad. U. Pa., 1968; m. Betty Stoutamire, Aug. 13, 1960; children—Steven, Mark. Dir. mktg. and research Perry Publs. and TV, West Palm Beach, Fla., 1957-62; v.p. William Wahl Assos. Research Agy., West Palm Beach, 1962-63; co-founder Metro Market Surveys, Princeton, N.J., 1963-66; v.p. Gallup Internat., Princeton, 1967-69; v.p. Gallup Orgn., Princeton, 1970-76, exec. v.p. sales and mktg., 1976—; mdm. bd. dirs. Gallup Orgn., Inc. Mem. Am. Mktg. Assn., Am. Assn. Pub. Opinion Research, Travel Research Assn. Episcopalian. Co-originator multi-client consumer survey research services. Home: 67 Robert Rd Princeton NJ 08540 Office: 53 Bank St Princeton NJ 08540

MAJESKE, LEONARD MICHAEL, educator; b. Detroit, Jan. 11, 1921; s. Samuel and Victoria (Rudy) M.; B.Aero. Engring., U. Detroit, 1943; M.Aero. Engring., Catholic U. Am., 1949; 4 children. Instr. aero. engring. Cath. U. Am., Washington, 1948-49; instr. engring. mechanics U. Detroit, 1949-53; pub. relations dir. Packard Motor Co., Detroit, 1954; Midwest editor Design News Mag., Detroit, 1955; editor Profl. Engring. News of Mich., 1956; cons., 1956-59; prof. math. Greater Hartford (Conn.) Community Coll., 1969—; cons. in engring. Served with USAF, 1944-46. Registered profl. engr., Mich., Ala. Unitarian. Contbr. articles to tech. jours. Home: 263 Grindlebrook Rd South Glastonbury CT 06073

MAJEWSKI, FRANK WALTER, ins. co. exec.; b. Warsaw, Poland, Jan. 4, 1922; s. Walter and Josephine (Michalski) M.; came to U.S., 1922, naturalized, 1940; B.B.A., St. John's U., 1947; m. Kathleen Curley, Aug. 13, 1949; children—Raymond, Kenneth. Sr. auditor, Jos. Fraggatt & Co., N.Y.C., 1947-51; audit mgr. Allstate Ins. Co., Newark, 1951-53, CIT Fin. Corp., N.Y.C., 1951-65, also treas. subs. Patriot Life Ins. Co., N. Am. Accident & Health Ins. Cos.; sr. cons. Frank Lang Assos., N.Y.C., 1965-67; founder, pres. A & M. Mgmt., Cranford, N.J., 1967—, also Auten Majewski, Monley & Assos., Cranford; co-founder, v.p. R.M. Donaldson Assos., 1967—, also dir. Active Boy Scouts Am.; pres. Colonial Gardens Civic Assn., 1960-64. Served with U.S. Army, 1943-46. Republican. Roman Catholic. Clubs: St. Vincent DePaul Soc., K.C. Home: 14 Denman Dr Fords NJ 08863

MAK, TY TSE-FAI, real estate exec.; b. Canton, China, Oct. 15, 1936; s. Kam Tai and Yuk Yue M.; came to U.S., 1957; B.Chem. Engring., City Coll., N.Y., 1962; M.Engring., N.Y. U., 1967; M.B.A., U. Conn., 1970; m. Susan P. Chan, Feb. 6, 1966; children—Julie, Ken, Aimee. Research engr. Gen. Foods, Tarrytown, N.Y., 1964-66; sr. project engr. Clairol Inc., Stamford, Conn., 1966-70; pres. Kam-Ross Properties, Inc., Stamford, 1970—. Chmn., founder Chinese Assn. of Fairfield County, 1974-75. Mem. Conn. Assn. Realtors, Stamford Bd. Realtors (dir.). Patentee in field. Home: 25 Chapin Ln Stamford CT 06903 Office: 917 High Ridge Rd Stamford CT 06905

MAKADOK, STANLEY, mgmt. cons.; b. N.Y.C., Mar. 30, 1941; s. Jack and Pauline (Speciner) M.; B.M.E., Coll. City N.Y., 1962; M.S. in Mgmt. Sci., Rutgers U., 1964; m. Lorraine Edith Dubin, Aug. 24, 1963; 1 son, Richard. Bus. systems analyst Westinghouse Electric Corp., Balt., 1964-65; project engr., corporate cons. Am. Cyanamid Corp., Pearl River, N.Y., Wayne, N.J., 1965-68; v.p., bus. devel. planning PepsiCo Inc. and affiliates, Purchase, N.Y., Miami, Fla., 1968-75; mgr. fin. and planning cons. Coopers & Lybrand, N.Y.C., 1975-77; pres. Century Mgmt. Cons., Inc., N.Y.C., 1977—. Contbr. articles to profl. jours. Home: 37 Grandview Ave Glen Rock NJ 07452

MAKAR, BOSHRA HALIM, educator; b. Sohag, Egypt, Sept. 23, 1928; s. Halim Khalil and Hakima (Mikhail) M.; B.Sc., Cairo U., 1947, M.Sc., 1952, Ph.D., 1955; m. Nadia Michel Eissa, Jan. 1, 1960; children—Ralph, Roger. Faculty Cairo U., 1948-65, asst. prof., 1955-60, asso. prof., 1960-65; vis. asso. prof. math. Am. U. Beirut, 1966; asso. prof. Mich. Tech. U., Houghton, 1967; prof. math. St. Peter's Coll., Jersey City, 1968—. Fellow Internat. Biog. Assn.; mem. Am. Math. Soc., N.J. Acad. Scis., AAAS, Community Leaders Am., Internat. Platform Assn., AAUP, Math. Assn. Am., Poetry Soc. Am., United Poets Laureate Internat. (v.p.). Home: 410 Fairmount Ave Jersey City NJ 07306

MAKAR, HARRY VLADIMER, metallurgist; b. Carnegie, Pa., Mar. 18, 1933; s. Michael and Mary (Drost) M.; B.S., Carnegie-Mellon U., 1955; m. Lee Ann Evancheck, July 16, 1960; children—Mary Ann, Gregory Leo, Diane Lee. Staff customer service, process control, research and devel. splty. steels Universal-Cyclops (now Cyclops Corp.), Bridgeville, Pa., 1955-56, 60-61, Titusville, Pa., 1958-59; quality control supr., research and devel., meltshop foreman stainless steels, high-temperature alloys Eastern Stainless Steel Corp., Balt. 1961-65; project leader scrap recycling U.S. Bur. Mines, College Park, Md., 1965-69, research supr. ferrous scrap refining, 1969-73, supr. metall. secondary resource recovery, from 1973—, now supr. secondary metals recovery research, also tech. rep. to Spain, 1973, 74, 75, mem. oil shale study Office Tech. Assessment, U.S. Congress, 1978. Pres. Chapelview Improvement Assn., Ellicott City, Md., 1975-76; chmn. Ukrainian Folk Festival Group, Pitts., 1960-61. Served with USMC, 1956-58. Mem. ASTM (chmn. com. nonferrous metals E-38, membership sec.), Am. Soc. Metals, Am. Inst. Mining, Metall. and Petroleum Engrs., League Ukrainian Catholics (nat. bd., editor newspaper). Contbr. articles on resource recovery, scrap metals recycling to profl. publs. Home: 3522 Belfont Dr Ellicott City MD 21043 Office: Bur Mines Avondale MD 20782

MAKAR, NADIA EISSA, educator; b. Cairo, Egypt, Oct. 7, 1938; d. Michel Issa and Yvonne Bitar; student Cairo U., 1958-59, 64-65; certificate Moscow U., 1964; B.A., St. Peter's Coll., 1969; Hon. Dr. Liberal Arts, Gt. China Arts Coll., 1973; m. Boshra Halim Makar, Jan. 1, 1960; children—Ralph, Roger. Tchr. chemistry Hudson Cath. High Sch., Jersey City, 1970-72, chmn. sci. dept., 1972—. Chmn. jr. poets Ann. Internat. Poetry Festival, 1973—; bd. dirs. N.J. Symphony, World Poets Resource Center, N.Y.C. Recipient Spl. award Poetry Soc. London, 1972; Regional award excellence in teaching chemistry Mfg. Chemists Assn., 1975; Leadership in Poetry crown 3d World Congress Poets, 1976; Nichols award, 1977, regional award for chemistry teaching Am. Chem. Soc., 1978; named outstanding secondary educator Am., 1973, Hudson County Woman of Achievement, 1975, Internat. Woman of Yr., 1976. Mem. AAAS, Nat., N.J. sci. tchrs. assns., Nat., N.J. sci. suprs. assns., Poetry Soc. London (life), Assn. for Edn. Tchrs. in Sci., Am. Chem. Soc., Centro Studi e Scambi Internaziolali (mem. internat. com. on sci. 1973—), United Poets Laureate Internat. (co-v.p.), N.Y., N.J. acads. sci., Internat. Platform Assn., Bus. and Profl. Women (v.p.). Home: 410 Fairmount Ave Jersey City NJ 07306 Office: 790 Bergen Ave Jersey City NJ 07306

MAKARETZ, JOHN, civil engr.; b. Tarnogrod, Poland, Feb. 22, 1907; s. Michael and Anna (Penko) M.; came to U.S., 1948, naturalized, 1953; Diploma Engr., Lwow Tech. Inst., Poland, 1932; m. Helen, Jan. 15, 1954; 1 son, Michael. Civil engr. Porombka (Poland) Dam Constrn., 1936-38; design engr. Negrelli Co., Vienna, Austria, 1938-44; engr. Thomas Worcester Co., Boston, 1948-57; civil engr. Badger-Am. Civil Engring. Cons., Cambridge, Mass., 1957—. Mem. ASCE, Ukrainian Engrs. Assn. Democrat. Ukrainian Orthodox. Contbr. articles to profl. jours.; watercolorist, 1960—. Home: 418 Mystic St Arlington MA 02174

MAKEPEACE, RUSSELL, agrl. co. exec.; b. May's Landing, N.J., July 9, 1904; s. Charles Denison and Pauline (Russell) M.; B.A., Williams Coll., 1925; m. Eleanor Morse, Nov. 1, 1930; children—Charles Denison II, Mary Zelinda. With Grand Union Co., N.Y.C., 1925-30; with A.D. Makepeace Co., Wareham, Mass., 1930—, pres., 1946—. Republican. Episcopalian. Clubs: Kittansett, Beverly Yacht (Marion, Mass.). Home: PO Box 655 Marion MA 02738 Office: PO Box 151 Wareham MA 02571

MAKER, JAMES HENRY, metallurgist; b. Barre, Vt., Dec. 21, 1917; s. Alfred Stafford and Ruth Pearl (Quinn) M.; A.B., Brown U., 1939; m. Marian Eldridge MacLean, Aug. 31, 1940; children—Kristin Maker Kiesel, Jeffrey MacLean. Lab asst., Washburn Wire Co., Phillipsdale, R.I., 1939-41; asst. metallurgist Watertown (Mass.) Arsenal, 1941-44; metallurgist B.F. Hirsch Co., N.Y.C., 1944-45, Hemphill Co., Pawtucket, 1946-47; metallurgist Wallace Barnes div. Associated Spring Corp., Bristol, Conn., 1947-62, chief metallurgist, 1962—. Served with USNR, 1945-46. Mem. ASTM, Am. Soc. Metals, Spring Mfrs. Inst. Patentee in field. Home: 1467 Stafford Ave Bristol CT 06010 Office: 18 Main St Bristol CT 06010

MAKHIJA, MOHANLAL CHHUGAMAL, radiologist, nuclear physician; b. Bombay, India, Oct. 1, 1941; s. Chhugamal V. and Bhagwanti M. (Nagpal) M.; came to U.S., 1969; student Jai Hind Coll., (India), 1957-59; G.S. Med. Coll., India, 1959-64; M.D., Bombay U., 1966. Intern, Bronx (N.Y.) Lebanon Hosp., 1969-70; resident Met. Hosp. Center, N.Y.C., 1971-77, Morristown (N.J.) Meml. Hosp., 1972-75, Yale-New Haven Hosp., 1975-76; postdoctoral fellow diagnostic radiology Yale U. Sch. Medicine, 1976-77; in-charge sect. nuclear medicine, attending radiologist Helene Fuld Med. Center, Trenton, N.J., 1977-78; asst. attending dept. radiology, dir. sect. nuclear medicine Monmouth Med. Center, Long Branch, N.J., 1978—; clin. sr. instr. Hahnemann Med. Coll. Diplomate Am. Bd. Nuclear Medicine, Am. Bd. Radiology. Fellow N.J. Acad. Medicine; mem. Am. Coll. Radiology, Radiol. Soc. N. Am., Royal Coll. Radiologists (U.K.), Soc. Nuclear Medicine, Am. Coll. Nuclear Physicians. Home: 900 Armstrong Blvd Ocean NJ 07712 Office: 300 2d Ave Long Branch NJ 07740

MAKHIJANI, SURESH PESSUMAL, metall. engr.; b. Karachi, India, Aug. 11, 1944; s. Pessumal Manghanmal and Ganga Tillumal (Jagtiani) M.; came to U.S., 1967; Dwitiya Praveshika in Indian Classical Music, Gandharva Sch. Music, 1959; B.Tech., Indian Inst. Tech., 1967; Inter.Sci., U. Bombay, 1963; M.S., U. Md., 1969; m. Nalini Arjandas Chandiramani, Jan. 9, 1974; 1 dau., Meena Suresh. Mgr. metallurgy and mech. testing labs. Tex. Instruments Inc., Attleboro, Mass., 1969-70; mgr. mfg. research and devel. Xerox Corp., Webster N.Y., 1972—. Mem. Am. Soc. Metals, Rochester Indsl. Engring. Soc. Home: 1242 LaBaron Circle Webster NY 14580 Office: 800 Phillips Rd Webster NY 14580

MAKOVER, HENRY BENEDICT, physician, educator; b. Balt., July 28, 1908; s. Bernard and Rose M.; A.B., Johns Hopdins U., 1929, M.D., 1933; m. Mildred Weinberg, July 6, 1931; children—Richard B., Michael E. Intern, Sinai Hosp., Balt., 1933-34, resident, 1934-36; practice medicine specializing in internal medicine, Balt., 1936-42; asso. med. dir. Montefiore Hosp., Bronx, N.Y., 1946-47; health and med. cons. Fedn. Jewish Charities of Phila., 1947-49; dir. med. survey Health Ins. Plan of Greater N.Y., 1949-50; med. dir. Central Manhattan Group of Health Ins. Plans of Greater N.Y., 1950-56; prof. preventive and environ. medicine Albert Einstein Coll., 1956-68, prof., then clin. prof. psychiatry, 1968-78, clin. prof. emeritus, 1978—; individual practice medicine specializing in psychiatry, Mamaroneck, N.Y., 1962—; supervising psychiatrist Bronx Psychiat. Center; vis. physician Bronx Municipal Hosp. Center, N.Y. Served with USPHS, 1942-46. Diplomate Am. Bd. Psychiatry and Neurology. Fellow Am. Pub. Health Assn., N.Y. Acad. Medicine, Am. Psychiat. Assn.; mem. N.Y. County Med. Soc., Internat. Epidemiological Assn., Westchester Acad. Medicine. Club: Johns Hopkins. Contbr. articles in field. Home and office: 3 Country Rd Mamaroneck NY 10543

MAKUCH, JAMES MICHAEL, univ. adminstr.; b. White Haven, Pa., Nov. 20, 1942; s. Michael James and Bertha Margaret (Ciesla) M.; B.S. with honors, U. Conn., 1964; M.B.A., U. Hartford (Conn.), 1968; m. Linda Susan Carter, June 18, 1966; children—Michael James, Mark David, Audra Linne. Mem. mgmt. staff U. Conn., Storrs, 1964—, asso. dir. food service dept., 1970-73, bus. mgr. phys. plant div., 1973—; cons. food service, 1967—; owner James M. Makuch Rental Properties, Willington, Conn., 1969—. Sec. zoning bd. appeals Town of Willington, 1970-73, mem. bd. edn., 1973, selectman, 1973-75, town parliamentarian, 1970—, mem. sch. bldg/renovation coms., 1973—. Mem. Profl. Employees Assn. (pres. 1976-77, exec. bd. 1975—), Nat. Assn. Coll. and Univ. Bus. Officers, Assn. Phys. Plant Adminstrs. Republican. Home: Old Farms Rd West Willington CT 06279 Office: U-38 Univ Conn Storrs CT 06268

MALABRE, ALFRED LEOPOLD, JR., journalist; b. N.Y.C., Apr. 23, 1931; s. Alfred Leopold and Marie (Leonard) M.; B.A., Yale U., 1952; m. Mary Patricia Wardropper, July 28, 1956; children—Richard C., E. Ann, John A. Copy editor Hartford (Conn.) Courant, 1957-58; successively reporter, Bonn bur. chief, econs. editor, news editor and Outlook columnist Wall St. Jour., 1958—, news editor, 1969—. Served with USNR, 1953-56; Korea. Poynter fellow, 1976. Mem. Authors Guild, Pilgrims Soc. U.S. Club: Union (N.Y.C.). Author: Understanding the Economy: For People Who Can't Stand Economics, 1976; America's Dilemma: Jobs vs. Prices, 1978. Address: 320 E 72d St New York City NY 10021

MALACH, HERBERT JOHN, lawyer; b. N.Y.C., Aug. 3, 1922; s. James J. and Therese (Lederer) M.; A.B., Iona Coll., 1951; J.D., Columbia U., 1955; m. Patricia Sweeny, Sept. 12, 1953 (dec. 1972); children—Therese, Herbert John, Helen. Admitted to N.Y. bar, 1957, D.C. bar, 1958, to U.S. Supreme Ct., 1961; practiced in N.Y.C., 1957-72, New Rochelle, N.Y., 1960—; lectr. bus. law Iona Coll., New Rochelle, 1957-59, asst. to pres. for community services, 1959-62. Vice chmn., exec. dir. Iona Coll. Westchester County Law Enforcement Inst.; spl. counsel N.Y. State Temporary Commn. on Child Welfare; mem. Westchester County Youth Adv. Council, 1969-73; mem. Law Enforcement Planning. Agy., New Rochelle, 1968-69; adv. counsel Westchester Police Youth Officers Assn.; mem. New Rochelle Narcotics Guidance Council, 1972-75; adv. council New Rochelle Salvation Army; legal adviser East-End Civic Assn.; law guardian Westchester County Family Ct.; referee New Rochelle City Ct.; arbitrator Civil Ct., Bronx. Bd. dirs. Art Inst., Iona Coll., mem. adv. bd. radio activities, adv. bd. criminal justice Iona Coll. Served with AUS, 1942-46. Recipient Patrick B. Doyle award for outstanding service, 1969, William B. Cornelia Founders award, 1976 (both Iona Coll.). Hon. dep. sheriff Westchester County. Mem. Am. (com. rights of family), N.Y. State (com. police), Bronx County (civil rights com.), Westchester County, New Rochelle bar assns., Am. Judicature Soc., N.Y. County Lawyers Assn. (family ct. com.), Criminal Cts. Bar Assn. Westchester County, Am. Fedn. Police, Internat. Narcotic Enforcement Officers Assn., Internat. Acad. Criminology, Am. Acad. Polit. and Social Sci., Am. Psychology-Law Soc., Internat., N.Y. State, Bergen County chiefs of police, Nat. Sheriffs Assn., Am. Soc. Internat. Law, Iona Coll. Alumni Assn., Inc. (pres., chmn. bd. dirs. 1958-60, 62-64, 72-76, dir. 1954-58, 68-72, 76—, v.p. 1966-68). Address: 105 Harding Dr New Rochelle NY 10801

MALACH, MONTE, physician; b. Jersey City, Aug. 15, 1926; s. Charles and Yetta (Pascher) M.; B.A., U. Mich., 1949, M.D., 1949; m. Ann Elaine Glazer, June 15, 1952; children—Barbara Sandra, Cathie Tara, Matthew David. Intern Beth Israel Hosp., Boston, 1949-50, resident, 1950-52; resident Kings County Hosp., Bklyn., 1954-55; practice medicine specializing in internal medicine and cardiology, Bklyn., 1955—; dir. coronary care unit Bklyn. Hosp., 1965—; pres. profl. staff Bklyn.-Cumberland Med. Center, 1966-69, chmn. med. bd., 1971-72; attending staff Caledonian Hosp.; cons. cardiology Samaritan Hosp., Kings County Hosp.; teaching fellow Tufts Med. Sch., 1951-52; instr. medicine Downstate Med. Center, Bklyn., 1955-59, clin. asst. prof. medicine, 1959-68, clin. asso. prof., 1969-76, clin. prof., 1976—. Kings County committeeman Democratic Party, 1964, 65. Served to ensign USNR, 1944-46; 1st lt. M.C., AUS, 1952-54. Diplomate Nat. Bd. Med. Examiners, Am. Bd. Internal Medicine. Fellow Am. Coll. Chest Physicians, A.C.P., Am. Coll. Cardiology; mem. N.Y. Heart Assn., AMA (vice chmn. sect. council for internal medicine), Am. (trustee 1975—), N.Y. State (pres. 1973-74, dir. 1966—, chmn. Bklyn. chpt., v.p. 1971, award of merit 1978), Bklyn. (mem. council 1965) socs. internal medicine, Med. Soc. State of N.Y. (chmn. sect. internal medicine 1976), Fed. Council for Internal Medicine. Address: 55 Rugby Rd Brooklyn NY 11226

MALANCHUK, JOHN LOUIS, educator; b. Mount Kisco, N.Y., Feb. 21, 1948; s. Dennis James and Mary Elizabeth (Smith) M.; B.S., State U. N.Y., 1970, M.A., 1972; Ph.D., U. Ga., 1979; m. Barbara Ellen White, June 13, 1970; children—Adriane Smith. Instr. environ. sci. State U. N.Y., Plattsburgh, 1972-74, asst. prof., 1977—; ecologist EPA, Athens, Ga., 1974-77. Mem. AAAS, Am. Inst. Biol. Scis. Roman Catholic. Home: Miner Center Chazy NY 12921 Office: Institute for Man and Environment State University of New York Plattsburgh NY 12901

MALCOLM, DANIEL CONNOR, govt. ofcl.; b. Yonkers, N.Y., Feb. 20, 1924; s. Andrew and Mary (Bradley) M.; student Furman U., 1945-46; B.S., S.D. Sch. Mines and Tech., 1951; M.S. (Univ. scholar) U. Cin., 1951; m. Veronica Majewski, Nov. 17, 1973. With Corps Engrs., N.Y. Dist., 1955-69; engr. agt. Internal Revenue Service, U.S. Treas., N.Y.C., 1969—. Instr. geology Bklyn. Coll., 1954-55, N.Y. U., N.Y.C., 1955-56. Served with USAAF, 1943-45. Registered profl. engr., Vt. Mem. Am. Inst. M.E., Am. Legion. Home: 101 Hazlet Ave Hazlet NJ 07730 Office: 120 Church St New York City NY 10007

MALDONADO, JUAN RAMON, physicist; b. Holguin, Cuba, May 6, 1938; s. Ramon Adriano and Edelmira Margarita (Learte) M.; came to U.S., 1961, naturalized, 1968; D. en Ciencias Fisico Matematicas, U. Havana, 1961; Ph.D., U. Md., 1968; m. Daria Cira Camacho, July 20, 1962; children—Daria, Diane, Janet. With CMQ-TV, Havana, Cuba, 1957-61; instr. physics dept. U. Havana, 1960-61; supr. electronics physics dept. U. Md., College Park, 1962-64, research asst., 1964-68; mem. tech. staff Bell Labs., Murray Hill, N.J., 1968—, mem. affirmative action com., 1973-78. Mem. Am. Phys. Soc., IEEE, Soc. Photo-optical Instrumentation Engrs., AAAS, U. Md. Alumni Assn., Sigma Xi, Sigma Pi Sigma. Contbr. articles in field to profl. jours.; patentee in field. Home: 32 Honeyman Pl Berkeley Heights NJ 07922 Office: 600 Mountain Ave Murray Hill NJ 07974

MALEK, JOSEPH VINCENT, mfg. co. exec.; b. Cicero, Ill., Apr. 16, 1924; s. John J. and Antoinette (Bozovsky) M.; B.S., U. Ill., 1950; m. Loretta Marilyn Cochran, Feb. 18, 1950; children—Joseph, Marie, Richard, Michael. Engr., designer Inland Steel Container Corp., Chgo., 1950-51; engr., prodn. mgr. Bunker Ramo Corp., Cicero, 1951-64, engr., mgr., Chatsworth, Calif., 1964-66, v.p. engring. and mfg., Janesville, Wis., 1966-69, div. pres., Roseland, N.J., 1969-71, pres., Scarborough, Ont., Can., 1971-73, div. pres., Danbury, Conn., 1973—. Served with USAAF and U.S. Army, 1943-46. Decorated Bronze Star; registered profl. engr., Ill., Wis. Mem. Am. Mgmt. Assn., Danbury C. of C. (dir. 1974—). Republican. Roman Catholic. Club: Ridgewood Country. Office: 33 E Franklin St Danbury CT 06810

MALER, ROGER, advt. exec.; b. Bklyn., Mar. 12, 1937; s. Lugero Roger and Rose (Sweet) Malerba; B.A., Bklyn. Coll., 1959; postgrad. N.Y.C. Community Coll., 1961-62; m. Wendy Friedman, May 5, 1970; children—Janine, Roger, Kyra, Paige. Advt. and promotion supr. Warner-Lambert Co., Morris Plains, N.J., 1969-72; creative dir. Victor & Richards, Inc., N.Y.C., 1968-69; pres. Thompson Maler, Inc., Morristown, N.J., 1972—, Maler, Miller & Brown, Morristown, 1977—. Vice-pres. Mt. Arlington (N.J.) Bd. Edn., 1974—. Served with Air NG, also USAF, 1962. Mem. Bus. Profl. Advt. Assn., Biomed. Mktg. Assn., Pharm. Advt. Club, N.J. Sch. Bds. Assn. Office: 161 Washington St Morristown NJ 07960

MALETZ, HERBERT NAAMAN, fed. judge; b. Boston, Oct. 30, 1913; s. Reuben and Frances (Sawyer) M.; A.B., Harvard U., 1935, LL.B., 1939; m. Catherine B. Loebach, May 8, 1947; 1 son, David M. Admitted to Mass. bar, 1939, D.C. bar, 1952; mem. staff Truman Com., U.S. Senate, 1941-42; atty. Anti-Trust div. Dept. Justice, 1946-50; with OPS, 1950-53, chief counsel, 1952-53; chief counsel anti-trust subcom. U.S. Ho. of Reps., 1955-61; commr. U.S. Ct. of Claims, 1961-67; judge U.S. Customs Ct., N.Y.C., 1967—. Served with AUS, 1942-46, to lt. col. Res., 1973. Home: 17 S Morris Ln Scarsdale NY 10583 Office: 1 Federal Plaza New York City NY 10007

MALEV, SHELDON, educator; b. N.Y.C., Aug. 1, 1938; s. Morris and Frances (Greenberg) M.; B.A., Queens Coll., 1960; M.A., San Francisco State Coll., 1963; postgrad. (fellow) Internat. Grad. Sch. Behavioral and Social Scis., Fla. Inst. Tech., 1974—. Research scientist U.S. Army Leadership Tng. Center, Monterey, Calif., 1961; instr. psychology Fairleigh Dickinson U., Rutherford, N.J., 1963-71; asst. prof. psychology Westchester Community Coll., Valhalla, N.Y., 1971—. Dir. psychol. services Tng. Services, Inc., Rutherford, N.J., 1968-71; fellow Morton Prince Clinic for Hypnotherapy, N.Y.C., 1970-73; profl. cons., lectr., demonstrator. Served with USAF, 1962.

NDEA fellow, 1966-67. Mem. Am. (asso.), Eastern psychol. assns., Soc. for Psychol. Study Social Issues, Psychologists for Social Action, United Fedn. Coll. Tchrs., Am. Soc. Psychosomatic Dentistry and Medicine, ACLU, Common Cause, Mensa, Alpha Epsilon Pi. Home: 31 Lawrence Dr North White Plains NY 10603 Office: Psychology Dept Westchester Community College Valhalla NY 10595

MALFATTI, ROGER ANDRE, JR., symphony exec.; b. N.Y.C., Sept. 10, 1940; s. Roger Andre and Janet Davidson (Mowat) M.; B.A. in Theatre Arts, Hofstra U., 1965; m. Marie Ann Cook, Dec. 26, 1964; children—Theresa, Jennifer. Recreation supr. Town Hempstead, N.Y., 1965-68, coordinator cultural arts, 1971-75; gen. mgr. L.I. Symphony, 1975—; sales rep. Weneger Corp., Owatonna, Minn., 1968-69, advt. mgr., 1969-70; sales engr. Century-Strand Theatrical Lighting, Clifton, N.J., 1970-71. Chmn. adminstrn. com. N.Y. sect. U.S. Inst. for Theatre Tech., 1971-73; chmn. bi-centennial com. Town of Hempstead, N.Y., 1973-77; program chmn. Nassau County (N.Y.) Council exploring div. Boy Scouts Am., 1973-76; chmn. arts dept. Nassau Council Chs., 1968-69. Recipient Theatre Arts award Hofstra U., 1963, Theatre Arts Citation of Merit, 1965, Outstanding Young Man Am., 1974, God and Country award Boy Scouts Am.; Distinguished Service award Nassau Library System, 1976. Mem. Nassau County Park and Recreation Soc., N.Y. State Recreation and Park Soc., U.S. Inst. for Theatre Tech., Am. Theatre Assn., Asso. Council on Arts, Am. Symphony Orch. League (chmn. mgrs. assn. Mid-Atlantic sect. 1976-78), Met. Orch. Mgrs. Assn. (1st v.p. 1978—). Home: 273 Hempstead Gardens Dr West Hempstead NY 11552 Office: LI Symphony 20 Dewey St Huntington NY 11743

MALIA, GERALD ALOYSIUS, lawyer; b. Blakley, Pa., Aug. 6, 1933; s. Anthony Francis and Mary Agnes (Kelly) M.; B.S., St. Peter's Coll., 1954; J.D., Georgetown U., 1958, LL.M., 1959; m. Mary Catherine Carolan, June 27, 1959; children—Mary Catherine, Carolan Elizabeth, Elizabeth Kelly, Gerald Anthony. Admitted to D.C. bar, 1959, also U.S. Supreme Ct.; legal asst. to chief judge D.C. Ct. Appeals, 1958-59; pvt. practice law, Washington, 1959—; partner Ragan & Mason; adj. prof. law Georgetown U. Law Center; mem. Jud. Conf. D.C., 1977. Served to 1st lt. U.S. Army, 1954-56. Mem. Am., D.C. bar assns., Maritime Adminstrv. Bar Assn. (pres. 1973-74), Maritime Law Assn. U.S., Phi Delta Phi. Roman Catholic. Club: Univ. (Washington). Author: Maritime Law, 1977; editor Georgetown Law Jour., 1958. Office: 900 17th St NW Washington DC 20006

MALIGNO, AMELIA, counselor; b. Bklyn., Nov. 20, 1948; d. Aurelius G. and Mary (Grecco) Mignone; student St. John's U., 1966-68; B.A. summa cum laude in Psychology, U. Guam, 1976; M.Ed., Boston U., 1978; m. Vincent J. Maligno, June 23, 1968; children—Julie Ann, Vincent, Melissa. Vol. counselor Personal Crisis Services, Omaha, 1971-73, Helpline, Offutt AFB, Nebr., 1971-73, Listen, Inc., Omaha, 1971-72; asst. tchr. in crisis intervention U. Guam, 1975; vol. counselor Helpline-Anderson AFB, Guam, 1974-76; drug/alcohol counselor Army Community Drug and Alcohol Center, Herzo Arty. Base, Germany, 1977, U.S. Army Hosp., Nurenberg, Germany, 1977—, counselor neuro-psychiat. clinic, 1977. Mem. Assn. Humanistic Psychology, Am. Personnel and Guidance Assn. Roman Catholic. Home: 69 Cambridge Ave Staten Island NY 10314 Office: ADCO/USMCA-NBG APO NY 09696

MALIGNO, VINCENT JOSEPH, psychologist; b. Queens, N.Y., Apr. 26, 1946; s. Joseph Anthony and Elizabeth Loretta (Fauci) M.; student Catholic U., 1963-66; B.A., Manhattan Coll., 1969; M.A., U. Okla., 1974; m. Amelia Mignone, June 23, 1968; children—Julie-Ann, Vincent Joseph, Melissa. Tchr., Xaverian Bros., Silver Spring, Md., 1963-66; psychology technician, Bronx, N.Y., 1966-68; store detective Saks Fifth Ave., N.Y.C., 1968; asst. mgr. Ace Sound Rental, N.Y.C., 1968-69; clin. dir. U.S. Army Drug/Alcohol Program, Nuremberg, Germany, 1976—; instr. U. Guam, 1974-76, U. So. Calif., 1976. Served to capt. USAF, 1969-76; capt. Res. Decorated D.F.C., Air medal, Meritorious Service medal, Joint Services Commendation medal, Air Force Commendation medal. Mem. Nat. Assn. of Social Workers, Am. Personnel and Guidance Assn., Nat. Assn. of Alcoholism Counselors, Air Force Assn., Guam Human Resources Assn., Nat. Assn. of Prevention Profls. Democrat. Roman Catholic. Home: 69 Cambridge Ave Staten Island NY 10314 Office: ADCO USMCA NBG APO New York City NY 09696

MALIN, CEDRIC K., interior designer; b. N.Y.C., Feb. 24, 1920; s. Louis and Ethel (Schuster) M.; B.A. cum laude, L.I. U., 1951; postgrad. Columbia U., 1953-54; m. Mary Kaem, Oct. 22, 1959. Asst. dir. evening schs. L.I. U., 1950, dir. Brookville Campus (now C.W. Post Coll.), 1951, instr. lit. and creative writing, 1950-51; free lance writer, artist, 1952-59; archtl. interior designer and sr. designer Cedric K. Malin Assos., Great Neck, N.Y., 1959-77; pres. Malin/Ross Assos. Inc., Great Neck, 1977—; cons. Great Neck and Seaford (N.Y.) town planning, 1976-78; lectr. in field. Recipient Nat. award Whitman Soc. Am., 1949. Mem. Assn. of Environ. Designers (pres. 1975—), Inst. Profl. Designers (London). Editor-in-chief Rev. Jour., 1949-51; contbr. articles to profl. jours.; columnist on design, Great Neck News mag., 1974-78, design editor, 1975—. Office: 310 Northern Blvd Great Neck NY 11021

MALIN, PAUL SAMUEL, tire and rubber co. exec.; b. N.Y.C., Oct. 29, 1943; s. Henry and Ruth (Pheffer) M.; B.S. in Biology, Pa. State U., 1965; postgrad. Baruch Sch. Bus., Coll. City N.Y., 1965-66; m. Gayle Ruth Scheinbach, Oct. 1, 1967 (div. 1976); children—Scott Hunter, Tobi Beth. With Broadway Tire & Rubber Co., Inc., River Edge, N.J., 1966—, v.p., 1973-78, pres., 1978—. Jewish. Home: 151 Prospect Ave 4B Hackensack NJ 07601 Office: 555 Hackensack Ave River Edge NJ 07661

MALINCONICO, S. MICHAEL, librarian; b. Bklyn., Mar. 12, 1941; s. Gennaro and Rosaria (Pappalardo) M.; B.S., Bklyn. Coll., 1962; M.A., Columbia U., 1964, S.L.S., 1976; m. Christine Cash, Aug. 5, 1968; 1 son, Michael. Lectr. dept. physics Bklyn. Coll., 1965-67; data/systems analyst NASA, Greenbelt, Md., 1967-69; systems analyst, mgr. systems analysis N.Y.C. Pub. Library, 1969-73, asst. chief systems analysis and data processing office, 1973-78, coordinator tech. services, 1978—; cons. in field; mem. evaluation teams Library Automation Studies, 1975—. NSF fellow, 1963-66; Joseph C. Pfister fellow, 1966-67. Mem. ALA (Esther J. Piercy award 1978), Am. Soc. Info. Sci., N.Y. Tech. Services Librarians, N.Y. Book Pubs. League., Melvil Dui Soc. Contbr. articles to profl. jours. Home: 1801 E 5 St Brooklyn NY 11223 Office: 8 E 40 St New York City NY 10019

MALINER, MYRON S., investment banking co. exec.; b. N.Y.C., Sept. 28, 1937; s. Sidney and Florence (Trachtenberg) M.; student Sorbonne U., 1954; B.A., Union Coll., 1958; postgrad. Bklyn. Law Sch., 1959-61; m. Carmenchita Villasanta Tuason, Sept. 28, 1964; children—Michael Lawrence, Mimi Suzanne. Order clk. Hardy & Co., N.Y.C., 1959, account exec., 1959-61; pres., chmn. M.S. Maliner & Co., Inc., Roslyn Heights, N.Y., 1961—. Mem. Assn. Investment Brokers (dir.), Nat. Assn. Securities Dealers, Am. Anthrop. Assn., Am. Assn. Phys. Anthropologists. Home: 16 Diana's Circle Roslyn Estates NY 11576 Office: PO Box 1373 Roslyn Heights NY 11577

MALINOSKI, BERNADINE MARIE, nursing exec.; b. Shenandoah, Pa., Aug. 16, 1927; d. John Stephen and Frances Clara (Stabinski) M.; R.N., Thomas Jefferson Med. Coll. Hosp., 1948; B.S. in Nursing, Boston Coll., 1955; M.P.H., U. N.C., 1963. Staff nurse VA Hosp., Coatesville, Pa., 1948-49; pub. health nurse Wayne County (Mich.) Health Dept., 1955-60; supr. pub. health nurses Delaware County State Health Center, Chester, Pa., 1960-65; instr. Sch. Nursing, U. Mich., Ann Arbor, 1965-66; asst. prof. nursing Pa. State U., Pitts., 1966-67; asst. dir. edn. Community Nursing Services of Phila., 1968-77; dir. nurses Frederick County (Md.) Health Dept., 1977—. Mem. Frederick County Sch. Health Council, Commn. on Aging, Md. Sch. Health Council. Served with Army Nurse Corps, 1949-51; Nurse Corps, USAF, 1951-53, col., USAFR, 1975—. Decorated Air Force Commendation medal. Mem. Am. Nurses Assn., Dist. 8 Nurses Assn., Am. Pub. Health Assn., Nat. League Nursing, Thomas Jefferson U. Alumni Assn., Boston Coll. Alumni Assn., Res. Officers Assn. Roman Catholic. Club: Zonta. Home: 328 W Oak St Shenandoah PA 17976

MALIONE, ANTHONY MICHAEL, pub. sch. adminstr.; b. Boston, June 1, 1935; s. Anthony and Ann Marie (Capodilupo) M.; B.A., Boston U., 1959; M.Ed., Boston State Coll., 1966, certificate Advanced Grad. Studies, 1970; m. Linda Capra, Oct. 16, 1960; children—Theresa, Ann. Dir. guidance dept. Everett (Mass.) Pub. Schs., 1971—; asso. prof. alcohol drug studies Boston State Coll.; bd. dirs. Tri-City Mental Health, Whidden Meml. Hosp., Everett (Mass.) Mental Health Div.; cons. Boston Sch. Dept. Served with Army N.G., 1949-56. Recipient ARC award, 1975. Mem. Am. Assn. Clin. Counselors, Am. Assn. Sch. Adminstrs., Am. Personnel and Guidance Assn. Contbr. articles to profl. jours. Home: 58 Bettinson Ave Everett MA 02149 Office: 548 Broadway Everett MA 02149

MALISZEWSKI, HENRY LOUIS, chemist; b. Batavia, N.Y., May 24, 1925; s. Keyser and Helen (Sudul) M.; B.S., Xavier U., Cin., 1950; postgrad. Ohio State U., 1950, Rutgers U., Newark, 1975-77; m. Mildred Lind, June 12, 1950; children—Thomas Gustav, Richard Paul, Jeanine, Rebecca Ann, Stephen Peter. Jr. chemist Airco Inc., Murray Hill, N.J., 1958-63, chemist, 1963-70, sr. research chemist, 1970-77, corporate indsl. hygienist, 1977—. Republican. Roman Catholic. Office: Airco Inc 100 Mountain Ave Murray Hill NJ 07974

MALITZ, SIDNEY, physician; b. N.Y.C., Apr. 20, 1923; s. Benjamin and Etta (Cohen) M.; student N.Y. U., 1940-42, Tulane U., 1942-43; B.M., Chgo. Med. Sch., 1946, M.D., 1947. Intern, St. Mary's Hosp., Huntington, W.Va., 1946-47; sr. intern Bethesda Hosp., Cin., 1947-48; resident N.Y. State Psychiat. Inst., N.Y.C., 1948-51, sr. research psychiatrist, 1954-56, acting prin. research psychiatrist, 1956-58, acting chief psychiat. research, chief dept. exptl. psychiatry, 1958-64, chief psychiat. research dept. exptl. psychiatry, 1964-72, dep. dir., 1972-75, acting dir., 1975-76, dep. dir., 1976-78; in charge psychiat. drug clinic Vanderbilt Clinic, Presbyn. Hosp., N.Y.C., 1956-75, asst. attending psychiatrist, 1960-66, asso. attending psychiatrist, 1966-71, attending psychiatrist, 1971—, acting dir. Psychiatry Service, 1975-76; asst. dept. psychiatry Coll. Phys. and Surgs. Columbia, 1955-57, asso., 1957-59, asst. clin. prof., 1959-65, asso. prof., 1965-69, prof., 1969—, vice chmn. dept. psychiatry, 1972-75, acting chmn., 1975-76, vice chmn., 1976-78; mem. panel impartial psychiat. experts N.Y. State Supreme Ct., 1960—; mem. adv. com. subcom.; cons. U.S. Pharmacopeia; mem. adv. com. subcom. health N.Y. State Constl. Conv.; cons. div. med. scis. NRC, Washington, 1967—; cons. Rush Found., Los Angeles, 1968—; mem. ad hoc rev. com. to select Nat. Drug Abuse Research Centers, Center Studies Narcotic and Drug Abuse, NIMH, 1972—. Diplomate Am. Bd. Psychiatry and Neurology. Fellow Am. Psychiat. Assn. (chmn. com. biol. psychiatry 1961-62, program com. 1961-62, sec-treas. chpt. 1962-63, mem. com. research 1966-68, pres. chpt. 1969-70), N.Y. Acad. Medicine, AAAS (council 1969—), Am. Coll. Neuropsychopharmacology, Collegium Internationale Neuropsychopharmacologicum, Am. (archivist-historian 1978—), Royal colls. psychiatrists, Am. Coll. Psychoanalysts; N.Y. Soc. Clin. Psychiatry, Assn. Research Nervous and Mental Disease, N.Y. State, N.Y. County med. socs., AMA (cons. council drugs 1960—), N.Y. Acad. Scis., Am. Psychopath. Assn., Soc. Biol. Psychiatry, Schilder Soc., N.Y. Psychiat. Soc. Contbr. numerous articles to profl. jours. Address: Coll Phys and Surgs Columbia Dept Psychiatry 161 Fort Washington Ave New York City NY 10032

MALKIN, MARTIN LOUIS, real estate exec.; b. Bklyn., July 15, 1924; s. Barnet and Kate (Werstein) M.; B.S., N.Y. U., 1950; m. Syma Werstein, Nov. 21, 1959; children—Barnet, Harwyn Joseph, Seth. Pvt. practice accounting, N.Y.C., 1950-63; investment dept. supr. C.B. Snyder, Jersey City, N.J., 1963-70; real estate broker, investor, Englewood Cliffs, N.J., 1970—. Licensed realtor, N.Y., N.J. Mem. Eastern Bergen Bd. Realtors. Club: K.P. Office: 601 Palisade Ave Englewood Cliffs NJ 07632

MALKIN, STANLEY LEE, neurologist; b. Pitts., Nov. 11, 1942; s. Maurice and Bessie Beatrice (Serbin) M.; B.A. with honors, U. Pa., 1964; M.D., U. Pitts., 1968; children—Justin Ross, Keith Richard. Intern, Montefiore Hosp., Pitts., 1968-69; resident in neurology Columbia-Presbyn. Med. Center, N.Y.C., 1969-72; chief neurology service Wright-Patterson AFB, Dayton, Ohio, 1972-74; practice medicine specializing in neurology, Englewood, N.J., 1974—; asso. attending staff Englewood Hosp.; asst. neurologist Presbyn. Hosp., N.Y.C.; instr. clin. neurology Columbia U.; dir. EEG lab. Englewood Hosp.; founder Bergen-Passaic Tomography Center, Fairlawn, N.J.; prin. Combined Sci. Resources Corp., Teaneck, N.J.; prin. Med. Resources Internat., N.Y.C. Co-municipal coordinator Ft. Lee Citizens for McGovern, 1972; mem. Edgewater Rent Control Bd., 1978. Served to maj. M.C., USAF, 1972-74. Diplomate Am. Bd. Psychiatry and Neurology. Fellow Acad. Medicine N.J.; mem. A.C.P., AMA (physicians recognition award), Am. Acad. Neurology, Am. Assn. Electromyography and Electro-diagnosis, Bergen County Med. Soc., Phi Delta Epsilon. Jewish. Office: 309 Engle St Englewood NJ 07631

MALLARY, GERTRUDE ROBINSON (MRS. R. DEWITT MALLARY), former state senator; b. Springfield, Mass., Aug. 19, 1902; d. George Edward and Jennie (Slater) Robinson; student Bennett Coll., 1922: student U. Conn., 1941-42; m. R. DeWitt Mallary, Sept. 15, 1923; children—R. DeWitt, Richard Walker. Co-owner, partner Mallary Farm, Bradford, Vt., 1936—. Mem. Vt. Ho. of Reps., 1953-56, sec. com. agr., 1953, mem. appropriations com., 1955; mem. Vt. Senate from Orange County, 1957-58, mem. appropriations com., sec. pub. health com., vice chmn. edn. com. Mem. Interim Commn. Study Nursing Problems Vt., 1958-59. Mem. Gov.'s Commn. to Study Library Service in Vt., 1966-67; regional v.p. Nat. Beef Council, 1960-64; mem. Vt. Bd. Recreation, 1959-65; Vt. chmn. Nat. Library Week, 1973; chmn. Fairlee (Vt.) Bicentennial Com., 1974-77, Spl. Mass. Council of Social Agys., 1938-40. Trustee Justin Smith Morrill Found., 1964-71, pres., 1968-71; trustee Asa Bloomer Found., 1963-71, Orange County 4-H Found., 1969-72; trustee Wesson Meml. Hosp., Springfield, 1937-42, chmn. com. on nursing, 1939-42; mem. core com. Gov.'s Conf. on Libraries, 1978—. Mem. N.E. State Holstein-Friesian Assn. (past sec.), Vt. Holstein Club (pres. 1951-53). Vt. Library Trustees Assn. (pres. 1965-67), Vt. Hist. Soc. (trustee 1964-69), Bradford Hist. Soc. (pres. 1965-69, 72-73, treas. 1976-78), Am. Antiquarian Soc. Editor: New Eng. Holstein Bull., 1947-50. Home: Mallary Farm Bradford VT 05033

MALLARY, RAYMOND DEWITT, lawyer; b. Lenox, Mass., Oct. 5, 1898; s. R. DeWitt and Lucy (Walker) M.; A.B., Dartmouth Coll., 1921; J.D., Harvard U., 1924; m. Gertrude Slater Robinson, Sept. 15, 1923; children—R. DeWitt, Richard Walker. Admitted to Mass. bar, 1924; partner firm Wooden, Small & Mallary, 1924-31, Mallary & Gilbert, 1931-51; pvt. practice, counsel to Richardson, Dibble & Atkinson, Springfield, Mass., 1951-56, Bulkley, Richardson, Godfrey & Burbank, 1956-64, Wilson, Keyser & Otterman, Chelsea and Bradford, Vt., 1961-63, Otterman & Allen, Bradford, 1965-70; dir. Vt. Electric Power Co. Inc., P.M. & G. Co., West Springfield, Mass.; dir., mem. exec. com. Central Vt. Pub. Service Corp. Chmn. bd. selectmen, Fairlee, Vt., 1953-57; chmn. Orange County Tax Appeal Bd., 1964-65; Vt. mem. New Eng. Govs.' Com. Pub. Transp., 1955—; mem. Conn. River Watershed Council, Inc.; trustee emeritus Am. Internat. Coll.; trustee, bd. dirs. Eastern States Expn., pres., 1954-57, chmn. bd., 1957-67, 1975—, hon. chmn. bd., chmn. Vt. bd. trustees, 1967-72; past chmn., now mem. exec. com. Green Pastures Com. New Eng.; trustee Hitchcock Found., Hanover, N.H. Recipient award Future Farmers Am., 1963, Hon. State Farmer; 4-H Outstanding Service award, 1965; award of achievement Internat. Assn. Fairs and Expns., 1967. Mem. Holstein-Friesian Assn. Am. (v.p.; dir. 1957-65, exec. com., pres. 1967-69; gen. chmn. 1970 conv.), New Eng. Fellowship Agr. Adventurers, Am., Vt., Hampden County, Orange County bar assns., New Eng. States Holstein-Friesian Assn. (past pres., dir.), Purebred Dairy Cattle Assn. Am. (pres. 1967-69). Home: Mallary Farm Bradford VT 05033 Office: Lower Plain PO Bradford VT 05033

MALLON, EDWARD JOHN, fin. service co. exec.; b. N.Y.C., July 2, 1944; s. Edward John and Helen (Will) M.; B.B.A., Pace Coll., 1968; postgrad. Baruch Coll., 1968-69; m. Frances Raye Simpson, Aug. 27, 1966; children—Kathryn Elaine, Melinda Mary, Edward John. Asst. controller Dishy Easton & Co., N.Y.C., 1966-68; control mgr. Glore Forgan, William R. Staats, Inc., N.Y.C., 1966-69; v.p., treas., chief operating officer ULAICO Equity Services, Inc., Concord, N.H., 1969-77, pres., chief exec. officer, 1977—; pres., chief exec. officer Hampshire Funding Inc., Concord, 1969—, also dir.; v.p. United Life and Accident Ins. Co., 1978—. Mem. investment com. Am. Coll., 1977—; mem. council fin. and adminstrn. N.H. Conf. United Methodist Ch., 1972-76; chmn. Concord chpt. N.H. Heart Assn., 1974; bd. regents Coll. Fin. Planning, 1977—; bd. dirs., clk. Central N.H. Community Mental Health Center, 1978—. C.L.U.; certified fin. planner. Mem. Concord C. of C. (v.p., dir.), Internat. Assn. Fin. Planners, Am. Coll. Life Underwriters, Nat. Assn. Life Underwriters, Nat. Assn. Security Dealers. Home: Surrey Dr Bow NH 03301 Office: One Granite Pl Concord NH 03301

MALLOUH, CAMILLE, physician; b. Beirut, June 13, 1930; s. Said and Laura Mallouh; came to U.S., 1958; naturalized, 1960; M.D., St. Joseph U., 1957; m. Vivian R. McGrath, June 3, 1961; children—Catherine, Stacy A. Intern, Elizabeth (N.J.) Gen. Hosp., 1958-59; resident N.Y. Med. Coll.-Met. Hosp. Center, N.Y.C., 1959-65; asso. dean, dir. med. edn., 1975—; chief urology Bird S. Coler Hosp., Roosevelt Island, N.Y., 1968-71; instr. urology and pathology N.Y. Med. Coll., 1965-68, asst. prof., 1968—, asst. dean, 1971-74; chief urology Met. Hosp., 1972—. Diplomate Am. Bd. Pathology, Am. Bd. Urology. Fellow A.C.S.; mem. AMA, Am. Urol. Assn., N.Y. Acad. Medicine. Home: 1106 Fedirko Ct Linden NJ 07036 Office: 1901 1st Ave New York City NY 10029

MALONE, JAMES DUANE, sporting goods co. exec.; b. Boston, Dec. 31, 1930; s. James Francis and Mary (Lillis) M.; B.S., Georgetown U., 1952; m. Maureen Donnelly, Aug. 20, 1964; children—Maura, James Duane. Nat. sales mgr. Raleigh Industries, Boston, 1966-67; market mgr. U.S. Envelope Co., Springfield, Mass., 1967-72; mgr. market research Am. Optical Co., Southbridge, Mass., 1972-75; v.p. mktg. O.F. Mossberg Co., North Haven, Conn., 1975—. Mem. Am. Mktg. Assn. (chpt. pres. 1971). Roman Catholic. Club: Woodland Country. Home: 344 Blueberry Hill Rd Longmeadow MA 01106 Office: 7 Grasso Ave North Haven CT 06473

MALONE, WILLIAM ROBERT, telephone co. exec.; b. Terre Haute, Ind., Apr. 15, 1936; s. Leander Alonzo and Dorothy Alice (Reveal) M.; A.B., Harvard U., 1958, J.D., 1962; m. Jane Helen Foulkes, June 25, 1959; children—Elizabeth, David, Christina. Admitted to Ind. bar, 1962, D.C. bar, 1963; law clk. U.S. Ct. Appeals for D.C. Circuit, 1962; lawyer firm Covington & Burling, Washington, 1963-70; resident att., v.p. Gen. Telephone & Electronics Corp., Washington, 1970—. Served with Signal Corps, U.S. Army, 1959. Mem. Computer Law Assn. (dir. 1972—), Am., Fed. bar. assns., Fed. Communications Bar Assn., IEEE. Republican. Methodist. Club: Internat. (Washington). Author: Broadcast Regulation in Canada, 1962. Home: 7205 Masters Dr Rockville MD 20854 Office: 1120 Connecticut Ave Suite 900 Washington DC 20036

MALONEY, JOAN MARIE, historian; b. Washington, May 7, 1931; d. Frank and Arline E. (Smith) M.; B.A., Trinity Coll., Washington, 1953; M.A., Georgetown U., 1958, Ph.D., 1961. Research asso. Center for Asian Studies, Seton Hall U., S. Orange, N.J., 1961-62; asst. prof. history Rosemont (Pa.) Coll., 1962-64; prof. Asian history Salem (Mass.) State Coll., 1964—; asso. dir. Research Inst. on Sino-Soviet Bloc, 1959—. Mem. Assn. Asian Studies, Am. Hist. Assn., AAUP, Phi Alpha Theta. Author: Communist China: The Domestic Scene 1949-67, 1967; Chinese Communist Impact on Cuba, 1962. Home: Box 364 North Chatham MA 02650 Office: Salem State Coll Salem MA 01970

MALONEY, MILFORD CHARLES, physician; b. Buffalo, Mar. 15, 1927; s. John Angelus and Winifred E. (Hill) M.; B.S., Canisius Coll., 1947, postgrad. in chemistry, 1947-49; M.D., U. Buffalo, 1953; m. Dione Sheppard, Sept. 2, 1950; children—Kevin, Michael, Diane, Rosemary, Brian, John, Carolyn, Patricia, Mark. Indsl. research chemist Buffalo Electrochem. Co., 1947-49; intern Mercy Hosp.-Georgetown U., Washington, 1953-54; resident in internal medicine Buffalo VA Hosp., 1954-56; resident in cardiology Buffalo Gen. Hosp., 1956-57; staff Mercy Hosp., Buffalo, 1959—, chmn. dept. medicine, 1972—, dir. residency tng. internal medicine, 1972—; faculty State U. N.Y. at Buffalo, 1960—, asso. clin. prof. medicine, 1972—; practice medicine specializing in internal medicine Buffalo, 1959—. Pres. Heart Assn. Western N.Y., 1969; bd. dirs. Health Care Plan Western N.Y., Erie Region Profl. Services Rev. Orgn. Served with M.C., U.S. Army, 1957-59. Diplomate Am. Bd. Internal Medicine. Fellow A.C.P.; mem. Western N.Y. (pres. 1968), N.Y. State (pres. 1974-75), Am. socs. internal medicine, State U. N.Y. at Buffalo Med. Alumni Assn. (pres. 1976), Am. Assn. Program Dirs. Internal Medicine (exec. com. 1978), Erie County Med. Soc. (exec. bd. 1976—), AMA, Am. Coll. Cardiology, C. of C. Orchard Park. Republican. Roman Catholic. Clubs: Buffalo, Buffalo Athletic, N.Y. Athletic, Orchard Park Country. Home: 6 Stonehenge Rd Orchard Park NY 14127 Office: Mercy Hosp 565 Abbott Rd Buffalo NY 14220

MALONEY, PAUL KEATING, JR., urologist; b. N.Y.C., Oct. 24, 1934; s. Paul Keating and Mary Veronica (Shanahan) M.; B.S., Holy Cross Coll., 1956; M.D., Georgetown U., 1960; m. Maureen Murphy,

Dec. 5, 1964; children—Jennifer Christie, Paula Christine, Edward Paul. Intern, St. Vincent's Hosp., N.Y.C., 1960-61, asst. resident in surgery, 1961-62; asst. resident in urology Squier Urol. Clinic, Columbia Presbyn. Med. Center, N.Y.C., 1962-64, in pediatric urology, 1964, resident in urology, 1964-65, fellow in pediatric urology, 1967, asso. in urology, 1967-72; lectr. U. Madrid Med. Sch., 1966; practice medicine, specializing in urology, Norwalk, Conn., 1967—; staff, med. bd. Darien Convalescent Center, Elmcrest Health Care Center; mem. staff Norwalk Hosp., sec. med. exec. com., 1976—; cons. Pub. Health Nursing Assn., Wilton, 1976-77. Trustee, Norwalk Med. Found.; mem. pres.'s council Georgetown U. Med. Sch., 1976, 77, 78. Served as capt. M.C., USAF, 1965-67. Diplomate Am. Bd. Urology. Fellow A.C.S.; mem. AMA, Conn. (del. 1976-78), Norwalk (sec.), Fairfield County med. socs., Am. Urology Assn., Holy Cross Alumni Club of Fairfield County (dir. 1977-78). Contbr. articles to profl. jours. Home: Wild Duck Rd Wilton CT 06897 Office: 12 Elmcrest Terr Norwalk CT 06850

MALONEY, RANDOLPH DAVID, peripheral vascular surgeon; b. Troy, N.Y., May 4, 1940; s. Randolph B. and Alice Mary M.; B.S. in Biology Georgetown U., 1963; M.D., N.Y. Med. Coll., 1967; m. Mary Alice Fisher, Oct. 12, 1968; children—Marielle, Claudine, Amanda. Intern, resident in gen. surgery St. Vincent's Hosp. & Med. Center, N.Y.C., 1967-72, chief resident in surgery, instr. in surgery St. Vincent's Hosp. & Med. Center-N.Y. U., 1971-72; clin., research fellow in vascular surgery Mass. Gen. Hosp.-Harvard Med. Sch., Boston, 1974-75; instr. in surgery Tufts U., 1975—; vis. surgeon Beverly (Mass.) Hosp., 1975—; chief dept. surgery Mass. Rehab. Hosp., Boston, 1975—; clin. asso. surgeon Mass. Gen. Hosp., Boston, research asso. Vascular Surgery Lab. Trustee Beverly Hosp., 1977—; bd. dirs. United Fund North Shore, 1975—; bd. dirs. North Bay council Boy Scouts Am., 1977—, chmn. adv. council Beverly Hosp. Explorer Post, 1978—. Served to lt. comdr., M.C., USN, 1972-74. Recipient Louis McCahill medal and Alpha Phi Omega award Georgetown U., 1963, Cor et Manus and Nat. Found. Merit awards N.Y. Med. Coll., 1967. Diplomate Am. Bd. Surgery. Fellow A.C.S.; mem. Mass. Med. Soc., Assn. Mil. Surgeons, Soc. Cryobiology, Am. Geriatrics Soc., Am. Heart Assn., Essex South Surg. Soc., Nat. Audubon Soc., New Eng. Soc. Vascular Surgery, Alpha Kappa Kappa. Clubs: Manchester Bath and Tennis (Mass.); Plantation Beach (Captiva Isle, Fla.). Home: 4 Bay View Ave Beverly Cove MA 01915 Office: Parkhurst Bldg Herrick St Beverly MA 01915

MALONEY, WILLIAM GERARD, investment co. exec.; b. Dansville, N.Y., Apr. 8, 1917; s. William J. and Fannie K. (Kirschner) M.; B.S., U. Pa., 1939; m. Katherine R. Kenney, Oct. 21, 1940; children—William J., Elizabeth Ann, Stephen G. Trainee, Hemphill, Noyes & Co., N.Y.C., 1939, mem. research dept., 1940-42, 44-45, mgr. corporate fin. dept., 1949, partner, 1951-63, co-mng. partner, 1963-64; co-ordinating partner Hornblower & Weeks-Hemphill, Noyes, N.Y.C., 1965-71, mgr. br. office adminstrn., 1969-71, vice chmn. exec. com., dir., 1972—; sr. mng. dir. Loeb Rhoades, Hornblower & Co., 1978—; dir. Servomation Corp., W.F. Hall Printing Co., Continental Investment Corp.; dir., vice chmn., Hanover Petroleum Corp., 1969-76. Served with AUS, 1942-43. Mem. N.Y. Soc. Security Analysts. Republican. Roman Catholic. Clubs: Met., India House, Assn. Knights and Ladies of Equestrian Order of Holy Sepulchre of Jerusalem, Knights of Malta. Home: 39 Louise's Ln New Canaan CT 06840 Office: 8 Hanover St New York City NY 10004

MALOOF, MITCHELL, speech pathologist, ednl. adminstr.; b. Boston, July 6, 1915; s. Assad J. and Hundumi (Najim) M.; B.A., Staley Coll., 1951, M.A., 1952, Ph.D., 1955; M.Ed., Boston Coll., 1954; Ed.D., Calvin Coolidge Coll., 1962; m. Ruth Stroum, May 29, 1949. Field rep. Kelley-Koett X-Ray Co., Boston, 1938-40; prof. speech and edn. Staley Coll., Brookline, Mass., 1951-57; prof. speech Harvard U. Extension, 1954-58; mem. psychiat. staff Boston State Hosp., 1955-57; dir. speech North Adams (Mass.) Sch. Dept., 1957—. Vis. speech pathologist North Adams Hosp., Plunkett Meml. Hosp., Adams, Mass. Bd. dirs. YMCA, 1961—, v.p., 1969-78. Served with M.C., AUS, 1941-45; ETO. Recipient Community Service award, 1969. Mem. Speech Assn. Am., Nat. Soc. Study Edn., N.E. Speech Assn., Mass. Speech Assn. Baptist. Clubs: Masons (Shriner), Rotary (pres. 1969). Research in speech therapy, 1955-57; pioneer in successful treatment of catatonic schizophrenia Boston State Hosp. Home: 517 Main St Williamstown MA 01267 Office: 206 E Main St North Adams MA 01247

MALOWANY, MOISES SALOMON, physician; b. Havana, Cuba, Aug. 10, 1934; s. Owszyja and Frima Gisia (Bard) M.; came to U.S., 1968, naturalized, 1973; B.S. summa cum laude, Instituto Vibora, 1953; M.D. summa cum laude, U. Havana, 1962; m. Rose Camus, Dec. 27, 1961; children—Israel, Daniel. Intern, Univ. Hosp., Havana, 1961-62, resident, 1962-63; dir. microbiology Hosp. A.A. Aballi, Havana, 1964-66; microbiologist in charge eneteric div. Pub. Health Lab., 1966-68; instr. dept. microbiology U. Havana Med. Sch., 1962-66; dir. microbiology Mt. Sinai Hosp. Services at Elmhurst (N.Y.) Hosp., 1968—; sr. instr. pathology Mt. Sinai Sch. Medicine, Elmhurst, N.Y., 1968—. Diplomate Am. Bd. Pathology. Mem. Coll. Am. Pathologists, Am. Soc. Clin. Pathologists, Am. Soc. Microbiology, N.Y. Acad. Sci., N.Y. State, Queens County med. socs. Republican. Jewish. Home: 181 Rutgers Rd E Orangeburg NY 10962 Office: 79-01 Broadway Elmhurst NY 11373

MALOY, CHARLES EDWARD, III, univ. adminstr., counselor; b. Altoona, Pa., May 14, 1942; s. Charles Edward and Natalie (Fleck) M.; B.A. in Polit. Sci., U. Fla., 1964, M.Ed. in Counseling, 1967; certificate advanced study adminstrn. in higher edn. Loyola Coll., Balt., 1975; m. Diane Carroll Lewis, Dec. 23, 1967; children—Charles Edward, IV, Molly Clark. Counselor, Towson State U. Counseling Center, 1967-71, asso. dir., 1971-73, dir., 1973—; asst. prof. psychology Towson State U., 1971—; tng. cons. U. Md., 1976; tng. cons. Md. Dept. Juvenile Services. Mem. Am. Assn. Higher Edn., Am., Md. personnel, guidance assns., Am., Md. (pres. 1974-75, certificate for meritorious service 1973) coll. personnel assns., Delta Tau Delta. Presbyterian. Home: 7906A Knollwood Rd Towson MD 21204 Office: Towson State U Towson MD 21204

MALSKY, STANLEY JOSEPH, physicist; b. N.Y.C., July 15, 1925; s. Joseph and Nellie (Karpinski) M.; B.S., N.Y. U., 1949, M.A., 1950, M.S., 1953, Ph.D., 1963; m. Gloria E. Gagliardi, Oct. 15, 1965; children—Randolph J., Roy W., Mark A. Nuclear physicist Dept. Def., 1959-54; chief physicist VA, 1954-63; adj. asso. prof., then prof. radiol. sci. Manhattan Coll., Bronx, N.Y., 1960-74; non-resident research collaborator med. div. Brookhaven Nat. Labs., Upton, N.Y., 1964-69; research prof. radiology N.Y. U. Sch. Medicine, 1975—; pres. Radiol. Physics Assn., White Plains, N.Y., since 1965. Served with U.S. Army, 1945-46. Recipient James Picker Found. award, 1963-67; Founder's Day award N.Y. U., 1964; Leadership award Manhattan Coll., 1969. Fellow Am. Pub. Health Assn., AAAS, Royal Soc. Health; charter mem. Am. Assn. Physicists in Medicine, Health Physics Soc. Roman Catholic. Author papers, chpts. in books.

MALTER, IRA JOEL, radiologist; b. N.Y.C., Apr. 14, 1943; s. Herman L. and Mary Elizabeth (Nose) M.; A.B., Columbia U., 1963; M.D., Harvard U., 1967; m. Geraldine Hass, Aug. 18, 1966; children—Harlan Mitchell, Evan Andrew. Pediatric intern, Univ. Hosps., Cleve., 1967-68; diagnostic radiology resident Barnes Hosp., St. Louis, 1968-71; chief nuclear medicine Day Kimball Hosp., Putnam, Conn., 1973-78; chief nuclear medicine Glover Meml. Hosp., Needham, Mass., 1978—; instr. radiology Brown U., Providence, 1973—. Mem. recreation commn., Pomfret, Conn., 1977—; trustee Temple Beth Israel, Killingly, Conn., 1974—. Served to maj. USAF, 1971-73. Diplomate Am. Bd. Radiology, Am. Bd. Nuclear Medicine. Mem. Am. Coll. Radiology, Am., New Eng. roentgen ray socs., Soc. Nuclear Medicine, Radiol. Soc. N.Am., Mass. Radiol. Soc., Conn. Med. Soc. Jewish. Contbr. articles to profl. jours. Home: 93 Dartmouth St West Newton MA 02165 Office: Glover Meml Hosp Needham MA 02192

MALTESE, JOHN ALBERT, metal finishing co. exec.; b. N.Y.C., Aug. 18, 1922; s. Joseph and Tina (Grasso) M.; grad. high sch.; m. Lyra Sue Swift, June 17, 1966; children—Jonathan J., Melissa Sue. Pres., co-founder Prodn. Spraying & Mfg. Corp., Deer Park, N.Y., 1955—, dir., 1956—; partner J. Maltese & Son, N.Y.C., 1946—; dir. Bank of Babylon (N.Y.). Served with USAF, 1942-45. Decorated D.F.C., Air medal with oak leaf clusters. Mem. Nat. Found. Health, Welfare and Pension Plans, Woods Hole Oceanographic Instn., Deep Sea Club (dir.). Clubs: Southward Ho Country, Ocean Reef. Address: Prodn Spraying & Mfg Corp Marcus Blvd Deer Park NY 11729

MAMULA, STEVEN NICHOLAS, JR., ins. broker; b. Pitts., Dec. 26, 1939; s. Steven and Minnie (Maravich) M.; B.S., Waynesburg Coll., 1961; M.A., U. W.Va., 1964. Ins. broker, owner Steven Mamula Agency, Carnegie, Pa., 1968—; v.p. Asso. Gen. Agy., Inc.; owner apt. complex. Mem. Fraternity Tchrs. of History, Pa. Assn. Notaries Pub., Pa. Assn. Ind. Ins. Agts., Nat. Assn. Ins. Agts., Delta Sigma Phi. Democrat. Serbian Orthodox. Clubs: Pitts. Athletic Assn., Lone Pine Country, Serbian, Moose, Elks. Home: 335 Thompson St Bridgeville PA 15017 Office: 217 E Main St Carnegie PA 15106

MANAHAN, KENNETH ROY, guidance counselor; b. Ridley Park, Pa., Dec. 2, 1930; s. Frederick Roy and Louise Mary (Edmunds) M.; B.S. in Edn., West Chester (Pa.) State Coll., 1957; M.S. in Ednl. Adminstrn., Temple U., Phila., 1970; certificate in guidance and counseling, Rutgers U., 1966; m. Lorna M. Fischer, Aug. 19, 1957; 1 son, Kenneth Roy. Tchr., Blackhorse Pike Regional Sch. Dist., Runnemede, N.J., 1957-59; tchr. Deptford Twp. Sch. Dist., West Deptford, N.J., 1959-65; guidance counselor West Deptford High Sch., Westville, N.J., 1965—; tennis coach. Mem. Deptford Twp. Sch. Bd.; adminstrv. bd. Almonesson Methodist Ch.; former library trustee; former exec. com. Boy Scouts Am.; former advisor Meth. Youth Fellowship; former umpire Little League Baseball. Served to staff sgt., USAF, 1949-53. Mem. NEA, N.J., West Deptford edn. assns., Am., Gloucester County personnel and guidance assns., Am. Sch. Counselors Assn., South Jersey Coaches Assn., Nat., N.J. sch. bds. assns. Democrat. Clubs: Haddonwood Tennis, Touchdown of So. N.J. Home: 51 Bruce Dr Deptford NJ 08096 Office: West Deptford High School Westville NJ 08093

MANCE, JULIAN CLIFFORD, JR., pianist-composer; b. Chicago, Oct. 10, 1928; s. Julian Clifford and Marie (McCollum) M.; student Roosevelt Coll., 1946-47; m. Beverlee Sylvia Stams, Sept. 20, 1958 (div. Dec. 1974); m. 2d, Marlene Dorrit Haertel, Dec. 3, 1975 (dec. Jan. 1978). Played and recorded with: Gene Ammons, 1947-49; Lester Young, 1949-50; Dinah Washington, 1954-55; Cannonball Adderley, 1956-57; Dizzy Gillespie, 1958-61; leader of own group (Junior Mance Trio), 1961—. Recordings for Verve, Riverside, Capitol, Atlantic, Polydor, East Wind record cos. Pres. Junito Music Pub. Co. Served with AUS, 1951-53. Recipient Downbeat Mag. New Star award, 1961. Mem. Nat. Acad. Rec. Arts and Scis. Author: How to Play Blues Piano, 1967. Address: 55 W 14th St New York City NY 10011

MANCINI, JOSEPH ANDREW, steel co. exec.; b. LeRoy, N.Y., Aug. 24, 1920; s. Chris J. and Sarah (Amato) M.; student U. Rochester, 1941-42; m. Anne Marie Lippa, Oct. 2, 1943; children—Joseph Chris, Julie Anne. With Burke Steel Co., Inc., 1940-55, beginning as laborer, successively asst. supt., 1940-50, mgr. forging ops., 1950-55; pres. Monroe Forgings, Inc. unit AMCA Internat. Corp., Rochester, N.Y., 1955—; pres. Certified Steels, Inc. Mem. Am. Soc. Metals, ASTM, C. of C., Am. Ordnance Assn., N.Y. State Conservation Council. Roman Catholic. Research and devel. in forging of super alloy metals. Home: 26 Harwood Ln East Rochester NY 14445 Office: PO Box 1111 Rochester NY 14603

MANCINI, LAWRENCE OTTO, microbiologist; b. Waterbury, Conn., Apr. 2, 1935; s. Lawrence and Josephine (Claricurzio) M.; B.S., U. Conn., 1958; M.S. magna cum laude, Coll. St. Rose, 1964; Ph.D. cum laude, U. R.I., 1968; m. Rosann Judith Mannello, June 10, 1961; children—Mark Joseph, Steven Lawrence, David Matthew. Diagnostic med. microbiologist St. Mary's Hosp., Waterbury, Conn., 1958-59; microbiologist Marshall Labs, Hamden, Conn., 1959-60; research asso. Sterling-Winthrop Research Inst., Rensselaer, N.Y., 1960-65; staff mem. virology U. R.I., Kingston, 1966-68; group leader Union Carbide Research Inst., Tarrytown, N.Y., 1968-73; pres. Biotest Labs., Ossining, N.Y., 1973-74; sect. chief microbiology dept. pathology Jersey City Med. Center, 1974-75; dir. microbiology, pathology dept. Middlesex Meml. Hosp., Middletown, Conn., 1975—; mem. profl. adv. panel Med. Lab. Observer, 1978—. Westchester County rep. Coll. St. Rose, Albany, N.Y. Mem. Am. Acad. Microbiology, Am. Soc. Microbiology, AAAS, Sigma Xi. Patentee avian encephalomyelitis vaccine. Home: 33 Somerset Dr Berlin CT 06037 Office: Middlesex Meml Hosp 28 Crescent St Middletown CT 06457

MANCINI, RONALD NOVEL, psychotherapist; b. Providence, Apr. 26, 1947; s. Camillo V. and Alyda (DeWilde) M.; B.A. in Psychology and Sociology, Roger Williams Coll., Providence, 1970; M.A. in Agy. Counseling, U. R.I., 1974. Social case worker R.I. Dept. Vets. Affairs, 1971-73; clin. social worker R.I. Vets. Home, Bristol, 1972-78; psychotherapist, Warren, R.I., 1978—; adj. faculty Roger Williams Coll., 1974—, Providence Coll., 1976—, U. R.I., 1978—; cons. Alcoholism Council Fall River (Mass.). Mem. Assn. Group Work Specialists, Internat. Transactual Analysis Assn., Am. Personnel and Guidance Assn., R.I. Conf. Social Work, R.I. Social Workers Alliance, Hope Council on Alcoholism, Am. Assn. Rehab. Counselors. Roman Catholic. Author articles. Home: 438 Almeida Ct Bristol RI 02809 Office: 1052 Main St Warren RI 02885

MANCUSO, LOUIS, recording co. exec.; b. N.Y.C., Jan. 22, 1944; s. Charles and Lena (Panzica) M.; student U. S.C., 1962-65, Middlesex County Coll., 1970-73; 1 son, Michael. Systems engr. IBM, N.Y.C., 1965-67; chief engr. A & B Duplications Ltd/Electro Sound, N.Y.C., 1967-75; v.p. and gen. mgr. ASR Rec. Services Inc., Fairfield, N.J., 1975—; audio visual cons. Served with USAF, 1961-65. Mem. Audio Engring. Soc. Roman Catholic. Club: Jaycees. Home: 16 River Rd Apt K Nutley NJ 07110 Office: 344 Kaplan Dr Fairfield NJ 07006

MANDARINO, MICHAEL PASCOL, orthopedic surgeon; b. Phila., Mar. 16, 1921; s. Michael J. and Genevieve (Pepe) M.; B.A., La Salle Coll., Phila., 1942; M.D., Hahnemann Med. Coll., Phila., 1945; m. Antoinette Marie (Dolly) Mandarino, Mar. 27, 1943; children—Stephanie, Michael J., Mariane. Intern, Hahnemann Hosp., Phila., 1945-46; resident orthopedic surgery Hahnemann Hosp., 1948-49, State Hosp. Crippled Children, Elizabethtown, Pa., 1949-50, Hosp. for Joint diseases, N.Y.C., 1950-51; chief dept. orthopedic surgery W. Park Hosp., Phila., 1963—; lectr., cons. in field. Licensed physician Pa. Diplomate Am. Bd. Orthopedic Surgery. Served to capt., M.C., U.S. Army, 1946-48, 51-53. Fellow Am. Acad. Orthopedic Surgeons, Am. Coll. Sports Medicine, Am. Fracture Assn., Am. Assn. Physicians and Surgeons, Luth. Med. Center, N.Y.; mem. AMA, Pa., Philadelphia County med. socs., Phila., Eastern orthopedic socs., other orgns. Address: 2832 Belmont Ave Philadelphia PA 19131

MANDEL, PERRY RICHARD, radiologist; b. N.Y.C., Sept. 19, 1927; s. Max and Pearl (Fox) M.; B.S., N.Y. U., 1950; M.D., N.Y. Med. Coll., 1954; m. Louise Wilensky, Dec. 25, 1952; children—Robert, Susan. Intern, Flushing (N.Y.) Hosp., 1954-55; resident in diagnostic radiology, Beth Israel Hosp., N.Y.C., 1955-57; resident in therapeutic radiology, Bellevue Hosp., N.Y.C., 1957-58; asst. radiotherapist, Queens Gen. Hosp., N.Y.C., 1958-59; chief dept. radiation therapy and nuclear medicine, Nassau Hosp., Mineola, N.Y., 1959—; cons., Nassau County Med. Center, So. Nassau Hosp., St. Francis Hosp.; asso. prof. clin. radiology, State U. N.Y., Stonybrook; research collaborator, Brookhaven Nat. Lab., 1975—; adj. prof. C.W. Post Coll., L.I. U., also med. dir. nuclear medicine tech. program C.W. Post health scis. dept. Served with U.S. Army, 1944-45. Regional med. program grantee, 1971-73. Diplomate Am. Bd. Radiology, Am. Bd. Nuclear Medicine. Fellow Am. Coll. Radiology; mem. Am. Soc. Therapeutic Radiology, Radiol. Soc. N.Am., Soc. Nuclear Medicine, N.Y. Roentgen Ray Soc., Am., L.I. (pres., 1965-66) radiol. socs., AMA, N.Y. State, Nassau County (pres. 1972-73) med. socs., Am. Cancer Soc. (pres. Nassau div. 1969-71, nat. award 1971). Contbr. articles to profl. med. jours. Office: Nassau Hospital 259 First St Mineola NY 11501

MANDELBAUM, MARK SAMUEL, editor; b. Bklyn., Jan. 2, 1950; s. Samson and Ruth (Korek) M.; B.A., Coll. City N.Y., 1972; m. Raellen Bernstein, Aug. 17, 1975. Supr., Lincoln Center for Performing Arts, N.Y.C., 1972-73; copy editor Am. Inst. Aeros. and Astronautics, N.Y.C., 1974-75, mng. editor scientific jours., 1975-77; exec. editor sci. jours. Assn. for Computing Machinery, N.Y.C., 1977—. Mem. AAAS, Assn. for Computing Machinery, Council Ednl. and Sci. Soc. Execs., Am. Mgmt. Assn. Home: 1561 Lemoine Ave Fort Lee NJ 07024 Office: Assn for Computing Machinery 1133 Ave of Americas New York City NY 10036

MANDELL, LEONARD CHARLES, cons. engr., forensic scientist; b. Providence, July 6, 1919; s. Charles Lawrence and Florence (Greenleaf) M.; B.S. in Mech. Engring., U. Ala., 1941; postgrad. U. So. Calif., 1942-44; M.S., Mass. Inst. Tech., 1946; M.S. in Occupational Health, Harvard U., 1953; m. Sylvia Evelyn Schwartz; children from previous marriage—Howard A., Linda R. Mandell Bennett, Mark S. Chief engr. Enginaire, Inc., Providence, 1945-54; cons. engr., Providence, 1954-67; pres., partner Leonard C. Mandell Assos., Providence, 1967-73; pres. Safety Services Inc., Providence, 1972—; adj. prof. USPHS extension div. U. R.I., 1949-53. Pres. Jewish Children's Home R.I.—Camp JORI, Point Judith, R.I., 1963-67; bd. dirs. R.I. Respiratory Disease Assn. Registered profl. engr., Mass., Conn., R.I., Maine. Diplomate Am. Acad. Environ. Engrs., Am. Bd. Indsl. Hygiene, Am. Acad. Forensic Scis. Mem. N.E. Air Pollution Control Assn. (founding pres. 1956—), Nat. Fire Protection Assn., ASTM, Am. Soc. Heating, Refrigerating and Air Conditioning Engrs., Info. Council Flammable Fabrics, ASME, Am. Inst. Chem. Engrs., Nat. LP Gas Assn., Am. Gas Assn., R.I. Soc. Profl. Engrs., Am. Soc. Safety Engrs., Sigma Xi. Clubs: Masons; Ledgemont Country (Seekonk, Mass.). Contbr. articles to profl. jours. Home: 441 Rochambeau Ave Providence RI 02906 Office: 140 Taunton Ave East Providence RI 02914

MANDIGO, JAMES ALLEN, cons. engr.; b. Kansas City, Mo., Oct. 25, 1911; s. Clark Rogers and Gladys Irene (Allen) M.; B.S. in Civil Engring., Kans. U., 1934; grad. Command and Gen. Staff Coll., U.S. Army, 1958; m. Helen Jedlicka, Apr. 13, 1935; 1 son, James Allen. Engr., Transcontinental and Western Airlines, Inc., Kansas City, Mo., 1935-36; asst. supr., chief draftsman J.F. Pritchard and Co., Kansas City, 1936-38; resident engr. Black and Veatch, Kansas City, 1938-40, engr., 1945-46; functional engr. Trans World Airlines, Kansas City, 1946-56, dir. facilities, 1956-57; project mgr. J.E. Greiner Co., Balt., 1957-59; exec. research div. FAA, Washington, 1959-60; dep. asst. tech. services Hdqrs. Air Force Systems Command, Washington, 1960-62, asso. dir. civil engring., 1962-63, asst. chief ops. and maintenance div., 1963-68; dir. master planning Airways Engring. Corp., Washington, 1968-69; project mgr. Landrum and Brown, Cin., 1969-72; dep. chief airport engr. Howard, Needles, Tammen, and Bergendoff, Balt., 1972-75; cons. engr. airport devel. and ops. Lutherville, Md., 1975—. Scoutmaster, committeeman Kansas City Area council Boy Scouts Am., 1923-57, engring. counselor Balt. Area council, 1972—; sec. Profl. Adv. Council State Energy Affairs Md. Served to lt. col. C.E., U.S. Army, 1940-45; ETO. Registered profl. engr., Md., Mo., N.Y. Fellow, life mem. ASCE and Md. Sect.; mem. Nat. Soc. Profl. Engrs. (membership com.), Md. Profl. Engrs. in Pvt. Practice (chmn.), Md. Soc. Profl. Engrs. (dir., officer Chesapeake chpt.), Soc. Am. Mil. Engrs. (dir. Balt. chpt.), Engring. Soc. Balt. (fin. adv., house, membership coms.). Republican. Roman Catholic. Club: Green Spring Inn (Md.). Home: 112 Martingale Rd Lutherville MD 21093

MANDL, ALEXANDER ERNST, physicist; b. Vienna, May 18, 1938; s. Otto and Sonja (Freilich) M.; came to U.S., 1938, naturalized, 1946; B.S., Coll. City N.Y., 1960; M.S., N.Y. U., 1963, Ph.D., 1967; m. Bette Greenwald, Nov. 23, 1960; children—Kenneth David, Jeffrey Elliot. Research scientist Nat. Bur. Standards, Gaithersburg, Md., 1967-69, Avco Everett Research Lab., Inc., Everett, Mass., 1969—. NSF fellow, 1965-66. Mem. Am. Phys. Soc., Phi Beta Kappa, Sigma Pi Sigma. Contbr. articles to profl. jours. Measured many of the basic properties of the alkali halides and the halogen negative ions. Home: 79 Clinton St Brookline MA 02146 Office: Avco 2385 Revere Beach Pkwy Everett MA 02149

MANES, DONALD RICHARD, borough pres. N.Y.C.; b. Bklyn., Jan. 18, 1934; s. Edward and Belle (Cohen) M.; student Bus. Adminstrn., Hofstra U.; J.D., Bklyn. Law Sch., 1957; m. Mariene Warshofsky, Dec. 25, 1955; children—Beth, Lauren, Eric. Admitted to N.Y. bar, 1957; practiced in N.Y.C., 1957-71; former mem. firm Baron, Harrison & Manes, Kew Gardens, N.Y.; borough pres., Queens, N.Y., 1971—. Asso. counsel to State Assembly majority leader Moses M. Weinstein, 1965; asst. dist. atty. Queens (N.Y.) County, 1961-64; mem. N.Y.C. Council, 1965-71, chmn. housing com., 1968-71, also mem. consumer affairs and legis. coms., chmn. Queens County Democratic Com., 1974—; mem. Nat. Dem. Com., 1975—. Mem. Turnpike Drug Council, 1971. Bd. dirs. Queens Child Guidance Center, Hillcrest Jewish Center. Mem. Brandeis Assn. (past pres.), Queens C. of C., Fedn. Jewish Philanthropies, K.P. Home: 162-01 71st Ave Flushing NY 11365 Office: 120-55 Queens Blvd Kew Gardens NY 11424

MANG, HENRY YANLING, physician; b. China, Sept. 9, 1940; s. Lie Ping and Yao Chin M.; M.B. B.S., U. Sydney (Australia), 1965; m. Juliane Patricia McDonnell, Mar. 20, 1967; children—Patrick, Caroline. Registrar, London Hosp. and Central Middlesex Hosp. (Eng.), 1968-70; staff radiologist VA Hosp., Bklyn., 1973; asst. attending radiologist Lutheran Med. Center, Bklyn., 1973-75; chief radiology dept. USPHS Hosp., S.I., N.Y., 1975—. Fellow Royal Coll. Radiologists; mem. Am. Coll. Radiology, Am. Coll. Nuclear Physicians, Am. Coll. Internat. Physicians. Office: USPHS Hosp Staten Island NY 10304

MANGAN, EDMUND LAWRENCE, engr., steel co. mgr.; b. Los Angeles, Dec. 20, 1938; s. Francis Aloysius and Edith Duell (Perry) M.; B.S., U.S. Naval Acad., 1960; M.B.A., Lehigh U., 1975; m. Suzanne Marie Yelle, Feb. 2, 1960; children—Alan Francis, Michele Marie, Meredith Kay. Engr., Curtiss Wright Corp., 1961-63, Weston Inst., 1963-64; research engr. measurement and control div. research dept. Bethlehem Steel Corp. (Pa.), 1964-70, research supr., 1970-76, asst. sect. mgr., 1976-78, spl. engr. gen. mgr. staff, 1978—. Served to ensign USN, 1960-61. Recipient Kelly award Assn. Iron and Steel Engrs., 1973. Mem. IEEE, Assn. Iron and Steel Engrs., Bethlehem Steel Club. Club: Bethlehem. Holder and co-holder 8 U.S. patents relating to indsl. dimensional measurement equipment. Office: Bethlehem Plant Office Bethlehem Steel Corp Bethlehem PA 18016

MANGANELLO, JAMES ANGELO, psychologist; b. Cambridge, Mass., Nov. 30, 1944; s. Almando and Carmella (Spera) M.; A.B., Eastern Nazarene Coll., Quincy, Mass., 1966; Ed.M., Suffolk U., 1969; A.M., Boston U., 1970, Ed.D., 1977; m. Rosemarie Bombara, Dec. 26, 1965. Instr. biology N.Y. Christian Acad., Bklyn., 1966-67; minister youth and edn. St. Paul Sch., Somerville, Mass., 1967-69; also founder, dir. Community Nursery Sch.; resident dir., instr. Malone Coll., Canton, Ohio, 1969-70; cons. psychologist E. Lindemann Mental Health Center, Boston, 1971-75; clin. and research fellow dept. psychiatry Mass Gen. Hosp., Boston, 1973-75; psychologist North Shore Counseling Center, Beverly, Mass., 1975—; instr. North Shore Community Coll., Beverly, 1975—; dir. Grace Chapel Health Center, Lexington, Mass., 1977—. Mem. Am. Psychol. Assn., AAAS, Am. Sci. Affiliation, Soc. Sci. Study Religion. Home: 14 Michael Rd North Beverly MA 01915 Office: 23 Broadway Beverly MA 01915 also Worthen Rd Lexington MA 02173

MANGEIM, DAVID STEPHEN, library adminstr.; b. S.I., N.Y., June 8, 1946; s. George and Eva (Kornstein) M.; B.A., Wagner Coll., 1968, M.A., 1972; M.L.S., Rutgers U., 1974. Congressional intern to Congressman John M. Murphy, 1966; tchr. S.I. Acad., 1967, 70, St. Louis Acad., S.I., 1969-70, Wagner Coll., 1970-71; fed. flood disaster loan officer SBA, S.I., 1971-72; reference librarian Rutgers U., New Brunswick, N.J., 1973-74; with Island Cycle Sales Inc., S.I., 1974, Bond's Inc., S.I., 1974-75; library dir. Neumann Preparatory Sch., Wayne, N.J., 1975-76; dir. Spotswood (N.J.) Pub. Library, 1976—; prof. history N.Y. Inst. Tech., S.I., 1977—. Served with U.S. Army, 1969. Recipient Verrazano Soc. award for excellence in geography, 1968. Mem. Am. Hist. Assn., N.J. Library Assn., N.Y. Motorcycle Coalition (exec. dir., pres.), Am. Motorcyclist Assn., Rutgers U. Grad. Sch. L.S. Alumni Assn., Phi Alpha Theta, Phi Mu Alpha Sinfonia. Editor, Rutgers U. Grad. Sch. L.S. Alumni Newsletter, 1977—; pub. relations columnist N.J. Libraries, 1978—; contbr. articles to profl. and motorcycle jours. Home: 339 Hart Ave Staten Island NY 10310 Office: 548 Main St Spotswood NJ 08884

MANGER, WILLIAM MUIR, physician; b. Greenwich, Conn., Aug. 13, 1920; s. Julius and Lilian (Weissinger) M.; B.S., Yale U., 1944; M.D., Columbia U., 1946; Ph.D., Mayo Found., U. Minn., 1958; student Washington and Lee U., 1940-41; m. Lynn Seymour Sheppard, May 30, 1964; children—William Muir, Lilian Wade, Stewart Sheppard, Charles Seymour. Intern, Presbyn. Hosp., N.Y.C., 1946-47, resident, 1949-50; fellow internal medicine Mayo Found., 1950-57; asst. physician Presbyn. Hosp., 1957, dir. Manger Research Found., 1961-77; clin. asst. vis. physician Columbia div. Bellevue Hosp., 1964-68, asst. attending, 1969-77, asso. attending, 1977—; instr. medicine Coll. Phys. and Surg., 1957-66, asso. medicine, 1966-70; asst. attending physician Presbyn. Hosp., 1966—; asst. clin. prof. medicine N.Y. U. Med. Center, 1968-75, asso. clin. prof. medicine, 1975—; mem. Internat. Med. Council on Drug Use, 1977—. Vice chmn. bd. Manger Hotels, Inc., 1957-73. Bd. govs. St. Albans Sch., Washington, 1958-64, 67-73, chmn., 1967-69; trustee Found. Research in Medicine and Biology, 1971-77, Buckley Sch., 1975—, Found. for Advancement Internat. Research in Microbiology, 1976—, Found. for Depression and Manic Depression, 1978—; bd. counselors Woodycrest, 1960-66. Served as lt. (j.g.) M.C., USNR, 1947-49. Recipient Meritorious Research award Mayo Found. Alumni, 1955. Diplomate Nat. Bd. Med. Examiners, Am. Bd. Internal Medicine. Fellow A.C.P., Acad. Psychosomatic Medicine, Am. Geriatric Soc., N.Y. Acad. Medicine (admission com. 1976—), Am. Coll. Cardiology, Am. Coll. Clin. Pharmacology, Royal Soc. Health, Am. Inst. Chemists; mem. Nat. Hypertension Assn. (chmn. 1977—), AMA, N.Y. State, N.Y. County med. socs., Am. Heart Assn. (fellow council on circulation, mem. council on high blood pressure research), Internat. Soc. Hypertension, Am. Thoracic Soc., N.Y. Acad. Scis., AAAS, Am. Physiol. Soc., Am. Chem. Soc., Am. Soc. Pharmacology and Exptl. Therapeutics, Am. Soc. for Clin. Pharmacology and Therapeutics, Med. Strollers, N.Y.C., Endocrine Soc., Pan Am. Med. Assn., Harvey Soc., Mayo Alumni (pres. N.Y. area 1970-71, sec.-treas. 1971—), Soc. Exptl. Biology and Medicine, S.R. (chmn. admissions com. 1959-67, bd. mgrs. 1959-67, 69-70), Research Discussion Group (sec.-treas. 1958—), Am. Fedn. Clin. Research, Am. Soc. Nephrology, Royal Soc. Medicine (affiliate), Fellows Assn. Mayo Found. (v.p., pres. 1953), Catecholamine Club (a founder, (sec.-treas. 1967—), Doctors Mayo Soc. (steering com.), New Eng. Soc., Sigma Xi, Nu Sigma Nu, Phi Delta Theta. Presbyterian (elder 1968-71, trustee 1962-72, deacon 1959-61). Clubs: Explorers, Meadow (L.I., N.Y.); University, Yale, N.Y. Athletic (N.Y.C.); Southampton Bathing Corp. Author: Chemical Quantitation of Epinephrine and Norepinephrine in Plasma, 1959; co-author: Pheachromocytoma, 1977. Editor, contbr. Hormones and Hypertension, 1966. Editor: Am. Lecture Series in Endocrinology, 1962-75. Contbr. articles to profl. and lay jours. Home: 8 E 81st St New York City NY 10028 Office: 400 E 34th St New York City NY 10016

MANGES, JAMES H., investment banker; b. N.Y.C., Oct. 8, 1927; s. Horace S. and Natalie (Bloch) M.; grad. Phillips Exeter Acad., 1945; B.A., Yale U., 1950; M.B.A., Harvard U., 1953; m. Joan Brownell, Oct. 1969 (div.); m. 2d, Mary Seymour, Mar. 28, 1974. With Kuhn, Loeb & Co., N.Y.C., 1954—, partner, 1967-77, mng. dir. Lehman Bros. Kuhn Loeb, Inc., N.Y.C., 1977—; dir. Baker Industries, Inc., Metromedia, Inc. Served with CIC, AUS, 1946-48. Clubs: Bond, Yale (N.Y.C.); City Midday, Century Country (Purchase, N.Y.). Home: 875 Park Ave New York NY 10021 Office: 1 William St New York NY 10004

MANGIERI, ROBERT PAUL, ins. cons.; b. N.Y.C., May 20, 1941; s. Frank and Augustine (DiMartino) M.; student Queens Coll., 1963; B.A., Coll. City N.Y., 1965; diploma U.S. Marine Corps Sch., 1968; certificate Pohs Inst. York Coll., 1970. Account exec. Marsh & McLennan, N.Y.C., 1975; ins. cons. Robert P. Mangieri Co., N.Y.C., 1975—; spl. asst. youth affairs Office of the Mayor, 1969; exec. sec. to chmn. transp. Community Planning Bd. #9. Legis. asst. N.Y.C. Council, 1970; pres. Bicentennial Adv. Bd. 1976; chmn. pub. relations Marine Corps Scholarship Found. Served with USMC, 1965-69. Hon. fire chief N.Y. State Fire Fighters Assn. Mem. Alumni Assn. City Coll. N.Y. Authur: The Pictorial History of Richmond Hill, Kew Gardens, Woodhaven, Ozone Park, 1976; Bicentennial columnist Leader-Observer; asst. editor Sea History. Home: 82-60 116th St Kew Gardens NY 11418

MANGLA, JAGDISH CHAND, gastroenterologist; b. Muktsar, Punjab, India, July 5, 1937; s. Hans Raj and Krishna Devi (Gupta) M.; came to U.S., 1966, naturalized, 1976; M.B.B.S., Punjab U., 1960, M.D., 1965; m. Sarla Gupta, May 19, 1963; children—Shailander Kumar, Neeraj Kumar. House officer, V.J. Hosp., Amritsar, Punjab, 1961, casualty med. officer, 1962; registrar, research asst. Postgrad. Med. Edn. and Research Inst., Chandigarh, Punjab, 1962-66; resident in internal medicine Highland Hosp., Rochester, N.Y., 1966-67; instr., asst. physician, research fellow gastroenterology U. Rochester/Strong Meml. Hosp., 1967-71, asst. prof. medicine, 1971-76, asso. prof., 1976—; acting dir. gastroenterology Monroe Community Hosp., 1970-72, dir., 1972—. Fellow Royal Coll. Physicians and Surgeons Can., ACP, Rochester Acad. Medicine, Royal Soc. Medicine (London); mem. Am. Gastroent. Assn., Am. Fedn. Clin. Research, AAAS, Med. Soc. Monroe County, Rochester Gut Club (pres. 1974-78), Sigma Xi. Hindu. Contbr. profl. jours. Home: 125 Clearview Dr Rochester NY 14526 Office: 435 E Henrietta Rd Rochester NY 14603

MANGOT, MICHAEL, elec. engr.; b. Warsaw, Poland, May 31, 1945; s. Jack Juda and Anna (Kielmanowitz) M.; came to U.S., 1956, naturalized, 1962; B.E., City Coll., City U. N.Y., 1966; M.S. in E.E., N.Y. U., 1970; M.B.A., U. Conn., 1975; m. Roselyn S. Lowenbach, Dec. 24, 1967; children—David Jeremy, Marc Benjamin. Elec. engr. Perkin Elmer, Wilton, Conn., 1966-71, engring. mgr., 1971-73, project dir. infrared spectroscopy, Norwalk, Conn., 1973-75, engring. mgr. chromatography mfg., 1978—; substitute tchr. Norwalk Tech. Inst., 1967. Bd. dirs. Congregation Agudath Sholom, 1978—, chmn. religious sch. bd. edn., 1978—. Regent scholar, 1962. Mem. IEEE, Stamford Engring. Soc., City Coll. of City U. N.Y. Alumni Assn. Jewish. Clubs: B'nai B'rith (v.p. Nutmeg lodge 1978—), Couples (pres. 1976-78). Home: 292 Haig Ave Stamford CT 06905 Office: Main Ave Norwalk CT 06856

MANGULIS, VISVALDIS, physicist; b. Tukums, Latvia, Nov. 25, 1930; s. Oskars Valdemars and Ieva Otilija (Sunins) M.; B.S., Bklyn. Coll., 1956; M.S., N.Y. U., 1958; m. Vija Blumfelds, Apr. 12, 1953; children—Mara, Antra. Physicist TRG div. Control Data Corp., Melville, N.Y., 1956-62, sect. head, 1962-68; mem. tech. staff Gen. Telephone & Electronics Labs., Bayside, N.Y., 1968; sr. staff cons. Computer Applications Inc., N.Y.C., 1968-70; v.p., sec./treas. Questek Inc., Roslyn, N.Y., also dir., 1970-75; prin. mem. engring. staff RCA Missile and Surface Radar div., Moorestown, N.J., 1975-78; mem. tech. staff RCA Labs., Princeton, N.J., 1978—. Served with USMC, 1951-53. Mem. IEEE, Am. Phys. Soc., Acoustical Soc. Am. Lutheran. Author: Handbook of Series for Scientists and Engineers, 1965. Contbr. articles to profl. publs. Home: 127 Ainsworth Ave East Brunswick NJ 08816 Office: RCA Labs David Sarnoff Research Center Princeton NJ 08540

MANICE, HAYWARD FERRY, architect; b. N.Y.C., Feb. 1, 1917; s. William DeForest and Harriet (Ferry) M.; grad. St. Mark's Sch., 1935; B.A., Yale, 1939, B.Arch., 1948; m. Beatrice Goelet, Feb. 7, 1948; children—John Hayward, Anne Guestier (Mrs. Edmond de la Haye Jousselin), Robert Goelet, Amelia Ferry, Pamela. Archtl. draftsman Harrison & Abramovitz, Architects, N.Y.C., 1948-49; archtl. planner NBC, N.Y.C., 1949-50; archtl. draftsman R.B. O'Connor & W.H. Kilham, Jr. Architects, N.Y.C., 1950-53; partner Hood & Manice, Architects, N.Y.C., 1954-59; project architect Rogers, Butler & Burgun, Architects, N.Y.C., 1960-68; partner Manice & Baker, Architects, N.Y.C., 1968-73; prin. Hayward F. Manice, architect, N.Y.C., 1973—. Pres. bd., chmn. exec. com. Christodora Found., N.Y.C., Northover, Inc., N.J.; bd. mgrs. St. Barnabas Hosp. for Chronic Diseases, Bronx; bd. dirs. Prescott Neighborhood House, N.Y.C.; former trustee Chapin Sch., Ltd., N.Y.C. Served with USNR, 1942-45. Registered architect, N.Y., N.J., Conn., Mass., R.I. Mem. AIA, N.Y. State Assn. Architects, Municipal Arts Soc. N.Y.C., Nat. Council Archtl. Registration Bds., St. Nicholas Soc. N.Y. Republican. Episcopalian. Clubs: Racquet and Tennis, Knickerbocker. Home: 4 E 72d St New York City NY 10021 Office: 342 Madison Ave New York City NY 10017

MANICE, WILLIAM DEF., former ins. broker; b. N.Y.C., May 14, 1914; s. William DeForest and Harriet (Ferry) M.; student Yale U., 1933-36; m. Olivia Ames, Sept. 10, 1944; children—William DeForest III, Oliver Ames. With Ins. Co. N.Am., N.Y.C., 1937-41; broker Marsh & McLennan, Inc., Boston, 1946-76; dir. Newport Electric Corp. (R.I.); corporator Provident Instn. For Savs. Chmn. advanced gifts Boston Community Fund, 1954, 69. Bd. dirs. Rogerson House, Seamen's Ch. Inst., Newport, R.I.; founder mem., regional v.p. for New Eng., U.S. Naval War Coll. Found.; trustee, mgr. Sears Fund, Children's Hosp. Med. Center Boston. Served to comdr. USNR, 1941-46. Decorated Bronze Star medal. Republican. Clubs: Brook (N.Y.C.); Country (Brookline, Mass.); Royal Bermuda Yacht; Tennis and Racquet, Somerset (Boston); Ida Lewis Yacht, Newport Country, Clambake, Newport Reading Room (Newport, R.I.). Home: 92 Orchard Ave Weston MA 02193

MANIKTALA, RAJINDAR KUMAR, cons. engr.; b. Sargodha, W. Punjab, India, May 10, 1936; s. Gobind Ram and Indra Vati (Narang) M.; came to U.S., 1960, naturalized, 1972; B.S. in Civil Engring., U. Nebr., 1962, M.S. in Structural Engring., 1963; m. Kamal Chowdry, Feb. 6, 1965; children—Arvin, Anita, Punam. Sr. engr. Bridge Design Div., Dept. of Rds., State of Nebr., Lincoln, 1962-69; supr. structural and archtl. sects. O'Brien & Gere Engrs., Inc., Syracuse, N.Y., 1969-71, mng. engr., 1971—. Dir., chmn. Internat. Service Com., 1975-78; mem. facilities com. N. Syracuse Central Sch. Dist., 1976-79; bd. dirs. UN Assn. of Central N.Y., 1975—. Registered profl. engr., Nebr., N.Y. Mem. Am. Water Works Assn. (mem. standards com. on prestressed concrete tanks 1974, chmn. ad hoc com. on post tensioned tanks 1975-76), ASCE, Am. Concrete Inst., Am. Mgmt. Assn., Am. Inst. Steel Constrn., Prestress Concrete Inst., Post Tensioning Inst. (mem. ad hoc com. on water tanks, silos and oil storage tanks). Club: Rotary (pres. 1974-75). Contbr. articles in field to profl. jours. Office: 1304 Buckley Rd Syracuse NY 13221

MANKA, DAN PAUL, chemist; b. Farrell, Pa., May 2, 1914; s. John Emil and Gizela (Bella) M.; B.S., Valparaiso U., 1936; postgrad. Carnegie-Mellon U., 1941-47; m. Louise Anna Wunderlich, Oct. 10, 1942; children—Paul D., Timothy E., John W., Dan P. Research chemist Koppers Co., Pitts., 1936-41; sr. research chemist Jones & Laughlin Steel Corp., Pitts., from 1941—; now cons. to fgn. and U.S. steel and non-ferrous producing cos., other related industries; lectr. to high sch. and coll. students; invited speaker 4th Internat. Conf. Analytical Chemistry, U. Birmingham (Eng.), 1977; mem. instructional staff 36th Appalachian gas measurement short course Robert Morris Coll., Pitts., 1976; invited speaker on sulfur analyses in gases symposium Chatham Coll., Pitts., 1976. Com. mem. Boy Scouts Am., 1955-60, review bd., 1956-64; sec. Regent Sq. Parents Assn., 1960-61. Accredited profl. chemist; named to Distinguished Speakers List, Instrument Soc. Am. Fellow Am. Inst. Chemists; mem. Soc. Analytical Chemists Pitts. (pres. 1975-76, invited symposium speaker 1976), Pitts. Conf. on Analytical Chemistry and Applied Spectroscopy (program chmn. 1975-76, exhibits chmn. 1976-78, publicity chmn. 1978—), Am. Chem. Soc., Eastern States Blast Furnace and Coke Oven Assn., Valparaiso U. Alumni Assn., Carnegie-Mellon U. Alumni Assn., Acad. Arts and Scis. Pitts., Nat. Audubon Soc., Audubon Soc. Western Pa., Nat., Internat. wildlife assns. Republican. Lutheran. Contbr. tech. presentations at profl. soc. meetings; patentee in field. Home: 1109 Lancaster Ave Pittsburgh PA 15218

MANKIN, HART TILLER, lawyer; b. Cleve., Dec. 26, 1933; s. Howard Edmonn and Fantine (Tiller) M.; student Northwestern U., 1950-52; B.A., U. South, 1954; J.D., U. Houston, 1960; m. Ruth A. Larson, Aug. 14, 1954; children—Margaret, Theodore, Susan. Admitted to Tex. bar, 1960, also D.C., U.S. Supreme Ct. bars; individual practice law, Houston, 1960-67; counsel, asst. to pres. Triumph Industries, Houston, 1967-69; gen. counsel GSA, Washington, 1969-71, Dept. Navy, Washington, 1971-73; v.p., gen. counsel Columbia Gas System, Wilmington, 1973—; dir. Del. Trust Co. Bd. dirs. Com. of 100, Del. Law Sch., Del. Humanities Council. Served with USAF, 1954-57. Recipient award GSA, 1970, Distinguished Pub. Service award Dept. Navy, 1973. Mem. State Bar Tex., D.C., Del., Am., Fed., Fed. Energy bar assns., Maritime Law Assn. U.S., Del. C. of C. (dir.). Episcopalian. Clubs: Greenville Country, Univ., Whist. Home: 1101 Westover Rd Wilmington DE 19807 Office: 20 Montchanin Rd Wilmington DE 19807

MANLEY, BROTHER EUGENE IGNATIUS, counselor; b. Scranton, Pa., Mar. 29, 1900; s. Patrick Joseph and Maria (Bohan) M.; student U. Pa., 1920-23, U. Scranton, 1924-25; B.S., LaSalle Coll., 1932; M.S., U. Pa., 1939; B.S. in Library Sci., Drexel U., 1944; certificate advanced studies in edn. Johns Hopkins U., 1971, postgrad., 1971-75; postgrad. Temple U., 1964-68. Secretarial, accounting positions various cos., Scranton, Pa., 1917-27; entered Christian Bros. Order, Roman Catholic Ch., 1927; tchr., librarian, bursar, adminstr. various schs., Beltsville, Md., Phila., Balt.; geriatric counselor, nutrition coordinator, lectr., tchr. phys. fitness for elderly Cath. Youth Assn., Adult Services, Pitts., 1975—; lectr. in field; asst. dir. Christian Bros., S.E. U.S. Novitiate, 1946-62. Recipient Citation, Comptroller, City of Balt., 1975, March of Dimes, 1977, U.S. Action Agy. for Volunteer Services, 1976; certificate of achievement Allegheny County (Pa.), 1978. Mem. Cath. Library Assn. (chmn. Phila. unit 1940), Am. Personnel and Guidance Assn., Nat. Vocat. Guidance Assn., Am. Sch. Counselors Assn., Am. Assn. Ret. Persons, Phi Delta Kappa. Roman Catholic. Contbr. articles in field to profl. jours. Home: 1000 McNeilly Rd Pittsburgh PA 15226 Office: Cath Youth Assn 286 Main St Pittsburgh PA 15201

MANN, CANDEE ANN MORICI, sch. counselor; b. N.Y.C., May 25, 1947; d. Anthony LoGalbo and Irene Ann (Rosenfeld) Morici; B.A. in Psychology, Coll. Notre Dame of Md., 1969; M.S., C.W. Post Center of L.I. U., 1973, P.D. in Counselor Edn. 1974; Guidance counselor Hauppauge (N.Y.) Pub. Schs., 1973-75; career guidance program coordinator BOCES II of Suffolk, Patchogue, N.Y. 1975-77; guidance counselor Babylon Pub. Schs., Babylon, N.Y. 1977—; cons., v.p. Life-Skills Center, Inc., Patchogue 1977—. Certified in life career devel. series, vocat. exploration group, gen. aptitude test. Mem. N.Y. Sch. Counselor Assn. (pres. 1978-79), W. Suffolk Counselors Assn. (pres. 1977-78), N.Y. State, Am. personnel and guidance assns., Am. Sch. Counselors Assn., N.Y. Vocat. Guidance Assn. (dir. 1978—), Phi Delta Kappa. Home: Manhasset NY 11030 Office: 50 Railroad Ave Babylon Jr-Sr High Sch Babylon NY 11702

MANN, HANNAH KOHL, counselor; b. Jersey City; d. Jacub and Rose (Rothberg) Kohl; B.S.Ed., Bklyn. Coll., 1946; M.A., N.Y. U., 1956; m. Sidney Mann, Mar. 11, 1933; 1 dau., Annette. Tchr. substitute N.Y.C. Schs., 1959-60; reading specialist Cranford (N.J.) Schs., 1959-60; supr. student tchrs. Bklyn. Coll., 1958-59; coordinator visual edn. Bklyn. Pub. Schs., 1945-50; guidance specialist Jersey City High Schs., 1970-79. Vice pres. Temple Emanuel, Jersey City. Served with USAAF, 1942-44. Mem. Am. Personnel and Guidance Assn., Hudson County Guidance Assn., N.J. Edn. Assn., Delta Chi Epsilon. Author: Use of Psycho-drama in Health Education 1961; contbr. children's plays to profl. jours. Office: Lincoln High School Jersey City NJ

MANN, MARGARET BLACKWELL (MRS. JAMES HAROLD MANN), civic worker; b. Orange, Va., Sept. 28, 1919; d. Price Barron and Mary (Gardner) Blackwell; student Averett Coll., 1936-37, George Washington U., 1943-44; m. James Harold Mann, Aug. 31, 1940; children—Margaret Blackwell, Judith Walker. Adminstrv. asst. Hecht Co., Washington, 1937-40. Active various community drives; exec. reservist Office Emergency Planning, 1967—. Pres., Woman's Suburban Democratic Club, Montgomery County, Md., 1959-61, Woman's Nat. Dem. Club, Washington, 1961-63, bd. govs., 1963—, chmn. ways and means com., 1973-74, hon. v.p., 1977; mem. Dem. Central Com. Md., 1964—; mem. inaugural com. Kennedy-Johnson, 1961; chmn. Woman's Speakers Bur. for Southwestern States, Johnson-Humphrey campaign, 1964, Humphrey-Muskie campaign, 1968; chmn. invitations and tickets com. Inaugural Balls Com., 1965; chmn. Nat. Dem. Women's Conf., Washington, 1966; chmn. Washington Area Friends of McGovern, 1971—; mem. spl. adv. com. women's activities Dem. Nat. Com., 1973—; trustee Washington Ednl. TV Assn.; bd. advisers Averett Coll., Danville, Va., 1969-72, bd. govs., 1972—; bd. visitors Frostburg (Md.) State Coll. Named Ky. col., 1969. Home: 14525 Montevideo Rd Poolesville MD 20837

MANN, MARY ELIZABETH, govt. agy. exec.; b. Pine Bluff, Ark., Mar. 13, 1924; d. Samuel Henry and Vivian Loraine (Moore) M.; A.B., Vassar Coll., 1945; postgrad. Cornell U. Law Sch., 1946; LL.B. (J.D.), Vanderbilt U., 1948. Admitted to Fla. bar, 1948, N.Y. bar, 19—; asso. firm Satterlee, Warfield & Stephens, N.Y.C., 1949-52; partner firm Mann, Harrison & Mann, St. Petersburg, Fla., 1952-56; cons. real property tax matters Govt. Affairs Found., N.Y. State Bd. Equalization and Assessment, Adv. Commn. on Intergovtl. Relations, 1956-65; asso. atty. N.Y. State Bd. Equalization and Assessment, 1966-76, dir. legal services, 1976-78; pres. N.Y.C. Tax Commn., 1978—. Mem. N.Y.C. Bar Assn., Order of Coif. Democrat. Presbyterian. Contbg. author: Role of States in Strengthening the Property Tax, 1963; author: (with Dr. Frederick C. Bird) State Constitutional Restrictions on Local Borrowing and Property Taxing Powers, 1965; comment editor Vanderbilt Law Rev., 1948. Office: 936 Municipal Bldg New York City NY 10007

MANN, ROBERT, physician; b. Vacz, Hungary, June 8, 1946; s. Adolph and Rozalie (Birnbaum) M.; came to U.S., 1952, naturalized, 1964; B.S. cum laude, Bklyn. Coll., 1968; M.D. cum laude, Downstate Med. Center, State U. N.Y., 1972; m. Etta Wieder, June 22, 1971; children—Jennifer, Jeffrey-Martin. Straight med. intern Maimonides Hosp., N.Y.C., 1972-73, resident in internal medicine, 1973-75, attending physician, 1975—; individual practice medicine, specializing in internal medicine Bklyn., 1975—. Diplomate Am. Bd.

Internal Medicine. Mem. A.C.P. Office: 1574 56th St Brooklyn NY 11219

MANN, ROBERT PAUL, lawyer; b. Pitts., July 24, 1929; s. O. Paul and Floy (Foster) M.; B.S., U. Md., 1951, LL.B., 1953; m. Dorothy Neeld, Sept. 4, 1953; children—Robin Duvall, Stewart Neeld. Admitted to Md. bar, 1954, since practiced in Towson; legal counsel Law Officers Assn. Baltimore County, Inc., 1964-79; trial magistrate, Fullerton, Md., 1958-59. Pres. Towson Library, 1963, bd. dirs., 1964—; pres. Friends of Artists Equity; mem. Historic Towson. Mem. Fed., Am., Baltimore County bar assns., Am. Trial Lawyers Assn., Am. Judicature Soc., Omicron Delta Kappa, Sigma Chi, Delta Theta Phi. Episcopalian. Home: 917 Rolandvue Rd Ruxton MD 21204 Office: Mann & Blair 413 Jefferson Bldg Towson MD 21204

MANN, ROY BERNARD, landscape architect, environ. planner; b. Mt. Vernon, N.Y., Jan. 25, 1933; s. Joseph and Rose (Bleiberg) M.; student N.Y. U., 1950-52, Cornell, 1952-54; B.S., U. Calif. at Davis, 1955; M.L.A., Harvard, 1967; m. Dorit Atzmon, Mar. 30, 1951; 1 dau., Hili Sonia; m. 2d, Carol Baum, Sept. 18, 1971. Landscape architect Sasaki, Dawson, DeMay Assos., Watertown, Mass., 1967; landscape architect Boston Redevell Authority, 1967; landscape architect Charles W. Eliot II, Cambridge, Mass., 1969; partner New Urban Landscape, Boston, 1969-70; pres. Roy Mann Assos., Inc., landscape architects, environ. planners, Cambridge, 1970—; coordinating landscape architect Boston Southwest Corridor Project, 1977—. Mem. Kibbutz, Israel, 1957-64; journalist, Jerusalem Post, 1963-64; lectr. Cambridge Center for Adult Edn., 1970-74; lectr. Harvard, Mass. Inst. Tech., Cornell U., Fla., others; originator Earth Crisis weekly environ. program WTBS, WBUR, WEEI radio, Boston, 1970—; mem. adv. com. Cambridge Center for Adult Edn., 1971-74, Boston Archtl. Center, 1973—. Chmn. Citizens Com. to Save the Fens, 1969; mem. Mass. Citizens Task Force on Energy Resources, 1972. Bd. dirs. Charles River Watershed Assn., 1969-71. Fulbright fellow, U.K., 1968; Nat. Endowment for Arts grantee, 1976. Mem. AIA, Boston Soc. Architects (research com. 1975—), Am. Soc. Landscape Architects (chmn. nat. com. on policies 1976-78), Cousteau Soc., Coastal Soc., Marine Technol. Soc. Author: Rivers in the City, 1973. Editor Connection mag., Harvard, 1965-66; book rev. editor Landscape Architecture, 1971-76. Office: 180 Franklin St Cambridge MA 02139

MANN, WILLIAM HOUSTON, sci. instrument distbn. co. exec.; b. Balt., June 13, 1926; s. Henry and Helen (Grimes) H.; A.B., Yale U., 1950; m. Mercedes Dewitt Spradling, Apr. 29, 1952; children—Monique, Paul, Mercedes, Alexandra, Maria. With R.W. Pressprich & Co., N.Y.C., 1950-52; v.p. E. Leitz Inc., Manca Inc., Northvale, N.J., Henry Mann Securities Corp., N.Y.C., 1952-68, pres., 1969—, also dir., Rochleigh, N.J., 1952—; dir. Riggs, Counselman, Michaels & Downes, ins. brokers, Balt. Vice-pres., Marsalin Inst., Holiston, Mass., 1958—, also bd. dirs.; mem. pres.'s com. Internat. Center Photography, N.Y.C., 1976—. Served with USNR, 1944-46. Clubs: Windham (N.Y.) Mount; Maidstone (East Hampton, N.Y.); Yale, Knickerbocker, City Midday (N.Y.C.); Frankfort (W. Ger.) Golf. Republican. Roman Catholic. Office: 40 E Leitz Inc Rockleigh NJ 07647

MANN, WILLIAM MARION, JR., psychiatrist; b. Enfield, N.C., Jan. 7, 1931; s. William Marion and Teressa Hope (Dickens) M.; B.S. cum laude, Wake Forest U., 1953; M.D., Bowman Gray Sch. Medicine, 1957; m. Vandelia Drew Smith, Aug. 1, 1960; children—William Marion, Benjamin Denton, William Oliver, Teressa Vandelia. Intern, Emory U. Hosp., 1957-58; resident internal medicine N.C. Baptist Hosp., Winston Salem, 1958-61; resident psychiatry Warren (Pa.) State Hosp., 1963-66; clin. dir. Crawford County Mental Health Center, Meadville, Pa., 1966-70; sr. psychiatrist Warren State Hosp., 1966-71, unit dir., 1971—; med. dir. Cameron-Elk-McKean-Potter counties Mental Health-Mental Retardation Clinic, Bradford, Pa., 1970-73, clin. dir. Counseling Center, 1973-76, psychiat. cons., 1976—. Bd. dirs. Warren County Mental Health Assn., 1970-77, v.p., 1974-76, pres., 1976-77; bd. dirs. Pa. Mental Health Inc., 1970-77, N.W. v.p., 1974-76, mem. exec. com., 1974-76. Served with M.C., AUS, 1961-63. Mem. AMA, Am. Psychiat. Assn., Soc. Cin., Soc. Descs. Knights Most Noble Order Garder, Order First Families Va., SAR, Jamestowne Soc., Soc. Colonial Wars. Home: PO Box 249 Warren PA 16365 Office: Warren State Hosp Warren PA 16365

MANNARELLI, JOHN EDWARD, osteo. physician; b. Lorain, Ohio, Nov. 9, 1918; s. Frank and Pasqua (Yacobozzi) M.; student Western Res. U., 1937-38, U. Buffalo, 1938-40, Gannon Coll., 1947-48; D.O., Kirksville Coll., 1943; m. Connie M. Gambatese, Sept. 28, 1940; children—Carol Kay Mannarelli Monaghan, John E. Pvt. practice osteo. medicine, Cerdo-Kenova, W.Va., 1943-46; teaching and research fellow Kirksville (Mo.) Coll. Osteo. Medicine, 1946-48; chief of anesthesia Erie (Pa.) Osteo. Hosp., 1950-76, also pres. staff; asso. med. dir. Erie County (Pa.) Hosp., 1962-73, med. dir., 1972-74, dir. med. services and facilities, 1973-74, adminstr., 1975-76; exec. dir. Erie County Geriatric Center, Girard, Pa., 1976—; cons. in long term care; mem. Pa. Bd. Examiners for Nursing Home Adminstrs. Fellow Am. Coll. Nursing Home Adminstrs.; mem. Am. Osteo. Assn., Am. Osteo. Coll. Anesthesiologists, Am. Soc. Anesthesiologists, Pa. Assn. County Affiliated Homes (exec. bd.), AAAS, Gerontol. Soc., Pa. Assn. Non-Profit Homes for Aged, Pa. Hosp. Assn., Pa. Osteo. Med. Assn. (trustee), Erie County Osteo. Soc. (pres.). Democrat. Roman Catholic. Clubs: Lake Shore Country, Univ., Profl. and Businessmen's. Home: 5630 King Rd Erie PA 16509 Office: RD 2 Girard PA 16417

MANNEY, DONALD MAXWELL, chiropractic physician; b. N.Y.C., Oct. 2, 1930; s. Irving and Pauline (Eiber) M.; B.A., N.Y.U., 1953; D. Chiropractic, Columbia Inst. Chiropractic (now N.Y. Chiropractic Coll.), 1958; M.B.A., Wagner Coll., 1968; m. Leah Schlomowitz, June 14, 1959 (div. 1977); children—Steven Paul, Rachel Deborah. Gen. practice chiropractic, N.Y.C., 1958-66, Rahway, N.J., 1976—; asst. adminstr. Montefiore Hosp. and Med. Center, N.Y.C., 1966-68; dir. profl. services Beekman-Downtown Hosp., N.Y.C., 1968-70; asso. adminstr. Maimonides Med. Center, Bklyn., 1970; exec. dir. Cath. Med. Center Affiliation Queens Hosp. Center, Jamaica, N.Y., 1970-73; adminstr. Williamsburgh Gen. Hosp., Bklyn., 1973-76; clin. instr. pub. health and physiology Columbia Inst. Chiropractic, N.Y.C., 1965; adj. prof. mgmt. bus. div. Coll. Ins., N.Y.C., 1971-73; adj. asst. prof. health care adminstrn. St. Francis Coll., Bklyn., 1973-76. Mem. Mayor's Community Planning Bd., 1968-70; mem. Bushwick Health Council, 1973-76. Fellow Royal Soc. Health; mem. Internat. Acad. Preventive Medicine, Huxley Inst. Biosocial Research, Internat. Acad. Chiropractic Nutritionists, Parker Chiropractic Research Found., Am. Hosp. Assn., Am. Coll. Hosp. Adminstrs., Am. Acad. Med. Adminstrs., Am. Pub. Health Assn., AAAS, Am., N.Y. State, N.J. State chiropractic assns., Pub. Health Assn. N.Y.C., Hosp. Execs. Club N.Y.C., Mensa, Intertel. Club: Mason. Office: 1271 Westfield Ave Rahway NJ 07065

MANNING, DAISY MAE PARKS, guidance counselor; b. Chattanooga, Tenn.; d. Cleve and Rebecca (Brittain) Parks; student Clark Coll., 1949-51; B.S., Miner Teachers Coll., 1955; student Howard U., 1956, 60, Am. U., 1963, N.Y. U., 1964, 66; M.A., Trinity Coll., 1973, postgrad., 1975, 76; postgrad. Md. U., 1973, George Washington U., 1977; Ph.D., U. Del., Walden U. Tchr., Orchard Knob Sch., Chattanooga, Tenn., 1954-60, Davis Sch., Washington, 1960-61, Draper Sch., Washington, 1961-62, Brentwood (Md.) Elem. Sch., 1962-64, Rudolph Elem. Sch., Washington, 1964-76; guidance counselor Taft Jr. High Sch., Washington, 1976—; instr. Trinity Coll., summer, 1977; cons. for tchrs. Mem. Am. Personnel and Guidance Assn., Assn. Counselor Edn. and Supervision, Nat. Vocat. Guidance Assn., Am. Sch. Counselor Assn., Nat. Congress Parents and Tchrs., Nat. Assn. Women Deans, Adminstrs., Counselors, AAUW, Bus. and Profl. Women, Va. Career Systems Assn., Instructional Devel. Inst., Greater Washington Reading Council. Baptist. Clubs: YWCA, Nat. Council Negro Women.

MANNING, EDWARD PETER, state legislator, lawyer; b. Providence, R.I., Nov. 16, 1924; s. John J. and Margaret M. (Cahir) M.; A.B., Iowa Wesleyan Coll., 1949; J.D., Cath. U. Am., 1952; m. Regina A. Fitzpatrick, May 11, 1957; children—John, Mary, Stephanie, Edward Peter, Amy, Melanie. Admitted to R.I. bar, 1953; mem. firm Slattery, Balkun & Mullen, Providence, 1953-64; Manning & West, Providence, 1964-70, Manning, West, Santaniello, Pari Providence, 1970—. Mem. R.I. Ho. of Reps., 1966—, speaker, 1977-78. Served with USAF, 1943-45. Mem. Am., R.I. bar assns., New Eng. Land Title Assn., Am. Legion, VFW. Democrat. Roman Catholic. Clubs: Serra, Elks. Home: Nate Whipple Hwy Cumberland RI 02864 Office: 711 Industrial Bank Bldg Providence RI 02903

MANNING, FERDINAND LARUE, lighting cons.; b. Cambridge, Mass., Oct. 1, 1925; s. George Charles and Blanche Marie (Larue) M.; B.A., Tulane U., 1948; M.F.A., Yale, 1951; m. Jean Marie Alexander, Nov. 10, 1951; children—Jill Alexander Manning Stockman, Patricia Larue, James Williams. Lighting dir. CBS-TV, 1951-62; head lighting dept. Ednl. Broadcasting Co., N.Y.C., 1962-63; lighting dir. Videotape Center, N.Y.C., 1963-68; freelance cons., 1968-70; pres., founder Acad. Lighting, East N.Y.C., 1970-76; founder, pres. Lyteman, Inc., N.Y.C., 1976—; dir. Martha Stuart Communications Inc.; instr. Grad. Sch. Edn. Fairfield U., 1969, Am. theatre Wing, 1956, 57; lectr. New Sch. Social Research, N.Y.C.; lighting cons. to White House and Republican Nat. Com., 1972-73, to Jimmy Carter Presdl. Campaign, 1976. Served with AUS, 1944-45, USNR, 1945-46. Mem. Soc. Lighting Dirs. (charter), Pi Kappa Alpha. Monthly columnist Lighting Dimensions mag.

MANNING, JAMES HUGH, actuary, fed. govt. ofcl.; b. Lansing, Mich., June 2, 1931; s. Stuart Moore and Carla Lucile (Kennedy) M.; B.A., Albion Coll., 1953; postgrad. U. Mich., 1957-58; m. Karen Hooper Gillis, July 3, 1978; children by former marriage—Deborah, James, William, Julie, John, Mary, Michael. Asst. actuary Peoples Life Ins. Co., Washington, 1960-62, exec. asst., asso. actuary, 1962-68, 2d v.p. computer services, 1968-70, asst. v.p., 1970; actuary, div. actuarial service Unemployment Ins. Service, U.S. Dept. Labor, Washington, 1970-75, chief div., 1975—. Pres. Ravensworth Sch. PTA, 1968; active Boy Scouts Am. Served with USNR, 1953-57; ETO. Recipient U.S. Dept. Labor spl. achievement award, 1975, distinguished achievement award, 1976, outstanding performance award, 1977. Mem. Am. Acad. Actuaries, Naval Res. Assn., Middle Atlantic Actuarial Club. Home: 4423 S 34th St Arlington VA 22206 Office: Unemployment Ins Service US Dept Labor 7410 601 D St NW Washington DC 20213

MANNING, WILLIAM GEORGE, mfrs. agt.; b. Haverhill, Mass., June 10, 1923; s. William George and Annie (Ingram) M.; B.S., Mass. Maritime Acad., 1944; m. Jen Lynch, Aug. 1, 1975; children—William G., Chris J. With Haverhill Electric Co., 1946-52; regional salesman Am. Paper Goods Co., 1952-53, Continental Can Co., 1953-54; pres., owner Bay Sales Td., Hyattsville, Md., 1954—. Served to lt. USNR, 1944-46. Mem. Md. Paper Trade Assn. Club: Army-Navy Country. Address: 115 Market St Annapolis MD 21401

MANNIX, HENRY, JR., surgeon; b. Bklyn., July 11, 1927; s. Henry and Mary Margaret (Friel) M.; B.S., Coll. Holy Cross, 1947; M.D., Cornell U., 1950; m. Margaret Mary Carney, Sept. 11, 1976. Intern, N.Y. Hosp., 1950-51, resident, 1951-59; practice medicine specializing in gen. surgery, N.Y.C. and Conn., 1959—; mem. staff N.Y. Hosp., 1959—; dir. surgery St. Francis Hosp., Hartford, Conn., 1971-77, vis. surgeon, 1971—; clin. asso. prof. surgery N.Y. Hosp., 1965—; asso. prof. U. Conn., 1971—; mem. Conn. Med. Exam. Bd., 1977—. Served to lt. U.S. Army, 1951-53. Mem. Hartford Med. Soc. (trustee), A.C.S., Holy Cross Alumni Assn. (pres. 1975-76), N.Y., New Eng. surg. socs. Republican. Roman Catholic. Clubs: Wampanoag Country, Mt. Kisco (N.Y.) Country. Contbr. articles to med. jours. Home: 31 Woodland St Hartford CT 06105 Office: 140 Woodland St Hartford CT 06105

MANOCCHIA, BENITO CESARE, journalist; b. Giulianova, Teramo, Italy, May 10, 1934; s. Francesco and Filomena (Spadacci) M.; came to U.S., 1955, naturalized, 1961; degree in journalism U. Urbino, 1955. Free-lance writer, 1950-72; fgn. corr. Rusconi Publs., Milano, Italy, 1972—, chief U.S. corr., N.Y.C., 19—. Served with Italian Air Force, 1953. Recipient award Italian Profl. Journalists, 1973. Roman Catholic. Author: Indagine su Dieci Squillo Di Lusso, 1971; Il Prete Di Cosa Nostra, 1971; Amore Voodo, 1973; Vivremo Duecento Anni, 1974.

MANOGUE, HELEN SMITH, redevel. planner; b. North Bergen, N.J., Dec. 14, 1931; d. William Casper and Teresa Elizabeth (Wulftange) Smith; B.A. summa cum laude (Rutgers scholar), Rutgers U. Newark Coll. Arts and Scis., 1975; m. Joseph F. Manogue, Nov. 28, 1959; children—Joseph Mark, Stephen James, Philip William. With Bonwit Teller, N.Y.C., 1949-61, buyer, 1959-61; project coordinator Center for Municipal Studies and Services, Stevens Inst., Hoboken, N.J., 1975; now program officer N.J. Mortgage Fin. Agy., Newark. Founder, chmn. Hoboken Environment Com., 1971—; founder, 1st coordinator Hudson Environ. Coalition; co-chmn. Hudson Toxic Substances Task Force; chmn. hist. sites com. Hoboken Bicentennial; trustee Central N.J. Lung Assn.; mem. N.J. Council Solid Waste Mgmt., 1976-78; co-founder, co-dir. Waterfront Coalition Hudson and Bergen; task force mem. Hudson Health Systems Agy.; mem. Liberty State Park Study and Planning Commn., 1977, Council on Future N.J., 1973. Mem. Phi Beta Kappa. Home: 610 River St Hoboken NJ 07030 Office: NJ Mortgage Finance Agy 1180 Raymond Blvd Newark NJ 07012

MANOLAKOS, DEMETRIUS, lawyer; b. Montreal, Que., Can., Mar. 4, 1935; s. Nicholas and Panagiota (Konstiantou) M.; B.A., Sir George Williams U., Montreal, 1956; LL.B., U. Montreal, 1963. Called to Que. Bd. Notaries, 1966; sr. partner firm Beaulieu, Manolakos & Bisante, Montreal, 1966—; city councillor City of Montreal, 1978-82; dir. numerous cos. Bd. dirs., v.p. Montreal Citizenship Council, Hellenic Canadian Trust; past pres. Hellenic Community of Montreal, Hellenic Cultural Inst., Montreal Stars Soccer Club; hon. pres. Hellenic Canadian Solidarity Com. for Cyprus; regional dir. Cyprus Relief Fund; hon. rover Boy Scouts Can.; mem. Canadian Consultative Council on Multiculturalism; bd. dirs. Canadian Council Christians and Jews; mem. Consultative Com. on Immigration for Que.; trustee Hellenic Coll., Holy Cross Greek Orthodox Theol. Sch. Decorated hon. officer Ecumenical Patriarchate Constantinople with title Archon Notarios; Cross Mt. Athos, Silver Jubilee medal for Coronation Queen Elizabeth II. Mem. Canadian Bar Assn., Assn. Notaries Que., League Greek Orthodox Stewards, Sir George Williams U. Alumni Assn. Greek Orthodox (mem. archdiocesan council). Club: Mount Stephen. Home: 1321 Sherbrooke St West Apt D-41 Montreal PQ H3A 2R7 Canada Office: 1010 Sherbrooke St West Suite 2301 Montreal PQ H2L 1L5 Canada

MANOR, FILOMENA ROBERTA, air force officer; b. Troy, N.Y., July 6, 1926; d. Gabriel Robert and Mary Carmina (Siciliano) Fusco; B.S., Russell Sage Coll., 1948; M.S., Ohio State U., 1960. Dietetic intern Peter Bent Brigham Hosp., Boston, 1949; commd. 2d lt. U.S. Air Force, 1950, advanced through grades to col., 1971—; served in dietetic services Mil. Airlift Command, Scott AFB, Ill., 1965-70; chief med. food service div., dir. dietetic internship Malcolm Grow USAF Med. Center, Andrews AFB, Washington, 1970—; asso. chief for dietetics and nutrition Air Force Surgeon Gen., Hdqrs. USAF, Washington, 1972—, cons. dietitian, nutritionist, 1973—; staff adviser for women in Air Force Biomed. Scis. Corps to Def. Adv. Com. on Women in the Services, 1972—; Air Force rep. to foods and nutrition bd. NRC, 1975—. Decorated Meritorious Service medal, Commendation medal; recipient Distinguished Alumnus award Ohio State U., 1973. Mem. Am. Dietetic Assn. (dietetic internship bd. 1972-75), Aerospace Med. Assn., Assn. Mil. Surgeons U.S. (McLester award 1962), Air Force Assn., Smithsonian Assos., Omicron Nu. Club: Home: 307 Yoakum Pkwy Apt 1104 Alexandria VA 22304 Office: Med Food Service Div Malcolm Grow USAF Med Center Andrews AFB Washington DC 20331

MANOS, GEORGE, pianist, conductor; b. Greensboro, N.C., Mar. 10, 1930; s. Spyros and Marina (Skalas) M.; diploma Peabody Conservatory Music, 1952; student Julliard Sch. Music, 1947. Dir. ProArte Chamber Orch., Washington, 1946-48, Peabody Opera Chorus, Balt., 1948-51, Nat. Assn. Am. Composers and Condrs. Chamber Orch., Nat. Oratorio Soc., Washington, 1957-67, D.C. Bach Festivals, 1960-67; founder, music dir., condr. Killarney Bach Festival, Republic of Ireland, 1971—; mem. tour Columbia Mgmt., 1957-58, European Athens Artist Bur., 1967-69; solo appearances; condr. Nat. Ballet, 1964-65; faculty Madeira Sch., 1964-67, Am. U., 1967, Cath. U., 1967-71, 74-76; exec. dir. Wilmington (Del.) Sch. Music, 1971-74. Vice pres. Kindler Found. Served with USMCR, 1948-52. Recipient ecclesiastic order Archbishop Australia for cultural contbn., 1957, commendation Royal House Greece, 1955. Clubs: Friday Morning Music Arts, Cosmos (Washington). Home: 6905 Millwood Rd Bethesda MD 20034

MANOS, JOHN GEORGE, banker, mayor; b. Paterson, N.J., Oct. 13, 1927; s. George and Katherine (Andrews) M.; student U. Mich., 1947-50; Stonier Grad. Sch. Banking, Rutgers U., 1961-63; m. Anna Konnon, June 6, 1954; children—George, Maria. With Atlantic Bank N.Y., N.Y.C., 1951-69; v.p., 1967-69, sec., 1965-69; v.p. Israel Discount Bank, N.Y.C., 1970-73, sr. v.p., 1973—. Lectr. N.Y. State Banking Dept. Mem. City Council Tenafly (N.J.), 1973-75, mayor, 1976—. Served with U.S. Army, 1945-47. Recipient Abraham Lincoln Brotherhood award JFK Library for Minorities, 1974, Presidents award St. John the Theologian Greek Orthodox Ch., 1975. Mem. Hellenic Am. C. of C. (dir.), N.Y. Creditmens Assn., Am. Hellenic Ednl. Progressive Assn. Republican. Greek Orthodox. Home: 74 Stonehurst Dr Tenafly NJ 07670 Office: 511 Fifth Ave New York City NY 10017*

MANOWITZ, NELSON, surgeon; b. Jersey City, May 27, 1924; s. Joseph and Bessie (Kominsky) M.; B.S., Tulane U., 1944, M.D., 1946; m. Judith G. Rosenthal, Feb. 1, 1948; children—Neil Robert, Marcia Ann. Intern, Newark Beth Israel Hosp., 1946-47; resident in surgery Flower Fifth Ave Hosp., N.Y.C., 1949-50, Newark City Hosp., 1950-53; practice medicine specializing in gen. surgery, Millburn, N.J., 1953—; attending surgeon Clara Maas Hosp., St. Barnabas Med. Center, Martland Hosp., N.J. Med. Coll.; asst. prof. surgery N.J. Coll. Medicine, Newark, 1969—. Served to capt. M.C., AUS, 1943-46, 47-49. Diplomate Am. Bd. Surgery. Fellow A.C.S.; mem. N.J., Essex County med. socs. Office: 120 Millburn Ave Millburn NJ 07041

MANROSS, WILLIAM WILSON, ret. historian; b. Syracuse, N.Y., Feb. 21, 1905; s. William Doane and Martha (Wilson) M.; B.A., Hobart Coll., 1926; M.A., Columbia U., 1930, Ph.D., 1938; M.Div., Gen. Theol. Sem., 1931; D.D., Phila. Div. Sch., 1973; m. Catharine Amelia Wisner, Jan. 25, 1936. Fellow, tutor Gen. Theol. Sem., N.Y.C., 1929-39; librarian, treas. Ch. Hist. Soc., Phila., 1948-56; lectr. ch. history Phila. Div. Sch., 1949-58, librarian, 1956-73, prof. ch. history, 1958-73; research fellow Gen. Theol. Sem., 1960-62; adj. prof. ch. history Temple U., 1963-64. Mem. Am. Hist. Assn., Am. Acad. Polit. and Social Sci., Am. Soc. Ch. History, Ch. Hist. Soc. (exec. bd.). Episcopalian. Author: The S.P.G. Papers in Lambeth Palace Library, 1974. Home: 221 Kathmere Rd Havertown PA 19083

MANSER, GORDON, assn. exec.; b. Lansford, N.D., Feb. 20, 1909; s. Percy L. and Clema (Johnson) M.; student Whitman Coll., 1927-31, Princeton U., 1931-32; M.S.W., U. So. Calif., 1948; m. Ellen Irene Pierson, Nov. 1, 1947; children—Marilyn, Janet, Norris, Clark. Caseworker, supr., county adminstr., field rep. Oreg. Pub. Welfare Commn., 1933-43, dir. pub. welfare Portland, 1943-46; asst. to dir., Community Chest Union County (N.J.), 1950; sec. to div. family and child care agencies, also asst. dir. Balt. Health and Welfare Council, 1951-55, dir. council, 1955-62; asso. exec. dir. Nat. Assembly Social Policy and Devel., Inc., N.Y.C., 1962-72, exec. dir., 1973-74; interim exec. dir. Assn. Jr. Leagues, Inc., N.Y.C., 1976-77; prin. cons. Acad. Ednl. Devel., N.Y.C., 1978—; cons. in field. Bd. dirs. Nat. Conf. Social Welfare, 1967-69; mem. sec.'s task force orgn. social services HEW, 1968-69; mem. bd. pensions United Presbyn. Ch., 1968-77, chmn., 1976-77; pres. Westchester (N.Y.) Young Actors Theatre, 1969-71. Mem. Nat. Assn. Social Workers, Acad. Certified Social Workers, Phi Kappa Phi, Beta Theta Pi. Club: Princeton. Author: (with R. Cass) Voluntarism at the Crossroads, 1976. Home: 5800 Arlington Ave Riverdale NY 10471 Office: Acad Ednl Devel 680 Fifth Ave New York City NY 10019

MANSI, JOSEPH ANNEILLO, pub. relations exec.; b. New Haven, Oct. 8, 1935; s. Joseph C. and Vinnie (Chirico) M.; B.S., N.Y. U., 1957; m. Mary P. Fusco, Aug. 1, 1959; children—Karen Marie, Jeanine. Newsman, Internat. News Service, UPI, 1953-58; mem. pub. relations staff Lawrence Orgn., 1960-63; account supr. Philip Lesly Co., 1963-67; dir. corporate communications Ward Foods, Inc., 1967-72; dir. pub. relations Metromedia, Inc., N.Y.C., 1973-75; pres. Corp. Relations Network, Inc., N.Y.C., 1975—; instr. Fairleigh Dickinson U., Rutherford, N.J. Served with AUS, 1958-60. Mem. Pub. Relations Soc. Am. (accredited), Silurians, Overseas Press Club, Theta Chi. Home: 10 Beatrice Ln Glen Cove NY 11542 Office: 280 Madison Ave New York City NY 10016

MANSKY, LEONARD, electronics engring. exec.; b. N.Y.C., Feb. 23, 1932; s. Harry and Rae (Abraham) M.; B.E.E., U. City N.Y., 1954; M.S. in Elec. Engring., Poly. Inst. N.Y., 1962; M.B.A., N.Y. U. Grad. Sch. Bus. Adminstrn., 1975; m. Elizabeth Kaufman, June 28, 1959; children—Janet Paula, Paul Abraham, Laura Marjorie Phyllis. Microwave sect. mgr. Maxson Electronics Corp., Great River, N.Y., 1956-61; mgr. antenna and microwave design Loral Electronic Systems, Yonkers, N.Y., 1961-65; engring. mgr., program mgr. Sedco

Systems Inc., Melville, N.Y., 1965—; also instl. investment adviser. Nassau Democratic County committeeman, 1963-69; pres. Greater Roslyn (N.Y.) Dem. Club, 1968; chmn. Roslyn Citizens for Humphrey, 1968; trustee Reconstructionist Synagogue of North Shore, 1974-77. Registered profl. engr., N.Y. Mem. IEEE (sr.), Antennas and Propagation Soc., Nat. Soc. Profl. Engrs., Tau Beta Pi, Eta Kappa Nu. Jewish. Home: 3 Regent Pl Roslyn NY 11576 Office: Sedco Systems Inc 65 Marcus Dr Melville NY 11746

MANSLEY, GREGORY ALLAN, retailing co. exec.; b. N.Y.C., July 20, 1946; s. Leslie and Anna Lillian (Bladwin) M.; B.A., State U. N.Y., Stony Brook, 1968, postgrad., 1968-72. Math. tchr. Syosset (N.Y.) High Sch., 1969-72; chief exec. officer Granado Co., Valley Stream, N.Y., 1972—. Mem. Valley Stream C. of C. (dir. 1973—). Republican. Episcopalian. Clubs: Kiwanis, Elks (Valley Stream). Home: Apt 3A 241-20 Northern Blvd Douglaston NY 11362 also Shore Rd Ammagansett East Hampton NY 11930 Office: 800 W Merrick Rd Valley Stream NY 11580

MANSON, FRANK ALBERT, orgn. exec.; b. Creek County, Okla., Dec. 26, 1920; s. Asa and Ella May (Eastham) M.; B.S., N.E. Okla. U., 1941; postgrad. U.S. Naval War Coll., 1958-59; m. Orie Lee Pickren, May 29, 1948; children—Frank Karig, Jennifer Joy, Barbara Lynne. Commd. ensign U.S. Navy, 1942; advanced through grades to capt., 1962; spl. asst. four chiefs naval ops., Pentagon, Washington, 1948-56, dir. plans and policies analysis naval ops., 1957-58; chief pub. relations, Europe, 1959-63, chief pub. affairs Supreme Allied Command Atlantic, NATO, 1964-68, chief mag. and books dept. of def., 1968-69, ret., 1969; dir. nat. security and fgn. affairs VFW, 1969-70; legis. asst. House of Reps., Washington, 1971-72; legis. asst. Res. Officers Assn., 1974-75; counsellor for fgn. relations The Am. Legion, 1976—; lectr. in field. Recipient Alfred Thayer Mahan award, U.S. Navy League for Literary Achievement, 1958; Silver Anvil award for Internat. Pub. Relations, Nat. Soc. Pub. Relations Am., 1964; Top Tau award for Community Service, Nat. Sigma Tau Gamma, 1970. Mem. Res. Officers Assn. Episcopalian. Clubs: VFW, Am. Legion. Author: (with Capt. W. Karig) End of an Empire, 1949, Victory in the Pacific, 1949; (with Capts. Karig and Cagle) War in Korea, 1951; The Sea War in Korea, 1957. Home: 5601 Seminary Rd Falls Church VA 22041 Office: 1608 K St NW Washington DC 20006

MANSOURI, FREYDOON, physicist, educator; b. Tehran, Iran, June 5, 1936; s. Hossein and Tadj (Panahi-Azar); came to U.S., 1960; B.A., U. Pa., 1962; M.A., Temple U., 1964; Ph.D., Johns Hopkins, 1969; 1 dau., Marina Shahrzad. Research asso. Enrico Fermi Inst., U. Chgo., 1970-72; J.W. Gibbs instr. physics Yale, 1972-74, asst. prof., 1974-79, asso. prof., 1979—. Mem. Am. Phys. Soc., Sigma Xi. Contbr. articles to profl. jours. Home: 145 Cottage St New Haven CT 06511 Office: Yale U Dept Physics New Haven CT 06520

MANSUY, MATTHEW MICHAEL, physician; b. Williamsport, Pa., Feb. 15, 1920; s. Michael M. and Helen A. (Eck) M.; B.S., Bucknell U., 1941; M.D., Temple U., 1944; m. Helen E. Logue, Nov. 17, 1944; children—Camille, Michele, Suzanne, Jacqueline, Francene, Michael, Kathryn. Intern, U.S. Naval Hosp., Phila., 1945-46; resident in internal medicine U. Pitts., 1946-50; chief med. service Williamsport and Divine Providence hosps., Williamsport, 1954—, chief cardiology, 1957—; instr. in medicine Hershey (Pa.) Med. Center, Pa. State U. Med. Center, 1978—; bd. dirs. Williamsport Hosp. Served with USNR, 1944-46, 52-54. Diplomate Am. Bd. Internal Medicine. Fellow Am. Coll. Cardiology, A.C.P., Am. Coll. Chest Physicians; mem. AMA, Lycoming County Med. Soc. (pres. 1976). Roman Catholic. Contbr. articles to med. publs. Home: 1155 Vallamont Dr NW Williamsport PA 17701 Office: 410 Locust St Williamsport PA 17701

MANTEL, HEINRICH, math. statistician; b. Rumania, Sept. 23, 1933; s. Lazar and Regina Mantel; came to U.S., 1962, naturalized, 1968; diploma in math. Univ. V. Babes, Clus, Romania, 1958; M.A. in Math. Statistics (Univ. fellow), Wayne State U., 1968; m. Eva B., 1969. Computer programmer computing center, then grad. asst. Wayne State U., Detroit, 1962-69; math. statistician U.S. Census Bur., Washington, 1969—. Mem. Am. Statis. Assn., Assn. for Computing Machinery. Author articles. Home: 8708 1st Ave Silver Spring MD 20910

MANUEL, THOMAS GEORGE, banker; b. Mineola, N.Y., Apr. 15, 1945; s. George Thomas and Vivian Evelyn (Anderson) M.; B.A., Wesleyan U., Middletown, Conn., 1967; M.B.A., Adelphi U., 1974; postgrad. N.Y. Law Sch., 1975; m. Karen Lee Kind, Dec. 21, 1968; children—Scott Thomas, Keith Anderson, Todd Gregory. With Chem. Bank, N.Y.C., 1972—, v.p. corporate bank, 1977—; chief exec. officer Elpa Mktg. Industries, Inc., 1978—. Chmn. bd. ushers Community Ch., 1976. Served with USN, 1968-72. Republican. Home: 36 Rilling Ridge New Canaan CT 06840 Office: 20 Pine St New York City NY 10015

MANUS, STEPHEN CHARLES, cardiologist; b. Phila., Apr. 15, 1947; s. Bernard and Marion Rose (Weiner) M.; B.A., Temple U., 1968, M.D., 1972; m. Dell Diane Christman, Sept. 25, 1970; 1 son, Christopher Mark. Intern, Springfield (Mass.) Hosp. Med. Center, 1972-73; resident in internal medicine Thomas Jefferson U. Hosp., Phila., 1973-75, cardiology fellow, 1975-77; practice medicine specializing in cardiology, Lewistown, Pa., 1977—; mem. attending staff Lewistown Hosp., 1977—; mem. coordinator Mifflin County (Pa.) Emergency Med. Techs., 1977—. Am. Heart Assn. grantee, 1975-76. Diplomate Am. Bd. Internal Medicine. Mem. A.C.P., Am. Coll. Cardiology, Am. Coll. Chest Physicians, Central Pa. Heart Assn. (pres. 1977-78). Club: Kiwanis. Contbr. articles, chpts. to med. jours., texts. Home and office: 200 Cider Ln Lewistown PA 17044

MANZI, ALBERT PETER, elec. contractor; b. Lawrence, Mass., Aug. 11, 1917; s. Michael and Angela (Grillo) M.; student Franklin Tech. Inst., 1938, Lowell Tech. Inst., 1941; D.C.S. (hon.), Merrimack Coll., 1962; m. Anna L. Mikolajczyk, Oct. 6, 1951; children—Albert, Annmarie, David, Paul, Lisa. With engring. dept. Pacific Mills, 1935-41, U.S. Naval Shipyard, Pearl Harbor, Hawaii, 1941, planning and engring., Boston, 1941-45; pres., gen. mgr. Manzi Elec. Corp., Lawrence, 1945—; dir. Arlington Trust Co. Lawrence; incorporator Lawrence Savs. Bank. Pres., Greater Lawrence Bus. Devel. Corp., 1959—; past pres. Lawrence Boys' Club. Adv. bd. Merrimack Coll. Decorated Knight of Malta, Knight of Holy Sepulchre (Roman Cath.). Mem. Lawrence C. of C. (dir.), I.E.E.E. (sr. mem.), Soc. Am. Mil. Engrs., Nat. Soc. Profl. Engrs., Bon Secours Hosp. Guild. Lion. Home: 440 Great Pond Rd North Andover MA 01845 Office: 217-221 Elm St Lawrence MA 01841

MAPLESDEN, DOUGLAS CECIL, chem. co. exec., veterinarian; b. Sandhurst, Kent, Eng., Oct. 30, 1919; s. Cecil Walker and Frances (Pantry) M.; D.V.M., Ont. Vet. Med. Coll., 1950; M.S.A., U. Toronto, 1957, Ph.D., Cornell U., 1959; m. Elizabeth Rawlings, Nov. 23, 1940; children—Anne Elizabeth (Mrs. John B. Hopkins III), John Douglas, Mary Jane, Joann Margaret. Veterinarian, Seaforth, Ont. Can., 1950-51, Walnut Springs, Tex., 1951-53; asso. prof. Ont. Vet. Coll., Guelph, 1953-59, prof., 1959-60; v.p. tech. services STB, London, Ont., 1960-63; dir. animal health research CIBA (acquired by E.R. Squibb & Sons 1969), Three Bridges, N.J., 1963—. Bus. mgr. Canadian Vet. Jour., 1959-61, editor, 1961-63. Served with RCAF, 1942-45. Mem. AAAS, N.Y. Acad. Sci., Am., N.J. vet. med. assns., Greater Flemington C. of C. (dir., pres. 1970-71). Author: Handbook of Nutrition, 1962. Home: Box 44 RD 2 Neshanic NJ 08853 Office: ER Squibb & Sons Inc Three Bridges NJ 08887

MARA, WILLIAM FRANCIS, accountant; b. N.Y.C., Sept. 2, 1927; s. John J. and Margaret (Coyne) M.; student Cathedral Coll. of Immaculate Conception, Bklyn., 1945-47; B.B.A., St. John's U., 1954. Clk. accounting dept. Desks, Inc., N.Y.C., 1947-50, 52-54; staff accountant, sr. tax accountant Harris, Kerr, Forster and Company, N.Y.C., 1954-66, supr., 1966, 73-75; supr. Patterson, Teele & Dennis, 1967-69; tax supr. Alexander Grant & Co., N.Y.C., 1969-72, Hurdman and Cranstoun, Penney & Co., N.Y.C., 1972-73; tax mgr. Sperduto, Priskie, Spector & Vanacore, N.Y.C., 1975-77, Oppenheim, Appel, Dixon & Co., N.Y.C., 1977—. Served with AUS, 1950-52. Mem. Am. Inst. C.P.A.'s, N.Y. State Soc. C.P.A.'s (pres. Richmond County chpt.), Am. Accounting Assn., Cath. Accountants Guild (pres.), Soc. for Advancement Mgmt., Internat. Platform Assn. Democrat. Home: One Lincoln Plaza 20 W 64th St New York NY 10023 Office: One New York Plaza New York NY 10004

MARACLE, NELSON PAUL, accountant; b. Rochester, N.Y., Dec. 7, 1931; s. Frank Charles and Evelyn (Gasser) M.; B.S., U. Rochester, 1959; m. Jean Eleanor Gage, July 29, 1967. Supr. tax dept., office mgr. Ernst & Ernst, Rochester, N.Y., 1959-70; self-employed Nelson P. Maracle, C.P.A., Rochester, 1970-75; mng. partner Maracle, Colway & Berretta, C.P.A.'s, Rochester, 1976—; sec.-treas., dir. Maracle Indsl. Finishing Co., Inc., Webster, N.Y., 1961—; pres., chmn. bd. Elcaram Realty, Inc., Webster, 1965-72. Mem. Henderson Bay Scenic Preservation Assn., Inc., 1966-72. Served with AUS, 1954-56. C.P.A., N.Y. Mem. Am. Inst. C.P.A.'s, N.Y. State Soc. C.P.A.'s, Estate Planning Council Rochester. Home: 1239 Imperial Dr Webster NY 14580 Office: 687 Monroe Ave Rochester NY 14607

MARAGOS, JAMES K., food service exec.; b. East Pittsburgh, Pa., Dec. 13, 1920; s. Kariofelis Peter and Katina (Tatelisa) M.; grad. bus. course Am. Mgmt. Assn., 1969; m. Jean Ella Zarr, Dec. 26, 1967; children—Rose Kathryn, Gerald Philip, Kenneth James. With John F. Davis Co., Scranton, Pa., 1946-56; regional v.p. and gen. mgr. ARA Services, Inc., Phila., 1957-70; dir. food service systems and mgr. indsl. sales Nat. Portion Control, Inc., Chgo., 1970-74; v.p. and gen. mgr. Cuisine Ltd., Phila., 1974-76; v.p. Food Service Engring. Co., Phila., 1976—; cons. in field. Trustee St. Luke's Greek Orthodox Ch., Broomall, Pa., 1975-76. Served with USNR, 1942-45. Decorated Purple Heart. Mem. Nat., Pa., Phila. restaurant assns., League Greek Orthodox Stewards, Food Service Execs. Assn., Internat. Food Mfrs. Assn. Clubs: Kiwanis, Order of Ahepa (past pres.). Home: 505 Kerr Ln Springfield PA 19064 Office: 1800 Chestnut St Philadelphia PA 19103

MARANZANO, MIKE FRANK, elec. engr.; b. Argentina, Aug. 14, 1941; s. Miguel and Nelida (Pizzini) M.; came to U.S., 1965; A.S., Pasadena City Coll., 1969. Designer, Ford Motor Co., Pico Rivera, Calif., 1967-68, Burroughs Corp., Pasadena, Calif., 1968-72; instrumentation engr. Sade Co., Buenos Aires, Argentina, 1972-74, Johnson Controls, Inc., Phila., 1978—. project engr. Ecosil Co., Buenos Aires, 1974-76, Perry Industries, Inc., Hicksville, N.Y., 1977-78; Mem. adv. com. N.Y. State Bd. Edn. Mem. IEEE. Contbr. article on indsl. digital controls to profl. jours. Office: 10601 Decatur Rd Philadelphia PA 19154

MARASCIULLO, DAVID LOUIS, clin. and sch. psychologist; b. Bklyn., Apr. 24, 1929; s. Joseph and Josephine Elizabeth (Maresca) M.; B.A. cum laude, Niagara U., 1957; M.A., Fordham U., 1959; Ph.D., St. Johns U., 1969; m. Margaret Rosella Devine, Sept. 1, 1962; children—Paul David, Janene Marie, Mark Joseph. Asst. prof. psychology Villanova (Pa.) U., 1959-61; research fellow psychology dept. U. Ark., Fayetteville, 1961-62; clin. psychologist Vocat. Adv. Service, N.Y.C., 1962-63; sch. psychologist Bur. Child Guidance N.Y.C. Bd. Edn., 1963-68; sch. psychologist, Huntington, N.Y., 1968-69, Merrick, N.Y., 1969—; vis. instr. grad. div. Hofstra U., 1969-71; adj. prof. psychology St. John's U., Jamaica, N.Y., 1971-72; cons. clin. psychologist Syosset (N.Y.) Hosp., 1974—; staff clin. psychologist S. Oakes Hosp., Amityville, N.Y., 1974—. Licensed psychologist, certified sch. psychologist, N.Y. Mem. Am., Nassau County (N.Y.) (dir. 1973—), Suffolk County psychol. assns., Nat. Registry Health Service Providers in Psychology. Contbr. to annotated bibliography on psychiatry and religion. Home and Office: 18 South Hollow Rd Dix Hills NY 11746

MARASCO, LOUIS JOSEPH, realtor; b. Jersey City, July 24, 1946; s. Joseph and Maria Josephine (Parisi) M.; B.A., U. Pitts., 1968; postgrad. Hofstra U., 1973; m. Rosemary Lee D'Acunto, July 31, 1971; 1 dau., Michelle Marie. Personnel adminstr. 1st Nat. City Bank, N.Y.C., 1968-70; adminstr. real estate investment trust Chase Manhattan Bank., N.Y.C., 1970-72; pres. Ramlaw Bldg. Corp., Island Park, N.Y., 1972—; v.p. Walmer Realty, Island Park, 1976—. Licensed real estate broker, N.Y. Mem. Nat. Assn. Real Estate Brokers, L.I. Bd. Realtors, Long Island Builders Assn., N.Y. Realtors Assn. Clubs: Masons. Home: 90 Washington Ave Island Park NY 11558 Office: 4043 Long Beach Rd Island Park NY 11558

MARASH, STANLEY ALBERT, mgmt. cons. exec.; b. Bklyn., Dec. 18, 1938; s. Albert and Esther (Cunio) M.; B.B.A., Coll. City N.Y., 1961; M.B.A., Bernard M. Baruch Coll., 1970; m. Muriel Sylvia Sutchin, June 24, 1961; children—Judith Ilene, Alan Scott. Statistician, Gen. Dynamics/Electric Boat, Groton, Conn., 1961-62, Idaho Nuclear Energy Lab., Idaho Fall, 1962-63; statistician, Memory Systems Operation, RCA, Needham, Mass., 1963-64, mgr. quality assurance, 1964-65, cons. engr., astro electronics div., Princeton, N.J., 1965-66; corp. mgr. quality assurance, Ideal Corp., Bklyn., 1966-68; mgr. quality assurance, Gen. Instrument, Signalite, Neptune, N.J., 1968; pres., STAT-A-MATRIX, Inc., Edison, N.J., 1968—, STAT-A-MATRIX Internat., Inc., Edison, 1975—; trustee, mng. dir. STAT-A-MATRIX-Inst.; adj. prof., statis. quality control, Middlesex County Coll., mem. indsl. tech. adv. com., quality tech. adv. com., 1971—; chmn. indsl. adv. com. for statistics dept., Rutgers U., 1977-78; vis. prof., Madrid Poly. U., 1975; U. Sao Paulo, Inst. Atomic Energy, 1974, 75, 77; instr. courses, Am. Mgmt. Assn., 1972—, FDA; cons. expert on quality and reliability assurance, Internat. Atomic Energy Agy. Mem. Edison Twp. ednl. goals com., 1977. Registered profl. engr. (quality), Calif. Mem. Am. Soc. Quality Control (sr., certified quality and reliability engr.), IEEE (sr., instr. courses 1973-77), Am. Statis. Assn., ASME, Am. Nuclear Soc., ASTM. Co-author textbooks in field; contbr. articles to profl. publs., papers to confs. Office: PO Box 2152 Menlo Park Station Edison NJ 08817

MARATHÉ, EKNATH V., physicist, educator; b. Bombay, India, June 1, 1923; s. Vyanktesh and Yamuna (Agashe) M.; came to Can., 1955, naturalized, 1965; B.Sc., U. Bombay, 1947; M.Sc., U. Poona (India), 1955; Ed.D., State U. N.Y. at Buffalo, 1978; m. Suniti Daté, June 5, 1952; children—Aruna, Sanjay. Demonstrator in physics Ferguson Coll., Poona, India, 1947-50; research physicist Kaycee Industries, Ltd., Poona, 1950-52, Nat. Chem. Lab. India, Poona, 1952-55, nuclear research lab. McMaster U., Can., 1955-56; lectr. physics U. Guelph, 1956-60; tchr. high sch., Ont., 1960—; head dept. sci. Grantham High Sch., St. Catherines, Ont., 1965—; asso. faculty Althouse Coll. Edn. and Brock U. Coll. Edn. Mem. Canadian Assn. Physicists, Am. Phys. Soc., Am. Assn. Physics Tchrs., AAAS, Nat. Sci. Tchrs. Assn., Am. Archaeol. Soc. Club: Torch. Contbr. articles to profl. jours. Home: 25 King's Grant Rd Saint Catharines ON L2N 2S1 Canada Office: 460 Linwell Rd St Catharines ON L2M 2P9 Canada

MARAZZI, WILLIAM CHARLES PIERRE, painter; b. France, Oct. 5, 1947; s. Pierre and Christiane (Velmonte Lecoq) M.; came to U.S., 1971. One-man shows: Avanti Gallery, N.Y.C., 1973, Seamen's Ch. Inst. Gallery, N.Y.C., 1974, Greene Gallery, New Rochelle, N.Y., 1975, Harkness Gallery, N.Y.C., 1975, Rowe House Gallery, Washington, 1976, Bodley Gallery, N.Y.C., 1977, Greene Gallery, 1977, Zion Episcopal Ch., Dobbs Ferry, N.Y., 1978, East-West Holistic Center, N.Y.C., 1978-79; group shows include: Greene Gallery, 1974, Evansville (Ind.) Mus. Art, 1975, Subways of World Exhibit, N.Y.C., 1976, Adams Davidson Gallery, Washington, 1976, Lowell Clay Gallery, N.Y.C., 1977, Sheridan (Wyo.) Gallery, 1977, Internat. Art Fair, Bologna, Italy, 1978, Scoop Gallery, Forest Hills, N.Y., 1978, Wingspread Gallery, Maine, 1978, P.S. One, N.Y.C., 1978; represented in permanent collections, including: Met. Mus. Art Costume Inst., N.Y.C., Tourist Commn., Guatemala City, Guatemala, LaGuardia Community Coll., N.Y.C., Rutgers U., Palm Springs (Calif.) Desert Mus., La. State U., Baton Rouge, Huntsville (Ala.) Mus. Art, Long Beach (Calif.) City Coll., Cdlumbia-Presbyn. Hosp., N.Y.C., N.Y. U. Med. Center. Artist Neighborhood Assn. to Preserve Fifth Ave. Houses, 1972—. Served as brig. French Cavalry, 1967-68. Mem. Found. for Peace through Culture, Internat. Soc. Artists. Photographer, designer: History and Architecture of 82nd Street From Fifth Avenue to Madison Avenue, 1975; translator (to French): Olt (K. Gangemi), 1972. Home: 2 E 82d St New York City NY 10028

MARBURY, BENJAMIN EDWARD, anesthesiologist; b. Farmington, Mo., May 23, 1914; s. Benjamin H. and Annie (Eversole) M.; A.B., U. Mo., 1939; M.S., La. State U., 1941; M.D., Washington U., 1944. Intern, St. Luke's Hosp., St. Louis, 1944-46; asst. resident N.Y. Hosp.-Cornell Med. Center, N.Y.C., 1948-49; practice medicine specializing in anesthesiology, N.Y.C., 1949—; prof. anesthesiology Cornell U. Med. Coll., N.Y.C., 1948—; staff N.Y. Hosp.-Cornell Med. Center, N.Y.C., 1948—. Served to capt., M.C., U.S. Army, 1946-48. Mem. AMA, N.Y. Acad. Medicine, N.Y. State, N.Y. County med. socs., Am., N.Y. socs. anesthesiology. Episcopalian. Club: Univ. (N.Y.C.). Home: 76 Flat Rock Hill Rd Old Lyme CT 06371 Office: 525 E 68th St New York City NY 10021

MARCANTONIO, ROBERT ALLAN, clergyman, psychologist; b. Providence, Nov. 30, 1942; s. Albert A. and Marjorie E. (Heath) M.; B.A., Our Lady of Providence Sem., Warwick, R.I., 1963; B.A., U. Louvain (Belgium), 1965, M.A., 1967; M.S., Iowa State U., 1973, Ph.D., 1975. Ordained priest Roman Cath. Ch., 1967; counselor, psychologist-intern Iowa State U., Ames, 1973-75; dir. counseling services Stonehill Coll., North Easton, Mass., 1975—; parttime asst. pastor St. John Vianney Ch., Cumberland, R.I., 1975—. Licensed psychologist, Mass., R.I. Mem. Am., Eastern, Mass. psychol. assns., Am. Personnel and Guidance Assn., Am. Coll. Personnel Assn., Assn. for Religious Values in Counseling. Home and office: Stonehill Coll North Easton MA 02356

MARCATANTE, JOHN JOSEPH, ednl. adminstr.; b. N.Y.C., Mar. 3, 1930; s. Joseph and Matilda Clara (Grasso) M.; student N.Y. U., 1948-50; A.B., Bklyn. Coll., 1955; M.S. in Edn., Hunter Coll., 1958. Tchr. English secondary schs., N.Y.C., 1955-72; asst. prin. Astoria Intermediate Sch., N.Y.C., 1967—; inst. Hunter Coll., 1963; lectr. in edn. Grad. Sch., Queens Coll., N.Y.C., 1965-67. Cons., Anglo-Am. Seminar on Teaching English, Dartmouth Coll., 1966, Anglo-Am. Seminar on Teaching the Disadvantaged, West Midlands Coll., Great Britain, 1968. Mem. Nat. Council Tchrs. English, N.Y.C. Tchrs. English, Council Supervisory Assns., N.Y. Soc. for Exptl. Study Edn., Catholic Tchrs. Assn., Columbia Assn. N.Y.C. Author: Identification and Image Stories, 1964; American Folklore and Legends, 1967; (with others) Macmillan Gateway English Series, 1969; also numerous articles in profl. jours., poetry. Editor: Fourteenth Yearbook N.Y. Society for Experimental Study for Education, 1970. Home: 34-51 9th St Long Island City NY 11106 Office: 31-51 21st St Long Island City NY 11106

MARCELLAS, THOMAS WILSON, electronics engr.; b. Owings, Md., June 22, 1937; s. Carroll Wilson and Mabel Ellice (Hardesty) M.; B. Engring. Sci., Johns Hopkins U., 1960; postgrad. George Washington U., 1976-78; m. Janet Fay Hardesty, June 20, 1964; children—David Carroll, Diane Elizabeth. Project engr. Bendix Radio Corp., Towson, Md., 1960-61, 63-66; electronic systems engr. Electronic Modules Corp., Hunt Valley, Md., 1966—. Served to 1st lt. U.S. Army, 1961-63. Mem. IEEE. Democrat. Methodist. Home: 13804 Princess Anne Way Phoenix MD 21131 Office: Box 141 Timonium MD 21093

MARCHENA, ISAAC (IMARC), artist; b. Dominican Republic, Dec. 11, 1937; s. Jules and Anna M.; came to U.S., 1959; Liberal Arts Degree, U. Santo Domingo, 1958, D.F.A. (hon.), 1958; m. Ellen Barron, Mar. 29, 1967. Painting Theory of the Emotions permanent display Nat. Mus. Beaux Arts, Dominican Republic, 1968—. Hon. doctorate, spl. order Pres. Dominican Republic, 1958. Address: PO Box 573 Wurtsboro NY 12790

MARCHI, JOHN J., state senator; b. S.I., N.Y., May 20, 1921; s. Louis B. and Alina (Girardello) M.; B.A., Manhattan Coll., 1942; J.D., St. John's U., 1950; J.S.D., Bklyn. Law Sch., 1953; LL.D., Manhattan Coll., St. John's U.; m. Maria Luisa Davini, Nov. 14, 1948; children—Joan Migliori, Aline Marchi. Mem. N.Y. State Senate, 1956—, chmn. finance com., chmn. legis. commn. on expenditure rev. Republican candidate for mayor N.Y.C., 1969, 73; mem. Nat. Adv. Council Drug Abuse Prevention. Served to comdr. USCGR, World War II. Decorated Order of Merit (Italy); recipient Mills G. Skinner award Nat. Urban League; award Anti-Defamation League, B'nai B'rith. Mem. Am., Richmond County bar assns., Am. Judicature Soc., Council State Govts. (chmn.), Am. Fedn. State, Municipal and County Employees (pub. service adv. bd.). Address: 358 St Marks Pl Staten Island NY 10301

MARCONIS, JOSEPH THOMAS, urologist; b. Phila., Nov. 15, 1916; s. Stanley T. and Regina M.; B.A., U. Pa., 1940; M.D., Hahnemann Med. Coll., 1942; m. Mary Nickel, 1950; children—Joseph, James, Carolyn. Intern, Hahnemann Hosp., Phila., 1942-43, resident in urology, 1947-50; resident in gen. surg. St. Francis Hosp., Wichita, Kans., 1946-47; practice medicine specializing in urology, Pottsville, Pa., 1950—; chief urology Pottsville and Good Samaritan hosps.; cons. Locust Mountain Hosp., Ashland State Hosp. Mem. corporate bd. trustees Hahnemann Med. Coll. Hosp., Phila.; chmn. Pottsville Charter Commn., 1967; mem. Pottsville Sch. Bd., 1975—. Served to capt. M.C., U.S. Army, 1943-46. Diplomate Am. Bd. Urology. Fellow A.C.S., Internat. Coll. Surgeons; mem. Am., Pa. (past pres.) urol. assns., AMA. Republican. Roman Catholic. Clubs: Schulylkill Country, Pottsville, Lions. Contbr. articles to med. jours. Home: 15th and Battery Sts Pottsville PA 17901 Office: 413 W Market St Pottville PA 17901

MARCOPLOS, TERRY (RUTH E.) SPEAR, counselor; b. Brockton, Mass., Aug. 3, 1926; d. G. Ernest and Annie Elizabeth (Riley) Spear; B.S., Boston U., 1948; M.S., Smith Coll., 1950; postgrad. U. N.H.; children—Mark Warren, Christianne Spear. Instr. phys. edn. The Brearley Sch., N.Y.C., 1948-49, Mary A. Burnham Sch., Northampton, Mass., 1949-50, Smith Coll., Northampton, 1950-52, Colby Jr. Coll., New London, N.H., 1953-55; field hockey lacrosse instr. Maryvale Trinity Prep. Sch., Stevenson, Md., 1961-63; dir. health and phys. edn., also student adviser Villa Julie Coll., Stevenson, 1964-67; health educator Towson (Md.) State Coll., 1967-70; counselor and dir. guidance services Londonderry (N.H.) and Auburn (N.H.) sch. dists., 1972-75; guidance counselor Windham (N.H.) pub. schs., 1975-76; elementary sch. guidance counselor Claremont (N.H.) Sch. Dist., 1976—. Vestrywoman St. Andrews Episcopal Ch., New London, 1978—. Mem. Am., N.H. (dir. 1977-78) personnel and guidance assns., Am., N.H. (del. 1976-77, pres. 1978-79) sch. counselors assns., AAUW, League of Women Voters (local dir. 1972-73), Council for Exceptional Children. Editorial bd. The School Counselor. Home: Main St New London NH 03257 Office: Claremont Jr High School 107 South St Claremont NH 03743

MARCOS, JOSE MARIANO, physician; b. Palencia, Spain, Mar. 19, 1930; s. Mariano and Encarnacion (Herrero) M.; came to Can., 1959, naturalized, 1973; B.A., La Salle Coll., Palencia, 1947; M.D., U. Valladolid (Spain), 1953; m. Teresa McInnis, June 5, 1965; children—Xavier, Vincent. Chest physician Ciudad Sanatorial de Tarrasa, Barcelona, Spain, 1953-54; gen. practice medicine, Rivas de Campos, Palencia, 1954-55, Noviercas, Soria, Spain, 1955-56; resident in radiology Residencia Sanitaria Fernando Primo de Rivera, Guadalajara, Spain, 1956-59; jr. intern Brantford (Ont., Can.) Gen. Hosp., 1959-60; sr. intern Scarborough (Ont.) Gen. Hosp., 1960-61; asst. resident in therapeutic radiology Princess Margaret Hosp., Toronto, Ont., 1962-64; chief resident therapeutic radiology Ont. Cancer Found., Kingston Cancer Clinic, 1964-68; gen. practice medicine, Windsor, Ont., 1968-72; chest physician Ont. Dept. Health, Ottawa, 1972-74; physician-in-charge Provincial Chest Clinic, Ottawa, 1975—. Mem. Ont. Thoracic Soc. Roman Catholic. Office: 1 1015 Merivale Rd Ottawa ON K1Z 6A6 Canada

MARCOTTE, MARCEL ERNEST, mktg. exec.; b. Sherbrooke, Que., Can., May 2, 1945; s. Gaston Arthur and Ernestine Leontine (LaVenture) M.; M.Comml. Sci., Sherbrooke U., 1969; m. Perusse Rose Ginette, Sept. 20, 1969; children—Marie-Claude, Phillippe. Sales rep. Office Products div. IBM Can., Sherbrooke, 1969; pricing and mktg. research analyst Que.-Telephone, Rimouski, 1969-71, budget sales analyst, 1971-74, market research specialist, 1974-76; mgr. mktg. services No. Telecom, Lachine, Que., Can., 1976-77; mktg. dir. Paragon Bus. Forms Ltd., Montreal, 1977-78; pres. Centre de Gestion Rive-Sud, Inc., St. Lambert, Que., 1978; markets mgmt. and planning dir. Telebec Ltd., Montreal, 1979—; faculty U. Que., Rimouski, 1971-73. Mem. Profl. Corp. of Chartered Adminstrs. Que. Roman Catholic. Contbr. articles in field to profl. jours. Home: 115 Blvd Des Champs Fleuris LaPrairie PQ Canada Office: 3232 Belanger E Montreal PQ Canada

MARCOUX, JULES EDOUARD, physicist, writer; b. Charny, Que., Jan. 26, 1924; s. Romeo Joseph and Atala (Fontaine) M.; B.A., Laval U., 1946, B.S., 1952; M.A., Toronto U., 1952, Ph.D. (Burton fellow), 1956; m. Hermina Manz, July 2, 1955; children—Daniel, Edouard, Elise, Vincent, Pierre, Paul. Research asso. U. Montreal (Que.), 1957; asso. prof. physics U. Laval, Quebec, Que., 1962-64; prof. physics Royal Mil. Coll., St.-Jean, Que., 1958-62, 64—. Postdoctoral fellow NRC Can., 1957. Mem. Am. Assn. Physics Tchrs., Can. Assn. Univ. Tchrs. Author in French: (with A. Ares) Physics Textbook, 6 vols., 1970-74; Astronauts and Astronautics, 1975; Energy: Its Sources, Its Future, 1976; contbr. articles to profl. publs. Home: 7 Charland St Iberville PQ J2X 2K8 Canada Office: Dept Physics Royal Mil Coll Jacques Cartier St Saint-Jean PQ J0J 1R0 Canada

MARCUS, AARON, graphic designer, educator; b. Omaha, May 22, 1943; s. Nathan and Libbie (Burstein) M.; A.B. in Physics, Princeton, 1965; B.F.A., M.F.A. in Graphic Design, Sch. of Art, Yale, 1968; m. Susan Wightman Douglas, Sept. 10, 1968; children—Joshua, Elisheva. Graphic designer Perspecta, Jour. Sch. Architecture, Yale, New Haven, 1968-69, vis. lectr., 1969-72, research asso. in the arts, 1972; asst. prof. visual arts program and sch. architecture and urban planning, Princeton, N.J., 1969-74, lectr., 1975-77, graphic designer, office of publs., 1975-77; sr. lectr. Bezalel Acad., Jerusalem, 1977-78; vis. lectr. Hebrew U., 1977-78; research fellow East-West Center, Honolulu, 1978; vis. lectr. Coll. Environ. Design, U. Calif., Berkeley, 1978—. cons. in computer graphics Bell Telephone Labs., Murray Hill, N.J., 1969-71; vis. lectr. lectr., Bezalel Acad. Art and Design, Jerusalem, Israel, 1975; cons. editor, Murphy Levy Wurman, Architects, Phila., 1974; exec. bd., Yale Arts Assn., Yale Art Sch., 1968-74; adv. bd., Am. Inst. Writing Research, 1974—; adv. bd., guest editor spl. issue, Visible Lang., 1974—. Mem. Am. Inst. Graphic Arts, Soc. Computer Arts. Democrat. Jewish religion. Author: Soft Where, Inc., 1975; computer graphics art work: Cybernetic Landscape I, 1971-73, Noise Barrier, (commd. Pratt Graphic Center, N.Y.C.), 1972-74; conceptual art works: A Zero-Circle Around the Earth, 1973, An X on America, 1972. Home: care Paul Douglas 48 Cleveland Ln Princeton NJ 08540 Office: Coll Environ Design U Calif Berkeley CA 94720

MARCUS, ALAN C., public relations counsel; b. N.Y.C., Feb. 26, 1947; s. Percy and Rose (Fox) M.; student Hun Sch., Princeton 1966; Dir. pub. relations Bergen County Republican Com., Hackensack, N.J., 1968-69; clk. N.J. Gen. Assembly, Trenton, 1969-70, sec. to majority party, 1970-71; pres. Regional Pub. Relations Inc., 1976—, Alan C. Marcus Assos., Newark, 1971—. Trustee Nat. Leukemia Assn., 1976, Am. Inst. Mental Studies, 1976, Hun Sch. of Princeton, 1977. Recipient World's Fair Journalism award N.J. Tercentenary Commn., 1964, Youth Enterprise award Jim Walter Corp., 1972. Mem. Pub. Relations Soc. Am. (pres. N.J. chpt. 1976-77), N.J. State C. of C., Greater Newark C. of C., N.J. Press Assn. Clubs: Essex, Apple Ridge Country; Capitol Hill (Washington). Office: 60 Park Pl Suite 1500 Newark NJ 07102

MARCUS, ALFRED ISRAEL, film producer; b. Manhattan, N.Y.C., Apr. 11, 1918; s. Joseph and Saide (Frommer) M.; student N.Y.U., 1938, 41; m. Naomi Brisk, Dec. 21, 1935; 1 dau., Janet (Mrs. Edward Zuckerman). Sales exec. B. V. D. Corp., N.Y.C., 1934-41; owner Airport TV Newsfilms, J.F. Kennedy Airport, N.Y.C., 1958—; partner Jack Marcus Men's Shops, Cedarhurst and Hewlett, N.Y., 1946-73, Community dir. Five Towns Civil Def. (N.Y.). Ofcl. cinematographer U.S. Olympic Com., 1956; sec., charter mem. U.S. Commn. Sports for Israel, 1950—; mem. health and phys. edn. com. Nat. Jewish Welfare Bd., 1957-75. Served with N.Y. NG, 1940-41, Signal Corps, U.S. Army, 1941-43. Recipient award San Francisco Film Festival, 1962. Mem. Overseas Press Club, Radio TV News Dirs. Assn., Nat. Press Photographers Assn. (life), Profl. Photographers Am., L.I. Press Photographers, Amateur Athletic Union U.S. (life), Zionist Orgn. Am. (life). Mason; mem. B'nai B'rith. Producer: World Maccabiah Olympic Films, Israel, 1953, 57, 61, 65, 69, Paraplegic Olympics, Israel, 1968, Amateur Athletic Assn. U.S. Indoor Nat. Championship Films, 1952-71, Olympic Games, 1952, 56, 60, Pan Am. Games, Mexico, 1955. Office: Airport TV Newsfilms Box 242 JF Kennedy Internat Airport New York City NY 11430 also Box 27142 Tucson Internat Airport Tucson AZ 85726

MARCUS, BRUCE WILLIAM, financial cons., author; b. N.Y.C., July 18, 1925; s. Louis David and Pauline (Lewis) M.; B.A. in Philosophy and Econs., New Sch. Social Research, 1951; m. Mana Balter, Nov. 27, 1962; children—David, Michael, Jonathan, Joseph, Lucy. Sr. asso. Ruder & Finn, Inc., N.Y.C., 1958-65, Mobil Corp., N.Y.C., 1965-67; pres. Bruce W. Marcus Co., N.Y.C., 1967-72, Campbell-Marcus, Inc., N.Y.C., 1968-71; sr. v.p. Financial Relations Bd., Inc., N.Y.C., 1972-77; pres. QOT Corp., N.Y.C., 1973-77; dir. ESP, Inc. Mem. mayor's adv. com. emergency housing, N.Y.C., 1972. Served with USAAF, 1941-46. Recipient Silver Anvil award Pub. Relations Soc. Am., 1957, Lucy Stoner award, 1959. Mem. New Sch. Social Research Alumni Assn. (dir., v.p.). Author: Competing for Capital, 1976; Report to the President on Interagency Task Force on Women Business Owners; Business Today, 1979; The Prudent Man, 1978; The Capital Markets, 1979; Marketing for Realtors, 1979; contbr. articles to mags. Home: 333 West End Ave New York City NY 10023

MARCUS, HELEN, photographer; b. N.Y.C.; d. Joseph M. and Augusta (Hittleman) M.; B.A., Smith Coll., 1947. TV casting CBS, N.Y.C., 1951; in charge subs. rights, play dept. MCA Mgmt., N.Y.C., 1952-54; program coordinator Names the Same TV show, N.Y.C., 1955, Two for the Money, 1955-57; asso. producer Beat the Clock, N.Y.C., 1958-61, Number Please, N.Y.C., 1961; casting dir. To Tell The Truth, Goodson-Todman Prodns., N.Y.C., 1962-68, What's My Line, 1968-75; free lance photographer, 1966—; work exhibited Parents' Mag. Gallery. Pres., Council of Phoenix Theatre, 1969-72; mem. adv. bd. Smith Coll. Theatre Dept., 1965—. Mem. Nat. Acad. TV Arts and Scis., Soc. Photographers in Communications, Am. Soc. Motion Pictures. Home: 120 E 75th St New York City NY 10021

MARCUS, MARIA LENHOFF (MRS. NORMAN MARCUS), lawyer; b. Vienna, Austria, June 23, 1933; d. Arthur and Clara (Gruber) Lenhoff; came to U.S., 1939, naturalized, 1944, B.A., Oberlin Coll., 1954; LL.B., Yale U., 1957; m. Norman Marcus, Dec. 23, 1956; children—Valerie Rae, Nicole Emily, Eric Arthur. Admitted to N.Y. bar, 1961; asso. counsel NAACP, N.Y.C., 1961-67; asst. atty. gen. N.Y. State, N.Y.C., 1967-78, chief Litigation Bur., 1976-78; adj. asso. prof. law N.Y. U., 1976-78; asso. prof. law Fordham U. Law Sch., N.Y.C., 1978—. Mem. Assn. Bar City N.Y. (chmn. com. 1972-75, judiciary com. 1975-76, exec. com. 1976-80), Am. (sect. adminstrv. law), N.Y. State (ho. of dels.) bar assns. Contbr. articles to legal, other publs. Home: 91 Central Park W Apt 4-D New York City NY 10023 Office: Fordham U Law Sch 140 W 62d St New York City NY 10023

MARCUS, MILDRED RENDL (MRS. EDWARD MARCUS), economist; b. N.Y.C., May 30, 1928; d. Julius and Agnes (Hokr) Rendl; B.S., N.Y. U., 1948, M.B.A., 1950; Ph.D. (Dean Bernice Brown Cronkhite fellow 1950-51), Radcliffe Coll., 1954; m. Edward Marcus, Aug. 10, 1956. Economist, Gen. Electric Co., 1953-56, Bigelow-Sanford Carpet Co., Inc., 1956-58; lectr. econs. Coll. City N.Y., evening sessions, 1953-58; research investment problems in tropical Africa, 1958-59; instr. econs. Hunter Coll., 1959-60; lectr. econs. Columbia U., 1960-61; research econ. devel. Nigeria, W. Africa, 1961-63; sr. economist Internat. div. Nat. Indsl. Conf. Bd., 1963-66; asst. prof. Grad. Sch. Bus. Adminstrn., Pace Coll., 1964-66; asso. prof. Borough of Manhattan Community Coll., City U. N.Y., 1966-71, prof., 1972—; participant Internat. Economical Meeting, Amsterdam, 1968. Bd. dirs. N.Y.C. Council on Econ. Edn., 1970—. Fellow Gerontol. Assn.; mem. Am. (vice chmn. ann. meeting 1973), Met. (sec. 1954-56) econ. assns., Indsl. Relations Research Assn., Allied Social Sci. Assn. (vice chmn. conv. 1973), AAUW, N.Y. U. Grad. Sch. Bus. Adminstrn. Alumni (sec. 1956-58). Club: Radcliffe. Author: (with husband) Investment and Development of Tropical Africa, 1959, International Trade and Finance, 1965, Monetary and Banking Theory, 1965; Economics, 1969; (with husband) Principles of Economics, 1969; Economic Progress and the Developing World, 1970; Economics, 1978; also monographs and articles in field. Econ. and internat. research in industrialization less developed areas. Address: POB 814 New Canaan CT 06840 Office: Manhattan Community Coll 1633 Broadway New York City NY 10019

MARCUS, MYLES MARTIN, engr.; b. Boston, July 29, 1927; s. Herbert Warren and Esther Harriet (Bergman) M.; B.B.A. in Elec. Engring./Mgmt., Northeastern U., 1959, M.B.A., 1967; m. Barbara Arleen Taylor, July 15, 1967; children—Linda, Josh. Designer and test engr., test methods mgr. Sylvania Electric Co., Waltham, Mass., 1955-60; sr. quality control engr., quality assurance mgr., reliability evaluation mgr. Raytheon Co., Mass. and R.I., 1960-73; product evaluation engring. mgr. National Cash Register, Cambridge, Ohio, 1974-77; mgr. electronics quality control Sybron/Taylor Instrument Co., Rochester, N.Y., 1977—. Served with USN, 1944-49, 50-51. Registered profl. engr., Calif. Mem. Am. Soc. Quality Control, Am. Radio Relay League. Home: 766 Newberry Ln Webster NY 14580 Office: Sybron/Taylor Instrument Co 95 Ames St Rochester NY 14601

MARCUS, ROSALIE, counselor, tchr.; b. Newark, July 5, 1947; d. Aaron and Edna Niomi (Nover) M.; B.S. in English, Monmouth Coll., 1969, M.S. summa cum laude in Student Personnel Services, 1972. Head resident Monmouth Coll., West Long Branch, N.J., 1968-69; tchr. English and journalism Long Branch (N.J.) Jr. High Sch., 1969-76, counselor, 1976-77; coordinator, counselor drop-out prevention program Long Branch Jr.-Sr. High Sch., 1977—, testing com., 1977-78, middle sch. steering com. 1976-77; instr. in field; facilitator reality therapy workshops, human relations tng. programs. Mem. exec. council Student-Tchr.-Parent Orgn. Long Branch Jr.-Sr. High Sch., 1976-78; vol. Riverview Hosp., Red Bank, N.J., 1973-74; supr. work-experience program Monmouth Med. Center, Long Branch, 1977-78; counselor Alt. Sch. for Socially Maladjusted/Emotionally Disturbed Youngsters, 1978. Certified counselor, tchr., N.J. Mem. Nat., N.J., Long Branch (chmn. dist. negotiations and labor relations 1975-79, corr. sec. 1977-79) edn. assns., Am. Personnel and Guidance Assn., Assn. Sch. Counselors, AAUW, Alpha Delta Kappa (past chpt. pres.; state chaplain 1978-80). Democrat. Clubs: Behavioral Sci. Club. Contbr. research studies in field; developer innovative programs to prevent drop-outs. Home: 460 E Ocean Blvd Long Branch NJ 07740 Office: Long Branch Jr High Counseling Suite Indiana Ave Long Branch NJ 07740

MARCUS, SIDNEY OTTMAR, JR., phys. scientist; b. Balt., May 18, 1918; s. Sidney Ottmar and Selma (Alexander) M.; student U. Md., U. Chgo., U. Melbourne (Australia); m. Lois Irene Hess, Mar. 11, 1944; children—Sidney O., John R., Kathryn L., Michael C., Wendy M., Susan I., Cynthia A. Meteorologist, analyst U.S. Weather Bur., Washington, 1952-56; weather, sea forecaster, Louis Allen Asso., 1956-57; oceanographer, forecaster U.S. Naval Oceanographic Office, Suitland, Md., 1957-62; oceanographer, phys. scientist Nat. Oceanographic Data Center, Washington, 1962—; cons. Marine Environ. Studies. Pres. Prince Georges Area Sci. Fair Exec. Com.; chmn. Cub Scout Com. Served in U.S. Army, 1941-45. Mem. Am. Meteorol. Soc., Am. Geophys. Union, Marine Tech. Soc. (com. chmn), VFW (past dist. comdr.), Chesapeake Bay Found. Democrat. Roman Catholic. Clubs: Chesapeake Ranch, Chesapeake Country. Editor English lang. translation Oceanology of USSR Acad. of Sci.; contbr. numerous publs. in field to profl. jours. Home: 2903 Lakehurst Ave Forestville MD 20028 Office: NOAA/NODC 2001 Wisconsin Ave Washington DC 20235

MARDAGA, THOMAS J., clergyman; b. Balt., May 14, 1913; s. Thomas J. and Agnes (Ryan) M.; B.A., St. Charles Coll., 1936; S.T.L., St. Mary's Sem., Balt., 1940; LL.D., Mt. St. Mary's Coll., 1968. Ordained priest Roman Catholic Ch., 1940; served St. Paul's Parish, Balt., 1940-46, Basilica of Assumption, 1946-62; named right reverend monsignor, 1963; aux. bishop Balt., 1967, vicar gen., 1967; bishop Wilmington (Del.), 1968—; dir. Archdiocesan Cath. Youth Orgn., 1946-55; dir., exec. sec. Archdiocesan Cath. Charity Fund Appeal, 1955; mem. Archdiocesan Bd. Consultors, 1966; alt. adminstrv. com. and bd. Nat. Conf. Cath. Bishops; regional rep. Cath. U. Louvain (Belgium), 1970, mem. bishops com. on doctrine, 1970, mem. Cath. U. com., 1972, chmn. Region IV, 1974-76; mem. com. budget and finance Nat. Conf. Cath. Bishops-U.S. Cath. Conf., 1972, adviser com. on doctrine, 1973, mem. com. on priestly life and ministry, 1974; mem. nat. hon. com. Black Catholics Concerned, 1972; chmn. Delmarva Ecumenical Agy., 1975; regional Episcopal adviser Region II, Cursillo Movement. Mem. bd. Greater Wilmington Devel. Council; bd. dirs. Cath. Diocese Found.; trustee Mt. St. Mary's Coll., Emmitsburg, Md. Home: 1307 N Bancroft Pkwy Wilmington DE 19806 Office: PO Box 2030 Wilmington DE 19899

MARDELLO, ALFRED FREDERICK, mech. engr.; b. Hackensack, N.J., Sept. 21, 1938; s. Isadore Nicholas and Margaret Domenica (Gennaro) M.; B.S. in Mech. Engring., Newark Coll. Engring., 1961; m. Alba Louise Natalicchio, Oct. 10, 1964; children—Lisa Ann, Karen Margaret. With U.S. Army, Picatinny Arsenal, Dover, N.J., 1961—, mech. engr., Army Armament Research and Devel. Command, 1977—. Recipient Army Research and Devel. award, 1977. Patentee in field; contbr. articles to profl. jours. Office: US Army Armament Research and Devel Command Dover NJ 07801

MARDEN, ARTHUR BUDGEN, realtor; b. Lunenberg, Mass., July 22, 1902; s. George Henry and Ida May (Budgen) M.; spl. student Mass. Inst. Tech., 1924-25, Harvard U., 1926-27; m. Florence May Illingworth, July 2, 1925; children—Edward A., Betty J. Marden Olivier, John C. Gen. contractor, Boston, 1925-50; mgr., owner Marden, N.H., Realty, Salem, N.H., 1925—. Mem. Sch. Bd. Salem, 1966-70, chmn., 1969-70; mem. N.H. Legislature, 1969-70; bd. dirs. Greater Lawrence (Mass.) Community Fund, 1966-69; bd. dirs., v.p. Salem Hist. Soc., 1972—. Mem. SAR, Salem Bd. Trade (dir., pres. 1963-69), Greater Lawrence C. of C. (dir. 1965-70). Republican. Methodist. Club: Masons. Address: 12 Millville Circle Salem NH 03079

MARDEN, PARKER GRIMES, sociologist; b. Worcester, Mass., Oct. 19, 1938; A.B., Bates Coll., Lewiston, Maine, 1961; A.M., Brown U., 1964, Ph.D., 1966; m.; 2 children. Research asst. Center for Aging Research, Brown U., summer 1962, dept. sociology, summer 1963, dept. preventive medicine Harvard U. Med. Sch., summer 1964; instr. sociology NSF Program for Superior Secondary Sch. Students, Goucher Coll., Towson, Md., summers 1964-65; research asso. sociology Center for Aging Research, Inst. for Health Scis., Brown U., 1965-66; asst. to asso. prof. sociology Coll. Arts and Scis., Cornell U., 1966-72, program asso. Internat. Population Program, 1966-72, dir. grad. studies, 1968-71, co-dir. Comprehensive Health Planning Tng. Program, 1968-72; asso. prof. sociology Lawrence U., Appleton, Wis., 1972-75; Charles A. Dana prof., chmn. dept. sociology St. Lawrence U., Canton, 1975—, dir. North Country Research Center, 1976—; dir. summer programs in population studies NSF Summer Insts. in Social Demography and Population Policy, Cornell U., 1972, Lawrence U., 1973; bd. dirs. Midwestern Area Alcohol Tng. and Edn. Program, 1974-75; cons. Ministry Pub. Health and Social Assistance, Republic of Honduras, 1967, Population Council, 1970-72, Div. Spl. Treat Treatment and Rehab. Programs, Nat. Inst. on Alcohol Abuse and Alcoholism, 1972—, KETC-TV, St. Louis, 1974-76, Midwestern Ae Area Alcohol Edn. and Tng. Program, 1975-78; cons. behavioral scientist Family Medicine Program, U. Miami Med. Sch., 1967. Recipient Bobbs-Merrill award in sociology, 1962, Babcock award Lawrence U., 1975. Hon. fellow Population Council, 1964-65. Mem. Phi Beta Kappa. Author: (with others) A Study Guide to Population and the American Future, 1973; Population Workbook: A Series of Learning Exercises in Population Studies for Undergraduates, 1975; editor: (with Dennis G. Hodgson) Population, Environment and the Quality of Life, 1974. Contbr. articles to profl. jours. Office: Dept Sociology and Anthropology St Lawrence U Canton NY 13617

MARDEN, RICHARD GUY, assn. exec.; b. Wolfeboro, N.H., Aug. 14, 1923; s. Guy and Ruby (Kent) M.; B.A., U. N.H., 1948; M. Govt. Adminstrn., U. Pa., 1949; m. Joanne Nelson, July 1, 1950; children—Kathleen Kent, Anne, Elaine. Town mgr. Ashland (N.H.), 1949-51; field rep. N.H. Taxpayers Fedn., Concord, 1951-54; exec. sec. N.J. Sch. Bd. Fedn., Trenton, 1954-57; exec. dir. N.H. Municipal Assn., Concord, 1957-59; asst. exec. dir. Pa. League Cities, Harrisburg, 1959-61, editor, 1959-63, exec. dir., 1962—; state corr. Pub. Mgmt., Nat. Municipal Rev., 1951-54; mem. Gov.'s Adv. Council Community Affairs. Bd. dirs. Pa. Tech. Assistance Agency; mem. bd. Pa. Intergovtl. Council. Served to maj. USAAF, 1942-46. Mem. Nat. Sch. Bds. Assn. (past sec.-treas. N.E. regional group), Holderness Sch. Alumni Assn. (past sec.-treas.), Am. Soc. Pub. Adminstrn., Nat. League Cities (dir.), Nat. Ski Patrol System. Editor Sch. Bd. Notes, 1954-57; N.H. Town and City, 1957-59; contbr. articles to edn. and govt. publs. Collector, dealer Early Am. antiques. Home: 3829 Club Dr Harrisburg PA 17110 Office: 2608 N 3d St Harrisburg PA 17110

MARDER, DORIE, painter, serigrapher; b. Nisko, Poland; d. Leisor and Esther (Jacobi) M.; came to U.S., 1940, naturalized, 1945; student Sorbonne, Paris, 1936-40. One-woman shows: Village Art Center, N.Y.C., 1961, 63, Studio Art Gallery, N.Y.C., 1965—, Fed. Savs. Bank, N.Y.C., 1966, High Point Gallery, Lennox, Mass., 1970, 71; exhibited in group shows: Riverside Mus., N.Y.C., 1960, Nat. Serigraph Soc., N.Y.C., 1958, Am. Color Print Soc., Phila., 1951, San Francisco Mus., 1957, Sweat Meml. Mus., Mdmphis, 1952, Printmakers So. Calif., 1952, Milw. Art Inst., 1955, Seattle Art Mus., 1950, Am. Contemporary Art Gallery, 1957, Audubon Artists, N.Y.C., 1970, Mus. N.J., 1966, Nassau Community Coll., 1971, Boston Printmakers, 1954, Portland (Oreg.) Mus., 1952, Nat. Arts Club, N.Y.C., 1963, Knickerbocker Artists, N.Y.C., 1956, N.Y. U., 1967, N.Y. Pub. Library, 1961, New Sch. for Social Research, 1954, NAD, 1970, Boston Mus. Fine Arts, 1954, Print Club Phila., 1951, Ohio U., 1955, Art Gallery Toronto, 1956, Stamford Mus., 1960, Tift Coll., 1961, Harding Coll., 1961, U. S.C., 1963, Mich. State U., 1962, Lehigh U., 1972, Women in Am. Art, Summit Gallery, 1977, Equitable Gallery, 1977, Union Carbide Gallery, 1977; exhibited abroad at Pollazzo Vechio, Florence, Italy, 1972, Pompeian Pavilion, Naples, Italy, 1972, Arts Gallery Manila, Philippines, 1960; represented in permanent collections: Safed Mus., Norfolk Mus., Roberson Center for Arts and Scis., Binghamton, N.Y., Idaho Mus., U.S. Dept. State, State U. N.Y. at Binghamton, Butler Inst. Am. Art Recipient first prize Village Art Center, 1959, 61, Clendenen prize for graphics Nat. Assn. Women Artists, 1961. Mem. Artist Equity, Am.

Color Print Soc., League Present Day Artists (dir. 1971—), Art Students League, Nat. Assn. Women Artists (Montag prize 1965). Home: 223 W 21st St New York City NY 10011 Office: 112-114 W 14th St New York City NY 10011

MARELLA, MEDEA MARIE, nursing adminstr.; b. Ascoli Piceno, Italy, June 30, 1927 (parents Am. citizens); d. Tancredi Giuseppi and Sebastiana M.; R.N., Uniontown (Pa.) Hosp., 1948; B.S. in Nursing, Fairleigh Dickinson U., 1969; M.A. in Nursing Service Adminstrn., Columbia U., 1970, Ed.M. in Nursing Edn., 1972, Ed.D. in Adminstrn. Higher Degree Programs in Nursing Adminstrn., 1974. Operating room supr. Uniontown (Pa.) Hosp., 1948-53, Mt. Sinai Hosp., N.Y.C., 1953-58; per diem nurse N.Y. Hosp., N.Y.C., 1958-59; inservice instr. Hosp. for Spl. Surgery, N.Y.C., 1960-61, nursing office supr., 1961-66; pvt. duty nurse, N.Y.C., 1967-70; clin. instr. Hunter Coll. Bellevue Sch. Nursing, N.Y.C., 1970-73; asst. prof. City U. N.Y., N.Y.C., 1973-76; asso. v.p., dir. nursing Sinai Hosp. Balt., 1976—; med. advisor CBS, The Guiding Light, 1972-73, The Nurses, 1965-66. Am. Jour. Nursing fellow, 1972-73. Mem. Am. Nursing Assn. (commn. on nursing services 1978—), Md. Nurses Assn., Nat. League Nurses (nat. forum for nursing service adminstrs.), Nursing Service Facilitators, Am. Soc. Nursing Service Adminstrs., Tchrs. Coll. Columbia U. Nursing Edn. Alumni Assn. (treas. 1976-78), Common Cause, Sigma Theta Tau. Democrat. Roman Catholic. Contbg. editor Jour. Nursing Service Adminstrs. Home: 349 Homeland Southway Apt 1-C Baltimore MD 21212 Office: Sinai Hospital of Baltimore 400 Belvedere Ave Baltimore MD 21215

MARELLI, JOHN VINCENT, astronomer, research co. exec.; b. Boston, Dec. 26, 1943; s. Carlo and Luisa (Balaschi) M.; student Boston U., 1961-62; student Tex. A. and M. U., 1962-64. Research asst. Regis Women's Coll., 1963, Air Force Cambridge Research Labs., Bedford, Mass., 1964, Research Calculations, Newton, Mass., 1964-67; weather forecaster Weather Services, Boston, 1965-68; research dir. John Marelli Meteorol. Assos., Boston, 1965—, also dir. Met. Brit. Interplanetary Soc., AAAS, Assn. Lunar, Planetary Observers, Royal Astron. Soc. Can., Astron. Soc. Pacific, Astron. League. Democrat. Research on dogma of psuedosci., 1974-76. Home and Office: 42 Chestnut St Charlestown MA 02129

MARESCA, TECKLA ANN, practical nurse, hosp. admnstr.; b. Plainfield, N.J., Oct. 3, 1944; d. Frances Mario Maresca and Lorraine Ruth (Hoblitzell) Maresca Olbrick; student Coll. of St. Elizabeth 1962-63, diploma in practical nursing Union County Tech. Inst., 1967; student in bus. admnstrn. County Coll. of Morris, 1978—. Nurse's aide Munlenberg Hosp., Plainfield, N.J. 1963-66, ward clk., 1966-67; operating room nurse Raritan Valley Hosp., N.J. Sch. Medicine and Dentistry, Green Brook 1967-70; central services supr. Raritan Valley Hosp., Green Brook 1970-71, Dover (N.J.) Gen. Hosp. 1971—; instr., founder central services technician program Morris County VoTech, Denville, N.J., 1978-79. Licensed practical nurse, N.J.; registered central services technician, N.J. Mem. Internat. Assn. Hosp. Central Services Mgmt., Am. Hosp. Assn. Central Services Mgmt. Home: 59 Pleasant Hill Rd Ironia NJ 07845 Office: Jardine St Dover Gen Hosp Dover NJ 07801

MARGOLIN, CARL M., psychotherapist; b. N.Y.C., Jan. 23, 1939; s. Samuel and Henrietta (Kressel) M.; B.A., CUNY, 1961; M.S.W., Columbia U., 1965; postgrad. Nat. Psychol. Assn. for Psychoanalysis, 1968-70; m. Susie Echols Watts, Feb. 10, 1964; children—Christopher, Andrew. Sr. psychiat. social worker W.J.C.S., White Plains, N.Y., 1964-76; psychotherapist Whitehill Counseling Service, Yorktown Hights, N.Y., 1973-76; pvt. practice psychotherapy, 1976—; tng. supr. Yeshiva U., 1972-76. Mem. exec. com. No. Westchester Mental Health Council, 1973-79, chmn. planning com., 1975-79. Cert. social worker, N.Y. State. Mem. Nat. Assn. Social Workers, Acad. Cert. Social Workers, Soc. Clin. Social Work Psychotherapists. Home: Route 124 Brewster NY 10509 Office: 344 E Main St Mount Kisco NY 10549

MARGOLIN, HAROLD, metallurgist; b. Hartford, Conn., July 12, 1922; s. Aaron David and Sonia (Krupnikoff) M.; B. Engring., Yale U., 1943, M.Engring., 1947, D.Eng. (Internat. Nickel fellow 1947-49), 1950; m. Elaine Marjorie Rose, July 4, 1946; children—Shelley, Deborah, Amy. Research asso., research scientist Research div. N.Y. U., N.Y.C., 1949-56; asso. prof. metall. engring., 1956-62, prof., 1962-73; prof. phys. metallurgy Poly. Inst. N.Y., Bklyn., 1973—; cons. in field. Served with USNR, 1944-46. Fellow Am. Soc. Metals (edn. award N.Y. chpt. 1967); mem. Am. Inst. Mining, Metall. and Petroleum Engrs., Metals Soc. (Brit.), Yale Engring. Assn., Sigma Xi. Democrat. Jewish. Contbg. author books; contbr. articles to profl. publs. Patentee in field. Home 19 Crescent Rd Larchmont NY 10538 Office: 333 Jay St Brooklyn NY 11201

MARGOLIN, SOLOMON, pharmacologist; b. Phila., May 16, 1920; s. Nathan and Fanny (Begelfor) M.; B.S., Rutgers U., 1941, M.Sc., 1943, Ph.D., 1945; m. Gerda Levy, Jan. 17, 1947; children—David, Bernard, Daniel. Grad. asst. Rutgers U., 1943-45; research biologist Silmo Chem. Co., Vineland, N.J., 1947-48; asst. dir. biol. research Schering Corp., Bloomfield, N.J., 1948-54, dir. pharmacological research, 1952-54; chief pharmacologist Maltbie Labs. div. Wallace and Tiernan, Inc., Belleville, N.J., 1954-56; dir. biol. research Wallace Labs. div. Carter-Wallace, Inc., Cranbury, N.J., 1956-64, v.p. biol. research, 1964-68; pres. AMR Biol. Research, Inc., 1968—. Mem. Soc. Animal Prodn., Endocrine Soc., Chem. Soc., Soc. Exptl. Biology, Pharmacological Soc., Pharm. Assn., N.Y. Acad. Scis., Am. Guernsey Cattle Club, Alpha Zeta. Lion. Home: RD 1 Box 440 Stockton NJ 08559 Office: PO Box 5700 Princeton NJ 08540

MARGOLIS, EUGENE, lawyer, city ofcl.; b. Bronx, Dec. 19, 1935; s. Louis and Minnie (Kaplan) M.; B.M.E., Rensselaer Poly. Inst., 1957; J.D., Georgetown U., 1960, M.Patent Law, 1962; m. Sally Fay Gellman, Sept. 22, 1962; children—Judith Miriam, Linda Aileen, Aaron Keith, Pamela June. Admitted to N.Y. bar, 1961, U.S. Supreme Ct. bar, 1969; patent examiner U.S. Patent Office, Washington, 1957-60; trial atty. antitrust div. U.S. Dept. Justice, Washington, 1960-66, N.Y.C., 1966-67; chief consumer protection div. N.Y.C. Dept. Law, 1967-71; gen. counsel Mayor's Interdeptl. Com. on Pub. Utilities, N.Y.C., 1972-73; spl. counsel to commr. N.Y.C. Dept. Gen. Services, 1974—; dir. N.Y.C. Office of Energy Conservation, 1975—; adj. prof. Cooper Union, 1978—; adj. asso. prof. Grad. Center, City U. N.Y., 1974—. Chmn. govtl. relations and grants com. Village of Larchmont, 1977—, mem. cable TV com., 1977—, tax base com., 1974—; chmn. Larchmont Democratic Com., 1976-77; mem. Westchester County Dem. Com., 1975-77. Mem. N.Y. State, Westchester County bar assns., ASME, Phi Delta Phi, Pi Delta Epsilon, Tau Epsilon Phi. Democrat. Jewish. Clubs: Rensselaer Alumni (sec. chpt. 1976-77), B'nai B'rith (lodge pres. 1976-78, 78—), Town and Village Synagogue Men's (pres. 1970-71). Editorial bd. Georgetown Law Jour., 1958-60. Home: 15 Bonnett Ave Larchmont NY 10538 Office: Dept Gen Services 1800 Municipal Bldg 1 Centre St New York City NY 10007

MARGOLIS, GERALD JOSEPH, psychiatrist, psychoanalyst; b. Bronx, N.Y., May 7, 1935; s. Max and Sophie (Siegel) M.; A.B., U. Rochester, 1957; M.D., U. Chgo., 1960; grad. Inst. Phila. Assn. Psychoanalysis, 1972; m. June Edelman Greenspan, July 13, 1976; children—David J., Peter S., Steven J. Intern, psychiat. resident, Upstate Med. Center, State U. N.Y., Syracuse, 1960-64, instr. in psychiatry, 1966-67; from instr. to asst. clin. prof., Med. Sch., U. Pa., Phila., 1967—; practice medicine specializing in psychiatry and psychoanalysis, Cherry Hill, N.J.; instr. psychotherapy demonstration course, 1976—. Mem. parents com. Wesleyan U. Served with M.C., USAF, 1964-66. Diplomate Am. Bd. Psychiatry and Neurology. Mem. Am. Psychoanalytic Assn. (certified), Am. Psychiat. Assn., AMA, Phila. Assn. for Psychoanalysis, U. Rochester Alumni Assn. (scholarship com., 1974—), Phi Beta Kappa. Clubs: Wesleyan of Phila., B'nai B'rith. Contbr. articles to profl. publs. Home: 103 Sussex Dr Cinnaminson NJ 08077 Office: 1 Cherry Hill Suite 920 Cherry Hill NJ 08002

MARGRO, ARTHUR LAWRENCE, educator; b. N.Y.C., Jan. 2, 1925; s. Vincent James and Margaret Elizabeth (Fortanascio) M.; student Iona Coll., 1946-47; B.A. in Philosophy, U. Notre Dame, 1951; postgrad. St. Francis Sem., 1951-56; M.S. in Edn., Fordham U., 1961, Ph.D. in Edn., 1973. Bank teller First Nat. City Bank of N.Y., N.Y.C., 1956-57; ins. adjuster, N.Y.C., 1952-58; tchr. Nanuet (N.Y.) pub. schs., 1958-62; tchr. Ossining (N.Y.) pub. schs., 1962—, tchr. English, coordinator English Middle Sch., 1971—. Founder, dir. The Castle, Nanuet. Served with USMCR, 1943-46. Mem. Am., N.Y. State, Fordham (1st v.p.) personnel and guidance assns., N.Y. State, Ossining (pres.) tchrs. assns., N.Y. Schoolmasters Club, Phi Delta Kappa (pres. Fordham chpt. 1975-76). Democrat. Roman Catholic. Club: Notre Dame (N.Y.). Home: 32 Badger St New City NY 10956 Office: Middle Sch Ossining NY 10562

MARGULIES, MARK ALAN, hosp. adminstr.; b. Bronx, N.Y., Feb. 22, 1949; s. Rubin and Rita (Horowitz) M.; B.S., Pratt Inst., 1971; M.S. in Hosp. Adminstrn., Columbia U., 1973; m. Susan Paley, June 20, 1970. Asst. adminstr. Goldwater Meml. Hosp., N.Y.C., 1973-74; dir. profl. services Peninsual Hosp. Center, Far Rockaway, N.Y., 1974—. Licensed nursing home adminstr. Mem. Am. Coll. Hosp. Adminstrs., Am. Coll. Nursing Home Adminstrs., Am. Hosp. Assn., Hosp. Execs. Club. Home: 1540 Hewlett Ave Hewlett NY 11557 Office: Peninsula Hosp Center 5115 Beach Channel Dr Far Rockaway NY 11691

MARGULIES, SELMA KOLATCH, speech pathologist; b. Bklyn., Aug. 10, 1931; d. Isidore Jack and Anna (Goldman) Kolatch; B.A., Hunter Coll., 1953; M.A. (Bergen County Tb and Health Assn. Scholar), Bklyn. Coll., 1956; certificate Inst. Myofunctional Therapy, 1971; children—Shira, Lisanne. Staff clinician dept. rehab. medicine Bellevue Hosp., 1953-58; speech pathologist fed. research project HEW, 1958-60; speech clinician Hunter Coll., N.Y.C., 1960-67, Harlem Hosp., N.Y.C., 1967-68, Hackensack Gen. Hosp. (N.J.), 1968-70; supr. speech pathology Flower & Fifth Ave. Hosp., N.Y.C., 1966-75, St. Clare's Hosp. & Health Center, N.Y.C., 1971-75, St. Clare's Hosp., 1975—; pvt. practice speech pathology, N.Y.C., 1971—. Mem. Am., N.Y. State speech and hearing assns., Dir. Hosp. Speech Pathology and Audiology, Myofunctional Therapy Assn. Am., Aphasia Study Group, Orton Soc. Home: 949 West End Ave New York City NY 10025 Office: St Clare's Hospital 415 W 51st St New York City NY 10019 also Lexington Profl Center 133 E 73d St New York City NY 10021

MARHOEFER, GILBERT LIONEL, real estate broker; b. Pitts., Oct. 6, 1925; s. Louis and Martha Maria (Bold) M.; B.S., U. Pitts., 1949, M. Litt., 1951, Ph.D., 1960; m. Lee Arthur, Oct. 1, 1975; children—Gilbert L.K., Sandra Louise. Owner, operator G.L. Marhoefer Realty, Pitts., 1949—; officer, dir. cos. Served with USAAF, 1944-46; PTO. Named hon. Ky. Col.; certified property mgr., Pa. Mem. Greater Pitts. Real Estate Bd., Nat. Real Estate Aviation Council, Inst. Real Estate Mgmt. Republican. Roman Catholic. Clubs: Pitts. Field, Duquesne (Pitts.); Tamarac Country (Ft. Lauderdale). Home: 18C Gateway Towers Gateway Center Pittsburgh PA 15222 Office: 4H Gateway Towers Gateway Center Pittsburgh PA 15222

MARIC, RADOSLAV, obstetrician, gynecologist; b. Croatia, Jan. 8, 1938; s. Ante and Ana (Ramljak) M.; came to U.S., 1971; M.D., U. Zagreb, 1963; m. Nada Trselic, July 4, 1964; children—Dubravka, Vlasta, Natalia. Intern, Univ. Clinic, Zagreb, 1964; gen. practice medicine, Croatia, 1965, 66-68; resident in obstetrics and gynecology, U. Clinic, Zagreb, 1968-69; intern, Winnipeg, Man., Can., 1970-71; resident in obstetrics and gynecology Stamford (Conn.) Hosp., 1971-73; practice medicine specializing in obstetrics and gynecology, Derby-Ansonia, Conn., 1973—. Served with M.C., Yugoslavian Air Force, 1965-66. Mem. Am. Coll. Obstetrics and Gynecology, Conn. State, New Haven County med. socs., Am. Fertility Soc., Nat. Interns and Residents Assn. Roman Catholic. Contbr. articles in Croatian lang. to med. publs. Office: 121 Wakelee Ave Ansonia CT 06401

MARIMOW, WILLIAM KALMON, journalist; b. Phila., Aug. 4, 1947; s. Jay and Helen (Gitnig) M.; B.A. in English, Trinity Coll., Hartford, Conn., 1969; m. Diane Katherine Macomb, Oct. 18, 1969; 1 dau., Ann Esther. Asst. editor Chilton Co., Bala Cynwyd, Pa., 1969-70; asst. to econ. columnist Phila. Bull., 1970; mem. staff dept. econs. Temple U., 1971-72; staff writer Phila. Inquirer, 1972—; instr. dept. urban studies U. Pa., 1979—. Recipient award for deadline reporting Phila. chpt. Sigma Delta Chi, 1977, Pub. Service award Phila. chpt., 1978, N.J. chpt., 1978, Nat. Pub. Service award, 1978; award for gen. reporting Pa. AP Mng. Editors, 1977, award for pub. service, 1978; 1st pl. award for team reporting Phila. Press Assn., 1977; 2d pl. award for investigative reporting Keysteon Press Assn., 1978, Print Journalism award Robert F. Kennedy Found., 1978, Roy Howard Pub. Service award Scripps Howard Found., 1978, Silver Gavel award Am. Bar Assn., 1978, Pulitzer prize for distng. public service, 1978. Home: 321 S 44th St Philadelphia PA 19104 Office: Phila Inquirer 400 N Broad St Philadelphia PA 19101

MARINACCIO, ANTHONY, educator, cons.; b. Bridgeport, Conn., Aug. 26, 1912; s. Paul and Louisa (DeLibero) M.; B.E., Conn. State Coll., 1937; M.A., Ohio State U., 1939; Ph.D., Yale U., 1949; LL.D., Parsons Coll., 1961; m. Elsie Kieps, Sept. 5, 1936 (dec. Sept. 1964); children—Warren, Karen Marinaccio Beacon, Dianna Marinaccio Carlisi, Nancy Marinaccio Wilber, Linda, Lee; m. 2d, M. Maxine Reynolds, Oct. 15, 1965. Tchr. jr. high sch., Hartford, Conn., 1935-41; elementary sch. prin., 1941-46; prof. edn., prin. campus sch. Tchrs. Coll., State U. N.Y. at Oswego, 1946-49; asst. supt. charge instrn. and supervision pub. schs., Peoria, Ill., 1949-53; supt. schs., Mexico, Mo., 1953-55, Kankakee, Ill., 1955-59, Davenport, Iowa, 1959-64; dean Parsons Coll., 1964-65; founding pres. The Hiram Scott Coll., Scottsbluff, Nebr., 1964-69; prof. higher edn. adminstrn. George Washington U., Washington, 1969—; professorial lectr. edn. George Washington U., summers 1952-69; prof. edn. Bradley U., part time, 1949-53, supervision of instrn. research extension courses, 1956-58; vis. prof. secondary edn. Ohio State U., summers 1953-54; dir. staff devel. program DODD Schs., 1978. Speaker various civic, bus., indsl. and ednl. groups; cons. colls. and sch. systems on orgn., adminstrn., accreditation. Active various local civic, religious and ednl. groups; organized South End Council, Hartford, 1944-46, Peoria Citizens Council for Pub. Schs., 1951-52, in service tchr. edn. program, Peoria, 1949-53; pres. Kankakee Community Chest (Ill.), 1957-58. Mem. Davenport (Iowa) Planning Commn., 1960-63; bd. dirs. Peoria Council Boy Scouts Am., 1951-53, ARC, Peoria, 1951-53; trustee Hiram Scott Coll., 1964-69, Palmer Found., 1974—; adviser to Palmer Coll. Bd. Dirs. Mem. Sheldon Forum, Phi Delta Kappa, Epsilon Pi Tau, Phi Sigma Phi, Psi Phi. Clubs: Masons, Shriners. Author: Exploring the Graphic Arts, 1959; Human Relations: The New Dimension in American Education, 1974; Human Relations and Cooperative Planning in Education and Management, 1977; contbr. articles to profl. publs. Home: 13919 Turnmore Rd Silver Spring MD 20906 Office: George Washington U Washington DC 20006

MARINAKOS, PLATO ANTHONY, hosp. adminstr.; b. Pitts., Dec. 26, 1935; B.S., in Zoology, U. Pitts., 1957, M.S. in Hosp. Adminstrn., 1961; postgrad Duquesne U., 1964; m. Vaselia Pecunes; children—Plato Anthony, Constantine, Theodore, Alexia. Asst. exec. dir. Allegheny Gen. Hosp., Pitts., 1961-65, asso. exec. dir., 1965-68, exec. dir., 1967-73; pres. Conemaugh Valley Meml. Hosp., Johnstown, Pa., 1973-77; exec. v.p. Mercy Catholic Med. Centre, Phila., 1977—, also dir.; dir. Delaware Valley Hosp. Council, 1977—. Bd. dirs. YMCA, 1975-78, Better Bus. Bur., Phila., 1978—. Recipient Hon. Biological award, U. Pitts. Mem. Hosp. Assn. Pa., Hosp. Council Western Pa., Am. Coll. Hosp. Adminstrs., Council Teaching Hosps., Del. Valley Hosp. Council, Delchester Consortium, Greater Del. Valley Health Care Assn., Gwynedd Mercy Coll., Catholic Conf. on Health Care, Am. Mgmt. Assn., Am. Pub. Health Assn., Nat. League for Nursing, U. Pitts. Alumni Assn., Rotary Internat. Greek Orthodox. Contbr. in field to med. jours. Home: 112 Ringwood Rd Rosemont PA 19010 Office: Lansdowne Ave & Baily Rd Darby PA 19023

MARINBACH, MARK GARY, dental lab. exec.; b. Bklyn., Feb. 14, 1940; s. Hyman C. and Ruth (Artzis) M.; student U. Buffalo, 1957-60, L.I. U., 1960-61; m. Susan Gutchin, Dec. 25, 1963; 1 son, Eric David. With Nu-Life Dental Lab., Inc., Bklyn., 1960-73, salesman, 1963-65, dir. sales and pub. relations, 1965-73; pres. chmn. bd. Nu-Life Restorations of L.I., Inc., 1973—; pres., chmn. bd. Hempstead Turnpike Dental Supply, Inc.; lectr. in field. Mem. Nat. Assn. Certified Dental Labs., L.I., N.Y. dental lab. assns., N.Y. Guild Dental Technicians, Am. Coll. Oral Implantology, United Cerebral Palsy Assn., Sigma Alpha Mu. Cert. dental technician. Republican. Clubs: Sheapshead Bay Tuna, Nat. Assn. Watch and Clock Collectors, Knights of Pythias. Home: 40 Valley Rd Old Westbury NY 11568 Office: 221 Hempstead Turnpike West Hempstead NY 11552

MARINELLI, ANTONIO MICHAEL, constrn. co. exec.; b. Bristol, Conn., Mar. 14, 1920; s. Michael and Francesca (Pistilli) M.; student N.Y. U., 1938-39; m. Phyllis Diorio, Mar. 28, 1948; children—Kim Maryann, Michael Xavier. With Intercounty Constrn. Corp., now subsidiary Westinghouse Electric Corp., Hyattsville, Md., 1941—, pres., 1969—. Served with arty. AUS, 1942-43. Decorated cavaliere Republic of Italy, 1973, cavaliere ofcl., 1975. Named Sons of Italy Citizen of Year, Washington, 1973; Man of Year, Lido Civic Club Washington, 1974. Mem. Nat. Utility Contractors Assn. (pres. 1967-69). Republican. Roman Catholic. Club: Congl. Country (Potomac, Md.). Home: 11908 River Rd Potomac MD 20854 Office: Intercounty Constrn Corp 4744 Baltimore Ave Hyattsville MD 20781

MARINO, ANTHONY JAMES, JR., communications co. exec.; b. Union City, N.J., Nov. 19, 1927; s. Anthony James and Virginia Rose (Petrocelli) M.; B.S. in Chemistry and Physics, Muhlenberg Coll., 1948; M.S. in Metallurgy, Stevens Inst. Tech., 1958; M.S. in Ceramics Engring., Rutgers U., 1974; m. Maureen Campbell, Nov. 30, 1974; children—Christopher, Maureen. Staff photographer Call Chronical Newspapers, Allentown, Pa., 1945-48; estate planner, ins. Mut. Benefit Life, N.Y.C., 1948-50; with ITT Fed. Communication Lab., now ITT Avionics, Clifton, N.J., 1952—, sr. project engr., 1964-67, mgr., lab. dir. Materials and Evaluation Facility and Environ. Testing Facility, 1967—; owner, operator Redmond Piano Co., Oradell, N.J.; chmn., dir., pres. Marine Research & Engring. Co., Inc., Oradell. Served with U.S. Army, 1950-52. Mem. Am. Ordnance Assn., ASTM, Am. Ceramic Soc., Am. Nat. Metric Council, U.S. Power Squadron, Keramos Soc., Sigma Xi, Alpha Tau Omega. Roman Catholic. Clubs: Rotary (pres. River Edge 1974-75, dist. gov. 1978-79); Palisades Yacht; Englewood. Patentee in field of semicondrs. and crystal growth. Home: 129 Copley Ave Teaneck NJ 07666 Office: 100 Kingsland Ave Clifton NJ 07013

MARINO, JOSEPH ANTHONY, razor co. exec.; b. Geneva, N.Y., Apr. 1, 1932; s. Anthony Rocco and Antoinette (DePalma) M.; B.B.A., Tri-State U., 1959; M.B.A., Mich. State U., 1960; m. Catherine Coville, Dec. 18, 1953; children—Joseph, Michael, Paul. Mgmt. trainee Gillette Co., Boston, 1960-64, exec. asst. to v.p. mktg., 1964-72, pres. Braun N.Am. div., 1972-76, corporate v.p. mktg.-safety razor div., 1976—; dir. OPUS, Inc., Boston. Vice-pres. exec. council Norumbega council Boy Scouts Am., Waban, Mass. Served in USAF, 1951-54. Recipient Honor award Fedn. Jewish Philanthropists N.Y., 1973. Mem. Internat. Photog. Council (pres. 1974), Am. Mgmt. Assn. Republican. Roman Catholic. Home: 110 Concord Rd Weston MA 02193 Office: Gillette Co Gillette Park Boston MA 02106*

MARINOVICH, MATO LUKO, physician; b. Dubrovnik, Yugoslavia, Dec. 17, 1921; s. Baldo and Maria Marquise (de Bona) M.; came to U.S., 1949, naturalized, 1955; student U. Zagreb (Yugoslavia), 1939-43; M.D., U. Rome, 1945; m. Daphne Mayo, July 1961; children—Matthew, Michael, Adrian. Intern French Hosp., N.Y.C., 1950-51; resident in internal medicine Bellevue Hosp., N.Y.C., North Shore Hosp., Manhasset, L.I., St. Vincent Hosp., N.Y.C.; practice medicine specializing in internal and preventive medicine N.Y.C., N.Y.C., 1956—; mem. staff Presbyn. Hosp., N.Y.C., Lenox Hill Hosp., 1964—, Doctor's Hosp., N.Y.C., 1974—; asst. in medicine Columbia U., 1956—; corp. med. dir. Lever Bros. Co., N.Y.C., 1972—. Served with Yugoslavian Army, World War II. Mem. N.Y. Acad. Scis., Am. Coll. Chest Physicians, Am. Occupational Med. Assn., N.Y. County, N.Y. State med. socs. Clubs: N.Y. Athletic; Meadow Club, Bathing Corp. (Southampton, N.Y.). Office: 178 E End Ave New York City NY 10028

MARION, BILL ALLAN, clergyman, counselor; b. Memphis, Jan. 17, 1930; s. Dewey Fleenor and Ruth (Richardson) M.; B.S. in Chemistry, Ga. Inst. Tech., 1951; postgrad. Va. Sem., 1955-57; M.S. in Edn., Fordham U. at Lincoln Center, 1978. With IBM, 1957-63; copywriter Benton & Bowles, N.Y.C., 1963-65; sr. writer Cunningham & Walsh, N.Y.C., 1965-67; creative supr. Lennan & Newell/Pacific, San Francisco, 1967-69; employment interviewer N.Y. State Dept. Labor, 1973—, employment counselor, 1977—, supr., 1978—; joined secular clergy, missions Old Catholic Ch. in America, 1959, ordained priest, 1960, archdeacon, 1974; pastor, missioner Unchurched Souls in N.Y.C. with Irremovable Status; pvt. practice religious and personal counseling; speaker, workshop leader on religion and homosexual, 1970—; Served to lt., j.g., USN, 1951-55. Mem. Am., N.Y. State, N.Y.C. personnel and guidance assns., Internat. Assn. Personnel in Employment Security. Home: 34-19 29th St Apt 2G Long Island City NY 11106 Office: NY State Employment Service 250 Schermerhorn St Brooklyn NY 11201

MARION, CLAUD COLLIER, educator; b. Ft. Pierce, Fla., July 4, 1913; s. James G. and Hattie (Jenkins) M.; B.S. in Agrl. Edn., Fla. A. and M. U., 1936; M.S. in Agrl. Edn., U. Minn., 1941; Ph.D., Cornell

U., 1948; postgrad. U. Cal. at Berkeley, 1953, Wash. State U., 1954; m. Evelyn Louise Young, June 17, 1946. Prin., Rosenwald Jr. High Sch., Midway, Fla., 1936-37, E.O. Douglas High Sch., Sebring, Fla., 1937-46; prof. agrl. edn., tchr. tng. U. Md. Eastern Shore, Princess Anne, 1948-70, asst. state dir., Md. Coop. Extension Service, 1970—. Guest prof. edn. Tenn. Agrl. and Indsl. U., 1951, Fla. A. and M. U., summers 1958-60, 65, 68-70. Mem. Pres.'s Conf. on Occupational Safety, Washington, 1960; cons., contbr. Nat. Lexicographic Bd., N.Y.C., 1952-60; speaker sch. banquets, P.T.A. orgns., 1948—; judge high sch. sci. fairs, 1956—; mem. Higher Edn. Commn., Peninsula Conf. United Meth. Ch., 1972—. Named Superior Tchr. Vocational Agr., Fla. Dept. Edn. Div. Vocational Edn., Tallahassee, 1941; recipient Superior Farmer degree New Farmers Am. Orgn., 1958; Hon. State Farmer degree Future Farmers Am., 1965, Am. Farmer degree, 1974. Mem. Am., Md. (award 1964) vacational assns., Agrl. Research Assn., Am. Assn. Tchr.-Educators in Agr., Md. Tchrs. Assn., AAUP, Phi Delta Kappa, Epsilon Sigma Phi, Alpha Tau Alpha, Phi Kappa Phi, Alpha Phi Alpha. Mason, Elk. Cons., contbr. New Wonder World Ency., New Wonder Book Ency. of World Knowledge, 1953, Illustrated Home Library Ency., 1957; contbr. Illustrated Ready Reference Ency., 1962; cons. New American Webster Handy College Dictionary, Illustrated World Ency., 1954-66, Fireside Dictionary, 1954. Contbr. articles to profl. jours. Home: POB 398 Princess Anne MD 21853

MARION, DAVID JEFFREY, psychologist; b. Newark, June 17, 1942; s. Saul Lionel and Anne Jacqueline (Muscat) M.; B.A., Cornell U., 1964, M.A., 1966; Ed.D., Boston U., 1971; m. Tovah Silver, Dec. 31, 1967; children—Jonathan Saul, Naomi Rachelle. Dir., Boston Colloquium for Philosophy of Edn., 1971-72; pres. Human Systems Devel., Inc., Boston, 1974—; staff psychotherapist Treatment Center, Boston Inst. for Psychotherapies, Inc., 1976-78; unit chief Greater Lawrence Area Inpatient Unit, Hawthorne, Mass., 1978—; lectr. Boston U., 1971-72; instr. Fitchburg State Coll., 1974-75; cons. Data Edn., Inc., Waltham, Mass., 1972-74. Chmn., bd. dirs. New Eng. Sch. Culinary Arts and Career Tng. Fellow Human Relations Center Boston U., 1969-71; Spencer research asso. Nat. Acad. Edn., 1971-72. Contbr. articles to profl. jours. Home: 61 Columbia St Brookline MA 02146

MARK, SANDRA FAY, educator; b. Bklyn., Dec. 1, 1940; d. Nathan and Bertha (Bell) M.; B.A., Ariz. State U., 1961; M.A., New Sch. for Social Research, 1971; postgrad. U. Rochester, 1975-79. Tchr. art and English, Hueneme High Sch., Oxnard, Calif., 1961-63, Yamato Am. High Sch., Tokyo, Japan, 1963-65; tchr. English, Ludwigsburg (Germany) Am. High Sch., Ludwigsburg, 1965-66; tchr. English, art King Jr. High Sch., Berkeley, Calif., 1966-69; asso. prof. psychology and sociology Genesee Community Coll., Batavia, N.Y., 1971—; cons. Faculty Council of Community Coll., State U. N.Y., 1977-78. Mem. planning com. Human Sexuality Conf., Genesee Regional Family Planning Council, Rochester, N.Y., 1973-77; Genesee Community Coll. rep. to Rochester Arts Council, 1972-75. Ariz. State U. scholar, 1957-61; New Sch. for Social Research scholar, 1969-71; U. Rochester scholar, 1976-77; NSF grantee, 1974-76. Mem. Am., Eastern, Genesee Valley psychol. assns., Assn. for Women in Psychology. Contbr. articles in field to profl. jours. Home: 140 Fairview Ave Rochester NY 14619 Office: Genesee Community Coll College Rd Batavia NY 14020

MARKARIAN, NOUBAR, textile co. exec.; b. Larnaca, Cyprus, Dec. 15, 1922; s. Paul and Gulenia (Torikian) M.; came to U.S., 1938; student Coll. S. Murat, Sevres, Frances, 1935-38; B.S., Sch. Engring., Columbia U., 1944; m. Judith Armistead Isley, Feb. 23, 1946; children—Judy, Beverly, Linda, Nancy, Amy, Richard. Partner, v.p. Mark Knitting Mills, Bergenfield, N.J., 1945—; v.p. Valette Undergarmets, Inc., Fajardo, P.R., 1958-61; sec.-treas. Johnson Corp., Bergenfield, N.J., 1961—. Vice chmn. bd. dirs. No. Valley chpt. ARC. Trustee Dwight Sch., Englewood, N.J. Mem. International House Assn. Episcopalian. Clubs: Bay Head (N.J.) Yacht; Englewood (N.J.) Field; Rotary (pres. Bergenfield 1962-63), Columbia Alumni of Bergen County (pres. 1957-58); Columbia of N.Y.; Mantoloking (N.J.) Yacht. Home: 71 Franklin St Englewood NJ 07631 Office: 26 Palisade Ave Bergenfield NJ 07621

MARKE, JULIUS JAY, educator, librarian; b. N.Y.C., Jan. 12, 1913; s. Isidore and Anna (Taylor) M.; B.S. in Sci., Coll. City N.Y., 1934; LL.B., N.Y. U., 1937, B.S. in L.S., Columbia U., 1942; m. Sylvia Bolotin, Dec. 15, 1946; 1 dau., Elisa Hope. Reference asst. N.Y. Pub. Library, 1937-42; admitted to N.Y. bar, 1938; pvt. practice, 3 years; prof. law, law librarian N.Y. U., 1949—; cons. World Peace Through Law, Ford Found.; cons. internat. trade br. legal div. UN, 1977—, Legal Services Corp., 1977—, Fed. Jud. Center, 1978—. Served from pvt. to sgt. U.S. Army, 1943-45, ETO. Decorated Bronze Star. Mem. Assn. Am. Law Schs., Council of Nat. Library Assns. (exec. bd. 1959, 60), Am. Assn. Law Libraries (pres. 1962-63, chmn. com. copy-right law), Law Library Assn. Greater N.Y. (pres. 1949, 50, chmn. joint com. on library edn. 1950-52, 60-69), Am. Bar Assn., Internat. Fedn. Library Assns. (chmn. internat. working com. on copyright law 1973—), Columbia U. Sch. Library Service Alumni Assn. (pres. 1973-74), Order of Coif (pres. N.Y. U. Sch. Law chpt. 1969—), Phi Delta Phi. Author: Vignettes of Legal History, 1965, 2d Series, 1977; Copyright and Intellectual Property, 1967; contbr. articles to profl. journals; editor: Modern Legal Forms, 1953; The Holmes Reader, 1955, 2d edit., 1964; The Docket Series, 1955—; Bender's Legal Business Forms, 4 vols., 1961; (with John G. Lexa) International Seminar on Constitutional Review, 1963; compiler, editor: A Catalogue of the Law Collection at N.Y. U.; with selected Annotations, 1953; Deans' List of Recommended Reading for Pre-Law and Law Students, 1958; (with E.J. Bander) Commercial Law, 1970; contbr. column legal research to N.Y. Law Jour., 1974—. Home: 4 Peter Cooper Rd New York City NY 10010

MARKER, LEONARD K., composer; b. Vienna, Austria; s. Joseph and Erna (Stamm) Kuhmarker; student harmony and counterpoint with Hans Gal; pvt. pupil composition Alban Berg, Vienna, 1930-34, Acad. Music, Vienna; m. Gertrude Osterer, Oct. 28, 1943; 1 son, James Steven. Came to U.S., 1942, naturalized, 1945. Mem. faculty Hunter Coll., N.Y.C.; composer symphony music, motion picture scores; musicals for stage: Tilted Hat, Max Reinhardt prodn., Ministry is Insulted and Why Do You Lie, Cherie? (7,000 performances in Europe, S.Am.); Twenty-Four Beautiful Hours; The Ant Hill; music for Bobino (play); music for various Erwin Piscator prodns.; also new arrangements of various operas including Wozzeck, Rosenkavalier, Love of Three Oranges. Mem. Broadcast Music Inc.; hon. mem. Alban Berg Soc. Co-author: (with Olin Downes) Ten Operatic Masterpieces; contbr. articles to N.Y. Times, Opera News, Musical Am., others. Address: 150 Claremont Ave New York City NY 10027

MARKEWICH, MAURICE ELISH (REESE), psychiatrist, musician; b. Bklyn., Aug. 6, 1936; s. Arthur and May (Elish) M.; A.B., Cornell U., 1958; M.S. in Social Work, Columbia U., 1960; M.D., N.Y. Med. Coll., 1970; certificate Center for Modern Psychoanalytic Studies, 1976; m. Linda Lawner, June 19, 1960; children—Jennifer Beth, Melissa Ann. Social worker Jewish Family Service, N.Y.C., 1961-64; resident Beth Israel Med. Center, N.Y.C., 1970-73; practice medicine specializing in psychiatry, N.Y.C., 1973—; mem. staff Beth Israel Med. Center; jazz musician, 1954—; pianist, flutist Reese Markewich Quintet, 1955-60; various appearances N.Y. State. Served with U.S. Army, 1960-61. Certified social worker, N.Y.; lic. physician, N.Y. Mem. Am. Psychiat. Assn., Med. Soc. County N.Y., Nat. Assn. Social Workers, N.Y. Soc. Clin. Social Work Psychotherapists, Conf. Advancement of Pvt. Practice in Social Work. Club: Masons. Author music books: Inside Outside, 1967; The Definitive Bibliography of Harmonically Sophisticated Tonal Music, 1970; The New Expanded Bibliography of Jazz Compositions Based on the Chord Progressions of Standard Tunes, 1974; Jazz Publicity II, 1974. Home: Bacon Hill Town of Mount Pleasant Pleasantville NY 10570 Office: 39 Gramercy Park N New York City NY 10010

MARKEY, EDWARD J., congressman; b. Malden, Mass., July 11, 1946; B.A., Boston Coll., 1968, J.D., 1972. Mem. Mass. Ho. of Reps., 1973-76; mem. 94th-96th Congresses from 7th Mass. Dist. Democrat. Office: 319 Cannon House Office Bldg Washington DC 20515

MARKEY, HOWARD THOMAS, chief judge U.S. ct.; b. Chgo., Nov. 10, 1920; s. Thomas Joseph and Vera Marie (Dryden) M.; J.D., cum laude, Loyola U., Chgo., 1949; M. in Patent Law, John Marshall Law Sch., 1950; m. Elizabeth Catherine Pelletier, Mar. 17, 1942; children—Jeffrey, Christopher, Thomas (dec.), Mary Frances. Admitted to Ill. bar, 1950, practiced in Chgo., 1950-72; partner firm Parker & Carter, later Parker, Markey & Plyer, 1956-72; chief judge U.S. Ct. of Customs and Patent Appeals, Washington, 1972—. Lectr. on jets, rockets, missiles and space, 1946-50, on U.S. Constitution, 1950—; instr. patent law Loyola U., 1970-71. Served to lt. col. USAAF, 1941-46, USAF, 1950-52; pioneer jet test pilot, 1944-46; maj. gen. Res. Decorated Legion of Merit, D.F.C., Soldier's medal, Air medal, Bronze Star (U.S.); Mil. Merit Ulchi medal (Korea); recipient George Washington Honor medal Freedoms Found., 1964. Mem. Am. Bar Assn., Am. Judicature Assn., Am. Legion (post comdr.), Air Force Assn. (pres. 1960-61, chmn. 1961-62). Republican. Club: Rotary. Home: 2350 King Pl NW Washington DC 20007 Office: 717 Madison Pl NW Washington DC 20439*

MARKEY, MARTIN JAMES, clin. psychologist; b. Jamaica, N.Y., May 4, 1938; s. Patrick and Christine (Dawson) M.; B.S., U. Nebr., 1965; M.S., U. Mass., Amherst, 1969, Ph.D., 1971; m. Sally Marie McTaggart, May 4, 1963; children—Patrick, Kevin, Joseph, Maureen, Eileen, Sean. Cons. clin. psychologist, Springfield, Mass., 1971—; pvt. practice psychotherapy and psychol. evaluation; biofeedback tng. Served to capt. USAF, 1959-67, maj. Res., 1967-76. Mem. Mass. Psychol. Assn., Am., New Eng. biofeedback socs. Contbr. articles to profl. jours. Address: 1767 Northampton St Holyoke MA 01040

MARKHAM, F. RICHARD, dental lab. exec.; b. Syracuse, N.Y., Nov. 23, 1944; s. Fredric H. and Ruth (Brown) M.; A.A.S. in Dental Tech., So. Ill. U., 1966; m. Diane E. Burlingame, May, 1972; children—Jill Elizabeth, Suzanne Clare. Dental technician, DeWitt, N.Y., 1966-67; pres. F.R. Markham Dental Studios, DeWitt, 1967-70, Markham Dental Studio Ltd., East Syracuse, N.Y., 1970—; instr. Carerrco Sch. for Para Profls., 1967-69. Mem. Nat. Assn. Dental Labs., 5th Dist. Dental Lab. Assn. (treas. 1973-76, ednl. chmn. 1976, v.p. 1976-77, pres. 1977-78), N.Y. State Assn. Certified Dental Labs., Onondaga Model Aircraft Club (treas. 1973, pres. 1974). Republican. Methodist. Club: Jaycees (past chpt. treas., v.p.). Home: 11 Edgewood Pkwy Fayetteville NY 13066 Office: 314 W Manlius St East Syracuse NY 13057

MARKHAM, MARY ELIZABETH THORNTON (MRS. REGINALD A. MARKHAM), state ofcl.; b. Haverhill, Mass.; d. John W. and Mary E. (Murphy) Thornton; B.A., Regis Coll., 1937; M.Ed., Salem State Coll., 1968; m. Reginald A. Markham, Feb. 26, 1954. With Mass. Div. Employment Security, 1937—, prin. counselor N.E. area Mass., Lawrence, 1965-70, mgr. concentrated employment program, Lowell, 1970-71, supervising mgr., 1971-75, supervising mgr. Haverhill/Newburyport area, 1975-77; with Lawrence Div. Employment Security, 1977—; mem. Greater Lawrence Community Services orgn., 1977—, Lawrence Com. for Employment of Handicapped, 1977—; mem. Regional Area Manpower Planning Bd., 1977—; past mem. Greater Lowell Adv. Com. Industry. Bd. dirs. Merrimack River council Girl Scouts Am., 1965-75, chmn. personnel com., 1965-75, v.p., 1972-75; sec. Medford Ancillary Manpower Planning Bd., 1972-73; past mem. steering com. project vol. power Malden Mayor's Com. for Employment of Handicapped, 1972-73; bd. dirs. Community Teamwork, Lowell, 1973-75; past bd. dirs. Greater Lowell Ancillary Manpower Planning Bd.; past chmn. selection com., mem. planning com. Greater Lowell Com. for Handicapped; bd. dirs. No. Essex Regional Community Action Commn.; adv. bd. Whittier Regional and Vocat. Tech. Sch.; mem. Merrimack Valley Econ. and Devel. Com., Haverhill Com. Employment Handicapped. Mem. Mass. Conf. Social Welfare, Am., Mass., Greater Boston personnel and guidance assns., Greater Lawrence C. of C., Internat. Assn. Personnel in Employment Security, Nat. Vocat. Guidance Assn., Nat. Employment Counselors Assn. Home: 83 Kenoza Ave Haverhill MA 01830 Office: 444 Canal St Lawrence MA 01840

MARKIN, JAMES STEIN, steel co. exec.; b. Rochester, N.Y., Dec. 16, 1931; s. E. Richard and Kathryn (Stein) M.; B.Mgmt. Engring., Rensselaer Poly. Inst., 1953; B.B.A., U. Mich., 1957; m. Sandra Wolk, Apr. 14, 1957; children—Louis Jeffrey, John Neal, Cynthia Ann, Theresa Louise. With Rochester Products div. Gen. Motors Corp., 1953-57; chmn., pres., chief exec. officer Markin Tubing Inc., Wyoming, N.Y., 1958—. Served to 1st lt. AUS, 1954-55. Republican. Unitarian (dir.). Mason, Rotarian. Home: 1 Benson Rd Wyoming NY 14591 Office: Pearl Creek Rd Wyoming NY 14591

MARKLE, GEORGE MICHAEL, entomologist; b. Riverside, N.J., Dec. 18, 1939; s. John and Palma (Bonatelli) M.; B.S., Cornell U., 1962; M.S., Rutgers U., 1970; m. Nancy Ann Lambert, June 27, 1964; children—John Michael, David Wayne, Nicole Ann. Asso. research prof., asst. coordinator entomology and interregional research project 4 nat. research unit Rutgers U., New Brunswick, N.J., 1965—; lectr. in field. Commr. Town of Middlesex (N.J.), 1973; chmn. Middlesex Bicentennial Com., 1975; scoutmaster Boy Scouts Am., 1977—; chmn. Dr. C.C. Compton Entomol. Trust Fund, 1977-78. Served with AUS, 1962-65. Recipient Tng. award Boy Scouts Am., 1977, also Scouter Key award, 1978. Mem. Middlesex Jaycees (blue chip pres. 1972-73, distinguished service award 1973), Entomol. Soc. Am., AAUP, Res. Officers Assn., Assn. U.S. Army, Alumni Assn. Cornell U., Am. Phytopath. Soc., Sigma Xi. Roman Catholic. Clubs: Am. Legion. Home: 305 Walnut St Middlesex NJ 08845 Office: Office of IR-4 Cook Coll Rutgers U New Brunswick NJ 08903

MARKLEY, KENNETH ALAN, psychologist, assn. ofcl.; b. Harrisburg, Pa., Sept. 30, 1933; s. Charles Donald and Gladys Elizabeth (Wallis) M.; B.A., Dickinson Coll., 1955; postgrad. Syracuse U., 1955-57; M.A., N.Y. U., 1959; postgrad. Ref. Episcopal Sem., 1966-68; H.H.D., Clarkesville Sch. Theology, 1976; m. Susan Watson, Sept. 14, 1957; children—Jennifer Elaine, Christopher David. Sch. psychologist Central Dauphin Schs., Harrisburg, 1959; exec. dir. United Cerebral Palsy Treatment Center, Camp Hill, Pa., 1960-64; eastern dir. Narramore Christian Found. and Rosemead (Calif.) Grad. Sch. Psychology, 1964—; mem. faculty Dickinson Coll., Carlisle, Pa., 1963-64; ordained chaplain Nat. Chaplains Assn., 1978; ordained to gospel ministry Evangelical Ch. Alliance, 1978. Bd. dirs. many community, civic, religious orgns. Served to 1st lt. Adj. Gens. Corps, AUS, 1955-57. Certified psychologist, Pa.; diplomate Am. Psychotherapy Assn. Mem. Nat. Chaplains Assn., Am. Acad. Human Services, Am. Psychol. Assn., Christian Assn. Psychol. Studies, Alpha Psi Omega, Assn. Christian Marriage Counselors, Phi Kappa Psi. Mem. Christian and Missionary Alliance Ch. (elder). Author: Our Speaker This Evening, 1974; contbr. to Psychology for Living mag. Address: Narramore Christian Found 104 N 26th St Camp Hill PA 17011

MARKOWITZ, ABE, lawyer; b. Reading, Pa., May 28, 1925; s. George and Sara Dora (Saracek) M.; B.S., Albright Coll., Reading, 1948; postgrad. Temple U., 1948-50, Pa. State U., 1951-52; LL.B., West Los Angeles Sch. Law, 1970; divorced; children—Janet Lynne, Susan Beth. Practice clin. psychology, 1950-54; realtor, 1957-70; admitted to Pa. bar, 1974, since practiced in Reading. Served with AUS, 1943-45. Mem. Am., Pa., Berks County bar assns., Am., Pa. trial lawyers assns., Nat., Pa., Greater Reading bds. realtors, Nat. Assn. Ind. Fee Appraisers, Nat. Assn. Home Builders, Travelers Protective Assn., Friendship Fire Co. Jewish. Clubs: Berkleigh Country, K.P., B'nai B'rith. Address: 534 Washington St Box #678 Reading PA 19603

MARKOWITZ, PHYLLIS FRANCES, counselor; b. Malden, Mass., Sept. 2, 1931, d. Abraham and Rose (Kaplan) Kalishman; B.A. cum laude in Extension Studies, Harvard U., 1972, M.Ed. (teaching fellow), 1974; children—Gary Keith, Carol Diane. Research asst. Boston Coll., Chestnut Hill, Mass., 1972-73; social worker, sr. citizen orgn. Combined Jewish Philanthropies, Boston, 1973-74; asso. in edn. Harvard U., 1974-75, counselor Commn. on Extension Studies, 1976-78, sr. counselor Bur. Study Counsel, 1974—; pvt. practice counseling, Newton, Mass., 1974—. Radcliffe Inst. grantee, 1972; certified in individual psychol. testing, secondary edn. in English and social studies. Mem. Am. Personnel and Guidance Assn., New Eng. Assn. Acad. Support Personnel, Soc. Family Therapy and Research, Northeastern Soc. Group Psychotherapy, Harvard Extension Alumni Assn. (steering com.), Phi Delta Kappa. Home: 59 Garland Rd Newton Centre MA 02159 Office: 5 Linden St Cambridge MA 02138

MARKS, ALBERT AUBREY, JR., broker; b. Phila., Dec. 19, 1912; s. Albert A. and Edythe (Lilian) M.; grad. Harrisburg (Pa.) Acad., 1928; student Williams Coll., 1928-30; B.S., U. Pa., 1932; m. Mary Kay Bryan; children—Albert Aubrey, Christina M., Robert B. Br. office mgr. Newburger & Co., Phila., 1934-42, gen. partner Newburger & Co., Atlantic City, N.J., 1946—, Advest Co.; dir. Guarantee Bank & Trust Co., Atlantic City, Anchor Savs. and Loan Assn.; allied mem. Am., N.Y., Phila., Balt. stock exchanges. Vice pres. N.J. Mid-Atlantic Farm Show, 1952-54; dir. Atlantic City Conv. Bur., 1951-54, treas., 1962; pres. Miss Am. Pageant, 1962-64, chmn. bd., 1966; chmn. Boardwalk Adv. Commn.; mem. Bd. Edn., Margate, N.Y.; vice chmn. Com. Adult Edn. So. N.J.; pres. Atlantic County Community Chest and Welfare Council, 1953; gen. campaign chmn. Community Chest, 1956; former pres. 4-Club Council; mem. exec. council Boy Scouts Am., Atlantic County; trustee So. N.J. Devel. Council, 1951-54; mem. N.J. Legis. Study Commn., Securities Adv. Com. N.J. State, Conflict Interest Com. Gov. Betty Bacharach Home Afflicted Children; chmn. Com. of 50, Atlantic City, 1972—, Atlantic County Improvement Authority, 1975. Served from 2d lt. to lt. col. USAAF, 1942-46. Named Citizen of Year, Atlantic City, 1953; Citizen of Decade, Elks, 1972. Mem. Investment Bankers Assn., Security Traders Assn., Nat. Assn. Security Dealers, Assn. Stock Exchange Firms, Atlantic City (pres. 1952-53), So. N.J. (chmn. devel. council 1951-54) C.'s of C., Atlantic City Centennial Assn. (v.p. 1953-54), Mil. Order World Wars (companion), Res. officers Assn., Air Force Assn., Newcomen Soc., Pa. Soc., Newcomen Soc. Roman Catholic. Clubs: Masons, Kiwanis (pres. 1954), Press, Haddon Hall Racquet, Osborne Beach; Williams, Marco Polo (N.Y.C.). Home: 1 N Osborne Ave Margate NJ 08402 Office: 20 S Tennessee Ave Atlantic City NJ 08401

MARKS, ARLYN CHARLES, univ. adminstr.; b. Edwardsville, Ill., Oct. 15, 1911; s. Charles Wesley and Edna (Kriege) M.; A.B., Ill. Coll., 1934; M.Ed., Harvard U., 1938; A.M., U. Ill., 1937, Ph.D., 1940; m. Charlotte Anita Hatch, Aug. 27, 1939 (dec. Nov. 1956); children—Richard Arlyn, Harriet Ann (dec.). Research asst. U. Ill., 1937-43, personnel sec., 1943-45, asst. dir. personnel, 1945-46; dir. personnel services U. Iowa, 1946-61; dir. nonacad. personnel, 1961-65, dir. univ. civil service system of Ill., Urban, 1961-68; dir. personnel Fordham U., 1968—; exec. sec. Coll. and Univ. Personnel Assn., N.Y.C., 1963-71. Pres. Hawkeye Area council Boy Scouts Am., 1959-61. Mem. Am. Mgmt. Assn., Coll. and Univ. Personnel Assn. (pres. 1955-56), Phi Beta Kappa. Methodist. Home: 2400 Johnson Ave Riverdale NY 10463 Office: Fordham University Bronx NY 10458

MARKS, ARTHUR, dentist; b. N.Y.C., June 5, 1920; s. Louis and Elizabeth (Levine) M.; A.B., N.Y.U., 1942, D.D.S., 1944; m. Ruth Flamberg, July 18, 1948; children—Pauline, Deborah, Frances. Practice dentistry, N.Y.C., 1947—; asso. vis. oral surgeon Sydenham Hosp., N.Y.C., 1947-75; mem. speakers bur. N.Y. Oral Hygiene Com.; dental rep. inter-profl. socs. adv. com. on Medicaid to commr. health N.Y.C.; admissions com. N.Y. U. Coll. Dentistry, 1976, 77. Hon. asst. chmn. Democratic State Conv., N.Y., 1966; mem. New Rochelle Dem. City Com. Served with Dental Corps, AUS, 1944-47. Recipient N.Y. U. Alumni Meritorious Service award, 1976. Mem. ADA, Am. Soc. Advancement Gen. Anesthesia in Dentistry, Am. Soc. Childrens Dentistry, Am. Dental Soc. Anaesthesiology, N.Y. Inst. Clin. Oral Pathology, Alumni Assn. N.Y.U. Dental Sch. (dir. 1961—, chmn. installation dinner 1963-64, 65, 67, chmn. constl. by-laws com. 1964-66, sec. 1968-69, pres. elect 1970-71, pres. 1971-72), Alumni Fedn. N.Y.U. (past pres., dir.), N.Y. Hort. Soc., Am. Acad. Polit. and Social Sci., Eastern Dental Soc. (pres. 1978), First Dist. Dental Soc. (dir., chmn. govt. funded health care com.), Empire Dental Polit. Action Com. (sec. 1976-77), Sydenham Hosp. Dental Clin. Soc. (pres. 1971-72), Grand St. Boys Assn., Assn. Mil. surgeons. Democrat. Club: N.Y. University College of Dentistry Century (organizing com. N.Y.C., dir. 1961-66). Home: 85 Hilary Circle New Rochelle NY 10804 Office: 601 W 139th St New York City NY 10031

MARKS, EDWARD BENNETT, internat. orgn. ofcl.; b. N.Y.C., Apr. 22, 1911; s. Edward Bennett and Miriam (Chuck) M.; A.B., Dartmouth Coll., 1932; M.A., Columbia U., 1938; m. Margaret Levi, June 20, 1940; children—Katharine, Thomas Edward. Asso. editor Am. Wine and Liquor Jour., 1938-39; dir. div. social adjustment Nat. Refugee Service N.Y., 1939-42; chief war refugee div. War Relocation Authority, Washington, 1942-46; community action specialist, adminstrv. analyst Nat. Housing Agy., Washington, 1946-47; dep. office chief Internat. Refugee Orgn., Geneva, 1947-50, chief of mission, Athens, Greece, 1950-52; chief of mission Intergovtl. Com. for European Migration, Athens, 1951-53, chief of mission, Belgrade, Yugoslavia, 1957, officer-in-charge, N.Y.C., 1954-59; exec. dir. U.S. Com. for Refugees, N.Y., 1959-62; now with AID, Dept. State, posts include, Washington, 1962-65, asst. dir. mission, Saigon, Vietnam, 1965-66, London, 1966-68, Lagos, Nigeria, 1968-71; coordinator emergency programs UNICEF, N.Y.C., 1971, spl. asst. to dir. European Regional Office, Paris and Geneva, 1972-73; dir. social devel. div. Asia Bur., AID, Washington, 1974-76; spl. cons. Office

Exec. Dir., UNICEF, N.Y.C., 1976-77, asso. dir. Internat. Year of the Child Secretariat, 1977—; lectr., participant confs. at Cornell U., Dartmouth Coll., Fordham U., Goucher Coll., other univs., also at Ditchley, Cambridge, U. Sussex, U.K.; del. UN confs., UNESCO Conf. on Cultural Integration Migrants; mem. U.S. del. UNICEF exec. bd. sessions, 1975-76; cons. Rockefeller Brothers Fund, N.Y.C. Bd. dirs. Am. Freedom from Hunger Com., U.S. Com. for Refugees and New Hope Housing, Washington. Recipient AID's Meritorious Honor award, 1970, Distinguished Career Service award, 1976. Contbr. articles to profl. lit., mags. Home: 333 E 46th St New York City NY 10017 Office: UNICEF UN New York City NY 10017

MARKS, EUGENE MELVIN, physician; b. Buffalo, July 5, 1921; s. Sidney M. and Marcia M. (Tritchler) M.; B.S. cum laude, U. Buffalo, 1943, M.D., 1946; m. Edna M. Aranibar, Nov. 25, 1943; children—James, Catherine, Joanne, Judith, Elizabeth, Edward. Intern, E.J. Meyer Meml. Hosp., Buffalo, 1946-47; plant physician E.I. duPont de Nemours & Co., Niagara Falls, N.Y., 1952-53; gen. practice medicine, Alden, N.Y., 1953-58; med. supr. E.I. duPont de Nemours & Co., Buffalo, 1958-68; med. dir. Remington Arms Co., Inc., Bridgeport, Conn., 1968—. Served with U.S. Army, 1943; to maj. M.C., U.S. Army, 1948-51; Korea. Fellow Am. Acad. Occupational Medicine, Am. Occupational Med. Assn., Am. Coll. Preventive Medicine. Republican. Mem. United Ch. of Christ. Club: Masons. Home: 22 Grand Pl Newtown CT 06470 Office: 939 Barnum Ave Bridgeport CT 06602

MARKS, GEORGE PEABODY, III, educator; b. Mobile, Ala., Apr. 4, 1923; s. George P. Marks, Jr.; B.A., Tulane U., 1943; M.A. in History, Columbia U., 1951; M.S. in L.S., 1952. Tech. asst. N.Y. Pub. Library, 1950-52; librarian Bklyn. Pub. Library, 1952-53; prof. history, library dir. Union Coll., Cranford, N.J., 1953—. Served with USAAF, 1943-45. Decorated Air medal. Mem. Am. Hist. Assn., Phi Beta Kappa. Author: The Black Press Views American Imperialism, 1898-1900, 1971. Contbr. articles in field to profl. jours. Home: 274 Cyrpess Dr Colonia NJ 07067 Office: Union Coll Cranford NJ 07016

MARKS, GERALD, physician; b. Bklyn., Apr. 14, 1925; s. Maurice and Lee (Leib) M.; grad. Villanova U., 1945; M.D., Jefferson Med. Coll., 1949; m. Barbara Ann Hendershot, Nov. 25, 1950; children—Richard M., James M., John H. Intern, Jefferson Med. Coll. Hosp., Phila., 1949-51, resident in surgery, 1952-57, resident in proctology, 1953-54; practice medicine specializing in gen. and colorectal surgery, Phila., 1957—; asst. dir. Tumor Clinic, Jefferson Med. Coll. Hosp., 1959-68; asst. chief surgery Phila. Gen. Hosp., 1957-70, chief Proctology Clinic, 1968-70, coordinator student surg. edn. Jefferson Surg. Service, 1970-71; asst. attending physician in surgery Thomas Jefferson U. Hosp., 1967—; instr. in surgery Jefferson Med. Coll., 1958-67, asso. in clin. surgery, 1967-68, clin. asso. prof. surgery, 1974-78, prof., 1978—; cons. in colon-rectal surgery VA Hosp., Coatesville, Pa., 1959—, VA Hosp., San Juan, P.R., 1968—, Dept. Army, Valley Forge Gen. Hosp., Phoenixville, Pa., 1971-73, VA Hosp., Wilmington, Del., 1977—, USN Regional Med. Center, Phila., 1977—, Pa. Hosp., 1978. Served with USN, 1943-46; to capt. USAF, 1951-52. Diplomate Am. Bd. Surgery, Am. Bd. Colon and Rectal Surgery. Fellow Pa. (v.p. 1975—), Am. socs. colon and rectal surgery, A.C.S., Coll. Physicians Phila.; mem. Phila. Acad. Surgery, Pa., Camden County, Phila. County (chmn. hosp. staff activities com. 1974—) med. socs., Soc. Surgery Alimentary Tract, Am. Soc. Gastrointestinal Endoscopy, AMA, Internat. Soc. Univ. Colon and Rectal Surgeons, Colostomy-Ileostomy Rehab. Assn. (med. adviser 1973—), Pan-Pacific Surg. Assn., Northeastern Soc. Colon and Rectal Surgeons, Jefferson Vol. Faculty Assn. (pres. 1973-74), Alpha Omega Alpha. Contbr. articles on colon-rectal surgery to profl. jours. Asso. editor Diseases of the Colon and Rectum, 1977—; cons. editor Pa. Medicine. Developed colonoscopic colon teaching model. Home: 45 Fairview Rd Narbeth PA 19072 Office: 111 S 11 St Philadelphia PA 19107

MARKS, HERBERT EDWARD, lawyer; b. Dayton, Ohio, Nov. 3, 1935; s. I.M. and Sarah (Schiff) M.; A.B., U. Mich., 1957; LL.B., Yale U., 1960; postgrad. George Washington U., 1966-69; m. Marcia Frager, June 5, 1966; children—Jennifer Lynn, Susan Elizabeth. Admitted to Ohio bar, 1960, D.C. bar, 1964; law clk. to chief judge U.S. Ct. Claims, Washington, 1964-65; practiced in Washington, 1965—; partner firm Wilkinson, Cragun & Barker, 1969—; asso. gen. counsel Presdl. Inaugural Com., 1969, 73. Sec., gen. counsel Am. Historic and Cultural Soc., Inc. Served to capt. USAF, 1961-64. Mem. Bar Assn. D.C. (chmn. ct. of claims com. 1974-75), Am., Fed. bar assns., Fed. Communications Bar Assn., Computer Law Assn. (pres. 1975-77), Phi Beta Kappa, Pi Sigma Alpha. Republican. Clubs: Lawyers, Army and Navy, Kenwood. Home: 5317 Cardinal Ct Bethesda MD 20016 Office: 1735 New York Ave NW Washington DC 20006

MARKS, HOWARD LEE, advt. exec.; b. Cleve., Feb 7, 1929; s. Archie M. and Belle (Parets) M.; student Ohio State U., 1946-48, Western Res. U., 1948-50; children—Melissa R., Andrew D. Pres., Howard Marks Advt., Inc., Cleve., 1956-64, Howard Marks Advt., Norman Craig & Kummel, Inc., N.Y.C., 1964-68; v.p. Norman, Craig & Kummel, Inc., N.Y.C., 1964-68; pres. Howard Marks Advt., Inc., N.Y.C., 1968—; chmn. Marks/Aucoin Prodns., Inc., N.Y.C., 1972—; pres. Hicks Marks Advt., Inc., London, Eng., 1971—; pres. Silver Mint Inc., also Glickman/Marks Mgmt. Corp., N.Y.C., 1976—. Chmn., United Appeal, Cleve., 1963, Cleve. Jewish Welfare Fund Campaign, 1962-64; trustee Cleve. Jewish Community Fedn.; bd. dirs. Cleve. Jewish Community Center, Cleve. Jewish Vocat. Service, Cleve. Community Fund, United Appeal. Served with AUS, 1951-53. Mem. Zeta Beta Tau, Am. Jewish Com. Club: B'nai B'rith. Home: 254 E 68th St New York City NY 10021 Office: 655 Madison Ave New York City NY 10021

MARKS, JOHNNY (JOHN D.), song writer; b. Mt. Vernon, N.Y., Nov. 10, 1909; s. Louis B. and Sadie (Van Praag) M.; B.S., Colgate U., 1931; m. Margaret Hope May, Oct. 25, 1947; children—Michael, Laura, David. Pres., St. Nicholas Music, Inc.; tour with USO-ASCAP, Far East, 1968. Trustee, chmn. pres.'s club Colgate U. Served as capt. AUS, 1942-46. Decorated Bronze Star with 4 battle stars; named Songwriter of Year by Songhits mag., 1949; Gold award for comml. Internat. Film and TV Festival of N.Y., 1967, Internat. Soc. Santa Claus award. Mem. ASCAP (dir. 1957—, bd. rev., adv. com.), Marshall Chess Club (dir.), Phi Beta Kappa, Kappa Phi Kappa, Mu Pi Delta. Composer popular songs including: Rudolph The Red-Nosed Reindeer (named to Songwriters Hall of Fame), Address Unknown, She'll Always Remember, Night Before Christmas Song, I Heard the Bells on Christmas Day, Rockin Around the Christmas Tree, A Holly Jolly Christmas, Anyone Can Move a Mountain. Editor and arranger two carol books. Originator of melody and harmony method of easy piano arrangements. Composer, lyricist 1 hr. ann. Christmas TV color spectacular Rudolph the Red-Nosed Reindeer with 8 songs for NBC (longest running TV Spl.), 1964—, TV spl. Ballad of Smokey the Bear, with 8 songs for NBC, 1965, 67, 68, TV spl. The Tiny Tree, NBC, 1975, 76, 77, 78; TV spl. Rudolph's Shiny New Year, ABC, 1976, 77, 78; also comml s. Gen. Electric Corp.; film Rudolph & Frosty. Home: 117 W 11th St New York City NY 10011 Office: 1619 Broadway New York City NY 10019

MARKS, LAWRENCE, lawyer; b. Montreal, May 9, 1908; s. Raphael and Bella M.; B.A., McGill U., 1929; LL.B., U. Montreal, 1933; m. Irene Marston, May 26, 1940; children—Isobel, Karin. Individual practice law, Montreal, 1935-76; named Queen's counsel, 1960; dir. Fin. Collection Agencies, Inc., Renmark Holdings Corp. Mem. Montreal Bar. Clubs: Montefiore, Lorraine Golf. Home: 400 Kensington Ave Apt 204 Montreal PQ H3Y 3A2 Canada*

MARKS, MARC LINCOLN, congressman; b. Farrell, Pa., Feb. 12, 1927; s. Benjamin H. and Myrtle S. M.; LL.B., U. Va., 1954; m. Jane London, June 22, 1952; children—Leslie, Patricia Mari. Admitted to Pa. bar; sr. partner firm Rodgers, Marks & Perfilio, Sharon; mem. 95th-96th Congresses from 24th Pa. Dist. Solicitor, Mercer County, 1960-66. Served with USAAF, 1945-46. Mem. Am., Pa., Mercer County bar assns., Am., Pa. trial lawyers assns. Republican. Jewish. Clubs: B'nai B'rith; Kiwanis. Office: 1127 Longworth House Office Bldg Washington DC 20515

MARKS, NORMAN CURTISS, clergyman, sch. adminstr.; b. Highspire, Pa., Feb. 11, 1937; s. Harry Curtiss and Rachel Ruth (Sides) M.; B.A., Bob Jones U., 1960, H.H.D.(hon.), 1976; m. Carol M. Ruth, Aug. 29, 1959; children—Deborah, David, Jonathan, Rebecca. Ordained to ministry Independent Fundamental Chs. Am., 1960; pastor Mountain View Bible Ch., Hummelstown, Pa., 1960—; tchr. Harrisburg (Pa.) Sch. of Bible, 1967—; pres. bd., 1975—; supervising prin. Mountainview Christian Ch., Hummelstown, 1974—. Mem. Eastern Ministerial Union Pa. (pres. 1975—), Organized Minorities Assn., Fundamental Bapt. Ass. Am., Bob Jones U. Alumni Assn., Am. Def. Preparedness Assn., Nat. Geog. Soc. Republican. Home: Box 83 RD 5 Hummelstown PA 17036

MARKS, ROBERT HUTCHINSON, assn. exec.; b. Bklyn., May 2, 1926; s. Robert John and Martha (Hutchinson) M.; B.S. in Civil Engring., Mass. Inst. Tech., 1947; m. Dorothy B. Alexander, Feb. 3, 1951. Application engr. Permutit Co. div. Sybron, Inc., N.Y.C., 1948-56, dist. mgr., 1960-62; asso. editor Power Mag., McGraw Hill, Inc., N.Y.C., 1956-60, mng. editor, 1962-69; mgr. pub. relations Michel-Cather, Inc., N.Y.C., 1969-70; asso. dir. pub. Am. Inst. Physics, Inc., N.Y.C., 1970—. Trustee Engring. Index, Inc.; bd. dirs. Nat. Fedn. Abstracting and Indexing Services. Bd. dirs. Bklyn. Meth. Home. Served to ensign USNR, 1945-46. Mem. AAAS, Am. Soc. C.E., Am. Soc. M.E., Am. Inst. Chem. Engrs., Nat. Assn. Corrosion Engrs., Am. Water Works Assn. Methodist (trustee). Mason. Home: 75 Henry St Brooklyn NY 11201 Office: 335 E 45th St New York City NY 10017

MARLAN, STANTON, clin. psychologist; b. Elizabeth, N.J., May 27, 1943; s. Jack and Sylvia (Boris) M.; B.A., Bard Coll., 1966; M.A., U. Hawaii, 1968; M.A., New Sch. for Social Research, 1970; postgrad. Duquesne U., 1970—; m. Janet DeVeber, Aug. 28, 1977; children by previous marriage—Dawn, Tori. Trainee, C. G. Jung Inst. Analytical Psychology, N.Y.C., 1968-70; instr. Jersey City State Coll., 1968-70; adj. lectr. New Sch. for Social Research, N.Y.C., 1969; psychologist Somerset (Pa.) State Psychiat. Hosp., 1970-71; staff psychologist Washington (Pa.) Green Mental Health Mental Retardation Clinic, 1971-72; chief psychologist Drug Abuse program Chartiers Mental Health/Mental Retardation, Bridgeville, Pa., 1972-74; dir. S. Hills Counseling Center, Pitts., 1974-77; co-dir., co-founder Pitts. Center for Psychotherapy, 1976-78, dir., 1978—; pvt. practice psychotherapy, Pitts., 1975—; candidate Inter-Regional Soc. Jungian Analysts, 1976—; faculty, exec. v.p. C. G. Jung Ednl. Center of Pitts., 1977—. Licensed psychologist, Pa.; Southwest Area Regional Tng. Council grantee, 1977-78. Mem. Wholistic Health Soc. Pitts. (charter; dir.), Am., Pa. psychol. assns., Greater Pitts. Psychol. Assn., Pitts. Psychoanalytic Center, Am. Acad. Psychotherapists, Western Pa. Soc. Clin. Hypnosis, C. G. Jung Found. Analytical Psychology. Contbr. articles to profl. jours. Home: 1043 Lancaster Ave Pittsburgh PA 15218 Office: Med Arts Bldg Suite 536 Fifth Ave Pittsburgh PA 15213

MARLOW, BRUCE ABBEY, communications co. exec.; b. Hartford, Conn., Dec. 1, 1946; s. George Henry and Wilma Ruth (Dubin) M.; A.B. cum laude, Tufts U., 1969; M.B.A., Columbia, 1971. Dir. merchandising and product mgmt. RCA Records, N.Y.C., 1971-73; dir. mktg. Novo Corp., N.Y.C., 1973-74; exec. v.p., chief ops. officer Novo Communications, Inc., N.Y.C., 1974-76, pres. chief exec. officer, 1976—. Mem. Am. Mgmt Assn., Am. Mktg. Assn., Columbia U. Club. Home: 319 E 85th St New York City NY 10018 Office: 733 3d Ave New York City NY 10017

MARLOW, DOROTHY JEANNETTE, pediatrician; b. N.Y.C., Oct. 30, 1922; d. Charles William and Edna Dorothy (Clarke) M.; B.A., Denison U., 1943; M.D., Woman's Med. Coll., 1947; m. June 14, 1947 (div.); children—Susan, Dorothy, John, Wendy. Intern, Queens Gen. Hosp., Jamaica, N.Y., 1947-48, resident 1951-52; resident in pediatrics Glen Cove Community Hosp., 1948-49, Willard Parker Hosp. Infectious Diseases, 1949-50; fellow N.Y.C. Health Dept., Babies Hosp., Presbyn. Med. Center, 1950; practice medicine specializing in pediatrics, Bedford Hills, N.Y., 1953-60; sch. physician Chappaqua (N.Y.) Pub. Schs., 1960-67; chief of pediatrics habilitation unit Letchworth Village, N.Y., 1967-75; dep. dir. Wassaic Developmental Center, N.Y., 1977—; med. dir. Frontiers Unlimited, 1973—. Recipient Physicians Recognition award AMA, 1975; named Outstanding Profl., Am. Acad. Human Services, 1974-75. Mem. AMA, Litchfield County, Conn. State med. socs., Am. Med. Women's Assn., Am. Assn. Mental Deficiency, AAUW (pres.). Congregationalist. Home: Box 339 Route 7 Kent CT 06757 Office: Box 305 Route 7 Kent CT 06757

MARMORA, SABATINO JOSEPH, security officer; b. Bklyn., Nov. 23, 1936; s. Joseph and Florence (Vezzuto) M.; B.A., St. John's U., 1958; postgrad. N.Y. Law Sch., 1962-64. Probation officer Cts. City of N.Y., 1961-69; sr. rep. narcotic edn. N.Y. State Narcotic Addiction Control Commn., 1967-69; supr. security Madison Detective Bur., N.Y.C., 1969-70; chief of security Lefrak Orgn. and Bklyn. Mus., 1971-73; mgr. protection services First Nat. City Bank, N.Y.C., 1973-77; mgr. security, real estate services dept., office bldgs. unit Mobil Oil Corp., N.Y.C., 1978—; pres. Praetorian Protection, Inc., Maspeth, N.Y., 1978—; lectr. security 2d U.S. Army Museum Conf., 1973. lectr. narcotic edn. Westchester County (N.Y.) Law Enforcement Seminars in Narcotic, 1968—. Mem. Internat. Criminal Justice Assn., Internat. Assn. Mus. Security Officers, Internat. Assn. Chiefs of Police, Am. Fedn. Police, Am. Soc. Indsl. Security, Internat. Narcotic Enforcement Officers Assn. Home: 118-18 Union Turnpike Kew Gardens NY 11415 Office: 150 E 42 St New York City NY 10017

MAROKO, PETER RICHARD, cardiologist; b. Kalisz, Poland, Sept. 27, 1936; s. Paul and Dora (Gelb) M.; B.S., Bandelrantes Coll., 1954; M.D., U. Sao Paulo, 1960, Ph.D., 1970; m. Cleuza Maria Mantovani, May 2, 1967; children—Robert T., Richard A., Andrew R. Intern, U. Sao Paulo (Brazil), 1960-61, resident in cardiology and medicine, 1961-62, asst. prof. medicine, 1963-67; fellow in cardiology Good Samaritan Hosp., Phoenix, 1967-68; asst. research cardiologist, asst. clin. prof. medicine U. Calif. at San Diego, 1968-72; asst. prof. medicine Harvard Med. Sch. and Peter Bent Brigham Hosp., Boston, 1972-75, asso. prof., 1975—. Fellow Am. Coll. Cardiology; mem. Am. Heart Assn. (editorial bd. Circulation 1975—), Am. Fedn. Clin. Research. Contbr. articles, abstracts to profl. publs. Home: 6 Bucknell Rd Wellesley MA 02181 Office: Harvard Med Sch Bldg A 25 Shattuck St Boston MA 02115

MARON, ARTHUR, pediatrician; b. Asbury Park, N.J., Apr. 15, 1933; s. Isidore Chaim and Sadie (Raskin) M.; B.S. in Biology, Rutgers U., 1954; M.D., Albany Med. Coll., 1958; m. Lynn Sunshine, Aug. 5, 1956; children—Stuart Glenn, Andrea Kim, Scott Michael. Intern, USPHS Hosp., Norfolk, Va., 1958-59; resident in pediatrics Babies' Hosp., Newark, 1961-63; practice medicine specializing in pediatrics, West Orange, N.J., 1963—; mem. staff St. Barnabas Med. Center, Livingston, N.J., Irvington (N.J.) Gen. Hosp., Newark Beth Israel Med. Center, Montclair (N.J.) Community Hosp.; clin. prof. pediatrics N.J. Med. Sch., Newark; mem. health adv. bd. Town of West Orange (N.J.), 1972—; chmn. child health tech. adv. com. N.J. Medicaid Program, 1973—; mem. child health planning com. N.J. State Health Coordinating Council, 1977—. Pres. Jewish Center of West Orange, 1973-74, editor Hayenu bull., 1977—. Served with USPHS, 1958-61. Diplomate Am. Bd. Pediatrics. Fellow Am. Acad. Pediatrics (chmn. N.J. chpt. 1975-78, alt. chmn. dist. III 1978—); mem. Essex County (N.J.) Med. Soc., Med. Soc. N.J. (chmn. pediatric sect. 1974-75). Club: B'nai B'rith. Editor 1958 Skull, Albany Med. Coll. yearbook. Home: 59 Woodland Ave West Orange NJ 07052

MARPLE, GARY ANDRE, mgmt. cons.; b. Mt. Pleasant, Iowa, Feb. 22, 1937; s. Kenneth Lowry and Truma Janice (Cook) M.; B.S., Drake U., 1959, M.B.A., Mich. State U., 1962, Ph.D. in Bus. Adminstrn., 1963; m. Ellen I. Metcalf, May 29, 1971; children—Brian E., Stephen L. Draftsman, Beling Engring Cons., Des Moines, 1956-58; asst. engr. John E. Brown, engring. cons., Des Moines, 1958-59; teaching asst. Mich. State U., East Lansing, 1960-62; Mass. Inst. Tech. postdoctoral fellow, 1962-63; cons. Arthur D. Little, Inc., Cambridge, Mass., 1963—; NDEA fellow, 1959-62. Mem. Am. Mktg. Assn., World Futures Soc. Club: Masons (Des Moines). Author: (with H. Wissmann) Grocery Manufacturing in the United States, 1968. Home: 47 Coolidge Ave Lexington MA 02173 Office: 35-356 Acorn Park Cambridge MA 02140

MARQUEZ, ERNEST DOMINGO, microbiologist, educator; b. Tranquillity, Calif., Nov. 13, 1938; s. Pedro and Jeronima (Ortiz) M.; B.A., Calif. State U., Fresno, 1961, M.S., 1967; Ph.D. (USPHS fellow), U. So. Calif., 1971; m. Antoinette Nastav, Nov. 26, 1974. USPHS postdoctoral fellow Scripps Inst. Oceanography, La Jolla, Calif., 1971-73; asst. prof. microbiology Pa. State U. Coll. Medicine, Hershey, 1973—; vol. instr. Internat. Latinam. Alliance, 1975. Served as officer USNR, 1962-65. Decorated Letter of Commendation. Mem. AAAS, Soc. Exptl. Biol. Medicine, Am. Soc. Microbiology, Smithsonian Assos., Phi Sigma, Beta Beta Beta. Author research papers. Office: Dept Microbiology Pa State Univ Coll Medicine Hershey PA 17033

MARR, CARMEL CARRINGTON (MRS. WARREN MARR II), state ofcl.; b. Bklyn.; d. William Preston and Gertrude Clementine (Lewis) Carrington; B.A., Hunter Coll., 1945; J.D., Columbia U., 1948; m. Warren Marr, II, Apr. 11, 1948; children—Charles Carrington, Warren Quincy. Admitted to N.Y. State bar, 1948; law asst. firm Dyer & Stevens, N.Y.C., 1948-49; practiced in N.Y.C., 1949-53; adviser legal affairs U.S. mission to UN, N.Y.C., 1953-67, sr. legal officer Office Legal Affairs, UN Secretariat, 1967-68; mem. N.Y. State Human Rights Appeal Bd., 1968-71; commr. N.Y. State Pub. Service Commn., 1971—; lectr. N.Y. Police Acad., 1963-67. Mem. N.Y. Gov.'s Com. Edn. and Employment of Women, 1963-64; mem. Nat. Gen. Services Pub. Adv. Council, 1969-71; mem. UN Devel. Corp., 1969-72. Bd. dirs. Amistad Research Center, New Orleans, Bklyn. Soc. Prevention Cruelty to Children, Indsl. Home for the Blind; bd. visitors N.Y. State Sch. Girls, Hudson, 1964-71; mem. exec. bd. Plays for Living, N.Y.C., 1968-75; pres. bd. dirs. Billie Holiday Theatre. Mem. Am., Bklyn., Bklyn. Women's bar assns., Nat. Assn. Women Lawyers, Nat. Assn. Regulatory Utility Commrs., Nat. Council Women, UN Assn. (gov.), Phi Beta Kappa, Alpha Chi Alpha. Republican. Contbr. articles to profl. jours. Office: Public Service Commn Two Wdrld Trade Center New York City NY 10047

MARR, EDWIN EUGENE, ednl. cons.; b. Aberdeen, Wash., Apr. 6, 1940; s. William John and Retta Arlita (Meeker) M.; B.A., Seattle Pacific U., 1964; M.A., U. Wash., 1966; m. Linda Kay Mace, Apr. 15, 1969; children—Keith LaVerne, Roger Alan, Erik Stephen. Research program officer NASA, Washington, 1967-71; v.p. devel. Innovative Scis. Inc., Stamford, Conn., 1971-76; pres. Tng. House Inc., Stamford, Conn., 1976—; ednl. cons. Layleader, Darien Methodist Ch., 1978—. Author: Applying Thinking Skills, 1975; The Cognitive Skills Manual, 1976-78. Address: 158 Sun Dance Rd Stamford CT 06905

MARR, THOMAS ALLEN, tech. co. exec.; b. Phila., May 19, 1949; s. Walter Webster and Agnes Evelyn (Simpson) M.; B.S., U. Md., 1973; m. Renee Martha Adams, Oct. 30, 1971; children—Michelle, Tamara, Jenelle Dianne. Engring. asst. Schnabel Engring. Co., Bethesda, Md., 1972; plant engr. Koppers Co. Inc., Forest Products div., Salisbury, Md., 1973-76, environ. project engr., Pitts., 1976-77, supr. environ. engring., 1977—. Served with USNR, 1971. Md. State scholar, 1968-72. Mem. ASME, Am. Wood Preservers Assn., Am. Wood Preserving Inst., Am. Paper Inst. Republican. Methodist. Home: 5734 Wilson Dr Bethel Park PA 15102 Office: K-927 Koppers Bldg Pittsburgh PA 15219

MARRA, BRUCE LAURENCE, bank exec.; b. Pitts., July 29, 1934; s. Louis Laurence and Florence Kathleen (Girton) M.; B.S. with honors, Lehigh U., 1956; M.B.A., U. Pitts., 1962; m. D. Janet Montgomery, Aug. 6, 1960; children—Susan, Lauren, Allison, Edward. With Mellon Bank, Pitts., 1960—, asst. v.p.-pension trusts, 1969-73, v.p.-personal trust investments, 1973—; guest instr. U. Pitts. Sch. Bus. Adminstrn., 1974-76. Mem. adv. bd. Bidwell Cultural and Tng. Center; bd. deacons Southminster Presbyterian Ch. Served with USNR, 1956-59. Fellow Inst. Chartered Fin. Analysts; mem. Pitts. Soc. Fin. Analysts (pres.'s award 1975), Pa. Bankers Assn. (chmn. trust investment com.). Club: Woodland Hills. Home: 1321 Redfern Dr Pittsburgh PA 15241 Office: Mellon Bank Mellon Sq Pittsburgh PA 15230

MARRA, DOROTHEA C. (MRS. MICHAEL D. MARRA), research chemist; b. Bklyn.; d. Salvatore and Mary (Faugiana) Polizzi; B.A., Bklyn. Coll., 1943; Ph.D., Dallas State Coll., 1974; m. Michael D. Marra, Jan. 11, 1947; 1 child, Jacques Marra. Research chemist Foster D. Snell, Inc., N.Y.C., 1944-69; v.p. Omar Research, Inc., N.Y.C., 1969—; chem. cons. to cosmetic, toiletry and pharm. cos. in U.S. and fgn. countries. Fellow Am. Inst. Chemists; mem. Sci. Research Soc. Am., Soc. Cosmetic Chemists, Sigma Xi. Patentee in field. Home: 107 Fernwood Rd Summit NJ 07901 Office: Omar Research Inc 200 Park Ave S New York City NY 10003

MARRA, MICHAEL, contractor, explosives cons.; b. Providence, Apr. 8, 1924; s. Anthony and Camella (Marotto) M.; B.S., R.I. Coll., 1976, M.Ed., 1978; m. Rosemarie DeLuise, Nov. 17, 1960; children—Anthony John, Gerianne and Marianne (twins). Gen. contractor specializing in heavy earthwork excavations, drilling and blasting rock, Providence, 1946—; pres. Statewide Freight Service

Inc., Providence, 1960—; explosives cons., 1963—; instr. diesel injection; lobbyist Indsl. Edn. Soc., 1976—; notary public, 1976—. Republican candidate R.I. Ho. of Reps., 1966; chmn. 5th ward U.S. senatorial campaign of John H. Chaffee, 1972, also mayoral campaign. Served with AUS, 1944-46: ETO. Recipient Order of Arrow, Scouters Key, Boy Scouts Am. Mem. Am. Welding Soc. (pres. 1971-72; sect. ednl. chmn. 1967-70), Assn. Diesel Specialists (nat. ednl. com. 1974—), Soc. Explosives Specialists, Providence Engring. Soc., Nat. Security Council, Am. Indsl. Arts Assn., R.I. Indsl. Arts Club, V.F.W. (nat. adv. bd.), D.A.V., R.I. Coll. Alumnae Assn., R.I. Rifle and Revolver Assn., Mil. Order Cootie, Wincheck Indians, Knights Yawgoog, Epsilon Pi Tau. Roman Catholic. Clubs: Elks, Stonybrook Rod and Gun. Address: 158 Gentian Ave Providence RI 02908

MARS, WITOLD TADEUSZ, artist, book illustrator; b. Rzesna, Poland, Sept. 1, 1912; s. Tadeusz Jozef and Stefania (Dunikowski) M.; grad. Acad. Fine Arts, Warsaw, 1934; m. Helene Bohusz, Dec. 29, 1960. Came to U.S., 1951, naturalized, 1957. Exhibited paintings in Poland, abroad, 1934-39; exhibited group shows at RBA Galleries, London, Nat. Gallery Scotland, London Group Exhbn., 1940-50; illustrator numerous books for leading pubs., N.Y.C., Boston, Chgo., 1951—; represented in permanent collection Polish State Collection, London, other collections, Gt. Britain, U.S.A.; executed murals Brit. Industry Fair, Festival of Britain. Trustee Comml. Arts Studio, London. Served with Polish Forces in Gt. Britain, 1940-45. Decorated Cross of Merit with swords (Polish); Croix du Combattant Volontaire (French); recipient Spl. Merit award 7th Book Jacket Competition, 1961; numerous others. Fellow Central Inst. Art and Design; mem. Polish Inst. Arts and Scis. N.Y.C. Address: 102-40 67th Rd Forest Hills NY 11375

MARSDEN, JOHN WARING, ins. cons.; b. Fall River, Mass., Nov. 6, 1927; s. William Grinrod and Sarah Roy (Waring) M.; Indsl. Engr., R.I. State Coll., 1949; m. Nancy Jane Jamrog, Mar. 5, 1974. Adjuster, Royal Globe Ins. Co., Boston, 1949-51; supt. Springfield Fire and Casualty Co. (Mass.), 1951-55; owner John W. Marsden Ins. Adjusters, Providence, 1955-75; pres. A.T. Parker & Co., Inc., North Attleboro, Mass., 1968-74; treas. JOMar Ins. Agy., North Attleboro, 1970—, pres. bd. dirs.; lectr. Boston U., 1966-67. Mem. Nat., S.E. Mass. (founder, past pres.) ind. agts. assns. Home: 5 Hixon Ct North Attleboro MA 02760 Office: 130 S Washington St North Attleboro MA 02760

MARSH, KENNETH STANLEY, shoe mfg. co. exec.; b. St. Albans, Eng., May 17, 1925; s. Cecil Stanley and Lucy (Tucker) M.; came to U.S., 1964, naturalized, 1973; ed. Kings Coll. Cambridge U., 1943-44, Royal Air Force Coll., Cranwell, Eng., 1944, Street (Eng.) Tech. Inst., 1953-54; m. Jeanne Carol Fink, Oct. 24, 1962; 1 son, Andrew Kenneth Laidlaw. Sr. indsl. engr. C & J Clark Ltd., Street, Eng., 1949-51, asst. prodn. mgr., 1951-53, chief tng. officer, 1953-64; chief engr. Hanover Shoe Inc. (Pa.), 1964—; mem. nat. council Brit. Boot and Shoe Instn., 1961-64; mem. edn. adv. com. Shoe and Allied Trades Research Assn., 1960-64; mem. edn. com. Brit. Footwear Mfrs. Assn., 1963-64; examiner City and Guilds of London, 1961-64. Bd. govs. Street Tech. Inst., 1957-64, Strode Tech. Coll., 1962-64; v.p. York-Adams council Boy Scouts Am., 1973-78. Served with RAF, 1944-49, 51. Registered profl. engr., Pa., W.Va. Fellow Brit. Boot and Shoe Instn.; mem. Brit. Inst. Mgmt., Guild of Cordwainers, Am. Def. Preparedness Assn., Am. Inst. Indsl. Engrs. (sr.), Am. Soc. Heating, Refrigerating and Air Conditioning Engrs., Nat. Soc. Profl. Engrs., Am. Mgmt. Assn. Episcopalian. Clubs: Royal Nat. Rose Soc., Am. Rose Soc., Internat. Wine Food Soc., Rotary, Hanover Country. Contbr. articles to profl. jours: author/editor tng. manuals for shoemakers, indsl. engrs., prodn. controllers, craft apprentices, pattern and last makers, others. Home: 990 McCosh St Hanover PA 17331

MARSH, LINDA KESSLER, psychologist; b. N.Y.C., Aug. 15, 1943; d. Max and Anna (Straus) Kessler; B.A., Queens Coll. City N.Y., 1964; M.S., Coll. City N.Y., 1966; Ph.D., N.Y. U., 1974; 1 dau., Allison Andra. Sch. psychologist Bur. Child Guidance, N.Y.C. Bd. Edn., 1968-70; staff psychologist, postdoctoral research fellow, clin. instr. in psychiatry dept. psychiatry N.Y. U. Med. Center, N.Y.C., 1974—; clin. extern in family psychotherapy Ackerman Inst. Family Therapy, 1977—. NIMH postdoctoral research fellow, 1974-76; Gralnick Found. grantee, 1977—; Walsh & Walsh, Inc. research grantee, 1977—. Mem. Am., Eastern, N.Y. State psychol. assns., Am. Orthopsychiat. Assn. Home: 2 E 67 St New York City NY 10021 Office: New York University Medical Center 550 1st Ave New York City NY 10016

MARSH, QUINTON NEELY, banker; b. Omaha, July 1, 1915; s. Arthur Judson and Rose Louise (Baysel) M.; B.C.S., Benjamin Franklin U., Washington, 1949, M.C.S., 1950; diploma Sch. Bank Adminstrn., U. Wis., 1959; postgrad. Am. Inst. Banking, 1945—, Am. U., 1950-51; m. Thelma M. Beck, Nov. 24, 1944. With Western Electric Co., Omaha, 1935-37, Lamson Bros. & Co., Omaha, 1937-39, C.A. Swanson & Sons, Omaha, 1939-42; with Am. Security & Trust Co., Washington, 1946-77, asst. auditor, 1956-58, auditor, 1958-69, security officer, 1968-77, gen. auditor, 1969-77, v.p., 1972-77, sr. officer in charge auditing div. and security; sr. v.p., cashier Bank of Columbia, N.A., Washington, 1977—; faculty Bank Adminstrn. Inst. Sch., U. Wis., 1961—; vice chmn. exam. com. Chartered Bank Auditor Program, 1968; lectr. banking schs., law enforcement groups and profl. convs., 1955—. Served with USNR, 1942-45. Certified bank auditor, certified internal auditor, certified protection profl. Mem. Inst. Internal Auditors (pres. D.C. 1962-63), Bank Adminstrn. Inst. (pres. D.C. 1966-67, auditing commn. 1968-70), D.C. Bankers Assn. (chmn. rewards and protective com. 1966-67), Internat. Assn. Chiefs of Police, Am. Soc. Indsl. Security (treas. D.C. 1963-65, chmn. nat. banking and fin. com. 1973-74), U.S. Naval Inst., Am. Legion, Am. Def. Preparedness Assn. Clubs: Masons (32 deg.), Shriners. Contbr. articles on banking and finance to profl. jours. Home: 4801 Connecticut Ave NW Apt 312 Washington DC 20008 Office: Bank of Columbia NA 1430 K St NW Washington DC 20005

MARSH, WALTON HOWARD, biochemist; b. Bay City, Mich., Mar. 26, 1919; s. Howard Daniel and May Louise (Baker) M.; A.B., Columbia U., 1940; M.S., Poly. Inst. N.Y., 1943; Ph.D., Case Western Res. U., 1951; m. Helen Ewart Rome, Feb. 5, 1944; children—Donald, Barbara. Clin. and med. research biochemist Crile VA Hosp., Cleve., 1951-54; mem. faculty State U. N.Y. Downstate Med. Center, Bklyn., 1954—, prof. pathology, 1966—; dir. clin. chem. labs. Kings County Hosp., 1954—, State Univ. Hosp., 1966-69. Served as pilot USAAF, 1943-45. Research grantee NIH, 1960—. Mem. Am. Soc. Biol. Chemists, Biochem. Soc. (Eng.), Am. Chem. Soc., Am. Assn. Clin. Chemists, N.Y. Acad. Scis., AAAS, Sigma Xi, Phi Lambda Upsilon. Author: Automation Clinical Chemistry, 1963; also articles. Home: 8 Sycamore Rd Glen Cove NY 11542 Office: State Univ NY Downstate Med Center Brooklyn NY 11203

MARSHALL, BARRY HAMILTON, fin. exec.; b. Cambridge, Mass., Oct. 25, 1944; s. Ivan and Ruth (Hamilton) M.; B.S. in Bus. Adminstrn., Northeastern U., 1967, M.B.A., 1969; M.S. in Taxation, Bentley Coll., 1978; m. Nancy Ellen Welteroth, Dec. 27, 1975. Staff accountant Price Waterhouse & Co., Boston, 1969-70, Elwynn J. Miller, C.P.A., Medford, Mass., 1970-71; sr. accountant Lambert, Levesque & Co., Framingham, Mass., 1971-72; in charge accountant Ernst & Ernst, Boston, 1972-74; sr. internal auditor USM Corp., Boston, 1974, asst. to machinery group controller, 1974-75; mgr. gen. accounting dept. Gen Rad, Inc., Concord, Mass., 1975-77, mgr. consol., compliance and taxation, 1977—; teaching asst. in accounting Northeastern U., 1968-69, part-time instr., 1976—; instr. in accounting Mass. Bay Community Coll., 1968. Pres. bd. mgrs. Village Condominium Assn., 1973-77; mem. Town Meeting, 1975-78; mem. Watertown Fin. Com., 1975-77. Mem. Am. Inst. C.P.A.'s, Mass. Soc. C.P.A.'s, Am. Accounting Assn., Northeastern U. Alumni Assn. (exec. com. 1976—, Telethon chmn. 1975, 76, v.p. 1977-79), Northeastern U. M.B.A. Assn. (v.p. membership 1975-76, rec. sec. 1974-76, sr. v.p. 1976-77, pres. 1977-79), Bentley Tax Alumni Assn. (dir. 1977—). Contbr. articles to Village Newsletters. Home: 4 Taft Ave Lexington MA 02173 Office: 300 Baker Ave Concord MA 01742

MARSHALL, BENJAMIN FRANKLIN, III, structural engr.; b. Grove City, Pa., July 2, 1935; s. Benjamin Franklin and Margaret Harris (Halderman) M.; B. Archtl. engring., Pa. State U., 1958; m. Alice Hunsberger, Dec. 27, 1958; children—Elizabeth Ann, Laura Kim, Margaret Alice. Design engr. Hunting, Larsen & Dunnells, Pitts., 1959-63; Deeter & Ritchey, Pitts., 1963-66; pvt. practice cons. structural engring., Pitts., 1966-70; partner firm Marshall & Brace, Pitts., 1970—. Registered profl. engr., Pa., N.Y., W. Va., Ohio, Md., Fla. Mem. Nat. Soc. Profl. Engrs., ASCE. Home: Spang Rd RD 1 Baden PA 15005 Office: 8980 Perry Hwy Pittsburgh PA 15237

MARSHALL, C(HARLES) HERBERT, physician; b. Washington, June 26, 1898; s. Charles H. and Pauline L. (Jennings) M.; Sc.B., Howard U., 1921, M.D., 1924; m. Esther Ophelia Tibbs, July 21, 1939; 1 son, Charles Herbert 3d. Intern Freedman's Hosp., Washington, 1924-25; pvt. practice medicine, Washington, 1925—; asst. instr. dept. medicine Howard U., Washington, 1925—; asst. instr. dept. medicine Howard U., Washington, 1928-32. Mem. Jr. Police and Citizens' Corps; mem. exec. bd. Nat. Capital area Boy Scouts Am.; mem. bd. Whipper Maternity Home; vice chmn. Commr.'s Youth Council, D.C., Citizens Joint Com. on Nat. Rep. D.C.; mem. Mayors Com. for Employment of Handicapped. Bd. dirs. Citizens Assn. of Georgetown, Citizens' Crime Commn. Met. Washington, So. Conf. Ednl. Fund, Met. Police Boys Club. Served with SATC, 1918. Recipient SSS Medal. Mem. Rock Creek Citizens Assn. (pres. 1935—), D.C. Fedn. Civic Assns. (pres. 1952-54), Nat. Med. Assn. (chmn. bd. trustees 1944-47, pres., 1949-50), NAACP, (D.C. pres. 1941-43). Baptist (trustee emeritus). Clubs: Kiwanis (Georgetown Kiwanian of Year 1974), Pigskin (v.p.). Home: 2710 P St NW Washington DC 20007

MARSHALL, DAVID, orthodontist; b. Syracuse, N.Y., Feb. 4, 1914; s. Moses and Fanny (Bagelman) Salutsky; B.S., Syracuse U., 1932-35; D.D.S., U. Md., 1938-42; postgrad. Columbia, 1943-45, Tufts Coll., Northwestern U.; m. Rita Stein, June 20, 1944; children—Robert Andrew, Howard Randy, Douglas S. (dec.), Susan Beth, Robin (dec.); m. 2d, Marjorie Kaufman, Sept. 7, 1973. Practicing orthodontist, Syracuse, N.Y.; mem. staff St. Joseph's Hosp., Crouse-Irving Hosp., University Hosp., Meml. Hosp.; mem. cons. School Speech, Syracuse U.; orthodontic cons. N.Y. State Health Dept.; lectr. in field, producer sci. exhbns. Recipient Hektoen medal AMA, 1970. Diplomate Am. Bd. Orthodontists. Mem. Am. Dental Assn., N.Y., Syracuse, 5th Dist. dental socs., Syracuse C. of C., Northeastern (qualifying com.), Am. orthodontists socs., Pierre Fauchard Acad. Contbr. articles to dental publs. Home: 1201 Meadowbrook Dr Syracuse NY 13224 Office: 1124 E Genesee St Syracuse NY 13210

MARSHALL, DAVID CHARLES, physician; b. Findlay, Ohio, June 9, 1932; s. John Hugh and Mildred Elizabeth (Neff) M.; student U. Mich., 1950-53; M.D., Harvard U., 1957; m. Rosemary Caroline Masi, Apr. 25, 1975; children by previous marriage—Hugh A., Anne C. Intern, Mary Hitchcock Hosp., Hanover, N.H., 1957-58, resident, 1958-59; asst. in surgery Peter Bent Brigham Hosp., Boston, 1959-61, resident in surgery, 1961-64; fellow in anatomy Harvard Med. Sch., 1960; pvt. practice surgery, New London, Conn., 1967-76; asst. clin. prof. surgery U. Conn. Med. Sch., 1978—; attending in surgery Lawrence and Meml. Hosps., New London; asso. dir. clin. research Pfizer, Inc., Groton, Conn., 1976—; cons. surgery Newington VA Hosp. Pres., Ledyard (Conn.) Hist. Soc., 1969-72; co-founder Ledyard Hist. Dist. and Commn.; chmn. Ledyard Conservation Commn., 1968-72; donor 100 acre nature preserve to Nature Conservancy, 1974; cons. restoration/hist. properties. Served to lt. comdr. USNR, 1964-67. Diplomate Am. Bd. Surgery; recipient Certificate of Commendation, Ledyard Bicentennial Commn., Ledyard Town Council, 1977. Fellow A.C.S.; mem. AMA, Conn., New London County med. socs., Conn. Conservation Assn. (v.p. 1966-67), Soc. for Preservation of New Eng. Antiquities (trustee 1969-72, mem. council 1976—), Antiquarian and Landmark Soc. Conn. (trustee 1969—). Clubs: Harvard (Boston); East Haddam (Conn.) Fishing and Game; Wadawanuck Yacht (Stonington, Conn.). Contbr. numerous articles to profl. jours. Home: 515 Pumpkin Hill Rd Ledyard CT 06339 Office: Pfizer Inc Central Research Eastern Point Rd Groton CT 06340

MARSHALL, FRANK IRVIN, steel co. exec.; b. Portersville, Pa., Oct. 13, 1917; s. Charles Irvin and Pearl Matilda M.; extension student Pa. State U., 1944; m. Ethel Bell Bloom, Sept. 22, 1936; children—Jean S. Marshall Arfield, Christine K. Marshall Anderson. Expeditor cold draw dept. Tubular Products div. Babcock & Wilcox Co. 1937-42, first helper steel mill, 1942-52, asst. melting supt. steel mill dept., 1952-54, melting supt., 1954-61, mgr. steel ops., 1961-68, asst. plant mgr., 1968-71, asst. to v.p., 1971—; v.p. 1st. Fed. Savs. & Loan Assn., Beaver Falls, Pa., 1973—. Mem. Chippewa Twp. Sch. Bd., 1949-55; mem. Chippewa Twp. Bd. Suprs., 1957-69; chmn. Upper Beaver Valley United Way, 1971. Mem. Electric Metal Makers Guild (pres. 1963-64), ASTM, Am. Iron and Steel Inst., Beaver County Indsl. Devel. Authority, Am. Inst. Metall. Engrs. Republican. Club: Masons. Home: 115 Oak Dr Beaver Falls PA 15010 Office: PO Box 401 Beaver Falls PA 15010

MARSHALL, JOHN ALOYSIUS, bishop; b. Worcester, Mass., Apr. 26, 1928; s. John A. and Katherine T. (Redican) M.; A.B., Coll. Holy Cross, 1949; student Sulpician Sem., Montreal; S.T.L., N. Am. Coll. and Pontifical Gregorian U., Rome, 1954; M.A. in Guidance and Psychology, Assumption Coll., 1964. Ordained priest Roman Catholic Ch., 1953, consecrated bishop, 1972; priest Our Lady of the Lake Ch., Leominster, Mass., 1954-56, St. Paul's Ch., Blackstone, Mass., 1956, St. Mary's Ch., Southbridge, Mass., 1956-57; asst. vice-rector, repetitor N. Am. Coll., Rome, 1957-61; faculty Acad. of the Sacred Heart, St. Stephen's High Sch., St. Vincent's Hosp. Sch. of Nursing, Worcester, Mass., 1961-62; headmaster St. Stephen's High Sch., 1962-68; chmn. Diocesan High Sch. Religion Com., 1964-68; spiritual dir. N. Am. Coll., 1968-69, bus. mgr., 1969-71; bishop, Burlington, Vt., 1972—. Office: 351 North Ave Burlington VT 05401

MARSHALL, KENNETH ALLAN, plastic and reconstructive surgeon; b. Boston, Dec. 28, 1938; s. Nathan Harold and Mary Elizabeth (Creagh) M.; A.B., Harvard U., 1960; M.D., Columbia U., 1964; m. JoAnne Theresa Burrows, Feb. 10, 1968; children—Torrey Alexander, Christopher Adrian. Intern, Harvard Surg. Service, Boston City Hosp., 1964-65, resident in gen. surgery, 1965-66, 69-72, resident and instr. in plastic surgery U. Va., Charlottesville, 1973-75; practice medicine specializing in plastic and reconstructive surgery, Boston and Cambridge, Mass., 1975—; clin. instr. in plastic surgery Harvard U. Served with M.C., USNR, 1966-69; Vietnam. Decorated Air medal, Navy Commendation; Am. Cancer Soc. grantee, 1970. Mem. AMA, Am. Burn Assn., Am. Soc. Plastic and Reconstructive Surgeons, Am. Assn. Hand Surgery, Plastic Surg. Research Council, Assn. Acad. Surgery, Mass. Med. Soc. Contbr. articles to profl. jours.; author (with others) profl. movies. Home: 203 Farm Ln Westwood MA 02090 Office: 300 Mount Auburn St Suite 306 Cambridge MA 02138

MARSHALL, KNEALE THOMAS, educator; b. Filey, Eng., Feb. 13, 1936; s. John Bertram and Winnifred Millicent (Taylor) M.; B.S., U. London, 1958; M.S., U. Calif., Berkeley, 1964; Ph.D., 1966; m. Dolores V. Bellig, Nov. 26, 1964. Metallurgist, Eldorado Mining & Refining, Sask., Can., 1958-62; mem. tech. staff Bell Labs., Holmdel, N.J., 1966-68; asst. prof. Naval Postgrad. Sch., Monterey, Calif., 1968-70, asso. prof., 1970-75, prof., 1975—; sci. adviser to dep. chief of naval ops. Dept. Navy, Washington, 1978—; cons. USMC, U. Calif.; vis. prof. U. Calif., Berkeley, 1972, London Sch. Econs., 1978. Named an Outstanding Young Man Am., 1969. Mem. Ops. Research Soc. Am. (past chmn. western sect.), Inst. Mgmt. Scis., Am. Inst. Indsl. Engrs. (sr.). Author: (with R.C. Grinold) Manpower Planning Models, 1977; editorial bd. Ops. Research, 1970-78, Jour. Applied Math., 1971-78. Office: DCNO (MPT) OP-01T Dept Navy Washington DC 20370

MARSHALL, MARA BLUMBERG (MRS. SYLVAN MITCHELL MARSHALL), artist; b. Nice, France, July 21, 1926 (parents Am. citizens); d. Joseph and Leah (Kristeller) Blumberg; grad. Scudder-Culver Jr. Coll., 1945, N.Y. Sch. Interior Decoration, 1946; Student Art Students League, N.Y.C., 1945-46; m. Sylvan Mitchell Marshall, Feb. 11, 1951; children—Douglas Wayne, Bradley Ross. One-woman show: First Fed. Gallery, Chgo., 1971, Nat. League Pen Women, Washington, 1972, Arts Club Washington, 1977; exhibited group shows Cosmos Club, Washington, Am. Art League Exhibit, Washington, Exhibit for Kennedy Center for Performing Arts, Washington, Julius Garfinckel & Co., Am. Art League Gallery, Washington, Washington Gallery Art, Nat. League Am. Pen Women, 1970, 72; pres. Park Exhibit, Washington; represented in permanent collections. Mem. bd. Salvation Army Aux., 1954-56; mem. Pan Am. Liaison Com. of Women's Orgns., 1954—; mem. Spanish-Portuguese Study Group, 1953—, mem. bd., corr. sec., 1956-57. Mem. Nat. League Am. Pen Women (Ann. award Biennial Contest in Art, D.C. br. 1967, 69, Ann. award, 1st prize oils nat. biennial contest 1969, exec. bd. D.C. br. 1968-70, corr. sec., 1968-70, pres. D.C. br. 1970-72, 1st prize accryllics 1971, chmn. hospitality nat. hdqrs. 1972-74, pres. D.C. 1974-76, co-chmn. bicentennial conv. 1974-76, mem. nat. art bd. 1976-78), Artists Equity Assn. Am. Art League, Nat. Soc. Arts and Letters (pres. Washington chpt. 1978-79), Miniature Painters, Sculptors and Gravers Soc. Washington. Home: 2929 Ellicott St NW Washington DC 20008

MARSHALL, MILDRED DELEVETT, former educator; b. Balt., Aug. 15, 1904; d. William Amoss and Lutie (Kemp) Delevett; grad. Balt. Tchrs. Tng. Sch., 1922; student Johns Hopkins, 1923-24, N.Y.U., 1927; m. William Harvey Marshall, Aug. 15, 1931 (dec.). Tchr. pub. schs., Balt., 1922-71; demonstration tchr.; mem. curriculum com. Balt. pub. schs.; mem. supt. com. ednl. tests and measurements. Supporting com. Walter's Art Gallery, Balt. Mus. Art; mem. women's Com. Balt. Symphony Orch. Mem. Pub. Sch. Tchrs. Assn., Md. Tchrs. Assn., N.E.A., Alumnae Assn. Samuel Ready Sch., Daus. Colonial Wars, Harford County Assn. (sec. 1950-52), Bishop's Guild, Md. Hist. Soc., Hist. Annapolis Inc., Nat. Trust Historic Preservation, English Speaking Union, Balt. Opera Guild, Soc. Preservation Md. Antiquities, D.A.R. Democrat. Episcopalian. Address: 3701 Edgewood Rd Baltimore MD 21215

MARSHALL, RAY, sec. labor; b. Oak Grove, La., Aug. 22, 1928; s. Thomas Jefferson and Virginia (Foster) M.; B.A., Millsaps Coll., 1949; M.A., La. State U., 1950; Ph.D., U. Calif., Berkeley, 1954; Fulbright research scholar U. Helsinki, 1955-56; Wertheim fellow, Harvard, 1960-61; Ford faculty research grantee, 1954-55; m. 1946; 5 children. Asst. prof., asso. prof. econs. U. Miss., 1953-57; asso. prof., prof. La. State U., 1957-62; prof. U. Tex., Austin, 1962-67, 69-77, dir. Center for Study Human Resources, 1969-77, chmn. dept., 1970-72; Alumni prof., chmn. dept. econs. U. Ky., 1967-69; mem. com. adminstrv. tng. programs HEW, 1967-68; mem. manpower adv. com. Dept. Labor, 1968-76, sec. labor, 1977—. Served with USN, 1944-46, to lt. comdr. Res., 1946—. Mem. Am., So. (exec. com. 1969-71, pres. 1973-74) econ. assns., Indsl. Relations Research Assn. (dir. 1969-72), Am. Arbitration Assn., Nat. Inst. Labor Edn. (dir.), AAUP (pres. Tex. chpt. 1966-67), Assn. for Evolutionary Econs., Beta Gamma Sigma, Omicron Delta Kappa, Phi Kappa Phi. Author: (with Paul Norgren and Samuel Hill) Toward Fair Employment, 1964; The Negro and Organized Labor, 1963; (with Allan M. Cartter) Labor Economics: Wages, Employment and Trade Unionism, 1967, rev. edit., 1972; Labor in the South, 1967; Negro and Apprenticeship; 1967; The Negro Worker, 1967; (with Vernon M. Briggs, Jr.) The Negro and Apprenticeship, 1967; (with Briggs) Equal Apprenticeship Opportunities: The Nature of the Issue and the New York Experience, 1968; (with Lamond Godwin) Cooperatives and Rural Poverty in the South, 1971; (with Sar Levitan and Garth Mangum) Human Resources and Labor Markets, 1972; (with Robert W. Glover) Compensation of Texas State Employees, 1972; (with Richard Perlman) An Anthology of Labor Economics, 1972; (with William S. Franklin and Glover) Training and Entry into Union Construction, 1974; Rural Workers in Rural Labor Markets, 1974; (with R. Lynn Rittenoure and James Walker) Human Resources Development in Rural Texas, 1974; (with Virgil Christian) Black Economic Progress in the South, 1974. Contbr. articles to profl. jours. Office: Dept Labor 200 Constitution Ave Washington DC 20210

MARSHALL, RICHARD DOUGLASS, educator; b. Washington, May 24, 1930; s. Garland Green and Ruby Elizabeth (Grymes) M.; A.B., Lincoln U., 1953; LL.B., Howard U., 1956; grad. Sch. Mortgage Banking Northwestern U.; m. Marie Bernadine Johnson, July 12, 1956. Mortgage loan appraiser Prudential Ins. Co. Am., Newark, then sr. personnel cons.; asso. dir. loans govt. Nat. Mortgage Assn., Dept. Housing and Urban Devel., 1971-72; prof. bus. adminstrn. grad. Sch. Bus. Adminstrn., Rutgers U., Newark, 1972—; cons. Urban Inst., Washington. Pres. Econ. Devel. and Planning com. Essex County, N.J.: mem. Newark Mayor's Task Force Edn.; chmn. bd. dirs. Newark Housing Devel. and Rehab. Corp. Trustee Lincoln U., Vocational and Guidance Assn. Mem. Mortgage Bankers Assn. Am., Am. Real Estate and Urban Econs. Assn. Urban League Essex County (past pres., dir.). Mason (Shriner). Home: 555 Mt Prospect Ave Newark NJ 07104 Office: 92 New St Newark NJ 07102

MARSHALL, ROBERT JAMES, religious assn. exec.; b. Burlington, Iowa, Aug. 26, 1918; s. Robert McCray and Margaret Emma (Gysin) M.; A.B., Wittenberg U., 1941, D.D., 1963; B.D., Chgo. Luth. Theol. Sem., 1944; D.D., Carthage Coll., 1961, Northwestern Luth. Sem., 1969, Waterloo U., 1970; L.H.D., Gettysburg Coll., 1965; LL.D., Augustana Coll., 1968; student U. Chgo., 1949-52; m. Alice Johanna Hepner, Feb. 6, 1943;

children—Robert Edward, Margaret Alice Marshall Niederer. Ordained to ministry Luth. Ch., 1944; pastor Grace Luth. Sch., Alhambra, Cal., 1944-47; instr. religion Muhlenberg (Pa.) Coll., 1947-49, head dept. religion, 1952-53; prof. O.T. interpretation Chgo. Luth. Theol. Sem., Maywood, Ill., 1953-62; pres. Ill. Luth. Ch. in Am., 1962-68; pres. Luth. Ch. in Am., N.Y.C., 1968-78; dir. mission, service and devel. Luth. World Ministries, 1978—; mem. exec. com. Luth. World Fedn.; mem. central com., exec. com., chmn. fin. com. World Council Chs.; mem. gen. bd. Nat. Council Chs. of Christ in U.S.A.; mem. exec. com. Luth. Council in U.S.A., 1968-78, mem. exec. council, 1964-68; chmn. on Evangelism Luth. Ch. Am., 1963-64; ann. prof. Am. Sch. Oriental Research, Jerusalem, Jordan, 1958-59; exec. bd. Chgo. Conf. on Religion and Race, 1964-68. Bd. dirs. Grand View Coll., 1966-68, Augustana Coll., 1963-68, Luth. Sch. Theology, 1963-68, Augustana Hosp., Chgo., 1963-68, Luth. Hosp., Moline, Ill., 1963-68. Mem. Chgo. Soc. Bibl. Research (sec. 1962-68), Nat. Assn. Profs. Hebrew, Soc. Bibl. Lit. and Exegesis. Author: The Mighty Acts of God. Home: 300 E 40th St Apt 31N New York City NY 10016 Office: 360 Park Ave S New York City NY 10010

MARSHALL, ROBERT WILSON, engring. cons.; b. Mpls., Nov. 20, 1912; s. Thomas and Margaret Agnes (Wilson) M.; B.S., in Elec. Engring., U. Minn., 1934; M.S., Columbia U., 1935; m. Alexandra Babcock Oct. 17, 1942; children—Robert, Carlile, Ann. Research asso. elec. engring. Columbia U., 1935-36; transmission and fgn. systems studies Bell Telephone Labs., 1936-41, radar systems devel., 1941-45, carrier telephone devel., 1945-53, underwater systems circuit and systems engring., 1953-59, edn. and tng. center, 1959—, head edn. and tng. dept., 1961-66, cons. switching systems, engring. div., 1966-70, supr. ops. research and quality assurance div., 1970-77, ret., 1977; cons., 1978—. Elder Presbyterian Ch.; mem. bd. devel. Princeton Sem. Registered profl. engr., N.Y. Mem. IEEE, Am. Soc. Engring. Edn., Sigma Xi. Republican. Contbr. articles to profl. jours. Patentee in field. Home: 155 Maple St Summit NJ 07901 Office: 155 Maple St Summit NJ 07901

MARSHALL, SYLVAN MITCHELL, lawyer, TV producer; b. N.Y.C., May 14, 1917; s. Louis H. and Kitty Markowitz; B.A., Coll. City N.Y., 1938; LL.B., Harvard U., 1941; m. Mara Byron, Feb. 11, 1951; children—Douglas Wayne, Bradley Ross. Admitted to N.Y. bar, 1946, Washington bar, 1953; mem. firm Garey & Garey, N.Y.C., 1946-51; spl. asst. to chief counsel OPS, Washington, 1951-53; partner Granik & Marshall, Washington, 1953-58; asst. producer Youth Wants To Know and Am. Forum, NBC-TV and radio, 1953-58; spl. dep. atty. gen., N.Y., 1946-50; pvt. practice Washington, 1958—; sr. partner law firm Marshall, Leon, Weill & Mahony, Washington; counsel Leon, Weill & Mahony, N.Y.C.; Washington counsel Community Fed. Savs. & Loan Assn., St. Louis, First Fed. Savs. & Loan Assn., Chgo., First Fed. Savs. & Loan Assn., Jacksonville, Fla., Standard Fed. Savs. & Loan Assn., Cin., First Savs. & Loan Assn. Wis., Milw., Sooner Fed. Savs. & Loan Assn., Tulsa, Diamond & Precious Stone Bourse, Idar-Oberstein, West Germany, also fgn. embassies. Hon. dep. police commr. N.Y.C., 1950-53; hon. consul Finland. Served from 2d lt. to lt. col., U.S. Army, 1941-46. Decorated knight comdr. Order of Falcon (Iceland); knight comdr. Order of Vasco Nunez de Balboa (Republic of Panama); comdr. Order of Lion (Finland); Order of Taj (Iran); comdr. Order Aztec Eagle (Mexico); Order of So. Cross (Brazil); Order of Ruben Dario (Nicaragua); comdr. Order of Lion and Sun (Iran.). Mem. Acad. TV Arts and Scis. Clubs: Internat., Cosmos (Washington). Home: 2929 Ellicott St NW Washington DC 20008 Office: 1825 K St NW Washington DC 20006 also 261 Madison Ave New York City NY 10016

MARSHALL, THERESA HOOPER, ednl. adminstr.; b. Newark, Sept. 30, 1939; d. Chester and Willie Belle (Sanders) Hooper; Mus.B., New Eng. Conservatory Music, 1961; M.A., Columbia U., 1972; Ed.D., Rutgers U., 1977, postgrad., 1978—; 1 dau., Erica. Adj. prof. Livingston Coll., Rutgers U., New Brunswick, N.J.; asso. examiner Ednl. Testing Service, Princeton, N.J., 1974-75; with N.J. Dept. Higher Edn., Trenton, 1977-78; coordinator student spl. services Upward Bound programs U. Del., Newark, 1979—. Mem. adv. bd. for women Douglass Coll., Rutgers U.; bd. dirs. aquatic div. YWCA, New Brunswick. Recipient awards United Community Corp., 1964, Newark Anti-Poverty Agy., 1966, Rutgers U., 1973. Mem. Music Educators Nat. Task Com., N.J. Music Educators Assn. (dir.), AAUW, Kappa Delta Pi, Phi Delta Kappa. Home: 4103 Golfview Dr Newark DE 19711

MARSHALL, THURGOOD, asso. justice U.S. Supreme Ct.; b. Balt., July 2, 1908; s. William and Norma (Williams) M.; A.B., Lincoln U., 1930, LL.D., 1947; LL.B., Howard U., 1933, LL.D., 1954; LL.D., Va. State Coll., 1948, Morgan State Coll., 1952, Grinnell Coll., 1954, Syracuse U., 1956, N.Y. Sch. Social Research, 1956, U. Liberia, 1960, Brandeis U., 1960, U. Mass., 1962, Jewish Theol. Sem., 1962, Wayne U., 1963, Princeton U., 1963, U. Mich., 1964, John Hopkins U., 1966; hon. degree Far Eastern U., Manila, 1968, Victoria U. of Wellington, 1968, U. Calif., 1968, U. Otago, Dunedin, New Zealand, 1968; m. Vivian Burey, Sept. 4, 1929 (dec. Feb. 1955); m. 2d, Cecelia S. Suyat, Dec. 17, 1955; children—Thurgood, John. Admitted to Md. bar, 1933; practice in Balt., 1933-37; asst. spl. counsel NAACP, 1936-38, spl. counsel, 1938-50, dir., counsel legal def. and ednl. fund, 1940-61; U.S. circuit judge for 2d Jud. Circuit, 1961-65; solicitor gen. U.S., 1965-67; justice U.S. Supreme Ct., 1967—. Civil rights cases argued include Tex. Primary Case, 1944, Restrictive Covenant Cases, 1948, U. Tex. and Okla. Cases, 1950, sch. segregation cases, 1952-53; visited Japan and Korea to make investigation of ct. martial cases involving Negro soliders, 1951. Cons. Constl. Conf. on Kenya, London, 1960; rep. White House Conf. Youth and Children. Recipient Spingarn medal, 1946; Living History award Research Inst. Mem. Nat., Am. bar assns., Bar Assn. D.C., N.Y.C. County Lawyers Assn. Alpha Phi Alpha. Episcopalian. Club: Masons (33 deg.). Home: Falls Church VA Office: Supreme Ct US Washington DC 20543*

MARSHALL, WILLOUGHBY MARKS, architect; b. Apalachicola, Fla., Sept. 16, 1923; s. John and Estelle Wefing (Marks) M.; B.F.A., U. Notre Dame, 1947, B.Arch., 1949; m. Marie Elizabeth Quigley, Aug. 28, 1967; children—William, Mary, John, James. Pvt. practice architecture, Fla., 1954-59; archtl. designer Franciscan Office of Art and Architecture, also exec. asst., N.Y.C., 1959-61; archtl. designer Architects Collaborative, Cambridge, Mass., 1961-64; pres., architect Willoughby Marshall, Cambridge, 1969—. Gen. chmn. Nat. Interfaith Conf. Religion and Architecture, Boston, 1976; bd. dirs. Newton YMCA, (Mass.) 1972-76. Recipient award Liturg. Conf. and Guild for Religious Architecture for Nativity Ch., Hollywood, Fla., 1967; St. Peter's Ch., Southwest Harbor, Maine, 1968; award Guild Religious Architecture for Newman Student Center, U. Maine, Orono, 1972; award for New Melleray Abbey, Dubuque, Iowa, 1976, also AIA honor award 1977; spl. mention for Excellence of Design, HUD Biennial Awards program, 1976. Mem. AIA (NE regional dir. Guild for Religious Architecture 1972-76, v.p. 1976-77, com. historic resources 1977—), Boston Soc. Architects, Mass. Assn. Architects, Soc. Preservation of New Eng. Antiquities. Club: Rotary. Contbr. articles to profl. publs.; work indexed in Maine Forms of American Architecture, 1976. Home: 164 Kirkstall Rd Newton MA 02160 Office: One Arnold Circle Cambridge MA 02139

MARSTELLER, WILLIAM A., advt. exec.; b. Champaign, Ill., Feb. 23, 1914; s. P.L. and Minnie (Finder) M.; B.S., U. Ill., 1937; m. Gloria Crawford, Apr. 22, 1938; children—Elizabeth A. Marsteller Gordon, Julie. Reporter Champaign News-Gazette, 1932-37; agy. counselor Mass. Mut. Life Ins. Co., Chgo., 1937-41; advt. and sales promotion mgr. Edward Valves, Inc., East Chicago, Ind., 1941-43, sec., 1943-45, v.p., dir., 1945-51; mgr. advt. and market research Rockwell Mfg. Co., Pitts., 1945-49, v.p., 1949-51; pres. Marsteller Research, Inc., Chgo., 1951—; pres. Marsteller Inc., 1951-60, chmn., 1960-75, chmn. exec. com., chief exec. officer, 1975—; chmn. Burson-Marsteller, Assos., 1953-68, Marsteller Internat., S.A., Geneva, Switzerland, 1961—. Bd. dirs. James Webb-Young Fund; trustee Whitney Mus. Am. Art, Barnard Coll. Recipient U. Ill. Achievement award, 1973, Pres.'s award, 1976. Mem. Am. Mgmt. Assn. (trustee), Am. Assn. Advt. Agys., Nat. Indsl. Advertisers Assn. (pres. 1947-49), Football Writers Assn. Am., U. Ill. Found., Art Inst. Chgo. (life), Sigma Chi. Clubs: Tavern, Arts (Chgo.). Author: The Wonderful World of Words, 1972. Contbr. articles to marketing and advt. publs. Home: 900 Lake Shore Dr Chicago IL 60611 also 1060 Fifth Ave New York City NY 10028 Office: 1 E Wacker Dr Chicago IL 60601 also 866 3d Ave New York City NY 10022

MARSTON, ALFRED J., economist; b. Silesia, Poland, July 22, 1924; s. Alovsius and Martha (Von Stackberg) M.; Ph.D., U. Paris, 1950; postgrad. Ecole des Sci. Politiques, 1945-47; m. Vilma Mercaldi, Nov. 30, 1956. Analyst, Internat. Pub. Opinion Research, N.Y.C., supr. European research operation, 1951-52; analyst, research supr. UNGRAN, N.Y.C., 1953-55; econ. analyst terminals Port of N.Y. Authority, 1956-60, asst. transp. economist, 1961-62, economist, 1962—. Vice pres. Manhattan Downtown Community Council; mem. steering com. Health Systems Agy. N.Y.C.; pres. bd. dirs. Chatham Towers; trustee, mem. adv. bd. Beekman Downtown Hosp.; mem., chmn. transp. com. N.Y.C. Local Planning Bd. Served with French Army, 1943-45. Mem. Am. Econ. Assn., Am. Statis. Assn., AAAS, Nat. Acad. Scis., Urisa (chmn. internat. sig. com.). Author: The French Legion of Haiti, 1952; contbr. to publs. in transp. field, articles to profl. jours. Home: 170 Park Row New York City NY 10038 Office: 1 World Trade Center New York City NY 10048

MARTAS, JULIA ANN, educator; b. Bronx, N.Y., July 30, 1949; d. Julio and Emilia Guerra de Martas; A.A., Bronx Community Coll., 1970; B.S. in Spl. Edn., City Coll. N.Y., N.Y.C., 1972, M.S. in Bilingual Edn., 1975. Sec., Premier Credit Finance Co., N.Y.C., 1967-71; bilingual tchr. for mentally retarded Pub. Sch. 43X, Bd. Edn. City N.Y., 1972—. Mem. N.Y. State Assn. for Retarded Children, N.Y. State Assn. for Tchrs. Retarded Nat. Assn. Humanities Edn., Nat. Council Basic Edn. Club: Odd Fellows. Licensed in teaching mentally retarded and bilingual classes kindergarten-6th grade, N.Y.C. Office: Public School 49X Room 238 Bronx NY 10454

MARTH, FRITZ LUDWIG, plating metal finishing co. exec.; b. Essen, Germany, Feb. 23, 1935; s. Fritz and Elizabeth (Dietrich) M.; came to U.S., 1952, naturalized, 1959; student pub. schs., Essen; m. Sonja Wiehl, June 17, 1964; children—Fritz Thomas, William Robert. Stock clk. Hamilton Art Metal Co., N.Y.C., 1952-55; with Keystone Metal Finishers, Inc., Secaucus, N.J., 1955—, asst. plant mgr., 1962-66, plant mgr., 1966—. Pres. N.J. State Soccer Assn., 1965-70; sec. So. N.Y. State Soccer Assn., 1972—; gen. sec. Cosmopolitan Soccer League, 1961—; mem. div. soccer U.S. Olympic Com. Served with U.S. Army, 1958-59; Korea. Lutheran. Club: Hoboken (N.J.) Soccer Football. Home: 121 W Passaic Ave Bloomfield NJ 07003 Office: 22 Raydol Ave Secaucus NJ 07094

MARTICORENA, ERNESTO JESUS, mech. engr.; b. Havana, Cuba, Mar. 14, 1941; s. Ernesto and Rosa (Rodil) M.; came to U.S., 1962, naturalized, 1977; student Villanova U., Havana, 1958-61; B. Engring. cum laude, Stevens Inst. Tech., 1968, M.M.E., 1970; m. Otilia Maria Mejias, Nov. 7, 1964; children—Ernesto Jesus III, Otilia. Design mech. engr. White Machine Co., Kenilworth, N.J., 1965-73, asst.chief engr., 1973-74; supt. plant engring. NL Industries, Sayreville, N.J., 1974-76; sr. chem. engr., sect. head C.F. Braun & Co., Murray Hill, N.J., 1976—. Registered profl. Engrs., Am. Chem. Soc., N.J. Mem. ASME, Nat., N.J. socs. profl. engrs., Am. Inst. Chem. Engrs, Stevens Alumni Assn. Roman Catholic. Club: Latin Am. Home: 937 Walnut St Elizabeth NJ 07201 Office: C F Braun & Co Diamond Hill Rd Murray Hill NJ 07974

MARTIMUCCI, RICHARD ANTHONY, engring. co. exec.; b. N.Y.C., Sept. 25, 1934; s. Dominic Ernest and Angela (Gentile) M.; student Coll. City N.Y., 1952-55; A.B., Syracuse U., 1960; m. Claudia Frances Reagan, Nov. 2, 1957; 1 dau., Lisa Felice. Sales engr. Morse-Boulger, Inc., N.Y.C., 1960-62; project engr. Nichols Research and Engring., N.Y.C., 1962-65; mgr. ops. Dorr-Oliver, Inc., Stamford, Conn., 1965-72; v.p. Environgenics Systems, Chemico div. Aerojet-Gen., El Monte, Calif., 1972-75; pres. RAM Engring., Inc., New Canaan, Conn., 1975—. Served with USAF, 1957-59. Registered profl. engr., Conn., N.Y., N.J., Calif. Mem. ASME, Nat. Soc. Profl. Engrs., Water Pollution Control Assn. Office: PO Box 1041 New Canaan CT 06840

MARTIN, AGNES HUDSON MACQUEEN (MRS. WILLIAM CLAYTON MARTIN), ret. librarian; b. Hummelstown, Pa., Jan. 3, 1900; d. James Michael and Emma Rachel (Martin) Macqueen; certificate Carnegie Library Sch., 1930; student U. Pitts., 1934-36; m. William Clayton Martin, Aug. 1, 1937; 1 stepdau., Mary (Mrs. Jay Crawford Painter). Asst., Sewickley (Pa.) Pub. Library, 1918-29; asst. children's dept. Carnegie Library of Pitts., 1929-38; librarian D.T. Watson Home for Crippled Children, Leetsdale, Pa., 1942-44; asst. Roselle (N.J.) Pub. Library, 1959-60; children's librarian Orange (N.J.) Pub. Library, 1960-75, ret., 1975. Mem. Am., N.J. library assns. Republican. Episcopalian. Home: 1280 Shetland Dr Union NJ 07083

MARTIN, ALBERTUS, bishop; b. Southbridge, Mass., Oct. 4, 1913; s. Arthur and Parmelie (Beaudoin) M.; B.A., Nicolet Coll., 1935; S.T.D. Laval U., 1941. Ordained priest Roman Catholic. Ch., 1939; prof. philosophy Nicolet Coll., 1939-46, dir., 1946-49; vicar gen. Diocese Nicolet, 1949-50, co-adjutor bishop, 1950, bishop, 1950—. Mem. commn. for liturgy Council Vatican II. Address: Bishop House PO Box 820 Nicolet PQ Canada

MARTIN, ALLEN, lawyer; b. Manchester, Conn., Aug. 12, 1937; s. Richard and Ruth Palmer (Smith) M.; B.A., Williams Coll., 1960; B.A., Oxford U., 1962; LL.B., Harvard U., 1965; m. Ina Lynch, July 10, 1965; children—Elizabeth Palmer, Samuel Bates. Admitted to Vt. bar, 1970; partner firm Downs, Rachlin & Martin, Burlington and St. Johnsbury, Vt., 1971—; mem. Vt. Bd. Jud. Responsibility, vice-chmn., 1978—. Trustee Franconia Coll., 1971-75; chmn. St. Johnsbury Republican Town Com., 1972-74. Mem. Am. Law Inst., Am., Vt. bar assns. Republican. Home: 10 Highland Ave Saint Johnsbury VT 05819 Office: 9 Prospect St Saint Johnsbury VT 05819

MARTIN, ANTHONY ALPHONSE, librarian, editor; b. Pitts., Aug. 18, 1920; s. John A. and Anna (Pocunis) M.; Ed.B., Duquesne U., 1942; B.S. in Library Sci., Carnegie Inst. Tech., 1946; postgrad. U. Pitts., 1946-48; m. Julia Claire Wallace, June 28, 1952; children—Michele, Anthony, Anita. Asst. bus. br. tech. dept., sr. librarian reference dept. Carnegie Library of Pitts., 1946-48, asst. head reference dept., 1949-52, adminstrv. asst. to dir., 1954-55, chief librarian Allegheny regional br., 1956-64, asst. dir. Carnegie Library of Pitts., 1964-69, dir., 1969—; chmn. bd. Pitts. Regional Library Center, Inc., 1970-72, 75; pres. N. Side City Pitts. Parking Corp.; dir. WQED Ednl. TV, OCLC, Inc.; part time instr. library sci. Duquesne U., 1959—; purchase analyst Westinghouse Airbrake Corp., 1953-54; librarian Bur. of Mines, Pitts. and Bruceton, Pa., 1956; editor Tech. Book Rev. Index, 1956-69; treas. Council Computerized Library Networks, 1974—; mem. Pa. State Advisory Council Library Devel., 1978—. Adv. bd. Internat. Poetry Forum; bd. visitors U. Pitts., 1976—, distinguished alumnus award, 1975. Served from aviation cadet to 1st lt., USAAF, 1943-45. Decorated 5 Air medals. Mem. World Affairs Council, Pitts. Bibliophiles, Am., Pa. library assns. Home: 3338 Sylvan Rd Bethel Park PA 15102 Office: Carnegie Library of Pitts 4400 Forbes Ave Pittsburgh PA 15213

MARTIN, BÉLANGER JOSEPH, philosopher, educator; b. Leclercville, Que., Can., Nov. 7, 1933; s. Alain and Marie Victoria (Hébert) M.; B.A., Laval U., Que., 1957; S.T.D., U. Montreal, 1965; M.A., Catholic U. Am., 1966, Ph.D., 1971. Ordained priest Roman Cath. Ch., 1961; prof. philosophy St-Boniface Coll., Man., Can., 1961-63, U. Montreal (Que.), 1963-65; prof. philosophy and theology, also ofcl. del. corp. Coll. André Grasset, Montreal, 1968—, chmn. philosophy and religious edn. dept., 1974—; co-founder Centre d'animation spirituelle, Montreal, 1968—; animator Personnalité et Relations Humaines Can., 1970—; pastoral counselor. Mem. Conseil de Direction, Commn. Pédagogique, Que. Philos. Assn. Address: Coll André Grasset 1001 E Crémazie St Montreal PQ H2M 1M3 Canada

MARTIN, CARL EATON, lawyer; b. Cornlea, Nebr., July 20, 1902; s. Linn S. and Nettie (Clark) M.; A.B., Brown U., 1923; LL.B., Yale U., 1925; m. Mildred V. Marvin, Feb. 14, 1928; children—Virginia A., Joan P. Martin Klee, Christine E. Admitted to N.Y. bar, 1926, since practiced in Troy; asso. Murphy, Aldrich & Guy, 1926-45; mem. Murphy, Aldrich, Guy, Broderick & Simon, 1945-66; sr. partner Martin, Hislop, Mackay and Shudt, 1966-71, Martin, Noonan, Hislop, Troue & Shudt, 1971—. Bd. dirs. Troy YMCA, 1962—. Mem. N.Y. State, Am. bar assns., Lambda Chi Alpha. Home: 2519 15th St Troy NY 12180 Office: 21 2d St Troy NY 12180

MARTIN, CHARLES, JR., educator, camp adminstr.; b. Orange, N.J., July 17, 1942; s. Charles and Concetta (Arcieri) M.; B.A., William Paterson Coll., 1965, M.A. Edn., 1970; prin. certificate Montclair State Coll., 1976; m. Lizabeth Martin; children—Suzanne, Charles. Tchr. elementary sch. Nutley (N.J.) Pub. Schs., 1965-68, spl. edn. workshop coordinator, 1968-76, coach baseball, basketball high sch., 1969-76; dir. Camp Hope for Retarded N.J. Assn. Retarded Citizens, East Orange, 1969—; mem. N.J. State Com. for Developmentally Disabled. Certified tchr., tchr. of handicapped, supr., N.J. Mem. Am. Camping Assn., Nat., N.J. (rep.) edn. assns., N.J. Assn. Retarded Citizens, Nutley Tchrs. Assn. Home: 584 Huyler St Teterboro NJ 07608 Office: Camp Hope for Retarded 62 N Walnut St East Orange NJ 07017

MARTIN, DAVID KENDALL, educator, assn. exec.; b. Troy, N.Y., June 23, 1933; s. George Elmer and Mary Viletta (Hutchins) M.; student U. St. Andrews, Scotland, 1953-54; A.B., Union Coll., Schenectady, 1955; M.A., N.Y. State U. at Albany, 1958; m. Patricia Roberts, June 16, 1956; children—Anne Kennedy, David Kendall, Elizabeth Viletta, Peter Stockwell. Tchr. English, Chazy (N.Y.) Central Rural Sch., 1958—; dir. Clinton County Hist. Assn., Plattsburgh, N.Y., 1964-77, pres., 1973-75; cons. genealogist, 1960—. Coordinator drama festivals N.Y. State U., Plattsburgh, 1971-74; mem. West Chazy Youth Commn., 1970-72, Clinton County Bicentennial Commn., 1971—, West Chazy Park and Recreation Commn., 1972—; bd. dirs. Clinton County Council on Arts, 1962-64. Served with AUS, 1955-57. Winston Churchill fellow, U. Cambridge (Eng.), 1975. Mem. Chazy Tchrs. Assn. (pres. 1963-64), N.Y. State United Tchrs. (zone chmn. 1961), English Speaking Union, Conn. Hist. Soc., New Eng. Hist. Geneal. Soc., N.Y. Geneal. Biog. Soc., Phi Sigma Kappa. Unitarian. Clubs: Adirondack Mountain, Lake George Assn. Author: (with N.J.B. Sullivan) A History of the Town of Chazy, 1970; Chazy and the Revolution, 1976; The 18th Century Zimmerman Family, 1976; contbr. articles to geneal. and hist. jours. Home: Mouse Hill West Chazy NY 12992

MARTIN, DONALD LLOYD, dairy farmer; b. Halifax. N.S., Can., June 25, 1938; s. Percy James and Eunice Louvane (Lloyd) M.; B.Sc. in Agr., MacDonald Coll., McGill U., Montreal, Que., Can., 1961; m. Carolyn Ella Watters, Sept. 8, 1962; children—Deborah, John, Barbara, James. Asst. agrl. rep. County of Elgin (Ont., Can.), 1961-65, City of Truro (N.S.), 1965-67; agrl. rep. City of Pictou (N.S.), 1967-74; dairy farmer, River Hebert, N.S., 1974—. Mem. Ayrshire Breeders Assn. Can. (dir. 1969), N.S. Ayrshire Breeders (sec. treas. 1965—), Atlantic Ayrshire Breeders (sec. treas. 1967—), N.S. Inst. Agrology. Home: PO Box 71 River Hebert NS B0L 1G0 Canada

MARTIN, DOUGLAS HARRY, cons. engr.; b. Hackensack, N.J., Aug. 10, 1929; s. Harry Edwin and Florence Hilma (Kellgren) M.; B.S. in Chem. Engring., Mass. Inst. Tech., 1950; M.Chem.Engring., N.Y. U., 1956, M.B.A., 1961; m. Christine Jacob, July 6, 1952; children—Pamela, Richard. Asst. to v.p. research Watson Elevator Co., Englewood, N.J., 1950-51; research engr., then process devel. engr. and process engr. M.W. Kellogg Co., 1953-61; planning engr., then mgr. mktg. services N.J. Zinc Co., 1961-70; asst. to v.p. Natural Resources Group, Gulf & Western Industries, Bethlehem, Pa., 1970-75; pres., dir., Winfield, Inc., Lincroft, N.J., 1970—; pres., dir. Douglas Martin & Assos. Inc., Allentown Minerals, Inc., 1977—. Alumni officer, mem. ednl. council Mass. Inst. Tech. Served with U.S. Army, 1951-53. Registered profl. engr., N.Y., N.J., Pa. Fellow AAAS; mem. Am. Chem. Soc., Am. Inst. Chem. Engrs., N.J. Acad. Sci., Nat. Soc. Profl. Engrs. Presbyterian. Patentee in field. Home: RD 7 Allentown PA 18103 Office: 119 Heather Dr RD 7 Allentown PA 18103

MARTIN, DOUGLAS RAY, state ofcl.; b. Gouverneur, N.Y., July 28, 1930; s. Lohvell H. and Florence Inez (Stickney) M.; B.S. cum laude, Am. U., 1964; M.P.A., N.Y. U., 1977; m. Alene Betty George, Oct. 25, 1952; children—Bruce Stuart, Tracy Lee. Accountant with S. Josef, pub. accountant, Syracuse, N.Y., 1952-56; auditor GAO, Washington, 1956-63; dir. internal auditing FDA and Smithsonian Instn., Washington, 1963-67; dir. accounting systems N.Y. State Dept. Audit and Control, Albany, 1967-70, dir. adminstrn. Office Parks and Recreation, 1970-72, adminstrv. dir. dept. audit and control, 1972—; cons. P.R. govt., Turkey govt.; instr. Siena Coll., 1972—, Albany Bus. Coll., 1969—; chmn. Nat. Council Govtl. Accounting; chmn. N.Y./N.J. Intergovtl. Audit Forum, 1978-79. Mem. com. Nat. Capitol area and Ft. Orange council Boy Scouts Am., 1966-71; mem. Gov.'s Mgmt. Adv. Council, 1971-72; asst. treas. Saratoga Performing Arts Center, 1973—. C.P.A., N.Y., Va. Mem. Am. Soc. Pub. Adminstrn. (chpt. council 1971-73, chpt. pres. 1975-76, nat. council 1976-80), Nat. Assn. Accountants, Fed. Govt. Accountants Assn., Inst. Internal Auditors, Phi Kappa Phi. Author: Workbook for Governmental Accounting, I, 1974. Home: 218 Westchester Dr Delmar NY 12054 Office: Dept Audit and Control A E Smith Office Bldg Albany NY 12236

MARTIN, EDWARD JOHN, factoring co. exec.; b. Utica, N.Y., Aug. 28, 1910; s. Edward Thomas and Alice (Nugent) M.; B.S.C., N.Y. U., 1934; m. Katherine Bennett, Nov. 19, 1938 (dec. June 1964); children—Katherine (Mrs. Henry P. Dougherty), Edward Joseph, Elizabeth M. (Mrs. Richard W. Burke), Patricia A. (Mrs. Willis Hartshorn IV); m. 2d, Grace B. Schwefel, July 25, 1966; stepchildren—Karen L. Schwefel, Charles A. Schwefel. With Irving Trust Co., N.Y.C., 1934-41; with John P. Maguire & Co., Inc., Factors, N.Y.C., 1941-43, 46-76, pres., 1974-76, cons., 1976—, past dir., cons.; dir. Lessing's Inc., Norwalk Powdered Metals, Inc., William T. Tonner, Inc., Sunbury Textile Mills, Inc., Troy Mills, Inc., Alexander Lee Wallau, Inc. Bd. dirs. Southside Hosp., Bay Shore, N.Y., 1952—. Served to lt. USNR, 1943-46. Mem. Friendly Sons of St. Patrick. Clubs: N.Y. Univ., Manhattan (N.Y.C.); Bayberry Yacht, Bayberry Bath and Tennis (Islip, N.Y.); Old Guard Soc. Palm Beach (Fla.) Golfers, Beach (Palm Beach); Southward Ho Country (BayShore, N.Y.).

MARTIN, EUGENE RONALD, chemist; b. Buffalo, Oct. 6, 1918; s. John Marion and Frances (Chojnacka) Marcinkiewicz; B.S., Canisius Coll., 1940; m. Dorothy Estelle Ochowiak, Jan. 17, 1942; children—Judith G., Michael E., Peter R., Sussan M., Stephen D., John P., Mary K., Mark A., Kathlein D. Process control mgr. foam rubber div., Hewitt Robins Inc., Buffalo, 1947-51, lab. mgr., 1951-54; asst. mgr. tech. dept. foam rubber div. Dunlop Tire and Rubber Corp., Buffalo, 1954-60, mgr. mill room control, 1960-62, asst. compounder and curing engr., 1962-63, chief chemist lab. mgr., 1963—; chmn. Buffalo Rubber Group, 1962. Aux. police, Buffalo, 1950-52; troop committeeman Boy Scouts Am., 1966. Served with U.S. Army, 1942-46. Mem. Am. Chem. Soc., Am. Indsl. Hygiene Assn., ASTM (corp., sub-com. chmn., 1973—), Am. Soc. Quality Control, Canisius Coll. Alumni Chem. Soc. (pres., 1959-60). Republican. Roman Catholic. Home: 345 Eggert Rd Cheektowaga NY 14225 Office: PO Box 1109 Buffalo NY 14240

MARTIN, FRANCIS JOSEPH, JR., social services agy. adminstr.; b. Phila., Feb. 1, 1936; s. Francis Joseph and Mary Josephine (Riley) M.; B.S., Widener Coll., 1969; M.B.A., U. Pa., 1972; m. Barbara Mae Witham, May 10, 1958; children—Patricia Lynn, John Francis. With Vertol div. Boeing Co., Springfield, Pa., 1960-68, asst. to gen. mgr., 1968; adminstr. out-reach programs The Children's Hosp. of Phila., 1968-70, asst. adminstr., 1970-71; exec. adminstr. Sch. Medicine U. Pa., Phila., 1972-77; dep. exec. dir. Phila. Psychiat. Center, 1977—; asso. in community medicine Sch. Medicine, U. Pa., 1972-78; lectr. Wharton Sch., U. Pa., 1976-77. Mem. Delaware County Planning Commn., 1970-71; v.p. Glen Acres Civic Assn., 1972-73; mem. adv. com. Chester County Boy Scouts Am. Served with USMC, 1954-60. Recipient Distinguished Service award U. Pa. Mem. Am. Hosp. Assn., Am. Public Health Assn., Pa. Public Health Assn., Pa. Assn. Pvt. Psychiat. Hosps., Am. Acad. Polit. and Social Scis., Am. Mgmt. Assn., Pi Gamma Mu. Republican. Roman Catholic. Contbr. articles to profl. jours. Home: 1160 Sylvan Rd West Chester PA 19380 Office: Ford Rd and Monument Ave Philadelphia PA 19131

MARTIN, HARROLD BERT, librarian; b. Cambridge, Pa., Mar. 8, 1916; s. David Hoover and Mary Edna (Wanner) M.; student Temple U., 1940-43; B.A., U. N.Mex., 1947; B.L.S., U. So. Calif., 1947; postgrad. U. Pa., 1949-50, 66. First asst. curator manuscripts and spl. collections Hist. Soc. Pa., Phila., 1948-62; librarian Phila. City Planning Commn., 1963—. Served with Spl. Service Corp, AUS, 1943, 44. Mem. Am., Pa. library assns., Council Planning Librarians, Byron Soc., Keats-Shelley Assn. Am., Browning Inst. (Charter), Classical Am. Soc., Silver Belle (Spiritualist) Assn., Friends of Casa Guidi, Friends of Harwood Found., Friends of Barnes Found. Home: 1928 DeLancey Pl Philadelphia PA 19103 Office: City Hall Annex 14th floor Philadelphia PA 19107

MARTIN, JOHN L., state legislator, educator; b. Eagle Lake, Maine, June 5, 1941; s. Frank and Edwidge (Raymond) M.; B.A. in History and Govt., U. Maine, Orono, 1963, postgrad., 1963-64. Mem. Maine Ho. of Reps., 1964—, minority leader, 1970-74, speaker of house, 1975—; tchr. Am. govt. and history Ft. Kent (Maine) Community High Sch., 1966-72; instr. polit. sci. U. Maine, Ft. Kent, 1972—; ins. agt. Union Mut. Life Ins. Co., Eagle Lake, 1968—. Pres. Maine Young Democrats, 1964-69; permanent chmn. Dem. State Conv. Maine, 1972-76; chmn. Maine Legis. Council, 1977; comptroller Sen. Edmund S. Muskie's Vice presdl. campaign, 1968. Mem. State Legis. Leaders Found. (dir., pres.), Eagle Lake C. of C. (dir. 1967-70). Roman Catholic. Clubs: K.C., Calumet. Home: Church St Eagle Lake ME 04739 Office: State House Augusta ME 04333

MARTIN, LEONA ELOISE, nurse; b. Scranton, Pa., Nov. 12, 1913; d. Clyde Lloyd and Ethel Geraldine (Lee) Gould; student Westminster Coll., 1931-32; R.N., Binghamton City Hosp., 1938; m. Arthur R. Martin, May 18, 1946 (dec.). Nurse, Binghamton (N.Y.) City Hosp. Sch. Nursing, 1938-40, labor and delivery rm., nursery, 1940-43; head nurse newborn nursery N.Y.C. Woman's Hosp., 1946-70; night nurse saline induction unit St. Luke's Hosp. Ctr., N.Y.C., 1970-73, supv. central supply, 1973—. Served as 1st. lt. with Nurse Corps, U.S. Army, 1943-46. Decorated EAMTO ribbon with 3 battle stars. Mem. Am. Nurses Assn., Am. Soc. Hosp. Central Service Personnel. Republican. Methodist. Office: Amsterdam Ave at 114th St New York City NY 10025

MARTIN, PAMELA JUNE NAULTY, social service ofcl.; b. Mt. Vernon, N.Y., Jan. 24, 1950; d. James Francis and Marjorie June (Acheson) Naulty; B.S., Drexel U., 1972; postgrad. Fairleigh Dickinson U.; m. Robert Lee Martin, Sept. 4, 1971. Various positions in store, kitchen and interior design, 1972-75; pvt. practice interior designer, 1975-76; coordinator Reassuring Calling Service, Monmouth County Bd. Social Services, Freehold, N.J., 1975—. Bd. dirs. Ret. Sr. Vol. Program, 1975—, Monmouth County Easter Seals, 1976—. Mem. Puppeteers of Am., Internat. Platform Assn. Home: 45 Salem Ln Little Silver NJ 07739 Office: PO Box 3000 Freehold NJ 07728

MARTIN, PATRICIA ANN, ednl. adminstr.; b. Indiana, Pa., Apr. 23, 1943; d. Edward J. and Marian Jean (Neurohr) M.; B.S. in Edn., Villa Maria Coll., 1965; Ed.M. in Guidance, Gannon Coll., 1973. Tchr., St. Joseph's Elementary Sch., Warren, Pa., 1961-63, parochial schs. of Erie (Pa.), 1965-70, pub. schs. of Anne Arundel County, Pasadena, Md., 1970-71; art instr. Gannon Coll., Erie, Pa., summers 1970-71; dir. student services Mercy Hosp. Sch. Nursing, Balt., 1971-74; student counselor, dir. admissions Union Meml. Hosp. Sch. Nursing, Balt., 1976—; play therapist and cons., Balt., 1973-76. Mem. Am., Md. personnel and guidance assns., Am., Md. coll. personnel assns., Nat. Cath. Guidance Conf., Am. Rehab. Counselor Assn. Home: B-7908 Knollwood Rd Baltimore MD 21204 Office: Union Memorial Hospital School of Nursing 201 E University Parkway Baltimore MD 21218

MARTIN, PETER BIRD, found. exec.; b. Phila., July 9, 1929; s. William Thornton and Virginia Evelyn (Bird) M.; B.A., Dartmouth Coll., 1951; children—William Thornton, Lucy Martin Halter. Reporter, St. Louis Post-Dispatch, 1951-53; fellow Inst. Current World Affairs, N.Y.C., 1953-55, exec. dir., Hanover, N.H., 1978—; contbg. editor Time mag., N.Y.C., 1955-61, asso. editor, 1961-63, sr. editor, 1963-70; asst. mng. editor Money Mag., N.Y.C., 1970-78; exec. dir. Am. Univs. Field Staff, Hanover, N.H., 1978—. Editor, contbr. numerous articles to mags., newspapers. Home: Bridge St Orford NH 03777 Office: PO Box 150 Hanover NH 03755

MARTIN, R. KEITH, educator; b. Seattle, Sept. 5, 1933; s. Jerome Milton and Winifred (Gifford) M.; A.B., Whitman Coll., 1955; M.B.A. with honors, Coll. City N.Y., 1965; Ph.D., U. Wash., 1973; m. Carolyn Joanne Carosella, June 15, 1957; children—Jefferson, Sean, Mary Jennifer, Katherine. Div. mgr. Campus Merchandising Bur., Inc., N.Y.C., 1955-56; sales rep. IBM, Seattle, 1956, N.Y.C., 1957-58; mgr. mgmt. adv. services Price Waterhouse & Co., N.Y.C., 1959-65, Seattle, 1965-67; dir. mgmt. systems dept. U. Wash., 1967-71, lectr. dept. accounting Sch. Bus. Adminstrn., 1971-73; prof. dept. accountancy Baruch Coll., City U. N.Y., 1973—; v.p. Eastalco Systems, 1971-72; faculty finance div. Am. Mgmt. Assn., 1963-64; part-time lectr. Bellevue Community Coll., 1967-69, Shoreline Community Coll., 1968-72, Seattle U., 1971-72. Mem. Citizens' Legis. Rev. Com., 1968-69; mem. City of Seattle EDP Adv. Com., 1968-71, chmn., 1968-69; mem. Citizens Adv. Com. Licensing and Consumer Affairs, 1970-73; chmn. indsl. engring. adv. com. Shoreline Community Coll., 1968-72; mem. mgmt. info. systems data element task force Western Interstate Commn. Higher Edn., 1968-70, adv. council, 1969-71; mem. com. for non-partisan nomination and election of Bronxville Sch. Bd. Trustees, 1976—, chmn., 1977—; cons. to Urban Acad., City N.Y., 1974—; chmn., pres. Loft Film and Theatre Center, Inc., 1977—. Recipient Certificate of Appreciation, Am. Mgmt. Assn., 1966, certificate of Merit for Distinguished Service to Mgmt. Scis., 1969, for Distinguished Service to Info. Systems Profession, 1973; Merit award Assn. Systems Mgmt., 1971, Achievement award, 1972; Certificate for service City of Seattle, 1973. Named Outstanding Young Man Am., 1970; Kellogg fellow, 1971-72; Price Waterhouse faculty fellow, 1976; registered profl. engr. Mem. Am. Inst. Indsl. Engrs. (dir. Seattle chpt. 1967-70, chmn. regional conf. 1969), Nat. Assn. Accountants (asso. dir. N.Y. chpt. 1963-64, 75—, Seattle chpt. 1967-70), Assn. Systems Mgmt. (pres. Pacific N.W. chpt. 1970-71), Data Processing Mgmt. Assn., Assn. Computing Machinery, Soc. Certified Data Processors, Soc. Mgmt. Info. Systems, AAUP, Am. Accounting Assn., Phi Delta Theta, Mu Gamma Tau, Phi Delta Kappa, Beta Alpha Psi. Co-author: Management Control of Electronic Data Processing, 1965; author: Management Information Systems in Higher Education: Case Studies at Three Universities, 1973; Effective Business Communications, 1976; Systems Development and Computer Concepts, 1977; also monographs and articles. Home: 2 Normandy Rd Bronxville NY 10708

MARTIN, RAYMOND SPENCER, JR., mech. engr.; b. Wilkes-Barre, Pa., June 18, 1928; s. Raymond Spencer and Augusta Matilda (Ecker) M.; B.S., Bucknell U., 1950; m. Joan Lee Woodruff, June 20, 1953; children—Eric Spencer, Kimberly Lee, Jeffrey Woodruff, Craig Kilgore, Kurt August. Test and design engr. Honeywell Inc., Phila., 1950-54; test engr. Pratt & Whitney Aircraft Co., East Hartford, Conn., 1954; design engr. Lacy, Atherton & Davis, architects and engrs., engrs., Wilkes-Barre, Pa., 1957-60; partner Martin & Fladd, cons. engrs., Wilkes-Barre, 1960—. Chmn. Dallas Area Municipal Authority, 1967—; council St. John's Luth. Ch., Wilkes-Barre, 1971—, organist and choirmaster, 1964—. Served with USN, 1954-56. Registered profl. engr., Pa. Mem. Am. Soc. Heating, Refrigerating and Air Conditioning Engrs., Pa. Soc. Profl. Engrs., ASME, Cons. Engrs. Council, Wilkes-Barre C. of C., Tau Beta Pi. Lutheran. Clubs: Rotary (past pres. Dallas, Pa. 1968-69), Masons, Shriners. Home: 185 Carverton Rd Trucksville PA 18708 Office: 25 N River St Wilkes-Barre PA 18702

MARTIN, RENEE COHEN, document examiner, graphologist; b. Bklyn., Feb. 26, 1928; d. Aref and Eleonora (Cofino) Cohen; student Bklyn. Coll., 1950, Coll. City N.Y., 1952, N.Y. U., 1954; Ph.D. (hon.), Ohio St. Matthew U., Columbus, 1971; m. Howard Martin Kessler, Dec. 24, 1950; children—Kenneth Samuel Kessler, Laurel Rose Kessler Orr, Elena Anna, Julia Mary. Pres., Organized Handwriting Cons., Inc., N.Y.C., 1955—; lectr. in field; TV and radio appearances; moderator radio show Psychic Scene, Sta. WHWH, Princeton, 1977-78; testified in ct. cases; cons. petition questions, unknown authorship documents. Active Am. Cancer Soc., pres. Mercer County Unit, 1974-76; vol. consumer affairs local assistance officer East Windsor Twp., Dept. Law and Pub. Safety, Consumer Affairs Bur. N.J., 1970-77. Mem. Nat. League Am. Penwomen (pres. So. Jersey 1976), Internat. Assn. Identification, Assn. Research and Enlightenment, Am. Psycho-synthesis Found., N.J. Fedn. Bus. and Profl. Women, Mensa. Liberal party. Jewish. Club: Bus. and Profl. Women's (pres. Hightstown, N.J. 1966-67, rec. sec. 1978-79). Author: Your Script Is Showing, 1969; Renee Martin's Secrets of Handwriting, 1972; Scriptease, 1976. Home: 20 Nassau St Princeton NJ 08540 Office: Handwriting Consultants 507 Fifth Ave New York City NY 10017

MARTIN, RICHARD EVERETT, architect; b. York, Pa., Nov. 29, 1922; s. Gilbert Drew and Cynthia Alice (Owens) M.; student Ecole Des Beaux Arts, Fontainebleau, France, 1958; student Tyler Sch., Temple U., Rome, 1966; m. Jacqueline Laura Loucks, June 8, 1946; children—Joy Christine, Richard Everett. Draftsman, Am. Chain & Cable Co., York, 1941-42; with Buchart Assos., Inc., York, Pa., 1946—, designer, dir. ch. dept., then v.p. to 1972, exec. v.p., 1972-76; self-employed cons. architect, 1976—. Served with USNR, 1942-45; ETO. Decorated Purple Heart. Mem. Am. Soc. Ch. Architecture. Episcopalian. Club: Masons. Home: 688 Florida Ave York PA 17404 Office: 120 S Beaver St York PA 17403

MARTIN, RICHARD HARRISON, art historian; b. Bryn Mawr, Pa., Dec. 4, 1946; s. Frank Harrison and Margaret (Dever) M.; B.A., Swarthmore Coll., 1967; M.A., Columbia U., 1969. Editor, Arts Mag., N.Y.C., 1974—; asst. prof. div. liberal arts Fashion Inst. Tech., State U. N.Y., 1973—; lectr. New Sch. Social Research; adj. lectr. Sch. Visual Arts, N.Y. U. Mem. Coll. Art Assn., Soc. Archtl. Historians, Victorian Soc. Am., Am. Soc. Aesthetics, Internat. Assn. Art Critics. Home: 235 E 22d St New York City NY 10010 Office: 23 E 26th St New York City NY 10010

MARTIN, RICHARD MILTON, philosopher; b. Cleve., Jan. 12, 1916; s. Frank Wade and Lena Beatrice (Bieder) M.; A.B., Harvard U., 1938; M.A., Columbia U., 1939; Ph.D., Yale U., 1941; m. Marianne von Winter, Oct. 23, 1948. Instr. math. Princeton U., 1942-44, U. Chgo., 1944-46; asst. prof. philosophy Bryn Mawr (Pa.) Coll., 1946-48; asst. prof. philosophy U. Pa., 1948, asso. prof., to 1959; prof. philosophy U. Tex., 1959-63, N.Y. U., N.Y.C., 1963-73, Northwestern U., Chgo., 1973—; guest prof. U. Bonn. (W. Ger.), 1960-61, U. Hamburg (W. Ger.), 1970-71; vis. prof. philosophy Yale U., 1964-65, New Sch. Social Research, 1972, Temple U., 1973; mem. Inst. Advanced Study, Princeton, N.J., 1975-76; research asso. Center for Philosophy and History of Sci., Boston U., 1977-79: cons., lectr. in field; exec. com. Conf. Method in Philosophy and Scis., N.Y., 1963—, chmn., 1970. John Simon Guggenheim Meml. Found. fellow, 1951-52, Fund for Advancement Edn. fellow, 1955-56, Am. Council Learned Socs. fellow, 1961; asso. fellow Clare Hall, Cambridge (U.K.) U., 1971—; research grantee NSF, 1958-74, Vaughn Found., 1970, 77. Mem. Assn. Symbolic Logic (exec. com., council 1950-53), Am. Philos. Assn. (exec. com. Eastern div. 1964-67), Charles S. Peirce Soc. (treas., pres.-elect 1978), N.Y. Philosophy Club (chmn. 1971-74), Fullerton Club (pres. 1955-56). Author: Truth and Denotation, A Study in Semantical Theory, 1958; The Notion of Analytic Truth, 1959; Towards a Systematic Pragmatics, 1959; Intension and Decision, A Philosophical Study, 1963; Belief, Existence, and Meaning, 1969; Logic, Language, and Metaphysics, 1971; Whitehead's Categoreal Scheme and Other Papers, 1974; Events, Reference, and Logical Form, 1978; Semiotics and Linguistic Structure. 1978; editor: (with Alan Anderson and Ruth Marcus) The Logical Enterprise, 1975; Peirce's Logic of Relations and Other Studies, 1979; Pragmatics, Truth, and Language, 1979; editorial bd. Ency. of Philosophy, 1967, various philos. jours.; contbr. articles, revs. to philos. publs. Address: 582 Blue Hill Ave Milton MA 02186

MARTIN, ROBERT LAWRENCE, educator; b. Washington, Nov. 18, 1933; s. Robert Fitz-Randolph and Thalia (Alden) M.; student Farmington State Tchrs. Coll., 1952-54, U. Colo., summers 1952, 53, 56; B.S. in Secondary Edn., U. Maine, 1956; postgrad. (NSF fellow) U. Md., summer 1957; M.S. in Zoology, Kans. State U., 1959; postgrad. U. Ill., 1959-61, (NSF fellow) U. Wash. at Friday Harbor, summer 1960; Ph.D. in Zoology, U. Conn., 1971; m. Shirley Ann Grunert, Dec. 23, 1955. Tchr. biology Madison Sr. High Sch., 1956-57; instr. zoology State U. N.Y. at Plattsburgh, 1961-63, asst. prof., 1963-64; asso. prof. biology U. Maine at Farmington, 1966-71, prof., 1971—; vis. scientist Whiteface Mountain Field Sta., Atmospheric Scis. Research Center, N.Y., summers 1962-65; research asso. Mt. Washington Obs., N.H., 1969-74, U. Conn. Chaco Boreal (Paraguay) Expdns., 1973, 74, 75; mem. U.S. Fish and Wildlife Service Ind. bat recovery team, 1975—; mem. bat specialist group Survival Services Commn., Internat. Union for Conservation Nature and Natural Resources. Recipient Distinguished Scholar award U. Maine, 1975. NSF fellow U. Conn., 1965; NASA fellow U. Conn., 1965-66. Fellow Zool. Soc. London, AAAS; mem. Am. Soc. Mammalogists (life), Australian Mammal Soc., Mammal Soc. Brit. Isles, N.Y. Acad. Scis., So. Calif. Acad. Scis., Nat. Rifle Assn. (life), Biol. Soc. Washington, Wildlife Soc., SAR (life), Soc. Mayflower Descs. (life), Explorers Club, Jaquar Drivers Club, Sigma Xi, Alpha Chi, Beta Beta Beta, Beta Kappa Chi, Phi Sigma, Phi Sigma Pi, Gamma Theta Upsilon, Kappa Delta Pi (Compatriot in Edn. award 1976). Editor-pub. Bat Research News, 1969-76. Contbr. numerous articles to profl. jours. Home: Cape Cod Hill New Sharon ME 04955 Office: Sci Research Annex U Maine Farmington ME 04938

MARTIN, ROBIN BRADLEY, broadcasting exec.; b. N.Y.C., Feb. 12, 1949; s. Alastair Bradley and Edith Godfrey (Park) M.; B.S. in Elec. Engring. cum laude, Rensselaer Poly. Inst., Troy, N.Y., 1972, M.S. in Communications, 1972. With Regional Broadcasters Group, Kingston, N.Y., 1966-74, exec. v.p., 1972-74; chief advanceman, dep. dir. scheduling to Vice Pres. Ford, 1974; staff asst. to President Ford, 1974-76; spl. asst. to chmn. Nat. Transp. Safety Bd., 1976-77; pres. bd. dirs. WOLF Broadcasting Service, Syracuse, 1976—, WRON, Inc., and WKGW/FM, Inc., Utica, N.Y., 1977—; pres., dir. Montachusett Broadcasting, Inc., Fitchburg, Mass., 1978—; v.p., dir. Telecommunications Cons., Inc., Kingston, 1969-74; adv. trustee Nat. Com. for Support Free Broadcasting, 1973-74. Regional coordinator N.E. N.Y. region Com. for Reelection of Pres., 1972; commr. Hudson River Valley Commn., 1974—; bd. dirs. Center Hudson River Valley, 1977-78; mem. council Rensselaer Poly. Inst., 1974—; dir. dist. 3, N.Y. State Young Republicans, 1973-74. Office: Suite 5D 210 E 53d St New York NY 10022

MARTIN, ROGER STOREY, state legis. research analyst; b. Medford, Mass., Jan. 26, 1932; s. Alexander W. and Katharine (Cole) M.; B.S. in Journalism, Boston U., 1953; m. Doreen Raynard, July 12, 1970; children—Karen, Stacy; children from previous marriage—Kathleen, Lisa, John Alexander. Reporter, Waltham (Mass.) News-Tribune, 1952, UP, 1953; reporter, sportswriter, columnist Worcester (Mass.) Telegram-Gazette, 1955-59; reporter New Bedford (Mass.) Standard-Times, 1960-64, polit. editor, columnist, 1964-73, editorial writer-editor, 1973-77; legis. research analyst Mass. State House, Boston, 1977—. Served to capt. AUS, 1953-55. Recipient news and feature writing awards AP, 1961, 69, UPI, 1964. Mem. Res. Officers Assn. (past chpt. pres.), Sigma Delta Chi. Home: 16 Vieira Ct South Dartmouth MA 02748 Office: Mass State House Boston MA 02133

MARTIN, RUTH MAY, nursing edn. adminstr.; b. Phila., Oct. 10, 1926; d. Clarence Reverdy and Erma Leona (Mutchler) Martin; R.N., Methodist Hosp. Sch. Nursing, 1948; student U. Pa., 1948-49; B.S., U. Cin., 1956, M.Ed., 1962. Staff nurse Meth. Hosp., Phila., 1948-49, Pa. Hosp., Phila., 1949-50, Cin. Gen. Hosp., 1950-52, Jewish Hosp., Cin., 1954-56; head nurse Cin. Gen. Hosp., 1952-54; instr. Jewish Hosp. Sch. Nursing, Cin., 1956-60, clin. coordinator, 1960-62, asst. dir., 1962-64; asst. dir. Capital City Sch. Nursing, Washington, 1964-68, asso. dir., 1968-72; asso. dir. nursing edn. D. C. Gen. Hosp., Washington, 1972—. Mem. Bowie Civic Assn., 1964-74. Mem. Am. Nurses Assn., Nat. League for Nursing, Am. Assn. Ret. Persons, Sigma Theta Tau. Republican. Presbyterian. Clubs: Nat. Travel, Club Internationale. Home: 3032 Belair Dr Bowie MD 20715 Office: DC Gen Hosp Washington DC 20003

MARTIN, THOMAS GEORGE, real estate appraiser; b. Tappan, N.Y., Aug. 31, 1935; s. Thomas J. and Wilma A. (Winstedt) M.; B.S., N.Y. U., 1958; LL.B., LaSalle Extension U., 1977; m. Alice J. Rea, Jan. 26, 1960; children—Teresa, Todd. Salesman, Frank T. Hurley, realtor, Spring Valley, N.Y. 1959; sr. partner Martin-Martin Real Estate Co., Valley Cottage, N.Y., 1960—; instr. real estate principles and appraising Rockland Community Coll., Suffern, N.Y., 1966—, Sullivan County Community Coll., Loch Sheldrake, N.Y., 1971-73, St. Thomas Aquinas Coll., 1972-74, Empire State Coll., Suffern, 1975, N.Y. State Grad. Realtors Inst., Ithaca, 1969-74; real estate broker Rockland County (N.Y.), 1959—. Pres. Valley Cottage PTA, 1963-65; bd. dirs. Rockland County Center for Phys. Handicapped. Mem. Appraisal Inst., Am. Inst. Real Estate Appraisers, 1974. Served as sgt., Signal Corps, U.S. Army, 1958-59, 61-62. Mem. Nat. Assn. of Realtors, N.Y. State Appraisers Soc. (editorial bd. 1972-75), Rockland County Soc. Real Estate Appraisers, Rockland County Bd. Realtors (pres. 1970-72), Realtors Nat. Mktg. Inst., Rockland County Rent Guidelines Bd. Lutheran. Home: 364A Kings Hwy Valley Cottage NY 10989 Office: 33 Route 303 Valley Cottage NY 10989

MARTIN, THOMAS GEORGE, III, health physicist; b. Boston, Jan. 14, 1931; s. Thomas George and Helen Celia (Cross) M.; B.S., Northeastern U., 1958; m. Beverly Ruth Curtis, May 20, 1951; children—Kathleen Martin Kearns, Dorothy Marie. Radiol. technologist Cancer Research Inst., Boston, 1954-58; head radiol. safety dept. Controls for Radiation Inc., Boston, 1958-62; radiochemist-health physicist Occupational Med. Service, Mass. Inst. Tech., Cambridge, 1962-63; radiation protection officer U.S. Army Natick (Mass.) Research and Devel. Command, 1963—; cons. in field. Served with AUS, 1951-54. Diplomate Am. Bd. Health Physics. Mem. Health Physics Soc., New Eng. Radiol. Physics Orgn., N.Y. Acad. Sci., Sigma Xi. Club: Southboro Rod and Gun. Home: 588 Winter St Framingham MA 01701 Office: US Army Natick Research and Devel Command Natick MA 01760

MARTIN, THOMAS VAN, satellite geodesist, computer scientist; b. Washington, Mar. 4, 1948; s. William Jennings and Sara Jane (Hendricks) M.; B.S. in Mech. Engring., U. Md., 1970; M.S. in Space Tech., Johns Hopkins, 1976. Analyst, EG and G/Washington Analytical Services Center, Inc., Wolf Research and Devel. Group, Washington, 1970-74, sr. scientist and mgr. sci. applications group, 1974—. Mem. Am. Geophys. Union, Pi Tau Sigma, Tau Beta Pi. Republican. Lutheran. Designed and programmed GEODYN Orbit and Geodetic Paramater Determination Program, 1971—. Home: 9418 Eldred Pl Seabrook MD 20801 Office: 6801 Kenilworth Ave Riverdale MD 20840

MARTIN, VERNON ANTHONY, realtor; b. Worcester, Mass., June 12, 1928; s. Lewis Orin and Anna (Sorel) M.; student Boston U., 1948-52; m. Yolanda Elso, Dec. 16, 1949; children—David, Karen, Cynthia, Michele. Pres., Vernon A. Martin, Inc., Lynn, Mass., 1952—; dir. for Mass. Realtors Nat. Inst.; tchr., lectr., cons. real estate. Bd. dirs. Jr. Achievement Eastern Mass., 1966-70, chmn. Greater Lynn, 1966; state dir. Am. Cancer Soc., 1966-69; mem. exec. bd. North area div. United Community Services, 1966-68; mem. Lynn Mayor's Advisory Com., 1968-69; bd. dirs. Greater Lynn chpt. ARC, 1966-68, Union Hosp., 66—. Served with U.S. Army, 1946-48. Named Realtor of Year Greater Lynn Bd. Realtors, 1969. Mem. Greater Lynn C. of C. (pres. 1969, del. U.S. C. of C. 1963-78), Greater Lynn Bd. Realtors (pres., dir. 1970), Internat. Real Estate Fedn. (Am. chpt.), Mass. Assn. Real Estate Bds. (dir.), Greater Boston, Greater Salem (dir. 1977-78), Rockingham (N.H.) bds. realtors, Republican. Office: 555 Boston St Lynn MA 01905

MARTINDALE, EDNA E., real estate co. exec.; b. N.Y.C., Jan. 10, 1942; d. Robert and Regina (Salami) Hallen; B.A., CUNY, 1964; M.B.A., SUNY, Fredonia, 1966; m. John W. Martindale, June 7, 1968; 1 son, John Simon. Real estate salesperson Smith Real Estate, Boston, 1966-70; broker, br. mgr. Riveler Realty, Brighton, Mass., 1970-73; owner, broker br. mgr. Riveler Realty Brighton, Mass., 1970-73; owner, broker LesCoel Realty, Cambridge, Mass., 1973—. Active Cambridge chpt. ARC; mem. Cambridge Bd. Edn., 1976—. Mem. Greater Boston Real Estate Bd., Cambridge C. of C. Democrat. Presbyterian. Club: Eastern Star. Address: 5 St Mary Rd Cambridge MA 02139

MARTINETTI, RAYMOND FREDERICK, psychologist; b. N.Y.C., Oct. 1, 1945; s. Raymond A. and Helen J. (Arzillo) M.; B.S., Coll. City N.Y., 1968; M.A., Fordham U., 1970; Ph.D., 1974; m. Rose Ann McKenna, June 22, 1968; children—Alana, Laura. Teaching fellow Fordham U., 1970-73; asst. prof. psychology Marywood Coll., Scranton, Pa., 1973-77, asso. prof., 1977—, chairperson dept., 1978—. Mem. Am. Psychol. Assn., AAUP, Am. Parapsychol. Research Found., Sigma Xi, Psi Chi. Roman Catholic. Author: College Testing and Study Techniques, 1977. Home: 417 Highland Ave RD 1 Clarks Summit PA 18411 Office: Marywood Coll PO Box 725 Scranton PA 18509

MARTINEZ, ELBA JOSEFA, physician; b. Ponce, P.R., Nov. 28, 1933; d. Antonio and Dolores (Colon) M.; B.S. cum laude, Catholic U. of P.R., 1955; B.S. cum laude, State U. N.Y., 1955; M.D. with excellence, U. P.R., 1959; m. Robert James Kirk, Mar. 11, 1967; 1 dau., Kathy. Intern, Harrisburg (Pa.) Hosp., 1959-60, resident in internal medicine, 1960-63; fellow in hematology The Cardeza Found. for Hematology Research, Thomas Jefferson U., Phila., 1963-64; clin. preceptor hematology and oncology Harrisburg Hosp., 1964-65; practice medicine specializing in internal medicine, Harrisburg, 1964-68, Silver Spring, Md., 1970-73, Potomac, Md., 1973—; hematologist Harrisburg Hosp., 1967-68; courtesy staff Washington Adventist Hosp., Takoma Park, Md., 1970—, Holy Cross Hosp., Silver Spring, Md., 1970—, Suburban Hosp., Bethesda, Md., 1973-75; acting asso. Suburban Hosp., Bethesda, 1975—; provisional active staff Washington Adventist Hosp., 1978—; med. officer Bur. of Hearings and Appeals, Social Security Adminstrn., HEW, 1969-75; physician adviser to Monntgomery County Profl. Standards Rev. Orgn., 1975-78; clin. asso. dept. family practice U. Md., 1975—. Bd. dirs. Montgomery County Med. Care Found., chairperson ops. com., 1976-78. Diplomate Am. Bd. Internal Medicine. Mem. A.C.P., Am., D.C. socs. internal medicine, Am. Soc. Hematology, Med. and Chirurg. Faculty Md., Montgomery County Med. Soc., AMA. Address: 8808 Hidden Hill Ln Potomac MD 20854

MARTINEZ, FERNANDO, translator, journalist; b. Tucuman, Argentina, Jan. 31, 1916; s. Melchor and Maria Luisa (Ungria) M.; diploma intermediate English, U. Popular, 1942; diploma advanced English, Inst. Argentino Estudios Ingleses, 1946; postgrad. N.Y. U., 1951-53. Translator lit. and tech. books Jackson, Inc., Emece Continental Service Editors, others, Buenos Aires, 1940-50; multilingual interpreter, translator City Bank, N.Y.C., 1952-53, U.S. Immigration Service, 1954; propr., dir. Iberia Translations, N.Y.C., 1955-63, Space Age Translations, W. Ger. 1968-76, N.Y.C., 1976—; interpreter Olympic Games, 1972; condr. world tours, lang. tchr., lectr., participant seminars. Recipient City medal Rüsselsheim, W. Ger. Mem. Deutsche-Amerikanischer Men's Club, Internat. Guides Club. Office: Space Age Translations care J R Longland 490 West End Ave Suite 2D New York City NY 10024*

MARTÍNEZ, RICHARD ISAAC, phys. chemist, govt. ofcl.; b. Havana, Cuba, Aug. 16, 1944; s. Joseph Louis and Susana (Nardea) M.; came to U.S., naturalized, 1951; B.Sc. in Chemistry, McGill U., Can., 1964; postgrad. San Diego State U., 1965-67; Ph.D. in Chemistry, U. Calif., Los Angeles, 1976. Lab. asst. DuPont of Can. Ltd., Maitland, 1962; teaching asst. dept. chemistry McGill U., Que., Can., 1964-65, San Diego State U., 1965-67; chemist Shell Chem. Co., Torrance, Calif., 1967-70; research chemist U. Calif., Los Angeles, 1971-76; NRC postdoctoral research asso. Nat. Bur. Standards, Washington, 1976-78, research chemist, 1978—. Mem. Am. Chem. Soc. Contbr. articles on reactions apposite to atmospheric chemistry to profl. jours. Established existence of dioxiranes. Office: A145 Chemistry National Bureau of Standards Washington DC 20234

MARTINEZ SOTO, WILLIAM E., hosp. adminstr.; b. Anasco, P.R., Oct. 13, 1930; s. Jesus Maria and Paula (Soto) Martinez; B.A., U. P.R., 1956; M.S., 1970; children—Hector E., Jose E., Carlos E. Coop. specialist Coop. Devel. Adminstrn., San Juan, P.R., 1956-62; exec. dir. Health Coop. of P.R., San Juan, 1962-67; asst. regional dir. Internat. Ladies Garment Workers Union, San Juan, 1967-72; asso. dir. Fordham Hosp., N.Y.C., 1973-76; asso. dir. North Central Bronx Hosp., Bronx, N.Y., 1976—. Mem. Neighborhood Assn. for P.R. Affairs, 1976—; v.p. Fedn. P.R. Vols., 1975—; pres. J.F.K. Ind. Democratic Club, 1976—. Served with USN, 1948-52. Mem. Am. Coll. Hosp. Adminstrs., Am. Hosp. Assn., Hosp. Exec. Assn. P.R., Hosp. Execs. Club N.Y. Democrat. Presbyterian.

MARTINI, CHARLES CONSTANTINE, ins. co. exec.; b. Phila., July 2, 1940; s. Louis Anthony and Elvira (Felizzi) M.; B.S. in Econ., Villanova U., 1962; M.B.A., U. Pa., 1964; m. children—Charles, Jason. Research asso. Chilton Research Services, Radnor, Pa., 1963-66; sr. mktg. analyst Standard Pressed Steel Co., Jenkintown, Pa., 1965-66; supr. consumer mktg. research Philco-Ford Corp., Phila., 1966-69; dir. mktg. services Colonial Pa. Group, Phila., 1969-74; asst. sec. mktg. Ins. Co. N. Am., Phila., 1974-78; dir. mktg. N.F.I., 1978—; tchr. Villanova U., 1971-78; Phila. Community Coll., 1976; cons. Delta Mktg. Research, Horsham, Pa., 1975—. Mem. Am. Mktg. Assn., Mktg. Research Assn., Soc. Ins. Research (Phila.), Am. Mktg. Assn. (dir.). Roman Catholic. Clubs: Toastmaster (Upper Darby) (pres., 1968-73). Contbr. articles, papers in field to profl. jours. and assns. Home: 113 Laurel Ln Broomall PA 19008 Office: 8049 West Chester Pike Upper Darby PA 19082

MARTINI, JOHN MELVIN, educator; b. Sauk Rapids, Minn., Aug. 17, 1903; s. John and Alicia (Dunn) M.; B.E., St. Cloud (Minn.) State U., 1934; grad. student Pa. State, U. Minn., U. Md., Johns Hopkins U.; m. Florence K. Dunn, Oct. 26, 1935 (dec.); 1 son, Melvin Robert; m. 2d, Mary R. O'heir, Dec. 30, 1968 (dec.). Salesman, Standard Oil Co. (Ind.), 1925-28; tchr., athletic coach pub. schs., Fairchance, Pa., 1930-34; tchr. evening sch. St. Cloud Tech. High Sch., 1934-35; engr. Greiner Engring. Co., Ft. Meade, Md., 1940-41; tchr. Laplata and Indian Head, Md., 1935-41, Balt. pub. schs., 1941-69; engr. Bethlehem Steel Co., Balt., summers 1944-45; engr. Md. Dry Dock Co., summers 1951—; master gen. electrician Baltimore County; notary public, real eatate salesman, 1966—. Mem. Real Estate Bd. Greater Balt., 1968—. Counselor, Boy Scouts Am., 1923—; v.p. Parkville Library Assn., 1961-62, 63—, pres., 1962-63, 74—; organizer, permanent pres. ex-officio Balt. County Libraries Assn., 1963—; mem. Md. Minute Men, 1942-45; pres. PTA, Parkville, 1943-44, 46-47; capt. Civil Def., 1945-52; mem. East Parkville Community Assn., 1972—; dir. Parkville Recreation Council, 1972-73. Democratic precinct exec. 14th dist. Balt. County, 1962-72; mem. 11th-14th Dist. Dem. Club. Mem. Balt. County Elec. Contractors Assn. (charter), Balt. City Pub. Sch. Tchrs. Assn., N.E.A., Md. Tchrs. Assn., Nat. Ret. Tchrs. Assn. Lion (sec. Parkville 1963—). Club: Eastern Yacht. Home: 7818 Bagley Ave Baltimore MD 21234

MARTINO, ROCCO LEONARD, mgmt. cons.; b. Toronto, Ont., Can., June 25, 1929; s. Domenic and Josephine (DiGiulio) M.; B.Sc., U. Toronto, 1951, M.A., 1952; Ph.D., Inst. Aerospace Studies, 1955; m. Barbara L. D'lorio, Sept. 2, 1961; children—Peter Domenic, Joseph Alfred, Paul Gerard, John Francis. Dir., Univac Computing Service Center, Toronto, 1956-59; pres. Mauchly Assos. Can. Ltd., Toronto, 1959-62, v.p. Mauchly Assos., Inc., Ft. Washington, Pa., 1959-61; mgr. advanced systems Olin Mathieson Chem. Corp., N.Y.C., 1962-64; dir. advanced computer systems Booz, Allen & Hamilton, N.Y.C., 1964-65; pres., chmn. bd. Info. Industries, Inc. and subs.'s, Wayne, Pa., 1965-70; chmn. bd., chief exec. officer XRT, Inc., Broomall, Pa., 1970—; asso. prof. math. U. Waterloo, 1959-62, prof. engring., dir. Inst. Systems and Mgmt. Engring., 1964-65; adj. asso. prof. N.Y. U., 1963-64, adj. prof. math., 1964-65, 66; lectr. on computers mgmt.; chmn. Gov. Ill. Task Force, 1970-71, Ill. Bd. Higher Edn. Task Force, 1971-72, Computer-Use Task Force FCC, 1972-73, Computer-Use Planning Task Force U.S. Postal Service, 1973-74. Mem. Assn. Computing Machinery, Ops. Research Soc. Am., Porfl. Engrs. Ont., Computing Soc. Can. Clubs: K.C., Lions, Overbrook Golf and Country, Yacht of Sea Isle City (commodore 1973-74), Commodores; S.Jerry Yacht Racing. Author books, most recent being: Resources Management, 1968; Dynamic Costing, 1968; Project Management, 1968; Information Management: The Dynamics of MIS, 1968; MIS-Management Information Systems, 1969; Decision Patterns, 1969; Methodology of MIS, 1969; Personnel Information Systems, 1969; Integrated Manufacturing Systems, 1972; contbr. numerous articles on mgmt., computers and planning in profl. publs.; designer, developer application program generator computer system, 1974-75. Home: 512 Watch Hill Rd Villanova PA 19085 Office: 85 Lawrence Rd Broomall PA 19008

MARTIS, JEROME MICHAEL, mech. engr.; b. Plymouth, Pa., Nov. 11, 1920; s. Michael Charles and Catherine Lillian (Khristman) M.; B.S. in Mec. Engring., Bucknell U., 1944; postgrad. Mass. Inst. Tech., summer 1953; m. Aileen Verna Beckley, July 29, 1945; children—Jerome Vincent, David Jerome. Sr. cons. engr., spl. projects div. N.Y. Engring. Office, ACF Industires, N.Y.C., 1945-57; sr. mech. engr., sr. scientist space communications and missile and surface radar RCA Astro div., RCA Missile and Surface Radar div., 1958-66; sr. cons. engr., Berwick Pa., 1967—; spl. research in advanced radiation tech., computers. Served with U.S. Army, 1942-43. Recipient spl. commendation NASA, 1964. Registered profl. engr., Pa. Mem. Nat., Pa. socs. profl. engrs., Profl. Engrs. in Pvt. Practice. Republican. Roman Catholic. Address: 618 E 10th St Berwick PA 18603

MARTON, EMERY, lawyer; b. Nasna, Rumania, Aug. 11, 1922; s. Julius and Esther (Fritsch) M.; brought to U.S., 1924, naturalized, 1930; student Queens Coll., 1940-42; B.S., U. Mich., 1947; M.S., Harvard, 1948; LL.B., N.Y. U., 1953, J.D., 1968; m. Marian C. Pruden, Dec. 25, 1948; children—Peter D., Elise J., Eric M., Susan A. Admitted to N.Y. bar, 1954. Instr., Newark Coll. Engring., 1948-51; engr. Belco Indsl. Equipment, Paterson, N.J., 1951-53; asst. gen. counsel Dorr Oliver, Inc., Stamford, Conn., 1953-63; v.p., corporate sec., house counsel Foster Grant Co., Inc., Leominster, Mass., 1963-77; now gen. counsel Am. Hoechst Corp., Somerville, N.J. Served with AUS, 1942-46. Mem. Am. Bar Assn., N.Y. Acad. Scis., Harvard Engring. Soc. Home: 40 Montadale Dr Princeton NJ 08540 Office: Route 202-206 N Somerville NJ 08876

MARTS, EDITH HAUGHTON, data processing services adminstr.; b. Pitts., Apr. 19, 1941; d. Harvey James and Loma Ida (Freudenberger) Haughton; B.A. in Bus. Edn., Grove City (Pa.) Coll., 1963; postgrad. Duquesne U., 1980—; m. James Merle Marts, Jan. 6, 1968. Part-time summer worker IBM, Pitts., 1959-63, systems engr., 1963-65; sr. analyst Blue Cross of Western Pa., Pitts., 1965-68; data processing mgr. West Pa. Adminstrn., Pitts., 1968-75; dir. data processing services Allegheny Gen. Hosp., Pitts., 1975—; instr. computer programming Computer Systems Inst.; cons. Carpenters Dist. Council of Western Pa.; speaker at seminars and before various bus. groups. Mem. bd., past pres. Women's Club of Grove City Coll. Mem. Assn. Systems Mgmt., Hosp. Fin. Mgmt. Assn., U.S. Senatorial Club. Republican. Lutheran. Office: 320 E North Ave Pittsburgh PA 15212

MARTY, FREDERICK NICHOLAS, physician; b. Syracuse, N.Y., Mar. 20, 1906; s. Frederick and Bertha Louise (Ehrmantraut) M.; A.B., Syracuse U., 1929, M.D., 1932; m. Hannah Virginia Bastable, June 22, 1938; children—Carol, Elizabeth, Frederick Stephen. Intern, Univ. Hosp., Syracuse, 1932-33; resident in medicine Fifth Avenue Hosp., N.Y.C., 1934-35; practice medicine specializing in internal medicine, Syracuse, 1936—; dir. univ. health service Syracuse U., 1948-72, asso. prof. clin. medicine, 1950-78, prof. health and preventive medicine, 1951-72; sr. attending physician Syracuse Meml. Hosp., 1961-78; staff physician Syracuse VA Hosp., 1972—; sec. Central N.Y. Blue Shield, 1945-61; co-founder Syracuse Regional Red Cross Blood Bank. Diplomate Am. Bd. Internal Medicine. Fellow A.C.P., Am. Coll. Health Assn., Royal Soc. Health, AMA; mem. Am. Acad. Allergy, N.Y. Trudeau Soc., Am. Soc. Internal Medicine, AAAS, Phi Kappa Psi. Republican. Episcopalian. Home: 326 Berkeley Dr Syracuse NY 13210 Office: 800 Irving Ave Syracuse NY 13210

MARVIN, JOHN GEORGE, clergyman, ch. orgn. exec.; b. Summit, N.Y., May 8, 1912; s. George and Caroline (Whitman) M.; B.S., Davidson Coll., 1933; Th.B., Princeton, 1936; D.D., Coll. Emporia, 1964; LL.D., Tarkio Coll., 1964; m. Elizabeth Anne Wheater, June 30, 1944; children—Caroline Wheater (Dorney), Elizabeth Anne, Martha Jane, Frances Alice. Ordained to ministry Presbyterian Ch., 1936; pastor, Windsor, N.Y., 1936-37, Montrose, Pa., 1937-44, Lewistown, Pa., 1944-52, Denton, Tex., 1952-61; presbytery exec. Greater Kansas City, Mo., 1961-65; pastor 1st Presbyn. Ch., Bartlesville, Okla., 1965-69; sr. minister Chevy Chase Presbyn. Ch., Washington, 1969-77, pastor emeritus, 1978—. Mem. exec. com. Pa. Council Chs., 1949-52, Tex. Council Chs., 1953-61; mem. exec. com., long range chmn. Greater Kansas City Council Chs., 1962-65; chmn. campus Christian Life Tex. Synod, 1958-61; chmn. nat. mission Pa. Synod, 1949-52; sec. nomination com. Gen. Assembly U.P. Ch., 1955-58, chmn. com. on baptized children, 1969-70, mem. com. of nine on synod bounderies, 1970-72; bd. dirs. Midwest Christian Counseling Center, 1963-69, Presbyn. Homes of Okla., Inc., 1966-69; mem. jud. commn. Synod of Okla.-Ark., 1966-69; mem. strategy com. Bd. Nat. Missions, 1968-70. Bd. dirs. Tarkio Coll., 1961-67; bd. dirs. Westminster Found., Pa. State U., 1945-52, N. Tex. State U., 1952-61; mem. ministerial relations com. Nat. Capital Union Presbytery, 1973—; bd. visitors Warren Wilson Coll. Mem. Beta Theta Pi. Republican. Rotarian. Contbr. articles to religious publs. Home: 14500 Elmhan Ct Silver Spring MD 20906

MARXE, MAXWELL, book mfg. cons.; b. N.Y.C., Feb. 29, 1912; s. Jack and Fanny (Goodman) M.; M.A., Columbia U., 1934; B.S., Bklyn. Coll., 1932; m. Sara Gollub, Feb. 21, 1935; children—Austin, Joan Marxe Bogdanoff. Supr. advt. makeup N.Y. Herald Tribune, 1932-45; v.p., dir. mfg. Pocket Books, Simon & Schuster, Inc., N.Y.C., 1945-75, cons., 1975—; pres. United Typographers, Inc.; tchr., cons. in field. Home: 151-17 26th Ave Flushing NY 11354 Office: Room 501 39-01 Main St Flushing NY 11354

MARZANO, ALBERT, artist; b. Phila., Aug. 22, 1919; s. Joseph and Philomena (Ricci) M.; student Phila. Graphic Sketch Club, 1934-39, Phila. Plastic Club, 1935-39; m. Gilda D'Ettorre, Jan. 29, 1944; children—Anton Gene, Arturo B. Designer-cons. Phila. Assn. Blind, 1953-56; art cons., graphic designer Phila. Pub. Health Dept., 1958-60; art dir., cons. J. Conninghan Cox Agy., Bala-Cynwyd, Pa., 1958—, Benn Assn. Agy., Phila., 1960—. Tchr. drawing, painting Sons of Italy in Am., Phila., 1965-70; exhibited in one-man shows in Phila., 1961, 64, 70, 71, 74, 75, 76, 77. Served with C.E., AUS, 1943-47. Recipient Gold medal awards Phila. Art Dirs. Club, 1954, 55, 56, Gold medal (fine art) Haddonfield (N.J.) Art Center, 1959, Gold medal (fine art) Nat. Soc. Painters in Casein, N.Y.C., 1961. Mem. Watercolor Club Phila., Phila. Art Alliance, Woodmere Art Gallery. Painted murals for Pub. Health Dept. Phila., 1967, 69. Home: 1809 Delancey Pl Philadelphia PA 19103 Office: 1949 Locust St Philadelphia PA 19103

MARZOCCO, LEONARD JOSEPH, real estate exec.; b. Bklyn., Dec. 17, 1942; s. Joseph and Rose (Parisi) M.; B.S., Poly. Inst. N.Y., 1964; m. Shelby Lynn Moore, 1972; 1 son, Joseph. Bldg. automation engr. Johnson Service Co., Long Island City, N.Y., 1966-70; real estate broker Breslin Realty, East Meadow, N.Y., 1971-75; dir. real estate and devel. Stackler & Frank, Hicksville, N.Y., 1975—, Mid Island Fashion Plaza, 1975—; real estate cons. Nathans Famous of Fla. Served to 1st lt. C.E., U.S. Army, 1964-66. Mem. Internat. Council of Shopping Centers, L.I. Assn. Commerce and Industry, L.I. Bd. Realtors. Home: 913 Park Ave Huntington NY 11743 Office: 3588 Mid Island Plaza Hicksville NY 11802

MASAOKA, MIKE MASARU, cons.; b. Fresno, Calif., Oct. 15, 1915; s. Eijiro and Haruye (Goto) M.; B.A., U. Utah, 1937; m. Etsu Mineta, Feb. 14, 1943; children—Midori Amano, Michael. Nat. sec. Japanese Am. Citizens League, 1941-43, Washington rep., 1945-72; pres. Masaoka-Ishikawa and Assos., Washington, 1953—; chmn. Impact Group, Inc., N.Y.C., 1965—; dir. Bank of Tokyo Trust Co. Mem. nationalities div. Democratic Nat. Com., 1948-76; cons. Pres.'s Com. on Civil Rights, 1948; observer Japanese Peace Conf., 1951; pres. Niesi Lobby, 1970—; officer Consumer Edn. Council on World Trade, 1970—. Served with U.S. Army, 1943-45. Decorated Legion of Merit, Bronze Star; Italian War Cross; recipient citations State of Hawaii, 1959, Los Angeles, 1967, Calif. State Legislature, 1970, White House, 1970; recipient Order of Rising Sun, Japan, 1968, Yamagata award Chgo. Japanese Am. Assn., 1940; named Japanese American of Year Nat. Japanese Am. Citizens League, 1950. Mem. Japan-Am. Soc. Washington (chmn. exec. com. 1964—), Am. Japanese Trade Com. (chmn. 1968—). Clubs: Internat., Nat. Press. Home: 5406 Uppingham St Chevy Chase MD 20015 Office: Suite 520 900 17th St NW Washington DC 20006

MASAPOLLO, WILLIAM MARIO, finance exec.; b. Phila., Oct. 7, 1937; s. Gaetano and Assunta Rosemary (Belmonte) M.; B.S., La Salle Coll., 1962; M.B.A., Drexel U., 1974; m. Patricia Marie O'Donoghue, May 3, 1969; children—Paul, Deirdre. Sr. auditor Arthur Andersen & Co., Phila., 1962-66; v.p.-controller Aldon Industries Inc., Concordville, Pa., 1966-71; v.p. fin. and ops., treas. Frances Denney Inc., Phila., 1971-73; v.p. fin. and planning IU Conversion Systems Inc., Phila., 1973-76; v.p. fin. Nat. Bottle Corp., 1976—. Served with U.S. Army, 1955-58. C.P.A., Pa. Mem. Greater Phila. C. of C., Pa. (accounting award 1962), Am. insts. C.P.A.'s, Alpha Epsilon. Club: Union League (Phila.). Home: 385 Contention Ln Berwyn PA 19312 Office: 1 Bala Cynwyd Plaza Bala Cynwyd PA 19004

MASCARI, FRANK, accountant; b. Paterson, N.J., Jan. 28, 1920; s. Edward and Mary M. Mascari; B.S., Fordham U., 1941; LL.B., John Marshall Law Sch., 1948; m. Phyllis Petrocine, Oct. 23, 1948; children—Edward, Charles, Elizabeth. Asst. controller Am. Fgn. Ins., N.Y.C., 1950-52; controller Wm. H. McGee, Inc., N.Y.C., 1954-67, Parker & Co. Internat. Inc., N.Y.C., 1967-69; dir. adminstrn.-finance, controller United Way Westchester, Inc., White Plains, N.Y., 1969—; adj. asst. prof. accounting Mgmt. Inst., N.Y. U., 1961-68; adj. asst. prof. Pace Coll., N.Y.C., 1968; instr. accounting Am. Inst. Banking, 1970-71; instr. finance and accounting Mercy Coll., 1976-77. Served to capt. AUS, 1941-45; ETO. C.P.A., N.Y., N.J. Mem. Am. Inst. C.P.A.'s, N.Y. State Soc. C.P.A.'s (chmn. careers com. Westchester chpt. 1967, chmn. data processing com. 1968, mem. com. accounting for non-profit orgns.), N.Y. State Assn. Professions, Nat. Assn. Accountants (socio-econ. dir. 1972; named Member of Yr. 1972; dir. communications 1973-74, v.p. edn. 1974-75, v.p. adminstrn. 1975-76, named most valuable dir. 1973-74), Westchester Personnel Mgmt. Assn. Club: Lion (past dir.). Home: 8 Larchmont St Ardsley NY 10502 Office: 158 Westchester Ave White Plains NY 10601

MASER, FREDERICK ERNEST, clergyman; b. Rochester, N.Y., Feb. 26, 1908; s. Herman A. and Clara (Krumm) M.; A.B., Union Coll., Schenectady, 1930; M.A., Princeton U., 1933, B.Th., 1933; D.D., Dickinson Coll., 1957; LL.D. (hon.), McKendree Coll., 1964; m. Anne S. Spangeberg, Aug. 3, 1933; m. 2d, Mary L. Jarden, Dec. 25, 1959. Ordained to ministry Meth. Ch., 1933; pastor Alice Focht Meml. Ch., Birdsboro, Pa., 1933-38, Central Ch., Frankford, Phila., 1938-45, St. James Ch., Olney, Phila., 1945-53; dist. supt. N.W. dist. Phila. Meth. Ann. Conf., 1953-58; pastor Old St. George's Ch., Phila., 1958-67, on sabbatical leave, Europe, 1967-68; acting dean students Conwell Sch. Theology, 1968-69; dir. pub. relations Eastern Pa. Conf. United Meth. Ch., 1969-72; exec. sec. World Meth. Hist. Soc., 1971-74; cons. commn. on archives and history United Meth. Ch.,

1974—; Tipple lectr. Drew U., Madison, N.J., 1977; rep. from N.E. Jurisdiction to TV Radio and Film Commn. Meth. Ch., 1952; exec. com. Am. Hist. Socs. of Meth. Ch., 1952; vice chmn. N.E. Jurisdictional Hist. Socs., 1948; chmn. div. evangelism Pa. Council Chs., 1953-58; mem.-at-large TV, Radio and Film Commn. Meth. Ch., 1960-64; del. Phila. Ann. Conf. to Jurisdictional Conf. of Meth. Ch., 1952; leader ministerial del. to Gen. Conf. Meth. Ch., Mpls., 1956; del. 9th World Conf. of Methodism, Lake Junaluska, 1956, 10th Conf., Oslo, 1961, 12th Conf., Denver, 1971, 13th Conf., Dublin, 1976; dir. pub. relations Phila. Meth. ann. conf., 1961-68; exec. sec. World Meth. Hist. Soc., 1971-74. Trustee George Ruck Trust; mem. adv. council Wesley Theol. Sem., Washington, 1960-72. Recipient St. George's Gold Medal award for distinguished service to Meth. Ch.; citation Temple U., 1971. Mem. Pa. Acad. Fine Arts (adv. council), Colonial Phila. Hist. Soc. (dir. 1956-64), Ch. History Soc., Jedidiah Smith Soc., Phi Alpha. Clubs: Union League, Philobiblon, Alpha, Peale, (Phila.); Mfrs. Golf and Country. Author: The Dramatic Story of Early American Methodism, 1965; The History of Methodism in Central Pennsylvania, 1971; Richard Allen, 1976; editor Meth. History, 1971-75; editor-in-chief Jour. Joseph Pilmore; editorial bd., author History American Methodism, 1964, Ency. World Methodism, 1974; contbr. articles to religious jours. Home: Apt 402 Cambridge Philadelphia PA 19144 Office: 1701 Arch St Philadelphia PA 19103

MASHECK, JOSEPH DANIEL, editor, art critic and historian; b. N.Y.C., Jan. 19, 1942; s. Joseph Anthony and Dorothy Anna (Cahill) M.; A.B., Columbia U., 1963, M.A., 1965, Ph.D., 1973. Instr. in art history Barnard Coll., Columbia U., 1971-73, asst. prof. art history, 1973—; editor Artforum Mag., N.Y.C., 1977—. Nat. Endowment for Arts art critics fellow, 1972-73, 75-76; John Simon Guggenheim Meml. Found. fellow, 1977. Mem. AAUP, Internat. Assn. Art Critics, Soc. Fellows in Humanities. Roman Catholic. Editor, contbg. author: Marcel Duchamp in Perspective, 1975; contbr. numerous articles, revs. to profl. publs. Office: Artforum Mag 667 Madison Ave New York NY 10021

MASISAK, DONALD JOSEPH, environ. planner; b. Reynoldsville, Pa., Mar. 10, 1946; s. Stephen Joseph and Angeline Marie (Alvetro) M.; student Mansfield State Coll., 1968-69; B.S., Indiana U. of Pa., 1972; postgrad. Pa. State U., 1976; student Nat. Rural Devel. Leaders Sch., 1976; m. Marcia Jean Miklos, Nov. 29, 1969; children—Lisa Ann, Jeffrey Paul. Phys. planner N. Central Pa. Regional Planning and Devel. Commn., Ridgway, 1972-75, project coordinator, 1975-76, program dir., 1976—. Mem. Ridgway Citizens Adv. Com., N.W. Pa. Environ. Health Task Force; chmn. N.W. Pa. Regional Rural Devel. Com., 1978-79; chmn. headwaters resource Conservation and Devel. Exec. Council, 1978-79. Served with 3d Armored div. U.S. Army, 1965-67. W.K. Kellogg Found. fellow, 1975-76. Mem. Nat. Water Pollution Control Assn., Pa. Environ. Council, Pa. Vector Control Assn., Alternative Waste Water Assn. Democrat. Roman Catholic. Home: 301 Ash St Ridgway PA 15853 Office: 122 Center St Ridgway PA 15853

MASKALERIS, STEPHEN NICHOLAS, lawyer; b. Newark, June 23, 1927; s. Nicholas S. and Kaliope (Pappas) M.; B.S. in Accounting, Seton Hall U., 1949; LL.B., Rutgers U., 1953; m. Corinne Pappas, Dec. 27, 1953; children—Carol Christine, Susan Corinne. Admitted to N.J. bar, 1953, U.S. Ct. Appeals 3d Circuit bar, 1963; U.S. Supreme Ct. bar, 1957; asso. firm Van Riper and Belmont, Newark, 1953-69; prin. firm Stephen N. Maskaleris and Assos., Newark and Athens, Greece, 1969—, Maskaleris & Berowitz, Morristown, N.J., 1977—. Lectr., Inst. continuing Legal Edn., Rutgers U., 1962—. Project chmn. Indigent Defender Project, Essex County, 1964; spl. rate counsel N.J. Pub. Utilities Commn.; arbitor Am. Arbitration Assn. Served with USAAF, 1944-46. Winner Personal Finance Competition, Conf. on Personal Finance Law, Am. Bar Assn., 1963. Mem. N.J. (chmn. jr. sect. 1959-61, trustee 1961-62, gen. council 1970—, chmn. pub. defender study com. 1978), Essex County, Morris County, Am. (chmn. jr. bar conf. client's security fund com. 1961-62, co-reporter spl. com. on def. of indigent persons accused of crime 1963-64, chmn. lawyers relationship com. econ. of law sect. 1978), Fed. bar assns., Advocate Soc., Comml. Law League Am., Am. Judicature Soc., Nat. Assn. Def. Lawyers in Criminal Cases, Assn. Trial Lawyers Am. (v.p. N.J. br. 1971-73, exec. council 1973—), Am. Arbitration Assn. Mem. Greek Orthodox Ch. (trustee 1949-50). Author: (with others) Defense of the Poor in Criminal Cases in American State Courts, 1965; Defending Persons Accused of Crime, 1966; Branch Offices of Lawyers, 1978; Branch Office Check List, 1978. Home: 2 Farley Rd Short Hills NJ 07078 Office: 744 Broad St Newark NJ 07102 also 30 Court St Morristown NJ also 23 Amerikis Athens Greece

MASLEY, PETER MICHAEL, physician; b. Clifton, N.J., Mar. 16, 1926; s. Michael Andrew and Antonina (Wujcicka) M.; A.B., Syracuse U., 1948; M.S., N.C. State Coll., 1951; M.D., N.Y. Med. Coll., 1955; student U. Chgo., 1945; m. Joan Marie Elso, Nov. 25, 1970. Research asst. N.C. State Coll., 1949-51; intern St. Mary's Hosp., Passaic, N.J., 1955-56; resident St. Vincent's Hosp., N.Y.C., 1956-59; practice medicine specializing in internal medicine, Clifton, 1959—; mem. staff, chmn. dept. medicine St. Mary's Hosp. Served with AUS, 1944-46. Diplomate Am. Bd. Internal Medicine. Fellow A.C.P.; mem. AMA, N.Y. Acad. Scis., AAAS, Am. Diabetes Soc., N.J. Acad. Medicine, Phi Kappa Phi, Sigma Xi. Contbr. articles to profl. jours. Home: 109 Churchill Dr Clifton NJ 07013 Office: 1050 Clifton Ave Clifton NJ 07013

MASLONA, PAUL MARK, chemist; b. Syracuse, N.Y., May 9, 1941; s. Stanley Paul and Sylvia Ann (Kruczkowski) M.; B.A. in Chemistry, Syracuse U., 1963; M.S. in Inorganic Chemistry, U. Dayton, 1966; m. Sandra Lee Zavoy, June 27, 1964; children—Mark, Michele. Chemist, Eastman Kodak Co., Rochester, N.Y., 1967—, sect. supr., Indsl. Lab., 1972—; faculty Rochester Inst. Tech., part-time, 1971—. Served to capt. USAF, 1963-67. Mem. Soc. Applied Spectroscopy, Soc. Photog. Engrs., Am. Soc. Quality Control. Roman Catholic. Home: 310 Heritage Dr Rochester NY 14615 Office: Indsl Lab Kodak Park Eastman Kodak Co Rochester NY 14650

MASLOWE, SHERWIN ALLAN, applied mathematician; b. Detroit, Oct. 23, 1938; s. Percy Arthur and Belle Teresa (Kessler) M.; B.S. in Mech. Engring., Wayne State U., Detroit, 1961; M.S., U. Calif., Los Angeles, 1965, Ph.D., 1970; m. Sheryl A. Weiss, Dec. 22, 1968 (div. Apr. 1974); 1 dau., Lisa A. Asso. engr. Boeing Co., 1961-62; teaching asst. aero. scis. U. Calif., Berkeley, 1962-63; sr. propulsion engr. Lockheed Co., 1963-70; instr. applied math. Mass. Inst. Tech., 1970-72; mem. faculty McGill U., Montreal, 1972—, asso. prof. math., 1976—; cons. to industry. Guggenheim fellow, 1978-79. Mem. Soc. Indsl. and Applied Math. Author articles on clear air turbulence, stability of stratified fluids, stability of rotating flows. Office: Burnside Hall McGill Univ Montreal PQ H3A 2K6 Canada

MASLYAR, GEORGE ANDREW, III, geophysicist; b. Plymouth, Ind., July 2, 1946; s. George Andrew and Phyllis June (Hoffman) M.; B.S. in Engring. Sci., Purdue U., 1968; M.S. in Physics, U. Md., 1974; doctoral student Johns Hopkins U., 1976—; m. Mary Jane Wright, June 8, 1970. Instr. mech. engring. and physics U. Asmara, Ethiopia, 1969-71; instr. physics U. Md., College Park, 1973-74; analyst, geophysicist in measurements, evaluation br. gravitational and magnetic field studies NASA Goddard Space Flight Center, Greenbelt, Md., 1974—. Served with U.S. Army, 1968-72. Mem. Am. Inst. Physics, Am. Phys. Soc. (mem. various divs.), Tau Beta Pi, Sigma Gamma Tau, Sigma Pi Sigma. Club: Goddard Chess. Contbr. articles to profl. jours. Home: 3941 Tynewick Dr Silver Spring MD 20906 Office: 10210 Greenbelt Rd Seabrook MD 20801

MASNICK, JEFFREY LEE, hosp. adminstr.; b. New Kensington, Pa., Feb. 12, 1943; s. Ignatius Anthony and Cloah Berlene (Moorhead) M.; B.A., Purdue U., 1965; M.B.A., U. Pitts., 1973, M.S., 1975; m. Sue Ann Baldwin, Apr. 4, 1970; children—Carey Ann, Jeffrey Allen. Dir. food service Broughton Food Services Inc., Bellermine-Ursuline U., Louisville, 1970-71; financial adminstr. Western Psychiat. Inst. and Clinic, Pitts., 1974-77, asst. dir-financial adminstr., 1977—; lectr. in field. Controller's com. Univ. Health Center Pitts., 1974—; bd. dirs. Arsenal Family and Children's Center. Served with USNR, 1966-69. Recipient Am. Legion award, 1958; Merit scholar, 1961-65. Mem. Pa., Am. hosp. assns., Hosp. Financial Mgmt. Assn., Pa. Assn. Notaries, Alumni Assn. Health Adminstrn., Sigma Chi. Democrat. Roman Catholic. Home: 116 Wincanton Dr New Kensington PA 15068 Office: 3811 O'Hara St Pittsburgh PA 15261

MASON, DONALD FRANK, accountant; b. Whitefield, N.H., Apr. 4, 1937; s. Homer Delphis and Theresa May M.; diploma Pierce Bus. Coll., 1957; m. Shirley Ann Baldi, July 15, 1961. Bookkeeper, Concord (N.H.) Dairy, Inc., 1955-59; partner John E. Rich & Co. Accountants, Concord, 1959—. Past treas. Concord ABC Program. Served with U.S. Army N.C., 1959. Mem. N.H., Nat. (certified in accounting, taxation) assns. pub. accountants, N.H. Golf Assn. (v.p.). Republican. Roman Catholic. Clubs: Concord Country, Bow Rotary. Home: Red Pine Dr Bow NH 03301 Office: 194A Pleasant St Concord NH 03301

MASON, ELI, accountant; b. N.Y.C., Nov. 16, 1920; s. David and Jennie (Ullman) M.; B.B.A., Baruch Coll., 1940, D.H.L., 1978; m. Claire Rosen, Aug. 9, 1942; children—Judith Ann Mason Berger, Nina Felice Mason Hirshfeld. Controller, Hydrawmatic Machine Corp., N.Y.C., 1943-45; sr. partner firm Mason & Co., N.Y.C., 1946—; pres. Found. Accounting Edn., Inc., 1973-74; mem. N.Y. State Bd. Pub. Accountancy, 1972—. Chmn. bd. advisers Baruch Coll., 1975—; trustee Baruch Coll. Fund, 1969—. Recipient Distinguished Service award U.S. Dept. Labor, 1975; Distinguished Service award Baruch Coll., 1974. C.P.A., N.Y. Mem. Am. Inst. C.P.A.'s (v.p. 1967-68), N.Y. State Soc. C.P.A.'s (pres. 1972-73), Am. Accounting Assn., Am. Arbitration Assn., Fin. Mgmt. Assn., Beta Gamma Sigma, Beta Alpha Psi. Office: 75 Rockefeller Plaza New York City NY 10019

MASON, FRANCIS SCARLETT, JR., museum adminstr., author; b. Jacksonville, Fla., Sept. 9, 1921; s. Francis Scarlett and Hattie Troupe (Spencer) M.; A.B., St. Johns Coll., Annapolis, Md., 1943; m. Patricia Millicent Michaels, Oct. 11, 1952; children—Spencer, Leslie Scarlett. Tutor, St. Johns Coll., 1946-47; info. specialist Internat. Broadcasting div. Dept. State, N.Y.C., 1948-54; cultural affairs officer U.S. embassies, Belgrade, Yugoslavia, London, Eng., 1954-65, asst. counselor for pub. affairs, London, 1959-60; chief East-West Exhbns., USIA, Washington, 1965-66, policy officer, office asst. dir. Europe, 1966; with Fgn. Service Inst., 1966-67; pres. Expts. in Art and Tech., 1968, mem. advisory council, 1970; asst. to pres. Steuben Glass Co., N.Y.C., 1968-75, mgr. market devel. and spl. projects, 1972-75; asst. dir. Pierpont Morgan Library, N.Y.C., 1975—. Pres. Martha Graham Center Contemporary Dance, 1974-75, chmn., 1975-76; v.p. Dance Research Found., 1969. Bd. dirs. St. John's Coll., Oratorio Soc. N.Y., Cunningham Dance Found., 1971-74, Am. Friends Covent Garden, Gallery Assn. N.Y., 1976; bd. dirs. N.Y. Studio Sch. Drawing, Painting and Sculpture, chmn., 1970-74; bd. dirs. Com. for Dance Collection N.Y. Pub. Library, chmn., 1970-72. Served to lt. (j.g.) USNR, 1943-46. Mem. Archtl. Assn. London. Author: (with George Balanchine) Balanchine's Complete Stories of the Great Ballets, 1954, 68, 77, 101 Stories of the Great Ballets, 1975, Balanchine's Festival of Ballet, 1978; editor: Steuben, 50 Years of American Glassmaking, 1974; Balanchine, The Early Years, 1976; contbr. Ency. of Dance and Ballet, 1977. Home: 46 Morton St New York NY 10014 Office: 29 E 36th St New York NY 10016

MASON, FRANK HERBERT, artist; b. Cleve., Feb. 20, 1921; s. Walter Harrison and Mildred Mary (Corbin) M.; student NAD, 1937-38, Art Students League, 1938-50; m. Anne Cary Crosby, Mar. 12, 1966; 1 child, Arden Harriman. Exhibited one-man shows: Ward Eggleston Galleries, Condon Riley Gallery, Wickersham Gallery, French & Co. (all N.Y.C.), Phoenix Mus. Fine Arts, 1962, Stony Brook (N.Y.) Mus., 1964, Gallery Internat., Cleve., 1966, Harbor Gallery, Cold Spring Harbor, N.Y., 1971, Nat. Arts Club, N.Y.C., 1973, John Pence Gallery, San Francisco, 1977; exhibited group shows: Asso. Artists Pitts., 1946, Nat. Arts Club Ann. Mem. Show, N.Y.C., 1950, 55, 61, 62, Internat. Exhbn., Monaco, 1968, others; paintings include portraits, landscapes, murals and figure compositions; 8 panels on life of St. Anthony of Padua, Ch. of San Giovanni di Malta, Venice, Italy; painting of San Rocco, Ch. of Santa Vittoria, Anticoli Corrado, Italy; instr. Art Students League, N.Y.C., 1950—; also tchr. pvt. classes, Stowe, Vt., summers. Served with AUS, 1945-46. Decorated Cross of Merit, Sovereign Mil. Order Malta Mem. NAD (asst. treas.), Nat. Soc. Mural Painters (exhbns. com.). Artistic work includes: Resurrection in Old St. Patricks Cathedral, N.Y.C., 1972. Home: 385 Broome New York City NY 10013

MASON, GEORGE ROBERT, surgeon; b. Rochester, N.Y., June 10, 1932; s. George Mitchell and Marjorie Louise (Hooper) M.; B.A., Oberlin Coll., 1955; M.D. with honors, U. Chgo., 1957; Ph.D. in Physiology (Giannini fellow 1966-67), Stanford U., 1968; m. Grace Louise Bransfield, Feb. 4, 1956; children—Douglas Richard, Marcia Jean, David William. Teaching asst. pathology U. Chgo., 1954-56; rotating intern U. Chgo. Clinics, 1957-58; teaching asst. surgery, NIH postdoctoral fellow, USPHS fellow surgery Stanford U., 1960-62; from asst. resident in surgery to sr. and chief resident in surgery Stanford Hosps., 1962-66; mem. faculty Stanford Med. Sch., 1965-71, asso. prof. surgery, 1970-71; prof. surgery, chmn. dept. U. Md. Med. Sch., 1971—, also prof. physiology. Served to capt. M.C., USAF, 1958-60. John Mary R. Markle scholar acad. medicine, 1968-74. Diplomate Am. Bd. Surgery (examiner 1977—), Bd. Thoracic Surgery. Mem. Am. Assn. Thoracic Surgery, AAUP, Am. Coll. Chest Physicians, A.C.S., AMA, Am. Physiol. Soc., Am., Pacific Coast, So. surg. assns., Assn. Acad. Surgery, Balt. Acad. Surgery (pres. 1977-78), Balt. Med. Soc., Halsted Soc., Med. and Chirurg. Faculty Md., Soc. Internat. de Chirurgie, Soc. Clin. Surgery, Soc. Surgery Alimentary Tract, Soc. Univ. Surgeons, Southeastern Surg. Congress, Sigma Xi, Alpha Omega Alpha. Contbr. to profl. jours., med. textbooks. Home: 112 Tunbridge Rd Baltimore MD 21212 Office: 22 S Greene St Baltimore MD 21201

MASON, HAYDEN, librarian; b. Westfield, N.J., Aug. 1, 1918; s. Roger and Irma Marguerite (Hayden) M.; B.A. (Coll. Library scholar), Haverford Coll., 1940; diploma Institut de Touraine Université de Poitiers (France), 1949; M.A., Harvard U., 1941; grad. Strategic Intelligence Sch., 1950, U.S. Command and Gen. Staff Coll., 1967; m. Jean Catherine Trace, June 17, 1950; children—Deborah Woolson, Dana Elliott, Diana Louise. Tchr. pub. schs., Mass., 1941-42, pvt. schs., Conn., Mass. and Pa., 1946-49; asst. headmaster Perkiomen Sch., Pennsburg, Pa., 1954-62; teaching fellow in French, Harvard U., 1952-54; librarian Nat. Fire Protection Assn., Boston, 1963-72, Nutter, McLennen & Fish, Attys. at Law, Boston, 1973, Chas. T. Main, Inc., Cons. Engrs., Boston, 1974—; research asso. Harbridge House, mgmt. cons., Boston, 1962; mem. staff terminology task adv. group Am. Soc. Safety Engrs., 1966; cons. Boston Environment, Inc. Mem. Weston (Mass.)/Rhombas Affiliation Com., 1957-58. Served with Intelligence Corps, U.S. Army, 1942-46, Pentagon, 1950-52; to col. Res. Mem. Spl. Libraries Assn., Res. Officers Assn. Republican. Club: Old Colony Harvard. Contbr. articles to profl. publs. Home: 881 Congress St Duxbury MA 02332 Office: Chas T Main Inc SE Tower Prudential Center Boston MA 02199

MASON, JOAN ELLEN, nurse; b. Reading, Pa., June 29, 1947; d. Richard Lenhart and Mary Jane (Miller) Fritz; R.N., Temple U. Hosp. Sch. Nursing, 1968; B.S. in Nursing Edn., Temple U., 1971, M.Ed. candidate; m. Wilbur Davis Mason, Feb. 12, 1977. Staff nurse Temple U. Hosp., 1968-71; nursing instr. Phila. Gen. Hosp. Sch. Nursing, 1971-76; coordinator staff devel. and patient edn. Meml. Hosp., Roxborough, Phila., 1976—; instr. cardiopulmonary resuscitation Am. Heart Assn.; voting mem. Health Systems Agy., W. Phila. Mem. Am. Nurses Assn., Pa. Nurses Assn. (exec. com. staff devel. conf. group 1977—), Nat. League Nursing, Delaware Valley Inservice Assn., Franklin Inst., Phila. Mus. Art. Republican. Lutheran. Co-developer patient edn. workshop, med. terminology course; developer self-learning packages for orientation. Home: 430 S 42 St Philadelphia PA 19104 Office: 5800 Ridge Ave Philadelphia PA 19128

MASON, KENNETH BERRY, JR., lawyer; b. Paterson, N.J., May 14, 1933; s. Kenneth Berry and Jeanette Adelaide (McCleary) M.; B.A., Cornell U., 1955, LL.B., 1960; m. Carol Adelaide Smith, May 30, 1960; children—Kenneth Berry, Marteena S. Admitted to N.Y. State bar, 1961, Ohio bar, 1969, U.S. Supreme Ct. bar, 1967; sr. litigating atty. Hawkins, Delafield and Wood, N.Y.C., 1960-63; asst. atty. gen. N.Y. State Dept. Law, 1963-65; asst. counsel, asst. sec. Schaefer Brewing Co., Bklyn., 1965-68; sr. litigating asso. Regan, Goldfarb, Powell & Quinn, N.Y.C., 1968-69; gen. counsel Rubbermaid Inc., Wooster, Ohio, 1969-73; sec., gen. counsel Schlegel Corp., Rochester, N.Y., 1973-74; individual practice law, Rochester, N.Y., 1974—; lectr., cons. in field; dir. Portable Channel Inc., Rochester. Mem. Pittsford (N.Y.) Com. Republican party, 1975—. Mem. Am. Arbitration Assn. (nat panel comml. arbitrators) Am., N.Y. State, Monroe County bar assns., Rochester Assn. Fin. Planners, Small Bus. Council, Rochester Area C. of C. Republican. Episcopalian. Clubs: Rochester City, Rotary (dir. Pittsford 1977—). Home: 20 Old Lyme Rd Pittsford NY 14534 Office: 5 S Fitzhugh St Rochester NY 14614

MASON, MADELINE, author, critic, poet; b. N.Y.C.; student lit. Arthur Symons, Eng.; student sci. Sir. Oliver Lodge, Eng.; pupil music Ernest Bloch; m. Malcolm Forbes McKesson, May 6, 1942. Poet in residence Shenandoah Coll., Winchester, Va., Delbrook Center for Advanced Studies, Riverton, Va., 1969—; dir. poetry workshops Poetry Soc. Am., N.Y.C., 1970-72, 75; poetry readings and recs. Harvard U., 1939-76, N.Y.C. Bd. Edn. Audio-Visual, 1960-70; books of poems include: Hill Fragments, 1936, The Cage of Years, 1949, also At the Ninth Hour, The Challengers, Sonnets in a New Form; prose (under pseudonym Tyler Mason); Riding for Texas, 1936; translator into French: Le Prophète (Gibran). Mem. PEN, Nat. League Am. Pen Women (Diamond Jubilee award 1958), Poetry Soc. Am. (v.p.), Composers, Authors, Artists Am. (past nat. v.p., N.Y. chpt. pres.), Nat. Assn. Composers, Pen and Brush Club, Nat. Arts Club, Authors League. Clubs: Jr. League, Harvard (N.Y.C.). Home: Hotel Seville 22 E 29th St New York City NY 10016

MASON, MARSHALL W., stage dir.; b. Amarillo, Tex., Feb. 24, 1940; s. Marvin Marshall and Lorine (Chrisman) M.; B.S. in Speech, Northwestern U., 1961. Dir. Little Eyolf, N.Y.C., 1964, Home Free!, 1965, The Hot L Baltimore, 1973, The Sea Horse, 1974, The Mound Builders, 1975, Knock Knock, 1976, The Farm, 1976, A Streetcar Named Desire, 1978; co-dir. Gemini on Broadway, 1977; televised WNET, The Moundbuilders, 1976, Home Free! and The Madness of Lady Bright, London, 1968; prodns. in Los Angeles, Chgo., Washington; founder, artistic dir., pres. bd. Circle Repertory Theater Co., Inc.; dir. Off-Off Broadway Alliance, Inc. Recipient OBIE awards for distinguished direction, Hot L Baltimore, 1973, Battle of Angels, 1974, The Mount Builders, 1975, Knock, Knock, 1976, Serenading Louie, 1976, TONY nominations for best dir., Knock Knock, 1976, Joseph Jefferson nominations for best dir. The Farm, 1975, Old Times, 1977; Vernon Rice award, 1974; Margo Jones award, 1977. Mem. Soc. Stage Dirs. and Choreographers, Dirs. Guild Am. Home: 165 Christopher St New York City NY 10014 Office: 186 W 4th St New York City NY 10014

MASON, PETER ANTHONY, ins. and real estate broker; b. Albany, N.Y., Jan. 8, 1947; s. Peter Patrick and Angela Rose (McCarty) M.; A.A.S., Hudson Valley Community Coll., 1967; B.S., Russell Sage Coll., 1972; m. Theresa Mary Streath, Sept. 27, 1975; 1 son, Peter Michael. Office service supr. Farm Family Ins. Co., Glenmont, N.Y., 1968-69; owner Mason Ins. Agy., Menands, N.Y., 1972—. Served with USAR, 1966-72. Mem. Colonie Jr. C. of C. (dir. 1973-74), Colonie C. of C., Life Underwriting Tng. Council. Democrat. Roman Catholic. Clubs: K.C., Men's Assn., Rotary. Home: 10 Hendrick Ave Menands NY 12204 Office: 243 Broadway Menands NY 12204

MASON, PETER LEONARD, real estate broker; b. Toronto, Ont., Can., July 4, 1944; s. W. Leonard and Ida Margaret (Moir) M.; degree York U., 1971; m. Dorothy Joan Jarvis, July 1, 1966; children—Sandra, Andrea, Joanna, Lesley. Accountant, Royal Bank Can., Toronto, 1963-65; appraisal and sales staff Webb & Mason, Ltd., Toronto, 1965-67; founder, pres. Picken & Mason Real Estate, Ltd., Don Mills, Ont., 1967—; pres. Toronto Real Estate Bd., 1977, chmn. fin. com., 1976, pres. elect, 1977; pres. Peter L. Mason, Inc., Gormley, Ont., 1974-76. Fellow Real Estate Inst. Can.; mem. Assn. Ont. Land Economists. Clubs: York Downs Golf and Country (Unionville, Ont.); Canadian Progress (Scarborough). Home: Rural Route 2 Gormley ON Canada Office: 1 Valleybrook Dr Suite 401 Don Mills ON M3B 2S7 Canada

MASON, ROBERT STANLEY, pub. affairs cons.; b. N.Y.C., Nov. 20, 1920; s. Irving and Belle (Solomon) M.; B.A., Harvard U., 1948; M.A., Columbia U., 1950; m. Abelle Dinkowitz, June 13, 1948; children—Peter Ian, Mark Evan. Washington corr. PM, 1940-42; propaganda analyst OWI, 1942-43; instr. English, Pa. State U., 1950-54; pub. relations asso. Westinghouse Electric Corp., N.Y.C., 1954-56; dir. editorial services N.Y. Life Ins. Co., N.Y.C., 1956-64; dir. communications McKinsey & Co., N.Y.C., 1964-71; v.p. communications Boston Co., 1971-73; pres. R.S. Mason Asso., Cambridge, Mass., 1973—; juror Loeb awards fin. journalism, 1972; seminar leader Am. Inst. Banking. Mem. adv. bd. Boston U. Med. Center, 1971-74; bd. dirs. Civic Center and Clearinghouse, 1972—. Served with AUS, 1943-46; ETO. Mem. Soc. Silurians, Pub. Relations

Soc. Am. Clubs: Harvard (N.Y.C.) (Boston). Contbr. articles to profl. publs. Address: 19 Garden St Cambridge MA 02138

MASSABNY, JUDITH TAYLOR, assn. exec.; b. Masontown, Pa., Apr. 20, 1941; d. Ray Jefferson and Georgia Muriel (Paris) Taylor; student Pa. State U., 1958-59, U. Va., 1960-64; m. Richard Joseph Massabny, Apr. 20, 1969. With Beaver County (Pa.) Times, 1955-58, Nov. Va. Sun, Arlington, 1960-64, Adler Advt. Agency, Washington, 1964-65, Washington World Mag. and Balt. Scene Mag., 1964-66, Falls Church (Va.) Globe, 1966-67; pub. relations dir. Nat. Grange, Washington, 1967—. Recipient Thoth award, 1977. Mem. Nat. Press Club, Pub. Relations Soc. Am. (dir. Nat. Capital chpt. 1977-78, sec. 1979), Nat. Assn. Farm Broadcasters, Am. Agrl. Editors Assn., Agrl. Relations Council. Coordinator Nat. Grange Bicentennial Year Cookbook, 1976. Home: 1950 N Calvert St Arlington VA 22201 Office: 1616 H St NW Washington DC 20006

MASSEY, DONALD AYRES, quality control engr.; b. Balston Spa, N.Y., July 24, 1931; s. Wesley Fulton and Margaret Jeanett (Levey) M.; B.S., U. Vt., 1953; M.S., Rensselaer Poly. Inst., 1976; m. Nancy Jane Keenan, Aug. 30, 1952; children—David Keenan, Mark Ayres, Sue Ann, Donna Janette, Daniel Glass. Mfg. trainee Gen. Electric Co., 1953-58, quality control engr., Pittsfield, Mass., 1958-63; chief quality engr. Chandler Evans div. Colt Industries, Inc., West Hartford, Conn., 1963-66; project quality engr. armament dept. Gen. Electric Co., Burlington, Vt., 1966-68, reliability program engr., 1968-69 process control engr., nuclear fuels div., Wilmington, N.C., 1970-73, quality control engr. mech. drive turbine dept., Fitchburg, Mass., 1973—; asst. mgr. quality control Maremont Corp., Saco, Maine, 1969-70. Founding pres. Town Planning Bd., New Lebanon, N.Y., 1961-63; asst. chmn. bd. missions Congregational Ch., 1964-66, deacon, 1975-77. Served with USAF, 1953-55. Mem. Am. Soc. Quality Control (past dir. No. Vt. sect.), Am. Mgmt. Assn., Am. Soc. Tool and Mfg. Engrs., Am. Ordnance Assn., Nat. Pilots Assn., Air Force Assn. Republican. Home: 73 Helena St Leominster MA 01453 Office: 166 Boulder Dr Fitchburg MA 01420

MASSIAS, JEANNETTE BERTHE, assn. exec.; b. Nice, France, June 3, 1919; d. Joseph and Elizabeth (MacLeod) Massias; grad. Nice Coll., France, 1939. Came to U.S., 1957. Exec. sec. Helicop-Air, Paris, 1949-57; adminstrv. asst. Nat. Bd. Med. Examiners, Phila., 1959-67, comptroller, 1967—. Served to capt. with Women Aux. Air Force of Free French Army, 1940-46. Decorated Legion d'Honneur, Croix de Guerre with Palm, Medaille de la Resistance, Medaille de l'Aeronautique; Def. Medal (England). Mem. Adminstrv. Mgmt. Soc. Home: 62-11 Drexelbrook Dr Drexel Hill PA 19026 Office: 3930 Chestnut St Philadelphia PA 19104

MASSIMINO, VITTORIO CARMELO, artist; b. N.Y.C., May 30, 1919; s. Carmelo and Rosaria Atheia (Nicolosi) M.; student Leonardo Di Vinci Art Sch., 1934, Art Students League, 1940-45, Pratt Inst., 1945, YMHA Fine Art Sch., 1948, Mus. Modern Art, 1962, Umberto Romano Art Sch., 1975. Instr. art Jones Center and Rheinlander Center, 1958-62; judge ann. art fair Boys' Clubs Am.; one-man exhbns. include Met. Mus. Art, 1932, U.S. Mcht. Marine traveling show, 1947, Prince George, 1957, Arts, 1957-58, Italia, 1958, Jones Center retrospective, 1960, Beaux Art, 1961, Gotham, 1961, First Fed. at Radio City, 1969, Excelsior, 1963-65, Steinway, 1966-67, Queensboro Art Soc., 1976; originator rhythmic emphasis technique; works include snow sculpture, floats, costumes, stage sets, murals and st. decorations. Served with U.S. Army, 1940-42, Mcht. Marine, 1943-50. Decorated Order Red Cross (Russia); recipient citation from Pres. Truman, prize Queens Borough Art Soc., plaque Prince George Art Show, 1957, also numerous others. Address: 2059 Steinway St Astoria NY 11105

MASSMANN, ROBERT ERNEST, librarian; b. Pittsburg, Kans., Apr. 2, 1924; s. Ernest A. and Rene (Anderson) M.; A.B., Kans. State Tchrs. Coll., 1947; A.M. in Library Sci., U. Mich., 1950; m. Eloise Coon, June 29, 1946; children—Charles Ernest, Richard Alan. Asst. law librarian Fed. Res. Bank N.Y., N.Y.C., 1950-51; dir. library services Central Conn. State Coll., New Britain, 1951—. Served as lt. (j.g.) USNR, 1943-46. Mem. Conn. Library Assn., Hist. Soc. New Britain. Methodist. Contbr. articles to profl. jours. Home: 478 Glen St New Britain CT 06051

MASSON, VICTORIN BERTRAND, anesthesiologist; b. St. Maurice, Que., Can., Oct. 12, 1924; s. Philippe and Valeda (Jalbert) M.; M.D., U. Laval, 1953; children—Pierre, Helene, Jacques. Intern, U. Laval Hosp., 1952-53, resident in anesthesiology, 1953-57; anesthesiologist Hosp. St. Sacrement, Quebec City, Que., 1959-71, Centre Hospitalier Robert Giffard and Mil. Hosp Valcartier (Que.), 1971—; indsl. physician Hydro Que., Quebec City, 1971—; physician U. Laval, 1953—; practice medicine, specializing in anesthesiology, Quebec City, 1953—. Mem. Can., Que. assns. anesthesists. Roman Catholic. Club: Golf Cap Rouge. Home: 1021 du Golf Cap Rouge PQ GOA 1KO Canada

MAST, WILLIAM RAY, physician; b. Hartly, Del., July 2, 1940; s. Clarence and Sylvia (Byler) M.; B.S., Ursinus Coll., Pa., 1962; M.D., U. Pa., 1966; m. Carolyn Rita West, Aug. 15, 1964; children—Valerie Anne, William Ray II, MariaLynne, Lisa Ellen. Intern, Misericordia Hosp., Phila., 1966-67; gen. practice medicine, pub. health officer El Milia, Algeria, 1968-69, med. dir., chief pub. health officer Civil Hosp., 1969-70; resident in surgery Presbyn.-U. Pa. Med. Center, Phila., 1970-71; resident in otorhinolaryngology U. Pa., 1971-74; practice medicine specializing in otorhinolaryngology, Dover, Del., 1975—, Phila., 1975—; mem. staff Kent Gen. Hosp., Dover, Hosp. of U. Pa., Phila.; cons. VA Hosp., Wilmington, Del., Sterck Sch. Hearing Impaired, Newark, Del., VA Hosp., Phila.; mem. Del. Gov.'s Interim Comprehensive Health Planning Commn., 1975-77; clin. instr. U. Pa. Med. Sch., 1975—. Trustee, elder Christian Life Center, Dover. Nat. Found. Health scholar, 1962-64. Diplomate Am. Bd. Otolaryngology. Fellow Pa. Acad. Ophthalmology and Otorhinolaryngology, A.C.S.; mem. Kent County Med. Soc., Med. Soc. Del., AMA (Physician's Recognition award 1973-77), Am. Acad. Ophthalmology and Otolaryngology, Phila. Soc. Facial Plastic Surgeons, Am. Acad. Plastic and Reconstructive Surgery. Home: RD 1 Box 196-B Hartly DE 19953 Office: 30 Division St E Dover DE 19901

MASTER, GERALD LOUIS, mech. engr.; b. Longswamp, Pa., Aug. 25, 1921; s. Robert D. and Estella Susan (Fenstermacher) M.; student N.C. U., 1943, Harvard U., 1946, Marietta Coll., 1942, Morris Harvey Coll., 1942; B.S. in M.E., Pa. State U., 1948; m. Marjorie Mae Lore, July 2, 1966; children—Eric, Steven, Susan, Melissa. Insp., Glen L. Martin Co., Balt., 1941-42; design engr. Babcock & Wilcox Co., Barberton, Ohio, 1948-49; mech. engr. Metropolitan Edison Co., Reading, Pa., 1949-62, staff engr., 1962-64, sr. staff engr., 1964—; chmn. Pa. Electric Assn., Power Generation Com., 1967-69. Treas., Windsor St. Meth. Sunday Sch., 1959-66; mem. Conestoga dist. com. Boy Scouts Am., 1964-65; Republican committeeman, 1976—; mem. regional Air Pollution Control Assn., 1964-67. Served with USN, 1942-46. Recipient Jr. C. of C. Spark Plug Award, 1954, 56; registered profl. engr., Pa. Mem. ASME (exec. com. 1959-63), Air Pollution Control Assn., Pa. Environ. Council (steering com. on Schuylkill River 1976—). Clubs: Lake Wynonah, Wodenschiere Country, Caterpillar. Author: Steam - Turbine Management and Governing, 1966. Home: 1546 Argonne Rd Reading PA 19601 Office: 2800 Pottsville Pike Reading PA 19603

MASTERS, HENRY GEORGE, psychologist; b. Rochester, N.Y., June 22, 1936; s. Henry Edward and Rose (Trapani) M.; B.A., U. Rochester, 1958; M.A., Emory U., 1961; Ph.D., Kan. State U., 1968; m. Pauline Ann Bianchi, July 25, 1959; children—Dana Rose, Robert Edward. Instr. psychology Washburn U., 1968; asst. prof. psychology Juniata Coll., Huntingdon, Pa., 1968-78, asso. prof., 1978—. Grantee Grass Found., 1970-73, Washburn U., 1967. Mem. Am. Psychol. Assn., Animal Behavior Soc., Am. Soc. Primatologists, Sigma Xi. Contbr. to profl. jours. Home: 3325 Blair Ave Huntingdon PA 16652

MASTERS, RICHARD E., mech. engr.; b. Bklyn., Mar. 15, 1928; s. William and Mollie (Beckerman) M.; B.M.E., Poly. Inst. N.Y., 1949; m. Joan Marilyn Hecker, Apr. 3, 1954; children—Cary, Amy, William. Engr., Nonpareil Concrete Constrn., 1949-50; cons. engr., partner Jaros, Baum & Bolles, N.Y.C., 1953—. Served to 1st lt. C.E., AUS, 1950-53. Decorated Bronze Star medal. Registered profl. engr., Calif., Conn., D.C., Fla., Ga., Ill., Mass., Md., Mich., Mo., N.C., N.Y., N.J., Ohio, Pa., R.I., Tex., W.Va. Fellow Am. Cons. Engrs. Council; mem. ASME, Am. Soc. Heating, Refrigeration and Air Conditioning Engrs., Nat. Soc. Profl. Engrs., N.Y. Assn. Cons. Engrs. (chmn. mech. code com. 1973, bd. govs. 1974), Soc. Fire Protection Engrs., Tau Beta Pi. Club: Metropolis Country (White Plains, N.Y.). Home: 3 Well House Ln Mamaroneck NY 10543 Office: 345 Park Ave New York City NY 10022

MASTERS, STUART JEFFREY, radiologist; b. Bklyn., June 18, 1943; s. Sigmond Stephen and Helen Masters; A.B. with honors, Hamilton Coll., 1964; M.D., Duke U., 1969; m. Ellen Susan Kahn, Aug. 13, 1966; 1 dau., Rachel Caryn. Intern, Duke U., Durham, N.C., from 1969, resident, then fellow in internal medicine, resident in diagnostic radiology, until 1974; asst. prof. radiology, head emergency radiology Yale-New Haven Hosp. and Yale U., 1974-76; attending radiologist Berkshire Med. Center, Pittsfield, Mass.; asst. clin. prof. radiology Yale-New Haven Hosp., U. Mass. Med. Sch., 1976—; lectr. in field. Yale U. grantee; teaching assistantship in biology State U. N.Y., Buffalo, 1964-65; diplomate Am. Bd. Radiology. Mem. Am. Coll. Radiology, Radiol. Soc. N. Am., Nat. Assn. Residents and Interns, Mass. Med. Soc., Mass. Radiologic Soc., Berkshire County Dist. Med. Soc. Contbr. articles to med. jours. Office: Berkshire Med Center 725 North St Pittsfield MA 01201

MASTRAN, JOHN LEO, orgn. and mgmt. counsel; b. Peekskill, N.Y., Mar. 29, 1920; s. John and Mary (Costella) M.; B.S. in Commerce, U. Va., 1942; Indsl. Adminstr., Harvard, 1943; m. Carol Ann Righter, Oct. 7, 1950; children—Mary Isabel, Elizabeth Righter. Orgn. planning adviser RCA, Camden, N.J., 1943-49, asst. to v.p. and to gen. plant mgr. RCA Electron Tube div., Harrison, N.J., 1949-53, mgr. orgn. planning and mgmt. devel., Camden, 1953-67, dir. orgn. planning and mgmt. devel., 1967-71, dir. orgn. planning, 1971—. Orgn. planning adviser 3d Internat. Conf. Mfrs. of N.A.M., 1956; chmn. adv. council on orgn. planning Nat. Indsl. Conf. Bd.; mgmt. course guest speaker Am. Mgmt. Assn. Mem. Orgn. Devel. Council (chmn., pres.), Harvard Bus. Sch. Assn., Beta Gamma Sigma, Alpha Kappa Psi. Clubs: Netherland Luncheon, Harvard (N.Y.C.); Moorestown Field (pres.). Home: 508 Stanwick Rd Moorestown NJ 08057 Office: 30 Rockefeller Plaza New York City NY 10020

MASTROROCCO, VIRGINIO PETER, optometrist; b. Bklyn., Nov. 12, 1923; s. Berardino and Rosa (Ruvolo) M.; B.S., Columbia U., 1945; O.D., Mass. Coll. Optometry, 1969; m. Ruth Alicia Flynn, Dec. 26, 1951; children—Diane Alicia, Susan Alicia. Pvt. practice optometry, Bklyn., 1949—; mem. optometric staff Holy Family for the Aged, Bklyn., 1967-69; lectr. clin. optometry, dept. optometry Columbia U., 1950-55; clin. examiner Bd. Examiners in Optometry, State N.Y., 1950-52, 69-70; mem. clin. staff Meth. Hosp. of Bklyn., 1975—. Bd. mgrs., 2d v.p. YMCA, Bklyn., 1966—; bd. dirs. Bklyn. Philharmonia at Bklyn. Acad. Music, 1973—; mem. adv. bd. Family Reception Center, Park Slope, 1973; chmn. Narcotic Addiction sect. Bay Ridge Area Bklyn. Mayor's Task Force, 1969-71. Fellow Am. Optometric Assn.; mem. Bklyn., N.Y. State optometric assns. Roman Catholic. Clubs: Lions, Montauk. Home: 881 54th St Brooklyn NY 11220 Office: 448 9th St Brooklyn NY 11215

MASTROTA, VINCENT FRANCIS, obstetrician; b. N.Y.C., Mar. 9, 1932; s. Vincent and Josephine (Dorsa) M.; B.S., Villanova U., 1954; M.D., Bologna U. (Italy), 1959; m. Maria Gale, Aug. 30, 1958; children—Valerie, Stephanie, Vincent, Lawrence. Intern, Kings County Hosp. Center, Bklyn., 1960-61; resident in pathology St. Catherine's Hosp., Bklyn., 1960-61; resident in obstetrics, gynecology North Shore Univ. Hosp., Manhasset, N.Y., 1961-62, sr. resident, chief resident, 1962-64; practice medicine specializing in obstetrics, Bayside, N.Y.; asso. dir. obstetrics and gynecology Whitestone Hosp., N.Y.C., 1964-69; asst. attending North Shore Univ. Hosp., Manhasset, N.Y., 1964-75, asso. attending, 1975—; cons. perinatologist South Nassau Communities Hosp., Oceanside, N.Y., 1975—; chief maternal fetal medicine Nassau Hosp., Mineola, N.Y., 1976-77, cons., 1977—; clin. instr. Cornell U. Med. Coll., N.Y.C., 1971-74, clin. asst. prof., 1974-76, asst. prof. obstetrics, gynecology and pediatrics, 1977—. Diplomate Am. Bd. Obstetrics and Gynecology. Fellow Am. Coll. Obstetricians and Gynecologists; mem. Soc. Perinatal Obstetricians. Contbr. articles to med. jours. Office: 214-10 24th Ave Bayside NY 11360

MASUBUCHI, KOICHI, naval architect; b. Otaru, Hokkaido, Japan, Jan. 11, 1924; s. Yosaku and Tomi (Ota) M.; B.S., U. Tokyo, 1946, M.S., 1948, Ph.D., 1959; m. Fumiko Kaneno, Oct. 24, 1950. Research engr. Transp. Tech. Research Inst., 1948-58; vis. fellow, cons. Battelle Meml. Inst., Columbus, O., 1958-62, research asso., fellow, tech. adviser, 1963-68, chief welding mechanics sect., welding div. Ship Research Inst., 1962-63; asso. prof. naval architecture Mass. Inst. Tech., 1968-71, prof. ocean engring. and materials sci., 1971—. Recipient Distinguished Service award Transp. Tech. Research Inst., Ministry Transp. Japan, 1959. Mem. Am. Welding Soc. (R.D. Thomas Meml. award 1977), Japan Welding Soc., Am. Soc. Metals, Soc. Naval Architects and Marine Engrs., Soc. Naval Architects Japan, Internat. Inst. Welding (commn. vice chmn.), Sigma Xi. Author: Materials for Ocean Engineering, 1970; co-author 3 books on residual stresses in weldments, materials for ocean engring.; contbr. tech. papers to profl. lit. Home: 34 Hamilton Rd Arlington MA 02174 Office: Mass Inst Tech Cambridge MA 02139

MATALIA, HARSHAD DILIPKUMAR, mech. engr.; b. Gondal, Gujarat State, India, June 7, 1943; s. Dilipkumar Vanechand and Dhanlaxmi Liladhar (Bhimani) M.; came to U.S., 1965; B. Engring. in Mech. Engring., Maharaja Sayajirao U., Baroda, India, 1965; M.S.M.E., N.C. State U., 1967; m. Taru Ratilal Choksi, June 10, 1973; children—Parag, Parul. Project engr. Fairchild Hiller Corp., Riverdale, Md., 1967-69, Gitchner Mobile System, Dallastown, Pa., 1970-71; plant mgr. Systems Engring. Co., Bombay, India, 1972; partner Technocrate Cons., Bombay, 1973-74; mech. engr. Mack Truck Co., Allentown, Pa., 1974; research asso. Am. Newspaper Pubs. Assn. Research Inst., Easton, Pa., 1975—. Mem. ASME. Patentee newsprint manual flying paster. Home: 907 George St Easton PA 18042 Office: 1350 Sullivan Tr Easton PA 18042

MATARAZZO, ANTHONY P., real estate broker, appraiser; b. Somerville, Mass., May 13, 1947; s. Anthony S. and Rose (Sottile) M.; B.B.A., U. Miami, 1969; m. Joan M. Fitzpatrick, Dec. 23, 1973; 1 son, Anthony Patrick. Gen. mgr., appraiser Matarazzo Real Estate, Nashua, N.H., 1971—; staff appraiser VA, Hillsborough County, 1977; pres. Hampshire Estates, Inc., 1976—, Downtown Realty, Inc., 1976—. Pres., Nashua Young Democrats, 1970-71; mem. Nashua City Democratic Com., 1971—; founder, pres. Italian Am. Club Greater Nashua, 1977—. Mem. Soc. Real Estate Appraisers, Am. Homebuilders Assn., Nashua C. of C. Roman Catholic. Home: 530 Broad St Nashua NH 03060

MATCZAK, SEBASTIAN ALEXANDER, educator, author; b. Warsaw, Poland, Jan. 20, 1914; s. Jan and Genowefa (Jagodzinska) M.; M.Ph., U. Cracov (Poland), 1938; M.Th., Warsaw U., 1944, M.A., 1945; Th.D., Gregorian U., Rome, Italy, 1951; Ph.D., Catholic Inst. Paris (France), 1956, U. Paris, 1963. Asst. to prof. Warsaw U., 1947-48; asst. prof. philosophy Manhattan Coll., 1956-57; professorial lectr. St. John's U., Jamaica, N.Y., 1957-59, asso. prof. philosophy Grad. Sch., 1959-65, prof., 1966—. Pres. Learned Publs., Inc., N.Y.C., 1968—. Mem. Am. Philos. Assn., Am. Cath. Philos. Assn., Cath. Theol. Soc. Am., History Sci. Soc., Polish Inst. Arts and Scis. in Am., Soc. for Sci. Study Religion, Acad. Religion and Mental Health. Author several books including: Karl Barth on God, 1962; A Select Classified Bibliography of Ethics, Economics, Law, Politics, Sociology, 1970; Philosophy: Its Nature, Method and Basic Sources, 1975; God in Contemporary Thought, 1977; also articles in profl. jours. Editor-in-chief Philos. Question Series, 1967—. Home: 83-53 Manton St Jamaica NY 11435

MATHESON, JOHN ROSS, judge; b. Arundel, Que., Can., Nov. 14, 1917; s. Alexander Dawson and Gertrude (McCuaig) M.; B.A., Queen's U., 1940; LL.M., U. Western Ont., 1954; M.A., Mount Allison U., 1975; m. Edith May Bickley, Aug. 4, 1945; children—Alexander Duncan, Wendy Jane (Mrs. Simpson), Margaret Jill, Donald Ross, Roderick Hugh, Murdoch Neil. Called to bar Ont., 1948, created Queen's Counsel, 1967; practiced in Brockville, 1949-68; partner Matheson, Henderson & Hart; mem. Ho. of Commons, 1961-68; del. 2d Commonwealth Law Conf., 1960; Canadian Parliamentary observer 16th Session UN Gen. Assembly, N.Y.C., 1961-62; del. 52d Interparliamentary Conf., Belgrade, 1963; chmn. standing com. external affairs 26th Parliament, 1963-65; parliamentary sec. to prime minister, 1966-68; judge Carleton County, Ont., 1968—. Life councillor Queen's U. Served to capt. Canadian Army, 1940-44; hon. col. 30th Field Regt., Royal Canadian Arty. Named Brockville Citizen of Yr., 1968. Knight of Justice, genealogist Venerable Order St. John; knight comdr. Order of St. Lazarus. Fellow Soc. Antiquaries (Scotland); life mem. Royal Order Scotland, Royal Canadian Arty. Assn. (life gov.), Canadian Bible Soc., Phi Delta Phi; mem. Canadian Olympic Assn., Canadian Amateur Boxing Assn. (hon. sec.), Heraldry Soc. Can. (founding life mem.), United Empire Loyalists Assn. Can. (hon. v.p.). Contbr. sect. on Canadian flag to Ency. Canadiana. Home: 2030 Thistle Crescent Ottawa KIH 5P5 ON Canada

MATHEWS, FREDERICK ANTHONY JOHN, pathologist; b. Halifax, N.S., Can., Jan. 17, 1933; s. Andrew Eusebius and Juanita Cox (Loomer) M.; student Dalhousie U., Halifax, 1950-56. With clin. cancer research group Med. Faculty, U. Dalhousie, 1954-56; research technician in phys. chemistry Fisheries Sta., Halifax, 1956-57; rotating extern Victoria Pub. Hosp., Fredericton, N.B., Can., 1956, St. Clare's Hosp., N.Y.C., 1957, Hotel Dieu de St. Joseph, Windsor, Ont., Can., 1958, U. Heidelberg (Germany) Clinics, 1959, U. Marburg (Germany) Clinics, 1959, U. Paris, 1960, U. Bonn (Germany), 1960-62; rotating intern Hôtel Dieu de St. Joseph, Windsor, 1963-64; med. and surg. intern Halifax Infirmary, 1965; resident pathology Hosp. of U. Pa., Phila. 1964, Ottawa (Ont.) Gen. Hosp., 1965-67, Toronto (Ont.) Gen. Hosp., 1967-68, New Mt. Sinai Hosp., Toronto, 1968-69, Winnipeg (Man.) Gen. Hosp., 1969, Md. Gen. Hosp., Balt., 1970-71; dir. labs., Port Colborne and Ft. Erie hosps., Ont., 1969-70; cons. pathologist St. John (N.B.) Regional Lab., 1971—, Camp Hill Hosp., Halifax, 1971—; Bridgewater (N.S.) Hosp., 1971—, Glace Bay and Sydney hosps., N.S., 1971—; demonstrator pathology med. schs. of U. Pa., 1964, U. Ottawa, 1965-67, U. Toronto, 1967-68; research fellow Inst. Exptl. Medicine and Surgery, U. Montreal Med. Sch., 1963-64; hon. mem. dept. Slavic studies U. Dalhousie, 1976—; pres., dir. Casa Morgagni Enterprises, Halifax, 1977—. Diplomate Am. Bd. Pathology. Mem. Medieval Soc. King's Coll., Halifax Med. Soc., Old Halifax S. End Community Assn., Kinsport Community Assn., Inst. Human Values St. Mary's U., German Soc. Pathologists. Roman Catholic. Home: 5784 Tower Terr Halifax NS B3H 1RS Canada

MATHEWS, HOWARD HUME, lawyer, engr.; b. Cumberland, Md., Nov. 30, 1911; s. John Lawrence and Edith (Tabler) M.; B.S., U. Md., 1933; postgrad. in electronics George Washington U., organic chemistry Seton Hall U., Georgetown U. Sch. Law, 1936-41; J.D., U. Conn., 1944; m. Helen Jones, Aug. 29, 1932; children—Philip Hume, John Addison, James Llewellyn. Chief engr. South Pittsburgh Coal Co., Morgantown, W.Va., 1933-35; mech. engr. Am. Radiator Co., Washington, 1935-36; patent examiner U.S. Patent Office, Washington, 1936-42; patent atty. United Aircraft Corp., East Hartford, Conn., 1942-47; mgr. legal dept. The Dentists Supply Co. of N.Y., York, Pa., 1947-49; mgr. patent dept. Air Reduction Co., Inc. (name now Airco, Inc.), Murray Hill, 1949-63, dir. patent trademark and licensing activities, 1963—, food and drug counsel, 1955—. Former chmn. Nat. Council Patent Law Assns.; founder Nat. Inventors Hall of Fame. Mem. Am., Fed., N.J. (past chmn. patent trademark, copyright law and unfair competition sect.) bar assns., Am., N.J. (past pres.) patent law assns., Assn. Corp. Counsel N.J., Assn. Corp. Patent Counsel, Amateur Radio Relay League, Aircraft Owners and Pilots Assn., Lambda Chi Alpha, Tau Beta Pi, Pi Delta Epsilon, Alpha Psi Omega. Club: Spring Brook Country. Home: Scott Rd Boonton Twp NJ 07005 Office: 16 Schuyler Pl Morristown NJ 07960

MATHEWS, J. ADDISON, lawyer; b. Washington, July 14, 1941; s. Howard Hume and Helen (Jones) M.; B.M.E., U. Md., 1963; J.D., Georgetown U., 1967; M.B.A., U. Rochester, 1975; m. Martha Jane Neil, Aug. 17, 1963; 1 son, Brian Philip. Examiner, U.S. Patent and Trademark Office, Washington, 1964-67; admitted to N.Y. bar, 1968; patent atty. Eastman Kodak Co., Rochester, N.Y., 1967-74, sr. patent atty., 1974—; mem. staff Pres.'s Commn. on Patent System, 1965-66; instr. U. Rochester Grad. Sch. Mgmt., 1976-78. Mem. Rochester Area C. of C., Rochester (sec., dir. 1976-77), Am. patent law assns., Am., N.Y. State, D.C. bar assns., Patent Office Soc., Beta Gamma Sigma, Phi Delta Phi. Republican. Methodist. Holder patents. Home: 18 High Point Trail Fairport NY 14450 Office: 343 State St Rochester NY 14650

MATHEWS, JAMES KENNETH, bishop; b. Breezewood, Pa., Feb. 10, 1913; s. James Davenport and Laura Mae (Wilson) M.; A.B., Lincoln Meml. U., 1934, D.D. (hon.), 1954; S.T.B., N.Y. Theol. Sem., 1937; grad. student Boston U. Sch. Theology, 1937-38; spl. student Cambridge (Eng.) U., 1955; Ph.D., Columbia, 1957; D.D., Wesleyan U., 1965, Colby Coll., 1971; L.H.D., Lycoming Coll., 1966, Ohio Wesleyan U., 1969, Norwich U., 1970; m. Eunice Jones, June 1, 1940; children—Anne, Janice (Mrs. William R. Stromsem), James Stanley.

Ordained to ministry Methodist Ch., 1938; missionary to India, 1938-42; asso. sec. div. world missions Meth. Bd. Missions, 1946-52, asso. gen. sec., 1952-60; bishop United Meth. Ch., resident in Boston Area, 1960-72, Washington area, 1972—; Frondren lectr. So. Meth. U., 1962; Lowell lectr. Boston U., 1964, Jones lectr., 1976; Gray lectr. Duke, 1967; Showers lectr. Lebanon Valley Coll., 1977; sec. Council of Bishops, 1972—; mem. bd. higher edn. and ministry United Meth. Ch., also mem. Gen. Commn. Archives and History; mem. exec. com. and governing bd. Nat. Council Chs.; mem. central com. World Council Chs.; mem. exec. com. World Meth. Council; chmn. United Christian Ashrams. Chmn. bd. dirs. Chs. Center for Theology and Pub. Policy; trustee Boston U., Western Md. Coll., Wesley Coll., Sibley Meml. Hosp. Asbury Meth. Home, Morgan Christian Center United Meth. Home, Providence, Nur Manzil Psychiat. Center, Lucknow, India, Morristown Coll.; chmn. bd. trustees Santiago (Chile) Coll., Am. U.; bd. govs., mem. exec. com. Wesley Theol. Sem.; bd. dirs. Friends of WCC Inc., Wesley Found., U. Del. Served to maj. AUS, 1942-46. Mem. Am. Oriental Soc. Club: Cosmos. Author: South of the Himalayas, 1955; To the End of the Earth, 1959; Eternal Values in a World of Change, 1960; A Church Truly Catholic, 1969. Editor: (with Eunice J. Mathews) Selections from E. Stanley Jones: Christ and Human Need, 1972; contbr. numerous articles to profl. jours. Home: 4120 48th St NW Washington DC 20016 Office: 100 Maryland Ave NE Room 400 Washington DC 20002

MATHIAS, CHARLES MCCURDY, JR., U.S. senator; b. Frederick, Md., July 24, 1922; s. Charles McCurdy and Theresa McElfresh (Trail) M.; B.A., Haverford Coll., 1944; student Yale, 1943-44; LL.B., U. Md., 1949; m. Ann Hickling Bradford, Nov. 8, 1958; children—Charles Bradford, Robert Fiske. Admitted to Md. bar, 1949; asst. atty. gen. of Md., 1953-54; city atty., Frederick, 1954-59; mem. Md. Ho. of Dels., 1958; mem. 87th-90th Congresses, 6th Dist. Md.; mem. U.S. Senate, 1968—. Trustee Episcopal Free Sch. and Orphan House. Served from seaman to capt. USNR. Republican. Episcopalian. Home: 3808 Leland St Chevy Chase MD 20015 also Frederick MD 21701 Office: Russell Office Bldg Washington DC 20510

MATHIEU, PETER LOUIS, JR., physician; b. Woodstock, Vt., June 23, 1924; s. Peter Louis and Ida (Racine) M.; B.S., Coll. of Holy Cross, 1946; M.D., St. Louis U., 1948; m. Betty Burkhardt, May 30, 1950; children—Elizabeth, Gretchen, Joan, Amy. Intern, R.I. Hosp., Providence, 1948-49, resident, 1949-50; resident in pediatrics Charles Chapin Hosp., Providence, 1950-51, Boston Children's Hosp., 1951-52, Providence Lying-In Hosp., 1952; practice medicine specializing in pediatrics and allergy, Providence, 1955—; mem. staff R.I., Providence Lying-In, Roger Williams hosps., R.I. Med. Center; dir. pediatrics St. Joseph's-Lady of Fatima Hosp. (all Providence); med. dir. Cath. Diocesan Social Welfare Service of R.I., 1958—, St. Vincent's Center, 1967; dir. metabolic diseases program R.I. Health Dept., 1960—; med. co-dir. R.I. Sch. for Deaf, 1968—; mem. bd. pediatric cons. Child Study Center, Brown U. Med. Sch., Providence, 1967—; asst. clin. prof. pediatrics Brown U.; dir. 1st Bank & Trust Co.; mem. Gov.'s adv. com. Child Welfare Service, 1959—, Gov.'s Children's Code Commn., R.I., 1967—. Served to capt. M.C., AUS, 1953-55. Diplomate Am. Bd. Pediatrics, Am. Bd. Clin. Allergy and Immunology. Fellow Am. Acad. Pediatrics; mem. Am., R.I. (pres.), Providence med. assns., Am. Med. Writers Assn., New Eng. Allergy Soc., Am. Acad. Allergy, Assn. Pres.'s Hosps. Med. Staffs R.I. (pres.). Asst. editor R.I. Med. Jour., 1960—; contbr. articles in field to profl. jours. Home and Office: 255 Waterman St Providence RI 02906

MATHISON, HAROLD RICHARD, diversified industry exec.; b. Bklyn., Nov. 16, 1926; s. Hans G. and Ruby E. (Dunham) M.; student N.Y. State Maritime Coll., 1946; m. Gloria Marian Hansen, Aug. 28, 1948; children—Carol Christine, Marian Elizabeth. Marine engr. Standard Oil of N.J., 1946-51; maintenance engr. Rapid Am. Corp., N.Y.C., 1963; corp. plant engr. Geigy Chem. Corp., N.Y.C., 1964-68; corp. dir. engring. USV Pharm. Corp., N.Y.C., 1968-70; corporate mgr. tech. services Xerox Corp., Stamford, Conn., 1970—; mem. pvt. cons. firm Plant Engring. & Maintenance Assos., Allandale, N.J., 1967—. Mem. com. for drafting and design Rockland County Center Tech., 1966—; mem. Citizen Adv. Com. for Ramapo I Sch. Dist., 1966-69. Served to lt. USNR, 1946-61. Recipient First award for excellence McGraw-Hill Factory Mag. Elec. Maintenance, 1967, First award for excellence McGraw-Hill Modern Mfg. Mag. in Plant Utilities, 1970. Mem. Nat. Assn. Power Engrs., Am. Inst. Plant Engrs. (chpt. pres., past regional v.p.), Air Pollution Control Assn., Soc. Am. Magicians. Contbr. sects. to McGraw Hill Facilities Management and Plant Engineering Handbook, 1970; Prentice Hall's Plant Engineering Manual and Guide, 1971. Contbr. articles to profl. jours. Patentee in field. Home: 1 Strawberry Hill Ave 9E Stamford CT 06902 Office: Long Ridge Rd Stamford CT 06905

MATHISON, STUART LLOYD, data communications exec.; b. Bklyn., Apr. 21, 1942; s. Ralph P. and Eleanor S. (Savage) M.; B.Engring. Physics, Cornell U., 1965; M.S. in Mgmt., Mass. Inst. Tech., 1968; m. June Goldstein, Sept. 14, 1968; children—Robin Jill, David Jay. Systems engr. IBM Corp., N.Y.C., 1965-67; mgmt. cons. Arthur D. Little, Inc., Cambridge, Mass., 1968-72; corporate staff Bolt Beranek & Newman, Inc., Cambridge, 1972-73; v.p., founder Telenet Communications Corp., Washington, 1973—, also dir. Lectr., Northeastern U. Grad. Sch. Engring., 1970-71; cons. Pres.'s Task Force on Communications Policy, 1968; cons. antitrust div. Justice Dept. Author: (with others) Computers and Telecommunications: Issues in Public Policy, 1970. Home: 1976 Lancashire Dr Potomac MD 20854 Office: Telenet Communications Corp 8330 Old Courthouse Rd Vienna VA 22180

MATHUR, KAILASH NATH, radiologist; b. Mussoorie, India, Sept. 16, 1936; s. Robert William and Ivy (Phillips) M.; came to U.S., 1966, naturalized, 1976; M.B.B.S., Christian Med. Coll. (India), 1963; m. Edna Marie Cotton, Jan. 18, 1969; children—Kailash Nath, Tina M., Raj Kumar. Intern, Resurrection Hosp., Chgo., 1966-67; resident, West Penn Hosp., Pitts., 1968-71; radiologist, Pottsville, Pa., 1972—. Diplomate Am. Bd. Radiology. Mem. Am. Med. Assn., Pa. Med. Soc., Am. Coll. Radiology, Pa. Radiol. Soc., Am. Coll. Nuclear Medicine. Home and Office: 78 Sherwood Rd Pottsville PA 17901

MATHUR, SURESH CHANDRA, educator; b. Fatehgarh, U.P., India, Mar. 23, 1930; s. Raghubansh Behari and Kamala (Devi) M.; came to U.S., 1958, naturalized, 1972; B.Sc., U. Lucknow, India, 1948, M.Sc., 1950; Ph.D., U. Tex., 1965; m. Padma Ramaswamy Iyengar, Jan. 2, 1963; 1 dau., Anu Radha. Tech. asst. Atomic Energy Dept., Govt. of India, New Delhi, 1950-52, asst. physicist, 1952-58; research scientist, then sr. research scientist Tex. Nuclear Corp., Austin, 1962-67; prof. physics U. Lowell, Mass., 1967—, dir. Computer Center, 1971—. Mem. Assn. Computing Machinery, Am. Phys. Soc. Democrat. Contbr. articles to profl. jours. Home: 1008 Ray St Manchester NH 03104 Office: Computer Center U Lowell Lowell MA 01854

MATIASEVIC, DOBROSAV, physician; b. Orasac, Yugoslavia, Oct. 5, 1928; s. Radivoje and Zorka M.; M.D., U. Zagreb (Yugoslavia), 1955; m. Ester Olga, June 10, 1961. Resident in medicine Met. Med. Center, N.Y.C., 1959-60, Kingsbrook Med. Center, N.Y.C., 1960-61, Meml. Hosp., N.Y.C., 1961-62, Maimonides Hosp., N.Y.C., 1962-63; fellow in endocrinology and metabolism N.Y. U., Bellevue Hosp., N.Y.C., 1963-65; research fellow in metabolism U. Basel Burgerspital, (Switzerland), 1965-66; asst. physician, mem. staff Flower Hosp., N.Y.C., 1966—; instr. medicine N.Y. Med. Coll., until 1972, asst. prof., 1972—; practice medicine specializing in internal medicine, N.Y.C., 1966—; mem. staff Met. Hosp., N.Y.C. Mem. Fedn. Am. European Med. Socs. (v.p.), Am. Yugoslav Med. Soc. (v.p.) A.C.P., AAAS, Am. Heart Assn., N.Y. Acad. Scis., N.Y. State, N.Y. County med. socs. Home: 321 78th St New York City NY 10021 Office: 1249 Fifth Ave New York City NY 10029

MATINZI, LOUIS FRANCIS, transp. exec.; b. Plymouth, Mass., Dec. 21, 1925; s. Ralph Francis and Bessie Rodgers (Holmes) M.; student Suffolk U., 1946-48, Northeastern U., Boston, 1953-54; m. Theodora Ann Tavares, Sept. 7, 1947; children—Paul A., Donald P. Asst. to gen. traffic mgr. Plymouth Cordage Co., 1950-59; dir. sales and traffic New Eng. Transp. Co., Boston, 1959-69; dir. transp. Ludlow Corp., Needham Heights, Mass., 1969—; dep. asst. dir. transp. Fed. Emergency Mgmt. Agy., Region 1, New Eng.-Nat. Def. Exec. Res., 1972—. Served to 1st lt. AUS, 1943-46, 48-50. Decorated Bronze Star medal, Purple Heart, Combat Inf. Badge. Mem. Am. Soc. Traffic and Transp., Am. Inst. Indsl. Engrs., Soc. Logistics Engrs., New Eng. Shippers Adv. Bd., Nat. Council Phys. Distbn., Nat. Indsl. Traffic League, Transp. Club New Eng. (dir.), Transp. Research Forum, Indsl. Mgmt. Soc., Mass. Chiefs of Police Assn. (asso.). Delta Nu Alpha. Club: Rod and Gun (Plymouth). Home: 68 Summer St Plymouth MA 02360 Office: 145 Rosemary St Needham Heights MA 02194

MATIS, JACOB DAVID, cardiologist; b. N.Y.C., Sept. 27, 1911; s. Joseph D. and Rose (Rand) M.; B.A., Cornell U., 1932; M.D., N.Y. State U., 1936; m. Rosaie Metzger, Oct. 12, 1942; children—George M., Nancy Joy. Intern, Muhlenburg Hosp., Plainfield, N.J., 1936-37; resident N.J. Sanatorium, Glen Gardner, N.J., 1937-39; practice medicine specializing in cardiology, N.Y.C., 1940—; sr. clin. cardiologist Mt. Sinai Hosp., 1940-70; attending physician Roosevelt Hosp., N.Y.C., 1964—; asso. medicine Columbia Coll. Physicians and Surgeons, 1971—. Served to lt. col. M.C., AUS, 1942-46. Fellow Royal Soc. Medicine, Am. Coll. Cardiology, A.C.P.; mem. Am. Coll. Compensation Medicine (bd. govs. 1968—). Jewish (trustee temple). Club: Masons. Contbr. articles to profl. jours. Address: 25 Central Park W New York City NY 10023

MATISSE, PIERRE, art dealer; b. Bohain, ain, France, June 13, 1900; s. Henri and Amelie Noelie (Parayre) M.; came to U.S., 1924 naturalized, 1942; educated privately; m. Alexina Sattler, Dec. 29, 1929; children—Jacqueline Matisse Monnier, Paul, Peter. Founder, 1931, since pres. Pietre Matisse Gallery, N.Y.C. Decorated knight Arts and Letters, Merite Nat. (France). Mem. Am. Art Dealers Assn. (pres. 1964-66). Clubs: N.Y. Yacht, N.Y. Athletic. Home: 167 E 64th St New York City NY 10021 Office: 41 E 57th St New York City NY 10022

MATSCHKE, ARTHUR LOUIS, JR., research co. exec.; b. Chgo., Nov. 16, 1927; s. Arthur Louis and Vera (Thomander) M.; student UCLA, 1945, Ill. Inst. Tech., 1958, Adelphi U., 1974; m. Elaine Louise Olson, Jan. 19, 1948; children—Kurt Louis, Gregg Lon, Rick Alan, Dawn Marie, Gwen Marguerite, Jeff Oscar, Brett Arthur, Ami Louise. Mfg. research Bell & Howell, 1951-57; experimentalist Fiber Optics, Armour Research Found., 1957-58; research project engr. Pyle Nat. Co-Sylvania joint project, 1958-59; automation research Bell & Howell, Matschke & Brooke Inc., AMF, MH and Zenith Radio Co., 1959-66; plant mgr. Zenith Rauland plants, 1966-69; dir. corporate product devel./mfg. Alloys Unltd., 1969-70; pres. Automatic Metal Products Co., Bklyn., also Kinetic Instruments Co., Bklyn., and Nat. Survey Info. Co. Inc., N.Y.C., 1971-72; founder, exec. v.p. Tele Speed Communications Co., Bklyn., 1972-74; founder, pres. Matschke Gen. Research Co., Westport, Conn., 1974-78; cons. hi-speed computer printing, 1972—. Mem. nat. advisory bd. Am. Security Council, 1977—. Served with U.S. Army, 1946. Mem. Mfg. Engring. Council (charter), Soc. Photog. Scientists and Engrs. Republican. Congregationalist. Patentee in field. Office: 21 Charles St Westport CT 06880

MATSUMIYA, YOICHI, neurophysiologist, psychologist; b. Tokyo, Mar. 6, 1934; s. Kazuya and Kaoruko (Ban) M.; A.B., Waseda U., Tokyo, 1957, M.A., 1959; Ph.D., Brown U., 1963; m. Yoshino Nakamura, Aug. 14, 1973; 1 son, Ray. Came to U.S., 1959. Research asso. George Washington U. Sch. Medicine, 1962-65, Yale Sch. Medicine, New Haven, 1965-69; prin. asso. Harvard Med. Sch., 1969—, also dir. spl. procedures in clin. neurophysiology Children's Hosp. Med. Center, Boston, 1969—. Okuma fellow, 1955-57; Fulbright fellow, 1959. Mem. Am., Eastern, Japan psychol. assns., Eastern Assn. Electroencephalographers, Am. Epilepsy Soc., Soc. Psychophysiol. Research, Sigma Xi. Home: 68 Almont St Winthrop MA 02152 Office: 300 Longwood Ave Boston MA 02115

MATSUOKA, SHIRO, physicist; b. Kobe, Japan, May 1, 1930; s. Teikichi and Matsuko M.; came to U.S., 1950, naturalized, 1971; M.E., Stevens Inst. Tech., Hoboken, N.J., 1955; M.S. in Engring. (Union Carbide fellow), Princeton U., 1957, Ph.D., 1959; m. Norma L.C. Chow, Aug. 3, 1957; children—Tama J., Bryce K., Timothy J.H. Mem. staff Bell Telephone Labs., Murray Hill, N.J., 1959—, group supr. plastics dept., 1972-74, head plastics research and devel. dept., 1974—; prof. chemistry Stevens Inst. Tech., 1963-69; vis. prof. Rutgers U., 1978—. Recipient Higley Math. award Stevens Inst., 1953. Fellow Am. Phys. Soc.; mem. Am. Chem. Soc., Soc. Plastics Engrs., Soc. Rheology, AAAS, Sigma Xi, Tau Beta Pi. Author: Dielectric Properties of Polymers; also articles. Home: 161 Thackeray Dr Millington NJ 07946 Office: 60 Mountain Ave Murray Hill NJ 07974

MATTEI, DAVID SAMUEL, hosp. adminstr.; b. Old Forge, Pa., July 23, 1932; s. David O. and Ella V. M.; B.S. in Pharmacy, Duquesne U., 1960; L.L.B., LaSalle Extension U., 1974; m. Evelyn M. Patrick, Oct. 19, 1957; children—David T., Patti Ann, Martin, James. Chief pharmacist St. Mary's Hosp., Scranton, Pa., 1961-66; instr. pharmacology Mercedian Sch. Practical Nursing and Mercy Hosp. Sch. Nursing, Scranton, Pa., 1961-66, dir. pharmacy Mercy Hosp., 1967-72, dir. pharmacy service, 1973-75, asst. adminstr., 1975—; adj. instructor pharmacy Duquesne U., 1976—; Temple U., 1977. Mem. Old Forge Sch. Bd., 1965—, pres., 1967-68; campaign chmn. Old Forge Dem. Com., 1969. Served with USN, 1955-57. Diplomate Am. Bd. Diplomates in Pharmacy. Fellow Am. Coll. Apothecaries, Royal Soc. Health; mem. Pa., Am. pharmaceutical assns., Am., Pa. socs. hosp. pharmacists, Hosp. Mgmt. Systems Soc., Am. Hosp. Assn., Hosp. Assn. Pa., Greater Scranton C. of C. Democrat. Roman Catholic. Contbr. articles papers to pharmaceutical jours. Home: 136 Brodhead Old Forge PA 18518 Office: 746 Jefferson Ave Scranton PA 18501

MATTEI, THOMAS JOSEPH, educator; b. Old Forge, Pa., Aug. 18, 1945; s. David Ottavio and Ella (Vincenti) M.; B.S., Duquesne U., 1968, Pharm.D., 1970; m. Judith Ann Yagle Aug. 16, 1969; children—Thomas Joseph, Todd Christopher, Michael Ryan. Clin. instr. Duquesne U., Pitts., 1971-73, also dir. ambulatory pharm. services Mercy Health Center, Pitts., 1971-73, asst. prof., chmn. clin. pharmacy dept. Duquesne U., 1973—, also asso. dir. clin. pharmacy services and edn. Mercy Hosp., also mem. Edn. for Justice Com., 1974—. Mem. Commn. Health Edn. of Allegheny County. Mem. Am. (vice chmn. council on therapeutics 1974-76, task force on accreditation and advanced residency tng.), Pa. (dir. 1973—, pres. 1976-77) socs. hosp. pharmacists, Am. (chmn.-elect Acad. Pharmacy Practice sect. clin. practice 1976-77), Pa. pharm assns., Rho Chi, Alpha Phi Delta, Phi Delta Chi. Club: Rosslyn Farms Men's. Editor: Drug Distribution in Hospitals, Volume III; contbg. editor Drug Intelligence and Clin. Pharmacy, 1975-78. Research on pharmacokinetics, health edn., also design of treatment protocols. Home: 26 Terrace Rd Carnegie PA 15106 Office: Pride and Locust St Pittsburgh PA 15219

MATTERN, ROBIN DONALD, fin. cons.; b. San Francisco, Apr. 16, 1950; s. John Donald and Jean Adrienne (Jepson) M.; student Boston U., 1968-70, Coll. Environ. Design, U. Calif., 1970-72. Asst. to pres. Mattern Constrn. Co., San Francisco, 1972-73; archtl. design asst. John Carl Warnecke & Assos., Washington, 1973-74; mktg. rep. Sci. Time Sharing Corp., N.Y.C., 1974-76, sr. fin. modeling cons., 1976—. Mem. Assn. Time Sharing Users, Assn. Computing Machinery. Episcopalian. Developer fin. reporting system. Home: 227 E 50th St Apt 17 New York NY 10022 Office: 747 3d Ave New York NY 10017

MATTESON, WILLIAM BLEECKER, lawyer; b. N.Y.C., Oct. 20, 1928; s. Leonard Jerome and Mary Jo (Harwell) M.; grad. Peddie Sch., 1946; B.A., Yale, 1950; J.D., Harvard, 1953; m. Marilee Brill, Aug. 26, 1950; children—Lynn, Sandra, Holly. Admitted to N.Y. bar, 1954; clk. to Judge Hand of U.S. Ct. of Appeals 2d Circuit, N.Y.C., 1953-54; clk. Justice Harold H. Burton, U.S. Supreme Ct., Washington, 1954-55; asso. Debevoise, Plimpton, Lyons & Gates and predecessor firms, N.Y.C., 1955-61, partner, 1961—, partner European office, Paris, 1973-78. Lectr. law Columbia, 1972-73, 77—. Trustee, Peddie Sch., 1968-73, Miss Porter's Sch., 1977—; mem. nat. council Salk Inst. Mem. Assn. Bar City N.Y. (chmn. securities regulation com. 1968-71), Fed., Internat., Am., N.Y. State bar assns. Clubs: Union (N.Y.C.); Sankaty Head (Nantucket); Circle Interallie (Paris). Office: 299 Park Ave New York City NY 10017

MATTEY, JOHN JOSEPH, analyst, appraiser; b. Mt. Pleasant, Pa., Nov. 8, 1927; s. John Michael and Dora Ethel (Polcha) M.; student U.S. Mcht. Marine Acad., 1945, St. Vincent Coll., 1945, U. Pitts., 1953-55, Duquesne U., 1953, Am. U. 1970, Tulane U., 1970, Tampa U., 1971, Del. U., 1968-76, Villanova U., 1973; m. Betty Ann Jacobs, Aug. 16, 1950; children—Marcia Mattey Cooley, Cynthia Mattey Howard, John D., James, Jerome, Joseph, Jeffrey. Mgr. real estate Bi-Lo Stations Gasoline Co., Lawrenceberg, Ind., 1960-66; exec. v.p. Colonial Investment Co., Ltd., Wilmington, Del., 1967-69; mgr. eastern region real estate Petroleum Cons., Louisville, 1969-73; designated sr. appraiser Jackson-Cross Co., Phila., 1973-78; project dir. valuation of Penn Central real estate taken by ConRail, 1976-77; pres. Del. Bond & Mortgage Co., Wilmington, 1968—, Del. Land and Investment Co., Wilmington, 1977—, Analysts and Appraisers, Inc., 1978—; lobbyist State of Del. senate, gen. assembly 1968—. Founder and bd. dirs. Friends of Lepers, Med. Charity, 1970—; pres. Cath. Men's Club, 1954-55. Mem. Am. Right of Way Assn., Am. Inst. Real Estate Appraisers, Appraisal Inst. Can., Assn. Fed. Appraisers, World Future Soc., Friends of Library of Am. Philos. Soc., Smithsonian Assos., Mensa. Republican. Roman Catholic. Club: Monroeville Am. Legion (pres., chaplain 1962-65). Home: 1209 Marsh Rd Wilmington DE 19803 Office: 3600 Silverside Rd Wilmington DE 19810

MATTHAEI, GAY HUMPHREY, interior designer; b. N.Y.C., Mar. 13, 1931; d. Robert Louis and Ethel Gladys Humphrey; B.A., Mt. Holyoke Coll., 1952; grad. Parsons Sch. Design, 1970; M.I.A., Columbia U., 1954; M.A., certificate Russian Inst. Columbia U., 1954; m. Konrad Henry Matthaei, Nov. 16, 1956; children—Marcella, Leslie, Konrad. Lectr., cons. NBC, 1956; dir. Radnick Prodns., Where Time Is a River, 1966-67; cons. N.Y.C. Parks Recreation and Cultural Adminstrn., 1970-72; asso. Pearl R. Mitchell A.S.I.D., 1972-74, owner, 1974-76; owner, mgr. Gay Matthaei East/West, N.Y.C., 1976—. Trustee Mt. Holyoke Coll., Young Audiences; mem. Commn. on State Capital Preservation and Restoration, Conn., 1977-82. Mem. Am. Soc. Interior Designers, Phi Beta Kappa. Christian Scientist. Clubs: River, Mt. Holyoke (N.Y.C.); Madison Beach (Conn.); Pink Sands (Harbour Island, Bahamas). Restorations include Town Farms Inn, 1978, State Capital of Conn., 1977-78. Home: 146 Chestnut Hill Rd Killingworth CT 06417 Office: 127 E 59th St New York NY 10022

MATTHEI, HERMAN, lawyer; b. Boston, Nov. 16, 1912; s. John and Eva (Hoffmann) M.; LL.B., Boston Coll., 1940; m. Edna L. Klein, Oct. 24, 1942; 1 dau., Diane G. Matthei Boden. Traffic mgr. Nat. Wool Mktg. Corp., Boston, 1933-35; asst. traffic mgr. W.F. Schrafft & Sons Corp., Charlestown, Mass., 1935-42; admitted to Mass. bar, 1942, to practice before ICC, 1946; practiced before state regulatory authorities in New Eng. and before fed. regulatory authorites, 1946—; chmn. standing rate com. New Eng. Motor Rate Bur., Inc., Burlington, Mass., 1946-48, gen. counsel, 1949—, gen. mgr., 1963—, treas., 1964—. Vice pres. Greater Boston council Camp Fire Girls, 1965-66, pres., 1967-68, dir., 1965-70. Served with AUS, 1943-45; ETO. Mem. Mass. Motor Truck Assn. (dir. 1964—), Nat. (past v.p.), New Eng. (past pres.) assns. ICC practitioners, Motor Carrier Lawyers Assn., Am. Soc. Traffic and Transp. (founder mem.). Clubs: Masons, Transp. New Eng. (Boston). Home: 36 Birch Tree Dr Westwood MA 02090 Office: New Eng Motor Rate Bur Inc 14 New England Exec Park Burlington MA 01803

MATTHEI, ROBERT THEODORE, mfg. co. exec.; b. Chgo., May 8, 1935; s. August H. and Theodora (Venn) M.; B.Sc., Loyola U., Chgo., 1958; postgrad. N.Y. U., 1962-63; m. Arline Clare Straka, July 13, 1965; children—Julia, Stacy. With Bell & Howell Co., Chgo., 1960-73; v.p. mktg. Singer Edn. Systems, Rochester, N.Y., 1973-77; v.p., gen. mgr. Nikon Photo div. Ehrenreich Photo-Optical Industries, Inc., Garden City, N.Y., 1977—. Mem. Nat. Audio Visual Assn. (dir. 1975-76), Am. Mktg. Assn., Rochester C. of C. Republican. Roman Catholic. Office: 623 Stewart Ave Garden City NY 11530

MATTHES, GERALD STEPHEN, advt. agy. exec.; b. Hamburg, Germany, Aug. 31, 1938; s. Stanley R. and Gerda E. (Spiro) M.; came to U.S., 1964, naturalized, 1977; grad. London Coll., 1962; m. Betsy Durkin, Aug. 22, 1965; 1 son, Peter Charlton. With various advt. agencies, London, Eng., 1959-64; with Doyle Dane Bernbach Inc., N.Y.C., 1964—, v.p. mgmt., supr., 1974—; lectr. London Coll., 1963-64. Mem. Advt. Assn. Gt. Britain. Democrat. Contbr. articles to profl. jours. Home: 145 E 35th St New York City NY 10016 Office: 437 Madison Ave New York City NY 10022

MATTHEWS, A. BRUCE, corporate exec.; b. Clarksburg, W.Va., Dec. 11, 1923; s. Ezra Wilson and Hilma (Nelson) M.; B.S., Ohio U., 1945; m. Marjorie Phillips, 1944 (div. 1962); children—Bruce, Thomas, Jennifer, David, Michelle, Bradford, Christopher; m. 2d, Marjorie Nelson, Dec. 31, 1963. Partner, Arthur Andersen & Co., Detroit, 1945-65, gen. partner, 1956, mng. partner, Denver, 1956-65; v.p. fin. and adminstrn. Communications Satellite Corp., Washington, 1965-70; pres., dir. Bliss & Laughlin Industries, Inc., Oak Brook, Ill., 1970-71; sr. v.p. CNA Fin. Corp., Chgo., 1972-75; chmn. bd., pres.

Larwin Group, Inc., Beverly Hills, Calif., 1974-75; chmn. bd., dir. Healthco, Inc., 1972-75, First Healthcare Corp., 1972-75, CNA Mgmt. Corp., 1973-75, Coaxial Communications, Inc., 1973-75; pres. The Matthews Group, Washington, Cairo, Egypt and London, Eng., 1975—; chmn. bd. Washington Communications Group, 1977—; dir. Gen. Fin. Corp., Employee Benefit Consultants, CNA Investors Group Ltd., 1972-75. Pres., Jr. Achievement Met. Denver, 1960-62, chmn. bd., 1962-64, chmn. bd. Western region, 1964-66, nat. exec. com., 1962—; pres. bd. trustees Graland Country Day Sch., Denver, 1960-61, trustee, 1959-65; treas. Denver Symphony Soc., 1964-65, trustee, 1958-65; chmn. Red Rocks Music Festival, 1960-61; trustee Nat. Symphony Orch., Washington, 1966-70; trustee Avery Coonley Sch., 1971-74, pres., 1973-74; bd. govs. Chgo. Symphony Orchestral Assn., 1972-75; treas., dir. Chgo. Crime Commn., 1970-72; bd. dirs. Health Edn. Inst., 1973-75. Served with U.S. Army, 1942-43. Mem. Fin. Execs. Inst., Am. Inst. C.P.A.'s, Am. Inst. Aeros. and Astronautics, Am. Mgmt. Assn. (Pres.'s Assn.), Nat. Assn. Bus. Economists, Newcomen Soc., Econ. Club Chgo. Clubs: Chicago, Mid-Am., Union League (Chgo.); Hinsdale Golf; Metropolitan Congl., Internat. (Washington); Sky (N.Y.C.). Home: 4970 Rockwood Pkwy NW Washington DC 20016

MATTHEWS, BURNITA SHELTON, U.S. dist. judge; b. Copiah County, Miss., Dec. 28, 1894; d. Burnell and Lora (Barlow) Shelton; LL.B., Nat. U. Law Sch., Washington, 1919, LL.M., M.P.L., 1920, LL.D. (hon.), 1950; LL.D. (hon.), Am. U., 1966; m. Percy Ashley Matthews, Apr. 28, 1917 (dec. Jan. 1969). Admitted to D.C. bar, 1920, Miss. bar, 1924, U.S. Supreme Ct. bar, 1924; pvt. practice, Washington, 1920-49; counsel Nat. Woman's Party, 1921; past mem. com. of experts on women's work ILO; del. Internat. Woman Suffrage Alliance, Paris, 1926; instr. Washington Coll. Law, 1933-37; U.S. dist. judge for D.C., 1949-68, sr. judge. 1968—; mem. legal research com. Inter-Am. Commn. Women, 1932-34. Bd. dirs. Med. Coll. Pa., 1953-75, past 1st v.p.; mem. nat. com. devel. Am. U., 1950; bd. stewards Mt. Vernon Pl. Methodist Ch., Washington, 1951-64; trustee Wesley United Meth. Ch., Washington, 1969-72. Recipient citation D.C. Fedn. Bus. and Profl. Women's Clubs, 1958; Alumni Achievement award George Washington U., 1968. Mem. Am., D.C. (Distinguished Service award 1968), D.C. Women's (pres. 1925-26) bar assns., Nat. Assn. Women Lawyers (pres. 1934-35, asso. editor jour. 1934-35), Internat. Assn. Women Lawyers, Nat. Fedn. Bus. and Profl. Women's Clubs, Am. Legion Aux. (past unit pres.), Kappa Beta Pi. Clubs: Women's City (pres. 1942-43), Pilot (Washington). Address: US District Ct 3d and Constitution Ave NW Washington DC 20001

MATTHEWS, DANIEL GEORGE, editor; b. Lawrenceville, Va., Dec. 18, 1932; s. George Daniel and Evelyn (Goodrich) M.; student George Washington U., 1956-64; m. Linda L. Fink, Oct. 25, 1975; 1 dau., Strelka Jamila. Analyst, VA, Washington, 1953-54; library asst. cataloging U.S. Dept. State, Washington, 1954-63, intelligence and research specialist, 1964-66; editor-in-chief African Bibliog. Center, Washington, 1963—, exec. dir., 1966—; editorial cons. Greenwood Press, N.Y.C., 1967—; pres. Washington Task Force on African Affairs, 1969—; mem. exec. com. coordinating council Internat. Ednl. Exchange, 1969—; lectr., cons. to acad. instns. on Africana collections and U.S. fgn. policy toward Africa. Served with AUS, 1950-53. Mem. African Studies Assn. (asso., award for outstanding contbn. to Africa 1975, mem. publs. com. 1974), African Heritage Studies Assn., ALA. Author: Soviet View of Africa, 1957, A Current Bibliography on Ethiopian Affairs, 1967, 72; editor-in-chief A Current Bibliography on African Affairs, 1963—; editor: African affairs for General Reader, 1967, Current Themes in African Hist. Studies, 1970; editorial bd. African Books in Print, Ife, Nigeria. Home: 1816 New Hampshire Ave NW Washington DC 20009 Office: 1346 Connecticut Ave NW Washington DC 20036

MATTHEWS, DOROTHEA ELIZABETH, lawyer; b. Englewood, N.J., June 12, 1947; d. John Clark and Dorothea (Kidd) M.; A.B. cum laude, Smith Coll., 1969; J.D., Fordham U., 1974. Admitted to N.Y. bar, 1975, U.S. Supreme Ct. bar, 1978; asso. firm Reid & Priest, N.Y.C., 1974—. Mem. Bar State N.Y., Am. Bar Assn., Smith Coll. Alumnae Assn., Fordham Law Alumni Assn., English-Speaking Union. Republican. Presbyterian. Office: 40 Wall St New York City NY 10005

MATTHEWS, MARTIN TAYLOR, retired govt. ofcl.; b. Mohawk, Tenn., Sept. 6, 1902; s. James Newton and Marietta C. (Shipley) M.; B.S., East Tenn. State Tchrs. Coll., 1926; Ed.M., Harvard, 1928; Ph.D., Columbia, 1937; m. Lula Margaret Robson, May 19, 1934. Prin. rural schs., Tenn., 1922-24; social research, tchr. social scis., colls., fed. agys., 1929-32, 34-39, 42-44, 47-48; social sci. analyst U.S. Dept. Agr., 1939-42, 44-47; field research dir. Miami Valley Mental Hygiene Survey, Hamilton, Columbus, Ohio, 1948-49; asso. prof. sociology U. Md. Overseas Program in Germany and Eng., 1949-53; community analyst Iraq, tng. officer Liberia and Thailand U.S. Fgn. Aid Program, 1954-62; social sci. research analyst Social Security Adminstrn., Balt., 1962-72. Mem. Am. Sociol. Assn. (emeritus), Rural Sociol. Soc. Club: Harvard-Radcliffe Md. Author: Experience Worlds of Mountain People, 1937. Contbr. articles to profl. jours. Home: 1629 Ingleside Ave Baltimore MD 21207

MATTHEWS, PAUL RANDOLPH, II, retail co. exec.; b. Wilmington, Del., Jan. 3, 1942; s. John S. and Veronica (Brand) M.; student Villanova U., 1959-60, N.Y. U., 1966; m. Sandra Ohlinger, Aug. 24, 1960 (div. Dec. 1970); children—Donna, Paul, Tina; m. 2d, Carla Carpenter, Mar. 26, 1971 (div. 1977). With Matthews, Inc., Wilmington, 1960-77, v.p., 1965-70, pres., 1970-77; founder, pres. Matthews Vending Programs and Matthews/Rampart, 1977—. Mem. Delaware Valley Stationers Assn. (pres. 1971), Adminstrv. Mgmt. Soc., Nat. Office Products Assn., Nat. Office Machine Dealers Assn., Del. C. of C. Home: Box 1561 Wilmington DE 19899 Office: 2505 W 6th St Wilmington DE 19805

MATTHIAS, GEORGE FRANK, educator; b. Greenport, N.Y., Aug. 22, 1934; s. George and Marguerite (Blanchard) M.; B.S., State U. N.Y. at Cortland, 1957; M.S., Syracuse U., 1962; M.A., Conn. Wesleyan U., 1970; m. Mary Jo Avery, Aug. 18, 1956; children—Todd Avery, Tara Lynn. Instr. secondary earth sci. Belleville (N.Y.) Acad., 1957-58, Croton-Harmon High Sch., Croton-on-Hudson, N.Y., 1961—; tchr./prin. Raquette Lake (N.Y.) Elementary Sch., 1958-61; mem. N.Y. State Earth Sci. Syllabus Revision Writing Commn., 1967-70; coordinator Bur. of Sci. Edn., N.Y. State Dept. Edn., 1971-72; instr. Finger Lakes Inst., Alfred U., 1970; cons. pub. schs. NSF grantee, 1963, 67-70; Shell merit fellow, 1971. Mem. Nat. Assn. Geology Tchrs., Nat. Assn. Research in Sci. Teaching, Research in Sci. Edn. Assn., Sci. Tchrs. Assn. N.Y. State, N.Y. State United Tchrs., Am. Fedn. Tchrs., Metric Assn. Clubs: Lions (Montrose, N.Y.); Masons. Author: (with Berey, Higham, Knabel, Maust) Observation and Interpreation in Earth Science, 1972; (with Daley and Higham) Earth Science: A Study of a Changing Planet, 1976; also articles. Home: 143 Dutch St Montrose NY 10548 Office: Old Post Rd S Croton-on-Hudson NY 10520

MATTIS, NOÉMI PERELMAN, psychologist; b. Lodz, Poland, Oct. 16, 1936; d. Chaim P. and Fela (Liwer) Perelman; B.A. magna cum laude, Université Libre de Bruxelles (Belgium), 1955, LL.D. magna cum laude, 1958; M.A., Columbia U., 1964, Ph.D., 1973; m. Daniel C. Mattis, Nov. 9, 1958; children—Michael, Olivia. Came to U.S., 1958, naturalized, 1962. Trainee VA Hosp., Montrose, N.Y., 1967-68, Bronx, N.Y., 1968-69; staff psychologist Cage Teen Center and Educage, White Plains, N.Y., 1973-76; pvt. practice, 1976—. Edn. chairperson Westchester Center for Psychol. Edn., 1977—; bd. dirs. Youth Shelter Westchester, Inc., 1977—. Certified psychologist, N.Y. State. Mem. Am., N.Y. State, Westchester County (sec. bd. 1977—) psychol. assns., Psi Chi, Kappa Delta Pi, Pi Lambda Theta. Home and Office: 26 Olmsted Rd Scarsdale NY 10583

MATTOX, DANIEL VALENTINE, JR., educator; b. Perryopolis, Pa., Feb. 13, 1922; s. Daniel and Julia Ann (Csábi) Mató; B.S., Pa. State U., 1943, M.Ed., 1955; profl. certificate U. Colo., 1958; Ph.D., Pa. State U., 1972; m. Anne Cleo Burkett, Aug. 25, 1956; children—Daniel Burkett, Jefferson Hoppenjahns, Richard Valen. Dir. guidance Austin E. Lathrop High Sch., Fairbanks, Alaska, 1955-57; asst. prof. Park Coll., Parkville, Mo., 1957-59; adminstr. Pratt County (Kans.) Schs., 1959-61; asst. prof. U. Tenn., Martin, 1961-62; asso. prof. Miss. State Coll. for Women, Columbus, 1962-69; asso. prof. Indiana (Pa.) U., 1969—, chmn. learning resources dept. sch. edn., 1972-77, prof., 1976—; vis. prof. summers Troy (Ala.) State U., 1964-67, Montevallo Coll., Ala., 1963, Kans. State Tchrs. Coll., Emporia, 1961, also Pa. State U., Miss. State U., U. Alaska, U. P.R. Served from pvt. to capt. U.S. Army, 1943-54. Decorated Combat Infantry Badge, Bronze Star; Nat. Teaching fellow, 1967-68. Mem. Am. Edn. Research Assn., Am. Psychol. Assn., NEA, Nat. Soc. for Study Edn., AAUP (chpt. pres. 1965-67), Assn. Edn. Communication and Tech., Pa. Learning Resources Assn. (chmn. tchr. edn. group 1972—), Pa. Edn. Assns., VFW, Am. Legion. Presbyterian. Clubs: Rotary, Masons, Shriners. Book rev. editor AudioVisual Instrn., 1966-74; contbr. articles to profl. jours., met. newspapers. Home: Route 2 Box 264-1 Homer City PA 15748 Office: Dept Edn Indiana U Indiana PA 15701

MATULAVAGE, PETER ANDREW, artist; b. Kingston, Pa., Sept. 23, 1915; s. Andrew and Veronica (Bainaravage) M.; grad. magna cum laude N.Y. Phoenix Sch. Design, 1951; 1 dau., Pamela. Foreman, Blue Ribbon Cake Co., Pa., 1931-34; supr. Seymour Mfg. Co., Conn., 1940-43; artist Illustrators, Inc., N.Y.C., 1951-54, Warsaw Studios, N.Y.C., 1957-73; free lance artist, 1954—; instr. N.Y. Phoenix Sch. Design, 1954-75, Pratt-Phoenix Schs. Design, 1976—, New Sch. Parsons Sch. Design, 1976—. Served with AUS, 1943-46. Decorated Purple Heart; recipient design awards N.Y. Phoenix Sch. Design, 1951, Wyoming Valley Sesquicentennial Watercolor award, 1957; Distinguished Service award DAR, 1976. Mem. Am. Artists Profl. League (dir. 1976—; Tristate watercolor award 1973, graphic award 1975), Allied Artists Am., Am. Watercolor Soc., Wilderness Soc., Nat. Art League (graphic award 1975, 77), New Rochelle Art Assn. (v.p., chmn. 1971-73, watercolor award 1974, 76, graphic award 1975), Hudson Valley Art Assn. (dir. 1976—), Salmagundi Club (co-chmn. jury of awards 1974-75, mem. curator's com. 1975—). Works include series of oil paintings for Cathedral Saints Peter and Paul, Ansonia, Conn. Home: 340 E 55th St New York City NY 10022

MATUNAS, MARIAN STARRETT (MRS. ANTHONY L. MATUNAS), psychoanalyst; b. Indpls., June 12, 1929; d. Wendell Holmes and Evalyn Elizabeth (Haig) Starrett; B.S., Northwestern U., 1950; M.A., N.Y. U., 1954, Ph.D., 1960; diploma in psychoanalysis Postgrad. Center for Mental Health, N.Y.C., 1970; m. Anthony L. Matunas, Nov. 7, 1956; 1 son, Anthony Laurence. From clin. psychologist to sr. psychologist Kings Park State Hosp., 1955-58; sch. psychologist Hicksville (N.Y.) Pub. Schs., 1958-60; staff psychologist Kings County Hosp., Bklyn., 1960-64; dir. psychol. services Jewish Meml. Hosp., N.Y.C., 1964-67; supervising clin. psychologist Postgrad. Center Mental Health, N.Y.C., 1967-69, faculty, 1975—; pvt. practice psychoanalysis and psychotherapy, N.Y.C., 1965—; adj. prof. Union Grad. Sch. at Antioch, 1969-74. Certified in child psychiatry, mental health consultation. Mem. Am., N.Y. State psychol. assns., Soc. Projective Techniques, Psi Chi, Pi Lambda Theta, Kappa Delta Pi. Home: 333 E 30th St Apt 3L New York City NY 10016 Office: 11 E 68th St Suite 1B New York City NY 10021

MATZ, DAVID JEROME, solar electric co. exec.; b. Phila., May 9, 1945; s. Benjamin and Claire (Whitman) M.; B.S., U. Pa., 1967; M.S., U. Wis., 1969, Ph.D., 1972; m. Roberta Rubenfein, Dec. 25, 1966; children—Paul, Jeremy. Mem. research staff Engring. Research Center, Western Electric Co., Princeton, N.J., 1972-76; project mgr. Solar Energy Systems, Newark, Del., 1976—. NSF fellow 1970-71; NDEA fellow, 1967-70. Mem. Am. Inst. Chem. Engrs., Soc. Polymer Engrs. Democrat. Jewish. Home: 4620 Talley Hill Ln Wilmington DE 19803 Office: One Tralee Industrial Park Newark DE 19711

MATZA, BRIAN, tech. sch. adminstr.; b. N.Y.C., Feb. 21, 1939; s. Morris and Molly (Prager) M.; A.A., State U. N.Y., 1958; postgrad. Queens Coll., 1962-65, U. Bridgeport; m. Nancy Hill, July 4, 1971; children—Evan David, Alexis Ruth. With M & M Refrigeration Co., N.Y.C., 1958-60, 62-66; tech. manual writer A.M.F. Co., Greenwich, Conn., 1960-62; flight and ground instr. Flight Safety Inc., Farmingdale, N.Y., 1966-69; owner, operator Climate Control Co., N.Y.C., 1969-70; tchr. N.Y.C. Bd. Edn., 1970-71; asst. to pres. New Eng. Tech. Inst., Providence, 1971-72; pres., dir. Associated Tech. Inst., Woburn, Mass., 1972—; asst. to vocat. dir. Manpower Devel. Program, N.Y.C. Certified flight instr., aviation ground instr., comml. pilot, FAA. Mem. Nat. Assn. Trade and Tech. Schs. Clubs: B'nai B'rith, Masons. Home: 148 Lincoln Rd Medford MA 02155 Office: 233 W Cummings Park Woburn MA 01801

MATZNER, ALEXANDRA MARIA, physician; b. Skarszewy, Poland; d. Mieczyslaw Jerzy and Pelagia Klara (Kasicka) Markiewicz; M.D., Med. Acad. Gdansk (Poland), 1952; m. Joseph M. Matzner, Mar. 5, 1961; 1 dau., Karen. Came to U.S., 1961, naturalized, 1964. Intern Med. Acad., Gdansk, 1952-53; resident Urbanowicz and Mielecki Hosp., Chorzow, 1953-60; practice medicine specializing in internal medicine and infectious diseases, Chorzow, 1953-60, specializing in radiology, Boston, 1966-70, Saugus, Mass., 1970—; radiologist Saugus Gen. Hosp., 1970—; mem. staff VA Hosp., Boston, 1966-70, Mt. Pleasant Hosp., Lynn, Mass. Home: 12 Forbes Ln Andover MA 01810 Office: 136 Boston St Lynn MA 01902

MAUCHLINE, DANIEL DONALD, ednl. and vocat. cons.; b. Pitts., Apr. 28, 1926; s. Daniel and Mitzi M.; B.Sc., Fla. State U., 1955; M.R.C., U. Fla., 1957; m. Ethel E. Mixon, Aug. 9, 1958; children—Pamela, Tracy, Gregory. Supr. counseling and selective placement Fla. Employment Service, 1955-57; project dir. Rehab. Center Greater St. Louis, 1958-60; project dir. Polk County (Iowa) Soc. Crippled Children and Adults, 1960-62; asst. exec. dir. Balt. League, 1962-66; cons. rehab., career planning and econs. of disability, 1966—; speaker on placement of handicapped; mem. Bowie City Council Mental Health Adv. Com., 1972-75. Served with USAAF, 1944-47, USAF, 1947-48. Decorated Air medal; Office Vocat. Rehab. fellow, 1957-58. Mem. Nat. Vocat. Guidance Assn., Am. Rehab. Counseling Assn., Nat. Employment Counseling Assn. Contbr. numerous articles on vocat. evaluation of disabled, vocat. placement of disabled to profl. jours. Home and Office: 2709 Federal Ln Bowie MD 20715

MAUGER, KARL FREDERICK, supt. schs.; b. Milton, Pa., Jan. 27, 1923; s. Wilbur Harry and Blanche Marguerite (Carl) M.; B.S., Bucknell U., 1953, M.S., 1956; Ed.D., Pa. State U., 1965; m. Mary Ann Shimer, June 24, 1950; children—Karen Ann, Frederick Scott, Karl Frederick. With Milton (Pa.) Sch. Dist., 1953-66, tchr., 1953-55, dean boys, 1954-55, guidance counselor, 1955-58, asst. prin. Milton Area High Sch., 1956-58, prin. Jr. High Sch., 1958-64, curriculum coordinator, 1964-66; supt. schs., Bellefonte, Pa., 1966-75, North Pocono Sch. Dist., Moscow, Pa., 1975—; lectr. edn. Bucknell U., 1963-66; mem. Gov.'s Commn. on Pub. Sch. Fin., 1967-68, Gov.'s Commn. on Basic Edn., 1972-73, Pa. Bd. Edn., 1970-76. Mayor, Milton, Pa., 1958-64; chmn. Bellefonte Area Indsl. Corp., 1970-75; chmn. Bellefonte chpt. ARC, 1970-75. Served with AUS and to maj. gen. Pa. 1940—. Decorated Bronze Star with two oak leaf clusters, Air medal with two oak leaf clusters. Mem. Am. Assn. Sch. Adminstrs., Assn. Supervision and Curriculum Devel., Mil. Order World Wars, N.G. Assn. U.S., Pa. Episcopal. Clubs: Masons, Elks. Home: Box 141 RD 4 Moscow PA 18444 Office: North Pocono Schs Church St Moscow PA 18444

MAUKE, OTTO RUSSELL, coll. pres.; b. Webster, Mass., Jan. 26, 1924; s. Otto G. and Florence (Giroux) M.; A.B., Clark U., 1947, A.M., 1948; Ph.D. (Kellogg fellow), U. Tex., 1965; m. Leah Louison, June 18, 1950. Tchr. history, academic dean Endicott Jr. Coll., Beverly, Mass., 1948-65; academic dean Cumberland County Coll., Vineland, N.J., 1966-67; pres. Camden County Coll., Blackwood, N.J., 1967—. Served with AUS, 1943-46; PTO. Home: PO Box 126 Blackwood NJ 08012

MAULDIN, ANITA JACKSON, sch. counselor; b. Betsy Layne, Ky., Sept. 18, 1921; d. James Henry and Edna Diew (Harris) Jackson; A.B., Columbia Union Coll., 1943; M.A., Peabody Coll. for Tchrs., 1958; postgrad. U. Md., 1965-70; m. Lloyd Wesley Mauldin, Sept. 19, 1943; children—Carol Anne Testerman, Lloyd William. Tchr. elementary grades Seventh-day Adventist Schs., Md., Ga., Nebr., 1943-47; instr. Seven-day Adventist preparatory and jr. coll., Indonesia, 1948-58; tchr. first grade Davidson County Pub. Schs., Nashville, 1958-60, Prince George's County Pub. Schs., Landover, Md., 1960-70, elementary counselor, 1970—; instr. coll. summer sch., county summer schs.; condr. workshops for tchrs., parents, church personnel. Chmn. Seventh-day Adventist Family Life Com., Met. Washington, 1977-78, chmn. vacation Bible Sch., leader Sabbath Sch. primary div., adult div. Recipient commendation awards, Prince George's County Assn., 1973, 76; NDEA grantee, 1971, 72; certified parent and tchr. effectiveness tng. instr. Mem. Am. Personnel and Guidance Assn., Nat. Vocat. Guidance Assn., Sch. Counselors Assn., Elementary Sch. Counselors Assn., Individual Psychology Assn., Group Work Assn., Assn. for Non-White Concerns, NEA. Co-author handbook for tchrs. of talented and gifted students, 1977. Home: 3905 Pitcairn Pl Laurel MD 20810 Office: 919 Hill Rd Landover MD 20785

MAUNEY, GLORIA JUANITA MEANS, librarian; b. Whitmire, S.C., Feb. 26, 1927; d. Barney Floyd and Sallie Coleman (Hunter) Means; B.S., Allen U., Columbia, S.C., 1950; M.S. in Library Sci., Cath. U. Am., 1968; m. Percy Eugene Mauney, Dec. 26, 1953; children—Shari Corinne, Louis Alvin. Reference librarian Natural History Library, Smithsonian Instn., Washington, 1960-64, br. librarian dept. entomology, 1965-68; librarian D.C. Pub. Schs., 1968—. Mem. ALA, D.C. Library Assn., D.C. Assn. Sch. Librarians, Smithsonian Assos., Alpha Kappa Alpha. Home: 23 Jefferson St NE Washington DC 20011 Office: 4501 Kansas Ave NW Washington DC 20011

MAURER, JOSEPH ABELE, educator; b. Bethlehem, Pa., Sept. 29, 1911; s. Andrew and Lydia (Abele) M.; A.B., Moravian Coll. Theol. Sem., 1932; M.A., Lehigh U., 1936; Ph.D., U. Pa., 1948; m. Kathleen E. Danneberger, Jan. 19, 1957. Instr. Latin and English, Moravian Coll., 1932-36, asst. prof., 1936-43; Latin master Princeton (N.J.) Country Day Sch., 1943-47; instr. Greek and Latin, Lehigh U., 1947-49, asst. prof., 1949-53, asso. prof. classical langs., 1953-55, head dept. classical langs., 1956-75, prof. classics, 1964-77, prof. emeritus, 1977—, asso. dean for langs., 1975-77, chmn. protem modern fgn. langs., 1975-77; lectr. N.T. Greek at Acad. New Church, Bryn Athyn, Pa., 1948-49. Mem. Am. Philol. Assn., Moravian Hist. Soc., Classical Assn. Atlantic States (pres. 1964-65), Phi Beta Kappa (hon.), Pi Gamma Mu, Phi Alpha Theta, Eta Sigma Phi, Alpha Chi Rho. Democrat. Episcopalian. Editor-in-chief The Classical World, 1968-71, asso. editor, 1971-73. Home: Bridle Path Woods D-12 400 Bridle Path Rd Bethlehem PA 18017

MAURER, LORETTA ANNA, educator; b. Bklyn., Sept. 2, 1936; d. Joseph and Anna (Mader) M.; diploma Bklyn. Hosp. Sch. Nursing, 1960; B.A. in Health Edn., Jersey City State Coll., 1970, M.A. in Health Adminstrn., 1973. Staff nurse S.I. (N.Y.) Developmental Center, 1963-66, head nurse, 1966-69, nurse instr., 1969—, coordinator rehab. unit, 1965. Mem. Phenylketonuria Screening Com.; del. postgrad. symposium Elwyn Inst., Media, Pa., 1973. Mem. N.Y. State Legis. Adv. Com., 1970—; mem. policy making seminars of Med. Adv. Bd. N.Y.C., 1969; mem. N. Shore Republican Club Richmond County, Women's Rep. Club N.Y. State, Fedn. Women's Rep. Clubs N.Y. State; mem. S.I. Consumer's Adv. Council on Mental Health, 1977—, Bard Ave. Residents Assn., Forest Regional Residents Civic Assn. Mem. Royal Soc. Health, Am. Nurses Assn., Am. Assn. on Mental Deficiency (in-service rep. regional 9 conf. Del. 1972), N.Y. State Mental Hygiene Employees Assn., Columbiettes K.C., NE Outward Bound Alumni Assn. Roman Catholic. Club: South Mountain Figure Skating. Home: 481 Bard Ave Staten Island NY 10310 Office: 2760 Victory Blvd Staten Island NY 10314

MAURER, RICHARD HORNSBY, physicist; b. Reading, Pa., Apr. 27, 1942; s. Samuel Forrest and Marian Elizabeth (Hornsby) M.; B.S., L.I. U., 1964; Ph.D., U. Pitts., 1970; m. Marian Ross Harvey, May 3, 1975; 1 son, Jonathan Harvey. Fellow Bartol Research Found. of Franklin Inst., Swarthmore, Pa., 1970-73; environmental test engr., physicist AMP, Inc., Harrisburg, Pa., 1973—; faculty classical mechanics Bartol Research Found., 1970-73; faculty elec. engring. University Center, Harrisburg, 1974-75. Asso. advisor explorers, Boy Scouts Am., Harrisburg, 1974-75. NASA fellow, 1966-69. Mem. Am. Phys. Soc., Optimates, Sigma Xi. Democrat. Methodist. Club: Central Pa. Pitt (sec.-treas.). Contbr. articles to profl. jours. Home: PO Box 469 Rural Delivery 1 Elizabethtown PA 17022 Office: 2100 Paxton St Harrisburg PA 17105

MAURETTI, GERALD JOSEPH, textile co. exec.; b. Fall River, Mass., July 13, 1943; s. Pasquale Joseph and Julia Louise (Hallisey) M.; B.S., Southeastern Mass. U., 1965; m. Nancy Ann Tacovelli, July 4, 1964; children—Lisa Jean, Thomas Gerald, Christine Ann. Product devel. engr. Am. Thread Co., Willimantic, Conn., 1965-68; mgr. cost and waste control Providence Pile Fabric Corp., Fall River, 1968; mgr. textile research labs. Leesona Corp., Warwick, R.I., 1968-74, market research specialist, 1974-75; tech. sales rep. and market research mgr. Laurel Products Corp., Phila., 1975—; vis. lectr. to colls. Pres. Watuppa Water Commn., 1978-79, Watuppa Water Bd., City of Fall River; mem. Fall River Community Fin. Corp. Mem. U.S. Jaycees (dir. Fall River chpt. 1969-70), Am. Assn. Textile Tech. (chmn. New Eng. chpt. 1976—), Am. Assn. Textile Chemists and Colorists, Am.

Mktg. Assn., ASTM, Textured Yarn Assn. Am. (charter), Internat. Textile Club, Textile Analysts Group, Southeastern Mass. U. Alumni Assn. Roman Catholic. Club: Westport (Mass.) Yacht (exec. com. 1977—). Contbr. numerous articles on processing, control and testing of textured textile yarns to profl. jours. Home: 41 Reservoir St Fall River MA 02723 Office: Laurel Products Corp 2600 E Tioga St Philadelphia PA 19134

MAURMEYER, ROBERT CARL, educator; b. Hanover, Germany, Apr. 30, 1902; s. Richard C. and Hilda (Christmann) M.; came to U.S., 1922, naturalized, 1928; B.S., Coll. City N.Y., 1928; A.M., Columbia, 1932; Ph.D., N.Y. U., 1939; m. Helga C. Maltan, Aug. 24, 1950; 1 dau., Evelyn Mary. Tutor chemistry Bklyn. Coll. City U. N.Y., 1929-36, instr. chemistry, 1936-48, asst. prof., 1948-58, asso. prof. 1958—71, prof. emeritus, 1971—, dep. chmn. dept. chemistry, summer sessions, 1956-65 Fellow AAAS, Am. Inst. Chemists; mem. Am. Chem. Soc., Am. Microchem. Soc., N.Y. Acad. Sci. (life), Sigma Xi. Club: N.Y. Athletic (N.Y.C.). Contbr. to profl. jours. Research in microchemistry functional group analysis. Home: 102-27 93d Ave Richmond Hill NY 11418

MAUSER, STEPHEN FREDERICK, elec. engr.; b. Seattle, July 12, 1946; s. Roy Kent and Harriet Linton (Maher) M.; B.E.E., Oreg. State U., 1969; M.S., U. Pitts., 1975; divorced; children—John Allen, Richard Lee, Stephanie Dawn. Counselor, Oreg. State U., 1967-68; with Westinghouse Elec. Advanced Systems Tech., E. Pitts., 1969—, mgr. devel. projects, 1978—; condr. seminars. Active local Boy Scouts Am. Recipient certificate of merit Johnstown (Pa.) VHF Soc., 1977. Mem. IEEE (vice chmn. Pitts. 1978-79), Irwin Area Amateur Radio Assn. Republican. Roman Catholic. Author papers. Office: 700 Braddock Ave East Pittsburgh PA 15112

MAVROS, CONSTANTIN, social and health services adminstr.; b. Athens, Greece, Oct. 13, 1941; s. Anargyros and Sophia (Kouthouridou) M.; M.A., Concordia U., 1975; m. Marie Louise Sichitig, Dec. 12, 1966; children—Myriam Sophia, Sylvia Martha, Aris. Dir. Community Center, Siegen, W. Ger., 1964-66; dir. Greek Canadian Radio Sta., Montreal, Que., Can., 1966-69; dir. Greek Canadian Citizen's Rights Assn., Montreal, 1969-74; dir. Multiethnic Community Centre Pilot A, Montreal, 1974—; cons. Sch. Social Work McGill U.; v.p. Univ. Settlement Montreal. Bd. Dirs. St. Mary's Hosp. Served with Greek Army, 1962-64. Sec. State grantee, 1974, Ministry Nat. Health and Welfare grantee, 1975, Manpower and Immigration Can. grantee, 1976. Mem. U.S. Capitol Hist. Soc., Nat. Council on Social Devel., Community Politics Soc. (sec.). Home: 469 Clarke Westmount PQ Canada Office: 4652 Jeanne Mance Montreal PQ H2Y 4J4 Canada

MAVROS, DONALD ODYSSEUS, clay worker, sculptor, educator, author; b. N.Y.C., Mar. 4, 1927; s. Peter Aristede and Elizabeth (Samiotakis) Mavrogenis; individual studies with ceramists in sculpture, pottery, 1944-45, 49-52. Exhibited one-man shows Pietrantonio Galleries, N.Y.C., 1956, Avant Garde Galleries, 1958, Nonagon Galleries, N.Y.C., 1959, 60, Galerie Nouvelle, Paris and Orleans, France, 1960, Wedgewood Galleries, Laurelton, N.Y., 1963, Bklyn. Mus. Art Sch., 1964, Alexander Gallery, 1967, Trias Gallery, N.Y.C., 1971, 72, 74, 75, Sculpture House Gallery, N.Y.C., 1973, Hazelton (Pa.) Art League Gallery, 1973, Greater Middletown (N.Y.) Arts Gallery, 1974, 77, 78; exhibited group shows including Syracuse Mus. Fine Arts, Met. Mus. Art, N.Y.C., Cin. Art Mus., Dayton Art Mus., Everson Mus., Syracuse, N.Y., Mus. for Decorative Arts, N.Y.C., U. Wis.; founder Mavros Workshop, N.Y.C., 1954—; represented in permanent collections; faculty New Sch. for Social Research, N.Y.C., 1960—; dir. Trias Gallery, N.Y.C., 1966—. Adviser Greater Middletown (N.Y.) Arts Council; mem. City of Unionville (N.Y.) Planning Bd., 1973—. Served with Chem. Corps, U.S. Army, 1945-49. Recipient sculpture awards Syracuse (N.Y.) Mus. and Am. Crafts Council, 1951, 52, 54, Pottery award Am. Crafts Council, 1954. Mem. Artist-Craftsmen N.Y. (v.p. 1968-69), Nat. Council Edn. Ceramic Arts, Am. Crafts Council. Author: Getting Started in Ceramics, 1970. Home: POB 547 Unionville NY 10988 Office: 49 W 28th St New York City NY 10001

MAVROULES, NICHOLAS, Congressman; b. Peabody, Mass., Nov. 1, 1929; student M.I.T. With Sylvania Corp., 1949-67; mayor Peabody, 1967-78; mem. 96th Congress from 6th Mass. dist. Office: 1204 Longworth House Office Bldg Washington DC 20515*

MAVROVIC, IVO, cons. engr.; b. Fiume, Italy, Dec. 5, 1927; s. Janko and Milica (Grgurina) M.; B.S., Tech. Faculty U. Zagreb (Yugoslavia), 1952, M.S. in Chem. Engring., 1954; m. Erna Gallian, Oct. 14, 1955; 1 son, Paul. Came to U.S., 1959, naturalized, 1964. Project engr. Dorr-Oliver, Milan, Italy, 1955-59, Stamford, Conn., 1959-60; process engr., group leader Chem. Constrn. Corp., N.Y.C., 1959-65; cons. engr., N.Y.C., 1965—; pres. Urea Techs., Inc., Hackensack, N.J. Registered profl. engr., N.Y. Mem. Am. Inst. Chem. Engrs. Patentee in field. Home and Office: 530 E 72d St New York City NY 10021

MAXWELL, MICHAEL, opera mgr.; b. Westport, N.Z., Jan. 6, 1936; s. Eric and Phyllis (Christian) M.; ed. King's Coll., Auckland, N.Z., 1949-53. Asst. program officer N.Z. Broadcasting Service, 1955-59; orch. mgr. Philharmonia Orch., London, 1960-63; tour mgr. Royal Philharmonic Orch., London, 1963; mgr. Princeton Chamber Orch., 1964-65; promotion dir. N.Y. Philharmonic, 1965-66; asst. mgr. Cleve. Orch., 1966-70, gen. mgr., 1970-76; mng. dir. Opera Co. of Boston, 1976—. Mem. recommendation com. Avery Fisher Artist Award Program; past trustee University Circle, Inc., Cleve.; past profl. adv. trustee Cleve. Music Sch. Settlement; past bd. dirs. Cleve. Ballet Guild. Mem. Am. Symphony Orch. League (patron, past dir.), Ohio Arts Council (former mem. music adv. panel), English-Speaking Union (former mem. jr. com. Cleve.). Home: 85 E India Row Boston MA 02110 Office: 711 Boylston St Boston MA 02116

MAXWELL, RICHARD ANTHONY, retail exec.; b. N.Y.C., Apr. 1, 1933; s. Arthur William and Mary Ellen (Winestock) M.; student N.Y. U., 1957-58, Acad. Advanced Traffic, 1959; m. Jacqueline Ann Creamer, Oct. 27, 1962. Import mgr. Asso. Merchandising Corp., N.Y.C., 1950-52, 56-65; divisional v.p. Asso. Dry Goods Corp., N.Y.C., 1965—. Served with USAF, 1952-56. Mem. Am. Importers Assn. (v.p., dir.), Shippers Conf. Greater N.Y. (pres., dir. 1975-77), Nat. Com. Internat. Trade Documentation (chmn. import com. 1972-75, vice chmn. gen. bus. com. 1975-78), Italy-Am. C. of C. (dir.), Transp. Assn. Am. Home: 47 Hardenburgh Ave Demarest NJ 07627 Office: 417 Fifth Ave New York City NY 10016

MAY, ARTHUR GLOVER, ret. oil co. exec.; b. Birmingham, Ala., Mar. 12, 1891; s. Lewis Alexander and Susie (Glover) M.; student Cornell U., 1911-12, U. Ala., 1912-13; m. Esther Boudo, Sept. 23, 1933; children—Suzanne, Arthur, Lewis. Ter. mgr. Standard Oil Co., of N.Y., China, 1916-30, N.Y. mgr. China div., 1930-39, London mgr., 1939-40, area mgr. China at N.Y., 1940-41; exec. sec. Fgn. Ops. Com. apptd. by Petroleum Adminstrn. War, 1941-45; area mgr. China Standard Vacuum Oil Co., 1946-50; sec. Standard-Vacuum Oil Co., 1951; exec. sec. Petroleum Supply Com. (Petroleum Adminstrn. for Def.), 1951, Middle East Emergency Com., 1956—; chmn. Fire Commn. Hon. life fire commr. Pound Ridge (N.Y.) Fire Dist.; councilman, Pound Ridge, 1959-63; chmn. Pound Ridge Park and Recreation Com., 1959-63; trustee, treas. Hiram Halle Meml. Library, pres. until 1962, now hon. life trustee. Served as 2d lt. F.A., U.S. Army, 1918. Recipient Good Neighbor award Town of Pound Ridge, 1958. Mem. Delta Tau Delta. Clubs: Am., Columbia Country (Shanghai); Tientsin, Tientsin Race, Tientsin Country (Tientsin, China); Cornell, Shanghai Tiffin (N.Y.); Tokeneke (Darien, Conn.). Home: RD 4 Pound Ridge NY 10576

MAY, DEAN EDWARD, pub. relations co. exec.; b. Lafayette, Ind., Oct. 31, 1944; s. Carl Eugene and Mary Louise (Miller) M.; B.S. in Agrl. Bus. Mgmt., Purdue U., 1967; m. Judy Gail Rozwat, June 26, 1971. Commodity buyer Quaker Oats Co., Chgo., 1967-72; mktg. specialist, resinite div. Borden Chem., N. Andover, Mass., 1972-76; chmn. bd. May Communications, Inc., Old Bridge, N.J., 1976—; mktg. cons. Chmn. environ com. N.J. Council Dive Clubs. Author: Great Diving-I, 1974; author, producer, underwater photographer: Diving in Roatan, 1973. Home: E1 Hillside Ct Highlands NJ 07732 Office: RD 1 206 Hwy 34 Matawan NJ 07747

MAY, HUGH JOHN, economist; b. Iron Mountain, Mich., May 9, 1918; s. Hugh J. and Lillian (Wallace) M.; student Park Coll., 1935-37. B.S., Northwestern U., 1941, M.A., 1942; m. Doris D. Double, June 12, 1944; children—John Arthur, James Philip. Statistician, FAA, Washington, 1945, various positions aviation statistics div., planning officer planning and devel. office, 1957-59, chief bus. analysis and forecast div. Bur. Nat. Capital Airports, 1959-67, staff asst. to dir., also industry economist, office of aviation econs., 1967-74, sr. industry economist, aviation forecast br., office of aviation policy, 1974—. Accredited airport exec. Am. Assn. Airport Execs. Mem. Soc. Govt. Economists, Nat. Geog. Soc. Clubs: Nat., Dulles Airport. Contbr. articles to profl. publs. Home: 2505 N Granada St Arlington VA 22207 Office: FAA 800 Independence Ave SW Washington DC 20591

MAY, JAMES, indsl. designer; b. Heilbronn, Germany, Feb. 27, 1921; s. Henry and Thekla (Saenger-lMai) M.; 1 dau., Vicki Barbara; came to U.S., 1936, naturalized, 1942. Vice-pres. Perspectives Inc., N.Y.C., 1948-49; dir. Inspire Industries Design Workshop, N.Y.C., 1950-58; pres. James May Orgn. Inc., N.Y.C., 1959—, also dir.; exhibited in group shows Cooper-Hewitt Mus., N.Y.C., 1978, Sarah Campbell Blaffer Gallery, U. Houston, 1979, Portland (Ore.) Art Mus., 1979, Art Inst. Chgo., 1979; TV guest appearances Pub. Broadcasting System, ABC, Miami, Fla., 1978; lectr., cons. Co-chmn. Friends to Save Mar-A-Lago. Served to capt., Signal Corps, U.S. Army, 1942-46. Mem. Nat. Soc. Indsl. Design (dir. 1967-70), Am. Assn. Textile Chemists and Colorists (sr.), Inter-Soc. Color Council, Carpet and Rug Inst. Club: Curzon House (London). Author: Carpet Printing, 1973. Developer polypropylene fibers indoor and outdoor carpeting, flatbed and rotary carpet printing. Office: James May Orgn Inc 137 E 36th St New York City NY 10016

MAY, SAMUEL CASAMERE, physician; b. Syracuse, N.Y., Sept. 19, 1920; s. Mark A. and Ruby C. (Patton) M.; B.S., Harvard U., 1942; M.D. cum laude, Yale U., 1945; m. Thelma Simmons, July 6, 1946; children—Mark G., Linda E. Intern, New Haven (Conn.) Hosp., 1945-46; asst. resident in surgery VA Hosp., Newington, Conn., 1948-49; asst. resident in surgery Univ. Hosp., Iowa City, 1949-52, resident in surgery, 1952-53; sr. surgeon Elliot Hosp., Manchester, N.H., 1954—, chief surgery, 1964-71, pres. staff, 1969-70; attending surgeon VA Hosp., 1954-57; courtesy staff surgery Sacred Heart Hosp., Notre Dame Hosp.; cons. surgeon Alexander Eastman Hosp., Derry, N.H., 1954—; sr. aviation med. examiner FAA, 1969—; trustee Elliot Hosp.; mem. N.H. Bd. Registration in Medicine. Active Am. Cancer Soc., 1956—; mem. N.H. Aeros. Com., 1974—, Air Transport Com. Served as capt. USAF, 1946-48. Diplomate Am. Bd. Surgery. Fellow A.C.S. (state liaison fellow cancer 1964; pres. N.H. chpt. 1974-75), Am. Coll. Chest Physicians, Am. Coll. Angiology, Am. Geriatrics Soc.; mem. Am. Thoracic Soc., Assn. Mil. Surgeons, Am. Trudeau Soc., Am. Inst. Aeros. and Astronautics, Pan Am. Med. Assn., Aerospace Med. Soc., N.H. State Med. Soc. (treas. 1965-66), New Eng. Surg. Soc. Clubs: Manchester Country. Address: 188 Tarrytown Rd Manchester NH 03103

MAYBERGER, HAROLD WOODROW, physician; b. Astoria, N.Y., Aug. 28, 1919; s. George Joseph and Grace Annie (Kemp) M.; student L.I. U., 1937-38; A.B., U. Ala., 1941; M.D., L.I. Coll. Medicine, 1944; m. Eva Marie Yerkovich, Mar. 10, 1951; children—Mary Grace, John Peter, James Francis. Rotating intern St. Johns Episcopal Hosp., Bklyn., 1944-45, 47-48, resident in obstetrics and gynecology, 1948-51; research fellow pathology Beth El Hosp., 1951-53; practice medicine, specializing in obstetrics and gynecology, Syosset, N.Y., 1953—, Glen Cove, N.Y., 1957—; staff mem., chief div. obstetrics-gynecology Community Hosp., Glen Cove; sometimes lectr.; cons. St. Johns Episc. Hosp., Bklyn.; asso. prof. clin. obstetrics and gynecology State U. N.Y., Stony Brook, 1974—. Served from lt. to capt. M.C., AUS, 1945-47. Diplomate Am. Bd. Obstetrics and Gynecology. Fellow A.C.S., Am. Coll. Obstetricians and Gynecologists, Am. Coll. Legal Medicine; mem. AAAS, AMA, N.Y. Acad. Sci., Nassau Obstet. and Gynecol. Soc., Nassau Surg. Soc., N.Y., Nassau County med. socs., Theta Kappa Psi. Contbr. articles to profl. jours. Home: Bear Ln Locust Valley NY 11560 Office: 99 Forest Ave Glen Cove NY 11542 also 99 Cold Spring Rd Syosset NY 11791

MAYER, ALFRED I., music synthesizer mfg. co. exec.; b. Newark, N.J., Nov. 11, 1921; s. Harry and Gussie (Erman) M.; B.S., Juillard Sch. Music, 1946; m. Annette R. Siegler, June 29, 1950; children—Bonnie Beth, Scott Brooks, Wendy Sue, Keith Jon. Chmn. accordion dept. Henry St. Settlement, 1946-53; mem. faculty dept. music Bklyn. Coll., 1950-62; pres. Alfred Mayer Organ Studios, Inc., 1945—; pres. Doric Organ Co., 1966-70; pres. Ionic Industries, Inc., Morristown, N.J., 1970—; condr. Alfred Mayer Orchs. Served with AUS, 1942-45. Mem. Am. Fedn. Musicians, Audio Engring. Soc., Accordion Tchrs. Guild Internat., Nat. Assn. Mus. Mchts. Clubs: Rotary, Masons. Patentee in field; composer, arranger, rec. artist. Contbr. articles to profl. jours. Address: 128 James St Morristown NJ 07960

MAYER, EDWARD FREDERICK, mgmt. cons.; b. Bklyn., Oct. 1, 1907; s. Frederick E. and Freda E. (Pless) M.; student Coll. City N.Y., 1925-27; m. Jean Blodwyn Wilson, July 12, 1947; children—Russell A., Patricia J., Carol B., Deborah J. Budget adviser Standard Oil Co. (N.J.), N.Y.C., 1924-64; dir. devel. C.W. Post Center of L.I. U., 1964-76, mem. exec. council, 1958-64. Founder, pres. Assn. Parents and Friends C.W. Post Coll., Inc., 1959-64; trustee Feiga Gory Remetier Found., Forest Hills. Decorated Grand Cross Eloy Alfaro Internat. Found. Pamama; recipient Pres.'s medal meritorious service C.W. Post Coll. Mem. Kappa Delta Rho. Club: Masons. Lutheran. Home: Blueberry Hill RD 1 Lebanon NH 03766

MAYER, JEFFREY ALAN, career apparel co. exec.; b. Bronx, N.Y., June 25, 1940; s. Joseph Henry and Cele (Brodsky) M.; grad. Peekskill Mil. Acad., 1958; m. Leslie Patricia Gordon, June 13, 1964; children—Jamie Alison, Jennifer Dawn, Casey Paige. Prodn. trainee Limelight Modes, Inc., N.Y.C., 1961-64; v.p. Mister Trio, Inc., pres. Fashion T, N.Y.C., 1965—. Active Harrison Non-Partisan Nominating Com. for Sch. Bd., 1976-77, Harrison Aux. Police, 1978—. Served with U.S. Army, 1959-61. Club: K.P. Home: 12 Rolling Hills Ln Harrison NY 10528 Office: 463 7th Ave New York City NY 10018 also 1350 Broadway New York City NY 10018

MAYER, KLAUS, internist; b. Mayence, Germany, May 21, 1924; s. Stephan Karl and Caecilie E.M. (Mueller) M; came to U.S., 1934; naturalized, 1941; B.S., Queens Coll., 1945; M.D., U. Groningen (Germany), 1950; m. Vera Strasser, May 6, 1950; children—Rulon Richard, Carla Christina. Intern, Hosp. of St. Raphael, New Haven, 1950-51; resident Meml. Sloan-Kettering Cancer Center, N.Y.C., dir. blood bank and hematology labs., 1966—. practice medicine specializing in internal medicine and hematology, N.Y.C., 1956—; mem. staffs Meml., N.Y., Manhattan Eye and Ear, Rockefeller U. hosps., Hosp. for Spl. Surgery; clin. asso. prof. medicine Cornell U. Med. Coll., N.Y.C., 1968—. Served with U.S. Army, 1943-46. Mem. Am. Assn. Blood Banks. (pres. 1973-74). Home: 45 Sutton Pl S New York City NY 10022 Office: 1275 York Ave New York City NY 10021

MAYER, ROBERT STANLEY, psychohistorian; b. Newark, Mar. 31, 1934; s. Barney and Mildred (Rappaport) M.; B.S., Rutgers U., 1956, M.A., 1965, Ph.D., 1968; grad. and fellow Am. Inst. Psychotherapy and Psychoanalysis, N.Y.C., 1970-77. Lectr., Rutgers U., New Brunswick, N.J., 1967-68; asst. prof. history Kean Coll. N.J., Union, 1968-72, asso. prof., 1972—; lectr. U.S. Army Signal Corps Sch., Fort Monmouth, N.J., 1969-72; faculty Am. Inst. Psychoanalysis and Psychotherapy, 1978—; staff therapist Community Guidance Service, 1974—, supr., 1977—; cons. in psychohistory. Certified psychotherapist, N.Y. Mem. Am. Hist. Assn., Internat. Psychohist. Assn., N.Y. State Assn. Practicing Psychotherapists, Am. Psychoanalytic Assn. Author: San Francisco: A Chronological and Documentary History, 1974; Los Angeles: A Chronological and Documentary History, 1976; San Diego: A Chronological and Documentary History, 1976; Psychobiographical Studies, 1978. Home and Office: 40 E 10th St New York City NY 10003

MAYER, SONDRA, printmaker; b. N.Y.C., July 12, 1933; d. Irving and Grace (Eil) Elster; B.A., Syracuse (N.Y.) U., 1954; M.A., Columbia U., 1955; postgrad. Pratt Inst., 1967-68, Art Students League, 1972-73; divorced; children—Howard Jeffrey, Jessica Beth. Group exhbns. include Artists Equity, 1972, 76, 77, Nat. Arts Club, 1977, Nat. Print Exhbn., 1977, Davidson Galleries, Seattle, 1976, Phila. Print Club, 1978, Dreyfuss Gallery, Ann Arbor, Mich., 1978; teaching asst. Ruth Leaf Studio, Douglaston, N.Y., 1976—; represented in permanent collections Albright-Knox Gallery, Buffalo, Los Angeles County Mus. Art, Syracuse U., Lowe Gallery, Bus. Com. for Arts, N.Y., Crocker Nat. Bank, San Francisco; works reproduced on greeting cards by Met. Mus. Art and Mus. Modern Art. MacDowell Colony fellow, 1978. Mem. Artists Equity, Phila. Print Club, Graphic Arts Council. Address: 6 Wooley Ln Great Neck NY 11023

MAYER, STUART DAVID, clin. psychologist; b. Montclair, N.J., Apr. 5, 1938; s. Milton and Helen (Buxbaum) M.; A.B., Columbia Coll., 1960; Ph.D., Adelphi U., 1967. Psychologist, VA Med. Center, East Orange, N.J., 1963—; co-adj. faculty mem. Rutgers U., 1968-76; individual practice clin. psychology, Clifton, N.J., 1966—; cons. Passaic (N.J.) Collegiate Sch., 1962-65, East Orange Pub. Schs., 1966, At-The-Cliffs Sch., Westwood, N.J., 1966-69, Paterson (N.J.) Orphanage, 1971-73. Mem. Clifton Juvenile Conf. Com., 1975—, sec., 1976-77. Adelphi U. Teaching fellow, 1962-63. Mem. N.J., Am., Eastern psychol. assns., Am. Congress Rehab. Medicine. Home: 207 Lincoln Ave Clifton NJ 07011 Office: Psychology Service VA Med Center East Orange NJ 07019

MAYERSON, DONALD JOEL, psychiatrist; b. Toronto, Ont., Can., Sept. 3, 1938; s. Sam and Minnie M.; came to U.S., 1944, naturalized, 1949; B.S. cum laude, Bklyn. Coll., 1958; M.D., State U. N.Y., Syracuse, 1963; m. Bonnie Mann, July 4, 1971; children—Katharine Mann, Louis Mann. Intern, L.I. Coll. Hosp., Bklyn., 1963-64; resident in psychiatry St. Vincent's Hosp., N.Y.C., 1964-66, 68-69; individual practice medicine specializing in psychiatry N.Y.C., 1969—; asst. dir. day hosp. Roosevelt Hosp. dept. psychiatry, 1969-71, dir., 1971-74, ward adminstr., inpatient unit, 1974-76; asst. adj. psychiatrist Lenox Hill Hosp., N.Y.C., 1976—; clin. instr. psychiatry Columbia U., N.Y.C., 1969—; attending psychiatrist St. Vincent's Hosp., 1969—, Cabrini Med. Care Center, N.Y.C., 1976—. Served to capt. USAF, 1966-68. Diplomate Am. Bd. Psychiatry and Neurology. Mem. Am. Psychiat. Assn., N.Y. Med. Coll. Psychiat. Soc., William Silverberg Soc., Mensa. Film, theatre critic The Villager, N.Y.C., 1968-71; film critic Cue mag., 1970-76. Office: 220 Central Park S New York City NY 10019

MAYERSON, MARJORIE KONWALER, counselor; b. Bklyn., May 9, 1949; d. Julius and Betty Konwaler; B.A. cum laude, Bklyn. Coll., 1970, M.S. in Counseling, 1973; postgrad. in social work Adelphi U., 1977—; m. Martin David Mayerson, June 29, 1969; children—Bruce, Cara. Early childhood tchr. N.Y.C. Bd. Edn., 1970; counselor Freeport (N.Y.) Family Service Center, summer 1976; corrections counselor in decision making Ossining (N.Y.) Correctional Facilities, 1976—; youth and family counselor Five Towns Community Center, Inwood, N.Y., 1978; bd. dirs. Long Islanders for Thresholds. Active Lawrence Cedarhurst Hadassah, 1974—, exec. v.p., bull. editor, 1976-77, pres., 1977—, named Woman of Year, 1977. Certified counselor, N.Y. Mem. Am. Personnel and Guidance Assn., Pub. Offenders Counselors' Assn., Kappa Delta Pi. Home: 409 Buckingham Rd Cedarhurst NY 11516

MAYES, EDYTHE BEAM, novelist, poet; b. Kings Mountain, N.C., May 9, 1902; s. Charles Lemuel and Mary Florence (McGinnes) Beam; ed. Lenoir Rhyne Coll., Juilliard Sch. Music, N.Y. U.; studied voice with Count Trabadello, Paris, Madam Cortesi, Milan, Italy; m. LeRoy H. Mayes, Sept. 26, 1926 (dec.). Former mem. staff N.Y. Times; in charge fgn. dept. Macfadden Publs., N.Y.C., 1924; active (with husband) in fund raising for colls., univs. and founds. Author: The Gift (containing Our Debt to the Negro, Prose Poem to Chardin), 1973; Washington. . . God's Workshop, 1973; Flesh is Grass, 1974; Never Too Old, 1974; Men Born Before Time, The Night's Sweet Bird, Seed Time and Harvest; Mrs. Patty's Pace, 1976; also numerous published poems, essays, short stories. Address: 358 Clark Ave Staten Island NY 10306

MAYES, STANLEY RYDER, pub. co. exec.; b. New Orleans, Sept. 21, 1926; s. Robert Morris and Evelyn Mabel (Ryder) M.; B.A., S.W. Mo. State U., 1951; m. Kathryn Weddle, Aug. 15, 1959 (dec.); 1 son, Jeffrey David. Advt. mgr., v.p. I.G.A.S., Inc., Springfield, Mo., 1951-59; with The Kiplinger Washington Editors Inc., 1959—, asst. to pres., dir. sales, 1969—, also dir.; speaker numerous direct mktg. confs. Adviser, Nat. Trust for Historic Preservation; patron Blue Ridge (Va.) Sch.; trustee Direct Mail Ednl. Found. Mem. Nat. Press Club, Am. Mgmt. Assn., 100 Million Club of N.Y., Direct Mktg. Club of Washington (Man of Year 1967, pres. 1969), Pres's. Club, Washington Bd. Trade, Advt. Club Met. Washington, Kappa Alpha. Democrat. Roman Catholic. Home: The Savoy Apt 701 1101 New Hampshire Ave NW Washington DC 20037 Office: 1729 H St NW Washington DC 20006

MAYHALL, JANE FRANCIS (MRS. LESLIE G. KATZ), author; b. Louisville, May 10, 1921; d. Howard Wesley and Loula Eliza (Bennett) M.; student Black Mountain Coll., 1937-40, Black Mountain Music Sch., 1944, Middlebury Music Sch., 1939, Longy Music Sch., 1940-41, New Sch. for Social Research, 1946-48, Claremont Coll., summer 1948; m. Leslie George Katz, June 4, 1940. Mem. faculty New Sch. for Social Research, N.Y.C., 1948; mem. summer workshop faculty Morehead (Ky.) State Coll., 1960-62, Alice Lloyd Coll., Pippa Passes, Ky., 1968; guest lectr. Ohio U., Athens, 1968, N.Y. U., 1950, New Sch. for Social Research, 1950. Fletcher Pratt prose fellow Breadloaf Sch. English, 1958, Yaddo fellow, Edward MacDowell fellow. Author: (play) Eclogue, 1954; Cousin to Human, 1960; Ready for the Ha-Ha, 1966; Givers and Takers, 1969; contbr. articles, poems, short stories, critical essays to various pubs. including Cross Sections, Best Am. Short Stories, Botteghe Oscure, New World Writing, N.Y. Times Book of Verse, Partisan Rev., Modern Lang. Quar., Nation, Harpers Bazaar, Aphra, Quar. Rev. of Lit., Paris Rev., O'Henry Prize Stories, others; translator: (with Otto Guth) Die Kluge, 1968. Home: 15 W 67th St New York City NY 10023

MAYLE, FRANCIS CARL, JR., physician; b. Newark, June 5, 1928; s. Francis C. and Pauline (Finkbeiner) M.; B.S., Georgetown U., 1949, M.D., 1953, M.S. in Neurophysiology, 1959; m. Barbara Mollach, May 30, 1953; children—Marjorie, Francis Carl, Katherine, Paul. Intern, U.S. Naval Hosp., St. Albans, N.Y., 1953-54; resident Georgetown U. Hosp., Washington, 1956-59, Mt. Alto VA Hosp., Washington, 1956-59, D.C. Gen. Hosp., 1957; practice medicine specializing in neurology, Bethesda, Md. and Washington, 1959—; mem. staffs Providence, Georgetown U. Children's, Sibley hosps., Washington Hosp. Center (all Washington), Suburban Hosp., Bethesda, Holy Cross Hosp., Silver Spring, Md.; asst. clin. prof. neurology Georgetown U. Sch. Medicine, 1959—. Chmn. regional adv. com. Met. Washington Regional Med. Programs, 1969-73; chmn. bd. Md. Med. Polit. Action Com., 1973-76. Served with USNR, 1953-56. Diplomate Am. Bd. Neurology. Fellow A.C.P., Am. Geriatric Soc.; mem. AMA, Am. Epilepsy Assn., Soc. Med. Assn., Montgomery County (v.p. 1972-73, pres. elect 1974-75, pres. 1975-76), D.C. med. socs., St. Luke's Soc., Georgetown Clin. Soc., Washington Med. and Surg. Soc., Am. Acad. Neurology (press and pub. relations chmn. 1969-73), Council Med. Chirurg. Faculty Md. (vice chmn. 1975-76, pres. 1978-79), Georgetown U. Alumni Assn. (senate). Club: K.C. Home: 4903 Scarsdale Rd Washington DC 20016 Office: 8212 Wisconsin Ave Bethesda MD 20014

MAYNARD, CATHERINE THERESA, educator; b. Worcester, Mass., July 28, 1945; d. Joseph Edward and Veronica Alice (Lundy) M.; A.B. in Biology, Anna Maria Coll., 1967; M.Ed. in Sci. Edn., Worcester State Coll., 1972. Mgr. lab. Anna Maria Coll., Paxton, Mass., 1967-69; tchr. chemistry biology and career oriented sci. Wachusett Regional High Sch., Holden, Mass., 1969—. Mem. Nat. Sci. Tchrs. Assn. (conv. speaker 1977), Mass. Tchrs. Assn., NEA, Wachusett Regional Tchrs. Assn. Roman Catholic. Home: 9 Maybrook Pl Worcester MA 01602

MAYNARD, DONALD NELSON, plant scientist; b. Hartford, Conn., June 22, 1932; s. Harry Ashley and Elsie Frances (Magnuson) M.; B.S., U. Conn., 1954; M.S., N.C. State U., 1956; Ph.D., U. Mass., 1963; m. Charlotte Louise Grybko, Mar. 23, 1974; 1 son, David Nelson. Instr. plant sci. U. Mass., Amherst, 1956-62, asst. prof., 1962-67, asso. prof., 1967-72, prof., 1972—, asst. dean, 1974-75; cons. Greenleaf, Inc., Hackensack, N.J. Recipient Aid to Edn. award Gulf Oil Corp., 1965. Mem. Am. Soc. for Hort. Sci. (Environ. Quality Research award 1975, Marion W. Meadows award 1977), Am. Soc. Agronomy, Sigma Xi., Phi Kappa Phi, Alpha Zeta, Phi Tau Sigma. Republican. Episcopalian. Asso. editor Jour. Am. Soc. Hort. Sci., also HortSci., 1975—. Home: 202 Strong St Amherst MA 01002 Office: Dept Plant and Soil Sci U Mass Amherst MA 01002

MAYO, RALPH ELLIOTT, chemist; b. Greenville, N.C., May 9, 1940; s. William Louis, and Mattie (Harris) M.; student E. Carolina U., 1958-60; B.S., Emory U., 1963, Ph.D., 1966; m. Tommie Nelda Humphries, Dec. 21, 1964; children—Jonathan Luke, Jane-Margaret. Sr. research chemist Perkin Elmer Corp., Norwalk, Conn., 1966-68; supr. methods devel. Air Products & Chemicals Co., Marcus Hook, Pa., 1968-78, mgr. analytical services, 1978—. Recipient chemistry award Am. Inst. Chemists, 1961, Chem. Rubber Co., 1959, physics award, 1960; NDEA fellow, 1963-65; Best Sci. scholar, 1958-59. Mem. AAAS, Am. Chem. Soc., Soc. Applied Spectroscopy, Catalyst Club. Contbr. articles in field to tech. jours. Home: 1231 Hawthorn Ln West Chester PA 19380 Office: PO Box 427 Marcus Hook PA 19061

MAYO, ROGER CARMELL, mfg. co. pres.; b. Milton, Fla., July 19, 1932; s. Clifford G. and Jessie Maye (Cox) M.; student Rice U., 1950-51; B.S. in Elec. Engring., U. Fla., 1954; postgrad. Northeastern U., 1970-71; m. Geraldine Rose Brill, July 6, 1956; children—Darryl, Cassandra. Communication, distbn., meter engr., div. sales mgr. Gulf Power Co., Pensacola, Fla., 1958-69; mgr. mktg. Anchor Electric, Manchester, N.H., 1969-71, v.p. mktg. Anchor Electric div. Sola Basic Industries, Manchester, 1971-73, pres. Sola Basic Ltd., Toronto, Ont., Can., 1973—, also dir. Served as aviator USNR, 1955-58. Mem. Canadian Elec. Mfrs. Assn., Met. Toronto Bd. Trade. Registered profl. engr., Fla., N.H. Presbyterian. Home: 991 Indian Rd Mississauga ON Canada Office: 377 Evans Ave Toronto ON Canada

MAYOCK, ROBERT LEE, internist; b. Wilkes-Barre, Pa., Jan. 19, 1917; s. John F. and Mathilde M.; B.S., Bucknell U., 1938; M.D., U. Pa., 1942; m. Constance M. Peruzzi, July 2, 1949; children—Robert Lee, Stephen Philip, Holly Peruzzi. Intern, Hosp. of U. Pa., Phila., 1943-44, resident, 1944-45, chief med. resident, 1945-46, attending physician, 1946—, chief pulmonary disease sect. 1955-72, sr. cons., 1972—; chief pulmonary disease sect. Phila. Gen. Hosp., 1959-72; asst. prof. clin. medicine U. Pa., 1959-70, prof. medicine, 1970—. Served to capt. U.S. Army, 1952-54. Diplomate Am. Bd. Internal Medicine. Fellow A.C.P., Am. Coll. Chest Physicians (regent, 1972—); mem. Pa., Phila. County med. socs., Physiology Soc. Phila., Laennec Soc. Phila., (pres. 1963-64), Am. Thoracic Soc., N.Y. Acad. Scis., AMA, Am. Fedn. for Clin. Research, Am. Lung Assn. Phila. and Montgomery County (dir. 1961—; pres. 1966-69), Am. Heart Assn., Pa. Lung Assn. (dir. 1976—), Alpha Omega Alpha, Sigma Xi. Clubs: Merion Cricket, Swiftwater Reserve. Contbr. articles in field to med. jours. Home: 244 Gypsy Ln Wynnewood PA 19096 Office: Hosp U Pa 214 Maloney Bldg Philadelphia PA 19104

MAZARAKIS, MICHAEL GERASSIMOS, physicist; b. Volos, Greece, Apr. 25, 1937; s. Gerassimos N. and Anthy M. (Kappatos) M.; B.S. in Physics summa cum laude (Greek Govt. fellow), U. Athens, 1960; Diplome d'Etudes Supérieures in Physics (French Govt. fellow), U. Paris, 1963, Ph.D. with honors in Physics, 1965; Ph.D. in Physics, U. Pa., 1971. Prof., Mil. Acad. Res. Officers, Athens, 1960-62; research asso. Greek Nuclear Center Democritos, Athens, 1960-62, 65-66, French Nuclear Center, Saclay, 1962-65; prof. Sibytanidios Coll., Athens, 1965-66; instr., research asso. Rutgers U., New Brunswick, N.J., 1971-72, sr. research asso., 1972-74; dir. exptl. program Migma Inst. High Energy Fusion, Princeton, N.J., 1973-77; dir. Fusion Energy Corp., Princeton, 1973-77, v.p., 1974-77; physicist Argonne Nat. Lab. (Ill.), 1978—. Served to lt. Greek Army, 1960-62. Mem. Am. Phys. Soc., IEEE, Am. Water Ski Assn., Sigma Xi. Mem. Greek Orthodox Ch. Contbr. numerous articles on nuclear physics, astrophysics and migma physics to sci. jours. Patentee migma fusion reactor; research in thermal neutron physics, nuclear physics, migma physics and nuclear astrophysics. Home: 307 Emmons Dr Princeton NJ 08540 Office: PO Box 2005 3684 US Route 1 Princeton NJ 08540

MAZEL, JOSEPH LUCAS, editor; b. Paterson, N.J., Oct. 1, 1939; s. Joseph Anthony and Anne (Kidon) M.; B.M.E., Newark Coll. Engring., 1960; m. Joyce Virginia Kronenberger, Apr. 20, 1968; children—Joseph William, Jeanne Eileen. Mech. engr. Austin Co., Roselle, N.J., 1960-61; engr. Western Electric Co., Newark, Atlanta, 1961-62; asst. asso., sr. editor Factory mag. McGraw-Hill Publs. Co., N.Y.C., 1962-71, editor-in-chief 33 Metal Producing mag., 1971—; guest lectr. Writers Conf., Newark Coll Engring., 1972-78. Mem. N.G., 1963-69. Recipient Apolloneer award Gen. Electric Co., 1966; Jesse H. Neal certificate of merit, 1977. Mem. Assn. Iron and Steel Engrs., Iron and Steel Soc., Inst. Mining, Metall. and Petroleum Engrs., Soc. Advancement Mgmt., Am. Inst. Indsl. Engrs., Am. Soc. Mag. Editors, Am. Soc. Bus. Press Editors. Clubs: K.C. (grand knight 1967-68, trustee); Pitts. Press. Home: 40-22 Tierney Pl Fairlawn NJ 07410 Office: 33 Metal Producing Mag McGraw Hill Bldg 1221 Ave of the Americas New York City NY 10020

MAZENAUER, ARTHUR JOHN, pub. co. exec.; b. Buffalo, Apr. 28, 1944; s. Arthur Francis and Dorothy Catherine (Powel) M.; student U. Buffalo, 1963-65, Millard Fillmore Coll., 1964-65; m. Barbara Lee Mitchell, Apr. 15, 1966; children—Heath John, Heather Leigh. With Grand Island Penny Savers (N.Y.), 1963—, pres., 1965—; editor, pub. Island Dispatch, 1978—. Chmn. bus. div. Grand Island United Funds, 1973; adv. bd. dirs. Neighbors Found. Recipient Young Man of Year award C. of C., 1975. Mem. Grand Island C. of C. (treas. 1973-74, sec. 1974-75, 2d v.p. 1975-76, 1st v.p. 1976-77, pres. 1977-78). Lutheran. Club: Rotary (local pres. 1973-74). Home: 2584 W Oakfield Rd Grand Island NY 14072 Office: 1869 Whitehaven Rd Grand Island NY 14072

MAZLEN, ROGER GEOFFREY, physician, clin. pharmacologist; b. Bklyn., Nov. 23, 1937; s. Henry Gershwin and Ann Kurland (Shapero) M.; B.S. in Biology, Rensselaer Poly. Inst., 1959; M.D., State U. N.Y., Bklyn., 1963; m. Sandra Phyllis Kuritzky, Aug. 7, 1960; children—James Edward, Vivien Gayle. Intern, Maimonides Med. Center, Bklyn., 1963-64; resident in medicine, 1964-65; research asso. NIH, Bethesda, Md., 1965-67; resident in med. ophthalmology Mt. Sinai Med. Center, N.Y.C., 1967-69; asso. med. dir. Pfizer Inc., N.Y.C., 1970-71; asst. dir. clin. research Ayerst Labs., N.Y.C., 1971-75; asso. dir. clin. research Schering Corp., Bloomfield, N.J., 1975-78; adj. asso. prof. biology Rensselaer Poly. Inst.; adj. asst. prof. medicine N.Y. Med. Coll.; sr. clin. asst. Mt. Sinai Sch. Medicine; med. dir. Clearview Nursing Home, Whitestone, N.Y.; med. cons. Profl. Children's Sch. Bd. dirs. Bayside Hills Civic Assn., 1970—; adv. mem. bd. dirs. U.S.A., Inc., 1970-72; founder, chmn. Queens County (N.Y.) Common Cause, 1972-75, vice chmn. N.Y. State, 1974-75. Served with USPHS, 1965-67. Fellow Am. Coll. Nutrition (sec.-treas.; chmn. council on nutrition and cardiovascular disease 1976—); mem. Am. Soc. Clin. Pharmacology and Therapeutics, Am. Soc. Parenteral and Enteral Nutrition, Am. Pub. Health Assn., AMA, N.Y. Cardiol. Soc. Republican. Club: Williams (N.Y.C.). Author: A New Manifesto for Middle America, 1972; (with others) Nutrition and Health Care; contbr. chpt. to Quick Reference to Clinical Nutrition. Office: 21 E 66th St New York NY 10021

MAZO, BERTRAND ROSS, metall. engr.; b. Bklyn., Dec. 16, 1941; s. Jack Lawrence and Francis (Gittelson) M.; B.S., Poly. Inst. N.Y., 1964; M.B.A., Hofstra U., 1968; m. Shirley Paula Holtz, Aug. 14, 1965; children—Eileen, Susan. Metall. engr. Charles Davidoff Inc., N.Y.C., 1964; with Ebasco Services, N.Y.C., 1964—, chief quality assurance engr., 1973—. Registered profl. engr., Calif. Mem. Am. Soc. Metals, Am. Inst. Metall Engrs., ASME (com. on nuclear quality assurance). Contbr. articles in field to profl. jours., tech. seminars and confs. Home: 9 Kenwood Ln Matawan NJ 07747 Office: 2 Rector St New York City NY 10006

MAZON, MEYER IRA, aerospace engr.; b. Bklyn., Jan. 25, 1922; s. Morris and Pearl (Spector) M.; A.A.S., Queensborough Community Coll., 1976; B.S., State U. N.Y., 1977; m. Sara Tuman, June 27, 1965; children by previous marriage—Patricia, Robert; stepchildren—Dennis, Martin. Designer, A. Johnson Machine Works, Bklyn., 1945-49, Joe Lowe Corp., N.Y.C., 1949-51, Cons. and Designers, Inc., N.Y.C., 1951-52; design engr. Am. Machine & Fdy. Co., Bklyn., 1952-55; engring. supr. Sunstrand-Turbo div., Pacoima, Calif., 1955-58; advanced engring. specialist Allstates Design & Devel. Co., Cin., 1958-59; mech. engr. Ziel-Blossom & Assoc., Cin. 1959-61; engr. Cons. and Designers, Inc., N.Y.C., 1961-63; engr. Grumman Aerospace Corp., Bethpage, N.Y., 1963—; cons. air pollution and bldg. constrn. Served with U.S. Army, 1939-45. Decorated Bronze Star; registered profl. engr., Ohio, N.Y. Mem. N.Y. Soc. Profl. Engrs. Jewish. Patentee in field. Address: 134-09 59 Ave Flushing NY 11355

MAZOR, DAVID MARK, urologist; b. Bklyn., May 29, 1938; s. Morris and Claire (Frankel) M.; A.B., U. Rochester, 1959; M.D., U. Bologna (Italy), 1965; m. Helen Server, Sept. 10, 1966; children—Eric S., Melissa S. Intern, L.I. Jewish-Queens Hosp. Center, Queens, N.Y., 1965-66, resident in urology, 1967-70; practice medicine specializing in urology, Great Neck, N.Y., 1970—; asso. urologist, North Shore Univ. Hosp., Manhasset, N.Y., 1970—; staff urologist L.I. Jewish-Hillside Med. Center, New Hyde Park, N.Y., 1970—; asso. vis. urologist Queens Hosp. Center, Jamaica, N.Y., 1970—; asst. attending urologist St. Francis Hosp., Roslyn, N.Y., 1975—; asst. clin. prof. surgery (urology) Cornell U. Med. Coll., 1977—. Diplomate Am. Bd. Urology. Fellow A.C.S.; mem. Am. Urol. Assn., AMA, N.Y. Acad. Medicine, Nassau Surg. Soc., Phi Delta Epsilon. Contbr. articles to urol. jours. and textbooks. Home: 14 Split Rock Dr Great Neck NY 11024 Office: 29 Barstow Rd Great Neck NY 11021

MAZUR, HELEN LOUISE JONES GROUTEN (MRS. ALBIN M. MAZUR), civic worker, med. sec.; b. Wilkinsburg, Pa., Aug. 2, 1923; d. Edward and Helen (Cooper) Jones; student Burroughs Secretarial Sch., 1941; m. Walter A. Grouten, July 21, 1946 (div. June 1961); 1 son, Barry Alan; m. 2d, Albin Mazur, Sept. 25, 1971; stepchildren—Dean Anthony, Kim Michael. Chief adminstr. United Fund, Avon, Conn., 1963-72, also bd. dirs.; med. sec. Fitzsimmons Gen. Hosp., Denver, 1942-46, Gilbert W. Heublein, M.D., Hartford, Conn., 1946-53, 59-67, Garner Lewis, M.D., Simsbury, Conn., 1959—. Pres., Tunxis council United Ch. Women, 1965-68, sec. Ch. Women United Conn., 1967; pres. Woman's Club, Avon, 1967; dir. pub. relations Conn. Yankee council, Girl Scouts U.S.A., 1966-67; bd. dirs. Conn. Health League; mem. Avon Pub. Health Nursing Bd.; mem. Avon Republican Town Com., 1964-72, sec., 1966-67, 68-72; justice of peace, Avon, 1968-72. Recipient Service award United Fund, Avon, 1966, Amblyopia Clinics, Conn. Soc. Prevention Blindness, 1965-68. Mem. UN Assn. Hartford (sec. 1968-78, pres. 1978—), Pub. Health Assn. Conn. (legis. chmn. 1966-67), Avon Pub. Health Nursing Assn. (dir. 1960-70), League of Women Voters Congregationalist. Club: Avon Woman's (editor newspaper 1968-71). Home: 88 Spring Ln West Hartford CT 06107 Office: 720 Hopmeadow St Simsbury CT 06070

MAZUR, RONALD MICHAEL, clergyman; b. Boston, May 14, 1934; s. Mitchell Michael and Blanche Marie (Mikanovich) M.; A.B., Boston U., 1955; M.Div., Harvard U., 1959; children—Michal Joyce, Nathan Ronald. Ordained to ministry Unitarian Universalist Ch., 1959; exec. dir. Unitarian Christian Fellowship, Boston, 1963-65; minister 1st Ch., Salem, Mass., 1965-70; pvt. practice sexuality counseling, Salem, 1970-72; dir. peer sexuality edn. program Univ. Health Services, U. Mass., Amherst, 1972—; cons. dept. edn. and social concern Unitarian Universalist Assn. Co-founder Citizens for Better Pub. Schs., Salem. NIMH grantee, 1973-74. Mem. Unitarian Universalist Ministers Assn., Nat. Council Family Relations, Am. Assn. Sex Educators, Counsels and Therapists, Am. Coll. Health Assn. Author: Commonsense Sex, 1968; The New Intimacy, 1973; editor: Training Peer Sex Educators, 1976; editor Sexual Health and Relationships, 1978—. Home: 32 Fruit St Northampton MA 01060 Office: Univ Health Center U Mass Amherst MA 01003

MAZUR, STELLA MARY, orgn. exec.; b. Lowell, Mass.; d. Stanley and Katherine (Cichowicz) M.; B.S.E., U. Lowell; student ARC Mgmt. Tng. Sch., Charlottesville, Va., 1962. USO club dir., Windsor Locks, Conn, 1942; gen. field rep. ARC, 1944, exec. dir., Waltham, Mass., 1944—; with Nat. Tng. Labs., Inst. Applied Behavioral Sci., 1963; spl. assignment graphic arts cultural exchange program USIA, Dept. State, Poland, 1965; instr. Lowell Coop. Learning Center. Mem. Lowell Seton Guild, 1935—, Lowell Museum Corp. Recipient Waltham Rotary Club Spl. Citation, 1952; ARC and Waltham Community Spl. 25 Year Service Anniversary Recognition award, 1969; dedication of report Waltham ARC, 1971; named to Women of Today, Waltham Bus. and Profl. Women's Club Publ., 1976. Mem. Internat. Platform Assn., U. Lowell Alumni Assn., Lowell Hist. Soc. Clubs: Vesper (Tyngsboro, Mass.); Longmeadow Golf (Lowell). Author, pub.: Roots and Heritage of Polish People in Lowell, 1976. Home: 170 Andover St Lowell MA 01852 Office: ARC 22 Appleton St Waltham MA 02154

MAZZA, PETER DOMENICK, lawyer, coll. adminstr.; b. West Springfield, Mass., Aug. 5, 1940; s. Peter and Mary (Valenti) M.; B.A., Am. Internat. Coll., 1962; M.Ed., Springfield Coll., 1967; J.D., Western New Eng. Coll., 1976; m. Arlene Joan Ayers, Nov. 28, 1963; children—Karen, Peter. Tchr., Agawam (Mass.) High Sch., 1962-68, guidance counselor, 1968-71; adminstr. Westfield (Mass.) State Coll., 1971—; admitted to Mass. bar, 1977; individual practice law, West Springfield, 1978—; vis. lectr. Sch. Law, Am. Internat. Coll., 1978. Mem. Town of Agawam Town Meeting, 1967-69; chmn. Agawam Bd. Library Trustees, 1969. Mem. Hampden County Bar Assn., Western Mass. Personnel and Guidance Assn. Roman Catholic. Home: PO Box 294 Feeding Hills MA 01030 Office: 1111 Elm St West Springfield MA 01089

MAZZACANE, JOHN ROYAL, hosp. ofcl.; b. New Haven, Apr. 4, 1944; s. James Vincent and Lena (Ciarleglio) M. Radiol. aide Yale-New Haven Med. Center, 1960-61, staff therapist, 1961-66, asst. chief respiratory therapy, 1966-67; tech. dir. Sch. Respiratory Therapy Scis., Hosp. St. Raphael, New Haven, 1967—. Mem. Nat. Bd. Respiratory Therapy (registered), Am. Assn. Respiratory Therapy, Conn. Soc. Respiratory Therapy, Nat. Soc. Cardiopulmonary Tech., Conn. Soc. Cardiopulmonary Technologists, Am. Assn. Physician Assts. Republican. Home: 14 Alling St West Haven CT 06516 Office: 1450 Chapel St New Haven CT 06511

MAZZATENTA, ROSEMARY DOROTHY, educator; b. Phila., Sept. 17, 1932; d. John and Aida Mary (Perucci) M.; B.S., U. Pa., 1953, M.S., 1956. Tchr., Haverford Twp. Sch. Dist., 1953-54; tchr. Phila. Sch. Dist., 1954-64, formerly elementary cons. tchr. Phila. Sch. Dist., asst. dir. prekindergarten program, 1965-68, asst. dir. Get Set Day Care, 1969—; social worker Pa. Hosp., 1957-59. Pres. U. Pa. Class 1953, 1958-73; bd. dirs. met. br. Phila. ARC, also chmn. Named Educator of Year, Phila. Edn. Assn., 1969; recipient Alumni award of distinction 1970, Alumni award of merit, 1975 (both U. Pa.). Mem. Phila. Tchrs. Assn. (v.p. 1965-67), Pa. Edn. Assn., Phila. Fellowship Commn., NEA, Phila. Area Profl. Panhellenic Assn. (pres. 1958-62), U. Pa. Alumnae Club Phila. (sec. 1957-59, v.p. 1962-68, pres. 1969-73), Kappa Delta Epsilon (N.E. regional dir. 1958-62, nat. v.p. 1962-72, nat. pres. 1972-76), Pi Lambda Theta (pres. alumnae chpt.). Roman Catholic. Club: Soroptimist of Phila. Home: 1014 Dickinson St Philadelphia PA 19147 Office: Stevens Adminstrn Center Spring Garden W 13th St Philadelphia PA 19123

MAZZOLA, JOHN WILLIAM, performing arts exec.; b. Bayonne, N.J., Jan. 20, 1928; s. Roy Stephen and Eleanor Burnett (Davis) M.; A.B., Tufts U., 1949; LL.B., Fordham U., 1952; m. Sylvia Drulie, Mar. 7, 1959; children—Alison Anthony, Amy. Admitted to N.Y. bar, 1952; asso. firm Milbank, Tweed, Hadley & McCloy, N.Y.C., 1952-64; sec., exec. v.p. Lincoln Center for Performing Arts, N.Y.C., 1964-68, gen. mgr., 1969-70, mng. dir., 1970-77, pres., 1977—; mem. adv. bd. Chopin Found. U.S., Van Cliburn Internat. Piano Competition, Avery Fisher Artist Awards; cons. to performing arts centers U.S., abroad. Bd. dirs. Maurice Ravel Acad., France, Broadway Assn., N.Y.C. Served with CIC, AUS, 1953-55. Decorated Knight officer Order of Merit of Italian Republic. Benjamin Franklin fellow Royal Soc. Arts. Episcopalian. Clubs: Century (N.Y.C.); Watch Hill (R.I.) Yacht; Misquamicut (R.I.). Home: 12 Beekman Pl New York City NY 10022 Office: Lincoln Center 140 W 65th St New York City NY 10023

MAZZONE, JOSEPH JOHN, pub. accountant; b. Schenectady, Apr. 24, 1923; s. John Joseph and Carmella Agatha (Castaldi) M.; grad. Bentley Coll., 1948; m. Mary Josephine Ciarmiello, June 21, 1947; children—John, Joseph John, Maria, James, Carmel. Accountant, Stone Webster Engring. Corp., Schenectady, 1948-50, Alco Products Co., Schenectady, 1950-54; pvt. practice pub. accounting, Schenectady, 1954—. Treas. Republican Town Com., Rotterdam, N.Y., 1974-77; finance chmn. Mt. Pleasant Boys Club 1975-76; 2d v.p. exec. bd. Big Bros., Schenectady, 1975-78, pres., 1978—; pres. Mt. Carmel Holy Name Soc., Schenectady, 1960-61, mem., pres. ch. parish council, 1975-77, recipient ch. merit award, 1963. Served with F.A., 3d Army, AUS, 1942-45; ETO. Recipient Outstanding Services certificate K.C., 1975; Ofcl. Citation award Mayor of Schenectady, 1975. Mem. N.Y. Soc. Ind. Accountants, VFW, Sons Italy, Italo-Am. Soc. (v.p. 1971-72). Clubs: Lions (pres. Schenectady 1974-75, certificate 1975, zone chmn. 1975-76), K.C. (grand knight Schenectady council 1974-75), 1st Friday. Home: 1021 Fairlane Rd Schenectady NY 12306 Office: 1821 Curry Rd Schenectady NY 12306

MAZZONE, V. DOMENICO, sculptor, painter; b. Rutigliano, Bari, Italy, May 16, 1927; s. Pietro and Cecilia (Defilippis) M.; came to U.S., 1966; student art sch., Treviso, Italy, 1950; m. Grace Romita, July 22, 1954; children—Cecila, Margret, Peter. Prin. works include Monument of Fra Diohisio, Barletta's Cathedral, Italy, 1970; Fountain of Knowledge Progett, Geneva, Switzerland, 1972; bust of Copernicus, 1973; bust of U Thant; bas-relief of Dag Hammarskjold, Southeast Mus., Brewster, N.Y., 1974; busts of Frau Laval, Bartholdi, Alexander Puskin, Cardinal Cooke, Toscanini, Edward Lamb;

bas-relief of The Emigrant; Spirito Olympic, Moscow; Drugs Enemy, Met. Mus., Miami, Fla.; Pretty Girl, Maitland, Fla., figure of Christ, Vatican residence, numerous other works exhibited and in permanent collections USSR, France, Austria, Japan, India, Greece, Italy, Poland and U.S.; instr. sculpture UN Internat. Sch., N.Y.C. Served with Italian Army, 1949. Decorated cavalier Ordineal Merito della Republica Italiana; recipient gold medal Viareggio (Italy) Exhbn., 1972; Silver medal Carrara (Italy) Exhbn. marble, 1962. Mem. Accademia Tiberina, Accademico Guglielmo Marconi, Italian Club of UN, Nat. Soc. Lit. and Art., Comply Soc., Internat. Acad. Sci., Letters and Arts, Leonardo di Vinci Letters, Academia of Merit, Internat. Burckhardt Akademie, Italian Assn. Arts, Acad. 500, Unione Scindacale Artisti Italiani Belle Arts. Address: 44 Lembeck Ave Jersey City NJ 07305

MAZZOTTA, LEON MICHAEL, dentist; b. Phila., Mar. 13, 1922; s. Charles and Rose (Cramasta) M.; D.D.S. cum laude, U. Md., 1945; m. Dolores Elizabeth Morse, Sept. 4, 1943; children—Charles Robert, James Ira. Served with USPHS, N.Y.C. and Balt., 1945-47; asst. prof. oral pathology U. Md., Balt., 1947-49; practice dentistry, Wildwood, N.J., 1949—; mem. staff Burdette Tomlin Meml. Hosp., Cape May Court House, N.J., 1950-77, co-chief dentistry, 1954, oral surgeon, 1958-77; chief surgery sect. U.S. Army Hosp., Camp Pickett, Va., 1951-52; mem. staff Mercy Hosp., Sea Isle City, N.J., 1953-70; chief dentist Leesburg (N.J.) State Prison, 1976-77. Mem. Wildwood Bd. Edn., 1955-59, pres., 1973-74; pres. Band Boosters Assn. of Wildwood High Sch., 1960-61; congl. del. to White House Conf. on Children, 1970; bd. dirs. South Jersey Homemakers Service, 1959-65, v.p., 1959-60. Mem. Atlantic Cape May County Dental Soc. (pres. 1974-75), ADA (del. 1976-78), N.J. Dental Assn. (trustee 1974-78, del. 1972-78), Am. Legion (chmn. scholarship com. 1958-60, del. state conv. 1960), Gorgas Odontological Soc., Psi Omega, Omicron Kappa Upsilon. Clubs: Rotary (v.p. 1957-58, pres. 1958-59, dir. 1955-59), K.C. (4 deg.). Address: 217 East Glenwood Ave Wildwood NJ 08260

MCAFEE, HORACE J., lawyer; b. Heflin, La., July 17, 1905; s. J. U. and Annie (Reeves) McA.; A.B., So. Meth. U., 1926; J.D., Columbia U., 1931; m. Kathryn Gage, July 6, 1931 (dec. Nov. 1972); children—Mary Ann McAfee Baxter, William Gage, Stuart Reeves; m. 2d, Jane Harrison Shaffer, Aug. 17, 1974. Admitted to N.Y. bar, 1932; with Simpson Thacher & Barlett, attys., N.Y.C., 1931—, partner firm, 1944-54, sr. partner, 1954-75; hon. dir. Sybron Corp. Mem. Irvington Bd. Zoning Appeals, 1951—, chmn., 1955—; trustee, sec. Irvington Pub. Library, 1948-61, pres., 1961-62. Mem. Assn. Bar City N.Y., Am. Bar Assn., N.Y. County Lawyers Assn., Am. Judicature Soc. Republican. Episcopalian. Clubs: Ardsley Curling, Ardsley Country (Ardsley-on-Hudson, N.Y.); Camp Fire of Am., Ch. (N.Y.C.). Home: Stoneleigh Matthiessen Park Irvington-on-Hudson NY 10533 Office: 1 Battery Park Plaza New York City NY 10004 also 350 Park Ave New York City NY 10022

MC AFEE, JERRY, petroleum co. exec.; b. Port Arthur, Tex., Nov. 3, 1916; s. Almer McDuffie and Marguerite (Calfee) McA.; B.S. in Chem Engring., U. Tex., 1937; Sc.D. in Chem. Engring., Mass. Inst. Tech., 1940; m. Geraldine Smith, June 21, 1940; children—Joe R., William M., Loretta M., Thomas R. Research chem. engr. Universal Oil Products Co., Chgo., 1940-45; tech. specialist Gulf Oil Corp., Port Arthur, Tex., 1945-49, v.p. engring., Pitts., 1955-60, v.p., exec. tech. adviser, 1960-64, dir. planning and econs., 1962-64, chmn. bd., chief exec. officer, 1976—, also dir.; dir. Chemistry div. Gulf Research & Devel Co., Harmarville, Pa., 1950-51, asst. dir. research, 1951-53, v.p., asso. dir. research, 1954-55; sr. v.p. Gulf Oil Corp., 1964-67, coordinator Gulf Eastern Co., London, Eng., 1964-67; exec. v.p. Brit. Am. Oil Co., Ltd., Toronto, Ont., 1967-69; pres., chief exec. officer, dir. Gulf Oil Can. Ltd., Toronto, 1969-76; dir. Mellon Bank, Pitts. Active Allegheny Conf. on Community Devel. Bd. dirs. Aspen Inst. Humanistic Studies, M.I.T. Corp., Pitts. Symphony Soc. Mem. Am. Inst. Chem. Engrs. (v.p. 1959, pres. 1960), Am. Petroleum Inst. (dir.), Am. Chem. Soc. Nat. Acad. Engring., Pitts. C. of C. (dir.). Clubs: Duquesne (Pitts); Toronto, York (Toronto); Laurel Valley Golf; Fox Chapel Golf; Rolling Rock; Links. Home: 4 Indian Hill Rd Pittsburgh PA 15238 Office: PO Box 1166 Pittsburgh PA 15230

MCALEER, WILLIAM KEARNS, engring. corp. exec.; b. Pitts., Aug. 14, 1921; s. William s. and Evelyn (Kearns) McA.; B.S., Carnegie Inst. Tech., 1942; M.S. in Indsl. Engring., U. Pitts., 1945; m. 2d, Felicia Lange, Mar. 20, 1976; 1 son, William H. Project engr. Mine Safety Appliances Co., Pitts., 1942-46; sales engr. McNally Pitts. Mfg. Corp., 1946-55; asst. sales mgr. Curtiss Wright Corp., Carlstadt, N.J., 1955-56; mgr. Latin Am. div. H.B. Maynard Inc., Pitts., 1956-66, v.p., 1966-67; v.p. Peter F. Loftus Corp., Pitts., 1967-70, pres., 1970—; chmn. Gurnham and Assos. Inc., pollution control consultants, Chgo., 1976—; pres. Peter F. Loftus Corp. (Ill.), Chgo., 1976—; lectr. indsl. engring. U. Pa., 1948-53. Registered profl. engr., Pa. Mem. ASME, Soc. Internat. Devel., Engrs. Soc. Western Pa., World Affairs Council, Andrew Carnegie Soc. (v.p. 1975-76). Clubs: Duquesne, Univ., Pitts. Press, St. Clair Country, Am. of Buenos Aires. Contbg. author Indsl. Engring. Handbook, 2d edit., 1963. Home: 651 Arden Ln Pittsburgh PA 15243 Office: Chamber of Commerce Bldg Pittsburgh PA 15219

MCALISTER, ISABEL MILEY (MRS. GEORGE ALEXANDER MCALISTER), health service adminstr.; b. Chambersburg, Pa., Jan. 29, 1906; d. Harry Mellvill and Orpah A. (Schaff) Miley; student Moore Inst. Illustration, 1926-28; diploma Phila. Sch. Occupational Therapy, U. Pa., 1935; m. George Alexander McAlister, June 24, 1942. Staff occupational therapist Norristown (Pa.) State Hosp., 1935-43, Spring Grove State Hosp., Catonsville, Md., 1955-57, also head occupational therapy, 1955-57; occupational therapist Washington County Soc. for Crippled Children and Adults, Washington, Pa., 1957-61; staff occupational therapist Montebello State Hosp., Balt., 1961-65; dir. occupational therapy, supr. of tng. aides South Mountain (Pa.) Restoration Center, 1965-77, phys. disability occupational therapist, 1977—. Mem. Am. Legion Aux., Am., Pa. occupational therapy assns., DAR (circle pres. 1949-51). Presbyterian (sec. missionary soc. 1945-46). Home: 79 N Main St Chambersburg PA 17201

MC ALLISTER, JOSEPH CHARLES, civil engr.; b. Mariners Harbor, S.I., N.Y., Aug. 25, 1928; s. Harry Eli and Blanche Edythe (Bergen) McA; Civil Engr., Coll. City N.Y., 1953; postgrad. Columbia, 1956-57; m. Anne Bargiuk, June 29, 1957; children—Rosanne, Joseph, Michael. Laborer, Brighton Marine Shipyard, S. I., 1944; carpenter Brewer Dry Dock Co., S.I., 1945; constrn. supt. Raymond Concrete Pile Co., 1953-55; soils and found. design engr. U.S. Army C.E., N.Y. dist., 1955-57, chief paving sect., 1957-62, chief fallout shelter updating sect., 1962-63, constrn. engr., 1963-68, asst. area engr. So. N.J. area, Wrightstown, 1968-71, chief office engr. sect. Secaucus Area, Jersey City, 1971-73, civil engr. N. Atlantic Div., N.Y.C., 1973—. Pres. Solutions to All U.S. and World Problems Found., Inc. Served with AUS, 1946-49. Recipient Sustained Superior Performance award C.E., 1963, Suggestion awards, 1969; Achievement award Civic Congress S.I., 1973. Registered profl. engr., Vt. Mem. Am. Soc. C.E., Rosicrucian Order. Democrat. Club: Banner. Author: (with Robert F. McAllister) Solutions to all United States and World Problems, Book 1, 1970, Book 2, 1976. Home: 125 Shirley Ave Staten Island NY 10312 Office: Army Corps Engrs Constrn Mgmt Branch 90 Church St New York City NY 10007

MC ALPINE, FREDERICK SENNETT, anesthesiologist; b. Monessen, Pa., June 16, 1929; s. Karl Sennett and Kathryn Helen (Schverhoff) McA.; A.B. with honors, St. Vincent Coll., Latrobe, Pa., 1950; M.D., U. Pitts., 1954; m. Barbara Ellen Adams, June 23, 1956; children—Christopher, Daniel, Karen. Intern, Bethesda Naval Hosp., 1954-55; resident anesthesia Mass. Gen. Hosp., 1955-57, chief resident, 1957; asst. chief anesthesia Bethesda Naval Hosp., 1957-60; anesthesiologist Lahey Clinic Found., Boston, 1960—, chmn. dept. anesthesia, 1971—; active staff New Eng. Deaconess Hosp., Chief dept. anesthesiology, 1978—; active staff Brooks, New Eng. Bapt. hosps. Served with M.C., USNR, 1954-60. Diplomate Am. Bd. Anesthesiology. Mem. AMA, Mass., Pa. med. socs., Am., Mass. (pres. 1971-72) socs. anesthesiologists, Internat. Anesthesia Research Soc., AAAS, Delta Epsilon Sigma. Home: 49 Arnold Rd Wellesley Hills MA 02181 Office: 605 Commonwealth Ave Boston MA 02215

MC ARTHUR, RUTH BELL, ednl. adminstr.; b. Manila, Philippine Islands, Oct. 5, 1938; d. Jose N. and Mary (Green) Bell; A.A., San Francisco Community Coll., 1958; B.S., San Francisco State Coll., 1960; M.S., San Francisco State U., 1970; m. Leroy McArthur, Aug. 27, 1960; children—Darryl Craig, Leroy Anthony, Maria Nicole. Med. sec. U. Calif. Med. Center, San Francisco, 1957-60; counselor Calif. State Sch. for the Blind, Berkeley, Calif., 1960-61; adminstrv. asst. Oceanview Merced Ingleside, San Francisco, 1962-65; counselor Neighborhood Youth Corps, San Rafael, Calif., 1966-68; acad. counselor San Francisco Community Coll., 1970-71; vocat. counselor/tchr. coordinator D.C. Sch. System, 1972—; cons. PUSH program, Washington, 1976-78. Sec., Winters Run Civic Assn., 1977-78. HEW grantee, 1968-70. Mem. Am. Personnel and Guidance Assn., Am. Rehab. Counselors Assn., Nat. Vocat. and Guidance Assn., Am. Bus. Women's Assn., League Women Voters. Home: 17212 Olde Mill Run Derwood MD 20855

MC AULEY, JOSEPH ANTHONY, surgeon; b. Grenada, West Indies, Mar. 23, 1940; s. Anthony and Rose (Somerson) McA.; came to U.S., 1959, naturalized, 1973; B.A., N.Y. U., 1964; M.D., State U. N.Y., 1968; m. Althea McIntosh, Dec. 27, 1977; children—Christopher, Yashana, Jolene. Intern, Kings County Hosp., Bklyn., 1968-69, resident, 1969-70, 72-75; practice medicine specializing in surgery, Bklyn., 1975—; mem. staffs St. John's Episcopal Hosp., Kings County Hosp., St. Mary's Hosp., Brookdale Hosp. Med. Center, Kingsbrook Jewish Med. Center; clin. asst. instr. surgery Downstate Med. Center, State U. N.Y., 1972-75, asst. prof., 1975—. Served to maj. AUS, 1970-72. Decorated Bronze Star, Army Commendation medal. Diplomate Nat. Bd. Med. Examiners, Am. Bd. Gen. Surgery. Fellow A.C.S.; mem. Bklyn. Surg. Soc., N.Y. Soc. Trauma, Bklyn. Soc. Trauma. AMA, N.Y., Kings County med. socs. Contbg. author: (with S. Kountz) Surgery Review, 1978. Office: 1310 President St Brooklyn NY 11225

MC AVOY, RITA CLOUTIER (MRS. GEORGE EDWARD MCAVOY), bus. exec., civic worker; b. Lewiston, Me., June 9, 1917; d. Gideon Edward and Eva Mary (Lambert) Cloutier; grad. High sch.; m. George Edward McAvoy, July 5, 1948; children—Richard Dixon, Suzanne Hopgood. Owner, operator Thayers Hotel, Littleton, N.H., 1949-69; operator, part owner Crawford House, Crawford Notch, N.H., 1969-73; postmaster Crawford House P.O., 1970-73; mem. gen. ct. Ho. of Reps., 1977-78. Pres. women's aux. Littleton Hosp., 1966-67, 71; sec., organizer fund drive Dollars for Scholars program, 1963—; mem. N.H. Network Fund Raising Com., 1968-74, Littleton Bicentennial Com., 1973-76, Pres.'s Assay Commn., 1970; legis. chmn. N.H. Assn. Hosp. Auxs., 1973—; mem. Dept. Def. selection com. Nat. Resources Conservation Awards, 1974-75; mem. N.H. Probation Commn., 1974—, Crime Commn. crime prevention adv. group, 1976—, Health Systems Agy. adv. com., 1976—; exec. dir. N.H. Gov.'s Commn. Status of Women, 1976; mem. N.H. State Health Coordinating Council, 1977—; mem. membership com. United Health Systems Agency, 1977—. Pres. Profile Republican Women's Club, 1957-58, 71; mem. N.H. State Rep. Com., 1950-76; women's chmn. Littleton Rep. Town Com., 1964-75; pres. N.H. Fedn. Rep. Women, 1974-75. Trustee Littleton Hosp., 1973—. Named Rep. Woman of Yr., Profile Rep. Women's Club, 1969, Woman of Yr., Colonial Club, 1972. Mem. N.H. Hotel and Motel Assn., N.H. Audubon Soc., Littleton Hist. Soc., League Women Voters. Clubs: Littleton Garden (pres. 1961-62), Littleton Colonial (pres. 1956-57). Address: Bethlehem Rd Littleton NH 03561

MC BRIDE, FRANK VINCENT, mech. contracting co. exec.; b. Paterson, N.J., Apr. 5, 1906; s. Frank A. and Alice (Nevin) M.; A.B., Holy Cross Coll., 1925; m. Margaret Mary Sweeney, Apr. 23, 1935; children—Frank Vincent, Daniel J., Mary Virginia, Timothy B. With Frank A. McBride Co., mech. contracting, 1925—, now chmn. bd., chief exec. officer; past chmn. bd., dir. N.J. Mfrs. Ins. Co.; dir. 1st Nat. Bank N.J., Paterson, N.J. Bell Telephone Co., Newark. Decorated knight St. Gregory (Pope Pius XII). Mem. Mech. Contractors Assn. Am. (nat. pres. 1961-62), N.J. Bus. and Industry Assn. (past chmn. bd.). Home: 335 Algnonquin Rd Franklin Lakes NJ 07417 Office: 233 Central Ave Hawthorne NJ 07506

MC BRIDE, HOWARD EARL, technol. products and services bus. exec.; b. Smoot, Wyo., Sept. 29, 1932; s. Cleao Wells and Fern Rose (Moffett) McB.; student Stanford, 1960-62; B.S. in Indsl. Mgmt., Brigham Young U., 1960; M.B.A., 1962; m. Lois Wilhelmina Ladner, Dec. 10, 1957; children—Stephen Charles, Kim Maree, Jolene Karen. Mgmt. trainee Standard Oil Co. of Calif., San Francisco, 1962-63; project leader Hughes Dynamics, Inc., Los Angeles, 1963-64; cons. to sr. cons. Mgmt. Tech., Inc. and Mgmt. Software Devel. Corp., Los Angeles, 1964-65, 67-69; v.p. Info. Processing Labs., Los Angeles, 1966; analyst Computer Usage Corp., Los Angeles, 1967; mgr. info. systems dept. Balt. Gas & Electric Co., 1969—; cons. in field. Served to 1st lt. AUS, 1956-59. Mem. Shared Program Application Devel. Effort. Republican. Mem. Ch. Jesus Christ of Latter-day Saints. Author: Impeach Justice Douglas, 1971; also articles. Home: 225 Solway Ct Timonium MD 21093 Office: 9117 Belair Rd Perry Hall MD 21236

MCBRIDE, LLOYD, union exec.; b. Farmington, Mo., 1916; student pub. schs., St. Louis; m. Dolores Neihaus, 1937; children—Larry, Sharon. Plant worker Foster Bros. Mfg. Co., St. Louis, 1930-38; mem. Steel Workers Organizing Com., St. Louis, 1936-38; pres. Local 1295 Steel Workers Am., St. Louis, 1938-40, organizer, staff rep., 1940-44, staff rep., Granite City, Ill., 1946-58, subdist. dir., 1958-65, dir. Dist. 34, Granite City, 1965-77, internat. pres., Pitts., 1977—; pres. St. Louis Indsl. Union Council CIO, 1940-42, Mo. State CIO Indsl. Union Council, 1942-44; del. Internat. Metalworkers Fedn., Geneva. Served with USN, 1944-46. Office: United Steelworkers Am Five Gateway Center Pittsburgh PA 15222

MCBRIDE, MILFORD LAWRENCE, JR., lawyer; b. Grove City, Pa., July 16, 1923; s. Milford L. and Elizabeth (Douthett) McB.; B.S., Grove City Coll., N.Y. U., 1944; J.D., U. Pa., 1949; m. Madeleine F. Coulter, Aug. 6, 1947; children—Marta, Brenda, Milford III, Randy, Barry. Admitted to Pa. bar, 1949, since practiced in Grove City; mem. firm McBride & McNickle, 1949—; mem. Grove City adv. bd. 1st Seneca Bank & Trust Co., 1962—, also dir. main bd.; pres., dir. Grove City Hotel Co., 1962—. Bd. dirs., past pres. Grove City Hosp.; bd. dirs. Grove City Indsl. Devel. Corp. Served with USAAF, 1943-46. Mem. Am., Pa. (treas. 1970-77), Mercer County bar assns. Clubs: University, Oakmont Country. Office: 211 S Center St Grove City PA 16127 Home: 316 E Washington Blvd Grove City PA 16127

MC BRIEN, ROD, singer, composer, producer; b. Amityville, N.Y., June 20, 1943; s. William Roger and Helen Lenore (Terry) McB.; ed. pub. schs.; m. Sarah Daly, May 3, 1969; 1 son, Roddy. Audio engr. Ultra-Sonic Rec. Studios, Hempstead, N.Y., 1962-64; chief engr. Roulette Records, N.Y.C., 1964-65; audio engr. Allegro Sound Studios, N.Y.C., 1966-68; songwriter M.R.C. Music, N.Y.C., 1968-69; ind. producer records and commls., N.Y.C., 1969-71; dir. Metromedia Records, N.Y.C., 1971-72; pres. Rod McBrien Prodns., Inc., N.Y.C., 1972—; pres. Star Spangled Music, Inc.; v.p. Stark & McBrien Enterprises, Inc.; rec. artist RCA records; writer popular songs and commls., including Look Up America. Served with USCGR, 1964-65. Recipient 1st prize 1st annual Am. Song Festival, 1974, Am. Song Festival Bicentennial Competition, 1975, Internat. Broadcasting Award for commls. Mem. AFTRA, Screen Actors Guild, Am. Fedn. Musicians, ASCAP. Club: U.S. Trotting Assn. Office: 405 Park Ave New York City NY 10022

MC BRYDE, FELIX WEBSTER, geographer, ecologist, cons.; b. Lynchburg, Va., Apr. 23, 1908; s. John McLaren and Flora O'N. (Webster) McB.; B.A., Tulane U., 1930, LL.D., 1967; Ph.D., U. Calif. at Berkeley, 1940; postgrad. (research fellow) U. Colo., 1930-31, Clark U., 1931-32; m. Frances Van Winkle, July 23, 1934; children—Richard Webster, Sarah Elva, John McLaren. Geographer-photographer 4th Tulane Expdn. across C.Am. Maya Area, 1927-28; field fellow Clark U.-Carnegie Inst., Washington, Guatemala, 1932; research fellow Middle Am. Research Inst., Tulane U., 1932-33; teaching asst. geography U. Calif. at Berkeley, 1933-35, 37; predoctoral field fellow social sci. Social Sci. Research Council N.Y., Guatemala and El Savador, 1935-36; instr. geography Ohio State U., 1937-42, U. Calif. at Los Angeles, 1940; field fellow NRC, Washington, also Berkeley, Guatemala, Mexico, 1940-41; expert cons., sr. geographer M.I., War Dept., Washington, 1942-45; lectr. geography Western Res. U., summer 1944; dir. Peruvian office Inst. Social Anthropology, Smithsonian Instn., Washington, Lima, 1945-47; spl. rep. Inst. Andean Research, Lima, 1947-48; prof. geography U. Md., 1948-59, cons. prof., 1959-63; geog. cons. internat. statistics U.S. Bur. Census, Washington and Latin Am., 1948-56; chief U.S. Census Mission, tech. advisor 1st Nat. Census of Ecuador, Quito, 1949-51; dir. regional planning Gordon A. Friesen Assos., Inc., Washington and Costa Rica, 1956-58; pres. F. W. McBryde Assos., Inc., Washington and Guatemala, 1958-64, Inter-Am. Inst. Modern Langs., Guatemala, 1963-66; Latin Am. cons. Inst. Modern Langs., Washington, 1963-66; chief phys. and cultural geography br., natural resources div. Inter-Am. Geodetic Survey, Fort Clayton, C.Z., 1964-65; field dir. Bioenvironmental Program, Atlantic-Pacific Interoceanic Sea-Level Canal Studies in Panama and Colombia, Battelle Meml. Inst., Columbus, Ohio, 1965-70, field dir. Andean ecology project, S.Am., 1967-69, dir. project devel. program, C.Am. and Mex., 1968-69; cons. in ecology, 1970—; founder-dir. McBryde Center for Human Ecology, 1969—; cons. in human ecology and Latin Am., Transemantics, Inc., Washington, 1970—; with UN Devel. Program, ecologist (tourism), expert Jamaica, W.I., 1971; hydrology ecologist, expert Parana River Nav. Improvement Project, Argentina, 1972; ecol. cons. Battelle Meml. Inst., Panama and Brazil, 1972; U.S. Bur. Census geography adviser to Govt. of Honduras on cartography for 1973 population census, 1972; Battelle cons., procedural analysis in internat. project devel., 1972; ecologist World Bank environ. impact analysis Bayano River Hydroelectric Project, one-man mission to Panama; Battelle cons., ecologist, prin. investigator and field coordinator, environ. impact study Darien Gap Hwy., Panama-Colombia for U.S. Dept. Transp., 1973; cons. Enviro Plan; expert ecologist (biology) Engr. Agy. Resources Inventories, C.E., U.S. Army, Washington, 1974; dir. recruitment, dir. internat. bus. intelligence, dir. office resources devel. and environ. services Transemantics, Inc., Washington, 1975—. Mem. nat. adv. bd. Am. Security Council. Mem. Am. Acad. Polit. and Social Sci., Am. Anthrop. Assn., AAAS, Am. Congress on Surveying and Mapping, Am. Ethnol. Soc., Am. Geog. Soc., Assn. Am. Geographers (founding pres., sec., treas., editor publs. 1943-44), Anthrop. Soc. Washington, Am. Geophys. Union, Am. Inst. Biol. Scis., Assn. Tropical Biology, Am. Soc. Photogrammetry, Ecuadorian Inst. Anthropology and Geography (founder dir. 1950-52, hon. dir. 1952—), Assn. Am. Geographers, Employment Mgmt. Assn., Inter-Am. Council (organizing sec. 1953-59, pres. 1959-62), Internat. Soc. for Tropical Ecology, Internat. Platform Assn., Lima Geog. Soc., Ohio Acad. Sci., Soc. Am. Archeology, Soc. Am. Mil. Engrs., Soc. for Med. Anthropology, Ecol. Soc. Am., Guatemalan Soc. History and Geography, Human Ecol. Soc., Internat. Oceanographic Found., Mexican Soc. Geography and Statistics, Phi Beta Kappa, Sigma Nu, others. Episcopalian. Club: Explorers. Author: Solola, 1933; Cultural and Historical Geography of Southwest Guatemala, 1947, Spanish edit., 1969; (with P. Thomas) Equal-Area Projections for World Statistical Maps, 1949; founding editor Profl. Geographer; contbr. numerous articles to profl. jours.; new map projections. Home: 10100 Falls Rd Potomac MD 20854

MC BRYDE, THOMAS HENRY, lawyer; b. New Albany, Miss., Oct. 26, 1925; s. Henry Thornton and Mary Catherine (Davis) McB.; B.S., U.S. Mil. Acad., 1946; LL.B., U. Va., 1952; m. Barbara White, Dec. 28, 1946; children—Elise McBryde Maloney, William Henry, John Thomas. Commd. 2d lt. U.S. Army, 1946, advanced through grades to capt., 1950; assigned Japan, ETO and U.S.; instr. law U.S. Mil. Acad., 1956-57; resigned, 1957; admitted to Va. bar, 1952, N.Y. State bar, 1959; asst. counsel N.Y. State Banking Dept., 1960-61; with firm Rogers & Wells, and predecessors, N.Y.C., 1957-60, 61—, partner, 1965—; chief counsel N.Y. State Joint Legis. Com. to Revise Banking Law, 1962-65, minority counsel, 1965-66; mem. comml. panel Am. Arbitration Assn., 1976—; mem. adv. com. supervision mut. instns. Office N.Y. Banking Supt., 1966-67. Mem. Am., Va., N.Y. State bar assns., Assn. Grads. U.S. Mil. Acad., N.Y. West Point Soc., Order of Coif. Republican. Episcopalian. Clubs: Am. Yacht (Rye, N.Y.); Union League, Sky (N.Y.C.). Home: 12 Mohawk St Rye NY 10580 Office: 200 Park Ave New York City NY 10017

MC CABE, CYNTHIA JAFFEE, curator; b. N.Y.C., Feb. 8, 1943; d. Harry and Pauline (Techefsky) Jaffee; B.A., Cornell U., 1963; M.A., Columbia U., 1967. Organizer fine arts sect., catalogue, bibliography Lower East Side: Portal to American Life (1870-1924), Jewish Mus., N.Y.C., Smithsonian Instn., Washington, 1966-67; research Nakian Retrospective, Mus. Modern Art, N.Y.C., 1966; organizer fine art sect. Erie Canal Sesquicentennial, N.Y. State Council Arts, 1967; research Venice 34, Nat. Collection of Fine Arts, Smithsonian Instn., 1968; curator painting and sculpture Hirshhorn Mus. and Sculpture Garden, Smithsonian Instn., 1967-76, curator exhbns., 1976—, organizer catalogues The Golden Door: Artist-Immigrants of Am., 1876-1976; 20th Century Sculptors and Their Drawings: Selections from the Hirshhorn Mus. collection, Smithsonian Instn. Traveling Exhbn. Service, 1979-80; asst. professorial lectr. George Washington U., 1975-76; lectr. Spoleto (S.C.) Festival, 1978. Mem. Internat. Council Museums, Am. Assn. Museums (curators com.; chmn.

credentials com. 1977-79), Coll. Art Assn. Am., Soc. Archtl. Historians, Women's Caucus for Art, N.E. Museums Conf. (program com. 1975-77). Art historian. Author: Henry Moore at the Hirshhorn Museum and Sculpture Garden, 1974; The Golden Door: Artist-Immigrants of America 1876-1976, 1976; Fernando Botero: A Retrospective Exhibition, 1979-80; others. Office: Hirshhorn Mus and Sculpture Garden Smithsonian Instn Washington DC 20560

MC CABE, EDWARD OWEN JAMES, publishing co. exec.; b. Bronx, N.Y., Mar. 30, 1947; s. Edward James and Ethel Gertrude (Corrigan) McC.; A.B., Cornell U., 1969; m. Julianne Susan Moneagle, June 25, 1969; children—Rachel, Edward, Michael, Benjamin. Tchr. history St. Raphael's Sch., Long Island City, N.Y., 1969-71; sales rep. Litton Automated Bus. Systems div. Litton Industries, White Plains, N.Y., 1971-73; asst. product mgr. Grolier Enterprises, Inc., Danbury, Conn., 1973-74, product mgr., 1975-77, dir. children's book clubs, 1977-78, asst. v.p. club mktg., 1978—. Office: Sherman Turnpike Danbury CT 06816

MC CABE, JAMES JOSEPH, lawyer; b. Phila., May 8, 1929; s. James J. and Marie (Seitz) McC.; A.B., LaSalle Coll., 1951; LL.B., Temple U., 1955; m. Dolores Anne Ruane, Sept. 18, 1954; children—Deirdre, Judith, James III. Admitted to bar Pa., 1956; asso. firm Duane, Morris & Heckscher, Phila., 1956-64, partner, 1964—; lectr. Practising Law Inst., N.Y.C.; adj. prof. med. law Thomas Jefferson U. Med. Coll. Mem. Am., Pa. (chmn. sect. ins., negligence and compensation), Phila. bar assns., Phila. Def. Counsel Assn. (past pres.), Def. Research Inst. (v.p. Atlantic region), Assn. Ins. Attys., Juristic Soc., Internat. Assn. Ins. Counsel, St. Thomas More Soc. (past pres.). Club: Phila. Cricket. Home: 817 E Gravers Ln Wyndmoor PA 19118 Office: Land Title Bldg Philadelphia PA 19110

MC CABE, JAMES PATRICK, coll. librarian; b. Phila., May 24, 1937; s. Felix and Josephine Theresa (Murtagh) McC.; A.B., Niagara U., 1963; M.A., U. Mich., 1966, Ph.D., 1968. Tchr., St. Francis de Sales High Sch., 1963-65; librarian Allentown Coll., Center Valley, Pa., 1968—. Sec.-treas. Greater Lehigh Valley Library Council, 1973-74. Mem. Beta Phi Mu. Roman Catholic. Author: Critical Guide to Catholic Reference Sources, 1971. Home: Allentown Coll Faculty Residence Center Valley PA 18034

MC CABE, JOSEPH CHARLES, pub. co. exec.; b. Plainfield, N.J., Jan. 16, 1914; s. Frank John and Margaret Mary (Ryan) McC.; B.E.E., Lehigh U., 1936; postgrad. Stevens Inst. Tech., 1941-42; m. Lucy Gloria Urello, Sept. 19, 1936; children—Frank J., Judith McCabe Koru, William Joseph. Cadet engr. Jersey Central Power & Light Co., 1936-37, tech. engr. power plants, 1937-43; field engr. Western Electric Co., 1943-45; asso. editor Power Mag., McGraw-Hill Pub. Co., N.Y.C., 1945-53; editor Combustion Mag., Combustion Pub. Co., N.Y.C., 1953—, v.p., 1958—. Mem. bd. edn., pres., Mountain Lakes, N.J., 1953-55; councilman Mountain Lakes, 1958-63. Served with USAAF, 1944-45; PTO. Registered profl. engr., N.J. Fellow ASME (chmn. fuels div. 1958-59). Home: 73 Woodland Ave Mountain Lakes NJ 07046 Office: 277 Park Ave New York City NY 10017

MCCABE, MARY ALEXANDRINE, accountant; b. Kearny, N.J., Aug. 4, 1920; d. Alexander Joseph and Mary Catherine (Brady) McC.; B.S. in Edn., St. Elizabeth Coll., 1955; diploma in acctg. Internat. Accountants Soc., 1975. Joined Sisters of Charity, Roman Catholic Ch., 1941; tchr. All Saints Sch., Jersey City, 1943-50, Sacred Heart Sch., Bloomfield, N.J., 1950-60, St. Rose of Lima Sch., Newark, 1960-62; treas. Acad. St. Aloysius, Jersey City, 1962—; chmn. Nike Club Acad. of St. Aloysius, 1971—. Mem. Am. Sch. Food Service Assn., N.J. Secondary Sch. Tchrs. Assn., N.J. Fedn. Bus. and Profl. Women's Clubs, Jersey City Bus. and Profl. Women's Club (pres. 1978—, treas. dist. VIII 1976-78). Home: 2495 Kennedy Blvd Jersey City NJ 07304 Office: Acad St Aloysius 2495 Kennedy Blvd Jersey City NJ 07304

MC CABE, THOMAS JOSEPH, mathematician; b. Central Falls, R.I., Nov. 28, 1941; s. John Joseph and Helen Francis (Taheny) McC.; A.B., Providence Coll., 1964; M.S., U. Conn., 1966; m. Linda May Szeliga, Aug. 29, 1964; children—Thomas, Timothy, Cathleen. Applied mathematician Nat. Security Agency, Ft. Meade, Md., 1969—; adj. faculty Howard Community Coll., Columbia, Md., 1969-74; cons. math. tech. Inst. for Advanced Tech., Control Data Corp., U. Calif., Mass. State Coll. System, 1971—; pres. McCabe & Assos., Inc., 1976—. Served with U.S. Army, 1967-69. Mem. Am. Math. Assn., Computing Machinery, IEEE. Club: Tennis (Columbia Md.). Home: 5380 Mad River Ln Columbia MD 21044 Office: Nat Security Agency Fort Meade MD 20755

MCCALLEY, ROBERT B(RUCE), JR., mech. engr.; b. Miami, Fla., Dec. 17, 1922; s. Robert Bruce and Ida (Castles) McC.; B.S. magna cum laude, U. S.C., 1947; M.C.E., Cornell U., 1949; Ph.D., 1952; m. Anita Baker, July 4, 1951. Research asso. Cornell U., 1948-51; engr. Applied Physics Lab., Johns Hopkins U., 1951-55; structural engr. Knolls Atomic Power Lab., Gen. Electric Co., 1955-57; reactor containment engineer AEC, 1958-59; cons. engr., 1960-63, mgr. stress analysis, 1963-68; mgr. structural mechanics Aircraft Engine group Gen. Electric Co., 1968-71, mgr. tech. ops., machinery apparatus ops., 1971-75, mgr. engring. support, 1976—. Served to 2d lt. AUS, 1943-46. Registered profl. engr., N.Y., Md. Mem. ASCE, ASME, N.Y. Acad. Scis., Phi Beta Kappa, Tau Beta Pi, Phi Kappa Phi. Episcopalian. Contbr. articles to profl. jours. Home: 826 Karenwald Ln Schenectady NY 12309 Office: Bldg 31 Gen Electric Co Schenectady NY 12305

MC CANDLESS, ANNA LOOMIS, club woman; b. Aspinwall, Pa., July 21, 1897; d. George Wilberforce and Estella (Loomis) McC.; B.S., Carnegie-Mellon U., 1919. Pres., Vis. Nurses Assn. Allegheny County (Pa.), 1955-57; mem. vis. com. Margaret Morrison Carnegie Coll., 1962-72; dir. Pitts. Hearing Soc., 1964-66; trustee emeritus Carnegie-Mellon U., 1966—. Mem. AAUW, Alumni Fedn. Carnegie-Mellon U. (v.p. 1963-66). Clubs: Twentieth Century (pres. 1956-58), Coll. Pitts., Univ. of Pitts., Appalachian Mountain. Home: Park Plaza Apts Pittsburgh PA 15213

MC CANDLESS, HUGH DOUGLAS, clergyman, fund raising cons.; b. N.Y.C., Oct. 21, 1907; s. Thomas and Beatrix (Sparks) McC.; B.A., Yale U., 1930; postgrad. Gen. Theol. Sem., 1930-31; B.D., Va. Theol. Sem., 1933, D.D., 1961; m. Dorothy Cutler Andrew, June 2, 1931; children—Hugh Andrew, Martha McCandless Durkee. Ordained priest Episcopal Ch., 1933; vicar St. Simon's-in-the-Clove, S.I., N.Y., 1933-39; rector Christ Ch. of Ramapo, Suffern, N.Y., 1939-45, Ch. of Epiphany, N.Y.C., 1945-72; past mem. dept. worship and the arts Nat. Council Chs. Trustee St. Barnabas' Hosp. Chronic Diseases. Mem. E. Mid-Town Ministers Assn., N.Y. Churchman's Clericus, Order St. John of Jerusalam, Sigma Chi. Republican. Clubs: Masons, Yale, Century Assn. Home: 83 Florence Rd Branford CT 06405

MC CANDLESS, RICHARD LEE, lawyer; b. Butler, Pa., May 30, 1934; s. Lee C. and Zella (White) McC.; A.B., Haverford Coll., 1955; M.Ed., Temple U., 1957; LL.B., Dickinson Sch. Law, 1960; m. Edith Lorraine Hagy, June 23, 1932; children—Mary Jo, Beth Ann. Tchr., Pennsburg Sch. System, Fairless Hills, Pa., 1955-57; admitted to Pa. bar, 1960, U.S. Tax Ct., 1964; practiced in Butler, 1960—; mem. firm Coulter, Gilchrist, Dillon & McCandless, 1970-76; partner firm Dillon, McCandless, King & Kemper, 1977—; dir. Butler Consumer Discount Co.; dir. Lawyers Abstract Co., 1968-76, v.p., 1971-74, pres., 1974-76. Mem. Butler County Soc. for Crippled Children and Adults, 1967-68; active Butler County United Fund, 1964-65, 71; chmn. fundraising United Cerebral Palsy of Butler and Lawrence Counties, 1972; bd. dirs. Butler County br. Pa. Assn. for Blind, 1970—, v.p., 1971—; trustee Pa. Elks Major Projects Found., 1968-74, 76—; bd. dirs. Butler County Fair and Agrl. Assn., 1974—, mem. exec. com., 1976—; Republican committeeman, 1964-66. Named Elk of Year, 1967-68. Mem. Am., Pa., Butler County (treas. 1965-69, chmn. legal services com. 1976-78) bar assns., Butler County Law Enforcement Assn., United Comml. Travelers, Pa. State Elks Assn. (fund raising com. Cerebral Palsy 1966-70, vice chmn. 1968-69, chmn. 1969-70; dist. dep. grand exalted ruler 1970-71, dist. sec. 1970-72), U.S. Trotting Assn., Pa. Harness Horseman Assn. (state dir., dir. W.Pa. chpt. 1975-77), Dickinson Sch. Law Alumni Assn. (dir. 1972-76), Butler County Meml. Hosp. Assn. Clubs: Masons, Elks (trustee 1972-74); mem. Fraternal Order of Police. Editor-in-chief Dickinson Law Rev., 1959-60. Home: 206 Blue Grass Dr Butler PA 16001 Office: 128 W Diamond St Butler PA 16001

MC CANN, JOHN THOMAS, civil engr.; b. Orange, N.J., Sept. 25, 1933; s. Thomas Aloysius and Ernstine Sophie (Mann) McC.; B.S., Newark Coll. Engring., 1958; M.B.A., Seton Hall U., 1968; m. Mary Patricia Kelly, Apr. 11, 1959; children—John, Karen, Maureen, Kelly Ann, Eileen. Pub. health engr. N.J. Dept. Health, 1958-59; borough engr. New Providence (N.J.), 1959-72; dir. pub. works, town engr. West Orange (N.J.), 1972—; cons. pub. works N.J. Dept. Community Affairs, 1969-70; mem. N.J. Bd. Profl. Engrs. and Land Surveyors. Served with USN, 1951-54. Mem. ASCE, Am. Pub. Works Assn., Nat. Soc. Profl. Engrs., Water Pollution Control Fedn., N.J. Soc. Profl. Planners, N.J. Soc. Municipal Engrs. (pres. 1975). Home: 151 Franklin Ave West Orange NJ 07052 Office: 66 Main St West Orange NJ 07052

MC CARTER, THOMAS N., III, investment counseling co. exec.; b. N.Y.C., Dec. 16, 1929; s. Thomas N., Jr. and Suzanne M. (Pierson) McC.; student Princeton, 1948-51; m. Nancy Kohler Alker, Sept. 23, 1955 (div. 1976); 1 dau., Nancy A.; m. 2d, Renate Bohne von Boyens, June 22, 1976. Sales exec. Mack Trucks, Inc., N.Y.C., 1952-59; partner Kelly, McCarter, D'Arcy Investment Counsel, N.Y.C., 1959-62; v.p., sec., dir. D'Arcy, McCarter & Chew, N.Y.C., 1962-66; v.p., dir., Trainer, Wortham & Co., Inc., N.Y.C., 1967-71, exec. v.p., 1972-76; chmn. Island Security Bank Ltd., Grand Cayman, B.W.I., 1976—; pres. Knottingham Ltd. N.Y., 1976—, Broad St. Fin. Mgmt., 1977—; dir. Fairmont Internat. Trade Co. Ltd., London. Mem. adv. bd. Mus. City N.Y. Charter trustee, Dalton Sch., N.Y.C., 1968-77, v.p., 1973-77; pres. Loyal Legion Found.; trustee Loyal Legion Meml. Fund; trustee Children's Aid Soc., N.Y.C., Found. for Am. Dance, 1973-77, City Center Joffrey Ballet, N.Y.C.; chmn. bd. trustees Christodora Found., Inc., N.Y.C. Mem. Mil. Order Loyal Legion U.S. (comdr. N.Y. State 1964-66, nat. comdr. in chief 1977—, mem. exec. com. commandry in chief Phila.). Clubs: Racquet and Tennis, Brook, Links, River (treas., gov.) St. Nicholas Soc., The Pilgrims U.S., New York City (N.Y.C.); Coral Beach and Tennis (Bermuda); Ivy (Princeton). Home: 823 Park Ave New York City NY 10021 Office: Knottingham Ltd care Laidlaw Adams & Peck 20 Broad St New York City NY 10005

MC CARTHY, DANIEL DONALD, III, advt. agy. exec.; b. Albany, N.Y., Apr. 8, 1944; s. Daniel Donald and Gail Mary (Langley) McC.; B.S. in Econs., Niagara U., 1967; m. Diane Patricia Ehlman, Nov. 30, 1968; 1 dau., Siobhan Gail. Media buyer Rumrill-Hoyt, Inc., Rochester, N.Y., 1968-70, market research analyst, 1970-72, asst. account exec., 1972-73, account exec., 1973-75, account supr., 1975-76; v.p., account supr., 1976; v.p., dir. media/market research Winterkorn, Hammond & Lillis, Inc., Rochester, 1976—. Served with USMCR, 1967-68. Mem. Bus./Profl./Advt. Assn., Rochester Advertisers Inc., Am. Research Assn., Am. Mgmt. Assn., Am. Mktg. Assn., U.S. Golf Assn. Roman Catholic. Club: Locust Hill Country. Home: 52 Cullens Run Pittsford NY 14534 Office: 311 Alexander St Rochester NY 14604

MC CARTHY, DANIEL JOSEPH, gross and microscopic anatomist, educator; b. Detroit, June 24, 1929; s. Daniel Joseph and Helen Ameila (Sorenson) McC.; Dr. Podiatric Medicine, Baldwin Wallace Coll., Ohio Coll. Podiatric Medicine, 1954; B. Ch. Ed., Grace Theol. Sem., 1962, M.R.E., 1963; M.A., Ind. U., 1963; postgrad. Mich. State U., 1967; Ph.D., U. Windsor (Ont.), 1974; m. LaRene Ann Clark, Sept. 16, 1950; children—Thomas J., Timothy J., Daniel W., David M. Practice podiatric medicine, Manistee, Mich., 1954-59, Elkhart, Ind., 1959-63, Bay City, Mich., 1963-74; prof. devel. and microscopic anatomy Ill. Coll. Podiatric Medicine, Chgo., 1975-76, chmn. dept., 1975-76; prof., chmn. dept. anatomy Pa. Coll. Podiatric Medicine, Phila., 1976-78; chief pediatric medicine VA Med. Center, Perry Point, Md. and coordinator pediatric research VA Central Office, Washington, 1978—. Served with USNR, 1945-54. Recipient Amour award in research, 1972, 78, Stickel Gold award, 1973, Bronze award, 1976, 78. Mem. Electron Microscopic Soc. Am., Ill., Am. podiatric assns., Am. Med. Writers Assn., Optimists. Spl. editor pathology Jour. Am. Podiatry Assn., 1972—. Researcher histology histochemistry, electron microscopy human skin scanning electron microscopy, rheumatology. Home: 1205 Bern Dr Havre de Grace MD 21078 Office: VA Washington DC

MCCARTHY, FREDERICK WILLIAM, investment banker; b. Boston, Nov. 25, 1941; s. Frederick William and Josephine Leona (Pannier) McC.; B.A. magna cum laude, Harvard U., 1963, M.B.A. with high distinction, 1967; m. Jeanette B. Champion, Sept. 2, 1967; children—Daniel Arthur, Frederick William III, Kathryn Elizabeth. Mgmt. cons. Booz Allen & Hamilton Inc., Chgo., 1967-70; 1st v.p. investment banking Shearson, Hammill & Co. Inc., N.Y.C., 1970-72, Chgo., 1972-74, Drexel, Burnham, Lambert Inc., Boston, 1974—. Served to 1st lt. U.S. Army, 1963-65. Home: 80 Whitelawn Ave Milton MA 02186 Office: Drexel Burnham Lamber Inc 1 Federal St Boston MA 02110

MC CARTHY, JOHN FRANCIS, JR., aerospace engr., educator; b. Boston, Aug. 28, 1925; s. John Francis and Margaret Josephine (Bartwood) M.; S.B. Mass. Inst. Tech., 1950, S.M., 1951; Ph.D., Calif. Inst. Tech., 1962; m. Camille Dian Martinez, May 4, 1968; children—Margaret Isabel, Jamie, Megan, Nicole, John III. Supr., air-ground communications TWA, Rome, Italy, 1946-47; project engr. aeroelastic and structures research lab., Mass. Inst. Tech., Cambridge, 1951-55; ops. analyst Strategic Air Command, USAF, Offutt AFB, Nebr., 1955-59; prin. scientist North Am. Aviation, Downey, Calif., 1961-62, tech. dir. space scis. Apollo, 1962, asst. chief engr., Apollo, 1962-63, dir. control systems, Apollo, 1963-65; dir. div. research and engring., 1965-66, v.p. research, engring. and test, 1966-68; v.p. research and engring. Rockwell Internat. Corp., Los Angeles, 1968-69, exec. v.p., 1969-70, v.p. systems engring., 1970-71; prof. dept. aeros. and astronautics, Mass. Inst. Tech., 1971—, dir. Center for Space Research, 1974—; cons. various indsl. firms; dir. Telcom, Inc., Vienna, Va., 1975—; cons. Office Sec. Def. dir. def. research and engring., Def. Sci. Bd., Washington, 1976; mem. Office of Aeros. and Space Tech., Research and Tech. Adv. Council-Panel on Space Vehicles, HQ NASA, Washington, 1974—, research adv. com. space vehicle aerodynamics, 1965-67; mem. joint strategic planning staff Sci. Adv. Group, Joint Chiefs Staff, 1976—; mem. sci. adv. bd. USAF, Washington, 1970—; chmn. div. adv. group Aero Systems Div. Wright-Patterson AFB, Ohio, 1971—. Campaign chmn. Downey (Calif.) Community Hosp. Fund Raising Campaign, 1968-69. Served with USAF, 1944-46. Recipient Apollo Achievement award NASA, 1969; Air Force Meritorious Civilian Service medal, 1973. Fellow Am. Inst. Aeros. and Astronautics (dir. 1975-76, tech. com. on entry vehicles 1963-66); Royal Aero. Soc. (asso.) (London); mem. Research Soc. Am., N. Am. Rockwell Corp. Mgmt. Club, Inc., Am. Mgmt. Assn. (research and devel. planning council 1968-78, pres.'s council 1978—), Am. Soc. Engring. Edn. (exec. com. aerospace div. 1969-72), Sigma Xi, Sigma Gamma Tau. Unitarian. Clubs: Toastmasters (dept. area gov. 1957-58, area gov. 1958). Contbr. numerous articles to profl. jours. Home: 53 Windsor Rd Wellesley Hills MA 02181 Office: Mass Inst Tech Room 37-241 Cambridge MA 02139

MC CARTHY, JOSEPH MICHAEL, historian; b. Lynn, Mass., Oct. 2, 1940; s. Joseph Donald and Johanna (Downing) McC.; A.B., St. John's Sem., 1961, postgrad., 1961-63; A.M., Boston Coll., 1968, Ph.D., 1972; m. Kathleen Theresa Wright, July 30, 1966; children—Joanna, Kristen, Erika, Joseph Michael. Tchr., Bishop Fenwick High Sch., Peabody, Mass., 1964-67; asst. dir. student fin. aid Boston Coll., 1967-69, 70-71; asst. dir. Inst. Human Scis., Chestnut Hill, Mass., 1969-70; lectr. in edn. Boston Coll., 1971-73; asso. prof. edn., dir. ednl. adminstrn. div. Suffolk U., 1973—; adj. lectr. Merrimack Coll., 1975, Boston Coll., 1974. Dir. III Pyramids Inc. Recipient Ahearn scholarship, 1959-61, fellowship, 1961-63. Mem. Am. Assn. for Higher Edn., Am. Assn. Sch. Adminstrs., Am. Cath. Hist. Soc. Phila., Am., Catholic hist. assns., History of Edn. Soc., History of Edn. Soc. Great Britain, Medieval Acad. Am., Orgn. Am. Historians, Phi Delta Kappa. Author: An International List of Articles on the History of Education, Published in Non-Educational Serials, 1965-74, 1977; Guinea-Bissau and Cape Verde Islands: A Comprehensive Bibliography, 1977; Humanistic Emphases in the Educational Thought of Vincent of Beauvais, 1976. Asso. editor The Urban and Social Change Review, 1969-72. Home: 344 West St Duxbury MA 02332 Office: Suffolk U Beacon Hill Boston MA 02114

MCCARTHY, KAREN A., ednl. adminstr.; b. Bklyn., Mar. 19, 1942. B.S. in Edn., Radford Coll., 1964; M.S. in Child Psychology magna cum laude, Coll. City N.Y., 1969; Ph.D. in Ednl. Psychology, U. City N.Y., 1975. Tchr. pub. schs., Tarrytown, N.Y., 1964-71; research asso. U. City N.Y., 1971-73; asso. dir. competancy based tchr. edn. program N.Y.C. Pub. Schs., 1973-74; dir. research, testing and evaluation White Plains (N.Y.) Pub. Schs., 1974-77; asst. supt. schs. Pelham (N.Y.) Pub. Schs., 1977—. Certified sch. dist. adminstr. Mem. Am. Edn. Research Assn., Am. Psychol. Assn., Nat. Council Measurement in Edn., Northeastern Research Assn., Am. Assn. Sch. Adminstrs. Co-author: Women and Educational Testing, 1974; Bd. High Edn. fellow. Home: 76 Broadway Hastings-on-Hudson NY 10706 Office: 17 Franklin Pl Pelham NY 10803

MC CARTHY, KEVIN JOHN, lawyer; b. N.Y.C., Apr. 8, 1941; s. Vincent Patrick and Mary Theresa (Hoffmeister) McC.; B.S., U. Md., 1963, J.D., 1966; m. Marianne Pitts, Nov. 5, 1966; children—Mary Rita, Kevin Joseph, Colin Michael. Admitted to Md., D.C. bars, U.S. Supreme Ct. bar; law clk. to asso. judge 7th Jud. Circuit Md., 1965-66; asso. partner firm Sasscer, Clagett, Channing and Bucher, Upper Marlboro, Md., 1966-75, Shipley, O'Malley, Miles, Farrington & McCarthy, Upper Marlboro, 1975—; mem. Products Liability Study Group for Md.; lectr. Washington retail security depts. Mem. Am., Prince George's County, Montgomery County, Anne Arundel County bar assns., Internat. Assn. Ins. Counsel, Am. Arbitration Assn., Def. Research Inst. Democrat. Roman Catholic. Club: Harbor Hills Yacht. Home: 3484 Olympia Rd Davidson MD 21035 Office: 9827 Central Ave Upper Marlboro MD 20870

MCCARTHY, ROLLIN HERBERT, consultant, former mfg. engr.; b. Cortland, N.Y., Jan. 17, 1899; s. John Henry and Nancy Elizabeth (Taylor) McC.; A.B., Cornell U., 1921, M.E., 1922, M.M.E., 1925; postgrad. Columbia U., 1935; m. Clara Frances Cheney, Aug. 19, 1925; children—Frances Ellen, Joan Taylor, Louise Robinson. Asst. prof. U. Nev., 1922-24, 25-28; instr. Cornell U., 1924-25; dir. mfg. engring., dir. bldg. design and constrn. Western Elec. Co., 1928-63; dir. bldg. planning and constrn. Ford Found., 1963-66; ret., 1966; cons. Nat. Inst. Higher Edn. (Ireland), VITA, Inc. (Bolivia), Internat. Exec. Service Corps (Indonesia). Bd. trustees Hartley Dodge Found., 1973—; chmn. bd. trustees Presbyterian Ch. of Madison, 1945; dir. Old Guard of Summit (N.J.), 1973. Served with U.S. Army, 1917-18. Registered profl. engr., N.Y., N.J. Fellow ASME; mem. Am. Soc. Engring. Edn., Phi Kappa Phi. Republican. Contbr. articles to profl. jours.

MCCARTHY, TERENCE ALAN, pub. relations exec.; b. Boston, Aug. 3, 1939; s. John Alfred and Agnes Mildred (Hovey) McC.; A.B., Georgetown U., 1962; M.A., Boston Coll., 1967; m. Marie Theresa Allen, May 28, 1966; children—Rebecca Marie, Nora Theresa. Staff writer N.Y. Central System, 1964-65; pub. relations rep., 1965-67; sr. writer Equitable Life Assurance Soc. U.S., N.Y.C., 1967-68; v.p., treas. Robert L. Bliss Inc., N.Y.C., 1968-71; exec. asst. N.Y. Stock Exchange, 1971-72; asso. dir. pub. info. Pub. Broadcasting Service, Washington, 1972-73; pres. Communique Inc., Boston, 1974-77; pres. McCarthy/Arnold Communications, 1977—; guest lectr. pub. relations Simmons Coll. Bd. dirs. Cohasset Community Center, 1974-75. Served with U.S. Army Res. Mem. Pub. Relations Soc. Am., Press Club Boston, Publicity Club Boston, Advt. Club Boston. Contbr. to local advt. and pub. relations media. Home: 45 Old Pasture Rd Cohasset MA 02025

MC CARTHY, THOMAS J., bishop; b. Goderich, Ont., Can., Oct. 4, 1905. Ordained priest, 1929, bishop, 1955; bishop of Nelson (B.C., Can.), 1955-58, St. Catharines (Ont.), 1958—. Office: 122 Riverdale Ave Saint Catharines ON L2R 4C2 Canada*

MC CARTNEY, EARL J., cons. atmospheric physics; b. Bucklin, Mo., June 29, 1908; s. Jesse and Sarah (Harper) McC; student U. Ia., 1925-27, 32, Ia. Wesleyan Coll., 1927-28, Coll. City N.Y., 1942-44; m. Marie Young, Oct. 10, 1936. Surveyor, U.S. Army C.E., Rock Island, Ill., 1936-41, elec. engr., Bklyn., 1941-44; electronics engr. Sperry Gyroscope Co., Great Neck, N.Y., 1944-71; adj. lectr. physics Hofstra Coll. Mem. Inst. Nav. (Burka award), IEEE, Optical Soc. Am., Am. Meteorol. Soc. Methodist. Republican. Author: Scattering: The Interaction of Light and Matter, 1966; Optics of Atmosphere: Scattering by Molecules and Particles, 1976. Contbr. profl. jours. Patentee in field. Home: 2 Winding Rd Rockville Centre NY 11570

MC CARTNEY, JOSEPH PHILIP, lawyer, actor, educator; b. N.Y.C., June 8, 1922; s. James Joseph and Anna (Sheridan) McC.; LL.B., St. John's U., 1952; m. Rita T. Pszczola, Nov. 11, 1955; 1 son, Mark J. With N.Y.C. Police Dept., 1947-49; admitted to N.Y. State bar, 1953, Fla. bar, 1974, U.S. Supreme Ct. bar, 1960; mem. staff N.Y. State Crime Commn., spl. agt. Office Naval Intelligence, N.Y.C., 1952-55; individual practice law Mineola, N.Y., 1955—; adj. prof.

criminal justice N.Y. Inst. Tech., 1975—. Extraordinary minister, lectr. St. Mary's Ch., Roslyn, N.Y., 1973—. Bd. dirs. No. Nassau Mental Health Center, Manhasset, N.Y. Served with USAAF, 1942-45; CBI; maj. Res. ret. Decorated Presdl. Unit citation, Bronze Star with cluster; knight comdr. Sovereign Order of Cyprus. Mem. Am., N.Y., Nassau County bar assns., Nat. Assn. Criminal Def. Lawyers, Catholic Lawyers Guild, AFTRA, Screen Actors Guild, Cath. Actors Guild, Delta Theta Phi. Rotary (pres. Roslyn 1973-74). Home: 41 Woodbine Rd Roslyn Heights NY 11577 Office: 1539 Franklin Ave Mineola NY 11501

MCCARTNEY, ROBERT CHARLES, lawyer; b. Pitts., May 3, 1934; s. Nathaniel H. and Esther S. (Smith) McC.; A.B. magna cum laude, Princeton U., 1956; J.D. cum laude, Harvard U., 1959; m. Janet Carolyn Moore, June 16, 1956; children—Ronald K., Sharon S., Carole J. Admitted to D.C. bar, 1959, Pa. bar, 1960; asso. firm Eckert, Seamans, Cherin & Mellott, Pitts., 1959-64, partner, 1965—; corporate sec., gen. counsel Ryan Homes, Inc., Pitts.; dir., v.p., sec., gen. counsel Holleran Services, Inc., York, Pa., 1974—; dir., sec., gen. counsel Washington Trotting Assn., Inc., Pitts. Mem. exec. com. Princeton (N.J.) Alumni Council, 1966-70, 75—; solicitor, alt. dir. North Pittsburgh Community Devel. Corp., 1968—; bd. dirs. United Meth. Found of Western Pa., 1972-78; trustee Otterbein Coll., Columbus, Ohio, 1975—; mem. corporate bd. North Hills Passavant Hosp., Pitts., 1976—. Mem. Am., Pa. Allegheny County bar assns., Golden Triangle YMCA, Princeton Alumni Assn. Western Pa. (pres. 1976-78). Republican. Methodist. Clubs: Allegheny, Downtown, Harvard-Yale-Princeton of Pitts. Home: 9843 Woodland Rd N Pittsburgh PA 15237 Office: 42d Floor 600 Grant St Pittsburgh PA 15219

MC CAULEY, H(ENRY) BERTON, city ofcl.; b. Duluth, Minn., Dec. 20, 1913; s. Henry Berton and Flora (Bourassa) McC.; diploma Balt. Poly. Inst., 1931; D.D.S., U. Md., 1936; m. Claire Ann Wolff, Dec. 20, 1937. Instr., oral roentgenology U. Md., 1936-40; Carnegie fellow in dentistry U. Rochester, 1940-43, asst. prof., 1943-45; dental research officer NIH, USPHS, 1945-49; dir. dental care Balt. City Health Dept., 1949-75, gen. adminstr. dept., 1977—; health adviser to mayor of Balt., 1976; cons. Manhattan Project, U.S. Army, Eastman Kodak Co., 1942-45. Trustee N. Balt. Mental Health Center. Served with USCG, 1945-46. Mem. Am. Soc. Dentistry for Children (Disting. Service award 1978), Md. Soc. Dentistry for Children (pres. 1954-55), Md. Pub. Health Assn. (pres. 1967), Md. State Dental Assn. (historian 1959—), Balt. City Dental Soc. (pres. 1973), Internat. and Am. assns. dental research, ADA (council on dental therapeutics 1943-48, chmn. pub. health sect. 1968), Am. Acad. History of Dentistry, Sigma Xi, Omicron Kappa Upsilon, Gorgas Odontol. Soc.; fellow AAAS, Am. Pub. Health Assn., Am. Coll. Dentists. Contbr. articles and research reports to pub. health and dental jours. Home: 3804 Hadley Sq E Baltimore MD 21218 Office: 111 N Calvert St Baltimore MD 21202

MC CLAIN, WILLIAM ANDERSON, psychologist; b. Phila., Oct. 24, 1942; s. William Anderson and Laura (McCourt) McC.; B.S., Temple U., 1965; M.Ed., U. Md., 1967, Ph.D., 1972; m. Dorie Sheryl Appel, Sept. 21, 1968. Counselor, U. Md., College Park, 1965-67; coordinator pupil services Bristol (Pa.) Sch. Dist., 1967-69; counseling psychologist D.C. Children's Center, Laurel, Md., 1969-72; supervisory psychologist Cheltenham Sch. Dist., Elkins Park, Pa., 1972—; pvt. practice psychotherapy, Phila., 1972—; lectr. psychology and ednl. psychology depts. Ogontz Campus, Pa. State U., Abington, 1974—; cons. Bethanna Home for Children, Beth Ayres, Pa., 1970—, Walden U., Naples, Fla.; lectr. in field. Mem. Am., Eastern, Pa. psychol. assns., Psi Chi, Phi Alpha Theta, Phi Delta Kappa. Asso. editor Newsletter div. The Sch. Psychologist, 1970. Contbr. articles to profl. jours. Home: 6006 Hasbrook St Philadelphia PA 19111 Office: Cheltenham Sch Dist Ashbourne Rd and Washington Ln Elkins Park PA 19117

MC CLANE, KENNETH ANDERSON, JR., poet, educator; b. N.Y.C., Feb. 19, 1951; s. Kenneth Anderson and Genevieve Dora (Greene) McC.; A.B., Cornell U., 1973, M.A. (Coll. scholar 1973, Univ. Grad. fellow 1973-74), 1974, M.F.A., 1976. Instr. English, faculty in residence Colby Coll., 1974-75; teaching fellow Cornell U., 1975-76, asst. prof., 1976—; humanities cons. Sta. WSKG, Elmira, N.Y.; author poetry books: Running Before the Wind, 1972; Out Beyond the Bay, 1975; Moons and Low Times, 1978. Recipient George Harmon Coxe award Cornell U., 1973, Corson Morrison Poetry prize 1973. Mem. AAUP, Phi Beta Kappa. Democrat. Editor Epoch, 1974-75, Watu, 1973-75, Rainy Day, 1970-73. Home: 316 Cascadilla St Ithaca NY 14850 Office: Dept of English Cornell U Ithaca NY 14850

MC CLARRIN, WILLIAM OTTO, govt. ofcl.; b. Atlanta, Apr. 11, 1918; s. Mozell and Geneva (Radden) McC.; B.A., Howard U., 1949; postgrad. Am. U., evenings, 1949-55, New Sch. Social Studies, N.Y.C., 1953, U. Notre Dame, 1969; m. Frances Justine Morsell, Feb. 14, 1942; children—Vaughn Otto, Lynn Frances. Reporter, artist Afro-Am., newspaper, Balt., 1936-40, copy editor, artist, 1940-41; publicity agt. Howard U., Washington, 1941-43, dir. pub. relations, 1947-56, 69-70; sr. artist, designer OPA, 1943; editor Newspic mag., Birmingham, Ala., N.Y.C., asst. editor Consumers Union Pubs., N.Y.C., 1946-47; pub. affairs officer USIA, Indonesia, 1956-58; chief info. office, illustrator U.S. Commn. on Civil Rights, 1958-62; pvt. practice pub. relations, U.S., Africa, 1962-66; dir. community relations community action program U.S. Office Econ. Opportunity, Washington, 1966-69, dir. spl. communications programs Office Pub. Affairs, 1970-72, dir. editorial div., 1972-74; coordinator agy.-wide recruitment Health Service Adminstrn., HEW, 1974-77, asso. adminstr. communications and pub. affairs, 1977—; pub. relations cons. to bus. and profl. orgns. Pub. relations com. Washington chpt. ARC, 1965—; chmn. pub. relations com. Health and Welfare Council Nat. Capital Area, 1967-69, UN Assn., Washington, 1971—; mem. citizens adv. com. Washington Zoning Commn., 1966—. Served with USAAF, 1943-45. Lucy E. Moten Travel fellow Howard U., 1941. Mem. Nat., Capital (Ann. awards 1948, 50, Newsman trophy 1960) press clubs, Pub. Relations Soc. Am., Coll. Pub. Relations Assn., Am. Alumni Council (Merit award 1949, 52), Advt. Club Met. Washington, Omega Psi Phi. Episcopalian. Clubs: Gourmets, Consorts (Washington). Editor Oracle mag., 1970—. Home: 1712 Allison St NW Washington DC 20011 Office: 5600 Fishers Ln Rockville MD 20857

MC CLARY, DAVID MICHAEL, mgmt. analyst fed. systems; b. W.Va., Aug. 29, 1943; s. Raymond Virgil and Isabelle (Moreau) McC.; Asso. degree U.S. Dept. Agr. Grad. Sch., 1969; B.A. in History and Anthropology, Am. U., 1972, M.P.A., 1975; postgrad. U. So. Calif. in D.C.; m. Gaynel Kegley Frizzell, Dec. 24, 1973; 1 son, Mark Edward. Explorer, adventurer CONUS, 1964-66; cartographer U.S. Dept. Agr., 1966; geodesist gravity analyst U.S. Army Map Service, Brookmont, Md., 1967-70; statis. wage analyst U.S. Dept. Labor, Washington, 1972-73; catalog delivery analyst Sears & Roebuck Catalog, Washington, 1973-77; mgmt. analyst Boulder labs. Commerce Dept., 1977-78; flood control analyst/surveyor, Boulder, 1978—. Adminstrn. officer CAP, 1977-78; mil. surveyor Colo. N.G., 1977-80; co-cir. Internat. Week, Am. U., 1973. Served with U.S. Army, 1962-63. Recipient awards various govt. agencies. Mem. Am. Hist. Assn., Am. Congress Mapping and Surveying, Am. Divers Assn., Am. Mgmt. Assn., Smithsonian Assos., Nat. Geog. Soc., Am. U. Alumni, Nat. Assn. Underwater Instrs., Nat. Rifle Assn. Democrat. Clubs: DAV, Boy Scouts Am., Wilderness Inst. Survival Edn. Researcher, writer for Nat. Geog., Smithsonian, Time and various newspapers. Home: PO Box 3281 Boulder CO 80307 Office: 4201 Massachusetts Ave NW Washington DC 20016

MC CLEAN, VERNON EMANUEL, educator; b. V.I., Sept. 17, 1941; s. Emanuel and Hilda (Leonard) McC.; B.A., St. Augustine's Coll., Raleigh, N.C., 1965; M.A., Atlanta U., 1967; certificate Inst. in So. and Black History, Johns Hopkins, 1969; Danforth Found. fellow Yale, 1972; Ed.D., Columbia, 1976; m. Freda Isaacs, Dec. 28, 1968; 1 dau., Malaika Nakupenda. Sec. to gov. V.I., St. Thomas, 1959-60; asst. advt. mgr. Episcopalian Mag., Inc., N.Y.C., 1960-61; instr. history Paine Coll., Augusta, Ga., 1966-67; asst. prof. history, dept. Black studies William Paterson Coll., Wayne, N.J., 1969—, dir. Inst. Black Studies, 1969-71, dir. CSP-Community Service Program, 1969-70, pub. Jour. Black Studies, editor Student Lit. Jour., asso. editor The Pen. Mem. African Heritage Studies Assn., Assn. for Study Negro Life and History, Am., So. hist. assns., Orgn. Am. Historians, Assn. Social and Behavioral Scientists, Phi Alpha Theta, Alpha Kappa Mu. Vernon E. McClean award named for him. Office: William Paterson Coll Wayne NJ 07470

MCCLELLAND, WILLIAM KELSEY, surgeon; b. Chgo., May 19, 1923; s. Dalton Finley and Mary Maud (Kelsey) McC.; B.A., Yale U., 1944, M.D., 1947; m. Betty Jean Weake, Sept. 18, 1948; children—Alan, Jean, James. Intern, Hartford (Conn.) Hosp., 1947-48, resident in surgery, 1948-50; asst. resident Children's Med. Center, Boston, 1953; surgeon Pondville State Cancer Hosp., Walpole, Mass., 1954-55, Mass. Gen. Hosp., Boston, 1954-55. Trustee Greenfield Public Library, 1963-66; pres. Pioneer Valley Symphony Orchestra, 1964. Served with M.C., U.S. Army, 1950-52. Mem. AMA, Mass. Med. Soc., N.E. Cancer Soc. Home: 4 Spring Terr Greenfield MA 01301

MC CLENATHAN, JAMES EDWARD, surgeon; b. Washington, Pa., Jan. 11, 1922; s. James Paul and Emma Romaine McC.; A.B., Washington and Jefferson Coll., 1943; M.D., U. Pitts., 1947; m. Evelyn Horner, June 17, 1944; children—James Horner, Donald Bruce, Robert Allen. Commd. lt. (j.g.) U.S. Navy, 1947, advanced through grades to capt. M.C., 1963; rotating intern U.S. Naval Hosp., Bethesda, Md., 1947-48, resident in gen. surgery, 1949-50, 51-54; fellow in surgery Georgetown U. Hosp., Washington, 1959; chief surgeon U.S. Naval Hosp., Guam, Marianas Islands, 1954-56; sr. staff surgeon U.S. Naval Hosp., Bethesda, Md., 1956-58; chief thoracic and cardiovascular surgery U.S. Naval Hosp., Nat. Naval Center, Bethesda, 1958-65, ret., 1965; practice medicine specializing in pediatric surgery, Washington, 1965-77; chief thoracic and cardiovascular surgery Children's Hosp., Washington, 1965-77, now cons. staff cons. Warner Hosp., Gettysburg, Pa.; asso. prof. surgery Med. Sch., George Washington U., Washington, 1966-73, prof. surgery, 1973-77, prof. child health and devel., 1973-77. Recipient Distinguished Service award Washington and Jefferson Coll., 1971. Washington Heart Assn. grantee, 1966-68. Diplomate Am. Bd. Surgery, Am. Bd. Thoracic Surgery. Fellow A.C.S., Am. Acad. Pediatrics, Am. Coll. Chest Physicians; mem. Am. Assn. Thoracic Surgery, Soc. Thoracic Surgeons, AMA (Physician's Recognition award 1973, 76), Am. Pediatric Surg. Assn., D.C. Thoracic Soc., Washington Heart Assn., Washington Acad. Surgery, Med. Soc. D.C., So. Thoracic Surg. Assn., Am. Trauma Soc., Adams County Med. Soc., Met. Washington Soc. Thoracic and Cardiovascular Surgery, Beta Theta Pi, Nu Sigma Nu. Methodist. Contbr. articles to med. jours. Home: 39 Winter Trail Carroll Valley PA 17320

MC CLINTOCK, SHIRLEY SPRAGUE, govt. ofcl.; b. Flushing, N.Y., Jan. 3, 1928; d. George Wilkie and Mary Dorothea (O'Rourke) Sprague; student Cornell U., 1949-51; m. John William McClintock, Sept. 22, 1951 (div. 1975); children—Barton, Charles, Scott. Analyst, Gen. Motors Overseas Ops., N.Y.C., 1965-68; personnel adminstr. Gen. Motors Corp., N.Y.C., 1952-54; spl. asst. to regional adminstr. HUD, N.Y.C., 1971—. Bd. dirs. Soc. for Prevention Cruelty to Children in Mass., 1962-64. Recipient Certificate for Superior Service, HUD, 1975. Mem. League Women Voters (sec. 1960-62), Cornell Alumni Assn. Home: 541 E 20th St New York City NY 10010 Office: 26 Federal Plaza New York City NY 10007

MC CLURE, DOUGLAS OLCOTT, headmaster; b. Scarsdale, N.Y., Dec. 16, 1929; s. Nathan Dixon and Louise Sheldon (Olcott) McC.; grad. Hotchkiss Sch., 1947; B.A., Yale, 1951; M.A., U. Conn., 1958; m. Kathleen Nelles, Feb. 2, 1952; children—Kathleen, Anne, Douglas, Peter. Instr., dir. admissions Pomfret (Conn.) Sch., 1955-63; headmaster Rockland County Day Sch., Congers, N.Y., 1963-66, Princeton (N.J.) Day Sch., 1966—; research asso. Princeton, 1969-71. Chmn. bd. Ind. Ednl. Services, 1971-75, bd. dirs., 1975—; trustee St. Mary's and Doane Acad., Burlington, N.J., 1968-75, Newark Acad., 1969—, Columbus Boy Choir Sch., Princeton, 1975—, St. Benedict's, Newark, 1976—. Served as submarine officer USNR, 1952-55. Mem. Country Day Sch. Headmasters Assn., Am. Acad. Polit. and Social Sci., Headmasters Assn., Headmistresses of East, Am. Hist. Assn., Am. Assn. Advancement Slavic Studies, Am. Assn. Sch. Adminstrs., Nat. Council Social Studies. Episcopalian (vestryman). Address: Princeton Day Sch POB 75 The Great Rd Princeton NJ 08540

MC CLUSKEY, WELDON JAMES, former YMCA exec.; b. Newton, Mass., June 20, 1913; s. James W. and Stella F. (Durland) McC.; B.S., Springfield Coll., 1935; postgrad. Temple U., 1960; m. Katherine Ellis, Sept. 23, 1939 (dec. 1976); children—James, Margery, Gail. Phys. dir. Elmira (N.Y.) YMCA, 1935-39, Kingston (N.Y.) YMCA, 1939-41, Asbury Park (N.J.) YMCA, 1941-42, Portland (Maine) YMCA, 1942-43; asso. exec. Poughkeepsie (N.Y.) YMCA, 1943-47; program dir. Montclair (N.J.) YMCA, 1947-51; exec. dir. Brookhaven YMCA, L.I., 1951-54; gen dir. Glocester County YMCA, Woodbury, N.J., 1954-78. Licensed dog show judge. Named Man of Year, Poughkeepsie, 1946. Mem. Assn. Profl. Dirs. YMCA, Greater Woodbury C. of C. (sec.), Am. Kennel Club, Borzoi Club Am., Gloucester County Kennel Club (past pres.), Delaware Valley, Greater N.Y. Borzoi clubs. Clubs: Rotary, Masons. Contbr. articles to profl. jours. Home: RR 3 Box 173 Sewell NJ 08080

MC COLL, JOHN ROME, JR., sports co. exec.; b. Glen Rock, N.J., Jan. 13, 1925; s. John Rome and Ellena Mackenzie (Heddle) McC.; B.A., Colgate U., 1949; m. Roberta J. Walker, June 30, 1956; children—John Rome, Susan G., Lauren E., Robin W. Sales rep. Shell Oil Co., Albany, N.Y., 1949-53; trainee Hendrix Heating Co., New Haven, 1953-55; founder McColl-Wade Inc., Branford, Conn., also pres., 1956—; co-founder Sports Assn. Inc. (New Haven Nighthawks), 1970—, v.p., 1970-73, pres., 1973—. Vice-pres., Greater New Haven Youth Hockey Assn., 1968-69, bd. dirs., 1969-75, founder midget program, 1973. Served to 1st lt., pilot, USAAF, 1943-45; ETO. ERDA grantee, 1977. Mem. Assn. Energy Engrs. (charter), Montgomery Pkwy. Assn. (pres. 1962-69), Branford C. of C. (dir. 1960-67), Am. Hockey League (alt. gov. 1974—). Republican. Mem. United Ch. Christ. Clubs: Lions (dir. Branford 1958-65), Am. Legion. Home: 25 Montgomery Pkwy Branford CT 06405 Office: PO Box 1444 New Haven CT 06506

MCCOLLOUGH, CLAIR R., broadcasting exec.; b. York, Pa., July 1, 1903; s. Austin E. and Pearl E. (Robinson) McC.; grad. Millersville State Coll., 1926; D.C.S., Franklin and Marshall Coll., 1955; D.Litt., Elizabethtown Coll., 1964; m. Velma A. Dilworth, July 12, 1926; 1 dau., Constance. In broadcasting industry, 1931—; pres., gen. mgr. (TV stas.) WGAL-TV, Lancaster, Pa., WTEV-TV, Providence, (radio stas.) WDEL, WSTW-FM, Wilmington, Del. Mem. U.S. Communications Mission to ETO, MTO, 1945; mem. Nat. Adv. Council to Study Broadcasting Practices in Post War Years, 1947; mem. Broadcast Adv. Council to Office Sec. Def. for Korean Conflict, 1950; chmn. radio and TV commn. U.P. Ch., N.Y.C., 1957-59; mem. Broadcasting Industry Nat. Red Cross Com., 1959-61, Nat. Conf. Christians and Jews, 1959-61, Radio Free Europe Com., 1961, Pa. State U. Adv. Com. on Broadcasting, 1961—; mem. Future of Broadcasting and Communications in Am. Com., Washington, 1963—; pres. Broadcasters' Found., N.Y.C., 1963—; chmn. Nat. TV Code Rev. Bd., Washington, 1964—; mem. U.S. Broadcasters Com. for UN, N.Y.C., 1965—; mem. Pa. Council on Crime and Delinquency, 1965—. Trustee Franklin and Marshall Coll., Ednl. Found. (AWRT), Inc., N.Y.C. Recipient Ambassador of U.S. Radio award Variety, 1950, U.S. Radio Silver Mike award, 1960, George Foster Peabody TV award, 1963, award for dedicated service to religious broadcasting U.P. Ch. in U.S., 1963, Alfred I. DuPont TV award, 1963; Golden Mike award Broadcast Pioneer and Broadcasters Found., 1969. Mem. Internat. Radio TV Soc. (pres.), Nat. (chmn. annual convs. 1953, 55, chmn. bd. dirs. 1961-63, chmn. new bldg. com. 1963—, chmn.; Distinguished Achievement award 1960), Pa. (founder-pres. 1932-43, Pioneer Pres. award 1958) assns. broadcasters, Broadcast Pioneers (dir.), Soc. TV Pioneers (dir.), NBC Affiliates Assn. (chmn. 1946-50), Radio Pioneers (pres. 1956-57), Sigma Delta Chi. Clubs: Nat. Press, Broadcasters (Washington); Megantic (Eustis, Me.). Home: 1021 Marietta Ave Lancaster PA 17603 Office: Telestation WGAL-TV Lincoln Hwy W Lancaster PA 17604

MC COLLOUGH, EDDIE CLARENCE, communications engring. co. exec.; b. Cleveland, Miss., Nov. 18, 1928; s. Ottis Calloway and Lyda Caroline (Williams) McC.; diploma Inst. Radio engrs., 1954; grad. Alexander Hamilton Inst., 1957; m. Evelyn Mary Bock, Sept. 14, 1957; children—Lynne, Kathleen, Calloway, Cynthia, Steven. In tech. mgmt. positions in communication systems RCA, 1953-61; v.p. engring. Com Tel Engring. Co., Menlo Park, Calif., 1961-62; v.p. mktg. Universal Services Inc., Seattle, 1962-63; mgr. West Coast div. Fed. Electric Corp. subs. ITT, Rome, Italy and Richland, Wash., 1963-66; dir. ops. Page Communications Engrs., Washington, 1966-70; founder, pres. engring., chmn., chief exec. officer McCollough and Co., Inc., Tehran, Iran, 1970—; cons. Ministry of Posts Telegraph and Telephone Iran, Nat. Iranian Oil Co. Served with U.S. Army, 1946-52. Mem. IEEE (sr.), Armed Forces Communications/Electronics Assn. (life), Iran Am. C. of C. Clubs: Imperial Country, French, Tehran (Tehran, Iran). Mgr. constrn. of systems for Iran, Tehran, 1970—. Home: 8513 Brickyard Rd Potomac MD 20854 Office: PO Box 41/1135 Tehran Iran

MC COMB, JOHN PAUL, JR., lawyer, b. Pitts., Oct. 7, 1922; s. John Paul and Katherine Elizabeth (McKinnon) McC.; A.B., Princeton, 1944; J.D., Harvard, 1948; m. Anne Mercur, Nov. 8, 1944; children—John Stewart, Sara Mercur, David Forbes, Richard Benson. Admitted to Pa. bar, 1948; asso. firm Griggs, Moreland, Blair & Douglass, Pitts., 1948-52; partner firm McComb & Wolfe, Pitts., 1952-58; dir., sec., gen. counsel J.H. Hillman & Sons Co., Pitts., 1958-63; partner Moorhead & Knox, Pitts., 1963—. Bd. dirs. World Affairs Council Pitts., 1952—; dir., sec. Action Housing, Inc., 1967—; trustee, vice chmn. Shadyside Hosp., 1958—. Served with USMCR, 1944-46, 51-52. Mem. Am., Pa., Allegheny County (Pa.) bar assns., Am., Pa. (exec. com. 1975-76) socs. hosp. lawyers. Republican. Presbyterian. Home: 207 Farmington Rd Pittsburgh PA 15215 Office: 4950 US Steel Bldg 600 Grant St Pittsburgh PA 15219

MC CONKY, WALTER BRADLEY, banker; b. Phila., Mar. 19, 1937; s. Kenneth W. and Helen T. (Bradley) McC.; B.A., Bowdoin Coll., 1959; postgrad. Pace Coll., 1962; postgrad. N.Y. U. Grad. Sch. Bus. Adminstrn., 1963; m. Nancy Bowser, Sept. 30, 1967; 1 dau., Elizabeth Patterson. With Bankers Trust Co., N.Y.C., 1962-71, asst. mgr., 1966-67, asst. treas., 1967-71; with First Nat. City Bank, N.Y.C., 1971-73, account officer, 1972-73; account officer Citicorp Factors, Inc., 1973; asst. v.p. City Nat. Bank of Conn., Bridgeport, 1973, v.p., mgr. real estate lending dept., 1974-76, dept. head, v.p. real estate lending, 1976—; lectr. Urban Reinvestment Task Force, 1978—. Bd. dirs. George Jr. Republic, N.Y.C., 1968-71, asst. treas., 1968-71; bd. dirs. Bridgeport Neighbor Housing Services, 1975-77, treas., 1975-76. Served to 1st lt. Intelligence Corps, U.S. Army, 1960-62; capt. Res., 1962-66. Mem. Nat. Assn. Rev. Appraisers (sr.), Mortgage Bankers Assn. (urban investment com. 1978), Soc. Real Estate Appraisers (asso.), New Eng. Land Title Assn., Conn. Bankers Assn. (mortgage com. 1973—, ad hoc com. on clear lang. 1978—, joint banking com. on alt. mortgages 1978—), Theta Delta Chi. Republican. Congregationalist. Home: The Meeting House Redding CT 06875 Office: 955 Main St Bridgeport CT 06602

MC CONNELL, ALAN EDWARD, newspaper exec.; b. Arnprior, Ont., Can., Mar. 10, 1928; s. John William and Violet Mildred (Diener) Mc C.; student pub. schs., Arnprior; m. Edith Alice Hussey, Dec. 11, 1953; children—Richard Alan, Ronald Darren. Advt. salesman Los Angeles Examiner, 1957-59; advt. salesman Toronto (Ont.) Star Ltd., 1944-57, nat. mgr. advt. Starweekly mag., 1959-68, Montreal mgr., 1969-71, gen. advt. mgr., 1971-75; exec. asst. to pres. Metro Market Newspapers Ltd., Toronto, Ont. 1976—. Mem. Toronto Advt. and Sales Club, Am. Mktg. Assn., Toronto Advt. Club. Episcopalian. Home: 71 Montgomery Rd Islington ON M9A 3H4 Canada

MC CONNELL, JOHN EDWARD, power systems engr., corp. exec.; b. Minot, N.D., July 28, 1931; s. Lloyd Waldorf and Sarah Gladys (Mathis) McC.; B.S. in Mech. Engring., U. Pitts., 1952; M.S., Drexel Inst. Tech., 1958; m. Carol Claire Myers, July 4, 1952; children—Kathleen Anne, James Mathis, Amy Lynn. With mktg., design dept. Westinghouse Electric Corp., Lester, Pa., 1954-60, 63-67, Pitts., 1960-63; mgr. power generation equipment activities in U.S. and regional mgr. power activities Middle Atlantic, Southeastern U.S. regions ASEA Inc., White Plains, N.Y., 1967—; adviser on energy matters to U.S. congressman 1968-74. Served to 1st lt. C.E., U.S. Army, 1952-54. Registered profl. engr., Pa. Mem. IEEE (sr.), Power Engring. Soc. (sr.), ASME, TAPPI (energy mgmt. com. membership chmn.). Republican. Contbr. numerous articles on energy topics to profl. jours. Home: 173 Remington Rd Ridgefield CT 06877 Office: 4 New King St White Plains NY 10604

MC CONNELL, JOHN HOWARD, mgmt. cons.; b. Highland Park, Mich., June 18, 1933; s. Melvin William and Dorothy Marie (Miller) McC.; B.S., Wayne State U., 1957, M.Ed., 1963; m. Dolores Ann Cooper, Oct. 29, 1955; children—Keith Ernest, Brian Howard, Eric William. Draftsman, Detroit Edison Co., 1951-57; tchr. Nichols Sch., Detroit, 1957-60; with Wolverine Tube Co., Detroit, 1960-69, plant indsl. relations mgr., 1965-68, mgr. devel., 1968-69; exec. dir. personnel Garan Inc., N.Y.C., 1969-70; pres. Assessment Centers Internat., Morristown, N.J., 1970-74, McConnell Simmons & Co.,

Morristown, 1974—. Pres., Rolling Hills Skyline Dr. Civic Assn., 1973-75; active Boy Scouts, PTA; bd. dirs. YMCA, Detroit, 1967. Mem. Am. Psychol. Assn., Am. Mgmt. Assn. Club: Internat. Brotherhood Magicians. Contbr. articles to profl. jours. Home and Office: 1 Skyline Dr Morristown NJ 07960

MCCONNON, JAMES CHARLES, lawyer; b. Pitts., Mar. 30, 1926; s. Myles and Myra V. (Steel) McC.; B.S., Cornell U., 1947; LL.B., U. Pa., 1951; m. Nancy Kern, 1953; children—James Charles, Linda J., Nancy K. Indsl./Engr. U.S. Steel Co., Pitts., 1947, Westinghouse Airbrake Co., Pitts., 1948; admitted to Pa. bar, 1952, Ct. of Customs and Patent Appeals bar, 1952; asso. firm Paul & Paul, Phila., 1952-58, partner, 1958—; mem. Nat. Transp. Policy Study Commn.; mem. Pa. Transp. Adv. Com., co-chmn. subcom. on local and area transp., 1971-76; mem. bd. Southeastern Pa. Transp. Authority, chmn., 1968-78; mem. bd. Inst. Rapid Transit, 1969-74, chmn. transp. of handicapped com., 1972-74; chmn. governing bds. com. Am. Transit Assn., 1972-73, mem. bd., exec. com., 1972-74; v.p. for rapid transit Am. Pub. Transit Assn., 1975-76; mem. bd. Transit Devel. Corp., Inc., 1972-76; mem. met. rys. com., mem. mgmt. com. Internat. Union Pub. Transport; mem. Pa. Gov.'s Com. for Transp., 1968. Chmn. com. legislation Montgomery County Indsl. Devel. Com., 1960-64; mem. Montgomery County Energy Adv. Com., Study Commn. Phila. Met. Area, Wynnewood Civic Assn.; chmn. exec. com., regional chmn. Montgomery County Republican Com. Served to ensign USN, 1944-46. Recipient recognition of service awards Greater Phila. C. of C., Am. Pub. Transit Assn. Mem. Am., Phila. bar assns., Am., Phila. patent law assns., Am. Legion. Roman Catholic. Clubs: Union League (Phila.); Seaview Country (N.J.). Home: 104 Anton Rd Wynnewood PA 19096 Office: 1800 Land Title Bldg Philadelphia PA 19110*

MC CORISON, MARCUS ALLEN, librarian; b. Lancaster, Wis., July 17, 1926; s. Joseph Lyle and Ruth (Mink) McC.; A.B., Ripon Coll., 1950; M.A., U. Vt., 1951; M.S., Columbia U., 1954; m. Janet Buckbee Knop, June 10, 1950; children—Marcus Allen II, Judith (Mrs. Jeffrey A. Gove), Andrew B., Mary Lyle, James R., Peter G. Librarian, Kellogg-Hubbard Library, Montpelier, Vt., 1954-55; chief rare books dept. Dartmouth Library, 1955-59; head spl. collections dept. State U. Iowa Libraries, 1959-60; librarian Am. Antiquarian Soc., Worcester, Mass., 1960—, dir., 1967—; lectr. Am. History Clark U., 1967—. Overseer Old Sturbridge Village, 1968—; mem. adv. com. Eleutherian Mills-Hagley Found., 1971-74; treas. Com. for New Eng. Bibliography, 1970-71. Served with USNR, 1944-46; 1st lt., inf. AUS, 1951-52. Mem. Am. Antiquarian Soc., Vt. (trustee 1956-60), Mass., hist. socs., Bibliog. Soc. Am. (1st v.p. 1978—), Ind. Research Libraries Assn. (chmn. 1972-73, 78—), Northeastern Soc. 18th Century Studies (pres. 1978-79), Colonial Soc. Mass., Beta Phi Mu. Clubs: Odd Volumes, St. Botolph, Grolier, Century. Author: Vermont Imprints, 1778-1820, 1963; The 1764 Catalogue of the Redwood Library, 1965; The History of Printing in America by Isaiah Thomas, 1970. Home: 4 Military Rd Worcester MA 01609 Office: Am Antiquarian Soc Worcester MA 01609

MC CORMACK, GEORGE HENRY, physician; b. N.Y.C., Jan. 24, 1925; s. George Henry and Natalie Josephine (Duffy) McC.; B.S., Coll. of Holy Cross, 1945; M.D., Columbia U., 1949; m. Joy Merchant Karn, May 31, 1963; children—Jane, Hugh, George, Julia. Intern, Presbyn. Hosp., N.Y.C., 1950-51, resident, 1951-54, now mem. staff; practice medicine specializing in internal medicine, N.Y.C., 1956—; mem. staff Roosevelt Hosp., N.Y.C.; instr. medicine Columbia U., N.Y.C., 1953-60, asso. in medicine, 1960-68, asst. prof. clin. medicine, 1968-72, asso. prof., 1972—. Served to capt. M.C., AUS, 1954-56. Mem. N.Y. Clin. Soc. Democrat. Roman Catholic. Home: 130 E 75th St New York City NY 10021 Office: 903 Park Ave New York City NY 10021

MC CORMACK, GRACE, microbiologist; b. Rochester, N.Y.; d. Walter and Maud (Brimacomb) McC.; A.B., U. Rochester, 1941; M.S., U. Md., 1951. Technician, U. Rochester Sch. Medicine and Dentistry-AEC, 1942-48; bacteriologist U.S. Fish and Wildlife Service, U.S. Dept. Interior, College Park, Md. and East Boston, Mass., 1948-53; asso. bacteriologist Md. Dept. Health, Balt., 1953-55; bacteriologist-technologist VA Hosp., Canandaigua, N.Y., 1955-66; tchr. biology dept. Monroe Community Coll., Rochester, 1966—. Recipient Sustained Superior Service award VA Hosp., 1963. Fellow Royal Soc. Health (Eng.), Am. Inst. Chemists, Intercontinental Biog. Assn.; mem. Soc. Microbiologists, Am. Chem. Soc., Am. Pub. Health Assn., Inst. Food Technologists, AAAS, Am. Inst. Food Technologists, Am. Inst. Biol. Scis., N.Y. Acad. Scis. Contbr. numerous articles to profl. jours. Home: 162 Raleigh St Rochester NY 14620

MC CORMACK, JOHN FRANCIS, JR., historian; b. Yonkers, N.Y., Apr. 30, 1935; s. John Francis and Margaret Elizabeth (O'Brien) McC.; B.S., Manhattan Coll., 1957; M.A. (N.Y. State 5th Year fellow), Coll. City N.Y., 1962; postgrad. N.Y. U., 1962-63, State U. N.Y., Binghamton, 1967, Villanova U., 1969-71, Nova U., 1974—; m. Mary Elizabeth Kirby, June 29, 1963; children—Sean Maurice, Maureen Ellen, Kevin Francis. Wire and cable insp. Phelps-Dodge Copper Products, Yonkers, N.Y., 1957-60; tchr., track and cross-country coach Sacred Heart High Sch., Yonkers, 1960-64, Rye Neck High Sch., Mamaroneck, N.Y., 1964-65; instr. Sullivan County Community Coll., S. Fallsburg, N.Y., 1965-67; prof., div. dean Del. County Community Coll., Media, Pa., 1963—. Pres., Irish-Am. Unified Soc. Yonkers, 1960-62; chmn. schs. com. and area rep. Marydell Farms Civic Assn., 1974-76; pres. E. Goshen Elementary Sch. Home and Sch. Assn., 1977-78. Fellow Co. Mil. Historians; mem. Del. County Community Coll. Assn. High Edn. (pres. 1977—), Pa. State Edn. Assn., Mil. History Soc. Ireland, Irish-Am. Cultural Inst., Am. Irish, N.Y., N.Y. State, Pa. hist. socs., Am. Hist. Assn., Am. Mil. Inst., Orgn. Am. Historians, NEA, Little Big Horn Assos., Nat. Rifle Assn. Democrat. Roman Catholic. Clubs: Order of Hibernians, K.C. Editor Research Rev., 1974—; author TV series America in Revolution, 1970-71; contbr. articles in field to profl. jours. Home: 1532 Bancroft Dr West Chester PA 19380 Office: Delaware County Community Coll Media PA 19063

MCCORMICK, J(OSEPH) CARROLL, bishop; b. Phila., 1907; student St. Charles Sem., Phila., Pontifical Roman Sem., Rome. Ordained priest Roman Catholic Ch., 1932; vice chancellor, later chancellor, Phila. archdiocese, 1936-44; pastor St. Stephen's Ch., Phila., 1944-60; titular bishop of Ruspe, aux. bishop of Phila., 1947-60; bishop of Altoona-Johnstown, Pa., 1960-67; bishop of Scranton, Pa., 1967—. Address: 315 Wyoming Ave Scranton PA 18503

MC CORMICK, JAMES CHARLES, mfg. co. exec.; b. Cleve., Jan. 23, 1938; s. Michael Patrick and Agnes Christine (Mortensen) McC.; B.S. in Accounting, Regis Coll., 1960; m. Claire A. Maskaly, Nov. 28, 1963 (div. June 1978); children—Kelly, Shannon. Accountant, Ernst & Ernst, Allentown, Pa., 1963-73; treas. Fuller Co., Catasauqua, Pa., 1973—. Dist. chmn. Minsi Trails council Boy Scouts Am., 1976—, treas., 1978—. Served with USNR, 1960-63. C.P.A., Pa. Mem. Am. Inst. C.P.A.'s. Club: Livingston (Allentown). Home: Spring Ridge Apts M-17 Whitehall PA 18104 Office 128 Bridge St Catasauqua PA 18032

MC CORMICK, JOSEPH FRANCES, engring. co. exec.; b. Springfield, Mass., Sept. 7, 1933; s. Frances Prendergast and Margaret Mary (O'Brien) McC.; B.S.M.E., Lowell Tech. Coll., 1959; m. Mary Anne Alerding, Sept. 15, 1956; children—Patricia, Jean, Michael, Joseph, James. Design engr. Raytheon Co., Waltham, Mass., 1958-60, Aerojet Gen. Co., Sacramento, Calif., 1960-62; applied scientist Gen. Dynamics Co., Rochester, N.Y., 1962-66; product mgr. Gar-Kenyon, Brewster, N.Y., 1966-70; engring. cons. in product devel. and mktg., Pawling, N.Y., 1970-74; pres. McCormick Servo Controls, Inc., Danbury, Conn., 1974—. Chmn., Young Republicans, 1964-65. Served with U.S. Army, 1953-55. Mem. Fluid Power Soc., Am. Mgmt. Assn., East Fishkill Hist. Soc. Clubs: Pawling Recreation Assn. Holder numerous patents on servo mechanisms. Home: North Quaker Hill Rd Pawling NY 12564 Office: 44 Backus Ave Danbury CT 06810

MC CORMICK, ROBERT LAWRENCE, ednl. adminstr.; b. Detroit; s. Thomas Daniel and Madeline Marie (Hicks) McC.; B.S., Columbia, 1962, postgrad., 1963-64; postgrad. U. Berlin, 1960-61; m. Barbara Jutta Baruschke, June 21, 1960; children—Danny, Mischa, Dylan. Co-dir. Camp Clarkston, 1958-60; tchr. Grosse Pointe Nursery, 1957-59; psychology research Psychiat. Inst., 1964-66; founder, dir. Open Community Sch., Claverack, N.Y., 1967—; headmaster Allegro Sch., Claverack. Bd. dirs. Allegro Learning Found., Open Community Camp. Home: Box 399 Claverack NY 12513

MCCORMICK-PICKETT, NANCY, assn. exec.; b. Dayton, Ohio, Apr. 20, 1951; d. George Alfred and Martha Jane McCormick; A.B. in Communication with distinction, Stanford U., 1972; M.A., Am. U., 1974; postgrad. Stanford Film and Broadcasting Inst., 1972; Spanish Lang. tng. Fgn. Service Inst. Dept. State, 1976; m. Richard R. Pickett, June 18, 197?. Fgn. service officer USIA, 1973-76; advance liaison Am. Embassy, The Hague, Netherlands, 1974; asst. dir. broadcast mgmt. Nat. Assn. Broadcasters, Washington, 1976-77, dir. employment clearinghouse, 1977-78; communications coordinator Cancer Coordinating Council for Met. Washington, 1978—; career counselor for young women entering communications industry. Mem. Media Task Force, Nat. Conf. Black Lawyers, Am. Women in Radio and TV, United Negro Coll. Fund, Arthritis and Rheumatism Assn. Met. Washington, Lupus Found. Met. Washington. Democrat. Roman Catholic. Author: Women on the Job, Careers in Broadcasting, 1978. Office: 1825 Connecticut Ave NW Washington DC 20009

MC COWAN, RICHARD JAMES, educator; b. N.Y.C., Oct. 10, 1931; s. Richard James and Veronica Mary (Quinn) McC.; B.A. cum laude, St. John's Coll., 1953; M.A., Niagara U., 1954, certificate, 1955; Ph.D., St. John's U., 1965; postgrad. State U. N.Y. at Buffalo, 1964-66, at Albany, 1967; m. Mary Elisabeth Coyle, Aug. 17, 1957; children—Mary Elisabeth, Kathleen Mary, Maura Ann, Sheila Coyle. Tchr., counselor Baldwin (N.Y.) Jr. High Sch., 1957-61; counselor Farmingdale (N.Y.) High Sch., 1961-64; dir. guidance Eden (N.Y.) Central Schs., 1964-66; chief Bur. Sch. and Cultural Research, N.Y. State Edn. Dept., 1966-68; dir. campus lab. sch., dir. ednl. research and devel., prof. edn. State U. N.Y. Coll. at Buffalo, 1968—; cons. numerous schs., agys. Adv. bd. BUILD Acad., 1968—, Erie Community Coll., City Campus, 1971—; mem. Woodlawn Adv. Com., 1973-74; campaign mgr. Republican mayoral candidate, Buffalo, 1973. Served with AUS, 1955-57. Mem. NEA, Am. Ednl. Research Assn., Nat. Soc. for Study Edn., Am. Personnel and Guidance Assn., Nat. Vocat. Guidance Assn., Am. Sch. Counselors Assn., N.Y. State Tchrs. Assn., AAUP, Phi Delta Kappa. Clubs: K.C., Rotary. Contbr. articles to profl. publs., poems. Home: 2466 W Oakfield Rd Grand Island NY 14072 Office: State U Coll at Buffalo Buffalo NY 14222

MC COY, JAMES FRANK, coll. librarian; b. Clarkton, N.C., Aug. 4, 1925; s. Frank and Gertrude Lee (Smith) McC.; B.A., Lincoln U., 1952; M.L.S., Rutgers U., 1956; certificate advanced studies U. Denver, 1973. Reference librarian N.J. State Library, N.J., 1956, Elizabeth (N.J.) Pub. Library, 1956; dir. Mercer County (N.J.) Community Coll., 1956-74; dir. learning resources Hudson Valley Community Coll., 1974—; sec. state U. N.Y. Council Head Librarians, 1977; advisory asso. Rutgers Grad. Sch. Library Service. Cons. Am. Coll., Paris, France, 1965; cons. library adminstrn. and ednl. tech. program United Bd. Coll. Devel., 1975. Mem. Trenton Mayor's Urban Renewal Advisory Com., 1966-68, Citizens Action Council, 1963-65, Mayor's Advisory Com. Model Cities, 1968—, North Trenton Neighborhood Council, 1970—, Trent House Commn., 1965—; bd. mgrs. Trenton Neighborhood Health Center, 1970-72, pres., 1971. Served with U.S. Army, 1944-46. Recipient Distinguished Alumni award Lincoln U., 1972. Mem. Am. (chmn. communications com. Community and Jr. Coll. Libraries sect. Assn. Coll. and Research Libraries 1975-77, editorial bd. CHOICE 1974—), N.J. (pres. coll. and univ. sect., archivist 1965, Distinguished Achievement award Coll. and Univ. sect. 1971) library assns., ALA, AAUP (pres. chpt. 1967-69, sec. N.J. conf. 1970-72), Rutgers U. Grad. Sch. Library Service Alumni Assn. (pres. 1975-76), N.J. Jr. Coll. Assns. (sec.-treas. 1960, 65), Council on Library Tech. (chmn. curriculum com.), Kappa Alpha Psi. Contbg. author: Bibliography of the Negro in New Jersey, 1967; Basic Books for Junior College, 1963. Home: 66 E Bishops Gate Guilderland NY 12084 Office: 80 Vandenburgh Ave Troy NY 12180

MC COY, KEVIN GEORGE, sales promotion co. exec., artist; b. N.Y.C., Jan. 7, 1941; s. Edgar William and Kathryn (Pappas) McC.; student Sch. Visual Art, 1962; B.A., Art Students League, 1964; 1 dau., Regan Kate. Artist, Twincraft Mfg. Co., 1960; art dir. Kevin G. McCoy Assos., 1961-63; pres. McCoy Weinreich Advt. Corp., 1963-67; exec. v.p. Pathmark Printing Corp., N.Y.C., 1967-70, pres., 1971; pres. J. Lampert Promotions, Inc., N.Y.C., 1972—, HarkGroup, Ltd., N.Y.C.; lectr. to profl. groups. Recipient award Art Dirs. Club, Printing Industries N.Y., 1964, Soc. Illustrators, 1964. Mem. Art Dirs. Club N.Y.C., Soc. Illustrators, Mktg. Communication Execs. N.Y. Roman Catholic. Clubs: Salmagundi, N.Y. Athletic (N.Y.C.). Home: 61 W 89 St New York City NY 10025

MC COY, LARRY DEAN, govt. ofcl.; b. Greeley, Colo., June 20, 1938; s. Dean H. and Josephine Ann (Sorenson) McC.; B.A., Calif. State U. at San Diego, 1964; M.P.A., Am. U., 1969; m. Eddymarie Navarrete, Aug. 24, 1963; 1 son, Kevin. Engring. aide Gen. Dynamics-Convair Corp., San Diego, 1958-61, master scheduling analyst, 1961-62, engring. adminstrv. asst., 1962-64; mgmt. technician Library of Congress, Washington, 1964-65, adminstrv. officer Reference Dept., 1965-68, mgmt. analyst Copyright Office, 1968-71; asst. chief Office Adminstrv. Services, GAO, Washington, 1971-72, asst. to dir. Office Fed. Elections, 1972-74, supr. mgmt. analyst Fin. and Gen. Mgmt. div., 1974-75; dep. asst. staff dir. Fed. Election Commn., Washington, 1975—. Recipient Comptroller Gen.'s Honor award Comptroller Gen. U.S., 1974; certified Inst. Certified Records Mgrs. Mem. Am. Records Mgmt. Assn., Nat. Microfilm Assn. Office: 1325 K St NW Washington DC 20463

MC CRACKEN, BLAIR, educator, author; b. Los Angeles, Nov. 12, 1933; d. Dwight Mason and Jean Elizabeth (Blair) McC.; B.A., George Washington U., 1957; M.A., Columbia U., 1965; m. Charles Ponce, 1970; 1 son, David Abrams. Tchr. pub. schs., Bowie, Md., 1955-56, Nanuet, N.Y., 1957-58, Syosset, N.Y., 1959-60; individual practice as remedial reading specialist, N.Y.C., 1965-69; dir. reading program YWCA Jr. Edn. and Tng. Program, N.Y.C., 1966; reading cons. Chapin Sch., N.Y.C., 1966-68; prin. elementary sch. Lenox Sch., N.Y.C., 1968-70; instr. Sch. Edn., Bklyn. Coll., N.Y. U., N.Y.C., 1970; sch. editor Holt, Rinehart & Winston Co., N.Y.C., 1970-72; state dir. div. curriculum resources Maine Dept. Ednl. and Cultural Services, Augusta, 1972-74, affirmative action com., 1973, ednl. cons. Mid-Coast Mental Health Clinic, 1976; sr. reading cons. McGraw-Hill Pub. Co., 1976; adminstr. curriculum div. Mass. State Dept. Edn., 1978—; mem. Indian edn. adv. com. to Maine Legislature, 1972; mem. Maine Profl. Standards Adv. Commn., 1973-74. Bd. dirs. Azoth Found., 1971-76; adv. bd. Center for Learning Disabilities, N.Y.C., 1969-70; mem. regional policy bd. Field Services Research Center Maine, 1973; mem. adv. council Community Sch., 1975-76; Maine del. alt. Nat. Women's Conf., 1977. Recipient Cutter prize for lit. George Washington U., 1957. Mem. Internat., New Eng. reading assns., NEA, Ednl. Research Assn., Maine Tchrs. Assn., Am. Psychol. Assn. Author: Bold Journeys, 1966; Joey's Secret, 1973; Stars are for Storytelling, 1973; Measure Me, Sky, Reading Components, 1975; Ginn & Co. Reading Series 720. Home: Cushing ME 04563 Office: Azoth Found Cushing ME 04563

MC CRACKEN, JERALD RUSSELL, ins. agt.; b. Rochester, N.Y., Nov. 23, 1930; s. George H. and Kathryn M. (Dyke) McC.; student SUNY, Geneseo, 1951-53; m. Ruth Slane, June 20, 1952; children—Daryl, Deborah, Darlene, Jerald Russell. Agt., Farmers & Traders Life Ins. Co., York, N.Y., 1953-55, gen. agt., Hornell, N.Y., 1955-59, regional supt. agts., Columbia, S.C., 1959-63, gen. agt., Rochester, N.Y., 1963, asst. to pres., Syracuse, N.Y., 1963-64, v.p., asst. to pres., 1964-66, v.p. data processing, Syracuse, 1966-67, gen. agt., Batavia, N.Y., 1967—. Chmn. Genesee County Commn. of Human Rights, 1972-73; bd. dirs. Grant Gilliam Found., 1975-78; mem. Genesee County Coop. Extension LongRange Planning Com., 1970-72; chmn. Community Resource and Devel. Com., 1975-78, mem. bd. dirs., 1977-78. Mem. Batavia Assn. Life Underwriters. Presbyterian. Clubs: Masons; Shriners (Rochester), Grange. Office: Farmers & Traders Life Ins Co PO Box 567 Batavia NY 14020

MC CRACKEN, STEWART, physician; b. Shanghai, China, May 9, 1922; s. Josiah Calvin and Helen (Newpher) McC.; B.A., U. Pa., 1942; M.D., Temple U., 1945; M.S. in Internal Medicine, U. Pa. Grad. Sch. Medicine, 1951; m. Joan Adamson Fernley, June 11, 1949; children—Ellen Clute, Stewart, Mary Newpher, James Christopher. Intern Pa. Hosp., Phila., 1945-46; mem. med. staff Temple U. Hosp., Phila., 1952—; instr. medicine Temple U. Med. Sch., 1952-63, asso. in medicine, 1964-69, clin. asst. prof., 1969—; research asso. in cancer chemotherapy group VA Hosp., 1956-75, cons. rheumatology VA Out-patient Clinic, 1975—. Served as lt. (j.g.) USNR, 1946-48. Mem. A.M.A., Am. Rheumatism Assn., Am. Soc. Clin. Oncology, Phila. Coll. Physicians, Phila. Rheumatism Soc. (pres. 1970-71), Sphinx Soc., Beta Theta Pi. Club: Cricket (Phila.). Home: 1300 Hickory Rd Plymouth Meeting PA 19462 Office: 33 E Chestnut Hill Ave Philadelphia PA 19118

MCCRANN, THOMAS EMMETT, bank exec.; b. Phila., May 30, 1943; s. Anthony Emmett and Elizabeth (Kline) McC.; B.A., U. Pa., 1965, M.B.A., 1967; m. Doreen Okumoto, May 4, 1974; 1 dau., Mari Elizabeth. With U.S. Trust Co., N.Y.C., 1967—, asst. v.p., 1974-78, v.p., 1978—. Served with AUS, 1968-70. Decorated Commendation medal. Mem. N.Y. Soc. Security Analysts, Fin. Analysts Fedn. Roman Catholic. Clubs: Princeton. Home: 186 Forest Way Essex Fells NJ 07021

MC CRARY, EUGENIA LESTER (MRS. DENNIS DAUGHTRY MCCRARY), civic worker, writer; b. Annapolis, Md., Mar. 23, 1929; d. John Campbell and Eugenia (Potts) Lester; A.B. cum laude, Radcliffe Coll., 1950; M.A., Johns Hopkins, 1952; postgrad. Harvard, spring 1953, Pa. State U., 1953-54, Drew U., 1957-58, Inst. Study USSR, Munich, Germany, 1964; m. John Campbell Howard, July 15, 1955 (dec. Sept. 1965); m. 2d, Dennis Daughtry McCrary, June 28, 1969. Grad. asst. dept. Romance langs. Pa. State U., 1953-54; tchr. dept. math. Brearley Sch., N.Y.C., 1954-57; dir. Sch. of Langs., Inc., Summit, N.J., 1958-69, trustee, 1960-69. Dist. dir. Eastern Pa., N.J. auditions Met. Opera Nat. Council, N.Y.C., 1960-66, dist. dir. publicity, 1966, nat. vice chmn. pub. relations, 1967-71, nat. chmn. pub. relations, 1972-75, hon. nat. chmn. pub. relations, 1976—. Mem. Mayflower Soc., Nat. Soc. Colonial Dames, Met. Opera Nat. Council, Jr. League Summit, Playhouse Assn. Summit, Pi Lambda Theta. Republican. Episcopalian. Clubs: Radcliffe N.J. (pres. 1959-61) (Summit); Colony (N.Y.C.). Home: 24 Central Park S New York City NY 10019

MC CRARY, VERNON EUGENE, optometrist; b. Greenville, S.C., Oct. 25, 1927; s. Charles Loyd and Blanche Angeline (Doggett) McC.; student optometry Furman U., 1945-46; O.D., No. Ill. Coll. Optometry, 1949; D. Ocular Sci. (hon.), Mass. Coll. Optometry, 1971, Ill. Coll. Optometry, 1972; m. Helen Victoria Horney, Nov. 24, 1951 (dec. Dec. 23, 1974); children—Wayne Eugene, Carolyn Joyce; m. 2d, Linda Lee Bready, Aug. 27, 1975; 1 dau., Rebecca Lynn. Practice optometry with father, Greenville, 1949-51; individual practice optometry, College Park, Md., 1953—; trustee Vision Care Services, Inc., Washington, 1970—, Optometric Center Md., Balt., 1977—; mem. Md. Bd. Examiners Optometry, 1959-63; cons. Office Econ. Opportunity, Project Headstart, 1965—, Bur. Health Manpower div. Allied Health Manpower, USPHS, 1967—. Mem. Pres.'s Com. Employment of Physically Handicapped, 1969—; mem. White House Conf. on Children and Youth, 1970, White House Conf. on Aging, 1970; nat. campaign chmn. Optometric Progress Fund, 1969-70; chmn. Cub pack com. Boy Scouts Am., merit badge counselor, 1958-64; mem. pedestrian safety com. Calvert Hills Citizens Assn., 1968; mem. College Park Boys Club, 1957, College Park Bd. Trade, 1956—, College Park Youth Adv. Bd.; chmn. bd. trustees Univ. Methodist Ch., mem. fin. com., 1967—, co-dir. fin. crusade, 1969. Served with USNR, 1945-46, 50-51. Named Noteworthy Practitioner Beta Sigma Kappa, 1958, Md. Optometrist of Year, 1969-70, hon. chief Otoe Indian Tribe of Oklahoma City, 1966; recipient Distinguished Service award Lions, 1956. Fellow Am. Acad. Optometry (pres. 1964, chmn. com. on fed. legis. 1970—, chmn. internat. affairs com.), AAAS; mem. Am. Pub. Health Assn., Nat. Health Forum, Better Vision Inst., Central Md. Optometric Soc. (founder 1954, pres. 1960-61), Am. Optometric Assn. (pres. 1965-66, dir. dept. nat. affairs 1967-70), Assn. Ophthalmic Opticians Ireland (overseas mem.). Home: 4500 Beechwood Rd College Park MD 20740 Office: 6901 Baltimore Blvd College Park MD 20740

MC CREA, JOHN COLES, assn. exec.; b. Sherbrooke, Que., Can., Nov. 24, 1937; s. Robert Perce and Maude Elizabeth (Coles) McC.; B.A., Sir George Williams U., 1966; M.Ed., McGill U., 1970; m. Patricia Ann MacDonald, Apr. 29, 1961; children—Heather Lynn, Ian Andrew. Tchr., Protestant Sch. Bd. Greater Montreal, 1962-68; v.p. Montreal Tchrs. Assn., 1968-69; exec. dir. Montreal Assn. Mentally Retarded and dir. gen. Peter Hall Schs., Inc., 1969—; vis. lectr. McGill U., 1974, intern thesis adviser, 1975. Bd. dirs. Camp Gatineau, Inc., 1973-76, Que. Assn. for Mentally Retarded, 1973-78; pres. Que. Assn. Sheltered Workshops, 1971-74; exec. com. Can.

Council Rehab. Workshops, 1972-74; sec. Found. for Mentally Retarded, 1972—. Recipient Vanier award as one of Five Outstanding Young Canadians, 1976; Outstanding Young Citizen award Montreal Lakeshore, 1977. Mem. Council Exceptional Children, Conseil de l'Enfance Exceptionnel du Que., Inst. Assn. Execs., Can. Coll. of Tchrs., Council Adminstrs. Spl. Edn. Home: 4895 Trenholme Ave Montreal PQ H4V 1Y2 Canada Office: 5915 boul Henri Bourassa Ouest St Laurent PQ H4R 1B7 Canada

MC CREEDY, RICHARD EUGENE, food broker; b. nr. Balt., Dec. 28, 1933; s. Edward Eugene and Helen Mae (Hopkins) McC.; B.S. in Mktg., U. Balt., 1959; m. Emma Jane Barnes, Oct. 16, 1954; children—Jennifer J., Richard J., Donna J. Salesman, Nat. Biscuit Co., Balt., 1954-55; dist. mgr. Dixie Cup div. Am. Can Co., Washington, 1955-60; pres. RMI, Inc., Elkridge, Md., 1960—. Mem. First Dist. County Council, Balt., 1962; pres. Medwick Civic Improvement Assn.; sec. Bon Secours Hosp. Guild. Bd. mgrs. YMCA. Served with USAF, 1952-54. Mem. Grocery Mfrs. Reps. of Balt. and Washington, Grocery Wheels of D.C., Chesapeake-Potomac Frozen Food Assn., Washington (past pres.), Md. food brokers assns. Democrat. Episcopalian. Home: 8037 Strauff Rd Towson MD 21204 Office: 6330 Howard Ln Elkridge MD 21227

MC CREEDY, WARREN THOMAS, educator; b. N.Y.C., Feb. 8, 1915; s. Thomas Burns and Louise Harriet (Rudolph) McC.; M.A., U. Chgo., 1949, Ph.D., 1961. Instr., U. Ind., Gary, 1950-53; lectr. Queens U., Kingston, Ont., Can., 1954-56; lectr. U. Toronto, Ont., 1956-60, asst. prof., 1960-64, asso. prof., 1964-69, prof., 1969—. Served with USAAF, 1940-45. Mem. Am. Assn. Tchrs. Spanish and Portuguese, Canadian Assn. Hispanists, Asociacion Internacional de Hispanistas. Author: La heraldica en las obras de Lope de Vega y sus contemporaneos, 1962; Bibliografia tematica de estudios sobre el teatro antiguo espanol, 1966; Lope de Vega: El mejor mozo de Espana, 1967. Editor: Bull. Comediantes, 1967-72. Office: Dept Hispanic Studies U Toronto Toronto ON M5S 1A1 Canada

MC CRENSKY, JONATHAN ALLEN, advt. agy. exec.; b. Providence, Apr. 23, 1939; s. Leo and Dora (Fishman) McC.; B.S., Boston U., 1961; m. Patricia McCrensky; children—Paige Sue, Glen, Debra, Robert, Toby Lea. Retail exec. Gimbels-Macy's-Bamberger for Hartz Mountain Corp., N.Y.C., 1964-66; account exec. Bo Bernstein Advt., Providence, 1966-68; account exec. Bloom Advt., Dallas, 1968-70; dir. advt. sales promotion, marketing Edward Trauner, Inc., Zodiac, Clebar & Vacheron Constantine watch cos., 1970-72; v.p. marketing Edward G. Coyne, Inc., N.Y.C., 1972-74; accounts supr. Rabin Advt., Valley Stream, N.Y., 1974-76, Halpern Advt., Garden City, N.Y., 1976; pres. Jonathan Allen Advt., 1976—; adj. prof. Suffolk County Community Coll. Served to capt. USAFR, 1961-64. Home: Lawn Ln Upper Brookville Oyster Bay NY 11771

MC CROHAN, KEVIN FRANCIS, educator; b. NYC, Apr. 7, 1944; s. Francis Howard and Edith Mary (McGrath) McC.; B.S., N.Y. U., 1967; M.B.A. in Internat. Bus. (grad. fellow), Baruch Coll., 1971, M.B.A., 1974; certificate in philosophy City U. N.Y., 1974, Ph.D., 1978; m. Veronica Joan O'Connor, May 22, 1966; children—Tara Marie, Kenneth Francis. Shipping coordinator Ametalco, Inc., N.Y.C., 1965-67, contract adminstr., 1967-69; instr. Baruch Coll., N.Y.C., 1971-75; asst. prof. U. New Haven, West Haven, Conn., 1975-78, asso. prof., chmn. dept. mktg. and internat. bus., 1978—; cons. edn. div. Xerox Corp., 1972, 1st Nat. City Bank N.Y.C., 1973-74. Mem. Friends of the Children of Vietnam, 1971-75; bd. dirs. Friends of All Children, 1975—. Served to capt. U.S. Army Res., 1971—. Recipient Baruch Coll. Alumni Award for Service to the Coll., 1972. Mem. Acad. Internat. Bus., Am., So. mktg. assns., Am. Polit. Sci. Assn., Assn. for Consumer Research, Spl. Forces Assn., Beta Gamma Sigma. Roman Catholic. Author monographs and articles in field. Home: 856 Leonard Dr Westbury NY 11590 Office: U New Haven 300 Orange Ave West Haven CT 06516

MCCUE, BRIAN JAMES, ednl. adminstr.; b. Elmhurst, Ill., Nov. 10, 1948; s. Al T. and Gertrude L. (O'Brian) McC.; B.S., U. Ill., 1970, M.S., 1971; postgrad. in public adminstrn. Nova U., 1978—. Adult Basic Edn./Gen. Edn. Diploma tchr. De Soto Correctional Instn., Arcadia, Fla., 1971-72; program adminstrn. Am. Lung Assn. S.W. Fla., Ft. Myers, 1972-73; health educator/sanitarian Collier County (Fla.) Health Dept., 1973-76; dir. community-univ. studies Sch. Continuing Edn., Indiana U. Pa., 1976—; mem. Pa. Emergency Med. Services Council; cons. Regional Police Tng. Acad., Indiana, Pa.; vol., mem. Citizens Ambulance Service, Indiana; developer nat. pilot demonstration project on emergency med. tech. tng. of coal mine personnel Office Deep Mine Safety, Pa. Dept. Environ. Resources, 1976—. Mem. Nat. Community Edn. Assn., Nat. Univ. Extension Assn., Adult Edn. Assn. U.S.A., Am. Assn. Univ. Adminstrs., Am. Public Health Assn., Soc. Public Health Edn., Am. Sch. Health Assn., Nat. Assn. Public Continuing and Adult Edn., Phi Delta Kappa. Club: Indiana U. of Pa. Rebounders (v.p.). Author: Human Sexuality and the Adult Male Offender—A Teaching Guide, 1972. Office: Uhler Hall Indiana U Pa Sch Continuing Edn Indiana PA 15705

MCCUE, DANIEL LAWRENCE, JR., educator; b. Somerville, Mass., Nov. 14, 1917; s. Daniel Lawrence and Mary Marguerite (O'Malley) McC.; A.B. cum laude, Boston Coll., 1940; M.A., Columbia U., 1947, Ph.D., 1974; m. Catherine Caroline Weaver, Nov. 25, 1954; children—Caroline Anne, Daniel Lawrence, Elizabeth Joan. Faculty Boston Coll., Chestnut Hill, Mass., 1953—, asso. prof. English; cons. in field. Served with U.S. Army, 1942-46. Mem. Modern Lang. Assn., AAUP, Edmund Burke Soc. Am., Am. Soc. 18th Century Studies, Conf. Brit. Studies. Contbr. articles in field to books and profl. jours. Home: 84 Bellefontaine Ave Framingham MA 01701 Office: 458 Carney Center Boston College Chestnut Hill MA 02167

MC CUE, JOHN B., lawyer; b. Pitts., June 22, 1921; s. Henry Michael and Mary Genevieve (McCrossin) McC.; B.A., Pa. State U., 1942; J.D., U. Pitts., 1948; m. Mary Helen Clapper, Nov. 5, 1949; children—Michael Brian, Patrick Alan. Admitted to Pa. bar, 1949, since practiced in Kittanning; mem. Pa. Ho. Reps. from 60th Dist., 1963-64, 71-76; now mem. firm McCue, Bertocchi & Heim. Served with USAAF, 1943-45, U.S. Army, 1950-52; brig. gen. Pa. N.G. (ret.). Decorated Air medal with 4 oak leaf clusters. Mem. Am., Pa. bar assns., N.G. Assn., Res. Officers Assn., Am. Legion, VFW. Republican. Roman Catholic. Clubs: Elks, Eagles. Home: RD 7 Kittanning PA 16201 Office: 217 Market St Kittanning PA 16201

MC CULLOUGH, JOSEPH LEE, mgmt. cons.; b. Bryn Mawr, Pa., Oct. 3, 1945; s. Leo Francis and Margaret Mary (Hart) McC.; A.B., Villanova U., 1967; M.A., Ohio State U., 1968, Ph.D., 1971. Teaching asst., then research asso. Ohio State U., 1967-69; asso. O.P.S. Assos., Columbus, Ohio, 1970-71; prin. Hay Assos., Phila., 1971—. Served with AUS, 1972. NDEA Title IV fellow, 1970; Univ. Dissertation Year fellow, 1971. Mem. Am., Eastern, Pa. psychol. assns. Co-author: The Acquisition of Information Across Cultures: I Persuasive Role-Play, Counterargument Attitude Changes, 1970; Repetition of Highly Similar Messages and Attitude Change, 1974. Home: K-16 Shirley Ln Lawrenceville NJ 08648 Office: One Dag Hammarskjold Plaza New York City NY 10017

MCCULLOUGH, KENDRICK, physician; b. Burlington, Vt., Dec. 20, 1904; s. Samuel H. and May (Kendrick) McC.; M.D., U. Vt., 1930; m. Margaret W. Lawrence, Nov. 8, 1940 (dec. Aug. 1960). Instr. pathology, U. Vt., 1931-35; pathologist Bishop de Goesbriand, Fanny Allen hosps., 1932-35; resident pathology Grasslands Hosp., Valhalla, N.Y., 1935-39; asst. dir. Bur. of Labs. City Yonkers, N.Y., 1940-43, dir. Feb. 1947; pathologist, dir. labs. St. John's Riverside Hosp., Yonkers, 1943-47; chief pathologist Peninsula Gen. Hosp., Salisbury, Md., 1947-74, pathologist, part-time 1974—; pathologist Nanticoke Meml. Hosp., Seaford, Del., 1952—. Diplomate Am. Bd. Pathology. Mem. A.M.A., Soc. Clin. Pathologists, Am. Coll. Pathologists, New Eng. Hist. Geneal. Soc., Internat. Acad. Pathology, Vt. Hist. Soc., Wicomico County Med. Soc. (pres. 1951), Royal Soc. Medicine (affiliate), Am. Acad. Forensic Scis. Episcopalian. Rotarian, Elk. Author (with Waters, Thomas) report on lingual thyroid Md. State Med. Jour.; articles in med. jours. on pathology. Home: Baileraghnaill RFD 1 Parsonburg MD 21849 Office: Peninsula Gen Hosp Salisbury MD 21801

MC CUNE, JAMES, structural engr.; b. Ballynahinch, No. Ireland, July 9, 1926; s. James and Margaret (McDowell) McC.; came to U.S., 1954, naturalized, 1959; B.A. and B.A.I. with honors, Trinity Coll. Dublin, 1949; postgrad. Northeastern U.; m. Evelyn Cornelia Marinus, June 16, 1956; 1 dau., Margaret Evelyn. Tech. officer Imperial Chem. Industries Ltd., Eng., 1949-53; chief engr. Lazarides, Lount & Partners, Toronto, Ont., Can., 1953-54; field engr. Rilco Laminated Products, Boston, 1954-55; foundation engr. Koppers Co., Pitts., 1955-57; asst. chief structural engr. Anderson Nichols Co., Boston, 1957-61; sr. asso. LeMessurier Assos., Cambridge, Mass., 1961-75; v.p. engring. Cannon Design Inc., Grand Island, N.Y., 1975—; mem. Bldg. Code Com., Wellesley, Mass., 1973-75. Mem. Bldg. Com. for Restoration of St. Paul's Cathedral, Buffalo, 1977—. Registered profl. engr., N.Y., Mass. Mem. ASCE, Am. Concrete Inst., Am. Inst. Steel Constrn. Episcopalian. Home: 2547 West River Pkwy Grand Island NY 14072 Office: 2170 Whitehaven Rd Grand Island NY 14072

MC CUNE, WILLIAM STANLEY, surgeon; b. Petoskey, Mich., June 4, 1909; s. William George and Helen Susan (Allen) McC.; B.A. with highest honors, Swarthmore Coll., 1931; M.D. cum laude, Harvard U., 1935; m. Doris Douglas, July 8, 1936; children—Carol McCune Hooker, Cynthia McCune Allen, Barbara, Mary McCune Mahoney; m. 2d., Mary C. Dykhouse, Mar. 22, 1975. House officer Mass. Gen. Hosp., Boston, 1935-37; asst. resident gen. surgery Peter Bent Brigham Hosp., Boston, 1937-39; house physician Boston Lying-in Hosp., 1939-40; practice medicine specializing in gen. surgery, Petoskey, 1940-43; clin. prof. surgery George Washington U., Washington, 1946-76; cons. surgery NIH, Walter Reed Army Hosp., Washington, 1946-76; chief staff VA Hosp., Batavia, N.Y., 1976—; clin. asst. prof. surgery U. Rochester (N.Y.), 1976—. Chmn. med. adv. bd. CARE/MEDICO, 1974-76. Served from capt. to maj., M.C., U.S. Army, 1943-46. Mem. Am. (v.p. 1963), So. (v.p. 1971) surg. assns., Soc. Surgery Alimentary Tract (founder), Southeastern Surg. Congress (pres. 1976), D.C. Med. Soc. (pres. 1965), Royal Soc. Medicine, Washington Acad. Surgery (pres. 1972), Phi Beta Kappa, Alpha Omega Alpha. Republican. Episcopalian. Club: Met. Washington. Author: (with Brian Blades) Nash's Surgical Physiology, 1953; (with Warren Cole) Cancer of Digestive Tract, 1968; contbr. articles to profl. publs. Home: VA Hosp Batavia NY 14020

MC CURDY, JOHN, physician; b. Coleraine, No. Ireland, Apr. 27, 1936; s. Marshall and Margaret Matilda (Thompson) McC.; Medicine B., B.A.O., B. Chir., Queens U., Belfast, 1960, D. Obstetrics, U. London, 1962; m. Margaret Rosemary Elaine Gilmore, Sept. 2, 1961; children—Shaun Marshall, Linda Anne. Intern, Belfast City Hosp., 1960-61; resident in obstetrics and gynecology Jubilee Maternity Hosp., Belfast, 1961-62; individual practice medicine, specializing in internal medicine and dermatology, Belfast, 1962-67, family practice, Brampton, Ont., Can., 1967—; med. registrar internal medicine and dermatology No. Ireland Hosps. Authority, Belfast, 1962-67; group med. practice, Brampton, 1967—; chief dept. family practice Peel Meml. Hosp., Brampton, 1974—. Served to capt. M.C., Royal Army, 1964-67. Serving Brother Order of St. John, 1964. Mem. Coll. Family Practice Can., North Peel Med. Soc. Clubs: Regency Racquets, Brampton. Home: 14 Derwent Ave Brampton ON L6W 1K4 Canada Office: 24 Queen St E Brampton ON L6V 1A7 Canada

MC CURDY, PATRICK PIERRE, editor; b. Angers, France, Sept. 14, 1928 (parents Am. citizens); s. Joseph Alexander and Constance Yolande (DeBoisferon) McC.; B.S. in Chem. Engring., Carnegie Inst. Tech., 1949; m. Eiko Yamada, May 30, 1953; children—Alan J., Wendy C., Alec J., Jeffrey R. Chem. engr. Humble Oil & Refining Co., Baytown, Tex., 1949-50, Callery Chem. Co. (Pa.), 1955-56; sr. chem. engr. research and devel. lab. U.S. Army, Fort Belvoir, Va., 1956-60; with Chem. & Engring. News, Washington, N.Y.C., Frankfurt, Germany, Tokyo, Japan, 1960-73, mng. editor, Washington, 1967-69, editor, 1969-73, editor-in-chief Chem. Week, N.Y.C., 1973—. Served to 1st lt. C.E., AUS, 1950-54. Mem. Am. Chem. Soc., Chemists' Club N.Y., Société de Chimie Industrielle (Am. sect.), Phi Kappa Phi, Tau Beta Pi, Theta Tau. Clubs: Overseas Press (N.Y.C.); Foreign Correspondents (Tokyo); Tokyo American. Home: 220-A Riverside Ave Riverside CT 06878 Office: 1221 Ave of Americas New York City NY 10020

MC CURDY, RICHARD CLARK, cons.; b. Newton, Iowa, Jan. 2, 1909; s. Ralph Bruce and Florence (Clark) McC.; A.B., Stanford, 1931, E.M., 1933; m. Harriet Edith Sutton, Sept. 11, 1933; children—Gregor, Richard, Carolyn, Robert. Engring. and prodn. Shell Oil Co., 1933-47; prodn. mgmt. Shell Caribbean Petroleum Co., 1947-50; gen. mgr. Shell Group Companies, Venezuela, 1950-53; pres. Shell Chem. Co., N.Y.C., 1953-65; dir., mem. exec. com. Shell Oil Co., 1955-69, pres., chief exec. officer, 1965-69; asso. adminstr. for orgn. and mgmt. NASA, Washington, 1970-73. Trustee United Seamans Service, 1954-70, Stanford U., 1965-70, Hood Coll., 1968—, Renssalaer Poly. Inst., 1974—. Recipient Distinguished Service medal NASA, 1972. Mem. Mfg. Chemists Assn. (bd. dirs. 1955-65, chmn. bd. 1961-62, chmn. exec. com. 1964-65), Am. Inst. Mining, Metall. and Petroleum Engrs., Am. Phys. Soc., Am. Petroleum Inst., Beta Theta Pi. Clubs: Tokeneke (Darien, Conn.); Noroton (Conn.) Yacht (commodore 1961-68); N.Y. Yacht, Links (N.Y.C.); St. Francis Yacht, Pacific Union (San Francisco). Home: 1 Weed Ln Contentment Island Darien CT 06820

MC CURDY, ROBERT VAUGHN, real estate appraiser; b. Muncie, Ind., July 19, 1914; s. Roy Earl and Minnie M. (Baugh) McC.; student pub. schs.; m. Doris Virginia Ennis, Dec. 1, 1943; 1 dau., Susan Ennis. Real estate broker, appraiser; proprietor Robert V. McCurdy & Co., real estate cons., Balt.; instr. real estate appraising Hagerstown Jr. Coll., 1962-63. Named Md. Realtor of yr. 1963. Mem. Am. Inst. Real Estate Appraisers (treas. Balt. 1961-62, v.p. 1966, pres. 1969-70, gov. 1971-73), Soc. Real Estate Appraiser (Md. pres. 1958), Am. Soc. Appraisers (internat. sec. 1961-62, gov. 1962-64), Am. Soc. Real Estate Counselors (gov. 1968-70, 1st v.p. 1975), Urban Land Inst., Real Estate Brokers Round Table Balt. (pres. 1960), Real Estate Bd. Greater Balt. (dir. 1959-60, 62, 63, pres. 1966), Am. Right of Way Assn. (v.p. Potomac chpt. 1960-61), Md. Real Estate Assn. (pres. 1958), Soc. Colonial Wars. Mason (32 deg.). Contbr. articles to profl. jours. Home: 4300 N Charles St Apt 7F Baltimore MD 21218 Office: Chesapeake Bldg 305 W Chesapeake Ave Towson MD 21204

MC DADE, JOSEPH MICHAEL, congressman, lawyer; b. Scranton, Pa., Sept. 29, 1931; s. John B. and Genevieve (Hayes) McC.; B.A., U. Notre Dame, 1953; LL.B., U. Pa., 1956; LL.D., St. Thomas Aquinas U., 1968, U. Scranton, 1969; m. Mary Teresa O'Brien, Mar. 31, 1962; children—Joseph, Aileen, Deborah, and Mark McDade. Admitted to Pa. bar, 1957; since practiced in Scranton and surrounding area; solicitor City of Scranton, 1962; mem. 88th to 96th congresses from 10th Pa. Dist. Mem. Am., Pa., Lackawanna bar assns. Home: 4006 N 27th St Arlington VA 22207 Office: Rayburn House Office Bldg Washington DC 20515

MC DANIEL, JAMES IRWIN, govt. ofcl.; b. Watertown, Mass., Nov. 3, 1946; s. James H. and Josephine Rose (Fantasia) McD.; B.A., Northeastern U., 1969; m. Michele Theresa Coursey, Aug. 2, 1970; children—James Paul, Jill Marie. Park ranger Minuteman Nat. Hist. Park, Concord, Mass., 1968-70, Grand Canyon Nat. Park, 1970-71; mgmt. asst. White House Liaison, Nat. Park Service, Washington, 1971-78, exec. asst., 1978—. Bd. dirs. Nat. Capital USO, 1976—. Recipient Outstanding Performance award Nat. Park Service, 1976. Mem. Nat. Recreation and Parks Assn. Office: 1100 Ohio Dr SW Washington DC 20242

MC DANIEL, JOHN PERRY, hosp. adminstr.; b. Findley, Ohio, Sept. 4, 1942; s. Oliver Perry and Bertha Lorraine (Schrading) McD.; B.S., Wittenberg U., 1964; M.H.A., U. Mich., 1966; m. Ellen Garb, June 18, 1966; children—Lorraine, Michael. Adminstrv. resident Del. Hosp., Wilmington, 1965-67, asst. adminstr., 1966; asst. adminstr. Community Hosp., Springfield, Ohio, 1967-68; asso. adminstr. Md. Gen. Hosp., Balt., 1968-72; exec. v.p., adminstr. Lutheran Hosp. of Md., Inc., Balt., 1972-78, pres., 1978—; pres. Md. Health Care System, Inc., 1977—. Mem. Am. Coll. Hosp. Adminstrs., Am. Hosp. Assn., Hosp. Execs. Assn., Protestant Hosp. Assn., Royal Soc. Health, Luth. Hosp. Assn. Am. Home: 235 Chancery Rd Baltimore MD 21218 Office: Lutheran Hosp Md 730 Ashburton St Baltimore MD 21216

MC DANNALD, CLYDE ELLIOTT, business exec.; b. N.Y.C., June 29, 1923; s. Clyde E. and Evelyn (Tunison-Morgan) McD.; B.A., Columbia U., 1948, M.B.A., 1949; m. Virginia Washington, Apr. 25, 1953; children—Leslie Ann McDannald Baxter, Clyde Elliott, Bruce Robert, Bonnie Washington, Brian Christopher, Laura Leigh. Market research analyst J. Walter Thompson Co., N.Y.C., 1948-50; asst. dir. market research Nat. Lead Co., N.Y.C., 1950-51; product research supr., account exec. Foote, Cone & Belding, Inc., N.Y.C., 1951-52; asst. advt. mgr., product mgr. Am. Safety Razor Corp., N.Y.C., 1953-54; account exec., account supr. Meldrum & Fewsmith, Inc., Cleve., 1954-56; sr. account exec. Young & Rubicam, N.Y.C., 1956-58; exec. asst. to v.p., advt. mgr. Brown & Williamson Tobacco Corp. subs. Brit.-Am. Tobacco Co., Ltd., Louisville, 1959-63; dir. advt. and mktg. services, dir. mktg. Miller Brewing Co., Milw., 1963-65; gen. mgr., div. v.p. consumer products, corporate v.p. Revere Copper & Brass Inc., N.Y.C., 1966-71; pres., chief operating officer H.H. Pott Distillers Ltd. U.S. subs. H.H. Pott NFGR, 1972-78, also dir.; dir. West Indies Distillers, Ltd.; vis. prof. Fairfield U., 1975-78. Mem. N.Y. Gov.'s Industry Commn., 1967-70; bd. dirs. Distilled Spirits Inst.; bd. govs. N.Y. Mil. Acad., 1970, trustee, 1975—. Served from pvt. to capt., inf. USAAF, 1942-45; ETO, ATO. Decorated D.F.C., Air medal with 4 oak leaf clusters. Mem. SAR, SR, Alumni Fedn. Columbia U., Am. Mgmt. Assn., NAM, Navy League, Sigma Chi (life), Alpha Chi Sigma. Presbyterian. Clubs: Columbia, Explorers, Univ. Home: 57 Canterbury Ln Wilton CT 06897

MC DAVID, FREDERICK RHODES, cons. mech. engr.; b. Sanford, N.C., Dec. 26, 1924; s. James Philip and Nora (Foy) McD.; B.M.E., N.C. State U., 1948; postgrad. Carnegie Inst. Tech., 1949; m. Janet Frances Smiley, Jan. 19, 1950; children—Frederick R., Philip A., Susan K., Nora J., Robert J. Process engr. U.S. Steel Corp., Pitts., 1947-49; design engr. Walter Hook & Assos., Charlotte, N.C., 1950-51, H.K. Ferguson Co., Cleve., 1951-53; partner McDavid Co., Washington 1954—; cons. engr. master plan Haile Selassie I Univ., Ethiopia. Chmn., Fairfax County (Va.) Bd. Plumbing Examiners and Appeals, 1968—; organizer, troop com. chmn. Nat. Capitol Area council Boy Scouts Am. Served with U.S. Army, 1944-46. Registered profl. engr., D.C., Va., Md., Pa., Ohio, Fla., Conn., N.Y., Ga., Tex., N.J., Minn. Mem. ASME, Cons. Engrs. Council, Am. Legion. Republican. Methodist (dir. 1960-61). Club: Elks. Home: 9321 Convento Terr Fairfax VA 22030 Office: 1319 F St NW Washington DC 20004

MC DERMOTT, IDARUTH MITCHELL (MRS. EDWARD BRIAN MCDERMOTT), business exec.; b. Hingham, Mass., Oct. 9, 1921; d. Henry Forrester and Rebecca (Gerrold) Mitchell; B.A., Radcliffe Coll., 1938; postgrad. N.Y. Inst. Finance, 1940, Am. Inst. Banking, 1942; m. Edward Brian McDermott, Feb. 11, 1939; children—Brian Emerson, Bruce Burnham, Diane Lee. Acting head investment dept., adminstrv. asst. to the trust officer Comml. Nat. Bank & Trust Co., N.Y.C., 1939-49; corp. sec.-treas. Specialized Components, Inc.; owner McDermott's Surgi-Clip, Inc. Mem. N.Y. Soc. Security Analysts, Nat. Soc. D.A.R. Address: 23 Flower ln Manhasset NY 11030

MC DERMOTT, NELSON JOSEPH, JR., casting mfg. co. exec.; b. Lowell, Mass., Aug. 25, 1923; s. Nelson Joseph and Josephine Dorothy (Donnellan) McD.; B.S., U.S. Naval Acad., 1945; children—Thomas Joseph, Linda Louise. With Gen. Electric Co., 1949-68, gen. mfg. mgr. large jet engine mfg. ops., Cin., Albuquerque, and Everett, Mass., 1964-68; with Hitchiner Mfg. Co. Inc., Milford, N.H., 1968—, pres., chief exec. officer, 1973—; chmn. bd. Hollis Engring. Co., Nashua, N.H.; dir. Bolton Emerson Co., Lawrence, Mass., Bellofram Co., Burlington, Mass., Babco Corp., Danver, Mass., Internat. Bus. Center of New Eng., Boston. Served with U.S. Navy, 1945-49, 51-53. Mem. Bus. and Industries Assn. N.H. (dir.). Home: Boston Post Rd Amherst NH 03031

MCDEVITT, RICHARD EGGLESTON, lawyer; b. Phila., July 14, 1919; s. Harry S. and Emily (Eggleston) McD.; B.S., Wharton Sch. U. Pa., 1940, J.D., 1943; m. Ann Khail Susskind, Mar. 3, 1957 (div. 1976); children—Todd, Bayne, Wade. Admitted to Pa. bar, 1943, since practiced in Phila.; mem. firm Montgomery, McCracken, Walker & Rhoads, 1943—; dir. Pa. and So. Gas Co., Sayre, Pa.; dir., v.p. Eagle Downs Racing Assn.; spl. hearing officer Dept. Justice, 1958-72. Commr. Charlestown Twp. Municipal Authority; exec. dir. Jud. Inquiry and Rev. Bd. Pa., 1969—; pres. Devon (Pa.) Horse Show and Country Fair, 1972—, Phila. Horse Show and Internat. Jumping Competition, 1971—; pres. Pa. Horse Breeders Assn., 1964-67, sec.-treas., 1969—; pres. Ludwigs Corner Horse Show, 1968—; mem. com. for equestrian events U.S. Olympic Com., 1970—; mem. endowment fund Shipley Sch., Phila.; bd. mgrs. Episcopal Hosp.; solicitor Glen Mills Schs. Served with USCG, 1942-43. Mem. Am. Judicature Soc. (dir. nat. adv. com. on jud. conduct orgns.), Am., Pa., Phila. bar assns., Assn. Def. Counsel, S.R., Union League of Phila., Juristic Soc., Brandeis Lawyers Soc. (bd. govs.) Lawyers Club Phila. (vice chmn., bd. govs.), Am. Horse Shows Assn. (pres., dir., com. chmn.; sr. judge, steward), Grand Prix Assn. U.S. (dir.), Nat.

Equestrian Fedn. U.S. (pres.), Phi Delta Theta. Republican. Clubs: Racquet, Union League, Sociolegal, Radnor Hunt Pony (pres. 1968-71), Sons of Revolution, Acadamy of Germantown (Pa.) Acadamy. Lectr.; contbr. articles to profl. jours. Home: Hillsover Farm 800 Conestoga Pike Malvern PA 19355 Office: 3 Parkway Philadelphia PA 19102

MC DEVITT, ROBERT JAMES, tech. co. exec.; b. Phila., May 24, 1942; s. James Aloysius and Margaret Catherine (Heim) McD.; B.S., Pa. State U., 1964: M.A., U. Scranton, 1970; m. Teresa Ann Lesko, Dec. 28, 1963; children—Robert James, Mary Agnes, Peter Anthony, Daniel Patrick. Chemist, Joseph E. Seagram & Sons, Inc., Relay, Md., 1964-65; asst.tech. dir. Miller Morton Co., Richmond, Va., 1965-68; mgr. quality assurance John H. Breck Inc., West Springfield, Mass., 1971-73; mgr. quality assurance Consumer Products div. Am. Cyanamid Co., Wayne, N.J., 1973-78, dir. quality assurance Shulton Inc. toiletries div., 1979—. Pres. Parent Tchrs. Orgn. Our Lady of Assumption Sch., 1972-73; active Little League, PAL, Boy Scouts Am. Teaching fellow U. Scranton, 1968-70. Mem. Am. Chem. Soc., Soc. Cosmetic Chemists, Am. Soc. Quality Control, Cosmetic, Toiletry and Fragrance Assn. (quality assurance com.), Chem. Splty. Mfrs. Assn. (comml. standards com. aerosol div.), Alpha Chi Sigma, Alpha Sigma Nu. Democrat. Roman Catholic. Home: 7 Van Riper Rd Wayne NJ 07470 Office: Am Cyanamid Co 759 Berdan Ave Wayne NJ 07470

MC DEW, CAROLYN HELEN, univ. adminstr.; b. Brocton, Mass., Dec. 7, 1923; d. Thomas J. and Meana Lucille (Stokes) McD.; B.A., Talladega Coll., 1946; M.A. (fellow), Syracuse U., 1956. Dean of women Fayetteville (N.C.) State Coll., 1958-61, psychiat. aide Inst. of Living, Hartford, Conn., 1961-65; teenage program dir. YWCA, New Britian, Conn., 1966-69; asst. dir. summer program U. Conn., Storrs, 1969—. Bd. corporators New Britian Gen. Hosp.; mem. minority bd. Sta. WFSB-TV 1975—. Mem. Nat. Assn. Women Deans, Counselors and Adminstrs., Am. Personnel and Guidance Assn., New Eng. Minority Women Adminstrs., AAUW (corporate rep.), New Britian Campus Ministry (dir. 1967-74), NAACP. Club: New Britian Coll. Home: 1204 Storrs Rd Storrs CT 06268 Office: PO Box U170 U Conn Storrs CT 06268

MC DONALD, ANDREW JEWETT, securities firm exec.; b. Cin., Sept. 7, 1929; s. Matthew Arnold and Jane (Jewett) McD.; grad. Hotchkiss Sch., 1947; grad. Yale, 1951. With firm Paine, Webber, Jackson & Curtis Inc., Boston, 1955—, dir. New Eng. region, 1972-73, sr. v.p., dir. Eastern div., 1973—; dir. F.W. Paine Found., 1973—. allied mem. N.Y. Stock Exchange, 1971—. Mem. Flight Safety Found., 1971—. Served with USAF, 1951-55. Club: Aero of New Eng., Federal, Down Town, Yale (Boston). Office: 100 Federal St Boston MA 02101

MC DONALD, CHARLES JACK, dermatologist; b. Tampa, Fla., Dec. 6, 1931; s. George B. and Bertha C. (Harbin) McD.; B.S. magna cum laude, A. and T. Coll. N.C., 1951; M.S., U. Mich., 1952; M.D. with highest honors, Howard U., 1960; m. Rosalyn J. Hodgins, Nov. 1, 1952; children—Marc S., Norman D., Eric S. Rotating intern Hosp. St. Raphael, New Haven, 1960-61, asst. resident in medicine, 1961-63; asst. resident in dermatology Yale U., 1963-65, spl. USPHS research fellow, chief resident in dermatology, 1965-66, instr. in medicine and pharmacology, 1966-67, asst. prof. medicine and pharmacology, 1967-68; asst. prof. med. sci. Brown U., 1968-69, asso. prof., 1969-74, prof., 1974—, dir. dermatology program, 1970—, head subsect. dermatology, 1974—; head div. dermatology Roger Williams Gen. Hosp., 1968—; cons. in field; com. and task force mem., chmn. task force on minority affairs Nat. Program Dermatology of Am. Acad. Dermatology; mem. dermatology adv. panel FDA; chmn. com. pub. edn., dir., v.p. R.I. div. Am. Cancer Soc., pres.-elect div.; bd. dirs. Planned Parenthood R.I.; lectr. for assns., univs., including Samuel Bluefarb lectr. Northwestern U., 1977; chmn. R.I. Gov.'s Task Force on Health, 1970-73; trustee Citizens Bank R.I. Bd. dirs. Providence Health Care Found. Served to maj. M.C. USAF, 1952-56. Recipient Distinguished Service award Hosp. Assn. R.I., 1971. Diplomate Am. Bd. Dermatology. Mem. Am., New Eng., R.I., N. Worcester dermatol. assns., Soc. Investigative Dermatology, Am. Fedn. Clin. Research, Am. Acad. Dermatology, Nat. (chmn. sect. dermatology 1973-75), Pan Am. (dermatology council) med. assns., AAAS, Am. Soc. Clin. Oncology, Dermatology Found. (chmn. sci. com. 1972-76), Assn. Profs. Dermatology, Sigma Xi, Alpha Omega Alpha, Alpha Kappa Mu, Beta Kappa Chi. Ind. Democrat. Contbr. numerous articles to med. publs. Office: 825 Chalkstone Ave Providence RI 02908

MC DONALD, JAMES EDWARD, paper co. exec.; b. Washington, Oct. 21, 1915; s. Robert Edward and Kathryn (Wilson) McD.; grad. Pace Coll., 1938; B.B.A., St. Johns U., 1940; m. Jean E. Tinkham, Jan. 19, 1962; children—Patrick Ann, Catherine M., Thomas Bancale. Sr. accountant Price Waterhouse & Co., N.Y.C., 1941-47; mgr. accounting Warner-Lambert Pharmacal Co., Morris Plains, N.J., 1948-56; v.p., treas. Hugo Stinnes Corp., N.Y.C., 1956-65; v.p. finance Oxford Pendaflex Corp., Garden City, N.Y., 1967-73, exec. v.p., 1973—, also dir. Served with USAAF, 1942-45. C.P.A., N.Y. Mem. Financial Execs. Inst. (sec.). Home: 67 Fairmount Blvd Garden City NY 11530 Office: 71 Clinton Rd Garden City NY 11530

MCDONALD, JOHN FRANCIS, educator; b. Narberth, Pa., Jan. 14, 1942; s. Frank Patrick and Lulu Ann (Hegedus) McD.; B.S. in Elec. Engring., Mass. Inst. Tech., 1963; M.Engring., Yale, 1964, Ph.D., 1969. Mem. tech. staff Bell Telephone Labs., 1965; lectr. Yale, 1969, asst. prof. elec. engring. 1970-74; asso. prof. elec. and systems engring. dept., and computer engring. div. Rensselaer Poly. Inst., Troy, N.Y., 1974—; cons. Argonne Nat. Lab., Westinghouse Hanford Engring. Devel. Lab., Gen. Electric Corp. Research and Devel. Center. Grantee Naval and Research Corp. Mem. IEEE (nat. chmn. computer design automation acad. affairs com., chmn. Schenectady sect. COM/ASSP tech. group 1978-79). Assn. Computing Machinery, Am. Inst. Physics. Home: 608 Crescent Village Apts Clifton Park NY 12065 Office: Rensselaer Poly Inst Troy NY 12181

MC DONALD, JOSEPH VALENTINE, neurol. surgeon; b. N.Y.C., June 7, 1925; s. Benedict and Catherine Eleanor (Chadney) McD.; A.B., Coll. Holy Cross, 1945; M.D., U. Pitts., 1949; m. Carolyn Alice Patricia Petersen, Apr. 30, 1955; children—Judith Catherine, Elizabeth Ann, Catherine Eleanor, Joseph Bede, David Randolph. Intern, St. Vincent's Hosp., N.Y.C., 1949-50; research fellow neuroanatomy Vanderbilt U., 1950-51; gen. surgery asst. resident Cushing VA Hosp., Boston, 1951-52; neurology extern Lenox Hill Hosp., 1952; asst. resident neurosurgery Johns Hopkins Hosp., 1953-55, resident neurosurgeon, 1955-56; practice medicine specializing in neurol. surgery, Rochester, N.Y., 1956—; prof. U. Rochester Med. Sch.; neurosurgeon-in-chief Strong Meml. Hosp.; cons. neurosurgery Genesee, St. Mary's hosps., Rochester, Thompson Meml. Hosp., Canandaigua, N.Y., Geneva (N.Y.) Gen. Hosp., Clifton Springs (N.Y.) Hosp., Wayne County Community Hosp., Newark, N.Y., Myers Meml. Hosp., Sodus, N.Y. Mem. Soc. Neurol. Surgeons, A.C.S., Acad. Neurology, Am. Assn. Neurol. Surgeons, Congress Neurosurgeons. Home: 800 Allens Creek Rd Pittsford NY 14618 Office: Rochester NY 14642

MC DONALD, KHLAR ELWOOD, surgeon; b. Clarington, Pa., Aug. 1, 1927; s. Carl Lincoln and Dorien Geraldine (Fitzgerald) McD.; student U. Pa., 1947-49; M.D., Temple U., 1953; m. Helen Shannon Hind, Mar. 5, 1949; children—Khlare Rene, Dennis Karl, Kathy Dorien, Kerry Alfred. Intern, Harrisburg (Pa.) Hosp., 1953-59; asst. surg. resident, Beverly (Mass.) Hosp., 1954-55; chief surg. resident, E.J. Meyer Meml. Hosp., Buffalo, 1960-61; research fellow in surgery, U. Buffalo, 1961-62; practice medicine specializing in surgery, Warren, Pa., 1962—; chief of surgery, Warren Gen. Hosp., 1975—; med. cons. to Armed Forces. Warren Boro Councilman, 1967—; chmn. pub. safety com., 1975-78; pres. Warren County United Fund, 1974-76; pres. Warren County Probation Assn., 1968; pres. Chief Cornplanter council Boy Scouts Am., 1971-72, Western Pa. camping chmn., 1977. Served with USN, 1954-57, to capt. M.C., USNR, 1969—. Recipient Silver Beaver and Silver Antelope awards, Boy Scouts Am. Diplomate Am. Bd. Surgery. Fellow A.C.S., Am. Coll. Chest Physicians; mem. AMA, Pa., Warren County med. socs., Royal Soc. Medicine (affiliate), Assn. Mil. Surgeons U.S., Pan Am. Med. Assn., U.S. Naval Inst. Repulbican. Methodist. Clubs: Conewango, Masons (master Joseph Warren Lodge, 1974—), Scottish Rite, Royal Arch Masons, Shriners. Home: 202 Redwood St Warren PA 16365 Office: 202 1/2 Pennsylvania Ave E Warren PA 16365

MC DONALD, MALCOLM WALKER, bus. exec.; b. Dedham, Mass., Aug. 4, 1920; s. James Francis and Maria Genevieve (McLane) McD.; student pub. schs.; m. Mary P. Lally, June 28, 1947; children—John Patrick, Peter Jude, Mary Louise, Sara Ann, Paula. With the Boston (Mass.) Naval Base, 1939-48; salesman Nat. Telephone Directory Corp. (formerly Von Hoffmann Corp.), Boston, 1948, sales mgr., 1948-53, gen. sales mgr. N.J., 1953-58, v.p., 1958-63, exec. v.p., 1963-66, pres., 1966—, also dir.; pres., dir. Victory Broadcasting Corp., N.J., 1968—. Served from pvt. to capt., AUS, 1942-46, ETO. Clubs: Seaview Country (Absecon, N.J.), Oyster Harbors (Osterville, Mass.); Tavistock Country (Haddonfield, N.J.). Home: 340 Knoll Top Ln Haddonfield NJ 08033 Office: 1050 Galloping Hill Rd Union NJ 07083

MC DONALD, OWEN PETER, govt. ofcl.; b. Yankton, S.D., June 5, 1916; s. Peter Joseph and Beatrice (Cogan) McD.; teaching certificate Black Hills Tchrs. Coll., 1936; B.A., Nebr. State Coll., 1939; M.A., Am. U., 1954; m. Elinor Dawn Johnson, Sept. 24, 1942; children—Kathleen Ann, John Owen, Lawrence Edward. Tchr., adminstr. Shannon County Pub. Schs., Danby, S.D., 1939-41; personnel classification analyst WPB, 1941-42; mem. planning staff, asst. adminstr. for constrn., supply and real estate VA, Washington, 1946-48; analyst mgmt. div. Hdqrs. USAF, Washington, 1948-51, chief systems and procedures br. mgmt. div., 1951-55; specialist for analysis and rev. properties and installations Office Asst. Sec. Def., Washington, 1955—, staff asst., 1955-56, chief mgmt. div., 1957-58, realty officer Dept. Def., 1958-65, chief mgmt. and reporting div. contract support services directorate, 1965-70, contract specialist, 1970—, with directorate of maintenance policy, 1977—; spl. asst. to adminstr. Gen. Services Adminstrn., Washington, 1956. Served from 2d lt. to capt., U.S. Army, 1942-46; CBI; col. USAF Res. ret. Decorated Bronze Star medal, Air Force Commendation medal. Mem. Am. Polit. Sci. Assn. Roman Catholic. K.C. Home: 9000 Linton Ln Stratford on the Potomac Alexandria VA 22308 Office: Pentagon Washington DC 20330

MC DONNELL, JOSEPH ANTHONY, sculptor; b. Detroit, Oct. 20, 1936; s. William Francis and Virginia Marie (Kirchner) McD.; B.F.A., U. Notre Dame, 1958, M.F.A., 1959; postgrad. Mexico City Coll., summers 1957, 58, Accademia delle Belli Arte, Florence, Italy, 1960-61; m. Ann Elizabeth Alexander, Dec. 22, 1961; children—Elizabeth Drew, Alexandra, Julia, Elena. One man shows Galleria L'88, Rome, 1961, Marble Arch Gallery, Miami, Fla., 1962, Galleria Pater, Milan, 1962, Florence Art Gallery, 1962, Galerie Fontainbleau, Miami, 1963, McNay Art Inst., San Antonio, 1964, John Wanamaker Fine Arts Gallery, Phila., 1970, others; exhibited in numerous group shows, U.S. and Europe; represented in pvt. collections; executed large monuments including Homage to Great Lakes Fountain, Milw. Pub. Mus., Gulls in Flight, 1st Fed. Bldg. Detroit, Fountain, Jamesville (Wis.) Mall. Home: Guard Hill Rd Bedford NY 10506 Office: 7 Railroad Ave Bedford Hills NY 10507

MC DONNELL, VIRGINIA BLEECKER (MRS. JOHN HENRY MCDONNELL), author; b. Short Hills, N.J.; d. J. Barclay and Helen Borden (Farley) Bleecker; R.N., Samaritan Hosp. Sch. Nursing, Troy, N.Y., 1941; postgrad. Russell Sage Coll., 1942; m. John Henry McDonnell, Feb. 13, 1954; 1 son, Gordon. Night supr. male surg. ward N.Y. Post Grad. Med. Sch. and Hosp., N.Y.C., 1942-43; co-dir. Gore Mountain Ski Sch., North Creek, N.Y., 1947-55; asst. to exec. dir. pubs. and pub. relations Grand Lodge, Free and Accepted Masons, N.Y.C., 1958; reporter, feature writer Macy Westchester Rockland Newspapers, Westchester County, N.Y., 1959-61, editor, 1961-63; free lance author, 1963—; asso. writer TV series The Guiding Light, 1977—. Mem. N.Y. State Winter Sports Council, 1950-60. Recipient citation Leukemia Soc., 1959, City of Hope, 1959. Mem. Authors' Guild and League, Mystery Writers Am., Writers Guild Am.-East. Author: Your Future in Nursing, 1963; Aerospace Nurse, 1966; The Irish Helped Build America, 1969; Careers in Hotel Management, 1971; Miscalculated Risk, 1972; Silent Partner, 1972; The Deep Six, 1973; The Long Shot, 1974; The Accident, 1975. others. Author numerous short stories and articles. Home: 79 Hudson Park Rd New Rochelle NY 10805

MC DONNELL, WILLIAM VINCENT, pathologist; b. Carbondale, Pa., Oct. 28, 1922; s. Patrick and Dorothy (Connolly) McD.; B.A., U. Scranton, 1943; M.D., Jefferson Med. Coll., 1947; m. Eileen Shanahan, Aug. 27, 1949; children—Brian, Kevin. Intern, Scranton (Pa.) State Hosp., 1947-48, resident in pathology, 1948-50; instr. pathology Jefferson Med. Coll., Phila., 1951-52, asst. prof., 1952-56, asso. prof., 1956-69, prof., 1969—, asst. pathologist, 1952-61; asst. dir. clin. lab. Methodist Hosp., Phila., 1952-60; dir. clin. lab. W. Jersey Hosp., Voorhees, 1961—, med. dir., chief of staff, 1969-72, v.p. med. affairs, chief of staff, 1972—; individual practice medicine, specializing in pathology, Voorhees, 1961—. Diplomate Am. Bd. Pathology. Fellow Coll. Am. Pathologists, A.C.P.; mem. Am. Soc. Clin. Pathologists, Am. Assn. Blood Banks, Am. Hosp. Assn., AMA, N.J., Camden County med. socs., N.J. Soc. Pathologists, Am. Acad. Med. Dirs. Office: W Jersey Hosp Evesham Rd Voorhees NJ 08043

MC DONOUGH, DANIEL JOHN, photographer; b. Hoboken, N.J., Dec. 19, 1943; s. Patrick Joseph and Margaret Mary (Bohan) McD.; m. Beverly Ann Grant, Dec. 19, 1969; 1 son, Daniel. With internat. div. Libby, McNeil & Libby, N.Y.C., 1962-66; office mgr. Johnson Motor Lines, Kearney, N.J., 1966-73; free lance comml. photographer, 1965-72; owner McDonough Studio, Jersey City, 1972—; permanent exhibit prints Bergen Community Art Mus. Recipient several local, state, nat. awards for photography. Mem. Photog. Soc. Am., Wedding Photographers Am., Profl. Photographers Am., Profl. Photographers N.J. (past pres. Bergen, Passaic, Hudson chpt.), Royal Photog. Soc. Gt. Britain. Club: Elks. Address: 3224 Kennedy Blvd Jersey City NJ 07306

MC DONOUGH, DONALD ARTHUR, city ofcl.; Phila., Apr. 12, 1935; s. Thomas B. and Elsie May (Wright) McD.; grad. high sch.; m. Concetta Mary Sassany, Apr. 16, 1960; children—Donna, Margot, Leslie. With Phila. Inquirer, 1953-72, staff reporter, writer, 1960-72; dir. port affairs Phila. Port Corp., 1972-74; editor, pub. port promotional bi-monthly mag. Destination: Phila., 1972-74; dep. exec. dir. Hosps. Authority of Phila., 1974—, Equipment Leasing Authority of Phila., 1976—; publicity dir. Ports of Phila. Maritime Soc. Served with U.S. Army, 1958. Recipient award for reporting reforms in govt. Sigma Delta Chi, 1968. Mem. Phila. Press. Assn. (pres. 1965-70, chmn. bd. 1971-75), Manuscript Soc., Phila. Pub. Relations Assn., Deltiologists Am., Smithsonian Soc., Baker St. Irregulars, Mason. Home: 428 Tanforan Dr Cherry Hill NJ 08034 Office: 10th Floor 1401 Arch St Philadelphia PA 19102

MC DONOUGH, FRANCIS ANTHONY, govt. data processing exec.; b. Lynn, Mass., Mar. 9, 1934; s. Anthony and Mary (Walsh) McD.; B.S., Boston U., 1956; M.A., George Washington U., 1962; m. Mary Alice Sallee, May 10, 1962. Systems analyst Navy Dept., Washington, 1962-64; head systems and programming Naval Research Lab., Washington, 1964-66; adv. systems analyst IBM, Gaithersburg, Md., 1966-70; dir. Office Systems Mgmt. Health Services and Mental Health Adminstrn., Rockville, Md., 1970-74; dir. Office Data Systems, Naval Oceanographic Office, Suitland, Md., 1974-76; dir. Office Computer Sci., Office Sec., Treasury Dept., Washington, 1976—; asso. adj. prof. Vanderbilt U., 1976; chmn. Interagy. Com. on ADP in Fed. Govt., 1978-79. Pres., High Point Civic Assn., Bethesda, Md., 1971-72, Winterset Citizens Assn., Potomac, Md., 1975. Served to lt. USNR, 1956-62. Recipient Outstanding Performance award Naval Research Lab., 1965; Superior Service award HEW 1973. K.C. Club: Toastmaster (treas. 1964). Home: 11800 Canfield Rd Potomac MD 20854 Office: Treasury Dept Washington DC

MCDONOUGH, JOHN MARTIN, lawyer; b. Ft. Smith, Ark., June 20, 1905; s. James B. and Sara (Mason) McD.; grad. Phillips Acad., Andover, Mass., 1922; A.B., Princeton, 1926; LL.B., Harvard, 1929; m. L. Norton Carroll, Mar. 17, 1945; children—J. Martin, Henry Carroll. Admitted to Md. bar, 1930, since practiced in Balt.; partner firm Piper & Marbury, 1933-75, of counsel, 1975-76, partner emeritus, 1977—; prof. corporate law U. Balt.; referee in bankruptcy, 1950-55. Past counsel, dir., chmn. bd. Balt. Legal Aid Soc. Served with USAAF, 1941-45. Mem. Am., Md., Balt. City bar assns., Balt. Assn. Commerce, Balt. Jr. Assn. Commerce (past pres., mem. legislative com.). Democrat. Episcopalian (vestryman, registrar). Clubs: Cap and Gown, Nassau (Princeton, N.J.); Merchants (Balt.); Princeton (N.Y.C.). Home: Sparks MD 21152 Office: 2000 First Maryland Bldg Baltimore MD 21201

MC DOUGAL, EDWARD FRANCIS, pub. relations exec.; b. Bklyn., Feb. 15, 1918; s. Jerome R. and Edna M. (DeRonde) McD.; student Hofstra U.; grad. N.Y. U., 1944; m. Elizabeth Carroll, June 16, 1970; children by previous marriage—Edward Francis, Peter J., Patrick G., Maureen (Mrs. Frederick Willets). Reporter, L.I. Press, also N.Y. World Telegram, 1936-41; instr. journalism N.Y. U., 1939-41; N.Y. State news dir. Treasury Dept., 1941-43; writer-producer TV shows NBC, 1945-47; dir. pub. relations Bankers Trust Co., N.Y.C., 1947-57; pres. Island Mgmt. Assos., Huntington, N.Y., 1956-67; exec. v.p. Am. Banker Inc., N.Y.C., 1967-68, pres., chief exec. officer, 1968-76; founding pub. Mideast Jour., Kuwait; exec. v.p. Jack Raymond and Co., N.Y.C. Chmn. bd. Nassau Clinic Mental Health, 1972-74. Bd. dirs. Washington Sq. Outdoor Art Show, 1972—. Served with USNR, 1943-45. Recipient citation from sec. Treasury Dept., 1970. Mem. Advt. Club N.Y.C., Bank Mktg. Assn., Fin. Advt. and Mktg. Assn. (pres. 1952). Clubs: N.Y. Athletic, City Midday, Salmagundi (treas., dir. 1972-73), Overseas Press (N.Y.C.); Northport Yacht. Author: Trylong and Perisites, 1939; also articles. Home: 27 Mariners Ln Northport NY 11768 Office: 488 Madison Ave New York City NY 10022

MC DOWELL, CHARLES W., obstetrician, gynecologist; b. N.Y.C., Nov. 3, 1933; s. Arthur Joseph and Frances Mary (McCarthy) McD.; B.S., Manhattan Coll., 1956; M.B., B.Ch., Nat. U. Ireland, 1965; m. Regina Jane Merrihue, Jan. 28, 1956; children—Maura Jean, Charles W., Francis Edward. Rotating intern St. Joseph's Hosp., Phoenix, 1965-66; resident in obstetrics and gynecology Boston City Hosp., 1966-69, Am. Cancer Soc. fellow in gynecol. oncology, 1969-70; clin. instr. obstetrics gynecology Boston U. Sch. Medicine, 1970-73; practice medicine specializing in obstetrics and gynecology, Swampscott, Mass., 1970—; past mem. obstet.-gynecol. adv. com. FDA. Diplomate Am. Bd. Obstetrics and Gynecology. Fellow A.C.S., Am. Coll. Obstetricians and Gynecologists; mem. Mass. Med. Soc., New Eng. Obstet. Soc., Am. Fertility Soc. Home: 30 Spray Ave Marblehead MA 01945 Office: 25 Pitman Rd Swampscott MA 01907

MC DOWELL, HARRY WALTER, chemist; b. York, Pa., June 9, 1923; s. Walter Alexander and Mae Augusta (Fried) McD.; student York Jr. Coll., 1946-48; B.S. with honors, Franklin and Marshall Coll., 1950; M.S., U. Del., 1951; M.S. in Environ. Scis., Rutgers U., 1977; m. Romaine Evelyn Weimer, Aug. 15, 1942; children—Harry Walter, Cathy Maureen. Analytical chemist E. I. duPont de Nemours & Co., Inc., Wilmington, Del., 1951-55, methods chemist, 1955-58, tech. shift supr., 1959-61, purchasing agt., 1962-65, area engr., 1966-72, sr. engr., 1973-76, plant coordinator environ. control and indsl. hygiene programs, 1976—. Mem. Union County Environ. Health Adv. Bd., 1971—, vice chmn., 1976-78; dist. adv. solid waste council of Union County, 1977—; v.p., dir. Fed. Credit Union, 1960-74; panel moderator N.J. Sch. Bds. Assn. workshops, 1972-74; panelist on radio and closed TV programs, 1968-78; mem. Rahway Bd. Edn., 1972-75, pres., 1974-75; bd. dirs. Rahway YMCA, 1971-77, v.p., 1974-77; trustee Rahway Day Care Center; pres., lay leader Zion Luth. Ch. Council, 1970-74, 76—; vol. worker United Fund, Heart Fund, others; den leader cub scouts Boy Scouts Am., 1957-60; coach City Basketball League, 1962-65, City Baseball League, 1960-62; organizer, first pres. Rahway High Sch. Choral Boosters, 1967-79; organizer, v.p. Rahway High Sch. Band Boosters, 1962-65, pres., 1965-67; charter mem., first pres. Community Edn. Group, Focus on Rahway Edn., 1967-69. Served with U.S. Army, 1943-46. Recipient plaque Rahway Bd. Edn., 1975; U. Del. grad. teaching assistantship, 1950-51. Mem. Water Pollution Control Fedn., N.J. Water Pollution Control Assn., C. of C., Smithsonian Assoc., Nat. Wildlife Fedn., Am. Chem. Soc. Republican. Lutheran. Clubs: Eastern Ltd. Edits. Collectors, Norman Rockwell, Ilderan Outing, Masons. Home: 284 Rudolph Ave Rahway NJ 07065 Office: EI duPont de Nemours and Co Inc Linden NJ 07036

MC DOWELL, WILLIAM GILES, pharm. co. exec.; b. Phila., Dec. 1, 1928; s. William Hunter and Caroline Agnes (Beck) McD.; B.S. in Econs., U. Pa., 1950; m. Margaret Ruth Carlson, Aug. 18, 1951; children—William Hunter II, Thomas Giles, John Baptie. Time study engr. Swift & Co., Inc., Phila., 1950-51, Sharp & Dohme, Inc., Phila., 1951-52; methods dept. mgr. Keasbey & Mattison, Ambler, Pa., 1952-55; indsl. engr. Sylvania Electric Products Co., Hatboro, Pa., 1955-56; with Merck Sharp & Dohme div. Merck & Co., Inc., West Point, Pa., 1956—, prodn. mgr. packaging and printing, 1972-73, dir. engring., 1973—. Mem. Tredyffrin Twp. Library Bd., 1970—, treas., 1972, pres., 1973-75; v.p. Tredyffrin Twp. Civic Council, 1960-61;

pres. Strafford Civic Assn., 1960; bd. dirs. Water Resources Assn. of Delaware River Basin Commn. Registered profl. engr., Pa. Mem. Am. Inst. Plant Engrs., Mineral. Soc. Pa., N. Pa. C. of C. (dir. 1977—). Home: 360 Hilltop Rd Paoli PA 19301 Office: Merck Sharp & Dohme West Point PA 19486

MC ELDOWNEY, ROBERT, JR., engr., land surveyor; b. Johnstown, Pa., Apr. 8, 1919; s. Robert and Helen Schuyler (Nicholson) McE.; B.S. in Engring., Princeton U., 1940, C.E. (Doty fellow), 1941; m. Mary Kinter, June 28, 1941; children—Alice McEldowney Jones, Henry Clay. Foundry mgmt. Taylor-Wharton Iron and Steel Co., High Bridge, N.J., 1941-50; pres. Studer and McEldowney, Clinton, N.J., 1950—; municipal engr. Bd. trustees Hunterdon Med. Center, 1958—; sec. class of 1940, Princeton U., 1960-65. Served with USMC, 1942-46. Mem. Nat., N.J. socs. profl. engrs., Am. Cons. Engrs. Council, Cons. Engrs. Council N.J., Am. Congress Surveying and Mapping, Sigma Xi, Tau Beta Pi. Republican. Presbyterian. Clubs: Beaver Brook Country, Copper Hill Country, Nassau, Rotary. Co-author: Moments in Flexible Arches, ASCE, 1941. Home: Box 25 Dogwood Dr Annandale NJ 08801 Office: 120 Highway 22 Clinton NJ 08809

MC ELROY, JAMES BENJAMIN, indsl. engr.; b. Zanesville, Ohio, Feb. 15, 1910; s. Joseph Edward and Mary Olive (Merrick) M.; B.S. in Indsl. Engring., Ohio State U., 1936; m. Alene Jones, Sept. 2, 1938; children—Patricia A. McElroy Carlson, James J., Michael D., William O. Chief engr. Nat. Radio, Republic of Guatemala, 1936-42; owner, chief engr. various broadcasting stations Guatemala City and Antigua, Guatemala, 1942-50; elec. design engr. U.S. Navy Bur. Ships, Mare Island Naval Shipyard, Vallejo, Calif., 1950-52; head low frequency devel. div. U.S. Naval Air Missile Test Center, Point Mugu, Calif., 1952-54; engring. cons. to chmn. FCC, Washington, 1954-59; mgr. NASA Frequency Mgmt. Program, Washington, 1959—; U.S. Dept. State del., various internat. confs.; NASA rep. to U.S. Interdept. Radio Adv. Com., 1959—, to World Adminstrv. Radio Conf., 1959, 63, 71—. Recipient Exceptional Service award, NASA, 1975. Mem. Sigma Nu. Contbr. articles to profl. jours. Home: 4301 Stanford St Chevy Chase MD 20015 Office: NASA Hdqrs Washington DC 20546

MC ELROY, JOHN HARLEY, electronics engr.; b. Marion, Ohio, June 27, 1936; s. Francis and Alice Marie (Braden) McE.; B.S., U. Tex., 1966; M.Electronics Engring., Cath. U. Am., 1973, Ph.D., 1978; m. Eleonore Hildegard Schmidt, Mar. 18, 1957. Research asst. Quantum Electronics and Plasma Dynamics Research Lab., U. Tex., Austin, 1963-66; electronics engr. NASA Goddard Space Flight Center, Greenbelt, Md., 1966-71, head laser heterodyne systems, 1971-75, head instrument electro-optics br., 1975-77, mgr. satellite communications tech. study, 1977-78, chief communications tech. div., 1978—; cons. in field. Served with U.S. Army, 1954-63. Recipient Apollo Achievement award, 1969. Fellow Am. Inst. Aeros. and Astronautics (asso.); mem. IEEE (sr.), Optical Soc. Am., Eta Kappa Nu, Tau Beta Pi, Omicron Delta Kappa. Contbr. numerous articles to profl. jours. Home: 1794 Stonegate Ave Crofton MD 21114 Office: Code 723 Goddard Space Flight Center Greenbelt MD 20771

MC ELWREATH, SALLY CHIN, airline exec.; b. N.Y.C., Oct. 15, 1940; d. Toon G. and Jean B. (Wong) Chin; B.A., Pace Coll., 1963, M.B.A., 1969; 1 son by previous marriage, Robert J. McElwreath III. Copywriter, O.E. McIntyre Co., 1963-64; writer Sinclair Oil Corp., N.Y.C., 1966-68, Atlantic Richfield Co., N.Y.C., 1968-69; account exec. Muller Jordan Herrick, N.Y.C., 1969-70; rep. pub. relations United Airlines, N.Y.C., 1971-74, asst. to dir., 1974-75, regional mgr. pub. relations, 1975—. Mem. mktg. com. Grad. Sch., Pace U., 1972—; mktg. rev. group Recruiting Command, U.S. Navy, 1974—. Served as lt. USNR Res., 1975—. Pace scholar, 1960-63. Mem. Aviation and Space Writers Assn., N.Y. Airline Pub. Relations Assn., Pub. Relations Soc. Am. Roman Catholic. Clubs: Wings; Ski of Gt. Britain, Naval and Mil. (London). Home: 109-14 Ascan Ave Forest Hills NY 11375 Office: United Airlines 1221 Ave of Americas New York City NY 10020

MC ENRUE, JAMES PETER, telephone testman; b. Montpelier, Vt., Jan. 28, 1928; s. James Harry and Katrina (Turney) McE.; student St. Michaels Coll., 1952; m. Catherine Ann Ryan, May 23, 1959; children—Kathleen, Jane, Paula, John. Meat cutter John McKenzie Packing Co., Burlington, Vt., 1947-55; with New Eng. Telephone Co., 1955—, central office supr., St. Johnsbury, Vt., 1963, testman, Burlington, 1968—. Chmn. North Burlington Democratic Com., 1974; chmn. Burlington Parks and Recreation Commn., 1975-76; candidate for alderman City of Burlington, 1975; mem. Jackson for Pres. Steering Com., Burlington, 1976; mem. Burlington Dem. Com., 1976—; v.p. St. Michaels Coll. Basketball Boosters; mem. exec. bd. Rice High Sch., Burlington; commr. Amateur Softball Assn. Vt. Served with U.S. Army, Korean War. Decorated Purple Heart. Mem. Telephone Workers Union (pres. Vt.), Friends of City Hall Park Project, Amateur Softball Assn. Am., Am. Rifle Assn., VFW, Am. Legion. Roman Catholic. Clubs: St. John's, Elks (chmn. Vt. com. youth activities 1976-79, Youth Activities award). Home: 49 Killarney Dr Burlington VT 05401 Office: 266 Main St Burlington VT 05401

MC EVOY, JAMES EDWARD, chem. co. exec.; b. London, Aug. 5, 1920; s. Edward James and Winifred Daisey (Robertson) McE.; came to U.S., 1925, naturalized, 1941; B.A., Temple U., 1955, postgrad., 1955-58; m. Edna May Wagner, July 5, 1941; children—Barbara, Edna McEvoy Barenbaum. Chemist, Houdry Process & Chem. Co. (acquired by Air Products and Chems., Inc., 1962), Allentown, Pa., 1962-64, project dir., 1964-68, group leader, 1968-71, asst. dir. research and devel., 1971-73, dir. contract research and devel., 1973-76, mgr. dept. govt. relations, 1976—. Served with U.S. Army, 1943-46. Decorated Bronze Star. Mem. Am. Chem. Soc., Catalysis Soc. N.Am., AAAS, Smithsonian Assos. Editor: Catalysts for Control of Automotive Pollutants, 1975. Contbr. articles to profl. jours. Patentee in field. Home: Rural Delivery 7 Quarter Mile Rd Bethlehem PA 18105 Office: POB 538 Allentown PA 18105

MC EVOY, RICHARD EUGENE, historian; b. N.Y.C., Nov. 12, 1943; s. Charles J. and Nelle (Fair) McE.; A.B. cum laude, Hiram Coll., 1965; postgrad. U. Md., 1969—. Corr. clk. U.S. Bur. Family Services, Washington, 1965-69; teaching asst. history U. Md., College Park, 1972-74, NDEA fellow, 1969-72, Am. Pub. Works Assn. bicentennial fellow, 1974-75. Mem. Am. Hist. Assn., Pub. Works Hist. Soc. Asso. editor Md. Historian, 1973-74. Home: 2730 Wisconsin Ave NW Washington DC 20007

MC EWAN, MARY CATHERINE FEE (MRS. IGNATIUS MCEWAN), psychiatrist; b. Glasgow, Scotland, May 4, 1919; d. Patrick and Bridget (McGovern) Fee; B.S., Glasgow U., 1939, M.B., Ch.B., 1942; m. Ignatius McEwan, Apr. 2, 1945; children—Patricia, Vincent, Veronica, Alex. Intern, Royal Hosp. Sick Children, Eastern Gen., Royal Maternity and Women's hosps., all Glasgow; resident Strathclyde Hosp., Lanarkshire, Scotland, Darnley Hosp., Renfrewshire, Scotland; med. officer in charge Antenatal Clinics, Renfrewshire, 1945-46; gen. practice medicine, Toronto, Ont., 1957-62; practice medicine specializing in psychiatry, Toronto, 1968—; mem. staff St. Michael Hosp., Toronto; partner mgmt. cons. firm Hickling Johnston, Toronto, 1978—. Pres., Acad. Medicine, Toronto, 1968-69; bd. dirs. P.S.I. Found., 1975—. Fellow Royal Coll. Physicians; mem. Ont. Med. Assn. (dir.). Home: 72 Dunvegan Rd Toronto ON M4V 2P7 Canada Office: 415 Vonge St 10th Floor Toronto ON M5B 2E7 Canada

MC EWEN, KENNETH LINDSAY, radiologist; b. Toronto, Ont., Can., Feb. 4, 1918; s. James Lindsay and Alma (Ward) McE.; B.S., Springfield Coll., 1943; M.D., Tufts U., 1946; m. Jane Helseth, Mar. 25, 1944; children—Nancy, Ann, Barbara. Intern, Springfield (Mass.) Hosp., 1949-52; chief radiology U.S. Army Hosp., West Point, 1948-49; resident Letterman Gen. Hosp., San Francisco 1949-52; chief radiology dept., U.S. Army Hosp., Ft. Belvoir, Va. 1952-54; practice medicine specializing in radiology, Springfield, Mass., 1954—; chief radiology services Wing Meml. Hosp., Palmer, Mass. 1959—; radiologist Baystate Med. Center, Wesson Meml. Div., Springfield, 1959—, Chest Clinic, Health Dept. of City of Springfield, Mass., 1954—; v.p. Radiol. Assoc., Inc., Springfield, 1967—. Served with U.S. Army, 1942-43, 43-46, to maj. with Med. Corps 1947-54. Recipient most improved award Tufts U. Med. Sch. 1946; Tarbell medallion, Springfield Coll. 1977. Fellow Am. Coll. Radiology, Royal Soc. of Health; mem. AMA, Mass., Hampden Dist. med. socs., New Eng. Roentgen Ray Soc., Mass., Conn. Valley radiol. socs., Radiol. Soc. of N. Am. Republican. Presbyterian. Clubs: Longmeadow Country, Carnoustie Golf (Scotland), Mason, Shriner, Jesters. Home: 163 Atwater Terrace Springfield MA 01107 Office: 130 Maple St Springfield MA 01103

MC EWEN, RICHARD CUSACK, educator, anthropologist, mgmt. specialist; b. Heber Springs, Ark. Nov. 19, 1920; s. William Richard and Lena Maude (Carey) McE.; B.S., Jackson Coll., 1952, M.A. 1958; B.A., U. Miss., 1959; M.A., Vanderbilt U., 1967; M.P.A., Nova U., 1975, D.P.A., 1976; m. Margaret Alice Berry, July 15, 1941; children—Margaret Ann, Mary Joan. Asso. prof. naval sci. Vanderbilt U., Nashville 1966-69, lectr. anthropology, 1968, history, 1969-70; asst. prof. sociology, anthropology Middle Tenn. State U., Murfreesboro, 1971-77; prof. mgmt. Robert Morris Coll., Coraopolis, Pa. 1977—. Non-resident dir. Navy Mut. Aid Assn., 1966-70. Served to comdr., aviator, USN, 1939-69. Decorated D.F.C., Air medal. Fellow Am. Anthrop. Assn.; mem. Soc. Advancement of Mgmt., Am. Soc. Pub. Adminstrn., Am. Security Council (nat. adv. bd.). Baptist. Clubs: Masons, Shriners. Author: Prayer in Primitive Religion, 1977; contbr. article in field to profl. jour.; mem. much decorated dive bombing squadron, USS Hornet, 1941-42. Home: 221 Baintree Rd Coraopolis PA 15108 Office: R Morris Coll Narrows Run Rd Coraopolis PA 15108

MCEWEN, ROBERT CAMERON, congressman; b. Ogdensburg, N.Y., Jan. 5, 1920; s. Robert H. and Mary (MacIntyre) McE.; student U. Vt., 1938-39, Wharton Sch. Finance, 1939-41. Albany Law Sch., 1941-47; m. Anita M. Sharples, July 26, 1952; children—Nancy, Mary. Admitted to N.Y. bar, 1947, since practiced in Ogdensburg; of counsel firm O'Connell, McEwen & DuPre; mem. N.Y. State Senate, 1954-64; mem. 89th to 95th Congresses, 30th Dist. N.Y. Mem. St. Lawrence County Bar Assn., Am. Legion, VFW, Phi Delta Theta. Republican. Clubs: Masons, Elks. Home: Route 2 Ogdensburg NY 13669 Office: Rayburn House Office Bldg Washington DC 20515

MC FADDEN, THOMAS J(OSEPH), lawyer; b. S.I., N.Y., May 1, 1900; s. Frank J. and Annie G. (McMenamin) McF.; A.B., Cornell, 1922, J.D., 1925; postgrad. Yale Law Sch., 1927-28. Admitted to N.Y. bar, 1928, D.C. bar, 1934, U.S. Supreme Ct. bar, 1935; spl. asst. to atty. gen. Dept. Justice, 1928-29; counsel mgr. Nat. Paint, Varnish and Lacquer Assn., Washington, 1929-33; partner firm Donovan, Leisure, Newton & Irvine, N.Y.C., 1934—. Served with U.S. Army, 1918; lt. comdr., naval air liaison officer, Sicily Invasion with 45th Inf. Div., USNR, 1942-45; chief Pacific Far East Morale Operations, O.S.S., Washington, 1943-44. Mem. Am. Soc. Internat. Law Fed., Am., N.Y. State bar assns., Catholic Lawyers Guild. Clubs: Nat. Lawyers (Washington); Cornell, Yale (N.Y.C.). Home: 183d and Pinehurst Ave Apt J33 New York City NY 10033 Office: 30 Rockefeller Plaza New York City NY 10020

MC FALL, ROBERT JOHN, realtor; b. Moscow, Pa., Nov. 19, 1939; s. Norman Smith and Mattie (Uhrhahn) McF.; Asso. Applied Sci., State U. N.Y., 1959; m. Elizabeth Halper, Nov. 20, 1971; children—Sarah Elizabeth, Simon Robert. Head gardener Dept. Floriculture, Cornell U., Ithaca, N.Y., 1959-61; mgr. Granite State Garden Centre, Concord, N.H., 1964-65; sales rep. Armour Agrl. Chem. Co., Carteret, N.J., 1965-68; owner N.S. McFall, real estate, Suncook, N.H., 1972—. Commr. Pembroke St. Village Dist., 1976, moderator, 1977, 78. Served with AUS, 1961-64. Named Realtor of Yr., Concord (N.H.) Bd. Realtors, 1974. Mem. Concord Bd. Realtors, N.H. (treas. 1976, pres. 1978), Nat. (dir. 1978-81) assns. realtors. Republican. Lutheran. Club: Kiwanis (v.p. Suncook Valley 1970). Home: Dearborn Rd Suncook NH 03275 Office: 114 Pembroke St Suncook NH 03275

MC FARLAND, CHARLES MANTER, chem. engr.; b. Dayton, Ohio, Jan. 11, 1920; s. Charles Brown and Lulu Alice (Manter) McF.; B.Chem. Engring. cum laude, U. Dayton, 1941; m. Dorothy Ruth Argo, Aug. 9, 1942; children—Lynn Ruth McFarland Schockner, Cynthia Lou McFarland Higgins, Patrice Eve. With N.J. Zinc Co., Palmerton, Pa., 1941-60, investigator, 1948-60; mem. research staff Gen. Electric Co., Schenectady, 1960-65, group liaison scientist, 1965-71, mem. staff, metallurgy lab., 1971—, mgr. separation tech. project, 1977. Vice pres. Sch. Bd. Towamensing Twp., Pa., 1949-56; chmn. fund drive ARC, Palmerton, 1960. Served to lt. (j.g.) USNR, 1944-46; PTO. Mem. Am. Chem. Soc., Am. Inst. Mining, Metall. and Petroleum Engrs., Am. Inst. Chem. Engrs. (asso.). Republican. Presbyterian. Clubs: Blue Ridge Country, Edison, Greenhouse and Indoor Plant Assn. Home: 835 Maxwell Dr Schenectady NY 12309 Office: PO Box 8 Schenectady NY 12301

MC FARLIN, HARRY HUGG, ins. broker, savs. and loan exec.; b. Phila., Oct. 5, 1911; s. Harry H. and Edith (McMillan) McF.; student Drexel Inst. Tech., 1936-37; m. Mary Louise Crocker, Nov. 5, 1966. Owner, McFarlin Ins. Agy., 1939—; pres. John Hanson Savs. and Loan Assn., Riverdale, Forestville, Laurel and Oxon Hill, Md., 1968—. Pres. Young Men's Democratic Club, Riverdale, 1966-68; commr. Town of Henlopen Acres, Del., 1972-76, 78. Served with USAAF, 1943-46. Mem. Md. Ins. Agts. Assn. (pres. 1956-57), Montgomery-Prince Georges Ins. Agts. (charter pres.). Methodist. Lion (pres. 1957-58), Tall Cedars, Elk. Clubs: Columbia Country (Washington); Henlopen Acres (Del.) Country. Home: 3310 Shirley Ln Chevy Chase MD 20015 Office: 7610 Pennsylvania Ave Forestville MD 20028

MC FARREN, GEORGE ALLEN, educator; b. Akron, Ohio, Nov. 2, 1930; s. Glenn Gilbert and Dorothy Constance (Courtney) McF.; B.A., Muskingum Coll., 1952; M.Ed., Kent State U., 1956; Ph.D., Ohio State U., 1962; m. Jean Ruth Finney, Aug. 10, 1957; 1 son, James Andrew. Tchr., Westfield High Sch., LeRoy, Ohio, 1954-55, Byron Jr. High Sch., Shaker Heights, Ohio, 1956-59; instr. Ohio State U., Columbus, 1960-62; asst. prof. Baldwin-Wallace Coll., Berea, Ohio, 1962-65; faculty State U. Coll. N.Y., Buffalo, 1965—, prof. social studies edn., 1967—. Bd. dirs. Wesley Found., Buffalo. Served with AUS, 1952-54. Mem. Nat. Council for Social Studies, Nat. Soc. for Study Edn., AAUP, Kappa Delta Pi, Phi Delta Kappa, Delta Tau Kappa. Methodist. Home: 11 Willow Lane Ct Tonawanda NY 14150 Office: 1300 Elmwood Ave Buffalo NY 14222

MC FEATERS, ARTHUR CHARLES, JR., dentist; b. Pitts., Feb. 11, 1932; s. Arthur C. and Minerva (Demetrius) McF.; B.S., Muskingum Coll., 1954; D.D.S., U. Pitts., 1958; m. Joanne E. Oellig, June 11, 1955; children—Lauren Joanne, Susan Jane, Arthur Charles III. Individual practice endodontics, Mt. Lebanon, Pa., 1960—. Mem. continuing edn. faculty U. Pitts. Sch. Dental Medicine, 1967—. Mem. devel. council Muskingum Coll., 1968-69; mem. admissions com. Sch. Dental Medicine, U. Pitts., 1971—, mem. univ. bd. visitors, 1976—. Served with Dental Corps, USNR, 1958-60. Recipient Outstanding Sr. award in oral radiography Am. Acad. Dental Radiology, 1958, award Pitts. Periodontal Soc., 1958. Diplomate Am. Bd. Endodontics. Fellow Am., Internat. colls. dentists; mem. ADA (council dental health and health planning 1975—), Odontological Soc. Western Pa. (pres. 1971, treas. 1971-72), Western Pa. Acad. Dentistry, Pa. Dental Assn. (dental adv. com. to Pa. Dept. Pub. Welfare, treas. 1972-76, trustee 1976—), Muskingum Coll. Alumni Assn. (pres. Pitts. chpt. 1967). Republican. Presbyn. (trustee, elder 1967-69, 71-74, 76-78, deacon 1962-64). Mason (Shriner). Club: St. Clair Country. Bus. mgr. Odontological Bull., 1971—, Pa. Dental Jour., 1975—. Home: 2355 Golfview Dr Pittsburgh PA 15241 Office: 20 Cedar Blvd Pittsburgh PA 15228

MC FEELEY, JOHN JAY, chem. engr.; b. Bklyn., Aug. 15, 1945; s. John Joseph and Maude May (Irvine) McF.; B.S., Poly. Inst. Bklyn., 1966, M.S., 1967, Ph.D., 1972; m. Jacquelyn Anne Ratzin, Oct. 30, 1971; children—Christine, John Jay. Engr., Polaroid Corp., Cambridge, Mass., 1971-72, sr. engr., 1972-74, sr. scientist, 1974-77, prin. engr. research and devel., 1977—; cons. Russo Cons., N.Y.C., 1969—. Mem. water supply study com. Town of Norfolk (Mass.), 1976-77, bicentennial com., 1975-76. NDEA fellow, 1969-71; NSF fellow, 1968-69, teaching fellow, 1967-68, research fellow, 1966-67. Mem. Am. Chem. Soc., Norfolk Jr. C. of C., Tau Beta Pi, Sigma Xi, Omega Chi Epsilon, Phi Lambda Upsilon. Democrat. Roman Catholic. Club: Lions (pres. 1977-78). Contbr. articles in field to profl. jours. Home: 10 Mohegan St Norfolk MA 02056 Office: 600 Main St Cambridge MA 02139

MC GAIL, ARNOLD RAYFIELD, JR., city govt. ofcl.; b. Rochester, N.Y., Aug. 5, 1946; s. Arnold Rayfield and Ruby May (Mowers) McG.; student Cornell State Coll., Brockport State Coll. Announcer, Sta. WCMF, Rochester, 1965-67; engring. technician Sta. WOKR-TV, Rochester, 1968; head buyer Rochester Radio Supply Co., Inc., 1968-71; asst. to dir. municipal parking City of Rochester, 1971—. Mem. Monroe County Democratic Com. Mem. Soc. Broadcast Engrs., Radio Engring. Soc., Am. Mgmt. Assn., Internat. Personnel Mgmt. Assn., Am. Soc. Pub. Adminstrn. Home: 9 Clarkes-Crossing Fairport NY 14450 Office: 119 E Main St Rochester NY 14604

MC GANN, JOHN RAYMOND, bishop; b. Bklyn., Dec. 2, 1924; s. Thomas Joseph and Mary (Ryan) McG.; student Cathedral Coll. Immaculate Conception, 1944, Sem. Immaculate Conception, Huntington, 1950; LL.D., St. Johns U., 1971. Ordained priest Roman Catholic Ch.; asst. priest St. Anne's Brentwood, 1950-57; asso. Cath. chaplain Pilgrim State Hosp., 1950-57; asst. chancellor Diocese of Rockville Centre, 1957-67; asst. sec. to Bishop Kellenberg, 1957-59; elevated to papal chamberlain, 1959; sec. to Bishop Kellenberg, 1959-70; apptd. titular bishop of Morosbisdus and aux. bishop of Rockville Centre, 1970—; Episcopal ordination, 1971. Del. Sacred Congregation for Religious to Marianists, 1973, Nat. Conf. Cath. Bishops, Rome. 1974; mem. adv. council U.S. Cath. Conf., 1969-70, mem. bishops' com. on health affairs, 1972-75; vicar gen. Diocese Rockville Centre, 1971—, episcopal vicar Suffolk County, 1971—; mem. U.S. Bishops' Com. for Apostolate of Laity, 1972—; mem. Rockville Centre Diocesan Bd. Consultors, 1969—; episcopal mem. N.Y. State Cath. Com., 1974—, chmn. N.Y. State Bishops' Com. on Elective Process, 1974—, Com. Religious Studies in Pub. Edn., 1974—. Bd. dirs. Good Samaritan Hosp., West Islip, N.Y., 1972—, St. Charles Hosp., Port Jefferson, N.Y., 1972—. Home and Office: 50 N Park Ave Rockville Centre NY 11570*

MCGANNON, DONALD HENRY, broadcasting exec.; b. N.Y.C., Sept. 9, 1920; s. Robert E. and Margaret (Schmidt) McG.; B.A., Fordham U., 1940, LL.B., 1947, L.H.D., 1964; L.H.D., U. of Scranton, 1963, Creighton U., 1965, Emerson Coll., 1966; D.Sc. (hon.), St. Bonaventure U., 1965, Temple U.; m. Patricia H. Burke, Aug. 22, 1942. Admitted N.Y., Conn. bars, 1947; practiced in N.Y.C., 1947-50, Norwalk, Conn., 1947-51; asst. to dir. broadcasting DuMont TV Network, 1951-52, gen. mgr., asst. dir. broadcasting, 1952-55; v.p., gen. exec. Westinghouse Broadcasting Co., Inc., N.Y.C., and Westinghouse Broadcasting Co., Inc. (Cal. Md.), 1955, pres., dir., 1955—, chmn. bd., 1963—; pres. Westinghouse Electric Corp.-Broadcasting, Learning & Leisure Time, 1968. Consultor to Pontifical Commn. for Social Communications. Chmn. Conn. Commn. for Higher Edn.; pres. Nat. Urban League. Mem. Conn. Democratic Central Com. Trustee N.L. Law Sch.; chmn. adv. council U. Notre Dame, Georgetown U.; trustee Ithaca Coll., Fordham U., Sacred Heart U., N.Y.U. Served as maj. CAC, AUS, 1941-46. Mem. Conn. Bar Assn., Nat. Assn. Broadcasters (Achievement award 1946). K.C., Knight St. Gregory. Clubs: Duquesne (Pitts.); Union League (N.Y.C.). Office: 90 Park Ave New York City NY 10016

MC GARVEY, JAMES FRANCIS, aerospace engr.; b. Rahway, N.J., Dec. 4, 1921; s. Robert Lee and Maude Henrietta (McMahon) McG.; student Ill. Inst. Tech., 1949-51; B.S., U. Minn., 1952; m. Miriam Katherine Bishop, Mar. 12, 1948; children—Robert, Kevin, Gerald, Shaun. Lab. technician Inst. Gas Tech., Chgo., 1949-51; research engr. Carpco,Jacksonville, Fla., 1954-55; aerodynamicist Republic Aviation, Farmingdale, N.Y., 1955-64; aerospace engr. Fairchild Hiller, Beltsville, Md., 1964-69, NASA Goddard Space Flight Center, Greenbelt, Md., 1969—. Tutor Bowie Youth Program. Served U.S. Army, 1943-46. Mem. Am. Inst. Aeros. and Astronautics. Clubs: Chess, Sailing, Astronomy (Goddard Space Flight Center). Home: 12510 Windover Turn Bowie MD 20715 Office: CODE 742 2 NASA Goddard Space Flight Center Greenbelt MD 20770

MC GAVIC, JOHN SAMUEL, ophthalmologist; b. St. Louis, Feb. 18, 1911; s. Hamilton and Anne (Wallbank) McG.; B.S., Iowa Wesleyan Coll., 1934; M.D., U. Iowa, 1934; M.S. in Surgery, U. Cin., 1937; children—John Dickinson, Derrick Everingham, Martha H. Barr. Fellow Columbia U., 1938-40; intern Cin. Gen. Hosp., 1934-35, resident in ophthalmology, 1935-37; attending ophthalmologist Wills Eye Hosp., Phila., 1965-72, civilian cons. Valley Forge (Pa.) Army Hosp., 1947-72; faculty Med. U. Pa., Phila., 1950-70, prof., 1955-70; faculty Temple U., Phila., 1947-53, prof., 1955-69; chief ophthalmologist Bryn Mawr (Pa.) Hosp., 1948-73; prof. ophthalmology Jefferson Med. Coll., Phila., 1971—, practice medicine, specializing in ophthalmology Rosemont, Pa., 1947—. Served to maj. M.C., AUS, 1944-46. Diplomate Am. Bd. Ophthalmology; mem. AMA, Am. Acad. Ophthalmology and Otolaryngology, Am. Ophthalmol. Soc., Verhoeff Soc., Alpha Omega Alpha, Phi Delta Theta. Republican. Presbyterian. Club: Union League Phila. Office: 1104 Montgomery Ave Rosemont PA 19010

MC GEACHIE, JOHN STEWART, data processing exec.; b. Buenos Aires, Argentina, Feb. 7, 1943; s. John C. and Doris E. (Raynes) McG.; came to U.S., 1961; A.B., Dartmouth, 1965, M.B.A. with highest distinction, Amos Tuck Sch., 1975; m. Emma C. Catalano, June 19, 1965; 3 children. Project leader, computer dept. Gen. Electric Co., Phoenix, 1965-66; dir. tech. services, Mandate Systems Inc., N.Y.C., 1966-69, dir. software devel., 1969-71, dir. data processing, 1971-75; dir. computing services Dartmouth, 1975-77; gen. mgr. First Data div. ADP Network Services, Inc., 1977—; cons., lectr. in field. Edward Tuck scholar, 1974. Mem. Assn. for Computing Machinery, IEEE, Assn. M.B.A.'s. Contbr. articles to profl. publs. Office: First Data Corp 40 2nd Ave Waltham MA 02181

MCGEE, DANIEL HUGH, soap co. exec.; b. Phila., Oct. 26, 1949; s. James Vincent and Dorothy (Vogt) McG.; B.A. (Merit Award scholar), U. Del., 1972; postgrad. Rutgers U., 1975—; m. Amy Elizabeth Holbert, June 26, 1971; children—Kathryn Cara, Daniel Hugh. Salesman, Colgate-Palmolive Co., Wilmington, Del., 1974-77, area sales mgr., Wilmington, Phila. and Lancaster (Pa.) area of Balt. dist., Wilmington, 1977—. Mem. Sigma Phi Epsilon. Roman Catholic. Home: 2221 Decatur Rd Wilmington DE 19810 Office: Colgate Palmolive Co 2600 Century Pkwy NE Suite 310 Atlanta GA 30345

MC GEE, DOROTHY HORTON, author, historian; b. West Point, N.Y., Nov. 30, 1913; d. Hugh Henry and Dorothy (Brown) McGee; ed. Cathedral Sch. of St. Mary, 1920-21; Green Vale Sch., 1921-28, Bearley Sch., 1928-29, Fermata Sch., 1929-31. Asst. historian Inc. Village of Roslyn, 1950-58; historian Inc. Village of Matinecock, 1966—. Author: Skipper Sandra, 1950; Sally Townsend, Patriot, 1952; The Boarding School Mystery, 1953; Famous Signers of the Declaration, 1955; Alexander Hamilton-New Yorker, 1957; Herbert Hoover: Engineer, Humanitarian, Statesman, 1959, rev. 1965; The Pearl Pendant Mystery, 1960; Framers of the Constitution, 1968; Colonies Vs. Crown (play), 1977; also booklets, articles on hist. and sailing subjects. Bd. dirs. Friends of Raynham Hall, Family Service Assn. Nassau County, 1958-69; treas. Family Welfare Assn. Nassau County, 1956-58; chmn. Oyster Bay Am. Revolution Bicentennial Commn., 1971—; mem. Nassau County Am. Revolution Bicentennial Adv. Commn. Recipient award N.Y. Assn. Elementary Sch. Prins., 1959, Nat. Soc. Children Am. Revolution, 1960; award N.Y. State Assn. Supervision and Curriculum Devel., 1961; Hist. award Town of Oyster Bay, N.Y. Recipient Founders medal Theodore Roosevelt Assn., 1976. Fellow Soc. Am. Historians; mem. Sagtikos Manor (dir. 1963-65), Oyster Bay (pres. 1971-75, chmn. 1975—), Nassau County, L.I. hist. socs., Nat. Trust Historic Preservation, Soc. Preservation of L.I. Antiquities (dir.), Soc. Mayflower Descs., N.Y. Geneal. and Biog. Soc., others. Republican. Club: Seawanhaka-Corinthian Yacht (N.Y.). Address: PO Box 142 Locust Valley NY 11560

MCGEE, GALE WILLIAM, ambassador to OAS; b. Lincoln, Nebr., Mar. 17, 1915; s. Garton W. and Frances (McCoy) McG.; B.A., Nebr. State Tchrs. Coll., 1936; M.A., U. Colo., 1939; Ph.D., U. Chgo., 1947; LL.D., U. Wyo., Eastern Ky. U., Am. U., Seton Hall U., Allegheny Coll.; m. Loraine Baker, June 11, 1939; children—David Wyant, Robert Merrill, Mary Gale, Lori Ann. Prof. Am. history Nebr. Wesleyan U., 1940-43, Iowa State U., 1943-44, U. Notre Dame, South Bend, Ind., 1944-45, U. Chgo., 1945-46, U. Wyo., 1946—; senator from Wyo., 1959-77; chmn. Post Office and Civil Service Com.; mem. Appropriations Com., mem. fgn. ops. subcom., chmn. Agr. Dept. and related agys. subcom., Interior Dept. and related agys. subcom., pub. works subcom., transp. subcom.; mem. Fgn. Relations Com., chmn. African affairs subcom.; permanent U.S. rep. to OAS, 1977—. Bd. visitors U.S. Mil. Acad. Mem. AAUP, Am. Hist. Assn., Mississippi Valley Hist. Assn., Am. Assn. UN, Council Fgn. Relations, Izaak Walton League. Democrat. Presbyterian. Club: Eagles. Address: US Mission to OAS 2201 C St NW Washington DC 20520

MC GEE, JAMES ROBERT, fed. govt. ofcl.; b. Phila., Dec. 21, 1936; s. James Joseph and Jean Winifred (Lecitski-Scholwinski) McG.; B.A., Villanova U., 1958; M.A., Central Mich. U., 1977; Ph.D. in Bus. Adminstrn., Calif. Western U., 1978; children—Steven James, Patricia Marie, Douglas Patrick. Mgr., Marriott Corp., 1963-64; spl. agt. FBI, 1964-67; chief of security, safety U.S. Mint, Dept. Treasury, Washington, 1971-75, U.S. Fish and Wildlife Service, Washington, 1975—; CAP cons., 1975-76. Served to capt. USAF, 1958-63, 67-71; now lt. col. Res. Decorated Bronze Star, Purple Heart; certified Safety Profl. of Ams., certified protection profl. Mem. Soc. Former Agts. FBI, Dept. Treasury, Dept. Interior safety councils, Fed. Safety and Health Council. Writer tng. programs, manuals; contbr. articles on safety, security to various publs. Office: 18th and C Sts NW Washington DC 20240

MC GEE, ROBERT CARLTON, JR., transp. and distbn. products mfg. co. exec.; b. Richmond, Va., May 24, 1936; s. Robert Carlton and Regina Katherine (O'Sullivan) McG.; B.Aero. Engring., U. Va., 1960; m. Mary Ann Peterson, Sept. 1959; children—Marjorie Ann, Robert Matthew, Mary Katherine, Lauren Paige. Sales engr. Sikorsky Aircraft Co., Stratford, Conn., 1962-63; Washington rep. Fairchild Hiller Corp., Washington, 1963-65, mgr. mil. marketing, 1965-67; pres. Forge Aerospace, Inc., Washington, 1967-73; v.p. All Am. Industries, Inc., Wilmington, Del., 1971-73; pres. Swan, Inc., Richmond, 1974—, now also chmn. bd.; chmn. bd. Millburn Corp. Bd. dirs. Richmond YMCA. Served with AUS, 1961-62. Recipient Achievement award Nat. Aviation Club, 1970; Army Commendation award, 1967. Mem. Am. Helicopter Soc., Am. Inst. Aeros. and Astronautics, Assn. U.S. Army, Army Aviation Assn. Am., Nat. Security Indsl. Assn., Navy League, A.I.M., Nat. Aviation Club, Eli Banana, Sigma Alpha Epsilon, Theta Tau. Home: 408 Lakeway Ct Richmond VA 23229 Office: Route 1 Box 111A-3 Powhatan VA 23139

MCGEE, TIMOTHY WILLIAM, social worker, psychoanalyst; b. N.Y.C., Nov. 5, 1945; s. James Edward and Norah Elizabeth (Russell) McG.; B.A. in Psychology, St. John's U., Jamaica, N.Y., 1969-72; M.S.W., Fordham U., 1972-74; certificate in psychoanalytic psycotherapy Washington Inst., 1974-77; postgrad. Columbia U. Psychiat. technician Jacobi Hosp., N.Y.C., 1968-69; mental health worker St. Vincent's Hosp., N.Y.C., 1969-74; dir. clin. services Assn. for Help Retarded Children, N.Y.C., 1974-77; pvt. practice psychotherapy, N.Y.C.; adj. prof. Fordham U.; adminstrv. asst. Jacobi Hosp. Served with USAF, 1965-68. Decorated Air Force Commendation, Bronze Star; recipient NIMH award, 1972-74. Mem. Nat. Accreditation Assn. Psychoanalysis, Acad. Cert. Social Workers, Soc. Clin. Social Workers. Democrat. Roman Catholic. Home: Two Adrian Ave Bronx NY 10463 Office: 77 Park Ave New York NY 10016

MC GEORGE, RONALD KENNETH, hosp. adminstr.; b. Fredericton, N.B., Can., June 7, 1944; s. Hubert Oswald and Ruth Johanna (Kolding) McG.; B.S., Houghton Coll., 1966; diploma in hosp. adminstrn., U. Toronto, 1969; m. Gail F. Mitchell, July 17, 1970; children—Ronald Millard Scott, Dacia Gail. Adminstrv. counsellor N.S. Hosp. Ins. Comm., Halifax, N.S., 1969-70; asst. exec. dir. Izaak Walton Killam Hosp. for Children, Halifax, 1970-72; v.p. Greater Niagara Gen. Hosp., Niagara Falls, Ont., 1972-74; chmn. Council Teaching Hosps.; exec. dir. Halifax (N.S.) Infirmary, 1974—; preceptor hosp. adminstrn. U. Ottawa; cons. in field. Mem. faculty Dalhousie U. Faculty Medicine. Mem. Can. Coll. Health Services Execs. (v.p.), N.S. Hosp. Assn. (dir.), Assn. Hosp. Adminstrs. of N.S. (pres.-elect 1972), N.S. Assn. Health Orgns. (dir.). Contbr. articles to profl. jours. Methodist. Home: 48 Briar Lynn Crescent Dartmouth NS B4G 143 Canada Office: 1335 Queen St Halifax NS B3J 2H6 Canada

MC GHEE, JOHN ROBERT, hosp. adminstr.; b. Minersville, Pa., Nov. 11, 1924; s. Clarence Edwards and Marie Olga (Gilger) McG.; B.A. in Econs., Dickinson Coll., 1949; certificate in indsl. relations St. Joseph's Coll.; m. June 18, 1947; children—John Robert, Michael Edward, Susan Louise. Prodn. and personnel mgr. in industry, 1949-59; with Chestnut Hill Hosp., Phila., 1959-63; adminstr. Coatesville (Pa.) Hosp., 1963-69; exec. dir. Met. Hosp., Phila., 1969-75; dir. Greater Paterson Gen. Hosp., Wayne, N.J., 1975—; cons. to ins. cos., nursing homes, hosps. Mem. vestry Trinity Episcopal Ch., Coatesville, 1965-68; chmn. Chinatown YMCA Cultural Com., 1974. Served with U.S. Army, 1943-45; ETO. Mem. Am., N.J. (council govt. relations) hosp. assns., Am. Coll. Hosp. Adminstrs., Bergen-Passaic Hosp. Adminstrs., Wayne C. of C. (v.p. 1977—). Club: Rotary. Home and Office: 224 Hamburg Turnpike Wayne NJ 07470

MC GIBBON, PAULINE MILLS, univ. chancellor, former Can. provincial ofcl.; b. Sarnia, Ont., Can., Oct. 20, 1910; d. Alfred William and Ethel (French) Mills; B.A., U. Toronto (Ont.), 1933, LL.D., 1975; LL.D., U. Alta., 1967, U. Western Ont., 1974, Queens U., 1974; D.Univ., U. Ottawa (Ont.), 1972, U. Laval (Que.), 1976; D.Hum.L., St. Lawrence U., N.Y., 1977; B.A.A. in Theatre Arts (hon.), Ryerson Poly. Inst., 1974; m. Donald Walker McGibbon, Jan. 26, 1935. Dir., IBM Can., 1972-74; chancellor U. Toronto, 1971-74; lt. gov. Province of Ont., Toronto, 1974-78; chancellor U. Guelph, 1977—. Pres. Dominion Drama Festival, 1957-59, Can. Conf. Arts, 1972-73, Children's Film Library Can., 1948-50; mem. Can. Council, 1968-71; mem. U. Toronto Senate, 1952-63; bd. dirs. duMaurier Council for Performing Arts, 1973—, Nat. Theatre Sch. Can., 1962-74; chmn. bd. dirs. Womens Coll. Hosp., 1970-74; bd. govs. Upper Can. Coll., 1971-74. Decorated officer Order of Can., 1967; dame of grace Order St. John Jerusalem; dame comdr. Order St. Lazarus Jerusalem; recipient Can. drama award, 1957; Centennial medal, 1967; civic award of merit City of Toronto, 1967; Centennial medal, 1967; Silver Jubilee medal, 1977; named hon. col. 25th Toronto Service Bn. Fellow Royal Coll. Physicians and Surgeons Can. (hon.); mem. Imperial Order Daus. of Empire (pres. nat. chpt. 1963-65), Royal Canadian Mil. Inst. (1st woman mem.), Royal Canadian Legion. Clubs: Heliconian, Empire, Ladies of Toronto, York (hon.), Nat. (hon; 1st woman), Granite (hon.), Blvd. (hon.). Home: 20 Avoca Ave Apt 2004 Toronto ON M4T 2B8 Canada Office: Queen's Park Toronto ON Canada

MC GILL, MANLEY, cell biologist; b. Amarillo, Tex., Feb. 15, 1940; s. Manley and Hallie (Weldon) McG.; B.S., Tex. A. and M. U., 1962; M.S. (NIH fellow), U. Tex. 1972, Ph.D., 1974; m. Ruth Adele Hardesty, Nov. 18, 1972; children—Weldon D., Laura J. Med. technologist depts. biochemistry and immuno-hematology Meth. Hosp. and VA Hosp., Houston, 1969-73; instr. and lectr. U. Tex. Med. Br., Galveston, 1974-75; research scientist ARC Blood Research Lab., Bethesda, Md., 1976—. Served to capt. U.S. Army, 1965-68. Mem. AAAS, Am. Soc. Cell Biology, Am. Soc. Clin. Pathologists, Washington Soc. Electron Microscopy, Cousteau Soc., Animal Nat. Geog. Soc., Sigma Xi. Republican. Contbr. chpts. to biol. publs. Home: 12719 Atherton Dr Silver Spring MD 20906 Office: 9312 Old Georgetown Rd Bethesda MD 20014

MC GILL, WILLIAM JAMES, univ. pres.; b. N.Y.C., Feb. 27, 1922; s. William E. and Edna (Rankin) McG.; A.B., Fordham Coll., 1943, A.M., 1947; Ph.D., Harvard U., 1953; m. Ann Rowe, June 14, 1948; children—Rowena, William. Teaching fellow Harvard U., 1948-49; staff mem. Lincoln Lab., Mass. Inst. Tech., 1951-54, asst. prof. psychology, 1954-56; asst. prof. psychology Columbia U., 1956-58, asso. prof., 1958-60, prof., 1960-65, chmn. dept., 1961-63, mem. grad. faculty pure sci., 1959-65, pres. univ., 1970—; prof. psychology U. Calif. at San Diego, 1965-68, chancellor, 1968-70, chmn. San Diego div. acad. senate 1967-68; dir. AT&T, McGraw-Hill, Texaco, Inc. Trustee, Trinity Sch.; mem. Fellowship panel CDRB, NIH, 1964—; chmn. N.Y. State Spl. Adv. Panel on Med. Malpractice, 1975-76; chmn. Carnegie Commn. on Future of Pub. Broadcasting, 1977—. Mem. Am., Eastern psychol. assns., Am. Statis. Assn., Biometric Soc., Psychometric Soc., Psychonomic Soc. (governing bd.), AAAS, N.Y. Acad. Scis., Am. Acad. Arts and Scis., Knights of Malta, Soc. Exptl. Psychologists, Am. Irish Hist. Soc. (exec. council 1973—), Phi Beta Kappa, Sigma Xi. Home: 60 Morningside Dr New York City NY 10027

MC GILLICUDDY, JOHN FRANCIS, banker; b. Port Chester, N.Y., Dec. 30, 1930; s. Michael J. and Anna J. (Munro) McG.; B.A., Princeton, 1952; LL.B., Harvard, 1955; L.H.D. (hon.), Coll. of New Rochelle, 1973; D.Sc. in Bus. Adminstrn. (hon.), Bryant Coll., 1975; m. Constance Burtis, Sept. 9, 1954; children—Michael Sean, Faith Burtis, Constance Erin, Brian Munro, John Walsh. With Mfrs. Hanover Trust Co., N.Y.C., 1958—, exec. v.p., asst. to chmn., 1969, vice chmn., dir., 1970, pres., 1971—; pres., dir. Mfrs. Hanover Corp.; chmn. Mfrs. Hanover, Ltd.; vice chmn., dir. Mfrs. Hanover Internat. Banking Corp., Mfrs. Hanover Internat. Finance Corp.; dir. AMF, Inc., Cities Service Co., Continental Corp., Kraft Inc., Sperry & Hutchinson Co., Westinghouse Electric Corp. Served to lt. (j.g.) USNR, 1955-58. Mem. Assn. Res. City Bankers. Roman Catholic. Clubs: Augusta Nat. Golf, Westchester Country; Blind Brook; Sky; Princeton of N.Y.; Madison Sq. Garden. Home: Hilltop Pl Rye NY 10580 Office: 350 Park Ave New York City NY 10022

MC GILLICUDDY, ROBERT LOUIS, civil engr.; b. Boston, Feb. 8, 1935; s. Cornelius Francis and Margaret Mary (O'Connor) McG.; S.B., Mass. Inst. Tech., 1956; M.S., Northeastern U., 1963; m. Mary Teresa McGrath, Aug. 26, 1961; children—Mary Teresa, Robert Louis, John Joseph, Kathleen Rose, Kara Lynn. Structural engr. Clarkson Engring. Co., Inc., Boston, 1957-59, Universal Engring. Corp., Boston, 1959-65; civil, structural engr. Sylvania Electric Products, Inc., Wakefield, Mass., 1965-69; v.p. Anderson-Nichols & Co., Inc., Boston, 1969—. Mem. permanent bldg. com., Winchester, Mass., 1970—; chmn. playground com. Winchester Pub. Schs., 1974—. Registered profl. engr. numerous states. Mem. Boston Soc. Civil Engrs., ASCE. Roman Catholic. Home: 24 Cox Rd Winchester MA 01890 Office: Anderson-Nichols & Co 150 Causeyway St Boston MA 02114

MC GINN, ALAN, animal welfare exec.; b. Murton, Eng., Nov. 30, 1928; s. Robert Ambrose and Elizabeth (Davison) McG.; came to Can., 1959; student Army Sch. Accountancy, Devizes, Eng., 1946-49; m. Janina Maria Skalska, May 27, 1965. Various corp. positions in Eng., 1946-59, accounting positions in Can., 1959-64; bus. mgr. Warrendale Instn., Newmarket, Ont., Can., 1964-65; sec.-treas. Ruston Diesels div. English Electric Co. Ltd., Toronto, Ont., 1965-69; exec. Soc. Prevention Cruelty to Animals, Toronto, 1970-71; founder, pres. Soc. for Animals in Distress, Toronto, 1971—; tchr., cons. in field. Served with Brit. Army, 1946-50. Office: 1721 Eglinton Ave W Toronto ON M6E 2H4 Canada

MC GINN, DONALD JOSEPH, educator; b. Indian Lake, N.Y., Apr. 1, 1905; s. James and Mary Elizabeth (McCarthy) McG.; A.B., Cornell U., 1926, M.A., 1929, Ph.D., 1930; m. Margaret Howley, June 27, 1940; children—Kathleen (Mrs. Donald P. Spring), Donald Joseph. With comml. dept. N.Y. Telephone Co., N.Y.C., 1926-28; head English dept. Rutgers Prep. Sch., 1930-36; instr. Rutgers U., New Brunswick, N.J., 1936-40, asst. prof., 1940-46, asso. prof., 1946-51, prof., 1951-73, prof. emeritus, 1973—; vis. prof. Georgian Ct. Coll., Lakewood, N.J., 1945-73, prof., 1973—. Mem. Coll. Council on English in Central Atlantic States (sec.-treas., chmn.), Modern Lang. Assn. Am., Shakespeare Assn. Am., Renaissance Soc. Am., Cath. Commn. on Intellectual and Cultural Affairs (chmn. 1970-71), Phi Beta Kappa. Author: Shakespeare's Influence on the Drama of His Age, 1938; The Admonition Controversy, 1949; Literature as a Fine Art, 1959; John Penry and the Marprelate Controversy, 1966. Home: 2 President Ave Lavallette NJ 08735 Office: Georgian Court Coll Lakewood NJ

MC GINNIS, JAMES DOUGLAS, state ofcl.; b. Chgo., Jan. 11, 1932; s. Philip A. and Evelyn Catherine (Mousel) McG.; student Balt. City Coll.; m. Mary Jane Richards, Aug. 25, 1951; children—Philip J., James E., Donna M. Mem. Del. Ho. of Reps., 1963-65, 73-77, majority leader, 1976-77; mem. Del. Senate, 1965-67; lt. gov. State of Del., 1977—. Pres., Kent County (Del.) Heart Assn., 1975. Served with N.G. Named Del.'s Outstanding Young Man of Year, 1965. Democrat. Roman Catholic. Clubs: Lions, Moose. Home: 148 Cooper Rd Dover DE 19901 Office: Legislative Hall Dover DE 19901*

MC GINNIS, THOMAS CHARLES, JR., managerial cons. firm exec.; b. Morehead City, N.C., Sept. 3, 1949; s. Thomas C. and Mary Y. (Kluttz) McG.; B.A., Wittenberg U., 1971; M.A., Fairleigh Dickinson U., 1977. Asst., Counseling and Psychotherapy Center, Fair Lawn, N.J., 1972-73, adminstr., 1974, adminstrv. v.p., 1975-76; pres. Profl. Adminstrv. Services Corp., Fair Lawn, 1977—. No. N.J. Coll. chmn. Nixon Campaign staff, 1971-72. Served as sgt. USAR, 1971-77. Mem. Biofeedback Research Soc., Nat. Council Family Relations. Presbyterian. Clubs: Rotary Internat., N.Y.C. Sea Gypsy's Inc. Author: The Early Years of Marriage, 1973; researcher: Open Family Living, 1976, Open Family and Marriage, 1975, Dynamics of Human Sexuality, 1974. Home: 346 Owen Ave Fair Lawn NJ 07410 Office: 0100 27th St Fair Lawn NJ 07410

MC GINNIS, THOMAS PETER, real estate and ins. agt. broker; b. Honesdale, Pa., June 29, 1933; s. Charles Peter and Verlo Ruth (Getz) McG.; B.S., Pa. State U., 1955; m. Patricia Marie Schmidt, Oct. 17, 1959; children—Peter Thomas, Craig Charles, Kevin Paul, Kimberly Marie, Jill Ann. Vice pres., dir. Sandy Shore Co., Inc., Lake Wallenpaupack, Pa., 1957—; owner, mgr. Thomas P. McGinnis Ins. and Real Estate Co., Honesdale, 1967—; pres., treas. Khee Land, Inc., Honesdale, 1969—, Seven Mountains, Inc., Honesdale, 1972—; pres. Beach Glen, Inc., Honesdale, 1972—; dir., 2nd v.p. N.E. Savs. and Loan Assn., Honesdale, Hawley, Matamoras, Pa. Vol., Protection Engine Co. No. 3, Honesdale; team mgr. Horesdale Little Baseball Assn.; active Beach Lake Community Center. Served with U.S. Army, 1955-57. Licensed real estate broker, N.Y., Pa., ins. agt., Pa., casualty and fire ins. broker, Pa., N.Y., N.J. Mem. Pa. State U. Alumni Assn., Phi Sigma Kappa. Republican. Roman Catholic. Clubs: Eagles, Lions, Honesdale, Golf, Honesdale Booster. Home: POB 167 Rural Delivery 3 Honesdale PA 18431 Office: 809 Main St Honesdale PA 18431

MC GIVERN, BERNARD EDWARD, JR., dentist; b. Cleve., June 6, 1936; s. Bernard Edward and Jeanne Frances (Hopkins) McG.; B.S., U. Notre Dame, 1958; D.D.S., Western Res. U., 1962; postgrad. N.Y. U., 1962-63; m. Diane Mary O'Neill, Sept. 2, 1961; 1 dau., Ryan Neill. Intern, Bellevue, N.Y. U., Med. Center, 1963-64, resident oral surgeon, 1964-65; practice dentistry specializing in oral surgery, S.I., N.Y., 1965—; asst. clin. prof. oral surgery N.Y. U., Coll. Dentistry; attending oral surgeon, asso. dir. Dental Intern Tng. Program S.I. Hosp., now chief oral surgery service, treas. exec. med. bd.; attending oral surgeon St. Vincents Med. Center, Beekman Downtown, Greenpoint hosps.; hon. cons. oral surgeon N.Y.C. Police Dept.; cons. USPHS. Past pres. Dongan Hills Improvement Soc., now bd. govs. Licensed D.D.S., Ohio, N.Y.; diplomate Am. Bd. Oral Maxillofacial Surgery, Am. Bd. Dental Examiners. Fellow Am. Dental Soc. Anesthesiology, Internat. Assn. Oral Surgeons, Am. Coll. Oral Maxillofacial Surgeons (regent); mem. Am. (del.), N.Y. State socs. oral maxillofacial surgeons, Am. Dental Assn., N.Y. State, Richmond County (trustee) dental socs., Bellevue Oral Surgery Soc., Am. Cancer Soc. (bd. advisors S.I. chpt.), Vizsla Club Am. (dir., del.), Vizsla Club Greater N.Y. (dir., past pres.). Clubs: Richmond County Country, American Kennel (del., judge), Westchester Kennel (dir.), Westminster Kennel, S.I. Kennel (past pres.). Contbr. articles to profl. jours. Home: 95 Westentry Rd Country Club Grounds Staten Island NY 10304 Office: 1460 Victory Blvd Staten Island NY 10304

MC GIVERN, JAMES SABINE, clergyman; b. Edmonton, Alta., Can., July 27, 1908; s. Richard James and Mary Ellen (Macdonald) McG.; B.A., Loyola U. at Montreal, 1931; Ph.D., Gregorian U., 1932; M.A., U. Toronto, 1949. Joined S.J., 1925; ordained priest Roman Catholic Ch., 1937; chaplain Canadian Army, 1940-64; archivist S.J., Toronto, 1964-70; archivist Roman Cath. Archdiocese Toronto, 1971—; historian, editor Martyrs' Shrine Message, Midland, Ont., 1964—, asso. lectr. Toronto Sch. Theology, 1970-79; nat. chaplain United Empire Loyalists; free lance writer on geneal., hist. and religious subjects. Bd. dirs. Multiple Sclerosis Soc., Ont., 1965-75; founder, RCE Mil. Mus., Chilliwack, B.C., 1955. Decorated Order Brit. Empire; knight Grand Cross Order St. John (Yugoslavia), knight comdr. Order St. Lazarus, chaplain Constantinian Order; recipient Silver Jubilee medal Can. Gov. Gen. Fellow Royal Geog. Soc., Soc. Antiquaries (Scotland); mem. Soc. Mayflower Descs. Author booklets; founding editor MS mag., 1968-69. Home: 71 Gough Ave Toronto ON M4K 3N9 Canada Office: 55 Gould St Toronto ON M5B 1G1 Canada

MC GLADE, DENNIS CULLEN, landscape architect; b. Chgo., Oct. 17, 1943; s. James Bernard and Loretta Marian (Schultz) McG.; student De Paul U., 1961-63; B.Landscape Architecture, U. Ill., 1967; M.Landscape Architecture, U. Pa., 1969. Landscape designer Vincent G. Kling & Partners, Architects, Phila., 1967-70; landscape architect, planner Wallace, McHarg, Roberts & Todd, Architects, Phila., 1970-78; landscape architect Hanna/Olin, Phila., 1978—. Ryerson traveling fellow U. Ill., 1967. Recipient award of merit Am. Soc. Landscape Architects, 1966. Mem. Pa. Hort. Soc. Home: 135 S 20th St Apt 1005 Philadelphia PA 19103 Office: 6 N 19th St Philadelphia PA 19103

MC GOUGH, WILLIAM EDWARD, psychiatrist; b. Union City, N.J., Nov. 12, 1928; s. Irving Victor and Minnie Mae (McAtee) McG.; B.S., St. Peter's Coll., N.J., 1950; M.D., Duke U., 1956. Intern, Duke U. Med. Center, Durham, N.C., Seton Hall Jersey City Med. Center, 1956-57; resident in psychiatry Yale-New Haven Hosp., 1957-60; instr., asst. prof. psychiatry Duke U., 1961-64; faculty Coll. Medicine and Dentistry of N.J., Rutgers Med. Sch., New Brunswick, 1965—, prof. psychiatry, 1972—, asso. dean Med. Sch., 1972-76; chief of psychiatry Raritan Valley Hosp., 1977—. Mem. Am., N.J. (pres. 1975-76) psychiat. assns. Roman Catholic. Clubs: Monmouth County Kennel (pres. 1967—), Camden County Kennel, Rock River

Valley Kennel. Contbr. articles on psychophysiology, cultural aspects of psychiatry, stuttering therapy, edn. fgn. med. grads. to profl. jours. Home: Laird Rd Colts Neck NJ 07722 Office: Coll Medicine and Dentistry of N J Rutgers Med Sch Piscataway NJ 08854

MC GOVERN, JOHN HUGH, urologist; b. Bayonne, N.J., Dec. 18, 1924; s. Patrick and Mary (McGovern) McG.; B.S., Columbia U., 1947; M.D., State U. Coll. Medicine N.Y., 1952; children—John Hugh, Robert, Ward, Raymond. Rotating intern Bklyn. Hosp., 1952-53; asst. resident surgery Bklyn. VA Hosp., 1953-54, surgery (urology), N.Y. Hosp., N.Y.C., 1954-56; resident, 1957-58, research asst. pediatric urology, 1958-59, asst. attending surgeon urology James Buchanan Brady Found., 1959-61, asso. attending surgeon, 1961-66, attending surgeon, 1966—; exchange surg. registrar W. London Hosp., 1956-57; asst. surgery Cornell U.; Med. Coll., N.Y.C., 1957-59, asst. prof. clin. surgery (urology), 1959-64, asso. prof., 1964-72, prof., 1972—; attending-in-charge Lenox Hill Hosp., N.Y.C., 1969—. Served to lt., M.C., U.S. Army. Diplomate Am. Bd. Urology, Pan Am. Med. Assn. Fellow N.Y. Acad. Medicine (exec. com. urologic sect.), A.C.S., Am. Acad. Pediatrics; mem. N.Y. State (chmn. urologic sect.), N.Y. County med. socs., AMA, Am. Orol. Assn. (chmn. residents essay com. N.Y. sect.). Home: 180 Central Park S New York City NY 10019 Office: 53 E 70th St New York City NY 10021

MC GOVERN, MICHAEL JOHN, educator; b. Allentown, Pa., Dec. 1948: s. James Michael and Mary Leona (Brotzman) McG.; B.S., Mt. St. Mary's Coll., 1970; M.A., Niagara U., 1972. Tchr., Phillipsburg (N.J.) High Sch., part-time, 1972-73, Allentown (Pa.) Central Cath. High Sch., 1974; asst. prof. history Alvernia Coll., Reading, Pa., 1974—; career counselor Mt. St. Mary's Coll., Emmetsburg, Md., 1976-78. Vol., Boy Scouts Am., Bethlehem, Pa., 1972-74. Mem. Am. Hist. Assn., Orgn. Am. Historians, Am. Name Soc., Mt. St. Mary's Alumni Assn., Phi Alpha Theta, Pi Delta Epsilon. Democrat. Roman Catholic. Club: K.C. Contbr. articles in field to profl. jours. Home: 1201 Penn Ave Wyomissing PA 19610 Office: Alvernia Coll Millmont Reading PA 19607

MC GOWAN, ALAN HUGH, sci. found. exec.; b. N.Y.C., Sept. 27, 1935; s. Frank Hugh and Evelyn (Hunt) McG.; B. Engring., Yale, 1957; m. Rochelle Schiff, Apr. 10, 1960; children—David Michael, Nina Rachel. Engr., Am. Electric Power Co., N.Y.C., 1957-59; tchr. physics, chemistry, biology and math. various high schs. N.Y. and Manhattan, 1960-69; program dir. Water Pollution Project, Tilton (N.H.) Sch., 1969-70; sci. adminstr. Center for Biology Natural Systems, Washington U., St. Louis, 1969-74; trustee, v.p. Inst. Environ. Edn., Cleve., 1971—; pres. Scientists Inst. Pub. Info., N.Y.C., 1973—. Chmn. subcom. alternative energy sources Gov.'s. Task Force on Energy Problems, N.Y.C., 1975-76; mem. N.Y. State Energy Research and Devel. Authority, N.Y.C. Mayor's Energy Policy Adv. Com. Mem. Yale Sci. and Engring. Assn. (exec. bd., chmn. activities com.), AAAS, Sigma Xi. Home: 66 W 94th St New York City NY 10025 Office: 355 Lexington Ave New York City NY 10017

MC GOWAN, CARL, judge; b. Hymera, Ind., May 7, 1911; A.B., Dartmouth Coll., 1932, LL.B., Columbia U., 1936; LL.D. (hon.), Northwestern U., 1976; m. Josephine V. Perry, Jan. 20, 1945; children—Mary, Rebecca, John, Hope. Admitted to N.Y. bar, 1936, Ill. bar, 1940, D.C. bar, 1948; sr. mem. firm Ross, McGowan, Hardies & O'Keefe, Chgo., 1953-63; gen. counsel C. & N.W. Ry., 1957-63; judge U.S. Ct. Appeals for D.C. Circuit, 1963—. Mem. Am., Ill., Chgo., D.C. bar assns., Am. Law Inst., Phi Beta Kappa. Home: 4717 Quebec Ave NW Washington DC 20016 Office: US Ct Appeals Washington DC 20442

MC GOWAN, DOLORES LOUISE, hosp. adminstr., nurse; b. Lewistown, Pa., Aug. 18, 1931; d. Herbert Everett and Kathryn Elizabeth (Burnett) Stull; diploma Bryn Mawr (Pa.) Sch. Nursing, 1953; student Villanova U., 1953-54; m. William Clayton McGowan, Sept. 9, 1955 (dec.); children—Michele, Susan, Kathryn. Pediatric nurse Bryn Mawr Hosp., 1953-55, 56-68, coordinator home care, 1968-70; pediatric nurse Univ. Hosp., Balt., 1955-56; dir. nursing Lewistown (Pa.) Hosp., 1970—; bd. dirs. Community Nursing Service, 1970-78, adv. com. profl. persons, 1972-78; bd. dirs. local chpt. ARC, 1976-78, United Community Fund, 1977-78; faculty asso. in nursing Coll. Human Devel., Pa. State U., 1975-76; mem. adv. com. Central Pa. Health Systems Agy., 1977, Mifflin-Juniata Sch. Practical Nursing, 1972-78; chmn. publicity United Community Fund, 1976-77; chmn. Lewistown Hosp. Horse Show and Fair, 1976-77. Mem. Am., Pa. (exec. com. 1974-78, pres. 1975-78) socs. hosp. nursing service adminstrs., Pa. Soc. Nursing Adminstrs., Am., Pa. hosp. assns., Dist. Pa. Nurses Assn. (pres. 1972-73), Hosp. Assn. Pa. (mem. Soc. of Presidents 1977). Presbyterian. Home: 440 W 4th St Lewistown PA 17044 Office: Lewistown Hosp Highland Ave Lewistown PA 17044

MC GOWAN, JOHN MALCOLM, physician; b. Kilmiur, P.E.I., Can., July 4, 1905; s. Malcolm Campbell and Jessie Murchison) McG.; came to U.S., 1933, naturalized, 1941; B.S., Dalhousie U., 1931, M.D.C.M., 1933; M.S. in Surgery, U. Minn., 1937; m. Euphemia Rennie, Mar. 31, 1934; children—John William, David Malcolm. Intern, Victoria Gen. Hosp., Halifax, N.S., Can., 1932-33; fellow in surgery Mayo Clinic, 1933-37; pvt. practice medicine, Quincy, Mass., 1938—; mem. staff Quincy City Hosp., surgeon in chief, 1950-60; vis. surgeon Cardinal Cushing, Boston City hosps.; asst. prof. surgery Tufts U., 1946-56. Served to lt. col. M.C., AUS, 1942-46. Fellow A.C.S., Royal Coll. Surgery (Can.); mem. Boston, New Eng. surg. socs., A.M.A. Republican. Presbyterian. Clubs: Surgeons Travel (pres. 1974), Masons. Mem. editorial bd. Yearbook of Health, 1973, Yearbook of Cancer, 1952-67. Contbr. articles to profl. jours. Research in biliary tract with reference to sphincter of Oddi. Office: 13 Presidents Ln Quincy MA 02169

MC GOWAN, PATRICK TERRANCE, mail order exec.; b. Bronx, N.Y., Dec. 30, 1941; s. Patrick Joseph and Bridget (Duggan) McG.; student N.Y. U., 1965-67, Parsons Sch. Design and Printing Industries Met. N.Y., 1968-76; m. Paula Kleinman, May 30, 1971; children—Lisa, Seth, Daniel. Asst. prodn. mgr. Lane Bryant Co., N.Y.C., 1970-74, prodn. mgr., 1975—; direct mail prodn. mgr. Rapp Collins, N.Y.C., 1974-75. Democrat. Home: 3 Burnham Pl Fairlawn NJ 07410 Office: 1500 Broadway New York City NY 10036

MC GRAIL, JOHN SIMON, physician; b. Eng., May 28, 1931; s. William Anthony and Dorothy (John) McG.; M.D., U. Manchester, 1955; D.L.O., U. London, 1957; M.S., U. Mich., 1964; m. Theresa Mary Jenkins, Apr. 4, 1959; children—Susan, Mark, Christopher, Justin. Practice medicine, specializing in otolaryngology, Toronto, Ont., Can., 1966—; otolaryngologist-in-chief Wellesley Hosp., 1966—; cons. Ont. Cancer Inst., 1966—; prof. otolaryngology U. Toronto, 1966—, asst. prof. anatomy, 1968—. Pres., Adult Fitness Centres, Toronto; bd. dirs. Integra Found., Toronto Arts Prodn. Served with M.C., Royal Army, 1956-58. Fellow Royal Coll. Surgeons (Can.); mem. Canadian, Ont. med. assns., Acad. Facial and Reconstructive Surgery (U.S.A.), Sports Medicine of Can. Roman Catholic. Author: Fitness for Fun; contbr. articles on head and neck cancer to med. jours. Office: 160 Wellesley St E Toronto 284 ON Canada

MC GRATH, GEORGE WILLIAM, JR., lawyer; b. Newark, Oct. 23, 1922; s. George William and Katherine M. (Brady) McG.; grad. Pingry Sch., 1940; A.B. magna cum laude, Princeton, 1943; LL.B. cum laude, Harvard, 1950; m. Fay Schmitt, Jan. 17, 1948; children—Bruce M., Brian F. Admitted to N.Y. State bar, 1951; asso. firm Sage Gray Todd & Sins, N.Y.C., 1950-57, partner, 1958—. Dir., East Riding Co., Inc., Huntington, N.Y. Served with AUS, 1943-46; ETO; maj. gen. Res. Mem. Am., N.Y. State bar assns., Assn. Bar City N.Y., Assn. U.S. Army, Res. Officers Assn., Mil. Order World Wars, 77th Inf. Div. Res. Officers Assn., Phi Beta Kappa. Elk. Clubs: Downtown Assn., Princeton (N.Y.C.); Bay; Huntington Crescent; Princeton Tower. Home: 172 Flowerhill Rd Huntington NY 11743 Office: 140 Broadway New York City NY 10005

MCGRATH, RICHARD T., bishop; b. Oderin, Placentia Bay, Newfoundland, Can., June 17, 1912; student St. Bonaventure's Coll., Meml. U., St. Augustine's Sem., Can.; M.A. in Sociology, Catholic U., U.S.A. Ordained priest Roman Catholic Ch.; asst. Cathedral Parish, St. Patrick's Parish, St. John's, Nfld., Can.; chancellor archdiocese of St. John's, sec. to archbishop, later vicar gen.; consecrated bishop, St. George's diocese, Nfld., Can., 1970; prof. ethics, moral theology, St. Bride's Coll., St. Clare's Mercy Hosp., St. John's. Asst. editor St. John's archidiocesan newspaper. Office: Bishop's Residence 16 Hammond Dr Corner Brook NF A2H 2W2 Canada*

MC GRATH, RUTH EHRIG, educator; b. Buffalo, Dec. 29; d. Ernest and Clara Catherine (Eichhorn) Ehrig; B.S., State Tchrs. Coll. Buffalo, 1930; postgrad. Merrill Palmer Inst., Detroit, 1930; Ed.M., U. Buffalo, 1950, Ed.D., 1953; m. John McGrath, Aug. 13, 1932; children—Garry Wayne, Earl James. Tchr. home econs. Northside High Sch., 1930-32; head tchr. lab. preschool, lectr. edn. U. Buffalo, 1938-50; dir. lab. preschool, asso. prof. edn. State U. N.Y. at Buffalo, 1959—. Cons., Headstart, 1967-69, Jewish Center, 1955-57, Jack and Jill Nursery of YWCA, 1965-70; mem. U.S. Nat. Com. for Early Childhood, 1972. Mem. Nursery Assn. Ont. (dir. 1957-63), World Orgn. Early Childhood Devel., N.Y. State Council Children (pres. 1970-71), N.Y. Assn. Edn. of Young Children (pres. 1968-70), Early Childhood Edn. Council Western N.Y. (pres. 1958-60, 64-66), Pi Lambda Theta (faculty adviser 1965—). Editor: (with Marna Burstein) Cooking with Children, 1969; (with Beth Graham) Tools Wood and Glue: An Invitation to Learn, 1976; Developing Concepts of Social Studies in Early Childhood, 1976; Developing Concepts of Safety in Early Childhood, 1977; Developing Concepts of Health in Early Childhood, 1977; contbr. articles profl. jours., encys. Home: 55 Marjann Terr Kenmore NY 14223 Office: 15 Christopher Baldy Hall Buffalo NY 14260

MC GRATH, WILLIAM THOMAS, assn. exec.; b. Pte du Chene, N.B., Can., Oct. 12, 1917; s. William Joseph and Maud (Tucker) McG.; B.A., Mt. Allison U., 1941; M.S.W., Toronto U., 1948; m. Flora MacDonald Wilkie, June 14, 1946; children—Patricia, Maude, Christine. Sch. tchr., N.B., 1936-38; with Dept. Pub. Welfare, N.S., Can., 1948-50; exec. dir. Canadian Criminology and Corrections Assn., Ottawa, Can., 1950—; chmn. bd. cons. dept. criminology U. Ottawa; nat. rep. for Can. Internat. Soc. Criminology; mem., sec. Canadian Commn. on Corrections; mem. Commn. Inquisition into Disturbances at Kingston Penitentiary. Served with Canadian Army, 1941-45. Named John Howard Man of Year, 1967. Author: Should Canada Abolish the Gallows and the Lash, 1956; Crime and Its Treatment in Canada, 1965, 2d edit., 1976; Youth and the Law, 1954, 2d edit., 1973; (with A.M. Kirkpatrick) Crime and You, 1976. Contbr. articles in field to profl. jours. Home: 296 1st Ave Ottawa ON K1S 2G8 Canada Office: 55 Parkdale Ave Ottawa ON K1Y 1E5 Canada

MC GUINNESS, ADELAIDE HELEN, sales exec.; b. Yonkers, N.Y., Mar. 19, 1922; d. James John and Adeline Isabelle (Kern) Kavanaugh; ed. Pa. State U.; div.; children—Kevin, Darcy. Sales coordinator Coopercraft Guild Subs. Armor Bronze & Silver, Taunton, Mass., 1960-62; co-orginator, sales mgr., Princess House, North Dighton, Mass., 1962-64; nat. v.p. sales, 1964—; dir. G.A. Rogers Inc., North Dighton, Baybank United, Taunton. Mem. Internat. Platform Assn. Home: 501 Fletcher Rd North Kingstown RI 02852 Office: 455 Somerset Ave North Dighton MA 02764

MC GUINNESS, JOHN SEWARD, managerial cons., actuary; b. Kingston, Pa., Mar. 12, 1922; s. John P. and Mary (Bogert) M.; student U. Wash., 1941-43, U. Pitts., 1943-44; B.S., U. Calif. at Berkeley, 1948, M.B.A., 1949; postgrad. U. Zurich, Switzerland, 1949-50; Ph.D., Stanford, 1955; grad. U.S. Army War Coll., 1971; m. Shirley Paige Campbell, Nov. 23, 1957; children—Brian B., Ann B., Lauren K. Ins. clk., underwriter, 1939-43; chief, automotive service br. EUCOM Exchange System, 1946-47; asso. actuary Allstate Ins. Co., 1955-58; casualty actuary MacArthur Ins. Group, 1958-61; budget dir., actuary Glens Falls Ins. Group, 1961-64; pres. John S. McGuinness Assos., Scotch Plains, N.J., 1964—. Served with AUS, 1943-46; col. Res. ret. Named Ky. col. Fellow Casualty Actuarial Soc., Canadian Inst. Actuaries, Soc. for Advancement Mgmt (internat. pres. elect 1979-80); mem. Ins. Soc. N.Y., Internat. Actuarial Assn., Am. Statis. Assn., Ops. Research Soc., Soc. Ins. Research (nat. pres. 1972), Soc. C.P.C.U.'s, Beta Gamma Sigma, Alpha Kappa Psi, Delta Tau Delta. Republican. Presbyterian (ruling elder). Author: Top-Management Organization and Control of Insurance Companies, 1954. Contbr. articles to profl. jours. Address: 15 Kevin Rd Scotch Plains NJ 07076

MC GUIRE, HEATHER PENNY, nurse; b. Orange, N.J., Dec. 6, 1951; d. James and Jeannie (Prentice) McGuire; R.N., St. Luke's Hosp. Sch. Nursing, 1972; B.A., Marymount Manhattan Coll., 1975; M.P.A., N.Y. U., 1978. Office mgr. pvt. physicians, 1970-72; staff nurse operating room St. Luke's Hosp., N.Y.C., 1972-74, mem. open heart surg. team, 1974-75; surg. head nurse operating room Long Beach (N.Y.) Meml. Hosp., 1976-78; asso. dir. nursing service, dir. hosp. operating room SUNY at Stony Brook, 1979—; chmn. ednl. seminar Assn. of Operating Room Nurses of N.Y., 1977-78. Health care rep. Com. for Re-Election of Judge Jack Mackston, 1977. N.Y. State scholar, 1969. Mem. N.Y. Nurses Assn., Am. Assn. Operating Room Nurses (del. to nat. congress 1978-79), Internat. Order of Rainbow. Home: 710 E Walnut St Long Beach NY 11561 Office: University Hosp SUNY Stony Brook NY 11749

MC GUIRK, RONALD CHARLES, banker; b. Balt., Dec. 9, 1938; s. Charles Francis and Grace Elizabeth (Delcher) M; student St. John's Coll., 1960; m. Katherine Sauer, Oct. 1, 1960; children—Frank David, Ann Elizabeth. With 1st Nat. Bank Md., Balt., 1960— sr. data processing officer, 1966-72, v.p. data processing, 1972-76, v.p. mktg., 1976—. Councilman, Anne Arundel County, Md., 1974—; trustee N. Arundel Hosp.; mem. govs. task force on inter-relationship of Md. and Fed. employment standards. Mem. Am. Banking Assn. (bank card standards com), Assn. for Computing Machinery, Md. Assn. Counties. Democrat. Roman Catholic. Home: 7970 Crownsway Glen Burnie MD 21061 Office: PO Box 1596 Baltimore MD 21203

MC GUIRL, MARLENE DANA, lawyer, educator, librarian; b. Hammond, Ind., Mar. 22, 1938; d. Daniel David and Helen Elizabeth (Baludis) Callis; A.B., Ind. U., 1959; J.D., DePaul U., 1963; M.A. in L.S., Rosary Coll., 1965; LL.M., George Washington U., 1978; m. James Franklin McGuirl, Apr. 24, 1965. Law library asst. DePaul Coll. Law Library, 1961-62, asst. law librarian, 1962-65; admitted to Ill. bar, 1963, Ind. bar, 1964, D.C. bar, 1972; reference law librarian Boston Coll. Sch. Law Library, 1965-66; librarian D.C. Bar Library, 1966-70; library cons. Nat. Clearinghouse on Poverty Law, OEO, 1967-69, Northwestern U. Nat. Inst. for Edn. in Law and Poverty, 1969, D.C. Office Corp. Counsel, 1969-70; instr. legal librarianship Grad. Sch., Dept. Agr., 1968; lectr. legal lit. and librarianship Grad. Dept. L.S., Catholic U., 1972-73, adj. asst. prof., 1973—; asst. chief Am.-Brit. Law div. Library, Congress Law Library Washington, 1970, div. chief, 1970—; instr. Ph.D. program in Am. civilization George Washington U., 1976—. Mem. Georgetown Citizens Assn.; trustee D.C. Law Students in Ct.; del. Ind. Dem. Conv., 1964. Recipient Meritorious Service cash award Library Congress, 1974. Mem. Am. (facilities of Law Library of Congress com. 1976-79), Fed. (chpt. council 1972-76), Ill., D.C. (inter-Am. bar relations com. 1968-70, memls. com. 1969-70), Women's (treas. 1970-72, pres. 1972-73, exec. bd. 73-77, parliamentarian 1975, chmn. constrn. and by-laws com. 1975-76) bar assns., D.C. Bar (election bd. 1973-75, specialization com. 1975-76), Am. Bar Found. (library service com. 1969-72), Nat. Assn. Women Lawyers (co.-chmn. legis. com. 1976-77), Internat. (program chmn. 1974), Am. (co-chmn. statistics com. 1970-72, chmn. legis. and legal devels. 1972-73, exec. bd. 1973-77) assns. law libraries, Law Librarian Soc. Washington (pres. 1971-73), Brit. and Irish Assn. Law Librarians, Assn. Am. Library Schs. (prison libraries com. 1975-76), Exec. Women in Govt., Nat. Lawyers Club. Contbr. articles to profl. jours. Home: 3416 P St NW Washington DC 20007 Office: Law Library Am-Brit Law Div Library Congress Washington DC 20540

MC HALE, EDWARD, JR., supt. schs.; b. Brattleboro, Vt., June 15, 1935; s. Edward G. and Marjorie Monica (Mitchell) McH.; B.A., Harpur Coll., 1958; postgrad. Cornell U., 1960-64; M.A., U. Mich., 1967, postgrad. (fellow), 1969-70; s. Nancy Jo Barnes, Aug. 11, 1956; children—Mary Colleen, Ellen Elizabeth, Edward G., III, Meghan P., Molly Ann. Tchr., English and Latin, Johnson City, N.Y., 1959, Moravia, N.Y., 1959-63, Auburn, N.Y., 1963-66, Aurora, N.Y., 1966-67; asso. dir. So. Tier Regional Edn. Center, Elmira, N.Y., 1967-68, exec. dir., 1968-73; supt. schs. Whitehall, N.Y., 1973—. Mem. Assn. Supervision and Curriculum Devel., Am. Assn. Sch. Adminstrs., Phi Kappa Phi. Democrat. Episcopalian. Club: Rotary. Home: Old Fair Haven Turnpike Whitehall NY 12887 Office: Buckley Rd Whitehall NY 12887

MC HALE, JOHN JOSEPH, baseball club exec.; b. Detroit, Sept. 21, 1921; s. John Michael and Catherine M. (Kelly) McH.; A.B. cum laude, U. Notre Dame, 1947; m. Patricia Anne Cameron, Feb. 15, 1947; children—Patricia Cameron II, John Joseph, Kevin K., Anne F., Brian F., Mary M. Profl. baseball player, 1941-42, 45-47; asst. dir. minor league clubs Detroit Tigers Baseball Club, 1948, asst. farm dir., 1948-53, dir. minor league clubs, 1954-55, dir. player personnel, 1956-57, gen. mgr., 1957-58; v.p., gen. mgr. Milw. Braves Baseball Club (became Atlanta Braves Baseball Club 1961), 1957-61, pres., gen. mgr., 1961-67; adminstrtv. asst. to commr. baseball, N.Y.C., 1967-68; pres. Montreal (Que., Can.) Baseball Club, 1968—; dir. Perini Corp.; dir. prevest Mut. Fund Ltd. Can. Club: National Monogram (U. Notre Dame). Office: PO Box 500 Sta M Montreal PQ H1V 3P2 Canada

MC HENRY, DONNEL MITCHEL, dentist; b. Sagamore, Pa., Nov. 19, 1918; s. Allan Robert and Vinie Maria (Haag) McH.; student Gettysburg Coll., 1936-38; D.D.S., Temple U., 1942; m. L. Ruth Deibert, Aug. 22, 1942; children—Donnel Mitchel, Janet Ruth. Dentist, Pa. Dept. Health, 1942-43; dental resident Harrisburg (Pa.) State Hosp., 1942-43; pvt. practice dentistry, Chambersburg, Pa., 1946—; mem. med. staff Chambersburg (Pa.) Hosp. Mem. Chambersburg Sch. Bd., 1954-56. Served with Dental Corps, USNR, 1943-46; PTO. Fellow Am. Coll. Dentists, Internat. Coll. Dentists; mem. Am., Pa. (pres. 1974), dental assns., 5th Dist. (past pres.), Cumberland Valley (past pres.) dental socs., Pierre Fauchard Acad., Acad. Gen. Dentistry (dir. Pa. polit. action com.), Am. Legion, Phi Delta Theta, Xi Psi Phi. Republican. Lutheran. Mason (Shriner), Rotarian. Home: 602 Montgomery Ave Chambersburg PA 17201 Office: 858 Lincoln Way E Chambersburg PA 17201

MC HENRY, ROBERT CLIFFORD, indsl. relations exec.; b. Phila., Apr. 22, 1932; s. Daniel James and Edna May (Carpenter) McH.; B.S., Temple U., 1963; m. Maureen Morris, Sept. 6, 1952; children—Maureen, Colleen, Robert Clifford, Eileen. With RCA, 1951—, compensation analyst, Cherry Hill, N.J., 1963-65, employment mgr., Bloomington, Ind., 1965-67, div. compensation mgr., Cherry Hill, N.J., 1967-69, div. compensation and benefits mgr., Indpls., 1969-71, indsl. relations mgr., Bloomington, Ind., 1971-75; v.p. indsl. relations RCA Global Communications, Inc., N.Y.C., 1975—; seminar instr. Ind. U., 1973-75. Chmn. United Fund, Bloomington, Ind., 1973-74; bd. dirs. Boys Club, Bloomington, Ind., 1972-75; adviser CYO, 1962-65, 67-69, 71-75. Roman Catholic. Clubs: K.C., Elks; Downtown Athletic (N.Y.C.). Home: 70 Spenser Dr Short Hills NJ 07078 Office: 60 Broad St New York City NY 10004

MC HUGH, MATTHEW, congressman; b. Phila., Dec. 6, 1938; s. Peter F. and Margaret M. (Whalen) McH.; B.S., Mt. St. Mary's Coll., 1960; J.D., Villanova U., 1963; m. Eileen Alanna Higgins, 1963; children—Alanna, Kelli, Meg. Admitted to N.Y. State bar, 1964; practiced in N.Y.C.; pros. atty. City of Ithaca (N.Y.), 1968; dist. atty. Tompkins County (N.Y.), 1969-72; mem. 94th-95th Congresses from 27th N.Y. Dist. Active numerous civic orgns. Mem. Am., N.Y. State, Tompkins County bar assns. Democrat. Home: 102 Willard Way Ithaca NY 14850 Office: 1204 Longworth House Office Bldg Washington DC 20515

MC ILHANY, STERLING FISHER, publishing co. exec.; b. San Gabriel, Cal., Apr. 12, 1930; s. William Wallace and Julia (Fisher) M.; B.F.A., U. Tex., 1953; student U. Calif. at Los Angeles, 1953-54, 55-57, Universita per Stranieri, Perugia, Italy, 1957; Rotary fellow Accademia Belle Arti, Rome, 1957-58. Teaching asst. art history U. Calif. at Los Angeles, 1953-54, 55-57; art supr. Kamehameha Prep. Sch., Honolulu, 1954-55; instr. Honolulu Acad. Arts 1955; asso. editor Am. Artist mag., N.Y.C., 1958-61, editor, 1969-70; condr. network series Books and the Artist, WRVR, N.Y.C., 1961-62; sr. editor Reinhold Book Corp., N.Y.C., 1962-69; pres. Art Horizons, Inc., N.Y.C., 1962—; instr. Sch. Visual Arts, N.Y.C., 1961-69. Recipient First award tour European art centers Students Internat. Travel Assn., 1952. Author: Banners and Hangings, 1966; Art as Design-Design as Art, 1970; Wood Inlay, 1972; Simbari, 1975; also articles. Address: 52 Morton St New York City NY 10014

MCILHONE, JOHN THOMAS, ednl. adminstr.; b. Montreal, Que., Can., Jan. 26, 1911; s. Robert Emmett and Ellen Eva (O'Rourke) McI.; B.A., Loyola Coll., Montreal, 1933; M.A., U. Montreal, 1939, B.Ed., 1940, Ph.D., 1942; m. Dorothy Agnes Quinn, June 20, 1942; children—Anne Marie (Mrs. R. Marc Huberdeau), Quinn. Prof. edn.

St. Joseph's Coll., Montreal, 1939-40, 45-48; dir. schs. Montreal Cath. Sch. Bd., 1948-73; dir. gen. Mt. St. Patrick Corp., Montreal, 1973—. Ednl. cons. Montreal Cath. Sch. Commn., 1973—; mem. Royal Commn. Enquiry into Edn., 1961-66. Active charity campaigns; trustee Loyola Coll., Concordia U.; bd. dirs. Canadian Cath. Trustees, Mt. St. Patrick. Served to comdr. RCAF, 1940-45. Decorated Grand Cross of Merit, Order of Malta. Recipient Coronation medal Govt. Can., 1952, Centennial medal, 1967; named comdr. Order of Sch. Merit, Que. Province, 1956. Mem. Can. (life), Nat. Cath. edn. assns., Can. Coll. Tchrs., Phi Delta Kappa. Club: Mount Stephen (Montreal). Contbr. articles to profl. jours. Home: 416 Barton Ave Mount Royal PQ H3P 1N4 Canada

MCILVAIN, DOUGLAS LEE, sculptor, educator; b. Mt. Holly, N.J., July 26, 1923; s. Edwin Hume and Elizabeth (Winton) McI.; B.F.A., Temple U., 1949, B.S., 1950; M.A., N.Y. U., 1967; m. Frances Haines, Feb. 7, 1948; children—Bonnie Jeanne, James Douglas. Tchr. art, head dept. Red Bank (N.J.) High Sch., 1950-68; asso. prof. art Georgian Ct. Coll., Lakewood, N.J., 1968—; art designer Monmouth Mus., 1978—; one-man shows include: Montclair State Coll., 1960, Rider Coll., 1971, Brookdale Coll., 1972, Guild Creative Arts, 1976, Thompson Park, 1977, Georgian Ct. Coll., 1978; group exhibitions include: Det. Inst. Art, Pa. Acad. Art, Newark Mus., Montclair Mus., Trenton State Mus., Monmouth Mus., Temple U., N.Y. U.; represented in permanent collections: Monmouth Coll., Tyler Sch., Rome, also pvt. collections. Served with USAAF, 1943-46. Mem. AAUP, N.J. Art Edn. Assn., Shore Area Art Educators Assn., Guild Creative Arts, Art Alliance, Internat. Sculpture Center, Monmouth Arts Assn. Home: 40 Whitman Dr Red Bank NJ 07701

MC ILVAIN, JESS HALL, architect; b. Denton, Tex., Mar. 29, 1933; s. Charles L. and Edith (Hall) McI.; B. Arch., Tex. Tech. U., 1959; m. Joni Wimberly, Aug. 23, 1959; children—James Sean, Sheila Maria. Designer, Nesmith & Lane, architects, El Paso, Tex., 1959, Garland & Hilles, architects, El Paso, 1960-63, William Metcalf, Architect, Washington, 1963; architect designer Cooper & Auerbach, architects, Washington, 1963-65, Bucher-Meyers, architects, Washington, 1966-67; project mgr. Weihe, Black, Kerr, architects, Washington, 1967-68; designer Callmer & Milstead, architects, Washington, 1968-69; dir. archtl. services Tile Council of Am., Inc., Washington, 1969—; lectr. on ceramic tile numerous colls. and univs. Third v.p. Woodacres PTA, 1975-76, treas., 1978-79; treas. Woodacres Citizens Assn., 1973-75, pres., 1975-76. Served with U.S. Army, 1953-55. Horizon Homes Regional award, 1962. Mem. AIA (dir. Washington chpt. 1968, mem. nat. codes and standards com. 1974-77), Constrn. Specifications Inst. (program chmn. D.C. Met. chpt. 1972-75, 3d v.p. 1974-76, award for excellent service award D.C. chpt. 1973, 75 pub. award region 2 1976, tech. commendation 1977, author specification series 09310 1971, 78), Am. Soc. for Testing and Materials, Bldg. Ofcls. and Code Adminstrn. Internat., Photographic Soc. Am., U.S. C. of C., Internat. Conf. Bldg. Ofcls., So. Bldg. Cod. Conf., Bldg. Industry Assn. (rep., sec. 1974-75, pres. 1976-77), Tex. Tech. U. Alumni Assn. (pres. Washington chpt. 1971-73, dist. rep. 1975-77), Sigma Chi. Republican. Methodist. Clubs: Kenwood Country, Bethesda Lions (pres. 1974-76, dir. 1976-78, sec. 1978-79), Tex. Tech. Century. Contbr. numerous articles on ceramic tile and installation standards to profl. jours.; architect of record 80 residences, residential remodelling and comml. stores, 1970-78. Home: 6012 Woodacres Dr Washington DC 20016 Office: 4801 Montgomery Ln Washington DC 20014

MC ILVAINE, RICHARD SCOTT, ednl. adminstr.; b. Rosemont, Pa., June 26, 1931; s. Donald and Elizabeth (Thomas) McI.; student W.Va. U., 1954-55; B.S., Cheyney State Coll., 1962; M.A., Columbia U., 1963; postgrad. U. So. Calif., 1970-71; m. Patricia Ann Burns, Feb. 15, 1958; children—Sarah R., Richard S., Steven D. Tchr., Chester County Pa. Bd. Sch. Dirs.-Physically Handicapped and Emotionally Disturbed Children and Retarded, 1956-60; tchr., curriculum chmn. Coatesville (Pa.) Area Schs. Slowlearners and Retarded, 1963-70, 72-78, supr. spl. edn. programs, 1978—; summer prin., dir. summer recreation day camp for educable mentally retarded Dept. Def. Overseas Schs., Kaiserslauten, Germany, 1970-71; guest lectr. spl. edn. Gen. Teaching Council Scotland, 1971-72. Served with AUS, 1951-54. Recipient Outstanding Service award Coatesville Area council PTA, 1968. Mem. NEA, Am. Assn. Mental Deficiency, Council Exceptional Children (chpt. legis. chmn. 1964-65), Overseas Edn. Assn. (faculty rep. 1970-71), Scottish Hist. and Research Soc. Delaware Valley, Chester County His. Soc. Mem. Religious Soc. of Friends (mem. ednl. com. 1968—). Clubs: European Motor Caravan (Inverness, Scotland); Camping of Great Britain and Ireland (London, Eng.); Family Motor Coach Assn. Home: 317 W Miner St West Chester PA 19380 Office: South Brandywine Jr High Sch RD 3 Box 121 Coatesville PA 19320

MC ILVEEN, WALTER, heating, ventilating and air conditioning engr.; b. Belfast, Ireland, Aug. 12, 1927; s. Walter Henry and Amelia (Thompson) McI.; M.E., Queens U., Belfast, 1948; Heating, Ventilating and Air Conditioning Engr., Borough Poly., London, 1951; m. Margaret Teresa Ruane, Apr. 17, 1949; children—Walter, Adrian, Peter, Anita, Alan. Came to U.S., 1958, naturalized, 1963. Mech. engr. apprentice Davidson & Co., Belfast, 1943-48; sr. contract engr. Keith Blackman Ltd., London, 1948-58; mech. engr. Fred S. Dubin Assos., Hartford, Conn., 1959-64; chief mech. engr. Koton & Donovan, West Hartford, Conn., 1964-66; prin. Walter McIlveen Assos., Avon, Conn., 1966—. Registered profl. engr., Conn., Mass., N.J., R.I., Fla., N.Y., Ohio, Vt., N.H. Home: 3 Valley View Rd Weatogue CT 06089 Office: 195 W Main St Avon CT 06001

MC INALLY, JOHN ANTHONY, physicist; b. N.Y.C., Oct. 3, 1929; s. John Anthony and Helen (Tarutis) McI.; B.A. in Physics, N.Y. U., 1957, postgrad., 1957-63; m. Mary E. Kealey, July 12, 1952; children—John F., Jeannette, Susan, Carol, Barbara, Robert. Physicist, Hanovia Lamp Co., Newark, 1956-61; sr. physicist Ford Instrument Co., N.Y.C., 1961-63; tech. specialist, project mgr. Xerox Corp., Rochester, N.Y., 1963—; cons. in field. Recipient Founders' Day award N.Y. U., 1957. Mem. Am. Phys. Soc. (plasma physics div., electron and atomic physics div., cosmic physics div.), Am. Assn. Physics Tchrs., Rochester Mus. and Sci. Center, Rochester Oratorio Soc., Rochester Civic Music Assn. Contbr. articles to tech. jours., papers to tech. confs. Patentee in field. Home: 58 Sawmill Dr Penfield NY 14526 Office: Xerox Corp Xerox Sq Rochester NY 14644

MC INTOSH, ROBERT EDWARD, JR., educator; b. Hartford, Conn., Jan. 19, 1940; s. Robert Edward and Natalie (Glynn) McI.; B.E.E., Worcester Poly. Inst., 1962; S.M., Harvard U., 1964; Ph.D., U. Iowa, 1967; m. Anne Marie Potvin, July 7, 1962; children—Robert E., Edgar J., Michael T., William P., Matthew P. Electromagnetics physicist NASA, Cambridge, Mass., 1967; asst. prof. U. Mass., 1967-70; asso. prof., 1970-73, prof., 1973—; vis. prof. U. Nijmegen, Netherlands, 1973-74; engr. cons., 1970—; proposal reviewer NSF, Dept. Def.; chmn. Internat. Symposium IEEE/AP-S and Internat. Radio Sci. Union/U.S. Nat. Com. Meeting; prin. investigator on grants from NSF, Air Force Office of Sci. Research, Army Research Office, NASA. Sr. mem. IEEE; mem. Internat. Radio Sci. Union (coms. B and C), Am. Phys. Sco. (div. plasma physics), Optical Soc. Am., Sigma Xi, Tau Beta Pi, Eta Kappa Nu, Phi Kappa Phi, Pi Delta Epsilon. Contbr. numerous articles to sci. jours; reviewer book and jour. publs. Democrat. Home: 138 Columbia Dr Amherst MA 01002 Office: Dept Elec & Comp Engr Univ Mass Amherst MA 01002

MC INTOSH, ROY LAWRENCE, dentist; b. Nashua, N.H., Feb. 26, 1921; s. George Victor and Ruth (Lawrence) McI.; student Boston U., 1940; D.M.D. cum laude, Harvard U., 1944; m. Anne Brock Langballe, Nov. 26, 1955; children—Scott Lawrence, Heather Lynn (dec.), Todd Brock, David Lawrence. Pvt. practice dentistry, Nashua, 1947—; pres. Family Dynamics, success motivation inst., Nashua; mem. N.H. Emergency Med. Services Coordinating Bd., 1975—. Pres. N.H. chpt. Am. Cancer Soc., 1970-72; mem. Nashua City Planning Bd., 1972—, now chmn.; bd. dirs. Meml. Hosp. Assn., Nashua. Served to capt. U.S. Army, 1944-46. Licensed airplane pilot. Mem. N.H. Assn. for Children with Learning Disabilities, ADA, N.H., Nashua Dist. dental socs., So. New Eng. Acad. Practice Adminstrn., Acad. Gen. Dentistry, Am. Soc. for Preventive Dentistry, Aircraft Owners & Pilots Assn., Mensa, Omicron Kappa Upsilon. Republican. Methodist. Home: Tinker Rd Nashua NH 03060 Office: 6 Concord St Nashua NH 03060

MCINTYRE, JAMES PHILIP, coll. adminstr.; b. Malden, Mass., Feb. 27, 1934; s. Peter Philip and Anne (Halloran) McI.; A.B., Boston Coll., 1957, M.Ed., 1961, Ed.D., 1967; m. Monica Flatley, Nov. 24, 1962; children—Mary Elizabeth, Peter Flatley, James Philip, Ann-Patrice, Karalyn, David Patrick. Asst. dir. admissions and fin. aid Boston Coll., 1959-66, exec. asst. to v.p. student affairs, 1966-68, v.p. student affairs, 1968-76, v.p. for univ. relations, 1976—, adj. prof. edn., 1960—. Adviser pres.'s com. on student affairs Temple U., 1973; exec. dir. Task Force on Open U., Commonwealth of Mass., 1973. Served with AUS, 1957-59. New Eng. Cath. Edn. Assn. research grantee, 1966. Mem. Am. Assn. Univ. Adminstrs., Phi Delta Kappa (chpt. v.p. 1966-67). Editor: A Changing Higher Education: How Will Student Personnel Survive the Storm (author with many others), 1972; editorial bd. Nat. Assn. Student Personnel Adminstrs. Jours., 1973; contbr. articles to profl. jours. Home: 83 McCormack St Malden MA 02148 Office: Brock House Boston Coll Chestnut Hill MA 02167

MC INTYRE, JAMES TALMADGE, JR., govt. ofcl.; b. Vidalia, Ga., Dec. 17, 1940; s. James T. McI.; B.S., J.D., U. Ga.; m. Maureen; 3 daus. Staff U. Ga. Inst. Govt.; individual practice law, Athens, Ga.; gen. counsel Ga. Municipal Assn., 1966-70; dep. revenue commr. State of Ga., 1970-72; dir. Ga. Office Planning and Budget, 1972-76; dep. dir. Office Mgmt. and Budget, Exec. Office of Pres., Washington, 1977, acting dir., 1977-78, dir., 1978—. Office: Office Mgmt and Budget Exec Office Bldg Washington DC 20503*

MC INTYRE, THOMAS JAMES, former U.S. senator; b. Laconia, N.H., Feb. 20, 1915; student pub. and parochial schs., Laconia; grad. Dartmouth Coll., 1937, Boston U. Law Sch., 1940; hon. degrees, Dartmouth Coll., U. N.H., Nathaniel Hawthorne Coll., Belknap Coll., New Eng. Coll.; m. Myrtle Ann Clement; 1 dau., Martha Grey. U.S. senator from N.H., 1962-78, elected to fill unexpired term, reelected 1966, 72, mem. armed services, banking, housing and urban devel. coms., select com. on small bus. Mayor, Laconia, 1949-51, city solicitor, 1953; Congressional candidate, 1954; del. Democratic Nat. Conv., 1956, 68; chmn. Laconia Dem. City Com. and Belknap County Dem. Com. Pres. bd. trustees Taylor Home for Aged, 1954-62; dir. Laconia Indsl. Devel. Corp., 1962. Served to maj. U.S. Army, 1942-46. Mem. VFW, Am. Legion, N.H., Belknap County (pres. 1961-63) bar assns., C. of C., Grange. Clubs: K.C., Kiwanis. Home: 2923 Garfield St NW Washington DC 20008

MCINTYRE, WILLIARD FRANCIS, graphics photog. co. exec.; b. Lost Creek, W.Va., Sept. 14, 1939; s. Ray L. and Lora Jean (Hayes) McI.; B.S. in Journalism, U. W.Va., 1960; M.A. (hon.), Purdue U., 1972; Ph.D. in Communications, U. Mo., 1978; m. Sharon Lee Smith, Apr. 30, 1970; children—Williard F., Christopher Lee. Asst. dir. sales promotion McCall Corp., Washington, 1961-63; chief Washington bur. Photo News Internat. Paris, 1961-65; asst. dir. photography Publishers Corp., Washington, 1963-67; dir. Washington region Delma Studios Inc., N.Y.C., 1967-76; pres., dir. Graphics Photo, Inc., Silver Spring, Md., 1976—; pres., dir. D.C. Publishers Inc., 1975—. Mem. U.S. Naval Inst., Mensa, Epsilon Delta Chi, U.S. Ho. of Reps. and U.S. Senate press galleries. Democrat. Presbyterian. Exhibited photography at Colorfax Galleries, Washington, Silver Spring, Md., 1974, 75; contbr. photos to Life and Look. Home: 13120 Clifton Rd Silver Spring MD 20904 Office: 7835 Eastern Ave Silver Spring MD 20910

MC KAY, DOUGLAS WILLIAM, orthopedic surgeon; b. Howland, Me., Mar. 10, 1927; s. Hugh Gordon and Elizabeth Mary (Jellison) McK.; B.A. with distinction, U. Maine, 1951; M.D., Tufts U., 1955; m. Elinor Caswell, Mar. 31, 1950; children—Ann Elizabeth, Hugh Gordon, Heather Jean. Intern, Eastern Me. Gen. Hosp., Bangor, 1955-56; resident in orthopedic surgery McKinney VA Hosp., Dallas, 1956-59, Newington Hosp. for Crippled Children, Newington, Conn., 1959-60; practice medicine, specializing in orthopedic surgery, Covington, Ky., 1960-61; chief surgeon Carrie Tingley Hosp. for Crippled Children, N.M., 1961-67; chief surgeon Shriner's Hosp. for Crippled Children, Shreveport, La., 1967-72; prof., head dept. orthopedic surgery La. State U., Shreveport, 1969-72; chmn. dept. pediatric orthopedic Surgery, Children's Hosp., Nat. Med. Center, Washington, 1972—; prof. orthopedic surgery George Washington U. Med. Sch., Washington, 1972—; lectr. in field. Served with Maine Maritime Acad., 1944-46. Diplomate Am. Bd. Orthopedic Surgeons. Mem. D.C. Med. Soc., Am. Acad. Orthopedic Surgeons, Pediatric Orthopedic Soc., Societe International de Chirurgie Orthopedique et de Traumatologie, Central, Russell Hibbs Soc., Washington Orthopedic Soc., Western orthopedic assns. Clubs: Little Orthopedic, Rotary. Contbr. articles to med. jours. Home: 10616 Red Barn Ln Potomac MD 20854 Office: 111 Michigan Ave NW Washington DC 20010

MC KAY, RICHARD JOSEPH, ednl. adminstr.; b. Webster, Mass., Nov. 12, 1934; s. James Henry and Anne (Harvanek) McK.; B.S. in History, Springfield Coll., 1956; M.Ed., Tufts U., 1957; m. Christine Leclaire, Sept. 3, 1957; children—Elizabeth, Laura, Peter, John, Mary, Richard, Andrea, Christopher, Douglas. Counsel, Black Horse Troop, Culver (Ind.) Mil. Acad., 1962-66; instr. guidance U. Va., Charlottesville, 1966-67; dean Clinch Valley Coll., Wise, Va., 1967-69; asst. supt. schs. Stoughton (Mass.), 1969-71; asst. supt. secondary edn. Arlington (Mass.) Pub. Schs., 1971-77; supt. schs. Holbrook (Mass.), 1977—; cons. Project Opportunity, Nelson County, Lovingston, Va., 1967; mem. ednl. adv. com. Boston Regional Office, Mass. Dept. Edn., 1971-77, chmn. Boston regional council, 1977—. Mem. New Eng., Mass. assns. sch. supts., Harvard Supts. Roundtable, Orton Soc. (nominating com. 1973—, dir. New Eng. Soc.), Nat. Council Social Studies, Am. Personnel and Guidance Assn., Am. Psychol. Assn., Assn. Supervision and Curriculum Devel., AAUP, Phi Delta Kappa, Nat. Assn. Amateur Oarsmen. Contbr. articles to profl. jours. Home: 225 4th St Stoughton MA 02072 Office: 227 Plymouth St Holbrook MA 02343

MC KAY, WINFIELD CLELAND, customs broker; b. Toronto, Ont., Can., Nov. 6, 1930; s. Winfield George and Jessie (Cleland) McK.; student Upper Can. Coll., 1945-48; m. D.A. Noreen Laing, May 2, 1959; children—Winfield Laing, Victoria Anne. With W.G. McKay, Ltd., Toronto, 1952—, pres., 1966—; pres. Asso. Customs Brokers; sec. Freight Consolidators of Can., Ltd.; chmn. bd. Lawson McKay & Assos., Ltd.; dir. Besser Can. Ltd. Chmn., Camp Vesle Skaugum, 1967-68, T.P. Loblaw Charity Trust Found., 1966, Gerrard Boys Club, 1959-60; nat. dir. Boys Clubs of Can., 1967—; chmn. Kiwanis Boys and Girls Clubs of Toronto, 1971-72; mem. Met. Toronto Police Commn., 1972—. Progressive Conservative party candidate for Parliament, Toronto, 1968. Mem. Young Pres.'s Orgn. (chpt. chmn. 1977-78). Clubs: Kiwanis (pres. Toronto 1965), Rosedale Golf, Badminton and Racquet, Lambton Golf. Home: 35 Old Forest Hill Rd Toronto ON Canada Office: 100 University Ave Toronto ON Canada

MC KEAGE, ARLINGTON BUD, bus. therapist; b. E. Angus, Que., Can.; s. Alexander and Lula (Willard) McK.; B.Commerce, Dalhousie U., Halifax, N.S., Can., 1950; B.A.M., U. Va., 1962. Supr., pricing sales Bell Can., Montreal, Que., 1950-59; mgr. planning and ops. AT&T, N.Y.C., 1959-64, exec. asst., regulation matters, 1964-68, dir. mktg. pricing policy, 1968-78; prin. Sombrero Enterprises, 1978—. Served with Can. Army, 1942-46. Mem. Am. Mktg. Assn., AIM, Acad. Polit. Sci., Creative Problem Solving Inst. State U. N.Y., Zeta Psi. Developer mgmt. tng. and problem-solving programs. Home: 299 W 12th St New York City NY 10014 Office: 195 Broadway New York City NY 10007

MC KEAN, ALEXANDER LAIRD, elec. research engr.; b. N.Y.C., Apr. 25, 1916; s. Alexander M. and Elizabeth A. (Burns) McK.; B.E.E., Poly. Inst. Bklyn., 1936, M.E.E., 1941; m. Elizabeth A. Gilchrist, Feb. 7, 1942 (dec. Dec. 1960); 1 son, Douglas S. With Phelps Dodge Cable & Wire Co., Yonkers, N.Y., 1936—, mgr. applications engring., 1950-52, chief devel. engr., power and communications cables, 1953-65, asso. dir. research and devel. labs., 1966—. Fellow IEEE; mem. ASTM, NRC, NAS, Nat. Assn. Corrosion Engrs., Congress Internat. Power Systems Engrs., Common Cause, Eta Kappa Nu. Club: Mens of Riverside Ch. Contbr. articles to profl. jours. Patentee in field. Home: 1 Lincoln Ave Ardsley NY 10502 Office: Phelps Dodge Cable and Wire Co PO Box 391 Yonkers NY 10702

MC KEAN, ANDREW, cons. criminal justice; b. Duluth, Minn., Mar. 14, 1926; s. Frank MacDonald and Elsie Allison (Miller) McK.; B.A., U. Minn., 1954; m. Mamie Lee Singleton, Jan. 16, 1953; children—Deborah Lee, Gerald Andrew. Dep. sheriff, Sioux Falls, S.D., 1950-51; policeman, Duluth, 1952-54; spl. agt. FBI, Washington, 1954-76; cons. criminal justice Rockville, Md., 1976—. Served with USN, 1943-47, 51-52; PTO. Mem. Internat. Assn. Chiefs Police, Nat. Sheriffs Assn. (project dir. 1976-78). Presbyterian. Club: Masons. Home: 307 Meadow Hall Dr Rockville MD 20851

MC KEAN, JOHN F., real estate cons.; b. Beaver Falls, Pa.; s. Arthur and Eleanor (Ferguson) McK.; m. Bette Rutkowski; children—Sandra (Mrs Paul Ogden), Susan Ferguson (Mrs. John Gibbs). Real estate dept. Manufacturers Trust Co.; real estate cons., 1945—; pres. Fish & Marvin, Peter Tare, Inc. Served as comdr. USNR, 1942-45. Decorated Bronze Star, Purple Heart, Legion of Merit. Member of S.R., Naval Order U.S. (comdr.), Mil. Order of World Wars, Delta Kappa Epsilon. Club: Williams (N.Y.C.). Home: 333 E 43d St New York City NY 10017

MC KEE, ADAM EMANUEL, JR., veterinarian; b. Fairfield, Ala., Apr. 12, 1932; s. Adam Emanuel and Lizzie (Brewton) McK.; A.B., Dillard U., 1954; D.V.M., Tuskegee Inst., 1958; m. Barbara Nance, Oct. 18, 1958; children—Adam E., Eric, Brett. Enlisted U.S. Air Force, 1958; advanced through grades to col.; base veterinarian, Istanbul, Turkey, 1958-60; sentry dog clinician, San Antonio, 1960-63; pathology resident Armed Forces Inst. Pathology, Washington, 1963-66, chief altitude chamber unit, 1966-67; chief veterinary pathology Biol. and Med. Scis. div. Naval Radiol. Def. Lab., San Francisco, 1967-69, dep. head exptl. pathology dept., 1969-74; chmn. exptl. pathology dept. Naval Med. Research Inst., Bethesda, Md., 1974—, chmn. policy adv. council, 1975-76; cons. scanning electron microscopy Armed Fores Inst. Pathology Med. Mus. Named Omega Man of Yr., Montgomery County, 1975, 2d Dist., 1976, 78; recipient Spl. Merit award Naval Med. Research Inst., 1976. Mem. AVMA, Washington Soc. Pathology, Internat. Acad. Pathology, Washington Soc. Scanning Electron Microscopy, Am. Soc. Microbiology, Wildlife Disease Assn., Am. Assn. Lab. Animal Sci., Am. Soc. Lab. Animal Practitioners, Tuskegee Vet. Med. Alumni Assn. (pres.), Omega Psi Phi (dist. rep. 1978). Baptist. Contbr. articles in field to profl. jours. Home: 14905 Bauer Dr Rockville MD 20853 Office: Naval Med Research Inst Bethesda MD 20014

MC KEE, DELBER L., historian; b. Superior, Nebr., Jan. 15, 1923; s. John K. and Lottie F. (Touzalin) McK.; A.B., Hastings (Nebr.) Coll., 1946; M.A., U. Wis., 1947; Ph.D., Stanford U., 1953; m. Margaret C. Carson, June 6, 1946; children—Richard H., Anne L., Mary F. Instr. history Simpson Coll., 1947-50; mem. faculty Westminster Coll., New Wilmington, Pa., 1952—, prof. history, 1958—, chmn. dept., 1956-79, acting dean, 1977. Bd. dirs. Wilmington Area Sch. Dist., 1971-77. Fulbright grantee, Taiwan, summer 1963. Served with USAAF, 1943-46. Mem. Am., Pa., Mercer County hist. assns., Orgn. Am. Historians, Asian Studies Assn., Soc. Historians Am. Fgn. Relations, AAUP, Phi Alpha Theta. Presbyn. Club: Rotary. Chinese Exclusion vs. the Open Door Policy, 1900-1906, 1977; also articles. Home: RD 3 PO Box 418 New Wilmington PA 16142 Office: Dept History Westminster Coll New Wilmington PA 16142

MC KEE, DUNCAN OLIPHANT, lawyer; b. New Philadelphia, Ohio, Nov. 2, 1931; s. Paul Harper and Anne McKennan (Oliphant) McK.; A.B., Coll. Wooster, 1953; LL.B., Duke U., 1956; m. Lois Mae Yale, June 20, 1953; children—Paul Harper, Susan, Martha, Glenn Yale, Duncan Oliphant. Admitted to Pa. bar, 1957; asso. firm Ballard, Spahr, Andrews & Ingersoll, Phila., 1956-64, partner, 1964—; dir. Bancroft Convertible Fund, Inc., First Nat. Stores, Inc. Mem. Scotch-Irish Soc. U.S.A., Am., Pa., Phila. bar assns. Republican. Presbyterian. Club: Coudersport Golf. Home: 15 Flagstone Pl Levittown PA 19056 Office: 30 S 17th St Philadelphia PA 19103

MC KEE, ELIZABETH BROOKS THAYER, club woman; b. Bklyn.; d. John Van Buren and Elizabeth B. (Chatfield) Thayer; grad. Bklyn. Hts. Sem., 1914; m. Waldo McCutcheon McKee, Oct. 3, 1925; children—Elizabeth Brooks (Mrs. J. Eugene Lewis), M. Jean. Hon. dir. Orphan Asylum, Bklyn.; past chmn. social service com. Cumberland Hosp., Bklyn.; past treas. Bklyn. Com. Met. Opera; past mem. com. N.Y. Philharmonic Soc.; mem. Cheshire Bicentennial Com. Bd. dirs. Womens Republican Club, Cheshire. Mem. Bklyn. Jr. League (past pres.), Nat. Soc. Colonial Dames (past v.p. State N.Y.), L.I., Cheshire (dir.), New Haven Colony hist. socs., Conn. Antiquarian and Landmarks Soc. Clubs: Civitas (past v.p.), Mrs. Fields Literary (past v.p.). Home: 532 S Brooksvale Rd Cheshire CT 06410

MC KEE, FRANCES GWENDOLYN MARTIN (MRS. DAVIS BELL MCKEE, JR.), nursing educator; b. Lawrence, Mass., Nov. 10, 1923; d. William Guy and Bertha Etta (Ferris) Martin; B.S., Merrimack Coll., 1958; M.S., Boston U., 1959, Ed.D., 1974; m. Davis Bell McKee, Jr., July 30, 1944; children—Linda Karen, Leslie Susan,

Davis Bell 3d, Guy Martin. Staff nurse Bon Secours Hosp., Methuen, Mass., 1955-69, Lawrence (Mass.) Gen. Hosp., 1970-78; prof. St. Anselm's Coll., Manchester, N.H., 1959—; instr. N.H. Coll., Manchester, 1971-72, Hesser Coll., Manchester, summer 1975; vis. prof. U. N.H., 1978; project dir. federal grant HEW, 1966-71. Woman's adviser Dist. 5 March of Dimes of N.H., 1972—. Trustee Manchester (N.H.) Area Family Planning Clinic, 1968-71, chmn. personnel com. 1968-71. Mem. Am. Nurses Assn., Nat. League for Nursing, VFW Aux. (pres. 1953-54). Home: New Boston Rd Bedford NH 03102 Office: St Anselm's Dr Manchester NH 03102

MC KEE, MARGARET JEAN, polit. analyst; b. New Haven, June 20, 1929; d. Waldo McCutcheon and Elizabeth (Thayer) McKee; A.B., Vassar Coll., 1951. Staff asst. United Republican Fin. Com., N.Y.C., 1952; staff asst. N.Y. Rep. State Com., N.Y.C., 1953-55; staff asst. Crusade for Freedom (name later changed to Radio Free Europe Fund), N.Y.C., 1955-57; researcher Stricker & Henning Research Asso. Inc., N.Y.C., 1957-59; exec. sec. New Yorkers for Nixon (name later changed to N.Y. State Ind. Citizens for Nixon Lodge), N.Y.C., 1959-60; asst. to Raymond Moley, polit. columnist, N.Y.C., 1961; asst. campaign com. Louis J. Lefkowitz for Mayor, N.Y.C., 1961; research programmer, treas. Consensus, Inc., N.Y.C., 1962-67; spl. asst. to U.S. Senator Jacob K. Javits, N.Y., 1967-73, adminstrv. asst. 1973-75; dep. acting adminstr. Am. Revolution Bicentennial Adminstrn., 1976-77; chief of staff Perry B. Duryea, Minority Leader N.Y. State Assembly, Albany, 1978—. Commr. N.Y. State Bingo Control Authority, 1965-72; pres. Bklyn. Heights Slope Young Republican Club, 1955-56; co-chmn. Bklyn. Citizens for Eisenhower-Nixon, 1956; chmn. 2d Jud. Dist. Assn. N.Y. State Young Rep. Clubs, Inc., 1957-58, vice-chmn., mem. bd. govs., 1958-60, v.p., 1960-62; pres., 1962-64; mem. exec. com. Fedn. Women's Rep. Clubs N.Y. State, Inc., 1960-64, mem. council, 1964—; mem. exec. com. N.Y. Rep. State Com., 1962-64; co-chmn. spl. assts. Rockefeller for Pres. Nat. Campaign com., N.Y.C., 1964; co-dir. N.Y. Rep. State Campaign Com., 1964; asst. campaign mgr. Kenneth B. Keating for Judge Ct. Appeals, N.Y., 1965; dir. scheduling Gov. Rockefeller campaign, 1966. Sen. Charles E. Goodell campaign, 1970; dir. scheduling and speakers bur. N.Y. Com. To Re-elect the Pres., 1972; bd. govs. Women's Nat. Rep. Club, N.Y.C., 1963-66. Mem. Jr. League Bklyn. (past dir.), Exec. Women in Govt., Nat. Women's Edn. Fund (mem. bd.), Nat. Soc. Colonial Dames, Am. Newspaper Women's Club. Episcopalian. Club: Vassar (past dir.) (Bklyn.). Home: 785 Park Ave New York City NY 10021 Office: 270 Broadway New York City NY 10007

MCKEEL, SAM STEWART, newspaper exec.; b. Wilson, N.C., Aug. 28, 1926; s. Henry Connor and Tryphenia (Mann) McK.; A.B., U. N.C., 1950; M.S., Columbia, 1952; m. Margarett Elizabeth Fields, June 14, 1952; children—Douglas, Karen, Stuart. Editor Northampton (N.C.) News, 1950-51; reporter Greensboro (N.C.) Daily News, 1952-54; reporter, personnel mgr. Charlotte (N.C.) Obs. and News, 1954-63; gen. mgr. Akron (Ohio) Beacon-Jour., 1964-71; pres. Phila. Inquirer and Daily News, dir., 1972—; dir. Met. Sunday Newspapers Inc. Pres. Akron Art Inst., 1968-71. Trustee, chmn. Phila. Coll. Art., Friends Hosp., Pop Warner Little Scholars. Served with USNR, 1943-46. Mem. Phila. C. of C. (dir., mem. exec. com.), Pa. Newspaper Pubs. Assn. (dir.). Presbyterian. Home: 1321 Pine Rd Rosemont PA 19010 Office: 400 N Broad St Philadelphia PA 19101

MC KEEVER, PAUL EDWARD, neuropathologist; b. Pasadena, Calif., Dec. 3, 1946; s. Lewis Goodell and Lillian Anne (Neuwirth) McK.; B.Sc., Brown U., 1968; M.D., U. Calif. at Davis, 1972; Ph.D., Med. U. S.C., 1976; m. Mary Olivia Gilchrist, June 19, 1971; children—Emily Rebecca, Lillian Marie. Pathology intern U. Calif. at San Diego, 1972-73; pathology resident Med. U. S.C., Charleston, 1973-74, neuropathology fellow, 1974-76; research asso. Lab. Microbial Immunity, Nat. Inst. Allergy and Infectious Diseases, NIH, Bethesda, Md., 1976—, neuropathology cons. Lab. Pathology, Clin. Center, 1976—; neuropathology instr. Med. U. S.C., 1976. Served with USPHS, 1976-78. Diplomate Am. Bd. Pathology. Mem. Internat. Acad. Pathology, Reticuloendothelial Soc., A.C.P., AAAS, Am. Assn. Neuropathologists, Alpha Omega Alpha. Contbr. articles to profl. jours. Home: 4621 Rosedale Ave Bethesda MD 20014 Office: Bldg 5 Room 237 NIH Bethesda MD 20014

MCKENNA, GERALD JAMES, psychiatrist; b. Beacon, N.Y., Nov. 11, 1940; s. Patrick Joseph and Elizabeth Patricia (McCallion) McK.; B.A. cum laude, Marist Coll., 1962; M.D., SUNY, Syracuse, 1966; m. Frances M. O'Brien, July 15, 1973; 1 son, Sean Patrick. Intern, San Francisco Gen. Hosp., 1966-67; resident in psychiatry Harvard Med. Sch.-Mass. Mental Health Center, 1967-70; dir. Boston City Hosp. Drug Detoxi- fication Unit, 1972-73; asso. dir. drug treatment services Cambridge/Somerville (Mass.) Mental Health Center, 1973-76, dir. Drug Problems Resource Center, Drug Treatment Services, 1976—; prin. investigator Nat. Inst. on Drug Abuse, research grantee Inst. in Psychiatry - Harvard Med. Sch. at Cambridge Hosp., 1973—, faculty primary care intern and residency program, 1975—. Served to maj. M.C., USAF, 1970-72. Recipient Distinguished Alumnus award Marist Coll., 1976; diplomate Am. Bd. Psychiatry and Neurology. Mem. Am., Mass. Psychiat. assns., Mass. Med. Soc. Roman Catholic. Contbr. numerous articles to med. jours. Home: 4808 Stearns Hill Rd Waltham MA 02154 Office: 1493 Cambridge St Cambridge MA 02139

MC KENNA, JAMES A(LOYSIUS), JR., lawyer, broadcaster; b. Poughkeepsie, N.Y., July 1, 1918; s. James Aloysius and Eleanor Frances (Mahoney) McK.; student Manhattan Coll., 1934-35; B.S., Cath. U. Am., 1938; LL.B., Georgetown U., 1942; m. Rebekah Ann Rial, Sept. 1, 1941; children—Michelle Marie (Mrs. Nassif), James Aloysius, Dennis M., Matthew M., Marc W., Aileen. Admitted to D.C. bar, 1941; counsel CAB, 1941-42; asst. to gen. counsel Office Alien Property Custodian, 1942-44; practiced in Washington, 1946—; mem. firm Haley, McKenna & Wilkinson, 1948-52; partner firm McKenna, Wilkinson & Kittner, 1952—; pres., dir., Stas. KQRS and KQRS-FM, Mpls., Sta. WCMB and WSFM, Harrisburg, Pa., Sta. WWQM and WMAD-FM, Madison, Wis.; v.p., dir. Sta. WAWA and WAWA-FM, West Allis, Wis. Served as lt. (j.g.) USNR, 1944-46. Recipient DuBois medal Mt. St. Mary's Coll., 1966; Outstanding Alumni award Cath. U. Am., 1978. Mem. IEEE, FCC Bar Assn., Georgetown U. Alumni Assn., Delta Theta Phi. Clubs: Internat., Army and Navy (Washington). Home: 5219 Oakland Rd Chevy Chase MD 20015 (summer) Annandale Rd Emmitsburg MD 21727 Office: 1150 17th St NW Washington DC 20036

MC KENNA, WILLIAM FRANCIS, lawyer; b. Meriden, Conn., May 14, 1910; s. Francis Joseph and Alice (Downes) McK; Ph.B., Yale, 1930, J.D., 1932; m. Catherine Agnes Donahue, June 25, 1935; children—William Francis (dec.), Daniel Joseph. Admitted to Conn. bar. 1932; asso. firm Buckley, Creedon & Danaher, Hartford, 1932-35; counsel, acting chief pub. loans sect. legal div. RFC, Washington, 1935-42; counsel Def. Supplies Corp., 1942; chief airports br. War Assets Adminstrn., 1945-47; counsel com. banking and currency U.S. Senate, 1947-57, U.S. Joint Com. Def. Prodn., 1950-51; adminstrv. asst. U.S. Senator William Benton, 1950; asso. Ford Motor Co. Washington Office, 1957-58; house counsel Nat. Assn. Mut. Savs. Banks, N.Y.C., 1958-59; dir.-counsel Washington office Nat. Assn. Mut. Savs. Banks, Washington, 1959-63; gen. counsel Nat. League Insured Savs. Assns. (name now Nat. Savs. and Loan League), Washington, 1963-75, v.p., 1971-75, sec., 1973-75; sec. Nat. League Internat., Inc., 1974-75; asso. firm Silver, Freedman, Housley and Taff, and predecessor, Washington, 1976—; lectr. on savs. and loans topics; dir. Knickerbocker Fed. Savs. and Loan Assn., N.Y.C., 1975—. Comdg. officer USNR Law Co. 5-11, Washington, 1956-57, 64-65. Pres. Conn. Democrats D.C., 1939-40; lector, server St. Matthew's Cathedral, Washington; cantor, extraordinary minister St. Michael's Ch., Silver Spring, Md. Served from lt. (j.g.) to lt., USNR, 1943-45, ret. capt. Mem. Inter-Am., D.C. bar assns., Bar Assn. D.C. (chmn. Latin-Am. ambassadors reception com. 1966, 78), Yale Law Sch. Assn., U.S. Senate Assn. Adminstrv. Assts. and Secs., Assn. Former Senate Aides, Lambda Alpha. Democrat. Clubs: Yale (N.Y.C.): University, Exchequer (Washington); Men's (Silver Spring, Md.). Author: National League Legal Bulletin Series, 1965-75. Editor: Manager's Manual, 1964-74. Home: 8004 Park Crest Dr Silver Spring MD 20910 Office: 1800 M St NW Washington DC 20036

MCKENNEY, FLORENCE REA (MRS. W. GIBBS MCKENNEY, JR.), civic worker, club woman; b. Canton, N.C., Nov. 6, 1914; d. William and Roberta (Payne) Rea; B.S., U. Md., 1936; m. W. Gibbs McKenney, Jr., July 17, 1939. Tchr. home econs. pub. schs., Balt., 1936-40, Washington, 1940-45. Asso. dir. Delta Delta Delta, 1958-62; chmn. orientation and tng. ARC, Balt., 1961-64, dir., 1961—, vice chmn. community relations, 1964-66, chmn. uniformed vols., 1966-67, vice chmn. vols. Balt. regional chpt. 1967-69, chmn. vols., 1969-72; mem. Hampton Nat. Historic Site Com., 1963—, chmn. trustees, 1976-77; 2d v.p. Balt. Civic Opera Guild, 1968-72; fin. sec. Cylburn Wildflower Preserve and Garden Center, 1971-77; bd. dirs. Meals on Wheels, YWCA, 1973-76; sec. bd. mgrs. J. Bennett Home, 1971, pres., 1974-76; dir. Central Atlantic region Nat. Council State Garden Clubs, 1977-79. Mem. Federated Garden Clubs Md. (dist. dir., state pres. 1967-69), Mortar Bd., Alpha Lambda Delta, Omicron Nu, Phi Kappa Phi. Methodist. Clubs: Baltimore Country, Lutherville Garden (pres. 1957-58), Woodbrook Murray Hill Garden, Woman's of Roland Park (gov. 1971-73). Home: 102 Estes Rd Baltimore MD 21212

MC KENNEY, JAMES FRANCIS, elec. mfg. co. exec.; b. Amsterdam, N.Y., June 21, 1914; s. James Keeley and Anna Beatrice (McNally) McK.; M.E., Rensselaer Poly. Inst., 1936; m. Frances Ann Burgess, June 21, 1947; children—Margaret, James Michael, Daniel, Mara. Student engr., design engr., then supervising engr. Gen. Electric Co., Pittsfield, Mass., 1936-58, mgr. engrng. documentation ordnance systems, 1962—; mgr. engring., mgr. engring., then mfg. producer goods Gen. Electric Argentina, 1958-62. Mem. fin. com. Town of Lenox (Mass.), 1971—, chmn., 1976—. Mem. ASME, Am. Def. Preparedness Assn., Sigma Xi (asso.). Democrat. Roman Catholic. Patentee in field. Home: 297 Old Stockbridge Rd Lenox MA 01240 Office: 100 Plastics Ave Pittsfield MA 01201

MC KENNEY, WALTER GIBBS, JR., lawyer, pub. co. exec.; b. Jacobsville, Md., Apr. 22, 1913; s. W. Gibbs and Mary (Starkey) McK.; student Williamsport Dickinson Sem., 1935-37; Ph.B., Dickinson Coll., 1939; LL.D. (hon.) Dickinson Sch. Law, 1964; LL.B., J.D., U. Va., 1942; m. Florence Roberta Rea, July 17, 1939. Admitted to Md. bar, 1942, since practiced in Balt. Partner Taxes and Estates, pub. co. Balt., 1946—; dir. Lutherville Supply & Equipment. Co., Equitable Trust Co., Equitable Bancorp., Alban Tractor Co. Lectr. Southwestern Grad. Sch. Banking, 1966-76. Pres. Balt. Estate Planning Council, 1963-64; dir. Balt. Civic Opera Co., 1963-68. Pres. Kelso Home for Girls, 1948—; pres. bd. child care Balt. Ann. Conf. Meth. Ch., 1961-64. Trustee Goucher Coll., Dickinson Coll., Lycoming Coll., Wesley Theol. Sem., Franklin Sq. Hosp. Served as lt. USNR, World War II. Mem. Am., Md., Balt. bar assns. Democrat. Methodist. Author (with J. Blake Lowe) Selling Life Insurance Through a Tax Approach, 1947. Editor of Taxes and Estates, 1946—; Minimizing Taxes, 1946—, The Educator, 1965—, The Patron, 1968—. Home: 102 Estes Rd Baltimore MD 21212 Office: Munsey Bldg Baltimore MD 21202

MC KENZIE, FRANCIS WALDO, asst. supt. schs.; b. West Somerville, Mass., Dec. 27, 1918; s. George Daniel and Leah Pearl (Thorne) McK.; B.S., Northeastern U., 1943; M.A., U. Chgo., 1945; Ph.D., Yale, 1957; m. Esther Horbal, June 5, 1943; children—Kendra Jean, Keith Thorne, Kristen Fraser. Dir. counseling service YMCA, Hartford, Conn., 1945-54; dir. guidance pub. schs., Darien, Conn., 1954-57, adminstrv. asst. for instrn., 1957-60, asst. supt., 1960-67; asst. supt. pub. schs., Brookline, Mass., 1967—. Vis. prof. psychology Trinity Coll., Hartford, 1950-54; lectr. U. Conn., Storrs, 1957-65, U. Bridgeport, (Conn.), 1958-67; co-dir. Brookline Early Edn. Project, 1971-72, sr. cons., 1972—; adj. prof. Boston U., 1973—, Boston Coll., 1978—; staff asso., invitational insts. for pupil personnel adminstrs. U.S. and Can., Harvard, summers 1963-69. Chmn. Darien Adv. Com. on the Gifted Child, 1955-57; mem. research and devel. com. Nat. Bd. YMCA N.Am., 1959-72. Bd. govs. YMCA, Darien, 1958-67; bd. dirs. Boston Project for Careers, 1972—, Boston Brookline Collaborative Center, 1972—, YMCA Counseling Services Greater Boston, 1967—. Recipient Alumni Key, The Acad., Northeastern U., 1963. Fellow Mass. Psychol. Assn.; mem. Am. Psychol. Assn., Am. Personnel and Guidance Assn., Nat. Assn. Pupil Personnel Adminstrs. (trustee), Mass. Assn. Pupil Personnel Adminstrs. (sec., 1973—, pres. 1974), Nat. Soc. Study Edn. Author: On Going to College, 1949; (with Seth Arsenian) Counseling in the YMCA, 1954; Life Plans of Intellectually S Superior Girls, 1957. Editor: Pupil Personnel Services: Goals and Services. Home: 85 Standish Rd Wellesley Hills MA 02181 Office: 333 Washington St Brookline MA 02146

MC KENZIE, MARY AGNES MUDD (MRS. TERENCE J. MCKENZIE), librarian, assn. exec.; b. Olton, Tex., Aug. 6, 1928; d. Benjamin Oliver and Annie Sallie (Herring) Mudd; B.A., N. Tex. State U., 1960; M.L.S., Cath. U. Am., 1970; m. Terence J. McKenzie, July 16, 1948; 1 son, Eric Francis. Asst. serial record and order divs. Library of Congress, 1949-50, head ordering unit, 1951-52, sr. editorial reviser East European Accessions Index, 1953-60, asst. head Am.-Brit. Exchange sect., 1961, editor Monthly Checklist of State Publs., 1962, asst. information officer, 1963-67; asst. librarian Conn. Coll., New London, 1967-68, librarian, 1968-74; exec. dir. New Eng. Library Bd., 1974-78; cons., writer, 1979—. Vice chmn. adv. council Conn. State Library, 1972-74; mem. Com. on Interracial Edn. and Coop., New London, 1971-73. Mem. Am. (sec. history sect., reference services div. 1969-71, councillor 1972-73), New Eng. (sec. 1970-71, v.p. 1971-72, pres. 1972-73), Conn. (sec. coll. and univ. sect. 1968-69, mem. steering com. plan for library devel. 1971-73) library assns., Assn. Coll. and Research Libraries (chmn. publs. com. 1975-77). Democrat. Contbr. articles to profl. jours. Home: Heritage Cove River Rd Essex CT 06426

MC KENZIE, RAY, anesthesiologist; b. Turua, N.Z., July 9, 1927; s. Robert Keith and Edith Harfield (Collingwood) McK.; student Hauraki Plains Coll., 1939-45; M.B. Ch.B., U. Otago, 1952; m. Barbara Mavis Snelling, Dec. 11, 1954; children—Robyn Kay, William Brett, Melvern Craig, Glenn Carrick. Intern, Auckland (N.Z.) Hosp., 1953, resident, 1954-56, cons. anesthetist, 1961-66; dir. anesthesia Mowasat Hosp., Kuwait, 1967-69; asst. prof. U. Pitts., 1969-71, asso. prof., 1971-77, prof., 1977—; dir. surg. anesthesia Magee-Women's Hosp., Pitts., 1971-73, dir. anesthesia, 1973—. Mem. Bro.'s Bro. Found., 1971—. Served with Royal N.Z. Air Force, 1957-59. Fellow Faculty Anesthetists Royal Coll. Surgeons (Eng.); mem. Internat. Research Soc., Pa. Med. Soc., Am., Pa., Western Pa. socs. anesthesiologists. Home: 1055 Devon Rd Pittsburgh PA 15213 Office: Magee-Women's Hosp Halket and Forbes Sts Pittsburgh PA 15213

MC KENZIE, WALTER LAWRENCE, pharm. chemist; b. Somerville, Mass., Apr. 6, 1938; s. Frank Joseph and Marion Gertrude (Sullivan) McK.; B.S., Mass. Coll. Pharmacy, 1960, M.S., 1962, Ph.D., 1971; m. Mary Dorothy Golden, Aug. 29, 1959; children—Walter Lawrence, Kevin, Jacqueline, Daniel. With Astra Pharm., Co., Worcester, Mass., 1963-72, sect. head; asso. dir. Eaton Labs., Norwich, N.Y., 1972-75; dir. Westwood Pharm., Inc., Buffalo, 1976—. Chmn. Community Devel. Com., Northboro, Mass., 1967-69. Bd. dirs. Youth Hockey Programs, 1969-75. Hoyt Pharm. Co., research grantee, 1961-62. Mem. Am. Chem. Soc., Parenteral Drug Assn. (dir. 1974-75, research com. 1971-75), Soc. Cosmetic Chemists (exec. com. 1966-68), Acad. Pharm. Scis., Proprietary Assn. (task group 1973-76, 76—), Pharm. Mfrs. Assn., Rho Chi. Home: 30 Belvoir Rd Williamsville NY 14221 Office: 468 Dewitt St Buffalo NY 14213

MC KERNAN, JANIS L(EIGH), nurse; b. New London, Conn., June 17, 1949; d. Joseph B. and Shirley M. McKernan; student Central Conn. State Coll., 1967-69; diploma Hartford Hosp. Sch. Nursing, 1969-72; student R.I. Coll., 1974—. Nurses' aide Westerly (R.I.) Nursing Home, 1968-72, grad. nurse, 1972, charge nurse, 1972-74; charge nurse neuro-psychiat. service R.I. Hosp., Providence, 1972-73; charge nurse psychiat. in-patient service, Providence, 1973-74; with R.I. Med. Center Inst. Mental Health, Cranston, 1974—, supervising registered nurse in-patient acute psychiat. services for females, 1975-77, supervising registered nurse rehab. unit, 1977—; pres. collective-bargaining unit of R.N.'s of R.I. Med Center, 1976—. Mem. Am., R.I. nurses's assns. Home: 81 Killey Ave Warwick RI 02889

MCKINLEY, DONALD BLACK, constrn. cons.; b. N.Y.C., Aug. 19, 1913; s. Joseph Andrew and Jennie Stewart (Black) McK.; B.C.E., Rensselaer Poly. Inst., 1936; m. Charlotte Louise Meurs, Oct. 1, 1938; children—Janet Meurs Horton, Susan Black Carpemter, Elizabeth Stewart Loomis. Chief engr. N.Y. State Postwar Planning Commn., 1943; partner Charles Sells & Donald McKinley, 1953-57; v.p. ops. Spencer White & Prentis, Inc., N.Y.C., 1957-78, also dir.; cons. Past commr. N.Y. State Pky. Authority; guest lectr. Cairo Conf. Tall Bldgs. Served to lt. C.E., USNR, World War II. Fellow ASCE; mem. Am. Soc. Mil. Engrs. Clubs: Stratton Country (Bondsville, Vt.); Timber Ridge Ski (Windham, Vt.); Quail Ridge County (Del Ray, Fla.). Contbr. articles to profl. publs. Home: RD 1 Chester VT 05143

MCKINLEY, JOHN KEY, petroleum co. exec.; b. Tuscaloosa, Ala., Mar. 24, 1920; s. Virgil Parks and Mary Emma (Key) McK.; B.S. in Chem. Engring., U. Ala., 1940, M.S. in Organic Chemistry, 1941, LL.D. (hon.), 1972; LL.D. (hon.), Troy State U., 1974; m. Helen Heare, July 19, 1946; children—John Key, Mark Charles. Chem. engr. Texaco Inc., Port Arthur, Tex., 1941, asst. supr. cracking research, 1953, supr., 1954, asst. dir. research, Beacon, N.Y., 1957, asst. to v.p. research and tech. dept., 1959, mgr. comml. devel., 1960, gen. mgr. petrochem. dept., N.Y., 1960, v.p. petrochems. dept., also v.p. in charge v.p. supply and distbn., 1967-71, sr. v.p. worldwide refining, petrochems. and supply and distbn., 1971, pres., dir., 1971—; chmn. bd. Texaco Devel. Corp., 1971—; dir. Burlington Industries. Bd. govs. Hugh O'Brian Youth Found. Served as maj. AUS, 1941-45; ETO. Decorated Bronze Star; recipient George Washington honor medal Freedoms Found., 1972. Andrew Wellington Cordier fellow Columbia U. Registered profl. engr., Tex. Fellow Am. Inst. Chem. Engrs.; mem. Am. Petroleum Inst. (dir.), Am. Chem. Soc., Mfg. Chemists Assn. (dir.), Sigma Xi, Tau Beta Pi, Gamma Sigma Epsilon, Kappa Sigma. Clubs: Wee Burn Country (Darien, Conn.); The Brook (N.Y.C.); Blind Brook Country (Port Chester, N.Y.); N.Y. Yacht, Cloud (N.Y.C.). Patentee in chem. and processing field. Home: 26 Parsons Walk Darien CT 06820 Office: 2000 Westchester Ave White Plains NY 10650

MCKINNEY, CHARLES MILTON, III, archeologist; b. Dallas, June 23, 1940; s. Charles Milton and Gladys Marie (Anderson) McK.; B.A., Am. U., 1969, M.A., 1974; m. Eileen Patricia Cherban, June 10, 1967; children—Rachel Lynne, Allison Marie. Research asso. Muse d'Bardo, Algiers, Algeria, 1964-66; archeologist, fellow Smithsonian Instn., Washington, 1967-70; archeologist Nat. Park Service, Dept. Interior, Washington, 1972-77, supervisory archeologist Heritage Conservation and Recreation Service, 1978—, mgr. Fed. Antiquities Program, 1973—. Bd. dirs. Sunfield Homeowners Assn., 1974-75. Served with USMC, 1961-66. Mem. Am. Soc. Conservation Archeology, Soc. Am. Archeology, Am. Quaternary Soc., Internt. Conf. Underwater Archeology, Soc. Hist. Archeology, Council Abandoned Mil. Posts. Republican. Lutheran. Contbr. articles to profl. jours. Home: 1125 Treeside Ln Herndon VA 22070 Office: Dept Interior 18th and C Sts NW Washington DC 20240

MC KINNEY, JAMES MORTON, chemist; b. Rochester, N.Y., Apr. 5, 1918; s. William Arthur and Esther Florence (Morton) McK.; B.A., Oberlin Coll., 1940; postgrad. U. Chgo., 1941. With Wis. Steel Co., Chgo., 1942; analytical chemist Am. Cyanamid Co., Bound Brook, N.Y., 1946—. Served with Signal Corps, U.S. Army, 1942-45. Address: 19 New Rd Kendall Park NJ 08824

MC KINNEY, JOHN FRANCIS, educator; b. Orange, N.J., July 9, 1931; s. Francis Thomas and Anna Rita (Sullivan) McK.; B.A., Seton Hall U., 1958, M.A., 1960; Ed.D., Fairleigh Dickinson U., 1978. m. Marie Catherine McGuire, June 3, 1961; children—Maureen, Christopher, Jacqueline, Peter. Asst. to rec. dir. Savoy Records, Newark, 1953-58; asso. prof. English and speech Seton Hall U., South Orange, N.J., 1959-65; asso. prof. English, Felician Coll., Lodi, N.J., 1958-72; prof. Bergen Community Coll., Paramus, N.J., 1972—; host Theme and Variations, Sta. WSOU, South Orange, 1972—. Vice pres. Fair Lawn Com. for Peace in Viet Nam, 1966-72; cons. to Democratic nominee for Congress Arthur Lesemann, 1970, 72. N.J. Dept. Higher Edn. grantee, 1974; Rutgers Inst. Jazz Studies grantee, 1975. Mem. Nat. Council Tchrs. English, Modern Lang. Assn., Cath. Poetry Soc. Am. (dir. 1963-68), Poetry Soc. Am. (dir. 1969-72), Craftsmen of N.Y., Nat. Assn. Jazz Educators. Republican. Roman Catholic. Club: K.C. Numerous poetry recordings for Spirit Records; contbg. author: Arts Catalog of New Jersey, 1978. Home: 172 Graham Terr Saddle Brook NJ 07662 Office: Bergen Community Coll Paramus NJ 07652

MCKINNEY, STEWART B., congressman; b. Pitts., Jan. 30, 1931; grad. Kent (Conn.) Sch., 1949; student Princeton, 1949-51; B.A. in Am. History, Yale, 1958; m. Lucie Cunningham; children—Stewart B., Lucie, Jean, Libby, John. Mem. Conn. Gen. Assembly, 1966-70, minority leader, 1969-70; mem. 92d-96th congress from 4th dist. Conn. Past pres. Fairfield br. A.R.C., Bridgeport Symphony. Bd. dirs. Bridgeport Hosp., Bridgeport Child Guidance Clinic, Eastern Fairfield County Rehab. Center. Republican. Home: Fairfield CT Office: Cannon House Office Bldg Washington DC 20515*

MC KINNON, JAMES JOSEPH, JR., hosp. adminstr.; b. New Haven, Conn., July 5, 1930; s. James Joseph and Rose Jane (Bump) McK.; grad. Culinary Inst. Am., 1954; m. Ernestine A. Weber, Dec. 23, 1950; children—James Joseph, Karen E., Catherine M., George E.G., Robert D.C., Michael J. Chef, St. Raphael Hosp., New Haven, 1954-57; food mgr. High Meadows, Hamden, Conn., 1957-69; dir. food services Vets. Home and Hosp., Rocky Hill, Conn., 1969—. Served with inf. U.S. Army, 1950-52. Mem. V.F.W. Home and Office: Veterans Home and Hospital Rocky Hill CT 06067

MC KINNON, LINDA MARY, bus. exec.; b. Manchester, N.H., Aug. 27, 1940; d. Charles E. and Flora B. (Cherry) Berry; B.S., Boston U., 1963; M.B.A., Rivier Coll., 1978; m. Archie C. McKinnon, Sept. 26, 1964; 1 son, Daniel J. Asst. chemist Kendall Co., Cambridge, 1962-64; librarian Monsanto Research Corp., Everett, Mass., 1964-67; materials engr. Sanders Assos. Inc., Nashua, N.H., 1967-70, mgr. tech. lit. research, 1970—. Mem. Am. Chem. Soc., Am. Soc. Metals, ASTM, ASME, Spl. Libraries Assn., Internat. Solar Energy Soc. Home: Courtland Ave RFD 3 Manchester NH 03103 Office: Sanders Assos Daniel Webster Hwy Nashua NH 03061

MC KISSICK, GAYLORD EDWARD, veterinarian; b. New Castle, Pa., July 27, 1932; s. Edward Lee and Opal Marie (Burdett) McK.; B.S., Westminster Coll., 1954; V.M.D., U. Pa., 1958, M.S., 1961; Ph.D., Purdue U., 1964; m. Barbara Jane Skiff, Aug. 25, 1956; 1 son, Eric Edward. Asst. pathologist Phila. Zool. Gardens, 1958-61; instr. virology, pathology, anatomy Purdue U., 1961-64; asst. prof. pathology Ohio State U., 1964-68, asso. prof., 1968-70; sr. research fellow Merck & Co., Ins., Rahway, N.J., 1970-76, asst. dir., Somerville, N.J., 1976—. Mem. Somerset Valley C. of C. (dir. 1977), Am. Coll. Vet. Pathologists, Am. Coll. Vet. Microbiologists, AVMA, Conf. Research Workers in Animal Disease. Presbyterian. Home: 108 Branch Rd Bridgewater NJ 08807 Office: 203 River Rd Somerville NJ 08876

MC KNIGHT, DANIEL FRANCIS, motor carrier co. exec.; b. N.Y.C., Nov. 25, 1916; s. John J. and Josephine (Dunn) McK.; B.S., Fordham U., 1938; m. Katherine G. Anderson, Apr. 19, 1941; children—Daniel F., Patricia A. Supr. customer services B. Altman & Co., N.Y.C., 1938-43; engaged in ops. United Parcel Service Am., N.Y., 1943-50, Pitts., 1950-52, Wis., 1952-55, N.Y., 1956-59, v.p. N.Y. ops., 1958-59, v.p. nat. labor relations, corp. hdqrs. group, 1959—, v.p. mgmt. devel., 1977—, dir., 1969—. Pres., West Lyon Farm Condominium Assn. Served with AUS, 1943-46. Mem. Am. Mgmt. Assn., N.Y.C. Chamber Commerce and Industry (nat. affairs com.). Club: N.Y. Athletic. Home: 112 W Lyon Farm Dr Greenwich CT 06830 Office: 51 Weaver St Greenwich CT 06830

MC KNIGHT, JOYCE SHELDON, counselor; b. Meadville, Pa., Oct. 12, 1949; d. Seth Carlyle and Juanita Bessie (Sheets) Sheldon; B.A. in Psychology and Sociology, Allegheny Coll., 1971; M.Ed. in Counseling, Gannon Coll., 1977: m. Hugh Frank McKnight, Aug. 22, 1970; 1 son, Frank Nathan. Asst. met. dir. Ecumenical Inst., Chgo. and Tulsa, 1970-73; health planner E. Okla. Devel. Dist., Muskogee, 1973; juvenile counselor Tulsa County Aftercare Program, 1973; program specialist psycho-social rehab. Counseling Services Center, Corry, Pa., 1975-77; counselor Adult Diploma Program, Corry, 1974—; dir. Anchor House Agy., Corry, 1977-78. Pres. Corry Concerned for Youth, Inc., 1975-77; pres. Community Care Council of Agys., Corry, 1976—, sec., 1975; mem. steering com. Vol. Action Center, Corry, 1977; bd. dirs. Erie County Citizens Coalition for Human Services, Erie, 1978—. Mem. Pa. Assn. Pub. Continuing Adult Edn. (dir. 1977-78), Rural Mental Health Assn., Nat. Assn. Social Workers, Am. Personnel and Guidance Assn., Commonwealth Prevention Alliance, Cory Bus. and Profl. Women. Methodist. Contbr. research, papers in field. Home and Office: 217 Fairview St Corry PA 16407

MCKOY, LATTICE ALICE, nursing adminstr.; b. Rose Hill, N.C., Mar. 22, 1926; s. Lewis Benjamin and Mary Alice (Herring) Boykin; grad. Community Hosp. Sch. Nursing, Wilmington, N.C., 1948; B.S., U. Md., 1958, M.S. in Nursing, 1960, postgrad., 1975-79; m. Romay McKoy, Aug. 29, 1969. Head nurse Community Hosp., Wilmington, N.C., 1948-49; staff nurse Meharry Med. Coll., Nashville, 1949-52; supr. Lincoln Hosp., Durham, N.C., 1952; staff nurse Freedmen's Hosp., Washington, 1952-53; head nurse pediatric unit Provident Hosp., Balt., 1954-58; instr. psychiat. nursing Seton Psychiat. Inst., Balt., 1960-66; dir. nursing Crownsville (Md.) Hosp. Center, 1966—. Mem. Adv. Council Balt. City Mental Health. Recipient various awards for poetry, 1972—. Mem. Am. Nurses Assn., Nat. League Nursing, Md. Nurses Assn. Democrat. Baptist. Home: Route 3 Box 958 Waterbury Dr Crownsville MD 21032 Office: Crownsville Hosp Center Crownsville MD 21032

MCKUSICK, VINCENT LEE, state chief justice; b. Parkman, Maine, Oct. 21, 1921; s. Carroll Lee and Ethel (Buzzell) McK.; A.B., Bates Coll., 1943; S.B., S.M., Mass. Inst. Tech., 1947; LL.B., Harvard U., 1950; LL.D., Colby Coll., 1976; m. Nancy Elizabeth Green, June 23, 1951; children—Barbara Jane, James Emory, Katherine, Anne Elizabeth. Admitted to Maine bar, 1952; law clk. to Chief Judge Learned Hand, 1950-51, to Justice Felix Frankfurter, 1951-52; partner Pierce, Atwood, Scribner, Allen & McKusick and predecessors, Portland, Maine, 1953-77; chief justice Maine Supreme Ct., 1977—; Mem. Supreme Jud. Ct. Adv. Com. Maine Rules of Civil Procedure, 1957-59, chmn., 1966-75; commr. on uniform state laws, 1968-76, sec. nat. conf., 1975-77. Trustee, Bates Coll.; mem. overseers vis. com. Harvard Law Sch.; past trustee Kent's Hill Sch., Maine Hist. Soc., Portland YMCA. Served with AUS, 1943-46. Manhattan Project, Los Alamos, 1945-46. Fellow Am. Bar. Found. (dir. 1977—); mem. Am. (chmn. fed. rules com. 1966-71, bd. editors Jour. 1971—, chmn. bd. editors 1976-77), Maine County bar assns., Am. Judicature Soc. (dir. 1976—), Am. Law Inst. (council 1968—), Maine Jud. Council (chmn. 1977—), Phi Beta Kappa, Sigma Xi, Tau Beta Pi. Republican. Unitarian. Clubs: Rotary (hon.; past pres. Portland), Harvard of N.Y. Author: Patent Policy of Educational Institutions, 1947; (with Richard H. Field) Maine Civil Practice, 1959, supplements 1962, 67, (with Richard H. Field and L. Kinvin Wroth) 2d edit., 1970, supplements, 1972, 74, 77, also articles in legal publs. Home: 1152 Shore Rd Cape Elizabeth ME 04107 Office: Cumberland County Courthouse PO Box 4910 Portland ME 04112*

MC LAIN, RICHARD LEE, educator; b. Colorado Springs, Colo., Nov. 28, 1939; s. Wade Charles and Vera Regena (Aschermann) McL.; B.A., U. Calif. at Berkeley, 1965, M.A., 1966, Ph.D., 1972; m. Catherine Roumasset, Apr. 3, 1966; children—David Lee, Christopher James. Prof., English and linguistics State U. N.Y. at Binghamton, 1972—, dir. expository writing, 1972—; Fulbright prof. theoretical linguistics U. Cluj (Romania), 1977-78. Served with AUS, 1958-61. Mem. Modern Lang. Assn., State U. Council on Linguistics, Linguistic Soc. Am. Editor: The Quire, 1965-67; Contemporary Stylistic Criticism in English: An Anthology, 1978. Contbr. poems and articles to profl. jours. Home: 4 Crestmont Rd Binghamton NY 13905 Office: Dept English State U NY Binghamton NY 13901

MC LAIN, WILLIAM TOME, educator; b. Washington, July 10, 1935; s. Ronald Alpha and Dorothy (Tome) McL.; B.A., U. Del., 1957; M.Ed., 1966; m. Meurial C. Webb, Nov. 20, 1977. Tchr. math., psychology Newark (Del.) High Sch., 1957-69, high sch. adminstrv. asst., 1969—. Mem. Del-Mar-Va council Boy Scouts Am., vice chmn. Lenape dist., recipient Silver Beaver, Order of Merit, Eagle Scout awards; trustee United Methodist Ch. Recipient Tchrs. medal Freedoms Found. at Valley Forge, 1968; Distinguished Service award Newark Jr. C. of C., 1968; Friend of Edn. award Newark Schs. Edn. Assn., 1976. Mem. Del. Assn. Sch. Adminstrs., Del. Assn. Sch. Bus. Ofcls., Assn. Sch. Bus. Ofcls. U.S. and Can., Nat., Del. assns. secondary sch. prins., Nat. Eagle Scout Assn. (past dir.), U. Del. Alumni Assn. (past dir.), Newark High Sch. Alumni Assn. (pres.), Internat. Platform Assn., Phi Delta Kappa. Home: PO Box 86 Newark DE 19711

MC LAUCHLIN, EVELYN FINK, state govt. ofcl.; b. Albany, N.Y., Feb. 19, 1934; d. Carl Samuel and Mary Magdalene (Zimmerman) Fink; student Empire State Coll., 1976—; children—John Scott, Jeffrey Channing. Successively ins. underwriter, installment loan officer, stock transfer agt. Schenectady Discount Corp., Albany, N.Y., 1950-69; asst. to dir. Legis. Commn. on Expenditure Review, State of N.Y., Albany, 1969—. Campaign coordinator United Way, Albany, 1970—; vol. Saratoga Performing Arts Center, N.Y., 1972—; blood program coordinator N.Y. State, 1970—; pres. N. Colonie Women's Republican Club, 1974-76. Mem. Women in State Govt., Purchasers Mgmt. Assn., N.Y. State Tng. Council. Lutheran. Clubs: Normanside Country; Mad River Ski; Tri-City Racquet. Home: 7 Chestnut Hill S Loudonville NY 12211 Office: 111 Washington Ave Albany NY 12210

MC LAUGHLIN, DONALD FRANCIS, tire distbr.; b. Patton, Pa., July 16, 1932; s. William Francis and Edith Elizabeth (Colberg) McL.; grad. high sch.; m. Marie Adoline Potter, May 17, 1954; children—Gregory, Maureen, Patrick, Brad, Erin. Retail sales Sears, Roebuck & Co., Salem, Ohio, 1950-52; saleman Boring Tire Service, Johnstown, Pa., 1952-58, gen. mgr., 1958-59, v.p., 1959-67, pres., chmn. bd., 1967—; mem. Eastern region Goodyear Dealer Council, 1971, 73, 76, chmn., 1976; mem. Nat. Goodyear Dealer Council, 1975-76; owner, operator McLaughlin Leasing Co. Served with AUS, 1950-52. Mem. Nat. Tire Dealer and Retreaders Assn., Am. Retreading Inst., Johnstown Area Regional Industries Assn., Western Pa. Tire Dealers Assn. Republican. Roman Catholic. Club: Elks. Home: 1118 Tener St Johnstown PA 15904 Office: 73 Hickory St Johnstown PA 15902

MC LAUGHLIN, EDWARD DAVID, surgeon; b. Ridley Park, Pa., Jan. 8, 1931; s. Edward D. and Catherine J. (Hilbert) McL.; B.S. magna cum laude, Georgetown U., 1952; M.D., Jefferson Med. Coll., 1956; m. Mary Louise Hanlon, June 20, 1959; children—Catherine, Louise, Edward, Patricia. Intern, Jefferson Med. Co.., Phila., 1956-57, resident in surgery, 1957-59; resident in surgery Jefferson Med. Coll. Hosp., Phila., 1962-64; practice medicine specializing in surgery; surg. asso. Nat. Cancer Inst., NIH, 1959-61, surgeon, 1961-62; teaching fellow Harvard Med. Sch., Boston and clin. research fellow Mass. Gen. Hosp., Boston, 1964-66; sr. surg. registrar Hawkmoor Chest Hosp., Davon, Eng., 1966-67; sr. surgeon Chestnut Hill Hosp., 1967-71; asst. prof. surgery Jefferson Med. Coll., 1968-72, asso. prof., 1972—, lectr. Jefferson Continuing med. edn. program, 1976-77; asso. chmn. of surgery Mercy Cath. Med. Center, Phila., 1972—. Chmn., Bethel Twp Planning Study Group, 1971-72, Bethel Twp. Sewer Authority, 1972-78. Served with USPHS, 1959-62. Recipient Mead Johnson award for research, 1962, Americus award K.C., 1963, Lindback award Jefferson Med. Coll., 1974; named Outstanding Prof. of 1976-77, Phi Alpha Sigma. Diplomate Am. Bd. Surgery. Fellow A.C.S.; mem. Phila. Acad. Surgery, N.Y. Acad. Scis., Med. Soc. State Pa., AAAS, Am. Soc. for Artificial Internal Organs, AMA, Pa. Thoracic Soc., Georgetown U. Alumni (dir. 1970-72, senator 1972—), Nu Sigma Nu, Alpha Kappa Kappa. Republican. Roman Catholic. Contbr. articles on research in cancer to med. jours. Home: 3112 Garnet Mine Rd Boothwyn PA 19061 Office: Misericordia Hosp 54th and Cedar Aves Philadelphia PA 19143

MC LAUGHLIN, HUGH DENNIS, JR., chemist, educator; b. Lindenwold, N.J., Dec. 21, 1935; s. Hugh Dennis and Florence Emma (Heartley) McL.; B.S. in Bus. Adminstrn., La Salle Coll., 1958, B.S. in Chemistry, 1970; m. Lucy Ann Flacco, May 7, 1960; children—Annamarie Jennine, Thomas, Michale. Sr. technician Shell Chem. Co., Woodbury, N.J., 1961-66; product devel. chemist Pennwalt Corp., King of Prussia, Pa., 1966-78; instr. chemistry and math. Student Edn. Center, Phila., 1978—. Fin. chmn. Somerdale Sch. Bd., 1970—; committeeman Boy Scouts Am., 1972-73. Served with U.S. Army, 1958-59, 60-61, to lt. col. Res. Mem. Am. Chem. Soc., Am. Soc. Metals, N.J. Sch. Bds. Assn., Res. Officers Assn., Assn. U.S. Army. Home: 633 W Somerdale Rd Somerdale NJ 08083 Office: 900 1st Ave King of Prussia PA 19406

MC LAUGHLIN, JOHN PATRICK, JR., advt. exec.; b. Morristown, N.J., July 13, 1932; s. John Patrick and Eleanor (Cox) McL.; A.B., Colgate U., 1954; m. Suzanne Roberts, Dec. 30, 1977; children by previous marriage—Mark John, Seth Nelson. With Compton Advt., N.Y.C., 1957-59, Ogilvy, N.Y.C., 1959-62, McCaffrey and McCall Inc., N.Y.C. 1962-64, Carl Ally, N.Y.C., 1964-66, Spade and Archer, N.Y.C., 1966-70; advt. exec., Keanan and McLaughlin Inc., N.Y.C., 1970-77; lectr. in field. Served with USN, 1955-57. Club: Essex County Country. Contbr. articles to Advt. Age. Home: 285 Glen Ave Short Hills NJ 07078 Office: 90 Park Ave New York City NY 10016

MC LAUGHLIN, WILLIAM EARLE, banker; b. Oshawa, Ont., Can., Sept. 16, 1915; s. Frank and Frankie L. (Houlden) McL.; B.A., Queen's U., Kingston, Ont., 1936; m. Ethel Wattie, July 20, 1940; children—William, Mary. With Royal Bank of Can., 1936—, mgr. Montreal br., 1951-53, asst. gen. mgr., 1953-59, asst. to pres., 1959-60, gen. mgr., 1960—, pres., 1960, chmn., pres., 1962-77, chmn. bd., chief exec. officer, 1977—; chmn. bd. Sun Alliance Ins. Co.; chmn. Canadian adv. com. Sun Alliance and London Ins. Group; trustee Sun Alliance & London Ins. Group, Canadian Staff Pension Plan; dir. Ralston Purina of Can., Ltd., Algoma Steel Corp., Ltd., Power Corp. Can., Ltd., Standard Brands, Inc., Genstar, Ltd., Met. Life Ins. Co., Security Reins. Corp. Ltd., Shawinigan Industries, Ltd., Adela Investment Co. S.A., Canadian Pacific Ltd., Royal Bank of Can. Trust Corp., Ltd., Gen. Motors Corp., Trans-Can. Corp. Fund, L'Air Liquide. Bd. govs. Royal Victoria Hosp. Clubs: Engineers, Royal Montreal Golf, Royal Montreal Curling, University, Mount Royal, Forest and Stream, St. James, Montreal; Seigniory (Montebello); Toronto, York (Toronto); Mt. Bruno Golf; Rideau (Ottawa, Can.); Canadian (N.Y.); Lyford Cay (Nassau); Mid-Ocean (Bermuda). Home: 67 Sunnyside Ave Westmount Montreal PQ H3Y 1C3 Canada Office: Royal Bank of Can Bldg Montreal PQ H3C 3A9 Canada

MC LAUGHLIN, WILLIAM LOWNDES, physicist; b. Stony Point, Tenn., Mar. 30, 1928; s. John Calvin Brown and Fanny Dargen (McCaa) McL.; student Potomac State Coll., 1945-47; B.S. in Physics, Hampden-Sydney Coll., 1949; postgrad Duke U., 1949-50, U. Tübingen, Germany, 1950-51; M.S. in Physics, George Washington U., 1963; m. Nancy Elizabeth Shepherd, Mar. 27, 1951; children—Peter Shepherd, David Wallace. Physicist, project leader Center for Radiation Research Nat. Bur. Standards, Washington, 1951—; cons. Risoe Nat. Lab., Roskilde, Denmark, Internat. Atomic Energy Agy., Vienna, Austria. Served with U.S. Army, 1954-56. Rotary Internat. fellow, 1950-51; Nat. Bur. Standards Fgn. Tng. grantee, 1970-71; recipient Dept. Commerce Silver medal, 1969. Mem. Soc. Photographic Sci. and Engring., Am. Phys. Soc., Optical Soc. Am., Health Physics Soc., Radiation Research Soc., N.Y. Acad. Sci., AAAS, Soc. Mfg. Engrs., ASTM. Presbyterian. Editor: International Journal of Applied Radiation and Isotopes, 1973—. Contbr. articles to profl. jours. Home: 3901 Albemarle St NW Washington DC 20016 Office: Center Radiation Research Nat Bur Standards Washington DC 20234

MC LEAN, ARLENE ELIZABETH ANDREWS (MRS. LEWIS FOLLETT MCLEAN), biometrician; b. nr. Coatesville, Pa., Nov. 11, 1941; d. William and Maude Elizabeth (Wheatley) Andrews; B.S. in Biology, Ursinus Coll., 1962; M.S. in Applied Statistics, Villanova U., 1967; Ph.D., Thomas Jefferson U., 1975; m. Lewis Follett McLean, Oct. 26, 1964. Research asst. Wyeth Labs., Radnor, Pa., 1962-64, adminstrv. asst., 1964-65; jr. statistician Merck, Sharp & Dohme Research Labs., West Point, Pa., 1966-67, statistician, 1967-69, sr. statistician, 1969-70, biometrician, 1970-71, head planning, coordination and analysis unit, 1971-76, dir. biologics evaluation and analysis, 1976—. Lectr. Villanova U., 1968-71. Mem. Am. Statis. Assn., Biometrics Soc., Am. Soc. Clin. Pharmacology and Therapeutics, Physiol. Soc. Phila., Soc. Neurosci., Sigma Xi. Home: 176 Kinsey Rd Harleysville PA 19438 Office: Merck Sharp & Dohme Research Labs Sumneytown Pike West Point PA 19486

MC LEAN, DONALD HOLMAN, JR., lawyer, med. center exec.; b. Elizabeth, N.J., Nov. 12, 1910; s. Donald Holman and Edna (Righter) McL.; grad. Phillips Acad., 1928; B.A., Amherst Coll., 1932, L.L.D. (hon.), 1977; LL.B., Yale, 1935; m. Martha Lamb, Sept. 2, 1939; children—Donald, Ruth (Mrs. James Lizotte), John, Barbara. Admitted to D.C. bar, 1936, N.Y. bar, 1938; practiced in N.Y.C., 1938-51, D.C., 1940-42; lawyer Milbank, Tweed, Hope & Hadley, N.Y.C., 1936-48; counsel Socony Vacuum Oil Co., N.Y.C., 1948-51; counsel, exec. John D. Rockefeller 3d, N.Y.C., 1951-65; pres. Lahey Clinic Found., Boston, 1965-75; dir. Summit and Elizabeth Trust Co., Summit, N.J., 1960-65; corporator Provident Inst. for Savs., Boston, 1965—; dir. Mass. Investors Trust, Mass. Investors Growth Fund, Inc., Mass. Income Devel. Fund, Inc., Mass. Capital Devel. Fund, Inc., Mass. Fin. Devel. Fund, Inc., Mass. Fin. Bond Fund, Inc., M.F.S. Managed Municipal Bond Fund. Mem. Council Fgn. Relations, N.Y.C., 1948—. Trustee Phillips Acad., pres. bd. 1968—; trustee Agrl. Devel. Council N.Y.C., chmn. 1973—. Served to lt. col. AUS, 1942-46. Decorated Legion of Merit with one oak leaf cluster. Mem. Am. Bar Assn. Clubs: University, Century (N.Y.C.); The Country Brookline, Mass.). Author: (with Francis T. Christy) The Transfer of Stock, 1940. Home: 187 Chestnut St Andover MA 01810

MC LEAN, LEWIS FOLLETT, neurophysiologist; b. Buffalo, Dec. 4, 1933; s. Lewis Follett and Anne Florence (Fitzsimmons) McL.; B.S., Canisius Coll., 1955; Ph.D., Thomas Jefferson U., 1972; m. Arlene E. Andrews, Oct. 26, 1964. Research asst. Roswell Park Research Inst., Buffalo, 1955-60; research asst. psychopharmacology dept. Wyeth Labs., Radnor, Pa., 1960-65; research asso. neurology dept. U. Pa., Phila., 1965-67; programmer computer systems Merck Sharp & Dohme, West Point, Pa., 1967-68, med. program coordinator, med. affairs, 1971-73, clin. asso., med. affairs, 1973—. Mem. Soc. Neurosci., Physiol. Soc. Phila., Mensa, Sigma Xi. Home: 176 Kinsey Rd Harleysville PA 19438 Office: Merck Sharp & Dohme Research Labs West Point PA 19486

MC LEAN, NELSON ALLEN, educator; b. Damariscotta Mills, Maine, Mar. 20, 1934; s. Harold J. and Leona (Oliver) McL.; B.S., U. N.H., 1954; M.Ed., U. Mass., 1963. Tchr. bus. Cushing Acad., Ashburnham, Mass., 1954-58; bus. and asst. headmaster Austin-Cate Acad., Center Strafford, N.H., 1958-59, headmaster, 1959—; bd. dirs. Teen Haven Home For Boys, 1974—, pres., 1978—. Bd. dirs., pres. Eastern dist. N.H. YMCA, pres. N.H. YMCA Assn. Mem. N.H. Edn. Assn. (sec. southeastern league 1963—). Home: Center Strafford NH 03815

MC LEAN, WILLIAM GEORGE, cons. engring. edn.; b. Scranton, Pa., Mar. 15, 1910; s. Michael and Matilda Marie (Geueke) McL.; B.S. in Elec. Engring., Lafayette Coll., 1932; M.S., Brown U., 1933. Head math. dept. West Scranton (Pa.) High Sch., 1934-37; asst. prof. mech. engring. Lafayette Coll., Easton, Pa., 1937-44; asst. to supr. spl. products div. Eastman Kodak Co., Rochester, N.Y., 1944-46; prof., head engring. sci. Lafayette Coll., 1946-75, dir. engring., 1962-75; cons. in field, 1950—. Chmn. Hugh Moore Park Commn., 1969—; mem. Am. Nat. Metric Practice Com., 1974—. Fellow ASME (nat. v.p. 1953-55, 70-72; Codes and Standards medal 1977); mem. Nat. Soc. Profl. Engrs. (pres. Pa. 1965-66), Am. Soc. Engring. Edn., Sigma Xi, Phi Beta Kappa, Tau Beta Pi, Eta Kappa Nu, Pi Tau Sigma, Kappa Delta Rho. Democrat. Roman Catholic. Author: (with E.W. Nelson) Engineering Mechanics, 1952, 3d edito., 1978; (with C.L. Best) Engring. Mechanics, 1965. Home and Office: 333 5th Ave Scranton PA 18505

MC LEAN, WILLIAM L., III, newspaper co. exec.; b. Phila., Oct. 4, 1927; s. William L. and Eleanor Ray (Bushnell) McL.; B.A., Princeton U., 1949; m. Elizabeth D. Peterson, Sept. 4, 1954; children—Elizabeth, William L. IV, Helen Brooke, Sandra, Warden. With Evening & Sunday Bull., Phila., 1949—, v.p., 1969-74, sr. v.p., 1974-75, editor, pub., 1975—. Mem. Pa. Newspaper Pubs. Assn. (chmn. fin. com., pres. 1964). Episcopalian. Club: Blooming Grove (Pa.) Hunting and Fishing. Office: Bulletin Co 30th and Market Sts Philadelphia PA 19101*

MC LEAN, WILMA CATHERN, pharmacist; b. Fort Wayne, Ind., Jan. 24, 1913; d. William and Sarah (Deahl) Fosler; B.S., Pharmacy, Purdue U., 1934; m. Donald I. McLean, Sept. 12, 1953; children—Jane S., Steven, Richard. Pharmacist Pranges Pharmacy, Fort Wayne, 1946-49; owner, pharmacist Fairfield Pharmacy, Fort Wayne, 1949-63; tchr. Westminster (Md.) pub. schs., 1965-66; dir. pharmacy Carroll County (Md.) Gen Hosp., Westminster, 1968—. Served with USN, 1944-45. Mem. Purdue Alumni Assn., Am., Ind., Md. pharm. assns., AAUW, Md., Am. socs. hosp. pharmacists, Balt. Met. Pharma. Assn., Alpha Chi Omega. Methodist. Home: 115 Smith Ave Westminster MD 21157 Office: Carroll County Gen Hosp 200 Meml Ave Westminster MD 21157

MC LEMORE, GEORGE AMMIE, JR., physician; b. Smithfield, N.C., July 4, 1925; s. George Ammie and Nell (Johnson) McL.; certificate medicine U. N.C., 1946; M.D., Harvard, 1948; m. Elizabeth Reinecke, Oct. 31, 1959; 1 dau., Elizabeth Johnson. Intern, Peter Bent Brigham Hosp., Boston, 1948-49, resident, 1954-55; research fellow U. London, 1950-51, Harvard, 1953-56; practice medicine specializing in internal medicine and cardiology, N.Y.C., 1956—; mem. staff N.Y., Drs. hosps., Meml. Center; clin. asst. prof. medicine Cornell Med. Coll., 1963—. Served as 1st lt. M.C., AUS, 1951-53. Diplomate Am. Bd. Internal Medicine. Fellow Am. Coll. Cardiology, A.C.P.; mem. A.M.A., Am. Soc. Internal Medicine. Presbyn. Clubs: Explorers, University (N.Y.C.). Contbr. articles to profl. jours. Research heart, lung diseases. Office: 728 Park Ave New York City NY 10021

MC LENDON, HEATH BRIAN, securities firm exec.; b. San Francisco, May 24, 1933; s. Jesse Heath and Clara Martha (Nelson) McL.; B.A., Stanford, 1955; M.B.A., Harvard, 1959; m. Judith Nelson Locke, May 30, 1959; children—Laurie, Eric, Brian and Michael (twins). Mgmt. trainee Standard Oil Calif., San Francisco, 1959-60; with Shearson Hayden Stone (and predecessor cos.), N.Y.C., 1960—, exec. v.p., 1971-77; pres. Bernstein-Macaulay Inc., Investment Advisors, 1977—. Trustee N.J. Shakespeare Festival, 1975—, Drew U. Served to lt. U.S. Army, 1955-57. Mem. N.Y. Soc. Security Analysts, Money Marketeers. Presbyterian. Club: Beacon Hill. Home: 17 Lenox Rd Summit NJ 07901 Office: 505 Park Ave New York NY 10022

MC LEOD, JOHN HENRY, physicist; b. Saltcoats, Sask., Can., Jan. 23, 1897; s. Donald and Mary Warwick Cowper (Meil) McL.; B.Sc., U. Sask., 1924; Ph.D., U. Toronto, 1929; m. Beatrice Elizabeth Wingrove, Aug. 17, 1928; children—Lorna Margaret, Donald Wingrove. Tutor physics Harvard U., 1929-34; researcher in optics and mechanics Eastman Kodak Co., Rochester, N.Y., 1934-68; ret., 1968. Served as fighter pilot Royal Flying Corps, 1918. Recipient David Richardson medal for work in optics and leadership, 1976. Fellow Optical Soc. Am. Presbyterian. Home: 110 Summit Dr Rochester NY 14620

MC LOUD, THERESA CLAIRE, radiologist; b. Boston, Jan. 5, 1944; s. Malcolm and Veronica Beatrice (Flynn) McL.; B.S., Boston Coll., 1964; M.D., McGill U., 1968. Intern, Royal Victoria Hosp., Montreal, Que., Can., 1968-69, resident 1969-73; asst. prof. radiology Yale U., 1974-76; staff radiologist Yale New Haven Hosp., New Haven, 1974-76; staff radiologist Mass. Gen. Hosp., Boston, 1976—; asst. prof. radiology Harvard U., 1976—. Winchester fellow, 1973-74. Mem. Am. Coll. Radiology, Assn. Univ. Radiologists, New Eng. Roentgen Ray Soc., Sigma Xi. Office: Dept of Radiology Mass Gen Hosp Boston MA 02114

MC MAHON, CAROL ELLEN, psychologist; b. Buffalo, Aug. 6, 1946; d. George Patrick and Helen Frances (Maloney) McM.; A.B., State U. N.Y., Buffalo, 1970; M.S., Pa. State U., 1972, Ph.D., 1973; m. Rajeev N. Parikh, Aug. 29, 1975; 1 dau., Monica McMahon. Postdoctoral fellow State U. N.Y., Buffalo, 1973-75, NIMH grantee, 1974-75, research asso., 1975—, Am. Philos. Soc. grantee, 1977-78; instr., invited lectr. in field. NSF trainee, 1972, 73. Mem. Am. Psychosomatic Soc., Am. Psychol. Assn., Soc. Psychophysiol. Research, History of Sci. Soc., Internat. Soc. History of Behavioral and Social Scis. Contbr. articles to profl. publs. Home: 8703 Lower East Hill Rd Colden NY 14033 Office: 4230 Ridge Lea Rd Amherst NY 14226

MC MAHON, GERALD FRANCIS, govt. ofcl.; b. Council Bluffs, Iowa, Nov. 7, 1922; s. James P. and Mary E. (White) McM.; B.A., U. Iowa, 1950; Fels fellow, U. Pa., 1950-51; m. Elsie Fox, Feb. 26, 1953; 1 dau., Gail Ann. Mil. govt. ofcl., Bavaria, W. Ger., 1945-49; adminstrv. asst. to county mgr. Warwick County (Va.), 1951-52; cons. to Va. cities and counties, 1952-53; asst. to city mgr. San Leandro (Calif.), 1953-56; city mgr. Martinez (Calif.), 1956-58; dept. chief adminstrv. officer Fresno (Calif.), 1958-62; city mgr. Fairbanks (Alaska), 1962-65; cons. pub. adminstrn., 1965-66; with FAA, Anchorage, 1966-75, specialist, Washington, 1975—. Charter commr. Greater Anchorage Borough, 1969-71; pres. Anchorage Citizens Council, 1971-72. Served to capt., inf., U.S. Army, 1942-47; ETO. Recipient Pub. Service award Anchorage Fedn. Execs. Assn., 1973; various awards FAA, 1971-76. Mem. Alaska City Mgrs. Assn. (pres. 1964). Contbr. articles to profl. jours. Home: 1819 N Brunswick Sterling Park VA 22170 Office: AAP-600 800 Independence Ave Washington DC 20591

MC MAHON, JOHN PATRICK, accountant; b. N.Y.C., Feb. 17, 1910; s. James Joseph and Mary (McHugh) McM.; B.A., Coll. City N.Y., 1937; m. Lucille Margaret Keating, Oct. 13, 1941; children—John James, Mary McMahon Cramer, Jane McMahon Kennedy, Margaret McMahon Lareau. Auditor, Brit. Purchasing Commn., N.Y.C., 1940-41; fgn. funds control investigator U.S. Dept. Treasury, N.Y.C., 1941-43, spl. agt. IRS, Boston, 1946-55; asso. prof. accounting Babson Coll., Babson Park, Mass., 1955-67; pvt. practice accounting Wellesley, Mass., 1955—. Served to comdr., USNR, 1943-46. C.P.A. Mem. Am. Inst. C.P.A.'s, Mass. Soc. C.P.A.'s. Roman Catholic. Club: Wardroom. Home: 98 Oak St Wellesley MA 02181

MC MAHON, JOSEPH JOHN, educator; b. N.Y.C., Nov. 15, 1933; s. John and Margaret (Kiernan) M.; B.A., Marist Coll., 1955; M.A. in Philosophy, Catholic U., 1962: M.A. in Counselling Psychology, Manhattan Coll., 1970; profl. diploma in counselling Fordham U., 1979; Ph.D., St. John's U., 1973; m. Joanna Dimocrati, Mar. 3, 1969; 1 child, Aris. Tchr. St. Helena High Sch., Bronx, N.Y., 1955-62; asst. prin. Marist Prep. Sch., Cold Spring, N.Y., 1962-63; registrar Marist Coll., Poughkeepsie, N.Y., 1966-67; dir. student devel. Harriman (N.Y.) Coll., 1972-73; asso. dean coll. continuing edn. State U. of N.Y. at Farmingdale, 1973-77; asso. prof. philosophy and edn. Unification Theol. Sem., Barrytown, N.Y., 1977—, v.p. Center for Law, Philosophy and Citizenship, 1975—; dir. Center for Pragmatic Living, N.Y.C., 1977—; co-dir. Marist Inst. Theol., Marist Coll., 1963-67. N.Y. Archdiocesan fellow U. Paris, 1967-68. Mem. Am. Personnel and Guidance Assn., Am. Catholic Philosophy Assn., Assn. for Humanistic Edn. and Devel., Kappa Delta Pi. Roman Catholic. Contbr. research study in field. Address: 38-24 Corporal Stone St Bayside NY 11361

MC MAHON, MICHAEL JAMES, systems analyst; b. Bklyn., July 15, 1951; s. James Joseph and Natalie Therese (Biasi) McM.; B.S., Poly. Inst. Bklyn., 1973; M.S. in E.E., Fairleigh Dickinson U., 1977; m. Mary Ann Vallone, Sept. 16, 1973; 1 dau., Maureen. Fin. analyst Citicorp, N.Y.C., 1973-74; elec. engr. U.S. Army Electronics Command, Fort Monmouth, N.J., 1974-78, Communications Research and Devel. Command, 1978—. Mem. Poly. Inst. N.Y. Alumni Assn. (asso. dir.). Club: Fort Monmouth Officers. Home: 36 Spruce Rd Howell NJ 07731 Office: CORADCOM Fort Monmouth NJ 07703

MC MAHON, WILLIAM JAMES, physician; b. Niagara Falls, N.Y., June 15, 1921; s. William and Madge McM.; B.A., Holy Cross Coll., 1943; M.D., Georgetown U., 1946; children—William Dan, Margaret. Intern, Gallinger Municipal Hosp., Washington, 1946-47, resident in pediatrics, 1950-51; resident in pediatrics Georgetown U. Hosp., 1949-50; practice medicine specializing in pediatrics, Niagara Falls, 1951—; head pediatrics St. Mary's Hosp., Niagara Falls, 1978—. Chmn., Am. Cancer Soc., 1975—. Served as flight surgeon USAAF, 1943-48. Fellow Am. Acad. Pediatrics. Roman Catholic. Address: 515 3d St Niagara Falls NY 14301

MC MANUS, EUGENE JOSEPH, mfg. co. exec.; b. Columbia, S.C., Jan. 19, 1936; s. Eugene Joseph and Minnie Grace (Kelly) McM.; B.S. in Engring. Physics, Auburn U., 1957; M.A. in Math., U. Ala., 1965; M.B.A., Clark U., 1972; m. Rene T. Thompson, May 7, 1960; children—Eugene Joseph, Peyton Meriwether, Porter Telfair. Solid state research physicist U.S. Army Missile Readiness Command, Redstone Arsenal, Ala., 1960-65; systems interface engr. missile systems div. Raytheon Co., Bedford, Mass., 1965-72, sr. systems analyst, 1972-76, tech. mktg. mgr., 1976—; asso. prof. mktg. Western New Eng. Coll., 1976—; adj. prof. mgmt. Fitchburg State Coll., 1972-78, vis. lectr. math., 1978. Sec., Stow (Mass.) Indsl. Devel. Commn., 1973-76; scoutmaster Algonquin council Boy Scouts Am., 1974-76; chmn. Stow Hist. Commn., 1976—. Served with U.S. Army, 1958-60. Recipient Eagle Scout award Boy Scouts Am., 1951, Scout Leader Wood Badge award, 1976. Mem. Am. Mgmt. Assn. Roman Catholic. Clubs: Lions (Stow); K.C. Papers reviewer IEEE Transactions Engring. Mgmt., 1969—. Home: 17 Wedgewood Rd Stow MA 01775 Office: Raytheon Co Hartwell Rd Bedford MA 01730

MCMANUS, THOMAS PATRICK, pediatrician; b. N.Y.C., May 19, 1919; s. James Francis and Ellen Mary (Cain) McM.; B.A., U. Notre Dame, 1941; M.D., State U. N.Y., Bklyn., 1944; m. Eileen McLaughlin, Oct. 30, 1946; children—Patricia, Suzanne, Siobhan, Thomas, Paul, John. Intern, St. Vincent's Hosp., N.Y.C., 1944-45, resident, 1945-46; resident Willard Parker Hosp., N.Y.C., 1948, St. Francis Hosp., Roslyn, N.Y., 1948-49; dir. pediatrics Mid Island Hosp., Bethpage, N.Y., 1955-56, Southside Hosp., Bayshore, N.Y., 1956—; practice medicine, specializing in pediatrics, West Islip, N.Y., 1947—; mem. Suffolk County Bd. Health, 1974—; asst. clin. prof. pediatrics State U. N.Y. at Stony Brook Med. Sch., 1971—. Served from 1st lt. to capt., M.C., USAF, 1946-48. Fellow Am. Acad. Pediatrics; mem. N.Y. State, Suffolk County med. socs., Suffolk County Pediatric Soc. (past pres.). Roman Catholic. Club: Southward Ho! Country. Office: 1111 Montauk Hwy West Islip NY 11795

MC MANUS, WILLIAM FRANCIS, psychologist; b. N.Y.C.; s. Michael Joseph and Mary Ann (Earley) McM.; B.A., Cath. U., Washington, 1943; B.D., St. Mary's U., Balt., 1948, S.T.L., 1951; M.S., St. John's U., N.Y.C., 1968, Ph.D., 1973; m. Mary C. O'Hara, July 15, 1972. Asst. dir. Holy Name Center, N.Y.C., 1957-62; asst. dir., dir. Family Life Bur., N.Y.C., 1962-67; counselor St. Michael's and St. Claire Acad., N.Y.C., 1968-70; asso. prof. psychology Mercy Coll., Dobbs Ferry, N.Y., 1970—; dir. Clin. Assos. Greater N.Y., Douglaston, 1973—; dir. grad. studies in counseling and guidance L.I. U., Dobbs Ferry, N.Y., 1977—; pvt. practice psychotherapy, Dix Hill, N.Y., 1975—; cons. Parish Counseling Services, Great Neck, N.Y., 1973—, Counseling Service for Religious Personnel, Rockville Center, N.Y., 1977—. Mem. AAUP, Biofeedback Soc., Am. Assn. Advancement Tension Control, Internat. Transactional Analysis Assn., Am., Eastern psychol. assns. Author: Marriage Guide for the Engaged, 1961. Home: 10 Knell Lane Dix Hills NY 11746

MCMASTER, GLORIA MAE BUGNI, mezzo-soprano, educator; b. Montreal, Wis.; d. Anton George and Rose (Gatto) Bugni; student U. Minn.; B.S., Juilliard Sch. Music, N.Y.C.; postgrad. Columbia U. Detroit, State U. N.Y., Brockport; Mus.M., Eastman Sch. Music, U. Rochester; m. Chester L. McMaster (dec. Dec. 8, 1972); children—Chester Anthony, Raymond Dale, Brian Monroe, Maureen Anne, Heather Lynn; m. 2d, Martin Juhn, II, July 30, 1977. Performed in concert, oratorio, opera throughout U.S., including solo appearances with Juilliard Opera Theater, Chautauqua Opera Assn., Rochester Opera Theater; appeared as soloist with Mpls. Symphony, Rochester (N.Y.) Philharmonic, Buffalo Philharmonic, Music Theater of Rochester, Eastman Rochester Symphony, Rochester, Hornell (N.Y.) Symphony; recitals at Youngstown, Ohio, Ironwood, Mich., Hornell, Alfred and Rochester, N.Y.; concerts Nazareth Art Center, Nat. Opera Assn., New Orleans; dir. Dansville (N.Y.) Music Theater; asst. prof. Youngstown State U., State U. Coll., Geneseo, N.Y.; now prof. music Houghton (N.Y.) Coll.; dir. Dansville Music Theater, 1972—. Appeared in title role Nat. Edn. Television prodn. The Medium. Mem. exec. com. Livingston County Young Republicans; mem. president's leadership council U. Rochester; mem. assos. U. Rochester. Mem. AAUW (past pres. Dansville area br.), AAUP (past chpt. exec. bd.), Nat. Opera Assn., Nat. Assn. Tchrs. Singing, Juilliard Alumni Assn., Eastman Alumni Assn., N.Y. Music Tchrs. Assn. (program dir. dist. 12). Home: 8470 Mt Morris Rd Dansville NY 14437 also 26 Bromley Rd Pittsford NY 14534

MC MASTER, THOMAS WILSON, former ednl. motion picture adminstr.; b. Phila., June 11, 1905; s. Arthur Ellsworth and Rae (Mayberry) McM.; B.S., Temple U., 1932; M.A., U. Pa., 1934; m. Frances Swartley, Sept. 11, 1939. Supervisory and curriculum work Sch. Dist. Phila., 1939-63, classroom instr., 1961-63; developer pilot study exchange sch. auditorium programs via internat. telephone in cooperation with Fox Film Corp. and Films Inc., N.Y.C., 1950-53; ednl. cons. Pa. State U., 1946-48; instr. film edn. St. Joseph's Coll., Phila., 1949-52; chmn. Phila. regional screening jury community affairs Council on Internat. Nontheatrical Events. Mem. U. Mus., Phila.; mem. screening com. The Free Library Phila. Fund for Advancement Edn. fellow, 1954-55. Mem. Soc. Motion Picture and TV Engrs., Nat. Com. Audio Visual Aids in Edn., Internat. Sci. Film Assn., Del. County Film Forum (pres. 1954-55), Hist. Soc. Pa., U. Pa. Mus., Kappa Phi Kappa, Phi Delta Kappa. Indsl. analyst Monthly Rev., Fed. Res. Bank Phila., 1937-39; contbr. articles to mags. Home: 101 D Locust St Moorestown NJ 08057 Office: POB 339 Moorestown NJ 08057

MC MENNAMIN, JOHN LAWRENCE, mfg. co. mktg. research exec.; b. Presque Isle, Maine, Sept. 8, 1936; s. Lawrence E. and Stella (McClean) McM.; B.A. in Polit. Sci., U. Idaho, 1958; postgrad. in sociology, N.Y. U., 1962, in Econometrics, New Sch. for Social Research, 1971; m. Camille Shelton, May 15, 1965; 1 dau., Deirdre Susanne. Research dir. P. Ballantine & Sons, Newark, 1960-66; mktg. exec. Young & Rubicam, N.Y.C., 1966-68; research mgr. new products Lever Bros. Co., N.Y.C., 1968-73; sr. v.p. Decisions Center, N.Y.C., 1973-75; v.p. research/new products Norton Simon Communications Co., N.Y.C., 1975—; coll. lectr. and speaker in field. Mem. Am. Mktg. Assn. (pres. N.Y. chpt. 1978, editorial rev. bd. Nat. JOur. Mktg. 1976—). Democrat. Unitarian. Clubs: Gipsy Trail (Carmel, N.Y.); Univ. (N.Y.C.). Home: 311 E 72d St New York NY 10021 Office: 230 Park Ave New York NY 10017

MC MILLAN, CAROLINE OSGOOD, mfg. co. exec.; b. Boston, July 23, 1929; d. John Endicott and Caroline (Cutter) McMillan; student N.Y. U., 1972. Sr. writer, editor J. Walter Thompson Co., N.Y.C., 1957-61; supr. financial and stockholder relations Schering Corp., Bloomfield, N.J., 1964-69; dir. pub. affairs Athlone Industries, Inc., Parsippany, N.J., 1972—. Trustee St. Mary's-in-the-Mountains, 1953-60; trustee White Mountain Sch., 1975—, also mem. bd. investment com., cons. fin. com. Asso. mem. alumnae presidents council Ind. Secondary Schs., 1958—. Mem. Am. Mgmt. Assn., Acad. Polit. Sci., Am. Acad. Polit. and Social Sci., NOW, Nat. Women's Polit. Caucus. Founding editor Investornews Mag., 1960-62. Home: 215 E 80th St New York City NY 10021

MC MILLAN, ROBERT LEE, psychologist; b. Wilson, N.C., Dec. 4, 1940; s. Joshua Way and Marlene McM.; B.S., D.C. Tchrs. Coll., 1966; M.A., Howard U., 1968; fellow in psychology State U. N.Y., 1970; 6th year advanced certificate N.Y. U., 1976; Ed.D., George Washington U., 1978; m. Sherlyn Elizabeth Green, Feb. 14, 1967; children—Eric Vincent, Elizabeth Marie. Tchr. pub. schs., Washington, 1965-67; curriculum coordinator Fed. City Coll., 1968-70; instr. Essex County Coll., 1970-73, asst. prof. counseling, 1974-76, asso. prof. coordinator research, 1976—; therapist Family Service and Child Guidance Center, Orange, N.J.; cons. D.C. Pub. Schs., Manpower and Tchr. Aid Tng. Recipient award Century Club of East Orange, N.J., 1973. Mem. Am. Personnel and Guidance Assn., Am. Assn. Higher Edn., Am. Coll. Personnel Assn., Am., N.J. psychol. assns., N.J. Acad. Psychology, Assn. Black Psychologists, Assn. Measurement and Evaluation in Guidance, PTA, Omega Psi Phi, Phi Delta Kappa. Contbr. to profl. jours., Civil Rights Commn. publs., also profl. reports and documents. Home: 437 Highland Ave Apt 2B Orange NJ 07050

MC MILLAN, ROBERT RALPH, lawyer, cosmetic co. exec.; b. N.Y.C., May 21, 1932; s. Harry and Vivian (Beatty) McM.; student Adelphi U., 1954-56; J.D., Bklyn. Law Sch., 1960; m. Jane Arbo, June 7, 1958; children—Robin Elizabeth, Karen Ann, Kenneth John. Admitted to N.Y. State bar, 1960; gen. atty. U.S. Dept. Justice, Washington, 1960; counsel to U.S. Senator Kenneth Keating of N.Y., 1960-62; govt. relations adviser Mobil Oil Corp., N.Y.C., 1962-63, 65-68; spl. asst. to Richard M. Nixon, 1964-65; dir. govt. and pub. affairs Avon Products, Inc., N.Y.C., 1968-72, gen. mgr., 1973, v.p. adminstrn., 1973-74, v.p. info. services, 1974—. Mem. N.Y. State Commn. on Powers of Local Govt., 1972-74, mem. U.S. del. Consumer Affairs Com., OECD, Paris, 1971, 72. Served to 1st lt. AUS, 1952-54. Decorated Bronze Star. Mem. Nassau Bar Assn., N.Y. C. of C. Republican. Home: 106 Goose Hill Rd Cold Spring Harbor NY 11724 Office: 9 W 57th St New York City NY 10019

MC MILLEN, LORING, mus. ofcl.; b. S.I., N.Y., Mar. 10, 1906; s. Harlow and Elizabeth Morton (Boyce) McM.; B.S. in Civil Engring., Union Coll., 1928, M.Litt., 1943; postgrad. in architecture Columbia, 1928-30, N.Y. U., 1931; m. Eleanor Marie Smith, Apr. 20, 1929; children—Harlow, William, Mary. Plant engr. N.Y. Telephone Co., 1928-66; sr. landmarks specialist N.Y.C. Landmarks Commn., 1966-67, also commr., 1960-66; dir. S.I. Hist. Mus., 1967—. Bd. dirs., exec. com. N.Y.C. Bicentennial Corp., 1970—. Recipient Distinguished Citizenship award Wagner Coll., 1956; named Am. of Year, U.S. Flag Found., 1973. Mem. Am. Scenic and Historic Preservation Soc. (dir., Pugsley medal), Soc. Preservation L.I. Antiquities (dir.), Early Am. Industries Assn. (dir.). Lion. Contbr. articles on historic bldg. preservation and restoration to publs. Home: 3531 Richmond Rd Staten Island NY 10306 Office: 302 Center St Staten Island NY 10306

MC MULLAN, JEAN FRANCES GENTRY, camp exec.; b. Hartford, Conn., June 7, 1926; d. Charles Burt and Kathleen (Moore) Gentry; B.A., U. Conn., 1947, Spl. certificate in Edn., 1948, M.A., 1949; m. Andrew J. McMullan, Jr., Mar. 31, 1950; children—Kathy Jean, Mark Andrew, Bruce Gentry (dec.), Keith Charles. Tchr., Coventry (Conn.) Country Day Sch., 1947-48; head counselor Camp Wyonegonic, Denmark, Maine, 1948-50, co-dir., 1950-62; supr. music Riverside (Conn.) Sch., Old Greenwich (Conn.) Sch., 1948-50; supr. music pub. elementary schs., Willimantic, Conn., 1950-51; owner, dir. Alford Lake Camp, South Hope, Maine, 1963-78; instr. grad. continuing edn. U. Maine, Portland, Gorham. Cellist, Willimantic Symphony, 1941-47, Portland (Maine) Symphony, 1955-72; asst. organizer Fund for Advancement Camping Durham Symposium, 1973. Trustee Fund for Advancement of Camping, 1975—, chmn. program council, 1978. Mem. Maine Camp Dirs. Assn. (pres. 1962-63, dir. 1940—), Am. (v.p. field service 1973-74, exec. com. 1970-74, nat. leadership chmn. 1975-76, chmn. nat. leadership cert. bd. 1976-77, inst. dean 1975), New Eng. (pres. 1970-71, dir.) camping assns., Mortar Bd., Phi Beta Kappa. Republican. Congregationalist. Home: 17 Pilot Point Rd Cape Elizabeth ME 04107 Office: Alford Lake Camp RFD 2 Union ME 04862

MC MULLEN, EDWIN DANIEL, composer, steel guitarist; b. N.Y.C., Oct. 21, 1911; s. Ward Daniel and Anna-Marie (Sheridan) McM.; LL.B., Blackstone Law Sch., 1962, J.D., 1968; m. Dorothy H. Sicina, May 11, 1956; children—Patrick, Annette-Marie, Mary-Ellen. Steel guitarist, 1927—; recorded with Eddy Arnold, Red Foley, Johnny Marvin, Radio City Music Hall, 1956, Ringling Bros., Barnum & Bailey Band, 1956; worked in motion pictures intermittently, 1946—; songs recorded by major cos. including Victor, Columbia, MGM, Decca; owner, instr. Sch. Hawaiian Steel Guitar, N.Y.C., 1940-43. Served with AUS, 1943-45. Decorated Purple Heart. Mem. Huntington Family Assn., Am. Fedn. Musicians, A.S.C.A.P. Composer: Game of Broken Hearts, 1949, Frivolette, 1952, Tipica Serenada, 1954, others. Address: 320 W 55th St New York City NY 10019

MC MULLEN, EDWIN WALLACE, JR., educator; b. Quincy, Fla., Dec. 8, 1915; s. Edwin Wallace and Della (Moore) McM.; B.A., U. Fla., 1936; M.A., Columbia U., 1939, Ph.D., 1950; m. Marian Elizabeth Hoper, June 9, 1946; children—William Wallace, Charles Edwin. Instr. English, Pa. State U., 1946-48, State U. Iowa, 1950-52; spl. instr. in report writing U.S. Dept. Def., Washington, 1953, sr. reporter, 1952-57; asst. editor Merriam Webster Dictionary Co., 1957; asst. prof. English, Lehigh U., 1957-61; asst. prof. English, Fairleigh Dickinson U., Madison, N.J., 1961-62, asso. prof., 1962-72, prof., 1973—, chmn. dept. lang. and lit., 1962-65, founder, dir. Names Inst., 1962—. Chmn. publs. subcom. Morris County Tercentenary Com., N.J., 1962-63. Served with Signal Corps, U.S. Army, 1942-46. Mem. Am. Name Soc. (pres. 1976), Modern Lang. Assn., Internat. Congress on Onomastic Scis., Internat. Linguistic Assn., Am. Dialect Soc., Nat. Council Tchrs. English, English Place-Name Soc., Morris County Hist. Soc. Democrat. Methodist. Author: English Topographic Terms in Florida, 1563-1874, 1953; editor Names, 1962-65, also articles. Home: 15 Rosewood Dr Madison NJ 07940 Office: English Dept Fairleigh Dickinson U Madison NJ 07940

MC MULLEN, FRANK JONES, ins. co. exec.; b. N.Y.C., Aug. 14, 1902; s. Adam and Agnes (Watson) McM.; B.S., Lafayette Coll., 1925, C.E., 1927; m. Clara A. Rigoulot, June 7, 1926; children—Cynthia (Mrs. Charles W. Fox), Barbara (Mrs. Walter M. Bieber). Civil engr. Structural Steel Post & McCord, N.Y.C., 1925-30; civil engr. N.Y. Fire Ins. Exchange, N.Y.C., 1930-35; engr. Fire Ins. Rating, N.Y.C., 1930-35; ind. ins. broker, 1935—; dir. Channing Mutual Funds, N.Y.C., 1952-73. Mem. N.Y. Assembly, 1945-60; commr. N.Y. Pub. Service, 1960-70; del. N.Y. State Republican Convs., 1946, 50, 54, 58, Nat. Convs., 1948, 52, 56, 60; mem. Mantoloking Bd. Adjustment; trustee Bay Head (N.J.) Chapel. Mem. Pi Kappa Phi. Presbyn. (elder). Clubs: Bay Head Yacht; Seagate Beach (Delray Beach, Fla.); Deerfield Country (Fla.). Home: 920 Lagoon Ln Mantoloking NJ 08738 Office: 4045 Amboy Rd Staten Island NY 10308

MC MULLEN, JOHN JOSEPH, naval architect, transp. cons., maritime co. exec.; b. Jersey City, May 10, 1918; s. Charles S. and Isabella V. (Oxley) McM.; B.S., U.S. Naval Acad., 1940; M.S. in Naval Constrn. and Engring., Mass. Inst. Tech., 1945; Dr. Tech. Sci., Swiss Fed. Inst. Tech., Zurich, 1950; m. Jacqueline Joy Everhart, Dec. 10, 1955; children—Peter Stuart, Catherine Joy, John Joseph. Commd. ensign U.S. Navy, 1940, advanced through grades to comdr., 1954; ETO, NATOUSA, PTO; resigned, 1954; chief office ship constrn. and repair Maritime Adminstrn., U.S. Dept. Commerce Washington, 1954-57; pres. John J. McMullen Assos., Inc., N.Y.C., 1957-68, chmn. bd., 1971—; pres., chief exec. officer Burmah Oil

Tankers Ltd., 1975; chmn. bd., pres., chief exec. officer U.S. Lines, Inc., N.Y.C., 1968-70; dir. Norton, Lilly & Co., Inc., Hudson Engring. Co., Perth Amboy Dry Dock Co., MPR Assos., Inc., Pacific Marine Corp., Dubai Dry Dock Co. Ltd., Cornell & Underhill, Inc., Am. Ship Bldg. Co. Trustee Boston Coll., Chestnut Hill, Mass., Georgian Court Coll., Lakewood, N.J. Decorated Am., Nat. Def. service medals, Silver Life Sav. medal; recipient Akroyd Stuart award Inst. Marine Engrs., London, Eng., 1957, 59, Distinguished Service medal citation Robert L. Hague Mcht. Marine Industries Post Am. Legion. Mem. Am. Soc. Naval Engrs., Navy League U.S., Am. Bur. Shipping (bd. mgrs.), Soc. Naval Architects and Marine Engrs. N.Y.C. Clubs: Whitehall Lunch, India House, Madison Square Garden (N.Y.C.); Pine Valley (N.J.) Golf; Montclair Golf; Oslo (Norway) Golf; Grasshopper (Zurich, Switzerland); Swiss Acad. Ski. Contbr. numerous articles to profl. jours. Home: 53 Undercliff Rd Montclair NJ 07042 Office: John J McMullen Assos Inc 1 World Trade Center Suite 3047 New York City NY 10048

MC MULLEN, ROBERT MICHAEL, marine scientist; b. Toronto, Ont., Can., Nov. 20, 1935; s. Robert Gascoigne and Kathleen Mary (Holt) McM.; student Upper Can. Coll., 1948-54, U. Toronto, 1954-55; B.Sc., U. Alta., 1957, M.Sc. (Shell Oil Grad. fellow in geology 1958-59), 1959; Ph.D., Reading (U.K.) U., 1964; m. Patricia Dora Beresford Brinkler, June 9, 1962; 1 dau., Catriona. Info. specialist Imperial Oil Ltd., Calgary, Alta., Can., 1959-61; subsurface geologist Imperial Oil Enterprises, Calgary, 1964-65, Hudson's Bay Oil and Gas Ltd., Calgary, 1965; marine geologist Govt. Can. Dept. Energy, Mines and Resources, Dartmouth, N.S., 1965-66, head. sci. info. services and library, 1966-70 dir. info. retrieval services Govt. Can. Dept. Communications, Ottawa, Ont., 1970-73; policy analyst and dir. policy and program coordination, ocean and aquatic scis., Govt. Can. Dept. Fisheries and Environment, Ottawa, 1973—. Treas. Pinecrest-Queensway Citizens Com., Ottawa, 1971-74. Fellow Geol. Soc. London (U.K.), Geol. Assn. Can.; mem. Am. Assn. Petroleum Geologists, Can. Assn. Info. Sci. (exec. Ottawa chpt. 1971-74, nat. exec. 1974-75), Inst. Info. Scientists (U.K.). Anglican. Mng editor Maritime Sediments, 1967-70. Contbr. papers to publs. Office: 240 Sparks St 8th Floor Ottawa ON K1A 0E6 Canada

MC MURTRY, JAMES GILMER, III, neurol. surgeon; b. Houston, June 11, 1932; s. James Gilmer and Alberta Elizabeth (Matteson) McM.; student Rice U., Houston, 1950-53; M.D. cum laude, Baylor U., Houston, 1957. Intern, Hosp. U. Pa., Phila., 1957-58; resident gen. surgery Baylor U. Affiliated Hosps., Houston, 1958-59; asst. neurol. surgery Coll. Physicians and Surgeons Columbia U., N.Y.C., 1959-60; asst. resident neurol. surgery and neurology Neurol. Inst. N.Y., Columbia Presbyn. Med. Center, N.Y.C., 1960-62, chief resident neurol. surgery, 1962-63; Nat. Inst. Neurol. Disease and Blindness spl. fellow neurol. surgery Coll. Physicians and Surgeons Columbia U., N.Y.C., 1963-64, instr. neurol. surgery, 1963-65, asso., 1965-68, asst. prof. clin. neurol. surgery, 1968-73, asso. prof., 1973—; asst. attending neurol. surgeon Neurol. Inst. N.Y., N.Y.C., 1964-73, asso. attending neurol. surgeon, 1973—; chief neurol. surgery clinic Vanderbilt Clinic, Columbia Presbyn. Med. Center, N.Y.C., 1964-68; attending-in-charge neurosurgery Lenox Hill Hosp., N.Y.C., 1970—; asso. cons. neurol. surgery Englewood (N.J.) Hosp., 1964—; asst. cons. neurol. surgery Harlem Hosp., N.Y.C., 1964—; cons. neurol. surgery Bronx (N.Y.) VA Hosp., 1964-65; mem. NIH Parkinson Research Group, Columbia U., 1965—. Jesse H. Jones scholar Baylor U. Coll. Medicine, 1953-57, Allen fellow dept. neurol. surgery Columbia U., 1964-65. Diplomate Am. Bd. Neurol. Surgery. Fellow ACS; mem. Am. Assn. Neurol. Surgeons, AAUP, AAAS, AMA, European Congress Pediatric Neurosurgery, Am. Soc. Stereotaxic Surgeons, Pan Am. Med. Assn., N.Y. State Soc. Surgeons, N.Y. State Neurosurgery Soc., N.Y. Acad. Sci., N.Y. Neurosurg. Soc., Med. Soc. State N.Y., N.Y. County Med. Soc., Osler Soc., Baylor U. Coll. Medicine Alumni Assn., Med. Strollers, Alpha Omega Alpha. Presbyn. Author: Medical Examination Review Book-Neurological Surgery, 1970, revised edit., 1975; Neurological Surgery Case Histories, 1975; contbr. articles in field to profl. jours. Home: 1 Cobb Lane Tarrytown NY 10591 Office: 710 W 168th St New York City NY 10032

MC NAIR, LOIS ISOBEL DINAH, educator; b. New Brunswick, Can.; d. George W. and Mary M. McNair; B.S. in Speech, Emerson Coll., 1967; M.Ed., Boston State Coll., 1969; postgrad. Boston U., 1974-75; came to U.S., 1963, naturalized, 1977. Radiographic technician Canadian Dept. Vets. Affairs, 1947-62; technician Radiology Group Greater Boston, 1964; tchr. speech and hearing Boston Sch. System, 1967-68; Manchester (N.H.) Sch. System, 1970, 71; tchr. speech and hearing therapy Houlton (Maine) Elementary Sch., 1972—. Mem. Am., Maine speech and hearing assns., Speech Communications Assn., Am. Personnel and Guidance Assn., Am. Sch. Counselors Assn., Am. Pub. Health Assn., Royal Soc. Health, Alexander Graham Bell Soc. Home: 71 Court St Houlton ME 04730

MC NALLEN, MARY FINDLE, dietitian; b. Irwin, Pa., July 17, 1919; d. Frank Joseph and Mary Mathilda (Flick) Findle; B.S., Seton Hill Coll., 1940; m. Donald J. McNallen, July 5, 1948 (dec.). Staff dietitian Jefferson Med. Hosp., Phila., 1941-44; head dietitian VA Hosp., Aspinwall, Pa., 1946-48; dir. in-plant cafeteria, gearing div. Westinghouse Electric Co., Pitts., 1948-53; dir. dietary dept. Suburban Gen. Hosp., Pitts., 1953—. Served with U.S. Army, 1944-46; ETO. Registered dietitian. Mem. Am., Pa., Pitts. (past pres.) dietetic assns., Am. Soc. Food Service Adminstrn., Dietary Adv. Hosp. Council Western Pa. Roman Catholic. Home: 710 Beaver St Sewickley PA 15143 Office: Suburban Gen Hosp Bellevue Pittsburgh PA 15202

MC NALLY, FRANK XAVIER, chem., elec. engr.; b. Berlin, N.H., Mar. 18, 1918; s. Frank Xavier and Lena (Cassidy) M.; B.S. in Chem. Engring., Johns Hopkins U., 1948; diploma in advanced engring. tech. Westinghouse Sch. Applied Engring. Sci., 1970; m. Mary Frances Mangum, July 15, 1957; children—Mary Martha, Frances Ruth. Chem. engr. Arcrods Corp., Balt., 1941-44; chem. engr. Rheem Mfg. Co., Balt., 1944-46; sr. materials processes engr., supv. Westinghouse Electric Corp., Balt., 1948-68, program mgr. 1969-70, sr. project engr., 1970-71, sr. engr., Pitts., 1971-72; cons., supv., sr. research scientist CSE Corp., Pitts., 1972-78; project mgr. Pitts. Environ. Corp., 1978—. Treas. West Baltimore County Republican Club, 1963-64. Served with U.S. Army, 1946-47. Registered profl. engr. Md. Mem. Engrs. Soc. Western Pa., Instrument Soc. Am., Toastmasters Internat. Club: K.C. Contbr. articles to profl. jours.; patentee numerous items. Home: 87 Bebout Rd Venetia PA 15367 Office: Pitts Environ and Energy System 67 Old Clairton Rd Pittsburgh PA

MC NAMARA, FRANCIS JOSEPH, JR., lawyer; b. Boston, Nov. 30, 1927; s. Francis Joseph and Louise (English) McN.; A.B., Georgetown U., 1949, LL.B., 1951; m. Noreen E. O'Connor, June 18, 1953; children—Francis Joseph III, Moira Patricia, John Allen, Kathleen Louise, Martha Jeanne, Mark Jeffrey. Admitted to Conn. bar, 1952; asso. firm Pullman, Comley, Bradley & Reeves, 1953; asst. U.S. atty., Conn., 1953-57; asso. firm Cummings & Lockwood, Stamford, Conn., 1957—, partner, 1959—. Mem. pres.'s council Fairfield (Conn.) U., 1967-69, trustee, 1969—. Trustee Charles E. Culpeper Trust, bd. dirs. Charles E. Culpeper Found., 1967—, chmn., 1968—. Served with USNR, 1946, 51-53. Fellow Am. Bar Found.; mem. Am., Fed. bar assns., Conn. Bar Assn. Conn. (ho. dels., gov. 1978—, chmn. fed. judiciary com. 1976—), Phi Delta Phi, Navy League U.S. Republican. Roman Catholic. Clubs: Yacht, Midtown, Landmark (Stamford); Noroton Yacht (Darien, Conn.); Univ. (N.Y.C.). Home: 16 Allwood Rd Darien CT 06820 also Belgo Rd Lakeville CT 06039 Office: 1 Atlantic St Stamford CT 06904 also 866 United Nations Plaza New York City NY 10017

MC NAMARA, J(OHN) DONALD, lawyer; b. Bridgeport, Conn., Feb. 28, 1924; s. John T. and Agnes (Keating) McN.; B.A., Dartmouth, 1945; M.A. in Govt., Harvard, 1947, LL.B., 1950; m. Shirley Addison Holdridge, Nov. 5, 1960. Admitted to Conn. bar, 1951, N.Y. bar, 1951; asso. firm Hall, Haywood, Patterson & Taylor, N.Y.C., 1951-53, 55-56; asst. U.S. atty. So. Dist. N.Y., 1953-55; asso. firm Wickes, Riddell, Bloomer, Jacobi & McGuire, N.Y.C., 1956-57; from asso. to partner firm Nottingham & McEniry and successor, N.Y.C., 1957-59; sec., gen. counsel Interpub. Group of Cos., Inc., N.Y.C., 1960—, dir., 1965—, sr. v.p., 1966-73, exec. v.p., 1973—, mem. exec. com., 1967—. Chmn., U.S. Nat. Tennis Championships, 1965. Served to lt. (j.g.) USNR, 1943-46. Mem. Am. Bar Assn. (com. on fgn. and internat. bus. law 1971—), Internat. Bar Assn. Clubs: River N.Y.C., West Side Tennis (gov. 1962-66, 78—, pres. 1964-66), University of N.Y.C., Metropolitan Opera; International (Washington). Home: 350 E 57th St New York City NY 10022 also Ethan Allen Rd Peru VT 05152 Office: 1271 Ave of Americas New York City NY 10020

MC NAMARA, JOHN JOSEPH, physician, pub. health adminstr., educator; b. Boston, Apr. 16, 1940; s. John James and Eleanor Ann (Quinn) McN.; B.S. magna cum laude, Boston Coll., 1961; M.D., Harvard, 1965; M.P.H., U. Calif. at Berkeley, 1969; m. Florence E. Goldmann, June 5, 1965; children—Mona, Rebecca, Susan, Katherine. Intern Vanderbilt U. Hosps., Nashville, 1965-66; jr. asst. resident, first asst. resident of children service Mass. Gen. Hosp., Boston, 1966-68; practice medicine specializing in pediatrics and preventive medicine; from teaching fellow pediatrics to clin. instr. pediatrics Harvard, 1967-71; asst. prof. pediatrics Albert Einstein Coll. of Medicine, N.Y.C., 1971-72; asst. prof. community medicine State U. of N.Y., Stony Brook, 1973-75; asst. prof. pub. health and pediatrics Columbia U., N.Y.C., 1975-77; asso. clin. prof. pediatrics, Boston U., 1977—; mem. staff Mass. Gen. Hosp., Boston, Lincoln Hosp., Bronx, N.Y., Queens Hosp. Center, Jamaica, N.Y., Babies Hosp., N.Y.C.; asst. dir. dept. pediatrics Lincoln Hosp., 1971; chief pediatrics Brockton (Mass.) Hosp., 1977—; chief children and youth unit Bur. M.C.H., Calif. Dept. Pub. Health, 1972-73; dir. community medicine Queens Hosp. Center, 1973-75; asso. commr. N.Y.C. Dept. of Health, 1975-77; dir. adolescent services Health Care of Southeastern Mass., Inc. Served to capt., M.C., USAF, 1969. Diplomate Am. Bd. Pediatrics, Am. Bd. Preventive Medicine. Fellow Am. Acad. Pediatrics, Am. Coll. Preventive Medicine, Mass., Boylston med. socs.; mem. AMA, Am. Pub. Health Assn., Med. Soc. of N.Y. State, Mass. Med. Soc., Am. Coll. Sports Medicine, Ambulatory Pediatric Assn. Democrat. Roman Catholic. Contbr. articles on pediatrics and pub. health to profl. jours. Home: 276 Prospect St Brockton MA 02401 Office: Brockton Hospital 680 Centre St Brockton MA 02402

MC NAMARA, KEVIN DAVID, nursing home adminstr.; b. Sydney, N.S., Can., Apr. 15, 1947; s. David Robert and Marguerita (Cogswell) McN.; B.S. in Commerce, St. Marys U., 1969; m. Eva Moore, Aug. 25, 1978. Social service worker N.S. Dept. Social Services, Can., 1969-70; social assistance worker Municipality of the County of Halifax, 1970-73; adminstr. Oceanview Manor, Halifax County, N.S., 1973—. Mem. N.S. Sr. Citizens Commn., 1975—; chmn. Dartmouth Housing Authority, 1973, Dartmouth Winter Carnival, 1975, 76; sec. Halifax Minor Hockey Assn., 1971-73; v.p. Halifax Little League Baseball Assn., 1972; pres. Asso. Homes for Spl. Care, 1975-76, Dartmouth South Liberal Assn., 1973-75; chmn. Dartmouth Community Contact Assn., 1977—; vice chmn. Dartmouth Housing Adv. Bd., 1977-78. Mem. Am. Coll. Nursing Home Adminstrs., Assn. N.S. Housing Authorities (pres. 1977—), Canadian Fedn. Long Term Care Assns. (v.p. 1977—), Canadian Gerontology Assn., N.S. Assn. Children with Learning Disabilities (sec. 1975). Club: Kiwanis. Home: 7 Lyngby Ave Dartmouth NS B3A 3T5 Canada Office: PO Box 130 Eastern Passage Halifax County NS Canada

MC NAMARA, ROBERT FRANCIS, clergyman, historian; b. Corning, N.Y., Nov. 3, 1910; s. Thomas Alexander and Helen (Dwyer) McN.; B.A., Georgetown U., 1932; M.A., Harvard U., 1933; Licentiate Sacred Theology, Gregorian U., Rome, 1937. Ordained priest Roman Catholic Ch., 1936; parish, journalistic work, Rochester, N.Y., 1937-38; faculty St. Bernard's Sem., Rochester, 1938—, prof. ch. history, 1974—; vis. prof. Toronto (Ont., Can.) Sch. Theology, 1971-72, 75-76; mem. Liturgical Commn. Diocese Rochester, 1965-76, diocesan archivist, 1976—. Mem. Liturgical Arts Soc. (dir. 1959-72), Am., Am. Cath. (2d v.p. 1970-71), N.Y. State hist. assns., Corning-Painted Post (N.Y.) Hist. Soc. (founder, 1st pres. 1947-48), Assn. State and Local History, Soc. Am. Archivists, Am. Soc. Ch. History. Author: A Century of Grace, 1948; The American College in Rome, 1855-1955, 1956; The Diocese of Rochester, 1868-1968, 1968; Catholic Sunday Preaching: The American Guidelines, 1791-1975, 1975. Editor: Essays in Honor of Joseph P. Brennan, 1976. Home and Office: 2260 Lake Ave Rochester NY 14612

MC NEIL, DONALD SOUTHWORTH, editor; b. Buffalo, Oct. 14, 1908; s. William D. and Irma Emily (Southworth) McN.; A.B., Hamilton Coll., 1930; m. Doris Campbell Mallory, July 3, 1936; children—Mary Chilton McNeil Rhodes, Alexander Mallory. News editor Adirondack Daily Enterprise, Saranac Lake, N.Y., 1930-33; reporter Syracuse (N.Y.) Herald, 1933-35; mng. editor Jewelers' Circular-Keystone, (div. Chilton Co.), N.Y.C., 1935-44, editor, Radnor, Pa., 1957-73, editor emeritus, 1973—; mng. editor Pathfinder Newsmag., Washington, 1944-54, Town Jour., Washington, 1954-57; cons. Jewelers' Book Club, 1977—. Recipient award for outstanding service to jewelry industry Golden Nuggets So. Calif., 1972, Neal award Am. Bus. Press, 1967, 68. Mem. 24 Karat Club City N.Y., Am. Gem Soc., Am. Watchmakers Inst., Conn. Hist. Soc., Conn. Soc. Genealogists, Soc. Mayflower Descs. Editor: Growing Desire for Diamonds, 1966; Sterling Flatware Pattern Index, 1970; Jewelers' Dictionary, 1976. Home: 621 Rosemont Plaza Rosemont PA 19010 Office: Jewelers' Circular-Keystone Chilton Co Radnor PA 19089

MC NEIL, HENRY SLACK, pharm. exec.; b. Phila., Apr. 22, 1917; s. Robert Lincoln and Grace F. (Slack) McN.; B.S., Yale, 1939; LL.D. (hon.), Phila. Coll. Pharmacy and Sci.; m. Lois A. Fernley, Oct. 4, 1941; children—Henry S., Barbara Joan, Marjorie Fernley, Robert Douglas. Dir., McNeil Labs., Inc., Phila., 1940—, v.p. sales and promotion, 1949-55, pres., 1955-60; v.p., dir. Johnson & Johnson, 1959-77; dir. Penguin Industries, Inc.; chmn. Claneil Enterprises Inc. Mem. devel. bd. Yale U.; mem. nat. council, adv. bd. Valley Forge council Boy Scouts Am.; mem. nat. adv. council Multiple Sclerosis Assn.; mem. fine arts com., chmn. fin. com. U.S. State Dept. Diplomatic Reception Rooms; asso. trustee U. Pa.; trustee Henry Francis duPont Winterthur Mus.; mem. council Am. Mus. in Britain; bd. dirs. Nat. Trust for Historic Preservation; trustee, pres. Pa. Acad. Fine Arts. Recipient Gold Medal Pa. Acad. Fine Arts. Mem. St. Andrew's Soc. Phila., Am. Pharm. Assn. (life), Hist. Soc. Pa., Clan MacNeil Assn. Am. (pres. 1962-72), Confrerie des Chevaliers du Tastevin, Newcomen Soc. N.Am., Omicron Delta Kappa (hon.). Clubs: St. Elmo (New Haven); Philadelphia, Sunnybrook Golf, Yale, Cricket, Racquet, Union League, Aviation Country, Corinthian Yacht (Phila.); Metropolitan (N.Y.C.); Metropolitan, Capitol Hill (Washington); Royal Danish Yacht (Copenhagen). Home: Plymouth Meeting PA 19462 Office: Suite 511 1 Plymouth Meeting Plymouth Meeting PA 19462

MC NEILL, JOHN MELVIN, chem. co. exec.; b. Birmingham, Mich., June 18, 1933; s. Thomas William and Helen (Melvin) McN.; B.S., Pa. State U., 1955; m. Sheila Hennessey, Apr. 8, 1961; children—Sean Butler, Mary Regan. Engr., duPont Co., Parlin, N.J., 1955-56; sales rep. Olin Corp., N.Y.C., 1958-61, sr. sales rep., 1961-64, prodn. mgr., 1964-67, mgr. mktg., 1967-69; pres., chief exec. Nat. Cryo-Chemics, Inc., Stamford, Conn., 1969—; v.p. Applied Tech. Co., Fort Worth, Synthetic Oil Corp. Am., N.Y.C., Charlyn Group, Stamford. Served with USAF, 1956-58. Mem. Am. Inst. Chem. Engrs., Am. Chem. Soc., Sales Exec. Club, Salesmen's Assn. Am. Chem. Industry, Navy League U.S. (dir.), Pi Kappa Alpha, Alpha Chi Sigma. Clubs: Stamford Yacht (fleet capt., dir.); Corinthians (N.Y.C.). Home and Office: 46 Saddle Rock Rd Stamford CT 06902

MC NELIS, FRANCIS LEO, physician; b. Pawtucket, R.I., Aug. 12, 1920; s. James and Catherine Agnes (Dalton) McN.; B.S., Providence Coll., 1942; M.D., Jefferson Med. Coll., 1945; m. Shirley Lucille Grube, June 21, 1947; children—Frances S., J. Kevin, Joanne Kathryn, Stephen F., Brian F., Marian E. Intern, Pawt;ucket Meml. Hosp., 1945-46; resident Jefferson Med. Hosp., Phila., 1949-51; practice medicine specializing in otorhinolaryngology, Providence, 1951—; dept. head R.I. Hosp.; asso. prof. surgery Brown U., Providence. Served as lt. (j.g.) USNR, 1946-48. Diplomate Am. Acad. Ophthalmology and Otolaryngology. Fellow A.C.S., Am. Acad. Facial Plastic and Reconstructive Surgery; mem. AMA, Am. Bronchoesophagological Soc., Am. Laryngol., Rhinol. and Otol. Soc., New Eng. Otolaryngology Soc. (past pres.). Republican. Roman Catholic. Clubs: Wannamoisett Country (East Providence); Gunstock Acres (Gilford, N.H.). Contbr. articles to med. jours. Home: 350 Wayland Ave Providence RI 02906 Office: 100 Dudley St Providence RI 02905

MC NELLY, THEODORE HART, educator; b. Lancaster, Wis., Dec. 27, 1919; s. Stephen S. and Caroline H. (Taylor) McN.; B.S. (Music Clinic Scholar), U. Wis., 1941, M.A., 1942; postgrad. Georgetown U., 1943-46; Ph.D., Columbia, 1952; m. Myra Mae Koehler, Sept. 4, 1960; children—Douglas Scot, Gale Anne. Instr. Kemper Mil. Sch., Boonville, Mo., 1942-43; research analytic specialist Army Security Agy., Arlington, Va., 1943-46; research analyst Civil Intelligence div. Far East Command, Tokyo, 1946-48; instr. polit. sci. Washington U., St. Louis, Mo., 1951-53; lectr. U. Md. European div., Heidelberg, Germany, 1953-58, U. Md. Far East div., Tokyo, govt. and politics U. Md., College Park, 1960—. Vis. asso. prof. Columbia, summer, 1963; discussion leader Johns Hopkins Peace Corps Tng. Program, Balt., summer, 1962. Recipient Medaille De Bronze French Ministry Fgn. Affairs, 1940, Meritorious Civilian Service award Dept. Army, 1947. Japan Found. fellow, 1973. U. Md. Gen. Research Bd. grantee, Summers 1961, 64, 66, 68, 76; Social Sci. Research Council binat. U.S.-Japan Study of Occupation of Japan grantee, 1976—; Mem. Assn. Asian Studies, Internat. Studies Assn., Am. Polit. Sci. Assn., Internat. House Japan, Asiatic Soc. Japan., Am. Assn. for Chinese Studies (dir. 1969—), Japan-Am. Soc. of Washington (trustee 1966—), Phi Kappa Phi, Pi Sigma Alpha. Author: Politics and Government in Japan, 1972. Editor: Sources in Modern East Asian History and Politics, anthology, 1967. Home: 14800 Cobblestone Dr Silver Spring MD 20904 Office: Dept of Govt and Politics U Md College Park MD 20742

MC NICHOL, JOHN AUGUSTUS, JR., exec. search cons.; b. Phila., Aug. 7, 1933; s. John Augustus and Amy Irene (Dress) Mc N.; B.A., LaSalle Coll., 1957; postgrad. Columbia, 1960-62. Reporter, Montgomery Pub. Co., Fort Washington, Pa., 1957-58; sr. tech. writer, editor Philco-Ford Corp., Willow Grove, Pa., 1958-60, 62-69; editor Chilton Co., Phila., 1969-73; editor Charette, Archimedia, Phila., 1973-74; mgmt. cons. Coxe Asso., Phila., 1974-76; exec. search cons. McNichol Assos., Phila., 1976—; guest lectr., Drexel U., Phila., 1973-74. Recipient Tom Campbell award. Mem. Am. Mktg. Assn., Am. Bus. Press, Inc., AIA (profl. affiliate). Author chpt. in Working with Words: Careers for Writers, 1977. Home: Apt 915 5450 Wissahickon Ave Philadelphia PA 19144

MCNIFF, PHILIP J., librarian; b. Cambridge, Mass., Feb. 10, 1912; s. Patrick J. and Catherine (Gralton) McN.; Boston Coll., 1933, L.H.D., 1969; B.S., Columbia U., 1940; m. Mary M. Stack, Nov. 28, 1935; 1 son, Brian S. Student asst. Brookline (Mass.) Pub. Library, 1926-33; circulation librarian Newton (Mass.) Free Library, 1933-35; librarian West Newton Br. Library, 1935-40, head catalog dept., 1940-42; reference asst. Harvard Library, 1942-43, supt. reading room, 1943-48, librarian Lamont Library, 1948-56, asso. librarian, 1956-65, mem. faculty Arts and Scis., 1957-65; chief librarian, dir. Boston Pub. Library and Eastern Mass. Regional Pub. Library System, 1965—. Archibald Cary Coolidge bibliographer Harvard Library; cons. to bds. trustees of libraries. Bd. dirs. Cambridge Center for Adult Edn., mem. Cambridge Social Union; mem. adv. bd. Newton Sacred Heart Coll., Newton Jr. Coll. Mem. Am., New Eng., Mass. (pres.), Cath. library assns., Assn. Coll. and Research Libraries (pres. 1969-70), Library Com. Lesley Coll. Democrat. Roman Catholic. Editor: Lamont Library Catalogue. Contbr. articles to profl. jours. Home: 101 Waban Hill Rd Chestnut Hill MA 02167 Office: Boston Pub Library and Eastern Mass Regional Library System Copley Sq Boston MA 02117

MCNITT, HAROLD AUSTIN, internat. economist; b. Cleve., Dec. 6, 1924; s. Harold Anson and Margaret (Austin) McN.; student Western Res. U., 1945; A.B., U. Mich., 1949, M.A., 1953, Ph.D., 1956; postgrad. (Fulbright fellow) U. Copenhagen, 1954-55, (SSRC fellow) U. Uppsala (Sweden), 1957-58; m. Roberta Frank, June 8, 1946. Instr. philosophy U. Mich., 1955-56, Western Res. U., 1956-57, Johns Hopkins U., 1958-59; European area specialist Dept. Commerce, Washington, 1961-75; economist Dept. Agr., Washington, 1975—; trade devel. officer U.S. Trade Mission to Sweden, 1963, dir., 1972. Served to 2d lt. USAAF, 1943-45. Mem. AAAS, Am. Econ. Assn., AAUP, Am. Philos. Assn., Am. Fgn. Service Assn., Phi Beta Kappa, Phi Kappa Phi. Club: Washington Philosophy. Contbr. articles to profl. jours. Home: 4918 Belt Rd NW Washington DC 20016 Office: US Dept Agr Washington DC 20250

MC NULTY, MATTHEW FRANCIS, JR., educator, health sci.-service adminstr.; b. Elizabeth, N.J., Nov. 26, 1914; s. Matthew Francis and Abby Helen (Dwyer) McN.; B.S., St. Peters Coll., 1938; law student Rutgers U., 1939-41; M. Hosp. Adminstrn., Northwestern U., 1949; M.P.H., U. N.C., 1952; Sc.D., U. Ala., 1969; D.H.L. (hon.), St. Peter's Coll., 1978; m. Mary Nell Johnson, May 4, 1946; children—Matthew Francis, Mary Lauren. Contract writer, mgmt. trainee actuarial div. Prudential Life Ins. Co. Am., N.J., 1938-41; dir. med. adminstrn. VA, 1946-54; adminstr. U. Ala. Hosp., Birmingham, 1954-63; gen. dir. U. Ala. Hosps. and Clins., 1963-66; prof. hosp.

adminstrn. U. Ala. Grad. Sch., 1954-69, vis. prof., 1969—, dir. grad. program hosp. adminstrn., 1964-66, prof. epidemiology and preventive medicine U. Ala. Sch. Medicine, Birmingham, 1964-69, vis. prof., 1969—; dean U. Ala. Sch. Health Services Adminstrn. 1966-69; dir. Council Teaching Hosps. and asso. dir. Assn. Am. Med. Colls., 1966-69; prof. community medicine and internat. health Georgetown U., Washington, 1969—, v.p. for med. center affairs, 1969-72, exec. v.p. med. center affairs, 1972-74, chancellor Med. Center, 1974—; chmn. bd. dirs. Univ. Affiliated Health Plan, Inc., 1974-78; chmn. bd. trustees Georgetown U. Community Health Plan, Inc., 1972—, W.K. Kellogg Found.; vis. prof. Central U. Venezuela, 1967; hosp. cons., 1953—; mem. spl. med. adv. group VA, 1978—, Spl. Higher Edn. Com. on Dental Schs. Curriculum, 1978-79; preceptor hosp. adminstrn. Northwestern U., George Washington U., U. Iowa, U. Minn., 1953-66; mem. nat. adv. com. health research projects Ga. Inst. Tech., 1959-65, 73—; nat. adv. com. health research projects U. Pitts., 1956-60; adv. com. W.K. Kellogg Found., 1960-65; vis. cons., lectr. Ministry of Health and Social Welfare, Venezuela, 1967-69. Bd. dirs. Blue Cross-Blue Shield of Ala., 1960-61, 65-68, Greater Birmingham United Appeal, 1960-66; trustee Jefferson County Tb Sanatorium, 1958-64; mem. Health Services Research Study Section, NIH, 1963-67; cons. com. on profl. nurse traineeships USPHS, 1959, 63; mem. White House Conf. on Health, 1965, White House Conf. on Medicare Implementation, 1966, Sec. Labor Conf. on Health Manpower, 1966, Nat. Conf. on Group Practice, 1967, Nat. Conf. on Costs of Health Care Facilities, 1967, mem. health services devel. grants study sect. NIH, 1971-75. Trustee, mem. exec. com. Group Hospitalization, Inc., Washington, 1973—, Nat. Council Internat. Health, 1975—; pres.-elect Nat. League Nursing, 1977-79. Served from pvt. to maj. USAAF, 1941-46. Recipient Northwestern U. Alumni Assn. Distinguished award, 1973. Fellow Am. Pub. Health Assn., Am. Coll. Hosp. Adminstrs. (bd. regents and council of regents, 1961-67; Distinguished Health Sci. Exec. award 1976); mem. Am. (life), Ala. (past pres.) hosp. assn., Ala. (past dir.), League for Nursing, Council Med. Adminstrn., Internat. Hosp. Fedn., Jefferson County Vis. Nursing Assn. (past pres.; Distinguished Service award), Ala. Pub. Health Assn. (past chmn. med. care sect.), Southeastern Hosp. Conf. (past dir.), Birmingham Hosp. Council (past pres.), Assn. Univ. Programs in Hosp. Adminstrn. (Distinguished award 1971), Greater Birmigham Area C. of C. (Merit award), Am. Assn. Med. Colls. (chmn. teaching hosp. council 1964-65, distinguished service mem.), Royal Soc. Health, Am. Systems Mgmt. Soc. (Distinguished award), Orgn. Univ. Health Center Adminstrs., AAAS, Santa Gertrudis Breeders Internat. Author articles in field. Clubs: Univ. (Ala.); Cosmos, City Tavern, Nat. Press (Washington). Home: 1602 Laurel Ln Annapolis MD 21401 Office: 3800 Reservoir Rd NW Washington DC 20007

MC NUTT, DAN JAMES, Canadian govt. ofcl.; b. Glace Bay, N.S., Can., Apr. 5, 1938; s. Howard Fulton and Isabel Evelyn (MacDonald) McN.; B.A., Mt. Allison U., 1967; M.A., U. Tex., El Paso, 1969; postgrad. U. Ky., 1969-70; Ph.D., Dalhousie U., 1974; m. J. Elaine Van Dyke, Apr. 25, 1968; children—Robert, William. Accountant Toronto Gen. Trust Corp. (Ont., Can.), 1958-59; miner Algoma Ore Properties, Jamestown, Ont., 1959-60; oilwell serviceman Pioneer Drilling Co., Hobbs, N.Mex., 1961; carman Canadian Nat. R.R., Toronto, 1963-64, 65; mill hand Anaconda Am. Brass Corp., Toronto, 1966; pub. relations officer Can. Post, Ottawa, Ont., 1974-75, chief communications, 1976—. Served with U.S. Army, 1961-63. Mem. Modern Lang. Assn. Author: The Eighteenth-Century Gothic Novel: An Annotated Bibliography of Criticism and Selected Texts, 1975. Home: 790 Springland Dr Apt 227 Ottawa ON K1V 6L7 Canada Office: Canada Post Hdqrs Ottawa ON K1A 0B1 Canada

MC PHEE, ALEXANDER HECTOR, mfg. co. exec.; b. Bklyn., Nov. 26, 1911; s. Alexander Hendry and Charlotte Elizabeth (Kraus) M.; student Pratt Inst., 1928-34, Bklyn. Poly. Inst., 1935-41; m. Cynthia Rose Agar, July 26, 1947; 1 son, Alexander Hector. Asst. chief engr. Peter Clark Inc., 1934-37; engr. U.S.S. Yorktown & Enterprise Airplane Elevators, 1930-37; partner Howard V. Harding & Co., 1937-38; asst. chief engr. Lukenweld div. Lukens Steel Co., 1938-44; partner McPhee & Johnston, 1945-48; pvt. practice cons. engr., 1948—; v.p. Hepworth Machine Co., Inc., Port Washington, N.Y., 1953-57, pres., 1957—, chmn. bd., 1962—, also dir. Designer 90 foot turntable for Aircraft Nuclear Propulsion Project, Idaho Falls, Idaho, 1953; engring. cons. mfr. movable auditorium ceiling Juilliard Sch. Music, 1967-69; mech. stage equipment John F. Kennedy Center for Performing Arts, 1968-71; gondola hoists and controls Nassau County Vets. Meml. Coliseum, 1972; mech. and elec. cons. Bronx Zoo Skyride, 1972-73; approved welding inspection agy. N.Y.C. Dept. Bldgs. Troop com. mem. Boy Scouts Am. Registered profl. engr., N.Y., N.J., Pa., Conn., D.C., P.R., W.Va., also nat. engring. certificate. Mem. ASME (life), Am. Soc. Testing and Materials, Am. Def. Preparedness Assn., Nat. Soc. Profl. Engrs., Nassau County Grand Jurors Assn., Pi Tau Sigma (hon.). Patentee flashwelding machine control, vertical conveyor, centrifugal machines, others. Home: 89 The Waterway Plandome Heights NY 11030 Office: Sagamore Hill Dr Port Washington NY 11050

MC QUADE, MARGARET ANN, mgmt. cons.; b. Newark, Apr. 28, 1931; d. Francis Andrew and Lucy Mary (Ford) McQ.; B.A. magna cum laude, Ladycliff Coll., 1959; M.A., Seton Hall U., 1965. Chmn. chemistry dept. Ladycliff Coll., Highland Falls, N.Y., 1960-62; elementary sch. tchr. N. Rockland Sch. Dist., Stony Point, N.Y., 1963-73, adminstrv. intern, 1971-72; pres., founder Human Resources Devel. Cons. Firm, Nyack, N.Y., 1973—; adj. asst. prof. psychology Pace U., 1974-76; guest instr. N.Y. U., 1974—. Recipient Outstanding Tchr. award St. Thomas Aquinas Coll., 1965. Mem. White Plains Regional, Nyack chambers commerce, N.Y. Orgnl. Devel. Network, AAUW, Sales and Mktg. Execs. Internat., Am. Soc. Tng. and Devel., Cons. Network. Roman Catholic. Contbr. articles in field to profl. jours. Home: 103 Gedney St Apt 4J Nyack NY 10960 Office: 103 Gedney St Nyack NY 10960

MC QUEARY, CHARLES EVERETTE, mech. engr.; b. Gordon, Tex., Sept. 1, 1939; s. Lilburn and Hazel Delano (Rexroat) McQ.; B.S., U. Tex., 1962, M.S., (NSF fellow), 1964, Ph.D., 1966; m. Cheryl Lee Bath, July 8, 1972; 1 dau., Joanna Lea. With Bell Labs., 1966—, head. advanced tech. dept., Whippany, N.J., 1976—. NASA fellow, 1963-66. Mem. Am. Def. Preparedness Assn., AAAS, Phi Eta Sigma, Pi Tau Sigma, Tau Beta Pi, Phi Kappa Phi. Republican. Office: 1 Whippany Rd Whippany NJ 07981

MC QUILLAN, ELIZABETH, ednl. adminstr.; b. Hudson, Mass., May 1, 1918; d. William A. and Julia A. (O'Neil) McQuillan; B.S., Regis Coll., 1940; M.Ed., Boston U., 1950; postgrad. Boston Coll., Framingham State Coll., Worcester State Coll. Tchr., Hudson High Sch., 1941-61, dir. guidance, 1961-68, asst. prin., 1968—; real estate broker, 1940—. Mem. Nat. Assn. Secondary Sch. Prins., Mass. Assn. Women Deans and Counselors, Mass. Sch. Counselors Assn., Am. Personnel and Guidance Assn., Middlesex County Tech. Assn. (exec. bd. 1964-67), Mass. Secondary Sch. Prins. Assn., Regis Coll. Alumnae Assn., Boston U. Alumni Assn., St. Michael's Ladies Sodality. Club: Regis (Framingham). Home: 8 Kathleen Rd Hudson MA 01749

MC QUILLIN, RICHARD JAMES, computer typesetting co. exec.; b. Tacoma, Wash., Dec. 31, 1932; s. James Alexander and Frances (Penlick) McQ.; B.Sc., U. Puget Sound, 1955; postgrad. Mass. Inst. Tech., 1956-57; M.Sc., Brown U., 1958; m. Mary Foss, May 22, 1959; children—Brian Robert and Barry Richard (twins). Mem. tech. staff Bolt Beranek & Newman, Inc., Cambridge, Mass., 1958-64; systems analyst Inforonics, Inc., Maynard, Mass., 1964-68, Info. Internat., Inc., Boston, 1968-69; pres. Composition Tech., Inc., Cambridge, 1970-74; systems analyst Camex, Inc., Boston, 1974-75; pres. Comptype, Inc., Winchester, Mass., 1975—. Mem. Assn. Computing Machinery (chmn. joint user group 1972—), Word Processing Assn., Digital Equipment Computer User Soc. (pres. 1968-73). Home and Office: 305 Highland Ave Winchester MA 01890

MCSHEA, JOSEPH, bishop; b. Lattimer, Pa., Feb. 22, 1907; s. Roger Aloysius and Jeanette (Beach) McS.; student St. Charles Sem., 1923-26; Ph.D., Pontifical Roman Sem., 1928, S.T.D., 1932. Ordained priest Roman Cath. Ch., 1931; prof. St. Charles Sem., Overbrook, Phila., 1932-35; ofcl. Sacred Oriental Congregation, Vatican City, 1935-38; sec. Apostolic Delegation. Washington, 1938-52; apptd. auxiliary bishop of Phila., 1952, 1st bishop Allentown diocese, 1961. Home: 2920 Chew St Allentown PA 18104 Office: 1729 Turner Ave Allentown PA 18104

MC SHERRY, MARY ELIZABETH, nursing adminstr.; b. Providence, Aug. 4, 1936; d. Bernard Joseph and Alice Madeline (McCann) McS.; diploma St. Joseph's Hosp. Sch. Nursing, Providence, 1960; B.S. in Nursing, Salve Regina Coll., Newport, R.I., 1964; M.S. in Nursing, Wayne State U., 1969; m. Joseph George Miller, Oct. 21, 1977; stepchildren—Nancy, Steven. Instr., Coll. Nursing, U. R.I., Kingston, 1971-73; asst. dir. nursing service dept. Kent County Meml. Hosp., Warwick, R.I., 1973-74, asso. dir. dept., 1974-75, asst. adminstr. dept., 1975—; tchr. continuing edn. workshops R.I. Jr. Coll., 1974-76. Mem. Am. Hosp. Assn., Nursing Dirs. Conf. of R.I. Hosp. Assn., Am. Cancer Soc. (chpt. dir.). Roman Catholic. Home: 15 Marquette Dr Warwick RI 02888 Office: 455 Tollgate Rd Warwick RI 02886

MCSHINE, KYNASTON LEIGH, curator; b. Port of Spain, Trinidad, Feb. 20, 1935; s. Austen H. McS., A.B., Dartmouth Coll., 1958; postgrad. U. Mich., 1958-59, Inst. Fine Arts, N.Y. U. 1960-64. Asst. prof. art history Hunter Coll., 1968-69; lectr. in art history Sch. Visual Arts, N.Y.C., 1969-76; curator of painting and sculpture Jewish Museum, N.Y.C., 1965-68, acting dir. mus., 1967-68; asso. curator painting and sculpture Mus. Modern Art, N.Y.C., 1968-71, curator painting and sculpture, 1971—; mem. visual arts com. N.Y.C. Cultural Council; mem. adv. com. Skowhegan Sch. Painting and Sculpture; mem. adv. com. Bennington Summers; dir. exhbns. Mem. Am. Fedn. Arts (trustee), Internat. Assn. Art Critics, Coll. Art Assn., Am. Assn. Mus.'s. Author catalogs: Josef Albers: Homage to the Square, 1964; Primary Structures, 1966; Information, 1970; editor, contbg. author catalogs: Marcel Duchamp, 1973; The Natural Paradise: Painting in America 1800-1950, 1976. Office: 11 W 53d St New York NY 10019

MCSORLEY, JAMES FRANCIS, social worker; b. Cambridge, Mass., Feb. 4, 1923; s. James Francis and Nora Teresa (Tully) McS.; A.B., Boston Coll., 1944, M.S.W., 1945; m. Charlotte Marie Duddy, May 17, 1947; children—Janet McSorley Leavee, James Francis III, David R. Social worker Cambridge Cath. Charitable Bur., 1945-48, Manchester (N.H.) VA Mental Hygiene Clinic, 1948-59; social worker Brockton (Mass.) VA Med. Center, 1959—. Mem. Abington (Mass.) Charter Commn., 1969-70; mem. Abington Park and Recreation Commn., 1974—; pres. Greater Brockton Community Services Inc., 1974-75; treas. Mass. Coalition for Social Work Licensure, 1973—; mem. profl. adv. bd. and clin. record rev. com. Abington Vis. Nurse Assn., 1976—. Mem. Acad. Cert. Social Workers, Nat. Assn. Social Workers (pres. S.E. chpt. 1970-72, chmn. regional steering com. 1978—). Democrat. Roman Catholic. Home: 1204 Washington St North Abington MA 02351 Office: VA Med Center Belmont St Brockton MA 02041

MC SPADDEN, THOMAS EDWARD, mfg. and service co. exec.; b. Palo Alto, Calif., Jan. 15, 1943; s. George Elbert and Natalia Jane (Allen) McS.; B.S. in Mech. Engring., George Washington U., 1967; m. Elisabeth Lee Weintraub, Nov. 1, 1970; children—Gail Frances, Ellen Renee. Cons. engr. MPR Assos., Inc., Washington, 1967-73; sr. quality assurance engr. Potomac Elec. Power Co., Washington, 1973-74; project mgr. Dept. Energy, Washington, 1974—; pres., dir. Arcola Enterprises, Inc., Silver Spring, Md., 1976—. Mem. ASME, Tau Beta Pi, Sigma Tau. Contbr. articles to tech. jours. Home: 901 Hoyt St Silver Spring MD 20902 Office: E 201 Dept Energy Washington DC 20545

MC SWEENY, WILLIAM FRANCIS, petroleum co. exec.; b. Haverhill, Mass., Mar. 31, 1929; s. William Francis and Mary Florence (Doyle) McS.; student Boston U., 1950; m. Dorothy Pierce, Jan. 20, 1969; children—William Francis, Cathy Ann, Ethan Madden Maverick, Terrell Pierce. Reporter, columnist, fgn. corr. Hearst Newspapers, 1943-67; dep. chmn., dir. pub. affairs Democratic Nat. Com., Washington, 1967-68; spl. asst. to postmaster gen. U.S., Washington, 1968-69; pres. Occidental Internat. Corp., Washington, 1969—. Bd. dirs. Arena Stage; bd. visitors Fletcher Sch. Law and Diplomacy; bd. advisers Tufts U., Sch. Fgn. Service Georgetown U. Served to capt., inf., U.S. Army, 1950-53. Named Boston's Outstanding Young Man, Jr. C. of C., 1961. Episcopalian. Clubs: Nat. Press, Cosmos, Internat. (Washington); Lotos (N.Y.C.). Author: Go Up For Glory, 1965; Violence Every Sunday, 1966; The Impossible Dream, 1967. Home: 2450 Virginia Ave NW Washington DC 20037 Office: 1747 Pennsylvania Ave NW Washington DC 20006

MC TAGUE, PETER JAMES, utilities exec.; b. Bklyn., May 3, 1928; s. Peter and Margaret Ann (Rae) McT.; B. Elec. Engring., Cornell U., 1948, J.D., St. John's U., 1954; postgrad. U. Calif.; m. Virginia Mae Kane, Nov. 14, 1954; children—Lois Claire, Bruce Christian. Admitted to N.Y., Conn. bars; Asst. v.p. Citizens Utilities Co., Stamford, Conn., 1957-60; engring. fin. cons. W.C. Gilman Co., N.Y.C., 1960-63; mgmt., fin. cons. Gilbert Assos., Inc., Reading Pa., 1963-73; pres., chief exec. officer Green Mountain Power Corp., Burlington, Vt., 1973—, also dir.; dir. Vt. Yankee Nuclear Power Corp., Vt. Electric Power Corp., Inc., Greater Burlington Indsl. Corp., Electric Council New Eng. Registered profl. engr., Pa., N.Y., Del.; chartered fin. analyst. Mem. Edison Electric Inst. (policy com. on energy conservation, mem. com. on financing new tech., adv. com. nat. bank policies and practices), Electric Vehicle Council (exec. com.), Electric Power Research Inst. (com. on energy mgmt. tech.), Am. Bar Assn., Inst. Chartered Fin. Analysts, IEEE, Nat. Assn. Accountants, N.Y. Soc. Security Analysts. Republican. Clubs: Bankers of N.Y., Ethan Allen (Burlington). Contbr. to various energy industry and gen. bus. publs. Home: Mt Philo Rd Charlotte VT 05445 Office: 1 Main St Burlington VT 05401

MC VERNON, JOHN JOSEPH, clergyman, drug cons.; b. N.Y.C., July 28, 1932; s. John Joseph and Regina Lillian (Hamilton) McV.; B.A., Cathedral Coll. Bklyn., 1954; grad. in Sociology, Immaculate Conception Sem., Huntington, L.I., 1954-58. Ordained priest Roman Catholic Ch., 1958; asst. pastor Sacred Heart Ch., Bklyn., 1958-65; dir. Community Boys Club, Queens, N.Y. 1965-70; asst. dir. youth project drug prevention program, N.Y.C., Bd. Edn., 1970-71; chaplain N.Y. State Drug Abuse Control Commn., N.Y.C., 1971-75; chief programs Inst. Advancement of Criminal Justice, N.Y.C., 1973-75; chaplain U. Tenn., Chattanooga, 1975-76; dir. community devel. Nat. Assn. Drug Abuse Problems, N.Y.C., 1976—; cons. in field, lectr. N.Y. State grantee early drug abuse, 1973-74. Mem. Am. Assn. Correctional Chaplains, Am. Social Health Assn., Cath. Campus Ministry Assn. Author: Journey Through Inner Space, drug usage handbook, 1967; Use Your Mind, 1968; The Counsellor and the Head, 1970. Home: 9-11 151st Pl Whitestone NY 11357 Office: 355 Lexington Ave New York City NY 10017

MC WETHY, JAMES ANDREW, investment co. exec.; b. Cleve., Jan. 4, 1941; s. John Adams and Mary Helen (Bell) McW.; B.A., Pomona Coll., 1963; M.B.A., U. So. Calif., 1969. Asst. mgr. 1st Western Bank, Long Beach, Calif., 1964-67; v.p. 1st Small Bus. Investment Co., Los Angeles, 1969-77; v.p. Security Pacific Capital, 1975-77, Security Pacific Venture Capital Adv. Corp., 1975-77; exec. v.p., gen. mgr. Irving Capital Corp., N.Y.C., 1977—. Served with USMC, 1963. Mem. Nat. Assn. Small Bus. Investment Cos., Beta Gamma Sigma. Republican. Congregationalist. Office: One Wall St New York City NY 10015

MC WHIRTER, JOHN RUBEN, chem. engr., diversified industry exec.; b. East St. Louis, Ill., Dec. 29, 1937; s. Walter James and Mildred Bernice (Johnson) McW.; B.S. in Chem. Engring., U. Ill., 1959; M.S. in Chem. Engring., Pa. State U., 1961, Ph.D., 1962; m. Gail Balthrope, June 28, 1958; children—John Winfield, Andrew James, Mark Steven, Brian Michael. Research engr. E.I. duPont de Nemours & Co., Wilmington, Del., 1962-63; mgr. research and devel. Mixing Equipment Co., Rochester, N.Y., 1963-66; gen. mgr. Linde div. Union Carbide Corp., N.Y.C., 1966—, also v.p., 1977—. Recipient Schoellkopf award, 1976. Mem. Am. Chem. Soc. (Chem. Innovator award 1971), Am. Inst. Chem. Engrs. (Outstanding Personal Achievement award 1970), Water Pollution Control Fedn., Water and Wastewater Equipment Mfrs. Assn., Alpha Chi Sigma, Tau Beta Pi, Delta Tau Delta. Patentee in field. Home: 75 Ledgebrook Dr Norwalk CT 06852 Office: 270 Park Ave New York City NY 10017

MCWILLIAMS, HARRY KENNETH, advt. exec.; b. Middlesboro, Ky., July 20, 1907; s. John William and Mattie S. (Bayliss) McW.; student U. Colo., 1927, numerous spl. courses Denver Sch. Tech., 1925-26; m. Rosa di Giulio, June 3, 1936; children—Rosanne (Mrs. Frank Rogala), Harry Kahle, Sarah Jane Fuller (Mrs. Gijs Van Stavern). Sales mgr. Acme Films, N.Y.C., 1930-32; owner Advt. Flag Co., 1930-37; publicity mgr. numerous chains, including Harry E. Huffman theatres and Paramount Publix Theatres, N.Y.C., Toledo, Denver, Dallas, 1926-30; advt. and publicity dir. Cin. Summer Opera, also publicity mgr. concert booker number leading personalities including violinist Rubinoff, and radio program, mgr. Benton and Bowles, Ted Bates, Inc., also advance agt. San Carlo Opera Co., Legitimate Theatre Corp., USO Camp Shows, 1937-45; dir. exploitation Columbia Pictures Corp., N.Y.C., 1945-53; dir. advt. and pub. relations Screen Gems, Inc., 1953-54; pres., sales mgr. Air Programs, Inc., 1954-55; asst. dir. advt. and pub. Ben-Hur at MGM, 1959; coordinator advt. and pub. King of Kings, 1960: dir. advt. and pub. Pepe at Columbia Pictures, 1960; dir. community relations U. Cin., 1961-62; pvt. pub. relations counsellor, N.Y.C., promotion, publicity co-ordinator 1959, 60, 61, Acad. Awards Telecast, Motion Picture Assn. Am., Inc.; asst. advt. and pub. dir. Magna Theatres Corp.; advt. exec. 20th Century Fox Film Corp.; asst. gen. mgr. The Original Amateur Hour; pres., gen. mgr. Original Amateur Hour de Mexico, S.A., pres., gen. mgr. Harry K. McWilliams Assos., Inc., 1964-75; owner, gen. mgr. Pyramid Press, 1966-75; pres., owner MCW Orgn., Inc., N.Y.C., 1975—; pub. relations cons. Nat. Assn. Theatre Owners. Recipient Silver Anvil award Am. Pub. Relations Assn., 1960. Mem. Assn. Theatrical Press Agt. and Mgrs. (gov., exec. com. 1955), Asso. Motion Picture Advertisers, Inc. (founder, pres. 1950-52; dir., dean sch. Showmanship, 1952-54), Pub. Relations Soc. Am. Home: 1509 Bunker Hill Dr Sun City Center FL 33570 Office: 342 Madison Ave Suite 2200 New York City NY 10017 also 1509 Bunker Hill Dr Sun City Center FL 33570

MEACHAM, CHARLES THOMAS, ophthalmologist; b. Kinston, N.C., Feb. 25, 1903; s. Charles Thomas and Susan Humphry (Pollock) M.; B.A., Duke U., 1925; M.D., U. Pa., 1930; m. Margaret T. Waterbury, July 21, 1951; children—Susan Jane, Elizabeth, Charles Thomas III. Intern, Chestnut Hill Hosp., Phila., 1930-31; served with USPHS, 1932-43, surgeon, 1941-43; resident in ophthalmology N.Y. Hosp., Cornell Med. Center, N.Y.C., 1944-45; practice medicine specializing in ophthalmology, Stamford, Conn., 1946—; clin. asst. surgeon N.Y. Eye and Ear Infirmary, N.Y.C., 1942-43; chief eye service St. Joseph's Hosp., Stamford, 1967-68, cons. staff, 1968—; surgeon to outpatients Cornell Med. Sch.-N.Y. Hosp., 1946-50; hon. attending Norwalk Hosp., 1969—; cons. staff Stamford Hosp., 1968—; instr. ophthalmology Cornell Med. Sch., 1944-45. Served to lt. comdr. M.C., USN, 1945-46; PTO. Mem. AMA, Conn., Fairfield County, Stamford med. socs., Am. Acad. Ophthalmology, Internat. Soc. Eye Surgeons, Internat. Corr. Soc. Ophthalmologists, Pan Am. Assn. Ophthalmology. Republican. Methodist. Clubs: Stamford Yacht, Midtown (Stamford); Darien Boat. Contbr. articles to profl. jours. Home: 14 Crane Rd Darien CT 06820 Office: 1911 Summer St Stamford CT 06905

MEAD, MARY ELLEN TERRY, Realtor; b. Balt., Sept. 4, 1935; d. Bernard Ennis and Ida Mae (Awalt) Terry; B.A., Mt. St. Agnes Coll., 1957; m. Robert Lawrence Mead, Aug. 9, 1958; children—M. Kathryn Mead, Robert Lawrence Mead, Christopher Mead, Daniel P. Mead. Real estate broker, pres. Terry/Mead Inc., Towson, Md., 1971—. Chmn. parish and community relations com. St. Pius Ch. Mem. Nat., Md., Greater Balt. bds. realtors., Woman's Council Realtors. Home: 427 Hopkins Rd Baltimore MD 21212 Office: 724 York Rd Towson MD 21204

MEAD, RUSSELL M., JR., ednl. cons.; b. Pueblo, Colo., Jan. 1, 1935; s. Russell M. and Marjorie (Mace) M.; A.B., Dartmouth, 1956; m. Marilyn Hunt Swanson, Sept. 19, 1976; children—Michael Evin, Judith Ann. Tchr., Woodstock County Sch., Vt., 1959-62; mem. faculty, adminstrn. Concord (Mass.) Acad., 1962-76, chmn. English, media, 1965-71, headmaster, 1971-76; pres. Saturday TV Corp.; chmn. The Editors, Inc. Mem. New Eng. Screen Edn. Assn. (charter pres.), Assn. Am. Rhodes Scholars. Author: If A Heart Rings, 1965; Tell Me Again About Snow White, 1966. Home: 30 Waterside Plaza 24J New York City NY 10010

MEADOWCROFT, JAMES ARTHUR, orthopaedic surgeon; b. Pitts., June 12, 1942; s. James Edward and Alberta Mae (Kessinger) M.; B.A., Allegheny Coll., 1964; M.D., Jefferson Med. Coll., 1968; m. Cheryl Jean Benford, Aug. 16, 1969; children—James Ward, Mark David. Intern, Harrisburg (Pa.) Polyclinic Hosp., 1968-69; resident Thomas Jefferson U. Hosp., 1969-73; orthopaedic surgeon Lankenau Hosp., Phila., 1973—; mem. teaching staff Thomas Jefferson U. Hosp. Served with U.S. Army, 1973-75. Mem. AMA, Pa., Montgromery County med. socs., Am. Acad. Orthopaedic Surgeons, Republican. Club: Merion Golf (Ardmore, Pa.). Home: 255 Lenape Dr Berwyn PA 19312 Office: 216 Lankenau Medical Bldg Philadelphia PA 19151

MEAGHER, ROBERT JOSEPH, solid waste mgmt. co. exec.; b. New Brunswick, N.J., Feb. 21, 1932; s. Edward A. and Helen (Morris) M.; grad. St. Peter's Coll., 1958; m. Marilyn Hayden, Oct. 17, 1953; children—Karen Helene, Sherrie Ann. Accountant, Celanese Corp., Summit, N.J., 1955; sec.-treas. Inmar Assos., Inc.; pres., dir. Scientific, Inc., 1965—, Kim Buc, Inc., 1966—, Eastern Indsl. Corp., Phila., 1967—, Mac San. Landfill, Inc., Deptford, N.J., 1968—, Arrow Realty, Inc., Revere, Pa., 1969—; dir. Nann Agy., Inc., Metuchen, N.J. Served with USNR, 1951-55. Mem. Nat. Assn. Accountants, A.I.M. Office: 1703 E 2d St Scotch Plains NJ 07076

MEANEY, JOSEPH THOMAS, ednl. adminstr.; b. Long Island City, N.Y., Dec. 4, 1934; s. John Michael and Mary (Morris) M.; B.S., Niagara (N.Y.) U., 1957, M.A. (fellow), 1965; m. Margaret Anne Connell, July 16, 1960; children—Kathleen Mary, Joseph Thomas, Timothy Michael. Tchr., Lake Shore Central Sch., Angola, N.Y., 1963-66, guidance counselor, 1966-73; adviser migrant edn. program, Angola, N.Y., 1969-70; instr. Sch. Bus. Adminstrn., Canisius Coll., Buffalo, 1969-71; asst. prof. Grad. Sch. Edn., St. Bonaventure U., Olean, N.Y., 1971-74; lectr. Grad Sch. Edn., Niagara U., 1972; supt. Pine Valley Central Sch. Dist., South Dayton, N.Y., 1973-77; asst. supt. for bus. Frontier Central Sch. Dist., Hamburg, N.Y., 1977—; adviser N.Y. State Migrant Edn. Program. Mem. Am. Assn. Sch. Adminstrs., Am. Assn. Curriculum and Devel., N.Y. State Council Chief Sch. Officers, N.Y. State Assn. Sch. Bus. Ofcls., Chautauqua County Chief Sch. Officers, U.S. and Can., Western N.Y. sch. bus. ofcls. assns. Author, co-author of studies of sch. bldgs. and supply statistics, scholastic analyses. Office: Frontier Central School Hamburg NY 14075

MEANS, CYRIL CHESNUT, JR., lawyer, educator; b. Phila., Dec. 21, 1918; s. Cyril Chesnut and Annette Thayer (Handley) M.; A.B., Harvard U., 1938, LL.M., 1948; J.D., Wayne State U., 1941; m. Rosaline S. Linn, Nov. 8, 1958; children—Elizabeth Rose, Annette Thayer, Cyril Chesnut. Admitted to Mich. bar, 1941; law sec. to Justice Henry M. Butzel, Mich. Supreme Ct., 1941-42; asso. prof. law Detroit Coll. Law, 1946-47; asst. prof. law Stanford U., 1948-50; legal adviser, Office of U.S. High Commr. for Germany, 1950-54; arbitration dir. N.Y. Stock Exchange, 1955-56; exec. v.p., dir. Tech. Studies, Inc., 1957—; chmn. bd. trustees Trent Sch., N.Y.C., 1963-64, dean, 1964-65; projects coordinator Western Australia Devel. Corp., 1965-66; asst. prof. N.Y. Law Sch., 1969-70, asso. prof., 1970-73, prof., 1973—; Am. co-founder Channel Tunnel Study Group; mem. N.Y. State Gov.'s Commn. to Review N.Y. State's Abortion Law, 1968. Chmn. legal com. Nat. Abortion Rights Action League, 1970—; mem. adv. com. population affairs, sec. HEW, 1973—; mem. Anglican Ch.; legal adviser Am. Ch. Union, 1962-65; chmn. N.Y. Met. Regional Br., 1963-64, lay canon Perth, Western Australia, 1966-67; vestryman Ch. of Resurrection, N.Y.C., 1975—. Served from ensign to lt. USNR, 1942-46. Mem. Am. Soc. Internat. Law, Assn. Bar City N.Y., Mich. State Bar, Am. Bar Assn., Selden Soc., Am. Soc. Legal History. Republican. Author: The Law of New York Concerning Abortion and the Status of the Foetus, 1664-1968: A Case of Cessation of Constitutionality, 1968; The Phoenix of Abortional Freedom, 1971. Home: 44 Fairview Ave Great Neck NY 11023 also Salt Island Rd Gloucester MA 01930 Office: 57 Worth St New York City NY 10013

MEANS, JOHN BARKLEY, educator; b. Cin., Jan. 2, 1939; s. Walker Wilson and Rosetta May (Miller) M.; B.A., U. Ill. at Urbana, 1960, M.A., 1963, Ph.D., 1968. U.S. Govt. research analyst on Latin Am., Washington, 1962-64; instr. Portuguese, U. Ill., 1965-67; asso. prof. Portuguese, Temple U., 1971—, co-chmn. dept. Spanish and Portuguese, 1971-75, dir. Center Critical Langs., 1975—; cons. on Portuguese and self-instructional fgn. lang. edn., 1968—. Served to 1st lt. AUS, 1960-61. NDEA fellow, 1962, 64; scholar State Dept. diplomat seminar, 1970. Mem. Nat. Assn. Self-Instructional Lang. Programs (exec. dir. 1977—), Modern Lang. Assn., Latin Am. Studies Assn., Am. Assn. Tchrs. Spanish and Portuguese, Am. Council Teaching Fgn. Langs., AAUP, Brazilian-Am. Soc., Am. Friends of the Middle East, S.R., Pi Kappa Phi (chmn. nat. future policy com.), Sigma Delta Pi, Phi Lambda Beta. Presbyterian. Editor: Essays on Brazilian Literature, 1971; contbr. articles to mags. Home: 1936 William Penn Annex Philadelphia PA 19105 Office: Humanities Bldg Box 38 Temple U Broad and Montgomery Sts Philadelphia PA 19122

MEANS, ROSALINE LINN (MRS. CYRIL CHESNUT MEANS, JR.), bus. exec., lectr.; b. Amoy, China; d. Chengpeng and Luchong (Sy) Linn; came to U.S., 1952, naturalized, 1962; A.A., U. Santo Tomas (Manila), 1949; B.S. in Comml. Edn., U. of East (Manila), 1951; M.A. in Edn., U. Ia., 1953; m. Cyril Chesnut Means, Jr., Nov. 8, 1958; children—Elizabeth Rose, Annette Thayer, Cyril Chesnut III. Tchr., Chinese Republican Sch., Manila, 1947-52; specialist in edn. physically handicapped children U. Hosp. Sch., Iowa City, 1952-53; corporate dir. and officer various cos. and corps. Lectr. State U. N.Y. Ednl. Opportunity Center, Bklyn., 1967—; adj. lectr. Community Coll. of City U. N.Y., 1969-72. Mem. profl. staff congress U. City N.Y., 1973—, also officer at large, 1973—, treas. Bklyn. chpt., 1975—. Mem. Internat. Platform Assn., United Fedn. Coll. Tchrs. (treas. Bklyn. Urban Center chpt. 1970-73) Secretarial Educators of N.Y. (membership chmn. 1972-74); individual mem. N.Y. State Assn. Jr. Colls., Bus. Tchrs. Assn. N.Y. State. Republican. Mem. Anglican Ch. Author: First Steps in Conversation, 1954. Home: 44 Fairview Ave Great Neck NY 11023 also Salt Island Rd Brier Neck Gloucester MA 01930 Office: State U NY Ednl Opportunity Center 470 Vanderbilt Ave Brooklyn NY 11238

MEANY, GEORGE, labor ofcl.; b. N.Y.C., Aug. 16, 1894; s. Michael Joseph and Anne (Cullen) M.; ed. pub. and high sch., N.Y.C.; LL.D., Seton Hall U., L.I. U., Cath. U., 1956, U. Pa., DePaul U., St. John's U., 1957, Boston Coll., 1959, U. Mass. 1963, Fordham U., Iona Coll., 1964, Georgetown U., 1965, Gonzaga Coll. High Sch., 1971; L.H.D., Oblate Coll., 1970; m. Eugenie A. McMahon, Nov. 26, 1919 (dec. 1979); children—Regina Clare Meany Mayer, Eileen Meany Lee, Genevieve Meany Lutz. Began career as an apprentice plumber, 1910, journeyman plumber, 1915; bus. rep. Plumbers Local Union No. 463, N.Y.C., 1922-34; pres. N.Y. State Fedn. of Labor, 1934-39; sec.-treas. AFL, 1940-52, pres., 1952; pres. combined orgn. AFL-CIO, 1955—. Mem. Nat. War Labor Bd., 1942—; bd. dirs. Communications Satellite Corp. Del. 12th, 14th Gen. Assembly UN. Recipient Laetare medal, 1955; Americanism award Amvets, 1963; Presdl. Medal of Freedom award, numerous others; decorated Cross of Merit with Star and Ribbon (W. Ger.); grand ofcl. Order of Merit (Italy). Democrat. Roman Catholic. Home: 7535 Cayuga Ave Bethesda MD 20034 Office: AFL-CIO 815 16th St NW Washington DC 20006

MEARS, DONALD BEAN, chiropractor; b. Milton, Vt., Jan. 23, 1905; s. Harry and Mary (Bean) M.; D.C., Ph.C., Palmer Sch. of Chiropractic, 1927; m. Florence Eleanor Armstrong, Mar. 28, 1928; 1 son, Donald Bean. Pvt. practice chiropractic, Swanton, Vt., 1928, St. Albans, Vt., 1933—; developed new technique for spinal adjustment, 1931; developed new technique for x-ray analysis of spine, 1937; lectr. Sch. Lyceums and State Socs., 1938—; granted patent on instrument for spinal analysis, 1939, on instrument to visually record certain types of spinal distortions, 1940; apptd. mem. Vt. Bd. of Chropractic Examiners by Gov. Wills, 1942, by Gov. Proctor, 1945, by Gov. Gibson. 1948, (chmn. 1942—) by Gov. Emerson, 1951; pres. Vt. Chiropractic X-ray Council, 1957, 58. Recipient D.D. Palmer Sci. award Palmer Coll. Chiropractic, 1968, Disting. Service award, 1974, 50 Yr. Service award, 1977. Vice comdr. USCG Aux., 1953, Flotilla Vol. comdr., 1954, life mem., 1968. Mem. Vt. Hist. Soc., Nat. Bd. Chiropractic Examiners (chmn. 1946-1951), Am. Chiropractic Assn., Vt. Chiropractic Assn. (legis. com. and pres., plaque for 30 years service 1968), AAAS, Delta Sigma Chi. Completed, 1950, study of X-rays showing postural defect of spine in 95 per cent of mental cases. Two chiropractic colls. teaching methods of X-ray analysis and adjustment, 1952. Author: Technique Textbook, 1976. Contbr. articles in Chiropractor the Jour. of Drugless Physicians, Voice of New England, Internat. Chiropractic Rev., N.Y. State Chiropractic Jour., Motor Boat, Prevention mag., Jour. Am. Chiropractic Assn., Chiropractic Econs. Home: 60 Bank Street Clinic 160 N Main St St Albans VT 05478

MEARS, JOHN HERBERT, JR., cattle breeder; b. Washington, Mar. 1, 1914; s. John Herbert and Annie Lind (Wilkins) M.; ed. pub. schs.; m. Sonya Marina Lawrence, Dec. 19, 1968; children by previous marriage—Sandra (Mrs. Wade Hampden Massie), Susan (Mrs. Michael Bennett), Nancy (Mrs. J.H. Lichtenstein), John Herbert III. Profl. golfer, 1932-37; founder, propr. Brookwood Farms Dairy, Balt., 1940—, Mears Plywood Co., 1945—, Monumental Millwork Corp., 1946—, Mears Aluminum Corp., 1955—, Universal Metal Mouldings Corp., 1957—; prop. Manor Vale Farm, 1950—, J.H. Mears & Co., real estate investments, 1964—, Mears Marina, 1966—; pres. Dorsey Motor Speedway, 1956—, Dorsey Ind. Park, 1958—, Dorsey Adminstrv. Services, 1960—, Eastport Marina, 1967—, Port Eastport Corp., 1968—; owner Easton (Md.) Plaza Shopping Center, 1977—, Yacht Haven, Oxford, Md., 1977—, Foxhall Farm, Flint Hill, Va., 1977—, Highland Manor Farm, Warrenton, Va., 1977—. Named adm. of Chesapeake Bay, Md. gov., 1970. Mem. Am. Hereford Breeders Assn., U.S. C. of C., Nat. Assn. Stock Car Auto Racing. Democrat. Episcopalian. Clubs: Severn River Yacht (past commodore), Anapolis Yacht, Ocean Reef, Ocean Reef Yacht, Turf Valley Country, Md. Capitol Yacht, Rolling Road Country, Gibson Island Yacht, Tred Avon Yacht, Talbot Country, Rotary. Patentee cushion glide sash balance, numerous others. Home: Sunset Hall Route 4 Easton MD 21601 Office: Easton Plaza Easton MD 21601

MEARS, WALTER ROBERT, journalist; b. Lynn, Mass., Jan. 11, 1935; s. Edward Lewis and Edythe Emily (Campbell) M.; B.A., Middlebury Coll., 1956; m. Sally Danton, Dec. 28, 1956 (dec. Dec. 1962); children—Pamela (dec.), Walter Robert (dec.); m. 2d, Joyce Marie Lund, Aug. 4, 1963; children—Stephanie Joy, Susan Marie, Newsman, AP, Boston, 1956, corr. Montpelier, Vt., 1956-60, state house corr., Boston, 1960-61, newsman, Washington, 1961-69, chief polit. writer, 1969-72, asst. chief Washington bur., 1973-74, spl. corr., 1975—; chief Washington bur. Detroit News, 1974-75; chief Washington bur. AP, 1977—, v.p., 1978—. Recipient ann. award AP Mng. Editors Assn., 1973; Pulitzer prize for nat. reporting, 1977. Mem. Phi Beta Kappa, Delta Kappa Epsilon. Clubs: Gridiron, Army Navy Country (Arlington, Va.). Home: 1338 Potomac School Rd McLean VA 22101 Office: Associated Press 2021 K St NW Washington DC 20006

MEBUS, CHARLES FILLMORE, II, state legislator, engring. co. exec.; b. Abington, Pa., June 15, 1928; s. George Brinker and Estelle Claston (Negus) M.; B.S. in Chemistry, Pa. State U., 1949, B.S. in Sanitary Engring., 1951; m. Joy Campbell Robbins, July 26, 1958; 1 dau., Lisa Jane Campbell. Jr. engr. George B. Mebus, Inc., Glenside, Pa., 1951, v.p., 1954-70, pres., Abington, 1970—. Mem. Pa. Ho. of Reps., 1965—, vice chmn. com. on appropriations, 1973-74, minority chmn. local govt. com., 1975-76. Served with C.E., AUS, 1951-53. Decorated NATO medal. Registered profl. engr., Pa., Del., N.J., Md., Va. Mem. ASCE, ASTM, Am. Water Works Assn., Water Pollution Control Fedn., Am. Cons. Engrs. Council, Sigma Alpha Epsilon. Episcopalian (vestryman 1957-60). Rotarian. Home: 214 Maple Ave Wyncote PA 19095 Office: 1560 York Rd Abington PA 19001

MECCA, WILLIAM ANTHONY, advt. exec.; b. N.Y.C., Feb. 8, 1944; s. William Anthony and Dorothy Teresa Mecca; B.B.A., Hofstra U.; M.B.A., L.I. U.; m. Kathleen Earley, May 8, 1971; 1 dau., Megan Elizabeth. Sr. sales rep. USV Pharm. Corp., N.Y.C., 1969-73; account exec. Rolf Werner Rosenthal Advt., N.Y.C., 1973-74; account supr. Robert A. Becker Advt., N.Y.C., 1974-77; v.p., group supr. Sudler & Hennessey Advt., N.Y.C., 1977—; mktg. cons. Active Am. Diabetic Assn., N.Y.C. Served with M.C., U.S. Army. Mem. Am. Mktg. Assn., Mgmt. Assn. Am., Pharm. Advt. Club. Editor, Introspection jour. Home: 109 Chestnut St Garden City NY 11530 Office: 130 E 59th St New York NY 10022

MECKLER, ALAN MARSHALL, publisher; b. Queens, N.Y., July 25, 1945; s. Herman Lewis and Lillian (Brodsky) M.; B.A., Columbia U., 1967, M.A., 1968, Ph.D., 1978; m. Ellen Laurie Finkelstein, Sept. 10, 1969; children—Naomi Anne, Catherine Sarah, Caroline Jill. Dir. mktg. Kennikat Press, Port Washington, N.Y., 1969-70, Greenwood Press, Westport, Conn., 1970-71; pres. Microform Rev., Weston, Conn., 1971—; dir., chmn. bd. Servco Leasing Corp. Mem. ALA, Nat. Micrographics Assn., Info. Industry Assn. Author: The Draft and Its Enemies, 1974; Oral History Collections, 1974; U.S. History to 1877 and to Present, 2 vols., 1975. Office: 520 Riverside Ave Westport CT 06880

MECKLEY, RAYMOND HENRY, mfg. engr.; b. Glen Rock, Pa., Oct. 13, 1915; s. Bertus S. and Lettie Alverta (Myers) M.; night student Pa. State Coll., 1937-54; m. Ethel Romaine Wildasin, Sept. 1, 1939; children—Joan Elaine, Elizabeth Ann, Alan Ray. Chief engr. Davey Products, Inc., Red Lion, Pa., 1951-59; v.p. Flinchbaugh Products, Inc., Red Lion, 1959-62; group leader prodn. engring. Honeywell Inc., Mpls., 1962-68; mgr. mfg. engring. York div. Am. Machine and Foundry Co., 1968-71; sr. mfg. engr. York div. Borg-Warner Corp., 1971—. Mem. Soc. Mfg. Engrs. (bd. dirs. 1964-68), Am. Soc. Metals. Contbr. to numerous tech. books in mfg. engring field. Home: 4233 Webster Dr York PA 17402 Office: Richland Ave York PA 17405

MEDEIROS, HUMBERTO SOUSA, clergyman; b. Arrifes, Sao Miguel, Azores, Oct. 6, 1915; s. Antonio Sousa and Maria de Jesus Sousa Massa (Flor) M.; came to U.S., 1931, naturalized, 1940; M.A., Catholic U. Am., 1942, S.T.L., 1946, S.T.D., 1952; LL.D., Stonehill Coll., Mass., 1959. Ordained priest Roman Catholic Ch., 1946; asst. St. John of God Parish, Somerset, Mass., 1946, St. Michael's Parish, Fall River, Mass., 1946-47, Our Lady of Health Parish, Fall River, 1947, St. Vincent de Paul Health Camp, 1948-49, Mt. Carmel Ch., New Bedford, Mass., 1949; research N.Am. Coll., Rome, 1949-50; asst. Holy Name Ch., Fall River, 1950-51; sec., asst. chancellor, chaplain Sacred Hearts Acad. and Vicar for Religious, 1951-53; vice-chancellor, chancellor Fall River (Mass.) Diocese, 1953-66; named domestic prelate, 1958; pastor St. Michael's Parish, 1960-66; consecrated bishop, 1966; bishop Diocese Brownsville, Tex., 1966-70; archbishop Archdiocese Boston, 1970—; named to Coll. Cardinals, 1973. Mem. U.S. Cath. Conf., Nat. Conf. Cath. Bishops. Address: 2101 Commonwealth Ave Brighton MA 02135

MEDICO, FRANK, govt. ofcl.; b. S. Braintree, Mass., Apr. 23, 1924; s. Domenic and Christine (Regatta) M.; B.C.S., Benjamin Franklin U., 1950; M.F.A., Columbus U., 1952; A.M.P., Harvard U., 1969; m. Billie Vaughnita Osborne, Feb. 9, 1947; children—Jane, Fred, Patricia. Staff accountant Def. Prodn. Adminstrn. and Dept. Agr., Washington, 1950-56; supervisory accountant U.S. GAO, Washington, 1956-66, asst. dir. gen. govt. div., 1966—. Mem. exec. bd. Waynewood Citizens Assn., 1969-76, pres., 1972; co-chmn. Mt. Vernon Council Citizens Assn., 1972-74, exec. bd. mem.; v.p. Taxpayers Alliance, 1978; exec. bd. Fairfax County Fedn. Citizens Assns., 1975, 76. Served with USN, 1942-46, 50. Recipient various govt. service awards, John L. Mitchel award Nat. Assn. Accountants, 1969. Mem. Am. Mgmt. Assn., Am. Soc. Pub. Adminstrn., Am. Inst. C.P.A.'s, Nat. Assn. Accountants, Harvard Bus. Club. Club: K.C. Home: 1000 Emerald Dr Alexandria VA 22308 Office: 441 G St Washington DC 20548

MEDIN, A. LOUIS, computer co. exec.; b. Balt., Oct. 2, 1925; s. Nathan and Bessie (Zell) M.; B.E., Johns Hopkins, 1948; Ph.D., Ohio State U., 1951; m. Julia A. Levin, Dec. 24, 1950; children—Douglas, David, Thomas, Linda. Chem. engr. AEC, Wilmington, Del., 1951-53; research engr. Ford Motor Co., Dearborn, Mich., 1953-55; chief nuclear reactor design ALCO Products, Schenectady, 1955-58; head nuclear applications U.S. Steel, Monroeville, Pa., 1958-62; project mgr. missile design AVCO Corp., Wilmington, Mass., 1963-65; sr. govt. analyst, mgr. IBM, Manassas, Va., 1965—; asst. dir. environment and life Dept. Def., 1972-74; lectr. in field. Mem. Monroeville Parks and Recreation Commn., 1960; chmn. Monroeville Mental Health Assn., 1961; mem. Monroeville Zoning and Planning Commn., 1960. Served with USN, 1944-46. Recipient award Am. Chem. Soc., 1957, IBM, 1969. Registered profl. engr., Md. Fellow Am. Inst. Chemists; mem. Nat. Security Indsl. Assn., Am. Inst. Chem. Engrs., Water Pollution Control Fedn., Am. Def. Preparedness Assn., Johns Hopkins, Ohio State U. alumni assns. Contbr. numerous articles to profl. jours. Home: 10912 Candlelight Ln Potomac MD 20854 Office: 9500 Godwin Dr Manassas VA 22110

MEDINA, HAROLD R., judge, author; b. Bklyn., Feb. 16, 1888; s. Joaquin A. and Elizabeth (Fash) M.; A.B., Princeton U., 1909 (highest honors in French); LL.B., Columbia U., 1912 (Ordronaux Prize); hon. degrees from 25 colls. and univs., 1947—; m. Ethel Forde Hillyer, June 6, 1911; children—Harold Raymond, Standish Forde. Admitted to N.Y. bar, 1912; practiced in N.Y.C.; prof. law Columbia U., 1915-40; judge U.S. Dist. Ct., So. Dist. N.Y., 1947-51, U.S. circuit judge Ct. Appeals, 2d Circuit, 1951-58, ret., 1958; now sr. circuit judge; presided, N.Y.C. over trial of 11 Communists charged with conspiracy to teach and advocate overthrow of U.S. govt. by force and violence, Jan.-Oct. 1949. Charter trustee emeritus Princeton U.; life trustee emeritus Tchrs. Coll., Columbia U. Awards and medals, Freedom Found., Holland Soc., N.Y. Bd. Trade, Nat. Inst. Social Sci., Eleanor Van Rensselaer Medal by Nat. Soc. Colonial Dames, VFW, Bklyn. Coll., Nat. Soc. New Eng. Women, S.A.R.; Am. Edn. award NEA, 1963; Golden Anniversary award Am. Judicature Soc., 1963, Justice award, 1971; award Tex. Bill Rights Found., 1964; Learned Hand medal Fed. Bar Assn. N.Y., N.J. and Conn., 1965; Columbia Law Sch. Alumni medal, 1965; Distinguished Service award Tchrs. Coll., Columbia U., 1966; Gold medal N.Y. State Bar Assn., 1967; Man of Year award Comml. Law League Am., 1970; honored at Columbia by establishment of new chair in law sch. Harold R. Medina professorship, 1973; James Madison award Nat. Broadcast Editorial Assn., 1976; Distinguished Pub. Service award Ohio Newspaper Assn., 1976; reported as only fed. judge still doing substantial ct. work at age 90 by N.Y. Times, 1978. Fellow Am. Acad. Arts and Scis.; mem., sometime officer, chmn. coms. several profl. assns. and orgns.; hon. mem. several state bars. Episcopalian. Clubs: Univ., Princeton (N.Y.C.); Lawyers (pres. 1942-48), Westhampton Country, Century, Church. Author numerous legal books, 1922—; those since 1950 include: Judge Medina Speaks, 1954; The Anatomy of Freedom, 1959. Contbr. to legal revs. Home: 14 E 75th St New York City NY 10021 also Westhampton NY 11977 Office: US Court House Foley Sq New York City NY 10007

MEDINA-SPYROPOULOS, ESPERANZA, cons. firm adminstr.; b. Mexico, Apr. 25, 1936; d. Jesus and Galdina (Sandoval) Medina-Villalobos; B.A., McMurry Coll., 1955; M.A., U. Tex., 1957; diplomas U. Vienna (Austria), 1961, U. Tours (France), 1963, Washington U., St. Louis, 1963; M.S., Georgetown U., Washington, 1970, Ph.D., 1972; married, May 28, 1965. Faculty Am. U., Georgetown U., U. Tex.; sr. scientist Human Resources Research Office, 1968-70; acad. coordinator World Instrn. and Transl., 1970-71; asso. dir. Right to Read Office, Hew-U.S. Office Edn., Washington, 1971-72; sr. research scientist in edn. Pres.'s Cabinet Com. on Opportunities for Spanish Speaking People, Washington, 1972-73; dir. acad. programs Devel. Assos. Inc., Washington, 1973—. Pres. Hope Assos., Inc.; del. Internat. Women's Year Conf., Mexico City, 1975. Mem. adv. bd. Planned Parenthood Assn. of Greater Washington; v.p. World Population Soc. Recipient award HEW-U.S. Office Edn., award NDEA. Univ. fellow Georgetown U. Mem. AAUW, League Women Voters, Sigma Delta Pi, Pi Delta Phi, Kappa Delta Pi, Sigma Tau Delta, Alpha Chi. Contbr. poems, articles on linguistics, multicultural-bilingual edn., culturally disadvantaged children, early childhood edn., women, population to profl. jours. Address: 2600 Virginia Ave NW Washington DC 20037

MEDLEY, KENNETH WAYNE, editor; b. Whitesboro, Tex., Mar. 8, 1921; s. Everett R. and Elsie Mae (Ragland) M.; B.A., So. Ill. U., 1947; postgrad. U. Mo., 1947-48; m. Katie Lee Knight, Dec. 25, 1943; children—Richard Wayne, Sharon Kay, Roger Kenneth. Reporter, copy editor St. Louis Globe Democrat, 1948-52; v.p. Mgmt. & Econs. Research Inc., Palo Alto, Calif., 1965-70; editor, pub. Assn. Mgmt., Washington, 1970-75; editor Nation's Business, Washington, 1975—. Served with USAF, World War II. Decorated Air medal; certified assn. exec. Mem. Nat. Assn. Bus. Economists. Methodist. Editor: The Law of Associations, 1973; The Principles of Association Management, 1975. Office: Nation's Business 1615 H St NW Washington DC 20036*

MEDOFF, WILLIAM, advt. exec.; b. N.Y.C., Aug. 26, 1903; s. Jacob and Sarah F. (Shroit) M.; student N.Y.U.; m. Sylvia Macnow, Apr. 13, 1926; children—Elinor Medoff Fisch, Betsy Ann Medoff Haveson. Advt. mgr. William Gluckin Co., N.Y.C., 1928; from advt. mgr. to v.p. to pres. Nat. Cellulose Corp., 1929-39; with Sitrue Inc., 1939-58, pres., 1954-58; cons. Doeskin products, 1960-62; mgr. unit mktg. pvt. brands Hudson Pulp & Paper Co., 1958-60; mem. tissue industry adv. com. OPA-WPB, World War II. Recipient Advt. Club Photography award, 1941-43, Am. Mgmt. Assn. award, 1937. Club: Advertising (N.Y.C.). Address: 6253 Dieterle Crescent Forest Hills NY 11374

MEDSGER, GERALD WILLIAM, educator, ret. army officer; b. Los Angeles, Aug. 18, 1927; s. Gerald Edgar and Evelyn (McGown) M.; B.S., U.S. Mil. Acad., 1948; M.S., Calif. Inst. Tech., 1957; M.S., N.Y. U., 1968; m. Margery Irene Bufano, June 9, 1948; children—Margery Susan, William Ronald. Commd. 2d lt. U.S. Army, 1948, advanced through grades to col., 1969; resident engr. USAF, Europe, 1949-52; instr. U.S. Army Engr. Sch., 1953; resident engr., Labrador, Nfld., Azores, 1954-55; asst. prof. mil. sci., tactics Mo. Sch. Mines, 1957-59; constrn. engr., operations officer, Europe, 1959-62; chief Electronics Projects br. U.S. Army Airborne, Electronics, Spl. Warfare Bd., Ft. Bragg, N.C., 1963-65; asso. prof.

math. U.S. Mil. Acad., West Point, N.Y., 1965-69, dir. Instl. Research, 1969-75; ret., 1975; dean U.S. Mil. Acad. Prep. Sch., Ft. Monmouth, N.J., 1975—. Fellow AAAS, ASCE; mem. Nat., Mo. socs. profl. engrs., Soc. Am. Mil. Engrs., Assn. Instl. Research, Am. Soc. Engring. Edn., Am. Assn. for Higher Edn., N.Y. Acad. Scis., Assn. U.S. Army, Am. Assn. Physics Tchrs., Math. Assn. Am., Mil. Ops. Research Soc., Soc. Indsl. and Applied Math., Sierra Club. Baptist. Home: 19 Morford Pl Apt 10I Red Bank NJ 07701 Office: Dean Academics US Mil Acad Prep Sch Fort Monmouth NJ

MEDWIG, THOMAS MICHAEL, mfg. co. exec., accountant; b. Pittsburgh, Sept. 23, 1941; s. Wassil and Nell (Telep) M.; B.S. in Bus., U. Minn., 1963; m. Margaret Esther Trottnow, Nov. 5, 1966; children—Michael, Christine, Mark, Brian. Accountant, Shell Oil Co., Chgo., 1963-64; tax accountant H.J. Heinz Co., Pitts., 1964-66, E.I. Du Pont de Nemours Corp., Wilmington, Del., 1966-68; tax mgr. Price Waterhouse & Co., Pitts., 1968-72; dir. taxes Joy Mfg. Co., Pitts., 1972—. Mem. Borough of Carnegie (Pa.) Council, 1972-74, chmn. fin. com., 1972-74; bd. dirs. Mt. Lebanon Civic League, 1975-77. Served with USAF, 1968. Honor scholar Marietta Coll., 1959-60; C.P.A. Mem. Pa., Am. insts. C.P.A.'s, Tax Execs. Inst. (pres. Pitts. chpt. 1977-78). Democrat. Ukrainian Catholic. Clubs: Pitts. Tax, Ukrainian-Am. Citizens, Elks. Home: 715 Pinetree Rd Pittsburgh PA 15243 Office: Henry W Oliver Bldg Pittsburgh PA 15222

MEECH, RICHARD CAMPBELL, lawyer; b. Portsmouth, Hampshire, Eng., Sept. 16, 1921; s. Richard George and Elizabeth (Campbell) M.; B.A., U. Toronto (Can.), 1946; postgrad. Osgoode Hall Law Sch., Toronto, 1950; LL.M., Harvard U., 1951; m. Carol Crockett, Oct. 6, 1951; children—Susan Crockett, Richard George, Peter, Sarah Elizabeth, Nancy Bingham. Admitted to Ont. bar, 1950; joined Borden & Elliot, Toronto, 1951—, sr. partner, 1957—; named Queen's counsel, 1960; hon. consul of Thailand, Toronto, 1967—; dir. Brit. Steel Corp. (Can.) Ltd., Budd Automotive Co. Can. Ltd., Drecona Industries Ltd., Howden Group Ltd., Harvey Hubbell Can. Ltd., RC Cola Can. Ltd., Stanton Pipes Ltd., Personal Ins. Co. Can.; dir., v.p., sec. Textron Can. Ltd.; dir., chmn. exec. com. Howden Canada Ltd.; dir., vice-chmn. Howden Group Canada Ltd.; dir., mem. exec. com. Slater Steel Industries Ltd.; dir., sec. Canabam, Ltd.; sec. Can. Securities Inst., Nat. Contingency Fund, Can. Depository for Securities Ltd. Mem. adv. council Ridley Coll.; mem. Met. Toronto adv. bd. Salvation Army; pres. Wellesley Coll. Can. Found.; trustee Sunnybrook Med. Centre, Toronto, Havergal Coll. Found., Toronto, chmn., 1972-74; trustee Can. Hemophilia Soc.; nat. chmn. Queen's U. Parents' Assn. Served as flying officer RCAF, 1942-46. Mem. Internat. Bar Assn. (sec. bus. sect.). Clubs: York, Badminton and Racquet, Nat., Toronto Golf, Harvard Law Sch. Assn. Ont. (pres. 1973-75), Lawyers, Canadian (pres. 1974-75), Empire, St. George's Soc. (Toronto); Glenmajor Angling, Harvard (N.Y.C.); Garden of the Gods (Colorado Springs); Coral Beach and Tennis (Bermuda). Home: 40 Stratheden Rd Toronto ON M4N 1E4 Canada Office: 250 University Ave Toronto ON M5H 3E9 Canada

MEEK, DONALD CHAMBERLIN, obstetrician, gynecologist; b. Los Angeles, Oct. 16, 1935; s. Joseph Alcinus and Clara Amy (Phillips) M.; B.A., Ohio Wesleyan U., 1957; M.D., Ohio State U., 1961; m. Julia Dyckman Stromsem, Oct. 29, 1977; children—Steven Scott, Lisa Lynn, John Emory. Intern, Phila. Gen. Hosp., 1961-62; resident in obstetrics and gynecology Kings County Hosp., Bklyn., 1962-63, Washington Hosp. Center, 1965-68; practice medicine specializing in obstetrics and gynecology, Washington, 1968—; clin. instr. obstetrics and gynecology Georgetown U. Sch. Medicine; chmn. bd. Childbirth Edn. Assn., 1970-72. Served with M.C., USAF, 1963-65. Diplomate Am. Bd. Obstetrics and Gynecology. Fellow Am. Fertility Soc.; mem. Am. Soc. Psychoprophylaxis in Obstetrics (pres. Washington chpt. 1975-77). Home: 6008 Highland Dr Chevy Chase MD 20015 Office: 5530 Wisconsin Ave Chevy Chase MD 20015

MEEKER, JOHN HARBECK, JR., pathologist; b. Orange, N.J., Mar. 7, 1918; s. John Harbeck and Adeline Helena (Medinger) M.; B.A., Drew U., 1940; M.D., George Washington U., Washington, 1952; m. Viola Mae Zinn, Apr. 29, 1950; children—Janet Harbeck, Pamela Southmayd. Intern, Hosp. Center Orange, N.J., 1952-53; practice gen. medicine, East Orange, N.J., 1953-55; resident pathology George Washington U., Washington, 1955-58; asst. pathologist Armed Forces Inst. Pathology, Washington, 1958-60; asso. pathologist Newton-Wellesley Hosp., Newton Lower Falls, Mass., 1960-74, chief pathologist, dir. labs., 1974—, dir. sch. med. tech., 1974—; asso. clin. prof. pathology Tufts U., Boston, 1977—. Served with USNR, 1942-46; ETO, PTO. Diplomate Am. Bd. Pathology, Nat. Bd. Med. Examiners. Mem. Coll. Am. Pathologist, Am. Soc. Clin. Pathologist, Am. Soc. Dermatopathology, AMA, Internat. Acad. Pathology, Am. Assn. Blood Banks, Longwood Cricket Club, Longwood Covered Cts. Republican. Episcopalian. Contbr. articles to profl. publs. Home: 19 Cornell Rd Wellesley MA 02181 Office: Newton-Wellesley Hosp 2014 Washington St Newton Lower Falls MA 02162

MEESE, HAROLD FREDERICK, scientist; b. Buffalo, Nov. 28, 1930; s. Harold F. and Mildred (Foulke) M.; student Allegheny Coll., 1948-50; B.E.E., Cornell U., 1954; m. Nadine Estelle VanTassel, 1951 (d. 1975); children—Jo Linda, Jan Leslie, Van Jeffrey. Engr., Airborne Instruments Lab., Inc., Mineola, N.Y. 1954-55; asst. engr. Cornell Aero. Lab., Inc., Cornell U., Buffalo, 1955-58, asso. physicist, 1958-60, research engr., 1960-62, staff prin. engring. physicist, 1962-64, head interscis. br., 1964-71; chmn. Interscience Assos., Buffalo, 1971—; cons. phys. scis. N.Y. riparian law; dir. Findley Lake Corp. (N.Y.). Mem. AAAS, IEEE, Am., Northeastern weed sci. socs., Chautauqua Lake Assn. (v.p. 1967-75), Sigma Xi. Home: 8625 Sunset Dr Williamsville NY 14221 Office: Interscience Assos Box 15 Buffalo NY 14221

MEGAHED, MOHAMED SALAH, neurologist; b. Mansurah, Egypt, Aug. 18, 1928; s. Ibrahim M. and Amouna A. (Naga) M.; came to U.S., 1964, naturalized, 1973; M.C., B.Ch., Cairo U., 1951, D.M., 1959; M.R.C.P., 1962; m. Mai Hathout, Apr. 1, 1954; children—Hatem, Amr, Nivine. Physician, Ct. of King Saud of Saudi Arabia, 1953-60; intern Cairo Univ. Hosp., 1950-51, Mecca Al Zaher Hosp., 1952-53; resident State U. N.Y. at Buffalo, 1964-67, asst. prof. neurology, 1967-72; chief neurology VA Hosp. Buffalo, 1972-73; practice medicine, specializing in neurology, N. Tonawanda, N.Y., 1973—; chief neurophysiology lab. Mt. St. Mary Hosp., Niagara Falls, 1973—; attending physician DeGraff Hosp., N. Tonawanda, 1973—, Kenmore (N.Y.) Mercy Hosp., 1973—, Deaconess Hosp., Buffalo, 1973—. Recipient Year Book award Med. Sch. Buffalo, 1971. Mem. AMA, N.Y. State, Niagara County med. socs., Am. Acad. Neurology. Moslem. Contbr. articles in field to med. jours. Home: 93 Telfair Dr Williamsville NY 14221 Office: 1089 Kinkead Ave North Tonawanda NY 14120

MEGERSON, JOHN S., law enforcement tng. adminstr.; b. Kansas City, Mo., Dec. 16, 1941; s. Shellvie E. and Mary K. (Boehm) M.; B.S. in Law Enforcement and Psychology, Central Mo. State U., 1967; M.S. in Counseling, Shippensburg (Pa.) State Coll., 1970; m. Nancy C. Harbison, June 19, 1965; children—Tracy Lynn, Kimberly JoAnn, John Steven. Police officer City of Independence (Mo.), 1963-67, detective, 1965-67; asst. prof. police adminstrn. Harrisburg Area (Pa.) Community Coll., 1967-70; chmn. law enforcement and criminal justice programs Des Moines Area Community Coll., Ankeny, Iowa, 1970-72; prof., dir. and coordinator Criminal Justice Tng. Center, Harrisburg Area Community Coll., 1972-78, dir. public safety, 1978—; cons. and lectr. Hocking Tech. Inst. Police Adminstrn. and workshops, Nelsonville, Ohio, 1972-74; coordinator Police Community Relations Inst. for police agys. in central Pa., 1970—; pres. Profl. Assos. Internat., Inc.; mem. law enforcement adv. com. Parsons Coll., Fairfield, Iowa, 1970-72, Drake U., Des Moines, 1971-72; tech. cons. on police tng. film for Batten, Batten, Hudson and Swab, Inc., Des Moines, 1972, Calif. State U., Long Beach, 1976. Mem. Harrisburg CSC, 1970. Recipient Service award Harrisburg Community Coll., 1970, Plaque of Appreciation award Crime Clinic of Greater Harrisburg, 1975. Mem. Internat. Assn. Chiefs of Police, Acad. Criminal Justice Scis., Lambda Alpha Epsilon. Contbr. articles in field to profl. publs. Home: RD 1 York Hill Rd Etters PA 17319 Office: Criminal Justice Training Center 3300 Cameron St Rd Harrisburg PA 17110

MEGHREBLIAN, ROBERT VARTAN, mfg. co. exec., physicist; b. Cairo, Egypt, Sept. 6, 1922; s. Vahan V. and Mary (Kurkjian) M.; came to U.S., 1923, naturalized, 1946; B.Engring. (Gotshall-Powell scholar), Rensselaer Poly. Inst., 1943; M.S. (Guggenheim fellow), Calif. Inst. Tech., 1950, Ph.D. (Guggenheim fellow), 1953; m. Mary J. Walton, Apr. 16, 1955; children—David V., Susan L. Lectr., Oak Ridge Nat. Lab., 1952-55, asso. project mgr., 1955-58; chief sect. physics jet propulsion lab. Calif. Inst. Tech., 1958-60, mgr. space scis. div., 1960-68, dep. asst. lab. dir., 1968-71, asso. prof. applied mechanics, 1960-61; v.p., dir. tech. Cabot Corp., Boston, 1971-77, v.p. research and engring., 1977—. Served to lt. (j.g.) USN, 1941-46; PTO. Fellow Am. Nuclear Soc., Am. Inst. Aeros. and Astronautics (asso.); mem. Indsl. Research Inst., Sigma Xi. Author: Reactor Analysis, 1960. Home: 1530 Beacon St Brookline MA 02146 Office: 125 High St Boston MA 02110

MEGNA, PHILIP LEWIS, JR., banker; b. Bklyn., Aug. 8, 1930; s. Philip Lewis and Mae Josephine (Spampinato) M.; B.A., Villanova U., 1952; postgrad. Pace Coll., 1956-59; m. Helene E. Kempner, Mar. 8, 1953; children—Joanne, Andrea, Julie. Treas., Megna Co., Inc., Elizabethport, N.J., 1954-62; mgr. data processing Howell Electric Motors Co., Plainfield, N.J., 1962-66; mgr. mining and mfg. systems Johns-Manville Co. (N.J.), 1966-69; dir. mgmt. services Permacel div. Johnson & Johnson Co., North Brunswick, N.J., 1969-72, Purolator, Inc., Rahway, N.J., 1972-76; with Chem. Bank, N.Y.C., 1976—; mktg. officer Domestic Depository Instns. Group, 1977—; pres. New Century Data Systems, Inc., 1966-69. Served with USN, 1952-54. Mem. Assn. Systems Mgmt., Am. Mgmt. Assn. Republican. Roman Catholic. Home: 36 Carriage Hill Dr Colts Neck NJ 07722 Office: 20 Pine St New York City NY 10005

MEGRUE, GEORGE HENRY, microanalytical systems co. exec.; b. Jamaica, N.Y., Mar. 23, 1936; s. Enoch Gest and Mildred Katherine (Marker) M.; A.B., Amherst Coll., 1957; A.M., Columbia U., 1960, Ph.D., 1962; m. Suzanne Jacobsen, Mar. 29, 1958; children—George Richard, Katherine Diane, Karen Lynn, Kevin Scott. Research asso. Brookhaven Nat. Lab., Upton, N.Y., 1962-64, research chemist, 1964-66; research scientist Smithsonian Astrophys. Obs., Cambridge, Mass., 1966-73; research fellow Harvard Coll. Obs., Cambridge, 1966-73; founder, pres. Megrue Microanalytical Systems, New Canaan, Conn., 1974—; co-founder Foxglove Sch., New Canaan, 1976; instr. State U. N.Y., Stony Brook, 1965-66. Nat. Geog. Soc. grantee for Ethiopian Rift Valley Expdn., 1969-72; NASA grantee for lunar rock analyses, 1970-73. Fellow AAAS; mem. Am. Geophys. Union, Am. Chem. Soc., Am. Mgmt. Assn. Lutheran. Clubs: Explorers, Rotary (sec. New Canaan club 1977-78). Patentee system and technique for gas analysis. Office: 130 Oenoke Ridge New Canaan CT 06840

MEHDI, MOHAMMAD TAKI, newspaper editor; b. Baghdad, Iraq, Jan. 6, 1928; s. Al Haj M. and Zahara (Moenni) M.; came to U.S., 1949; B.A., U. Calif. at Berkeley, 1953, M.A., 1954, Ph.D., 1960; m. Beverlee Turner, June 20, 1953; children—Anisa, Janan, Laila. Teaching asst. U. Calif., 1958-60; dir. Arab Information Center, San Francisco, 1960-63; founder, sec. gen. Action Com. on Am.-Arab Relations, 1964—; exec. editor Action Newspaper, N.Y.C., 1969—. Adviser to Arab dels. to UN, 1963-64; lectr. Arab and Middle East Affairs, 1960—. Recipient Book of Year award Soc. of Friends of Book in Beirut, 1963. Mem. Am. Polit. Sci. Assn., Am. Soc. for Legal and Polit. Philosophy. Author: Constitutionalism, Western and Middle Eastern, 1961; A Nation of Lions Chained, 1963; Peace in the Middle East, 1967; Kennedy and Sirhan: Why?, 1968. Editor: Palestine and the Bible, 1970; Peace in Palestine, 1976. Address: PO Box 416 New York City NY 10017

MEHL, ROGER HOWARD, elec. engr., transp. cons.; b. Chgo., Dec. 2, 1943; s. Paul Theodore and Anita Marie (von Fange) M.; B.S. in Elec. Engring., U. Ill., 1966, M.B.A., 1968; m. Carol E. Groves, Nov. 26, 1977; 1 dau. Jessica Aline. Operations research analyst, Penn Central Transp. Co., N.Y.C., Phila., 1968-70; sr. indsl. engr., 1970-72; sr. systems engr. Transp. & Distbn. Assos., Media, Pa., 1972-76; dir. planning support Conrail, Phila., 1976—. Mem. Transp. Research Forum, Phi Eta Simga, Sigma Iota Epsilon. Democrat. Developed gen. freight yard simulation model; simulated high-speed passenger train service in N.E. Corridor. Contbr. articles in field to profl. jours. Home: 240 Quince St Philadelphia PA 19107 Office: Conrail 1434 Six Penn Center Plaza Philadelphia PA 19103

MEHLMAN, MYRON A., biochemist, environ. health adminstr., corp. exec.; b. Zaleschiki, Poland, Dec. 21, 1934; came to U.S., 1948, naturalized, 1953; B.S., Coll. City N.Y., 1957; Ph.D. (NIH fellow), Mass. Inst. Tech., 1964; m. Constance L. Lloyd, Sept. 5, 1960; children—Mara Elizabeth, Hope, Alison. Asso. prof. biochemistry Rutgers U., 1967-69; prof. biochemistry U. Neb. Coll. Medicine, 1969-74; chief biochem. toxicology FDA, Washington, 1972-73; spl. asst. for toxicology, environ. affairs, and nutrition Office Asst. Sec. Health, HEW, Washington, 1973-75, spl. asst. to asso. dir. for program planning and evaluation NIH, Bethesda, Md., 1975-76, intragy. liaison officer, from 1976; corp. exec., dir. environ. health and toxicology Mobil Oil Corp., N.Y.C. Served with U.S. Army, 1958-60. Recipient NIH grants, 1967-72. NIH postdoctoral fellow, 1964-67. Mem. Am. Soc. Pharmacology and Exptl. Therapeutics, Am. Soc. Biol. Chemists, Am. Physiol. Soc., Am. Soc. Nutrition, Soc. Toxicology, Endocrinology Soc., Biochemical Soc., Am. Coll. Toxicology (pres. 1978—), Am. Indsl. Hygiene Soc. Editor: Jour. of Toxicology and Environmental Health, 1975—; Advances in Modern Nutrition, 1974—; Advances in Modern Toxicology, 1974-85; Symposia on Metabolic Regulation, 1969-75; Jour. Environ. Pathology and Toxicology. Contbr. articles profl. jours. Home: 62 Cayuga Way Short Hills NJ 07078 Office: Mobil Oil Corp Medical Dept 150 E 42nd St New York City NY 10017

MEHTA, MOHAN L., accountant, educator; b. Udaipur, India, Aug. 8, 1935; s. Pyar Chand and Jhamkudevi M.; came to U.S., 1966; LL.B., U. Rajasthan (India), 1964; M.B.A., Ohio U., 1967; M.B.A., City U. N.Y., 1976; m. Asha Mehta, Feb. 9, 1953; children—Anita, Ashok, Alok, Alka. Asst. prof. fin. S.C. State Coll., Orangeburg, 1967-68; prof. bus. adminstrn. Fairfield (Conn.) U., 1970-76; prof. accounting Christopher Newport Coll. of Coll. William and Mary, Newport News, Va., 1976-77, So. Conn. State Coll., New Haven, 1977—; cons. silver futures trading Am. Bd. Trade, N.Y.C., 1968—. Recipient award N.Y. Bank for Savs., 1968; C.P.A. Mem. Am. Fin. Assn., Am. Inst. C.P.A.'s, Conn., N.Y., Va. socs. C.P.A.'s, Nat. Assn. Accountants, Am. Accounting Assn., India Assn. of Conn. (treas. 1974-76). Mem. Ralph Nader's study group on ICC. Home: 195 Summit St Bridgeport CT 06606

MEHTA, SUNIL KUMAR, internist; b. Mandsaur, India, Jan. 26, 1939; s. Chandmal Jawaharlal and Javer Bai (Patangia) M.; came to U.S., 1969, naturalized, 1973; B.Sc., Ramnarain Ruia Coll., 1957; M.B., B.S., Mahatma Gandhi Meml. Med. Coll., 1962, M.D., 1968; m. Usha Shah, May 22, 1966; children—Kiran, Prabhat, Nisha. Intern, Maharaja Yeshwant Rao Hosp., Indore, India, 1962-64; resident in internal medicine Kingsbrook Jewish Med. Center, Bklyn., 1969-72; fellow in cardiology Montefiore Hosp. and U. Pitts., 1972-73; emergency rm. physician, dir. outpatient clinic Butler Meml. Hosp., Butler, Pa., 1973-74; practice medicine, specializing in internal medicine, Grove City, Pa., 1975—; chief dept. internal medicine Bashline Meml. Hosp., Grove City, also cons. physician, cardiologist, 1975—. Mem. AMA, Mercer County, Pa. med. socs. Hindu. Home: 104 Overhill St Grove City PA 16127 Office: Oakland Ave Grove City PA 16127

MEIENHOFER, JOHANNES ARNOLD, organic chemist; b. Dresden, Germany, Mar. 3, 1929; s. Emil August and Katharine Marie (Gabriel) M.; came to U.S., 1957, naturalized, 1978; Diplom-Chemiker, U. Heidelberg (Ger.), 1954, Dr.rer.nat., 1956; m. Katharina Bredol, Aug. 10, 1963; children—Johannes, Peter Eugen. Research asso. V. du Vigneaud, Cornell U. Med. Coll., N.Y.C., 1957-59, Hormone Research Lab., U. Calif., Berkeley, 1959-60; research asso. Wollforsch. Inst., Technische Hochschule, Aachen, Ger., 1961-64; insulin project leader Farbenfabriken Bayer AG, Elberfeld, Ger., 1961-64; asso. Children's Cancer Research Found., Boston, 1965-73; research sect. chief Hoffmann-LaRoche Inc., Nutley, N.J., 1973—; lectr. biol. chemistry Harvard U. Med. Sch., Boston, 1969-73. Mem. AAAS, Am. Chem. Soc., N.Y. Acad. Sci., Gesellschaft Deutscher Chemiker, Gesellschaft für Biologische Chemie. Co-editor 5 books; contbr. articles and revs. to profl. jours. Home: 35 Glenwood Rd Upper Montclair NJ 07043 Office: 340 Kingsland St Nutley NJ 07110

MEIER, LOUIS LEONARD, JR., lawyer, naval officer; b. Hawthorne, Cal., Oct. 12, 1918; s. Louis Leonard and Celestine Helen (Gabriel) M.; B.S., U.S. Naval Acad., 1942; LL.B., Georgetown U., 1951; m. Donna Eleonora Tomacelli, June 5, 1954; children—Renee, Sharon, Catherine, Marina. Commd. ensign USN, 1941, advanced through grades to capt., 1961; admitted to Va. bar, 1951, Supreme Ct. bar, 1970; legal and legis. asst. to Chmn. Joint Chiefs Staff, Washington, 1965-67; comdr. squadron guided misslie destroyers Atlantic Fleet, 1967-69; mem. policy planning staff Sec. of State, Washington, 1969-72; ret., 1972; asst. sec., Washington counsel Am. Soc. C.E., 1972—. Decorated Legion of Merit. Mem. Am. Bar Assn., Am. Soc. Internat. Law, Am. Soc. C.E., Mid-Atlantic Club. Clubs: N.Y. Yacht; Chevy Chase (Md.); Metropolitan (Washington). Comd. warships receiving battle efficiency awards: U.S.S. Gherardi, 1951; U.S.S. John S. McCain, 1959, 60. Home: 5132 Baltan Rd Washington DC 20016 Office: 1625 Eye St NW Washington DC 20006

MEIJER, ROBBY, plastic surgeon; b. Pontianak, Indonesia, July 9, 1931; s. John Kroese and Louise (Hummelgens) M.; came to U.S., 1955, naturalized, 1961; M.D., State U. Leiden, The Netherlands, 1955; m. Dorothy J. Sieglinger, July 28, 1956; children—Carol A., Linda J., Robert C., Clifford J. Intern, The Bklyn. Hosp., 1955-56, resident, 1957-59, St. Barnabas Hosp., Newark, N.J., 1959-61; practice medicine specializing in plastic surgery, Livingston, N.J., 1963—; attending plastic surgeon St. Barnabas Med. Center, Livingston, 1961—, dir. Rehab. Center for Speech and Hearing, 1975—, dir. Cleft Palate Center, 1974—, bd. trustees, 1975—; attending plastic surgeon Morristown (N.J.) Meml. Hosp., 1977—; clin. asst. prof. plastic surgery Coll. Medicine and Dentistry of N.J.-Rutgers Med. Sch., Piscataway, N.J. Served with Royal Dutch Army. Diplomate Am. Bd. Plastic Surgery. Fellow A.C.S., Acad. Medicine of N.J.; mem. Am. Soc. Plastic and Reconstructive Surgery, Am. Soc. Aesthetic Plastic Surgery, Am. Cleft Paltate Assn., N.J. Soc. Plastic Surgeons, N.Y. Regional Soc. Plastic and Reconstructive Surgery, N.J. State Med. Soc. Contbr. articles to profl. jours. Home: 99 Oak Ln Essex Fells NJ 07021 Office: 349 E Northfield Rd Livingston NJ 07049

MEILLEUR, PAUL ANDRE, physician; b. Ottawa, Ont., Can., May 19, 1928; s. J. Honore and Florida (Hurtubise) M.; A.B., B.P.H., U. Ottawa, 1950, M.D., 1955; postgrad., U. Mich., 1955-61; m. Fernande Bouvier, Oct. 22, 1955; children—Martine, Daniele, Dominique, Simon, Christian. Intern, Ottawa Gen. Hosp., 1955-56, resident in internal medicine and hematology, St. Lawrence Hosp., Lansing, Mich., also Simpson Meml. Hosp.-U. Mich., Ann Arbor, 1955-61; chief of medicine, Sacre Coeur Hosp., Hull, Que., Can., 1963-66, chief med. staff, 1966-70, chief specialized medicine, chief oncology clinic, 1970—; pres., Corp. Hôpital Pierre Janet Hull, 1970, pres., consul d'administration, 1970; v.p. Regional Health Council, 1972-76. Decorater officier de l'ordre du Merite du Sénécal, Order of 24th Anniversary of Queen. Mem. Assn. des Medicins de Langue Francaise du Can. (pres. 1975-78, conseil gen. 1977-78), Assn. des Medicins de Langue Francaise de France (dir.), Conseil Permanent Canadien. Home: 47 Lacasse Hull PQ J9A 1K1 Canada Office: 4 Taschereau Suite 330 Hull PQ J8Y 2V5 Canada

MEINECKE, WILLARD HENRY, mgmt. cons.; b. Marysville, Kans., Aug. 19, 1916; s. Louis P. and Katherine S. (Shierkolk) M.; B.S. Milling Engring., Kans. State U., 1941; postgrad. Okla. U., 1942; sr. student econs. Johns Hopkins, 1969; m. Mary Jane Lewis, June 13, 1941; children—Joel, Steve, Douglas. Milling engr., mgr., Gen. Mills Corp., various locations, 1941-62; dir. AID, State Dept., Ethiopia, 1962-66, dir. N. African affairs, Washington, 1966-69, dir. E. Asia affairs, 1969-70, dep. asst. adminstr. E. Asia, 1970-72, dep. asst. adminstr.-mgmt., 1972-74; asst. dir. Action, 1974-77; mgmt. cons., 1977—; tchr. vocat. ednl. high sch., 1948-52. Recipient Distinguished Ser. award Kans. State U., 1971. Mem. Assn. Operative Millers (pres. 1954), Sigma Mu, Alpha Zeta. Kiwanian. Home: 8604 Burning Tree St Bethesda MD 20034

MEISCH, KATHERENE LOUISE, educator; b. Penn Yan, N.Y., Nov. 17, 1936; d. Howard Olden and Sarah Emily Tuttle; B.A. cum laude, Keuka Coll., 1958; postgrad. U. Rochester, 1961-63, Ohio State U., 1962, U. Calif. Berkeley, 1963, Brown U., 1964, Rochester Inst. Tech., 1970, 76, 77, Finger Lakes Community Coll., 1973, 74, Geneseo State Tchrs. Coll., 1974; m. John Harper Meisch, Dec. 18, 1965. Tchr. chemistry Webster (N.Y.) Central Sch., 1958-78. Recipient award Lions Club, 1962; NSF grantee, 1962, 63, 64; named Chemistry Tchr. of Year, Rochester chpt. Am. Chem. Soc., 1976. Mem. Webster Tchrs. Assn., New Eng. Assn. Chemistry Tchrs., N.Y. State United Tchrs., Am. Fedn. Tchrs., Chi Beta Phi, Delta Kappa Gamma (chmn. personel growth com. Eta chpt.), Keuka Coll.

Alumnae Club (chmn. Webster chpt.). Republican. Methodist. Home: 2792 Saint Paul Blvd Rochester NY 14617

MEISEL, DAVID DERING, astronomer, educator; b. Fairmont, W.Va., Mar. 28, 1940; s. Louis David and Dorothy Margaret (Dering) M.; B.S., W.Va. U., 1961; M.S., Ohio State U., 1963, Ph.D., 1967; m. Carolyn Mae Conrad, Aug. 25, 1962; children—Grace Margaret, Catherine Elise. Instr. astronomy U. Va., Charlottesville, 1965-68, asst. prof., 1968-70; asst. prof. State U. N.Y., Coll. at Geneseo, 1970-76, asso. prof., 1976—; asso. C.E.K. Mees Obs., U. Rochester (N.Y.), 1973—; dir. planetarium State Coll. Geneseo, 1970—; cons. NASA, 1966—, Radio Can. Internat., 1970—; vis. astronomer Kitt Peak Nat. Obs. State U. N.Y. research fellow, 1971-72; research grantee NASA, 1973—, Nat. Acad. Sci. NRC sr. research asso. NASA Goddard Space Flight Center, 1977-78; guest investigator Copernicus Space Telescope, Princeton Obs., 1974—; instructional grantee NSF, 1976-77, review panelist, 1978—. Fellow AAAS, Royal Astronom. Soc.; mem. Am. Meteor Soc. (nat. dir. 1973—), Am. Astronom. Soc., Astronom. Soc. Pacific, Internat. Astronom. Union, Internat. Sci. Radio Union, Soc. Photo Instrumentation Engrs., Royal Astronom. Soc. Canada, Meteoritical Soc. Contbr. articles to profl. jours. Office: Dept Physics and Astronomy State Univ Coll Geneseo NY 14454

MEISEL, JOSEPH THOMAS, city ofcl.; b. Balt., Feb. 13, 1919; s. Casper and Anna Agnes (Bunn) M.; B.S. in Chemistry cum laude, Loyola Coll. of Balt., 1941; m. Faun Marlow, June 6, 1951; children—David M., Donna M., Paul A., Carl T., Robert A. Research chemist Crown, Cork & Seal Co., 1941-42, Continental Oil Co., 1942-44, Catalyst Research Inc., 1944-45, Rheem Research Products, Inc., 1945-46; self-employed, 1946-48; research chemist Chem. Test Labs., City of Balt., 1948-53, chief test labs., 1953-76, chief Div. of Tests, Bur. Constrn. Mgmt., 1976—. Mem. Am. Electroplaters Soc., Internat. Acad. Sci. (award), Am. Chem. Soc., Md.-Del. Sewage Assn., ASTM, Am. Pub. Words Assn., Am. Water Works Assn., Am. Assn. Ret. Persons. Democrat. Roman Catholic. Contbr. articles to profl. publs. Office: Room 1103 Municipal Bldg Holliday and Lexington Sts Baltimore MD 21202

MEISEL, LOUIS KOENIG, art dealer exec.; b. Bklyn., Sept. 4, 1942; s. Sidney and Grace Elizabeth (Moak) M.; student Tulane U., 1960-62, Columbia, 1963, New Sch., 1964; m. Susan Pear, Mar. 26, 1966. With Capital Paper Co., Inc., N.Y.C., 1962-65; owner, pres. Eminent Publ., N.Y.C., 1963-78; owner, dir. Meisel Gallery, N.Y.C., 1963-72, owner, dir. Louis K. Meisel Gallery, N.Y.C., 1972—. Served with U.S. Army, 1964-65. Mem. Am. Power Boat Assn. Jewish religion. Author: The Photo-Realism Address: 141 Prince St New York City NY 10012

MEISEL, MARTIN HUGH, mgmt. cons. co. exec.; b. Bklyn., Jan. 31, 1933; s. Clarence A. and Seraphine S. (Sanft) M.; B.A., N.Y. U., 1954, M.P.A., 1958; postgrad. Syracuse U., 1954; m. Lola H. Preiss, June 12, 1960. Asst. salary adminstr. B. Altman & Co., N.Y.C., 1956-60; asst. dir. personnel, Bache & Co., N.Y.C., 1960-62; pres. Exec. Talent Inc., N.Y.C., 1962-68, Martin H. Meisel Assn., Inc., N.Y.C., 1968—, Faith Prodns. Inc., entertainer mgmt. and movie prodn., 1978—. Fund raising cons. Democratic presdl. candidates, 1968, 72, 76. Served with AUS, 1954-56. Mem. Ams. for Dem. Action (dir. 1973—), Am. Soc. Pub. Adminstrn., ACLU, Am. Friends Service Com., Internat. Platform Assn., Phi Beta Kappa, Pi Sigma Alpha. Club: Town. Author: Televisomania Fantasy 2050, 1950. Office: 55 E 87th St New York City NY 10028

MEISEL, MICHAEL S., lawyer; b. Cin., Feb. 24, 1944; s. Edward and Miriam (Stein) M.; B.A., Miami U., Oxford, Ohio, 1966; J.D., George Washington U., 1969; m. Tobie Garth, June 18, 1967; children—John Garth, Amanda Lee, Elizabeth Nancy. Admitted to N.J. bar, 1969; law sec. to Judge Morris Pashman, 1969-70; asso. firm Cole, Berman & Belsky, Paterson, N.J., 1970-73, partner, 1974—; del. Jud. Conf. 3d Circuit Ct. Appeals, 1974-77; trustee Passaic County Legal Aid Soc., 1975-76; sec. Passaic County Ethics Com., 1976-77. Mem. Am., N.J. (chmn. fidelity and surety law com. 1978—), Passaic County (trustee 1974—) bar assns., Am. Judicature Soc. Home: 23 Pontiac Dr Pines Lake Wayne NJ 07470 Office: 365 W Passaic St Rochelle Park NJ 07661

MEISENHEIMER, DANIEL THOMAS, JR., mfg. co. exec.; b. Bklyn., Nov. 2, 1927; s. Daniel Thomas and Marion Frances (Wiseman) M.; B.S. in Mech. Engring., U. Bridgeport, 1950, M.S. in Mech. Engring., 1966; postgrad. U. Conn., 1951-55, U. New Haven, 1955-56; m. Mary Ellen Broderick, July 29, 1950; children—Daniel Thomas III, Richard Charles. With Spectrum Assos., Inc., Milford, Conn., 1958—, founder-owner, pres., treas., 1958—; pres., treas., subsidiary Spectrum Pressurestat Co., Inc., Milford, 1965—; mgr. subsidiary Squareline Controls Co., Milford 1962—. Cons. to A.C. Gilbert Co., 1957-58, Harvey Hubbell Co., 1962-68, Haydon Switch Co., 1958-61, Schick Safety Razor Co., 1965-66. Local chmn. Boy Scouts Am., 1960-67, scoutmaster, 1968-71. Served with AUS, 1946. Mem. Nat. Soc. Profl. Engrs. (sr. asso.), ASME, Instrument Soc. Am., Am. Inst. Aeros. and Astronautics, Soc. Exptl. Stress Analysis, AAAS, C. of C. (dir.). Episcopalian. Clubs: Milford (sec. 1971-77, pres. 1977), Landmark, Rotary, Masons. Patentee in field. Home: 404 Longmeadow Rd Orange CT 06477 Office: 525 Boston Post Rd Milford CT 06460

MEISLAHN, HARRY POST, lawyer; b. Bklyn., Apr. 5, 1938; s. Harry E.P. and Marjorie (Findley) M.; A.B. cum laude, Princeton, 1960; J.D., Cornell U., 1966; m. Meredith Lee Gowdy, May 2, 1970; children—Brooke Louise, Leigh Marjorie, Christopher Post. Admitted to N.Y. bar, 1966, Fed. bar, 1966, U.S. Supreme Ct. bar, 1974; asso. firm Whalen, McNamee, Creble & Nichols, Albany, N.Y., 1966-70; prin., dir. McNamee, Lochner, Titus & Williams P.C., and predecessors, 1973—; dir. Hudson Valley Paper Co., 1972—, Albany Legal Aid Soc. Inc., 1972—; lectr. N.Y. Bar Assn. Bd. dirs., Albany Boys Clubs, Inc., 1967—, v.p., 1974—. Served with USN, 1960-63. Mem. Albany County, N.Y. State bar assns. Republican. Presbyterian. Home: 16 Axbridge Lane Delmar NY 12054 Office: 75 State St Albany NY 12207

MEISTER, STEVEN GERARD, cardiologist; b. Boston, Sept. 13, 1937; s. Harry and Edith (Segal) M.; B.A., Bowdoin Coll., 1958; M.D., Tufts U., 1962; m. Carol Anne Ross, Jan. 28, 1966; children—Laura Ilise, Elizabeth Lee. Intern in medicine Ind. U. Med. Center, Indpls., 1962-63; asst. resident in medicine Boston VA Hosp., 1965-66, resident in medicine, 1966-67; research fellow in medicine Boston City Hosp., 1967-68; research fellow in medicine Peter Bent Brigham Hosp., Boston, 1968-70; research fellow in cardiology Tufts U., Boston, 1967-68, Harvard U., 1968-70; practice medicine specializing in cardiology, Phila., 1970—; dir. cardiac catheterization lab. Presbyn.-U. Pa. Med. Center, 1970-73; dir. cardiac catheterization lab. Med. Coll. Pa. and Hosp., 1973—, acting dir. cardiology div., 1978-79; asst. prof. medicine U. Pa., Phila., 1970-73; asso. prof. medicine, Med. Coll. Pa. and Hosp., 1973-78, prof., 1978—; cons. in cardiology Frankford, Phila. VA hosps. Served to capt. U.S. Army, 1963-65. Diplomate Am. Bd. Internal Medicine. Fellow A.C.P., Am. Coll. Cardiology; mem. Am. Fedn. Clin. Research, Am. Heart Assn. (Upper Atlantic research com. 1977—), Phila. Acad. Cardiology. Jewish. Contbr. 77 articles on cardiology and electrocardiology to profl. jours. Office: Medical College Pa 3300 Henry Ave Philadelphia PA 19129

MEIXNER, ARTHUR WARREN, educator; b. Orange, N.J., Apr. 29, 1930; s. Arthur and Angela (Carlock) M.; A.B., The Citadel, 1952; postgrad. Oxford U. (Eng.), 1954; Ph.D., N.Y.U., 1978. Instr. polit. sci. Fairleigh Dickinson U., Rutheerford, N.J., 1958-68, asst. prof. polit. sci., 1968-74, asso. prof., 1974—. Cons. on transp. problems to mayor Rutherford, 1967-68; mem. working com. Gov.'s Econ. Evaluation Com. for an Intercontinental Jetport for N.J., 1969-70. 1st v.p. Wolf Lake, Inc., 1970-73, pres., 1973—. Mem. East Orange Model Cities Council, 1969-72, vice chmn., 1970; v.p. Planning Assn. North Jersey, 1970-73, pres., 1973—; vice chmn. East Orange Planning Bd., 1973—. Bd. dirs. Passaic Valley Citizens Planning Assn. Serviced to 1st lt. U.S. Army, 1952-54. Mem. Am. Polit. Sci. Assn., Pi Sigma Alpha. Club: Wolf Lake (pres. 1971—). Home: 320 S Harrison St East Orange NJ 07018 Office: Fairleigh Dickinson U Rutherford NJ 07070*

MEKLER, ARLEN B., lawyer, chemist; b. N.Y.C. May 4, 1932; s. Lev A. and Ethel (Fox) M.; B.S. in Chemistry, Reed Coll., San Jose State U., 1953; M.S. in Organic Chemistry, Iowa State U., 1955; Ph.D., Ohio State U., 1958; J.D. Temple U., 1972; m. Marianne Harriette Eckerström, Nov. 4, 1961; children—Jeffrey Arlen, Rebecca Ann, Ann-Marie Laura, Victoria Arlene, Lamar Adam, Lars Arlen. Sr. research chemist E.I. du Pont de Nemours & Co., Wilmington, Del., 1958-69; admitted to Del. bar, 1972, Pa. bar, 1972, U.S. Supreme Ct. bar, 1976; practiced in Wilmington, 1972—; State Laws, mem. firm Mekler and Siebold, 1977—; chief of appellate div. Office of Pub. Defender, State of Del., 1973-77; pres. Del. Law Center, Wilmington, 1973—; instr. constl. law Wilmington Coll., 1973-75; adj. prof. criminal law/procedure Del. Law Sch., Widener Coll., 1976—. Pres. Mental Health Center for Gov. Bacon Health Center, 1964-66; mem. Citizens Conf. for Modernization of State Legislatures, 1964-68; state chmn. Reform Commn. for Modernization of Polit. Party Rules, 1965-68; pres. Del. Citizens for Fair Housing, 1965-69; state commr. Nat. Conf. on Uniform State Laws, 1972—; pres. Democratic Forum of Del., 1966-70; mem. Democratic State Platform Com., 1966, 68, 72, 76; research dir. Del. Citizens for Humphrey-Muskie, 1968, Citizens for Biden, 1972, 78; mem. 3d Circuit Ct. of Appeal Jud. Nominating Commn., 1977—, 3d Circuit Ct. Appeal Jud. Conf.; mem. social action com. Unitarian Ch., Wilmington, 1962-68. Recipient Keyman award, 1964, 65; State Govtl. Affairs award, 1964, 65. Mem. Am., Del. (mem. com. on rules of criminal procedure 1973-74, supreme ct. com. on revision of criminal law 1973—, supreme ct. com. on rules of evidence 1976—, mem. com. on revised rules of Del. Supreme Ct. 1974—), Pa. bar assns., Am. Chem. Soc., ACLU (dir.), N.Y. Acad. Scis., Chem. Soc. of London, AAAS, Catalyst Club Phila., Del. Jaycees (state chmn. govtl. affairs com. 1963-65), Sigma Xi, Wilmington Organic Chemists Club, Phi Alpha Delta. Unitarian. Contbr. monographs to legal publs. Home: 1007 Barley Mill Rd Westover Hills Greenville DE 19807 Office: 1700 Farmers Bank Bldg Wilmington DE 19801

MELATO, MARION URSULA, aircraft test equipment co. exec.; b. Bklyn., Sept. 16, 1929; d. Nicholas Joseph and Rose Marie (Risolio) Melato; diploma Washington Sch. for Secs. and Bus., 1949; student Bklyn. Coll. With Greer Hydraulics, Inc., Bklyn., 1948-64, staff asst. spl. projects, 1956-60, mgr. Eastern regional office, 1960-64; co-founder, co-owner, controller, sec.-treas., gen. mgr., dir. Applied Hydro-Pneumatics, Inc., Valley Stream, N.Y., 1964—. Conservative Republican. Roman Catholic. Office: North Plaza Bldg Valley Stream NY 11580

MELBY, JAMES CHRISTIAN, physician, educator; b. Duluth, Minn., Feb. 14, 1928; s. Leonard and Frances (Sullivan) M.; B.S., U. Minn., 1951, M.D., 1953; m. Mary E. O'Brien, June 25, 1955; children—Christian Leonard, Elizabeth Ann. Intern dept. medicine U. Minn. Hosps., Mpls., 1953-54, resident, 1955-58; part-time practice medicine specializing in internal medicine, endocrinology and metabolism Univ. Hosp., Boston, 1962—; instr. U. Minn., 1958-59; asst. prof. U. Ark., 1959-62, asso. prof., 1961-62; asso. prof. medicine Boston U. 1962-69, prof., 1969—; head sect. endocrinology and metabolism Univ. Hosp., Boston U. Med. Center; vis. physician Boston City Hosp., Univ. Hosp.; mem. VA merit rev. bd. in endocrinology. Served with AUS, 1946-48. Diplomate Am. Bd. Internal Medicine. Mem. A.M.A., Assn. Am. Physicians, Am. Diabetes Assn., Am. Soc. Clin. Investigation, Endocrine Soc., Am. Fedn. Clin. Research, Central Soc. Clin. Research AAAS, Am. Coll. Clin. Pharmacology, AAUP, Sigma Xi, Alpha Omega Alpha. Mem. editorial bd. Jour. Clin. Endocrinology and Metabolism; cons. editor Am. Jour. Medicine; editor Jour. Steroid Biochemistry. Contbr. articles to profl. jours. Home: 26 Meredith Circle Milton MA 02186 Office: University Hospital 75 E Newton St Boston MA 02118

MELCHER, GEORGE W., JR., physician; b. Portsmouth, Va., Aug. 24, 1922; s. George W. and Estelle (Rea) M.; B.A., Colo. Coll., 1943; M.D., Columbia, 1946; children—Merrick, Paula, Ellen, Laura, George III, John G. Practice medicine specializing in internal medicine, N.Y.C.; formerly instr. Columbia U. Sch. Pub. Health, now asso. clin. prof. internal medicine; asso. attending physician Presbyn. Hosp., N.Y.C.; treas. Health Care Inst. N.Y.C.; pres. Group Health Inc., N.Y.C.; pres. Group Health Ins. of N.J., North Brunswick. Pres. Nat. Genetics Found., N.Y.C., Council of Mgmt., Internat. Fedn. Health Service Funds, Dublin, Ireland; dir. West Side Assn. of Commerce, N.Y.C. Bd. dirs. Health Systems Agy. of N.Y.C. Served as capt. AUS, 1947-49. Diplomate Am. Bd. Internal Medicine. Fellow N.Y. Acad. Medicine; mem. A.C.P., N.Y. County (censor), N.Y. (del.) med. socs., AMA. Clubs: N.Y. Athletic, N.Y. Univ. Contbr. articles to med. jours. Home: 230 W 41st St New York City NY 10036 Office: 326 W 42d St New York City NY 10036

MELIA, JAMES LEE, indsl. machinery appraiser; b. Pitts., June 11, 1933; s. Martin Joseph and Lena May (Fryer) M.; student Duquesne U., 1951-54; m. Kathleen Mary Scanlon, Sept. 5, 1960; children—Christine, Patrick, Maureen, Megan, Michael, Matthew. Owner, Melia Hardware, Crafton, Pa., 1953-65; sr. appraiser machinery and equipment Indsl. Appraisal Co., Pitts., 1966—, also tng. dir. Active Pa. Assn. for Retarded Citizens, 1966-76. Served with AUS, 1956-58. Registered Appraiser, Pa., Gen. Services Adminstrn., Register of Appraisers. Mem. Am. Soc. Appraisers (sr., chmn. edn. fund Pitts. chpt. 1974-75, program chmn. 1974-75, v.p. 1976-77, pres. 1977-78). Democrat. Roman Catholic. Home: 604 Broadhead Ave Pittsburgh PA 15205 Office: 222 Blvd of Allies Pittsburgh PA 15222

MELLINGER, LOUIS TODHUNTER, geol. engr.; b. Pitts., Nov. 20, 1939; s. Frank Millin and Helen Emeline (Todhunter) M.; student Ohio State U., 1959-61; B.S. in Geology, U. Cin., 1963; postgrad. U. Pitts., 1963-64; m. Evelyn Nancy Brennemann, July 20, 1963; children—Rebecca, Andrew. Grad. teaching asst. U. Pitts., 1963-64; geol. engr. E. D'Appolonia Cons. Engrs., Inc., Pitts., 1964-73; chief geol. engr. Fetterolf Coal & Constrn Inc., Boswell, Pa., 1973-76; pvt. practice geol. engring., 1977—. Asst. scoutmaster Boy Scouts Am., Madeira, Ohio, 1963. Served with USAR, 1957-58. Mem. Am. Inst. Profl. Geologists, Assn. Engring. Geologists, Geol. Soc. Am. Home: 645 W Main St Somerset PA 15501 Office: Low Vol Fuels Somerset PA 15501

MELLIS, JOHN GEORGE, elec. engr.; b. Weirton, W.Va., Apr. 6, 1935; s. George John and Mary Kaliope (Makricosta) M.; Asso. Sci. in Elec. Engring., Central Tech. Inst., 1956; m. Helen Chris Giovanakis, July 9, 1961; 1 dau., Maria Elena. Systems engr. UNIVAC, St. Paul, 1956-64; sr. engr. design group Gen. Dynamics/Electronics, San Diego, Calif., 1964-67; system analyst Maritime Adminstrn., Washington, 1967—. AUS, 1957-59. Recipient Commendation for Apollo Project, Gen. Dynamics Corp., 1967, Spl. Achievement award Maritime Adminstrn., Dept. Commerce, 1973, 75, 77. Registered profl. engr., mfg. engr., Calif. Mem. Am. Soc. Naval Engrs., IEEE. Greek Orthodox. Club: Masons. Home: 7886 Bastile Pl Severn MD 21144 Office: Code M-340 14th and E Sts NW Washington DC 20235

MELLO, JOSEPH MICHAEL, microbiologist; b. West Warwick, R.I., Jan. 1, 1931; s. Antonio and Maria (Couto) M.; B.S., U. R.I., 1954; med. technologist R.I. Inst. Pathology, 1957; postgrad. Brown U., 1965; m. Pauline Simon Lecuivre, Sept. 18, 1954; children—Michele, Peter, Jeffery, Mathew, Andrew. Biophysicist, R.I. Hosp., Providence, 1958-60; microbiologist Davol Inc., Cranston, R.I., 1960—; pres., incorporator Ethide Sterilizing Corp., Coventry, R.I., 1958—; also dir.; pres., treas. Ethide Labs., Coventry, 1973—; mem. adv. council Coventry Vocational Tech. High Sch., 1969—. Pres., Coventry Baseball Jr. League, 1973—. Served to 1st lt. AUS, 1954-56. Mem. Inst. for Environmental Scis. (sr.), Am. Soc. Microbiology, Soc. Indsl. Microbiology, Am. Soc. Clin. Pathologists, Tau Kappa Epsilon, Parenteral Drug Assn. K.C. Home: Hill Farm Rd Coventry RI 02816 Office: Box D Providence RI 02901

MELMED, RONALD MARTIN, psychiatrist; b. Middleberg, Union of South Africa, July 20, 1930; s. David and Eva (Cohen) M.; student N.Y. U., 1948-50; B.A., Lafayette Coll., 1952; M.D., Jefferson Med. Coll., 1956; came to U.S., 1933, naturalized, 1958; m. Marilyn Cohen, May 14, 1960; children—Carey, Fran. Intern, Atlantic City Hosp., 1956-57; resident in psychiatry Manhattan VA Hosp., 1957-58, Phila. Psychiat. Center, 1960-62; practice medicine specializing in psychiatry, Stamford, Conn., 1962-69, Greenwich, Conn., 1964—; mem. staff Greenwich Hosp.; co-founder, med. dir. Fly Without Fear, 1969—; co-founder, co-dir. Cardiac Comprehensive Care 77—; dir. Biofeedback and Behavior Therapy Centers of Conn. Served with USNR, 1958-60. Mem. AMA, Am. Psychiat. Assn., Am. Group Psychotherapy Assn., Greenwich, Fairfield County, Conn. med. socs., AAAS, Internat. Assn. Study Pain, Am. Pain Soc., Acad. Psychosomatic Medicine, Biofeedback Soc. Conn. (founding mem., pres.), Biofeedback Soc. Am. (chmn. council of state socs.), Am. Holistic Med. Assn. (founding), Assn. Advancement of Behavior Therapy. Jewish. Home: 71 Strawberry Hill Ave Stamford CT 06902 Office: 38 Lake Ave Greenwich CT 06830

MELNITCHENKO, EUGENE, investment co. exec.; b. Ukraine, Mar. 8, 1937; s. B.A., City U. N.Y., 1966; M.A., N.Y. U., 1973, M.B.A., 1973; m. Valentina, Jan. 22, 1961; children—Dereck, Mark. With U.S. Trust Co. N.Y., N.Y.C., 1961-73, 74—, v.p., 1975—; asst. to pres. ICN Pharms., Irvine, Calif., 1973-74. Served with USMC, 1955-58. Chartered fin. analyst. Mem. N.Y. Soc. Security Analysts, Inst. Chartered Fin. Analysts, Am. Chem Soc., Med. Group N.Y. Home: 143 Kilburn Rd Garden City NY 11530 Office: 45 Wall St New York City NY 10005

MELTZER, ABRAHAM, physician; b. Passaic, N.J., Nov. 27, 1935; s. Hymen and Rose M.; B.A., Rutgers U., 1957, postgrad., 1958; M.D., N.Y. Med. Coll., 1962; m. Susan Rosenberg, Nov. 20, 1966; children—Jeffrey, Franklin. Intern, Newark Beth Israel Hosp., 1963; resident internal medicine St. Michael's Hosp., Newark, 1965-67, resident cardiology, 1967-68, asst. attending cardiology St. Michael's Med. Center, 1968—; asso. electrocardiographer Perth Amboy (N.J.) Gen. Hosp., 1968—, dir. medicine, 1978—. Pres., Middlesex County chpt. Am. Heart Assn., 1977—. Served to lt., M.C., USNR, 1963-65. Recipient physicians recognition award AMA, 1969, 72, 76. Diplomate Am. Bd. Internal Medicine. Fellow A.C.P., Am. Coll. Cardiology (asso.); mem. Am., N.J. socs. internal medicine. Contbr. articles to profl. publs. Office: 280 Hobart St Perth Amboy NJ 08861

MELTZER, MILTON, physician, psychoanalyst; b. Rochester, N.Y., May 11, 1923; s. Louis and Clara (Ratner) M.; B.A. cum laude, Ohio State U., 1943, M.D., 1946; grad. Washington Psychoanalytic Inst., 1960; m. Sallie Rabinoff, Mar. 23, 1946; children—Gail Miriam, Steven Marc. Intern, St. Elizabeth's Hosp., Washington, 1946-47, resident psychiatry, 1947-50; chief med. officer Alcatraz Fed. Penitentiary, 1951-52; gen. practice psychoanalysis and psychiatry Washington, 1952—; psychiatric cons. D.C. Dept. Vocational Rehab., 1953-73; tng. and supervising analyst Washington Psychoanalytic Inst., 1965—; clin. prof. psychiatry and behavioral scis. George Washington U. Sch. Medicine and Health Scis., 1973—. Served wtih USPHS, 1951-53. Fellow Am. Psychiat. Assn.; mem. Am. (mem. exec. council 1967-73), Wash. (pres. 1975-77) psychoanalytic assns., Washington Psychiatric Soc. (pres. 1967-68), Washington Assn. Pscyhoanalytic Edn. (chmn. 1977—) Phi Beta Kappa, Alpha Omega Alpha. Address: 2934 Fessenden St NW Washington DC 20008

MELTZER, YALE LEON, economist; b. Bklyn., Nov. 3, 1931; s. Benjamin and Ada (Luria) M.; A.B., Columbia U., 1954, postgrad. Sch. Law, 1954-55; M.B.A., N.Y. U., 1966; m. Annette Schoenberg, Aug. 7, 1960; children—Benjamin Robert, Philippe David. Asst. to chief patent atty. Beaunit Mills, Inc., Elizabethton, Tenn., 1955-56, prodn. mgr., 1956-58, research chemist N.Y. Med. Coll., N.Y.C., 1958-59; research chemist H. Kohnstamm & Co., Inc., mfg. chemists, N.Y.C., 1959-66, mgr. comml. devel., market research, patents and trademarks, 1966-68, sr. security analyst Harris, Upham & Co., Inc., 1968-70; instr. dept. econs. N.Y. U., 1972—; adj. asst. prof. dept. accounting, finance and mgmt. Pace U., N.Y.C., 1974—; lectr. bus., fin., econs., sci. and tech. Mem. AAAS, Am. Chem. Soc., Am. Econ. Assn. Author: Soviet Chemical Industry, 1967; Chemical trade with the Soviet Union and Eastern European Countries, 1967; Chemical Guide to GATT, The Kennedy Round and International Trade, 1968; Phthalocyanine Technology, 1970; Hormonal and Attractant Pesticide Technology, 1971; Urethane Foams—Technology and Applications, 1971; Water-Soluble Polymers: Technology and Applications, 1972; Economics, 1974; Water-Soluble Resins and Polymers: Technology and Applications, 1976; Putting Money to Work: An Investment Primer, 1976. Contbr. articles to profl. publs. Translator, Russian and German tech. lit. Home: 141-10 82d Dr Jamaica NY 11435

MELUCCI, RICHARD CHARLES, research inst. adminstr.; b. Oceanside, N.Y., July 17, 1946; s. Richard Joseph and Marcia Jane (Lockwood) M.; B.S., Adelphi U., 1968, M.B.A., 1971; m. Rosanne Alice Kessel, Dec. 15, 1968; children—Christine Ann, Donna Marie, Richard Paul. Planning engr. Sperry Gyroscope Co., Great Neck, N.Y., 1967-70; planning adminstr. PRD Electronics, Inc., Syosset, N.Y., 1970-73, program adminstr., 1973-74; sr. staff asst. Brookhaven Nat. Lab., Upton N.Y., 1974—; adj. asst. prof. bus. adminstrn. Dowling Coll., Oakdale, N.Y., 1978—. Home: 29 Patricia Ln South

Setauket NY 11720 Office: Brookhaven Nat Lab Bldg 510A Upton NY 11973

MELVILLE, GREVIS WHITAKER, artist; b. Damariscotta, Maine, Dec. 23, 1904; s. George Henry and Alice (Jones) M.; scholarship student Yale U., 1929-32, N.Y. Art Students League, 1932-33, 38-41, 52, 53-54. Exhibited one man shows Bowdoin Coll. Mus., Smith Coll. Mus.; exhibited in group shows Ogunquit (Maine) Art Center, Pa. Soc. Art, Portland Soc. Art, Salmagundi Club, Am. Fine Arts Soc., Shore Studio Gallery, Boston, Provincetown, Boston Arts Festival, others; represented in collections Farnsworth Mus., Rockland, Maine, Pierson Coll., Yale, Damariscotta Info. Bur.; represented by Green Mountain Gallery, N.Y.C., Ogunquit (Maine) Gallery, Jacques Seligmann Galleries, N.Y.C.; resident artist Hackley Sch., Tarrytown, N.Y., 1941-42; exec. dir., treas. Damariscotta Region Info. Bur., 1934—, sec.-treas. Chapman-Hall House Preservation Soc., Damariscotta, 1959-66, v.p., 1966, clk., 1969—. Exec. com., mem. Maine Art Gallery, Wiscasset, 1968-69, 76—. Mem. citizens adv. com. Damariscotta Bd. Selectman, 1968-69; mem. Damariscotta Conservation Commn., 1972-75; treas. Damariscotta River Assn., 1974—, pres., 1975—. Bd. dirs. Pemaquid Group of Artists. Served with USNR, 1942-45. Mem. Walker Art Mus. Assn. (Bowdoin Coll.), Friends of Art (Colby Coll.), Portland Soc. Art, N.Y. Art Students League (life), Mus. Modern Art, Am. Legion. Address: 38 Main St Damariscotta ME 04543

MELVILLE, LARRY SCOTT, judge; b. N.Y.C., Oct. 25, 1933; s. Lawrence Albert and Vivienne (Scott) M.; A.B., N.Y. U., 1956; LL.B., Howard U., 1962; m. Sonja Douglas, May 25, 1963; children—Sonja-Lisa, Scott Douglas, Douglas Lawrence. Admitted to Conn. bar, 1962, U.S. Supreme Ct. bar, 1967; partner Merchant & Melville, Bridgeport, Conn., 1962-66; exec. dir., chief atty. Waterbury (Conn.) Legal Aid and Referal Service, 1966-68; partner Merchant, Melville, Spear & Seymour, Bridgeport, 1968-72; individual practice law, Bridgeport, 1972-77; judge Conn. Ct. Common Pleas, 1977-78, Conn. Superior Ct., 1978—; asst. city atty., Bridgeport, 1976-77. Cons. Northeastern Region Legal Services Program, 1967-69. Pres., Bishop's Commn. on Human Relations, Bridgeport, 1972—; hearing examiner State Commn. on Human Rights and Opportunities, 1965—. Bd. dirs. Goodwill Industries Southwestern Conn., 1969-71, Action or Bridgeport Community Devel., 1966-72, Fairfield County Council Boy Scouts Am., NAACP, Bridgeport, United Way Eastern Fairfield County, SW Conn. Health Systems Agy., Bridgeport Area Found. Served with ASUS, 1956-58. Mem. Conn. (ho. of dels. 1971—), Bridgeport (exec. bd.), Nat. bar assns., Pi Lambda Phi. Roman Catholic. Home: 100 Chatham Terr Bridgeport CT 06606 Office: Superior Court Bldg Main St Bridgeport CT 06604

MELVIN, A(RTHUR) GORDON, author; b. Halifax, N.S., Can., Dec. 19, 1894; s. Arthur Leander and Bessie (Warner) M.; came to U.S., 1919, naturalized, 1931; B.A., Dalhousie U., Halifax, 1916; A.M., Columbia U., 1920, Ph.D., 1923; m. Lorna Reade Strong, 1931; children—Alice Branch, Mary Lorna. Tchr., Provincial Normal Coll., Truro, N.S., 1916; fellow English, Columbia U. Trhrs. Coll., 1920-22; prod. Edon Central China Tchrs. Coll., Wuchang, 1924-27; asso. prof., then prof. edn. Coll. City N.Y., 1928-55; author: Adventures on Midsummer Evenings, 1951; Mexico Travel Guide, 1956; Gems of World Oceans, 1964; Sea Shells of the World, 1966; Sea Shell Parade, 1973; also books on teaching, curriculum materials adv. council CBS Sch. of Air, 1946; hon. curator Ernesto Santos Galindo Malacological Museum, Mex., 1973—. Mem. Movement Fedn. Americas (v.p. continental council), Assn. Arts in Childhood (pres. 1945-47), Am. Edn. Fellowship (life), AAUP, Am. Malacological Union. Clubs: Columbia U. Faculty; Malacological (Boston). Address: 863 Watertown St West Newton MA 02165

MENACHEM, NEAL JAY, accountant; b. N.Y.C., Dec. 23, 1941; s. Louis and Pearl (Herbert) M.; B.B.A. cum laude, Adelphi U., 1963; m. Barbara Joan Bedine, Nov. 17, 1968; children—Andrew Jonathan, Fredric Jason, Seth Jared, Mara Joy. Auditor, Aronson & Oresman, C.P.A.'s, N.Y.C., 1963-65, G. Hyman & Co., C.P.A.'s, N.Y.C., 1965-68; auditor Ernst & Ernst, C.P.A.'s, N.Y.C., 1968—, mgr., 1971—. Bd. trustees Hartman YMHA; v.p. Woodmere Park Civic Assn., 1975—. C.P.A., N.Y. State. Mem. Am. Inst. C.P.A.'s, N.Y. State Soc. C.P.A.'s, Nat. Accounting Assn., P.R. C. of C. in U.S. (dir., chmn. legis. com.). Home: 897 Lakeside Dr Woodmere NY 11598 Office: Ernst & Ernst Citicorp Center 153 E 53d St New York City NY 10022

MENARD, MARCEL, physician; b. Quebec, Can., Apr. 24, 1921; s. Joseph Xavier and Adélaide (Chevrier) M.; B.A., Coll. Bourget, Rigaud, 1943; M.D., U. Montreal, 1950; m. Jeannette Denis, Sept. 4, 1950; children—Luc, Sylvain. Intern, Hotel-Dieu de Montréal, Hôpital Notre-Dame, Hôpital Ste-Jeanne d'Arc (all Montreal, 1948-50; pvt. practice medicine, Montebello, Que., Can., 1950—; part-time anaesthetist, Centre Hospitalier du Buckingham. Roman Catholic. Home and Office: 18 rue Saint Joseph Montebello PQ J0V 1L0 Canada

MENCHER, ALEXANDER, lawyer; b. Bklyn., Sept. 30, 1902; s. Max and Anna (Weisman) M.; A.B., Columbia, 1923, A.M., 1924; J.D., N.Y.U., 1927; m. Mildred Heidt, Sept. 7, 1934; children—Howard, Bonnie. Admitted to N.Y. bar, 1928; mem. firm. Merin & Mencher, N.Y.C., 1929-32, Juhass & Mencher, 1932-34; pvt. practice, N.Y.C., 1934—; patent and engrng. counsel Modern Adhesives & Electronics, Inc.; patent counsel Am. Safety Equipment Corp.; dir., counsel Internat. Patent Exchange, Ltd., Del. Mem. N.Y., Queens County bar assns., N.Y. Patent Law Assn., Columbia Engring. Sch. Alumni. Author articles in field. Home: 69-42 Ingram St Forest Hills NY 11375 Office: 150 Broadway New York City NY 10038

MENDELL, EDWARD JOEL, mfg. co. exec.; b. N.Y.C., Nov. 28, 1920; s. M. Lester and Malvina W. (Cohen) M.; B.S., N.Y. U., 1943; m. Renee Lazarus, Jan. 24, 1954; children—Richard, Alan, Gary, Robert, Victoria. Founder, pres., chief exec. officer Edward Mendell Co. Inc., Carmel, N.Y., 1946—. Cons. Bank Leumi le-Israel, 1964—; lectr. numerous univs. in U.S., fgn. countries, 1958—; chmn. tech. symposia, Switzerland, Eng., France, Spain, Italy, Australia, South Africa, 1960—. Chief officer New Rochelle (N.Y.) Office CD, 1957-64. Served with AUS, 1942-46. Mem. Am. Pharm. Assn., Walter Reed Soc., CPS Assos. Jewish religion (pres. temple 1973—). Contbr. articles to profl. publs. Home: Rural Route 2 Box 104-A South Salem NY 10590 Office: Route 52 Carmel NY 10512

MENDELSOHN, FREDERIC ANTHONY, neurologist; b. N.Y.C., June 9, 1946; s. Fred Vincent and Phyllis (Galgano) M.; A.B., Hofstra U., 1966, M.A., 1969; M.D., U. Louisville, 1971; m. Sonia Conza, June 20, 1971; children—Jason Frederic, Adam Michael. Intern, Nassau County (N.Y.) Med. Center, 1971-72, resident, 1972-75; gen. staff St. Charles Hosp., Port Jefferson, N.Y., 1975—, Mather Hosp., Port Jefferson, 1975—; practice medicine specializing in neurology, Port Jefferson, N.Y., 1975—; med. adv. com. Multiple Sclerosis Soc. Diplomate Am. Bd. Psychiatry and Neurology. Mem. Suffolk County, N.Y. State med. socs. Roman Catholic. Contbr. papers Am. Acad. Cerebral Palsy, 1974; contbr. article to med. jour. Office: 120 N Country Rd Port Jefferson NY 11777

MENDELSOHN, JOHN, historian, archivist; b. Berlin, Oct. 19, 1928; s. Hans E. and Hedwig Mendelsohn; came to U.S., 1951, naturalized, 1954; B.A., U. Md., 1961, M.A., 1967, PH.D., 1974; m. Elizabeth A. Rathjens, Aug. 27, 1963; children—Michael L., Elizabeth S. Chmn. social studies dept. Augusta Mil. Acad., Ft. Defiance, Va., 1961-68; lectr. German, summers, Am. U., 1961-63; asst. U. Md., 1968-70, asso. prof. history, 1977—; archivist Nat. Archives and Records Service (Washington). Served with USAF, 1952-60. Mem. Am. Hist. Assn., Conf. Group Central European History, Conf. Group German Politics. Home: 10404 Hayes Ave Silver Spring MD 20902 Office: Federal Record Center Suitland MD 20409

MENDELSOHN, MONROE LEONARD, market research exec.; b. Detroit, Dec. 15, 1924; s. Maurice S. and Sylvia (Rosenfeld) Davis; M.B.A., U. Chgo., 1948; m. Frieda Catherine McGrath, Dec. 24, 1951; children—Monroe Leonard, Sylvan McGrath, Timothy William. Research fellow Grad. Sch. Bus. U. Chgo., 1948-49; instr. mktg. Drake U., 1949-50; Southwestern mgr. Gould, Gleiss & Benn, Inc., Chgo., 1950-52; v.p. Internat. Research Assos., Inc., Rio de Janeiro, Brazil, 1952-58; pres. Monroe Mendelsohn Research, Inc., N.Y.C., 1958—. Served with USN, 1943-46; PTO. Mem. World, Am. assns. pub. opinion research, Am. Mktg. Assn., N.Y. Rug Soc. Republican. Jewish religion. Author: The Marketing Plan in Action, 1965. Office: 352 Park Ave S New York City NY 10010

MENDELSON, SOL, scientist, educator; b. Checonovska, Poland, Oct. 10, 1926; s. David C. and Frieda (Cohen) M.; came to U.S., 1927, naturalized, 1948; B.M.E. cum laude, Coll. City N.Y., 1955; M.S., Columbia, 1957, Ph.D., 1961. Sr. scientist Sprague Electric Co., North Adams, Mass., 1962-64, Airborne Instruments Lab., Melville, N.Y.., 1964-65, Bendix Research Lab., Southfield, Mich., 1967; adj. prof. physics and engring. City U. N.Y., 1972—; research, scientist and cons. Prof. engring. Coll. City N.Y., 1955-58; vis. prof. physics Williams Coll., Williamstown, Mass., 1962-63. Mem. Am. Physics Soc., ASM, Metall. Soc. of AIME, Am. Assn. Physics Tchrs., AAAS, Fedn. Am. Scientists, Sigma Xi, Tau Beta Pi, Pi Tau Sigma. Contbr. articles to profl. jours. Home: 446 W 25th St New York City NY 10001

MENDENHALL, DONNA JUNE MACMILLAN, info. scientist; b. Calif., Aug. 2, 1925; d. Robert S. and Emma (Nikkel) MacMillan; B.S., So. Conn. State Coll., 1972, M.S. in L.S., 1975; div.; 1 son. Tech. librarian Carlisle Chem. Works, Cin., 1962-65, Good Samaritan Hosp., Cin., 1965, Hoechst Pharm., Cin., 1966; tech. info. scientist Uniroyal Chem. Co. div. Uniroyal Inc., Naugatuck, Conn., 1967—. Mem. peer rev. panel NSF, 1976 Pres. West Hill Condominium Assn., 1975-76. Mem. Am. Chem. Soc. (position referal chmn. div. chem. info. 1974-75), Am. Soc. Info. Sci., Chem. Notation Assn., ALA, Spl. Libraries Assn., Med. Library Assn., Met. Opera Guild. Home: 617 Millville Ave Condo 8-6 Naugatuck CT 06770 Office: Library Uniroyal Chemical Naugatuck CT 06770

MENDENHALL, THOMAS CORWIN, II, coll. pres.; b. Chgo., June 4, 1910; s. Charles Elwood and Dorothy (Reed) M.; B.A., Yale, 1932, Ph.D., 1938; B.A., Oxford U., 1935, B.Litt., 1936; m. Cronelia Isabel Baker, June 4, 1938; children—Bethany, Mary, Cornelia. Instr. history Yale, 1937-42, asst. prof., 1942-46, asso. prof., 1946-59, asst. to provost, 1942-50, dir. fgn. area studies, 1944-46, master Berkeley Coll., 1950-59, dir. Office Tchr. Tng., 1958-59; pres., prof. history Smith Coll., 1959-75. Research fellow Huntington Library, 1956. Author: (with B. D. Hennings, A. S. Foord) Ideas and Institutions in European History, 1948; Quest for Principle of Authority, 1948; Shrewsbury Drapers and Welsh Wool Trade, 1953. Home: RFD Vineyard Haven MA 02568

MENDEZ, RUBEN P., UN ofcl.; b. Manila, Philippines, June 28, 1933; s. Mauro and Paz (Policarpio) M.; A.B. cum laude, Harvard U., 1953; M.A. in Econs., Columbia U., 1959; m. Matilda Currier McEwen; children—Katherine McEwen, Tomas Currier. Economist and fin. analyst planning dept. Merrill Lynch, Pierce, Fenner & Smith, N.Y.C., 1959-63; project officer UN Spl. Fund, N.Y.C., 1963-68, investment officer UN Devel. Programme, N.Y.C., 1968-72, sr. area officer, 1972-77, prin. officer, asst. dir. UN Environment Programme, 1978—. Mem. Am. Econ. Assn., Soc. Internat. Devel. Clubs: Harvard of N.Y.C.; Riverdale Yacht; United Kenya. Contbr. articles on econs. to profl. publs. Office: United Nations New York City NY 10017 also UN Environment Programme Nairobi Kenya

MENDRICK, RONALD JAY, coll. admnstr.; b. Mpls., Nov. 10, 1949; s. Donald Daniel and Lela (Carver) M.; B.A magna cum laude Fredonia State Coll. of N.Y., 1971; M.S. State U. of N.Y. at Albany 1972; m. Nancy Sturcey, Aug. 21, 1971. Asst. dean Geneseo State Coll., Geneseo, N.Y. 1972-74; career development coordinator Castleton State Coll., Castleton, Vt. 1974-76; dir. placement Slippery Rock State Coll., Slippery Rock, Pa. 1976—; cons. career planning and placement, leadership. Program dir. Slippery Rock Jaycees 1977—. Recipient 2 grants in career devel.; certified tchr., N.Y.; certified counselor Vt. Mem. Am. Personnel and Guidance Assn., Am. Coll. Personnel Assn., Middle Atlantic Placement Assn., Middle Atlantic Assn. of Sch., Coll. and U. Staffing. Democrat. Home: RD 6 White Oak Rd Mercer PA 16137 Office: Maltby Ctr Slippery Rock State Coll Slippery Rock PA 16057

MENETREZ, JEAN HUGUES, psychiatrist, psychoanalyst; b. Hericourt, Haute-Saone, France, Feb. 18, 1924; s. Camille Celestin Charles and Mariette Suzanne (Caillet) M.; M.D., McGill U., 1950; m. Janet Ruth Babigan, June 29, 1962; children—Jennifer, Frank, Carole. Intern, St. Mary's Hosp., Montreal, Que., Can., 1950-51; resident obstet.-gynec. surgery Royal Victoria Hosp., Montreal, 1951-52, Queen Mary Vets. Hosp., Montreal, 1952-53, Boston Lying-in Hosp., 1953-54; resident in psychiatry St. Anne's Hosp., Ste Anne de Bellevue, Que., 1954-55, N.C. Meml. Hosp., 1955-57; psychiatrist, Washington Inst. Mental Hygiene, 1957-58; chief alcoholic rehab. div. D.C. Dept. Pub. Health, Washington, 1958-60; physician mem. D.C. Commn. on Mental Health of U.S. Dist. Ct. for D.C., 1963-69; practice medicine specializing in psychoanalysis and psychiatry, Washington, 1957—; asso. clin. prof. psychiatry George Washington U. Sch. Medicine, Washington, 1972—; faculty Washington Psychoanalytic Inst., 1966—. Bd. dirs. Met. Acad. Ballet, Bethesda, Md., 1977—. Served with French Air Force, 1944-46. Fellow Am. Psychiatric Assn., Royal Soc. Health, Am. Acad. Psychoanalysis; mem. Am. Med. Assn., Md. Med. and Chirurgical Soc., Washington Psychoanalytic Soc., Washington Psychiatric Soc. Clubs: Univ., Bethesda Country. Home: 7440 Arrowwood Rd Bethesda MD 20034 Office: 2141 K St NW Suite 303 Washington DC 20037 also 7440 Arrowhead Rd Bethesda MD 20034

MENG, MARY TYLER, nurse, hosp. exec.; b. Tampa, Fla., Sept. 2, 1924: d. Arthur M. and Jessie (Williams) Tyler; B.S., Tchrs. Coll. Columbia U., 1967; M.S., Nova U., 1972. Asst. dir. nursing service Mt. Sinai Hosp., N.Y.C., 1964-70; asst. adminstr. nursing services Meml. Hosp., Hollywood, Fla., 1970-73; asst. v.p., dir. nursing Bklyn. Hosp., 1973-77: asso. v.p., dir. nursing Roosevelt Hosp., N.Y.C., 1977—. Mem. Am. Soc. Nursing Service Adminstrs., Am. Nurses Assn., Nat. League Nursing, Am. Hosp. Assn. Democrat. Home: 205 West End Ave New York City NY 10023 Office: 435 W 58th St New York City NY 10019

MENG, MAURICE, physician; b. Blackpool, Eng., Mar. 3, 1914; s. Mathias and Margarite (Swarbrick) M.; B.Sc. in Engring., U. Manchester (Eng.), 1935, M.Sc. in Engring., 1937; S.M. in San. Engring., Harvard U., 1938; B.A., Concordia U. (Can.), 1945, B.Com., 1947; M.A., U. Ottawa (Can.), 1948; M.D., C.M., McGill U. (Can.), 1951; diploma in Indsl. Health, Royal Coll. Physicians and Surgeons, 1964; m. Jean Fransham, Apr. 30, 1949. Cons. engr. Robert A. Rankin & Co., Montreal, Que., Can., 1944-47; intern Queen Elizabeth Hosp., Montreal, 1951-52; med. officer Canadian Nat. Rys., Air Can., Montreal, 1952-75, regional med. dir., 1975—. Diplomate Am. Bd. Preventive Medicine. Fellow Royal Soc. Health. Home: 6550 Duncan Ave Montreal PQ H4B 1E9 Canada Office: 935 Lagauchetiere St Montreal PQ H3C 3N4 Canada

MENG, RALPH HARVEY, psychiatrist, clin. adminstr.; b. Little Rock, Mar. 9, 1918; s. William Lucius and Eleanor (Lovejoy) M.; B.S., U. Md., 1939; M.D., Hahnemann Med. Coll., 1943; m. Frances Nilsson, Mar. 25, 1943; children—Mary Margaret (Mrs. Alan Chittick), Ellen Bernice (Mrs. Timothy Byron), William Lawrence, David Ralph, John Nilsson, Ann Frances (Mrs. Ann Row); m. 2d, Lois Perry Jones, Feb. 21, 1966. Intern, Hahnemann Hosp., Phila., 1943; resident Traverse City (Mich.) State Hosp., 1946-49; staff physician Haven Sanitarium, Rochester, Mich., 1949-54, Pontiac (Mich.) Gen. Hosp., 1954; clin. dir. Crownsville (Md.) State Hosp., 1954-56, supt., 1956-57; asst. supt. Mental Health Inst., Clarinda, Iowa, 1958-61; supt. Springfield State Hosp., Sykesville, Md., 1961-63; mem. staff Prince Georges Gen. Hosp., Cheverly, Md., 1964-67; practice medicine specializing in psychiatry, Chevy Chase, Md., 1957-58, Bethesda, Md., 1963-76; chief mental health clinic VA Center, Togus, Maine, 1976—; mem. staff Washington Sanitarium and Hosp., Sibley Meml. Hosp.; chief psychiatry Suburban Hosp., 1966-71. Council commr. S.W. Iowa council Boy Scouts Am., 1959-60. Chmn., Suburban Mental Health Found., 1973-76. Served from 1st lt. to capt., AUS, 1944-46. Diplomate Am. Bd. Neurology and Psychiatry. Fellow Am. Psychiat Assn., Am. Coll. Psychoanalysts, Eastern Psychoanalytic Assn. (treas. 1970-73, v.p. 1973-74, pres. 1974—), Am. Coll. Psychiat. Physicians; mem. AMA, Knox County Med. Soc., Washington Psychiat. Soc. (chmn. suburban Md. chpt. 1972-74), Maine Psychiat. Soc. Home: Sherman's Cove Camden ME 04843 Office: VA Center Mental Health Clinic Togus ME 04330

MENG, TING-TUNG, toxicologist, biochemist; b. Hoipei, China, Aug. 27, 1938; s. Chi Siang and Yei (Liu) M.; came to U.S., 1965, naturalized, 1977; B.S., Chung Hsing U., 1962; postgrad. Ohio State U., 1966-68, (fellow), Jefferson Med. Coll., 1968-69, U. Nebr., 1969-70, Med. U. S.C., 1970-71; M.S., Youngstown State U., 1975; postgrad. (fellow) Poly. Inst. N.Y., 1975-76. med. technologist Yu-Ying Hosp. and Sch., Taiwan, 1957-62; teaching fellow Wayne State U. Med. Sch., Detroit, 1965-66; biochemistry technician Ohio State U. Hosps., Columbus, 1966-68; research fellow biochemistry Med. Sch., U. Nebr., Omaha, 1969-70; research fellow immunology and biochemistry Med. U. S.C., Charleston, 1970-71; teaching asst. clin. chemistry lab. Youngstown (Ohio), State U., 1974-75: teaching fellow analytical chemistry lab. Poly. Inst. N.Y., Bklyn., 1975; supr., asst. to dir. labs. Rolling Hill Hosp., Elkins Park, Pa., 1976-77: supr. toxicology and radioimmunology Met. Hosp., Phila., 1977—. Mem. Am. Assn. Clin. Chemists, Am. Soc. Clin. Pathologists (certified chemistry specialist). Home: 235 W Rittenhouse St Philadelphia PA 19144

MENGEL, ARTHUR CLAYTON, mgmt. cons.; b. Schenectady, Oct. 18, 1915; s. Arthur Clayton and Maude Ethelred (Thomas) M.; B.A., Union Coll., Schenectady, 1937; m. Winifred Margaret Roberts, Sept. 29, 1945; children—Loretta Susan, Margaret Maude, Arthur Clayton III. Rate clk. Del & Hudson R.R. Corp., Albany, N.Y., 1937-39; supr. water trans. Republic Steel Corp., Cleve., 1940-52; asst. mgr. crane vessel dept. Columbia Transp. Co., Cleve., 1953-55; exec. dir. Port of Oswego (N.Y.) Authority, 1955-64; mgmt. cons. in traffic and transp., 1964-70; exec. dir. Research and Devel. Center, St. Lawrence U., 1966—. Trustee St. Pauls Sch.; pres., trustee Taylor Center Controlled Reading and Research. Mem. Am. Assn. Port Auth., Nat. Assn. Devel. Orgns. (dir.), Internat. Assn. Great Lakes Ports (dir. 1963-64), N.Y. State Waterways Assn. (mem. exec. com. 1960-64). Episcopalian. Home: 14 Prospect St Canton NY 13617 Office: St Lawrence U Canton NY 13617

MENKEN, ROBERT CARL, mfg. co. exec.; b. Omaha, June 25, 1923; s. Carl William and Alma Betty (Dice) M.; B.S.M.E., U. Ill., 1948; m. Emma Louise Edgar, Jan. 9, 1944; children—Gail, John, Sue. Design engr. Quaker Oats Co., Chgo., 1948-51; plant engr. David Bradley Mfg. Co. div. Sears Roebuck Corp., Kankakee, Ill., 1952-63, prodn. mgr., 1955-61, mdse. mgr., 1961-63; plant mgr. Carnes Co., Madison, Wis., 1964-65; with Winchester (Ont., Can.) Group, Olin Corp., 1965—, v.p., 1973-75, pres., 1975—, gen. mgr., 1976—, pres. subs. Turner Co., Sycamore, Ill., 1975-76. Exec. dir. Jr. Achievement, Kanakee, Ill., 1953-64; campaign chmn. various state candidates from Kankakee County, 1958-63. Served with USAAF, 1943-45: ETO; with USAF, 1951-52. Decorated Air medal with 6 oak leaf clusters. Mem. ASME, Res. Officers Assn. Clubs: Dalewood Gold and Curling, Rotary, Elks. Home: 399 Lakeshore Dr Cobourg ON K9A 1S2 Canada

MENNEG, PAUL EDWARD, publishing co. exec.; b. N.Y.C., Nov. 26, 1916; s. Francis Walter and Margaret Mary (Carlon) M.; B.A., Notre Dame U., 1940; m. Barbara Ann Garrett, May 1, 1942; children—Karlin, Paul Edward, Richard. Reporter N.Y. Daily News, 1940-41; reporter, editor Fairchild Publs., N.Y.C., 1946-48; dir. pub. relations Burlington Industries, N.Y.C., 1948-58; v.p. McCann Erickson, N.Y.C., 1955-60; v.p. Rogers & Cowan, N.Y.C., 1960-67; v.p., asso. publisher Golf Digest, N.Y. Times, 1967—. Mem. Town Meeting Greenwich, Conn., 1950-54. Served with AUS, 1941-46. Decorated Legion Merit, Bronze Star, Purple Heart. Mem. Met. Golf Writers (pres. 1974-75), Pub. Relations Soc. Am., Textile Mfgs. Assn., Ret. Officers Assn. Roman Catholic. Clubs: Milbrook, Hamlet, West Lake. Home: 124 W Lyon Farm Dr Greenwich CT 06830 Office: 495 Westport Ave Norwalk CT 06856

MENNIN, MIRIAM JULIET KOBRIN, career and coll. counselor; b. Bklyn., Jan. 7, 1940; d. Sydney and Jennie (Papier) Kobrin; B.A. in English (Regents scholar), Bklyn. Coll., 1960: M.A. in English and Am. Lit., U. Pa., 1963; M.A. in Counseling Psychology, Manhattan Coll., 1970; m. Gerald S. Mennin, Nov. 12, 1967; children—Danielle Susan, Douglas Steven. Publicity dir. Dover Publs., N.Y.C., 1960-61; tchr. English, Benjamin Franklin High Sch., N.Y.C., 1963-67; guidance counselor William F. Niles Jr. High Sch., South Bronx, 1968-69, Hartsdale (N.Y.) Sch., 1976-77; career counselor for handicapped students Francis Lewis High Sch., Queens, N.Y., 1977-78; pvt. practice, Yonkers, N.Y.; instr. English and academic and admissions counselor Mercy Coll., Dobbs Ferry, N.Y., 1977—. Treas. Edgemont Community Com. on Edn., 1977-79; legal rep. Edgemont Elementary PTA, 1977-78. Mem. Am. Personnel and Guidance Assn., Nat. Vocat. Guidance Assn., Nat. Council Tchrs. English. Jewish. Editor: (Edgemont Bicentennial publ.) Poor

Richard's Almanac, 1976. Choreographer Cactus Flower prodn. Greenville Community Theatre, 1977. Home: 33 Andrea Ln Scarsdale NY 10583 Office: 45 Ludlow St Yonkers NY 10705

MENNIN, PETER, composer, music conservatory adminstr.; b. Erie, Pa., May 17, 1923; s. Attilio and Amelia (Benacci) M.; student Oberlin Conservatory, 1940-42; Mus.B., Mus.M., Eastman Sch. Music, 1945, Ph.D., 1947; studied with Howard Hanson; studied conducting with Serge Koussevitsky at Tangelwood, Mass., 1946; m. Georganne Bairnson, Aug. 28, 1947; children—Felica, Mark. Tchr. composition Juilliard Sch. Music, 1947-58, pres., 1962—; dir. Peabody Conservatory Music, Balt., 1958-62. Mem. adv. panel USIA, 1916; adv. com. arts State Dept., 1963—; mem. exec. com. Internat. Music Council, Paris, 1956, Nat. Fedn. Music Clubs Commn., 1957. Bd. dirs. Walter W. Naumburg Found. Served with USAAF, 1943. Recipient award Am. Acad. Arts and Letters; Guggenheim award; Bearns prize Columbia, First Gershwin Meml. award; Koussevitsky award; Dallas Symphony Commn.; Juilliard Found. commn.; Collegiate Chorale commn.; NBC Radio commn.; League of Composers commn.; Prot. Radio commn.; Columbia Record's Chamber Music award, 1952; Naumburg Found. Am. Composition award, 1952; Elizabeth Sprague Coolidge Found.-Library of Congress Chamber Music commn., 1952; Nat. Fedn. Music Clubs commn., 1956; Cleve. Symphony commn., 1957; others. Mem. League Composers (dir.). Composers' Forum (dir.), Nat. Music Council (pres. 1968—), Nat. Inst. Arts and Letters, Am. Music (dir.), Am. Soc. Composers, Authors and Pubs. (dir.), Phi Mu Alpha. Composer: First Symphony, 1942; String Quartet, 1942; Concertino for Flute, Strings and Percussion, 1945; Second Symphony, 1945; Folk Overture, 1945; Fantasia for Strings (Canzona and Tocata), 1946; Third Symphony, 1946; (for piano) Divertimento, 1947, Partita (5 movements), 1949; (for mixed chorus) The Gold-Threaded Robe, Crossing the Han River, In the Quiet Night, Song of the Palace, 1948; (women's chorus) Tumbling Hair, Bought Locks, 1949; Fourth Symphony for Chorus and Orch., 1949; A Christmas Cantata for Chorus, Soloists and Chamber Orch., 1949; Violin Concerto, 1950; Second Quartet, 1950; Fifth Symphony, 1950; Concertato for Orch. (Moby-Dick), 1952; Sixth Symphony, 1953, Cello Concerto, 1955, Sonata Concertante for Violin and Piano, 1956, Piano Concerto, 1957, Canto for Orch., 1957, Symphony No. 7, 1964, Piano Sonata, 1964, Sinfonia for Orch. 1971, Cantata de Virtute, 1969, Symphony No 8. 1974, Voices for Soprano and Chamber Ensemble, 1976, others. Works performed by N.Y. Philharmonic Soc., NBC Symphony Orch., Columbia Broadcasting Orch., Boston; Chgo., San Francisco, Nat., Cin. WOR, Rochester (N.Y.), Mpls., Dallas, Houston, Los Angeles, Phila., Pitts., Detroit orchs., Götesburg Symphony Orch. of Sweden, orchs. in Europe, S.A., Orient and Far East; in music festivals, Rochester, N.Y., Tanglewood, Mass., Yaddo (Saratoga Springs, N.Y.), Colorado Springs and Seattle. Office: Juilliard School Lincoln Center New York City NY 10023

MENTER, A. SOLOMON, lawyer; b. Syracuse, N.Y., Sept. 23, 1910; s. Benjamin and Sarah (Kosmovitch) M.; B.S., Syracuse U., 1947, LL.B., 1932; m. Charlotte Sandler, Oct. 25, 1936; children—Roberta Greene, Lois Joan Zachary, Joyce Baron. Admitted to N.Y. bar, 1933; since practiced in Syracuse. Pres., Menter, Rudin & Trivelpiece, P.C. Mem. pres.'s assos. Le Moyne Coll., 1968—. Mem. N.Y. State (mem. continuing legal edn. com.; lectr.), Am., Fed., Bankruptcy bar assns., Am. Trial Lawyers Assn., Comml. Law League Am. (vice chmn bankruptcy com.), Am. Judicature Soc., Zionist Orgn. Am. (pres. Syracuse dist. 1963-66), Onondaga County Bar (chmn. bus. lawyers sect. 1967-69, continuing legal edn. com. 1972-74), Syracuse Assn. Credit Mgmt. (pres. 1973-74), Louis Marshall Law Soc. Jewish (v.p. temple, pres. Men's Club). Mem. B'nai B'rith (dist. pres. 1965-66). Home: 770 James St Syracuse NY 13203 Office: Univ Bldg Syracuse NY 13202

MEOLA, JOHN MICHAEL, clin. chemist; b. Guordioregia, Italy, Feb. 24, 1929; s. Nicholas and Nicholina (Pallota) M.; came to U.S., 1946, naturalized, 1947; B.S., St. Michael Coll., 1953; m. Gladys Jean Hunter, Feb. 27, 1957; children—Nicholina, John, Nancy, Mark. Asst. dir. clin. chemistry Albany (N.Y.) Med. Center Hosp., 1953—; instr. biochemistry Albany Med. Coll., 1976—. Certified clin. chemist Nat Registry Clin. Chemistry. Mem. Am. Assn. for Clin. Chemists, Am. Acad. Clin. Toxicologists. Republican. Roman Catholic. Contbr. articles in field to profl. jours. Home: 321 Highland Dr Schenectady NY 12303 Office: Albany Med Center Hosp Albany NY 12208

MERABI, SHARI JOHN, pharmacist; b. Kerman, Iran, Jan. 15, 1923; s. Jamshid Esfandiar and Firozeh Rostam (Mehrab) M.; M.S., Columbia, 1957; D. Pharmacy, Tehran U., 1954; m. Mehrdokht, June 21, 1959; children—Holly, Helga. Came to U.S., 1955, naturalized, 1962. Sr. pharmacist Lederle Labs., Pearl River, N.Y., 1957-61; mgr. drug and pharm. devel. Rexall Drug Co., Los Angeles, 1961-68; group mgr. med. diagnostic ops. Xerox Corp., Pasadena, Calif., 1968-69; sr. research investigator Bristol Myers Co., Hillside, N.J., 1969—. Trustee, Darl Mehr Zoroastrian Temple. Mem. Am. Pharm. Assn., Acad. Pharm. Sci., Soc. Cosmetic Chemists, Amateur Astronomers, Rho Chi. Home: 144 Pine Way New Providence NJ 07974 Office: 1350 Liberty Ave Hillside NJ 07207

MERCER, SHERWOOD ROCKE, former ednl. adminstr.; b. Manchester, Conn., June 27, 1907; s. Robert and Mary Elizabeth (Rocke) M.; A.B., Wesleyan U., 1929, A.M., 1930; postgrad. Yale U., 1933-38, Harvard U., 1943-44; LL.D., Phila. Coll. Textiles and Sci., 1957; m. Rowena Nichols, Aug. 14, 1933; children—Alexander, Caroline (Mrs. Christopher B. Robbins), Elizabeth (Mrs. Curtis C. Roseman). Tchr. social studies high sch., Middletown, Conn., 1930-42, dir. adult edn., 1938-42; instr. social sci., Wesleyan U., Middletown, 1939; sec. com. on gen. edn. in a free soc. Harvard U., Cambridge, Mass., 1943-44; chmn. div. applied arts Elmira (N.Y.) Coll., 1944-45; cons. in higher edn. Conn. State Dept. Edn., 1945-46; dean of faculty Mulhenberg Coll., Allentown, Pa., 1946-54; dean Phila. Coll. Osteopathic Med., 1954-69, v.p. ednl. affairs, 1965-76, dean, v.p. ednl. affairs emeritus, also prof. history of medicine emeritus, 1976—. Treas. Girl Scouts U.S.A. of Del. County, Pa., 1965-68. Bd. dirs. Greater Del. Valley, Pa. Regional Med. Program, 1969-76, chmn. fin. com., 1969-76. Mem. Am. Assn. Colls. Osteo. Medicine (bd. govs. 1970—, pres. 1974-75), Scotch Irish Soc. U.S.A. (pres. 1977—), Alpha Chi Rho, Phi Delta Kappa, Omicron Delta Kappa. Presbyterian (elder 1968—). Club: Union League (Phila.). Home: 13 Thompson Dr Havertown PA 19083 Office: Phila Coll Osteopathic Medicine 4150 City Ave Philadelphia PA 19131

MERCOUN, DAWN DENISE, mfg. co. exec.; b. Passaic, N.J., June 1, 1950; d. William S. and Irene F. (Micci) Mercoun; B.S. in Bus. Mgmt., Fairleigh Dickinson U., 1978. Personnel payroll coordinator Bentex Mills, Inc., East Rutherford, N.J., 1969-72; employment mgr. Inwood Knitting Mills, Clifton, N.J., 1972-75; gen. mgr. Consol. Advance, Inc., Passaic, N.J., 1975-76; personnel mgr. Gemini Industries, Inc., Clifton, 1976—. Mem. Am. Soc. for Personnel Adminstrn. Episcopalian. Office: 140 Delawanna Ave Clifton NJ 07014

MERCURE, JULIEN GILLES, clergyman, psychotherapist; b. Hearst, Ont., Can., Mar. 17, 1933; s. Albert George and Florence (Villemaire) M.; M.A., Ottawa U., 1962; M.A., Catholic U. Louvain, Belgium, 1968. Dir. family sect. Novalis, Ottawa, Can., 1962-69; prof. Postoral Inst., St. Paul U., Ottawa, 1970—; prof. faculty psychology Ottawa U., 1972—. Mem. Assn. Conseillers Matrimoniaux de Que., Am. Group Psychotherapy Assn., Ont. Group Psychotherapy Assn., Ont. Assn. Marriage and Family Counsellors, Am. Assn. Marriage and Family Counselors, Internat. Group Psychotherapy Assn., Internat. Transactional Analysis Assn. Roman Catholic. Author: Projet Mariage, 1969; Counselling Engaged Couples, 1973. Home: 291 Nelson Ottawa ON K1N 7S1 Canada Office: 223 Main Ottawa ON K1S 1C4 Canada

MERCURIO, PAT ANTHONY, hosp. adminstr.; b. N.Y.C., Aug. 15, 1933; s. James Gregory and Carmela (D'Argenio) M.; grad. U.S. Mcht. Marine Acad., 1956; B.S. in Bus. Admnstrn., Adelphi U., 1969; M.B.A., Wagner Coll., 1971; doctoral student N.Y. U., 1971—; m. Catherine Caligiuri, Nov. 24, 1958; children—Gregory James, Anthony James, Marisa Elena. Asst. admnstr., dir. personnel Brookhaven Meml. Hosp., Patchogue, N.Y., 1962-69; asso. dir. Sea View Hosp., S.I., N.Y., 1969-76; spl. asst. to corporate officer N.Y.C. Health & Hosps. Corp., 1976-77; admnstr. Gouverneur Hosp. Skilled Nursing Facility, N.Y.C., 1975-76; dep. exec. dir. Harlem Hosp. Center, N.Y.C., 1977-79, acting exec. dir., 1979—; prof. bus. and hosp. adminstrn. U. City N.Y., 1970—, Coll. of S.I., 1976—, St. Francis Coll., N.Y., 1976—. Bd. dirs. Community Bd. 3. S.I., 1971-73; pres., bd. dirs. Italian Club of Profl. and Businessmen, S.I., 1970—; mem. S.I. Community Chest, 1971-76, United Hosp. Fund, N.Y.C., 1976-78. Served with USNR, 1951-56. Recipient Borough Pres. certificate of merit Health System Agy. Dist., 1974. Mem. Health Systems Agy (bd. dirs. 1971-77), Am. Coll. Hosp. Adminstrs., Am. Hosp. Assn., Hosp. Edn. and Research Trust, World Future Soc. Clubs: Mason. Contbr. research and articles in field. Home: 9 Diana Trail Staten Island NY 10304 Office: 506 Lenox Ave New York City NY 10037

MEREDITH, DOROTHY MAE, author; b. South Hill, Va., May 19, 1927; d. John Lee and Rebecca M.; grad. Sch. Music, Chgo., Lincoln Sch. Practical Nursing, Los Angeles, Nat. Sch. Dress Design, Chgo., 1949. Ch. organist St. Mary's Episcopal Ch., La Crosse, Va., 1940-45; practical nurse, 1969—; author: (poetry) Dear Willie, 1974; (lyrics) Guide Me, Dear Lord, 1975, Suddenly Baby, 1977. Mem. Music Educators Nat. Conf., Black Writers Conf., Nat. Guild Piano Tchrs., Tomorrows Songwriters Club. Address: 1429 Columbia Rd NW Apt 46 Washington DC 20009

MEREDITH, EDWARD JOHN, accountant; b. Bklyn., June 19, 1941; s. Walter A. and Dorothy Alice (White) M.; B.S., Fordham U., 1963; m. Cathy Stephens, July 23, 1976; children by previous marriage—Edward W., Susan, Lori, Daniel. Auditor, Arthur Andersen & Co., N.Y.C., Newark, 1963-68; controller Mattel, Inc., South Plainfield, N.J., 1969-71; controller Electronic Assos., Inc., West Long Branch, N.J., 1971-74; pres. Analog Tng. Computers, Inc. subs. Electronic Assos., West Long Branch, 1974-76; partner firm Grippo, Meredith & Co., C.P.A.'s, Woodbridge, N.J., 1976—. Mem. Am. Inst. C.P.A.'s, N.J. State Soc. C.P.A.'s. Roman Catholic. Club: K.C. Home: 26 Courtland Ln Matawan NJ 07747 Office: 57 Green St Woodbridge NJ 07095

MEREDITH, GEORGE (MARLOR), writer, assn. exec.; b. Somerville, N.J., Apr. 21, 1923; s. Gilbert Judson and Dorothea (Pope) M.; student Columbia, 1940-41; m. Elizabeth Jean Moore, Nov. 15, 1955; children—Gilbert Judson III, Scott Arthur. Mng. editor Mast, 1944-47; editor Premium Practice, 1947-55; partner, editorial dir. Meredith Assos., 1955-67, pres. 1967—; pres. Meredith Research Corp., 1962-74; exec. sec. Nat. Premium Sales Execs., 1957-67, exec. dir., 1967-74, pub. relations dir., 1972—; exec. sec. Nat. Assn. Food Equipment Mfrs., 1957-59; exec. dir. Nat. Premium Mfrs. Reps. 1963-66, dir. research programs, 1964-67; dir. Marketing News Bur., 1973— (all Union, N.J.). Coordinator, moderator Premiums and Incentives Conf., N.Y. U., 1972; pub. relations dir. Soc. Incentive Travel Execs., 1974—. Recipient Premium Man of Year award Nat. Premium Mfrs. Reps., 1973; Nat. Premium Sales Execs. Past Pres.'s award, 1966; Distinguished Achievement award Premium Advt. Assn. Am., 1963. Mem. Asso. Bus. Writers Am., Advt. Club N.Y., Hon. Order Ky. Cols., Am. Soc. Assn. Execs., Inst. Assn. Mgmt. Cos., Nat. Premium Sales Execs., Sales Execs. Club N.Y., Sales and Mktg. Execs. Internat., Premium Merchandising Club N.Y. Lion. Author: Effective Merchandising with Premiums, 1962; Creative Application of Sales Incentive Plans, 1972; (film) The Caine Coil, 1973; Incentives in Marketing, 1977. Editor: Premiums in Marketing, 1971; exec. editor, research dir. Incentive Marketing Facts, 1968—; editor, pub. Sales Motivation Letter, 1973-74. Contbr. articles to profl. publs. Home: 7 Oyster Bay Dr Rumson NJ 07760 Office: 1600 Route 22 Union NJ 07083

MEREDITH, SCOTT, authors' rep.; b. N.Y.C., Nov. 24, 1923; s. Henry and Esta (Meredith); pvt. edn.; m. Helen Kovet, Apr. 22, 1944; children—Stephen Charles, Randy Beth. Writer numerous mag. stories; established Scott Meredith Lit. Agy., Inc., N.Y.C., 1940, pres., 1942—. Served with USAAF, World War II. Clubs: Three Oaks Tennis, Spectator, Rare Book Soc. (N.Y.C.). Author: Writing to Sell, 1950, rev. 1960, 2d rev. edit., 1974; George S. Kaufman and His Friends, 1974; Louis B. Mayer and His Enemies, 1978; also stories, novelettes, serials and articles. Editor: The Best of Wodehouse, 1949; The Best of Modern Humor, 1951; Bar One Roundup, 1951; (with P.G. Wodehouse) The Week-End Book of Humor, 1952; Bar Two Roundup, 1952; Bar Three Roundup, 1954; Bar Four Roundup, 1955, (2d series), 1956; Bar Five Roundup, 1956; (with Ken Murray) The Ken Murray Book of Humor, 1957; Bar Six Roundup, 1957; (with Henry Morgan) The Henry Morgan Book of Humor, 1958; (with Sidney Meredith) The Best from Manhunt, 1958; The Bloodhound Anthology, 1960; The Fireside Treasury of Modern Humor, 1963; Best Western Stories, 1964; Best Western Stories For Young People, 1965; (with P.G. Wodehouse) The Best of Humor, 1965; (with P.G. Wodehouse) A Carnival of Modern Humor, 1966. Contbr. articles on humor to Ency. Brit., 1954-59, articles on fiction writing to Oxford Ency., 1960-61. Frequent guest TV, radio shows; expert witness copyright cases. Home: Kings Point NY 11024 Office: 845 3d Ave New York City NY 10022 also 44 Great Russell St London WC1 England

MERIAM, PHILIP WITHINGTON, library adminstr.; b. Lincoln, Mass., Nov. 26, 1929; s. Richard S. and Alice G. (O'Brien) M.; B.A., Alfred U., 1958; M.L.S., Rutgers U., 1959; 1 dau., Anne F. Asst. library dir. Wellesley (Mass.) Free Library, 1962-66; dir. Dedham (Mass.) Pub. Library, 1966-70; dir. Wilmington (Mass.) Meml. Library, 1970—. Served with USCGR, 1952-56. Mem. Am., Mass. library assns., Boston Library Adminstrs., Men's Library Club. Home: Wells Rd Lincoln MA 01773 Office: Wilmington Memorial Library Middlesex Ave Wilmington MA 01887

MERINGOFF, BRIAN NILS, radiologist; b. Passaic, N.J., July 18, 1940; s. Saul S. and Bertha Yvonne (Coopersmith) M.; student U. Md., 1958-61; M.D., U. Miami, 1965: m. Marlene Barbara Meringoff, July 15, 1962; children—Jodi, Tracy, Andy. Intern in medicine Jackson Meml. Hosp., Miami, Fla., 1965-66, resident in radiology, 1966-69; radiologist, chief diagnostic ultrasound Fairfax HOsp., Falls Church, Va., 1971-74; practice medicine specializing in radiology, nuclear medicine and diagnostic ultrasound, Gaithersburg, Md., 1974—; mem. staff Suburban Hosp. Served with USPHS, 1969-71. Diplomate Am. Bd. Radiology, Am. Bd. Nuclear Medicine. Mem. Am. Coll. Radiology, AMA, Soc. Nuclear Medicine, Radiol. Soc. N.Am., Am. Inst. Ultrasound in Medicine, Am. Coll. Nuclear Medicine, Am. Coll. Nuclear Physicians, Am. Heart Assn., Md., Montgomery County, Va. med. socs., Am. Coll. Sports Medicine, Am. Med. Joggers Assn., Phi Delta Epsilon, Alpha Omega Alpha, Phi Kappa Phi. Jewish. Home: 11100 Korman Dr Potomac MD 20854 Office: 19241 Montgomery Village Ave Gaithersburg MD 20760

MERJAVE, CHARLES MICHAEL, elec. engr.; b. Bklyn., Oct. 6, 1945; s. Julius Michael and Mary Stella (Wensek) M.; A.A.S., N.Y.C. Community Coll., 1973; B.S. cum laude, N.Y. Inst. Tech., 1977. Lab. engring. technician Freed Tranformer Co., Bklyn., 1964-66; elec. engr. Ebasco Services Inc., N.Y.C., 1968—. Commr. of Deeds, N.Y.C.; v. chmn. Community Planning Bd. Number 1, 1976-78, chmn., 1978—; past parliamentarian Greenpoint Hosp. Community Bd.; chmn. 58th dist. Rep. Party county com., 1978—; pres. Regular Rep. Club 58th Assembly Dist., candidate State Senate, 1976; past vice chmn. Greenpoint-Williamsburgh Neighborhood Facilities Corp. Served with Signal Corps, U.S. Army, 1966-68. Recipient Norman Robins award N.Y.C. Community Coll.; Generoso Pope Meml. Scholarship award Columbus Citizen's Com., 1963. Mem. IEEE, Illuminating Engring. Soc. N.Am., Tau Phi Sigma. Roman Catholic. Home: 73 Guernsey St Brooklyn NY 11222 Office: 2 Rector St New York City NY 10006

MERKLEN, KENNETH ELMER, lawyer, patent atty.; b. N.Y.C., May 11, 1923; s. Alfred V. and Grace (Bichsel) M.; LL.B., St. John's U., 1954; postgrad. Bridgeport U., 1957-58, N.Y. Law Sch., 1961-62; m. Helen Tripler, Sept. 5, 1964 (div. 1966); m. 2d, Vilma Morabito, May 11, 1968. Admitted to N.Y. bar, 1955, U.S. Supreme Ct. bar, 1964; registered patent atty.; practice law, Ossining, N.Y., 1955-64, N.Y.C., 1964-73; patent atty. G.P.L Aerospace div. Gen. Precision Inc., Pleasantville, N.Y., 1964-66; patent counsel AEL Systems, Inc., Stamford, Conn. 1966-70; asso. patent counsel Gulf & Western Industries, Inc., 1971—; sec., dir. Sensor Corp., Greenwich, Conn., 1964-72; gen. and patent counsel. Exec. dir., sec., gen. counsel World Youth Culture, New Canaan, Conn., 1964-71. Served with USAAF, 1943-46. Mem. Internat. Platform Assn., Am. Bar Assn., Delta Theta Phi (dean Boston alumni senate 1960-64). Home: 133 Hillcrest Park Rd Cos Cob CT 06807

MERLE, JANE MALLOY, assn. exec.; b. Youngstown, Ohio, July 17, 1924; d. Henry I. and Annabel M. (Doyle) Malloy; B.A., State U. N.Y., 1945; m. Burton J. Merle, Nov. 22, 1947; children—James H., Patricia Ann, Joel Burton, Jeanne Elizabeth. Tchr., Letchworth Central Sch., Gainesville, N.Y., 1945-65; free lance writer, 1955—; co-dir. Info. Div., N.Y. Farm Bur., Glenmont, N.Y., 1971-72; asso. editor N.E. Agr., Glenmont, 1972; lectr. in field; dir. pub. relations Western N.Y. Apple Growers Assn., Victor, N.Y., 1971—. Bd. dirs. Wyoming County Community Hosp., 1971-77; pres. Letchworth Central PTA, 1970; bd. dirs. Wyoming County Cooperative Extension Service, 1970-75; chmn. Wyoming County Farm Bur. Women's Com., 1974. Recipient N.Y. State Agrl. Soc. Journalism Certificate of Excellence, 1978. Mem. N.Y. Horticultural Soc., Pub. Relations Soc. Am., Retired Tchrs. Assn., N.Y. Farm Bur., Western N.Y. Writers Assn. Republican. Roman Catholic. Contbr. articles various mags. and journals including Redbook Mag., Am. Agriculturist, Am. Girl, Buffalo Evening News, others. Home: 5888 Sheppard Rd Bliss NY 14024 Office: 7645 Main St Victor NY 14564

MERLINO, ANTHONY FRANK, orthopaedic surgeon; b. Providence, Jan. 21, 1930; s. Anthony Frank and C. Mildred (Campagna) M.; B.S., Providence Coll., 1951; M.S., U. Conn., 1952; M.D., Jefferson Med. Coll., 1956; m. Dolores Mary Aucello, Nov. 22, 1956; children—Christa Marianne, Paula Nicole. Intern St. Joseph's Hosp., Providence, 1956-57; resident orthopedic surgery VA Hosp., Phila., 1959-63; practice medicine specializing in orthopaedic surgery, Phila., 1963-68, Providence, 1968—; asst. attending staff in orthopedics St. Joseph's Hosp., Providence, pres. med. staff, 1974-75, trustee, 1973-76; asst. attending staff Our Lady of Fatima Hosp., North Providence, R.I.; vis. orthopaedic surgeon R.I. State Hosp., Howard; asst. orthopaedic surgery Hahnemann Med. Coll., Phila., 1965-69; cons. orthopaedic surgeon Roger Williams Gen. Hosp., Providence, 1969—; v.p. R.I. Orthopaedic Group, Inc., Providence, 1969—; team physician hockey and basketball teams Providence Coll.; mem. R.I. Gov.'s Med. Malpractice Commn., R.I. Bd. Examiners in Chiropractic, 1977—; mem. study commn. R.I. Med. Rev. Bd., 1977—; mem. corp. Blue Cross/Shield R.I., 1976—. Served to capt. M.C., USAF, 1957-59. Diplomate Am. Bd. Orthopedic Surgery. Fellow Am. Acad. Orthopaedic Surgeons, A.C.S., Internat. Coll. Surgeons, Latin Am. Soc. Orthopaedics and Traumatology; mem. Orthopaedic Research and Edn. Found. (life), Am. Fracture Assn., Pan-Pacific Surg. Assn., New Eng., R.I., Eastern orthopedic socs., Jefferson Orthopaedic Soc., AMA, R.I. Med. Soc. (commr. profl. relations 1976, ho. of dels. 1976), Providence Med. Assn., Am. Profl. Practice Assn., Am. Acad. Compensation Medicine, Am. Coll. Sports Medicine, Am. Med. Photography Assn., Internat. Soc. Orthopaedics and Traumatology, Am. Soc. Law and Medicine, Thomistic Inst. Drs. Guild, R.I. Hist. Soc., R.I. Audubon Soc. Roman Catholic. Clubs: Boston Orthopaedic, Mal Brown. Contbr. articles to profl. publs. Home: 2 Countryside Dr North Providence RI 02904 Office: 655 Broad St Providence RI 02907

MERMELSTEIN, JACOB, clin. psychologist; b. Vienna, Austria, Feb. 3, 1925; s. Abraham and Minna (Blum) M.; came to U.S., 1942, naturalized, 1949; rabbi Mesifta Rabbinical Sem., Bklyn., 1949; Ed.M., Rutgers U., 1960, Ed.D., 1964; m. Renee Weitman, Feb. 25, 1951; children—Chana Esther (Mrs. Moshe Berg), Joseph T., Chaya, Shoshana, Tobi. Rabbi, Congregation Beth Halevi, Bronx, N.Y., 1948-51; prin. Hillel Sch., Asbury Park, N.J., 1951-64; coordinator, asst. prof. Kingsborough Community Coll., City U. N.Y., 1964-66; pvt. practice clin. psychology, 1965—; chief psychologist Operation Head Start Torah U., 1965-67; mem. adj. faculty Rutgers U., 1964-65, Seton Hall U., South Orange, N.J., 1969-70, Richmond Coll. City U. N.Y., 1967; cons. and lectr. in field, 1965—; mem. commn. Survey Edn. State Israel Nat. Soc. Hebrew Day Schs., 1965. Hon. cons. Or Hachayim Home Girls, Bene Beraq, Israel. N.J. regional v.p. Nat. Assn. Hebrew Day Sch. Prins., 1960-62; chmn. commn. psychol. services Nat. Soc. Hebrew Day Schs., 1965—. Diplomate Am. Bd. Profl. Psychology. Mem. Am., N.J. psychol. assns. Contbr. numerous articles to profl. jours. Columnist Psychol. Issues, Jewish Parent mag., 1964—. Home: 336 Hicksville Rd Far Rockaway NY 11691 Office: 650 Central Ave Cedarhurst NY 11516 also 2833 Ocean Pkwy Brooklyn NY 11235

MEROLA, EMMA M. VARVARO, physician; b. N.Y.C., Jan. 1, 1908; d. Ettore and Anna (Borghini) Varvaro; B.S., Douglass Coll., 1930; student Woman's Med. Coll., 1930-33; M.D., Middlesex Coll., 1936; m. Joseph F. Merola, Nov. 30, 1939; children—Frank, Joseph, Henry, Anthony, Marianne. Intern, Glens Falls (N.Y.) Hosp., 1936-37; X-ray, lab. work Victory Meml. Hosp., Bklyn., 1937-39; practice, Waltham, Mass., 1939—; staff Waltham Hosp. Tchr. elementary sch., 1964-65; instr. in Teaching English as Fgn. Lang. program, 1968-69. Leader Girl Scouts and Boy Scouts. Mem. adv. bd. Salvation Army of Waltham, 1961-65; mem. Am. Med. Polit. Action

Com. Mem. A.M.A., Mass. Med. Soc., Middlesex Aux. Mass. Med. Soc., Am. Med. Women's Assn. (pres. 1960), Douglass Boston Alumnae Club (pres. 1959), League Women Voters, Grapho-Analyst Study Group, Charles River Med. Soc., Charles River Aux., Internat. Platform Assn., St. Luke's Guild Mass. Cath. Physicians, Am. Police Acad. Club: College. Home: 114 Church St Waltham MA 02154 Office: 117 Summer St Waltham MA 02154

MEROLLA, MICHELE EDWARD, chiropractic physician; b. Providence, Feb. 20, 1940; s. Joseph and Viola (Horne) M.; B.Sc., Bryant Coll., 1961; D.C., Chiropractic Inst. N.Y., 1965; L.H.D., Logan Chiropractic Coll., St. Louis, 1973; m. Joan Ellen Williams, July 18, 1964; children—Michele Edward, Matthew Joseph, Samantha Joan. Pvt. practice chiropractic medicine, New Bedford, Mass., 1965—. Producer variety shows for charitable orgns., 1966—; mem. New Bedford City Council, 1969-73, New Bedford Airport Commn., 1972-75, New Bedford Sch. Com., 1978—; pres. New Bedford Aid Center, 1977. Recipient Service award New Eng. Chiropractic Council, 1973. Mem. South Eastern Mass. (bd. dirs.), Mass. chiropractic socs., Am. Chiropractic Assn., N.Y. Acad. Sci. Clubs: Moose, Lions. Editor: New Eng. Jour. Chiropractic, 1965—. Home and Office: 100 Bedford St New Bedford MA 02740

MEROWITZ, MARTIN, psychiatrist; b. N.Y.C., Sept. 28, 1940; B.A., Columbia U., 1961; M.D., N.Y. U., 1966. Cons. editor Grolier Inc., N.Y.C., 1961-72; intern Montefiore Hosp., N.Y.C., 1966-67; resident in psychiatry Mass. Mental Health Center, Boston, 1967-69, Beth Israel Hosp., Boston, 1969-70; fellow Harvard Med. Sch., Boston, 1967-70; dir. community geriatrics Boston State Hosp., 1972-73, dir. clin. affairs, 1973-76; dir. residency tng. and staff edn. Boston VA Outpatient Clinic, 1976—; individual practice medicine, specializing in psychiatry, Wellesley, Mass., 1972—; asso. clin. prof. psychiatry Tufts U., Boston, 1976—; clin. instr. psychiatry Harvard Med. Sch., 1976—; mem. staff Mass. Gen., McLean, Leonard Morse, Glover hosps. Bd. dirs. SW Boston Sr. Services Inc., 1973-75. Served to maj. M.C., U.S. Army, 1970-72. Mem. Mass. Psychiat. Soc., Mass., Charles River med. socs., Boston Soc. Gerontologic Psychiatry (dir. 1975—). Editorial bd. Jour. Gerontologic Psychiatry, 1978—. Home and Office: 1 Mayo Rd Wellesley MA 02181

MERRIAM, DANIEL F(RANCIS), geologist; b. Omaha, Feb. 9, 1927; s. Faye Mills and Amanda Frances (Wood) M.; B.S., U. Kans., 1949, M.S., 1953, Ph.D., 1961; M.Sc., Leicester U., 1969, D.Sc., 1975; m. Annie Laura Young, Feb. 12, 1946; children—Beth Ann Merriam Wissman, John Francis, Anita Pauline, James Daniel, Judith Diane. Geologist, Union Oil Co. of Calif., Rocky Mountains and W. Tex., 1949-51, summer, 1952; asst. instr. U. Kans., 1951-53, instr., 1954, research asso., 1963-71; geologist Kans. Geol. Survey, 1953-58, div. head basic geology, 1958-63, chief geologic research, 1963-71; Jessie Page Heroy prof. geology, chmn. dept. Syracuse (N.Y.) U., 1971—; vis. research scientist Stanford, 1963; Fulbright-Hays Sr. Research fellow, U.K., 1964-65; chmn. supply-tech. adv. com. FPC, 1975-77; dir. Am. Geol. Inst.'s Internat. Field Inst. to Japan, 1967; vis. prof. geology Wichita State U., 1968-70; Am. Geol. Inst. vis. geol. scientist, 1969; U.S. del. UNESCO-IUGS Internat. Geol. Correlations Program, Budapest, 1969; chmn. U.S. Nat. Com. for IGCP, 1976—, participant Project COMPUTE, Dartmouth, 1974. Served with USNR, 1945-46. Mem. Am. Assn. Petroleum Geologists (academic adv. com. 1973-77, ho. of dels. 1974-76, computer applications in geology com. 1971—), Geol. Soc. Am. (gen. chmn. 10th ann. meeting Northeastern sect. 1975, publs. com. 1973-76), Soc. Econ. Paleontologists and Mineralogists (nominating com. 1972-73, chmn. research group in computer tech. com. 1970-75), Classification Soc. (membership com. 1968-71, dir. 1968-71), Internat. Assn. Math. Geology (council 1968-72, sec.-gen. 1972-76, pres. 1976—), N.Y. State Geol. Assn. (exec. sec. 1972-77, pres. 1977-78, dir. 1978—), Rocky Mountain Assn. Geologists (research com. 1966-69), Kans. Acad. Sci. (program chmn. geology sect. 1959), Geologists Assn. (Eng.) (field trip dir. 1965), AAAS, Kans. Geol. Soc. (dir. 1964), Leicester Geol. Soc. (hon. life), Nat. Assn. Geology Tchrs. Sigma Xi, Sigma Gamma Epsilon (chpt. pres. 1952-53). Editor-in-chief: Math. Geology, 1969-76, Computers & Geoscis., 1975—; editorial cons. Geosystems, 1971—; co-editor: Pacific Geology, 1971—; editor: Syracuse U. Geology Contributions, 1973—; editorial rev. bd. Colo. Sch. Mines Quar., 1974—; editorial com. Syracuse U. Press, 1978—; corr. Open Earth, 1978—. Contbr. articles to sci. jours. Home: 12 Drumlins Terr Syracuse NY 13224 Office: Dept Geology Syracuse U Syracuse NY 13210

MERRILL, ARTHUR ALEXANDER, analyst, writer; b. Honolulu, June 17, 1906; s. Arthur Merton and Grace (Dickey) M.; B.S., U. Calif. at Berkeley 1927; M.B.A., Harvard U., 1929; m. Elsie Louise Breed, Aug. 17, 1929; 1 dau., Anne Louise (Mrs. Robert Breiling). With Gen. Electric Co., Schenectady and N.Y.C., 1928-61; pres. Merrill Analysis, Inc., Chappaqua, N.Y., 1961—. Served with USAAF, 1925-27. Mem. Market Technicians Assn. (4th Ann. award), N.Y. Soc. Security Analysts, Fin. Analysts Fedn., Soc. for Investigation Recurring Events, Soc. for Preservation and Encouragement Barbershop Quartet Singing, SAR, Mensa. Republican. Congregationalist. Club: Harvard. Author: Behavior of Prices on Wall Street, 1966; Filtered Waves Basic Theory, 1977; Seasonal Tendencies in Stock Prices, 1975; How Do You Use the Slide Rule?, 1961; Chess Openings Simplified, 1974; Circumpolar Constellations, 1962; Battle of White Plains, 1975; Revolutionary War Calendar, 1976. Contbr. articles to profl. jours. Home: 25 Commodore Rd Chappaqua NY 10514 Office: Box 228 Chappaqua NY 10514

MERRILL, JAMES, author; b. N.Y.C., Mar. 3, 1926; s. Charles Edward and Hellen (Ingram) M.; grad. Lawrenceville Sch., 1943; B.A., Amherst Coll., 1947. Author: First Poems, 1951; (play) The Immortal Husband, 1956; The Seraglio, 1957; (poetry) The Country of A Thousand Years of Peace, 1959; (play) The Bait, 1960; (poetry) Water Street, 1962; The (Diblos) Notebook, 1965; (poetry) Nights and Days, 1966 (Nat. Book award 1967); (poetry) The Fire Screen, 1969; (poetry) Braving the Elements, 1972, The Yellow Pages, 1974, Divine Comedies (Pulitzer prize), 1976. Recipient Bollingen prize in poetry, 1973. Mem. Nat. Inst. Arts and Letters. Served with U.S. Army, 1944-45. Home: Stonington CT 06378*

MERRILL, LAWRENCE JOHN, former motor transp. co. exec.; b. Mpls., Dec. 12, 1911; s. Lawrence Amos and Margaret (McAdams) M.; student Acad. Advanced Traffic, 1946-49; m. Theresa Hudos, Nov. 23, 1944; children—Margaret Rae (Mrs. Robert Chavanne), Lawrence Robert. Shipping supr. Lorr Labs., Paterson, N.J., 1936-47; rate analyst Barrett div. Allied Chem. & Dye Co., N.Y.C., 1947-52; supr. rates Engle Oostdyk Inc., East Paterson, N.J., 1952-77. Served with AUS, 1942-46; PTO. Mem. Assn. ICC Practitioners, Traffic Club North Jersey. Presbyn. (elder 1952-58). Home: 22 9th Ave Hawthorne NJ 07506

MERRILL, WALTER WILLIAMSON, city auditor; b. St. Louis, July 27, 1914; s. Walter Williamson and Mary Adalyn (Haldeman) M.; A.B., Princeton U., 1936; M.B.A., Harvard U., 1938; m. Jane Scott Webster, Jan 13, 1945; children—Margaret Spencer Merrill Loutrel, George Webster, William Emery. Accounting supr. Procter & Gamble Co., Cin., 1938-50; mgr. adv. services Price Waterhouse & Co., Boston, Maracaibo, Venezuela, and N.Y.C., 1950-60; corp. controller Hot Shoppes Inc. (now Marriott Corp.), Bethesda, Md., 1960-62; dir. adminstrv. services Wolf Research Co., West Concord, Mass., 1962-65; dir. mgmt. adv. services Price Waterhouse & Co., Boston, 1965-73; city auditor City of Boston, 1973—. Served to lt., USNR, 1942-45. C.P.A. Mem. Am. Inst. C.P.A.'s, Mass. Soc. C.P.A.'s, Mass. Municipal Accountants and Auditors Assn., Soc. Colonial Wars, Phi Beta Kappa, Sigma Xi. Republican. Clubs: Harvard Boston, Wellesley Country (treas. 1970—). Contbr. articles to profl. publs. Home: 67 Elmwood Rd Wellesley Hills MA 02181 Office: City Auditor Boston MA 02201

MERRIMAN, HENRY, physician; b. N.Y.C., May 1, 1910; s. Merritt Heminway and Sally Mallory (Betts) M.; B.A., Yale U., 1932; M.D., Columbia U., 1936; m. Marjorie Duke Flint, June 18, 1949; children—Katharine F. Merriman Nichols, Henry, John Croswell. Intern, Bellevue Hosp., N.Y.C., 1937-38; resident in otolaryngology New Haven Hosp., 1939-42; practice medicine specializing in otolaryngology, Waterbury, Conn., 1946—; mem. staff Waterbury Hosp., 1946—, chief staff, 1959-61, pres. med. staff, 1970, bd. incorporators, 1974, trustee, 1979—; cons. numerous other hosps.; asst. clin. prof. Yale Sch. Medicine, 1952-73; mem. med. adv. bd. Waterbury Area Rehab. Center, 1959-62. Pres. Waterbury chpt. Am. Cancer Soc., 1972. Served with U.S. Army, 1942-46. Diplomate Am. Bd. Ophthalmology and Otolaryngology. Fellow A.C.S. (past chpt. pres.); mem. Conn. State Med. Soc. (past pres.), New Eng. Otolaryngol. Soc., Pan Am. Surg. Assn. Oto-Rhino-Laryngology and Broncho-Esophagology (founder), Am. Rhinological Soc. (founder), AMA. Republican. Episcopalian. Clubs: Waterbury, Yale of N.Y., Tunxis, SAR, Soc. Colonial Wars (past state gov.). Home: 5 Pleasant St Woodbury CT 06798 Office: 134 Granview Ave Waterbury CT 06708

MERRIN, SEYMOUR, venture capital and new businesses co. exec.; b. N.Y.C., Aug. 13, 1931; s. Joseph and Esther Bella (Manelis) M.; B.S., Tufts Coll., 1952; M.S., U. Ariz., 1954; Ph.D., Pa. State U., 1962; m. Elizabeth Jenifer Slack, Oct. 12, 1963; children—Charles Seymour, Mariamne Jenifer. With Magma Copper Co., Superior, Ariz., 1954; chemist IBM, Poughkeepsie, N.Y., 1962-64; mgr. package devel. and reliability Sperry Semicondr. div. Sperry Rand Corp., Norwalk, Conn., 1965-67; cons. in materials tech. relating to semi-condr. industry, Fairfield, Conn., 1967-69; pres., v.p., dir. Innotech Corp., Norwalk, 1969-74; project and div. mgr. Emdex div. Exxon Enterprises, N.Y.C., 1974—. Mem. Republican Town Com., Fairfield, 1968-71. Served with AUS, 1954-56. Fellow Geol. Soc. Am., Am. Inst. Chemists; mem. Am. Crystallographic Assn., Mineralogic Soc. Am., Internat. Soc. Hybrid Crystallographic Assn., Mineralogic Soc. Am., Internat. Soc. Hybrid Microelectronics, Am. Ceramic Soc. Patentee in field. Home: 235 Old Spring Rd Fairfield CT 06430 Office: 540 New Haven Ave Milford CT 06460

MERRISS, PHILIP RAMSAY, JR., banker; b. N.Y.C., June 7, 1948; s. Philip Ramsay and Elisabeth (Paine) M.; A.B. in Economics magna cum laude, Lafayette Coll., 1970, M.B.A. (Tuck scholar, Gulf Oil fellow), Dartmouth Coll., 1972; m. Janet Henry Hylan, Oct. 27, 1973. Asso. corporate fin. dept. A.G. Becker and Co. Inc., N.Y.C., 1972-73; fin. analyst corporate banking dept. Chase Manhattan Bank, 1973, asst. treas. N.Y.C. dist., 1974-75, 2d v.p. mining and metals div., 1976-78, 2d v.p. petroleum div., 1978—. Served to 1st lt. U.S. Army, 1973; capt. Res. Mem. Am. Econ. Assn., Phi Beta Kappa. Republican. Episcopalian. Clubs: Yale (N.Y.); Weston (Conn.) Gun. Home: 100 Hills Point Rd Westport CT 06880 Office: Chase Manhattan Bank One Chase Manhattan Plaza New York City NY 10015

MERSAND, JOSEPH, educator; b. Zbaraz, Austria-Hungary, July 30, 1907; s. Nathan and Mollie (Stein) M.; came to U.S., 1909; B.S., N.Y. U., 1928, M.A., 1929, Ph.D., 1934; postgrad. Columbia U., St. Johns U.; m. Estelle Joy Himmelstein, Aug. 20, 1950. Teaching fellow German, N.Y. U., 1930-31; instr. English, speech Boys High Sch., Bklyn., 1931-43; chmn. English dept. L.I. City High Sch., 1943-53; curriculum coordinator sr. high schs., N.Y.C., 1953-54; prin. James K. Paulding Jr. High Sch., 1954-55; chmn. English dept. Jamaica High Sch., 1955-72; faculty Queens Coll., 1956-61, Coll. City N.Y., 1956-61, Hunter Coll., 1961-63, Yeshiva U., 1959, adj. prof., 1972; lectr. Hofstra U. Sch. Edn., 1970-72, Fairleigh Dickinson U., 1972-73; asso. prof. York Coll. of City U. N.Y., 1973-77; specialist English, secondary schs. sect. U.S. Office Edn., 1963; summer sessions various colls., univs. Served with AUS, 1943-45. Mem. N.Y. English Council (pres. 1952-53), N.Y.C. high sch. English syllabus rev. com. Mem. Nat. Council Tchrs. English (2d v.p. 1953-54, pres. 1958-59, chmn. adv. council 1960), N.Y. Soc. for Exptl. Study Edn. (exec. com., editor Yearbook 1953-63, 73—), N.Y.C. Assn. Tchrs. English (exec. com. 1953-56), Am. Ednl. Theatre Assn. (chmn. audio-visual project 1953), Eastern Communications Assn. (chmn. elementary speech edn. com.), First Yale Conf. Teaching English (com. mem.), Linguistic Soc. Am., Modern Lang. Assn., Coll. English Assn., Speech Communication Assn., Assn. Supervision and Curriculum Devel., NEA, Nat. Assn. Secondary Sch. Prins., Internat. Reading Assn. Author: Chaucer's Romance Vocabulary, 1937; Traditions in American Literature, 1939; American Drama, 1930-40, 1941: The Play's the Thing, 1941; (with Francis Griffith) One-Act Plays for Today, 1945, The American Drama Since 1930, 1949; Modern One-Act Plays, 1951; English Grammar and Composition, Grade 11, 1977; Attitudes Toward English Teaching, 1960; Index to Plays 1966; Teaching the Drama in Secondary Schools, 1969; Spelling Your Way To Success, rev. edit., 1974; also writer pamphlets, articles. Editor: Guide to Play Selection, 3d edit., 1975; A Tale of Two Cities, 1960; Pickwick Papers, 1960; Three Comedies of American Family Life, 1961; Three Dramas of American Individualism, 1961; Three Dramas of American Realism, 1961; Three Plays About Doctors, 1961; Three Plays about Married Life, 1962; David Copperfield, 1962; The Crisis, 1962; The Stars Look Down, 1963; Three Plays about Business, 1964; Great Short American Biographies, 1966; Sonnets from the Portuguese, 1966; A Shropshire Lad, 1966; Great Narrative Essays, 1968; (with Frank Griffith) Eight American Ethnic Plays, 1974; Key Ideas in English, vols. 1, 2, 3, 1974. Home: 166-05 Highland Ave Jamaica NY 11432

MERSKEY, MARIE GERTRUDE FINE (MRS. CLARENCE MERSKEY), librarian; b. Kimberley, South Africa, Oct. 10, 1914; d. Herman and Annie Myra (Wigoder) Fine; came to U.S., 1960, naturalized, 1965; grad. Underwood Bus. Sch., Cape Town, South Africa, 1934; B.A., U. Cape Town, 1958, diploma librarianship, 1960; m. Clarence Merskey, Oct. 8, 1939; children—Hilary Pamela (Mrs. Robert Nathe), Susan Heather, Joan Margaret (Mrs. Mark Schneiderman). Sec., Chief Rabbi Israel Abrahams, South Africa, 1945-49, Jewish Sheltered Employment Council, 1954-56; reference librarian New Rochelle Pub. Library, 1960-63; research librarian Consumers Union, Mt. Vernon, 1963-66; asst. readers services, head union catalog Westchester Library System, 1966-69, mem. adult services com., 1973-74; dir. Harrison Pub. Library and West Harrison Br., 1969—. Recipient Brotherhood award B'nai B'rith, 1974. Mem. Am., Westchester, N.Y. (mem. adult edn. com. for continuing edn. 1971-75) library assns., Pub. Library Dirs. Assn. (tech. services com. chmn. Westchester county 1971, exec. bd. 1974-75, vice chmn. 1975), Harrison Women's Club, Harrison Hist. Soc. (founder), Hadassah, Van Riebeeck Soc. (Cape Town), USCG Aux. Contbr. articles to local newspapers. Home: 316 S Barry Ave Mamaroneck NY 10543 Office: Bruce Ave Harrison NY 10528

MERTENS, WILLIAM, judge; b. N.Y.C., May 20, 1910; s. William and Emma (Kane) M.; A.B., Wesleyan U., 1931; J.D., Harvard U., 1934; m. Carmen Wielich, Aug. 21, 1940; children—Diane, Patricia, Victoria. Admitted to N.Y. bar, 1934; dep. asst. dist. atty. New York County, 1938-41; dep. supt. Banks of N.Y. State, gen. counsel N.Y. State Banking Dept., 1945; pvt. law practice, N.Y.C., 1946-66; judge N.Y.C. Civil Ct., 1967—; counsel, N.Y. State Joint Legis. Com. Installment Financing, 1947-49; justice City Ct., N.Y.C., 1950; spl. counsel N.Y. State Ins. Dept., 1951-53; asso. counsel N.Y. Joint Legis. Com. Ct. Reorgn., 1959-61. Mem. exec. com. N.Y. County Republican Com., 1942-50, 51-66; mem. Rep. State Com. 1951-63; alt. del. Rep. Nat. Conv., 1944, 56; del. Rep. State convs., 1942-62, Rep. presdl. elector, N.Y. State, 1952; acting state supreme ct. justice, 1971, 73, 74—, pres. Nat. Rep. Club, 1959-62; campaign mgr. Rep. City Com., 1957. Mem. Bar Assn. City N.Y., Am., N.Y. bar assns., N.Y. County Lawyers Assn., Am. Judges Assn. (award 1975), Am. Judicature Soc., Nat. Conf. Spl. Ct. Judges (chmn. 1972-73), Phi Beta Kappa, Sigma Nu, Delta Sigma Rho. Club: Harvard. Home: 630 Park Ave New York City NY 10021 Office: 111 Centre St New York City NY 10017

MERTHAN, LAWRENCE CASPER, lawyer; b. St. Paul, Sept. 25, 1918; s. Casper Matthew and Theresa Martha (Laber) M.; B.A. cum laude, Coll. St. Thomas, St. Paul, 1941; J.D., U. Minn., 1949; LL.D. (hon.), Iowa Wesleyan Coll., 1967; m. Rita R. Chapowicki, Oct. 13, 1964; 1 dau., Mary Elizabeth. Admitted to D.C. bar, 1964, Minn. bar, 1949; practice law, St. Paul, 1949-55, Washington, 1978—; legis. counsel to U.S. Senator Eugene McCarthy, also staff dir. Spl. Senate Com. Unemployment Problems, Washington, 1959-65; dir. govt. relations Pfizer Inc., Washington, 1965-68; sr. v.p. Hill and Knowlton Co., Washington, 1968-74; exec. v.p. Carpet and Rug Inst., Washington, 1974-78; mem. firm Hedrick & Lane, Washington, 1978—; dir. N.Y. Venture Fund. Vice-chmn. St. Paul Housing and Redevel. Authority, 1952-55. Served with USAAF, 1941-45; ret. col. Res. Decorated D.F.C., Air medal. Mem. Minn., Ramsey County, Fed. bar assns., Assn. Trial Lawyers Am. Democrat. Roman Catholic. Clubs: Internat. D.C., Capitol Hill. Home: 2230 46th St NW Washington DC 20007 Office: 1211 Connecticut Ave Suite 700 Washington DC 20036

MERTZ, ALFRED STEPHEN, clergyman; b. Allentown, Pa., Aug. 18, 1910; s. Stephen Joseph and Sarah (Vogenitz) M.; A.B., Moravian Coll., 1932, postgrad., 1937-38; B.D., Lancaster Theol. Sem., 1935; m. Norma Jane Snyder, Jan. 17, 1937; children—Christine Mertz Henson, Clayton Alfred. Ordained to ministry United Ch. Christ, 1937; pastor Fullerton-Greenawalds Ch., Allentown, 1937-49, Old Zionsville, Pa., 1949-63, Huffs and St. Peters Ch., Alburtis, Pa., 1949-74, Jerusalem United Ch. Christ, 1974—; tchr. pub. schs., Allentown, 1942-43, Coplay, Pa., 1958-63, Upper Perkiomen Dist. Schs., Pennsburg, Pa., 1963-65. Active Lehigh and Hawk Mountain councils Boy Scouts Am., 1937—; mem. spl. edn. adv. com. Quakertown (Pa.) Joint Schs., 1970-72. Address: 627 N West End Blvd Quakerstown PA 18951

MERTZ, PIERRE, communications engr.; b. Paris, Apr. 2, 1897; s. Cornelius and Fanny (Nery) M.; came to U.S., 1902; A.B., Cornell U., 1918, Ph.D., 1926; m. Eunice H. Hanhart, June 27, 1923; children—Harvey, Robert, Lawrence. Communications engr. AT & T, N.Y.C., 1919-22, 26-34; with Bell Telephone Labs., N.Y.C., 1934-58; with Rand Corp., Los Angeles, 1959-67; cons., Hightstown, N.J., 1967—, cons. Office Sci. Research and Devel., 1942-45. Recipient certificate of appreciation Office Sci. Research and Devel., 1948, 51. Fellow IEEE (Paper award 1962), Soc. Motion Picture and TV Engrs. (mem. bd. editors jour. 1954-77, David Sarnoff Gold medal 1962, hon. mem. 1971—), Optical Soc. Am.; mem. Am. Phys. Soc., Inter-Soc. Color Council, Sigma Xi, Phi Kappa Phi. Republican. Contbr. articles to profl. publs. and handbooks. Home: Meadow Lakes 901 Hightstown NJ 08520

MERWIN, ROBERT FREEMAN, mfg. co. chmn.; b. Erie, Pa., Dec. 21, 1913; s. Orange F. and Louise (Regal) M.; B.A., Hiram Coll., 1936; m. Betty Moreland MacKay, June 22, 1940; 1 son, Richard A. Original partner, Eriez Mfg. Co. (now Eriez Magnetics), Erie, Pa., 1942, pres., 1951-70, chmn. bd., 1971—; dir. 1st Nat. Bank Pa., Erie; mem. Regional Export Expansion Council Dept. Commerce, 1967-69. Mem. Erie Sch. Bd., 1957-63; trustee Hamot Med. Center, 1972, YMCA, 1973, Gannon Coll., Erie, Pa., Hiram Coll.; bd. dirs. Nat. Hearing Assn. Recipient Job Makers' award C. of C., 1965, Export E award, 1965; Outstanding Achievement award Hiram Coll., 1972. Mem. 1st Christian Ch. Clubs: Shrine, Duquesne, University, Kahkwa. Patentee magnetic equipment. Home: 6501 W Heidler Rd Fairview PA 16415 Office: Eriez Magnetics Asbury Rd at Airport Erie PA 16512

MESCAVAGE, ALEXANDER ANTHONY, JR., psychologist; b. Bklyn., Dec. 7, 1946; s. Alexander Anthony and Constance (Loggia) M.; B.A., State U. Coll. N.Y., Oneonta, 1969; M.A., C.W. Post Coll., 1971; m. Jackuelyn Zaso, Apr. 28, 1973. Tchr., counselor Suffolk County Center for Emotionally Disturbed Children, Bay Shore, N.Y., 1971-72; narcotics addiction control counselor Ridge Hill Rehab. Center, Yonkers, N.Y., 1972-73; psychologist N.H. Hosp., Concord, 1973-77; psychol. cons. Franklin Regional Sch. Dist., Franklin, N.H., 1977-78; psychologist Harlem Valley Psychiat. Center, Wingdale, N.Y., 1978—; co-dir. Derry (N.H.) Counseling Services, 1974-75. Mem. Internat. Transactional Analysis Assn., N.H. Psychol. Assn., N.H. Affiliation Mental Health Practitioners (alt. chmn. 1976), Am. Personnel and Guidance Assn. Home and Office: 16 F 7 Scuppo Rd Danbury CT 06810

MESHREKI, MAKRAM HABIB, chemist; b. Alexandria, Egypt, Oct. 27, 1936; s. Habib Bishai and Wadida Basta (Michael) M.; came to U.S., 1968, naturalized, 1978; B.S. with honors, Alexandria U., 1958, M.S., 1962, Ph.D., 1965; m. Yvonne Labib Mitry, Sept. 22, 1968; children—Samer M., Lotus M. Instr. chemistry Alexandria U., 1958-66, asst. prof., 1966-68; postdoctoral fellow, research asso. chemistry Ohio State U., Columbus, 1968-71, U. Mont., Missoula, 1971-72, biochemistry, Purdue U., Lafayette, Ind., 1972-73; sr. research chemist G.D. Searle & Co., Chgo., 1973-76; research chemist ICI Ams. Inc., Wilmington, Del., 1976—. Mem. Am. Chem. Soc., Inst. Food Technologists, Sigma Xi. Coptic Orthodox. Contbr. articles to profl. publs., lectr. profl. orgns. Home: 2524 Channin Dr Wilmington DE 19810 Office: Concord Pike and Murphy Rd Wilmington DE 19897

MESKAUSKAS, JOHN ALGIMANTAS, ednl. psychologist; b. Kaunas, Lithuania, Sept. 7, 1941; s. Juozas and Jone (Petrulis) M.; came to U.S., 1948, naturalized, 1955; B.S., Ill. Inst. Tech., 1964, M.S., 1966; postgrad. U. Pa., 1973—; m. Audrone Virgilija Petrulis, July 6, 1963; 1 dau., Ruta. Project dir. Sci. Research Assos., Chgo., 1966-69; asst. dir. Nat. Bd. Med. Examiners, Phila., 1969-74; asso. dir. for psychometrics Am. Bd. Internal Medicine, Phila., 1974—; lectr. in edn. U. Pa. Mem. Am. Ednl. Research Assn., Assn. of Am. Med. Colls., Am. Psychol. Assn., Nat. Council for Measurement in Edn., Nat. Soc. for the Study of Edn., Psychometric Soc. Democrat. Contbr.

articles to profl. jours. and presentations to profl. meetings. Home: 236 Valley Rd Merion PA 17235 Office: 3624 Market St Philadelphia PA 19104

MESMER, ROGER EDWARD GEORGE, psychiatrist; b. Buffalo, May 16, 1932; s. Edward George and Eleanor Lindsay (Roberts) M.; B.A., U. Buffalo, 1953; M.D., McGill U. (Can.), 1956; m. Christina Sandblade, Aug. 22, 1969; children—Sara Lindsay, Thomas Gregory Lathbury, Rachel Maria. Intern, Millard Fillmore Hosp., Buffalo, 1957-58; gen. practice medicine, San Luis, Colo., 1960-63; resident in psychiatry Warren (Pa.) State Hosp., 1963-66, sr. psychiatrist, 1966-68, dir. community psychiatry, 1969-74, dir. western unit, 1971-74, 76—, dir. adolescent unit, 1976—, dir. med. edn., 1976—; med. dir. Oaklawn Psychiat. Center, Elkhart, Ind., 1975; founder, pres. bd. Warren Sr. Center, 1968-74; instr. abnormal psychology U. Pitts., 1968, adj. asst. prof. psychiatry, 1971—. Mem. Bishop's Commn. for Selection of Clergy, Erie, Pa., 1975, Commn. on Ministry, 1976; mem. Commn. for Human Services for Warren and Forest Counties. Diplomate Am. Bd. Psychiatry and Neurology (asso. examiner 1978). Fellow Am. Psychiat. Assn.; mem. Pa. Assn. State Mental Hosp. Physicians (founding pres. 1970), Pa., Warren County med. socs., AMA, Pa. Psychiat. Soc., Am. Assn. Dirs. Psychiat. Residency Programs, Assn. for Acad. Psychiatry. Republican. Episcopalian. Home: 312 W 5th Ave Warren PA 16365 Office: PO Box 249 Warren PA 16365

MESNEY, DOROTHY TAYLOR, mezzo-soprano, pianist, composer, educator; b. Bklyn., Sept. 15, 1926; d. Franklin and Kathryn Ross (Munro) Taylor; diploma Berkeley Inst., 1934; B.A., Sarah Lawrence Coll., 1938; postgrad. Columbia, 1938-41, Juilliard Sch. Music, 1963-71, Manhattan Sch. Music, 1971-73; m. Peter Michael Mesney, Oct. 15, 1942; children—Douglas, Kathryn, Barbara. Mezzo-soprano, operetta, concert and oratorio soloist in various churches, N.Y.C., 1956—; debuts include: N.Y. Cultural Center, 1971, Carnegie Recital Hall, 1974; leading roles with local opera groups and with Gilbert and Sullivan Soc., Douglaston, L.I.; rec. artist Folkways Records; founder American Experience ensemble; tchr. piano and singing, Douglaston, 1958—, also tchr. music classes; founder children's series Concerts for children; founder Introduction to Music for preschoolers; co-founder The Elizabethan Experience, musical lectr. series. Com. chmn. PTA, Douglaston, 1952-55; den mother Greater N.Y. council Cub Scouts Am., 1953-56; Brownie leader Greater N.Y. council Girl Scouts U.S.; bd. dirs. Community Concerts Assn. of Great Neck, N.Y. Mem. Nat. Piano Tchrs. Guild, Nat. Fedn. Music Clubs (N.Y. chpt.), Met. Opera Guild, Tuesday Morning Music Club (publicity chmn. 1968-74, v.p. 1975-77. Democrat. Congregationalist. Composer hymns, songs and ballades including Spread Your Wings and Fly, 1960, Walk Into the Promised Land, 1964, Song of Creation, 1974, Zion's Hill, 1975. Address: 324 Manor Rd Douglaston NY 11363

MESSER, THOMAS M., museum dir.; b. Bratislava, Czechoslovakia, Feb. 9, 1920; s. Richard and Agatha (Albrecht) M.; exchange student Inst. Internat. Edn., 1939; student Thiel Coll., Greenville, Pa., 1939-41; B.A., Boston U., 1942; degree U. Sorbonne (Paris), 1947; M.A., Harvard, 1951; D.F.A. honoris causa, U. Mass., 1962; m. Remedios Garcia Villa, Jan. 10, 1948. Came to U.S., 1939, naturalized, 1944. Dir. Roswell (N.Mex.) Mus., 1949-52; asst. dir. Am. Fedn. Arts, N.Y.C., 1952-53, dir. exhbns., 1953-55, dir., 1955-56, trustee, 1972-76; dir. inst. Contemporary Art, Boston, 1957-61, The Solomon R. Guggenheim Mus., N.Y.C., 1961—; adj. prof. Harvard, 1960, Barnard Coll., 1966, 71. Mem. vis. com. on art Museums and Fine Arts Dept., Harvard; mem. com. on art Port Authority of N.Y. and N.J.; trustee Internat. Com. for Museums and Collections Modern Art of Internat. Council Museums, 1977-79; pres. MacDowell Colony Inc., 1977—; trustee Am. Arts Alliance, Wooster Sch., Center for Inter Am. Relations, N.Y.C. chmn. Internat. Exhbns. Com., Washington, 1976-79; vice chmn. council Am. Assn. Museums/Internat. Council Museums, 1978—. Decorated knight Royal Order St. Olav (Norway); Order Leopold II (Belgium); officers cross Order of Merit (Fed. Republic Germany); spl. fellow for study in Brussels, Belgian-Am. Ednl. Found., 1953; sr. fellow Center Advanced Studies, Wesleyan U., 1966. Mem. Assn. Art Mus. Dirs. (pres. 1974-75). Clubs: Met. Opera, Century Assn. (N.Y.C.). Author: Edvard Munch, 1973. Contbr. to mus. catalogues, art jours. Home: 1105 Park Ave New York City NY 10028 Office: 1071 Fifth Ave New York City NY 10028

MESSINA, GIACOMO ANTHONY, surgeon; b. Bklyn., Oct. 4, 1922; s. Bernardo and Frieda (Sinacore) M.; B.S., Fordham U., 1943; M.D., L.I. Coll. Medicine, Bklyn., 1946; m. Petrina Barbara La Rosa, Nov. 9, 1946; children—Leonard, Maria. Intern, L.I. Coll. Hosp., Bklyn., 1946-47; fellow surg. pathology Columbia-Presbyn. Med. Center, N.Y.C., 1947-48; resident surgery Wyckoff Heights Hosp., Bklyn., 1948-51; clin. instr. surgery Downstate Med. Center, State U. N.Y., N.Y.C., 1951-59; attending surgery Wyckoff Heights Hosp., 1951—; individual practice medicine, specializing in gen. surgery, Bklyn., 1951—; cons. in field. Served with M.C., U.S. Army, 1943-46. Diplomate Am. Bd. Surgery. Fellow A.C.S., AMA, N.Y. State, Queens County med. socs., Queens Surg. Soc. Republican. Roman Catholic. Clubs: N. Hills Country (Manhasset, N.Y.) (pres. 1969), Bushwick, 20 Queens. Home: 215-15 86th Ave Queens Village NY 11427 Office: 149 St Nicholas Ave Brooklyn NY 11237

MESSINEO, PAUL JOSEPH, civil engr.; b. Turtle Creek, Pa., Dec. 15, 1936; s. Samuel and Margaret (Franciullo) M.; B.S., Northwestern U., 1958; m. Marie E. Harcarik, Oct. 5, 1963; children—Paul Joseph, Michele. Party chief Thompson Survey, Monroeville, Pa., 1958-59, Siefers Surveying, Wilkinsburg, Pa., 1959-60; project engr. Branna Constrn. Co., Pitts., 1960-68; sr. project mgr. Dick Corp., Pitts., 1968—; cons. VISTA. Pres. parish council, chmn. bldg. com. St. Colmans Roman Catholic Ch., pres. Parent Tchrs. Guild, 1973-74. Mem. ASCE (sr.), Am. Soc. Hwy. Engrs. (sr.), Soil Mechanics of Pitts. (dir., chmn.). Democrat. Clubs: K.C., Ancient Order of Hybernians. Home: 107 Larchwood Dr Turtle Creek PA 15145

MESSNER, JOSEPH ANTON, child welfare dir.; b. Halli, Tirol, Austria, Mar. 1, 1924; s. Josef Franz and Maria Anna (Kiniger) M.; came to Can., 1952; Diplom Dolmetscher, Ferdinand Franzens U., Innsbruck, Austria, 1949; m. Magdalena Schreder, Jan. 14, 1944 (dec.); m. 2d, Herlinde Ingeborg Ohm, Mar. 28, 1952; children—Peter, William, Patricia. Investigator, U.S. Displaced Person Screening Mission, Austria, 1950; sect. head, Internat. Refugee Orgn., Austria, 1951; lectr. U.S. Info. Center, Austria, 1952; social worker Cath. Welfare Bur., Hamilton, Ont., Can., 1952-54; exec. dir. Cath. Children's Aid Soc., Hamilton, 1954-65; spl. lectr. sci. German, McMaster U., Hamilton, 1954-65; exec. dir. Childrens Aid Soc., Ottawa, Ont., 1965—, mem. bd., 1975—; exec. dir. Friends of SOS Childrens Villages, Can. Inc., Ottawa, 1969—, mem. bd., owner Mesle Can. Reg'd. Importer, Ottawa, 1972—. Mem. Ont. Assn. Childrens Aid Socs. (dir., chmn. legislation com.), Child Welfare League Am., Can. Waterski Assn. Club: Outaouis Hang-Gliding. Author: Day Care-Right or Remedy?; Canadian Welfare. Home: Box 666 Rural Route 5 Ottawa ON K1G 3N3 Canada Office: 1370 Bank St Ottawa ON Canada

MESSNER, ROBERT THOMAS, lawyer, retail trade exec.; b. McKeesport, Pa., Mar. 27, 1938; s. Thomas M. and Cecelia Mary (McElhinny) M.; A.B., Dartmouth Coll., 1960; LL.B., U. Pa., 1963; m. Anne Margaret Lux, Dec. 3, 1966; children—Megan Anne, Michael Thomas. Admitted to Pa. bar, 1965; asso. firm Rose, Schmidt and Dixon, Pitts., 1965-68; asst. dir. employee relations G.C. Murphy Co., McKeesport, 1968-70, asst. sec., 1970-74, corp. sec., 1974-75, corp. sec. and gen. counsel, 1975—, v.p., 1976—; lectr. Nat. Investor Relations Conf., N.Y.C.; dir. G.C. Murphy Co. Found. Adv. bd. Pa. Human Relations Commn., 1968-69; registration chmn. Republican Com. Allegheny County, Pa., 1967; bd. dirs. McKeesport YMCA. Served with U.S. Army, 1963-65. Mem. Am., Pa., Allegheny County bar assns., Am. Soc. Corp. Secs. (pres. Pitts. regional group), McKeesport C. of C. (dir. 1972-73). Clubs: University (Pitts.); Nat. Lawyers (Washington); Dartmouth of Western Pa. Home: 1061 Blackridge Rd Pittsburgh PA 15235 Office: 531 Fifth Ave McKeesport PA 15132

MESSNER, WAYNE KENNETH, air force officer; b. Troy, N.Y., Mar. 22, 1936; s. Lee Kenneth and Kathryn Beatrice (Snyder) M.; B.S., U.S. Naval Acad., 1959; M.B.A., Pa. State U., 1972; grad. Def. Systems Mgmt. Coll., 1976; m. Janice Ann Millett, Jan. 25, 1958; children—Susan, Kimberly, Kristina. Commd. 2d lt. USAF, 1959, advanced through grades to lt. col., 1975; service in Korea; chief bus. mgmt. div. Hdqrs. Electronics Systems Div., Hanscom AFB, Mass., 1976-78; assigned Naval War Coll., 1978—. Mem. Chelmsford (Mass.) Village Improvement Assn. Decorated Joint Service Commendation medal, Air Force Commendation medal, Meritorious Service medal. Mem. U.S. Naval Acad., Pa. State U., St. Lawrence U. alumni assns., Air Force Assn., U.S. Naval Athletic Assn., Beta Gamma Sigma. Republican. Episcopalian. Author articles. Office: Naval War Coll Newport RI 02840

METCALF, HARLAN GOLDSBURY, educator; b. Elyria, Ohio, July 29, 1899; s. Harlan Paul and Zarena (Goldsbury) M.; B.A., Oberlin Coll., 1921; M.A., Tchrs. Coll., Columbia U., 1924; Ph.D., N.Y. U., 1934; m. Margaret Wyer, Apr. 9, 1925; 1 son, Harlan James. Dir. individual phys. edn., Ohio State U., Columbus, 1928-36, asst. prof. phys. edn., 1928-32, asso. prof., 1932-36; prof., chmn. dept. health phys. edn. Peabody Coll. Tchrs., Nashville, 1936-42; asst. exec. dir. FSA, Washington, 1942-44, exec. dir., com. phys. fitness, 1944-45; spl. rep. Nat. Recreation Assn., 22 northeastern states, 1945-47; prof. recreation edn. State U. N.Y., Cortland, 1947-69, chmn. dept. recreation edn., 1947-67; cons. on outdoor edn. numerous nat. outdoor edn. workshops, 1955-75. Chmn. recreation com. Cortland County Council Social Agy., 1950-51, pres., 1952-53; mem. nat. adv. com. Fitness U.S.A., 1941-45; mem. adv. bd. Cortland Youth Bur., 1952-55; elder Presbyterian Ch., Cortland, 1953-56; bd. dirs. Cortland YMCA, Cortland Salvation Army, Cortland County Council Chs. Recipient Outstanding Contbn. award L.I. Recreation and Parks Assn., 1965, Golden award N.Y. State Outdoor Edn. Soc., 1968, Spl. Youth Service award Gov. of N.Y., 1968, Hall of Fame award N.Y. State Life-Time Sports, 1975, Lit. award N.Y. State Outdoor Edn. Assn., 1974, Distinguished Fellow award Nat. Soc. Park and Recreation Educators, 1974, others. Mem. AAHPER (past v.p. recreation eastern dist., nat. v.p. 1965, chmn. recreation div. 1965), Am. Recreation Soc., Nat. Recreation Assn., N.Y. State Recreation and Parks Assn. (life, award 1963, 65), Izaak Walton League, Nat. Field Archery Assn., Cortland Coll. Alumni Assn. (hon. life, Distinguished alumnus award 1973). Club: Rotary (hon.). Author: Physically Fit for Production, 1944; (with A.O. Haugen) Field Archery and Bowhunting, 1963; Whittlin Whistles and Thingamajigs, 1974; contbr. numerous articles on recreation and outdoor recreation to profl. publs. Home: 6 Levydale Park Cortland NY 13045 also Assembly Park RD 2 Tully NY 13159

METCALF, HARRY LEONARD, physician; b. Buffalo, Dec. 3, 1934; s. Jack Stewart and Evelyn (Seaner) M.; B.A., U. Buffalo, 1956, M.D., 1960; m. Kaaren Jean Heim, Apr. 13, 1957; children—Marc, Eric, Christine. Intern, Phila. Naval Hosp., 1960-61; resident U.S. Naval Hosp., Kenitea, Morocco, 1961-64; practice family medicine, Buffalo, 1964—; full attending family practice Deaconess Hosp., Lockport Hosp.; asst. clin. prof. family medicine State U. N.Y., Buffalo, 1975—, dir. admissions, 1977—; moderator and lectr. Telephone Lecture Network Operation, Communications and Learning, Inc., 1972—; pres. Research and Edn. Found., N.Y. State Acad. Family Physicians, 1977—. Mem. Narcotics Guidance Council Erie County (N.Y.), 1973-75. Served to lt., M.C., USN, 1960-64. Diplomate Am. Bd. Family Practice. Fellow Am. Acad. Family Physicians (del. N.Y. state 1975—, chmn. com. mental health 1976-77); mem. Buffalo Acad. Medicine, N.Y. State Acad. Family Physicians (chmn. commn. environ. medicine 1970-73, mem. commn. legis. 1973—), N.Y. State, Erie County med. socs., Am. Soc. Clin. Hypnosis, Soc. Tchrs. Family Medicine. Republican. Episcopalian. Club: Country of Buffalo. Contbr. articles in field to med. jours. Home: 55 Parkledge Dr Snyder NY 14226 Office: 3435 Bailey Ave Buffalo NY 14215

METREY, GEORGE DAVID, social worker; b. Milw., July 23, 1939; s. Richard Joseph and Catherine (Evans) M.; A.B., Marquette U., 1961; M.S.W., Fordham U., 1963; Ph.D., N.Y. U., 1970; m. Cheryl Ann Mosca, June 21, 1969. Social worker N.J. Diagnostic Center, Edison, 1963-64; asst. social work supr., 1964-66, dir. psychiat. social work, 1966-70; coordinator undergrad. social work program Kean Coll. N.J., 1970-73, asso. prof. social work, 1970-74, prof., 1974—, chmn. dept. sociology, anthropology and social work, 1973-77, dir. social work program, acting asso. dean Sch. Arts and Sci., 1977—; field instr. Fordham U. Sch. Social Service, 1966-70, adj. prof., 1969-77; adj. asso. prof. Rutgers U. Grad. Sch. Social Work, 1972-73. Mem. Nat. Assn. Social Workers (chmn. central Jersey unit 1971-75, mem. state exec. bd., v.p. state chpt. 1975-76, pres., 1976, pres. elect 1976-78, pres. 1978—, mem. nat. task force on B. in Social Work 1975-76, chmn. 1976-77, nat. 2d v.p. 1978—), Council on Social Work Edn., Assn. Program Dirs. (sec.-treas. 1977-79) N.J. Assn. Undergrad. Social Worker Educators, Acad. Certified Social Workers, Nat. Registry Clin. Social Workers, Am. Soc. Pub. Adminstrs., Alpha Phi Omega, Gamma Pi Mu, Alpha Delta Mu (regional v.p.). Roman Catholic. Home: 42 Devon Dr E Piscataway NJ 08854 Office: Kean Coll New Jersey Union NJ

METSCH, ARTHUR DAVID, def. procurement exec.; b. N.Y.C., Sept. 20, 1913; s. Benjamin and Clara (Linder) M.; B.S. in Bus. Adminstrn. cum laude, City U. N.Y., 1938; M.B.A., N.Y. U., 1957; m. Evelyn Martin, Oct. 23, 1938; children—Lawrence, Jonathan, Victor. Office mgr. B. Goldstein & Co., N.Y.C., 1930-41; supervisory auditor USAAF, N.Y.C., 1941-43; termination negotiator and contracting officer USAF, N.Y.C., 1946-50; chief contract div. AF Dist. covering Pa., N.J., Md., Del., Va. and N.C., 1950-54; mgr. contracts W.L. Maxson Corp., 1954-59, Loral Electronics, N.Y.C., 1959-64, Superior Mfg. & Instrument Corp., N.Y.C., 1965-74; contracting officer Def. Logistics Agy., Garden City, N.Y., 1974-76; contracting officer for Navy Dept., Sperry Div., Great Neck, N.Y., 1974—; instr. business mgmt. N.Y. U. Grad. Sch. Bus. Adminstrn., 1960-67. Mem. B'nai B'rith Anti-Defamation League. Served with USAAF, 1943-46. Mem. AF Assn., Am. Def. Preparedness Assn., Jewish War Vets, Beta Gamma Sigma, Torch and Scroll. Democrat. Clubs: B'nai B'rith, K.P. Contbr. handbook on govt. procurement. Address: 60-05D 194th St Flushing NY 11365

METSISTO, TAUNO JAMES, info. systems cons.; b. Springfield, Mass., Apr. 16, 1944; s. Tauno O. and Mary J. (Gallerani) M.; B.S.E.E., Lowell Technol. Inst., 1965; M.S. in Mgmt., Rensselaer Poly. Inst., 1966; m. Diana Drucas, Sept. 21, 1969; 1 dau., Nicole. Advanced research engr. Sylvania Research Lab., Waltham, Mass., 1966-70; cons. Corporate Tech Planning, Inc., Waltham, 1970-73; mgr. Arthur Young & Co., Hartford, Conn., 1973-76, prin., Boston, 1976—; instr. in statistics Rensselaer Poly. Inst., Troy, N.Y., 1965-66. Mem. IEEE, Data Processing Mgmt. Assn., Assn. Computing Machinery. Club: Satuit Boat. Office: 1 Boston Pl Boston MA 02102

METSON, GRAHAM, artist, writer; b. London, June 24, 1934; s. Sydney Walter and Maude Florence (Moore) M.; ed. London U.; m. Cheryl Lean, Sept. 1977; children—Mark, Oliver. Thirty one-man exhbns., including London, N.Y., Toronto, Can., 1959—; also numerous group exhbns.; represented in numerous pvt. collections. Bd. dirs. Visual Arts N.S. Served with RAF. Recipient prizes and commendations including Can. Council, U. London. Author: The Halifax Explosion, 1978. Home: Sanford North Medford RR2 Canning Kings County NS B1P 1HD Canada

METZ, EDWARD, elec. engr.; b. Crown Point, Ind., June 3, 1921; s. Russell and Minnie (Kaiser) M.; E.E., Purdue U., 1943; m. Sophie Kish, Nov. 21, 1943; children—Diana L. Metz Giannini, Cheryl A., Gregory R. Asst. lab. supr. Bryant Electric Co., Bridgeport, Conn., 1945-52; with Leviton Mfg. Co., Inc., Little Neck, N.Y., 1952—, dir. research and devel., 1957-75, dir. engring. services, 1975—. Served with C.E., USAAF, 1943-45. Mem. Purdue Alumni Assn., ASTM, Am. Soc. Metals, IEEE, Nat. Rifle Assn. Republican. Greek Catholic. Club: Bridgeport Rifle. Home: 141 Sturbridge Ln Monroe CT 06611 Office: 59-25 Little Neck Pkwy Little Neck NY 11362

METZ, VERNON WAHL, educator; b. Zelienople, Pa., Oct. 25, 1917; s. Lester Cameron and Alma (Wahl) M.; A.B., Capital U., 1938; M.Litt., U. Pitts., 1940. Chmn. speech dept., dir. advanced placement and student activities North Hills Sch. Dist., Pitts., 1939-69; prin. North Hills Intermediate High Sch., 1969-73; instr. speech Pa. State U., U. Pitts.; speech cons. Pitts. Savs. & Loan, Industry (Pa.) Dept. Pub. Instrn. Served with AUS, 1943-45. Recipient Freedoms Found. medal, 1960, Pa. Dept. Pub. Instrn. citation, 1967. Mem. NEA, Pa. Edn. Assn., Am., Eastern States, Pa. speech assns., Nat. Forensic League (nat. dir.), Tau Kappa Alpha, Phi Alpha Theta, Phi Delta Kappa. Republican. Lutheran. Clubs: Masons, K.T., Rotary. Author: Primary Sources in Teaching and Interpreting American History, 1967. Home: 810 Harden Dr Pittsburgh PA 15229 Office: Pa State U Beaver Campus Monaca PA 15061

METZGER, ALAN FAIRFIELD, mfr., elec. engr.; b. Montclair, N.J., Feb. 28, 1906; s. Elmer Eugene and Mina (Burgess) M.; B.S., Yale U., 1929; m. Nathalie Elizabeth Whitten, June 15, 1935; children—Alan Whitten, Joan Elizabeth. Test course Gen. Electric Co., 1929-31, design engr., motors, 1931-36, application engr., New Eng. dist., 1936-43; asst. elec. engr. Electric Boat Co., 1943-45, chief elec. engr., 1945-51; v.p., dir. Ideal Windlass Co., 1951-55; pres., treas. Edward Parkingson Mfg. Co., 1956-71, pres., 1971-76, now chmn. bd., dir.; pres. Hope Industries, 1957-61; dir. Web Systems, Inc. Mem. exec. bd. com. United Fund Southeastern New Eng., 1968—. Mem. Am. Inst. E.E., Soc. Naval Architects and Marine Engrs., Am. Soc. Naval Engrs., Providence Engring. Soc., R.I. Soc. Profl. Engrs. (named Engr. of Year), Marine Hist. Assn., Yale Engring. Assn., U.S. Power Squadron (tchr. nav., piloting, boat handling 1940—), USCG Aux. (tchr. boating courses 1959—). Club: Weckford Yacht. Home: Pojac Point RFD 2 North Kingstown RI 02818 Office: Edward Parkinson Mfg Co Esmond RI 02917

METZGER, ERNEST HUGH, aerospace scientist; b. Nurnberg, Germany, Oct. 22, 1923; s. Paul Arthur and Charlotte Babette (Kann) M.; came to U.S., 1939, naturalized, 1943; B.S., Coll City N.Y., 1949; M.S., Harvard U., 1950; m. Sarah Temple Grinnell, Nov. 19, 1956; children—Lisa Temple, Charlotte Ann, George Grinnell. Automatic control engr. Bell Aerospace Co., div. Textron, Buffalo, 1950-54, tech. dir. inertial nav. systems, 1954-60, chief engr. inertial instruments, 1960-70, research mgr. advanced inertial systems, 1970—; mem. NASA accelerometer criteria com. Trustee Unitarian-Universalist Ch. of Buffalo, 1959-62, chmn. 1962. Served with AUS, 1943-46. Recipient Aerospace Pioneer award Niagara Frontier sect. Am. Inst. Aeros. and Astronautics, 1977. Mem. IEEE, Inst. Nav., AAAS, Air Force Assn., Sigma Xi, Tau Beta Pi, Eta Kappa Nu. Club: Harvard, Buffalo Ski. Patentee in field; contbr. articles in field to profl. jours. Home: 90 High Park Blvd Buffalo NY 14226 Office: PO Box 1 Buffalo NY 14240

METZGER, WILLIAM HENRY, JR., chemist; b. Richmond, Va., Feb. 17, 1922; s. William Henry and Emma Elizabeth (Hasker) M.; B.S., U. Richmond, 1943; m. Marion Jane Grant, Nov. 19, 1949. Chemist, Nat. Bur. Standards, Washington, 1943-69; chief chemist, fed. supply service, materials evaluation and devel. lab. GSA, Washington, 1969-77; cons. chemist, 1977—. Served to lt. (j.g.) USNR, 1944-46. Fellow Am. Inst. Chemists; mem. Am. Chem. Soc., Am. Electroplaters Soc. (pres. 1955), ASTM, Phi Kappa Sigma. Lutheran. Clubs: Cosmos, Potomac Archers (Washington); SW Anglers (Fla.). Patentee in field. Home and office: PO Box 148 Port Clyde Rd Tenants Harbor ME 04860

METZMAN, FRANCES SCHUMAN, sculptor, art cons.; b. Phila., June 18, 1937; d. Lewis and Sarah (Brenner) Schuman; student Temple U., 1955-58; B.F.A., Moore Coll. Art, 1974; m. Milton Metzman, Jan. 8, 1961; children—Ross Adam, Carla Jane. Real estate agt. Lenny Agency, Phila., 1966-69; exhibited in 1-woman shows Community Center, Cherry Hill, N.J., 1973-75, Wallnuts Gallery, Phila., 1974, Rogue's Gallery Phila. and Cherry Hill, 1975; numerous group shows throughout U.S.; represented in permanent collections; cons., coordinator art Wallnuts Gallery, 1977—; artist agt. Vol. tchr. reading skills to culturally deprived children. Mem. Am. Crafts Council, Clay Studio Phila. Jewish. Home: 27 Spring Mill Ln Cherry Hill NJ 08003 Office: 2018 Locust St Philadelphia PA 19103

MEYBURG, ARNIM HANS, transp. engr.; b. Brenerhaven, W. Ger., Aug. 25, 1939; s. Friedel and Auguste (Kleeberg) M.; came to U.S., 1965; student U. Hamburg, 1960-62, Free U. Berlin, 1962-65; M.S. (Fulbright travel grantee), Northwestern U., 1968, Ph.D., 1971; m. Lee Denise Stollerman, June 18, 1967. Research asso., Transp. Center, Northwestern U., Evanston, Ill., 1968-69; asst. prof. transp. engring., Cornell U., Ithaca, N.Y., 1969-75, asso. prof., 1975-78, prof., 1978—, acting dept. chmn., 1977-78; vis. mem. faculties U. Calif. at Irvine, Tech. U. Munich (Germany); Humboldt Found. research fellow Tech. U. Munich, 1978-79; mem. Transp. Research Bd., 1970—, Transp. Research Forum, 1972—; prin. investigator projects U.S. Dept. Transp., Nat. Coop. Hwy. Research Program. NSF Research Initiation grantee, 1973. Mem. ASCE, Ops. Research Soc. Am., Regional Sci. Assn. Author: Urban Transportation Modeling and Planning, 1975; Transportation Systems Evaluation, 1976. Home: 30 St Joseph Ln Ithaca NY 14850 Office: 305 Hollister Hall Cornell U Ithaca NY 14853

MEYER, CARL EDWIN, JR., aviation corp. exec.; b. Flushing, N.Y., Aug. 6, 1928; s. Carl Edwin and Eunice Clifton (Taylor) M.; B.A., Amherst Coll., 1950; M.B.A., N.Y. U., 1955; m. Ruth Leslie Oddy, Sept. 21, 1957; children—Jeffrey S., William D. Mgr., Harris, Kerr, Forster & Co., N.Y.C., 1953-65; asst. treas. Eastern Airlines, 1965-68; pres., chief airline exec. Trans World Airlines, N.Y.C., 1968—, also dir.; dir. Hilton Internat., Canteen Corp., Med. Testing Systems, Inc. Trustee Midwest Research Inst. Served with AUS, 1950-53. Mem. Am. Inst. C.P.A.'s, Air Transport Assn. (dir.). Clubs: Sky (N.Y.C.); North Hempstead Country (Port Washington). Office: Trans World Airlines Inc 605 3d Ave New York NY 11016*

MEYER, CORNELIUS CHARLES, educator; b. Buffalo, Aug. 29, 1942; s. Cornelius Charles and Mildred Mary (Roth) M.; B.A., State U. N.Y. at Buffalo, 1964; M.A., Conn. Coll. at New London, 1966; Ph.D., U. Waterloo (Ont., Can.), 1968; m. Olita Nogobods, Aug. 6, 1966; children—Jesse Cornelius, Aaron Arturs. Prof. psychology and biology Quinnipiac Coll., Hamden, Conn., 1968—. Prin. investigator NIMH, 1970-75, NSF, 1977—. Research grantee USPHS, 1970-75. Mem. AAAS, Animal Behavior Soc., Am. Psychol. Assn., Psychonomic Soc. Contbr. articles to profl. jours. and books. Home: 35 Arrowleaf Ct Cheshire CT 06410 Office: Dept Psychology Quinnipiac Coll Hamden CT 06518

MEYER, E(MMA) DOROTHEA, educator; b. Bklyn.; d. Richard C. and Ida D. (Mueller) Meyer; B.S., Susquehanna U., 1933; M.A., N.Y. U., 1943; Ed.D., N.Y. U., 1953. Tchr. high sch., South Fork, Pa., 1934-37, jr. high sch., pvt. bus. schs., Syracuse U., 1937-46; chmn. bus. and secretarial edn. Mitchell Coll., New London, Conn., 1946-52; faculty Hofstra U., Hempstead, N.Y., 1954—, asso. prof. bus. communications, 1955—; instr. office workers Standard Oil Co. of N.J., Island of Aruba, 1953. Cons. tng. programs. Mem. Adminstrv. Mgmt. Soc. (v.p. 1968, Merit award 1969), Am. Bus. Writing Assn., Eastern Bus. Tchrs. Assn., Nassau County Bus. Edn. Assn., Hempstead Heights Civic Assn., Beta Alpha Psi, Delta Pi Epsilon, Pi Gamma Mu, Pi Lambda Theta. Club: Hofstra U. (sec. 1976—). Asso. editor Transitions, 1975, editor, 1976—. Contbr. articles to ednl. jours. Home: 3 Commander St Hempstead NY 11550 Office: Fulton Ave Hempstead NY 11550

MEYER, EDWARD HENRY, advt. exec.; b. N.Y.C., Jan. 8, 1927; s. I.H. and Mildred (Driesen) M.; B.A. with honors in Econs., Cornell U., 1949; m. Sandra Raabin, Apr. 26, 1957; children—Margaret Ann, Anthony Edward. With Bloomingdale's div. Federated Dept. Stores, 1949-51, Biow Co., agy., 1951-56; with Grey Advt., Inc., N.Y.C., 1956—, exec. v.p., 1963-68, pres., chief exec. officer, 1968—; dir. Merrill Lynch Spl. Value Fund, Merrill Lynch Ready Assets Trust, Trans Lux Corp., Jim Pattison Group Inc. Trustee Asso. Y's of N.Y., Am. Health Found. Served with USCGR, 1945-47. Clubs: Cornell, Harmonie, Economic (N.Y.C.); Century Country. Home: Rockwood Ln Greenwich CT 06830 also 40 E 88th St New York City NY 10028 Office: 777 3d Ave New York City NY 10022

MEYER, ELMER EPHRAIM, JR., univ. dean; b. Green Bay, Wis., Jan. 4, 1928; s. Elmer E. and Irma D. (Heins) M.; B.A., Carroll Coll., 1950; M.S., U. Wis., 1955, Ph.D., 1965; certificate Inst. Edn. Mgmt., Harvard U., 1977; m. Nancy S. Ramsay, June 26, 1954; children—Marc Ramsay, Megan Christina, Rene Jean. Admissions counselor Carroll Coll., Waukesha, Wis., 1950, 52-54; research asst. U. Wis. Extension, 1954-55; counselor Integrated Liberal Studies, U. Wis., Madison, 1955-57, asst. to dir. tchr. placement, 1956-57, activities adviser, 1952-63, asst. dean students, 1963-66; asst. chancelor student affairs U. Wis. Center System, 1966-68; dean of students, asst. v.p. student affairs Cornell U., Ithaca, N.Y., 1968-72, dean of students, asst. v.p. campus affairs, 1972—; mem. adv. bd. CHOICE, 1978-79. Chmn. parent-tchr. bd. Ithaca Elementary Sch., 1971-72; trustee Ithaca Montessori Soc., 1970-75. Served with U.S. Army, 1950-52. Mem. Am. Assn. Higher Edn., Am. Coll. Personnel Assn., Am. Personnel and Guidance Assn., Nat. Assn. Student Personnel Adminstrs., Council Student Personnel Assns. in Higher Edn. (chmn. 1974-75), Phi Delta Kappa. Mem. United Ch. Christ. Club: Ithaca Yacht. Contbr. articles to profl. jours. Home: 214 Cascadilla Park Ithaca NY 14850 Office: 103 Barnes Hall Cornell U Ithaca NY 14853

MEYER, FRED CHARLES, cons. mech. and elec. engr.; b. Paterson, N.J., Sept. 21, 1907; s. Fred John and Madelena (Scheldorfer) M.; B.S. in Elec. Engring., Newark Coll. Engring., 1933; m. Regina Ruszkowski, Nov. 30, 1935; children—Regina (Mrs. P. Dituri), Fred Charles. Draftsman Okonite Co., Paterson, 1926-30, chief draftsman, devel. engr., 1932-39; design engr. Wright Aero Co., Paterson, 1939-45; devel. engr. U.S. Rubber Co., 1945-47; partner Grady & Meyer, cons. engrs., Teaneck, N.J., 1947-58; cons. engr. Meyer & Luongo Assos., Saddle Brook, N.J., 1958-75; cons. engr. as Fred C. Meyer Cons. Engr., 1975—. Tchr. Rutger U., Teaneck, 1942-46. Registered profl. engr., N.J. Mem. I.E.E.E., Am. Soc. Heating, Refrigeration and Air Conditioning Engrs., Nat. Soc. Profl. Engrs., Am. Cons. Engrs. Council, Cons. Engrs. Council N.J. (chmn. bldg. code com. 1969-70). Patentee in field. Home: 717 Birchwood Dr Wyckoff NJ 07481 Office: 717 Birchwood Dr Wyckoff NJ 07481

MEYER, GEORGE F., JR., ednl. adminstr.; b. New Brunswick, N.J., Jan. 24, 1938; d. George F. and Helen (Troger) M.; B.A. in Indsl. Edn., Trenton State Coll., 1962, M.A. in Indsl. Edn., 1969; now postgrad. in Adminstrn. Rutgers U.; m. Barbara F. Meyer; children—George F. III, Keith P., Kristen Ann. Adminstr. Monmouth County (N.J.) Vocat. Schs., Freehold, 1968-69; dir. vocat. edn. pub. schs., New Brunswick, 1969-71, dir. Gov. N.J. career devel. program, 1971-73, dir. career edn., 1973-78; asst. supt./dean Somerset County Vocat.-Tech. Schs., 1978—; chmn. Nat. Advisory Council Career Edn., 1976-77. Vice chmn. N.J. Youth Correction Complex, 1978-79. Mem. Nat. Adv. Council Career Edn.; trustee N.J. Youth Correction Complex. Mem. Am. Vocat. Assn., N.J. Indsl., Vocat. Assn., Nat., N.J. edn. assns., Phi Delta Kappa, Epsilon Pi Tau. Home: 245 Colfax Rd North Brunswick NJ 08902 Office: Somerset County Vocat-Tech Schs Bridgewater NJ 08807

MEYER, HAROLD ROBERT, packaged goods co. exec., bus. cons.; b. N.Y.C., Mar. 11, 1944; s. Herbert and Shirley (Robins) M.; B.B.A., 1968, M.B.A., 1970; postgrad. Baruch Grad. Sch. Bus., Columbia U., Germain Sch. Photography, Harvard U., Hunter Coll., Rochester Inst. Tech. Mktg. specialist Navy Resale System Office, N.Y.C., 1970-74; mgr. hobbies, crafts and games div. Mitsubishi Internat. Corp., N.Y.C., 1974-76; mktg. mgr. Wilkinson Sword, Inc., Berkley Heights, N.J., 1976-76, Hicks & Greist, Inc., N.Y.C., 1977—; cons. to numerous orgns. in pub. and pvt. sector. Mem. exec. com. Big Bros.; mem. Central Park Community Fund, Municipal Art Soc. N.Y., Mus. Modern Art. Mem. Am. Mktg. Assn., Am. Mgmt. Assn. Home: 215 W 75th St New York City NY 10023

MEYER, IRWIN STEPHEN, lawyer, accountant; b. Monticello, N.Y., Nov. 14, 1941; s. Ralph and Janice (Cohen) M.; B.S., Rider Coll., 1963; J.D., Cornell U., 1966; m. Leslie J. Mazor, July 10, 1977; 1 dau. by previous marriage, Kimberly B. Accounting tax mgr. Lybrand Ross Bros. & Montgomery, N.Y.C., 1967-71; admitted to N.Y. State bar, 1966; tax atty. Ehrenkranz, Ehrenkranz & Schultz, N.Y.C., 1971-74; prin. Irwin S. Meyer, Atty., C.P.A., N.Y.C., 1974-77, Levine Honig Eisenberg & Meyer, 1977—. Mem. Am., N.Y. State bar assns., Am. Inst. C.P.A.'s, N.J. Soc. C.P.A.'s, Am., N.Y. assns. Attys.-C.P.A.'s. Home: 370 E 76th St New York City NY 10021 Office: 125 Maiden Ln New York City NY 10038

MEYER, JOHN HENRY, educator; b. Kiel, Wis., Apr. 10, 1945; s. Walter Joseph and Lorretta (Wagner) M.; B.S. in Econs., St. Norbert Coll., 1967; M.S., U. Wis., 1978—; postgrad. Sch. Edn. Boston U. Vol., Peace Corps, Gambia, West Africa, 1967-69, pub. affairs ofcl., Rochester, N.Y., 1969-71; ednl. dir. Shirley Pre-release Center, Mass. Correctional System, 1972-74; asst. dir. human services program, instr. social edn. Boston U., 1977—, adminstr. community counseling program; cons. community-based social service and ednl. programs. Sec., S.W. Corridor Coalition, Boston. Mem. North Atlantic Regional Assn. Suprs. and Counselor Edn., Am. Personnel and Guidance Assn.

MEYER, KENNETH ARTHUR, ednl. counselor; b. N.Y.C., June 28, 1926; s. Jack and Regina (Mast) M.; B.S., N.Y. U., 1949, M.A., 1950, profl. diploma, 1956; m. Riva, June 16, 1957; children—Sari Allyn, Jonathan Allan. Tchr. pub. schs., Seabright, N.J., 1949, Westfield, N.J., 1953-55; counselor pub. schs., Middletown, N.Y., 1955-56; coordinator elementary guidance pub. schs., Hicksville, N.Y., 1956-59; guidance counselor S.H. Calhoun High Sch., Merrick, N.Y., 1959—. Pres. Hampshire Coop. Apts., Flushing, N.Y., 1963-64, Seaford (N.Y.) Republican Club, 1971-72; mem. Hempstead (N.Y.) Republican Com.; mem. Congressman Norman Lents Com. to Assist in Screening for Nominees to U.S. Naval Acad. and Kings Point. Served with USN, 1944-46, 51-53; PTO, Korea. Mem. Ret. Officers Assn., Naval Res. Assn., Naval Acad. Found., Nat. Vocat. Guidance Assn. (profl.), Am. Personnel and Guidance Assn., Internat. Reading Assn., Grand St. Boys Assn., Am. Sch. Counselors Assn., Am. Legion, Epsilon Pi Tau. Club: K.P. Home: 2411 Maple St Seaford NY 11783 Office: SH Calhoun High Sch State St Merrick NY 11566

MEYER, MARSHALL MORISS, investigation agy. exec.; b. Chgo., Dec. 24, 1919; s. Edward Alex and Fanny (Eisman) M.; student U. So. Calif., 1950-51, McCoy Coll., 1952-53, USAF Inst., 1948-49, Army Police Officers Sch., 1943, Army Counter-Intelligence Sch., 1949; m. Madeleine Roveda, Apr. 19, 1952; children—Michele, Michael. Commd. 2d lt. U.S. Army, 1941, advanced through grades to lt. col., 1960; maj. assignments include: chief spl. ops. counterintelligence, chief br. P.O.W. div. 1st U.S. Army Hdqrs.; ret., 1953; chief exec. officer Inter-State Bur. Investigation, Inc., Balt., 1953—, also dir.; v.p. Globe Security Group, Inc., Balt., Inter-State Security Equipment Co., Balt., Nat. Research Service, Balt., Chmn. Gov's Com. Jud. Selection, 1971-72; mem. Mayor's Task Force on Criminal Justice, 1966-67; chmn. Md. Criminal Injuries Bd., 1970-72; pres. Exchange Club Balt., 1968. Decorated Bronze Star medal, Purple Heart. Fellow Am. Acad. Registered Criminologists; mem. Soc. Profl. Investigators, Investigators and Security Assn. Md., Advt. Club Balt., Am. Soc. Indsl. Security (certified security specialist), Council Internat. Investigators, World Assn. Detectives. Democrat. Roman Catholic. Contbr. profl. jours. Home: 117 W Lake Ave Baltimore MD 21210 Office: PO Box 5646 725 Deepdene Rd Baltimore MD 21210

MEYER, RICHARD B., former investment co. exec.; b. Hoboken, N.J., Jan. 2, 1909; s. Richard and Adelaide (Glander) M.; student N.Y. U., 1933-36, 45-47; grad. N.Y. Stock Exchange Inst. Finance, 1941; m. Elizabeth Hedwig Toth, Dec. 11, 1954; 1 dau., Elaine Richelle. With Merrill Lynch, Pierce, Fenner & Smith, N.Y.C., 1935-74, mgr. accounting, 1942-48, mgr. planning and analysis, 1949-53, cashier mgr., 1954-55, asst. to chief exec., 1956-74, v.p., 1969-74; mem. N.Y. Stock Exchange Spl. Com. on Industry Capital. Mem. exec. bd. Boy Scouts Am., 1968-72, v.p., 1972; chmn. Hillsdale (N.J.) Zoning Bd., 1962; mem. Hillsdale Planning Bd., 1963-65; councilman Hillsdale, 1963-65, council pres., 1965; pres. Hillsdale Republican Club, 1962; trustee, pres., mem. exec. com. Pascack Valley Hosp. Home: 61 Twin Brooks Rd Saddle River NJ 07458

MEYERS, BARBARA EUNICE, sci. communications researcher; b. Passaic, N.J., July 28, 1953; d. Eugene Richard and Matilda Theresa (Mycek) M.; B.A. in Journalism, George Washington U., 1975, M.A. in Sci., Tech. and Pub. Policy, 1976. Mem. exec. bd. Forum for Advancement of Students in Sci. and Tech., Washington, 1974-75, dir. news service, asst. editor, 1974-75; writer Nat. Acad. Scis., Washington, 1976, cons., 1976; research asso. Capital Systems Group, Inc., Rockville, Md., 1976-78, project dir., 1977-78, asso. editor, 1977-78; info. research asso. research and devel. dept. Am. Chem. Soc., Washington, 1978—. Recipient Bausch & Lomb Hon. Sci. award, 1971. Mem. Soc. Scholarly Pub. (dir. 1978—), ASIS, Cousteau Soc., Early Am. Soc., AAAS, Sigma Delta Chi. Roman Catholic. Contbr. articles on sci. communication to various publs. Home: 4977 Battery Ln Bethesda MD 20014 Office: 1155 16th St NW Washington DC 20036

MEYERS, ERNEST STANLEY, lawyer; b. N.Y.C., Apr. 19, 1910; s. Arthur Jay and Miriam (Schweriner) M.; A.B., U. Pa., 1931; LL.B., Yale U., 1934; m. Shirley Rosalind Scheuer, Aug. 26, 1938; children—Nancy Irene, Eric Barton. Admitted to N.Y. bar, 1934, since practiced in N.Y.C.,; admitted to D.C. bar, 1947, U.S. Supreme Ct. bar, 1945; with firm Hartman & Craven, 1934-35; atty. SEC, 1935-36, FCC, 1936-37, N.Y. State Constn. Conv. Com., 1937, Fed. Power Commn., 1938; spl. asst. U.S. atty. gen., chief consent decree sect., anti-trust div. Dept. Justice, 1938-46; sr. partner Meyers, Tersigni Kaufman Debrot Feldman & Gray, and predecessor firm, 1946—; adviser, U.S. State Dept. del. Rome Conf., 1961, Intellectual Property Conf., Stockholm, 1967, Geneva, 1971, internat. copyright panel, 1969—; cons. Librarian of Congress on Gen. Revision Copyright Law, 1956-77; lectr. Practicing Law Inst., also bus. seminars; exec. dir. Am. Dye Mfrs. Inst.; sec. Woolens and Worsteds Am. Trustee Roger Williams Coll., 1973-76, Copyright Soc. U.S., 1973-76. Mem. Fed., Am. (mem. antitrust, trade assn. coms., chmn. copyright div. sect. patent, trademark and copyright law), N.Y. State bar assns., Lawyers Club N.Y.C., Assn. Bar City N.Y. (copyright com.), Am. Soc. Assn. Execs., Am. Judicature Soc., Tau Epsilon Phi. Club: Beach Point (pres. 1965-68 Mamaroneck, N.Y.). Asso. editor Antitrust Bull., 1956-66. Contbr. articles to profl. jours. Home: 40 Birchall Dr Scarsdale NY 10583 Office: 630 3d Ave New York City NY 10017

MEYERS, JOHN FRANCIS, assn. exec.; b. Altoona, Pa., July 26, 1930; s. George and Magdalene (Keller) M.; A.B., Pontifical Coll. Josephinum, Columbus, Ohio, 1952, M.Div., 1975, D.Litt. (hon.), 1976; M.A., Catholic U. Am., 1959; postgrad. N.Y. U., 1961-62; Ed.D., N.Tex. State U., Denton, 1964. Ordained priest Roman Catholic Ch., 1956; asst. pastor Holy Name Parish, Ft. Worth, 1956-58; dean students, lectr. U. Dallas, 1959-61; asst. supt. schs. Diocese of Dallas, 1960-61, supt., 1961-67, diocesan Newman dir., 1964-67; pastor Immaculate Conception Parish, Tyler, Tex., 1967-68; exec. sec. dept. chief adminstrs. Cath. edn. Nat. Cath. Ednl. Assn., Washington, 1968-74, v.p. div. fundamental edn., 1970-74, acting pres., 1972-74, pres., 1974—; mem. assembly of pres.'s Interam. Confedn. for Cath. Edn., Panama, 1973, Brazil, 1974, Venezuela, 1975, Peru, 1976, Costa Rica, 1977, bd. dirs., 1977—; mem. com. on edn. U.S. Cath. Conf., 1974; mem. Diocesan Sem. and Vocations Bd., 1962-66, Diocesan Bldg. Commn., 1962-67, Diocesan Bd. Consultors, 1966-68; mem. nat. adv. com. for ednl. labs. and research and devel. centers U.S. Office Edn., 1966-68; sec. Diocesan Priests Senate, 1967-68, pres., 1968; mem. Cath. Internat. Edn. Congress, Zaire, 1971, Philippines, 1976, Colombia, 1978. Bd. dirs. Council for Am. Pvt. Edn., Inc., 1974, Clergy Relief Assn., 1962-67; trustee Joint Council on Econ. Edn., 1974, Pontifical Coll. Josephinum, 1973—; bd. advisers Presdl. Classroom for Young Ams., 1974; mem. adv. bd. St. Paul Sch. Nursing, 1965-67. Served to lt. USNR, 1963-69. Mem. Am. Assn. Sch. Adminstrs., Religious Edn. Assn., Internat. Cath. Ednl. Assn. (dir. 1978—), Phi Delta Kappa. Author: (with Thomas Sullivan) Focus on American Catechetics: A Commentary on the General Catechetical Directory, 1972; co-editor: Boards of Education: A Primer, 1972; exec. editor Criteria for the Evaluation of Religious Education Programs, 1970, A Curriculum Guide for Continuous Progress in Religious Education, 1973, The Qualities and Competencies of the Religion Teacher, 1973; contbr. sects. to Cath. Ency. for School and Home, 1975, The New Catholic Ency., 1978, also articles to profl. publs. Address: Nat Catholic Edn Assn 1 Dupont Circle Suite 350 Washington DC 20036

MEYERS, MARTIN DANIEL, advt. exec.; b. Phila., Sept. 21, 1904; s. Harry M. and Amelia (Kahrweiler) M.; B.S. in Econs., U. Pa., 1926; grad. Advt. Splty., Nat. Assn. Mgmt. Tng. Seminar, Western Res. U., 1961; m. Dorothy A.D. French, Mar. 17, 1947; step-children—Mary E. French Hall, Forrest J. French. Asst. prom. mgr. John Clark Sims Co., advt., Phila., 1926-28; dist. mgr. Whitehead & Hoag Co., advt., Phila., 1928-32; propr. Martin Meyers Co., splty. advt., Phila., 1932-41, partner, 1946-62, exec. v.p., 1962-73, sr. v.p., 1974-76, adv. cons., 1976—. Mem. Delaware Valley com. Freedoms Found. Valley Forge, 1961—, Com. of One Thousand, 1971; mem. nat. bd. Am. Security Council, 1971—; bd. mgrs. Armed Service br. YMCA, 1971—, chmn. bd., 1975-77; bd. dirs. USO, Phila., 1975—. Served from capt. to col. AUS, 1941-46; col. AUS ret. Decorated Bronze Star; named Hon. Ky. col., 1964; Hon. citizen New Orleans, 1963, named to Legion of Honor, Chapel of 4 Chaplains, Phila., 1977. Mem. Advt. Splty. Nat. Assn. (v.p. 1961-62, pres. 1962-63), Exclusive Advt. Assos. (pres. 1958), Mil. Order World Wars (comdr. 1965-66 Pa. comdr. 1970, Nat. Comdr-in-Chief citation 1969), Ret. Officers Assn. U.S. (pres. Phila. chpt. 1972-73), LeCoin d'Or (sec. 1960-63), Germantown Hist. Soc., Pa. Hist. Soc. Phila., Phila. Mus. Art, Res. Officers Assn. (pres. Phila. chpt. 1957-58), Navy League U.S., U. Pa. Museum, Pa. Soc. (N.Y.C.), Am. Legion, Mil. Order Fgn. Wars, Nat. Sojourners (pres. 1975-76), Sovereign Mil. Order Temple Jerusalem. Clubs: Bachelors Barge, Germantown Cricket, Poor Richard, Union League, Brit. Officers', Masons. Home: 3422 Warden Dr Philadelphia PA 19129 Office: PO Box 5645 Philadelphia PA 19129

MEYERS, ROBERT TOWNSEND, JR., author; b. N.Y.C., Sept. 3, 1943; s. Robert Towsend and Roslyn (Willinger) M.; B.A., U. Calif. at Los Angeles, 1965; m. Tanna Kaljakin, Apr. 18, 1970 (div. Aug. 1976). Free-lance writer, 1970-76; asst. press. sec. U.S. Senator Alan Cranston of Calif., 1972; writing cons. Andrus Gerontology Center, U. So. Calif., 1974; reporter Washington Post, 1976—. Mem. Author's Guild, Soc. Mag. Writers, Shakespearean Authorship Soc., Shakespeare-Oxford Soc. Author: Like Normal People, 1978. Contbr. Washington Post, Newsweek, Sat. Rev., Rolling Stone, TV Guide, others. Address: 1150 15th St NW Washington DC 20071

MEYERSON, MARTIN, univ. pres.; b. N.Y.C., Nov. 14, 1922; s. S. Z. and Etta (Berger) M.; A.B., Columbia, 1942; M.C.P. (Wheelwright fellow), Harvard U., 1949; m. Margy Ellin Lazarus, Dec. 31, 1945; children—Adam, Laura, Matthew. Mem. staff Am. Soc. of Planning Ofcls., 1943-44; staff Phila. City Planning Commn., 1944-45, Michael Reese Hosp., Chgo., 1945-47; asst. prof. planning program Coll. Soc. Scis., U. Chgo., 1948-52; asso. com. on nat. policy Yale, 1948; asso. prof. city and regional planning, asso. research prof. urban studies U. Pa., 1952-56, prof., 1956-57, pres., 1970—; exec. dir., research dir. Am. Council to Improve Our Neighborhoods, 1955-56, v.p., 1956-60, vice chmn. bd., 1961—; Williams prof. city planning and urban research Harvard, 1957-63, acting dean Grad. Sch. Design, 1963; dir. Joint Center for Urban Studies, Mass. Inst. Tech. and Harvard U., 1959-63; became dean, prof. urban devel. Coll. Environmental Design, U. Calif. at Berkeley, 1963, acting chancellor, 1965; pres. State U. N.Y. at Buffalo, 1966-70. Cons. to govts., pvt. firms of U.S. and abroad, UN missions to Japan, Indonesia, Yugoslavia, 1958—; adviser Arthur D. Little, Inc., 1958—, Sears, Roebuck Found., 1958—, adv. com. U.S. Census, 1958-61, housing panel White House Office Sci. and Tech., 1962-63, area devel. com. Com. for Econ. Devel., 1962—; mem. U.S. delegation UN Conf. on Sci. and Tech. for Less Developed Areas, 1963. Vis. com. Washington U., 1962—; mem. Air Conservation Commn., 1962—. Fellow AAAS; mem. Am. Acad. Arts and Scis., Am. Soc. Planning Ofcls. (dir.), Am. Inst. Planners (past gov.), Am. Soc. Archtl. Historians, Am. Soc. Pub. Adminstrn., Japan Soc. Urban Relations (hon.). Club: Cosmos (Washington). Author: (with E. C. Banfield) Politics, Planning and the Public Interest, 1955; Housing, People and Cities, 1962; Face of the Metropolis, 1963. Address: Office of Pres Univ of Pa Philadelphia PA 19104

MEYLER, WILLIAM ANTHONY, chem. co. exec.; b. Newark, Oct. 29, 1944; s. Raymond Francis and Margaret (Loveless) M.; B.S., St. Joseph's Coll., 1966; M.B.A., Fairleigh Dickinson U., 1974; m. Dana Irene Brennan, May 3, 1975. Sr. accountant Ernst & Ernst, Trenton, N.J., 1970; dir. accounting Baker Industries, Inc., Parsippany, N.J., 1971-72; mgr. corp. accounting Witco Chem. Corp., N.Y.C., 1973-75, asst. to controller, 1976, asst. controller, 1977—; asst. adj. instr. Rutgers U., fall 1975. C.P.A., N.J. Fellow N.J. Soc. C.P.A.'s; mem. Am. Inst. C.P.A.'s, Am. Accounting Assn. Home: 30 Southview Terr S Middletown NJ 07748 Office: 277 Park Ave New York City NY 10017

MEYNER, HELEN STEVENSON, former congresswoman; b. N.Y.C., Mar. 5, 1929; d. William Edward and Eleanor (Bumstead) Stevenson; B.A. in History, Colo. Coll., 1950, LL.D., 1973; m. Robert B. Meyner, Jan. 19, 1957. With ARC, Korea, 1950's; later with UN, N.Y.C.; then consumer adviser TWA; staff Adlai E. Stevenson; columnist Newark Star Ledger, 1962-69; hostess TV interview program, 1965-68; mem. 94th-95th Congresses from 13th N.J. Dist. Opened N.J. gov.'s mansion Morven to pub.; mem. N.J. Rehab. Commn., 1961—. Bd. dirs. Newark Mus., N.J. Symphony Orch.; trustee Rider Coll. Mem. N.J. Democratic Policy Council; congl. candidate from 13th N.J. dist., 1972. Mem. UN Assn. (dir. N.J. chpt.), Phi Beta Kappa. Home: 372 Lincoln St Phillipsburg NJ 08865

MEZER, ROBERT ROSS, physician; b. Boston, Feb. 2, 1923; s. Joseph Henry and Evelyn (Cabitt) M.; A.B., Harvard U., 1942; M.D., Tufts U., 1945; m. Lois Sternlieb, Apr. 10, 1949; 1 son, Harry Cabitt. Intern, Boston City Hosp., 1945-46; psychiat. resident Bedford and Cushing VA hosps., 1946-48, Boston Psychopathic Hosp., 1948-49; practice medicine specializing in psychiatry, Boston, 1949—; sr. staff psychiatrist Southard and Community Clinics, Mass. Mental Health Center; instr. Harvard Med. Sch., 1949-59, Mass. Gen. Hosp. Sch. Nursing, 1951-59; clin. dir. Parole Clinic, 1956-59; asst. prof. Boston U. Schs. Medicine and Law, 1959-60. Mem. Nat. Council on Crime and Delinquency, 1959-60. Served to capt., M.C., AUS, 1946-48. Diplomate Am. Bd. Psychiatry and Neurology. Fellow Am. Psychiat. Assn. (com. law and psychiatry 1960—), Mass. Med. Soc. (councillor

1960—); mem. AMA, Greater Boston (exec. bd. 1967-68), Norfolk Dist. (chmn. com. on mental health 1960—, pres. 1977-78) med. socs., Phi Delta Epsilon. Author: Dynamic Psychiatry in Simple Terms, 4th edit., 1970; Elements of Psychiatry for Nurses, 1965. Home: 205 Tappan St Brookline MA 02146 Office: 160 Commonwealth Ave Boston MA 02116

MEZROW, RALPH RAYMOND, dentist; b. Phila., June 25, 1920; s. Samuel and Ruth (Fineberg) Goldstein; D.D.S., Temple U., 1943; postgrad. Columbia U., 1947; m. Lora Kamens, July 24, 1958; children—Gail, Steven, Craig. Practice dentistry specializing in oral reconstrn., Merion, Pa., 1946—; attending oral surgeon Albert Einstein Med. Center, Phila., 1970—, chief dental transplant and implantology, 1972—; lectr. oral pathology Temple U. Sch. Dentistry, 1960—. Served with AUS, 1943-45. NIH grantee. Diplomate N.Y. Bd. Oral Surgery. Fellow Am. Acad. Implant Dentistry; mem. N.Y. Acad. Scis., Phila. Soc. Periodontology, Phila. Soc. Clin. Oral Pathology (sec. 1962-64), Internat. Assn. Dental Research, Am. Acad. Oral Pathology, AAAS, ADA, Internat. Anesthesiology Research Soc. Contbr. numerous articles to dental sci. jours. including Jour. Oral Surgery and Oral Medicine, Oral Pathology, Jour. Dental Research. Research in dental transplantation field. Home: 1220 Rock Creek Rd Gladwyne PA 19035 Office: 6 Old Lancaster Ave Merion PA 19066

MICHAEL, PHYLLIS CALLENDER (MRS. ARTHUR L. MICHAEL), hymnwriter; b. nr. Berwick, Pa., Dec. 24, 1908; d. Bruce Miles and Emma (Harvey) Callender; grad. Bloomsburg Coll., 1928; B.Mus., U. Extension Conservatory, Chgo., 1953; m. Arthur L. Michael, Aug. 21, 1933; children—Robert Bruce, Keith Winton. Elementary tchr. Berwick Schs., 1928-33; substitute tchr. Shickshinny and Northwest Area, Pa., 1954-66; tchr. Northwest Area High Sch., 1966-71; gen. tchr. piano, organ, theory and voice, 1943—; hymnwriter, poet, author, composer, 1943—. Recipient first place in Nat. Favorite Hymns contest for Take Thou My Hand, 1953, and others. Mem. Internat. Platform Assn., Hymn Soc. Am. Author: Poems for Mothers, 1963; Poems From My Heart, 1964; Beside Still Waters, 1968; Fun To Do Showers, 1970; Bridal Shower Ideas, 1972; Is My Head On Straight, 1976; contbr. songs, articles, poems to hymnbooks, booklets, mags. Address: Oak Haven RFD 3 Shickshinny PA 18655

MICHAEL, STANLEY THEODORE, educator, physician; b. Pitts., Jan. 20, 1912; s. Anthony and Albina (Dubsky) M.; M.D., U. Prague, 1937; m. Cornelia Wathen, June 10, 1972; children—Faidon, Robert, Eloise, Andrea. Research fellow Mass. Gen. Hosp., Boston, 1940-41; asst. pathologist Worcester (Mass.) State Hosp., 1941-43; fellow Inst. Living, Hartford, Conn., 1944-45; resident Butler Hosp., Providence, 1945-46; instr. Yale Med. Sch., 1946-48; asso. psychiatrist N.Y. Psychiat. Inst., N.Y.C., 1949-53; prof. psychiatry Cornell U. Med. Coll., N.Y.C., 1954-77; research asso. prof. psychiatry N.Y. Med. Coll., Valhalla, 1978—; practice medicine specializing in psychiatry. Diplomate Am. Bd. Psychiatry and Neurology, Nat. Bd. Med. Examiners. Fellow Am. Psychiat. Assn.; mem. AMA, Assn. Research in Nervous and Mental Diseases, Soc. Biol. Psychiatry, World Fedn. Mental Health. Author: (with others) Cornell Midtown Manhattan Study, 2 vols., 1962, 63. Contbr. articles to profl. jours. Home: 100 Pines Bridge Rd Ossining NY 10562

MICHAELIS, PAUL CHARLES, engring. physicist; b. Bronx, N.Y., June 18, 1935; s. Paul Frederick and Rose (landsbury) M.; B.S.E.E., Newark Coll. Engring., 1964, M.S. in Physics, 1967; m. Geraldine Ann DeCuollo, June 29, 1958; 1 son, Paul Charles, Draftsman, Bell Telephone Labs., Murray Hill, N.J., 1953-59, technician, 1959-63, asso. mem. tech. staff, 1963-67, mem. tech. staff, 1967—; lectr. USSR Acad. Scis., 1972. Mem. IEEE (Morris N. Liebmann award 1975), Am. Inst. Physics, AAAS, U.S. Naval Inst. Club: Lions (Watchung, N.J.) (pres. 1976). Contbr. articles to profl. jours.; patentee single wall domain memory tech., electronics, magnetics and mechanics. Home: 103 High Tor Dr Watchung NJ 07060 Office: Bell Labs 600 Mountain Ave Murray Hill NJ 07974

MICHAELS, ABRAHAM, cons. san. engr.; b. Bklyn., Nov. 6, 1919; s. Jack and Fanny (Kramer) M.; student evenings Coll. City N.Y., 1935-38; B.M.E., N.C. State Coll., 1942; postgrad. pub. adminstrn. U. Pa., 1954-56; m. Enid Hope Olenick, Jan. 1, 1944; children—Jill Michaels Shusterman, Eric Philip, Mark David. Structural engr. Chance Vought Aircraft, Stratford, Conn., 1942-47, The Tex. Co., N.Y.C., 1947-48, Skidmore, Owings, Merrill, N.Y.C., 1948-49; asst. city engr. Long Beach, N.Y., 1949-53; village engr., Dobbs Ferry, N.Y., 1953-54; refuse disposal engr., dep. street commr. City Phila., 1954-66; cons. san. engr., Phila., 1966-77; supt. pub. works Town of Barnstable (Mass.), 1977—; cons. WHO, EPA, HEW, Interior Dept.; adj. prof. Drexel U., Phila., 1966-68; guide prof. World Open U. Mem. Winchester Park Civic Assn., 1960-64, Soc. Hill Civic Assn., 1972—; pres. troop com. Boy Scouts Am., 1958-60. Bd. dirs. br. com. Neighborhood Center, N.E. Phila., 1960-63. Recipient Charles Walter Nichols award, 1961. Diplomate Am. Acad. Environ. Engrs. Mem. Inst. Solid Waste (pres. 1966-67), Am. Pub. Works Assn., ASME, Phila. Engrs. Club, Nat. Conf. on Air Pollution (chmn. solid waste panel, 1965), Air Pollution Control Assn. Editor Solid Waste Forum in Public Works. Inventor manually operated sweeper. Home: 45 Marston Ave Hyannisport MA 02647 Office: Dept Public Works Town of Barnstable Hyannis MA 02601

MICHAELS, GEORGE, lawyer; b. Boston, Sept. 16, 1923; s. Arthur and Ida (Levitt) M.; LL.B., J.J.D., Boston U., 1948; postgrad. Yale U., 1949; m. Barbara Gould Etelman, Jan. 26, 1951; children—Julia Susan, Faith India. Admitted to Mass. bar, 1949, to bars U.S. Supreme Ct., U.S. Dist. Ct.; practiced in Boston, 1949—; mem. firm George Michaels, P.C., 1961—; asst. atty. gen., Mass., 1953-58; officer ABT Assos., Inc., Nibur Realty Trust; dir. N.Am. Plastics Corp., Lion Precision Corp., Maric, Inc., Eldacare, Inc. Officer Council for Applied Social Research; mem. Gov.'s Com. to Study Pre-trial Publicity; Republican candidate for atty. gen. Mass., 1960; mem. Newton Rep. City Com.; pres. Friends Newton Free Library, regional bd. Anti-Defamation League. Served with inf. AUS, 1943-45. Mem. Fed., Am., Boston bar assns., Am., Mass. trial lawyers assns., Am. Judicature Soc., Boston U. Sch. Law Alumni Assn. (exec. com.), Tau Epsilon Rho, Tau Epsilon Phi. Home: 195 Islington Rd Newton MA 02166 Office: 25 New Charnon St Boston MA 02114

MICHAELS, LINDA ANN, savs. and loan exec.; b. Pitts., Aug. 20, 1945; d. Stanley John and Anne Dolores (Fleisher) Michaels; B.A., Duquesne U., 1967; certificate in pub. relations Allegheny Community Coll., 1970; M.Pub. Adminstrn., U. Pitts., 1973; certificate in mgmt. devel. Pa. State U., 1973-76; certificate in mgmt. for women Chatham Coll., 1975; certificate in mktg. U. Wis., 1977. Editor-in-chief Signal-Item, newspaper, Carnegie, Pa., 1967-68; exec. sec., community orgn. specialist for Fed. Code Enforcement Program, Borough of Carnegie, 1968-72; dir. pub. relations Century Fed. Savs. & Loan Assn., Pitts., 1972-75, dir. mktg., 1975—. Com. chmn. United Fund, Pitts., 1972; mem. exec. bd. Carnegie Community Action Com., 1971-72; bd. dirs. Holy Family Inst., 1978; directing mem. Boys Clubs Am., 1968-69. Recipient forensic degree excellence, 1963; certificate of merit in journalism, 1964; certificate of commendation for community service Boys Clubs Am., 1967; citation for contbns. in journalism to Heart Fund, 1967; Journalism award Pa., 1968; Carnegie Day plaque for community service, 1968; commendation for excellence in journalism U.S. Army, 1968; commendation for creative reporting U.S. Sec. Dept. Forest and Waters, 1969. Mem. Exec. Women's Council Greater Pitts., Savs. Instns. Mktg. Soc. Am., Women in Communications. Home: Essex House Apt 1610 Essex Sq Pittsburgh PA 15206 Office: 5912 Penn Mall Pittsburgh PA 15206

MICHAELS, PETER EDWARDS, fine arts conservator; b. Kansas City, Mo., May 3, 1929; s. Eldon Wilson and Gertrude Martha (Edwards) M.; A.B. (teaching fellow), Oberlin Coll., 1952; M.A. (teaching fellow), U. Mich., 1958; postgrad. U. Freiburg (Germany), 1954-56, 58-59; m. Barbara Lawyer, May 16, 1962 (div. Mar. 1972); children—Karen, Janet, Susan. Conservator, Walters Art Gallery, Balt., 1959-74; pres. Twelve Oaks Regional Fine Arts Conservation Center, Balt., 1971—; cons. conservator U.S. Capitol, Washington, 1972—, also Md. Hist. Soc., Balt., Cummer Gallery, Jacksonville, Fla., Ringling Mus. Art, Sarasota, Fla., Meml. Art Mus., Rochester, N.Y.; adj. prof. Goucher Coll., Towson, Md., 1973—. Served with AUS, 1952-54. Hon. fellow Friends of Art, Milan, Italy. Fellow Internat. Inst. for Conservation (London), Am. Inst. Conservation (chmn. com. on profl. relations, 1973-77), AAUP, Am. Soc. Appraisers (sr.), Washington Conservation Guild. Club: Balt. Choral Arts Soc.; Nat. Arts (N.Y.C.). Address: 1922 South Rd Baltimore MD 21209

MICHAELSON, JULIUS COOLEY, former state ofcl.; b. Salem, Mass., Jan. 26, 1922; s. Carl and Celia (Cooley) M.; LL.B., Boston U., 1948; M.A., Brown U., 1967; m. Rita Caslowitz, Nov. 20, 1950; children—Mark C., Jeffrey S. Admitted to R.I. bar, 1948; partner firm Abedon, Michaelson, Stanzler & Biener, Providence, 1968-75; mem. R.I. Senate from 3d Dist., 1963-74, dep. majority leader, 1971-72, chmn. judiciary com., 1973; atty. gen. R.I., 1975—; past mem. R.I. Bd. Bar Examiners. Served to 1st lt. U.S. Army, World War II. Recipient Charles Carroll Citizenship award R.I. Edn. Assn., 1969; Liberty Under Law award Eagles Club, 1976. Mem. Am., R.I. (past pres.) bar assns. Democrat. Jewish. Home: 78 Lorraine Ave Providence RI 02906 Office: Providence County Courthouse Providence RI 02903

MICHANOWSKY, GEORGE, research found. exec., author; b. Yalta, Russia, Mar. 9, 1920 (Am. citizen); s. Ilya and Eleonora M.; student Mont. Coll., Rome U. Founder, pres. Amazonia Found., N.Y.C., 1952. Originator prep. research, leader Amazonia Found. expdns. to unexplored Andes and Upper Amazon areas, resulting in mapping of legendary River of Writing and prehistoric roads; discoverer of new data on ancient scripts; organizer dir. 1st aerophotog. reconnaissance of pre-historic Tihuanacu ruins; originator ultraviolet reconnaissance technique for clear air turbulence detection approved for investigation by U.S. Navy Dept. and Air Transport Assn. Am. Dir. spl. ultraviolet flight safety project, Kennedy Internat. Airport, N.Y.; dir. ultraviolet study of jet engine pollutants, FAA, cons. Aviation Rev. Conf. Dir. spl. ultraviolet research project on wake turbulence, U.S. Nat. Aviation Facilities Exptl. Center. Decorated Comdr. Order of Condor of the Andes (Bolivia); recipient spl. citation inter-Am. Hist. Municipal Congress, spl. avalanche research citation Peru, citation from Bolivian Govt. and Parliament in fields of photogrammetry, flight safety, cultural activities and historical research; 100th Anniversary citation for contbn. to ency. Funk & Wagnalls. Hon. mem. Archeol. Soc. Bolivia; mem. U.S. Naval Inst., Saint-Georges de Bourgogne, Am. Inst. Aeros. & Astronautics. Club: Explorers (mem. sci. adv. bd.). Author: (book) The Once and Future Star, 1977. Author articles on archeology of Western Hemisphere countries in Funk & Wagnalls New Ency.; author Special Ultraviolet Effect as Clear Air Turbulence Detector, The Potential of Ultraviolet Reconnaissance as a Remote Detector of Invisible Nitric Oxide; Ultraviolet Reconnaissance as a Remote Detector and Tracker of Wake Turbulence; Cuneiform Clues to an Ancient Starburst, 1975; Ankh Symbol of Ancient Egypt linked to Supernova, 1978; contbr. article The Remote Detection of Air Pollutants to Ency. of Environmental Sci. and Engring. Initiator concept infrared and ultraviolet aerophotography for archeol. purposes and gen. Andean studies. Discoverer of references to Vela X supernova explosion in Sumero-Akkadian cuneiform texts. Address: Box 651 New York City NY 10023

MICHAUD, ALPHEE MARTIAL, bus. exec.; b. St. Quentin, N.B., Can., Nov. 13, 1938; s. Napoleon and Alpheda (Deschenes) M.; M.D., Laval U., 1965; postgrad. in econs. McGill U., 1973; m. Claudette Gingras, July 4, 1964; children—Marie, Claude, Harold, Isabelle. Intern, Hotel-Dieu and Hosp. St. Sacrement, Quebec City, Que., 1964-66; resident in internal medicine Hosp. St. Sacrement, Quebec City, 1966-67; gen. practice medicine, Caraquet, N.B., 1968-71; pres., owner Les Pharmacies Populaires Ltd., Caraquet, 1971—; pres. Les Entreprises Ami Ltd., Caraquet, 1972—; pres. Radio-Acadie Ltd., Caraquet, 1976-77, sec., 1977—; med. editor weekly newspaper Le Voilier, 1972-76, pub., 1977—; pub. Le Point, 1977—, Laviron, 1978—; dir. N.B. Devel. Corp. Bd. dirs. Tracadie Assn. Mental Disease, 1973-77, N.B. Indsl. Devel. Bd., 1976—; pres. Le Festival Acadien Caraquet, 1974-76. Mem. Can., N.B. med. assns., Assn. Med. De Langue Francaise, Caraquet Bd. of Trade, Atlantic C. of C. (v.p. 1978—). Roman Catholic. Home: 316 A Boulevard St Pierre Ouest Caraquet NB E0B 1K0 Canada Office: Place Caraquet Caraquet NB E0B 1K0 Canada

MICHAUD, PATRICK ARNOLD, safety engr.; b. Madawaska, Maine, Feb. 26, 1931; s. Wilfred Magloire and Mary Ann (Cyr) M.; A.S. in Constrn. Tech., 1957; B.S. in Indsl. Tech., U. Maine, 1976; certificate in occupational safety and health tng. Ind. U., 1976; cert. in loss control Internat. Loss Control Inst., 1978; cert. in indsl. hygiene Nat. Loss Control Inst., 1978; children—Michael, Patrice, Martin. Materials mgr. Walsh Constrn. Co., Portland, Maine, 1954-55; constrn. supr. W.H. Hinman Co., Portsmouth, Maine, 1957-58; prodn. mgmt. positions Portsmouth Naval Shipyard, 1958—, dir. indsl. safety, 1975—; safety instr. U. So. Maine, 1978, U.S. Navy, Boy Scouts Am. Chmn. disaster control York County (Maine); dist. chmn. Sanford (Maine) Town Meeting, 1961-74. Served with USN, 1950-54; Korea. Recipient Superior Accomplishment award Navy Dept., 1964, 65, 76. Certified sr. engring. technician, Nat. Soc. Profl. Engrs.; certified safety engr., Calif. Mem. Naval Civilian Adminstrs. Assn., Maine Fed. Safety Council (chmn.), Nat. Safety Council, Maine Safety Council, VFW. Roman Catholic. Club: Fred Bear Sports. Home: Box 148 Sanford ME 04073 Office: Portsmouth Naval Shipyard Portsmouth ME 03801

MICHAUD, ROBERT JEAN, cardiologist; b. St. Hyacinthe, Que., Can., July 23, 1927; s. Jean Baptiste and Robertha (Robert) M.; B.A., St. Hyacinthe Coll., 1948; M.D., Laval U., 1954; m. Louise Beaudet, June 26, 1954; children—Nicole, Claude, Evelyne. Intern, Hôpital St.-Luc, Montreal, Que., 1953-54; resident in internal medicine St. Alexis Hosp., Cleve., 1954-55, Cleve. Clinic., 1955-57; practice medicine specializing in internal medicine and cardiology, St. Hyacinthe, 1958-65, in cardiology, Montreal, 1965—. Fellow Royal Coll. Physicians Surgeons Can., Am. Coll. Chest Physicians; mem. A.C.P. (asso.). Roman Catholic. Home: 616 Powell St Mount Royal PQ Canada Office: 2459 E Fleury St Montreal PQ Canada

MICHEL, HENRY LUDWIG, cons. engring. firm exec.; b. Frankfurt, Germany, June 18, 1924; s. Max and Charlotte (Hepner) M.; student Queens Coll., 1941-43; B.C.E., Columbia U., 1949; m. Mary Elizabeth Strolis, June 5, 1954; children—Eve Musette, Ann Elizabeth. Design engr. powerplants United Engrs., Phila., 1949-53; resident engr. oil refineries M.W. Kellogg Co., Ohio and Can., 1953-54; project mgr. aviation facilities DMJM, Grad, Seelye Co., Eng., 1954-60; pres. Engring. Co. Internat. and Enconi Spa, Italy, Africa, Mid-East, 1960-65; pres., chief exec. Parsons, Brinckerhoff, Quade & Douglas Inc., N.Y.C., 1965—, also dir. subs. corp.; dir. Internat. Road Fedn., Agribus. Council, Inc.; vis. prof. grad. sch. mgmt. Colo. State U. Served with U.S. Army, 1943-46. Mem. Soc. Am. Mil. Engrs. (dir.), ASCE, Am. Inst. Mgmt., Am. Water Works Assn., Am. Cons. Engrs. Council, Am. Soc. Profl. Engrs., Newcomen Soc., Columbia Alumni Soc., Sierra Club. Clubs: Empire State, Drug and Chem., Mid-Town Tennis. Contbr. numerous articles in field to tech. publs. Home: 45 East End Ave New York City NY 10028 Office: 1 Penn Plaza New York City NY 10001

MICHEL, ROBERT EMORY, wholesale co. exec.; b. Balt., Dec. 19, 1911; s. Ambrose Emory and Mary Elizabeth (Wood) M.; LL.D., U. Balt., 1935; m. Mary Ellen Michel, Dec. 29, 1934; children—Suzanne Michel Twells, Robert E., Greer Michel Haines, John W. H. Admitted to Md. bar, 1936; pres. R.E. Michel Co., Inc., Balt., 1950—, also dir.; dir. Michel Real Estate Corp. Bd. govs. Balt. Symphony Orch.; bd. dirs., pres. Star Spangled Banner Flag House Assn.; bd. dirs. U.S. Frigate Constellation Found.; mem. maritime com. Md. Hist. Soc., Balt. Mem. Balt. C. of C. Republican. Episcopalian. Clubs: Balt. Country, Md., Gibson Island. Home: 4327 Wickford Rd Baltimore MD 21210 Office: 2801 W Patapsco Ave Baltimore MD 21230

MICHELE, MARY ELLEN, communications co. exec.; b. N.Y.C., Mar. 29, 1945; d. Arthur Albert and Rose (LaCerva) M.; B.A., Bethany Coll., 1967; M.A., San Jose (Calif.) State U., 1969. Instr., Santa Clara (Calif.) Sch. Dist., 1967-69; sales agt. Pan Am. Airways, N.Y.C., and Atlanta, 1969-73, sr. systems analyst, N.Y.C., 1973-75; with AT&T, 1975—, mktg. industry analyst transp., Morristown, N.J., 1975-78, mktg. communications, 1978—. Mem. Am. Mgmt. Assn., Am. Trucking Assn., Phi Mu. Club: Indian Lake Community. Office: 1776 On the Green Morristown NJ 07960

MICHELI, LYLE JOSEPH, orthopaedic surgeon; b. LaSalle, Ill., Aug. 19, 1940; s. Prodie Joseph and Margaret Frances (Garcia) M.; A.B. cum laude, Harvard Coll., 1962; M.D., Harvard U., 1966; m. Linda Ross McJennett, June 16, 1964; children—Elizabeth Ross, Amanda Ross. Intern, U. Hosp., Cleve., 1966-68; resident Mass. Gen. Hosp., Boston, 1968-72; asst. clin. prof. George Washington U., Washington, 1972-74; asso. in orthopaedic surgery Children's Hosp. Med. Center, Boston, 1974—, dir. div. sports medicine, 1975—; instr. orthopaedic surgery Med. Sch., Harvard U. Served as maj. M.C., USAF, 1972-74. Mem. Am. Acad. Orthopaedic Surgeons, Am. Acad. Pediatrics, Am. Coll. Sports Medicine, Herodicus Soc. Contbr. articles to profl. publs. Office: 300 Longwood Ave Boston MA 02115

MICHELIS, MICHAEL FRANK, physician; b. Bklyn., Dec. 11, 1938; s. Michael and Gisella (Gammer) M.; B.A., Columbia U., 1959; M.D., George Washington U., 1963; m. Mary Ann Wolak, July 28, 1973. Intern, resident Lenox Hill Hosp., N.Y.C., 1963-65; resident Hosp. Med. Coll. Pa., Phila., 1965-67; fellow in renal disease Dept. Medicine, U. Pitts. Sch. Medicine, 1969-70, asst. prof. medicine, 1971-75; chief renal diagnostic unit VA Hosp., Pitts., 1971-75; asst. prof. clin. medicine N.Y.U. Med. Sch., 1975—; chief nephrology sect. Lenox Hill Hosp., N.Y.C., 1975—; spl. lectr. Georgetown U. Med. Sch., 1973—; lectr. Western Pa. Continuing Edn. for Physicians, 1972-75, vis. prof., 1976; mem. merit rev. bd. VA, 1973-76. Served to maj. M.C., AUS, 1967-69. Decorated Army Commendation medal, 1969; grantee Health, Research and Services Found., 1970, 72, 74. Mem. AMA (invited lectr. 1973-75), A.C.P., Am. Fedn. Clin. Research, Am. Soc. Nephrology, Internat. Soc. Nephrology, Central Soc. Clin. Research. Greek Orthodox. Contbr. articles to profl. jours. and textbooks. Home: 55 Woodland Park Dr Tenafly NJ 07670 Office: Lenox Hill Hosp 100 E 77th St New York City NY 10021

MICHELS, EDWARD HERBERT, JR., educator; b. Jersey City, Oct. 17, 1944; s. Edward H. and Thelma E. (Engelhardt) M.; B.A. cum laude, Montclair (N.J.) State Coll., 1967; M.A., Rutgers U., 1972; postgrad. N.Y. U., 1972—; m. Susanna M.B. Helmers, Feb. 20, 1972. Tchr. history Pascack Hills High Sch., Montvale, N.J., 1967-68, Ridgefield Park (N.J.) High Sch., 1968—. Mem. Am. Hist. Assn., Orgn. Am. Historians, NEA, N.J., Bergen County, Ridgefield Park edn. assns., Pi Gamma Mu, Kappa Delta Pi. Republican. Mem. Reformed Ch. in Am. Office: Ridgefield Park High School Ridgefield Park NJ 07660

MICHELSEN, CHRISTOPHER BRUCE HERMANN, surgeon; b. Boston, Aug. 18, 1940; s. Jost Joseph and Ingeborg Elizabeth (Dilthey) M.; B.A., Bowdoin Coll., 1961; M.D., Columbia U., 1969; m. Geraldine Gay Stilp, Mar. 23, 1968; children—Heidi Elizabeth, Matthew Christopher. Intern Columbia Presbyn. Med. Center, N.Y.C., 1969-70, resident, 1970-71, now asso. orthpaedic surgeon; orthopedic resident N.Y. Orthopedic Hosp., N.Y.C., 1971-73, jr. Anne C. Kane fellow, 1973-74, sr. Anne C. Kane fellow and hip fellow, 1974-75, traveling fellow, 1975-76; postgrad. fellow in biomechanics, instr. biomed. engring. Case-Western Res. U.; asso. in clin. orthopaedic surgery Columbia Coll. Physicians and Surgeons. Served with AUS, 1961-63. Diplomate Am. Bd. Orthopaedic Surgery. Fellow A.C.S., N.Y. Acad. Medicine. Home: 160 Donnybrook Dr Demarest NJ 07627 Office: 622 W 168th St New York City NY 10032

MICHELSON, DAVID SCOTT, city planner; b. N.Y.C., Jan. 4, 1953; s. Stanley and Naomi (Greenwald) M.; B.A. with honors, Fairleigh Dickinson U., 1974; postgrad. Columbia U., 1976. Asst. to dep. city planner City of Hackensack, N.J., 1973-74; project coordinator Dept. City Planning, N.Y.C., 1974; planning cons. Community Planners, Inc., Mineola, N.Y., 1975; sr. planner City of Stamford, Conn., 1976—; adj. prof. State U. N.Y., Old Westbury, 1977. William F. Kinne Traveling fellow, 1975. Mem. Am. Inst. Planners, Nat. Assn. Housing and Redevel. Ofcls., Assn. Architects & Engrs. in Israel, Columbia Archtl. and Planning Alumni Assn., Conn. Community Devel. Assn. Contbr. articles in field to profl. jours. Home: 105-55 62d Dr Forest Hills NY 11375 Office: 429 Atlantic St Stamford CT 06901

MICHELSON, LESLIE PAUL, physicist; b. N.Y.C., June 23, 1943; s. Leonard Richard and Josephine (Elfenbein) M.; B.S., Adelphi U., 1966, M.S., 1968, Ph.D., 1975; m. Laura Mayron, Jan. 25, 1970; children—Emily, David, Daniel. Tech. asst. in physics Adelphi U., 1965-73, lectr. physics, 1966-74; research collaborator physics dept. Brookhaven Nat. Lab., Upton, N.Y., 1973-74; sr. lab. systems analyst Coll. Medicine and Dentistry N.J., Newark, 1975—; lectr. dept. psychiatry and mental health services N.J. Med. Sch., Newark. Mem. IEEE, Am. Phys. Soc. Contbr. articles to sci. jours., papers at sci. soc. meetings. Home: 29 Norfolk Ave Maplewood NJ 07040 Office: Coll Medicine and Dentistry NJ 100 Bergen St Newark NJ 07103

MICHIE, DANIEL BOORSE, JR., lawyer; b. Phila., July 28, 1922; s. Daniel Boorse and Mae (Mueller) M.; B.S., Harvard, 1943; LL.B., U. Va., 1948; m. Barbara F. Maddox, Aug. 29, 1970. Admitted to Pa. bar, 1949; practice law, Phila., 1949—; asso. firm Harry J. Alker, Esq., 1949, Kephart & Kephart, 1950-51; asso. firm Fell & Spalding, 1952-53, partner, 1954-68; partner Fell, Spalding, Goff & Rubin, 1969—. Pres., Phila. Council Internat. Visitors, 1957-60, Phila. Crime Commn., 1960-63, Phila. Fellowship Commn., 1970-71; chmn. Pa. Adv. Com. on Probation, 1966—, Bd. Phila. Prisons, 1968-71; pres. Nat. Assn. Citizens Crime Commns., 1961-62, Unitarian Universalist Service Com., 1969-72; regional co-chmn. NCCJ, 1967-71, nat. bd. govs., 1971—. Spl. master U.S. Ct. Appeals for 3d Circuit, 1970—; solicitor Twp. of Abington, Pa., 1958-78. Bd. dirs. Valley Forge council Boy Scouts Am., 1955—. Served to lt. USNR, 1943-46. Mem. Phila. (gov. 1970-72), Pa. (ho. dels. 1971—), Am. (chmn. organized crime com. 1964-65), Fed. bar assns., Am. Judicature Soc., Navy League (dir. Phila. 1967-73, v.p. 1973-76, pres. 1976—, nat. dir. 1977—), St. Andrew's Soc., Friendly Sons of St. Patrick, S.A.R. Unitarian Universalist (ch. pres. 1961-62, dist. pres. 1966-69). Republican. Clubs: Huntingdon Valley Country, Down Town, Union League (Phila.). Home: 1129 Wrack Rd PO Box 8 Meadowbrook PA 19046 Office: 510 Walnut St Philadelphia PA 19106

MICHIELLI, DONALD WARREN, scientist, educator; b. Queens Village, N.Y., Aug. 15, 1934; s. James and Marie (LaBelle) M.; B.S., Springfield Coll., 1957; M.A., Ohio State U., 1961, Ph.D., 1965. Research asst. div. aviation physiology Ohio State U., Columbus, 1963-64; chmn. dept. phys. edn. Franklin Jr. High Sch., Columbus, 1965-66; faculty L.I. U., Bklyn., 1966-71, asso. prof. phys. edn., 1970-71, adj. asso. prof. dept. health scis., 1978—; adj. asso. prof. health and phys. edn. Hunter Coll., City U. N.Y., 1970; adj. asso. prof. N.Y. U., 1970-74; asso. prof., dir. Lab. Work Physiology, Bklyn. Coll., City U. N.Y., 1971—. Served with AUS, 1957-59. Fellow Am. Coll. Sports Medicine; mem. AAHPER, N.Y. Acad. Sci., Am., N.Y. heart assns., AAAS. Home: 77 Patterson Ave Hempstead NY 11550

MICHMAN, RONALD DAVID, educator; b. Hartford, Conn., Oct. 31, 1931; s. Morris and Rose B. (Garber) M.; B.S., N.Y. U., 1953, M.A., 1957, Ed.D., 1966; m. Ruth Krefting, Sept. 5, 1955; children—Laura, Carol. Asst. prof. mktg. U. N.H., 1960-64; prof. mktg. Syracuse U. Utica Coll., 1964-75; prof. mktg. Shippensburg State Coll., 1975—; cons. in field. Served with U.S. Army, 1954-56. Found. for Econ. Edn. fellow, 1967; AFL-CIO Am. Fedn. of Tchrs. grantee, 1971. Mem. Am. Mktg. Assn., AAUP, Midwest Bus. Adminstrs. Assn. Author: Marketing Channels, 1974; Strategic Advertising Decisions, 1976; Marketing Channel Strategy, 1976; Market Segmentation, 1977. Home: 203 Sherwood Dr Chambersburg PA 17201

MICKEL, HUBERT SHELDON, physician; b. Bridgeton, N.J., Aug. 27, 1937; s. Ralph Andrew and Lillian Almeda (Burkett) M.; B.S. summa cum laude, Eastern Nazarene Coll., 1958; M.D., Harvard, 1962; m. Betty Jane Harris, Oct. 2, 1961 (div. Dec. 1972); children—Paul David, Deborah Elizabeth, Pamela Marie. Intern, Mary Fletcher Hosp., Burlington, Vt., 1962-63; resident internal medicine Royal Victoria Hosp., Montreal, Que., Can., 1963-64; resident neurology, neurol. unit Boston City Hosp., 1964-67; NIH spl. fellow in chemistry Harvard, 1967-68; practice medicine specializing in neurology, Boston, 1970—, Concord, Mass., 1971-73; instr. neurology Harvard Med. Sch., Boston, 1970-71, asst. prof. neurology, 1971-77, asst. clin. prof. neurology, 1977—; instr. neurology Boston U. Sch. Medicine, 1970—; research asso. neurosurgery Children's Hosp. Med. Center, Boston, 1970-71, asst. neurology, 1970-77, asso. in neurology, 1977—; dir. Wrentham State Sch. div., dept. neurology Children's Hosp. Med. Center, Boston, 1973-76; asst. neurology Beth Israel Hosp., Boston; pre-med. adviser Leverett House, Harvard U., Cambridge, Mass., 1971—, hon. research asso., dept. chemistry, 1977—; chief physician, dir. med. research Wrentham (Mass.) State Sch., 1973-76. Served to maj. M.C., USAF, 1968-70. Diplomate Am. Bd. Psychiatry and Neurology. Fellow Internat. Biog. Assn.; mem. Am. Acad. Neurology, N.Y. Acad. Sci., AAAS, Assn. Research in Nervous and Mental Diseases, Assn. Harvard Chemists, Boston Soc. Psychiatry and Neurology, Mass. Med. Soc., Am. Chem. Soc., Am. Oil Chemists Soc., Internat. Soc. for Fat Research, Undersea Med. Soc., Pan Am. Med. Soc. (N.Am. v.p. sect. on neurology), Am. Assn. on Mental Deficiency, Am. Coll. Emergency Physicians, Univ. Assn. Emergency Medicine, Internat. Platform Assn. Home: Leverett House G-107 Cambridge MA 02138 Office: Children's Hosp Med Center Boston MA 02115

MICKEVICH, WALTER CHARLES, psychologist; b. Boston, Nov. 24; s. Walter Paul and Amelia M. (Lawcewicz) M.; B.S., Suffolk U., 1964; M.Ed., Boston State Coll., 1969; J.D., Western New Eng. Coll., 1972. Coordinator spl. edn. Franklin (Mass.) Sch. System, 1968-71; tchr. Marlborough (Mass.) Pub. Schs., 1971—; vis. lectr. div. grad. edn. and spl. programs, asso. prof. dept. psychology Worcester (Mass.) State Coll., 1976—. Mem. Am. Psychol. Assn., Nat. Assn. Sch. Psychologists. Home: 37 Sarah St Randolph MA 02368

MICUNIS, GORDON JULES, designer; b. Lynn, Mass., June 16, 1933; s. Morris and Ida (Gordon) M.; A.B. cum laude, Tufts U., 1954; M.F.A., Yale U., 1959. Freelance scenic and costume designer, 1959—, including Stratford Shakespeare Festival, 1967, N.Y.C. Opera, 1960-77, Opera Soc. Washington, 1959-64, Charles Playhouse, Boston, 1962, Boston Opera, 1962, Atlanta Arts Alliance, 1963, Balt. Opera Soc., 1964-68, Tyrone Guthrie's Theatre, Mpls., 1970; asso. Peter Wolf Assos., Dallas, 1969-74: interior designer George Nelson & Co., N.Y.C., 1974-75; pres. Gordon Micunis Interiors, Inc., Stamford, Conn., 1976—; asst. prof. theatre design C.W. Post Coll., 1971-73; instr. theatre Barnard Coll., 1967-77; instr. costume design Fashion Inst. Tech., 1977, Lester Polikov's Forum Scenic and Costume Design, 1977—; one-man show theatre designs: Wright Hepburn Gallery, N.Y.C., 1970; group shows: Smithsonian Exhibit and tour Am. Designers, 1976—, students of Donald Oenslager, Lincoln Center, N.Y.C., 1976. Served with U.S. Army, 1954-56. Mem. United Scenic Artists (trustee display and diorama 1970-77), Am. Soc. Interior Designers (asso.). Jewish. Designer for Am. premier plays, operas and revivals. Home: One Rogers Rd Stamford CT 06902

MIDDLEKAUFF, JAMES HOLAN, chem. co. exec.; b. Cleve., July 16, 1938; s. Roger David and Ella Marie (Holan) M.; B.S., Mass. Inst. Tech., 1960; M.B.A., Boston U., 1964: children by previous marriage—Scott H., Lee M. Sales engr. Trane Co., Boston, 1960-64; rep. comml. devel. Am. Cyanamid Co., Wakefield, Mass., 1964-67, mgr. comml. devel., bldg. products div., 1967-68; asst. to v.p. Watts Regulator Co., Lawrence, Mass., 1968-70; mgmt. analyst comml. devel. div. Am. Cyanamid Co., Wayne, N.J., 1970-72, project coordinator internat. div., 1972-74, mgr. comml. planning med. products, 1974-75, mgr. pharm. div., 1975-76, mgr. strategic planning internat. div., 1976—; instr. Merrimac Coll., Mass., 1968-70. Mem. Town of Lynnfield (Mass.) Charter Commn., 1968-70. Served with U.S. Army, 1961. Mem. Wyckoff Jaycees (v.p.), Road Runners Club of N.J. Clubs: Mass. Inst. Tech. of N.J., Toastmasters of Clifton (N.J.) (v.p.). Entrant Boston Marathon, 1974, 75, 78. Home: 942 Pines Lake Dr W Wayne NJ 07470 Office: Berdan Ave Wayne NJ 07470

MIDDLETON, DAVID, physicist, applied mathematician, educator; b. N.Y.C., Apr. 19, 1920; s. Charles Davies Scudder and Lucile (Davidson) M.; grad. Deerfield Acad., 1938; A.B. summa cum laude, Harvard U., 1942, A.M., 1945, Ph.D., 1947; m. Nadea Butler, May 26, 1945 (div. 1971); children—Susan Terry, Leslie Butler, David Scudder Blakeslee, George Davidson Powell; m. 2d, Joan Bartlett Reed, 1971. Teaching fellow electronics Harvard U., 1942, spl. research asso. radio research lab., 1942-45, predoctoral fellow physics NSF, 1945-47, research fellow electronics, 1947-49, asst. prof. applied physics, 1949-54; cons. physicist, Cambridge, Mass., 1954—, Concord, Mass., 1957-71, N.Y.C., 1971—, also Johns Hopkins U., Rand Corp., Air Force Cambridge Research Center, industry, Communication Satellite Corp., Lincoln Lab., NASA, Raytheon, Sylvania, Sperry-Rand, Inst. Def. Analyses, Office Naval Research, Applied Research Lab. U. Tex., Gen. Electric Co., Honeywell, Transp. Systems Center of Dept. Transp., Dept. Commerce Office Telecommunications, Nat. Oceanographic and Atmospheric Adminstrn., Office Telecommunications Policy of Exec. Office Pres., Nat. Telecommunication and Info. Adminstrn., others; adj. prof. elec. engring. Columbia U., 1960-61; adj. prof. applied physics and communication theory Rensselaer Poly. Inst., Hartford Grad. Center, 1961-70; prof. communication theory U. R.I., 1966—; mem. Naval Research Adv. Com., 1970-77, mem. Naval Research Adv. Coms. Lab. Adv. Bds. for Undersea Warfare, for Research; mem. exploitation adv. bd. USN Office Chief Naval Ops.; mem. adv. bd. for command, control, communication and intelligence NRAC. NRC Predoctoral fellow, 1945-47; recipient award (with W.H. Huggins) Nat. Electronics Conf., 1956; Wisdom award of honor, 1970; prize paper awards IEEE Electromagnetic Compatability Group, 1978, Inst. Telecommunication Scis., 1978. Fellow Am. Phys. Soc., IEEE, AAAS, Explorers Club; mem. Acoustical Soc. Am., Optical Soc. Am., Am. Math. Soc., Soc. Indsl. and Applied Math., AAUP, N.Y. Acad. Sci., Authors Guild Am., Inst. Math. Statistics, Phi Beta Kappa, Sigma Xi. Clubs: Stone Horse Yacht (Harwich Port, Mass.); Harwich Port Tennis Assn.; Concord (Mass.) Country; Harvard (N.Y.C.); Cosmos (Washington). Author: Introduction to Statistical Communication Theory, 1960; Russian edit. Soviet Radio Moscow (2 vols), 1962; Topics in Communication Theory, 1965 (Russian edit., 1966). Mem. editorial bd. Information and Control, Advanced Serials in Electronics and Cybernetics, Contbr. tech. jours. Research in radar, telecommunications, underwater acoustics, oceanography, seismology, systems analysis, communication theory. Home: 127 E 91st St New York City NY 10028 Office: 127 E 91st St New York City NY 10028 also 35 Concord Ave Cambridge MA 02138

MIDDLETON, JOHN THOMAS, educator; b. Olney, Tex., Feb. 19, 1926; s. Benjamin Franklin and Ola Aurora (Davenport) M.; B.S., Hardin Coll., 1948; postgrad. N. Tex. State Tchrs. Coll., 1948, So. Meth. U., 1948-49, Southwestern Med. Sch., 1955-56; Ph.D., Fla. State U., 1968; m. Betty Judith Hill, July 16, 1950 (dec. July 1963); children—Karen, Marsha, Valeda, Holly; m. Claire M.A.J. Bastien, Jan. 21, 1965; children—Thomas, Frank, John. Chief clin. psychologist Terrell (Tex.) State Hosp., 1949-53, chief social service, 1955; dir. psychiat. social services, coordinator out patient psychiatry clinics Austin (Tex.) State Hosp., 1956-66; prof. family life-marriage counseling State U. N.Y., Plattsburgh, 1968—; pvt. practice in marriage-family counseling and psychotherapy, 1953—, West Chazy, N.Y., 1968—. Mem. Bastrop County (Tex.) Devel. Com., 1962-66; founding chmn. Champlain Valley (N.Y.) Birthright and Right to Life Com., 1970-72; vice-chmn. N.Y. State Right to Life, 1972, chmn., 1973; pres. N.Y. State Right to Life Ednl. Found., 1973; pres. Family Life Found., 1977-78; founding life mem., clin. mem., pres. Northeastern region Nat. Alliance for Family Life, 1975-77, dir.-at-large, nat. sec., 1976-78. Served with USNR, 1943-45. Recipient Pres. Spl. award State U. Coll., Plattsburgh, 1970; Research grantee Lake Champlain-Lake George Devel. Com., 1970, Innovation Teaching award State U. N.Y., Plattsburgh, 1971; Edgar P. Wadhams award Wadhams Hall Sem. and Coll., 1973; accredited family life educator, supr. counseling Nat. Alliance for Family Life. Mem. AAUP (pres. 1970-71), Am. Assn. Marriage and Family Counselors (approved supr.), Am. Sociol. Assn., Am. Edn. Assn. (dir. 1976). Roman Catholic. K.C. Home: PO Box 243 West Chazy NY 12992 Office: State U NY Plattsburgh NY 12901

MIDURA, MIECZYSLAW JOZEF, physician; b. Chorzow, Poland, Apr. 2, 1938; s. Jozef Stanislaw and Elizabeth (Pluta) M.; M.D., Med. Acad. Cracow, Poland, 1964; m. Barbara Maria Manka, Mar. 16, 1968; children—Michael Andrew, Anne Katherine. Intern, VA Hosp., Bklyn., 1968-69; resident N.Y. Hosp.-Cornell Med. Center, 1970-72; anesthesiology fellow Meml. Hosp. Cancer, N.Y.C., 1972-73; asst. attending anesthesiologist Victory Meml. Hosp., Bklyn., 1973—; mem. staff Drs. Hosp., S.I., N.Y. Fellow anesthesiology Cornell Med. Coll., N.Y.C., 1970-73. Mem. Am., N.Y. State socs. anesthesiologists, N.Y. State, Kings County, Polish-Am. med. socs. Home: 9601 Shore Rd Brooklyn NY 11209 Office: 9036 7th Ave Brooklyn NY 11228

MIELE, PHILIP HARGREAVES, communications cons., educator; b. Jersey City, Aug. 24, 1922; s. Philip Joseph and Grace (Hargreaves) M.; A.B., Princeton U., 1948; M.A., New Sch. Social Research, 1972; m. Marjorie Schilbe, Apr. 3, 1947; 1 dau., Grace Miele Owen. Press relations mgr. Western Electric Co., 1948-50; asst. mgr. pub. relations Am. Cyanamid Co., 1951-56; pres. Miele, Stone Inc., N.Y.C., 1958-65; pub relations dir. Ametek Inc., N.Y.C., 1965-66; cons. communications, 1966—; asst. prof. communication arts N.Y. Inst. Tech., N.Y.C., 1971—. Served with AUS, 1942-45. Co-author: (with Benjamin S. Frank) Doctor Frank's No-Aging Diet, 1976. Contbr. articles to profl. publs. Home: 145 E 15th St New York City NY 10016

MIGLIORE, SALVATORE ANTHONY, orthodontist; b. Wilkinsburg, Pa., Dec. 18, 1931; s. Salvatore and Clara Clementina (Pergola) M.; B.S., U. Pitts., 1961, D.M.D., 1961; postgrad. Harvard Sch. Dental Medicine, 1961-64; m. Patricia A. Dowling, Jan. 9, 1960; children—Salvatore Anthony, Debra Lee, Lisa Ann, Tina Marie, Michael Paul, Francesca Lynn. Research fellow in bacteriology U. Pitts., 1958-61, asst. prof. orthodontics Sch. Dental Medicine, research asso. in microbiology, instr. microbiology, lectr. grad. histology, 1964-68; research fellow in orthodontics, NIH postdoctoral research fellow Harvard Sch. Dental Medicine, 1961-64, instr. orthodontics, 1963-64; practice dentistry specializing in orthodontics, North Hills, Pa., 1964. Lectr. histology Forsythe Dental Center Sch. for Dental Hygienists, 1961-63, lectr. functional dental anatomy, 1962-63. Served with AUS, 1954-56. Fellow Internat. Coll. Dentists); mem. Am., Pa. dental assns., Am. Assn. Orthodontists, Pa., Pitts. (sec. 1972, pres. 1973), orthodontic socs., Odontological Soc. Western Pa., North Dental Club (treas. 1971, sec. 1972, pres. 1973). Club: Harvard (Boston). Contbr. articles to dental jours. Home: 2209 Ben Franklin Dr Pittsburgh PA 15237 Office: 6000 Babcock Blvd Pittsburgh PA 15237

MIGNAULT, ROBERT DUVAL, electronic co. exec.; b. Montreal, Que., Can., Mar. 19, 1929; s. Bertrand and Jessie Bruce (Emslie) M.; B.E.E., McGill U., Montreal, 1951; m. Cecile McGovern, June 7, 1952; children—Louise, Peter, Michele. Electronics engr. C.D. Howe Co., 1951-57; pres. Mansions Car Radio, Ltd., 1957-62; pres., dir. Pye Electronics, Ltd., Pye Leasing, Ltd. (all Montreal). Active youth centers and sch. coms. Fellow Radio Club Am.; mem. Corps. Engrs. Que. Clubs: Kiwanis (dir.); Royal St. Lawrence Yacht (Dorval, Que.). Home: 6 Manresa Ct Beaconsfield PQ H9W 5H6 Canada Office: Pye Electronics Ltd 8580 Darnley Rd Montreal PQ H4T 1M6 Canada

MIHALIK, FRANK MELVYN, realty co. exec.; b. Aliquippa, Pa., Feb. 20, 1927; s. Michael K. and Mary K. M.; B.A., Duquesne U., Pitts., 1949; m. Mona Jo Haney, Aug. 25, 1962; children—Jeffrey Mark, Marisa Ann. Feature writer Pitts. Post-Gazette, 1949; sports editor Beaver Valley Times, Aliquippa, 1944-45; publicity dir. contest bd. Am. Automobile Assn., 1949-51; screen writer MGM, Hollywood, Calif., 1951-52; publicity dir. Switch and Signal div. Westinghouse Air Brake Co., 1952-53; pub. relations dir. Instrument Soc. Am., 1953-54; sales promotion mgr. Catranel Constrn. Co., Pitts., 1954-59; v.p. Penn Internat. Inc., Pitts., 1959-70; pres. Comml. Realty Mktg., Inc., Monroeville, Pa., 1970—, Shortway-Freeway Land Corp., 1962—. Served with USNR, 1945-46. Mem. Nat. Assn. Corp. Real Estate Execs. (chpt. edn. chmn. 1976-78), Nat. Assn. Rev. Appraisers, Urban Land Inst., Am. Mgmt. Assn., Internat. Council Shopping Centers, Internat. Platform Assn. Roman Catholic. Office: Monroe Complex Bldg 1 Mosside Blvd Monroeville PA 15146

MIHRAM, GEORGE ARTHUR, systemic scientist; b. Norman, Okla., Sept. 21, 1939; s. Russell George and Ella Lee (Stanaland) M.; B.S. summa cum laude, U. Okla., 1960; postgrad. Wash. State U., 1960-61; Fulbright scholar, U. Sydney (Australia), 1964; M.S. (NSF fellow), Okla. State U., 1962, Ph.D., 1965; m. Danielle Redibaum, Dec. 22, 1965. Operational researcher Ops. Research, Inc., Silver Springs, Md., 1965-66; systems analyst Joint Chiefs Staff, Washington, 1966-68; mem. faculty U. Pa., Phila., 1968-74, asst. prof., 1968-74. Cons., IBM, 1973, Office Asst. Sec. Def., 1969, Hdqrs. USAF, 1968-69, Acad. Natural Scis., 1970-71, Ops. Research, Inc., 1972, U. So. Calif., 1978. Served with AUS, 1966-68. Recipient Joint Service Commendation medal Joint Chiefs of Staff. NSF research initiation grantee, 1970-72, internat. travel grantee, 1975; NATO travel grantee, 1977. Mem. AAAS, Am. Soc. Engring. Edn., Am. Math. Soc., Biometric Soc., Am. Statis. Assn., IEEE, Inst. Math. Statistics, Ops. Research Soc. Am., Soc. Computer Simulation, Soc. Gen. Systems Research, Soc. Indsl. and Applied Math., Soc. Sci. Study Religion, Sigma Xi. Author: Simulation: Statistical Foundations and Methodology, 1972; An Epistle to Dr. Benjamin Franklin, 1974; A Critique of World Models, 1975; co-author: Human Knowledge: Role of Models, Metaphors and Analogy, 1974. Asso. editor Simulation, 1973-75, Internat. Jour. Gen. Systems, 1973—; Modeling and Simulation, 1974—. Contbr. articles to profl. jours. Address: PO Box 234 Haverford PA 19041

MIKOLJI, BORIS HRVOJE, educator; b. Visoko, Yugoslavia, Jan. 24, 1926; s. Vincent and Helena (Vrbica) M.; came to U.S., 1951, naturalized, 1956; student Karl Franzens U., Graz, Austria 1947-51; M.A., Western Res. U., 1955, Ph.D., 1961; m. Adele Christine Tacher, Nov. 28, 1952; children—Helen, Dorothy, Vera-Marie. Research and adminstrv. staff McDowell-Wellman, Inc., Cleve., 1955-63; asst. prof. sociology Concord Coll., 1963-64, Nazareth Coll., 1964-67; asso. prof. urbanization and sociology Rochester Inst. Tech., 1967, chmn. social sci., 1970-72, chmn. sociology, 1976—, prof. sociology, 1977—; cons. govtl. agys., social agys. Trustee Diocesan Charities. Recipient Eisenhart award for outstanding teaching, 1977; NSF research fellow, 1973-74. Mem. Am., N.Y. (pres. 1976-77) sociol. assns., Pi Gamma Mu, Delta Tau Kappa. Author: Ethnicity and Politics in Urban Community, 1971; also articles. Home: 20 Sunset Trail Fairport NY 14450 Office: 06-1311 Rochester Inst Tech 1 Lomb Meml Dr Rochester NY 14623

MIKULSKI, BARBARA ANN, congresswoman; b. Balt., July 20, 1936; d. William and Christina Eleanor (Kutz) Mikulski; B.A., Mt. St. Agnes Coll., 1958; postgrad. Loyola Coll. at Balt., 1961; M.S.W., U. Md., 1965; LL.D., Goucher Coll., 1973, Hood Coll., 1978. Tchr., Mt. Saint Agnes Coll., 1969, Community Coll. Balt., 1970-71, VISTA Tng. Center, 1965-70, St. Mary's Sem., 1971; with Balt. Dept. Social Services, 1961-63, 66-70, York Family Agy., 1964, Asso. Cath. Charities, 1958-61; past city councilwoman 1st dist. Balt.; mem. 95th-96th Congresses from 3d Md. Dist., mem. Interstate and Fgn. Commerce Com., Mcht. Marine and Fisheries Com. Adj. prof. Loyola at Balt.; cons. orgns. including Nat. Center Urban Ethnic Affairs, HUD, U.S. Senate Com. on Aging, Md. Higher Edn. Council on Urban Affairs, Balt. Dept. Edn., Anne Arundel County Dept. Mental Hygiene, U. Md. Sch. Library Sci. and Pub. Information. Mem. Polish Women's Alliance, Polish Am. Congress, Citizen Planning and Housing Assn., S.E. Community Orgn.; chmn. commn. community devel. Archiocesan Urban Commn. Mem. Nat. Women's Polit. Caucus; mem. nat. com. Muskie for Pres., 1971-72; chairperson commn. del. selection and party structure Democratic Nat. Com. Nat. bd. dirs. Urban Coalition; bd. dirs. Valley House. Named One of Outstanding Young Women in Am.; Md. Outstanding Young Woman of Year, 1968. Mem. Am. Fedn. Tchrs., Nat. Assn. Social Workers, League Women Voters, Mems. Congress for Peace through Law. Contbr. articles to N.Y. Times, U.S. Steelworker Jour., Red Book and others. Home: Fell's Point Baltimore MD Office: 1414 Federal Bldg Baltimore MD 21201

MIKURIYA, TADAFUMI, civil structural engr.; b. Saga, Kyushu, Japan, Jan. 3, 1899; s. Hiromi and Haru (Shigetomi) M.; came to U.S., 1923, naturalized, 1953; student Kumanoto Engring. Coll., 1918-21; B.S., U. Pa., 1926, M.S., 1927, C.E., 1935; m. Anna S. Schwenk, June 10, 1929; children—Tod, Mary Jane, Beverly Anne. With Am. Bridge Co., Phila., 1927-45; chief engr. Keystone Structural Steel Co., Trenton, N.J., 1945-48; structural cons. engr., Trenton, 1948—; profl. planner, 1967—. Life mem. ASCE, Nat. Soc. Profl. Engrs., Nat. Cons. Engrs. Council, Japanese Am. Citizens League. Club: Rotary. Contbr. articles to profl. jours. Developed theory of influence equations for analysis of indeterminate structures. Home: 1102 Buckingham Way Morrisville PA 19067 Office: 19 Peace St Trenton NJ 08608

MILANO, HEATHER CASEY, educator; b. St. John, N.B., Can., Mar. 2, 1934; married, 2 children. B.A. in L.S., St. Francis Xavier U., Antigonish, N.S., Can., 1956; M.Sc. in Audiovisual Edn., Western Conn. State Coll., Danbury, 1976. Librarian various schs., 1957-59; library media specialist Putnam Valley (N.Y.) Central Sch. Dist. 2, 1972—. Mem. cultural com. Putnam Valley Pub. Library, 1972-74; media council rep. to Bd. Coop. Ednl. Services, Yorktown Heights, N.Y., 1973—. Mem. NEA, N.Y. State United Tchrs., Sch. Librarians of Southeastern N.Y. Pi Lambda Theta. Certified library media specialist, N.Y. State. Home: 2730 Quaker Church Rd Yorktown Heights NY 10598 Office: Putnam Valley Middle Sch Peekskill Hollow Rd Putnam NY 10579

MILAZZO, JOSEPH JAMES, optometrist; b. Wyoming, Pa., June 13, 1923; s. Louis and Theresa (Martorana) M.; Dr. Optometry, Pa. Coll. Optometry, 1952; m. Theresa DiGian, Sept. 28, 1958; 1 son, Joseph James. Practice optometry, Chambersburg, Pa., 1952—; cons. S.Mountain Restoration Eye Clinic, 1969—; dir. Vision Service Assos. Bd. dirs. Beacon Lodge Camp for Blind, Art Alliance; chmn. adv. council Corpus Christi Cath. Ch. and Sch. Served with USAAF, 1943-46. Recipient Am. Legion award, 1965, Lions award, 1967, Freedoms Found. award, 1971, Humanitarian award Lions Club, 1976. Mem. Am., Pa., Central Pa. optometric assns., Am. Legion.

Roman Catholic. Clubs: Lions Internat. (dir.); Elks. Home and office: 75 W Queen St Chambersburg PA 17201

MILBANK, JEREMIAH, finance co. exec.; b. N.Y.C., Mar. 24, 1920; s. Jeremiah and Katharine (Schulze) M.; B.A., Yale U., 1942; M.B.A., Harvard U., 1948; L.H.D. (hon.), Ithaca Coll., 1976; m. Andrea Hunter, July 19, 1947; children—Jeremiah III, Victoria M. Doelger, Elizabeth, Joseph H. Pres., JM Found., N.Y.C., Cypress Woods Corp.; dir. Internat. Minerals and Chems. Vice pres. Boys' Clubs Am.; pres. I.C.D. Rehab. and Research Center; trustee, treas. Robert A. Taft Inst. Govt.; fin. chmn. Republican Nat. Com., 1969-72, 75-77. Served to lt. USNR, 1943-46. Clubs: Madison Sq. Garden, Univ., Round Hill (Greenwich, Conn.), Racquet and Tennis, River. Author: First Century of Flight in America, 1942. Home: 620 Round Hill Rd Greenwich CT 06830 Office: 60 E 42d St New York City NY 10017

MILBOURNE, WALTER ROBERTSON, lawyer; b. Phila., Aug. 27, 1933; s. Charles Gordon and Florie Henderson (Robertson) M.; A.B., Princeton U., 1955; LL.B., Harvard U., 1958; m. Georgena Sue Dyer, June 19, 1965; children—Gregory Broughton, Karen Elizabeth, Walter Robertson. Admitted to Pa. bar, 1959; asso. firm Pepper, Hamilton & Sheetz, Phila., 1959-65; asso. firm Obermayer, Rebmann, Maxwell & Hippel, Phila., 1965-67, partner, 1968—; dir. Pa. Lumbermens Mut. Ins. Co., 1972—, Phila. Reins. Corp., 1976—. Chmn. mental health budget sect. Phila. United Fund, 1967-70. Served with Pa. N.G., 1958-59. Fellow Am. Coll. Trial Lawyers; mem. Am., Pa., Phila. bar assns., Internat. Assn. Ins. Counsel, Assn. Def. Counsel. Republican. Clubs: Union League (Phila.); Merion Cricket, Princeton, Idle Hour Tennis (pres. 1968-69), Phila. Lawn Tennis Assn. (pres. 1969-70). Home: 689 Fernfield Circle Strafford PA 19087 Office: 14th Floor Packard Bldg 15th and Chestnut Sts Philadelphia PA 19102

MILCH, ROBERT AUSTIN, physician; b. N.Y.C., May 24, 1929; s. Henry and Pearl (Salzberg) M.; A.B., Columbia U., 1949, M.D., 1953; M.B.A., Loyola Coll., Balt., 1977; m. Margot Wurtzburger, Aug. 14, 1960; children—Pamela Alexandra, Thomas Andrew. Research fellow in medicine Sloan Kettering Inst. Meml. Cancer Center, N.Y.C., 1953-54; surg. house officer Peter Bent Brigham Hosp., Boston, 1954-55; clin. asso. in surgery Nat. Cancer Inst., 1955-57; asst. resident surgeon Peter Bent Brigham Hosp., 1957-58; asst. resident in orthopaedic surgery Johns Hopkins Hosp., Balt., 1958-60, chief resident, 1960-61, asst. prof. orthopaedic surgery Johns Hopkins U. Sch. Medicine, 1961-64, asso. prof., 1964-67; spl. asst. for health and life scis., chmn. interagency com. on internat. health Office Sci. and Tech., Exec. Office of Pres., Washington, 1967-68; study dir., chmn. panel on internat. affairs Bd. of Medicine, Nat. Acad. Scis., Washington, 1968-69; acting asso. dir. collaborative studies Nat. Heart Inst., 1969; pres. Bioengineering Corp., Washington, 1969; chmn. bd., chief exec. officer U.S. Health Corp., Balt., San Francisco, 1969-71; prin. Peat, Marwick, Mitchell & Co., Washington, 1971-77; prof. bus. adminstrn., dir. program in health care mgmt. Loyola Coll., Balt., 1977—. Bd. visitors Columbia Coll., N.Y.C.; Bd. dirs. Gessell Inst. Child Devel., New Haven, Balt. Symphony Orch., Md. Ballet Co., Md. Acad. Scis., Loyola-Notre Dame Library Corp., Balt. Diplomate Am. Bd. Orthopaedic Surgery. Fellow A.C.S., Am. Pub. Health Assn., Royal Soc. Health; mem. Soc. Univ. Surgeons, Am. Acad. Orthopaedic Surgeons, Am. Acad. Polit. and Social Sci., AAAS, Am. Coll. Preventive Medicine, Am. Mgmt. Assn., AMA, others. Author: (with H. Milch) Fracture Surgery, A Textbook of Common Fractures, 1959; also numerous articles. Editor 3 books. Home: Overlook Pikesville MD 21208 Office: Grad Dept Bus Adminstrn Loyola Coll 4501 N Charles St Baltimore MD 21210

MILCH, ROBERT JEFFREY, writer, editor; b. N.Y.C., Oct. 7, 1938; s. Sam and Mathilde (Sokol) M.; B.A., Bklyn. Coll., 1960; M.A., N.Y. U., 1964; diploma Center Study Polish Culture and Lang., U. Warsaw, 1969; m. Adele Leokadia Krause, Apr. 20, 1965; children—Aleksander Boleslaw, Dimitri Yofi. Cons. editor Twayne Pubs., Inc., 1964-74; editor on micropaedia project internat. devel. div. Ency. Brit., Inc., 1969-70; contbg. editor Holy Bible Ency., 1969-70; editor Ktav Pub. House, 1973—; N.Y. State Regents coll. teaching fellow, 1960. Mem. Authors Guild. Jewish. Author: How to Be an American Jew, 1969; also notes for Cliff's Notes series, 1962-67; editor: New Comprehensive Jewish Ency., 1978; contbr. Keystone One-Volume Ency., Ency. Judaica, Young Students Illustrated Ency., Cadillac Modern Ency., also mags. Address: 9 Millbrook Dr Stony Brook NY 11790

MILCH, RONALD BARRY, hosp. adminstr.; b. N.Y.C., Sept. 6, 1933; s. Samuel S. and Ann C. (Cherkofsky) M.; m. Susan N. Schlesinger, June 14, 1959; children—Donna, Douglas, David. Adminstrv. asst. Meml. Hosp., Sloan-Kettering, N.Y.C., 1958-64; asst. to dean U. N.C. Sch. Medicine, Chapel Hill, 1966-67; research coordinator Montefiore Hosp. and Med. Center, Bronx, 1964-66, asst. adminstr., 1967-71; adminstr. Beth Abraham Hosp., Bronx, N.Y., 1971-74; exec. dir. Beth Israel Hosp., Passaic, N.J., 1974—. Trustee Bergen-Passaic Health Systems Agy. Served with U.S. Army, 1956-58. Mem. Am. Coll. Hosp. Adminstrs., Am. Pub. Health Assn., Am., Greater N.Y. hosp. assns., Am. Soc. Pub. Adminstrn., Hosp. Execs. Club N.Y., Hosp. Adminstrs. Forum-N.J., N.J. Hosp. Assn. (chmn., trustee ins. and pension, chmn. council on planning). Democrat. Jewish. Home: 119 Cherry Ln Teaneck NJ 07666 Office: 70 Parker Ave Passaic NJ 07055

MILDE, HELMUT INGO, physicist; b. Uttendorf, Austria, Dec. 3, 1934; s. Ingo Maria and Emmy (Mueller) M.; came to U.S., 1960, naturalized, 1962; diploma Tech. U. Graz, 1960, Ph.D., 1967; M.S., Mass. Inst. Tech., 1962; m. Leslie F. Faunce, Dec. 28, 1961; children—Inge Elizabeth, Ursula Sabina. Research scientist Brown Boveri Co., Baden, Switzerland, 1964-67; sr. physicist Ion Physics Corp., Burlington, Mass., 1967-73, v.p., mgr., 1973—; cons. high voltage pulse power tech. Mem. IEEE, Sigma Xi. Patentee field electrostatic precipitation. Home: 110 Middleton Rd Boxford MA 01921 Office: S Bedford St Burlington MA 01803

MILES, HORACE CLINTON, mgmt. cons.; b. Pitts., Nov. 2, 1934; s. Horace Chapman and Florence Estella (Boston) M.; B.A., Washington and Jefferson Coll., 1952-56; postgrad. math. Carnegie-Mellon U., 1960-65, mgmt. sci. U. Cal. at Los Angeles, 1972, pub. and internat. affairs U. Pitts., 1976; m. Esther Clauselle, Dec. 15, 1956; 1 son, Christopher Chapman. With Mellon Bank, Pitts., 1958-63; sci. coordinator Computer Oriented Research and Engring., Pitts., 1963-64; systems supr. Anderson & Gilbert, Inc., Greensburg, Pa., 1964-66; v.p. Ecco Cons. Inc., Pitts., 1966—, also dir. mgr. Glass Research Computer Center PPG Industries, Pitts., 1970-71; cons. Mid-Am. Producing, Omaha, 1974, Duquesne U. Computing Group, Pitts., 1973. Mem. Allegheny County planning subcom. Health Systems Agy. Western Pa.; trustee Pitts. Child Guidance Center. Served to capt. Ordnance Corps, AUS, 1956-58. Mem. Assn. Computing Machinery, Ops. Research Soc. Am., Am. Soc. Pub. Adminstrs., Internat. Platform Assn., World Affairs Council of Pitts., Aircraft Owners and Pilots Assn., Alpha Phi Alpha. Club: Pitts. Press. Home: 154 Suncrest Dr Verona PA 15147 Office: 607 Washington Rd Pittsburgh PA 15228

MILETTE, PIERRE CHARLES, diagnostic radiologist; b. Montreal, Que., Can., Nov. 18, 1943; s. Paul Leo and Jeanne (Piquette) M.; B.A. magna cum laude, U. Montreal, 1963, M.D. magna cum laude, 1967; m. Diane Bigras, Aug. 3, 1968; 1 son, Jean-Luc. Intern, Saint-Luc Hosp., Montreal, Montreal Gen. Hosp., 1967-69; resident in diagnostic radiology and neuroradiology Notre-Dame Hosp., Montreal, Maisonneuve Hosp., Montreal, Montreal Heart Inst., Montreal Children's Hosp., Montreal Neurol. Inst., 1969-73; mem. staff dept. diagnostic radiology Saint-Luc Hosp., Montreal, 1973—; cons. neuroradiologist Sainte-Jeanne D'Arc Hosp., Montreal, 1974—, Hopital-du-Haut-Richelieu, Saint-Jean, Que., 1975—; asso. prof. dept. radiology U. Montreal, 1974—; pres. Varad, Inc., pvt. x-ray office, 1974-78. Fellow Royal Coll. Physicians and Surgeons Can. (certified specialist in diagnostic radiology); mem. Association des Medecins de Langue Francaise du Canada, Can., Que. med. assns., Can., Que. assns. radiologists, French-Canadian Soc. Radiology (treas. 1977—), Am. Soc. Neuroradiology (sr.). Home: 307 Ave de Bretagne Longueuil PQ J4H 1R2 Canada Office: 235 Dorchester E Suite 700 Montreal PQ H2X 1N8 Canada

MILEWSKI, STANISLAW ANTONI, ophthalmologist, educator; b. Bagrowo, Poland, June 16, 1930; s. Alfred and Sabina (Sicinska) M.; came to U.S., 1959, naturalized, 1967; B.A., Trinity Coll., U. Dublin (Ireland), 1954, M.A., 1959, B. Chir., M.B., B.A.O., 1956; m. Anita Dobiecka, July 11, 1959; children—Andrew, Teresa, Mark. House surgeon Hammersmith Hosp. Postgrad. Sch. London, 1958; intern St. Raffael Hosp., New Haven, 1960-61; resident in ophthalmology Gill Meml. Hosp., Roanoke, Va., 1961-64; mem. staff Manchester (Conn.) Meml. Hosp., 1964-71, chief of ophthalmology, 1971—; asst. clin. prof. ophthalmology U. Conn., 1972—. Clin. fellow Montreal (Que., Can.) Gen Hosp., McGill U., 1971-72, Mass. Eye and Ear Infirmary, Harvard Med. Sch., Boston, 1974; diplomate Am. Bd. Ophthalmology. Fellow A.C.S.; mem. Am., Conn. (sec.-treas.), Brit. med. assns., New Eng. Ophthal. Soc. Republican. Roman Catholic. Home: 127 Lakewood Circle S Manchester CT 06040 Office: 191 Main St Manchester CT 06040

MILICI, JOHN ATTILIO, psychiatrist; b. N.Y.C., Oct. 25, 1924; s. Attilio and Marguerite Adele (Goggin) M.; A.B., Yale U., 1947; B.S. in Med. Sci., U. Geneva (Switzerland), 1951, M.D., 1957; m. Nora Johnson, Apr. 18, 1964; children—Justin John, Jonathan Francis. Intern, St. Vincent's Hosp., N.Y.C., 1957-58; resident in psychiatry Westchester div. N.Y. Hosp., White Plains, 1958-59; asst., then chief resident in psychiatry St. Luke's Hosp., N.Y.C., 1959-61, attending psychiatrist, 1961—, resident supr., 1961—; fellow in psychiatry Roosevelt Hosp., N.Y.C., 1961; acting univ. psychiatrist, dir. student mental health Columbia U., N.Y.C., 1961-63, univ. psychiatrist, dir. student mental health, 1963-74, cons. Internat. House, 1974—, asst. clin. prof. psychiatry Coll. Physicians & Surgeons, 1972—; asst. psychiatrist Vanderbilt Clinic Presbyn. Hosp., 1962—; practice medicine specializing in psychiatry, N.Y.C., 1961—. Served with USN, 1943-46. NIMH grantee, 1970-75; diplomate Am. Bd. Psychiatry and Neurology. Fellow Am. Psychiat. Assn.; mem. Am. Coll. Psychiatrists, Am. Coll. Health Assn., Met. Coll. Mental Health Assn. (past pres.), N.Y. County Med. Soc. Club: Yale (N.Y.C.). Office: 642 Park Ave New York NY 10021

MILKE, DENIS JEROME, psychiatrist; b. Cleve., Nov. 2, 1938; s. Merle J. and Kathleen R. (Schaeffer) M.; B.S., Pa. State U., 1960; M.D., Hahnemann Med. Coll., 1965; m. Sandra Lamont, Dec. 29, 1962; children—Dana Lynne, Christopher Denis. Intern, Harrisburg Hosp., 1965-66; resident in psychiatry Western Inst. and Clinic, U. Pitts., 1966-69; now practice medicine specializing in pscyiatry, Camp Hill, Pa.; dir. outpatient psychotherapy Harrisburg (Pa.) Hosp. Mental Health Center; asst. prof. psychiatry Milton S. Hershey Med. Center. Served with U.S. Army, 1969-72. Diplomate Am. Bd. Psychiatry and Neurology. Mem. Pa. (del.), Am. psychiat. assns., Pa. State, Dauphin County med. socs., AMA, Soc. Clin. and Exptl. Hypnosis. Club: West Shore Country. Office: 890 Poplar Church Rd Camp Hill PA 17011

MILL, CHARLES STUART, publishing exec.; b. Dedham, Mass.; s. William Robbie and Margaret (Watson) M.; m. Jane Baggott; children—Charles Stuart, Jeffrey Joseph. With McGraw-Hill, 1945-63; v.p., dir., gen. mgr. mag. pub. div. R.H. Donnelley Corp., 63-70; pres. Am. Bus. Press, Inc., 1970—; past treas. Bus. Publs. Audit of Circulation. Served with AUS, 1941-45. Mem. Advt. Council (dir.), Berkeley in Scarsdale Assn., St. Andrews Soc., Burns Soc. Clubs: Nat. Press; Scarsdale Town, Scarsdale Golf. Home: 17 Taunton Rd E Scarsdale NY 10583 Office: 205 E 42d St New York City NY 10017

MILLARD, CHARLES WARREN, III, mus. curator; b. Elizabeth, N.J., Dec. 20, 1932; s. Charles Warren and Constance Emily (Keppler) M.; A.B. magna cum laude, Princeton U., 1954; M.A., Harvard U., 1963, Ph.D., 1971. Asst. to dir. Fogg Art Mus., Harvard U., 1963-64; asst. to dir. Dumbarton Oaks, Washington, 1965-66; dir. Washington Gallery Modern Art, 1966-67; curator 19th century European art Los Angeles County Mus. Art, 1971-74; chief curator Hirshhorn Mus. and Sculpture Garden, Smithsonian Instn., 1974—; teaching fellow Harvard U., 1968-69; chmn. vis. com. to fine arts dept. Boston U., 1977—. Served with USN, 1956-59. Author: The Sculpture of Edgar Degas, 1977; art editor Hudson Rev., 1972—; contbr. articles to profl. jours. Home: 2853 Ontario Rd NW Washington DC 20009 Office: Hirshhorn Museum 8th St and Independence Ave SW Washington DC 20560

MILLARD, WILLIAM ANDREW, chemist; b. Plymouth, Pa., May 17, 1942; s. Abner Pike and Edith (Cosslett) M.; B.A., Lafayette Coll., 1965; M.A., Lehigh U., 1967, M.S., 1971; m. Donna L. Recicar, Dec. 26, 1964; children—William Andrew, Carrie Ann, Jennifer Lynn. Tchr. chemistry Summit (N.J.) High Sch., 1965-69; sr. research chemist Asarco Inc., Central Research Dept., South Plainfield, N.J., 1971—. Served with U.S. Army, 1959-60, 61-62. NSF grantee Bowdoin Coll., 1968. Mem. Sigma Xi. Methodist. Home: 128 Blackford Ave Piscataway NJ 08854 Office: Asarco Inc Central Research Dept Park Ave and Oak Tree Rd South Plainfield NJ 07080

MILLER, ALAN HARVEY, metall. engr.; b. Hartford, Conn., June 26, 1931; s. Harry and Julia (Stone) M.; B.S., Rensselaer Poly. Inst., 1953; postgrad. U. Pa., 1956, Stevens Inst. Tech., 1967; m. Charlotte Helene Wiener, Jan. 9, 1954; children—Lisa Ann, Scott Andrew. Metall. engr. Kaiser Fleetwings Inc., Bristol, Pa., 1957-61, ITE Circuit Breaker Co., Phila., 1961-63; metall. engr. DeLaval Turbine Inc., Trenton, N.J., 1963-70, chief materials engr., 1970—; cons. Mem. advisory com. Mercer County Vocational-Tech. Sch., 1975—. Served with U.S. Army, 1955. Mem. Am. Soc. Metals (Silver certificate award 1977), ASME, Am. Welding Soc. (chmn. Del. Valley sect.), ASTM, Rensselaer Alumni Assn., Alpha Epsilon Pi. Jewish. Club: Trenton (N.J.) Engrs. Patentee. Office: 853 Nottingham Way Trenton NJ 08602

MILLER, ALAN JAY, investment co. exec.; b. Bklyn., July 11, 1936; s. Louis and Claire (Maltz) M.; B.A., Cornell U., 1957; m. Susan Ruth Morris, Oct. 29, 1961; children—Laurie Ann, Adam Louis. Pres., Analysis-In-Depth, Inc., N.Y.C., 1965-67; mng. editor Value Line Investment Survey, N.Y.C., 1967-68; research dir. Emanuel Deetjen & Co., N.Y.C., 1968-69; exec. v.p., dir. Intersci. Capital Mgmt. Corp., N.Y.C., 1969-71; pres., dir. ICM Equity Fund Inc., ICM Fin. Fund Inc., N.Y.C., 1970-71; v.p., asso. research dir. Bache & Co., Inc., N.Y.C., 1972, G.H. Walker & Co. Inc., N.Y.C., 1972-73; 1st v.p., asso. research dir. Blyth Eastman Dillon & Co., Inc., N.Y.C., 1974-76; sr. v.p., research dir. E.F. Hutton & Co. Inc., N.Y.C., 1976—; adj. asso. prof. Columbia Grad. Sch. Bus., N.Y.C.; mem. faculty N.Y. Inst. Fin. Chartered fin. analyst. Mem. N.Y. Soc. Security Analysts, Fin. Analysts Fedn., Am. Statis. Assn., Nat., N.Y. assns. bus. economists. Office: 1 Battery Park Plaza New York City NY 10004

MILLER, ALAN MANNING, lawyer; b. N.Y.C., July 24, 1934; s. Philip and Sylvia (Lubash) M.; A.B., Syracuse U., 1955, LL.B., 1958, J.D., 1968; m. Ferne M. Steckler, Jan. 13, 1978; children by previous marriage—Neil, Peter, Stephanie, Douglas. Admitted to N.Y. bar, 1958, Mass. bar., 1970; individual practice law; adj. faculty N.Y. State Inst. Tech., Westbury, 1974-75, Nassau Community Coll., 1978—, Hofstra U. Law Sch., 1979—. Mem. N.Y. State Democratic Com., assembly dist. leader 11th Assembly Dist., 1965-77. Mem. Am., Mass., N.Y. State, Nassau County, Berkshire County, Criminal Courts bar assns., Nat. Assn. Criminal Def. Lawyers, Am. Arbitration Assn. Jewish religion. Home: 35 Wood Ln S Woodsburgh NY 11598 Office: 1 Old Country Rd Carle Place NY 11514

MILLER, ALBERT JAY, librarian, educator; b. Beaver Falls, Pa., Dec. 7, 1928; s. Joseph Jefferson and Alberta Fae (Shaffer) M.; B.A., Geneva Coll., 1952; M.S. in L.S., Rutgers U., 1958; advanced certificate in library sci. U. Pitts., 1967. Librarian, West Allegheny Jr. High Sch., Imperial, Pa., 1961-62, Butler (Pa.) Area High Sch., 1963-68; librarian, media specialist Pa. State U., New Kensington, Pa., 1968—; library staff Seattle World's Fair, 1963; library cons. secondary schs. Western Pa.; instr. continuing edn. div. Pa. State U.; library cons. Monroeville Sch. Bus., 1977—. Bd. dirs. Allegheny-Kiski Sr. Citizens Center, New Kensington, 1975—; mem. water safety div. ARC, New Kensington, 1972-75; mem. Allegheny-Kiski Human Relations Council, New Kensington, 1975—. Recipient Service award Cub Scouts Am., 1974. Mem. NEA, Pa. Edn. Assn., Am. Soc. Indexers, Pa. Library Assn. Democrat. Presbyterian. Author: A Selective Bibliography of Existentialism in Education and Related Topics, 1969; Confrontation, Conflict, and Dissent; A Bibliography of a Decade of Controversy, 1960-1970, 1972; (with M.J. Acri) Death: A Bibliographical Guide, 1977. Book and media rev. editor Learning Today, 1978. Home: 417 Charles Ave New Kensington PA 15068 Office: Pa State U 3550 7th St Rd New Kensington PA 15068

MILLER, ALBERT RAYMOND, JR., economist; b. Detroit, July 19, 1913; s. Albert Raymond and Virginia Ann M.; A.B. in Econs., George Washington U., 1939, M.A. in Econs., 1941; M.A. in Econs., Harvard U., 1946, Ph.D. in Econs., 1958; m. Catherine Lavinia Newcomer, Oct. 26, 1946; children—Albert Matthew, Winston Brian. Teaching fellow econs. George Washington U., 1939-40, asst. prof. econs., 1946-52; economist OPA, 1941-43, War Food Adminstrn., 1943-44; dir. research Nat. Found. Consumer Credit, 1952-57; dep. sec. Md. Dept. State Planning, 1957—; chmn. Gov. Md. Potomac River Basin Adv. Com.; adviser to Gov. on Susquehanna River Basin Commn.; mem. evening sch. faculty Johns Hopkins U., Loyola Coll., Balt. Episcopalian. Club: Johns Hopkins Faculty. Contbr. articles to profl. publs. Home 3700 N Charles St Baltimore MD 21218 Office: 301 W Preston St Baltimore MD 21201

MILLER, ARNOLD, data processing exec.; b. Bklyn., May 3, 1928; s. Nathan and Amelia (Kapel) M.; student N.Y. U., 1945-47; m. Margery Beth Neinken, July 9, 1952; children—John, Robert, Julie. Mgr. programming John Felix Asso., N.Y.C., 1957-65; asst. v.p. market research Datamation Services, Inc., N.Y.C., 1965-75; mgr. research and devel. Datatab, Inc., N.Y.C., 1975-76; v.p. Computerite/Air Tariffs Inc., Port Washington N.Y., 1976—. Served with AUS, 1950-52. Mem. Am. Mktg. Assn. Trustee, mem. sch. bd. Temple Emanuel, New Hyde Park, N.Y., 1975—. Contbr. articles in field to profl. jours. Home: 2 Lake Dr Manhasset Hills NY 11040 Office: 800 Port Washington Blvd Port Washington NY 11050

MILLER, BARRY, state ofcl.; b. N.Y.C., Dec. 25, 1942; s. Jack and Ida (Kaplan) M.; B.S., Bklyn. Coll., 1965; M.S., Villanova U., 1967; Ph.D. (Maurice Falk fellow 1969-70, coll. fellow 1970-71), Med. Coll. Pa., 1971; m. Francine Judith Pelzman, Aug. 22, 1965; children—Eric, Arianne. Acting head exptl. psychology br., dept. psychology U.S. Naval Air Devel. Center, Johnsville, Pa., 1967-68; asst. dir. behavioral scis. Eastern Pa. Psychiat. Inst., Phila., 1971-73, dir. bur. research and tng., mental health, 1973—; lectr. Villanova (Pa.) U., 1971-74; pvt. practice psychotherapy, Phila., 1971—; asst. prof. psychiatry dept. U. Pa. Med. Sch., 1975—; cons. research adv. group NIMH, 1976, Mich. Dept. Mental Health, 1977, NIMH Research Task Force Nat. Plan, 1978. Bd. dirs. Intercommunity Action, Inc. community mental health center, Phila., 1969-73; mem. Lafayette Hill Civic Assn., 1973—. Grantee Geigy Pharm., 1973, Lakeside Labs., Milw., 1973, Pfizer Pharm., 1973, Roche Labs., 1973, Sandoz Pharm., 1973, E.R. Squibb & Sons, Inc., 1973, NIMH-HEW, 1975, Health Care Financing Adminstrn., HEW, 1977, Office Family Assistance, HEW, 1978. Mem. Am., Pa., Eastern. psychol. assns., AAAS, Assn. Mental Health Adminstrs., N.Y. Acad. Scis. Contbr. articles to profl. jours. Home: 4139 Jackson Dr Lafayette Hill PA 19444 Office: Bur Research and Tng Mental Health Eastern Pa Psychiat Inst Henry Ave and Abbottsford Rd Philadelphia PA 19129

MILLER, BRUCE ALAN, mfg. co. exec., mech. engr.; b. N.Y.C., Aug. 3, 1930; s. William A. and Martha B. (Brunner) M.; B.S., U.S. Naval Acad., 1952; M.B.A., Adelphi U., 1962-63; m. Joan Constance Carl, Dec. 16, 1957; children—Dawn, Susan, Bruce Alan, Laura. Various prodn. engring. positions L.I. Lighting Co., Port Jefferson, N.Y., 1957-64; mgr. bus. devel. Sanderson & Porter, Inc., engrs., mgmt. cons., N.Y.C., 1964-66, asst. v.p., 1966-68, v.p., 1968-77; v.p. ops. Sid Harvey Industries, wholesale distbn. and mfg., Garden City, N.Y., 1977—. Mem. bd. advisers King's Coll., Briarcliff Manor, N.Y., 1966—. Served to lt. USN, 1952-57. Mem. Am. Soc. Naval Engrs., Am. Soc. M.E., Assn. of Iron and Steel Engrs. Baptist (mem. bd. deacons 1960—). Clubs: Army Navy of Washington, Downtown Athletic of New York City. Home: 23 Bob-O-Link Ln Northport NY 11768 Office: 605 Locust St Garden City NY 11530

MILLER, CAROL MILLER, shipping co. exec., music educator; b. Chgo., Feb. 18, 1931; d. Charles Edward and Gladys Ilene (Birker) Miller; B.Music Edn., Northwestern U., 1953, Mus.M., 1954; m. Robert Bernard Miller, Mar. 7, 1957. Dir. instrumental music schs. in Chgo., Highland Park, Highwood and Lake Forest, Ill., 1954-61; 1st flutist West Suburban Symphony Orch., Cook County, Ill., 1956-58; asst. 1st flutist Evanston (Ill.) Symphony Orch., 1956-61; Flute and Fiddle Club, Highland Park, 1956-61; v.p., dir. Sealanes Internat., Inc., Chgo., 1956-68, Trade Routes Inc., Conn. and N.Y., 1968—. Mem. Phi Beta (nat. pres. 1974—; scholarship 1954, 3 achievement awards), Alpha Chi Omega. Republican. Presbyterian. Clubs: Viking Yacht (pres. aux. 1976-77) (Norwalk); Eastern Packard. Address: Shorefront Park South Norwalk CT 06854

MILLER, CHARLES NORMAN, educator; b. Balt., Nov. 7, 1943; s. Joseph S. and Elizabeth A. (Hill) M.; B.S., Towson State Coll., 1965, postgrad., 1965-67; M.Ed., Johns Hopkins U., 1967, certificate Advanced Study in Edn., 1969; postgrad. Loyola Coll., Balt., Towson State Coll., 1969—. Admissions/registrations asst. Towson State

Coll., Balt., 1961-65; hydrologic field asst. U.S. Geol. Survey, 1964-65; tchr. geography, U.S. history, world affairs, counselor Balt. City Schs., 1965-70; tchr., vocat. and career devel. counselor, job placement coordinator Bd. Edn. Baltimore County, Balt., 1970—. Mem. Dundalk Drug Abuse Com., 1972—. Mem. Am. Personnel and Guidance Assn., Nat. Vocat. Guidance Assn., Am. Vocat. Assn., Am. Assn. Geographers, Am. Geog. Soc., Towson State Coll. Alumni Assn. (dir.), Phi Delta Kappa (editor univ. frat. Bull. 1971—), Gamma Theta Upsilon. Democrat. Baptist. Club: Masons (32 deg.). Asso. editor Directory of Educational Specialists, 1972. Home: 1900 Weyburn Rd Baltimore MD 21237

MILLER, CHARLES RICHARD, coll. dean; b. Elmira, N.Y., May 1, 1924; s. Charles Hooker and Florence Rena (Brand) M.; B.A., Hobart Coll., 1949; M.Ed., St. Lawrence U., 1952; postgrad. (Esso Safety Found. fellow), N.Y. U., 1954-58; m. Gwendolyn Virginia Davis, June 29, 1946; children—Charles Edward, Carol Ann Miller Carlin. Tchr., Elmira Free Acad., also Southside High Sch., Elmira, N.Y., 1949-56; vice prin. Southside High Sch., Elmira, 1956-58; supr. N.Y. State Edn. Dept., Albany, 1958-60; prin. Maine-Endwell Sr. High Sch., Endwell, N.Y., 1960-65, asst. supt. Maine-Endwell Central Schs., 1965-67; supt. schs. Sodus (N.Y.) Central Sch. Dist., 1967-68, Carol Morgan Schs., Santo Domingo, Dominican Republic, 1968-69; dean of admissions Elmira Coll., 1969—, mem. continuing edn. faculty, criminal justice program, 1976—, acting coordinator criminal justice program, 1977—. Pres. Chemung County Safety Council, 1954-56; organizer, dir. Traffic Violators Sch., Elmira, 1956-58; v.p. Chemung County PTA, Elmira, 1957-58; chmn. Elmira Traffic Safety Bd., 1954-58; mem. Gov.'s Traffic Safety Com., 1958-60; chmn. Chemung County Disaster Preparedness Com., 1975—, Chemung County Traffic Safety Bd., 1976—. Served with USAAF, 1942-45; prisoner of war Germany; with USAFR. Decorated Air medal, Purple Heart; named Young Man of Year, Elmira, 1957. Mem. NEA, N.Y. Edn. Assn., N.Y. Sch. Adminstrs. Assn., Nat., N.Y. State assns. coll. admissions counselors, Am. Assn. Collegiate Registrars and Admissions Officers, European Council Internat. Schs., N.Y. State, Chemung County deps. assns., N.Y. State Sheriffs Assn., C. of C. Elmira (dir. 1972-74), Am. Legion. Republican. Congregationalist. Clubs: Rotary (pres. 1978), Elmira Country, Masons (Elmira). Home: 88 Greenridge Dr W Elmira NY 14905 Office: Elmira Coll Elmira NY 14901

MILLER, DALE LLOYD, electronics engr.; b. Lebanon, Pa., Nov. 21, 1941; s. Lloyd H. and Kathryn M. (Clay) M.; B.S.E.E. (Pa. Senatorial scholar), Pa. State U., 1963, postgrad. Capitol campus, 1975—; m. Marion L. Kitchen, Sept. 10, 1966; children—Ruth-Anne, Stephen L. Engring. trainee Olmsted AFB, Pa., summers 1962, 63; electronics engr. U.S. Naval Research Lab., Washington, 1963-64; cons. for industry Gatter & Diehl Inc., Harrisburg, Pa., 1965-66; devel. engr. Buell Envirotech, Lebanon, Pa., 1967; project engr. Terryphone Corp. div. ITT, Harrisburg, 1968—; vol. adviser to Pa. and U.S. govts. Tchr. electronics Keystone Area council Boy Scouts Am., 1974—; mem. nominating com. Ridgeway Ch. of Brethren, Harrisburg, 1973-76. Recipient award Nat. Math. Assn., 1959, Young Citizens' award Optomists Club, 1952; registered profl. engr., Pa. Mem. Am. Security Council Found., IEEE, Triangle Engring. Frat. Ind. Republican. Patentee resettable over current-protected D.C. power supply. Home: 1419 Ford Ave Harrisburg PA 17109 Office: ITT 300 E Park Dr Harrisburg PA 17111

MILLER, DAVID THOMAS, broadcasting exec.; b. Chgo., July 13, 1925; s. William Henry and Doris Marie (Jones) M.; B.S., Loyola U., Chgo., 1950; postgrad. U. Chgo., 1950-51; L.H.D., St. John's U., 1974; m. Miriam Therese Koenig, May 16, 1953; children—Thomas, William, Mary, Julia, Lawrence. Asst. research dir. ABC, Chgo., 1950-51; sales service mgr. CBS Television Network, Chgo., 1951-53; account exec. CBS-TV, N.Y.C., 1954-61; v.p., gen. mgr. WLS-TV, Chgo., 1961-66; asst. to pres. CBS Broadcast Group, N.Y.C., 1966-70, v.p., 1977—; pres. CBS TV Stas. div. CBS, Inc., N.Y.C., 1970-77. Bd. dirs. Big Brothers, Inc., Catholic Apostolate of Radio, Television and Advt. Served to 2d lt. USAAF, 1943-46. Mem. Internat. Radio and Television Soc. (dir.), Television Bur. Advt. (dir.), Advt. Council (dir.). Roman Catholic. Clubs: Bronxville (N.Y.) Field; Winged Foot Golf (Mamaroneck, N.Y.). Home: 25 Ridge Rd Bronxville NY 10708 Office: 524 W 57th St New York City NY 10019

MILLER, DONALD LE SESSNE, mfg. co. exec.; b. N.Y.C., Jan. 10, 1932; s. John Hill and Mamie (Johnson) M.; B.A. with high honors, U. Md., 1967; postgrad. Harvard U., 1969; m. Ann Davie, Aug. 12, 1951; children—Lynn Ann, Mark Lamar. Commd. 2d lt. U.S. Army, 1956, advanced through grades to maj., 1966, ret., 1968; spl. asst. to pres. Inmont Corp. N.Y., N.Y.C., 1968-70; v.p. indsl. relations Seatrain Shipbldg. Corp., Bklyn., 1970-71; dep. asst. sec. def. Dept. Def., Washington, 1971-73; v.p. for personnel mgmt. Columbia U., N.Y.C., 1973-78; dir. personnel devel. and adminstrn. Internat. Paper Co., N.Y.C., 1978—; dir. Bank of N.Y. Co., Bank of N.Y. Mem. adv. com. BEEP Program Nat. Urban League, 1970—; bd. dirs. Greater N.Y. Fund, N.Y.C.; mem. nat. bd. govs. USO, Washington; trustee Pace U. Decorated Legion of Merit; recipient Distinguished Civilian Service medal Dept. Def., 1973. Mem. Alpha Phi Alpha, Sigma Pi Phi, Pi Sigma Alpha, Alpha Sigma Lambda, Phi Kappa Phi. Author: An Album of Black Americans in the Armed Forces, 1969. Office: 220 E 42d St New York NY 10017

MILLER, ELAINE JULIA, chiropractor, occupational therapist; b. Trenton, N.J., Aug. 21, 1950; d. Alexander and Bertha (Kovacs) Miller; A.A., Bucks County Community Coll., 1970; B.S. in Occupational Therapy, Temple U., 1972; student Columbia Inst. Chiropractic, 1973-76; Occupational therapist Hosp. of U. Pa., 1972-73; intern Columbia Inst. Chiropractic. Mem. Am. (registered), Pa. occupational therapy assns., Am. (council roentgenology), Internat., N.Y., N.J., Pa., Bucks County chiropractic assns., So. N.J. Chiropractic Soc. (editor newsletter, sec. 1976-77), World Fedn. Occupational Therapists, Met. Sacro Occipital Therapy Research Assn. (treas. 1977-78), Council Women Chiropractors, Parker Chiropractic Research Found., Assn. Research and Enlightenment, Sacro Occipital Research Soc. Internat., Bucks County Community Coll. Alumni, Temple U. Alumni, Club: Union Fire Co. Women's Aux. Home: 714 Crown St Morrisville PA 19067 also 24 Wilkins Ave Haddonfield NJ 08033 Office: 24 Wilkins Ave Haddonfield NJ 08033

MILLER, ELLEN LOUISE, librarian; b. Newark, Feb. 26, 1947; d. Frederick Lindsey and Helen Rita (Fitzpatrick) Miller; A.B., Chestnut Hill Coll., 1968; M.L.S., Columbia U., 1972. Asst. librarian First Boston Corp., 1968-74; head librarian White, Weld & Co., Inc., N.Y.C., 1974-78; mgr. research service Booz, Allen & Hamilton, N.Y.C., 1978—. Mem. Spl. Libraries Assn. (treas. N.Y. chpt.), N.Y. Library Club (mem. council). Home: 40 East End Ave Apt 3C New York City NY 10028 Office: 245 Park Ave New York City NY 10017

MILLER, FRANCES ELIZABETH, ednl. adminstr.; b. Lunenburg County, Va., July 5, 1938; d. Walter Woodrow and Janie Bell (Wallace) Watson; diploma Roanoke Meml. Hosp., 1959; B.S. in Nursing, U. Md., 1977; m. Douglas C. Miller, Sept. 20, 1969; children—Angela, Kimberly. Staff nurse Union Meml. Hosp., Annapolis, Md., 1961-63; staff nurse Anne Arundel County Health Dept., Annapolis, 1963-64; bldg. supr. Crownsville (Md.) State Hosp., 1964-65; staff nurse, instr., nursing supr. Anne Arundel Gen. Hosp., 1965-77: adminstr. ednl. programs div. licensing and certification Dept. Health and Mental Hygiene, Balt., 1977—. Mem. Am., Md. nurses assns. Home: 306 Cypress Creek Rd Severna Park MD 21146 Office: 201 W Preston St Baltimore MD 21201

MILLER, FREDERICK, pathologist; b. N.Y.C., Apr. 5, 1937; s. Alex and Sarah M.; B.S., U. Wis., 1956; M.D., N.Y. U., 1961; m. Emilie J. Kronish, June 2, 1962; children—David, Allison. Intern, Bellevue Hosp., N.Y.C., 1961-62, resident, 1962-63; practice medicine specializing in pathology, 1965—; clin. asso., attending physician Nat. Inst. Arthritis and Metabolic Diseases, 1963-65, resident, chief pathology dept. N.Y. U. Med. Center, 1965-67; attending pathologist Bellevue and U. Hosps., N.Y.C., 1967; asst. prof. pathology N.Y. U., 1967-70, asso. prof., 1970; asso. prof. pathology State U. N.Y., Stony Brook, 1970-75, prof., 1975—, acting chmn. dept. pathology, 1977—, dir. lab for arthritis and related diseases, 1976—; dir. labs. Univ. Hosp., Stony Brook, 1978—. Served with USPHS, 1963-65. Recipient Bausch & Lomb Medal for Research, 1961; Am. Soc. Clin. Pathologists award, 1961; NIH grantee, 1963—. Diplomate Am. Bd. Pathology. Mem. Harvey Soc., Am. Soc. Exptl. Pathology, Reticuloendothelial Soc., AAAS, Am. Assn. Pathol. Bacteriology. Contbr. articles in field to med. jours. Hort. authority on roses. Home: 46 Manchester Ln Stony Brook NY 11790 Office: Dept Path HSC-SUSB Stony Brook NY 11794

MILLER, G(EORGE) WILLIAM, govt. ofcl.; b. Sapulpa, Okla., Mar. 9, 1925; s. James Dick and Hazle Deane (Orrick) M.; B.S., USCG Acad. 1945; J.D. U. Calif., Berkeley, 1952; m. Ariadna Rogojarsky, Dec. 22, 1946. Admitted to Calif. bar, 1952, N.Y. bar, 1953; with firm Cravath, Swaine & Moore, N.Y.C., 1952-60; with Textron Inc., Providence, 1956-78, v.p., 1956-57, treas., 1958-59, pres., dir., 1960-74, chmn., chief exec. officer, dir., 1974-78; chmn. bd. govs. FRS, Washington, 1978—; dir. Fed. Res. Bank Boston, 1971-78, Allied Chem. Corp., 1973-78, ConRail, 1976-78, Federated Dept. Stores, 1977-78. Chmn. adv. council Pres.'s Com. on Equal Employment Opportunity 1963-65; mem. council Nat. Found. on Humanities, 1966-67; bd. dirs. USLG Acad. Found., 1969-78, pres., 1973-77, chmn., 1977-78; chmn. U.S. Indsl. Payroll Savs. Bond Com., 1977, Pres.'s Com. on HIRE; co-chmn. Polish-U.S. Econ. Council. Mem. State Bar Calif., Nat. Alliance Businessmen (dir. 1968-78, chmn. 1977-78), Conf. Bd. (trustee 1972-78, chmn. 1977-78), Order of Coif, Phi Delta Phi. Clubs: Lyford Cay (Nassau, Bahamas): Acoaxet (Westport, Mass.); Squantum Assn., Hope, Turks Head, University, Agawam Hunt (Providence); Brook (N.Y.C.). Office: Fed Res Bd Washington DC 20551

MILLER, (RICHARD) GUY, sculptor, ret. mil. officer, educator; b. Pitts. Oct. 27, 1917; s. John Thomas and Florence Ann (Sohner) M.; B.A. in Chemistry, U. Conn., 1956; postgrad. Heatherley Sch. of Fine Arts, also City and Guilds of London Art Council, London, 1958, Art Students League, N.Y.C., 1961-63; M.F.A., Pratt Inst., 1965; m. Gertrude Ann Hinst, Dec. 28, 1948; 1 son, Richard Guy. Commd. 2d lt. USAAF, 1943, advanced through grades to lt. col. USAF, 1955; engring. officer U.K. and Europe, 1943-49; asso. prof. AFROTC, U. Conn., 1950-54; exec. officer, dep. chief staff installations 3d Air Force, London, 1955-59; airbase engr. Stewart AFB, N.Y., 1960-63, ret., 1963; instr. sculpture Pratt Inst., Bklyn., 1965, West Long br. Monmouth (N.J.) Coll., 1966-69; artist-in-residence Friends World Coll., Huntington, N.Y., 1977-78; one-man shows of sculpture include: Pratt Inst., Bklyn., 1965, Caravan Gallery, N.Y.C., 1967, 68, Shelter Rock Library, 1972, Syosset (N.Y.) Library, 1972, Manhasset (N.Y.) Pub. Library, 1974, Ward-Nasse Gallery, N.Y.C., 1976, 78; group shows include: Royal Soc. Water Colorists, London, 1956, Bethlehem Art Gallery, New Windsor, N.Y., 1960, El Paso, Tex., 1962, State U. Coll., New Paltz, N.Y., 1963, Monmouth Coll., 1967, 68, Selected Artists Gallery, N.Y.C., 1970, Maury Mark Gallery, Great Neck, N.Y., 1970, Patrick Galleries, P.R., 1973, Nantucket Gallery, 1973, Trianon Gallery, N.Y.C., 1975, Lever House, N.Y.C., 1976, Parish Mus., Southampton, N.Y., 1976, Elsen Gallery, N.Y.C., Himplefarb Gallery, Watermill, N.Y., 1977, Caumsett Park, Huntington, N.Y., 1978, Lincoln Center, N.Y.C., 1978; represented in permanent collections: Pratt Inst., State U. N.Y., New Paltz, Jericho (N.Y.) Pub. Library, Betty Parsons, N.Y.C., Manhasset Pub. Library, New Sch., N.Y.C., also pvt. collections. Louis Comfort Tiffany Found. grantee, 1966; MacDowell Colony fellow, 1968; certified tchr., N.Y. State. Mem. Art Students League (life). Address: 25 Minetta Ln New York City NY 10012

MILLER, HAROLD, cons. engr., developer; b. Poughkeepsie, N.Y., June 8, 1916; s. Samuel and Esther (Rolnick) M.; B.S. in Civil Engring., U. Mo., 1940; m. Anne Oqul, July 24, 1942; children—James Philip, Paul Alan, Jane Ellen. Field engr. Stone & Webster Engring. Co., Boston, 1940-43; pres., constrn. mgr. S.H. Miller Constrn. Co., Inc., Poughkeepsie, 1947-65; pres. Harold Miller Enterprises, Poughkeepsie, 1965—; dir. Electronic Missiles & Communications, Inc., Square Buff, Inc. Registered profl. engr. and land surveyor, N.Y. Mem. Poughkeepsie C. of C. (treas.), N.Y. State Soc. Profl. Engrs. Home: 26 Miller Rd Poughkeepsie NY 12603 Office: 85 Market St Poughkeepsie NY 12601

MILLER, HARRY, JR., hosp. adminstr.; b. Balt., June 24, 1943; s. Harry and Earline Miller; B.A. in Sociology, U. Md., 1971; postgrad. Johns Hopkins U., 1975-76; m. Mattie L. Turner, July 1, 1976; 1 son, Gregery Wade. Personnel asst. Rosewood State Hosp., Center, Owings Mills, 1973-77; dir. personnel Walter P. Carter Center, Balt., 1977—. Served with AUS, 1965-68; Vietnam. Mem. Internat. Personnel Mgmt. Assn., Am. Soc. Tng. and Devel., United Properties Assn., N.W. Civic Forum, Nat. Black Vets. Orgn. Baptist.

MILLER, HELENA A., educator; b. Rudolph, Ohio, Apr. 25, 1913; d. Royal James and Bertha (Hansen) Miller; B.A., Ohio State U., 1935, B.S. in Edn., 1935, M.S., 1938; Ph.D., Radcliffe Coll., Harvard U., 1945. Tchr., dean of girls Montgomery Twp. High Sch., Wayne, Ohio, 1935-37; asst. botany Ohio State U., Columbus, 1938-39; lectr. biology Hiram Coll. (Ohio), 1939; biology instr. Milton (Mass.) Acad., 1939-40, biology instr., head sci. in lower sch., 1940-41; teaching fellow in biology Radcliffe Coll., Cambridge, Mass., 1942-43, Harvard U., 1943-44; cons. to War Dept., 1944; botany instr. Conn. Coll. Women, New London, Conn., 1944-45, Wellesley Coll., Wellesley, Mass., 1945-48; asso. prof. biology Duquesne U., Pitts., 1948-59, prof., 1959-78, asst. dean of Coll. of Arts and Sci. for advt., 1966-76, asst. dean spl. studies, 1976-78. Mem. Bot. Soc. Am. (vice chmn. teaching sect. 1966, chmn. 1967), Taxonomic Soc. Am., Nat. Geog. Soc., Am. Assn. U. Adminstrs. (com. growth devel.), Nat. Sci. Tchrs. Assn., Internat. Assn. Plant Morphologists, Pa. Cath. Round Table Sci. (past exec. sec.-treas.), Western Pa. Conservancy, Phi Beta Kappa, Sigma Xi, Alpha Epsilon Delta, Sigma Pi Sigma, Phi Epsilon Phi. Contbr. numerous articles to profl. jours. Home: 532 Highview Rd Pittsburgh PA 15234

MILLER, HENRY, III, coll. ofcl.; b. Tuskegee, Ala., Mar. 3, 1948; s. Henry and Annie B. (White) M.; B.A., Talladega Coll., 1971; M.Ed., Tuskegee Inst., 1976. Grad. asst. to dean Sch. Edn., Tuskegee Inst. (Ala.), 1972-73; lab. technician N.Y. U., N.Y.C., 1973-75; asst. to registrar Western Md. Coll., Westminster, 1977—. Tuskegee Inst. grad. fellow, 1972-73. Mem. Am. Personnel and Guidance Assn., Am., Middle State assns. collegiate registrars, Kappa Delta Pi. Methodist. Office: Office of Registrar Western Md Coll Westminster MD 21157

MILLER, HENRY GEORGE, lawyer; b. Bklyn., Feb. 18, 1931; s. Henry A. and Anne T. (Withers) M.; B.A., St. John's U., Bklyn., 1952, J.D., 1959; postgrad. Columbia U., 1954-55, N.Y.U., 1960; m. Helena M. McCarty, Aug. 2, 1958; children—Jennifer, Henry, Matthew, Margaret. Admitted to N.Y. bar, 1959; mem. firm Lawless and Lynch, N.Y.C., 1959-62; partner firms Bachkoff, Miller & Steger, N.Y.C., 1962-67, Clark Gagliardi & Miller, White Plains, N.Y., 1967—; lectr. in field. Served with U.S. Army, Korea. Fellow Am. Coll. Trial Lawyers, Internat. Acad. Trial Lawyers, Am., N.Y. bar founds.; mem. Am., N.Y. State, Westchester County (pres. 1975-77) bar assns., Internat. Assn. Ins. Counsel, Fedn. Ins. Counsel, Assn. Trial Lawyers Am., N.Y. State Trial Lawyers Assn. (dir.), Def. Assn. N.Y. (dir.). Roman Catholic. Contbr. articles to profl. pubis. Office: Inns of Court 99 Court St White Plains NY 10601

MILLER, IRVING WILLIAM, pub. accountant, fin. cons.; b. Bklyn., Dec. 15, 1914; s. Louis L. and Lina (Levinson) M.; B.B.A., Dowling Coll., 1973; m. Sylvia Finkelstein, June 8, 1941; children—Gale Miller Fingerman, Andrew M. Examiner municipal affairs N.Y. state comptroller, 1944-56; chief audits and accounts for Suffolk County, Riverhead, N.Y., 1956-72; dir. fin. mgmt. Suffolk County Med. Assistance Adminstrn., Hauppauge, N.Y., 1973—. Pres., Suffolk Fed. Credit Union, 1968-78. Mem. Assn. Govt. Accts., Met. Solar Energy Soc., Nat. Assn. Accts. Republican. Jewish. Club: Elks. Compiler manual of fiscal procedures for local govts. Home: 39 Chestnut St Huntington NY 11743

MILLER, JASON, psychiatrist; b. N.Y.C., Dec. 26, 1913; s. Samuel and Cecelia (Keshin) M.; B.S., Columbia, 1935; M.D., Royal Coll. Physicians and Surgeons Edinburgh, 1940; certified analyst Am. Inst. Psychoanalysis, 1959; Ph.D., Southeastern U., 1972; m. Barbara Adelman, Sept. 20, 1947 (div.). Intern, Met. Hosp., N.Y.C.; resident psychiatry State U. N.Y., 1946-49; sr. psychiatrist Bellevue Hosp. Center, 1952-72, also mem. med. bd.; pvt. practice psychiatry and psychoanalysis, N.Y.C., 1949—; asst. attending psychiatrist U. Hosp., 1965-73; faculty N.Y. U. Sch. Medicine, 1965-73; prof. clin. edn. Southeastern U., 1971-72; asst. clin. prof. psychiatry Albert Einstein Coll. Medicine, 1972-74; vis. prof. New Sch. Social Research, 1971—; dir. psychiatry Bklyn. Correctional Instn. N.Y. Dept. Health, 1974—; lectr. Am. Inst. Psychoanalysis, 1964—. Served with USPHS, 1942-46. Diplomate Am. Bd. Psychiatry and Neurology. Fellow Am. Acad. Psychoanalysis, Am. Psychiat. Assn., Internat. Soc. for Existential Psychiatry (pres.), Royal Coll. Physicians and Surgeons, Am. Assn. Psychoanalytic Physicians. Office: 147 E 50th St New York City NY 10022

MILLER, JEANNE-MARIE ANDERSON (MRS. NATHAN JOHN MILLER), educator, adminstr.; b. Washington, Feb. 18, 1937; d. William and Agnes Catherine (Johns) Anderson; B.A., Howard U., 1959, M.A., 1963, Ph.D., 1976; m. Nathan John Miller, Oct. 2, 1960. Instr. dept. English Howard U., Washington, 1963-76, asst. prof., 1976—, also asst. dir. Inst. Arts and Humanities, 1973-75, asst. acad. planning office v.p. for Acad. Affairs, 1976—; cons. Am. Studies Assn., 1972—, Silver Burdett Pub. Co., Nat. Endowment for Humanities, 1978—; adv. bd. D.C. Library for Arts, 1973—, John Oliver Killens Writers Guild, 1975—, Afro-Am. Theatre, Balt., 1975—. Mem. Washington Performing Arts Soc., 1971—, Friends of WETA-TV, 1971—, Mus. African Art, 1971—, Arena Stage Assos., 1972—. Ford Found. fellow, 1970-72; So. Fellowships Fund fellow, 1972-74; Howard U. research grantee, 1975-76; Am. Council Learned Socs. grantee, 1978-79. Mem. Nat. Council Tchrs. of English, Coll. English Assn., Am. Studies Assn., Am. Theatre Assn., AAUP, AAUW, D.C. LWV, Common Cause, Civil Liberties Union, Am. Acad. Polit. and Social Sci., Coll. Lang. Assn., Modern Lang. Assn., Am. Assn. Higher Edn., Friends Kennedy Center for Performing Arts. Democrat. Episcopalian. Contbr. articles in field to profl. jours. Home: 1100 6th St SW Washington DC 20024

MILLER, JOEL ROBERT, psychologist; b. Gadsen, Ala., May 22, 1944; s. Raymond and Frances (Bratman) M.; B.A., Hawthorne Coll., 1967; M.S., Kan. State Coll., 1968; D.Psychology, Rutgers U., 1978; children—Cammie, Scott. Clin. intern psychologist Am. Inst. Mental Studies, Vineland, N.J., 1968-69, staff psychologist, 1969-70; sch. psychologist, Bridgeton (N.J.) Pub. Schs., 1970-71; clin. psychol. cons. Leesburg (N.J.) State Prison, 1971-75; sch. psychologist, dir. spl. edn. Pleasantville (N.J.) Pub. Schs., 1971-72; chief psychology cons. White House Spl. Action Office for Drug Abuse Prevention, Exec. Office of Pres., Washington, 1973-74; dir. psychol. services NARCO, Atlantic City, 1973-76; cons. CETA-Atlantic County, N.J. Vocat. Rehab. Commn., 1974—, Resource Planning Corp., Washington, 1976—, Atlantic County Youth Service Shelter, 1976—, Manor Woods Acad., Estelle Manor, N.J., 1977—, Atlantic City Probation Dept., 1977—; also pvt. practice psychology. Pres. Cumberland City Drug Abuse Council; mem. adv. bd. Atlantic County Mental Health Bd.; bd. dirs. Family Services, 1977—. Mem. Council Exceptional Children (past pres. South Jersey chpt.), Am. Assn. Mental Deficiency, Nat. Assn. Sch. Psychologists, Am. Acad. Psychotherapists, Nat. Rehab. Assn., Royal Soc. Health. Home: 151 N Annapolis Ave Atlantic City NJ 08401

MILLER, JOHN A(DALBERT), ins. co. exec.; b. Wilkes-Barre, Pa., June 14, 1927; s. Joseph and Marie (Arenova) M.; A.B. in Econs., Columbia U., 1948; postgrad. Cornell U., 1949; m. Margaret Hausler, Aug. 14, 1945; children—Cynthia Miller Hibbert, Jeffrey, John, Kristen. Agt., Aetna Life and Casualty Co., 1949-58, acting gen. agt., 1956-58; cons. to v.p. co. relations Life Ins. Mktg. and Research Assn., Hartford, Conn., 1958-72; with Provident Mut. Life Ins. Co., 1972—, pres., chief operating officer, 1976-78, pres., chief exec. officer, 1978—; dir. Phila. Nat. Bank, Phila. Nat. Corp. Co-chmn. devel. fund campaign YMCA of Phila. and Vicinity, 1976-77, chmn. met. bd. dirs., 1978-79; elder Bryn Mawr (Pa.) Presbyterian Ch.; bd. dirs. Children's Hosp. Phila., Food Distbn. Center, Phila., Phila. Drama Guild, Univ. City Sci. Center, Phila. Served with USMC, 1945-46. C.L.U. Mem. Ins. Fedn. Pa. (exec. com., dir.). Republican. Club: Overbrook. Author: What You Should Know About Permanent Life Insurance, 1962; Getting More Out of Life, 1968; contbr. articles to periodicals. Home: 1946 Montgomery Ave Villanova PA 19085 Office: PO Box 7378 4601 Market St Philadelphia PA 19101

MILLER, JOHN LEWIS, health care adminstr.; b. Phila., Sept. 24, 1940; s. Malcolm White and Elaine (Crossett) M.; B.A., Westminster Coll., New Wilmington, Pa., 1964; M.B.A. in Health Care Adminstrn., George Washington U., 1967; m. Susan Hale, June 18, 1965; children—Jonathan Lee, Matthew White. Asst. adminstr. Dauphin County Hosp., Harrisburg, Pa., 1967-69; dir. Westmoreland Manor, Greensburg, Pa., 1969-70; adminstr. Broomall (Pa.) Presbyterian Home, 1970-77; v.p. Phila. Presbytery Homes, Inc., 1977-78; exec. v.p. Maine Health Care Assn., Augusta, 1978—; founder, 1968, since pres. Geriatric Mgmt. Assos.; lectr. Elizabethtown Coll., others; cons. in field. Fellow Am. Coll. Nursing Home Adminstrs.; mem. Am., Pa. hosp. assns., Am. Health Care Assn., Pa. Assn. Non-Profit Homes for Aging, Alumni Assn. George Washington U., Chi Psi, Alpha Alpha. Author papers in field. Home:

County Rd RFD 2 Box 20 Richmond ME 04357 Office: 99 Western Ave Augusta ME 04330

MILLER, JOHN NELSON, banker; b. Youngstown, Ohio, Sept. 15, 1948; s. W. Frederic and Julia Elizabeth (Lohman) M.; Mus. B. in Cello, Westminster Coll., 1970; M.B.A. in Finance, Wharton Sch. Finance, U. Pa., 1974; m. Lynnette McDonald, May 31, 1974. Asst. br. mgr. Mahoning Nat. Bank, Youngstown, 1970-72; asst. dir. fin. services dept. Mellon Bank N.Am., Pitts., 1974-75; dir. cash mgmt. div. Md. Nat. Bank, Balt., 1976-77; v.p. Bank of Am., 1978—, also head cash mgmt. div. N.Y. office; lectr. Wharton Grad. Sch., Am. Mgmt. Assn., cash mgmt. seminars; speaker Payment Systems Inc., also mem. corp. payment task force; mem. Corporate EFT Cost/Benefit Task Force, Bank Adminstrn. Inst. Mem. Wharton Grad. Alumni Assn. (pres., local club, rep.), Am. Nat. Standards Inst., Cash Mgmt. Inst. (dir.), Omicron Delta Kappa. Clubs: Merchants, University of Pitts., Balt. Rotary. Contbr. articles to profl. publs. Office: 299 Park Ave New York City NY 10017

MILLER, JOHN PETER (JACK), newspaper columnist; b. Peterborough, Ont., Can., Aug. 3, 1928; s. Wesley and Margaret (Baker) M.; ed. Welland and Toronto, Ont.; m. Helen DeMars, July 30, 1949; 1 son, Gregory. Sports editor to front page editor Welland Evening Tribune, 1949-53; with Hamilton (Ont.) Spectator, 1953-71, radio and TV columnist, 1955-71; radio and TV columnist Toronto (Ont.) Daily Star, 1971—, frequent TV and radio appearances. Named leading daily columnist Western Ont., 1968. Mem. Sigma Delta Chi, Chgo. Journalistic Soc. Contbr. stories to mags. Home: 44 Charles St W Apt 3809 Toronto ON Canada Office: 1 Yonge St Toronto ON Canada

MILLER, JOHN ROBINSON, JR., publisher; b. La Grange, Ill., Jan. 19, 1914; s. John Robinson and Helen Dora (Smythe) M.; student St. Paul's Sch., Garden City, N.Y., Goldey Bus. Coll., Wilmington, Del., 1933-34; m. Helen Elizabeth Fulton, June 14, 1935; children—Dale Dunlap, John Robinson III, Mark Fulton. With Hearst Magazines, Inc., N.Y.C., 1934—, successively clk. circulation dept., agy. mgr., trade mgr., subscription sales dir., asst. treas., asst. gen. mgr., 1934-55, v.p., circulation dir., asst. gen. mgr., 1955-62, v.p., gen. mgr. 1962-67, exec. v.p., gen. mgr., 1967-73, exec. v.p. The Hearst Corp., 1973-74, pres., chief exec., 1975—, also dir.; v.p. Internat. Circulation Co., N.Y.C., 1945-50; asst. treas. Hearst Corp., 1952-55; v.p., asst. treas., dir. Periodical Publishers Service Bur., Inc., Sandusky, Ohio, 1953-55, pres., dir., 1963-70, chmn. bd., 1970-71, v.p., dir. Popular Mechanics Co., 1958-59, Science Digest Co., 1958-59, Good Housekeeping, Inc.; dir., chmn. bd. Nat. Mag. Co., London; dir. S.W. Forest Industries, Am. Home Products Corp. Trustee St. Paul's Sch., Garden City, William Randolph Hearst Found., The Hearst Found. Dir., vice chmn. Audit Bur. Circulations, chmn. bd. central registry, 1957-58, dir., 1958; bd. dirs. Nat. Better Bus. Bur., 1961-70, chmn. bd., 1966-68; bd. dirs. ABBI, 1968-70; bd. dirs. Council of Better Bus. Burs., 1970-71. Recipient Pub. Industry Anti-Defamation League award, 1972, Lee C. Williams award, 1975; Henry T. Zwisner Meml. award, 1976. Episcopalian. Club: Cherry Valley Golf (Garden City); Metropolitan (N.Y.C.). Home: 18 Wellington Rd Garden City NY 11530 also Falls Drive Buck Hill Falls PA 18323 Office: 959 8th Ave New York City NY 10019

MILLER, JOSEPH ARTHUR, elec. mfg. co. exec.; b. Irvington, N.J., June 16, 1932; s. Charles W. and Josephine M. (Koermaier) M.; B.S.E.E., Newark Coll. Engring. (now N.J. Inst. Tech.), 1960; m. Kathleen M. Kelly, Sept. 7, 1963; children—Colleen, Joseph, Mark, Patricia. Order service clk. Gen. Electric Co., Newark, 1948-52, price edit clk., 1952-54, sales engrs. asst., 1956-60, sales engr. power transmission, 1960-77; pres. High Voltage Breakers Inc., Phila., 1977—, also dir.; U.S. del. Internat. Conf. Large High-Voltage Electric Systems (CIGRE). Mem. exec. council Shongum Lake Property Owners Assn., 1972-73. Served with U.S. Army, 1954-56. R.H. Rice scholar, 1950. Mem. IEEE, Phi Eta Sigma, Tau Beta Pi. Roman Catholic. Club: Engrs. Phila. Home: 1108 Wooded Way Dr Media PA 19063 Office: High Voltage Breakers Inc 6901 Elmwood Ave Philadelphia PA 19142

MILLER, KENNETH LEWIS, aerospace engr.; b. Bellefonte, Pa., Mar. 30, 1952; s. Robert Leon and Lois (Hoy) M.; B.S., Pa. State U., 1974. Aerospace engr. Naval Air Devel. Center, Warminster, Pa., 1974—. Mem. Am. Inst. Aeros. and Astronautics. Home: English Village Apts Bldg 11 Room A-8 North Wales PA 19454 Office: Naval Air Devel Center Code 403413 Warminster PA 18974

MILLER, KENNETH MICHAEL, electronics co. exec.; b. Chgo., Nov. 20, 1921; s. Matthew and Tillie (Otto) M.; student Ill. Inst. Tech., 1940-41, U. Calif. at Los Angeles, 1961; m. Dolores June Hagstrom, Jan. 16, 1943 (dec. Dec. 1968); children—Barbara Anne Woodcock, Nancy Jeanne Hathaway, Kenneth Michael II, Roger Allan; m. 2d, Sally J. Ballingham, June 20, 1970. Electronics engr. Rauland Corp., Chgo., 1941-48; gen. mgr. Lear, Inc., Santa Monica, Calif., 1948-59; v.p., gen. mgr. Motorola Aviation Electronics, Inc., Culver City, Calif., 1959-60; v.p., gen. mgr. Instrument div. Daystrom, Inc. subsidiary Schlumberger, Inc., Los Angeles, 1961; gen. mgr. Metrics div. Singer Co., Bridgeport, Conn., 1962-65; v.p., gen. mgr. Lear Jet Corp., 1965-66; pres., dir. Infonics Inc., 1967-68; v.p., gen. mgr. Computer Industries, Inc., 1968-69; dir. operations, tech. products group Am. Standard Corp., McLean, Va., also v.p., gen. mgr. Wilcox Electric div., Kansas City, Mo., 1969-71; pres., dir. Wilcox Electric, Inc. subsidiary Northrop Corp., 1971-73; v.p., dir. Worldwide Wilcox, Inc., McLean, Va.; pres., chief exec. officer, dir., mem. exec. com. Penril Corp., Rockville, Md., 1973—. Mem. regional planning council Community Mental Health Services, Bridgeport, 1964, mem. Bridgeport Capital Fund Com.; trustee Park City Hosp., bd. dirs. U. Bridgeport. Recipient Job Makers award Mfrs. Assn. Bridgeport, 1963. Mem. Aircraft Owners and Pilots Assn., Am. Inst. Aeros. and Astronautics, Am. Mgmt. Assn., Armed Forces Communications and Electronics Assn., Electronic Industries Assn., IEEE, Instrument Soc. Am., Nat. Aero. Assn., Soc. Non-Destructive Testing, Soc. Automotive Engrs., Air Force Assn., Am. Radio Relay League, Quarter Century Wireless Assn., Mfrs. Assn. Bridgeport (dir.), Bridgeport Engring. Inst., C. of C. (pres., 1964). Clubs: Rolling Hills Country (Wichita); Algonquin (Bridgeport). Contbr. articles to profl. jours. Home: 16904 George Washington Dr Rockville MD 20853 Office: Penril Corp 5520 Randolph Rd Rockville MD 20852

MILLER, LOIS ANDERSON, cons., former newspaper editor; b. Morgantown, W.Va., Mar. 24, 1928; d. George A. and Jean (Long) Anderson; student Indiana U. of Pa., 1948-49; B.A., Temple U., 1951, M.S. in Edn., U. Pa., 1951; m. Willard E. Miller, Apr. 19, 1974; children by previous marriage—Alan Hepler, Harold Hepler, Margaret Jean Hepler. News editor, reporter Canonsburg Daily Notes, Ind. Evening Gazette, Germantown Courier and Montgomery Pub. Co., 1941-78; mng. editor Montgomery Pub. Co. (Jenkintown Times Chronicle, Glenside News, Huntingdon Valley Globe), Jenkintown, Pa., 1971-78; journalism cons., free lance writer, Jenkintown, 1978—; cons. Temple U. Sch. Journalism. Mem. ad hoc police study commn., Jenkintown, 1976, 77. Recipient Pa. Newswoman of Yr. award, 1965, 72, 73; recipient numerous state and nat. press competition awards; recipient citation Pa. Ho. of Reps., 1969. Mem. Pa. Women's Press Assn., Pa. Soc. Newspaper Editors, Internat. Press Club, Phila Press Assn., DAR, Ga. Air N.G. (hon.), Old York Rd. Hist. Soc., Sigma Delta Chi. Democrat. Home and Office: 416 Leedom St Jenkintown PA 19046

MILLER, LOTHAR KURT, apparel co. exec.; b. Phila., Mar. 5, 1944; s. Lothar Helmut and Margaret (Thorp) M.; A.B. in Econs., Muhlenberg Coll., 1965; A.B. in Psychology, Temple U., 1966; m. Doris Judith Baker, June 19, 1965; children—Stephen, Katherine, David. Dir. mfg. Miss Quality Inc., Phila., 1966-76; asst. to pres. Penn Pad Co., Phila., 1976—; bd. chmn., pres. S.K.M. Investments Inc., Hatboro, Pa., 1968--. Address: 233 E Moreland Ave Hatboro PA 19040

MILLER, MARGARET ELLIS, counselor, adminstr.; b. Peoria, Ill., Apr. 26, 1922; d. William Edward and Marie (Allton) Ellis; B.A. in Psychology, Bradley U., 1950; M.A. in Guidance and Counseling, Columbia U., 1968; m. Vincent A. Miller, Feb. 12, 1944; children—Pamela, Patrice, Carl. Guidance dir. Escola Americana do Rio de Janeiro (Brazil), 1963-66; tchr. psychology UN Internat. Sch., N.Y.C., 1966-76, dir. counseling, 1966—, chmn. sch. and coll. relations com. Internat. Baccalaureate, mem. Common Application Steering Com., 1977—; cons. entrance to foreign univs., fgn. student admission to Am. univs.; cons. on socio-affective edn. UNESCO, Hamburg, Germany, 1972, Tremsbuttel, Germany, 1973, Levy, Quebec, Can., 1973. NSF fellow in animal behavior State U. N.Y. at Potsdam, 1970, in psycho-biology Vanderbilt U., 1971. Mem. Am., N.Y. State, N.Y.C. personnel and guidance assns., Am. Sch. Counselor Assn., Assn. Measurement and Evaluations in Guidance, Nat. Assn. Coll. Admission Counselors, N.Y. State Assn. Coll. Admission Counselors, Nat. Assn. Fgn. Student Affairs, Am. Psychol. Assn. Presenter, lectr. and panelist to profl. confs.; contbr. book review, numerous articles in field to profl. jours. Home: 306 E 96th St New York City NY 10028 Office: 24-50 E River Dr New York City NY 10010

MILLER, MARIE DI STEFANO (MRS. PHILLIP MILLER), sociologist; b. Elizabeth, N.J., Feb. 13, 1942; s. Joseph and Philomena (Di Maggio) Di Stefano; B.A., Rutgers U., 1962; M.A., N.Y. U., 1967, also postgrad.; m. Phillip Miller, Mar. 15, 1970; 1 son, Douglas Stephen. Research asst. Union County (N.J.) Dist. Ct., 1961-62; tchr. 14th Ave. Sch., Newark, 1962-65; instr. sociology Caldwell (N.J.) Coll., 1965-67; asst. prof. Hartwick Coll., Oneonta, N.Y., 1967-70, Rutgers U., New Brunswick, N.J., 1970-73; adj. prof. sociology Seton Hall U., 1966-67, Kean Coll., 1971-72; pub. rep. bd. examiners N.J. Ophthalmic Dispensers and Ophthalmic Technicians, 1976—; head county tng. unit N.J. Dept. Corrections Officers Tng. Sch., Trenton, 1978—. Vice-chmn. Hillsborough (N.J.) Democratic municipal com., 1975-76; Dem. candidate for sheriff, N.J., 1976. NDEA fellow, 1963; NSF fellow, 1969. Mem. Eastern Sociol. Soc., Am. Sociol. Assn., Am. Correctional Assn., Nat. Inst. Criminology and Delinquency, LWV, Alpha Kappa Delta. Home: 3 Walker Dr Belle Mead NJ 08502

MILLER, MARY EMILY, historian; b. Wilmington, Del., Mar. 7, 1934; B.A. in History with distinction, U. Del., 1955; certificate Harvard-Radcliffe Program Bus. Adminstrn., 1956; M.A., Boston U., 1959, Ph.D., 1962. Sec. research com. Lemuel Shattuck Hosp., Harvard U., 1956-58; mem. staff registrar's office Radcliffe Coll., 1958-59; resident asst. Boston U., 1959-61; asst. prof. history, dean women Methodist Coll., Fayetteville, N.C., 1962-64, chmn. history dept. and social sci. area, 1963-64; asst. prof., dean women Park Coll., Parkville, Mo., 1964-66, acting chmn. dept., 1965; prof. history Salem (Mass.) State Coll., 1966—, coordinator grad. history programs, 1976-77, coordinator East European and Russian studies, 1978—; coordinator Mass. State Colls. Consortium, 1969-71; mem. Cumberland County (N.C.) Tercentennary Commn., 1963-64. Mem. Fayetteville Symphony Orch., 1962-64, St. Joseph Symphony Orch., 1964-66. Mem. Am. Hist. Assn., Orgn. Am. Historians, Am. Personnel and Guidance Assn., Am. Coll. Personnel Assn., Mass. Personnel Assn., Nat. Assn. Women Deans, Adminstrs. and Counselors, New Eng. Hist. Assn., New Eng. Women's Hist. Assn., Berkshire Conf., Soc. History Discoveries, N.Am. Oceanic History Assn., U.S. Naval Inst., Peabody Museum, Medieval Conf. New Eng., Renaissance Conf. New Eng., Renaissance Assn., AAUP (chpt. pres.), Phi Alpha Theta, Delta Tau Kappa. Contbr. articles to profl. publs. Address: 68 Washington St Marblehead MA 01945

MILLER, MAX, physician; b. N.Y.C., Jan. 28, 1911; s. Abraham and Sarah R. (Miller) M.; B.S., N.Y. U., 1931; M.D., U. Vienna (Austria), 1936; M.M.Sc. in Cardiology, U. Pa., 1940; m. Marion Miller. Intern, Beth David Hosp., N.Y.C., 1937-38, asst. vis. cardiologist, 1940-41, asso. attending, 1944-50, attending in charge cardiology, 1951-58; pvt. practice medicine specializing in cardiology, N.Y.C., 1940—; staff mem. Trafalgar Hosp., N.Y.C., now med. dir.; staff mem. Lincoln Hosp., N.Y.C., Grand Central Hosp., N.Y.C.; courtesy staff Drs. Hosp., N.Y.C.; asso. attending St. Clare's Hosp. and Med. Center, 1975—; instr. N.Y. U., 1946-58, asst. clin. prof., 1958—; cons. Mary Manning Walsh Home, N.Y.C., 1955—, N.Y.C. Sch. Health Service, 1945-46. Fellow Am. Coll. Cardiology; mem. N.Y. Cardiol. Soc. (pres.), N.Y. Power Squadron (comdr.) AMA, Am., N.Y. heart assns., N.Y. County, Rudolf Verchow med. socs., Am. Soc. Internal Medicine, Assn. Am. Med. Colls. Home: 169 E 88th St New York NY 10028 Office: 829 Park Ave New York NY 10021

MILLER, NORMAN ADAM, coll. dean; b. Belleville, Mich., Sept. 7, 1924; s. Norman Adam and Hazel Marie (Dolph) M.; A.B. in Edn., U. Mich., 1948, A.M. in History, 1949; certificate Western State Coll., Gunnison, Colo., 1959; Ed.D., Stanford U., 1967; m. Maria Bonanno, Sept. 2, 1967; children—Marc, Debbi, Kip, Loree, Preston, Kelly. Tchr., then elem. sch. prin., Pueblo, Colo., 1949-61; with Pa. Dept. Edn., Harrisburg, 1962-67, asst. commnr. basic edn., 1966-67; prof. edn., chmn. dept. Beaver Coll., Glenside, Pa., 1967-77, dean grad. and evening studies, 1977—. Served with USNR, 1944-46. Ray Lyman Wilbur doctoral fellow, 1961. Recipient Bro. Azarias award Pa. Assn. Liberal Arts Colls., 1966. Mem. NEA (life), Am. Ednl. Research Assn., Pa. Assn. Colls. Tchrs. Edn. (pres. 1975-76), Phi Delta Kappa. Home: PO Box 233 Glenside PA 19038 Office: Beaver Coll Glenside PA 19038

MILLER, PATRICK MICHAEL, research co. exec.; b. Maple City, Mich., June 2, 1936; s. William Aloysius and Evelyn Nesbit (Svoboda) M.; B.S., Mich. State U., 1957; M.S., 1960, Ph.D., 1966; m. Dolores Anne Osterman, Dec. 28, 1957; children—Mary, Brenda, Suzanne, P. Michael. Tchr. math. high sch., East Lansing, Mich., 1957-60; research engr. Ford Motor Co., Dearborn, Mich., 1960-62; asst. dir. edn. Soc. Mfg. Engrs., Dearborn, Mich., 1962-63; instr. engring. mechanics Mich. State U., East Lansing, 1963-66; asst. head dept. Calspan Corp. (formerly Cornell Aero, Lab.), Buffalo, 1966-77; pres. MGA Research Corp., 1977—; lectr., cons. in field; witness before congl. coms., govt. task forces on automotive transp.; former mem. transp. adv. com. Fed. Energy Adminstrn. Mem. ASME, Soc. Automotive Engrs., Phi Kappa Phi, Sigma Xi. Roman Catholic. Home: 1049 Boncliff Dr Alden NY 14004 Office: 4245 Union Rd Buffalo NY 14225

MILLER, REX ARNOLD, YMCA ofcl.; b. Lexington, Mo., Nov. 4, 1937; s. Ernest R. and Hazel M. (Shinn) M.; B.A. in Child Psychology, U. Minn., 1963; M.A. in Ednl. Psychology, Mich. State U., 1973; M.B.A. candidate, Rutgers U., 1977—; children—Scott, Colleen, Stefanie. Youth dir. Knox County YMCA, Galesburg, Ill., 1965-67; community program dir. East Side Br. YMCA, Mpls., 1967-70; asst. exec. dir. camping and program devel. YMCA, Lansing, Mich., 1970-74; asso. dir. program and ops. Holiday Hills YMCA, Pawling, N.Y., 1974-75; exec. dir. Camp Speers-Eljabar YMCA, Westfield, N.J., 1975-77, West Nassau (N.Y.) YMCA, 1978—; chmn. nat. YMCA task force on outdoor edn., 1975-78. Served with USN, 1963-65. Mem. Assn. Profl. Dirs., Am. Camping Assn. (dir. Mich. sect.), N.Y. State Outdoor Edn. Assn. (pres.). Lutheran. Contbr. articles in field to profl. jours. Office: 34 Monroe St Franklin Square NY 11010

MILLER, RICHARDS THORN, naval architect and engr.; b. Jenkintown, Pa., Jan. 31, 1918; s. Herman Geistweit and Helen Buckman (Thorn) M.; B.S. in Naval Architecture and Marine Engring., Webb Inst. Naval Architecture, 1940; Naval Engr., Mass. Inst. Tech., 1951; m. Jean Corbat Spear, Sept. 13, 1941; children—Patricia (Mrs. Charles G. Fishburn), Linda (Mrs. John X. Carrier). Commd. ensign U.S. Navy, 1940, advanced through grades to capt., 1960; specialized work design oceanographic research ships, mine sweepers, torpedo boats, destroyers; ret., 1968; mgr. ocean engring., Oceanic div. Westinghouse Electric Corp., 1969-75, adv. engr., 1975—; cons. Gibbs & Cox, naval architects, 1968—. Mem. com. naval architecture Am. Bur. Shipping, 1960-63, mem. ship structure com., 1966-68. Decorated Navy Legion of Merit. Registered profl. engr., Md. Mem. Soc. Naval Architects and Marine Engrs. (chmn. S.E. sect. 1965-66, chmn. marine systems com. 1970-77; chmn. tech. and research steering com. 1977—, v.p., mem. council 1976—, mem. exec. com. 1977—; Capt. Joseph H. Linnard prize 1964), Am. Soc. Naval Engrs. (mem. council 1976-78), U.S. Naval Inst., Sigma Xi. Clubs: N.Y. Yacht (N.Y.C.); Annapolis Yacht. Author: (with R.G. Henry) Sailing Yacht Design, 1963; also sects. in books, articles. Home: 975 Melvin Rd Annapolis MD 21403 Office: Oceanic Div Westinghouse Box 1488 Annapolis MD 21404

MILLER, RITA, diecasting co. exec.; b. Bklyn., Jan. 15, 1925; d. Joseph and Etta M.; B.A., Bklyn. Coll., 1947; M.A., Boston U., 1949; children—Erika Greenwald, Roy Barnet Glickman. Personnel officer, sec. to pres. Marine Elec. Corp., Bklyn., 1943-47; script writer Song Debut, Boston, 1949-50; dir. Writers' Workshops, interviewer pub. opinion surveys, New Rochelle, N.Y., 1962-64; mgr. employee relations Gries Reproducer Co. div. Coats & Clark, Inc., New Rochelle, 1966—. Mem. Am. Soc. Personnel Adminstrn., Westchester Personnel Mgmt. Assn. (dir.), Personnel Council New Rochelle, Nat. Sociology Hon. Soc. Editor: The Management Consultant (George Kenning), 1965; contbr. articles to profl. jours. Office: 125 Beechwood Ave New Rochelle NY 10802

MILLER, ROSE MARY, educator; b. Peacham, Vt., Nov. 23, 1911; d. Frank Andrew and Margaret (Whitehill) Miller; B.S., Middlebury Coll., 1933; Ed.M., U. Vt., 1949; post master's certificate advanced study U. Me., 1957. Tchr., Peacham Acad., 1937-41, prin., 1942-44; tchr. Exeter (Me.) High Sch., 1941-42; instr. Vt. Coll., Montpelier, 1944-56, dean women, 1953-56; asso. prof. math. Monmouth Coll., West Long Branch, N.J., 1957-77. Trustee Peacham (Vt.) Library, 1977—, Whitehill Homestead Assn., 1977—. Recipient Distinguished Teaching award Monmouth Coll., 1975. Mem. Am. Math. Soc., Nat. Council for Tchrs. Math., AAUW (liaison officer 1964-77), Am. Assn. Colls. for Tchr. Edn. (instl. rep. 1963-74), Peacham Hist. Assn. (treas. 1977—). Club: Order Eastern Star. Congregationalist. Home: South Peacham VT 05870

MILLER, RUTH LOUISE, found. exec.; b. Akron, Ohio, July 11, 1915; d. Arthur W. and Elizabeth (Pfeiffer) Miller; B.S., U. Akron, 1939; M.A., Hartford Sem. Found., 1941. Nat. sec. girls missionary work United Brethren Ch., Dayton, Ohio, 1942-46; coordinator non-Western dels. to World Conf. Christian Youth, Oslo, Norway, 1946-47; adminstrv. sec. Japan Internat. Christian U. Found., N.Y.C., 1948—, exec. dir., 1963—. Mem. Japan Soc. N.Y.C., Religious Pub. Relations Council. Presbyterian. (elder). Home: 180 West End Ave New York City NY 10023 Office: 475 Riverside Dr New York City NY 10027

MILLER, RUTH MARY HELEN (MRS. WILLIAM H. FERGUSON), physician; b. La Crosse, Wis.; d. Carl Frederick and Helen Adelaide (Klosheim) Miller; student Rosary Coll., 1936-38; B.A., U. Wis., 1941, M.D., 1945; postgrad. Los Angeles State Coll., 1956; certificate N.Y. Polyclinic Med. Sch. and Hosp., 1958; Ph.D., Belin U., 1959; M.A. in Med. Sci., Northwestern U., 1972, Ph.D., 1975; m. William H. Ferguson, Mar. 28, 1943 (dec. Jan. 1944). Concert pianist throughout Mid-West, 1939-41; intern Goldwater Meml. Hosp., Welfare Island, N.Y.C., 1944-45, resident neurology, 1945-47; practice medicine, Avon Park, Fla., 1948-51, specializing in neurology and internal medicine, Fall River, Mass., 1959-66, Somerset, 1966—. Mem. Mass. Citizen's Rights Com., Mass. Council Pub. Justice. Served to lt. col. M.C., AUS, 1951-55; now col. Res. Fellow Internat., Am. colls. angiology, Am. Geriatrics Soc., Acad. Psychosomatic Medicine; mem. AMA, Am. Med. Womens Assn., Am. Coll. Emergency Physicians, Assn. Mil. Surgeons, Mass. Bar Assn. (asso.), Internat. Soc. Comprehensive Medicine, NOW, Wilderness Soc., AAUW, Humane Soc. U.S., League of Women Voters, Res. Officers Assn., WAC Vets Assn. (hon.), Rosary Coll., U. Wis. alumnae assns., Internat. Platform Assn., Royal Soc. Health Eng., Alpha Epsilon Iota, Phi Sigma, Psi Chi. Clubs: Order Eastern Star, Order White Shrine Jerusalem (officer), Order Ct. of Amaranth (officer). Home: 161 Johnson St Somerset MA 02726

MILLER, SAMUEL CLIFFORD, museum ofcl.; b. Roseburg, Ore., May 6, 1930; s. Loren and Blanche (Baron) M.; B.A., Stanford, 1951; postgrad. N.Y. U., 1962-64; D.F.A. (hon.), Seton Hall U., 1976; m. Nell Schoellkopf Ely (dec.); m. 2d, Rosetta Averill. Asst. to dir. Nat. Serigraph Soc. and Meltzer Gallery, 1955-62, Albright-Knox Art Gallery, Buffalo, 1964-67; asst. to dir. Newark Mus., 1967-68, dir. 1968—, also trustee; bd. govs. NE Museums Conf.; mem. Port Authority Com. on Art; mem. art com. Coll. Medicine and Dentistry N.J. Mem. James St. Adv. Bd., Newark, Newark Preservation and Landmarks Com. Served with U.S. Army, 1951-53. Mem. Assn. Art Mus. Dirs., Am. Assn. Museums, Museums Council N.J. Club: Essex. Home: 375 Mt Prospect Ave Apt 6B Newark NJ 07104 Office: 43-49 Washington St Newark NJ 07101

MILLER, SONIA KAY FLICKER, psychologist, counselor; b. Reading, Pa., Jan. 9, 1936; d. George Edwin and Ida Mae (Cranage) Flicker; B.S., Albright Coll., 1957; M.Ed., Lehigh U., 1964, postgrad., 1964-67; m. Robert Levi Miller, Dec. 28, 1957; children—Robert Levi, Ida Mae. Tchr., Reading Sch. Dist., 1957-58; substitute tchr./counselor Pottsville (Pa.) Area Sch. Dist., 1963-65; psychol. examiner Lincoln Consultation Center, Bethlehem, Pa., 1965-66; adminstr. Reading Child Devel. Program, 1966-68; psychologist/couselor Exeter Twp. (Pa.) Sch. Dist., 1968—; workshop leader for in-service programs for educators; leader Human Devel. Tng. Inst. Bd. dirs. Big Bros. Am., 1967-68; sec., bd. dirs. Soroptimist Internat. of Reading, 1970's. Mem. Am., Pa. psychol. assns., Am. Personnel and Guidance Assn., Am. Sch. Counselors Assn., Am. Assn. Spl. Educators, Nat. Assn. Women Deans, Adminstrs. and Counselors, Berks Area Psychologists Soc., NEA, Pa.

State Edn. Assn. Methodist. Home: 3624 East Ave Reiffton Reading PA 19606 Office: 3650 Perkiomen Ave Reading PA 19606

MILLER, STANLEY, govt. ofcl.; b. N.Y.C., Nov. 14, 1929; s. Philip and Florence Joyce (Mann) M.; B.S.S., Coll. City N.Y., 1950; M.S., U. Wis., 1953, Ph.D., 1967; m. Karola Miller, Mar. 26, 1962; children—Suzanne C., Daniel J. Instr., U. Md., 1957-64; asso. prof. U. State Coll., N.Y., 1964-65; economist Dept. Labor, Washington, 1965-66, Econ. Devel. Adminstrn., 1967-68; economist Fed. Hwy. Adminstrn., Dept. Transp., 1968-73, Dept. Interior, 1973—; instr. U.S. Dept. Agr. Grad. Sch., Washington, 1965—. Served with U.S. Army, 1954-55. Mem. Am. Econ. Assn., Regional Sci. Assn. Contbr. articles to regional sci., transp. jours; co-author Energy perspectives. Home: 11116 Nicholas Dr Silver Spring MD 20902 Office: 18th and D St NW Washington DC 20240

MILLER, STANLEY ALLEN, state ofcl.; b. Harrisburg, Pa., Aug. 3, 1928; s. Sigmund and Molly (Abrams) M.; U. Pa., 1946-47; m. Shirley Tuck, Jan. 2, 1949; children—Marlene, Elliott. Pres., treas. Miller's Auto Supplies, Inc., Harrisburg, 1952—, Stanley Distbg. Co., Harrisburg, 1952—; dir. Automotive Assos.; hon. dir. Woodhill Chem. Co.; mem. Health Ins. Benefits Adv. Council. Mem. nat. council Joint Distbn. Com., 1967—; asso. chmn. Jewish Nat. Fund; state sec. pub. welfare, mem. gov.'s cabinet, 1970-71. Mem. advisory council Harrisburg, Polyclinic hosps., 1953—; sec. exec. com. United Jewish Community, Harrisburg, 1956-58; mem. bd. Am. Jewish Com., 1956—; fin. chmn. Susquehanna dist. Boy Scouts Am., 1960-64, mem. exec. council Keystone Area, dist. chmn., 1964-66; dir. Child Guidance Center, United Fund; pres., bd. Harrisburg Community Theatre; sec. Pa. Human Relations Commn., 1969; gov.'s rep. human affairs, 1967-70; del. White House Conf. on Children and Youth, 1970; mem. State Council Human Services, 1970-71, State Council CD, 1970-71, State Exec. Bd., 1970-71; mem. Dauphin County Republican Finance Com.; trustee Rep. Club, 1st ward Susquehanna Twp. Recipient Order of Merit award Boy Scouts Am., Distinguished Service award Am. Histadrut Devel. Found., 1970, numerous others. Mem. Toy Wholesalers Am. (past v.p.), Automotive Accessories Industries (pres. 1948—), C. of C. (past v.p.), Pa. Soc. Jewish. Clubs: Elks, Masons, Lions, Second Generation (dir., past founder and 1st pres., chmn. nominating com.), Blue Ridge Country, Reciprocity of Am. (v.p. Harrisburg chpt.), Tuesday, Century. Editorial adv. bd. Home and Auto Retailer.) Home: 4713 Galen Rd Harrisburg PA 17110 Office: 200 S 18th St Harrisburg PA 17105

MILLER, STANLEY NORMAN, coll. educator; b. La Crosse, Wis., Mar. 1, 1929; s. Louis William and Ida Willhelmena (Foesher) M.; ed. U. Wis., 1947-51, George Peabody Coll., 1954-56; m. Miriam Adalia Mac Lachlan, June 28, 1952; children—Rebecca Lynn, Stephen Lee. Tchr., Balsam Lake (Wis.) High Sch., 1951-52; asst. prof. polit. sci. La. Poly. Inst., Ruston, 1956-59; asst. prof. social scis. Kans. State U., Manhattan, 1959-60; curriculum planning spl. Penn. Dept. Edn., Harrisburg, 1960-62, dir. Bur. Gen. and Academic Edn., 1962-66; prof. social sci. and edn., head social sci. programs Pa. State U. Capital Campus, Middletown, 1971—; instr. summers Tufts U., Carnegie-Mellon U., Temple U. Served with USN, 1952-54. Mem. Nat. Council Tchrs. Social Studies. Lutheran. Author publs. in field. Home: RD 3 PO Box 153A Dillsburg PA 17919 Office: Pa State U Capitol Campus Middletown PA 17057

MILLER, STEPHEN HERSCHEL, physician, educator; b. N.Y.C., Jan. 12, 1941; s. Morris Louis and Mildred Lily (Beller) M.; student U. Chgo., 1957-58, U. Ga., 1958-59, Tulane U., 1960-61; M.D. cum laude, U. Calif. at Los Angeles, 1964; m. Carol Susan Shapiro, Dec. 18, 1965; children—Mark, David. Intern, U. Calif. at Los Angeles, 1964-65, resident gen. surgery, 1965-67; resident gen. surgery U. Calif. at San Diego, 1967-69; resident plastic surgery U. Calif. at San Francisco, 1969-71; research fellow in plastic surgery African Med. Research Found., Kenya, 1971-72; research fellow head and neck program Roswell Park, Buffalo, 1972; practice medicine specializing in plastic surgery, San Francisco, 1973-74, Hershey, Pa., 1974—; asst. prof. surgery U. Calif. at San Francisco, 1973-74, exec. head div. plastic surgery, 1973-74; chief plastic surgery San Francisco Gen. Hops., 1973-74, VA Hosp., San Francisco, 1973-74; co-dir. burn unit San Francisco Gen. Hosp., 1973-74; asso. prof. surgery Pa. State U., Milton S. Hershey Med. Center, Hershey, 1974-78, prof. surgery, 1978—, asso. chief div. plastic surgery, 1974—, asso. mem. grad. faculty, 1975—; cons. in plastic surgery Elizabethtown State Crippled Childrens Hosp., 1976—. Recipient Physicians Recognition award AMA, 1976—; Pacinian Corpuscle Regeneration study grantee, 1974-75; Am. Soc. Surgery of Hand grantee, 1974-75. Licensed physician, Pa., Calif.; diplomate Am. Bd. Surgery, Am. Bd. Plastic Surgery. Mem. AMA, Am. Trauma Soc., Am. Soc. Plastic and Reconstructive Surgery, ACS, N.Y. Acad. Scis., Robert H. Ivy Soc., Assn. Am. Med. Colls., Am. Fedn. Clin. Research, Am. Burn Assn., Wainwright Tumor Clinic Assn., Pa., Dauphin County med. socs., Soc. for Cryobiology, Plastic Surgery Research Council, Soc. Head and Neck Surgeons, Internat. Soc. Clin. Plastic Surgeons, Am. Soc. Aesthetic Plastic Surgery, Israel Assn. Plastic and Reconstructive Surgery, Assn. for Acad. Surgery, Am. Assn. Plastic Surgeons, Am. Assn. for Surgery of Trauma, Am. Soc. for Surgery of Hand, Pan-Pacific Surg. Assn., Soc. Neurosci., Nat. Burn Fedn., Sigma Xi. Contbr. numerous articles in field to med. jours. Home: 98 Woodbine Dr Hershey PA 17033 Office: 500 University Dr Hershey PA 17033

MILLER, WAYNE DUNBAR, speech pathologist, audiologist; b. Brockton, Mass., Dec. 26, 1934; s. Wilford Eugene and Doris Mae (Dunbar) Miller; B.A. in Speech Pathology, Staley Coll., Brookline, Mass., 1958; M.Ed. in Counseling, Psychotherapy, Suffolk U., Boston, 1971; m. Helen Louise Grant; children—Valerie-Gail, Wilford Gordon. Supr. speech therapy and hearing Paul A. Dever State Sch., Taunton, Mass., 1961-70; practice neuro-communi-pathology (aphasiology) Goddard Meml. Hosp., Stoughton, Mass., and Sturdy Meml. Hosp., Attleboro, Mass., 1977—; founder Speech, Lang. and Hearing Clinic Morton Hosp., 1968. Registered speech pathologist, audiologist, Fla.; certificate clin. competence speech pathology and audiology Am. Speech and Hearing Assn. Mem. Am. Speech and Hearing Assn., Am. Audiology Soc., Mass. Speech and Hearing Assn., Am. Soc. of Group Psychotherapy and Psychodrama. Home: 76 Short St South Easton MA 02375 Office: 76 Short St South Easton MA 02375 and Speech Dept Bliss Sch Park St Attleboro MA 02703

MILLER, WAYNE ELWOOD, physician; b. Trevorton, Pa., Apr. 2, 1934; s. Marlin Elwood and Laura Eleanor (Bohner) M.; A.B., Susquehanna U., 1955; M.D., Temple U., 1959; m. Frances Ann Rhoads, June 28, 1958; children—Jonathan, Jeffrey, Ann. Intern, Northeastern Hosp., Phila., 1959-60; resident U.S. Army Hosp., Okinawa, 1961-63; family practice medicine, Orange, Mass., 1963—; asst. clin. profl. family practice U. Mass., Worcester, 1975—; mem. Bd. Health Orange (Mass.), 1964-72, chmn., 1965-72; chmn. pub. relations Central Mass. Health Planning Council, 1972-73. Mem. Orange Recreation Assn., 1966-73, pres., 1967-73; mem. Packard Pond Assn., 1964-78, pres., 1972-74; mem. Orange Airport Commn., 1977—. Served with U.S. Army, 1960-63. Diplomate Am. Bd. Family Practice. Fellow Am. Acad. Family Physicians; mem. AMA, New Eng. Soc. Clin. Hypnosis, Mass. Med. Soc., Aircraft Owners and Pilots Assn., Am. Soc. Psychic Research. Methodist. Clubs: Athol-Orange Aero, Home: 300 Pleasant St Orange MA 01364 Office: 10 Fountain St Orange MA 01364

MILLER, WILLIAM ARCH, JR., social worker, marriage and family psychotherapist; b. Cumberland, Md., Sept. 5, 1934; s. William Arch and Gussie (Catherman) M.; A.A., Mars Hill Coll., 1954; B.S., Wake Forest U., 1958; M.S.W., W.Va. U., 1960; postgrad. Indiana (Pa.) State U., 1962-63; Ph.D., Rutgers U., 1975; m. Barbara Ann Thuss, Aug. 3, 1956; children—William Arch III, Lynne Michele. Psychiat. social worker, adminstrv. asst., dir. Ridgway (Pa.) Area Psychiat. Center, 1960-64; cons. DuBois Office Pa. Bur. Vocat. Rehab., 1963-64; exec. dir. Atlantic Mental Health Center, Atlantic City, 1964-77; marriage and family counselor, Ridgway and Absecon, N.J., 1963—; pres. Miller/Human Relations Consultants, 1977—; cons. Seashore House, Atlantic City, 1977—; instr. Cumberland County Coll., Vineland, N.J., 1968-69; instr. psychology dept. Atlantic Community Coll., 1969-70; coordinator, instr. field work Rutgers U., 1967—; cons. N.J. Rehab. Commn., 1972—. Bd. dirs. Sarah W. Leeds Found., Atlantic City, 1974-77; chmn. welfare com. City of Absecon. Served with USNR, 1954-56. Mem. Nat. Assn. Social Workers (chpt. exec. bd. 1969-70), Acad. Certified Social Workers, N.J. Assn. Alcoholism Counselors, N.J. Assn. Mental Health Agys. (exec. bd. 1966-71, 72—; past pres.). Club: Lions (v.p.) (Absecon). Columnist, Dealing with Feelings, Mainland Jour., Pleasantville, N.J.; Daily Observer, Toms River, N.J., 1977—; producer, broadcaster The Best of Mental Health, Sta. WFPG, Atlantic City. Home and office: 18 W Bayview Dr Absecon NJ 08201

MILLER, WILLIAM CHARLES, lawyer; b. Jacksonville, Fla., Aug. 6, 1937; s. Charles and Mary Elizabeth (Kiger) M.; B.A., Washington & Lee U., 1958, LL.B., 1961; LL.M., N.Y. U., 1963; m. Hadmut Gisela Larsen, June 10, 1961; children—Monica Lee, Charles Andreas. Admitted to Fla. bar, 1961, U.S. Supreme Ct. bar, 1968; counsel to electrochem., elastomers and internat. depts. E.I. du Pont de Nemours and Co., Wilmington, Del., 1963-66; counsel S. Am. ops. Bristol-Myers Co., N.Y.C., 1967-69; internat. counsel Xerox Corp., Stamford, Conn., 1969—; prof. internat. law U. Md., Munich, Germany, 1962. Bd. dirs. Southwestern Legal Found., 1975—. Fulbright scholar, 1959-60, Ford Found. fellow, 1961-62, German Govt. grantee, 1962-63, Hague Acad. fellowship, 1963, Kappa Sigma scholar, 1959. Mem. Westchester Fairfield County Corp. Counsel Assn. (chmn. internat. com.), Practicing Law Inst. (internat. workshop chmn. corp. counsel), Internat., Am., Fla. bar assns., Phi Beta Kappa. Clubs: Masons, Elks. Home: 130 Cheese Spring Rd Wilton CT 06897 Office: High Ridge Park Stamford CT 06905

MILLER, WILLIAM EDWARD, supt. schs.; b. Trenton, N.J., Feb. 1, 1917; s. Milton Edward and Ida (Ross) M.; B.S., N.J. State Coll. at Trenton, 1938; M.A. in Edn., Columbia U., 1940; postgrad. Advance Sch. Tchrs. Coll., 1942-44, Rutgers U., 1950-54; m. Thelma Swenson, Nov. 27, 1942; children—John Willian, Sven Otis, Ida Marie. Tchr. pub. schs., Chatham, Highland Park, N.J., 1938-42; asst. prof. edn. N.J. State Coll., 1942-46; prin. Vine St. Sch., Bridgeton, N.J., 1946-50, Clara Barton Sch., Edison, N.J., 1950-56, Edison High Sch., 1956-58; supt. schs., Manasquan, N.J., 1958—. Camp dir. George Washington council Boy Scouts Am., 1934-39, com. mem. Monmouth council, 1957—; pres. Monmouth County (N.J.) Audio-Visual Aid Commn., 1957—. Served with USNR, 1944-47. Mem. Monmouth County Roundtable (pres.), Monmouth County Supts. Assn. (pres.), Bapt. Camping Fedn. Phila. (exec. dir.), Manasquan C. of C. (dir., pres.), Am. Math. Soc., Am. Assn. Sch. Administrs., N.J. Edn. Assn., N.J. Council Edn., N.J. Schoolmasters, South Jersey Sch. Masters, N.J. Sch. Adminstrs. Assn., Kappa Delta Pi, Phi Delta Kappa. Clubs: Kiwanis (sec.), Torch. Producer film on research in outdoor edn., 1949. Home: PO Drawer M 47 Cowart Ave Manesquen NJ 08736

MILLER, WILLIAM JOHN, JR., state ofcl.; b. Wilmington, Del., Feb. 5, 1917; s. William John and Mary A. (Durkin) M.; B.S., Drexel Inst. Tech., 1954; m. Helen Virginia Hughes, Aug. 7, 1942; children—Mary Ann, Judith Ellen, Sarah Louise, William John III. Dir. Del. State Hwy. Dept., Dover, 1961-64; dir. Del. River & Bay Authority, New Castle, Del., 1964—. Bd. dirs. Del. Safety Council, 1947—, Del. Racing Assn., 1965—, Internat. Road Fedn., 1972—. Served to capt. C.E., AUS, 1942-46. Mem. Internat. Bridge, Tunnel and Turnpike Assn. (past pres., dir. 1964—), Del. Motor Club (pres. 1976—). Roman Catholic. Home: Manor Dr Moore's Lake Dover DE 19901 Office: PO Box 71 Delaware Meml Bridge New Castle DE 19720

MILLER, WILLIAM RUSSELL, hosp. equipment mfg. co. exec.; b. Bklyn., Dec. 16, 1928; s. William Albert and Claudia Anna (Ballagh) M.; B.S., Mass. Inst. Tech., 1952, M.S., 1952; m. Marlene Christine Sullivan, July 21, 1961; children—Claudette Patrice, Kathleen Brenda. Engr., Gen. Electric Co. Erie, Pa., 1954-62, supr. devel. engring., 1962-65, mgr. advance engring., 1965-66, mgr. product engring., 1966-71, mgr. engring., 1971-72; gen. mgr. systems div. Am. Sterilizer Co., Erie, Pa., 1972-75, v.p. research and devel., 1975—; dir. Armor Electric, Inc. Bd. corporators, mem. planning com. St. Vincents Health Center, 1970—; mem. engring. adv. bd. Gannon Coll., 1976—, co-chmn. 1977. Served with USAF, 1952-54, capt., 1959. Registered profl. engr., Pa. Mem. Tau Beta Pi, Eta Kappa Nu, Sigma Xi. Clubs: Erie Jaycees (v.p. 1960), Presque Isle Rotary, Kahkwa, Maennechor, Westwood Racquet. Patentee in field. Home: 4950 Wolf Rd Erie PA 16505 Office: 2424 W 23d St Erie PA 16512

MILLER, WILLIAM SANFORD, mgmt. cons.; b. N.Y.C., May 28, 1918; s. Carl August and Charlotte Sanford (Baker) M.; A.B., Yale U., 1941; m. Anne Hopkins, June 23, 1951; children—William Sanford, Blair, Carolyn Ten Eyck, Catherine, Carl A., Charlotte. Copywriter, J. Walter Thompson Co., 1946-51, mng. dir., Mexico City, 1951-55; area mgr. for Middle East, Ford Motor Co., Beirut, 1955-60; v.p., mng. dir. Kenyon & Eckhardt de Mex., Mexico City, 1960-67; v.p., mng. dir. Boyden Latin Am. S.A., Mexico City, 1967-77; sr. v.p., internat. dir. Boyden Assos. Inc., N.Y.C., 1977—, also dir.; mem. council Internat. Exec. Service Corps, 1977—. Served to lt. USNR, 1941-46; ETO. Mem. Yale Alumni Assn. (dir. 1951-55), Bus. Council Internat. Understanding (dir. 1952-60). Assn. Ex-Mems. Squadron A, St. Nicholas Soc., Soc. Colonial Wars, Mil. Order Fgn. Wars, Mil. Order Loyal Legion. Republican. Episcopalian. Clubs: Adirondack League, Racquet and Tennis, Yale (N.Y.). Home: 433 E 51st St New York City NY 10022 Office: Boyden Assos Inc 260 Madison Ave New York City NY 10016

MILLER, YVETTE ESPINOSA, educator; b. Lota, Chile; d. Oscar Norberto and Rosalba Denise (Dufeu) Espinosa; B.A., U. Concepcion; M.A., U. Pitts., Ph.D. (Andrew Mellon fellow); m.; children—Lisette, Paul, William Kenneth, Clinton, Brian. Lectr., U. Pitts., 1966, Chatham Coll., Pitts., 1969; asso. prof. Carnegie-Mellon U., Pitts., 1967—. Inst. Internat. Edn. fellow, 1949-50; Falk grantee, 1974. Mem. Center Inter-Am. Women Writers (pres.), Women Writers from Latin Am. (symposia dir.), Modern Lang. Assn., Am. Assn. Tchrs. Spanish and Portuguese, Instituto Internacional Literatura Iberoamericana, Assn. de Literatura Femenina Hispanica. Author: La Novelistica de Gabriel Miro, 1975; Latin American Women Writers, Yesterday and Today, 1976; editor: Latin Am. Lit. Rev. Home: 246 Sunset Dr Pittsburgh PA 15235 Office: Carnegie Mellon University Dept Modern Language Pittsburgh PA 15213

MILLET, JOHN BRADFORD, surgeon; b. Buffalo, Aug. 8, 1916; s. John Alfred Parsons and Alice Jeannette (Murrell) M.; B.S., Harvard Coll., 1938; M.D., Harvard U., 1942; m. Constance Hopkins Dallas, Nov. 1974; children—John Bradford, David Francis, Polly Watson Millet Barnard. Surg., intern, Mass. Gen. Hosp., Boston, 1942-43, surg. resident, 1946-49; chief thoracic surgery, partner Slocum Dickson Clinic, Utica, N.Y., 1949-55; practice medicine specializing in surgery, Utica, 1955—; sr. attending surgeon, St. Luke's Meml. Hosp. Center, Utica, 1955—, chief dept. surgery, 1969-70; cons. surgeon, Herkimer Meml. Hosp., Rose Hosp., Rome, N.Y., Marcy State Hosp., Marcy, N.Y.; med. advisor to Vis. Nurse Assn.; dir. Health Systems Agy. Central N.Y., Med. Securities Fund, 1964-65, Med. Funds Mgmt. Corp., 1964-65, Digimetrics Inc.; med. adv. com. Planned Parenthood of Mohawk Valley, Presbyn. Home. Dir. Oneida County Cancer Soc., Mohawk Valley Assn. for Progress, Oneida County Indsl. Devel. Corp., Homogenous Metals Inc., 1970-75, Urban Reclamation Technologies Inc., Mohawk Valley Comets, Engine II, chief, 1966-67; pres. Midstate Com. on Area Wide Health Planning, 1966-72; co-chmn. citizens com. on devel. of med. sch. in Utica area; co-developer Brookside Racquet Club, Wedgewood Apartments, Treadway Resort, Meadows. Served to maj. M.C. AUS, 1943-46. Fellow A.C.S., Am. Coll. Chest Physicians; mem. Am. Thoracic Soc., Am. Bd. Surgery, Coll. Angiology, Central N.Y. Surg. Soc., Mohawk Valley Surg. Soc. (pres., 1968-69), Central N.Y. Acad. Medicine, Oneida County (chmn. edn. com., 1968-69), N.Y. State Med. Socs., AMA, Pan-Am. Med. Assn., Pan Pacific Surg. Assn., Utica Med. Club (pres. 1960-61). Republican. Episcopalian. Clubs: Night Stick (chief, 1965-66), Harvard Club of Mohawk Valley (pres. 1951-66), Harvard Coll. Alumni (Fund area chmn.), Ft. Schuyler, Sadaquada Golf, Adirondack League, Ideal Flying, Rotary, Masons, Shrine. Home: 5 Tennyson Circle New Hartford NY 13413 Office: 1624 Genesee St Utica NY 13502

MILLIE, HAROLD RAYMOND, editor; b. Mpls., July 19, 1930; s. Odin Larsen and Aagot (Skaftun) M.; B.A., Claremont Men's Coll., 1955, M.A., 1960; m. Elena Gonozalez, Aug. 8, 1969. Resident teaching fellow Brown U., Providence, 1961-63; research asso. Nat. Planning Assn., Washington, 1964-65; operations research analyst Nat. Bur. Standards, Washington, 1965-70, Gen. Services Adminstrn., Washington, 1971-73; editor Bur. Mines, Dept. Interior, Washington, 1974—. Served with U.S. Army, 1949-50. Mem. Am. Inst. Mining, Metall. and Petroleum Engrs. Episcopalian. Editor: Minerals and Materials/A Monthly Survey, 1976—. Home: 4633 River Rd Chevy Chase MD 20016 Office: 2401 E St NW Washington DC 20241

MILLIGAN, JOHN DRANE, historian, educator; b. N.Y.C., Oct. 11, 1924; s. Carl Glover and Hazel Gray (Drane) M.; B.A., U. Mich., 1952, M.A., 1953, Ph.D., 1961; m. Joyce Mary Jervis, Nov. 16, 1946; children—Jacqueline M., Paula J., Mary M., Elizabeth Y. Teaching asst. U. Mich., Ann Arbor, 1951-52, teaching fellow, 1954-56; from asst. prof. to prof. history State U. N.Y. at Buffalo, 1962—, dir. grad. programs in history, 1963-68; vis. prof. McMaster U., Hamilton, Ont., Can., summer 1964, 69-70. Exec. bds. Ann Arbor chpt. NAACP, 1956-61, ACLU, 1959-61; mem. campaign coms. for various candidates for local and nat. office, 1960-76; mem. Buffalo Housing Opportunities Made Equal, Citizens Council on Human Relations; faculty chmn. United Fund drive, 1977; active Foster Parents Plan, 1955—. Served with USAAF, 1943-46. James B. Angell scholar U. Mich.; grantee Research Found. of State U. N.Y., U.S. Naval Inst. Mem. Am. Hist. Assn., Assn. Am. Historians, So. Hist. Assn., Buffalo and Erie County Hist. Soc., Buffalo Council for Responsiblity in Fgn. Policy (founding), Soaring Soc. Am., Aircraft Owners and Pilots Assn., Niagara Soaring Club. Author: Gunboats Down the Mississippi, 1965; From the Fresh-Water Navy, 1861-1864, 1970; also chpts. in books, articles in jours., encys. Home: 21 Allenhurst Rd Buffalo NY 14214 Office: History Dept State U NY Buffalo NY 14216

MILLIGAN, REX VINCENT, mech. engr.; b. Smithfield, Utah, Sept. 14, 1925; s. James Henry and Emma Christina (Johnson) M.; B.S.C.E., Utah State U., 1953; M.S. in Applied Mechanics, Rensselaer Poly. Inst., 1956; m. Carol LeFevre, Sept. 1, 1954; children—Cheri, Karen, Linda, Christine, Valerie. Teaching asst. Rensselaer Poly. Inst., 1953-56, instr., 1956-58, research asso., 1958-61; research mech. engr. U.S. Army Watervliet (N.Y.) Arsenal, 1961—. Pres. Albany br. Ch. Jesus Christ of Latter-day Saints, 1962-67, pres. Hudson br., 1968-77. Served with USCGR, 1943-46. Mem. ASME, Soc. Exptl. Stress Analysis, AAAS, Sigma Xi, Sigma Tau. Contbr. articles in field to sci. jours. Home: RD 1 Ghent NY 12075 Office: Watervliet Arsenal Bldg 115 Watervliet NY 12189

MILLIGAN, ROBERT HARRY, wholesale fabric co. exec.; b. Pitts., Sept. 3, 1924; s. John Chester and Betty (Gardner) M.; B.A., Oklahoma City U., 1947; M.S.W., Tulane U., 1950. Psychiat. social worker VA, Houston, 1950-51; supr. employment Crucible Steel Co. Am., Pitts., 1951-55; dir. personnel devel. Joy Mfg. Co., Pitts., 1955-68, mgr. personnel services, 1968-70; sec., treas. Decorator & Upholstery Supply, Inc., 1959—, also dir.; trustee Decorator & Upholstery Supply, Inc. Profit Sharing Trust, 1966—. Served with AUS, 1943-45. Decorated Purple Heart. Presbyterian. Home: 2315 Caswell Dr Bethel Park PA 15102 Office: 100 Vista Park Dr Pittsburgh PA 15205

MILLIKEN, ELVA GARDINER (MRS. JAMES R. MILLIKEN), radiologic technologist, educator; b. Fillmore County, Minn., June 10, 1911; d. Allen J. and Mabel M. (Bernard) Gardiner; B.S. in Social Sci., Boston Coll., 1946; postgrad. Rivier Coll.; m. James R. Milliken, June 27, 1959 (dec.). X-ray technologist Mayo Clinic, Rochester, Minn., 1936-39; chief radiologic technologist Meml. Hosp., Nashua, N.H., 1939-65, tech. dir. Sch. Radiologic Tech., 1965-77, instr. Sch. Nursing, 1957-61; instr. Sch. Radiologic Tech., Notre Dame de Lourdes Hosp., Manchester, N.H., 1958-68. Mem. Am. Registry Radiologic Technologists, Am. (affiliate com. 1958-60, by laws com.), N.H. (counselor Am. soc. 1955-58, pres. 1957-58, sec. 1964-65) socs. radiologic technologists, New Eng. Conf. Radiologic Technologists (sec. 1958-59), N.H. Congress Career Women (chmn. 1970-71), Nashua Bus. and Profl. Women's Club (pres. 1969-70, Woman of Year 1977), N.H. Bus. and Profl. Women's Clubs Inc. (dist. dir. 1973-74), Quota Internat. (1st v.p. Nashua 1970-71, pres. 1972-74), Cath. Daus. Am., Nashua Hist. Soc. Home: 46 Dunbarton Dr Nashua NH 03060

MILLMAN, NEAL ALLEN, psychotherapist; b. N.Y.C., Oct. 25, 1942; s. Joseph Jerome and Evelyn Yvette (Schechter) M.; B.A., Adelphi U., 1964; postgrad. Western Mich. U., 1964-65; M.S.W., Hunter Coll., 1969; m. Barbara Schuessler, July 3, 1976; children by previous marriage—Daniel, Scott. Psychiat. social worker Kings Park State (N.Y.) Hosp., 1967-71; psychotherapist Mid Nassau Community Guidance Center, Hicksville, N.Y., 1969-72; Huntington (N.Y.) Mental Health Clinic, 1971-72, East Plains Mental Health Center, Hicksville, 1972—; pvt. practice psychotherapy, 1969—; field instr. Adelphi U., 1976—. Certified social worker, N.Y. State. Fellow Soc. Clin. Social Work Psychotherapists; mem. Am. Assn. Marriage and Family Counselors, Nat. Assn. Social Workers, Acad. Certified Social Workers. Office: 7 Wood Ave Massapequa NY 11758

MILLMAN, SANDY KEITH, golf equipment co. exec.; b. Poughkeepsie, N.Y., Mar. 23, 1930; s. Morris and Rosalie (Josephson) M.; A.B., U. Miami, 1952; postgrad. New Paltz State Tchrs. Coll., 1953, New Sch. Social Research, 1963; m. Ellin S. Bainder, Aug. 30, 1953; children—Jode Susan, Stuart Lawrence. With pub. relations Pan Am. World Airways, 1952; with Kabriko Internat., Inc., N.Y.C., 1953-76, pres., 1962-74; pres. Nat. Athletic Products, N.Y.C., 1962—, Tempo Golf & Tennis, Inc., 1976—; v.p. Weimann Internat, Inc., N.Y.C., 1963—; cons. to commr. trade Honduras UN Trade Commn., 1966—. Intelligence team U.S. State Dept., 1947. Mem. U.S. Power Squadron, Aircraft Owners and Pilots Assn., Mid-Hudson Power Squadron, U.S. Trotting Assn., N.Y. State Sheriff's Assn., Alpha Delta Sigmn. Club: Atrium (N.Y.C.). Home: 7 Adriance Ave Poughkeepsie NY 12602 Office: 15 W 27th St New York City NY 10001

MILLS, CLIFFORD WHEELER, physician; b. Worcester, Mass., May 5, 1913; s. Clifford Frank and Gertrude (Estabrook) M.; A.B., Dartmouth, 1935, med. certificate, 1936; M.D., Cornell U., 1938; m. Letha Lucille Jones, Jan. 18, 1943; children—Marilyn, Nancy, Clifford Wheeler, Letha, Richard. Intern, Norwalk Hosp., Conn., 1938-39; resident Bellevue Hosp., N.Y.C., 1939-40, French Hosp., 1940-41; practice medicine specializing in obstetrics and gynecology, Norwalk, Conn., 1945-59, specializing in gynecology, 1959—; sr. attending physician gynecology and tumor clinic Norwalk Hosp., 1952—; surgeon, 2d Co. Gov.'s Footguard, 1965—; chmn. Aspetuck Valley Health Dist., 1966-72, dir., 1972—; school physician Westport Sch. System, 1972—. Adv. bd. Conn. Nat. Bank, Westport, Conn., 1959—, also chmn., hon. bd. dirs.; dir. Fairfield County Publs., 1957-72. Chmn. Westport Republican Town Com., 1960-61, 72; rep. Westport Town Meeting, 1956-58; mem. Zoning Bd. Appeals, Westport, 1961-63; mem. citizens adv. com. Radio Sta. WMMM, 1961-62; dir. Norwalk Med. Soc. Found., 1954-58; pres. Fairfield County Football Found. and Hall Fame; chmn. Westport chpt. Leukemia Soc.; bd. govs. Shriners Hosp. Crippled Children; trustee Pop Warner Scholar Athletes, 1970—. Served from lt. to maj., M.C., AUS, 1941-45. Recipient Plaque award, citizens of Westport as Outstanding Citizen, 1961. Citizenship award Sportsmen of Westport, 1968. Fellow Am. Coll. Obstetricians and Gynecologists (Eng.), Internat. Coll. (Eng.); mem. New Eng. Obstet. and Gynecol. Soc., Internat. Coll. Surgeons; mem. New Eng. Obstet. and Gynecol. Soc., Soc. Abdominal Surgeons, World Med. Assn., Am. Sch. Health Assn., Nat. Environ. Health Assn., Acad. Health Adminstrn., Conn. Dirs. Health Assn., Internat. Union Helth Edn., Internat. Fertility and Sterility Assn., Com. on Maternal Care (life mem.), Am. Geriatrics Soc., Pan Am. Med. Assn. (life mem.), Pan Am. Cytology Assn., AMA, Nat. Med. Vets. Soc., Aero Med. Soc., N.Y. Acad. Scis., Conn. (ho. dels. 1956—, chmn. legis. com. 1958-62, rep. to Mass. Med. Soc. 1958-62), Norwalk (pres. 1957-58) med. socs., Fairfield County Med. Assn. (ho. of dels. 1956-63), New Eng., Am., Conn. pub. health assns., Conn. Environ. Health Assn., Res. Officers Assn. Western Conn. (pres. 1961-62), Mil. Order World Wars, Order of Lafayette, Circus Saints and Sinners (v.p. 1966, chmn. bd. 1968—), Air Force Assn., Navy League U.S. (v.p. Bridgeport chpt.), Assn. Mil. Surgeons, AAAS, Am. Legion, VFW, Norwalk C. of C. Republican. Congregationalist. Clubs: Mason (32 deg.) K.T., Shriners, (potentate 1964); Nat. Sojourners, Lambs of N.Y.; Twilight of Conn., Norwalk Catholics, Officers of Conn.; Touchdown of N.Y.; Sportsman of Westport (pres. 1974-75). Home: 1 Yankee Hill Rd Westport CT 06880 Office: 65 East Ave Norwalk CT 06851

MILLS, EDWARD WARREN, lawyer; b. N.Y.C., Apr. 7, 1941; s. Foy Fitzhugh and Isabelle Marie (Vega) M.; B.S. in Commerce, Washington and Lee U., 1962; M.B.A., Hofstra U., 1974; J.D., N.Y. Law Sch., 1977; m. Maria Parascandolo, Sept. 19, 1971. Accountant, Wassermann & Taten, N.Y.C., 1962-69; exec. v.p. L.H. Keller Co., Inc., N.Y.C., 1969-73, Hugo P. Keller, Inc., 1969-73; pres. Gen. Ruby & Sapphire Corp., N.Y.C., 1973—, Qualistar Corp., N.Y.C., 1973—; admitted to N.Y. State bar, 1978, since practice in N.Y.C. C.P.A., N.Y. Mem. Am. Bar Assn., N.Y. State Bar Assn., N.Y. County Lawyers Assn., Am. Inst. C.P.A.'s, N.Y. State Soc. C.P.A.'s, Sigma Phi Epsilon. Clubs: Hofstra U., 60 East., Downtown Athletic (N.Y.C.). Contbr. to Suburban Econ. Network, 1977. Home: 271 Cold Spring Rd Syosset NY 11791 Office: 60 E 42d St New York City NY 10017

MILLS, GEORGE MARSHALL, state ofcl.; b. Newton, N.J., May 20, 1923; s. J. Marshall and Emma (Scott) M.; B.A., Rutgers U., 1943; M.A., Columbia, 1951, Profl. Certificate, 1952; m. Dorothy Lovilla Allen, Apr. 21, 1945; children—Dianne (Mrs. Thomas McKay III), Dorothy L.A. (Mrs. Edward Sphatt). Pres. George M. Mills Inc., North Brunswick, N.J., 1946-75; risk mgr. N.J. Hwy. Authority, Woodbridge, 1975—. Dir. Nat. Interfraternity Conf., 1973, v.p., 1977—; bd. dirs. Alpha Chi Rho Ednl. Found. Served with USNR, 1943-46. C.L.U., C.P.C.U. Mem. Am. Coll. Life Underwriters, Am. Coll. Property Liability Underwriters, Internat. Bridge, Tunnel and Turnpike Assn. (vice chmn.), English Speaking Union, New Brunswick Hist. Soc., Alpha Chi Rho (nat. councillor 1964-70, nat. pres. 1970-73, treas. 1975—), Kappa Kappa Psi, Tau Kappa Alpha, Phi Delta Phi. Mem. Reformed Ch. Am. Club: Rutgers Alumni-Faculty (New Brunswick, N.J.). Home: 1054 Hoover Dr North Brunswick NJ 08902 Office: NJ Hwy Authority Woodbridge NJ

MILLSTEIN, SIDNEY NELSON, dentist; b. Paterson, N.J., Feb. 26, 1936; s. Philip and Anne E. (Fis) M.; B.A. in Psychology, Rutgers U., 1957; D.D.S., U. Pa., 1961; m. Bethanie Noel Bauchner, Apr. 9, 1972; 1 son, Daniel E.; children by previous marriage—Andrew W., Edward W., Eric W. Practice dentistry, Atlantic City, 1964-67, Margate City, N.J., 1967—; dental staff Hebrew Old Age Center, Atlantic City. Chmn. dental adv. com. Atlantic County Vocat. High Sch., 1972—; mem. dental adv. com. Medicaid Program, State of N.J., 1970—; dental plan rev. dentist N.J. Service Plan, 1971—, dist. commr., 1973—. Bd. dirs. Jewish Community Center, Margate, also pres., 1977—; bd. mgrs. N.J. Y Camps; v.p. Congregation Beth Israel, Margate, 1975—. Served to Dental Corps, USAF, 1961-63. Mem. Am. (del.), N.J. (ho. of dels 1970—, trustee 1974—) dental assns., Atlantic Cape May County Dental Soc. (v.p. 1971-72, pres. 1972—). Club: Kiwanis. Editor: Dental Record, 1961; asso. editor Bull. Atlantic Cape May County Dental Soc., 1970-71. Home: 500 N Douglas Ave Margate NJ 08402 Office: 8500 Ventnor Ave Margate NJ 08402

MILNE, DAVID WILSON, ednl. adminstr.; b. Pittsfield, Mass., Jan. 28, 1942; s. Alexander Wilson and Caroline May (Chown) M.; B.A. in Polit. Sci., Am. Internat. Coll., Springfield, Mass.; M.A. in Polit. Theory, U. Maine, Orono; m. Joyce Harris; stepchildren—Arson Blake Gardner III, Toby Reeve. Asst. to co-dirs. Bement Sch., Old Deerfield, Mass., 1968-70; asst. to headmaster Walnut Hill Sch. and Sch. of Performing Arts, Natick, Mass., 1970-72; dir. admissions, devel., alumni affairs and pub. relations Colorado Springs Sch., 1972-74; headmaster Garland Sch., Chester, N.J., 1974-78; headmaster, founder, owner HighCroft Sch., Williamstown, Mass., 1978—. Mem. Nat. Assn. Ind. Schs., Council on Basic Edn., Orter Soc. Home and Office: HighCroft Sch Gale Rd PO Box 167 Williamstown MA 01267

MILNE, FRANK EMMETT, educator; b. Halifax, Nova Scotia, Can., Mar. 31, 1935; s. Frank Alden and Lillian May (Emmett) M.; B.S., Dalhousie U., 1956; B.E., 1957; M.A., Saint Mary's, 1962; postgrad. (Shell Merit fellow) Cornell, 1965. Tchr. math. Queen Elizabeth High Sch., Halifax, 1957-62; television tchr. math N.S. Dept. of Edn., 1962-74; vice prin. extension services N.S. Inst. Tech., 1974—; lectr. math. Dept. of Edn., Saint Mary's U., Halifax, 1968—. Trustee Dr. R.E. Marshall Scholarship Fund, 1970—. Mem. Dalhousie U. Alumni Assn. (pres. 1969-70), N.S. Math. Tchrs. Assn. (pres. 1962-63). Clubs: Waegwoltic (past pres.); Masons (32 deg.), Shriners, Rotary (dir. 1969-70), Kiwanis (v.p. 1978-79). Home: 6110 Roxton Rd Halifax NS B3H 1H8 Canada Office: PO Box 483 Halifax NS B3J 2R7 Canada

MILNE, GEORGE HECTOR FANJOY, hosp. supply co. exec.; b. New Glasgow, N.S., Can., Nov. 23, 1926; s. James Andrew and Mary Evelyn (Fanjoy) M.; B.Commerce, McGill U., 1948, B. Engring., 1953; m. Carolyn Boyd Wiseheart, Mar. 18, 1968; children—Mary (Mrs. Lee Pillsbury), James, Catherine, Malcolm, Christopher, Elizabeth. Came to U.S., 1961. Successively plant mgr., sec.-treas., dir. Horton Steel Works, Ltd., Ft. Erie, Ont., Can., 1953-61; controller Duriron Co., 1961-64; mgr. corp. accounting, then mgr. corp. systems and data processing Xerox Corp., 1964-69; exec. v.p., treas., dir., mem. exec. com. Scholastic mags., 1969-75; corp. v.p., treas., dir. fin. and adminstrn. IPCO Hosp. Supply Corp., 1975—; dir. H.M. Boyd Co., Cheyenne, Wyo., Transnat. World Trade Corp., asso. dir. Peoples Trust Co., Hackensack, N.J. Chartered accountant, Que., Ont.; C.P.A., Ohio; registered profl. engr., Que., Ont. Mem. Nat. Assn. Accountants, Fin. Execs. Inst., Engring. Inst. Canada, ASME. Clubs: N.Y. Yacht (N.Y.C.); Palisades Yacht (Englewood, N.J.), Masons. Home: 110 Summit St Englewood NJ 07631 Office: 1025 Westchester Ave White Plains NY 10604

MILNER, CHARLES FREMONT, JR., mfr.; b. Durham, N.C., July 21, 1942; s. Charles Fremont and Eloyse (Sargent) M.; B.A., Guilford Coll., 1963; M.B.A., Harvard, 1965; m. Molly Franc Wakefield, Aug. 28, 1965; children—Bernadette Ann, Eloyse Lee. Asst. to comptroller Harvard, 1965-66; instr. Northeastern U., Boston, 1965-66; with Burlington Hosiery Co. div. Burlington Industries (N.C.), 1966-71, asst. v.p., 1970-71; exec. v.p. Parklane Hosiery Co., Inc., Great Neck, N.Y., 1971-74, also dir.; pres. Rudin & Roth, Inc., N.Y.C., 1974-75, also dir.; v.p. apparel group M. Lowenstein and Sons, Inc., N.Y.C., 1975-76; pres., chief exec. officer Bacon Baker Commack and Camp divs., pres. hosiery group Genesco, Inc., N.Y.C., 1974—. Trustee Friends Acad., Locust Valley, N.Y., 1974—. Home: 6 Libby Dr Glen Head NY 11542 Office: 1290 Ave of Americas New York City NY 10019

MILNES, JOHN HERBERT, fuel oil co. exec.; b. Toronto, Ont., Can., Aug. 9, 1912; s. James Herbert and Isabel Bansley (Sinclair) M.; student Ridley Coll., 1928-29, Upper Can. Coll., 1929-32, U. Toronto. With The Milnes Coal Co. Ltd., Toronto, 1937-48; with Standard Fuel Co. Ltd., Toronto, 1949-74, exec. v.p., 1961-71, pres., 1971-74; with Milnes Fuel Oil Ltd., Toronto, 1950-61, exec. v.p., 1961-67, pres., 1967—; with Milnes Holding Co., Toronto, pres., 1971—. Served with Intelligence Corps, Canadian Army, 1942-46. Mem. Toronto Bd. Trade, Phi Kappa Phi. Mem. Ch. Eng. Clubs: Granite, Speakers Club of Toronto. Home: 22 Deer Park Crescent Toronto 12 ON M4V 2C2 Canada Office: 1815 Yonge St Toronto ON M4T 2A4 Canada

MILONOPOULOS, ANTHONY, acct.; b. Cambridge, Mass., Jan. 9, 1941; s. Nicholas and Georgia (Copanas) M.; A.S.A., Bentley Coll., 1961, B.S.A., 1970; m. Constantina A. Giannapoulos, Nov. 8, 1970; children—Jane, Irene, Elizabeth. Controller, Kenmore Hosp., Boston, 1970-76; mgr. cost reimbursement, internal auditor Faulkner Hosp., Boston, 1976—; pvt. practice gen. acctg. and income tax, Jamaica Plain, Mass. Pres., Greek Orthodox Ch., W. Roxbury. Served with USAF, 1961-65. Mem. Nat. Assn. Accts., Hosp. Fin. Mgmt. Assn. Greek Orthodox. Address: 80 Keystone St West Roxbury MA 02132

MILOTTE, LOUIS HENRY, JR., mgmt. accountant, bus. cons.; b. New Bedford, Mass., July 14, 1934; s. Louis Henry and Isabelle Beatrice (Betty) M.; B.C.S., Southeastern U., Washington, 1962; m. Cynthia Edith Avila, May 16, 1953; children—Louis Henry, C. Marie, Melissa Ann, Annette Suzanne, John Paul. Controller, Arlington Iron Works, Manassas, Va., 1956-58, Riverton Corp. (Va.), 1968-69, Bus. Equipment Mfg. Assn., Washington, 1969-71, Richard Neel & Co., C.P.A.'s, Alexandria, Va., 1971-73; pres. Mgmt. Adv. Services, Inc., Washington, 1973—, MAS Internat. Ltd., Sterling, Va., 1978—; lectr. Strayer Coll., 1970-74, No. Va. Community Coll., 1975—. Mem. Com. Econ. Devel., Loudon County, Va.; bd. dirs. Small Bus. Mgmt. Inst. Served with USMC, 1952. Certified mgmt. cons. Mem. Nat. Assn. Accountants, Nat. Soc. Pub. Accountants, Loudon C. of C. (treas. 1978), Sterling Mchts. and Profl. Assn. (pres. 1978), Inst. Mgmt. Cons. Club: Kiwanis (pres. Sterling). Home: 105 N Ithaca Rd Sterling VA 22170 Office: PO Box 17346 Dulles Internat Airport Washington DC 20041

MILSTEIN, RICHARD SHERMAN, lawyer; b. Westfield, Mass., May 9, 1926; s. Abraham and Sarah (Yudman) M.; A.B., Harvard U., 1948; J.D., Boston U., 1952. Admitted to Mass. bar, 1952; practice in Springfield, Mass., 1954—; asso. firm Ely, King, Kingsbury and Corcoran, 1954-58, partner, Ely, King, Kingsbury, Corcoran, Milstein and Beaudry, 1958—; instr. Western New Eng. Law Sch., Springfield, 1962-65, 74—; dir. Mass. Continuing Legal Edn., Inc., 1969-76; exec. dir. New Eng. Law Inst., 1975-76, Mass. Continuing Legal Edn.-New Eng. Law Inst. Inc., 1976—. Mem. Mass. Gov.'s Jud. Nominating Commn., 1975-78, Gov.'s Spl. Com. to Revise Mass. Securities Laws, 1970-73; chmn. City of Westfield (Mass.) Personnel Policy Bd., 1962-67; v.p. WGBY Pub. TV, 1975—; incorporator Springfield Symphony Orch., 1977—; dir. Stage West, Springfield, 1978—; life mem. Springfield Library Museums Assn., 1976—; mem. trustees com. Springfield Fine Arts Mus., 1978—. Served to lt. comdr. USCGR, 1952-54. Mem. Am. Law Inst., Am., Mass. bar found., Am., Mass. (adminstr. com. on continuing legal edn. of bar 1960-69, mem. edn. com. 1976-78, future planning com. 1976-78, council corp. law sect. 1978—), Hampden County (mem. exec. com. 1963-70, 72-78, grievance com. 1967-70), Boston (corp. law com. 1971—) bar assns., Assn. Continuing Legal Edn. Adminstrs. (exec. com. 1967-68, sec. treas. 1969-71), Boston U. Law Sch. Alumni Assn. Clubs: Harvard (pres. 1965-67), Colony (Springfield). Editorial bd. Mass. Law Quar., 1960-76. Home: 140 Chestnut St Springfield MA 01103 Office: 1387 Main St Springfield MA 01103

MILSTOCK, MAYER, pathologist; b. Iasy, Romania, Dec. 14, 1920; s. Leib and Iahat (Marovici) M.; came to U.S., 1961, naturalized, 1966; grad. Nat. Lyceum (Romania), 1939; M.D., U. Bucharest, 1950; m. Gilda Rachmuth, May 25, 1945. Asst. research Inst. of Research in Antibiotics, Bucharest, 1951-55, chief of lab., 1955-57; asst. prof. Med. Sch., Bucharest, 1954-56; chief of lab. Colentina Hosp., Bucharest, 1957-61; asst. pathologist Montefiore-Morrisania Hosp., N.Y.C., 1966; asst. prof. pathology N.Y.U., 1967-72, asso. prof. clin. pathology, 1972—; dir. lab. N.Y.U.-Goldwater Meml. Hosp., N.Y.C., 1969—. Recipient Physician Recognition award AMA, 1974. Diplomate Am. Bd. Pathology. Mem. Am. Soc. Clin. Pathologists, Coll. Am. Pathologists, N.Y. State Soc. Pathology, N.Y. Pathol. Soc., N.Y. Acad. Scis., Internat. Acad. Pathology, Sigma Xi. Jewish. Contbr. articles to profl. jours. Home: 370 76th St New York City NY 10021 Office: Goldwater Meml Hosp Roosevelt Island NY 10044

MILTENBERGER, FREDERICK WILLIAM, surgeon; b. Cumberland, Md., May 2, 1933; s. James Edward and Mary Agnes (Rephann) M.; B.S., Washington Coll., Chestertown Md., 1953; M.D., Med. Coll. Va., 1957; m. Mary F. Coffey, June 11, 1955; children—Francine, Lawrence, Julia, Beth, Matthew, Bernard, Rosalynn. Intern, Ohio Valley Gen. Hosp., Wheeling, W.Va., 1958; resident in surgery W.Va. U. Hosp., 1961-67; practice medicine specializing in thoracic, vascular and gen. surgery, Cumberland, 1967—; mem. staff Sacred Heart Hosp.; pres. staff Cumberland Meml. Hosp., 1977-79; bd. dirs. Med. Mut. Liability Ins. Soc. Md., 1975-81; pres. Region I Emergency Med. Services Advisory Council, 1977. Mem. Md., W. Md. profl. standards rev. orgns., 1977. Served with M.C., USAF, 1958-61. Mem. Allegany County (Md.) Med. Soc., Med. and Chirurg. Faculty State Md., AMA, A.C.S., Bernard Zimmerman Surg. Soc., Am. Coll. Angiology. Republican. Roman Catholic. Clubs: El Fidel, K.C. Contbr. articles to med. jours. Home: Route 2 Box 605 Cumberland MD 21502 Office: 122 S Centre St Cumberland MD 21502

MILTNER, JOHN ROBERT, assn. exec.; b. Conneaut, Ohio, Sept. 6, 1946; s. Robert John and Grace Evelyn (Hall) M.; B.S., Bowling Green U., 1968; m. Carol Lee Herd, Oct. 27, 1973; children—William, Kelli, Bryan, Tiffany, Robert. Exploring dir. Boy Scouts Am., Toledo, 1968-72, dir. exploring, N.Y.C., 1975-76, dir. devel., 1977—; mktg. mgr. IBM Corp., Toledo, 1972-73; regional mktg. mgr. Docutel Corp., Boston, 1974. Bd. dirs. Am. Humanics Found. Bd., Pace U., N.Y.C., 1977—. Mem. Nat. Soc. Fund Raising Execs. (dir. 1977—). Congregationalist. Home: 107 Summit Ave Upper Montclair NJ 07043 Office: Boy Scouts of America 345 Hudson St New York City NY 10014

MILTON, LEONARD, electronics mfg. co. exec.; b. N.Y.C., July 26, 1917; s. Israel M. and Sadie (Kranes) M.; E.E., Pratt Inst., 1939, D.Sc., 1965; m. Hilda Lozner, Dec. 29, 1946; children—Donn, Ilo, Cindy, Rand. Chief engr. Solar Mfg. Corp., Bayonne, N.J., 1940-46; v.p., chief engr. Filtron Co., Inc., Flushing, N.Y., 1946-56, pres., 1956-70, chmn. bd., 1970—, pres., chmn. bd., Bethpage, N.Y., 1977—; chmn. bd. APC Inc., Bethpage, 1975—; dir. Starrett Housing Corp., N.Y.C., 1967—. Pres. People to People Sports Com., 1966—; pres. L. Milton Found., 1950—; bd. govs. St. Huberts Soc.; trustee Pratt Inst. Mem. IEEE, Tau Beta Pi. Clubs: Shikar Safari, N.Y. African Safari; Glen Head Country (L.I.); Explorers, Adventurers (N.Y.C.). Author: Radio Interference in Aircraft Systems; Radio Interference in Aircraft Electrical and Electronic Systems; Electromagnetic Analysis of the Arctic; Interference Reduction Guide for Design Engineers. Patentee in field. Home: Windsor Gate Great Neck NY 11020 Office: 98 Cuttermill Rd Great Neck NY 11021

MILUTINOVICH, JUGOSLAV SRBOLJUB, educator; b. Belgrade, Yugoslavia, Sept. 10, 1935; s. Srboljub Milan and Jelena Vasa (Petrovich) M.; came to U.S., 1962; naturalized, 1968; B.Sc., U. Belgrade, 1957; M.B.A. with distinction (Harry Hopf fellow 1968-69), N.Y. U., 1969, Ph.D., 1970; m. Dragica Calvovic, Dec. 18, 1973; 1 dau., Yelena-Tiana. Exec. v.p. Betonite Mines, Petrovac na Moru, Monte Negro, Yugoslavia, 1957-60; buyer Duga Paints, Belgrade, 1960-62; asst. to gen. mgr. J. Felsenfeld Co., Inc., wholesale jewelers, N.Y.C., 1962-64; research asst. N.Y. U., 1965-68; asso. prof. mgmt. Temple U., 1969—; cons. to industry. Recipient Founders Day award N.Y. U., 1970, Univ. Honors scholar, 1971; Faculty research grantee Temple U., 1970, 75; recipient Fulbright-Hays Faculty research award, 1975. Mem. Acad. Mgmt., Am. Psychol. Assn., Internat. Assn. Applied Psychology, Am. Inst. Decision Scis., Ops. Research Soc. Am., Inst. Mgmt. Scis., Delta Pi Sigma, Mu Gamma Tau, Beta Gamma Sigma, Omicron Delta Epsilon. Republican. Mem. Eastern Greek Orthodox Ch. Co-author: Decision Making in Administration: Text, Critical Incidents and Cases, 1979. Contbr. numerous articles to profl. jours., monographs. Home: 6120 Brockton Rd Hatboro PA 19040 Office: Dept Mgmt Sch Bus Adminstrn Temple Univ Philadelphia PA 19122

MIMM, ROBERT FRANKLIN, govt. ofcl.; b. Lancaster, Pa., Oct. 18, 1924; s. Paul Kinaley and Violet Marie M.; student West Chester State Coll., 1946-47; B.S. in Edn., Millersville State Coll., 1950; M.Ed., Rutgers U., 1956; M.A., Trenton State Coll., 1974; postgrad. U. Wis., 1974; m. Theresa Beatrice Symanowicz, Aug. 22, 1953; children—Bonita Marie Mimm Phillips, Randolph Robert, Roberta Eileen, Noreen Adrienne, Clifford Robert, Douglas Robert. Sch. tchr., Bareville, Morrisville and Langhorne, Pa., 1952-59; with U.S. Post Office, Levittown, Pa., 1959-62; edn. services officer Edn. Center, U.S. Army, Fort Dix, N.J., 1962-65, edn. dir., Augsburg, Germany, 1965-67, chief mil. occupational specialty vocat. tech. sect. Edn. Br., Fort Dix, 1967-77, chief student services and adminstrn. sect., 1977—; adj. instr. social scis. Burlington County Coll. Served with USAAF, 1943-46, AUS, 1950-52. Mem. Assn. U.S. Army, Am. Def. Preparedness Assn., Armed Forces Mgmt. Assn. (v.p. Delaware Valley chpt. 1965-66, program chmn. 1963-65), Civilian Mgrs. and Profls. Assn. (chmn. steering com. Fort Dix chpt. 1973), Criminal Investigation Div. Agts. Assn. (bd. govs. 1977, v.p. 1978), Am. Legion, VFW. Clubs: Shore Athletic, AAU, U.S. Olympic Assn., N.Y. Masters Sports Assn. Nat. AAU Masters Track champion, 1975-78; N.Am. Masters Track champion, 1978; mem. U.S. Olympic Team, 1960. Home: 44 Endwell Ln Willingboro NJ 08046 Office: Edn Br DPCA Fort Dix NJ 08640

MIMS, GEORGE L., coll. adminstr.; b. Batesburg, S.C., Feb. 27, 1934; s. George W. and Mary Aletha (Corley) M.; B.S., Fla. A. and M. U., 1955; M.A., Columbia U., 1957, profl. diploma, 1967; Ed.D., Rutgers U., 1976; m. Clara Ann Twigg, Aug. 12, 1961; children—Cheryl Ann, Carla Aletha. Head resident, instr. Fisk U., Nashville, 1959-61; dean of students Volusia County Community Coll., Daytona Beach, 1961-63; asst. placement dir. Hunter Coll., Bronx, N.Y., 1963-67; dir. spl. programs Pace U., N.Y.C., 1968—. Pres. HEOP-Profl. Orgn., N.Y. State, 1971-73, 76-77, Better Edn. Orgn. Lakeview, N.Y., 1977-78; mem. 100 Black Men of Nassau-Suffolk Counties, 1976—. Served with U.S. Army, 1957-59. Mem. Am., N.Y. personnel and guidance assns., Assn. Non-White Concerns, Am. Coll. Personnel Assn., Am. Edn. Research Assn., Kappa Delta Pi, Phi Delta Kappa, Alpha Phi Alpha, Alpha Phi Omega. Home: 885 Seneca Rd West Hempstead NY 11552 Office: Office of Spl Programs Pace U New York City NY 10038

MIN, DAVID BYONG, food scientist; b. Seoul, Korea, Sept. 12, 1942; s. Yun Shik and Soon Duk (Yun) M.; came to U.S., 1965, naturalized, 1972; B.S. magna cum laude, Seoul Nat. U., 1965; M.S., U. Minn., 1969; Ph.D., Rutgers U., 1973; m. Linda Lou Gieseke, June 14, 1969; children—Peter Kee, Stephen Kee. Research fellow chemistry Rutgers U., New Brunswick, N.J., 1970-73; sr. flavor chemist John Stuart Research Lab., Quaker Oats Co., Barrington, Ill., 1973-76; instr. chemistry Ill. Inst. Tech., Chgo., 1976; prin. scientist Best Foods Research Center, CPC Internat., Union, N.J., 1976—; hon. asst. prof. chemistry Rutgers U., New Brunswick, 1977—. Gen. Foods research fellow, 1973. Mem. Am. Oil Chemists Soc. (research awardee 1972, 73, dir. NE sec. 1976—), Inst. Food Technologists,

Am. Soc. Mass Spectrometry, Am. Chem. Soc., Sigma Xi, Phi Tau Sigma, Alpha Zeta. Club: Toastmaster. Contbr. articles to profl. publs. Home: 19 Northview Rd New Providence NJ 07974 Office: 1120 Commerce Ave Union NJ 07083

MIN, LEO YOON-GEE, educator, research adminstr.; b. Seoul, Korea, Nov. 1, 1933; s. Byung Chan and Kyung Soon (Hong) M.; came to U.S., 1965; B.A., Seoul Nat. U., 1956, M.Ed., 1965; M.S., Stanford U., 1968, Ph.D., 1970; m. Sook Ja Bang, May 14, 1972; children—Richard Kyunglib, Sarah Kyungok. Sr. researcher Central Edn. Research Inst., Seoul, 1958-65; mathematician Stanford Research Inst. Menlo Park, Calif., 1968-70; sr. statistician Center Applied Linguistics, Arlington, Va., 1974-75; asst. prof. edn. Cath. U. Am., 1970-76, cons. instl. research and planning, 1974-75, dir. Div. Research and Evaluation MSSD Gallandet Coll., 1976—; cons. Nat. Planning Assn., 1971-72. Internat. Devel. fellow East-West Center, Honolulu, 1965. Mem. Am. Ednl. Research Assn., Am. Psychol. Assn., Am. Statis. Assn., Ops. Research Soc. Am., Inst. Mgmt. Sci. Contbr. articles in field. Home: 6022 Forrest Hollow Lane Springfield VA 22152 Office: 4001 Harwood Rd NE Washington DC 20017

MINA, GEORGE MICHAEL, orthopedic surgeon; b. Cairo, Egypt, Feb. 20, 1939; s. Michael G. and Rose Fam (Fanous) M.; came to U.S., 1966, naturalized, 1969; M.B., B.Ch., Cairo U., 1965; m. Mary George Kazazis, Feb. 25, 1967; children—Anthony, George Michael. Intern, St. Clare's Hosp., N.Y.C., 1966-67; resident Kings County Hosp. Center and Downstate Med. Center, Bklyn., 1967-69, 70-72; asst. instr. surgery Downstate Med. Center, Bklyn., 1968,72; practice medicine specializing in orthopedic surgery, Potsdam, N.Y., 1972—; mem. staffs Potsdam Hosp., State Hosp. at Ogdensburg, N.Y. Served with M.C., AUS, 1969-71. Decorated Commendation medal. Diplomate Am. Bd. Orthopedic Surgery. Fellow Am. Acad. Orthopedic Surgery, A.C.S. Home: 10 Wellings Dr Potsdam NY 13676 Office: 1 Riverview Dr Potsdam NY 13676

MINADAKIS, NICHOLAS JOHN, library dir.; b. Island of Chios, Greece, Jan. 22, 1924; s. John N. and Charikleia (Mavroudis) M.; came to U.S., 1958, naturalized, 1971; Proficiency in English, English Lang. Inst. U. Mich., 1957; B.A., Boston U., 1962; M.L.S., Simmons Coll., 1964; m. Irene Xydelis, 1976; 1 son, John Nicholas. Sales mgr. United Africa Co. Ltd., Ghana, West Africa, 1953-57; tchr. modern Greek lang., Assumption Sch., Somerville, Mass., 1958-62; library intern Baker Library Harvard, 1962-64; library dir. Hellenic Coll., 1964-68; library dir. Chelsea (Mass.) Pub. Library, 1969—; corporator Atlantic Bank of Chelsea and Revere (Mass.), 1972-78, trustee, 1978—. Served with Greek Armed Forces, 1951-53. Mem. Am., New Eng., Mass. library assns., Men Librarian's Club, Center of Byzantine and Neohellenic Studies of Belmont (Mass.). Mem. Greek Orthodox Ch. Rotarian. Clubs: Hellicon, Pancretan (Boston). Contbr. articles to profl. jours. Home: 8 St Paul St Cambridge MA 02139 Office: 569 Broadway St Chelsea MA 02150

MINA-MORA, DORISE OLSON, artist; b. N.Y.C., June 8, 1932; d. Arthur E. and Anna (Karlsson) Olson; student Trapnagen Sch. Design, 1949-51, Art Students' League, 1952-56; m. Raul J. Mina-Mora, Oct. 27, 1967. Exhibited one-man shows Parrish Art Mus., Southampton, L.I., 1972, Bklyn. Mus., 1970, Nat. Art League, 1970, Caravan House Gallery, N.Y.C., 1973, State U. N.Y., Stony Brook, 1978, ann. show Nat. Arts Club, N.Y.C.; exhibited group shows Nat. Acad., N.Y.C., Met. Mus. Art, N.Y.C.; illustrations for West Vaco, N.Y.C., Holt-Rhinehart-Winston pubs., N.Y.C.; demonstrator techniques for art socs.; represented in permanent collections Southampton High Sch., William Cook Shipping Co., R. Chapdelaine & Co., also numerous pvt. collections. Recipient Knickerbocker Artists Gold medal of honor, 1968, Am. Legion Spirit of '76 Exhibit 1st pl., 1969, Nat. Art League Gold medal, 1970, Nat. Art League 1st pl. watercolors, 1970, Nat. Arts Club Grumbacher award, 1970, 1st pl. Greenwich Savs. Bank, 1st pl. watercolors Burr Artists, 1975, Malverne Artists, 1976, Windsor and Newton award, 1976, 77, numerous awards Washington Sq. Outdoor Art Shows. Mem. Catharine Lorillard Wolfe Art Club, Allied Artists of Am., Burr Artists, Nat. Artists Profl. League, Knickerbocker Artists, Nat. Soc. Painters in Casein and Acrylic., Art Students League, Nat. Art League, Audubon Artists, Nat. Arts Club. Home: 87 Central Blvd Oakdale NY 11769

MINA-MORA, RAUL JOSÉ, artist; b. Santa Ana, El Salvador, Mar. 13, 1915; s. Carlos and Isabel (Rodrigues-Vides) Mina-M.; student San Francisco Sch. Design, 1938, Rudolph Shaffer Sch. Design, 1939, N.Y. Art League, 1950; m. Dorise Olson, Oct. 27, 1967. Came to U.S., 1924, naturalized, 1940. One man shows Wickford Gallery, 1971, 72, 73, 74, Parish Art Mus., 1973-74, Caravan House, N.Y.C., 1973; exhibited in group shows Parish Art Mus., 1972-73, Bklyn. Mus., 1972, Springfield (Mass.) Mus., 1973, Berkshire Mus., 1974, Met. Mus. Art, N.Y.C., 1977, also Salmagundi Club, Nat. Acad., Union Carbide Gallery, Lever House Gallery, Nat. Art League, N.Y.C. Represented in permanent collection Freiden Calculator Co., N.Y.C., South Hampton (N.Y.) High Sch. Instr. design and visual architecture Rudolph Shaffer Sch. Design, San Francisco, 1939; dir. Wank & Wank Advt., San Francisco, 1939-40; creative dir. Hannah Advt. Agy., San Francisco, 1946-47; cons. art dir. Blow Advt. Co., San Francisco, 1948-49, Roma Wines Co., San Francisco, 1949-50; cons. art dir. designer, illustrator, advt. agencies San Francisco, N.Y., Phila., Chgo.; illustrator ednl. books and outerspace books. Served with 65th Inf. Div., AUS, World War II. Recipient Gold medal finest fgn. architecture San Francisco World's Fair, 1939, Pan Am. prix for abstract art, 1939, Grand Prix for Internat. competition in Modern Art, Pan Am. Soc., San Francisco, 1939, Silver medals oils Nat. Art Club, 1970, Kupferman award Nat. Art Soc. Casine and Acrylic, 1971, Frank Monahan Meml. award for acrylics Nat. Arts Club, 1971, and others. Mem. Salmagundi Club, Burr Artists, Am. Artist Profl. League (Winsor and Newton award, Grand prize), Nat. Soc. Painters in Casein (dir.), Nat. Art League (Gold medal watercolor 1973, 1st prize oils 1974), Knickerbocker Artists (pres. 1974-76), Nat. Arts Club. Home: 87 Central Blvd Oakdale NY 11769

MINASI, JOSEPH, physician; b. Scilla, Calabria, Italy, Sept. 9, 1919; s. Salvatore and Angela (Neri) M.; M.D., U. Genoa, Italy, 1945; diploma in surgery U. Turin U. Genoa, 1951; m. Angela Victoria Lo Faro, Oct. 20, 1951; children—Louis Robert, Joseph Paul, John Salvatore, Marc Anthony. Came to U.S., 1953, naturalized, 1956. Intern, St. Barnabas Hosp., Newark, 1953-54, Unity Hosp., Bklyn., 1954-55; resident Mount Sinai Hosp., N.Y.C., 1967-69; gen. practice medicine, 1956-67, specializing in anesthesiology, 1967—, N.Y.C., 1956-59, Lynbrook, N.Y., 1959—; mem. staffs South Nassau Communities Hosp., Oceanside, N.Y. (sec. med. staff 1974-76), Mercy Hosp., Rockville Centre, N.Y. Trustee Our Lady of Peace Ch., Lynbrook. Diplomate Am. Bd. Anesthesiology. Fellow Am. Coll. Anesthesiologists; mem. Nassau County Med. Soc., Nassau County Acad. Medicine, Am. Soc. Anesthesiology, N.Y. State Soc. Anesthesiologists (dist. v.p. 1973-74, pres. 1974-76), Acad. Romana di Cultura. Home: 121 Hempstead Ave Lynbrook NY 11563 Office: 165 N Village Ave Rockville Centre NY 11570

MINASY, ARTHUR JOHN, aerospace and electronic detection systems exec.; b. N.Y.C., July 19, 1925; s. John and Esther (Horvath) M.; B.S. in Adminstrv. Engring., N.Y. U., 1949, M.S. in Indsl. and Mgmt. Engring., 1952; postgrad. Case Inst. Tech., 1953-55; m. Jayne Marion Leary, June 29, 1946; children—Karen Lynn, Keith Leary, Kathy Jayne. Asst. gen. mgr. def. div. Bulova Watch Co., Maspeth, N.Y., 1950-53; chief indsl. engr. Standard Products Co., Cleve., 1953-55; gen. mgr. ops. Gruen Industries, Cin., 1955-57; mgmt. cons. Booz-Allen & Hamilton, N.Y.C., 1957-60; mfg. mgr. Sperry Gyroscope Co., Great Neck, N.Y., 1960-62; v.p. ops. Belock Instrument Co., College Point, N.Y., 1962-64; pres. Detection Devices, Inc., Hicksville, N.Y., 1963—, KNOGO Corp., Hicksville; dir. KNOGO Internat. Corp. and KNOGO Europe Ltd., Brussels, Belgium, KNOGO Italia S.r.l., Milan, Italy; prin. Arthur J. Minasy & Assos., Mgmt. Cons., 1957-62; adv. bd. Abilities, Inc. Lectr. sci. law enforcement, detection systems. Bd. dirs., mem. adv. bd. Human Resources Found.; trustee Rehab. Inst. Served with AUS, 1943-46. Mem. Am. Inst. Indsl. Engrs., Am. Ordnance Assn., Am. Mgmt. Assn., Tau Beta Pi, Alpha Pi Mu. Patentee in field. Home: 15 Hunting Hill Rd Woodbury NY 11797 Office: KNOGO Corp Hicksville NY 11801

MINER, LISBETH (MRS. ALASDAIR WILLIAM SPENS-THOMSON), writer, editor, photographer; b. Litchfield, Conn., Oct. 14, 1915; d. Ellsworth Frost and Mary Helen (Kennard) Miner; B.A., Ohio Wesleyan U., 1937; postgrad. N.Y. U., 1938, U. Conn., 1973; m. Alasdair William Spens-Thomson, Sept. 19, 1949 (dec. 1977); children—Alasdair William, Shena Elisabeth. Mem. editorial staffs Soundings, Essex, Conn., 1964—, Fairfield County, Westport, Conn., 1977—; works pub. Boatings, Motorboating and Sailing, Sailing, Yachting, Yachting Racing, N.Y. Times, Bridgeport (Conn.) Post; tchr. lang. arts and communications, 1966-75. Recipient certificate of Appreciation, USCG Aux., 1972; Dir.'s award merit Nat. Assn. Engine and Boat Mfrs., 1973; named 1st in sports category Nat. Fedn. Press Women. Mem. Women in Communications, Nat. Fedn. Press Women, Boating Writers Internat. Home and office: Sylvester Ct East Norwalk CT 06855

MINER, (THEODORE) RICHARDSON, JR., hosp. adminstr.; b. Bklyn., July 15, 1936; s. Theodore R. and Florence (Carroll) M.; A.B., Middlebury (Vt.) Coll., 1958; M.A., Trinity Coll., Hartford, Conn., 1964; m. Barbara Alice Weeks, June 12, 1976; 1 dau., Meredith Weeks; 1 dau. by previous marriage, Robin. Tchr., Kingswood Sch., West Hartford, Conn., 1962-64, head lower sch., 1967-69; tchr., adminstr. Frankfurt Internat. Sch., Oberursel, Germany, 1964-67; asst. to pres. Middlebury Coll., 1969-77, sec., 1977-79; dir. devel. Lahey Clinic, Boston, 1979—; bd. corporators Burlington Savs. Bank (Vt.). Auditor, Town of Cornwall, Vt., 1971-74, selectman, 1974-79; chmn. bd. dirs. Health Policy Council, State of Vt., 1976-77, bd. dirs. Vt. Health Policy Corp., 1977-79; chmn. Statewide Health Coordinating Council, 1978-79; bd. dirs. Porter Med. Center, Middlebury, 1972-79, pres., 1975-79; bd. dirs. Addison County (Vt.) chpt. ARC, 1970—. Served with USN, 1958-62. Home: 151 Plainfield Rd Concord MA 01742 Office: Lahey Clinic 605 Commonwealth Ave Boston MA 02215

MINER, SAMUEL NORTON, architect; b. Salisbury, Conn., Mar. 28, 1911; s. Samuel Corning and Fanny Maria (Peckham) M.; grad. Hotchkiss Sch., 1930; B.Arch., Mass. Inst. Tech., 1936; m. Isabel Keller, June 1937; children—1 dau. Linda (Mrs. Malcolm MacLaren, Jr.). Apprentice, Perry M. Duncan, architect, N.Y.C., 1938-41; site planner Corps Engrs., 1941-43; individual practice architecture, N.Y.C., 1938-41, Lakeville, Conn., 1946—; cons. architect on airport site valuation for Nfld. with O'Connor, Kilham, N.Y.C., 1946; prin. work includes design and reconstrn. Northwestern Conn. towns and neighboring towns in N.Y. and Mass.; chmn. Historic Dist. Commn. Salisbury, 1977—; chmn. Salisbury Cemetery Assn., 1970—; sec., treas. Salisbury Parks and Forest Commn., 1968—; chmn. N.W. Conn. region for Gov. Conn. Task Force Housing, 1971-73; chmn. N.W. Conn. Region for Housing Assistance Council Conn. Dept. Community Affairs, 1974—; selectman Town of Salisbury, 1977—; trustee Scoville Meml. Library, 1950-70; chmn. Salisbury Republican Town Com., 1970. Served to lt. USNR, 1943-45. Fellow Am. Registered Architects; mem. AIA, Conn. Soc. Architects. Congregationalist (chmn. trustees 1971-78). Home: Top of the Hill Lakeville CT 06039

MING, SI-CHUN, educator, pathologist, b. Shanghai, China, Nov. 10, 1922; s. Sian-Fan and Jan-Teh (Kuo) M.; came to U.S., 1949, naturalized, 1964; M.D., Nat. Central U. Coll. Medicine, China, 1947; m. Pen-Ming Lee, Aug. 17, 1957; children—Carol, Ruby, Stephanie, Michael, Jeffrey, Eileen. Resident pathology Mass. Gen. Hosp., Boston, 1952-56; asso. pathologist Beth Israel Hosp., Boston, 1956-67; asst. prof. pathology Harvard Med. Sch., 1965-67; asso. prof. U. Md. Med. Sch., Balt., 1967-71; prof. pathology Temple U. Med. Sch., Phila., 1971—. Nat. Cancer Inst. sr. fellow Karolinska Inst., Stockholm, Sweden, 1964-65. Mem. Internat. Acad. Pathology, Am. Assn. Pathologists, AAAS, N.Y. Acad. Scis. Author: Tumors of the Esophagus and Stomach, 1973. Office: 3400 N Broad St Philadelphia PA 19140

MINGOLLA, COSMO EDWARD, constrn. co. exec.; b. Worcester, Mass., Sept 8, 1914; s. Joseph John and Stella (Favulli) M.; student Northeastern U., 1932-34; L.H.D., Assumption Coll., 1965; m. Elaine F. Toombs, Apr. 30, 1938; 1 son, Edward J. With Bayer & Mingolla Industries, Inc., Worcester, 1934—, exec. v.p., 1950-71, pres., 1971-74, chmn. bd., 1974—; treas. Lincoln-Worcester Assos., Worcester, 1971—; chmn. bd. Pleasant Valley Corp., 1974—; dir. Freedom Fed. Savs. & Loan Assn., Worcester, Old Colony Bank of Worcester County, N.A., New Eng. Electric System. Trustee Assumption Coll., Worcester, St. Camillus Hosp., Whitinsville, Mass.; trustee, mem. exec. com. St. Vincent Hosp., Worcester, 1960—. Recipient Isaiah Thomas award Worcester Advt. Club, 1969; Jimmy Fund award, Children's Cancer Research Found., 1971; Pub. Service award SBA, 1973; Star Solidarity, Republic of Italy, 1971; Good Neighbor award Beth Israel Brotherwood, Worcester, 1974; Man of Yr. award New Eng. Profl. Golf Assn., 1977. Mem. Worcester Area C. of C., New Eng. Rd. Builders Assn. (past pres.). Roman Catholic. Clubs: Gridiron (Boston), Pleasant Valley Country (Sutton, Mass.). Home: 18 Malden St West Boylston MA 01583 Office: PO Box 991 Worcester MA 01613

MINIFIE, JAMES MACDONALD, JR., architect; b. Paris, France, Apr. 14, 1934; s. James MacDonald and Helen Ursula (Gordon) M.; came to U.S., 1940, naturalized, 1946; A.B. cum laude, Harvard U., 1956, M.Arch., 1962; m. Lola Josephine Ham, Nov. 12, 1966; children—Sarah Hale, Margaret Chapin. Jr. draftsman several Boston offices, 1962-66; job capt. Arthur H. Brooks, Jr., and Assos., Cambridge, Mass., 1966-67; project mgr., office mgr. Integrated Design Services Group, Cambridge, 1967-71; project mgr. Hoyle, Doran & Berry, Architects, 1971-73; pvt. archtl. practice, Boston, 1973—; resident cons. architect Coffin & Richardson, Inc.; architect residential bldgs., renovations and additions, including Gilbert House, Newton, Mass.; architect for renovation town hall, also new library, East Millinocket, Maine, also archtl. design water and sewage treatment plants, Newburyport, Mass. and Bath, Maine; design cons. Ondine Gallery, Boston; instr. Boston Archtl. Center, 1970-74. Team capt. archtl. div. United Fund, 1972; vol. Project 70, Brighton, Mass.; mem. Democratic Ward Com., Cambridge, 1976. Served to lt. arty., AUS, 1956-58. Recipient certificate of merit Dracut Housing Competition, 1975. Registered architect, Mass., Fla., Maine; certified Nat. Council Archtl. Registration Bds. Mem. Boston Soc. Architects (urban design com.), Nat. Trust Hist. Preservation, Carpenter Center for Visual Arts Assn., Charles River Basin Com. Clubs: Harvard (Boston), Speakers. Home: 51 Ellery St Cambridge MA 02138 Office: Suite 902 141 Milk St Boston MA 02109

MINIKES, STEPHAN MICHAEL, lawyer, banker; b. Berlin, Aug. 28, 1938; came to U.S., 1949, naturalized, 1957; B.S., Cornell U., 1961; J.D., Yale U., 1964; m.; 1 child. Admitted to N.Y. bar, 1965, U.S. Supreme Ct. bar, 1973, D.C. bar, 1977; asso. firm Milbank, Tweed, Hadley & McCloy, N.Y.C., 1964-68, Borden & Ball, N.Y.C., 1968-72; counsel to spl. cons. for energy Pres. of U.S., 1973; counsel to chief Naval Ops., Washington, 1972-74; sr. v.p. Export-Import Bank of U.S., Washington, 1974-77; partner firm Butler, Binion, Rice, Cook & Knapp, Houston and Washington, 1977—; Treas., Nat. Com. for Responsible Health Care; mem. exec. com. Yale Law Sch.; chmn. fin. com. Washington Opera Mem. Am., Fed., D.C. bar assns., Assn. Bar City N.Y., Am. Soc. Internat. Law, Am. Arbitration Assn. (nat. panel), Cornell U., Yale U. alumni assns. Washington. Clubs: Univ., Yale (Washington). Contbr. articles to profl. jours. Office: 818 Connecticut Ave Washington DC 20006

MINISH, JOSEPH GEORGE, congressman; b. Throop, Pa., Sept. 1, 1916; s. George and Angeline (Nardozzi) Minish; ed. pub. schs.; m. Theresa LaCapra, June 15, 1943; children—George, James, Joyce. Polit. action dir. dist. 4, L.U.E., AFL-CIO, 1953-54; exec. sec. Essex W. Hudson Labor Council, 1954-61, exec. sec.-treas., 1961-62; mem. 88th-96th Congresses, 11th Dist. N.J.; mem. banking, finance and urban affairs com., chmn. subcom. on gen. oversight and renegotiation, mem. internat. devel. instns. and finance, consumer affairs subcoms.; mem. house adminstrn. com., mem. accounts, personnel and police subcoms. Served in World War 2. Roman Cath. K.C. Home: 66 Sheridan Ave West Orange NJ 07052 Office House Office Bldg Washington DC 20515

MINK, PATSY T., ofcl. Dept. State; b. Paia, Maui, Hawaii, Dec. 6, 1927; d. Suematsu and Mitama (Tateyama) Takemoto; B.A., U. Hawaii, 1948; J.D., U. Chgo., 1951; hon. degrees Lindenwood Coll., Wilson Coll., Duff's Inst.; m. John Francis Mink,; 1 dau., Gwendolyn R. Lectr., U. Hawaii, Honolulu, 1952-56, 59-62; atty. Ter. Hawaii Ho. of Reps., 1955; mem. Hawaii Ho. of Reps., 1956-58, Hawaii Senate, 1958-64; mem.-at-large 89th to 94th Congresses from Hawaii; mem. Edn. and Labor Com., mem. edn. gen. subcom., equal opportunities subcom., edn. select Subcom.; mem. Interior and Insular Affairs Com., chmn. mines and mining subcom., nat. parks and recreation subcom., territorial and insular affairs subcom.; asst. sec. for oceans and internat. environ. and sci. affairs Dept. State, Washington, 1977—. Charter pres. Young Democrats of Oahu (Hawaii), 1954; 1st territorial pres. Hawaii Young Dems., 1956; nat. v.p. Young Dem. Clubs Am., 1957; bd. dirs. Hawaii Assn. to Help Retarded Children, rural Oahu chpt. YMCA, Honolulu Symphony, Lanakila Crafts, Hawaii chpt. Am. Assn. UN. Recipient Sch. Bell award Overseas Edn. Assn., 1967, Leadership for Freedom award Roosevelt Coll., Chgo. Mem. Mems. of Congress for Peace Through Law (chmn. U.S.-China relations com.), Democratic Study Group (chmn. region IV). Club: 89th Dem. Congressional (sec.) (Washington). Office: Dept State 2201 C St NW Washington DC 20520

MINKOFF, JEFFREY, orthopedic surgeon; b. Bklyn., July 28, 1943; s. Sidney and Sylvia (Jacobson) M.; A.B., Western Res. U., 1963; M.D., State U. N.Y. Downstate Med. Center, 1967; children—Amy Melissa, Sheri Gail. Intern, Bronx (N.Y.) Municipal Hosp., 1967-68, surg. resident, 1968-69; resident in orthopedics Lenox Hill Hosp., N.Y.C., 1969, 71-72, staff, 1972—, cons. Inst. Sports Medicine and Athletic Trauma; resident St. Charles div. Cath. Med. Center, N.Y.C., 1970; staff House of St. Giles the Cripple, N.Y.C., 1977-78; dir. sports medicine N.Y. U., 1978—; cons. U.S. Olympic Fencing Team; team physician N.Y. Islanders, N.Y. Knickerbockers, N.Y. Cosmos; asso. attending physician Lenox Hill Hosp. Diplomate Am. Bd. Orthopedic Surgery. Fellow Am. Acad. Orthopedic Surgeons; mem. N.Y. County Med. Soc., AMA, Internat. Arthoscopic Soc. (charter), Am. Acad. Pediatrics (affiliate fellow), N.Y. State Soc. Orthopedic Surgeons, N.Y. Acad. Medicine, Heirodicus Soc., Am. Acad. Orthopedic Surgeons Soc. Sports Medicine. Contbr. book sect., articles to profl. jours. Address: 115 E 64 St New York City NY 10021

MINKOW, JULIUS, machine co. exec.; b. Bklyn., June 17, 1911; s. Robert and Ida (Flaxer) M.; M.E., Stevens Inst. Tech., 1932; m. Barbara Brill, Sept. 25, 1940; children—Roger and Peter (twins). Salesman, Hobbs Sales & Service N.Y.C., 1932-36; insp. Lockheed Aircraft, Burbank, Cal., 1937; engr. Minco Prod. Corp., N.Y.C., 1938, v.p. in charge, 1945-46, pres., Long Island City, Bklyn., 1951—; chief insp. Fairchild Camera & Instrument Co., Jamaica, N.Y., 1939-45; pres. Ropet Sales & Devel. Co., Long Island City, N.Y., 1947-51. Pres., treas. Fairfield Park Civic Assn., 1951-52; dist. chmn. Nassau County Boy Scouts Am. 1962. Recipient Order Arrow, Boy Scouts Am., 1962. Mem. Pi Lambda Phi. Clubs: Cache, Fish & Game (Quebec, Can.). Patentee in field. Home: 61 Overlook Terr Roslyn Heights NY 11577 Office: 69 Washington St Brooklyn NY 11201

MINKOWITZ, MARTIN, lawyer; b. Bklyn., Feb. 7, 1939; s. Jacob and Marion (Kornblau) M.; A.A., Bklyn. Coll., 1960, B.A., 1961; LL.B., Bklyn. Law Sch., 1963, LL.M., 1965, J.D., 1967; m. Helen Barbara Chesler, Feb. 14, 1965; 1 son, Stuart Allan. Admitted to N.Y. bar, 1963, U.S. Supreme Ct. bar, 1967, U.S. Tax Ct. bar, 1974, also fed. dist. cts.; sr. partner firm Minkowitz, Hagen & Rosenbluth, N.Y.C., 1964-76; spl. counsel to N.Y. Assembly Com. on real estate property tax, 1975—; gen. counsel N.Y. State Workmen's Compensation Bd., 1976—; instr. bus. law Kingsborough Community Coll. City U. N.Y., 1975—. Analyst cons. N.Y.C. Council, 1969; presiding hearing officer N.Y.C. Transp. Adminstrn., 1970-76; lectr. Brotherhood in Action, N.Y.C., 1972—; bd. dirs., mem., pres. Shore Terr. Coop. Housing Corp., Bklyn.; mem. met. council Am. Jewish Congress, 1977—. Mem. N.Y. State (chmn. lawyer referral com. 1973-76, acting chmn. com. on unlawful practice law 1976—), Am. bar assns., N.Y. County Lawyers Assn., Assn. Bar City N.Y., Bklyn. Law Sch. Alumni Assn. K.P. Author: (with others) Rent Stabilization and Control Laws, 1972. Editor: Bklyn. Law Sch. Newspaper, 1962-63. Home: 3655 Shore Pkwy Brooklyn NY 11235 Office: 2 World Trade Center New York City NY 10047

MINNA, JOHN DORRANCE, physician; b. San Francisco, Dec. 19, 1941; s. John and Roberta M.; B.A. with distinction, Stanford U., 1963, M.D., 1976; m. Myrna Lynn McElhany, July 23, 1964; children—Laura, Leslie. Predoctoral trainee USPHS, Stanford Med. Sch., 1963-67; intern Mass. Gen. Hosp., Boston, 1967-68, asst. med. resident, 1968-69; research asso. lab. biochem. genetics Nat. Heart and Lung Inst., NIH, Bethesda, Md., 1969-73, head sect. somatic cell genetics, 1973-75; chief med. oncology br. div. cancer treatment Nat. Cancer Inst.-VA, NIH, Washington, 1975—. Diplomate Am. Bd. Internal Medicine. Fellow A.C.P.; mem. Am. Assn. Cancer Research, Am. Soc. Clin. Oncology, Am. Soc. Hematology, Am. Soc. Human Genetics, Am. Soc. Cell Biology, AMA. Office: NCI-VA Med Oncology WVAMC 50 Irving St Washington DC 20042

MINNER, ARTHUR ROBERT, architect; b. N.Y.C., May 17, 1937; s. Fred and Barbara (Dittrich) M.; B.Arch., Pratt Inst., 1960; postgrad. Hunter Coll., N.Y. U.; m. Monique M. St. Laurent, May 14, 1966; children—Eric, Karl. Archtl. asst. William C. Humpries, AIA, N.Y.C., 1957-60, James O. Marshall, AIA, Lawton, Okla., 1962-63, Victor H. Bisharat, AIA, Stamford, Conn., 1965-68; architect-planner Arthur R. Minner, AIA, Irvington-on-Hudson, N.Y., Fort Lauderdale, Fla., 1963—; bd. advisors Am. Modular Communities; archtl. dir. Radice Realty, Wendover Devel. Corp. Served with AUS, 1961-63. Certified Nat. Council Archtl. Registration Bds.; registered architect N.Y., Conn., Wis., Fla., N.J. Mem. AIA, N.Y. State Assn. Architects. Architect-planner condominiums Whitehall South, Boca Raton, Fla., Environ of Inverrary, Fort Lauderdale, Fla.; townhouses Abbotsford, Irvington-on-Hudson, N.Y.; Montauk Yacht Club and Inn, L.I., N.Y.; asst. urban renewal projects, Stamford, Conn., various corp. headquarters. Contbr. articles in field to various mags., also chpts. in books. Office: Irvington-on-Hudson NY 10533

MINNICH, ELI BLAUSSER, elec. engr.; b. York, Pa., Nov. 17, 1926; s. Eli Franklin and Bertha Francis (Olewiler) M.; B.Sc., Pa. State U., 1954; m. Gloria Jean Eckenrode, Sept. 3, 1960; children—Timothy Allan, Patrick David. Engring. trainee ITE Circuit Breaker Co., Phila., 1954-55; chief elec. engr. Buchart Assos., York, 1955-63; elec. engr. Jno. Z. Barton Co., York, 1963-64; chief elec. engr. Nicholas Cowley Assos., Harrisburg, Pa., 1964-68; sec.-treas. Filson-Minnich & Assos. Inc., Harrisburg, 1968—. Served with USAF, 1946-49. Registered profl. engr., Pa., Del., R.I., Ga. Mem. Nat., Pa. socs. profl. engrs., Illuminating Engring. Soc., Constrn. Specifications Inst. Democrat. Roman Catholic. Home: 1125 Eric Dr Harrisburg PA 17110 Office: 2426 N 2d St Harrisburg PA 17110

MINNICH, LEONARD LORRAINE, sales engr.; b. Hegins, Pa., Dec. 3, 1922; s. Charles Ward and Lula Ruth (Kimmel) M.; grad. pub. schs.; m. Florence Dorothy Hacker, Aug. 30, 1942. Field engr. McKay Co., York, Pa., 1957-66; sales engr. Dow Chem. Co., Camden, N.J., 1966-68; rep. Wootten Welding Supplies, Salisbury, Md., 1969-72; sales engr. Amsco div. Abex Corp., Delmar, Md., 1972—. Tri-chmn. United Fund, 1971. Mem. Am. Welding Soc. (chmn. 1971-72), Am. Mgmt. Assn. Democrat. Home: R D 3 Mallard Dr Delmar MD 19940 Office: Abex Corp R D 3 Delmar MD 19940

MINNICH, SARAH ELY, psychologist; b. Lansford, Pa., Feb. 11, 1903; d. William Franklin and Dora (Huber) Ely; student Westchester State Coll., West Chester, Pa., 1920-22; B.S., Muhlenberg Coll., 1938; M.Ed., Pa. State U., 1944; m. Albert George Munnich, Sept. 3, 1928; children—William R., Albert B. Dir. art Lancaster (Pa.) schs., 1922-28, 35-54; pvt. practice psychology, Hazleton, 1944-54; supr. spl. edn. Lebanon County (Pa.) Schs., Lebanon, 1954-69; pvt. practice psychology, Lebanon, 1969—; psychologist, bd. dirs. Lebanon County Workshop, Inc., 1969—. Bd. dirs. Easter Seal Soc., Lebanon, Family and Childrens Services, Lebanon, Friends of Retarded, Lebanon. Mem. Pa., Am. psychol. assns. Home: PO Box 160 Cornwall PA 17016 Office: 704 Mentz Dr Lebanon PA 17042

MINNICK, ADRIENNE KAVANAGH, youth agency exec.; b. Evanston, Ill., Dec. 8, 1921; d. Clarence Henry and Elizabeth Victoria (Ashenden) Kavanagh; B.S., Northwestern U., Evanston, Ill., 1949; M.A., U. Mich., 1958, Ph.D., 1972; m. Richard Donald Minnick, Mar. 7, 1942; 1 son, Richard Donald II. Exec. dir. Girl Scouts Bartholomew County, Columbia, Ind., 1945-49, Girl Scouts Sheboygan, Wis., 1949-51, field supr., dir. research Girl Scouts Met. Detroit, 1951-72, orgn. project dir. Girl Scouts U.S.A., N.Y.C., 1972-74, research dir., 1974—. Research and devel. com. Nat. Bd. YMCA's, N.Y.C., 1976—; research and devel. task group Nat. Assembly Nat. Vol. Health and Social Welfare Orgns., N.Y.C., 1977—. Mem. Assn. Vol. Action Scholars, Assn. Girl Scout Exec. Staff, AAUW, Phi Kappa Phi, Pi Lambda Theta. Roman Catholic. Home: 200 N Barry Ave Mamaroneck NY 10543 Office: Girl Scouts USA 830 3d Ave New York NY 10022

MINNOCK, JEANNE B., city ofcl.; b. New Bedford, Mass., Jan. 8, 1920; d. Romeo Joseph and Laura Mary (Gravel) Bouvouloir; student Housatonic Community Coll., 1975-76, Sacred Heart U., 1972, 75, 77; m. Charles Joseph Minnock, June 30, 1941; children—Charles Joseph, Marie Gertrude, Jeannette Ann, Thomas Orien, John Vianney, Paul Henry. Purchasing and traffic clk. Sikorsky Aircraft, Stratford, Conn., 1955-57; assessing clk. City of Bridgeport (Conn.), 1957-62; purchasing agt. Town of Trumbull (Conn.), 1962—. Certified purchasing officer, purchasing mgr., emergency ops. planner. Mem. Pub. Purchasing Assn. Conn. (pres. 1971-72, program chairperson 1969-70), Nat. Purchasing Inst. (nat. sec. 1976-77, dir. 1974-76), Nat. Inst. Govtl. Purchasing, Conn. Assn. Purchasing Mgmt., Council Cath. Women, Am. Legion Aux. (past pres.). Roman Catholic. Club: Altrusa of Bridgeport (rec. sec. 1972-73). Home: 3005 Reservoir Ave Trumbull CT 06611 Office: Town Hall 5866 Main St Trumbull CT 06611*

MINNS, ALBERT EDWARD, JR., ret. army officer, pharmacist; b. Buffalo, Mar. 13, 1907; s. Albert Edward and Elizabeth (Sparks) M.; Ph.G., U. Buffalo, 1926; B.S., U. Md., 1961; m. Nordy E. Christensen, Aug. 2, 1931. Clk., Bell-Williams, Inc., Buffalo, 1921-26; pharmacist, mgr. Allendel Pharmacy, Buffalo, 1926-41; commd. 2d lt. AUS, 1941, advanced through grades to col., 1958, ret. 1961; curator Med. Mus., Armed Forces Inst. Pathology, 1958-61; staff pharmacist Roswell Park Meml. Inst., Buffalo, 1961-69, sr. staff pharmacist, 1969-73; chief pharmacist Niagara Luth. Home, Inc., 1973-77. Chief Brighton Vol. Fire Co. 5, Town of Tonawanda, N.Y., 1940; hon. mem. nat. adv. council Cleve. Health Mus. Decorated Bronze Star medal. Fellow Buffalo Soc. Natural Scis. (asso.); mem. Res. Officers Assn., Ret. Officers Assn., Am. Assn. Ret. Persons, Assn. Mil. Surgeons U.S., Western N.Y. Hosp. Assn., Kappa Psi. Republican. Episcopalian. Clubs: Masons, Shriners, Order Eastern Star. Home: 27 Southwood Dr Town of Tonawanda Buffalo NY 14223

MINTURN, BENJAMIN BRADSHAW, psychotherapist, counselor; b. Chgo., Mar. 7, 1929; s. Benjamin E. and Jeannette (Tate) M.; B.A., Trinity Coll., Hartford, Conn., 1951; M.Div., Va. Theol. Sem., 1954; m. Roberta Parker Schuette, 1951 (div. 1975); children—Judith, William, Peter; m. 2d, Lynda B. Batchelder, Apr. 3, 1976. Ordained to ministry Episcopal Ch., 1954; dir. dept. edn. Episc. Diocese Washington, 1963-66; rector Ch. of Ascension, Silver Spring, Md., 1957-64; dir. exec. Chesapeake Found., Washington, 1965-70; v.p. Marriage and Family Inst., Washington, 1970-74, pres., 1974—. Mem. Am. Assn. Marriage and Family Counselors (clin. chmn. nat. com. on legis. and pub. policy), Am. Assn. Marriage and Family Therapy (clin.). Democrat. Home: 4620 N Park Ave Chevy Chase MD 20015 Office: 1500 Massachusetts Ave NW Washington DC 20005

MINTZ, FRED, mech. engr.; b. N.Y.C., June 30, 1918; s. Sam and Dora (Feinbaum) M.; B.S., George Washington U., 1940; M.E., 1946; M. Engring., U. Calif., Los Angeles, 1965; m. Shirley R. Pomerantz (dec.); children—Susan Ellen Mintz Super, Robert Edward; m. 2d, Elaine K. Prensky, Feb. 22, 1976. Acoustical physicist U.S. Dept Navy, Washington, 1942-49; acoustical engr., supr. Armour Research Found., Chgo., 1949-55; mgr. various research lab. depts. Lockheed Calif. Co., Burbank, 1955-73; environ. control specialist, program mgr. EPA, Washington, 1973—. Pres. Community Concert Assn., Burbank, 1971-73. Recipient Silver medal EPA, 1977. Fellow Acoustical Soc. Am. (chmn. coms.). Jewish. Pioneer in testing high intensity sound on electronic components. Home: 4601 N Park Ave Chevy Chase MD 20015 Office: Crystal Mall #2 Crystal City Washington DC 20460

MINTZ, GILBERT, data processing cons.; b. Bklyn., Apr. 28, 1933; s. David and Lena (Kobulnick) M.; B.A., Coll. City N.Y., 1954, M.B.A., 1961; m. Joan Feingold, June 10, 1956; children—Harold Phillip, Steven Glen. Pub. accountant Irving Schwartz & Co., C.P.A.'s, Norwalk, Conn., 1955-58, Joseph Mandel C.P.A., N.Y.C., 1956; controller Colorforms, Norwood, N.J., 1958-63; controller Automatic Data Processing, Inc., Clifton, N.J., 1963-67, treas. 1967-69, v.p., treas., 1969-73; pres. Broadview Assos., Inc., Fort Lee, N.J., 1973—. Part time faculty Fairleigh Dickinson U., Teaneck, N.J., 1964-68, lectr. bus. systems, 1961—. C.P.A., N.J. Mem. Am. Inst. C.P.A.'s, N.J. Soc. C.P.A.'s, Beta Alpha Psi. Home: 55 Fairview Ave Woodcliff Lake NJ 07675 Office: 2125 Center Ave Fort Lee NJ 07024

MINTZ, NORMAN NELSON, univ. adminstr.; b. N.Y.C., Sept. 18, 1934; s. Alexander and Rebecca (Nelson) M.; A.B., Bucknell U., 1955; Ph.D., N.Y. U., 1966; m. Marcia Lynn Belford, Aug. 27, 1960; children—Geoffrey Belford, Douglas Nelson. Asst. prof. fin. Syracuse (N.Y.) U., 1965-69; asst. prof. econs. Columbia U., N.Y.C., 1969-72, asso. dean grad. sch. arts, scis., 1972-77, dep. provost, 1977-78, acting provost, 1978—, economist U.S.-P.R. Commn. on Status P.R., 1965-66; dir. Conf. Jewish Social Studies, 1975—; cons. various corps., U.S. govt. Served to lt. U.S. Army, 1955-57. Earhart Found. fellow, 1963-65. Mem. Am. Econ. Assn., Am. Fin. Assn., Royal Econ. Soc., AAUP. Author: Monetary Union and Economic Integration, 1970. Contbr. articles to profl. jours. Home: 35 Claremont Ave New York NY 10027 Office: 205 Low Library Columbia U New York NY 10027

MINTZ, ROBERT ALAN, fin. co. exec.; b. N.Y.C., Nov. 5, 1940; s. Harold S. and Hilda (Silvertein) M.; B.S., U. Tampa, 1965; M.B.A., Pace U., 1969; m. Rita Mae Grennan, Oct. 22, 1962; children—Dana Sheryl, Craig Aaron. Jr. accountant Chase Manhattan Bank, N.Y.C., 1965-66; sr. aerospace and electronics analyst, registered rep. H. Hentz & Co., N.Y.C., 1966-69; sr. instl. analyst Scheinman, Hochstin & Trotta, N.Y.C., 1969-70; asst. dir. research, sr. instl. analyst Filor, Bullard & Smyth, N.Y.C., 1970-73; dir. research, syndicate mgr. corp. fin. com., mgr. gold coin dept. Muller & Co., N.Y.C., 1973-76; v.p. research Phillips, Appel & Walden, N.Y.C., 1976—; cons. Lanchart Industries, Wichita Falls, Tex., Cinemation Industries, N.Y.C., Biometric Testing Inc., Englewood Cliffs, N.J., Internat. Cine Film, N.Y.C., Haber Instruments, Palisade Park (N.J.) Shade Tree Commn. Active Upper Saddle River (N.J.) PTA, Bicentennial Com. Mem. Fin. Analysts Fedn., N.Y. Soc. Security Analysts, Research Dirs. Forum, Fin. Analysts Research Found. Contbr. articles to fin. jours. and newspapers. Home: 58 Hampshire Hill Rd Upper Saddle River NJ 07458 Office: 111 Broadway New York City NY 10004

MINTZ, SAMUEL ISAIAH, humanist, educator; b. N.Y.C., Nov. 20, 1923; s. Nathan and Anna (Sheinkman) M.; B.A., Bklyn. Coll., 1948; M.A., Columbia U., 1949; Ph.D., 1958; postgrad. (Fulbright fellow) Cambridge (Eng.) U., 1955-56; m. Eleanor Streichler, Mar. 2, 1947; children—Joel, Jonathan. Faculty Coll. City N.Y., N.Y.C., 1948—, asst. prof. 1960-65, asso. prof., 1965-69, prof. English, 1969—, dir. grad. program in English, 1966-72; vis. prof. English, Guggenheim fellow, Fulbright research scholar Cambridge U., 1964-65; vis. prof. Columbia U., 1967-68; vis. fellow Wolfson Coll., Oxford (Eng.) U., 1972-73. Served with USAAF, 1943-46. Mem. Conf. on Brit. Studies, Milton Soc. Am., Modern Lang. Assn. Author: The Hunting of Leviathan, 1962. Editor History of Ideas News quar., 1950-55. Home: 628 Standish Rd Teaneck NJ 07666 Office: Dept English Coll City NY New York City NY 10031

MIR, JUAN ENRIQUE, interior designer; b. Havana, Cuba, Aug. 12, 1936; s. Enrique Mir y Ortiz and Pilar Alvarez y Rodriguez; came to U.S., 1960, naturalized, 1970; student Havana U., 1959, Villanueva U., 1959; B.A. in Interior Design, Pratt Inst., 1972. Interior designer R.H. Macy's, N.Y.C., 1961-68, Bloomingdales, N.Y.C., 1968-70; asso. Edward Benesch Interior Design, N.Y.C., 1970-72; pres., prin. Juan E. Mir, Interior Design Inc., N.Y.C., 1972—. Mem. Am. Soc. Interior Designers. Roman Catholic. Home and Office: 205 E 63 St New York City NY 10021

MIRA, JOHN FRANCIS, psychiatrist; b. Emporium, Pa., June 19, 1945; s. Dominic Earnest and Josephine Leona M.; M.D., Creighton U., 1970; m. Dec. 19, 1976. Intern, St. Paul and Parkland hosps., Dallas, 1970-71; resident Strong Meml. Hosp., Rochester, N.Y., 1971-74; staff psychiatrist Naval Regional Med. Center, Phila., 1974-76; chief inpatient staff psychiatrist Albert Einstein Med. Center, No. div., Phila., 1976—, acting chmn. adult psychiatry, 1978—. Served with USN, 1974-76. Diplomate Am. Bd. Psychiatry and Neurology. Mem. Am. Psychiat. Assn., Nat. Assn. Residents and Interns. Republican. Office: Div Psychiatry Albert Einstein Med Center Old York and Tabor Rds Philadelphia PA 19141

MIRABELLI, ANDRE ROBERT, performing arts center exec.; b. Bronx, N.Y., Aug. 26, 1941; s. Angelo and Fay Bernadette (Basso) M.; B.S., Fordham U., 1963; m. Marlene Frances Latronica, May 17, 1969; 1 son, Robert. Sr. accountant Peat Marwick, Mitchell & Co., N.Y.C., 1964-68, supr. White Plains, N.Y., 1968-71; controller Lincoln Center Performing Arts, Inc., N.Y.C., 1971-73, dir. bus. affairs, corp. sec., 1973—; cons. Nat. Com. for Cultural Resources, Concerned Citizens for Arts; guest lectr. Hofstra U., Tampa U. Served with U.S. Army, 1963-64. Mem. Am. Inst. C.P.A.'s, Nat. Assn. Accountants, Am. Mgmt. Assn., Fordham U. Bus. Sch. Alumni Assn. (dir.). Home: 2 Sylvan Ln Scarsdale NY 10583 Office: Lincoln Center Plaza 140 W 65th St New York NY 10023

MIRABITO, JOHN ARMAND, meteorologist; b. Somerville, Mass., May 16, 1917; s. Joseph and Mary Concetta (Cincotta) M.; B.S., Wake Forest U., 1941; certificate in Aerological Engring., Mass. Inst. Tech., 1943; m. Helen Whitfield Way, July 19, 1939. Commd. ensign USN, 1942, advanced through grades to comdr., 1956; sr. meteorologist, sci. adviser Operation Deep Freeze, 1954-59; sr. meteorologist, oceanographer for comdr. 6th Fleet, 1959-63; ret., 1963; with U.S. Weather Bur., 1963-65, Environ. Sci. Services Adminstrn., 1965-70; program analyst Nat. Oceanic and Atmospheric Adminstrn., Rockville, Md., 1970—; exec. sec. Working Group VIII U.S.-USSR Bilateral on Protection of The Environment, 1975—. Mountain range in Antarctica named Mirabito Range. Mem. Am. Meteorol. Soc. (chmn. Washington chpt.), Am. Geophys. Union, AAAS. Roman Catholic. Home: 4713 Jasmine Dr Rockville MD 20853 Office: 6010 Executive Blvd Rockville MD 20853

MIRANDA, VINCENT BUZ, artist, educator, visual communications specialist; b. Buffalo, June 24, 1939; s. Vincent Louis and Rose Marie (Nitto) M.; student N.Y. State U., 1959; certificate graphics and pub. N.Y. U., 1961; m. Barbara Zawierucha; children by previous marriage—Lisa Ruth, Raymond Vincent. With various pub. cos., N.Y.C., 1961-65; with advt. and graphic design cos., Buffalo, 1965-71; operator Photo Design & Coop. Graphics, Buffalo, 1971-74; asso. prof. graphics and communications Sch. Architecture and Environ. Design, State U. N.Y., Buffalo, 1973-75; partner, creative dir. Visual Communications Group, Buffalo, 1975-78; exec. art dir. Lloyd Mansfield Advt., Buffalo, 1978—; one-man shows: Coffee Encores Gallery, Buffalo, 1961, 62; numerous group exhbns.; univ. lectr., demonstrator in field; pres., dir. Kenmore Art Soc., Cheektowaga Art Guild. chmn. art com. Unitarian Ch.; v.p. Cheektowaga Cultural Soc.; publicity chmn. Midsummer Nights Group; organizer Del.-Allen Businessmen's Assn.; bd. dirs. Allentown Community Center. Mem. Am. Soc. Mag. Photographers, Art Dirs. and Communicators Club Buffalo. Home: 810 Richmond Ave Buffalo NY 14222

MIRANTE, THOMAS ANTHONY, composer; b. Utica, N.Y., Oct. 11, 1931; s. John and Catherine (Cerro) M.; B.S., State U. Coll., Potsdam, N.Y., 1954; M.S., Ithaca Coll., 1955; postgrad. Colgate U., 1964; m. Lucy Fiore, Aug. 11, 1962; children—Anne Catherine, Mary Jo. Music tchr. Oneida (N.Y.) Schs., 1960—. Mem. Oneida Area Arts Council, 1973—. Served with AUS, 1955-57. Meet the Composer grantee Am. Music Center, grantee Martha Baird Rockefeller Fund for Music, 1975. Mem. Am. Music Center, Composer: Piano Sonata, 1964; Eight Recital Solos, 1967; A Musical Journey, Prelude and March, 1967; I Am, 1968; Andante and Allegro, 1968; The House on the Hill, 1968; Symphony, 1968; Eight Recital Encores, 1968; Silent Snow, 1971; String Quartet, 1970; Concerto for Viola and Orchestra, 1971; Portrait for Strings, 1972; The War Poems of Walt Whitman (commd. by Oneida Area Civic Choral), 1975; The Stream of Life, 1976; This Is All, 1976. Home: 208 N Main St Canastota NY 13032

MIRCHANDANI, DILIP, engring. firm exec.; b. Sukkur, Pakistan, Jan. 17, 1937; s. Khanchand and Savitri (Wadhwani) M.; came to U.S., 1962, naturalized, 1973; B.Engring., Ind. Inst. Tech., 1966; M.Engring., City U. N.Y., 1971; m. Usha Sajnani, Aug. 6, 1972. Dir. tech. services Mohammad Qasim Argani, Khouram Shahr, Iran, 1957-58; adminstr., tchr. Fazalbhoy Sch. Refrigeration and Air Conditioning Engring., Bombay, India, 1960-62; environ. project. mgr. Ebasco Services Inc., N.Y.C., 1977—. Environ. task force coordinator Internat. Youth Center, 1970-71. Mem. ASME. Democrat. Hindu. Contbr. tech. papers to profl. lit. Home: 210 E 47th St New York City NY 10017 Office: 19 Rector St New York City NY 10006

MIREAULT, JEAN-MARC, clergyman; b. Quebec, Que., Can., Dec. 12, 1943; s. Patrice and Marie-Louise (Lafreniere) M.; B.A., U. Man., 1966; T.Th., Laval U., 1969, M.Th., 1970; D.D. (hon.), London Inst. Research, 1974. Ordained priest Roman Catholic Ch., 1966; pastor chs. in Peterborough, Ont., 1966-71; adminstr. St. Vital (Man.) Parish, 1971-72, Our Lady of Mercy, Port Hope, Man., 1972-73; chaplain in residence Ontario Hosp., Cobourg, 1971-74; dir. pastoral services D'Arcy Pl. Developmental Centre, Ministry Community and Social Services, Govt. Ont., Cobourg, 1972-78; instr. oral French, U. Waterloo, 1970, St. Peter's High Sch., Peterborough, 1969; chaplain Monarchist League Can., 1975, local council K.C., 1970; judge Toronto Regional Tribunal, 1978—. Recipient certificate of merit K.C., 1974, Queen's Jubilee medal, 1977. Mem. Am. Assn. Mental Deficiency, Ont. Hosp. Assn. (certificate of merit 1974), Assn. Mental Deficiency, Can. Cath. Chaplains Assn., Assn. Clin. Pastoral Edn., Nat. Apostolate for Retarded, Am. Assn. Mental Health Chaplains, Religious Certification for Retardation, Canadian Canon Law Soc. Mem. Progressive Conservative Party. Club: K.C. (4 deg., hon. life) Author: Religious Education for the Developed Mentally Handicapped, 1978. Home: 1515 Bathurst St Toronto ON M5P 3H8 Canada Office: 67 Bond St Suite 231 Toronto ON M5B 1X5 Canada

MIRKIN, GABE BARON, physician; b. Brookline, Mass., June 18, 1935; s. Mitchel and Vera (Baron) M.; A.B., Harvard U., 1957, M.D., 1961; m. Irene Mannheimer, June 2, 1961; children—Gene, Jan, Jill, Geoffrey. Intern Michael Reese Hosp., Chgo., 1961; resident in pediatrics Mass. Gen. Hosp., Boston, 1962-63; fellow Johns Hopkins Med. Sch., 1963-65; practice medicine specializing in allergy and dermatology, Silver Spring, Md., 1965-68, 70—; asst. prof. sports medicine U. Md., 1977—; commentator Dr. Gabe Mirkin on Fitness CBS radio stas. network, also Radio Sta. WCAU, Phila. Competitive marathon runner, 1963—; nat. chmn. boys long distance running Amateur Athletic Union, 1972—. Served with AUS, 1968-69. Diplomate Am. Bd. Pediatrics, Am. Bd. Allergy and Immunology, Am. Bd. Pediatric Allergy. Mem. Am. Acad. Allergy, Road Runners Club Am. Author: The Sportsmedicine Book, 1978; also articles; syndicated columnist on sports medicine N.Y. Times Spl. Features, 1978—. Home: 11109 Rosemont Dr Rockville MD 20852 Office: 9900 Georgia Ave Silver Spring MD 20902

MIRON, TSIPORA, musician, music pub. exec., composer; b. Olevsk, U.S.S.R., July 27, 1923; d. Shalom and Chaya (Schindler) Tchetchik; diploma N. Balfour Coll., Tel Aviv, 1939; B.A., Israel Conservatoire Acad. Music, Tel Aviv, 1944; m. Issacher Miron, Jan. 25, 1944; children—Ruth Miron Schleider, Shlomit Miron Sholem, Miriam Miron Bowers. Mem. piano faculty Israel Conservatoire Acad. Music, music editor Mills Music Inc., N.Y.C., 1959-64; profl. dir., exec. pres. Star Record Co. Enterprises, including McRon Music Co., Main Floor, N.Y.C., 1964; concert organist and pianist, recording artist; translator music from Hebrew to English; composer: Mirages (piano etudes), 1959, Lonely Hill, 1964, On Riddle, Meditation and Dance, 1965. Mem. ASCAP, Am. Guild Authors Composers, Am. Fedn. Musicians. Home: 515 West End Ave New York NY 10024 Office: 521 5th Ave New York NY 10017

MIRSKY, STANLEY, physician; b. Yonkers, N.Y., June 19, 1929; s. Jacob and Sarah (Barschi) M.; B.S. cum laude, U. Mich., 1951; M.D., Northwestern U., 1955; m. Susan Ellen Schur, Jan. 24, 1963; children—Jennifer Lynn, Jonathan Stephen. Intern, St. Lukes Hosp., Chgo., 1955; rotating fellow Lahey Clinic, Joslin Clinic, and New Eng. Deaconess Hosp., Boston, 1956, Joslin Clinic fellow, 1957; resident Mt. Sinai Hosp., N.Y.C., 1958, mem. staff, 1961—; practice medicine specializing in internal medicine, N.Y.C., 1965—; mem. staff Lenox Hill Hosp., Doctors Hosp.; asst. clin. prof. metabolic diseases Mt. Sinai Sch. Medicine. Bd. dirs. Boys Harbor, N.Y.C. and East Hampton, N.Y., 1963—. Served as capt. USAF, 1959-61. Fellow A.C.P.; mem. Am., N.Y. (dir. 1970—, chmn. clin. soc. 1976-77) diabetes assns., N.Y. Soc. Medicine, Phi Beta Kappa, Pi Kappa Epsilon. Republican. Jewish. Contbr. articles to med. jours. Home: 911 Park Ave New York NY 10021 Office: 4 E 70th St New York NY 10021

MIRTO, VALENTINE DOMINICK, constrn. co. exec.; b. Bklyn., Oct. 27, 1918; s. Joseph and Sabina (Saracini) M.; B.C.E., Rensselaer Poly. Inst., 1950; postgrad. N.Y. U., 1950-51; m. Gilda Theresa Gallo, Aug. 28, 1948; children—Lawrence, Valentine. Design engr. Pullman Kellogg Co., engrs. and contractors, N.Y.C., 1950-56; design supervising engr., mgr. plant design engring. Treadwell Corp., N.Y.C., 1956—, also v.p. TRC subs., N.Y.C., 1970—. Troop asst. scoutmaster Union council Boy Scouts Am., 1966-68. Served with USN, 1938-46; ETO, CBI. Registered profl. engr., N.Y., N.J.; licensed master rigger, N.Y.C. Fellow ASCE; mem. Nat. Soc. Profl. Engrs., Am. Concrete Inst., Am. Welding Soc., Am. Inst. Steel Constrn., Chi Epsilon. K.C. Home: 1774 Columbia Terr Union NJ 07083 Office: 1700 Broadway New York City NY 10019

MISCHLER, FORREST CLAIR, surgeon; b. Elk Creek Twp., Pa., Feb. 5, 1939; s. J. Lockwood and Winifred Esther (Joslin) M.; B.A., Gannon Coll., 1962; student Allegheny Coll., 1957-60; M.D., U. Cin., 1967; m. Shirley Ann Eaton, Aug. 22, 1962; children—Paul Bryan, Deborah Marie, Michael Forrest. Intern, Hamot Med. Center, Erie, Pa., 1967-68, gen. surg. resident, 1968-71, chief resident, 1971-72, attending staff, Dept. Surgery, 1973—, chmn. Dept. Surgery, 1977—; practice medicine, specializing in surgery, Erie, Pa., 1972—. Med. advisor disaster com. ARC 1972-74; adv. bd. Gannon Coll., 1974—; bd. dirs. Erie chpt. Am. Cancer Soc., 1976—, Emergency Med. Services Council, Nothwestern Pa., 1977—. Diplomate Am. Bd. Surgery. Fellow A.C.S.; mem. AMA, Pa., Erie County med. socs., Nat. Assn. Residents and Interns, Am. Burn Assn., Am. Trauma Soc., Am. Soc. Abdominal Surgery. Republican. Roman Catholic. Clubs: Aviation, Lakeshore Country. Home: 409 Hardscrabble Blvd Erie PA 16505 Office: 104 E 2nd St Erie PA 16507

MISHLER, JACOB, fed. judge; b. N.Y.C., Apr. 20, 1911; s. Abraham and Rebecca (Heller) M.; B.S., N.Y. U., 1931, J.D., 1933; m. Helen Shillet; children—Alan J., Susan R. Admitted to N.Y. State bar, 1934; practiced in Long Island City, N.Y., 1934-59; justice N.Y. Supreme Ct., 10th Jud. Dist., 1959-60; U.S. dist. judge Eastern Dist., N.Y., 1960-69, chief judge, 1969—. Mem. Electoral Coll., 1952. Bd. dirs. Boys Club Queens. Mem. Queens County Bar Assn. Club: Masons. Home: Birchwood Towers Forest Hills Queens NY 11827 Office: Courthouse 225 Cadman Plaza E Brooklyn NY 11201*

MISHOE, LUNA ISAAC, coll. pres.; b. Bucksport, S.C., Jan. 5, 1917; s. Henry and Martha (Oliver) M.; B.S., Allen U., 1938; M.S., U. Mich., 1942; Ph.D., N.Y. U., 1953; postgrad. Oxford (Eng.) U., 1955-56; m. Hattie B., 4 children. Prof. math. and physics Kittrell Coll., 1939-42; prof. math. and physics Del. State Coll., Dover, 1946-48, pres., 1960—; asso. prof. physics Morgan State Coll., Balt., 1948-54, prof., 1954-60, chmn. div. natural sci., 1956-60; research mathematician Ballistics Research Lab., Aberdeen Proving Ground, summers 1952-57, cons., 1957-60; mem. adv. bd. Farmers' Bank Del., 1972—. Served from pvt. to 2d lt. USAAF, 1942-46. Recipient Gold Good Citizenship medal Del. Soc. S.A.R., 1974. Trustee U. Del., 1969—; bd. dirs. University City Sci. Center, Phila., 1970—; adv. bd. USCG Acad., 1972—; pres. jud. council African Methodist Episcopal Ch., 1964—; mem. Edn. Commn. of States, 1970—, Higher Ednl. Aid Adv. Commn.; bd. dirs. Nat. Assn. for Equal Opportunity in Higher Edn., 1972—; mem. exec. com. Mid-Eastern Athletic Assn., 1st chmn. presidents' council Mid-Eastern Athletic Conf.; state chmn. Council of Presidents Pub. Instns. Higher Edn., 1970-71; mem. Del. Gov.'s Cabinet representing higher edn., 1970-71; bd. dirs. WHYY-TV, 1974—; chmn. Del. Postsecondary Edn. Commn., 1974-78; mem. Gov.'s Task Force on Cost-of-Living Pay Increase Formulas, 1974. Mem. Am. Math. Soc., Math. Assn. Am., Del. Acad. Sci. (pres. 1967-68), Alpha Phi Alpha, Phi Kappa Phi, Beta Kappa Chi, Delta Mu Delta, Phi Alpha Theta. Clubs: Rotary, Masons. Author: Eigenfunction Expansions Associated with Non-Self-Adjoint Differential Equations, 1964; also articles in math. jours. Address: Delaware State Coll Office of Pres Dover DE 19901

MISIEK, MARTIN, microbiologist; b. Buffalo, Sept. 6, 1919; s. John and Elizabeth (Kristofik) M.; A.B., U. Buffalo, 1943; M.S., Syracuse U., 1949, Ph.D., 1955; m. Elizabeth Eleanor Hudson, Oct. 27, 1945; children—Marte, Joy. With Bristol Labs., Syracuse, N.Y., 1943—, sr. microbiologist, 1955-64, sr. research scientist and project leader, 1964-77, asst. dir. microbiology research, 1977—. Mem. Community Council, Baldwinsville, N.Y., 1961, 66; pres. PTA, 1961, Am. Field Service, 1968-69; mem. Citizens Adv. Com. on New Community Devel., 1971-72; trustee Sch. Bd., 1965—. Mem. Am. Soc. Microbiology., Sigma Xi. Methodist. Contbr. articles to profl. jours. Home: 70 Maple Rd Baldwinsville NY 13027 Office: PO Box 657 Syracuse NY 13201

MISSON, GEORGE WILLIAM, mech. engr.; b. Ottawa, Ont., Can., Aug. 23, 1913; s. George Douglas and Mary Veronica (Mulvey) M.; B.S. in M.E., The Cooper Union, 1942; postgrad. Poly. Sch. Bklyn., 1947-48; came to U.S., 1930, Naturalized, 1939; m. Alice Louise Chesnut, Sept. 15, 1945 (dec. Dec. 1968); children—Barbara Anne, Frances Louise; m. Martha Collete Staub, June 20, 1970. Employed in nat. def. industries, 1939-44; supervisory engr. Austin Co., N.Y.C., Chgo., Roselle, N.J., 1944-58; supervisory research engr., staff engr. P.P.G. Industries, Harmarville, Pa., Pitts., 1958-78. Registered profl. engr., Ill., N.J., Pa. Mem. ASME, AAAS, Pa. Soc. Profl. Engrs. Republican. Roman Catholic. Elks. Patentee in field. Home: Hickory Stick Farm RD 7 Butler PA 16001

MISTLER, ROSE MARIE, automotive parts and service co. exec.; b. St. Louis, Aug. 25, 1933; d. Karl and Marie Katherine (Wiesler) Ratz; grad. pub. schs.; div.; children—Stephen, David, Sandra, Deborah, Craig. Bookkeeper, Krey Pkg. Co., St. Louis, 1951-53; bookkeeper People's 905 Liquors, St. Louis, 1960-62; bookkeeper Newton (N.J.) Meml. Hosp., 1964-69; office mgr. Sussex County Battery Sta., Newton, 1969—. Mem. Am. Soc. Notaries. Roman Catholic. Club: Women's Internat. Bowling Congress. Home: 41 Woodside Ave Newton NJ 07860 Office: 134 Water St Newton NJ 07860

MITCHELL, ALAN EDWARD, systems design specialist; b. Bayonne, N.J., Oct. 20, 1949; s. Alfred Edward and Margaret M. (O'Shea) M.; B.S. in Math., St. Peter's Coll., 1971; M.M.S. in Mgmt. Sci., Stevens Inst. Tech., 1974; M.B.A. in Fin., St. John's U., 1978; m. Maryann K. Kennelly, Nov. 9, 1968; 1 child—Deana Marie. Programmer, Gen. Cable Corp., N.Y.C., 1971-73; programmer-analyst Royal Globe Ins. Co., N.Y.C., 1973-74; systems design specialist Equitable Life Assurance Co., N.Y.C., 1974-77, Smith, Barney, Harris & Upham, N.Y.C., 1977-79; software cons. CGA Computer Assos., Cranford, N.J., 1979—. Served with N.J. N.G., 1970-76. Mem. Am. Mgmt. Assn., Omicron Delta Epsilon. Democrat. Roman Catholic. Club: Recreational Life Center. Home: 89 Ave E Bayonne NJ 07002 Office: 25 Commerce Dr Cranford NJ 07016

MITCHELL, BRADFORD WILLIAM, ins. co. exec., lawyer; b. Lewiston, Maine, Aug. 14, 1927; s. William Henry and Marietta Edna (Ramsdall) M.; student U. Maine, 1947-49; LL.B., Boston U., 1952; m. Frances T. Cantwell, June 20, 1953; children—Mark, Scott, Patrick, Paula, Kirsten. Admitted to Maine bar, 1952, Mass. bar, 1952, N.H. bar, 1967, U.S. Supreme Ct. bar, 1971, U.S. Ct. Mil. Appeals, 1974, Pa. bar, 1976; asst. gen. counsel Am. Mut. Liability Ins. Co., Wakefield, Mass., 1959-67, asst. v.p., 1963-67; gen. counsel Nat. Grange Mut. Ins. Co., Keene, N.H., 1967-73, dir., 1967-75, corporate sec., 1971-75, exec. v.p., 1973-75; pres., chief exec. officer, dir. Harleysville Mut. Ins. Co. (Pa.), 1976—, Harleysville Life Ins. Co., 1976—. Chmn. automobile ins. com. Am. Mut. Alliance, 1972-73; mem. N.H. Gov.'s Com. on Automobile No-Fault Legis., 1974-75; pres. Keene PTA, 1970; chmn. City of Keene Sunday Sales Com., 1971; campaign chmn. Am. Cancer Soc., Keene, 1973, Monadnock United Fund, Keene, 1974. Served with USNR, 1945-46; served to capt. Judge Adv. Corps, U.S. Army, 1952-59, lt. col. Res. ret., 1972. Mem. Am., N.H. bar assns., Wakefield (Mass.) C. of C. (pres. 1973), Nat. Assn. Ind. Insurers (bd. govs. 1977). Republican. Episcopalian. Club: Masons. Contbr. articles on ins. to various jours. and newspapers. Home: 54 Water Crest Dr Doylestown PA 18901 Office: 355 Maple Ave Harleysville PA 19438

MITCHELL, CHARLES ALFRED, indsl. hygienist; b. Broughton, Ill., Nov. 9, 1924; s. George Alfred and Rachael Mae (McQuay) M.; B.S., Shurtleff Coll., 1954; M.S., Harvard U., 1960; m. Virginia Rose Rye, June 1, 1946; children—Aleta Charlene, Sherry Lynn. Prodn. clk. Western Cartridge Co., East Alton, Ill., 1946-52; asst. control chemist Dow Chem. Co., Madison, Ill., 1954-59; with Gen. Electric Co., Lynn, Mass., 1960—, indsl. hygienist, radiation Safety officer, 1960-78, mgr. occupational hygiene and safety Indsl. & Marine Steam Turbine div., 1978—; research asst. to head dept. indsl. hygiene Harvard Sch. Pub. Health, 1962-66. Served with inf. AUS, 1943-46. Decorated Bronze Star, Purple Heart. Mem. Am. Indsl. Hygiene Assn., Health Physics Soc., Am. Acad. Indsl. Hygiene, Am. Acad. Certified Safety Profls. Congregationalist. Club: Mason. Home: 105 Locksley Rd Lynnfield MA 01940 Office: 1100 Western Ave Lynn MA 01910

MITCHELL, CLAUDE, psychologist; b. Bossier City, La., July 25, 1935; s. Willie Bryant and Lorrie Louise (Johnson) M.; B.A. in Psychology, So. U., 1959; M.S., Howard U., 1964; Ph.D. in Exptl. Psychology, U. Minn., 1976; m. Velma Elaine McLin, June 29, 1968; children—Gary Delano, Joyce Marie. Teaching asst. Howard U., Washington, 1961-62, instr., 1964; human engr. Gen. Electric Co., Washington and Phila., 1965-67, N.Am. Rockwell, Inc., Columbus, Ohio, 1967-69, Honeywell, Inc., Mpls., 1969-71; research asst. U. Minn., 1974; asso. prof. psychology Cheyney (Pa.) State Coll., 1976—, chmn. dept., 1977—. Served with U.S. Army, 1959-61. Mem. Human Factors Soc., Am. Psychol. Assn. Office: Dept Psychology Cheyney State Coll Cheyney PA 19319

MITCHELL, DONALD J., congressman; b. Ilion, N.Y., May 8, 1923; student Hobart Coll., 1946-47; B.S. in Optometry, Columbia, 1949, M.A. in Edn., 1950; m. Margaretta Wilson Levee, 1945; children—Gretchen, Cynthia, Allen. Practice optometry, Herkimer, N.Y., 1950-72; mem. 93d-96th congresses from N.Y.; mem. House Com. on Armed Services; asst. regional Whip of Republican Party. Councilman, Town of Herkimer, 1954-56; mayor, Village of Herkimer, 1956-59; pres. Mohawk Valley Conf. Mayors, 1959; apptd. to Herkimer Zoning Bd. of Appeals, 1963; mem. N.Y. State Assembly, 1965-72, majority whip, 1968-72. Bd. dirs. Herkimer chpt. ARC, Cancer Soc., Washburn Meml. Library Boy Scouts Am., Cub Scouts. Served with USNR, 1942-45, 51-53. Recipient Pub. Service award, 1965; named Optometrist of Year, N.Y. State Optometric Assn., 1971. Mem. Nat. Soc. State Legislators (bd. govs. 1971). Am. Legion, V.F.W., C. of C., Herkimer County Extension Service. Republican. Methodist. Clubs: Masons, Elks, Kiwanis, Rod and Gun, East Herkimer Fish and Game. Home: Herkimer NY 13350 Office: 1527 Longworth House Office Bldg Washington DC 20515

MITCHELL, FREDERICK MYRON, auto and truck spring service co. exec.; b. Hackensack, N.J., July 18, 1925; s. Roger Irving and Anna Louise (Deatrick) M.; B.E.E., Cornell U., 1948; m. Ruth Elizabeth Morrison, Nov. 8, 1952; children—Martha, Kenneth, Jeanne, Julia. Treas., dir. Jenson & Mitchell, Inc., Newark, 1947—, sec., 1959-66, pres., 1967—, chmn. bd., 1975—; chmn. bd. Cutler Controls, Inc., Horsham, Pa., 1972-77; pres. Somerset Spring & Alignment Inc., Raritan, N.J., 1972-76; v.p., sec. The Train Station Inc., Mountain Lakes, N.J., 1974—. Mem. Mountain Lakes Vol. Fire Dept.; trustee Community Ch. of Mountain Lakes, 1977—. Served with USNR, 1943-46, U.S. Army, 1950-52. Mem. U.S., N.J., Newark, Jersey City, Paterson chambers commerce, N.J. Motor Truck Assn., Nat. Fedn. Ind. Bus., Council Fleet Specialists, U.S. Indsl. Council. Clubs: Mountain Squares, Lakeland Squares, Mountain Lakes Glee. Home: 4 Point View Pl Mountain Lakes NJ 07046 Office: 400 New St Newark NJ 07103

MITCHELL, HESTER LOUISE, librarian; b. Plainfield, N.J., Dec. 8, 1915; d. Henry Sayen and Maude Frances (Raymond) M.; spl. courses U. Va., 1937, London Regent Inst., 1939, U. N.H., 1939, 40, 48, 51, Harvard U., 1941, 42, Boston U., 1941, 46, 47, 50, 52, 53, U. Okla., 1961-62 and 64. Asst. high sch. library, Beverly, Mass., 1934, children's asst. pub. library, 1935-40, adult asst., 1940-48; literary staff Springfield (Mass.) Rep. Newspaper, 1941-45; head children's dept. pub. library, Everett, Mass., 1948-51; head librarian pub. library, Ipswich, Mass., 1951-67; librarian Addison-Wesley Pub. Co., Inc., Reading, Mass., 1967—. Pres. Cable Meml. Hosp. Aux., 1958. Mem. ALA, N.E., Mass. (exec. bd. 1952, 53, 56, com. mem. 1963-64), Merrimac Valley (past pres.) library assns., Mass. State Aid to Libraries (sec. to adv. bd. N.Met. region 1963-64), Spl. Libraries Assn., Ipswich Hist. Soc., Women's Nat. Book Assn., Am. Security Council, Internat. Platform Assn., D.A.R., Marquis Biog. Soc. (adv. mem.), Swampscott (Mass.) Improvement Soc. Episcopalian. Clubs: Woman's (Ipswich, Mass.); Book Review (treas. 1957) (Boston); Order Eastern Star. Author articles in mags. and newspapers. Book reviewer A.L.A. Reference Quar., 1969—. Home: 88 Stetson Ave Swampscott MA 01907 also 7503 NW 70th Terr Fort Lauderdale FL 33319 Office: Addison-Wesley Pub Co Inc Reading MA 10867

MITCHELL, IRA CANFIELD, III, ret. film co. exec.; b. Bklyn., Oct. 16, 1911; s. Ira C. and Helen (Cloud) M.; student Rensselaer Poly. Inst., 1930-32; B.S., N.Y.U., 1933; m. Florence C. Holmes, Sept. 5, 1934 (dec.); children—Ira Canfield IV, Martha M.; m. 2d, Marion R. Blace, Apr. 13, 1974. With Eastman Kodak Co., 1935-75, successively chem. engr., personnel mgr., prodn. supr., 1935-55, plant mgr. Kodak Processing Lab., Fair Lawn, N.J., 1956-75. Active Boy Scouts; bd. dirs. Bergen County United Fund, campaign chmn., 1969, Distinguished Service award, 1973, now pres.; v.p. N.J. affiliate Am. Diabetic Assn. Bd. dirs. Valley Hosp.; trustee Indsl. Fund; mem. Bergen County Charter Commn. Recipient Silver Beaver award Boy Scouts Am., 1950. Mem. Bergen County (dir.), Fair Lawn (pres. dir.) chambers commerce, Rotary Internat. (dist. gov. 1966-67), Lambda Chi Alpha. Mason, Rotarian (pres. Fair Lawn, 1962-63). Club: Hackensack Golf. Home: 35 Twin Brooks Rd Saddle River NJ 07458

MITCHELL, JAMES RICHARD, mus. dir.; b. Madison, Wis., June 26, 1938; s. Quentin Nicholson and Ruth (Schmidt) M.; B.A., U. Wis., 1963; M.A. (Winterthur fellow), U. Del., 1965; m. Johanna Martha Giese, June 22, 1963; children—Fredericka Anne, James Richard, Nicholas John. Asst. curator Bennington (Vt.) Mus., 1965-67; curator decorative arts State Mus., Trenton, N.J., 1967-73; curator Carborundum Mus. Ceramics, Niagara Falls, N.Y., 1973-76; dir. William Penn Meml. Mus. Pa. State Mus., Harrisburg, 1976—. Mem. Am. Ceramic Circle, Am. Assn. Museums. Lutheran. Home: 15 N 24th St Camp Hill PA 17011 Office: PO Box 1026 Harrisburg PA 17120

MITCHELL, JOHN PATRICK, sheriff, bookseller, detective agy. exec.; b. Phila., July 4, 1915; s. Thomas Joseph and Mary Ann (McManus) M.; grad. Pa. Police Acad., 1937; student bus. adminstrn. U. So. Calif., 1976-77; m. Muriel Dicken-Mitchell, Nov. 18, 1939; children—Beverly Ann (Mrs. Lawrence A. Wiley), William John. With Pa. State Police, Doylestown, 1936-62; owner Mitchell Detective Agy., Doylestown, 1950—, Mitchell's Old & Rare Book Shop, Doylestown, 1962—; sheriff Bucks County (Pa.), 1974—. Mem. Fraternal Order Police (pres. 1956-58), Bucks County Chiefs of Police Assn., Central Bucks County C. of C. (dir.). Democrat. Roman Catholic. Club: Moose. Home: 198 Shewell Ave Doylestown PA 18901 Office: Bucks County Courthouse Doylestown PA 18901

MITCHELL, JOHN THOMAS, JR., food co. exec.; b. Bklyn., July 14, 1929; s. John T. and Ella B. (Neylon) M.; A.B., Niagara U., 1951; postgrad. Harvard Bus. Sch., 1953-54; m. Marilyn E. Merolla, May 25, 1963; children—Denise, Douglas. Account exec. Benton & Bowles Advt., N.Y.C., 1958-62; sales mgr. Franklin Sugar Co., Phila., 1962-66; mktg. mgr. Standard Packaging, N.Y.C., 1966-69; v.p. mktg. Nabisco, Inc., East Hanover, N.J., 1969—. Pres., Independence Day Assn., 1970-71; pres. Village Players Community Theater, 1971-75. Served with AUS, 1951-53. Decorated Bronze Star medal. Mem. Internat. Foodservice Mfrs. Assn., Nat. Automatic Merchandisers Assn. Roman Catholic. Clubs: Mountain Lakes; K.C. Home: 34 Arden Rd Mountain Lakes NJ 07046 Office: 100 DeForest Ave East Hanover NJ 07936

MITCHELL, MARK BRENDAN, architect; b. London, Eng., May 16, 1934; s. Edward Arnold and Isla Mai (Dwyer) M. came to U.S., 1946, naturalized, 1954; B.A., Dartmouth Coll., 1956; M. Arch. (Markoe scholar), Harvard U., 1962; m. Sarah Lincoln Lorenz, June 22, 1957; children—Christopher Brendan, Adam Pearsall, Benjamin Lincoln. Project mgr. John Carl Warnecke & Assos., Honolulu, 1963-66; sr. designer Eero Saarinen & Assos., Hamden, Conn., 1966-67; sr. architect, planner Dober, Paddock, Upton & Assos., Cambridge, Mass., 1967-69, Gourley, Richmond & Mitchell, Cambridge, 1969—. Pres., Nuuanu Valley (Hawaii) Community Assn., 1965-66. Bd. dirs. Hill House, Beacon Hill, Mass., 1970-74, pres., 1971-73; bd. dirs. Fayerweather St. Sch., Cambridge, Vols. for Internat. Tech. Assistance. Served with AUS, 1956-58. Mem. AIA, Soc. Coll. and U. Planners. Important archtl. works include: Mass. State Library, Wheaton Coll. Library, Smith Coll. Library, recreation bldg. Mass. Hosp. Sch. (1st prize design competition, commn.), 15 schs. City Boston, other schs., social centers. Home: 31 Brewster St Cambridge MA 02138 Office: 18 Brattle St Cambridge MA 02138

MITCHELL, NEAL BURGESS, JR., structural engr., bldg. constrn. cons.; b. Salem, Mass., Aug. 3, 1934; s. Neal B. and Jean D. (Spear) M.; B.S. in Engring., Brown U., 1958; M.S. in Structural Engring., Mass. Inst. Tech., 1959; m. Kristin Hall, Jan. 28, 1957; children—Neal Burgess III, Jennifer Scott Allen. Pres., Internat. Constrn. & Mktg. Co., Lexington, Mass., 1960—, Mitchell Systems, Inc., Sudbury, Mass., 1965—, Structural Programming Inc., Sudbury, 1970—; cons. constrn. engr., 1967—; prof. Harvard Grad. Sch. Design, Boston, 1961-70, dir. archtl. tech. workshop, 1963-70; mem. faculty Cornell U., 1959-61; lectr. on structures, housing and constrn. at numerous Am. univs., 1961—. Registered profl. engr., Mass.; Milton Research fellow, 1963-64; recipient award of merit Nat. Assn. Home Builders, 1965. Mem. ASCE, Boston Soc. Civil Engrs., Am. Concrete Inst., Nat. Soc. Profl. Engrs. (mem. com. on structures), Sigma Xi. Contbr. articles on structural engring. to profl. jours.; patentee in field. Home: 122 Prides Crossing Rd Sudbury MA 01776 Office: 83 Boston Post Rd Sudbury MA 01776

MITCHELL, PARREN JAMES, congressman; b. Balt., Apr. 29, 1922; A.B., Morgan State Coll., 1950; M.A., U. Md., 1952. Formerly prof. sociology, asst. dir. Urban Studies Inst., Morgan State Coll.; mem. 92d-96th Congresses from 7th dist. Md. Mem. Balt. Area Council on Alcoholism, Md. Com. Day Care Children; pres. Balt. Neighborhoods, Inc. Bd. dirs. Martin Luther King Parent-Child Center, Ams. for Democratic Action, Com. for Sane Nuclear Policy. Served with AUS, 1942-45. Decorated Purple Heart. Mem. NAACP, Nat. Assn. Community Devels., Balt. Urban League, Am. Sociol. Soc., Am. Acad. Polit. and Social Scis., Met. Balt. Assn. Mental Health. Democrat. Episcopalian. Home: 1805 Madison Ave Baltimore MD 21217 Office: US Ho of Reps Washington DC 20515

MITCHELL, STEPHEN EDWARD, physicist; b. Olney, Ill., Aug. 20, 1946; s. Carl Edward and Carrie Marie (Simms) M.; B.S., Rose Holman Tech. Inst., 1968; m. Judith Ann Barsell, Sept. 26, 1970; 1 son, Michael Edward. Chemist, chem. engr. Naval Ordnance Sta., Indian Head, Md., 1968-77, physicist, 1977—. Mem. Am. Def. Preparedness Assn. Methodist. Contbr. articles to profl. jours. Home: Route 2 Box 2061C La Plata MD 20646 Office: Naval Ordnance Station Indian Head MD 20640

MITCHELL, WILLIAM JOSEPH, surgeon; b. Pitts., Oct. 16, 1928; s. William Joseph and Marie (Moore) M.; M.D., Georgetown U., 1955. Intern, D.C. Gen. Hosp., 1955-56; resident in orthopedics Georgetown U., Washington, 1956-60; practice medicine specializing in orthopedic surgery, Uniontown, Pa.; orthopedic cons. to Surgeon Gen. USAF, Europe, 1963-66; mem. staff Brownsville, Charleroi hosps.; pres. med. staff Uniontown Hosp., 1972-73, chief of orthopedic dept., 1967-78; cons. to U.S. Steel, 1970-78; mem. cons. staff Brownsville, Waynesburg hosps.; asso. prof. Internat. Inst. Hand Surgery, Rome, 1964-74; dir. First Nat. Bank & Trust Co., Washington, Pa. Served to maj. M.C., USAF, 1960-66. Diplomate Am. Bd. Orthopedic Surgery. Fellow Am. Acad. Orthopedic Surgeons, A.C.S.; mem. Pa., Fayette County (pres. 1976-77) med. socs. Contbr. articles on orthopedic surgery to med. jours. Home: 63 Stockton Ave Uniontown PA 15401 Office: Professional Plaza Bldg Delaware Ave Uniontown PA 15404

MITCHEM, HORACE FOSTER, JR., dentist; b. Elizabeth, N.J., Nov. 7, 1925; s. Horace Foster and Rena (Stetson) M.; student Princeton U., 1943, U. Manchester (Eng.), 1945, Rutgers U., 1947-48; D.D.S., U. Pa., 1952, postgrad., 1960, 64; grad. Inst. for Grad. Dentists N.Y.C., 1960; postgrad. U. London (Eng.), 1968, U. Zurich (Switzerland), 1968; m. Nancy Glendenning, July 2, 1955; children—Jill Rena, Laurie Nan. Practice gen. dentistry, Kenilworth, N.J., 1952—; sch. dentist Harding Pub., St. Theresa Parochial schs., both Kenilworth. Served with inf. AUS, 1944-45. Decorated Bronze Star. Fellow Soc. Oral Pathology and Occlusion, Acad. Gen. Dentistry; mem. ADA, Union County (treas. 1967-69), N.J. (mem. ho. of dels. 1967-70) dental socs., Am. Soc. for Study Orthodontics, Internat. Assn. Begg Study Groups (treas. 1969-71, certified 1975), Chi Psi, Delta Sigma Delta. Home: 4 Woods Hole Rd Cranford NJ 07016 Office: 409 Boulevard St Kenilworth NJ 07033

MITRIK, LEONARD JOHN, pharmacist; b. Elizabeth, N.J., Oct. 19, 1939; s. John and Mary (Kocak) M.; B.S. in Pharmacy, St. John's U., 1962; m. Mary Ann Seaman, Aug. 7, 1965; 1 dau., Kathryn Marie. Product research pharmacist Reed & Carnrick, Kenilworth, N.J., 1963-64; jr. scientist, product formulation chemist Sandoz Pharms., Hanover, N.J., 1964-67; asst. chief pharmacist Elizabeth (N.J.) Gen. Hosp., 1967-68; chief pharmacy services Rutgers Med. Sch.-Raritan Valley Hosp., Green Brook, N.J., 1968—, clin. pharmacy coordinator, 1976—. Mem. Am., N.J. socs. hosp. pharmacists, Am. Pharm. Assn., N.J. State Pharmacists Group. Home: 1415 Summit Terr Linden NJ 07036 Office: 275 Greenbrook Rd Green Brook NJ 08812

MITSAKOS, CHARLES LEONIDAS, cons. curriculum; b. Lowell, Mass., Oct. 17, 1939; s. Leonidas and Vasiliki (Sampatakakis) M.; B.S., U. Lowell, 1961; M.Ed., Boston U., 1963, D.Ed., 1977; m. Stella Martakos, June 23, 1963; children—Charles Leonidas, Andria Estelle. Tchr. social studies, pub. schs. Lexington, Mass., 1961-66, team leader

Bridge Sch., 1966-67; cons. social studies curriculum pub. schs. Chelmsford, Mass., 1967-78; asst. supt. schs. Andover (Mass.), 1978—; vis. lectr. social studies edn. Brandeis U., Boston Coll., Boston U., U. N.C. at Greensboro, Rider Coll., R.I. Coll., Erdiston Tchrs. Coll. Barbados; part-time instr. Rivier Coll., 1977—; cons. staff devel. for sch. desegregation programs N.J., Va., S.C.; cons. sch. dists. 14 states, Boston Children's Mus., Ministry of Edn., Antigua, W.I., Am. Sch., Warsaw, Poland, Fgn. Policy Assn., Colombia Peace Corps Tng. Program; mem. acad. council Intercultural Action Learning Program, Princeton, N.J., 1973-76. Mem. coordinating com. Lowell Council Chs., 1970-73; vice chmn. home rule adv. com. Town Chelmsford, 1972—; trustee Old Chelmsford Garrison House Assn., 1975—. Mem. Social Sci. Edn. Consortium, Nat. Council Social Studies (field services bd. 1972-75, publs. bd. 1975-77, mem. ho. of dels. 1967-73, dir. 1975-76), Social Studies Suprs. Assn. (pres. 1972, dir.), Mass. Council Social Studies (pres. 1971-72, editor newsletter 1972-75), U. Lowell Alumni Assn. (dir. 1976-80, pres. 1977-79). Co-author: Study America, 1976; Successful Models and Materials for Elementary Social Studies, 1976; America! America!, 1977. Author, gen. editor The Family of Man, elementary sch. multi media social studies program, 1972-77; editorial cons. A Social History of The United States, filmstrip series, 1975. Home: 13 Housatonic Ave Chelmsford MA 01824 Office: 36 Bartlet St Andover MA 01810

MITTEL, JOHN J., economist, business exec.; b. L.I., N.Y.; s. John and Mary (Leidolf) M.; B.B.A., U. City N.Y. Researcher econs. dept. McGraw Hill & Co., N.Y.C.; mgr., asst. to pres. Indsl. Commodity Corp., J. Carvel Lange Inc. and J. Carvel Lange Internat., Inc., 1956—, corp. sec., 1958—, v.p., 1964—; pres. I.C. Investors Corp., 1972—; pres. I.C. Pension Advisory, Inc., 1977—; trustee Combined Indsl. Commodity Corp. & J. Carvel Lange Inc. Pension Plan, 1962—, J. Carvel Lange Internat. Inc. Profit Sharing Trust, 1969—, Combined Indsl. Commodity Corp. & J. Carvel Lange Inc. Employees Profit Sharing Plan, 1977—; mem. grad. adv. bd. Bernard M. Baruch Coll., U. City N.Y., 1971. Mem. Conf. Bd., Am. Statis. Assn., Newcomen Soc. N.Am. Club: Union League (N.Y.C.). Co-author: How Good A Sales Profit Are You?, 1961; The Role of the Economic Consulting Firm; also numerous market surveys. Office: Room 1206 122 E 42d St New York NY 10017

MITTELMAN, JAY ARNOLD, surgeon; b. Hartford, Conn., July 14, 1925; s. Reuben and Hilda C. (Zucker) M.; M.D., U. Pa., 1948; m. Barbara Katz, Dec. 21, 1958; children—Gary Lee, Robert Todd. Intern, St. Francis Hosp. and Med. Center, Hartford, 1948-49; resident pathology Duke U. Hosp., Durham, N.C., 1949-50; resident surgery N.Y. U. Bellevue Med. Center, 1950-56; practice medicine specializing in surgery, Bloomfield, Conn., 1956—; mem. staffs Mt. Sinai Hosp., St. Francis Hosp. Served to 1st lt. M.C., AUS, 1951-52. Diplomate Nat. Bd. Med. Examiners, Am. Bd. Surgery. Mem. Conn., Hartford med. socs. Club: Tumble Brook Country. Home: 81 Beacon Hill Dr West Hartford CT 06117 Office: 701 Cottage Grove Rd Bloomfield CT 06002

MITTL, RAINER NORBERT, ophthalmologist; b. Munich, W.Ger., Mar. 19, 1939; s. Joseph and Maria (Schwickert) M.; came to U.S., 1965; M.D., U. Munich, 1964; m. Janice J. Janoski, June 28, 1970. Intern, E. Orange (N.J.) Gen. Hosp., 1966; resident in ophthalmology N.Y. Med. Coll., 1967-70; fellow Johns Hopkins Hosp., 1972-73; practice medicine, specializing in ophthalmology, N.Y.C., 1973—; mem. staff St. Vincent's Hosp., N.Y. Eye and Ear Infirmary. Mem. Am. Acad. Ophthalmology, AMA. Club: N.Y. Athletic. Office: 1001 Park Ave New York City NY 10028

MITTMAN, BRUCE JOEL, advt. exec.; b. Bklyn., Nov. 29, 1949; s. John and Ethel Fava; student Nassau Community Coll., 1968-69; B.S., Northeastern U., 1972. Prodn. asst. Arnold Advt. Co., Boston, 1971-73, account supr., 1976—; account exec. Marvin & Leonard Advt. Co., Boston, 1973-76; cons. in field. Mem. Boston Advt. Club. Office: 1111 Park Sq Bldg Boston MA 02116

MOAKLEY, JOHN JOSEPH, congressman; b. Apr. 27, 1927; LL.B., Suffolk U., 1956; m. Evelyn Duffy, 1957. Admitted to Mass. bar, 1957; practiced in Boston, 1957-72; mem. 93d-96th congresses from 9th Mass. Dist., majority whip at large, mem. rules com.; mem. Ho. of Reps., 1953-60; Democratic majority whip, 1957; mem. Mass. Senate, 1964-70; mem. Boston City Council, 1971-72, chmn. com. on appropriations and finance. Served with USNR, 1943-46. Address: Cannon House Office Bldg Washington DC 20515

MOAN, CHARLES EDWARD, JR., state ofcl.; b. Providence, Dec. 5, 1924; s. Charles Edward and Mary Alice (Doyle) M.; B.S., Providence Coll., 1952; M.P.A., U. R.I., 1963; m. Barbara B. Block, Oct. 6, 1956; children—Patricia A., Michael C., Eileen M., Mary C., Maureen E. Personnel analyst R.I. Div. of Personnel, Providence, 1954-56, sr. personnel analyst, 1956-60, chief of tng., 1960-70, chief of classification and tng., 1970-75, dep. state personnel adminstr., 1975—, acting state personnel adminstr., 1975-76; adj. prof. pub. adminstrn. U. R.I. Grad. Sch.; instr. govt. New Eng. State Police Staff Coll.; cons. Warwick Civil Service Study Commn., R.I. Council Community Services. Sec., State Vets. Council, 1953; state comdr. Dept. R.I., Marine Corps League, 1952. Served with USMC, 1943-46, 50-51. Decorated D.F.C., Air medal (U.S.); Royal War Cross (Yugoslavia); recipient Past Pres. award St. Peter's Parish Council, 1973; Service awards for conducting AID internship programs. Mem. Internat. Personnel Mgmt. Assn. (pres. R.I. chpt. 1976-77), Am. Soc. Tng. and Devel., Providence Coll. Alumni Assn., Nat. Assn. State Personnel Execs., Nat. Polit. Sci. Honor Soc., Pi Sigma Alpha. Roman Catholic. Clubs: Gaspee Point Yacht, K.C. Author: Employee Training on State Level in U.S., 1965; contbr. articles in field to govt. publs. Home: 143 Audubon Rd Warwick RI 02888 Office: 289 Promenade St Providence RI 02908

MOCHARY, MARY VERONICA (MRS. STEPHEN E. MOCHARY), lawyer; b. Budapest, Hungary, Sept. 7, 1942; d. Alexander and Elisabeth (Aranyi) Kasser; came to U.S., 1949, naturalized, 1957; B.A., Wellesley Coll., 1963; J.D., U. Chgo., 1967; m. Stephen E. Mochary, Sept. 25, 1965; children—Alexandra, Veronica, Matthew Neal, Translator, trainee Bank of Am., Internat. Hdqrs., San Francisco, 1963-64; admitted to Ark. 1968, N.J. bar, 1970; pvt. practice law, Fayetteville, Ark., 1968; partner Mochary & Mochary, Montclair, N.J., 1970—. Bd. dirs. Manhattan Indsl. Home for Blind League; bd. dirs. Kasser Art Found., mgr., 1969—. Mem. Am., Ark., N.J. bar assns., League Women Voters, Confrerie de la Chaine des Rottiseurs. Republican. Mem. Ref. Ch. Clubs: N.J. Wellesley (pres.), Essex Fells Country. Home: 60 Undercliff Rd Montclair NJ 07042 Office: 26 Park St Montclair NJ 07042

MOCHIZUKI, JOHN TSUNETERU, trading co. exec.; b. Tokyo, Sept. 15, 1930; s. Tomoyuki and Nami (Koguchi) M.; grad. Tokyo Coll. Fgn. Affairs, 1951; postgrad. Fairleigh Dickinson U., 1976; m. Noriko Takimoto, May 30, 1965; children—George, Ray. Partner, Fair World Mdse. Co., N.Y.C., 1963-67; v.p. TNS Mills, Inc., Blacksburg, S.C., 1967-69; pres. Takigen Corp., Port Washington, N.Y., 1971—. Com. mem. Am. Field Service. Recipient citation S.C. State Devel. Bd., 1969. Mem. Am. Translators Assn., Nippon Club, Inc. Home: 22 South Court Port Washington NY 11050

MOCIUK, YAR WASYL, corp. exec.; b. Mylowannia, Ukraine, Jan. 26, 1927; s. Mykola and Ewdochia (Hawrysh) M.; came to U.S., 1950, naturalized, 1956; B.A., N.Y.C. U., 1957; M.Psychology, Jackson (Miss.) State U., 1968; Ph.D., World U., Tucson, 1972; L.H.D., Peoples U., 1973; m. Irene Groch, Apr. 12, 1959; children—Daria N., Natalie M. Plant mgr. Comprehensive Service Corp., N.Y.C., 1955-65; pres. C & M Film Service Corp., 1965-73, Filmtreat Internat. Corp., N.Y.C., 1973—; asst. dean communications Peoples U. of Americas, N.Y.C. Sec. St. Michaels PTA, Yonkers, N.Y. Mem. Soc. Motion Picture TV Engrs., Ukranian Cinema Assn. Am. (pres.), Univ. Film Assn., Ukranian Inst. Am. Greek Catholic. Patentee method and apparatus for treating film. Home: 2 Essex Pl Bronxville NY 10708

MOCK, ERNEST LEIGHTON, physician; b. Bluffton, Ind., Oct. 9, 1896; s. George Augustus and Emma Myrtle (Falk) M.; student Huntington Bus. U., 1914-15; LL.B., Hamilton Coll. Law, Chgo., 1922; B.S., Ind. U., 1928, M.D., 1930, M.D. cum laude, 1931; m. Mary Lucille Halsey, May 15, 1918; 1 son, Ernest Leighton; m. 2d, Elsie Mae Davis, Feb. 20, 1934; children—Charles Robert, James Edward. With operating div. Erie R.R., Huntington, Ind., 1916-17, spl. agent claims dept., Marion, Ohio, then div. claim agent, Dunmore, Pa. and Chgo., 1917-19; admitted to Huntington County, Ind. bar, 1918, Tex. bar, 1945; individual practice law, Huntington, 1919; sec.-treas. Service Motor Truck Co., treas. Service Aviation Tng. & Transp. Co., dir. Ind. Hotel Corp., Wabash, Service Motors of Ill., Chgo., atty. Service Truck Co., Kansas City, Mo., 1919-24; extern Ind. Christian Hosp., Indpls., 1929-30; intern, resident Univ. Hosps., Indpls., 1930-32; practice medicine specializing in eye, ear, nose and throat, Decatur, Ind., 1932-33, Bicknell, Ind., 1933-34; appointed med. officer USPHS, 1934; acting asst. surgeon div. mental hygiene, Leavenworth, Kans., 1934-36; asso. med. officer VA Facility, Wadsworth, Kans., 1937; med. officer VA Hosp., Huntington, W.Va., 1937-40; sr. med. officer VA Hosp., Dallas, 1940-44; served as maj., M.C., AUS, 1944-46; regional med. officer U.S. Civil Service Commn. 10th Region, New Orleans, 1946-50; staff mem. Central Office dept. medicine and surgery VA, Washington, 1950-65; ret., 1965. Chmn. ofcl. bd. Mt. Rainier (Md.) United Meth. Ch., 1961, 66; lay rep. Balt. Conf. U.N. Meth. Ch., 1968—; pres. Meth. Men, 1965; mem. exec. com. Northwestern High Sch. PTA, Hyattsville, Md., 1954-58, treas., 1957, pres., 1958; chmn. Mt. Rainier council Boy Scouts Am., 1959; life mem. Prince Georges Sci. Fair Assn.; active Mt. Rainier Citizens Assn., Md. Soc. Prevention Blindness, United Meth. Hist. Soc. Diplomate Am. Bd. Ophthalmology. Mem. AMA, Med. and Chirurg. Faculty of Md., Prince Georges County Med. Soc., Assn. Mil. Surgeons of U.S. (life), Tex., Dallas bar assns., Ind. U. Alumni Assn. (life), Am. Legion, DAV, Phi Beta Pi-Theta Kappa Psi Alumni Assn. Clubs: Masons (32 deg.), Shriners; Modern Woodmen of Am.; Craftsmens of VA, VA Alumni. Home: 4212 29th St Mount Rainier MD 20822

MOCK, ROBERT CLAUDE, architect; b. Baden, Germany, May 3, 1928; s. Ernest and Charlotte (Geismar) M.; came to U.S., 1938, naturalized, 1943; B.Arch., Pratt Inst., 1950; M.Arch., Harvard U., 1953; m. Belle Carol Bach, Dec. 23, 1952 (div.); children—John Bach, Nichole Louise; m. 2d, Marjorie E. Reubenfeld, Dec. 1964. Architect, Guided Missile Center, George C. Marshall Space Center, Huntsville, Ala., 1950-51; archtl. critic Columbia Sch. Architecture, N.Y.C., 1953-54; dir. facility design Am. Airlines, N.Y.C., 1955-60; founder Robert C. Mock & Assos., architects and engrs., N.Y.C., 1960—. Recipient 1st prize motel category for Shine Motor Inn, Queens C. of C., 1961. Registered architect, N.Y. State, Nat. Council Archtl. Registration Bds. Mem. Am. Arbitration Assn. Prin. works include: Shine Motor Inn, Queens, N.Y., 1961; Eastern Air Lines Shuttle Terminal Bldg., La Guardia Airport, N.Y., 1961, United Airlines and Trans World Airlines Cargo Bldgs., Kennedy Airport, N.Y., Bridgeport (Conn.) Airport, 1961; Eastern Air Lines Med., Center, Kennedy Airport, 1962. Trans World Airlines Fifth Ave. Ticket Office, N.Y.C., 1962; Eastern Air Lines and Trans World Airlines Terminal Bldg., La Guardia Airport, N.Y., 1963; Ambassadors Club, La Guardia Airport, 1964; Lufthansa German Air Lines, Swissair Cargo Terminals, 1972; Mfrs. Hanover Trust Co. Banks, 1966-70; FAA Nat. Prototype Air Traffic Control Towers, 1967; Happyland Nursery Sch., 1967; Lufthansa German Airlines; Irish Internat. Airlines, Varig Brazilian Airlines, El Al Israel Airlines passenger terminals, Kennedy Airport, 1968-72; Lufthansa Computer Center, 1968; El Al Israel Airlines Cargo Terminal, Kennedy Airport, 1974; Govt. of Israel Lab. Bldg., N.Y.C., 1975; Argentine Airlines N.Am. Hdqrs., N.Y.C., 1975. Argentine Airlines passenger terminal Kennedy Airport, 1977; Sky-Chefs hdqrs., N.Y.C., 1977; Norel-Ronel Indsl. Park, Hollywood, Fla., 1978; Verig Brazilian Airlines N.Am. hdqrs., N.Y.C., 1978. Clubs: Harvard, City (N.Y.C.). Home: Greenwich CT 06830 Office: 185 Byram Shore Rd Greenwich CT 06830

MOCKRIDGE, NORTON, columnist, author; b. N.Y.C., Sept. 29, 1915; s. Frank Walter and Fredricka (Apfel) M.; student pub. schs., Mt. Kisco, N.Y.; m. Valborg Palmer, 1963; children—Philip, Nancy Mockridge Miner, John. Journalist, 1933—; with World-Telegram, N.Y.C., 1940-66, city editor, 1956-63; syndicated humor columnist Scripps-Howard newspapers, also United Feature Syndicate, 1963—; editor Litton Publs., Oradell, N.J., 1971—; lectr. Keedick Lecture Bur.; star daily show Sta. WCBS, 1963-64, CBS radio network show; judge Miss Am. Pageant, 1967-71, Maj. Armstrong FM Radio Awards, 1970—. Served to 1st lt., M.I., AUS, 1942-45. Mem. 7th Regt. Vets. Assn., Silurian Soc., Sigma Delta Chi. Clubs: Players, Dutch Treat, River, Coffee House, Regency, Casino (Chgo.); Cuernavaca Racquet (Mex.). Author: Fractured English; Scrawl of the Wild; This Is Costello; The Big Fix; Mockridge, You're Slipping!; others; contbr. numerous articles to mags. Address: Beach Ln Wainscott NY 11975

MODERACKI, EDMUND ANTHONY, educator, condr.; b. Hackensack, N.J., July 18, 1946; s. Edmund Joseph and Helen Theresa (Fisher) M.; B.A., Montclair State Coll., 1968, postgrad., 1970-71; M.A., Hunter Coll., 1970, postgrad., 1970-72; postgrad. Newark State Coll., 1969-70, Seton Hall U., 1970, Rutgers U., 1976. Center for Understanding Media, 1973. Tchr. music, audio-visuals pub. schs., River Vale, N.J., 1968—; asst. condr. Ridgewood (N.J.) Symphony Orch., 1969—, also trustee; tuba soloist Rutherford Community Band, 1970-71, Ridgewood Village Band, 1973, Waldwick Band, 1976; founding mem. Collegium Musicum Montclair State Coll., 1971—; condr. Waldwick Band, 1978. Recipient Fellowship award Bergen County PTA, 1976. Mem. Music Educators Nat. Conf., N.J. Edn. Assn., NEA, Ednl. Media Assn. N.J., Assn. for Ednl. Communications and Tech., Phi Mu Alpha Sinfonia, Kappa Delta Pi. Home: 531 Westwood Ave River Vale NJ 07675 Office: Holdrum Sch River Vale NJ 07675

MODICA, ALFRED JOSEPH, mktg. communications mgmt. co. exec.; b. Riverdale, N.Y., Jan. 22, 1925; s. Vincent J. and Agatha S. (Nicosia) M.; certificate Morton Schs. Real Estate, N.Y.C., 1963; certificate Henry George Sch. Social Sci., N.Y.C., 1966; LL.B., Blackstone Sch. Law, Chgo., 1965, J.D., 1968; B.S. in Bus. Adminstrn., Empire State Coll. State U. N.Y., 1976; postgrad. L.I. U.; m. Teresa D. O'Donnell, Sept. 7, 1947; children—Christopher, Stephen, Eugene. Sales mgr. Electrolux Corp., N.Y.C., 1946-49; freelance mktg. dir., 1949-54; pres., dir. Meadowstone, Inc., N.Y.C., 1954-62; mkgt. communications cons. on franchise programming, 1962-66; exec. v.p. Seltz Franchising Devel., Inc., N.Y.C., 1967-69; pres., dir. OFI Corp Corp., Mespeth, N.Y., 1969—, Lee Myles Assos. Corp., Maspeth, 1970—; exec. v.p., dir. Lee Myles Corp., Maspeth, 1970—, Alfred J. Modica Assos., 1974—; instr. group area dir. mgmt. Mercy Coll., 1974—, also ednl. work shop sessions for minority groups, workshop session and seminars for fed. and state govts., bus., 1970—, group leader sch. of continuing edn., div. of bus. and mgmt. N.Y. U. Served with USMCR, 1943-46. Mem. Inst. for Applied Communications (dir.), Am. Acad. Consultants, Mid-Hudson Inst., Nat. Small Bus. Assn., Am. Mktg. Assn., C. of C. U.S., Internat. Platform Assn., Alpha Psi Omega, Kappa Delta Pi. Asso. editor Franchising Around the World mag., 1970—. Contbr. articles to profl. Publs. Home: 700 Scarsdale Ave Scarsdale NY 10583

MODNY, CYNTHIA JEAN, dermatologist; b. Glen Ridge, N.J., Jan. 23, 1945; d. Michael Theodore and Mary (Tabaka) Modny; B.A., Mount Holyoke Coll., 1967; M.D., U. Va., 1971; postgrad. Stanford U., 1971. Intern, Lenox Hill Hosp., N.Y.C., 1971-72; resident N.Y. Hosp.-Cornell U. Med. Center, N.Y.C., 1972-75; practice medicine specializing in dermatology, Montclair, N.J., 1976—; clin. instr. dermatology Cornell Med. Center, N.Y.C., 1976—. Diplomate Am. Bd. Dermatology. Mem. AMA, Am. Med. Women's Assn., Essex County Med. Soc., Med. Soc. State N.J., Am. Soc. for Dermatologic Surgery, Am. Acad. Dermatology, U. Va. Med. Alumni Assn. (co-chmn. alumni activities com.). Republican. Ukranian Orthodox. Clubs: Mount Holyoke (N.Y.C.), Princeton (N.Y.C.); Montclair Golf. Contbr. articles in field to med. jours. Office: 36 Hawthorne Pl Montclair NJ 07042

MOELLER, CARL WILLIAM, chemist; b. Carroll, Iowa, Mar. 2, 1924; s. Carl William and Leila Helen (Selzer) M.; B.S., Harvard U., 1949; Ph.D., U. Southern Calif., 1954; m. Lois B. balken, Oct. 4, 1952; children—Eric M., Niel B. Mem. faculty U. Conn., Storrs, 1955—, prof. chemistry, 1978—. Served with AUS, 1943-46. Fulbright fellow, Tubingen U., 1954-55. Mem. Am. Chem. Soc., AAUP, AAAS, Sigma Xi, Phi Lambda Upsilon. Democrat. Episcopalian. Contbr. articles to profl. jours. Home: 112 Puddin Ln Mansfield Center CT 06250 Office: Dept Chemistry Univ Conn Storrs CT 06268

MOELLER, GEORGE ROSSWORN, govt. adminstr.; b. Queens, Mar. 25, 1935; s. George and Helen (Rossworn) M.; A.B., Hunter Coll., 1957, postgrad., 1960-63; M.S.W., Fordham U., 1966; postgrad. N.Y. Med. Coll., 1973; certificate in Family, Marital Therapy, N.Y. Med. Coll., 1973; m. Betty Carol La Fountaine, July 9, 1966. With N.Y.C. Dept. Social Services, 1958—, ednl. coordinator, 1971—; psychotherapist Fifth Av. Center Counseling and Psychotherapy, N.Y.C., 1971—; child therapist Bleuler Psychotherapy Center, 1974; pvt. practice psychotherapy and marriage counseling, 1974—; cons. Flushing Consultation Service (N.Y.), 1969-71; field tchr. Sch. Social Work Columbia U., 1970-71. Mem. West End Civic Assn., Floral Park Village (N.Y.), 1969—; bd. dirs. N.Y. State Opera Soc. Served with AUS, 1957. N.Y.C. Dept. Social Services fellow, 1963-66. Mem. Acad. Certified Social Workers, Am. (clin. mem.), N.Y. (clin. mem.) assns. marriage and family counselors, Nat. Assn. Social Workers, Am. Assn. Psychiat. Services for Children, Fordham U. Alumni Assn. Nassau County. Episcopalian. Home: 244 Floral Blvd Floral Park NY 11001 Office: 109 E 16th St New York City NY 10004

MOELLERING, ROBERT CHARLES, JR., physician; b. Lafayette, Ind., June 9, 1936; s. Robert Charles and Irene Pauline (Nolde) M.; B.A., Valparaiso U., 1958; M.D. cum laude, Harvard U., 1962; m. Mary Tigg Johnston, June 14, 1964; children—Anne Elizabeth, Robert Charles III, Catherine Irene. Intern Mass. Gen. Hosp., Boston, 1962-63, resident, 1963-64, 66-67, postdoctoral fellow infectious diseases, 1967-70, mem. infectious disease unit and asst. physician, 1970-76, asso. physician, 1976—, cons. bacteriology, 1972—; instr. medicine Harvard Med. Sch., 1970-72, asst. prof., 1972-76, asso. prof., 1976—. Served with USPHS, 1964-66. USPHS grantee. Diplomate Am. Bd. Internal Medicine. Fellow ACP; mem. Infectious Diseases Soc. Am., Am. Soc. Microbiology, Am. Fedn. Clin. Research, Mass. Med. Soc., Alpha Omega Alpha, Phi Kappa Psi. Research in cardiovascular epidemiology, mechanism of antibiotics, automated techniques for clin. microbiology. Contbr. articles to profl. jours. and books. Mem. editorial bd. New Eng. Jour. Medicine, 1977—, Antimicrobial Agents and Chemotherapy, 1977—. Home: 76 Wellesley St Weston MA 02193 Office: Infectious Disease Unit Mass General Hospital Boston MA 02114

MOENCH, JOHN CHRISTOPHER, neurologist; b. Boston, Nov. 18, 1921; s. John Christopher and Margaret Charlotte (Borden) M.; B.A., Amherst Coll., 1945; M.D., U. Rochester, 1945; m. Mary Jane Detzer, June 22, 1950; children—Susan Moench Art, Margaret D. Moench Mellman, Robert B. Intern U. Minn. Hosps., 1945-46; asst. resident Yale Hosp., 1948; resident Dartmouth Grad. Med. Program, 1948-51; clk. Nat. Hosp. Queens Sq., London, Eng., 1951-52; practice medicine specializing in neurology, New Haven, 1955—; asso., clin. instr. Yale Sch. Medicine, 1954-60, asst. clin. prof., 1960-74, asso. clin. prof., 1974—; attending physician Yale New Haven Hosp., Hosp. St. Raphael; cons. Gaylord, Meriden, Meriden Meml., Griffin hosps., Elmcroft Psychiat. Inst.; chmn. med. adv. com. Gaylord Hosp., 1968—; mem. med. bd. Yale-New Haven Med. Center, 1972-75; chmn. Conn. Gov.'s Com. for Study Epilepsy Facilities, 1967-69. Mem. Conservation Commn., Guilford, Conn., 1967-70; trustee New Haven Found. Med. Care. Served from 2d lt. to capt. AUS, 1943-47, capt. USAF, 1952-54. Fellow A.C.P., Am. Acad. Neurology; mem. New Haven County Med. Assn. (chmn. study com. 1967-68). Home: 132 Old Quarry Rd Guilford CT 06437 Office: 111 Park St New Haven CT 06511

MOFFETT, ANTHONY TOBY, congressman; b. Holyoke, Mass., Aug. 18, 1944; s. Anthony John and Mary (Romenius) M.; B.A. in Polit Sci., Syracuse U., 1966; M.A. in Urban Affairs, Boston Coll., 1968; 1 dau., Julia. Liaison to urban st. gangs, Washington, 1968; dir. U.S. Office Students and Youth, Washington, 1969; aide to Senator Walter Mondale of Minn., 1970; dir. Conn. Citizen Action Group, 1971; tchr. pub. schs., Boston; mem. 94th-96th Congresses from 6th Conn. dist. Democrat. Author: The Participation Put-On; Reflections of a Disenchanted Washington Youth Expert, 1970; Nobody's Business: The Political Intruder's Guide to Everyone's State Legislature, 1973. Home: 622 C St SE Washington DC 20003 Office: 1008 Longworth Office Bldg Washington DC 20515

MOFFETT, HENRY CLAY NICK, pub. relations exec., floraculturist; b. Camden, N.J., Nov. 30, 1908; s. Charles Chauncey and Melissa Lawrence (Arthur) M.; student Fordham U., 1946, Rutgers U., 1947-48; m. Dorothy Claire Deering, Feb. 4, 1939; 1 dau., Betty Marie Moffett Terres. Free-lance accountant, Camden, 1931-39; sales mgmt. staff Met. Life Ins. Co., Camden and Haddonfield, N.J., 1939-63; chief fin. officer City of Woodbury (N.J.), 1963-72; v.p. pub. relations firm Most Co. Inc., 1972—; pres. N.Am. Gladiolus Council, 1962-64; judge, dir. All Am. Gladiolus Selections, 1962—; lectr. gladiolus culture; TV and radio commentator gladiolus culture. Chmn. Gloucester County (N.J.) Econ. Stblzn. Bd., 1968—; commr. Gloucester County Tax Bd., 1972; pres. Woodbury Republican Club, 1958; Rep. campaign mgr. Gloucester County, 1958-71; trustee, adminstr. treas. Woodbury Pub. Library, 1963-72.

Served with AUS, World War II; PTO. Named Man of Year 4-H Gloucester County, 1968; recipient Gold medal award N. Am. Gladiolus Council, 1964. Mem. N.J. Gladiolus Soc. (pres. 1960-62), Gloucester County Holy Name Soc., St. Patrick's Soc., St. Vincent de Paul Soc. (pres. 1948-67), Met. Vets. Assn. N.J., Royal Brit. Hort. Soc. (hon.), Gloucester County Hist. Soc. (trustee 1972—), Am. Legion, VFW. Clubs: Rotary, Woodbury Men's Catholic (pres. 1946-69). Home: 428 Hemlock Terr Woodbury NJ 08096 Office: 44 Delaware St Woodbury NJ 08096

MOFFITT, AUGUSTINE EDWARD, JR., toxicologist, chemist; b. Pottsville, Pa., Oct. 2, 1945; s. Augustine Edward and Margaret Dolores M.; B.A. cum laude, LaSalle Coll., 1967; M.S., Harvard U., 1969, Sc.D. (USPHS fellow), 1973; m. Joanne Klatko, Sept. 16, 1967; children—Christopher A., Amy E. Toxicologist, Nat. Inst. Occupational Safety and Health, Cin., 1972-73, chief biochem. pharmacology unit, 1972-74; sr. environ. health chemist, toxicologist Bethlehem Steel Corp. (Pa.), 1974-76, dir. environ. chemistry and toxicology, 1976—; mem. environ. studies adv. com. Northampton Area County Community Coll.; expert ILO Meeting on Limits of Exposure to Dangerous Airborne Substances, Geneva, 1977; lectr. Indsl. Health Found., Pitts., Thomas Jefferson U., Phila. Served with USPHS, 1969-71. Mem. Soc. Toxicology, Am. Indsl. Hygiene Assn., Soc. Occupational and Environ. Health, AAAS, ASTM, Sigma Xi. Contbr. articles to profl. jours. Office: Martin Tower B 252 Bethlehem PA 18016

MOFFITT, ROBERT JAMES, indsl. engr.; b. Springfield, Mass., May 13, 1943; s. James Joseph and Clare Edna (Lyons) M.; B.S. in Mech. Engring., U. Notre Dame, 1968; m. Mary Catherine Connor, Aug. 27, 1966; children—Catherine Casey, Robert Lyons. Mech. engr. Naval Ship Systems Command, Dept. Navy, Washington, 1968-72; naval architect Naval Sea Systems Command, 1972-74; dep. chief Indsl. Support Services div. SBA, 1974—, also mem. interagy. quality control and reliability com., fed. agy. metric coordinator, also mem. interagy metrication policy com. Recipient Outstanding Performance and Spl. Achievement award Dept. Navy, 1970; Spl. Achievement award Dept. Navy, 1971; Outstanding Performance award SBA, 1977. Mem. Assn. of Sr. Engrs., Am. Soc. Naval Engrs. Roman Catholic. Clubs: West Potomac Rugby Football (v.p. 1977), Jocques Football, Lorsac Athletic (v.p.) (Washington). Home: 112 Weymouth St Upper Marlboro MD 20870 Office: 1441 L St NW Washington DC 20416

MOGEL, ERNEST H., clin. psychologist; b. N.Y.C., July 6, 1929; s. Maurice and Mary (Schulman) M.; B.A., U. Conn., 1951, M.A., 1952; m. Suzanne T. Nicholl, July 1, 1966; children—Brian, Laurie, Julie, Melinda. Program dir. Boston Jr. Achievement, 1955-58; psychologist Center Club, rehab. inst., Boston, 1959-61, Jewish Vocat. Service, Boston, 1961-63, Mass. Dept. Mental Health, 1963-74; pvt. practice psychology, Haverhill, Mass., 1966—; cons. community agencies. Served with AUS, 1953-55. Mem. Am., New Eng., Mass. psychol. assns., Mass. Assn. State Psychologists. Jewish. Club: Masons. Home: 1 Bellevue Rd Swampscott MA 01907 Office: 215 Summer St Haverhill MA 01830

MOGLIA, FRED ANDREW, chemist; b. Montclair, N.J., Feb. 12, 1945; s. Fred Andrew and Elvera (Zanelli) M.; B.S., Fairleigh Dickinson U., 1971, M.S., 1975; m. Marie Grace Catalano, June 27, 1965; 1 dau., Gina Marie. Asst. dir. research and devel. Royal Lubricants Co., East Hanover, N.J., 1963—. Fellow Am. Inst. Chemists; mem. Am. Chem. Soc., Am. Soc. Lubrication Engrs., ASTM, Soc. Automotive Engrs. Home: 31 Bridgeton Dr Lake Parsippany NJ 07054 Office: Royal Lubricants Co River Rd East Hanover NJ 07936

MOHL, ALLAN SUSSMAN, social worker; b. Passaic, N.J., Feb. 10, 1933; s. Milton and Ruth (Meisler) M.; B.A., N.Y. U., 1954, M.A., 1956, M.S.S., 1960; m. Judith Klein, Dec. 21, 1958; children—Barbara, Eric, Adam. Group leader Project Enable, Bronx, N.Y., 1965-67; pvt. practice, Scarsdale, N.Y., 1966—; social service supr. Daus. of Jacob Geriatric Center, Bronx, 1967-70; unit dir. Childrens Village, Dobbs Ferry, N.Y., 1971-77; dir. residential social services Queens (N.Y.) Diagnostic Center, 1977—; instr. sociology Mercy Coll., Dobbs Ferry, 1977—. Mem. Ardsley (N.Y.) Youth Council, 1966-67; coach Ardlsey Little League, 1975, 76, co-mgr., 1977, 78. Served with U.S. Army, 1956-58. NIMH grantee, 1958-60; cert. social worker, N.Y. State. Mem. Nat. Assn. Social Workers, Acad. Cert. Social Workers, N.Y. State Soc. Clin. Social Work Psychotherapists, Am. Assn. Marriage and Family Therapists, Camp Becket Dads Assn. Democrat. Contbr. articles to profl. publs. Home: 8 Shorthill Rd Ardsley NY 10502 Office: 340 Ardsley Rd Scarsdale NY 10583

MOHL, ROBERT CHARLES, city ofcl.; b. Paterson, N.J., Aug. 1, 1933; s. Irving and Fannie (Weiss) M.; A.A., Rutgers U., 1972; B.S., William Paterson Coll., 1974; m. Connie Nunziato, Feb. 29, 1960; children—Laurell, Tracy, Davia. Patrolman, Police Dept., Paterson, N.J., 1957-65, detective, 1965, detective sgt., 1965-68, patrol sgt., 1968-70, warden Passaic County Jail, 1970-71, patrol sgt., 1971, comdr. antirobbert squad, 1971-72, lt., comdr. vice-squad, 1972—, detective squad leader, 1973, comdr. C watch patrol, 1973-74, capt., 1974—, capt. in command B Watch, patrol div., 1975-76, dep. police chief in command field ops., 1978—; instr. criminal law Paterson Police Acad. Served with U.S. Army, 1957-59. Recipient Policeman of Year award Jr. C. of C., 1967, Mayor's Valor medal, 1965, 66, Revolver, Paterson Businessmen's Assn., 1965,66, Distinguished Service ribbon Police Commrs., 1965, 66, 67, 71. Mem. Internat. Assn. Chiefs Police, Honor Legion-State N.J., Acad. Pub. Safety Scis., Policemen's Benevolent Assn., Am. Law Enforcement Officers Assn., Internat. Conf. Police Assn., Rutgers Alumni Assn. Home: 124 Arlington Ave Paterson NJ 07502 Office: 111 Washington St Paterson NJ 07509

MOHNEN, VOLKER ARMIN, physicist; b. Stuttgart, Germany, Mar. 11, 1937; s. Otto and Maria M.; came to U.S., 1967; B.S., U. Karlsruhe, 1959; M.S., U. Munich, 1962, Ph.D., 1966; m. Ilse Balcke, Mar. 30, 1963; children—Jorg, Heiner. Research asso. U. Munich (Germany), 1963-66; asso. prof. dept. atmospheric sci. State U. N.Y., Albany, 1967-77, research prof., 1977—, asso. dir. Atmospheric Scis. Research Center, 1972-74, acting dir., 1974-75, dir., 1975—; cons. air pollution, aerosol physics and atmospheric scis. to various corps. Trustee Inst. on Man and Sci., Rensselaerville, N.Y., 1974—; mem. internat. commn. on atomspheric electricity, internat. Assn. Meteorology and Atmospheric Physics, 1975-79; mem. NASA-Ames Research Center Sci. Steering Group for Airborne Atmospheric Experiments, 1977—. Recipient Outstanding Young Man award Schenectady Jr. C. of C., 1970. Fellow AAAS, N.Y. Acad. Scis.; mem. Am. Chem. Soc., Am. Geophys. Union, Am. Meteorol. Soc., Am. Phys. Soc., Air Pollution Control Assn., Am. Inst. Aeros. and Astronautics, Deutsche Physikalische Gesellschaft. Contbr. articles to profl. jours. Home: 105 Governor Dr Scotia NY 12302 Office: 1400 Washington Ave Albany NY 12222

MOHORICH, HELEN MARIE, naval officer; b. Pueblo, Colo., Apr. 23, 1937; d. Joseph John and Rose (Panepinto) M.; B.A. in Polit. Sci., U. Colo., 1959; M.S. in Mgmt., Naval Postgraduate Sch., 1972; postgrad Nat. Def. U., 1977-78. Commd. ensign U.S. Navy, 1960, advanced through grades to comdr., 1975; regimental comdr. Recruit Tng. Command for Women, 1967-68, dir. ops. policy and procedures Command Naval Telecommunications, Washington, 1972-74, dir. programs, 1974-77, head program devel. and appraisal, 1978—; chmn. ABM Investments. Roman Catholic. Home: 6710 Capstan Dr Annandale VA 22003

MOHR, LIONEL CHARLES, mktg. exec.; b. N.Y., Dec. 18, 1927; s. Lionel C. and Emma Ann (Stohldrier) M.; came to Can., naturalized, 1967; A.B., Wesleyan U., 1950; M.B.A., Harvard, 1959; m. Patricia Margaret Sinclair, Aug. 24, 1968; children—Lionel Thomas, Deborah Susan, Sharon Patricia, Deborah Anne, Douglas Tredwell, John David Edward. Retail salesman Scott Paper Co., N.Y.C., after 1950, then retail dist. sales mgr., Binghamton, N.Y., advt. staff asst., Phila., 1959-60, asst. merchandising mgr., Phila., 1960-61; mgr. consumer products div. E.B. Eddy Co., Ottawa, Ont., Can., 1961-62; product mgr. Gen. Foods, Ltd., Toronto, Ont., 1962, sales promotion mgr., 1963-64, product planning mgr., 1964, sr. product mgr., 1965; cons. Stevenson & Kellogg Co., Toronto, 1966, prin., 1967, then prin. in-charge of mktg.; dir. mktg. Toronto Star Ltd., 1971, v.p. mktg., 1974-77; v.p. Torstar Corp., 1977—, also dir.; chmn., dir. Comac Communications Ltd.; dir. Toronto Star Newspapers Ltd., Metromarket Newspapers Ltd. Founding dir. Peel Family Services, 1970, 73-75, treas., 1974-75, mem. exec. com., 1974-76; pres. Can. Opera Co., 1978—, bd. govs., 1977—, operating bd. dirs., mem. fin. cabinet, 1976; chmn. bd. of stewards Christ Ch. United Clarkson, 1963, elder, 1964—; nat. chmn. dept. planning assistance United Ch. of Can., 1971-72. Served to sgt., Transp. Corps, U.S. Army, 1950-52. Mem. Internat. Circulation Mgrs. Assn., Am. Mktg. Assn. (dir. Toronto chpt. 1965-69), Internat. Newspaper Advt. Execs. (chmn. mktg. mgmt. com.), Can. Daily Newspaper Pubs. Assn. (dir.), Newspaper Readership Council. Mem. United Ch. Can. Clubs: Rotary (mem. internat. services com. 1973—), Nat., Ont. Racquet, Empire, Canadian, Mississaugua Golf and Country. Home: 1674 Ruscombe Close Mississauga ON L5J 1Y3 Canada Office: One Yonge St Toronto ON M5E 1P9 Canada

MOHTASHEMI, HORMOZ, physician; b. Tehran, Iran, Jan. 10, 1939; s. Lotfolah and Touran (Mansour) M.; came to U.S., 1966, naturalized, 1972; M.D., Tehran U., 1964; m. Shamsi Gazinoori, Nov. 1, 1967; children—Negar, Payman. Resident internal medicine VA Hosp., N.Y.C., 1967-69, Nassau County Med. Center, East Meadow, N.Y., 1969-70; resident gastroenterology Montefiore Hosp. and Med. Center, Bronx, N.Y., 1970-72; practice medicine specializing in gastroenterology, Wayne, N.J., also Clifton, N.J., 1972—; med. attending staff St. Joseph's Hosp. and Med. Center, Paterson, N.J., also Greater Paterson Gen. Hosp., Wayne, N.J. Mem. A.C.P., Am. Gastroenterology Assn., Am., N.J. socs. gastrointestinal endoscopy, Am., N.J., Passaic County med. socs. Home: 34 Cathyann Ct Wayne NJ 07470 Office: 220 Hamburg Turnpike Wayne NJ 07470 also 187 Lakeview Ave Clifton NJ 07011

MOILES, WILLIAM HENRY, JR., journalist; b. Worcester, Mass., June 10, 1914; s. William Henry and Cathryn Irene (Candlin) M.; student Emerson Coll., 1934-35; m. Mary Elizabethe Kendall, June 30, 1951; children—Christopher A., Susan L. Columnist, reporter Worcester Evening Post, 1937-38; reporter Worcester Telegram, 1939-47, columnist, 1948—; editor Los Alamos (N.Mex.) Times, 1946. Democrat. Home: 19 Monroe Ave Worcester MA 01602 Office: 20 Franklin St Worcester MA 01613

MOLAN, JOHN EDWARD, clergyman; b. Manchester, N.H., Apr. 24, 1927; s. John E. and Katherine (Maher) M.; student St. Anselm's Coll., 1944-45, 47; A.B., St. Mary's Sem., 1949, S.T.B., 1951; M.S.W., Boston Coll., 1962. Ordained priest Roman Cath. Ch.; asst. pastor St. Joseph Cathedral, Manchester, 1953-60; asst. dir. N.H. Cath. Charities, Manchester, 1958-63, dir., 1963-75; diocesan coordinator health affairs, 1963—; pastor Immaculate Conception Ch., Portsmouth, N.H.; papal chamberlain monsignor, 1965, prelate of honor, 1970. Bd. dirs. Catholic Med. Center, St. Joseph Hosp., Pope John XXIII Med.-Moral Research and Edn. Center. Served with AUS, 1945-46. Mem. Acad. Certified Social Workers. Home: 98 Summer St Portsmouth NH 03801 Office: 215 Myrtle St Manchester NH 03105

MOLANDER, DAVID JOHN, mktg. exec.; b. Exeter, Eng., Sept. 25, 1945; s. Walter Harold and Phyllis Rosemary (Webb) M.; (parents Am. citizens); A.S.B.A. with high honors, Burdett Coll., 1968; B.S.B.A. cum laude, Suffolk U., 1973, M.B.A., 1976; m. Carolyn M. Sarro, July 15, 1967; children—Eric J., Scott D. Asst. cost mgr. Rust Craft Greeting Cards, Dedham, Mass., 1969-72; mktg. admnstr. Bell & Howell Communications, Burlington, Mass., 1972-76; asst. product mgr. Am. Biltrite Inc., Cambridge, Mass., 1976—; instr. mktg. and sales dept. Newbury Jr. Coll., Boston, 1976—. Congregationalist. Home: 91 Beech St Dedham MA 02026

MOLDENKE, HAROLD NORMAN, naturalist, botanist; b. Watchung, N.J., Mar. 11, 1909; s. Charles Edward and Sophia Meta (Heins) M.; B.S., Susquehanna U., 1929; M.A., Columbia U., 1932, Ph.D., 1934; m. Alma Lance Ericson, Sept. 2, 1942; 1 son, Andrew Ralph. Biology asst. Susquehanna U., 1926-29; fellow N.Y. Bot. Garden, N.Y.C., 1929, asst., 1929-32, asst. curator, 1932-37, asso. curator, 1937-48, curator, adminstr. herbarium, 1949-52, hon. curator, 1973—; supr. nature activities Union County Park Commn., Elizabeth, N.J., 1952-60, dir. Trailside Nature and Sci. Center, Mountainside, N.J., 1952-67; instr. grad. faculty Columbia U., 1936-42, 46-52; instr. Hunter Coll., 1947-50, N.J. State Tchrs. Coll., 1951-54; prof. dept. biol. scis. William Paterson Coll. of N.J., Wayne, 1967-72; co-founder bot. jour. Phytologia, N.Y.C., 1933, co-editor, 1933—, pub., 1952—; asso. editor Plant Life and Herbertia, La Jolla, Calif., 1947-78; corr. editor Chronica Botanica, Waltham, Mass., 1939-63; collaborator Biol. Abstracts, Phila., 1933-78. Fellow N.Y. Acad. Sci., AAAS; mem. Bot. Soc. Am., Internat. Assn. Plant Taxonomy, Nat. Audubon Soc., Centro de Estudiantes del Doctorado en Ciencias Naturales, Sociedad Amigos Flora Brasilica, Sociedad Botanica de Mex., Sociedad Cubana de Botanica, Instituto Ecuatoriano de Ciencias Naturales, Sigma Xi, Pi Gamma Mu. Author: American Wild Flowers, 1949; (with wife) Plants of the Bible, 1952; A Fifth Summary of Verbenaceae, Stilbaceae, Dicrastylidaceae, Symphoremaceae, Nyctanthaceae, and Eriocaulaceae, 1971. Contbr. articles to profl. jours. Home: 303 Parkside Rd Plainfield NJ 07060

MOLINARI, PIETRO FILIPPO, hematologist; b. Mestre-Venice, Italy, Sept. 9, 1923; s. Roberto and Clelia (Colla) M.; came to U.S. 1964, naturalized, 1969; B.S., Lyceum M. Foscarini, Venice, 1948; D.V.M., Milan U., 1952, Ph.D., 1960; m. Simona Maria Teresa Casolari, Aug. 9, 1956; children—Barbara, Roberto. Clin. vet. pathologist Milan (Italy) U., 1952-56, asst. prof. vet. medicine, 1956-60, asso. prof., 1960-64; asso. in research Mason Research Inst., Worcester, Mass., 1964-68, prin. investigator, 1968-70; asst. dir., div. hematology-oncology St. Vincent Hosp., Worcester, 1971—; practice vet. medicine, Whitinsville, Mass., 1973—; asst. prof. medicine U. Mass. Med. Sch., Worcester, 1975—. Served with Italian Army, 1943. Mem. Endocrine Soc., N.Y. Acad. Scis., Internat. Soc. Exptl. Hematology, Mass. Vet. Med. Assn., Sigma Xi. Contbr. articles in field to profl. jours. Home: 7 Hancock Hill Dr Worcester MA 01609 Office: 25 Winthrop St Worcester MA 01610

MOLITOR, GRAHAM THOMAS TATE, lawyer; b. Seattle, Apr. 6, 1934; s. Robert Franklin and Louise Margaret (Graham) M.; B.S., U. Washington, 1955; LL.B., Am. U., 1963; m. Carlotta Jean Crate, July 30, 1960; children—Graham Thomas Tate, Jr., Anne Therese, Christopher Robert. Research asst. U. Wash., Seattle, 1957; bailiff U.S. Criminal Ct. for D.C., 1958-59; admitted to D.C. bar, 1963, legis. counsel U.S. Ho. of Reps., Washington, 1961-63; dir. candidate research Rockefeller for Pres. com., 1963-64, 68; D.C. counsel, asst. dir. govt. relations Nabisco, Inc., Washington, 1964-70; dir. govt. relations Gen. Mills, Inc., Washington, 1970-77; pres., chief exec. officer Public Policy Forecasting, Inc., Potomac, Md., 1977—; adj. prof. Grad. Sch. Bus. Am. U., Washington, 1969-75; dir. research White House Conf. on Indsl. World Ahead, 1971-72; mem. White House Adv. Com. on Social Indicators, 1975-76; guest lectr. numerous univs. Del. White Confs. on Food, Nutrition and Health, 1969-71, White House Conf. on Youth, 1970. Served to 1st lt. U.S. Army, 1958-61. Recipient Distinguished Service award Grocery Mfrs. Am., 1974-73, Nat. Consumer Info. Center, 1974, Am. Mgmt. Assn., 1973. Mem. Washington Bus.-Govt. Relations Council, Washington Indsl. Rountable, E.D. Export Council, World Future Soc. (gen. chmn. 2d Gen. Assembly 1975, Distinguished Service award 1975), Phi Kappa Sigma, Phi Alpha Delta. Republican. Presbyterian. Clubs: University. Contbg. editor Food Tomorrow Newsletter, 1976-77; contbr. articles to profl. jours.; bd. editors Hudson Inst. Study of World Food Problems, 1975-77; editorial bd. Bus. Tomorrow Newsletter, 1977-79. Home and Office: 9208 Wooden Bridge Rd Potomac MD 20854

MOLIVER, MARTIN, educator; b. Phila., Aug. 17, 1913; s. David Levi and Anna (Soibalis) M.; B.A. (mayor's scholar), U. Pa., 1934, M.A. (NSF grantee 1959-60), 1964; Ed.M., Temple U., Phila., Ed.D., 1977; m. Emma Klempner, Aug. 17, 1936; children—Joanne Moliver Neff, Nina Moliver Hornbacher. Tchr. math. high schs., Phila., 1935—; head math. dept. Overbrook High Sch., 1970—; prin. King Standard Eve. High Sch., 1968—. AAAS fellow, 1961-63. Mem. Math. Assn. Am., Nat. Council Tchrs. Math., Am. Fedn. Tchrs., Assn. Tchrs. Math. Phila. and Vicinity, Pi Mu Epsilon, Phi Delta Kappa. Democrat. Jewish. Home: 7901 Henry Ave Apt F505 Philadelphia PA 19128 Office: Overbrook High Sch 59th and Lancaster Ave Philadelphia PA 19131

MOLL, CLARENCE RUSSEL, coll. pres.; b. Chalfont, Pa., Oct. 31, 1913; s. George A. and Anna A. (Schmidt) M.; B.S., Temple U., 1934, Ed.M., 1937; L.H.D., Pa. Mil. Coll., 1949; Ph.D., N.Y. U., 1955; LL.D., Temple U., 1963; Sc.D., Chungang U., Seoul, Korea, 1969; LL.D., Swarthmore Coll., 1970; Litt.D., Del. Valley Coll., 1976; m. Ruth E. Henderson, Nov. 19, 1941; children—Robert Henderson, Jonathan George. Instr. physics and chemistry Conshohocken (Pa.) High Sch., 1935-37; instr. sci. Freehold (N.J.) High Sch., 1937-38; instr. physics, chemistry Meml. High Sch., Haddonfield, 1938-42; instr. electronics and radar USN, Phila., 1942-43; asso. prof. physics Pa. Mil. Coll. (name changed to Widener Coll.), Chester, 1943-45, registrar, coordinator engring. program, 1945-47, dean admissions, student personnel, prof. edn., 1947-56, v.p. coll., 1956-59, pres. coll., 1959—, also trustee; chief exec. Del. Law Sch., Wilmington, 1975—; pres. Brandywine Coll., 1976—; instr. electronics Temple U., 1944-46; headmaster Pa. Mil. Prep. Sch., 1945-47; dir. Fedders Corp.; mem. Pa. Assn. Colls. and Univs., pres., 1970-71; past chmn. Ind. Colls. Pa., Found. Ind. Colls. Pa. Bd. dirs. Crozer Chester Med. Center, Hero Scholarship Fund, Chester Group, Univ. City Sci. Center, Phila. Recipient Horatio Alger award, 1962; Man of Year awards City of Chester, 1964, Delaware County, 1964; Distinguished Alumnus award Temple U., 1964; B'nai B'rith Citizen Service award, 1966; Distinguished Citizen award Deleware County Real Estate Bd., 1971; Themis award Delaware County Bar, 1976; Good Citizenship award Phila. bar, 1976. Mem. Assn. Mil. Colls. and Schs. (past pres.), Am. Soc. Engring. Edn., AIM (Exec. of Year award 1978, dir.), Tau Beta Pi, Phi Delta Kappa. Lutheran. Clubs: Springhaven (Wallingford, Pa.); N.Y. U., Univ., Harvard (N.Y.C.); Racquet (Phila.); Greenville (Del.) Country; Univ. and Whist (Wilmington); Masons. Author: History of Pennsylvania Military College. Home: 10 Church St Wallingford PA 19086 Office: Widener Coll Chester PA 19013 also Brandywine Coll Wilmington DE 19803

MOLLENKOTT, VIRGINIA RAMEY, educator; b. Phila., Jan. 28, 1932; d. Robert Franklin and May (Lotz) Ramey; B.A., Bob Jones U., 1953; M.A., Temple U., 1955; Ph.D., N.Y. U., 1964; m. Friedrich H. Mollenkott, June 17, 1954 (div. July 1973); 1 son, Paul Friedrich. Chmn. English dept. Shelton Coll., 1955-63, Nyack Coll., 1963-67; prof. English, William Paterson Coll. of N.J., Wayne, 1967—, chmn. dept. English, 1972-76. Asst. editor Seventeenth-Century News, 1965-74; stylistic cons. New Internat. Bible Translation Com.; guest speaker various colls., civic and religious groups. Recipient Andiron award, 1964, Penfield fellowship, 1963, Founders Day award, 1964 (all from N.Y. U.). Mem. Modern Lang. Assn. (regional del.), Milton Soc. Am. (mem. exec. com.), Conf. Christianity and Lit. (chief bibliographer, dir.). Author: Adamant and Stone Chips: A Christian Humanist Approach to Knowledge, 1967; In Search of Balance, 1969; Adam Among the Television Trees, 1971; Women, Men, and the Bible, 1976; Is the Homosexual My Neighbor?, 1978; editorial asso. The Other Side; contbg. editorial asso. Faith at Work mag.; contbr. articles to profl. jours. Home: Route 3 Box 1139 Hewitt NJ 07421 Office: William Paterson Coll of NJ Wayne NJ 07470

MOLLOW, BENJAMIN RICHARD, physicist, educator; b. Trenton, N.J., Nov. 26, 1938; s. William and Rose (Ginsberg) M.; A.B., Cornell U., 1960; Ph.D., Harvard U., 1966; children—Anna, David. Postdoctoral fellow Brandeis U., 1966-68, asst. prof., 1968-69; asst. prof. physics U. Mass. at Boston, 1969-73, asso. prof., 1973—. NSF fellow, 1960-63; Woodrow Wilson fellow (hon.), 1960-61. Mem. Am. Phys. Soc., Am. Assn. Physics Tchrs., Phi Beta Kappa. Contbr. articles in field to profl. jours. Home: 67 Court St Newtonville MA 02160 Office: Dept Physics U Mass Harbor Campus Boston MA 02125

MOLNAR, AUGUST JOHN, found. exec.; b. Cleve., Mar. 24, 1927; s. August and Mary (Petro) M.; B.A., Elmhurst Coll., 1949; M.A., U. Mich., 1950; B.D., Lancaster Theol. Sem., 1952; postgrad. Columbia U., 1954-61, Rutgers U., 1969—; m. Priscilla B. Arvay, June 14, 1952; children—August John, Katherine Marie. Asst. prof. history, chmn. dept. Hungarian studies Elmhurst (Ill.) Coll., 1952-59; lectr. Hungarian studies Rutgers U. New Brunswick, 1959-65; pres. Am. Hungarian Studies Found., New Brunswick, 1955-72, exec. dir., 1972-75; pres. Am. Hungarian Found., 1975—; cons. lang. resources project U. Pa., 1961-63. Bd. dirs. Mason W. Gross Found. Cholnoky fellow, Columbia, 1954, 55. Mem. Am. Hist. Assn., Modern Lang. Assn., Am. Assn. U. Profs. Mem. United Ch. of Christ. Editor: Hungarian Writers and Literature, 1964; asso. editor American Hungarian Dialect Notes, 1962; chmn. editorial com., contbr. chpt. The New Jersey Ethnic Experience, 1977. Home: 59 Pennington Rd New Brunswick NJ 08901 Office: 177 Somerset St New Brunswick NJ 08903

MOLZ, ROBERT JOSEPH, chemist; b. Yonkers, N.Y., Mar. 15, 1937; s. Philip and Maria Hilda (Geist) M.; B.S., City Coll. N.Y., 1960, M.A., 1966; Ph.D., N.Y. Med. Coll., 1969; m. Diane Ruth Horowitz, July 31, 1960; children—Jennifer Ann, Erica Beth. Research biochemsit E.I. DuPont De Nemours & Co., Inc., Wilmington, Del., 1969-71, tech. services supr., 1971-73, product mgr., 1973-75, research mgr. Automatic Clin. Analysis Div., 1976—; instr. N.Y. Inst. Tech., 1968-69. Pres., Arbour Park Civic Assn., 1971-72. Mem. Am. Chem. Soc., Am. Assn. for Clin. Chemistry. Roman Catholic. Home: 306 Dove Dr Newark DE 19713 Office: Concord Plaza Wilmington DE 19898

MONAGHAN, JAMES MATTHEW, III, radiologist; b. Atlantic City, Mar. 26, 1926; s. James Matthew and Anna Margaret (Farne) M.; student Villanova U., U. Pa.; M.D., Jefferson Med. Coll., 1950; m. Jean Mary Pritchard, June 3, 1950; children—Kathleen, Kevin, Brian, Sean, Justin, Clare. Intern, St. Lukes Hosp., Cleve., 1950-51; resident Jefferson Med. Coll. Hosp., Phila., 1951-52, Columbia Presbyn. Hosp., N.Y.C., 1954-56; practice medicine specializing in radiology, Short Hills, N.J., 1956—; attending staff Hosp. Center at Orange (N.J.), 1956—, dir. radiology, 1968—, trustee, 1974—; mem. staff Irvington (N.J.) Gen. Hosp.; pres. X-ray Technician Bd. N.J., 1969-73. Served with USNR, 1944-46, U.S. Army, 1952-54. Fellow AMA, Am. Coll. Radiology; mem. Radiol. socs. N.A., N.J. (pres. 1976-77), Med. Soc. N.J. Roman Catholic. Home: 12 Wells Ln Short Hills NJ 07078 Office: 85 Woodland Rd Short Hills NJ 07078

MONAHAN, JOHN FRANCIS, mgmt. cons.; b. Worcester, Mass., Nov. 25, 1930; s. Francis A. and Mildred Elizabeth (Murphy) M.; A.B. in Mathematics, Holy Cross Coll., 1953; J.D., Boston Coll., 1956; m. Marion Teresa Wall, Dec. 15, 1956; children—Joseph Francis, Mary Elizabeth. Contract negotiator Raytheon, Portsmouth, R.I., 1960-63, contracts product line mgr., 1963-67, chief negotiator, 1968-73; contracts mgr. United Engrs., Phila., Pa., 1973-74, v.p., United Engrs. Internat., 1975—; owner, cons. J. F. Monahan Mgmt. Cons., Radnor, Pa., 1976—; sec., treas. Energy Cons., Inc.; cons. in field; asso. prof. Roger Williams Coll. Pres., v.p. PTA, Barrington, R.I., 1972-74, exec. com., 1972-73; coach, mgr. Little League, 1974-76. Served as lt. USN, 1956-60. Mem. Contract Mgmt. Assn., Raytheon Advisory Mgmt. Assn., U.S. Naval Reserve Honary. Roman Catholic. Home: 2559 Crum Creek Drive Berwyn PA 19312 Office: Box 35 Radnor PA 19087

MONAHON, PHILIP CHRISTOPHER, constrn. corp. exec., cons.; b. Newton, Mass., June 4, 1929; s. Arthur Thomas and Ruth (Tulis) M.; B.S., Mass. Maritime Acad., 1952; m. Joan Skillin Mills, July 18, 1953; children—P. Christopher, Gregory, Hilary, Catherine, Laura. Vice pres. Monahon Corp., Watertown, Mass., 1955—; pres. Nat. Home Inspection Service New Eng., Inc., 1969—; constrn. cons. Served as lt. USNR, 1953-55; Korea, Vietnam. Recipient United Fund awards, 1965, 66; Mem. of Year award Mass. Maritime Acad. Alumni Assn., 1962. Mem. Asso. Gen. Contractors Mass. (past pres. and dir., award 1965), Asso. Gen. Contractors Am. (dir.), Am. Inst. Constructors, Am. Soc. Home Insps. (nat. dir.), Am. Arbitration Assn. (arbitrator). Republican. Club: Lakewood Tennis (Newton). Contbr. articles and book revs. to Constructor mag.; author: Planning Committee Report for Asso. Gen. Contractors (Mass.), 1976. Contbr. to First Printings of Am. Authors. Home: Five Chester St Newton Highlands MA 02161 Office: 2 Calvin Rd Watertown MA 02172

MONATH, NORMAN, publishing co. exec.; b. Toronto, Ont., Can., July 3, 1920; came to U.S., 1924, naturalized, 1944; A.B., N.Y. U., 1941; m. Pauline K. Farber, Aug. 30, 1952 (dec. Feb. 1972); children—Richard, Robert, Bruce. Export sales mgr., music and chess editor Simon & Schuster, Inc., N.Y.C., 1954-57, dir. subs. rights, 1957-59, now cons.; founding pres. Cornerstone Library Inc., N.Y.C., 1960—, also dir.; dir. Paperback Affiliates Inc., N.Y.C. Served with Signal Corps, AUS, 1942-45. Mem. ASCAP. Clubs: Saltaire (N.Y.) Yacht; Town Tennis, Marshall Chess (N.Y.C.). Inventor Bali word game, 1954. Composer. Home: 40 5th Ave New York City NY 10011 Office: 630 5th Ave New York City NY 10020

MONCURE, ASHBY CARTER, surgeon; b. Richmond, Va., Dec. 27, 1934; s. Powhatan and Maude Leah (Carley) M.; student U. Va., 1953-56, M.D., 1960; m. Patricia Juanita Leighton, June 21, 1960; children—Diana Carley, Ann Marie, Ashby Carter, Elizabeth Leighton. Intern Mass. Gen. Hosp., Boston, 1960-61, asst. resident in surgery, 1961-62, 64-67; locum sr. registrar to sr. thoracic cons. S.W. Regional Hosp. Bd., Bristol, Eng., 1967; chief surgical resident Mass. Gen. Hosp., 1968, asst. in surgery, 1969-71, asst. surgeon, 1971, asso. vis. surgeon, 1973—; instr. surgery Harvard U. Med. Sch., 1969-71, asst. prof., 1971—. Served with U.S. Army, 1962-64. Diplomate Am. Bd. Surgery, Am. Bd. Thoracic Surgery. Fellow A.C.S.; mem. Am. Assn. Acad. Surgery, Am. Assn. Thoracic Surgery, Eastern Surg. Soc., Boston Surg. Soc., Internat. Cardiovascular Soc., Alpha Omega Alpha. Episcopalian. Clubs: Union Boat, Weston Golf. Home: 116 Plain Rd Wayland MA 01778 Office: Mass Gen Hosp 32 Fruit St Boston MA 02114

MONDALE, JOAN ADAMS, wife of v.p. U.S.; b. Eugene, Oreg., Aug. 8, 1930; d. John Maxwell and Eleanor Jane (Hall) Adams; B.A., Macalester Coll., 1952; m. Walter Frederick Mondale, Dec. 27, 1955; children—Theodore, Eleanor Jane, William. Asst. slide librarian Boston Mus. Fine Arts, 1952-53; asst. in edn. Mpls. Inst. Arts, 1953-57; profl. tour guide Washington Whirl-Around, 1974—. Active Jr. League Washington; active Women's Nat. Democratic Club Washington, bd. dirs., 1967-71; vol. tour guide Nat. Gallery Art. Presbyterian. Author: Politics in Art, 1972. Home: Vice President's House Washington DC 20501

MONDALE, WALTER FREDERICK, v.p. U.S.; b. Ceylon, Minn., Jan. 5, 1928; s. Theodore Sigvaard and Claribel Hope (Cowan) M.; B.A. cum laude, U. Minn., 1951, LL.B., 1956; m. Joan Adams, Dec. 27, 1955; children—Theodore, Eleanor, William. Admitted to Minn. bar, 1956; pvt. practice law, 1956-60; atty. gen. State of Minn., 1960-64; senator from Minn., 1964-76; v.p. U.S., 1977—. Served with AUS, 1951-53. Named Outstanding Young Man of Year in Minn., 1960. Mem. Am., Minn., Hennepin County bar assns., Minn. Safety Council, Am. Assn. UN, Am. Legion. Mem. Democratic Farm Labor Party. Presbyterian. Mem. editorial bd. Minn. Law Rev., 1955-56. Home: House of Vice Pres Washington DC 20501 also 3421 Lowell St NW Washington DC 20016 Office: The White House Washington DC 20500

MONET, JACQUES, clergyman, historian; b. St. Jean, Que., Jan. 26, 1930; s. Fabio and Anita (Deland) M.; B.A., U. Montreal, 1955, Ph.L., 1956, Th.L., 1967; M.A., U. Toronto, 1961, Ph.D., 1964. Ordained priest Roman Catholic Ch., 1966; asso. prof. history U. Ottawa, 1969—, chmn. dept., 1972-76; attache Gov. Gen. Can., 1976—. Mem. Heritage Found. Ont., Canadian Hist. assn. (pres. 1975-76), Institut d'Histoire d l'Amerique francaise. Author: The Last Cannon Shot: A Study of French Canadian Nationalism, 1969. Contbr. articles to profl. jours. Home: 2104-211 Wurtemborg St Ottawa ON K1N 8R4 Canada Office: Dept History Univ Ottawa Ottawa ON K1N 6N5 Canada

MONG, FRANK FOWLER, educator; b. Dawson, Pa., May 28, 1923; s. Albert Vanhorn and Irene (Brothers) M.; A.B. cum laude, Waynesburg Coll., 1948; postgrad. Western Theol. Sem., 1948-49; M.A., U. Pitts., 1950. Tchr., Greensburgh (Pa.) High Sch., 1950-53; instr. Latin, Waynesburg Coll., 1953; asst. prof. Latin, capt. N.Mex. Mil. Inst., 1953-58; Latin master St. Albans Cathedral Sch., Washington, 1958-60; sr. lang. tchr. Hatboro (Pa.) High Sch., 1960-78; ret., 1978; ind. research and study, 1978—. Served with AUS, 1943-45. Recipient award of appreciation and excellence Hatboro-Horsham Sch. Dist., 1978. Mem. Am. Philol. Assn., Am. Oriental Soc., Phila. Classical Assn., Am. Classical League, SAR, Assn. Internationale de Papyroloques, Am. Soc. Papyroloqists, VFW. Presbyterian. Home: Box 240 Dawson PA 15428

MONIOS, CONSTANTINE MICHAEL, clergyman; b. Monessen, Pa., Oct. 25, 1933; s. Michael Constantine and Amalia (Christy) M.; B.A. in Orthodox Theology, Holy Cross Theol. Sch., Hellenic Coll. 1957; S.T.M. in Religious Edn. (Taylor scholar, Univ. scholar), Boston U., 1960; m. Mary N. Christodoulou, July 15, 1956; children—Amalia, Harry, Athena, Michael, Nikki. Ordained to ministry Greek Orthodox Ch., 1956; priest Assumption Ch., Manchester, N.H., 1957-60; priest Holy Cross, Mt. Lebanon, Pitts., 1960-75; dean Annunciation Cathedral, Balt., 1975—. Mem. Archdiocese Presbyter's Council, 1970-74, Diocesan Spiritual Ct., 1965-75; mem. Youth Commn., Fgn. Missions and Nat. Pension program Greek Orthodox Archdiocese. Mem. steering com. Christian Assos. Southwestern Pa., 1963-65; religious adviser Bd. Planned Parenthood, Pitts., 1966-69; chaplain Woodville State Hosp., Bridgeville, Pa., 1960-73. Bd. dirs. South Hills Child Guidance Center, Conf. Christians and Jews, Southwestern Pa.; mem. bd. Md. Chs. United, Md. region NCCJ; pres. Cooley's Anemia Chpt. Md., Central Chs. of Balt.; bd. dirs. Ecumenical Inst. Balt. Named Economos, Archbishop Iakovos, 1971. Mem. Greek Orthodox Clergymen's Assn. (pres.), Orthodox Clergy Assn. Greater Pitts. (past pres.). Contbr. articles to religious jours. Home: 10832 Sandringham Rd Cockeysville MD 21030 Office: 24 W Preston St Baltimore MD 21201

MONK, ABRAHAM, educator; b. Buenos Aires, Argentina, Dec. 27, 1931; s. Jose and Maria (Ginzburg) M.; came to U.S., 1967, naturalized, 1972; B.A., Nat. U. and La Plata (Argentina), 1956; M.A., Columbia, 1959; Ph.D., Brandeis U., 1969; m. Raquel Helman, Nov. 3, 1951; children—Liliana B., Daniel B., Rebeca D. Dir., Inst. Human Relations, Buenos Aires, 1962-66; asso. prof. Nat. U. of La Plata, 1964-67, Nat. U. of Buenos Aires, 1965-67; prof. social work and gerontology State U. N.Y., Buffalo, 1969-77; Brookdale prof. geontology Columbia U., N.Y.C., 1977—; cons. Erie County Office for Aging. Fulbright Hays sr. scholar, 1975-76. Fellow Gerontol. Soc.; mem. Nat. Assn. Social Workers, Council Social Work Edn., Am. Sociol. Assn., Nat. Conf. Social Welfare, N.Y. State Assn. Gerontol. Edn. Jewish. Clubs: Jewish Center Greater Buffalo, Faculty. Author: Social Welfare Planning: Issues, Values and Policy Directions, 1972; (with Arthur G. Cryns) The Rural Aged: An Analysis of Key Providers of Services to the Elderly, 1976. Contbr. articles to profl. jours. Home: 4-21 Brennan Ct Fairlawn NJ 07410 Office: Columbia U Sch Social Work 622 W 113th St New York NY 10025

MONK, IVAN, strategic planning inst. exec.; b. Funston, Ga., Jan. 6, 1912; s. Jeremiah Bryant and Balma (Stephenson) M.; B.S., Ga. Inst. Tech., 1934; postgrad. Harvard Bus. Sch., 1956; m. Eleanor Elizabeth Yarbro, Oct. 2, 1937 (dec. Aug. 3, 1973); children—Juanita Elizabeth (Mrs. Bradley Hosmer), Ivan Stanley; m. 2d, Janet Roman, Feb. 2, 1974; 1 dau., Robin Roman. Commd. ensign USN, 1934, advanced through grades to capt. 1956; ret. 1960; mem. process selection bd. Office Saline Water, Dept. Interior, 1957-60; dept. mgr. turbine div. De Laval Turbine Inc., 1961-64, asst. gen. mgr. turbine div., 1965, v.p., gen. mgr. div., 1966-68, v.p., asst. group mgr. heavy equipment group, 1969, group v.p., 1970-71, exec. v.p., dir., 1972, pres., chief exec. officer, 1972-74, vice chmn. bd., 1975-78, also dir.; pres. PIMS Assos., strategic planning inst., 1978—. Decorated Legion of Merit, Bronze Star. Registered profl. engr., D.C. Fellow Am. Soc. M.E. (chmn. Trenton sect.); mem. Soc. Naval Architects and Marine Engrs. (chmn. Phila. sec.), Am. Soc. Naval Engrs., pres., council mem.), Newcomen Soc., Phi Sigma Kappa, Pi Tau Sigma. Presbyn. (mem. session). Clubs: Rotary, Nassau, Harvard Bus. (Princeton, N.J.); Engineers (Trenton, N.J.). Contbr. articles to profl. jours. Patentee in field. Home: 50 Wittmer Ct Princeton NJ 08540 Office: PO Box 2072 Princeton NJ 08540

MONSKY, MARK B. VON SOMMER, TV exec.; b. N.Y.C., Aug. 28, 1941; s. Leo Clement and Irma (Reinhold) M.; student Columbia U., 1959-62; m. Beverly DuBose, May 2, 1965; children—Alexander Reinhold DuBose, Eric Demarest DuBose. Reporter N.Y.C. newspapers, 1961-66; producer, reporter CBS News., N.Y.C., 1966-69; mng. editor WNEW-TV, N.Y.C., 1970-74, news dir., 1975, v.p. news., 1976—; instr. journalism New Sch. for Social Research, N.Y.C., 1973-74. Co-chmn. com. on TV in cts., Admnstrv. Bd., N.Y. State Supreme Ct., 1973—. Served with U.S. Army, 1962-63. Recipient Emmy award, Nat. Acad. TV Arts and Scis., 1973, 1977; merit award Am. Bar Assn., 1977, 78; gold shield award N.Y. Press Club, 1975, gold typewriter, 1976. Mem. Radio and TV News Dirs. Assn., N.Y. Press Club. Author: LookOut for Number One, 1975; chief undercover film operations Knapp Commn. on Police Corruption, NYC, 1971. Office: 205 E 67th St New York City NY 10022

MONTAGUE, JAMES LEE, artist; b. New Rochelle, N.Y., May 6, 1906; s. James Jackson and Helen Lee (Hageny) M.; A.B., Dartmouth, 1928; student Art Students League, N.Y.C., Academie Moderne, Paris; pvt. study with Guy Pene Du Bois, N.Y.C.; m. Josephine Dodge, July 24, 1939; 1 son, James J. Comml. artist, muralist, N.Y.C., 1932-38; with Newsweek mag., 1935-37, Travel mag., 1936-37; with U.S. Coast and Geodetic Survey, also Boston Navy Yard, World War II; exhibited paintings, prints in New Eng. including Boston Arts Festival, Madison Sq. Garden, N.Y.C., Balt., Portland, Me.; represented in permanent collections So. Vt. Artists, U.S. Mil. Acad., West Point; dir. Sharon (N.H.) Art Center, 1956-68; dir. So. Vt. Art Center, Manchester, 1964-74, sec., 1975—. Recipient exhbn. prizes, Fitchburg, Mass., Keene, N.H., Northfield, Vt., Albany, N.Y., others. Mem. Artists Equity, Nat. Arts Club, Burr Artists, Print Club of Albany, Art Students League (life). Club: Salmagundi (N.Y.C.). Contbr. verse to newspapers, mags. Home and Studio: Overlook Rd Manchester Center VT 05255

MONTAGUE, LAWRENCE MICHAEL, JR., village ofcl.; b. Tarrytown, N.Y., Sept. 24, 1943; s. Lawrence Michael and Margaret Ann (Melrose) M.; B.S. in Accounting, Fordham U., 1967. Accountant, Ticker & Trager, Ossining, 1967-71; treas., tax collector, Ossining, 1971—. Bd. dirs. Ossining Jr. Baseball League, 1964—, pres., 1972-76; adminstr. Ossining Babe Ruth League, 1964-68, team mgr., 1963-66; mgr. team Am. Legion Baseball, 1965-70; adviser, coach Catholic Youth Orgn.; chmn. spl. gifts Ossining United Way 1970, chmn. campaign, 1971-73; mem. parish council St. Augustine's Roman Cath. Ch., 1973-75; bd. dirs. Ossining Children's Center, 1972—, No. Westchester United Way, 1973-74, Ossining Little League Football, 1975-77; pres. Assn. A. League Softball Players, 1975-77. Recipient Distinguished Service award Ossining Jaycees, 1975. Mem. Assn. Municipal Officers N.Y. State. Republican. Clubs: Rotary, Elks. Home: 210 N Highland Ave Ossining NY 10562 Office: 16 Croton Ave Ossining NY 10562

MONTAIGNE, SANFORD HOWARD, educator; b. Phila., Dec. 23, 1935; B.S., Temple U., 1957, Ed.M., 1962, M.A., 1967; Ed.D., U. Sarasota, 1976; m. Genevieve Bialczak, Jan. 1, 1967; children—Hugh Scott, David Sanford, Lauren Fern. Tchr., Sch. Dist. of Phila., 1957—; tchr. social studies Germantown High Sch., Phila., 1966—, acting dept. head social studies, 1976—; adj. prof. Northland Open U., 1978—, Canadian Sch. Mgmt., 1978—, Pa. State U., 1979—. Mem. exec. bd. Upper Moreland Homeowners Assn., 1975. Mem. Western Writers Am., U. Sarasota Alumni Assn., Phi Alpha Theta. Author: Blood Over Texas: The Truth About Mexico's War with the United States, 1976; contbr. to The Cattleman, Ft. Worth, Del. Valley Community Living, The Educator. Home: 24 Overlook Ave Willow Grove PA 19090

MONTAMBAULT, LEONCE, telephone co. exec.; b. Montreal, Que., Can., May 27, 1932; s. Louis and Lydia (Giroux) M.; B.A., B.Sc. in Civil Engring., Laval (Que.) U., 1957; m. Colette Nadeau, May 31, 1958; children—Ann, Claire, Louis. With Bell Can., 1957—, supr., Ottawa, Ont., Can., 1961-63, Montreal, Que., 1965-66, v.p., Quebec City, 1971—, v.p. Montreal, 1976—; dir. Telebec Inc., Montreal. Vice pres., exec. com. Que. Diabetes Assn.; mem. Ecole de Technologie Supérieure de l'Université du Québec. Mem. Jeunes Chambres du Can. Français (grand conseil consultatif), Centre des dirigeants d'entreprises, Internat. Centre for Research and Studies in Mgmt., Can. C. of C., C. de C. Provinciale, Que. Assn. Profl. Engrs., Montreal C. of C. Roman Catholic. Club: St. Denis (Montreal). Address: 1060 Universite St Montreal PQ Canada

MONTER, GERALD, builder, developer; b. Bklyn., June 2, 1921; s. Nathan Louis and Dorothy G. (Moiel) M.; B.S., N.Y. U., 1942, postgrad., 1947-51; m. Ruth Danoff, May 19, 1946; children—Elliot, Marilyn. Tchr. vocat. edn. N.Y.C. Pub. Schs., 1942-51; pres. Holiday Park Properties, Roslyn Heights, N.Y., 1951—; pres. Selden Water Co. (N.Y.), 1963-75, Holiday Mgmt. Assos., Roslyn Heights, 1967—. Vice pres. Nassau div. Am. Cancer Soc., 1964—, recipient Humanitarian award, 1964, Div. award, 1968. Served to 1st lt. U.S. Army, 1942-45. Decorated Bronze Star, Purple Heart. Mem. L.I. Builders Inst. (pres. 1965-66), Nat. Assn. Home Builders (life dir.), N.Y. State Builders Assn. (dir. 1964-74). Mem. Temple Beth Sholem, Roslyn. Clubs: B'nai B'rith (v.p. 1970), Lions. Office: 393 Willis Ave Roslyn Heights NY 11577

MONTERO, DARREL MARTIN, sociologist; b. Sacramento, Mar. 4, 1946; s. Tony and Evelyn (Hash) M.; A.B., Calif. State U., 1970; M.A., U. Calif., Los Angeles, 1972, Ph.D., 1974; m. Tara Kathleen McLaughlin, July 6, 1975; 1 son, David Paul. Postgrad. researcher Japanese Am. Research Project, U. Calif., Los Angeles, 1971-73, asso. head Program on Comparative Ethnic Studies, Survey Research Center, 1973-75, dir. research Japanese Am. Research Project, 1973-75; asst. prof. urban studies, research sociologist Pub. Opinion Survey, dir. urban ethnic research program U. Md., College Park, 1976—; cons. research sect. Viewer Sponsored Television Found., Los Angeles, Berrien E. Moore Law Office, Inc., Gardena, Calif., 1973. Served with U.S. Army, 1966-72. Mem. Am. Sociol. Assn., Am. Assn. Pub. Opinion Research (exec. council, standards com.), Am. Ednl. Research Assn., Soc. Study of Social Problems, D.C. Sociol. Soc., Am. Soc. Pub. Adminstrn. Author: The Japanese American Community: A Study of Changing Patterns of Ethnic Affiliation Over Three Generations, 1978; Urban Studies, 1978; Vietnamese Americans: Patterns of Resettlement and Socioeconomic Adaptation in the United States, 1978; editorial bd. Humanity and Society, 1978—. Home: 8238 Canning Terr Greenbelt MD 20770 Office: 2112 Woods Hall U Md College Park MD 20742

MONTESI, RICHARD LEWIS, supt. schs.; b. Mar. 5, 1935; B.S. in Edn., Western Conn. State Coll., Danbury, 1956, M.S. in English, 1960; Ph.D. in Ednl. Adminstrn., U. Conn., Storrs, 1967; married; 2 children. Prin., Darien (Conn.) pub. schs., 1960-63; prin. Simsbury (Conn.) pub. schs., 1963-67, Quaker Ridge Sch., Scarsdale, N.Y., 1967-72; supt. Pocantico Hills Central Sch. Dist., North Tarrytown, N.Y., 1972—; cons. Edn. Commn. of States, 1972-73, also cons. sch. dists. and pvt. industry. Mem. Am. Assn. Sch. Adminstrs., Nat. Assn. Elementary Sch. Prins., Assn. for Supervision and Curriculum Devel., NEA, Kappa Delta Pi, Phi Delta Kappa. Contbr. articles to profl. jours. Office: Bedford Rd North Tarrytown NY 10591

MONTGOMERY, CLAUDE, painter; b. Portland, Maine, Jan. 25, 1912; s. Geo. W. and Lillian (Bangs) M.; student Portland Sch. Fine Arts, 1931-35, N.A.D., N.Y.C., 1935-36, Am. Acad., Rome, Italy, 1938-39, Pratt Inst., 1941; m. Louise Kreuzer, July 5, 1941; children—Richard Bruce, Nancy Louise, Susan Elizabeth. Portrait painter, 1940—, water color artist 1937—, studios at Tulsa and Georgetown, Maine; one-man shows Radio City, N.Y., 1935, Soc. Am. Etchers, 1935, Paris Internat. Exposition, 1937, NAD, 1937-38, Am. Watercolor Soc., 1942, Portland Art Mus., 1946, Philbrook Art Mus., Tulsa, 1948, 60, Jr. League Gallery, Tulsa, 1948, Oklahoma City Art Center, 1949, Oklahoma City Mus., 1949-61, Gilcrease Mus., 1960, Tulsa Arts Festival, 1965, Mus. Conservative Art, Oklahoma City, 1965; exhibited Muscogee Art Ann. (grand prize portrait, 1st prize water color), 1962, Tulsa Arts Fair, 1962, 63, Peter Bent Brigham Hosp., Boston, 1961, Denver Art Mus., 1963, Oklahoma City Art Mus. (purchase prize), 1961, Bartlesville Ann., 1965, N.Y. World's Fair, 1964-65, Philbrook Art Mus., Tulsa, 1963, 66, others; traveling show Maine Artists, 1963-66, nationwide traveling show to museums and univs. Am. Watercolor Soc., 1970-71; represented permanent collections Portland Art Mus., Colgate U., Gilcrease Art Mus., Tulsa, 1962, Mid-Am. Print Show, St. Louis, 1963; also many pvt. collections; portrait of John F. Kennedy for Harvard Club, Boston, Senator Edmund Muskie, Gov. Kenneth Gurtis for Maine State Capitol, Augusta. Mem. Gov.'s Conf. on Arts, 1966. Recipient Suydam Silver medal, Nat. Acad., 1935; Silver medal, Paris (France) Expn., 1937; Baxter prize, Portland Art Mus., 1934, Portrait prize Montreal, Que., Can., 1952; Ruskin prize Philbrook Art Mus., 1963, 66; portrait award Springfield, Mo., 1967; grand prize for best painting, also 2nd prize watercolor, 3d for drawing and honorable mention Redbridge Mus. Conservative Art, 1967, Hewgley prize, 1966; 1st watercolor prize Mexican Watercolor Soc., 1969, Grand prize for portrait Susan Spiva Art Mus., 1973. Hon. life mem. Portland Soc. Art; mem. Southwestern Art Assn., Am., Maine watercolor socs., English-Speaking Union (bd. Tulsa 1961), Royal Soc. Art (London), Kennebec County Hist. Soc. Clubs: Cumberland, Portland Yacht (Portland); Salmagundi (N.Y.C.). Author, illustrator: Majorca Sketchbook. Address: Indian Point Georgetown ME 04548

MONTGOMERY, DEAN CHRISTOPHER, office machine mfg. co. exec.; b. Chgo., Nov. 22, 1940; s. Samuel Dean and Virginia Natalie (Wood) M.; B.S., Loyola U., 1965; m. Marcia Marie Scarbeck, Feb. 27, 1965; children—Maureen, Michele, Peter. Technician, Am. Inst. Baking, Chgo., 1960-62; chemist A.B. Dick Co., Chgo., 1962-64, Addressograph Multigraph Co., Mt. Prospect, Ill., 1965-66; lab. mgr. Alberto Culver Co., Melrose Park, Ill., 1967-70, Am. Photocopy Corp., Evanston, Ill., 1970-74; product engr. reprographics and organic coatings Olivetti Corp. Am., Harrisburg, Pa., 1974—; cons.

fine art graphics. Mem. TAPPI, ASTM, Inst. Graphic Communication, Fine Arts 260, Assn. Am. Artists, Original Print Collectors Group. Roman Catholic. Author articles. Address: 6 Redwood Ct Camp Hill PA 17011

MONTGOMERY, EVERETT FRANCIS, JR., mail order pub. co. exec.; b. Hartford, Conn., Oct. 14, 1952; s. Everett Francis and Thelma (Baldwin) M.; student Eastern Conn. State Coll., 1971-73; children—Charise, Jason Ra-Shad. With Nat. Cash Register, Hartford, Conn., 1973-74; welder Pratt & Whitney Aircraft, E. Hartford, Conn., 1974; salesman United Consumers Clubs of Am., E. Hartford, 1975; pres. Montgomery Enterprises, Hartford, 1976—; profl. model Ophelia Dewre Sch. Modeling, 1973—; with Royal Bus. Machines, Hartford, 1978—. Mem. New Eng. Basketball Assn. Baptist. Address: 132 Edgewood St Hartford CT 06112

MONTGOMERY, HENRY EDWARD, JR., naval officer; b. Lexington, Ky., July 7, 1946; s. Henry Edward and Agnes Luella (Callebs) M.; B.A., Berea Coll., 1968; Ph.D., U. Ky., 1971. Commd. ensign U.S. Navy, 1971, advanced through grades to lt., 1975; instr. Naval Nuclear Power Sch., Bainbridge, Md., 1971-76; asst. prodn. engring. officer Phila. Naval Shipyard, 1976; instr. chemistry dept. U.S. Naval Acad., Annapolis, Md., 1976—. Naval Acad. Research Council grantee, 1977-78. Mem. Am. Chem. Soc., Am. Inst. Physics, U.S. Parachute Assn., Sigma Xi, Phi Kappa Phi. Democrat. Mem. Disciples of Christ Ch. Club: Naval Acad. Sport Parachute (officer rep.). Contbr. articles on quantum chemistry to profl. jours. Home: BOQ US Naval Acad Annapolis MD 21402 Office: Chemistry Dept US Naval Acad Annapolis MD 21402

MONTGOMERY, RICHARD MILLAR, chemist; b. Cleve., Apr. 19, 1941; s. Allen Marshall and Dorothy (Millar) M.; B.S., Carnegie Inst. Tech., 1968; M.S., U. Pitts., 1973, Ph.D., 1974; children—Ian Bruce, Patrick Woodward. Criminalist, Pitts. and Allegheny County Crime Lab., Pitts., 1972-73; dir. lab. services Mylan Splty. Procesees, Pitts., 1973-75; mgr. characterization center Mellon Inst., Pitts., 1975—; cons. chem. analysis problems; expert witness, cons. drug analysis cases. Served with USN, 1962-67. Mem. Soc. for Analytical Chemists of Pitts., Am. Soc. for Mass Spectroscopy, ASTM, Soc. for Applied Spectroscopy, AAAS, Forensic Sci. Soc. (Eng.), Am. Chem. Soc., Am. Radio Relay League (life), Sigma Xi. Republican. Episcopalian. Clubs: Carnegie Tech Radio (faculty adviser); Chemists of Pitts. Office: Mellon Inst 4400 5th Ave Pittsburgh PA 15213

MONTI, FRANK ANTHONY, optical co. exec.; b. Providence, Mar. 13, 1948; s. Stanley Angel and Lucy Louise (DiMaio) M.; B.S., Providence Coll., 1970; m. Mary Elizabeth Mellone, Dec. 5, 1970; 1 son, Justin Philip. Jr. accountant Pascarella & Trench, C.P.A.'s, Providence, 1967-68; staff accountant Anthony T. Allegretti & Co., C.P.A.'s, Providence, 1968-70; mgr. Price Waterhouse & Co., Providence, 1970-75, N.Y.C., 1975-76, London and Providence, 1976-78; dir. acctg., asst. treas. Am. Optical Corp., Southbrige, Mass., 1978—; guest lectr. Providence Coll., 1976-78. C.P.A. Mem. Providence Coll. Gridiron Alumni Assn. (treas. 1970-75, v.p. 1976-78), Nat. Assn. Accountants (Man of Year 1974-75, dir. Providence chpt. 1976-78). Am. Inst. C.P.A.'s (spl. task force on basic tng. for auditors 1976), NE Controllers Assn., Am. Accounting Assn. Home: 94 Rumstick Rd Barrington RI 02806 Office: 14 Mechanic St Southbridge MA 01550

MONTIGNY, RICHARD WARREN, social services assn. exec. dir.; b. Charlottetown, P.E.I., Can., Aug. 20, 1948; s. Louis Alfred and Ruth Frances (Hood) M.; B.B.A., U. P.E.I., 1971; m. Sadie Marion Campbell, Apr. 16, 1976. Office mgr. Bruce Steward Ltd., Charlottetown, 1972-73; exec. dir. Atlantic Cerebral Palsy Assn., Charlottetown, 1973-76, P.E.I. Council of the Disabled, Charlottetown, 1976—. Pres. P.E.I. New Democratic Party, 1974-75; bd. dirs. P.E.I. United Way; mem. St. John Ambulance Brigade. Mem. Occupational Tng. Center (dir.), P.E.I. Recreation and Sports Assn. for Disabled, Can. (1st v.p.), P.E.I. (pres.) cerebral palsy assns. Presbyterian. Clubs: P.E.I. Numismatic Assn., Lions, Jaycees. Home: 1 Fountain Dr Charlottetown PE C1A 6L9 Canada Office: POB 2128 147 Pownal St Charlottetown PE C1A 7N7 Canada

MONTNEY, RUSSELL LEON, city planning cons.; b. Linden, Mich., Feb. 5, 1923; s. Elmer H. and Grace A. Montney; B.S., Mich. State U., 1950; m. Kathleen M. Dalton, Sept. 8, 1951; 1 son, Paul A. Mem. staff Detroit City Planning Commn., 1950-51; planning cons. Russell Vannest Blak, New Hope, Pa., 1951-54; mem. staff Rochester (N.Y.) City Planning Commn., 1954-56; dir. county planning Middlesec County, N.J., 1956-61; dir. planning and urban renewal City of Rockville, 1961-63; v.p. Robert Catlin & Assos., planning cons., Denville, N.J., 1963—. Trustee Rockaway Pub. Library, 1973—. Served with USAF, 1942-45. Mem. Am. Inst. Planners (past pres. N.J. chpt.), Am. Soc. Planning Ofcls., N.J. Fedn. Planning Bds. Presbyterian. Club: Masons. Home: 27 Hemlock Rd Rockaway NJ 07866 Office: 2 Valley Rd Denville NJ 07834

MONTOURI, WARREN KENDALL, banker, investor; b. Washington, July 6, 1929; s. Felix Carl and Drusilla L. (Kendall) M.; A.B.A., Am. U., 1959, B.S. in Fin., 1961; m. Ann Yerrick, Jan. 10, 1959; children—Anne Kendall, Elisabeth Allyn. With Shannon & Luchs Co., Washington, 1958—, broker, appraiser, 1960-69, v.p., 1970—; dir. D.C. Nat. Bank, Commonwealth Title Co., Internat. Developers Inc., Westwood Mgmt. Corp. Mem. Washington Bd. Tax Appeal, 1971-75; trustee Norwood Sch., Bethesda, Md. Served with CIC, U.S. Army, 1952-54. Mem. Am. Inst. Real Estate Appraisers, Internat. Soc. Real Estate Appraisers, Mortgage Bankers Assn., D.C. Bankers Assn. Clubs: Congresional, University, Internat. Home: 8801 Bradley Blvd Potomac MD 20854 Office: 900 17th St NW Washington DC 20006

MONTOYA, JUAN, design co. exec.; b. Bogota, Colombia, May 7, 1945; s. Alberto Montoya Willianson and Ines Blanca Isaacs Montoya; came to U.S., 1965; student in Architecture, U. Gran Colombia, 1965; degree in Parsons Sch. Design, 1972. Spl. rep. Western Union Internat., 1966-67; jr. designer Ford & Earl Design Assos., N.Y.C., 1970-72; free-lance designer, Paris, 1972-73; sr. designer archtl. dept. Durable Dental Co., N.Y.C., 1973-74; pres./owner, mgr. Juan Montoya Design Corp., N.Y.C., 1975—; mem. ad. faculty Kean (N.J.) Coll., 1975—; lighting cons., 1975—. Recipient Resources Council Product Design award, 1977, also others. Mem. Am. Soc. Interior Designers, Roman Catholic. Contbr. articles to profl. publs., mags., newspapers. Home: 299 W 12th St New York City NY 10014 Office: 80 8th Ave New York City NY 10011

MOODY, BARBARA GAREY, nursing educator; b. Medford, Mass., June 23, 1931; d. DeMelle and Mildred (Holman) Garey; B.A., William Jewell Coll., Liberty, Mo., 1953; M.Ed., Northeastern U., Boston, 1964; m. Richard H. Moody, May 15, 1954; children—Meredith, Heather, Richard B., Janice. Dir. personnel P.W. Moody Co., Andover, Mass., 1954-70; guidance counselor Lawrence (Mass.) Gen. Hosp. Sch. Nursing, 1971-77; adminstrv. asst. New Eng. Deaconess Hosp., Boston, 1977—. Dir., sec. Gale Systems, 1972-74; dir. Coulter Fibers, Inc.; asso. dir. Lawrence Coop. Bank. Pres. Andover Vis. Nurse Assn., 1964-74; mem. Andover Sch. Com., 1963-66; v.p. Greater Lawrence Family Service, 1973—; bd. Andover Girl Scouts, 1956-60, Andover YMCA, 1968-73, Andover Family Services, 1973-76, Merrimack Valley Family Planning, Inc. Mem. Nat. Assn. Women Deans, Adminstrs. and Counselors, League Women Voters, Nat. League Nursing, Am. Personnel and Guidance Assn., Pi Kappa Delta. Mem. United Ch. Christ (clk.). Club: Andover Tennis. Home: 12 Suncrest Rd Andover MA 01810 Office: 1 General St Lawrence MA 01842

MOOERS, EDWARD ALLEN, bus. exec.; b. Towanda, Pa., Apr. 26, 1896; s. Charles W. and Margaret C. (Allen) M.; Ch.E., Lehigh U., 1920; L.H.D., Keuka Coll., 1971; m. E. N. H. Welles, Sept. 23, 1918; children—Mary Welles Mooers Smith, Katherine Nelson Mooers van den Blink. Asst. supt. Elmira (N.Y.) plant Thatcher Glass Mfg. Co., 1921-25, supt., 1925-28; dir.-gen. mgr. Hilliard Corp., Elmira, 1928—, SEC, 1928-42, v.p., 1942-47, pres., 1948-64, chmn. bd., 1964—; dir. Schweizer Aircraft Corp.; past pres. Chemung County Devel. Corp. Past pres. Elmira Neighborhood House, Chemung County Council Social Agys., Elmira Symphony and Choral Soc., Capabilities, Inc.; bd. dirs. Jr. Achievement, Community Concert Assn., Bethany Retirement Center; trustee Robert Packer Hosp., Nat. Soaring Mus. Mayor, Elmira, 1956-61. Mem. labor-mgmt. com. War Manpower Commn., 1943-44. Served as 1st lt. flying instr. and flight comdr. AAF, 1917-18. Recipient (Great Britain) Kings medal for service in cause of freedom, Alumnus award Lehigh U., 1968, Excalibur award Elmira Star-Gazette, 1969, Mem. Elmira Assn. Commerce (past pres.), Chemung County History Soc. (past pres.), Newcomen Soc., Soc. Anon de Philippe-Hilco-Europe (dir., v.p.), Psi Upsilon, Tau Beta Pi. Republican. Presbyterian. Clubs: Rotary, Elmira City, Country, Torch. Home: 861 College Ave Elmira NY 14901 also (summer) Lake Wesauking Towanda PA 18848 Office: 100 W 4th St Elmira NY 14901

MOOK, KENT WALKER, communications co. exec.; b. Rochester, N.Y., Mar. 29, 1938; s. Kenneth Campbell and Leone Belle (Walker) M.; B.A., Syracuse U., 1960; B.B.A. in Bus. Mgmt., Pace U., 1967, M.B.A. in Profl. Mgmt., 1971; m. Martha Ann Phyfe, Feb. 11, 1961; children—Jeffrey Kent, Caroline Ann, Bradley Lloyd. Asst. sales mgr. Thomas Doran Co., White Plains, N.Y., 1960-65; sr. programmer-analyst N.Y. Telephone Co., 1965-66; project mgr., leader sabre system Am. Airlines, Briarcliff Manor, N.Y., 1966-69; account mgr. Electronic Data Systems, Inc., N.Y.C., 1969-70, IBM, 1970-73; sr. corp. cons. ITT, N.Y.C., 1973—; mgmt. devel. cons., dir. IBM, 1971. Capt., Westchester County (N.Y.) United Way, 1969-74; co-founder, treas., bd. dirs., mem. adv., exec. coms. Continuing Edn. of Briarcliff, 1969-75; co-pres. Briarcliff PTA, 1974-76; founder Explorer post 747 Boy Scouts Am., named outstanding scout leader, 1967. Mem. Am Mgmt. Assn., Am. Industry Mgmt., Am. Prodn. and Inventory Control Soc., Sigma Phi Epsilon. Republican. Episcopalian. Home: 14 Briarwood Ln Pleasantville NY 10570 Office: ITT 320 Park Ave New York City NY 10022*

MOOMJIAN, MARTIN, banker; b. Boston, June 18, 1928; s. Kevork and Aznive (Ayvazian) M.; student accounting Burdett Coll., 1950; B.B.A., Northeastern U., 1958; postgrad. Am. Inst. Banking, 1958-63, Rutgers U., 1969-71; m. V. Elizabeth Bogosian, May 7, 1961; children—Mark, Gregg, Jeffrey. Accountant, Touche Niven, Bailey & Smart, C.P.A.'s, Boston, 1952-53; budget analyst Provident Instn. Savs., Boston, 1953-63; asst. treas. 1st Bank & Trust Co., Haverhill, Mass., 1963-65; v.p. Lafayette Bank & Trust Co., Bridgeport, Conn., 1965—; past dir., treas Barnum Festival Soc. Served with U.S. Army, 1951-52; Korea. Mem. Bank Adminstrn. Inst. (pres., dir.), Nat. Assn. Credit, Bridgeport, Fairfield, chambers commerce Fairfield Bd. Realtors. Armenian Orthodox. Clubs: H. Smith Richardson Golf Bridgeport Exchange (past pres.). Home: 243 Short Hill Ln Fairfield CT 06430 Office: 345 State St Bridgeport CT 06603

MOON, JAY, artist, poet; b. White Plains, N.Y., Mar. 7, 1934; s. James Clayton and Bertha L. (Hardwick) M.; student Pratt Inst., 1952-53, 55-56; m. Anna Kaufman, Dec. 1969; 1 dau., Janay. Represented in permanent collections Nat. Gallery, Mus. of Mod. Art, Fogg Mus. of Harvard U., Mus. Fine Arts, Boston, Library of Congress, Nat. Collection, Washington, Bibliotheque National, Paris, N.Y. Pub. Library Print Dept., Boston Pub. Library Print Dept., Syracuse U. Served with U.S. Army, 1953-55. Recipient Purchase award Library of Congress. Address: 311 Van Duzer St Staten Island NY 10304

MOON, JOHN ROBERT, dentist; b. Fort Wayne, Ind., Nov. 13, 1926; s. John Leslie and Marguerite Eleanor (Rosekrans) M.; B.S., Union Coll., 1949; D.D.S., N.Y. U., 1953; m. Elisabeth Elyette Bertol, Apr. 1, 1955; 1 son, John Malcolm. Intern, Rochester Gen. Hosp., 1953-54; pvt. practice dentistry, Schenectady, 1954—; staff St. Clare's, Ellis hosps. Vice chmn., mem. exec. com. Schenectady County Conservative party, 1963—; chmn. Town of Niskayuna Conservative Com. Served with USNR, 1944-46; bd. dirs. Capitol Area Health Maintenance Orgn. Planning Council, Inc. Mem. ADA, Schenectady County, 4th Dist. (past pres.) dental socs., Dental Soc. State N.Y., Empire State Soc., SAR (sec. Adm. Browne chpt.), Xi Psi Phi, Phi Delta Theta. Rotarian. Club: Dental Study, Conservative. Home: 907 St David's Ln Schenectady NY 12309 Office: 2215 Nott St Schenectady NY 12309

MOONE, EVERETT CHARLES EDWARD, civil engr.; b. Chgo., Sept. 18, 1937; s. Everett Edward and Germaine Marguerite (Sire) M.; B.S.C.E., Ind. Inst. Tech., 1966; postgrad. Northwestern U., 1966-67; m. Sharon Kay Voisard, July 15, 1967; children—Charles Rollin, Meri Elizabeth, Jason Marcel. Asst. supr. street design D.C. Dept. Hwys. and Traffic, 1959-60; project engr. W.P. Campbell Constrn. Co., Frederick, Md., 1960-61; with Rummel, Klepper & Kahl, Balt., 1960-61, 62—, dir. computer services, 1969—, asso., 1974—; v.p. Comp-Tron Inc., 1970—; guest lectr. Cornell U., 1978; bd. dirs. Neighborhood Design Center, Inc., 1977—. Served with U.S. Army, 1961-62. Recipient Maharaj trophy, Kekiongan Feather, Ind. Inst. Tech., 1966. Mem. ASCE (Certificate of Merit 1966), Engring. Soc. Balt. (pub. service com.), Soc. Computers in Engring., Planning and Architecture (pres. 1976), Iota Tau Kappa. Home: 512 Woodside Rd Baltimore MD 21229 Office: 1035 N Calvert St Baltimore MD 21202

MOOR, EDGAR JACQUES, mgmt. cons. corp. exec.; b. Charlottenburg, Austria, June 6, 1912; s. Ernest and Henriette Caroline (Goldschmidt) M.; student Sorbonne, Paris, 1931; Dipl. Ing. cum laude, Tech. U., Berlin, 1937; M.B.A., Harvard U., 1942; m. Joan Rothwell, Aug. 5, 1950. Came to U.S., 1941, naturalized, 1946. Indsl. engr. Chrysler Corp., Johannesburg, South Africa, 1938-39; asst. to pres. Holtzer-Cabot div. First Indsl. Corp., Boston, 1942-46; v.p. USMC (Internat.), Geneva, also dir. internat. planning USM Corp., Boston, 1947-64; pres. Multinat. Bus. Assos., Inc., Cambridge, Mass., 1966—; dir. MBA, Inc.; spl. cons. U.S. Dept. Commerce, Washington, 1968-70, Overseas Pvt. Investment Corp., Washington, 1971. Mem. commerce com. Alliance for Progress, Washington, 1962-64; mem. Gov. Volpe's Task Force, Boston, 1965; bd. dirs. Spanish Cultural Inst., 1978—. Fellow Internat. Acad. Law Sci., Royal Soc. Arts, Manufacture and Commerce London; mem. Pan Am. Soc. New Eng. (gov. 1971—, pres. 1971-73), Am. Mktg. Assn. (sec. Boston chpt. 1949-55), Boston Com. Fgn. Relations, Multinat. Bus. Council (co-chmn. Cambridge 1968—), World Affairs Council (dir., mem. pres.'s com.). Clubs: Cosmos (Washington); Harvard (Boston, N.Y.C.). Contbr. articles in multi-nat. corporate mgmt. to profl. jours. Home: Taborknoll Lincoln MA 01773 Office: Suite 010 Lower Level 545 Technology Sq Cambridge MA 02139

MOOR, JOAN THORNTON ROTHWELL (MRS. EDGAR JACQUES MOOR), biochemist; b. Lynn, Mass., Feb. 19, 1921; d. Paul Taylor and Adeline (Magrane) Rothwell; A.B., Vassar Coll., 1942; S.M., Mass. Inst. Tech., 1945; m. Edgar Jacques Moor, Aug. 5, 1950. Instr., Vassar Coll., Poughkeepsie, N.Y., 1946; research asst. Children's Hosp., Boston, 1947-48; research asst. New Eng. Deaconess Hosp., Boston, 1949-51; staff div. sponsored research Mass. Inst. Tech., Cambridge, 1952—; treas., dir. Multinational Bus. Assos., Inc., Cambridge, 1967—. Fellow Internat. Acad. Law and Sci.; mem. Am. Chem. Soc., AAAS, AAUW, Boston Council Fgn. Relations (exec. com.), Pan Am. Soc. New Eng., Inc. New Eng. Council Latin Am. Studies (hon.), Sigma Xi. Republican. Roman Catholic. Contbr. articles to profl. jours. Home: Taborknoll Lincoln MA 01773

MOORE, ACEL, journalist; b. Phila., Oct. 5, 1940; s. Jerry A. and Hura Mae (Harrington) Acel; student Settlement Music Sch., 1958, Charles Morris Price Sch., 1966-67; m. Cheryl Rice, Oct. 1975; 1 son, Acel. Copyboy, Phila. Inquirer, 1962-64, editorial clk., 1964-68, staff reporter, 1968—; co-producer weekly news program Black Perspective on the News, PBS, 1972—. Served with U.S. Army, 1959-61. Recipient Phila. Bar Assn. award, 1970; Community Service award Youth Devel. Center, 1976; Pulitzer prize for local reporting, 1977; Robert F. Kennedy Journalism prize, 1977; Heywood H. Broun prize, 1977; Pa. Prison Soc., Ann. Paul Robeson and Clarion awards, 1977; Humanitarian award House of Umoja, 1977; Journalism award Phila. Party, 1977; Media award Mental Health Assn., 1977. Mem. Nat., Phila. (pres.) assns. Black journalists, Sigma Delta Chi (Phila. chpt. Public Service award 1972, 77, Reporting award 1977). Office: Phila Inquirer 400 Broad St Philadelphia PA 19101*

MOORE, ADAM GILLESPIE NICHOL, physician; b. Boston, Oct. 21, 1931; s. Merrill and Ann Leslie (Nichol) M.; student Milton Acad.; grad. Phillips Andover Acad., 1950; A.B., Harvard U., 1955; M.B., U. Aberdeen, Scotland, 1964, Ch.B., 1964; grad. advanced asso. course A.M.S.S., Ft. Sam Houston, Tex.; m. Rosamie Alexander, 1966; children—Fiona Alexander, Andrew Mathieson, Emily Kathleen. Resident physician, later casualty officer Aberdeen Royal Infirmary, 1964-65; resident pediatrics Carney Hosp., Boston, 1965-66; practice medicine specializing in community care, Squantum, Mass., 1968—; mem. staff Harvard Health Service, Carney, Quincy City hosps. Sec. Booth Meml. Home Bd., 1967-69, chmn., 1969-72; mem. Greater Boston adv. bd. Salvation Army, 1969-72. Served to maj. Med. Service Corps, AUS. Recipient Struthers Gold medal U. Aberdeen, 1959, Munday Prize, 1962; AMA Physicians Recognition award, 1970—. Diplomate Am. Bd. Family Practice. Certified librarian, Mass. Fellow Boston Med. Library (life; trustee 1975—, v.p. 1976-78), Mass. Med. Soc.; mem. Boston Athenaeum, Nat. Geog. Soc., AAAS, U.S. Naval. Inst., Assn. Mil. Surgeons, Brit. Med. Assn., Am., Mass. acads. family physicians, N.Y. Acad. Scis., Greater Boston Hosp. Council (trustee rep. 1968-72), Mass. Physicians Art Soc. (sec.-treas. 1976—), Countway Assos. Clubs: Aberdeen U. Rugby Football (v.p. 1960—); Harvard Faculty (Cambridge Mass.). Mem. contbg. adv. bd. Internist Reporter, Family Practice Reporter. Contbr. to Dorland's Illustrated Med. Dictionaries, Dictionary Med. Abbreviations, articles to profl. jours. Home: 10 Crabtree Rd Squantum MA 02171 Office: 319 Bellevue Rd Squantum MA 02171 also State St Bank & Trust Co Q-2-E Box 351 Boston MA 02101

MOORE, ANDREW GIVEN TOBIAS, II, lawyer; b. New Orleans, Nov. 25, 1935; s. Emmett and Hazel Pauline Moore; B.B.A., Tulane U., 1958, J.D., 1960; m. Ann Elizabeth Dawson, June 5, 1965; children—Cecily Elizabeth, Marianne Dawson. Admitted to La. bar, 1960, Del. bar, 1963; law clk to chief justice Del., Dover, 1963; asso. firm Killoran & Van Brunt, Wilmington, Del., 1964-70, partner, 1971-76; partner firm Connolly, Bove & Lodge, Wilmington, 1976—; mem. Del. Bd. Accountancy, 1965-72, Del. Bd. Bar Examiners, 1975—, Del. Judicial Selection Commn., 1977—; mem. law com. Del. Gen. Corp., 1969—. Trustee Del. Home and Hosp. for the Chronically Ill, Smyrna, Del., 1966-70; mem. New Castle County Historic Rev. Bd., Wilmington. Served with JAG Dept., USAF, 1960-63. Mem. Am., La., Del. (v.p. 1976-77) bar assns. Democrat. Presbyterian. Clubs: Greenville Country, Wilmington, Nat. Lawyers. Home: 11 Red Oak Rd Wilmington DE 19806 Office: 1800 Farmers Bank Bldg Wilmington DE 19899

MOORE, CHARLES HENKEL, research assn. exec.; b. New Market, Va., Oct. 25, 1915; s. Charles Henkel and Meta (Burke) M.; B.S., U. Va., 1936, M.S., 1937; Ph.D., Cornell U., 1940; m. Elsie W. Davis, 1939 (div. 1962); children—Sandra Lee, C. Donald; m. 2d, Virginia Barber, Sept. 16, 1962; 1 dau., Carla Elizabeth. Instr., Cornell U., 1937-40; chief petrographer Carborundum Co., Niagara Falls, N.Y., 1940-43; asst. prof. mineralogy Pa. State U., 1943-45; with Nat. Lead Co., 1945-51, tech. dir., cin, 1951; mgr. metals and rectifier divs. P.R. Mallory and Co., Indpls., 1951-55, exec. dir. corporate research and devel., 1956-60; tech. dir. Internat. Copper Research Assn., N.Y.C., 1960-63, exec. v.p., 1963-76, pres., 1976—; founder Titania Gem Industry; vis. prof. Rutgers U., 1946-49. Fellow AAAS; mem. Am. Inst. Mining, Metall. and Petroleum Engrs., Newcomen Soc. N.Am., Keramos, Sigma Xi, Phi Kappa Phi. Clubs: Ardsley (N.Y.) Country and Curling; Mining, Cornell (bd. govs.) (N.Y.C.). Author, patentee in field. Home: Copperwood Cricket Ln Dobbs Ferry NY 10522 Office: 708 3d Ave New York City NY 10017

MOORE, DANIEL EDMUND, sch. adminstr.; b. Pitts., Dec. 31, 1926; s. John Daniel and Alma Helen (Goehring) M.; B.S.Ed., Duquesne U., 1949, M.Ed., 1952; postgrad. California (Pa.) State Coll., 1954-56, U. Pitts., 1958-59, Mt. Mercy Coll., 1959-60, Cath. U. Am., 1966, W.Va. U., 1970-72; m. Rose Marie Blunkosky, Nov. 11, 1949; children—Catherine Moore Lawrence, Claire Marie Moore Caveney, Mary, Suzanne, Elizabeth. Tchr. math., Cecil Twp. Sch. Dist., McDonald, Pa., 1949-52, Pitts. pub. schs., 1952-53; with Mt. Lebanon Twp. (Pa.) Sch. Dist., 1953—, psychologist, 1954-71, coordinator pupil personnel services, 1971—. Lectr. ednl. psychology Grad. Sch. Edn. Duquesne U., 1957—; ednl. cons. St. Francis Schs. Nursing, New Castle and Pitts., 1959—; psychol. cons. Peters Twp. Sch. Dist., McMurray, Pa., 1961—; mem. test adv. bd. Ednl. Records Bur., 1976—; hearing officer Right to Edn. Office, Dept. Edn., Harrisburg, Pa., 1975—. Mem. Chartiers Valley Sch. Dist. Bd., 1963—, pres., 1971; mem. Pkwy. West Tech. Sch. Bd., 1965-67. Bd. dirs. secondary sch. research program Ednl. Testing Service, Princeton, 1971—; bd. dirs. Robert E. Ward Home for Children, 1975—. Served with USNR, 1945-48. Henry C. Frick grantee, 1970, 73. Mem. Am., Pa. psychol. assns., Council Exceptional Children (pres. 1957), Phi Delta Kappa (pres. chpt. 1974-75). Roman Catholic. Home: 213 Station St Bridgeville PA 15017 Office: 7 Horsman Dr Mt Lebanon Sch Dist Pittsburgh PA 15228

MOORE, DAVID LEONARD, historian, social scientist; b. Charleston S.C., Oct. 21, 1945; s. Joe and Florence (Justine) M.; B.A., Voorhees Coll., 1968; postgrad. City Coll. City U. N.Y., 1969—. Tchr.

social studies W.E. Parker High Sch., Edgefield, S.C., 1968-69, Newark Prep. Sch., 1970-71, Weequahic High Sch., Newark, 1972-78, Barringer High Sch., Newark, 1978—. Mem. Newark Tchrs. Union, Am. Hist. Assn., Nat. Trust Historic Preservation, Am., N.J. fedn. tchrs. Democrat. Episcopalian. Club: White Rose. Office: 90 Parker St Newark NJ 07112

MOORE, DOROTHY HEYECK, lawyer; b. Orange, N.J., Mar. 25, 1939; d. John Charles and Elsie Amelia (Goellner) Heyeck; A.B., Coll. St. Elizabeth, N.J., 1961; J.D., Seton Hall U., 1964; m. Alan James Moore, 1968; children—Laura, Gregory, Sharon. Admitted to D.C. bar, 1965, U.S. Supreme Ct. bar, 1969; atty. Fgn. Claims Settlement Commn. U.S., Washington, 1964-68; chmn. Property Tax Assessment Appeal Bd. for Montgomery County (Md.), 1974—. Pres., L'Enfant Club, Washington, 1969-70; program chmn. State Fedn. Bus. and Profl. Women, Washington, 1970-71. Mem. D.C. Bar Assn., Women's Bar Assn. D.C., Kappa Beta Pi. Roman Catholic. Office: 51 Monroe St Unibank Bldg Rockville MD 20850

MOORE, EARLE KENNEDY, lawyer; b. Buffalo, Dec. 8, 1921; s. Frank Charles and Velma (Kennedy) M.; A.B., Harvard U., 1943, LL.B., 1948; m. Sarah Clarissa Burt, Feb. 15, 1947 (div. Nov. 1964); children—Arthur B., Frank C., Rebecca T., Elizabeth K.; m. 2d, Katherine Fusako Muto, Feb. 3, 1968. Admitted to N.Y. bar, 1948, U.S. Supreme Ct. bar, 1954; atty. firm Goldstein, Judd & Gurfein, N.Y.C., 1948-60, partner, 1960-68; partner firm Moore, Berson & Lifflander, N.Y.C., 1968—. Dir. P & F Ind, Inc., Great Neck, N.Y. Chmn., Town and Village Com. Against Discrimination, N.Y.C., 1952; mem. Great Neck Com. on Human Rights, 1960-63, Nassau County Ethics Commn., 1963; cons. N.Y. State Temporary Commn. on Estates, 1967—; vice chmn. Citizens Union, N.Y.C., 1967-72; chmn. Civil Service Reform Assn., N.Y.C., 1967-73; trustee Community Service Soc., N.Y.C., 1974—, Nat. Citizens Com. Broadcasting, 1969-76, Shalkenbach Found., 1970-76, Action Children's TV, 1974—, Tri-State Media Ministry, 1976—, Citizens Union Research Found., 1976—, Am. Jour. Econs. and Sociology, 1975—; mem. gen. communication and interpretation com. Nat. Council Chs. of Christ in U.S.A., 1970—; mem. media com. ACLU, N.Y.C., 1972-76; mem. Com. for Municipal Broadcasting, 1973-75. Mem. Assn. Bar City N.Y., N.Y. Law Inst. Mem. United Ch. of Christ (Churchmanship award 1969). Home: 185 E 85th St New York City NY 10028 Office: 555 Madison Ave New York City NY 10022

MOORE, EDWARD FREDERICK, investor; b. Detroit, Feb. 1, 1900; s. George Frederick and Walfrid Louisa (Brudin) M.; B.S. in Mech. Engring., U. Mich. 1922, B.A. with distinction, 1923; M.S.E., U. Mich., 1923; postgrad. Columbia U., 1935-37, Union Theol. Sem., 1936-37. Mech. engr. Gen. Motors Corp., Detroit, 1923-26; fin. engr. nat. gas pipeline financing P.W. Chapman & Co., N.Y.C., 1926-28; fin. engr. W.Va., Ohio, Ky., Tex., 1928-33; asso. Dr. Alexis Carrel, 1937-41; founder, pres. Found. for Future of Man, Inc., N.Y.C., 1972—. Mem. ASME, Phi Beta Kappa, Sigma Xi, Tau Beta Pi. Republican. Congregationalist. Club: University (N.Y.C.). Author, designer: Deep Water Salvage, 1923; Encyclopedia of Unknown, 1973, 77, Charting the Future, 1978. Home: 341 Mountain Rd Englewood NJ 07631 Office: 39 Broadway New York City NY 10006

MOORE, JAMES ROBERT, govt. ofcl.; b. Williamsburg County, S.C., Nov. 23, 1927; s. William M. and Elizabeth (McFadden) M.; A.B., Lincoln U., 1953; certificate human relations U. Pa., 1959, postgrad., 1962; m. Joyce Elizabeth Newcomer, Nov. 23, 1968; children—Amy Elizabeth, David James. Chemist, City of Phila., 1953-56, juvenile aid investigator, 1956-61; tchr. sci. and math pub. schs., Phila., 1961-64; human relations investigator State of Pa., 1964-66; chief Title VIII sect., conciliator HUD, Region II, N.Y.C., 1966—. Chmn., Delaware County Fair Housing Council, 1962-65, also bd. dirs.; area coordinator Unitarian-Universalist Service Com., 1974—; chmn. Social Responsibility Com., Cherry Hill, 1974-76. Served with AUS, 1946-49. Recipient Entermann Chanian award for social responsibility Unitarian-Universalist Service Com., 1976. Mem. Am. Mgmt. Assn., Nat. Assn. Intergroup, Alpha Phi Alpha. Democrat. Unitarian. Home: 1101 W Valleybrook Rd Cherry Hill NJ 08034 Office: 26 Federal Plaza New York City NY 10007

MOORE, JANE ROSS, librarian; b. Phila., Apr. 24, 1929; d. John William and Mary (McClure) Ross; A.B., Smith Coll., 1951; M.S. in L.S., Drexel U., 1952; postgrad. Columbia U.; M.B.A. with distinction, N.Y. U., 1965; Ph.D., Case Western Res. U., 1974; m. Cyril Howard Moore, Jr., June 1, 1956 (div. Mar. 1967). Cataloguer, Yale U. Library, 1952-54; chief tech. processes librarian Lederle Labs., Am. Cyanamid Co., Pearl River, N.Y., 1954-58; chief serials catalog librarian Bklyn. Coll. Library, 1958-65, asst. prof., chief catalog div., 1965-70, asso. prof., chief catalog div., 1971-73, asso. prof., asso. librarian for adminstrv. service, 1973-76; prof., chief librarian Grad. Sch. and Univ. Center, City U. N.Y., 1976—; vis. lectr. Syracuse U. Grad. Sch. Library Sci., summer 1967, 69; lectr. Queens Coll. Grad. Sch., 1967-69, adj. asso. prof., 1974-76, adj. prof., 1977—. HEW Title IIB fellow Case Western Res. U. Sch. L.S., 1970-72. Mem. ALA (membership com. 1967-71, dir. resources and tech. services div. 1968-70, 75-76, chmn. council of regional groups 1968-69, chmn. cataloging and classification sect. 1975-76), N.Y. Tech. Services Librarians (pres. 1963-64), AAUP, Spl. Libraries Assn., N.Y. Library Assn. (councilor, sect pres. 1966-67, v.p. 1975-76), N.Y. U. Grad Sch. Bus. Adminstrn. Alumni Assn. (rec. sec. 1967-69, dir. 1969-70, 75—), Phi Kappa Phi. Presbyterian (elder 1973—). Clubs: N.Y. Library (sec. 1964-66, council 1966-70, 73—); Smith Coll. (pres. Bklyn. 1966-68, class treas. 1976—), Civitas. Home: 35 Schermerhorn St Brooklyn NY 11201 Office: 33 W 42d St New York City NY 10036

MOORE, JEAN-MARIE, health adminstr.; b. N.Y.C., July 24, 1934; d. Patrick and Jane (Phillips) Moore; diploma Mary Immaculate Hosp. Sch. Nursing, 1955; B.S., Adelphia U., 1959; M.A., N.Y. U., 1962. Staff nurse John T. Mather Hosp., Port Jefferson, N.Y., 1955-58; clin. instr. Bellevue and Mills Schs. Nursing, N.Y.C., 1958-62; instr. Nassau Community Coll., Garden City, N.Y., 1962-63; asst. prof. Skidmore Coll., N.Y.C., 1963-68; nurse edn. adviser to Phong Dinh Province Nursing Sch., Can Tho, Vietnam Mission, AID, Dept. of State, Washington, 1968-69; asst. dir. devel. and research, N.Y. U. Hosp., N.Y.C., 1970-75; sr. PSRO specialist USPHS, N.Y.C., 1975—. Mem. Nat. League Nursing, Am. Pub. Health Assn., League Women Voters, Am. Soc. Pub. Adminstrn., Am. Heart Assn., Soc. Social and Polit. Sci., N.Y. U. Alumni Assn. Home: 531 E 20th St New York City NY 10010 Office: 26 Federal Plaza Room 3821 New York City NY 10007

MOORE, JOHNNIE ADOLPH, govt. ofcl.; b. Cuero, Tex., Sept. 28, 1929; s. Nelson and Eva Mae (Jones) M.; B.S., Tuskegee Inst., 1950; postgrad. George Williams Coll., Chgo., 1957; m. Tommye Dalphine Jordan, July 9, 1961. Pub. relations dir. Lane Coll., Jackson, Tenn., 1951-52; mng. editor Dallas Star-Post, 1952-53, 55-56; exec. sec. Gibson br. YMCA, Galveston, Tex., 1957-58; bur. editor Jour. and Guide, Norfolk, Va., 1958-59; night editor Chgo. Daily Defender, 1959-61; pub. info. specialist Pres.'s Com. Govt. Contracts, Washington, 1960-61; exec. dir. Nat. Ins. Assn., Chgo., 1961-62; mng. editor Internat. Personnel Mgmt. Assn., Chgo., 1963-66; pub. info. officer Dept. Labor, Chgo., 1966-67, CSC, Washington, 1967—; mem. adv. com. Howard U. Sch. Communications. Served to 1st lt. USAF, 1953-55. Recipient Image Maker award Nat. Assn. Media Women, 1976; Commr.'s Spl. citation CSC, 1978. Mem. Nat. Assn. Govt. Communicators, Pub. Relations Soc. Am., Internat. Communication Assn., Am. Soc. Pub. Adminstrn., Internat. Personnel Mgmt. Assn., Suburban Md. Fair Housing, NAACP, Nat. Urban League, Kappa Alpha Psi. Methodist. Clubs: Capital Press (pres. 1972-74; Pearlie Cox Harrison award 1974), Nat. Press (Washington). Contbr. articles to profl. jours. Home: 2212 Westview Ct Silver Spring MD 20910 Office: USCSC-OPA 1900 E St NW Washington DC 20415

MOORE, LUCILLE CASS, hosp. adminstr.; b. Laconia, N.H., Oct. 24, 1919; d. Frank Henry Whipple and Eleanor Nora (Davis) Cass; grad. high sch.; m. Alfred Edwin Moore, June 15, 1945; children—Sheryl Lynne Moore Scott, Marilyn Eleanor Moore Guimond. Operator, New Eng. Telephone Co., Laconia and Portsmouth, N.H., also Newport, R.I., 1939-46; co-owner, mgr. Moore & Emerson Bottled Gas Co., Inc., Newport, N.H., 1947-67; with Newport (N.H.) Hosp., 1967—, asst. asso. adminstr., 1975—, interim adminstr., 1978-79. Mem. Am., New Eng. socs. for hosp. personnel adminstrn., N.H. Hosp. Assn., Newport Bus. and Profl. Women's Club. Republican. Congregationalist. Club: Order Eastern Star (recipient Grand Cross of Color Internat. Order Rainbow for Girls 1965, worthy matron 1958-59, grant rep. N.H. 1975-77). Home: PO Box 238 Newport NH 03773 Office: 167 Summer St Newport NH 03773

MOORE, PATRICK LEWIS, cell biologist; b. Schenectady, July 5, 1947; s. John Joseph and Mary Dolores (Cuttle) M.; B.S., St. Lawrence U., 1969; Ph.D. in Cell Biology, State U. N.Y. at Albany, 1975; m. Judith Lee Luborsky, Sept. 1, 1974. Postdoctoral fellow in pathology Med. U. S.C., Charleston, 1974-76, instr., 1975-76; postdoctoral fellow biology dept. and dept. internal medicine Yale U., 1976—. NIH trainee, 1969-74; NIH fellow 1977—. Mem. Am. Soc. Cell Biology, Electron Microscopy Soc. (Presdl. scholar in biol. scis. 1974), Southeastern Soc. Electron Microscopists, S.C. Electron Microscopy Soc. Contbr. articles to profl. jours. Office: Yale U Med Sch New Haven CT 06510

MOORE, PAUL, JR., bishop; b. Morristown, N.J., Nov. 15, 1919; s. Paul and Fanny Weber (Hanna) M.; grad. St. Paul's Sch., Concord, N.H., 1937; B.A., Yale, 1941; S.T.B., Gen Theol. Sem., N.Y.C., 1949, S.T.D. (hon.), 1960, D.D. (hon.), 1964; m. Jenny McKean, Nov. 26, 1944 (dec.); children—Honor, Paul III, Adelia, Rosemary, George Mead, Marian Shaw, Daniel Sargent, Susanna McKean, Patience; m. 2d, Brenda Hughes, May 16, 1975. Ordained to ministry Episcopal Ch., 1949; mem. team ministry Grace Ch., Jersey City, 1949-57; dean Christ Ch. Cathedral, Indpls., 1957-64; suffragan bishop, Washington, 1964-69; bishop coadjutor, N.Y.C., 1969-72, bishop N.Y., 1972—. Lectr. St. Augustine's Coll., Canterbury, Eng., 1960. Mem. commn. Delta Ministry Nat. Council Chs., 1964—; mem. urban div., nat. exec. council Episcopal Ch., 1952—; dep. to Gen. Conv., 1961, Anglican Congress, 1963. Mem. Yale Corp.; chmn. George W. Henry Found.; chmn. com. 100, legal def. fund NAACP; mem. nat. bd. Nat. Recreation Bd. Trustee Gen. Theol. Sem., Bard Coll., Trinity Sch. Served as capt. USMCR, 1941-45; PTO. Decorated Navy Cross, Silver Star, Purple Heart. Mem. Urban League Washington (dir.), Council Fgn. Relations. Author: The Church Reclaims the City, 1964. Home: 1047 Amsterdam Ave New York City NY 10025

MOORE, RALPH JOSEPH, JR., lawyer; b. St. Paul, Sept. 29, 1932; s. Ralph Joseph and Dorothy Louise (Noll) M.; B.A. summa cum laude, Yale U., 1954; LL.B., U. Calif., Berkeley, 1959; postgrad. Cambridge U., 1961; m. Coralie Z. Berman, July 15, 1956; children—Laurie Alison, Leslie Ellen, Kenneth Evan. Admitted to Calif. bar, 1961, U.S. Supreme Ct. bar, 1963, D.C. bar, 1965, Md. bar, 1972; law clk. Chief Justice Earl Warren, 1959-60; individual practice law, Oakland, Calif., 1960, 61-62; mem. policy planning sect., anti-trust div. U.S. Dept. Justice, 1963; mem. firm Shea & Gardner, Washington, 1963—. Bd. dirs. Md. Assn. Retarded Citizens, Centers for Handicapped, Montgomery County Assn. Retarded Citizens, Coop. Sch. for Handicapped Children; chmn. citizens adv. bd. Rosewood State Hosp. (Md.), 1972-73; mem. Gov.'s Commn. on Edn. Handicapped, 1975-76; mem. Md. Bd. Edn. adv. com. on edn. Severely and profoundly handicapped, 1975-77, spl. edn. consumer satellite com., 1977—. Mem. Am., Md., bar assns., Bar Assn. D.C., State Bar Calif., Order of Coif, Phi Beta Kappa, Phi Alpha Delta. Contbr. to profl. jours. Home: 6805 Laverock Ct Bethesda MD 20034 Office: 734 15th St NW Washington DC 20005 also 7315 Wisconsin Ave Bethesda MD 20014

MOORE, RICHARD LATHROP, mfg. co. exec.; b. Fort Lee, N.J., Nov. 11, 1923; s. Robert Jerome and Sarah G. (Gardiner) M.; A.B., Bucknell U., 1947, M.A., 1948; m. Dorothy Jean Dillenback, Sept. 13, 1944; children—Diana (Mrs. Paul A. Newman), Pamela, Richard Lathrop. With Foster D. Snell Inc., chem. cons., N.Y.C., 1948-56, asst. treas., dir. pub. relations and advt., 1951-56; with W.R. Grace & Co., N.Y.C., 1956—, dir. pub. relations 1960-71, v.p. corp. communications div., 1971—; dir. Fanning Enterprises Inc. personnel agy., N.Y.C., First Fed. Savings and Loan Assn., Montclair, N.J.; dir. N.Y. Bd. Trade, 1977; mem. pub. relations com. Ave. of Ams. Assn., 1976—, Fla. Phosphate Council, 1977—. Bd. dirs. Union Devel. Corp., urban housing, Montclair, N.J., 1973, Appeal of Conscience Found., N.Y., 1976—; bd. dirs., chmn. nominating com. Laymen's Nat. Bible Com., 1976—. Served to lt (j.g.) USNR, 1943-46; PTO, CBI. Mem. Pub. Relations Soc. Am. (mem. N.Y. exec. com. 1977—), Chem. Pub. Relations Assn. N.Y. (pres. 1970-72), Chemists Club N.Y. (trustee, treas. 1976-77), Mfg. Chemists Assn. (chmn. pub. relations com. 1965-68, mem. exec. com. 1965—), Soc. Plastics Industry (chmn. pub. relations com. 1974-77), NAM (pub. relations com. 1977), West Side Assn. Commerce (dir. 1977), Broadway Assn. (dir. 1977), 100 Year Assn. N.Y., Trinidad and Tobago C. of C. (v.p. 1967-71), Am. Inst. Chemists (chmn. editorial bd. 1976—), Alpha Chi Sigma, Sigma Chi. (v.p. N.Y. alumni 1977). Episcopalian (vestryman). Clubs: Chemists; Montclair Golf; Overseas Press, Union League (N.Y.C.). Contbr. articles to profl. jours. Home: 82 Stonebridge Rd Montclair NJ 07042 Office: 1114 Ave of Americas New York City NY 10036

MOORE, ROBERT CHALMER, engring. co. exec.; b. Harrisburg, Pa., Jan. 25, 1929; s. Chalmer Grove and Adaline L. (Burris) M.; B.S., Pa. State U., 1953; m. Jeanne Catherine Baer, Sept. 17, 1949; children—Robin Gary, Michael Alan, Diane Louise, Linda Jeanne, David Scott. Research and staff engr. HRB-Singer, State College, Pa., 1954-70; tech. sales coordinator C-Cor Electronics, State College, 1970-72; prin. engr. Scitek, Inc., State College, 1972-75; prin. engr., mgr. Marinco Ltd., Falls Church, Va., 1975-78; v.p. product devel. Accubar Engring. Co., Alexandria, Pa., 1978—. First aid instr. ARC, 1963—. Served with USAAF, 1945-49. Decorated D.F.C., Bronze Star, Air medal, Purple Heart; registered profl. engr., Pa.; recipient Silver Beaver award Boy Scouts Am., 1968. Mem. Assn. U.S. Army, Am. Def. Preparedness Assn., DAV. Contbr. articles in field to profl. jours. Home: 530 W Main St Boalsburg PA 16827 Office: Box 350 Woolverton Way Alexandria PA 16611

MOORE, ROBERT EDMUND, electronic engr.; b. Orange, N.J., Dec. 11, 1925; s. Edmund James and Helene Mathilde (Meyer) M.; B.S., N.J. Inst. Tech., 1948; M.S., Rensselaer Poly. Inst., 1950; M.E., Pa. State U., 1956; m. Leona Ann Levey, Aug. 30, 1952; 1 son. James Davenport. Devel. chemist MacDermic, Inc., Waterbury, Conn., 1950-51; devel. chemist F. Gumm Chem. Co., Kearny, N.J., 1951-54, sales eng., 1954-56; engr., semicondr. div. Gen. Electric Co., Syracuse, N.Y., 1956-60, cons. engr., 1960-66, cons. engr. space systems, King of Prussia, Pa., 1966-69, program mgr. ordnance systems, Pittsfield, Mass., 1970—. Active Boy Scouts Am. Served in U.S. Army, 1944-46. Mem. Sigma Xi, Omicron Delta Kappa, Phi Lambda Upsilon. Research in intermetallic diffusion and compound formation; microelectronic processes. Home: 68 Gravesleigh Terr Pittsfield MA 01201 Office: 100 Plastics Ave Pittsfield MA 01201

MOORE, ROBERT PAUL, educator, lawyer, writer; b. S.I., N.Y., Jan. 28, 1948; s. Barnett Mark and Lillian (Nelson) M.; A.B., Bklyn. Coll., 1970; J.D., Bklyn. Law Sch., 1974; m. Carol Rose Peckio, June 5, 1971; 1 son, Robert Paul. Tchr., N.Y.C. Pub. Sch. System, Bklyn., 1970—; admitted to N.Y. bar, 1975; asso. firm Vittoria, King and Parker, N.Y.C., 1976-78; individual practice law, Bklyn., 1978—; instr. Am. Bus. Inst., N.Y.C.; author: Welcome to #57; Four Years of Teaching and Learning in Bedford-Stuyvesant, 1975. Recipient Am. Jurisprudence award Lawyer's Coop. Pub. Co., 1974. Mem. Am. Bar Assn., United Fedn. Teachers (del. 1971-74, 76, 78, chpt. chmn. 1975). Home: 2235 E 57th Pl Brooklyn NY 11234

MOORE, ROGER ALLAN, lawyer; b. Framingham, Mass., Aug. 8, 1931; s. Ralph Chester and Mabelle (Taft) M.; A.B. cum laude, Harvard U., 1953, LL.B., 1956; m. Barbara Lee Wildman, July 4, 1955; children—Marshall Christian, Elizabeth Lee, Taft Hayden Davis, Allan Baron. Admitted to Mass. bar, 1956, since practiced in Boston; asso. firm Ropes & Gray, 1956-66, partner, 1967—. Chmn. bd. Nat. Rev., Inc.; clk. L.S. Starrett Co., Wrentham Steel Products Co. Former chmn. bd. dirs. Beacon Hill Civic Assn.; former mem. Bd. Fgn. Scholarships, U.S. Dept. State; bd. dirs., clk. Historic Boston; clk. Bostonian Soc. Recipient Endicott Peabody Saltonstall prize Harvard U., 1953, Boylston prize, 1952. Mem. Am., Mass., Boston bar assns., Old South Assn. (pres.). Episcopalian (mem. corp., warden). Home: 26 W Cedar St Boston MA 02108 Office: 225 Franklin St Boston MA 02110

MOORE, SHIRLEY THROCKMORTON (MRS. ELMER LEE MOORE), accountant; b. Des Moines, July 3, 1918; d. John Carder and Jessie (Wright) Throckmorton; student Iowa State Tchrs. Coll., summers 1937-38, Madison Coll., 1939-41; M.C.S., Benjamin Franklin U., 1944; m. Elmer Lee Moore, Dec. 19, 1946; children—Fay Moore-Sines, Lynn Dallas. Asst. bookkeeper Sibley Hosp., Washington, 1941-42, Alvord & Alvord, 1942-46, bookkeeper, 1946-49, chief accountant, 1950-64, financial adviser to sr. partner, 1957-64; dir. Allen Oil Co., 1958-74; pvt. practice in accounting, 1964—. Mem. sch. bd. Takoma Acad., Takoma Park, Md., 1970—; bd. dirs. Washington Adventist Hosp., 1971—. Recipient Distinguished Grad. award Benjamin Franklin U., 1961. C.P.A., Md. Mem. Am., D.C. insts. C.P.A.'s, Am. Women's Soc. C.P.A.'s, Bus. and Profl. Women's Club, Benjamin Franklin U. Alumni Assn. (Distinguished Alumni award 1964), DAR, Md. Assn. C.P.A.'s (charter mem. Montgomery Prince George County). Mem. Seventh Day Adventist Ch. Contbr. articles to profl. jours. Home and office: 1007 Elm Ave Takoma Park MD 20012

MOORE, SIDNEY RICHARDS, govt. ofcl.; b. Monroe, La., Aug. 20, 1924; s. Sidney Richards and Betty (O'Niell) M.; B.A., La. State U., 1949; postgrad. Tulane U., U. Md., Roosevelt U., U. So. Calif.; m. Diana Tarr, Apr. 28, 1952; children—Roderick, Shawneen, Pamela, Monica, Brett. Asst. field dir. ARC, 1950-51; mgr. advt. Am. Brewing Co., New Orleans, 1955-56; commd. ensign U.S. Naval Res., 1949, advanced through grades to lt. comdr., 1960; info. officer, Washington, 1956-59, Great Lakes, Ill., 1959-63, New London, Conn., 1963-64, Philippines, 1964-65, Vietnam, 1965, Taiwan, 1965-67, Washington, 1967-70, also Ft. Slowm, N.Y. and New Orleans; ret., 1970; info. officer U.S. Dept. Agr., Washington, 1970—. Roman Catholic. Home: 7229 Burroughs Ln Falls Church VA 22043 Office: US Dept Agr Room 1140 South Bldg Washington DC 20250

MOORE, SONIA, author, theatre dir., drama coach; b. Gomel, Russia; d. Evser and Sophie (Pasherstnik) Shatzov; student U. Kiev, U. Moscow, 1918-20, Drama Studio Solovzo Theatre, Kiev, 1919-20, Studio of Moscow Art Theatre, 1920-23; diploma Alliance Française, Paris, 1927, Istituto Interuniversitario Italiano, Rome, 1938, Reale Conservatorio de Musica Santa Cecilia, 1939, R. Accademia Filarmonica, Rome, 1939; m. Leon Moore, May 11, 1926 (dec. Mar. 1957); 1 dau., Irene Moore Jaglom; came to U.S., 1940, naturalized, 1946. Appeared at Russian Theatre in Germany, 1923-26; Off-Broadway dir., co-producer The Painted Days, 1961; dir. Sharon's Grave prodn. Irish Players, 1961; dir. Sonia Moore Studio of Theatre, N.Y.C., 1961—; founder, pres. Am. Center for Stanislavski Theatre Art, Inc., 1964, artistic dir. Am. Stanislavski Theatre, 1970—, prodns. include The Cherry Orchard, Desire Under the Elms, The Man With the Flower in his Mouth, The Stronger, The Crucible, A Streetcar Named Desire, My Poor Marat, Long Days Journey Into Night, others; lectr. series on Stanislavski System, Library and Museum of the Performing Arts at Lincoln Center, 1967-68; lectr. on WNYC-FM, 1968-69, 73; supr. Stanislavski System Workshop under auspices Recreation and Cultural Affairs Adminstrn. City N.Y., seminar Stanislavski Canadian Govt., 1969, 73; also various univs. and workshops. Author: The Stanislavski Method, 1960; The Stanislavski System, 1965, rev. edit., 1974; Training an Actor: The Stanislavski System in Class, 1968; editor, adapter: Stanislavski Today, 1973; author: The Logic of Speech on Stage, 1976; contbr. articles to profl. jours.; articles on Stanislavski to Ency. Brit., 1974. Address: 485 Park Ave New York City NY 10022

MOORE, STANFORD, biochemist; b. Chgo., Sept. 4, 1913; s. John Howard and Ruth (Fowler) M.; B.A., Vanderbilt U., 1935; Ph.D., U. Wis., 1938, D.Sc., 1974; M.D. (hon.), U. Brussels, 1954; Dr. honoris causa, U. Paris, 1964. U. Wis. Alumni Research Found. fellow, 1935-39; asst. Rockefeller Inst. Med. Research, 1939-42, asso., 1942-49, asso. mem., 1949-52, mem., prof., 1952—; tech. aide Nat. Def. Research Com., OSRD, 1942-45; vis. prof. U. Brussels, Belgium, 1950-51; vis. investigator U. Cambridge (Eng.), 1951; chmn. panel on proteins, com. on growth NRC, 1947-49; sec. commn. on proteins Internat. Union Pure and Applied Chemistry, 1953-57. Trustee Vanderbilt U., 1974—. Co-recipient Nobel prize in chemistry, 1972, Linderstrom-Lang medal, Copenhagen, 1972. Mem. Am. Chem. Soc. (chromatography award 1963, Richards medal 1972), Am. Soc. Biol. Chemists (pres. 1966-67), Brit., Belgian biochem. socs., Harvey Soc., AAAS, Nat. Acad. Scis., Am. Acad. Arts and Scis., Belgian Royal Acad. Medicine (fgn. corr.), Fedn. Am. Socs. Exptl. Biology (pres. 1970-71), Phi Beta Kappa, Sigma Xi. Mem. editorial bd. Jour. Biol. Chemistry, 1950-60. Contbr. tech. articles to profl. jours. Home: 200 E 66th St New York City NY 10021 Office: Rockefeller U 66th St and York Ave New York City NY 10021

MOORE, TALMADGE LEE, guidance counselor; b. Great Falls, S.C., May 1, 1920; s. Benjamin and Juanita M.; B.A., Howard U., 1960; M.A., Fed. City Coll., 1971; m. Carliss Spears, Sept. 28, 1946; 1 dau., Karen J. Correctional officer Nat. Tng. Sch. for Boys, Washington, 1957-63; tchr. D.C. Pub. Schs., 1963-73; counselor Bell Vocat. Sch., Washington, 1973—, acting asst. prin., 1976-77; prin.

Phelps Adult Evening Sch., Washington, 1973-76. Commr., Boy Scouts Am., Washington, 1968-69; elder Presbyn. Ch., Washington, 1967—, ch. sch. supt., 1969-71; mem. Brookland Civic Assn., 1963—. Served to lt. col. USAR, 1942-45, 50-57. Mem. NAACP, Am. Secondary Sch. Counselors, Am. Personnel and Guidance Assn., D.C. Counselor Assn., D.C. Sch. Counselors Assn., Howard U. Alumni Assn., D.C. U. Alumni Assn., U.S. Army Res. Officers Assn. Democrat. Presbyn. Clubs: Walter Reed Officers, Research. Home: 1512 Newton St NE Washington DC 20017

MOORE, WALTER CALVIN, mgmt. cons.; b. Oklahoma City, Oct. 21, 1910; s. Walter A. and Mary Helen (Hingeley) M.; student chem. engring. U. Okla., 1927-31; diploma nuclear engring. tech. Capitol Radio Engring. Inst., 1963, diploma in servomechanisms and computers, 1967; m. L. Erma McKee, Aug. 21, 1931; children—Annalee (Mrs. Mikell), Carol Sue (Mrs. Samuel Jordan), Lawrence Calvin. Asst. chief engr. gaseous diffusion plant Union Carbide Nuclear Co., Oak Ridge, 1951-54, asst. plant supt. Y-12 plant, 1954-58; project mgr. exptl. beryllium oxide reactor devel. Gen. Atomic div. Gen. Dynamics Corp., San Diego, 1959-62; v.p., dir. engring., research York div. Borg-Warner Corp., York, Pa., 1962-76; self-employed mgmt. cons., 1976—. Mem. Am. Inst. Chem. Engrs., Am. Soc. Heating Refrigerating and Air Conditioning Engrs., Am. Nuclear Soc. Club: Rotary. Contbr. articles to profl. jours. Home: 360 Tri-Hill Dr York PA 17403

MOORE, WILL TERRY, hwy. engr., educator; b. Selmer, Tenn., Nov. 14, 1941; s. Leonard Augusta and Mozelle (Kendall) M.; B.S. in Civil Engring., Tenn. State U., 1963; M.A. in Regional Sci., U. Pa., 1977. With Fed. Hwy. Adminstrn., 1963—, hwy. engr., Washington, Lincoln, Nebr., San Francisco, 1963-66, hwy. research engr. urban planning div., Washington, 1966-76, community planner, 1976—; adj. asst. prof. transp. dept. civil engring. Howard U., 1975—; tennis instr. (part-time), 1977—. Mem. urban activity systems com. Transp. Research Bd.; vol. Red Cross, 1977—. Served with U.S. Army, 1961-63. Mem. Regional Sci. Assn., Ops. Research Soc. Am., Internat. Platform Assn., Am. Inst. Planners, ASCE, U.S. Profl. Tennis Assn., Alpha Kappa Mu. Club: Toastmasters (Washington). Author: Selected Available Land Use Models, 1974; Introduction to the Empiric Activity Allocation Model and the Projective Land Use Model, 1975; (with others) An Introduction to Urban Development Models and Guidelines for their Use in Urban Transportation Planning, 1975; Land Use Forecasting Techniques For Use in Small Urban Areas, 1977. Home: 5225 Pooks Hill Rd Apt 226-S Bethesda MD 20014 Office: 400 7th St SW Washington DC 20590

MOORE, WILLIAM EDWARD, psychoanalyst; b. N.Y.C., Oct. 17, 1945; s. Edward V. and Sally (O'Leary) M.; B.A., Bklyn. Coll., City U. N.Y., 1970; Ph.D. in Psychology, Union Grad. Sch., 1975; postgrad. Option Method Inst., N.Y., 1973-76. Sociologist, Met. Applied Research Center, N.Y.C., 1970-71; instr. sociology Southampton Coll., L.I. U., N.Y., 1971-72; tng. officer City of Plainfield (N.J.), 1972-73; researcher and program planner Office Dean Univ. and Spl. Programs, Grad. Sch., City U. N.Y., 1973-75, organizer, adminstr. Urban Acad. Learning Center, 1973-75; asst. prof. counseling York Coll., City U. N.Y., 1977—; cons. psychologist Community Youth Service Center, New Brunswick, N.J., 1977—; psychoanalyst Center for the Person, N.Y.C., 1976—; organizer, dir. Inst. Personal and Profl. Devel., Southampton Coll., L.I. U., 1978—; cons. Office Mayor N.Y.C., 1975. Mem. Am. Personnel and Guidance Assn., N.Y. State Assn. Practicing Psychotherapists, N.Y. Option Method Assn. Office: 40 E 10th St New York City NY 10003

MOORES, FRANK D., Canadian govt. ofcl.; b. Carbonear, Nfld., Can., Feb. 18, 1933; s. Silas W. and Dorothy (Duff) M.; student St. Andrew's Coll.; LL.D. (hon.), Regional Coll., Meml. U., 1975; m. Janis Johnson, Aug., 1973; 1 son, Tomas Stefan; children by previous marriage—Stuart William, Susan Joyce, Deborah Joan, Michele Jan, Elizabeth Jill, Nicole Jane, Andrea Dorothy. Engaged in fishing industry, Harbour Grace, Nfld., 1953-58; pres. N.E. Fish Industries Ltd.; dir. Avalon Telephone Co. Ltd.; elected of House of Commons, Ottawa, Ont., 1968; premier Nfld. and Labrador, 1972—. Mem. Royal Commn. on Nfld.'s Econ. Prospects; pres. Harbour Grace Recreation Centre; bd. dirs. Fisheries Council Can., Atlantic Provinces Econ. Council; bd. govs. Coll. of Fisheries; pres. Nat. Progressive Conservative party, 1969-70; leader Progressive Conservative party, Nfld. and Labrador, 1970—. Clubs: Kiwanis (pres.); Masons (Carbonear). Home: Mount Scio House St John's NF Canada Office: Office of Premier St John's NF Canada

MOORHEAD, DAVIS TATUM (DAVE), patent examiner; b. Orlando, Fla., Sept. 12, 1929; s. Charles C. and Annie M. (Chandler) M.; B.S., Clemson U., 1954; M.A., Central Mich. U., 1975; m. Joyce Marie Weekly, Dec. 12, 1959; children—Ann Marie, Susan Lee. With U.S. Patent and Trademark Office, Dept. Commerce, Washington, 1957—, asst. examiner, 1957, GS-7 patent examiner, 1957-67, primary examiner, 1967-70, primary examiner-expert, 1970—. Mem. N.W. Annandale Civic Assn., 1966-76. Served with U.S. Army, 1954-56; col. Res. Mem. Am. Def. Preparedness Assn. (dir. Washington chpt. 1975—), Patent Office Soc. (exec. com. 1958—, pres. 1964, 66), Assn. Indsl. Coll. Armed Forces (2d v.p. 1976-77), S.C. State Soc. (pres. 1968), Res. Officers Assn. U.S. (pres. D.C. chpt. 1977), Civil Affairs Assn., Clemson Alumni Assn. (v.p. 1975-76, pres. 1977-78). Methodist. Club: Army-Navy Country (Arlington, Va.). Home: 1901 Army-Navy Dr Arlington VA 22202 also 919 Cutter Ct Hilton Head Island SC 29948 Office: US Dept Commerce Patent and Trademark Office Washington DC 23231

MOORHEAD, ROBERT GEORGE CHADBOURNE, financial exec.; b. Omaha, Oct. 2, 1937; s. Harley Green and Elizabeth Ward (Speir) M.; A.B., Amherst Coll., 1959; postgrad. Yale Law Sch., 1959-60; M.B.A., N.Y. U., 1968; m. Helen Rudisill Kirkpatrick, Jan. 10, 1970. With Mfrs. Hanover Trust Co., N.Y.C., 1964-74, mem. investment research dept., 1968-70, mem. investment scis. com., 1969-70, head investment scis. group, 1969-70, head budget and planning group personal trust ops., 1970-74; with Moorhead Assos., 1974-75; adminstr. pension fund, investment mgr. Chesapeake and Potomac Telephone Co., 1975-77; pension fund mgr. Asarco, Inc., 1977—. Served from ensign to lt. (j.g.), USNR, 1961-64. Named Outstanding Young Man Am., 1973. Mem. N.Y. Soc. Security Analysts, Washington Soc. Investment Analysts, Fin. Analysts Fedn., Am. Statis. Assn., Ops. Research Soc. Am., Inst. Mgmt. Scis., Naval Res. Assn., U.S. Naval Inst., N.Y. Naval Militia. Presbyterian. Club: Univ. Home: 303 E 83 St New York City NY 10028 Office: 120 Broadway New York City NY 10005

MOORHEAD, WILLIAM SINGER, congressman; b. Pitts., Apr. 8, 1923; s. William Singer and Constance (Barr) M.; student Shady Side Acad., Pitts., 1929-38, Phillips Acad., Andover, Mass., 1938-41; A.B., Yale, 1944; J.D., Harvard, 1949; m. Lucy Galpin, Dec. 23, 1946; children—William Singer III, Lucy Perrin Galpin, Stephen Galpin, James Barr. Admitted to Pa. bar, 1949, since practiced in Pitts.; partner Moorhead & Knox, 1952-70; mem. 86th-87th congresses 28th Pa. dist., 88th-96th congresses from 14th Pa. dist., mem. com. on banking, fin. and urban affairs, chmn. subcom. econ. stblzn., com. on govt. ops., joint econ. com., co-chmn. subcom. fiscal and intergovtl. policy; asst. city solicitor Pitts., 1954-57; sec. Allegheny County Housing Authority, 1956-59. Bd. dirs. Tb League Pitts., 1952-74, Pitts. Child Guidance Center, 1957-63, Western Pa. Conservancy, 1958-64, Pitts. Park and Playground Soc., 1951—. Served as lt. (j.g.) USNR, World War II. Mem. Am., Pa., Allegheny County bar assns. Democrat. Episcopalian. Club: Pitts. Golf. Home: Bigelow Apts Pittsburgh PA 15219 Office: 2467 Rayburn House Office Bldg Washington DC 20515

MOORTHY, RAVI KRISHNA, elec. engr.; b. Madurai, India, Oct. 27, 1944; s. K. Krishnamoorthy and Janaki K. Moorthy; came to U.S., 1974; B.Engring. with honors, U. Jabalpur (India), 1966; M.E.E., U. Del., 1978; m. Lakshmi Moorthy, Nov. 2, 1973; children—Satya Narayan and Satish Kumar (twins). Asst. mgr. Garg Assos. P. Ltd., India, 1968-74; research engr. W.L. Gore & Assos. Inc., Newark, Del., 1974—. Mem. IEEE. Office: PO Box 8734 555 Paper Mill Rd Newark DE 19711

MOOS, WALTER ANTON, gallery ofcl.; b. Karlsruhe, Germany, Sept. 6, 1926; s. Friedrich and Klara (Kadisch) M.; came to U.S., 1947; dip. Ecole Supérieure de Commerce, Geneva, Switzerland, 1946; student New Sch. Social Research, 1950-52; m. Martha Wegmueller, July 6, 1962; children—Michel André, David Alfred. Asst. to export mgr. New Am. Library, N.Y.C., 1952-59; pres. Gallery Moos Ltd., Toronto, Ont., Can., 1959—; v.p. Arts Mag., 1977—. Mem. Can. Eskimo Arts Council, 1974—. Mem. Profl. Art Dealers Assn. Can. (pres. 1971-74). Office: 136 Yorkville Ave Toronto ON M5R 1C2 Canada

MOOSE, JAMES SAYLE, economist; b. Teheran, Iran, Dec. 24, 1940; s. James Sayle and Eleanor Duncan (Wood) M.; B.A., Harvard U., 1961, Ph.D., 1967; M.A., Oxford U., 1963; m. Claudia Stanley, Dec. 6, 1975. Petroleum cons. Arthur D. Little, Cambridge, Mass., 1967-70; economist, v.p., partner Loomis Sayles & Co., Inc., Boston, 1970—; mem. Mass. gov.'s com. New Eng. Regional Commn. on Capital and Labor Markets, 1975. Rhodes scholar, 1961-63; NSF fellow, 1964-67. Mem. Fin. Analysts Fedn., Am. Econ. Assn., Am. Fin. Assn. Presbyterian. Home: 18 Ravine Rd Winchester MA 01890 Office: 225 Franklin St Boston MA 02110

MOOSE, RAY STANLEY, coll. adminstr.; b. High Point, N.C., Jan. 24, 1947; s. Price and Gladys (Brown) M.; B.A. in Polit. Sci., N.C. Central U., 1969; M.A. in Student Personnel Service, Montclair State Coll., 1977; m. Justine Elizabeth Evans, Mar. 20, 1969. Tchr. Cleveland Elem. Sch., Newark, 1970-72; recreation specialist Essex County (N.J.) Park Commn., 1971-76, supr., 1974-76; counselor intern Essex County Coll., 1976; counselor Ednl. Opportunity Fund program Bloomfield (N.J.) Coll., 1977, asst. dean students, 1977—, dir. housing and career planning and placement, 1977—. Bd. dirs. Passaic County Community Council, Paterson, N.J., Mem. Am. Personnel and Guidance Assn., Middle Atlantic Placement Assn., Nat. Assn. Student Personnel Adminstrs., Coll. Placement Council. Address: 72 Monroe Pl Bloomfield NJ 07003

MOOT, AGNES BRUMBAUGH (MRS. EARLE O. MOOT), home economist; b. Henrietta, Pa.; d. Moses R. and Florence (Stuard) Brumbaugh; B.S., Pa. State U., 1935; student Juniata Coll., 1923-25; m. Earle O. Moot, Feb. 2, 1946; 1 dau., Linda. Tchr., Greenfield Twp. High Sch., Claysburg, Pa., 1927-36; extension home economist Washington County, Washington, Pa., 1936-39; asst. state 4-H Club leader, University Park, Pa., 1939-40; state supr. home econs. Pa. Extension, University Park, 1940-41, state leader home econs., 1941-46; extension home economist Lebanon County, Lebanon, Pa., 1952-68; substitute tchr. No. Lebanon High Sch., 1968-74; interviewer Gallop Poll, 1969-74. Mem. Lebanon County Welfare Council, 1966-68, Lebanon County Family and Children's Service, 1966-68, Mental Health Bd. Lebanon County, 1968—. Mem. Nat., Pa. assns. extension home economists, Nat. Grange, Nat., Pa., Lebanon County (pres. 1965-66) home econs. assns., C. of C. Safety Council, Soc. Farm Women, Kappa Delta Alumni, Epsilon Sigma Phi. Republican. Presbyterian. Clubs: Soroptimist (pres. 1966-68), Lionettes. Columnist, Lebanon Daily News, 1960-68. Home: Rural Route 2 Box 965 Lebanon PA 17042

MORAHAN, DANIEL MICHAEL KEVIN, economist, polit. cons., writer; b. Washington, Aug. 15, 1940; s. John J. and Eileen Alice (McKeown) M.: A.A., George Washington U., 1963, B.B.A., 1965. Occupational analyst U.S. Employment Service, Washington, 1965-66; employment service advisor Bur. Employment Security, Washington, 1966-67; economist Dept. Labor, Bur. Labor Statistics, Atlanta, N.Y.C., Phila., 1967-68; position classification specialist Office Chief Staff, Dept. Army, Washington, 1968-72; wirter-editor printed media Adjutant Gen.'s Office, Washington, 1973; personnel officer Office Chief Staff, Army, Washington, 1972-74; pres. Manpower Economic counselor, writer Metra Ltd. Enterprises, Landover Hills, Md., 1974—; sales rep. Tiffany div. Am. Lubriacants Co., Dayton, Ohio, 1978—; chmn., pres. M-METRA Ltd. Enterprises; student tchr. English, music Herbert Hoover Jr. High Sch., Potomac, Md., 1975. Adv. bd. Drug Intervention Counseling Action program, Prince George's County, Md. Health Dept., 1977—; participant 2nd nat. conf. on Need Assessment in Health and Human Services, U. Louisville, 1978. Mem. Am. Inst. Mgmt. (exec. council 1969—), Am. Def. Preparedness Assn., Am. Security Council (nat. Adv. bd. 1969—), Am. Conservative Union, M.B.A. Execs. Assn., Am. Enterprise Inst. for Pub. Policy Research, Phi Sigma Kappa, Delta Nu Alpha. Democrat. Roman Catholic. Clubs: Gaslight, George Washington Univ., Poets, Capitol Hill. Contbr. articles in field to profl. jours. Home: 4005 74th Pl Bellemead Landover Hills MD 20784

MORALES, ALVARO, urol. surgeon; b. Bogota, Colombia, Oct. 21, 1938; s. Jorge Enrique and Emma Maria (Gomez) M.; M.D. cum laude, Javeriana U. (Colombia), 1964; m. Diane Lynn Dilworth, July 4, 1970; children—John Charles, Andrea Christine. Intern, Mil. Hosp., Bogota, 1964-65; resident Washington Hosp. Center, 1965-67, Tufts U., Boston, 1968, Queen's U., Kingston, Ont., Can., 1968-70, Toronto (Ont.) Gen. Hosp., 1971-72; practice medicine, specializing in urol. surgery, Kingston, 1972—; lectr. dept. urology Queen's U., 1972-75, asst. prof., 1975—; Ont. Cancer Found. research grantee, 1973-78; guest investigator, lab. immunodiagnosis Nat. Cancer Inst. NIH, Bethesda, Md., 1975-76; cons. urologist Kingston Gen. Hosp., Hotel Dieu Hosp., St. Mary's Lake Hosp., Armed Forces Hosp. Mem. Royal Coll. Physicians Surgeons Can., A.C.S., Can., Am., Colombian, Brit. urol. assns., Assn. Acad. Surgery, Can. Oncology Soc. Roman Catholic. Contbr. articles to profl. jours. Home: 796 Wartman Ave Kingston ON K7M 4M4 Canada Office: Dept Urology Queen's U Kingston ON K7L 3N6 Canada

MORALES, RAUL, physician; b. Havana, Cuba, Feb. 5, 1931; s. Antonio and Valeria (Vazavez) M.; came to U.S., 1957, naturalized, 1964; M.D., U. Havana, 1957; postgrad. N.Y. Polyclinic Med. Sch., 1972-74; m. Blanca Morales, July 5, 1957; children—Alice, Albert. Intern, Cooper Hosp., Camden, N.J., 1957; intern in medicine Trafalgar Hosp., N.Y.C., 1958-60; research fellow Inst. Applied Biology, N.Y.C., 1960-62; rotating intern St. Joseph Hosp., Yonkers, N.Y., 1964-65, mem. staff, 1965—; practice medicine specializing in family medicine, Yonkers, 1965—; mem. staffs Yonkers Profl. Hosp., Yonkers Gen. Hosp. Recipient Physician's Recognition award AMA, 1969, 72, 75, 78. Diplomate Am. Bd. Family Practice. Lic. physician, Miss., N.Y., N.J. Fellow Am. Acad. Family Physicians, Wetchester Acad. Medicine; mem. AMA, N.Y. Vet. Police Assn. Home: 42 Anderson Ave Englewood Cliffs NJ 07632

MORAN, CHARLES A., banker; b. Chgo., Feb. 7, 1943; s. Charles W. and Rose B. (Sutcher) M.; A.B., Princeton U., 1964; J.D., U. Mich., 1967; m. Donna L. Orbach, Sept. 2, 1967; children—Scott Alan, Erin Lizabeth. Pension trust officer, adminstrv. officer, officer in charge new bus. devel., pension div. Chase Manhattan Bank, N.Y.C., 1967-70; sr. v.p., sr. adminstrv., fin. officer trust div. bank coms. Manufacturers Hanover Trust Co., N.Y.C., 1971—; lectr. bus., econs. Bloomfield Coll.; formerly lectr. sociology, fin. employee benefits C.W. Post Coll., L.I. U., Am. Inst. Banking; cons. Urban Vol. Cons. Group, Inc.; adv. council U.S. Dept. Labor; dir. Lionel D. Edie & Co., Inc.; chmn. Employees Retirement Income Security Act of 1974 Rountable. Mem. Am. Pension Conf. (treas.), N.Y. State Bankers Assn. (employees trust com.), Am. Bankers Assn. (chmn. employee trust com.), AAUP, N.Y. C. of C. (task force on pub. pensions). Contbr. articles to profl. jours. Home: 16 Holland Terr Montclair NJ 07042 Office: 600 Fifth Ave New York City NY 10020

MORAN, HAROLD JOSEPH, lawyer; b. N.Y.C., Feb. 21, 1907; s. Thomas J. and Leonore M. F. (Geoghegan) M.; A.B. cum laude, Holy Cross Coll., 1928; LL.B., Fordham U., 1932, J.D., 1968; m. Geraldine D. Starkey, July 12, 1956. Admitted to N.Y. bar, 1934; practiced in N.Y.C., 1934-42, Bklyn., 1949-57, Malverne, N.Y., 1977—; law dept. Title Guarantee & Trust Co., Bklyn., 1945-48; sr. atty. real property bur. N.Y. State Law Dept., Albany, 1957-63, N.Y.C., 1963-77; ret., 1977; spl. dept. atty. gen. for election frauds, 1973. Title closer City Title Co., Bklyn., 1949-52; U.S., P.R. mortgage loan examiner Cadwalader, Wickersham & Taft, N.Y.C., 1952-56, 9th Fed. Savs. & Loan Assn., N.Y.C., 1971—; instr. law St. John's U. Sch. Commerce, Jamaica, N.Y., 1956-57. Served with AUS, 1942-45. Decorated Knight Holy Sepulchre, 1967. Mem. Am. Bar Assn., Bar Assn. Nassau County, Am. Judicature Soc., N.Y. County Lawyers Assn., Cath. Lawyers Guild. Democrat. Roman Catholic. Clubs: Hempstead Golf and Country; Southward Ho Country. Home: 974 Gardiner Dr Bay Shore NY 11706 Office: 277 Hempstead Ave Malverne NY 11565

MORAN, JAMES JOSEPH, drug co. exec.; b. Jersey City, Nov. 28, 1942; s. James Anthony and Catherine Cecelia (Murphy) M.; B.S. in Accounting, St. Peter's Coll., 1964; M.B.A., Pace Coll., 1974; m. Cordelia Gottiaux, Oct. 13, 1972; children—Jaymie, James. Controller, House of Revlon, N.Y.C., 1966-67; mgr. accounting P. Ballantine & Sons, Newark, 1967-69; budget and cost dir. Block Drug Co., Jersey City, 1969—; prof. accounting and fin. Passaic County Community Coll. Evening Div., 1979—; mem. fin. adv. bd. Hudson County Coll. Fin. adviser Boro of Beachwood, N.J. Club: Middlesex County Chess. Home: 853 Ocean Ave Beachwood NJ 08722 Office: 257 Cornelison Ave Jersey City NJ 07302

MORAN, JULIETTE M(AY), chem. co. exec.; b. N.Y.C., June 12, 1917; d. James Joseph and Louise Moran; B.A., Columbia, 1939; M.S., N.Y. U., 1948. Research asst. Columbia, 1941; jr. engr. Signal Corps Lab. AUS, 1942-43; with GAF Corp., 1943—, jr. chemist process devel. dept., tech. asst. to N.Y. process devel. dept., tech. asst. to dir. Central Research Lab., tech. asst. to dir. comml. devel., 1953-55, supr. tech. service, comml. devel. dept., 1955-59, sr. devel. specialist, 1959-60, mgr. planning, 1961, asst. to pres., 1962-67, v.p., 1967-71, sr. v.p., 1971-74, exec. v.p., 1974—, also dir. corp. and various subsidiaries. Trustee Empire Savs. Bank. Fellow AAAS, Am. Inst. Chemists; mem. Am. Chem. Soc., Comml. Devel. Assn. Clubs: Econ. of N.Y., Hemisphere. Office: GAF Corp 140 W 51st St New York City NY 10020

MORAN, MARTIN JOSEPH, fund raising co. exec.; b. Bklyn., Nov. 3, 1930; s. Dominick and Mary (Lydon) M.; B.A., St. John's U., 1952; m. Mary Therese Schofield, June 5, 1954; children—Martin Joseph, John P., Maureen M., Thomas S., Robert P., William M., Maria M. With Community Counselling Service, fund raising firm, N.Y.C., 1956-64, v.p., 1960-62, head nat. sales and operations, 1962-64, asst. to pres., 1962-64; founder Martin J. Moran Co., Inc., N.Y.C., 1964—, pres., 1964-74, chmn. bd., 1974—. Mem. Cardinals Com. for Edn. N.Y.C., 1970—; mem. Am. Revolution Bicentennial Commn., Town of Oyster Bay. Mem. Zoning Bd. Appeals, Massapequa Park, N.Y., 1972—, Ethics Commn., 1969-72. Trustee Notre Dame Coll., S.I., 1969-72, La Salle Acad., N.Y.C., 1971—; mem. pres. council Cath. U. P.R., Ponce, 1966-71. Served as aviator USNR, 1952-56. Decorated knight Order Holy Sepulchre, Pope Paul VI, 1969, Knight of Malta, 1974. Mem. Navy League, Naval Hist. Assn., Am. Assn. Fund Raising Counsel (dir. 1970—), Friendly Sons of St. Patrick. Roman Catholic. K.C. Club: Madison Square Garden. Home: 1300 Lake Shore Dr Massapequa Park NY 11762 Office: One Penn Plaza New York City NY 10001

MORAN, WILLIAM ARNOLD, JR., pharm. co. exec.; b. Jackson Heights, N.Y., Nov. 27, 1947; s. William Arnold and Catherine Frances (Cleary) M.; A.S., State U. N.Y., 1978; m. Leta Jean Casper, June 12, 1971; children—William Christopher, Lisa Kathleen. Chem. weigher Barrows Labs., Inwood, N.Y., 1970-71; chem. weigher, compounder Endo Labs., Garden City, N.Y., 1971; packaging supr. Evsco Veterinarian Pharm., Oceanside, N.Y., 1971-75; packaging supr. Ketchum Labs., Amityville, N.Y., 1975-77; plant mgr. Corwood Labs., Hauppage, N.Y., 1977—. Served with USAF, 1966-70. Mem. Am. Legion. Home: 427 17th St West Babylon NY 11704

MORANO, PASQUALE FRANCIS, educator; b. Brockton, Mass., June 7, 1926; s. Domenic and Amelia (Venti) M.; B.F.A. in Painting, R.I. Sch. Design, Providence, 1953; M.Ed., Bridgewater (Mass.) State Coll., 1955. Supr. art edn. N. Attleboro (Mass.) Pub. Schs., 1955-58, 59-60; dir. art edn. Sherwood, Genoa and Kings Ferry (N.Y.) Pub. Schs., 1958-59; dir. art edn. Brockton (Mass.) Pub. Schs., 1960—, dir. arts, 1974—. State chmn. Mass. Scholastic Art awards; mem. com. devel. Mass. Curriculum Art Guide. Mem. Mass. (pres.) Nat. art edn. assns., NEA, Music Edn. Nat. Conf., Mass. Dirs. Art Edn. Home: 92 Wyman St Brockton MA 02401 Office: Brockton Pub Schs 43 Crescent St Brockton MA 02401

MORE, EILEEN MARIE, security analyst; b. Bridgeport, Conn., Apr. 10, 1946; d. Maurice Joseph and Muriel Marie (Fitch) Farrell; student U. Bridgeport, 1965-67; m. Ronald More, Sept. 17, 1966; children—Robert, Donna. Analyst, Wright Investors Service, Bridgeport, 1964-67, sr. security analyst, asst. investment officer, 1972-78; dr. research Oak Mgmt. Co., Darien, Conn., 1979—; tax cons. H & R Block, Nashua, N.H., 1968-69. Chartered fin. analyst. Mem. Fin. Analysts Fedn., N.Y. Soc. Security Analysts, Hartford Soc. Security Analysts. Home: Rock Ridge Rd Easton CT 06468 Office: 500 State St Bridgeport CT 06604

MORELL, DAVID LOUIS, polit. scientist; b. N.Y.C., Oct. 17, 1939; s. Samuel Allan and Elsa Marie (Bohmrich) M.; B.A., U. Wis., 1961; M. Pub. Affairs (Helen Wessel fellow, Archibald A. Gulick fellow), Princeton U., 1963, Ph.D. in Pub. and Internat. Affairs, 1974; children—Thomas, Julia, Nicholas, Anne. Research program dir. Research Analysis Corp., McLean, Va. and Bangkok, Thailand, 1965-68; research project mgr. Am. Insts. Research, Pitts. and Bangkok, 1968-70; vis. prof. Asian Inst. Tech., Chulalongkorn U.,

Bangkok, 1970-72; dir. Office Transp. and Land Use Policy, U.S. EPA, Washington, 1972-74; research polit. scientist, lectr. politics and urban planning Princeton U., 1974—; mem. research adv. bd. N.J. Marine Scis. Consortium; mem. exec. com. Thai Univ. Research Assos.; cons. AID, UNICEF, Devel. Counsellors Internat. Ltd., U.S. Nat. Security Council. Bd. dirs. Parent Tchr. Orgn., Riverside Sch., Princeton. Served to lt. AUS, 1963-65. Rockefeller Found. grantee, 1975. Mem. Am. Polit. Sci. Assn., Urban Land Inst., Assn. Asian Studies, Siam Soc., Social Sci. Assn. Thailand, Stony Brook-Millstone Watersheds Assn., N.J. League for Conservation Legislation, Asia Soc. (chmn. Thailand council), Council Fgn. Relations (S.E. Asia rev. group), Delta Sigma Pi, Phi Eta Sigma. Democrat. Unitarian. Co-author: Six Slums in Bangkok, 1972; Issues in Clustered Nuclear Siting, 1976; author: Who's in Charge: Capabilities of Government Institutions to Make Energy Facility Siting Decisions in New Jersey; Thailand: Domino by Default?, 1978; co-editor: Political Participation Under Military Regimes, 1976; contbr. articles in field to profl. jours. Home: 10 Howe Circle Princeton NJ 08540 Office: Center for Environ Studies Princeton U Princeton NJ 08540

MORENCY, RENALD MICHEL, pathologist; b. Quebec, Que., Can., Oct. 13, 1943; s. Andre and Angeline (Brouard) M.; B.A., Coll. Des Jesuites, 1963; M.D., Laval U., 1967; postgrad. in oral pathology Eastman Dental Hosp., London, 1973-74; m. Colette Carmichael, Aug. 23, 1965; children—Chantale, Claude, Marie-Josee, Michele. Intern, St.-Sacrement Hosp., Quebec City, 1967-68; resident in internal medicine Chus, Sherbrooke, P.Q., 1968-69; resident in pathology Enfant-Jesus Hosp., Quebec City, Chus, Sherbrooke, Hotel-Dieu Hosp., Quebec City, 1969-73; pathologist Enfant-Jesus Josp., Quebec, P.Q., 1974—; tchr. oral pathology Laval U. Fellow Royal Coll. Physicians (C.); mem. Internat. Acad. Pathology, Royal Soc. Medicine, Canadian Assn. Pathologists. Roman Catholic. Home: 8255 Trudelle St Quebec PQ G1G 5C1 Canada Office: 1401 18th St Quebec PQ G1J 1Z4 Canada

MORENO, JOHN HENRY, rehab. counselor; b. N.Y.C., Feb. 24, 1948; s. Peter Henry and Marguerite Theresa (Cusack) M.; B.A., Villanova U., 1970; M.A., Montclair State Coll., 1972; m. Victoria Kuczynski, Apr. 23, 1977. Patient rep. Morrisania City Hosp., Bronx, N.Y., 1972-73; rehab. counselor div. vocat. rehab. State of N.J., Rahway, 1973-75, East Orange, 1975-77, Newark, 1977—; rehab. counselor Rehab. Edn. and Career Advisement and Planning Group, 1978—; cons. Turning Point Alcohol Rehab. Center. Cert. rehab. counselor, alcohol counselor. Mem. Am. Personnel and Guidance Assn., Am. Rehab. Counseling Assn., Nat. Rehab. Assn. Roman Catholic. Home: 59 Long Hill Rd Oakland NJ 07436

MORERE, JEAN MARIE, nurse; b. Paterson, N.J., June 1, 1938; d. Alexis Emil and Myra Charlotte (Pullins) Morere; R.N., Jersey City Med. Center, 1959; B.S. in Nursing, Seton Hall U., 1969; M.A., N.Y. U., 1977; postgrad. Tex. Women's U., 1971; certificate in hosp. mgmt. Rutgers U. Extension Div., 1979. Staff nurse operating rm. Jersey City (N.J.) Med. Center, 1959-60; staff nurse Greater Paterson (N.J.) Gen. Hosp., 1960-63, asst. supr., 1963-65, supr. operating rm. 1965-74, coordinator scheduling and admitting, 1974—. Active Girl Scouts, U.S.A., Paterson, N.J., 1948, recipient leaders awards, 1970, 75. Mem. Assn. Operating Room Nurses, Am. Nurses Assn., Jersey City Med. Center Alumnae Assn., Sigma Theta Tau. Roman Catholic. Home: 205 Mt Pleasant Ave West Paterson NJ 07424 Office: 224 Hamburg Turnpike Wayne NJ 07470

MORGAN, COLIN JOHN, cosmetics co. exec.; b. London, Aug. 20, 1935; s. Clifford and Eveline (Bartlett) M.; B.A., Oxford (Eng.) U., 1959; m. Rosario Sanjurjo Regueiro, Nov. 2, 1963; children—Benjamin Luis, Richard Joseph. Exec. trainee Colgate Palmolive Co., London, 1950-59, resident mgr., Nigeria, 1960-62, new products mgr., London, 1962-65, mktg. dir., Madrid, 1965-68; gen. mgr. Revlon P.R. and Caribbean, 1968-72, mng. dir. Revlon Spain, Madrid, 1972-77, v.p. mktg. Latin Am., Revlon Internat. Corp., N.Y.C., 1978—. Served with Royal Navy, 1954-56. Roman Catholic. Home: 18 Eno Ln Westport CT 06880 Office: Revlon Internat Corp 767 5th Ave New York City NY 10022

MORGAN, DAVID HOWELL, architect; b. Wales, 1886; s. Howell Thomas M.; came to U.S., 1907, naturalized, 1914; grad. Royal Inst. Brit. Architects, London, 1907. Asso. Cope & Stewardson, Phila., 1907-08, Olds & Puckey, Wilkes Barre, Pa., 1908-10, George D. Mason, Detroit, 1910-11, Albert Kahn, Detroit, 1911-12, Donaldson & Meier, Detroit, 1912-13, Edward H. Davis, Scranton, Pa., 1913-16; pvt. practice architecture, Phila., 1916-74, ret., 1974; mem. Pa. Bd. Licensing of Architects, 1927-41, chmn., 1936-41. Rellow AIA (pres. Phila. chpt. 1954-55). Home: Park Towne Pl Apt 1608 N 2200 Benjamin Franklin Pkwy Philadelphia PA 19130

MORGAN, FRANK THOMAS, personnel exec.; b. Mt. Carmel, Pa., July 8, 1944; s. Burgess Sherman and Marion Regina (Lewis) M.; A.B. cum laude, Princeton U., 1966; M.S. in Psychology, Pa. State U., 1967; postgrad. Stevens Inst. Tech.; m. Nancy Ida Bishop, May 30, 1970; children—Elizabeth Marion, Douglas Bishop. Plant personnel mgr. Gen. Foods, Jacksonville, Fla., 1967-69, asso. placement mgr., White Plains, N.Y., 1969-70, sales personnel devel. mgr., 1970-71; mgr. organizational devel. Berol Corp., Danbury, Conn., 1971-74, dir. human resources, 1974-76, v.p. human resources, 1976—; adj. faculty W. Conn. State Coll., Danbury, 1977—. Trustee Danbury Hosp., 1972—, bd. dirs., chmn. personnel com. 1972-77; bd. dirs. United Way N. Fairfield County, Danbury, 1973-75; mem. Adv. Council on Career Edn., Danbury, 1974—. Certified tng. asso. Lifework Planning Assos. Mem. Am. Psychol. Assn., Am. Soc. Tng. and Devel., Nat. Orgn. Devel. Network, Lifework Planning Assos., Psi Chi. Republican. Episcopalian. Research and publs. in field. Office: Berol Corp Internat Hdqrs Danbury CT 06810

MORGAN, JEAN ELIZABETH, surgeon; b. Washington, July 9, 1947; d. William James and Antonia Mary (Bell) M.; B.A. magna cum laude, Harvard U., 1967; M.D., Yale U., 1971. Research fellow dept. medicine Oxford (Eng.) U., 1970; resident in surgery Yale-New Haven Hosp., 1971-73; sr. surg. resident, chief surg. resident Tufts-New Eng. Med. Center, Boston, 1973-76; fellow plastic surgery Yale-New Haven Hosp., 1976-77; plastic surgery fellow Harvard Med. Sch.-Cambridge City Hosp., 1977—; columnist Cosmopolitan mag., 1973—; Trustee Schefer Sch., Falls Church, Va. Diplomate Am. Bd. Surgery. Mem. AMA, Mass. Med. Soc., English Speaking Union. Episcopalian. Clubs: Brit. Commonwealth, Harvard, Yale. Home: 33 Pond Ave #B-1116 Brookline MA 02146 Office: Dept of Surgery 1493 Cambridge St Cambridge MA 02139

MORGAN, LEROY TUTTLE, farmer; b. Washington, March 20, 1928; s. Charles Carroll and Adelaide LeRoy (Tuttle) M.; B.A., Yale U., 1949; m. Carolyn Diana Mary Makins, June 1, 1956; children—Diana Vivian, Teresa Adelaide, Eleanora Carroll, Cecilia Hay, Maria Abell, Olivia Dudley. Ops. dir. NBC, Washington, 1951-57; asst. to sec. of commerce, Washington, 1958-60; asst. to bd. govs. FRS, Washington, 1961-74. Trustee Com. of 100 on the Fed. City, Georgetown Day Sch., Grace Episcopal Ch. Clubs: Chevy Chase, Met., Potomac Boat, Pamet Harbor Yacht and Tennis, Mory's. Author: Smatterings of Aversity, 1945. Home: Alodialea 25214 Peach Tree Rd Clarksburg MD 20734

MORGAN, LORRAINE LEE, ednl. cons.; b. Carrolltown, Pa., 1930; married, 3 children. B.S. in Elementary Edn., U. Pitts., 1956, M.Ed. in Elementary Edn., 1961, Ed.D. in Reading and Lang. Arts, 1967. Tchr., U. Pitts. Falk Lab., 1961-64; research asso., lectr. U. Pitts., 1964-66; chmn. dept. edn. Chatham Coll., Pitts., from 1970; now ednl. cons. Bd. dirs. Reading is Fundamental. Mem. Internat. Reading Assn., Nat. Council Tchrs. of English, Nat. Soc. Study of Edn., AAUP, Adminstrv. Women in Edn. Author: Developmental Activities for the Primary Classroom; Auditory Skills. Specialist in reading, lang. arts, child devel., urban edn. Home: 6909 Meade St Pittsburgh PA 15208 Office: Woodland Rd Pittsburgh PA 15232

MORGAN, WALTER EDWARD, mgmt. cons.; b. Hempstead, N.Y., Nov. 19, 1940; s. Edward Alexander and Anne Cecelia (Wright) M.; A.B., Morgan State Coll., 1962; M.A., U. Md., 1969; m. Lorraine Roberson, June 1, 1962; children—Walter Edward, Gary Leroy, Cheryl Elise. Sr. asso. A.L. Nellum and Assos. Inc., Washington, 1969-71; dir. tng. Skill Upgrading Inc., Balt., 1968-69; adminstrv. specialist Social Security Adminstrn., Columbia, Md., 1966-68; v.p., Pagan and Morgan, Balt., 1971-74; pres. Morgan Mgmt. Systems, Columbia, 1974—. Chmn. affirmative action com. United Way Central Md., 1978—, also bd. dirs.; bd. dirs. G. James Fleming Scholarship Fund, pres., 1977—. Served to 1st lt. U.S. Army, 1962-66. Certified mgmt. cons. Mem. Am. Mgmt. Assos., Am. Soc. Pub. Adminstrn., Omega Psi Phi, Alpha Kappa Mu, Inst. Mgmt. Cons.'s. Home: 10730 Evening Wind Ct Columbia MD 21044 Office: 301 Clark Bldg Columbia MD 21044

MORGENSTERN, DAN MICHAEL, mag. editor; b. Munich, Germany, Oct. 24, 1929; s. Soma and Ingeborg Henrietta (von Klenau) M.; came to U.S., 1947, naturalized 1947; student Brandeis U., 1953-56; m. Elsa Schocket, Mar. 31, 1974; 1 son, Adam Oran. Editor, Brandeis U. Justice, 1955-56; editorial asst. N.Y. Post, 1957-58; N.Y. corr. Jazz Jour., London, 1958-61; asso. editor, then editor-in-chief Metronome, 1961; editor Jazz, 1962-64; asso. editor Down Beat, 1964-67, editor, 1967-73; producer ann. 10-concert series Jazz in the Garden, Museum Modern Art, N.Y.C., 1961-66; co-producer concert series Jazz on Broadway, 1963, Just Jazz, 10 program TV series Pub. Broadcasting Service, 1971; lectr. jazz history Peabody Instn., Balt., 1978—; dir. Inst. Jazz Studies, Rutgers U., 1976—. Bd. dirs. Jazz Inst. Chgo., N.Y. Jazz Mus. Served with U.S. Army, 1951-53. Grammy award best album notes, 1973, 74, 76; ASCAP Deems Taylor award, 1977. Mem. Nat. Acad. Rec. Arts and Scis. (gov. 1971—, trustee 1976—), Nat. Endowment for Arts (chmn. jazz adv. panel 1971-73, cons. music programs 1973—), Music Critics Assn., P.E.N., Authors Guild. Author: The Jazz Story: An Outline History, 1973; Jazz People, 1976. Translator, editor: (Joachim E. Berendt) The New Jazz Book, 1962, rev. edit., 1975. Home: 365 West End Ave New York City NY 10024 Office: Inst Jazz Studies Rutgers U Newark NJ 07102

MORGENSTERN, STEPHEN, optometrist; b. Bklyn., Mar. 2, 1940; s. Abraham and Yetta (Steiger) M.; B.S. in Pharmacy, Bklyn. Coll. Pharmacy, 1961; B.S., Pa. Coll. Optometry, 1969, O.D., 1970; m. Marcia Mandel, Oct. 11, 1970; children—Andrew Seth, Rebecca Jill, Lauren Dayna. Instr., Bklyn. Coll. Pharmacy, 1961; registered pharmacist, 1961-62; resident orthoptics and vision tng. Optometric Center N.Y., 1970, engaged in myopia research project, 1970; developmental optometrist N.Y. Center Learning Disorders, 1970-71; pvt. practice developmental optometry, East Northport and Port Jefferson, N.Y., 1970—; optometrist staff mem. Suffolk County Assn. Retarded Children, 1973—; cons. in field. Served to 1st lt. USAF, 1962-65. Fellow Coll. Optometrists in Vision Devel.; mem. Am., N.Y. State, Suffolk County optometric assns., Optometric Extension Program (clin. asso.), Internat. Myopia Prevention Assn., Assn. Children with Learning Disorders, Council Exceptional Children, N.Y. Assn. Brain Injured Children, Suffolk County Mental Health Assn. Club: K.P. Home: 6 Norman Ct Dix Hills NY 11746 Office: 554 Larkfield Rd East Northport NY 11731 also 640 Belle Terre Rd Port Jefferson NY 11777

MORGENTHAU, ANTHONY REGINALD, stockbroker; b. London, Eng., Mar. 21, 1945 (father Am. citizen); s. Edwin Franklin and Joan Annette (Tuck) M.; B.A., Westminster Coll., Fulton, Mo., 1968; m. Elizabeth Ann Coulter, June 21, 1969. With Stein Bros. & Boyce, Balt., 1969-70, F.I. DuPont, Balt., 1970-73; pres. Morgenthau & Assos., Balt., 1973—, also dir.; dir. MORMAC, Ltd., Wil-Co Exploration, Inc. Mem. Nat. Assn. Security Dealers, Balt. Engrs. Club., Classic Car Club U.S.A. Republican. Episcopalian. Clubs: Towson (Md.); Johns Hopkins, Center (Balt.). Home: 5200 Springlake Way Baltimore MD 21212 Office: 900 Sun Life Bldg Baltimore MD 21201

MORIARTY, EUGENE VINCENT, chem. engring. co. exec.; b. Chgo., Aug. 5, 1924; s. Michael Joseph and Catherine Marie (Meller) M.; B.S.Chem. Engring., Northwestern U., 1947, postgrad. Bus. Sch., 1948-50; m. Virginia Marie Shaw, Mar. 8, 1958; children—Kathleen Hill, Kevin Shaw. Asst. plant engr. G.D. Searle & Co., Chgo., 1947-53; asst. mgr. Lummus Co., Chgo., 1953-58; mgr. new chem. projects Vitro Engring. Co., N.Y.C., 1958-60; asst. v.p. Sci. Design Co., N.Y.C., 1960-66, v.p., 1966-67; v.p. Vyplex Corp., N.Y.C., 1967; dir. corp. sales Lummus Co., Bloomfield, N.J., 1967-71, v.p., 1971-76, sr. v.p., 1973—. Served as lt. inf., AUS, 1942-44. Mem. Am. Inst. Chem. Engrs., Am. Chem. Soc., Licensing Execs. Soc. Clubs: Union League (N.Y.C.); Montclair (N.J.) Golf. Home: 10 Crestmont Rd Montclair NJ 07042 Office: 1515 Broad St Bloomfield NJ 07003

MORIARTY, JAMES BRENDAN, coll. dean; b. Southbridge, Mass., Sept. 3, 1943; s. Michael Eugene and Rita (Hurley) M.; B.B.A. in Mgmt., Nichols Coll., Dudley, Mass., 1966; M.B.A. in Fin., U. Bridgeport (Conn.), 1972; m. Janet Ruth Antenucci, Aug. 7, 1971; children—Tara Susan, Brendan David. Accountant, auditor Am. U., 1970-71; staff accountant Nat. Tech. Inst. Deaf, Rochester, N.Y., 1972-73; dean fin. and adminstrv. services Community Coll. Finger Lakes, Canandaigua, N.Y., 1973-78; dean of bus. and fin. affairs Ocean County Coll., Toms River, N.J., 1978—. Chmn. fund drive DeSalles High Sch., Geneva, N.Y., 1974-75. Served with USAF, 1966-70; Vietnam. Mem. Eastern Assn. Coll. Aux. Services, N.Y. State Community Coll. Bus. Officers Assn., Rochester Area Colls. Consortium Bus. Mgrs. Group (chmn. 1977-78), Am. Legion. Democrat. Roman Catholic. Home: 1505 Baltimore Ave Lavalette NJ 08735 Office: Ocean County Coll College Dr Toms River NJ 08753

MORIN, MORTON EDWIN, govt. ofcl.; b. Worcester, Mass., Oct. 29, 1925; s. Jacob and Gertrude (Greenburg) M.; B.S., U. Mass., 1950; postgrad. Worcester State Coll., 1962-63; spl. courses Holy Cross Coll., 1958-60, Springfield Coll., 1967, U. Colo., 1971; children—Michael D., Peter L., Richard A., Andrea L. Pres., Morin Landscape Service, Worcester, 1951-56, Landscape Service, Inc., Shrewsbury, Mass., 1956-58; chief supr. Commn. Mass. Div. Employment Security, Boston, 1957—. Pres., Employment Security, Conf., 1972—. Served with USNR, 1943-46. Mem. Internat. Assn. Personnel in Employment Security (pub. relations chmn. Mass. chpt. 1971—, past pres. Mass. chpt.), Am. Soc. Indsl. Security, Boston Gun and Rifle Assn. (instr., chief range master 1977—), N.E. Aquarium Socs., Inc. (pub. relations chmn. 1968-70). Club: Worcester Aquarium (pres. 1966-67, dir. 1962-71). Editor, asso. Worcester Aquarist, 1960-72; editor N.E. Council News, 1968-70, The Minuteman, 1971—. Home: 63 Glencliff Rd Roslindale MA 02131 Office: CF Hurley Employment Security Bldg Govt Center Boston MA 02114

MORIN, RAYMOND GERALD, music critic, editor; b. Fitchburg, Mass., Dec. 28, 1910; s. Francis Xavier and Anna (Cauchon) M.; student New Eng. Conservatory Music, 1927-28, Inst. Mus. Art, N.Y.C., 1929; Mus.B., U. Mich., 1932; L.H.D., Anna Maria Coll., 1969; Mus.D. (hon.), Assumption Coll., 1974; D.F.A., Central New Eng. Coll. Tech., 1975. Appearances in concerts and radio, East, Middle West, Can.; music critic Worcester (Mass.) Telegram, 1940-75; music commentator Sts. WTAG, Worcester, 1952-61; head music dept. Beeker Jr. Coll., 1941-72; faculty St. Gabriel Sch. Music, 1953-64, U. Lowell (Mass.) Grad. Sch., 1978—. Mem. program coms. for various civic activities. Trustee (with Boston Safe Deposit & Trust Co.) Susan Glover Hitchcock Fund, Young Artists Awards. Served with USAAF, 1942. Mem. Am. Guild Organists, Worcester County Mus. Assn. (hon.), Phi Eta Sigma. Editor: Critics Criteria, 1959-63. Contbr. various articles to N.Y. Herald Tribune, Phila. Inquirer, Etude, Mus. Digest, other popular mags. Home: 45 West Hill Dr Worcester MA 01609 Office: 20 Franklin St Worcester MA 01601

MORISSETTE, GUY JEAN, orthopedic surgeon; b. Mont-Joli, Que., Can., Mar. 14, 1929; s. Xavier Joseph and Gertrude (LaFrance) M.; B.A., U. Ottawa 1951, M.D., 1955; m. Madeleine Charbonneau, Aug. 6, 1955; children—Guy, Andree, Elaine, Carole, Michel. Intern, Ottawa Gen. Hosp., Columbus, Ohio, 1955-56; resident in orthopedic surgery, 1956-59; resident in orthopedic surgery Shriner's Hosp., Montreal, Que., 1959-60; practice medicine specializing in orthopedic surgery Hull, Que., 1960—; chief staff Sacred Heart Hosp., Hull, 1971—; prof. orthopedic surgery U. Que.; co-owner Hull Festivals Jr. B. Hockey Team, 1975—; founder, pres. Outaouais Jr. Hockey League, 1976—; rep. Outaouais to Que. Ice Hockey Fedn., 1975—, also provincial sec.; pres. Hull Olympics Hockey Club; mem. provincial appeal com. Que. Ice Hockey Fedn.; Que. rep. for jr. hockey Canadian Amateur Hockey Assn. Pres. Hull Crippled Children Soc., 1964-70; pres. Legal Aid Commn. Outaouais Region, Commn. Inquiry on Welfare People; mem. Outaouais a L'Urgence. Recipient Julien-Daoust: Sportsman of Year trophy, 1977; Queen Elizabeth II medal. Licenciate Med. Council Can., certified specialist Que. Mem. Can. Assn. Sports Medicine, Canadian Orthopaedic Assn., other orgns. Club: Seignory (Montbello, Que.). Home: 22 Thibault St Hull PQ J9A 1H3 Canada Office: 4 Taschereau Hull PQ J7A 1H3 Canada

MORITZ, DONALD IRWIN, utility exec.; b. McKeesport, Pa., Oct. 23, 1927; s. Maurice Louis and Rose (Klein) M.; B.S., U. Pitts., 1948, J.D., 1951; m. Janet Papernick, Nov. 9, 1952; children—Paula, Laurie, J. Kenneth. Admitted to Pa. bar, 1952; with Equitable Gas Co. and subs.'s, 1952—, asst. to pres., 1967-72, exec. v.p., 1972-77, pres., 1977—, chief exec. officer, 1978—, also dir.; dir. subs.'s Equitable Gas-Energy Co., Pitts., Ky. W.Va. Gas Co., Ashland, Ky., Ky. Hydrocarbon Co., Maytown, Phila. Oil Co., Berea Gathering Co.; trustee Inst. Gas Tech. Mem. Versailles Twp. Sch. Bd. (now McKeesport Area Sch. Bd.), 1965-66; bd. dirs. Congregation Tree of Life, McKeesport, pres., 1967-69. Mem. Am., Pa. (pres., dir.) gas assns., Pa., Allegheny County bar assns., Pitts. C. of C., U. Pitts. Law Alumni Assn., Order of Coif, Tau Epsilon Rho, Phi Eta Sigma, Beta Gamma Sigma. Republican. Jewish. Clubs: B'nai B'rith; Pitts. Athletic Assn.; Pitts. Press. Home: 2004 Monongahela Blvd McKeesport PA 15132 Office: 420 Blvd Allies Pittsburgh PA 15219

MORLINO, MICHAEL ROBERT, cons. engr.; b. Phila., Nov. 29, 1947; s. Michael James and Josephine Rita (Freda) M.; B.S., Drexel U., 1970; M.C.E., Villanova U., 1975; m. Jeanne Carol Landis, Sept. 11, 1971. San. engr. Gannett-Fleming-Corddry & Carpenter Engrs., Inc., Harrisburg, Pa., 1970-73; asst. project engr. Betz Converse Murdoch, Inc., Plymouth Meeting, Pa., 1973, project engr., 1975, sr. engr., 1976, tech. cons. concept devel. and ops. dept., 1978-79; project engr. Frito-Lay, Inc., Irving, Tex., 1979—; adult edn. instr. Pa. Dept. Community Affairs, 1976—. Mem. Lower Providence Twp. Planning Commn., 1977—; mem. citizens adv. council Methacton Sch. Dist., 1978; mem. Pa. Wastewater Adv. com., 1977—. Mem. Water Pollution Control Fedn., Pa. Soc. Profl. Engr., Nat. Soc. Profl. Engrs., Pa. Water Pollution Control Assn., Eastern Pa. Water Pollution Control Operators Assn. (exec. com.), Am. Mgmt. Assn., Nat. Foreman's Inst. Contbr. articles to profl. jours. Home: 3211 Sunset Ave Eagleville PA 19408 Office: PO Box 2231 900 N Loop 12 Irving TX 75060

MORMILE, JUDE MARIE, counselor educator; b. N.Y.C., June 19, 1923; d. Frank Paul and Florence Gertrude (Cocorese) M.; B.S. in Edn., Fordham U., 1962, M.R.E., 1967, M.S. in Counselor Edn., 1972. Tchr. elementary grades Holy Rosary Sch., N.Y.C., 1956-63, asst. prin., 1963-69, guidance counselor, 1969-72; guidance dir. Holy Rosary Acad. N.Y., Union City, 1972-74; counselor educator Harriamn (N.Y.) Coll., 1974—. Recipient various fellowships. Mem. Am. Personnel and Guidance Assn., Nat. Vocat. Guidance Assn., Nat. Cath. Guidance Assn. Roman Catholic. Home and Office: Harriman College Harriman Hts Rd Harriman NY 10926

MORNINGSTAR, ANN SCOTT (MRS. ROBERT P. MORNINGSTAR), pub. relations exec.; b. Huntington, W.Va.; d. Paul W. and Pearl (McNeill) Scott; A.B., Ohio State U., 1932; M.A., W.Va. U., 1936; m. Robert P. Morningstar, Nov. 15, 1946. First v.p. Phoenix News Bur., Inc., 1946-50; founder, owner, Morningstar Prodns., Inc., N.Y.C., 1951—. Bd. dirs. Community Chest, Huntington, W.Va., 1938-39, Jr. League, 1932—, Huntington Horse Show, 1938-43. Pres. W.Va. Fedn. Women's Rep. Clubs, 1939-40. Recipient Kappa Kappa Gamma Alumnae Achievement award, 1958. Mem. Am. Women in Radio and Television, Pub. Relations Soc. Am., Nat. Fedn. Women's Rep. Clubs (v.p. 1940-41), Women in Communications, Kappa Kappa Gamma (chmn. pub. relations com. 1954-74), Phi Beta Kappa. Home: Friendly Acres Milford PA 18337 Office: 52 E 41st St New York City NY 10017

MORRELL, WAYNE BEAM, JR., artist; b. Clementon, N.J., Dec. 24, 1923; s. Wayne Beam and Martha L. (Plack) M.; grad. Lincoln Prep. Sch.; student Drexel Inst., Phila. Sch. Indsl. Art.; grad. Famous Artist Sch., Westport, Conn.; m. Lillian Eunice Major, July 14, 1952; children—David Wayne (dec.), Lisa Anne. Exhibited one-man show Washington County Art Mus., Hagerstown, Md., 1973; exhibited nat. group shows including NAD, Conn. Acad. Fine Arts, Wadsworth Atheneum, Addison Gallery Am. Art, Mus. Fine Arts, Columbus, Ga., New Britain Mus., Smithsonian Inst., Expn. Intercontinental, Monoco, France; indsl. exhibitor, designer John Oldham Studios, 1955-58, art dir., 1958-61; designer Paris and Brussells Worlds Fairs, other maj. exhibits; designer cover Reader's Digest, 1967. Served with AUS, 1949-52. Recipient Louis Seley purchase award; Gold medal Jordan Marsh, Boston; award Council Am. Art Socs., 1971; Carelli Gold Medal award Academic Artists Assn., 1974; others. Mem. Allied Artists Am. (Jane Peterson award 1969, 74), Am. Artists Profl. League, Am. Vet. Soc. Artists, Springfield Acad. Fine Arts, Rockport Art Assn. (Gold medal honor), Guild Boston Artists, North Shore Art Assn., New Eng. Artist Group, Grand Central Art Galleries, Newman Galleries Phila. Club: Salmagundi (Gwynne Lennon prize 1971, Phillip J. Ross award 1971, 1st hon. mention 1971). Home: 153 Main

St Rockport MA 01966 Office: Wayne Morrell Gallery 153 Upper Main St Rockport MA 01966

MORRILL, WILLIAM FRANK, lawyer; b. N.Y.C., Sept. 20, 1938; s. Albert Harrison and Eleanor (Tench) M.; B.A., Cornell U., 1960; J.D., Columbia U., 1966; m. Mary Sue Robinson, Aug. 31, 1963. Mgmt. trainee Morrill & Morrill, N.Y.C., 1961-63; admitted to N.Y. bar, 1967, Conn. bar, 1972; staff atty. IBM Corp., Armonk, N.Y. and Princeton, N.J., 1966-70; exec. dir., counsel Berkshire-Litchfield Environ. Council, Lakeville, Conn., 1970—; legal counsel environment com. Conn. Gen. Assembly, Hartford, 1974-76; individual practice law, Lakeville, 1973-76, 78—; partner firm Wagner, Morrill & Yoakum, Lakeville, 1976-77. Bd. dirs., corporate sec. Salisbury (Conn.) Village Housing, Inc., 1974-77; alt. Salisbury Planning and Zoning Commn., 1973—; mem. Salisbury Forest and Park Commn., 1973—; Mem. adv. com. Conn. Solar Energy Alliance, 1978—; mem. adv. com. N.E. Energy Congress, 1978—. Served with USMC, 1960-61. Mem. Conn., Litchfield County bar assns., Conservation Law Found. New Eng. (dir. 1976—), Salisbury Taxpayers Assn. (trustee 1976-78), Sierra Club (exec. com. S. N.J. group 1968-70, Conn. chpt. 1973-75), Appalachian Mountain Club (conservation com. 1971-73), Housatonic Audubon Soc. (dir. 1972-76, 77—). Club: Rotary. Home: Belgo Rd Lakeville CT 06039 Office: Belgo Rd Lakeville CT 06039

MORRIS, BERNARD NEWTH, clergyman; b. Phila., Nov. 11, 1919; s. George Newth and Virginia (Calahoun) M.; A.B., Eastern Baptist Coll., St. Davids, Pa., 1943; S.T.B., Temple U., Phila., 1953, S.T.M., 1973; m. Lorraine Louise Weiderhold, June 7, 1941; children—Faith Ann, Bernard Newth, Hope Louise, Grace Miriam. Ordained to ministry Am. Bapt. Ch., 1943; pastor chs. in Pa., 1947-53; chaplain USN, 1953-61; pastor 1st Bapt. Ch., Schenectady, 1961-70, Pine City Bapt. Ch., 1970-73; with coop. extension Cornell U., 1973-77; adminstr. Bapt. Retirement Center, Scotia, N.Y., 1977—; vis. faculty div. continuing edn. Elmira (N.Y.) Coll. Vice chmn. Human Service Com. Southerntier; mem. N.Y. State Central Regional Planning and Devel. Com. Mem. Am. Coll. Nursing Home Adminstrs. Author: (poetry) Harmony of Words, 1965, Harmony of Truth, 1972, Harmony of Sermons, 1973, Harmony of Hope, 1974. Home: Box 202 RD 1 Rock Stream NY 14878 Office: 297 N Ballston Ave Scotia NY 12302

MORRIS, CALVIN MILYARD, ins. co. exec.; b. Salida, Colo., Oct. 21, 1934; s. Charles Lee and Margaret Naomi (Milyard) M.; B.A., Beloit Coll., 1953-57; M.Ed., U. Va., 1969, E.Ed., 1974; student Naval Intelligence Sch., 1968-61, Command, Staff Coll., 1968-69; m. Karen Lynn Hansen, Sept. 8, 1956; children—Diane, Calvin, Scott, James. Commd. 2d lt. U.S. Marine Corps, 1957, advanced through grades to lt. col., 1974; head academics Marine Corps Officer Candidate Sch., 1966-68; chief analyst N. Vietnam, China desk U.S. Mil. Asst. Command, Vietnam, 1969-70; asso. prof. naval sci. dept. U. Va., 1970-74; dir. Instructional Mgmt. Sch. Marine Corps Edn. Center, Quantico, 1974-77; ret., 1977; head human resources devel. div. Met. Property and Liability Ins. Co., Warwick, R.I., 1977—. Decorated Bronze Star, Purple Heart. Mem. Nat. Profl. Edn. Soc., Am. Personnel and Guidance Assn., Am. Soc. Tng. and Devel., Phi Delta Kappa, Kappa Delta Pi. Office: 700 Quaker Ln PO Box 350 Warwick RI 02887*

MORRIS, CAROLINE JANE MCMASTERS STEWART (MRS. FRANCIS J. MORRIS), librarian; b. Ridley Park, Pa., Sept. 14, 1923; d. James Sterrett and Mildred M. (McCloskey) Stewart; B.S. in Commerce, Drexel U., 1950; M.S. in L.S., 1964; m. Francis Joseph Morris, Feb. 3, 1950; 1 son, Edward James Stewart. Adminstrv. trainee John Wanamaker, Phila., 1946-50; serials librarian Penn Morton Colls., Chester, Pa., 1964-65; dir. libraries Pa. Hosp., Phila., 1965—; instr., leader several library workshops Am. Hosp. Assn., Cath. Hosp. Assn., Med. Library Assn. Mem. Emergency Aid Pa., 1960—. Served with WAVES, 1943-45. Mem. Nat. Med. Library Assn. (sect. chmn. 1970), ALA, Spl. Libraries Assn. (nat. chmn. biol. scis. div.), Med. (local chpt. pres. 1969-70), Prospect Park library assns., AAUP, D. of R. (pres. Pa. chpt. 1947—), Victorian Soc. Am., Delaware County Hist. Soc., Historic Delaware County, Valley Forge Hist. Soc., Geneal. Soc. Pa., Hort. Soc. Pa., Dames Loyal Legion (state pres. 1966-68), Phila. Mus. Art, Inst. Contemporary Art, Drexel U. Alumni Assn. (pres. 1969-71). Club: Art Alliance (Phila.). Home: 555 13th Ave Prospect Park PA 19076 Office: 8th and Spruce Sts Philadelphia PA 19107

MORRIS, DAVID MARK, acct.; b. Ellwood City, Pa., Jan. 13, 1949; s. William Leroy and Janice Faye (Strutt) M.; B.S. in Mech. Engring., Case Inst. Tech., 1970; M.B.A., U. Mich., 1972; m. Mary Elaine Norton, Dec. 30, 1972. Staff acct. Price Waterhouse & Co., N.Y.C., 1972-75, sr. acct., 1975-78, audit mgr., 1978—. C.P.A., N.Y. Mem. Am. Inst. C.P.A.'s, N.Y. State Soc. C.P.A.'s, Am. Acctg. Assn., Am. Mgmt. Assn., Sigma Alpha Epsilon. Presbyterian. Club: N.Y. Athletic. Home: 1060 Park Ave Apt 4G New York NY 10028 Office: 153 E 53d St New York NY 10022

MORRIS, DONALD ARTHUR, ophthalmologist, educator; b. N.Y.C., Oct. 24, 1934; s. Robert I. and Betty C. (Greenberg) M.; A.B. summa cum laude, Columbia, 1956; M.D., N.Y. U., 1960; m. Anne Marie Pierré, June 26, 1968; children—Alexander Paul, Stephanie Marie-Fleur. Intern, Mt. Sinai Hosp., N.Y.C., 1960-61; resident in ophthalmology N.Y. U. Coll. Medicine, N.Y.C. 1964-67, fellow ophthalmic pathology, 1967-68, dir. ophthalmic pathology, clin. asst. prof. ophthalmology 1971-73; dir. ophthalmology Morrisania Hosp., 1973-76; asst. clin. prof. ophthalmology Albert Einstein Coll. Medicine, N.Y.C., 1973-78, asso. clin. prof. ophthalmology, 1978—; dir. ophthalmology North Central Bronx Hosp., 1976—; asso. attending surgeon Univ. Hosp., 1968-73, N.Y. Eye and Ear Infirmary, Montefiore Hosp. Served with U.S. Army, 1962-64. Diplomate Am. Bd. Ophthalmology. Fellow ACS, Am. Acad Ophthalmology and Otolaryngology; mem. AMA, N.Y. State, N.Y. County med. socs., Am. Soc. for Contemporary Ophthalmology, Am. Intra-Ocular Lens Soc., N.Y. Soc. Clin. Ophthalmology, N.Y. Ophthal. Soc., Ophthal. Soc. U.K., Phi Beta Kappa. Contbr. articles to ophthal. jours. Office: 104 E 40th St New York City NY 10016

MORRIS, EDWARD LAURENCE, JR., educator; b. Lowell, Mass., Oct. 10, 1944; s. Edward Laurence and Marie Denyse (Reardon) M.; B.A. in English, St. Anselm's Coll., 1966; M.A., Assumption Coll., 1972; postgrad. U. Mass., 1971-73; J.D., Suffolk U. Law Sch., 1976; m. Joanne Mulligan, June 17, 1967; children—Jonalyn Patricia, Bethany Denise, Edward Laurence. Tchr. secondary sch. Greater Lowell Regional Vocat. Sch., 1974—; atty. Mem. Lowell Planning Bd., 1972—, No. Middlesex Area Commn., 1974—. Mem. Greater Lowell Tchrs. Orgn. (exec. bd. 1974—), Lowell Tchrs. Orgn. (exec. bd. 1969-74). Roman Catholic. Democrat. Home: 124 Wentworth Ave Lowell MA 01852 Office: Greater Lowell Regional Vocat Tech Sch Tyngsboro MA 01879

MORRIS, ERNEST BROUGHAM, lawyer; b. Rensselaer, N.Y., May 11, 1908; s. John W. and Minnie (Brougham) M.; A.B., Union Coll., 1928; J.D., Albany Law Sch., 1931, LL.D., 1971; m.; children—Alice (Mrs. Karl H. Schrade), Robert, David; m, 2d, Barbara Middaugh, Aug. 26, 1961. Admitted to N.Y. bar, 1932; practiced in Albany, N.Y., 1932-65; spl. counsel N.Y. State Tax Commn., 1943-45; dep. atty. gen. N.Y., 1944; dist. atty. Albany County, 1944; dir. Adirondack Trust Co. Chmn. bd. Saratoga Harness Racing. Trustee Saratoga Performing Arts Center; trustee Hall Fame Trotter, Grayson Found. trustee, past pres. Albany Law Sch.; past pres. bd. govs. Union U.; trustee emeritus Albany Med. Coll. Mem. Saratoga County Bar Assn., U.S. (dir.), Internat. (pres. 1977—) trotting assns. Republican. Presbyterian. Clubs: Fort Orange; Saratoga Golf. Address: PO Box 356 Saratoga Springs NY 12866

MORRIS, HARVEY SETH, clin. psychologist; b. Bklyn., Apr. 29, 1943; s. Sam and Sylvia (Bachman) M.; B.A., Queens Coll., 1965; Ph.D. (NIMH fellow), U. Nebr., 1970; children—Amanda, Brooke, Matthew. Instr., U. Nebr., Lincoln, 1969; intern Columbia-Presbyn. Med. Center, N.Y.C., 1969-70; supervising psychologist Coney Island Hosp., N.Y.C., 1970-74; dir. Psychol. Inst., N.Y.C., 1972—; pvt. practice clin. psychology, N.Y.C., 1972—. Psychol. cons., N.Y.C., 1972—. Bd. dirs. Paraprofl. Tng. Inst. for Social Services, N.Y.C., 1973—. Mem. Am., Westchester County, Bklyn. psychol. assns., AAAS. Office: 40 E 89th St New York NY 10028

MORRIS, J(OSEPH) ANTHONY, govt. ofcl.; b. nr. Marboro, Md., Sept. 6, 1918; s. Charles Lafayette and Essie (Stokes) M.; B.S., Cath. U. Am., 1940, M.S., 1942, Ph.D., 1947; m. Ruth Savoy, Nov. 1, 1942; children—Carol Ann, Marilyn T., Joseph A., Larry A. Asst. scientist Josiah Macy, Jr. Found., N.Y.C., 1943-44; virologist, Depts. Agr., Interior, Laurel, Md., 1944-47; virologist, chief hepatitis virus research Walter Reed Army Inst. Research, Washington, 1947-56; virologist, asst. chief, dept. virus and rickettsial diseases U.S. Army Med. Command, Japan, 1956-59; virologist chief sect. respiratory viruses, div. biologics standards NIH, Bethesda, Md., 1959—, dir. slow, latent and temperate virus br. FDA, Bethesda, 1972—. Cons., Commn. on Influenza, Armed Forces Epidemiologic Bd., 1960—; Nat. Inst. Neurol. Diseases and Blindness, 1962—. Mem. Soc. Tropical Medicine and Hygiene, Soc. Am. Microbiologists, Soc. Exptl. Biology and Medicine, Am. Assn. Immunologists, N.Y. Acad. Sci. Discoverer of respiratory sycytial virus; research on infectious hepatitis, respiratory diseases of virus etiology and zoonosis. Home: 23-E Ridge Rd Greenbelt MD 20770 Office: NIH Campus Bethesda MD 20014

MORRIS, JAMES STEPHEN, psychologist; b. N.Y.C., July 15, 1940; s. George Richard and Marie Teresa (Lynch) M.; B.A., Fordham U., 1962; Ph.D. in Psychology (Research fellow), Cornell U., 1966; m. Kathleen P. Caulfield, Aug. 19, 1961; children—Joan, Veronica, Catherine. Mgr., Riverside Research Inst., N.Y.C., 1971-72, McKinsey & Co., N.Y.C., 1972-76; dir. Orgn. & Mgmt. Resources, Indian Head, N.Y., 1976-78; v.p. Profl. Examination Service, N.Y.C., 1970-71, Drake-Beam & Assos., N.Y.C., 1978—; instr. Cornell U., Ohio State U., U. Md.; cons. State Dept., Dept. Defense. Cons. United Way of Am., Assn. of Jr. Leagues. Served to capt. U.S. Army, 1966-68. Decorated Bronze Star, Vietnamese Medal of Honor; recipient certificate of appreciation Office of Sec. of Defense, 1969; N.Y. State fellow, 1962-64. Mem. Met. N.Y. Assn. for Applied Psychology, Am. Psychol. Assn., Am. Soc. Tng. and Devel., Orgn. Devel. Network, N.Y. Personnel Mgrs. Assn., Sigma Xi. Contbr. articles in field to profl. jours. Home: 350 E Pine St Long Beach NY 11561 Office: 277 Park Ave New York City NY 10017

MORRIS, JILL CARLOTTA, phychotherapist; b. N.Y.C., June 25, 1931; d. Joseph J. and Della P. M.; student Goucher Coll., 1952-56; B.A., N.Y. U., 1957, M.A., 1958; postgrad. Center for Modern Psychoanalytic Studies, 1973—, Calif. Grad. Inst., 1976—. Asst. editor, writer Mademoiselle mag., N.Y.C., 1956-59; asso. editor, writer Camera 35 mag., N.Y.C., 1959-61; features editor, feature writer U.S. Camera mag., N.Y.C., 1961-65; asso. editor, feature writer Steelways mag., N.Y.C., 1966-68; psychotherapist, N.Y.C., 1976—; co-founder Washington Sq. W. Assos., psychotherapy group, N.Y.C., 1977—; exhibited art one-woman shows: Hudson Park Library, N.Y.C., 1973, D'Lower Gallery, N.Y.C., 1971, group shows including Lincoln Center shows, N.Y.C., 1975. Sinclair scholar art, 1965. Mem. Joint Council Mental Health Services, Nat. Accreditation Assn. Psychoanalysis, Am. Personnel and Guidance Assn., Women's Mus. Group. Author: Time and Timelessness in Virginia Woolf, 1977; contbr. feature articles, profiles on celebrities and photographers to newspapers and nat. mags., including Pageant, Image, Scholastic Roto.

MORRIS, JOHN EDWARD, lawyer; b. N.Y.C., Sept. 30, 1916; s. John and Honora C. (Long) M.; A.B., Coll. City N.Y., 1937; A.M., Columbia, 1938; LL.B., Harvard, 1942; m. Patricia E. Grojean, Oct. 14, 1943. Admitted to N.Y. bar; asso. Clarke & Reilly, N.Y.C., 1946-50; pvt. practice, N.Y.C., 1950—; def. trial atty. Meml. Hosp., N.Y.C. Active St. Labre (Mont.) Indian Sch., 1960—. Served to lt. USCGR, 1942-46. Mem. New York County Lawyers Assn., Am. Bar Assn., Internat. Assn. Ins. Counsel. Roman Catholic. Clubs: N.Y. Athletic, Harvard, N.Y. Athletic (N.Y.C.); Great Dane of Am. Home: 9 Meadowlark Dr West Nyack NY 10994 Office: 233 Broadway New York City NY 10007

MORRIS, JOSEPH PAUL, JR., free lance agt.; b. Phila., Dec. 27, 1922; s. Joseph Paul and Emma (Montgomery) M.; student Haverford Coll., 1941-42, 46, 49; m. Rebecca Polk Darnall, Apr. 16, 1955; children—Sarah, Martha. Pvt. studies, writing in fgn. affairs, 1951—; free-lance agt. fgn., domestic industry, 1958—. Mem. 1st troop Phila. City Cavalry, 1948-50; active Heart Fund drives, Haverford, Pa., 1954-59, Am. Fund for Westminster Abbey, Phila., 1954; treas. Episcopal Cooperating Com., 1967-72; guarantor Bach Choir of Bethlehem, 1957—. Bd. dirs. Chinese Christian Ch. and Center, 1968-72. Vol. ambulance driver Brit. Army, Am. Field Service, Middle East and Italy, 1943-45. Decorated Africa Star, Italy Star, Victory Medal (Eng.). Mem. Hist. Soc. Pa., Welcome Soc., Colonial Soc. Pa., S.R., Pa. Soc., Zool. Soc. Phila., Navy League U.S., Atheneaum of Phila., C.C. Morris Cricket Library Assn., Cricket Soc. London (hon.), Friends of Independence Nat. Hist. Park, Friends of Wyck, Mil. Order Fgn. Wars U.S. Republican. Episcopalian. Mem. publs. com. Morris Family of Phila., 1957—. Address: PO Box 218 Ambler PA 19002

MORRIS, KENNETH BAKER, banker; b. Bklyn., Feb. 12, 1922; s. Clarence E. and Mabel (Baker) M.; student bus. adminstrn. Manhattan Coll., 1940-43, B.C.E., 1949; postgrad. Inst. Design, 1959-62; m. Dorothy E. Kohler, Sept. 3, 1960; children—Laura Susan, Sandra Lee. Asst. to pres., chief engr. Kretzer Constrn. Corp., N.Y.C., 1956-58; cons. engr. Kenneth B. Morris P.E., N.Y.C., Augusta, Ga., 1958-61; dir. plant and properties N.Y. U., 1961-66, bus. mgr., 1966-68; v.p. Cooper Union Univ., N.Y.C., 1968-74; v.p. East River Savs. Bank, N.Y.C., 1974—. Pres., bd. dirs. Grammercy Greenwich Corp., N.Y.C.; bd. dirs. Wash. Sq. S.E. Served with USAAF, 1943-45. Registered profl. engr., N.Y., N.J., Conn., Pa., Mass., Ga., Can.; lic. profl. planner, N.J. Mem. N.Y. Real Estate Bd. (city planning com., edn. com., internat. real estate com., taxes and assessments com.), N.Y. State Soc. Real Estate Appraisers, A.I.M., N.Y.C.'s East Side C. of C. (chmn. bd.), Am. Soc. Appraisers, N.Y. State C. of C. (edn. com.). Contbr. articles to newspapers and mags. Home: 38 Cedar Dr W Briarcliff Manor NY 10510 Office: East River Savs Banks Exec Offices 26 Cortlandt St New York City NY 10007

MORRIS, PATRICIA JOSEPHINE COLLINS (MRS. JOHN F. MORRIS), educator; b. Mpls., Jan. 15, 1912; d. Patrick and Kathryn (Hennessy) Collins; B.S., U. Minn., 1933, M.A., 1941; Ed.D., Temple U., 1960; m. John F. Morris, Dec. 21, 1951. Asst. prof. phys. edn. Temple U., Phila., 1938-52; tchr. Springside Sch., Chestnut Hill, Pa., 1953-57; asso. prof. phys. edn. Trenton (N.J.) State Coll., 1961-71, prof., 1971-76, prof. emeritus, 1976—. Recipient Honor award N.J. Assn. Health, Phys. Edn. and Recreation. Fellow Am. Coll. Sports Medicine; mem. Am. Assn. Coll. Women Tchrs. Phys. Edn., AAHPER, N.J. Edn. Assn., AAUP, Psi Chi, Delta Psi Kappa (service pin 1960), Sigma Kappa. Research on somatotypes and body structure. Home: Box 154 Croydon PA 19020 Office: Packer Hall Trenton State Coll Trenton NJ 08625

MORRIS, RICHARD COOK, JR., educator; b. Swedesboro, N.J., Feb. 10, 1945; s. Richard Cook and Blanche (Trullender) M.; A.B., Glassboro State Coll., 1968, M.A., 1976. Tchr. sixth grade, Upper Pittsgrove Sch., Monroeville, N.J., 1968-76, tchr. gifted edn. program, 1976—. Camping chmn. Beaver Dist. Boy Scouts Am.; trustee Salem County Juveniles in Need of Supervision Center; mem. Salem County Hist. Soc. Recipient Silver Stag award Boy Scouts Am., 1974, Order of Arrow, 1975, Award of Merit, 1974, Silver Beaver, 1975; N.J. Dept. Edn. grantee, 1974-75, 77-78. Mem. Upper Pittsgrove (v.p.), Salem County, N.J. edn. assns., NEA. Methodist. Club: Order of Arrow (Apatukwe Lodge 107). Home: Route 1 Alloway Rd Salem NJ 08079

MORRIS, RICHARD JULES, physician, clin. dir.; b. Atlantic City, N.J., Sept. 9, 1930; s. Maurice and Rose E. Morris; A.B., Temple U., 1951, M.D., 1955; m. Cecily Gusman, July 29, 1956; children—Stacy Jill, Meredith, Debra Sue. Intern, Chester (Pa.) Hosp., 1955-56; gen. practice family medicine, Chester, 1958—; preceptor family practice Hahnemann Med. Coll., Phila., 1975—; active staff Crozer-Chester Med. Center, 1958—; courtesy staff Sacred Heart Hosp., Riddle Meml. Hosp.; med. dir. Chester Extended Care Center, 1976—. Served with M.C., USAF, 1956-58. Diplomate Am. Bd. Family Practice. Mem. Med. Surg. Assn. So. Delaware County (Pa.) (med. dir.), Am., Pa. acads. family practice. Republican. Jewish. Home: 301 Colonial Dr Wallingford PA 19086 Office: 2304 Edgmont Ave Chester PA 19013

MORRIS, ROGER RAY, chem. co. exec.; b. Aaron's Fork, W.Va., June 2, 1943; s. Charles Sinnett and Mary Elizabeth (Pauley) M.; B.A., Morris Harvey Coll., 1966; M.S., U. Ill., 1967; m. Lowella Laverne Alford, Jan. 14, 1966. Supplement editor Charleston (W.Va.) Gazette, 1964-66; instr. mass communications Ariz. State U., Tempe, 1967-70; asst. dir. pub. relations George Washington U., Washington, 1970-72; rep., editor in pub. relations DuPont Co., Wilmington, Del., 1972—; lectr. English and enology U. Del.; mem. adv. bd. Del. Today. Del. publicity chmn. United Way, 1974. Recipient awards Edn. Press Assn. Am., 1972, 74. Mem. Am. Soc. Journalists and Authors, Internat. Assn. Bus. Communicators (Gold Quill award 1975, 78), Del. Writers Group (founder). Democrat. Contbr. to profl. jours., also New Republic, TV Guide, Parents; wine columnist Washington Star. Home: 900 Pickett Ln Newark DE 19711 Office: 1007 Market St Wilmington DE 19898

MORRIS, TERRY LESSER (MRS. EUGENE J. MORRIS), writer; b. N.Y.C., Feb. 19, 1914; d. Samuel and Lena (Weissmann) Lesser; B.A., Hunter Coll., 1933, M.A., 1937; m. Eugene J. Morris, Mar. 29, 1934; 1 son, Richard Samuel. Tchr. English, N.Y.C. High Schs., 1937-43; feature writer Battle Creek (Mich.) Enquirer and News, 1943-44; writer, producer radio series WKZO, Kalamazoo, 1944-45; writer short stories, mag., articles for publs. including McCall's, Good Housekeeping, Woman's Home Companion, Cosmopolitan, Family Weekly, Life, New Republic, Redbook, Saga, This Week, Family Circle, Reader's Digest, 1945—. Lectr. mag. article writing N.Y. U., 1958-59; guest lectr. mag. article writing New Sch. Social Research, N.Y.C., 1960-61; lectr. Queens Coll., Bklyn., 1966-67. Recipient Blakeslee award for mag. article Am. Heart Assn., 1964. Mem. Am. Soc. Journalists and Authors (v.p. 1961, chmn. 1968, exec. council 1968-71, chmn. membership com. 1973-74, pres. 1974-75). Author: No Hiding Place, 1945; Cross Section (short story anthology), 1947; Strange Desires (short story anthology), 1954. Editor, contbr.: Prose by Professionals, 1961; Dr. America: The Story of Tom Dooley, 1963; Shalom, Golda, 1971; A New You: How Plastic Surgery Can Change Your Life, 1977. Address: 200 Central Park S New York City NY 10019

MORRIS, THOMAS JEFFERSON, ret. judge; b. Pearson, Ga., Apr. 17, 1910; s. John Warren and Mary Frances (Lipsey) M.; B.A., Rollins Coll., 1929-33; LL.B., Yale, 1933-36; m. Elizabeth Adele Currier, Dec. 29, 1934; children—Anne D., Mary D., Eleanor C., Richard C., Elizabeth W. Admitted to N.H. bar, 1937; pvt. practice law, Portsmouth, N.H., 1937-57; judge Rye (N.H.) Municipal Ct., 1955-57; asso. justice N.H. Superior Ct., 1957-75, ret., 1975. Instr., asst. to pres. Stoneleigh Coll., Rye Beach, N.H., 1936-43; County solicitor Rockingham County, N.H., 1951-52. Served from lt. (j.g.) to lt. USNR, 1943-46. Mem. Internat., Inter-Am., Am., N.H., Rockingham County bar assns., Am. Judicature Soc. Home: 11 Washington Rd Rye NH 03870

MORRISON, A.H., assn. exec.; b. North Little Rock, Ark., July 8, 1916; s. Alph and Emma (Smith) M.; B.A., U. Tenn., 1938; Engaged in fed. law enforcement, 1939-53; practice astrology, 1954—; exec. sec. Congress Astrological Orgns., N.Y.C., 1973—; founder Overseas Astrologers Club, 1973; tchr., lectr. in field. Served with U.S. Army, 1945-46. Mem. Am. Fedn. Astrologers, Astrological Assn. Gt. Britain, numerous others orgns. Editor, Astrological Rev., 1970; CAO Times quar., 1975—; pub. Void of Course Moon Ephemeris ann., 1970—. Address: Box 75 Old Chelsea Sta New York City NY 10011

MORRISON, CHARLES FREDERICK, hosp. engr.; b. Brunswick, Md., Apr. 1, 1916; s. Frank Thomas and Emma Elizabeth M.; student Mon. 1939. Fireman-engr. B. & O. R.R., 1948-53; safety dir. Washington County (Md.) Dept. Roads, 1954-56; mem. staff Church Home and Hosp., Balt., 1956—, asst. chief engr., 1968, dir. plant ops., 1969—; chmn. engr.'s com. Hosp. Cost Containment, 1970; chmn. engrs. selection com. for group purchasing Hosp. Services and Supply Center, 1971; speaker, cons. in field. Mem. Balt. CSC, 1967, 69. Served with AUS, 1937-44. Recipient certificates and awards in field. Mem. Am. Hosp. Assn., Am. (regional rep. 1972—, pres.-elect 1978), Chesapeake Area (a founder, past pres.) socs. hosp. engring., Am. Inst. Plant Engrs., Royal Soc. Health, Nat. Fire Protection Assn., Environ. Mgmt. Assn. (chpt. pres. 1972-73), Am. Hosp. Assn., Carroll County Kennel Club (past v.p.), Safety Council Md., Fells Point, Washington-Hill improvement assns., Md. Fire Protection Assn. Democrat. Methodist. Club: Paint and Powder. Address: 918 S Wolfe St Baltimore MD 21231

MORRISON, DONALD KEITH, contract food co. exec.; b. Harrisburg, Pa., July 7, 1943; s. Donald E. and Alice L. Gillen) M.; B.S., Pa. State U., 1965, M.S., 1966; m. Marilyn M. Morrison, Feb. 21, 1970; children—Pamela, Donald. Grad. assts. Pa. State U., 1965-66; mgmt. trainee, dir. food service Saga Adminstrv. Co., 1966-67; asst. dir. food services Norwalk Hosp., 1967-69; motel gen. mgr. N.B.O. Industries, Princeton, 1969-71; dir. food services ARA

Service, White Plains, N.Y., 1971-75, dist. mgr., 1975-78; with contract food service div. Marriott. Corp. Vol. fireman; coronary paramedic; trustee Fire Dept., Liverpool, N.Y., 1972-75. Certificate coronary paramedic, N.Y. Mem. Am. Dietetic Assn. (registered dietitian). Am. Hosp. Assn., Pa. Hotel and Restaurant Soc., N.Y. State Fire Police Assn. Home: 5767 Flagflower Pl Columbia MD 21045 Office: 4701 Sangamore Rd Washington DC 20058

MORRISON, DONALD WILLIAM, obstetrician, gynecologist; b. Bklyn., Oct. 2, 1915; s. Armitage and Emily Augusta (Wilson) M.; A.B., Columbia, U., 1937, M.D., 1940; m. Ruth Constance Tiffin, Apr. 4, 1941 (div. 1978); children—Donald A., Bonnie Lynn, Douglas Jay; m. 2d, Diane Helen Flath, May 12, 1978. Intern, Paterson Gen. Hosp., 1940-42; resident Manchester (Conn.) Meml. Hosp., 1945-47, mem. staff, 1949—; resident Jersey City Med. Center, 1947-48; practice medicine specializing in obstetrics and gynecology, Manchester, Conn., 1949—; pres. Drs. Morrison & Walden, P.C., 1976—. Chmn. Manchester Community Coll. Regional Council, 1965-73; pres. Manchester Community Coll. Found., Inc., 1966—. Served with M.C., U.S. Army, 1942-45. Diplomate Am. Bd. Obstetrics and Gynecology. Fellow Am. Coll. Obstetrics and Gynecology; mem. AMA, Am. Soc. Colposcopy and Colpomicroscopy, Conn., Hartford County, Manchester (pres. 1963-64) med. assns., Conn. Soc. Am. Bd. Obstetricians and Gynecologist (pres. 1963-64), Manchester C. of C. Democrat. Home: 39 Florence St Manchester CT 06040 Office: 17 Haynes St Manchester CT 06040

MORRISON, FRANK STROUSS, lawyer; b. Danville, Pa., Feb. 28, 1946; s. James A. and Helen I. (Strouss) M.; B.A., U. Pitts., 1968; J.D., Villanova U., 1971; m. Cheryl Ann Hartman, Apr. 8, 1972; children—Christie Lyn, Julie Ann. Admitted to Pa. bar, 1971; mem. firm Strouss, Morrison & Strouss, Mt. Carmel, Pa., 1971—; solicitor Borough of Mt. Carmel, 1972—; asst. dist. atty. Northumberland County (Pa.), 1976—; adv. bd. 1st Nat. Trust Bank, 1978—. Solicitor, Mt. Carmel Municipal Sewer Authority, 1972—, Mt. Carmel Municipal Recreation Authority, 1972—, Borough of Centralia. Mem. Am., Pa., Northumberland County bar assns., Pa. Dist. Attys. Assn., Pa. Trial Lawyers Assn., Pa. Borough Solicitors Assn., Mt. Carmel C. of C. (v.p. 1976-77). Clubs: Fountain Springs Country, Mt. Carmel Rotary, Elks, K.C. Home: 1 N Walnut St Mount Carmel PA 17851 Office: 202 Guarantee Trust Bldg Mount Carmel PA 17851

MORRISON, HOWARD IRWIN, computer cons. co. exec.; b. Bklyn., Aug. 16, 1929; s. Philip O. and Anne (Eisler) M.; B.A., George Washington U., 1951; m. Barbara May Kraut, Dec. 5, 1959 (dec. Feb. 1967); children—Peter Keith, Scott David; m. 2d, April Keil, Dec. 8, 1968 (div.); 1 dau., Dina Helen; m. 3d, Joyce Simone, June 18, 1977. Research asst. Harvard Research Found., Washington, 1951; statistician U.S. Govt., Washington, 1951-52; buyer Lansburgh's Dept. Store, Washington, 1954-56; economist, adminstr. CEIR, Inc., Washington, 1956-61; pres. Computer Concepts, Inc., Washington, 1961-66; v.p. Computer Applications, Inc., N.Y.C., 1964-68, pres. Information Scis. div., 1968-70, also dir.; pres., chmn. bd. Policy Mgmt. Systems, Inc., 1970-71; chmn. bd. Dewey, Irwin & Co., Inc., N.Y.C., 1970-71; exec. v.p., gen. mgr. Auerbach Pubs., Inc., Phila., 1971-76; pres., dir. ADL Systems Inc., Subsidiary Arthur D. Little, Burlington, Mass., 1976—; chmn. bd. Delphi Assos. Inc., 1976—; dir. Pilgrim Health Applications. Served with USNR, 1952-53. Mem. Assn. for Computing Machinery, Colonials, Am. Newcomen Soc., Phi Epsilon Pi, George Washington U. Alumni Assn. Democrat. Home: 227 Mossman Rd Sudbury MA 01776 Office: 10 New Eng Exec Park Burlington MA 01803

MORRISON, IAN ALASTAIR, educator; b. Glasgow, Scotland, Apr. 22, 1924; s. William John and Alexandrina (Smith) M.; came to U.S., 1932, naturalized, 1937; B.A. (Grad. fellow 1948), Wagner Coll., S.I., N.Y., 1948, L.H.D., 1968; M.A., Columbia, 1950, M.S., 1958, Ed.D., 1961; D.H.L., Bard Coll., 1968; m. Naida Brown, Apr. 19, 1946; children—Craig William, Sheila Elise. Asso. prof. history, dean students Wagner Coll., 1949-56; exec. Inter Royal Corp., N.Y.C., 1956-57; exec. sec. Greer Sch., Millbrook, N.Y., 1958-61, exec. dir., 1961-72; pres. Greer-Woodycrest Children's Service, N.Y.C., 1972—; pub. Residential Group Care quar.; dir. Bank of Millbrook. Pres. Eastchester (N.Y.) Bd. Edn., 1962-66, Unionvale (N.Y.) Bd. Edn., 1969—; mem. advisory council Dutchess County Coll. Served with AUS, World War II; ETO. Decorated Purple Heart (2). Mem. N.Y. State Assn. Child Care Agencies (pres. 1969), N.Y. State Assn. Children's Inst. (chmn. edn. com. 1961-68, pres. 1968), Nat. Assn. Homes for Children (dir. 1975—, pres. 1977-78, chmn. pub. affairs com. 1975, 76-78, author code of ethics), Child Welfare League Am., Fgn. Policy Assn., St. Andrews Soc., Nat. Assn. Homes for Children, Nat. Assn. Fundraisers, Aircraft Owners and Pilots Assn. Democrat. Clubs: Union League (N.Y.C.); Shenerock Shore; Millbrook Golf and Tennis; Binghamton (N.Y.); Bradenton (Fla.) Yacht. Author: Higher Education in World War II, 1950; American Political Parties: Political Science Handbook, 1953; Foster Care in the United States, 1975; also articles. Address: Hope Farm Millbrook NY 12545

MORRISON, JAMES WILLIAM, JR., govt. ofcl.; b. Bluefield, W.Va., Jan. 14, 1936; s. James William and Winnie Ella (Hendricks) M.; B.A., W.Va. State Coll., 1957; M.P.A., U. Dayton (Ohio), 1970; m. Marva Elizabeth Tillman, Aug. 8, 1957; children—Traquita Renee, James William. Inventory mgr. Dayton Air Force Depot/Def. Electronics Supply Center, 1959-63; mgmt. specialist Air Force Logistics Command, Dayton, 1963-72; exec. asst. to dir. mgmt. systems NASA, Washington, 1972-74; sr. mgmt. asso. Exec. Office of Pres., Office Mgmt. and Budget, 1974—; vis. lectr. pub. exec. project State U. N.Y., Albany, 1974-76. Mem. adv. com. Dayton Bd. Edn., 1971. Served to 1st lt. U.S. Army, 1957-59. Recipient Sustained Superior Performance award Def. Supply Agy., 1963; Exceptional Service award Exec. Office Pres., Office Mgmt. and Budget, 1977; Distinguished Service award U.S. CSC, 1978. Mem. Alpha Phi Alpha, Pi Delta Phi, Pi Alpha Alpha. Democrat. Presbyterian. Contbr. articles to profl. jours. Home: 5634 Gulf Stream Row Columbia MD 21044 Office: New Exec Office Bldg Washington DC 20503

MORRISON, JEFFREY STEVEN, chem. engr.; b. Bronx, N.Y., Mar. 23, 1947; s. Milton and Ruth (Shay) M.; B.S., Columbia U., 1968, M.S., 1970; M.B.A., Fairleigh Dickinson U., 1979; m. Irene Merle Wagner, Dec. 18, 1971; children—Stacy Renee, Caryn Melissa. Sect. head chem. devel. pilot plant Burroughs-Wellcome & Co., Inc., Tuckahoe, N.Y., 1968-70; project engr. Exxon Research & Enginrg. Co., Florham Park, N.J., 1970-77, staff engr.-supr. synthetic fuels research, 1977—; owner-partner Calculator Games Co., Lake Hiawatha, N.J., 1977—. NSF fellow, 1968-69. Mem. Am. Inst. Chem. Engrs., Am. Chem. Soc., Sigma Xi, Tau Beta Pi, Phi Lambda Upsilon, Delta Mu Delta, Sigma Alpha Mu. Home: 8 Wolf Pl Parsippany NJ 07054 Office: PO Box 101 Florham Park NJ 07932

MORRISON, JOHN DOANE, lawyer, r.r. exec.; b. Albany, N.Y., Mar. 26, 1927; s. J. Cayce and Grace D.; student Swarthmore Coll., 1943-45; A.B., U. Pa., 1946; LL.B., Harvard, 1951; m. Barbara Lewis, June 27, 1953; children—Jeffrey Lewis, Christopher Doane. Admitted to N.Y. bar, 1952, Mich. bar, 1962, Ill. bar, 1967; atty., commerce counsel, asst. to v.p.-law N.Y. Central R.R., 1951-62; mem. firm Badgley, Domke, Morrison, McVicker & Marcoux, Jackson, Mich., 1962-67; gen. atty., gen. solicitor Ill. Central R.R., 1967-72; dir., gen. counsel Bessemer & Lake Erie R.R., 1972—, sec., 1973—; dir., gen. counsel, sec. Carbon County Ry., Duluth, Missabe and Iron Range Ry., Elgin, Joliet and Eastern Ry., Johnstown and Stony Creek R.R., Lake Terminal R.R., McKeesport Connecting R.R., Newburgh and S. Shore Ry., Northampton and Bath R.R., Union R.R., Youngstown and Northern R.R., Pittsburgh and Conneaut Dock Co., Birmingham So. R.R. Served to lt. j.g., USNR, 1944-47. Mem. Am. Bar Assn., ICC Practitioners Assn., Pi Gamma Mu, Phi Delta Theta. Clubs: Duquesne, Allegheny Country. Home: RD 4 Blackburn Rd Sewickely PA 15143 Office: PO Box 536 Pittsburgh PA 15230

MORRISON, LAYTON ARTHUR, forest products machinery co. exec.; b. Syracuse, N.Y., Sept. 12, 1923; s. Charles Markland and Adeline LaVera (Auberten) M.; student mech. engring., Internat. Corr. Schs.; m. Gloria J. Chaufty, Apr. 28, 1946. With Carthage Machine Co. (N.Y.), 1942—, v.p., 1965-68, pres., 1968—; dir. Carthage Savs. & Loan Assn. Bd. dirs. Jefferson County Industries, 1970-71. Trustee Village of Carthage, 1957-61; mem. Carthage Planning Commn., 1970—; trustee Jefferson Community Coll., 1977—. Served with USAAF, 1943-45. Mem. Paper Industry Mgmt. Assn., Am. Legion, Air Force Assn. Republican. Methodist. Elk. Club: Carlowden Country (Denmark, N.Y.). Home: 1 Morrison Ln Carthage NY 13619 Office: 571 West End Ave Carthage NY 13619

MORRISSEY, CHARLES DAVID, civil engr.; b. N.Y.C., Apr. 28, 1926; s. Charles Patrick and Agnes Mary (Brownregg) M.; B.S. in Civil Engring., Manhattan Coll., 1949; M.C.E., N.Y. U., 1952; m. Monica Dolan, July 7, 1950; children—David, Karen, James, Christine. Instr. civil engring. N.Y. U., N.Y.C., 1949-52; partner Praeger Kavanagh Waterbury, cons. engrs., N.Y.C., 1960-70; exec. v.p. URS/Madigan-Praeger, Inc., cons. engrs., N.Y.C., 1970-74, pres., 1974—; chmn. Coverdale & Colpitts, Inc.; adj. asst. prof. civil engring. Manhattan Coll. Mem. Planning Bd. Ardsley, N.Y., 1960-65. Served with USMC, 1943-46. Named Engr. of Year N.Y. Soc. Profl. Engrs., 1973. Fellow Am. Cons. Engrs. Council, ASCE; mem. Am. Concrete Inst., Soc. Am. Mil. Engrs., N.Y. Soc. Cons. Engrs., Chi Epsilon, Sigma Xi. Roman Catholic. Clubs: Ardsley Country (past pres.), Yale, Pinnacle. Designer buildings, bridges, wharves, communications facilities. Home: 15 Woodfield Rd Briarcliff Manor NY 10510 Office: URS Madigan Praeger Inc 150 E 42nd St New York City NY 10017

MORRISSEY, JAMES JOSEPH, JR., hosp. adminstr.; b. Albany, N.Y., Oct. 20, 1938; s. James Joseph and Mary Agnes (Dailey) M.; B.S. in Pharmacy, Albany Coll., 1965. Chief pharmacist Champlain Valley Hosp. Plattsburgh, N.Y., 1965-68; dir. material mgmt. Champlain Valley Physicians Hosp. Med. Center, Plattsburgh, 1968-73; asst. adminstr. Leonard Hosp. Troy, N.Y., 1973-75, asso. dir., 1975—. Served with USN, 1956-59. Mem. Albany Coll. Pharmacy Alumni Assn. (certificate appreciation 1971), Am. Hosp. Assn., Northeastern N.Y. Health Care Mgrs. Assn. (past pres.), Am. Pharm. Assn. Am. Soc. Hosp. Pharmacists, Champlain Valley Pharm. Assn. past pres., certificate appreciation 1969). Roman Catholic. Home: 852 Chestnut St Albany NY 12203 Office: New Turnpike Rd Troy NY 12182

MORRISSEY, MADELEINE MARIA, perfume co. exec.; b. N.Y.C., Jan. 8; d. Joseph Lawrence and Madeleine Catherine (Curran) M.; B.A. in Sociology, Notre Dame Coll., N.Y.; postgrad. N.Y. U.; m. Francis Klabouch; 1 dau., Meryn. Vice pres. Grant Advt., N.Y.C., 1960-65; copy chief consumer div. Hazard Advt., N.Y.C., 1965-69; copy supr. Ketchum, MacLeod & Grove Advt., N.Y.C., 1969-71; pres. Capricorn Communications, N.Y.C., 1971-73; dir. advt. and pub. relations Dana Perfumes Corp., N.Y.C., 1973—. Mem. parish council St. Thomas More Ch., N.Y.C., 1973—, also founder, editor-in-chief More ch. newspaper; chmn. Yorkville Cath.-Jewish Council, 1976—; bd. dirs. Yorkville Outreach. Home: 60 East End Ave New York City NY 10028 Office: 625 Madison Ave New York City NY 10022

MORRISSEY, THOMAS JEROME, investment banker; b. Racine, Wis.; s. Patrick William and Lillian (Mitchell) M.; Ph.B., U. Wis., 1940; certificate U. Ill., 1942; postgrad. U.S. Naval Acad., 1942; m. Clovene Marie Nogel, Feb. 21, 1957. Merchandising trainee Vick Chem. div. Richardson-Merrill, Inc., N.Y.C., 1940-41, sales promotion asst., 1941-42, mgr. mil. sales, 1942; pvt. practice as mktg., fin. cons., N.Y.C., 1952-54; dir. mktg. research Pharmacraft Labs. div. Seagrams Distillers, Inc., N.Y.C., 1946-48, mgr. sales promotion, 1948-49, gen. sales mgr., 1949-52; asst. to pres. Turner-Smith Drug Co., N.Y.C., 1954-55, sales mgr., Smithtown, L.I., N.Y., 1955-57; mgr. advt. and sales Denver Chem. Mfg. Co., Stamford, Conn., 1957-58, N.Y.C., 1958-59; v.p., dir. mktg., account exec. Ralph Allum Advt. Agy., N.Y.C., 1959-67; v.p. Community Sci., Inc., 1959-67; account exec. Walston & Co., Inc., N.Y.C., 1967-74, Harris, Upham & Co., Inc., 1974-76, Smith, Barney, Harris, Upham & Co., N.Y.C., 1976—. Served to lt. USNR, 1942-46. Decorated Silver Star. Mem. The Marketeers (pres. 1963-66), Astoria Park Tennis Assn. (pres. 1967-70), Eastern Lawn Tennis Assn. (del. 1967-70), Met. Badminton Assn. (del. 1968—), Sigma Chi. Clubs: Dutch Treat (chmn. 1960-61), Army and Navy (gov.), Central Badminton (pres. 1971—), West Side Tennis (Forest Hills). Research in field. Home: 865 United Nations Plaza New York City NY 10017 Office: 120 Broadway New York City NY 10005

MORROW, DAVID WARREN, grocery chain exec.; b. Hood River, Oreg., Aug. 11, 1931; s. Claude W. and Etta Elfreda (Brown) M.; student Coll. Idaho, 1949; exec. program Stanford U., summer 1968; m. Patricia Ann Ballard, Apr. 16, 1949; children—Kelly, Kristi, Jodi. With Albertsons, Inc., Boise, Idaho, 1949-77, exec. v.p., 1975-76, pres., chief operating officer, 1976-77; pres., chief operating officer Gt. Atlantic & Pacific Tea Co., Inc., Montvale, N.J., 1977—, also dir. Mem. Food Mktg. Inst. (dir.). Office: Gt Atlantic & Pacific Tea Co Inc 2 Paragon Dr Montvale NJ 07645

MORROW, GLENN DAVIS, economist, govt. ofcl.; b. Madisonville, Ky., Mar. 4, 1911; s. Charlie Lee and Willie (Hughes) M.; A.B. in History, Econs., Polit. Sci. and Philosophy, Murray State U., 1933; M.A. in Econs., Sch. Adminstrn. and Polit. Sci., George Peabody Coll., 1940; postgrad. in econs., pub. adminstrn. and law U. Ky., 1941-44, in econs., U. Chgo., 1967-68; m. Mary B. Folwell, June 10, 1935; 1 son, Dan F. High sch. tchr., grade sch. prin. pub. schs. State of Ky., 1934-41; research asst. bur. bus. research U. Ky., 1941-44, asst. research prof., 1945-49; asst. adminstr. gen. Iran; mem. Am. Fin. Mission to Iran, Tehran, 1944-45; tax specialist U.S. Army Far East Command, Tokyo, 1949-51; spl. asst. to commr. revenue Ky. Dept. Revenue, Frankfort, 1951-52; dep. commr. finance Ky. Dept. Finance, Frankfort, 1952-54; cons. to mayor City of Louisville, 1953; cons. legis. reference service Library of Congress, Washington, 1954; research asso. Commn. on Intergovtl. Relations, Washington, 1954; cons. Philippines Govt. Survey and Reorgn. Commn., Manila, 1955-56; tax adminstrn. advisor ICA Mission to Korea, Seoul, 1957; cons. Com. Econ. Devel., Washington, 1958; social sci. analyst Social Security Adminstrn., Washington, 1958-63; sr. economist SBA, Washington, 1963-67, supervisory economist, 1967-74, dir. div. econ. research and statistics office advocacy planning and research, 1974—; speaker in field. Recipient prize Henry A. Simons Meml. Essay Contest, 1943. Mem. U. Ky. Research Club, Beta Gamma Sigma. Republican. Contbr. articles to profl. publs. Home: 4750 Chevy Chase Dr Chevy Chase MD 20015 Office: 1441 L St NW Washington DC 20416

MORROW, SCOTT IMLAY, chemist; b. Oklahoma City, Sept. 11, 1920; s. Walter Alexander and Blanche (Teape) M.; student Middlebury Coll., 1938-39; B.S., Case-Western Res. U., 1946, M.S. (Office of Naval Research fellow, DuPont fellow), 1947, Ph.D., 1951; children—Sarah Lee, Paul Alexander, Charles Scott. Chemist, Monsanto Chem. Co., Everett, Mass., 1951-54, Mobil Oil Corp., Paulsboro, N.J., 1954-56, Thiokol Chem. Co., Denville, N.J., 1956-66; research chemist ARRADCOM LCWL Energetics, U.S. Army, Dover, N.J., 1966—; asst. prof. chemistry Fairleigh Dickinson Coll., Madison, N.J., County Coll. of Morris, Dover, N.J. Served with USNR, 1942-56; PTO. Mem. Am. Chem. Soc., Am. Inst. Physics, Am. Crystallographic Assn., Phi Gamma Delta. Contbr. articles to profl. jours. Patentee in field. Home: 36 E Shore Rd Denville NJ 07834 Office: ARRADCOM LCWL Energetics Dover NJ 07801

MORROW, WILLIAM EARL, govt. ofcl.; b. Perryopolis, Pa., Oct. 22, 1923; s. Robert Ferguson and Daisy (Johnson) M.; B.S. in Psychology, Waynesburg Coll., 1948; M.A., U. Pitts., 1953; postgrad. U. Md., Exec. Seminar Center, 1969, Indsl. Coll. Armed Forces, 1969-70; m. Danna Katunaric, Apr. 26, 1958; children—Jamie Johnson, Tammara Marie, Kim Ina, William Joseph, Geoffrey Sean. With Survey Research Center, U. Mich., 1947; auditor, employment interviewer, then asst. dir. personnel Jones & Laughlin Steel Corp., 1948-54; exec. coordinator Peoples Cab Co., 1954; labor-mgmt. adviser, policy coordinator Arabian Am. Oil Co., Saudi Arabia, 1954-57; personnel expert ILO, Switzerland and Yugoslavia, 1957-58; cons., 1958-59; tng./program officer AID, Eastern Caribbean, 1959-65; adminstrv. officer Bur. Internat. Labor Affairs Labor Dept., 1965-68, dep. div. chief, 1968-72, projects dir. Latin Am. and Caribbean, 1973—, now asst. dir.; guest prof. U. Coll. W.I., 1960-64; lectr. Prince George's Community Coll., 1965—; lectr. U. Md., 1967—. Mem. Tantallon (Md.) Civic Assn. Served with USAF, 1942-44. Mem. Indsl. Relations Research Assn., Prince George's County Bd. Realtors, Am. Fedn. Govt. Employees, Am. Soc. Tng. Dirs., Am. Legion, D.A.V., Psi Chi Iota, Phi Alpha Theta, Delta Sigma Phi. Methodist. Clubs: Masons, Shriners, Tantallon Country; U. Md. Faculty. Home: 1220 Swan Harbour Circle Tantallon Washington DC 20022 Office: Bur Internat Affairs Labor Dept Washington DC 20210

MORROW, WILLIAM LEE, chemist; b. Athens, Ala., Oct. 8, 1921; s. William G. and Isabel (Ingram) M.; B.A., Fisk U., 1949; m. Gwendolyn Blackburn, June 24, 1951; children—Jared Kevin, Charles William. Clk., VA, Washington, 1950-52; cartographer U.S. Navy Hydrographic Office, Suitland, Md., 1952-53; research chemist Nat. Bur. of Standards, Washington, 1953-68; sr. chemist Gen. Services Adminstrn., Washington, 1969—. Vice chmn. Samuel Kelsey Scholarship Found., 1975-78; sgt.-at-arms North Portal Civic League, 1976-78; bd. dirs. Sigma Systems, sec., treas., 1970-78. Served with U.S. Army, 1943-46; ETO, PTO. Recipient Spl. Achievement award U.S. Govt., 1976. Mem. Am. Chem. Soc., Chem. Soc. of Washington, Am. Standards for Testing Materials, NAACP, Washington Urban League. Democrat. Contbr. articles on pulp and paper industrial processes to tech. jours. Home: 1697 Tamarack St Northwest Washington DC 20012 Office: Reno Rd and Van Ness St NW Washington DC 20405

MORSE, DEAN WEBER, economist, educator; b. N.Y.C., Aug. 31, 1920; s. Sterne and Isabelle (Weber) M.; A.B., Harvard U., 1941; Ph.D., Columbia U., 1965; m. Joanne Ryan, Aug. 6, 1955. Instr. econs. Yale U., 1948-50; instr. history The Fieldston Sch., 1954-59; asst. prof. econs. Columbia U., 1965-69, asso. prof. bus., 1970-71, sr. research asso., 1976—; prof. social scis. Fordham U., 1971—. Sec. Columbia Seminar on Tech. and Social Change, 1963-69. Dir. Morningside Citizens Coalition; bd. dirs. Inst. Intercultural Studies. Served to 1st lt. inf., U.S. Army, 1942-46. Decorated Silver Star, Bronze Star Purple Heart. Mem. Am. Econ. Assn., Econ. History Assn. Author: The Peripheral Worker, 1969; (with Boris Yavitz) the Labor Market: An Information System. Editor: The Impact of Science on Technology; The Environment of Change; Technological Innovation and Society. Home: Timber Lake Rd Sherman CT 06784 Office: Conservation of Human Resources Columbia U New York City NY 10025

MORSE, JOHN JOSEPH, educator; b. Framingham, Mass., Sept. 30, 1938; s. John Thomas and Elizabeth Marie Morse; B.A., Coll. of Holy Cross, 1960; M.B.A., Harvard U., 1966, D.B.A., 1969; div.; 1 son, Christopher Jon. Prof. organizational behavior UCLA, 1969-78; prof. organizational behavior Babson Coll., Babson Park, Mass., 1979—. Served as lt. USN, 1961-64. Named Tchr. of Yr., UCLA, 1973; NDEA fellow, 1966-69. Mem. Am. Sociol. Assn., Acad. of Mgmt., Assn. Humanistic Psychology, Harvard Assn. Bus. and Mgmt. Sci. Author: Organizations and Their Members: A Contingency Approach, 1974; reviewer for various jours.; contbr. articles to profl. jours. Office: Babson College Babson Park MA 02157

MORSE, JOSEPH LOUIS, dermatologist; b. N.Y.C., Feb. 22, 1899; s. Philip and Dinah (Rosenthal) M.; M.D., Rufts U., 1923; m. Elsa Schreider, May 12, 1925; children—Flora Diane, Joan Shirley, Intern, Beth Israel Hosp., Boston, 1923-24; asso. with Dr. George M. MacKee, Prof. Dermatology, N.Y. Postgrad. Med. Sch. and Hosp., N.Y.C., 1926-32, staff, 1926-27; staff N.Y. Skin and Cancer Hosp., N.Y.C., 1927-57; asso. prof. dermatology N.Y. Skin and Cancer Hosp., 1945-57; prof., chmn. dept. dermatology N.Y. Med. Coll., 1957-68, prof. emeritus dermatology, 1968—; cons. dermatologist Flower Fifth Ave. Hosp., 1957—, Met. Hosp., 1957—, Hosp. for Joint Diseases, 1950—. Diplomate Am. Bd. Dermatology. Mem. Am. Med. Assn., N.Y. Med. Soc., N.Y. Acad. Medicine, Am. Acad. Dermatology, Soc. Investigative Dermatology, Greater N.Y. Dermatol. Soc., Soc. Tropical Dermatology, Am. Acad. Compensation Medicine, Tau Epsilon Phi. Jewish. Clubs: Masons, Physicians Sq. Address: 15 Central Park W New York City NY 10023

MORSE, LEON WILLIAM, phys. distbn. exec.; b. N.Y.C., Nov. 13, 1912; s. Benjamin and Leah (Shapiro) M.; B.S., N.Y.U., 1935; student Acad. Advanced Traffic, 1937, 54; D.B.A.; m. Goldie Kohn, Mar. 30, 1941; children—Jeffrey W., Saul J. Individual bus. and traffic mgmt. cons., Phila., 1950-58; gen. traffic mgr. W.H. Rorer, Inc., Ft. Washington, Pa., 1958-77; partner Morse, Stoner, Travis & Assos., consultants phys. distbn. and logistics, Phila., 1978—; instr. econs. of transp., logistics Pa. State U. Ogontz campus, 1963-78; mem. adv. council Pa. SBA; formerly chmn. exec. com. Drug and Toilet Preparations Traffic Conf. Served to capt. Transp. Corps, AUS, World War II. Recipient Del. Valley Traffic Mgr. of Year award, 1963. Mem. Traffic and Transp. Club of Phila., Am. Soc. Internat. Execs., Canadian Assn. Phys. Distbn. Mgmt., Assn. ICC Practitioners, Am. Soc. Traffic and Transp. (founder mem.), Nat. Council Phys. Distbn., Del. Valley Drug Traffic Assos. (chmn.), Soc. Logistics Engrs. Clubs: Traffic (Phila. and Norristown, Pa.). Mason (Shriner). Home: 14086 Kelvin Ave Philadelphia PA 19116 Office: 3220 PSFS Bldg 1250 12th St Philadelphia PA 19107

MORSE, RICHARD VAN TUYL, advt. agy. exec.; b. N.Y.C., May 7, 1931; s. Norvell Van Tuyl and Julia Mary (Lominska) M.; B.S. in Econs., U. Pa., 1953; M.Bus. Edn., N.Y. U., 1958; m. Florence Katharine Denby, June 26, 1953; children—Stuart Van Tuyl, Andrew Denby. Media buyer Young & Rubicam, Advt., N.Y.C., 1953-59; v.p., account supr. SSC & B Advt., N.Y.C., 1960-67; mgmt. group supr. Wells, Rich, Greene Advt., N.Y.C., 1968-70; v.p., mgmt. supr. Norman, Craig & Kummel Advt., N.Y.C., 1970-73; sr. v.p. account services F. William Free & Co., Advt., N.Y.C., 1974—; advt. cons.; tchr. communications U. Pa., Toastmasters Internat., N.Y.C., 1970—. Exec. com. Westfield High Sch. Boosters Assn., 1974-77; deacon Reformed Ch. Am., Oradell, N.J., 1963-66; Union County (N.J.) Rep. County committeeman, 1970-74. Served to 1st lt. U.S. Army, 1954-56. Mem. Am. Mktg. Assn., U. Pa. Alumni Assn. Republican. Presbyn. Clubs: Vanderbilt Toastmasters (pres. 1976), Toastmasters Internat. (area gov. 1977-78), Spray Beach Yacht, Echo Lake Country. Home: 849 Knollwood Terr Westfield NJ 07090 Office: 400 Park Ave New York City NY 10022

MORSE, THOMAS SMYTH, life ins. co. cons.; b. Isleford, Maine, July 4, 1912; s. Frederick W. and Mary (Smyth) M.; B.A., U. Maine, 1934; postgrad. U. Iowa, 1935; m. Emeline Hamilton, June 24, 1941; children—Maureen (Mrs. John Gruber), Peter, Anne, Theresa (Mrs. Henry Connor), Timothy. Agt., Phoenix Mut. Life, Ellsworth, Me., 1936-41, sales tng. dept., Hartford, Conn., 1945—, dir. estate research, 1971—; instr., lectr. life ins. U. Conn. Sch. Ins., 1948—; C.L.U. instr., 1949-60. Served to maj. AUS, 1941-45. Mem. Nat. Assn. Life Underwriters, Soc. C.L.U., Am. Risk and Ins. Assn. Home: Olde House Islesford ME 04646 Office: 66 College Ave Orono ME 04473

MORTENSEN, RALPH, publisher; b. Mankato, Minn., Jan. 29, 1894; s. Jacob and Christine (Strand) M.; B.A., Augsburg Coll., 1913; student Augsburg Sem., 1913-16, Oslo U., 1916-17; M.S.T., Hartford Sem., 1918, Ph.D., 1927; m. Petra Helland, June 3, 1918 (dec. Nov. 1942); children—Ralph Helland (dec.), Agnes Carolyn (Mrs. Donald Paul Mosling), Margaret Christine Anne (Mrs. George Boine Anderson); m. 2d, Esther Elizabeth Tappert, Jan. 19, 1946. Tchr. Luth. Boys' Sch., Kweiteh, Honan, China, 1919-21; pub. Luth. Bd. Publ., Hankow, China, 1930-42; China rep. Am. Bible Soc., Chungking, 1944-45, Shanghai, 1945-53; pastor Bethel Luth. Ch., LaCrosse, Wis., 1921-25; asso. pastor Emanuel Luth. Ch., Manchester, Conn., 1925-27, Battle Lake Parish, Minn., 1927-30; acting pastor Community Ch., Shanghai, China, 1946, 51; rep. Am., Brit., Scottish Bible socs. as traveling sec. East Asia, 1954-58; field sec. Am. Bible Soc., N.Y.C., 1958-65, spl. sec., 1966-67, spl. rep., 1968—; v.p. Research Center for Religion and Human Rights in Closed Societies, N.Y.C., 1976—. Mgr. Lord's Day Alliance U.S., 1966-71; treas. Hymn Soc. of Am., 1967-76; lectr., gen. sec. Internat. Red Cross for Central China, Hankow, China, 1939-41; chmn. coordinating com. Fgn. Refugees, Shanghai, China, 1948-52; chaplain, commr. S.E. dist. Long Rivers council Boy Scouts Am., 1967-77. Charter mem. Cheshire (Conn.) Com. on Aging, 1972-78. Recipient Distinguished Alumnus Citation Augsburg Coll., 1964, Bronze medal, 1969, Service award Inst. Chinese Culture, 1972; Silver Beaver award Boy Scouts Am., 1977. Fellow Royal Asiatic Soc., Hymn Soc. Am.; mem. Am. Oriental Soc., Asia Soc., Tibet Soc., Norsemen's Fedn. Oslo. Republican. Clubs: Rotary (sec.-treas. Fellowship Overseas Rotarians, N.Y.C., 1962-77, chmn. 1977—) (N.Y.C.); Shanghai Tiffin. Home: Riverbound Farm on Quinnipiac 1881 Cheshire St RFD 1 Southington CT 06489 Office: RCDA Interchurch Center 475 Riverside Dr New York City NY 10027

MORTON, DONALD JOHN, librarian; b. Bklyn., Jan. 11, 1931; s. Ellwood Stokes and Gladys (Hassler) M.; B.S., U. Del., 1952; M.S., La. State U., 1954; Ph.D., U. Calif. at Berkeley, 1958; M.S. in L.S., Simmons Coll., 1969, D. Arts in L.S., 1976; m. Ann Mayo Tilden, Aug. 16, 1958; children—Saundra Kay, Donald John, Mary Ann. Asst. prof. botany N.M. State U., Las Cruces, 1957-58; asst. prof. plant pathology N.D. State U., Fargo, 1959-61; plant pathologist Agr. Dept., Tifton, Ga., 1961-65; asso. prof. plant pathology U. Del., Newark, 1965-68; librarian Northeastern U., Boston, 1968-70; library dir., asso. prof. library sci. U. Mass. Med. Sch., Worcester, 1970—; tchr. med. librarianship Worcester State Coll., 1974—; pres. North Atlantic Health Scis. Libraries, 1974-76, Worcester Med. Library, Worcester Area Coop. Libraries, 1974-75; mem. Oliver Wendell Holmes endowment com. Boston Med. Library; mem. coop. staff Worcester Found. Exptl. Biology; chmn. Council Developing Med. Libraries, 1974. Mem. U. Mass. Bicentennial Com. cons. sci. libraries. Mem. Worcester Art. Mus., Worcester Hist. Soc., Northboro Hist. Soc., Am. Assn. Univ. Adminstrs., Am. Soc. Information Sci., ALA, Mass., Med. library assns., Simmons Coll. Library Sch. Alumni Assn. (pres. 1975-76), Mycol. Soc. Am., Spl. Libraries Assn., New Eng. Coll. Librarians, Sigma Xi, Phi Kappa Phi, Delta Tau Delta, Phi Sigma Soc. Contbr. articles to profl. jours. Home: 97 Main St Northboro MA 01532 Office: U Mass Med Sch Library Worcester MA 01605

MORTON, EUGENE DANIEL, corporate exec.; b. Jacksonville, Fla., May 16, 1931; s. Frederick Samuel and Shan Witherspoon (Daniel) M.; B.S., Davidson (N.C.) Coll., 1955; student Harvard Bus. Sch., 1956-57; m. Maria Consuelo Gimenez, Dec. 16, 1967; children—Thomas, Scott, Paul, Daniel. Analyst, Am. Airlines, 1955-56; gen. traffic mgr. Northeast Airlines, 1958-61; dir. devel. planning Eastern Airlines, 1961-69; v.p., dir. Alliance One, N.Y.C., 1969-74, sr. v.p., 1974, pres., 1974—; pres., dir. PetroAir Trading Inc.; cons. strategic planning, aviation econs., mergers and acquisitions. Mem. exec. council Norwalk (Conn.) P.T.A., 1965. Served to 1st lt. AUS, 1954. Decorated Army Commendation medal. Mem. N.Y. Soc. Security Analysts, Airline Analysts Soc., Sigma Phi Epsilon. Republican. Presbyn. (moderator 1965-66). Clubs: Wings, Bankers, Harvard (N.Y.C.). Contbg. author: Air Transportation—1975 and Beyond, 1968. Home: 180 Riverbank Dr Stamford CT 06903 Office: 280 Park Ave Suite 3400-W New York City NY 10017

MORTON, JAY ROBERT, energy equipment mfg. co. exec.; b. Tarrytown, N.Y., July 24, 1914; s. Jay Daniel and Sara (Skerritt) M.; A.B., Syracuse U., 1936, M.S., 1937; student Alexander Hamilton Inst., 1939; m. Barbara Louise Tyler, Feb. 8, 1941; children—Jay Robert II, Wellington Charles, Linda Joy. With Vega Industries, Inc. (formerly San-Equip, Inc.), 1937-60, traffic mgr., 1937-46, gen. traffic mgr., 1946-58, asst. to the pres., 1958-60; gen. traffic mgr., Combustion Engring., Inc., Stamford, Conn., 1960-66, dir. corporate traffic and transp., 1966-70, v.p. corporate transp. and distbn., 1970—. Mem. Atlantic States Shippers Adv. Bd. Pres. Myasthenia Gravis Found. Named Conn. Transp. Man of Yr., 1977. Mem. Nat. Def. Transp. Assn. (regional v.p.), Nat. Indsl. Traffic League (past pres.), Newcomen Soc. N.Am., Nat. Def. Exec. Res., Nat. Freight Traffic Assn. (past v.p.), Traffic Club N.Y., Am. Soc. Traffic and Transp. (past regional v.p.), Charter Oaks Shippers Assn., Am. Boiler Assn. (past chmn. traffic com.), Am. Mgmt. Assn., Stamford Area Commerce and Industry Assn. (past chmn. mass transit com.), Delta Nu Alpha (past regional v.p.), Sigma Phi Epsilon (dir.). Episcopalian (vestryman). Clubs: Masons, City, Wampanoag Country (West Hartford). Home: 108 Gray Farms Rd Stamford CT 06905 Office: 900 Long Ridge Rd Stamford CT 06902

MORTON, THOMAS GRANT, ednl. adminstr.; b. White Plains, N.Y., Feb. 16, 1948; s. Harry Smith and Elizabeth Catherine (Sedlak) M.; B.A., Iona Coll., 1970; M.A., Fairfield U., 1975; postgrad. N.Y. U., 1977—; m. Monica Wenderoth, June 13, 1970; children—Adam, Jacob, Brent, Kira. Sr. child care dir. Cardinal McClosky Home and Sch., N.Y.C., 1969-70; coach, instr. and counselor Archbishop Stepinac High Sch., White Plains, N.Y., 1970-76; asst. dean, dir. counseling Washington Bus. Inst., N.Y.C., 1976—; group counselor Nat. Found. for Sudden Infant Death, 1976-78, acting counselor, 1976-78, asst. to pres., 1976-78. Mem. Am. Personnel and Guidance Assn., Assn. Non-White Concerns, Nat. Vocat. Guidance Assn. Democrat. Roman Catholic. Contbr. articles to profl. jours. Home: 555 Ridgeway White Plains NY 10605 Office: 19 Union Sq West New York NY 10003

MORTON, THOMAS GREGORY, educator; b. Birmingham, Ala., Oct. 6, 1941; s. Thomas Grey and Iris (Spearman) M.; B.S. in Bus. Adminstrn., High Point Coll., 1964; M.B.A. (Bus. Found. grantee), U. N.C., 1965; Ph.D. (NDEA fellow), Syracuse U., 1973; postgrad. (fellow) Sch. Savs. Banking, 1978; m. Pamela Sain Morton, Oct. 23, 1947; children—Scott Gregory, Jeffrey Lawrence. Adminstrv. asst., asst. investment officer State Treas. N.C., Raleigh, 1966-69; instr. dept. finance U. Syracuse (N.Y.), 1971-72; asst. prof. U. Conn., Storrs, 1972-77, asso. prof., 1977—. Vol. worker United Fund, Winston Salem, N.C., 1965-66. Recipient Student Achievement award Wall Street Jour., 1964. Mem. Am., Eastern, So. finance assns., Fin. Mgmt. Assn., Am. Real Estate and Urban Econs. Assn., Soc. for Advancement Mgmt. (pres. 1963-64), High Point Coll. Alumni Assn. (past pres.). Democrat. Contbr. articles to profl. jours. Home: 32 Beech Rd Tolland CT 06084 Office: U Conn Storrs CT 06268

MOSCHETTI, GUY ANTHONY, radiologist; b. N.Y.C., Nov. 6, 1934; s. Vincent de Pascale and Elizabeth C. Moschetti; B.S., St. Francis Coll., 1955; M.D., U. Bologna (Italy), 1961; m. Cecelia O'Brien, Oct. 18, 1964; children—Elizabeth, Guy, John. Intern, L.I. Coll. Hosp., Bklyn., 1962-63, resident, 1963-64; resident radiology St. Luke's Hosp., N.Y.C., 1964-66, research fellow, 1968-69; asso. radiologist Bronx Lebanon Hosp. Center, 1972—; asst. prof. radiology Albert Einstein Coll. Medicine, Bronx, 1972—. Diplomate Am. Bd. Radiology, Am. Bd. Nuclear Medicine. Mem. AMA, Radiol. Soc. N. Am., Am. Coll. Radiology, N.Y. Roentgen Soc., Bronx County Med. Soc. Roman Catholic. Contbr. articles in field to profl. jours. Office: Fulton Ave at 168th St Bronx NY 10456

MOSELEY, GEORGE THOMAS, lawyer; b. Buffalo, June 20, 1918; s. George Thomas and Isabella (Pelton) M.; grad. Choate Sch., 1937; A.B., Harvard, 1941; J.D., Buffalo Sch. Law, 1948; m. Elizabeth Keating, Apr. 2, 1957; 1 dau., Georgia Barnum. Admitted to N.Y. bar, 1949; dispute settlement adminstr. and counsel Better Bus. Bur. Western N.Y., Buffalo. Bd. dirs. Psychiat. Clinic of Buffalo, 1953-63, pres., 1962-63; bd. dirs. Mental Health Assn. Erie County, 1964-69, pres., 1966-67. Served to maj. CIC, AUS, 1941-45; ETO. Decorated Bronze Star (U.S.); Croix de Guerre (France). Mem. Bar. Assn. Erie County, Newcomen Soc., Asmodeus Lit. Soc. Clubs: Harvard, Saturn. Founder, music dir. Didymus Mus. Saw Quartet, 1968—. Home: 17 Cleveland Ave Buffalo NY 14222 Office: 775 Main St Buffalo NY 14203

MOSER, HAROLD DEAN, historian; b. Kannapolis, N.C., Oct. 31, 1938; s. Walter Glenn and Angie Elizabeth (Allen) M.; A.A., Wingate Coll., 1959; B.A. cum laude, Wake Forest U., 1961, M.A. (Univ. fellow), 1963; Ph.D. (Ford fellow), U. Wis., 1977; m. Carolyn Irene French, Mar. 28, 1964; children—Andrew Paul, Anna Elizabeth. Tchr., Robert B. Glenn High Sch., Winston-Salem, N.C., 1961-62; instr. history Chowan Coll., Murfreesboro, N.C., 1963-65; teaching asst. dept. history U. Wis., Madison, 1967-69; research asso., history of Wis. project State Hist. Soc. Wis., Madison, 1968-71; Nat. Hist. Publ. Commn. fellow The Papers of Daniel Webster, Dartmouth Coll., Hanover, N.H., 1971-72, asst. editor, 1972-73, asso. editor, 1973-76, co-editor, 1976-77, editor corr. series, 1978—. Mem. Am., So. hist. assns., Orgn. Am. Historians, Phi Alpha Theta, Eta Sigma Phi, Phi Theta Kappa. Democrat. Contbr. articles to profl. jours. Home: 67 E Wheelock St Hanover NH 03755 Office: Hinman 6025 Baker Library Dartmouth College Hanover NH 03755

MOSES, DONALD ALLEN, psychiatrist; b. Bklyn., Feb. 8, 1938; s. Edward and Evelyn (Roberts) M.; student Bates Coll., 1954-58; M.D., N.Y. Med. Coll., 1962; m. Sarah Mosley Dean, Dec. 6, 1957; children—Richard David, Erik Alan. Intern, Queen's Hosp., Honolulu, 1962-63; resident in psychiatry Hillside Hosp., Glen Oaks, N.Y., 1965-68; pvt. practice medicine, specializing in psychiatry, Greenvale, N.Y., 1968—; staff psychiatrist L.I. Jewish-Hillside Med. Center, 1968—, North Shore Univ. Hosp.; cons. in field. Served with M.C., USAF, 1963-65. Mem. AMA, Am. Psychiat. Assn., Nassau Psychiat. Soc., Royal Soc. Health (London), Am. Acad. Clin. Psychiatrists. Clubs: Beaver Dam Skating, Glen Cove Soccer, Stratton Mountain Ski, Matingcock Rod and Gun. Author: Are You Driving Your Children to Drink?, 1975. Home: 9 Southland Dr Glen Cove NY 11542 Office: 90 Glen Cove Rd Greenvale NY 11548

MOSES, ELBERT RAYMOND, JR., educator; b. New Concord, Ohio, Mar. 31, 1908; s. Elbert Raymond and Martha (Miller) M.; A.B., U. Pitts., 1932, M.S., U. Mich., 1934, Ph.D., 1936; m. Mary Miller Sterrett, Sept. 21, 1933; 1 son, James Elbert. Instr. U. N.C., 1936-38; asst. prof. Ohio State U., 1938-46; asso. prof. Eastern Ill. State U., 1946-56; asst. prof. Mich. State U., 1956-59; prof. Clarion State Coll., 1959-72, prof. emeritus, 1972—, chmn. dept. speech and dramatic arts, 1959—; Fulbright lectr. Cebu Normal Sch., Cebu City, P.I., 1955-56; vis. prof. phonetics U. Mo., summer 1968; del. 3d World Congress Phoneticians, Tokyo, 1976. Mem. nat. adv. com. Fgn. Students and Tchrs., Health, Edn. and Welfare. Del. to Internat. Congress Phonetic Scis., Helsinki, 1961; del. to 13th Congress Internat. Soc. Logopedics and Phoniatrie, Vienna, 1965. Liason rep. of Peace Corps. Pres. County Library bd.; past exec. dir. Clarion County (Pa.) United Fund; commr. Boy Scouts Am., 1976-77; pres. Venango County Adv. Council for Aging, 1978-79. Served from 1st lt. to maj. AUS, 1942-46, from major to lt. col. ret. Recipient certificate of appreciation Nicaraguan Dept. Pub. Health, 1974, Silver Beaver award Boy Scouts Am., 1978. Mem. AAAS, Assn. Phonetique Internat., Nat. Assn. Fgn. Student Advisers, Internat. Soc. Phonetic Scis., S.A.R. (chpt. pres., mem. state bd. mgmt.), Clarion County Hist. Soc. (pres. 1977-78), Internat. Platform Assn., VFW, Clarion C. of C. (dir.), Tau Kappa Epsilon, Theta Xi, Phi Delta Kappa (Service Key 1978). Clubs: Masons, Order Eastern Star (worthy patron), Rotary (dist. gov. internat. 1973-74), White Shrine Jerusalem. Author: Handbook of Persuasion, 1940; Guide to Effective Speaking, 1957; Phonetics: A History and Interpretation, 1964. Author weekly newspaper column, From the Four Corners. Contbr. articles to profl. jours. Home: 18 Fairview Ave Clarion PA 16214

MOSES, FRANK LAMBERTH, timber co. exec.; b. Roanoke, Va., Nov. 7, 1945; s. Abdo Joseph and Lucy Ellen (Hudgins) M.; A.S. magna cum laude, Va. Western Community Coll., 1973; B.S. with distinction, U. Va., 1975; m. Cheryl Elaine Deyerle, June 14, 1969; 1 dau., Kristen Deyerle. Chief right-of-way agt. Roanoke County Pub. Service Authority, Salem, Va., 1971-73; treas.'s asst. Seabrook Blanching Co., Edenton, N.C., 1975-76; supr. acctg. ITT Continental Baking Co., Washington, 1976-78; corp. controller Whitewater, Inc., Washington, 1978—. Served with U.S. Army, 1966-68. Decorated Bronze Star medal with V, Purple Heart with one oak leaf cluster. Mem. Alpha Kappa Psi, Phi Theta Kappa. Roman Catholic. Clubs: U. Va. Alumni, Berwyn Rod and Gun. Home: 3 Orchard Dr Gaithersburg MD 20760 Office: 1835 K St Washington DC 20006

MOSES, JOHN GABRIEL, ednl. cons.; b. New York Mills, N.Y., Dec. 21, 1912; S. Gabriel and Julia (Chamoun) M.; B.A., Hamilton Coll., 1934; M.A. (fellow 1934-35), Columbia U., 1935, postgrad., 1936-45; postgrad. N.Y. U., Syracuse U.; m. Mabel Koury, June 9, 1935; children—Gerard, Clement. Tchr. history and fgn. langs. Utica Free Acad., Proctor High Sch., Utica, N.Y., 1935-45; editorial staff Utica Observer-Dispatch, 1943-60; counselor Proctor High Sch., 1945-55, prin., 1968-69; dir. guidance Utica Pub. Schs., 1955-65, dir. pupil personnel, 1966-75; mem. staff Colgate U., 1958-73, ednl. cons., 1975—. Mem. N.Y. State, Am. personnel and guidance assns., Nat. Vocat. Guidance Assn., Nat. Assn. Pupil Personnel Adminstrs. Clubs: K.C., Torch.

MOSHER, GILES EDMOND, banker; b. Boston, Jan. 1, 1933; s. Giles Edmond and Mary A. (Downs) M.; B.S. in Bus. Adminstrn., Boston Coll., 1955; postgrad. Northwestern U. Sch. Fin. Pub. Relations, 1963; Stonier Grad. Sch. Banking, Rutgers U., 1965; m. Thelma A. Doyle, Sept., 1956; children—Mary Beth, Susan M., Michelle, Giles E., III, Alison, Caitlyn. With Newton-Waltham Bank and Trust Co., Waltham, Mass., 1955—, mgr. credit dept., 1959-60, asst. treas., 1960-62, asst. v.p., 1962-64, v.p., 1964-65, sr. v.p., 1965-68, exec. v.p., 1968-70, pres., 1970—, chmn., pres., 1971—; dir. Mass. Bus. Devel. Corp. Mem. fin. and adminstrn. advisory council Archdiocese of Boston; past pres. Newton (Mass.) Boys Club; mem. advisory bd. Emmanuel Coll.; mem. pres.'s advisory council Bentley Coll.; trustee Catholic Charitable Bur., Fessenden Sch., Newton-Wellesley Hosp.; trustee, mem. endowment investment com. Boston Coll.; trustee, chmn. adminstrn. and finance com. St. Elizabeth's Hosp. Recipient Bronze medallion Boys Clubs of Am., 1964; Distinguished Community award Brandeis U., 1975; named Young Man of Year, City of Newton, 1960; one of Ten Outstanding Young Men of Greater Boston, 1964; one of Four Outstanding Young Men of Mass., 1965; one of Five Outstanding Young Men New Eng., 1966. Mem. Newton Bankers Assn. (past pres.), Newton Taxpayers Assn. (dir.), Boston Coll. Alumni Assn. (past pres.), Newton C. of C. (past pres.), Alpha Gamma Sigma (hon.). Clubs: Brae Burn Country (bd. dirs., chmn. fin. com.) (West Newton, Mass.). Home: 227 Windsor Rd Waban MA 02168 Office: 880 Main St Waltham MA 02154*

MOSHER, PETER DAVID, lawyer; b. N.Y.C., Mar. 14, 1931; s. Max and Lillian (Einsohn) M.; A.B., Kenyon Coll., 1952; J.D., Harvard U., 1955. Admitted to N.Y. bar, 1955, U.S. Supreme Ct. bar, 1974, U.S. Ct. Appeals bar, 1960, also fed. dist. cts. Republican committeeman, 1959—; pres. Larchmont Babe Ruth League (pres. 1974-75). Mem. Am., N.Y. State, Mamaroneck-Harrison-Larchmont (v.p.), Westchester bar assns., Kenyon, Harvard Law Sch. alumni assns., N.Y. Jaycees (past dist. pres., past legal counsel, past nat. dir.), Phi Beta Kappa. Clubs: B'nai B'rith (past pres. Larchmont-Mamaroneck); Elks; Masons; Lions (pres. 1972-73, zone chmn. 1973-74, dep. dist. gov. 1978-79); Beach Point (Mamaroneck, N.Y.). Home: 17 N Chatsworth Ave Larchmont NY 10538 Office: 2001 Palmer Ave Larchmont NY 10538

MOSHIER, DAVID IRWIN, univ. adminstr.; b. Roanoke, Va., Sept. 14, 1954; s. Emery Irwin and Evelyn Mae (Kunkel) M.; student George Washington U., 1972—. Research asst. mkgt. dept. Clarendon Bank & Trust, Arlington, Va., 1974, collection agt. installment loans, 1974-75; fed. student loan collection officer George Washington U., Washington, 1975-77, sr. fed. loan collection officer, 1977—. Lay reader, St. Georges Episcopal Ch., Arlington, Va., 1975—, adult edn. com., 1975, seminary com., 1978-79; mem. campaign staff Arlington County Republican Com., 1974-77. Mem. Nat. Geog. Soc., Nat. Trust Historic Preservation, Soc. Va., Okla. State Soc. of Washington, U.S. Naval Inst. (asso.), Va. State Sheriff's Assn. (hon.). Club: George Washington. Home: 1308 N Herndon St Arlington VA 22201 Office: 2121 I St NW Washington DC 20052

MOSIER, MAURICE LEE, assn. exec.; b. Pittsburg, Kans., June 20, 1925; s. John Lee and Nellie Velma (Ledenham) M.; B.S. in Math., Kans. State Coll., 1949. m. Flossie Irene Ballock, Jan. 22, 1946; children—John Tate, Patti Lynne, Michael Curtis, Stacy Anne. Personal mgr. Kans. Ordnance Plant, Parsons, 1951-55; mgr. labor relations Kaiser Aluminum, Baton Rouge, 1955-64; dir. indsl. relations Kaiser Aluminum, Spokane, Wash., 1964-68; dir. labor relations Kaiser Engr., Oakland, Calif., 1968-71; dir. industry relations Litton Shipbldg. Co., Pascagoula, Miss., 1971-72; pres. Nat. Constructors Assn., 1972—; mem. Construction Industry Stblzn. Com., 1973-74, Fed. Energy Adminstrn. Advisory Bd., Presidents Collective Bargaining Com. in Construction; dir. Am. Council for Construction Edn. Chmn. Piping Industry Training Trust. Served with USN, 1943-46. Mem. Am. Inst. Constructors, Am. Soc. of Assn. Execs., Am. Legion. Clubs: Nat. Assn. Exec., Nat. Press. Home: 724 Carlisle Dr Arnold MD 21012 Office: 1101 15th St NW Washington DC 20005

MOSKI, BRUNO ALBERT, mgmt. engr.; b. New Haven, Apr. 17, 1906; s. Bruno and Mary (Sowinski) M.; B.S. in Indsl. Engring. cum laude, Yale U., 1927; m. Geraldine Twomey, July 4, 1941. Cadet engr. Consol. Gas Co., N.Y.C., 1927-30; chief indsl. engr. Wilson H. Lee, Orange, Conn., 1930-35; time study engr. Wester Electric Co., 1935-40; methods engring. supr. Sperry Gyroscope Co., 1940-42; chief indsl. engr. Sargent Co., New Haven, 1942-44; chief prodn. engr. Colt Industries, Kensington, Conn., 1944-45; plant mgr. Am. Paper Goods Co., Conn., 1946-49; dir. indsl. engr., corp. cons. Baton, Yale & Towne Co., 1950-70; pres. Bruno A. Moski Assos., mgmt. engrs., Pennlyn, Pa., 1970—; lectr. Grad. Sch., Drexel U., Phila., 1952-60. Mem. Soc. Advancement Mgmt. (pres. Phila. 1954-55, 67-68; Materials Handling award 1972). Club: Yale (Phila.). Author handbook, articles. Address: 110 Nottoway Dr Pennlyn PA 19422

MOSKOWITZ, M. L. (CHIC), health care products co. exec.; b. Boston; s. Frank Gedalia and Esther Belasco (Simons) M.; student N.Y. U., 1940-41, Coll. City N.Y., 1941-43, Rutgers U., 1962-63; m. Frances Singer, June 10, 1945; children—Sophia Simone Moskowitz Turkus, Rosalinda Moskowitz Saltiel, David. Technician, United Aircraft Co., Stratford, Conn., 1943-44; inspection foreman Emerson Radio Co., N.Y.C., 1944-48; actor, dir. Village Theatre, 1949; quality control mgr. Gen. Aviation Corp., N.Y.C., 1949-55; chief inspection mgr. quality assurance Emertron, Jersey City, 1955-63; with Johnson & Johnson Co., New Brunswick, N.J., 1963—, quality assurance coordinator, tech. info. services coordinator. Vice pres. Players Pyramid; dir. Apron Theatres; dir. Community Theatre; dir., tchr. St. Josephs Players of Carteret, Clark Players. Mem. Am. Soc. Quality Control. Democrat. Jewish. Home: 15 Westminster Pl Edison NJ 08817

MOSS, ARTHUR JAY, cardiologist; b. White Plains, N.Y., June 21, 1931; s. Abraham L. and Ida (Bank) M.; A.B., Yale, 1953; M.D., Harvard, 1957; m. Joy Folkman, June 23, 1957; children—Katherine,

Deborah Rose, David Abraham. Intern, Mass. Gen. Hosp., Boston, 1957-58, resident in medicine, 1960-61, Am. Heart Assn. research fellow, 1962-65; asst. prof., asso. prof. medicine, U. Rochester (N.Y.) Sch. Medicine and Dentistry, 1966-71, clin. asso. prof. medicine, 1971—; cons. in cardiology, Batavia (N.Y.) VA Hosp., Canandiagua (N.Y.) VA Hosp. Mem. bd. trustees, Genesee Valley Heart Assn., N.Y. Heart Assembly, Temple B'Rith Kodesh. Served with M.C. USN, 1958-60. Gleason Meml. Fund, Heart Research Follow-up Program grantee, 1972-77, Am. Heart Assn. advanced research fellow, 1962-66; recipient Monroe County Med. Soc. research prize award, 1962. Diplomate Am. Bd. Internal Medicine. Mem. A.C.P., Boylston Med. Soc., Am. Fedn. Clin. Research Soc., Am. Physiol. Soc., AMA, Genessee Valley Heart Assn., N.Y. Heart Assembly, Am. Coll. Cardiology, Am. Heart Assn. (council on clin. cardiology), Alpha Omega Alpha. Jewish. Author: Antiarrhythmic Agents, 1973. Home: 581 Claybourne Rd Rochester NY 14618 Office: 877 Elmwood Ave Rochester NY 14620

MOSS, DORIS FITZER, adminstr., counselor, educator; b. N.Y.C.; d. Louis and Bertha Freda (Romm) Fitzer; B.A., Bklyn. Coll., M.A., 1964; Ed.D., N.Y. U., 1972; m. Ira Lloyd Moss; children—Steven Alan, Marjorie Louise. Asst. program dir. Office of Career Edn., N.Y.C. Bd. Edn., 1965-67, program dir., 1967-76; exec. v.p. The Womanschool, N.Y.C., 1976-77; founder, exec. dir. Interpersonal Counseling Center of N.Y., Inc., N.Y.C., 1976—; exec. dir. Nat. Assn. for Div. Women, N.Y.C., 1978—; press sec. Congressman James H. Scheuer, 1978—; cons. N.Y. State Dept. Edn.; tchr. Bklyn. Coll. Sch. Gen. Studies, 1964-65, Tchrs. Coll., Columbia U., 1974—. Sec., Rockaway (N.Y.) Community Council, 1962-64; mem. Mayor's Task Force on Rape and Battered Women. Mem. Nat. (Social Justice Commn. award 1975), N.Y. assns. pub. and continuing edn., Eastern Sociol. Assn., Am. Personnel and Guidance Assn., Doctorate Assn. N.Y. Educators, N.Y. Assn. Women Bus. Owners, Phi Delta Kappa. Clubs: Women's City, B'nai B'rith. Contbr. articles to profl. jours. Home: 176 Beach 146 St Neponsit NY 11694 Office: 200 Park Ave Suite 303 E New York City NY 10017

MOSS, EDGAR GEORGE ERNEST, newspaper pub.; b. London, July 31, 1906; s. Ernest J. and Edith (Murray-Campbell) M.; B.A., N.Y. U., 1931; m. Ada Alberta Long, Dec. 20, 1977; 1 son, Ronald Edgar. Mdse. mgr. N.Y. Post; advt. mgr. Lambertville Bergen newspaper, Hunterdon Rev., v.p. Twin-ets Mfg. Co.; asst. advt. mgr. classified advt. N.Y. Times, N.Y.C.; owner, pub. New Brunswick (N.J.) Spokesman, 1972—. Scoutmaster, dist. committeeman, campmaster Boy Scouts Am. Mem. N.J. Bulldog Club, Bulldog Club Am., Hunterdon Hills Kennel Club, Dog Writers Am. Episcopalian. Clubs: New Brunswick Lions (pres. 1978), K.T., Masons. Home: 44 Old Mountain Rd Lebanon NJ 08833 Office: 90 Bayard St PO Box 1266 New Brunswick NJ 08903

MOSS, HUGH MACMILLAN, ophthalmologist; b. Mpls., June 22, 1928; s. John Hugh and Mary Margaret (Quinn) M.; A.B., Harvard, 1952; M.D., U. Pa., 1956; m. Elaine Jean Bordeau, Sept. 28, 1957; children—James, William, Shaun, Eric, Heather, Heidi. Intern, resident in medicine Hartford (Conn.) Hosp., 1956-58; resident in ophthalmology Columbia-Presbyn. Med. Center, N.Y.C., 1958-61, Heed fellow in ophthalmology, 1961; attending ophthalmologist Presbyn. Hosp., N.Y.C., 1961—; asst. clin. prof. ophthalmology Columbia, 1974—; dir. Motility Clinic, Edward S. Harkness Eye Inst., N.Y.C., 1961—; practice medicine specializing in ophthalmology, Hackensack, N.J., 1961—; cons. in field. Com. chmn. Bergen County council Boy Scouts Am., 1966-70, unit commr., 1971-72. Served with U.S. Army, 1946-48. Diplomate Am. Bd. Ophthalmology. Mem. AMA, Bergen County Med. Soc., Am. Acad. Ophthalmology and Otolaryngology, Am. Assn. Ophthalmology. Contbr. articles to profl. publs. ocular motility, ptosis and orbit. Home: 54 Everett Rd Demarest NJ 07627 Office: 430 Union St Hackensack NJ 07601

MOSS, ROBERT SHERIFFS, lawyer; b. Milw., July 15, 1908; s. Roy M. and Cornelia M. (Sheriffs) M.; B.S., Northwestern U., 1929; J.D., U. Wis., 1932; LL.M., Georgetown U., 1964; m. Bernice M. Pfeifer, Aug. 24, 1946; children—Marilyn, Karen. Admitted to Wis. bar, 1932, D.C. bar, 1947, also U.S. Supreme Ct.; pvt. practice, Milw., 1932-43, Washington, 1947—; counsel materials div. Office Gen. Counsel, Navy Dept., 1946-47; with Elmore, Moss & Moore, Washington, 1948-50; partner firm Hart, Moss & Tavenner, 1962-70; individual practice, 1970-71; prin. atty. Robert Sheriffs Moss & Assos., Chartered, 1971-76; partner firm Sullivan, Beauregard, Clarkson, Moss, Brown & Johnson, 1976—; gen. counsel Graphic Arts Assn. Wis., 1936-43; lectr. Columbus U., 1950-54, Cath. U., 1945-55, Tax Practice Inst., 1955-58. Sec. Mayor's Adv. Adv. Council, Milw., 1936-37; bd. govs. Nat. Grad. U., 1978—; pres. Milw. YMCA Toastmasters Club, YMCA Speakers' Bur. Mem. Am. (chmn. regional program com. 1965-67, chmn. pub. contracts com. 1953-55; mem. council, sect. pub. contract law 1968-71, sec. 1971-72, chmn. com. bd. contract appeals 1972—), Wis., Fed. (nat. council 1968-69, 71-72) bar assns., Bar Assn. D.C. (chmn. taxation com. 1954-55, steering com. sect. govt. contracts; chmn. adminstrv. law sect. 1975-76, dir. 1975-76), Wranglers, Scribes, Phi Delta Phi. Clubs: Univ., Army and Navy, Nat. Lawyers. Author: Cases and Materials on the Law of Government Contracts; Flaherty's District of Columbia Practice; articles on law. Home: 8521 Doter Dr Waynewood Alexandria VA 22308 Office: 1800 M St NW Washington DC 20036

MOSZYNSKI, JERZY ROBERT, mech. engr., educator; b. Lwow, Poland, May 12, 1925; s. Stanislaw Karol and Miroslawa Helena (Sterzynska) M.; came to U.S., 1955, naturalized, 1966; B.Sc. in Engring. with 1st class honors, U. London, 1949, M.Sc., 1952, Ph.D., 1958; m. Barbara Magdalena Trzaska-Durska, Dec. 16, 1950; children—Stanislaw Karol, Catherine Irene. From asst. lectr. to lectr. U. London, 1949-54; sr. design engr. English Electric Co., Leicester, Eng., 1954-55; research asso. Brown U., Providence, 1955-58; asst. prof. Case Inst. Tech., Cleve., 1958-60, asso. prof., 1960-63, prof., 1963-66; prof. mech. engring. U. Del., Newark, 1966—; cons. TRW Inc., Babcock and Wilcox Co., Argonne Nat. Lab., Nat. Bur. Standards. Served with Polish Underground Army, 1942-45. NSF research and travel grants; recipient Alexander von Humboldt Found. Marshall prize, 1974-75. Mem. ASME, Am. Soc. Engring. Edn., Instn. Mech. Engrs., AAUP, Polish Vets. in Exile Assn. Contbr. articles to profl. jours. Home: 501 Country Club Dr Newark DE 19711 Office: Dept Mech and Aero Engring U Del Newark DE 19711

MOTLEY, JOHN PAUL, psychiatrist; b. Carbondale, Pa., July 5, 1927; s. Joseph Adrian and Lillian (McCormick) M.; B.S., Georgetown U., 1951; M.D., Hahnemann Med. Coll., Phila., 1955; m. Barbara Bennett Mitchell, Feb. 1, 1958; children—Marianne, Patricia, Kathleen, John Paul, Elizabeth, Joseph A. III, Grace, Michael. Intern, Hahnemann Med. Coll. Hosp., Phila., 1955-56; resident in psychiatry Inst. of Living, Hartford, Conn., 1956-59; practice medicine specializing in psychiatry, Point Pleasant, N.J., 1961—; mem. staff Jersey Shore Med. Center, 1961-72, chief of psychiatry, 1970-72; mem. staff Point Pleasant Hosp., 1961—, chief of psychiatry, 1961—; cons. in forensic psychiatry to various cts. and agys.; dir. Moat Corp. Served with U.S. Army, 1944-47; ETO. Diplomate Am. Bd. Psychiatry and Neurology. Fellow Am. Psychiat. Assn.; mem. AMA, Royal Coll. Psychiatry, N.J. Psychiat. Assn. (pres. elect). Clubs: Springlake Golf; Scranton Country (Clarks Summit, Pa.). Office: 3822 River Rd Point Pleasant NJ 08742

MOTT, CHARLES HARVEY, accountant, educator; b. Norwich, Conn., Nov. 29, 1930; s. Charles H. and Mabel E. (Lambert) M.; B.S. in Accounting magna cum laude, U. Conn., 1956; M.B.A., U. Hartford, 1966; postgrad. Am. U., 1969—; m. Madeline Margaret Leary, Feb. 16, 1952; 1 dau., Karen Elizabeth. Cost accountant Pratt & Whitney aircraft div. United Aircraft Corp., East Hartford, Conn., 1956-57, asst. chief cost accountant, Middletown, Conn., 1957-58, chief cost accountant, 1958-63, budget and cost controller, East Hartford, 1963-67, staff asst., controller's office, 1967-68; research and devel. controller Black and Decker Mfg. Co., Towson, Md., 1969-70, mgr. fin. planning, 1970-71; div. controller L. Greif & Brother div. Genesco Inc., Balt., 1971-73, v.p. fin., 1973-75; facility controller Curtis Bay (Md.) facility Davison Chem. Co., 1975-76; controller Contee Sand & Gravel Co., Laurel, Md., 1976-77, treas., 1977—; partner firm Jeffers and Mott, Pasadena, Md., 1975—; instr. accounting U. Balt., 1974-75, asst. prof. accounting, 1975—. Vol., United Fund of Central Md., 1971. Served with U.S. Army, 1950-52. C.P.A., Md. Mem. Nat. Assn. Accountants (Best Article award Balt. chpt. 1973, award for contbn. to lit. 1977), Am. Inst. C.P.A.'s, Md. Soc. C.P.A.'s, Am. Inst. Corporate Controllers, Planning Execs. Inst. (v.p. 1974), Am. Accounting Assn., Phi Kappa Phi. Democrat. Roman Catholic. Contbr. articles to profl. publs. Home: 3904 Rayton Rd Randallstown MD 21133 Office: PO Box 1000 Laurel MD 20810

MOTT, GEORGE FOX, mgmt., internat. affairs cons.; b. Riverside, Calif., June 4, 1907; s. George Fox and Alice (Way) M.; A.B., Stanford U., 1929, A.M., 1931; Ph.D., U. Minn., 1938; m. Dorothy Hale Williams, Feb. 12, 1944; children—David Edward Way, Jonathan Loren Gould. Dean, prof. English and polit. sci. San Diego Army and Navy Acad. and Jr. Coll., 1929-33; dean, prof. edn. and polit. sci. Emerson Jr. Coll., Chgo., 1933-35; asst. to pres. Hancher Orgn., Chgo., 1935-36; asst. prin., critic instr. Univ. High Sch., Coll. Edn., U. Minn., 1936-38; dean students, publicity dir. N.Mex. State U., 1938-39; cons., asst. dir. Kansas City Sch. Survey, 1939; cons. Mayors Survey Coms., St. Louis, Houston, 1939-40; chief analyst, adv. council War Assets Adminstrn., 1946-48; mng. partner, sr. cons. Mott of Washington & Assos., 1948—; chmn. Mott Research Group, 1952—; pres., chief exec. officer Wold Air Brush Mfg. Co.; cons. Bilger Monorail Internat. Inc., 1975—; vis. prof. U. Md., 1949, Fla. State U., 1950; adj. prof. Am. Univ., 1964-70; internat. lectr. in field. Alt. mem. adv. council to Com. on Fund Raising within Fed. Services, 1959-66; bd. dirs., to 1977, since bd. counsellors and chmn. Greater Washington council United Bd. for Christian Higher Edn. in Asia. Bd. dirs., founding mem. Am. Korean Found., 1952-62, spl. cons., 1962-67; hon. mem. Noyes Sch. Rhythm Found.; mem. Am. Symphony Orch. League. Mem. arty. U.S. Army, Res., 1928-63; served as col. U.S. Army, 1940-46, with Insp. Gen.'s Office, 1941-45, insp. gen. Am. Forces-in-Korea, 1945-46. Decorated Bronze Star with cluster, Commendation Ribbon; Distinguished Service citation Republican of Korea, 1962. Mem. AIM (pres.'s council), AAAS, Am. Acad. Polit. and Social Sci., Am. Polit. Sci. Assn., Nat. Def. Transp. Assn., Res. Officers Assn. (past Md., Va. and D.C. dept. pres., past nat. chmn. army affairs com., nat. resolutions com.; past nat. and dept. officer, minuteman), Nat. Rifle Assn. (trustee Pinwheel Jr. Rifle Club), Mil. Order World Wars (past comdr. D.C. chpt., mem. nat. gen. staff), Sino-Am. Soc. (dir. 1966), Mil. Order Fgn. Wars, Am. Legion (past post comdr., chmn. dept. resolutions com.), Ill. Mfg. Assn., Chgo. Trade and Commerce (dir. 1975—), Nat. Art Materials Trade Assn., Phi Delta Kappa (life). Clubs: Elks, Army and Navy. Author: San Diego Politically Speaking, 1932; History of the Middle Ages, 1933, rev., 1950; Survey of Journalism, 1937; Housing of College Students in the U.S., 1938; New Survey of Journalism, 1950, rev., 1965; U.S. Government Jobs, 1950; Survey of U.S. Ports, 1951; mil. engring. series, 1952-54; Miami's Marine Destiny, 1955; The Panama Canal: Today's Decision-Tomorrow's Security (A Case History 1963 to 1977), 1977; editor: Transportation Renaissance, 1963; Transportation Century, 1967; Urban Change and the Planning Syndrome, 1973; Wold Airbrush Artist series, 1975—. Home: 3220 Rittenhouse St NW Washington DC 20015 Office: Dupont Circle Bldg Washington DC 20036 also 2171 N California Ave Chicago IL 60647

MOTT, VINCENT VALMON, educator; b. Washington, La., Sept. 18, 1916; s. Lucius and Marie (LeDoux) M.; A.B., Xavier U., 1938; M.A., Fordham U., 1947, Ph.D., 1956; m. Margaret McDonald, June 19, 1948; children—Vincent Valmon, Helene Virginia, John Michael. Instr. social sci. U. Scranton (Pa.), 1947-51; instr. econs. Seton Hall U., South Orange, N.J., 1952-53, asst. prof., 1954-58, asso. prof., 1958-66, prof. mktg., 1966—; adj. asso. prof. sociology St. Peters Coll., Jersey City, 1955-60. Pres., Florham Park Press, Madison, N.J., 1957—; mem. bd. LePlay Research, Inc. Mem. bd. advisers Scranton Inst. Indsl. Relations, 1949-50. Served with AUS, 1940-45. Mem. AAUP, Am. Mktg. Assn. Author: The American Matriarchy, 1970; The American Consumer, 1972; (with N. Chirovsky) Philosophy in Economic Thought, 1972, Philosophical Foundations of Economic Doctrines, 1978; editorial bd. Jour. Acad. Marketing Sci., N.J. Gerontol. Soc. Contbg. editor N.J. Bus. Mag., 1955-56; editor Jour. Bus., Seton Hall U., 1963—. Home: 12 Leslie Ave Florham Park NJ 07932 Office: Seton Hall U South Orange NJ 07079

MOTTA, JOHN RICHARD, profl. basketball coach; b. Salt Lake City, Sept. 3, 1931; s. Ambrose and Zelda (Squires) M.; B.S., Utah State U., 1953, M.A., 1960; m. Janice Fraser, June 4, 1954; children—Kip A., Jodi, Kirt Glen. Jr. high sch. basketball coach, Grace, Idaho, 1953, high sch. basketball coach, 1956-59; basketball coach Weber State Coll., Ogden, Utah, 1961-68; basketball coach Chgo. Bulls, 1969-76, gen. mgr., dir. player personnel, 1973-76; coach Washington Bullets, 1976—. Served with USAF, 1954-56. Named Coach of Yr., Nat. Basketball Assn., 1971. Office: care Washington Bullets Capital Centre Landover MD 20786*

MOTTER, ROBERTA LEE, state ofcl.; b. Honolulu, Mar. 8, 1936; d. Donald D. and Florence B. (Downie) Reed; student Cornell U., summer 1956, various other courses; children—Eddie, Lori, Lisa. Dir. personnel Hawaiian Village Hotel, Honolulu, 1956-59; office mgr. Fisher Constrn. Co., Honolulu, 1960-61; paymaster, computer specialist Gate City Steel, Omaha, 1961-64; payroll supr., accounts receivable supr. Mayflower Hotel, Washington, 1966-67; computer specialist, dir. personnel Alan M. Voorhees & Assos., McLean, Va., 1968-71, adminstrv. mgr. PRC Computer Center subs., 1972-73; conversion specialist accounts payable system Medenco, Inc., Houston, 1973-74; personnel dir., office mgr. Summit Ins. Co. of N.Y., Houston, 1974-75; dir. personnel and adminstrn. N.Y. State Ins. Dept. Liquidation Bur., N.Y.C., 1975—. Mem. Am. Soc. Personnel Mgrs., N.Y. Purchasing Mgmt. Assn., Beta Sigma Phi. Democrat. Home: 21 Dameo Pl Short Hills NJ 07078 Office: 116 John St New York City NY 10038

MOTTLEY, CHARLES CRANSTON, investment co. exec.; b. Vancouver, B.C., Can., Apr. 6, 1934; s. Charles McCammon and Jean Dow (Cranston) M.; came to U.S., 1938, naturalized, 1958; B.S., Hampden Sydney Coll., 1956; B.D., Union Theol. Sem., Richmond, Va., 1959; m. Geraldine I. Frederick, Dec. 13, 1970; children—Marcia, Douglass, Joshua, Jed. Tchr., coach St. Christopher's Sch., Richmond, 1958-62; football coach U. Va., 1962-63; v.p., sales mgr. A.E. Finley & Assos. Va., constrn. equipment sales, 1963-67; founder, 1968, since pres., owner Mottley Industries, Inc., and predecessor, venture capital investments, Gt. Falls, Va.; founder, pres. Man to Man, Inc., 1973-75. Democratic candidate for U.S. Congress, 1974; mem. Gov. Va. Adv. Com. Volunteerism; vice chmn. Offender Aid and Restoration U.S.A., 1975-77. Mem. Fairfax County C. of C. Club: Kiwanis. Author: Now, 1970; The Parables of Jesus, 1972; co-author: The Mustard Seed, 1977. Columnist, Charlottesville (Va.) Daily Progress, 1974-75. Home: 420 River Bend Rd Great Falls VA 22066 Office: PO Box 17401 Dulles Airport Washington DC 20041

MOUAT, ROBERT HARROWER, JR., employment agy. exec.; b. Southampton, N.Y., July 17, 1946; s. Robert Harrower and Pamela Lane (Sharretts) M.; B.Sc.E., Britannia Royal Naval Coll., Eng., 1968; m. Abigail Alta Cornell, Feb. 19, 1969; children—William John-Thomas, Perrin Ray. Sales rep. Curtis Pub. Co., 1969-70; cons. to tech. industry, 1970-74; owner, mgr. Norwalk (Conn.) div. Snelling & Snelling, tech. placement, 1974—; pres. Abro Realty Co., 1974—, Most Devel. Co., 1977—. Served with Royal Navy, 1965-69. Mem. Nat. Employment Assn., Norwalk C. of C., Air Force Assn., Rolls Royce Owners Club. Democrat. Presbyterian. Home: 60 Cross Hwy Redding CT 06896 Office: 64 Wall St Norwalk CT 06850

MOULTON, ELLIOTT JAN, consulting co. exec.; b. Grand Haven, Mich., Nov. 5, 1936; s. Elliott Glen and Gladys Fern (Seiler) M.; B.E.E., Clarkson Coll. Tech., 1958; M.B.A., Harvard U., 1965. Mgmt. trainee telephone operating group ITT, Havana, Cuba, 1958, Santiago, Chile, 1959-60; mem. tech. staff Space Tech. Labs., Redondo Beach, Calif., 1960-61; asso. sta. mgr. Hughes Aircraft Corp., Culver City, Calif. and Johannesburg, S. Africa, 1962-63; mgr. African and Near East devel. Communications Satellite Corp., Washington, 1965-68, asst. to v.p. fin., 1968-69; dir. and treas. Teleconsult, Inc., Washington, 1970-78. Mem. Republican com. of Washington, 1971-72. Served to lt. Signal Corps, U.S. Army, 1960-67. Mem. S.R., Nat. Huguenot Soc., Founders and Patriots Am., Tau Beta Pi, Eta Kappa Nu, Delta Upsilon. Clubs: Harvard (N.Y.); Univ. (Washington). Home: 1061 Thomas Jefferson St NW Washington DC 20007

MOULTON, JOHN KNIGHT, educator; b. Hartford, Conn., July 8, 1914; s. Jasper Roland and Edith (Knight) M.; A.B., Harvard, 1936; Ed.M., 1940; A.M., Bowdoin Coll., 1962, Ed.D. (hon.), 1970; m. Miriam Hoagland, June 26, 1937; children—Miriam (Mrs. Anthony O. Tyler), Deborah. Tchr. math., Brookline, Mass., 1945-62; lectr. math. Northeastern U., 1959-62; mem. staff Bowdoin Coll. Summer Insts., 1966-69; prof. math. U. Maine, 1962-78; ret., 1978; editorial cons. Addison-Wesley Pub. Co. Mem. speakers bur. for secondary schs. Math. Assn. Am. Named Mass. Tchr. of Year, U.S. Office Edn. and Council Chief State Sch. Officers, 1967. Mem. NEA, Assn. Advanced Placement Math. Tchrs. (past pres.), Phi Delta Kappa. Conglist. (deacon 1972-73). Co-author: College Freshman Mathematics, 1968; Elementary Calculus from an Advanced Viewpoint, 1967; Five Modules in College Geometry, 1975. Home and office: Box 316 Yarmouth ME 04096

MOULTON, PAUL (PETE) DOUGLAS, systems engr.; b. Binghamton, N.Y., Sept. 1, 1944; s. Fredrick Douglas and Helene Marjorie (Cole) M.; B.S. in Math., Clarkson Coll. Tech., 1966, M.S. in Indsl. Mgmt., 1968; (N.Y. Regent scholar); children—Susan Jenifer, Jeremy Matthew. Instr. indsl. mgmt. Clarkson Coll. Potsdam, N.Y., 1967-68; tech. staff Sanders Data Systems, Inc., Nashua, N.H., 1968-71; grad. asst. Pa. State U., University Park, 1971-72; computer specialist Nat. Weather Service, Silver Spring, Md., 1972; mgr. Info. and Communication Applications, Inc., Rockville, Md., 1972-75; mgr. Rehab. Group, Inc., Arlington, Va., 1975-77; systems engr. U.S. Senate, Washington, 1977—; speaker at interface, 1977, 78; cons. and lectr. in field. Mem. Am. Inst. Indsl. Engrs. (sr.). Contbr. articles to profl. jours. Home: 9453 Greco Garth Columbia MD 21045 Office: Senate Computer Center 400 N Capitol St Washington DC 20510

MOULTRIE, JAMES, artist; b. Lakeland, Fla., July 13, 1941; s. Alfred and Florie Mae (Washington) M.; student Art Students League, 1961-62, Frank J. Reilly Sch. Art, N.Y.C., 1961-64; diploma Art Instrn. Schs., Mpls., 1964, Bur. Cartooning, Colorado Springs, 1974, Cartoonerama, Branford, Conn., 1975; A.A., Pels Sch. Art, N.Y.C., 1976; m. Marlene McClary, Oct. 23, 1971. Free lance comml. and fine arts artist, 1967-74; beauty portrait artist Florie Roberts, Inc., Farmingdale, N.J., 1975-76; police officer N.Y.C. Transit Police Dept., 1965—; works exhibited Atlantic City Art Show, 1977, Allied Artists Am., 1976, Art Instrns. Sch. Ann., 1965, Lakewood Arts and Crafts Show, 1976; T.A. Art Assn. Show, 1975, Rego Park (N.Y.) Outdoor Show, 1968; represented in permanent collections Art Instrns. Sch., Bur. Cartooning, numerous pvt. collections. Served with AUS, 1958-60. Recipient numerous awards in fine arts. Mem. Soc. Internat. Soc. Artists (charter), Soc. N.Am. Artists. Baptist. Home: 131 Governors Rd Lakewood NJ 08701

MOUNT, WADSWORTH WALTON, inventor; b. Wheaton, Minn., July 22, 1907; s. William Henry Hooten and Louise (Wadsworth) M.; A.B., Amherst Coll., 1928; m. Doris Ogden, Aug. 1, 1945; children—John Wadsworth, William Ogden, Keith Alden, Wendy Elizabeth. Various positions in investment banking, accounting, mgmt. of mfg. bus., printing and pub., 1928-37; asst. dir. research Commerce and Industry Assn. N.Y.C., 1938-41, mgr. indsl. bur., 1941-43; inventor, promoter new products, 1946—. Recipient Naval Ordnance Devel. award for new weapon U.S. Navy, 1945. Mem. Am. Ordnance Assn., Am. Rocket Soc. (former dir. N.Y. chpt.), Delta Upsilon. Baptist. Club: Deer Lake. Contbr. articles on econs., sci. to jours.; developer Consol. Bus. Tax plan (plan by which bus. collects fed. taxes by levying true added value defined as cash receipts less cash payments to outsiders), 1941; inventor line throwing rockets, cable and reel (rep. in Nat. Air and Space Museum-Smithsonian Inst.); holder over 20 U.S., fgn. patents. Home and Office: 154 Mountain Ave Warren NJ 07060

MOUNT, WARD (PAULINE WARD), artist, painter, sculptor; b. Batavia, N.Y.; d. Fred Kendall and Nellie L. (Dowsey) Ward; student N.Y. U., Art Students League; pupil of Gertrude Gardner, Kenneth Hayes Miller, Albert P. Lucas, Joseph P. Pollia; m. Elmer M. Mount; 1 son, Marshall Ward. Former head dept. oil painting and sculpture N.J. State Tchrs. Coll.; former mem. faculty Acad. Allied Arts, N.Y.C.; dir., instr. Ward Mount Art Classes; dir. art Jersey City Med. Center; represented by paintings and sculptures in Pa. Acad. Fine Art, Delgado Mus., Carlebach Galleries, Hudson River Mus., Medalic Art, Brentanos, Roosevelt Mus., Montclair Art Mus., Los Angeles Mus., Trenton State Mus., Jersey City Mus., Nat. Acad. of Design, Library of Congress, Nat. Sculpture Soc., Archtl. League (N.Y.), Verona Pub. Library, N.Y. Pub. Library, Municipal Art Galleries, Allied Artists Am., Grand Central Palace, Acad. of Allied Arts (N.Y. City), Am. Brit. Art Center, N.Y. Hist. Mus., Essex, Sussex & Warren and Monmouth hotels (Spring Lake, N.J.), Berkley Carteret (Asbury Park, N.J.), Terry Art Inst. (Miami, Fla.), Smithsonian Inst., Audubon Artists (N.Y.C.), Jersey City Med. Center, Mus. Modern Art, Madison Sq. Garden, Carlebach Galleries, N.Y. Hist. Mus., Nat. Arts Club, N.Y.C., Lever House, N.Y.C.; represented by painting N.Y. World's Fair, 1965, F. D. Roosevelt Mus., Archives Am. Art, Eng.;

one of two largest contbns. of Louis Comfort Tiffany Exhbn. held at Mus. Contemporary Crafts, 1958; Riverside Mus., Finch Coll. Mus., N.Y.C., France, Germany, Italy, Switzerland, others; represented in many pvt. collections, including the late Franklin D. Roosevelt, Charles B. Howard of Can., George Timkin Fry, Bernard U. Gimbel, Leonard Wood Hall, Westchester Art Assn., Archives Am. Art, Eng., Franklin D. Roosevelt Mus., others. Recipient 1st prize for water-color Jersey City Art Exhbn., 1923; 1st prize for oil painting Jersey City Mus., 1941; 1st prize sculpture Painters and Sculptors Soc. N.J., 1943; Clayton E. Freeman 1st prize sculpture, ann. state exhbn. Montclair Art Mus.; 1st prize sculpture N.J. Artists (Union, N.J.); 1st prize sculpture Asbury Park Soc. Fine Arts; 1st prize for sculpture Kearny Mus.; Favrile and Flowers purchased by Jersey City Mus. for permanent collection; 1st prize for sculpture Art Fair, N.Y.C.; 1st prize for sculpture Painters and Sculptors Soc. N.J., Jersey City Mus.; Gold medallion as woman of achievement Jersey Jour.; designed, executed bell of Am. Bell Assn., Christmas Card Am. Heart Assn., 1971. Fellow Internat. Inst. Arts and Letters (life), Royal Soc. Arts Eng., Internat. Platform Assn., Knight Mark Twain; founder Painters and Sculptors Society N.J. (pres. 12 years, now hon. pres.); mem. Artists Equity Assn., DAR, Knight of Mark Twain. Collector Tiffany Favrile glass and art. Contbr. exhbn. Mus. Contemporary Art, N.Y.C., 1958, Finch Coll. Mus. Home: 72 Sherman Pl Jersey City NJ 07307 Studio: 74 Sherman Pl Jersey City NJ 07307

MOUNTAN, ALBERT WAYNE, veterinarian; b. Westmoreland County, Pa., Sept. 25, 1927; s. Albert Earl and Lulu Jane (Johnson) M.; student St. Vincent Coll., 1945-47; V.M.D., U. Pa., 1951; m. Sara Jane Bender, June 20, 1951; children—Gregory Alan, Cheryl Lynn, Deborah Ann, Amy Leigh. Pvt. practice veterinary medicine, Latrobe, Pa., 1953—; mem. Westmoreland County Agrl. Extension Exec. Com., 1969-73. Mem. Latrobe C. of C., Pa. (past pres., past chmn. bd.), Western Pa. (past pres.) veterinary med. assns., Am. Animal Hosp. Assn., Am. Assn. Equine Practitioners. Republican. Methodist. Clubs: Masons, Elks, Lions, Ligonier Country. Address: 809 Monastery Dr Latrobe PA 15650

MOUTRAN, JULIA SPENCER, sch. adminstr.; b. Raleigh, N.C., Mar. 17, 1947; d. Carl Baxter and Julia Mills (Farish) Spencer; student Mary Washington Coll., 1965-67; B.S., U. Va., 1969; M.A., U. Conn., 1975, postgrad., 1975—; m. Alan Wayne Moutran, Apr. 14, 1978. Tchr. Pub. Schs. Knoxville (Tenn.), 1969-70; tchr. West Hartford (Conn.) Pub. Schs., 1970-72, coordinator, 1972—. Mem. Phi Kappa Phi, Phi Delta Kappa, Pi Lambda Theta, Zeta Tau Alpha. Home: 36 Rosewood Rd Avon CT 06001 Office: 35 Barksdale Rd West Hartford CT 06117

MOWAD, JOSEPH JAMES, urologist; b. Scranton, Pa., July 2, 1935; s. James Thomas and Hind Marie (Yamin) M.; B.S. magna cum laude, U. Scranton, 1957; M.D., Creighton U., 1961; m. Josephine M. Cardillo, June 24, 1961; children—Christen, Nicole. Intern, Harrisburg (Pa.) Hosp., 1961-62; resident in gen. surgery U. Md., Balt., 1964-65, resident in urologic surgery, 1965-68; asso. urology Geisinger Med. Center, Danville, Pa., 1968—. Mem. Pa. Gov.'s Advisory Com. on Renal Disease, 1973—; mem. Advisory Bd. on Drug and Alcohol, Montour County, Pa., 1973—, Montour County Child Welfare Service, 1972—; del. to renal disease council Susquehanna Valley (Pa.) Regional Med. Program, 1973—. Alternate service with USPHS, 1962-64. Diplomate Am. Bd. Urology. Fellow A.C.S.; mem. AMA, Am., Central Pa., Pa. urol. assns., Montour County Med. Soc. Democrat. Roman Catholic. Clubs: Elks, Frosty Valley Country (bd. dirs.). Home: Frosty Hills Dr RD 4 Danville PA 17821 Office: Geisinger Med Center Danville PA 17821

MOWER, GEORGE RICHARDSON, dairy farmer; b. Bangor, Maine, July 31, 1903; s. Frank Lester and Mildred Mae (Richardson) M.; student U. Maine, 1922-23; m. Harriet Elizabeth Vickery, Oct. 27, 1928; children—George H., Frank E., Charles M., Donald L., Emily Mower Doble, Martin A., Priscilla Mower Hodsdon, Caroline Mower Doane, Harold E. Mail carrier U.S. Post Office, Bangor, 1923-58; dairy farmer, Bangor, 1927—; notary pub.; justice of peace. Active Boy Scouts Am.; mem. Maine Legislature, 1963-64; treas. Penobscot County, 1973-74; treas. Penobscot County Republican Com., 1970—, chmn. ward 5 Bangor, 1965-75. Recipient Farmer of Yr. award Maine Grange, 1972. Mem. Grange (state dep. 1936-43), Farm Bur. (county pres. 1958-62, county dir. 1954—, state dir. 1961-62), Nat., Maine Ayrshire assns., Phi Mu Delta. Conglist. Clubs: Kiwanis (chmn. agrl. com.), Masons (past master), Shriners. Home: RFD 1 Bangor ME 04401

MOWITZ, ARNOLD MARTIN, chemist; b. N.Y.C., Jan. 14, 1923; s. Isidore and Mamie Lillian (Rittenberg) M.; B.S., Coll. City N.Y., 1943; M.A., U. Buffalo, 1953; m. Clare Levine, Sept. 22, 1946; children—Ira Jeffrey, Sandra Karen. Chief analytical research chemist Nat. Aniline div. Allied Chem. & Dye Corp., Hopewell, Va., 1946-55; tech. mgr. research services dept. Inmont Corp., Clifton, N.J., 1955-77, mgr. indsl. toxicology, 1977—. First aid instr., ARC; dist. commr. Boy Scouts Am., 1971-76, recipient Scouters Key award, Shofar award; pres. Little League Teaneck, 1964; trustee Teaneck Jewish Center, 1977—. Served with AUS, 1943-46. Mem. Am. Microchem. Soc. (nat. chmn. 1961), Am. Chem. Soc., Soc. Applied Spectroscopy, Am. Inst. Chemists, AAAS, N.Y. Acad. Sci., ASTM, Sigma Xi. Jewish religion. Club: Masons. Patentee in gas chromatography instrumentation. Home: 1111 Falmouth Ave Teaneck NJ 07666 Office: 1255 Broad St Clifton NJ 07015

MOWRY, DAVID THOMAS, chemist; b. Pyengyang, Korea, Mar. 11, 1917 (parents Am. citizens); s. Eli Miller and Lois (Thomas) M.; B.A., Coll. Wooster, 1938; M.S., Ohio State U., 1940, Ph.D., 1941; m. Dorothy Bernice Robins, Oct. 16, 1971; children—Lynn Mowry Cox, Sarah Lois, Thomas Cassel. Teaching fellow Ohio State U., 1938-41; research group leader Monsanto Co., Dayton, Ohio, 1941-52, devel. mgr., St. Louis, 1952-58, dir. gen. devel. dept., 1958-61, devel. mgr. plastics div., 1961-64; mng. dir. Monsanto Japan Ltd., Tokyo, 1964-74; mgr. East Asia, internat. div. NUS Corp., 1974-77; patent licensing specialist, nat. tech. info. service U.S. Dept. Commerce, Washington, 1977—; dir. Ryoko Chemstrand, Japan EPC Ltd.; cons. Am. Planning Corp. Chmn. bd. dirs. Bluff Hosp., Yokohama, Japan, 1970-73. Mem. Am. Chem. Soc., Comml. Devel. Assn., Licensing Execs. Soc., Am. Nuclear Soc., Chem. Soc. (London), U.S. Power Squadron (comdr. Yokohama 1973), Phi Beta Kappa, Sigma Xi. Clubs: Chemists (N.Y.C.); Internat., Cosmos (Washington); Tokyo, Press (Tokyo). Contbr. articles to various jours. Patentee. Home: 2737 Devonshire Pl NW Apt 408 Washington DC 20008 Office: 5285 Port Royal Rd Springfield VA 22161

MOXEY, LOUIS WHITE, III, cons. elec. engr.; b. Phila., Jan. 8, 1908; s. Louis White and Emma Christine (Boettger) M.; grad. high sch.; m. Myrtle Stehlig, June 20, 1931; children—Richard Todd, Ronald Louis. With Keller-Pike Co., Phila., 1926-51, sec., 1928-43, pres., 1943-51; cons. engr., Phila., 1951-62; partner Louis W. Moxey III & Assos., Phila., 1962-71; pres., treas. Moxey Assos., Inc., New Britain, Pa., 1971-75; cons., 1975—. Registered profl. engr., Pa., N.J., Del. Mem. IEEE (life, sr.), Nat. Soc. Profl. Engrs. Home: 201 Braeburn Terr Lansdale PA 19446 Office: 31 N Tamanend Ave New Britain PA 18901

MOXEY, RICHARD TODD, elec. engr.; b. Phila., Sept. 20, 1932; s. Louis W. and Myrtle L. H. (Stehlig) M.; B.S.E.E., Drexel U., 1956; m. Lorraine Anne Flindt, Feb. 2, 1957; children—David Todd, Susan Lynn. Draftsman, Walker-Yeomans Assos., Inc., Phila., 1952-53, Louis W. Moxey, Phila., 1954-56, project engr., 1957-61; partner Louis W. Moxey & Assos., Jenkintown, Pa., 1962-70; v.p., sec. Moxey Assos., Inc., Hatboro, Pa., 1970-75, pres., 1975—. Served with C.E., U.S. Army, 1957. Registered profl. engr., Pa., N.J., N.Y., Conn., Md., Del., Va. Mem. IEEE, Profl. Engrs. in Pvt. Practice, Illuminating Engring. Soc., Nat., Pa. socs. profl. engrs. Home and Office: 31 N Tamanend Ave New Britain PA 18901

MOYER, ARLINGTON SCHULER, mfg. co. exec.; b. Easton, Pa., July 17, 1915; s. Arlington Clinton and Catherine Elizabeth (Schuler) M.; M.E., Internat. Sch., 1938; m. Helen Elizabeth Kuhns, Feb. 6, 1932; children—Mary Jane, Carol, Diane. With Mack Trucks Inc., 1935—, v.p., gen. mgr. Allentown (Pa.) ops., 1971-78; ret., 1978. Pres. East Pa. Sch. Dist. Bd. Edn., 1950-62, Lehigh County Bd. Edn., 1961-62; trustee Lehigh County Community Coll., 1965—. Mem. Soc. Mfg. Engrs., Soc. Automotive Engrs., Am. Def. Preparedness Assn., Automotive Orgn. Team, Smithsonian Inst. Republican. Mem. United Ch. of Christ. Clubs: Mason, Lehigh Country, Shepherd Hills Country, Lehigh Valley, Pilots. Home: 32 Shepherd Hills Ave Wescosville PA 18106 Office: 2100 Mack Blvd Allentown PA 18105

MOYER, F. STANTON, stock broker; b. Phila., June 7, 1929; s. Edward T. and Beatrice (Stanton) M.; B.S. in Econs., U. Pa., 1951; m. Ann P. Stovell, May 16, 1953; children—Edward E., Alice E. Registered rep. Smith, Barney & Co., Phila., 1951-54, Kidder, Peabody & Co., Phila., 1954-60; mgr. corp. dept. Blyth Eastman Dillon & Co., Inc. (formerly Eastman Dillon, Union Securities & Co.), Phila., 1960-65, instnl. sales mgr., 1965-67, gen. partner, 1967-71, 1st v.p., 1971-74, sr. v.p., 1974—. Mem. Bond Club Phila., Financial Analysts Phila., Phila. Securities Assn., Delta Psi Clubs: Racquet, Philadelphia, St. Anthony (Phila.); Merion Cricket (Haverford, Pa.); Gulph Mills Golf (King of Prussia, Pa.). Republican. Episcopalian. Home: 37 Evans Ln Haverford PA 19041 Office: 3 Girard Plaza Philadelphia PA 19102

MOYER, JOHN HENRY, physician; b. Hershey, Pa., Apr. 1, 1919; s. John H. and Anna Mae (Gruber) M.; B.S., Labanon Valley Coll., 1939, Sc.D. (hon.), 1968; M.D., U. Pa., 1943; m. Mary Eliabeth Hughes, Sept. 3, 1948; children—John Henry IV, Michael Warren, Carl Frederick, Anna Mary, Nancy Elizabeth, Mary Louise, Mathew Timothy. Intern, Pa. Hosp., Phila., 1943; resident in Tb and contagious diseases Belmont Hosp., Worcester, Mass., 1944-45; resident in medicine Brooke Gen. Hosp., San Antonio, Tex., 1947; fellow in pharmacology and medicine U. Pa. Sch. of Medicine, Phila., 1948-50; practice medicine specializing in internal medicine Houston, 1950-57, Phila., 1958-74, Johnstown, Pa., 1975—; asst. instr. in Tb and contagious diseases U. Vt., 1944-45; asst. prof. medicine and pharmacology Baylor U. Coll. Medicine, Houston, 1950-52, asso. prof., 1952-56, prof., 1956-57; prof., chmn. dept. medicine Hahnemann Med. Coll. and Hosp., Phila., 1957-72, exec. v.p. acad. affairs, 1971-73; dir. profl. and ednl. affairs Conemaugh Valley Meml. Hosp., Johnstown, 1974—; prof. medicine, dir. regional affairs Temple U. Sch. Medicine, Phila.; cons. Bd. Veterans Appeals, 1963—, Pa. Med. Soc. Council on Edn. and Sci., 1974—, Pa. Med. Care Found., 1976—, VA Hosp., Houston, Tex., 1950-57, VA Hosp., Phila., 1958-68, Phila. Naval Hosp., 1958-74, Phila. Gen. Hosp., 1958-74; attending physician Meth. Hosp., Houston, 1950-52, sr. attending physician, 1952-57, Jefferson Davis Hosp., Houston, 1952-57; prof. medicine Hahnemann Hosp., Phila., 1957-74. Trustee U.S. Pharmacopeia, Inc., 1970—, pres., 1970-75. Recipient Susan and Theodore R. Cummings Humanitarian award, 1962, 65, 66, Honors Achievement award Angiology Research Found., 1965, Trustees award Hahnemann Med. Coll., 1964; diplomate Am. Bd. Internal Medicine. Fellow A.C.P. (mem. subcom. on hosp. clinics 1969-72), Am. Coll. Chest Physician (mem. com. on hypertension 1962-70), Am. Coll. Cardiology (mem. publs. com. 1962-70), N.Y. Acad. Scis., Am. Soc. Clin. Pharmacology and Therapeutics (chmn. com. on med. edn. 1969-72), Oscar B. Hunter award 1959, pres. 1965-66); mem. Am. Soc. for Pharmacology and Exptl. Therapeutics (mem. com. on toxic reactions to drugs 1964-67), Assn. of Am. Med. Colls., Pa., Cambria County med. socs., Pa. Thoracic Soc., Am. Acad. Med. Dirs., Soc. for Explt. Biology and Medicine, Am. (mem. med. advisory bd. 1962-64), Pa. heart assns., Soc. of Med. Consultants to the Armed Forces, Physiol. Soc. of Phila., Central Soc. for Clin. Research, AMA (del. sect. clin. pharmacology and therapeutics 1972—), Am. Med. Authors, Peruvian Soc. of Cardiology (hon. mem.), Hellenic Soc. of Cardiology (hon. mem.), AAAS, So. Soc. Clin. Research, All Pa. Coll. Alumni Assn. (Alumnus citation award 1971), Sigma Xi. Mem. United Ch. Christ. Club: Union League (Phila.). Contbr. numerous articles on renal pathology, cardiology, clin. pharmacology and pulmonary diseases to med. jours.; editor-in-chief Cyclopedia of Medicine, 1963-65, Today's Clinician, 1977—; editorial bd. Family Practice News, 1971—, Internal Medicine News, 1969—. Home: 556 Colgate Ave Johnstown PA 15905 Office: Conemaugh Valley Memorial Hospital 1086 Franklin St Johnstown PA 15905

MOYER, KENNETH HAROLD, metall. engr.; b. Wappingers Falls, N.Y., Oct. 1, 1929; s. William Leander and Charlotte (Cronk) M.; B.S., Poly. Inst. Bklyn., 1959, M.S., 1962; m. Carol Louise Rauch, Sept. 12, 1965; children—Tawnie Chi, Julie Ellen, Renee Marie, Kenneth Harold. Head heat treatment dept., paint line and quality control U.S. Hoffman Machinery Corp., Poughkeepsie, N.Y., 1953-54; supr. paint line Internat. Nickel Research Lab., Bayonne, N.J., 1954-55; jr. engr. quality control lab. Grumman Aircraft Engring. Corp., Bethpage, N.Y., 1955-58; mgr. quality control lab. Sylvania-Corning Nuclear Corp., Bayside, N.Y., 1958-60; project engr. Beryllium Corp., Reading, Pa., 1960-62; mgr. beryllium operations Gen. Astrometals Corp., Yonkers, N.Y., 1962-66; mgr. spl. alloys Hoeganaes Corp., Riverton, N.J., 1966—; instr. Temple U., 1969-75, Spring Garden Coll., 1974—; info. officer U.S. Naval Acad., 1974—. Served with USN, 1948-50. Fellow Am. Soc. Metals (chmn. Phila. chpt. 1976-77), Am. Inst. Mining, Metall. and Petroleum Engrs., Am. Ordnance Assn., Soc. Mfg. Engrs., AAAS, Vols. Internat. Tech. Assistance, N.Y. Acad. Scis. Registered profl. engr., Pa., N.J. Episcopalian. Clubs: Cinnaminson Community Chorus, Church Bowling League. Contbr. articles in field to profl. jours. Home: 4 Green Briar Lane Cinnaminson NJ 08077 Office: River Rd and Taylors Lane Riverton NJ 08077

MOYLAN, DERMOT BRENDAN, retail corp. exec.; b. Kanturk, Ireland, Feb. 5, 1935 (parents Am. citizens); s. Michael Francis and Margaret (Kennealy) M.; B.B.A., St. Johns U., 1961, postgrad. Coll. Ins., 1962; m. Jannis Marie Bonnett, Oct. 4, 1958; children—Michael, Linda, David. With Zayre Corp., discount dept. store, Framingham, Mass., 1967—, mgr. ins. benefits adminstrn., 1967-73, asst. sec., 1973—. Served with AUS, 1953-55. Mem. Nat. Safety Mgmt. Soc., Am. Soc. Ins. Mgmt., Nat. Fire Protection Assn., Adjusters Roundtable Boston, Mass. Ins. Buyers Assn. Club: Milford Country. Home: 138 Stagecoach Rd Holliston MA 01746 Office: 770 Cochituate Rd Framingham MA 01701

MOYLAN, FERGUS MICHAEL BLAKE, physician; b. Dublin, Ireland, Sept. 23, 1944; s. Donough Patrick and Hanora Margaret (Canning) M.; came to U.S., 1968, naturalized, 1973; M.B., B.Ch., B.A.O., Nat. U. Ireland, 1968; m. Kathleen Ann Kelly, Aug. 9, 1969; children—Aislin Balfour, Clifford Kelly. Intern, Mt. Carmel Mercy Hosp., Detroit, 1968-69; resident in pediatrics Bellevue Hosp., N.Y.C., 1969-71, Mass. Gen. Hosp., Boston, 1971-72, asso. dir. pediatric intensive care unit, 1973-77; asso. dir. neonatology New Eng. Med. Center Hosp., Boston, 1977—; fellow Harvard Med. Sch., 1972-73, instr., 1973-77; asst. prof. pediatrics Tufts U. Sch. Medicine, 1977—; cons. staff St. Margaret's Hosp. for Women; lectr. pediatrics Boston U. Sch. Medicine. Diplomate Am. Bd. Pediatrics. Fellow Am. Acad. Pediatrics; mem. Soc. Critical Care Medicine, Am. Thoracic Co., New Eng., Irish-Am. pediatric socs. Contbr. articles to profl. jours. Home: 295 Commonwealth Ave Boston MA 02116 Office: 171 Harrison Ave Boston MA 02111

MOYNIHAN, DANIEL PATRICK, U.S. senator; b. Tulsa, Mar. 16, 1927; s. John Henry and Margaret Ann (Phipps) M.; student City Coll. N.Y., 1943; B.A. cum laude, Tufts U., 1948, M.A., Fletcher Sch. Law and Diplomacy, 1949, Ph.D., Fletcher Sch. Law and Diplomacy, 1961, LL.D., 1968; Fulbright fellow London (Eng.) Sch. Econs. and Polit. Sci., 1950-51; A.M. (hon.), Harvard, 1966; LL.D., La Salle Coll., 1966, Seton Hall Coll., 1966, Catholic U. Am., 1968, Ill. Inst. Tech., 1968, New Sch. Social Research, 1968, Duquesne U., 1968, St. Louis U., 1968, U. Calif., 1969, U. Notre Dame, 1969, Fordham U., 1970, St. Bonaventure U., 1972, U. Ind., 1975, St. Anselm's Coll., 1976, Boston Coll., 1976, Ohio State U., 1976, Adelphi U., 1976, Hebrew U., 1976; D.Pub. Adminstrn., Providence Coll., 1967; L.H.D., U. Akron, 1967, Hamilton Coll., 1968. D.S.Sc., Villanova U., 1968; D.H., Bridgewater State Coll., 1972; D.Sc., Mich. Technol. U., 1972; m. Elizabeth Therese Brennan, May 29, 1955; children—Timothy Patrick, Maura Russell, John McCloskey. With Internat. Rescue Com., 1954; successively asst. to sec., asst. sec., acting sec. to gov. State of N.Y., 1955-58; mem. N.Y. State Tenure Commn., 1959-60; dir. N.Y. State Govt. Research Project, Syracuse U., 1959-61; spl. asst. to sec. labor, 1961-62, exec. asst. to sec., 1962-63, asst. sec. labor, 1963-65; dir. Joint Center for Urban Studies, Mass. Inst. Tech. and Harvard U., 1966-69; prof. edn. and urban politics Kennedy Sch. Govt., Harvard U., 1966-73, sr. mem., 1966—, prof. govt., 1973—; asst. for urban affairs to Pres. U.S., 1969-70, counsellor to Pres. U.S., mem. Cabinet, 1969-70, cons. to Pres. U.S., 1971-73; mem. U.S. del. 26th Gen. Assembly, UN, 1971; mem. Pres.'s Sci. Adv. Com., 1971-73; ambassador to India, New Delhi, 1973-75; U.S. permanent rep. to UN, N.Y.C., 1975-76; U.S. Senator from N.Y., 1977—. Vice chmn. Pres.'s Temp. Commn. on Pennsylvania Avenue, 1964-73; chmn. adv. com. traffic safety dept. HEW; fellow Center Advanced Studies, Wesleyan U., 1965-66; hon. fellow London Sch. Econs. and Polit. Sci., 1970—. Sec. pub. affairs com. N.Y. State Democratic Com., 1958-60; del. Dem. Nat. Conv., 1960, 76. Vice chmn. Woodrow Wilson Internat. Center for Scholars, 1971—; chmn. bd. trustees Joseph H. Hirshhorn Mus. and Sculpture Garden, 1971—. Served with USN, 1944-47. Recipient Centennial medal Syracuse U., 1969. Mem. Am. Philos. Soc., Nat. Acad. Pub. Adminstrn., AAAS (vice chmn. 1971, dir. 1972-73), Catholic Assn. Internat. Peace, Am. Acad. Arts and Scis. (chmn. seminar on poverty). Clubs: Century, Harvard (N.Y.C.); Federal City (Washington). Author: Maximum Feasible Misunderstanding, 1969; The Politics of a Guaranteed Income, 1973; Coping: On the Practice of Government, 1974; co-author: Beyond the Melting Pot (Anisfield award 1963), 1963. Editor: The Defenses of Freedom, 1966; On Understanding Poverty, 1969; Toward a National Urban Policy, 1970; co-editor: On Equality of Educational Opportunity, 1972; Ethnicity: Theory and Experience, 1975. Editorial bd. Am. Scholar, Pub. Interest. Contbr. articles to profl. publs. Home: Waldorf Towers Apt 42A 50th St and Park Ave New York City NY 10022 Office: 1109 Dirksen Senate Office Bldg Washington DC 20510

MOZO, WILLIAM BRANTLY, JR., dentist; b. Cheyenne, Wyo., Jan. 9, 1950; s. William Brantly and Naomi Ruth (Berry) M.; D.D.S., U. Mo., 1975; m. Elizabeth Faria, June 27, 1976; 1 son, Adam Brant. Resident, Englewood (N.J.) Hosp., 1975-76; pvt. practice dentistry, Plainfield, N.J., 1976—; mem. staff Muhlenberg Hosp.; instr. oral pathology Middlesex County Coll. Chmn. dental div. United Way, 1977-78; mem. Hillside Ave. Citizens Group, 1978-79. Mem. Am., N.J., Plainfield dental socs., Acad. Gen. Dentistry. Methodist. Home: 1118 Hillside Ave Plainfield NJ 07060 Office: 829 Park Ave Plainfield NJ 07060

MPELKAS, CHRISTOS CHARLES, plant physiologist; b. Lynn, Mass., Apr. 16, 1920; s. Charles and Katherine (Thomas) M.; A.S., Essex A. and T. Inst., Mass., 1942; B.S., U. Mass., 1949; M.S., U. Conn., 1950; m. Angela Vlahakis, June 8, 1947; children—Charles, John, William, Katherine. Research produce mgr. Star Supermarkets, Newtonville, Mass., 1950-52; research technician Mass. Agrl. Expt. Sta., Waltham, 1952-53; head vegetable crops dept. Essex A. and T. Inst., Hathorne, Mass., 1953-61; with Sylvania Lighting Products, Danvers, Mass., 1961-71, sr. applications engr., 1971-77; resource devel. specialist U. Mass., Amherst, 1971-77; plant physiologist, mktg. mgr. GTE Agronomics div. GTE Sylvania, 1977—. With Lynn Conservations Service, 1974—. Served with USAF, 1943-46. Mem. Am. Soc. Agrl. Engrs., Am. Inst. Biol. Scis., Am. Soc. Plant Physiologists, Am. Soc. Hort. Sci., Bot. Soc. Am., Illuminating Engring. Soc. Greek Orthodox. Clubs: Nahout Lions; Amity Masons (Danvers, Mass.). Home: 12 Mansfield St Lynn MA 01904 Office: 100 Endicott St Danvers MA 01923

MRAZ, RUTH REED, univ. ofcl.; b. Ft. Fairfield, Maine, Feb. 8, 1927; d. Walter Manley and Eva Ruth (Seeley) Reed; student R.I. Sch. Design, 1945-46; A.A., Erskine Coll., 1948; student Boston U., 1946-48; m. Arthur J. Mraz, Aug. 7, 1948; children—Randall, Nancy. Feature writer, dist. corr. Gannett Pub. Co., Portland, Maine, 1959-70; dir. univ. relations U. Maine, Presque Isle, 1970—. Free-lance writer, 1959—; cons. pub. relations, also antiques and restorations. Mem. Maine Potato Blossom Festival Com., 1960-78; mem. Gov.'s Task Force for Rehab., 1968-69, Maine State Museum Commn., 1966-77; mem. exec. com. Council for Advancement and Support of Edn., 1976—; mem. Gov.'s Positive Action Com., 1976-78; mem. Maine planning com. White House Conf. on Libraries, 1978—. Bd. dirs. N.E. Dist. YMCA, 1968-71, Maine YMCA, 1969-72; bd. dirs. Found. U. Maine at Presque Isle, 1973—, clk., 1972—. Recipient Woman of Yr. award Philomathian Club, 1968. Mem. Am. Coll. Pub. Relations Assn. (New Eng. membership chmn. 1973-76, hospitality chmn. 1973-74), Council for Advancement and Support Edn. (exec. com. 1977), Beta Sigma Phi (hon.), Kappa Mu (hon.). Club: Philomathian (pres. 1952-53, 77—) (Fort Fairfield, Maine). Home: Monson Pond Fort Fairfield ME 04742 Office: U Maine at Presque Isle Presque Isle ME 04769

MROCZEK, WILLIAM JOSEPH, research physician; b. N.Y.C., Aug. 9, 1940; s. William and Helena (Federowicz) M.; B.A., Seton Hall U., 1962; M.D., N.J. Coll. Medicine, 1966; children—Michelle Anne, Melissa Lynn; m. Christine Landegger, Apr. 7, 1979. Intern, St. Michael Hosp., Newark, 1966-67; resident Georgetown U. med. div. D.C. Gen. Hosp., 1967-69; fellow in cardiovascular disease Georgetown U. Sch. Medicine, 1969-70, asst. prof. medicine, 1972-77; chief dept. hosp. clinics Ft. Campbell, Ky., 1970-72; asso.

prof. medicine Howard U., Washington, 1977—; dir. hypertension and hemodynamics lab. D.C. Gen. Hosp., 1972—. Bd. dirs. Nations Capitol affiliate Am. Heart Assn., 1976—. Served to maj. U.S. Army, 1970-72. Diplomate Am. Bd. Internal Medicine. Fellow Am. Coll. Cardiology, Am. Coll. Angiology, Am. Coll. Geriatrics; mem. Am. Fedn. Clin. Research, Am. Soc. Nephrology, Am. Soc. Clin. Pharmacology and Therapeutics, Nat. Kidney Found., AMA. Contbr. numerous articles to med. jours. Office: 19th and Massachusetts Ave SE Washington DC 20003

MRUK, WALTER FREDERICK, physicist; b. McKees Rocks, Pa., Jan. 9, 1928; s. Walter Joseph and Katherine (Zabawa) M.; B.S.E.E., Carnegie Inst. Tech., 1949; M.S. in Physics, U. Pitts., 1954; Ph.D. in Physics, U. Tenn., 1963; m. Claudia Urban, May 7, 1949; 1 dau., Celeste Claudia. Research asst. Mine Safety Appliances Co., Pitts., 1949-54; sr. scientist Oak Ridge Nat. Lab., 1954-65; dir. physics research Honeywell Corp., Ft. Washington, Pa., 1965-67; cons. med., glass and textile measurements, Phila., 1967-75; chmn. dept. electronics, asst. prof. electronics Community Coll. Phila., 1975—; mem. faculty LaSalle Coll., N.Y. Inst. Tech.-Old Westbury. Served with USN, 1945-46. Mem. Instrument Soc. Am., Am. Phys. Soc., Electrostatic Soc. Am., Franklin Inst., Sigma Xi. Clubs: Quadradox Aero.; Sons of Copper Beeches; Phila. Piloting, Vesper (Phila.). Research on fission fragment times of flight; velocity of ultrasonic pulses in water. Office: 1600 Spring Garden St Philadelphia PA 19130

MUCCARI, FRANK GREGORY, educator; b. Squillace, Italy, July 13, 1928; s. Joseph and Antonette (Ferraro) M.; B.S., Temple U., 1959; M.S., U. Pa., 1961. Tchr., Overbrook Regional High Sch., Clementon, N.J., 1959-61, NE Cath. High Sch., Phila., 1961-62; tchr. social studies North Penn High Sch., Lansdale, Pa., 1962—. Served with USAF, 1950-53. Mem. Am. Hist. Assn., NEA. Roman Catholic. Home: 1150 Emerald Ave Lansdale PA 19446 Office: Valley Forge Rd Lansdale PA 19446

MUCENIEKS, PAUL RAIMOND, chemist; b. Latvia, Feb. 3, 1921; s. Robert and Anna (Keirs) M.; student U. Latvia, 1940-43; M.A., Johns Hopkins U., 1961, Ph.D., 1964; m. Ella Arendt, May 17, 1956; 1 dau., Jasmím Rebecca. Prin. physicist Litton Systems, Silver Spring, Md., 1962-64; sr. research chemist FMC Corp., Princeton, N.J., 1964—. Gilman fellow, 1959-64. Mem. Am. Chem. Soc., Electrochem. Soc., Phi Lambda Upsilon. Patentee in field. Home: Glenn Ave Lawrenceville NJ 08648 Office: PO BOX 8 Princeton NJ 08540

MUCHNICK, RICHARD STUART, ophthalmologist; b. Bklyn., June 21, 1942; s. Max and Rae (Kozinsky) M.; B.A. with honors. Cornell U., 1963, M.D., 1967; m. Felice Dee Greenberg, Oct. 29, 1978. Intern medicine N.Y. Hosp., N.Y.C., 1967-68; resident in ophthalmology, 1970-73; individual practice medicine, specializing in ophthalmology, notably strabismus and ophthalmic plastic surgery N.Y.C., 1974—; attending staffs N.Y., Manhattan Eye, Ear and Throat hosps., N.Y.C.; clin. asst. prof. ophthalmology Cornell U., N.Y.C., 1977—. Served with USPHS, 1968-70. Recipient Coryell Prize Surgery Cornell U. Med. Coll., 1967. Diplomate Am. Bd. Ophthalmology, Nat. Bd. Med. Examiners. Fellow A.C.S., Am. Acad. Ophthalmology and Otolaryngology; mem. Am. Soc. Ophthalmic Plastic and Reconstructive Surgery, Am. Assn. Pediatric Ophthalmology and Strabismus, N.Y. Soc. Clin. Ophthalmology, AMA, Alpha Omega Alpha, Alpha Epsilon Delta. Clin. researcher strabismus, ophthalmic plastic surgery, 1973—. Office: 111 E 65th St New York City NY 10021

MUCK, DARREL LEE, chemist, mktg. exec.; b. Larned, Kans., Jan. 26, 1938; s. Howard Fred and Florence Lulu (Pritchett) M.; B.S. in Chemistry (indsl. research scholar 1955-57), Wichita State U., 1959, M.S., 1962; Ph.D. in Phys. Organic Chemistry, U. Fla., 1965; certificate in bus. gmt. Villanova U., 1978; m. Judith Ann Meyer, June 4, 1960; children—Jay Curtis, Brian Lee. Teaching and research fellow U. Fla., 1962-65; research chemist Procter & Gamble Co., Miami Valley Labs., 1965-71; tech. service specialist Pfizer, Inc., N.Y.C., 1971-72; tech. mgr. Phila. Quartz Co., Primos, Pa., 1972-74; mgr. polymer additives PQ Corp., Valley Forge, Pa., 1974—. Mem. Soc. Plastics Industry, Soc. Plastic Engrs., Am. Ceramic Soc., Am. Chem. Soc., Soc. Preservation and Encouragement Barbershop Quartet Singing in Am. (adminstrv. v.p., asst. chmn. internat. contest and conv. 1977). Republican. Presbyterian. Contbr. articles to profl. jours. Home: 19 Oak Hill Circle Malvern PA 19355 Office: PO Box 840 Valley Forge PA 19482

MUELLER, CLAUS, sociologist; b. Berlin, Germany, July 23, 1941; s. Wilhelm and Dorothea Elisabeth (Milsch) M.; B.A., U. Cologne, 1964; M.A., New Sch. Social Research, 1966, Ph.D., 1970; C.E.P., Institut de'Etudes Politques, Paris, 1967; m. Carol Coe Conway, Sept. 1968 (div.); m. 2d, Martha A. Link, June 1976 (div.). Photog. editor W. Ger. TV, Cologne, 1963-64; sales analyst Avon, Inc., N.Y.C., 1964-65; custodian New Sch. Art Gallery, N.Y.C., 1969-70; cons. Herder & Herder, N.Y.C., 1970-72, Casriel Inst. Group Dynamics, N.Y.C., 1973, Vision of Asia, N.Y.C., 1977—, Brockton (Mass.) Art Center, 1978—, NSF, 1979; exec. producer VideoSociology, Manhattan Cable TV, N.Y.C., 1974-76; asst. prof. sociology Hunter Coll., N.Y.C., 1970-74, asso. prof., 1974—, dir. masters in social research program, 1976—; partner Media Resource Assos., N.Y.C., 1978—. Mem. Am. Sociol. Assn., Inst. Internat. de Sociologie, Assn. Ind. Video and Film Makers, Univ. Film Assos., Center for Inter-Am. Relations, Nat. Acat. TV Arts and Scis. Author: The Politics of Communications, 1973. Home: 420 E 64th St W2H New York City NY 10021 Office: Hunter Coll 695 Park Ave New York City NY 10021

MUELLER, HANS JACOB, engineer; b. Schwenningen, Germany, Dec. 14, 1919; s. John and Elise (Banholzer) M.; came to U.S., 1925, naturalized, 1932; student Oliver Wolcott Tech. Sch., 1934-38, U. Conn., 1939-41, Waterbury State Tech. Sch., 1966; m. Agnes Krayeski, Jan. 29, 1944; children—Thomas John, James Paul. Apprentice tool maker Seth Thomas Clock Co., Thomaston, Conn., 1939-41; tool and die maker Scovill Mfg. Co., Waterbury, Conn., 1941-47; die maker, model maker E. Ingraham Co., Bristol, Conn., 1947-52; tool maker, model marker Technicraft Labs., Thomaston, 1952-57; production engr. Microtech, Inc., Cheshire, Conn., 1957-61; engring. mgr. Electronic Specialty Co., Thomaston, 1961-66; chief engr. Tech Systems Corp., Thomaston, 1966—; cons. New Opportunities of Waterbury, 1975—. Vice pres., team mgr. Thomaston Little League, 1958-65; awards com. chmn. Boy Scouts Am., Thomaston, 1958-65; council St. Thomas Roman Cath. Ch., 1975—. Served with USN, 1944-50. Mem. Soc. Mfg. Engrs., Internat. Electromech. Com., Electronic Industries Assn., Am. Soc. Metals, Am. Legion, Smithsonian Assos. Home: 115 Clay St Thomaston CT 06787 Office: 401 Watertown Rd Thomaston CT 06787

MUELLER, HARRY LOUIS, pediatric allergist; b. Steubenville, Ohio, May 28, 1908; s. Charles Louis and Mary Elizabeth (Rarick) M.; B.S., Harvard Coll., 1930, M.D., 1934; m. Lyna Christopher, Apr. 23, 1964; children—Gretchen, Sandra, Harry. Intern, Mass. Gen. Hosp., Boston, Children's Hosp., Boston, 1934-37; resident in pediatrics Children's Hosp. Mich., Detroit, 1937; pediatrician Commonwealth Fund, East Ala. Health Dist., 1938-39; vis. pediatrician Mass. Gen. Hosp., 1939-41; instr. Harvard Med. Sch., 1941-52, clin. asso., 1952-56, asso. clin. prof. pediatrics, 1957-74; asst. pediatrician Childrens Hosp., Boston, 1946-52, asso. allergist, 1952-56, allergist in chief, 1952-74, asso. clin. allergist in chief emeritus, 1974—, also prof. emeritus. Diplomate Am. Bd. Pediatrics (chmn. Am. Bd. Pediatric Allergy (1966-68). Fellow Acad. Pediatrics, Acad. Allergy; mem. New Eng. Soc. Allergy (past pres.), New Eng. Pediatric Soc., AMA, Mass., N.H. med. socs. Republican. Congregationalist. Clubs: Rotary. Author textbook in field, also research papers. Home: Cricket Farm Boston Post Rd Amherst NH 03031 Office: 300 Longwood Ave Boston MA 02115 and 2 4 Prospect Ave Nashua NH 03060

MUELLER-HEUBACH, EBERHARD AUGUST, physician, educator; b. Berlin, Feb. 24, 1942; s. Heinrich Gustav and Elizabeth (Heubach) Mueller; came to U.S., 1968; M.D., U. Cologne, 1966; m. Cornelia Uffmann, Feb. 6, 1968. Intern, U. Cologne, W. Ger., 1967-68, Middlesex Hosp., New Brunswick, N.J., 1968-69; research fellow obstetrics, gynecology Columbia U., N.Y.C., 1969-71; resident, chief resident obstetrics, gynecology Sloane Hosp. Women, N.Y.C., 1971-75; asst. prof. obstetrics, gynecology U. Pitts., 1975—; individual practice medicine, specializing in obstetrics, gynecology Pitts., 1975—. Diplomate Am. Bd. Obstetrics and Gynecology. NIH research fellow, 1969-71. Mem. Soc. Gynecol. Investigation, Soc. Perinatal Obstetricians. Fellow Am. Coll. Obstetricians and Gynecologists. Researcher fetal, maternal physiology; contbr. articles to med. publs. Home: RD 2 Box 254 Venetia PA 15367 Office: Magee-Women's Hosp Forbes Ave and Halket St Pittsburgh PA 15213

MUENKER, LOUIS THOMAS, guidance counselor; b. Phila., Dec. 3, 1950; s. Louis Joseph and Helen Agnes (Uzar) M.; B.A. in Psychology, Kutztown State Coll., 1972, M.Ed. in Guidance and Counseling, 1973; postgrad. Pa. State U.; m. Margaret Theresa Roethke, Aug. 9, 1975. Home and sch. visitor Phila. Sch. Dist., 1973, sch. counselor, 1973-74; dir. guidance Mt. Carmel (Pa.) Area Sch. Dist., 1974—, also tchr. career edn. classes, supr. testing program. Mem. Am., Pa. personnel and guidance assns., Am., Pa., Susquehanna Valley sch. counselors assns., Pa. Assn. Counselor Edn. and Supervision, Mt. Carmel Area Edn. Assn. (sec. 1975-76, v.p. 1976-77), Iota Alpha Delta. Club: Lions (v.p. 1977-79). Home: 227 W 3d St Mount Carmel PA 17851 Office: W 5th St Mount Carmel PA 17851

MUFFLER, JOHN PAUL, clergyman; b. Washington, Aug. 17, 1948; s. John Paul and Marie Ellen (Tracey) M.; B.A., St. Mary's Sem. and U., Balt., 1970, M.Div., 1974; postgrad. U. Notre Dame, 1976; M.A. candidate Johns Hopkins U., 1978. Ordained priest Roman Catholic Ch., 1974; asso. pastor St. Bernardine Ch., Suitland, Md., 1974—; mem. intermediate dept. faculty Mt. Calvary Sch., Forestville, Md., 1975-78; mem. jr. high faculty Sts. Paul and Augustine Sch., Washington, 1978—; mem. Senate of Priests, 1975—. Bd. dirs. New Directions, 1974-77. Certified in manual communication and sign lang. Mem. Am. Personnel and Guidance Assn., Am. Sch. Counselors Assn., Nat. Cath. Guidance Conf., Cath. Com. on Urban Ministry. Democrat. Club: K.C. Home: 13000 Evanston St Rockville MD 20853 Office: 1425 V St NW Washington DC 20009

MUGAVERO, FRANCIS J., clergyman; b. Bklyn., June 8, 1914; ed. Cathedral Coll., Bklyn.; Immaculate Conception Sem., Huntington, N.Y., Fordham U. Ordained priest Roman Catholic Ch., 1940; bishop of Bklyn., 1968—. Address: 75 Greene Av Brooklyn NY 11238

MUIR, J(OHN) DAPRAY, lawyer; b. Washington, Nov. 9, 1936; s. Brockett and Helen Cassin (Dapray) M.; student McGill U., 1954-55; A.B., Williams Coll., 1958; LL.B., U. Va., 1964; m. Louise Rutherfurd Pierrepont, July 16, 1966; children—John Dapray, Christopher Bryant, Sophia Stuyvesant. Admitted to D.C., Md., Va., U.S. Supreme Ct. bars; law clk. U.S. Dist. Ct. for D.C., 1964-65; practiced in Washington, 1965-71; staff asst. Exec. Office of Pres., 1971; asst. legal adviser for econ. and bus. affairs Dept. State, 1971-73; gen. practice, Washington, 1974—. Mem. U.S. del. Joint U.S./USSR Comml. Commn., 1972. Served to lt. (j.g.) USNR, 1958-61. Mem. Am. (co-chmn. com. on internat. econ. orgns., internat. law sect.), Fed., D.C. bar assns., Am. Soc. Internat. Law, The Barristers. Clubs: Metropolitan (Washington); Chevy Chase (Md.). Bd. editors Va. Law Rev., 1963-64; bd. advisers Jour. Internat. Law and Econs., 1974—. Home: 2905 Woodland Dr Washington DC 20008 Office: 1819 H St NW Washington DC 20006

MUIRHEAD, GEORGE ROBERTSON, coll. adminstr.; b. Waterloo, Iowa, Feb. 10, 1925; s. James Alexander and Margaret Drynan (Dodd) M.; B.A., Coe Coll., 1945; M.A., U. Iowa, 1947, Ph.D., 1951; m. Ann Maloney, July 4, 1964; children—Paul, Margaret, Mary, Sara. Instr. history U. Iowa, Iowa City, 1948-49; instr. Central Conn. State Coll., New Britain, 1949-53, asst. prof., 1953-57, asso. prof., 1957-66, prof., 1966—, dir. div. social sci., 1969-73, asst. to v.p. academic affairs, 1974—; exchange lectr. Bingley Coll., Yorks, Eng., 1973-74. Past pres. mem. bd. dirs. New Britain Repertory Theatre, 1963—. Danforth postdoctoral fellow, 1963. Mem. Am., New Eng. hist. assns. Democrat. Unitarian. Home: 91 Farmington Chase Crescent Farmington CT 06032 Office: Central Conn State Coll New Britain CT 06050

MUIRHEAD, GLEN D., ret. supt. schs.; b. Pitts., Dec. 7, 1917; s. William and Marion (Glenn) M.; B.A., Muskingum Coll., 1939; M.Ed., U. Pitts., 1948; postgrad. U. W.Va., 1940, U. Del., 1960-61, U. N.C., 1941, U. Cin., 1952; m. Wilma Dean Croft, June 2, 1943; children—Dean (Mrs. Manning L. Crump), Beverly Jean (Mrs. Demmon F. Canner), Marilyn (Mrs. David W. Boucher). Tchr. various schs., 1940-53; supervising prin. Amwell Twp. Sch. Dist., Amity, Pa., 1953-60, John M. Clayton Sch. Dist., Dagsboro, Del., 1960-63; supt. schs. Saucon Valley Sch. Dist., Hellertown, Pa., 1963-70, North East Sch. Dist., North East, Pa., 1970-75, ret., 1975. Sec. Vol. Fire Co., Marianna, Pa., 1950-58, pres., 1959-60; active Boy Scouts Am., 1932-52. Treas. Lehigh U. Sch. Bd. Conf., 1968-70. Served with AUS, 1942-46. Mem. NEA, Pa., Del. edn. assns., Am. Assn. Sch. Adminstrs., Pa. Assn. Sch. Adminstrs. (pres. 1971), Kappa Sigma, Phi Delta Kappa. Presbyterian (elder 1961—). Lion. Home: 95 Tannery St North East PA 16428

MUKAI, CROMWELL DAISAKU, chemist; b. Bostonia, Calif., Apr. 13, 1917; s. Tasaburo and Fusae (Tsujino) M.; student San Diego State Coll., 1937-39; B.S., U. Calif., Berkeley, 1943; postgrad. U. Nebr., 1943-44, Wayne U., 1945-46; lM.S., N.Y. U., 1949, Ph.D., 1955; m. Kyoko Hoshiga, Oct. 26, 1944; children—Robert Lawrence, Thomas Victor, David Daisaku, Margret Kyoko. Devel. chemist Gelatin Products Corp., Detroit, 1944-46; with Boyle-Midway div. Am. Home Products Corp., Cranford, N.J., 1946-75; mgr. Analytical Lab. and Lithographic Varnish Devel. Lab., Polychrome Corp., Yonkers, N.Y., 1975—. Mem. Am. Chem. Soc., Soc. Applied Spectroscopy, Sigma Xi. Methodist. Home: 26 Brook St Berkeley Heights NJ 07922 Office: 137 Alexander St Yonkers NY 10702

MUKERJI, JATINDRA NATH, librarian; b. Allababad, India; s. Rajendra Nath and Pusparenu (Chatterji) M.; came to U.S., 1962; M.A., LL.B., Allababad U.; B.L.S., Aligarh U.; M.Law Librarianship, U. Wash., Seattle, 1964. Asst. law librarian Multnomah County Law Library, Portland, Oreg., 1964; asst. prof. law, law librarian Williamette U. Coll. Law, Salem, Oreg., 1965-69, asso. prof. law, 1969-75; dir. library services Seton Hall U. Law Library, Newark, 1975—. Mem. Am. Assn. Law Libraries, Am. Trial Lawyers Assn., Conf. Law Sch. Library Dirs. Greater N.Y., Phi Delta Phi. Co-author: Legal Periodical Management Data, Vol. 1, 1978. Home: 830 Main St Apt D Belleville NJ 07109 Office: 1111 Raymond Blvd Newark NJ 07102

MUKHERJEE, ASIT BARAN, educator; b. Suri, India; s. Shyama Pada and Savasona (Chatterjee) M.; came to U.S., 1963, naturalized, 1969; B.S., U. Utah, 1965, M.S., 1966, Ph.D., 1968; m. Tapani Ghoshal, July 9, 1970; 1 son, Deepro. Teaching asst. U. Utah, Salt Lake City, 1965-67, univ. research fellow, 1967-68; research asso. Upstate Med. Center, Syracuse, N.Y., 1968-69; postdoctoral fellow Columbia, 1969-70; instr. Albert Einstein Coll. Medicine, N.Y.C., 1970-72; asst. prof. dept. biol. scis. Fordham U., Bronx, N.Y., 1972-77, asso. prof., 1977—. NIH fellow, 1969-70; W. Alton Jones Found. fellow, 1973—; Herman and Ruth Goodman Found. grantee, 1974-75; Fordham U. Faculty research grantee, 1973—. Mem. AAAS, Am. Soc. Cell Biology, Tissue Culture Assn., Sigma Xi, Phi Sigma. Contbr. articles to profl. jours. Home: 2100 Eastchester Rd Bronx NY 10461 Office: E Fordham Rd Bronx NY 10458

MULDER, DAVID STEVENSON, cardiovascular surgeon; b. Eston, Sask., Can., July 28, 1938; s. Peter and Laura Mulder; M.D., U. Sask., 1962; M.Sc., McGill U., 1964; m. Norma D. Johnston, Aug. 19, 1961; children—Scott David, Lizabeth Jane, John Christopher. Tng. in gen. surgery Montreal Gen. Hosp., 1962-67, cardiac surgery U. Iowa Hosp., 1967-69; research tng. McGill U. Med. Sch., 1969-70, prof. surgery, 1980—; mem. staff Montreal Gen. Hosp., also mem. exec. com., surgeon-in-chief; staff Montreal Children's, Montreal Chest, Royal Victoria hosps.; team physician Montreal Jr. Canadians. Fellow Royal Coll. Surgeons Can.; mem. A.C.S. Contbr. articles to med. jours. Home: 751 Upper Lansdowne Crescent Westmont PQ Canada Office: Room 633 Montreal Gen Hosp Montreal PQ Canada

MULDER, FREDERICK SASSER, state ofcl.; b. nr. Alexander City, Ala., Nov. 24, 1932; s. William S. and Sarah (Sasser) M.; student Auburn U., 1951; B.S., U. Ala., 1955; certificate U. Paris, 1955; M.S., N.Y. U., 1965, postgrad., 1965—; postgrad. Columbia U., 1962-63, New Sch. for Social Research, 1971-72; certificate state edn. dept. State U. N.Y. With N.Y. State Dept. Mental Hygiene and Social Service, N.Y.C., 1958—, exec. dept. Div. Youth, 1971—; psychiat. admitting officer N.Y. U. Med. Center-Bellevue Psychiat. Hosp., 1967-75, N.Y.C. Health and Hosp. Corp., 1973-75; dir. West Bklyn. Counseling Services. Trustee Tng. Center for Social Workers, 1976-78. Served to 1st lt. AUS, 1956-58. Mem. Assn. Mil. Surgeons, Soc. Descs. Knights of Most Noble Order Garter, SAR, Colonial Order Crown, Ala., Elmore County hist. assns., Police Res. Assn. N.Y.C. (sponsor), Am. Soc. Pub. Adminstrn., Res. Officers Assn., U. Ala. Nat. Alumni Assn. Clubs: Nat. Trust; Nat. Democratic (N.Y.C.). Author: Samuel Whatley, R.S., 1762-1826. Home: 1482 York Ave New York City NY 10021 Office: 50 Court Brooklyn NY 11201

MULDER, HERMAN, coal co. exec.; b. The Hague, Netherlands, June 7, 1946; s. Herman and Wilma (Prijs) M.; came to U.S., 1977; M.L.L., U. Rotterdam, 1969, B.Econs., 1972; m. Hillegrien F. Horring, May 15, 1970; children—Alexander, Jan-Maarten, Michiel. Asst. treas., fin. analyst Pakhoed Holding Co., Rotterdam, 1972-76, project mgr. mergers and acquisitions, 1977; devel. mgr. coal Pakhoed Coal Co., Blue Bell, Pa., 1977—. Home: 114 Executive Dr Ambler PA 19002 Office: 650 Skippack Pike Blue Bell PA 19422

MULE, SALVATORE JOSEPH, pharmacologist; b. Trenton, N.J., Apr. 7, 1932; s. Vincent P. and Frances (Palmere) M.; B.A., Coll. of Wooster, 1954; M.S., Rutgers U., 1955; Ph.D., U. Mich., 1961; m. Anne C. Haney, Apr. 28, 1956; children—Marc, Timothy, Jeffrey, Martine. USPHS postdoctoral fellow U. Wis., 1961-63; research pharmacologist NIMH Addiction Research Center, Lexington, Ky., 1963-68; lab. dir., asst. commr. Drug Abuse Control Commn., Bklyn., 1968—. Cons. to govt. and industry including WHO. Served with AUS, 1956-58. Mem. Am. Soc. Pharmacology, Am. Chem. Soc., N.Y. Acad. Sci., AAAS, Am. Inst. Chemists, Am. Soc. Clin. Chemistry, Am. Mgmt. Assn., Fedn. Am. Scientists, Am. Acad. Forensic Sci. Editor books, also editor in chief Drug Abuse Series. Contbr. articles to profl. jours. Home: 204 Arborlea Ave Yardley PA 19067 Office: DSAS Testing and Research Lab 80 Hanson Pl Brooklyn NY 11217

MULERT, HOWARD MAX, ins. broker; b. Pitts., Feb. 19, 1929; s. Carl J. and Thelma M. (Salkeld) M.; student U. Nev., 1947-49; m. Jeanne P. Vaux, June 20, 1950; children—Sandra J., Jeffrey S. Trainee The London Assurance, N.Y.C., 1949-50; with Justus Mulert Co., Pitts., 1950-64, v.p., dir., 1955-64, pres., 1970—; v.p. Edwards, George & Co., Ebbert, Grant & Kakel, Pitts., 1964-66; v.p., dir. Strothman & Mock, Inc., Pitts., 1966-70; v.p. 900 Washington, Inc. Bd. dirs. Golden Triangle YMCA, 1962—, chmn. bd., 1968-70; chmn. bd. Mt. Lebanon (Pa.) Community Center, 1968-69. Past bd. dirs., v.p. adminstrn. Civic Light Opera Assn. Greater Pitts.; bd. dirs. Greater Pitts. Bus. Devel. Corp., 1977—. Mem. Nat. Assn. Life Underwriters, Nat. Assn. Ins. Agents, Greater Pitts. Assn. Ind. Ins. Agents and Brokers (past v.p.), Mass Marketing Ins. Inst. (charter; dir., past v.p.), Nat. Assn. Ins. Brokers, Pitts. Alumni Assn., Internat. Platform Assn., Sigma Alpha Epsilon (past pres.). Republican. Episcopalian. Mason (32 deg., Shriner, Jester). Clubs: Allegheny, Duquesne, St. Clair Country, Allegheny (dir. 1971—), Rotary. Home: 137 Mayfair Dr Pittsburgh PA 15228 Office: Union Bank Bldg Pittsburgh PA 15222

MULFORD, DONALD LEWIS, publisher; b. Montclair, N.J., Apr. 22, 1918; s. Vincent S. and Madeleine (Day) M.; A.B., Princeton, 1940; m. Frances Root, Aug. 9, 1940 (div.); children—Marcia M., Sally E., Sandra D.; m. 2d, Josephine M. Abbott Davisson, Apr. 23, 1954 (dec. Mar. 24, 1956); stepchildren—Lee, Joanne, Sue; m. 3d, Emily L. Enbysk, Dec. 29, 1958. With Montclair Times Co., 1940—, exec. v.p., 1950-64, asso. pub., 1964-71, pres., co-publisher, 1971-79, pres., publisher, 1979—; pres., co-publisher Verona-Cedar Grove Times, Inc., 1971-79, pres., publisher, 1979—. Served to capt., AUS, 1942-46. Mem. Phi Beta Kappa. Rotarian. Clubs: Nat. Press (Washington); Overseas Press of America; Princeton of N.Y.; Montclair Golf. Home: 260 Highland Ave Upper Montclair NJ 07043 Office: 114 Valley Rd Montclair NJ 07042

MULHALL, JOHN MICHAEL, data processing co. exec.; b. Lansing, Mich., July 21, 1938; s. Joseph Henry and Cecilia Elizabeth; B.B.A., U. Notre Dame, 1960; M.B.A. with honors, N.Y. U., 1966; m. Maureen Rose Finnegan, Sept. 11, 1965; 1 son, Kevin John. Systems engr., adv. systems engr. IBM, Cranford, N.J., 1963-69; mgr. installation services Shared Med. Systems, King of Prussia, Pa., 1969-71, v.p. installation services, 1971-74, v.p. customer support, 1974—. Served with Signal Corps, U.S. Army, 1961-62. Recipient Patriotic Service award U.S. Treasury Dept., 1976. Republican. Roman Catholic. Clubs: N.Y. Athletic, K.C. Home: 450 Donalyn Ln Berwyn PA 19312 Office: 650 Park Ave King of Prussia PA 19406

MULL, WALTER RAY, electric co. ofcl.; b. Lancaster, Pa., Mar. 8, 1922; s. Levi Homer and Ruth Gertrude (Kochel) M.; grad. J.P. McCaskey High Sch., Lancaster Pa., 1940; m. M. Jane Esbenshade, June 4, 1949; 1 dau., Denise Ann. Clk., Pa. Power & Light Co., Lancaster, 1940-55, insp. line and right-of-way maintenance, 1955-64, right-of-way rep., 1964-72, right-of-way agt., 1972—. Active United Fund, Am. Heart Assn. Methodist. Club: Masons. Home: 111 Eisenhower Blvd Lancaster PA 17603 Office: 1701 Manheim Pike Lancaster PA 17604

MULLANEY, RICHARD LANGLEY, JR., chemist, adminstr.; b. South Bend, Ind., Sept. 20, 1926; s. Richard Langley and Eleanor Marie (Niven) M.; A.B. in Chemistry cum laude, St. Anselm's Coll., 1947; postgrad. St. Joseph's Coll., 1961-64, Renessalaer Poly. Inst. Conn., 1973; m. Helene Marie Lavoie, Sept. 6, 1948; children—Richard, Sean, Helene, Kathleen, Martha, Michael, Elizabeth, James, Eugene, Mary, Timothy. Supr. plating and polishing dept. Trumbull Electric Co., Plainville, Conn., 1947-49; chemist St. Francis Hosp., Hartford, Conn., 1949-51, Pratt and Whitney Aircraft Corp., East Hartford, Conn., 1951-53; sr. chemist Hubbard Hall Co., Waterbury, Conn., 1953-56; chief chemist MacDermid of Bristol, Inc., Terryville, Conn., 1956-59; supr. chem. lab. Emhart Corp., Bloomfield, Conn., 1959-67; supr. research Enthone, Inc., West Haven, Conn., 1967-72; supr. analytical chemistry lab., project mgr. environ. contract services, TRC, Wethersfield, Conn., 1972-75; chief chemist, project adminstr. Rutland Fire Clay Co. (Vt.), 1976—; environ. cons. Mem. Am. Electroplaters Soc., Am. Indsl. Hygienists Assn., Nat. Air Pollution Control Assn. Democrat. Roman Catholic. Patentee autocatalytic chem. plating and treatment systems. Home: 286 Ivy Dr Bristol CT 06010 Office: 96 Curtis Ave Rutland VT 05701

MULLEN, FRANK ALBERT, assn. exec.; b. Lafayette, Ind., Apr. 7, 1931; s. Albert Edwin and Bernice (Weidlich) M.; A.B., Wabash Coll., 1953; B.D. (Henry B. Wright fellow), Yale, 1956, M.Div., 1956; m. Ruth Ackerman, May 28, 1960 (dec. Oct. 1969). Ordained minister, 1956; exec. dir. YMCA, Wilmington, Del., 1956-60; with YMCA Greater N.Y., N.Y.C., 1960-74, exec. dir. William Sloane House YMCA, 1970-74; Yale research fellow, 1974-75; asso. dir. Campaign for Yale, N.Y.C. office, 1975—. Instr., Yale, 1954-56, Union Theol. Sem., N.Y.C., 1960-63; faculty So. Conn. Coll., New Haven, 1955-56, Springfield (Mass.) Coll., 1966-69. Pres., alumni council Div. Sch., Yale, 1972-75. Recipient Liberty Bell award Queens County Bar Assn., 1969; Community Leader Am. award News Pub. Co., 1970; Alumni Merit award Wabash Coll., 1970. Charter mem. Assn. Yale Alumni. Mem. Christian Ch. (elder). Mason, Rotarian, Lion. Home: 178-33 Croydon Rd Jamaica Estates NY 11432

MULLEN, JOSEPH JAMES, psychiatrist; b. Cleve., Aug. 11, 1927; s. Hugh James and Zita Therese M.; B.S., John Carroll U., 1950; M.D., Ohio State U., 1954. Rotating intern, St. Luke's Hosp., Cleve., 1954-55, resident internal medicine, 1955-56; resident adult psychiatry, Western Res. U., Cleve., 1956-57, Boston State Hosp., 1959-61; resident child psychiatry Children's Hosp. Med. Center, Boston, 1961-63, sr. asso. in psychiatry, 1972—, dir. psychiatry tng. program, 1977—; Judge Baker Guidance Center, Boston, 1963, chmn. dept. psychiatry, 1973—, clin. dir. child abuse project, 1976—; cons. psychiatrist, Mass. Youth Service Bd., 1963-64; Residential Treatment Unit Jewish Family and Children's Services, 1963-65; dir. psychotherapy, Manville Sch. and Resident, Judge Baker Guidance Center, 1965-71; psyciat. cons., N.Eng. Home for Little Wanderers, Boston, 1966-76; cons. psychiatrist, Newton (Mass.) Mental Health Center, 1968-69; clin. instr. psychiatry, Harvard Med. Sch., 1969—. Served with USNR, 1957-59. Diplomate Am. Bd. Psychiatry and Neurology, also subsplty. in child psychiatry. Mem. AMA, Am. Ortho psychiat. Assn., Am. Acad. Child Psychiatry, Am. Psychiat. Assn. Office: 295 Longwood Ave Boston MA 02115

MULLEN, WILLARD FRANKLIN, ret. assn. exec.; b. Dresden, Ohio, Mar. 9, 1914; s. Clyde A. and Florence (Pritchard) M.; B.S., Rutgers U., 1936; M.S., Pa. State U., 1948, Ceramic Engr., 1951; m. Myrtle Greenwood, July 10, 1937; children—Robert Lawrence, Catherine Elizabeth (Mrs. Donald Flick), Doris Elaine (Mrs. Robert Roth). Ceramic engr. E.I. du Pont de Nemours Co., Perth Amboy, N.J., 1936-42; project coordinator Curtiss-Wright Corp., Caldwell, N.J., 1942-45; research asso. Pa. State U., University Park, 1945-52; exec. dir. Pa. State Producers Guild, Pen. Argyl, 1952-76. Mem. U.S. Dept. Commerce Middle Atlantic Nat. Def. Exec. Res. Mem. Am. Soc. Testing and Materials, Phi Beta Kappa. Author trade publs. Home: 120 Hillview Ave State College PA 16801

MULLER, ALFRED, physician; b. N.Y.C., Apr. 14, 1942; s. Kenneth Coe and Dorothy (Parton) M.; A.B. cum laude, Princeton U., 1962; M.D., Columbia U. 1966. Intern, St. Luke's Hosp., N.Y.C., 1966-67, resident, 1967-70; pvt. practice internal medicine, Washington, 1973—; asst. clin. prof. medicine George Washington U., Washington, 1973—, Georgetown U., Washington, 1975—. Chmn., Friendship Heights Village Council, 1975—; usher Nat. Cathedral, Washington, 1973—. Served to maj. U.S. Army, 1970-72; Vietnam. Diplomate Am. Bd. Internal Medicine. Mem. A.C.P., Phi Beta Kappa. Democrat. Episcopalian. Clubs: Princeton (Washington) (N.Y.C.). Home: 4450 S Park Ave Chevy Chase MD 20015 Office: 3301 New Mexico Ave Washington DC 20016

MULLER, DOROTHEA ROSALIE, educator; b. Bklyn., Oct. 29, 1924; d. William Thomas and Anna Muller; B.A., Hunter Coll., 1946; M.A., U. Wis., 1948; Ph.D., N.Y. U., 1956. Temporary tutor Hunter Coll., 1948-50, 56; tchr. N.Y.C. pub. schs., 1950-53, White Plains (N.Y.) High Sch., 1953-54; asst. prof. C.W. Post Coll. of L.I. U., 1957-62, asso. prof., 1962-71, prof. history, Greenvale, N.Y., 1971—; reader papers Metropolitan N.Y. Am. Studies Assn., 1958, Orgn. Am. Historians Conv., spring, 1963. Recipient Founders Day award, N.Y. U., 1956; N.Y. U. Alumni Club award, 1953, 56; N.Y. U. fellow, 1951-52, 52-53; AAUW fellow, 1964-65; U. Wis. scholar, 1946-47, teaching asst., 1947-48. Mem. Am. Hist. Assn., Orgn. Am. Historians, Am. Studies Assn., Western History Assn., Am. Soc. Ch. History, AAUP, AAUW, Nat. Council of Women of U.S., Nat. Trust for Historic Preservation, Wyo. Hist. Soc., Am. Teilhard Assn. for Future of Man. Christian. Contbr. articles in field to profl. jours. Office: C W Post Coll Greenvale NY 11548

MULLER, GARY WILLIAM, ins. co. exec.; b. Queens, N.Y., Jan. 13, 1941; s. Howard Peter and Helen Rose (Tubbiola) M.; B.B.A., Fairfield U., 1962; M.B.A., St. John's U., 1964; postgrad. N.Y. U., 1965—; m. Noreen Mullen, June 6, 1964; children—Anne Marie, Nancy Elizabeth, Barbara Jeanne. Grad. asst., chmn. mgmt. dept. St. John's U. Grad. Sch. Bus. Adminstrn., Jamaica, N.Y., 1962-64; mgmt. trainee Asso. Hosp. Service of N.Y., N.Y.C., 1964-65, exec. asso. to v.p., 1965-72, asst. to exec. v.p., 1972, asst. to pres., 1972-74; asst. v.p. Subscriber Service, Blue Cross & Blue Shield of Greater N.Y., N.Y.C., 1974—; adj. prof. Pace U. Grad. Sch. Bus. Adminstrn., N.Y.C., 1976-77. Recipient Mgmt. award, Bus. Adminstrn. Soc., 1964; St. John's U. grad. assistantship, 1962-64. Mem. Adminstrv. Mgmt. Soc. N.Y. (dir. 1975-77, Merit Mgmt. award 1977), Acad. Mgmt., Beta Gamma Sigma, Omicron Delta Epsilon. Roman Catholic. Contbr. articles in field to profl. jours. Home: 1362 E 28th St Brooklyn NY 11210 Office: 622 3d Ave New York City NY 10017

MULLER, PETER, publishing co. exec.; b. Tallinn, Estonia, July 11, 1939; s. Karl and Irene (Krisch) M.; B.A., Western Res. U., 1960; M.A., U. Calif., Berkeley, 1964; m. Anne Inga Jackson, Mar. 19, 1976. Programmer/analyst M.A.I., N.Y.C., 1966-67; data processing cons. S.D.I., N.Y.C., 1967-70, E.C.S., Oak Brook, Ill., 1970-72, C.P.C., N.Y.C., 1972-75; programming mgr. Prentice Hall Inc., Englewood Cliffs, N.J., 1975—; adj. lectr. N.Y. U., 1972—. Served with U.S.A. Army, 1962-63. Mem. Adabas User Group. Mem. Unity Ch. Author: (with others) Business Data Programming, 1974. Home: 530 E 89th St New York City NY 10028 Office: Route 9W Englewood Cliffs NJ 07632

MULLER, RICHARD JOHNSON, automotive corp. exec.; b. Westfield, N.J., Nov. 28, 1928; s. Julius Frederick and Ethel Mae (Johnson) M.; student Kenyon Coll., 1947-49; A.B., Bard Coll., 1951; m. Barbara Alice Reading, Oct. 11, 1952; children—Melissa Ann, Richard Johnson, David Webster. Intelligence officer CIA, 1951-54; asst. news editor Sta. WICH, Norwich, Conn., 1954-57; news dir. Sta. WHCT-TV, Hartford, Conn., 1958, Sta. WNBC-TV, West Hartford, Conn., 1959, Sta. KDKA-TV, Pitts., 1960-61; mgr. radio-TV, Chrysler Corp., Detroit, 1961-65, mgr. field pub. relations, 1965-67, dir. div. and field pub. relations, 1967-68, dir. pub. relations services, 1968-75, dir. nat. and internat. media relations, 1975, dir. pub. relations, Washington, 1976—; chmn. pub. relations com. Motor Vehicles Mfrs. Assn., 1974-75. Vestryman Episcopal Ch., 1972-74, lay reader, 1969-75. Mem. Nat. Press Club, Radio-TV News Dirs. Assn., Pub. Relations Soc. Am. Club: George Town (Washington), Aircraft Owners and Pilots Assn. Lic. pvt. pilot. Office: 1100 Connecticut Ave NW Washington DC 20036

MULLER, STEVEN, univ. and hosp. pres.; b. Hamburg, Germany Nov. 22, 1927; s. Werner A. and Marianne (Hartstein) M.; B.A., U. Calif., Los Angeles, 1948; B.Litt. Oxford U., 1951; Ph.D., Cornell, 1958; m. Margie Hellman, June 19, 1951; children—Julie, Elizabeth, Vis. prof. polit. sci. U. Calif. at Los Angeles, summer 1957; asst. prof. polit. sci. Haverford Coll., 1956-58; asst. prof. govt. Cornell U., Ithaca, N.Y., 1958-61, dir. Center for Internat. Studies, asso. prof. govt., 1961-66, v.p. for pub. affairs, 1966-71; provost Johns Hopkins U., Balt., 1971-72, pres., 1972—; pres. Johns Hopkins Hosp., 1972—; cons. on Western European polit. affairs U.S. Arms Control and Disarmanent Agy., 1962-67; cons. internat. security affairs Dept. Def., 1962-67; dir. Comml. Credit Co., Fed. Res. Bank Richmond, Chessie System, Inc., Blue Cross Md. Trustee Balt. Mus. Art, Whitney Mus. Am. Art, Dermatology Found.; bd. dirs. ARC, Balt., Council for Fin. Aid to Edn.; mem. bd. Nat. Assn. Ind. Colls. and Univs.; mem. Pres.'s Commn. on White House Fellowships; vice chmn. Pres.'s Commn. World Hunger. Served with AUS, 1954-55. Mem. Council on Fgn. Relations, Inst. for Strategic Studies, Md. Acad. Sci. (trustee), Am. Polit. Sci. Assn., Am. Assn. Rhodes Scholars, Phi Beta Kappa. Clubs: Cosmos, Univ. Author: Documents on European Government, 1963. Home: 1405 Harper House Village Cross Keys Baltimore MD 21210 Office: Johns Hopkins U Charles and 34th Sts Baltimore MD 21218

MULLESTEIN, WILLIAM ERNEST, steel co. exec.; b. St. Gallen, Switzerland, Aug. 22, 1911; s. Christoph and Hulda Hitz (Lehmann) M.; C.E., Cornell U., 1932; postgrad. N. Y. U. Law Sch., 1933-35; m. Louise Pforzheimer, Jan. 25, 1941; children—Mary (Mrs. Harry L. Shuford), Linda (Mrs. William Barry). Constrn. engr., supt. Austin Co., N.Y.C., 1939; sec. bldg. code com. Am. Iron and Steel Inst., N.Y.C., 1939-42; dir. constrn. div. WPB, Washington, 1942-43; asst. supt. Dewey & Almy Chem. Co., Cambridge, Mass., 1943-44; with Lukens Steel Co., 1944—, v.p. adminstrn., 1957-61, v.p., gen. mgr., 1961-69, pres., chief operating officer, 1969-73, pres., chief exec. officer, 1973-74, chmn. bd., pres., chief exec. officer, 1974-76, chmn., chief exec. officer, 1976-78, now dir.; pres., dir. Pennock Realty Co.; dir. Provident Nat. Corp., Provident Nat. Bank, Phila., Carpenter Tech. Corp., Ogden Corp. N.Y.; chmn., dir. Alleghany Ore and Iron Co., Fior de Venezuela, S.A.; pres., dir. Lukens Steel de Venezuela, C.A.; mem. exec. res. Bus. Def. Services Adminstrn.; mem. listed co. adv. com. N.Y. Stock Exchange. Mem. Brandywine Valley Assn., Cornell U. Council. Mem. U.S. Strategic Bombing Survey, ETO, 1945. Mem. Western Chester County C. of C., Am. Iron and Steel Inst. (dir.), Steel Plate Fabricators Assn., Soc. Cornell Engrs., Am. Mgmt. Assn. Clubs: Cornell (N.Y.C. and Phila.); Racquet, Sunday Breakfast (Phila.); Mohawk (Schenectady); Rolling Rock (Ligonier, Pa.); Tower (Cornell U.). Home: Valley Creek Farm RD 1 West Chester PA 19380

MULLETTE, PAUL STANLEY, sales rep.; b. Sydney, Australia, Nov. 24, 1946; s. Ronald Stanley and Sheila (Phillips) M.; B.A., Rutgers U., 1968; m. Lona-Lee Whitmarsh, Jan. 9, 1972; 1 dau., Jaime Suzanne. Sales rep. Manhattan Shirt Co., N.Y.C., 1972-73, Katzenbach & Warren, N.Y.C., 1973—. Served with U.S. Army, 1969-71; Vietnam. Named Salesman of Year, 1977. Mem. Mass. Fair Share. Golf instr. Home: 67 Jersey St Marblehead MA 01945

MULLIGAN, ANDREW PHILLIP, ednl. adminstr.; b. N.Y.C., Nov. 10, 1927; s. John Joseph and Jeanette Florence (Wilton) M.; B.S., Fordham U., 1951, M.S., 1953, Ph.D., 1959; m. Agnes T. Katzmarski, Oct. 20, 1951; children—Andrew Killian, Jean Marie, Kathleen, Margaret Mary, John. Tchr. pub. schs., N.Y.C., 1952-54; tchr. Uniondale (N.Y.) Pub. Schs., 1954-56, dept. chmn., 1956-57, adminstrv. asst., 1957-58, asst. high sch. prin., 1958-61, prin., 1961-68; supt. schs. Park Ridge (N.J.) Pub. Schs., 1968-70; supt. schs. Frankfort-Schuyler Central Schs., Frankfort, N.Y., 1970-76, Cheektowaga (N.Y.) Central Schs., 1976—; adj. prof. Fordham U., St. Johns U., Hofstra U., Herkimer County Community Coll., State U. N.Y., Utica-Rome. Dir. Herkimer County Area Devel. Corp. Served with AUS, 1946-47. Mem. Am. Assn. Sch. Adminstrs., Nat. Assn. Secondary Sch. Prins., N.Y. State Council, Erie-Niagara sch. dist. adminstrs. Roman Catholic. Home: 260 Nagel Dr Cheektowaga NY 14225 Office: Cheektowaga Central Sch 3600 Union Rd Cheektowaga NY 14225

MULLIGAN, ELINOR PATTERSON, lawyer; b. Bay City, Mich., Apr. 20, 1929; d. Frank Clark and Agnes (Murphy) Patterson; A.B., U. Mich., 1950; J.D., Seton Hall U., 1970; m. John C. O'Connor, Oct. 28, 1950; children—Christine, Valerie, Amy, Christopher Criffan; m. 2d, William G. Mulligan, Dec. 6, 1975. Editorial asst. Silver Burdett Pub. Co. subs. Time, Inc., Morristown, N.J., 1964-65; asst. publicity mgr. Worthington Corp., 1965-67; dir. devel. and pub. relations Children's Aid and Adoption Soc. N.J., 1967-68; admitted to N.J. bar, 1970; practiced in Newark, 1970, Morristown, 1971, Springfield, 1972, Hackettstown, 1972—; partner firm Mulligan & Jacobson, N.Y.C., 1973—, Mulligan & Mulligan, Hackettstown, 1976—; atty. Hackettstown Planning Bd., 1973—, Green Twp. (N.J.) Zoning Bd., 1973-77, Blairstown Twp (N.J.) Zoning Bd., 1973—; municipal prosecutor Blairstown Twp., 1974-75. Sec. Warren County Ethics Com., 1976-78. Mem. Am., Warren County, Morris County bar assns., Assn. Bar City N.Y., Kappa Alpha Theta. Republican. Clubs: Panther Valley Country; Harvard, Union League (N.Y.C.); Baltusrol Golf (Springfield, N.J.). Home: Panther Valley Hackettstown NJ 07840 also 35 Park Ave New York City NY 10036 Office: 480 Hwy 517 Hackettstown NJ 07840

MULLIGAN, HUGH AUGUSTINE, journalist; b. N.Y.C., Mar. 23, 1925; s. John Joseph and Jeanette (Wilton) M.; B.A. summa cum laude, Marlboro Coll., 1948, L.H.D. (hon.), 1973; M.A. in English Lit., Harvard U., 1951; M.S. in Journalism, Boston U., 1951; m. Brigid Mary Murphy, Jan. 14, 1948. With AP, 1952—, feature writer, N.Y.C., 1956-65, fgn. corr., Vietnam, 1965-68, Biafra, Middle East, Paris Peace Talks, 1968-69, Cambodia, Laos, 1971, No. Ireland, Nigeria, Middle East, China, Russia, Persian Gulf, Iceland, 1971-75, The Sahel, Angola, Ulster, Svalbard, Iran, 1975-77, columnist, N.Y.C., 1977—, spl. corr., 1966—. Served with U.S. Army, 1944-46. Recipient Gold medal Am. Newspaper Pubs. Assn., 1951; award for feature writing Nat. Headliners, 1963, award for fgn. coverage, 1967; award for internat. reporting Overseas Press Club, 1967, award for fgn. corr. Sigma Delta Chi, 1970, Mng. Editor's award for top reportial performance AP, 1972, 78. Mem. Authors League, Authors Guild. Roman Catholic. Clubs: Overseas Press, Dutch Treat. Author books, the most recent being: No Place to Die, The Agony of Vietnam, 1967; (with Sid Moody, John Barbour) Lightning Out of Israel; (anthologies) How I Got That Story, 1967, Reporting, Writing from Front Row Seats, 1971; editor: The World in 1964, 1965; as fgn. corr. covered wars in Vietnam, Middle East, Biafra-Nigeria, Oman, Upper Volta-Mali, No. Ireland, Lebanon, Cyprus, Angola. Home: 50 Crest Rd Ridgefield CT 06877 Office: 50 Rockefeller Plaza New York City NY 10020

MULLIGAN, JAMES MARION, lawyer; b. Wilmington, Del., Sept. 5, 1932; s. James Marion and Marie D. (Burke) M.; B.S., St. Joseph's Coll., 1954; J.D. (Owen J. Roberts scholar), U. Pa., 1957; m. Caroline Butler, Aug. 10, 1957; children—James Marion III, Theresa, Claire, Joseph. Admitted to Del. bar, 1958, Pa. bar, 1958, U.S. Supreme Ct. bar, 1965; asso. firm Pepper, Bodine, Frick, Sheetz & Hamilton, Phila., 1957-58; asso. firm Connolly, Bove & Lodge, Wilmington, 1958—, partner, 1964—; instr. accounting Wharton Sch. Fin. and Commerce, U. Pa., Phila., 1955-57. Asst. city solicitor, Wilmington, 1958-64. Mem. Am., Pa., Del. bar assns., Am. Judicature Soc. Roman Catholic. Home: 510 Kerfoot Farm Rd Wilmington DE 19803 Office: 1800 Farmers Bank Bldg 919 Market St Wilmington DE 19899

MULLIGAN, WILLIAM G(EORGE), lawyer; b. N.Y.C., July 16, 1906; s. William George and Agnes (Murphy) M.; A.B., Hamilton Coll., 1927; LL.B., Harvard, 1930; m. Dorothy K. Zimmer, Jan. 27, 1928; 1 dau., Maura Elaine; m. 2d, Mary Luciel McGookey, Sept. 6, 1942; children—Don John, Luciel Laurene; m. 3d, Elinor Patterson O'Connor, Dec. 6, 1975. Asst. Wickersham Crime Commn., 1929-30; admitted to N.Y. bar, 1931, N.J. bar, 1976; asst. Hon. Samuel Seabury, 1931-32; asso. White & Case, 1932-34; asst. corp. counsel City N.Y., 1934-38; asso. counsel Bd. Transp., 1939-40; mem. various law firms, 1940-50; gen. counsel War Materials, Inc. (fed. material procurement agy.), Pitts., 1942-43; dir. Foster D. Snell, N.Y.C., Am. Flange & Mfg. Co., Inc.; sr. partner Mulligan & Jacobson, N.Y.C.; mem. firm Mulligan & Mulligan, Hackettstown, N.J. Fellow Am. Coll. Trial Lawyers; mem. Assn. Bar City N.Y. (chmn. com. state cts. superior jurisdiction; mem. com. judiciary and mem. com. on grievances), N.Y. County Lawyers Assn. (mem. com. on matrimonial law), Am., N.Y. State, N.J. bar assns., S.A.R. (bd. mgrs. N.Y.C. chpt.), Theta Delta Chi. Clubs: Union League, Harvard (N.Y.C.); Baltusrol Golf (Springfield, N.J.); Panther Valley Country (Allamuchy, N.J.). Home: Panther Valley Hackettstown NJ 07840 also 35 Park Ave New York City NY 10016 Office: 36 W 44th St New York City NY 10036

MULLIGAN, WILLIAM HUGHES, fed. judge; b. N.Y.C., Mar. 5, 1918; s. Stephen Hughes and Jane (Donahue) M.; A.B. cum laude, Fordham U., 1939, LL.B. cum laude, 1942, LL.D. (hon.), 1975; LL.D. (hon.), St. Peters Coll., Jersey City, 1966, Bklyn. Law Sch., 1972, Iona Coll., 1972, Villanova U., 1974; L.H.D., Siena Coll., 1967; m. Roseanna Connelly, Oct. 20, 1945; children—Anne O'Boyle Mulligan Hartmere, William Hughes, Stephen Edward. Admitted to N.Y. bar, 1942; lectr. law Fordham U., 1946-52, asso. prof., 1953-54, asst. dean, prof. law, 1954-56, dean Law Sch., 1956-71, Wilkinson prof. law, 1961-71; judge U.S. Ct. Appeals, 2d circuit, 1971—. Mem. Law Revision Commn. State N.Y., 1958-71; chmn. exam. bd. Manhattan and Bronx Surface Transit Operating Authority, 1964-71; mem. N.Y. State Commn. on Constl. Conv., 1965; mem. adv. council Labor and Mgmt. Improper Practices Act, 1968-71; mem. State Commn. Rev. Legislative and Jud. Salaries, 1970-71; mem. Com. Adminstrn. Cts., 1970-71; internat. arbitrator; legal cons. counsel various state and local coms.; chmn. Citizens Com. of Reapportionment Gov. Rockefeller, 1964; gen. counsel Republican del. N.Y. State Constl. Conv., 1967. Served as spl. agt. CIC, AUS, 1942-46. Recipient St. John de La Salle medal Manhattan Coll., 1967, Encaenia medal Fordham Coll., 1966, Fordham Law Alumni medal, 1971. Mem. Am., N.Y. bar assns., Friendly Sons of St. Patrick, Gamma Eta Gamma. Roman Catholic. Clubs: Knights of Malta; Nat. Lawyers; Mchts. Contbr. articles to profl. publs. Home: 7 Sturgis Rd Bronxville NY 10708 Office: US Ct of Appeals One Federal Plaza New York City NY 10007

MULLINIX, EDWARD WINGATE, lawyer; b. Balt., Feb. 25, 1924; s. Howard Earl and Elsie (Wingate) M.; student St. John's Coll., 1941-43; J.D. summa cum laude, U. Pa., 1949; m. Virginia Lee McGinnes, July 28, 1944; children—Marcia Lee (Mrs. James R. Ladd), Edward Wingate. Admitted to Pa. bar, 1950; asso. law firm Schnader, Harrison, Segal & Lewis, Phila., 1950-55, partner, 1956—. Mem. adv. bd. Antitrust Bull. Served with USMCR, 1943-44; to lt. (j.g.) USNR, 1944-46. Fellow Am. Bar Found., Am. Coll. Trial Lawyers; mem. Juristic Soc., Am. Counsel Assn., Am. Judicature Soc., Am. (spl. com. on complex and multidist. litigation 1969-73, co-chmn. 1971-73, mem. council, sect. litigation 1976—), Pa., Phila. bar assns., Lawyers Club Phila., Order Coif. Republican. Presbyn. Clubs: Socialegal, Down Town (Phila.); Aronimink Golf (Newtown Sq., Pa.); Bald Peak Colony (Melvin Village, N.H.). Home: 251 Chamounix Rd St Davids PA 19087 Office: Packard Bldg Philadelphia PA 19102

MULROONEY, JOHN PATRICK, real estate cons.; b. N.Y.C., May 20, 1929; s. Michael Francis and Catherine (Cullinan) M.; B.B.A., Manhattan Coll., 1953; m. A. Patricia Mortimer, May 16, 1959; children—John, Stephen, Kevin. Vice pres. Leonard J. Beck, Inc., N.Y.C., 1954-56; sr. real estate cons. 1st Nat. City Bank, N.Y.C., 1966-76; exec. N.Y. Life Ins. Co., N.Y.C., 1977—; dir., pres., treas. 52d St. Realty Corp., 1968-76; v.p. Peggy Equities Corp., 1970-76; pres. North Shore Realty Co. Licensed real estate broker, N.Y. Mem. Real Estate Bd. N.Y., Inst. Real Estate Mgmt. (certified), Nat. Assn. Rev. Appraisers (certified). Home: 23 High St East Williston NY 11596 Office: 51 Madison Ave New York City NY 10010

MULROY, EDWARD TIMOTHY, ednl. adminstr.; b. New Castle, Pa., Aug. 1, 1946; s. Reardon Duane and Marie Jean (Algier) M.; B.S.B.A., Tri-State U., 1968; m. Deidrea Ann Palmer, May 16, 1970; children—Kara, Erin, Ryan. Field auditor Sch. Audit Bur., Commonwealth of Pa., Harrisburg, 1970-75; bus. mgr. Mars (Pa.) Area Schs., 1975-76; bus. mgr. Churchill Area Schs., Pitts., 1976—; part-time accountant Fombell Fabricating & Welding, Inc. (Pa.), 1970-78. Mem. Pa. Assn. Sch. Bus. Ofcls. Democrat. Roman Catholic. Club: Lions. Home: RD 2 Box 141A Gregg Dr Harmony PA 16037 Office: Churchill Area Sch Dist 4240 Greensburg Pike Pittsburgh PA 15222

MULVEY, MARY CROWLEY (MRS. GORDON F. MULVEY), ednl adminstr.; b. Bangor, Maine; d. Michael Joseph and Ann Loretta (Higgins) Crowley; B.A., U. Maine, 1930; M.A., Brown U., 1953; Ed.D., Harvard U., 1961; m. Gordon F. Mulvey, 1940. Tchr., dir. drama and music Berwick Acad. South Berwick, Maine, 1930-32, Madawaska (Maine) High Sch., 1935-38; tchr. Latin and math. Elmhurst Acad., Providence, 1946-48, 50-56; tchr. math. Classical High Sch., Providence, 1957-59; guidance counselor Hope High Sch., Providence, 1959-61, 63-65; supr. adult edn. Providence Sch. Dept., 1965—; dramatics coach, supr., personnel dir. Universal Producing Co., N.Y.C., 1932-35; lectr. on preparing for retirement U. R.I. extension, Providence, 1963—; part-time faculty Roger Williams Coll., 1971-72; cons. and lectr. on adult edn., gerontology and women for various colls. and nat. orgns; dir. adult basic edn. Tchr. Trainer Inst. U. Maine, summer 1967, Adminstr. Div. Aging R.I., 1961-63; cons. PHA, HHFA (now HUD), R.I., 1963-65; conducted series Edn. Later Maturity, sta. WJAR-TV, 1957, also lectr. radio and TV programs adult edn., geronotology; mem. nat. adv. com. White House Conf. Aging, 1958-61; chmn. R.I. Com. Aging, 1953-64; pres. Sr. Citizens Edn. and Research Center, Washington, 1963-68, 75—; mem. tech. rev. com. tng. grants Adminstrn. Aging, U.S. Dept. HEW, 1965-70; mem. Nat. Task Force on Edn., White House Conf. on Aging (chmn. subcom. on edn.), 1971; participant nat. sem. innovation edn. U.S. Office Edn. and Kettering Found., Hawaii, summer 1967; dir. Providence Sr. Aides Project, 1968—; dir. Adult Referral and Info. Service in Edn., 1966—; project dir. Sr. Opportunities and Services, 1972-74; dir. Model Cities Adult Basic Edn. Project, 1972-75; mem. State Manpower Planning Council, 1973-74, commn. study R.I. Tax Reform, 1973-75, Nat. Citizens for Tax Reform in 1978, Gov.'s Task Force to Monitor Nursing Home Inspections, 1973-75, 76—; mem. Task force on Adult Edn., Corp. for Pub. Broadcasting, 1974-75; dir. confs., programs, workshops, orgns. adult edn., aging; active pub. relations fields Medicare, Social Security, sr. citizens housing. Chmn. R.I. Com. for Nat. Health Security, 1974—; active R.I. campaigns Kennedy, 1960, Johnson, 1964, Humphrey, 1968, Carter, 1976. Bd. dirs., Providence Model Cities Edn. Coalition. Fellow Gerontol. Soc.; mem. Ind. Schs. Assn. R.I. (sec., treas. 1951-71), Nat. Council Sr. Citizens (co-founder, dir. 1961—, v.p.); New Eng. Gerontol. Assn. (co-founder, pres. 1955-57, 1958-60). Adult Edn. Assn. (exec. bd. R.I. chpt., R.I. legis. chmn. 1966-69, mem. planning com. nat. pilot inst. edn. for aging 1966-67, chmn. sect. on edn. for aging 1969-72, regional membership chmn.), Nat. Assn. Pub. Continuing and Adult Edn., Assn. Providence Pub. Sch. Staff and Adminstrs., Am., R.I. personnel and guidance assns., New Eng. Assn. for Measurement and Evaluation in Guidance. (charter), Internat. Reading Assn. (mem. com. on reading for aging 1969-72), AAUW, Nat. Council Aging U. Maine Alumnae Assn. (past pres. R.I. chpt.), Harvard Grad. Sch. Edn. Alumni, Pi Lambda Theta, Delta Delta Delta. Club: Soroptimist (gerontology research fellow 1957, 59, 61), Women Educators of R.I. Contbr. articles to profl. jours. Developer, editor 74 learning activity packages Library Adult Basic Edn., 1977. Home: 95 Plymouth Rd East Providence RI 02914 Office: 396 Smith St Providence RI 02908

MULVIHILL, JOSEPH GREGORY, banker; b. Carbondale, Pa., Mar. 5, 1948; s. Francis James and Virginia Iona (Mac donald) M.; B.S. in Finance, Long Island U., 1973; m. Margaret Galinis, Nov. 25, 1972; 1 dau., Colleen Marie. Loan and credit adminstrn. officer Marine Midland Bank, N.Y.C., 1973-77; loan rev. officer United Jersey Bank, 1977—; lectr. on finance various pub. sch. systems. Fin. advisor 83rd Assembly Dist. Rep. party, 1974—. Served with U.S. Army, 1966-70. Decorated Bronze Star, Air medal (8), Purple Heart; recipient Horowitz-Blatt award, Horowitz-Blatt Assos., 1972; Sr. Service certificate L.I. U., 1973, Consumer and Mercantile Credit award, 1973. Mem. Bank Credit Assn., N.Y. Inst. of Credit, Am. Inst. Banking, Young Ams. for Freedom. Republican. Roman Catholic. Clubs: Finance Soc., Boulevard Rep. Home: 65 King St Fanwood NJ 07023 Office: 210 Main St Hackensack NJ 07602

MUMFORD, HERBERT WINDSOR, III, mech. engr.; b. Washington, Feb. 10, 1945; s. Herbert Windsor and Mildred Aliza (Goold) M.; B.S. in Mech. Engring., Duke U., 1967; m. Ruth Arlene Connor, Nov. 8, 1969; children—Christine Ann, Jeffrey Herbert. Jr. engr. Bechtel Corp., Gaithersburg, Md., 1966-67, engr., 1967-69, lead engr., 1969, sr. engr., 1969-74; engring. supr. SNUPPS project (nuclear plants) Bechtel Power Corp., Gaithersburg, 1974—; v.p., dir. Ramsey Inc., Deale, Md., 1978—. Tribal chief YMCA Indian Guides, 1977—. Mem. Instrument Soc. Am., IEEE (nuclear power engring. com., ops., surveillance and testing subcoms.). Republican. Methodist. Contbr. to profl. pubs. Office: 15740 Shady Grove Rd Gaithersburg MD 20760

MUMFORD, ROBIN BRUCE, chem. co. exec.; b. London, June 20, 1931; s. Ivor Ross James and Hannah (Robinson) M.; B.S., London U., 1952; came to U.S., 1962; m. Shirley Handisyde, Dec. 29, 1954; children—Roger Andrew, Richard James. Sr. scientist Rubber Producers Assn., 1959-60; mgr. tech. services Flaytex Ltd., 1960-62; project leader Allied Chem. Corp., Morristown, N.J., 1962-68, dir. mktg. apparel, 1968, v.p. indsl. ops., fibers div., 1973-77, dir. tech. ops., 1977—; group pres. Duplan Corp., N.Y.C., 1971-72. Served as 2d lt. Royal Signals, 1954-56. Mem. Rubber and Plastics Inst. Clubs: Princeton (asso.), Channel. Patentee in field. Home: 43 Blackbriar Dr Colts Neck NJ 07722 Office: PO Box 2064R Morristown NJ 07960

MUMMA, ALBERT GIRARD, JR., architect; b. Long Beach, Calif., July 2, 1928; s. Albert Girard and Carmen (Braley) M.; B.Arch., U. Va., 1951; m. Janeal Thomas Woolf, Dec. 24, 1973; children by previous marriage—Eugenia Suzanne, Albert Girard, Peter Brenaman. Designer, McLeod, & Ferrara, Architects, Washington, 1951-56; asso. Deigert & Yerkes, Architects, 1956-62; prin. Mumma & Assos., Washington, 1962—. Served with USMCR, 1945-47. Recipient AIA medal, 1951; Design award Washington Bd. Trade, 1964. Mem. AIA. Presbyn. Prin. archtl. works include: Nat. Arboretum Hdqrs. Bldg., 1961, Finnmark Square, Silver Spring, Md., 1964, Inverness townhouses, Potomac, Md., 1971, Post Office and Fed. Bldg., Elkins, W.Va., 1971, U.S. Trade Fairs in Spain, Finland, Japan, El Salvador, USSR, 1963-72, Fallswood housing project, Falls Church, Va., 1972, Bristow Village townhouses, Annandale, Va., 1972-73, pvt. residences, subdivision and townhouse projects, Washington, Md., Va., Pa., 1962-78. Home: 816 Whann Ave McLean VA 22101 Office: Mumma & Assos 1071 Wisconsin Ave NW Washington DC 20007

MUNASINGHE, MOHAN P. C., economist, engr.; b. Colombo, Sri Lanka, July 25, 1945; s. Peter De Silva and Flower R. (Wickramasinghe) M.; B.A. with honors, Cambridge (Eng.) U., 1967, M.A., 1968; S.M., Mass. Inst. Tech., 1969, E.E., 1969; Ph.D. in Elec. Engring., McGill U., 1973; M.A. in Econs., Concordia U., 1975; m. Sria N. Gooneratne, May 8, 1970; children—Anusha D., Ranjiva M. Research officer Sri Lanka Inst. Sci. and Indsl. Research, 1969-70; vis. prof. elec. engring. U. Sri Lanka, 1969-70; research asso. and cons. Internat. Inst. Quantitative Econs., Concordia U., Montreal, Que., Can., 1972-75; economist-engr. World Bank, Washington, 1975—; vis. prof. econs. Am. U., Washington, 1977—; v.p. and dir. Canifex Internat. Socio-Econ. Devel. Centre, Montreal, 1975—; dir. Sri Lanka Overseas Found., Washington, 1977—; research adviser Inst. Applied Econ. Research, Concordia U., Montreal, 1975—. J.W. Beauchamp scholar, 1966-67; Albert M. Grass entrance fellow, 1967-68. Mem. Inst. Elec. Engrs. (U.K.) (charter engr.), IEEE, Am. Econ. Assn., Sri Lanka Assn. Washington (dir.), Sri Lanka Assn. Advancement of Sci. (life), World Future Soc., Sigma Xi. Author: Economics of Power System Reliability: Theory and Case Study; contbr. articles to physics, engring. and econs. jours. Home: 4201 East-West Hwy Chevy Chase MD 20015 Office: World Bank 1818 H St NW Washington DC 20433

MUNDY, DAVID HORTON, assn. exec., former air force officer; b. Somerville, N.J., Sept. 25, 1928; s. George Horton and Bertha Sanger (Bodine) M.; student U. Md., 1952-55; Command and Staff Sch., Air U., Montgomery, Ala., 1964; m. Lois M. Metzler, Mar. 10, 1951; children—David H., Donald H. Enlisted U.S. Air Force, 1946-48; commd. 2d lt. and rated pilot, 1948, advanced through grades to dir. ops. and tng., 307th Air Refueling Wing, 1966; dist. Scout exec. Boy Scouts Am., Wayne, N.J., 1966-70; exec. dir. Skyline YMCA, 1970—; asst. prof. Air Sci. Stevens Inst. of Tech., 1955-58. Decorated D.F.C., Air Medal. Mem. Ret. Officers Assn., Assn. of Profl. Dirs., YMCA. Mem. Ponds Reformed Ch. Club: Rotary (Wayne) (pres. 1976-77, sec. dist. 749 1978-79). Home: 48 Cherokee Trail Oakland NJ 07436 Office: 216 Colfax Rd Wayne NJ 07470

MUNDY, MARK JAMES, hosp. adminstr.; b. N.Y.C., July 8, 1942; s. Archibald and Madge M.; B.S. in History, Murray State U., 1966; M.S. in Hosp. Adminstrn., Columbia U., 1970; m. Caryl Ann Eisenfelder, Nov. 27, 1965; children—Timothy, Todd. Asst. dir. St. Vincent's Hosp. and Med. Center, N.Y.C., 1970-73; asso. adminstr. Nassau Hosp., Mineola, N.Y., 1973—; guest lectr., residency preceptor Columbia U.; speaker on health care at nat., regional, state meetings. Served to capt. U.S. Army, 1966-68. Lic. nursing home adminstr., N.Y. Mem. Am. Coll. Hosp. Adminstrs., Columbia U. Sch. Pub. Health Alumni Assn. (pres. 1976-77), Met. (N.Y.) Health Adminstrs. Assn. (pres. 1972-73). Club: Masons (Nutley, N.J.). Home: 114 Kingsbury Rd Garden City NY 11530 Office: 259 1st St Mineola NY 11501

MUNIN, MARTIN IRVING, dentist; b. Phila., Aug. 18, 1929; s. William and Jean (Weinstein) M.; A.B., Temple U., 1952, D.D.S., 1956; m. Norma T. Sharf, May 14, 1961; children—Michael, Robert. Gen. practice dentistry, Malvern, Pa., 1959—; cons. Devereau Sch. Handicapped Children, W. Chester, Pa., 1960-64, Malvern Prep. Sch., 1961—, Phelps Sch., Malvern, 1962—. Vice pres. Malvern Bus. and Profl. Assn., 1966-68; mem. bd. Middle Atlantic region Nat. Fedn. Men's Clubs, 1971-77. Served to capt. USAF, 1956-58. Fellow Harry S. Truman Library. Fellow Royal Soc. Health; mem. Am., Pa., Main Line, Chester County, Philadelphia County dentals assns., Am. Acad. Gen. Dentistry, Am. Soc. Preventive Dentistry, Fedn. Dental Internationale, Temple U. Alumni Assn., Temple U. Assos. Soc., Sigma Epsilon Delta, Alpha Sigma Pi. Republican. Jewish (bd. dirs. temple 1971—, pres. men's club 1971-72). Mem. B'nai B'rith. Home: 1736 Josie Ln Havertown PA 19083 Office: Malvern Shopping Center Malvern PA 19355

MUNLEY, JANE KRAVITZ, educator; b. Hazleton, Pa., Jan. 19, 1954; d. William B. and Ilean (Augustitus) Kravitz; B.S. in Law Enforcemnt and Corrections, Pa. State U., 1974; M.S. in Rehab. Counseling, U. Scranton, 1976; m. James M. Munley, Aug. 13, 1977. Police intern Freeland (Pa.) Police Dept., 1973; counselor intern Scranton (Pa.) Community Service Center, 1974; casework intern Vols. in Probation, Scranton, 1976; instr. criminal justice and psychology Luzerne County Community Coll., Nanticoke, Pa., 1976—. Mem. Am. Personnel and Guidance Assn., Am. Coll. Personnel Assn., Am. Rehab. Counseling Assn. Home: 34 Oak Dr Mountaintop PA 18707 Office: Prospect St and Middle Rd Nanticoke PA 18634

MUNOZ, JOHN RIVERS, JR., pharm. mfg. co. exec.; b. Manila, Philippines, Nov. 23, 1932 (parents Am. citizens); s. Juan R. and Matilde (Rivers) M.; B.S. in Chem. Engring., De La Salle Coll., 1955; M.B.A., Fairleigh Dickinson U., 1973. Plant mgr. Sterling Drug Inc., N.Y.C., 1958-64; sr. project engr. Bristol Lab. Inc., Syracuse, N.Y., 1965; chief chem. engr. Burroughs Wellcome & Co. Inc., Tuckahoe, N.Y., 1966-67; dir. engring. Block Drug Co. Inc., Jersey City, 1968-77; mgr. processing and packaging Life Savers Inc. div. Squibb Corp., N.Y.C., 1977—. Mem. North Cortlandt (N.Y.) Neighbors Assn. Mem. Am. Inst. Chem. Engrs., Am. Chem. Soc., Am. Mgmt. Assn. Home: 10 Mountain View Rd RFD 2 Peekskill NY 10566 Office: 257 Cornelison Ave Jersey City NJ 07302

MUNSON, HAROLD EDWIN, mech. engr.; b. Jamestown, N.Y., Dec. 2, 1924; s. Edwin and Lucy Emma (Bragg) M.; B.A. magna cum laude, Alfred U., 1949; m. Doris Jean Carlberg, Sept. 5, 1964; children—Robert Harold, Katherine Jean. With Bell Aircraft Corp., Buffalo, 1951-56; lab. technician Marlin Rockwell Corp., Jamestown, N.Y., 1956-62; adminstr. research lab. Marlin Rockwell div. TRW Inc., Jamestown, 1962-68, supr. project engring., 1968—. Pres. Bd. Edn., Fewsburg (N.Y.) Central Sch., 1960-72; town historian Town of Carroll (N.Y.), 1962-68. Served with F.A., U.S. Army, 1944-46. Mem. Chautauqua County Sch. Bds. Assn. (pres. 1967-68). Republican. Baptist. Home: 286 Bragg Rd Frewsburg NY 14738 Office: 402 Chandler St Jamestown NY 14701

MUNTERS, MANFREDS, orthopedic surgeon; b. Riga, Latvia, Dec. 11, 1936; s. Karlis and Ilga M.; came to U.S., 1950, naturalized, 1957; B.S. cum laude, City Coll. N.Y., 1958; M.D., State U. N.Y., Downstate Med. Center, 1962. Intern, Kings County Hosp., Bklyn., 1962-63, resident in orthopedic surgery, 1963-68; practice medicine specializing in orthopedic surgery, Bklyn., 1969—; asst. prof. orthopedic surgery State U. N.Y. Downstate Med. Center, Bklyn. Served to capt. USAF, 1966-68. Mem. Am. Acad. Orthopedic Surgeons, A.C.S., N.Y. Acad. Medicine, N.Y. State, Eastern orthopedic assns., Am. Trauma Soc., Phi Beta Kappa. Address: 451 Clarkson Ave Brooklyn NY 11203

MURANAKA, RICHARD GEORGE, govt. ofcl.; b. Waimea, Kauai, Hawaii, May 14, 1930; s. Peter Kenichi and Ethel Kimiye (Yamamoto) M.; student U. Hawaii, 1948-50, U. Chgo., 1950-51; B.S., Ind. State U., 1956, M.S., 1957; M.Nuclear Engring. (NSF Sci. Faculty fellow), U. Okla., 1963; postgrad. Internat. Sch. Nuclear Sci. and Engring., 1963-64; m. Evelyn Louise Tuck, Oct. 4, 1952; children—Lori, Peter, R. Todd. Instr., Flint (Mich.) Community Coll., 1957-62; spl. instr. U. Okla., 1962; sr. nuclear engr. U.S. NRC, Washington, 1963-66, br. chief, 1968—; sr. nuclear engr. Navy Dept., 1966-68. Bd. dirs. Montgomery County Scholarship Fund. Served with AUS, 1952-54. Mem. Am. Nuclear Soc. (exec. com. reactor operations div.), Research Soc. Am., AAAS, Hawaii State Soc., Sigma Xi, Phi Kappa Psi. Home: 14400 Brad Dr Rockville MD 20853 Office: Office Mgmt Info and Program Control US NRC Washington DC 20555

MURARKA, SHYAM PRASAD, materials scientist; b. Jaynagar, India, Mar. 13, 1940; s. Bihari Lal and Suti M.; came to U.S., 1966, naturalized, 1974; B.S. with honors (Dir. Pub. Instruction Merit Scholar), Bihar (India) U., 1958, M.S., 1960; Ph.D. in Metall., Materials Sci., U. Minn., 1970; Ph.D. in Chemistry, Agra (India) U., 1970; m. Saroj Goel, May 21, 1962; children—Sumeet, Amal. Lectr. chemistry Bihar (India) U. and Univ. Grants Commn. research scholar, 1960-61; sci. officer Atomic Energy Establishment, Trombay, India, 1962-66; research asso. U. Minn., Mnpls., 1970-72; mem. tech. staff Bell Labs., Murray Hill, N.J., 1972—. Recipient Gold medal Bihar U., 1960. Mem. Am. Soc. Metals, Electrochem. Soc., Am. Vacuum Soc., Am. Inst. Mining Engrs. Langat Singh Coll. Chem. Soc. (hon. life mem.). Hindu. Contbr. articles in field to sci. jours. Office: 600 Mountain Ave Murray Hill NJ 07974

MURCHISON, DAVID CLAUDIUS, lawyer; b. N.Y.C., Aug. 19, 1923; s. Claudius Temple and Constance (Waterman) M.; student U. N.C., 1942-43; A.A., George Washington U., 1947, J.D. with honors, 1949; m. June Margaret Guilfoyle, Dec. 19, 1946; children—David Roderick, Brian Cameron, Courtney Virginia, Bradley Duncan, Stacy Constance. Admitted to D.C. bar, 1949; with Dorr, Hand & Dawson, N.Y.C., 1949-50; partner Howrey, Simon, Baker & Murchison, Washington, 1956—; legal asst. under sec. of army, 1949-51; counsel motor vehicle, r.r. equipment, textile, aircraft and ordnance and ship-bldg. divs., NPA, 1951-52; asso. gen. counsel Small Def. Plants Adminstrn., 1952-53; legal adv. and asst. to chmn. FTC, 1953-55, legal adv. to U.S. delegation to UN Econ. and Social Council. Served with AUS, 1943-45. Mem. Am. (chmn. com. internat. restrictive bus. practices, sect. antitrust law 1954-55, sect. litigation, sect. adminstrv. law), Fed., N.Y. bar assns., Bar Assn. D.C., Order of Coif, Phi Delta Phi. Republican. Clubs: Metropolitan, Chevy Chase. Home: 5417 Blackstone Rd Westmoreland Hills MD 20016 Office: 1730 Pennsylvania Ave NW Washington DC 20006

MURDAUGH, NOVEREE, counselor; b. Ashton, S.C., Dec. 21, 1927; d. Alphonso Cardosar and Ollie (Carter) M.; B.S. in Edn., Claflin Coll., 1957; postgrad. Cheyney State Coll., 1962-63, Temple U., 1964—; M.Ed., Antioch Coll., 1974. Tchr. pub. schs., Seabrook Island, S.C., 1946-47, McMichael Sch., Phila., 1961-75; guidance counselor James Rhoads Sch., Phila., 1975—. Named Miss Alumni, Claflin Coll., 1977. Mem. Phila. Fedn. Tchrs., Am. Personnel and Guidance Assn., Claflin Coll. Alumni Assn., NAACP, James R. Shockley Meml. Com., Black Ednl. Forum, Nat. Vocat. Guidance Assn., Pa. Sch. Counselors Assn., Sigma Gamma Rho. Democrat. Methodist. Home: 1951 N 61st St Philadelphia PA 19151

MURDOCH, KEITH RUPERT, pub. corp. exec.; b. Melbourne, Australia, Mar. 11, 1931; s. Keith and Elisabeth Joy (Greene) M.; came to U.S., 1974; M.A., Worcester Coll., Oxford, Eng., 1953; m. Anna Maria Torv, Apr. 28, 1967; children—Prudence, Elisabeth, Lachlan, James. Chmn., City Post Pub. Corp., pub. N.Y. Post, N.Y. mag., New West mag., Village Voice, 1977—; chmn. News Am. Pub. Inc.; pub. The Star, San Antonio Express & News, News Internat. Ltd. Group, London; chief exec., mng. dir. News Ltd. Group & Assos. Cos., Australia. Office: N Y Post Corp 210 South St New York NY 10002*

MURDOLO, MICHAEL ANTONIO, interior designer; b. Caulonia, Italy, Nov. 21, 1934; s. John and Angela Assunta (Albanese) M.; came to U.S., 1956, naturalized, 1961; student of Ilario Geregitano (Italy), 1945-56, Francesco Gallo (Italy), 1945-56; student Ilario Lavorata Sch. Art and Design (Italy), 1945-56, Traphagen Sch. Fashion and Design, N.Y.C., 1971-74, Isabel O'Neil Studio, N.Y.C., 1974-77; m. Frances Trombetta, Oct. 28, 1962; children—John, Loriann. Pvt. practice interior design, Summit, N.J., 1967—; restorations include Acorn Hall Morris County Hist. Soc. hdqrs., Morristown, N.J., 1973, Speedwell Village, Morristown, 1975. Roman Catholic. Home: 14 Floral St Chatham NJ 07928 Office: Summit NJ 07901

MURPHEY, WILLIAM MEREDITH, govt. nuclear researcher; b. Washington, Aug. 16, 1936; s. Henry Schuldt and Elizabeth (Bunn) M.; A.B., Princeton U., 1958; m. Leigh Fitler Wood, July, 1960 (div. 1975); m. 2d Dorothy Ann Barranger, Oct. 1976; children—William Meredith, Sarah Elizabeth. Physicist neutron physics sect. Center for Radiation Research, Nat. Bur. Standards, Washington, 1954-69, project leader nuclear materials safeguards project tech. analysis div., 1969-74; chief plans and analysis div. safeguards and security ERDA, Washington, 1974-75; chief tech. support div. safeguards, environ. and fuel cycle research Nuclear Regulatory Commn., Washington, 1975-78; nuclear safeguards staff, nonproliferation bur. ACDA, Washington, 1978—. Mem. Am. Phys. Soc., Ops. Research Soc., Inst. Nuclear Materials Mgrs., Sigma Xi. Democrat. Episcopalian. Contbr. research reports in field. Home: 13417 Crispin Way Rockville MD 20853 Office: Washington DC

MURPHY, ANDREW PHILLIP, JR., lawyer; b. Swampscott, Mass., Sept. 27, 1922; s. Andrew Philip and Irene Mary (O'Connell) M.; A.B., Harvard U., 1943; LL.B., Boston U., 1949; m. Ann Marie O'Hagan, Feb. 13, 1954; children—Sean Francis, Andrew Philip, Chrystal Ann, James Bryne, Paul Clarke. Admitted to Mass. bar, 1949, D.C. bar, 1957; practiced in Lynn. Mass., 1949-50; with Econ. Stablzn. Agy., 1951-53, Office Chief Counsel, WSB, 1951, counsel R.R. and Airline Wage Bd., 1952, alt. mem., counsel Nat. Enforcement Commn., 1953; indsl. relations adv. Office Chief Ordnance, U.S. Army, 1954; labor relations dir. Nat. Assn. Home Builders 1954-60; pvt. law practice, 1960—. Alt. mem. Constrn. Industry Joint Conf., 1960-61; sec.-treas. U.S. Expn. Sci. and Industry, 1960-74; alt. mem. Constrn. Industry Stblzn. Com., Washington, 1971-74; mem. Collective Bargaining Com. in Constrn. Presdl. Commn., 1975-77. Served as lt. (j.g.) USNR. Mem. Fed. Bar Assn. (treas. D.C. chpt. 1952-53, 2d v.p. 1953-54, nat. council 1954-59), U.S. C. of C. (labor relations com. 1955-59). Clubs: Harvard (N.Y.C.); Metropolitan (Washington); Belle Haven Country (Alexandria); Annapolis (Md.) Yacht; Farmington Hunt (Va.); Gibson Island (Md.), Gibson Island Yacht Squadron. Editor in chief Fed. Bar Jour., 1952-59; co-editor Research and Development Procurement, 1958. Home: 1815 Edgehill Dr Alexandria VA 22307 also Skywater Rd Gibson Island MD 21056 Office: 1133 15th St NW Washington DC 20005 also 40 Court St Boston MA 02109

MURPHY, AUSTIN JOHN, former state senator Pa.; b. North Charleroi, Pa., June 17, 1927; s. Austin John and Evelyn Frances (Spence) M.; B.A., Duquesne U., 1949; LL.B., U. Pitts., 1952; m. Eileen Ramona McNamara, Feb. 7, 1953; children—Colleen, Brian, Sheila, Erin, Holly, Maureen. Admitted to Pa. bar, 1952; gen. practice law; solicitor for 10 municipalities; auditor, councilman, Borough of Speers, 1952-56; asst. dist. atty. Washington County, 1957; mem. Pa. Ho. of Reps. from 48th Dist., 1959-70, Pa. Senate from 46th Dist., 1970-77; mem. Pa. Local Govt. Commn. Mem. Charleroi Sch. Dist., 1956; mem. Monongahela Democratic Com., 1952. Served with USMCR, 1944-46. Recipient Thomas Chrostwaite award Pa. Assn. Boroughs, 1973. Mem. law rev. staff U. Pitts., 1965. Home: 699 Maple Dr Monongahela PA 15063

MURPHY, BARBARA JANE, educator; b. Bklyn., Nov. 13, 1938; d. Salvatore J. and Rose M. (Capalbo) Tartaglia; B.A. in English, St. Joseph's Coll., N.Y.C., 1960; M.S. in Edn., Wagner Coll., N.Y.C., 1965; m. Daniel J. Murphy; children—Martin, Christopher, Sean Patrick. Reading specialist Hopatcong (N.J.) Boro Schs., 1969-72; state aid reading specialist Our Lady of the Lake, Mt. Arlington, N.J., 1972-73; dist. supr. reading Sparta (N.J.) Pub. Schs., 1973—, dir. Right to Read program; project mgr. Sussex County office N.J. Dept. Edn. Chairperson Boro Nat. Heart Assn., 1972-73, area chairperson Cerebral Palsy, 1974. Cert. tchr., supr., prin., N.J. Mem. Internat.

Reading Assn. Initiated Cross Age Teaching in elementary sch. Home: 20 Bettino Dr Ogdensburg NJ 07439 Office: Sparta Bd Edn 328 Sparta Ave Sparta NJ 07871

MURPHY, BRIAN JOHN, restaurant exec.; b. Concord, Mass., Nov. 22, 1951; s. Daniel James and Dorothea Rosalyn (Whitelock) M.; student nights Springfield (Mass.) Tech. Community Coll., 1971-72, Nathaniel Hawthorne Sch., 1976-77; m. Wendy Sanderson, May 27, 1978. Asst. mgr. Friendly Ice Cream Corp., Springfield, 1972-74, mgr., 1974-76; dist. mgr., personnel mgr. Idlenot Farm Restaurants, Inc., Springfield, Vt., 1976—; also dir.; cons. pub. relations Level-All Corp. Served with Mass. Air N.G., 1970-71. Mem. Am. Mgmt. Assn., Smithsonian Assos., New Eng. Ice Cream and Sandwich Shop Owners and Operators Assn. Roman Catholic. Home: PO Box 175 North Springfield VT 05150 Office: Idlenot Farm Restaurants Inc Springfield Shopping Plaza Springfield VT 05156

MURPHY, CHARLES FRANCIS, artist, carver; b. Boston, Jan. 31, 1924; s. Walter Ray and Ellen Margaret (Shea) M.; grad. Sch. Practical Art, 1944; grad. Watertown Arsenal Apprentice Sch., 1947; student Mass. Inst. Tech., 1947-49; m. Jean Chandler Garvin, 1944; children—Janeen Marie, Lynn Ellen, Norma Jean; m. 2d, Dorothy Barbara Menard, June 15, 1959; children—Adam Sean, Joshua Brett. Engr. Am. Machine & Fdy. Co., Boston, 1949-53; project engr. Gen. Telephone & Electronics, Waltham, Mass., 1953-63; configuration mgr. Raytheon Co., Bedford, Mass., 1963-65; mgr. optical systems div. configuration mgmt. Itek Corp., Lexington, Mass., 1965-71; owner pvt. art studio The Sneak Box Studio, Concord, Mass., 1971—; one man show carvings Concord Art Assn., Concord, Mass., 1971; exhibited in group shows at First Internat. Decoy Carvers Exhibit, Thousand Island Mus., Clayton, N.Y., 1969, World Championship Wildfowl Carving Competition, Civic Center, Salisbury, Md., 1976; represented in numerous pvt. collections; tchr. decoy carving Sneak Box Studio, Concord Mass., 1971—; antique decoy restorer, appraiser. Recipient award, Internat. Decoy Contest, 1969, U.S. Nat. Decoy Show, 1971, 72, 74, 75, Midwest Decoy Contest, 1969. Registered profl. engr., Mass. Mem. Concord Art Assn., Nat. Woodcarvers Assn., New Eng. Woodcarvers Assn. Home: 297 Laws Brook Rd Concord MA 01742 Office: PO Box 1055 101 Commonwealth Ave Concord MA 01742

MURPHY, CORNELIUS F., radiologist; b. Tilton, N.H., Sept. 1, 1920; s. Dennis and Esther (Carroll) M.; B.S. in Physics, Boston Coll., 1943, postgrad., 1946-47; postgrad., Hofstra Coll., N.Y. U., 1951-52; M.D., Georgetown U., 1956; m. Betty Southard, May 1, 1965; children—Ann Southard, Cornelius F. Health physicist Brookhaven Nat. Lab., L.I., 1947-52; instr. radiology George Washington U., Washington, 1960-62, asst. prof., 1962-65, asso. prof., 1965-72, asso. clin. prof., 1972—, dir. div. nuclear medicine dept. radiology, 1964-72, dir. radiology univ. clinic, 1969-71, chmn. med. isotopes com., 1964-72; staff radiologist U.S. VA Hosp., Washington, 1972—; mem. various univ. hosp. coms.; lectr. in radiology technicians program Washington Tech. Inst., 1970—, chmn. advisory com., 1970-71; lectr. Nuclear Medicine Inst., Cleve., 1970. Served with U.S. Army, 1943-46; ETO. Certified Am. Bd. Radiology, Am. Bd. Nuclear Medicine; diplomate Nat. Bd. Med. Examiners. Mem. AMA, So. Med. Assn., Am. Coll. Radiology, Med. Soc. D.C., Soc. Nuclear Medicine, Health Physics Soc., Am. Inst. Physics, AAAS. Contbr. articles in radiology to med. jours. Office: 40 Irving St NW Washington DC 20422

MURPHY, EDMOND LAWRENCE, trust co. exec.; b. Bklyn., Apr. 1, 1931; s. Frank Joseph and Clara Margaret (Nelson) M.; B.A., Bklyn. Coll., 1952; M.B.A., N.Y. U., 1956; m. Carol Mae Hornbeck, Oct. 17, 1953; children—Stephen, Paul, Janice, Gail. Mem. research and investment adv. depts. First Nat. City Trust Co., N.Y.C., 1952-62; investment counselor Delafield & Delafield, N.Y.C., 1962-68; v.p. Fiduciary Trust Co. N.Y., N.Y.C., 1968—. Chmn. property trustees Incarnation Lutheran Ch., Pompton Lakes, N.J., 1968-72. Mem. Stoneleigh Homeowners Assn. (pres. 1970-72). Republican. Lutheran. Home: 91 Highland Ave Riverdale NJ 07457 Office: 2 World Trade Center New York City NY 10048

MURPHY, EILEEN MARIA, coll. adminstr.; b. Boston, July 31, 1941; A.B., Boston U., 1964; M.S., Syracuse U., 1969; doctoral candidate Harvard U., 1975—; m. June 4, 1966. Intern grad. student personnel Syracuse (N.Y.) U., 1968-69; tng. specialist Bache & Co., N.Y.C., 1969; dir. student employment Simmons Coll., Boston, 1970-75, dir. summer session, 1972-75. Cons. on women in employment; mem. Mayor's Commn. to Improve Status of Women, 1975-76, chmn. employment task force. Served as officer USAF, 1965-67. Mem. Boston C. of C., Personnel Mgrs. Club (mem. exec. com. 1972-75), Eastern Coll. Personnel Officers, Nat. Assn. Women Deans, Adminstrs. and Counselors, Nat. Assn. Summer Sessions, Coll. and U. Personnel Assn., NOW (mem. nat. task force for credit), Phi Delta Kappa (exec. bd. Harvard chpt. 1977—). Home: 945 Centre St Boston MA 02130

MURPHY, FRANCIS TIMOTHY, JR., judge; b. Bronx, N.Y., Apr. 21, 1927; s. Francis Timothy and Bess (Varick) M.; B.S., Fordham Coll., 1949; LL.B., N.Y. Law Sch., 1952; m. Sheila T. Casey, July 4, 1959; children—Francis T. III, Eileen J., Kathleen A., Sheila M., Anne Marie. Admitted to N.Y. bar, 1952; asst. dist. atty. Bronx County (N.Y.), 1953-55; law sec. to judge Supreme Ct. State N.Y., 1955-58; justice Municipal Ct., N.Y.C., 1958-62, Civil Ct., N.Y.C., 1962; justice Supreme Ct. State N.Y., 1962-71, asso. justice Appellate Div., 1st Dept., 1971-77, presiding justice, 1977—. Served with USNR, 1944-46. Recipient Distinguished Alumnus award N.Y. Law Sch. Alumni Assn., 1971. Mem. Am., N.Y. State, Bronx County bar assns., Assn. Bar City N.Y., Emerald Lawyers Soc., VFW, Ancient Order Hibernians, Guild Cath. Lawyers, Friendly Sons St. Patrick. Democrat. Roman Catholic. Home: 2 Split Rock Rd Bronx NY 10464 Office: Appellate Div Court House 27 Madison Ave New York City NY 10010

MURPHY, GEORGE EDWARD, med. research, educator; b. Kansas City, Mo., Aug. 22, 1918; s. Franklin Edward and Cordelia (Brown) M.; A.B., U. Kan., 1939; M.D., U. Pa., 1943; m. Annette Forbes Cross, June 12, 1943. Intern U. Kan. Med. Center, 1943; asst. resident, resident pathologist Johns Hopkins Hosp., 1944-45; asst. in pathology Johns Hopkins Med. Sch., 1944-45; asst. physician Hosp. of The Rockefeller Inst. for Med. Research, 1946-53; asso. prof. pathology Cornell U. Med. Coll., N.Y.C., 1954-68, prof. pathology, 1968—; asst. attending pathologist N.Y. Hosp., 1954-60, asso. attending pathologist, 1961-67, attending pathologist, 1968—. Mem. Am. Heart Assn. Council Arteriosclerosis and Council Cardiovascular Disease in Young, 1945-46. Bd. dirs. Cross Found., Stanley M. Isaacs Neighborhood Center, Burden Center for Aging; chmn. bd. dirs. Asphalt Green, youth sports center, N.Y.C. Served as lt. (j.g.), M.C., USNR. Recipient William Osler medal Am. Assn. History Medicine, 1943, Lederle Med. Faculty award, 1954-57; Golden Doughnut award Salvation Army, 1974. Fellow Life Ins. Med. Research Fund, 1946-49, Helen Hay Whitney Found., 1949-53. Mem. Am. Soc. Exptl. Pathology, Harvey Soc., Am. Assn. Pathologists and Bacteriologists, Soc. for Exptl. Biology and Medicine, N.Y. Acad. Sci., N.Y. Acad. Medicine, Sigma Xi, Nu Sigma Nu, Beta Theta Pi. Contbr. exptl. and histologic investigations on the nature of rheumatic fever, rheumatic heart disease, glomerulonephritis and arteriosclerosis. Home: 130 East End Ave New York City NY 10028 Office: 1300 York Ave New York City NY 10021

MURPHY, JAMES DANIEL, engr.; b. N. Providence, Sept. 4, 1921; s. Louis Walter and Clare Rita (Meenan) M.; B.M.E., U. R.I., 1949; M.S. in Power and Fuels Engring. (fellow), Va. Poly. Inst., 1950; m. Helen Veronica Norton, July 24, 1944; children—Donna Marie, Helen Ann, James Daniel. Tech. asst. Worcester County (Mass.) Electric Co., 1950-56; results engr. Del. Power & Light Co., Delaware City, 1956-57; prin. engr. cons. div. Ebasco Services Inc., N.Y.C., 1957-64; dir. plant ops. Somerset Hosp., Somerville, N.J., 1964-78; dir. engring. services Perth Amboy (N.J.) Gen. Hosp., 1978—; instr. Worcester Jr. Coll., 1952-56. Councilman, Borough of S. Bound Brook (N.J.), 1964-67. Served with U.S. Army, 1943-45. Mem. Am. Soc. Hosp. Engrs., Tau Beta Pi. Democrat. Roman Catholic. Home: 11 Von Steuben Ln S Bound Brook NJ 08880 Office: Perth Amboy Gen Hosp Perth Amboy NJ 08861

MURPHY, JAMES STEPHEN, paper, bldg. materials and chems. co. exec.; b. Newark, Jan. 4, 1934; s. William Henry and Margaret (Crehan) M.; B.S. in Chem. Engring., Newark Coll. Engring., 1957; M.B.A., Rutgers U., 1962; Ph.D., New Sch. for Social Research, 1972; m. Eunice Ruth June, Dec. 8, 1956; children—James S., Paul T., Eileen R. Mgr. planning Allied Chem. Corp., Morristown, N.J., 1962-70; asst. to v.p. Sperry & Hutchinson Co., N.Y.C., 1970-71; mgr. long range and econ. planning W.R. Grace & Co., Fords, N.J., 1971-73; dir. corp. devel. Bowater Inc., Old Greenwich, Conn., 1973—; dir. Terrain Inc.; asst. prof. econs. County Coll. of Morris; lectr. in econs. Fairleigh Dickinson U. Mem. Boro Mountain Lakes Adv. Com.; mem. fin. com. Boro of Mountain Lakes. Served with U.S. Navy, 1953-55. Jr. C. of C. scholar, 1951; N.J. Inst. Tech. fellow, 1975. Mem. N.Am. Soc. Corp. Planning, Am. Mktg. Assn. Contbr. articles in field to profl. jours. Home: 124 Lake Dr Mountain Lakes NJ 07046 Office: 1500 E Putnam Ave Old Greenwich CT 06870

MURPHY, JOHN ANTHONY, editor; b. Everett, Mass., July 10, 1936; s. John Francis and Emanuela Josephine (Ofria) M.; B.Sc., Mass. Inst. Tech., 1958; m. Grace Helen Wells, Feb. 17, 1968. Research scientist, Mpls. Honeywell, Riviera Beach, Fla., 1959-60; research and devel. engr. Raytheon, Newton, Mass., 1960-61; v.p., mng. editor Cambridge, Communications, Washington, 1961-70; tech. editor Modern Data mag., Framingham, Mass., 1970-74; mng. editor Datapro Research div. McGraw Hill, Delran, N.J., 1974-78, editorial dir., 1978—. Served with U.S. Army, 1958-59. Mem. Am. Inst. Physics, IEEE, Nat. Micrographics Assn. Home: PO Box 126 Lindenwold NJ 08021 Office: 1805 Underwood Blvd Delran NJ 08075

MURPHY, JOHN JAMES, comml. fin. co. exec.; b. Bayonne, N.J., July 28, 1947; s. John J. and Carmelia (Massarelli) M.; B.S., Seton Hall U., 1969; m. Karen A. Kolakowski, Apr. 20, 1974; 1 son, David John. Sr. staff auditor S.D. Leidesdorf & Co., N.Y.C., 1969-73; chief analyst James Talcott Inc., West Orange, N.J., 1973-74, new bus. devel., 1974-77; v.p., div. leader comml. financing div. Franklin Comml. Corp., Somerset, N.J., 1977—. C.P.A., N.J. Mem. N.J. Soc. C.P.A.'s, Am. Inst. C.P.A.'s, Bankers Comml. Fin. Assn., Nat. Comml. Fin. Conf. Home: 1035 Soldier Hill Rd Oradell NJ 07649 Office: 630 Franklin Blvd Somerset NJ 08873

MURPHY, JOHN JOSEPH, toy mfg. and importing co. exec.; b. Bklyn., Feb. 3, 1932; s. John Joseph and Mary Magdelene (Reddy) M.; B.B.A. in Acctg., Pace U., 1965; m. Arlene Frances Gagliardi, June 4, 1955; children—Loretta, Caryn, Craig. With Charles E. Quincey & Co., N.Y.C., 1955-56, Joel E. Mitchell & Co., N.Y.C., 1956-65, Tenco div. Coca Cola Co., Linden, N.J., 1965-68, Dayco Corp., Dover, N.J., 1968-69, Tappins Inc., Newark, 1969-70, Gulton Industries Inc., Metchuchen, N.J., 1970-71, Vita Food Products Co., Bronx, N.Y., 1971-74, Fischer Casting Co., Dunnellon, N.J., 1974; with Lesney Products Corp., Moonachie, N.J., 1974—, controller, 1977—. Coach, Mt. Olive Jr. Baseball, Flanders, N.J., 1971-74. Served with USN, 1951-55. Recipient citation for athletic activities Mt. Olive Twp., 1973. Mem. Nat. Assn. Accountants. Home: 8 Graydon Pl Flanders NJ 07836 Office: 141 W Commercial Ave Moonachie NJ 07074

MURPHY, JOHN MICHAEL, congressman; b. S.I., N.Y., Aug. 3, 1926; s. Frank and Florence (Sullivan) M.; student Amherst Coll.; B.S. in Civil Engring., U.S. Mil. Acad., 1950; m. Kathleen Johnson; children—Deirdre, John, Eve, Mark, Emily, Elizabeth. Commd. 2d lt. U.S. Army, 1945, resigned as capt., 1956; mem. 88th Congress from 15th N.Y. dist., 89th to 92d congresses from 16th N.Y. dist., 93d-95th congresses from 17th Dist.; chmn. Mcht. Marine com.; mem. Interstate and Fgn. Commerce com., chmn. subcom. consumer protection and fin.; chmn. adhoc select com. on outer continental shelf. Parliamentarian Democratic Nat. Conv., 1968; bd. dirs. Community Chest S.I. Club. Decorated D.S.C., Bronze Star with oak leaf cluster, Purple Heart. Mem. Assn. Grads. U.S. Mil. Acad. (trustee), N.Y. Soc. Mil. and Naval Officers World War, Res. Officers Assn., Am. Legion, VFW. Roman Catholic. Home: 150 Mada Ave Staten Island NY 10310 Office: Rayburn House Office Bldg Washington DC 20515

MURPHY, JOSEPH SAMSON, coll. pres.; b. Newark, Nov. 15, 1933; s. Joseph and Doris (Milgram) M.; student U. Colo., 1951-53; A.B. with honors in Philosophy, Olivet Coll., 1955; postgrad. (Graham Kenan fellow, Woodrow Wilson fellow), U. N.C., 1955-56; M.A. (grad. fellow), Brandeis U., 1958, Ph.D., 1961; m. Margaret Herrick, Dec. 19, 1954; children—Lisa Jean, Suzanne Ruth, Peter Mesfin. Instr. in philosophy Brandeis U., Waltham, Mass., 1957-61, asst. prof. politics, 1961-65; dir. V.I. Peace Corps Tng. Center, St. Croix, 1965-66; confdl. asst. to sec. Dept. HEW, Washington, 1966-67; asso. dir. Job Corps, OEO, Washington, 1967-68; dir. Peace Corps, Ethiopia, 1968-70; vice-chancellor for Higher Edn. State of N.J., Trenton. 1970-71; pres. Queens Coll. of City U. N.Y.. Flushing, 1971-77, Bennington (Vt.) Coll., 1977—; pres. Coll. Pub. Agy. Council, N.Y.C., 1973; vice-chmn. Regents Regional Coordinating Council Post-Secondary Edn., N.Y.C., 1973; cons. Dir. Peace Corps., 1961-65; cons. V.I. Econ. Opportunity Program, 1965-66; vis. prof. Coll. V.I., St. Thomas, 1965-66. Recipient U.S. Fgn. Service merit award, 1965. Mem. Am. Philos. Assn., Am. Polit. Sci. Assn., Mind Assn. U.K., Am. Orthopsychiat. Assn., AAAS, AAUP, Brandeis U. Alumni Assn. (council 1961-65). Author: The Theory of Universals in Eighteenth Century British Empiricism, 1961; Political Theory: A Conceptual Analysis, 1968. Office: Bennington Coll Bennington VT 05201

MURPHY, LAWRENCE ERIC, ednl. adminstr.; b. Queens County, N.Y.C., July 2, 1947; s. Walter Clifford and Mamie Lea (Germaine) M.; A.B., Oberlin Coll., 1969; M.A. (Univ. fellow), Columbia U., 1971. Program dir. Youth Services Agy., Office of Mayor, N.Y.C., 1970-71; supervising counselor, instr. Bklyn. Coll., 1971-73; asst. dir. admissions, coordinator minority affairs Oberlin Coll., 1973-75; adminstr. M. L. King Jr. scholarship program N.Y. Inst. Tech., 1975-76; dir. coll. placement and student services Friends Sem., N.Y.C., 1976—; research asst. Columbia U., 1969-70; intern N.Y. Urban Coalition, 1968-69; cons. Central Bklyn. Model Cities; bd. dirs. East Harlem Coll. and Career Counseling Program. Dir. music, organist Friendship Baptist Ch., Jamaica, N.Y. Mem. Oberlin Coll. Alumni Assn. (coordinator alumni admission rep. program, mem. class pres's. council, mem. alumni admissions advisory council of alumni bd., pres. N.Y.C. Alumni Club), Nat. Assn. Coll. Admissions Officers, Am. Personnel and Guidance Assn., Assn. Nonwhite Concerns in Personnel and Guidance, Am. Sch. Counselors Assn., AAUP, Gospel Music Workshop Am. Democrat. Home: 200 W 90th St New York City NY 10024

MURPHY, LEONARD EDWARD, transp. co. exec.; b. Boston, May 20, 1916; s. Edward Francis and Agnes Louise (Gavin) M.; student Boston U., 1948, Mich. State U., 1956-57; m. Mary Regina Clancy, July 6, 1946; children—Robert, Thomas, Maureen, Gregory. Asst. traffic mgr. Westinghouse Electric Corp., Boston, 1947-51; traffic and sales rep. P.B. Mutrie Motor Transp. Co., Boston, 1951-56; traffic mgr. Frank Cosgrove Transp., Inc., 1956-63; mgr. New Eng. Main Trucking and Rigging Co., Boston, 1963-67; mgr. New Eng. Nat. Car Rental System, Boston, 1967-69; gen. mgr. traffic and sales Roy Bros., Pinehurst, Mass., 1969—. Chmn. Personnel Bd. Scituate (Mass.), 1968-70. Served with U.S. Army, 1943-46. Mem. Transp. Club New Eng., Nat. Def. Exec. Res., Delta Nu Alpha. Roman Catholic. Club: K.C. Home: 2 Curtis Ave Scituate MA 02066 Office: 764 Boston Rd Pinehurst MA 01866

MURPHY, PAUL FRANCIS, elec. engr.; b. Cambridge, Mass., Oct. 8, 1941; s. Francis Xavier and Marie Grace (Porter) M.; B.S., Northeastern U., 1968; postgrad. Northeastern U. Grad. Sch. Bus. Adminstrn., 1968-70; m. Jeanette D. Bell, July 16, 1966; children—Robert Allen, Shannon Marie. Asso. engr. Tupper Trent Co., 1960-65; asso. engr. Honeywell Radiation Center, Brighton, Mass., 1965-66; engr. infrared detection dept. Mithras, Inc., Cambridge, Mass., 1966; with Sanders Assos., Inc., Nashua, N.H., 1968—, mgr. infrared detection group, 1974—; cons. in infrared detection applications, 1976—. Mem. Am. Mgmt. Assn. Democrat. Roman Catholic. Club: Irish Am. Home: 66 Hume Ave Medford MA 02155 Office: 95 Canal St Nashua NH 03060

MURPHY, RALPH EDGAR, bus. exec.; b. Manchester, N.H., Aug. 14, 1931; s. Charles Joseph and Dorothy May (Leslie) M.; B.S. in Edn., Plymouth State Coll. (U. N.H.), 1956; m. Marjorie Anne Miller, July 4, 1964 (div. Nov. 1977); 1 dau., Margaret Leslie. Bus. instr. Anne Arundel County, Md., 1956-58; traffic specialist Chemstrand Corp., N.Y.C., 1958-60, Greenville, S.C., 1960-61, transp. mgr., N.Y.C., 1961-64; audit supr. Monsanto Co., St. Louis, 1964-70; audit supr. Microdot Inc., Greenwich, Conn., 1970-74, asst. to v.p. operational analysis, 1974-75; dir. fin. Malco, a Microdot Co., Montgomeryville, 1975-77; controller, asst. sec. Malco Mfg. Can. Ltd., acting controller Microdot Ltd., Tokyo; controller Microdot connector group, Montgomeryville, Pa., 1977—. Treas., Fellowship of Concerned Churchmen, also asso. editor The Certain Trumpet, Amherst, Va.; bd. dirs. Fountainville (Pa.) Hist. Farm Assn. Served with U.S. Army, 1948-52. Certified internal auditor, Conn., Pa. Mem. Inst. Internal Auditors. Democrat. Anglican. Home: Box 12 New Britain PA 18901

MURPHY, ROBERT BLAIR, mgmt. cons. co. exec.; b. Phila., Jan. 19, 1931; s. William Beverly and Helen Marie (Brennan) M.; B.S., Yale U., 1953; m. Mary Emily Eckart, June 24, 1953; children—Stephen, Emily, Julia, David, Catherine. Indsl. engr. Dupont Corp., Aiken, S.C., 1953-55; mgr. sales can div. Reynolds Metals Co., Richmond, Va., 1955-69; gen. mgr. corrugated div. Continental Can Co., N.Y.C., 1969-73; v.p. and gen. mgr. beverage div. Am. Can Co., Greenwich, Conn., 1973-75; asso. Hendrick & Struggles, Inc., N.Y.C., 1976-78, v.p., 1978; v.p., prin. and mgr. Stamford (Conn.) office Spencer Stuart & Assos., Inc., 1978—. Clubs: Round Hill, Riverside Yacht (Greenwich); Yale (N.Y.C.). Home: 11 Tomahawk Ln Greenwich CT 06830 Office: Four Landmark Sq Stamford CT 06901

MURPHY, ROBERT C., judge; b. 1926; grad. U. Md. Admitted to bar, 1952; chief judge Md. Ct. Appeals, 1972—. Office: Md Ct Appeals 361 Rowe Bldg Annapolis MD 21401*

MURPHY, ROBERT JOHN, obstetrician, gynecologist; b. N.Y.C., Oct. 18, 1933; s. James Francis and Jean (Lazarus) M.; A.B., Middlebury Coll., 1955; M.D., Johns Hopkins U., 1959; m. Joan Drutman, Oct. 25, 1969; 1 dau., Rachel Judith. Intern, Johns Hopkins Hosp., Balt., 1959-60; resident Met. Hosp., N.Y.C., 1962-65; practice medicine specializing in obstetrics and gynecology, N.Y.C., 1965—; chmn. med. records com. Flower Fifth Ave. Hosp. Served with M.C., USAR, 1960-62. Diplomate Am. Bd. Obstetrics and Gynecology. Fellow Am. Coll. Obstetrics and Gynecology; mem. N.Y. Gynecol. Soc., Obstetrical and Gynecol. Soc. N.Y. Med. Coll. (v.p.). Home: 530 E 90th St New York City NY 10028 Office: 1103 Park Ave New York City NY 10028

MURPHY, THOMAS DANIEL, JR., chem. co. exec.; b. Franklin, Pa., Apr. 30, 1934; s. Thomas Daniel and Deborah (Wallace) M.; B.S. in Chem. Engring., U. Md., 1957; M.S. in Statistics, Rutgers U., 1964; m. Judith Bolton Powell, Sept. 27, 1958; children—Katherine Bolton, Jason David, Thomas Daniel. With Hercules, Inc., various locations, 1957-67, supr. prodn., Franklin, Va., 1959-60, lab. supr., Parlin, N.J., 1960-67; cons. statistics, supr. statis. analysis Am. Cyanamid Co., Bound Brook, N.J., 1967—. Instr. dept. statistics Rutgers U. Extension Div., New Brunswick, N.J., 1969—, Center Profl. Advancement, Somerville, N.J., 1973—. Mem. Am. Inst. Chem. Engrs. (N.J. chmn. 1969-70), Am. Soc. Quality Control (councilor region III chem. div. 1977—), Am. Statis. Assn., Sigma Xi (asso.), Alpha Chi Sigma, Sigma Nu. Episcopalian (vestryman). Home: 308 Ellis Pkwy Piscataway NJ 08854 Office: Main St Bound Brook NJ 08805

MURPHY, THOMAS PAUL, columnist, cons.; b. Evanston, Ill., May 22, 1927; s. Thomas Ritter and Doris M. (Ambler) M.; B.A., U. Iowa, 1948; M.B.A., Harvard U., 1953; m. Countess Viviane de Jonghe D'Arodye, Feb. 16, 1976; 1 dau., Victoria; children by previous marriage—Thomas, Ellen. Asso. editor Fortune Mag., 1955-60; mng. editor Think Mag., IBM Corp., 1960-70, spl. asst. to chmn. World Trade Corp., 1965-70; spl. asst. to U.S. Ambassador, Dept. State, Paris, 1970-72; pres. Partnership Dankist, Stamford, Conn., 1975—; dir. Neotec Inc., Actmedia Inc. Mem. Conn. Venture Capital Group (founder). Republican. Presbyterian. Columnist, Forbes Mag., 1976—. Author: A Business of Your Own, 1955. Contbr. articles on bus. to profl. jours. Address: 48 Alma Rock Rd Stamford CT 06903

MURPHY, WILLIAM PARRY, physician; b. Stoughton, Wis., Feb. 6, 1892; s. Thomas Francis and Rose Anna (Parry) M.; A.B., U. Oreg., 1914; M.D., Harvard U., 1920; D.Sc., Gustavus Adolphus Coll., 1963; m. Harriet Adams, Sept. 10, 1919; children—Priscilla Adams (dec.), William Parry. Intern, R.I. Hosp., Providence, 1920-22; asst. resident physician Peter Bent Brigham Hosp., Boston, 1922-23, from jr. asso. to sr. asso. in medicine, 1923-58, cons. hematology, 1958—; asst. in medicine Harvard U., 1923-28, instr. medicine, 1928-35, asso. in medicine, 1935-48, lectr. medicine, 1948-58, lectr. emeritus, 1958—; pvt. practice medicine, Brookline, Mass., 1923—; cons. internal medicine Melrose, Quincy hosps., Emerson Hosp., Concord (all Mass.), Del. State Hosp., Franhurst; research on diabetes and diseases of blood especially pernicious anemia; discoverer (wtih Dr. George R. Minot) liver treatment for pernicious anemia. Dir. Cordis Corp. Served with M.C., U.S. Army, 1917-18. Recipient Cameron prize, 1930; Nobel prize in Medicine, 1934; comdr. Order of White Rose 1st rank (Finland), 1934; gold medal Humane Soc. State Mass., 1935; Distinguished Achievement award City of Boston, 1965; Nat. Order of Merit, Carlos J. Finlay (Cuba); Internat. Bicentennial Symposium award, 1972; Gold badge Mass. Med. Soc., 1973; 50-Year Service award Peter Bent Brigham Hosp., 1975. Diplomate in Internal Medicine. Mem. U. Oreg. Med. Alumni Assn. (hon.), AMA (Bronze medal for sci. exhibit 1934), Am. Soc. Clin. Investigation, Assn. Am. Physicians, AAAS, Internat. Soc. for Research on Civilization Diseases and Vital Substances (hon.), N.Y. Acad. Scis., Soc. Finnish Physicians For Internal Diseases (hon.), Nat. Inst. Social Scis., Kaiserlich Leopold Caroline deutsche Acad. der. Naturforscher, Sigma Xi, Alpha Kappa Kappa. Republican. Congregationalist. Clubs: Rotary, Harvard, Aesculapian. Author: Anemia in Practice Pernicious Anemia, 1939. Contbr. sci. articles to med. jours. Home: 97 Sewall Ave Brookline MA 02146 also 1101 Beacon St Brookline MA 02146

MURRAY, ALBERT EDWARD, JR., tech. info. specialist; b. Phila., Aug. 25, 1935; s. Albert Edward and Ruth Baker (Johnson) M.; B.S., Rutgers U., 1958; M.S., U. Ill., 1960; Ph.D., Pa. State U., 1970. Hackett fellow U. Ill., Urbana, 1958-59; Mercer fellow Harvard U., Cambridge, Mass., 1965; research asso. Cornell U., Ithaca, N.Y., 1968-69; editor Am. Horticultural Soc. Plant Records Center, Lima, Pa., 1970-71, Kalmia, 1969—; editor Holly Soc. Am., 1978—; tech. info. specialist U.S. Naval Air Devel. Center, Warminster, Pa., 1971—; faculty U. Pa., Phila., summers, 1963-67. Served with U.S. Army, 1960-62. Mem. Del. Valley Iris Soc. (founder), Phila. Daffodil Soc. (founder), Phila. Area Daylily Soc. (pres. 1969-73), Am. Hemerocallis Soc. (regional v.p. 1970-72), Royal Horticultural Soc., Internat. Assn. for Plant Taxonomy, Pa. Horticultural Soc., Am. Soc. Plant Taxonomists, Am. Soc. Hort. Sci., Sigma Xi, Pi Alpha Xi, Phi Epsilon Phi, Phi Mu Alpha. Contbr. articles in field to profl. jours.; author: A Monograph of the Aceraceae, 1970. Home: PO Box 2067 Warminster PA 18974 Office: 5031 Software and Computer Directorate Naval Air Devel Center Warminster PA 18974

MURRAY, ANTHONY HARRY, JR., lawyer, land devel. co. exec.; b. Bethleham, Pa., June 7, 1926; s. Anthony Harry and Johanna (Sullivan) M.; B.S., St. Joseph's Coll., 1950; J.D., Temple U., 1957; m. Wilma Ann Bruhns, Dec. 26, 1949; children—Susan, Anthony III, Kenneth, Virginia, Michael. Admitted to Pa. bar, 1958; practiced in Phila.; program planner Redevel. Authority, Phila., 1950-56; dep. regional dir. urban renewal adminstr. HHFA, Phila., 1956-60; exec. v.p. Walker-Murray Assos., Planning and Urban Renewal Cons., 1960-67; v.p. Land devel. The Korman Corp., Jenkintown, Pa., 1967-74; individual practice law. 1974—; dir., chmn. bd. Neshaming Valley Bank, Bucks County, Pa. Mem. housing and urban renewal com. Phila. Citizens Council on City Planning, 1968-70; mem. urban renewal council Urban Land Inst. Mem. adv. bd. Gwynedd-Mercy Coll., Gwynedd, Pa., 1967-70. Served to rear adm. USNR, 1946-47, 51-53; chmn. nat. bd. U.S. Naval Sea Cadet Corps, 1976—. Mem. Phila. Bar Assn., Navy League (nat. v.p. 1976—). Roman Catholic. Layman, Nat. Assn. Housing and Redevel. Ofcls. (chpt. pres. 1961-63; mem. regional bd. 1963—; mem. nat. met. com. 1968-70). Republican. Club: Union League. Home: 3035 Winchester Ave Philadelphia PA 19136

MURRAY, CAROLINE FISH, psychologist; b. Buenos Aires, Argentina, Mar. 28, 1920; d. Alfred DuPont and Caroline Johnston (Ramsay) Chandler; A.B. magna cum laude, Smith Coll., 1942; M.Ed., U. N.H., 1962; Ed.D., Boston U., 1967; m. Henry A. Murray, May 17, 1969; children by previous marriage—Caroline Davis Janover, Alexander M. Davis, Ann Kelso Davis MacLaughlin, Quita Davis Palmer, Maude I. Fish. Exec. sec. to dir. Alfred I. DuPont Inst., Wilmington, Del., 1953-55; tchr. Kingston (N.H.) Pub. Schs., 1962-63; instr. Boston U., 1966-67, asst. prof., 1967-71, co-dir. psychoednl. clinic, 1966-70, coordinator Headstart Evaluation and Research Center, 1966-69; practice psychology for schs. and clinics, Boston, 1971—. Bd. dirs. Douglas A. Thom Clinic, Boston, 1974-77, pres., 1977; bd. dirs. Wediko Children's Services, Boston; chmn. bd. Ariel Chamber Music, Cambridge, Mass.; bd. dirs. Shaker Community, Inc., Hancock, Mass., Mass. Children's Lobby. NEA grantee, 1964-67. Mem. Am., Eastern, Mass. psychol. assns., Mass. Sch. Psychology Assn., Soc. Research in Child Devel., Jean Piaget Soc., Assn. Advancement of Psychology, N.Y. Acad. Scis., Fedn. Am. Scientists, Assn. Autistic Children, Medieval Acad. Am. Democrat. Author novels. Home: 22 Franics Ave Cambridge MA 02138

MURRAY, CATHERINE ELAINE, mech. engr.; b. McKeesport, Pa., Jan. 5, 1947; d. Willis Edward and Wilma Elsie (Diosegy) M.; B.S., U. Pitts., 1968; m. John Thomas Flaherty, May 21, 1977; 1 son, Michael Murray. Jr. product engr. Elliott Co., Jeannette, Pa., 1968-73, asso. product engr., 1973-75, product engr., 1975-78, sr. product engr. oil systems, 1976-78; cons., Gibsonia, Pa., 1978—. Mem. ASME, Soc. Women Engrs. Republican. Roman Catholic. Home and Office: 5089 Lakewood Dr Gibsonia PA 15044

MURRAY, FLORENCE KERINS (MRS. PAUL F. MURRAY), state justice; b. Newport, R.I., Oct. 21, 1916; d. John X. and Florence (MacDonald) Kerins; A.B., Syracuse (N.Y.) U., 1938; LL.B., Boston U., 1942; student R.I. Coll. Edn., 1942, Ed.D. (hon.), 1956; grad. Nat. Coll. State Trial Judges, 1966; LL.D. (hon.), Bryant Coll., 1956, R.I. U., 1963, Mt. St. Joseph Coll., 1972, Providence Coll., 1974; m. Paul F. Murray, Oct. 21, 1943; 1 son, Paul F. Admitted to Mass., R.I., U.S. Supreme Ct. bars; pvt. law practice with husband, under name Murray & Murray, Newport, 1942-56; asso. justice R.I. Supreme Ct., 1956-78; presiding justice Superior Ct. R.I., 1978—; first woman judge State of R.I.; staff, faculty adviser Nat. Coll. Judiciary, Reno, Nev., 1971-72, dir., 1975—; legal adviser R.I. Girl Scouts; sec. Commn. Jud. Tenure and Discipline, 1975—. Mem. R.I. Senate, 1948-56, chmn. spl. legislation com.; mem. Newport Sch. Com., 1948-57, chmn., 1951-57; mem. Gov.'s Jud. Council, 1950-60, White House Conf. Youth and Children, 1950, Ann. Essay Commn., 1952, Nat. Def. Adv. Com. on Women in Service, 1952-58, Gov.'s Adv. Com. Mental Health, 1954, R.I. Alcoholic Adv. Com., 1955-58, R.I. Com. Youth and Children, Gov.'s Adv. Com. on Revision Election Laws, Gov.'s Adv. Com. Social Welfare, Army Adv. Com. for 1st Army Area; mem. civil and polit. rights com. Pres.'s Commn. on Status Women, 1960-63; chmn. R.I. Com. Humanities, 1972—, Family Ct. Study Com.; chmn. R.I. com. Nat. Endowment Humanities; bd. dirs. Newport YMCA; sec. Bd. Physicians Service; bd. visitors Law Sch., Boston U.; mem. edn. policy and devel. com. Roger Williams Jr. Coll.; trustee Syracuse U.; pres. Newport Girls Club, 1974-75. Served to lt. col. WAC, World War II. Decorated Legion of Merit, Army Commendation Ribbon; recipient Arents Alumni award Syracuse U., 1956; Carroll award R.I. Inst. Instruction, 1956; Regina medal Salve Regina Coll., 1962; Alumni award Boston U., 1965; Outstanding Woman award Bus. and Profl. Women, 1972. Mem. Am. Arbitration Assn., Nat. (state chmn. membership com., sec. exec. com.), New Eng. (com. chmn. 1967) trial judges confs., Am. Bar Assn. (chmn. credentials com. nat. conf. state trial judges 1971-73), Am. Judicature Soc. (dir.), Boston U. Alumni Council, Am. Legion (judge adv. post 7, mem. nat. exec. com.), AAUW (chmn. state edn. com. 1954-56), Bus. and Profl. Women's Club (past state v.p., past pres. Newport chpt., past pres. nat. legis. com.), Alpha Chi Omega, Kappa Beta Pi. Club: Quota (past gov. internat., past pres. Newport chpt.). Home: 2 Kay St Newport RI 02840 Office: Court House Providence RI 02903

MURRAY, JAMES JOSEPH, clergyman; b. N.Y.C., Jan. 29, 1926; s. Joseph and Rose (Vallely) M.; student Fordham Coll., 1942-44, A.B., 1948, J.D., 1951, M.Social Service, 1958; postgrad. St. Josephs Sem., 1951-56. Admitted to N.Y. bar, 1951; practiced in N.Y.C., 1951-53; staff N.Y. Cath. Charities, 1956-69, asst. dir. family service, 1965-66; asst. exec. dir. Cath. Home Bur.. N.Y.C.. 1956-65, dir. social research, 1966-69; sec. to His Eminence Terence Cardinal Cooke, N.Y.C., 1969-73; exec. dir. Cath. Charities archdiocese of N.Y., 1973—. Atty., N.Y. State Crime Commn., 1952; mem. Mayor's Com. of Religious Leaders, 1966-69. Bd. dirs. Astor Home for Children, Mt. Carmel Home, St. Patricks Home, Calvary Hosp., Mission of Immaculate Virgin, Pius XII Sch., others, v.p., dir. McMahon Meml. Shelter; sec. Mary Manning Walsh Home. Served with AUS, 1944-46. Mem. Am. Bar Assn., Acad. Certified Social Workers, Delta Theta Psi. Roman Catholic. K.C. Home: 348 E 55th St New York City NY 10022 Office: 1011 First Ave New York City NY 10022

MURRAY, JOSEPH DANIEL, clin. psychologist, air force officer; b. Elgin, Ill., Nov. 29, 1938; B.S. in Psychology, St. Louis U., 1962, M.S. in Psychology, 1964; Ph.D. in Clin. Psychology, U. Okla., 1971. Commd. 2d lt. U.S. Air Force, 1965, advanced through grades to Maj., 1976; clin. psychologist Wilford Hall USAF Med. Center, Lackland AFB, Tex., 1965-66, USAF Hosp. Elmendorf, Anchorage, 1966-69, 3415 Spl. Tng. Group, Lowry AFB, Colo., 1971-72, USAF Hosp., Wiesbaden, Germany, 1972-73, Office of the Command Surgeon, Europe, Ramstein, Germany, 1973-75, staff biomed. scientist Office of the Surgeon Gen. USAF, Washington, 1975—; instr. dept. of psychology U. Alaska, Anchorage, 1967-69; mil. cons. to the Surgeon Gen., USAF, 1976—. Diplomate in clin. psychology. Mem. Am., D.C., Colo., Va. psychol. assns., Assn. of Mil. Surgeons of the U.S., Soc. of Air Force Psychologists. Contbr. articles on clin. psychology and med. programs to profl. jours. Home: 7774 Dove Dr Alexandria VA 22306 Office: Hdqrs USAF/SGHP Bolling AFB Washington DC 20332

MURRAY, JOSEPH FRANCIS, JR., social worker; b. Cambridge, Mass., May 2, 1933; s. Joseph F. and Constance (Whitney) M.; B.A., Northeastern U., 1958; M.S.W., Columbia U., 1960; M.B.A., Northeastern U., 1975; m. Marlene L. Zepp, Mar. 25, 1961; children—Evan, Gayle. Community organizer Pillsbury Citizens Service (Minn.), 1960-63; program dir. Norfolk House, Roxbury, Mass., 1963-66; dep. dir. community and ops. dept. Action for Boston Community Devel., 1966-67; exec. dir. South Boston (Mass.) Neighborhood House and dir. coordinator W. Broadway Multi-Service Center, South Boston, 1967—. Active various community drives; bd. mem. South Boston Area Planning Action Council, 1967—; mem. adv. com. to trustees Boston City Hosp., 1969—; mem. adv. com. Tenants' Policy Council of Boston, 1968—. Served with AUS, 1953-56. Mem. Nat. Assn. Social Workers, Acad. Certified Social Workers, Mass. Conf. Social Welfare, Met. Boston Settlement Assn. (chmn. tng. 1968—), Nat. Fedn. Settlements (mem. nat. adv. bd. tng. center 1968—). Club: Kiwanis. Office: 62 Joyce-Hayes Way South Boston MA 02127

MURRAY, LAWRENCE ALLEN, theatrical adminstr.; b. Hempstead, N.Y., Oct. 7, 1939; s. Walter Lawrence and Ruth Alice (Pearce) M.; student Northeastern U., 1960, Harvard, 1961. With Warner Bros., N.Y.C., 1957-58, Bernard Plastics, L.I. City, 1958-59; copywriter Jack Alan Advt., Boston, 1963; account exec. John M. Lord & Co., Boston, 1963-64; free lance publicity writer, 1964; dir. advt. Sweetheart Plastics div. Md. Cup Corp., Wilmington, Mass., 1965-68; dist. dir. Muscular Dystrophy Assn., 1968; v.p. Turner Assos., Pub. relations, Boston, 1968-69; free lance writer, 1969-72; sales promotion exec. Modern Talking Picture Service, 1972-73; dir. devel. Pocket Mime Theatre, Boston, 1973-77; dir. mktg. Boston Ballet Co., 1977—; founder, dir. Compel, Inc., Cambridge, Mass., 1964—. Founder, Youth Workshops, Woburn, Mass., 1972-73; mem. Met. Cultural Alliance, 1973—. Committeeman, Nassau (N.Y.) Democratic Party, 1973-74; city chmn. McGovern Campaign, Woburn, 1972-73. Served with USNR, 1959-60. Bd. dirs. Muscular Dystrophy Assn., 1967-68, Citizens Scholarship Found., Fall River, Mass., 1964. Named Advt. Man of Year, Boston Jr. Advt. Club, 1968; Citizen of Year, Woburn Kiwanis and Key Club, 1972. Mem. Advt. Club Boston. Kiwanian. Contbr. to various mags. Home: 206 Hanover St Boston MA 02113 Office: 19 Clarendon St Boston MA 02116

MURRAY, PATRICIA ANN, educator; b. Providence, Aug. 16, 1922; d. Raymond L. and Mary Winifred (McNulty) M.; A.B., Salve Regina Coll., 1954; M.A., U. Notre Dame, 1959; postgrad. U. Pa., 1963—, Walden U., 1978—. Tchr., East Providence, Providence and Pawtucket, R.I., 1942-57; from instr. to asso. prof. sociology Salve Regina Coll., Newport, 1957-71, chmn. dept. sociology, 1968-71; dir. social service Newport (R.I.) Hosp., 1971-76; vis. lectr. sociology Misericordia Hosp., Phila., 1965-67; research asst. U. Pa., 1969; nursing home cons., 1975-76, 78-79. Bd. dirs. Tonomy Hill Day Care Center, 1974—, Girls Club Newport. NIH grantee, 1963-64. Mem. Am. Sociol. Assn., Am. Catholic Sociol. Assn., Social Work Dirs. Hosp. Assn. R.I., Social Work Dirs. of Am. Hosp. Assn. Democrat. Roman Catholic. Home: 220 Carroll Ave Newport RI 02840 Office: Salve Regina College Newport RI 02840

MURRAY, ROBERT LEE, union ofcl.; b. Brownsville, Pa., Oct. 5, 1926; s. William Robert and Ada (McCoy) M.; grad. Brownsville Sr. High Sch., 1944; m. Shirley Mae Mortland, Mar. 9, 1949; children—Cheryl Lee, Robert Lynn. Brakeman, Monongahela Ry. Co., Brownsville, 1947, flagman, 1956, condr., 1956, extra train dispatcher, 1958-68, regular train dispatcher, 1968—; vice-chmn. grievance com. Brotherhood Railroad Trainmen Local 703, 1958-61; gen. chmn. Am. Train Dispatchers Assn., 1969—. Fire chief Brownsville Fire Co. 1, 1966-71, pres. 1975-77; mem. central com. 5th Ward Democratic Com., 1973-74; pres. Brownsville Fireman's Relief Assn., 1956-58, sec. 1969-70, treas. 1972-73. Served with USAF, 1944-46; ETO. Mem. Fayette County (pres. 1969-70), Western Pa. firemen's assns., Southwestern Pa. Fire Chiefs and Asst. Chief's Assn. (pres. 1968). Methodist. Clubs: Fraternal Order of Police, United Fraternal Order of Fire Fighters. Home: 301 Front St Apt B Brownsville PA 15417 Office: Room 203 Union Sta Bldg Brownsville PA 15417

MURRAY, ROBIN RIVERS BARDEN, librarian; b. Shediac Cape, N.B., Can., Aug. 27, 1921; s. Alexander Archibald and Gwendoline Rosa May (Rivers) M.; B.A., U. Toronto, 1948; B.L.S., McGill U., 1949; librarian's certificate, N.Y. State U., 1950; m. Eldred Maud MacAlpine, Aug. 17, 1957; children—Laurie Elizabeth, Pamela Gwynne, Sharlan Alison, Jan Klyne MacDonald. Came to U.S., 1955. Reference librarian Bklyn. Pub. Library, 1949-50; br. librarian NRC-Can., Ottawa, 1950-53; chief librarian St. John (N.B.) Free Pub. Library, 1953-55; research librarian Central Research Lab., Crucible Steel Co. Am., Pitts., 1955-59; dir. Scholes Library Ceramics, N.Y. State Coll. Ceramics, Alfred U., 1959—. Served with Canadian Army, 1938-44. Mem. Spl. Libraries Assn. (nat. adv. council 1965-67, pres. Upstate N.Y. chpt. 1966-67), Canadian, N.Y. State library assns., Delta Sigma Phi (chpt. treas. 1960-67). Mason. Author numerous articles in field. Home: 113 S Main St Almond NY 14804 Office: Scholes Library Ceramics NY State Coll Ceramics Alfred U Alfred NY 14802

MURRAY, THOMAS HAROLD, info. scientist; b. Chgo., June 3, 1926; s. Thomas Grover and Grace Viola (Cotes) M.; B.S., Ill. Inst. Tech., 1956; M.S., Ga. Inst. Tech., 1966; Ph.D. in Pub. Adminstrn., Am. U., 1978; m. Jeanne Victoria Morris, June 19, 1964; children—Thomas G., William H. Served as enlisted man U.S. Army, 1944-46; commd. 2d lt. U.S. Army, 1952, advanced through grades to lt. col., 1966, ret., 1972; sr. info. scientist, office of tng. CIA, Washington, 1972—; adj. faculty U. Va., Am. U. Decorated Legion of Merit with oak leaf cluster, Air medal, Bronze Star medal; recipient George Griffin Meml. award Ga. Inst. Tech., 1963. Mem. Am. Soc. for Cybernetics (exec. dir. 1970), Soc. for Gen. Systems Research (dir. Middle Atlantic region 1972-74), U.S. Coast Guard Aux., Washington Acad. Sci., Am. Soc. for Pub. Adminstrn., Am. Soc. for Info. Sci., U.S. Navy Sailing Assn. Club: Army and Navy (Washington). Author: Interdisciplinary Aspects of General Systems Theory, 1974. Home: 2915 27th St N Arlington VA 22207 Office: CIA Office of Tng Info Sci Center Washington DC 20505

MURRAY, THOMAS PATRICK, physicist; b. Pitts., May 11, 1919; s. Thomas and Bridget (Loughnane) M.; B.S., Carnegie Inst. Tech., 1951, M.S., 1955; m. Dorothy Thase, Aug. 27, 1951. Jr. physicist Carnegie Inst. Tech., Pitts., 1951-55; physicist Jones & Laughlin Steel Corp., 1955-61; sr. scientist Westinghouse Astronuclear Lab., 1961-64, U.S. Steel Corp., Monroeville, Pa., 1964—; research cons. temperature measurement. Served with Transp. Corps, AUS, 1942-46. Recipient IR-100 award Indsl. Research Mag., 1967. Mem. Am. Phys. Soc., Am. Assn. Physics Tchrs., Instrument Soc. Am., Tau Beta Pi. Inventor automatic ellipsometer, 1962, polaradiometer and duoradiometer, temperature measuring instruments. Home: 2525 Collins Rd Pittsburgh PA 15235 Office: US Steel Corp Monroeville PA 15146

MURRAY, WARREN JAMES, educator; b. St. Paul, Dec. 3, 1936; s. James Bernard and Louis (Robertson) M.; student St. Thomas Coll., 1954-55; B.A. in Chemistry, Wis. State Coll., River Falls, 1962, B.Ph. in Philosophy, Universite Laval (Que., Can.), 1964, Ph.L., 1965, scolarite Ph.D., 1966; m. Mary Ann McAulay, July 18, 1959; children—Mark, Anne, Kathleen. Analytical chemist 3M Co., St. Paul, 1957-61, research chemist, 1961-63; prof. philos. sci. University Laval, Sainte-Foy, 1966—; vice dean, 1979—. Invited prof. Faculte de philosophie Comparee, Paris, France, 1969, 72, Université libre des sciences de l'homme, Paris, 1975—, Ecole des hautes Études, Paris, 1976; fgn. exchange teaching grantee Province Que., 1969. Mem. Am. Phys. Soc., Canadian Philos. Assn., Soc. Aristotelian Studies (pres.), Canadian Soc. History and Philosophy of Sci. (v.p.). Editorial bd. Laval Theologique et Philosophique, 1969—. Home: 1221 Rousseau St Quebec PQ 6 Canada Office: Faculte de Philosophie Universite Laval Sainte-Foy PQ 10 Canada

MURRAY, WILLIAM BRUCE, lyric baritone; b. Schenectady, Mar. 13, 1935; s. John Allison and Jessie Crystal (Gray) M.; B.A., Adelphi U., 1956; m. Nancy Lee Adams, Mar. 1, 1958; children—John Horton, Christopher Andrew, Judith Leora. Debut in Secreto di Susanna, Spoleto, Italy, 1957; appeared in world premiers Love's Labour's Lost, Brussels, 1973, Jumeaux, Brauschweig, Ger., 1963, Sim Tjong, Munich, 1972; performances in N.Y. State Theatre, La Scala, Milan Geneva, Brussels, Copenhagen, Rome, Barcelona, and others; leading lyric, Italian baritone; premieres include Telezky in Queen of Spaces, others. Served with U.S. Army, 1958-60. Fulbright fellow, Rome, 1956-57. Home: RFD Sparrowbush NY 12780 Office: Deutsche Oper Richard Wagner Strasse Berlin Germany

MURTAGH, JAMES P., lawyer; b. N.Y.C., Feb. 26, 1911; s. Thomas and Mary (Mee) M.; A.B., Coll. City N.Y., 1931; J.D., Harvard, 1934; m. Roberta Virginia Flaherty, Aug. 30, 1947; children—Melinda, James, Robert, Hilary, Richard, Kenneth. Admitted to N.Y. bar, 1935; asst. U.S. atty., So. Dist. of N.Y., 1934-36; asso. with and partner Simpson Thacher & Bartlett, 1936—. Mem. N.Y.C. Bd. of Higher Edn., 1948-52. Served from 2d lt. to lt. col. AUS, 1942-45. Mem. Am. Bar Assn., Bar Assn. City N.Y., N.Y. County Lawyers Assn., Delta Sigma Phi, Phi Beta Kappa. Clubs: Marco Polo, Larchmont Shore. Home: 9 Huguenot Dr Larchmont NY 10538 Office: 350 Park Ave New York NY 10022

MURTAGH, THOMAS JOHN, investment banker; b. San Francisco, July 25, 1930; s. James Joseph and Teresa (Murphy) M.; B.S., U.S. Naval Acad., 1953; postgrad. bus. adminstrn. N.Y. U., 1959-62; m. Maurine M. Mills, Feb. 3, 1973; children—Sean Travis, Hugh Keenan. Vice-pres., dir. Smith Barney & Co., N.Y.C., 1959-72; mng. dir. Western Am. Bank, London, 1973-74; sr. v.p., dir. Dean Witter & Co., N.Y.C., 1975—; dir. Puritan Bennet Corp. Served with USN, 1953-58. Clubs: Brook, Knickerbocker, Maidstone. Home: 200 E 66th St New York City NY 10021 Office: Dean Witter & Co 130 Liberty St New York City NY 10004

MURTAUGH, WALTER ANGELUS, educator; b. Providence, Apr. 7, 1903; s. Patrick Joseph and Brigdet (Bowie) M.; A.B., Providence Coll., 1924; M.S., Cath. U. Am., 1943; honorary degrees, M.A., 1953, D.Sc., 1964. Entered Dominican Order, 1925; ordained priest Immaculate Conception Coll., Washington, 1932; tchr. math. and physics Aquinas Coll. High Sch., Columbus, Ohio, 1934-43; prof. physics Providence Coll., 1943-68, chmn. dept. physics, 1943-68; asso. prof. physics R.I. Coll. Pharmacy, 1944-60; cons. work aeros., 1932—; conducted research counter rotating propellers and stability. Mem. R.I. AEC Commn. Mem. Am. Phys. Soc., Am. Assn. Physics Tchrs., IEEE, Assn. Edn. by Radio-TV, Nat. Assn. Better Radio and TV, Nat. Aeros. Assn. Author: Physics Laboratory Manual, 1947; Physics Text for Non-Science Students, 1948; also articles on aeros. and physics. Address: Providence Coll Providence RI 02908

MURTHA, JOHN PATRICK, congressman; b. New Martinsville, W.Va., June 17, 1932; s. John Patrick and Mary Edna (Ray) M.; student Washington and Jefferson Coll., 1950-51; B.A., U. Pitts., 1961; postgrad. Indiana U. Pa., 1962-65; m. Joyce Bell, June 10, 1955; children—Donna Sue, John Mark, Patrick Clark. Mgr. Johnstown Minute Car Wash (Pa.), 1958-62, pres., 1962-70; sec.-treas., chmn. bd. U.S. Nat. Car Wash, 1966—; mem. 93d-95th Congresses from 12th Pa. Dist.; mem. exec. bd. U.S. House Steel Caucus, 1977—. Mem. Pa. Ho. of Reps., 1969-73. Bd. dirs. Mecy Hosp., Wood Council Boy Scouts Am., Community Nursing Service. Served with USMC, 1952-55, 66-67; Vietnam. Decorated Am. Spirit Honor medal, Bronze Star, Purple Heart (2); Cross of Gallantry (Vietnam); recipient Pa. Distinguished Service medal, 1977; Pa. 2d highest award for service to community, 1977; named Distinguished Alumni, U. Pitts. at Johnstown, 1977, also scholarship established in his name. Mem. Res. Officers Assn. (past pres.). Home: 109 Colgate Ave Johnstown PA 15905 Office: 431 Cannon House Office Bldg Washington DC 20515

MUSA, FRANK JAMES, social worker; b. N.Y.C., Mar. 15, 1922; s. Louis and Rose (Persani) M.; B. Social Scis., St. Peter's Coll., Jersey City, 1947; M.S.W., U. Mich., 1950; m. Martha Stryker, Oct. 15,

1949; children—Louis, Susan, Anne, Rosemary. Psychiat. social worker Mental Health Clinic, Health Inst., U.A.W.-C.I.O., Detroit, 1949-52; dir. psychiat. social work dept. Brisbane Child Treatment Center, Farmingdale, N.J., 1952-60; asst. chief bur. community mental health services div. mental health and hosps. N.J. Dept. Instns. and Agys., Trenton, 1960-67, chief bur. devel. and evaluation mental health programs, 1967-75; asst. to dir. N.J. Div. Mental Health, 1975-77; ret., 1977; chief social worker, clin. coordinator Jersey Shore Med. Center, Community Mental Health Center, Neptune, N.J., 1977—; cons. NIMH-ADAMA Region II, 1975—. Mem. nat. adv. com. outpatient clinic statistics biometrics br. Nat. Inst. Mental Health, 1961-63; marriage counselor Family Service Agy., part-time 1961-68; individual practice marriage counseling, Trenton, 1968-70. Served with AUS, 1943-46. Mem. Conf. Social Workers in State and Territorial Mental Health Programs (chmn. nominating com. 1974). Home: 23 Coral Way Neptune NJ 07753 Office: Jersey Shore Med Center Community Mental Health Center Neptune NJ

MUSIC, JACK FARRIS, mgmt. cons. co. exec.; b. Childress, Tex., Oct. 5, 1921; s. Rondo William and Madeline Callie (Hanson) M.; B.A. in Chemistry with honors, U. Tex., 1946, Ph.D. in Phys. Chemistry with honors, 1951; m. Barbara Ellen Isett, Sept. 20, 1942; children—Barbara Helen, Elizabeth Ann. With Gen. Electric Co., Richland, Wash., 1951-60, research scientist, internal cons.-research and devel. mgmt., Schenectady, 1960-62, strategic planning for def. and space info. systems groups, King of Prussia, Pa., 1962-71; pres. Strategic Mgmt., Inc., Paoli, Pa., 1971—. Mem. Am. Chem. Soc., Am. Phys. Soc., Inst. Mgmt. Scis., Sigma Xi, Phi Beta Kappa, Phi Lambda Upsilon. Author: The Logic of Business Success . . . And How To Apply It, 1978. Home: 590 Bair Rd Berwyn PA 19312

MUSICUS, MILTON, city ofcl.; b. Russia, Feb. 23, 1913; s. Boris and Sofia (Dorfman) M.; B.S., Coll. City N.Y., 1933; M.A., Columbia, 1934; M.P.A., N.Y. U., 1941; m. Marjorie E. Fine, July 5, 1940; children—Josephine N., Barbara J. Examining asst. N.Y.C. Civil Service Commn., 1937-42; asst. dir. salary standardization N.Y. State Civil Service Commn., Albany, 1942-49; asst. commr. adminstrn. N.Y. State Dept. Edn., 1949-59, 61-63; asst. sec. to gov. for adminstrn., Albany, 1959-61; exec. dir. N.Y. State Health Facilities Corp., Albany, 1964-70; adminstr. municipal services N.Y.C., 1970-74, dir. city constrn., 1970-74; vis. prof. State U. N.Y. at Albany, 1974—. Cons. on adminstrn. Dominican Govt., Ecuador, Honduras, P.R., Turkey, N.Y. State Charter Revision Commn.; cons. on energy N.Y. Senate Finance Minority Com., N.Y. State Emergency Fuel Office, 1974; asso. Inst. Pub. Adminstrn., N.Y.C., 1974; asso. Clapp and Mayne, Inc., P.R., 1974—; cons. UN, 1978. First v.p. Council Community Services, Albany, 1968-69; mem. Gov.'s Constrn. Adv. Com., Interdepartmental Com. on Mgmt. Improvement, State Adv. Purchasing Council, N.Y. State Standardization Bd.; chmn. N.Y.C. Mayor's Interdeptl. Com. Pub. Utilities, 1970-74; chmn. Mayor's Flatbush Task Force, 1970-74; mem. City Univ. Construction Fund, 1970-72. Bd. govs. Bldg. Congress, 1970-74. Recipient A.E. Smith award outstanding pub. adminstrn., 1959. Mem. Am. Soc. Pub. Adminstrn. (dist. pres. 1956, dir. nat. council 1957), Phi Delta Kappa, Phi Beta Kappa. Home: 4 Harvard Ave Albany NY 12208

MUSIL, MARGARET HOOKER KIRKLAND (MRS. RALPH A. MUSIL), religious educator; b. Essex, Conn., Oct. 5, 1915; d. Henry Burnham and Helen (Mays) Kirkland; student Mills Coll., 1935-37; B.A., Bklyn. Coll., 1959, M.S., 1962; M.R.E., Bibl. Sem. N.Y., 1962; m. Ralph A. Musil, June 5, 1937; children—Marjorie Anne, Robert Kirkland. Tchr. Tudor City Sch., N.Y.C., 1937-42; dir. Hudson View Gardens Nursery Sch., 1942-44; dir. religious edn. children Nassau Council Chs., Christ, 1956-61, v.p., Hempstead, N.Y., 1961-63; mem. bd. Christian edn. N.Y.C. Assn. Congl. Christian Chs., 1954-57, 58-61, N.Y.C. Assn. United Ch. Christ, 1962-63; tchr. Nassau Sch. Religion, 1952-62; tchr. Summer Leadership Schs., U.P. Ch. in U.S.A., 1953-60, 64, Bd. Christian Edn. Synods Washington, Pa., Balt., N.J., N.Y., 1953-60; dean Nassau County Sch. Religion, 1964; instr. Bergen Council Chs., N.J., 1959-63, Queens Fedn. Chs., N.Y., 1957-63, Protestant Council N.Y., Bklyn. div., 1960-64, N.Y.U. Sch. Edn., dept. religious edn., 1964-65, Protestant Council, Manhattan div., 1965-66; dir. Christian edn. Congl. Ch. of Rockville Centre, 1965-71, also dir. nursery sch. TV series: Exploring Our Churches, 1962; adj. asst. prof. edn. C.W. Post Center L.I.U., 1971-74. Mem. women's planning com. Japan Internat. Christian U. Found.; chmn. dept. religious edn. children Nassau Council Chs., 1953-65; chmn. children's work com. Met. Assn. United Ch. Christ, 1963-70, mem. Christian edn. com., 1963-70, rec. sec., 1967-69, v.p., 1971—, mem. ch. and ministry com., 1978—, also dir.; alt. del. Synod; trustee Garden City Community Ch., 1972-78; mem. Christian edn. com N.Y. conf. United Ch. Christ, 1964—, ch. life and leadership com., 1978—; mem. com. on church and econ. life dept. Social Justice Nat. Council Chs., 1967—; mem. New Dimensions commn.-Church Women United Ecumenical Assembly, 1967. Recipient award for services to blind Indsl. Home for Blind, Bklyn., 1957; Centennial citation Wilson Coll., 1969. Mem. Magna Charter Dames, D.A.R. (chpt. dir. 1955-61, chmn. approved schs., 1951-58, chmn. good citizens com. 1965—), Nat. Trust for Historic Preservation, Soc. for Preservation New Eng. Antiquities, Soc. for Preservation L.I. Antiquities, World Alliance Ref. Chs. (chmn. task force N.Am. area 1965-66), N.Y. State Assn. for Edn. of Young Children, Nat. Doll and Toy Collectors Club. Club: Garden City Community (chmn. Americanism com. 1979—). Author articles in field. Home: 69 Kenwood Rd Garden City NY 11530

MUSKIE, EDMUND SIXTUS, U.S. senator; b. Rumford, Maine, Mar. 28, 1914; s. Stephen and Josephine (Czarnecki) M.; A.B., Bates Coll., Lewiston, Me., 1936; LL.B., Cornell, 1939; hon. degrees U. New Brunswick, Middlebury Coll., St. Anselm's Coll., William and Mary Coll., U. Md., Alliance Coll., U. N.H., Northeastern U., John Carroll U., Providence Coll., Boston U., Syracuse U., Bates Coll., U. Maine, Suffolk U., Bowdoin Coll., Colby Coll., Lafayette Coll., U. Notre Dame, Hanover Coll., Cornell U., George Washington U., U. Buffalo, Nasson Coll., Husson Coll.; m. Jane Frances Gray, May 29, 1948; children—Stephen Oliver, Ellen (Mrs. Ernest M. Allen), Melinda, Martha, Edmund Jr. Admitted to Mass. bar, 1939, Maine bar, 1940; practice of law in Waterville, Maine, 1940, 45-51, 1952-54; mem. Maine Ho. of Reps., 1947-51, Democratic floor leader, 1949-51; gov. Maine, 1955-59; U.S. senator from Maine, 1959—, asst. majority whip, 1966—, chmn. senate com. on budget, sub. on environ. pollution, chmn. subcom. on intergovtl. relations, others; exec. dir. Am. Vets., 1951; dist. dir. OPS, Maine, 1951-52. chmn. Roosevelt Campobello Internat. Park Commn.; Maine chmn. citizens com. for Hoover report, 1950; chmn. platform com. Mem. Dem. Conv., 1948, 50, Dem. Nat. Com., 1952-55; chmn. Dem. senatorial campaign com., 1967-69; Dem. vice presdl. nominee, 1968. Served as lt. USNR, 1942-45. Mem. Am. Legion, VFW, Amvets (post comdr. 1947, nat. exec. com.-man. 1947-48), Phi Beta Kappa. Office: US Senate Washington DC 20510

MUSSARI, ANTHONY JOSEPH, educator; b. Wilkes-Barre, Pa., Mar. 18, 1942; s. Angelo L. and Jane R. (Petro) M.; B.A., King's Coll., Wilkes-Barre, 1963; M.A., Niagara (N.Y.) U., 1964; postgrad. Kent State U., 1964-66; Ph.D., U. Iowa, 1978; postgrad. Lehigh U., Bethlehem, Pa., 1975; children—Elena Jacqueline, Anthony Joseph. Mem. staff Niagara U., 1964; teaching fellow Kent (Ohio) State U., 1964-68, Mt. Mercy Coll., Cedar Rapids, Iowa, 1966-68; asst. prof. history King's Coll., 1968—; mem. staff Congressman John C. Culver, 1966-68; exec. dir. civil def., Wilkes-Barre, 1976—. Pres. Wilkes-Barre Area Bd. Edn., 1971-76; mem. joint operating com. Wilkes-Barre Vocat. and Tech. Sch.; mem. Luzerne County Flood Study Commn., 1975-76. Recipient various service awards. Mem. Nat. Sch. Bds. Assn., Pa. Sch. Bd. Assn. Author Appointment With Disaster. Contbr. articles to newspapers, profl. jours. Home: 150 S Grant St Wilkes-Barre PA 18702 Office: Box 1503 King's Coll Wilkes-Barre PA 18702

MUSSELMAN, FRANCIS HAAS, lawyer; b. Utica, N.Y., Aug. 3, 1925; s. John Joseph and Kathryn Agnes (Haas) M.; A.B., Hamilton Coll., 1950; J.D., Columbia, 1953; m. Marjorie Louise Balme, June 22, 1948; children—Martha Christina (Mrs. Paul W. Sheridan), Kathryn Ann (Mrs. Richard Bourbonniere), Carol Elizabeth (Mrs. Robert Kuntz), John Francis. Admitted to N.Y. State bar, 1954; asso. firm Milbank, Tweed, Hadley & McCloy, N.Y.C., 1953-60, mem., 1960—; dir. Arbank Farms, Inc., Coral Gables, Fla., Panfield Nurseries, N.Y.C., Fla. Cane Co., Inc., Lake Harbor, Fla. Pres., dir. Panfield Corp., N.Y.C., 1961—. Bd. dirs. Milbank Meml. Fund, 1960—, Memton Fund, 1958—; trustee Wadhams Hall Sem. Coll., Ogdensburg, N.Y., 1977—, vice chmn., 1978—; trustee Kirkland Coll., Clinton, N.Y., 1971-78, chmn., 1972-78; trustee Hamilton Coll., Clinton. Served with USNR, 1943-46; PTO. Mem. N.Y. Law Inst., Am. Judicature Soc., Am. Law Inst., Internat., Am., N.Y. State, Nassau County bar assns., World Assn. Lawyers, Soc. Computers and Law, Assn. Bar City N.Y., Phi Delta Phi, Lambda Chi Alpha. Roman Catholic. Clubs: Union League, Wall Street (gov. 1978—), World Trade Center (N.Y.C.). Home: Oak Point Hammond NY 13646 Office: 1 Chase Manhattan Plaza New York NY 10005

MUSSER, BENJAMIN GARBER, cardiovascular and thoracic surgeon; b. Columbia, Pa., Apr. 15, 1921; s. Alvin K. and Clara W. (Schlosser) M.; B.S., Elizabethtown Coll., 1941; M.D., Hahnemann Med. Coll., 1944; m. Vera Blinn Shoop, Aug. 1, 1943; children—Philip, Pamela, Lynne, Cynthia. Intern Lancaster (Pa.) Gen. Hosp., 1944-45, Riverside Hosp., Toledo, Ohio, 1945-46; resident in gen. surgery Walter Reed Army Hosp., 1947-48, Tripler Army Hosp., Honolulu, 1948-52; resident in thoracic surgery Hahnemann Med. Coll. and Hosp., Phila., 1953-56; practice medicine specializing in cardiovascular and thoracic surgery, Harrisburg, Pa., 1956—; clin. asso. prof. surgery Hahnemann Med. Coll., 1956—; clin. asso. prof. surgery Hershey Med. Coll., 1972—. Trustee Elizabethtown Coll., 1965—. Served with U.S. Army, 1942-53. Decorated Bronze Star. Nat. Heart Inst. fellow, 1954-56. Diplomate Am. Bd. Surgery, Am. Bd. Thoracic Surgery. Mem. A.C.S., Am. Coll. Cardiology, Soc. Thoracic Surgery, Pa. Assn. Thoracic Surgery, Pa., Dauphin County med. socs., AMA, Am. Coll. Chest Physicians, Am. Med. Writers Assn., Assn. Advancement of Med. Instrumentation, Soc. Preservation and Encouragement of Barbershop Quartet Singing. Republican. Presbyn. Contbr. articles to med. jours. Home: 95 Greenwood Circle Wormleysburg PA 17043 Office: 2247 N Front St Harrisburg PA 17110

MUSSER, JAY CHARLES, cons. chemist; b. Elizabethtown, Pa., Sept. 5, 1917; s. Charles Klugh and Ada Bertha (Coble) M.; student Lebanon Valley Coll., 1935-37; B.S., Franklin and Marshall Coll., 1940, M.S., 1953; m. Mary Ruth Hertzler, Sept. 9, 1944; children—Susan, Charles, James, Janet. Chemist, Klein Chocolate Co., Elizabethtown, 1941-42, chief chemist, 1946-55, v.p. research and devel., 1955-58, v.p. mfg., 1958-61, exec. v.p., 1961-70; freelance cons. chemist Mt. Joy, Pa., 1970—. Mem. Donegal Sch. Bd., 1954-70, v.p., 1966-70, pres., 1964-65. Served with Ordnance Corp. U.S. Army, 1942-46; ETO, PTO. Mem. Am. Assn. Candy Technologists (Stroud Jordan award 1967), Pa. Mfg. Confectioners Assn. (research chmn. 1958—), Am. Chem. Soc., Am. Soc. Cost Engrs., Inst. Food Technologists, ASTM, Chocolate Mfrs. Assn. Methodist. Rotary (pres. Mt. Joy 1970—). Researcher chocolate, confectionery, 1953—. Patentee in field. Home and Office: 214 Marietta Ave Mt Joy PA 17552

MUSSER, WILLIAM LLOYD, JR., investment co. exec.; b. N.Y.C., Dec. 12, 1942; s. William Lloyd and Phyllis (Person) M.; A.B., Princeton, 1964; M.B.A. (Fulbright scholar), Harvard, 1967; m. Linda Swanberg, Sept. 10, 1966; children—Philip Adrian, Lila Ruth. Securities analyst F. Eberstadt & Co., N.Y.C., 1967-69; v.p. Cannell, Breed & Musser, 1969-71; v.p., dir. Cotty, Felleman & Co., 1971-74 (merged with New Court Securities), sr. v.p., 1974—; dir. New Court Capital Mgmt. Co., West Fork Coal Co. Mem. N.Y. Soc. Security Analysts. Episcopalian. Club: Racquet and Tennis. Home: 167 E 82d St New York City NY 10028 Office One Rockefeller Plaza New York City NY 10020

MUSTIAN, ALFRED PLUMMER, JR., govt. ofcl., forester; b. Roanoke Rapids, N.C., Aug. 15, 1925; s. Alfred Plummer and Katherine Mae (Parker) M.; B.S.F., N.C. State U., 1949; postgrad. Emory U., 1963-64; m. Gussie Pierce Evans, Mar. 22, 1947; children—Cheryl Mustian Rice, Charles Alfred, Gary Russell. With U.S. Forest Service, 1949—, forester, Ala. and La., 1949-53, dist. ranger, La. and Tex., 1953-57, asst. forest supr., Tallahassee, Fla., 1957-60, br. chief timber mgt., Atlanta, 1960-64, staff specialist legis. affairs, Washington, 1965-70, asst. dir. timber mgmt., Washington, 1970-75, dep. dir., 1975—. Served with U.S. Army, 1944-46. Decorated Purple Heart. Mem. Soc. Am. Foresters, Soil Conservation Soc. Am., Am. Polit. Sci. Assn., Nat. Rifle Assn., Xi Sigma Pi. Baptist (deacon). Home: 4405 Rockcrest Dr Fairfax VA 22032 Office: 14th and Independence Ave Washington DC 20250

MUSTO, DAVID FRANKLIN, physician, historian; b. Tacoma, Jan. 8, 1936; s. Charles Hiram and Hilda Marie (Hanson) Mustoe; B.A., U. Wash., 1956; M.A., Yale U., 1961; M.D., U. Wash., 1963; m. Emma Jean Baudendistel, June 2, 1961; children—Jeanne Marie, David Kyle, John Baird, Christopher Edward. Spl. asst. to dir. NIMH, Bethesda, Md., 1967-69; vis. asst. prof. history Johns Hopkins U., Balt., 1968-69; asst. prof. psychiatry and history Yale U., New Haven, 1969-73, asso. prof., 1973-78, sr. research scientist, 1978—, lectr. history and Am. studies, 1978—; intern Pa. Hosp., Phila., 1963-64; resident in psychiatry Yale Med. Center, 1964-67; program dir. Nat. Humanities Inst., 1977-78; cons. in field. Mem. White House Strategy Council, 1977—; historian Pres.'s Commn. Mental Health, 1977—; mem. U.S. Del. UN Narcotics Commn., 1978. Recipient William Osler medal Am. Assn. History Medicine, 1960, Kremers award Am. Inst. History Pharmacy, 1974. Fellow Am. Psychiat. Assn. (chmn. history commn. 1973-77); mem. Am. History Assn., Conn. Med. Soc., Group for Advancement Psychiatry, Conn. Trust Historic Preservation, N.Y. C.S. Lewis Soc. Author: Historical Perspectives on Mental Health and Racism, 1973; The American Disease: Origins of Narcotic Control, 1973; Adv. editor Yale edits. papers James Boswell, 1975—. Office: Yale Child Study Center 333 Cedar St New Haven CT 06510

MUSUMECI, THOMAS, hosp. adminstr.; b. Milily, Sicily, Italy, Nov. 26, 1942; s. Joseph and Vincenza (Di Mauro) M.; Asso. in Accounting, Becker Jr. Coll., 1964; B.B.A., Nichols Coll., 1970; certificate of procurement U. Conn., 1967; m. Jeri Lee Carpenter, Dec. 5, 1964; children—Brian, Scott, Gina, Joey. Cost accountant Emhart Corp., New Britain, Conn., 1964-65; auditor John Meyers, C.P.A., Danielson, Conn., 1966—; purchasing agt. Belding Heminway, Inc., Putnam, Conn., 1966-72; materials mgr. Day Kimball Hosp., Putnam, 1973—. Active local youth orgns., 1966—. Mem. Internat. Material Mgmt. Soc., Nat. Assn. Hosp. Purchasing Mgmt., Conn. Hosp. Purchasing Mgmt. Assn. Club: Elks (Putnam, Conn.). Home: Box 71B Dukeland Dr Woodstock CT 06281

MUZAC, ANDRE J., surgeon; b. Haiti, June 9, 1934; s. Juvigny and Eden (Lafortune) M.; came to U.S., 1963, naturalized, 1971; B. Degree, Lycee A. Petion, Haiti, 1954; M.D., Faculte Medecine D'Haiti, 1960; m. Suzy Monsanto, Dec. 29, 1961; children—Jean-Edouard, Henry-Robert, Martine. Intern in surgery Ste. Justine Hosp., Montreal, Que., Can., 1962-63; rotating intern St. Johns Episcopal Hosp., Bklyn., 1963-64, resident in surgery, 1964-68, asso. dir. surgery, 1976—; resident in surgery Kings County Hosp., Bklyn., 1965; clin. instr. surgery Downstate Med. Center State U. N.Y., 1977—. Fellow Am. Coll Surgeons (com. unnecessary surgery Bklyn. L.I. chpt.), mem. AMA (Continuing Edn. award 1977). Office: 363 Eastern Pkwy Brooklyn NY 11216

MYERHOLTZ, EARL FREDERICK, metals co. exec.; b. Oak Harbor, Ohio, Oct. 12, 1923; s. Ernest Henry and Viola Louise (Foreman) M.; B.S., Va. Poly. Inst., 1948; m. Betsy Jane Draper, June 20, 1946; children—Suzanne (Mrs. David Cameron), Pamela Jean (Mrs. Norman Brose). With Gen. Electric Co., 1948-64, mgmt. trainee, Lynn, Mass., 1948-51, mfg. mgmt., Evendale, Ohio, 1951-61, mgr. mfg. engring., 1961-64; with TRW, 1964—, dir. mfg. engring., v.p., gen. mgr., mech. products div., Cleve., 1966-71, v.p., gen. mgr. Marlin Rockwell div., Jamestown, N.Y., 1971—; dir. 1st Nat. Bank Jamestown. Bd. dirs. YMCA, Jamestown, 1973—, WCA Hosp., Jamestown. Served as sgt. AUS, 1942-46. Decorated Bronze Star. Mem. Anti-Friction Bearing Mfrs. Assn. (dir. 1971—, chmn. 1976), Jamestown Mfg. Assn. (dir. 1972-74, pres. 1976, Am. Inst. Indsl. Engrs., Soc. Automotive Engrs. Club: Moon Brook Country (Jamestown). Home: 48 W Fairwood Dr Lakewood NY 14750 Office: 402 Chandler St Jamestown NY 14701

MYERS, ALFRED FRANTZ, state ofcl.; b. Crooked Creek State Park, Pa., Feb. 19, 1936; s. Jacob Alfred Jr. and Ida Gertrude (Schaeffer) M.; B.A., Lehigh U., 1958, M.A., 1966; postgrad. George Peabody Coll., 1971-72. Instr., Culver Mil. Acad. (Ind.), 1966-68, Kiskiminetas Springs Sch., Saltsburg, Pa., 1968-71; asst. prof. social studies Ind. State U., Terre Haute, 1972-73; div. trainer Ency. Britannica, Rochester, N.Y., 1973-75; mgr. Rupp's, Kittanning, Pa., 1976-77; criminal justice system planner Pa. Commn. on Crime and Delinquency, Harrisburg, 1977—. Social work Dominican Rep., 1958. Served to 1st lt. with USAF, 1958-63. Mem. Nat. Council Social Studies, Am. Acad. Polit. and Social Sci., AAUP, Assn. for Supervision and Curriculum Devel., Hist Assn. (London), Am. Hist. Assn., Caribbean Studies Assn., Assn. Am. Geographers, Latin Am. Studies Assn., Nat. Braille Assn., Phi Beta Kappa, Phi Delta Kappa. Republican. Methodist. Home: 849 Melissa Ct Enola PA 17025

MYERS, ANDREW BREEN, educator; b. N.Y.C., Sept. 28, 1920; s. Andrew Jefferson and Margaret (Breen) M.; A.B., Fordham Coll., 1940; postgrad. Biarritz Am. U. (France), 1945-46; M.A., Columbia, 1947, Ph.D., 1964; m. Margaret Helen Lohrmann, July 4, 1949; children—Cathleen, Christopher, Andrew. Trainee, Wall St. Jour., N.Y.C., 1941; geometry tchr. Regis High Sch., N.Y.C., 1942-43; from instr. to asso. prof. Fordham U., Bronx, N.Y., 1946-75, mem. grad. faculty, 1958—, asso. dir. devel., 1964-66, pres. faculty senate, 1969-72, mem. editorial bd. univ. press, 1973—, prof., 1975—, chmn., 1978—; research cons. Sleepy Hollow Restorations, Tarrytown, N.Y., 1970—. Fellow Pierpont Morgan Library, N.Y.C., 1963—, Pintard fellow N.Y. Hist. Soc. (council mem., vice chmn. 1977—). Served with AUS, 1943-46. Recipient Achievement in Edn. award Fordham Coll. Alumni Assn., 1970; grantee Am. Philos. Soc., 1964, Nat. Endowment for Humanities, 1968. Mem. AAUP, Am. Studies Assn. Modern Lang. Assn. Manuscript Soc., Melville Soc., Thoreau Soc., Bibliog. Soc. Am. (sec., council mem.). Democrat. Roman Catholic. Clubs: Century, Grolier (council mem.), Lotos. Editor: Washington Irving, A Tribute, 1972, the Knickerbocker Tradition, 1974, The Worlds of Washington Irving, 1974, A Century of Literary Criticism of Washington Irving, 1976, Poems (1972) By Nathaniel Evans, 1976; Washington Irving's Old Christmas, 1977. Home: 144-89 38th Ave Flushing NY 11354 Office: English Department Dealy Hall Fordham University Bronx NY 10458

MYERS, CAROLINE CLARK (MRS. GARRY CLEVELAND MYERS), mag. exec.; b. Morris, Pa., July 14, 1887; d. Charles Edgar and Elizabeth (Boyd) Clark; grad. Bloomsburg State Tchrs. Coll., 1905; student Ursinus Coll., 1907-08, Juanita Coll., 1912-13, Merrill Palmer Sch. Detroit, 1930-31, Tchrs. Coll., Columbia, summers 1931-34; m. Garry Cleveland Myers, June 26, 1912 (dec. July 1971); children—Jack E., Elizabeth (Mrs. Kent L. Brown), Garry C. (dec.). Laura Spellman Rockefeller scholar, 1930; dir. parent edn. and family life Cleve. Welfare Fedn., 1931-41; instr. family life and child devel. Cleve. Coll., Western Res. U., 1931-41; instr. U. Wash., Seattle, summers 1938-41; instr. Oreg. State U., 1942; leader pub. forums U.S. Office Edn. 1937; asso. editor Children's Activities, 1941, 46; co-founder, mng. editor Highlights for Children, Honesdale, Pa., also v.p.; dir. Highlights for Children, Inc., 1946—. Co-chmn. Community Fund campaign Wayne County Meml. Hosp., 1947, bd. dirs., 1946—. Recipient Distinguished Service award Bloomsburg State Tchrs. Coll., 1953, Nat. award Freedoms Found., 1976. Mem. Nat. Council Family Relations. Co-author: Myers Mental Measure, 1920; Language of America 1921; My Work Book in Arithmetic, 1926; Homes Build Persons, 1950; Your Child and You, 1970. Contbr. articles and chpts. to profl. publs. Home: Milanville PA 18443 Office: 803 Church St Honesdale PA 18431

MYERS, CHARLES F., pub. co. exec.; b. Long Island City, N.Y., Sept. 28, 1941; s. Frank J. and Beatrice Myers; B.S., Fordham U., 1963; m. Lorraine Muller, Dec. 28, 1963; children—Debra, David. Mgr. audit dept. S.D. Leidesdorf & Co., N.Y.C., 1963-73; dir. internal audit Gulf & Western Industries Inc., N.Y.C., 1973-75; exec. v.p. Simon & Schuster Inc., N.Y.C., 1975—, also dir. C.P.A. Mem. Am. Inst. C.P.A.'s, N.Y. State Soc. C.P.A.'s, Beta Alpha Psi. Home: 35 Grant St Haworth NJ 07641 Office: Simon & Schuster Inc 1230 Ave of Americas New York City NY 10020

MYERS, EDWIN NELSON, electronic engr.; b. Sayre, Pa., Jan. 26, 1924; s. Everett Harding and Edith (Lane) M.; B.S., Okla. State U., 1956; M.S., Mass. Inst. Tech., 1961; m. Marian Louise Engler, Aug. 29, 1944; children—Metta Lou Mari Anne. Commd. 2d lt. USAAF, 1944, advanced through grades to lt. col., 1963; iwth Continental Weather Wing, 1946-54, asst. chief systems engr. Sage P.O. Air Research and Devel. Command, N.Y.C., 1956-59, research and devel. program mgr. Radar Techniques and Lasers, Pentagon, 1961-65; ret., 1965; staff asst. electronic devices and lasers Office Dir. of Def. Research and Engring., Office Sec. Def., 1965-70, staff asst. to asst. dir. electronics and phys. scis., 1971-72, staff specialist electronic scis., 1972-76, sr. staff specialist electronic devices and search systems, 1976—. Recipient Meritorious Civilian Service medal Sec. Def., 1977. Mem. IEEE, Am. Radio Relay League, Mil. Affiliate Radio System, Sigma Xi, Phi Kappa Phi, Eta Kappa Nu, Pi Mu Epsilon. Home: 1010

Priscilla Ln Alexandria VA 22308 Office: Sec of Defense Washington DC 20301

MYERS, EUGENE EKANDER, art adminstr.; b. Grand Forks, N.D., May 5, 1914; s. John Q. and Hattye Jane (Ekander) M.; B.S. in Edn., U. N.D., 1936, M.S. in Edn., 1938; postgrad. U. Oreg., summer 1937; M.A., Northwestern U., 1940, Columbia U., 1947; advanced mgmt. program Harvard U., 1953; certificate Cambridge (Eng.) U., 1958; postgrad. U. Md., 1958-61, Oxford (Eng.) U., 1964; diploma various mil. schs.; m. Florence Hutchinson Ritchie, Sept. 9, 1974. Student asst. U. N.D., 1935-36, instr. summer sessions, 1936, 37, asst., 1936-37; instr. N.D. Tchrs. Coll., 1938-40, Tchrs. Coll., Columbia U., 1940-41; prof. U. Vt., summer 1941, 42; commd. 1st lt. USAAF, 1942, advanced through grades to col., 1951; dir. personnel plans and tng. Hdqrs. Air Force Systems Command, Washington, 1959-60, dir. personnel research and longrange plans, 1960-62, head dept. internat. relations Air War Coll., Air U., Maxwell AFB, Ala., 1962-63, dir. curriculum, dean, 1963-65, dir. res. affairs Hdqrs. Air Res. Personnel Center, Denver, 1965-66; dean Corcoran Sch. Art, Washington, 1966-69; v.p. Corcoran Gallery Art, Washington, 1970-72; art. cons., vis. art dir. Palm Beach, Fla. and Washington, 1972—; adv. D.C. chpt. Nat. Soc. Arts and Letters; bd. asso. Artists Equity. Recipient Sioux award U. N.D., 1978. Bd. dirs. World Arts Found., N.Y.C., Columbia (Md.) Inst. Art. Mem. Nat. Soc. Study Communication (hon.), U. N.D. Alumni Assn. (pres. Washington 1959), Mil. Classics Soc., Titanic Soc., Co. Mil. Historians, St. Andrews Soc., Clan Donnachaidh (Perthshire), Mil. Order of Carabao, Order of Lafayette (dir.), English Speaking Union, Mil. Order World Wars, Delta Omicron Epsilon, Lambda Chi Alpha, Delta Phi Delta, Phi Delta Kappa, Phi Alpha Theta. Republican. Presbyn. Clubs: Lions; Curzon House, Royal Over-Seas League (London); Union (hon.) (Manchester, Eng.); New (asso.) (Edinburgh, Scotland); Army and Navy, Army and Navy Country, Nat. Aviation, George Town, City Tavern, Harvard Bus. Sch. (Washington); Met., Salmagundi, Wings, Explorers (fellow), Harvard (N.Y.C.); Mpls., Everglades, Beach, Sailfish of Fla. (Palm Beach, Fla.); Fairmont Field Country (Fairmont, W.Va.). Author: (with Paul E. Barr) Creative Lettering, 1938; (with others) The Subject Fields in General Education, 1939; Applied Psychology, 1940; contbr. articles and reports in mags. and profl. publs. Address: 3320 Volta Pl NW Washington DC 20007 also 1 Royal Palm Way Palm Beach FL 33480

MYERS, GARY ARTHUR, former congressman; b. Toronto, Ohio, Aug. 16, 1937; s. Arthur Hamilton and Dorothea Carolyn (Isaly) M.; M.E., U. Cin., 1960; M.B.A., U. Pitts., 1964; m. Elaine J. Roppolo, Apr. 20, 1963; children—Michele Renee, Mark Christopher. Mech. engr. coop. student Armco Steel Corp., 1955-60, mech. engr., 1960-61, indsl. engr., 1961-65, turn foreman hot strip mill, 1965-74; mem. 94th-95th Congresses from 25th Pa. dist. Served with USAFR, 1961-68. Home: 106 Shady Dr Butler PA 16001

MYERS, JEAN ANN, ednl. adminstr.; b. Freeland, Pa., Nov. 7, 1925; d. John M. and Gladys (Seylar) Stevens; A.B., MacMurray Coll., 1947; M.Ed., Pa. State U., 1963; certificate Western Md., 1971; m. Richard F. Myers, June 1, 1946; children—Reba Ann Myers Walking, Amy Lei, Steven A. Tchr., Lafayette Sch., Jacksonville, Ill., 1947-48; dir. Vallamont Child Care Center, Williamsport, Pa., 1948-49; tchr. Pine Tree Day Sch., York, Pa., 1955-57, Dover (Pa.) Elementary Sch., 1957-61, Ferguson Sch., York, 1961-63; reading supr. West York Area Schs., York, 1963-68, coordinator, 1968-70, prin. Lincolnway Sch. and Loucks Sch., 1970-76; instr. developmental reading and children's lit. Pa. State U., York Center, part-time 1970-73, York Coll. Pa., 1975; mem. Middle Atlantic States Elementary Sch. Evaluation Team. Mem. Pa. Congress Parents and Tchrs. (hon. life), Pa. Congress Sch. Adminstr., York County Schoolman's Club, Pa. Assn. Supervision and Curricular Devel., Internat. Reading Assn. (council), Delta Kappa Gamma. Methodist. Home: 1050 Rohlers Church Rd Dover PA 17315 Office: 1731 W Philadelphia St York PA 17404

MYERS, JO ANNE, plastics co. exec.; b. Detroit, Sept. 12, 1940; d. Gilbert Joseph and Geraldine (Stanley) M.; B.A., Douglass Coll., 1963; M.A., N.Y. U., 1966. Elementary tchr. Internat. Sch., Bangkok, Thailand, 1959-60; instr. English, U. Mex., 1963; elementary tchr. Am. Sch., Manila, 1963-64; bilingual sec. Master Builders Co., Manila and Madrid, 1963-65; tchr. Spanish, W. Orange (N.J.) High Sch., 1965-69; instr. Spanish Bloomfield (N.J.) Coll., 1969-72; adminstrv. exec. Nat. Assn. Small Bus. Investment Cos., Washington, 1972-74; sales rep. Celanese Plastics Co., Chatham, N.J., 1974—. N.J. Fedn. Women's Club scholar, 1963. Mem. Soc. Plastics Engrs. (dir. Newark sect. 1976—, sec. 1978-79; Woman of Year award Newark sect. 1977). Home: 7 Morris Pl Madison NJ 07940 Office: 26 Main St Chatham NJ 07928

MYERS, JOHN HENRY, oil co. exec.; b. Lancaster, Pa., Oct. 30, 1930; s. Jay Russell and Anna Elizabeth (Ransing) M.; ed. trade sch.; m. Teresa Ann Quinn, June 5, 1954; children—Teresa Ann, Ellen Elizabeth, Colleen Mary, John Henry. Foreman Peach Bottom Power Plant, 1968-74; supr., Saudi Arabia Bechtel Co., Lancaster, Pa., 1975-78. Served to sgt., USAF, 1950-54. Mem. Am. Rifleman Assn., Am. Def. Preparedness Assn. Democrat. Roman Catholic. Home: 213 E Liberty St Lancaster PA 17602

MYERS, LAWRENCE, agrl. economist; b. Humboldt, Iowa, July 14, 1898; s. George A. and Mary (Barrett) M.; B.S., U. Minn., 1922, postgrad., 1923-27; M.S., Iowa State Coll., 1923; m. Anne Cornelia Henkel, July 15, 1924; children—Margaret Mary Myers Rast, Dorothy Helen Myers Sampas. Instr. agrl. econs. U. Minn., St. Paul, 1925-27; economist Bur. Agr. Econs., U.S. Dept. Agr., Washington, 1927-33; economist, div. dir. AAA, Washington, 1933-39; div. dir. CCC, Washington, 1939-46; dir. textiles and raw materials UNNRA, Washington, 1946; asst. to sec. agr., Washington, 1946; dir. sugar div. U.S. Dept. Agr., Washington, 1947-63; chmn. bd. Nat. Molasses Corp., Washington, 1963-68; Washington rep. C. Brewer & Affiliates, 1968-71; econ. cons., 1972—; cons. Philippine Sugar Commn., 1973—; chmn. Internat. Sugar Council, 1955. Served with U.S. Army, 1918. Recipient certificate of merit Dept. Agr., 3 times, Distinguished Service award 1955. Republican. Clubs: Cosmos (Washington); Potomac (Md.) Hunt. Home: 4301 Massachusetts Ave NW Washington DC 20016 Office: 1001 Connecticut Ave NW Washington DC 20036

MYERS, LEGH RICHMOND, sculptor; b. Ventnor, N.J., Nov. 11, 1916; s. Legh Richmond and Emma (Hautman) M.; student Pa. State U., 1935-36, Lehigh U., 1936-39 student J. Wallace Kelly, Phila., 1952-54; m. Gloria Glenn Fitzsimons, Sept. 26, 1962; children—Legh Richmond, Laura Marie Myers Hudspeth. One-man shows: Madison Gallery, N.Y.C., 1961, Ruth White Gallery, N.Y.C., 1965, Chapman Sculpture Gallery, N.Y.C., 1969, Alonzo Gallery, N.Y.C., 1976; two-man shows: Madison Gallery, N.Y.C., 1960, Key Gallery, N.Y.C., 1963, Sculpture House, N.Y.C., 1966; group shows include: Audubon Artists Ann., 1960, 62, 63, 64, 70, 71, 72, 73-78, 79, Nat. Arts Club, N.Y.C., 1957, 59-63, 68, 70-73, Lever House, N.Y.C., 1971-77, Gen. Electric Hdqrs., Fairfield, Conn., 1977, Sculpture Guild. Ann., 1978; represented in pvt. collections. Served to lt. (s.g.) USNR, 1942-46. Mem. Artists Equity Assn. N.Y., Sculptors Guild N.Y. (dir., exec. com., sec.), Audubon Artists Nat. Acad. (Margaret Hirsch Levine Meml. prize 30th Ann. Exhbn. 1972, medal for creative sculpture 28th Ann. Exhbn. 1970), Knickerbocker Artists, Nat. Arts Club. Work reviewed in art publs. Home and Office: 9 S Mansfield Ave Margate NJ 08402

MYERS, MICHAEL, congressman; b. Phila., May 4, 1943; student pub. and parochial schs.; m. Ethel P. Sutherland. Mem. 95th Congress from 1st Pa. Dist. Office: 1331 Longworth Bldg Washington DC 20515 also 1725 S Broad St Philadelphia PA 19148

MYERS, MOREY M., lawyer; b. Scranton, Pa., Aug. 5, 1927; s. Samuel Zigman and Libbye (Kaplan) M.; A.B., Syracuse U., 1949; LL.B., Yale, 1952; m. Sondra Gelb, Nov. 26, 1956; children—Jonathan S., David N. Admitted to Pa. bar, 1953, U.S. Supreme Ct. bar, 1960; practice law, 1952—; asst. city solicitor, Scranton, 1957-61; dept. atty. gen. Pa., 1962-63; partner firm Gelb & Myers, Scranton, 1960—. Chief counsel Pa. Milk Control Commn., 1962-63; vis. prof. Marywood Coll. Sch. Social Work, Scranton, 1969-71; cons. Presdl. Commn. on Campus Unrest, 1970. Chmn., Lackawanna United Fund, 1968; mem. nat. cabinet United Jewish Appeal, 1972—. Chmn., Scranton Democratic Com., 1968-70. Trustee Keystone Jr. Coll., Scranton, United Israel Appeal. Served with USNR, 1945-46. Mem. Am. Bar Assn., Am. Judicature Soc. Jewish. Home: 1121 Myrtle St Scranton PA 18510 Office: Scranton Life Bldg Scranton PA 18503

MYERS, ROBERT JOHN, mag. publisher; b. Elkhart, Ind., Jan. 1, 1924; s. Hallet Frederick and Grace (Mattern) M.; student DePauw U., 1942-43; M.A., U. Chgo., 1948, Ph.D., 1959; m. Elizabeth Lauchlin Watson, Sept. 21, 1953; children—Timothy, Holly, Lynn. Area analyst Dept. Army, Japan, 1949-55; 2d sec., Indonesia and Cambodia, 1956-65; co-founder, pub. Washington mag., 1965-68; pub. New Republic mag., Washington, 1968—; v.p., dir. Liveright Pub. Co., N.Y.C., 1969-74; v.p. The New Republic Books, Inc. Mem. Madeira Sch. Bd., Greenway, Va., 1970—, pres., 1975—. Served with U.S. Army, 1943-46; CBI. Mem. Asia Soc., Phi Beta Kappa. Author: The Tragedy of Richard II, 1973; The Coming Collapse of the Post Office, 1975; The Cross of Frankenstein, 1975. Home: 2318 44th St Washington DC 20007 Office: 1200 19th St Washington DC 20036

MYERS, THOMAS ANDREWS, mfg. co. exec.; b. Latrobe, Pa., Mar. 24, 1949; s. Clarence Rolland and Mary Ruth M.; B.A., Allegheny Coll., 1971; postgrad. Clarion State Coll., 1972; Asst. dir. Cable TV-13 Meadville Pa., 1971-73; mgr. advt. and pub. relations Teledyne Vasco, Latrobe, 1973—, advt. cons. Teledyne Allvac, Monroe, N.C., 1976—. Chmn. adv. com. publicity and publs. Seton Hill Coll. Bd. dirs. Adelphoi Village, Latrobe, 1977; mem. admissions adv. council Allegheny Coll., Meadville, Pa., 1978—. Mem. Latrobe Area C. of C. (chmn. publicity com. 1976), Laurel Highlands Advt. Assn. (dir. 1975—, pres. 1978-79). Home: 1240 Mission Rd Apt 26 Latrobe PA 15650 Office: PO Box 151 Latrobe PA 15650

MYERS, THOMAS KROMER, advt. agy. exec.; b. Pasadena, Calif., June 9, 1932; s. Norval F. and Elizabeth (Miles) M.; B.A., Dartmouth, 1954; M.B.A., Harvard, 1958; m. Birgit Enlund, June 6, 1955; children—Thomas Kromer, James M., John P. Area supr. Colgate Palmolive Internat., 1958-59; product mgr. Colgate-Palmolive Ltd., London, 1960-61; mktg. mgr. Colgate-Palmolive, Stockholm, Sweden, 1961-64; product mgr. Gen. Foods U.S., White Plains, N.Y., 1964-66; mktg. dir. Norman, Craig & Kummel, Inc., N.Y.C., 1964-70, exec. v.p., 1971-73, pres., 1973-76, chmn., 1976—, also dir.; dir. NCK Orgn. Served to capt. USAF, 1955-57. Mem. Am. Assn. Advt. Agys. (dir.), Nat. Found. Conservation and Environ. Officers (dir.), Silvermine Art Guild (dir.), Beta Theta Pi. Republican. Episcopalian. Clubs: Ocean Reef; Harvard Bus. Sch. (dir.); Dutchess Valley; Met.; New Canaan Field. Home: 9 Summit Ridge Rd New Canaan CT 06840 Office: 919 3d Ave New York City NY 10022

MYERS, WAYNE ALAN, psychiatrist; b. N.Y.C., Dec. 13, 1931; s. Harry and Eve (Posnansky) M.; B.S. with high honors, U. Ark., 1952; M.D., Columbia U., 1956; Psychoanalyst, N.Y. Psychoanalytic Inst., 1962-69; m. Joanne Jackson, Mar. 23, 1969; children—Tracy Victoria, Blake Andrew. Intern, Bellevue Hosp., N.Y.C., 1956-57; asst. resident in psychiatry Payne Whitney Clinic of N.Y. Hosp., 1957-59, 61-62; clin. instr. Cornell U. Med. Center, 1962-72, psychiatrist outpatients New York Hosp., 1962-72, clin. asst. prof., asst. attending pscyhiatrist Cornell U.-New York Hosp. Med. Center, 1972-77, asso. prof. psychiatry, asso. attending psychiatrist, 1977—; mem. faculty Columbia U. Center for Psychoanalytic Study and Research, 1977—; practice medicine specializing in psychiatry and psychoanalysis, N.Y.C., 1962—. Served with M.C., U.S. Army, 1959-61. Fellow Am. Psychiat. Assn.; mem. Am., Internat. psychoanalytic assns., N.Y. Psychoanalytic Soc. and Inst., Assn. Psychoanalytic Medicine, AMA, N.Y. State Med. Soc., Med. Soc. County N.Y., N.Y. Soc. Clin. Psychiatry, N.Y. Acad. Sci., AAAS. Contbr. articles to med. jours. Office: 1385 York Ave New York City NY 10021

MYLER, DAVID DONALD, mfg. co. exec.; b. Claremont, N.H., July 21, 1944; s. Donald Raymond and Lucy (Guay) M.; B.B.S., N.H. Coll., 1969; postgrad. U. N.H., 1969-76; m. Wendy Stevens, Aug. 9, 1969; 1 son, Benjamin Michael. Dir. personnel Northeast Electronics, Concord, N.H., 1970-75; div. dir. personnel and indsl. relations Edison Electronics, Manchester, N.H., 1975—; tchr. N.H. Vocat. Tech. Sch., 1971-76. Bd. dirs. Red Cross, Concord, 1973-75; trustee N.H. Coll., 1975—; active United Fund, 1971—. Served with USNG, 1963-72. Mem. Greater Manchester Personnel Assn., N.H. Coll. Alumni Assn., So. N.H. Survey Group, Am. Soc. Personnel Adminstrn. Roman Catholic. Home: Schoolhouse Rd Amherst NH 03031 Office: Grenier Field Manchester NH 03103

MYLROIE, VICTOR LAVONNE, chemist; b. Ogden, Utah, Feb. 7, 1937; s. George Ernest and Alice Arlene (Lester) M.; B.S., Brigham Young U., 1965, M.S., 1968; m. Gloria Francis Darland, May 25, 1962; children—J. Robert, Natasha K., V. Shane, Cameron K., Michelle L. Egg prodn. mgr. Woodward Bros. Poultry, Franklin, Idaho, 1965-67; research chemist Research Labs., Eastman Kodak Co., Rochester, N.Y., 1968-70, supr. high pressure lab., 1971-72, research chemist spl. organic synthesis group, 1972-74, project engr., film group, 1974-78, supr. high pressure lab. catalytic hydrogenation for synthetic chems., 1978—. Active Boy Scouts Am., 1959—; young men's pres. Ch. of Jesus Christ of Latter-day Saints, 1970-74; pres. Patriots Club Am., 1977—. Cleve. Refractory Metals Co. grantee, 1966-68. Mem. Am. Chem. Soc., N.Y. Acad. Sci., Assn. Heterocylic Chemists, Soc. Photog. Scientists and Engrs., Conf. on Catalytic Hydrogenation. Republican. Home: 812 Lithuanica Ln Webster NY 14580 Office: Eastman Kodak Co Kodak Park Rochester NY 14650

NACE, EDGAR PAUL, psychiatrist; b. Collegeville, Pa., Oct. 14, 1939; s. Kenneth Beyer and Sara (Grater) N.; B.S. magna cum laude, Muhlenberg Coll., 1961; M.D. (Appel award psychiatry), U. Pa., 1965; m. Carol Charlat, June 5, 1965; children—Bradford Winston, Randolph William. Intern, Univ. Hosps., Madison, Wis., 1965-66; resident in psychiatry Inst. of Pa. Hosp., Phila., 1966-70; research psychiatrist Drug Dependence Treatment Center, Phila. VA Hosp., 1973-76; asst. prof. clin. psychiatry U. Pa., Phila., 1973—; dir. alcoholism treatment program Pa. Hosp., Phila., 1973—; mem. faculty U. Pa. Served to maj. M.C., U.S. Army, 1970-73. Mem. Am. Psychiat. Assn., Am. Med. Soc. Alcoholism, Soc. Exptl. and Clin. Hypnosis, Alcoholism Assn. Pa., Alcohol and Drug Problems Assn., Pa. Psychiat. Soc. Republican. Presbyterian. Researcher alcoholism drug abuse, hypnosis. Home: 300 Cherry Ln Wynnewood PA 19096 Office: 111 N 49th St Philadelphia PA 19139

NACHTIGALL, LILA EHRENSTEIN, physician; b. N.Y.C., Feb. 23, 1934; d. Irving and Adele Pearl (Holzer) Ehrenstein; A.B., Bklyn. Coll., 1955; M.D., N.Y. Med. Coll., 1960; m. Richard Henry Nachtigall, Dec. 24, 1957; children—Margaret, Lisa, Ellen. Intern Bellevue Hosp., N.Y.C., 1960-60, resident 1961-64; instr. medicine N.Y. U. Med. Center, 1964-66, asst. prof. obstetrics and gynecology, 1966-74, asso. prof., 1974—, dir. endocrinology Goldwater div., 1966—, dir. Gynecology-Endocrinology Out Patient Dept., 1973—; vis. lectr. Booth Meml. Hosp., Lenox Hill Hosp. Chmn. fund-raising Bank St. Coll. Sch. Children, 1969-74. Recipient Karl Harpuder award in phys. medicine N.Y. Med. Coll., 1960. Mem. A.M.A., Am. Med. Women's Assn., Soc. Study Reprodn., Am. Fertility Soc., Endocrine Soc. Research developed test for estriol determination in human plasma. Home: 355 Riverside Dr New York City NY 10025 Office: 566 1st Ave New York City NY 10016

NADEEM, RAPHAEL GEORGE, dept. store exec.; b. Pawtucket, R.I., Apr. 5, 1926; s. George Raphael and Adel (Samra) N.; student pub. schs., Pawtucket. Asst. display mgr. Strawbridge & Clothiers, Ardmore, Pa., 1950-55; dir. display Snellenburghs, Phila., 1955-61; dir. visual presenta[tion Litt Bros., Phila., 1961-67; dir. display Lansburgh's Washington, 1969-73; corporate v.p. dir. visual presentation The Hecht Co., Washington. Served with USN, 1944-46; PTO. Recipient award Nat. Assn. Display Industries. 1976. Home: 512 S Pitts St Alexandria VA 22314 Office: F St at 7th NW Washington DC 20004

NADEL, BARBARA ANNE, architect; b. Bronx, N.Y., June 13, 1953; d. George and Ruth Lillian (Friedman) N.; student Cornell U., 1973, Hofstra U., 1974; B.A. with honors, SUNY at Binghamton, 1975; B.F.A., R.I. Sch. Design, 1977, B.Arch. with honors, 1978. Electro-mech. draftsperson Avionics Research Corp., Plainview, N.Y., 1974; intern Crandell Assos., Architects and Planners, Vestal, N.Y., 1974, Binghamton Commn. Arch. and Urban Design, 1975; research asst. Nassau County (N.Y.) Planning Commn., 1975, Soc. Preservation of L.I. Antiquities, Setauket, N.Y., 1976; archtl. designer H.W. Markoff, P.E., Providence, 1977; architect VA Hosp., Providence, 1978, Keyes Assos., Architects, Engrs. and Planners, Providence and Waltham, Mass., 1978—; planner, designer R.I. Med. Center/Health Care Services Bldg.; designer, renovator intensive care unit and operating room suite VA Hosp., 1978. Mem. Alliance of Women in Arch., Nat. Trust Hist. Preservation, Soc. Preservation L.I. Antiquities, Friends of Cast Iron Arch. Democrat. Jewish. Home: 53 Pasadena Dr Plainview NY 11803

NADEL, BENJAMIN IRVING, historian; b. Petrograd, Russia, Nov. 1, 1918; s. Isaac and Esther (Truboczyst) N.; came to U.S., 1969, naturalized, 1975; student U. Vilno, 1936-39; diploma with distinction, Belorussian U., Minsk-Saratov, 1941; postgrad. U. Leningrad, 1945-47; advanced degree in history Acad. of Scis. USSR, Leningrad, 1947; m. Mirra Kopzywa, Jan. 16, 1947; children—Isaac-Robert, Eleanora Nadel Golobic. Chair of Latin, asso. prof. Herzen Coll., Leningrad, 1949-57; chair of ancient and medieval history U. Gdansk (Poland), 1958-62; dozent of classics U. Lodz (Poland), 1962-68; vis. asso. prof. humanities U. Chgo., 1969-70; vis. prof. history No. Ill. U., 1970-71; prof. European history and classics Franconia (N.H.) Coll., 1972-78, dir. curriculum devel., 1974-75; exec. dir. Bund Archives of Jewish Labor Movement, 1978—. Bd. dirs. Jewish Hist. Inst., Warsaw, Poland, 1964-68. Mem. Sci. Soc. Gdansk, Sci. Soc. Lodz, Polish Acad. Scis. (com. 1969-68), Am. Hist. Assn., Assn. Ancient Historians. Contbr. articles to history jours. Home: 150-39 61st Rd Flushing NY 11367 Office: 25 E 78th St New York City NY 10021

NADEL, MICHAEL, editor; b. Glasgow, Scotland, Feb. 20, 1901; s. Lazar David and Etta (Gillies) N.; student lit. and writing Coll. City N.Y., 1921-24; m. Frances Muchnick, Mar. 4, 1932; 1 dau., Heidi (Mrs. Ellis Stanley Kempner). Naturalized citizen, 1928. Corporate sec. East Coast Shipyards, Inc., N.Y.C., 1947-55; asst. exec. dir. The Wilderness Soc., Washington, 1955-71, corporate sec., 1964-72, spl. cons., 1971—, editor The Living Wilderness, 1964-71, editor emeritus, 1971—. Lectr. on Wilderness Perservation. Mem. adv. com. fish and game N.Y. State Commr. Conservation, 1945-49; v.p., dir. N.Y. State Conservation Council, 1944-45; dir. Citizens Com. on Natural Resources, Washington, 1971; pres. Chesapeake and Ohio Canal Assn., Washington, 1967-68; chmn. steering com. Rock Creek Park, Washington, 1963-66; trustee Friends of Forest Preserve, N.Y. State, 1944-45; v.p., dir. Mineral. Soc. D.C., 1966-69, 71; mem. profl. working com. U.S.A.-U.S.S.R. Environmental Program Cooperation, 1973—; mem. Fed. Interagy. Subcom. on Internat. Environment Edn., 1977—; mem. mus. com. Lake George (N.Y.) Inst. History, Art and Sci.; past mem. adv. com. open space to chmn. Fairfax County (Va.) Bd. Suprs. Mem. library com. Hudson Guild, N.Y.C., 1923. Recipient certificate of merit for exceptional service to conservation, 1953. Mem. Wilderness Soc. (historian, life mem.), Constitutional Council for Forest Preserve (bd. advisers 1974—), Southwestern Assn. Indian Affairs, Md. Acad. Sci. (hon.), Thoreau Soc., Audubon Naturalist Soc. Central Atlantic States, Thoreau Lyceum, Wildlife Soc., Am. Fisheries Soc., Izaak Walton League Am. (chpt. 1st v.p. 1956-57), Mus. Am. Indian, Smithsonian Assos. Club: Potomac Appalachian Trail (Washington). Author: Scenic, Historic and Natural Sites in Origins of American Conservation, 1966; Revision of Parks and Wilderness in America's Natural Resources, 1967; Eight Biographies for Leaders of American Conservation, 1971; also numerous editorials and articles on environ. matters, wilderness and parks. Editor: Wildlife Restoration sect. Game Breeder and Sportsman mag., 1944-45; also various club bulls. Participated in devel. legislation resulting in Wilderness Act of 1964. Home: 4427 N Pershing Dr Arlington VA 22203 Office: 1901 Pennsylvania Ave NW Washington DC 20006

NADEL, MONROE STANLEY, architect, landscape architect; b. Bronx, N.Y., July 24, 1922; s. Joseph Paurice and Rae Ruth (Gross) N.; B.S. in Social Sci., Coll. City N.Y., 1949; B.Arch., Columbia, 1956, M.Arch., 1975; m. Evelyn Feldman, Sept. 6, 1953; children—Jonathan Oren, Jeremy Adam. Practice architecture, N.Y.C., 1960—, landscape architecture, 1964—; adminstrv. architect, div. sch. bldgs. Bur. Facilities Planning and Design, N.Y.C. Bd. Edn., 1965—, chief archtl. design sect., 1969-76, asst. chief archtl. sect., 1976—. Active Bronx Assn. for Better Community, Community Center Israel, Bronx. Mem. AIA (oculus com., 1976—, architects in govt. com.), Am. Soc. Landscape Architects, Hochheiser Family Circle. Home: 2343 Mickle Ave Bronx NY 10469 Office: 28-11 Queens Plaza N Long Island City NY 11101

NADICH, JUDAH, clergyman; b. Balt., May 13, 1912; s. Isaac and Lena (Nathanson) N.; B.A., Coll. City N.Y., 1932; M.A., Columbia U., 1936; Rabbi, Jewish Theol. Sem. Am., 1936, M.H.L., 1949, D.H.L., 1953, D.D. honoris causa, 1966; m. Martha Hadassah Ribalow, Jan. 26, 1947; children—Leah N. Meir, Shira Adina Levin, Nahma Meira. Rabbi, Temple Beth David, Buffalo, 1936-40, Anshe

Emet Synagogue, Chgo., 1940-42, Kehillath Israel, Brookline, Mass., 1947-57, Park Ave. Synagogue, N.Y.C., 1957—; lecture tours in U.S., Union South Africa, Rhodesia, 1946; led religious retreats for Jewish chaplains, Viet Nam, Japan, 1971, Germany, 1974. Past pres. Jewish Book Council Am.; chmn. Commn. on Jewish Chaplaincy; mem. exec. com. Jewish Theol. Sem.; past pres. Rabbinical Assembly; bd. dirs. Jewish Theol. Sem., Jewish Braille Inst., 92d St. YM-YWHA, Jewish Welfare. Bd. Served as chaplain, lt. col. AUS, 1942-46; sr. Jewish chaplain ETO, adviser to Gen. Eisenhower on Jewish affairs ETO. Decorated Order Brit. Empire, Croix de Guerre, Israel Warriors medal, Am. Victory medal, Occupation of Germany, ETO medal with battle star. Mem. Jewish War Vets U.S. (past nat. chaplain), Am. Jewish Hist. Soc., Mil. Chaplains Assn., Assn. Jewish Chaplains Armed Forces (past pres.), Phi Beta Kappa. Mason. Author: Yom Kippur, 1952; Eisenhower and the Jews, 1953; Jewish Legends of the Second Commonwealth, 1979. Editor: Hebrew Essays (Louis Ginzberg); The Flowering of Modern Hebrew Literature by M. Ribalow, 1959. Contbr. articles to mags. Home: 993 Park Ave New York City NY 10028 Office: 50 E 87th St New York City NY 10028

NADLEY, HARRIS JEROME, accountant; b. Phila., July 6, 1926; s. Michael and Celia (Millman) N.; B.S., Wharton Sch. Commerce, U. Pa., 1950; M.A., Harvard, 1952; m. Barbara A. Malone, June 28, 1953; children—Jennifer Beth, Amy Jane, Adam Christopher. Asst. trust officer Provident Trust Co., Phila., 1949; exec. trainee Merrill, Lynch, Pierce, Fenner & Smith, N.Y.C., 1950; pres. Michael Nadley Co., C.P.A.'s, Phila., 1952—. Teaching fellow Harvard, 1952; instr. finance Wharton Sch., Phila., 1953-54; adj. prof. bus. adminstrn. St. Joseph's Coll., Phila., Acad. Food Mktg., Pa. Inst. C.P.A.'s, Am. Inst. C.P.A.'s; cons. Control Data Corp., 1971; participant Current Strategy Forum, Naval War Coll., 1978. Gen. chmn. Marine Corps Birthday Ball, Phila., 1973. Bd. dirs. Montgomery County Assn. for Retarded Children, Cruiser Olympia Assn.; trustee Lesley Coll., Cambridge, Mass.; pres. adv. council Wharton Sch., U. Pa., 1950. Served with USMCR, 1944-46; PTO. Mem. Am. Radio Relay League, Fraternal Order Police (hon.), Econometric Soc., Am. Econ. Soc., Mil. Order Fgn. Wars, Preservation Soc. Newport County, St. Joseph's Coll. Acad. Food Marketing (founder), Quarter Century Wireless Assn., Marine Corps Res. Officers Assn., Pa. Soc., Beta Gamma Sigma, Pi Gamma Mu, Beta Sigma Rho. Mason. Clubs: Union League, Harvard, Harvard Faculty, Mercedes-Benz, Urban (Phila.). Author: A Covey of Peacocks, 1969. Contbr. articles to profl. jours. Home: 1024 Lindsay Ln Rydal PA 19046 also 89 Spring St Newport RI 02840 Office: Suburban Station Bldg Philadelphia PA 19103

NAGARAJ, HOLAVANAHALLY SESHACHAR, research scientist; b. Markonahally, Karnataka, India, Sept. 14, 1949; s. Holavanahally Krishnachar Seshachar and Holavanahally Sechachar Subhadramma; B.E. (Nat. Merit scholar), Bangalore U., 1970; M.E. (scholar), Indian Inst. Sci., 1972; Ph.D., Ga. Inst. Tech., 1977; m. Vimala Devi Nagaraj. Teaching asst. Ga. Inst. Tech., Atlanta, 1973, research asst., 1973-76, State U. N.Y., Stony Brook, 1972; research analyst Mech. Tech. Inc., Latham, N.Y., 1977—. Mem. ASME, Am. Soc. Lubrication Engrs. Hindu. Contbr. articles on numerical control of machine tools, elastohydrodynamic lubrication to sci. jours. Home: 3 Winding Brook Dr Apt 2G Guilderland NY 12084 Office: 968 Albany Shaker Rd Latham NY 12110

NAGEL, CARL EDWARD, JR., mgmt. cons.; b. St. Paul, Nov. 15, 1915; s. Carl Edward and Helen Ruby (Pringle) N.; B.A., Stanford, 1937; m. Grace Wilkie, July 20, 1940; children—Jan (Mrs. James Arthur Clarkson III), Dawn (Mrs. Richard Barry Fiss). Dir. tech. pub. relations Westinghouse Elec. Corp., 1940-48; v.p. McGraw-Hill Book Co., 1948-61; partner Antell, Wright & Nagel, N.Y.C., 1961—. Mem. Bd. Edn., Mamaroneck, N.Y.; councilman, Mamaroneck. Bd. dirs., Camp Fire Girls, Inc. Served with USNR, 1943-46. Clubs: Union League (N.Y.C.); Larchmont Yacht, Larchmont University. Home: 430 Orienta Ave Mamaroneck NY 10543 Office: 230 Park Ave New York City NY 10017

NAGLE, FREDERICK FLOYD, banker; b. Greenwich, Conn., July 10, 1943; s. Smyser Floyd and Vera (Curtis) N.; B.A., Yale, 1966; postgrad. Cornell U. Law Sch., 1969; M.B.A., Fordham U., 1974; m. Susan Nelson, Dec. 10, 1977. Investment reviewer State Nat. Bank Conn., 1967-68; investment officer Citibank, N.Y.C., 1971-78; 2d v.p. Chase Manhattan Bank, N.A., N.Y.C., 1978—. Active Yale alumni fund; asst. class agt. Taft Sch. Served to capt. Ordnance Corps, U.S. Army, 1968-71. Mem. N.Y. Soc. Security Analysts (sr. security analyst), Fedn. Fin. Analysts. Republican. Roman Catholic. Club: Greenwich Field. Home: 725 Old Post Rd Bedford NY 10506 Office: 1211 Ave of Americas New York City NY 10030

NAGLER, ARNOLD L., pathologist, scientist, educator; b. N.Y.C., Aug. 18, 1935; s. Max and Esther (Finkel) N.; B.S., Coll. City N.Y., 1953; M.D., N.Y. U., 1958, Ph.D., 1960; m. Rosalie Groden, Feb. 18, 1961; children—Stephen Marc, Melissa Sue. Research asso. Mt. Sinai Hosp. N.Y.C., 1960-61; mem. faculty Albert Einstein Coll. Medicine, Bronx, 1961—, asso. prof. pathology, 1975—, asso. prof. surgery, 1975—; cons., prof. chairperson pathology dept., dean pre-clin. medicine N.Y. Coll. Osteopathic Medicine, 1978—. Chmn. Boy Scouts Am., 1971-73. Served with AUS, 1953-55. Grantee NIH, 1961—. Licensed dir. labs., N.Y.C. Mem. N.Y. Acad. Sci., N.Y. Acad. Medicine, AAAS, Am. Trauma Soc. (founder). Republican. Jewish. Editorial bd. Circulatory Shock. Contbr. articles to profl. jours. Home: 72 Hazelwood Dr Jericho NY 11753 Office: 1300 Morris Park Ave Bronx NY 10461 also PO Box 170 Wheatley Rd Old Westbury NY 11568

NAGLER, LEON GREGORY, lawyer, mgmt. cons., bus. exec.; b. Buenos Aires, Argentina, Jan. 29, 1932 (parents Am. citizens); s. Morris and Jennie (Golden) N.; B.S. cum laude, Boston U., 1953, M.B.A., 1954; J.D. cum laude, Cleve. State U., 1961; m. F. Elise Charness, Dec. 20, 1953; children—Jeri Lynn, Sandra Michelle. Supr. employment and tng. Jones & Laughlin Steel Corp., Cleve., 1957-65; exec. dir. indsl. relations Charles Corp., Cleve., 1965-67; dir. personnel ITT Service Industries Corp., Cleve., 1967-72; v.p. personnel Builder Service Corp., Bellaire Bluff, Fla., 1972-73; v.p. adminstrn. Damon Corp., Needham Heights, Mass., 1973-77; pres. Nagler & Co., Newton Centre, Mass., 1977—; admitted to Ohio bar, 1961. Sec., Zoning Bd. Appeal, Mayfield Heights, Ohio, 1963-65; mem. Planning and Zoning Commn., Mayfield Heights, 1965-67; pres. NE Ohio region Am. Jewish Congress, 1972-73, mem. nat. governing council, 1972-73; bd. dirs. New Eng. region Anti-Defamation League, 1977—, Jewish Vocat. Service, 1977—; trustee Temple Beth Avoda, 1978—. Served with AUS, 1955-57. Mem. Ohio, Cleve. bar assns., Am. Soc. for Tng. and Devel., Am. Soc. for Personnel Adminstrn., Boston U. Alumni Assn. (pres. chpt. 1969-73, nat. council 1973—). Democrat. Jewish. Club: Masons. Home: 72 Westgate Rd Newton Centre MA 02159 Office: 72 Westgate Rd Newton Centre MA 02159

NAGORSKI, ZYGMUNT, writer, polit. scientist; b. Warsaw, Poland, Sept. 27, 1912; s. Zygmunt Julian and Maria (Cederbaum) N.; came to U.S., 1948, naturalized, 1953; M.A., U. Cracow (Poland), 1935; postgrad. U. Geneva, 1937-38, Internat. Inst. Trade and Patents, Berne, Switzerland, 1937-38, U. Paris, 1938; m. Marie Bogdaszewski, Nov. 22, 1938; children—Maria, Andrew, Teresa. Reporter, Chattanooga Times, 1948; editor-in-chief Fgn. News Service, Inc., N.Y.C., 1949-56; chief Internat. Br. Office Research, USIA, Washington, 1956-59; fgn. service officer, Cairo, 1959-61, Seoul, 1961-64, Paris, 1964-66; spl. asst. to pres. Fgn. Policy Assn., Inc., N.Y.C., 1966-68; mem. profl. staff Hudson Inst., Inc., 1968-69; dir. Members Meetings Program, Council on Fgn. Relations, N.Y.C., 1969-78; v.p. Lehrman Inst., 1978—; spl. adviser Aspen Inst.; adj. asst. prof. polit. sci. dept. Queens Coll., 1974-75; guest lectr. Wilton Park, Sussex, Eng., Fgn. Service Inst., Center for Study Human Values, Tanglewood, N.C., Expt. in Internat. Living (Vt.), also numerous univs. Pres., Am. Friends of Wilton Park, 1967-70, Mid-Atlantic Club of New York, 1972—; bd. dirs. Scarsdale Adult Sch., 1968-72, Internat. U. Found., Nat. Office for Social Responsibility. Served with Polish Army, 1939-45. Decorated Brit. War medal, officer's cross Order of Merit (W. Ger.); recipient Meritorious Service award USIA, 1965. Mem. Am. Acad. Polit. Sci., Council on Fgn. Relations, Am. Polit. Sci. Assn., Internat. Studies Assn., Polish Inst. Arts and Scis., Am. Fgn. Service Assn. Democrat. Roman Catholic. Clubs: University (N.Y.C.); Dacor House (Washington). Author: Armed Unemployment, 1945; The Psychology of East-West Trade, 1975. Contbr. articles to newspapers and mags. Home: 91 Central Park W New York City NY 10023 Office: 42 E 71st St New York City NY 10021 also 717 Fifth Ave New York City NY 10022

NAGY, BRIAN ROBSON, psychiatrist; b. Cleve., May 31, 1937; s. Franklyn Harold and Cecile Enid (Robson) N.; B.A., DePauw U., 1959; M.D., Cornell U. Med. Coll., N.Y.C., 1963; m. Pattie Leigh Wilson, June 8, 1963; children—Kevin Andrew, Kristopher Sheldon, Seth Hamilton. Intern, Roosevelt Hosp., N.Y.C., 1963-64; resident in psychiatry Strong Meml. Hosp., Rochester, N.Y., 1964-67; practice medicine specializing in psychiatry, Elmira, N.Y., 1969—; mem. staff St. Joseph's Hosp.; mem. cons. staff Arnot Ogden Hosp.; med. dir. So. Tier Alcoholism Rehab. Service, Elmira; mem. med. advisory com. Chemung County (N.Y.) Health Center, Elmira; clin. asst. prof. psychiatry U. Rochester, 1976—; cons. on alcoholism U.S. Air Force; cons. on profl. edn. Elmira Psychiat. Center; cons. in field. Served to capt. USAF, 1967-69. Diplomate Am. Bd. Psychiatry and Neurology. Mem. Am. Psychiat. Assn., AMA, Med. Soc. State N.Y., Am. Med. Soc. on Alcoholism, Chemung County Med. Soc., Chemung County Council on Alcoholism. Home: 4289 Fairway Ln Horseheads NY 14845 Office: Elmira Med Arts Center Elmira NY 14901

NAGY, FRANK ANDREW, chemist; b. Perth Amboy, N.J., Nov. 20, 1942; s. Frank and Mary (Horvath) N.; B.S. in Chemistry, Rutgers U., 1973, M.S. in Packaging, 1978; m. Margaret Herlitschek, Apr. 4, 1964; children—Regina, Steven. With Central Research and Devel. Labs., Mobil Chem. Co., Edison, N.J., 1963—, coatings chemist, 1973-76, research chemist, 1976-78, sr. research chemist, 1978—. Mem. Soc. Mfg. Engrs., Assn. Finishing Processes, Packaging Inst. Democrat. Roman Catholic. Home: 63 Garden St Edison NJ 08817

NAIDER, FRED ROBERT, educator; b. Manhattan, N.Y., Jan. 31, 1945; s. Leonard and Molly (Schwebel) N.; B.Ch.E. with distinction, Cornell U., 1965, M.Ch.E (Standard Oil of Calif. fellow 1965-66), 1966; Ph.D., Bklyn. Poly. Inst., 1970; m. Anita Joy Serle, Dec. 23, 1967; children—Avraham Zvi, Shoshana Esther, Rachel Yaffa. Vis. scientist Weizmann Inst. Sci., Rehovot, Israel, 1971-73; asst. prof. Richmond Coll., 1973-75; asso. prof. chemistry Coll. S.I., City U. N.Y., 1975—. NSF Research grantee, 1973-76, NIH Research grantee, 1975-78, 78-81, Am. Cancer Soc. Research grantee, 1975-77; recipient Research Career Devel. award HEW, 1975—. Mem. Am. Chem. Soc., Am. Soc. Microbiology, AAAS. Democrat. Jewish. Contbr. articles to sci. jours. Home: 419 Buchanan Ave Staten Island NY 10314 Office: 50 Bay St Staten Island NY 10301

NAIDORF, IRVING JOSEPH, educator, dentist; b. Bklyn., Oct. 19, 1915; s. Zelig and Sarah (Breslau) N.; B.A., N.Y. U., 1937; D.D.S., Columbia U., 1941; m. Blanche Goodman, June 18, 1942; children—Michael William, Kenneth Fredric. Pvt. practice dentistry, N.Y.C., 1946—; instr. dentistry Columbia, 1952-58, asst. clin. prof., 1959-67, asso. clin. prof. dentistry, 1967-71, clin. prof. dentistry, 1971-75, prof. dentistry, 1975—, head microbiology sect. Sch. Dental Hygiene, 1958-71, dir. postgrad. endodontics, 1969—, dir. postdoctoral edn., 1972—, asst. dean for postdoctoral edn., 1974—, acting dir. oral biology, 1975-78; cons. in endodontia VA, Montrose and Kingsbridge hosps., 1960—; faculty continuing edn. Sch. Dental Medicine, U. Pa., 1972-73, vis. prof., 1974—; vis. lectr. Boston U. Sch. Grad. Dentistry, 1978—; asso. attending dental surgeon Columbia Presbyn. Hosp., 1972-76, attending, 1976—. Served from lt. to maj. AUS, 1942-46. Recipient Meritorious Service award Columbia U. Assn. Dental Alumni, 1967. Diplomate Am. Bd. Endodontics (dir. 1973—, sec. 1976-78, pres. 1978—). Fellow Am. Assn. Endodontists (chmn. membership com. 1967-68, mem. exec. com. 1970-72, mem. editorial bd. 1969-75, chmn. budget and finance com. 1971-72, long range planning 1972), Royal Soc. Health, Royal Soc. Medicine, Am. Coll. Dentists (chmn. N.Y. sect. 1978-79), L.I. Acad. Odontology, N.Y. Acad. Dentistry, Acad. Dentistry Internat.; mem. ADA (cons. to councils on dental edn. and hosp. dental service, mem. adv. commn. on accreditation), Soc. Am. Bacteriologists, AAAS, N.Y. Acad. Sci., Tri State Soc. Endodontics (chmn. 1967-68), Internat. Assn. Dental Research, Assn. Dental Alumni Columbia (treas. 1971-72), Sigma Xi, Omicron Kappa Upsilon (pres. chpt. 1975-76). Contbg. author: Pharmacotherapeutics of Oral Disease, The Biology of the Human Dental Pulp; The Dental Clinics of North America and Current Therapy in Dentistry and Clinical Dentistry; former asso. editor Jour. Oral Therapeutics and Pharmacology; author: Oral Microbiology Laboratory Manual, Endodontic Microbiology Laboratory Manual; contbr. articles to profl. jours. Research in bacteriology and immunology of root canal. Home: 100 Haven Ave New York City NY 10032 Office: 30 Central Park S New York City NY 10019

NAIDU, JANAKIRAM RAMASWAMY, ecologist; b. Bangalore, India, Nov. 15, 1931; s. Govind Ramaswamy and Ahalyabai Naidu; came to U.S., 1969, naturalized, 1976; B.S., Bombay U., 1955; M.S., U. Wash., 1963; Ph.D., Oreg. State U., 1974; m. Veena Cupala, May 1, 1964. Grad. asst. Oreg. State U., Corvallis, 1969-74; project ecologist Dames & Moore, Los Angeles, 1974-75; ecologist Brookhaven Nat. Lab., Upton, N.Y., 1975—; adj. prof. oceanography State U. N.Y., Stony Brook, 1976—. Served with inf. Indian Army, 1951-52. Mem. Marine Biol. Assn. of U.K., Health Physics Soc. Home: 4 Thornwood Circle Setauket NY 11733 Office: Brookhaven National Lab Upton NY 11973

NAIMAN, JAMES, psychiatrist, educator; b. Berlin, Ger., Sept. 23, 1926; s. Emmanuel and Sophie (Strasbourg) N.; B.A., McGill U., Montreal, Que., Can., 1945, M.D., 1949; m. Janina Schwarz, Oct. 25, 1970; children—Linda, David, Robin. Intern, Bellevue Hosp. N.Y.C., 1949; resident in psychiatry Queen Mary Vets. Hosp., Montreal, 1950, Neurol. Inst., Montreal, 1951, Royal Victoria Hosp., Montreal, Montreal Gen. Hosp., 1954; practice medicine, specializing in psychiatry, Montreal, 1955—; demonstrator in psychiatry McGill U., 1956-61, lectr., 1961-65, asst. prof., 1965-69, asso. prof. psychiatry, 1969—; dir. psychiatry Queen Elizabeth Hosp., Montreal, 1972-78; pres. bd. examiners psychiatry, Que. Fellow Royal Coll. Physicians Can., Am. Psychiat. Assn.; mem. Internat. Psychoanalytical Assn., N.Y. Acad. Sci., Canadian Psychiat. Assn., Canadian Med. Assn., Assn. Psychophysiol. Study of Sleep. Jewish. Contbr. articles to psychiat. and psychoanalytic jours. Home: Apt 707 3495 Mountain St Montreal PQ Canada Office: Apt 3 4330 Sherbrooke W Montreal PQ Canada

NAIMARK, GEORGE MODELL, advt. agy. and publishing exec.; b. N.Y.C., Feb. 5, 1925; s. Myron S. and Mary (Modell) N.; B.S., Bucknell U., 1947, M.S., 1948; Ph.D., U. Del., 1951; m. Helen Anne Wythes, June 24, 1946; children—Ann, Richard, Jane. Research biochemist Brush Devel. Co., Cleve., 1951; dir. quality control Strong, Cobb & Co., Inc., Cleve., 1951-54; dir. sci. services White Labs., Inc., Kenilworth, N.J., 1954-60; v.p. Burdick Assos., Inc., N.Y.C., 1960-66; pres. Naimark & Barba, Inc., N.Y.C., 1966—, Rajah Press, Summit, N.J., 1963—; dir. Chemotronics Internat. Inc., Ann Arbor, Mich.; mem. adv. bd. Center Profl. Advancement, Somerville, N.J. Served with USNR, 1944-46. Fellow A.A.A.S., Am. Inst. Chemists; mem. Am. Chem. Soc., N.Y. Acad. Scis., Am. Mktg. Assn., Edinburgh Bibliog. Soc. Author: A Patent Manual for Scientists and Engineers, 1961; Communications on Communication, 1971, 2d edit., 1978; also articles in profl. jours. Home: 87 Canoe Brook Pkwy Summit NJ 07901 Office: 130 E 40th St New York City NY 10016

NAIMI, SHAPUR, cardiologist; b. Tehran, Iran, Mar. 28, 1928; s. Mohsen and Mahbuba (Naim) N.; came to U.S., 1959, naturalized, 1968; M.B., Ch.B., Birmingham (Eng.) U., 1953; m. Amy Cabot Simonds, May 11, 1963; children—Timothy Simonds, Susan Lyman, Cameron Lowell. House physician Royal Postgrad Med. Sch. London, 1955; sr. house officer Inst. Diseases of the Chest, London, 1956; fellow in grad. tng. New Eng. Med. Center and Mass. Inst. Tech., 1961-64; cardiologist Tufts New Eng. Med. Center, Boston, 1966—, dir. intensive cardiac care unit, 1973—, asso. prof. Med. Sch., 1970—. Recipient Distinguished Instr. award, 1972, Teaching citation, 1976 (both Tufts Med. Sch.); diplomate Royal Coll. Physicians London, Royal Coll. Physicians Edinburgh, Am. Bd. Internal Medicine (subsplty. bd. cardiovascular disease). Fellow Royal Coll. Physicians (Edinburgh), A.C.P., Am. Coll. Cardiology; mem. Am. Soc. Exptl. Biology and Medicine, Am. Heart Assn., Mass. Med. Soc. Clubs: Country Brookline; Cohasset Yacht. Contbr. to profl. jours. Home: 265 Woodland Rd Chestnut Hill MA 02167 Office: 171 Harrison Ave Boston MA 02111

NAISMITH, GRACE AKIN, writer; b. Ft. Collins, Colo., Nov. 20, 1904; d. A.I. and Nellie (Taylor) Akin; student William Woods Coll., 1920-22, D.Sc., 1969; student U. Colo., 1922; m. John Naismith, 1922; children—James A., Stuart D.; m. 2d, Edward Pierce, 1943; m. 3d, John Devlin, Nov. 23, 1960. Reporter, Rocky Mountain News, 1929-30; info. and edn. specialist U.S. Dept. Agr. 1936; editor, writer med. subjects Reader's Digest, N.Y.C., from 1938, cons. editor, to 1976. Recipient Internat. Health Found. award for health journalism, 1973. Mem. Nat. Assn. Sci. Writers, Am. Soc. Journalists and Authors, Women in Communications, Overseas Press Club (sec.), Woman Pays Club, Alpha Phi. Author: Private and Personal, 1966; (with John C. Devlin) The World of Roger Tory Peterson, 1977. Contbr. articles to popular mags. Home: Westview Ln South Norwalk CT 06854 Office: 51 East 42d St New York City NY 10017

NAKANO, MICHIO, trading co. exec.; b. Tokyo, Japan, Oct. 6, 1931; s. Toshio and Aiko (Ito) N.; came to U.S., 1952, naturalized, 1956; B.S., Columbia U., 1958; m. Sachiko Tanaka, Sept. 19, 1955. With Mitsubishi Internat. Corp., N.Y.C., 1958—, projects dir., 1972—; chief exec. officer Canyon W. Corp., Palm Springs, Calif., 1972-75; chief exec., operator Fleming Joffe Jentra, Moonachie, N.J., 1975-77; pres. Canyon Club, Armonk, N.Y., 1973—; chmn. Chelsea Co. Ltd. Recipient citation, Japanese Ceramic Tile Exporters Assn., 1963. Clubs: Scarsdale Golf (Westchester); Canyon Country (Palm Springs); Nippon (N.Y.C.). Home: 2500B Johnson Ave Riverdale NY 10463

NALL, THOMAS MARTIN, allergist; b. Fulton, Ky., Apr. 12, 1933; s. Martin Carl and Emily Helen (McDonald) N.; B.A., Wesleyan U., Middletown, Conn., 1955; M.D., Cornell U., 1959. Intern, Barnes Hosp., St. Louis, 1959-60; resident in medicine and allergy Roosevelt Hosp., N.Y.C., 1963-66; practice medicine specializing in allergy and immunology, N.Y.C., 1968—; asso. in medicine Columbia Coll. Physicians and Surgeons. Served to lt. comdr., M.C., USNR, 1966-68. Diplomate Am. Bd. Allergy and Immunology. Fellow Am. Acad. Allergy, Am. Coll. Allergists; mem. Phi Beta Kappa, Sigma Xi, Sigma Chi. Home: 17 Mt Green Rd Croton-on-Hudson NY 10520 Office: 121 E 60th St New York City NY 10022

NAMBA, TATSUJI, physician, researcher; b. Changchun, China, Jan. 29, 1927; s. Yosuke and Michino (Hinata) N.; M.D., Okayama U. (Japan), 1950, Ph.D., 1955. Came to U.S., 1959, naturalized, 1968. Asst., lectr. medicine Okayama U. Med. Sch. and Hosp., 1955-62; research asso. Maimonides Med. Center, Bklyn., 1962-66, dir. neuromuscular labs., 1966-70, dir. neuromuscular disease div., head electromyography clinic, 1966—; instr., asst. prof., asso. prof. medicine State U. N.Y., Bklyn., 1959-76, prof., 1976—; mem. med. adv. bd. Myasthenia Gravis Found., 1968—. Recipient commendation for research and clin. activities on insecticide poisoning Minister Health and Welfare, Japanese Govt., 1958. Fellow A.C.P.; mem. A.M.A., Am. Acad. Neurology, Am. Soc. Pharmacology and Exptl. Therapeutics, Am. Soc. Clin. Pharmacology and Therapeutics, N.Y. State Med. Soc. Office: 4802 10th Ave Brooklyn NY 11219

NAMIAS, JEAN E., statistician; b. Warsaw, Poland; s. William and Minna (Sklar) N.; B.S. in Edn. and Econs., Coll. City N.Y., 1946; M.A. in Econs. and Statistics, N.Y. U., 1948, Ph.D. in Econs., Statistics, Mktg. and Finance (Univ. scholar), 1958; postgrad. Wharton Sch. U. Pa., 1961-62. Research economist Chilean Devel. Corp., N.Y.C., 1945-48; statistician, comptroller Com. on Service to Fgn. Born, N.Y.C., 1948-55; statis. analyst Engring-News Record, N.Y.C., 1955-56; econ. analyst Nat. Indsl. Conf. Bd., N.Y.C., 1956-57; research statistician, economist Nat. Bur. Econ. Research, N.Y.C., 1960-61; statistician Group Health Ins., N.Y.C., 1961-62; research statistician N.Y. Regional Statis. Center, N.Y.C., 1965-66; lectr. Bklyn. Coll., 1956-57; instr. statistics Fairleigh Dickinson U., 1957-59; asst. prof. econs. Adelphi U., 1957-58; prof. statistics St. John's U., 1958-76; prof. statistics Montclair State Coll., 1976—; cons. in field; asso. Columbia U. Seminar, 1965—. Mem. Am. Statis. Assn. (exec. council 1975-77, v.p. N.Y. chpt. 1977—, editor N.Y. Statistician 1973—), Am., Met. (chmn. com. collegiate relations 1973-74) econ. assns., Am. Mktg. Assn., Am. Soc. Quality Control (initiator, chmn. 1st and 2d Ann. Conf. on Quality Control and Statistics in Bus., Finance, Industry 1976, 77, Met. sect. award for faithful service, contbn., quality achievement 1977), Alpha Kappa Psi, Delta Pi Sigma. Author: (with John I. Griffin) Fact Book: The New York Metropolitan Region, 1965; Handbook of Selected Sample Surveys in the Federal Government with Annotated Bibliography, 1969; editor: Applications of Quantitative Methods of Business Decisions, 1974; contbr. articles to profl. publs. Home: 700 Columbus Ave Apt 20F New York City NY 10025 Office: Montclair State Coll Upper Montclair NJ 07043

NAMROW, ARNOLD, psychiatrist; b. N.Y.C., Aug. 1, 1924; S. Samuel and Mary (Becker) N.; A.B., Washington U., 1943, M.D., 1947; m. Lillian Coe, Dec. 3, 1950; children—James, Andrew, Laurel, David. Intern, St. Elizabeth's Hosp., Washington, 1947-48; resident in psychiatry Perry Point (Md.) VA Hosp., 1948-50; staff psychiatrist Fairfax County, VA., 1953-54, VA Mental Hygiene Clinic, Washington, 1953-54; practice medicine specializing in psychiatry and psychoanalysis, Washington, 1953—; clin. asso. prof. psychiatry Georgetown U. Med. Sch., Washington, 1954—; faculty Washington Psychoanalytic Inst., 1970—; cons. Jewish Social Service Agy., 1970-76. Served with USN, 1951-53. Recipient Vicennial Medal, Georgetown U., 1974. Fellow Am. Psychiatric Assn.: mem. Washington Psychiatric Soc., Am. Psychoanalytic Soc., Am. Acad. Psychoanalysis. Jewish. Contbg. author: The Dream in Clinical Practice, 1978. Home: 6406 E Halbert Rd Bethesda MD 20034 Office: 4501 Connecticut Ave NW Washington DC 20008

NANAY, JULIA, oil co. exec.; b. Budapest, Hungary, Mar. 15, 1951; d. Andrew and Marta (Medvegy) N.; came to U.S., 1957, naturalized, 1965; B.A. magna cum laude, U. Calif., Los Angeles, 1973; M.A., Fletcher Sch. Law and Diplomacy, Tufts U., 1975. With Northeast Petroleum Industries, 1976—, pub. policy analyst, Washington, 1978—. Mem. Phi Beta Kappa. Lutheran. Author: Transylvania: The Hungarian Minority in Rumania, 1977. Home: 1233 29th St NW Washington DC 20007 Office: 1700 Pennsylvania Ave Suite 300 Washington DC 20006

NANCE, ROY ALFRED, mech. engr.; b. Allentown, Pa., Apr. 9, 1931; s. James Emmett and Hilda Lorene (Baker) N.; B.M.E., Ga. Inst. Tech., 1954; m. Billye Jane Fox, June 12, 1954; children—Karen Rene, Mark Todd. Research and devel. engr. Oak Ridge Nat. Lab., 1956-60; mgr. nondestructive testing engring. Budd Co., Phila., 1960-68; mgr. nondestructive testing systems Automation Industries, Danbury, Conn., 1968-69; mgr. inspection devel. Westinghouse Bettis Atomic Power Lab., Pitts., 1969—; guest lectr. Temple U., Phila., 1963-68. Served with AUS, 1954-56. Registered profl. engr., Calif. Fellow Am. Soc. Nondestructive Testing. Republican. Mem. Ch. of Christ. Author, patentee in field. Home: 206 Trinity Dr McMurray PA 15317 Office: Box 79 West Mifflin PA 15122

NANTEL, ALBERT JOHN, physician; b. Montreal, Que., Can., Feb. 13, 1939; s. Gaston and Laurette (Bellavance) N.; B.A., U. Montreal, 1959, M.D. magna cum laude, 1964, M.Sc. in Pharmacology, 1966; m. Anne-Marie Thibodeau, Dec. 26, 1963; children—Andre, Francois (twins), Jean-Pierre. Jr. intern U. Montreal Hosps., 1963-64, research fellow pharmacology, 1964-65, instr. pharmacy, 1964-66; asst. resident cardiology Notre-Dame Hosp., Montreal, 1965-66; research fellow clin. pharmacology Emory U., Atlanta, 1966-67; research fellow pharmacology and therapeutics McGill U., Montreal, 1967-68; asst. prof. pharmacology and medicine U. Sherbrooke (Que.), 1968-72; dir. regional toxicology center, chief provincial poison control program, chief provincial program in indsl. toxicology U. Laval, Sainte-Foy, Que., Can., 1972—; vis. prof. U. Que., 1974. Mem. Nat. Com. Bioavailability, Health and Welfare. Med. Research Council of Can. fellow, 1964-65; Can. Found. Advancement Therapeutics fellow, 1965-67. Certified Am. Acad. Clin. Toxicology. Mem. Canadian, Que. (pres.) acads. sports medicine, Can. Assn. Sports Scis. Mem. editorial adv. bd. Rx Bull., 1970-71. Contbr. articles to profl. jours. Home: 2734 De lAnse St Sainte Foy PQ G1W 2G5 Canada Office: 2705 Laurier Blvd Sainte Foy PQ G1V 4G2 Canada

NAPIER, ROBERT JON, architect; b. Bklyn., Dec. 2, 1934; s. John and Anna Constance (Turuta) N.; B.Arch., Pratt Inst., 1957, M.Arch., 1959; m. Susan Anne Colquhoun, Apr. 5, 1969; children—Jason, Kristina Anne, Julia Anne. Pvt. practice architecture, University Park, Pa., 1963-66; asso. William N. Breger Assos., architects, N.Y.C., 1966-69; prin. Unger/Napier Assos., N.Y.C., 1970-73; v.p. project devel., chief architect Kraus Enterprises, Inc., N.Y.C., 1973—. Asst. prof. architecture Pa. State U., 1959-66, vis. lectr. dept. pub. information, 1960-65; vis. critic dept. architecture Pratt Inst., 1967-69; adj. asst. prof. City U. N.Y., 1972-73; cons. several radio, tv stas. Mem. AIA, AAUP, N.Y. State Soc. Architects. Home: Box 63 RD1 Stockton NJ 08559 Office: Kraus Enterprises Inc 445 Park Ave New York City NY 10022

NAPLES, JOHN DANIEL, obstetrician and gynecologyst; b. Buffalo, Aug. 23, 1934; s. John Dominic and Anne Gabrielle (Sorgi) N.; A.B., Canisius Coll., 1955; M.D., Georgetown U., 1959; m. Jeanne Migliore, June 28, 1958; children—Maria, Christopher, Jill. Intern, Buffalo Gen. Hosp., 1959-60; resident in obstetrics and gynecology State U. N.Y., Buffalo, 1960-64; practice medicine specializing in gynecology, infertility and obstetrics, Buffalo, 1964-66, 68—; mem. staff Buffalo Gen., Sisters of Charity, St. Francis, Children's, Meyer Meml. hosps.; mem. clin. faculty State U. N.Y. Med. Sch. at Buffalo. Mem. bd. regents Canisius Coll. Served with M.C. USN, 1966-68. Recipient Pediatric medal Georgetown U., 1959, Physician Recognition award AMA, 1970; diplomate Am. Bd. Obstetrics and Gynecology. Mem. Am., N.Y. State, Erie County (N.Y.) med. socs., Am. Coll. Obstetricians, Gynecologists, A.C.S., Am. Cancer Soc., Western N.Y. Obstetrical-Gynecol. Soc., Am. Soc. Gynecol. Laparoscopists. Roman Catholic. Contbr. articles to med. publs. Home: 58 Dan Troy Dr Buffalo NY 14221 Office: 2900 Main St Buffalo NY 14214

NAPOLITANO, ERNEST GEORGE, chiropractor, coll. pres.; b. N.Y.C., Feb. 20, 1914; s. Cesare and Catherine (Faggella) N.; Dr. Chiropractic, Palmer Sch. Chiropractic, 1942; Philosopher of Chiropractic (hon.), Atlantic State Chiropractic Inst., 1955, D.Sc. (hon.), 1956, Ph.D. (hon.), 1958; LL.B., Blackstone Coll. Law, 1960; LL.D. (hon.), Brantridge Coll., 1970, Universidad Internacional Montezuma, 1971; D.Sc., N.Y. Inst. Tech., 1978; m. Helen Jean Iddings, June 11, 1945; 1 dau., Catherine Emily. Practice chiropractic medicine, N.Y.C., 1943—; pres. N.Y. Chiropractic Coll. (formerly Columbia Inst. Chiropractic), Old Brookville, N.Y., 1959—; cons., adviser Aetna Life and Casualty Ins. Co., N.Y.C., 1970—, Kentuckiana Children's Center for Edn., Health and Research, Louisville, 1968—, Kyoto Pain Control Inst., Japan, 1969—; faculty dept. anatomy Atlantic States Chiropractic Inst., 1952-59; lectr. in neuroanatomy, jurisprudence and social scis. to various civic and profl. groups, 1946—. Seved with M.C., U.S. Army, 1943-46. Decorated Bronze Star, Purple Heart. Recipient award of honor Queens Secondary Sch., 1964, Distinguished Service award Atlantic States Chiropractic Inst., 1956, Pontifical Lateran Cross, 1960, Distinguished Service Cross, Gov. of N.Y. State, 1970; named to Nat. Chiropractic Hall of Honor, also fellow. Fellow Internat. Chiropractors Assn. (mem. bd. control 1950-59), Internat. Coll. of Chiropractors, Am. Coll. Chiropractors, Am. Chiropractic Soc., Internat. Acad. Pain Control, Nat. Soc. Audiometry, London Soc. Physiologists; mem. Am. (citation 1968; mem. council diagnosis and internal disorders), N.H., Mass., P.R. chiropractic assns., Nat. Acad. Clinicians, Chiropractic Press Guild (pres. 1969-74), Columbia Assn. Nassau County (chmn. adv. bd. 1968), Internat. Pain Control Inst., Am. Soc. Audiometrists, Am. Council Chiropractic Roentgenologists, Acad. Chiropractic (award of merit 1962), N.Y. Acad. Scis., VFW, Mil. Order of Purple Heart, Am. Legion, Navy League U.S., Am. Assn. Studies UN, Am. Judicature Soc., Acad. Polit. Sci., Queensborough C. of C. (mem. pub. health com. 1970-73), Delta Sigma Chi, Beta Omega Chi, Alpha Chi Sigma, Alpha Omega Chi. Roman Catholic. Clubs: K.C., Cath. Youth Orgn. Men's, Nat. Travel. Contbr. numerous articles on chiropractic, jurisprudence and the family community to various profl. publs. Address: 86-18 Jamaica Ave Jamaica NY 11421

NAPOLITANO, PAT, union ofcl.; b. N.Y.C., Feb. 1, 1916; s. Giuseppe and Anna (Liquori) N.; adult edn. courses Fordham U., 1944-47; m. Beatrice G. Gagliardo, Apr. 25, 1959. With tech. facilities dept. Western Union, 1943—; former mem. exec. bd. Comml. Telegraphers Union, A.F.L.; sec.-treas. local 1177 Communications Workers Am. AFL-CIO, 1966-69, del. L.I. Fedn. Labor, AFL-CIO, 1966-76; free-lance writer. Mem. N.Y. Police Coordinating Councils, 1940-55, N.Y. Civilian Def., 1943-55; sch. visitor N.Y. Adult Edn. Council, Inc., 1945-55; active Boy Scouts Am., 1938-55. Mem. Nassau County (N.Y.) Democratic Com.; pres. New Hyde Park Democratic Club, 1969-70. Trustee Ch. Most Precious Blood, 1942-59. Mem. Assn. Catholic Trade Unionists, Sons of Italy (charter lodge), Ams. of Italian Descent, Father Drumgoole Alumni Assn. (pres. 1965-73, chmn. bd. officers 1974—), Nat. Council Catholic Men, Holy Name Soc., Third Order St. Francis. Democrat. Roman Catholic (lector, usher, extraordinary minister of eucharist). K.C. Home: 1062 N 7th St New Hyde Park NY 11040 Office: 2 Aerial Way Syosset NY 11791

NAPOR, CARL ANTHONY, sales and engring. dir.; b. Jersey City, Feb. 3, 1921; s. Anthony and Josephine (Ojcienaszewski) N.; B.S., Newark Coll. Engring., 1942; postgrad. physics N.Y. U., 1951-53; m. Catherine Marion Pogoda, June 2, 1945; children—Carl John, Janet Lois, Cathy Lynn, Robert James. Asst. chief engr. Linde Air Products div. Union Carbide & Carbon, Tonawanda, N.Y., 1942-46, devel. engr., Newark, 1946-51; sect. head Sylvania Elec. Products, Hicksville, N.Y., 1951-53; chief engr. Ronson Corp., Newark, 1953-56; works mgr. Aeroflex Labs., N.Y.C., 1956-62; cons. engr. Automatic Mfg., Glen Ridge, N.J., 1962-67; v.p. Arkwin Industries, Westbury, N.Y., 1966-67; dir. sales and engring. Kahle Engring. Co., Union City, N.J., 1967—; instr. physics Newark Coll. Engring., 1942-43. Mem. I.E.E.E. (sr. mem., chmn. adminstrn. com., chmn. tech. ops. dept., mem. awards and recognition com.), Indsl. Application Soc., past chmn. glass industry com.). Contbr. articles to profl. jours. Patentee in field. Home: 19 Victor Ave Glen Ridge NJ 07028 Office: 3322 Hudson Ave Union City NJ 07087

NARAYANAN, MADAYATH, physicist; b. Valoor, Kerala, India, Dec. 6, 1937; s. Meleth Kunju and Ekkave Amma M.; B.Sc., Kerala U., India, 1959; M.Sc., Bombay U., India, 1964; M.Tech., Brunel U., Eng., 1970; m. Prameela Menon, Sept. 8, 1969; children—Satish Menon, Nisha. Exptl. officer Telecomm-Research dept., London, 1967-72; supr. failure analysis lab. Gen. Instruments Microelectronics, Hicksville, N.Y., 1972-74; semicondr. device physicist Motorola Applications and Research Lab., Mesa, Ariz., 1974-75; mgr. materials and device analysis, cons. semiconductor device Digital Equipment Corp., Maynard, Mass., 1975—. Mem. IEEE. Cons., adv. editor Jour. Solid State Tech., 1977—. Home: 12 Banbury Dr Westford MA 01886 Office: 146 Main St Maynard MA 01754

NARCISI, ROCCO SANDY, research physicist; b. Bristol, Pa., Apr. 4, 1931; s. Domenico and Maria (Antonelli) N.; B.S. with honors, Pa. State U., 1953; A.M., Harvard, 1955, Ph.D., 1959; m. Mary Elizabeth Howard, June 15, 1957; 1 dau., Elizabeth Mary. Research asso. Harvard, Cambridge, Mass., 1953-57, teaching fellow, 1957-58; project scientist Air Force Cambridge Research Labs., Hanscom Field, Mass., 1958-60, Wentworth Inst., Boston, 1960-63, br. chief, supervisory research physicist, Hanscom AFB, 1963—; advisor Def. Nuclear Agency, 1965—; mem. Atmospheric Effects Com. for Space Shuttle; cons. Dept. Transp. on Climatic Impact Assessment Program; NASA cons. for selection of experiments on Pioneer Venus; chmn. Rocket Site Selection Com. for Upper Atmosphere Obs. Recipient USAF Exceptional Civilian Service Award, 1972, Guenter Loeser Meml. Award, 1970, Marcus D. O'Day Award, 1966. Mem. Am. Geophys. Union, AAAS, N.Y. Acad. Scis., Phi Beta Kappa, Sigma Xi, Phi Kappa Phi, Sigma Pi Sigma. Pioneer ionospheric expts., measurements; contbr. numerous articles to profl. jours. Home: 20 Putnam Rd Bedford MA 01730 Office: USAF Geophysics Labs Hanscom AFB MA 01731

NARDI, THOMAS JAMES, psychologist; b. N.Y.C., Feb. 27, 1949; s. Gaetano Thomas and Enes Dorothy; B.A. in Psychology, Manhattan Coll., 1970; M.S. in Edn., St. John's U., 1972; profl. diploma in Sch. Psychology, 1972, Ph.D. in Child Psychology, 1977; m. Lynette Guardino, Aug. 21, 1971; 1 son, Thomas Paul. Spl. edn. tchr. Bronx Children's Psychiat. Center, N.Y., 1970-73, staff psychologist, 1973—; pvt. practice psychotherapy, Saddle River, N.J. 1977—; lectr. psychology Mercy Coll., 1974—. Certified permanent tchr., sch. psychologist, rational emotive psychotherapist, N.Y. State Mem. Am. Psychol. Assn., Nat. Assn. Sch. Psychologists, Psi Chi. Contbr. presentations at profl. meetings, articles to profl. jours. Office: 188 E Saddle River Rd Saddle River NJ 07458

NARDIN, MARIO, sculptor; b. Venice, Italy, Mar. 17, 1940; s. Giacomo and Ines (Fuins) N.; student Academia Belle Arte, Venice. Came to U.S., 1962, naturalized, 1973. Asst. to Fiore de Henriquez, artist, Eng. and U.S., 1960-64; asst. to Jacques Lipchitz, artist U.S., 1964-72; asst. mgr. Avnet-Shaw Art Foundry, Plainview, L.I., N.Y., 1964-73, Joel Meisner Co. Art Foundry, Plainview, L.I., N.Y., 1973-76; one-man shows at Hudson River Mus., 1964, 72, Atelier Gallery, N.Y., 1968, Fordham U., 1969, Lesnick Gallery, 1970, State U. N.Y. Coll. Plattsburgh, 1971, Sindin Gallery, 1977, Lincoln Center, 1978, Fine Art Gallery at Gallimaufry, 1978; represented in permanent collections Hudson River Mus., Fordham U., pvt. collections U.S. and abroad. Recipient award New Rochelle Art Assn., 1967, Greenburgh Arts and Culture Com., 1971, 72, Mamaroneck Artists Guild, 1973. Home and studio: 184 Warburton Ave Hastings-on-Hudson NY 10706

NARDONE, DON D., fin. co. exec.; b. N.Y.C., Feb. 10, 1924; s. Sebastian and Mary (Genero) N.; B.S. in Econs. and Fin., City Coll. N.Y., 1948; m. Maryalice Clark, Feb. 5, 1955; children—Karin, Michael, Nora. Account exec. Charles Plohn & Co., N.Y.C., 1962-70; v.p. Thomson McKinnon Securities, Inc., N.Y.C., 1970—; lectr. on fin. products, 1963—. Served to 1st lt. inf. U.S. Army, 1943-46. Club: Shelton Rock Tennis (Manhasset, N.Y.). Contbr. articles to profl. jours. Home: 34 Shrub Hollow Rd Roslyn NY 11576 Office: One New York Plaza New York City NY 10004

NARDONE, VINCENT JOSEPH, artist, educator; b. South Orange, N.J., Oct. 19, 1937; s. Joseph V. and Michelina (Magliaro) M.; B.A., Contclair State Coll., 1961; M.F.A., U. So. Calif., 1966; diploma Paris Am. Acad. Fine Arts, France, 1978. Instr. gifted children's program U. So. Calif., 1965-66; painting instr. Adult Sch., Maplewood, N.J., 1966-70; adj. faculty Seton Hall U., 1968-73; illustrator/art cons. N.J. Music and Arts mag., 1969-73; previewer Film News mag., N.Y.C., 1972—; tchr., art specialist Tuscan Sch., South Orange/Maplewood sch. dist., 1961—. Mem. Essex County Cultural and Heritage Commn., 1971-73; bd. dirs. Art Guild South Orange and Maplewood, 1961-79. Served with Armed Forces, 1961-62. Recipient numerous art awards include Prix de Paris Raymond Duncan medal, 1977, 78, Queen Fabiola Prix Rubens medal, 1978. Mem. Les Surindependants Soc. Paris., Societe des Artistes Francais, Art Guild South Orange and Maplewood, Art Educators N.J., Irvington Art Assos., N.J. Edn. Assn. Roman Catholic. Club: Village Players. Address: 75 Essex Ave Maplewood NJ 07040

NARVELL, DAVID BROWN, JR., sales rep.; b. Wilmington, Del., June 27, 1939; s. David Brown and Alice Faye (Sharp) N.; student N.Mex. State U., 1959-60, Computer Programming Inst. Del., 1969; m. Jane Elizabeth Kane, Sept. 21, 1963; children—Todd, Kimberly, Gregg, Gary. Salesman, Speakman Co., Wilmington, 1962-63; estimator, salesman Wilco Plumbing & Heating Supplies, Wilmington, 1963-73; sales rep. Climate Control div. Singer Corp., Wilmington, also Phila. and So. N.J., 1973—. Served with USAF, 1958-62. Methodist. Clubs: Masons, Shriners. Home and Office: 6 Clyde Circle New Castle DE 19720

NARWICZ, CHARLES ANTHONY, marine transp. cons.; b. Bklyn., Sept. 12, 1927; s. Louis and Antoinette (Weskiewicz) N.; B.S., U.S. Mcht. Marine Acad., 1949; m. Loretta Krasno, June 16, 1949; children—Susan, Charles, John, Laura, Christina. Engr./officer refrigerated ship United Fruit Co., 1949-50; world mgr. marine system service Gen. Electric Co., 1952-69; engring. asst. to pres. Stanwick Co., Washington, 1969-71; mgr. container engring. U.S. Lines, Inc., N.Y.C., 1971-74; pres. Arthur Tickle Engring. Works, Inc., Bklyn., 1974-76; pvt. marine systems cons. Charles A. Narwicz & Co., N.Y.C., 1976—. Trustee Pop Warner Football League. Served with USN, 1950-52; now comdr. Res. Mem. Navy League U.S., Soc. Naval Architects and Marine Engrs. (advanced planning com. research and devel. energy conservation, reliability maintainability ship systems), Am. Soc. Naval Engrs., Res. Officers Assn., Am. Bur. Shipping, Naval Res. Assn., Naval Order U.S., Am. Legion, Kosciuszko Found. Republican. Roman Catholic. Clubs: Whitehall, Ft. Hamilton Officers, Raquette at Oldfields. Patentee bulk carriage in intermodal containers. Home: 4 Grace Ct Greenlawn NY 11740 Office: 17 Battery Pl New York City NY 10006

NASADUKE, IRENE, ophthalmologist; b. Oct. 29, 1945; d. Nicholas and Anna (Chronowicz) N.; B.A., Barnard Coll., 1966; M.D., Albert Einstein Coll. Medicine, 1970. Intern in surgery N.Y. Hosp., Cornell Med. Center, N.Y.C., 1970-71, resident in surgery, 1971-72; resident in ophthalmology N.Y. U. Med. Center, N.Y.C., 1972-75, retinal fellow, 1975-76; practice medicine specializing in ophthalmology, Jamaica Estates, N.Y., 1977—; ophthalmologist to outpatients N.Y. Hosp., N.Y.C., 1976; asso. attending LaGuardia Hosp., 1977; asst. attending Queens Hosp. Center, 1977, Flower & Fifth Ave. Hosps., 1977—. Diplomate Nat. Bd. Med. Examiners, Am. Bd. Ophthalmology. Mem. Am. Assn. Ophthalmology, Am. Acad. Ophthalmology and Otolaryngology. Address: 181-23 Kruger Rd Jamaica Estates NY 11432

NASH, HAROLD EDWARD, JR., surgeon; b. Boston, July 5, 1921; s. Harold E. and Rose (Brady) N.; A.B., Boston Coll., 1942; M.D., Tufts U., 1945; m. Mary G. Costello, June 20, 1951; children—Mary Ellen (Mrs. Michael Gordon), Harold III, Barbara, Elizabeth, Christopher, Edward, John, Stephen, Joseph, Rosemary, Philip, Joanne, Christine. Intern, Carney Hosp., Boston, 1945-46, jr. vis. surgeon, 1953-59, asst. vis. surgeon, 1960-68, vis. surgeon, 1968—; intern St. Elizabeth Hosp., Boston, 1948-49, surg. resident, 1949-52, fellow surgery, 1953, grad. asst., 1954-58, asst. surgeon, 1958-59, asst. vis. surgeon, 1959-69, vis. surgeon, 1969—, staff pres., 1971-73; resident Pondville Cancer Hosp., Norfolk, Mass., 1952-53; asst. clin. prof. surgery Tufts U., Medford, Mass., 1960; cons. surgeon St. Margaret's Hosp., Boston, 1960—; surg. staff Youville Hosp., Cambridge, pres. staff, 1969-70. Served to capt., M.C., AUS, 1946-48. Diplomate Am. Bd. Surgery. Fellow Mass. Med. Soc. (councillor), A.C.S.; mem. Am., New Eng. Cancer Socs., Boston Surg. Soc., Norfolk Dist. Med. Soc. (pres. 1970-71). Home: 99 Grayfield Ave West Roxbury MA 02132 Office: 23 Bay State Rd Boston MA 02215

NASH, PETER HOWARD, physician, pharm. co. exec.; b. Sidcup, Kent, Eng., Feb. 20, 1917; s. George Howard and Clarice (Mills) N.; B.A., Cambridge U., 1938, M.B., 1941, M.A., 1945, M.D., 1950; D.P.H., London Sch. Hygiene and Tropical Medicine, 1947, D.I.H., 1953; postgrad. Harvard, 1948; m. A. Elizabeth Phillips, Oct. 13, 1951; children—Sarah Elizabeth, Jane Alexandra, Anne Louise, Edward Peter Howard. Intern, Middlesex Hosp., London, 1942; resident Met. Hosp., London, 1949-50; Rockefeller fellow preventive medicine, 1946-48; research fellow Harvard Med. Sch., 1948; chief asst. Slough Indsl. Health Service, 1950-53; lectr. London Sch. Hygiene, 1950-53; regional med. dir. Bell Telephone Co. Can., 1954-47; with Abbott Labs., Ltd., Montreal, 1957—, now dir. sci. affairs, med. dir.; asst. physician Royal Victoria Hosp., Montreal; exec. dir. Canadian Found. Advancement Clin. Pharmacology; Divisional surgeon St. John Ambulance Brigade, 1950-53; chmn. indsl. sect. Health League Can., 1955-57. Served to capt. Royal Army M.C., 1942-46. Mem. Canadian Assn. for Research in Toxicology (pres. 1972), Pharm. Mfrs. Assn. Can. (chmn. med. sect. 1961-62), N.Y. Acad. Scis., Canadian Med. Assn. Home: 228 Portland Ave Montreal PQ H3R 1V2 Canada Office: PO Box 6150 Montreal PQ H3C 3K6 Canada

NASHED, M. ZUHAIR, mathematician; b. Aleppo, Syria, May 14, 1936; s. Zaki M. and Nabiha (Musalati) N.; came to U.S., 1954, naturalized, 1974; S.B., Mass. Inst. Tech., 1957, S.M. in Elec. Engring., 1958; Ph.D. in Math., U. Mich., 1963; m. Ragda Yagan, Dec. 23, 1959; children—Ziad, Zaki, Zane. Asst. prof. math. Ga. Inst. Tech., Atlanta, 1963-65, asso. prof., 1965-69, prof., 1969-71, 72-76; prof. U. Del., Newark, 1977—; asso. prof. Am. U., Beirut, Lebanon, 1967-69; vis. asso. prof. Math. Research Center, U. Wis., Madison, 1967, vis. prof., 1970-72, summer 1973; vis. prof. U. Mich., Ann Arbor, 1976-77; cons. to govt., indsl. and ednl. instns.; lectr. univs., Europe, N.Am. and Middle East; speaker internat. symposia. Recipient Ford award Math. Assn. Am., 1967; Faculty Research award Ga. Inst. Tech., 1965, 73, Sustained Research award, 1976. Mem. Am. Math. Soc., Soc. Indsl. and Applied Math. (vis. lectr. 1972-75), Math. Assn. Am., London Math. Soc., Ops. Research Soc. Am., AAAS, AAUP, Sigma Xi. Author: Generalized Inverses and Applications, 1976; Functional Analysis Methods in Numerical Analysis, 1977; Recent Applications of Generalized Inverses, 1978; editor-in-chief Jour. Numerical Functional Analysis and Optimization; editor Jour. Integral Equations; editorial bd. mem. Jour. Computer and System Scis., Jour. Nonlinear Analysis, Jour. Applicable Analysis, Jour. Engring. Scis.; contbr. articles to profl. jours., chpts. to books. Home: 312 Dove Dr Newark DE 19713

NASPINSKY, CASIMER ANDREW, educator; b. McKeesport, Pa., July 12, 1946; s. Casimer and Mazzetta (Casteel) N.; B.A., Waynesburg Coll., 1967; M.A., Ohio U., 1969; postgrad. U. Pitts., 1968-69; m. Penny Ann Strawn, Dec. 21, 1967. Teaching fellow U. Pitts., 1968-69; lectr. Community Coll. of Allegheny County (Pa.), South Campus, part-time, 1971, instr. full time, 1971-73, asst. prof. social scis., 1973—, sec., campus curriculum com., 1972-74, mem. campus reorgn. com., 1975-77. Recipient Waynesburg Coll. History Dept. award, 1967; Ohio U. grad. scholar, 1967; U. Pitts. teaching fellow, 1968. Mem. Am. Hist. Assn., Phi Alpha Theta, Xi Psi Epsilon. Contbr. articles in field to coll. publs. Home: 1005 Kentucky Blue Dr

West Mifflin PA 15122 Office: 1750 Clairton Rd West Mifflin PA 15122

NASSIF, SHAKEEB JOSEPH, theatrical producer; b. Cedar Rapids, Iowa, Aug. 30, 1938; s. Samuel Joseph and Mary (Slaman) N.; B.A., Grinnell Coll., 1960; M.F.A., Yale, 1963; Ph.D., U. Denver, 1973; m. Michelle Marie McKenna, Aug. 29, 1964; children—Jonathan James, Alexandra Marie. Founder, producer Montowese Theatre, Branford, Conn., 1961-63; producer-dir. Yale Summer Theatre, 1964; prof. theatre U. Mont., Missoula, 1965-66; prof. English, U. So. Calif., Los Angeles, 1966-67; producer Westinghouse Broadcasting Co., Pitts., 1967-69; exec. producer Pitts. Playhouse, 1969-75; dir., partner SJN & Sons Mgmt. Co., Pitts., 1975—. Guest lectr. U. Evansville (Ind.), U. Pitts., Hollins Coll., State U. Coll. at Brockport (N.Y.), Rollins Coll., U. Mich., Cornell U., Ithaca, N.Y. Mem. Pitts. Council on the Arts, 1968-75, Pa. Council on the Arts, Theatre Adv. Panel, 1971, Greater Pitts. Council on Orthodoxy, 1970—, Pitts. Council on Higher Edn., 1971-74; adv. com. Chautauqua Instn., N.Y., 1972—. Trustee Erwin Piscator Found. N.Y., Pitts. Ballet Theatre; bd. dirs. St. George Greek Orthodox Cathedral, Pitts., 1976. Recipient Nat. citation for Documentary on Anti-Smoking, Am. Tb Assn.-Am. Heart Assn., 1968, Nat. citation for Excellence for Documentary The New Disciple, Nat. Council of Chs., 1969; named Man of Year in Entertainment, Pitts. C. of C., 1971. Mem. Am. Theatre Assn., Speech Assn., Am., ANTA, Actors' Equity Assn. Clubs: Harvard-Yale-Princeton Pittsburgh Athletic Assn. Home: 5122 Pembroke Pl Pittsburgh PA 15232 Office: 5115 Centre Ave Pittsburgh PA 15232

NAST, CHARLES COUDERT, lawyer; b. Tuxedo, N.Y., July 23, 1903; s. Conde and J. Clarisse (Coudert) N.; B.A., Harvard, 1925; LL.B., Columbia, 1927; grad. advanced course Inf. Sch., Ft. Benning, Ga.; grad. U.S. Army Command and Gen. Staff Coll., Ft. Leavenworth; m. Charlotte B. Brown, Dec. 6, 1928; 1 son, Peter C. (dec.). Admitted to N.Y. State bar, 1928; asso. firm Miller, Otis, Farr & Henderson, N.Y.C., 1927-28; dep. asst. N.Y. State atty. gen., 1928-29; asso. firm DeWitt, Nast, Diskin & Martini and predecessor firm, N.Y.C., 1929-37, partner, 1937-74; gen. counsel Condé Nast Publs. Inc., N.Y.C., 1975—. Served to lt. col. AUS, 1940-46; maj. gen. Res. ret.; chief of staff, later asst. div. comdr., then div. comdr. 42d Inf. Div., 1949-63. Mem. Am., N.Y. State bar assns., New York County Lawyers Assn., Assn. Bar City N.Y., Coffee House, Psi Upsilon. Republican. Roman Catholic. Clubs: Harvard (N.Y.C.), Racquet and Tennis, Outrigger Canoe (Honolulu). Home: 501 Lexington Ave New York City NY 10017 Office: 350 Madison Ave New York City NY 10017

NATALE, ANTHONY PAUL, coll. adminstr.; b. Trenton, N.J., June 17, 1925; s. Domenic Anthony and Maria Josephine (Porfirio) N.; B.S., Villanova U., 1973; M. in Adminstrn., Rider Coll., 1976; m. Frances Lucy Daloisio, July 1, 1951; children—Robert Allen, John Anthony. With U.S. Steel Corp., Trenton, N.J., asst. to works engr., appropriations engr., wire rope prodn. foreman, 1951-70; budget coordinator N.J. Dept. Transp., 1970; adminstrv. asst. bus. and fin. Trenton State Coll., 1971-74, purchasing officer, 1974-78, adminstrv. analyst, bus. services supr., 1978—, asst. prof. bus., 1977—, also mem. speakers bur. Bd. dirs. Lower Bucks Regional Confraternity of Christian Doctrine Roman Catholic Ch., 1974-78, asst. prin. adminstrn., 1978—. Served with AUS, 1943-46, 50-51. Decorated Combat Infantrymans Badge. Mem. Am. Def. Preparedness Assn., Purchasing Agts. Club Trenton, Villanova U., Rider Coll. alumni assns., Smithsonian Assos., Cousteau Soc. Club: K.C. Home: 299 Hicory Rd Morrisville PA 19067 Office: PO Box 940 Pennington Rd Trenton NJ 08625

NATALE, SAMUEL MICHAEL, clergyman, psychotherapist, educator; b. Phila., May 5, 1943; s. Samuel Michael and Anne (Vanore) N.; D.Phil., Oxford U., 1972. Joined S.J., 1973; ordained priest Roman Catholic Ch., 1979; exec. dir. Archdiocesan Consultation Center, Washington, 1975-76; dir. tng. Nat. Found. for Ednl. Research, Eng., Wales, 1971-72; prof. psychology Grad. Sch. Religion, Fordham U., Bronx, N.Y., 1978—; cons. Archdiocese of Balt. and Phila., 1973—. Mem. Am. Psychol. Assn., British Psychol. Soc., Am. Assn. Pastoral Counsellors. Author: An Experiment in Empathy, 1972; Pastoral Counselling, 1977. Contbr. numerous articles to profl. jours. Home: Jesuit Community Fordham U Bronx NY 10458 Office: Dept Psychology Grad Sch Religion Fordham U Bronx NY 10458

NATALI, ALFRED MAXIM, clergyman; b. Genoa, Italy, Mar. 9, 1915; s. Amilcare Salvatore and Victoria Lavinia (Daziani) N.; came to U.S., 1928, naturalized, 1937; B.A., Villanova U., 1940, M.A., 1944; postgrad. in theology St. Augustine Coll., Washington, 1941-44. Ordained priest Augustinian Order, 1943; asst. priest Holy Rosary Ch., Lawrence, Mass., 1944, pastor, 1962-71; missionary, N. Queensland, Australia, 1944-52; asst. priest St. Nicholas Ch., Phila., 1952-53, 77—, Our Lady of Good Counsel Ch., S.I., N.Y., 1953-56, 71-72, St. Augustine Ch., Lawrence, 1956-62, Our Lady of Pompeii, Vineland, N.J., 1974; missionary tchr. Gulf of Carpentaria, Cairns, Innisfail, Tully, Australia. Recipient Commonwealth of Mass. citation, 1968. Mem. Order of St. Augustine, Order of Alhambra, Bucks County Writers Guild. Club: K.C. Author: Italians in America, 1973; Jonathan Scroll, 1974. Composer: The Workingman's Prayer, 1974, A Wandering Priest, 1974; Mamma Giovanna, 1974. Home: 38 Avery Dr Williamstown NJ 08094 Office: 910 Watkins St Philadelphia PA 19148

NATHANS, DANIEL, educator, biologist; b. Wilmington, Del., Oct. 30, 1928; s. Samuel and Sarah (Levitan) N.; B.S., U. Del., 1950; M.D., Washington U., 1950-54; m. Joanne E. Gomberg, Mar. 4, 1956; children—Eli, Jeremy, Benjamin. Intern, Presbyn. Hosp., N.Y.C., 1954-55, resident medicine, 1957-59; clin. asso. Nat. Cancer Inst., 1955-57; guest investigator Rockefeller U., N.Y.C., 1959-62; prof. microbiology Sch. Medicine, Johns Hopkins, 1962-72, prof., dir. dept. microbiology, 1972—. Home: 2227 Crest Rd Baltimore MD 21209

NATHANSON, CHARLES CONRAD, planning and devel. cons. co. exec.; b. Bklyn., Sept. 6, 1930; s. Simon and Bella (Alter) N.; B.A. in Geography, Coll. City N.Y., 1952; M.A. in Geography, Columbia U., 1955; certificate in real estate Fordham U., 1956; m. Helene Klein, June 26, 1960; children—Shari Lee, Mitchell Jay, Amy Ilene. Research analyst U.S. Corps Engrs., Washington, 1955-57; rep. N.Y. Central R.R., N.Y.C., 1957-58; prin. planner N.J. Div. State and Regional Planning, Trenton, 1958; spl. asst. planning and devel. to N.J. Commr. of Conservation and Econ. Devel., Trenton, 1959-61; adminstr. N.J. Area Devel. Adminstrn., Trenton, 1961; exec. dir. Jersey City Redevel. Agy., 1961-66; dir. planning and devel. City Trenton, N.J., 1966-70; dir. housing and devel. McKee-Berger-Mansueto, Inc., N.Y.C. 1970-72; pres. Blau-Lasser-Nathanson Co., Newark, N.J., 1972; now pres. Charles C. Nathanson & Assos., P.A., Trenton. Exec. dir. N.J. Meadowlands Regional Devel. Agy., Trenton, 1959-63; project officer N.J. Pub. Market Commn., Trenton, 1960-61; dir. N.J. Small Bus., Trenton, 1959-61; Jersey City commr. to Meadowlands Regional Devel. Agy., 1960-65; mem. Govs. Task Force on Housing and Urban Renewal, Trenton, 1965—; mem. N.J. Pub. Broadcasting Authority. Served with USAF, 1952-54. Mem. State Bd. Profl. Planners (pres.), Am. Inst. Planners, Nat. Assn. Housing and Redevel. Ofcls. (chpt. pres. 1968-71). Jewish. Editor: Develop the Meadows, 1960. Contbr. articles to various publs. Home: 216 Renfrew Ave Trenton NJ 08618 Office: 865 Lower Ferry Rd Trenton NJ 08628

NATTERSTAD, JERRY H., educator; b. Urbana, Ill., Aug. 8, 1938; s. Harold Walter and Lucille Jeanette (Gullett) N.; B.S., So. Ill. U., 1960, M.A. (univ. teaching assistantship), 1961, Ph.D. (univ. grad. dissertation fellow), 1972; M.A., N.Y. U., 1967; 1 son, Gregory Michael. Grad. teaching asst. English, So. Ill. U., Carbondale, 1960-61; instr. English, U.S. Air Force Acad., Colorado Springs, Colo., 1961-64; instr. English, U. Conn., Waterbury, 1965-67, So. Ill. U., Carbondale, 1967-68, 70; asst. prof. English, Framingham (Mass.) State Coll., 1973—. Mem. council Danforth Mus., Framingham, 1977—. Served to lt., USAF, 1961-64. So. Ill. U. grad. research fellow, 1970. Mem. Modern Lang. Assn., Am. Com. for Irish Studies, Phi Kappa Phi, Kappa Delta Pi, Pi Sigma Alpha. Author: Francis Stuart, 1974; editor Jour. Irish Lit., 1976; contbr. articles in field to profl. jours. Home: 14B Winthrop Terr Framingham MA 01701 Office: Dept English Framingham State Coll Framingham MA 01701

NAUGHTON, ETHEL MAY (MRS. CLIFFORD ZEISS), physician; b. N.Y.C., Oct. 11, 1919; d. Thomas Joseph and Elizabeth (Carey) Naughton; B.A., Hunter Coll., 1941; M.D., N.Y. Med. Coll., 1944; m. Clifford J. Zeiss, May 12, 1944; 1 dau., Holly Elizabeth. Intern, resident Nassau Hosp., Mineola, N.Y., 1944-46; practice medicine, Valley Stream, N.Y., 1948-76; staff physician N.Y. Telephone Co., 1948-52; hon. staff Nassau Hosp., Mineola; indsl. physician N.Y. Telephone Co., 1976—. Diplomate Nat. Bd. Med. Examiners. Mem. AMA, N.Y. State, Nassau County med. socs., Am. Acad. Family Physicians. Address: 63 N Cottage St Valley Stream NY 11580

NAUGHTON, FRANK CHRISTOPHER, chem. engr.; b. North Bergen, N.J., Nov. 8, 1924; s. Christopher and Catherine (Natoli) N.; B.Chem. Engring., Poly. Inst. Bklyn., 1947, M.Chem. Engring., 1952, postgrad., 1955; postgrad. Jersey City State Coll., 1972-73; m. Marian Wende, Aug. 8, 1950; children—Stephen, Christopher, Barbara Anne. Research engr. Nat. Lead Co. Research Labs., Bklyn., 1947-50; research and devel. engr. Baker Castor Oil Co., Bayonne, N.J., 1950-56, mgr. devel. dept., 1958-73; supervisory engr. Revlon Inc., Passaic, N.J., 1957; mgr. product and process devel. NL Industries Inc., Hightstown, N.J., 1973-75, mgr. specialty chems. lab., 1975-78, tech. mgr., 1978—; instr. Pratt Inst., Bklyn.; cons. Jasonols Chem. Corp. Pres. Hillside (N.J.) Little League, 1967-68; sec., treas. Hillside Pop Warner League, 1965-68; commr. Hillside Pool and Recreation Bds., 1968-69. Served with U.S. Army, 1945-47. Mem. Am. Oil Chemists Soc. (Merit award 1977, mem. governing bd., treas. 1978-79), Soc. Plastics Engrs., Holy Name Soc. (pres.). Roman Catholic. Clubs: Columbian, K.C. Contbr. articles to profl. jours. Patentee in field. Home: 338 Old Grove Rd Mountainside NJ 07092

NAVIA, LUIS EDUARDO, educator; b. Cali, Colombia, Jan. 28, 1940; s. Jose Vicente and Juanita (Loboguerrero) N.; came to U.S., 1957, naturalized, 1963; B.A., Queens Coll., 1963; M.A., N.Y. U., 1966, Ph.D., 1972; m. Alicia Stella Cadena, July 28, 1973; 1 dau., Monica Stella. Instr. modern langs. Hofstra U., 1965-67; lectr. philosophy N.Y. U., 1970, Queens Coll., 1965-70; asso. prof. philosophy N.Y. Inst. Tech., 1968—. Mem. vis. team Middle States Assn. Colls., 1974; asso. dir. Jour. Pre-Coll. Philosophy, 1975—. Named Man of Year, N.Y. Inst. Tech., 1973; N.Y. State Teaching fellow, 1965; Borden Parker scholar, 1964. Mem. Am. Philos. Assn., AAAS, L.I. Philos. Soc. (exec. com.), Nat. Council Critical Analysis, Ancient Astronaut Soc. (adv. bd.), Phi Beta Kappa, Sigma Delta Pi. Author: A Guide to the Problems of Philosophy, 1973; Unsere Wiege steht im Kosmos: Das Weltbild eins und heute, 1976. Contbr. articles to profl. jours. Office: New York Institute of Technology Old Westbury NY 11568

NAWY, EDWARD GEORGE, educator, civil engr.; b. Bagdad, Iraq, Dec. 21, 1926; s. George M. and Ava (Marshall) N.; D.I.C., Imperial Coll. Sci. and Tech., London, Eng., 1951; C.E., Mass. Inst. Tech., 1959; D.Engring., U. Pisa (Italy), 1967; m. Rachel E. Shebbath, Mar. 23, 1949; children—Ava Margaret, Robert M. Came to U.S., 1957, naturalized, 1966. Head, hydraulic structures div. Israel Water Planning Authority, Tel-Aviv, 1952-57; mem. faculty Rutgers U., 1959—, distinguished prof. civil engring., 1966—, mem. grad. faculty, 1961—, mem. univ. Senate, 1973—, faculty mem. bd. govs.; vis. prof. Stevens Inst. Tech., Hoboken, N.J., 1968-72; guest prof. Nat. U. Tucuman (Argentina), summer 1963, Imperial Coll. Sci. and Tech., summer 1964; cons. to industry, 1958—; cons. FAA, Washington, also cons. energy div. GAO, Washington; chmn. Conf. on Deflection and Crack Control, Mexico City, 1976. Mem. Civil Engring. Tech. Adv. Council N.J., 1966—. Vice pres. Berkeley Twp. Taxpayers Assn., Ocean County, N.J., 1966-70; mem. Task Force N.J. Dept. Higher Edn. 1980-90 Master Plan Higher Edn. Recipient merit citation and award N.J. Concrete Assn., 1966; Henry L. Kennedy award Am. Concrete Inst., 1971; Gulbeakian Found. fellow (Portugal), 1972. Registered profl. engr., N.J., N.Y., Pa. Fellow ASCE (mem. joint com. on slabs), Am. Concrete Inst. (pres. N.J. chpt. 1966, 77—, 1st v.p. N.J. chpt. 1976-77, chmn. nat. com. on cracking 1966-73; rep. to Internat. Commn. on Fracture; mem. joint com. on slabs; Achievement award N.J. chpt. 1972, Nat. Activities award 1978), Instn. Civil Engrs. (London); mem. Prestressed Concrete Inst. (Bridge Competition award 1971), Nat. Soc. Profl. Engrs., Am. Soc. Engring. Edn., AAUP, N.Y. Acad. Scis., Sigma Xi, Chi Epsilon (hon.), Tau Beta Pi. Rotarian. Author research papers in field. Home: 347 Felton Ave Highland Park NJ 08904 Office: Civil Engring Dept Rutgers Univ New Brunswick NJ 08903

NAZARENO, JOSE POBLETE, pathologist; b. Naic, Cavite, Philippines, Nov. 29, 1925; s. Maximino A. and Aurea P. (Poblete) N.; came to U.S., 1954, naturalized, 1960; M.D., Manila Central U., 1953; m. V. Charlene Boardman, Aug. 3, 1973; 1 son, Christopher. Intern, Mt. St. Mary Hosp., Niagara Falls, N.Y., 1954-55; resident Our Lady of Lourdes Hosp., Binghamton, N.Y., 1955-56; resident pathology Binghamton (N.Y.) Gen. Hosp., 1956-57, Roswell Park Meml. Hosp., Buffalo, 1957-59, Deaconess Hosp., Buffalo, 1959-60; asst. pathologist Binghamton (N.Y.) Gen. Hosp., 1960-64, asso. pathologist, 1964-69; dir. labs. Binghamton Psychiatric Center, 1965—; owner, dir. So. Tier Med. Lab. Inc., Johnson City, N.Y., 1969—. Diplomate Am. Bd. Pathology. Fellow Am. Coll. Pathologists, Am. Soc. Clin. Pathologists; mem. AMA, N.Y. Med. Soc., N.Y. Soc. Pathologists, N.Y. Soc. Acupuncture for Physicians and Dentists, Am. Pathology Found., Assn. Philippine Practicing Physicians of Am. Democrat. Roman Catholic. Club: Binghamton Country. Office: 240 Riverside Dr Johnson City NY 13790

NAZEM, FEREYDOUN F., investment co. exec.; b. Tehran, Iran, Dec. 29, 1940; s. Hassan and Afsar; came to U.S., 1960, naturalized, 1976; B.Sc., Ohio State U., 1964; M.Sc., U. Cin., 1967; M.B.A., Columbia U., 1971; m. Susie Gharib, Jan. 20, 1973. Sr. research chemist Matheson Coleman & Bell, Norwood, Ohio, 1967-68; asst. v.p. and investment analyst Irving Trust Co., N.Y.C., 1969-74; v.p., venture capital officer Charter N.Y., N.Y.C., 1974-75; exec. v.p. fin. Tehran (Iran) Cement Co., 1975-76; pres. Collier Enterprises, N.Y.C., 1976—; dir. Delka Corp., Newton, Mass., Thershold Tech., Delran, N.J. Recipient several sch. fellowships and scholarships. Mem. N.Y. Soc. Security Analysts, N.Y. Venture Capital Forum, Am. Chem. Soc. Author: The Chemical Industry and the Energy Shortage, 1973; contbr. research reports on securities; photography exhibitor, 1963, 64, 66, 67. Home: 1185 Park Ave New York City NY 10028 Office: 1270 Ave of Americas New York City NY 10020

NAZZARO, ROCCO MICHAEL, chemist; b. Paterson, N.J., May 4, 1905; s. Anthony and Eugenia (DeGise) N.; B.S., Leonardo Da Vinci Tech. Inst., Rome, Italy, 1927; Ph.D., U. Rome, Italy, 1933; m. Ada Marie De Rogatis, June 7, 1930; children—Eugenia Angela, Lois Elaine, Anthony Donald. Vice pres. Victory Finishing Co., 1933-37; pres. Garden State Chem. Co., 1933-36; pres. Pan-Am. Color and Chem. Co., 1936-40; pres. Am. Processing Corp., Paterson, N.J., 1939—. Mem. Am. Chem. Soc., Am. Assn. Textile Chemists and Colorists. Home: 610 Doremus Ave Glen Rock NJ 07452 Office: 18 Market St Paterson NJ 07501

NEAL, MANSFIELD C., JR., lawyer; b. Washington, Apr. 16, 1939; s. Mansfield C. and Adelaide L. (Stewart) N.; B.A., Amherst Coll., 1961; LL.B., U. Pa., 1964; m. Cheryl L. Taylor, June 11, 1966; children—David, Jonathan. Admitted to Pa. bar, 1965; asso. firm Norris, Brown & Hall, Phila., 1965-68; pvt. practice law, Phila., 1968-71; counsel Re-entry and Environ. System div. Gen. Electric Co., Phila., 1971-72, counsel Elec. Utility Sales div., N.Y.C., 1972-74, counsel AEP litigation, Fairfield, Conn., 1974-77, div. counsel Indsl. & Marine Steam Turbine div., Lynn, Mass., 1977—; asst. city solicitor, Phila., 1967-68; dir. govt. relations Model Cities Program, Phila., 1970-71. Vice pres., bd. dirs. Diversified Community Services, Phila., 1968-74; bd. dirs. Phila. Architects Workshop, 1968-74, Heritage House of Phila., 1968-74. Mem. Nat., Am., Pa., Phila. (vice chmn. pub. service com. 1971) bar assns. Home: 236 Follen Rd Lexington MA 02173 Office: Gen Electric Co 1100 Western Ave Lynn MA 01910

NEAL, ROBERT CHESTER, educator; b. Lexington, Ky., Dec. 1, 1924; s. Chester and Gippie Dupree (Norton) N.; B.A., U. Va., 1947; M.A., Johns Hopkins U., 1958; m. Elizabeth Maynadier Scott Boyle, Apr. 5, 1951; children—Carbery, Roger, Julia, Letitia, Susannah. With Glenburn Farm, Taneytown, Md., 1951—, owner, 1972—; faculty Mt. St. Mary's Coll., Emmitsburg, Md., 1962—. Democratic candidate Md. Ho. of Dels., 1974. Served with USNR, 1942-46. Methodist. Home: Glenburn Farm Taneytown MD 21787

NEALE, F. BRENT, investment banker; b. N.Y.C., Aug. 28, 1919; s. G. Brent and Sophie Hill (Hamilton) N.; student N.Y. Inst. Finance, 1938-41, St. Peter's Coll., 1950, N.Y. U. Grad. Sch. Bus., 1954-58, Coll. Fin. Planning, 1978-80; m. Elizabeth M. Rowan, Apr. 25, 1953. Asst. syndicate mgr. Loeb Rhoades Co., N.Y.C., 1945-54; syndicate mgr. Parrish & Co., N.Y.C., 1954-58; salesman Lehman Bros., N.Y.C., 1958-62; sales mgr. and v.p. Blair Granbery Marache & Co., N.Y.C., 1962-64; asso. mem. N.Y. Stock Exchange, 1962-64; asst. v.p. sales E.F. Hutton Co., N.Y.C., 1965-71; salesman Riter Pyne Kendall & Hollister, Inc., N.Y.C., 1971-72; instl. sales Hayden Stone Co., N.Y.C., 1972-74; investment banking and instl. sales Hoppin Watson Inc., N.Y.C., 1974-76; salesman Smith Barney, Harris Upham & Co., Inc., Tinton Falls, N.J., 1976—; dir. Pkwy. Plastics Co., Piscataway, N.J., 1960—, Neale Assos., 1978—. Mgr. tobacco farm, 1945-54. Chmn. Monmouth (N.J.) Ocean Damage Control Bd., 1958-64; chmn. Central Rd.-Seaview Ave.-Monmouth Beach Project, 1975—; mem. planning bd. Boro of Monmouth Beach, 1976-77, 78-81, commr. revenue and fin., 1977-78, mayor, 1978-81; campaign mgr. Monmouth County Republican primary candidates, 1958, 62; trustee Ch. of Precious Blood, Monmouth Beach. Served with AUS, 1941-45. Decorated Purple Heart medal, Bronze Star medal, Combat Infantryman's Badge; recipient citations Fairleigh Dickinson U., 1954, 56, Kiwanis Internat., 1950, Internat. Lions Clubs, 1951, Catholic Action medal, 1950. Mem. Md. Soc., N.Y. Soc. (pres. 1951-54, 70-74), So. Soc. (trustee 1970-74), Wall Streeters (pres. 1958-76), SAR, Order Magna Charta (baron), Order Descs. Charlemagne, Sovereign Order Temple Jerusalem (knight), Manor Lords Md., Bond Club N.Y., Channel Club, City Midday Club, Money Marketeers, Soc. 1st Div., Cath. War Vets. (N.J. trustee 1948-50, comdr. Hudson County 1949-50), Monmouth Beach Bus. Men's Club. Clubs: K.C., Monmouth Beach Bath and Tennis (trustee 1972-75). Home and Office: 94 Ocean Ave Monmouth Beach NJ 07750

NEALE, JOSEPH HAMILTON, container mfg. co. exec.; b. Balt., Nov. 10, 1922; s. G. Brent and Sophie (Hamilton) N.; A.B., Loyola U., Balt., 1947, M.A., 1953; grad. Advanced Mgmt. Program, Harvard Bus. Sch., 1967; Licentiate in Philosophy, Gregorian Inst., Rome, 1948; m. Kathleen F. O'Shea, Nov. 21, 1953; children—James H., Patricia B. Indsl. sales Charles F. Hubbs Corp., Hillside, N.J., 1952-53; indsl. sales Union Camp Corp., Trenton, 1953-55, sales service mgr., 1955-57, asst. sales mgr., 1957-59, sales mgr., Chgo., 1960-63, asst. div. sales mgr., N.Y.C., 1963, div. sales mgr., 1964-65, Eastern region gen. mgr., N.Y.C., 1966-67, gen. mgr. container div., 1967—, corporate v.p., 1968—. Pres., River Glen Civic Assn., Yardley, Pa., 1962-63; chmn. edn. com. Country Club Civic Assn., Short Hills, N.J., 1965-66. Mem. Fibre Box Assn. (dir., exec. com., chmn. 1976-77), Am. Paper Inst. Home: 19 Kenilworth Dr Short Hills NJ 07078 Office: 1600 Valley Rd Wayne NJ 07470*

NEALL, ROBERT RAYMOND, state legislator Md.; b. Balt., June 26, 1948; s. William Wesley and Doris Virginia (McGinnis) N.; student U.S. Mil. Acad., 1968; A.A., Anne Arurdel Community Coll., 1971; B.A., U. Md., 1979; m. Margaret Lindsay Glendinning, Sept. 18, 1970; children—Robert R., David G. Mgr., Davidsonville Supply Co. (Md.), 1969—; legis. asst. to Md. Senate minority leader, 1973-74; mem. Md. Ho. of Dels., 1974—, minority whip, 1978—. Pres. Young Republicans, Annapolis, 1973-74. Served with USN, 1967-68. Named Man of Year, Anne Arurdel County Young Reps., 1973, Christian Citizen of Year, United Christian Citizens Md., 1975. Episcopalian. Home: 771 W Central Ave Davidsonville MD 21035 Office: 215 House Office Bldg Annapolis MD 21404

NEALON, WILLIAM JOSEPH, U.S. judge; b. Scranton, Pa., July 31, 1923; s. William Joseph and Ann Cannon (McNally) N.; student U. Miami (Fla.), 1942-43; B.S. in Econs., Villanova U., 1947; LL.B., Cath. U. Am., 1950; LL.D., U. Scranton, 1975; m. Jean Sullivan, Nov. 15, 1947; children—Ann, Robert, William, John, Jean, Patricia, Kathleen, Terrence, Thomas, Timothy. Admitted to Pa. bar, 1951; with firm Kennedy, O'Brien & O'Brien, and predecessor, Scranton, 1951-60; mem. Lackawanna County Ct. Common Pleas, 1960-62; U.S. dist. judge Middle Dist. Pa., Scranton, 1962-76, chief judge, 1976—; lectr. bus. law and labor law U. Scranton, 1951-59. Mem. Scranton Registration Commn., 1953-55; hearing examiner Pa. Liquor Control Bd., 1955-59; campaign dir. Lackawanna County chpt. Nat. Found., 1961-63; mem. Scranton-Lackawanna Health and Welfare Authority, 1963—; pres. Father's Club, Scranton Prep Sch., 1966; pres. bd. dirs. Cath. Youth Center; chmn. bd. trustees U. Scranton; vice chmn. bd. trustees Lackawanna Jr. Coll., Scranton; asso. bd. Marywood Coll., Scranton; trustee St. Michael's Sch. for Boys, Hoban Heights; bd. dirs. Lackawanna County unit Am. Cancer Soc., Lackawanna County Heart Assn., Lackawanna County chpt. Pa.

Hosp., 1963-68, subsequently clin. dir.; chief Oswego County unit Marcy Psychiat. Center, 1968-74, asst. dep. dir., after 1977. Served with Turkish Army, 1949-50. Mem. Am., No. N.Y. Dist. psychiat. assns., Nat. Geog. Soc. Moslem. Clubs: New Seabury Country, Falmouth Hosp. Assn. Contbr. articles to med. jours. Home: PO Box 177 Waquoit MA 02536 Office: Medfield State Hosp Medfield MA

OKUN, MILTON RAPHAEL, dermatologist; b. Phila., Oct. 25, 1928; s. William and Dora (Perlman) O.; B.A., U. Pa., 1950; M.D., Jefferson Med. Coll., 1954. Intern, Phila. Gen. Hosp., 1954-55; resident in dermatology Boston City Hosp., 1957-59, Mass. Gen. Hosp., 1959-60; practice medicine specializing in dermatology, Needham, Mass.; mem. staff Boston City Hosp.; mem. faculty Med. Sch., Tufts U., Boston, 1961—, now asso. prof. dermatology; chmn. Dermatopathology Found. and Press. Served with USPHS, 1955-57. Med. Found. Boston grantee, 1965-67. Mem. AMA, Am. Acad. Dermatology, Am. Soc. Dermatopathology, New Eng. Dermatol. Soc., Mass. Med. Soc., Boston Dermatology Club. Author: (with L Edelstein) Gross and Microscopic Pathology of the Skin, 1976. Contbr. articles to med. jours. Patentee method for treating psoriasis, 1976. Home: 47 Commercial Wharf Boston MA 02110 Office: 91 Dedham Ave Needham MA 02192

OLABISI, OLAGOKE, plastics engr.; b. Oshogbo, Nigeria, Sept. 25, 1943; s. Onoolapo Joseph and Maria (Olapade) O.; came to U.S., 1965; B.S. in Chem. Engring., Purdue U., 1969, B.S. in Indsl. Mgmt., 1969; M.S. in Chem. Engring., U. Calif., Berkeley, 1971; Ph.D. in Macromolecular Sci., Case Western Res. U., 1973; m. Gail Yvette, Sept. 5, 1970; children—Olatoke, Olaronke, Olanrewaju. Project scientist Union Carbide Corp., Bound Brook, N.J., 1973—. Chmn. curriculum com. Nyerere Edn. Inst., 1975-76. Recipient Clarence Lottes Meml. award for most promising chem. engr. Purdue U., 1969. Mem. Am. Chem. Soc., Am. Phys. Soc., N.Y. Acad. Scis., Soc. Plastics Engrs., Material Research Soc., Sigma Xi, Tau Beta Pi, Omega Chi Epsilon. Contbr. articles to profl. jours. Patentee in field. Office: Union Carbide Corp Research and Devel Dept 1 River Rd Bound Brook NJ 08805

OLAFSSON, THOMAS ROBERT, chem. co. exec.; b. Boston, Oct. 9, 1932; s. Hogni Peter and Katherine (Savage) O.; B.S. in Chemistry, Tufts U., 1959; M.B.A. in Fin., Babson Coll., 1977; m. Barbara L. Soley, June 20, 1959; children—Thomas Robert, Michael. Tech. sales rep. Celanese Corp. Am., 1959-61; new bus. devel. specialist Carter's Ink Co., Cambridge, Mass., 1962-64; pres., founder Chromex Chem. Corp., Bklyn., 1964-72, Butler Labs., Inc., N.Y.C., 1971-72; v.p., gen. mgr. Brotherhood Corp., Washingtonville, N.Y., 1972-73; founder, pres. Environex Corp., Boston, 1973—; dir. Diversified Chem. Corp., Union, N.J., Beautiline, Inc., N.Y.C. Served with Mil. Police Corps, AUS, 1953-55. Mem. Am. Chem. Soc, Inst. Mgmt. Accounting. Club: N.Y. Athletic. Home: 180 St Paul St Brookline MA 02146 Office: 84 State St Boston MA 02109

OLDAY, CHARLES HAROLD, aviation and health safety products co. exec.; b. Buffalo, N.Y., May 15, 1934; s. Harold John and Edith Georgia (Sneck) O.; B.S., U. Buffalo, 1965; children—Susan Faye, Douglas Charles, Matthew Campbell. Controller, Graphic Controls Corp., Buffalo, 1958-71; corp. controller Foseco, Inc., Cleve., 1971-72; v.p., controller, asst. sec. Scott Aviation, div. A-T-O, Lancaster, N.Y., 1972—. Mem. faculty Erie County Community Coll., 1965-71. Served with USMCR, 1952-56. Mem. Planning Execs. Inst. (pres. Buffalo chpt. 1969-70), Fin. Execs. Inst., Buffalo C. of C., Delta Sigma Pi. Home: 98A Foxberry Dr Getzville NY 14068 Office: 225 Erie St Lancaster NY 14086

OLDENBURG, HENRY, educator, agrl. and polit. geographer; b. Fillmore, N.Y., Mar. 10, 1938; s. Carl and Dorothea (Hedwig) O.; student Houghton Coll., 1956-57; B.A. with honors, U. Mont., 1961, M.A., 1967; m. Pauline Betty Bourquin, Aug. 8, 1971. Teaching asst. U. Mont., Missoula, 1961-62; project asst. U. Wis., Madison, 1967-68; instr. U. Wis., Whitewater, 1969, U. Wis., Oshkosh, 1970-72; agri./estate mgr. Fillmore, 1962—; pvt. cons. floodplain mgmt. and devel., 1973—. W.K. Kellogg Found. fellow, 1975-77. Mem. AAUP, Assn. Am. Geographers, Nat. Council for Geog. Edn., Phi Kappa Phi, Gamma Theta Upsilon, Kappa Delta Pi. Elk. Author: Naval Planning for the German Invasion of Norway, 1967. Home: 30 E Main St Fillmore NY 14735

OLDENBURG, RICHARD ERIK, museum dir.; b. Stockholm, Sept. 21, 1933; s. Gösta and Sigrid Elisabeth (Lindforss) O.; came to U.S., 1936, naturalized, 1959; A.B., Harvard U., 1954; m. Harriet Lisa Turnure, Dec. 17, 1960. Mgr. design dept. Doubleday & Co., Inc., N.Y.C., 1958-61; mng. editor trade div. MacMillan Co., Inc., N.Y.C., 1961-69; dir. publs. Mus. of Modern Art, N.Y.C., 1969-72, dir. mus., 1972—. Served with U.S. Army, 1956-58. Office: 11 W 53d St New York NY 10019

OLDS, RICHARD J., cons.; N.Y.C., Mar. 27, 1911; s. John J. and Isabel (Guth) G.; A.B., Colgate U., 1932; m. Barbara Moses, Apr. 13, 1940; children—Robert R., John T., Nancy (Mrs. Benson B. Sloan III). Spl. asst. to pres. Bklyn. Trust Co., 1941-43; mgr. housing Agy. Savs. Bank Trust Co., 1943-47; asst. to pres. George A. Fuller Co., Inc., 1948-54; adminstrv. v.p. Fischbach & Moore, Inc., 1954-56; asst. to pres. Turner Constrn. Co., 1956-60; v.p. George A. Fuller Co., Inc., 1961-69; asso. dir. N.Y. Hosp.-Cornell Med. Center, N.Y.C., from 1969; now Cons. Fischbadd & Moore, N.Y.C. Trustee exec. com. Manhattan Eye, Ear and Throat Hosp., 1954-69, 76—; dir. Colgate U. Alumni Corp., 1967—, pres., 1973-76; mem. exec. com., trustee Colgate U.; trustee, v.p. Seamen's Ch. Inst. of N.Y. Recipient Distinguished Service award Colgate U., 1973. Mem. The Moles, N.Y. Bldg. Congress (gov. 1961-64, 73-76). Republican. Episcopalian. Clubs: Univ. (N.Y.), The Creek. Constrn. cons. The Frick Collection and Winifred Masterson Burke Relief Found. Home: 200 E 66th St New York City NY 10021 Office: Fischbadd & Moore Inc 485 Lexington Ave New York City NY 10017

OLDSEY, BERNARD STANLEY, educator, editor, author; b. Wilkes-Barre, Pa., Feb. 18, 1923; s. Frederick and Mary (Chohol-Moroz) O.; B.A. in Journalism and English, Pa. State U., 1948, M.A. in English, 1949, Ph.D., 1955; m. Ann Marie Re, Sept. 21, 1946; children—William Frederick, Jan Marie. Faculty dept. English, Pa. State U., University Park, 1950-69, asst. prof., 1957-63, asso. prof., 1963-69; prof. English, West Chester (Pa.) State Coll., 1969—. Sr. Fulbright prof. Am. lit. U. Zaragoza, Spain, 1964-65; vis. prof. U. Md., 1965. Editor Coll. Lit. jour., 1973—. Served with inf. AUS, 1942-45. Decorated 3 Battle Stars, Purple Heart. Mem. Modern Lang. Assn., Kappa Delta Rho. Author: From Fact to Judgment, 1957, 63; Visions and Revisions in Modern American Literary Criticism, 1962; The Art of William Golding, 1965; The Spanish Season, 1970. Writer mil. publs. in Italy, including Stars and Stripes. Home: 1003 Woodview Ln West Chester PA 19380

OLDSHUE, JAMES YOUNG, equipment co. exec.; b. Chgo., Apr. 18, 1925; s. James and Louise (Young) O.; B.S. in Chem. Engring., Ill. Inst. Tech., 1947, M.S., 1949, Ph.D., 1951; m. Betty Weirsema, June 14, 1947; children—Paul F., Richard J., Robert W. Chem. engr. Los Alamos Labs., 1945-46; devel. engr. Mixing Equipment Co., Rochester, N.Y., 1950-52, head devel engring. 1952-54, dir. research, 1954-63, tech. dir., 1964-70, v.p. mixing tech., 1970—; instr. U. Rochester, 1954-57. Chmn. YMCA, Irondequoit, N.Y., 1960-62 pres. Parent's Forum, Irondequoit High Sch., 1970; mem. bd. world missions, mem. exec. com. gen. program council Reformed Ch. in Am.; del. N.Am. area World Alliance Reformed and Presbyn. Chs.; del. uniting council World Alliance Reformed and Presbyn. Chs. and Internat. Congl. Council, 1970. Mem. men's com. Japan Internat. Christian U. Found. Bd. dirs. internat. div. Nat. YMCA, Rochester YMCA; mem. exec. forum Genesee Ecumenical Ministries, Rochester. Served with AUS, 1944-46. Registered profl. engr., N.Y. Fellow Am. Inst. Chemists, Am. Inst. Chem. Engrs. (pres., past dir.); mem. Am. Chem. Soc., Engrs. Joint Council (chmn. metric commn.), Internat. Platform Assn., Sigma Xi, Tau Beta Pi. Mem. Reformed Ch. Adv. bd. Internat. Chem. Engring. Contbr. articles to profl. jours. Research in field. Home: 141 Tyringham Rd Rochester NY 14617 Office: 135 Mt Read Blvd Rochester NY 14611

O'LEARY, EDWARD CORNELIUS, bishop; b. Bangor, Maine, Aug. 21, 1920; student Holy Cross Coll., Worcester, Mass., St. Paul's Sem., Ottawa, Ont., Can. Ordained priest Roman Catholic Ch., 1946, consecrated bishop, 1971; appointed titular bishop Moglena and aux. bishop, Portland, Maine, 1971; bishop, Portland, 1974—. Office: 510 Ocean Ave Portland ME 04103

O'LEARY, JEREMIAH DANIEL, JR., urban planner; b. Summit, N.J., Sept. 25, 1929; s. Jeremiah Daniel and Marguerite Maude (Wolfe) O'L.; A.B. with honors, Harvard U., 1952; M. City Planning, Harvard Grad. Sch. Design, 1957; m. Barbara Cherrix Adkins, Sept. 4, 1962. Urban planner Planning Council Greater Balt. Com., 1957-62; govt. adminstr. Housing and Home Finance Agy., Washington, 1962; partner Marcou, O'Leary & Assos., Washington, 1962-74, exec. v.p., dir., 1969—, asset mgr., financial analyst, 1974—; vis. critic urban planning Harvard U., Tulane U. Served with USN, 1952-55. Mem. Am. Inst. Planners. Club: Rehoboth Beach Country. Contbr. articles in field to profl. jours. Home: PO Box 202 Rehoboth Beach DE 19971

O'LEARY, K(EITH) DANIEL, educator, clin. psychologist; b. West Chester, Pa., Oct. 3, 1940; s. Daniel Keith and Alma Rose (Boyer) O'L.; B.A., Pa. State U., 1962; M.A. (USPHS fellow), U. Ill., 1965, Ph.D., 1967; m. Susan Gilbert, Aug. 7, 1964; children—Michael Boyer, Kathryn Searls. Asst. prof. State U. N.Y. at Stony Brook, 1967-70, asso. prof., 1970-73, prof. clin. psychology, 1973—, chmn. dept. psychology, 1978—. Cons. Nat. Inst. Mental Health, 1972-75; Dir. Point of Woods Lab. Sch., Stony Brook, 1969-73. U.S. Office of Edn. grantee, 1969; NIMH grantee, 1971. Fellow Am. Psychol. Assn.; mem. Soc. for Research in Child Devel., Phi Beta Kappa, Phi Kappa Phi. Author: (with O'Leary) Classroom Management: The Successful Use of Behavior Modification, 1972; (with G.T. Wilson) Behavior Therapy: Application and Outcome, 1975. Editor Jour. Applied Behavior Analysis, 1977-78; asso. editor Jour. Abnormal Child Psychology, 1973—; mem. editorial bd. Jour. Cons. and Clin. Psychology and Behavior Therapy. Contbr. articles to profl. jours. Home: 236 Christian Ave Stony Brook NY 11790

O'LEARY, RICHARD A., broadcasting exec.; b. San Francisco; grad. U. So. Calif.; married; 4 children. With ABC, 1955—, account exec. KABC-TV, Los Angeles, 1955-59, sales mgr., 1959-60, gen. sales mgr., 1960-66. v.p., gen. mgr. WLS-TV, Chgo., 1966-70, pres. ABC owned TV stas., N.Y.C., 1970—. Served with USNR, World War II; ETO, PTO. Office: 1330 Ave of Americas New York City NY 10019

O'LEARY, WILFRED LEO, educator; b. Boston, July 3, 1906; s. Daniel Joseph and Frances Marie (O'Hara) O'L.; grad. Boston Latin Sch., 1925; A.B., Boston Coll., 1929, A.M., 1930; Ed.M., State Coll. at Boston, 1938; Ed.D., Calvin Coolidge Coll., 1954; m. Gertrude Margaret Cashman, June 26, 1938; 1 dau., Ann Marie O'Leary Gessner. Master, Boston Latin Sch., 1934-42, 46-48; head history dept. Jeremiah E. Burke High Sch., Dorchester, Mass., 1948-57; asst. prof. edn. Calvin Coolidge Coll., 1952-57; headmaster Roslindale High Sch., Mass., 1957-64, Boston Latin Sch., 1964-76. Vice pres., dir. Roslindale Coop. Bank. Mem. adv. bd. Scholastic Mag. 1960-64; mem. Mass. Adv. Council on Edn. Bd. dirs. Boston chpt. ARC; ho. of dels. Easter Seal Soc. Mass. Served with USAF, 1942-46; col. Res. ret. Mem. New Eng. History Tchrs. Assn. (sec.-treas. 1952-64, v.p. 1965, pres. 1966-67), Boston Headmasters Assn. (pres. 1963-65), Boston Latin Sch. Assn. (sec. 1973—, librarian 1964—), Am. Hist. Assn., Boston Athenaeum, Nat. Council Social Studies Tchrs. Mass. Assn. Secondary Sch. Prins., Bostonian Soc., Mil. Order Fgn. Wars U.S., Boston Headmasters' and Prins. Assns. (pres. 1966-69), Mass. Schoolmasters' Club (pres. 1964-65), Head Masters Assn. (trustee 1975-76, pres. 1976-77). Author: (with others) Communism vs. Democracy, 1955; Philosophy of the Mass. Secondary School Principals Assn., 1960. Home: 4 Calvin Rd Jamaica Plain MA 02130 Office: Boston Latin School 78 Ave Louis Pasteur Boston MA 02115

O'LEARY, WILLIAM ALOYSIUS, san. engr.; b. Elizabeth, N.J., Feb. 28, 1901; s. John J. and Mary (O'Donnell) O'L.; B.S. in Civil Engring., Villanova U., 1922; m. Margaret Claire Smith, Feb. 10, 1928. Designer sewer constrn. N.Y. Subway Constrn., 1923-33; project engr. Bur. Water Pollution Control, Dept. Pub. Works, City N.Y., 1935-48, chief design, 1948-54, dir. water pollution control, 1954-65; cons. Camp, Dresser & McKee, Boston, 1966-76; also ind. cons. engr. Served from lt. to lt. comdr. CEC, USNR, 1942-46. Mem. ASCE (life), Fedn. Water Pollution Control (life), Am. Acad. Environmental Engrs. (life), Municipal Engrs. City N.Y. (life, dir. 1962-65), N.Y. (life, dir. Met. sect. 1960-63), New Eng. water pollution control assns. Home: Short Woods Rd PO Box 8801 New Fairfield CT 06810

OLEKSIW, MICHAEL NICHOLAS, II, art service co. exec.; b. Evanston, Ill., June 4, 1945; s. Jerome J. and Mary Beston (Fullerton) O.; B.A., St. Lawrence U., 1968; postgrad. U. Ariz., 1968-69; M.A., U. Del., 1972; m. Susan Prince Ryan, Aug. 19, 1967. Pres., chmn. bd. J.F.O. Art Ltd., Wilmington, Del., 1974—; cons. artists, galleries, art-related businesses, groups and schs.; cons., research on individual creative artist Mass. Arts and Humanities Found., Boston, 1977—. Served to capt. AUS, 1971-73. Recipient Steinmen Art Festival award, 1968. State of Del. grantee, 1970-71. Mem. Artists Equity Assn. Sculptor Sculptural Environment II, commd. by State of Del., 1971. Editor, J.F.O. Newsletter. Office: 1 E 5th St Wilmington DE 19801

OLENDER, JACK H., lawyer; b. McKeesport, Pa., Sept. 8, 1935; s. Benjamin and Kate (Harris) O.; A.B. summa cum laude, U. Pitts., 1957, J.D., 1960; LL.M., George Washington U., 1961; m. Lovell V. Ruckman, July 15, 1962. Teaching fellow George Washington U. Law Sch., Washington, 1960-61; admitted to D.C. bar, 1961, Md. bar, 1966; prin. Jack H. Olender & Assos., Washington, 1961—; lectr. Southeastern U., Washington, 1965-67. Diplomate Am. Bd. Profl. Liability Attys. Mem. Am., Md., Montgomery County bar assns., Assn. Plaintiffs' Trial Attys. (pres. 1969-70), Bar Assn. D.C., Am. Trial Lawyers Assn. (asso. editor Torts 1965—, mem. state com. for D.C. 1970-73, bd. govs. 1973-76), Am. Judicature Soc., Md. Trial Lawyers Assn. (v.p. 1973), Inner Circle of Advocates, Pitts. Inst. Legal Medicine, Am. Arbitration Assn., Scribes, World Peace Through Law, Phi Beta Kappa. Contbr. articles to profl. jours. Office: 1725 K St NW Washington DC 20036

OLENICK, ARNOLD JEROME, educator; b. N.Y.C., Sept. 2, 1918; s. Jesse and Eleanor (Rothenberg) O.; B.S. in Accounting, N.Y. U., 1940, M.B.A., 1947; m. Bernice Rosenblum, Nov. 4, 1945; children—Philip R., Steven E. With Eisner & Lubin, C.P.A.s, N.Y.C., 1939-40; mktg. research analyst Dun & Bradstreet Inc., N.Y.C.; partner Rosenblum, Olenick & Needleman, C.P.A.s, N.Y.C. 1948-62; prin. Arnold J. Olenick, C.P.A., N.Y.C., 1962-73; asso. prof. N.Y. Inst. Tech., 1966-71; asso. prof. S.I. Community Coll., City U. N.Y., 1971-76; vis. asso. prof. U. Mass., Boston, 1976-77, prof., 1977—; cons. taxation N.Y.C. Council, 1975. Treas. Manhasset-Great Neck Econ. Opportunity Council, 1968-70; chmn. Great Neck Com. Human Rights, 1964-65; treas. Kensington Civic Orgn., Great Neck, 1962. Served to major, USAAF, 1940-45. C.P.A., N.Y., Mass. Mem. Am. Inst. C.P.A., N.Y., State, Mass. socs. C.P.A.'s, Am. Accounting Assn., AAUP (chapt pres. 1970-71), Accountants for Pub. Interest, Inc. N.Y. (pres. 1975-76) Mass. Accountants Pub. Issues (pres. 1978—). Author: Managing the Company Tax Function, 1976. Editor: Teachers of Accounting in Two-Year Colls. Jour., 1975-76. Home: 303A Commonwealth Ave Boston MA 02115 Office: College of Professional Studies University Massachusetts Harbor Campus Boston MA 02125

OLER, WESLEY MARION, III, physician; b. N.Y.C., Mar. 8, 1918; s. Wesley Marion, Jr. and Imogene (Rubel) O.; grad. Phillips Andover Acad., 1936; A.B., Yale U., 1940; M.D., Columbia, 1943; m. Virginia Carolyn Craemer, Dec. 8, 1951; children—Helen Louise (dec.), Wesley Marion IV, Stephen Scott. Intern, Bellevue Hosp., N.Y.C., 1944, resident, 1948-50; fellow Hosp. U. Pa., 1951; practice medicine, specializing in internal medicine, Washington, 1952—; sr. attending physician, vice chmn. dept. medicine Washington Hosp. Center, 1962-64, v.p. med. bd., 1971-72, trustee, 1973—; clin. prof. medicine Med. Sch., Georgetown U. Founder, pres. Washington Recorder Soc.; bd. dirs. Am. Recorder Soc. Served to maj. M.C., U.S. Army, 1944-47. Fellow A.C.P.; mem. Mensa, Osler Soc. Washington (past pres.). Republican. Episcoplian. Clubs: Metropolitan, Cosmos, Chevy Chase. Contbr. to jours. on old musical instruments. Home: 4800 Van Ness St NW Washington DC 20016 Office: 3301 New Mexico Ave NW Washington DC 20016

OLGAS, KASSIE ANN, nurse; b. Manchester, N.H., Dec. 4, 1923; d. John G. and Jennie K. (Karavas) O.; R.N., Elliot Hosp. Sch. Nursing, 1948; B.S., St. Anselm's Coll., 1960. Supr. operating room VA Hosp., Manchester, 1950-60, VA Hosp., Bklyn., 1960-67, coordinator operating room VA Hosp., Hines, Ill., 1967-72, VA Hosp., Boston, 1972—, cons. operating room VA and pvt. instns. Recipient numerous profl. awards. Mem. Assn. Operating Room Nurses, Am. Nurses Assn., Nat. League for Nursing. Republican. Eastern Orthodox. Author, dir. film Care of the Neurosurgical Patient, 1971. Home: 780 Boylston St Boston MA 02199 Office: 150 S Huntington Ave Boston MA 02130

OLIN, STEPHEN, chemist; b. Mansfield, Ohio, Dec. 23, 1919; s. Edwin Mason and Edna Francis (Munro) O.; B.A., DePauw U., Greencastle, Ind., 1941; M.A., Ohio State U., 1943, Ph.D., 1948; m. Lois Saunders, Dec. 26, 1942; children—Phillip, Patricia. Research chemist Miles Labs., Elkhart, Ind., 1948-58; sr. investigator Miles Chem. Co., 1958-61; with Ayerst Lab., N.Y.C., 1961—, asso. dir. quality control, 1964-66, dir. devel. and quality control, 1966-76, dir. quality assurance, 1976-77, v.p. quality assurance, 1977—. Served with USNR, 1944-46. Mem. Am. Chem. Soc., AAAS, Acad. Pharm. Sci., Am. Soc. Quality Control. Bd. editors Analytical Profiles, 1971-74. Home: 623A Heritage Village Southbury CT 06488 Office: 685 3d Ave New York City NY 10017

OLIPHANT, S. PARKER, constrn. co. exec.; b. Washington, Oct. 26, 1927; s. Abner Chambers and Ruth Parker (Larner) O.; grad. St. Albans Sch., 1945; B.S. in Engring., Princeton, 1949; m. Martha Carmichael, June 2, 1962; children—Leonard Carmichael, Samuel Duncan. Chainman subdiv. #43 Pa. R.R. Co., Lewistown, Pa., 1948; with William P. Lipscomb Co., Inc., Washington, 1949—, field engr., 1949-50, payroll clk., 1950, supt., 1951-53, estimator, 1950-54, project mgr., 1953-69, treas., 1967—, pres., 1971—; v.p. House Realty & Devel. Co., Arlington, Va., 1971—; partner firm Mills, Oliphant & Truland, Washington, 1961—; dir. Chevy Chase Land Co. Vice pres. Spring Valley-Wesley Heights Citizens Assn., 1971-73, pres., 1973-74; mem. D.C. Republican com., 1956—; bd. dirs. Columbia Hosp. for Women, 1967—, pres., 1971-73; bd. dirs. Children's Hosp., 1970-72; mem. Nat. Presbyn. Sch. Bd., 1973-76; bd. dirs. Presbyn. Home D.C., 1975—; mem. adv. bd. Textile Mus., 1974—; mem. Maret Sch. Bd., 1976. Mem. Washington Bldg. Congress, Asso. Gen. Contractors. Presbyn. Clubs: Metropolitan (dir.) (Washington); Chevy Chase (Md.). Home: 4977 Glenbrook Rd Washington DC 20016 Office: 2731 N Washington Blvd Arlington VA 22201

OLITSKI, JULES, artist; b. Snovsk, Russia, Mar. 27, 1922; s. Jevel and Anna (Zarnitsky) Demikovsky; came to U.S., 1923, naturalized, 1943; student Acad. de la Grande Chaumiere, Paris, 1949-50; B.S., N.Y. U., 1952, M.A., 1955; student Beaux Arts Inst., N.Y.C., 1940-42, N.A.D., N.Y.C., 1940-42; m. Gladys Katz, 1944 (div. 1951); 1 dau., Eve; m. 2d, Andrea Hill Pearce, Jan. 21, 1956 (div. 1975); 1 dau., Lauren. One man exhbns. include Galerie Huit, Paris, 1950, Iolas Gallery, N.Y.C., 1958, French & Co., N.Y.C., 1959-61, Poindexter Gallery, N.Y.C., 1961-68, Bennington (Vt.) Coll., 1962, Richard Gray Gallery, Chgo., 1964, Kasmin, Ltd., London, 1964-72, Galerie Lawrence, Paris, 1964, David Mirvish Gallery, Toronto, Ont., Can., 1964-74, Corcoran Gallery, Washington, 1967, 74, Am. Pavillion, Venice Biennale Art Exhbn., 1966, Inst. Contemporary Art U. Pa., 1968 Andre Emmerich Gallery, 1973-74, Laurence Rubin Gallery, N.Y.C., 1969-73, Knoedler Contemporary Arts, N.Y.C., 1974—; group exhbns. include Carnegie Internat., Pitts., 1961, 65, Washington Gallery Modern Art, 1963, Los Angeles County Mus., 1964, Fogg Art Mus., Harvard, 1965, Pasadena (Cal.) Art Mus., 1965, 69, Mus. Basle (Switzerland), 1965, Venice Biennale, 1966 Corcoran Gallery Art, 1967, Tokyo Biennale, Japan, 1967, Instituto Torcuato di Tella, Buenos Aires, 1967, Found. Maeght, France, 1968, Met. Mus. Art, 1969; retrospective exhbn. sculpture Boston Mus. Fine Arts, 1977, Hirshorn Mus., Washington, 1977; represented in permanent collections Mus. Modern Art, Art Inst. Chgo., Whitney Mus., Norman MacKensie Art Gallery, Regina, Can., Dayton (Ohio) Art Inst., Cleve. Mus., Corcoran Art Gallery, Chrysler Mus., Norfolk, Va., Albright-Knox Art Gallery, Buffalo, Met. Mus. Art, N.Y.C., Hirschhorn Mus., Washington; asst. prof. art State U. N.Y. Coll. at New Paltz, 1954-55; asso. prof. coordinator fine arts div. C.W. Post Grad. Coll., L.I. U., Greenvale, N.Y., 1956-63; tchr. Bennington Coll., 1963-67. Recipient 2d prize Carnegie Internat., 1961; 1st prize Corcoran Biennale, Washington, 1967.

OLIVEIRA, MILTON DIAS, corrosion engr., cons.; b. Jaguarao, Brazil, Mar. 18, 1939; s. Protestato Dias Oliveira and Maria Dorvalina; came to U.S., 1968; B.S., Fed. U. Rio Grande do Sul, Brazil, 1963; M.S., Fed. U., Bahia, Brazil, 1965; M.S., N.Y.U., 1972; m. Liana Bloisi, Oct. 23, 1968. Cons. for drilling and prodn. crude oil Petrobras, Salvador, Bahia, Brazil, 1965-68; protective coatings and materials specialist Ebasco Services Inc., N.Y.C., 1968—; also cons.

Registered profl. engr., Calif. Mem. Nat. Assn. Corrosion Engrs., Am. Inst. Metall. Engrs., Iron and Steel Soc., Am. Water Works Assn., Brazilian Assn. Profl. Engrs. Home: 345 E 56th St New York City NY 10022 Office: 2 Rector St New York City NY 10006

OLIVER, CHARLES, consulting firm exec.; b. Cohocton, N.Y., May 12, 1915; s. Charles and Fannie Elizabeth (Snyder) O.; A.B. in Edn., U. Ala., 1936; m. Constance Marium Crites, Mar. 5, 1942; children—Charles, Mary Constance, Thomas George, Theodore Kent. With Corning Glass Works, Corning, N.Y., 1936-72, mgr. market research Indsl. and Tech. Products Div., 1960-72; pres. Charles Oliver Co., Corning, 1972—. Pres. Steuben Area council Boy Scouts Am., 1966-67; pres. Corning Painted Post Hist. Soc., 1973-74; mem. mayor's com. Market St. Restoration, Corning; historian Steuben County, 1976—. Recipient Silver Beaver award Boy Scouts Am., 1960. Mem. Am. Mktg. Assn. (Spl. Achievement award 1970), Med. Surg. Market Research Group, Assn. Records Mgrs. and Adminstrs. Club: Kiwanis. Home and office: 66 Catherine St Corning NY 14830

OLIVER, ROBERT EDWARD, communications cons.; b. Brough, Eng., Oct. 1, 1913; s. Harry Ernest and Lilian (Vincent) O.; came to Can., 1914, naturalized, 1945; student pub. schs. Ottawa, Ont., Can.; m. H. Winnifred Colton; children—Douglas Robert, Margaret Ellen. Prin. Bear Brook Continuation Sch., Carleton County, Can., 1936-39; sect. head Govt. of Can., Ottawa, 1939-43; advt. mgr. R. L. Crain Ltd., Ottawa, 1943-46; asst. pub. relations mgr. Bank of Montreal (Que.), 1946-48; research mgr. office pub. relations Ford Motor Co. of Can., Windsor, Ont., 1948-50, asst. dir. office pub. relations, 1950-56; supr. pub. relations and advt. Bank of N.S., (Can.), Toronto, 1956-66; prin. Robert E. Oliver & Assn., Toronto, 1966—; pres. Canadian Advt. Advisory Bd., Toronto, Ont., 1967—. Vice-pres. Ont. Welfare Council, 1960-63; bd. dirs. Canadian Mental Health League, 1964-66. Recipient Gold Medal award Assn. Canadian Advertisers, 1974; named Advt. Person of Year Canadian Advt. and Sales Assn., 1976. Mem. Canadian Club, Inst. Assn. Execs., Canadian Pub. Relations Soc., Toronto Bd. Trade, Canadian Council Internat. C. of C. Club: Toronto Press. Author: A Canadian Christmas Carol, 1967; Shopping Sense, 1976; (with M.J. Daypuk) Money Matters 1974—; (with R.B. Collett) Advertising At Work In The Modern Marketplace, 1976. Home: 52 Chelford Rd Don Mills ON M3B 2E5 Canada Office: 1240 Bay St Suite 302 Toronto ON M5R 2A7 Canada

OLIVER, ROBERT ROBINS, advt., pub. relations exec.; b. N.Y.C., Oct. 20, 1912; s. Elmer Wesley and Edith Isabel (Robins) O.; B.A., Colgate U., 1935; student economics, journalism Columbia, 1936-37; m. Mary Lucas Hart, May 12, 1944; children—Judith Oliver Gordon, Robert R. Copy writer, account exec. N.W. Ayer & Co., N.Y.C., 1937-39; exec. asst., advt. mgr. Internat. Flavors & Fragrances Inc., N.Y.C., 1939-54; pres., prin. Oliver-Beckman Inc., N.Y.C., 1954—; also dir. subsidiaries in Italy, Germany, U.K.; dir. Palmer & Oliver Inc. Mem. Brookhaven Indsl. Devel. Commn., 1963—; dep. mayor, trustee, commr. Village of Shoreham, N.Y., 1960-72; founding dir. N.Y. State Job Devel. Bank, Brookhaven/Suffolk County. Served to lt. comdr. USCG, 1941-45. Mem. Pub. Relations Soc. Am., Nat. Trust Historic Preservation, Smithsonian Inst. (asso.), Asia Soc. (mem. council), Sons of Revolution, U.S. Coast Guard Assn., Vet. Corps Artillery (7th Regiment N.Y. Nat. Guard), Scotch-Irish Soc. Am., Royal Yachting Assn. (U.K.), English Speaking Union. Republican. Episcopalian. Clubs: Overseas Press, N.Y. Yacht, Shoreham Country (pres., dir.), Royal Ulster Yacht (U.K.). Home: 250 E 73d St New York City NY 10021 Office: 120 E 56th St New York City NY 10022

OLIVERE, PETER JOHN, radiologist; b. Wilmington, Del., July 14, 1913; s. Peter C. and Mary C. O.; M.D., Georgetown U., 1934, M.D., 1937; postgrad in radiology U. Pa., 1946; m. Mary A. Davolos, Dec. 19, 1946; children—Peter J. 3d, Christina M., Mary Lucia. Intern, Del. Hosp., Wilmington, 1937-38, Union Meml. Hosp., Balt., 1938-39; resident Grad. Hosp. U. Pa., 1945; asst. radiologist Del. Hosp., Wilmington, 1939-42, asso. radiologist, 1945-46; dir. radiology St. Francis Hosp., Wilmington, 1946-69; practice medicine specializing in diagnostic radiology, Wilmington, 1946—; cons. radiologist Del. State Hosp. Served with U.S. Army, 1942-45. Deplomate Am. Bd. Radiology. Mem. Am. Coll. Radiology, Radiol. Soc. N. Am., AMA, Med. Soc. Del., New Castle County Med. Soc., Radiol. Soc. Del. Home: 304 Rockwood Rd Wilmington DE 19802 Office: 1003 Delaware Ave Wilmington DE 19806

OLIVERE, RAYMOND LOUIS, artist; b. Wilmington, Del., Aug. 31, 1924; s. Louis Ronald and Natalie Adele (Caldara) O.; student Wilmington Acad. Art, 1934, N.C. Wyeth, Frank Schoonover, 1939-40, Art Students League, 1947-48; m. Kathryn Howett, May 9, 1949 (dec. 1964); children—Marc, Laura, Gina; m. 2d, Betty Field, Mar. 22, 1968 (dec. 1973). Exhibited paintings Audubon Artists Assn., N.Y.C., 1972, NAD, N.Y.C., 1973, Nat. Arts Club, N.Y.C., 1975, 76, 77, Allied Artists Am., N.Y.C., 1976, Am. Soc. of Painters in Casein and Acrylics, N.Y.C., 1977; also numerous exhbns., N.Y. and Wilmington; portrait painter numerous stage celebrities; illustrator nat. mags., advt. tchr. painting. Served to 1st lt. as med. illustrator, artist with entertainment unit AUS, World War II. Howard Pyle scholar, 1934-41. Home: 1435 Lexington Ave New York City NY 10028

OLMSTED, ROBERT AMSON, civil engr.; b. N.Y.C., Nov. 7, 1924; s. Harold M. and Sophia (Amson) O.; student Princeton U., 1943-44; B.C.E., Cornell U., 1946; M.C.E., Poly. Inst. Bklyn., 1953; m. Pauline Weiner, June 25, 1949; children—Elizabeth, Alan, Lawrence. Jr. civil engr. Triborough Bridge and Tunnel Authority, 1946-49; civil engr. Port of N.Y. Authority, 1949-51; engr. Tippetts-Abbett-McCarthy-Stratton, 1951-62; transp. engr. N.Y. State Office Transp., 1962-67; asst. dir. planning Met. Transp. Authority, N.Y.C., 1967—; lectr. transp. planning Poly. Inst. Bklyn., 1966-70; adj. prof. Manhattan Coll., 1975—. Served with AUS, 1943-46. Mem. ASCE (exec. com. N.Y. met. transp. group 1969-74, sec. N.Y. met. urban planning group 1971—, dir. met. sect. 1974-76), Inst. Transp. Engrs., Met. Assn. Urban Designers and Environ. Planners (v.p., dir. 1970—). Home: 33-04 91st St Jackson Heights NY 11372 Office: 1700 Broadway New York City NY 10019

OLNEY, JULIAN FREDERICK, JR., investment exec.; b. White Plains, N.Y., Dec. 24, 1929; s. Julian Frederick and Dorothy (McGrayne) O.; B.A., Dartmouth, 1951; M.B.A., N.Y. U., 1955; m. Andrea Helen Dombrowski, Oct. 5, 1968; children—Julianna, Cheryl. Comml. banker Chem. Bank, 1953-57; investment banker Arnold Bernhard & Co., Inc., 1957-60, A.G. Becker & Co., Inc., 1961-62, F. Eberstadt & Co., Inc., 1965-68; chief fin. officer Creative Playthings, Inc., 1962-65, Telecheck Internat., 1970; venture capitalist, investor, 1968-70; assn. with others as investor, Warwick, R.I., 1971—; dir. CompuScan, Inc. Active YMCA; founder Warwick Mus. Served with CIC, U.S. Army, 1951-53. Mem. N.Y. Soc. Security Analysts, Inst. Chartered Fin. Analysts. Roman Catholic. Home: 5 Loewen Ct Rye NY 10580

OLNEY, WILLIAM SALISBURY, univ. ofcl.; b. Rochester, N.Y., June 14, 1924; s. Burt Cady and Harriet Edith (Salisbury) O.; A.B., Harvard U., 1946, postgrad. Inst. Ednl. Mgmt., 1970; m. Diana S. Forbes Rogers, Apr. 14, 1956; children—Diana S., Cynthia F.; stepchildren—William Bowditch Rogers, IV, Peter M. Rogers, John F. Rogers. Retail rep. Life Mag., Time Inc., N.Y.C., 1947-49, asst. to pub. Life Mag., 1951-52, asst. to pres. Time Inc., 1949-51; account exec. Batten Barton Durstine & Osborne, N.Y.C., 1952-55, Benton & Bowles, N.Y.C., 1956-62; staff asso. pub. relations Earl Newsom & Co., N.Y.C., 1955-56; univ. devel. officer Harvard U., 1962—. Asst. treas. Nat. Citizens Commn. for Pub. Schs., 1949-50; pres. Winsor Sch. Corp., Boston, 1970-72. Served to lt. (j.g.) USNR, 1942-46. Mem. Soc. Colonial Wars, Council Advancement, Support Edn. Clubs: Amateur Ski of N.Y.; Harvard (N.Y.C. and Boston); North Haven (Maine) Yacht. Home: 900 High St Dedham MA 02026 Office: Holyoke Center 700 75 Mount Auburn St Cambridge MA 02138

O'LOANE, J(AMES) KENNETH, physicist; b. Walla Walla, Wash., Dec. 12, 1913; s. Kenneth and Mary Gertrude (Hoffman) O'L.; B.S., St. Benedict's Coll., 1935; M.S., U. Wash., 1944; M.A., Harvard, 1947, Ph.D., 1950; m. Barbara Gearhart, Mar. 31, 1943; children—Anne, Lawrence, Marian, Philip. Jr. chemist Shell Devel. Co., Emeryville, Calif., 1943-45; asst. prof. U. N.H., Durham, 1948-54, asso. prof., 1954; with Eastman Kodak Co., Rochester, N.Y., 1954—, research asso., chem. div., research labs., 1964—. Mem. lay adv. bd., supt. schs. Diocese of Rochester, 1962-68, mem. diocesan pastoral council, 1975—; mem. lay adv. bd. Catherine McAuley Coll. Rochester, 1966-69; mem. N.Y., Nat. bds. Citizens for Ednl. Freedom, 1962—. Served with AUS, 1938-41. Mem. Am. Chem. Soc., Am. Phys. Soc., Optical Soc. Am., Urban League, Common Cause, Cath. League Religious and Civil Rights, Sigma Xi, Phi Lambda Upsilon, Pi Mu Epsilon. Democrat. Home: 331 Seneca Pkwy Rochester NY 14613 Office: Eastman Kodak Co Research Labs B81 Rochester NY 14650

OLOFFSON, WERNER OLAF, advt. cons., artist; b. Haiti, June 21, 1905; s. Walter Gustav and Margot (Tippenhauer) O.; grad. high sch.; Practical Aviation certificate N.Y. U., 1933. Came to U.S., 1929, naturalized, 1935. Tech. purchasing accounts. Pan Am.-Grace Airways, N.Y.C., 1931-37; profl. service dir., export mgr. Wyeth Labs, Phila., 1938-45; v.p. Cortez F. Enloe, Inc., 1954-57; copy and tech. cons. Ogilvy & Mather, Inc., 1959-62; copy chief, sci. dir. med. div. Ted Bates & Co., William Douglas McAdams, N.Y.C., 1962—. Cons. in field; exhibited one man shows painting, Hamburg, Germany, 1958, Monte Carlo, 1959, N.Y.C., 1960, 61, 74; exhibited numerous group shows including Jury Shows, N.Y.C., 1942—, Phila., 1961—. Mem. Queens County Criminal Grand Jury, 1964—. Mem. Am. Watercolor Soc., Assn. Psychophysiol. Study Sleep, Nat. Soc. Lit. and Arts, Am. Artists Profl. League, N.Y. Acad. Scis., AAAS, Pharm. Advt. Club. Club: Salmagundi. Address: 35-33 83d St Jackson Heights NY 11372

O'LOUGHLIN, ALIDA J. KOLK, ednl. exec.; b. The Hague, Holland, May 21, 1930; d. Sieger Jacob and Wilhelmina (Olijslag) Kolk; M.A., U. Mass., 1953; postgrad. N.Y. U.; m. Francis J. O'Loughlin, 1955 (div. 1969); children—Wilhelmina Agnes, Joseph Seeger, Janna Margaret. Hydraulic engring. asst. Hydraulic Lab., Delft, Holland, 1947-51; FLES instr. French Lesley-Ellis Sch., Cambridge, 1962-64; exec. sec. Boston office Expt. in Internat. Living, 1963-64, dir., 1964-70; dir. Cambridge Center for Adult Edn., 1970—; cons. Action for Boston Community Devel., 1970—. Chmn. Harvard Sq. Devel. Task Force; v.p. Met. Cultural Alliance; bd. dirs. Cambridge Community Services; mem. adv. bd. Cambridge Arts Council, New Eng. Folk Arts Center. Mem. Harvard Sq. Bus. Assn., N.A.A.C.P., World Affairs Council, Netherlands Acad. Circle, Am. Acad. Polit. and Social Sci., Adult Edn. Assn., NOW. Home: 101 Aberdeen Ave Cambridge MA 02138 Office: 42 Brattle St Cambridge MA 02138

O'LOUGHLIN, THOMAS JOSEPH, JR., freight co. exec.; b. Lowell, Mass., May 24, 1927; s. Thomas Joseph and Margaret (Drumm) O'L.; certificate Internat. Corr. Schs., 1948; student Boston U., 1949-50, Northeastern U., 1950-54, St. Anselm's Coll., 1959; m. Jeanne A. Demers, June 10, 1950; children—Deborah, Amy, Thomas Joseph, Matthew. Asst. traffic mgr. Johns Manville Corp., Nashua, N.H., 1945-50; traffic mgr. Wonalancet Co., Nashua, 1950-51; traffic mgr. Law Motor Freight, Inc., Nashua, 1951-64, v.p. traffic, 1964—; v.p. traffic Bulk Haulers, Inc., Nashua, 1964—; gen. mgr. Law Warehouses, Inc., Nashua, 1955—; pres. HaT Enterprises, Inc., Nashua, 1967—; pres. L.H. Hardy Book Bindery, Inc., Hudson; dir. Lawpool, Inc., Nashua; lectr. distbn.-traffic mgmt. St. Anselm's Coll., 1957—, chmn. Ann. Transp. Seminar, 1958—. Troop chmn. Boy Scouts Am., Hudson, N.H., 1954-56; chmn. Nashua/Hudson Heart Fund drive, 1960; mem. Citizens Task Force N.H., 1969. Mem. Assn. ICC Practitioners (pres. New Eng. dist. 1 chpt. 1976-77), Nat. Def. Transp. Assn., New Eng. Shipper-Carrier Conf. (pres. 1973), Eastern Central Motor Carriers Assn. (gen. rate com. 1960—), New Eng. Council (chmn. traffic com. 1976—), Traffic Club N.Y., Delta Nu Alpha. Republican. Roman Catholic (mem. pastoral council 1972—, diocesan council laity 1970-71). Clubs: K.C., Serra (pres. 1969 Nashua). Contbr. column to PFM mag., 1972—. Home: 18 Baker St Hudson NH 03051 Office: Airport Rd Nashua NH 03060

OLSEN, DOUGLAS RAYMOND, stationer, bookseller; b. S.I., N.Y., Oct. 9, 1932; s. Trygve and Cecelia (Matheson) O.; B.Ch.E., Poly. Inst. Bklyn., 1953; m. Janet Irene Ernst, Mar. 3, 1956; children—Mark, Susan. Research engr. Allied Chem. Co., Morristown, N.J., 1953, 55-59; process engr. FMC Corp., N.Y.C., 1959-62, program engr., 1962-67, supr. engring. services, 1967-70; mgr. div. Kinser Assos., ednl. material, Pawling, N.Y., 1970-71; owner, operator Kent Stationery (Conn.), 1971—; lectr., cons. on cost and schedule control methods for maj. capital projects. Republican committeeman, Richmond, N.Y., 1965-68; mem. Pawling Sch. Bd., 1973—; pres. Christ the King Luth. Ch., Pawling, 1974, 75. Served with U.S. Army, 1953-55. Mem. Am. Booksellers Assn., Nat. Office Products Assn., Kent C. of C., Lambda Chi Alpha. Publisher: The Appalachian Trail Through Kent, Connecticut, 1972. Patentee chem. engring. Home: North Quaker Hill Pawling NY 12564 Office: PO Box 216 Kent Green Kent CT 06757

OLSEN, HERMAN ELMER, chiropractor; b. Gilford, N.H., Apr. 16, 1925; s. Elmer Herman and Marion Kathryn (Hoyt) O.; Dr. Chiropractic, Palmer Coll. Chiropractic, 1952; m. Evamarie Covey, June 19, 1946; children—Nancy Sonja Olsen Smith, Katherine Marion (dec.), Gregory David. Practice chiropractic, Berlin, N.H., 1952-54, Meredith, N.H., 1954—. Chmn. finance com. YMCA, Meredith; past chmn. finance com. Daniel Webster council Boy Scouts Am., 1957-62. Served with U.S. Army, 1943-46; ETO. Fellow Internat. Coll. Chiropractic; mem. Am. (past chmn. ins. cons. div., past chmn. commn. ins.; v.p. 1977-78), N.H. (v.p. 1960-62, pres. 1962-64, dir. 1956-60, del. to Am. Chiropractic Assn. 1970-77, chmn. continued edn., mem. peer rev. com.) chiropractic assns. Clubs: Jesters (dir.), Masons (32 deg.), Rotary (pres. 1963-64). Home and Office: 37 Main St Meredith NH 03253

OLSEN, ROBERT JOHN, savs. and loan assn. exec.; b. N.Y.C., July 8, 1928; s. Christian Marinius and Agnes Geraldine (Jensen) O.; B.S., Strayer Coll., D.C., 1956; m. Lois Claudette Trumble, Apr. 18, 1959; children—Duanne Mara, Bradley Stephen, Russell John. Supervisory agt. Fed. Home Loan Bank Bd., N.Y.C., 1956-65; pres., dir. Keystone Savs. & Loan Assn., Asbury Park, N.Y., 1965—; chmn. bd., pres. Rapid Money Services Inc., Deal, N.J., 1977—; dir. Central Corp. Savs. and Loan Assns., Newark; N.J. trustee Savs. and Loan Found. Councilman, Borough of Oceanport, N.J., 1971-73, 77—; bd. dirs. Econ. Devel. Corp., Asbury Park, N.J., 1972—; police commr. Borough of Oceanport (N.J.), 1972—; mem. Zoning Bd. of Adjustment, Oceanport, 1969-70; dir. Monmouth and Ocean Devel. Council, Eatontown, N.J., 1974-77; mem. Citizen's Adv. Council, Oceanport, N.J., 1975-76. Served with USMC, 1946-48, 1950-56. Mem. N.J. Savs. League (pres. chpt. 1966-67, chmn. electronic funds transfer com. 1971—), U.S. Savs. League (chmn. com. on remote service units, vice chmn. com. on internal ops.), Nat. Soc. Controllers and Fin. Officers, Monmouth County, Ocean County realtors assns., Nat. Assn. State Savs. and Loan Suprs. (asso. rep. N.E. U.S. to adv. council), Nat. Soc. Fin. Execs., Brevet Provost Marshal's Guild, C. of C. Asbury Park, Navy League, AUS Aux. Clubs: Rotary, Channel (Monmouth Beach, N.J.); Wheelmans (Asbury Park); World Trade (N.Y.C.). Home: 67 Hiawatha Ave Port-au-Peck NJ 07757 Office: 440 Cookman Ave Asbury Park NJ 07712

OLSEN, ROBERT LESLIE, banker; b. Boston, Feb. 13, 1928; s. Otto E. and Iva (Brown) O.; grad. arts scis. U. Me., 1946-48; grad. Stonier Sch. Banking, Rutgers State U., 1960-63; m. Phyllis Hope Brow, Nov. 28, 1950; children—Sally Phyllis, Cheryl Ann. With Phoenix Mut. Life Ins. Co., 1948-49, Comml. Credit Corp., 1950-55, Ashuelot-Citizens Nat. Bank, Keene, N.H., 1955-59; with Tompkins County Trust Co., Ithaca, N.Y., 1959-73, v.p., 1964-73; exec. v.p. Citizens Central Bank, Arcade, N.Y., 1973, pres. 1974-76; pres., chief exec. officer, trust officer, dir. First Nat. Bank of Hancock (N.Y.), 1976—. Instr., Am. Inst. Banking, 1950—. Treas., Ithaca (N.Y.) YMCA, 1960; pres. West Ithaca Civic Assn., 1969-70; chmn. bus. div. United Fund, Ithaca, 1962; chmn. adv. bd. Salvation Army, Ithaca, 1973—; mem. Wyoming County Health Orgn., 1974—; mem. Wyoming County Bd. Health, 1975—. Mem. City Council Keene, 1958-59. Trustee Tompkins County Meml. Hosp., Ithaca, 1964—, pres. bd. trustees, 1967—, mem. bd. mgrs., 1973-74. Served with USNR, 1945-46, USMCR, 1950-51. Recipient Outstanding Service award United Fund, 1964. Mem. N.Y. State Bankers Assn. (div. chmn. 1971), Gen. Alumni Assn. U. Me. (chpt. pres. 1969-70, mem. alumni council 1974—). Republican. Methodist (treas. bd. trustees 1967—). Mason (32 deg.). Clubs: Delaware County Shrine (pres. 1977—), City (Ithaca, v.p. 1970-73). Home: 6 Risley St Hancock NY 13783 Office: First Nat Bank Hancock Main St Hancock NY 13783

OLSEN, THEODORA EGBERT PECK (MRS. SEVERT ANDREW OLSEN), artist; b. Union, N.J., Sept. 6, 1909; d. Edward Egbert and Theodorea G. (Tucker) Peck; student N.Y. Sch. Design, 1928-29, Phoenix Art Inst., N.Y.C., 1929-32, Coll. City N.Y., 1955; m. Ray Sheldon Wilbur, Sept. 8, 1933 (dec. Aug. 1966); 1 dau., Margaret Anne (Mrs. Prudhomme); m. 2d, Severt Andrew Olsen, July 17, 1967 (dec. Feb. 1975); stepchildren—Arlene Christine, Severt Eugene. Exhibited at Contemporary Gallery, Newark, 1932, S.I. Mus., 1947-65, N.Y.C. Fedn. Women's Clubs exhibit, 1961, Island Art Center Gallery, New Dorp, S.I., 1961, 33d N.J. Exhbn., Montclair Art Mus., 1964, Summit (N.J.) Art Center, 1965; outdoor shows at Sailors Snug Harbour, S.I., 1956-63, Greenwich Village, N.Y.C., 1961-64, Southhampton and Westhampton (L.I.) Beach, 1964, Summit Art Center, N.J., 1967, Spring Festival Arts, Staten Island, 1968; represented in permanent collection at Wagner Coll., S.I.; prin. works include View From Guild Hall, Show Case, Variation on Theme VIII, Long Island Expressway, Seed Pods, Emergence from Chrysalis. Cons., lectr., pvt. tchr., 1934—; tchr. painting YWCA, S.I., 1971-72. Active fund-raising Richmond Mem. Hosp., 1946-54, com. to beautify halls Tottenville (S.I.) High Sch., 1958-60. Recipient S.I. Mus.-Wagner Coll. Purchase award, 1958—; Julius Weisglass award S.I. Mus., 1960, 65; 1st prize and Honorable mention N.Y.C. Fedn. Women's Clubs competition, 1961. Founder, hon. life mem. S. Shore Artists Group (pres. 1946-47, 49-61, 2d v.p 1965-66); mem. S.I. Inst. Arts and Scis., S.I. Hist. Soc. Women's Aux., S.I. Hist. Soc., Pratt-Phoenix Art Inst. Alumni (jury awards 1949), Epsilon Nu Sigma. Clubs: South Shore Garden, Prince Bay Women's (pres. 1969-71); Coast Guard Officer's Wives. Home: 72 Bayview Ave Prince Bay NY 10309

OLSON, CARL ERIC, lawyer; b. Center Moriches, N.Y., May 19, 1914; s. August William and Sophie (Maiwald) O.; A.B., Union Coll., 1936; LL.B., Yale U., 1940; m. Ila Dudley Yeatts, May 31, 1945; children—Carl E., William Yeatts, Nancy Dudley. Admitted to Conn. bar, 1941, N.Y. State bar, 1947; asso. firm Clark, Hall & Peck, New Haven, 1940-41; asso. firm Reid & Priest, N.Y.C., 1946—, mem. firm, 1956—. Served with AUS, World War II. Mem. Am., N.Y., Inter-Am., Internat. bar assns., Soc. Internat. Law, City Bar Assn. N.Y., Am. Judicature Soc., Phi Beta Kappa, Delta Upsilon. Clubs: Lawyers, Yale (N.Y.C.). Home: 99 Birch Ln Manhasset NY 11030 Office: 40 Wall St New York City NY 10005

OLSON, CHARLES ERIC, economist; b. Wausau, Wis., June 2, 1942; s. Roland Anthony and Lois (Erickson) O.; student U. Wis., Marathon County, 1960-62; B.B.A. with honors, U. Wis., Madison, 1964, M.S., 1966, Ph.D. (Vilias fellow), 1968; m. Pamela Ann Templin, July 1, 1967 (div. Oct. 1973), children—Sonja Anne, Erika Christine; m. 2d, Carole Emily Collesian, Dec. 1, 1973; 1 dau., Cora Elizabeth. Instr., U. Wis., Madison, 1966-68; asst. prof. U. Md., College Park, 1968-71, asso. prof. bus. adminstrn., 1971-76; sr. economist H. Zinder & Assos., Washington, 1976—, v.p., 1977—. Cons. Devel. Advisory Service, atty. gens. N.C., Minn., Ky., Mass., Va. U.S. Postal Rate Commn., Dept. Def., City N.Y. Testified numerous pub. utility rate cases, before Senate Subcom. on Inter-govtl. Relations; mem. advisory com. research and devel. and energy conservation Fed. Power Commn., 1973-74, vice chmn. rate design task force, 1976—. Mem. Prince Georges County (Md.) Citizens Airpark Advisory Com., 1970-71. Inst. Pub. Utilities grantee, 1967-68; U. Md. grantee, 1970, 76. Mem. Am. Econ. Assn., Transp. and Pub. Utilities Group, Assn. for Evolutionary Econs., Am. Soc. Traffic and Transp. (dir. 1977—), Delta Sigma Pi. Author: Cost Considerations for Efficient Electricity Supply, 1970. Contbr. chpts. to books, articles to profl. jours. Home: 10822 Alloway Dr Potomac MD 20854 Office: 1828 L St NW Washington DC 20036

OLSON, DON CHARLES, civil engr.; b. Paton, Ia., Aug. 5, 1935; s. Leonard Melvin and Lucille Honor (Stark) O.; B.S. in Civil Engring., Ia. State U., 1956; M.S., Purdue U., 1972; m. Anna Solveig Margareta Lindgren, Oct. 24, 1970; children—Deanna Lynn, Deborah Ann, Anna Gabriella. Staff engr. Am. Oil Co., Whiting, Ind., 1956-67; project engr. Great Lakes Carbon Corp., Harnosand, Sweden, 1967-70, Berthierville, Que., Can., 1970-72, Niagara Falls, N.Y., 1972-77; project mgr. Carborundum Co., Niagara Falls, N.Y., 1977—. Bd. dirs. Jr. Achievement Niagara Frontier, 1972—, v.p. finance, 1976-77. Mem. Nat. Grape Growers Assn., U.S. Trotting Assn., Niagara Coop. Extension, W. N.Y. Harness Horsemen's Assn. Republican. Home: 3822 Lower Mountain Rd Lockport NY 14094 Office: PO Box 423 Niagara Falls NY 14302

OLSON, HAROLD ROY, mfg. co. exec.; b. Escanaba, Mich., Apr. 8, 1928; s. Roy A. and Sara Calla Margarita (Carlson) O.; B.A. in Journalism and Advt., Mich. State U., 1950; m. Angela Davis Hennessy, Sept. 26, 1959. Mail clk. McCann Erickson Co., N.Y.C., 1950, 52-53; book promotion specialist, mgr. mag. promotion McGraw-Hill, N.Y.C., 1953-56; mgr. mag. promotion Reinhold

Publishing Co., N.Y.C., 1956-58; space salesman McCall Corp., N.Y.C., 1959-60; pres. Visual Identity, Inc., N.Y.C., 1960-68; mktg. rep. Honeywell Info. Systems, Inc., N. N.Y.C., 1969—. Served with U.S. Army, 1950-52. Republican. Episcopalian. Home: 12 Stony Point Rd Westport CT 06880 Office: 1211 Ave of the Americas New York City NY 10036

OLSON, HARRY AXEL, psychologist; b. Phila., Dec. 5, 1944; s. Axel Niklas and Mary Dorothy (Ruffee) O.; student Phila. Coll. Bible, 1962-64; A.B., Temple U., 1966, Ed.M., 1968; student Lutheran Theol. Sem., Phila., 1966-67; Ph.D. (Nonservice fellow 1969-71), U. Tenn., 1972; m. Carol Wayne Martin, May 20, 1967; 1 son, David Barclay. Dir. residental treatment services Luth. Social Services, Balt., 1972-73; psychologist Spring Grove Hosp. Center, Catonsville, Md., 1973-74; dir. tng. Walter Pl Carter Center, Balt., 1974-78; practice psychology, Reisterstown, Md., 1973—; faculty Morton Prince Inst. Hypnotherapy, Md.-D.C. div., 1978—; part-time faculty mem. Johns Hopkins U., 1975—; vis. prof. Adler-Dreikurs Inst., Bowie (Md.) State Coll., 1976—; pres. Assos. for Profl. Devel., Inc.; co-founder, dir. Cons. to Encouragement, Inc., Balt. Fellow Md. Psychol. Assn. (chmn. human affairs com. div. 2, 1977-78); mem. Am. Psychol. Assn., Balt. Assn. Cons. Psychologists, N.Am. Soc. Adlerian Psychology, Individual Psychology Assn. Greater Washington, Encouragement, Inc. Lutheran. Club: Kiwanis. Author: Early Recollections: Their Use in Diagnosis and Psychotherapy, 1978; contbr. articles to profl. jours. Home: 708 Church Rd West Reisterstown MD 21136 Office: 313 Main St Reisterstown MD 21136

OLSON, JERRY CARL, supt. schs.; b. Brookville, Pa., Aug. 16, 1932; s. Carl and Charlotte (Knappenberger) O.; B.S., California (Pa.) State Coll., 1957; M.Ed., U. Pitts., 1960; Ph.D., Ohio State U., 1964; m. Virginia Haugh, Nov. 10, 1955; children—Phillip, Elizabeth Ann. Asst. supt. occupational-vocat.-tech. edn. Pitts. Pub. Schs., 1968-70, asst. supt. system-wide programs and services, 1970-73, acting supt., 1973, supt., 1973—; vis. prof. Oreg. State U., Corvallis, summers 1968-70, U. Minn., Mpls., summer 1971; adj. prof. U. Pitts., 1974-76; mem. edn. steering com. Graphic Arts Tech. Found., 1965-72. Bd. dirs. Jr. Achievement S.W. Pa., 1971—, Psychol. Service of Pitts., 1971—. Served with U.S. Army, 1953-54. Recipient spl. citation for leadership Wayne State U., 1968, certificate of recognition indsl. arts curriculum project Ohio State U., 1971, certificate of leadership recognition Am. Soc. Tng. and Devel., 1971. Mem. Epsilon Pi Tau, Phi Delta Kappa. Club: Pitts Press. Author: Plastics Technology: A Curriculum Resource Study, 1962; Graphic Communication Series, 8 textbooks, 1970. Mem. editorial advisory bd. Sch. Shop, 1970-72. Home: 5449 Fair Oaks St Pittsburgh PA 15217 Office: Pitts Pub Schs 341 S Bellefield Ave Pittsburgh PA 15213

OLSON, RALPH ARTHUR, neurosurgeon; b. Chgo., Jan. 1, 1927; s. Arthur G. and Margaret M. (Kumlin) O.; student U. Calif. at Berkeley, 1946; B.S., U. Ill., 1950, M.D., 1952, M.S., 1954; m. Lynn Hautman, Aug. 19, 1967; children—Kathleen, Leslie, Jonathan. Intern, U. Ill. Research and Ednl. Hosps., 1952-53; resident Northwestern U. Med. Center, 1953-55, Royal Victoria Hosp., Montreal, Que., Can., 1955-56, Neurol. Inst., Columbia Presbyn. Hosp., 1956-58; practice medicine specializing in neurosurgery, N.Y.C., 1958—; chief service Cabrini Med. Center; mem. staff Bellevue, St. Vincents, N.Y. Eye and Ear, Doctor's hosps.; asso. prof. clin. neurosurgery N.Y. U. Bd. dirs. Am. Cancer Soc., N.Y.C. Served to ensign USNR, 1944-46; now col. U.S. Army Res. Fellow A.C.S. Internat. Coll. Surgeons (past pres. N.Y. State surg. div. U.S. sect.); mem. Harvey Cushing Soc., N.Y. Neurosurg. Soc., Congress Neurol. Surgery, Am. Acad. Neurology, Aerospace Med. Assn., Soc. U.S. Army Flight Surgeons, Vet. Corps Arty. N.Y., N.Y. County Med. Soc., AMA, Order of Jerusalem, Order of Lafayette (dir.), Confederation des Anciens Combattants, Order Knights Hospitallers St. John, Sigma Xi. Clubs: Leash; Squadron A; Clay Hill; Paris-American. Address: 652 Park Ave New York City NY 10021

OLSON, ROBERT EDWARD, coal co. exec.; b. Phila., Aug. 5, 1927; s. Oscar E. and Marie B. (Kilgallen) O.; student U. Richmond, 1945, Duke, 1945-46, U. Pa., 1946; B.S. in Mining Engring., Pa. State U., 1952; m. Jean Emilie Wadsworth, Dec. 31, 1955; children—Grace, Nancy, Karen. Indsl. engr. Island Creek Coal Co., Holden, W.Va., 1952-55; treas., sr. asso. Coal Standards, Inc., mgmt. cons., Charleston, W.Va., 1955-61; v.p. adminstrn. Rochester & Pitts. Coal Co., Indiana, Pa., 1961—; dir. Helvetia Coal Co.; pres., dir. Iselin Preparation Co. Bd. dirs., vice chmn. Indiana County Municipal Service Authority; study advisory com. Southwestern Pa. Regional Planning Commn.; bd. dirs. Indiana County (Pa.) Devel. Corp., Pitts. Coal Mining Inst. Am.; mem. Indiana County Republican Exec. Com. Served with USNR, 1945-47. Mem. Central Pa. Coal Producers Assn. (dir.), Indiana County C. of C. (past pres., dir.). Episcopalian (past vestryman, sr. warden). Rotarian. Clubs: Indiana Country, Ingleside. Home: 250 N 12th St Indiana PA 15701 Office: 655 Church St Indiana PA 15701

OLSON, RONALD LEROY, fin. cons.; b. Waynesboro, Pa., Jan. 20, 1939; s. Tilman and Birdillia Ruth (Robertson) O.; B.S., Shippensburg State Coll., 1960; M.B.A., Ind. U., 1962, D.B.A., 1964; m. Margaret Joyce McNair, June 3, 1961; children—David M., Bradley T., Jennifer J. Asso. prof. finance and accounting U. Md., 1964-69; pres. Olson Research Assos., Silver Spring, Md., 1969—; mem. profl. adv. council Coll. Bus. and Mgmt., U. Md.; dir., trustee Inter City Hosp. Corp. Mem. exec. com. PTA, 1968—, Cub Scouts, 1970—. Mem. Am. Accounting Assn., Am. Inst. C.P.A.'s, Nat. Assn. Accountants. Republican. Methodist. Home: 2135 Edgewater Pkwy Silver Spring MD 20903 Office: 10750 Columbia Pike Silver Spring MD 20901

OLSON, WILLIAM CANNICOTT, educator; b. Oak Park, Ill., Aug. 1, 1943; s. Howard Kenneth and Grace (Cannicott) O.; B.A., Duke, 1965; M.A., U. N.C., 1968, Ph.D., 1974; 1 dau., Amanda Elizabeth. Tchr. social studies George Washington High Sch., Danville, Va., 1965-70; asso. prof. history Marist Coll., Poughkeepsie, N.Y., 1970—, chmn. dept. history, polit. sci. and criminal justice, 1975—; adj. prof. polit. sci. Ladycliff Coll., Highland Falls, N.Y., 1977—; cons. U.S. Office Edn. HEW, 1978—; bd. dirs. Rehab. Programs Inc., Poughkeepsie, N.Y., 1975—. Nat. Endowment for Humanities fellow, 1974. Mem. Am. Hist. Assn., Am. Polit. Sci. Assn., Soc. for Historians of Am. Fgn. Relations, Bus. History Conf., Phi Alpha Theta. Home: 14 W Dogwood Dr Poughkeepsie NY 12601 Office: Dept History and Polit Sci Marist Coll Poughkeepsie NY 12601

OLUGEBEFOLA, ADEMOLA, artist, educator; b. Charlotte Amalie, St. Thomas, V.I., Oct. 2, 1941; s. Harold Alexander Thomas and Golda Valencia (Matthias) O.; grad. Fashion Inst. Tech., 1961, Yoruba Acad., 1966; Ph.D. in Fine Art Devel. and History, Weusi Acad., 1969; m. Dec. 28, 1963 (div.); children—Mona, Monica, Tanyeni, Olori Rahim, Khari, Solar. Art dir. Pomusicart Inc., N.Y.C., 1962-65, Black Theatre Publs., N.Y.C., 1969-72; resident designer New Lafayette Theatre, 1969-72; dir. ednl. dept. Weusi Acad., N.Y.C., 1971—; artistic presentor Smithsonian Instn., 1976—; numerous exhbns. U.S., Africa, Caribbean. Bd. dirs. N.Y. Arts Consortium. Bd. dirs. Benin Enterprises. Recipient Achievement award Afro-Arts Cultural Center, 1968; Louis Noel Jones award Carnegie Inst., 1972. Mem. St. Croix Art Soc., Harlem Cultural Council (dir.), Nat. Conf. Artists, Nat. Arts Consortium. Fine and graphic artist; illustrator; book cover designer; set designer for theatrical and film prodns. Studio: Tetrahedron 250 W 72d St Suite 37 New York City NY 10023

OLYMPIA, JOSIE LIM, psychiatrist; b. Or. Mindoro, Philippines, Feb. 9, 1944; d. Pedro Gastro and Consuelo Roxas (Lim) Olympia; came to U.S., 1967; A.A., U. Philippines, 1962, M.D., 1967. Rotating intern Mt. Sinai Hosp., Milw., 1967-68; resident in psychiatry Buffalo Psychiat. Center, 1968-71; health officer designee Erie County, N.Y., 1973—; cons. psychiatrist N.Y. State Bur. Disability, 1974—; attending psychiatrist Western N.Y. Psychiat. Group, Niagara Falls Meml. Med. Center, 1975—; psychiatrist III, Buffalo Psychiat. Center, 1977—, dir. med. edn., 1977—; cons. Corp. II Mental Health Clinics; asst. clin. prof. State U. N.Y. Med. Sch., Buffalo. Diplomate Am. Bd. Psychiatry and Neurology. Mem. Am. Psychiat. Assn., N.Y. State Assn. Physicians and Dentists, Filipono-Am. Assn. Western N.Y. (v.p.). Roman Catholic. Home: 3342 Baseline Rd Grand Island NY 14072 Office: 400 Forest Ave Buffalo NY 14213

OMABOE, NARH, obstetrician and gynecologist; b. Accra, Ghana, Feb. 1, 1930; s. Nii Okwei and Emelia Aba (Schandorf) O.; came to Can., 1963; B.S., Wayne State U., 1955; M.D., U. Geneva, 1960; D.T.M., U. Marsailles, 1962; children—Nortey John, Norley Olga, Norkor, Cecil. Intern, St. Joseph's Hosp., Toronto, Ont., Can., 1960-61; resident Victoria Gen. Hosp., Halifax, N.S., Can., 1963-66; head dept. obstetrics and gynecology Trenton (Ont.) Meml. Hosp., 1970-74, pres. med. staff, 1976—; cons. in field, Trenton Meml. Hosp., Belleville (Ont.) Gen. Hosp. Diplomate Am. Bd. Obstetrics and Gynecology. Fellow Royal Coll. Obstetrics and Gynecology Can.; mem. Ont. Med. Assn., Soc. Obstetrics and Gynecology Can. Lodges: Flumen Luminis, Anemasse, France, Alpha, Toronto (affiliate). Contbr. articles to med. jours. Office: 30 King St Trenton ON K8V 5R5 Canada

O'MALLEY, EDWARD JOSEPH, JR., ednl. adminstr.; b. Flushing, N.Y., Jan. 4, 1942; s. Edward Joseph and Elsie Anne (Ende) O'M.; B.S., Widener Coll., 1963; M.B.A., St. Johns U., Jamaica, N.Y., 1976; m. Iris Theresa Hill, Aug. 10, 1975; stepchildren—James, Marc. Ins. agt. Liberty Mut. Ins. Co., N.Y.C., 1966-67; supr. group home Children's Village, Bayside, N.Y., 1967-69; unit head N.Y. Narcotic Addiction Control Commn., N.Y.C., 1970-71; exec. dir., sch. dist. drug abuse program, Howard Beach, N.Y., 1971—. Chmn., N.Y.C. Coalition Sch. Based Drug Prevention Programs; vice chmn. Comprehensive Health Planning Agy., Queens, N.Y.; mem. Queens Community Planning Bd.; past v.p. Flushing (N.Y.) Boys Club; past chmn. bd. dirs. Regular Democratic Club, Rockaway, N.Y.; mem. N.Y. State Dem. Com.; chmn. Rockaway Ind. Dems.; mem. St. Camillus Parish Council, Rockaway Task Force on Arts, Jamaica Bay Council, Far Rockaway chpt. NAACP; bd. dirs. Queens chpt. ARC. Mem. Emerald Assn. L.I., Beta Gamma Sigma. Roman Catholic. Club: Rockaway Kiwanis (past pres.). Home: 107 10 Shore Front Pkwy Rockaway Park NY 11694 Office: Howard Beach NY 11414

O'MALLEY, EDWARD PAUL, county ofcl.; b. Hudson, N.Y., May 30, 1926; s. Thomas Patrick and Helen Mary (Cornell) O'M.; B.S., St. John's U., 1949; M.S., Loyola U., Chgo., 1953, Ph.D., 1954; M.D., State U. N.Y., 1958; postgrad. Columbia U. Sch. Community Psychiatry, 1969. Intern, St. Vincent's Hosp., N.Y.C., 1958-59; resident Bronx VA Hosp., also N.Y. State Psychiat. Inst., Columbia-Presbyn. Med. Center, N.Y.C., 1959-62; psychiatrist Rikers Island Dept. Corrections, Bronx, N.Y., 1962-66, Riverside Hosp., Bronx, 1962-63, N.Y.C. Bur. Child Guidance, 1963-68, Catholic Charities Guidance Inst., N.Y.C., 1962-68; med. dir. West Nassau Mental Health Center, 1967-68; exec. dir. Suffolk County Community Mental Health Services, Farmingville, N.Y., 1968-70; commr. Orange County Dept. Mental Health, Goshen, N.Y., 1970—; asst. clin. prof. in psychiatry N.J. Med. Sch.; asst. psychiatrist St. Vincent's, N.Y.C., St. Francis Hosp., N.Y.C.; treas., bd. dirs. Neurol. Disease Found., 1964-68; asso. attending psychiatrist Bronx Lebanon Hosp.; courtesy staff psychiatrist Southampton Hosp. Mem. Suffolk County Narcotic Control Commn., 1968-70; asst. clin. prof. psychiatry State U. N.Y. Med. Sch. at Stony Brook, 1971—. Trustee United Fund L.I. Served to lt. comdr. USNR, 1959-62; now comdr. Res. USPHS fellow, 1953-54; Joseph Collens Found. scholar State U. N.Y. Downstate Med. Center, 1954-58. Diplomate Am. Bd. Psychiatry and Neurology. Fellow Am. Psychiat. Assn.; mem. AMA. Club: Orange County Golf. Contbr. articles to tech. jours. Home: 360 Central Park W New York City NY 10025 Office: Harriman Dr Goshen NY 10924

O'MALLEY, FRANCIS EDWARD, oral surgeon; b. Framingham, Mass., Feb. 20, 1917; s. Edward Francis and Margaret Louise (Desmond) O'M.; B.S., Boston Coll., 1943; D.D.S., Georgetown U. Med. Center, 1948; postgrad. Tufts New Eng. Med. Center, Boston, 1974-75. Oral surgery intern Kings County Hosp., Bklyn., 1948-49; practice oral surgery, Framingham, 1952—; chief dept. oral surgery Bethany Hosp., Framingham, 1963—, sec. med. staff, 1971—; staff Leonard Morse Hosp., Natick, Mass., 1971—, Framingham Union Hosp. Mem. Mountain Rescue Service, N.H. Served to 1st lt. AUS, 1951-52. Mem. Caths. United for Faith, Mt. Washington Obs., West Met. Dental Soc., Young Ams. for Freedom. Clubs: Appalachian Mountain (Boston); Randolph (N.H.) Mountain. Home: Randolph Hill Randolph NH 03593 Office: 151 Edgewater Dr Framingham MA 01701

O'MALLEY, JOHN EDWARD, child psychiatrist; b. Detroit, Oct. 27, 1942; s. Jack Patrick and Anne (Jones) O'M.; M.D., U. Mich., 1967; m. Carol Ann Dellicolli, Aug. 22, 1964; children—Dawn, April. Pediatric intern Johns Hopkins Hosp., 1967-68; resident child psychiatry Hawthorn Center, 1968-69; gen. psychiatry fellow Harvard Med. Sch., Mass. Gen. Hosp., 1969-71; child psychiatry research fellow, 1971-72; asst. prof. Harvard Med. Sch., Boston, 1974—; project dir. Sidney Farber Cancer Inst., Boston, 1975—; dir. continuing edn. Children's Hosp. Med. Center, Boston, 1977—; bd. mem. Thom Clinic, Boston, 1977—; cons. Emerson Hosp., Concord, Mass., 1975—. Served with U.S. Army, 1972-74. Johns Hopkins Med. Sch. fellow, 1967-68; Psychosocial Sequelae of Childhood Cancer grantee, 1975—. Diplomate Am. Bd. Psychiatry and Neurology. Mem. Am. Acad. Child Psychiatry, Am. Orthopsychiat. Assn., Am. Psychiat. Assn., New Eng. Council Child Psychiatry. Home: 300 Border Rd Concord MA 01742 Office: Sidney Farber Cancer Inst Boston MA 02115

O'MALLEY, JOHN WILLIAM, electronics co. exec.; b. Scranton, Pa., Sept. 5, 1932; s. William and Catherine Elizabeth (Mackin) O'Malley; B.S., U. Scranton, 1954; M.S., U. Del., 1956; postgrad. Loyola Coll., 1976—; m. Jo Etta Russell, Dec. 7, 1957; children—Mark, Sean, Megan. Design engr. Sperry Gyroscope Co., Great Neck, N.Y., 1956-57; sales engr. Ingersoll Rand Corp., Scranton, 1957-60; instr. physics U. Scranton, 1958-59; with IBM Corp., 1960—, various positions, Owego, N.Y. and Bethesda, Md., 1960-78, v.p. shipboard and def. systems, Manassas, Va., 1978—. Mem. Air Force Assn., Army U.S.A. Assn., Navy League, Nat. Space Club, Nat. Security Indsl. Assn., Am. Def. Preparedness Assn., Aerospace Industries Assn., Am. Inst. Aeros. and Astronautics, Electronic Industries Assn., Armed Forces Communications and Electronics Assn. Roman Catholic. Clubs: Lakewood Country, K.C., Elks. Home: 9616 Falls Bridge Ln Potomac MD 20854 Office: IBM Corp 9500 Godwin Dr Manassas VA 22110

O'MALLEY, RITA HELEN, mfg. co. exec.; b. Worcester, Mass., May 19, 1913; d. William and Bridget (Reynolds) O'M.; grad. Becker Bus. Coll., 1932. With L. Farber Co., South Worcester, 1934—, adminstrv. mgr., 1939—, traffic mgr., 1943—; v.p., clk. Nacy Enterprises, Inc., Ogunquit, Maine; dir. Progressive Shippers, Inc., Worcester. Mem. Worcester Democratic City Com., sec. Ward 3; former mem. Mass. Dem. State Com. for 2d Worcester dist.; trustee Mental Health Assn. Worcester. Recipient Achievement award Worcester chpt. Sons of Italy. Mem. Adminstrn. Mgmt. Assn. (past pres., Diamond merit award), Self-Made Millionaires Charitable Soc. (New Eng. chpt.), Worcester Profl. Bus. Women's Club, Internat. Mgmt. Soc., Cath. Daus. Am. (past grand regent Bishop O'Leary ct.), Calvary Guild Pasionist Fathers Retreat Center (past pres.), Worcester Sci. Center, Worcester Art Mus., Worcester Mechanics Hall Assn., Altrusa, Delta Nu (past pres. Worcester chpt.). Clubs: Cath. Women's (past pres.); Lehigh (Fla.) Acres Country. Home: 23 Duncannon Ave Worcester MA 01604 also Estes Lak Sanford ME 04073 Office: 158-60 Fremont St South Worcester MA 01603

O'MARA, JOSEPH JAMES, clin psychologist; b. Meadville, Pa., Jan. 29, 1938; s. Thomas Joseph and Ada Rosanna (Riordan) O'Mara Shiffer; B.A., Allegheny Coll., 1959; M.A., Kent State U., 1964; Ph.D., Duquesne U., 1973. Clin. psychologist Polk (Pa.) State Sch. and Hosp., 1962-66; asst. dir. psychology Western State Sch. and Hosp., Cannonsburg, Pa., 1966-69; clin. psychologist Hamot Community Mental Health Center, Erie, Pa., 1970-77, clin. team leader adult outpatients, 1973-77; asst. dir. psychology, chief geriatric psychology Warren (Pa.) State Hosp., 1977—. Research dir., socio-legal subcom. Pa. Supreme Ct. Com. on Proposed Standard Jury Instructions, 1969—. Treas. N.W. Pa. Cleft-Palate Inst., Hamot Med. Center, 1970-77; bd. dirs. Pa. Mental Health, Inc., Phila., 1971-78. Recipient Pa. Profl. Edn. stipend, 1962, 63, 64. Mem. Am., Pa., N.W. Pa. psychol. assns., Am. Assn. Mental Deficiency. Club: Aviation Country (Erie). Contbr. articles to profl. jours. Home: 301 Bird Ave Warren PA 16365 Office: Warren State Hosp Warren PA 16365

OMATA, ROBERT ROKURO, govt. ofcl.; b. Hanford, Calif., Nov. 3, 1920; s. George Jitsuzo and Kane (Okazaki) O.; A.B., U. Calif. at Berkeley, 1944; M.S., U. Minn., 1946, Ph.D. (NIH predoctoral fellow), 1949; m. Hiroko Kamikawa, Nov. 25, 1948; children—Douglas, Roberta, Donna. Research asso. Nat. Inst. Dental Research, NIH, USPHS, Bethesda, Md., 1949-53, 53-60, USPHS, 1953—; sci. adminstr. div. research grants, 1960-63, sci. adminstr. office internat. research, 1963-68, asst. chief NIH Pacific office U.S. Embassy, Tokyo, Japan, 1964-67, head internat. fellowship sect. Fogarty Internat. Center, Bethesda, 1968-74; internat. program specialist, office internat. affairs Nat. Cancer Inst., 1974—, also exec. sec. U.S.-Japan coop. cancer research program. Am. Dental Assn. postdoctoral fellow, 1949-53. Mem. Am. Soc. Microbiology, AAAS, Sigma Xi. Office: Office Internat Affairs Nat Cancer Inst NIH Bethesda MD 20014

O'MEARA, FRANCIS EDMUND, govt. ofcl.; b. N.Y.C., Aug. 8, 1923; s. Dennis S. and Frances (Kennedy) O'M.; B.S., U. Mich., 1947; m. Alwine Johanna Moritz, Nov. 23, 1944 (div. 1971); children—Kathleen, Terese, Dennis, Tyche, Christine, Michael. Physicist, Nuclear Energy for Propulsion Aircraft Project, Oak Ridge, 1947-51, Bendix Research Lab., Detroit, 1951-54; ops. analyst Dept. Def. and AEC, Omaha, 1954-57, Washington, 1957-63; mgr. evaluation missile and space system div. McDonnell-Douglas Corp., Santa Monica, Calif., 1963-71; dir. programs and budget NOAA, 1972—. Investment counsel Calif., 1965-71. Served to 1st lt. USAAF, 1943-46. Fellow AAAS, Am. Inst. Aeros. and Astronautics (asso.). Author: The New Age, 1962. Contbr. articles to profl. jours. Home: 203 Mannakee St Rockville MD 20850 Office: 6010 Executive Blvd Rockville MD 20852

O'MEARA, PETER HUGUET, state ofcl.; b. Boston, Sept. 6, 1946; s. Daniel L. and Yvonne (Huguet) O'M.; A.B., Villanova U., 1968; M.Social Planning, Boston Coll., 1972; postgrad. Boston State Coll., Wiedener Coll., Pa. State Coll., U. Pitts.; m. Susan Lamantia, May 21, 1976. Program specialist Mass. Dept. Pub. Welfare, 1970-72; dir. social and rehabilitative services Pa. Dept. Pub. Welfare, Spring City, 1972—; v.p. cons. div. Medacert Inc.; instr. Pa. State U. Mem. Chester County Task Force on Spl. Edn. Licensed nursing home adminstr., Pa. Mem. Am. Inst. Mental Deficiency. Home: Tara PO Box 264 Hereford PA 18056 Office: Pennhurst Center Spring City PA 19475

OMMAYA, AYUB KHAN, neurosurgeon; b. Pakistan, Apr. 14, 1930; s. Sultan Nadir and Ida (Counil) Khan; came to U.S., 1961, naturalized, 1968; M.D., U. Punjab (Pakistan), 1953; M.A., Oxford (Eng.) U., 1956; children—David, Alexander, Shana. Intern, Mayo Hosp., Lahore, Pakistan, 1953-54; resident in neurosurgery Radcliffe Infirmary, Oxford, 1954-61; vis. scientist NIH, Bethesda, Md., 1961-63, asso. neurosurgeon, 1963-68, head sect. applied research, 1968-74, chief neurosurgery, 1973—; clin. prof. George Washington U. Med. Sch., 1970—; cons. VA, Armed Forces Radiobiology Research Inst.; mem. panel psychosurgery Nat. Commn. Protection Human Rights in Med. Research. Rhodes scholar, 1954-59; recipient J.W. Kirkdaldy prize Oxford U., 1956. Mem. Soc. Neurosci., Pan Am. Med. Assn. (life), Am. Assn. Neurol. Surgeons, Research Soc. Neurosurgeons, ASME, Brit. Soc. Neurol. Surgeons (corr.), Internat. Brain Research Orgn. Moslem. Author articles, chpts. in books. Home: 8901 Burning Tree Rd Bethesda MD 20034 Office: 5454 Wisconsin Ave Chevy Chase MD 20015

O'MORRISON, KEVIN, playwright; b. St. Louis, May 25, 1916; s. Sean E. and Dori Elizabeth (Adams) O'M.; privately educated; m. Linda Soma, Apr. 30, 1966. Author: (plays) The Realist, 1968, Three Days Before Yesterday, 1965, Requiem, 1969, The Morgan Yard, 1970, A Report to Stockholders, 1975, Ladyhouse Blues, 1975, Dark Ages, 1978; (TV plays) The House of Paper, 1959, A Sign for Autumn, 1962, And Not a Word More, 1960, Pompeii . . . One Day before Yesterday; (radio version) Ladyhouse Blues; (novel) Something Perfect; actor (film) The Set-Up, 1948, in PBS prodn. The Watergate Coverup Trial, 1975; vis. prof. U. Mo., Kansas City, 1976; artist-in-residence numerous univs. and colls. Served with USAAF, 1943-45. Creative Artists Pub. Service fellow, 1975. Mem. Dramatists Guild, Writers Guild Am., Actors Equity Assn., Screen Actors Guild, AFTRA. Clubs: Players, Lambs (N.Y.C.). Address: The Players 16 Gramercy Park New York City NY 10003

ONA, FERNANDO VILLALOBOS, physician; b. Philippines, July 1, 1944; s. Melchor and Martina O.; came to U.S., 1967; M.D., U. Santo Tomas (Philippines), 1967; m. Celia, June 14, 1969; children—Eric, Mel Angelo. Intern, Perth Amboy (N.J.) Gen. Hosp., 1967-68; resident in internal medicine VA Hosp., Boston, 1968-70, resident in gastroeneterology, 1970-71, resident in gastroenterology Boston City Hosp., 1971-72, New Eng. Center Hosp., Boston, 1972-73; clin. asst. prof. medicine U. N.C., Chapel Hill, 1973-74; head gastro-intestinal unit, asst. prof. medicine U. Rochester, 1974—. Diplomate Am. Bd. Internal Medicine with Subsplty. in gastroenterology. Mem. A.C.P., Am. Gastroenterology Assn. Roman

Catholic. Home: 70 Deer Creek Rd Pittsford NY 14534 Office: 89 Genesee St Rochester NY 14611

O'NAN, MARTHA, educator; b. Shelbyville, Ky., June 28, 1921; d. Samuel Gross and Mary S. (Mays) O'Nan; B.A., Agnes Scott Coll., 1941; M.A., U. Ky., 1942; Ph.D., Northwestern U., 1952; diploma Universite de Paris, 1953. Instr. Spanish, Pikeville Coll., 1942-44, Jacksonville Coll., 1944-46; asst. prof. Centre Coll., 1946-48; chmn. French, Elmhurst Coll., 1951-54; asso. prof. to chmn. modern langs. Millikin U., 1956-63; asso. prof., then prof. modern langs. Ohio U., asst. chmn. modern langs., 1964-69; prof., chmn. fgn. langs. State U. N.Y., Brockport, 1969—; evaluator Middle States Assn. Colls. and Schs., 1978—. French Govt. fellow, 1952-53; State U. N.Y. grantee improvement undergrad. edn., 1976. Mem. Am. Assn. Tchrs. French, Am. Assn. Tchrs. Spanish and Portuguese, Modern Lang. Assn. Am. (del. 1976-77), Assn. des Amis d'Andre Gide, Claudel Soc. Am., Eta Sigma Phi, Phi Sigma Iota Phi Kappa Phi (chpt. pres.), Delta Kappa Gamma (chpt. v.p.). Democrat. Episcopalian. Author: The Role of Mind in Hugo, Faulkner, Beckett and Grass, 1967. Gen. editor Folio, 1970—. Contbr. French Rev., 1954, 58, Ky. Fgn. Lang. Quar., 1957, Symposium, 1958 and others, Hispania, 1959, Instants: Poems, 1964; book revs. Books Abroad, 1954—. Home: 29 Ellis Dr Brockport NY 14420

ONEAL, GLEN, JR., physicist; b. Great Falls, Mont., Feb. 2, 1917; s. Glen and Marion (Sherrard) O.; B.S., Mont. State Coll., 1940; M.S., U. Pa., 1947; m. Lois Fay, May 23, 1941 (div. Aug. 1968); 1 dau., Fay (Mrs. W. James Redwine); m. 2d, Evelyn Spies Hessenbruch, May 5, 1975. Jr. engr. physicist Pub. Rds. Adminstrn. Washington, 1941; asso. physicist Naval Ordnance Lab., Washington, 1941-45; physicist Sun Oil Co., Newtown Square, Pa., 1947-55; research physicist Am. Viscose Corp., Marcus Hook, Pa., 1955-63; research physicist Am. Viscose div. FMC Corp., 1963-70, chem. group research, 1970—. Research asso. Nat. Bur. Standards, 1968-70. Prodn. chmn. Rose Valley Chorus, Media, Pa., 1950-67. Bd. dirs. Media (Pa.) Fellowship House, Mem. Am. Phys. Soc., ASTM, IEEE, Sigma Xi. Mem. Soc. of Friends. Home: 128 Yale Ave Swarthmore PA 19081 Office: Chem Group Research and Devel Lab FMC Corp PO Box 8 Princeton NJ 08540

O'NEAL, RONDALD ANSON, community devel. co. exec.; b. Marion, N.C., Apr. 9, 1950; s. Sidney James and Eleanor Marie O'Neal; B.A., Lehman Coll., City U. N.Y., 1978; children by previous marriage—Rondald Anson, Marc Damon, Philip Amiri. Housing coordinator City of Lewiston (Maine), 1969-71; chief planning officer City of New Haven Model Cities Agy., 1971-72; exec. dir. Mt. Vernon (N.Y.) City Demonstration Agy., 1972-76; v.p., exec. dir. Grace Community Devel. Corp., Mt. Vernon, 1976-78, also bd. dirs.; pres. Anderson Research Group, Inc., 1978—; exec. dir. First Harlem Mgmt. Corp., 1978—, Camden Bus. Devel. Orgn., 1978—. Recipient Community Service award Grace Bapt. Ch., 1978. Mem. NAACP, Pi Sigma Alpha. Home: 5028 Erringer Pl Philadelphia PA 19144 Office: 211 N 5th St Camden NJ 08102

O'NEIL, BONNIE SANDRA, financial exec.; b. N.Y.C., July 2, 1945; d. Milton and Lorraine (Rosenthal) Seidt; B.A. summa cum laude, L.I. U., 1966; m. John E. O'Neil, Nov. 29, 1975. Research analyst F. I. DuPont & Co., Inc. and successor firms, N.Y.C., 1966-67, portfolio analyst, 1967-70, mgr. Portfolio dept., 1970-74; v.p., dir., investment mgr. Grace Capital Inc., N.Y.C., 1974—; pres. Dirs. Mgmt. Corp., Calif., 1977—; sec. Dirs. Capital Fund, Del., 1977—; dir. Grace Metro Enterprises, N.Y.C., 1974—. N.Y. U. fellow, Columbia fellow; New Sch. Social Research fellow. Mem. N.Y. Soc. Security Analysts, Financial Analysts Fedn. Home: 185 E 85 St New York City NY 10028 Office: One Gulf and Western Plaza New York City NY 10023

O'NEIL, JAMES WALTER, indsl. security cons.; b. Boston, Feb. 8, 1927; s. Bernard Joseph and Sarah Ann (Fahey) O'N.; A.B. cum laude, Boston Coll., 1950; m. Jean Carol Quintiliani, May 1, 1955; children—Christopher James, Barbara Jean, Peter Stephen. Spl. agt. FBI, San Francisco and Springfield, Ill., 1951-52; spl. agt. Thoroughbred Racing Protective Bur., Mass., R.I., N.H., N.Y., N.J., N.Y.C., 1953-56; corp. security dir. EG & G Inc., Bedford, Mass., 1956-69, S.S. Pierce Co., Boston, 1970-72; indsl. security cons., pvt. investigator James W. O'Neil, Inc., Braintree, Mass., 1972—; lectr. law enforcement and security Northeastern U., Boston, 1970—. Served with USN, 1945-46. Mem. Am. Soc. Indsl. Security, Soc. Former Spl. Agts. FBI, Mass. Chiefs of Police, Nat. Fire Protection Assn., Nat. Assn. Sch. Security Dirs., Soc. Profl. Mgmt. Cons.'s. Roman Catholic. Address: 25 Massachusetts Ave Braintree MA 02184

O'NEIL, JOSEPH FRANCIS, lawyer; b. Boston, Jan. 29, 1929; s. Edward W. and Anna (Sullivan) O'N.; B.S., Coll. Holy Cross, 1950; LL.B., Boston Coll., 1953; m. Elinor R. Swide, 1969; children—Allison M., Jennifer E. Admitted to Mass. bar, 1956; practiced in Boston, 1956—; gen. counsel, dir. Lincoln Trust Co. (Mass.), 1966—, Mass. Bankshares, Inc., Mortgage Shops, Inc., Quantum-Detector Tech., Inc. Instr. law Boston Coll. Law Sch., 1969—. Served with AUS, 1954-56. Mem. Am. (com. immigration and naturalization), Mass. (chmn. immigration and naturalization law com. 1975—) bar assns., Assn. Immigration and Nationality Lawyers (chmn. Mass. and R.I. chpt. 1975—, gov. 1976—), Fellows of Boston Coll. Law Sch. (v.p. 1971—). Home: 104 Colwell Dr Dedham MA 02026 Office: 116 Lincoln St Boston MA 02111

O'NEIL, MARIANNE E., publishing co. exec.; b. Oyster Bay, N.Y., Oct. 1, 1936; d. Liveo L. and Donetta E. (Leon) Principe; student pub. schs., Oyster Bay; m. John J. O'Neil, III, June 11, 1967; children—Robyn, Jody, Tricia. Asst. mgr. Community Newspapers, Inc., Glen Cove, N.Y., 1963-65, classified advt. mgr., 1965—, v.p., 1975—; lectr. in field; chmn. bd. advisers ANCAM Newspaper Assn., 1975, past mem. Action Com.; classified industry rep. adv. bd. Nat. Assn. Recruitment Advt. Agencies, 1974. Campaign mgr. Howard Blankman, Republican candidate N.Y. State Assembly, 1978—; bd. govs. Port Washington Rep. Club, 1977-79; v.p. pub. relations Port Washington Chpt. Cancer Care, Inc.; mem. council of advisers Broadway Drama Guild. Recipient numerous awards N.Y. State Press Assn., 1967-75; certificate of appreciation Pa. Newspaper Pubs. Assn., 1975. Mem. N.Y./N.J. Met. Newspaper Assn., Nat. Speakers Assn., Bus. Profl. Advt. Assn., Am. (dir. 1973-74, distinguished service award 1975), Northeastern (pres. 1975-76, numerous awards 1969-71) classified advt. mgrs. assns., L.I. Advt. Club. Roman Catholic. Home: 40 Middle Neck Rd Port Washington NY 11050 Office: 29 Continental Pl Glen Cove NY 11542

O'NEIL, TERENCE QUINN, TV producer; b. Natrona Heights, Pa., July 8, 1949; s. Joseph Emmett and Mary Louise (Quinn) O'N.; B.A. in Communication Arts, U. Notre Dame, 1971; M.S. in Journalism, Columbia U., 1974. Summer Olympics researcher ABC Sports TV, 1972, producer, N.Y.C., 1975—. Co-recipient Emmy award for Olympic Sports coverage, 1972, 76. Mem. Writers Guild Am., Sigma Delta Chi. Author: Fighting Back, 1975. Home: 7 Mary Austin Pl Norwalk CT 06851 Office: 1330 Ave of Americas New York City NY 10019

O'NEILL, ANNE FRANCES, mathematician, educator; b. Troy, N.Y., Aug. 21, 1915; d. Dennis Patrick and Sarah Anne (Strong) O'Neill; B.A., Vassar Coll., 1938; M.A., Radcliffe Coll., 1939, Ph.D., 1942. Instr. math. Smith Coll., Northampton, Mass., 1942-47, asst. prof. math, 1947-52; asst. prof. math Wheaton Coll., Norton, Mass., 1952-54, asso. prof., 1954-60, prof., 1960—. NSF faculty fellow U. Calif. at Berkeley, 1961-62. Mem. Am. Math. Soc., Math. Assn. Am., Am. Statis. Assn., Phi Beta Kappa, Sigma Xi. Author: (with N.H. McCoy and R.E. Johnson) Introduction to Mathematical Analysis, 1962. Home: PO Box 264 7 Pine St Norton MA 02766

O'NEILL, DANIEL J., educator; b. Groton, Conn., May 15, 1931; s. James F. and Catherine A. (Clark) O'N.; B.S., Boston U., 1957, M.Ed., 1957; Ed.D. (teaching fellow), 1964; m. Dorothy F. Drew, Aug. 20, 1955; children—Catherine, Daniel J. Instr. U. R.I., Kingston, 1963-64; asst. prof. Boston U., 1964-66; prof. psychology Bristol Community Coll., Fall River, Mass., 1968—. Pvt. practice counseling and psychotherapy New Bedford, Fall River, Hyannis, Mass., 1969—. NSF grantee, 1959. Mem. Am. Psychol. Assn., Brit. Royal Soc. Health, Am. Personnel and Guidance Assn., AAUP. Club: Wamsutta (New Bedford). Author: The Change of Life, 1971. Home: 225 Ryan St New Bedford MA 02740 Office: Bristol Community College Fall River MA 02720

O'NEILL, MARY JANE, assn. exec.; b. Detroit, Feb. 24, 1923; d. Frank R. and Kathryn C. (Rice) Kilcoyne; Ph.B., U. Detroit, 1944; postgrad., U. Wis., 1949-50; m. Michael J. O'Neill, May 31, 1948; children—Michael, Maureen, Kevin, John, Kathryn. Editor, East Side Shopper, Detroit, 1939-45; club editor, Detroit Free Press, 1946-48; reporter United Press, 1949; dir. pub. relations, Fairfax-Falls Church (Va.) Community Chest, 1955-60; copy editor, Falls Church Sun-Echo, 1958-60; free lance writer, 1960-63; asso. editor, Med. World News, Washington, 1963-67; dir. pub. relations Westchester Lighthouse, N.Y. Assn. for the Blind, White Plains, N.Y., 1967-71, dir. pub. edn., Lighthouse, N.Y.C., 1971-73, pub. relations dir., 1973—; advisory pub. relations com. Nat. Council on Social Welfare. Bd. dirs. Scarsdale Family Counseling Service, 1972—. Mem. Pub. Relations Soc. Am., Women in Communications, Publicity Club N.Y., Am. Assn. Workers for the Blind (chmn. pub. relations com. 1975-77), Community Agencies Pub. Relations Assn. Home: 23 Cayuga Rd Scarsdale NY 10583 Office: 111 E 59th St New York City NY 10022

O'NEILL, TERRENCE MICHAEL, physician; b. Toledo, Dec. 5, 1938; s. Marcus George and Ursula Matilda (Navarre) O'N.; B.S., Xavier U., 1961; M.D., State U. N.U. Upstate Med. Center, Syracuse, 1965; m. Roberta A. Dawson, Aug. 24, 1963; children—Darcy Ann, Sean Patrick, Devin Michael. Intern, Akron (Ohio) City Hosp., 1965-66, resident in obstetrics and gynecology, 1966-70; practice medicine Associated Obstetricians and Gynecologists, Inc., Springfield, Mass., 1970—, bd. dirs., 1972—; clin. instr. Tufts U. Med. Sch., 1975—, U. Mass. Med. Sch., 1975—. Mem. Bd. Health West Springfield, Mass., 1973—, chmn., 1975-76; mem. Sch. Com., West Springfield, 1978—. Served to capt., M.C., AUS, 1973—. Mem. AMA, Mass., Hampden Dist. med. socs., Am. Coll. Obstetricians and Gynecologists, New Eng. Obstetrics and Gynecology Soc. Republican. Roman Catholic. Clubs: West Springfield Men's, Springfield Country. Home: 18 Nonotuck St West Springfield MA 01089 Office: 125 Liberty St Springfield MA 01104

O'NEILL, THOMAS P., congressman; b. Dec. 9, 1912; s. Thomas P. and Rose Anne (Tolan) O'N.; ed. St. John's High Sch. and Boston Coll.; m. Mildred Anne Miller, June 17, 1941; children—Rosemary, Thomas III, Susan, Christopher, Michael Tolan. Engaged in ins. bus., Cambridge, Mass.; mem. Cambridge Sch. Com., 1946, 47; mem. Mass. Legislature, 1936-52, minority leader, 1947, 48, speaker of house, 1948-52; mem. 83d-87th Congresses 11th Mass. Dist., 88th-96th Congresses from 8th Mass. Dist., majority whip, 1971-73, majority leader, 1973-77, speaker, 1977-79. Democrat. Address: Room 2231 Rayburn House Office Bldg Washington DC 20515

O'NEILL, THOMAS P., III, lt. gov. Mass. Office: Lt Gov State Capitol Boston MA 02133*

O'NEILL, WILLIAM A., state ofcl.; b. Hartford, Conn., Aug. 11, 1930; student New Britain Tchr.'s Coll., U. Hartford. Formerly owner, mgr. O'Neill's Restaurant, East Hampton, Conn.; served with Democratic Com., Town of East Hampton; later mem. Conn. Ho. of Reps., asst. majority leader, 1971-72, asst. minority leader, 1973-74, majority leader, 1975-76, 77-78; lt. gov. Conn., 1979—. Served with USAF, 1950-53 (Korea). Named outstanding legis. leader Conn. dept. Am. Legion, 1974. Office: Office of Lt Gov State Capitol Room 304 Hartford CT 06115*

O'NEILL, WILLIAM LAWRENCE, historian; b. Big Rapids, Mich., Apr. 18, 1935; s. John Patrick and Helen Elizabeth (Marsh) O'N.; A.B., U. Mich., 1957; M.A., U. Calif., Berkeley, 1958, Ph.D., 1963; m. Elizabeth Carol Knollmueller, Aug. 20, 1960; children—Cassandra Leigh, Catherine Lorraine. Asst. prof. history U. Colo., 1964-66; asst. prof. history U. Wis., 1966-69, asso. prof., 1969-71; prof. history Rutgers U., New Brunswick, N.J., 1971—; vis. asst. prof. U. Pitts., 1963-64; vis. asso. prof. U. Pa., 1969-70. Mem. Am. Hist. Assn., Orgn. Am. Historians. Author: Divorce in the Progressive Era, 1967; Everyone Was Brave: The Rise and Fall of Feminism in America, 1969; Coming Apart: An Informal History of America in the 1960s, 1971; The Last Romantic: A Life of Max Eastman, 1978. Home: 232 Harrison Ave Highland Park NJ 08904 Office: Dept History Rutgers U New Brunswick NJ 08903

ONETT, TRAYON, chem. co. exec.; b. Pitts., June 5, 1930; s. Trayon and Marie Onett; B.S., U. Pitts., 1951, M.S., 1957; m. Norma C. Oriolo, Oct. 26, 1930; children—Marianne, Trayon Philip. Sales engr. Union Carbide Corp., 1951; sales mgr. Fisher Sci. Co., Pitts., 1959-63, ops. mgr., 1963-67; mgr. research Koppers Co., Pitts., 1967-69, mgr. comml. devel., 1969-70, mgr. reinforced plastics, 197173; pres. Odi Inc., Pitts., 1973—; lectr. in field. Active Boy Scouts Am., 1967—; registrar, hockey coach, also bd. dirs. Mt. Lebanon (Pa.) Hockey Assn., 1973—; mem. adv. com. Nat. Acad. Sci., 1970—. Served to lt. (j.g.), USNR, 1947-49; ETO. Mem. Am., Pitts. (gov. 1967—), chem. socs., Soc. Plastic Industry, Am. Concrete Inst., Soc. Am. Mil. Engrs., Assn. Bridge Constrn. and Design. Office: Odi Inc Lytle St Pittsburgh PA 15207

ONG, STEPHEN TJINLOK, physician; b. Indonesia, July 3, 1943; s. Hoen Tjig and Boen Tjwe O.; came to U.S., 1970, naturalized, 1978; A.B., Philippine Union Coll., 1965; M.D., Univ. of the East, Philippines, 1970; M.P.H. in Maternal and Child Health and Health Adminstrn., Loma Linda (Calif.) U., 1971. Rotating intern, Prince George's Gen. Hosp., Cheverly, Md., 1972, resident in obstetrics and gynecology, 1973; practice family medicine, Oxon Hill, Md., 1974—. Diplomate Am. Bd. Family practice. Fellow Am. Acad. Family Physicians; mem. Am. Fertility Soc., Am. Coll. Obstetrics and Gynecology, Prince George's County Med. Soc., Med. and Chirurgical Faculty Md. Office: 6188 Oxon Hill Rd Oxon Hill MD 20021

ONNE, ROBERT GARY, human services trainer; b. N.Y.C., Dec. 7, 1941; s. Tsing My and Tih Lou (Tasi) O.; B.S., Johnson (Vt.) State Coll., 1969; M.Ed., Springfield (Mass.) Coll., 1970; m. Jeanne Malachowski, May 29, 1971. Counselor, Springfield Coll. Big Bros. Program, 1969-70; mem. faculty Community Coll. Vt., Newport, 1972-73; residence dir. group foster home NE Kingdom Mental Health Services, Newport, 1972-73; tchr.-counselor Happy Day Child Center, Waterbury Center, Vt., 1973-74; community-sch. guidance facilitator Orange-Washington Supervisory Union, E. Barre, Vt., 1974-76; dir. social services, tng. supr. Champlain Valley Family Devel. Corp., Winooski, Vt., 1976—; group cons., workshop leader, also psychol. cons. Served with USAF, 1963-65. Mem. Am., Vt. (area rep.) personnel and guidance assns., Assn. Humanistic Edn. and Devel., Johnston State Coll. Men's Ensemble. Club: Barre Fish and Game. Home: RFD 3 Montpelier VT 05602 Office: 6 Maple St Winooski VT 05404

ONODY, STEPHEN KENNETH, scientist; b. Ridgewood, N.J., Mar. 14, 1953; s. Lawrence Stephen and Doris (Engelke) O.; B.S., Seton Hall U., 1975; M.B.A. in Pharm. Mktg., Fairleigh Dickinson U., 1979; m. Phyllis Ann Reilly, Apr. 2, 1977. Scientist, asst. to mgr. analytical services dept. Sandoz, Inc., East Hanover, N.J., 1977—. Mem. Am. Chem. Soc., AAAS, Am. Mgmt. Assn., Am. Assn. Certified Scuba Divers, Florham Park Jaycees (v.p. 1978, publicity chmn.). Home: 39 Townsend Dr Florham Park NJ 07932 Office: Sandoz Inc Route 10 East Hanover NJ 07936

ONTHANK, JOHN BONTIES, candy and soft drink co. exec.; b. Greenwich, Conn., Apr. 12, 1936; s. Pierce and Nancy (Fuller) O.; B.A. in Econs., Yale, 1957; m. Judy Howse, Nov. 2, 1957; children—Robert Pierce, Christopher Howse, John Bonties. Mktg. exec. Can. Dry Corp., N.Y.C., 1960-68, Coca-Cola U.S.A., Atlanta, 1968-71, mktg. exec. Schweppes U.S.A., Stamford, Conn., 1971-75, pres., 1976—; pres. Cadbury Schweppes U.S.A. Inc., Stamford, 1976-78, Schweppes N.Am., 1977—, Rondo Beverage Corp., 1978—. Served to lt. USN, 1957-60. Mem. Am. Mgmt. Assn., Pres.'s Assn. Republican. Episcopalian. Club: Wilton Riding. Home: 18 Turner Ridge Ct Wilton CT 06897 Office: 1200 High Ridge Rd Stamford CT 06905

ONUFER, GEORGE ROBERT, guidance counselor; b. Passaic, N.J., Mar. 8, 1936; s. George J. and Helen K. O.; B.A., Seton Hall U., 1958, M.A., 1964; postgrad. (Gen. Electric guidance fellow) Boston U., 1966, Rutgers U., 1968, Temple U., 1968-71, Trenton State Coll., 1959-62, Glassboro State Coll., 1965-67; children—Todd P., Tobiellen. Tchr., St. Brendan's Elementary Sch., 1956-58, Montgomery Twp. Schs., Skillman, N.J., 1960-64; guidance counselor Oakcrest Regional High Sch., 1964-72; co-dir. human relations workshop Greater Egg Harbor Regional High Sch. Dist., 1972, dir., head facilitator human relations workshop, 1973; coordinator placement services Oakcrest High Sch., 1965-68, coordinator group dynamics project, 1968-74; guidance counselor Absegami High Sch., Mays Landing, N.J., 1972—; mem. adj. faculty psychology dept. Atlantic Community Coll., 1973—; psychology instr. Kelly Security Acad., 1977—; cons. counseling and testing Atlantic County Jail, 1973—; cons. Nat. Inst. on Role of Youth Orgns. in Vocat. Edn., Rider Coll., 1969; cons., dir. workshop Midwinter Conv. United Synagogue South Jersey, Ventnor, 1973. Bd. dirs. Community Nursery Sch., 1971-74. Served with U.S. Army, 1958-60. Recipient Charles Tabler award N.J. Personnel and Guidance Assn., 1974; Gen. Electric guidance fellow, 1966. Mem. NEA, Am., N.J. (pres. 1976-77) personnel and guidance assns., Atlantic-Cumberland County Personnel and Guidance Assn. (sec.-treas. 1969-70), Am. Secondary Sch. Counselors Assn., Nat. Vocat. Guidance Assn., Assn. Specialists in Group Work, Pub. Offender Counselor Assn., N.J. Edn. Assn., Oakcrest-Absegami Tchrs. Assn., Brigantine Jr. C. of C. (Halloween parade chmn. 1971). Club: K.C. Home: 31 Wesley Ave Ocean City NJ 08226 Office: Absegami High Sch Mays Landing NJ 08330

OPEIL, DIANE KACER, nurse; b. Scranton, Pa., Mar. 25, 1952; d. John George and Emma B. (Harrison) Kacer; B.S.N. magna cum laude, Coll. Misericordia, Dallas, Pa., 1974; M.S. (grantee), U. Scranton, 1976, postgrad., 1977—; m. Andrew Joseph Opeil, July 23, 1976. Child care worker Keystone City Residence, Scranton, 1973, vol., com. to establish spl. interest group alcoholism counseling, 1977—; psychiat. nurse Community Med. Center, Scranton, 1974, VA Hosp., Wilkes Barre, Pa., 1974—, tchr., 1976—. Pres., Young Democrats, Coll. Misericordia, 1973-74; vol., student help center Coll. Misericordia, 1971-74; vol. Big Sister-Little Sister Program, Lourdesmont Sch., Clarks Summit, Pa., 1973-74; bd. dirs. Northeastern Pa. chpt. Am. Heart Assn., 1978—. Recipient Incentive award VA Hosp., Wilkes Barre, 1978. Mem. Am. Personnel and Guidance Assn., Am. Rehab. Counseling Assn., Am., Pa. nurses assns., Nat. Vocat. Guidance Assn., Inst. for Rational Living, Scott Softball Assn., Kappa Gamma Pi. Roman Catholic. Researcher suicidal patients and their fear of death, 1976. Home: 23 Falls Rd Blakely Village Blakely PA 18447 Office: VA Hosp Wilkes Barre PA 18711

OPEL, JOHN ROBERTS, data processing co. exec.; b. Kansas City, Mo., Jan. 5, 1925; s. Norman J. and Esther (Roberts) O.; A.B., Westminster Coll., 1948; M.B.A., U. Chgo., 1949; m. Julia Carole Stout, Dec. 28, 1953; children—Robert, Nancy, Julia, Mary, John. Salesman, IBM, Armonk, N.Y., 1949-64, v.p. mktg., 1964-69, sr. v.p. fin. and planning, 1969-70, sr. v.p., chmn. mgmt. com., 1970-74, pres., 1974—; dir. Pfizer, Inc., Bank of N.Y. Nat. adviser Nat. Tech. Inst. Deaf; trustee Westminster Coll., Inst. for Advanced Study and Joint Council on Econ. Edn.; bd. govs. United Way Am. Served with U.S. Army, 1943-45. Office: IBM Corp Old Orchard Rd Armonk NY 10504

OPHER, PHILIP, economist; b. R. Valcea, Rumania, Sept. 30, 1930; s. Naftaly and Fany (Segal) Herscovici; M.A., U. Bucharest, 1957; M.A., N.Y. U., 1971, Ph.D., 1973; m. Eugenie Amadu, Oct. 21, 1950; 1 dau., Elana. Came to U.S., 1967. Sr. examiner State Comptroller Israel, Tel-Aviv, 1962-63; econ. journalist Daily Newspaper Haaretz, Tel Aviv, 1963-67; econ. adviser Govt. Israel Investment and Export Authority, N.Y.C., 1967-71; exec. v.p. Am.-Israel C. of C. and Industry, N.Y.C., 1971—; sec.-treas. Assn. Secs. of Chambers of Fgn. Commerce in U.S.A., 1971—. Pres., Philip Opher & Assos. Inc., internat. trade and investments cons., N.Y.C., 1973—. Mem. Am. Econ. Assn. Editor, Am. Israel Econ. Horizons, 1971—. Home: 340 E 51st St New York City NY 10022 Office: Am-Israel Chamber Commerce and Industry 500 Fifth Ave New York City NY 10036 also Philip Opher & Assos Inc 340 E 51st St New York City NY 10022

OPPEDAHL, PHILLIP EDWARD, naval officer; b. Renwick, Iowa, Sept. 17, 1935; s. Edward and Isadore Hannah (Gangstead) O.; B.S. in Naval Sci., Navy Postgrad. Sch., 1963, M.S. in Nuclear Physics, 1971; M.S. in Systems Mgmt., U. S.C., 1978; m. Sharon Elaine Ree, Aug. 3, 1957; children—Gary Lynn, Tamra Sue, Sue Ann, Lisa Kay. Commd. ensign U.S. Navy, 1956, advanced through grades to capt., 1977; with Airborne Early Warning Squadron, 1957-59, Anti-Submarine Squadron, 1959-65; asst. navigator USS Coral Sea, 1965-67; basic jet flight instr., 1967-69; student Armed Forces Staff Coll., 1971; test group dir. Def. Nuclear Agy., 1972-74; weapons officer USS Oriskany, 1974-76; program mgr. for armament Naval Air Systems Command, Washington, 1977—. Decorated Meritorious Service Medal, S. Vietnam Distinguished Service Medal, 2 Navy Unit Commendations, 2 Vietnam Service Medals. Mem. Naval Inst., Am. Nuclear Soc., Am. Def. Preparedness Assn., Aircraft Owners and Pilots Assn., Tailhook Assn. Lutheran. Author: Energy Loss of High Energy Electrons in Beryllium, 1971; Understanding Contractor Motivation and Incentive Contracts, 1977. Home: 4924 Althea Dr Annandale VA 22003 Office: NAVAIR SYSCOM AIR 532 Dept of Navy Washington DC 20361

OPPENHEIM, ADOLPH DAVID, city ofcl.; b. Hanau, Germany, Feb. 15, 1918; s. Joseph Mordecai and Malka Rose (Oppenheim) O.; came to U.S., 1939, naturalized, 1947; B.S. magna cum laude, Coll. City N.Y., 1947; M.City Planning, Mass. Inst. Tech., 1949; m. Julia Frankenhuis, Dec. 12, 1950; children—Joseph, Aaron. Head research sect. Tel Aviv (Israel) Town Planning Dept., 1955-60; project chief Pa.-Jersey Transp. Study, 1960-61; head small area population analysis sect. N.Y.C. Dept. City Planning, 1961-78, head housing statistics and analysis sect., 1978—. Mem. Am. Inst. Certified Planners, Am. Soc. Planning Ofcls., Assn. Orthodox Jewish Scientists (bd. govs. 1964—), Soc. for Promotion Jewish Edn. (dir.), Phi Beta Kappa. Home: 66 Overlook Terr New York City NY 10040 Office: 2 Lafayette St New York City NY 10007

OPPENHEIM, JUSTIN SABLE, business exec.; b. N.Y.C., Aug. 17, 1923; s. Ferdinand S. and Esther D. (Hirsch) O.; B.S., N.Y. U., 1943; postgrad. Cambridge U., 1945, New Sch. for Social Research, 1963; m. Joyce Marrits, June 26, 1949; children—Janet, Judi, Jeffrey. Vice pres. Consol. Mercantile Industries, N.Y.C., 1946-52; adminstrn. and mgt. Norden div. United Aircraft Co., 1952-60; pres., gen. mgr. Potentiometer div. Litton Industries, Floral Park, N.Y., 1960-68, pres. Office Products Centers div., 1968-70, v.p. Litton Industries, 1970—, also v.p. Litton Bus. Systems, Inc., Litton Bus. Equipment Ltd. (Can.), Standard Desk Ltd. (Can.); pres., dir. Streater Industries Ltd.; dir. Atal S.A. (France). Lectr. on advt. N.Y. U., Coll. City N.Y., 1954-57; mem. adv. com. N. Hempstead Housing Authority, 1956-59. Mem. Nassau County Republican Com., 1961-73. Served with AUS, 1943-45. Hon. Adm. Tex. Navy, 1969. Mem. SAR, Actor's Fund (life), Alpha Epsilon Pi. Jewish. Clubs: Masons (32 deg.), Lambs (N.Y.). Contbr. articles to profl. jours. Home: 14 Sherwood Ln Roslyn Heights NY 11577 Office: 267-06 Hillside Ave Floral Park NY 11004

OPPENHEIMER, BERTRAM JAY, hosp adminstr.; b. N.Y.C., Mar. 10, 1922; s. Leopold and Kate Blanche (Rosenwasser) O.; B.A., Cornell U., 1943; B.S., N.Y. U., 1944; M.D., Wash. U., 1950; m. Leatryce Powell Clarke, Feb. 14, 1976; children by previous marriage—Martin, George, Betty, Joseph; stepchildren—Valerie, Cleveland, Gregory. Intern, Kings County Hosp., Bklyn., 1950-51; resident Montefiore Hosp., Bronx, N.Y., 1951-54; practice medicine specializing in gastroenterology, to 1976; asso. adminstr. Yonkers (N.Y.) Gen. Hosp., 1976-77, adminstr., 1977—; clin. asst. prof. medicine N.Y. Med. Coll., 1973—. Served with USAAF, 1943-46. Diplomate Am. Bd. Internal Medicine. Mem. AMA, N.Y., Westchester County med. socs. Office: Yonkers Gen Hosp Two Park Ave Yonkers NY 10703

OPPENHEIMER, FRED R., fin. cons.; b. Frankfurt-Main, Germany, June 14, 1910; s. Eugen and Rosa (Epstein) O.; Abitur, Frankfurt U. and Philantropin (Germany), 1931; m. Dorothee Spiegel, 1963; children—Paul E., Miriam, Anton. Came to U.S., 1936, naturalized, 1939. Jr. exec. Frankfurter Zeitung, 1931-35; pres. Fadex Comml. Corp., N.Y.C., 1938-60; pres. Transcontinental Motors, Inc., N.Y.C., 1960-71, Ludwig Motor Corp., 1961-71, Fanta Motors, Inc., 1953-70; financial cons., Port Washington, N.Y., 1973—. Lectr. internat. trade Coll. City N.Y., 1946-50, Practicing Law Inst., 1946-54. Bd. dirs. United Community Fund, Great Neck, N.Y., 1970—. Club: Princeton (N.Y.C). Home: Great Neck NY 11023

OPPENHEIMER, GERDI, interior designer; b. Wuppertal-Elberfeld, Germany, July 22, 1925; d. Ernest and Pauly (Mathias) Baum; came to U.S., 1939, naturalized, 1945; student Johns Hopkins U., 1944-46; A.B., Loyola U., 1974, postgrad., 1974-77; certificate N.Y. Sch. Interior Design, 1955; m. Alfred S. Oppenheimer, Mar. 19, 1944; children—Leslie Joan, Kenneth R. Asst. humanities dept. Enoch Pratt Free Library, Balt., 1944-48; design asso., Zaid, Inc., Balt., 1956-67; interior design cons. Rouse Co., Columbia, Md., 1968-69; interior designer, design cons. to corps., Balt., 1969—; joint projects: Balt. Mus. Art, Balt. Symphony, Center Stage. Bd. dirs. Sisterhood of Har Sinai Congregation, 1957-58, del. to World Conf. for Reform Judaism, 1964; active fundraising Associated Jewish Charities, United Fund, Heart Assn., Mental Health, Multiple Sclerosis, 1950-75; tng. in psychotherapy Spring Grove State Hosp., 1975. Recipient commendation for HUD-sponsored Housing Project for Elderly, 1978; housing won nat. lighting award. Mem. Am. Soc. Interior Designers (corp.; dir. Md. chpt.). Democrat. Jewish. Clubs: Green Valley Swimming and Tennis (charter), City-County Garden (pres., 1956). Chmn. project for nat. profl. involvement in inner-city prototype house, 1968; condr. research on early environment on young child, effect of environment on human behavior; designer innovative model homes for Columbia, Md., project including fine arts rental throughout. Monthly columnist; contbr. articles to profl. jours. Home: 3219 Timberfield Ln Baltimore MD 21208

OPPENHEIMER, SELMA LEVY (MRS. REUBEN OPPENHEIMER), artist; b. Balt.; d. William and Beatrice (Stern) Levy; A.B., Goucher Coll., 1919; student Md. Inst., 1920-22; m. Reuben Oppenheimer, June 26, 1922; children—Martin J., Joan (Mrs. Stanley Weiss). One-woman show: Har Sinai Synagogue, 1977; group shows at Balt. Mus. Art, 1935-61, also invitational exhbn., 1968, Peale Mus., 1938-66, Phila. Art Alliance, 1940, So. State, 1947, Hagerstown Mus. Fine Arts, Pa. Acad., 1938, Chgo. Art Inst., 1952, Phillips Meml. Gallery, 1938, Corcoran Gallery, 1941-47, 51, 56, 57, 60, Va. Mus. Fine Arts, 1938, Ringling Mus. Art, 1960, Calif. Palace Legion Honor, San Francisco, 1938, Mus. Modern Art, N.Y.C., 1933, Smithsonian Instn., 1956, NAD, N.Y.C., 1938-66, Royal Acad. Galleries, Edinburgh, Scotland, 1963, Royal Birmingham (Eng.) Soc. Artists Galleries, 1963, Johns Hopkins Med. Residence Hall, 1961, Goucher Coll., 1965, Jewish Community Center, 1967; 1st juried artist equity exhbn., 1978; with traveling exhbn. U.S., 1963-65, Scotland (Edinburg), 1964, France, 1965; represented in permanent collection Balt. Pub. Schs., Loyola Coll. Chmn. art com. Jewish Community Center, Balt., 1958-65, bd. dirs., 1958-64; corr. sec. Balt. br. Council Jewish Women; publicity chmn. Md. Fedn. Women's Clubs; sec-treas. Balt. Art Festival; vice chmn. artists com. Balt. Mus. Art, 1950, artists com., trustee, 1961-71, chmn. classical arts accessions com., 1969-70. Recipient medal Md. Inst., 1933, Balt. Mus. Art, 1935, 38, Balt. Water Color Club, 1959, award oil painting Nat. Assn. Women Artists, 1952, 60, 65, purchase award Loyola Coll., 1967. Mem. Nat. Assn. Women Artists, Artists Equity Assn. (past pres. Md. chpt.), Am. Fedn. Arts, Balt. Watercolor Club. Clubs: Hamilton Street (Balt.); Suburban (Pikesville, Md.). Address: 7121 Park Heights Ave Baltimore MD 21215

ORAM, THOMAS FELIX DENNYS, pathologist; b. London, Dec. 26, 1926; s. Roy Algur and Dulciebella Adelaide (Denny) O.; came to U.S., 1957, naturalized, 1966; B.A. in Natural Scis. with honours, Cambridge U., 1948, M.A., M.B., B.Chir. (Kitchener scholar 1948-52), U., 1952; M. Joanne Elizabeth Merendo, Jan. 5, 1974; 1 dau., Cara Lynn; children by previous marriage—Felicity, Robert. House officer, causalty officer Middlesex Hosp., London, 1952-53; resident, then chief resident in medicine Ellis Hosp., Schenectady, 1957-59, resident, then chief resident in pathology, 1959-62, sr. asso. pathologist, 1964—; fellow in pathology N.Y. State Dept. Health, 1962-63; instr. pathology Albany (N.Y.) Med. Coll., 1963-67, clin. asso. prof. pathology, 1973—, adj. asso. prof. microbiology, 1973—; mem. Narcotics Guidance Council Schenectady County; cons. Drug Info. Center Schenectady County; pathologist Med. Examiners Office, Schenectady.; vol. physician, Vietnam, 1967. Served with M.C., Brit. Overseas Civil Service, 1953-56. Recipient Golden Apple award Albany Med. Coll., 1971. Fellow Coll. Am. Pathologists, Am. Soc. Clin. Pathologists; mem. Am., Panam. med. assns., N.Y. State, Schenectady County med. socs., Kitchener Assn., Old Eastbournian Assn. Democrat. Clubs: Overseas (London); Union (Cambridge U.). Contbr. med. jours. Office: Ellis Hosp Schenectady NY 12308

ORANGE, ALLAN HERBERT, dentist; b. N.Y.C., Oct. 29, 1934; s. Irving and Rose (Danoff) O.; B.A., U. Mich., 1955; D.D.S., N.Y. U., 1959; m. Amy Lynne Wolfe, Sept. 4, 1966; children—Jordan Scott, Lisa Shawn. Pvt. practice dentistry, N.Y.C., 1961—. Operative clin. asst. Mt. Sinai Hosp., N.Y.C., 1964-67; asso. attending dept. oral surgery Jacque Lowes Found. Hosp., N.Y.C., 1963-68. Served with Dental Corps, AUS, 1959-61. Mem. Mil. Surgeons U.S., Acad. Gen. Dentistry, Am. Acad. Oral Medicine, Fedn. Dentaire Internat., Am. Analgesia Soc., Am. Soc. Geriatric Dentistry, Internat. Acad. Orthodontics, Am. Soc. for Preventive Dentistry, Am. Soc. Dentistry for Children, Am. Hypnodontic Soc., Pierre Fauchard Acad., Acad. Dentistry for Handicapped, Am. Acad. Orthodontics for Gen. Practitioner, N.Y. State Assn. Professions (charter), Alpha Omega. Mason. Home: 23 Hilltop Dr W Great Neck NY 11021 Office: 200 Park Ave S New York City NY 10003

ORBAN, KURT, fgn. trade co. exec.; b. S.I., N.Y., Aug. 6, 1916; s. Kurt and Gertrude (Astfalck) Orbanowski; grad. steel fgn. trade course U.S. Works, Duesseldorf, Germany, 1938; m. Elizabeth Arnold, Feb. 28, 1945; children—Robert Arnold, Robin Ann; m. Katrina Orban; children—Kurt Matthew, Jonathan Seyppel. Fgn. trade corr. Stahlunion, Dusseldorf, 1938, rep., Bulgaria, 1938-40; steel export trader Steel Union Sheet Piling Co., N.Y.C., 1941; v.p. North River Steel Co., N.Y.C., 1941; pres. Kurt Orban Co., Inc., Wayne, N.J., 1946—, Kurt Orban Can., Ltd., Montreal, Que., Kurt Orban Co. Bruxelles, Brussels, Belgium, Orban Export Corp., Wayne, Kurt Orban (U.K.) Ltd., London; chmn. Kurt Orban Japan Ltd., Tokyo. Mem. field hockey games com. U.S. Olympic Com., 1948-61; playing mgr. U.S. Field Hockey Team, London, Eng., 1948, playing coach, Melbourne, Australia, 1956; U.S. rep. Bur. Internat. Hockey Fedn., Brussels, 1954-62. Served to 1st lt. USAAF, 1943-45. Mem. Am. Inst. Imported Steel (pres. 1966-68, 78-79; dir. N.Y.C.), Am. Importers Assn. (pres. 1970-72). Home: 1 Orban Way Wayne NJ 07470 Office: Kurt Orban Co Inc Box 79 Wayne NJ 07470

ORCHARD, BASIL CYRIL LAURENCE, psychiatrist; b. Toronto, Ont., Can., July 17, 1934; s. George Henry and Doris Viola (Rathbone) O.; M.D., U. Toronto, 1961, D.Psychiatry, 1964; m. Miriam Ann Melville, Dec. 15, 1961; children—Christopher, Kevin, Ian, Heather. Intern St. Michael's Hosp., Toronto, 1962; chief resident forensic clinic Toronto Psychiat. Hosp., 1965-66; staff psychiatrist Penstanguishene (Ont.) Mental Health Centre, 1966, dir. regional div. and cons. Oak Ridge div., 1967; staff psychiatrist forensic psychiatry Clarke Inst. Psychiatry, Toronto, 1967—; asst. prof. U. Toronto Med. Sch., 1971—. Fellow Royal Coll. Physicians Can.; mem. Canadian, Ont. (council) med. assns., Med.-Legal Soc. Toronto, Canadian (founding mem. forensic psychiatry sect.), Ont. (founding mem. forensic sect.) psychiat. assns. Club: U. Toronto Faculty. Address: 250 College St Toronto ON M9C 1P7 Canada

ORCHARD, ROBERT JOHN, theatre exec., educator; b. Maplewood, N.J., Dec. 3, 1946; s. Robert and Beatrice Anne (Gould) O.; B.A., Middlebury Coll., 1969; M.F.A. (fellow), Yale U., 1972; m. Pamela Marcy Pritchard, Sept. 6, 1969; 1 son, Christopher Bryant. Gen. mgr. Peterborough (N.H.) Players, 1967-70; asst. mng. dir. Yale Repertory Theatre, New Haven, 1971-72, artistic adminstr., 1972-73, mng. dir., 1973—, asst. prof. theatre adminstrn., 1973—. Served with N.G., 1969-75. Mem. League Resident Theatres. Home: 49 Hidden Ln Guilford CT 06437 Office: 222 York St New Haven CT 06520

ORDWAY, JOHN AMOS, psychiatrist-psychoanalyst; b. Bronxville, N.Y., Jan. 31, 1920; s. George Theodore and Eliza Brookhouse (Perkins) O.; A.B., Harvard Coll., 1942; M.D., Columbia U., 1951; postgrad. Harvard U., 1946-47, Cornell U., 1946-47; certificate Inst. Psychoanalysis, Chgo., 1966; m. Janet Marie Eddy, May 27, 1950; children—John Amos, Wendy, Sarah, Abigail, Susan. Tchr., Shady Hill Sch., Cambridge, Mass., 1939-42, 46-47; athletic instr. Harvard U., Cambridge, Mass., 1946-47; intern Dartmouth Med. Center, 1951-52; resident U. Cin. Med. Sch., 1952-55, asst. clinician, 1952-55, clinician, 1956-70, instr., 1955-58, asst. prof., 1958-65, asso. clin. prof., 1965-70; asst. and attending psychiatrist Cin. Gen. Hosp., 1959-71; attending and cons. psychiatrist Hamilton County Home for Aged, Daniel Drake Meml. Hosp., 1955-56; staff psychiatrist, asso. chief neuropsychiatry VA Hosp., 1955-58; founding dir. Municipal Ct. Clinic and Div. Mental Health, Cin., 1957-70; attending psychiatrist, Eastern Maine Med. Center, Bangor, 1971—, chief psychiatry, 1973—; cons. U.S. Bur. Hearings and Appeals, 1977-78, Fed. Bur. Prisons, 1960-66; asst. health commr., Cin., 1962-64, 67-71; dir. mental health, Cin., 1962-64, 67-71. Dir. Episcopalian clin. services Protestant Episcopal Diocese So. Ohio, 1969-71; chmn. pastoral devel. com. province V, Protestant Episcopal Ch., 1969-71; founding pres. Queen City Found., Cin., 1969-70; dir. Community Commitment, 1968-71. Served with USN, 1942-46. Diplomate Nat. Bd. Med. Examiners, Am. Bd. Neurology and Psychiatry. Fellow Am. Psychiat. Assn. (del. to assembly); mem. AMA, Am. Psychoanalytic Assn., AAUP, Tri-State Group Psychotherapy Soc. (past pres.), Maine Psychiat. Assn. (past pres.), Maine Med. Assn. (past del.). Republican. Clubs: Cincinnati Country; Spee; Harvard Varsity. Contbr. articles in field to profl. jours. Home: Route 4 Box 53 Bangor ME 04401 Office: 489 State St Bangor ME 04401

OREM, CHARLES ANNISTONE, boiler mfg. co. exec.; b. Bryn Mawr, Pa., Apr. 1, 1929; s. Howard Emery and Elizabeth Clements (Stone) O.; B.S. in Engring., U.S. Naval Acad., 1950; M.S.E.E., USN Postgrad. Sch., 1960; nuclear engr. U.S. Naval Nuclear Power Program, 1962; postgrad. George Washington U., 1968-69; m. Gerry Morgan Wellborn, June 15, 1951; children—Nancy Elizabeth, Catherine Stone, Sarah Annistone. Commd. ensign U.S. Navy, 1950, advanced through grades to comdr.; served in U.S.S. Seawolf, 1957, navigator U.S.S. Abraham Lincoln, exec. officer U.S.S. Thomas Jefferson; commanded nuclear powered ballistic missile submarine, 1965-68; submarine specialist Office Chief Naval Ops., 1968-70; ret., 1970; various mgmt. and exec. positions with Babcock & Wilcox Co., 1970-77, dir. corp. planning and devel. at corp. hdqrs., N.Y.C., 1977—; profl. lectr. on mgmt. principles. Past v.p. Civic Assn., Annadale, Va. Decorated Meritorious Service medal, Polaris Patrol award with 6 stars. Mem. Navy League U.S., U.S. Naval Inst., Am. Inst. Aeros. and Astronautics, IEEE, Ret. Officers Assn., Am. Mgmt. Assn., Sigma Xi. (asso.). Republican. Clubs: Fairlawn Country (Akron, Ohio); Army-Navy Country (Arlington, Va.). Home: 44 Fanton Hill Rd Weston CT 06883 Office: 161 E 42d St New York City NY 10017

ORENT, HERBERT LEONARD, shoe store chain exec.; b. Springfield, Mass., July 15, 1925; s. Maurice David and Mae (Kaufman) O.; student St. Vincent Coll., Latrobe, Pa., 1943-44; B.S. in Bus. Adminstrn., Boston U., 1949; m. Daisy Rubin, Sept. 18, 1949; children—Clifford, James Michael, Thomas. Pres., Mason's Dept. Store, Arlington, Mass., 1949-60; merchandising coordinator John Irving Shoe Corp., Boston, 1960-61; with Mortons Shoe Stores Inc., Boston, 1961—, sr. v.p., 1966—, pres. footwear merchandising service div. and Orbit Shoe Co., 1968—, mem. corporate operating com., steering com., 1969—. Pres., PTA, Claflin Sch., 1961, Warren Jr. High Sch., 1964; mem. exec. bd. Friends Amherst Coll. Music, 1970—. Served with USAAF, 1943-46. Mem. Am. Mgmt. Assn., 210 Assos., Arlington C. of C. (pres. 1959-60), Lock Honor Soc. (Boston U.), Phi Epsilon Pi. Mason. Home: 1595 Commonwealth Ave West Newton MA 02165 also Freedom NH 03836 Office: 647 Summer St Boston MA 02210

OREOPOULOS, DIMITRIOS, physician; b. Alexandroupolis, Greece, May 24, 1936; s. George and Antigoni (Antoniadou) O.; came to Can., 1969; M.D., U. Athens (Greece) Sch. Medicine, 1960; Ph.D. (Brit. Council scholar), Queen's U. (No. Ireland), 1969; m. Nancy Hooker, Sept. 19, 1971; children—George and Philip (twins), Antigoni. Intern, U. Athens, 1960-61, resident, 1961-62, sr. resident, 1963-66; sr. registrar Queen's U. of Belfast (No. Ireland), also Belfast City Hosp., 1966-69; sr. research fellow Toronto Western Hosp., 1969-70; asst. prof. medicine U. Toronto, 1970-75, asso. prof. medicine, 1975—; dir. peritoneal dialysis unit, also Stone Clinic, Toronto Western Hosp., 1970—. Served with M.C., Greek Army, 1960-62. Med. Research Council of Can. grant, 1970-75. Fellow Royal Coll. Physicians (Can.), A.C.P.; mem. Internat., Can., Am. socs. nephrology, Am. Soc. Artificial Internal Organs, Can. Soc. Clin. Investigation, European Dialysis and Transplant Assn., Calcium Bone Club Toronto. Home: 10 Ladywood Dr Rexdale ON Canada Office: 399 Bathurst St Toronto ON M5T 2S8 Canada

ORESKES, IRWIN, biochemist; b. Chgo., June 30, 1926; s. Herman and Clara (Rubenstein) O.; B.S. in Chemistry, Coll. City N.Y., 1949; M.A. in Phys. Chemistry, Bklyn. Coll., 1956; Ph.D. in Biochemistry, City U. N.Y., 1969; m. Susan E. Nagin, June 18, 1949; children—Michael, Daniel, Naomi, Rebecca. Chemist, Tech. Tape Co., Bronx, N.Y., 1949; technician N.Y. U. Sch. Medicine, 1950-51; phys. chemist Kingsbrook Jewish Med. Center, 1951-56; research fellow Poly. Inst. N.Y., 1957-58; research asso. Mt. Sinai Hosp., N.Y., 1959-68; research asst. prof. Mt. Sinai Sch. Medicine, 1969-74, research asso. prof., 1974—; asso. prof. biochemistry Hunter Coll. Sch. Health Scis., City U. N.Y., 1970-73, prof., 1973—, dean Sch. Health Scis., 1977—; vis. prof. Johns Hopkins U. Sch. Health Services, 1976-77; cons. to diagnostic reagent and instrument mfrs., 1961—; mem. Internat. Sci. Council, Albert Einstein Research Inst., Buenos Aires, Argentina, 1969—, mem. bd. examiners for clin. labs. N.Y.C. Dept. Health, 1973-75. Served with U.S. Army, 1944-46. Nat. Inst. Arthritis and Metabolic Diseases grantee, 1960-69; Arthritis Found. grantee, 1961-65, 69, 72; Lupus Fedn. grantee, 1975-77; certified clin. lab. dir., N.Y. Mem. Am. Chem. Soc., Am. Rheumatism Assn., AAAS, N.Y. Acad. Scis., Am. Assn. Immunologists, Harvey Soc., Nat. Acad. Clin. Biochemistry, Nat. Acad. Clin. Lab. Physicians and Scientists, Sigma Xi, Phi Lambda Upsilon. Contbr. numerous articles to profl. jours. Home: 670 West End Ave New York City NY 10025 Office: 105 E 106th St New York City NY 10029

ORLANDO, FRANK PETER, accountant; b. Pittston, Pa., July 5, 1943; s. Onofrio Louis and Frances Olga (Lamson) O.; B.S., King's Coll., 1965; m. Sandra Jean Williams, June 24, 1972. Sr. accountant Haskins & Sells, Wilkes-Barre, Pa., 1965-71; partner Parente, Randolph, Orlando, Carey & Assos., Wilkes-Barre and Scranton, Pa., 1971—. Bd. govs. King's Coll. Alumni. Served with USAR, 1965-71. Mem. Am. Inst. C.P.A.'s, Pa. Inst. C.P.A.'s (chpt. pub. relations dir.). Roman Catholic. Clubs: K.C., Westmoreland, King's Coll. Century. Home: 57 N Pioneer Ave Shavertown PA 18708 Office: Suite 800 First Eastern Bank Wilkes-Barre PA 18701

ORLIN, HARVEY, physician; b. Bklyn., June 22, 1938; s. Philip and Minnie (Epstein) O.; student N.Y. U., 1954-57; M.D. summa cum laude, State U. N.Y., 1961; m. Roslyn Rader, June 18, 1961; children—Caryn, Paul. Intern, Boston City Hosp., 1961-62; asst. resident in gen. surgery Bellevue Hosp., N.Y.C., 1962-63; asst. resident in orthopedic surgery N.Y. Orthopedic Hosp., Columbia Presbyn. Med. Center, N.Y.C., 1963-65, resident and Jr. Anne C. Kane fellow in orthopaedic sur[gery, 1965-66; mem. orthopaedic staff Franklin Gen. Hosp., Valley Stream, N.Y., 1968—, South Nassau Communities Hosp., Oceanside, N.Y., 1968—; asst. attending Presbyn. Hosp., Vanderbilt Clinic, Columbia Presbyn. Med. Centers, N.Y.C., 1969—; clin. asso. orthopaedics Coll. Physicians and Surgeons, Columbia Presbyn. Med. Center, N.Y.C., 1969—; practice medicine specializing in orthopaedics, L.I. Orthopaedic Group, Valley Stream, 1968—. Served to capt. M.C., U.S. Army, 1966-68. Diplomate Am. Bd. Orthopaedic Surgery. Fellow ACS, Am. Acad. Orthopaedic Surgeons; mem. N.Y. State, Nassau County med. socs., Nassau Acad. Medicine, Nassau Surg. Soc., Alpha Omega Alpha. Office: 30 S Central Ave Valley Stream NY 11580

ORMAND, DWIGHT HENRY, systems analyst; b. Gastonia, N.C., Apr. 13, 1943; s. Robert Shetley and Eva Blanche (Matthews) O.; A.A., Gardner-Webb Coll., 1965; B.S., E. Tenn. State U., 1968; m. Madeline Jean Mathis, June 17, 1967; children—Christopher Daryl, Benjamin Scott. Mem. info. systems staff Western Electric Co., SAFEGUARD, Madison, N.J., 1968-74, DIR/ECT, Murray Hill, N.J., 1974-76, systems tng. dept., 1976—. Mem. Assn. Systems Mgmt. (edn. and research com. Garden State chpt. 1970, chmn. hospitality and reservations com. 1973-74, sec. 1974-75, v.p. 1975-76, pres. 1976-77, chmn. edn. and publ. com. div. 24, 1974-76, 77-78; named Systems Man of Year 1977-78), Math. Assn. Am., IEEE. Home: 437 E Main St Somerville NJ 08876 Office: Bell Telephone Labs 6 Corporate Pl Piscataway NJ 08854

ORMANDY, EUGENE, music dir.; b. Budapest, Hungary, Nov. 18, 1899; s. Benjamin and Rosalie O.; student Royal State Acad. of Music 1904-13, B.A., 1913 state diploma for violin as prof., 1915; student U. of Budapest, 1917-1920; Mus.D., Hamline U., 1934, U. Pa., 1937, Phila. Acad. Music, 1939, Curtis Inst. Music, 1946, U. Mich., 1952; LL.D., Temple U., 1949; Dr. honoris causa, Clarke U., 1957, Miami U., Oxford, O., 1959, Rutgers U., 1960, L.I. U., 1965; L.H.D., Lehigh U., 1952, C.W. Post Coll., 1965; Litt.D., Lafayette Coll., 1966; Mus. D., Villanova U., 1968, Peabody Inst. Music, 1968, Rensselaer Polytechnic Inst., 1968, U. Ill., 1969 came to U.S., 1921, naturalized, 1927; m. Steffy Goldner, 1922 (dec.); m. 2d, Margaret Frances Hitch, May 15, 1950. Toured Hungary as child prodigy, later toured Central Europe; apptd. head of master classes, State Conservatorium of

Music, Budapest, at age of 20; substituted for Toscanini as condr. Phila. Orch.; condr. Mpls. Symphony Orch., 1931-36; condr. and music dir. Phila. Orch., 1936—. Decorated commandeur French Legion Honor, 1958; knight Order of Dannebrog, 1st class. Denmark, 1952; Order of Merit of Juan Pablo Duarte, Dominican Republic, 1945; knight Order of White Rose, comdr. Order of Lion (Finland); Honor Cross for Arts and Sci. (Austria); recipient citation distinguished service in music, Boston U., 1957; Sibelius medal, 1965; Nicolai medal Vienna Philharmonic, 1967; Presdl. Medal of Freedom, 1970; Phila. award, Nat. Recognition award, 1970. Mem. Mahler Soc., Bruckner Soc. Address: care Phila Orchestra 1420 Locust St Philadelphia PA 19102

ORMONT, LOUIS ROBERT, psychologist; b. Phila., June 16, 1918; s. I. and Goldie (Mittmann) O.; B.A., Temple U., 1941; postgrad. Washington and Jefferson U., 1942, Washington and Lee U., 1943; M.A., Western Res. U., 1945; M.F.A., Yale U., 1949; Ph.D., Columbia U., 1960; m. Joan Connor, Aug. 28, 1959; children—Marian, Michael. Tchr., counselor pub. schs., 1939-42; vocat. guidance counselor Vocat. Guidance Service, Cleve., 1945-46; writer playwright, New Haven, N.Y.C., 1946-50; psychotherapist, N.Y.C., 1950—, Lectr., Columbia Tchrs. Coll., 1957-68; faculty Nat. Psychol. Inst. for Psychoanalysis, 1970—, Center for Modern Psychoanalytic Studies, 1971—, Boston Center Psychotherapeutic Studies, 1973—, N.Y. Center for Psychoanalytic Tng., 1973—, Phila. Sch. Psychoanalytic Studies, 1974—; clin. prof. psychology Inst. Advanced Psychol. Studies, Adelphi U., 1974—, Internat. Grad. U., 1976—. Served with AUS, 1942-45. Fellow Am. Group Psychotherapy Assn.; mem. Am., N.Y. State, Eastern psychol. assns., Eastern Group Psychotherapy Assn., Council for Psychoanalytic Psychotherapists, Nat. Conf. Family Relations, Nat. Psychol. Assn. for Psychoanalysis (sr. mem., tng. analyst). Author: The Talking Cure, 1964; Conjoint Therapy, 1978. Contbr. articles to profl. jours. Office: 55 Central Park W New York City NY 10023

ORMSBY, JOHN CARTER, educator; b. Bath, N.Y., Nov. 15, 1934; s. J. Raymond and Marion C. O.; B.A. in History, Colgate U., Hamilton, N.Y., 1956, M.A. in Social Sci., 1958; postgrad in Guidance, Alfred (N.Y.) U., 1966; married; children—Katharine, Adam, Qynn. Tchr. Haverling Central Sch., Bath, N.Y., 1958-59, dir. guidance, 1967—; asst. dean Stevens Inst. Tech., Hoboken, N.J., 1959-60; asst. dir. admissions Colgate U., 1960-64. Dir. United Fund, 1973-75. Recipient Counselor of the Year award Alfred State Coll., 1972. Mem. Am., N.Y. State (pres. 1972) personnel and guidance assns., N.Y. State Sch. Counselors Assn., N.Y. State Assn. Coll. Admissions Counselors. Club: Rotary (pres. 1976-77). Home: RD 2 Bath NY 14810 Office: Haverling Central Sch Bath NY 14810

ORNER, ROBERT LEROY, ednl. cons.; b. Clearfield, Pa., Jan. 31, 1947; s. Allen Leroy Jr. and Wilma Alice (Brown) O.; B.S. in Elementary Edn., Edinboro (Pa.) State U., 1968, M.E. in Reading, 1970; elementary prin. certificate Westminster Coll., 1978. With Titusville (Pa.) Area Sch. Dist., 1968—, dir. reading clinic, 1971—, reading cons., 1971—; grad. faculty Westminster Coll., Summer 1978. Mem. Titusville, Pa. State edn. assns., NEA, Internat., Seneca reading assns., Christian Educators Fellowship, Phi Delta Kappa. Home: Rural Delivery 3 Box 38 Titusville PA 16354 Office: 302 E Walnut St Titusville PA 16354

O'ROURKE, JOHN JOSEPH, JR., aerospace co. exec.; b. Boston, Jan. 10, 1933; s. John Joseph and Julianna (Scannell) O'R.; B.A. in Math., Boston Coll., 1954; M.B.A. in Econs., Northeastern U., 1970; m. Madelyn Wilkins, Oct. 29, 1955; children—Gerard, Julianna, John Joseph III, Denise, Justin. Engring. services staff Sikorsky Aircraft, Bridgeport, Conn., 1957-58; mktg. mgr. AMF, Inc., Santa Barbara, Calif., 1958-65; dir. mktg. Avco Systems div. Avco. Corp., Wilmington, Mass., 1965—; dir. Photographic, Inc., Boston. Vice pres. Stoneham Youth Hockey Assn., Stoneham Little League. Served to 1st. lt. U.S. Army, 1954-56. Mem. Am. Inst. Aeros. and Astronautics, Tech. Mktg. Soc. Am., Nat. Security Indsl. Assn., Air Force Assn., Am. Def. Preparedness Assn., Assn. U.S. Army, VFW, Am. Legion. Club: K.C. Writer, producer more than 25 indsl. motion pictures. Home: 6 Rustic Rd Stoneham MA 02180 Office: 201 Lowell St Wilmington MA 01887

ORRMONT, ARTHUR, writer, editor; b. Albany, N.Y., July 3, 1922; s. William and Leona (Kaufman) Goldberg; student U. Ala., 1941, U. Mich., 1942-45, Cornell U., 1945; m. Lora Orenstein, Oct. 4, 1956 (div. 1965). Asso. editor, editorial dept. head Farrar, Straus & Co., N.Y.C., 1945-51; sr. editor Popular Library, N.Y.C., 1951-55; exec. editor Fawcett Books, N.Y.C., 1955-57; lectr. creative writing Coll. City of N.Y., 1961; Columbia U., N.Y.C., 1967; pres., editorial dir. Author Aid Assos., N.Y.C., 1968—; editor Nat. Hall of Fame Biography Series, 1970-72; author: Love Cults and Faith Healers, 1962; (with Marion Aten) Last Train Over Rostov Bridge, 1961; Indestructible Commodore Matthew Perry, 1962; Amazing Alexander Hamilton, 1964; Master Detective: Allan Pinkerton (Jr. Literary guild), 1965; Chinese Gordon, Hero of Khartoum, 1966; Fighter Against Slavery; Jehudi Ashmun, 1966; Mr. Lincoln's Master Spy: Lafayette Baker, 1966; Diplomat in Warpaint: Chief Alexander McGillivray of the Creeks, 1967; Fearless Adventurer; Sir Richard Burton, 1969; James Buchanan Eads, 1970; (with Father Joseph Lauro) Action Priest, 1970; Requiem for War: The Life of Wilfred Owen, 1972. Served with AUS, 1942. Recipient Avery Hopwood awards, 1943, 44, 45; recipient special citation N.J. Tchrs. of English, 1967. Clubs: Jamesians (N.Y.C.), Chichester (N.Y.C.). Home and Office: 340 E 52d St New York City NY 10022

ORSER, DAVID ALAN, chemist; b. Rochester, N.Y., Apr. 29, 1942; s. W. Donald and Florence Bertha (Hufeland) O.; B.S., Houghton Coll., 1964; postgrad. Union Coll., 1964-65; m. Edna Grace Lovestrand, July 11, 1964; children—Donald Louis, Thomas Alan, William David. Organic chemist research tech. program Gen. Electric Co., Schenectady, 1964-66, design chemist, Syracuse, N.Y., 1966—. Bd. dirs. Youth for Christ, Schenectady, 1965-66, Syracuse, 1971-73; mem. Mid East Conf. Christian Edn. Bd., Evang. Covenant Ch., 1975—. Mem. Am. Chem. Soc. Republican. Editor The Syracuse Chemist, 1978—. Patentee in field. Home: 7637 Harbor Circle Liverpool NY 13088 Office: Electronics Park 6 304 Syracuse NY 13201

ORSETTI, ROBERT FRANCIS, med. communications ofcl.; b. N.Y.C., Feb. 13, 1942; s. Olinto Charles and Eleanor Marie (Rosasco) O.; B.S. in English, St. Peter's Coll., Jersey City, 1965; M.A. cum laude in Sci., Fairleigh Dickinson U., 1972; m. Marianne Therese Doyle, Aug. 21, 1965; children—Kim, Karen, Kathleen. Supr. med. data processing Carter-Wallace Inc., Cranbury, N.J., 1965-69; coordinator biomed. documentation Schering Corp., Kenilworth, N.J., 1969-71; dir. med. communications and lit. services Ciba-Geigy Corp., Summit, N.J., 1971—. Lector St. Anthony's Roman Cath. Ch., Hightstown, N.J. Fellow Am. Med. Writers Assn. (pres., dir., Distinguished Service award); mem. Soc. Tech. Communication (Achievement award), Drug Info. Assn., Am. Soc. Info. Sci. Roman Catholic. Club: K.C. Contbr. articles to med. jours. Home: 10 Valley Rd Englishtown NJ 07726 Office: 556 Morris Ave Summit NJ 07901

ORSINI, JOSEPH EMMANUEL, clergyman, educator; b. Bayonne, N.J., June 1, 1937; s. Giuseppe and Carmela Consolata (Amore) Orsini; B.A., Seton Hall U., 1960, M.A., 1965; Ed.D., Rutgers U., 1973. Ordained priest Roman Catholic Ch., 1964; tchr. St. John's Sem., Little Rock, 1960-64, Camden Cath. High Sch., Cherry Hill, N.J., 1964-68, Paul VI High Sch., Haddon Heights, 1968-70, Don Bosco Coll., Newton, 1970-71; tchr. Gloucester Cath. High Sch., Gloucester City, 1972-76. Dir.-consultor Bayonne Charismatic Community, 1970-72, New Life Community, Haddon Heights, 1972—; consultor Cath. Charismatic Renewal, Diocese of Camden, 1972—. Recipient distinguished service award Unico Nat., 1965-67. Mem. Unico Nat. (nat. chaplain 1965—). Author: Hear My Confession, 1971; The Anvil, 1974; An Educational History of the Pentecostal Movement, 1973; Papa Bear's Favorite Italian Dishes, 1976; The Cost in Pentecost, 1977. Home: 42 W 50th St Bayonne NJ 07002 Office: 239 Stanton Ave Franklinville NJ 08322

ORT, MIROSLAV JAN, pediatrician; b. Miloslavov, Czechoslovakia, June 9, 1929; s. Josef and Josefa (Duskova) O.; came to Can., 1968, naturalized, 1974; M.D., Charles U., Prague, 1952, Ph.D., 1959; m. Stefana Gocalova, June 20, 1953; 1 son, Jan Zdenek. Asst. prof. pediatrics Charles U., Prague, Czechoslovakia, 1958-68; fellow in pediatric nephrology Michael Reese Hosp., Chgo., 1965-67; resident in pediatrics Ottawa (Ont., Can.) Gen. Hosp., 1968-70; practice medicine specializing in pediatrics, Oshawa, Ont., 1970—; bd. dirs. Children's Aid Soc., Oshawa, 1972-74; Crippled Children's Soc., Oshawa, 1974—. Certified pediatrician, Can. Diplomate Am. Bd. Pediatrics. Mem. Can., Ont. med. assns., Am., Toronto socs. nephrology. Baptist. Contbr. articles in field to med. jours. Home: 26 Brant Ct Oshawa ON L1G 4M9 Canada Office: 117 King St Oshawa ON L1H 1B9 Canada

ORT, PAUL LANNING, cons., appraiser; b. Hackettstown, N.J., May 31, 1917; s. Charles C. and Jeanette E. (Gulick) O.; grad. Jordon Engring. Sch., Phila., 1938; hon. Ph.D. in Bus. Adminstrn.; m. Mildred H. Vey, June 21, 1938; children—Michael P., Thomas W. With Thomas Motors, Hackettstown, 1938-40, William G. Vey & Sons, 1940-42; propr. Paul L. Ort, Hackettstown, N.J., 1945—; chmn. adv. bd. Nat. Community Bank of N.J., Hackettstown; real estate counselor. Chmn. Hackettstown Parking Authority, 1956—; past chmn. Hackettstown Planning Bd., Juvenile Conf. Com., Hackettstown, 1955-58; past pres. 1st Aid and Rescue Squad; past chmn. Hackettstown Zoning Bd. Adjustment; chmn. Hackettstown Planning Bd.; mem. adv. council N.W. County unit N.J. Planning Officials. Bd. dirs. Warren County unit Retarded Children Assn.; pres. Healthvillage. Served with USCGR, World War II. Recipient Community Service award Warren County Realtors, 1970. Mem. Nat. Inst. Real Estate Brokers (dist. rep.), Nat. Assn. Real Estate Counselors, Nat. Assn. Rev. Appraisers, Nat. Assn. Real Estate Appraisers, Nat. Assn. Ind. Fee Appraisers, Warren County Bd. Realtors (past pres.), N.J. Assn. Real Estate Bds. (past v.p.), VFW (past comdr.), Internat. Platform Assn. Presbyn. (elder; past dir. N.J. Presbyn. Homes). Rotarian (past pres. Hackettstown). Clubs: Vista Royale Country, Warren County C, Panther Valley Country. Home and office: 410 Moore St Hackettstown NJ 07840

ORTH, RICHARD CONRAD, JR., aero. engr.; b. Mineola, N.Y., Oct. 4, 1937; s. Richard Conrad and Margaret Dorothy (Holzberger) O.; B.M.E. cum laude, Princeton U., 1959; M.S., Columbia U., 1961; postgrad. U. Md., 1966-71; m. Marsha Judith Harris, Sept. 5, 1959; children—Richard Kevin, Michael David, Paul James. Engr., applied physics lab. Johns Hopkins U., Laurel, Md., 1965-68, sr. engr., 1968-78; adminstr. member services Am. Inst. Aeros. and Astronautics, N.Y.C., 1978—; instr. aerospace engring. U. Md., 1968-69. Pres., Stonecrest Civic Improvement Assn., 1967; treas. Howard County Young Republicans, 1968. Served to capt. C.E., AUS, 1959-65. Asso. fellow Am. Inst. Aeros. and Astronautics (mem. council Nat. Capital sect., chmn. soc. and aerospace tech. tech. com.); mem. U.S. Environment and Resource Council (treas.), Am. Personnel and Guidance Assn., Assn. Humanistic Psychology. Contbr. articles in field to profl. jours. Home: 210 E 47th St New York City NY 10017 Office: Am Inst Aeros and Astronautics 1290 Ave of Americas New York City NY 10017

ORTIZ, JOHN WILLIAM, banker; b. Lynn, Mass., Jan. 29, 1924; s. Michael and Bridget Teresa (Heaney) O.; B.B.A., Northeastern U., 1954; m. Marie Corbo, June 28, 1952; children—Anita, John, Michael, Stephen, Mary. With S. Shore Bank, Quincy, Mass., 1942—, now v.p., sr. loan officer; dir. Heath Consultants, Inc., Stoughton. Past bd. dirs., treas. S. Shore Mental Health Assn.; bd. dirs. Mass. Higher Edn. Loan Assistance Corp. Served with U.S. Army, 1943-45. Mem. Robert Morris Assos. (past pres. New Eng. chpt.). Roman Catholic. Clubs: Pembroke Country, Lions (pres. 1958-59). Home: 85 Central St South Weymouth MA 02190 Office: 1400 Hancock St Quincy MA 02169

ORTIZ-SQUILLACE, ALTAGRACIA, historian; b. Cayey, P.R., Jan. 21, 1941; d. Benigno Ortiz and Matilde Ortiz (Rodriguez) Ramos; B.A., Hunter Coll., 1964, M.A. (grad. fellow), 1965; Ph.D., City U. N.Y., 1977; m. Thomas N. Squillace, June 30, 1968; 1 dau., Nicolè Anne. Adj. lectr. Queens Coll., City U. N.Y., 1966-67; lectr. history City Coll. N.Y., 1969-72; asst. prof. John Jay Coll. Criminal Justice, 1972-77, chairperson Puerto Rican studies dept., 1974-78. NDEA fellow, 1965-66. Mem. Am. Hist. Assn., Caribbean Historians Assn., Nat. Conf. Puerto Rican Women. Home: 54 2d Ave Brentwood NY 11717 Office: 446 W 59th St New York City NY 10019

OSATHANONDH, RAPIN, obstetrician and gynecologist; b. Bangkok, Thailand, Jan. 20, 1943; s. Jajaval and Dusadee (Panyarachun) O.; came to U.S., 1968; M.D., Mahidol U., (Thailand), 1967. Intern in surgery Sirraj Hosp., Bangkok, rotating intern Meml. Hosp., Worcester, Mass.; resident in surgery St. Elizabeth's Hosp., Boston; resident in obstetrics and gynecology Boston Hosp. Women, practice medicine specializing in obstetrics and gynecology, Boston, 1977—; asst. prof. obstetrics and gynecology Harvard Med. Sch., Boston, 1977—; obstetrician and gynecologist Boston Hosp. for Women, 1977—; dir. prenatal clinic Crittenton-Hastings House of the Florence Crittenton League of Am., 1977—. Ford Found. fellow, 1975-77. Diplomate Am. Bd. Obstetrics and Gynecology. Mem. Am. Fertility Soc., AAAS, Am. Assn. Gynecol. Laparoscopists, Am. Coll. Obstetricians and Gynecologists, AMA, Am. Fedn. for Clin. Research, Endocrine Soc., Am. Soc. Abdominal Surgeons, Mass. Med. Soc., Med. Assn. Thailand, N.Y. Acad. Scis. Buddhist. Club: Harvard. Contbr. articles in field to med. jours. Home: 10 Halsey Ave Wellesley MA 02181 Office: 221 Longwood Ave Boston MA 02115

OSAWA, YOSHIO, biochemist, research adminstr.; b. Tokyo, Japan, May 28, 1930; s. Rihei and Natsu (Morita) O.; came to U.S., 1967; B.S., Tokyo Met. U., 1953; M.S., U. Tokyo, 1955, Ph.D., 1959; m. Michiko Morita, Mar. 26, 1955; children—Yoichi, George. Research scientist Teikoku Hormone Mfg. Co., Ltd., Kawasaki, Japan, 1956-58, chief div. total synthesis of steroids, 1958-60, 63-64, prin. research scientist, 1964-67; exchange vis. scientist dept. medicine Roswell Park Meml. Inst., Buffalo, 1960-63; asso. research scientist Med. Found. of Buffalo, 1967-69, head steroid biochemistry lab., 1969-71, head steroid biochemistry dept., 1971-75, head endocrine biochemistry dept., 1975—, asso. dir. postdoctoral tng. program in endocrinology research, 1970—; cons. clin. staff Roswell Park Meml. Inst., Buffalo, 1973—, breast cancer research unit, 1975—; asst. research prof. biochemistry dept. State U. N.Y., Buffalo, 1974—; vis. research prof. Nihon U. Sch. Medicine, Tokyo, 1977. Recipient Am. Cancer Soc. Faculty award 1972; USPHS grantee, 1970—. Mem. Am. Chem. Soc., Chem. Soc. Japan, AAAS, Endocrine Soc., Am. Soc. Biol. Chemists, N.Y. Acad. Sci., Sigma Xi. Contbr. numerous articles on biochem. research to sci. publs. Patentee in field. Home: 145 Elmhurst Dr Orchard Park NY 14127 Office: 73 High St Buffalo NY 14203

OSBORNE, EUGENE FIELDING, lawyer, engr.; b. Peach Bottom, Pa., Mar. 10, 1922; s. Isom Virgil and Rosa (Miller) O.; student Franklin and Marshall Coll., 1946-47; B.S. in E.E., U. Del., 1949; M.S., Pa. State U., 1951; LL.B., U. Md., 1964, J.D., 1969; m. Jennye Alyce Gladding, Dec. 29, 1946; children—Janet Louise, Eugene Fielding. Admitted to Md. bar, 1977; lab. mechanic War Dept., Aberdeen, Md., 1941-42; design engr. Curtiss-Wright Corp., Carlstadt, N.J., 1951; sr. engr. Aeronca Mfg. Corp., Balt., 1952-56; fellow engr. Westinghouse Electric Corp., Balt., 1957-67; staff engr. Applied Physics Lab., Johns Hopkins U., 1967-77; individual practice law, Westminster, Md., 1978—; owner Camargo Enterprises, Westminster, 1976—. Foreman grand jury Carroll County (Md.) Cts., 1971-72; trustee Black Rock Ch. and Cemetery, Butler, Md., 1976—. Served to 2d lt. USAAF, 1943-45. Registered U.S. patent atty. Mem. Am., Md. State bar assns., IEEE, Smithsonian Assos., Nat. Geog. Soc., Engring. Alumni Assn. U. Del. (bd. dirs. 1977—), Tau Beta Pi, Delta Theta Phi. Author: Global Timing Systems. . . Using Satellite References, 1970. Contbr. articles to profl. jours. Patentee in field. Home: 3000 Old Taneytown Rd Westminster MD 21157 Office: PO Box 423 Westminster MD 21157

OSBORNE, GEORGE ROGER, indsl. hygienist; b. Danbury, Conn., July 3, 1942; s. Frank Cromwell and Ethel Doris (White) O.; B.S. in Veterinary Medicine, Mich. State U., 1965, postgrad., 1965-68; M.S. in Indsl. Hygiene, Wayne State U., 1976; m. Paula Jean Hannah, Aug. 15, 1975. Research technician Henry Ford Hosp., Detroit, 1968-69; meat insp. Mich. Dept. Agr., Detroit, 1970-76; indsl. hygienist Babcock & Wilcox, Apollo, Pa., 1977—. Mem. Am. Indsl. Hygiene Assn. (chmn. edn. com. Pitts. sect.), Health Physics Soc., Am. Nuclear Soc., Nat. Fire Protection Assn., Am. Soc. Safety Engrs. Office: 609 N Warren Ave Apollo PA 15613

OSBORNE, MERRILL JOHNSTON, paper co. exec.; b. West Palm Beach, Fla., Dec. 29, 1921; s. Cindillian and Evelyn (Travis) O.; student Palm Beach Jr. Coll., 1939; B.S., Ga. Sch. Tech., 1944; m. Sara Nelle McElreath, June 21, 1944; children—Evelyn Anne (Mrs. Dean Kilpatrick), Travis McElreath, Merrill Johnston, Mary Nelle. Elec. engr. Tenn. Eastman Corp., 1944-45; 2d engr. on turbo-electric tankers Am. Trading & Prodn. Co., 1945-46; elec. engr. Crossett Paper Mills (Ark.), 1946-52; elec. supt. Bowaters So. Paper Corp., Calhoun, Tenn., 1952-60, chief engr., 1960-65; v.p., chief engr., 1965-70, v.p., dir. engring., 1970; dir. engring. Bowater, Inc., Old Greenwich, Conn., 1970—. Mem. Athens (Tenn.) Utility Bd., 1959-70, Athens City Council, 1969-70. Served with U.S. Maritime Commn., 1941-42. Mem. TAPPI (pres., chmn. bd., First Engring. Div. award), IEEE (Pulp and Paper Industry award), Canadian Pulp and Paper Assn. (tech. sect.), Briarian Soc., Tau Beta Pi, Eta Kappa Nu. Home: 42 Blue Spruce Circle Weston CT 06883 Office: 1500 E Putnam Ave Old Greenwich CT 06870

OSBORNE, RAYMOND LESTER, physician; b. N.Y.C., Apr. 20, 1910; s. Nat and Mary (Bellow) O.; A.B., Columbia, 1932, M.D., 1936, M.A., 1936. Intern Roosevelt Hosp., N.Y.C., 1936-37, Bellevue Hosp., 1941; resident nueropsychiatry Rockland State Hosp., Orangeburg, N.Y., 1937-39; fellow neuropsychiatry Neuropsychiat. Inst. of Hartford (Conn.) Retreat, 1939-41; asso. resident, resident neurologist Bellevue Hosp. neurol. and neurosurg. service Cornell U., 1941-42; chief resident neurologist Cornell U., 1942; sr. alienist psychiat. div. Bellevue Hosp., 1942-46; sr. psychiatrist Psychiat. Clinic, Ct of Gen. Sessions, N.Y., 1942-46; asst. vis. neurologist neurol. and neurosurg. service Bellevue Hosp., 1946-50; sr. clin. neuropsychiatrist Lenox Hill Hosp., N.Y., 1946-48; asst. vis. neurologist Mt. Sinai Hosp., N.Y.C., 1946—, fellow in neurology, 1946-51; cons. surgeon N.Y. Police Dept.; sr. med. examiner FAA. Served from capt. to maj., M.C., AUS, 1942-46. Licensed comml. pilot. Fellow Am. Acad. Neurology, N.Y. Acad. Medicine; mem. Am. Psychiatric Assn., AMA, Am. Psychopathol. Assn., Assn. for Research in Nervous and Mental Diseases, Internat. League Against Epilepsy, Am. Geriatric Soc., N.Y. Acad. Scis., N.Y. Neurol. Soc., N.Y. Soc. Clin. Psychiatry, Am. Assn. Automotive Medicine, Am. Guild Authors and Composers, ASCAP, Flying Physicians Assn., Aerospace Med. Assn., Airplane Owners and Pilots Assn., Nat. Pilots Assn., Nat. Aero. Assn., Civil Aviation Med. Assn., Airplane Owners and Pilots Assn., Quiet Birdmen, Air Force Assn., Nat. Bus. Aircraft Assn. (Million Miler Safety award), Antique Auto Club, Allard Owners Club (London), Internat. Order Characters (v.p.), Wings Club, Sigma Xi. Contbr. papers to profl. publs. Office: 27 N Woodland St Englewood NJ 07631

OSBORNE, SALLY RUTH, psychologist; b. St. Anthony, Nfld., Can., Nov. 2, 1932; d. Frederick Gilbert and Margaret Ruth (Heidger) Osborne; came to U.S., 1950; naturalized, 1955; B.S., with honors, U. Iowa, 1966; Ph.D., State U. N.Y., Stonybrook, 1971. Clin. psychologist VA Hosp., Northport, N.Y., 1971-74, Manchester, N.H., 1974—. Mem. Am., Canadian psychol. assns., N.H. Soc. Psychologists, Mensa, ACLU, Fortune Soc. Home: 11 Ray Dr Hooksett NH 03106 Office: Smyth Rd Manchester NH 03104

OSGOOD, ALAN A., chem. engr.; b. Belgium, Oct. 15, 1922; s. Claude J. and Flora B. (Lepret) O.; B.S. in Chem. Engring., Purdue U., 1951; m. Marci F. Gardner, June 25, 1949; children—Ken, Don, Claude, Sue. Group leader Uniroyal Co., Malaysia, 1951-60; sr. engr. Thiokol Co., Elkton, Md., 1961-73; sr. engr. demil/disposal officer Aberdeen (Md.) Proving Group, 1974—; cons. rocket propellant rheology. Served with USMCR, 1942-46. Registered profl. engr., Del. Asso. fellow Am. Inst. Aeros. and Astronautics; mem. Am. Inst. Chem. Engrs., Nat. Soc. Profl. Engrs., U.S. Parachute Assn. Club: Alta Skydiving Center. Author: Rocket Propellant Rheology. Patentee in field. Home: 32 Woodhill Dr Fairfield Crest Newark DE 19711 Office: US Armament Research & Devel Command Chem Systems Lab DRDAR-CLW-E Aberdeen Proving Ground MD 21010

OSGOOD, JEANNETTE AUSTIN, civic worker; b. Cleve.; d. Charles Taylor and Margaret (Montgomery) Austin; A.B., Wellesley Coll., 1930; postgrad. Columbia, 1957-59; m. John Harrison Hosch, Jr., Oct 21, 1931 (dec. Oct. 1956); 1 son, John Harrison III (dec.); m. 2d, William Broadwell Osgood, Aug. 28, 1964. Chmn. provisional program Jr. League, Stanford, Conn., 1940, vice chmn. placement, 1941; chmn. Y-Teen com. YWCA, Greenwich, Conn., 1944-46, chmn. young adult com., 1947-49; pres. P.T.A., Old Greenwich, Conn., 1943; trustee John H. Hosch, Jr. Trust Fund, Conn., 1956—; worker in women's div. Legal Aid Soc., N.Y.C., 1958-66; tchr. reading program Pub. Edn. Assn. N.Y., 1962-74. Congregationalist. Club: Wellesley (N.Y.C.). Address: 31 Perkins Rd Greenwich CT 06830 also 139 E 63d St New York City NY 10021

OSGOOD, PETER GREER, pub. relations firm exec.; b. Waltham, Mass., Dec. 26, 1940; s. Ernest Hamilton and Katherine (Greer) O.; B.A. in Journalism and Polit. Sci., Syracuse U., 1965; m. Theodora Jean Stewart, July 2, 1966; children—Greer Elizabeth, Blaire Stewart. With Newsome & Co. Inc., Boston, 1965—, exec. v.p., 1969-75, pres., 1975—, treas., 1972-75, also dir. Instr., Boston U., 1970-71, 74—, Simmons Coll., Boston, 1972—. Mem. pub. affairs adv. council Mayor Boston, 1972—. Mem. Wellesley Republican Town Com., 1972—. Served with AUS, 1959-62. Mem. Pub. Relations Soc. Am. (mem. exec. com. counselors sect., chmn. counselors sect.), Nat. Investor Relations Inst. (nat. dir., chmn. ethics and univ. relations coms., past pres. N.E. chpt.), Publicity Club Boston, Sigma Phi Epsilon. Episcopalian. Club: Brae Burn Country. Editor: New England Business mag., 1967-68. Home: 94 Elmwood Rd Wellesley MA 02181 Office: 225 Franklin St Boston MA 02110

O'SHEA, JOHN ROBERT, marine biologist; b. S.I., N.Y., Sept. 27, 1946; s. Thomas Joseph and Marie Elizabeth (Flannigan) O'S.; A.B., St. Anselm Coll., 1968; M.S., U. N.H., 1978, postgrad., 1978—; m. Mary Ellen Archer, Oct. 2, 1976. Marine biologist Normandeau Assos., Inc., Portsmouth, N.H., 1975—; instr. phytoplankton ecology and taxonomy N.H. Coll. and U. Council. Served to 1st lt. U.S. Army, 1968-71; to capt. U.S. Army Res., 1971—. Am. Cancer Soc. fellow, 1965. Mem. AAAS, Am. Soc. Limnology and Oceanography, Phycological Soc. Am., New Eng. Estuarine Research Soc., Nat. Marine Edn. Assn., Res. Officers Assn. Republican. Roman Catholic. Clubs: Army & Navy, Officers' Open Mess, K.C. Authority on phytoplankton of Gulf of Maine. Home: Wheelwright Hall Phillips Exeter Acad Exeter NH 03833 Office: 15 Pickering St Portsmouth NH 03801

OSINSKI, HENRY JOSEPH, banker; b. Buffalo, Sept. 9, 1911; s. Stanislaus and Amelia (Goniszewski) O.; B.S., Canisius Coll., 1935; postgrad. U. Buffalo, 1937-43, Fordham U., 1935-36, Am. Inst. Banking, 1952-54; L.H.D., Canisius Coll., 1962; m. Antoinette Lopian, Sept. 5, 1938; children—Elizabeth Louise, Paul, Peter. Sr. social worker State Dept. Social Work, 1936-43; exec. sec. Am. Relief of Poland, Chief of Missions for Am. Relief in Poland, 1943-50; mem. exec. com. Am. Council Fgn. Vol. Agys., 1943-48; sec. gen. Polish Union Am., Buffalo, 1950-51, dir., 1951—; chmn. Fgn. Council Vol. Agys. in Poland, 1946; office mgr. Mfrs. & Traders Trust Co., Buffalo, 1951-64, asst. v.p., 1964-69, v.p., 1969—; mem. Adv. Commn. East and West Trade Dept. Commerce, 1974-75. Bd. regents Canisius Coll., 1954—; mem. State Youth Council, 1956—; mem. Nat. Cath. Resettlement Council; trustee Cath. Charities and United Fund; treas. Supreme Council Polish, German and Italian Fedns.; chmn. com. for Celebration of Milinium Christianity in Poland; mem. council Seek program; mem. Diocesan Pastoral Council; chmn. Villa Maria Coll. Drive Fund; mem. Nat. Council Voluntary Services; trustee Villa Maria Coll.; mem. task force United Way. Decorated knight Papal Order St. Gregory, Order St. Andrew, Greek Orthodox Ch.; recipient Americanization medal VFW, Am. Legion, 1952, Bishop's Plaque, Buffalo Diocesan Labor Mgmt. Coll., 1965, Brotherhood award citation NCCJ, 1968; Gold Service Cross (Poland), 1977. Mem. Profl. Businessmen's Assn., C. of C., Polish Nat. Alliance, Polish Roman Catholic Union, Central Council Polish Orgns. (past pres.), Polish Am. Congress (dir. 1972—), N.Y. State Fraternal Congress (mem. exec. com.), Buffalo Urban League, Am. Inst. Banking. Roman Catholic. Home: 175 Parkside St Buffalo NY 14214 Office: 175 Parkside Buffalo NY 14214

OSIUS, GARY EUGENE, glass artist, mfg. co. exec.; b. Detroit, Aug. 4, 1943; s. Walter Frederick and Leona (Novak) O.; B.A., U. Mich., 1965; postgrad. Wayne State U., 1966; postgrad. in Art, George Washington U., 1966-67; m. Isobel Feltner Goldstein, Nov. 25, 1975. Aide to Senator P. Hart, Washington, 1966-67; news asst./reporter Washington bur. N.Y. Times, 1967-68; reporter The Providence Jour.-Evening Bull., 1968-69; co-founder, v.p. New Arts Mgmt., Inc., N.Y.C., 1969; computer programmer Realtronics, Inc., N.Y.C., 1969-70; founder, pres. Osius-Macfarlane Glassworks, Ltd., N.Y.C., 1970—. Home: 440 W 34th St New York NY 10001 Office: 89 Horatio St New York NY 10014

OSMAN, MARY ELLA WILLIAMS, jour. editor; b. Honea Path, S.C.; d. Humphrey Bates and Jennie Louise (Williams) Williams; student Coll. William and Mary, Ga. State Coll. for Women, Richmond Profl. Inst.; A.B., Presbyn. Coll., 1939; B.S. in L.S., U. N.C., 1944; m. John Osman, Oct. 22, 1936. Asst. librarian Presbyn. Coll., Clinton, S.C., 1936-38, Union Theol. Sem., Richmond, Va., 1938-44; sr. cataloger, asst. librarian Southwestern Coll., Memphis, 1944-52; asst. test cities project Ford Found. Fund for Adult Edn., N.Y.C., 1952-57, asso. dir. office of info., 1957-61, exec. asst. to pres., sec. to bd. dirs., 1960-61; asst. librarian AIA, Washington, 1962-68, asst. editor AIA Jour., 1969-72, asso. editor, 1972-77, sr. editor, 1978—. Mem. Chi Delta Phi, Kappa Delta. Republican. Presbyn. Contbr. to various mags. Home: 2500 Que St NW Washington DC 20007 Office: AIA 1735 New York Ave Washington DC 20006

OSMER, DENNIS, colorimetry scientist; b. Patterson, N.J., June 25, 1947; s. Erwin W. and Grace E. (Anderson) O.; B.A. in Math., Fairleigh Dickinson U., 1976; m. Donna M. Munson, June 30, 1973; 1 son, Eric John. Supr. spectrophotometry lab. Crompton and Knowles Corp., Fair Lawn, N.J., 1969-73; sr. research asst. in charge colorimetry lab. pigments dept. Ciba-Geigy Corp., Ardsley, N.Y., 1974-76, mgr. colorimetry lab., 1976—. Co-recipient award for paper Dry Color Mfrs. Assn., 1977. Mem. Inter-Soc. Color Council, Optical Soc. Am., Colour Group (U.K.), Fedn. Socs. Coatings Tech., Soc. Plastics Engrs. (1st color and appearance div. award 1978). Methodist. Office: Sawmill River Rd Ardsley NY 10502

OSOFF, JEFFREY ARLIN, printing exec.; b. Everett, Mass., June 5, 1936; s. Meyer and Minerva (Cogan) O.; B.A., Bowling Green State U., 1958; M.S., Columbia, 1959; m. Arlene Shuman, Sept. 23, 1962; children—Judith Robin, David Eric. Reporter Boston Post, 1955-56; reporter Boston Globe, 1956-62, rewriteman, 1962-63, acting asst. city editor, 1963-64; dir. News Bur. Brandeis U., Waltham, Mass., 1964-67, asst. dir. pub. affairs, 1967-69, dir. pub. affairs, 1969-74; co-founder, owner Jansson, Inc., Waltham, 1974—; also lectr. in journalism and pub. relations cons. First v.p. Dysautonomia Found., 1965-66, 74—, bd. dirs., 1965—, pres., 1973-74; bd. dirs. New Eng. region Anti-Defamation League. Served with USAF, 1961-62. Recipient citation for outstanding journalistic reporting Mass. N.G., 1961; several awards for high achievement in graphics. Mem. New Eng. Press Assn., Internat. Thermographic Assn., Printing Industries Am., Printing Industries New Eng., Am. Coll. Pub. Relations Assn., Jewish Pub. Relations Soc. Am., Pub. Relations Soc. Am., Publicity Club Boston, Sigma Delta Chi, Zeta Beta Tau. Jewish (trustee, bd. dirs. temple). Home: 67 Sherburne Rd Lexington MA 02173 Office: Jansson Inc 411 Waverley Oaks Rd Waltham MA 02154

OSOFSKY, BARNETT, shipping co. exec.; b. N.Y.C., Sept. 15, 1922; s. Samuel and Annie (Kavaleer) O.; certificate Pohs Inst. Ins., 1947; diploma Traffic Mgrs. Inst., 1948; m. Marion Tuchman, Aug. 30, 1947; children—Lynn Susan (Mrs. Adrian Mazurek), Marci (Mrs. John De Rario). Vice pres. Inter Maritime Forwarding Co., Inc., N.Y.C., 1946—; treas. Gen. & Maritime Brokerage Inc., N.Y.C., 1952—. Lectr. internat. trade Fordham U., N.Y.C., 1966—, Hofstra U., Westbury, L.I., 1965—. Bd. dirs. Occupational Center Hudson County, Jersey City, 1959—. Served with AUS, 1943-45. Decorated Purple Heart, Combat Inf. Badge (U.S.); Fouraguerre (France). Licensed ins. broker, N.Y.; ICC practicioner. Mem. ICC Practitioners Assn., Nat. Def. Transp. Assn., DAV (comdr. 1958-59, Distinguished Comdrs. award 1959), Jewish War Vets. U.S. Contbr. articles on freight forwarding and containerization to transp. jours. Instituted innovative methods of tng. and rehab. for sheltered workshops for mentally retarded. Home: 167 W 27th St Bayonne NJ 07002 Office: 1 World Trade Center Suite 2147 New York City NY 10048

OSOL, ARTHUR, chemist, former coll. pres.; b. Riga, Latvia, Dec. 1, 1905; brought to U.S., 1906, naturalized, 1915; s. Peter and Caroline (Irbit) Osol; grad. Northeast High Sch., Phila., Pa., 1923; Ph.G., Phila. Coll. Pharmacy and Sci., 1925, B.S. in chemistry, 1928; M.S. in chemistry, U. Pa., 1931, Ph.D., 1933; LL.D., Eastern Baptist Coll., 1964; Sc.D., Thomas Jefferson U., 1971; m. Amelia Virginia Lebo, Dec. 28, 1928. With Phila. Coll. Pharmacy and Sci., 1928—, asst. in chemistry, 1928-30, instr., 1930-33, asst. prof., 1933-34, asso. prof., 1934-37, prof. 1937-75, prof. emeritus, 1975—, dir. chem. labs., 1937-43, dir. chemistry dept., 1943-63, dean sci., 1959-63, pres., 1963-75, pres. emeritus, 1975—; prescription editor Am. Druggist Mag., N.Y.C., 1933-45; editorial cons. Blakiston-McGraw-Hill, N.Y.C., 1944-73. Dir., University City Sci. Center Corp.; pres. West Phila. Corp. Chmn. com. on phys. chemistry Nat. Conf. on Pharm. Research, 1934-41. Collaborating research worker League of Nations Health Com. investigating methods of analysis of opium and coca, 1933-37. Mem. sci. adv. com. Smaller War Plants Corp., World War II; mem. U.S. Pharmacopeia Rev. Com., 1950-70; chief chem. br. Phila. Tech. Def. Div. Trustee Chapel of Four Chaplains, Internat. House, Phila. Recipient Procter Gold medal Phila. Drug Exchange, 1975. Fellow Am. Inst. Chemists (Honor Scroll 1954), AAAS; mem. Am. Chem. Soc. (chmn. Phila. sect., 1943-44; councilor, dir.), Am. Electrochem. Soc. (chmn. Phila. sect. 1949-51), Am. Pharm. Assn. (pres. Phila. sect. 1939-40), Franklin Inst., Am. Acad. Polit. and Social Sci., N.Y. Acad. Scis., Phila. Sci. Council (v.p., dir.), Sigma Xi, Phi Delta Chi, Rho Chi. Republican. Presbyn. Clubs: Engineers, Bala Golf, Metachemical, Rotary (dir. Phila.). Asso. editor: U.S. Dispensatory, 22d edit., 1937, and supplement, 1940, co-editor (with Horatio C. Wood, Jr.) 23d edit., 1943, and supplement, 1944, editor-in-chief 24th-27th edits., 1947-73; chmn. editorial bd. Remington's Pharmaceutical Scis., 14th edit., 1970, 15th edit., 1975; co-editor Blakiston's New Gould Medical Dictionary, 1949, 2d edit., 1955, 3d edit., 1971; Blakiston's Illustrated Pocket Medical Dictionary, 3d edit., 1973; contbr. to sci. jours. Home: 128 Colwyn Ln Bala-Cynwyd PA 19004 Office: 43d St and Kingsessing Ave Philadelphia PA 19104

OSOL, VIRGINIA LEBO (MRS. ARTHUR OSOL), assn. exec., artist; b. Phila. Feb. 21, 1908; d. Frank Clayton and Amelia (Howell) Lebo; student Phila. Coll. Pharmacy and Sci., 1926-29; m. Arthur Osol, Dec. 28, 1928. Editorial asst. Dispensatory of U.S.A. and other reference works, 1934—; one-man show Bala-Cynwyd Women's Club, Women's University Club, also Panoras Gallery, New York, Twentieth Century Club of Lansdowne, Women's City Club, Phila., Annie S. Kemerer Mus., Bethlehem, Pa.; exhibited in group shows Phila. Art Alliance, Woodmere Art Gallery, Phila. Sketch Club, Wayne Art Center. Recipient Award Phila. Sketch Club 100th Ann. Exhibition. Mem. Aux. for Phila. Orch., Women's Club of Phila. Coll. Pharm. and Sci. (pres. 1945-49), Profl. Panhellenic Assn. (pres. Phila. Area, 1956-60), Nat. League Am. Pen Women (state art show winner 1977), Republican Women of Pa., Phila. Art Alliance, Pa. Acad. Fine Arts, Lambda Kappa Sigma (nat. pres. 1940-46, nat. editor, 1942-52, bus. mgr. 1952-54, nat. hon. adviser 1954-68). Club: Peale. Home: 128 Colwyn Ln Bala-Cynwyd PA 19004

OSORIO, CARMEN, educator, social worker; b. San Juan, P.R.; d. Lino and Maria L. (Travecier) Osorio; B.S., L.I. U., 1954; M.S.W., Fordham U., 1957. Caseworker, Cath. Charities N.Y., N.Y.C., 1954-55, ct. cons., ct. rep. Manhattan Family Ct., 1957-62; social worker, therapist, community organizer Lower Eastside Info. Center, Moblzn. for Youth, N.Y.C., 1962-64; instr. Albert Einstein Coll. Medicine, Yeshiva U., Lincoln Hosp. Mental Health Services, N.Y.C., 1964-67; community mental health rep., narcotic addiction Bur. Accreditation and Contract Services, N.Y. State Narcotic Addiction Control Commn., N.Y.C., 1967-71, sr. field rep. Office Pub. and Pvt. Agy. Affairs, 1971-72; asst. prof. Fordham U. at Lincoln Center Grad. Sch. Social Service, N.Y.C., 1972-76; dir. social services CABS Health Related Facility, Bklyn., 1976; now asst. dir. social work service dept. Letchworth Village Developmental Center, Thiells, N.Y. Bd. dirs. Puerto Rican Family Inst., N.Y.C.; bd. dirs. Puerto Rican Ednl. Projects, treas., 1971—; bd. dirs. Puerto Rican Bd. Guardian, treas., 1972—. Fellow Am. Orthopsychiat. Assn.; mem. Acad. Certified Social Workers, Nat. Assn. Social Workers (dir. N.Y.C. chpt. 1976—), Nat. Conf. Social Welfare, World Fedn. Mental Health, NCCJ, AAAS, Fordham U. Grad. Sch. Social Service Alumni Assn. (dir. 1975—), Assn. Spanish Speaking Cath. Social Workers (pres. 1960-70), N.Y. Assn. Puerto Rican Social Workers (pres. 1965-68), UN Assn. U.S., Council on Social Work Edn. Home: 387 Cumberland St Englewood NJ 07631 Office: Letchworth Village Devel Center Thiells NY 10984

OSSERMAN, RICHARD ALLEN, lawyer; b. N.Y.C., May 21, 1930; s. Harold Aaron and Letty Henrietta (Tonkonogy) O.; A.B., Hobart Coll., 1951; J.D., Columbia, 1954; LL.M., N.Y. U., 1961; m. Linda Adler Chalt, Apr. 15, 1974; children—Eric, Steven, Joel, Robert. Admitted to N.Y. bar, 1954; practice law, N.Y.C., 1954—; partner firm Weisman Cellar Allan Spett & Sheinberg, 1956-72, Pryor Cashman & Sherman, 1972—. Lectr. in field. Chmn. younger lawyers div. United Jewish Appeal; mem. budget, finance coms. Nat. Jewish Welfare Bd. Bd. dirs. N.Y.C. chpt. Nat. Multiple Sclerosis Soc. Mem. Fed. Bar Council (taxation com.), N.Y. State Bar Assn. (tax com.), N.Y. U. Tax Study Group. Served with AUS, 1954-56. Author: (with Joseph Ruskay) Halfway to Tax Reform, 1970. Home: 22 Baldwin Farms N Greenwich CT 06830 Office: 410 Park Ave New York City NY 10022

OSTBERG, HENRY DEAN, marketing co. exec.; b. Bocholt, Germany, July 21, 1928; s. Fred and Lotte (Hertz) O.; came to U.S., 1939, naturalized, 1945; LL.B., N.Y. Law Sch., 1950; M.B.A., Ohio State U., 1953, Ph.D., 1957; 1 son, Neal. Admitted to N.Y. bar, 1952; asso. prof. mktg. N.Y. U., N.Y.C., 1954-63; pres. H.D. Ostberg Assos., N.Y.C., 1950—; chmn. bd. Admar Co., N.Y.C., 1968—; dir. Self-Instructional Devel. Corp., Porter Industries, Inc. Served to capt. USAF, 1950-53. Mem. Inst. Mgmt. Scis., Am. Mktg. Assn., Assn. Pub. Opinion Research. Jewish. Contbr. articles in law and advt. to profl. jours. Home: 278 Fountain Rd Englewood NJ 07631 Office: 44 E 23 St New York NY 10010

OSTER, KURT ALEXANDER, cardiologist; b. Cologne, Germany, Apr. 20, 1909; s. Benno and Regine (Vyth) O.; came to U.S., 1938, naturalized, 1944; M.S. in Chemistry, Berlin U., 1932; M.D., Cologne U., 1934; m. Jean G. Baum, July 22, 1945; children—Pamela Regine Oster Harrison, Jeffrey Benjamin. Intern, Fairview Park Hosp., Cleve., 1939-40; resident Jewish Hosp., Berlin, 1935-36; research fellow Mt. Sinai Hosp., N.Y.C., 1940-42, Columbia U., 1942-43; med. dir. McKesson Labs., Fairfield, Conn., 1943-74, cons. med. dir., 1974—; practice medicine specializing in internal medicine and cardiology, Bridgeport, Conn., 1943—; chmn. dept. medicine Park City Hosp., Bridgeport, 1949-69, chief cardiology, 1949-74, dir. electrocardiograph lab., 1949-74; adj. asso. prof. U. Bridgeport, 1949-64; adj. research prof. Fairfield U., 1972—; med. cons. Nat. Commn. on Egg Nutrition, 1975. Diplomate Am. Bd. Internal Medicine. Fellow A.C.P. (life), Am. Coll. Cardiology, Am. Coll. Clin. Pharmacology, Am. Coll. Nutrition; mem. Bridgeport, Fairfield County med. assns., Conn. State Med. Soc., AMA, Soc. Exptl. Biology and Medicine, Conn. State Adv. Com. Food and Drugs, Greater Bridgeport (pres. 1963-64), Fairfield County (dir.) heart assns., Internat. Soc. Heart Research, AAAS, Am. Numismatic Soc. Contbr. chpts. to pharmacology textbooks, articles to sci. and med. jours.; condr. research in atherosclerosis and heart disease; internat. patentee creation of enzyme-free milk and treatment of atherosclerosis. Home: 468 Valley Rd Fairfield CT 06432 Office: 881 Lafayette Blvd Bridgeport CT 06604

OSTER, MARTIN WILLIAM, physician; b. N.Y.C., Apr. 9, 1947; s. Joseph A. and Bella O.; B.A. summa cum laude, Columbia U., 1967, M.D., 1971; m. Karen A. Strauss, May 18, 1975; 1 dau., Bonnie Felice. Intern, resident in medicine Mass. Gen. Hosp., Boston, 1971-73; clin. asso. div. of cancer treatment Nat. Cancer Inst., Bethesda, Md., 1973-76; asst. prof. medicine Columbia Coll. Physicians and Surgeons, 1976—, asst. prof. medicine Cancer Research Center, Columbia U., 1976—; asst. attending physician Columbia-Presbyn. Med. Center, N.Y.C., 1976—. Served with USPHS, 1973-76. Diplomate Am. Bd. Internal Medicine and Subsplty. med. oncology. Mem. A.C.P., N.Y. Cancer Soc., Am. Soc. Clin. Oncology, Phi Beta Kappa, Alpha Omega Alpha. Office: 161 Fort Washington Ave New York City NY 10032

OSTER, RALPH JOHN, JR., accountant; b. Cleve., Feb. 4, 1919; s. Ralph John and Pauline (Moffett) O.; B.S., Miami U., Oxford, Ohio, 1943; M.B.A., Duquesne U., 1972; M.Pub. Adminstrn., U. Pitts., 1976; m. Marcella Lorraine Riehl, Sept. 14, 1945; children—Karen Joan Martindill, Vicki Ann Mains. Agt., IRS, Pitts., 1945-50, appellate conferee, 1950-75; asst. prof. accounting Grove City (Pa.) Coll., 1975-78; dir. Oster Mfg. Co., Cleve.; instr. accounting Robert Morris Coll., Pitts.; sec. Chartiers Valley Sch. Dist., Pitts., 1966-78. Pres., Bower Hill Civic League, 1963-71, treas., 1971-75. Served with USMC, 1943-45. C.P.A., Pa. Mem. Am., Pa. insts. C.P.A.'s, Scott Twp. Sch. Dist. Authority, Pa. S. Central Spl. Sch. Authority. Democrat. Episcopalian (sr. warden 1978—). Clubs: Rotary (Grove City); Elks. Home: 408 W Washington Blvd Grove City PA 16127 Office: Grove City Coll Grove City PA 16127 Died Jan. 22, 1979

OSTERGAARD, PAUL BLUME, acoustical engr.; b. Erie, Pa., Nov. 11, 1924; s. Christian and Elizabeth (Blume-Knudsen) O.; S.B., Mass. Inst. Tech., 1949, S.M., 1950, postgrad., 1953-54; m. Jacqueline M. McKnight, Nov. 24, 1951; children—Trisha Ann, Hans Paul, Niels Christian, Lisa Marie. Acoustical specialist Carrier Corp., Syracuse, N.Y., 1954-59; sr. engr. Lewis S. Goodfriend & Assos., Montclair, N.J., 1959-63; v.p. Goodfriend-Ostergaard Assos., cons. in acoustics, Cedar Knolls, N.J., 1964-71; v.p. Zurn Industries, Erie, 1969-71; pres. Ostergaard Assos., cons. in acoustics, Caldwell, N.J., 1971—; chmn. Environmental Acoustical Resources, Inc., Caldwell, N.J. Fellow Acoustical Soc. Am., Inst. Acoustics (Gt. Brit.); mem. Am. Soc. Heating, Refrigerating and Airconditioning Engrs. (chmn. sound and vibration com. 1967-68), ASME (performance test code com. 1967—), ASTM (environ. acoustics com.), Am. Meteorol. Soc. (asso.), Audio Engring. Soc., Am. Arbitration Assn., Inst. Noise Control Engring. (founding), Sigma Xi, Theta Xi. Presbyn. Mason. Home: 10 Glenwood Way West Caldwell NJ 07006 Office: 115 Bloomfield Ave Caldwell NJ 07006

OSTERKAMP, ANNEMARGRET LEWENZ (MRS. F. EMILE OSTERKAMP), social worker; b. Dresden, Germany, Sept. 4, 1910; d. Hans Leo and Ella Henriette (Arnhold) Lewenz; came to U.S., 1938, naturalized, 1948; M.S.W., U. Pa. Sch. Social Work, 1951; m. F. Emile Osterkamp, Apr. 15, 1942; 1 son, George. Caseworker, Children's Aid Soc. Montgomery County, Norristown, Pa., 1951-54; supr. Child Study Center, Pa. Hosp., Phila., 1954-56; supr. Eastern Pa. Psychiat. Inst., Phila., 1956-62; chief social worker Center for Child Guidance, Phila., 1962-64; unit dir. Charles Peberdy Child Psychiatry Clinic, Hahnemann Med. Coll. and Hosp., Phila., 1964-74, chief child psychiat. social worker children's services, 1974-75, asst. prof., 1971-75; pvt. practice, 1975—. Counselor, counseling service, family relations com. Phila. Yearly Meeting of Friends, 1958—. Mem. corp. Friends Hosp., Phila., 1970. Fellow Am. Orthopsychiat. Assn.; mem. Nat. Assn. Social Workers, Nat. Conf. Social Welfare, Internat. Conf. Social Welfare, Acad. Certified Social Workers, Women's Internat. League for Peace and Freedom, Women's Nat. League for Peace and Freedom. Mem. Soc. of Friends. Author papers in field. Home and office: Foulkeways Gwynedd PA 19436

OSTERWEIL, SUZANNE EVE, artist; b. N.Y.C., June 22, 1940; d. Fredrick and Lillian (Simon) Lesser; B.S., Pratt Inst., 1961, M.S. in Art Edn. (Sch. Art League scholar, Deans scholar), 1964; postgrad. City U., 1963-67, (Nat. Edn. Def. Act Title I fellow) N.Y. U., 1963-69, Pratt Graphic Center, 1972-74; M.S. in Adminstrn. and Supervision with distinction, Pace U., 1976. Exhibited one-woman show paintings, prints Alonzo Gallery, N.Y.C., 1965, Westbroadway Gallery, N.Y.C., 1977; exhibited art in group shows at Alonzo Gallery, Avnet-Hechlinger Gallery, Avanti Gallery, Nat. Assn. Women Artists nat. and internat. shows, USIA Traveling Graphics, Nat. Assn. Artists in Casein and Acrylics Shows, Hunterdon Art Center Print Show, Pratt Graphic Center, Townhouse Gallery; tchr. fine arts, chairwoman dept. James Madison High Sch., Bklyn., 1963—, coordinator high sch. self renewal project, 1977; chmn. dept. Bklyn. Mus., summer 1969; licensed supr. art, N.Y.C.; free lance graphic designer, 1968—. Recipient prize for painting Nat. Assn. Women Artists, 1972, 75, prize for graphics, 1973. Mem. Nat. Assn. Women Artists (graphics jury 1974-75), N.Y. State Art Tchrs. Assn., Assn. Art Suprs. and Adminstrs., Phi Delta Kappa. Mem. editor staff, art interviewer Bennington Rev. Home and Studio: 479 Broome St New York City NY 10013

OSTIGUY, JEAN PAUL WILSON, investment dealer; b. Montreal, Que., Can., Mar. 4, 1922; s. Paul Emile and Marguerite (Wilson) O.; student U. Montreal Faculty Commerce, 1938-39; grad. Royal Mil. Coll. Can., 1942, LL.D. (hon.), 1978; m. Michelle Bienvenu, Oct. 15, 1946; children—Marc, Claude, Danielle, Denyse, Suzanne. Rep., Stevenson & Kellogg Ltd., Montreal, 1945-47; v.p., dir. Casgrain & Co. Ltd., Montreal, 1948-56; pres. Morgan, Ostiguy & Hudon, Inc., Montreal, 1956-72; pres., chief exec. officer, dir. Crang & Ostiguy, Inc. (merged with Bankers Securities Can. Ltd. 1974, with Greenshields Inc. 1977), mems. Montreal, Canadian, Toronto, Winnipeg, Vancouver, Phila.-Balt.-Washington stock exchanges, Montreal, 1972—; chmn. bd. Greenshields Inc., 1977—; dir., mem. exec. com. Canadian Imperial Bank Commerce, Kerr Addison Mines Ltd.; dir. Canadian Pacific Airlines, Ltd., Canadian Pioneer Ins. Co., Ciba-Geigy Can. Ltd., Canadian Canners Ltd., Procor Ltd., Quemont Mines Ltd., Dominion Life Assurance Co. Can., Ford Motor Co. of Can., Sintra Ltd., Scottish Canadian Assurance Corp., Gen. Accident Assurance Co. Can. Pres., La Maison des Etudiants Canadiens a Paris, 1964—; co-chmn. brotherhood week Canadian Council Christian and

Jews, 1964-65, co-chmn. council, 1974-76; mem. exec. com. of council Montreal Mus. Fine Arts, 1964-66; chmn. compaign policy com. Federated Appeal Greater Montreal, 1966-67; mem. adv. com. Minister Industry, Trade and Commerce, 1971-74. Bd. dirs. Que. Hosp. Assn., 1961-63, Regie de la Place des Arts, Montreal, 1969-73, Les Feux-Foliets, Montreal Symphony Orch., Nat. Youth Orch. Assn. Can., Jr. Achievement Can., 1967-69, Can. Com., 1970-71, Council Bus. and Arts Can., 1974—; chmn. bd. dirs. Jean Talon Hosp., 1961-67, Combined Health Appeal Greater Montreal, 1965-66; bd. govs. Canadian Mental Health Assn., 1964—, Royal Victoria Hosp., 1972—, Hockey Can., 1973—; chmn. bd. trustees Nat. Museums of Can., 1968-73; co-chmn. Canadian U. Service Overseas, 1964-65. Served to capt. Canadian Army, 1942-45. Decorated officer Order of Can.; Star of Italy; Centennial medal; knight Mil. and Hospitaller Order of St. Lazarius of Jerusalem; knight Sovereign and Mil. Order of Malta. Mem. Investment Dealers Assn. Can. (chmn. Quebec dist. 1962-63, pres. 1965-66), Montreal C. of C. (pres. 1966-67, chmn. bd. dirs. 1967-68), Mt. Royal Property Owners Assn. (past dir.), Young Presidents Orgn., Montreal Bond Traders' Assn. (hon. pres. 1969—), Clubs: St. James's, Mount Royal (Montreal); Toronto; Royal Military College of Can. (pres. 1967-68). Home: 318 Geneva Crescent Mount Royal Montreal PQ H3R 2A9 Canada Office: 4 Pl Ville Marie Montreal PQ H3B 2E8 Canada

OSTRANDER, DALE HOWARD, clergyman, counselor; b. Pasadena, Calif., Oct. 26, 1938; s. Smith Wallace and LaVerne Francis (Hurter) O.; B.A., Stanford U., 1961; M.Div., Union Theol. Sem., N.Y.C., 1965; certificate profl. clin. tng. Inst. Pastoral Psychotherapy, Washington, 1968, Spring Grove State Hosp., Balt., 1973; m. Judith Ann Kolterjohn, Sept. 21, 1963; children—Leslie Therese, Stephen Christopher. Ordained to ministry United Church of Christ, 1968; asst. pastor, Lincoln Temple, Washington, 1965-68; counselor Manpower Redevel. Tng. Program, Washington, 1968; asso. pastor Cleve. Park Congl. Ch., Washington, 1968-70; marriage and family counselor, center dir., Pastoral Counseling Centers, Washington, 1968-74; pvt. practice marriage and family counseling, Milford, N.H., 1974—; supr. students Inst. Pastoral Psychotherapy, Washington; lectr. Hesser Coll., Manchester, N.H., Franklin Pierce Coll., Rindge, N.H.; cons. Child Family Service, Fitchburg, Mass. Trustee, Wadleigh Meml. Library, Milford, 1976-79; bd. dirs. Souhegan Valley Scholarship Council, N.H., 1975-78. Mem. Am. Assn. Marriage and Family Counselors (pres. No. New Eng. region), Nat. Alliance Family Life, Am. Assn. Sex Educators Counselors, Sigma Chi. Democrat. Home: 46 Summer St Milford NH 03055 Office: 74 Nashua St Milford NH 03055

OSTROM, BARBARA DIANE, interior designer; b. Jersey City, Nov. 28, 1942; d. Robert Clarence and Doris Harriet (Schubert) Mead; B.F.A., N.Y. U., 1964; M.S. in Interior Design, Pratt Inst., 1967; certificate N.Y. Sch. of Interior Design, 1965, Traphagen Sch. of Fashion, 1969; m. Roy Daniel Ostrom, Sept. 19, 1964; 1 dau., Meredith Joy. Interior designer Roslyn Rosier, N.Y.C., 1960-64; dir. design Katzman Assos., Inc., N.Y.C., 1964-70; dir. design Copeland, Novak and Israel Co., N.Y.C., 1970-71; interior designer, home fashion coordinator model rooms Bloomingdales, N.Y.C., 1971-73; pres. Barbara Ostrom Assos., Inc., Upper Saddle River, N.J., 1973—. Recipient Major Design award AIA, 1969. Mem. Am. Soc. Interior Designers (state sec. 1976-77), NOW. Republican. Club: Altrusa (dir. 1975—). Columnist The Town Jour. newspaper, 1978—. Home and office: 28 Hopper Farm Rd Upper Saddle River NJ 07458

OSTROM, ROBERT BINGHAM, lawyer; b. Morristown, N.J., May 3, 1944; s. Charles Warren and Phyllis (Harrison-Berlitz) O.; B.A., U. Vt., 1966; J.D., Georgetown U., 1969; m. Anne Dietrich, June 25, 1966; children—Jill Marie, Dawn Michele, Robin Anne. Admitted to Md. bar, 1969; asso. firm De Paul, Willoner & Kenkel, P.A., and predecessor, College Park, Md., 1969-72, partner, 1973, 75-78; dep. county atty. Prince George's County (Md.), 1973-75, county atty., 1978—; instr. in bus. law U. Md., 1970-73. Deacon, Riverdale Presbyterian Ch., University Park, Md., 1974-77; bd. govs. Holy Trinity Episcopal Day Sch., 1974-79, chmn., 1977-79; elder Hope Presbyn. Ch., Michellville, Md., 1979—. Mem. Am. Bar Assn., Md. Bar Assn. (chmn. sect. young lawyers 1976-77), Prince George's County Bar Assn. Republican. Home: 4920 Smithwick Ln Mitchellville MD 20716 Office: 7100 Baltimore Ave College Park MD 20740*

OSTROY, JOSEPH, educator; b. Novoarchangelsk, Russia, July 4, 1917; s. Max M. and Tillie R. (Robinovic) O.; came to U.S., 1923, naturalized, 1929; B.A., N.Y. U., 1952, M.A., Sch. Edn., 1953; prof. diploma Columbia U., 1966; Ph.D., 1972; m Alexandra Leontina Kruger, Dec. 22, 1944. Charge product promotion and publicity L. Kruger & Co., N.Y.C., 1945-49; tchr. English, journalism, dramatics pub. and pvt. schs., New Orleans, 1954-55, Mohegan Lake, N.Y., 1958-59; dir. guidance services Dannemora (N.Y.) High Sch., 1962-66; asst. prin. and guidance director Ft. Ann (N.Y.) Central Sch., 1966—; sr. guidance counselor, dir. ednl. vocational counseling Brewster High Sch.; sr. high sch. guidance dir. Roosevelt (N.Y.) Pub. Schs., 1969—; columnist on sch. counseling and edn. writer L.I. Jour., Long Beach, N.Y.; city editor Homestead Daily Messenger, Pitts., 1944, Claremont (N.H.) Daily Eagle, 1944-45. Mem. steering com. Champlain Valley Sch. Devel. Council, 1963—; cons., adv. com. N.Y. State Senate Com. on Health, 1969—; mem. Ednl. Resources Information Center; guidance commentator Radio Sta. WPUT, 1969—; pub. adv. com. Upward-Bound program Hofstra U. Served with AUS, World War II. Mem. Personnel and Guidance Assn., Nat. Vocat. Guidance Assn. (del. assembly N.Y. State), Am. Ednl. Theatre Assn., Am. Sch. Counselor Assn. (New Eng. editor Newsletter), Am. Acad. Polit. and Social Sci., Am. (nat. coordinator pub. relations, Writer of Year award 1971), N.Y. State (del. 1969-71) sch. counselors assns., Nat. Assn. Sch. Counselors (N.Y. State del.), N.Y. Personnel and Guidance Assn., Internat. Platform Assn., State Counselors Assn., N.Y. State Tchrs. Assn., Columbia, Washington Square (dean's com.) alumni fedns., N.Y.U. Alumni Assn. (past pres. New Orleans), DAV (N.Y. State committeeman 1963-64, sr. vice-comdr. chpt.). Kappa Delta Pi, Phi Delta Kappa. Home: 453 W Walnut St Long Beach NY 11561 Office: Roosevelt Public Schools Roosevelt NY 11575

O'SULLIVAN, JAMES THOMAS, retail shoe co. exec.; b. Providence, June 21, 1945; s. John Francis and Helen Ethel; B.S., Ind. U., 1967; M.B.A. in Mktg.-Fin., 1969; m. Marsha Schulz, Morrison, Aug. 7, 1970; children—Steven David, Lisa Catherine. Gen. mdse. mgr. Jewel Cos., Inc., (Turnstyle, Inc.), Chgo., 1969-76; v.p., gen. mgr. R.W. Shipley Assos., Elmhurst Ill., 1976; v.p. ops. Ideal Shoe Co., Phila., 1976—, also exec. com.; retail cons. Fragments, Inc., Oak Park, Ill., Gilmores, Inc., Oak Park, OK Bazaars, S. Africa. Active Little League Baseball, Glen Ellyn, Ill., 1973-75; dir. Glen Ellyn Jaycees, 1974; chmn. Residential Crusade of Mercy, Glen Ellyn, 1975; budget rev. com. United Fund, 1976. Named Outstanding Jaycee, Glen Ellyn, 1974; recipient Service award United Fund, 1976. Mem. Am. Mgmt. Assn., Nat. Mass. Retailers Inst. Congregationalist. Clubs: Springhaven Golf, Jaycees. Home: 202 Pembroke Rd Wallingford PA 19086 Office: 3175 John F Kennedy Blvd Philadelphia PA 19014

O'SULLIVAN, RENEE BENNETT, physician; b. Boston, July 13, 1929; d. Paul Lloyd and Jessie (Bennett) O'S.; B.A., Bennington Coll., 1951; M.D., Med. Coll. Pa., 1955; children—Rebecca Bennett, Jennifer Letitia, Kimberley Lloyd. Intern in pathology Children's Hosp. Med. Center, Boston, 1955-56, asst. resident in pediatrics, 1957-58, Mass. Gen. Hosp., Boston, 1956-57; asst. resident in gen. surgery Boston VA Hosp., 1958-60; sr. resident plastic surgery Bronx (N.Y.) VA Hosp., 1960-61, N.Y. Hosp., Cornell Med. Center, N.Y.C., 1960-62; practice medicine specializing in plastic surgery Djakarta, Indonesia, 1962-64, Wellesley, Mass., 1964-78; cons. in plastic surgery Indonesian Naval Hosp., 1962-64, Am. embassy, Djakarta, 1962-64, Seventh Day Adventist Hosp., Bandung, Indonesia, 1962-64; mem. staff Boston City Hosp., Faulkner Hosp., Newton-Wellesley Hosp., Glover Meml. Hosp., New Eng. Med. Center Hosp., Cambridge (Mass.) City Hosp., Leonard Morse Hosp., St. Elizabeth's Hosp., Emerson Hosp.; asst. surgeon med. dept. Milit., Cambridge, 1966-68, asso. surgeon, 1968-76; clin. instr. in surgery Harvard Med. Sch., Boston, 1972-78. Diplomate Am. Bd. Plastic Surgery. Fellow A.C.S.; mem. Am. Soc. of Plastic and Reconstructive Surgeons, New Eng. Soc. of Plastic and Reconstructive Surgery, Mass. Soc. Plastic Surgery, Am. Soc. for Aesthetic Plastic Surgery, Mass., Am. Hand Assn., Charles River Dist. med. socs., Am. Trauma Soc. (v.p. Mass. chpt. 1974-75), Am. Med. Women's Assn. (pres. New Eng. br. 1970-71), AMA, Boston Hand Soc., Conway Soc. Republican. Episcopalian. Clubs: White Mountain Ski Runners; Woods Hole Yacht, Quissett Yacht; Harvard; Wellesley College. Contbr. articles on plastic surgery to med. jours. Home: 14 Denton Rd Wellesley MA 02181

OSWALD, DONALD CLIFFORD, civil engr.; b. Olcott, N.Y., June 25, 1925; s. M. Clifford and Ima B. (Gilbert) O.; A.A.S., Erie Community Coll., 1949; m. Lois K. Veen, Apr. 14, 1944; children—David Clifford, Douglas Charles, Dale Craig, Darrell Clifton, Lynda Kim, Drew Christian. Draftsman/surveyor, successively designer, project mgr., sr. project mgr., safety officer Wendel Engrs., Lockport, N.Y., 1948—; instr. pipeline installation Cornell U., 1971, 72, 73. Bd. dirs. Inter-Community Meml. Hosp., 1961—, v.p., 1963-67, chmn. planning and bldg. com., 1963-73, chmn. joint conf. com., 1973-77; chmn. Newfane Town Fire Prevention Bur., 1975—; fire policeman Wrights Corners Fire Co., 1952—, chaplain, 1966—, photographer, 1975—; organizing pres., tng. officer Niagara County Vol. Fire Police Assn., 1963—, chaplain, 1963-76; fire police com. chmn. Western N.Y. Firemans Assn., 1971-76, chaplain, 1976—; charter mem. Vol. Fire Police Assn. State of N.Y., 1953, dir. 1965-67, v.p., 1967-69, pres., 1969-71, chaplain, 1970—; emergency med. technician. Served with USN, 1943-44. Hon. life mem. Erie County Vol. Fire Police Assn., Vol. Fire Police Assn. State of N.Y. (Fire Policeman of Year 1974). Recipient Scouters Key, Lewiston Trail council Boy Scouts Am., 1952. Mem. Niagara County Water Works Assn., Western N.Y. Water Works Conf. Republican. Author: Fire Police Handbook for Vol. Fire Police Assn. of N.Y. State Home: 3786 Olcott Rd Lockport NY 14094 Office: 7405 Canal Rd Lockport NY 14094

OSWALD, JOHN WIELAND, univ. pres.; b. Mpls., Oct. 11, 1917; s. Wieland L. and Isabel (Duhn) O.; A.B., Depauw U., 1938, LL.D., 1964; Ph.D., U. Calif. at Berkeley, 1942; LL.D., Centre Coll., 1966, U. Louisville, 1966, U. Calif. at Davis, 1967; Sc.D., Temple U., 1971; D.H.L., Juniata Coll., 1973, Gettysburg Coll., 1974; m. Rosanel Owen, Oct. 20, 1945; children—Elizabeth, Nancy, John Wieland. Mem. faculty and staff U. Cal. at Berkeley, 1945-63; chmn. dept. plant pathology, 1954-59, prof. plant pathology, 1957-63, v.p., exec. asst to pres., 1961-62, v.p. adminstrn., 1962-63; pres. U. Ky., 1963-68; exec. v.p. U. Calif., 1968-70; pres. Pa. State U., 1970—; cons. NSF, 1957-67; pres. Assn. Am. Univs., Pa. Assn. Colls. and Univs., 1976. Served to lt. (s.g.) USNR, World War II. Decorated Letter Commendation sec. navy; Distinguished Service Cross (Britain); Fulbright research grantee, 1953-54. Mem. Am. Phytopathol. Soc., Am. Council Edn. (dir. 1970-72, chmn. 1973—), Nat. Assn. State Univs. and Land Grant Colls. (exec. com.), Phi Beta Kappa, Sigma Xi, Phi Kappa Psi. Episcopalian (vestry, sr. warden). Contbr. articles to profl. jours. Discoverer virus diseases in cereals in Calif. Home: 639 Kennard Rd State College PA 16801

OTA, HAJIME, agrl. engr.; b. San Gabriel, Calif., Aug. 9, 1916; s. Koichi and Tomi (Miyasako) O.; B.S., Mich. State U., 1948; M.S., U. Minn., 1951; m. Mary Haruko, Apr. 5, 1942; children—Loren, Alan. Asst. engr. grain storage research U.S. Dept. Agr., Redwood Falls, Minn., 1950, project engr., Beltsville, Md., 1951—. Pres., Prince Georges Area High Sch. Sci. Fair Assn., 1972. Served with AUS, 1942-45. Recipient grants Brit. Egg Mktg. Bd., Japanese Poultry Assn. Mem. Orgn. Profl. Employees U.S. Dept. Agr. (dir. 1976). Am. Soc. Agrl. Engrs. (sect. pres. 1973), Am. Soc. Heating, Air Conditioning and Refrigerating Engrs., Poultry Sci. Assn., Animal Sci. Assn., World Poultry Sci. Assn., AAAS, Washington Acad. Scis., Washington Soc. Engrs., Tau Beta Pi, Internt. Soc. Biometeorology, Am. Legion. Presbyterian. Home: 5708 64th Ave Riverdale MD 20840 Office: Bldg 200 BARC-E Beltsville MD 20705

OTELSBERG-GOODWIN, JONAH, statistics adminstr.; b. Warsaw, Poland, Aug. 6, 1932; d. Abraham and Esther Otelsberg; came to U.S., 1962, naturalized, 1968; M.B.A., Baruch Coll., 1967; Ph.D., City U. N.Y., 1976; m. Peter D. Goodwin, Feb. 15, 1976. dir. planning Govt. Israel Central Bur. Statistics, 1958-59; budget dir. City of Tel Aviv, 1959-62; research mgr. Nat. Knitted Outerwear Assn., N.Y.C., 1963-66; project dir. Schwerin Research, N.Y.C., 1966-67; mgr. statis. design and methods McGraw Hill Info. Systems Co., N.Y.C., 1967-76; project dir. Research Found., Center for Social Research, City U. N.Y., 1976—. Mem. Am. Statis. Assn. (chmn. com. small area statistics), Am. Pub. Health Assn., Internat. Inst. Survey Statisticians, Sierra Club, Adirondack Mountain Club, Appalachian Mountain Club. Home: 45 W 54th St New York City NY 10019 Office: 2 W 45th St New York City NY 10036

OTEY, ORLANDO, mus. exec., educator, pianist; b. Mexico City, Mexico, Feb. 1, 1925; s. Ponciano O. and Dolores (Olin) O.; D. Mus., U. Mexico, 1945; student Curtis Inst. Music, Phila., 1945-48; also studied with Luis Moctezuma, Vladimir Sokoloff, Walter Gieseking, Manuel M. Ponce, Gian-Carlo Menotti; m. Diane E. McAnney, Feb. 22, 1974; 1 son, Nathaniel; children by previous marriage—Olivia, Alexander. Pianist appeared in Mexico, U.S., recitals and with orchs., 1929—; faculty mem. Nat. Sch. Music, U. Mexico, 1941-45, Jenkintown Music Sch.; faculty Wilmington (Del.) Mus. Sch., 1965-70, exec. dir., 1966-70; musical dir. Brandywine Pops Orch., 1969-74, Jewish Community Center Orch., 1974-78; dir. Otey Music Sch., 1970—. Gen. mgr. Am. Trade Export Corp., 1960-63; tech. translator export dept. S.S. White Co. (Pennwalt), 1957-60; one of 3 U.S. pianists at Chopin Centennial Festival, Warsaw, Poland, 1949; organist, choirmaster St. John's Episcopal Ch., Bala-Cynwyd, Pa., 1962-64, Christ Episcopal Ch., Media, Pa., 1965-67, Mt. Salem United Meth. Ch., Wilmington, Del., 1973—. Composer: Mexican Fantasy, 1941, Etudes for Piano, 1941, Sonata Tenochtitlan, 1948, Arabesque, 1950, (songs) Sinfonia Breve, 1956, Suite for Strings, 1957, Tzintzuntzan for strings, 1958, Poetica for Soprano and orch., 1958; Poetica for solo trumpet and orch., 1970. Program chmn. Tri-County Concerts Assn., Wayne Pa., 1955-57; v.p. Main Line Symphony Orch., 1956-58; mem. steering com. Cultural Center Commn. Wilmington. Bd. dirs. Del. Symphony Orch. Mem. Nat. Assn. Composers U.S.A. (pres. Phila. chpt. 1959-61), Nat. Edn. Assn. Jazz Educators, Am. Guild Organists, Am. String Tchrs. Assn. (life), Pan-Am. Assn., Curtis Inst. Music Alumni Assn. (life), Postal Commemorative Soc., Am. Symphony Orch. League, Phila. Art Alliance, Mus. Fund Soc. Phila., Nat., Phila., Del. music tchrs. assns., Advancement Mus. Edn., Smithsonian Assos., Nat. Hist. Soc. (charter), Del. Classical Guitar Soc., Wilmington Soc. Fine Arts, Del. Art Mus., Phila. Franklin Inst., Salem County (life), Valley Forge (life) hist. socs., Music Educators Nat. Conf., Internat. Platform Assn. Club: Rotary (pres. local club 1973). Author: Otey Music Teaching Method, 1973. Home: PO Box 5053 Wilmington DE 19808 Office: 2391 Limestone Rd Wilmington DE 19808

OTHMER, DONALD FREDERICK, chem. engr., educator; b. Omaha, May 11, 1904; s. Frederick George and Fredericka Darling (Snyder) O.; student Ill. Inst. Tech., Chgo., 1921-23; B.S., U. Nebr., 1924; M.S., U. Mich., 1925, Ph.D., 1927; D. Engring. (hon.), U. Nebr., 1962, Poly. Inst. N.Y., 1977, N.J. Inst. Tech., 1978; m. Mildred Jane Topp, Nov. 18, 1950. Devel. engr. Eastman Kodak Co. and Tenn. Eastman Corp., 1927-31; instr. Poly. Inst. N.Y., 1932-33, prof., 1933—, head dept. chem. engring., 1937-61, sec. grad. faculty, 1948-58, distinguished prof., 1961—, hon. prof. U. Conception, Chile, 1951; licensed chem. engr. in N.Y., N.J., Ohio, Pa.; dir. several indsl. corps.; cons. chem. engr. and licensor of process patents, 1931—, to numerous cos., also to govtl. depts. U.S., Can., Mexico, Cuba, Puerto Rico, Central and S.Am., Norway, Sweden, Finland, Denmark, Germany, France, Eng., Belgium, Switzerland, Italy, Spain, S. Africa, India, Burma, Yugoslavia, Korea, Taiwan, Japan, Iran, Philippine Islands, United Arab Emirates, Poland in fields of chem. manufacture, transport pipe lines, also sea-water desalting, pollution control, pigments, extractive metallurgy, petrochemicals, plastics, energy devel.; cons. UN, WHO, U.S. Dept. Interior, Nat. Materials Adv. Bd., NRC, Chem. Corps. and Ordance Dept., U.S. Army, spl. devices div. U.S. Navy; sci. adv. bd. U.S. Army Munitions Command., WPB, Dept. of State, WHO, and other depts. U.S. govt., also financial instns., fgn. govts.; dir. indsl. corps. Sr. gas officer Bklyn. Citizens Def. Corps. Trustee or regent several hosps., univs., founds. Recipient Profl. Achievement award Ill. Inst. Tech., 1978. Fellow AAAS, Am. Inst. Cons. Engrs., N.Y. Acad. Scis. (hon. life, chmn. engring. sect. 1972-73), Am. Inst. Chemists (Honor Scroll 1970, Chem. Pioneer award 1977), ASME (chmn. process industries div. 1956), Am. Inst. Chem. Engrs. (chmn. N.Y. sect. 1944, dir. 1956-59; Tyler award 1958; profl. devel. com., internat. relations com.); mem. Am. Chem. Soc. (council 1945-47, E.V. Murphree award 1978), Soc. Chem. Industry (Perkin medal 1978), Engrs. Joint Council (dir. 1956-59), Japan Soc. Chem. Engring., Soc. de Chem. Industrie (pres. Am. sect. 1973-74), Chemurgic Council (member board directors 1963—, chmn. research com.), Assn. Cons. Chemists and Chem. Engrs. (award of merit 1975), Newcomen Soc., Am. Soc. Engring. Edn. (Barber Coleman award 1958), Am. Arbitration Assn. (panel mem.), Sigma Xi, Tau Beta Pi, Phi Lambda Upsilon, Iota Alpha, Alpha Chi Sigma, Lambda Chi Alpha; hon. mem. Deutsche Gesell. fur Chem. Appar. Clubs: Chemists (pres. 1974-76), Norwegian (N.Y.C.); Rembrandt. Designer of plants and processes for numerous corps. in U.S. and fgn. countries. U.S. and fgn. patentee on methods, processes and engring. equipment in mfg. of synthetic fibers, plastics, petrochems., pipe line heating, refrigeration, wallboard, chems. from pulping liquors, water desalination, sewage treatment, extractive metallurgy, solar energy utilization, etc. Contbr. numerous articles to tech. jours. Co-editor: Kirk-Othmer Ency. Chem. Technology 17 vols., 1947-60, 24 vols., 2d edit., 1963-71, vols. 1-4, 3d edit., 1978; editor of Fluidization, 1956. Co-author: Fluidization and Fluid Particle Systems, 1960. Mem. adv. bd. Perry's Chemical Engineer's Handbook; tech. editor UN report Tech. of Water Desalination, 1964. Lectr. sci. and engring. fields; lectr. U.S. Army War Coll., 1964, Swiss univs. for Am. Swiss Found. Sci. Relations, 1950; lecture tour Chem. Inst. Can., 1944-52, India, 1952, Japan, 1955, Am. Chem. Soc.; hon. del., 1961, Fedn. Chem. Engrs., Athens, Greece, 1962. Hon. del. ACHEMA, Frankfurt, Germany, 1958, 61, 64, 67, 70, 73, 76, CHISA Czechoslovakia, 1962, 69, 72, 75, Internat. Congresses Soc. de Chimie Industriel, Belgrade, 1963, 70, Warsaw, 1964, 67, 69, 73, Madrid, 1968, Argentina, 1969, France, 1948, 68, 72, P.R., 1965, Turkey, 1969, Bucharest, 1970, Iran, 1973, Internat. Symposium Freight Pipe Lines, 1976, Arab Petroleum Congresses, Kuwait, 1971, Algiers, 1972, Dubai, 1975, Abu Dhabi, 1976. Home: 140 Columbia Heights Brooklyn NY 11201 also Coudersport PA 16915 Office: 333 Jay St Brooklyn NY 11201

O'TOOLE, EDWARD THOMAS, JR., microbiologist, educator; b. Frederick, Md., July 7, 1933; s. Edward Thomas and Margaret Russelle (Dorsey) O'T.; B.S., U. Md., 1958; postgrad. Balt. Med. Campus, 1959-66, Loyola Coll., 1960; Sc.M., Johns Hopkins Sch. Hygiene and Pub. Health, 1971; Ph.D., Union Grad. Sch., 1977; m. Edith Hellen Stimson, Apr. 19, 1958; children—Shirley Hope, Edward Thomas III, Eugene Stanley. Tchr., dept. chmn., audio-visual coordinator Baltimore County Bd. Edn., Towson, Md., 1958-60; chief microbiologist St. Joseph Hosp., Balt., 1960-64; cons. microbiologist Hosp. for Women of Md., Balt., 1964-65; microbiologist Becton, Dickinson & Co., Cockeysville, Md., 1964-65, chief microbiologist Biol. Safety and Control Labs., 1965-68; dir. sterility services and clin. lab. Huntingdon Research Center, Inc., Balt., 1968-72; tchr. biology and health Balt. City Bd. Edn., 1972—; microbiologist FDA, 1978—; sr. partner firm E Squared Plus 3, Lutherville, Md., 1969—; cons. sterility services and clin. lab., also microbial limits. Vol. instr. cardio-pulmonary resuscitation. Served with AUS, 1956-58. Registered microbiologist, specialist microbiologist Nat. Registry. Mem. Am., Md. socs. med. technologists, Am. Soc. Clin. Pathologists, Am. Soc. Cytology, AAAS, Am. Inst. Biol. Scis., Am. Soc. Microbiology (sec.-treas. Md. br. 1969-74, spl. chmn. clin. meeting 1970, mem. archives com. 1974—), Inst. Food Tech. Roman Catholic. Address: Thornton Ridge Rd Riderwood MD 21139

O'TOOLE, JOHN E., advt. exec.; b. Chgo., 1929; B.S. in Journalism, Northwestern U., 1950; m. Phyllis O'Toole, 1955; children—Sally, Ellen. With Batten, Barton, Durstine & Osborn, 1953-54; with Foote, Cone & Belding Advt., 1954—, successively copy writer, copy supr., asso. copy dir., Chgo., 1954-61, v.p., 1961-64, v.p., creative dir., Los Angeles, 1964-67, Chgo., 1967-68, sr. v.p., dir., 1968-69, pres., dir., N.Y.C., 1969—; pres. Foote, Cone & Belding Communications, Inc., 1970—. Bd. dirs. Advt. Council; mem. Citizens Com. N.Y.C.; trustee Greenwich Acad., Am. Ballet Theatre; mem. U.S. Internat. Com. Served with USMCR, 1951-53, ret. Res., 1956. Mem. Am. Assn. Advt. Agencies (dir.). Home: Greenwich CT Office: 200 Park Ave New York City NY 10017

OTT, WALTER RICHARD, ceramic engr.; b. Bklyn., Jan. 20, 1943; s. Harold Vincent and Mary Elizabeth Ott; B.S., Va. Poly. Inst., 1965; M.S., U. Ill., 1967; Ph.D., Rutgers U., 1969; m. Jeannette Winter, June 27, 1964; children—Regina Winter, Christina Winter, Walter Richard. Process engr. Corhart Refractories, Buckhannon, W.Va., 1965-66; teaching asst. U. Ill., Urbana, 1966-67; research asst. Rutgers U., New Brunswick, N.J., 1967-69, asst. prof. ceramic sci. and engring., 1970-74, asst., asso. dean Coll. Engring., 1974-77, asso. prof., 1973—, grad. dir. Coll. Engring., 1974—; staff research engr. Champion Spark Plug Co., Detroit, 1969-70; engring. cons., 1970—; course developer Center for Profl. Advancement, 1973—. Supt. Sunday sch. St. Pauls Episcopal Ch., Bound Brook, N.J., 1977—.

Recipient Ralph Teetor award Soc. Automotive Engrs., 1973, Profl. Achievement in Ceramic Engring. award Nat. Inst. Ceramic Engrs., 1974. Registered profl. engr., Pa., N.J. Mem. Am. Ceramic Soc. (pres. ceramic ednl. council 1976-77), Am. Soc. Engring. Educators (campus activity coordinator 1975-76, exec. bd. materials div. 1972-76), Ceramic Assn. N.J. (exec. bd.), Soc. Glass Tech., Internat. Confedn. Thermal Analysis, N.Am. Thermal Analysis Soc., Sigma Xi, Sigma Gamma Epsilon. Contbr. articles to profl. jours. Home: 267 Beechwood Ave Middlesex NJ 08846 Office: Dept Ceramics Coll Engring Rutgers U New Brunswick NJ 08903

OTTENSTEIN, ARTHUR BENJAMIN, heavy machinery mfg. co. exec.; b. Bklyn., Apr. 8, 1935; s. Nathan and Shirley (Gilman) O.; B.B.A., Coll. City N.Y., 1957; m. Rosalie Wininger, June 9, 1956; children—Thomas, Nancy, James. Audit supr. Touche Ross & Co., N.Y.C., 1961-65; asst. comptroller Studebaker-Worthington, Inc., N.Y.C., 1965-69; v.p. Masonelilan Internat., Norwood, Mass., 1969-78, sr. v.p., 1978—; pres. Masoneilan Regulator Co., Norwood, 1972—. C.P.A., N.Y., N.J. Mem. Fin. Execs. Inst. Office: 63 Nahatan St Norwood MA 02062

OTTINGER, RICHARD LAWRENCE, congressman; b. N.Y., Jan. 27, 1929; s. Lawrence and Louise (Loewenstein) O.; A.B., Cornell, 1950; LL.B., Harvard, 1953; postgrad. Georgetown U., 1960-61; children—Ronald, Randall, Lawrence, Jenny Louise. Admitted to N.Y. bar, 1955; practice in N.Y.C., 1955-60; contract mgr. ICA, 1960-61; founder, staff mem. Peace Corps, dir. Programs West Coast S.Am., 1961-64; mem. 89th to 91st Congresses, from 25th N.Y. Dist., 94th-95th Congresses from 24th N.Y. Dist. Dir. Friends of the Earth; mem. nat. adv. com. Nat. Rivers and Harbors Congress, 1965—; bd. dirs. Environ. Def. Fund, Tuskegee Inst. Nat. Adv. Council; mem. council Cornell U.; bd. sponsors Zero Population Growth. Served to capt. USAAF, 1953-55. Mem. Internat., Inter-Am., N.Y. bar assns., Assn. Bar City N.Y., Am. Legion, Am. Civil Liberties Union, Cortlandt Conservation Assn., Am. Vets. Com., Friends of Hudson, Common Cause, Nat. Audubon Soc., Sierra Club. Club: Golden Retriever Am. Home: 235 Bear Ridge Rd Pleasantville NY 10570

OTTMAN, JOHN BUDLONG, fin. co. exec.; b. N.Y.C., Nov. 14, 1922; s. DeWitt F. and Julia Menck (Budlong) O.; B.A., Yale, 1944; postgrad. Mass. Inst. Tech., 1944; M.B.A., Harvard, 1947; m. Joan Sidley Kennedy, Oct. 20, 1951; children—Josephine, John Budlong. Advt. mgr. Stewart Warner Corp., Chgo., 1947-52; advt. and sales promotion mgr. Admiral Corp., Chgo., 1952-56; asst. dir. advt. Sunbeam Corp., Chgo., 1956-58; dir. advt., merchandising and pub. relations Skil Corp., Chgo., 1958-63; merchandising mgr. Bristol-Myers Corp., N.Y.C., 1963-70; v.p. investment research C.J. Lawrence Inc., N.Y.C., 1970—. Served to capt. USAAF, 1943-46. Mem. N.Y. Soc. Security Analysts. Republican. Episcopalian. Club: Field. Home: 10 North St Greenwich CT 06830 Office: 115 Broadway New York City NY 10006

OTTO, CALVIN PETER, paper mfg. co. exec.; b. Detroit, Apr. 19, 1930; s. John I. and Myrtle M. (Soncrant) O.; B.B.A., U. Mich., 1958; m. Patricia R. Reed, Mar. 6, 1954; children—Sharon Lynn, James Reed. With Prentice-Hall, Inc., Englewood Cliffs, N.J., 1958-63, asst. v.p., 1962-63; mgr. ednl. div. Bolt Beranek & Newman, Inc., Cambridge, Mass., 1963-72; pres., chmn. bd. Wood Flong Corp., Hoosick Falls, N.Y., 1971—, Wood Graphics Ltd., Eng., 1973—; pres. Wood Flong Internat. Corp., 1972—; chmn. Joseph Batchelor Ltd., Eng., 1972—. Trustee So. Vt. Coll. Served with AUS, 1950-53. Mem. Ephemera Soc. London (dir. N. Am. unit), Delta Sigma Pi. Methodist. Author: (with Rollin Glaser) Management of Training, 1970; Publick Occurrences: The First American Newspaper, 1975; Treaty of Paris: 1783, 1976; The Battle of Bennington, 1977; contbg. author The Shires of Bennington, 1975. Home: 124 Elm St Bennington VT 05201 Office: Wood Flong Corp Davis St Hoosick Falls NY 12090

OTTO, GILBERT FRED, zoologist, educator; b. Chgo., Dec. 16, 1901; s. Martin and Fredericka Christina (Rose) O.; A.B., Kalamazoo Coll., 1926; M.S., Kans. State U., 1927; Sc.D., Johns Hopkins, 1929; m. Loudale Simmons, Dec. 20, 1932; children—Sandra Otto Abbott, Frederick Simmons. Instr. Johns Hopkins U., Balt., 1929-31, asst. prof., 1931-42, asso. prof., 1942-53, asst. dean Sch. of Pub. Health, 1940-47; dir. Parasitology Lab. of Med. Clinics, Johns Hopkins Hosp., Balt., 1946-53; mgr. Parasitology Research Div., Abbott Labs., North Chicago, Ill., 1953-61, dir. of agrl. and vet. research, 1961-66; prof. zoology U. Md., College Park, 1966-72, adj. prof., 1972—. Cons. Naval Med. Research Inst., 1948-54; mem. sci. adv. bd. biology dept., U. Notre Dame, 1958-67; vis. prof. U. Mich. Biol. Sta., summers, 1946-53; cons. NIH, 1945-50, WHO, 1952-75; sec. gen. 2d Internat. Congress Parasitology, 1970. Chief judge High Sch. Sci. Fairs, Prince Georges County (Md.), 1967-70. Chmn. bd. B.H. Ransom Meml. Trustee Fund, 1956—. Named Distinguished Alumnus Kalamazoo Coll., 1951. Fellow AAAS, Royal Soc. Tropical Medicine and Hygiene; mem. Ill. Mosquito Control Assn. (pres. 1960-61), Am. Soc. Tropical Medicine, Am. Heartworm Soc. (sec. treas. 1974—, asso. editor 1974—, pres. 1977-80), Internat. Soc. Tropical Dermatology, World Assn. Advancement Vet. Parasitology, Am. (treas. 1937-41, 44, v.p. 1955, pres. 1957), Brit. socs. parasitologists, Poultry Sci. Assn., Helminthological Soc. Washington (pres. 1936, editor 1952-66), Am. Micros. Soc. Contbr. numerous articles on parasitology to sci. jours; contbr. chpts. to med. and vet. texts. Developer treatment for heartworm in dogs. Home: 10506 Greenacres Dr Silver Spring MD 20903 Office: Zoology Dept University of Maryland College Park MD 20742

OTTO, ROSALIE THERESE, educator; b. Middletown, Conn., Sept. 4, 1914; d. Adam Steven and Mary Barbara (Dedick) Wolak; student Radcliffe Coll., 1934-36; B.A., U. Chgo., 1939; student Meschini Inst., Rome, 1947-48; M.A., Wesleyan U., 1959, Trinity Coll., 1968; postgrad. U. Guadalajara, Mexico, summers 1955-57; m. Robert Edward Otto, July 1, 1944 (dec.); 1 son, Donald Philip. Pvt. sec. Aero Ins. Underwriters, N.Y.C., 1939-40, United Aircraft, East Hartford, Conn., 1940-41; research asst. Van Vleck Obs., Middletown, 1941-43; aerologist Weather Central, Washington, 1943-44; tchr. pub. schs. Great Mills, Md., 1951-53, Deep River, Conn., 1953-57, Meriden, Conn., 1957—; instr. Community Coll., Middletown, 1965-69. Leader Girl Scouts U.S.A., 1940-43; pres. Homeowners Assn., Harrison, Maine, 1971-78. Served with WAVES, 1943-44. Mem. Am. Assn. Tchrs. Spanish and Portuguese, Sociedad Honoraria Hispánica (nat. dir.). Republican. Congregationalist. Club: Garden. Home: 688 Middle St Middletown CT 06457 Office: Platt High Sch Coe Ave Meriden CT 06450

OTTO, THOMAS HERBERT, engring. co. exec.; b. N.Y.C., Nov. 11, 1938; s. Erich Alfred and Charlotte (Wilhm) O.; B.C.E., Rensselaer Poly. Inst., 1960; postgrad. in civil and indsl. engring. Columbia U., 1962-64. Engr., Tippetts, Abbett, McCarthy, Stratton, N.Y.C., 1960-66; asst. head soil and found. dept. Frederic R. Harris, Inc., Engrs., N.Y.C., Stamford, Conn., 1966-68; dept. head Storch Engrs., East Orange, N.J., 1968-69; dept. head, project mgr. Van Houten Assos., Inc., Cons. Engrs., N.Y.C., 1969-71; partner, founder Thor Engrs., Newark, 1971-77; founder Thomas H. Otto & Assos., Fort Lee, N.J., 1977—. Served with C.E., AUS, 1961-63. Mem. Am. Soc. C.E., Nat., N.J. (trustee Bergen County chpt.) socs. profl. engrs., Rensselaer Poly. Inst. Alumni Assn., Alpha Chi Rho. Office: 2337 Lemoine Ave Fort Lee NJ 07024

OTTOMANELLI, GENNARO ANTHONY, psychologist; b. N.Y.C., June 12, 1939; s. Joseph and Angelica (Moligano) O.; B.S., Manhattan Coll., 1961; M.A., Fordham U., 1966; Ph.D., N.Y. U., 1973; m. Helen Dirscherl, Apr. 30, 1964; children—Douglas, Michael. Rehab. counselor N.Y. State Narcotic Addiction, N.Y.C., 1968-70; adminstr. Outpatient Methadone Program, Downstate Med. Center, Bklyh., 1970-71, asso. dir. Div. Drug Dependence, 1971—, clin. asst. prof. depts. psychiatry and biol. psychology. lectr. in field. Licensed psychologist, N.Y. Mem. Am., Eastern Suffolk County psychol. assns. Contbr. articles in field to profl. jours. Home: 47 Village Ln Hauppauge NY 11787 Office: K Bldg PO Box 9 Code 24 600 Albany Ave Brooklyn NY 11203

OUELLET, GILLES, archbishop; b. Bromptonville, Que., Can., Aug. 14, 1922; s. Joseph Adelard and Armande (Biron) O.; B.A., Sherbrooke Sem. Ordained priest Roman Catholic Ch., 1946; archbishop of Rimouski, Que., 1973—. Address: PO Box 730 Rimouski PQ Canada

OUELLETTE, ANDRE, clergyman; b. Salem, Mass., Feb. 4, 1913; s. Amedee and Celina (Ouellette) O.; B.A., Laval U., 1934, L.Th., 1946. Ordained priest Roman Catholic Ch., 1938; prof. philosophy and theology Sem. Trois-Rivieres, Que., 1938-56; rector Major Sem., Trois-Rivieres, 1948-53, Minor Sem., Trois-Rivieres, 1953-57; pres. La Fedn. des Colls. Classiques, 1956; aux. bishop Diocese Mont. Laurier, Que., 1957-63, adminstr., 1963-65, bishop, 1965—. Mem. central commn. Canadian Cath. Conf., 1967-69, pres. theology commn., 1967-70, mem. social action and liturgy commn., 1965-69, co-pres. family com., 1969-71; pres. social action commn. Assembly of Bishops of Province of Que., 1969-71. Address: 435 dela Madone Mont-Laurier PQ J9L 1S1 Canada

OUSSANI, JAMES JOHN, stapling co. exec.; b. Bklyn., Jan. 3, 1920; s. John Thomas and Clara (Tager) O.; B.M.E., Pratt Inst., 1938-42; m. Lorraine G. Tutundgy, Apr. 25, 1954; children—James J., Gregory P., Rita C. Dir. research, mfg. Supertronic Co., N.Y.C., 1943-46; sr. partner Perl-Oussani Machine Mfg. Co., N.Y.C., 1946-49; founder, pres. Staplex Co., Bklyn., 1949—; dir. Lourdes Realty Corp., Junros Corp., Gregrita Realty Corp., Republic Nat. Bank N.Y., Republic N.Y. Corp. Producer air sampling equipment for radioactive fallout AEC, 1951—. Mem. Pres.'s Council on Youth Opportunity; mem. Cardinal's Com. for Edn.; mem. bishop's com. Catholic Charities; founder-dir. Oussani Found.; trustee Ch. Virgin Mary. Recipient Blue Ribbon Mining award, Sch. Mgmt. award, Bur. Research Air Pollution Control, and Aerospace Pride Achievement award; named Knight Holy Sepulchre. Mem. Office Execs. Assn., Nat. Office Machine Mfg., Assn. Adminstrv. Mgmt. Soc., Office Adminstrn. Assn., Nat. Statis. and Office Equipment Assn., Our Lady Perpetual Help, Holy Name Soc., Bus. Equipment Mfrs. Assn., Nat. Office Products Assn. Rotarian. Clubs: Salaam (N.Y.C.); Mahopac Golf (Lake Mahopac, N.Y.). Inventor automatic electric stapling machine. Patentee in field. Office: 777 Fifth Ave Brooklyn NY 11232

OVERCASH, STEPHEN JAY, psychologist; b. Chambersburg, Pa., July 17, 1945; s. Charles Jay and Mary Virginia (Manning) O.; B.S., Dickinson Coll., 1968; M.Ed., U. Del., 1973; Ed.D., U. Va., 1974; m. Elise Claire Suppan, June 20, 1970; children—David, Michael. Tchr., counselor, coach Westminster Sch., Simsbury, Conn., 1968-71; Headstart tchr. SPHERE, Hartford, Conn., 1970-71; counselor Learning Skills Center, U. Del., Newark, 1971-72, research asst., 1972, grad. asst., 1972-73, univ. examiner, 1972-73; intern, clin. psychology trainee VA Hosp., Elsmere, Del., 1972-73; intern in counseling U. Del., Newark, 1973-74; testing cons. Ednl. Testing Service, Princeton, N.J., 1973; counseling psychologist U. Del., Newark, 1973; grad. asst. Counselor of Edn. Lab., U. Va., Charlottesville, 1974, cons. Ednl. Evaluation Service, 1974; cons. Welfare Agy. of Charlottesville, Va., 1974, Chambersburg Area Schs., 1974—, Scotland Sch. for Vet. Children, 1974—, Franklin County Prison and Detention Center, 1974—, Occupational Services, Inc., Chambersburg, Pa., 1975—, Community Living Arrangement, 1975—, Headstart of Franklin County, 1977—, many others; pvt. practice psychology, Chambersburg, Pa. Democrat. Presbyterian. Club: Rotary. Contbr. articles in field to profl. jours. Home: 1030 Wallace Ave Chambersburg PA 11201 Office: 1035 Wayne Ave Chambersburg PA 11201

OVERS, RONALD ROLAND, inventor, mfg. co. exec.; b. Buffalo, Nov. 18, 1931; s. Charles F. and Beatrice O.; student St. Bonaventure U., 1951, U. Buffalo, 1953; m. Barbara Quane, 1969; children—April, Cheryl, Randall, Lauren, Ronald Roland, Gordon, Ingrid, Audrey. Dist. sales mgr. J.C. Virden Co., Cleve., 1954-58; pres. Overs Assos., Inc., Williamsville, N.Y., 1958—; pres. Electro Marine Systems, Inc., East Amherst, N.Y., 1970—, Electro Marine Systems Internat., Inc., East Amherst, 1973—; v.p. Overs, Ltd., Toronto, Ont., Can., 1974—; pres. Emsco Electronics, Inc., Buffalo, 1973—; dir. RB II Corp.; cons. Hoovercraft Bell Aerospace, 1976 Olympics. Recipient President's award J.C. Virden Co., 1956, 57. Mem. IEEE, Boating Industry Assn., Internat. Yacht Racing Assn., Buffalo Zool. Soc., Fox Hunt Farms Civic Assn. Clubs: Buffalo Yacht, Buffalo Canoe, Rolls Royce Owners, Classic Corvette. Patentee marine instruments; designer cardiac med. equipment. Home: 96 Fox Hunt Ln East Amherst NY 14051

OVIATT, VINSON ROMERO, environ. engr., govt. ofcl.; b. Huron, S.D., Aug. 4, 1926; s. Herbert Vinson and Mathilda Joan (Romero) O.; B.S.C.E. S.D. State U., 1949 (W.K. Kellogg Found. fellow); M.P.H., U. Mich., 1953; m. Carla Brown, Aug. 29, 1948; children—Stephen Vinson, Mark Dale. Asst. pub. health engr. Calhoun Health Dept., Battle Creek, Mich., 1949-50; pub. health engr. Barry County (Mich.) Health Dept., 1950-54; hosp. engr. cons. Mich. Dept. Health, Lansing, 1954-64, chief phys. plant unit, 1964-65; chief sect. environ. health services HEW, Silver Spring, Md., 1965-69; chief br. environ. safety NIH, Bethesda, Md., 1969—; Eminent Engrs. lectr. S.D. State U., 1972; preceptor Rackham Grad. Sch. U. Mich.; spl. lectr. pub. health U. Minn.; mem. council pub. health consultants Nat. Sanitation Found. Chmn. com. Troop 1340, Nat. Capital Area council Boy Scouts Am., 1966-73; pres. Winston Churchill High Sch. PTA, Potomac, Md., 1969-71; elder, deacon Geneva United Presbyterian Ch., Rockville, Md. Served with USAAF, 1945. Registered profl. engr., Mich. Mem. AAAS, Am. Hosp. Assn., Am. Acad. Environ. Engring. (diplomate), Am. Pub. Health Assn., Am. Soc. Hosp. Engrs., Internat. Fedn. Hosp. Engring., Nat. Soc. Profl. Engrs., Conf. Fed. Environ. Engrs., Blue Key. Contbr. articles on environ. and hosp. engring. to profl. jours., 1956—. Home: 8505 Victory Ln Potomac MD 20854 Office: NIH Bldg 13 3K04 Bethesda MD 20014

OWEN, ARCHIBALD ALEXANDER, mfg. co. exec.; b. Nashville, Oct. 4, 1932; s. Archibald Alexander and Elizabeth Fairchild (Spyker) O.; B.S., in Chem. Engring., Bucknell U., 1954; M.B.A., George Washington U., 1968; m. Glenn Allen Brown, Dec. 30, 1958; children—Archibald Alexander, Carter Brown, Henry Spyker. With Celanese Corp., 1959-71, prodn. mgr., Lanaken, Belgium, 1963-65, devel. supt., Rock Hill, S.C., 1966-71; mgr. mfg. Gen. Electric Co., Selkirk, N.Y., 1971-73, Pittsfield, Mass., 1973-74; mgr. mfg. FMC Corp., Parkersburg, W.Va., 1974-75, dir. mfg. film, Phila., 1975—; instr. marine engring. U.S. Naval Acad., Annapolis, 1957-59. Served with USN, 1954-59. Mem. Am. Inst. Chem. Engring (sec. Carolinas sect. 1967-68), Toastmasters Internat. (pres. local chpt. 1969-70, regional gov., 1970-71, named Man of Year S.C., 1970), Bucknell Engring. Alumni Assn. (dir. 1971—, pres. 1977—), Phi Gamma Delta. Republican. Presbyterian. Home: 225 Mystic Ln Media PA 19063 Office: 2000 Market St Philadelphia PA 19103

OWEN, CHLOE, soprano, educator; b. Raleigh, N.C.; Mus.B., U. Chattanooga, 1939; postgrad. Peabody Conservatory, Balt. Opera tour of European cities including Bern, Switzerland, Dusseldorf, Germany, Augsburg, Germany, Milan and Spoleto, Italy, Salzburg, Austria, 1953-64; performed radio concerts, Germany, Italy and Switzerland; asso. prof. voice, Boston U.; performed with Little Orch. Soc., N.Y.C., Pitts. Opera Co.; N.Y. Singing Tchrs. Assn., Am. Guild Mus. Artists, condr. master classes various locations. Mem. Nat. Assn. Tchrs. Singing, Mass. Music Tchrs. Assn., Nat. Opera Assn., faculty summer vocal inst. Am. Inst. Mus. Studies, Graz, Austria; AAUP. Studio: 41 W 86th St 3E New York City NY 10024 Office: Boston U SFA 855 Commonwealth Ave Boston MA 02215

OWEN, DWIGHT HALL, printing co. exec.; b. Lewiston, Maine, July 11, 1914; s. Herbert W. and Harriet Ethlyn (French) O.; student U. Hawaii, 1933-35; LL.D., George Washington U., 1939; m. Kathryn Gehan Owen, Sept. 24, 1941; children—Dwight Hall, John Russell, Robert Winslow. Investigator, U.S. Ho. of Reps., Washington, 1939-41; personnel mgr. Cranston Print Works Co. (R.I.), 1941-42, v.p. corporate relations, 1945—; instr. bus. Brown U., 1946-48. Mem. R.I. Civil Service Adv. Com., 1958-59; chmn. R.I. Joint Bus./Legis. Com., 1959-61; bd. dirs. Children's Friend and Service, 1957-63; mem. R.I. Govt. Mgmt. Task Force, 1978; trustee Cranston Found., Textile Workers, Machine Printers, United Textile Workers pension funds. Served to lt. USNR, 1942-45. Decorated Legion of Merit. Mem. R.I. Textile Assn. (pres. 1959-62), Am. Textile Mgmt. Inst., Am. Mgmt. Assn., Am. Arbitration Assn. Republican. Congregationalist. Clubs: Agawan Hunt, Hope, Personnel Execs. (pres. 1950-51). Home: 140 Arlington Ave Providence RI 02960 Office: 1381 Cranston St Cranston RI 02920

OWEN, H. MARTYN, lawyer; b. Decatur, Ill., Oct. 23, 1929; s. Honore Martyn and Virginia (Hunt) O.; grad. Phillips Exeter Acad., 1947; A.B., Princeton, 1951; LL.B., Harvard, 1954; m. Candace Catlin Benjamin, June 21, 1952; children—Leslie Woodruff, Peter Hunt, Douglas Parsons. Admitted to Conn. bar, 1954; asso. firm Shipman & Goodwin, Hartford, Conn., 1958—, partner, 1961—. Dir., Village Water Co. of Simsbury, Inc. (Conn.), Cushman Industries, Inc. Mem. Simsbury Zoning Bd. Appeals, 1961-67, Simsbury Zoning Commn., 1967—; sec. Capitol Region Planning Agy., 1965-66; dir. Symphony Soc. Greater Hartford, 1967-73. Trustee Renbrook Sch., West Hartford, Conn., 1963-72, treas., 1964-68, pres., 1968-72, hon. life trustee, 1972—; trustee Simsbury Free Library, Hartford Grammar Sch.; corporator Inst. of Living, Hartford. Served to lt., Supply Corps, USNR, 1954-57. Clubs: Hartford; Princeton (N.Y.C.); Ivy (Princeton, N.J.). Republican. Episcopalian. Home: 44 Pinnacle Mt Rd Simsbury CT 06070 Office: 799 Main St Hartford CT 06103

OWEN, HARRISON HOLLINGSWORTH, educator; b. Evanston, Ill., Dec. 2, 1935; s. Raymond Smith and Mary Crawford (Siter) O.; B.A., Williams Coll., 1957; B.D., Va. Sem., 1960; M.A., Vanderbilt U., 1965; m. Ethelyn Rose Abbott, July 20, 1967; children—Mary Christine, Harrison Hollingsworth. Ordained minister Episcopal Ch., 1960; Episcopal chaplain Johns Hopkins U., 1960-62; asso. fellow Inst. for Policy Studies, Washington, 1966-67; exec. dir. Adams Morgan Community Council, Washington, 1965-67; asso. dir. Peace Corps, Liberia, 1967-69; dir. Nassau Suffolk Regional Med. Program, 1969-74; program coordinator Heart Inst., NIH, Bethesda, Md., 1974-77; confidential asst. to chief med. dir. VA, Washington, 1977—, exec. dir. VA Scholars Program, 1977—. Mem. Am. Public Health Assn., Soc. for Dirs. of Continuing Med. Edn. Democrat. Author: When the Devil Dances, 1971; Red Dust on Green Leaves, 1973. Home: 8225 Stone Trail Dr Bethesda MD 20034 Office: VA 810 Vermont Ave Washington DC 20034

OWEN, JACK WALDEN, hosp. assn. exec.; b. Union City, Pa., Sept. 21, 1928; s. Wallace A. and Rosamond E. (Walden) O.; B.S., Western Mich. U., 1951, B.A., 1953; M.B.A., U. Chgo., 1957; m. Charlotte E. Keller, Sept. 14, 1957; children—Linda, Lisa, Jack Walden II. Occupational therapist Vets. Hosp., Battle Creek, Mich., 1953; asst. dir. Am. Hosp. Assn., Chgo., 1957-63; pres. N.J. Hosp. Assn., Princeton, 1963—, Hosp. Research and Ednl. Trust, 1964—, N.J. Hosp. Service Corp., 1972—; chmn. bd., pres. N.J. Hosp. Assn. Underwriters, Inc., 1975—; mem. bd. First Nat. Bank Central N.J., 1977—. Treas., Regional Med. Program, 1967-73. Mem. Sch. Bd. Rocky Hill, N.J., 1966—. Bd. dirs. Westfield Children's Hosp. Served with M.C., AUS, 1953-55. Dept. Health, Edn. and Welfare grantee, 1963-74. Mem. Hosp. Soc. N.Y., N.J. State Hosp. Assn. (pres. exec. forum 1971), U. Chgo. Hosp. Alumni Assn. (pres. 1973-74), N.J. Med. Malpractice Reins. Assn. (dir. 1976—). Club: Nassau (Princeton, N.J.). Home: 12 Lemore St Rocky Hill NJ 08553 Office: 760 Alexander Rd Princeton NJ 08540

OWEN, JOHN LAVERTY, mfg. co. exec.; b. Mayfield, Ky., July 28, 1923; s. John Clarence and Lydia (Laverty) O.; B.A. magna cum laude, Westminster (Mo.) Coll., 1944; postgrad. Purdue U., 1945; M.S. in Psychology, Pa. State U., 1951; m. Marjory Clara Wallace, June 29, 1946; children—John Wallace, David William, Jeffrey Daniel. With Hamilton Watch Co., Lancaster, Pa., 1944—, personnel research supr., 1946-58, personnel selection and devel. mgr., 1958-63, staff personnel services dir., 1963-70, corporate employee relations dir. HMW Industries, Inc., 1970-77, human resources dir., 1977—. Bd. dirs. United Way of Lancaster County, Lancaster chpt. Nat. Urban League. Licensed psychologist, Pa. Mem. Am., Eastern, Pa. psychol. assns., Am. Mgmt. Assn., Am. Soc. for Personnel Adminstrn. (accredited exec. in personnel), Lancaster Assn. Commerce and Industry, Omicron Delta Kappa, Psi Chi, Phi Kappa Phi, Delta Tau Delta. Republican. Presbyn. Home: 948 Pleasure Rd Lancaster PA 17601 Office: 901 Columbia Av Lancaster PA 17604

OWEN, RICHARD, fed. judge; b. N.Y.C., Dec. 11, 1922; s. Carl Maynard and Shirley (Barnes) O.; A.B., Dartmouth Coll., 1947; LL.B., Harvard U., 1950; m. Lynn Rasmussen, June 6, 1960; children—Carl R., David R., Richard. Admitted to N.Y. State bar, 1950; practiced in N.Y.C., 1950-74; asso. firm Willkie, Owen, Farr, Gallagher & Walton, 1950-53, Willkie, Farr, Gallagher, Walton & Fitzgibbon, 1958-60; individual practice, 1960-65; partner firm Owen & Aarons, 1965-66, Owen & Turchin, 1966-74; asst. U.S. atty. So. Dist. N.Y., 1953-55; antitrust div. Dept. Justice, 1955-58; judge U.S. Dist. Ct. for So. Dist. N.Y., 1974—; asst. prof. N.Y. Law Sch., 1951-53; asso. counsel N.Y. State Moreland Com. on Alcoholic Beverage Control Laws, 1963-64. Trustee Manhattan Sch. Music, N.Y.C.; bd. dirs. Hudson Valley Philharmonic; chmn. bd. Maine Opera Assn., Inc. Served to 1st lt. USAAF, 1942-45. Decorated D.F.C. with oak leaf cluster, Air medal with 3 oak leaf clusters. Mem. ASCAP, Maine Opera Assn. (chmn. bd.). Republican. Quaker. Clubs: Met. Opera; Gipsy Trail; Pine Pond Yacht (commodore 1967-70). Composer- librettist operas: A Moment of War, 1958; A Fisherman

Called Peter, 1965; Mary Dyer, 1975. Office: US Courthouse Foley Sq New York City NY 10007

OWEN, STEPHEN FREDERICK, JR., lawyer; b. Springfield, Mass., Apr. 9, 1934; s. Stephen Frederick and Stephanie (Jack) O.; B.S. in Elec. Engring., U. Mass., Amherst, 1955; Certificate in Bus. Mgmt., U. Pitts., 1959; J.D., Cornell, 1962; LL.M. in Taxation, Georgetown U., 1964; m. Mary Lani, Apr. 4, 1964; children—Tara Ann, Stephen Frederick III, Meredith Diane, Jonathan James. Sales engr., dir. systems dept. Westinghouse Elec. Corp., Pitts., 1955-59; admitted to D.C. bar, 1962, U.S. Supreme Ct. bar, 1966; atty., adviser div. corp. finance SEC, Washington, 1962-64; asso. mem. law firm Loomis, Owen, Fellman & Howe, Washington, 1964-69, partner, 1969-77, sr. partner, 1977—. Gen. counsel to seven nat. trade assns. Mem. Planning and Zoning Commn., South Bethany, Del., 1977-78. Registered profl. engr., Mass. Mem. Fed., Am. (chmn. com. on uniform rules of practice and procedure 1974, vice-chmn. food and drug law com. 1975—, mem. council adminstrv. law sect. 1976—), D.C. bar assns., Nat. Lawyers Club, Phi Delta Phi. Clubs: University, Kenwood Country, Capitol Hill. Contbr. articles in field to profl. jours. Home: 5610 Knollwood Rd Bethesda MD 20016 Office: 2020 K St NW Washington DC 20006

OWEN, THOMAS LLEWELLYN, investment exec.; b. Patchogue, N.Y., June 24, 1928; s. Griffith Robert and Jeanette Roberts (Hatfield) O.; A.B. in Econs., Coll. William and Mary, 1951; postgrad. Columbia, 1952; postgrad. N.Y. Inst. Finance, 1960-62; M.B.A., N.Y. U., 1966. Exec. trainee Shell Oil Co., N.Y.C. and Indpls., 1951-59, supr., 1958-59; investment analyst Paine, Webber, Jackson & Curtis, N.Y.C., 1959-62; sr. investment analyst DuPont Investment Interests, Wilmington, Del., N.Y.C., 1962-66, asst. dir. research, 1964-66; with Nat. Securities & Research Corp., N.Y.C., 1966-75, sr. investment officer, mem. policy, investment coms., 1969-75; with F. Eberstadt & Co., Inc., N.Y.C., 1975—. Mem. N.Y. Soc. Security Analysts, Assn. Energy Economists, Nat. Assn. Petroleum Investment Analysts, Oil Analysts Group N.Y., Am. Econ. Assn., Investment Assn. N.Y., Am. Petroleum Inst. Contbr. chpt. to Fin. Analysts Handbook, 1975. Home: 251 E 32d St New York City NY 10016 Office: 61 Broadway New York City NY 10006

OWENS, CHESTER DANIEL, penologist, educator; b. Buffalo, Dec. 27, 1907; s. Daniel Webster and Theresa Jessie (Altmann) O.; A.B., Bucknell U., 1933; M.A., N.Y. U., 1945; m. Louise Ethel Anthes, Aug. 22, 1934; 1 dau., Faith Ethel (Mrs. Richard C. Evans). Tchr., supr. edn. Woodbourne (N.Y.) Correctional Inst., 1937-45; dir. edn. Elmira (N.Y.) Reformatory, 1945-53; asst. supt. Reception Center, Elmira, 1953-63, supt., 1963-76. Instr., St. Lawrence U., 1950-54, Elmira Coll., 1956—; cons. on objectives, orgn., prins., policies of reception centers. Mem. Planning Bd., Horseheads, N.Y., 1962—; mem. Youth Commn., Horseheads, 1964—. Mem. Am. Correctional Assn. (com. on classification and treatment), Correctional Edn. Assn. (hon. life, past pres.), Kappa Phi Kappa, Tau Kappa Alpha, Tau Kappa Epsilon. Baptist. Mason (33 deg.), Rotarian. Editor: Jour. Correctional Edn., 1948-55; mem. editorial staff Jour. Criminal Psychopathology, Jour. Clin. Psychopathology and Psychotherapy; asso. editor Handbook on Correctional Classification, 1978. Contbr. numerous articles to profl. jours. Home: 109 Orchard Knoll Dr Horseheads NY 14845

OWENS, GARLAND CHESTER, educator; b. Wilson, N.C., Dec. 12, 1922; s. James F. and Leona (Owens) O.; B.S., U. Richmond, 1947; M.S., Columbia, 1948, Ph.D., 1956; m. Mary Elizabeth Wade, June 19, 1948; 1 dau., Lynn Carol. Accountant, Arthur Young & Co., C.P.A.'s, N.Y.C., 1950-53; mem. faculty Columbia Grad. Sch. Bus., N.Y.C., 1956—, prof., 1964—, asso. dean, 1962-70; program dir. Mgmt. Devel. Center, Belo Horizonte Minas Gerais, Brazil, 1973-75. Controller Arctic Inst. N.Am., 1957-77. Mem. bd. edn. Union Free Sch. Dist. 5, Greenburgh, N.Y., 1964-69, v.p., 1965-68, pres., 1968-69; mem. NE Regional Postmaster Selection Bd., U.S. Postal Service, 1969-75. Served to capt. USAAF, 1942-45. Decorated D.F.C., Air medal. C.P.A., N.Y. Mem. Am. Inst. C.P.A.'s, N.Y. State Soc. C.P.A.'s, Am. Accounting Assn., Beta Gamma Sigma. Presbyterian. Author: Cost Basis in Business Combinations, 1956; (with James A. Cashin) Auditing, 1963. Home: 2 Woods Ln Scarsdale NY 10583 Office: Uris Hall Columbia Univ New York City NY 10027

OWENS, GUY, neurosurgeon, educator; b. Amarillo, Tex., Jan. 25, 1926; s. Guy Fitzhugh and Mary Virgin O.; B.S. magna cum laude, Tufts U., 1946; M.D., Harvard, 1950; m. Janet Parkinson, June 11, 1949; children—Victoria Anne, Guy Parkinson. Intern, Vanderbilt U. Hosp., Nashville, 1950-51, resident, 1951-52, 54-55, Rockefeller fellow NRC, Nashville, 1957-58; practice medicine specializing in neurosurgery, Nashville, 1958-60; chief dept. neurosurgery Roswell Park Meml. Inst., Buffalo, 1960-68; prof. surgery U. Conn., 1968; mem. staff New Britain (Conn.) Gen. Hosp., 1970—, chief neurosurgery, 1975—; mem. staffs U. Conn. Hosp., VA Hosp., Newington, Conn.; cons. to hosps. Served with USN, 1952-53. Markle scholar, 1958-65; NIH grantee, 1970-75; Squibb grantee, 1973—. Mem. Soc. Univ. Surgeons, Am. Physiol. Soc., Am. Soc. Clin. Oncology, A.C.S., Am. Soc. Neurol. Surgeons, Hartford County (Conn.) Med. Soc. Republican. Congregationalist. Club: Shuttle Meadow Country. Contbr. numerous articles to profl. publs. Home: 41 Main St Farmington CT 06032 Office: 40 Hart St New Britain CT 06052

OWENS, THOMAS FRANCIS, oral surgeon; b. Mt. Carmel, Pa., Oct. 18, 1932; s. Thomas Francis and Anna (Hrabovsky) O.; student Pa. State U., 1950-53; D.D.S., U. Md., 1957; postgrad. Grad. Sch. Medicine, U. Pa., Phila., 1962-63; m. Helen Mary Scerbak, July 28, 1962. Intern oral surgery Mt. Sinai Hosp., N.Y.C., 1959-60; resident in dental anesthesiology Kingsbrook Med. Center, Bklyn., 1960-61; resident in oral surgery Cornell Med. Center Hosp., N.Y.C., 1961-62; practice dentistry specializing in oral surgery, Springfield, Pa., 1964—. Diplomate Am. Bd. Oral Surgery. Mem. Am. Dental Assn., Chester-Delaware County Dental Soc., Am. Soc. Oral Surgeons, Am. Dental Soc. Anesthesiology. Office: 1050 Baltimore Pike Springfield PA 19064

OWENS, THOMAS WEBSTER, lawyer; b. Cape May, N.J., Jan. 13; s. James F. and Ethel O.; B.S., Ind. U., 1956, M.Pub. Adminstrn., 1961; J.D., U. Conn., 1974. Housing asst. Pitts., 1957-59; sr. city planner Hartford (Conn.), 1962-64, prin. city planner, 1964-68, asst. planning dir., 1968-75; admitted to Pa. bar, 1974; atty. Hartford Nat. Bank & Trust Co., 1975—; tchr. Miss Porters Sch., Farmington, Conn., 1972-75. Loaned exec. United Way, 1977; adv. bd. Greater Hartford Salvation Army. Mem. Am., Pa., Phila. bar assns., Am. Inst. Planners. Home: 7 Highland St # 3 West Hartford CT 06119 Office: 777 Main St Hartford CT 06115

OWENS, WILLIAM ROBERT, mfg. co. exec.; b. Syracuse, N.Y., May 12, 1932; s. William James and Florence Elizabeth (Haar) O.; B.B.A., Lemoyne Coll., 1953; grad. student Syracuse U., 1957-60; m. Lois Ruth Gumprecht, Apr. 7, 1956; children—William Michael, Robert Joseph, Steven Patrick. Service technician Carrier Corp., Syracuse, 1953, Porter-Cable Power Tool Co. div. Rockwell Mfg. Co., Syracuse, 1955-61; mgr. corporate systems devel. Crouse-Hinds Co., Syracuse, 1961—; instr. Sair Aviation Flight Sch., Syracuse 1975—; instr. systems and data processing Auburn (N.Y.) Community Coll., 1967—, cons. data processing adv. com., 1969-75; guest lectr. Syracuse U. Sch. Mgmt., 1977. Served with U.S. Army, 1953-55. Recipient Merit award Assn. Systems Mgmt., 1970, Nat. Achievement award, 1971; certified flight and ground sch. instr., N.Y. Mem. Assn. Systems Mgmt. (pres. Central N.Y. chpt. 1968-69), CAP (asst. squadron comdr. 1975-76), Central N.Y. Pilots Assn. (pres. 1973-74), Syracuse Systems Execs. Assn. (co-founder 1971). Author booklet on aviation, 1978. Home: 4062 Pawnee Dr Liverpool NY 13088 Office: c/o Crouse-Hinds Co Wolf at 7th N St Syracuse NY 13201

OXFORD, HARRY JAMES, athletics director; b. Port Chester, N.Y., Nov. 9, 1936; s. Harry James and Dorthory Rita (Smith) O.; A.A., B.S., George Washington U., 1961; m. Roberta A. Keenan, Apr. 15, 1961; children—Harry James, Keenan Andrew, Karen Amelia. Dir. athletics, Maret Sch., Washington, 1961-63; dir. phys. edn. Beavoir Elementary Sch., Washington, 1963-72; sports coordinator, Army's World Wide program, U.S. Army, Washington, 1972-75; dir. athletics Peddie Sch., Hightstown, N.J., 1975—; head coach, St. Albans, Sidwell Friends, & Landon; head coach All-Army Womens Basketball Team, 1976, 77; cons. to U.S. vice president's Operation Champ, 1968; coordinator for Phys. Edn. for Pub. Info. Program. Recipient Exceptional Meritorius Service award Dept. of Army, 1975. Mem. AAHPER, AAU (bd. dirs., chmn. com. pub. rels. for Potomac Valley), Am. Assn. Football Coaches, U.S. Olympic Coms., 1973-75. Roman Catholic. Contbr. articles to athletics jours. Home and Office: Dept Athletics The Peddie School Hightstown NJ 08520

OYEWOLE, GODWIN GBOLADE, broadcasting cons. and producer; b. Lagos, Nigeria, Apr. 23, 1942; s. Benjamin Ajibola-Olufayo and Mabel Olubunkola (Shokoya) O.; came to U.S., 1960; B.A., State U. N.Y., 1964; M.B.A., Loyola U., Chgo., 1970; Ph.D., U. Mass., 1972; m. Saundra Elaine Herndon, Mar. 21, 1970; children—Ayodeji Babatunde Olusegun, Kolade Olufayo. Research asst. Russ Johnson Assos., Chgo., 1964-67; claim examiner Prudential Ins. Co., Chgo., 1966-70; dir. bus. affairs and devel. WFCR-FM, Amherst, Mass., 1966-72, gen. mgr., 1972-78; exec. editor Georgetown Law Weekly, 1977—; dir. Asso. Pub. Radio Sta., 1972-73, Nat. Pub. Radio, 1973-76; pres. Eastern Pub. Radio Network, 1973-76; adj. prof. communication U. Mass., Amherst, 1976-77; instr. mgmt. Western New Eng. Coll., Springfield, Mass., 1972-77; TV host Hello Nigeria, 1974, Salute by Satellite, USIA Bicentennial TV program; mem. adv. panel on essentials for effective minority programming CPB, 1974-75, mem. task force on minorities in pub. broadcasting, 1977-78. Mem. Nat. Assn. Ednl. Broadcasters, Am. Mktg. Assn., Educators Travel to Africa Assn. Anglican. Home: 50 Overlook Dr Amherst MA 01002 Office: WFCR-FM Univ of Mass Amherst MA 01002

OZARK, DANIEL LEONARD, athletics mgr.; b. Buffalo, Nov. 26, 1923; s. Leo and Margaret (Cieslewicz) O.; grad. high sch. Buffalo; m. Virginia Zdinski, Feb. 19, 1949; children—Dwain, Darlene. Player, Los Angeles Dodgers, mgr. minor league, coach, to 1972; mgr. Phila. Phillies, 1972—. Served with U.S. Army. Decorated Purple Heart. Bronze Star (5). Clubs: Elks, Moose. Home: 2737 Ocean Dr Villa 25 Vero Beach FL 32960 Office: Philadelphia Phillies Broad and Patterson Sts Veterans Stadium Philadelphia PA 19148

OZAWA, SEIJI, conductor, musical dir.; b. Hoten, Manchuria, Sept. 1, 1935; s. Kaisaku and Sakura Ozawa; student Toho Sch. Music, Tokyo, Japan, 1953-59; studied with Eugene Bigot, Herbert Von Karajan, Leonard Bernstein. One of three asst. condrs. N.Y. Philharmonic, 1961-62 season; music dir. Ravinia Festival, 1964-69; permanent condr. Toronto (Ont., Can.) Symphony Orch., 1965-69; music dir. San Francisco Symphony Orch., 1970-76; dir. Berkshire Music Festival, Tanglewood, 1970—; music dir. Boston Symphony Orch., 1973—; guest condr. major orchs. throughout world. Office: Columbia Artists Mgmt Inc 165 W 57th St New York City NY 10019

OZIMEK, RICHARD THOMAS, markets researcher, publishing co. exec.; b. Newark, Aug. 22, 1929; s. Peter and Mary O.; A.B. in Chemistry, Rutgers U., 1951; postgrad. Wharton Grad. Sch. Fin. and Commerce, U. Pa., 1954-55; m. Phyllis Blake, May 5, 1962; children—Kimberley, Elizabeth. Civilian research chemist Picatinney Arsenal U.S. Army, N.J., 1951-52; market research analyst Allied Chem. Co., N.Y.C., 1955-56; supr. market research Comml. Solvents Corp., N.Y.C., 1956-59; markets editor Chem. Week Mag., McGraw Hill Pub. Co., N.Y.C., 1960-66; dir. research, sr. analyst N.Y. Securities Co., N.Y.C., 1966-68; sr. instl. cons. F.I. DuPont Co., N.Y.C., 1968-70; v.p. instl. services Janney Montgomery Scott, N.Y.C., 1971-73; v.p. research Laidow Coggeshall, N.Y.C., 1973-74, Rosenkrantz, Ehrenkrantz, Lyon and Ross, N.Y.C., 1975—; pres., dir. Ozimek Data Corp., Rye, N.Y., 1976—. Served to 2d lt. USAF, 1972-73. Home and Office: 92 Mendota Ave Rye NY 10580

PAASWELL, ROBERT EMIL, civil engr., educator; b. Red Wing, Minn., Jan. 15, 1937; s. George and Evelyn (Cohen) P.; B.A. (Ford Found. fellow), Columbia, 1956, B.S., 1957, M.S., 1962; Ph.D., Rutgers U., 1965; m. Rosalind Snyder, May 31, 1958; children—Judith Marjorie, George Harold. Field engring. asst. Spencer White & Prentis, Washington, 1954-56, engr., N.Y.C., 1957-59; research scientist Davidson Lab., N.J., 1964; research fellow Greater London Council, 1971-72; research and teaching asst. Columbia, 1959-62; asst. prof. civil engring. State U. N.Y., Buffalo, 1964-68, chmn. bd. govs. Urban Studies Coll., 1973-76, asso. prof., 1968-76, prof. civil engring., 1976—; faculty-on-leave U.S. Dept. Transp., 1976-77; v.p. Faculty Tech. Consultants, Inc.; cons. transp. planning and soil mechs.; spl. cons. to Congressman T. Dulski, 1973. Mem. Buffalo Environ. Mgmt. Comm., 1972-74; mem. Area Com. for Transit, Mayor's Energy Adv. Bd., 1974; chmn. com. on transp., mem. rev. adv. bd. Research and Planning Council Western N.Y. Recipient U.S. Dept. Transp. award, 1977. State U. N.Y. faculty fellow, 1965-66. Mem. ASCE (pres. Buffalo sect.), Transp. Research Bd., AAAS, Sigma Xi. Author: Problems of the Carless, 1977. Bd. editors of Jour. Environ. Systems, 1971—, Jour. Urban Systems, 1974—, Transportation, 1978—. Contbr. articles to profl. jours. Home: 277 Woodbridge Ave Buffalo NY 14214 Office: Dept Civil Engring State U NY Buffalo NY 14214

PABARCIUS, ALGIS, investment co. exec.; b. Telsiai, Lithuania, May 1, 1932; s. Vacius and Brone (Ziuryte) P.; came to U.S., 1950, naturalized, 1956; B.S., U. Ill., 1955; M.S., Ill. Inst. Tech., 1958, Ph.D., 1964; postgrad. Technische Hochschule Muenchen, Germany, 1962; m. Eleanor A. Rakovic, Aug. 18, 1956; children—Nina, Lisa, Algis. Engr., Esso Research & Engring. Co., Linden, N.J., 1955-56; instr. U. Ill., Chgo., 1956-59, asst. prof., 1959-64; partner Zubkus, Zemaitis & Assos., Architects and Engrs., Chgo., Washington, 1959-67; v.p. Garden Hotels Investment Co. and Whitecliff Corp., Lanham, Md., 1967-75; pres. Aras Investment Corp., 1975—. Profl. engr. Ill., D.C.; structural engr. Ill. Danforth Found. grantee, 1960-61, NSF faculty fellow, 1961-62. Mem. Am. Soc. C.E., Sigma Xi, Tau Beta Pi, Sigma Tau, Chi Epsilon, Phi Kappa Phi. Home: 10020 Hall Rd Potomac MD 20854 Office: 9301 Annapolis Rd Lanham MD 20801

PACCO, CHARLES BERNARD, savs. and loan exec.; b. Corinth, N.Y., Apr. 17, 1918; s. Charles P. and Agnes M. (Cohan) P.; grad. high sch.; m. Mary Agnes Mooney, Sept. 14, 1943; children—Jeanne, Richard, Carol, Loraine, Paul. Asst. dept. supr. Internat. Paper Co., 1940-54; treas.-mgr. Hudson River Fed. Credit Union, Corinth, 1954—. Mem. Saratoga County Selective Service Bd., 1962—; treas. Corinth Indsl. Devel. Agy., 1977—. Mem. Credit Union Assn. (dir. Adirondack dist. 1957—), N.Y. State Credit Union League (dir. 1958—, past pres.), Empire State Credit Union Execs. Soc. (treas.), Credit Union Execs. Soc., Mgrs. Soc. Clubs: Elk, Rotary. Home: RD 1 Box 55 Corinth NY 12822 Office: 312 Palmer Ave Corinth NY 12822

PACE, OMAR THOMAS, surgeon; b. Rackett, Nebr., Aug. 28, 1917; s. William T. and Myrtle (Kelleher) P.; B.S., State U. Iowa, 1940, M.D., 1943; m. Audrey Brown, Oct. 31, 1941; children—Pamela, Gregory, Lawrence. Intern, County Hosp., U. Utah, Salt Lake City, 1943; resident in surgery Franklin Sq. Hosp., Balt., 1944-45, Gen. Hosp., U. Louisville, 1945-46; resident, asst. supt. State Cancer Hosp., Westfield, Mass., 1946-49; practice medicine specializing in surgery, Springfield, Mass., 1949—; chief cancer staff, surgeons in chief Western Mass. State Cancer Hosp., Westfield, 1964-70; sr. staff mem. Springfield Hosp. Med. Center (now Baystate Med. Center, 1949—; clin. instr. surgery Tufts Med. Sch., 1956-60, Albany (N.Y.) Med. Sch., 1962-65. Mem. Western Mass. Health Planning Council, 1967-77, dir., 1967-76, pres., 1972-74; mem. Gov.'s Adv. Council for Comprehensive Health Planning, 1972-73; mem. nat. task force on cancer of colon and rectum Am. Cancer Soc., 1973—; mem. Interstate Cancer Council of New Eng.; pres. Am. Cancer Soc., Mass. div., 1970-72, dir., 1960—, dir. nat. div., 1972—. Diplomate Am. Bd. Surgeons. Fellow A.C.S.; mem. Springfield Acad. Medicine (past pres.), Mass. Med. Soc., AMA, New Eng. Surg. Soc., N.E. Med. Assn. Republican. Club: Rotary. Contbr. chpts. to med. textbooks. Home: 1428 Longmeadow St Longmeadow MA 01106 Office: 281 State St Springfield MA 01105

PACICCO, ROBERT RUDOLPH, diamond dealer, jeweler; b. Jersey City, Aug. 22, 1952; s. Alfred Michael and Leatrice Theresa (Cacioli) P.; B.A. with honors, St. Peter's Coll., Jersey City, 1975; postgrad. Fordham U. Law Sch., 1978. Supr., Leonia (N.J.) Recreation Commn., 1968-72; mgr. Manor Beverage Corp., Leonia, 1972-75; legal paraprofl. firm Donovan, Leisure, Newton & Irvine, N.Y.C., 1975-76; v.p. P&P Jewelers, N.Y.C., 1976—; lectr., cons. in field. Councilman, Borough of Leonia, 1978—; Democratic dist. coordinator 9th Congl. Dist., 1978—. Mem. Jewelers Bd. Trade, Diamond Club Am., Registered Jewelers Assn., Nat. Assn. Physically Handicapped (hon.), Phi Alpha Theta, Alpha Phi Omega. Club: Leonia Lions. Home: 550 Grandview Terr Leonia NJ 07605 Office: 29 W 47th St New York City NY 10036

PACIFICO, RICHARD DOMENIC, art gallery exec.; b. Corning, N.Y., Jan. 28, 1933; s. Joseph and Adeline Treasa (Santoro) P.; diploma Washington Sch. Music, 1952; student Lowell State Tchrs. Coll, 1956-60; Mus.B., Eastern Nazarene Coll., 1962; m. Gail Alice Pitcher, Apr. 10, 1954; children—Gail Adrienne, Deanna Marie, Richard Joseph. Owner, Pacifico Restaurant, Somerville, Mass., 1963-65; music supr. elementary schs., Somerville, 1967-69; now pres., dir. Pacifico Art Gallery, Boston; condr. Dick Pacific Orch. Served with USAF, 1951-53. Mem. Music Educators Nat. Conf. Home: 94 Hutchinson Rd Arlington MA 02174 also 617 Surf Dr Falmouth MA 02144 Office: Pacifico Galleries Inc 395 Commercial St Boston MA 02109

PACIK, PETER THOMAS, physician; b. N.Y.C., May 19, 1940; s. Erik and Kitty (Storm) P.; M.D., State U. N.Y., Downstate Med. Center, 1965; m. Mia Jacobson, June 14, 1964; children—Deborah, Nadine, Danielle. Intern, Beth Israel Med. Center, N.Y.C., 1965-66, resident in surgery, 1966-67; resident Grasslands Hosp., Westchester, N.Y., 1967-70; resident in plastic surgery Upstate Med. Center, Syracuse, N.Y., 1970-72; practice medicine specializing in plastic surgery, Manchester, N.H., 1972—; mem. staff Catholic Med. Center, Manchester, Elliot Hosp., Manchester. Diplomate Am. Bd. Surgery, Am. Bd. Plastic and Reconstructive Surgery. Fellow A.C.S.; mem. Am., New Eng. socs. plastic and reconstructive surgeons, Am. Cleft Palate Assn., Internat. Soc. Clin. Plastic Surgeons, N.H. Med. Soc. Home: 11 Shirley Park Goffstown NH 03045 Office: 540 Chestnut St Manchester NH 03101

PACINELLI, RALPH NICHOLAS, govt. ofcl.; b. Downingtown, Pa., Oct. 6, 1934; s. Ralph and Josephine Katherine (Shaw) P.; B.S., Villanova U., 1956; M.Ed., Pa. State U., 1958, Ed.D., 1968; m. Patricia Ann Piersol, Jan. 3, 1959. Counselor, supr. Pa. Bur. Vocat. Rehab., Williamsport and Harrisburg, 1958-64; cons. rehab. services adminstrn. Dept. HEW, Washington, 1964-66; dir. edn. and research Internat. Assn. Rehab. Facilities, Washington, 1968-72; dir. devel. and community edn. Elwyn (Pa.) Inst., 1972-73; research officer Social and Rehab. Service, HEW, Phila., 1973-74, dir. Office Rehab. Services, Region III, 1974—. Mem. Am. Personnel and Guidance Assn., Nat., Pa. rehab. assns., Assn. Rehab. Facilities, Am. Rehab. Counseling Assn., Nat. Assn. Rehab. Adminstrn., Assn. Educators of Rehab. Facility Personnel (pres. 1970), Phi Delta Kappa. Editor: Internat. Newsletter, 1969-72, Cost Control in Rehabilitation Centers, 1969, Work Evaluation, 1969, 70, Research Utilization in Rehab. Facilities, 1971; cons. editor Jour. Rehab. Adminstrn. Home: 600 Old School House Dr Springfield PA 19064 Office: 3535 Market St Philadelphia PA 19101

PACKARD, ALBERT GIBSON, JR., orthopedic surgeon; b. Balt., Nov. 7, 1927; s. Albert Gibson and Eva (De Ford) P.; A.B., Johns Hopkins U., 1950; M.D., U. Md., 1954; m. Mary Frances Reeves, June 23, 1951; children—Albert Gibson, 3rd, Stanley R., Mary Tracy. Intern, U. Hosp., Balt., 1954-55, asst. resident in gen. surgery, 1955-56; hosp. resident Columbia Presbyn. Med. Center, N.Y.C., 1956-59; practice medicine specializing in orthopedic surgery, Balt., 1959-70; mem. staffs John Hopkins, Children's hosps., Balt.; chief orthopedic sect. dept. surgery Meml. Hosp., Easton, Md., 1971-76; cons. Children's Orthopedics, Balt. City Hosp., 1967-70; owner Midshore Welding Corp. Served to 2d lt., C.E., AUS, 1946-47. Diplomate Am. Bd. Orthopedic Surgery. Fellow Am. Acad. Orthopedic Surgeons. A.C.S.; mem. Eastern Orthopedic Assn., Md. Orthopedic Soc. (pres. 1966-67), Assn. Bone and Joint Surgeons, Chesapeake Orthopedic Assn. (pres.), Am. Welding Soc., Am. Soc. Metals, Midshore Welding Corp. (pres.), Dress Circle (v.p.), Nu Sigma Nu (pres. Beta Alpha chpt. 1954). Editor sect. Md. State Med. Jour. Home: Route 4 Box 119 Waverly Island Easton MD 21601 Office: 32 S Washington St Easton MD 21601

PACKER, SAMUEL, ophthalmologist; b. N.Y.C., Jan. 26, 1941; s. Frank and Thelma (Miller) P.; B.A., N.Y. U., 1962; M.D., State U. N.Y. at Bklyn., 1966; m. Barbara Gale Karlow, June 16, 1963; 1 dau., Heidi Ann. Med. intern Kings County Med. Center, Bklyn., 1966-67; resident Yale-New Haven Hosp., 1967-71; attending ophthalmologist Albert Schweitzer Hosp., Deschepelles, Haiti, 1971, N. Shore Univ. Hosp., Manhasset, N.Y., 1971—; chief ophthalmology St. Albans (N.Y.) Naval Hosp., 1971-73; vis. clinician Med. Research Center, Brookhaven Nat. Lab., Upton, N.Y., 1972—; chief ocular tumor service N. Shore Univ. Hosp., 1973—; practice medicine specializing in ophthalmology, Manhasset, 1972—; clin. asst. prof. surgery Cornell U. Med. Coll. Served with USN, 1971-73. Nat. Cancer Inst. grantee, 1974—. Fellow A.C.S.; mem. Am. Acad. Ophthalmology and Otolaryngology, Assn. Research in Vision and Ophthalmology, Soc. Nuclear Medicine, N.Y. State Med. Soc., Nassau Surg. Soc., Psi Chi. Jewish religion. Author articles and textbook chpts. on eye tumors. Home: 55 Twin Ponds Ln Syosset NY 11791 Office: 300 Community Dr Manhasset NY 11030

PACKWOOD, CYRIL OUTERBRIDGE, librarian; b. Paget, Bermuda, Nov. 22, 1930; s. Cyril A. and Gladys M. (Outerbridge) P.; came to U.S., 1946, naturalized, 1960; A.B., Fisk U., 1953; M.S. in L.S., Western Res. U., 1954; M.A., Hunter Coll., 1972; m. Dorothy Cunningham, Nov. 15, 1958; 1 dau., Cheryl. Librarian, N.Y. Pub. Library, N.Y.C., 1957-68; chief librarian Borough of Manhattan Community Coll., N.Y.C., 1968—; Founder's Day speaker Berkeley Ednl. Soc., Bermuda, 1976; speaker Bermuda Writers Club, 1977. Bd. dirs. Am. Forum for Internat. Study. Served with U.S. Army, 1955-57. Mem. ALA, N.Y. State Library Assn., Library Assn. City U. N.Y., ALA Black Caucus, Beta Phi Mu. Democrat. Author: Chained on the Rock, Slavery in Bermuda, 1975, Detour - Bermuda, Destination - U.S. House of Representatives, Life of Joseph Rainey, 1977. Home: 303 W 66th St New York City NY 10023 Office: 1633 Broadway Borough of Manhattan Community College New York City NY 10019

PADDACK, WILLIAM ARTHUR, accountant; b. Waterville, Maine, Apr. 22, 1947; s. Melvin Arthur and Priscilla Yvette (Belanger) P.; B.B.A., Thomas Coll., 1969; m. Janet Linda Igoe, May 30, 1976. Sr. accountant Arthur Young & Co., Boston, 1971-75; audit mgr. Seidman & Seidman, Boston, 1975-77; partner McManus & Paddack, Boston, 1977—. Served with AUS, 1969-71. C.P.A., Mass. Mem. Am. Inst. C.P.A.'s, Mass. Soc. C.P.A.'s, Nat. Assn. Accountants, Am. Accounting Assn., Kappa Delta Phi. Roman Catholic. Home: One Summer Dr Reading MA 01867 Office: 1 Bulfinch St Boston MA 02114

PADDISON, GARY WAYNE, physicist; b. York, Pa., Feb. 14, 1946; s. Arthur John and Sara Kathryn (Fields) P.; B.S., Millersville State Coll., 1969; m. Cynthia Ann Myers, Aug. 12, 1967; children—Lisa Ann, Kimberly Lynn. Asso. chemist Armstrong Cork Co., Lancaster, Pa., 1967-69, research chemist, 1969-77, research scientist,. 1978—, mem. supervisory team to Pa. State U., 1976-78. Mem. Am. Inst. Chemists. Contbr. articles in field to profl. jours. Home: 211 Maplewood Dr Dover PA 17315 Office: 2500 Columbia Ave Lancaster PA 17604

PADULA, WILLIAM VINCENT, mil. arsenal adminstr.; b. Bayonne, N.J., Dec. 4, 1918; s. Irvin Vincent and Mae Agnes P.; certificate criminal investigation Delehanty Inst. N.Y., 1938; student Pratt U., N.Y.C., 1939; m. Dec. 3, 1944; 1 son, William Vincent II. Marine draftsman Gibbs & Cox, Inc., naval architects, N.Y.C., 1939-43; civil service marine draftsman Transp. Corps, Research and Devel. Bd., U.S. Army, Bklyn. Army Base Terminal, 1946-50; naval architect design div., sci. dept. N.Y. Naval Shipyard, N.Y.C., 1950-53; designer furniture for mfrs., Hickory, N.C., 1953-55; writer tech. publs. Raritan Arsenal, Metuchen, N.J., 1955-61; editor tech. publs. Picatinny Arsenal, U.S. Army, Dover, N.J., 1961-76, supr. conventional ammo tech. publs. sect., 1976—. Served as spl. agt. CIC, U.S. Army, 1943-45. Patentee Munitions systems field. Home: 299 Manor Ave Cranford NJ 07016 Office: Conventional Ammo Tech Publs Sect Picatinny Arsenal US Army Dover NJ 07801

PADWA, VLADIMIR, composer, pianist, educator; b. Krivyakino, Russia, Feb. 8, 1900; s. Michael and Maria (Schneidmann) P.; student Imperial Conservatory, Petrograd, Russia, 1917, State Conservatory, Berlin, Germany, 1921-27, Leipzig (Germany) Conservatory, 1924; pupil Ferruccio Busoni; D.Mus. (hon.), Thiel Coll., 1978; m. Natalie J. Lozier, Dec. 18, 1947; children—Tatiana, Thomas Matthew. Came to U.S., 1932, naturalized, 1948. Co-founder, mem. faculty State Conservatory, Tallinn, Estonia, 1918-21; accompanist Mischa Elman, 1934-48; mem. faculty N.Y. Coll. Music, 1945-68, chmn. dept. piano, 1967; asso. prof. music edn. N.Y. U., 1967—; dir., performer first broadcast all-electronic music, Berlin, 1932; concertized U.S., Can., Europe, Far East, S.Am., South Africa; founder, mem. First Piano Quartet, 1941-50; adjudicator Que. (Can.) Music Festival, 1961—, N.B. (Can.) Competitive Music Festivals, 1965—, others. Recipient N.Y. Madrigal Soc. award, 1934, Musical Am. award, 1948, Peabody award, 1949, award merit Nat. Fedn. Music Clubs, 1973, others. Mem. ASCAP (awards 1968-78), Am. Music Center, Music Tchrs. Nat. Assn., Coll. Music Soc., N.Y. Music Tchrs. League, Piano Tchrs. Congress N.Y. Club: Bohemians. Compositions include orchestral suite ballet Tom Sawyer, Concerto for 2 Pianos and Strings, Symphony in D, String Symphony, Symphony for Concert Band, Trio for Clarinet, Cello and Piano, Sonatas for Cello, Clarinet, Bassoon, Concerto for Clarinet, also songs and choral works. Contbr. articles to music jours. Home: 736 Riverside Dr New York City NY 10031

PAEK, UN-CHUL, mech. engr.; b. Korea, Dec. 2, 1934; s. Dahan and Bunduck Paek; came to U.S., 1963, naturalized, 1976; B.S., Korean Mcht. Marine Acad., 1957; M.S. in Mech. Engring., U. Calif., Berkeley, 1965, Ph.D., 1969; m. Jaehack Lee, June 10, 1963; 1 dau., Heyun. Mem. research staff Engring. Research Center, Western Electric Co., Princeton, N.J., 1969—. Served from ensign to lt. Korean Navy, 1957-63. Mem. ASME, Am. Optical Soc., Sigma Xi. Contbr. articles to profl. jours. Home: 8 Lake Shore Dr RD 1 Lawrenceville NJ 08648 Office: PO Box 900 Princeton NJ 08540

PAELET, DAVID, univ. dean; b. New Haven, Sept. 26, 1935; s. Sidney and Eva P.; B.S., City Coll. N.Y., 1960, M.S., 1963; Ph.D., U. Conn., 1973; m. Judith Anne Martin, Oct. 5, 1962; children—Lawrence, Stephen. Sch. psychologist, dir. spl. edn. Darien (Conn.) pub. schs., 1966-73; asso. prof. psychology, coordinator community psychology grad. program U. New Haven, 1973-77, asso. dean Grad. Sch., 1977—; cons. to various orgns. Served with U.S. N.G., 1962. Mem. Am., Conn. psychol. assns., Nat., Conn. assns. sch. psychologists, Phi Delta Kappa, Phi Kappa Phi. Unitarian. Home: 18 Pheasant Ln Madison CT 06443 Office: 300 Orange Ave West Haven CT 06505

PAGAN, RAYMOND, real estate exec.; b. San Juan, P.R., May 23, 1914; A.B., Tufts U., 1937; spl. certificate German lang. and area study U. Pitts., 1944; LL.B., Am. Extension Sch. Law, 1959; spl. certificate in econ. devel. SAIS Johns Hopkins, 1960; m. Theresa Grace DeCarlo, Aug. 27, 1942; children—Daniel Leverett, Virginia Grace, Roxane Ruth. With Alexander Smith & Co., 1939-42; German publs. officer U.S. War Dept., 1945-47; dep. chief publs. div., chief publs. div. High Commr. of Germany, Wiesbaden, 1947-49; entered fgn. service Dept. State, 1949; asst. editor Die Neue Zeitung, Berlin, Germany, 1949-53; info. officer Am. embassy, Cairo, Egypt, 1953-54, info. specialist USIA, Washington, 1954-55, info. officer FOA, ICA, Saigon, Vietnam, 1955-57; communications media officer ICA, Am. embassy, Beirut, Lebanon, 1959-60, asst. program officer, Kabul, Afghanistan, 1960-62, Afghan desk officer AID, 1962-67, program officer population, Washington, 1967-75; mgr. Croyden-Irvin Realty, Bethesda, Md., 1975-78; realtor asso. Schwartz Realty, Prince Frederick, Md., 1978—. Chmn. refugee com. Chevy Chase (Md.) Methodist Ch., 1974-78. Served with M.I., AUS, 1942-45. Mem. Am. Fgn. Service Assn., Montgomery County, So. Md. bd. realtors. Republican. Contbr. articles to newspapers and mags. Office: Schwartz Realty Prince Frederick MD 20678

PAGANELLI, RICHARD GREGORY, biologist; b. Phila., July 31, 1926; s. Americus Julius and Lucy Katherine (Finn) P.; B.S., Pa. Mil. Coll., 1951; m. Berniece Grace Slezak, Apr. 11, 1953; 1 dau., Pamela Ann. Ofcl. processed products insp. U.S. Dept. Agr., N.Y.C., 1951-53; supermarket exec. Empire Market, Inc., Schenectady, 1953-58; ins. cons. Met. Life Ins. Co., Poughkeepsie, N.Y., 1959-66; tech. mgr. Taconic Farms, Inc., Germantown, N.Y., 1966-73, sales and tech. dir., 1974—, v.p. for sales, tech. dir., 1977—; microbiol. cons.; research cons. Served with AUS, 1944-46. Decorated Purple Heart medal. Mem. Upstate N.Y., Am. assns. lab. animal sci., VFW. Club: Elks. Home: Rural Delivery 2 Germantown NY 12526 Office: Hover Ave Germantown NY 12526

PAGANO, FRANK XAVIER, agrl. exec.; b. Bklyn., Mar. 1, 1931; s. Joseph R. and Janet (Maribito) P.; B.A., St. Johns' U., Bklyn., 1960; m. Doris L. Heinzman, Dec. 27, 1952; children—Joseph, Frank Xavier, George, John, Michael, Donna, Christopher, Deborah, Diana. Jockey agt. thoroughbred racing, 1965-67; horse owner, 1970—; asst. trainer horses 1967-70, trainer, 1970—; gen. mgr. Goldmill Farms Inc., Old Westbury, N.Y., 1969—; cons. in field. Membership chmn. Am. Com. Italian Migration, 1974—. Served with USCG, 1951-54; Korea. Mem. N.Y. State Thoroughbred, Fla. breeders assns., Sons of Italy. Republican. Roman Catholic. Clubs: Hempstead Golf and Country, Businessman's Internat., Rotary. Home, office: 154 Old Westbury Rd Old Westbury NY 11568

PAGE, EDGAR JOSEPH, chemist; b. Putnam, Conn., Nov. 7, 1919; s. Eugene J. and Mary (Durand) P.; B.S., Marianapolis Coll., 1943; m. Eleanor B. Cournoyer, May 12, 1945; children—Mary Jeanne, Denise Anne, Marc Robert. Instr. Marianapolis Acad., 1945-46; chemist Belding Heminway Co., Putnam, 1943—, chief chemist, 1951—. Sec. Putnam Community Concert Assn., 1947—. Mem. Am. Chem. Soc., ASTM, N.Y. Acad. Scis. Lion, K.C. Home: PO Box 85 South Woodstock CT 06267 Office: Belding Heminway Co Putnam CT 06260

PAGE, (CHARLES) GETTY, (JR.), med. assn. exec.; b. Bklyn., Apr. 21, 1913; s. Charles Getty and Geraldine Diven (Lee) P.; B.S., Syracuse U., 1936, M.S., 1940; postgrad., 1940-43; m. Ann Elizabeth Ball, June 27, 1940; children—Heather Page Martin, Nancy Page Smith, John M., Jean Page Patoine. Field dir. ARC, Africa, Europe, 1943-47; dean student, prof. biology Rutland (Vt.) Jr. Coll., 1947-49; exec. dir. Vt. State Med. Soc., Rutland, 1949—; exec. coordinator Health Care Found. Vt., Town Health Officer, Mendon, Vt., 1970-72, selectman, 1972-74; mem. state Republican platform com. Decorated Presdl. medal of Freedom, 1946. Mem. Am. Assn. Med. Soc. Execs., AMA (affiliate), Vt. State Med. Soc. (hon.), New Eng. Pub. Health Assn. (pres. 1968-69), New Eng. Health Edn. Assn. (pres. 1974-76). Episcopalian (lay reader diocese Vt. 1956—). Clubs: Rotary, S.R., Mil. Order of the Loyal Legion. Editor Newsletter Vt. State Med. Soc., 1949—. Home: Eastridge Acres Rural Free Delivery 2 Mendon VT 05701 Office: Bd Med Practice 100 State St Montpelier VT 05602

PAGE, JOHN FREDERIC, mus. exec.; b. Ringoes, N.J., Aug. 3, 1935; s. Norman F. and Charlotte K. (Tunney) P.; B.A., U. N.H., 1958; M.A., Coll. William and Mary, 1969; m. Ruth Yvonne Cox, July 23, 1966; children—David Hamilton, Christopher Walker. Tchr., Suffield (Conn.) Acad., 1959-63; curator Conn. Hist. Soc., Hartford State House, 1964-66; dir. Litchfield (Conn.) Hist. Soc., 1966-69, N.H. Hist. Soc., Concord, 1969—. Mem. bd. overseers Strawbery Banke, Inc., Portsmouth, N.H., 1970-74; bd. dirs. Com. for New Eng. Bibliography; mem. N.H. Council for Humanities, 1977—. Mem. Nat. Trust Historic Preservation, Soc. Archtl. Historians, Am. Assn. Museums, Am. Assn. State and Local History. Author: Litchfield County Furniture, 1730-1850, 1969; Decorative Arts of New Hampshire: A Sesquicentennial Exhibition, 1973. Home: 10 Wildemere Terr Concord NH 03301 Office: 30 Park St Concord NH 03301

PAGE, LORNE ALBERT, physicist; b. Buffalo, July 28, 1921; s. John Otway and Laura May (Stewart) P.; B.Sc., Queen's U., Kingston, Ont., Can., 1944; Ph.D., Cornell U., 1950; m. Muriel Emily Jamieson, Sept. 7, 1946; children—J. Douglas, Kenneth L., James F., Donald S., David K. Asst. prof. U. Pitts., 1950-53, asso. prof., 1953-58, prof., 1958—; vis. scientist Lawrence Livermore Lab., 1970. Served to lt. Can. Navy, 1943-45. Guggenheim fellow, 1957-58; A. P. Sloan fellow, 1961-63. Fellow Am. Phys. Soc.; mem. Sigma Xi. Episcopalian. Contbr. articles to profl. jours. Home: 157 Lloyd Ave Pittsburgh PA 15218 Office: Physics Dept Univ Pittsburgh Pittsburgh PA 15260

PAGE, PHILIP POWERS, JR., cons. engr.; b. Evanston, Ill., July 17, 1923; s. Philip Powers and Scott Alleyne (McCabe) P.; student Washington and Lee U., 1941-43, Syracuse U., 1943-44; B.C.E., Cornell U., 1947; M.S. in Civil Engring., Newark Coll. Engring., 1959; m. Barbara Ann Fickenscher, Apr. 6, 1964; children—John, Kenneth, Lawrence; children from previous marriage—Scott, James. With firm Seelye, Stevenson, Value & Knecht, cons. engrs., N.Y.C., 1947-61, asso., 1956-61; partner firm Goldreich, Page & Thropp, cons. engrs., N.Y.C., 1961—. Served with AUS, 1943-46. Mem. ASCE, Am. Concrete Inst., N.Y. Assn. Cons. Engrs., Am. Cons. Engrs. Council, Am. Arbitration Assn. (nat. panel arbitrators). Mem. United Ch. of Christ. Home: 5 Roberts Dr Mountain Lakes NJ 07046 Office: 257 Park Ave South New York City NY 10010

PAGE, ROBERT BICKNELL, neurosurgeon; b. Phila., Nov. 17, 1937; s. William Hansel and Frances Warner (Bicknell) P.; B.A., Amherst Coll., 1959; M.D., Columbia U., 1963. Intern, Bellevue Hosp., N.Y.C., 1963-64, resident, 1964-65; resident Yale-New Haven Med. Center, 1967-71; asst. prof. neurosurgery Yale U., 1971-72; asst. prof. M.S. Hershey Med. Center, Pa. State U., 1972-77, asso. prof. neurosurgery and anatomy, 1977—. Served to lt. M.C., USN, 1965-67. USPHS spl. fellow, 1969-70, 71-72, NIH. Tchr. Investigator awardee, 1976-81. Mem. AMA, A.C.S., Congress Neurol. Surgeons, Am. Assn. Neurol. Surgeons, Am. Assn. Anatomists, Research Soc. Neurol. Surgeons, Assn. Acad. Surgery, AAAS, Sigma Xi. Home: 8 Brandywine Briarcrest Gardens Hershey PA 17033 Office: MS Hershey Med Center Hershey PA 17033

PAGE, WALTER HINES, banker; b. Huntington, L.I., N.Y., July 7, 1915; s. Arthur W. and Mollie H. (Hall) P.; grad. Milton (Mass.) Acad., 1933; A.B., Harvard, 1937; m. Jane N. Nichols, Jan. 24, 1942; children—Jane N., Walter Hines, Mark N. With J.P. Morgan & Co., Inc., N.Y.C., 1937-59, chmn., chief exec. officer, 1977—, also dir.; bank merged with Guaranty Trust Co., 1959; v.p. Morgan Guaranty Trust Co., N.Y.C., 1959-64, sr. v.p., 1964-65, exec. v.p., 1965-68, vice chmn. bd., 1968-71, pres., 1971-77, also dir.; dir. Merck & Co. Inc., Kennecott Copper Corp. Pres. L.I. Biol. Assn. Bd. dirs. Fgn. Policy Assn., N.Y. Urban Coalition; trustee Cold Spring Harbor Lab., Carnegie Instn. Washington. Home: Cold Spring Harbor NY 11724 Office: 23 Wall St New York City NY 10015

PAGET, ALLEN MAXWELL, investment co. exec.; b. Karuizawa, Japan, Sept. 12, 1919 (parents Am. citizens); s. Allen Maxwell and Mary (Baum) P.; B.S. in Bus. Adminstrn., Lehigh U., 1941; m. Dorothy A. Lord, Dec. 22, 1941. With C. L. Emmert & Co., 1955-58; investment mgr., distbr. united group of mutual funds Waddell & Reed, Inc., 1958-68, regional mgr., resident v.p., Harrisburg, Pa., 1961-68; v.p. Mark Securities, Inc., 1968—; chmn. bd. pres., treas., dir. Penn-Ben, Inc., 1969—; chmn. bd., pres., treas., dir. Paget-San Enterprises, Inc., 1973—; v.p. Gamma Lambda Corp., 1973-78. Served to comdr. Supply Corps, USN, 1941-55; capt. Res., ret. 1972. Mem. Internat. Assn. Financial Counselors (charter), Am. Philatelic Soc., Navy League U.S., Res. Officers Assn. (pres. Central Pa. chpt. 1972-73), Nat. Sojourners, Heroes of '76, Navy Supply Corps Sch. Alumni Assn. (founding mem.), Harrisburg Area, West Shore Area chambers commerce, Mil. Order World Wars, Legion of Honor, Mid Atlantic Shrine Clown Assn., Pa. Shrine Assn. (pres. 1978-79), Zembo Shrine Clowns, Lambda Mu Sigma (founder), Pi Kappa Alpha (treas.), Alpha Phi Omega, Pi Delta Epsilon. Presbyn. (trustee). Clubs: Rotary (dir.), Masons (K.T.; master 1968), Shriners (potentate Zembo temple 1978), Zembo Luncheon, Central Pa. Lehigh (pres. 1966), also numerous Pa. Shrine Clubs. Home: Keiseian 308 Lamp Post Ln Pine Brook Camp Hill PA 17011 Office: 2517 Paxton St Harrisburg PA 17111

PAGLEY, CARMELLA, nurse; b. Midland, Pa., Feb. 9, 1932; d. James and Amelia (Gentile) Crappio; R.N., St. Francis Hosp. Sch. Nursing, 1953; postgrad. Youngstown State U., 1976—; m. Donald Pagley, Oct. 19, 1957; 1 son, Donald; legal guardian, Joseph Charles, David, Deborah Retort. Operating room nurse St. Francis Hosp. of New Castle (Pa.), 1953-66, head nurse in charge operating room, 1966—; asst. instr. students and new employees in operating room. Recipient 20 years service in nursing award St. Francis Hosp., 1974. Mem. Pa., Am. nurses assns., Assn. Operating Room Nurses. Democrat. Roman Catholic. Contbr. procedure to publ., 1969. Home: 1203 Miller Rd New Castle PA 16101 Office: South Mercer at Phillips St New Castle PA 16101

PAGLIACCIO, JOHN VALENTINE, mfg. co. exec.; b. Buffalo, Feb. 14, 1935; s. Frank and Josephine (Sperduto) P.; Asso. Applied Sci., Erie Community Coll., 1954; m. Carol A. Friend, May 14, 1960; children—Michael A., Gina M., James E. Technician, Moog Inc., East Aurora, N.Y., 1956-62, sr. quality engr. technician, 1962-63, 66-70, supr. final assembly, 1963-66, supr. quality engring. and data mgmt., 1970-78, mgr. product assurance, 1978—. Scoutmaster, Boy Scouts Am., East Aurora, N.Y., 1960—; sec. Vol. Fire Dept., 1960-70; team capt. Vol. First Aid Squad, 1963-70; mem. East Aurora (N.Y.) Sch. Bd., 1970-73; deacon Presbyterian Ch., 1969-72, elder, 1975—. Recipient Silver Beaver award Boy Scouts Am., 1970, Community Leader's award Boys Clubs Am., 1976. Mem. Inst. Environ. Sci. Republican. Home: 409 Girard Ave East Aurora NY 14052 Office: Jamison Rd East Aurora NY 14052

PAHIDES, STEVE PETER, banker; b. Marcus Hook, Pa., July 6, 1931; s. Peter S. and Despina (Helios) P.; B.S., Pa. Mil. Colls., 1963; m. Florence Krupp, Aug. 14, 1954; children—Stephen, Susan. Teller, Delaware County Nat. Bank (name now changed to S.E. Nat. Bank Pa.), Chester, 1955-57, discount dept. mgr., 1957-60, br. asst., 1960-61, br. mgr., 1961-63, asst. cashier, 1963-67, asst. v.p., 1967-70, regional v.p., 1970-75, v.p. trust bus. devel., 1975—. Mem. allotment com. United Way S.E. Delaware County; asst. treas. Central Delaware County Sch. Authority, 1964-74; treas., chmn. Middletown Twp Sewer Authority, 1966-70; supr. Middletown Twp., 1970-72; vice-chmn. Middletown Twp. Zoning Bd., 1972-74; mem. Rose Tree Media Sch. Bd., 1974—, pres. sch. dist., 1978. Served with USN, 1951-55. Recipient Service award YMCA, 1966-67, Service award Pa. Mil. Coll., Alumni, 1971, Past Pres. award Indian Lane Parent Tchrs. Group, 1973-75. Mem. Delaware County C. of C., Estate Planning Councils Delaware and Chester Counties, Robert Morris Assos. Republican. Greek Orthodox. Clubs: Concord Country, Paoli Malvern Berwyn Rotary. Home: 12 Springhouse Ln Media PA 19063 Office: SE Nat Bank Pa 17 N High St West Chester PA 19380

PAHL, IRWIN RUSSELL, obstetrician, gynecologist; b. Springfield, Mass., Aug. 25, 1926; s. Irwin Alfred and Sybil Pearl (Gilman) P.; B.S. in Engring., USCG Acad., 1949; postgrad. Harvard U., 1954-55; M.D., Tufts U., 1959; m. Apr. 9, 1962; children—Russell, Karen, Christian. Enlisted man USNR, 1944-45; commd. cadet U.S. Coast Guard, 1945, advanced thorugh grades to comdr., 1969; various assignments at sea and ashore, Boston, 1949-54; intern Springfield Hosp., 1959-60; resident Albany (N.Y.) Hosp., 1960-64; practice medicine specializing in obstetrics and gynecology, Springfield, 1964—; mem. staff Hampden County Obstetricians & Gynecologists, Inc., Baystate Med. Center, Springfield, Wing Meml. Hosp., Palmer, Mass.; pres. staff obstetrics-gynecology dept. Wesson Women's Hosp., Springfield; asso. prof. obstetrics and gynecology U. Mass., 1973—; asso. clin. prof. Tufts U., 1976—. Mem. Mass., Hampden Dist. med. socs., Western Mass. Obstet. and Gynecol. Soc. (treas.), Am. Coll. Obstetricians and Gynecologists. Club: Masons. Contbr. articles to med. jours. Home: 77 Fair Hill Dr Longmeadow MA 01106 Office: 110 Maple St Springfield MA 01105

PAIGE, KENNETH LEE, educator; b. Canonsburg, Pa., June 12, 1941; s. Thomas and Ethel (Lowe) P.; Asso. Sci., Robert Morris Jr. Coll., 1964; B.S. in Bus. Adminstrn., Duquesne U., 1968; M.S., Kent State U., 1969; postgrad. U. Pitts., 1972—; m. Lynn Elaine Hairston, Jan. 28, 1966; 1 son, Dale. Accountant, Ernst & Ernst, Akron, Ohio, 1968-69; instr. Robert Morris Coll., Pitts., 1970-72; lectr. accounting U. Pitts., 1972—. Bd. dirs., treas. Glen Canon Homes Assn., 1972-73. Served with USAF Res., 1966-71. C.P.A., Pa.; Am. Accounting Assn. fellow, 1975-76, Price Waterhouse & Co. grantee, 1975-77, Ernst & Ernst grantee, 1976-77, Leopold Shepp Found. scholar, 1975-76. Mem. Nat. Assn. Black Accountants, Nat. Alliance Businessmen, Am. Inst. C.P.A.'s, Pa. Soc. C.P.A.'s, Beta Alpha Psi. Democrat. Baptist. Home: 2329 Weston Dr Pittsburgh PA 15241 Office: Grad Sch Bus U Pitts Pittsburgh PA 15260

PAIGE, RICHARD E., inventor; b. N.Y.C., Dec. 30, 1904; s. Louis and Florence (Elias) P.; student Voltaire Sch. Music, Grand Central Sch. Art; m. Evelyn Kitz, Apr. 26, 1931. Profl. musician, orchestra leader, sometimes radio sta. WHN, N.Y.C., vaudeville performer; composed and sold some of earliest theme songs and singing commls.; mem. Band of a Thousand Melodies, WJZ, N.Y.C.; salesman Reproduction Products, Bklyn., 1929-31; idea man, constrn. expert Display Finishing Co., L.I. City, N.Y., 1931; created profession of cardboard engr.; granted the only basic patents in field of paper manufacture, inventions introduced through Gen. Elec. Co., Coty, Seagram, Calvert, Colgate, Gen. Foods, other nat. advts., 1931-34; entered field of folding boxes, 1934; v.p. Display Finishing Co., 1936-40; established Richard E. Paige, Inc., N.Y.C., 1940; guest lectr. Am. Mgmt. Assn., Pratt Inst.; exhibit New Frontiers of Modern Design, Pratt Inst.; inventor instructional sighting device used by U.S. Army, USMC, World War II; founded Paige Tng. Aids, 1944, Paige Lab., 1946, The Paige Co., 1948, Paige Co. Internat., Rotor-Sensor Co., 1973; developed can carriers Container Corp. American; developed corrugated floor display stands; with Hallmark Cards, Inc., 1960—; chmn. bd. Paper Products Devel. Corp., 1964—; research steel foil Behlehem Steel Co., 1964-65; partner Merchandising

Studios, Tokyo, Japan; guest lectr. New School for Social Research; engring. cons. Proctor & Gamble Co. Judge nat. competition Folding Paper Box Assn., 1967, Canadian Packaging Assn., 1968; judge intercollegiate package design competition St. Regis Paper Co., 1969. Recipient Bronze Plaque, Advertising Club of Greater Providence C. of C., 1956; Top Design award Design Mag.; inducted into Packaging Hall of Fame, 1975. Mem. Point of Purchase Advt. Inst. Club: Advertising (N.Y.C.). Author: Complete Guide to Making Money with Your Ideas and Inventions. Patentee talking book, protective labeling. Home: 215 E 68th St New York City NY 10021 Office: 432 Park Ave S New York City NY 10016

PAIGE, ROSLYNE GROSS, advt. agy. exec.; b. Chgo., May 26, 1926; d. Benjamin and Clara (Sniderman) Gross; student U. Chgo., 1943-45; m. Robert D. Stern, June 5, 1978; children by previous marriage—Sandra Weber, Barbara Taylor-Sharp, Elizabeth Paige. Profl. model, 1954-55; profl. singer, 1947-58; account exec. Interstate United, Chgo., 1953-58; with Getting To Know You Internat. Ltd., Great Neck, N.Y., 1963—, exec. v.p., 1971—; sales cons. Rudor Consol., N.Y.C., 1978—, Danad Pub. Co., N.Y.C., 1978—. Active various local polit. campaigns. Mem. Pub. Relations Soc. Am., L.I. Ad Club, LWV. Democrat. Jewish. Home: Pirates Cove Mamaroneck NY 10543 Office: 49 Watermill Ln Great Neck NY 11022

PAINTER, GERALDINE VIRGINIA, nurse, educator; b. Knoxville, Md., July 4, 1922; d. Franklin P. and Nellie M. (Leopold) Webber; R.N., King Daughters Hosp., 1943; B.S. Nursing Edn., U. Pitts., 1945; M.Ed., Duquesne U., 1968; m. Clarence S. Painter, July 29, 1949; 1 dau., Susan Geraline. Staff nurse Eye and Ear Hosp., Pitts., 1943-45; nursing instr. South Side Hosp., Pitts., 1945-49; nursing instr. Allegheny Valley Hosp., Tarentum, Pa., 1949-56, dir. nursing edn., 1956-59; instr. Braddock (Pa.) Hosp., 1963-64; chmn. nursing I, instr., guidance counselor McKeesport (Pa.) Hosp., 1964-71, asso. dir. nursing edn., 1971-73, dir. staff devel. and continuing edn., 1973—; nursing cons. Harmerville Rehab. Hosp., 1963-65. Mem. Am., Pa. nurses assns., Nat. League Nursing, Western Pa. Nurse Adminstrs. Group, Inservice Interest Group Southwestern Pa., Hosp. Christian Fellowship Group, Alpha Tau Delta. Home: 602 Harrison City Rd Trafford PA 15085 Office: McKeesport Hospital 1500 5th Ave McKeesport PA 15132

PAINTER, MICHAEL JAMES, pediatric neurologist; b. Detroit, Nov. 30, 1939; s. James E. and Elizabeth M. (Melvin) P.; B.S., Georgetown U., 1961; M.D., U. Mich., 1965; m. Nancy Long, June 8, 1963; children—William, Elizabeth, Michael. Intern, Children's Hosp. Pitts., 1965-66, resident, 1966-68; resident Neurol. Inst. N.Y., 1970-73; fellow pediatric neurology Columbia U., N.Y.C., 1970-73; practice medicine specializing in pediatric neurology, Pitts., 1973—; mem. staffs Children's Hosp. Pitts., Magee Women's Hosp.; asst. prof. pediatrics and neurology U. Pitts., 1973. Served with USAF, 1968-70. Mem. Am. Epilepsy Soc., Am. Acad. Pediatrics and Neurology. Home: 3037 Swansea Circle W Allison Park PA 15101 Office: Forbes and Halket St Pittsburgh PA 15113

PAINTER, ROBERT LOWELL, physician; b. Winchster, Ind., Jan. 13, 1934; s. Lowell Walter and Lillian Genevieve (Pierson) P.; A.B., Earlham Coll., 1955; M.D., Ind. U., 1959; m. Esther Reece, Jan. 22, 1957 (div.); children—Elizabeth Anne, Bradley Robert, Robert Reece, Andrew Lowell. Intern, Hartford (Conn.) Hosp., 1959-60, resident in surgery, 1960-65; resident in thoracic surgery Baylor Coll. Medicine, 1966-68; practice medicine specializing in surgery, Putnam, Conn., 1968—, Webster, Mass., 1976—; chief surgery Day Kimball Hosp., Putnam, 1976—; cons. thoracic and vascular surgery Hartford Hosp., 1968—, Hubbard Regional Hosp., 1976—; asst. clin. prof. surgery U. Conn. Med. Sch., 1978—. Served with USAF, 1965-67. Diplomate Am. Bd. Thoracic Surgery, Am. Bd. Surgery. Fellow ACS; mem. Conn. Soc. Am. Bd. Surgeons, Conn. Med. Soc. Republican. Home: Box 143 Pomfret CT 06258 Office: Professional Bldg 320 Pomfret St Putnam CT 06260

PAISNER, CLAIRE VIVIAN, journalist; b. Boston, Apr. 10, 1933; d. Philip and Hilda Marian (Benjamin) P.; B.A. cum laude, Cornell U., 1955; M.A., Harvard U., 1958; postgrad. Inst. de Scis. Politiques, Paris, 1962-66; m. Julien Serge Doubrovsky, June 17, 1956; children—Renee Anne, Catherine Louise. Instr. polit. sci. Suffolk U., Boston, 1959-61, Mt. Holyoke Coll., S. Hadley, Mass., 1961-62; exec. editor N.Y. Voice, N.Y.C., 1969-76; coordinator public affairs Consol. Edison Co. of N.Y., 1977—; speech writer for Manhattan Borough Pres. Percy Sutton, 1977; adv. com. writing York Coll., City U. N.Y. Recipient Community award Ministerial Council Race Relations, 1973; Journalism award Nat. Newspaper Pubs. Assn., 1970, 71, 74; Investigative Reporting awards Lincoln U., 1975, 76, 77. Mem. Nat. Assn. Media Women, Bus. and Profl. Women, NAACP, Urban League, Phi Beta Kappa. Home: 138-17 78th Rd New York NY 11367

PAK, HYUNG WOONG, publisher; b. Ham-Hoong, Korea, Nov. 6, 1932; s. Kyung-Koo and Myung-Sook (Lee) P.; A.B., U. Chgo., 1958. Editor, pub. Chgo. Rev., 1958-63, cons., 1963-65; asso. editor Ency. Britannica Press, 1963-64, sr. editor social scis. and humanities, 1964-66; dir. instl. materials div. and sales mgr. sch. and coll. div. Bantam Books, Inc., N.Y.C., 1966-69; v.p., editorial dir. Instl. Media Am., Inc., N.Y.C., 1969-70; gen. mgr. sch. dept. Appleton-Century-Crofts/New Century, N.Y.C., 1970-72; v.p., editorial dir. D. Van Nostrand Co., N.Y.C., 1972-74, pres., 1974-76; pres. Chatham Sq. Press, Inc., N.Y.C., 1976—; pub. Urizen Books, Inc., N.Y.C., 1978—. Instr. Japanese, U. Chgo., 1962. Served with Republic Korea Army, 1950-54. Mem. Mus. Modern Art, Met. Mus. Art, Friends Am. Ballet Theatre, ACLU, Friends of City Center, Arts Club Chgo. Home: 1015 Sharpless Rd Melrose Park PA 19126 Office: 401 Broadway New York City NY 10013

PAKAN, WALTER STEPHEN, cons. engr.; b. Little Falls, N.Y., Apr. 19, 1918; s. Stephen and Susan (Dubrava) P.; B.S. in Mech. Engring., Va. Poly. Inst., 1944; m. Anna Devan, July 5, 1943; children—Mildred S. (Mrs. Paul Sivacek), Robert W. Facilities engr. Norton Abrasives Co., Troy, N.Y., 1946-61; partner Hayward & Pakan Assos., Poughkeepsie, N.Y., 1961—. Mem. archtl. design curriculum adv. com. Dutchess Community Coll., 1965-66, 73—. Served with AUS, 1942-46. Registered profl. engr., N.Y. Mem. Am. Arbitration Assn., Nat. Soc. Profl. Engrs., Cons. Engrs. Council, Instrument Soc. Am., Am. Soc. Heating, Refrigeration and Air Conditioning Engrs., Nat. Fire Protection Assn. Lutheran (trustee ch.). Kiwanian. Home: 13 Valley View Rd Hyde Park NY 12538 Office: 54 Market St Poughkeepsie NY 12601

PALACE, FRED MILTON, radiologist; b. N.Y.C., Aug. 1, 1935; s. Irving and Estelle (Cabot) P.; B.A. with honors, Johns Hopkins U., 1956, M.A. 1956; M.D., Yale U., 1960; m. Ruth Goldner, June 29, 1958; children—Susan D., Jay M. J.H. Brown research fellow Yale U., 1959; intern in medicine N.C. Meml. Hosp., Chapel Hill, 1960-61; resident in radiology Yale-New Haven Med. Center, 1961-64; practice medicine specializing in radiology, Morristown, N.J., 1966—; attending staff, vice chmn. dept. radiology, chief nuclear medicine Morristown Meml. Hosp.; cons. staff nuclear medicine Community Med. Center and Hackettstown Community Hosp.; asst. clin. prof. radiology N.J. Coll. Medicine and Dentistry, Newark, N.J. Med. Sch. Rutgers U., Piscataway; adj. prof. allied health Fairleigh Dickinson U.; cons. in field. Mem. Morris Twp. (N.J.) Bd. Edn., 1969-72; bd. dirs. United Way, Morris County, 1974—. Served as capt. M.C. USAF, 1964-66. Decorated Air Force Commendation medal; diplomate Am. Bd. Radiology, Am. Bd. Nuclear Medicine. Fellow Am. Coll. Radiology; mem. Morris County Med. Soc. (pres. 1976-77, mem. exec. com. 1970-78), Radiol. Soc. N.J. (pres. 1977-78), Soc. Nuclear Medicine, Am. Coll. Nuclear Physicians, AMA, Radiol. Soc. N.Am. Home: Overlook Ln Mendham NJ 07945 Office: 101 Madison Ave Morristown NJ 07960

PALADE, GEORGE EMIL, educator, scientist; b. Jassy, Romania, Nov. 19, 1912; s. Emil and Constanta (Cantemir) P.; Bachelor, Hasdau Lyceum, Bazau, Romania; M.D., U. Bucharest (Romania); m. Irene Malaxa, June 12, 1941 (dec. 1969); children—Georgia Teodora, Philip Theodore; m. 2d, Marilyn G. Farquhar, 1970. Came to U.S., 1946, naturalized, 1952. Instr., asst. prof., then asso. prof. anatomy Sch. Medicine, U. Bucharest, 1935-45; vis. investigator, asst. asso., prof. cell biology Rockefeller U.; now prof. cell biology Yale; correlated biochem. and morphological analysis cell structures. Recipient Albert Lasker Basic Research award, 1966, Hurwitz prize, 1970, Nobel prize, 1974. Fellow Am. Acad. Arts and Scis.; mem. Nat. Acad. Sci. Author sci. papers. Office: Biology Sect Yale U New Haven CT 06510

PALADINO, PATRICK JOSEPH, accountant, fin. exec.; b. Bklyn., Aug. 17, 1943; s. Pasquale Alfredo and Josephine Mary (Muti) P.; B.B.A., Iona Coll., 1965; M.B.A., U. Conn., 1976; m. Oct. 8, 1966; children—Patrick Joseph Jr., Joseph James, Laureen Marie. Jr., semi-sr., sr. and heavy sr. accountant Harris, Kerr, Forster & Co., N.Y.C., 1964-71; sr. internal auditor, sr. tax accountant GTE Service Corp., N.Y.C., 1971-74, mgr. consolidation accounting GTE Info. Systems Inc., Stamford, Conn., 1974-75, mgr. fin. ops. Latin Am., 1976—, mgr. fin. planning budgets and analysis, 1977—. Certified internal auditor. Mem. Inst. Internal Auditors, N.Y. State Soc. C.P.A. Candidates. Republican. Roman Catholic. Club: Cos Cob Revolver and Rifle. Home: 44 Calass Ln North Stamford CT 06903 Office: One Stamford Forum Stamford CT 06904

PALANK, GARY PETER, dentist; b. Washington, Mar. 5, 1948; s. Edward Anthony and Antoinette (Lonien) P.; B.S. in Biology, Mt. St. Mary's Coll., 1970; D.D.S., U. Md., 1974; m. Sharon L. O'Neil, July 29, 1972; 1 son, Gary Peter. Resident in gen. dentistry VA Hosp., Washington, 1974-75; practice gen. dentistry, Gaithersburg, Md., 1976-77, Hagerstown, Md., 1976—; staff dentist VA Hosp., Washington, 1975-76, Washington County Hosp., Hagerstown, 1978—; clin. instr. dept. operative dentistry Georgetown U. Sch. Dentistry, Washington, 1975-76; chmn. adv. com. Dental Assisting Program of Career Studies Center, Hagerstown, 1977-78; cons. Ravenwood Lutheran Nursing Home, Hagerstown, 1978—, Washington County and Frederick County dental hygienists assns., 1978—; asst. chmn. Nat. Children's Dental Health Week, Washington County, 1977; mem. com. Concerned Vets. Adminstrn. Dentists, 1975. Chmn., Nat. Children's Dental Health Week, Washington County, Md., 1978. Recipient Achievement award for Excellence in Pedodontics, Md. Soc. Dentistry for Children, 1974. Diplomate Nat. Bd. Dental Examiners. Mem. ADA, Md. State (dental trade and lab. relations com. 1978), Washington County dental assns., Acad. Gen. Dentistry, Am. Cancer Soc. (dir. 1977-80), Beta Beta Beta. Roman Catholic. Clubs: Elks, Lions, K.C. (council local chpt. 1978—). Home: 25 Bittersweet Dr Hagerstown MD 21740 Office: 138 E Antietam St Hagerstown MD 21740

PALATTA, LARRY MICHAEL, priest; b. Washington, Feb. 10, 1921; s. John A. and Rose P.; B.A., Rochdale Coll., 1970; D.D., Ministry of Christ Sem., 1974; M.D., United Am. Med. Coll., 1977. With patrolman's div. N.Y.C. Housing Authority, 1952-78, police chaplain, spl. patrolman, 1978; ordained priest Roman Catholic Ch., 1974; oblate Order St. Benedictines, St. Mary's Abbey, N.J.; chaplain N.Y. Vets. Police Assn., 1976-78, N.Y. State Assn. Chiefs Police, 1976; col. Nat. Chaplains Assn., Tenn., 1977-78; retired. Recipient Chaplain's Legion of Honor award Nat. Chaplains Assn., Am. Law Enforcement Officers Assn. award, 1978; Am. Parapsychol. Research fellow. Mem. N.Y. Vets. Police Assn., N.Y. State Police Benevolent Assn., Nat. Assn. Chiefs Police. Home: 74-02 Metropolitan Ave Middle Village NY 11379

PALEFSKY, LOUIS BENJAMIN, counselor; b. Queens, N.Y., Oct. 16, 1948; s. Mayer and Pauline (Kozak) P.; student City U. Coll. Center in Manhattan, 1966-67; A.A., Queensborough Community Coll., 1970; B.A., Herbert H. Lehman Coll., 1972; M.A., N.Y. U., 1975; m. Elsa Crespi, Oct. 29, 1977. Counselor, staff Student Activities/Human Devel. Center, La Guardia Community Coll., City U. N.Y., L.I. City, 1975-77, financial aid counselor Fin. Aid Office, 1977—. Mem. Am. Personnel and Guidance Assn., Am. Coll. Personnel Assn. Office: 31-10 Thomson Ave Long Island City NY 11101

PALEY, ALFRED IRVING, electronics Co. ofcl.; b. Monticello, N.Y., Apr. 12, 1927; s. Max and Dora P.; B.E.E., Poly. Inst. Bklyn., 1949; m. Sylvia Tiffel, June 26, 1949; children—Maureen, Howard, Doreen. Test engr. Fairchild Guided Missiles, Farmingdale, N.Y., 1949-50; sr. engr. W.L. Maxson Corp., N.Y.C., 1950-58; chief engr. Acoustica Assos., Plainview, N.Y., 1958-60; staff scientist Am. Bosch Arma, Garden City, N.Y., 1960-62; chief engr. Janus Products, Syosset, N.Y., 1962-63; sect. mgr. Gyrodyne Co. Am., St. James, N.Y., 1963-67; mgr. cost and value control Loral Electronic Systems, Yonkers, N.Y., 1967—; mem. faculty Poly. Inst. Bklyn., 1956-63, Hofstra U., 1976-78, Am. Mgmt. Assn., 1977-78. Bd. dirs., v.p. Suburban Temple. Served with USNR, 1945-46. Mem. Soc. Am. Value Engrs. (certified), AAAS, Acoustical Soc. Am., Am. Helicopter Soc., Soc. Info. Display (sec. N.Y. chpt.). Contbr. articles on acoustics and value engring. to profl. jours. Patentee in field. Home: 14 Downhill Ln Wantagh NY 11793

PALEY, WILLIAM S., broadcasting exec.; b. Chgo., Sept. 28, 1901; s. Samuel and Goldie (Drell) P.; grad. Western Mil. Acad., Alton, Ill., 1918; student U. Chgo., 1918-19; B.S., U. Pa., 1922, LL.D., 1967; LL.D., Adelphi U., 1957, Bates Coll., 1963, Columbia, 1975, Brown U., 1975; m. Dorothy Hart Hearst, May 11, 1932; children—Jeffrey, Hilary; m. 2d, Barbara Cushing Mortimer, July 28, 1947; children—William Cushing, Kate Cushing. Vice pres., sec. Congress Cigar Co., Phila., 1922-28; pres. CBS, Inc., 1928-46, chmn. bd., 1946—; life trustee Columbia U., 1950-73, trustee emeritus, 1973—; trustee Mus. Modern Art, 1937—, pres., 1968-72, chmn., 1972—; mem. Com. for White Ho. Conf. on Edn., 1954-56; gen. chmn. United Hosp. Fund campaign, 1942; chmn. Pres.'s Materials Policy Commn. which produced report Resources for Freedom, 1951-52; chmn. N.Y.C. Task Force Urban Design, 1967; chmn. Urban Design Council City N.Y., 1968-71; mem. exec. com. Resources for the Future, Inc., 1952-69, chmn., 1966-69, hon. dir., 1969—; pres., dir. William S. Paley Found., Inc., Greenpark Found., Inc.; co-chmn. bd. trustees emeritus North Shore Univ. Hosp.; life trustee Fedn. Jewish Philanthropies; trustee Museum of Modern Art, pres. 1968-72, chmn. 1972—; trustee Columbia U., 1950-73, emeritus, 1973—; bd. dirs. Bedford-Stuyvesant D & S Corp., 1967-72; mem. Commn. Critical Choices Am., Council Fgn. Relations, Commn. Cultural Affairs City N.Y., Internat. Exec. Service Corps. Served as col. AUS, World War II; dep. chief Psychol. Warfare Div., S.H.A.E.F., dep. chief Info. Control Div. U.S.G.C.C. Decorated Legion of Merit, Medal for Merit; officer Legion of Honor, Croix de Guerre with Palm (France); Order Crown of Italy; recipient medallion of honor City of N.Y., 1965; Keynote award Nat. Assn. Broadcasters; Gold medal award Nat. Planning Assn.; Skowhegan Gertrude Vanderbilt Whitney award. Mem. Pilgrims of U.S., Acad. Polit. Scis., Nat. Inst. Social Scis. Clubs: River, Turf and Field, National Golf, Links Golf, Deepdale Golf; Century Assn.; Meadowbrook; Lyford Cay (Nassau); Bucks (London). Home: Kiluna Farm Manhasset NY 11030 Office: 51 W 52d St New York City NY 10019

PALGEN, JACK JOSEPH ODILON, UN ofcl.; b. Leuven, Belgium, May 6, 1920; s. Alphonse Rene and Cecile (Lebrun) P.; came to U.S., 1968, naturalized, 1973; m. Mimi Maisonneuve, Nov. 11, 1965; children—Michel, Carine. Asso. prof. geodesy and photogrammetry al-Hikma U. of Baghdad, 1958-64, Baghdad State U., 1960-64; vis. prof. Am. U. Beirut, 1963-64; research asso. Dept. of Photogrammetry Laval U., Quebec, Can., 1966-68; sr. research scientist State U. N.Y., Stony Brook, 1968; sr. research scientist Allied Research Assoc., Greenbelt, Md., 1969-72; dir. African programs NASA Goddard Space Center, ERTS project, Earth Satellite Corp., 1973-76; sr. regional advisor in remote sensing UN Econ. Commn. for Africa, N.Y.C., 1976-79; cons. to NASA Goddard Space Center, 1970-72, Bolivia, 1974. Alexander van Humbold Stiftung (Germany) Fellow, 1966; NRC (Can.) fellow, 1966-68. Mem. Am. Soc. Photogrammetry, Pattern Recognition Soc., Internat. Assn. For Math. Geology, Soc. for Internat. Devel., Assn. des Experts de la Cooperation Internationale. Home: Claridge House 2445 Lyttonsville Rd Silver Spring MD 20910 Office: UNECA Pouch 3-B1 Addis PO Box 20 New York City NY 10017

PALISI, ANTHONY THOMAS, psychologist, educator; b. Rahway, N.J., Mar. 8, 1930; s. Anthony Francis and Marianne Catherine (Picone) P.; B.S., Seton Hall U., 1947, M.A., 1958; Ed.D., Temple U., 1973; m. Dyane Cassidy, Apr. 19, 1954; children—Jane, Anthony Francis, II, Phyllis, Damian-Marie. Tchr., coach, pub. schs., Rahway, 1953-60; sports editor Rahway News-Record, 1950-60; prin. elementary pub. sch., Franklin Twp., N.J., 1960-65; asst. prof. edn. Seton Hall U., 1965-73, asso. prof., 1974-77, prof., 1977—, acting grad. dean, 1976-77, dir. VA guidance services, 1969—; indsl. cons. group dynamics, 1967—; mem. Rahway Bd. Edn., 1961-62. Mem. Rahway Bd. Library Trustees, 1961-68, pres., 1967-68. Recipient award N.J. Sportswriters' Assn., 1953; certified secondary tchr., elementary prin., psychologist, rehab. counselor, N.J. Mem. Am. Psychol. Assn., Am. Personnel and Guidance Assn., AAUP, Nat. Soc. Study Edn., N.J. Council Edn., Center Italian Culture, N.Y. Acad. Scis. Roman Catholic. Research, publs. on counseling, group dynamics. Home: 25 S Crescent Maplewood NJ 07040 Office: 55 Morris Ave Springfield NJ

PALLADINO, CHARLES FREDERICK, food co. exec.; b. Pottstown, Pa., May 5, 1948; s. Charles Angelo and Malvina Marie (Roberts) P.; B.S. in Bus. Adminstrn. (Eastern Frosted Foods Found. scholar), St. Joseph's Coll., Phila., 1970; m. Gail Lynne Daminski, June 26, 1971. Dist. mgr. Eastern Pa., Mrs. Smith's Pie Co., Pottstown, 1970-72, nat. sales mgr. in-store bakery products, 1972-74, mktg. mgr. food service products, 1974-78, interim mktg. mgr. retail consumer pie products, 1976-77, mktg. mgr. Eggo consumer products, 1978—. Bd. dirs. Pottstown Meml. Med. Center, 1976—. Mem. Frozen Food Assn. Del. Valley. Republican. Roman Catholic. Club: K.C. Home: 1447 Shaner Dr Pottstown PA 19464 Office: South and Charlotte Sts Pottstown PA 19464

PALLADINO, NEIL MARIO, physician; b. Bloomfield, N.J., Feb. 24, 1927; s. Mario and Lena P.; student Union Coll., Schenectady, 1945-47; M.D., Harvard U., 1951; children by former marriage—Karen, Neil, Kathleen. Intern, Phila. Gen. Hosp., 1951-52, resident pediatrics, 1952-54; individual practice medicine specializing in pediatrics Plainview, N.Y., 1954—; asso. attending pediatrics Nassau County (N.Y.) Med. Center; dir. pediatrics Central Gen. Hosp., Plainview, N.Y., 1961—, chmn. exec. bd., 1967, 77; asst. prof. clin. pediatrics State U. N.Y. at Stony Brook, 1973—. Diplomate Am. Bd. Pediatrics. Fellow Am. Acad. Pediatrics; mem. Nassau County, N.Y. State med. socs., Nassau County Pediatric Soc., AMA. Roman Catholic. Club: Rotary (pres. 1959). Home: 1 Stauber Dr Plainview NY 11803 Office: 25 Central Park Rd Plainview NY 11803 also 206 Water Lane S Levittown NY 11756

PALLAGROSI, ANTONIO UGO, physician; b. Isola Del Liri, Italy, Mar. 2, 1925; s. Paolo and Berenice (Coppola) P.; came to U.S., 1953, naturalized, 1958; B.A., Liceum Virgilo, Rome, 1944; M.D., U. Rome, 1952; m. Judith L. Pfleeger, Nov. 18, 1967; children—Antonio, Christine, Deborah. Gen. practice medicine, Rome, Italy, also asst. prof. obstetrics and gynecology, Inst. Regina Elena, Rome, 1952-53; intern Paterson (N.J.) Gen. Hosp., 1953-54; resident in surgery St. Joseph's Hosp., Phila., 1954-55; chief resident Point Pleasant Hosp., N.J., 1955-59; Research Inst. fellow in gravitational strain pathology, N.Y.C., 1959-60; physician State of Md., Hagerstown, 1960-66; dir. med. edn. Merck, Sharp & Dohme Internat., Rahway, N.J., 1966-74; asso. dir. clin. research Schering-Plough Internat., Kenilworth, N.J., 1974—. Mem. AMA (N.Y.), Acad. of Scis., Am. Med. Colls., Am. Assn. Fgn. Med. Grads. Roman Catholic. Contbr. articles to profl. jours. Home: 532 Lenox Ave Westfield NJ 07090 Office: 2000 Galloping Hill Rd Kenilworth NJ 07033

PALLEY, REESE, art dealer, mktg. cons.; b. Atlantic City, N.J., Jan. 26, 1922; s. Max and Anne (Rosenberg) P.; B.A. in Economics, New Sch., 1948, postgrad., 1948-49; postgrad. London Sch. of Economics, 1949-52; children—Gilbert, Diane, Toby. Owner, operator Reese Palley Inc., Atlantic City, N.J., San Francisco, 1968, Palm Beach, Fla., 1976; lectr. Mem. N.J. State Dem. Policy Council, 1970-72; mem. Atlantic City Pub. Relations Com., 1974-76; commr. Atlantic County Charter Study, 1974; treas. Atlantic County Dem. Com., 1975-76; chmn. N.J. State Lottery, 1977-79; trustee Coll. Osteopathic Medicine and Surgery, Des Moines, 1976-79, dir., 1977-79; dir. Coll. Medicine Dentistry N.J., 1977-79, Met. Hosp., 1977-79; chmn. fellows Center for Ocean Studies. Served with U.S. Army, 1942-46. Recipient many civic awards. Mem. Slocum Soc., Oceanic Soc. (dir.). Jewish. Clubs: Margate Yacht, Cruising Assn. (London). Author: The Porcelain Art of Edward Marshall Boehm, 1976. Home: 151 N Annapolis Ave Atlantic City NJ 08401 Office: 1201 Boardwalk St Atlantic City NJ 08401

PALLONE, ADRIAN JOSEPH, scientist; b. Lille, France, Apr. 8, 1928; s. Giovanni and Laurina P.; came to U.S., 1946, naturalized, 1954; B.Aero. Engring., Poly. Inst. N.Y., 1952, M.Aero. Engring., 1953, Ph.D. in Applied Mechanics, 1959; m. Teresa M. Violino, June 12, 1954; children—John M., Anne Marie, Janet M., Joan L. Research scientist Bell Aerospace Systems, 1954-55; research asso. Poly. Inst. N.Y., 1955-59; chief exptl. and theoretical aerodynamics sect. Avco Systems Div., Wilmington, Mass., 1959-63, mgr. aerophysics dept., 1963-66, dir. tech., 1967-77, chief scientist, 1977—; prof. aerospace engring. N.Y. U., 1966-67. Asso. fellow Am. Inst. Aeros. and Astronautics, N.Y. Acad. Scis., Sigma Xi, Sigma Gamma Tau. Home: 1 Rennie Dr Andover MA 01810 Office: 201 Lowell St Wilmington MA 01887

PALLOP, ANTS, veterinarian; b. Tartu, Estonia, May 4, 1928; s. Juhan and Linda (Vatsar) P.; came to U.S., 1949, naturalized, 1956; B.S., Miss. State U., 1952; D.V.M., Cornell U., 1962; m. Anita Parna, Nov. 28, 1959; children—Eric Ain, Tarmo Ants. Asso. veterinarian Plainfield (N.J.) Animal Hosp., 1962-64; owner, dir. Bernardsville (N.J.) Animal Hosp., 1964—. Mem. Bernards Twp. Bd. Health, 1967-74, pres., 1969. Mem. AVMA, Assn. for Advancement of Baltic Studies. Republican. Lutheran. Club: Rotary (pres. 1973-74). Home: 71 Old Fort Rd Bernardsville NJ 07924 Office: 41 Morristown Rd Bernardsville NJ 07924

PALLOZZI, DENNIS PETER, educator; b. Paterson, N.J., Nov. 2, 1947; s. Harold N. and Viola (Spacciapoli) P.; B.S. in Edn., Seton Hall U., 1968; M.A. in Am. History, Montclair State Coll., 1972, M.A. in Edn. Adminstrn. and Supervision, 1976; m. Patricia Cryor, Aug. 12, 1973. Tchr. pub. schs., Paterson, 1968-70; tchr. Central Middle Sch., Montville, N.J., 1970-76, adminstrv. trainee, 1974-76; asst. prin. Hudson Maxim Sch., Hopatcong, N.J., 1976—; cons. Middle Sch. Orgn. and Curriculum. Mem. N.J. Assn. Supervision and Curriculum Devel., Nat. Assn. Secondary Sch. Prins., Am. Hist. Assn., Nat., N.J. assns. elementary sch. adminstrs., Sigma Alpha Beta (pres. 1966-67). Home: 216 Tomahawk Trail Route 2 Sparta NJ 07871

PALMATIER, SUSAN MAY, librarian; b. Nyack, N.Y., Aug. 28, 1944; d. John Lambert and Esther Elizabeth (White) Palmatier; A.B., Mt. Holyoke Coll., 1966; M.S. in L.S., Case Western Res. U., 1967. Indexer, H.W. Wilson Co., Bronx, N.Y., 1967; librarian Fed. Res. Bank of N.Y., N.Y.C., 1968-70, sr. librarian, 1970-72, asst. chief librarian, 1972-75; S.W. dist. cons. N.H. State Library, Keene, 1975—; instr. pub. library techniques Continuing Edn. Div., U. N.H., 1976—. Sec. statewide library devel. program SW Dist. Adv. Council, 1975—; mem. task force on bus. info. services New Eng. Library Bd., 1976—; mem. State Library Staff Devel. Com., 1977—; mem. regional meeting subcom. of core com. N.H. Conf. on Libraries, 1978. Mem. Spl. Libraries Assn. (chpt. nominating com. 1971-72, nat. teller's com. 1971-72, chmn. N.Y. chpt. spl. libraries directory com. 1972-74), ALA, N.H. Library Assn., New Eng. Library Assn., Monadnock Community Chorus. Editor: Granite State Libraries, 1977—. Home: Old Ashuelot Rd Ashuelot NH 03441 Office: NH State Library Dist Office King Ct Keene NH 03431

PALMER, ALLISON WRIGHT POST, real estate co. exec.; b. N.Y.C., June 10, 1935; s. Josiah Culbert and Katharine (Post) P.; B.A., Yale, 1957; m. Anna Maria Caracciolo Di Brienza, Feb. 20, 1960; children—James Culbert, Lucius Noyes, Elisabeth C., Katharine P. Asst. cashier, loan officer First Nat. City Bank, N.Y.C., 1961-68; account exec., corp. DeHaven & Townsend, Crouter & Bodine, N.Y.C., 1968-78; account exec. Janney Montgomery Scott, Inc., N.Y.C., 1978—; pres. Beekman Family Assn., N.Y.C., 1970—, also dir.; pres. Beekman Estate, Inc., N.Y.C., 1970—, also dir., mem. exec. com.; dir. Sheltering Arms Childrens Service. Served to lt., USNR, 1957-60. Presbyn. Clubs: Union (N.Y.C.); Down Town Assn. Editor: The Principle Stock Exchanges of the World, 1964. Home: 1170 Fifth Ave New York City NY 10029 Office: 420 Lexington Ave New York City NY 10004

PALMER, ANTHONY JOSEPH, psychologist, clin. dir.; b. Pitts., Jan. 21, 1943; s. Anthony Joseph and Kimberly Ann P.; B.A., Muskingum Coll., 1963; M.A., Bowling Green (Ohio) State U., 1965; Ed.D., W.Va. U., 1973; m. Mikal Lynn Glass, Dec. 3, 1977. Staff psychologist Toledo (Ohio) State Hosp., 1965, Osawatomie (Kans.) State Hosp., 1965; staff psychologist Woodville State Hosp., Carnegie, Pa., 1966—, dir. psychology dept., 1976—; cons. Goodwill Industries Pitts., 1967—, Byzantine Cath. Sem. U.S., 1967—; grad. instr. psychology Duquesne U., Pitts., 1969—; pvt. practice clin. psychology, Mt. Lebanon, Pa., 1973—; mem. United Mental Health Allegheny County (Pa.). Mem. Am., Pa., Pitts. psychol. assns., Nat. Register Mental Health Providers. Home: 13 Fawn Ridge Dr McKees Rocks PA 15136 Office: Woodville State Hospital Psychology Dept Carnegie PA 15106

PALMER, BERNARD BARNEY, city ofcl.; b. Phila., Sept. 21, 1911; s. Samuel and Rose (Seidenberg) P.; B.S. in Edn., Temple U. (Phila.), 1933, M.S., 1935; m. Dinah Kaufman, Dec. 15, 1940; 1 dau., Linda C. Personnel officer VA, Wilkes-Barre, Pa., 1946-52; personnel officer Water Dept. City Phila., 1952-57, adminstrv. services dir., 1957—. Instr., Phila. Govt. Tng. Inst., U. Pa. Fels Inst., U. Pa., Phila., 1959-66. Active charitable drives, Phila. Served with AUS, 1942-46. Mem. Am. Acad. Polit. and Social Scis., Internat. Personnel Mgmt. Assn., Am. Soc. Pub. Adminstrn., Am. Pub. Works Assn. Home: Penn Towers Apt 626 1801 JFK Blvd Philadelphia PA 19103 Office: Municipal Services Bldg Philadelphia PA 19107

PALMER, CHESTER RALPH, accountant; b. Thetford, Vt., Nov. 25, 1921; s. Ralph Alden and Ruth Esther (Cadwell) P.; B.A., Dartmouth Coll., 1949; M.A. in History, U. Ill., 1953; m. Natalie Elizabeth Barrup, Jan. 17, 1964; children—Pamela R., Craig B. Tchr., prin. Lyme (N.H.) Schs., 1949-51; tchr., New Rochelle and Mohopac, N.Y., 1951-53; office mgr. Southworth's Garage, Norwich, Vt., 1955-63; prop. Maple Grove Farm Nursery, East Thetford, Vt., 1958-63; office mgr. Kelton Motors, Inc., Thetford, 1963-64; accountant William H. Corsner & Co., Lebanon, N.H., 1964-67; pub. accountant, Lebanon, 1967—. Chmn., Thetford Sch. Planning and Bldg. Com., 1957-63; mem. Thetford Planning Commn. Served with AUS, 1942-45; PTO. Mem. Nat., N.H. (pres.) socs. pub. accountants. Congregationalist. Clubs: Thetford Lions (past pres., treas.), Nat. Grange. Home: Maple Grove Farm East Thetford VT 05043 Office: 211 National Bank Bldg Park St Lebanon NH 03766

PALMER, DAVID CHEETHAM, librarian; b. Washington, Aug. 26, 1925; s. Roy Massey and Theodosia Josephine (Walter) P.; student Peabody Conservatory of Music, 1943-52; B.S., Johns Hopkins, 1953; M.L.S., Rutgers U., 1956; m. Marion Louise Chamberlin, Dec. 4, 1965. Reference asst. Enoch Pratt Free Library, Balt., 1956-57; exec. sec. Pa. Library Survey, Harrisburg, 1957-59; exec. dir. Gov.'s Commn. on Pub. Library Devel. in Pa., Harrisburg, 1959-61; field cons., dir. library devel. div. Pa. State Library, Harrisburg, 1961-65; asst. dir. N.J. State Library, Trenton, 1965—, acting state librarian, 1975-78. Adj. prof. library adminstrn. Rutgers U., 1965-69; cons. library devel. State of Pa., 1966-67, State of Md., 1972-73, State of Tenn., 1967; cons. library statistics U.S. Office Edn., 1969-72. Mem. Trenton (N.J.) Bicentennial Com., 1973-74; adv. bd. Rutgers Grad. Library Sch., 1972—; pres. State House Historic Dist. Assn., Trenton, 1977—. Recipient citation for distinguished service Pa. Adv. Council on Library Devel., 1965. Mem. Am., N.J., Pa., N.Y. library assns., Am. Soc. Pub. Adminstrn., Civil Liberties Union. Editor: Planning for a Nationwide System of Library Statistics, 1970. Contbr. to publs. in field. Home: 336 W State St Trenton NJ 08618 Office: State Dept Edn NJ State Library 185 W State St Trenton NJ 08625

PALMER, EDWARD, ednl. adminstr.; b. Williamsburg, Va., July 26, 1928; s. Louis and Amelia P.; A.B. in Sociology, Va. State Coll., 1962; M.S., Coll. City N.Y., 1967; postgrad. Columbia U., 1975—; m. Edith E. Maginley, July 30, 1960; children—Karen Allison, Brian Edward. Technician, Pacific Telephone & Telegraphy Co., Los Angeles, 1955-58; dormitory supr., counselor Youth House, Bronx, N.Y., 1958-60; tchr., counselor N.Y.C. Bd. Edn., 1960-68; lectr., asst. higher edn. officer City U. N.Y., 1968-70; asso. regional dir. Coll. Entrance Exam. Bd., N.Y.C., 1970—; mem. adv. com. on tchr. edn. and certification N.Y. State Bd. Regents. Area dir. Operation Crossroads Africa (West Africa), 1969; bd. dirs. Logos Drug Rehab. Center, N.Y.C., 1972-74. Served with U.S. Army, 1950-53; ETO. Mem. Am. Personnel and Guidance Assn., N.Y. State Fin. Aid Adminstrs. Assn., N.Y. State Personnel and Guidance Assn., Nat. Assn. Fgn. Student Advisors. Democrat. Home: PO Box 1116 Teaneck NJ 07666 Office: 888 7th Ave New York City NY 10019

PALMER, JAMES ROBERT, electronic mfg. exec.; b. Elm Creek, Nebr., Dec. 13, 1923; s. Charles Andrew and Margaret Eleanor (Mitchell) P.; B.S., Iowa State U. 1944; postgrad. U.S. Navy Officers PreRadar and Radar Schs., Bowdoin Coll., Mass. Inst. Tech.; postgrad. advanced engring. program Gen. Electric Co. 1947; m. Barbara M. Raeder, Aug. 21, 1948; children—Janet Palmer Lipcon, David, Charles. Project engr. Gen. Electric Co., Phila. 1946-51; elec. engr. United Engrs. and Constructors, Inc., 1951-53; project engr. Haller, Raymond and Brown, Inc., State College, Pa. 1953-56; pres. Centre Video and subs., State College, 1956-72, C-COR Electronics, State College, 1956—. Bd. dirs. Allegheny Ednl. Broadcast Council, 1966-74. Registered profl. engr., Pa., S.C. Mem. Nat. Cable TV Assn. (dir. 1965-68, chmn. various coms.), Pa. Community Antenna Assn. (pres. 1966-67, dir. 1960-66), IEEE (sr.), Tau Beta Pi, Eta Kappa Nu, Phi Kappa Phi. Presbyterian (elder). Patentee in field. Home: 324 Homan Ave State College PA 16801 Office: 60 Decibel Rd State College PA 16801

PALMER, PAUL RICHARD, librarian; b. Cin., Jan. 21, 1917; s. Gardner O. and Sarah Ellen (Christy) P.; B.A., U. Cin., 1949; M.S. in Library Service, Columbia, 1950, M.A., 1955. Br. asst. Bklyn. Pub. Library, 1950-51; librarian Burgess-Carpenter classics Paterno Philosophy libraries, Columbia U., N.Y.C., 1951-67, librarian Sch. Library Service, 1968, curator Brander Matthews Dramatic Mus., also theatre arts librarian, 1969-72, bibliographer Avery Archtl. Library, 1972-75, curator Columbiana Collection, 1975—. Cons. for research reprint com. ALA, 1954-59. Served with AUS, 1942-45. Mem. AAUP, Internat. Com. of Museums Assos., Univ. and Coll. Theatre Assn., Theatre Library Assn. (rec. sec., mem. exec. bd. 1975—), Am. Film Inst., Nat. Trust for Historic Preservation, ALA, Phi Beta Kappa. Home: 560 Riverside Dr New York City NY 10027 Office: Columbiana Collection 210 Low Meml Library Columbia University New York City NY 10027

PALMER, RALPH CONRAD, rolling bearings and automotive parts co. exec.; b. Phila., Nov. 16, 1920; s. Ralph C. and Isabella M. (Shive) P.; B.S., U. Pa., 1951; m. Dorothy E. Thies, Oct. 21, 1944; children—Ralph, Frederick. Indsl. engr. SKF Industries, Inc., Phila., 1940-50, mgmt. in indsl. relations and pub. relations, 1950-72, v.p. indsl. relations, 1972-76, v.p. indsl. relations and pub. relations, 1976—. Served to lt. USCG, 1942-46. Mem. Indsl. Relations Research Assn., Indsl. Relations Assn. Phila., Labor Relations Council, Indsl. Relations Council Machinery and Allied Products Inst., N.A.M. (mem. multi-nat. labor relations com.), Mfrs. Assn. Delaware Valley (mem. indsl. relations com.), Anti-Friction Bearing Mfrs. Assn. (mem. indsl. relations com.), U.S., Pa., Phila. chambers commerce. Republican. Roman Catholic. Clubs: Phila. Country, Rotary (Phila.). Home: 1130 Robin Rd Gladwyne PA 19035 Office: 1100 1st Ave King Prussia PA 19406

PALMER, RICHARD WARE, lawyer; b. Arlington, Mass., Oct. 20, 1919; s. George Ware and Ruth French (Judkins) P.; A.B., Harvard, 1942, LL.B., 1948; m. Nancy Fernald Shaw, July 8, 1950; children—Richard Ware, John Wentworth, Anne Fernald. Admitted to N.Y. bar, 1950, Pa. bar, 1959; sec., dir. N.Am. Mfg. Co., Natick, Mass., 1946-48; asso. firm Burlingham, Veeder, Clark & Hupper, Burlingham, Hupper & Kennedy, N.Y.C., 1949-57; partner Rawle & Henderson, Phila., 1958—; sec., dir. Underwater Technics, Inc., Camden, N.J., 1967—. Adviser on admiralty law to U.S. delegation Inter-Governmental Maritime Consultative Orgn., London, 1967; mem. U.S. Shipping Coordinating Com., Washington. legal sub-com., 1967—; adviser admiralty law to U.S. delegation 6th working session UN Conf. on Internat. Shipping Legislation, Geneva, 1974; U.S. del. 30th Internat. Conf. Comité Maritime Internationale, Hamburg, Germany, 1974, 31st Internat. Conf., Rio de Janeiro, 1977; mem. adv. bd. Tulane Admiralty Law Inst., New Orleans. Chmn., Phila. com. Harvard Law Sch. Fund, 1972-74, area chmn. Pa., N.J., Del. for Class of 1942, 1967—; trustee, pres. Seamen's Ch. Inst., Phila.; bd. dirs. Phila. Council for Internat. Visitors; pres. Haverford (Pa.) Civic Assn. Served to lt. comdr. USNR, 1942-46. Mem. Am. (chmn. standing com. on admiralty and maritime law), N.Y.C., Phila. bar assns., Am. Judicature Soc., Maritime Law Assn. (chmn. limitation liability com.), Assn. Average Adjusters, Port of Phila. Maritime Soc. Republican. Episcopalian. Clubs: Union League, Downtown, Merion Cricket, Phila. Skating (Phila.); India House, Whitehall Lunch (N.Y.C.); Harvard (N.Y.C., Phila.). Home: 318 Grays Ln Haverford PA 19041 Office: Packard Bldg Philadelphia PA 19102

PALMER, STUART HUNTER, educator; b. N.Y.C., Apr. 29, 1924; s. Herman G. and Beatrice (Hunter) P.; B.A., Yale, 1949, M.A., 1951, Ph.D., 1955; m. Anne Barbara Scarborough, June 22, 1946; 1 dau., Catherine. Asst. to dean Yale Coll., New Haven, 1949-51; instr. sociology New Haven Coll., 1949-51, 53-55; faculty U. N.H., Durham, 1955—, prof., 1964—, chmn. dept. sociology, 1964-69; Distinguished vis. prof. State U. N.Y., Albany, 1970-71; vis. behavioral scientist N.H. Div. Mental Health; vis. prof. U. Sussex (Eng.), 1976, U. Ga., 1977. Cons. U.S. Office Edn., USPHS, U.S. Office Delinquency and Youth Devel., U.S. Dept. Justice. Mem. adv. com. for sociology Com. on Internat. Exchange of Persons; mem. exec. com. N.H. Gov.'s Commn. on Crime and Delinquency. Trustee New Eng. Aero. Inst. Served to lt. AC, AUS, 1942-45, USAF, 1951-53. Decorated Air medal with 3 oak leaf clusters; Henry Page fellow, 1953-55. Mem. Am. Sociol. Assn., Eastern Sociol. Soc., Internat. Soc. Criminology, A.A.A.S., Am. Acad. Polit. and Social Scis., N.Y. Acad. Scis., Am. Assn. Suicidology, Soc. for Cross-Cultural Research, Am. Soc. Criminology, Sigma Xi, Alpha Kappa Delta. Author: Understanding Other People, 1955; A Study of Murder, 1960; (with Brian R. Kay) The Challenge of Supervision, 1961; Deviance and Conformity, 1970; (with Arnold S. Linsky) Rebellion and Retreat, 1972; The Violent Society, 1972; The Prevention of Crime, 1973. also articles. Home: Riverview Dr Durham NH 03824 Office: Social Sci Center U NH Durham NH 03824

PALMER, THEODORE HAROLD, JR., orgn. exec.; b. Milford, Del., Mar. 6, 1942; s. T. Harold and Elsie (Evans) P.; B.S., U. Del., 1964, M.S., 1971; m. Carole Marvel, Sept. 7, 1963; children—Robert Ross, Darree Lynn. Asst. sales mgr. Townsend's Poultry, Inc., Millsboro, Del., 1964-65; tchr. sci. Milford Sch. Dist., 1965-68; county agrl. agt. U. Del. Coop. Extension Service, Georgetown, 1968—; notary pub. Past vestryman St. John the Baptist Episcopal Ch., Milton, Del., St. Peter's Episcopal Ch., Lewes, Del. Mem. Nat. Assn. Ext. 4-H Agts., Lewis Hist. Soc., Sussex County Bd. Realtors, Epsilon Sigma Phi, Alpha Zeta. Republican. Clubs: St. Peter's Mens, Rehoboth Art League, Elks. Home: 221 2d St Lewes DE 19958 Office: Route 2 Box 48 Georgetown DE 19947

PALMER, WINTHROP BUSHNELL, educator, writer; b. N.Y.C., Sept. 14, 1899; d. Ericsson Foote and Bertha Tudor (Thompson) Bushnell; student Barnard Coll., Columbia, N.Y. U.; Litt.D. (hon.), L.I. U., 1956; m. Carleton H. Palmer, Oct. 2, 1919; children—Carleton H., Lowell M. II, Winthrop (Mrs. James Boswell), Rosalind (Mrs. Henry G. Walter Jr.). Pres. Nat. Assn. Jr. Leagues Am., 1926-28; rep. New Eng. states Eleanor Roosevelt's Reporter Plan Com., 1932; asso. editor Dance News, N.Y.C., 1940; exec. com., faculty English, C.W. Post Coll., Brookville, N.Y., 1955-74; trustee L.I. (N.Y.) U., 1969—, chmn. bd. trustees, 1974-75, chmn. emerita, 1975—; lectr. in field. Mem. Poetry Soc. Am. (exec. council 1974-78), Acad. Am. Poets, Joyce Soc., Alliance Française, PEN, Poets and Writers. Clubs: Piping Rock, Seawanhaka, Met. Author: Theatrical Dancing in America, 1945, rev. edit., 1978; The New Barbarian, 1951; Beat the Wind, 1960. Asso. editor Confrontation, 1973—. Home: 435 E 52d St New York City NY 10022

PALMERSHEIM, THERESA ANN, communications exec.; b. Rockford, Ill., Aug. 29, 1950; d. John P. and Ellen L. (McNeil) McHugh; B.A., St. Catherine's Coll., St. Paul, 1972; postgrad. Am. U., 1977—; m. Lawrence A. Palmersheim, June 17, 1972. Reporter, Catholic Bull. Newspaper, St. Paul, 1971-72; editor Allstate Ins. Co., Northbrook, Ill., 1972-75; mgr. employee publs. McCormick & Co., Inc., Hunt Valley, Md., 1975—. Mem. Internat. Assn. Bus. Communicators, Balt. Pub. Relations Council, Pub. Relations Soc. Am., N.Y. Publicity Club, Sigma Delta Chi (awards 1972). Home: 212 Gaywood Rd Baltimore MD 21212 Office: 11350 McCormick Rd Hunt Valley MD 21031

PALMIERI, LUCIEN EUGENE, librarian; b. Cambridge, Mass., Nov. 8, 1921; s. William Maria and Elvina (David) P.; B.S., U. Wis., 1947, M.S., 1949, Ph.D., 1953, M.S. in L.S., 1956; m. Valerie Doreen Tremlin, Sept. 18, 1948 (div.); children—Joanne Valerie, Candida Elvina (Mrs. Robert Walker), Maxim Russell. Instr., U. Wis., Madison, 1949-51, instr. extension div., 1953-56; head librarian Chgo. Tchrs. Coll., 1956-62; cons. Ministry of Edn., Dar es Salaam, Tanzania, 1962-66; prof. philosophy Northeastern Ill. State U., Chgo., 1966-67; dir. Butler Library, State U. Coll., Buffalo, 1967-74, head Office for Collection Devel., 1974—. Trustee Western N.Y. Library Resources Council, 1967-77. Served with AUS, 1942-46. Mem. Am. Philos. Assn., ALA, AAUP (Chgo. pres. 1959-61), Mind Assn., State U. N.Y. Librarians Assn. Club: University (Buffalo). Author: Language and Clear Thinking, 1960. Contbr. articles to profl. jours. Home: Hotel Lenox 140 North St Buffalo NY 14201 Office: 1300 Elmwood Ave Buffalo NY 14222

PALMIERI, SAM VINCENT, accountant; b. Bayonne, N.J., Mar. 14, 1942; s. Frank Anthony and Yolanda (Doria) P.; B.S., St. Peter's Coll., 1963; M.B.A., Fairleigh Dickinson U., 1968. Supervising sr. accountant Touche Ross & Co., Newark, N.J., 1967-73; controller Joseph J. Brunetti Constrn. Co., Oldbridge, N.J., 1973—; part-time accounting instr. Hudson County Community Coll. Mem. fin. com. Our Lady of Assumption Ch., 1976—. C.P.A., N.J. Mem. Am. Accounting Assn., Am. Mgmt. Assn., Eastern Fin. Assn., Nat. Assn. Accountants, Am. Inst. C.P.A.'s, N.J. Soc. C.P.A.'s (com. on mems. in industry and commerce), Am. Taxation Assn., Fin. Mgmt. Assn. Democrat. Roman Catholic. Club: K.C. Home: 193 W 26th St Bayonne NJ 07002 Office: 200 Route 9 Old Bridge NJ 08857

PALO, JOHN, chiropractor; b. N.Y.C., Feb. 27, 1920; s. Joseph and Frances (La Cascia) Palazzotto; B.S., Queens Coll., 1956; D.C. Nat. Coll. of Chiropractic, 1950; m. Fern May Raybon, June 13, 1961. Gen. practice chiropractic medicine, Ozone Park, N.Y., 1950—; asst. dir. chiropractic div. N.Y.C. Dept. Health, 1976-77; instr. USAF, 1941-42. Served with USAF, 1941-46. Fellow Am. Coll. Chiropractors; mem. Am., N.Y. State chiropractic assns. Clubs: Rosicrucian. Author: While Passing Through, 1954; New World Mystics, 1976; contbr. articles in various fields including Am. Indian Music to profl. jours; Composer Suite Master Jesus. Lectr., song. recitalist. Editor Chiropractic Psychotherapy, 1957-58. Office: 55 W 42d St New York City NY 10036

PALUHA, JAROSLAW, computer co. exec.; b. Ginsburg, Germany, July 14, 1946; s. Roman and Paraskewia K.P.; came to U.S., 1950, naturalized, 1968; B.S., Quinnipiac Coll., 1968; M.B.A., U. Bridgeport, 1976. Accountant Bua, Simione & Co., New Haven, Conn., 1968-71; sr. accountant Kuriansky & Co., Stamford, Conn., 1971-75; tax audit specialist Nat. CSS Inc., Norwalk, Conn., 1975-78; pvt. practice, 1978—; dir., treas. Richard Martin Inc., Westport, Conn. Recipient New Haven Scholarship award, 1964. C.P.A., Conn. Mem. Am. Inst. C.P.A.'s, Conn. Soc. C.P.A.'s, Stamford Area C.P.A.'s. Ukrainian Catholic. Home and office: 9 Avery Pl Westport CT 06880

PALUMBO, THOMAS ANTHONY, electrochem. engr.; b. Newark, Sept. 22, 1938; s. Thomas Samuel and Veronica (Ciunowicz) P.; B.S. in M.E., Newark Coll. Engring., 1960; postgrad. Stevens Inst. Tech., 1962-63; m. Margaret E. Moffitt, May 16, 1964; children—Alice, Andrea. Chief chemist and quality control mgr. Platronics, Inc., Linden, N.J., 1960-68; mem. tech. staff and supr. electrodeposition group Bell Telephone Labs., Murray Hill, N.J., 1968—. Recipient Gold Metal award, Am. Electroplaters Soc., 1971. Mem. ASTM, Am. Electroplaters Soc. Office: 600 Mountain Ave Murray Hill NJ 07974

PALUSZEK, JOHN LAWRENCE, pub. relations cons.; b. Bklyn., Nov. 3, 1933; s. John and Sophie Gladys (Mahnick) P.; B.A. in Mgmt., Manhattan Coll., 1955; m. Jean Evelyn Murphy, June 18, 1955; children—Michael, Stephen, Patricia, Christopher, Matthew, Mary, Julie, Amy, Jennifer. Asso. editor Petroleum Week, N.Y.C., 1955-60; exec. v.p. Basford Pub. Relations, N.Y.C., 1960-71; pres. Paluszek & Leslie Assos., also subs. Corporate Social Action, Inc., N.Y.C., 1971—; lectr. N.Y. U., Georgetown U., Am. Mgmt. Assn., Syracuse U. Recipient service awards Manhattan Coll. Mem. Pub. Relations Soc. Am. (accredited, past pres. N.Y. chpt.), Manhattan Coll. Alumni Soc. (pres.). Democrat. Roman Catholic. Author: Will The Corporation Survive?, 1977; contbr. articles profl. jours. and periodicals. Home: 47 Red Ground Rd Old Westbury NY 11568 Office: 1500 Broadway New York City NY 10036

PAMILLA, JEANNE ROSE, orthopedic surgeon; b. N.Y.C., Apr. 2, 1943; d. Salvatore Charles and Josephine Serafina (Di Gregorio) Pamilla; B.S., St. John's U., 1964; M.D. (Alpha Omega Alpha fellow), Woman's Med. Coll. Pa., 1968. Intern, Lenox Hill Hosp., N.Y.C., 1968-69; gen. surg. resident, 1969-70; orthopaedic surg. resident, 1970-72, chief orthopedic resident, 1972-73; fellow in children's orthopedics and cerebral palsy Hosp. Spl. Surgery, Cornell Med. Center, N.Y.C., 1973-74, sr. fellow, 1974-75; instr. surgery Cornell U. Med. Sch., 1973-78, clin. asst. prof., 1978—; clin. cons. in orthopedics N.Y.C. Dept. Health, 1973—; asst. attending orthopedic surgeon Hosp. for Spl. Surgery, 1975—, N.Y. Hosp.-Cornell Med. Center, 1975—. Recipient Physicians Recognition award, annually 1972—; diplomate Am. Bd. Orthopedic Surgery. Mem. Am. Med. Women's Assn., N.Y. Acad. Scis., Am. Acad. for Cerebral Palsy, N.Y. State, N.Y. County med. socs., Alumni Assn. Med. Coll. Pa., Delta Epsilon Beta. Contbr. articles to med. jours. Editor: IATRIAN, yearbook Woman's Med. Coll. Pa., 1968. Home: 320 E 57th St New York City

NY 10022 Office: Hosp for Spl Surgery 535 E 70th St New York City NY 10021 also 520 E 72d St New York City NY 10021

PAN, HUO-HSI, educator; b. Foochow, China, Nov. 11, 1918; s. Bai-Ming and Won-Ching (Chen) P.; came to U.S., 1948, naturalized, 1973; B.M.E., Nat. S.W. Asso. U. (China), 1943; M.M.E., Tex. A. and M. Coll., 1948; M.S. in Applied Mechanics, Kans. State Coll., 1950; Ph.D., U. Calif., 1954; m. Chao Pan, June 4, 1960; children—Lillian, Nina. Mem. tech. staff to head inspection dept. 21st Arsenal, Kunming, China, 1943-47; asso. in mech. engring. U. Calif. at Berkeley, 1952-53; research engr., research labs. Portland Cement Assn., Skokie, Ill., 1954; asst. prof. U. Toledo, 1954-55; asst. prof. U. Ill., Urbana, 1955-57; asst. prof. engring. mechanics N.Y. U., 1957-59, asst. prof. applied mechanics, 1959-63, asso. prof., 1963-69, prof., 1969-73; prof. applied mechanics Poly. Inst. N.Y., Bklyn., 1973-74, prof. mech. engring., 1974-76, prof. mech. and aerospace engring., 1976—, adminstrv. officer dept. mech. engring., 1975-76; cons. in field. NSF grantee, 1964-67; NASA grantee, 1966-69. Mem. ASME, Am. Acad. Mechanics, Soc. Indsl. and Applied Math., Soc. Engring. Sci., Am. Inst. Aeros. and Astronautics, AAUP, Sigma Xi, Phi Kappa Phi, Pi Tau Sigma, Pi Mu Epsilon. Contbr. articles and revs. to profl. jours.; reviewer Applied Mechanics Rev. Home: 76 Edgars Ln Hastings-on-Hudson NY 10706 Office: Dept Mech and Aerospace Engring Poly Inst NY 333 Jay St Brooklyn NY 11201

PANARO, VICTOR ANTHONY, radiologist; b. Buffalo, Aug. 7, 1928; s. Anthony and Teresa P.; B.A. summa cum laude, U. Buffalo, 1948, M.D., 1952; m. Virginia Spann, Dec. 4, 1954; children—Denise, Lynn, Stephen. Intern, E. J. Meyer Meml. Hosp., Buffalo, 1952-53, resident, 1953-54, 56-58, resident Roswell Park Meml. Hosp. Cancer Inst., Buffalo, 1956-57; practice medicine specializing in radiology, Buffalo, 1961—; mem. staff E.J. Meyer Hosp., Buffalo, 1961—, asso. dir. radiology dept., 1972—; mem. staff Westfield (N.Y.) Meml. Hosp., 1959—, dir. radiology dept., 1959—; mem. staff Buffalo Psychiat. Inst., 1974—, dir. radiology dept., 1974—; cons. nuclear medicine and radiology Brooks Meml. Hosp., 1970—; prof. radiology and nuclear medicine State U. N.Y., Buffalo. Served as capt. M.C., U.S. Army, 1954-56. Diplomate Am. Bd. Radiology, Am. Bd. Nuclear Medicine, Am. Bd. Med. Examiners. Fellow Am. Coll. Radiology; mem. AMA, N.Y. State, Erie County med. socs., Radiol. Soc. N.Am., Buffalo Radiol. Soc., Gibson Anatomical Soc., Cath. Physicians Guild Western N.Y., Phi Beta Kappa, Phi Chi. Republican. Roman Catholic. Club: Baccelli Med. Home: 25 Elmhurst Rd Buffalo NY 14226 Office: Erie County Med Center 462 Grider St Buffalo NY 14209

PANCELLA, JOHN RAYMOND, educator; b. Dunbar, Pa., June 24, 1931; s. Joseph and Angela Carmela (Tominio) P.; B.S. (Alumni scholar), Indiana (Pa.) U., 1953; postgrad. U. Pitts., 1955-56, Wesleyan U., 1960; M.S. (Nat. Sci. Found. summer grantee 1957-60, AEC summer research asst. 1961, NSF grantee 1962), U. Md., 1962, Ed.D., 1970. Instr. Penn Hills High Sch., Pitts., 1955-60; grad. asst. zoology U. Md., 1960-61, asst. instr., 1961-62, instr. edn., 1962-65; instr. biology Montogomery County Pub. Sch., Rockville, Md., 1965-68, supr. sci., 1968-71, asst. dir. for devel., 1971-76, coordinator sci., 1976—; vis. prof. Western Md. Coll., 1969, U. Md., Balt., 1971; asst. dir. Am. U. NSF Summer Insts., 1970-71, dir. Title IV gifted sci. project, 1977—. Served with U.S. Army, 1953-55. Mem. Sons of Italy of Am., Sigma Xi, Phi Sigma. Democrat. Roman Catholic. Clubs: Gaslight, Les Amis du Vin, Elks. Author: Studying Teaching, 1967, 71; Behavioral Objectives in Concept-Seeking; 1970; Toward Individualized Instruction, 1973; Individualized Learning Packages for Elementary Science, 1973; also articles on invertebrate zoology; book revs. for profl. jours., research in freshwater zoology and sci. teaching. Home: 1209 Veirs Mill Rd Rockville MD 20851 Office: 850 Hungerford Dr Rockville MD 20850

PANCHAL, PRAVIN D., physician; b. Ahmedabad, India, Sept. 16, 1941; s. D.A. and Kamalaben D. Panchal; came to U.S., 1968, naturalized, 1973; M.D., B.J. Med. Coll., 1964; m. Joan Dauginikas, June 20, 1970; children—Nita, Sheila, Lisa. Intern, South Side Hosp., Pitts., 1968-69; VA Hosp., Bronx, N.Y., 1969-71; chief rehab. med. services VA Hosp., Pitts., 1971—; dir. rehab. services Negley House Inc., Pitts., 1974—; chief rehab. services Central Med. Pavallion, Pitts., 1974—; physiatrist South Side Hosp., Pitts., 1977—. Diplomate Am. Bd. Phys. Medicine and Rehab. Mem. Am. Congress Rehab. Medicine, Am. Acad. Rehab. Medicine, Internat. Med. Soc. Parapalegia, Am. Geriatric Soc., Pa. State Med. Soc. Contbr. research papers in field. Home: 1017 Beechwood Blvd Pittsburgh PA 15206 Office: 1400 Center Ave Pittsburgh PA 15219

PANDISCIO, JOSEPH ROBERT ANTONIO, JR., real estate broker; b. Fitchburg, Mass., Aug. 31, 1942; s. Joseph R. A. and Rachel S. (Lastella) P.; B.A. in Bus., St. Louis U., 1964; m. Carol A. Zink, Oct. 3, 1965; children—Christine M., Joseph R. A. Pres., gen. mgr., constrn. engr. Bay State Engring. & Constrn. Co., Inc., 1968—; pres. Lake Shirley Realty, Inc., 1968-72; pres. Pandiscio Realty of Cape Cod Inc., South Yarmouth, Pandiscio Assos., South Yarmouth, Pandiscio, Inc., Fitchburg and Harvard; owner Pandiscio, Realtors, South Yarmouth, Fitchburg and Harvard. Real estate broker, Mass., N.H.; ins. broker, Mass. Mem. Nat. Assn. Realtors (dir.), Soc. Real Estate Appraisers (asso.), Mass. Bd. Real Estate Appraisers, Mass. Assn. Realtors (past v.p.; fin. chmn., trustee polit. action com., exec. com.), Worcester County Bd. Realtors (past pres.). Club: Elks. Home: 289 Mount Elam Rd Fitchburg MA 01420 Office: 1060 South St Fitchburg MA 01420

PANE, PHILIP, town ofcl.; b. Adami, Italy, Mar. 31, 1913; s. Antonio M. and Rachela P.; came to U.S., 1921, naturalized, 1933; diploma engring. Lowell Inst., 1934; student U. Maine, 1942, Harvard U., 1943, Northeastern U., 1944; m. Edythe Fairbanks, Aug. 17, 1940; children—Philip Anthony, James Andrew, Ann Marie. Sales rep. B. F. Goodrich Co., Watertown, Mass., 1939-42; supr. Jenney Mfg. Co., Boston, 1946-47; indsl. specialist Boston Ordnance Dist., 1942-45; treas. Town of Watertown, 1968—, mem. sch. com., 1949-55, selectman, 1959-68; mem. Mass. State Interstate Commn., 1960-64. Recipient Certificate of Commendation, U.S. Army, 1945. Mem. Am. Ordnance Assn. (life), Mass. Collectors and Treas.'s Assn. (pres.), Watertown C. of C. (hon.). Republican. Roman Catholic. Clubs: Rotary, Sons of Italy, Elks, K.C. Home: 37 Orchard St Watertown MA 02172 Office: Main St Watertown MA 02172

PANG, YUNG-SOO, physician; b. Shanghai, China, Aug. 9, 1943; s. Hwa-Ill and Hong-Sook (Paik) P.; came to U.S., 1970, naturalized, 1976; M.D., Yon-Sei U., Seoul, Korea, 1967; m. Jung-Sook Pang, Dec. 17, 1970; children—Debbie, Joy, Philip. Intern, S. Balt. Gen. Hosp., 1970; resident Detroit Gen. Hosp.-Wayne State U., 1972; practice medicine specializing in internal medicine, Lyons, N.Y., 1974—; mem. staffs Newark-Wayne Community Hosp., Clifton Springs Hosp. and Clinic. Served with Republic of Korea Navy, 1967-70. Mem. A.C.P., AMA, N.Y. Cardiological Soc. Presbyterian. Home: 133 Oak Dr Newark NY 14513 Office: 45 Phelps St Lyons NY 14489

PANIAGUA, ALEJANDRO DARIO, psychiatrist; b. Santo Domingo, Dominican Republic, Jan. 8, 1927; s. Alejandro and Rosa Maria (Rodriguez) P.; M.D., U. Santo Domingo, 1952; postgrad. N.Y. U., 1955-56; came to U.S., 1952, naturalized, 1976; m. Maria Giove, June 23, 1956; 1 dau., Rosa Maria. Intern, Jersey City Med. Center, 1953-54; resident Phila. Gen. Hosp., 1954-55, N.J. State Hosp., Ancora, 1960-64; practice medicine specializing in psychiatry, Santo Domingo, Dominican Republic, 1964-70, Bronx, N.Y., 1970—, Paterson, N.J., 1975—; mem. staff Corona Elmhurst Guidance Center, Jackson Heights, N.Y., 1974—; clin. instr. psychiatry N.Y. Med. Coll., 1977. Licensed physician, Conn., N.Y., N.J. Mem. Am., Bronx County psychiat. assns., N.Y. State, Bronx County med. assns., Spanish Am. Med. Soc., Asociacion Medica Dominicana N.Y., Asociaciones Dominicanas, Profesionales Dominicanos, Grupo Benefico Dominicano (founder, pres. 1976-78). Roman Catholic. Editor: Los Dominicanos, 1969. Home: 1136 Fifth Ave New York City NY 10028

PANITZ, DANIEL ROBERT, psychologist; b. Bklyn., May 1, 1945; s. Daniel and Lillian (Rodman) P.; B.A., Rutgers U., 1968, M.A., 1970; postgrad. N.Y. U., 1978; m. Joan M. Campbell, Jan. 21, 1968; children—Daniel Thomas, Damian Jon. Personnel mgr. Daniels Security Systems, Bklyn., 1969-70; psychologist N.Y. State Drug Abuse Control Commn., S.I., 1970-76, N.Y. State Dept. Mental Hygiene, Rockland, 1976-77; chief services Alcohol div. N.Y. State Alcohol Rehab., Albany, 1977—. Mem. subcom. on alcoholism adv. com. N.Y. State Senate, 1977-78. Recipient Queens County Good Citizenship award, 1970-71; New Sch. for Social Research fellow, 1970. Mem. Nat. Assn. Social Workers, Am. Personnel and Guidance Assn., Assn. Alcoholic Councils, Assn. Humanistic Psychology. Home: 51-13 Van Loon St Elmhurst NY 11323

PANITZ, LAWRENCE, physician; b. Bklyn., Apr. 30, 1928; s. Max and Gussie (Gorenstein) P.; B.A., N.Y.U., 1962, M.D., 1966; m. Adrienne Ruth Luke, June 20, 1965; children—Jennifer, Michael. Intern, St. Joseph's Hosp., Syracuse, N.Y., 1966-67; practice gen. medicine, Elmsford, N.Y., 1967—; mem. staff St. Agnes Hosp., White Plains, Phelps Mem. Hosp., N. Tarrytown, Dobbs Ferry Hosp.; police surgeon, Tarrytown, Elmsford. Served with U.S. Army, 1946-48. Diplomate Am. Bd. Family Practice. Fellow Am. Acad. of Family Physicians, AMA, Med. Soc. of the State of N.Y., Westchester County Med. Soc., Westchester Acad. of Medicine. Jewish religion. Clubs: Shriners, Masons. Home: 49 Roundabend Rd Tarrytown NY 10591 Office: 132 S Central Ave Elmsford NY 10523

PANNIZZO, FRANK JOSEPH, bioengr.; b. Hackensack, N.J., Oct. 16, 1948; s. Frank and Josephine (Baiada) P.; diploma Inst. Audio Research, N.Y.C., 1970; B.S. in E.E., U. New Haven, 1974; M.S., Fairleigh Dickinson U., 1978. Instr. math. and sci. Abeel Sch., Hackensack, N.J., 1970-71; rec. engr. Ampex Corp., Hackensack, 1971; engr. Paradell Co., Ridgewood, N.J., 1974-75; mem. faculty math. and electronics County Coll. of Morris, Dover, N.J., 1975-76; project engr. ESP, Inc., Norwood, N.J., 1976-77; research asso. Montefiore Hosp. and Med. Center, Bronx, N.Y., 1977—. Dep. municipal dir. N.J. CD and Disaster Control Emergency Communications, Oradell, 1964-66. Mem. IEEE, Am. Assn. Advancement Med. Instrumentation, Am. Def. Preparedness Assn. Home: 670 Oradell Ave Oradell NJ 07649 Office: 111 E 210th St Bronx NY 10467

PANUZIO, NICHOLAS ARTHUR, cons.; b. Bridgeport, Conn., Oct. 28, 1935; s. Nicholas Louis and Carmella (Petrucelli) P.; B.S., U. Bridgeport, 1957; m. June Ann Bartram, Aug. 29, 1959; children—Susan Ann, Nicholas Arthur, Thomas Edward. Asst. dir. adminstrn. U. Bridgeport, 1957-58, asst. to bus. mgr., 1958-62, dir. purchasing, 1962-68, dir. Student Center, 1968-71, devel. adminstr., 1971; mayor City of Bridgeport, 1971-75; commr. Pub. Bldgs. Services, GSA, 1975-77; pres. Panuzio Assos., Washington, 1977—. Mem. Pres.'s Commn. on Continuing and Higher Edn., Conn. Gov.'s Drug Adv. Council; dir. Conn. Resource Recovery Authority; adv. bd. Conn. Dept. Community Affairs; exec. bd. Planning Council for Criminal Adminstrn. Co-chmn. Republican Action League, 1968-72. Pres. EBTCA Hall Housing Devel., Hall Neighborhood House, John Winthrop P.T.A., Big Bros. Greater Bridgeport, Model Cities Commn.; mem. Gov.'s Clean Air Task Force; trustee U. Bridgeport. Recipient Conn. Jr. C. of C. Key award, 1967, Presdl. award, 1968; named Bridgeport's Outstanding Young Man, 1966. Mem. Conn. (past pres.), Bridgeport (past pres.) jr. chambers commerce, Jr. C. of C. Internat. (senator). Home: 3117 Northwood Rd Fairfax VA 22030 Office: Suite 628 Barr Bldg 910 17th St NW Washington DC 20006

PANZARINO, SAVERIO JOSEPH, surgeon; b. E. Orange, N.J., Nov. 29, 1930; s. Joseph Saverio and Pasqua Olympia (Binetti) P.; A.B., Columbia U., 1952; M.D., U. Rome, 1957; m. Suzanne D. Laico, May 24, 1958; 1 dau., Laura Kathleen. Intern, St. Vincent's Hosp., N.Y.C., 1957-58; resident in surgery Manhattan VA Hosp., N.Y.C., 1958-62; fellow in pediatric surgery Hosp. for Sick Children, London, 1962-63; practice medicine specializing in pediatric surgery, Short Hills, N.J., 1963—; staff Overlook Hosp., Summit, N.J., St. Barnabas Med. Center, Livingston, N.J. Sec., Oak Knoll Fathers Club, 1976. Bowen-Brooks fellow, 1962-63. Diplomate Am. Bd. Surgery, Am. Bd. Pediatric Surgery. Mem. Summit (past pres.), Essex County med. socs., N.Y. Soc. Pediatric Surgery, N.J. Acad. Medicine; fellow A.C.S., Am. Acad. Pediatrics. Republican. Roman Catholic. Club: Racquets (Short Hills). Home: 51 Keats Rd Short Hills NJ 07078 Office: 553 Millburn Ave Short Hills NJ 07078

PAO, HSIEN PING, civil engr.; b. Ningpo, Chekiang, China, July 1, 1935; s. Cheying and Wen (Chang) P.; came to U.S., 1958, naturalized, 1971; B.S. in Engring., Taiwan U., Taipei, Formosa, 1956; Ph.D. in Fluid Mechanics (Univ. fellow, Ford Found. fellow), Johns Hopkins U., 1963; m. Chia-Ming Chen, Dec. 18, 1965; children—Jean Y., Lucy Y. Mech. engr. Hsin-Chu Air Base, Chinese Air Force, Taiwan, Formosa, 1957-58; design engr. Kuo-hwa Engring. Corp., Taipei, 1958; research asst. Johns Hopkins U., 1958-63, research asso., 1963-64; asst. prof. Sch. Engring. Architecture, Cath. U. Am., Washington, 1964-66, asso. prof., 1966-70, prof., 1970—, NASA Am. Soc. Engring. Edn. faculty fellow, 1973, 74; dir. P & L Assos., Inc., Silver Spring, Md.; cons. Flow Research, Inc., Kent, Washington, Integrated Systems, Rockville, Md., MERDOC Research Labs. U.S. Army, Ft. Belvoir, Va., Singer Info. Services Co., Washington, Applied Sci. Div. Litton Systems, Inc., Silver Spring, Md.; prin. investigator research grants NSF and Office Naval Research; dir. govt. research projects; lectr. in field. Mem. ASCE, Am. Phys. Soc., Am. Meteorol. Soc., Sigma Xi. Reviewer, Applied Mechanics, 1973-75; contbr. articles in field to profl. jours. Home: 12903 Autumn Dr Silver Spring MD 20904 Office: Sch Engring Arch Cath U Am Washington DC 20064

PAO, JAMES SHIH-KUO, educator; b. Chingshan, China, Sept. 29, 1926; s. Shen Fu and Tsao Shih Pao; came to U.S., 1951, naturalized, 1964; B.S., U. Santo Tomas, 1949; M.A., U. Mich., 1952; LL.D. (hon.), S.China U., 1971; m. Sandra Kuo, Jan. 11, 1963; children—Lincoln, Linda, James, Duke. Instr., LaSalle Extension U., Chgo., 1954-59; asst. prof. Chiang Kai Shek Coll., Manila, 1960-65; asso. prof. Prince George's Community Coll., Largo, Md., 1966—; lectr. Bowie (Md.) State Coll., 1977—. Mem. Am., Eastern econ. assns., AAUP, Orgn. Chinese Ams. (sec. 1972-73), Soc. Internat. Devel., Atlantic Econ. Soc., Rho Psi Soc. (Washington-Balt. chpt. pres. 1975-76). Contbr. articles to profl. jours. Home: 3304 Beret Ln Wheaton MD 20906 Office: 301 Largo Rd Largo MD 20870

PAOLIN, JOHN RAYMOND, advt. agy. exec.; b. Akron, Ohio, Sept. 10, 1936; s. Louis Gerard and Ann Marie (Hand) P.; student Rutgers U., 1956-59, Temple U., 1959-61; m. Dolores Elaine Wilkinson, Sept. 7, 1957; children—Nancy, Joan, Cheryl, Susan, John. Investigator Travelers Ins. Co., Camden, N.J., 1961-64; adjuster Allstate Ins. Co., Phila., 1964-67; owner, proprietor Paolin & Sweeney Advt., Inc., Collingswood, N.J., 1967—; partner Paolin-Carleton Co., Cherry Hill, 1973—, Tork Transmission, Maple Shade, 1970—. Adj. prof. communications Glassboro (N.J.) State U., 1974—. Mem. Cherry Hill Businessmen's Club (charter). Home: 852 Waterford Dr Delran NJ 08075 Office: 900 Haddon Ave Collingswood NJ 08108

PAOLINO, RONALD MARIO, clin. psychologist, psychopharmacologist; b. Providence, R.I., Mar. 15, 1938; s. Lawrence and Maria Corinne (Guglielmi) P.; B.S., U. R.I., 1959; M.S., Purdue U., 1961, Ph.D., 1963; m. Eileen Quimby, June 18, 1960; children—Lisa Katherine, David Lawrence. NIMH fellow Yale U., 1963-65; asst. prof. pharmacology U. Conn., 1965-67; asso. prof. psychopharmacology Purdue U., 1967-74; psychology intern U. Okla. Med. Center, 1974-75; asso. prof. psychiatry Brown U. Med. Program, 1975—; dir. drug dependence treatment program, dir. biofeedback clinic and lab. VA Hosp., Providence, R.I., 1975—. Mem. R.I. Gov.'s Premanent Council on Drug Abuse Control; bd. dirs. Samaritans, Inc. Mem. Am. Soc. Pharmacology and Exptl. Therapeutics, Soc. Biol. Psychiatry, Am., R.I. psychol. assns., Internat. Soc. Devel. Psychobiology, AAAS, Soc. Neuroscience, Sigma Xi. Contbr. articles to profl. jours. Office: Psychiatry Service VA Hosp Providence RI 02908

PAOLUCCI, ANNE ATTURA, educator, author; b. Rome, July 31, 1926; d. Joseph and Lucy (Guidoni) Attura; came to U.S., 1934; B.A., Barnard Coll., 1947; M.A., Columbia U., 1950, Ph.D., 1963; Fulbright scholar U. Rome, 1951-52; m. Henry Paolucci, 1949. Mem. faculty Brearley Sch., N.Y.C., 1957-59, Coll. City N.Y., 1959-69; Univ. research prof. St. John's U., Jamaica, N.Y., 1969-78, prof. English, 1978—, acting head dept. English lit., 1974; Fulbright lectr. Am. drama U. Naples (Italy), 1965-67; spl. lectr. Renaissance Inst., Ashland, Oreg., 1973, 74; founder, editor Rev. Nat. Lits., 1970—; founder, exec. dir. Council Nat. Lits., 1974—; writer-in-residence Yaddo, 1965; author: Pirandello's Theater: The Recovery of the Modern Stage for Dramatic Art, 1974; From Tension to Tonic: The Plays of Edward Albee, 1972; Hegel on Tragedy, 1962; Machiavelli's Mandragola, 1962; Poems Written for Sbek's Mummies, Marie Menken, and Other Important People, Places and Things, 1977; Eight Short Stories, 1977. Garibaldi scholar, 1948-50; grantee Columbia U., 1963, 64, 65; Woodbridge fellow, 1961-62; recipient Drama award Medieval and Renaissance Inst., 1972; named Distinguished Alumna in News, Barnard Coll. mag., 1973; Woman of Year, Dr. Herman Henry Scholarship Found., 1973; Woman of Year, AMITA, 1970; other citations and awards. Mem. Dante Soc. Am. (v.p.), Pirandello Soc. Am. (v.p.), World Centre Shakespeare Studies (dir.), Conf. Editors Learned Jours. (exec. com.), Nat. Soc. Lit. and Arts, Internat. Shakespeare Assn., Shakespeare Assn. Am., Renaissance Soc. Am., Renaissance Inst. Japan, Internat., Am. comparative lit. assns., Am., Internat. Byron socs. (adv. bds.), PEN. Office: Dept English St John's Univ Jamaica NY 11439

PAONE, JAMES, govt. ofcl.; b. Spangler, Pa., Aug. 15, 1925; s. Domenick and Grace (Antonazzo) P.; B.S., Pa. State U., 1951; M.S., George Washington U., 1970; grad. Nat. Def. U., 1970; grad. Fed. Exec. Inst., 1976; m. Joan Westover, Aug. 18, 1951; children—Mary Grace, Antoinette, Patricia. Mining engr. Cambria div. Bethlehem Mines Corp. (Pa.), 1951-55; mining research engr., program mgr. U.S. Bur. Mines, Minn. and Washington, 1955-72, chief div. ferrous metals, Washington, 1972-74, chief div. environment, Washington, 1974—; mining cons. Def. Dept., 1958-68, NASA, 1961-68, Bur. Pub. Rds., 1962-65. Served with USAAF, 1943-46. Recipient Dept. Interior Meritorious award, 1976, performance awards, 1963, 65, 66, 68, 1971, 74. Mem. Am. Legion (comdr. 1947-48), St. Vincent De Paul Soc. (v.p. 1973-78), Soc. Mining Engrs., Am. Inst. Mining, Metall. and Petroleum Engrs. Contbr. articles to profl. jours. Office: US Bur Mines 2401 E St NW Washington DC 20241

PAONE, JOHN, city ofcl.; b. Phila., June 19, 1947; s. Gregoro and Angelina (Vertrella) P.; B.A. in Polit. Sci., Pa. State U., 1969; M.A. in Pub. Adminstrn., Am. U., 1971. Adminstrv. intern City of Phila., 1972-73, adminstrv. analyst II, 1973-74, chief housing statistics, 1974-75, housing preservation analyst, 1975-76, housing program adminstr., 1976—; part-time instr. pub. adminstr. Temple U., Phila.; mem. bd. Phila. Neighborhood Housing Services Corp., 1976—. Mem. East Mt. Airy Neighbors Civic Assn., 1976. Mem. Nat. Assn. Housing and Redevel. Ofcls. (dir.), Phila. Mummers Assn., Am. Soc. Pub. Adminstrn., Am. Soc. Planning Ofcls., Am. Polit. Sci. Assn., Internat. Personnel Mgmt. Assn., Nat. Pi Sigma Alpha. Co-author computer statis. game Urban Law, 1971. Home: 327 E Mount Airy Ave Philadelphia PA 19119 Office: City Hall Annex Philadelphia PA 19107

PAONE, JOSEPH VERINO, ins. co. exec.; b. Syracuse, N.Y., July 14, 1951; s. Anthony Nicholas and Zella Elizabeth P.; B.S. in Mktg. Mgmt., Syracuse U., 1973. Bus. service rep. Marine Midland Services Corp., Syracuse, 1973-74; sr. benefits rep. Equitable Life Assurance Soc., Syracuse, 1974-77; asst. adminstrv. mgr. Agway Ins. Co., E. Syracuse, 1977—. Bd. dirs. East Area Vol. Emergency Service, 1975—; officer Lyncourt Fire Dept., 1972—. Mem. Central N.Y. Life and Health Claims Assn. (sec. 1976-77, v.p. 1977-78, dir.), Onondaga Community Coll. Alumni Assn. Republican. Roman Catholic. Home: 727 Hillside St Syracuse NY 13208 Office: PO Box 4851 Syracuse NY 13224

PAPA, PHILIP ANTHONY, export co. exec.; b. San Lupo, Italy, Mar. 9, 1947; s. Umberto and Alessandra Papa; came to U.S., 1961, naturalized, 1962; B.S. in Bus. Adminstrn., St. Peter's Coll., 1970; m. Josephine A. Ippolito, July 9, 1977. Mgr. intermodal ops. Am. Export Lines, Inc., N.Y.C., 1968-78; asst. mgr. adminstrn. and cost control Farrell Lines, Inc., N.Y.C., 1978—. Home: 48 Terrace Ave Jersey City NJ 07307 Office: 1 Whitehall St New York City NY 10004

PAPADIMITRIOU, DIMITRI BASIL, economist, coll. adminstr.; b. Salonica, Greece, June 9, 1946; s. Basil John and Ellen (Tacas) P.; came to U.S., 1965, naturalized, 1974; B.A., Columbia, 1970; M.A., New Sch. Social Research, 1974, postgrad., 1974—; m. Vasiliki Fokas, Aug. 26, 1967; children—Jennifer E., Elizabeth R. Vice pres., asst. sec. ITT Life Ins. Co. N.Y., N.Y.C., 1970-73; v.p., sec., treas. William Penn Life Ins. Co. N.Y., N.Y.C., 1973-77, also dir.; v.p. Bard Coll., Annandale-on-Hudson, N.Y., 1977—; adj. lectr. econs. New Sch. Social Research; dir. Bankers & Shippers Ins. Co. N.Y., Hallmark Retirement Plan Services, Inc. Vice pres. Hellenic Soc. of Columbia, 1966-67. Mem. Am. Econ. Assn., Royal Econ. Soc., Am. Fin. Assn., Am. Statis. Assn. Home: Box 40 Annandale-on-Hudson NY 12504 Office: Bard Coll Annandale on Hudson NY 12504

PAPADOPOULOS, SPYRIDON GEORGE, mech. engr.; b. Athens, Greece, July 14, 1945; s. George Anthony and Georgia Vassiliou (Germanos) P.; came to U.S., 1963; naturalized, 1969; Asso., So. Tech. Inst., 1966; B.S.M.E., Northeastern U., 1970; M.E.A., George Washington U., 1976; m. Mary Cathleen Campbell, Sept. 9,

1964; children—Georgia, Mary, Irene. Mech. engr. Ganteaume & McMullen, Inc., Boston, 1966-71; project engr. Gen. Engring. Assn., Washington, 1971-74; sr. engr. Syska & Hennessy, Inc., Washington, 1974-76; chief mech. engr. A. Epstein & Sons, Inc., Chgo., 1976-77; prin. engr. Alphatec, Washington, 1977—; course dir., lectr. environ. engring. Prince's George Community Coll., Largo, Md., 1973-76. Registered profl. engr., D.C., N.Y., Md., Va., Ill. Mem. ASME, ASHRAE, Order Am. Hellenic Ednl. Progressive Assn. (chpt. bd. govs. 1975—), Pi Tau Sigma. Greek Orthodox. Club: Cleveland Park (Washington). Researcher psychrometrics. Home: 3430 34th St NW Washington DC 20008 Office: Alphatec 4301 Connecticut Ave NW Washington DC 20008

PAPAGEORGIOU, JOHN CONSTANTINE, educator; b. Kallithea, Greece, Nov. 22, 1935; came to U.S., 1969, naturalized, 1975; B.Sc., Athens (Greece) Sch. Econs. and Bus. Scis., 1957; diploma tech. sci., U. Manchester (Eng.), 1963, Ph.D., 1965; m. Thalia Christidou, 1969; 4 children. Lectr., Athens Sch. Econs. and Bus. Scis., also Postgrad. Inst. Bus. Adminstrn., Athens, 1966-68; asst. prof. Faculty Adminstrv. Studies, York U., Toronto, Ont., Can., 1968-69; asst. prof. mgmt. Wayne State U., Detroit, 1969-71; asso. prof. mgmt. scis. St. Louis U., 1971-72; vis. prof. ops. research Athens Sch. Econs. and Bus. Scis., 1972-73; asso. prof. ops. analysis U. Toledo, 1974-76; asso. prof. mgmt. sci. and coordinator Coll. Profl. Studies, U. Mass., Boston, 1976-78, prof. and coordinator, 1978—; head dept. econ. research Agrl. Bank Greece, 1966-67; ops. analyst Esso-Pappas Indsl. Co., Greece, 1967-68; spl. adviser Center Planning and Econ. Research, Greece, 1972-73; cons. in field, condr. seminars. Served to 2d lt. Greek Army, 1958-60. Greek Govt. scholar, 1962-65; NATO postdoctoral fellow, 1965. Fellow AAAS, Internat. Biog. Assn.; mem. Ops. Research Soc. Am., Inst. Mgmt. Scis., Am. Statis. Assn., Hellenic Ops. Research Soc., Internat. Platform Assn., Sigma Xi. Author: Introduction to Operations Research (in Greek), 1973; Fundamentals of Operations of Research, 1973; co-author: Data on the Greek Economy, 1966; contbr. to profl. jours. Address: 44 Outlook Rd Marshfield MA 02050

PAPANOS, STANLEY, turfgrass agronomist; b. New Haven, Oct. 28, 1918; s. William and Lillian (Rogers) P.; B.S. U. Conn., 1942, M.S., 1952; m. Mary Frances Beebe, May 14, 1943; children—Robert, William, Richard, Thomas, Charles. Research asst. U. Conn., 1946-50; farm planner Soil Conservation Service, Rockville, Conn., 1951-53; county agt., Hartford, Conn., 1952-76; turfgrass specialist U. Conn. Extension Service, 1965-76; agronomist Cadwell and Jones, Manchester, Conn., 1977—; instr. pesticides U. Conn., 1975-76. Served with USCG, 1942-46. Recipient Distinguished Service award Nat. Assn. County Agrl. Agts., 1967, N.E. County Agt. award of merit, 1971, Scott Turfgrass regional award, 1974. Mem. Am. Soc. Agronomy, Am. Chem. Soc., Am. Inst. Biol. Scis., Council Agrl. Sci. and Tech., Gamma Sigma Delta, Sigma Phi Epsilon. Contbr. articles on lawn care to profl. jours. Home: 57 N River Rd Coventry CT 06238

PAPARELLA, JULIA MARIE BOLAND (MRS. BENEDICT A. PAPARELLA), nurse, educator; b. Penllyn, Pa.; d. James and Ellen (Mullen) Boland; diploma Abington Meml. Hosp. Sch. Nursing, 1942; B.S. in Nursing Edn., U. Pa., 1954, M.S. in Edn., 1956; M.L.S., Villanova U., 1975; m. Benedict A. Paparella, Dec. 28, 1957; 1 son, Thomas E. Head nurse Abington Meml. Hosp., 1942-43; surg. office nurse Pfeiffer Surg. Group, 1946-52; mem. faculty Villanova (Pa.) U. Coll. Nursing, 1955—, asso. prof. nursing, 1965—, acting dean Coll. of Nursing, 1971-72; mem. staff 361st Evacuation Hosp., 1972-75; acting chief nurse 348 Gen. Hosp., 1978—. Mem. state council CD Montgomery County (Pa.) Med. Health Service, 1965—; mem. Health and Welfare Council Montgomery County Dist. Pa.; dir. Family Service Montgomery County; mem. Montgomery County Task Force on Aging, 1971-72, Montgomery County Task Force on Older Adults, 1972—; Pa. del. White House Conf. on Aging, 1971. Ann. giving class agt. U. Pa., Phila., 1960—. Served to capt. Army Nurse Corps, 1943-46; maj. U.S. Army Res., 1972—. Mem. Nat. (Pa. sec. 1966-68), Southeastern Pa. (chmn. nursing edn. com. 1961-64, mem. planning com. 1964-66, rep. collegiate nursing, nursing and health careers com. 1965-67) leagues for nursing, AAUP, Pa. Assn. Women Deans and Counselors, Sigma Theta Tau. Club: Soroptimists (dir. 1975-76, v.p. 1976-77, pres. 1977—). Home: 1607 County Line Rd Villanova PA 19085

PAPARELLO, FRANK NICHOLAS, pub., educator; b. N.J., July 9, 1928; s. Cosmo and Louise (De Taranto) P.; B.S., Seton Hall U., 1949, M.A., 1954; Ph.D. (NSF fellow), Columbia, 1960; m. Elizabeth Petrozzello, Oct. 1954; children—Stephanie, Scott, Kimberley. Tchr. sci., math. Montclair (N.J.) Pub. Schs., 1954-59; instr. biol. scis., psychology Seton Hall U., Newark, 1954-60, Columbia, N.Y.C., 1960-62; exec. sci. editor Holt, Rinehart & Winston, N.Y.C., 1960-66; v.p., editor-in-chief Ency. Brit. Ednl. Corp., Chgo., 1966-68; v.p., gen. mgr. D.C. Heath & Co., Lexington, Mass., 1968-73; pres., owner PSG Pub. Co., Littleton, Mass., 1974—; cons. ednl. TV network, Columbia, S.C., Royal Sci. Soc., Jordan, Right to Read Commn. Mass.; guest lectr. in sci. edn. Mem. Internat. Med./Sci. Pubs. Assn., AAAS, Am. Assn. Pubs., Phi Delta Kappa. Democrat. Roman Catholic. Club: Concord (Mass.) Kiwanis (pres.). Home: 581 Hayward Mill Rd Concord MA 01742 Office: 545 Great Rd Littleton MA 01460

PAPAS, PAUL NICHOLAS, II, ins. exec.; b. Boston, Feb. 15, 1951; s. Nicholas M. and Bessie Papas; B.S. in Criminal Justice, Northeastern U., 1976, M.A. in Fin., 1977; m. Marguerite A. Scott, Sept. 8, 1974; children—Erica M., Paul Nicholas, III. With Centre Assos., real estate, Dedham, Mass., 1970—, owner, 1971—; founder, 1974, since owner Paul N. Papas, II, ins. agy., Dedham; founder, 1977, since owner Bay State Appraisers, Dedham; founder, 1976, since owner Concept Leasing, Dedham; founder, 1977, since owner Capital Investment Adv. Services, Dedham. Trustee Ch. of the Annunciation, Greek Orthodox Ch., Boston, 1977; Justice of peace, 1972—; chmn. Dedham Republican Town Com., 1973-76. Named Republican of Year, Young Rep. Club, 1973. Mem. Nat. Assn. Life Underwriters, Dedham C. of C. Club: Masons. Office: PO Box 253 Dedham MA 02026

PAPITTO, RALPH RAYMOND, corp. exec.; b. Providence, Nov. 1, 1926; s. Giovanni and Maria (Davide) P.; B.S. in Accounting and Fin., Bryant Coll., 1947; student law Suffolk Law Sch., 1947-48; children—Andrea Papitto Crump, Aurelia, David John. Auditor, Arthur Andersen, also Ernest & Ernst, Providence, 1948-51; v.p. fin. Ritz Products, Inc., Providence, 1951-55; founder, pres., chmn. bd. GTI Corp., Providence, 1955-66; chmn. bd. HI-G, Inc., Windsor Locks, Conn., 1965-66; founder, pres., chief exec. officer, dir. Nortek, Inc., Cranston, R.I., 1967—; dir. 1st Mut. Fund, Inc. Trustee Roger Williams Coll., 1969—; bd. dirs. Meeting St. Sch., 1969-70. Named Man of Year, R.I. Jaycees, 1961. Democrat. Roman Catholic. Clubs: Turks Head, Alpine Country, Aurora Civic Assn., Surf (Fla.). Office: 815 Reservoir Ave Cranston RI 02910

PAPP, JOSEPH, theatrical dir., producer; b. Bklyn., June 22, 1921; s. Samuel and Yetta (Morris) Papirofsky; grad. Actors Lab., Hollywood, Calif., 1948; D.Arts, Columbia Coll., Chgo., 1971, Northwestern U., 1972; children by previous marriages—Susan, Michael; m. Peggy Marie Bennion, Oct. 27, 1951; children—Miranda, Anthony. Founder, 1953, since producer-dir. N.Y. Shakespeare Festival; founder, producer, dir. Pub. Theater, 1966—; producer-dir. numerous prodns., 1951—, including: Much Ado About Nothing, 1961, 72, The Merchant of Venice, 1962, King Lear, 1962, Antony and Cleopatra, 1963, Twelfth Night, 1963, Hamlet, 1964, Troilus and Cressida, 1965, All's Well That Ends Well, 1966, King Henry V, 1965, 68, Taming of the Shrew, 1965, Hamlet (modern version), 1967, The Memorandum, 1968, Romeo and Juliet, 1968, King John, 1967, Stock Up on Pepper Cause Turkey's Going to War, 1967, Black Hamlet, 1968, Huui, Huui, 1968, Mod Donna, 1970; dir. operatic version Hamlet, 1962; adapted libretto and directed Mozart's opera Idomeneo, 1963; producer numerous prodns., 1951—, including Delacorte Dance Festival, 1962-72, The Tempest, 1962, Rebekah Harkness Found. Dance Festival, 1962-69, Macbeth, As You Like It, 1963, The Winter's Tale, 1963, Othello, 1964, Electra, 1964, A Midsummer Night's Dream, 1964, The Shoemaker's Prodigious Wife, The Puppet Theater of Don Cristobal (Spanish), 1964, Love's Labor Lost, 1965, Coriolanus, 1965, Ethnic Poetry Nights, 1965-66, Romeo and Juliet (Spanish), 1965, We Real Cool, 1965, Newport Folk Festival, 1965-66, Measure for Measure, 1966, King Richard III, 1966, Macbeth (Spanish), 1966, Potluck (children's show), 1966, Comedy of Errors, 1967, Titus Andronicus, 1967, Volpone, 1967, Volpone (Spanish), 1967, Lallapalooza, A Big Show for Little Kids, 1967, Hair, 1967, Ergo, 1968, Henry IV, Parts 1 and 2, 1968, Take One Step, 1968, Cities in Bezique, 1968, No Place To Be Somebody, Black Electra, 1969, Peer Gynt, 1969, Henry VI, Parts 1, 2 and 3, 1970, Timon of Athens, 1971, Two Gentlemen of Verona, 1971, Cymbeline, 1971, Ti-Jean and His Brothers, 1972, Invitation to A Beheading, 1969, Stomp, 1970, The Happiness Cage, 1970, Trelawney of the Wells, 1970, Slag, 1970, Subject to Fits, 1970, The Basic Training of Pavlo Hummel, 1971, Sticks and Bones, 1971, Iphigenia, 1971, Older People, 1972, Black Terror, 1972, Black Visions, 1972, That Championship Season, 1972, Winning Hearts and Minds, 1972, Wedding Band, 1972, The Children, 1972, Siamese Connections, 1973, The Cherry Orchard, 1973, The Orphan, 1973, King Lear, 1973, The Boom-Boom Room, 1973, The Tempest, 1974, What the Wine Sellers Buy, 1974, The Killdeer, 1974, The Last Days of British Honduras, 1974, A Midsummer Night's Dream, 1975, Fishing, 1975, others; produced for TV, Romeo and Juliet, 1972, Much Ado About Nothing, 1973, Sticks and Bones, 1973. Distinguished seminar prof. L.I.U. Distinguished Lecture Series, 1965-66; adj. prof. directing Yale Sch. Drama, 1966-67; adj. prof. play directing Columbia, 1967-69; vis. fellow humanities Colo. U., Feb., 1965; mem. nat. screening com. Fulbright-Hays awards, 1962-67; mem. adv. com. N.Y. Edn. Task Force on Performing Arts Center, 1962—; mem. N.Y. Adv. Com. on Arts and Culture, 1972; mem. theater adv. panel Nat. Endowment for Arts, 1971-72; mem. Ad Hoc Com. To Save Theater at Lincoln Center, 1971; mem. playwrights nominating com. Rockefeller Found., 1971—. Bd. dirs. Harlem Cultural Com.; bd. overseers theater arts Brandeis U.; mem. adv. council Jr. League N.Y.C. Served with USNR, 1942-46. Recipient Obie award Village Voice, 1955, 56; Tony awards, 1957-58, 72, 73; Shakespeare Club N.Y.C. award, 1958; ann. award distinguished service Tchrs. Union N.Y.C., 1962; Creative Arts award Brandeis U., 1963; Outstanding Creative Achievement award Am. theater New Eng. Theater Conf., 1963; Outstanding Contbn. to Theater award L.I. U., 1964; Distinguished Citizen award Queen's div. Am. Jewish Congress, 1964; Nat. Poetry Day award N.Y. State, 1964; Finley award City Coll. N.Y. Alumni Assn., 1964; citation women's div. Fedn. Jewish Philanthropies, 1965; Distinguished Service to N.Y.C. award New Sch. Social Research, 1965; award of merit Lotos Club, 1968; Outer Circle Critics citations 1957, 58, 68, 71, 72; Vernon Rice award Drama Desk, 1968; Albert S. Bard award, 1968; Pulitzer prize, 1970; Handel medallion N.Y.C., 1971; N.Y. Drama Critics Circle awards for best play and best musical, 1972; numerous others. Mem. ANTA (pres. 1969, dir., ann. award 1965), Nat. Theatre Conf. (Man of Year citation 1969), Dirs. Guild Am., Internat. Theatre Inst., Actors Equity Assn., Sigma Alpha Delta (hon.). Editor: (with others) Troilus and Cressida, 1967; The Naked Hamlet, 1969. Contbr. articles to mags. Address: NY Shakespeare Festival 425 Lafayette St New York City NY 10003*

PAPP, LASZLO GEORGE, architect; b. Debrecen, Hungary, Apr. 28, 1929; s. Joseph and Gizela (Szoboszlai) P.; Degree Archtl. Engring., Polytech. U. of Budapest, 1955; M.Arch., Pratt Inst., 1960; m. Judith Liptak, Apr. 12, 1952; children—Andrea, Laszlo-Mark (dec.). Came to U.S., 1956, naturalized, 1963. Architect-designer Inst. for Residential Devel., Budapest, Hungary, 1950-56; designer Harrison & Abramovitz, Architects, N.Y.C., 1958-63; partner Whiteside & Papp, Architects, White Plains, N.Y., 1963-67; prin. Papp Assos., Architects, White Plains, N.Y., 1968—; pres. L.P. Designs, Inc., White Plains. Vice chmn. New Canaan (Conn.) Planning and Zoning Commn., 1971—; mem. New Canaan Inland Wetland Commn.. 1973—. Mem. AIA (chpt. dir. 1967-69, chpt. treas. 1971-73, pres. 1976-77), White Plains C. of C. (dir. 1969-72). N.Y. State Assn. Architects (v.p. 1977—), Hungarian U. Assn. (pres. 1958-60). Home: 1197 Valley Rd New Canaan CT 06840 Office: 222 Mamaroneck Ave White Plains NY 10605

PAPPACHEN, ANDREWS KORAH, chemist; b. Kerala, India, May 17, 1948; s. Korah P. and Lucy I. Andrews; came to U.S., naturalized, 1973; M.S. in Analytical Chemistry, Kerala U., India, 1969; postgrad. environ. sci. Stevens Inst. Tech., Hoboken, N.J., 1976; m. Saramma Mathew, May 28, 1973; 1 dau., Simmy S. Lectr. chemistry Kerala U., India, 1969-70; prodn. supr. in rubber factory, Kerala, 1970-71; chemist Madras Rubber Factory (India), 1971-73; water chemist City of Newark, 1974—. Home: 32 Laura Ave Nutley NJ 07110

PAPPAS, CHARLES NICHOLAS, dentist; b. Phila., Jan. 14, 1936; s. Charles Nicholas and Marie (Pero) P.; student U. Colo., 1953-55; D.D.S., Northwestern U., 1959; m. Edith Basedow, Aug. 24, 1974. Asso. practice dentistry, South Weymouth, Mass., 1962; pvt. practice dentistry, Weymouth Heights, Mass., 1962-65; pub. health dentist Dept. Health and Hosps., Boston, 1965-70; asso. practice, Weymouth, 1965-68, Brookline, Mass., 1969; practicing clin. dentist Harvard, 1970-71, clin. instr. operaive dentistry, 1967-71; clin. research asst. Forsyth Dental Center, 1972; asst. prof. restorative dentistry U. Pa., 1972—; clin. instr. Tufts U., 1965. Served to capt. AUS, 1960-62. Mem. Harvard Odontological Soc., ADA, Mass., Philadelphia County dental socs., Pa. Assn. Dental Surgeons, Goethe Soc. New Eng., English-Speaking Union, 4001 Lit. Union (founder, faculty advisor), Lambda Chi Alpha, Xi Psi Phi. Episcopalian (program, fund raising chmn. Phillips Brooks Club 1965-66). Club: Northwestern U. of Delaware Valley (pres. 1978) (Phila.). Author pamphlet: Self-Control of Tooth Decay, 1967. Contbr. articles to profl. pubs. Home: 234 S 20th St Philadelphia PA 19103 Office: U Pa Sch Dental Medicine 4001 Spruce St Philadelphia PA 19104

PAPPAS, GEORGE WILLIAM, mktg. and sales cons.; b. Woodbridge, N.J., July 11, 1930; s. William Peter and Caroline Sarah (Brown) P.; student Juilliard Music Sch., N.Y.C., 1947, 48, Monmouth Coll., 1962-64; grad. U.S. Navy Sch. Music, 1949; m. Margaret Valeria Elyar, July 27, 1952; children—William George, George William, Margaret Carolyn. Dist. sales mgr. Allied Processing Corp., Newark, 1956-63, dir. sales, 1963-68; pres. Pappas & Assos., mktg. and sales cons., Fords, N.J., 1968—; pres. Colorcraft Photographers Inc., 1960—. Mem. guiding faculty Hallmark Inst. Photography. Served with USN, 1948-52. Recipient Distinguished Salesman award Sales Execs. Club N.Y., 1955, Art Asher award for sales excellence Profl. Photographers Soc. N.Y., 1963, Profl. Photographers of Pa. conv. lectr. awards (2), 1972. Mem. Profl. Photographers Am., Profl. Photographers Assn. N.J., Am. Fedn. Musicians (bus. agt., officer exec. bd. Local 373, 1971—), Wedding Photographers Internat. (advisory bd.). Author: Salesmanship! The Answer to Bridal Photography Success, 1968, rev. edit., 1973. Contbg. editor Rangefinder mag., 1968—. Home: 31 Soren St Fords NJ 08863 Office: 537 New Brunswick Ave Fords NJ 08863

PAQUET, EDMOND, physician; b. Que., Can., Apr. 11, 1925; s. Edmond and Beatrice (Boucher) P.; B.A., U. Laval, 1945, M.D., 1950; postgrad. U. Pa. Sch. Medicine, 1952; m. Thérèse Brousseau, Aug. 19, 1950; 1 dau., Christine. Intern, Hotel Dieu de Québec, Que., 1951; resident Hopitaux de Paris, 1952-55; chief dept. medicine St. Ambroise Hosp., Loretteville, Que., 1962—; cons. in internal medicine R. Samuel McLaughlin Found. fellow, 1954-55. Fellow Am. Coll. Chest Physicians, Royal Coll. Physicians Can.; mem. Can. Med. Assn. Roman Catholic. Home: 2755 Liegeois Blvd Sainte Foy Quebec 10 PQ Canada Office: Hospital Saint Ambroise Loretteville PQ Canada

PARASCOS, EDWARD THEMISTOCLES, utilities exec.; b. N.Y.C., Oct. 20, 1931; s. Christos and Nina (Demitrovich) P.; B.S. in Mech. Engring., Coll. City N.Y., 1956, M.S., 1958; predoctoral ops. research N.Y. U., 1964—. Design engr. Ford Instrument, 1957-61; reliability engring. supr. Kearfott div. Gen. Precision Inc., 1961-63; staff cons. Am. Power Jet, 1963-64; reliability mgr. Perkin Elmer Corp., 1964-66; dir. system effectiveness CBS Labs., Stamford, Conn., 1966-72; pres., dir. engring. DIPAR Cons. Services, Ltd., 1970—; quality assurance and reliability engring. cons. Consol. Edison Co. N.Y., Ind., N.Y.C., 1972—; pres., chmn. bd. Lapa Trading Corp., 1973—, Ram Power Power Engring. Cons. Ltd. Registered profl. engr., Calif. Mem. Am. Soc. Quality Control (sr. mem., vice chmn. 1968-70), Am. Mgmt. Assn., ASME, Am. Statis. Assn., Inst. Environ. Scis., Edison Engring. Soc. Home: 34-47 88th St Jackson Heights NY 11372 Office: 4 Irving Pl New York City NY 10003 also 30-02 83d St East Elmhurst NY 11370

PARCO, SALVADOR ABONAL, educator; b. Nabua, Camarines Sur, Philippines, Jan. 3, 1934; s. Eulogio Almazan and Anacleta Dorosan (Abonal) P.; came to U.S., 1967; A.B., Ateneo de Naga, Philippines, 1955; M.S. (AID fellow), Cornell U., 1963; Ph.D., Pa. State U., 1973; m. Alicia Tan Uy, Dec. 22, 1957; children—Maria-Laura, Farolito, Maria-Stella, Salvador, William. Journalist community newspapers, radio stas. southern Philippines, editor sch. newsmag., annual, 1950-56; instr., adminstr., supr. community devel. program Pres. Ramon Magsaysay, Philippines, 1956-62; asst. prof. rural sociology U. Philippines Coll. Agr., Los Baños, Laguna, 1964-65; asso. prof. behavioral scis., chmn. dept., asso. prof. sociology and anthropology Ateneo de Manila U., Philippines, 1965-67; lectr. rural sociology Nat. Rural Devel. Tng. Center, Royal Govt. Afghanistan under auspices of The Asia Found., 1967; asst. prof. sociology Behrend Coll., Pa. State U., Erie, 1970-77; cons. State Civil Service Commn., Commonwealth of Pa.; cons. in Philippines to Exec. Devel. Acad., Land Reform Tng. Center, Inst. Social Order, Jr. C. of C. Asia Found. travel grantee, 1967; AID travel grantee, 1963. Mem. Am. Sociol. Assn., Philippine Sociol. Soc., Rural Sociol. Soc., Alpha Kappa Delta, Gamma Sigma Delta. Mem. Ch. of Jesus Christ of Latter-Day Saints. Editor Philippine Sociol. Rev., 1966. Contbr. articles in field to profl. jours. Home: 655 E 41st St Erie PA 16504 Office: Gen Electric Co 2901 E Lake Rd Erie PA 16511

PARDEE, JOHN PERRY (JACK), profl. football coach; b. Exira, Iowa, Apr. 19, 1936; B.A., Tex. A. and M. Coll., 1957. Football player Los Angeles Rams, 1957-64, 66-71; asst. coach Tex. A. and M. Coll., 1965; player Washington Redskins, 1972, asst. coach, 1973, head coach, gen. mgr., 1978—; head coach Fla. Blazers, 1974, Chgo. Bears, 1975-77; host TV show. Named Coach of Yr., 1976. Office: care Washington Redskins 13832 Redskin Dr PO Box 17247 Dulles Internat Airport Washington DC 20041*

PARE, MARIUS, clergyman; b. Montmagny, Que., Can., May 22, 1903; s. Joseph and Lucie (Boulet) P.; B.A., U. Laval, 1923; student U. Laval en Theologie, 1923-27. Ordained priest Roman Catholic Ch., 1927; priest Coll. Sainte-Anne-de-la-Pocatiere, 1927-56, tchr.-dir., 1933-52, rector, 1952-56; aux. bishop Chicoutimi, 1956, coadjutor-bishop, 1960, bishop, 1961—. Mem. commn. for clergy Canadian Cath. Conf.; mem. commn. edn. 2d Vatican Council, 1962-66; consultor Sacred Congregation Cath. Edn., Rome, 1968-78. Decorated knight grand cross Order Edquestre du Saint-Sepulcre de Jerusalem. K.C. (4th deg.). Address: 602 E Racine St Chicoutimi PQ Canada

PARE, THOMAS ANOTHONY, psychologist; b. N.Y.C., Dec. 25, 1941; s. Robert Edward and Gladys (Routh) P.; B.A., Earlham Coll., 1965; M.Ed., Miami U., Oxford, Ohio, 1966; postgrad. U. Iowa, 1968; m. Cheryl Ann Gritman, Feb. 14, 1977. Sch. counselor Sault Ste. Marie (Mich.) High Sch., 1966-67; coordinator of counseling, project upward bound Lake Superior State Coll., Sault Ste. Marie, 1967; coordinator of counseling, adult edn. div. Area X Community Coll., Cedar Rapids, Iowa, 1967-68, so. supr., adult edn. dir., 1968, personal adjustment counselor, rehab. facility, 1968-69; psychologist, children services div. N.E. Kingdom Mental Health Service, St. Johnsbury, Vt., 1969-70, psychologist, med. psychiat. div., 1970-74, chief psychologist, chief treatment substance abuse and aftercare div., 1974—; cons. tng. evaluation program devel. Vt. Dept. Corrections; cons. St. Johnsbury Child Health Center. Served with USCG, 1963-64. Licensed psychologist, Vt. Mem. Am. (asso.), Vt. psychol. assns., Am. Personnel and Guidance Assn., Am. Psychology and Law Soc., Vt. Alcohol Counselors Assn. (certified alcohol counselor, pres. 1977—, clin. preceptor Vt. Eastern area alcohol edn. 1977—). Home: RFD 1 Lyndonville CT 05851 Office: Northeast Kingdom Mental Health Service Railroad St Saint Johnsbury VT 05819

PARIS, HERBERT, hosp. adminstr.; b. Boston, May 6, 1934; s. William and Rose Elizabeth (Yassen) P.; A.B. in Biology, Brandeis, U., 1956; M.H.A., Med. Coll. Va., 1962; m. Harriet Hemleben, Jan. 18, 1958; children—Jonathan, David. Resident in hosp. adminstrn. Grace-New Haven (Conn.) Community Hosp., 1961-62; adminstrv. asst. Yale-New Haven Hosp., 1962-65, asst. dir., 1965-70, dir. ambulatory services, 1968-78, asso. dir., 1970-78; dir. Regional Meml. Hosp., Brunswick, Maine, 1978—; lectr. in pub. health Yale U. Sch. Medicine, 1965—; pre-med. adviser Yale Coll., 1972-75; mem. adv. com. Conn. Ambulatory Care Study, 1974-77. Mem. social legis. com. Community Council of Greater New Haven, 1965-68; bd. dirs. New Haven Health Care, Inc., 1974-76, Shirley Frank Found., New Haven, 1975—, New Haven Rehab. Center, 1976—, New Haven Symphony Orch. Assn., 1977—, Planned Parenthood of New Haven, 1967-69, New Haven Inst. Allied Health Careers, Inc., 1972-75; trustee Brandeis U., 1977—. Served to lt. (jg.) USN, 1957-60. Fellow Berkeley Coll., Yale U., 1970—. Mem. Am. (chmn. com. on med. records 1973-75), Conn. hosp. assns., Am. Pub. Health Assn., Am. Heart Assn., New Eng. Hosp. Assembly. Home: 17 Dionne Circle Brunswick ME 04011 Office: Regional Memorial Hosp 58 Baribeau Dr Brunswick ME 04011

PARISER, BERTRAM, physicist, mgmt. cons.; b. Long Beach, N.Y., July 18, 1940; s. Michael and Dora (Duckman) P.; B.S., Mass. Inst. Tech., 1961; M.S., Columbia U., 1963, Ph.D., 1965; m. Lora Sue Doppelt, Sept. 2, 1976; children—Carl Lisa, Julie Beth, Stephanie Ivy, Jason David. Research asso. Columbia U., 1966; founder, pres. M.I.T.C.U. Corp., Long Beach, N.Y., 1966—; pres. Capital Auxetics, Inc., N.Y.C., 1968-71; v.p. Pauleon Holding Co., Inc., 1971-73; v.p. corporate finance Herzog & Co. Inc., 1975-76; dir. Adelphi Research Center, Inc. Cons. Am. Inst. Physics, 1966-67, Adelphi U., to Dep. Mayor City N.Y., 1966-67, to dean Sch. Engring. Columbia U., 1966-68, to Thayer Lindsley Lab., Columbia U., 1968-74, Philips Appel & Walden, Inc., Health Delivery Systems, Inc., Heat Systems-Ultrasonics, Inc., Interstate Dental Co., Inc., R.M. Smythe & Co. Inc., Silicon Tech. Corp., Union Analytical Labs., Inc. Mem. Sci. and Tech. Adv. Council to Mayor N.Y.C., 1966-73. Mem. Friends of Fin. Edn., Am. Phys. Soc., Sigma Xi. Office: 475 Long Beach Blvd Long Beach NY 11561

PARISER, RUDOLPH, chemist; b. Harbin, China, Dec. 8, 1923; s. Ludwig Jacob and Lia (Rubinstein) P.; B.S., U. Calif. at Berkeley, 1944; Ph.D., U. Minn., 1950; m. Margaret Louise Marsh, July 31, 1972. Research chemist Organic Chems. dept. E.I. DuPont de Nemours & Co. Inc., Wilmington, Del., 1950-54, research supr., 1954-59, div. head Elastomer Chems. dept., 1959-63, asst. lab. dir., 1963-67, lab. dir., 1967-70, dir. exploratory research, mgr. research and devel., 1970-72, mgr. market research and market devel., 1972-74, dir. pioneering research, 1974—. Served with U.S. Army, 1944-46. Recipient Outstanding Achievement award U. Minn., 1976. Mem. Am. Chem. Soc., Soc. Rheology, AAAS, N.Y. Acad. Sci., Am. Phys. Soc., Sigma Xi, Phi Labmda Upsilon. Clubs: Phila. Interlocutors (pres. 1972-76), DuPont Country. Asso. editor Jour. Chem. Physics, 1966-69, Chem. Physics Letters, 1967-70, Du Pont Innovation, 1969-75; contbr. articles to profl. publs. Home: RD 2 Box 106 Old Public Rd Hockessin DE 19707 Office: Elastomer Chems Dept Exptl Sta E I Du Pont de Nemours & Co Inc Wilmington DE 19898

PARISI, RONALD FREDERICK, constrn. engr.; b. Passaic, N.J., Jan. 31, 1945; s. Charles Seminaro and Dorothea Theresa (Holford) P.; B.Eng., Stevens Inst. Tech., 1967; m. Alberta Vivian Bellofatto, Feb. 24, 1968; children—Ronald, Nicole, Jeannine. Engr., Bechtel Corp., N.Y., Calif., Ill., N.J., 1967-72; constrn. mgr. MDC Corp., Cherry Hill, N.J., 1972-76; constrn. planning mgr. Burns & Roe, Inc., Oradell, N.J., 1976—. Registered profl. engr., N.Y., N.J. Mem. Am. Assn. Cost Engrs., Nat. Wildlife Fedn., Delta Tau Delta. Office: 550 Kinderkamack Rd Oradell NJ 07649

PARK, CHANG HWAN, urologist; b. Korea, Apr. 11, 1935; s. Young Kyl and Ok Hi (Yang) P.; came to U.S., 1964; M.D., Yonsei U. Coll. Medicine, 1960; m. Jun Hi Kim, June 19, 1965; children—Stephen, Joanne, Roger. Intern Misericordia Hosp., Bronx, N.Y., 1964-65; chief resident in urology Francis Delafield Hosp. Columbia U., N.Y.C., 1968-70; practice medicine specializing in urology, Cortland, N.Y., 1971—. Served with Korean Navy, 1961-64. Diplomate Am. Bd. Urology. Fellow A.C.S. Mem. AMA, Am. Urol. Assn., Am. Fertility Soc., N.Y. Med. Soc., Cortland County Med. Soc. (past pres.). Club: Cortland Country. Home: 9 Crestwood Ct Cortland NY 13045 Office: 6 Euclid Ave Cortland NY 13045

PARK, CYNTHIA, sociologist, artist cons., educator; b. Schenectady, Feb. 7, 1925; d. Robert Hirum and Miriam Elizabeth (Nelson) P.; student N.Y. Sch. Design, 1944-45, Greenwich House Music Sch., 1946-48, Greenwich House Pottery Sch., 1949-50, Columbia U., 1952-54; B.A., New Sch. Social Research, N.Y.C., 1959, postgrad. in sociology, 1969—; M.S., Yeshiva U., 1961; M.A., Hunter Coll., 1968; m. Robert Wentworth Christy, May 7, 1955 (div. 1970). Salesperson, Met. Mus. Art, N.Y.C., 1956-58, Bennett Bros. Jewelry, N.Y.C., 1953-55; tchr. social studies N.Y.C. Bd. Edn., 1961-67; prof. sociology Bloomfield Coll., 1967-70, Manhattan Community Coll., 1970-71, Quinnipiac Coll., 1971-73, U. New Haven, 1973-75; dir. Westerly Gallery, N.Y.C., 1963-65; producer, dir. Finnish music records, 1957-59; gen. grip, cons. film Finnegan's Wake, 1966-67; claims interviewer Conn. Dept. Labor, 1975; self-employed cons. to musicians and artists, New Haven, 1976—. Election dist. capt. Lexington Democratic Reform Club, 1963-66; election bd. registration ofcl., N.Y.C., 1961-66; mem. New Haven Chorale, 1974-76; cellist Little Symphony, 1973-75, So. Conn. Symphonic Pops, 1977—, New Haven Civic Symphony, 1972-74; mem. Gilbert and Sullivan Soc., summer 1976, Yale U. Bach Aria Soc., 1978—. Fulbright travel grantee U. Helsinki and Sibelius Acad., Finland, 1959-60. Mem. Am. Sociol. Assn., AAUP, Am. Fedn. Musicians, The Parke Soc. (hon.). Address: 59 Trumbull St New Haven CT 06510

PARK, DOROTHY GOODWIN DENT (MRS. ROY HAMPTON PARK), broadcasting, newspaper exec.; b. Raleigh, N.C.; d. Walter Reed and Mildred (Goodwin) Dent; student Peace Jr. Coll., 1925-33; A.B., Meredith Coll., 1936; m. Roy Hampton Park, Oct. 3, 1936; children—Roy Hampton, Adelaide Hinton Park Gomer III. Sec., dir. RHP, Inc., Ithaca, N.Y., 1945—, Roy H. Park Broadcasting of Va., Inc., Sta. WTVR-TV-AM-FM, Richmond, 1965—, Roy H. Park Broadcasting of Tri-Cities, Inc., Sta. WJHL-TV, Johnson City, Tenn., 1964—. Roy H. Park Broadcasting of Tenn., Inc., Sta. WDEF-TV-AM-FM, Chattanooga, 1963—, Park Broadcasting, Inc., Ithaca, 1942—, Roy H. Park Broadcasting, Inc., Sta. WNCT-TV-FM, Greenville, N.C., 1962—, Roy H. Park Radio, Inc., Sta. WNCT-AM, Greenville, 1963—, Park Found., Inc., Greenville, 1966—, Cobb House of Rock Hill, S.C. Inc., 1967—, Roy H. Park Broadcasting of Midwest, Inc., Sta. WNAX-AM, Yankton, S.D., 1968—, Roy H. Park Broadcasting of Roanoke, Inc., Sta. WSLS-TV, 1969—, Roy H. Park Broadcasting of Utica-Rome, N.Y., Inc., Sta. WUTR-TV, 1969—, Park Newspapers, Inc., Ithaca, 1972—, Park Outdoor Advt. of Scranton-Wilkes-Barre, Inc., Park Newspapers of Ga., Inc., 1972—. KWJJ-AM, Portland, Ore., 1973—, RHP Newspapers, Inc., Ithaca, 1973—, Roy H. Park Broadcasting of Birmingham (Ala.), Inc., 1973—, Park Newspapers Va., Inc., 1973—, Birmingham TV Corp., Sta. WBMG-TV, 1973—, Lockport Publs., Inc., Ithaca, 1973—, Lockport (N.Y.) Union Sun & Jour. Inc., 1973—, Prince William Pub. Co., Inc., Manassas, Va., 1973—, Roy H. Park Broadcasting of Lake County, Inc., Sta. KFMX-FM, St. Louis Park, Minn., 1974—, Roy H. Park Broadcasting of Minn., Inc., Sta. KRSI-AM, St. Louis Park, 1974—, Contemporary FM, Inc., Sta. KJIB-FM, Portland, 1974—, Roy H. Park Broadcasting of Syracuse, Inc., WHEN-AM, Syracuse, N.Y., 1976—, Roy H. Park Broadcasting of Wash., Inc., Sta. KEZX-FM, Seattle, 1975—, Roy H. Park Broadcasting of the Finger Lakes, Inc., WONO-FM, Syracuse, 1977, Park Newspapers of Neb., Inc., Ithaca, 1975—, Press Printing Co., Nebraska City, Neb., 1975—, Park Newspapers of Fla., Inc., Brooksville, 1975—, Park Newspapers of St. Lawrence, Inc., Ithaca, 1975—, Northern N.Y. Pub. Co., Odensburg, 1975—, Courier-Freman, Inc., Potsdam, N.Y., 1975—, Massena (N.Y.) Observer Pub. Co., 1975—, St. Lawrence Plaindealer, Inc., Canton, N.Y., 1975— Park Newspapers of Ind., Inc., The Pilot News, Plymouth, Ind., 1977, Park Newspapers, of Norwich, Inc., The Evening Sun, Norwich, N.Y., 1977, Park Newspapers of Okla., Inc., The News-Capital and Democrat, 1978. Bd. visitors Peace Coll., Raleigh, 1968—. Mem. D.A.R. (1st vice regent 1955-57), Daus. Am. Colonists, Nat. Soc. Magna Charta Dames, Sovereign Colonial Soc. Ams. Royal Descent, Desc. Knights of Garter, Colonial Order of Crown, Service League Ithaca. League Women Voters. Presbyterian. Clubs: Garden (Ithaca), Ithaca Woman's. Home: 205 Devon Rd Ithaca NY 14850 Office: Terrace Hill Ithaca NY 14850

PARK, JAE KYUN, obstetrician, gynecologist; b. Seoul, Korea, Jan. 26, 1938; s. Byung Sun and Ok Nam (Lee) P.; M.D., Seoul Nat. U., 1962; m. Jung Sook Park, June 13, 1965; children—Judy, John, Jason. Intern, Altoona (Pa.) Hosp., 1965-66; resident in obstetrics and gynecology Wilmington (Del.) Med. Center, 1966-69; fellow in gynecologic endocrinology N.Y. Med. Coll., N.Y.C., 1969-71; practice medicine specializing in obstetrics and gynecology, Milford, Del., 1971—; mem. staff Milford Meml. Hosp. Diplomate Am. Bd. Obstetrics and Gynecology. Fellow Am. Coll. Obstetrics and Gynecology; mem. AMA, Del., Sussex County med. socs., Assn. Am. Gynecol. Laparoscopy. Home: RD 3 Box 591 C Milford DE 19963 Office: 505 Lakeview Ave Milford DE 19963

PARK, JON KEITH, dentist, educator; b. Wichita, Kans., May 26, 1938; s. William Ray and Eleanor Jeanette (Cunningham) P.; D.D.S., U. Mo., 1964; B.A., Wichita State U., 1969; M.S. in Dental Edn., U. Mo., 1971. Gen. practice dentistry, Wichita, 1964-67; chmn. dept. dental hygiene Wichita State U., 1967-72; asso. prof. oral diagnosis, coordinator dental radiology Balt. Coll. Dental Surgery, U. Md., 1972, program dir. U. Md. dental externship, 1974—; lectr. Essex Community Coll., Harford County Community Coll. Mem. bd. dirs. Univ. One Residents' Assn., 1975—. Recipient U. Md. Media Achievement award, 1977. Mem. Am., Md. dental assns., Balt. City Dental Soc., Orgn. Tchrs. Oral Diagnosis, Am. Theater Organ Soc., Kans. Dental Hygienists Assn. (hon.), Balt. Music Club, Am. Acad. Dental Radiology (editorial bd.), Am. Assn. Dental Schs., Psi Omega. Episcopalian. Patentee pivotal design dental chair. Office: University of Md School Dentistry Baltimore MD 21201

PARK, LEE CRANDALL, psychiatrist; b. Washington, July 15, 1926; s. Lee I. and Alice (Crandall) P.; grad. Putney (Vt.) Sch., 1944; B.S. in Zoology, Yale, 1948; M.D., Johns Hopkins, 1952; m. Barbara Anne Merrick, July 1, 1953;children—Thomas Joseph, Jeffrey Rawson. Intern medicine Johns Hopkins Hosp., Osler Clinic, Balt., 1952-53; resident psychiatry USN Hosp., Oakland, Calif., 1954, Henry Phipps Psychiat. Clinic, Johns Hopkins Hosp., 1955-59; asst. psychiatrist out patient dept. Johns Hopkins Hosp., 1955-59, staff psychiatrist, 1959—, asso. staff dept. medicine, 1970—, dir. psychiat. outpatient services and community psychiatry program, 1972-74, asst. dir. clin. services (psychiatry), 1973-74, deptl. council (psychiatry), 1974-76; fellow psychiatry Johns Hopkins U., 1955-59, instr. in psychiatry, 1959-63, asst. prof., 1963-71, asso. prof., 1971—, physician charge psychiat. services student health service, 1961-66, sr. psychiat. cons., 1966-73; vis. psychiatrist Balt. City Hosp., 1960-61; co-prin., prin. investigator NIMH Psychopharmacology Research Br. Outpatient Study of Drug-Set Interaction, 1960-68, co-dir. (with Eugene Meyer) Time-Limited Psychotherapy Research Grant, 1969-73; pvt. practice psychiatry, 1964—; cons. Met. Balt. Assn. Mental Health, 1961-63, Bur. Disability Ins., Social Security Adminstrn., 1964—; attending staff Seton Psychiat. Inst., 1966-73, exec. bd., 1970-73; courtesy staff Sheppard and Enoch Pratt Hosp., 1974—. Served to lt. M.C., USNR, 1953-55, div. psychiatrist 1st Marine Div., Korea, staff psychiatrist USN Hosp., Camp Pendelton, Calif., 1954-55. Diplomate Nat. Bd. Med. Examiners, Am. Bd. Psychiatry and Neurology. Fellow Am. Psychiat. Assn., AAAS; mem. Md. Psychiat. Soc. (pres. 1978-79), Am. Psychosomatic Soc., AMA, Am., Md. Socs. adolescent psychiatry, Soc. Psychotherapy Research, N.Y. Acad. Scis., Med. and Chirurg. Faculty Md., Balt. City, Baltimore County med. socs., Johns Hopkins Med. and Surg. Assn., AAUP, Md. Assn. Pvt. Practicing Psychiatrists, Am. Coll. Neuropsychopharmacology, Phi Beta Pi. Clubs: Johns Hopkins (Balt.); Metropolitan (Washington); Farmington Country (Charlottesville, Va.); Chevy Chase (Md.) Country. Research includes controlled studies of interrationships of psychotherapy and psychopharmacotherapy, time ltd. psychotherapy, subjective experiences of research patients, ethical considerations in clin. research. Contbr. articles to profl. jours. and books. Home: 8218 Thornton Rd Baltimore MD 21204 Office: Johns Hopkins Hosp 550 N Broadway Baltimore MD 21205 also 1205 York Rd Lutherville MD 21093

PARK, YOUNG HO, physician; b. Hamhung, Korea, Jan. 20, 1930; s. Tae-Yun and Kyu-Jun (Kim) P.; came to U.S., 1963, naturalized, 1976; M.D., Seoul Nat. U., 1957; m. Chi Hyun Yeum, Oct. 15, 1960; children—Hae-Sue, Hae-Yun, David, Aileen. Intern, Delaware County Meml. Hosp., Drexel Hill, Pa., 1964; resident Muhlenberg Hosp., Plainfield, N.J., 1965-69; practice medicine specializing in pathology, Plainfield, N.J., 1969—; mem. staff Muhlenberg Hosp.; clin. asso. prof. pathology Rutgers Med Sch., New Brunswick, N.J., 1970—. Served to capt. Korean Air Force, 1957-61. Diplomate Am. Bd. Pathology and Nuclear Medicine. Mem. AMA, Am. Soc. Clin. Pathologists, Coll. Am. Pathologists, Soc. Nuclear Medicine, N.J. Med. Soc., N.J. Soc. Pathologists. Home: 9 Helen St Warren NJ 07060 Office: Muhlenberg Hospital Plainfield NJ 07061

PARKE, DAVID WILLIAM, ophthalmologist; b. Hartford, Conn., Nov. 19, 1922; s. David Wilkin and Elizabeth Emily (Crampton) P.; B.S., Aurora Coll., 1946; M.D., Ohio State U., 1950; m. Joyce Eunice Erikson, Sept. 19, 1945; children—David Wilkin II, Marna Joyce, Lissa Ann. Rotating intern Univ. Hosp., Columbus, Ohio, 1950-51; resident in internal medicine Meriden (Conn.) Hosp., 1951-52; resident in ophthalmology Wilmer Inst. Johns Hopkins Hosp., 1952-55; practice medicine specializing in ophthalmology, Meriden, 1955—; chief ophthalmology Meriden-Wallingford (Conn.) Hosp., 1960—, chief staff, 1966-76, sec. bd. dirs., 1971—; mem. faculty Nat. Hosp. Staff Conf.; dir. Physicians Edn. Netwark, Inc. Bd. dirs. United Way, Bradley Home for Aged; chmn. com. Hosp. Conf. of Chief of Staffs, Comprehensive Health Planning "B" Agy., 1972-75, Health Systems Agy. Sub Area Council, 1975—, Police and Fire commns., Meriden, 1970, 72. Served with M.C., U.S. Army, 1942-46. Diplomate Am. Bd. Ophthalmology and Otolaryngology. Fellow Am. Acad. Ophthalmology; mem. Conn. Soc. Prevention Blindness (dir.), Conn. Soc. Eye Physicians, AMA, Conn. Med. Soc., Pan-Pacific Surg. Assn., Internat. Soc. Eye Surgeons, Am. Intraocular Implant Soc., Conn. Hosp. Assn., Wilmer Alumni Assn. Republican. Congregationalist. Club: Meriden Home. Mem. editorial adv. bd. Ophthalmology Times, 1976—; contbg. editor The Pen, 1977. Home: 133 Preston Dr Meriden CT 06450 Office: 477 S Broad St Meriden CT 06450

PARKER, CLIFFORD MAXWELL, textile, apparel co. exec.; b. N.Y.C., July 31, 1942; s. Arthur Leon and Bertha (Neuhaus) P.; B.S. in Accounting and Fin., N.Y. U., 1964. Sales trainee Venice Knitting Mills, N.Y.C., 1964; salesman Bobbie Brooks, Cleve., 1965-66; sales mgr. Venice Industries, N.Y.C., 1967-69, v.p., 1969-73, pres., 1973—. Active Am. Jewish Com.; active Assn. for Help of Retarded Children; active Beth Rivka Schs. Recipient leadership awards from community groups. Home: 211 E 62d St New York City NY 10021 Office: 1400 Broadway New York City NY 10018

PARKER, ELLEN, arts cons.; b. Columbus, Ohio, Feb. 18, 1949; d. Milton Marvin and Harriet Sylvia (Hyman) P.; student N.C. Sch. Arts, 1967-68, U. Pa., 1970; certificate Inst. Arts Adminstrn., Harvard U., 1976; B.A. (Univ. Honors scholar), N.Y. U., 1978, Lesley Jane Rosen scholar Grad. Sch. Public Adminstrn., 1978—. Dancer, Pa. Ballet, 1968-72; adminstr. Manhattan Sch. Music Summer Chamber Music Center, 1972, 73; 1st intern dance program Nat. Endowment Arts, Washington, summer 1974; asst. to dir. for performance Manhattan Sch. Music, 1973-76; dir. continuing edn. and community services Minskoff Cultural Center, N.Y.C., 1976-77; performing arts cons. N.Y. State Council Arts, 1975—; bd. dirs., sec. Performing Arts Dance Fund, N.Y.C., 1977—; sec., bd. dirs. Pauline Koner Dance Consort, N.Y.C., 1976—. Mem. Nat. Assn. Regional Ballet, Am. Dance Guild, N.Y. State Dance Assn., Am. Council for Arts. Home: 175 W 79th St New York NY 10024

PARKER, FRANK DOUGLAS, ins. co. exec.; b. Hartford, Conn., Sept. 12, 1919; s. Frederick L. and Mary Esther (Porter) P.; B.S., Springfield Coll., 1941; m. Elizabeth Bryant, Aug. 16, 1947; children—Deborah J., Douglas H. Field scout exec. Charter Oak council Boy Scouts Am., Hartford, 1945-47; sales engr. Eaton Mfg. Co., N.Y.C., 1947-53; pres. Parker Ellingwood Agy. Inc., Windsor, Conn., 1953-58. Mem. Windsor Town Council, 1959-63, 1954-69; mem. Town of Windsor Charter Revision Commn., 1967-69, chmn., 1967; active Civil Def. Dept. Bd. dirs. Windsor chpt. ARC, 1954—, vice chmn., 1955—; mem. Windsor Republican Town Com., 1954—. Served with Signal Corps, AUS, World War II; CBI. Decorated Bronze Battle Star; named Rep. of Yr., 1970. Mem. Am. Legion (adj. 1954-55), Windsor C. of C. (pres. 1957, sec. 1959-78, award of merit 1962, Jerry Hallas meml. award 1976, sec.), Windsor Hist. Soc. Mason, Elk. Republican. Home: 77 Elm St Windsor CT 06095 Office: 176 Broad St Windsor CT 06095

PARKER, GENEVIEVE FISH (MRS. E.M. PARKER), mus. ofcl.; b. Punxsutawney, Pa., Sept. 25, 1903; d. John Charles and Ollie Jane (Van Dyke) Fish; grad. high sch.; m. E.M. Parker, June 21, 1923; children—Earl M., Walter E. (dec.). Cashier, J.H. Fink Co., Punxsutawney, 1920-23; curator E.M. Parker Indian Mus., Brookville, Pa., 1925—. Mem. Jefferson County Hist. and Geneal. Soc., Dames of Malta Lodge. Clubs: Order Eastern Star, Order of Amarantha. Home and Office: 247 E Main St Brookville PA 15825

PARKER, HENRY GRIFFITH, III, ins. co. exec.; b. Plainfield, N.J., Oct. 27, 1926; s. Henry Griffith and Ruth Martin (Van Auken) P.; grad. Lawrenceville Sch., 1944; A.B., Princeton, 1948; postgrad. U. Pa. Sch. Law, 1949; m. Audrey Lansing Turner, May 11, 1957; children—Henry Griffith IV, Elizabeth Wright. With Chubb & Son, Inc., N.Y.C., 1949—, sr. v.p., dir., 1971—; sr. v.p. Fed. Ins. Co., 1972—, Vigilant Ins. Co., 1966—, mgr. internat. div., 1967—; dir. La Federacion Compania de Seguros C.A., Caracas, Venezuela, 1969, Eberhard Faber, Inc., La Federacion European D'Assurances, Brussels, Belgium, Bolivar Compania de Sequros, Ecuador, Al Saudia Ins. & Reins. Co., Luxembourg. Chmn. Internat. Ins. Advisory Council, U.S. C. of C., 1970-73, dir. internat. com. Chmn. ins. advisory com. Borough of Madison, N.J., 1970—. Dir. Nat. Fgn. Trade Council, chmn. ins. com., chmn. declarations com.; chmn. U.S. delegation to Hemispheric Ins. Conf., Vina Del Mar, Chile, 1969, Asuncion, Paraguay, 1971. Trustee, chmn. bd. Overlook Hosp., Summit, N.J.; trustee Drew U., Madison, N.J. Served as lt. (j.g.) USNR, 1944-46. Mem. Down Town Assn. N.Y., Psi Upsilon. Republican. Episcopalian. Clubs: Morris County (N.J.) Golf; Morristown Field; Princeton, River (N.Y.C.); Devon Yacht. Contbg. author: Annals of Hemispheric Insurance Conference, Jour. Commerce, Internat. Ins. Monitor, others. Home: 38 East Ln Madison NJ 07940 Office: 100 William St New York City NY 10038

PARKER, J(ACK) ROYAL, engring. exec.; b. N.Y.C., Apr. 25, 1919; s. Harry and Clara (Saxe) P.; student Bklyn. Poly. Inst., 1943; D.Sc., Pacific Internat. U., 1956; m Selma Blossom, Dec. 8, 1946; children—Leslie Janet, Andrew Charles. Instr. Indsl. Tng. Inst., 1938-39; engr. Brewster Aero. Corp., 1939-40; pres. Am. Drafting Co., 1940; design engr. U.S. Navy Dept., 1941-44, also supervising instr. N.Y. Drafting Inst., 1941-43; instr. Gasoline Handling Sch. U.S.N.T.S., 1944-46; cons. Todd Shipyards Corp., 1947-54; tech. adviser to pres. Rollins Coll., 1949-50; v.p. Wattpar Corp., 1947-54; pres. Parco Co. of Can., Ltd., 1951-55; partner, dir., chief project mgr. Parco Co., N.Y.C., 1947-75; pres. Par-Con, Inc., Royalpar Industries, Inc.; v.p. Parkise Realty, Inc.; former pres., sec., dir. Vernitron Corp., past v.p., dir. Amsterdam fund, European Securities Publ., Inc.; v.p., dir., founder Refinadora Costarricense de Petroleo, S.A., San Jose, Costa Rica, 1963—; pres. Parco Chem. Services, Inc., 1965-69, Guyana Oil Refining Co. (Brit. Guiana), 1966-69; pres., dir. Parco Internat., Inc., 1965—; developer with Robert B. Anderson, Zones of Internat. Commerce and Industry, Costa Rica, 1963—; dir. with Robert B. Anderson, Resources Iberica, S.A., Madrid, Spain, 1964—; dir. Marlin Lines and Commerce Marine Lines, N.Y.C., Internat. Capital Devel., Ltd., Nassau, and B.W.I. C/M Worldwide Personnel Cons., Inc.; cons. Dominican Republic Puerto Plata Free Port, 1964; cons. pres. Repbulic Costa Rica Zones of Internat. Commerce and Industry, 1964-65; cons. Malta Indsl. Devel. Study Co., Ltd., 1965-69, Hambro-Am. Bank & Trust Co.; gen. mgr. Kellex Power Services-Pullman Kellog Co., Wayne, Pa., 1975-77; pres. J. Royal Parker Assos., Inc., 1977—. Lectr. One World Club, Cornell U., 1963. Mem. drafting commn. Bd. Edn., City N.Y. Trustee Coll. Advanced Sci., Canaan, N.H., 1958-60; mem. mus. com. U.S. Mcht. Marine Acad., Kings Point, N.Y., 1976—. Decorated Order St. John Jerusalem, Knights Malta, 1974; recipient Humanitarian award Fairleigh Dickinson U., 1975. Fellow A.A.A.S.; mem. Inst. Engring. Designers (London, U.K.), Am. Petroleum Inst., Soc. Am. Mil. Engrs., Am. Inst. Chem. Engrs., Am. Inst. Design and Drafting, Marine Tech. Soc. Mason. Author: Gasoline Systems, 1945. Contbr. articles tech. jours. Patentee in field; inventor Lazy Golfer. Home: 106 The Mews Haddonfield NJ 08033 Office: 900 Haddon Ave Collingswood NJ 08108

PARKER, JACK STEELE, corp. exec.; b. Palo Alto, Calif., July 6, 1918; s. Wwilliam L. and Mary I. (Steele) P.: student Menlo Jr. Coll., 1935-37, B.S., Leland Stanford Jr. U., 1939; LL.D., Clark U.; D.B.A., S.E. Mass. Inst. Tech.; m. Elaine Simons, 1946; 1 dau., Kaaren Lee, Mech. engr. Western Pipe & Steel Co. Calif., San Francisco, 1939-40; marine surveyor Am. Bur. Shipping, Seattle, 1940-42; asst. gen. supt. Todd Shipyards, Inc., Houston, 1942-44, gen. supt. outfitting, San Pedro, Calif., 1944-46; asst. chief engr. Am. Potash & Chem. Co., Trona, Calif., 1946-50: asst. mgr. design and constrn. Gen. Electric Co., Richland, Wash., 1950-52, ops. mgr. aircraft nuclear propulsion project, Cin., 1952-53; gen. mgr. small aircraft engine dept., Lynn, Mass., 1953-54, gen. mgr. aircraft gas turbine div., Cin., 1955-57: v.p. Gen. Electric Co., 1956-68, v.p. relations services, exec. office, 1957-61: v.p., group exec. aerospace and def. group, 1961-68, exec. v.p., 1968, vice chmn. bd., exec. officer, 1968—. Bd. dirs. Travel Program for Fgn. Diplomats, Inc.; trustee St. Louis U., 1967-69, Rensselaer Poly. Inst., Grand Central Art Galleries, Conf. Bd. (chmn. 1972-74, counselor for life), Council Fin. Aid to Edn.; bd. overseers Hoover Instn., chmn., 1973—: mem. adv. council Stanford Grad. Sch. Bus. Asso. fellow Royal Aero. Soc.: fellow Am. Inst. Aeros. and Astronautics (sr.), Inst. Jud. Adminstrn.; mem. ASME, NAM (dir. 1958-62), Aerospace Industries Assn. (chmn. bd. govs. 1966), Nat. Security Industry Assn. (trustee), Soc. Automotive Engrs., Air Force Assn., U.S. C. of C. (continental group), Newcomen Soc., Conquistadores Del Cielo. Clubs: Augusta Nat. Golf; Burning Tree, George Towne Washington); Commonwealth, Queen City, comml.

(Cin.); Econ., Univ., Sky, Links (N.Y.C.); Question: Blind Brook; Rolling Rock; Pauma Valley Country; Camp Fire of America: Round Hill; Clove Valley Rod and Gun; Lyford Cay; Bohemian (San Francisco); Boone and Crockett. Home: Round Hill Club Rd Greenwich CT 06830 Office: 3135 Easton Turnpike Fairfield CT 06431

PARKER, JEROME LEE, journalist; b. Kansas City, Mo., Aug. 14, 1939; s. Roy W. and Lucilee (Bisby) P.; B.A., U. Iowa, 1961. Gen. assignment reporter Miami (Fla.) Herald, 1961-66; feature writer specializing in arts, reporter N.Y. Bur., Newsday, N.Y.C., 1966—. Democrat. Contbr. articles to Cosmopolitan mag., Nat. Air Lines in-flight mag. Aloft, Dallas Times Herald, Los Angeles Times, Chgo. Tribune, Detroit Free Press. Home: 340 E 57th St New York NY 10022 Office: 1500 Broadway New York NY 10036*

PARKER, JOHN OSMYN, hosp. adminstr.; b. Denver, May 31, 1919; s. George Lindsey and Marie Walker (Bloedorn) P.; B.S. in Bus., U. Colo., 1942; m. Judith Fehr, July 20, 1942; children—Craig Steven, John Fehr, Diane, Newton Lindey. Jr. indsl. engr. U.S. Steel Corp., Gary, Ind., 1942-43; mgr. personnel research Trans World Airlines, Kansas City, Mo., 1945-55; mgmt. cons. Douglas Williams Assos., N.Y.C., 1955-56; dir. personnel Central Hudson Gas & Electric Corp., Poughkeepsie, N.Y., 1956-69, United Hosp., Port Chester, N.Y., 1969-78, Mountainside Hosp., Montclair, N.J., 1978—; mgmt. cons., instr. mgmt. devel. Rutgers U. Chmn. budget div., bd. dirs. United Way, Dutchess County, N.Y., 1963-69. Served with U.S. Army, 1943-45; ETO. Mem. Am. Soc. Personnel Adminstrn. (research awards com. 1958—, accredited exec. in personnel), Am. Soc. Tng. Dirs., Am. Mgmt. Assn., Phi Kappa Psi. Republican. Presbyterian. Clubs: Rotary (dir. Rye, N.Y. 1975-78, pres. 1977-78; mem. Montclair); Landmark (Stamford, Conn.). Home: 9 Oates Terr West Caldwell NJ 07006 Office: Mountainside Hospital Montclair NJ 07042

PARKER, LAWRENCE CRAIG, coll. adminstr.; b. Auburn, Maine, Aug. 24, 1910; s. George H. and Lucy Steele (Craig) P.; A.B., Bates Coll., 1932; M.A., Tufts U., 1935; postgrad. Yale U., 1957-58, N.Y. U. 1961-62; m. Virginia M. Moulton, May 12, 1934; children—L. Craig Jr., Judith A. (Mrs. John E. Cole III). Asst. gen. mgr. The Lionel Corp., Irvington, N.J., 1936-44; gen. mgr. Oxford Wood & Plastics Co., West Paris, Maine, 1944-46; prodn. mgr. A.C. Gilbert Co., New Haven, 1946-56; dir. devel. U. New Haven, West Haven, Conn., 1956-70, dir. devel., alumni relations and govtl. relations, 1970-78; cons. U. New Haven, The Dodds Found., New Haven, 1965—. Treas., dir. Motor Club Ins. Agy., Inc., 1968—. Motor Club Finance Co., Inc. Bd. dirs. Conn. Motor Club (AAA), 1965—, treas., 1966—; bd. dirs. Conn. Radio Found. (sta. WELI), sec., 1967-71; bd. dirs. Jr. Achievement of Greater New Haven, Quinnipiac council Boy Scouts Am., Univ. Research Inst. Conn. Mem. Newcomen Soc. N.Am., Delta Sigma Rho. Kiwanian (pres. New Haven chpt. 1962). Clubs: Landmark (Stamford); Yale, Quinnipiack, Graduate (New Haven). Home: 137 Hotchkiss Grove Rd Branford CT 06405 also Whitingham VT 05361 Office: 300 Orange Ave West Haven CT 06516

PARKER, NANCY KNOWLES (MRS. CORTLANDT PARKER), pub. co. exec.; b. Buffalo, Aug. 30, 1929; d. Ward Emerson and Barbara Louise (Bull) Knowles; student Chevy Chase Jr. Coll., 1949; m. Cortlandt Parker, Sept. 8, 1951; children—Elizabeth, Cortlandt, Stephen, Nancy Gray. Copy girl Washington Evening Star, 1947-49; reporter Newark Evening News, 1949-51; asst. pub. relations dir. Newark Community Chest, 1951-52; writer Suburban Life mag., Summit, N.J., 1952-55; co-founder, asso. editor Observor Tribune, Mendham, N.J., 1955-59; womans editor, v.p. Recorder Pub. Co., Bernardsville, N.J., 1960—. Trustee Somerset Hills Community Chest, North Jersey Tng. Sch., Totowa, Virginia Day Nursery Summer Home, Bernardsville; former trustee Morris-Somerset chpt. UN Assn., Vis. Homemaker Service of Somerset County (N.J.). Mem. Bus. and Profl. Women, Nat. Soc. Arts and Letters, Jr. League, Pen and Brush N.Y.C. Episcopalian. Home: Mine Mount Rd Bernardsville NJ 07924 Office: 17 Morristown Rd Bernardsville NJ 07924

PARKER, ROBERT ORION, cons. engr.; b. Big Pool, Md., Dec. 24, 1915; s. Orion Horace and Frances Lenore (Furry) P.; B.S. Chem. Engring., Carnegie Inst. Tech., 1936; M.S., Columbia U., 1943; D.Eng., N.Y. U., 1959; m. Elizabeth Porter Simonelli, Nov. 13, 1976; 1 stepdau., Lynn Paustenbach. Engr., Freedom Oil Co. (Pa.), 1936-37; test engr. Griscom Russell Co., N.Y.C., and Massillion, Ohio, 1937-45, dir. research, 1945-55; instr. Hillyer Coll., Hartford, Conn., 1957; instr. chem. engring. N.Y. U., N.Y.C., 1957-59, asst. prof., 1959-62, asso. prof., 1963-68, prof. chem. and nuclear engring., 1969-73; pvt. practice cons. engr., N.Y.C., 1972—. Registered profl. engr., N.Y. Fellow Am. Inst. Chemists; mem. Am. Nuclear Soc., Nat. Fire Protection Assn., Am. Inst. Chem. Engrs., N.Y. Acad. Scis., Sci. Research Soc. Am., Sigma Xi, Tau Beta Pi, Phi Lambda Upsilon. Roman Catholic. Contbr. articles to profl. jours. Home and Office: 800 E 85th St New York City NY 10028

PARKER, ROLLAND SANDAU, psychologist; b. N.Y.C., Dec. 31, 1928; s. Irving and Stella (Sandau) Pocker; A.B., N.Y.U., 1948, Ph.D., 1959. Various trainee positions, 1948-53; intern Mt. Sinai Hosp., N.Y.C., 1953-54; clin. and sr. clin. psychologist N.Y. State Dept. Mental Hygiene, 1955-59; pvt. practice clin. psychology, 1960—; ward clin. psychologist VA Hosp., Northport, N.Y., 1960-62; clin. psychologist VA Outpatient Clinic, N.Y.C., 1962-70; dir. psychol. services Exec. Research Internat., N.Y.C., 1970-71; supervising psychologist Lincoln Inst. Psychotherapy, 1971-72. Lectr., Bklyn. Coll., 1959-60; adj. asso. prof. grad. sch. L.I. U., 1966-67, faculty group relations ongoing workshops, 1969-73; supervising psychologist, dept. psychiatry Jersey City Med. Center, 1974—; dir. Center for Emotional Common Sense, 1973—. Diplomate in clin. psychology Am. Bd. Profl. Psychology. Fellow Soc. for Projective Techniques; mem. Am. Group Psychotherapy Assn., AAAS, N.Y. Acad. Scis., Am., N.Y. State psychol. assns. Author: Emotional Common Sense, 1973; Effective Decisions and Emotional Fulfillment, 1977; Careers in Psychology and Counseling, 1977; Living Single Successfully, 1978. Contbr. pubis. in areas of psychotherapy, psychodiagnosis, psychotherapy tng. Editor: The Emotional Stress of War, Violence and Peace, 1972. Address: 50 W 96th St Apt 9C New York City NY 10025

PARKER, ROSCOE J., former city ofcl.; b. Annapolis, Md., May 23, 1912; s. James and Katie (McGowan) P.; diploma Cortez Peters Bus. Coll., 1948; student Va. Union U., 1932-35, LaSalle Extension U., Chgo., 1965-66. Mgr. Parker's Bus. and Accounting Service, Annapolis, Md., 1949-74; mgr. George Thomas Realty, Annapolis, 1956-58; acting dir. N.W. St. Br. YMCA, Annapolis, 1951-52; chmn. Annapolis Taxicab Commn., 1966-73; Annapolis city councilman, 1953-73. Resident mgr. Newtowne Housing project, Annapolis, 1972-73; Sec., Republican City Central Com., Annapolis, 1949-52; del. Rep. state conv., 1948-52. Recipient Merit certificate K. C., 1973; Honor award NAACP, 1953, Afro-Am. Newspapers, 1953, Kappa Alpha Psi, 1973, City Annapolis, 1973, N.W. St. Br. YMCA, 1965, Elks, 1973. Mem. Frontiers Internat., Kappa Alpha Psi. Mem. A.M.E. Ch. (trustee). Home: 100 W Washington St Annapolis MD 21401 Office: 4 Clay St Annapolis MD 21401

PARKER, WILLIAM HOOPER, III, cons. environ. engr.; b. Westbrook, Maine, May 4, 1937; s. William Hooper and Anne Marnie (Delaney) P.; B.S., U. Maine, 1960; M.S. in Civil Engring., Northeastern U., 1966; m. Joan Moody Currier, June 17, 1959; children—Laurie, Michael, Suzan, Julie. Engr., Camp Dresser & McKee, Cons. Engrs., Boston, 1962-66, project engr., 1966-70, project mgr., 1970-71, v.p., 1971-75, 77—; v.p. Camp Dresser & McKee Internat., Camp Dresser & McKee Ltd.; asso. partner Camp, Dresser & McKee; v.p. Edward C. Jordan Co., Portland, Maine, 1975-77. Chmn. Reading (Mass.) Planning Bd., 1971, mem., 1966-72; mem. Reading Municipal Light Bd., 1973—. Served to 1st lt. C.E., AUS, 1960-62. Registered profl. engr., Maine, Mass., R.I., Vt., N.H., N.Y., Fla. Mem. ASCE, Maine Wastewater Control Assn., New Eng. Water Pollution Control Assn., New Eng. Water Works Assn., Soc. Am. Mil. Engrs., Mass. Soc. Profl. Engrs. (named Young Engr. of Year 1971), Maine Cons. Engrs. Council, Inst. of Engrs. (Singapore), Chi Epsilon. Home: 12 Sturdivant Rd Cumberland Foreside ME 04110 Office: One Center Plaza Boston MA 02108

PARKET, IRWIN ROBERT, educator, mktg. cons.; b. N.Y.C., May 23, 1931; s. Samuel and Anna (Noble) P.; B.B.A., City Coll. N.Y., 1953, M.B.A., 1964; Ph.D., Columbia, 1969; m. Reba Soberman, June 3, 1962; children—Jeffrey, Allison. Vice-pres. Quality Electronics Co., N.Y.C., 1956-62; pres. Merrell Electronics Co., N.Y.C., 1962-64; lectr. mgmt. St. John's U., Jamaica, N.Y., 1966-69; asso. prof. Baruch Coll., N.Y.C., 1969—; cons. in field. Mem. Am. Mktg. Assn., Soc. Advancement Mgmt., Nat. Assn. Purchasing Mgmt., Beta Gamma Sigma, Pi Sigma Epsilon, Psi Chi. Author: Statistics for Business Decision Making, 1974. Researcher indsl. mktg. and purchasing, consumer behavior, social responsibility. Home: 56 Cedar Dr Great Neck NY 11021 Office: 17 Lexington Ave New York City NY 10010

PARKINSON, THOMAS IGNATIUS, JR., lawyer; b. N.Y.C., Jan. 27, 1914; s. Thomas I. and Georgia (Weed) P.; A.B., Harvard, 1934; LL.B., U. Pa., 1937; m. Geralda E. Moore, Sept. 23, 1937; children—Thomas Ignatius III, Geoffrey Moore, Cynthia Moore. Admitted to N.Y. bar, 1938, since practiced in N.Y.C.; asso. Milbank, Tweed, Hope and Hadley, 1937-47, partner, 1947-56; pres. Mar Ltd., 1951; pres. Breecom Corp., 1951—; dir., mem. exec. com. Pine St. Fund, N.Y.C. Trustee State Communities Aid Assn., 1949—; dir. Fgn. Policy Assn., 1949-53, Milbank Found. Mem. Am. Bar Assn., Assn. Bar City N.Y., Brit. War Relief Soc. (officer), Met. Unit Found. (officer), Pilgrims U.S., Phi Beta Kappa. Clubs: Knickerbocker, Union, Down Town Assn. (N.Y.C.); Piping Rock. Home: 215 Lakeview Ave W Brightwaters NY 11718 Office: 25 Broadway New York City NY 10004

PARKISON, ED HOYT, research engr.; b. Ventura, Calif., Feb. 10, 1932; s. Hoyt S. and Hila (Clifford) P.; B.S. in Mech. Engring., U. Wyo., 1953; J.D., U. Md., 1962; m. Shirley Regina Dixon, Dec. 4, 1954; children—Mark Hoyt, Regina Ann, David Clifford. Test engr. Koppers Co., Balt., 1955-57, sr. test engr., 1957-59, supr. sound control lab., 1959-61; sr. engr. Martin Marietta Corp., Balt. Div., 1961-64, mgr. support operations RIAS Div., 1964-74, mgr. engring. Martin Marietta Labs., 1974-77, prin. engr. parent co., 1977—. Treas. Catonsville PTA, 1964-66, v.p., 1966-67, treas., 1972-74; treas. Hillcrest PTA, 1968-70, pres., 1970-71; treas. pub. edn. nominating com. Baltimore County, 1973-75. Served with AUS, 1953-55. Recipient Exceptional Achievement award Martin Marietta Corp., 1974. Mem. Md. Acad. Sci. (sci. council), Am. Soc. Mass Spectrometry, ASME (dir. 1965-67, sec. 1970-71, chmn. 1972-73), Acoustical Soc. Am., Aluminum Assn. (chmn. 1975-77), Inst. Noise Control Engring., Catonsville Hist. Soc., Wyo. State Soc., Md. Hist. Soc., Kappa Sigma. Mem. Ch. Latter-Day Saints. Developed isotope ratio mass spectrometer for extra-terrestrial life detection, 1966; developed upper atmospheric gun launched probe for project HARP, 1967; developer noise suppression systems for U.S. Army, 1973-74; inventor, developer novel mineral benefication process, 1972-74. Home: 1211 Brandford Rd Baltimore MD 21228 Office: 1450 S Rolling Rd Baltimore MD 21227

PARKS, DANA, JR., genealogist; b. Newton, Mass., Oct. 30, 1910; s. Dana and Ragnhild Amalie (Aune) P.; student Northeastern U., 1932-35, Am. U., 1967; m. Gladys Elizabeth Rogers, Sept. 4, 1933; children—Dana, Shelley Diane (Mrs. Rodney Morey Huntoon). With Lee Higginson & Co., Boston, 1929-32; with Provident Instn. for Savs., Boston, 1932-42, teller, 1935-42; field mgr. IBM Corp., Boston, also Concord, N.H., 1942-70; engaged in geneal. research, 1930—; pres., chief exec. officer Salisbury (N.H.) Hist. Soc., Inc., 1966-74. Moderator, Town of Salisbury, 1960-76, trustee of town funds, 1960-74. Bd. dirs. Concord Mental Health Center, 1966-72, Havenwood Retirement Community, 1970-74; trustee N.H. Conf. United Ch. of Christ, 1970-77; vice chmn. Merrimack Valley Regional Sch. Bd., 1966-70; chaplain, lay preacher N.H. chpt. Nat. Camping Travelers. Recipient pub. service awards Am. Radio Relay League, 1955, 72. Certified Am. lineage specialist. Mem. New Eng. Historic Geneal. Soc., Nat. Geneal. Soc., S.A.R., Soc. Colonial Wars. Mason (Shriner). Club: Concord (N.H.) Brasspounders Amateur Radio. Home: Box 47 Salisbury NH 03268 winter 705 Country Park Clearwater FL 33516

PARKS, EARLE CHARLES, lawyer; b. Montague, Mass., Mar. 27, 1904; s. Charles Warren and Adelaide (Cramm) P.; J.D., Boston U., 1925; m. Bernice Downs, June 29, 1935; 1 dau., Judith (Mrs. Robert Anderson). Admitted to Mass. bar, 1926, U.S. Dist. Ct. of Mass. bar, 1927, U.S. Supreme Ct. bar, 1937; asso. Adams & Blinn, Boston, 1925-39; propr. firm of Parks & Hession, 1939-71; propr. firm Parks, Carroll & Sullivan, 1975—; of counsel Provident Instn. for Savs. in Town of Boston. Mem. sch. com. Belmont, 1944-47; town counsel Belmont, 1947-63; pres., gen. counsel Masonic Casualty Co., 1956-67. Chmn. legal and legislative com. N.E. Fed. League of Savs. and Loan Assns., 1943-45. Mem. bd. Selectmen for Belmont, 1963-69, chmn., 1964-69. Served as capt. Mass. Militia, on Judge Adv. Staff, 1943-45. Trustee Boston U., 1971-74. Recipient Alumni award Boston U., 1967, Silver Shingle award, 1971. Mem. Am., Mass., Middlesex County bar assns., Mass. Trial Lawyers (pres. 1967-68), City Solicitors and Town Counsels Assn. Mass. (pres. 1956-57), Mass. Conveyancers Assn., Boston U. Law Sch. Alumni Assn. (pres. 1964-65), Boston U. Nat. Alumni Council (chmn. 1968-73), Phi Delta Phi. Republican. Conglist. Mason (Shriner, past master, past comdr.). Clubs: Boston City (pres. 1950-51), Bay (Boston); Annisquam Yacht (sec. 1952-56) (Gloucester, Mass.). Home: 49 Hill Rd Belmont MA 02178 Office: 28 State St Boston MA 02109

PARKS, JAMES NICHOLAS, state ofcl., rec. co. exec.; b. Manchester, N.H., Oct. 31, 1924; s. Nicholas D. and Angela (Boritsos) Psarakis: student Columbia U., 1948, 49; Asso. Bus. Sci., N.H. Coll. Accounting and Commerce, 1952; m. Georgette Poirier Psarakis. Song plugger Lewis Music Pub. Co., N.Y.C., 1947-49: gen. mgr. Marvel Records, 1949-50; freelance producer London Records, 1950-53; Am. rep. W & G Record Processing Co. Pty. Ltd. Australia, 1953-58, v.p. Am. operations, 1958-61, exec. v.p. Am. ops., 1961-68, dir. W & G Group; control dir. Internat. Jaspar Music Group Ltd., 1967; state indsl. agt. at large Office of Indsl. Devel., State of N.H. 1967-68, supr. comml. devel. and research dept. resources and econ. devel., 1968-75, supr. fgn. trade and comml. devel., 1975—; dir. Taylor Industries Ltd., Toronto, Ont., Can.; personnel mgr. The Brandywine Singers and Mar-Vels, 1964—, The Seekers, 1965-68, Danny Gravas, Bambi Lynn, 1967-75, Marc Denny, 1968—; writer column Record Round Up, N.H. Sunday News, 1955-73. Bd. dirs. St. George Greek Orthodox Cathedral. Served with USNR, 1945-46. Mem. Internat. Record Mfrs. Assn. (sec. 1958), Am. Hellenic Ednl. Progressive Assn., A.F.M. (hon. life). Northeast Indsl. Devel. Assn., Profl. Musicians Union Australia (hon. life), League of Greek Orthodox Stewards. Mem. Greek Orthodox Ch. Lion. Club: NOA. Home: 188 Highland St Manchester NH 03104 Office: 852 Elm St Manchester NH 03101

PARKS, JOHN SCOTT, pediatric endocrinologist: b. Washington, Oct. 14, 1939; s. John Louis and Mary Dean (Scott) P.: A.B. magna cum laude (Gen. Motors Nat. scholar), Amherst Coll., 1961; M.D., (Am. Cancer Soc. grantee 1963-64, NIH grantee 1963-64), U. Pa., 1966, Ph.D. (NIH grantee 1966-67), 1971; m. Georgia Agnes Bigley, May 7, 1959; children—Stephanie, Paige, John. Intern, Children's Hosp., Phila., 1967-68; resident in pediatrics, 1967-69, fellow in pediatric endocrinology, 1971-72, asso. dir. pediatric endocrinology, 1972—; clin. asso. endocrinology br. NIH, Bethesda, Md., 1969-71; asst. prof. pediatrics U. Pa., 1972—. Bd. dirs. Hill Top Prep. Sch., Rosemont, Pa., 1976-78. Served with USPHS, 1969-71. NIH grantee, 1971-78. Mem. Soc. Pediatric Research, Endocrine Soc., Lawson Wilkins Pediatric Endocrine Soc. Democrat. Methodist. Research, numerous publs. on bacterial gene control, 1970-71, pediatric endocrinology, 1971-78, growth hormone mechanism of action, 1976-78. Home: 423 Bryn Mawr Ave Bala Cynwyd PA 19004 Office: One Children's Center Philadelphia PA 19104

PARKS, PAUL, state ofcl.; b. Indpls., May 7, 1923: s. Cleab Jiles and Hazel (Crenshaw) P.; B.S. in Civil Engring., Purdue U., 1949; postgrad., Mass. Inst. Tech., 1958; m. Virginia Loftman, Sept. 18, 1971: children—Paul, Pamela, Stacey. With Ind. State Hwy. Commn., Indpls., 1949-51; designer Stone & Webster Engring., Boston, 1951; Fay, Spofford & Thorndike, Boston, 1951-52; missile designer Chance Vought Aircraft, Boston, 1952-53; nuclear engr. Pratt & Whitney Aircraft, Boston, 1953-57; partner architecture and engring. firm, Boston, 1957-67: adminstr. Boston Model City Adminstrn., 1968-76; sec. ednl. affairs Commonwealth of Mass., Boston, 1976—. Lectr. Tufts U. Sch. Civil Engring., 1968—; cons. gen. accounting office, Mayor's Com. for Adminstrn. of Justice; mem. Atty. Gen.'s Adv. Com. on Civil Rights, 1969-71; mem. health task force Boston Fed. Exec. Bd.; adviser Boston Mothers for Adequate Welfare, 1966-68; speech therapist Vets. Lang. Clinic, Mass. Gen. Hosp., 1964-66; mem. Mass. Adv. Council on Edn., 1968-71, Mass. Com. on Children and Youth, 1962-67; chmn. Mass. adv. com. to U.S. Civil Rights Commn., 1961-73; chmn. urban affairs com. Mass. Fedn. Fair Housing and Equal Rights, 1961-67; mem. Community Ednl. Council, 1961-73; pres. Com. for Community Ednl. Devel., Inc., 1968-74. Adult leader youth programs Roxbury YMCA, 1951-58. Trustee, Peter Bent Brighm Hosp.; bd. dirs. Mass. Planned Parenthood Assn., Mass. Mental Health Assn., Mass. Soc. Prevention of Blindness, Boston Coll. Upward Bound Program. Served with C.E., AUS, 1943-46; ETO, PTO. Registered profl. engr., Mass. Mem. ASCE, Nat. Soc. Profl. Engrs., Nat. Acad. Pub. Adminstrn., N.A.A.C.p. (co-chmn. edn. com. 1960-68, v.p. Boston br. 65-70), Boston C. of C., Americans for Democratic Action (nat. bd. 1971-74, state bd. 1970-74). Mem. United Ch. of Christ (mem. nat. social action bd. 1963-68). Home: 78 Woodhaven St Mattapan MA 02126 Office: John W McCormack Bldg One Ashburton Pl Boston MA 02108

PARKS, ROBERT LLOYD, mathematician, physicist, educator; b. Miami, Mar. 14, 1954; s. Robert Lloyd and Shirley Mabel (Albertelli) P.; B.A. with honors, Gettysburg Coll., 1976. Computer operator, Math lab. asst., tutor math. and physics Gettysburg (Pa.) Coll., 1973-76; teaching fellow physics U. Va., Charlottesville, 1976—. Mem. Am. Phys. Soc., Soc. Physics Students, AAAS. Democrat. Lutheran. Home: 6413 Darlington Ave Harrisburg PA 17111 Office: Physics Dept U Va Charlottesville VA 22901

PARMER, MICHAEL ANDREW, surgeon; b. N.Y.C., June 1, 1939; s. Benjamin Franklin and Lillian Helen (Marks) P.; B.A., Cornell U., 1960; M.D., N.J. Med. Sch., 1964; m. Margaret Alice Ham, Jan. 7, 1967; children—Alissa, Diana. Intern, Med. Center, Jersey City, 1964-65; resident and chief resident in surgery Univ. Hosps., Boston, Mass., 1965-69; chief gen. surgery Gen. Leonard Wood Army Hosp., 1969-70; chief surgery, chief profl. services 8th Field Hosp., Republic of Vietnam, 1970-71; staff surgeon St. Francis Hosp., Port Jervis, N.Y., 1971-75, chief surgery, 1976; clin. asst. prof. surgery N.J. Med. Sch., 1974—. Served with U.S. Army, 1969-71. Decorated Bronze Star; diplomate Am. Bd. Surgery. Fellow A.C.S.; mem. AMA. Producer, co-host Take Five for Health, Sta. WDLC, Port Jervis, 1974-76. Home: Box 92 RD 3 Port Jervis NY 12771 Office: 21 E Main St Port Jervis NY 12771

PARO, TOM EDWARD, broadcasting exec.; b. Belleville, Ill., July 7, 1923; s. Edward Westermann and Alice Jane (Price) P.; B.J., U. Mo., 1948; m. Aileen Nance, Oct. 1, 1955; children—Jeffrey, Daniel, Kathleen. With MBS, 1948-54; with sales dept. NBC, 1955-59; dir. sales WRC-TV, Washington, 1960-62, sta. mgr., 1962-65, v.p., gen. mgr., 1965-77; sta. mgr. WNBC-TV, 1966-69; v.p. Nat. Broadcasting Co., 1969-77; exec. v.p. Assn. Maximum Service Telecasters, Inc., 1977-78, pres., 1978—; adv. bd. Riggs Nat. Bank. Bd. dirs. Washington Bd. Trade, NCCJ, Jr. Achievement, Heart Assn., Boy Scouts Am., Meridian House, D.C. Crippled Children, Capital Area United Way. Served to lt., AUS, 1943-46; ETO; to capt., 1951-53. Kiwanian. Clubs: Burning Tree Country, Congl. Country, International; National Broadcasters. Home: 5913 Searl Terr Washington DC 20016 Office: 1735 DeSales St NW Washington DC 20036

PARR, ALBERT F. W., sci. instrument co. exec.; b. Tauberbischofsheim, Germany, Jan. 9, 1923; s. Ferdinand Franz and Hildegard Marie (Hessler) P.; came to U.S., 1926, naturalized, 1932; B.S., City U. N.Y., 1943; certificate display engring. Harvard U., 1944; M.S., Mass. Inst. Tech., 1951; certificate space optics U. Calif. at Los Angeles, 1962; certificate ednl. tech., U. Calif. at Berkeley, 1974; m. Dorothy Adele Hennesey, June 12, 1948; children—Stephen Joseph, Virginia Katherine, Andrew Albert, William Raymond. Project engr. instrumentation lab., Mass. Inst. Tech., Cambridge, 1946-52; program mgr. combined systems Gen. Precision Lab., Pleasantville, N.Y., 1952-55: head systems dept. Norden div. United Techs. Co., Norwalk, Conn., 1955-58; dir., v.p. mgr. engring. Powertronics, Inc., New Rochelle, N.Y., 1958-61; div. mgr. control instrument prodn. Farrand Optical Co., Valhalla, N.Y., 1961—. Served from 2d. lt. to 1st. lt., tech. intelligence, U.S. Army, 1943-46; ETO. Mem. Instrument Soc. Am., IEEE, Soc. Motion Picture and TV Engrs., Assn. Edn. and Communication Tech. div. NEA, Sigma Xi. K.C. Patentee in field. Home: Beech Pl Pine Knolls Valhalla NY 10595 Office: 117 Wall St Valhalla NY 10595

PARRACK, EDWARD TAYLOR, advt. exec.; b. Atlanta, Mar. 7, 1914; s. Ernest E. and Mabel (Taylor) P.; A.B., U. Pitts., 1936; m. Elizabeth Rees Felix, Aug. 17, 1940; 1 son, Edward Taylor. With Ketchum, MacLeod & Grove, Inc., Pitts., 1936—, beginning as account asst., successively asst. to pres., v.p., 1936-55, exec. v.p. service, 1955-62, pres., chief exec. officer, 1962-70, chmn. bd., chief exec. officer, 1970—, also chmn. exec. com.; Lend Lease officer for Middle East, 1942-43; asst. to sec. U.S. delegation San Francisco Peace Conf., 1945. Trustee Carnegie Inst., Pitts. Episcopalian. Clubs: Fox Chapel Golf; Duquesne (Pitts.); Rolling Rock, Laurel Valley Golf (Ligonier, Pa.); Pinnacle (N.Y.C.); Pittsburgh Golf. Home: Park Mansions 5023 Frew Ave Pittsburgh PA 15213 Office: Four Gateway Center Pittsburgh PA 15222

PARRELLA, JULIUS CARL, consumer products co. exec.; b. Plainfield, N.J., Oct. 28, 1938; s. Julius and Anna Marie (Flanagan) P.; B.S., Seton Hall U., 1960; m. Mary Linda Lombardi, June 25, 1960; children—Karen, Kevin, Keith. With Chicopee, New Brunswick, N.J., 1964—, dist. sales mgr., 1969-71, asst. product dir., 1972-73, product dir., 1974-75, mdse. mgr., 1975—. Mem. Warren Recreation Commn., 1969-76, sec., 1971-76; mem. Warren Baseball Assn., 1973-76. Served with USMC, 1960-64. Mem. Sales and Mktg. Execs. Club, Am. Mktg. Assn. Democrat. Roman Catholic. K.C. (4 degree). Home: 77 Ferguson Rd Warren NJ 07060 Office: 301 George St New Brunswick NJ 08903

PARRETT, DANIEL JOSEPH, mgmt. cons.; b. N.Y.C., Jan. 1, 1951; s. Woodrow James and Margaret (Cremins) P.; B.M.E., Manhattan Coll., 1972; M.B.A., N.Y. U., 1974. Asst. product mgr. Handy & Harman Co., N.Y.C., 1974-77; cons. Booz Allen & Hamilton, Florham Park, N.J., 1977—. Home: 46-08 30th Ave Astoria NY 11103 Office: 66 Hanover Rd Florham Park NJ 07932

PARROTTA, MICHAEL ANDREW, research chemist; b. Trenton, N.J., Apr. 30, 1950; s. Umberto Joseph and Maria Louisa P.; B.S., Lamar U., 1972; M.S., Rutgers U., 1977; m. Lynda Ann Jarvie, Sept. 25, 1976; 1 son, Michael Jacob. Asst. chemist Congoleum Industry, Trenton, N.J., 1972-73; chief chemist Nat. Automotive Fiber Ind. div. Chris-Craft Co., Trenton, 1973-76; project supr. Nat. Starch & Chem. Co., Bridgewater, N.J., 1976-77; group leader Moore Bus. Form Ltd., Grand Island, N.Y., 1977—. Named Man of Year Hamilton Twp. Jaycees, 1975; Fullbright-Hayes fellow, 1972-73. Mem. N.Y. Rubber Group (cons.), Am. Chem. Soc., TAPPI, Am. Mktg. Assn., N.J. Dist. (v.p. 1975-76), Hamilton Twp. (dir. 1975-76) jaycees, Fermi Fedn. Democrat. Roman Catholic. Patentee foams. Home: 298 Belmont Ct E North Tonawanda NY 14120 Office: 300 Lang Blvd Grand Island NY 14072

PARRY, JOHN ROBERT, geophysicist; b. Vancouver, B.C., Can., Sept. 22, 1941; s. John Pearson and Lilian Alice (Harris) P.; B. Applied Sci., U. B.C., 1964; M.Sc., U. Calif., Berkeley, 1965, Ph.D. (Jane Lewis fellow, Sinclair Oil fellow), 1969; m. Julia Ann Veltman, June 18, 1966; children—John Preston, Barbara Brooke. Geophysicist, Newmont Mining Corp. Can., Toronto, 1969-70, sr. geophysicist, Danbury, Conn., 1970-76, staff geologist Newmont Mining Corp., N.Y.C., 1976—. Vice pres. Brookfield Town and Home Assn., 1975; dir. Eliot Pratt Edn. Center, 1976—, v.p., 1977—. Mem. Am. Inst. Mining Engrs., Soc. Exploration Geophysicists, IEEE, Sigma Xi. Home: 8 White Pine Dr Brookfield Center CT 06805 Office: 300 Park Ave New York City NY 10022

PARSI, EDGARDO J., chem. engr.; b. Ponce, P.R., Oct. 19, 1928; s. Julio Esteban and Rosa Maria (Arce) P.; B.S. in Chem. Engring., Mass. Inst. Tech., 1950, Sc.D., 1960; m. Catherine C. Cahill, Apr. 16, 1966; children—Carolyn, Robert, Stephen. Chem. Engr., IONICS Inc., Watertown, Mass., 1950-60, chief product devel., 1960-69, dir. research, 1969—. Mem. Mass. Research Mgrs. Assn. (bd. govs.), Boston Research Dirs. Club, Sigma Xi. Holder 11 patents in fields membrane and electro-chem. tech.; contbr. several articles to profl. jours. and encys. Home: 21 Justin St Lexington MA 02173 Office: 65 Grove St Watertown MA 02172

PARSONS, DONALD SPENCER, chem. engr.; b. Westfield, N.J., May 31, 1930; s. Guy Cook and Edith Georgina (Miller) P.; B.S. in Chem. Engring., Bucknell U., 1951, M.S., 1971; m. Patricia Ann Wiley, Sept. 20, 1952; children—Daniel Guy, Edith Jane, Lucy Elaine. Product engr. chem. and metall. div. GTE Sylvania, Towanda, Pa., 1951-55, engr. semi-conductors, 1958-62, sr. engr. metals research, 1962-69, sr. engr. computers-applied math., 1969-70, devel. engr. hard materials, 1970-73, head phys. testing lab., 1973—; cons. powder particle size and distbn., analysis and interpretation. Committeeman, Boy Scouts Am., 1970-78, Explorer post committeeman, 1970-71. Served with Ordnance Corps, AUS, 1955-58. Mem. Am. Inst. Chem. Engrs. (bd. dirs. Central Pa. sect. 1962—, nat. admissions com. 1978—), AAAS, Am. Powder Metallurgy Inst. (chmn. N.Y.-Pa. sect. 1967-68), Fine Particle Soc., Bucknell Engring. Alumni Assn. (bd. dirs. 1973—), Am. Mus. Natural History (asso.), Alpha Chi Sigma, Phi Mu Alpha, Sigma Phi Epsilon. Republican. Methodist. Club: Lions (pres. Towanda 1969-70, zone chmn. 1970-71). Patentee in field. Home: RFD 5 Box 295A Towanda PA 18848 Office: GTE Sylvania Co Hawes St Towanda PA 18848

PARSONS, GERALD JAMES, librarian; b. Syracuse, N.Y., June 30, 1924; s. George and Valeria Ann (Wilson) P.; A.B., Syracuse U., 1949, M.S. in L.S., 1950. Asst., local history div. Rochester (N.Y.) Pub. Library, 1950-53, head, edn. and religion div., 1953-58; head local history and genealogy dept. Onondaga County Pub. Library, Syracuse, 1958—. Served with U.S. Army, 1943-46. Fellow Am. Soc. Genealogists; mem. N.Y. Library Assn., Pi Gamma Mu, Beta Phi Mu. Republican. Methodist. Contbg. editor, The American Genealogist, 1952—. Contbr. articles to profl. jours. Home: 224 Arnold Ave Syracuse NY 13210 Office: 335 Montgomery St Syracuse NY 13202

PARTEE, WOODIE AUGUSTUS, JR., banker, lawyer; b. Washington, Ga., Oct. 3, 1921; s. Woddie Augustus and Edna (Chafin) P.; A.B., U. Ga., 1943; postgrad. Fletcher Sch. Law and Diplomacy, 1949-50; J.D., George Washington U., 1962; LL.M. in Taxation, Georgetown U., 1966. With Riggs Nat. Bank, Washington, 1951—, v.p. cridit, 1970—; law clk. to Judge Marvin Jones U.S. Ct. Claims, 1962-63; admitted to D.C. bar, 1963. Served with Transp. Corps, U.S. Army, 1945-49. Mem. Am., Fed. bar assns., Bar Assn. D.C., Robert Morris Assos., Order of Coif, Blue Key, Sphinx, Phi Beta Kappa, Phi Kappa Phi, Omicron Delta Kappa, Phi Eta Sigma, Phi Delta Phi, Sigma Chi. Club: Nat. Lawyers. Home: 2480 16th St NW Washington DC 20009 Office: 1503 Pennsylvania Ave NW Washington DC 20005

PARTIN, JAMES JENNINGS, transp. co. exec.; b. Paris, Ark., Oct. 26, 1938; s. Jay Virnie and Laura Mae (Jones) P.; B.A., Ark. Poly. Coll., 1960; B.D., So. Bapt. Theol. Sem., 1965; A.M., Ind. U., 1966, Ph.D., 1967; m. Patricia Ann Dargie, July 22, 1972. Dir. staff devel. and community edn. Ft. Wayne (Ind.) State Hosp., 1967-69; mgr. tng. and orgn. devel. RCA Astro-Electronics div., 1969-71; mgr. orgn. and mgmt. devel. Zenith Radio Corp., 1971-73; dir. human resources Intercraft Industries Corp., 1973-74; dir. orgn. and mgmt. devel. IU Internat. Mgmt. Corp., Phila., 1974—. Fellow Internat. Soc. Orgn. Devel.; mem. Internat. Registry Orgn. Devel. Profls., Orgn. Devel. Network, Phila. Orgn. Devel. Network, Human Resource Planning Soc. Author, editor in field. Address: 110 Westbury Ct Marlton NJ 08053

PARTNOY, RONALD ALLEN, lawyer; b. Norwalk, Conn., Dec. 23, 1933; s. Maurice and Ethel Marguerite (Roselle) P.; B.A., Yale U., 1956; LL.B., Harvard U., 1961; LL.M., Boston U., 1965; m. Diane Catherine Keenan, Sept. 18, 1965. Admitted to Mass. bar, 1962, Conn. bar, 1966; atty. Liberty Mut. Ins. Co., Boston, 1961-65; asso. counsel Remington Arms Co., Bridgeport, Conn., 1965-70, gen. counsel, 1970—. Served with U.S. Navy, 1956-58, to capt. USNR, 1956—. Mem. Sporting Arms and Ammunition Mfrs. Inst. (chmn. legis. and legal affairs com. 1971—), Am., Conn., Bridgeport bar assns., Westchester-Fairfield Corp. Counsel Assn., Am. Judicature Soc., U.S. Navy, League (pres. Bridgeport council 1975-77, nat. dir., Conn. pres. 1977—). Clubs: Chancery, Harvard Club Boston, Yale Club N.Y.C. Home: 135 Parkwood Rd Fairfield CT 06430 Office: 939 Barnum Ave Bridgeport CT 06602

PASCALL, ROSS WILLIAM, investment co. exec.; b. Orange, N.J., Mar. 22, 1945; s. Ross Mandaville and Viola Ann (Schroeder) P.; B.S. in Bus. Adminstrn., Widner Coll., 1967. Pres. RWP Assos., Inc., West Caldwell, N.J., 1973-75; pres. Austin-Daley Ltd., Ridgefield Park, N.J., 1975—; v.p., dir. Unitron Industries, Inc.; dir. N.Y. Petro-Min Corp. Continental Dynamics Inc., Wesco Equities Inc., Dathar Acoustics Inc., Consol. Capitol Corp.; dir., cons. Central Corporate Reports Services Inc. Served to 1st lt. AUS, 1968-70. Decorated Bronze Star medal, Purple Heart, South Vietnamese Honor medal; Knight of Malta; knight comdr., Order of St. John. Club: President's of Widner Coll. (Chester, Pa.). Home: Suite 2009 380 Mountain Rd Union City NJ 07087 Office: POB 296 Ridgefield Park NJ 07660

PASCARELLI, EMIL FRANCIS, physician, health care adminstr.; b. N.Y.C., July 19, 1930; s. Carlo Maria and Anna Carmela (Di Milta) P.; B.A., Columbia, 1952; M.D., U. Pavia, Italy, 1958; m. Dolores Lorraine Klein, Jan. 12, 1962; children—Claudia, Eric. Intern, Roosevelt Hosp., N.Y.C., 1958-59, resident in medicine, 1959-60, 61-63, in pathology, 1960-61; practice medicine specializing in internal medicine, N.Y.C., 1963-68; dir. community health dept. ambulatory care Roosevelt Hosp., N.Y.C., 1968-74; chief dept. ambulatory care Beekman Downtown Hosp., N.Y.C., 1974—, also attending physician dept. medicine; adj. clin. prof. Sch. Pub. Health, N.Y. Hosp.-Cornell Med. Center; asso. sch. pub. health Columbia Coll. Physicians and Surgeons; vis. cons. Roosevelt Hosp. Diplomate Am. Bd. Family Practice. Mem. AMA, N.Y. State, N.Y. County med. socs., Am. Pub. Health Assn., Pub. Health Assn. N.Y.C., Scientists Inst. Pub. Info., Gerontol. Soc., Am. Geriatric Soc., Vis. Nurse Service N.Y. (advisory com.). Contbr. articles in field to profl. jours.; developer programs for emergency care and treatment of drug dependence. Office: 170 William St New York City NY 10014

PASHKE, GREGORY FRANCIS, accountant; b. North Tonawanda, N.Y., Jan. 26, 1948; s. Raymond LeRoy and Edna Margaret (Kodosky) P.; B.S., Gannon Coll., 1969; M.B.A., U. Pitts., 1970; m. Janet Fromknecht, Aug. 23, 1969; children—Kimberly, Kristen. Sr. accountant Ernst & Ernst, Pitts., 1970-73; v.p. finance Keystone Asros. Corp., Pitts., 1973-74; mng. partner Fargo-Dowling Pashke & Twargowski, C.P.A.'s, Erie, Pa., 1974—. C.P.A.; certificate in mgmt. accounting. Mem. Nat. Assn. Accountants (dir. Erie chpt. 1977-78), Soc. for Advancement Mgmt. (charter pres. Erie chpt.), Am. Mgmt. Assn., Inst. Mgmt. Accounting, Am., Pa. insts. C.P.A.'s. Clubs: Sertoma Service (dir. Erie 1975-77), Erie Maennerchor, Univ. of Erie. Home: 4636 Budd Dr Erie PA 16506 Office: 1306 Baldwin Bldg Erie PA 16501

PASKUS, JOHN MARTIN, educator; b. Long Branch, N.J., July 25, 1946; s. Lindley Garrison and Gertrude W. (Weinheimer) P.; B.A., U. Pitts., 1968; M.A., U. Mass., 1971, Ph.D. (Nat. Endowment Humanities grantee), 1973; m. Kathleen Snyder, Dec. 26, 1968; 1 dau., Laura Christine. Instr. dept. English, U. Mass., Amherst, 1969-72; asst. prof. English, career opportunity program N.Y. U., 1972; Fulbright lectr. English, Yale, 1973; asst. prof. dept. English, Simon's Rock Coll., Great Barrington, Mass., 1973—; cons. Nat. Endowment Humanities. Recipient Fulbright-Hays research award, 1973; Woodrow Wilson fellow, 1968-71. Mem. Modern Lang. Assn. Am., Milton Soc., Melville Soc., NE Modern Lang. Assn., Phi Beta Kappa, Phi Kappa Phi. Author: Not Less But More Heroic: Milton's Christian and Classical World, 1977; editor: Massachusetts Studies in English, 1971-72. Home and office: Simons Rock Coll Great Barrington MA 01230

PASQUARELLI, JOSEPH JEROME, engring. and constrn. co. exec.; b. N.Y.C., Mar. 5, 1927; s. Joseph and Helen (Casabona) P.; B.C.E. cum laude, Manhattan Coll., 1949; m. JoAnne Brienza, June 20, 1964; children—Ronald, Richard, June, Joy. Engr., Madigan-Hyland, N.Y.C. and Burns & Roe Inc., N.Y.C., 1949-56; sr. engr., asst. to exec. dir. Office of Sch. Bldgs., N.Y.C. Bd. Edn., 1956-67; dir. design and constrn. mgmt. City U. N.Y., 1967-72; dir. constrn. mgmt. Morse/Diesel Inc., N.Y.C., 1972-76; dir. constrn. Burns & Roe Indsl. Services Corp., Paramus, N.J., 1976—; instr. Mechs. Inst., N.Y.C. Community Coll. Applied Arts, Sci., 1955-58. Chmn. United Fund R. for Morse/Diesel Inc., 1973-75; mem. Cardinal's Com. of Laity for Roman Catholic Charities of N.Y.C., 1967-77; mem. North Caldwell (N.J.) Skating Pond Com. Served with U.S. Army, 1945-46. Licensed profl. engr., N.Y. Fellow ASCE; mem. N.Y. Bldg. Congress (chmn. legis. com.), Nat. Soc. Profl. Engrs., Soc. Am. Mil. Engrs., Municipal Engrs., Am. Arbitration Assn. (panel of arbitrators), Chi Epsilon. Contbr. articles to profl. jours. Home: 38 Oak Pl North Caldwell NJ 07006 Office: 283 Route 17 S Paramus NJ 07652

PASQUARIELLO, PETER JOSEPH, chemist, educator; b. Paterson, N.J., Mar. 18, 1929; s. Cosmo and Lena P.; B.S., Seton Hall U., 1952; M.A., Tchrs. Coll. Columbia U., 1956; m. Dolores Vermeulen, June 4, 1953; children—Frank, Peter, Paula, David, Eric. Tchr. chemistry Eastside High Sch., Paterson, N.J., 1956-69, Lakewood (N.J.) High Sch., 1969—; adj. instr. chemistry Ocean County Coll., Toms River, N.J., 1975—; NSF chemistry grantee Kenyon Coll., Gambier, Ohio, 1962—. Mem. Am. Chem. Soc. (Tchr. of Month award 1964), NEA, N.J. Ednl. Assn. Home: 508 Kingsley Ct Toms River NJ 08753 Office: Lakewood High School Science Dept Lakewood NJ 08701

PASQUIER, ARTHUR LOUIS, glass co. exec.; b. Fleurus, Belgium, Sept. 6, 1893; s. Achille August and Marie Celine (Brousmiche) P.; civil mining engr. Ecole Poly., 1920; m. Jeanne de Rasse, June 21, 1922; 1 dau., Marie Jeanne (Mrs. Robert Wallace Miller). Came to U.S., 1933, naturalized, 1943. With Franklin Glass Co., Butler, Pa., 1933—, now pres.; dir. Butler Savs. & Trust Co. Decorated knight of Crown, knight Order of Leopold, officer Order of Leopold II (Belgium). Mem. Royal Soc. Engrs. Clubs: Duquesne, University (Pitts.); Country (Butler). Home: 427 N Main St Butler PA 16001 Office: PO Box 150 Butler PA 16001

PASS, CAROLYN JOAN, dermatologist; b. Balt., May 14, 1941; d. Isidore Earl and Rhea (Koplowitz) Pass; B.S., U. Md., 1962, M.D., 1966; m. Richard Malcolm Susel, June 23, 1963; children—Steven, Gary. Rotating intern USPHS Hosp., Balt., 1966-67; med. resident St. Agnes Hosp., Balt., 1967-68; dermatology resident and fellow U. Md. Sch. Medicine Hosps., 1968-71; pvt. practice specializing in dermatology, Balt. and Ellicott City, Md., 1971—; mem. staff Howard County Gen. Hosp., Columbia, Md., James Lawrence Kernan, St. Agnes, South Baltimore Gen., Lutheran Gen. and Bon Secours hosps.; vol. dermatology clinics U. Md., St. Agnes hosps.; asst. clin. prof. dermatology U. Md. Sch. Medicine, 1978—; mem. exec. com. adv. bd. Nat. Program in Dermatology, 1975. Diplomate Am. Bd. Dermatology. Mem. AMA, Med. and Chirurgical Faculty Md., Balt. City Med. Soc. (del. 1974), Am. Women's Med. Assn., Am. Acad. Dermatology (award exhibit 1970), Soc. Investigative Dermatology, Md. Dermatology Soc. (sec.-treas. 1974-76, pres. 1976—), Soc. Contemporary Medicine and Surgery. Jewish. Clubs: Suburban Country (Balt.); Country Garden. Gourmet. Home: Timberlane 8410 Park Hts Ave Extension Pikesville MD 21208 Office: St Agnes Med Center Suite 301 3455 Wilkens Ave Baltimore MD 21229

PASSARELLI, FRANK ANDREW, ins. agt.; b. Paterson, N.J., Apr. 6, 1941; s. Albert Henry and Madeline Mary (Tiscione) P.; student Wake Forest U., 1958-60; B.S. in Accounting, Fairleigh Dickinson U., 1965. Sr. accountant, Peat, Marwick, Mitchell & Co., N.Y.C., 1965-70, sr. cons., Washington, 1970-72; fin. cons. Nat. Endowment for Arts and Humanities, Washington 1972, Am. Standard Co., Pitts., 1973; controller, v.p. finance MBS, Washington, 1973-74; agt. N.Y. Life Ins. Co., Washington, 1974—. Cons. Bishop Ireton High Sch., Alexandria, Va.; trustee D.C. chpt. Cystic Fibrosis Found., 1975—; coordinator Washington Met. Area Food Stamp Program; 8th dist. financial coordinator various polit. campaigns, Alexandria; coordinator speakers bur. Boy Scouts/Goodwill Industries Clothing Drive, 1975-76; state program dir. Hugh O'Brien Found., 1977-78. Served with Army N.G., 1965-73. Recipient Service award Cystic Fibrosis Found., 1976, 77, 78. Mem. Nat. Assn. Life Underwriters, U.S. Jaycees, D.C. Life Underwriters Assn., Va. Jaycees (State Key Man award 1976, life mem.; internat. senator 1978), Annandale Jaycees, Order Sons Italy in Am. Democrat. Roman Catholic. Club: Bishop Ireton Boosters (Alexandria). Editor New Dominion mag. Va. Jaycees, 1977. Home: 4701 Kenmore Ave Alexandria VA 22304 Office: 600 New Hampshire Ave NW Washington DC 20036

PASSERI, ANDREW JOSEPH, hosp. adminstr.; b. Revere, Mass., Apr. 1, 1938; s. Andrew and Mary (Riccio) P.; B.S., Mass. Coll. Pharmacy, 1960; M.B.A., Wagner Coll., 1970; m. Rosanne Marie La Mendella, June 27, 1964; children—Andrew Joseph III, Christine M., Jonathan J. Commd. ensign USPHS, 1960, advanced through grades to capt., 1976; asso. dir. hosp. services USPHS Hosp., Staten Island, N.Y., 1976—. Mem. Am. Coll. Hosp. Adminstrs., Am. Hosp. Assn., Commd. Officers Assn. Office: USPHS Hospital Bay St and Vanderbilt Ave Staten Island NY 10304

PASSOJA, DANN EINAR, research scientist; b. Chgo., Jan. 28, 1941; s. Einar A. and Leon G. (Van Schuck) P.; B.S., Purdue U., 1963; Ph.D., Reselaer Poly. Inst., 1968; postgrad. U. Manchester (Eng.), 1968-69; m. Margaret Lewin, Dec. 6, 1963; 1 son, Erick Allen. Metall. trainee Gleason Works, Rochester, N.Y., 1964; metall. cons. Fusion Lab., Chicopee, Mass., 1964-68; v.p. dir. research Ebtec Corp., Agawam, Mass., 1969-70; research scientist Kennecott Copper Co., Cleve., 1970-71, Union Carbide Corp., Tarrytown (N.Y.) Tech. Center, 1971—. Allegheny Ludlum fellow, 1967, Reynolds Aluminum fellow, 1969. Mem. Am. Inst. Mining and Metall. Engrs., ASTM (chmn. com.), Alpha Sigma Mu. Contbr. numerous publs. to profl. jours.

PASSOW, MICHAEL JOEL, educator; b. Buffalo, May 6, 1948; s. Aaron Harry and Shirley (Siegel) P.; diploma Horace Mann Sch., 1966; B.A., Columbia, 1970, M.A. in Teaching, 1971, Ed.D., 1974; m. Nancy Reinish, June 7, 1970; 1 dau., Kate Elizabeth. Tchr. New Lincoln Sch., N.Y.C., 1970-72; instr. earth scis. Pace Coll., N.Y.C., 1971-72; instr. earth scis. Fairleigh Dickinson U., Rutherford, N.J., 1971-77; tchr. Horace Mann Sch., 1976—. Mem. Geol. Soc. Am., Am. Meteorol. Soc., Nat. Assn. Geology Tchrs., N.J. Acad. Sci., Flat Rock Brook Nature Assn. (dir. 1974-75, 77—). Jewish. Contbr. articles to profl. jours. Home: 296 Central Ave Englewood NJ 07631 Office: 231 W 246th St Bronx NY 10471

PASSWATER, RICHARD ALBERT, biochemist; b. Wilmington, Del., Oct. 13, 1937; s. Stanley Leroy and Mabel Rosetta (King) P.; B.S., U. Del., 1959; Ph.D., Bernadean U., 1976; m. Barbara Sarah Gayhart, June 2, 1964; children—Richard Alan, Michael Eric. Supr. instrumental analysis lab. Allied Chem. Corp., Marcus Hook, Pa., 1959-64; tech. services rep. F & M Sci. Corp., Avondale, Pa., 1965; dir. applications lab. Am. Instrument Co., Silver Spring, Md., 1965-77; dir. Am. Gen. Enterprises, Minn. Bd. dirs. Sci. Documentation Center, Dunfermline, England, Union U. Fellow Am. Acad. Preventive Medicine; mem. Am. Chem. Soc., Gerontology Soc., Am. Geriatric Soc., Am. Aging Assn., Soc. Applied Spectroscopy, ASTM, Captial Chem. Soc., Pi Kappa Alpha. Author: Guide to Fluorescence Literature, vol. 1, 1967, vol. 2, 1970, vol. 3, 1974; Supernutrition: Megavitamin Revolution, 1975, paperback edit., 1976; Cancer: Nutritional Therapies, 1978; Super Calorie and Carbohydrate Counter, 1978; Supernutrition for Healthy Hearts, 1977, paperback, 1978; The Perfect No-Flab Diet, 1979. Editor Fluorescence News, 1966-77; editorial bd. Nutritional Perspectives, 1978—. Patentee in field. Office: 529 Southview Ave Silver Spring MD 20904

PASTERNAC, ANDRÉ, cardiologist, educator; b. Toulouse, France, July 22, 1937; s. Jacques and Régine (Modry) P.; came to Can., 1971, naturalized, 1978; adv. math. Lycée Henri IV, Paris, 1956; B.A. in Polit. Sci., Toulouse U., 1963, M.D., Med. Sch., 1968. Intern, Toulouse Univ. Hosp., 1962-63, resident, 1963-64, 66-68; resident Edouard-Herriot Hosp., Lyon, France, 1965-66; Fulbright scholar in cardiology Harvard U., 1968-71; research fellow Peter Bent Brigham Hosp., Boston, 1968-69; Milton fellow Children's Hosp., Boston, 1969-71; fellow in cardiology Toronto (Ont., Can.) U., 1971-72; staff cardiologist Montreal (Que., Can.) Heart Inst., 1972—; asst. prof. medicine U. Montreal, 1972-78, clin. asso. prof., 1978—; vis. asso. prof. McGill U., Montreal, 1975-76; vis. lectr. U. Liège (Belgium), 1977, U. Madrid, 1977, U. Warsaw, 1979. Am. Field Service grantee, Oreg., 1954-55; specialist in cardiology, Paris, Montreal. Mem. French Cardiac Soc., Canadian Cardiovascular Soc., Am. Coll. Cardiology, Am. Heart Assn., Internat. Soc. Heart Research, Am. Fedn. Clin. Research. Research in ventricular wall motion during myocardial ischemia, stress-related myocardial dysfunction. Home: 3465 Redpath St Montreal PQ H3G 2G8 Canada Office: Montreal Heart Inst 5000 Belanger E Montreal PQ H1T 1C8 Canada

PASTERNAK, EUGENIA, instn. adminstr.; b. Ukraina, Jan. 8, 1919; d. Mychail and Maria (Okonska) Nowakiwsky; student philosophy, Goethe U., Germany, 1945-47; certificate Shaw Bus. Coll., Toronto, Ont., Can., 1956; diploma McMaster U., 1971; m. Eugene Pasternak, July 19, 1944. Came to Can., 1948, naturalized, 1955. Tchr., prin. jr. coll., Galitzia, Ukraina, 1939-42; exec. relief coms., also A.R.C. during and after World War II; exec. Multoblitz Photog., Toronto, 1955-57; accountant Legal Humenick and Romanko, Toronto, 1958-63; pres. Ukrainian Home for Aged, Toronto, 1961-73; dir., adminstr. Ivan Franko Homes, Toronto, 1964—. Mem. Ont. Inter Group Com.; commr. for taking affidavits Province Ont. Recipient medal and scroll Ukrainian Canadian Com., 1962, medal and scroll Ukrainian Free Cossacks, 1978. Fellow Internat. Biog. Assn. (life). Club: Ukrainian

Pensioner's (pres. 1975). Address: 767 Royal York Rd Toronto ON M8Y 2T3 Canada

PASTUSHAK, ROMAN JOSEPH, psychologist; b. Znaim, Germany, Mar. 16, 1945; s. Constantine and Michalina P.; came to U.S., 1951, naturalized, 1960; B.A. (class of 1920 scholar 1966), Pa. State U., 1967, M.Ed. (Vocat. Rehab. Adminstrn. trainee 1968-69), 1969; Ph.D. (fellow), Temple U., 1978; m. Lida L. Kwashynsky, July 6, 1974. Placement mgr., rehab. counselor Goodwill Industries, Phila., 1969-70; rehab. counselor West Phila. Community Mental Health Consortium, Phila., 1972-73; psychology intern Friends Hosp., Phila., 1975-76; dir. psychol. services Northwestern Inst. Psychiatry, Fort Washington, Pa., 1977—, mem. adj. profl. staff, 1978—; adj. asst. prof. counseling psychology Temple U., 1978—. Served with U.S. Army, 1970-72; Vietnam. Decorated Bronze Star; certified rehab. counselor; lic. psychologist, Pa. Mem. Am. Psychol. Assn., Am. Personnel and Guidance Assn., Nat. Rehab. Counseling Assn., Pa. Psychol. Assn., Phila. Soc. Clin. Psychologists, Am. Assn. Marriage and Family Therapy. Home: 67 Cynthia Dr Richboro PA 18954 Office: 450 Bethlehem Pike Fort Washington PA 19034

PATCH, VERNON DUANE, psychiatrist, educator; b. Wayzata, Minn., May 29, 1929; s. Edgar Mansfield and Chloe (Whittemore) P.; B.A. cum laude, Harvard, 1951, M.D., 1958; m. Ann Sutherland Ramsay, 1977; children by previous marriage—Carol, Cynthia, Jonathon. Intern, Johns Hopkins Hosp., Balt., 1958-59; resident Mass. Mental Health Center, 1959-62; practice medicine specializing in psychiatry, Boston City Hosp., 1962—; instr. psychiatry Harvard Med. Sch., 1962-68, asst. prof., 1968-72, asso. prof., 1972—; founder Coll. Mental Health Center of Boston, Inc., 1965, clin. dir., 1965—; founder, pres. Drug Abuse Found. of Boston Inc., 1970; dir. Boston Drug Treatment Program, 1970-76; cons. White House Spl. Action Office for Drug Abuse Prevention; mem. Mass. Gov.'s Drug Rehab. Adv. Bd., 1970-73; mem. Boston Mayor's Com. Coordinating Council on Drug Abuse, 1970-74. Served with USN, 1951-54. HEW grantee, 1965; NIMH grantee, 1972. Fellow Am. Psychiat. Assn. (Silver Achievement award 1969); mem. Mass. Med. Soc., Am. Coll. Health Assn. Clubs: Harvard, Engrs. (Boston). Author: (with P. Solomon) Handbook of Psychiatry, 1968. Contbr. articles to profl. jours. Editor: Handbook of Psychiatry, 1974 (transls. into 5 langs.). Home: 318 Commonwealth Ave Boston MA 02115 Office: 4360 Prudential Center Boston MA 02199

PATCHETT, ISABEL STEDMAN (MRS. EDWARD PATCHETT), statistician; b. Hartford, Conn., July 2, 1924; d. Lewis H. and Margaret L. (Wilson) Stedman; B.S. in Indsl. Mgmt., U. Conn., 1951; M.B.A. in Mktg., U. Hartford, 1965; m. Edward Patchett, June 14, 1947; 1 son, Lewis. Supr. group dept. Travelers Ins. Co., Hartford, 1952-65; mktg. research analyst Royal Typewriter Co., Hartford, 1965-68; econ. statistician Scovill Mfg. Co., Waterbury, Conn., 1968-76; v.p. Profl. Mgmt. Inst., Hartford, 1976—. Regional mktg. dir. Quest Adventures, Inc. retail travel agy., Atlanta, 1972-73. Campaign mgr. Republican candidate for congress, Farmington, Conn., 1961; mem. Rep. Town Com., Farmington, 1962-64; mem. alumni council U. Hartford, 1978—. Mem. U. Conn. Alumni Assn. (treas., 1960-63), U. Hartford Alumni Assn., Am. Marketing Assn. (treas., 1970-71), League Women Voters. Episcopalian. Mem. Order Eastern Star. Home: 146 W Avon Rd Unionville CT 06085 Office: 630 Oakwood Ave West Hartford CT 06110

PATEL, ASHOK ZAVERBHAI, mech. engr., engring. mgr.; b. Palitana, Gujarat, India, Feb. 15, 1940; s. Zaverbhai H. and Maniben L. (Lakhani) P.; came to U.S., 1963, naturalized, 1972; B.E. Mech. Engring., S.V. U. (India), 1962; M.S. in Mech. Engring., U. Mo., 1964; m. Parul S. Patel, Jan. 17, 1971; children—Nealesh, Rupesh. Mech. engr. Atlantic Cement Co., Revena, N.Y., 1964-66; sr. design engr. Hamilton Standard, Windsor Locks, Conn., 1967-69; successively devel. engr., chief devel. engr., engring. mgr. Torin Corp., Torrington, Conn., 1969—. Registered profl. engr., Conn. Mem. ASME, Am. Soc. Heating, Refrigerating and Air Conditioning Engrs., Nat., Conn. socs. profl. engrs. Patentee on propeller fan. Home: 24 Francis St Avon CT 06001 Office: Torin Corp Kennedy Dr Torrington CT 06790

PATEL, MAHESH SOMABHAI, metallurgist; b. Bhadran, Gujarat State, India, Dec. 31, 1939; s. Somabhai C. and Maniben (Patel) P.; came to U.S., 1960, naturalized, 1977; B.S., Sardar Vallabhbhai U., Anand, India, 1960; B.S., Mo. Sch. Mines, 1963; M.S., N.Y. U., 1970: m. Yadunanda G. Amin, May 7, 1967; children—Shveta, Manish. Research metallurgist Alloy Inc., Melville, N.Y., 1963-65; research engr. Arwood Corp., Bklyn., 1965-67; engr. Metco, Inc., Westbury, N.Y., 1967-70; mgr. metall. powder devel. Eutectic Corp., Flushing, N.Y., 1970—. Mem. Am. Soc. Metals, Am. Powder Metallurgy Inst., Am. Welding Soc. Patentee in field of flame spray materials, Coating Materials. Home: 17 Oak Ridge Ln Albertson NY 11507 Office: Eutectic Corp 40-40 172d St Flushing NY 11358

PATEL, PINAKIN SHANABHAI, chem. engr.; b. India, Dec. 12, 1952; s. Shanabhai G. and Zaverben S. Patel; came to U.S., 1975; B.S. in Chem. Engring., M.S. U., India, 1975; M.S. (research fellow Dept. Energy 1975-77), Ill. Inst. Tech., 1977. Cons. chem. engring., New Field, India, 1973-75; research asst. petroleum oil recovery Group Ill. Inst. Tech., 1975-76; research asso. energy conversion systems analysis Inst. Gas Tech., Chgo., 1976-77; project engr. fuel cells Energy Research Corp., Danbury, Conn., 1977—. Mem. fund raising com. S.P. Trust, 1976—. Served with Indian Air Force, 1969-71. Nat. Merit scholar, 1969-75. Mem. Am. Inst. Chem. Engrs., Electrochem. Soc. Author reports. Home: 122 Hammersmith Apts Danbury CT 06810 Office: 3 Great Pasture Rd Danbury CT 06810

PATERSON, ROBERT WILLIAM, fluid dynamicist; b. Newark, Jan. 19, 1939; s. Archie and Lila Mae (Stoeckel) P.; B.S. in Engring., Princeton U., 1960; M.A. (NSF fellow, Watson Grad. fellow), Harvard U., 1965, Ph.D., 1969; m. Joyce Mae Pero, Aug. 12, 1967; 1 son, Robert William. Nuclear power engr. AEC, Washington, 1960-64; research asst. Harvard U., Cambridge, Mass., 1964-69; research engr. United Technologies Research Center, East Hartford, Conn., 1969-73, supr. aeroacoustics and exptl. gas dynamics group, 1973—. Served to lt. USN, 1960-64. Mem. Am. Inst. Aeronautics and Astronautics, Phi Beta Kappa, Sigma Xi. Contbr. articles to tech. jours. Home: 4 Pinecrest Dr Simsbury CT 06070

PATIL, MADHUKAR YASHWANTRAO, research scientist; b. Jalgaon, India, Feb. 11, 1942; s. Yashwantrao Govind and Anusaya Deoram (Mahajan) P.; B.Sc. with honors U. Poona (India), 1962; B.Pharmacy, U. Nagpur (India), 1965; M.S., Phila. Coll. Pharmacy and Sci., 1967; m. Sushila Krishnarao Rane, Dec. 12, 1969; children—Nayana, Reshama. Came to U.S., 1965. Research pharmacist Cooper Labs. Inc., Wayne, N.J., 1967-71; research phamacist McNeil Labs. Inc., Fort Washington, Pa., 1971—. Mem. Acad. Pharm. Scis., Am. Pharm. Assn., Lehigh Valley Indian Assn., English Speaking Union. Contbr. research publ. to Jour. Pharm. Scis. Home: 1908 Muhlenberg Dr Lansdale PA 19446 Office: McNeil Labs Inc Camp Hill Rd Fort Washington PA 19034

PATRICK, DOUGLAS ARTHUR, philatelist, journalist; b. Hamilton, Ont., Can., Mar. 17, 1905; s. Arthur and Emma Alberta (Yaeger) P.; student comml. art Hamilton Tech. Art Sch., 1926; m. Mary Ellen Powell, Aug. 15, 1929; 1 son, Robert John. With retail drug firms, 1924-29, F.W. Woolworth Co., St. Catharines and Hamilton, 1929-37; with Charters Pub., newspapers, Toronto, Ont., 1938-41, Gen. Foods, Toronto, 1941-46; free-lance advt., 1946-52; advt. salesman Globe & Mail newspaper, Toronto, 1952-70, stamp columnist, 1952—; host Canadian Broadcasting Corp. Stamp Club, radio network show, 1950-71; curator philately Royal Ont. Mus., Toronto, 1963-75. Recipient Bronze medal Polish Internat. Stamp Show, 1973, Founder's medal Canadian Assn. Israel Phiately, 1973. Fellow Royal Philatelic Soc London, Royal Philatelic Soc. Canada; mem. Am. Philatelic Soc. (Writers Hall of Fame 1976), Soc. Israel Philatelists. Am. Philatelic Congress (fgn. mem., council), Author books including: Postage Stamps-Postal History of the United Nations, 1955; International Guide to Stamps and Stamp Collecting, 1962; Canada's Postage Stamps, 1964; Stamp Collectors' Dictionary, 1972; Stamp Bug, 1978. Contbr. stamp column to various Canadian newspapers. Home: 1616 Applewood Rd Mississauga ON L5E 2M3 Canada Office: Globe & Mail 440 Front St W Toronto ON Canada

PATRINACOS, NICON DEMETRIUS, clergyman; b. Sparta, Greece, Mar. 19, 1911 (came to U.S. 1950; naturalized 1955); s. Demetrius Christy and Angelica (Salvara) P.; student Sch. Theology U. Athens (Greece), 1931-35; B.A., U. Queensland, Australia, 1945, M.A. with 1st class honors in Philosophy, 1947; Ph.D., Oxford (Eng.) U., 1950. Ordained as priest Greek Orthodox Ch., 1936, accorded rank Archimandrite, 1937; head Greek Orthodox communities, So. Queensland, 1937-48; head community, St. Louis, 1950-53; dean Greek Orthodox Sch. Theology, Boston, 1953-55; chmn. dept. Archdiocesan Edn. North and South Am., N.Y.C., 1968—; ecumenical officer Greek Orthodox Ch. in U.S.A., 1975—; tchr. psychology of religion Washington U., St. Louis, 1950-53; tchr. philosophy St. Basil's Inst., Garrison, N.Y., 1961-74. Bd. dirs. Nat. Council Chs. of Christ in U.S.A., 1976—. Author: The Individual and His Orthodox Church, 1970; The Orthodox Liturgy, 1973; The Orthodox Church and Birth Control, 1976. Editor: The Orthodox Observer, 1967-72. Home: 20 Salem Rd White Plains NY 10603 Office: 10 E 79th St New York City NY 10021

PATTEE, ELIZABETH GREENLEAF, ret. architect, landscape architect; b. Quincy, Mass., June 7, 1893; d. William Greenleaf Appleton and Laura (Saltonstall) P.; B.A., Mass. Inst. Tech., 1916. Tchr. Lowthorpe Sch. Landscape Architecture, Groton, Mass., 1918, 23-45; tchr. landscape architecture R.I. Sch. Design, 1945-63, prof., to 1960; pvt. practice architecture, landscape architecture, Boston, 1918-45, East Greenwich, R.I., 1945-60; lectr. to garden clubs, New Eng., N.Y. Fellow Am. Soc. Landscape Architecture; mem. AIA. Democrat. Episcopalian. Contbr. articles to Landscape Architecture. Home: Meadow Lakes Apt 23-08 Hightstown NJ 08520

PATTEN, EDWARD JAMES, congressman; b. Perth Amboy, N.J., Aug. 22, 1905; s. Nathan and Mary (Crowe) P.; B.S. in Edn., Rutgers U., 1928, LL.B., 1926; m. Anna Quigg, Feb. 22, 1936; 1 dau., Catherine Mary. Tchr., Perth Amboy and Elizabeth, N.J., schs., 1927-34; admitted to N.J. bar, 1927; pvt. practice, Perth Amboy, 1927—; sec. of state N.J., 1954-62; mem. 88th-96th congresses from 15th Dist. N.J. Dir., past counsel Woodbridge Nat. Bank (N.J.). Pres., Raritan Bay Area United Fund, 1960—, Perth Amboy Salvation Army, 1934—. Mayor, Perth Amboy, 1934-40; county clk. Middlesex County, 1940-54; mem. N.J. Democratic Com., 1954—; campaign mgr. for Gov. Meyner, 1953, 57. Recipient Outstanding Citizenship award Am. Heritage Found., 1960, Brotherhood award B'nai B'rith, 1958. Mem. Am. Judicature Soc., Nat. Conf. Christians and Jews, Perth Amboy C. of C., NAACP. K.C. (past N.J. advocate), Elk, Eagle, Kiwanian, Moose. Home: 270 Market St Perth Amboy NJ 08861 Office: Rayburn House Office Bldg Washington DC 20515

PATTERSON, CHARLES MEADE, geologist, author; b. Waynesburg, Pa., June 24, 1919; s. Robert Meade and Margaret (Milligan) P.; B.A., Coll. Wooster, 1940; M.A., Columbia, 1942; M.S., Calif. Inst. Tech., 1943; Ph.D., Columbia, 1947; m. Florence Arnelda Leach, June 16, 1943 (div. Jan. 1947); m. 2d, Constance Jacqueline Lawson, June 1947 (annulled 1950); m. 3d, Anna Marie Hibbs, Oct. 26, 1967. Geologist, Gulf Research & Devel. Co., Pitts., 1947-53; antique firearms specialist and staff editor Nat. Rifle Assn. Am., Washington, 1953-57; lime and calcium specialist Bur. Mines, Washington, 1957-63, sci. editor, 1964-67; marine geologist U.S. Naval Oceanographic Office, Washington, 1967—. Hon. curator West Point Mus., 1952-58. Served to capt. USAAF, 1942-46. Fellow Co. of Mil. Historians; mem. Geol. Soc. Am., Pa. Gun Collectors Assn. (pres. 1950-51), Potomac (pres. 1955-57), Md. (pres. 1965-66) arms collectors assns., Sigma Xi. Author: (with Paul F. Kerr) Alteration of Santa Rita, N.M., Copper Mine, 1947; (with J.M. Kalman) A Pictorial History of U.S. Single Shot Martial Pistols, 1957. Sci. staff editor A Dictionary of Mining, Mineral and Related Terms, 1963-67; editor Gun Report, 1959—. Home: PO Box 784 Hyattsville MD 20783 Office: US Naval Oceanographic Office Washington DC 20390

PATTERSON, EDITH JERRY, guidance counselor; b. Doswell, Va., Nov. 18, 1945; d. Joseph Louis and Deanna (Kelly) Jerry. B.S., Va. Union U., 1968; M.Ed. in Guidance and Counseling, Bowie State Coll., 1975; m. Ralph Elwood Patterson, Mar. 17, 1973; children—Ralph Elwood II, Robert Eric. Social adjustment tchr. Stuart Jr. High Sch., Washington, 1968-69; adult edn. tchr. Roosevelt Adult Evening Sch., Washington, 1969-73; tchr. biology Hart Jr. High Sch., Washington, 1969-73; tchr. sci. John Hansen Middle Sch., Waldorf, Md., 1973-74; guidance counselor Charles County Community Coll., La Plata, Md., 1974—; program coordinator Tri-County Career-Coll. Day Fairs. Chmn. task force on edn. Charles County Commn. for Women, 1978—. NSF summer program grantee, 1969, 70, 71, 72; NSF sci. tchrs. grantee, 19—. Mem. Am., Md. personnel and guidance assns., Assn. Non-White Concerns in Personnel and Guidance, Charles County Bus. and Profl. Womens Club, Democrat. Methodist. Home: 2715 Preston Ln Pomfret MD 20675 Office: Box 910 Mitchell Rd La Plata MD 20646

PATTERSON, ELLMORE CLARK, banker; b. Western Springs, Ill., Nov. 29, 1913; s. Ellmore Clark and Harriet Emma (Wales) P.; B.S., U. Chgo., 1935; m. Anne Hyde Choate, Sept. 28, 1940; children—Michael Ellmore, Arthur Choate, Robert Ellmore, David Choate, Thomas Hyde Choate. With J.P. Morgan & Co., Inc., N.Y.C., 1935-39, 39-41, 46-59, v.p., 1951-59; exec. v.p. Morgan Guaranty Trust Co. N.Y. (merger J.P. Morgan and Guaranty Trust Co.), 1959-65, dir., chmn. exec. com., 1967-68, pres., 1969-71, chmn., 1971-77, chmn. exec. com., 1978—; with Morgan Stanley & Co., 1939; dir. Gen. Motors Corp., Can. Life Assurance Co., A.T. & S.F. Ry., COMSAT, Inc., Standard Brands, Inc., J.P. Morgan & Co. Inc., Bethlehem Steel Corp., Schlumberger Ltd. Mem. Presdl. Commn. on Financial Structure and Regulation, 1970-72; bd. mgrs. Meml. Hosp. Cancer and Allied Diseases, N.Y.C.; trustee Alfred P. Sloan Found., Sloan-Kettering Inst. Cancer Center, N.Y.C., U. Chgo., Mass. Inst. Tech. Served from ensign to lt. comdr., USNR, 1941-46. Mem. Council Fgn. Relations, Psi Upsilon. Episcopalian. Clubs: Links (N.Y.C.); Chicago; Bedford (N.Y.) Golf and Tennis; Jupiter Island (Hobe Sound, Fla.); Fishers Island Country; Links Golf; Augusta Nat. Golf. Home: Hook Rd Bedford Village NY 10506 Office: 23 Wall St New York City NY 10015

PATTERSON, JERRY EUGENE, author; b. Fort Worth, May 2, 1931; s. Charles Edward and Lois (Pruitt) P.; B.A., U. Tex., 1952, M.A., 1955; postgrad. Yale, 1955-57, Columbia, 1958-60. Asst. editor Hispanic Am. Hist. Rev., 1954; manuscript. div. librarian Yale U. Library, 1955-57; cataloguer Edward Eberstadt & Sons, N.Y.C., 1958-61; with Parke-Bernet Galleries, N.Y.C., 1962-68, asst. v.p., 1964-65, v.p., 1965-68; U.S. rep. Christie, Manson & Woods, N.Y.C., 1968-71. Cons. Library of Congress, 1964-67. Mem. N.Y. Hist. Soc. (Pintard fellow 1967), bibliog. socs. Am., Eng., Va. Oxford, Cambridge. Republican. Episcopalian. Author: Autographs, a Collectors Guide, 1973; A Collector's Guide to Relics and Memorabilia, 1974; Antiques of Sport, 1975; The City of New York, 1978; mng. editor Artnewsletter, 1975-78. Contbr. to Auction Antiques Ann., 1971; also articles on rare books and manuscripts to Am. and fgn. periodicals. Home: 176 E 77th St New York City NY 10021

PATTERSON, KENNETH FRANCIS, educator; b. Ogdensburg, N.Y., Aug. 6, 1946; s. Wilbert John and Marie (LaVanture) P.; A.A.S., State U. N.Y., Canton, 1968; B.S., State U. N.Y., Plattsburgh, 1971; postgrad. State U. N.Y., Oswego, 1974—; m. Marlene Ann Delduchetto, Aug. 23, 1969; children—Andrew, Jeremy. Tech. asst. State U. N.Y., Canton, 1968-70; tchr. physics Plattsburgh High Sch., 1973-74, Chittenango (N.Y.) High Sch., 1974—; owner, Kenmar Electronics, Chittenango, 1977—. Chmn., Village of Chittenango Planning Bd., 1978—. Served with USNR, 1971-73; now lt. Res. Mem. Am. Assn. Physics Tchrs., Sci. Tchrs. N.Y., N.Y. State United Tchrs., Nat. Sci. Tchrs. Assn., Am. Assn. Sci. Tchrs., Naval Res. Assn., Electronic Technician Dealers. Democrat. Roman Catholic. Clubs: Lions, Jaycees. Home: 510 Valley Dr Chittenango NY 13037 Office: Chittenango High Sch Genesee St Chittenango NY 13037

PATTERSON, M. CLARE, JR., hosp. adminstr.; b. Binghamton, N.Y., Dec. 3, 1934; s. Marion Clare and Mary Alice P.; B.A., John Brown U., 1956, B.S., 1956; children—Lawrence W., David C., Becky L., Charles A., Betsy A. Asst. purchasing agt. Simmons Co., Munster, Ind., 1960-62; purchasing agt. Grant Hosp., Chgo., 1962-64; dir. purchasing Louis A. Weiss Meml. Hosp., Chgo., 1964-66, MacNeal Meml. Hosp., Berwyn, Ill., 1966-70; dir. of stewardship Practical Bible Tng. Sch., Johnson City, N.Y., 1970-74; dir. purchasing Charles S. Wilson Meml. Hosp., Johnson City, 1974—. Dir. CD, Highland, Ind., 1958, 59; v.p. Johnson City Part Time Patrolmen, 1973-75. Fellow Nat. Assn. Hosp. Purchasing Mgmt.; mem. Am. Hosp. Assn., Internat. Materials Mgmt. Soc., Am. Soc. Hosp. Materials Mgmt., Central N.Y. Hosp. Purchasing Agts. Assn. (pres.), Central N.Y. Hosp. Assn. (chmn. com. on group purchasing). Mem. Christian and Missionary Alliance Ch. Club: Rotary (Johnson City). Home: Route 2 Grippen Hill Rd Vestol NY 13760 Office: 33-57 Harrison St Johnson City NY 13790

PATTERSON, POLLY REILLY (MRS. W. RAY PATTERSON), ret. communications co. exec., civic worker; b. Wilkinsburg, Pa.; d. Thomas L. and Margaret (Coughey) Reilly; grad. high sch.; student U. Pitts.; m. W. Ray Patterson, Sept. 2, 1943. With Bell of Pa., Pitts., 1925-71, clk., mgmt. positions, 1935-64, staff asso. pub. relations staff, 1965-71 Asst. treas. Allegheny County Soc. for Crippled Children, 1962-66, v.p., 1966-70; bd. dirs. Jr. Achievement, Inc. of S.W. Pa., 1950-71; bd. dirs. Pa. Soc. Crippled Children and Adults, 1960-68, YWCA, 1964-72; dir. Chatham Village Homes, Inc., 1973-76. Named One of Pitts.'s Ten Outstanding Women, Pitts. Sun Telegraph, 1959, Pitts. Advt. Woman of Year, 1958; recipient Crystal Prism award Am. Advt. Fedn., 1972, 75. Mem. Pitts. Bus. Clubs (dir. 1946—, pres. 1952-53), Pitts. Advt. Club (v.p., sec. 1929-69), Altrusa Internat., Bus. and Profl. Women, Telephone Pioneers Am. Home: 402 Olympia Rd Pittsburgh PA 15211

PATTERSON, ROBERT ALLAN, univ. adminstr.; b. Turtle Creek, Pa., Nov. 5, 1917; s. Robert and L. (Naysmith) P.; B.S. in Commerce, Grove City Coll., 1939; grad. Traffic and Transp. Sch. Pitts., 1942; postgrad. Duquesne U., U. Tenn., Cornell U., U. Wash.; M.B.A., N.Y.U., 1949; m. Nancy Evans, Feb. 5, 1939; 1 dau., Anne St. Clair. With Pa. R.R. Co., Pa., also Ohio, 1935-36, 40-46, Ry. Express, Inc., Pitts., 1939-40, Eastern Air Lines, Inc., N.Y., 1946-50; traffic rep. L.I. R.R. Co., Jamaica, N.Y., 1950-52, gen. passenger agt., 1952-55, mgr. research, 1956-62, sec., treas., 1962-68; v.p. for fin., treas. Pa. State U., 1968-71, sr. v.p., 1971—; dir. Mid-State Bank and Trust Co.; tchr. Investments Grad. Sch. Bus., N.Y.U., 1962-67. Trustee Grove City Coll. Served with USNR, 1944-46. Republican. Mason (Shriner). Club: N.Y. Home: 1640 Cherry Hill Rd State College PA 16801 Office: 208 Old Main St University Park PA 16802

PATTERSON, ROGER THOMAS, mfg. co. exec.; b. Mineola, N.Y., Apr. 18, 1928; s. Joseph Armstrong and Esther Beck (Vroom) P.; student N.Y. State Inst. Applied Arts and Scis. (now Mohawk Coll.), 1947-48; m. Barbara Anne White, Aug. 20, 1949; children—Christopher, Brian, David, Andrew, William. Tech. illustrator Raymond Corp., Greene, N.Y., 1955-59; graphic arts supr. Milford Rivet and Machine Co. (Conn.), 1959-62; advt. mgr. Whitney Blake Co., New Haven, 1962-65; advt. mgr. Internat. Packings Corp., Bristol, N.H., 1965-69; account exec. Davis Advt., Worcester, Mass., 1969-70; advt. and sales promotion mgr. Internat. Packings Corp., Bristol, 1970—, dir. mktg. services, 1973—. Mem. adv. council Bristol Community Center. Mem. Automotive Market Research Council, N.H. Advt. Club (past pres.), Nat. Press Photographers Assn., Automotive Service Industry Assn., Bus. and Profl. Advt. Assn. (bd. dirs.). Republican. Home: 7 Prospect St Bristol NH 03222 Office: Route 104 Bristol NH 03222

PATTERSON, WILLIAM HOWELL, aerospace co. exec.; b. Fort Benton, Mont., Nov. 11, 1918; s. John Hawkins and Nell Margaret (Harris) P.; B.S., Whittier Coll., 1939, M.S., 1941; postgrad. U. Calif. at Los Angeles; m. Alma Frances Schreiber, June 20, 1945; children—Gail, Vaudene, Evelyn, Carolyn, William. Research physicist Gen. Dynamics, San Diego, 1946-51, chief project engr., 1951-55, dep. program gen. mgr., 1955-61, v.p., 1961-65; gen. mgr. research and engring. ops. Gen. Electric Co., Valley Forge, Pa., 1966-73, dir. govt. affairs for energy and def. programs, Washington, 1973—. Served with U.S. Army, 1941-46. Decorated Bronze Star. Mem. Am. Inst. Aeros. and Astronautics, Air Force Assn., Am. Def. Preparedness Assn., Nat. Energy Resources Orgn. Clubs: Capitol Hill, 116, Pisces, Congl. Country. Home: 9720 Brimfield Ct Potomac MD 20854 Office: Suite 1000 777 14th St NW Washington DC 20005

PATTON, ELDA CLAYTON, physician; b. Hartford, Ky.; d. Clayton Lunsford and Lena Rivers (Miller) Patton; B.A., U. Evansville (Ind.), 1942, Hum.D. (hon.), 1971; M.A., Columbia U., 1950; M.D., U. Padua (Italy), 1959; m. Nathaniel Ned Herts. Tchr. pub. schs., Ind., 1930-33, 38-43, N.J., 1950, N.Y., 1953-54; translator, interpreter U.S. Fgn. Service, Buenos Aires, Argentina, 1945-47; intern N.Y. Polyclinic Hosp., N.Y.C., 1959-60; resident Central Islip (N.Y.) State Hosp., 1960-62; sr. psychiatrist Manhattan State Hosp., N.Y.C., 1962-65, asst. to met. unit chief, 1970-72; supervising psychiatrist Lower Manhattan Narcotic After Care Clinic, N.Y.C., 1965-67; practice medicine specializing in psychiatry, N.Y.C., 1961—; mem. staff Gracie Sq. Hosp., N.Y.C.; supervising psychiatrist Bayview Rehab. Center, N.Y.C., 1967-70; psychiatrist in charge Kirby Manhattan State Hosp. Out Patient Clinic, 1972-75; cons. Puerto

Rican Family Inst., 1967—. Mem. drug-abuse sub-com. Pub. Health Com., County N.Y. Med. Soc., 1965—. Diplomate Am. Bd. Neuropsychiatry. Fellow Am. Acad. Psychiatry and Neurology; mem. AMA, Am. Psychiatry Assn., Am. Womens Med. Soc., Womens Med. Soc. N.Y. State. Author: Sarmigivto in the United States, 1976. Home: 37 W 12th St New York City NY 10011 Office: 25 Leroy St New York City NY 10014

PATTON, JAMES STEPHEN, cons. engr.; b. Washington, Pa., Jan. 25, 1942; s. J. Donald and Priscilla Ann (Johnson) P.; B.S., Swarthmore Coll., 1963; M. City Planning, U. Pa., 1966; m. Penelope Schoyer Yeo, June 22, 1968; 1 son, Jonathan Knight. Dir. urban renewal and dir. Pitts. office Kendree & Shepherd, Phila. and Pitts., 1969-72; v.p. to pres. Engelhardt-Power & Assos., Cons. Engrs., Washington, Pa., 1972—; chmn., owner Walnut Center for Design, Ltd.; dir. R.G. Johnson Co., Walnut Ridge, Inc. Engr., City of Washington, 1973-76. Served to lt. C.E.C., USNR, 1966-69. Registered profl. engr., Pa., Md. Mem. Am. Inst. Planners, ASCE, Nat. Soc. Profl. Engrs. Presbyterian. Clubs: University, Gibson Island, Gibson Island Yacht Squadron. Home: 10 Midway Rd Pittsburgh PA 15216 Office: 125 S College St PO Box 8 Washington PA 15301

PATTON, JOHN MICHAEL, lawyer; b. Washington, Sept. 3, 1947; s. Earl Richard and Frances Anne (Basar) P.; B.A. in History, George Washington U., 1969, J.D., 1974. Naval historian U.S. Navy Dept., Washington, 1969-72; admitted to D.C. bar, 1974; tax law specialist (exempt orgns.) IRS, Washington, 1972—. Served with U.S. Army, 1970. Mem. Am., Fed. bar assns. Roman Catholic. Home: 3725 Macomb St Washington DC 20016 Office: 1111 Constitution Ave Washington DC 20224

PATTON, RICHARD BOLLING, food co. exec.; b. Pitts., Jan. 8, 1930; s. Melvin Gerald and Anne (King) P.; B.A., Yale U., 1952; M.B.A., Harvard U., 1954; m. Mary Ann Bickford, June 8, 1963; children—Pamela Watson, Edward Bickford, Richard Randolph, Jennifer Bolling. Product mgr. H.J. Heinz Co., Pitts., 1958-62, gen. mgr. mktg. div., Australia, 1964-66; account exec. Ogilvy & Mather, N.Y.C., 1962-64; asst. v.p. Ogden Corp., N.Y.C., 1966-68; v.p. passenger sales and services programs Trans World Airlines, Inc., N.Y.C., 1968-70; pres. N. Am. Cunard Line, Ltd., N.Y.C., 1970-73, also, dir., comml. dir.; v.p. mktg. and sales H.J. Heinz, 1973—, v.p. tomato products and condiments div., 1976, pres. Heinz U.S.A., 1976—. Trustee Shadyside Hosp., Leukemia Soc. Am.; bd. dirs. United Way Allegheny County. Clubs: Yale of Pitts. (bd. govs.), Fox Chapel Golf, Duquesne, Pitts. Golf; Yale of N.Y.C.; Buck's (London); John's Island (Fla.). Home: 109 Royston Rd Fox Chapel Pittsburgh PA 15238 Office: HJ Heinz USA PO Box 57 Pittsburgh PA 15230

PATTON, ROBERT FREDERICK, lawyer; b. New Castle, Pa., Dec. 9, 1927; s. Wylie E. and Lena Francis (Gardner) P.; A.B., Westminster Coll., N. Wilmington, Pa., 1950; J.D., Harvard, 1953; m. Virginia Lee Reehl, Aug. 15, 1952; children—Thomas E., Barbara L., Susan G., Laura L. Admitted to Pa. bar, 1954; asso. firm Buchanan, Ingersoll, Rodewald, Kyle & Buerger, Pitts., 1953-60, partner, 1960—; dir. Union Nat. Bank Pitts., Armstrong Cork Co.; adj. prof. U. Pitts. Law Sch. Trustee Westminster Coll., 1976—; elder Southminster Presbyterian Church, 1965-68; pres. United Mental Health, 1970-73; chmn. Allegheny County Mental Health/Mental Retardation Bd., 1977—. Served with U.S. Army, 1945-47. Mem. Am. Law Inst., Am., Pa., Allegheny County Bar Assns. Republican. Clubs: Duquesne, Harvard-Yale-Princeton, Chartiers Country. Home: 293 Dixon Ave Pittsburgh PA 15216 Office: 57th floor 600 Grant St Pittsburgh PA 15219

PATUKAS, PETER (EPAMINONDAS) CONSTANTINOS, physician; b. Homori, Nafpaktos, Greece, Dec. 23, 1933; s. Charles Constantinos Theodore and Spirythoula Panayiotou (Skiadas) P.; came to U.S., 1947, naturalized, 1954; B.S., Franklin and Marshall Coll., 1958; M.D., Hahnemann Med. Coll., 1962; m. Phyllis Jane Smith, July 14, 1963; children—Constantina, Demetri Peter. Intern, Harrisburg (Pa.) Hosp., 1962-63; family practice medicine, Coatesville, Pa., 1963—; indsl. physician Phila. Electric Co., Coatesville, 1968—; mem. staff Coatesville Hosp., 1963—, pres. med. staff, 1977—; clin. lectr. family and community medicine Hershey Med. Sch., Pa. State U., 1975-76. Bd. dirs. Coatesville Dist. United Charities, 1978-79. Diplomate Am. Bd. Family Practice. Mem. Pa., Chester County (v.p. 1978-79) med. socs., AMA (Physician's Recognition award 1972, 75, 78), Am. Assn. Physicians and Surgeons, Nat. Assn. Ind. Bus., Hellenic Council Am., Alumni Assn. Hahnemman Med. Coll. (gov. Class of 1962). Greek Orthodox. Club: Hellenic Univ. Home: 7 Downing Rd Downingtown PA 19335 Office: 10th Ave and Olive St Coatesville PA 19320

PAUL, DAVID LEWIS, real estate developer; b. N.Y.C., May 1, 1939; s. Isadore and Ruth (Goldstein) P.; B.S. in Econs., U. Pa., 1961; M.B.A., Columbia U., 1965, J.D., 1967; Ph.D., Harvard U., 1968; children—David J., Michael M. Pres., Paul Properties, Great Neck, N.Y., 1971—; adj. prof. Grad. Sch. Architecture, City U. N.Y. Trustee Mt. Sinai Med. Center, City U. N.Y., Mt. Sinai Hosp., Mt. Sinai Sch. Nursing, Neustadter Convalescent Center; bd. dirs., governing mem. Lincoln Center Repertory Theatre. Home: 800 Park Ave New York City NY 10021 Office: 17 Maple Dr Great Neck NY 11021

PAUL, EDWARD CHARLES, power plant engr.; b. New Brunswick, N.J., Oct. 11, 1932; s. Edward Charles and Marie (Fischer) P.; grad. New Brunswick pub. schs., 1952; m. Temilda Gonzalez, Mar. 3, 1966; children—Margaret, Paul. Power plant engr. U.S. Gypsum Co., Jersey City, 1960-66; power plant engr. Bristol-Myers Co., Hillside, N.J., 1966—. Adviser New Brunswick Youth Council, 1951-52, Fedn. of N.J. Taxpayers, 1969-70. Served with USN, 1952-56. Decorated Korean medal, Chinese medal, Nat. Def. medal; recipient award New Brunswick Optimist Club, 1952. Mem. SAR, Am. Def. Preparedness Assn., N.Y. Geneal. Soc., Assoc. of Nat. Archives, Fleet Reserve Assn., New Eng. Hist. Geneal. Soc. Club: VFW. Proposer resolutions on N.J. State Income Tax; geneal. researcher. Home: 1111 Salem Rd Union NJ 07083 Office: 225 Long Ave Hillside NJ 07207

PAUL, GEORGE HARVEY, city ofcl.; b. Ft. Dodge, Iowa, May 19, 1925; s. Dwight and Morrie (Schultz) P.; grad. high sch.; m. Rita Lorraine Terrenzi, Aug. 25, 1946; children—Donna Kipp, Susan DiMarino, Dianne. Mem. Boston Fire Dept., 1948—, chief, 1970—; tchr. Boston Fire Dept. Fire Coll.; cons. in field. Served with USNR, 1943-46. Author articles. Home: 7 John Alden Rd West Roxbury MA 02132 Office: 115 Southampton St Boston MA 02118

PAUL, HERBERT MORTON, accountant, lawyer; b. N.Y.C., July 17, 1931; s. Julius and Gussie Paul; B.B.A., Baruch Coll., 1952; J.D., Harvard U., 1955; M.B.A., N.Y. U., 1956, LL.M., 1960; m. Dec. 26, 1954; children—Leslie Beth, Andrea Lynn. Partner, dir. tax services-N.Y., exec. nat. service dir-CSO, nat. coordinator tax practice devel. Touche Ross & Co., N.Y.C., 1957—; prof. N.Y. U. Co-chmn. accountants div. Fedn. Philanthropies; adv. bd. Tax Mgmt. div. Bur. Nat. Affairs; adv. bd. Internat. Inst. Tax and Bus. Planning, Inst. Fed. Taxation; mem. com. on trusts and bequests Rockefeller U. Trustee Asso. Y's of N.Y. Served with AUS, 1954-56. C.P.A., N.Y. Mem. N.Y. State Soc. C.P.A.'s (chmn. com. on fed. taxation, mem. gen. tax com., com. relations IRS, chmn. furtherance com.), Am. Inst. C.P.A.'s (taxation div.), N.Y.U. Tax Study Group, Nat. Assn. Accountants (v.p.), N.Y. U. Tax Soc. (chmn. com. tax shelters), New York County Lawyers Assn., Estate Planning Council N.Y. (dir.), Pension Club, Accountants Club Am., Empire State C. of C. (tax com.), Alumni Assn. Grad. Sch. Bus. N.Y. U. (treas.). Clubs: Wall Street, City Athletic. Author: Ordinary and Necessary Expenses. Contbr. articles to profl. jours. Contbg. editor: Federal Income Taxation of Banks; adv. editor The Practical Accountant. Home: 775 Oakleigh Rd North Woodmere NY 11581 Office: 1633 Broadway New York City NY 10019

PAUL, HERMAN LOUIS, JR., valve mfg. co. exec.; b. N.Y.C., Dec. 30, 1912; s. Herman Louis and Louise Emilie (Markert) P.; student Duke U., 1931-32, Lehigh U., 1932-33; m. Janath Powers; children—Robert E., Charles Thomas, Herman Louis III. Power plant engr. Paul's Machine Shop, N.Y.C., 1935-43; pres., chief engr. Paul's Machine Shop, N.Y.C., 1943-48; v.p., chief engr. Paul Valve Corp., East Orange, N.J., 1948-54; pres., chief engr. P-K Industries, Inc., North Arlington, N.J., 1954-59; v.p., dir. research Gen. Kinetics, Englewood, N.J., 1959-62; engring. cons., N.Y.C., 1962-65; v.p., dir. Hudromatics, Inc., Bloomfield, N.J., 1965-67; with P.J. Hydraulics, Inc., Myerstown, Pa., 1967—, pres., chief engr., 1968—. Mem. ASME, Instrument Soc. Am. Club: Heidelberg Country (Bernville, Pa.). Patentee in field. Office: Box 187 Ramona Rd Myerstown PA 17067

PAUL, NORMAN HENRY, French scholar, educator; b. Holyoke, Mass., June 6, 1922; s. Henry John and Eva Marie (Nolin) P.; B.A., Syracuse (N.Y.) U., 1949, M.A., 1956; Ph.D., N.Y.U., 1961. Radio announcer Sta. WMUR, Manchester, N.H., 1941-42; camp mgr. Byrne Constrn., Turkey, 1952-53; newscaster Radio Hilversum, Holland, 1954; asst. French, Syracuse (N.Y.) U., 1954-56, N.Y.U., N.Y.C., 1956-58; tutor French, Queens Coll., Flushing, N.Y., 1958-61, instr., 1961-65, asst. prof., 1966-69, asso. prof., 1970—; resident dir. Study Abroad, Reims, France, 1965-66, Nice, France, 1966-67; dir. internat. summer seminar, Ajaccio, France, 1967-71; lectr. NDEA Summer Inst., Mich. State U., 1960-61, Hollins (Va.) Coll., 1962. Served with USAAF, 1942-45. Decorated Bronze Star medal; French Govt. fellow U. Strasbourg (France), 1949-51. Mem. Modern Lang. Assn., Assn. Am. Tchrs. French, Société Professeurs Français D'Amérique, Société d'Histoire du Théâtre, Amis de Jacques Copeau, Amis d'André Gide. Democrat. Roman Catholic. Contbr. articles, revs. and critical bibliographies to scholarly publs. Office: Dept Romance Languages Queens Coll Flushing NY 11367

PAUL, PHYLLIS OSTRUM, physician; b. Phila., June 9, 1926; d. Samuel B. and Rose (Shay) Ostrum; B.A., Temple U., 1946; M.D., Hannemann Coll., 1950; m. Gerson S. Paul, June 24, 1951; 1 dau., Sindy Michelle. Intern Hahnemann Hosp., Phila., 1950-51, now mem. staff; practice medicine specializing in internal medicine, Phila., 1951-54, 55-56, USAF Hosp., Elmendorf Air Force Base, Anchorage, Alaska, 1951—; mem. staff Phila., Albert Einstein Med. Center, Oxford Hosp., Rolling Hill Hosp., John F. Kennedy Meml. Hosp.; instr. medicine Hahnemann Med. Col., 1951-58; sec., treas. Gyneco Products, Inc., Bay Pharm. Co., Inc., 1962—. Diplomate Nat. Bd. Med. Examiners. Mem. AMA, Am. Heart Assn. (SE Pa. chpt.), Am. Med. Women's Assn., Pa. State, Phila. County med. socs., Am. Geriatric Soc., Pa. Thoracic Soc., Am. Acad. Gen. Practice, Nat. Steeplechase and Hunt Assn., Am. Horse Show Assn., Pa. Horse Breeders Assn. Home: 1710 Woodland Rd Abington PA 19001 also 29 N Overbrook Ave Longport NJ 08403 Office: 2001 Knoor St Philadelphia PA 19149

PAUL, RICHARD CHADWICK, research co. exec.; b. Salt Lake City, Mar. 27, 1920; s. James Pettegrew and Velma (Mackay) P.; B.A. in Biology, Lehigh U., 1942, M.S., 1946; m. Lois Johanna Dick, June 15, 1961; children—Patricia Ann, Katherine, Richard, David. Lab. dir. Paul Labs., York, Pa., 1947—. Instr. dept. biology York Jr. Coll. (now York Coll. of Pa.), 1953-56, dept. bacteriology York Hosp., Pa. State U. Sch. Nursing, 1962-67. Served to lt. Med. Service Corps, USNR, 1943-46; PTO. Diplomate Am. Bd. Bioanalysis. Fellow Royal Soc. Health (London, Eng.); mem. Pa. Assn. Clin. Labs. (pres. 1951-52), Am. Assn. Bioanalysts (dir. states activities, govtl. affairs and profl. relations), Am. Acad. Microbiology (specialist microbiologist), AAAS, Am. Soc. Microbiology, Am. Pub. Health Assn., Nat. Council Health Lab. Services (sec.-treas. 1977—, chmn. 1979—). Rotarian. Club: Country (York). Home: 321 Old Orchard Ln York PA 17405 Office: PO Box 1802 476 W Market St York PA 17405

PAUL, ROBERT ARTHUR, steel co. exec.; b. N.Y.C., Oct. 28, 1937; s. Isadore and Ruth (Goldstein) P.; A.B., Cornell U., 1959; J.D., Harvard, 1962, M.B.A., 1964; m. Donna Rae Berkman, July 29, 1962; children—Laurence Edward, Stephen Eric, Karen Rachel. With Ampco-Pitts. Corp. (formerly Screw & Bolt Corp. Am.), 1964—, v.p., dir. 1969-71, exec. v.p., dir., 1972-73, exec. v.p., treas., dir., 1973—; v.p., dir. Steel Trading Corp., Dover Securities, Inc.; v.p., asst. sec., asst. treas., dir. Parkersburg Steel Corp., Louis Berkman Co., Follansbee Steel Corp., Louis Berkman Realty Co., 1st Dyna Corp., 1st Nat. Bank of Washington (Pa.); dir. Rust Craft Greeting Cards, Inc.; gen. partner Romar Trading Co. Instr., Carnegie Mellon U. Grad. Sch. Indsl. Adminstrn., 1966-69. Trustee H.L. and Louis Berkman Found.; trustee, sec. Montefiore Hosp.; trustee, treas. YM and YWHA of Pitts.; trustee Vocational Rehab. Center Allegheny County; trustee, v.p. Riverview Apts. for Elderly; trustee, treas. Jewish Chronicle; trustee, treas. Ampco-Pitts. Found. Mem. Am., Mass. bar assns., Soc. Security Analysts. Republican. Jewish religion. Clubs: Harvard (Boston); Harvard (N.Y.C.); Concordia, Press, Harvard-Yale-Princeton (Pitts.); Westmoreland Country (Export, Pa.). Home: 1236 Squirrel Hill Ave Pittsburgh PA 15217 Office: Porter Bldg Pittsburgh PA 15319

PAULIN, JOHN MICHAEL, chemist; b. Summit Sation, Pa., Mar. 19, 1940; s. John and Mary (Kachur) P.; student U. Mass., 1958-61, Am. Internat. Coll., 1961-62, Holyoke Community Coll., 1976, 77; m. Elaine Gertrude Stevens, Feb. 14, 1961; children—Karen Ann, John Dennis, Christopher Michael. Quality control technician Scott Graphics Inc., South Hadley, Mass., 1960-63, research technician, 1963-65, research profl., 1965-70, research group leader, 1970-78, plant mgr., 1978—, pres. Employees Assn., 1962, 63. Recipient Indsl. Research 100 award Indsl. Research Mag., 1973. Roman Catholic. Home: 31 Michael Dr South Hadley MA 01075 Office: 28 Gaylord St South Hadley MA 01075

PAULSON, EDGAR GARHEART, chem. engr.; b. Pitts., Sept. 12, 1925; s. John and Clementine (Schibeck) P.; B.S., U. Pitts., 1949, M.S., 1950; m. Marie Nelson, July 28, 1948; children—Linda (Mrs. Russell Roscoe), Larry M., Mark G., Marsha C. With Calgon Corp., Pitts., 1954-72, mgr. environ. engring., 1960-70, tech. cons. environ. group, 1970-72; asst. tech. dir. environ. tech., ITT, N.Y.C., 1972-75; v.p., tech. dir. Indsl. Pollution Control, Inc., Westport, Conn., 1976—. Served with AUS, 1946-47, 50-53. Mem. Pa. Water Pollution Control Assn., Am. Inst. Chem. Engrs., Air Pollution Control Assn., N.A.M. (chmn. ednl. com. 1966-70). Contbr. profl. jours. Research water mgmt. and waste water treatment. Republican. Presbyterian. Home: 22 Arlen Rd Weston CT 06883 Office: 45 Riverside Ave Westport CT 06880

PAULSON, JOHN FREDERICK, chemist; b. Providence, Oct. 29, 1929; s. Frederick Holroyd and Doris (Kerfoot) P.; A.B., Haverford Coll., 1951; Ph.D., U. Rochester, 1958; m. Marjorie Johnson, Sept. 24, 1955; children—David Frederick, Suzanne Elizabeth. Project asso. U. Wis., 1958-59; research chemist Air Force Geophysics Lab., Hanscom AFB, Mass., 1959—. Recipient sci. achievement award AF Systems Command, 1970. Mem. Am. Chem. Soc., Am. Phys. Soc., Am. Soc. Mass Spectrometry, Sigma Xi. Contbr. chpts. in books, articles tech. jours. Research in ion chemistry. Home: 93 Carlisle Pines Carlisle MA 01741 Office: Air Force Geophysics Lab Hanscom Air Force Base MA 01731

PAULUS, JOHN DOUGLAS, pub. relations and advt. exec.; b. Canton, Ohio, July 6, 1917; s. James and Helen (Pateas) P.; B.A., U. Pitts., 1936; postgrad. Georgetown U.; m. Mildred Hankey, Dec. 4, 1937. Sports editor Washington Post, 1936-40; editorial exec., Pitts. Press, 1940-45; promotion dir., asso. pub. Bklyn. Eagle, 1945-47; sr. account exec., Ketchum Inc., 1947-51; dir. pub. relations and advt. Jones & Laughlin Steel Corp., Pitts., 1951-57; dir. pub. relations Firestone Tire & Rubber Co., 1957-58; pres. Hankey, Paulus & Co., pub. relations, fund raising, advt.; lectr. editing, pub. relations, U. Pitts., 1945-53; v.p. pub. relations Allegheny Ludlum Steel Corp., 1958-70; v.p. pub. relations and pub. affairs Allegheny Ludlam Industries, Inc., 1971—. Book editor Am. Metal Market, daily newspaper, 1960-70, Mid-Continent Feature Syndicate, 1953—. Cons., Task Force on Water Resources and Power, 2d Hoover Commn., 1953-55. Trustee Mercy Hosp., Pitts., Duquesne U., Pitts., Pitts. Ballet Theater, ARC, Pitts. Council Internat. Visitors, Point Park Coll., Pitts., Seton Hall Coll., Greensburg, Pa. Recipient Putnam medal for advt., 1954, Golden Quill, 1962. Mem. Internat. Iron and Steel Inst. (com. on pub. affairs and pub. relations 1968—, chmn. com. 1971—), Am. Iron and Steel Inst. (sr. v.p. 1970-71), Sigma Delta Chi, Omicron Delta Kappa. Episcopalian. Clubs: Duquesne, University, Press. Author: Pittsburgh in Music, 1949; Our Dollar in Danger, 1961; For Whom the (Steel) Bell Tolls, 1962; Rome Wasn't Bilked in a Day, 1963; House Organs—Sour Notes and Lullabies, 1966; Carrying Kumquats to Khartoum, 1972; The Curious Case of the Busted Back, 1973; Toward Economic Chaos-Via Majority Vote, 1973; Of Sheiks and Shahs and Commissars, 1974; Whither Trade Unionism in Industrial Democracies?, 1977. Home: 826 N Meadowcroft Ave Pittsburgh PA 15216 Office: 2 Oliver Plaza Pittsburgh PA 15222

PAVESI, WALTER ALBERT, ret. city ofcl.; b. Bronx, Oct. 23, 1919; s. Lino and Ida (Guagnini) P.; grad. high sch.; m. Antonina Borrello, Dec. 16, 1973. With Dept. Sanitation, N.Y.C., 1943-77, asst. chief staff, 1970-74, chief staff, 1974, dir. ops., 1974-77, ret., 1977. Served with AUS, 1942-45. Recipient Pub. Service award N.Y.C., 1973. Mem. Am. Legion, V.F.W. Club: Van Nest Recreation Center (Bronx). Home: 1627 Van Buren St New York City NY 10460

PAVIS, JESSE ANDREW, social scientist, educator; b. Washington, Sept. 15, 1919; s. Abraham and Ethel (Raine) P.; A.B., George Washington U., 1943; M.A., Howard U., 1947; Ph.D., N.Y. U., 1969; m. Mary Margaret Monahan, May 9, 1964; children—Amaranth, Athar, Arne, Andrea, Deidre, Shira. Constrn. office mgr. Am. Bridge div. U.S. Steel Corp., Pitts., 1954-64; prof. social sci. Borough Manhattan Community Coll., City U. N.Y., N.Y.C., 1964—; faculty New Sch. Social Research, N.Y.C., 1973—. Served with U.S. Army, 1943-45. Mem. Am. Sociol. Soc., Am. Soc. Psychical Research, Am. Soc. Psychophysiol. Study Sleep, Soc. to Conquer Mental Illness, Order Artus, Pi Gamma Mu. Democrat. Home: 35 Clark St Brooklyn NY 11201 Office: 1633 Broadway St New York City NY 10020

PAVLAKIS, CHRISTOPHER, musician, publisher; b. Haverhill, Mass., Mar. 26, 1928; s. Nicholas and Panayota (Theophilos) P.; B.Music, Chgo. Mus. Coll., 1954; M.Music, DePaul U., 1956; m. Betty M. Bohlken, May 5, 1956; children—Ann Elizabeth, John Christopher. Tchr. music Chgo., 1956-58; co-editor Who Is Who in Music, Chgo., 1958; tchr. theory, history, music composition, piano pvt. music schs. Chgo., 1958-63; editor, advt. mgr. Instrumentalist mag., Evanston, Ill., 1963-64; lectr. music Northeastern Ill. State Coll., Chgo., 1963-64; pres. music importing, subscription service firm N.Y.C., 1964-71; co-founder, v.p. Univ. Music Edits., N.Y.C., 1967—, High Density Systems Inc., N.Y.C., 1969—, Molex Microfilm Products Inc., N.Y.C., 1973—; profl. writer on music, 1962—. Served with AUS, 1946-48. Recipient Distinguished Alumni award DePaul U., 1974. Mem. Music Library Assn., Am. Musicol. Soc., Am. Music Center, Central Opera Service, Nat. Micrographic Assn. Democrat. Greek Orthodox. Author: The American Music Handbook; The Free Press, 1974. Contbr. articles, revs. to profl. publs. Composer chamber opera, orchestral works, choral works, chamber instrumental works. Office: Box 52 Inwood Station New York City NY 10034

PAVONE, PAUL JOSEPH, educator, counselor; b. Bklyn., Jan. 18, 1949; s. Joseph and Nicoletta Rose (DiGiore) P.; B.A., Hunter Coll., 1970; M.S., Richmond Coll., 1977; m. Janice Yodice, June 19, 1971. Tchr. math., coach St. Michael High Sch., Bklyn., 1970-73; tchr. math., advisor and counselor Tottenville High Sch., S.I., 1973—; exec. dir., owner Busy Bee Montessori Sch., S.I., 1976—. NSF grantee, 1971-73. Mem. Am. Personnel and Guidance Assn. Home: 57 Chestnut Ave Staten Island NY 10305 Office: 97 Guyon Ave Staten Island NY 10306

PAWELEC, WILLIAM JOHN, electronics co. exec.; b. Hammond, Ind., Feb. 15, 1917; s. John and Julia (Durnas) P.; B.S. in Accounting, Ind. U., 1939; m. Alice E. Brown, May 30, 1941 (dec. Dec. 1970); children—William John, Betty Jane Pawelec Conover; m. 2d, June Anderson Shepard, Nov. 27, 1976. Statistician, Ind. State Bd. Accounts, 1939-41; with RCA, 1941—, mgr. accounting and budgets internat. div., 1957-61, controller internat. div., 1961-68, corporate mgr. internat. finance ops. and controls, 1968-75, dir. internat. accounting, 1975 mgr. corporate accounting, 1977—; controller, treas., dir. RCA Internat., Ltd.; treas. RCA Disc Corp., 1975; controller Electron Ins. Co. Active Westfield United Fund, 1967—. Mem. Nat. Assn. Accountants (past nat. v.p.), Nat. Fgn. Trade Assn., Watchung Power Squadron, N.J. State C. of C., N.Y. Chamber of Commerce and Industry, Stuart Cameron McLeod Soc., Ind. U. Alumni Assn. (past pres. N.J. club), Beta Gamma Sigma, Sigma Epsilon Theta. Club: Echo Lake Country. Home: 86 New England Ave Summit NJ 07901 Office: RCA Corp 30 Rockefeller Plaza New York City NY 10020

PAWL, WALTER STANLEY, lawyer, research and devel. co. exec.; b. Chgo., May 13, 1894; s. Wladyslaw and Teodora (Surowiecki) Pawlowski; B.S. in Mech. Engring., Armour Inst. Tech., 1921; LL.B., Wash. Coll. Law, 1931, M.P.L. 1932; m. Georgina Kral, Sept. 21, 1927 (dec. 1976); m. 2d, Myra L. Goodwin, Apr. 3, 1978. Examiner, U.S. Patent Office, Washington, 1928-41; supervisory patent atty. Office Naval Research, Dept. Navy, Washington, 1941-54; admitted to Md. bar, 1954; patent atty. Helitarics, research and devel., Adelphi, Md., 1954—; v.p. Gregoire Engring. and Devel. Co., Newport, Pa., 1962-72; propr. Z-Loc Block Co., Adelphi, 1973—; pres. Inventors Co-op, Inc., Washington, 1969—. Served with C.E., U.S. Army, 1915-19. Mem. Am. Judicature Soc., Am., Md. bar assns., Patent Office Soc., Am. Patent Law Assn., Am. Inst. Aeros. and Astronautics, Air Force Assn., Sigma Nu Phi. Club: Masons. Research in helical planetary mechanics. Address: 4407 Ridge St Chevy Chase MD 20015

PAXTON, RALPH ROBERT, chem. engr.; b. Zion, Ill., Mar. 4, 1920; s. James Robert and Hazel Marie (Lawrence) P.; B.S. in Chem. Engring., U. Ill., 1943; Sc.D. (Gerard Swope fellow), Mass. Inst. Tech., 1949; m. Mary Louise Espy, Oct. 16, 1943; children—Nancy, Anne. Engr., Standard Oil Co., Whiting, Ind., 1943-45; instr. chem. engring. U. Colo., Boulder, 1945-47; asst. prof. Stanford, 1949-55; sr. engr. Gen. Electric Co., Pittsfield, Mass., 1955-58; chief engr. Pure Carbon Co., St. Marys, Pa., 1958—. Cons., Permanente Cement Co., Los Gatos, Calif., Standard Oil Co., San Francisco. Pres., Elk County Music Assn., 1959-60. Mem. Am. Chem. Soc., Am. Inst. Chem. Engrs., Am. Inst. Chemists, Electrochem. Soc., Am. Soc. Lubrication Engrs., Am. Soc. Testing and Materials (sec. carbon div. 1968-74). Unitarian (moderator 1957-58). Kiwanian (pres. 1962). Patents, publs. in field. Home: 627 Sherry Rd St Marys PA 15857 Office: 441 Hall Ave St Marys PA 15857

PAYACK, PAUL J.J., author; b. Boonton, N.J., Jan. 3, 1950; s. Peter Paul and Florence Marie (Marcello) P.; student Bucknell U., 1968-71; A.B., Harvard, 1974, postgrad., 1976—; m. Millie Lorenzo, Apr. 19, 1974. Author: A Ripple in Entropy, 1973; Legend of the Shaman, 1974; Solstice, 1975; Mythomania, 1977; The Unexpected Twist Series & Solstice II, 1976; The Black Lists, 1977; Solstice III, 1977; Microtales, 1979; The Land of Orth, 1978; Uncollected Early Works, 1979; A Short History of Chess, 1979, also short stories, essays, poetry, metafictions; editor Chthon Press, Westford, Mass., 1973—; admissions counselor Newbury Coll., Boston, 1975, sr. admissions officer, 1976, asst. dir. admissions, 1977-78, asst. to pres., 1978; software writer Digital Equipment Corp., Tewksbury, Mass., 1978—. Mem. adv. bd. Inst. for Profl. Studies, Boston. Mem. Modern Lang. Assn., Sci. Fiction Writers Am. Home: Ten Mark Vincent Dr Westford MA 01886 Office: 1925 Andover Rd Tewksbury MA 01876

PAYACK, PETER, poet, editor, environ. artist; b. Boonton, N.J., Jan. 3, 1950; s. Peter Paul and Florence (Marcello) P. Writer poetry, satire and short fiction; books include: No Free Will in Tomatoes, 1976; A Brief Guide to the Theory of Relativity, 1977; The Evolution of Death, 1977; Rainbow Bridges, 1978; contbr. poetry to more than 125 periodicals including The Village Voice, Christian Sci. Monitor, New Voices, Isaac Asimov's Sci. Fiction Mag., Paris Rev., N.Y. Times; environ. artist; works include Elec. Poetry, 1977; Star Poems, 1978; founder, editor Phone-A-Poem, 1976—; poetry cons. Cambridge Arts Council, 1977—; poetry coordinator Cambridge River Festival, 1977, 78; poetry chmn. Boston's First Night, 1979. Recipient awards Cambridge Arts Council, 1976, 77, 78, citation of commendation Cambridge City Council, 1977. Home and office: 64 Highland Ave Cambridge MA 02139

PAYETTE, THOMAS MARTIN, architect; b. Grand Rapids, Mich., Aug. 9, 1932; s. Robert J. and Mary (Kay) P.; B.S. in Structural Engring., Mich. State U., 1956; M.Arch., Harvard, 1960; m. Virginia Carson, Sept. 4, 1954; children—Scott Carson, Monte Martin, Shelly Kellog, Jennifer Jennings. Archtl. designer Markus & Nocka, Boston, 1960-65; asst. prof. R.I. Sch. Design, 1964-65; pres. Payette Assos., Inc., and predecessor, Boston, 1965—; mem. com. to establish guidelines and minimal criteria for intensive care units and coronary care units Mass. Dept. Pub. Health, 1971—; prin. works include Emerson Hosp., 1970, Leonard Morse Hosp., 1969, Eastern Maine Med. Center, 1974, Aga Khan Hosp. and Med. Coll., Karachi, Pakistan, 1976, Joslin Diabetes Found., 1977. Julian Appleton traveling fellow, 1960. Registered architect, Mass., Ky., Fla., Ga., Pa., R.I., Maine, Minn., N.H., N.Y., Conn., Mich., Vt.; certified Nat. Council Archtl. Registration Bds. Fellow AIA; mem. Boston Soc. Architects (chmn. edn. com. 1970-72, 74—), Am. Hosp. Assn., New Eng. Hosp. Assembly, Royal Inst. Brit. Architects, Chi Epsilon Phi, Phi Kappa Phi, Tau Beta Phi. Home: 283 Upland Rd Cambridge MA 02140 Office: 40 Isabella St Boston MA 02116

PAYNE, MABEL LOUISE, coll. counselor; b. N.Y.C., Oct. 24, 1949; d. Lawrence and Elaine Augusta (Philips) P.; B.A. in Social Scis. (Jewish Found. for Edn. Girls scholar), State U. N.Y., Binghamton, 1971; M.S. in Edn., ednl. specialist certificate (grad. minority student fellow) State U. N.Y., Albany, 1974, career counseling certificate, 1977. Career counselor div. continuing edn. N.Y.C. Community Coll., Bklyn., 1975-77, gen. counselor Voorhees Campus, N.Y.C., 1977—; mem. adv. council, planning com. McKinney Jr. High Sch., Bklyn., 1976—. Founding mem., sec. Our Future, ch. based service orgn., 1977—. Recipient scholar-incentive award N.Y. State Bd. Regents, 1967-74. Mem. Am. Personnel and Guidance Assn. Episcopalian. Home: 1523 Unionport Rd Bronx NY 10462 Office: 450 W 41st St New York City NY 10036

PAYNE, MARGARET JUNE BUTTIMER (MRS. MORLEY ELDON PAYNE), owner rest home; b. Salmon Beach, N.B., Can., May 25, 1919; d. Allen and Ada Pearl (Knowles) Buttimer; student pub. schs.; m. Morley Eldon Payne, July 15, 1940; children—Lillian Grace Pearl (Mrs. Raymond Joseph Russell), Marjorie Frances (Mrs. Rodney Hubert Sealy), George Allen, Dorothy Edna (Mrs. Donald Ramsey), Margaret June. Owner, operator Paynes Rest Home for Sr. Citizens, Bathurst, N.B., Can., 1964—. Mem. United Ch. of Can. Home: Box 585 Rural Route 1 Bathurst NB E2A 3Y5 Canada

PAYNE, S. HOWARD, prosthodontist, educator; b. Buffalo, May 4, 1914; s. S. Howard and Zola (Mitchell) P.; D.D.S., U. Buffalo, 1937; m. Margaret White; children—ZoAnn Payne Landen, Cheryl Payne Rogers, Jennifer, Denise. Faculty U. Buffalo, 1937—, instr. prosthodontics, 1937-40, asst. prof., 1941-46, asso. prof., acting chmn., 1946-48, prof., chmn. dept. prosthodontics, 1948-64, asst. dean, 1950-64, part-time prof. prosthodontics, 1964—, also practice prosthodontics, 1937—. Dir. Amherst Records, Inc., Buffalo, 1960—. Nat. cons. prosthodontics to the VA; cons. Meyer Meml. Hosp., 1965-73. Recipient Thomas Hinman award, 1956, 69; dean's medal U. Buffalo, 1968; named Man of Year, U. Buffalo Alumni, 1964. Diplomate Am. Bd. Prosthodontics (pres. 1958-59, examiner 1953-59). Fellow Am. Coll. Dentists, Acad. Denture Prosthetics (pres. 1967), Greater N.Y. Acad. Prosthodontics; mem. Am. Prosthodontic Soc., Prosthodontic Soc. South Africa (hon.), Omicron Kappa Upsilon. Asso. editor removable prosthodontic sect. Jour. Prosthetic Dentistry, 1969—. Contbr. numerous articles in field to profl. jours. Presentations and TV clins. U.S. and abroad. Home and office: 396 Porter Ave Buffalo NY 14201

PAYNE, STAN LEE, ednl. adminstr.; b. Trenton, N.J., July 18, 1941; s. Stanley J. and Roxie Julia (Lamar) P.; apprenticeship Tool/Die Making, Trenton Vo-Tech., 1963; B.S. in Edn., Temple U., 1972, now doctoral candidate; M.A. in Guidance and Counseling, Villanova U., 1975; 1 dau., Penni Leah. Machine shop instr. Trenton (N.J.) Evening Adult Sch., 1964; machine tool ops. instr. Trenton MDTA Multi-Skill Center, 1966-69; instr. vocat. edn. Chester-Upland Sch. Dist., 1970-72, dean of students, 1972—; mem. long term community planning adv. com. Bd. Youth in Action; chmn. exec. bd. Comprehensive Delivery of Services to Youth. Trenton Women's Civic League Coll. scholar, 1959-60; certified, registered tool/die maker; certified machine shop and tool/die instr., coordinator Vocat. and part-time coop. edn., supr./dir. vocat. edn., secondary guidance counselor, elementary/secondary prin. Mem. Am., Pa. vocat. assns., NEA, Pa. State, Chester-Upland edn. assns., Am. Personnel and Guidance Assn., Nat. Vocat. Guidance Assn., Am. Sch. Counselors Assn., Assn. Non White Concerns, NAACP. Club: Optimist of S. Chester. Home: 111 MacDade Blvd Folsom PA 19033 Office: 18th and Melrose Ave Chester PA 19013

PAYNTER, DOROTHY KAY, educator; b. Albuquerque, July 1, 1935; d. Howard Kenneth and Catherine Mae (Krema) P.; B.A., State U. Coll. of N.Y., 1973; M.S. in Edn., State U. N.Y., 1975; Ed.D., Syracuse U.; children by previous marriage—Catherine, Margaret, David, Andrew. Tchr. aide Barker Rd. Jr. High Sch., Pittsford, N.Y., 1970-72; acad. adviser Office of Continuing Edn., State U. N.Y. Coll. at Brockport, 1973-74; counselor continuing studies for women Rochester (N.Y.) Inst. Tech., 1974-75, asst. prof. bus. and community studies, 1975-77, cons. program devel., 1977—; cons. to women's groups, bus. and industry, 1974—. Mem. Am. Personnel and Guidance Assn., Nat. U. Extension Assn., Adult Edn. Assn., AAUW, Am. Humanist Assn., World Future Soc. Contbr. articles on edn. to lit. mags. Home: 5 Cross Ridge Rd Pittsford NY 14534 Office: Rochester Inst of Technology College of Continuing Education One Lomb Memorial Dr Rochester NY 14625

PAYSON, HENRY EDWARDS, forensic psychiatrist, educator; b. N.Y.C., May 12, 1925; s. Aurin Eliot and Lois Elizabeth (Chickering) P.; B.S., Harvard U., 1948; M.D., Columbia U., 1952; M.S.L., Yale, 1978; m. Barbara Louise Jarvis, M.D., Mar. 29, 1958; children—Ann Elizabeth, John Eliot, Sally Lynn, Susan Gail. Intern, Osler Clinic Johns Hopkins Hosp., 1953-54; resident in psychiatry Phipps Clinic, 1955-58; resident in internal medicine Duke U. Hosp., Durham, N.C., 1954-55; asst. prof. psychiatry and medicine Yale, also attending physician Yale-New Haven Med. Center, 1958-63; asst. prof. psychiatry Dartmouth Coll., 1963-68, asso. prof., 1968-78, prof., 1978—; attending psychiatrist Hitchcock Clinic, Mary Hitchcock Hosp.; chief in-patient service Dartmouth-Hitchcock Mental Health Center, 1969-72; cons. VA, Vt. Crime Commn., N.H. Prisons; dir. Disturbed Offender Project of N.H., 1972-73. Served with AUS, 1943-46. NIMH career tchr., 1961-63. Fellow Am. Psychiat. Assn.; mem. N.H. Psychiat. Soc. (pres. 1977-78), Am. Acad. Academic Psychiatry, Am. Acad. Forensic Scis., Am. Acad. Psychiatry and Law, Am. Psychosomatic Soc., Am. Polled Hereford Assn., Am. Soc. Psychophysiol. Study of Sleep, Grafton County Med. Soc., AAAS. Mem. Ch. of Christ. Club: Harvard (N.Y.C.). Contbr. articles to profl. books and jours. Home: 17 N Balch St Hanover NH 03755 Office: Dartmouth Medical School Hanover NH 03755

PEABODY, CHARLES NEWTON, surgeon; b. Detroit, Aug. 4, 1925; s. Charles William and Miriam (Church) P.; student Harvard, 1942-44, Boston U. Sch. Medicine, 1944-46; M.D., Harvard, 1948; postgrad. Nuffield Inst., Oxford (Eng.) U. Worcester Coll., 1950-51; m. Claude-Noele Fonthier, Oct. 10, 1952; children—Carol-Ann, Charles William, Norbert Worthington. From intern to chief resident Mass. Meml. Hosps., Boston, 1948-56; asst. to attending physician U.S. Capitol, Washington, 1952; asst. clin. prof. surgery Boston U. Sch. Medicine; practice medicine specializing in surgery, Framingham, Mass., 1957—; vis. surgeon Framingham Union Hosp.; surgeon Univ. Hosp., Boston. Trustee Boston Med. Library, Fay Sch., Southborough, Mass. Served with USNR, 1943-46, 52-54; comdr. M.C. Res. Recipient research grants USPHS, 1959-60. Diplomate Am. Bd. Surgery. Fellow A.C.S.; mem. AMA, Mass. Med. Soc., New Eng., Boston surg. socs., Oxford Society. Republican. Clubs: Harvard; Hasty-Pudding Institute of 1770, Fox (Cambridge, Mass.); Aesculapian. Contbr. sci. articles to tech. jours. Editor: Harvard Crimson, 1942-43; mng. editor Harvard Service News, 1943-44. Home: 265 Belknap Rd Framingham MA 01701 Office: 16 Evergreen St Framingham MA 01701

PEABODY, VELTON LESTER, newspaper editor; b. Beals, Maine, July 27, 1936; s. Clyde Bertram and Arlene Aseliah (Beal) P.; A.A., Graceland Coll., 1957; B.J., U. Mo., 1965; m. Marilyn Blanchard, Apr. 28, 1962. Corr. Bangor (Maine) Daily News, 1951-54, editorial staff, 1955-56, 58-63; copy desk Rochester (N.Y.) Times-Union, 1965-68; night wire editor Buffalo Evening News, 1968—. Mem. Sigma Delta Chi, Kappa Tau Alpha. Democrat. Mem. Reorganized Ch. Jesus Christ Latter Day Saints. Author: Tall Barney's People, 1974; Tall Barney: Giant of Beals Island, 1975. Editor Mormonia: A Quar. Bibliography works Mormonism, 1971-73. Home: 50 Williamstowne Ct Cheektowaga NY 14227 Office: One News Plaza Buffalo NY 14240

PEACE, JOHN H., advt. exec.; b. N.Y.C., Nov. 20, 1922; s. Thomas G. and Ella (Curry) P.; m. Agnes Cross, Mar. 7, 1942; children—Kathleen, Ellen, John, Mary, James, William. With William Esty Co., Inc., N.Y.C., 1941—, successively v.p., media dir., account exec., 1st v.p., 1941-58, chmn. operating com., 1958-60, pres., 1960-67, chmn. bd., 1967-74, chmn. exec. com., 1974—. Clubs: Siwanoy, Bronxville (N.Y.); Spring Lake (N.J.) Golf and Country; Sky (N.Y.C.). Home: 8 Richbell Close Scarsdale NY 10583 Office: William Esty Co 100 E 42d St New York City NY 10017

PEAKS, MARY JANE (MRS. ROBERT MALCOLM POLK), orthodontist; b. N.Y.C., Aug. 19, 1916; d. Archibald Garfield and Emilie Henrietta (Stauderman) Peaks; D.D.S., U. Pa., 1939; orthodontic certificate Columbia U., 1974; certificate interior design N.Y. U., 1977; m. Robert Malcolm Polk, Sept. 29, 1942; children—Robert, Mary Moneen (Mrs. Frank Forster Gilmore), Eileen. Individual practice dentistry specializing in orthodontics, N.Y.C., 1939-52, Garden City, N.Y., 1950—. Fellow Royal Soc. Health; mem. Am. Assn. Orthodontists, Am. Dental Assn., A.S.C.A.P., N.Y. Soc. Orthodontists, N.Y. Assn. Professions. Soroptimist Internat., Am. Guild Authors and Composers, Songwriters Hall of Fame. Composer: I Told A Lie, 1954. Home: 152 W 11th St New York City NY 10011 Office: 520 Franklin Ave Garden City NY 11530

PEARCE, WILLIAM HOWARD, land devel. and property mgmt. co. exec.; b. Buffalo, Sept. 26, 1922; s. Howard William and Frances Deborah (Ryan) P.; A.B., Rutgers U., 1943; M.B.A., Harvard, 1946; m. Elizabeth Ward, Oct. 22, 1955; children—William Howard, Elizabeth F., Nina. With Ford Motor Co., Detroit, 1946; with Pearce & Pearce Co., Inc., Buffalo, 1947—, v.p., 1947-49, exec. v.p., 1949-68, pres., 1968—; dir. Bank of N.Y.-Western Region, Half Moon Bay, Ltd. Bd. dirs. Millard Fillmore Hosp., Buffalo Fine Arts Acad.; trustee United Way Buffalo, Buffalo Sem.; bd. regents Canisius Coll., Buffalo. Served to capt. AUS, 1943-46; ETO. Mem. Niagara Frontier Builders Assn. (pres. 1954-55), Greater Buffalo Bd. Realtors, Buffalo C. of C., Chi Psi. Clubs: Buffalo (past pres., dir.), Country of Buffalo (dir.), Saturn (Buffalo); Harvard (N.Y.C.). Home: 101 Farmington Williamsville NY 14221 Office: 900 Niagara Falls Blvd Buffalo NY 14223

PEARINCOTT, JOSEPH VERGHESE, educator, physiologist; b. Travancore, India, May 26, 1929; s. George F. and Elizabeth (Kottakaram) P.; B.Sc., Travancore U., 1949; M.Sc., Aligarh U., 1951; Ph.D., Fordham U., 1959; m. Michaeleen Ferrara, May 1, 1958; 1 son, George Joseph. Came to U.S., 1952, naturalized, 1959. Instr. biology Fordham U., N.Y.C., 1952-56; postdoctoral fellow Columbia Coll. Physicians and Surgeons, N.Y.C., 1959-61; research asso., dept. physiology and pharmacology N.Y. Med. Coll., N.Y.C., 1961-62; asst. prof. biology Northeastern U., Boston, 1962-68, asso. prof. biology, 1968—. Mem. N.Y. Acad. Scis., AAAS, Am. Soc. Zoologists, Entomol. Soc. Am., AAUP, Sigma Xi. Home: 61 Webb St Lexington MA 02173 Office: 360 Huntington Ave Boston MA 02115

PEARL, HARVEY, psychologist; b. N.Y.C., July 11, 1930; s. Louis and Blanche (Birnbaum) P.; B.S., N.Y. U., 1953, M.A., 1957; Ph.D., Syracuse U., 1970; m. Dorothy Morrison, June 20, 1953; children—Stuart Ray, Lesley, Andrea. Tchr. indsl. arts pub. schs., Elizabeth, N.J., 1955-56; workshop supr. United Cerebral Palsy Assn., Roosevelt, N.Y., 1956-58; workshop dir. Jewish Vocat. Service, Cin., 1958-61; dir. work tng. center Assn. for Retarded Children, Rochester, N.Y., 1961-63; asst. exec. dir. Consol. Industries Greater Syracuse (N.Y.) 1965—; instr. Cornell U., Ithaca, N.Y., 1970—; cons. Social Security Adminstrn., 1962—. Bd. dirs. Jewish Family Service Bur., 1974—; adv. council Cazenovia Coll., 1977—, Occupational Edn., Syracuse City Sch. Dist., 1971—. Served with U.S. Army, 1953-55. Recipient citation of merit Syracuse U. Sch. Social Work, 1972; certified rehab. counselor. Mem. Nat. Rehab. Assn., Am. Personnel and Guidance Assn., Am. Rehab. Counseling Assn., Nat. Vocat. Guidance Assn. Author: (with A. Speiser, A. Staniec) Bibliography of Work Evaluation in Vocational Rehabilitation, 1966. Office: 541 Seymour St Syracuse NY 13204

PEARL, JOHN JOEL, consumer products co. exec.; b. Orange, N.J., July 28, 1936; s. Jacob and Bertha Mary (Slaseman) P.; B.S., Fairleigh Dickinson U., 1961; M.B.A., Seton Hall U., 1965, postgrad. Law Sch., 1965-67; m. Sheila Slade, May 25, 1962; children—Jamie, Jill. With Pepsico, 1967—, dir. personnel Frito-Lay, Inc., Dallas, 1971-74, dir. employee relations Pepsi-Cola Co., Purchase, N.Y., 1974-75, v.p. personnel Pepsi-Cola Co. and Pepsi-Cola Bottling Group, Purchase, 1975—; cons., lectr. personnel labor relations. Served with U.S. Army, 1955-57. Mem. Am. Arbitration Assn., Employment Mgmt. Assn., Am. Mgmt. Assn., Phi Alpha Delta. Clubs: Rolling Hills Country; Dallas Athletic. Office: Pepsi Cola Co Anderson Hill Rd Purchase NY 10577

PEARLMAN, LUCY FRIEDLANDER, family planning counselor; b. Bklyn., May 9, 1932; d. Percy and Gladys (Sammet) Friedlander; B.A., Vassar Coll., 1954; M.A., N.Y. U., 1973; m. Hubert S. Pearlman, Nov. 14, 1954; children—Frederick Lee, Henry, George. Adminstrv. asst. Council Fin. Aid to Edn., 1955; substitute tchr. N.Y.C. Bd. Edn., 1962-65; family planning counselor Planned Parenthood N.Y.C., 1966—. Mem. Queens (N.Y.) Community Planning Bd. 14, 1977—. Mem. Am. Personnel and Guidance Assn., Nat. Vocat. Guidance Assn., Nat. Assn. Sch. Counselors, LWV, PTA. Democrat. Jewish. Club: N.Y. Vassar. Home: 134-16 Cronston Ave Belle Harbor NY 11694

PEARLMAN, ROBERT EUGENE, advt. exec.; b. Boothwyn, Pa., Sept. 16, 1939; s. Max and Ruth Viola (Foster) P.; student Temple U. Tyler Sch. Fine Arts, 1957-58, Mus. Coll. Art, Phila., 1958-61; m. Ruth Himelfarb, Jan. 15, 1958; children—Scott Anthony, Ilana; m. 2d, Gail Ann Ash, Apr. 12, 1975; 1 dau., Ashley Beth. Jr. med. illustrator Smith Kline & French Labs., Phila., 1958-62; owner design firm Mixed Media, N.Y.C., 1963-69, partner, 1970-74; resident, Palinuro, Italy, 1969-70; pres. Cavalieri Kleier Pearlman, Inc., advt. agy., N.Y.C., 1974—; lectr. Marymount Coll., Tarrytown, N.Y., 1965-70; film critic Sta. WBAI-FM, N.Y.C., 1967-68; conducted field expdn. to analyze Masai lang. and symbols, Kenya, 1973. Mem. Citizens Com. for Democratic Nat. Conv., N.Y.C., 1976—. Recipient awards Jour. Comml. Art, N.J. Art Dirs. Club, N.Y. Art Dirs. Club, Soc. Illustrators, Am. Film Festival Mem. Am. Mgmt. Assn., Am. Mktg. Assn., Travel Research Assn., Am. Inst. Archaeology. Club: Explorers. Author: (with Ruth Himelfarb Pearlman) Feeding Your Baby, 1972; co-discover Greek shipwreck dated 175 B.C., Sicily, 1970. Home: 400 E 56th St New York City NY 10022 Office: 777 3d Ave Ave New York City NY 10017

PEARLSTEIN, SEYMOUR, artist; b. Bklyn., Oct. 14, 1923; s. Morris Lazarus and Anna (Bassiur) P.; certificate Pratt Inst., Bklyn., 1950, Art Students League of N.Y., 1954; student Jack Potter; m. Toby Tessie Rubinstein, Mar. 21, 1943; children—Judith Helene Pearlstein Weltman, Lawrence Jonathan. Owner, artist, designer Sy Pearlstein Advt. Art Studio, N.Y.C., 1946-71; artist-painter rep. by Far Gallery, N.Y.C., 1968—; asst. prof. N.Y.C. Community Coll., Bklyn., 1971—; vis. lectr. Pratt Inst., 1975; one-man shows: Grace Gallery, N.Y.C. Community Coll., 1971, Silvermine Guild of Artists, New Canaan, Conn., 1973, Far Gallery, 1973, 75, 78, Klitgord Center, N.Y.C. Community Coll., 1974, De Mers Gallery, Hilton Head, S.C., 1975; group shows: A.M. Sachs Gallery, N.Y.C., 1971, Springfield (Mo.) Art Mus., 1971, Am. Acad. Arts and Letters, N.Y.C., 1975, 76, 77, NAD, N.Y.C., 1975, Butler Inst. Art, Ohio, 1975, Ball State U., Queens Mus., N.Y.C., U.S. Dept. State Art In Embassies Program, Am. Watercolor Soc., N.Y.C., Audubon Artists, N.Y.C., Allied Artists Am., N.Y.C., Phila. Mus. Sales and Loan Gallery, Nat. Arts Club, N.Y.C., others; represented in permanent collections at Mus. N.Mex., Santa Fe, Mint Mus. Art, Charlotte, N.C., NAD, N.Y.C. Served with AUS, 1942-46. Recipient Gold medal Nat. Acad. Design, 1969, Hassam Fund Purchase award Am. Acad. Arts and Letters, 1969, 77, Gold medal of honor Nat. Arts Club, 1970, Ranger Fund Purchase award NAD, 1971, Gold medal Soc. Illustrators, 1972, Nat. Inst.-Am. Acad. Arts and Letters grant, 1975. Mem. Am. Watercolor Soc. (Watercolor U.S.A. award 1971), Art Students League of N.Y. (life), Allied Artists Am. (dir. 1976-79, E. Lowe award 1969), Audubon Artists (Grumbacher Meml. award 1971, award for realistic painting 1976), NAD, Silvermine Guild Artists, Alliance Figurative Artists (chmn. 1976-77), Profl. Staff Congress. Home: 52 Dartmouth St Forest Hills NY 11375 Office: 300 Jay St Brooklyn NY 11201

PEARSON, DAVIS, architect; b. Bryn Mawr, Pa., June 10, 1925; s. Rodney Stockton and Bertha Elizabeth (Bott) P.; B.Arch., U. Pa., 1950; m. Priscilla Joan Ball, May 15, 1954; children—Leslie Buchanan, Davis, Donald Stockton. Architect, Kneedler, Mirick & Zantzinger, 1952-61; partner Kneedler, Mirick, Zantzinger, Pearson, Ilvonen, Batcheler, Architects, 1962-71, Mirick, Pearson, Ilvonen, Batcheler, Phila., 1972—. Dir. Devon Manor Corp. Mem. Lower Merion Twp. Planning Commn., 1969—. Bd. dirs. Merion Community Assn.; pres. Merion Civic Assn., 1975-76; bd. mgrs. Saunders House, 1962—; trustee Episcopal Acad., 1974—; mem. Carpenters Co. City and County of Phila. Served with AUS, 1943-45. Decorated Purple Heart. Mem. AIA (dir. Phila. chpt. 1974-76), Tau Sigma Delta. Clubs: Racquet (Phila.); Avalon (N.J.) Yacht (commodore 1976—). Home: 71 Merbrook Ln Merion PA 19066 Office: 3 Parkway Philadelphia PA 19103

PEARSON, ELVER THOMAS, ins. trade assn. exec.; b. Newark, N.J., June 20, 1928; s. Elver Eric and Catherine Margaret (Morrissey) P.; B.A., Johns Hopkins U., 1950; J.D., U. Minn., 1954; m. Beverly Reynolds Busick, July 13, 1968; children—Sara E., Martin E., Lindley C. Admitted to N.D. bar, 1954, Supreme Ct. U.S., 1966; partner firm Zuger, Zuger & Pearson, Bismarck, N.D., 1954-60; atty. U.S. Fidelity and Guaranty Co., Balt., 1960-68; counsel, Am. Ins. Assn., N.Y.C., 1968-70, mgr. Washington office, 1970-71; sec. Surety Assn. of Am., N.Y.C., 1971-73, gen. mgr., 1973—; lectr. ins. law, U. Balt., 1965-68.

Justice of the Peace, Burleigh County, N.D., 1956-57. Mem. Am. Bar Assn., N.Y. County Lawyers Assn., Am. Soc. of Assn. Execs. Clubs: Internat. Club of Washington, D.C., Johns Hopkins, Bankers Club of Am., Drug and Chem. (N.Y.C.). Home: 8 Belknap Ln Rumson NJ 07760 Office: 100 Wood Ave S Iselin NJ

PEARSON, GEORGE BERNARD, business exec.; b. Mercedes, Tex., Feb. 19, 1938; s. Bernard and Agatha (Peterson) P.; B.A., U. Tex. 1959, M.B.A., 1961; m. Margaret Jean Royall, May 1, 1965; 1 dau., April Michele. Statistician, Bur. Bus. Research, U. Tex., Austin, 1959-60; sales engr. IBM Corp., Endicott, N.Y., also Dallas, 1959; lead engr. Ling-Temco-Vought, Inc., Dallas, 1961-65, engring. specialist, 1965-67; sr. ops. research analyst Pan-Am. World Airways, 1967-68, mgr. operations research, 1969, mgr. ops. research and systems planning, 1970-71, dir. system planning, 1971-72, dir. system devel., 1972-74, dir. planning systems and adminstrn., 1974-75; v.p. planning and research Beneficial Mgmt. Corp., Morristown, N.J., 1975—. Mem. study group on flight in atmosphere USAF. Mem. Ops. Research Soc. Am. (treas., membership chmn. N. Tex. sect. 1965-66), U. Tex. Alumni Assn. Lutheran. Contbr. articles to profl. jours. Home: 100 Carriage House Rd Bernardsville NJ 07924 Office: Beneficial Bldg 200 South St Morristown NJ 07960

PEARSON, PETER ROBB, film dir. and writer; b. Toronto, Ont., Can., Mar. 13, 1938; s. Charles Todd and Dorothy (Robb) P.; B.A. in Polit. Sci., U. Toronto, 1961; postgrad. Centro Sperimentale di Cinematografia, Rome, 1963; m. Suzanne Nicole Vachon, June 15, 1974; 1 son, Louis-Charles de Beauce. Producer-dir. This Hour Has Seven Days, CBC, Toronto, 1964-66; dir. Nat. Film Bd., Montreal, Que., Can., 1966-68; free lance dir., writer, producer, 1968—; films include: Best Damn Fiddler from Calabogie to Kaladar (Canadian Film of Year), 1969; Paperback Hero (3 Canadian Film awards), 1973, Along These Lines (Best Theatrical Short), 1975; author screenplays: The Insurance Man From Ingersoll (Best Original Screenplay, Assn. Canadian TV and Radio Artists, 1977, One Man (Best Original Screenplay, Canadian Film Awards), 1977; mem. adv. com. Sec. State Can., 1972-75; mem. Toronto Arts Council, 1974-76. Mem. Dirs. Guild Can. (pres. 1972-75), Council Canadian Filmmakers (chmn. 1973-75). Home: Rural Route 3 Mansfield ON L0N 1M0 Canada

PEARSON, ROGER, corp. dir.; b. London, Aug. 21, 1927; s. Edwin and Beatrice May (Woodbine) P.; came to U.S., 1965; B.S. with honors, U. London, 1951, M.S., 1954, Ph.D., 1969; m. Marion Primrose Simms, June 3, 1959; children—Edwin, Sigrid, Emma, Rupert. Chmn., Pakistan Tea Assn., 1954; mng. dir. Octavius Steel & Co. of Pakistan, Ltd., Chittagong, East Pakistan, 1959-65; chmn. Plummer Bros., Ltd., Chittagong, 1959-65, Chittagong Warehouses, Ltd., 1960-65; chmn. dept. sociology and anthropology Queens Coll., Charlotte, N.C., 1970-71; chmn. dept. anthropology U. So. Miss., Hattiesburg, 1971-74; dean acad. affairs, dir. research Mont. Coll. Mineral Sci. Tech., Butte, 1974-75. Exec. dir. Council on Am. Affairs, Washington, 1975—. Served to lt. Brit. Indian Army, 1945-48. Fellow Inst. Chartered Secs. Adminstrs. (London), Royal Anthrop. Inst. (London). Author: Eastern Interlude, 1954; An Introduction to Anthropology, 1974; A History of Social Thought, 1978; editor Sino-Soviet Intervention in Africa, 1977; editor publisher Jour. Indo-European Studies, 1973—, Jour. Social and Polit. Studies, 1976—. Office: 1716 New Hampshire Ave NW Washington DC 20009

PEARSON, WILLIAM HENRY, metal mfg. co. ofcl.; b. Toronto, Ont., Can., Nov. 7, 1927; s. John David and May Pearson; ed. Ryerson Inst. Tech., 1944-48; m. Jean Doreen McDonald, Nov. 25, 1950; children—Glenn, Beverly, Grant. Mgr., Coulter Copper & Brass So., Toronto, 1950-64, Supreme Aluminum Industries, Scarborough, Ont., 1964-65; mgr. projects Atlas Alloys Co. div. Rio Algom Ltd., Etobicoke, Ont., 1965—; cons. in field. Recipient Dr. Bell award United Ch. Can. Mem. Soc. Mfg. Engrs. (internat. dir.), Calif. Profl. Engrs. in Mfg. Engring., Am. Soc. Metals (exec. council, Achievement award 1974). Mem. United Ch. Can. Contbr. to metalworking books. Home: 59 Montvale Dr Scarborough ON M1M 3E5 Canada Office: 161 West Mall Etobicoke ON M9C 4V8 Canada

PEARSON, WILLIAM ROWLAND, chem. engr.; b. New Bedford, Mass., Sept. 30, 1923; s. Rowland and Nellie (Hilton) P.; B.S., Northeastern U., 1953; postgrad. U. Ohio, 1960; m. Arlene Cole Loveys, June 14, 1953; children—Denise, Robert, Rowland, Nancy. Engr., Goodyear Atomic Corp., Portsmouth, Ohio, 1953-63, Cabot Titania Corp., Ashtabula, Ohio, 1963-64; supr. United Nuclear, Wood River, R.I., 1964-72; sr. engr. Nuclear Materials and Equipment Co., Apollo, Pa., 1972-74; engr. U.S. Nuclear Regulatory Commn., Rockville, Md., 1974—. Served with USNR, 1942-45. Decorated Air medal. Mem. Am. Nuclear Soc., Am. Inst. Chem. Engrs. (chmn. 1966-67), AAAS. Republican. Baptist. Mason, Elk. Home: 19108 Dowden Circle Poolesville MD 20837 Office: Fuels Process Systems Standards Br Office Standards Devel US Nuclear Regulatory Commn Washington DC 20555

PEASE, EDMUND W., banker; b. Boston, Jan. 30, 1934; s. Edmund Waldo and Mary Ann (Harvie) P.; student Mass. Inst. Tech., 1952-55; B.A., Columbia, 1957, postgrad., 1957-58. Sr. analyst Merrill, Lynch, Pierce, Fenner & Smith, N.Y.C., 1958-65; with Chase Manhattan Bank, N.Y.C., 1965—, v.p., 1971—, trust investment div. exec., 1973-76, investment services group exec., 1976-77, staff exec. trust and fiduciary dept., 1977—; dir. Vance Finance and Holding Corp., Wilmington, Del. Mem. alumni trustee nominating com. Columbia U., 1970-75, mem. univ. senate, 1975-79, chmn. senate alumni relations com., 1975-77, mem. budget com., mem. search com. for new dean of sch. gen. studies; treas. Smadbeck Found., 1965-75; trustee St. Lawrence Found., Rochester, N.Y., 1965-76, pres., 1978—; trustee Unitarian Universalist Assn., 1963-71; trustee Starr King Sch. for Ministry, Grad. Theol. Union, Berkeley, Calif., 1977—, chmn. bd., 1978—; bd. dirs. Martha Graham Center for Contemporary Dance, 1974—, also treas., v.p., 1975-77, mem. exec. and finance coms., chmn. long range planning com. Mem. N.Y. Soc. Security Analysts, Inst. Chartered Fin. Analysts, Fin. Analysts Fedn. Mason. Club: Internat. Wildlife Fedn. Office: 1211 Ave of Americas New York City NY 10036

PEASE, ELEANOR THOMPSON (MRS. DONALD CARGILL PEASE), lawyer; b. Bucyrus, Ohio, Mar. 28, 1923; d. Edgar William and Mary (Bliss) Thompson; B.A., Vassar Coll., 1944; J.D., Yale, 1946; m. Donald Cargill Pease, Sept. 9, 1949; 1 son, William Thompson. Admitted to Dist. Ct., D.C., Ct. Appeals, D.C., 1947; corp. lawyer E.I. DuPont Co., 1947-49. By-laws chmn. Jr. League, Wilmington, Del., 1951-53, bd. dirs., 1951-53, mag. chmn., 1959-60, edn. com., 1961-62; pres. Jr. League of Wilmington Sustainers Garden Club, 1969-70; by-laws chmn., bd. dirs. Del. Soc. Prevention Cruelty to Animals, 1950-52; chmn. Winterthur Mus. Jr. League Day, 1955-61; del., class rep. Vassar Alumnae Council, 1954; parliamentarian Girl Scouts, Wilmington, 1957, 59; pres. Del. Vassar Club, 1960-62; area chmn. United Fund, 1960-62; exec. com. Women's Coll. Information Program, 1961; docent Del. Art Mus., 1961-63; mem. Courts Task Force of Del. Agy. to Reduce Crime, 1968-71. Bd. dirs. vol. bur. Del. Welfare Council, 1950-52. Mem. Del. Hist. Soc., Nat. Trust for Historic Preservation, Soc. Colonial Dames Am. (pres. Del chpt. 1976—), Roger Williams Family Assn. Republican. Presbyn. (deacon). Home: 804 Princeton Rd Westover Hills Wilmington DE 19807

PEASE, SAMUEL FRANCIS, analytical chemist; b. Steelton, Pa., July 4, 1923; s. Louis and Louise P.; B.S., Mt. St. Mary's Coll., 1949; m. Louise Marie Trombino, July 31, 1950; 1 son, Christopher Joseph. Analytical chemist Central Iron and Steel, Harrisburg, Pa., 1950-51; asst. chief chemist A. S. McCreath and Sons, Harrisburg, 1953-69; supr. analytical chemistry AMP Inc., Harrisburg, 1969—. Active local Roman Catholic Ch.; high sch. tchr. Confrat. of Christian Doctrine. Served with U.S. Army, 1943-45. Mem. Am. Chem. Soc., Am. Legion. Republican. Home: 719 Paxton Rd Steelton PA 17113 Office: 2100 Paxton St Harrisburg PA 17105

PEASLEE, CHARLOTTE HOFFMAN, mag. editor; b. N.Y.C., July 13, 1931; d. Edmund Witherbee and Emily (Delafield) Peaslee; student Radcliffe Coll., 1949-52; B.J., U. Mo., 1958. Reporter, Paterson (N.J.) Morning Call, 1958; editorial asst. Electronic and Appliance Specialist, N.Y.C., 1958-60, Palmerton Pub. Co., N.Y.C., 1960-61; asst. editor in charge prodn. Sci. Digest, Hearst Mag. div., N.Y.C., 1961-64; writer Consol. Edison Co., N.Y.C., 1964-69; tech. editor Nat. Elec. Mfrs. Assn., N.Y.C., 1969-70; free-lance writer, copy editor, 1970-71; mng. editor Lady's Circle mag. Lopez Publs., N.Y.C., 1971-75; free-lance writer, editor Charlotte Peaslee Freelance Assos., 1976—. Mem. Women in Communications, NOW (N.Y. exec. v.p. 1972, dir. 1973), N.Y. Assn. Women Bus. Owners, Kappa Tau Alpha, Kappa Alpha Mu. Club: Overseas Press (N.Y.C.). Home: 165 E 72d St New York City NY 10021

PECAUT, ROBERT EUGENE, banker; b. Sioux City, Iowa, June 16, 1932; s. John Harold and Ethel Lillian (Horne) P.; B.A., Morningside Coll., 1958; LL.B., U. S.D., 1960; m. Janice Claire Metcalf Spencer, Feb. 24, 1956; children—Gregory Spencer, Mark Alan. Admitted to Iowa bar, 1960, S.D. bar, 1960, Fed. bar, 1960; trust officer First Nat. Bank, Sioux City, 1960-63, v.p., sr. trust officer, 1963-70; v.p., sr. trust officer Northeast Bank & Trust Co., Bangor, Maine, 1970-73; sr. v.p. Harvard Trust Co., 1973-77; v.p., trust officer Hempstead Bank, Garden City, N.Y., 1977—; v.p. Northeast Bankshare Assn., Lewiston, Maine, 1970-73; former dir. Harbeck Footwear, Grants Dairy Co., Rathbun Co., Rathbun Realty Co., Rathbun Lumber Co. Guest lectr. U. S.D. Law Sch., 1965-67. Chmn., Speakers Bur., Sioux City, 1964-65; mem. adv. bd. St. Joseph Hosp., 1968-70; mem. Bangor Dist. Nurses Adv. Bd.; chmn. finance com. Bangor Half-Way House; treas., mem. investment com. Community Girl Scouts; scoutmaster Boy Scouts Am. Mem. investment adv. com., City of Bangor, 1970-73. Former mem. bd. dirs. Harriett Ballou New Hope Center, Siouxland Assn. for Retarded Children, Sioux City Council Chs.; past pres. Siouxland Estate Planning Council. Served with USAF, Intelligence Service, 1952-56. Mem. Am. (probate, pension and profit sharing com.), Iowa bar assns., Am. Bankers Assn. (mem. community banks com., chmn. subcom. on community banks), Sudbury Pub. Health Nursing Assn. (past dir.), Mass. Bankers Assn. (chmn. edn. com.), Sudbury Minute Militia (capt.), State Bar S.D., State Bar Iowa, C. of C., Jr. C. of C. (dir.), Pi Kappa Delta (past pres.), Delta Theta Phi. Republican. Lutheran (past trustee). Mason. Club: Exchange. Home: 8 Tower Pl Smithtown NY 11787 Office: 1035 Stewart Ave Garden City NY 11530

PECK, EDWARD LIONEL, fgn. service officer; b. Los Angeles, Mar. 6, 1929; s. Alexander George and Rae (Lee) P.; B.S., U. Calif. at Los Angeles, 1956; M.B.A., George Washington U., 1973; m. Ann Day Slevin, May 5, 1974; children—Heather Anne, Brian Michael, Thomas William. With mktg. dept. Mobil Oil Co., 1956-57, Shell Oil Co., 1957; commd. fgn. service officer Dept. State, 1957; economics trainee, Washington, 1958-59; polit./economic officer, Sweden, 1960-61; lang. trainee, Morocco, 1962-63; economic officer, Tunisia, 1964-65; prin. officer, Oran, Algeria, 1967-68; internat. relations officer, Washington, 1969-71; spl. asst. to U/SEC, 1972-74; economic/comml. counsellor, Egypt, 1974-74; prin. officer, Iraq, 1977—. Served with U.S. Army, 1946-49, 51-52. Recipient various State Dept. awards; recipient Rivkin award Am. Fgn. Service Assn., 1973. Mem. Am. Fgn. Service Assn., Am. Mgmt. Assn., Alpha Tau Omega. Home and Office: Baghdad Dept of State Washington DC 20520

PECK, HUBERT RAYMOND, JR., mfg. exec.; b. Newark, Feb. 23, 1923; s. Hubert Raymond and Helen O. (White) P.; B.A., U. Pa., 1947; B.S., N.C. State U., 1949; m. Barbara Smith, Sept. 7, 1946; children—Hubert Raymond, Thomas, Laura H., Sarah E., Mary Tucker. Salesman, L.P. Muller & Co., Inc., Valley Forge, Pa., 1948-59, mgr. N.Y. office, 1959-63, partner, 1960, v.p., 1961, exec. v.p., 1974—; dir., v.p. Peck Mfg. Co., Warrenton, N.C., 1965—, Clayton Spinning Co. (N.C.), 1965—; dir., mem. fin. com. Windsor Life Ins. Co. Am., N.Y.C., 1966-77. Served with USAAF, 1943-45. Decorated Air Medal with six oak leaf clusters. Mem. Phila. Tennis Assn. (pres. 1971-73), Phila. Patrons Tennis Assn. (v.p. 1974—), Varsity Club, Sphinx Sr. Soc., Phi Gamma Delta. Republican. Episcopalian. Clubs: Merion Cricket, Martins Dam, Haverford Tennis. Home: 1272 Upper Gulph Rd Radnor PA 19087 Office: PO Box 486 Wayne PA 19087

PECK, RALPH HAROLD-HENRY, author; b. N.Y.C., May 9, 1926; s. Harold Lyman and Margaret Loretta (Dowdle) P.; grad. Cornell U., 1951; postgrad. U. Leyden (Netherlands), 1948, Sorbonne, Paris, 1948-49, N.Y. U., 1951-52; m. Martha Elizabeth Hunt, May 29, 1954. Author: Getaway Guides to Hong Kong, 1969-76, Las Vegas, 1969-76, Washington, 1969-76; The World of Plants, 1979; World Erosion, 1979; Travel Careers, 1976; Hotel and Motel Careers, 1977; freelance writer for Travel and Leisure, Gentlemen's Quar., Cleve. Mag., Town and Country, Mainliner, Vista/U.S.A., N.Y. Times, Buffalo News, others; advt. copywriter Cunningham & Walsh, N.Y.C., 1961-62, Caples Co., N.Y.C., 1957-61; dir. pub. relations Pan Am. World Airways, N.Y.C., 1953-57, Spanish Ministry Info. and Tourism, N.Y.C., 1966-69; dir. Greater Niagara Vacationland Tourism Agy. Mem. Beautification and Revitalization Com. Orchard Park. Served with U.S. Army, World War II. Decorated Silver Star, Bronze Star, Purple Heart with oak leaf clusters; recipient Man Who Did the Most for Buffalo citation C. of C., 1977. Mem. Soc. Am. Travel Writers (chmn. freelance council 1978), Cornell Alumni Assn., Zeta Psi. Presbyterian. Home and office: 51 Harvard Pl Orchard Park NY 14127

PECKHAM, JOHN MUNROE, III, real estate exec.; b. Abington, Mass., July 25, 1933; s. John Munroe and Mildred (Davis) P.; A.B., Tufts U., 1955; postgrad. Law Sch. Columbia, 1956; m. Joyce Mercier, July 14, 1962; children—Lisa M., Holly E. Pres. Data Realty Cos. Inc., Boston, 1965-74, Boston, 1974—; editor, pub. Real Estate Investment Newsletter, 1968-76; editor Real Estate Investor, also Real Estate Investor Letter, 1972—; columnist, cons., lectr. in field. Trustee several real estate trusts; chmn. fund raising Nat. Jewish Hosp., 1975—. Served with USNR, 1956-62. Named one of 10 outstanding young men Boston, 1969, Realtor of yr. Mass., 1969. Mem. Nat. Assn. Realtors (dir. 1973—), Realtors Nat. Mktg. Inst., C.C.I.M. (v.p. 1970-74), Nat. Inst. Farm and Land Brokers (v.p. 1975—), Internat. Real Estate Fedn., Real Estate Securities and Syndication Inst., Inst. Real Estate Mgmt., Mass. Assn. Realtors (pres. 1979). Baptist. Club: Ex-Ten Boston (pres. 1975—). Author: Master Guide to Income Property Brokerage, 1968; 101 Questions and Answers on Investing in Real Estate, 1971. Home: Charles River Park Boston MA 02114 Office: 358 Chestnut Hill Ave Boston MA 02146

PECKHAM, LAUREN AUGUSTUS, pipe organ and automatic instrument service exec.; b. Apulia Station, N.Y., Dec. 22, 1935; s. Augustus Newton and Dona Burton (Colebrook) P.; ed. pub. schs.; m. Joyce Lorraine Weitz, Dec. 20, 1958; children—David Scott, Kent Sheldon. Electronic technician Westinghouse Electric Corp., Elmira, N.Y., 1954-71; free-lance pipe organ and automatic instrument service and restoration. Mem. Am., Rochester (N.Y.) theatre organ socs., Antique Wireless Assn. (v.p., bd. chpt. vacuum tube com., editor Fact Sheet, Houck award 1978), Empire State Theatre and Musical Instruments Mus., Antique Radio Club Am. (dir.), Ind. Hist. Radio Soc. Methodist. Home: Ormiston Rd Breesport NY 14816

PECOR, RAYMOND CHARLES, JR., ferry boat transp. co. owner, mobile home co. owner; b. Burlington, Vt., May 18, 1939; s. Raymond C. and Lorraine T. (Tupper) P.; student Nichols Coll. Bus. Adminstrn., 1959, U. Vt., 1961; m. Jean Gianarelli, Sept. 15, 1962; children—Stacey, Raymond Charles III. Pres., Ray's Mobile Homes, Inc., Winooski, Vt., 1961—, Ray's Devel., Inc., Burlington, 1962—, Ray's Motor Sales, Inc., Barlington, 1947—, Ray's Mobile Homes, Ltd., St. John's, N.B., Can., 1971—, Can. Mobile Home Bus., St. Johns, 1971—, Lake Champlain Transp. Co., 1976—; dir. McAuliffe, Inc., Burlington, Mchts. Bank, Burlington. Bd. dirs. YMCA, United Fund, Greater Burlington Indsl. Corp. Mem. Young Pres.'s Orgn., Greater Vt. Assn., New Eng. Mobile Home Assn. (dir.), U. Vt. Alumni Assn. (dir. 1969—). Methodist. Club: Ethan Allen, Burlington Country (Burlington). Home: Pine Haven Shore Shelburne VT 05482 Office: King St Dock Burlington VT 05401

PEDERSEN, MARGUERITE, travel agy. exec.; b. N.Y.C.; d. Gustave and Gunhild (Pedersen) Olsen; student Trinity Coll., Chgo., 1930-32; m. Thomas Pedersen, June 6, 1936; children—Thomas Keith, David Alan. Realtor, Pedersen Agy., Inc., Nanuet, 1946—; pres. Pedersens Travel Agy. Inc., New City, N.Y., 1960—; tchr. adult edn. North Rockland Schs., 1960-78. Pres., Organized Taxpayers Assn. Inc.; past pres. units PTA Clarkstown Central Sch. Dist. Named Women of Year Rockland County by Rockland Bus. and Profl. Women's Club, Inc., 1977. Mem. Nanuet C. of C. (past pres.), Bd. Realtors, Rockland County Ins. Agts. Assn., Assn. Westchester Travel Agts., N.Y. State Soc. Real Estate Appraisers, Rockland Bus. and Profl. Womens Club. Mem. Mission Ch. and Evang. Free Ch. Am. Club: Soroptimist. Office: 135 S Main St New City NY 10956

PEDERSEN, WESLEY NIELS, ofcl. USIA; b. South Sioux City, Nebr., July 10, 1922; s. Peter Westergaard and Mary Gertrude (Sorensen) P.; student Tri-State Coll., Sioux City, Iowa, 1940-41; B.A. summa cum laude, Upper Iowa U.; postgrad. George Washington U., 1958-59, Fgn. Affairs. Exec. Seminar, Fgn. Service Inst., 1975; m. Angela Kathryn Vavra, Oct. 17, 1948; 1 son, Eric Wesley. Editor, writer Sioux City Jour., 1941-50; corr. N.Y. Times, Time, Life, Fortune, 1948-50; editor Dept. State, 1950-53, fgn. service officer, Hong Kong, 1960-63; fgn. affairs columnist, roving corr. USIA, 1953-60, chief, worldwide spl. publs. and graphics br., 1963-69, chief Office Spl. Projects, Washington, 1969-78; chief Office Spl. Projects, Internat. Communication Agy., Washington, 1978—; lectr. Upper Iowa U., 1975, George Washington U., 1975, 76, U.S. Dept. Transp., 1976, Pub. Relations Inst., Am. U., 1976, N.Y. U., 1976, 78; cons. pub. relations, editorial and design. Chmn. bd. Inst. for Govt. Pub. Info. Research, 1978—. Served with USAAF, 1943-46. Recipient 2 awards for journalistic excellence AP Mng. Editors Assn. Iowa, 1949; Meritorious Service award USIA, 1963; Mead Papers award 1969; named Most Outstanding Info. Ofcl. in Exec. Br. Govt., Govt. Info. Orgn., 1975; 1st prizes Soc. Tech. Communications, 1974, 75, 76. Mem. Fed. Editors Assn. (awards 1970, 74, 75), Am. Fgn. Service Assn., Internat. Assn. Bus. Communicators (nat. co-chmn. govt. relations com. 1976-78, awards 1973, 76, 78 chmn. nat. capital dist. conf. 1977, Communicator of Yr. award 1978), Nat. Assn. Govt. Communicators (chmn. profl. devel. 1976-77, pres. 1978—, Communicator of Yr. award 1977), Pub. Relations Soc. Am. (speaker nat. conf. New Orleans 1978). Episcopalian. Author: Legacy of a President, 1964; editor: Escape At Midnight and Other Stories (Pearl S. Buck), 1962, Macao (Richard Hughes), 1963; China's Urban Commoners (Henry Lethbridge), 1963; China's Men of Letters (K.E. Priestley), 1963; Children of China (Pearl S. Buck, Margaret Wylie), 1963; Quest for Greatness (Hubert H. Humphrey), 1967; The Americans and the Arts (Howard Taubman), 1969; The Dance in America (Agnes DeMille), 1969; Bounty from the Land (Dorothy Lafferty, Thomas Clemens), 1970; contbr. to American Heroes of Asian Wars, 1969, Principles and Practices of Public Relations (Fraser P. Seitel), 1978; mem. editorial bd. Fgn. Service Jour., 1975—; contbr. articles to profl. jours. Home: 5214 Sangamore Rd Washington DC 20016 Office: Internat Communication Agy 1776 Pennsylvania Ave NW Washington DC 20547

PEDREIRA, FRANK ALAN, pediatrician; b. New Brunswick, N.J., July 19, 1937; s. Frank and Mary Antonia (Fernandez) P.; A.B., Rutgers U., 1959; M.D., State U. N.Y., 1963; m. Anita Marie Michelle Perry, Aug. 4, 1962; children—Mark, Tracy, David, Christina. Intern, Upstate Med. Center, Syracuse, 1963-64, resident, 1964-66, chief resident in pediatrics, 1966, fellow in infectious disease, 1966; research virologist NIH, Bethesda, Md., 1966-69; practice medicine, specializing in pediatrics, Gaithersburg, Md., 1969—; clin. asso. prof. pediatrics, George Washington U. Sch. Medicine, Washington, 1975—; cons. infectious disease of children. Trustee Research Found., Children's Hosp. Nat. Med. Center, 1977—; bd. dirs., vice chmn. House of Ruth, Washington, 1976—. Served with USPHS, 1966-69. Recipient Honor's Thesis award Upstate Med. Center, 1963; AMA Physician Recognition award, 1973-76, 76-79. Diplomate Am. Bd. Pediatrics. Fellow Am. Acad. Pediatrics; mem. AMA, Montgomery County Med. Soc., Montgomery County Pediatric Soc., Med. and Chirurg. Faculty Md. Democrat. Club: Optimist (dir. 1971). Contbr. articles in field to profl. jours.; editorial bd. Clin. Proc., Children's Hosp. Nat. Center, 1976—. Home: 18919 Diary Rd Gaithersburg MD 20760 Office: 19251 Montgomery Village Gaithersburg MD 20760

PEEBLER, CHARLES DAVID, JR., advt. exec.; b. Waterloo, Iowa, June 8, 1934; s. Charles David and Marry E. (Barnett) P.; student Drake U., 1954-56; m. Susie Jacobs, June 5, 1958; children—David Jacobs, Mark Walter. Asst. to exec. v.p. J.L. Brandeis & Sons, Omaha, 1956-58; with Bozell & Jacobs, Inc., 1958—, v.p., mem. plans bd., 1960-65, pres. mid-continent ops., Omaha, 1965-67, pres., chief exec. officer, N.Y.C., 1967—, now also chmn. Mem. Covered Wagon Council Boy Scouts Am., 1962—; asso. chmn. Coll. Worlds Series, 1966; co-chmn. primary gifts div. Creighton U. New Goals Program, 1963; chmn. Omaha area Drake U. Bldg. Fund drive, 1960, 72; bd. dirs. United Community Services Omaha, 1963—, drive chmn., 1966-67; bd. dirs. United Funds and Councils of Am., 1967, chmn. pub. relations adv. com., mem. exec. com., 1968; bd. dirs. Omaha Jr. Achievement, 1964—, treas., mem. exec. com., 1965-66, pres., 1972-74; bd. dirs. Omaha chpt. NCCJ, 1962-65, chmn. ann. dinner, 1963; trustee Creighton-Omaha Regional Health Care Corp., 1972-73; pres. trustees Brownell-Talbot Sch. Mem. Young Pres.'s Orgn. (internat. dir.), Omaha Advt. Club (bd. dirs. 1964—), Omaha C. of C. (chmn. edn. com. 1962-64, bd. dirs. 1965—), Omaha Indsl.

Mgmt. Club (adv. bd. mgmt. 1960-62), Omaha Sales and Mktg. Execs. (bd. dirs. 1962), Ad Sell League Omaha (pres. 1972, chmn. exec. bd.), Nebr. Wildlife Fedn. (pres.). Clubs: Marco Polo (N.Y.C.); Bermuda Dunes Country (Palm Springs, Calif.); Omaha Press, Omaha Plaza, Highland Country (Omaha). Office: One Dag Hammarskjold Plaza New York City NY 10017

PEEL, JAMES EDWIN, chem. engr.; b. Lonaconing, Md., Dec. 26, 1924; s. Thomas Roscoe and Agnes Ferguson (Kirkpatrick) P.; B.S. in Chem. Engring., Carnegie Inst. Tech., 1953; m. Camilla Ellen Macaluso, June 25, 1955; children—James Edwin, David Thomas. Div. engr. U.S. Steel Chems. Co., Pitts., 1955-59, 67-71; project mgr. Pitts. Plate Glass Co., 1959-67; owner, operator Peel Engring. & Constrn. Co., cons. engring., Pitts., 1971—. Cub Scout master Allegheny Trails council Boy Scouts Am., 1965-69; mgr. Pony League Baseball, Leetsdale, Pa., 1967-71. Served with C.E., AUS, 1942-45. Decorated Bronze Star, Purple Heart; registered profl. engr., Pa. Mem. Pa. Soc. Profl. Engrs., Am. Inst. Chem. Engrs. Democrat. Roman Catholic. Designer, builder, operator waste treatment facilities for maleic acid waste liquors, 1956, developer energy conservation system, 1977. Home: 713 Harbaugh St Sewickley PA 15143 Office: 814 Eight Allegheny Center Pittsburgh PA 15212

PEGRAM, ROGER MILLER, communications exec.; b. Charlotte, N.C., May 13, 1930; s. James Roger and Mary Lilly (Sossomon) P.; student Ga. Inst. Tech., 1946-47; A.B. in Journalism and History, U. N.C., 1947-50. Sr. mktg. specialist Conf. Bd., N.Y.C., 1956-60, 63-72; asso. editor McGraw-Hill Pub. Co., N.Y.C., 1960-63; dir. communications Hay Assos., mgmt. cons., Phila., 1972—; instr. mktg. Fairleigh-Dickinson U., 1962. Served with C.E., AUS, 1951-53; Korea. Recipient Crain Found. gold medal for best indsl. original mktg. research, 1964; Outstanding Citizenship-Leadership award St. Bartholomew's Community Club, 1965. Mem. Am. Mktg. Assn., Am. Mgmt. Assn., S.A.R. (mem. nat. bicentennial commn. 1976—, state exec. bd. Pa., 1976—, bd. mgmt. Phila-Continental chpt.), Pa. Huguenot Soc. (sec. 1975—), Pa. Hist. Soc., S.R., Barons Order Magna Charta, Soc. Mayflower Descs., Colonial Order Acorn, Phila. Art Alliance, Order of Colonial Wars, Mil. Order Crusades, Am. Legion. Republican. Episcopalian. Clubs: St. Bartholomew's, Nine Plus (N.Y.C.); Vanguards Motoring (Phila.). Author: Selecting/Evaluating Distributors, 1964; Selling/Servicing National Accounts, 1972, others; Mgmt. Memo monthly bus. treatise, 1972—; articles on purchasing, mktg., gen. bus. mgmt., patriotic newsletters. Home: 1500 Locust St Philadelphia PA 19102 Office: 1845 Walnut St Philadelphia PA 19103

PEIKER, ALFRED STEPHEN, systems design engr.; b. Hartford, Conn., Mar. 12, 1936; s. Alfred Louis and Mildred Marie (Abrahamson) P.; B.E.E., Swarthmore Coll., 1959; postgrad. U. N.H., 1963-65; m. Sharon Lynne Maurer, Sept. 8, 1962 (div. Mar. 1974); children—Kathleen Marie, Jennifer Lynne. Jr. engr. The Perkin-Elmer Corp., Norwalk, Conn., 1959; nuclear instrumentation engr. E. G. and G., Inc., Boston, 1960; sr. engr. AVCO Corp., Lawrence, Mass., 1966-68; sr. project design engr. N.E. Electronics Corp., Concord, N.H., 1971-74; systems design engr. Aerotronic Assos., Inc., Contoocook, N.H., 1975—. Mem. Manchester Choral Soc., Concord Community Players. Mem. Jaycees (v.p. local chpt. 1970, state v.p. 1971, life mem. Senate 1972). Methodist. Developed infra-red baby warmer for hosp. use. Home: 18 N Spring St Concord NH 03301 Office: Riverside Dr Contoocook NH 03229

PEIPERL, ADAM, kinetic artist; b. Sosnowiec, Poland, June 4, 1935; s. Jacob and Fanny (Alster) P.; Came to U.S., 1953, naturalized, 1958; B.S. in Chemistry, George Washington U., 1957; postgrad. Pa. State U., 1959; m. Martha Rose Dorf, June 15, 1958; children—Maury, Laurence, Linda. One man shows at Balt. Mus. Art, 1969, Pa. Acad. Fine Arts, 1969, Smithsonian Mus. History and Tech., 1972, Marlborough Gerson Gallery, N.Y.C., 1969, Phila. Art Alliance, 1978; exhibited in group shows Washington Gallery Modern Art, 1968, Corcoran Gallery, 1968, Kent State U., 1969, McNay Art Inst., San Antonio, 1969, NASA Manned Spacecraft Center, Houston, 1970-71, U. Rochester, 1978; represented in permanent collections Pa. Acad. Fine Arts, Nat. Mus. History and Tech., Nat. Collection Fine Arts, Smithsonian Instn., Museum Boymans-van Beuningen, Rotterdam, Holland, John F. Kennedy Center for Performing Arts, Mus. Electricity in Life, Mpls., also prominent pvt. collections; created first kinetic polarized-light sculpture in water, 1968. Cons. in Russian lang. sci. lit. Library Congress, Washington, 1959-61, 66-67; chemist Nat. Bur. Standards, Washington, 1961-63. Address: 1135 Loxford Terr Silver Spring MD 20901

PEIZER, MAURICE SAMUEL, advt. co. exec.; b. Hartford, Conn., Aug. 21, 1912; s. David I. and Mary (Pomerantz) P.; B.A., U. Pa., 1933; postgrad. in Journalism Columbia, 1945, 49, 50; m. Marjorie Knowlton, Aug. 25, 1951; children—Joy Denise, Miriam Frances, Jessica Cathleen (dec.). Asst. to acting chief POW dept. U.S. Office of Censorship, N.Y.C., 1943-45; med. advt. writer Paul Klemtner & Co., Inc., Newark and N.Y.C., 1946-52, asst. copy chief, 1952-53, tech. dir. of copy, 1953-57, tech. dir., 1957-58, copy chief, 1958-62; sr. writer, pharm. copy chief, Hutchins Advt. Co., Rochester (N.Y.), 1962-67; group copy supr. William Douglas McAdams Inc., N.Y.C., 1967—. Pres. Nutley (N.J.) Little Theatre, 1957-59; co-founder Penfield (N.Y.) Players, pres., 1967; mem. publicity com. Nutley (N.J.) Citizens for Kennedy, 1960; mem. ofcl. bd. Methodist Ch., Penfield, N.Y., 1963-67; chmn. missions com. Community Ch., Cedar Grove, N.J., 1969-71, long-range planning com., 1972-74. Fellow Am. Med. Writers Assn. (pres. Met. N.Y. chpt. 1975-76, dir. 1973—, chmn. fellowships awards com. 1976-77, mem. exec. com. 1977-78, dir. dept. membership affairs 1977-79; Distinguished Service award 1978); mem. Pharm. Advt. Club of N.Y., AAAS, N.Y. Acad. Scis. Home: 135 Sunrise Terr Cedar Grove NJ 07009 Office: William Douglas McAdams Inc 110 E 59th St New York City NY 10022

PELELLA, JOHN VINCENT, JR., pharmacist; b. Newburgh, N.Y., Dec. 26, 1951; s. John Vincent and Lillian C. (Villa) P.; B.S. in Pharmacy, Union U. Albany Coll. Pharmacy, 1974; postgrad. in Health Care Adminstrn. C.W. Post Center, L.I. U., 1976—; m. Margaret Juliet Rogan, June 22, 1975; 1 son, Christopher John. Pharmacy intern Cassidy's Pharmacy, Newburgh, 1974; grad. pharmacist Dixx Drugs, Newburgh, 1974-75; staff pharmacist Cornwall (N.Y.) Hosp., 1975-76, dir. pharmacy, 1976—; preceptor Union U. Albany Coll. Pharmacy; lectr. on over-the-counter drugs to sch. and adult groups. Recipient Scholarship key Kappa Psi, 1971, certificate of appreciation Albany Coll. Pharmacy Alumni Assn., 1977. Fellow Am. Coll. Apothecaries; mem. Am. Soc. Hosp. Pharmacists, Am. Pharm. Assn., Am., Mid-Hudson Valley (sec.) socs. hosp. pharmacists, N.Y. State Council Hosp. Pharmacists. Roman Catholic. Home: 234 Summit Dr New Windsor NY 12550 Office: Cornwall Hosp Laurel Ave Cornwall NY 12518

PELL, ANTHONY DOUGLAS, fin. mgmt. co. exec.; b. Washington, July 2, 1938; s. Robert Thompson and Thecla Caroline (Barker) P.; A.B., Princeton, 1960; J.D. with honors, George Washington U., 1976; m. Katharine Murphey, Sept. 27, 1962; children—Theodore, Katherine. Admitted to N.Y. bar, 1966, Washington bar, 1966; atty., firm Coudert Bros., N.Y.C., 1966-68, firm Cadwalader, Wickersham & Taft, N.Y.C., 1968-72; v.p. The Boston Co., 1972-75, sr. v.p. fin. strategies, 1975—; dir. Fin. Strategies, Inc., Boston. Mem. Weston (Mass.) Planning Bd., 1976—. Served to lt. USN, 1960-64. Episcopalian. Club: Brookline (Mass.) Country. Home: 2 Willow Rd Weston MA 02193 Office: 1 Boston Pl Boston MA 02106

PELL, CLAIBORNE, U.S. senator; b. N.Y.C., Nov. 22, 1918; s. Herbert Claiborne and Matilda (Bigelow) P.; student St. George's Sch., Newport, R.I.; A.B. cum laude, Princeton U., 1940; A.M., Columbia U., 1946; 12 hon. degrees; m. Nuala O'Donnell, Dec., 1944; children—Herbert Claiborne III, Christopher T. Hartford, Nuala Dallas, Julia Lorillard Wampage. Enlisted USCG Res., 1941; served as seaman, ensign, North Atlantic, also Africa, Italy; hospitalized to U.S., 1944; instr. Navy Sch. of Mil. Govt., Princeton, 1944-45; lectr. Army Civil Affairs tng. schs., Harvard, Yale and Stanford, 1944-45; promoted to capt., 1963; on loan to Dept. State at San Francisco Conf., 1945, Dept. State, 1945-46, U.S. embassy, Czechoslovakia, 1946-47, established consulate gen., Bratislava, 1947-48; consulate gen. Genoa, Italy, 1949; with Dept. State, 1950-52; U.S. del. Inter-Govtl. Maritime Consultative Orgn., 1959; U.S. senator from R.I., 1961—. Dir., v.p. Internat. Rescue Com., Am. Immigration and Citizenship Conf., World Affairs Council R.I., F.D. Roosevelt Found. Cons. Dem. Nat. Com., 1953-60, exec. asst. to Dem. state chmn. R.I., 1952-54; chmn. R.I. Dem. fund drive, 1952; chmn. Dem. nat. registration drive, 1956, co-chmn., 1962. Decorated Legion of Honor (France); Knight Crown of Italy; Red Cross of Merit (Portugal); Order of Merit with Crown, Knights of Malta Grand Cross Order Merit (Liechtenstein). Mem. R.I. Soc. of Cincinnati (v.p.). Episcopalian. Clubs: Hope (Providence); Knickerbocker, Racquet and Tennis, Brook (N.Y.C.); Metropolitan (Washington); Travellers (Paris); Reading Room (Newport); St. James (London). Author: Megalopolis Unbound; (with Harold L. Goodwin) Challenge of The Seven Seas: Power and Policy. Address: Ledge Rd Newport RI 02840 Office: Senate Office Bldg Washington DC 20510

PELLICANO, VICTOR LOUIS, physician; b. Niagara Falls, N.Y., Mar. 26, 1912; s. Nicholas Alfred and Amalia Maria (Petito) P.; M.D., U. Buffalo, 1936; m. Eulalie M. Vincent, Sept. 10, 1938; children—Vicki Ann, Mary Susan. Intern, Buffalo City Hosp., 1936-37; resident internal medicine E.J. Meyer Meml. Hosp., Buffalo, 1937-40; individual practice medicine, specializing in internal medicine Niagara Falls, N.Y., 1940—; mem. staffs Mt. St. Mary's Hosp., Lewiston, N.Y., Niagara Falls Meml. Med. Center. Served from lt. to maj., U.S. Army, 1941-46. Diplomate Am. Bd. Internal Medicine. Fellow A.C.P.; mem. Niagara Falls Acad. Medicine (pres. 1950-51), Niagara County Med. Soc. (pres. 1955-56), Western N.Y. Soc. Internal Medicine (pres. 1953-54), Western N.Y. Heart Assn. (pres. 1975-76), AMA, Am. Soc. Internal Medicine; fellow Internat. Acad. Preventive Medicine, Internat. Coll. Applied Nutrition. Republican. Roman Catholic. Clubs: Niagara, Century. Home: 1317 Throndale Ave Niagara Falls NY 14305 Office: 760 Main St Niagara Falls NY 14301

PELTIER, HUBERT CONRAD, pharm. co. exec.; b. N.Y.C., Apr. 6, 1925; s. Hubert Whitmel and Margaret Cecile (Trainor) P.; student Manhattan Coll., 1943; student Ind. U., 1943-44, M.D. 1948; m. Joan Theresa Schroeder, Apr. 14, 1952; children—Mark, Jan, Marcia, Karen, Bret, Jeffrey. Intern, Sch. Medicine, Ind. U., 1948-49; resident James Whitcomb Riley Hosp. for Children, 1950-52; research physician Upjohn Co., Kalamazoo, 1956-59, chief clin. devel., 1959-62, mgr. clin. research, 1962-64; v.p., med. dir. Bristol Labs., Syracuse, N.Y., 1964-68; sr. dir. med. research Merck Sharp & Dohme Research Labs., West Point, Pa., 1968-70, exec. dir. med. affairs, 1970, v.p. med. affairs, 1971-78, sr. v.p. for med. affairs, 1978—. Served with M.C., AUS, 1943-46, USAF Res., 1948-50. Diplomate Am. Bd. Pediatrics. Mem. Am. Diabetes Assn., AMA, Am. Acad. Pediatrics, Am. Soc. Clin. Pharmacology and Therapeutics, Am. Rheumatism Assn., Pa. Med. Assn. (sci. adv. com.). Republican. Club: Glen Hardie Country (Wayne, Pa.). Home: 639 Gulph Rd Wayne PA 19087 Office: Merck Sharp & Dohme West Point PA 19486

PELZ, EDWARD JOSEPH, newspaper co. exec.; b. Seattle, May 26, 1918; s. Victor Hugo and Lois (Campbell) P.; B.A., Colo. Coll., 1938; postgrad. Columbia, 1940-42, 43; m. Caroline Lockwood Duncombe, July 11, 1942; children—Caroline C. (Mrs. Peter H. Elbow), Margaret L., Patricia C. (Mrs. Richard T. Hart), Sanford M. Office mgr. Pubs. Assn. of N.Y.C., 1938-45; personnel dir. N.Y. Times, N.Y.C., 1946-70, personnel benefits dir., 1970—. Served to lt. USNR, 1942-45. Mem. Am. Econ. Assn., Newspaper Personnel Relations Assn., Am. Assn. Rhodes Scholars, Phi Beta Kappa, Sigma Chi, Alpha Kappa Psi. Episcopalian. Home: 55 E 87th St New York City NY 10028 Office: 229 W 43d St New York City NY 10036

PEMBERTON, SANDI MACPHERSON, govtl. policy analyst, historian; b. St. Kitts, W.I.; s. Abraham Ebenezer and Rachel Adeiaide (Benjamin) P.; came to U.S., 1961, naturalized, 1978; Fulbright scholar in Ednl. Adminstrn., U. Utah, 1961-62; M.A. in History (Can. Govt. scholar), U. Alta., Edmonton, 1966; Ph.D. in History and Philosophy of Edn. (U. scholar 1967-68), U. Calif., Berkeley, 1969; m. Janette Emelda Matthew, Apr. 15, 1973. Sch. prin., St. Kitts, 1958-61; researcher Carnegie Commn. on Higher Edn., Berkeley, 1967-68, Office Instl. Research U. Calif., Berkeley, 1968-69; research asso. NEA, Washington, 1969-70; research dir., asst. prof. higher edn. U. Pitts., 1970-71; sr. researcher, project officer Nat. Inst. Edn., HEW, Washington, 1973-76; liaison rep. for program evaluation Bur. Postsecondary Edn., Office Edn., Washington, 1976-77; spl. asst. to asst. sec. for edn. HEW, Washington, 1977—; assigned White House Task Force on Internat. Cultural Programs, 1978; Nat. Inst. Edn. rep. to 1st Internat. Conf. on Gen. Cultural Theory Edn., Wis., 1973; dep. commr. higher edn. rep. to Fedn. Adv. Council on State Statistics, 1977; asst. sec. for edn. rep. Nat. Council Ednl. Research, 1978; mem. adv. panel for statis. analysis group edn. project Nat. Center Edn. Statistics; vis. scholar Harvard U., 1969. Recipient First Class certificate Erdiston Tchrs'. Coll., Barbados, W.I., 1958, Summer award Lincoln U., 1962; Carnegie Commn. Higher Edn. grantee, 1967. Mem. Center for Study of Presidency, Internat. Platform Assn., AAAS, Am. Hist. Assn., Nat. Trust Hist. Preservation, Met. Opera Guild, Nat. Symphony Orch. Assn. (asso.), Phi Beta Kappa. Adventist. Author: Disestablishment and Educational Equity in Ireland, 1869-1879, 1979. contbr. articles to profl. pubis. Home: 4404 Sunflower Dr Rockville MD 20853 Office: HEW North Bldg Washington DC 20202

PENA, JESUS J., hosp. adminstr.; b. Calabazar de Sagua, Cuba, May 4, 1938; s. Juan J. and Rosario M. (Valdes) P.; came to U.S., 1963, naturalized, 1969; J.D., Havana U., 1961; M.P.A., N.Y. U., 1971; m. Beatriz A. Meilan-Prat, Sept. 3, 1964. Mgr. laundry prodn. Mt. Sinai Hosp., N.Y.C., 1963-68; dir. bldg. services Jewish Meml. Hosp., N.Y.C., 1968-70; asst. dir. Lincoln Hosp., N.Y.C., 1970-72; asso. dir. Knickerbocker Hosp., N.Y.C., 1972-74; dep. dir. adminstrn. Central Islip (N.Y.) Psychiat. Center, 1974—; vice chmn. Planning Bd. No. 1, Bronx, N.Y., 1971-74; founder, co-chmn. Comprehensive Planning Health Bd., Bronx, 1969-71. Mem. Am. Hosp. Assn., Assn. Mental Health Adminstrs., Am. Pub. Health Assn., Hispanic Assn. Health Service Execs. (pres. 1976-77), N.Y. Hosp. Execs. Club, Royal Soc. for Promotion Health, N.Y. U. Alumni Assn. Democrat. Roman Catholic. Home: 3333 Henry Hudson Pkwy Riverdale NY 10463 Office: Carleton Ave Central Islip Psychiatric Center Central Islip NY 11722

PENDER, MICHAEL ROGER, county ofcl.; b. Bklyn., Feb. 18, 1926; s. Horace G. and Lilian (Higgins) P.; A.B., Dartmouth, 1947, M.S., 1950; m. Francina Joan Krosschell, June 4, 1949; children—Michael Roger, William J., Robin Jane, Richard A., John A. Civil engr. N.H. Hwy. Dept., 1948; project engr. Madigan-Hyland, Inc., cons. engrs., N.Y.C., 1950-60; exec. asst. to exec. v.p. and dir. state exhibits N.Y. World's Fair 1964-1965 Corp., N.Y.C., 1960-65; commr. pub. works Town of Hempstead, N.Y., 1965-73; commr. gen. services Town of Hempstead, 1974-77; commr. pub. works County of Nassau, 1978—. Sec., asst. treas. Hempstead Indsl. Devel. Corp., 1967—; mem. Traffic Safety Bd. Nassau County, 1973—, vice chmn., 1975-77; mem. Garden City Adv. Com. on Edn., 1965-69, pres., 1968-69; mem. Men's Assn. Garden City High Schs., 1964—, v.p., 1970-73; past pres. Garden City Paid and Vol. Employment Service; mem. Nassau-Suffolk Bi-County Planning Bd. Named One of Top Ten Pub. Works Ofcls. in U.S., 1973; Profl. Engr. of Year Nassau County, 1976; L.I. Civil Engr. of Year, 1978. Registered profl. engr., N.Y. Fellow ASCE (past br. pres., past sect. pres.), Inst. Transp. Engrs.; mem. Nat., N.Y. (v.p.) socs. profl. engrs., Inst. Municipal Engrs. (pres.), Inst. for Transp., Am. Pub. Works Assn. (regional dir., pres. N.Y. Chpt. 1974), Am. Rd. and Transp. Builders Assn. (exec. com. transp. ofcls. div.), Am. Water Works Assn., N.Y. State Assn. Traffic Safety Bds. (pres. 1975-77), Assn. Indsl. Devel. Agys. N.Y., N.Y. State Assn. Towns (v.p. 1975-78), Permanent Internat. Assn. Nav. Congresses, L.I. Water Conf., N.Y. State County Hwy. Supts. Assn., Nat. Assn. County Engrs., Dartmouth Soc. Engrs., Dartmouth Alumni Assn. L.I. (pres. 1962-64, sec. 1960-62, 67—), World's Fair Collectors Soc. (founder, 1st sec.-treas. 1968-75, pres. 1976-77), Garden City Hist. Soc. Rotarian. Contbr. articles to profl. jours. Home: 148 Poplar St Garden City NY 11530 Office: 1 West St Mineola NY 11501

PENDLETON, OTHNIEL ALSOP, fund raiser, clergyman; b. Washington, Aug. 22, 1911; s. Othniel Alsop and Ingeborg (Berg) P.; A.B., Union Coll. (N.Y.), 1933; B.D., Eastern Bapt. Theol. Sem., 1936; M.A., U. Pa., 1936, Ph.D., 1945; postgrad. Columbia U., 1937-38; m. Flordora Mellquist, May 15, 1935; children—John, James, Thomas, Ann, Susan. Ordained to ministry Bapt. Ch., 1936; pastor chs., Jersey City, 1935-39, Phila., 1939-43; dean Sioux Falls (S.D.) Coll., 1943-45; fund raiser Am. Bapt. Ch., N.Y.C., 1945-47, Mass. Bapt. Ch., Boston, 1947-54; fund raiser, Seattle, Chgo., Boston, Washington and N.Y.C., 1955-64, Westwood, Mass., 1971—; staff Marts & Lundy, Inc., N.Y.C., 1964-71; lectr. Andover-Newton Sem., Newton, Mass., 1958, Boston U. Sch. Theology, 1958, Harvard U., Cambridge, Mass., 1977-78. Mem. Am. Hist. Assn., Phi Beta Kappa. Democrat. Baptist. Contbr. articles in field to profl. jours.; author: New Techniques for Church Fund Raising, 1955. Address: 411 Hartford St Westwood MA 02090

PENNELL, CARROLL EDWARD, II, banker; b. Brunswick, Maine, Aug. 12, 1934; s. Andrew Simpson and Alice Maria (Coffin) P.; A.B., Bowdoin Coll., 1956; M.B.A., N.Y. U., 1973; m. Nancy Wheelan Sutliff, Sept. 3, 1966; children—Andrew Sutliff, Samuel Stuart. Project supr. Cole, Layer-Trumble Co., Dayton, O., 1959-63; adminstrv. asst. Investors Central Mgmt. Corp., N.Y.C., 1963-64; chief real estate appraiser Empire Savs. Bank, N.Y.C., 1964-73; real estate officer New England Merchants Nat. Bank, Boston, 1973—; instr. lectr. real estate, fin. analysis Univ. Coll. Northeastern U., Boston; cons. in field. Served with U.S. Army, 1957-58. Mem. Columbia Soc. Real Estate Appraisers, Beta Theta Pi. Republican. Congregationalist. Clubs: Sons of Am. Revolution, Bowdoin (Boston). Home: 12 Cottonwood Rd Wellesley MA 02181 Office: 28 State St Boston MA 02106

PENNEY, ALPHONSUS LIGOURI, bishop; b. St. John's, Nfld., Can., Sept. 17, 1924; s. Alphonsus Ligouri and Catherine (Mullaly) P.; L.Ph., U. Ottawa, 1945, L.Th., 1949. Ordained priest Roman Catholic Ch., 1949, named vicar forane, 1960, vicar gen., 1971, prelate of honour, 1971; asst. priest, then parish priest, 1949-72; bishop of Grand Falls (Nfld.), 1973—. Mem. sch. bd., Burin Peninsula, Nfld., 1957-69, St. John's, 1969-71; mem. Cath. Edn. Com., 1973—. Served with RCAF, 1952-57. Address: Cathedral Residence Box 771 8A Church Rd Grand Falls NF A2A 2J8 Canada*

PENNEY, CHARLES RAND, lawyer, civic worker; b. Buffalo, July 26, 1923; s. Charles Patterson and Gretchen (Rand) P.; B.A., Yale U., 1945; LL.B., U. Va., 1951; J.D., U. Va., 1970. Admitted to Md. bar, 1952, N.Y. bar, 1958; U.S. Supreme Ct. bar, 1958; law sec. to U.S. Dist. Judge W.C. Coleman, Balt., 1951-52; mem. firm Penney & Penney, Buffalo, 1958-61; pvt. practice, Niagara County, N.Y., 1961—. Dir. devel. office Children's Hosp., Buffalo, 1952-54; sales mgr. Amherst Mfg. Corp., Williamsville, N.Y., 1954-56, also Delevan Electronics Corp., East Aurora, N.Y. Mem. art com., hon. bd. mgrs. Meml. Art Gallery, U. Rochester (N.Y.); trustee Buffalo Soc. Artists. Served to 2d lt. AUS, 1943-46. Life mem. Niagara County Antiques Club (hon.), Albright-Knox Art Gallery, Buffalo, Patteran Artists (hon.), Niagara County Hist. Soc., Buffalo Museum Sci., Buffalo and Erie County Hist. Soc.; mem. Niagara County (N.Y.) bar assns., Assn. Am. Artists, Niagara Council Arts, Niagara Falls Area C. of C., Smithsonian Instn., M.H. de Young Meml. Mus., Asso. Art Orgn. Western N.Y. Historic Lockport (life), Nat. Trust Historic Preservation, Gallery Assn. N.Y., Kenan Center, Met. Mus. Art, Mus. Modern Art, Asian Art Mus., Calif. Palace Legion of Honor, Archives of Am. Art, Historic Lewiston, Old Fort Niagara Assn. (life), Victorian Soc. in Am., Cobblestone Soc., Intrepids Club, Internat. Mus. Photography, Chi Psi, Phi Alpha Delta. Presbyterian (deacon). Clubs: Masons (32 deg.), Automobile; Zwicker Aquatic (Lockport, N.Y.). Editorial bd. The Art Gallery mag. Address: 343 Bewley Bldg Lockport NY 14094

PENNIE, JOHN CRAIGANS, holding co. exec.; b. London, Ont., Can., June 1, 1939; s. Kenneth James and Marjorie Alberta (Tennant) P.; C.I.M., U. Westen Ont., 1964; m. Ellen Cook Nichols, Oct. 8, 1977; children by previous marriage—Todd Leland, Ryan Richardson. Merchandising mgr. Can. Gen. Electric Co., Montreal, Que., 1967-70, mktg. mgr., Toronto, Ont., 1970-72; dir. mktg. GSW Ltd./Limitee, Toronto, 1972—; pres. Omnibus Corp., Toronto, 1975—; chmn. Omnibus Inc., Los Angeles; dir. Omnibus Corp., London, Image West Inc., Los Angeles, Dynatrex Holdings Ltd., Guelph, Ont., Image Graphics Ltd., Omnibus Communications Ltd., London, Ont. Mem. Can. Inst. Mgmt. Home: 935 Meadow Wood Rd Mississauga ON L5J 2S8 Canada Office: 92 Jarvis St Toronto ON M5C 2H5 Canada

PENNINGTON, DENNIS IRA, geochemist; b. Bklyn., Dec. 27, 1949; s. George Albert and Elizabeth (Barr) P.; B.A. in Geology, State U. N.Y., Potsdam, 1971; M.S. in Geochemistry (Research fellow) Pa. State U., 1973; m. Mary Lou Schrom, Sept. 27, 1975. Project engr. Sanders and Thomas, Pottstown, Pa., 1973-75; project coordinator Jack McCormick & Assos., Inc., Berwyn, Pa., 1975-76; project mgr. Richard Cowan & Assos., Inc., Quakertown, Pa., 1976—. Bd. dirs. Potsdam Coll. Devel. Fund, 1970-71; active Pa. Assn. Retarded Children. Served with Air N.G., 1971-76. Mem. Assn. Profl. Geol. Scientists (editor newsletter, mem. exec. com.), Soc. Mining Engrs.,

Am. Inst. Mining Engrs., Geochem. Soc., Soc. Environ. Geochemistry and Health, Assn. Geoscientists for Profl. Devel., AAAS, Water Pollution Control Fedn., Water Pollution Control Assn. Pa., Nat. Water Well Assn. Methodist. Contbr. articles to profl. jours. Home: 59 Dewsbury Ln Quakertown PA 18951 Office: 128 E Broad St Quakertown PA 18951

PENNISTEN, JOHN WILLIAM, actuary; b. Buffalo, Jan. 25, 1939; s. George William and Lucy Josephine (Gates) P.; A.B., Hamilton Coll., 1960; NSF fellow Harvard, 1960-61; postgrad. U.S. Army Lang. Sch., 1962-63. Asst. actuary Mass. Gen. Life Ins. Co., Boston, 1966-68; actuarial asst. New Eng. Mut. Life Ins. Co., Boston, 1965-66; actuarial asso. John Hancock Mut. Life Ins. Co., Boston, 1968-71; asst. actuary George B. Buck Cons. Actuaries, Inc., N.Y.C., 1971-75; asst. actuary Martin E. Segal Co., N.Y.C., 1975—. Served with AUS, 1961-64. Mem. Soc. Actuaries (asso.), Internat. Actuarial Assn., Am. Risk and Ins. Assn., Am. Pension Conf., Actuaries Club N.Y., Am. Math. Soc., Math. Assn. Am., Phi Beta Kappa. Home: 135 Willow St Brooklyn NY 11201 Office: 730 Fifth Ave New York City NY 10019

PENNOCK, DONALD WILLIAM, engr.; b. Ludlow, Ky., Aug. 8, 1915; s. Donald and Melvin (Evans) P.; B.S. in Mech. Engring., U. Ky., 1940, M.E., 1948; m. Vivian C. Kern, Aug. 11, 1951; 1 son, Douglas. Stationary engring., constrn. and maintenance Schenley Corp., 1935-39; mech. equipment design engr., mech. lab. U. Ky., 1939; exptl. test engr. Wright Aero. Corp., Paterson, N.J., 1940, 41, investigative and adv. engr. to personnel div., 1941-43; indsl. engr. Eastern Aircraft, div. Gen. Motors, Linden, N.J., 1943-45; factory engr. Carrier Corp., Syracuse, N.Y., 1945-58, sr. facilities engr., 1958-59, corp. staff engr., 1959-60, corp. material handling engr., 1960-63, mgr. facilities engring. dept., 1963-65, mgr. archtl. engring., 1966-68, mgr. facilities engring. dept., 1968-78; faculty mem. Indsl. Mgmt. Center, 1962; staff mem. U. Kans. Extension Material Handling Analysis Course, 1959-67. Mem. munitions bd. SHIAC, 1950-52. Named to Exec. and Profl. Hall of Fame, 1966; registered profl. engr., Ky., N.J., D.C. Mem. Soc. Advancement Mgmt. (nat. v.p. material handling div. 1953-54), ASME, Am. Material Handling Soc. (dir. 1950-57, chmn. bd., pres. 1950-52), Am. Soc. Mil. Engrs., Nat. Soc. Profl. Engrs., Am. Mgmt. Assn. (mem. packaging council 1950-55; life mem. planning council), Nat. Material Handling Conf. (exec. com. 1951), Internat. Material Mgmt. Soc. (life), Tau Beta Pi. Mng. editor Materials Handling Engring. (mag. sect.), 1949-50; mem. editorial adv. bd. Modern Materials Handling (mag.), 1949-52. Contbr. articles to tech. jours. Contbg., cons. editor: Materials Handling Handbook, 1958. Home: 24 Pebble Hill Rd Dewitt NY 13214

PENNOCK, GEORGE IRVING, chem. engr.; b. Laconia, N.H., Apr. 17, 1948; s. George Ayer and Helen Belle (Grace) P.; B.S. in Chem. Engring., U. N.H. Gen. Electric Extension, 1966, tool and die makers certificate, 1970; m. Marie Joanne St. Pierre, Aug. 3, 1968; 1 dau., Robin Amy. Mem. mfg. and engring. acad. program Gen. Electric Co., Somersworth, N.H., 1966-72; shift supr. Gallant Mfg. Co., Newmarket, N.H., 1972-73; ops. chem. engr. Atlantic Terminal Corp., Newington, N.H., 1973—. Home: 7 Bernier St Somersworth NH 03878 Office: PO Box 1288 Old Dover Rd Newington NH 03801

PENSIERO, NICHOLAS FRANCIS, mfg. co. exec.; b. Phila., Mar. 4, 1918; s. Frank J. and Maria Antonia (Zenobio) P.; B.S., magna cum laude, La Salle Coll., 1940; m. Dorothy Connors, July 1, 1950; children—Ted, James, Mary Ann, Mark, Nicole, Benjamin. With RCA Corp., Moorestown, N.J., 1940-53, 62—, dir. mktg. services and pub. affairs, 1962—; asst. to pres., mgr. mdse. devel. Oxy Catalyst, Inc., Devon, Pa., 1953-S9; v.p., gen. cons. Dibrell & Co., Phila., 1959-60; mgr. mktg. adminstrn. Philco Corp. Computer div., Willow Grove, Pa., 1960-62; instr., lectr. bus., LaSalle Coll., 1946-61; guest lectr. Temple U., 1974-76, Stockton State Coll., 1975-76. Mem. La Salle Coll. Endowment Found.; chmn. bd. trustees So. N.J. chpt. Nat. Multiple Sclerosis Assn., 1975-76. Served with USAAF, 1942-46, USAF, 1951-53. Decorated Legion of Merit. Mem. Pub. Affairs Council (chmn. 1976—), Aerospace Industries Assn., Phila. Public Relations Assn., Air Force Assn., Assn. U.S. Army, Armed Forces Communications and Electronic Assn., N.J. Press Assn. (dir. 1972-76), Pub. Relations Soc. Am., Alpha Epsilon. Clubs: Riverton (N.J.) Country; National Space, National Press, Army and Navy (Washington). Home: 433 Paul Dr Moorestown NJ 08057 Office: RCA Cherry Hill Bldg 201 1 Camden NJ 08101

PENSIS, ALBERT ETIENNE, home furnishing co. exec.; b. La Hulpe, Belgium, June 12, 1937; s. Albert F. and Madeleine (Doppee) P.; A.A., Mitchell Coll., 1959; postgrad. Parsons Sch. Design, 1959-62. Staff designer H. Chambers Co., Balt., 1962-64; v.p. in charge design and merchandise mgr. Louise Mazor, Inc., Balt., 1964-69; sr. v.p. interior design W & J Sloane, Inc., N.Y.C., 1969—. Recipient Nat. Retail Design award Am. Soc. Interior Design, 1977. Home: 200 CPS New York NY 10019 Office: 414 Fifth Ave New York NY 10018

PENTA, IRENE PLATT (MRS. WALTER E. PENTA), nurse, club woman; b. Concord, N.H., Jan. 2, 1920; d. Frank Bishop and Ida Louisa (Cable) Platt; student Portland Jr. Coll., 1939; R.N., Dr. Drummond's Hosp. Nursing Sch., Portland, Maine, 1942; m. Walter E. Penta, Sept. 25, 1943; 1 son, Donald Platt. Nurse, Maine Med. Center, Portland, 1942-43, Mercy Hosp., Portland, 1943, Boston City Hosp., 1943-44, Beth Israel Hosp., Boston, 1944, Mass. Gen. Hosp., Boston, 1944, Deaconess Hosp., Boston, 1943, Meth. Hosp., Dallas, 1944-45, Med. Arts, Dallas, 1944-45, So. Bapt. Hosp., Dallas, 1944-45. Sec., Woman's Aux. Maine Med. Assn., Portland, 1955-56, v.p., 1956-57, pres.-elect, 1957-58, pres., 1958-59, bd. dirs., 1955—, internat. health chmn., 1967-69; v.p. Ladies of Kiwanis, Portland, 1958, pres., 1959, bd. dirs., 1957—, welfare chmn., 1968-69, activities chmn., 1972-74; active Hosp. Aux. Maine Med. Center; mem. organizational com. Tri-State Health Careers Research Group, Portland, 1960-61; rural health chmn. region one, Women's Aux. to AMA, 1960—, internat. health chmn. Maine Women's Aux., 1968-71. Mem. Am., Maine nurses assns., Dr. Drummonds Hosp. Alumni Assn. (pres. 1964-66), Nat. Soc. Daus. Founders and Patriots Am., Internat. Platform Assn., Wives' Wing Aerospace Med. Assn., Maine Hist. Soc., Am. Water Ski Assn., Nat. Soc. Women Descs. Ancient and Hon. Arty. Company (v.p. Maine chpt. 1973—, color bearer 1975—). Congregationalist (pres. Jr. Guild 1956). Club: Woodfords (Portland). Home: 316 Woodford St Portland ME 04103

PENZIAS, ARNO ALLAN, astrophysicist, electronics co. exec.; b. Munich, Germany, Apr. 26, 1933; s. Karl and Justine (Eisenreich) P.; came to U.S., 1940; naturalized, 1946; B.S., Coll. City N.Y., 1954; M.A., Columbia U., 1958, Ph.D., 1962; Dr. honoris causa, l'observatoire de Paris, 1976; m. Anne Pearl Barras, Nov. 25, 1954; children—David Simon, Mindy Gail, Laurie Ruth. Mem. tech. staff Bell Labs., Holmdel, N.J., 1961-72, head radiophysics research dept., Holmdel, N.J., 1972-76, dir. radio research lab., 1976—. Lectr., Princeton U., 1967-72, vis. prof., 1972—; asso. Harvard Coll. Obs., Cambridge, Mass., 1968—; adj. prof. State U. N.Y., Stony Brook, 1974—. Trustee, Trenton (N.J.) State Coll., 1977—. Served to lt. Signal Corps AUS, 1954-56. Recipient Henry Draper medal Nat. Acad. Sci., 1977; Herschel medal Royal Astronom. Soc., 1977, Nobel prize in Physics, 1978. Mem. Nat. Acad. Scis., Am. Astron. Soc., Am. Acad. Arts and Scis., Am. Phys. Soc., Internat. Astron. Union. Republican. Jewish. Club: E. Brunswick Country Swim. Contbr. numerous articles to profl. jours. Home: 419 S 5th Ave Highland Park NJ 08904 Office: Crawford Hill Holmdel NJ 07733

PEOPLES, VERNON DANIEL, JR., econ. cons., speech writer; b. Chgo., Dec. 22, 1949; s. Vernon Daniel and Margarette (Wende) P.; B.A. in Polit. Sci., Wittenberg U., 1971; M.A. in Internat. Econs., (Sch. Advanced Internat. Studies grantee) Johns Hopkins, 1975. Researcher, writer, cons. dept. internat. econ. affairs Nat. Assn. Mfrs., Washington, 1974-75; mgr. pub. affairs planning and research Internat. Paper Co., N.Y.C., 1975—. Served with AUS, 1971-73. Mem. Nat. Forensics Soc. (hon.), Pi Sigma Alpha, Pick and Pen, Am. Polit. Sci. Assn., Phi Eta Sigma. Home: 229 E 81st St New York City NY 10028 Office: 220 E 42d St New York City NY 10017

PEPPER, ADELINE ELIZABETH, author, photographer; b. Madison, Wis.; d. John William and Emmeline (Able) Pepper; B.A., U. Wis. Med: writer A.M.A., A.C.S.; asst. advt. mgr. Mead Johnson & Co., Evansville, Ind., publicity dir. Com. on Care of Children in Wartime, Evansville, 1945; radio advt. writer Knox Reeves, Inc., Mpls.; pub. relations Pa. R.R. Centennial, 1946; advt. writer L. W. Frohlich Agy., N.Y.; med. advt. writer and designer E. R. Squibb & Sons, Ciba Pharm.; owner Pep, Inc., advt. service, 1956—. Mem. Authors League Am., Am. Med. Writers Assn., Phi Kappa Phi. Author: Tours of Historic New Jersey (N.J. Tercentary medal 1964), 1965, rev. edit., 1973; N.J. vol. Fodor's Guide to the U.S.A., 1966; The Glass Gaffers of New Jersey and Their Creations (award N.J. Assn. Tchrs. English 1972, award of Merit Am. Assn. State and Local History 1972), 1971. Contbr. articles on travel, history, and decorative arts to mags. and maj. met. newspapers. Address: 221 W Colfax Roselle Park NJ 07204

PEPPER, JAMES, realtor, investor; b. Wilmington, Del., Aug. 17, 1933; s. Thomas A. and Pauline C. (Carpenter) P.; grad. Goldey Beacom Real Estate Sch., 1970; m. Shirley A. Rogers, Feb. 25, 1953; children—Robert, Colleen, Keith, Darryl. Engaged as home builder, 1957-65; with retail kitchen cabinet bus., 1965-67; realtor, 1965—; pres. Pepper Real Estate Co., Inc., Georgetown, Del., 1965—, also Harris-Hanby of Dover (Del.); sec. treas. chpt. Nat. Assn. Home Builders, 1964. Served with USAF, 1953-57; Korea. Licensed comml. multi-engine pilot. Mem. Nat. Assn. Realtors, Del. Assn. Realtors (pres. 1978), Sussex County Bd. Realtors (pres. 1974), Georgetown C. of C. (pres. 1965). Republican. Methodist. Club: Georgetown Lions (pres. 1964). Home: 11 W Pine St Georgetown DE 19947 Office: 105 Depot St Georgetown DE 19947

PEPPER, ROLLIN ELMER, microbiologist, educator; b. Glens Falls, N.Y., June 8, 1924; s. Henry Orville and Ruby Mae (Tucker) P.; B.A., Earlham Coll., 1950; M.S., Syracuse U., 1953; Ph.D., Mich. State U., 1963; m. Lucille Beverly Blackman, May 30, 1953; children—Roger R., Barbara Pepper Moquin, Susan B. Asso. scientist Ethicon, Inc., Somerville, N.J., 1951-60; research asso. Mich. State U., East Lansing, 1963-64; asst. prof. dept. biology Elizabethtown (Pa.) Coll., 1964-65, asso. prof., 1965-68, prof., 1968—, chmn. dept., 1968-77; vis. prof. biology U. Zambia, 1972-73; microbiol. cons. R. Schattner Co., Washington. Pres. Elizabethtown Bd. Health. Postdoctoral fellow Mich. State U., 1963-64. Mem. Am. Soc. Microbiology, AAUP, Am. Sci. Affiliation, Internat. Graphoanalysis Soc., Nat. Campers and Hikers Assn. Mem. Brethren in Christ Ch. Club: Rotary. Contbr. articles to profl. jours., chpt. to book. Patentee in field. Home: 420 N Mt Joy St Elizabethtown PA 17022 Office: Elizabethtown College Elizabethtown PA 17022

PEPYNE, EDWARD WALTER, educator, lawyer, psychologist; b. Springfield, Mass., Dec. 27, 1925; s. Walter Henry and Frances A. (Carroll) P.; B.A., Am. Internat. Coll., 1948; M.S., U. Mass., 1951; prof. diploma U. Conn., 1964, student N.Y. U., 1952-55; Ed.D., U. Mass., 1968; J.D., Western New Eng. Coll., 1978; m. Carol Jean Dutcher, Aug. 2, 1958. Prin., tchr. Gilbertville Grammar Sch., Hardwick, Mass., 1948-49; sch. counselor West Springfield (Mass.) High Sch. 1949-53; instr. N.Y. U., 1953-54; supt. schs., New Shoreham, R.I., 1954-56; asst. prof. edn. Mich. State U., 1956-58; sch. psychologist, guidance dir. Pub. Sch. System, East Long, Mass., 1958-62; lectr. Westfield State Coll., 1961-65; dir. pupil services Chicopee Pub. Sch., 1965-68; asso. prof. counselor edn. U. Hartford, West Hartford, 1968-71, prof., 1971—, dir. Inst. Coll. Counselors Minority and Low Income Students, 1971-72, dir. Div. Human Services, 1972-77. Cons. Aetna Life & Casualty Co., Hartford, 1962-75; exec. dir. Sinapi Assos., 1959-78. Chief Welfare Services, Civil Defense, Levittown, N.Y., 1953-54. Mem. Am. Personnel and Guidance Assn., New Eng. Personnel and Guidance Conf. (dir.), New Eng. Ednl. Research Orgn. (pres. 1971), Am. Assn. Sch. Adminstrs., Am. Bar Assn., Mass. Bar Assn., Mass. Acad. Trial Attys., Am. Psychol. Assn., Am. Ednl. Research Assn., Phi Delta Kappa. Co-author: Better Driving, 1958. Asso. editor Highway Safety and Driver Education, 1954; chmn. editorial com. Man and the Motor Car, 5th edit., 1954. Contbr. numerous articles to profl. jours. Home: Box 31 Suburban Dr Ashfield MA 01330 Office: 200 Bloomfield Ave West Hartford CT 06117 also PO Box 345 Ashfield MA 01330

PERALES, CESAR AUGUSTO, govt. ofcl.; b. N.Y.C., Nov. 12, 1940; s. Francisco and Manuela P.; B.A., Coll. City N.Y., 1962; LL.B., Fordham U., 1965; m. Gladys Pena, Aug. 30, 1970; children—Nina, Diana. Admitted to N.Y. State bar, 1966; atty.-in-charge Williamsburg Neighborhood Legal Services, Bklyn., 1968-70; gen. counsel N.Y.C. Model Cities Adminstrn., 1970-72; exec. dir. Puerto Rican Legal Def. and Edn. Fund, N.Y.C., 1972-74; dir. Criminal Justice Coordinating Council, Office of Mayor N.Y.C., 1976-77; prin. regional official HEW, N.Y. Region, 1977—; adj. asso. prof. polit. sci. L.I. U., 1976; adj. lectr. Bklyn. Coll., 1971-72. Candidate Dem. Primary Election, Congress 14th Dist. Bklyn., 1974. Home: 218 Wyckoff St Brooklyn NY 11217 Office: HEW 26 Federal Plaza New York City NY 10007

PERCHARD, ROBERT JOSEPH, research and devel. cons.; b. Boston, Dec. 7, 1909; s. John Richard and Agnes Theresa (Houston) P.; A.B., Boston Coll., 1933, M.A. in Biol. Scis., 1934; postgrad. Boston U., 1934-35; m. Katherine Avis Pheeny, June 15, 1935; children—Robert Anthony (dec.), Avis Marion, Susan Elizabeth. Asso. in pharmacy Lynch Drug Co., Hyde Park, Mass., 1935-37; profl. service rep. E.R. Squibb & Sons, Boston, 1937-40, hosp. rep., 1940-43, profl. service mgr., N.Y.C., 1946-56; med. asso. Squibb Inst. for Med. Research, New Brunswick, N.J., 1956-59, clin. research asso., 1959-65; cons. in research and devel. programs USCG; pres. Therm-X-Glo, Ltd., Providence, 1973—; vis. lectr. biology Northeastern U., Boston, 1949; guest lectr. Conn. Coll. Pharmacy, New Haven, 1948; guest speaker R.I. Soc. Hosp. Pharmacists, Providence, 1956, N.E. Dental Soc., Swampscott, Mass., 1954. Vice chmn. Conservation Commn., Town of Bourne (Mass.), 1974—, Mashnee Dike Com., 1974—. Served with USNR, 1943-46; ETO. Mem. AAAS, Am. Soc. Cell Biology, Soc. Nuclear Medicine, Am. Pharm. Assn., U.S. Naval Inst., Am. Inst. Biol. Scis., Mass. Pub. Health Assn. Roman Catholic. Home: 159 Presidents Rd Gray Gables MA 02532 Office: care James M Sloan III 1309 Turks Head Bldg Providence RI 02903

PERCIACCANTE, RONALD GEORGE, pediatrician; b. N.Y.C., Mar. 26, 1938; s. James Vincent and Mary (Frigiola) P.; B.S., Georgetown U., 1959, M.D., 1963; m. Celia Fay, May 25, 1963; children—Marianne, Janet, Nancy, James, Megan, Thomas. Intern, St. Vincent's Hosp. and Med. Center, N.Y.C., 1963-64, resident, 1964-66; dir. Cystic Fibrosis Clinic, House of Good Samaritan, Watertown, N.Y., 1971—, attending staff, 1968—; practice medicine, specializing in pediatrics as partner Lustick & Perciaccante, Watertown, 1968—; attending staff Mercy Hosp., Watertown, 1968—, chief pediatrics, 1978—; chmn. med. adv. com. Jefferson County Pub. Health Nursing Service, 1973—. Bd. dirs. St. Lawrence Valley chpt. Cystic Fibrosis Found., 1971—, Sacred Heart Found., 1977—; bd. dirs. Jefferson County chpt. Am. Cancer Soc., 1972-78, pres., 1974-75. Served as capt. M.C., USAF, 1966-68. Diplomate Nat. Bd. Med. Examiners, Am. Bd. Pediatrics. Fellow Am. Acad. Pediatrics; mem. N.Y. Heart Assn., C. of C., Soc. Medicine State of N.Y., AMA, Jefferson County Med. Soc. (sec. 1972-74). Mem. N.Y. State Conservative Party. Roman Catholic. Contbr. articles to profl. jours. Home: RD 5 Watertown NY 13601 Office: 145 Clinton St Watertown NY 13601

PERDUNN, RICHARD FRANCIS, mgmt. engr.; b. Trenton, N.J., Dec. 12, 1915; s. Francis R. and Edith (Nogle) P.; B.S., Lehigh U., 1939; postgrad. student U. Pitts., 1939-40, Johns Hopkins, 1941-42; m. Eugenia E. Morel, June 7, 1941; 1 dau., Justine Reneau. With U.S. Steel Co., also Glenn L. Martin, 1939-43, supt. machine and assembly, 1941-43; partner Nelson & Perdunn, engrs. and cons., also v.p. Penco Corp., 1947-49; with Merck & Co., 1949-54, mgr. adminstrn., 1951-54; with Stevenson, Jordan & Harrison, mgmt. engrs., N.Y.C., 1954-70, exec. v.p., 1962-64, pres., 1964-70; partner, v.p. Golightly & Co. Internat., Inc., N.Y.C., 1970—, also dir., mem. exec. com.; dir. W. Point & Annapolis Text Book Pub. Co., 1948—. Indsl. Edn. Films Inc., 1966—, Eldun Corp., 1964—, Security Nat. Bank, Newark, 1964—, Suburban Life Ins. Co., 1966—, Mainstem Inc., 1965—, Greenhouse Decor Inc., 1961—, Neuwirth Fund, 1975—; pres., chief exec. officer, dir. Bachman-Jack's, Inc., Reading, Pa. Lectr. on finance and mfg. in U.S., Can., Eng., Sweden. Bd. drs. Inst. Better Confs., Internat. Inst. Bus. Devel., Inst. Urban Affairs; dir. finance Assn. Help for Retarded Children. Served with USAAF, 1942-47. Mem. N.Y.C. C. of C., Council Econ. Devel. Am. Mgmt. Assn., Reading Berks County C. of C., AIM (pres.'s council), Newcomen Soc. N. Am., Systems and Procedures Assn. Am., Soc. Advancement Mgmt. Club: Manasquan River Country. Author articles in field. Asso. editor Systems and Procedures Quar., 1948-51. Home: 407 Kenli Ln Brielle NJ 08730 Office: Golightly & Co Internat Inc 1 Rockefeller Plaza New York City NY 10020

PEREIRA, GEORGE ANTHONY, dentist; b. Holyoke, Mass., Sept. 27, 1918; s. Louis Jerome and Helena Lily (Metzler) P.; B.S., U. Mass., 1939; D.D.S., N.Y.U. Coll. Dentistry, 1943; postgrad. N.Y.U. Coll. Dentistry, Tufts U. Coll. Dentistry; M.S. in Psychology, Springfield Coll., 1974; m. Leona Mercedes Beauchamp, Oct. 30, 1943. Practice dentistry Belchertown, Mass., 1946-57, Holyoke, 1946—; mem. dental staff Holyoke, Wing Meml. hosps.; instr. dental psychology Holyoke Hosp. Pres. Holyoke League Arts and Crafts, 1953. Served from 1st lt. to maj., AUS, 1943-46. Fellow Internat. Coll. Dentists, Am. Soc. Psychosomatic Dentistry and Medicine, Springfield Acad. Medicine, Acad. Gen. Dentistry, Royal Soc. Health (Eng.); mem. Am. Soc. Psychomatic Dentistry and Medicine (pres. 1966-68), Am. Soc. Clin. Hypnosis, Am. Dental Assn., Am. Legion, Vets. Fgn. Wars, Acad. Gen. Dentistry, Fedn. Dentaire Internationale, Psi Omega. Elk, Lion (pres. Holyoke 1957, dep. dist. gov. 1959). Contbr. articles in field to technical journals. Home: 16 Old Jarvis Rd Holyoke MA 01040 Office: 323 Appleton St Holyoke MA 01040

PEREL, JULES, publishing exec.; b. Buenos Aires, Argentina, Nov. 5, 1934; s. Adolph and Bella (Silberberg) P.; came to U.S., 1950, naturalized, 1955; A.S., Miriano Moreno-Buenos Aires, 1949; B.B.A., Columbia U., 1954; m. Sheila B. Balsam, Jan. 20, 1957; children—Andrew J., Erica G., Melissa C. Bus. mgr. book div. Billboard Publs., Inc., N.Y.C., 1962-70, gen. mgr. Am. Artist div., 1970-72, v.p. Billboard Publs., Inc., 1972-76, sr. v.p. Art and Design Publs. group, 1976—, dir., 1976—, exec. v.p., 1978—; dir. Tell-Time/London. Trustee Tappan Library. Served in U.S. Army, 1954-56. Mem. Mag. Pubs. Assn., Am. Bus. Press, Assn. Am. Pubs. Democrat. Jewish. Club: Yale. Contbr. articles to jours. Home: 29 Musket Rd Tappan NY 10983 Office: 1515 Broadway New York City NY 10036

PERELLE, IRA B., psychologist; b. Mt. Vernon, N.Y., Sept. 16, 1925; s. Joseph Yale and Lillian (Schaffer) P.; student U. Tex.; grad. study R.C.A., Inst., 1951, Iona Coll.; B.S., M.S., Ph.D., Fordham U.; children—Ronnie Jean, Robert Jeffrey. Prodn. mgr. Arden Jewelry Case Co., 1946-49; became chief engr. Westlab Electronic Service Engrs., 1949; partner Westlab, 1954; pres. Westlab, Inc., 1955-64, chmn. bd., 1956; pres. Westchester Research and Devel. Labs.; exec. dir. Interlink, Ltd.; dir. Internat. Valve Corp., Stamford, Conn.; cons. ednl. research Fordham U., Catholic U. of P.R., Bayamon (P.R.) Central U., World U., San Juan, P.R., John Jay Coll., N.Y.C., Rockland Community Coll., N.Y.; research cons. So. Westchester County Bd. Coop. Ednl. Services; mem. faculty dept. psychology N.Y. U.; asso. prof. dept. bus. and econs., dept. psychology Mercy Coll., Dobbs Ferry, N.Y.; past mem. faculty S U NY, Purchase, Fordham U., N.Y.C.; faculty adv. com. Mercer County Coll., 1969-73; conf. leader Nat. Conf. Ednl. Tech., 1971-73. Mem. staff Civil Def., 1954-74; bd. dirs. Mid-Hudson Inst., Dobbs Ferry, N.Y. Served as radio instr. USAAF, 1943-46. Mem. IEEE, N.Y. Zool. Soc., Assn. Ednl. Communication and Tech., N.Y. State Ednl. Communication Assn., Audio Engring. Soc., Acoustical Soc. Am., Am. Inst. Physics, Am. Psychol. Assn., Am. Ednl. Research Assn., AAAS, Animal Behavior Soc. Author: A Practical Guide to Educational Media for the Classroom Teacher, 1974; also articles. Discoverer Perelle Phenomenon, psychology-attention. Home: 1234 Midland Ave Bronxville NY 10708 Office: Mercy Coll Dobbs Ferry NY 10522

PERERA, PHILLIPS, pvt. investment banker; b. Boston, Sept. 26, 1933; s. Guido Rinaldo and Faith (Phillips) P.; A.B., Harvard, 1955; diplôme in Indsl. Mgmt., Centred' Etudes Industrielles, 1961; m. Frederica Plimpton Drinkwater, Dec. 22, 1962; children—Phillips, Frederica Sophia, Christopher Davis, Alexander Lorenzo. Trainee Morgan et Cie., Paris, Am. Export Lines, N.Y.C., First Nat. Bank of Boston, 1958-63; indsl. economist Arthur D. Little Inc., Cambridge, Mass., 1963-68; dir. authorizations and acting dep. dir. ops. Office of Fgn. Dir. Investment, Dept. Commerce, Washington, 1968-69; pres. Internat. Liquidities Inc., fin. cons., Washington, 1971-72; v.p. corporate devel. Am. Express Co., N.Y.C., 1972-74; sr. v.p., dir. Donaldson, Lufkin, Jenrette and Co., N.Y.C., 1975; pres. Phillips Perera & Co., Inc., N.Y.C., 1976—; former dir. Am. Express Investment Mgmt. Co., 1972-74; dir. Club Med. Inc., 1972-74; spl. cons. UN, 1967-68, AID, 1969; cons. Orgn. Am. States on Devel. Fin., 1976. Served to capt. USAF, 1956-58. Clubs: Knickerbocker (N.Y.C.); Met. (Washington); Somerset (Boston). Contbr. articles to profl. jours.; author: Development Finance-Institutions, Problems and Prospects, 1968. Home: 150 Sarles St Mount Kisco NY 10549 Office: Suite 270 200 Park Ave New York City NY 10017

PEREY, JOAN SAWYER, real estate broker, devel. cons.; b. Brunswick, Maine, Aug. 27, 1933; d. Pacifique Amedee and Catherine May (Jean) Sawyer; student Colby Coll., Waterville, Maine, 1951-52; divorced; children—Katherine A. Sec., bookkeeper Sawyer Agy., Brunswick, 1953-57, real estate broker, partner, 1958-70, owner, 1971—; v.p. J.S.P. Corp. Republican del. Maine Conv., 1968. Mem. Androscoggin Valley Bd. Realtors, Brunswick C. of C. (dir.). Roman Catholic. Home: 18 Elm St Topsham ME 04068 Office: 5 Bank St Brunswick ME 04011

PEREZ, ISIDORO JOSE, chemist; b. Pinar del Rio, Cuba, Mar. 9, 1945; s. Isidoro Manuel and Hilda Maria (Canal) P.; B.S., Moravian Coll., 1967; m. LaMae Karen Fegely, May 27, 1967; children—Monica, Matthew. Scientist, Schering-Plough Corp., Kenilworth, N.J., 1967-72, sr. registration scientist, 1972, tech. mgr., internat. regulatory affairs, 1972—. Mem. Am. Chem. Soc., Am. Pharm. Assn., Acad. Pharm. Scis. Roman Catholic. Office: 2000 Galloping Hill Rd Kenilworth NJ 07033

PEREZ, LOUIS ANTHONY, physician; b. N.Y.C., June 11, 1939; s. Salvatore Lawrence and Valvadina Rose (Ruscillo) P.; B.E.E. (scholar), Manhattan Coll., 1962; M.D., State U. N.Y., Downstate Med. Center, 1966: m. Catherine Ann Larney, June 11, 1961; children—Lisa A., Gregg A., Nicole A. Intern, Kings County Hosp., Bklyn., 1966-67: resident Bronx (N.Y.) Municipal Hosp. Center, 1967-70; practice medicine specializing in nuclear medicine, Norwalk, Conn., 1975—; attending radiologist, instr. Albert Einstein Coll. Hosp., Bronx, 1970-71; attending radiologist Misericordia Hosp. Med. Center, Bronx, 1971-75; cons. dept. radiol. health and sci. Manhattan Coll. Radiol. Inst., 1974-77; chief, sect. nuclear medicine Norwalk (Conn.) Hosp., 1975—; instr. radiology Albert Einstein Coll. Medicine, 1971-76, asst. clin. prof., 1977—. Served to lt. comdr. USN, 1962-77. Recipient Physicians Recognition awards AMA, 1974, 77—. USPHS grantee, 1974-75, Am. Cancer Soc. grantee, 1968-70, Adria Corp. grantee, 1976-77, Proctor & Gamble grantee, 1976-77. Diplomate Nat. Bd. Med. Examiners, Am. Bd. Radiology, Am. Bd. Nuclear Medicine. Mem. Am. Coll. Radiology, Radiol. Soc. N.Am., Conn. Soc. Nuclear Medicine (bd. govs. 1976—). Club: Explorers. Contbr. articles to med. jours. Home: Blackacre Thornwood NY 10594 Office: Norwalk Hosp 24 Stevens St Norwalk CT 06856

PEREZ, ROBERT CLAUDE, investment co. exec.; b. Bklyn., Oct. 18, 1926; s. Claude Thomas and Gertrude (Royce) P.; B.A., Yale U., 1950; M.B.A., N.Y. U., 1956, Ph.D., 1966; m. Mary Jean Howard, Sept. 30, 1950; children—Barbara, Frederic, Moira. Vice pres. Chem. Fund, Inc.; v.p., voting stockholder F. Eberstadt & Co., Inc., 1950—; adj. prof. Baruch Coll. Grad. Div. City U. N.Y., 1966-72; mem. pub. info. and edn. com., pension com. Investment Co. Inst., Washington. Club: Yale (N.Y.C.). Home: 115 Central Park W New York City NY 10023 also Cherryfield ME 04622

PEREZ-PARIS, EDUARDO ENRIQUE, advt. exec.; b. Caracas, Venezuela, Dec. 26, 1951; s. Eduardo Perez-Alfonzo and Alicia Margaita Paris de Perez-Alfonzo; came to U.S., 1975; student Escuela de publicidad y Mercades, 1970-71, Instituto Superior de Mercadeo, 1971-73, Instituto de Extension Gerencial, 1973-74, Instituto de Estudios Superiores de Administrn., 1974; B.S., Bobson Coll., 1979; m. Mercedez de Perez-Paris, Dec. 12, 1974; 1 son, Enrique Eduardo. Salesman, Emeve Publicidad, Caracas, 1971-74; sales exec., mktg. adviser ARS Publiciada, Caracas, 1974—; cons. mktg. communications Hauser & Assos., Caracas. Grantee ARS, 1975-79. Mem. Fedn. Venezuelan Advt. Agencies, Am. Mktg. Assn., Assn. Nacional de Anuncisntes. Home: 11 Guild Rd Needham MA 02192 Office: ARS Publicidad Edificio ARS Los Rvices Caracas Venezuela

PERFALL, ARTHUR GEORGE, banker, journalist, communicator; b. Jamaica, N.Y., Apr. 26, 1927; s. Arthur Anthony and Helen E. (Guldhardt) P.; B.A., Hofstra U., 1951; children—Alison Ellen, Arthur Clayton, Faye Francesca. Reporter, L.I. (N.Y.) Daily Press, 1948-50; asst. city editor Nassau Daily Rev. Star, Rockville Centre, N.Y., 1950-51; organizer, staff writer Seafarers Internat. Union AFL, N.Y.C., 1951-54; with Newsday, Inc., Garden City, N.Y., 1954-72, fgn. corr., feature editor, picture editor, mng. editor, asso. editor; sr. v.p. Franklin Nat. Bank, N.Y.C., 1972-74; sr. v.p. European-Am. Bank & Trust Co., 1974-77; dir. public affairs N.Y. State Met. Transp. Authority, N.Y.C., 1978—; adj. lectr. journalism C.W. Post Coll., L.I. U., 1962-64. Chmn. L.I. region Nat. Alliance Businessmen, 1974-75. Bd. dirs. Nassau County Manpower Council, Day Care Council Nassau County; mem. adv. bd. Hofstra U.; mem. steering com. Law Sch., Hofstra U.; mem. adv. bd. Poly. Inst. N.Y. Served with USNR, 1944-46. Recipient numerous awards including Pulitzer Prize for community service, 1970. Mem. Overseas Press Club, Acad. Polit. Sci., Deadline Club N.Y., Nat. Headliners Club, Bank Mktg. Assn., Am. Mktg. Assn., Pub. Relations Soc. Am., L.I. Advt. Club, U.S. Naval Inst., Am. Acad. Social Polit. Scis., Sigma Delta Chi. Club: Indian Hills Country. Contbr. to various mags. Home: 1 Haig Dr Dix Hills NY 11746 Office: 1700 Broadway New York NY 10019

PERFECKY, BOHDAN ANDRIJ, accountant; b. Lviv, Ukraine, Dec. 12, 1913; s. Eugene and Maria (Kapko) P.; came to U.S., 1949, naturalized, 1955; LL.B., U. Lviv, 1935; grad. M. Lysenko Music Inst. (Ukraine), 1935; m. Natalia Czolij, Sept. 17, 1938; 1 son, George A. Accountant Albert Einstein Med. Center, Phila., 1965—; asst. dir. fiscal affairs Ukrainian Music Inst. Am., Phila., 1960—, also bd. dirs.; piano tchr., Phila., 1952—; pianist, accompanist Andrij Dobrjanskyj and Charlotte Ordassy, Met. Opera Co. Mem. Ukrainian Lawyers Assn. U.S.A. Musical reviewer America Ukrainian Cath. Daily, Phila., 1951—. Home: 5022 11th St Philadelphia PA 19141 Office: Albert Einstein Med Center York and Tabor Sts Philadelphia PA 19141

PERFECKY, GEORGE ALEXANDER, educator; b. Piotrkow, Poland, May 27, 1940; s. Bohdan Andrew and Natalia (Czolij) P.; came to U.S., 1949, naturalized, 1955; B.A., U. Pa., 1963; M.A., Columbia, 1966, Ph.D., 1970; m. Christine Konaszewycz, June 20, 1964; children—Tanya Maria, Marta Christina. Instr. Russian LaSalle Coll., Phila., 1965-68, asst. prof. Russian, 1968-73, asso. prof., 1973—; vis. lectr. German, Temple U., Phila., 1968-69. Mem. Am. Assn. Tchrs. Slavic and East European Langs., Am. Assn. Advancement Slavic Studies, Shevchenko Sci. Soc. Author: The Galician-Volynian Chronicle-An Annotated Translation, 1973. Reviewer, Slavic and East European Jour. Home: 621 Garden Rd Glenside PA 19038 Office: Olney Hall La Salle Coll 20th and Olney Sts Philadelphia PA 19141

PERKINS, EDDIE LEE, med. techonolgist; b. Delhi, La., Jan. 11, 1938; s. Jerome and Lillie Mae (Atkins) P.; B.S., U. Ark., 1965; M.S., George Washington U., 1974; m. Neta Mae Parker, Dec. 26, 1964; Med. technologist Bionetic Research Lab., Falls Church, Va., 1965-70, McCoy, et al., Med. Lab., Marlow Heights, Md., 1969-71, Cafritz Hosp., Washington, 1971-74, St. Elizabeth's Hosp., Washington, 1974—. Served with USAF, 1958-62. Registered technologist, Nat. Registry in Clin. Chemistry, Am. Soc. Clin. Pathologists. Baptist. Club: Masons. Home: 317 Quarry Ave Capitol Heights MD 20027 Office: 2700 Martin L King Ave Washington DC 20032

PERKINS, MARVIN EARL, health services dir.; b. Moberly, Mo., June 1, 1920; s. Marvin Earl and Nannie Mae (Walden) P.; A.B., Albion Coll., 1942; M.D., Harvard U., 1946; M.P.H. (USPHS fellow), Johns Hopkins U., 1956; L.H.D., Albion Coll., 1968; grad. U.S. Army Command and Gen. Staff Coll., 1966, U.S. Army War Coll., 1972; m. Mary MacDonald, May 24, 1943; children—Sarah, Cynthia, Marvin, Mary, Irene. Intern, Henry Ford Hosp., Detroit, 1946-47; post surgeon, hosp. comdg. officer Fort Eustis, Va., 1948; resident physician psychiatry Walter Reed Army Hosp., Washington, 1949-52; chief psychiatry br., psychiatry and neurology cons. div. Office U.S. Army Surgeon Gen., Washington, 1952-53, chief records rev. br., 1953-55; chief psychiat. services div. D.C. Dept. Pub. Health, 1955-58, chief bur. mental health, 1959-60; dir. N.Y.C. Community Mental Health Bd., 1960-68, commr. mental health services, 1961-68; lectr. Johns Hopkins U., Balt., 1960-65; adj. prof. Columbia U., 1961-67; prof. psychiatry Mt. Sinai Sch. Medicine of City U. N.Y., 1967-72; clin. prof. psychiatry Coll. Physicians and Surgeons, Columbia U., 1972-77; prof. psychiatry N.Y. Coll. Medicine, 1977-78; dir. psychiatry Beth Israel Medical Center, N.Y.C., 1967-72, dir. Morris J. Bernstein Inst., 1968-72; dir. Community Mental Health Services Westchester County, 1972-77; dir. psychiatry Westchester County Med. Center, 1977-78. Served with AUS, 1943-46; col. M.C. Res. Diplomate in psychiatry Am. Bd. Psychiatry and Neurology; certified mental hosp. adminstr. Am. Psychiat. Assn. Fellow Am. Psychiat. Assn., N.Y. Acad. Medicine; mem. AAAS, Group Advancement Psychiatry, Westchester County Med. Soc., Nat. Geneal. Soc., New Eng. Hist. Geneal. Soc., Am. Assn. State and Local History, N.Y. Psychiat. Soc., State Hist. Soc. Mo. (life), N.Y. Hist. Soc., Res. Officers Assn. (life), Schilder Soc., N.Y. Geneal. and Biog. Soc. Home: Route 2 Box 190A Fincastle VA 24090

PERKINS, RUSSEL GORDON, safety engr.; b. Goldendale, Wash., Oct. 18, 1919; s. Shields Herbert and Elsie Elizabeth (McCullough) P.; B.S., Washington State U., 1941; m. Josephine Bonita Welmaker, Dec. 27, 1942; children—Russel Gordon, Mary Averil Perkins Riley. Examiner, U.S. Civil Service Commn., Washington, 1941-42; ordnance engr. Bur. Ordnance, Dept. Navy, 1942-46; safety engr. Dept. Def. Explosives Safety Bd., Washington, 1946-73, dir. tech. programs div., 1973-78; cons., 1978—. Recipient Meritorious Civilian Service awards, U.S. Govt., 1966, 78. Mem. Am. Inst. Mining, Metall. and Petroleum Engrs., Soc. Am. Mil. Engrs., Am. Def. Preparedness Assn., Huguenot Soc. of D.C. Presbyterian. Home and Office: 1101 La Grande Rd Silver Spring MD 20903

PERKINS, THOMAS LEWIS, dentist; b. Greensburg, Pa., Dec. 10, 1937; s. Thomas Curtis and Dorothy Alberta (Lewis) P.; B.S., U. Pitts., 1959, D.M.D., 1965; m. Susan Loretta Baker, June 1, 1962; children—Gretchen, Thomas, Roger, Hallie. Instr. restorative dentistry U. Pitts., 1965-69, asst. prof. pedodontics; 1969-77; practice gen. dentistry, Bradford Woods, Pa., 1965—. Councilman, Borough Bradford Woods, 1970-82; mem. Police Commn. Bradford Woods, Marshall Twp. and Pine Twp.; trustee Bradford Woods Community Ch. and Ch. Council. Served with USNR, 1959-61. Fellow Acad. Gen. Dentistry (state dir.), Am. Coll. of Internat. Coll. Dentistry; mem. Am., Pa. dental assns., Am. Acad. Dental Practice Adminstrn., Am. Soc. Dentistry for Children (sec.-treas., pres. Western Pa.), Western Pa. Practice Mgmt. Club, Odontological Soc. Western Pa. (exec. sec., past pres.), Pitts. Acad. Dentistry, North Dental Club (past pres.), U. Pitts. Dental Alumni Assn. (dir.), Pi Kappa Alpha Alumni, Psi Omega Alumni. Mason (32 deg., Shriner). Clubs: Gas Light (Pitts.); Century, Golden Panther. Address: 195 Bradford Rd Bradford Woods PA 15015

PERKINS, WILLIAM E(DWARD), microbiologist; b. Seattle, Nov. 9, 1925; s. William E. and Letitia Ellen (Larkin) P.; B.S., U. Wash., 1950; married, six children. Chief chemist Gen. Brewing Corp., Vancouver, Wash., 1951-54; bacteriologist Berkeley (Calif.) Lab., Nat. Canners Assn., 1955-60, head bacteriology and processing dept., 1960-65; research technologist Campbell Soup Co., Camden, N.J., 1965-72, sr. research scientist, 1972-75, dir. process devel., 1975—; research asso. lab. research canning industry U. Calif., 1962-65; cons. Calif. Dept. Pub. Health, 1962-63. Served with USNR, 1944-46. USPHS research grantee, 1960-65. Mem. Am. Soc. Microbiology, Inst. Food Technologists. Researcher food microbiology, bacterial spores, heat processing of foods, food poisoning, food processing equipment, formulation of foods. Address: 18 Robin Rd Moorestown NJ 08057

PERKONS, AUSEKLIS KARLIS, forensic sci. cons.; b. Riga, Latvia, Mar. 13, 1932; s. Eduards and Marija (Asenbergs) P.; B.A. Sc., U. Toronto, 1958, M.A. Sc., 1960, Ph.D., 1965, Cert. in Criminology, 1971; m. Rasma Aina Buka, Jan. 21, 1957; children—Dzintra Rudite, Zaiga Rota, Zintis Rusins. Research scientist Centre of Forensic Scis., Toronto, Ont., Can., 1960-69; nuclear expert Internat. Atomic Energy Agy., Ceylon, 1969-70, Venezuela, 1971-72, India, 1973; asso. prof. Universidad Simon Bolivar, Caracas, Venezuela, 1972-74; prof., head dept. chemistry Universidad De Tachira, San Cristobal, Venezuela, 1975-76; dir. Forensic Sci. Cons., Toronto, 1977—; spl. lectr. dept. criminology U. Toronto, 1969; spl. lectr. forensic sci. Seneca Coll., Toronto, 1972. Fellow Am. Indian acads. forensic scis.; mem. Forensic Sci. Soc. (Eng.), Am. Nuclear Soc., AAAS. Contbr. articles to sci. jours. Home and office: 158 Upper Canada Dr Willowdale ON M2P 1S8 Canada

PERL, WILLIAM R., clin. psychologist; b. Prague, Czechoslovakia, Sept. 21, 1906; s. Rudolph and Camilla (Fischer) P.; M.A., U. Vienna, 1927, Ph.D. in Correctional Psychology, 1930; M.A., Columbia, 1951; m. Lore Rollig, Apr. 18, 1938; children—Raphael F., Solomon M. Came to U.S., 1940, naturalized, 1943. Dir. New Zionist Resettlement Center, Vienna, 1935-39; founder chmn. AF Alpi, rescue com. for Jews to emigrate to Palestine (now Israel), 1937-40; practicing psychologist, N.Y.C., 1947-51; chief clin. psychologist U.S. Disciplinary Barracks, Ft. Leavenworth, Kan., 1951-55; chief psychol. sect. U.S. Army Hosp., Munich, Germany, 1955-58; chief psychol. dept. Laurel Child Center, D.C. Dept. Welfare, 1958-68; pvt. practice, also cons. U. Md., College Park, 1971-75; professorial lectr. George Washington U., 1962—; cons. to govt., 1965—. Del. White House Conf. Children and Youth, 1960; U.S. del. Internat. Congress Psychology, Moscow, 1966. Nat. chmn. Jewish Def. League, 1973-74, chmn. internat. adv. council, 1975—. Served to lt. col. AUS, 1942-47. Mem. Am. Psychol. Assn., Am. Assn. Correctional Psychologists (pres. 1954), Internat. Soc. Criminology. Contbr. articles to profl. jours. Home: 3901 Harrison Rd Beltsville MD 20705

PERLBERG, WILLIAM, chem. co. exec.; b. N.Y.C., July 30, 1933; s. Samuel and Pearl (Pulver) P.; B.S. in Chemistry, Coll. City N.Y., 1954, M.B.A., 1963; m. Muriel Rhoda Spiegel, Nov. 21, 1954; children—Mark Craig, Elyssa Laine. Research chemist Colgate Palmolive Co., Jersey City, 1956-60; mgr. product devel. Airkem, Inc., 1960-64; asst. dir. research Revlon Inc., 1964-68; v.p. research and devel. control Airwick Industries, Inc., Carlstadt, N.J., 1968-73, also dir.; corporate v.p. Hartz Mountain Corp., 1973—. Served with AUS, 1954-56. Mem. Am. Pub. Health Assn., Air Pollution Control Assn., Am. Chem. Soc., Soc. Cosmetic Chemists, Royal Soc. Health. Patentee in field. Office: 700 S 4th St Harrison NJ 07481

PERLBERG, ZELMA, educator; b. Balt.; d. Philip and Ida (Gumnitzky) Perlberg; B.A., U. Md., 1952, M.A., 1954, postgrad., 1960-66; postgrad. Johns Hopkins, 1960. Social worker Balt. Dept. Welfare, 1953-54; tchr. spl. edn. Balt. Dept. Edn., 1954-59, counselor emotionally disturbed, educable, mentally retarded adolescents, Balt., 1959-77; chmn. guidance dept. High Sch. Alternative Learning Center, Balt. City Dept. Edn., 1977—. Mem. Am. Orthopsychiat. Assn., Nat. Assn. Sch. Counselors, NEA, Assn. for Mental Health Aid to Israel, Md. Personnel and Guidance Assn. (Balt. chpt.), Md. Tchrs. Assn., Phi Kappa Phi. Home: 2506 Smith Ave Baltimore MD 21209 Office: Fayette and Calhoun Sts Baltimore MD 21223

PERLESS, ROBERT L., sculptor; b. N.Y.C., Apr. 23, 1938; s. Meyer and Ethel (Glassman) P.; student U. Miami, 1955-59; m. Ellen R. Kaplan, July 2, 1965. One man shows at Bodley Gallery, N.Y.C., 1968, 70, Galerie Simonne Stern, New Orleans, 1969, Bernard Danenberg Gallery, N.Y.C., 1970, 72, Bonino Gallery, N.Y.C., 1976; exhibited in group shows at Bodley Gallery, 1970, Whitney Mus., N.Y.C., 1970, Forum Gallery, N.Y.C., 1975, Bonino Gallery, N.Y.C., 1975, Houston Gallery, 1975, Aldrich Mus., 1978; represented in permanent collections Whitney Mus. Am. Art, Aldrich Mus. Contemporary Art, Ridgefield, Conn., Chrysler Mus., Norfolk, Va., Everson Mus., Syracuse, N.Y., Okla. Art Center, Oklahoma City, Phoenix Art Mus. Club: Northeast Harbor (Maine) Fleet. Home: 43 Greenwich Ave New York City NY 10014 Office: 412 6th Ave New York City NY 10011

PERLEY, JOHN STEPHEN, banker; b. Laconia, N.H., Jan. 6, 1937; s. John Russell and Melba Dixie (Beagle) P.; B.A., Dartmouth Coll., 1959; M.B.A., Dartmouth Coll., 1960; m. Sally Judith Payne, June 27, 1959; children—Linda Elaine, Stephen Russell. Asst. v.p. Chem. Bank, N.Y.C., 1961-69; sr. v.p. comml. banking and mktg. Amoskeag Nat. Bank, Manchester, N.H., 1969—; also dir.; dir. Greater Manchester Growth Co., Inc. Bd. dirs. Manchester Inst. Arts and Scis., Palace Theater Trust, Manchester Indsl. Council, Child and Family Services N.H., NCCJ, Animal Rescue League Manchester; trustee Capital Res. & Trust Funds City Manchester. Served with USAR, 1960-61. Mem. Bank Mktg. Assn., Am. Bankers Assn., Am. Inst. Banking, N.H. Bankers Assn. Republican. Congregationalist. Clubs: Rotary, Manchester Chess. Home: 150 Steinmetz Dr Manchester NH 03104 Office: 875 Elm St Manchester NH 03101

PERLIS, HARLAN JAY, elec. engr.; b. Union City, N.J., June 12, 1924; s. William and Florence Rae (Jacobson) P.; B.E.E., Clarkson Coll. Tech., 1950; M.S., Stevens Inst. Tech., 1952; D.Engring. Sci., N.Y. U., 1963; m. Marie Josephine Lisanti, Dec. 20, 1963; children—Jay, Robert, Anthony. Broadcast engr. Sta. WICY, Sta. WMSA-AM-FM, 1947-49; jr. engr. Coles Signal Engring. Lab., 1949; sr. engr., group head A.B. DuMont Labs., 1950-56; sr. specialist Emerson Radio & Phonograph Corp., 1956-58; instr., exec. asst., elec. engring. dept. N.Y. U., 1958-63; asso. prof. Rutgers U., 1963-68; prof. elec. engring. N.J. Inst. Tech., Newark, 1968—; cons. elec. engring.; dir. Electro Mech. Corp.; co-dir. Environ. Instrumentation Systems Lab.; gen. chmn. Joint Automatic Control Conf., 1978. Scoutmaster, Alexander Hamilton council Boy Scouts Am., 1946-50. Served with U.S. Army, 1942-46; PTO. Recipient Founders Day award N.Y. U., 1974. NSF grantee, 1964-72; EPA grantee, 1977-78. Mem. IEEE, Instrument Soc. Am., Armed Forces Communications and Electronics Assn., Soc. Indsl. and Applied Math., Am. Soc. Engring. Edn., N.Y. Acad. Scis., Am. Geophys. Union, Water Pollution Control Assn., Nat. Soc. Profl. Engrs., Theta Chi. Club: Saddle Ho Riding (Fairlawn, N.J.). Contbr. articles to profl. jours. Home: 791 Hartwell St Teaneck NJ 07666 Office: 323 High St Newark NJ 07102

PERLMAN, BERNARD BENJAMIN, neurol. surgeon; b. Bklyn., May 23, 1927; s. David and Lillian (Reitman) P.; B.S. magna cum laude, L.I. U., 1949; postgrad. Rockefeller Inst., 1949-50, U. Fribourg (Switzerland), 1950-51; M.D., State U. N. N.Y., Bklyn., 1955; m. Trude Schwarz, June 28, 1953; children—David Bruce, Elizabeth Ruth, Linda Karen. Intern, St. John's Episc. Hosp., Bklyn., 1955-56; resident Columbia Neurol. Inst., 1961-62, N.Y. Kingsbridge VA Hosp., Bronx, 1956-61, 62-63; pvt. practice neurol. surgery, Forest Hills, N.Y., 1961—; attending neurosurgeon Booth Meml. Med. Center, Flushing (N.Y.) Med. Center; clin. asso. prof. neurol. surgery N.Y. U., 1975—. Served to capt. M.C., U.S. Army, 1956-62; served with U.S. Mcht. Marine, 1944-46. Diplomate Am. Bd. Neurol. Surgery. Fellow N.Y. Acad. Medicine, A.C.S. (examiner); mem. Am. Assn. Neurol. Surgeons, Congress Neurol. Surgeons, N.Y. Seurosurg. Soc., Am. Epilepsy Assn., Am. Coll. Angiology, AMA, N.Y. State Med. Soc., N.Y. Acad. Sci., AAAS. Author: Congenital Anomalies of the Spine, 1972; Brain Death and Coma, 1977; Head Injuries, 1978; contbr. poetry to mags. and anthologies. Office: 109-33 71st Rd Forest Hills NY 11375

PERLMAN, ELLIS SHERMAN, transit ofcl.; b. Chgo., Aug. 15, 1913; s. J.S. and Jeannette Charlotte (Gorove) P.; student Central Coll., Chgo., 1932-33, Chgo. Art Inst., 1933-34, Trl State Coll., 1942, Ind. Inst. Tech., 1943, Baldwin Wallace Coll., 1943; m. Leonarda Mortash; children—John Niels, Inga Jeanne, Robert Jessen. With Economist Papers, 1935-37; owner Perlman Advt. and Pub. Relations Agy., 1937-41; with Office of Sec. of War, War Dept., 1944-46; chief speakers and publs. War Assets Adminstrn., 1946-47; advt., pub. relations mgr. Indsl. Rayon Corp., 1947-49; v.p. Coleman Todd & Assos., 1949-54; mng. dir. Ohio Trucking Assn., 1954-61; spl. asst. to adminstr. Nat. Capitol Transp. Agys., Washington, 1961-66, 66-67; spl. legis. asst. Office of Dir., Office Econ. Opportunity, 1966; dir. govt. relations Washington Met. Area Transit Authority, 1967—. Active ARC, Cancer Soc., Community Chest. Served with USAAC, 1941-44. Mem. Advt. Fedn. Am. (v.p. 1953-54), Pub. Relations Soc., Assn. Trade Assn. Execs. Home: 1629 Dryden Way Crofton MD 21114 Office: 600 5th St NW Washington DC 20001

PERLMAN, EVELYN BERNICE, psychologist; b. Boston, Dec. 8, 1928; d. Joseph and Anna (Wallace) Kushner; A.B., Bates Coll., Lewiston, Me., 1949; M.A., Radcliffe Coll., 1950; grad. student psychology Boston U., 1951-54; m. Sumner Earl Perlman, June 23, 1956; children—Andrew Jay, Walter Lew, Gary David. Therapeutic tutor and tester Browne and Nichols Sch., Cambridge, Mass., 1951-54; psychologist Mass. Youth Service Bd., Lancaster Sch. Girls, 1954-56, Quincy (Mass.) Pub. Schs., 1956-58; part-time psychologist, psychol. counseling dept. Arlington (Mass.) Pub. Schs., 1960—, supr. staff psychologists, 1974—; pvt. practice clin. psychology, 1976—; cons. pub. schs. Chairperson study group League Women Voters, Waltham, Mass., 1957-58, corr. sec., 1956-57; pre-sch. program chairperson Lexington (Mass.) PTA, 1960-62; co-advisor Temple Youth Group. Certified sch. psychologist; licensed psychologist. Mem. Mass. Sch. Psychologists Assn. (charter), Mass. (chairperson child devel. group 1971-72), Am. psychol. assns., Parent Counseling Assn. New Eng. (publicity chair 1978), Women's Am. ORT (dir., chairperson study groups 1965-69). Co-author: The K-Q The Kindergarten Questionnaire (pre-sch. screening). Home: 10 Tyler Rd Lexington MA 02173 Office: 23 Maple St Arlington MA 02174

PERLMAN, JOHN NIELS, poet, critic, editor, educator; b. Alexandria, Va., May 13, 1946; s. Ellis Sherman and Bertha Elaine (Jessen) P.; B.A., Ohio State U., 1969; m. Janis Lynn Hadobas, May 26, 1967; 1 dau., Nicole. Author: Nicole, 1976; Self Portrait, 1976:

from The Hudson: a weave, 1975; Notes Toward A Family, 1975; Dinner 650 Warburton Ave., 1974; Three Years Rings, 1972; Kachina, 1971; Swath, 1978; Two Poems, 1978; The Vineyard, 1978; 15 Poems, 1978; poems published many mags, including Grosseteste Review (Eng.), Origin (Japan), Survivor's Manual, Madrona, The Ohio Jour., Sparrow, Broadway Boogie; anthologized in My Music Bent, 1973; The Doctor Generosity Poets, 1975; editor Shuttle Mag., 1972—; co-ordinator The Mamaroneck Poetry Series, 1975; cons. poetry Nat. Endowment for the Arts, 1972; poet-in-residence Wyo. Community Colls., 1972-73; vis. instr. creative writing Ohio State U., 1973; vis. instr. poetry Northfield-Mt. Herman Sch., Northfield, Mass., 1975; vis. poet Poets-in-the-Schools, N.Y., Ga., Cal., Wyo., Minn., 1972-76. Recipient Vanderwater Poetry prize, 1969; Acad. of Am. Poets prize, 1969. Home and Office: 1632 Mamaroneck Ave Mamaroneck NY 10543

PERLMAN, KONRAD JOSEPH, city planning adminstr.; b. N.Y.C., Oct. 6, 1936; s. Alexander Konne and Florence (Stern) P.; A.B., Colgate U., 1958; M. City Planning, (Alumni fellow), Yale U., 1960; m. Norma Tila Davidoff, Aug. 1, 1976. Community planning analyst Ebasco Services, Inc., N.Y.C., 1960; city planner Raymond & May Assos., Pleasantville, N.Y., 1961; sr. planner Boston Redevel. Authority, 1962-64; project planner Daniel, Mann, Johnson & Mendenhall, Los Angeles, 1964-67; urban planner, chief of planning Redevel. Land Agency, Washington, 1967-75; acting dep. chief planning and research D.C. Dept. Housing and Community Devel., Washington, 1975—; lectr. in field. Mem. Am. Planning Assn., Am. Assn. Housing and Redevel. Ofcls. Contbr. articles to profl. jours. Developer computerized info. system for urban research and planning. Home: 1111 G St SE Washington DC 20003 Office: 1325 G St NW Washington DC 20005

PERLMAN, MATTHEW S., psychologist; b. Bklyn., Aug. 4, 1938; s. Bernard R. and Sara (Kessin) P.; B.A., Bklyn. Coll., 1960; Ph.D., U. Rochester, 1965; children—Deborah, David, Eric. Staff psychologist Convalescent Hosp. for Children, Community Mental Health Center, Rochester, N.Y., 1964-69, dir. preventive and consultative services, 1969-78; pvt. practice clin. psychology, Rochester, 1966—, Buffalo, 1976—; asso. clin. instr. dept. psychiatry U. Rochester Med. Sch., 1972-75, clin. asst. prof. psychiatry, 1975—; regional asso. William Glasser's Educator Tng. Center, Los Angeles, 1974—. Chmn. Psychologists for Senator Laverne Com., 1972. Mem. Am., Genesee Valley (pres. 1970-72), N.Y. State (dir. 1972—, council of reps. 1972—) psychol. assns. Home: 40 Long Meadow Circle Pittsford NY 14534 Office: 2075 Scottsville Rd Rochester NY 14623

PERLMAN, SOL, electronics engr.; b. Bklyn., Apr. 22, 1906; s. Alexander and Anna (Marcus) P.; B.E.E., Poly. Inst. Bklyn., 1929, M.E.E., 1947; m. Judith Katz, Aug. 1, 1937; children—Janet Esther, David Allen. Chief electronics engr. Mfrs. Machine & Tool Co., Mt. Vernon, N.Y., 1947-49; electronics project engr. Rome Air Devel. Center (N.Y.), 1949-56; staff engr., cons. U.S.A. Radio Propagation Agy., Fort Monmouth, N.J., 1956-66; tech. dir. Fort Monmouth Facility of Stratcom, 1966-67; radio propagation cons. Electronics CMD, Avionics Lab., Fort Monmouth, 1967-75, cons. radio communication flight tests, 1977—; cons. radio antennas, radio propagation effects on radio communications systems. Recipient letter of commendation Comdr. Gen. Stratcom for solving problems in radio interference in Western Pacific, 1966. Mem. Assn. Computing Machinery, AAAS, IEEE (life), Am. Geophys. Union. Democrat. Jewish. Club: B'rith Abraham. Contbr. articles in field to profl. jours. Home: 174 Franklin Ave Long Branch NJ 07740

PERLOFF, ROBERT, educator, psychologist; b. Phila., Feb. 3, 1921; s. Myer and Elizabeth (Sherman) P.; A.B., Temple U., 1949; M.A., Ohio State U., 1949, Ph.D., 1951; m. Evelyn Potechin, Sept. 22, 1946; children—Richard Mark, Linda Sue, Judith Kay. Instr. edn. Antioch Coll., 1950-51; with personnel research br. Dept. Army, 1951-55, chief statis. research and cons. unit, 1953-55; dir. research and devel. Sci. Research Assos., Inc., Chgo., 1955-59; vis. lectr. Chgo. Tchrs. Coll., 1955-56; mem. faculty Purdue U., 1959-69, prof. psychology, 1964-69, field assessment officer univ. Peace Corps Chile III project, 1962; cons. in field, 1959—; prof. bus. adminstrn. and psychology Grad. Sch. Bus., U. Pitts., 1969—, dir. research programs, 1969-77, mem. bd. dirs. Book Center, 1969-72; v.p. Senior Citizens Service Corp., 1972—; cons. HEW; mem. adv. com. on assessment of exptl. manpower research and devel. labs., Nat. Acad. Scis., 1972-73. Served with AUS, World War II; PTO. Decorated Bronze Star. Diplomate Am. Bd. Profl. Psychology. Fellow AAAS, Am. (mem.-at-large exec. com., div. consumer psychology 1964-67, mem. council reps. 1965-68, pres. div. consumer psychology 1967-68, chmn. sci. affairs com. 1968-71, mem. edn. and tng. bd. 1969-72, treas., dir. 1974—), Eastern (chmn. program com. 1973-74, dir. 1977—) psychol. assns.; mem. Am. Mktg. Assn., Assn. for Consumer Research (pres. 1970-71), Am. Assn. Pub. Opinion Research, Internat. Assn. Applied Psychology, N.Y. Acad. Scis., ACLU (chpt. dir. 1970-71), Soc. Psychol. Study Social Issue, Thoreau Soc., Am. Ednl. Research Assn., Authors Guild, Authors League Am., Evaluation Research Soc. (pres. 1977—), Sigma Xi, Psi Chi. Contbr. profl. jours. Editor: Indsl. Psychologist, 1963-65; book rev. editor Personnel Psychology, 1952-55; editorial bd. Inst. Personality and Ability Testing, 1962-69; cons. editor Jour. Applied Psychology, 1970-74, Am. Jour. Community Psychology, 1972—, Am. Psychologist, 1974—; guest editor American Psychologist, May 1972; book reviewer Pitts. Press, 1971-73. Home: 815 St James St Pittsburgh PA 15232

PERLS, LAURA POSNER, psychotherapist; b. Pforzheim, Ger., Aug. 15, 1905; d. Rudolf and Toni (Eber) Posner; came to U.S., 1947, naturalized, 1955; D.Sc. in Psychology, U. Frankfurt/Main, 1932; student Frankfurt Psychoanalytical Inst., 1928-30, Berlin Psychoanalytic Inst., 1930-33; m. Frederick S. Perls, Aug. 23, 1930; children—Renate, Stephen R. Pvt. practice psychotherapy, Ger. and U.S., 1933-73; co-developer Gestalt therapy, co-founder N.Y. Inst. Gestalt Therapy, 1952, pres., 1958—; tchr., cons. U.S., Can. and Europe. Mem. Am. Psychol. Assn., Am. Acad. Psychotherapists, Assn. Humanistic Psychology, Assn. Advancement Psychology, N.Mex. Group Therapy Assn., N.Y., Cleve. insts. Gestalt therapy. Author articles. Address: 7 W 96th St New York City NY 10025

PERMUT, STEPHEN ROBERT, physician; b. Olympia, Wash., Sept. 24, 1945; s. Max L. and Ruth (Epstein) P.; A.B., U. Pa., 1967; M.D., Temple U., 1972; m. Marylene Quiambao, Apr. 20, 1974; children—Laura Q., Irene Q. Intern, Ind. U. Med. Center, Indpls., 1972-73, resident, 1973-75; practice medicine specializing in internal medicine, Wilmington, Del., 1975—; mem. staff Wilmington Med. Center; dir. family practice residency program St. Francis Hosp., Wilmington, 1976—. Bd. dirs. Del. League Planned Parenthood, 1977—, Del. Council Crime and Justice, Latin Am. Community Center. Diplomate Am. Bd. Internal Medicine, Am. Bd. Family Practice. Mem. A.C.P. Home: 309 Cox Rd Newark DE 19711 Office: 1219 W 8th St Wilmington DE 19806

PERNA, ALBERT FREDRIC, podiatrist, educator; b. Concord, Mass., Dec. 30, 1915; s. Joseph and Rachel (Mangone) P.; D. Podiatric Medicine, Temple U., 1946; Ed.M., Framingham State U., 1965; m. Elizabeth Annie Dugas, Apr. 18, 1942; children—Susan Elizabeth, John Joseph. Gen. practice podiatry, Waltham, Mass., 1946—; staff podiatrist Waltham Hosp., 1947—; prof. anatomy and physiology, also philosophy Bay State Jr. Coll., 1966—; prof. philosophy Fitchburg (Mass.) State Coll., 1968—. First aid instr. ARC, Waltham, 1959-75; mem. Waltham Sch. Bd., 1956-76, vice chmn., 1957, 58, 75; past bd. dirs. Waltham Boys Club; past chmn. YMCA, Cancer Fund, Heart Fund, Cerebral Palsy Fund. Served with AUS, 1941-42, as combat glider pilot USAAF, 1942-45, Mass. Air N.G., 1945-66; Korea; lt. col. Res. ret. Recipient D.S.C.; City Keys, Mobile, Ala. Mem. Am. Philos. Assn., Philosophy of Sci. Assn., Acad. Podiatry (pres. 1967-69), Soaring Soc. Am., Mass. N.G. Alumni Assn. Roman Catholic. Clubs: Waltham Rotary (pres. 1957-58), VFW. Author: The Glider Gladiators, 1970; Glider Warfare Diary, 1978; editor The Glider Rag, summer 1942; Glider Gazette, fall 1942; footnote editor Mass. Chiropody Soc. jours., 1947-51. Home: Waltham MA 02154 Office: Waltham MA 02154

PERNA, FRANCIS JOHN, town ofcl., civil engr.; b. Greenwich, Conn., Sept. 7, 1918; s. James F. and Annie (Morano) P.; B.C.E., Clemson U., 1940; M.S. (Univ. fellow), U. Tenn., 1941; m. Edith Jane Gunter, June 4, 1942; children—Anida Vivian Mims, Francis John, William Lee, Kathryn Jane, Georgette Jamie. Engr. of tests S.C. Hwy. Dept., Columbia, 1940; jr. profl. engr. TVA, Knoxville, 1941; supt., asst. sec. for constrn. firm, Greenwich, 1945-48, asst. treas., 1953; asst. commr. pub. works Town of Greenwich, 1953-67, commr., 1968—. Served from 2d lt. to maj. U.S. Army, 1941-45; PTO; to col., 1948-52; Korea. Decorated Bronze Star. Registered profl. engr. and land surveyor S.C., Conn. Mem. ASCE, Soc. Am. Mil. Engrs., S.C. Soc. Profl. Engrs., Am. Pub. Works Assn., Conn. Soc. Civil Engrs. (dir. 1970-72). Clubs: Rotary (pres. Cos Cob 1961), Masons, Order Eastern Star. Home: 75 Valleywood Rd Cos Cob CT 06807 Office: Town Hall Annex Havemeyer Pl Greenwich CT 06830

PERNA, GEORGE D., mgmt. cons.; b. Concord, Mass., Aug. 24, 1911; s.; Joseph and Rachel (Mangone) P.; ed. Boston U., Northeastern U., Harvard U.; Ph.D., U. Mass.; m. Marie Rosalie Pineau, Mar. 25, 1935; children—Marcia Ann (Mrs. S. Greene), Nancy Jean (Mrs. W. Jarvis), George Donald, Malcolm Joseph, Richard, J. David. Methods, prodn., sales div. Ford Motor Co., 1933-39; prodn. asst. Watertown Arsenal, 1939-41; mgr. Autosyn Motor div. Bendix Aviation Corp., 1941-45. Publicity and dramatic writer; art dir.; editor and pub. Hyde Park Gazette-Times, 1945—; editor, pub. Milton-Mattapan News, 1945—; pres. Norfolk Press., Inc. 1946—; prodn. mgr. Nat. Pneumatic Co., also Holtzer-Cabot div., 1951-56; mgmt. engr. Dyer-Lundberg Assos. cons. engrs., 1956-58; systems and procedures Raytheon Mfg. Co., 1958-63; corp. systems mgmt. AVCO Corp., DIPG Mgmt. Center, 1963—; advt. service, specialized couns., copy, pub. relations, sales cons., 1934—; pub. relations, J.P. Denton, Inc.; course instr. integrated and advanced mgmt. systems Northeastern U. and Systems Procedures Assn.; dir. Allied Machinists, Norwood; Mem. Bd. of Trade. Dir. journalism and dramatic presentations by various community orgns.; Norfolk County Orch., Norwood PTA, pres. Winslow-West PTA, pres. Sr. High Sch. PTA, Norwood Band-Orch., Parents Club. Norwood Cub Scouts; chmn. Norwood Council PTA; active Boy Scouts Am., v.p. Old Colony Council, fin. chmn. Massasoit Dist., chmn. Scouters Assn., corp. sec. Hale Reservation, instl. chmn. Cub Scouts; career conf. chmn. Mass. Accounting Careers Council; gen. chmn. Norwood Red Cross; pub. info. Community Fund and Council; chmn. Hale Camping Reservation. Rep. Norwood Town Meeting; exec. adviser Air Squadron, Naval Air Sta., Weymouth; chmn. New Eng. Systems Seminar. Recipient Silver Beaver award Boy Scouts Am.; award Mass. Bay United Fund. Registered profl. engr. Mem. Assn. Systems Mgmt. (certificate of merit 1972), AIM (pres.'s council), Am. Mgmt. Assn., Internat. Systems and Procedures Assn. (treas. Bay State chpt., award for outstanding services in systems edn.), Nat. Assn. Accountants (dir. ednl. activities, Manuscript award, certificate of merit). Home: 8 Kennedy Ln Walpole MA 02081 Died Mar. 11, 1978.

PERNECKY, PAUL, accountant, former govt. ofcl.; b. Chgo., Feb. 1, 1912; s. Paul and Marie (Orth) P.; B.S., Northwestern U., 1934; M.A., George Washington U., 1941; m. Elsie L. Phelps, Oct. 1, 1941; 1 dau., Elsie Marie. With HEW, 1936-43, Dept. Commerce, 1943-50, Dept. Interior, 1950-55, Dept. Navy, 1955-57, HUD, Washington, 1957-66; C.P.A., Silver Spring, Md. Mem. Third Order St. Francis; permanent deacon for the deaf Archdiocese Washington, Catholic Deaf Center, Washington. Mem. Nat. Assn. Accountants, Ill. Soc. C.P.A.'s, Am. Inst. C.P.A.'s. Home and office: 3499 S Leisure World Blvd Silver Spring MD 20906

PEROSKY, WAYNE FREDERICK, office supply co. exec.; b. Peekskill, N.Y., Jan. 17, 1947; s. Arthur Ferdinand and Lucy Beatrice (Tompkins) P.; student Victor Comptometer Bus. Machines Sch., 1966; m. Lee Ann Ackerley, July 17, 1971. Service mgr., v.p. Jensen Office Products Co., Mohegan Lake, N.Y., 1963—. Served with USAF, 1966-70. Mem. Nat. Office Machine Dealers Assn., Nat. Office Products Assn. Republican. Methodist. Home: 1 Stephen Pl Beacon NY 12508

PERR, IRWIN, psychiatrist, lawyer, medicolegal cons.; b. Newark, Mar. 4, 1928; B.S., Franklin and Marshall Coll., 1946; M.D., Jefferson Med. Coll., 1950; J.D., Cleve. State U., 1961; m. Dec. 13, 1952; children—Hilary, Geoffrey, Andrea, Jonathan. Chmn. dept. psychiatry Huron Rd. Hosp., Cleve., 1966-72; clin. prof. legal medicine Case Western Res. U. Sch. Law, Cleve., 1971-72; adj. prof. law Rutgers U. Law Sch., Newark; prof. psychiatry and community medicine Rutgers U. Med. Sch., Piscataway, N.J. Served to capt. USAF, 1952-54. Diplomate Am. Bd. Forensic Psychiatry. (v.p. 1977—). Mem. Am. Psychiat. Assn., AMA, Am. Acad. Forensic Scis. (v.p. 1975-76), Am. Acad. Psychiatry and Law (pres. 1977—), Am. Coll. Legal Medicine. Contbr. numerous articles to profl. jours. Home: 14 Liberty Bell Ct East Brunswick NJ 08816 Office: Dept Psychiatry Rutgers Med Sch Piscataway NJ 08854*

PERRAULT, CHARLES, cons.; b. Montreal, Que., Can., Sept. 22, 1922; s. Jean Julien and Laurette (Beaubien) P.; B.Eng., McGill U., 1943, M.Eng., 1945; m. Lucette Benington, June 30, 1947; children—Raymond, Jean, Jacques, Gabrielle, Suzanne. Personnel mgr. Que. Iron & Titanium Corp., Sorel, Que., 1950-54; gen. mgr. Casavant Freres, Limitee, St. Hyacinthe, Que., 1958, pres., 1961-69, chmn., 1969—; pres. Conseil ou Patronat du Que., Montreal, 1969-76; pres. Perconsult Ltd., Montreal, 1976—; dir. Avon Products Ltd., Beaubran Corp., Quaker Oats Co. Can., Ltd., Celanese Can., Ltd., BP Can. Ltd., Molson Cos. Ltd., Taurus Fund Ltd., Canron Ltd., No. Telecom Ltd., Oshawa Group Ltd., Gaz Met. Inc., N.Am. Life Assurance Co. Bd. dirs. C.D. Howe Research Inst. Served to lt. Royal Canadian Elec. and Mech. Engrs., 1943-45. Club: Cercle Universitaire (Que.). Home: 11355 James Morrice St Montreal PQ H3M 2E6 Canada Office: 2050 Mansfield St Montreal PQ H3A 1Y9 Canada

PERRAULT, RENE ALBERT FRANCOIS, physician; b. St. Hyacinthe, Que., Can., Oct. 3, 1932; s. Antonio and Andree (Gavard) P.; B.A., Coll. Breboeuf (Montreal, Que.), 1952; M.D., U. Montreal, 1957; m. Colette Benoit, May 26, 1956; children—Marie, Francois, Philippe. Resident in surgery Notre Dame Hosp., Montreal, 1957-61; gen. surgeon Honore Mercier Hosp., St. Hyacinthe, Que., 1962—, chief of staff dept. surgery, 1972—; dir. Le Centre Medico Chirugical de St. Hyacinthe Inc. Fellow Royal Coll. Surgeons; mem. Que. Profl. Corp. Physicians, Que., Can. med. assns., Que. Assn. Gen. Surgeons, Association des Medecins de langue Francaise. Home: 2905 Girouard St Hyacinthe PQ J2S 3B7 Canada Office: 2780 Raymond St St Hyacinthe PQ J2S 5W7 Canada

PERRETTE, JEAN RENE, banker; b. Dinan, France, May 24, 1931; s. Rene Jean and Marie Cecile (Ollivier) P.; came to U.S., 1961; LL.D., U. Paris, 1955; D. Econs., 1959; m. Virginia Moore Schott, Sept. 8, 1962; children—Virginie-Alvine, Clarisse, Jean-Briac, Julien-Yannick. Asst. to gen. mgmt. Worms CMC, Paris, 1959-61, U.S. rep. N.Y.C., 1961-65; U.S. rep. Banque Worms, N.Y.C., 1965—; pres. Permal Internat. Inc., U.S. reps. Messrs. Worms & Cie., Paris, other European cos., N.Y.C., 1965—; dir. several cos.; cons. French pub. group, 1967-71. Served with French Navy, 1956-59. Mem. HEC Bus. Sch. U.S. Alumni Assn. (pres. 1975-76), French C. of C. in U.S. (exec. com. 1975—). Clubs: Union (N.Y.C.), India House (N.Y.C.). Home: 14 E 90th St New York City NY 10028 Office: 919 3d Ave New York City NY 10022

PERRIN, LESLEY DAVISON (PSEUDONYM LESLEY DAVISON), writer, composer, performer; b. London, Sept. 7, 1930; d. Edward and Natalie (Weiner) Davison; B.A., Brown U., 1951; m. Forrest G. Perrin, May 3, 1961; children—Wendy Elizabeth, Christopher Scott. Appeared as singer-guitarist, Blue Angel, Playboy Club, 1959—; writer Julius Monk's Plaza 9 revues, Upstairs at the Downstairs, Crystal Palace, Aspen, Colo., Wit's End, Atlanta, Cherry Lane Theatre, N.Y., 1959—; writer TV shows, including Laugh In, Dean Martin, Merv Griffin, Jack Paar, Today, Tonight also Not So Much A Programme, BBC, London, Mavis Bramston Show, Australia; also for recordings; composer: Ping Pong; Alma, Whatsa Mater?; Ten Percent Banlon; Cover-Up; The Jackie Look; Lady Bird; Silent Majority Waltz; Cook's Tour; Cries in the Common Marketplace; Las Vegas East; Lust in My Heart; Marching for Peace; also contbr. Julius Monk's Baker's Dozen; contbr. poems, lyrics to pop. mags., recordings, revues. Home and Office: 162 W 54th St New York City NY 10019

PERRONE, ANTHONY JOSEPH, research scientist; b. Westerly, R.I., July 12, 1926; s. Angelo Michael and Annuizala (Marchese) P.; student R.I. Sch. of Electronics, 1948-50, Pa. State U., 1968—, Mass. Inst. Tech., 1968, U. of R.I., 1969, RCA, 1969; m. Susie C. Chiaradio, Oct. 16, 1948; children—Anthony J., Diane, Angela, Suzanne. Radio engr. Sta. WERI, Westerly; lab technician Sperry Products Co., Danbury, Conn., 1951-52; research project leader Navy Underwater Systems Center, New London, Conn., 1952—. Served with USN, 1944-46. Recipient numerous superior accomplishment and pub. awards. Fellow Acoustical Soc. of Am. (Narragansett chpt.), VFW. Contbr. articles in field to profl. jours. Home: 98 East Ave Westerly RI 02891 Office: Ft Trumbull New London CT 06320

PERRONE, SAMUEL JOSEPH, physician; b. Worcester, Mass., Aug. 20, 1918; s. Joseph Santo and Matildha Rosa (Intriere) P.; A.B., Clark U., 1940; M.D., Tufts U., 1943; m. Sophia Rosa Gnoza, Jan. 21, 1940; children—John R., Samuel Joseph, Paula A. Perrone Neumann. Intern. Worcester (Mass.) City Hosp., 1943-44; sr. physician, St. Vincent Hosp., Worcester, 1971—; attending physician, Doctors Hosp., Worcester, 1948—; practice family medicine, Worcester, 1947—; dir. Doctors Hosp., 1948-76, pres. bd. dirs., 1964-66, chief of staff, 1968-70, chief pediatrics, 1970-75, chief of medicine, 1976—; preceptor family practice, Med. Sch., U. Mass., Worcester; bd. govs. Mass. Acad. Family Practice, 1973—. Dir. Central Mass. Lung Assn., 1958—, pres., 1977; dir. Central Mass. Health Care Found., 1974—; dir. Central Mass. Profl. Standards Review Orgn., 1976—; dir. Worcester Boys Clubs Am., 1965—. Served to capt. M.C. U.S. Army, 1944-47. Diplomate Am. Bd. Family Physicians. Fellow AMA (Physician Recognition award 1973), Mass. Med. Assn., Worcester Dist. Med. Soc., Am. Acad. Family Physicians; mem. N.Y. Acad. Scis. Clubs: U.S. Power Squadron N, Boston Navigators, Italian Am. Profl. Bus. Mens Assn. (dir.), Bishops Fund Profl. Com. (chmn. 1974-75), Century Clark U., M Club Tufts U. Home: 9 Beeching St Worcester MA 01602 Office: 82 Hamilton St Worcester MA 01604

PERROTTA, FIORAVANTE GERALD, lawyer; b. Lynbrook, N.Y., July 26, 1931; s. Ercole John and Frances (Raimondi) P.; B.A., St. John's Coll., 1952, J.D., 1955. Admitted to N.Y. State bar, 1955, U.S. Supreme Ct. bar; asst. U.S. atty. So. Dist. N.Y., 1955-57; asso. firm Jackson Nash Brophy Barringer & Brooks, 1957-58; asst. counsel to Gov. Rockefeller, 1959-60, spl. asst., 1961-62; asso. firm Simpson Thacher & Bartlett, 1960-61; dep. supt., gen. counsel N.Y. State Ins. Dept., 1963, 1st dept. supt., 1964-66; v.p. USLIFE Holding Corp., 1966-67; v.p., dir. South Coast Life Ins. Co., Houston, 1966-67, Commonwealth Life Ins. Co., Pasadena, Cal., 1966-67; exec. asst. to Mayor Lindsay, 1968; fin. adminstr. N.Y.C., 1969-70; partner firm Rogers & & Wells, 1970—; dir. Bankers Life Ins. Soc., 20 Sutton Pl. South, Inc., Charter Indemnity Co.; commr. State Ins. Fund, 1971-77. Dir. Gov. Rockefeller re-election campaign, 1970; N.Y.C. campaign dir. re-election Pres. Nixon, 1972; trustee N.Y. Foundling Hosp., Mercy Coll., 1972. Mem. exec. com. N.Y.C. Fusion Adv. Council, 1970. Named Young Ins. Man of Year, 1966. Mem. Assn. Bar City N.Y., Am., N.Y. bar assns., Am. Arbitration Assn. (panel arbitrators), Phi Delta Phi. Republican. Roman Catholic. Home: 20 Sutton Pl S New York City NY 10022 Office: 200 Park Ave New York City NY 10017

PERRY, ANTHONY JOHN, cons. engr.; b. Boston, Sept. 7, 1905; s. Anthony A. and Ellen M. (Connors) P.; A.B., Boston Coll., 1926; S.B., Mass. Inst. Tech., 1929. Civil and elec. engr. Bur. Reclamation, Dept. of Interior, specializing in design and constrn. hydro-electric power and high tension transmission, 1930-65. Cons. engr. electric generation and transmission; spl. assignments include Point 4 program, Iran, Iraq, Lebanon and Italy, 1952, ICA, Cambodia, 1958; cons. govts., Brazil, 1964, Republic Korea, 1966, Bolivia, 1967-68, UN, AEC, pvt. engring. firms. Registered profl. engr., Colo., D.C. Fellow ASCE (life); mem. Nat. Soc. Profl. Engrs., Am. Def. Preparedness Assn. Democrat. Roman Catholic. K.C. Address: 4000 Massachusetts Ave NW Washington DC 20016

PERRY, CHARLES NORVIN, union ofcl.; b. Balt., Mar. 3, 1928; s. William Raymond and Hazel Leona (Schmidt) P.; student pub. schs., Balt. with P.P.G. Industries, Inc., Balt., 1944—; chmn. exec. com., fin. officer, local chpt. United Steelworkers Am., Balt., 1969—. Chief emergency rescue service Office Disaster Control, Civil Def. Balt.; chief emeritus Balt. Vol. Rescue Squad; mem. Regional Planning Commn. Emergency Med. Service, 1975—; rescue instr. Fed. Civil Def.; pres. local Democratic orgn.; mem. Dem. Nat. Com. Served with USN, World War II. Selected Outstanding Citizen P.P.G., 1968-69, 72, Presdl. citation, 1975; commendation Mayor of Balt., 1956, 62, 75, 76, 77; named Balt.'s Best, 1977. Mem. Md. Ambulance Rescue Assn. (v.p., life mem., outstanding achievement award 1977), Internat. Rescue First Aid Assn. Lutheran. Editor: Md. Rescue Jour., 1972—. Author emergency med. service publs. Home: 2405 Tionesta Rd Lansdowne MD 21227 Office: 360 S Dukeland St Baltimore MD 21223 also PO Box 3052 Baltimore MD 21229

PERRY, DANIEL DEVERELL, architect; b. Buffalo, Aug. 29, 1905; s. George Daniel and Emma (Deverell) P. B.Arch., Syracuse U., 1930; student Fonteinbleau Sch. Fine Arts, France, 1930; m. Mary Jean K.

Smoak, Dec. 14, 1932; children—Mary Jean, George Daniel II. Individual practice architecture, Port Jefferson, N.Y., 1931-62; partner Perry & Bergmark architects, 1962-75; prin. Daniel Perry architect, 1975—; project engr. Scintilla Magneto div. Bendix Aviation Corp., Sidney, N.Y., 1941-46. Mem. AIA (past pres.), N.Y. State Assn. Architects, Archtl. League, Soc. Preservation Long Island Antiquities. Club: Setauket Yacht. Architect, Sterling and Francine Clark Art Inst., Williamstown, Mass., 1953, Sunrest Nursing Home, Port Jefferson, 1965, James E. Allen Learning Center, 1974. Home and office: 1213 Main St Port Jefferson NY 11777

PERRY, DARRELL DELMAR, math. statistician; b. Fertigs, Pa., Dec. 7, 1933; s. Ora Benton and Marion June P.; B.S., Clarion State Coll., 1961; postgrad. George Washington U., 1963-68; m. Kathryn Elizabeth Davis, Jan. 26, 1963; children—Gregory Alan, Lori Alison. Tchr. Valley Grove Schs., Franklin, Pa., 1961-63; statistician Naval Ordnance Sta., Indian Head, Md., 1963-66, mgr. reliability and statistics, 1966—. Exec. com. Matthew Henson PTA, 1977, v.p. Pomonkey PTA, also del. county council, 1972; sec. North Indian Head (Md.) Estates Civic Assn., 1973. Served with USAF, 1953-57. Mem. Am. Statis. Assn., Am. Ordnance Assn., So. Md. Choral Soc. Clubs: Methodist Mens, Naval Ordance Sta. Golf (gov. 1977—). Home: 215 Amherst Rd Bryans Road MD 20616 Office: Naval Ordnance Station Indian Head MD 20640

PERRY, EDWARD JOSEPH, supt. schs.; b. Rome, N.Y., Aug. 20, 1923; s. Nicholas and Esther (Festa) P.; B.A. cum laude, Syracuse U., 1948; postgrad Colgate U.; m. Mary Ann Decotis, June 24, 1950; children—Edward M., Deborah B. With Utica (N.Y.) Pub. Schs., 1948—, jr. high sch. prin. 1963-66, dep. supt. schs., 1966-68, supt., 1968—. Guest lectr. Utica Coll., Cortland Grad. Sch., 1971-73; moderator weekly program radio sta. WIBX, Utica. Dir. Blue Cross. Mem. Mayor's adv. com., Utica, 1968—, Mohawk Valley Ednl. Planning Bd., 1968—, mem. exec. bd. Region 7 Vocational-Occupational Edn. Com.; Mohawk Valley Com. Prevention Alcoholism. Bd. dirs. Cerebral Palsy Clinic. Served with USAAF, 1942-45. Named Outstanding Educator of Am., Am. Acad. Educators, 1973. Mem. Mohawk Valley Chief Sch. Officers (exec. bd.), Nat. Council Bus. Men, Kappa Phi Kappa. Club: Exchange (Utica). Contbr. articles to profl. jours., newspapers. Home: 139 Proctor Blvd Utica NY 13502 Office: 13 Elizabeth St Utica NY 13501

PERRY, EDWARD (TED) SAMUEL, educator/adminstr.; b. New Orleans, June 4, 1937; s. Edward Severa and Gertrude Morris (Stevens) P.; B.A., Baylor U., 1960; M.A., U. Iowa, 1966, Ph.D., 1968; m. Miriam Moody, July 14, 1961; children—Melissa Kathryn, Megan Stevens, John Myles, Edward Thaddeus. Writer-dir. films So. Baptist Conv. Radio-TV Commn., 1961-64; free-lance writer-dir., 1964; instr., asst. prof. dept. speech and dramatic art U. Iowa, 1964-69; asso. prof., dir. grad. studies dept. radio/TV/film Sch. Communication, U. Tex., Austin, 1969-71; asso. prof. N.Y. U., 1971-72, prof., 1972-75, chmn. dept. cinema studies, 1971-75; dir. dept. film Mus. Modern Art, N.Y.C., 1975-78; den arts and humanities Middlebury (Vt.) Coll., 1978-79; dir. Brit. Film Inst., London, 1979—; vis. Henry Luce prof. Harvard U., spring 1976; vis. lectr. theatre arts State U. N.Y., Purchase, 1972-73; co-dir. Interplay, 1969; creator, writer, co-producer JOT, animated films, 1969; dir., writer numerous TV films; mem. Commn. Archives in Developing Countries, Internat. Fedn. Film Archives; mem. bd. dirs. Collective for Living Cinema, Learning about Learning Found.; lectr. in field, 1964—; project dir. Nat. Endowment for Arts, 1971-76, Jerome Found., 1972-76, N.Y. State Council on Arts, 1972-76; judge Western Heritage Awards, 1972; mem. steering com. 3d Internat. Congress on Religion, Architecture and Arts, Jerusalem, 1973; mem. arts adv. com. Library of Congress; co-dir. Am. Film Inst. Seminar on Film, Center for Advanced Film Study, Los Angeles, 1972; mem. adv. bd. Univ. Film Found.; mem. adv. council Nat. Project Center on Film and Humanities. Recipient blue ribbon Am. Film Festival, 1972, 18th ann. Chris award Film Council Greater Columbus, 1970. Nat. Endowment for Humanities grantee, 1973-75; Gottesman Found. grantee, 1974-76. Mem. Theatre Library Assn. (ex-officio dir.), Speech-Communication Assn. (research bd. 1972-75), Univ. Film Assn. (dir. 1970), Danforth Fedn. (asso.), Media Educators Assn. (adv. council), Soc. for Cinema Studies, Am. Fedn. Arts (adv. com. on film), Nat. Com. on Film and TV Resources and Services. Club: University (N.Y.C.). Author: (play) Go Where the Ducks Are, 1966; Fellini's 8 1/2, 1974; (with Richard Dyer MacCann) The Film Index, 1975. Editor: Performing Arts Resources, vols. I-III, 1975-77; asso. editor Communication Quarterly. Contbr. articles to profl. publs. Home: 43 South St Middlebury VT 05753 Office: 127 Charing Cross Rd London WC2H OEA England

PERRY, EDWARD THOMAS, constn. and bldg. materials cons.; b. Attleboro, Mass., June 7, 1898; s. Charles Henry and Elizabeth (Murray) P.; student Brown U., 1923-26; m. Lisabella Clare, Apr. 7, 1921. Adminstrv. v.p., dir. New Haven Trap Rock Co. (Conn.), 1951—; dir. Dunning Sand and Stone Co. (Conn.), 1951—; dir. Dunning Sand and Stone Co., Wauregan, Conn., Foxon Concrete Co., New Haven, M.F. Roach Co., North Eastham, Mass. Served with U.S. Army, World War I. Mem. Nat. Hwy. Research Bd. (Washington), R.I. Road Builders Assn. (past sec., dir.), R.I. Hwy. Assn., Nat. Asphalt Pavement Assn. (hon.; bd. govs., chmn. awards com.), Conn. Bituminous Concrete Assn. (past pres., hon. mem.), Conn. Crushed Stone Assn. (past pres.). Clubs: Quinnipiack, Country (New Haven); New York Yacht; Triton (Que., Can.). Home: 3205 Diamond Hill Rd Cumberland RI 02864 Office: 221 Church St New Haven CT 06510

PERRY, G. DANIEL, architect; b. Port Jefferson, N.Y., Sept. 3, 1940; s. Daniel Deverell and Mary Jean (Smoak) P.; A.B., Princeton U., 1962, M.F.A., 1964; diploma Ecole d'Art Americaine Fontainebleau, 1963; m. Georgia Kathleen Asher, July 1, 1966; children—George Asher, Thomas Asher. Architect, U.S. Peace Corps, Tunisia, 1964-66, Eisenman & Graves, Architects, Princeton, N.J., 1966-67, Michael Graves, Architect, Princeton, 1967; with Mitchell/Giurgola Architects, N.Y.C., 1967—, partner, 1974—. Mem. AIA, Constrn. Specifications Inst., Urban Land Inst., Archtl. League N.Y. Project architect Mission Park Residential Houses, Williams Coll., Williamstown, Mass., 1970; Sherman Fairchild Center for Life Scis., Columbia, 1976, U.S. Car Mfg. div. Volvo of Am. Corp., Chesapeake, Va., 1976. Home: 95 W 95th St New York City NY 10025 Office: Mitchell/Giurgola Architects 170 W 97th St New York City NY 10025

PERRY, GEORGE ELEUTHERIOS, librarian, editor; b. N.Y.C., Aug. 27, 1929; s. Gus and Cleo (Panagatos) Pierratos; B.A. in English Lit. with honors, Cornell U., 1952; M.Internat. Affairs, Columbia U., 1956, postgrad. dept. pub. law and govt., 1956-58, student Russian Inst., 1954-56, M.Phil., 1975; m. Sophie Livadas, Oct. 4, 1953; children—Clio Irene, Constance Maria. Acquisitions librarian Columbia U., 1956-61; mem. staff Library of Congress, 1963-77, curator Slavic room, 1964-68, head Slavic room 1968-74, Greek area specialist, 1971-77; editor Ethnic Racial Rev., 1975—; founder, pres. Ethnic Employees of Library of Congress, 1973—; chmn. com. ethnic affairs Library of Congress Employee Union, 1973; gen. counselor Black Employees Library of Congress, 1974—. Mem. U.S. Bicentennial com. Greek Orthodox Archdiocese N. and S. Am., 1972-76; asso. Nat. Center Social Research, Greece, 1973-74, Center Neo-Hellenic Studies, Austin, Tex., 1969-76; sec., bd. dirs. Fountainhead Towers Condominium Assn., 1973-74. Recipient Meritorious Service award Library of Congress, 1965; Ford Found. fgn. area fellow Soviet Union and Eastern Europe, 1954-56. Mem. A.L.A. (sec., mem. exec. com. Slavic and E. European subsect. 1966-69), Modern Greek Studies Assn., Phi Beta Kappa, Phi Kappa Phi. Republican. Mem. Greek Orthodox Ch. Clubs: Cornell (Washington); Order Ahepa (chmn. Am. Revolution Bicentennial com. 1972-76). Author, compiler in field. Home and office: 6100 East View Kenwood Park Washington DC 20034

PERRY, GEORGE FRANCIS, educator; b. Taylor, Pa., Apr. 1, 1923; s. George and Helen (Kaschak) Perosh; B.A. cum laude, U. Scranton, 1948; M.A., Cath. U. Am., 1950; Ph.D., Fordham U., 1971; m. Mary Ellen Dean, Aug. 28, 1963. Radio announcer, dir. Sta. WARM, Scranton, Pa., 1943-48; instr. speech, dir. drama Georgetown U., Washington, 1949-51; instr. speech and drama Marywood Coll., Scranton, 1951-54, asst. prof. speech and drama, 1954-59, asso. prof. drama, 1959-62, prof. drama, grad. lectr. English, 1962—. Incorporator, Northeastern Pa. Ednl. TV Assn., 1963, bd. dirs., 1963-74, sec., 1965-69; bd. dirs. Scranton Philharmonic Orch., 1954-60; mem. com. on theatre Pa. Council for Performing Arts, 1971. Recipient Vicennial medal for distinguished service Marywood Coll., 1971. Mem. AAUP (pres. Marywood Coll. chpt. 1973-74), Modern Lang. Assn., Am. Theatre Assn., Speech Communication Assn., Pa. Speech Assn. (chmn. speech arts div. 1962-63). Catholic. Co-author: History of the Theatre—A College Syllabus, 1961. Producer, lectr. History of Drama course WNEP-TV, Scranton, 1955; producer theatre prodns., 1949—. Home: 109 Sturbridge Rd Clarks Summit PA 18411 Office: Dept Communication Arts Marywood Coll Scranton PA 18509

PERRY, GORDON CLARK, cons. agrl. engr., govtl. assn. exec.; b. Penn Yan, N.Y., Oct. 19, 1924; s. Claude S. and Faith (Eveland) P.; B.S. in Agrl. Engring., Cornell U., 1949, M.S. in Elec. Engring. and Thermodynamics, 1961; Ph.D. in Engring./Adminstrn., U. Sarasota, 1971; m. Edith Marie Palmer, June 12, 1948; children—Nancy Irene, David Lyle, Beth Lorraine, Janine Marie, Geoffrey Gordon. Owner, operator Dairy Farm, Yates County, N.Y., 1949-54; extension agrl. engr. Cornell U., Ithaca, N.Y., 1954-61; field engr. G.L.F. Exchange, Inc., Ithaca, N.Y., 1961-63; 63; dir. agrl. engring. research Agway, Inc., Syracuse, 1964-65; dir. systems devel. Environment Controlled Systems, Weedsport, N.Y., 1966-77; cons. on research and ednl. prodn. facilities and waste disposal Columbia U. Physicians and Surgeons, Rockefeller Inst., Mt. Sinai Hosp. and Med. Research Center, Montefiori Hosp. Med. Research Center, Squibb Pharmaceuticals, Johns Hopkins U. Med. Sch., numerous others, 1965-77; exec. dir. N.Y. State Conf. Mayors, 1978—. Mem. N.Y. State Com. Intergovtl. Cooperation, Senator Javitt's Advisory Com. Local Govt., Gov.'s Commn. Human Rights, Gov.'s Conf. Com. Energy Conservation, Cayuga County Traffic Safety Bd.; mem. exec. com. N.Y. State Conf. Mayors, 1974-77. Republican committeeman Town Italy, Yates County, N.Y., 1952-54; mayor Village of Weedsport, 1972-78, also trustee. Served with Inf., 1943-46. Mem. Am. Soc. Agrl. Engrs., Engrs. Joint Council, N.Y. Milk and Food Sanitarians Assn., Internat. Assn. Milk, Food and Environmental Sanitarians, Am. Assn. for Lab. Animal Sci., Am. Forestry Assn. Mason, Lion. Republican. Baptist. Home: 316 State St Albany NY 12210 Office: 6 Elk St Albany NY 12207

PERRY, HENRY ALEXANDER, materials engr.; b. Newton, Mass., Mar. 21, 1913; s. Henry A. and Emma G. (Henderson) P.; B.S. in Chem. Engring., Northeastern U., 1936; postgrad. Mass. Inst. Tech., 1944-45, U. Md., 1947-49; m. Alice C. Krans, June 17, 1944; 1 dau., Carolyn Julie Perry Shipp. Research engr. Kinney Mfg. Co., Boston, 1940-42; safety engr. Ordnance Corps., U.S. Army, Chgo., 1942-44; radome engr. Radiation Lab., Mass. Inst. Tech., Cambridge, 1944-45; materials engr. Ordnance Lab., U.S. Navy, Silver Spring, Md., 1945-54; project mgr. Massive Glass Hulls for Deep Submergence. Cons. on materials, 1954-78; pres. Marine Materials Corp., Annapolis, Md., 1971—. Mem. adv. council on materials U.S. Navy, 1960-64; mem. com. on composites NRC, 1962-63, Engring. Found., N.Y.C., 1963—. Councilman Town Laytonsville, 1966-69. Charter pres. Laytonsville (Md.) Vol. Fire Dept., 1954-55; mem. Anne Arundel County (Md.) Bicentennial Com., 1976. Recipient Meritorious Civilian Service award U.S. Navy, 1956. Mem. ASTM, Soc. Plastics Engrs., Soc. Plastics Industry, Soc. Washington Engrs., Am. Ceramics Soc., Inst. Ceramics Engrs. Clubs: Lions (charter Laytonsville, pres. 1964-65, pres. Anne Arundel 1976-77), Classic Yacht Am., Windjammers of the Chesapeake. Author: Adhesive Bonding of Reinforced Plastics, 1960. Patentee materials, weapons systems. Home and Office: 4077 Waterview Dr Edgewater MD 21037

PERRY, JACQUELINE CHERYL, govt. ofcl.; b. Bronx, N.Y., Aug. 29, 1947; d. James Edward and Jessie Mae (Footmon) P.; B.A., Hunter Coll. of City U. N.Y., 1970; M.S., U. Utah, 1976. Mgmt. trainee GSA, N.Y.C., 1970-71, inventory mgmt. specialist, 1971-72, equal opportunity specialist, 1972-78, supervisory equal opportunity specialist, 1978—. Race relations officer U.S. Army Res. NSF grantee in computer applications to psychol. research, 1969. Mem. Am. Soc. Pub. Adminstrn., Conf. Minority Pub. Adminstrs., Am. Personnel and Guidance Assn., Nat. Employment Counselors Assn., Assn. Non-White Concerns in Personnel and Guidance, Res. Officers Assn. (life), Federally Employed Women Inc. (coordinator regional), Nat. Council Negro Women, Bklyn. Urban League, Dance Theatre Found. Inc., WAC Mus. Soc. (life). Office: 26 Federal Plaza New York City NY 10007

PERRY, JOHN RICHARD, historian, marine artist: b. Rockland, Maine, Jan. 29, 1945; s. Robert Lee and Doree Elizabeth (Knowles) P.; student pub. schs., Rockport, Mass.; m. Marilyn Brown, May 8, 1976; children from previous marriage—John Richard Perry Jr., Dianne Louise Perry; stepchildren—David Brown, DiannaBrown, Douglass Brown, Deanna Brown, Derek Brown. Detail draftsman Gloucester Engring. Inc. (Mass.), 1968-70; sr. artist, dir. art dept. Keezer Mfg. Inc., Plaistow, N.H., 1970-73; profl. artist, 1973—; marine artist, historian, partner Perry's Ship Gallery, Salisbury, Mass., 1976—; adviser North East Cultural Arts Inc. Served with USAF, 1965-69; Vietnam. Recipient 1st place Greater Haverhill Arts Assn., 1977, 78. Mem. Greater Haverhill Art Assn. (pres), Nat. Maritime Hist. Soc., Soc. N.Am. Artists, Copley Soc. Research and authentically-detailed portraits of sailing ships; represented in permanent collections USCG Acad., pvt. collections Pres. . Gerald Ford, Queen Elizabeth II, others. Home and Studio: 5 S Pleasant St Merrimac MA 01860

PERRY, RICHARD BERNARD, internist; b. Washington, Feb. 20, 1930; s. Roy Montgomery and Genevieve Loretta (McMahon) P.; B.S., Georgetown U., 1951, M.D., 1955; m. Maureen Brennan Canning, Apr. 21, 1956 (dec. 1977); children—Richard Bernard, Mark X. Michael J., Maureen Leigh; m. 2d, Valda Berzins Strong, June 9, 1978. Intern, D.C. Gen. Hosp., 1955-56; resident Georgetown U. Hosp., Washington, 1956-58; fellow pulmonary disease D.C. Gen. Hosp., 1958-59; fellow cardiology Georgetown U., 1961-62; practice medicine specializing in internal medicine, Washington, 1962—; mem. staffs Georgetown U., Sibley hosps., Washington Hosp. Center; asst. clin. prof. medicine Georgetown U., 1968-78. Mem. parish council Our Lady of Mercy Roman Cath. Ch., Washington, 1974-75; sec.-treas. Osler Soc., 1973. Served to capt. USAF, 1959-61. Diplomate Am. Bd. Internal Medicine. Fellow A.C.P. (sec. 1969; sec.-treas., gov.'s council Met. D.C. chpt.); mem. AMA, D.C. Med. Soc., Am. Heart Assn., Clin. Pathology Soc. D.C. Republican. Clubs: Bethesda Country; Internat. (Washington). Contbr. articles to med. jours. Home: 10100 Iron Gate Rd Potomac MD 20854 Office: 1145 19th St NW #600 Washington DC 20036

PERRY, VERNON MCGLENN, JR., utility ofcl.; b. Norfolk, Va.; s. Vernon McGlenn and Mildred (Bishop) P.; B.S. in Math., Elizabeth City State U., 1966; postgrad. Marist Coll., Poughkeepsie, N.Y.; m. Portia Perry, Dec. 19, 1964; children—Vernon McGlenn, Vera. Mathematician, NASA, Langley, Va., 1966; nuclear systems engr. Newport News Shipbldg. & Drydock Co. (Va.), 1966-70; supt. nuclear power plant constrn. and testing Consol. Edison Co., Indian Point, N.Y., 1970-76, supt. Elec. Bur., 1976-78, supt. contract inspection and pub. improvement, 1978—; vis. prof. Black Exec. Exchange Program, Urban League. Exec. bd. South Ave Sch. PTA, Cub Scouts Am., 1973; co-chmn. bd. deacons Baptist Temple (Newburgh, N.Y.). Recipient Black Achievers in Industry award, 1973. Mem. Am. Nuclear Soc., Alpha Phi Alpha. Home: 18 Doran Dr Hopewell Junction NY 12533 Office: 315 Old Sawmill River Rd Eastview Vallhalla NY 10595

PERRY, WILLIAM RUSSELL, govt. ofcl.; b. Provincetown, Mass., Apr. 20, 1916; s. Albert J. and Elizabeth Agnes Perry; B.Ed., Conn. State Tchrs. Coll., 1939; M.Ed., Hartford U., 1951; m. Alice F. Sullivan, Apr. 23, 1942; children—William Russell, Patrick A. Tchr., prin., schs. in Scotland and Weston, Conn., 1939-41; regional sales supr. Republic Aviation Co., Farmingdale, N.Y., 1946-51; dep. dir. Conn. Pub. Sch. Bldg. Commn., 1951-55; exec. and career devel. and tng. officer Air Force, Washington, 1959—, Directorate of Civilian Personnel, 1973—; chmn. Weather br. Annapolis Power Squadron, 1976-78. Served with USAF, 1942-66. Certified tchr., Conn. Mem. Am. Soc. for Tng. and Devel. (pres. Canaveral br. 1964-66), Am. Assn. Sch. Adminstrs., Systems Application of Learning Tech., Am. Mgmt. Assn., Nat. Assn. Ednl. Communication, Ret. Officers Assn. Republican. Roman Catholic. Club: Pentagon Rod and Gun. Contbr. articles on flight instruction and tech. to profl. publs. Home: 144 Berrywood Dr Severna Park MD 21146 Office: HQ/USAF Forrestal Bldg Washington DC 20314

PERRYMAN, CHARLES R., radiologist; b. Elliot, Iowa, Sept. 21, 1916; s. Raymond H. and Mery Gertrude (Weir) P.; B.S., Dartmouth, 1938; M.D., Cornell U., 1942; D.Sc., U. Pa., 1947; m. Charlene Omen, Aug. 23, 1940; children—Richard W., Charles A. Intern Bellevue Hosp., N.Y.C., 1942-43; fellow dept, radiology Hosp., U. Pa., 1943-46, mem. staff dept. radiology, 1946-49; radiologist Baton Rouge Gen., Greenwell Springs Tb Hosps., 1949-51; dir. dept. radiology Mercy Hosp., Pitts., 1951-63, dir. Sch. X-Ray Technique, 1952-63; dir. Philip Murray Radiation Therapy Center, 1954-63; now practice medicine specializing in radiology, Pitts.; asst. prof. radiology U. Pitts. Med. Sch., 1951-56, asso. prof., 1956—. Partner, sec. treas. Metro Co. Bd. dirs. Pitts. Opera, Inc. Recipient Citation OSRD, 1948. Diplomate Am. Bd. Radiology. Fellow Royal Soc. Health Scis.; mem. A.M.A., Am. Radium Soc., Am. Coll. Radiology, Radiol. Soc. N.Am., Am., Phila. roetgen ray socs., Pa. State., La. State, Allegheny County med. socs., Pa. Radiol. Soc., Pitts. Acad. Medicine, Soc. Nuclear Medicine, Rocky Mountain Radiol. Soc., N.Y. Acad. Scis., Sigma Xi. Contbr. articles to profl. jours. Home: 640 Osage Rd Pittsburgh PA 15243 Office: 1501 Locust St Pittsburgh PA 15219

PERSELL, CHARLES BOWEN, JR., bishop; b. Lakewood, N.Y., Mar. 4, 1909; s. Chas. Bowen and Berenice (Caskey) P.; A.B., Hobart Coll., 1931, S.T.D., 1963; grad. Gen. Theology Sem., N.Y.C., 1934, S.T.D., 1963; m. Emily Elizabeth Aldrich, July 8, 1936 (dec. Sept. 1968); children—Charles Bowen III, Carolyn Ruth, William Dailey, Peter Michael; m. 2d, Dorothy Lorenz Patterson, Nov. 28, 1969. Ordained deacon Episcopal Ch., 1934, priest, 1935; pastor in Scottsville and Caledonia, N.Y., 1934-37, Avon, N.Y., 1937-42, Holcomb, N.Y., 1937-41, Honeoeye Falls, N.Y., 1941-42, Ch. of Epiphany, Rochester, N.Y., 1942-44; archdeacon, exec. sec. Diocese Rochester, 1944-50; editor diocesian newspaper The Episcopalian, 1947-50; rector St. John's Ch., Massena, N.Y., 1950-61; archdeacon of Albany, N.Y., 1961-63, suffragan bishop, 1963-77. Dep. to Gen. Conv. Episcopal Ch. from Rochester 1949, from Albany, 1952-55; instr. Rochester Youth Conf., 1934-44, dir., 1940-43; bd. dirs. Fingers Lake Conf., 1944-46, 61—; trustee Diocese Rochester, 1949-50; dean St. Lawrence Deanery, 1952-59; mem. Albany Diocesan Council, 1952-69; canon to ordinary Albany, 1961; chmn. dept. promotion Albany Diocese, 1960-61, chmn. dept. missions, 1961-69; mem. Presiding Bishop's Com. Town and Country Work, 1962—; bd. dirs. N.Y. State Council Chs., Capital Area Council Chs.; Episcopal Ch. rep. on Christians United in Mission. Mem. adoption sect. Council Social Agys. Rochester, 1945-50; bd. dirs. Rochester Better Housing Assn., 1943-50, Albany United Appeal, ARC, St. Margaret's House and Hosp. for Babies, 1963-77, mem. adv. bd., 1977—; bd. dirs. Child's Hosp., 1963-77, Nelson House, 1963-77; bd. dirs. Mary Warren Free Inst., Troy, N.Y., 1965—, pres., 1975. Clubs: University (Albany); Crater, Split Rock Yacht (Essex, N.Y.). Home: 10 DeLucia Terr Loudonville NY 12211 Office: 62 Swan St Albany NY 12210

PERSIANI, CARMINE, chemist; b. Bklyn., Mar. 20, 1931; s. Anthony Paul and Nancy P.; B.S. in Chemistry, Coll. City N.Y., 1953; M.S. in Chemistry, C.W. Post Coll., 1966; m. Irene Del Gardo, Nov. 22, 1958; children—Denise, Jeanette, Geraldine, Anthony. Tech. asso. Brookhaven Nat. Lab., Upton, N.Y., 1955-62; sr. materials engr. Republic Aviation Corp., Farmingdale, N.Y., 1962-64; chemist GTE Research Lab., Waltham, Mass., 1964—. Active Boy Scouts Am., various civic assns. Served with U.S. Army, 1953-55. Mem. Am. Chem. Soc., Am. Nuclear Soc., Sigma Xi. Roman Catholic. Clubs: Photography, Chess. Contbr. articles on analytical chemistry, chromatography, nuclear chemistry to research jours. Home: 36 Whipowill Ln Milford MA 01757 Office: 40 Sylvan Rd Waltham MA 02154

PERSICO, DANIEL FRANCIS, chemist; b. Boston, Sept. 9, 1955; s. I. Frank and Louise Elizabeth (McLaughlin) P.; B.S., Boston Coll., 1977. Research asst. Boston Coll., 1976-77; research chemist U. Tex., Austin, 1978—, grad. teaching asst., 1977—; undergrad. teaching asst. Boston Coll., 1976-77. Named Outstanding Sr. Chemist, Boston Coll., Mass. Inst. Chemists, 1976-77. Mem. Am. Chem. Soc. (analytical chemistry award 1975-76), AAAS. Democrat. Roman Catholic. Home: 141 Edgewood Rd Westwood MA 02090 Office: 5-110 Welch Hall Austin TX 78712

PERSKY, ROBERT SAMUEL, lawyer; b. Jersey City, Jan. 5, 1930; s. Benjamin and Ethel (Soman) P.; B.A., N.Y. U., 1949; LL.B., J.D., Harvard, 1952; children—Steven David, Joshua Soman, Laura Rachel. Admitted to N.Y. bar, 1953; law sec. to judge U.S. Dist. Ct., Eastern Dist. N.Y., 1954-56; asst. counsel Waterfront Commn. N.Y. Harbor, 1956-57; partner Harold, Luca, Persky & Mozer, N.Y.C., 1957-65, Amen, Weisman, Finley and Butler, N.Y.C., 1965-68, Finley, Kumble, Underberg, Persky, Roth & Grutman, 1968-73, Persky & Jarblum, P.C., 1973-75; pres. Soroban Corp., 1975—; dir. Images Gallery. art gallery. Vice pres. Friends Henry St. Settlement, 1954-55; bd. dirs. N.Y. Young Democratic Club, 1955-60, Am. Com.

for Weitzman Inst., 1975—; treas. Com. Elect Ryan to Congress, 1960-72. Served with AUS, 1952-54. Mem. N.Y. County Lawyers Assn. Club: Harvard. Home: 322 W 57th St New York City NY 10019 Office: 11 E 57th St New York City NY 10022

PERSON, JOHN ELMER, JR., newspaper exec.; b. Williamsport, Pa., Aug. 22, 1918; s. John Elmer and Lenna Mae (Braddock) P.; student Dickinson Coll., 1936-39, Rochester Inst. Tech., 1939-41, Babson Inst., 1941-42; m. Charlotte Louise Tepel, Feb. 1, 1947; children—John, Michael, Thomas, David. With Sun-Gazette Co., Williamsport, 1942—, clk., apprentice pressman, 1942-63, pres., 1963—; dir. No. Central Bank. Mem. Family and Children's Service Bd., 1946-52, pres., 1951; mem. Williamsport Sch. Bd., 1949-55, v.p., 1954-55; campaign chmn. Community Chest, 1951, pres., 1952; treas. Lycoming United Way, 1956-62; trustee Lycoming Found., 1956—; bd. mem. (Lycoming chpt. ARC, 1949-54, fund chmn., 1948; trustee YWCA, 1965—; bd. mem. Williamsport Hosp., 1959—, exec. com., 1965—, vice chmn., 1975—; bd. and exec. com. mem. Lycoming Housing Corp., 1970—; chmn. Williamsport Redevel. Authority, 1960-73; trustee Lycoming Coll., 1970—; chmn. Williamsport Found., 1976—. Served to capt. U.S. Army, 1942-46. Named Young Man of Year, Jaycees, 1952; recipient Grit award Ind. Sunday Newspaper, 1958. Mem. Beta Theta Pi, Alpha Delta Sigma. Republican. Methodist. Clubs: Williamsport Country, Grays Run Hunting and Fishing, Masons. Home: 139 Lincoln Ave Williamsport PA 17701 Office: Sun-Gazette Co Williamsport PA 17701

PERSONS, EDWARD B., former govt. ofcl.: b. N.Y., May 3, 1916; B.A., Antioch Coll., 1938; m. Janet Wilson. Asst. budget examiner Bur. Budget, 1940-41; field office mgr., asst. chief, chief field office sect.; civilian personnel div. Dept. War, 1941-43; asst. coordinator internat. coop. programs Dept. Commerce, 1947-48; chief internat. labor orgn. div. Dept. Labor, 1948-56; chief mgmt. analysis staff HEW, 1956-59, asst. dir. personnel, 1959-63; fgn. affairs officer Dept. State, Washington, 1963-71; asso. dep. under sec. Labor for internat. affairs, 1971-76; dir. Washington br. Internat. Labor Office, 1976—. Served to lt. (j.g.) USNR., 1943-47. Recipient Meritorious Service award Dept. Labor, 1953, Merit citation Nat. Civil Service League, 1955, Meritorious Honor award Dept. State, 1968. Home: 6318 Avalon Dr Washington DC 20016 Office: IL Washington Br Office 1750 New York Ave NW Washington DC 20006

PESCATELLO, MICHAEL, investment co. exec.; b. Stonington, Conn., Dec. 24, 1907; s. Orazio and Antonina (Muni) P.; student U.S. Naval Acad., 1927-29; A.B., Temple U., 1933, M.B.A., Harvard, 1935; m. Edith W. Flaacke, June 25, 1941; children—Edward, Michael, Mary, Marjorie, Anita, Paul. Investment officer Carnegie Corp. N.Y., 1935-47; v.p., investment officer Central Trust Co., Cin., 1947-49; investment officer First Nat. Bank N.Y., 1949-55; v.p. First Nat. City Bank, N.Y.C., 1955-72; pres. M. Pescatello & Co., Inc., N.Y.C., 1973—; dir. Cordis Corp., Miami; instr. econs. Coll. City N.Y., Baruch Sch. Bus., U. Cin. Mem. Soc. Security Analysts. Roman Catholic. Clubs: Harvard, Harvard Bus. Sch. Contbr. articles in field to profl. jours. Office: 130 Liberty St New York City NY 10006

PESCOW, JEROME KENNETH, educator, accountant; b. N.Y.C., Dec. 25, 1929; s. Samuel and Anna (Zwerin) P.; B.B.A., Coll. City N.Y., 1952; M.S., Columbia U., 1957; m. Anita Ruth Cohen, June 29, 1958; children—Michael James, Steven Howard. Jr. accountant, Lopez, Edwards, Frank & Co. C.P.A.'s, N.Y.C., 1952; sr. accountant Robert Gold & Co., N.Y.C., 1954-57, 58; accounting analyst, internal auditor N.Y. Central System, N.Y.C., 1957-58; supr. accounting Crown Cork & Seal Co., Inc., Chgo., 1958; account investigator Internat. Ladies Garment Works Union, N.Y.C., 1958-59; sr. editor Prentice Hall Inc., Englewood Cliffs, N.J., 1959-62; lectr. Rutgers U., 1961; asso. prof. accounting Hofstra U., Hempstead, N.Y., 1962—; partner J.K. Pescow & Co., C.P.A.'s, Roslyn Heights, N.Y., 1960—; pres. Linear Systems Inc., Glen Head, 1972—. Served as sgt. AUS, 1952-54. Recipient Shell research award, 1966. C.P.A., N.Y. Mem. Am. Inst. C.P.A.'s, Am. Accounting Assn., N.Y. State Soc. C.P.A.'s, Nat. Assn. Accountants, C.W. Post Tax Inst., Am. Taxation Inst., AAUP. Author: (with J. Horn and M. Bachman) Handbook of Successful Data Processing Applications, 1973; Getting More Out of Your Social Security, 1965. Contbr. to profl. jours. Editor various books, also Ency. Accounting Systems, 3 vols., 1976. Home: 12 Rini Rd Glen Head NY 11545 Office: 99 Powerhouse Rd Roslyn Heights NY 11577

PESIN, EDWARD, lawyer; b. Jersey City, Sept. 23, 1924; s. Samuel and Libby (Weisman) P.; A.B. with high honors, Rutgers U., 1947; J.D., Harvard, 1950; LL.M. in Taxation, N.Y. U., 1957; m. Helene Sylvia Rattner, June 22, 1952; children—Ella Michele, Samuel Richard. Admitted to bar, N.J., 1949, N.Y., 1950; trial atty. office chief counsel Internal Revenue Service, Phila., 1951-55; with J.K. Lasser & Co., N.Y.C. 1955-57; pres. Edward Pesin P.A., with offices for practice of fed. tax law, Newark, N.Y.C. 1957—. Taxation lectr. N.Y.U. Inst. Fed. Taxation, 1958, 62, 64, Inst. Continuing Legal Edn., Rutgers Law Sch., 1961—; N.J. State Bar Assn. del. to Lawyers Liaison Com. of Mid Atlantic Internal Revenue Region, 1960-74; mem. N.J. Supreme Ct. Com. on Profl. Corps., 1969. Traffic safety coordinator Hudson County, N.J., 1958-63; bd. dirs. N. Hudson chpt. ARC, 1963—, Jewish Hosp. and Rehab. Center N.J., 1972—; chmn. North Bergen (N.J.) ARC campaign, 1963; mem. Hudson County Charter Study Commn., 1973-74. Served from pvt. to 2d lt. AUS, 1943-46. Recipient Loyal Sons Rutgers award, 1962. Mem. Am., N.J. (chmn. com. on fed. taxation 1960-63, chmn. com. on legal assistance to elderly 1975—), N.Y. State, Essex, Hudson County (chmn. com. on fed. taxation 1963—) bar assns., N.Y. County Lawyers Assn., Phi Beta Kappa. New Decisions Editor: Jour. Taxation, 1955. Home: 5-75th St North Bergen NJ 07047 Office: 744 Broad St Newark NJ 07102 also 444 Madison Ave New York City NY 10022

PESIN, STUART GEORGE, obstetrician, gynecologist; b. N.J., Feb. 9, 1943; s. Harry and Molly (Singer) P.; B.S., St. Peter's Coll., 1964; M.D., N.J. Coll. Medicine, 1968; m. Regina Anne Simpson, 1969; children—Stephen James, Laura Michele. Intern, St. Michael's Med. Center, Newark, 1968-69; resident in obstetrics and gynecology N.J. Coll. Medicine, 1969-72, chief resident and clin. instr., 1972; practice medicine specializing in obstetrics and gynecology, Winchester, Mass., 1977—; mem. staff Malden (Mass.) Hosp., Winchester Hosp.; clin. instr. Boston U., 1974—; cons. to hosps. Served as maj. M.C. U.S. Army, 1972-74. Diplomate Am. Bd. Obstetrics and Gynecology. Fellow Am. Coll. Obstetricians and Gynecologists, A.C.S., Am. Fertility Soc.; mem. AMA, North Boston Obstet. Soc., Mass., Middlesex East med. socs., PTA. Democrat. Club: Temple Emunah Brotherhood. Home: 18 Suzanne Rd Lexington MA 02173 Office: 63 Shore Rd Winchester MA 01890

PETCH, JOHN FRANK, lawyer; b. Kitchener, Ont., Can., June 25, 1938; s. Lorne Franklin and Margaret Mary (Dietrich) P.; B.A., U. Western Ont., 1960; LL.B., U. Toronto, 1963; children—Andrea, Alisa, Britton. Admitted to Ont. bar, 1965; partner firm Osler, Hoskin & Harcourt, Toronto, Ont., 1975—. Instr. bar admission course Osgoode Hall, Toronto, 1967-69; dir. Na-Churs Internat. Ltd., London, Ont., 1970—, Na-Churs Plant Food Co., Marion, Ohio, 1970—. Bd. dirs. Madame Vanier Childret's Services, London, 1965-71, pres. bd. dirs., 1970-72; chmn. bd. dirs. King's Coll., U. Western Ont., 1968-70; bd. dirs. United Community Services, London, 1968-71. Recipient Gold medal U. Toronto, 1963, Treasurer's Gold medal, Law Soc. Upper Can., 1965. Mem. Canadian, York bar assns., Canadian Tax Found. Club: Toronto-Albany. Home: 177 Roxborough St E Toronto ON M4W 1W3 Canada Office: PO Box 50 67th Floor First Canadian Pl Toronto ON M5X 1B8 Canada

PETER, PHILLIPS SMITH, elec. product co. exec.; b. Washington, Jan. 24, 1932; s. Edward Compston and Anita Phillips (Smith) P.; B.A., U. Va., 1954, J.D., 1959; m. Jania Jayne Hutchins, Apr. 8, 1961; children—Phillips Smith Peter Jr., Jania Jayne Hutchins. Admitted to Calif. bar, 1959; asso. mem. firm McCutchen, Doyle, Brown, Enerson, San Francisco, 1959-63; with Gen. Electric Co. and subsidiaries, various locations, 1963—, v.p. corp. bus. devel., 1973-76, v.p., Washington, 1976—. Mem. leadership com. United Fund, Darien, Conn., 1974—, finance com. Republican Town Com., Darien, 1974—. Served with Transp. Corps, U.S. Army, 1954-56. Mem. Calif. Bar. Assn., Elfun Soc., Order Coif, Omicron Delta Kappa. Episcopalian. Clubs: Wee Burn (Darien); Eastern Yacht (Marblehead, Mass.); Farmington Country (Charlottesville, Va.); Ponte Vedra (Fla.); Lago Mar (Fort Lauderdale, Fla.); Racquet (Miami Beach, Fla.); Landmark (Stamford, Conn.; Congl. Country (Bethesda, Md.); Georgetown, F Street (Washington); Coral Beach and Tennis (Bermuda). Mem. edit. bd. Va. Law Rev., 1957-59. Home: 10805 Tara Rd Potomac MD 20854 Office: 777 14th St NW Washington DC 20005

PETERNEL, ARTHUR FREDERICK, civil engr.; b. Willock, Pa., Mar. 13, 1915; s. Joseph Bernard and Frances (Dolence) P.; student Pa. State U., 1935, Harvard, 1944; m. Frances Patricia Zele, Jan. 26, 1957; children—Arthur Frederick II, Frances Ellen. Civil engr. and surveyor, various cos., 1931-42; chief constrn. engr. Ben Constrn. Co., Inc., Pitts., 1946-51; hwy. constrn. engr. Calif. Dept. Hwys., 1947, sr. engr. Peternel-McGuire Co., Pitts., 1951-54; gen. supt. Easton Constrn. Co., Pitts., 1954-61; pres., mgr. Peternel Engring. and Constrn. Co., Library, Pa., 1961-71; borough engr. Borough Bethel Park, Pa., 1971—. Served to capt. C.E., AUS, 1942-46; ETO. Mem. ASCE, Am. Soc. Hwy. Engrs., Nat. Utilities Contractors Assn., Am. Soc. Mil. Engrs., Slovenian Nat. Benefit Soc. Roman Catholic. Clubs: Lakeview Country, Library Social. Home: 5069 Sherwood Rd Bethel Park PA 15102 Office: 5100 W Library Ave Bethel Park PA 15102

PETERS, ALBAN GERARD, physician; b. Bklyn., Oct. 19, 1915; s. William Warren and Mary Frances (Conlon) P.; B.A., Columbia U., 1937; M.D., N.Y. U., 1940; m. Joan Bassler, June 7, 1942; 1 dau., Harriette. Intern, resident in medicine St. Vincent's Hosp., N.Y.C., 1940-42, asst. attending physician, 1950-54; asst. attending physician Bellevue Hosp., N.Y.C., 1950-52; practice medicine specializing in internal medicine, Paterson, N.J., 1950—; attending physician St. Joseph's Hosp., Paterson 1950-75, cons., 1975—. Commr. Bd. Health, Paterson, N.J., 1970-74. Served to capt. M.C., AUS, 1942-45. Diplomate Am. Bd. Internal Medicine. Mem. A.C.P., Royal Soc. Physicians, Internat. Coll. Physicians, AMA, Am. Rheumatism Assn., Alpha Omega Alpha. Club: North Jersey Country. Home: 309 E 38th St Paterson NJ 07504 Office: 599 Broadway Paterson NJ 07514

PETERS, ALTON EMIL, lawyer; b. Albany, N.Y., Mar. 21, 1935; s. Emil and Winifred (Rosch) P.; grad. Phillips Exeter Acad., 1951; A.B. cum laude, Harvard, 1955, LL.B., 1958; m. Elizabeth Irving Berlin, Feb. 27, 1970; 1 dau., Rachel Canfield; 1 stepdau., Emily Anstice Fisher. Admitted to N.Y. Bar, 1958, U.S. Dist. Court for the So. Dist. N.Y., 1963; asso. firm Bleakley, Platt, Schmidt & Fritz, N.Y.C., 1958-65, partner 1965—. Bd. dirs. The Am. Friends of Covent Garden and Royal Ballet, N.Y.C., 1971—, v.p., 1971—; chmn. U.S. council Am. Museum in Britain, Bath, Eng., 1970—; bd. dirs. Goodwill Industries of Greater N.Y., Inc., 1966—, pres., 1971—; mem. adv. com. Lamont Gallery, Phillips Exeter Acad., Exeter, N.H., 1970—; bd. dirs. Met. Opera Assn., N.Y.C., 1968—, sec., 1974—; bd. dirs. Met. Opera Guild, 1965—, first v.p. 1971—; trustee Signet Assos., Cambridge, Mass. Mem. Assn. Bar City N.Y., N.Y. State Bar Assn., Am. Judicature Soc., Am. Bar Assn., English-Speaking Union U.S. (dir. 1968—, mem. exec. com. 1973—, chmn. N.Y. br. 1972—). Episcopalian (mem. adv. council Episcopal Ch. Found. 1967—). Clubs: Church, Century Assn., Downtown Assn., Knickerbocker, The Pilgrims (N.Y.C.); Odd Volumes (Boston). Home: 1185 Park Ave New York City NY 10028 Office: 120 Broadway New York City NY 10005

PETERS, ANTHONY JOSEPH, realtor; b. Portsmouth, N.H., Mar. 15, 1916; s. Joseph and Carmela (Cuoio) P.; student pub. schs., N.Y.C.; m. Mary Fitzpatrick, (dec. May 1972); children—Mary Ann Peters Giffuni, Patrician Peters Cavanagh, Kathleen, Elizabeth, Carol, Robert, John, Anthony Joseph; m. 2d, Marie Ann Kelly Johnston, Feb. 9, 1974; children—Nancy Johnston Elting, John Johnston, David Johnston, Peter Johnston. With Cushman & Wakefield, Inc. real estate, N.Y.C., 1933—, pres., chief operating officer, 1971-76, chmn. bd., 1976—. Mem. Cardinal's Com. for Edn. Served with USAF, 1942-46. Recipient Most Ingenious Deal of Year award, 1954, 59. Mem. Downtown Lower Manhattan Assn., Real Estate Bd. N.Y. Clubs: Bankers, Boca Raton Hotel and Club; World Trade Center, Columbus Citizens, N.Y. Plaza, N.Y., N.Y. Rifle, Board Room, Metropolitan (Chgo.). Home: 14 Sutton Pl S New York City NY 10022 Office: 529 Fifth Ave New York City NY 10017

PETERS, CAROL BEATTIE TAYLOR (MRS. FRANK ALBERT PETERS), mathematician; b. Washington, May 10, 1932; d. Edwin Lucius and Lois (Beattie) Taylor; B.S., U. Md., 1954, M.A., 1958; m. Frank Albert Peters, Feb. 26, 1955; children—Thomas, June, Erick, Victor. Group mgr. Tech. Operations, Inc., Arlington, Va., 1957-62, sr. staff scientist, 1964-66; supervisory analyst Datatrol Corp., Silver Spring, Md., 1962; project dir. Computer Concept, Inc., Silver Spring, 1963-64; mem. tech. staff, then mem. sr. staff Informatics Inc., Bethesda, Md., 1966-70, mgr. systems projects, 1970-71, tech. dir., 1971-76; sr. tech. dir. Ocean Data Systems, Inc., 1976—. Mem. Assn. Computing Machinery, IEEE Computer Group. Home: 12321 Glen Mill Rd Potomac MD 20854 Office: 6000 Executive Blvd Rockville MD 20852

PETERS, CHARLES HENRI, personnel exec.; b. Ithaca, N.Y., Feb. 7, 1914; s. John A. and Charlotte E. (Bowers) P.; B.S., Cornell U., 1940; m. Idamae Hamer, Sept. 9, 1944. Jr. indsl. engr., Beaver Falls, Pa. and Camden, N.J., 1943-47; sr. indsl. engr. Armstrong Cork Co., Camden, 1948-50, plant indsl. engr., 1950-53; chief indsl. engr. Raybestos Manhattan, Inc., Manheim, Pa., 1953-59, mgr. indsl. relations, 1959-65; mgr. employment and indsl. relations AMP, Inc., Harrisburg, Pa., 1965-76, personnel specialist, 1976—; tchr. indsl. relations Community Coll., Temple U., Phila., 1950-51. Gen. chmn. United campaign, Lancaster, Pa., 1965; treas., mem. vestery St. Thomas Episcopal Ch., Lancaster, 1958-65; bd. dirs. Jr. Achievement, Lancaster County 1956-59, Community Chest, Lancaster County, 1957-65, Lancaster Guidance Clinic, 1962-65. Fellow Soc. for Advancement of Mgmt. (pres. Lancaster chpt. 1958); mem. Am. Mgmt. Assn., Am. Soc. Personnel Adminstrs. (accredited exec. in personnel), Inst. of Mgmt. (pres. Lancaster County chpt. 1960). Republican. Episcopalian. Clubs: Elks, Masons (32 deg.). Home: 2364 Middlegreen Ct Lancaster PA 17601 Office: PO Box 3608 Harrisburg PA 17105

PETERS, GEORGE ANTHONY, educator; b. Pitts., May 9, 1951; s. George A. and Ellen V. (Ricci) P.; B.A., W.Va. U., 1972, M.S., 1973, Ed.D., 1976; m. Joan Bernotas, Aug. 5, 1972. Psychologist, Junction, Inc., Westminster, Md., 1973-74; asst. prof. Seton Hall U., South Orange, N.J., 1977—; psychologist West Ridge Center for Counseling and Psychotherapy, West Orange, N.J., 1977—. Mem. Am. Personnel and Guidance Assn., Nat. Soc. Adlerian Psychology, Nat. Rehab. Assn. Contbr. articles to profl. jours. Home: RD 1 Box 704C Newton NJ 07860 Office: Dept Counseling and Spl Services Seton Hall U South Orange NJ 07079

PETERS, HARRIET AUERBACH, career services adminstr.; b. Buffalo, June 15, 1936; d. Carlton William and Mary Winifred (Congreve) Auerbach; B.S., State U. N.Y., Buffalo, 1959; M.S., Cornell U., 1975; m. Earl Peters, July 6, 1957; children—David, Laura, Deborah. Seminar coordinator James Farr Assos., Greensboro, N.C., 1972-73; teaching asst. Cornell U., Ithaca, N.Y., 1973-75, career counselor, 1975-76; dir. career services Wells Coll., Aurora, N.Y., 1977—; mem. adv. bd. Council for Career Planning Inc.; cons. personnel dept. tng. and devel. sect. Cornell U. Active Family Life Council, Greensboro; vol. chmn. Mobile Meals. Mem. Am. Assn. Higher Edn., AAUW, Nat. Council Career Educators, Internat. Mgmt. Council, Eastern Coll. Placement Officers, Kappa Delta Pi. Home: 125 Burleigh Dr Ithaca NY 14850 Office: 200 Macmillan Hall Wells College Aurora NY 13026

PETERS, HENRY FREDERICK, cons. chem. engr.; b. N.Y.C., Jan. 5, 1918; s. August and Rose Anna (Frank) P.; B.S. in Chem. Engring., Cooper Union, 1941; m. Mary F. Flynn, June 8, 1940; children—Walter F., Rosemary M., Clair I. Field constrn. engr. Caye Constrn. Co., Bklyn., 1935-41; process engr. M.W. Kellogg Co., N.Y.C., 1942-48; sr. v.p. Sci. Design Co., N.Y.C., 1948-72; cons. chem. engr. H.F. Peters Assos., South Jamesport, N.Y., 1972—. Mem. Am. Chem. Soc., Am. Inst. Chem. Engrs., Nat. Soc. Profl. Engrs., Am. Petroleum Inst. Author: (with R. Landau) The Chemical Plant, 1970; contbg. author: Ency. of Chemistry. Home: 12 Dunlookin Ln South Jamesport NY 11970 Office: H F Peters Associates PO Box 183 South Jamesport NY 11970

PETERS, HENRY JOHN, baseball club exec.; b. St. Louis, Sept. 16, 1924; s. Henry J. and Estelle (Biehl) P.; m. Dorothy Kleimeier, Nov. 21, 1950; children—Steven, Sharon. Asst. farm dir. St. Louis Browns, 1946-53; gen. mgr. Burlington (Iowa) Baseball Club, 1954; farm dir. Kansas City A's, 1955-60, asst. gen. mgr., 1962-64, gen. mgr., 1965; farm dir. Cin. Reds, 1961; v.p., dir. player personnel Cleve. Indians, 1966-71; pres. Nat. Assn. Profl. Baseball Leagues, St. Petersburg, Fla., 1972-75; exec. v.p., gen. mgr. Balt. Orioles, 1976—. Served with U.S. Army, 1943-45. Recipient Good Guy award Cleve. chpt. Baseball Writers Assn., 1970. Republican. Lutheran. Clubs: Elks, St. Petersburg Yacht. Home: 328 Boca Ciega Point Blvd S St Petersburg FL 33708 Office: Meml Stadium Baltimore MD

PETERS, JOHN C., data processor; b. Buffalo, Oct. 2, 1914; s. John L. and Mary (Bartlemes) P.; student State Tchrs. Coll., Buffalo, 1932-34; B.S., Canisius Coll., 1956. Chem. research asst. Buffalo Electro-Chem. Co., Inc., 1936-43, 46-47, jr. chem. engr., 1947-54; sr. engring. technician FMC Corp., Buffalo, 1954-67, chem. analyst, data processor, 1967—. Served with 83d Inf. Div., AUS, 1943-46. Decorated Purple Heart. Mem. Am. Chem. Soc., Am. Inst. Chem. Engrs. (chmn. Western N.Y. sect. 1971-72, auditor Western N.Y. sect. 1973-74), Internat. Mgmt. Council. Roman Catholic. Home: 89 S Union Rd Williamsville NY 14221 Office: FMC PO Box 845 Buffalo NY 14240

PETERS, LEONARD LECKEL, physician; b. Paterson, N.J., Nov. 18, 1940; s. Leonard and Ottilia Bertha (Leckel) P.; B.A., Va. Mil. Inst., 1963; M.D., U. Rochester, 1967; m. Ruthanna Margaret Williams, June 26, 1965; children—Karen Margaret, Betsy Ellen. Intern, Greenwich (Conn.) Hosp., 1967-68; resident in surgery W.Va. U. Hosp., 1970-74, instr. surgery, 1975—; practice medicine specializing in gen. and vascular surgery, Franklin, Pa., 1975—. Served with AUS, 1968-70. Clin. fellow Am. Cancer Soc., 1972-74, clin. faculty Fellow, 1974-75. Diplomate Nat. Bd. Med. Examiners, Am. Bd. Surgery. Mem. AMA, Am. Trauma Soc. Home: 320 16th St Franklin PA 16323 Office: 150 Prospect Ave Franklin PA 16323

PETERSEN, MARTIN ROSS, consumer affairs cons.; b. Bakersfield, Calif., Aug. 14, 1944; s. Peter Arthur and Valerie A. (Swink) P.; B.A. in Govt., Calif. State U., Sacramento, 1969. Asst. dir. govtl. affairs Calif. State Univs. and Colls., Sacramento, 1967-72; exec. sec. council continuing edn. Calif. Dept. Consumer Affairs, 1972-74, exec. sec. consumer council, adminstr. div. consumer services, 1974-75; dir. Office External Liaison, U.S. Office Consumer Affairs, Washington, 1975-77; v.p. Virginia Knauer and Assos., Inc., 1977—. Recipient Quality Performance award U.S. Office Consumer Affairs, 1976. Mem. Acad. Polit. Sci., Western Govtl. Research Assn., Consumer Fedn. Calif., Soc. Consumer Affairs Profls. in Bus. (pres. Washington chpt. 1977-78), Nat. Consumers League, Common Cause. Home: 2018 Hillyer Pl NW Washington DC 20009 Office: 2033 M St NW Suite 502 Washington DC 20036

PETERSEN, ROGER DUDLEY, tng. specialist; b. Boise, Idaho, Jan. 6, 1942; s. Dudley Reilly and Faye Louise (Cully) P.; B.A., U. Oreg., 1963; postgrad. (Woodrow Wilson fellow 1964-65), Cornell U., 1964-67; m. Janiece Avery, Aug. 18, 1972; 1 son, Laurence Russell. Asst. prof. psychology Washington Coll., Chesterton, Md., 1967-70; research psychologist Bur. Standards, Gaithersburg, Md., 1971-72; freelance cons., Washington, 1972-76; tech. coordinator Fed. Programs and Assistance Project adminstered by Nat. Assn. for Retarded Citizens, Washington, 1976—; mem. Pres.'s Com. on Employment Handicapped, 1978—. Bd. dirs. Nat. Capital Area Coalition of Citizens with Disabilities, 1978—; mem. elctronics aids com. Am. Council of Blind, 1978—. Mem. Soc. Advancement of Handicapped, Nat. Braille Assn., Ind. Living for Handicapped, Internat. Travel Soc., Smithsonian Assos., Phi Beta Kappa, Sigma Xi. Democrat. Home: 1629 Columbia Rd NW #800 Washington DC 20009 Office: 1522 K St Suite 1030 Washington DC

PETERSEN, SUSAN JANE, publishing co. exec.; b. Akron, Ohio, Oct. 9, 1944; d. Christian Henry and Susan Elizabeth (Wigand) Petersen; B.A. cum laude, Vassar Coll., 1966; M.F.A., N.Y. U., 1969; m. Bruce Harris, Aug. 4, 1973; 1 son, Petersen Nathaniel. Producer, Calliope Films Co., N.Y.C., 1970-73; mgr. promotion and advt. Avon Books, N.Y.C., 1973-74; dir. promotion and advt. Ballantine Books, N.Y.C., 1974-76, v.p., mktg. dir., 1978—; v.p. promotion and advt. Pocket Books, N.Y.C., 1976-78. Mem. Publishers Advt. Club (dir.), Am. Assn. Publishers. Lutheran. Office: 201 E 50th St New York City NY 10022

PETERSON, A.E.S. (MRS. CARL U. PETERSON), artist; b. Northampton, Mass., June 30, 1908; d. Albert Hobart and Louise Josephia (Lenardson) Sanderson; pvt. study painting; m. Carl U. Peterson, May 1, 1937. Exhibited one-man shows Attleboro (Mass.) Mus., Providence (R.I.) Water Color Club, Providence Art Club, Newport (R.I.) Art Assn., Ch. Gallery, Meeting House; exhibited group shows NAD, Nat. Arts Club, N.Y.C., Riverside Mus., N.Y.C., Bristol (R.I.) Art Mus., Attleboro Art Mus., Springfield (Mass.) Art

Mus., Jersey City Mus., Butler Inst. Am. Art; represented in permanent collections Nat. Shawmut Bank, Boston, R.I. Hosp. Trust Co., Providence, Grant Capital Mgmt. Corp., Providence, Tillinghast-Stiles Co., East Providence. Recipient Am. Watercolor Soc. awards, 1968; Nat. Soc. Painters in Casein medal, 1968, awards, 1970, 73; Audubon Artists award, 1969, Nat. Art League awards (2), 1969, 73; Painters and Sculptors Soc. N.J. award, 1970, medal, 1973; awards Allied Artists Am., 1970, 73, 76, Catharine Lorillard Wolfe Art Club, 1970, Greater Fall River Art Assn., 1970, 71, 76; gold medal Catharine Lorillard Wolfe Art Club, 1971, 75, 77, numerous local and regional awards. Mem. Am. Watercolor Soc., Nat. Soc. Painters in Casein and Acrylic (dir. 1970-77, chmn. traveling exhbns. 1971—, chmn. awards 1974-76), Allied Artists Am., Painters and Sculptors Soc. N.J. (v.p. for watercolor), Knickerbocker Artists N.Y., Catharine Lorillard Wolfe Art Club, Nat. Assn. Women Artists, Audubon Artists, Nat. Art League, Providence Art Club (mem. ladies adv. bd. 1965-68), Providence Water Color Club (treas. 1962-70, rec. sec. 1971—), Attleboro Mus., Bristol Art Mus., Internat. Platform Assn. Home and studio: 27 Holbrook Ave Rumford RI 02916

PETERSON, ANN SULLIVAN, physician, univ. adminstr.; b. Rhinebeck, N.Y., Oct. 11, 1928; A.B., Cornell U., 1950, M.D., 1954. Intern, Bellevue Hosp., N.Y.C., 1954-55, resident, 1955-57; fellow in medicine and physiology Meml.-Sloan Kettering Inst., Cornell Med. Coll., N.Y.C., 1957-60; instr. medicine Georgetown U. Sch. Medicine, Washington, 1962-65, asst. prof., 1965-69, asst. dir. clin. research unit, 1962-69; asso. prof. medicine U. Ill., Chgo., 1969-72, asst. dean, 1969-71, asso. dean, 1971-72; asso. prof. medicine, asso. dean Coll. Physicians and Surgeons, Columbia U., N.Y.C., 1972—; cons., mem. admissions com. Sackler Med. Sch., Tel Aviv U.-N.Y. State program, 1976—; mem. working group nat. task force on postgrad. med. edn., Assn. Am. Med. Colls., 1978. John and Mary R. Markle scholar, 1965-70; diplomate Am. Bd. Internal Medicine. Fellow A.C.P.; mem. Am. Fedn. Clin. Research, Nat. Group on Student Affairs of Assn. Am. Med. Colls., Mortar Bd., Alpha Omega Alpha, Alpha Epsilon Delta. Contbr. articles to med. jours. Office: 630 W 168th St New York City NY 10032

PETERSON, BERTRAM HAROLD, JR., moving co. exec.; b. Chgo., Sept. 17, 1924; s. Bertram Harold and Lilie (Bloom) P.; B.A., Coll. City N.Y., 1950; m. Alice Marion Peterson, Jan. 2, 1945; children—Bertram Harold, Harold Bertram. Mem. customer relations staff Mo. Kan. Tex. R.R., N.Y.C., 1943-45; market analyst U.S. Steel Corp., N.Y.C., 1946-48; asst. v.p. Asso. Transport, N.Y.C., 1948-53; v.p. nat. accounts McLean Trucking Co., N.Y.C., 1953-57; traffic sales coordinator Johnson Motor Lines, N.Y.C., 1957-61; exec. v.p. Fisher & Brother, N.Y.C., 1961-75, 77-78; exec. v.p. Coventry Moving & Storage, Inc., N.Y.C., 1978—; pres. Free Enterprises Unltd., Inc., N.Y.C., 1976-77. Leader seminars for various profl. assns., 1969-71. Mem. exec. bd. Manhattan council Boy Scouts Am., 1968-71; mem. Mayor's Com. for a Better N.Y., 1970-72; chmn. Sr. Citizens Cons. Com., 1966-68. Served with AUS, 1945-46. Recipient Merit award Adminstrv. Mgmt. Soc., 1971, Profl. Mgmt. citation Soc. Advancement Mgmt., 1973. Mem. Adminstrv. Mgmt. Soc., (pres. 1971, dir. 1970—, chmn. internat. bldg. services, layout and design com. 1969-72), Am. Soc. Traffic and Transp. (founder, pres. 1951), Sales Execs. Club, N.Y. Bd. Trade (chmn. membership com. 1968-71), ICC Practitioners Assn., Am. Mgmt. Assn., VIP Execs. Club (pres. 1969), Assn. Records Execs., Bldg. Owners and Mgrs. Assn., Traffic Club N.Y., Real Estate Bd. N.Y. (asso.), Nat. Export Traffic League, Am. Indsl. Devel. Council, Delta Nu Alpha. Rotarian. Clubs: Men's Forum, Touchdown, N.Y. Athletic. Contbg. author: Handbook of Modern Office Management and Administrative Services, 1972. Contbr. to profl. jours. Home: 1920 E 17th St Brooklyn NY 11229 Office: 711 3d Ave New York City NY 10017

PETERSON, GLEN ROBERT, color lab. exec.; b. Kalamazoo, Mar. 4, 1908; s. Elias and Effie (Van Worden) P.; student photography Lake Sch. Photography, 1929-33; m. Barbara Kruger, Feb. 3, 1969; 1 son, Glen Karl. Indsl. photographer Kalamazoo Vegetable Parchment Co., 1932-43; color photo engraver Wayne Color Plate, Dayton, Ohio, 1944-46, Rogers Engraving, N.Y.C., 1946-47; pres. Peterson Color Lab. Inc. (merged with Berkey K & L to become Peterson, K & L Color Lab.), Bronxville, N.Y., 1948—; tech. sales rep. Colorite, N.Y.C., 1977—. Bd. dirs., pres. Kalamazoo Art Inst., 1940-44. Served as comdr. CAP, 1941-44. Mem. Dye Transfer Assn. N.Y. (pres. 1968-71), Soc. Photog. Scientists and Engrs., Sterosocopic Soc., Theater Organ Soc., Internt. Photo Engravers Assn. Mem. Ref. Ch. Photographer, Golden Books, 1974, UNICEF, 1973; stereo cameras on permanent exhbn. Eastman House and Photog. Mus. Patentee in field. Office: 113 E 31st St New York City NY 10016

PETERSON, JAY BRYAN, JR., orthopedic surgeon; b. Greensburg, Pa., Aug. 28, 1931; s. Jay Bryan and Grace Ellen (Laughlin) P.; A.B., Washington and Jefferson Coll., 1953; M.D., Temple U., 1957; m. Mary Ann; children—Diane Louise, Eric David. Intern, Hamod Hosp., Erie, Pa., 1957-58; orthopedic resident Allegheny Gen. Hosp., Pitts., 1959-60; comd. Capt. U.S. Army, 1960, advanced through grades to maj., 1967; staff Tripler Gen. Hosp., Honolulu, 1961-64, Honolulu Shriner's Crippled Children Hosp., 1964; resigned, 1967; practice orthopedic surgery, Greensburg, 1967—; med. dir. Westmoreland County Soc. for Crippled Children and Adults, 1968—. Bd. dirs. Westmoreland County chpt. Am. Arthritis Found. Served with AUS, 1960-67. Diplomate Am. Bd. Orthopaedic Surgery. Fellow A.C.S.; mem. Am. Acad. Orthopaedic Surgeons. Methodist. Home: 28 Windihill St Greensburg PA 15601 Office: 662 N Main St Greensburg PA 15601

PETERSON, MARY ANN, hosp. exec.; b. Holton, Kans., Aug. 26, 1932; d. Dan Alfred and Lois Mary (Johnson) Peterson; student Park, Coll., Mo., 1950-52; R.N., John Hopkins Hosp., 1955, B.S., 1955; M.S., Boston U., 1964. Head nurse Johns Hopkins Hosp., Balt., 1955-58; staff nurse Loch Raven Veterans Hosp., Balt., 1958-63; supr. Mass. Gen. Hosp., Boston, 1964-67; project dir. USPHS coronary nurse tng., asst. prof. nursing Boston U., 1967-69; nurse trainer coronary care Boston City Hosp., 1969-70; continuing edn. coordinator Mass. Rehab. Hosp., Boston, 1970-71, acting dir. nursing, 1971; dir. med. nursing, asst. prof. U. Mich. Hosp., Ann Arbor, 1971-74; asst. dir. nursing Mount Auburn Hosp., Cambridge, Mass., 1974-75, dir. nursing, 1975—. Mem. Am., Mass. hosp. assns., Soc. Hosp. Nursing Service Dirs., Sigma Theta Tau. Republican. Presbyterian. Co-author: Acute Coronary Care, 1971. Home: 15 Strathmore Rd Braintree MA 02184

PETERSON, MILLER HARRELL, chemist; b. Darlington, S.C., Jan. 3, 1925; s. John Hiram and Pauline (Kelly) P.; B.S., Clemson U., 1944; M.A., U. N.C., 1951; m. Suzanne Waldrop, June 3, 1950; children—Sarah Harrell, Susan Daly, Marsha Ann. Chemist, U.S. Naval Ordnance Lab., 1951-54; chemist, research chemist U.S. Naval Research Lab., Washington, 1954—, head marine corrosion sect. Served with USNR, 1944-46. Registered profl. engr., Calif. Fellow Am. Inst. Chemists; mem. electrochem. Soc., Am. Chem. Soc., Nat. Assn. Corrosion Engrs., AAAS, Sigma Xi. Contbr. articles to profl. jours. Office: Code 6386 Naval Research Lab Washington DC 20375

PETERSON, ROGER GEORGE, ins. co. exec.; b. New Britain, Conn., Dec. 28, 1925; s. George Edward Eugene and Mildred Amanda (Casperson) P.; A.B., Brown U., 1946; postgrad. U. Conn. Law Sch., 1949-51; m. Jane Rowell Burkle, June 18, 1960; children—Jay Lars, Petter Eric. Budget officer Am. Mut., Boston, 1957-58; treas. N. Am. Assurance Soc., Richmond, Va., 1959-61; prin. mgmt. services div. Joseph Frogatt & Co., N.Y.C., 1962-65; sr. v.p. Nat. Liberty Life Ins. Co., Valley Forge, Pa., 1966-67; pres. Am. Progressive Ins. Co., Mt. Vernon, N.Y., 1968-72; pres., dir. Gerber Life Ins. Co., White Plains, N.Y., 1973—. Served to lt. Supply Corps, USNR, 1946-47, 51-53. Mem. Am. Council Life Ins., Health Ins. Assn. Am., Life Cos. of N.Y., Direct Mktg. Advt. Assn., Direct Mktg. Ins. Council. Contbr. articles to profl. jours. Home: 5 Candlelight Pl Greenwich CT 10601 Office: 66 Church St White Plains NY 16830

PETIT, LEO ARSENE, JR., hosp. adminstr.; b. Chicopee, Mass., June 30, 1938; s. Leo Arsene and Sonya Antoinette (Wojtasiewicz) P.; B.S., Babson Coll., 1959; M.S., Columbia, 1961; m. Virginia Ann Spencer, May 22, 1965; children—Ann Louise, Joan Arsene. Asst. adminstr. Met. Hosp., N.Y.C., 1964-66; adminstr. Little Falls (N.Y.) Hosp., 1966-69, Project HOPE Teaching Hosp., SS HOPE, Tunis, Tunisia, 1969-70; exec. dir. R.I. Group Health Assn., Providence, 1970-72; coordinator-cons. Tri-State Regional Med. Program, Springfield, Mass., 1972-73; hosp. dir. Springfield Municipal Hosp., 1973—; cons., lectr. Sch. Health Scis., U. Mass., Amherst, 1973—, preceptor, Dept. Community Medicine, Sch. Medicine, Worcester, 1973—; mem. Western Mass. Health Planning Council, 1973-77, vice-chmn. adv. com., 1974-77. Pres., Crescent Lake Assn., 1972-74; mem. Springfield Council on Aging, 1973—; bd. dirs. Home Care Corp., Springfield, Mass., 1975—, mem. exec. com., 1977—. Served to 1st lt. USAF, 1961-64. Mem. Am. Coll. Hosp. Adminstrs., Am. Hosp. Assn., Internat. Hosp. Assn., Am. Pub. Health Assn., Alpha Kappa Psi. Roman Catholic. Contbr. articles in field to profl. jours. Home: RD 2 Crescent Lake East Longmeadow MA 01028 Office: Springfield Municipal Hosp 1400 State St Springfield MA 01109

PETIT-CLAIR, ALFRED JOSEPH, JR., lawyer; b. Newark, N.J., Jan. 20, 1944; s. Alfred Joseph and Geraldine Martha (Peet) P.; B.A., Rutgers U., 1966; J.D., Seton Hall U., 1971; m. Dianne A. Wozniak, Nov. 19, 1966; 1 dau., Adrienne Jeanne. Admitted to N.J. bar, 1971, D.C. bar, 1974, U.S. Supreme Ct. bar, 1974; wage collection hearing examiner N.J. Dept. of Labor and Industry, Trenton, N.J., 1967-71; individual practice Law, Perth Amboy, N.J., 1971—; gen. counsel Middlesex County AFL-CIO Council, 1974—, vol. attorney ACLU, 1972-75; trustee, Middlesex County Legal Services Corp., 1975—; bd. mem. Lawyers Com. Against Am. Policy in Vietnam, 1974-75; founder U.S. Supreme Court Hist. Soc., 1975; mem. N.J. Supreme Court Com. on the Admission of Foreign Attorneys, 1976. Mem. Am., N.J. State, Middlesex County bar assns., Am. Judicature Soc., Am. Trial Lawyers Assn. Independent Democrat. Roman Catholic. Contbr. articles to profl. jours. Clubs: Moose, Rutgers Univ. Scarlet R, Elks. Home: 408 East Ave Sewaren NJ 08861 Office: 313 State St Perth Amboy NJ 08861

PETONE, ARTHUR JOSEPH, brokerage exec.; b. Somerville, Mass., May 23, 1927; s. Antonio and Rosina (Agresti) P.; certificate in accounting Bentley Sch. Accounting and Finance, 1953; m. Alma Marsilii, July 8, 1950; 1 dau., Cheryl Lee. Bookkeeper firm Hutchins & Parkinson, Boston, 1948-53; accountant firm Leslie Banks & Co., Boston, 1953-59; partner firm Burgess & Leith, Boston, 1959-69, Tucker Anthony & RL Day, 1969—. Served with AUS, 1945-46. Club: Oakley Country (Watertown, Mass.). Home: 8 Christine Rd Arlington MA 02174 Office: 1 Beacon St Boston MA 02108

PETRI, HERBERT LEON, exptl. psychologist; b. Hamilton, Ohio, Dec. 3, 1944; s. Herbert Leon and Estelle Ruth (Klein) P.; A.B., Miami U., Oxford, Ohio, 1967; M.A., Johns Hopkins U., 1969, Ph.D., 1971; m. Janice Lynn Wills, Dec. 19, 1965; children—Stephanie, Kathleen, Estelle. Asst. prof. dept. psychology Towson (Md.) State U., 1971-76, asso. prof., 1976—, undergrad. coordinator dept. psychology. Trustee Hunts United Meth. Ch., Riderwood, Md. Mem. Am., Eastern psychol. assns., AAAS, Animal Behavior Soc., Sigma Xi. Contbr. articles to profl. publs., papers to confs. Home: 8107 Rider Ave Towson MD 21204 Office: Dept Psychology Towson State U Towson MD 21204

PETRIE, PETER LEE, potter; b. Poniac, Mich., May 22, 1935; s. Henry Harrison and Jane Irene (Clegg) P.; apprentice to Pat Miller, Detroit, 1964-66, later to Hon. James Campbell, Eng.; student Escuela National de Arte, Spain; m. Marjorie Susan Clemons, June 25, 1977. Group shows include Internat. Pavillion of Humour, 1978.

PETRIE, STEWART JUDSON, obstetrician and gynecologist; b. New Haven, July 15, 1923; s. Arthur Judson and Emma Stewart (Robinson) P.; B.S., U. Conn., 1946; M.D., Temple U., 1950; m. Mary Daphne Pizzi, Sept. 10, 1967; children—Stewart Judson, Cynthia, Gwen, Suzanne. Intern, Worcester (Mass.) City Hosp., 1950-52; resident Yale-New Haven Hosp., 1952-55; practice medicine specializing in obstetrics and gynecology, Derby, Conn., 1955—; mem. staff Griffin Hosp.; chief obstetrics-gynecology St. Raphael's Hosp. Editor, Issues and Insight, New Haven, 1971—. Diplomate Nat. Bd. Med. Examiners. Mem. A.C.S., Am. Coll. Obstetrics and Gynecology, Am. Fertility Assn., AMA, Conn., New Haven County med. socs., New Haven Obstet. Soc. Home: 16 Wolf Tree Dr Woodbridge CT 06525 Office: 56 Minerva St Derby CT 06418

PETRILLA, STEPHEN THOMAS, resource tchr.; b. Hazle Brook, Pa., June 5, 1911; m. Mary Kopfinger; children—Karyn, Caroline, John, Tamala. B.S. in Edn., Social Sci., Biology, English, State Tchrs. Coll., Bloomsburg, Pa., 1936; M.A. in Edn., Supervision and Adminstrn., N.Y. U., 1938; postgrad. State Tchrs. Coll., Montclair, N.J., 1949-50, State Tchrs. Coll., Trenton, N.J., 1963-69. Asst. supt., N. Jersey Tng. Sch., Totwa, N.J., 1948-51; asst. supt., State Colony, New Lisbon, N.J., 1951-56; dir. Industries Ltd. Workshop for phys. and mentally handicapped, Lindenwold, N.J., 1956-59; dir. resource center, Lawrenceville Elementary Sch., Lawrenceville Twp. Sch. Dist., Trenton, N.J., 1960—. Council mem. Boy Scouts Am., 1973—. Fellow Am. Assn. Mental Deficiency; mem. NEA, N.J. Edn. Assn., Lawrenceville Twp. Edn. Assn., Smithsonian Instn. Assos. Certified in sch. adminstrn. in elementary, spl. edn., guidance, Pa.; adult workshop, spl. edn., N.J. Home: 4223 Nottingham Way Hamilton Square NJ 08690

PETROCELLI, ORLANDO RALPH, publisher; b. N.Y.C., Oct. 10, 1930; s. Lucio and Carmela (Carrione) P.; student Bklyn. Coll., 1948-50; m. Kathleen Fontana, Oct. 23, 1960; children—Lucio, Joseph, Neil. Bus. mgr. D. Van Nostrand Pub. Co., N.Y.C., 1948-67; controller Stein & Day Pubs., Scarborough, N.Y., 1967-69; v.p. Auerbach Pub. Co., Phila., 1969-73; pres. Mason-Charter Pubs. Inc., N.Y.C., 1973-76, Petrocelli Books, Inc., Petrocelli Enterprises, 1976—. Treas., Republican Club, Princeton, N.J., 1965-67. Mem. Assn. Am. Pubs., Author's Guild, Assn. Computing Machinery, Am. Booksellers Assn. Roman Catholic. Club: Players. Author: The Pact, 1973; Olympia's Inheritance, 1975; Match Set, 1977; Five Days to Paradise, 1978. Editor: Best Computer Papers of 1971. Home: 174 Brookstone Dr Princeton NJ 08540 Office: 384 Fifth Ave New York City NY 10018

PETRONKO, MICHAEL ROMAN, psychologist; b. Elizabeth, N.J., Sept. 25, 1944; s. John and Mary (Flyesta) P.; B.A., Seton Hall U., 1966; M.A., Miami U., Oxford, Ohio, 1967; Ph.D., Fla. State U., 1971; m. Patricia Ann Panzarino, Aug. 13, 1966; children—Michael Roman, Nadine. Clin. psychology fellow Harvard, 1970-71; pvt. practice psychology, Easton, Pa., 1971-75, Vineland, N.J., 1976-77; dir. div. psychol. services Fairleigh Dickinson U., Teaneck, N.J., 1975—; chief clin. psychologist Am. Inst. for Mental Studies, Vineland, N.J., 1972-75, chief div. emotional disturbance, 1972-75, cons. editor Tng. Sch. Bull., 1972-75. Adj. prof. Stockton Coll., Pomona, N.J., 1973-75. Mem. Am. Psychol. Assn., Am. Assn. on Mental Deficiency, N.J., Eastern psychol. assns. Contbr. articles to profl. jours. Home: RD2 Longview Rd Lebanon NJ 08833

PETROSKAS, JOHN ALFRED, metallurgist; b. Boston, Nov. 26, 1910; s. Christopher and Mary Tamulen (Phelps) P.; B.S., Mass. Inst. Technology, 1938; m. Margaret E. Young, July 25, 1943; children—Elizabeth Petroskas Robinson, John Alfred, Suzanne Petroskas Nelson, James W. Chief metallurgist, Midvale Co., Phila., 1950-54; supt. melting forging and heat treatment Fairmount Penncoyd Steel Co., Phila., 1954-55; chief metallurgist Phoenix Steel Corp., Phoenixville, Pa., from 1955, now ret.; cons. product liability, steel melting, casting, heat treatment. Served to maj., AUS, 1940-46. Mem. ASTM, Am. Soc. Metals, Am. Inst. Metal. Engrs., Mass. Inst. Tech. Alumni Assn., Am. Petroleum Inst. Republican. Home: 105 Forest Ln Swarthmore PA 19081

PETROVIC, NJEGOS MASAN, educator; b. Vucitrn, Yugoslavia, May 20, 1933; s. Masan Savov and Zivka Grigorija (Bozovic) P.; came to U.S., 1965, naturalized, 1971; B.A., U. Belgrade (Yugoslavia), 1953; M.A. (French Govt. scholar), U. Montreal (Que., Can.), 1962, Ph.D., 1967; m. Klara Szwarc, Nov. 10, 1960; children—Tamara, Jasmina, Petar. Instr. French, Classical Coll. St. Jean, Que., 1961-64, Royal Mil. Coll. St. Jean, Que., 1964-65; asst. prof. French, Nebr. Wesleyan U., Lincoln, 1965-67; asso. prof. French lit. U. Scranton (Pa.), 1967-74, founder, chmn. concert and theater series, 1969—, prof., 1974—. Advisor, Commonwealth Pa. Council on Arts, Harrisburg, 1973-76; bd. dirs. Museum Assn. Scranton, 1971—, Scranton Philharmonic Orch. Soc., 1972—. Publ. grantee Govt. Que., 1969, performing arts grantee Pa. Council on Arts, 1972, 74. Mem. Modern Lang. Assn. Am., AAUP, l'Alliance Internat. des Anciens de l'Univ. de Paris, Alpha Sigma Nu. Democrat. Author: Ivo Andric, l'Homme et l'oeuvre, 1969, Everhart Museum Catalog, 1974, also numerous articles, essays and poems published in lit. jours. and mags. in U.S., Can., Yugoslavia and France. Home: 1010 Monroe Ave Scranton PA 18510 Office University Scranton Scranton PA 18510

PETRUCCI, PASQUALE MICHAEL, diagnostic co. exec.; b. New Haven, Conn., Oct. 7, 1938; s. Louis and Anna Elizabeth P.; student Providence Coll., 1956-58; B.S., Quinnipiac Coll., 1962; M.S., So. Conn. State Coll., 1965; M. Maureen A. Murphy, Oct. 15, 1965; children—Anne Marie, Louis, Anthony. Clin. chemist Bridgeport (Conn.) Hosp., 1963-67; lab. dir. Columbia Med. Lab., Bridgeport, 1967-68; v.p. Gen. Sci. Corp., Bridgeport, 1968-72; v.p. research and devel. J.T. Baker Instrument Co., Milford, Conn., 1972-76; dir. research and devel. Clay Adams div. Becton-Dickinson & Co., Parsippany, N.J., 1976-78, v.p. research and devel., 1978—; lectr., cons. in field; dir. Gen. Sci. Corp., 1970-72. Mem. Am. Soc. Clin. Pathologists, Am. Assn. Clin. Chemists, Am. Soc. Med. Technologists, Registry Med. Technologists, Phi Theta Kappa, Lambda Tau. Roman Catholic. Club: K.C. Patentee in field. Home: 9 Raskin Rd Morristown NJ 07960 Office: 299 Webro Rd Parisippany NJ 07054

PETRUCELLI, R. JOSEPH, II, physician, med. historian, educator; b. Meriden, Conn., Sept. 20, 1943; s. Rocco J. and Marguerite (Colwell) P.; A.B., Yale U., 1965; M.D., Harvard U., 1969. Intern, Mt. Sinai Med. Center, N.Y.C., 1969-70, resident in medicine, 1970-72; fellow in nephrology U. San Francisco Med. Center, 1972-74; chief nephrology New Rochelle (N.Y.) Hosp. Med. Center, 1975—; asst. prof. physiology and biophysics Mt. Sinai Sch. Medicine, N.Y.C., 1975—. Recipient Richard Cabot prize, 1969; diplomate Am. Bd. Internal Medicine. Fellow N.Y. Acad. Medicine; mem. Phi Beta Kappa. Author: An Illustrated History of Medicine, 1978. Home: 167 Country Ridge Dr Rye Town NY 10573 Office: 140 Lockwood Ave New Rochelle NY 10801

PETTIBONE, JOHN WOLCOTT, adminstr.; b. Springfield, O., Jan. 30, 1942; s. John Howard and Joan (Morrison) P.; student Wittenberg U., 1962-63, Cleveland Inst. Art (Ford Found. scholar), 1963-65. Asst. curator Rockport (Mass.) Art Assn., 1969-74, curator, 1974-78; adminstr. John Woodman Higgins Armory Mus., Worcester, Mass., 1978—; Exhibited in group shows Rockport Art Assn., 1971-76, Am. Fortnight Exhbn., Hong Kong, 1973; represented in permanent collection ARC, Washington, Town Rockport; instr. art Hammond Mus., Gloucester, Mass., 1971-73; instr. drawing pub. schs. Rockport, 1973-78. Mem. Rockport Traffic Com., 1971-73, Rockport Bd. Trade Governing Bd., 1971-73, 75-77. Mem. Rockport Art Assn., Mediaeval Acad. Am., Co. Mil. Historians. Lutheran. Clubs: Japanese Sword; Arms and Armour Soc. (London, England). Home: PO Box 109 Holden MA 01520 Office: 100 Barber Ave Worcester MA 01606

PETTINE, RAYMOND JAMES, judge; b. Providence, July 6, 1912; s. James and Alvina (Caruole) P.; student Providence Coll., 1931-34; LL.B., Boston U., 1937, LL.M., 1940; LL.D., Our Lady of Providence Sem., 1967; m. Lidia Golini, Sept. 6, 1941; 1 dau., Lydia A. Admitted to R.I. bar, 1940, U.S. Supreme Ct. bar; practiced in Providence, 1946-61; spl. counsel atty. gen. Dept. State R.I., 1948-52; asst. atty. gen., 1952-61; U.S. Atty. dist. R.I., Providence, 1961-66; U.S. Dist. Court judge for R.I., 1966—, now chief judge. Vice pres., treas. Italian Collection and Reading Room Com., 1957-58; mem. R.I. Commn. to Encourage Morality in Youth, 1958-60. R.I. Family Ct. Study Commn., 1956-57. Bd. dirs., exec. com. R.I. Philharmonic Orch. Served to maj. U.S. Army, 1941-46. Mem. R.I. Bar Assn., Italian-Am. Vets., Res. Officers Assn. R.I. (past pres.), Nat. Assn. Christians and Jews (dir.), Amvets (past judge adv. R.I.), Order Sons Italy. Club: Serra Internat. Home: 400 Angell St Providence RI 02906 Office: Federal Bldg Providence RI 02903

PETTIT, HORACE, former physician; b. Phila., Jan. 28, 1903; s. Horace and Katherine (Howell) P.; B.S., Harvard Coll., 1927; M.D., 1931; m. Millicent Lewis, Nov. 22, 1924; children—Emily Sargent (Mrs. Condon), Horace, Deborah (Mrs. Herbert L. Myers), Norman; m. 2d, Jane Mann Hiatt, May 13, 1950; 1 adopted dau., Barbara (Mrs. Jeffrey R. Hall). Intern, Bryn Mawr Hosp., 1933-34; asst. instr., instr., asso. bacteriology U. Pa. Sch. Medicine, 1932-39, instr. medicine, 1939-53; pvt. practice of allergy, 1940-42, 1947-75; cons. in allergy Bryn Mawr Hosp.; cons. allergist Bryn Mawr Coll. Served from maj. to lt. col. AUS, 1942-46. Fellow Coll. Physicians of Phila.; mem. Am. Acad. Allergy, Am. Soc. Microbiology, Phila. County, Pa. med. socs., AMA, Phila. Allergy Soc. (pres. 1958-59), United World Federalists (mem. nat. exec. council 10 years), St. Andrew's Soc. Phila. Unitarian. Clubs: Harvard (Phila.); Merion Cricket (Haverford, Pa.); Camden (Maine) Yacht. Home and Office: 123 Kennedy Ln Bryn Mawr PA 19010

PETTIT, JANUSZKA RYMSZA (MRS. HORACE PETTIT, JR.), psychologist; b. Edinburgh, Scotland, June 25, 1942; d. Janusz Gozdawa and Sonia (Lee-Rayner) Gozdawa de Lilio Rymsza; B.A., U. B.C., 1962; M.A. Edn., 1966; Ph.D., Fla. State U., 1968; m. Horace Pettit, Jr., Dec. 5, 1970; children—Andrew John Lee-Rayner, Katherine Vaughan, Iaian Gozdawa Franklin. Came to U.S., 1966, naturalized, 1975. Dir. kindergarten Alert Bay, B.C., Can., 1963-65; mem. faculty Fla. State U., Tallahassee, 1966-68; asst. clin. dir. Vanguard Sch., Haverford, Pa., 1969-70; researcher Edward N. Hay & Assos., Phila., 1970-71, also psychotherapist Delaware County Child Guidance Clinic, Media, Pa.; psychodiagnostician Chester Sch. Dist. (Pa.), 1970-73; psychologist Mitchell-Main Line Day Sch., Haverford, 1970—; psychotherapist St. Edmond's Home for Crippled Children, Bryn Mawr, Pa., 1971—; individual practice psychotherapy for children, adolescents and adults. Lectr. Villanova (Pa.) U., 1970-71, Pa. State U. at King of Prussia, 1969-72. Nat. Inst. Mental Health fellow Devereux Found., Devon, Pa., 1968-69. Mem. Archtl. League of Phila. Art Alliance, Yellow Springs Found. Chester County, Friends of Independence Nat. Hist. Park. Mem. Am., Pa., Eastern psychol. assns., Assn. Children with Learning Disabilities, Phila. Soc. Clin. Psychologists, Internat. Transactional Analysis Assn., Assn. Humanistic Psychology, Eastern Inst. Transactional Analysis and Gestalt, Silva Mind Control Assn., Orton Soc. Children with Learning Disabilities, Phi Delta Pi. Club: Photography Place. Home and office: 301 Windsor Ave Wayne PA 19087

PETTY, JOHN ROBERT, bank exec.; b. Chgo., Apr. 16, 1930; s. Dewitt Talmage and Beatrice (Worthington) P.; A.B., Brown U., 1951; postgrad. N.Y. U., 1953-54; m. H. Lee Mills, May 11, 1957; children—L. Talmage, Robert D., George D., George M., Victoria Lee. With Chase Manhattan Bank, N.Y.C., Paris, 1953-66, v.p., 1964-66; dep. asst. sec. Dept. Treasury, Washington, 1966-69, asst. sec. for internat. affairs, 1969-72; partner Lehman Bros., N.Y.C., 1972-76; pres., chmn. exec. com. Marine Midland Banks, Inc., Buffalo, 1976—, Marine Bank, 1976—; dir. RCA Corp., NBC, 1973—, Hercules, Inc., 1974—. Served with USNR, 1951-53. Mem. Council Fgn. Relations (pres.), Fgn. Bondholders Protective Council. Office: Maine Midland Banks Inc One Midland Marine Center Buffalo NY 14203*

PETTY, ROBERT ETHAN, chem. engr.; b. Columbus, Ohio, Aug. 26, 1926; s. Ethan Chalmers and Golda Margaret (Imler) P.; student Ohio Wesleyan, 1944-45; B.Chem. Engring., Ohio State U., 1948; postgrad. U. Pitts., 1952-59; m. Marjorie Edwards, Oct. 24, 1953; children—Douglas, David. Sr. engr. Koppers Co., Pitts., 1951-62; sr. engr. Bechtel Corp., San Francisco, 1962-63, Westinghouse Corp., Pitts. Bettis Atomic Power Lab., 1963—. Asst. leader Cub Scouts, 1966-67. Block capt. Republican party, Pitts., 1961-62. Served with USNR, 1944-46. Registered profl. engr., Pa. Mem. Am. Inst. Chem. Engrs., Ohio State Alumni Club, Phi Delta Theta. Presbyn. Invention award selective adsorption of radioactive wastes on a two stage bed. Home: 865 Lovingston Dr Pittsburgh PA 15216 Office: PO Box 79 West Mifflin PA 15122

PETVAI, STEVE ISTVAN, mech. engr.; b. Budapest, Hungary, Oct. 13, 1929; s. Sandor and Olga (Fenaisz) P.; came to U.S., 1956, naturalized, 1962; M.S.M.E., Tech. U. Budapest, 1953; m. Carol Francies Starkey, Aug. 12, 1961; children—John Victor, James Williams. Mech. engr. Keithley Instrument Corp., Cleve., 1964; project engr. The Bunker Ramo Corp., Cleve., 1965-66, Gilmore Industries, Inc., Cleve., 1967; adv. engr. IBM Corp., System Product Div., Hopewell Junction, N.Y., 1968—. Elder, First Presbyn. Ch., Wappingers Falls, N.Y., 1973-76. Certified mfg. engr., N.Y.; registered profl. profl. engr., N.Y. Mem. Am. Vacuum Soc., Soc. Mfg. Engrs., Nat. Soc. Profl. Engrs. Contbr. articles in field to profl. jours. Home: 2 Bell Air Ln Wappingers Falls NY 12590 Office: Bldg 320 Zip 69E Rt 5 Hopewell Junction NY 12533

PEUGEOT, DAVID ERNEST, pub. relations cons.; b. Buffalo, June 26, 1902; s. David E. and Margaret (Divins) P.; B.S., Hobart Coll., 1924; m. Violette M. Williams, Sept. 19, 1931; children—Patricia J., Peter D., Suzanne Marie Louise. Tchr. history Bennett High Sch., Buffalo, 1925-29; reporter Buffalo Evening News, 1925, asst. promotion editor, 1929-32, promotion editor, 1932-72; v.p., treas. P.M. Sales, Buffalo, 1973-75. Lectr., Am. Press Inst., Columbia, N.Y.C., 1965. Chief, Buffalo Aux. Fire Corps, 1950-65; chmn. Erie County Fire Adv. Bd., 1962—; mem. Buffalo Bd. Fire Awards, 1943-74, adv. commn. Civil Def., Erie County, 1966—; life mem. Buffalo Pub. Library; bd. dirs. Crippled Children's Camps, Buffalo, 1946—, treas., 1955—; bd. dirs. Fresh Air Mission Buffalo, Western N.Y. Sci. Congress; trustee Maud Holmes Arboretum, Garden Center Inst., Buffalo. Named friend of 4-H, Erie County, 1957, Western N.Y. chpt. 4-H, 1958, Nat. Friend award nat. chpt., 1966; recipient Distinguished Service award Sci. Tchrs. Assn. N.Y. State, 1973, 74. Mem. Western N.Y. Interscholastic Press Assn. (founding dir.), Lit. Clinic Buffalo (pres. 1962-64, 67-68), Buffalo Hist. Soc., Hobart Coll. Alumni Assn. (past pres.), Grosvenor Soc., Kappa Sigma, Scalp and Blade. Republican. Episcopalian. Mason (Shriner, K.T.). Clubs: Buffalo Torch (charter), Central Park Men's (dir.). Author: Newspaper Helps to Learning, 1961. Editor: Buffalo Evening News Almanac and Fact Book, 1933-72. Address: 666 W Ferry St Buffalo NY 14222

PEYSER, PETER A., congressman; b. Cedarhurst, N.Y., Sept. 7, 1921; s. Percy A. and Rubye (Hoeflich) P.; B.A., Colgate U., 1943; m. Marguerite Richard, Dec. 23, 1949; children—Penny, Carolyn, Peter, James, Tommy. Mgr., Mut. N.Y. Ins. Co., N.Y.C., 1956-70; mayor, Irvington, N.Y., 1963-70; mem. 92d to 94th congresses from 25th N.Y. Dist., mem. edn. and labor com., edn. gen. subcom., edn. select subcom., labor select subcom., house task force drug abuse, task force on aging; mem. 96th Congress from 23d Dist. N.Y.; mem. N.Y. Congl. Del. Steering Com. Bd. dirs. Nat. Com. Student Vote; trustee Colgate U. Served with U.S. Army, 1943-46. Decorated Bronze Star, Belgian Fourragere. Democrat. Episcopalian. Home: Sunnyside Ln Irvington NY 10533 Office: US Ho of Reps The Capitol Washington DC 20515*

PEYTON, SARAH MARGARET, physician; b. Crisfield, Md., Dec. 29, 1895; d. William John and Margaret Edith (Adams) Peyton; A.B., Goucher Coll., 1916; M.D., Johns Hopkins U., 1923. Intern New Eng. Hosp. for Women and Children, Boston, 1923-24; physician Playground Athletic League Md., 1924-25; gen. practice medicine, Crisfield, 1925—; mem. staff McCready Meml. Hosp., Crisfield, chief physician, 1970. Mem. welfare bd. Somerset County, Md., 1963-69. Named Citizen of Year, Crisfield C. of C. 1940; recipient A.B. Robins Co. award Med. and Chirurgical Faculty of Md., 1976. Mem. AMA, Am. Acad. Family Physicians, Md. Hist. Soc., Md., Crisfield med. assns., Phi Beta Kappa, Delta Delta Delta. Democrat. Methodist (trustee 1966-70). Club: Women Civic (pres. 1946-48) (Crisfield). Home and office: 33 W Main St Crisfield MD 21817

PEZZULICH, ROBERT ANTHONY, surgeon; b. N.Y.C., Oct. 3, 1939; s. Anthony John and Anna (Pratka) P.; A.B., Cornell U., 1961, M.D., 1965; m. Helen Elizabeth Hunfeld, June 6, 1964; children—Lisa Marie, Matthew Carl. Intern in surgery N.Y. Hosp.-Cornell Med. Center, 1965-66, resident in gen. surgery, 1966-70, chief resident, 1970-71; practice medicine, specializing in gen. and vascular surgery, Bennington, Vt., 1973—; mem. staff Putnam Meml. Hosp.; cons. Mary McClellan Hosp., Cambridge, N.Y.; mem. steering com. Vt. Regional Cancer Center. Pres., Bennington County chpt. Am. Cancer Soc., 1977—; v.p. bd. trustees United Counseling Service, Bennington, 1976—. Served to maj. USAF, 1971-73. Diplomate Am. Bd. Surgery. Fellow A.C.S.; mem. AMA, Vt., Bennington County med. socs. Roman Catholic. Home: Meadowbrook Dr Bennington VT 05201 Office: 140 Hospital Dr Bennington VT 05201

PFAFFLIN, JAMES REID, educator, civil engr.; b. Connersville, Ind., Dec. 3, 1930; s. Theodore Frederick and Mottie Marie (Reid) P.; B.S., Ind. State U., 1952; B.E.S., Johns Hopkins U., 1956, M.S., 1957; Ph.D., U. Windsor, 1972; m. Sheila Honoré Murphy, Sept. 7, 1957. Design engr. Rummel, Klepper & Kahl, Balt., 1957-58, Md. State Health Dept., Balt., 1958-59; research scientist N.Y. U., 1959-61; instr. civil engring. Cooper Union, 1961-65; asst. prof. Poly. Inst. of Bklyn., 1965-70; asso. prof. Stevens Inst. of Tech., 1973-77, N.J. Inst. of Tech., Newark, 1977—; cons. in field. Mem. sch. bd. Passaic Twp., N.J., 1977—; tech. bd. Am. Boat and Yacht Council, 1969—. Served with U.S. Army, 1953-55. Profl. engr., Ont., Can.; chartered engr., Eng. Fellow Royal Soc. of Health, Inst. of Fuel; mem. Canadian Soc. Civil Engrs., Engring. Inst. of Canada, IEEE, AAUP, Sigma Xi. Democrat. Roman Catholic. Club: Raritan Yacht. Editor: (with E.N. Ziegler) The Encyclopedia of Environmental Science and Engring., 1976, Advances in Environmental Science and Engineering (ann.); (with M. Levy) Resource Management and Optimization, 1978; (with J. McK. Ellison) Theoretical and Environmental Reviews, 1978; contbr. over 30 articles to profl. jours. Home: 173 Gates Ave Gillette NJ 07933 Office: 323 High St NJ Inst of Tech Newark NJ 07102

PFALTZ, HUGO M., JR., lawyer; b. Newark, Sept. 23, 1931; s. Hugo M. and Mary Elizabeth (Horr) P.; B.A., Hamilton Coll., 1953; LL.B., Harvard, 1960; LL.M. in Taxation, N.Y.U., 1965; m. Marilyn M. Muir, Sept. 29, 1956; children—Elizabeth W., William M., Robert L. Admitted to N.J. bar, 1960; asso. firm McCarter & English, Newark, 1960-61; mem. firm Bourne and Noll, Summit, N.J., 1961-74; individual practice law, Summit, 1974—. Del. N.J. Constl. Conv., 1966; mem. N.J. Gen. Assembly, 1967-71; mem. Gov.'s Tax Policy Com.; mem. Uniform Consumer Credit Code Study Com. Served to lt USNR, 1953-62. Mem. Am., N.J. (chmn. banking law sect., mem. gen. council), Union County (trustee, 1970—, mem., chmn. ethics com., 1967-70), Summit (pres. 1976-77), Essex County bar assns., Phi Beta Kappa. Republican. Unitarian. Clubs: Baltusrol Golf, Beacon Hill. Editor: N.J. Law Jour., 1965—. Home: 118 Prospect St Summit NJ 07901 Office: 382 Springfield Ave Summit NJ 07901

PFEFFER, CHRISTIAN JACKSON, business cons.; b. St. Louis, Dec. 29, 1942; s. Jackson and Lora (Doolen) P.; B.S., So. Ill. U., 1969; M.B.A., Rochester Inst. Tech., 1973; m. Karen Jean Selfridge, Oct. 8, 1977; 1 dau., Susan Christian. Analyst customer accounts Reinhold Gardner Investment Bankers, St. Louis, 1963-64; program planner McDonnell Douglas Corp., St. Louis, 1964-69; planning and control, new product devel. Xerox Corp., Rochester, N.Y., 1969-74, mgr. planning and analysis Office Systems div., Dallas, 1974-76, bus. cons. to group v.p. Info. Products group, Greenwich, Conn., 1977—; presdl. interchange exec. Exec. Office of Pres., Washington, 1976-77; lectr. in field. Mem. Presdl. Interchange Exec. Assn., So. Ill. U., Rochester Inst. Tech. alumni assns., Xerox Mgmt. Assn. Methodist. Club: Wolfpit Running (Ridgefield, Conn.). Home: 1100 Stillwater Rd Stamford CT 06902 Office: Two Pickwick Plaza IPG Greenwich CT 06830

PFEFFER, SUSAN BETH, writer; b. N.Y.C., Feb. 17, 1948; d. Leo and Freda (Plotkin) Pfeffer; B.A., N.Y. U., 1969. Free-lance writer novels, reviews, articles, short stories, 1970—; lectr. children's lit.; instr. Orange County Community Coll., Middletown, N.Y., 1972. Bd. dirs. New Country Theater, Ridgebury, N.Y., 1972. Author: Just Morgan, 1970; Better Than All Right, 1972; Rainbows and Fireworks, 1973; The Beauty Queen, 1974; Whatever Words You Want to Hear, 1974; Marly the Kid, 1975; Kid Power, 1977. Home: 14 S Railroad Ave Middletown NY 10940 Office: care Curtis Brown Ltd 575 Madison Ave New York City NY 10022

PFEIFER, DONALD, clin. social worker; b. Bklyn., Sept. 14, 1946; s. Donald Herman and Mary Concetta (Mosso) P.; B.A., L.I. U., 1969; M.S.W., Fordham U., 1973; postgrad. Inst. Study of Psychotherapy, 1976; m. Dorothy Simolo, Oct. 10, 1970. Caseworker Angel Guardian Home, Bklyn., 1970-74; psychotherapist Mercy Guidance Clinic, Angel Guardian Home, 1974-78; pvt. practice psychotherapy, Bklyn., 1976—; psychotherapist Mercy Hosp., Rockville Center, 1977—, Bleuler Psychotherapy Center, Queens, N.Y., 1978—; field instr. Fordham U. Sch. Social Service, 1978—. Fellow N.Y. State Soc. Clin. Social Work Psychotherapists; mem. Nat. Assn. Social Workers, Acad. Certified Social Workers. Office: 2022 W 5th St Brooklyn NY 11223

PFEIFFER, CARL, oil co. exec.; b. Steelton, Pa., Dec. 20, 1924; s. Thomas William and Louise (Schmick) P.; B.S., Pa. State U., 1946, M.S., 1947; m. Jane Marie Neiman, Jan. 24, 1953; children—Carl, Cheryl, Cathy, Carol. Chem. engr. Houdry Process Corp., Linwood, Pa., 1947-52; prin. engr. Catalytic Constrn. Co., Phila., 1952-59; chief process engr. Sun Olin Chem. Co., Phila., 1959-62; mgr. process design Sun Oil Co., Phila., 1962—. Served to lt. USNR, 1944-45. Registered profl. engr., Pa. Mem. Am. Inst. Chem. Engrs., Am. Chem. Soc., Am. Legion, Triangle Fraternity. Republican. Roman Catholic. Home: 913 Penn Valley Rd Media PA 19063 Office: 1608 Walnut St Philadelphia PA 19103

PFEISTER, RAYMOND LYNN, ins. co. exec.; b. Cape Girardeau, Mo., May 31, 1946; s. Herman Joe and Imogene Elsie (Groseclose) P.; B.S., U. Ill., 1969, M.B.A., 1971; Ph.D., Baruch Coll., City U. N.Y., 1978; m. Susan Jane Selby, July 1, 1969; 1 son, Joseph Robert. Sales analyst Koppers Co., Magnolia, Ark., 1969-70; instr. bus. U. Ill., Urbana, 1971; spl. agt. Prudential Ins. Co. Am., Champaign, Ill., 1971, div. mgr., Balt., 1971-74, mktg. specialist, mgr. group pension, Newark and N.Y.C., 1974; account exec. Alexander & Alexander Inc., N.Y.C., 1974-76, asst. v.p., 1976-78, v.p., 1978—; founder, chmn., pres. Pfeister Corp., Wilmington, Del., 1977—; lectr., cons. in field. Pres. Jr. Achievement, Denver, 1963-64; active Boy Scouts Am., 1964—, United Fund, 1973. Named outstanding young man Am., U.S. Jaycees, 1977. Mem. Vernon (Conn.) C. of C., Acad. Mgmt., Am. Psychol. Assn., Nat. Eagle Scout Assn., Soc. Am. Foresters, Forest Products Research Soc., Nat. Life Underwriters Assn., Nat. M.B.A. Assn., U. Ill. Alumni Assn. (life)(v.p. 1974—), Sigma Iota Epsilon. Club: N.Y. Athletic. Home: 73 Kensington Rd Bronxville NY 10708 Office: Alexander & Alexander Inc 1185 Ave of Americas New York City NY 10036

PFISTER, LINDA ARLENE, ednl. cons.; b. Lima, Ohio, July 11, 1947; d. Clare Russell and Beulah Pauline (Zeisloft) Pfister; B.S., Bowling Green State U., 1969, M.A., 1971; m. Joseph E. Keilholtz, July 20, 1968. Curriculum specialist, bus. and office edn. tchr. Toledo (Ohio) pub. schs., 1969-71; project asso., comprehensive career edn. model Center for Vocat. and Tech. Edn., Ohio State U., 1971-72; supr. career devel., div. vocat. edn. Ohio Dept. Edn., Columbus, 1972-75; program service officer Coll. Entrance Exam. Bd., N.Y.C., 1974—. Mem. Am. Vocat. Assn., Nat. Vocat. Guidance Assn., Am. Personnel and Guidance Assn. Home: PO Box 62 Sterling Forest NY 10979 Office: 888 7th Ave New York City NY 10019

PFLIEGER, JOHN ELY, publishing exec.; b. N.Y.C., Feb. 18, 1930; s. John James and Janet (McNeir) P.; grad. Yale U., 1953; m. Donna Rae Carlson, Apr. 17, 1956; children—John Ely, Robert McKay. Asso. dir. market research House & Home mag. Time Inc., N.Y.C., 1953-56, asst. circulation mgr., 1956-58, circulation dir., 1958-63; asst. dir. edn. Time Inc., N.Y.C., 1963-65, sales supr. Time mag., 1965-73, divisional sales mgr., Washington, 1973-76, dir. govt. affairs Time Inc., 1976—. Mem. adv. com. Fed. Nat. Mortgage Assn., 1972, 73, 75, 76, 78—, Home Owners Warranty Corp., 1975-78; mem. exec. com. and adv. bd. Joint Center for Urban Studies of Mass. Inst. Tech. and Harvard, 1971—, chmn. exec. com., 1974, chmn. adv. bd., 1975, mem. vis. com., 1978. Republican. Episcopalian. Clubs: Chevy Chase, 1925 F St., City Tavern, Capitol Hill. Home: 5303 Falmouth Rd Washington DC 20016 Office: Time Inc 888 16th St NW Washington DC 20006

PFLUM, WILLIAM JOHN, physician; b. N.Y.C., July 30, 1924; s. Peter Arthur and Caroline (Schmidt) P.; B.S., Georgetown U., 1947; M.D., Loyola U., Chgo., 1951; m. Roseann Sarah Stubing, Oct. 13, 1956; children—Carol Jean, Jeannine, Suzanne, Denise, Peter. Intern, St. Vincent's Hosp., N.Y.C., 1951-52, resident in internal medicine, 1954-55; resident in internal medicine N.Y. U. div. Goldwater Meml. Hosp., N.Y.C., 1952-53; resident in allergy Inst. Allergy, Roosevelt Hosp., N.Y.C., 1956; attending internal medicine (allergy and immunology) Overlook Hosp., Summit, N.J., 1958—; asso. attending Inst. Allergy, Immunology and Infectious Diseases, Roosevelt Hosp., N.Y.C., 1957—; pvt. practice medicine, specializing in allergy and immunology, Summit, 1957—; cons. in field. Served with USAAF, 1943-45; ETO. Decorated Purple Heart, Air medal with two clusters. Diplomate Am. Bd. Allergy and Immunology. Fellow Am. Acad. Allergy, Am. Coll. Allergists, Am. Assn. Clin. Immunology and Allergy.; mem. Robert A. Cooke Allergy Alumni Assn., Summit Med. Soc., Am. Assn. Clin. Immunology and Allergy (pres. Mid-Atlantic region 1975-76), World Marathon Runners Assn. Roman Catholic. Home: Lake Trail W Mt Kemble Lake Morristown NJ 07960 Office: 332 Springfield Ave Summit NJ 07901

PHELAN, ARTHUR JOHN, JR., savs. and loan exec.; b. Washington, June 8, 1934; s. Arthur John and Elton Frances (Taylor) P.; student Holy Cross Coll., Worcester, Mass., 1952-54; B.A., Yale, 1956, M.A., 1957; m. Wanda Mathias, Dec. 11, 1965; children—Arthur John III, Margaret Anne. Securities research Merrill Lynch, Pierce, Fenner & Smith, N.Y.C., 1957; investment broker, cons. to several cos., 1959-64; dir., sec.-treas. Govt. Services Savs. & Loan, Inc., Bethesda, Md., 1964-67, v.p., mng. officer, 1967-70, exec. v.p., 1970-71, pres., 1971-75, chmn. bd., chief exec. officer, 1973—. Mem. com. Md. Savs.-Share Ins. Corp. Mem. Chevy Chase Village Land Use Adv. Bd., 1972—; sec. Montgomery County Arts Council, 1977—. Served with USAF, 1957-59. Mem. U.S. (legis. com.), Md. (dir.) savs. and loan leagues, Bethesda-Chevy Chase C. of C. Republican. Roman Catholic. Clubs: Metropolitan (Washington); Chevy Chase Country; Yale (N.Y.C.). Office: 7200 Wisconsin Ave Bethesda MD 20014

PHELAN, HOWARD TAYLOR, financial co. exec.; b. Washington, Oct. 19, 1936; s. Arthur John and Elton (Taylor) P.; B.S., Yale, 1958, M.A. (hon.), 1968; postgrad. U. Freiburg (Germany), 1958-59; m. Mary Elizabeth Voss, July 4, 1964; children—Elizabeth Andre, Victoria Taylor. Gen. partner Phelan & Co., N.Y.C., 1957-63; asst. instr. physics Yale, 1959-60; cons. NASA, Washington, 1960-62; staff cons. Arthur D. Little, Inc., 1960-65; dir. mgmt. ops. and univ. devel. Yale, 1965-70; pres., chief exec. officer, dir. Welsbach Corp., New Haven, Conn., 1970-76; pres. Howard T. Phelan & Co., Greenwich, Conn., 1976—, Moran Stahl Boyer Assos., Inc., N.Y.C., 1978—; chmn. bd., chief exec. officer TWC Holding Corp., Greenwich, 1971-76; chmn. AZCO Equipment Corp., Westbury, N.Y., 1970-76, Eastern Trout Farms Corp., Portland, Maine, 1978—; chmn. exec. com. Jamaica Water Supply Co., 1970-76; dir., exec. com. 1st New Haven Nat. Bank, 1969-77. Trustee St. Thomas More Corp., 1964-69, Found. Religion and Mental Health, Briarcliff, N.Y., 1976—; asst. chmn., dir. Yale Alumni Fund, 1960-67, mem. Yale Devel. Bd., 1970—; bd. overseers com. on adminstrn. and accounts Harvard, 1967-71. Mem. Greenwich Riding and Trails Assn. (pres., dir. 1974-77). Clubs: Innis Arden (Greenwich); Met. (Washington); Yale (N.Y.C.). Home: 44 Benjamin St Old Greenwich CT 06870 Office: 41 W Putnam Ave Greenwich CT 06830

PHELAN, JOSEPH FRANCIS, found. exec.; b. Wareham, Mass., June 28, 1939; s. Joseph Foley and Lillian Verna (Lewis) P.; B.A., U. N.H., 1961; M.A. in Edn., Morehead State U., 1966; m. Brenda Jane Heath, Aug. 26, 1961; 1 dau., Colleen Gale. Tchr., Bristol (N.H.) Meml. High Sch., 1961-62; asst. prin., chmn. English dept. Newfound Meml. High Sch., Bristol, 1963-65; New Eng. regional dir. Citizens Scholarship Found. Am., Concord, N.H., 1967-68, exec. dir., 1968—. Mem. Sch. Bd. Auburn (N.H.), 1973-76; dir. Auburn Village Players, 1970-75. Mem. Tau Kappa Epsilon, Tau Kappa Alpha. Democrat. Congregationalist. Contbr. to profl. jours. Home: Chester Rd Auburn NH 03032 Office: 1 South PO Box 636 Concord NH 03303

PHELAN, WILLIAM FRANCIS, ednl. cons.; b. Pompey, N.Y., Jan. 19, 1906; s. John and Catherine (Kinney) P.; B.A., Niagara U., 1928, M.A., 1934; postgrad. Buffalo State Tchrs. Coll., summer 1936, Buffalo U. Sch. Edn., 1936-40; Ed.D., Tchrs. Coll., Columbia U., 1949; m. Hilda Clements, June 26, 1929; children—Margaret Jane (Mrs. Daniel J. O'Connell), Elizabeth Ann (Mrs. Richard Amari). Tchr., coach, asst. prin. Lewiston (N.Y.) pub. schs., 1928-34; supervising prin. North Collins (N.Y.) pub. schs., 1934-43; supt. Depew (N.Y.) Pub. Schs., 1943-57; dist. prin. North Babylon (N.Y.) Pub. Schs., 1957-62; dist. supt. schs. 2d supr. dist. Suffolk County, Patchogue, N.Y., 1962-74; ednl. cons., 1974—; vis. prof. Buffalo State Tchrs. Coll. Grad. Sch., 1948-50, Buffalo U. Grad. Schs., summers 1950, 57, Niagara U. Grad. Sch., 1950-57; vis. instr. St. John's U., 1958-62; ednl. cons. N.Y. State Fedn. Womens' Clubs, 1952-54; mem. L.I. Citizens Com. on Sch. Finance, 1959-62, pres., 1960, v.p., 1960-62; v.p. L.I. Ednl. Leadership Conf., 1963-64; adv. bd. Erie County Vocat. and Ednl. Extension Bd., 1954-57; mem. Congress Sch. Dist. Adminstr. Orgns., 1971-74, pres., 1972-73. Chmn. adv. bd. Family Service Soc. Buffalo and Erie County, 1956-57, bd. dirs., 1956-57; mem. L.I. Regional Mental Health Planning Com.; pres. Lancaster Town Planning Commn., 1954-55; bd. dirs. Depew Boys' Club, Inc., 1945-55, Community Chest Buffalo and Erie County, 1945-55, Suffolk County Mental Health Assn., 1963—; mem. Commr.'s Adv. Council Sch. Suprs., 1968-73, Suffolk County Econ. Opportunity Commn., 1964-67; mem. Suffolk County Interdept. Welfare Adv. Commn. Mem. N.Y. State Assn. Sch. Dist. Adminstrs. (chmn.; legis. com. 1964-67), N.Y. State Council Sch. Dist. Adminstrs. (chmn. legis. com. 1968-71, v.p. 1970-71, pres. 1971-72, Distinguished Service award 1974), Am. Assn. Sch. Adminstrs. (Distinguished Service award 1978). Club: Rotary (1st pres. Eden-N. Collins, N.Y. 1940-41). Home: 45 Orchard Dr Brightwaters NY 11718

PHELEN, DAVID, veterinarian; b. Mo., June 19, 1936; s. Thomas Herman and Anna Louise (Peters) P.; B.S. in Agr., U. Mo., 1963, D.V.M., 1963; m. Diane Louise Carter, Jan. 26, 1974; 1 son, Christopher. children by previous marriage—Karen Phelen Ditch, Susan, Diane. Asst. dir. profl. services Affiliated Labs, East St. Louis, Ill., 1963-66, research veterinarian, White Hall, Ill., 1966-68; supt. dept. lab. animal resources Merck & Co., West Point, Pa., 1968-72; mgr. dept. lab. animal sci. Smith Kline Corp., Phila., 1972—; co-owner New Dawn Enterprises, New Dawn Arabians, 1973—. Editor, Smithton (Ill.) News, community newsletter, 1964-66; chmn. church survey com. St. James Episcopal Ch., 1974-75, chmn. refugee com., 1975—. Pres. Smith Kline Employees Fed. Credit Union, 1978—. Served with U.S. Army, 1954-57. Fellow Am. Coll. Veterinary Pharmacology and Therapeutics; mem. Am., Pa. vet. med. assns., Am. Assn. Lab. Animal Sci., Indsl. Veterinarians Assn., Lab. Animal Practitioners Soc. Republican. Club: Arabian Horse. Home: 86 Sunset Rd Limerick PA 19468 Office: 1500 Spring Garden St Philadelphia PA 19101

PHELPS, FLORA L(OUISE) LEWIS, editor, anthropologist, photographer; b. San Francisco, July 28, 1917; d. George Chase and Louise (Manning) Lewis; student U. Mich.; A.B. cum laude, Bryn Mawr Coll., 1938; A.M., Columbia U., 1954; m. C(lement) Russell Phelps, Jan. 15, 1944; children—Andrew Russell, Carol Lewis, Gail Bransford. Acting dean Cape Cod Inst. Music, East Brewster, Mass., summer 1940; asso. social sci. analyst, U.S. Govt., 1942-44; co-adj. staff instr. anthropology Univ. Coll., Rutgers U., 1954-55; mem. editorial bd. Americas, Pan Am. Union, Washington, 1960—, sr. editor, 1963-71, editor English edition, 1971—, mng. editor, 1974—. N.J. vice chmn. Ams. Democratic Action, 1950; mem. Dem. County Com. N.J., 1948-49. Mem. Am. Anthrop. Assn., Anthrop. Soc. Washington, Am. Ethnol. Soc., AAAS, Soc. Woman Geographers. Club: Woman's Nat. Democratic. Author articles in field of anthropology, art, architecture, edn. Office: Gen Secretariat OAS Washington DC 20006

PHELPS, PETER WILMOT, noise control engr.; b. Pitts., Dec. 22, 1946; s. Preston Erle and Amelia Marie (Wilmot) P.; B.S., in M.E., Ohio U., Athens, 1969; M.B.A., Loyola Coll., Balt., 1977. Asst. project engr. Koppers Co., Inc., Balt., 1969-72; sr. environ. engr. Martin Marietta Labs., Balt., 1973—; cons. noise abatement. Officer Jeffers Glen Community Assn., 1973-74. Mem. Acoustical Soc. Am., Inst. Noise Control Engring., ASME. Episcopalian. Author: (with others) Portable Air Compressor Noise Reduction, 1974. Home: 9053 Watchlight Ct Columbia MD 21045 Office: 1450 S Rolling Rd Baltimore MD 21227

PHILBIN, JAMES EDWARD, pilot, aerospace co. exec.; b. N.Y.C., June 28, 1931; s. James Francis and Anna Theresa (Monaghan) P.; B.A., St. John's U., 1953; postgrad. Adelphi U., 1968; P.M.D., Harvard U., 1970; children—Susan Marie, Kathleen Ann, Joyce Eileen. Mgr. mil. liaison Wright Aero. Co., Woodridge, N.J., 1957-58; asst. chief pilot, dir. fleet requirements, dir. Israeli ops. Grumman Aerospace Corp., Bethpage, N.Y., 1958—, also dir. Mayor, Belle Terre Village, 1973-77, trustee, 1971-73, police commr., 1969-73, youth programs mgr., 1958-68; active Save the Children orgn. Served with USN, 1953-57. Mem. Soc. Exptl. Test Pilots. Home: 294 Captains Dr West Babylon NY 11704 Office: 4A Chisson St Entrance B Tel Aviv Israel

PHILIP, A.G. DAVIS, astronomer, educator; b. N.Y.C., Jan. 9, 1929; s. Van Ness and Lilian (Davis) P.; B.S., Union Coll., Schenectady, 1951; M.S., N.Mex. State U., 1959; Ph.D., Case Inst. Tech., 1964; m. Kristina Drobavicius, Apr. 25, 1964; 1 dau., Kristina Elizabeth Elanor. Tchr. physics, math., chemistry Brooks Sch., 1954-59; instr. Case Inst. Tech., 1962-64; asst. prof. astronomy U. New Mex., 1964-66; asst. prof. astronomy State U. N.Y., Albany, 1966-67, asso. prof., 1967-76, mem. exec. com Arts and Scis. Council, 1975-76; prof. Union Coll., 1976—; astronomer Dudley Obs., 1967—; vis. Prof. Yale, 1972, 73, vis. fellow, 1976; vis. prof. La. State U., 1973, 76, Acad. Scis. Lithuania, USSR, 1973, 76, Stellar Data Center, Strasbourg, France, 1978; Harlow Shaply lectr. Am. Astron. Soc., 1973-78; sec.-treas., dir. N.Y. Astron. Corp. Served with AUS, 1951-53. Fellow Royal Astron. Soc., AAAS; mem. Am. Phys. Soc., Am. Astron. Soc., Internat. Astron. Union (sec. commn. galactic structure 1973-76, organizing com., sec. commn. radial velocities 1973—, mem. working group commn. stellar spectra and multicolor indices 1976—), N.Y. Acad. Sci., Astron. Soc. Pacific, Astron. Soc. N.Y. (sec.-treas. 1974—, editor Newsletter), Sigma Xi. Author: (with M. Cullen, R.E. White) UBV Color—Magnitude Diagrams of Galactic Clusters. Editor: The Evolution of Population II Stars; Multicolor Photometry and the Theoretical HR Diagram; (with D.S. Hayes) Galactic Structure in the Direction of the Galactic Polar Caps; (with M.F. McCarthy) Spectral Classification of the Future; (with McCarthy and Coyne) In Memory of Henry Norris Russell; The HR Diagram: The One-Hundredth Anniversary of Henry Norris Russell; (with D.S. Hayes) Problems in Calibration of Multicolor Systems; Dudley Observatory Report Series; contbr. chpts. to books, articles profl. jours. Home: 1125 Oxford Pl Schenectady NY 12308 Office: 69 Union Ave Schenectady NY 12308

PHILIP, ANTHONY FRANCIS, psychologist; b. N.Y.C., Oct. 9, 1927; M.A., Columbia U., 1954; Ph.D., N.Y. U., 1959; m. Rina De Russi, Sept. 2, 1951; children—Daria, Carla, Alida. Postdoctoral fellow Austen Riggs Center, Stockbridge, Mass., 1959-62; dir. counseling service and human devel. dept. Columbia U., N.Y.C., 1965—; pvt. practice clin. psychology, N.Y.C. and Teaneck, N.J., 1962—. Served with U.S. Army, 1945-47. Diplomate Am. Bd. Clin. Psychology. Mem. Am. Psychol. Assn., AAAS, Am. Coll. Health Assn.

PHILIPS, PARIS JOHN, urologist; b. Volos, Greece, Dec. 4, 1929; s. John Philip and Katherine S. (Kapetanias) Philippidjis; immigrated to Can., 1963, naturalized, 1969; M.D., Nat. U. Athens, 1953; m. P.G.A. McArter, Aug. 24, 1968; children—John Paris, Katherine Elizabeth. Rotating intern Oak Park (Ill.) Hosp., 1957-58; resident in surgery Baroness Erlanger Hosp., Chattanooga, 1958-60; resident in urology Univ. Hosp., Balt., 1960-63; research in pediatric urology Hosp. Sick Children, Toronto, Can., 1963-64; fellow urology St. Joseph's Hosp., Toronto, 1964-65; urology cons. York Central Hosp., Richmond Hill, Ont., 1966—. Served as officer Greek Army, 1953-56. Fellow Royal Coll. Surgeons Can., U. Md. Surg. Soc.; mem. Royal Surg. Soc., Ont. Med. Assn., Toronto Acad. Medicine, Hellenic Canadian Cultural Soc., AHEPA (officer 1965). Greek Orthodox. Contbr. med. jours. Home: 5 Portree Crescent Thornhill ON L3T 3G1 Canada Office: 10271 Yonge St Richmond Hill ON L4G 3G5 Canada

PHILLIPS, ANTHONY FRANCIS, lawyer; b. Hartford, May 18, 1937; s. Frank A. and Lena (Malone) P.; B.A. with distinction, U. Conn., 1959; J.D., Cornell U., 1962; m. Rosemary Karran McGowan, Jan. 28, 1967; children—Karran A., Antonia M., Justin F. Admitted to N.Y. State bar, 1963, since practiced in N.Y.C.; asso. firm Willkie, Farr & Gallagher, N.Y.C., 1963-69, partner, 1969—. Served with AUS, 1962-63. Mem. Order of Coif, Phi Beta Kappa. Home: 21 Greenfield Ave Bronxville NY 10708 Office: Citicorp Center 153 E 53d St New York City NY 10022

PHILLIPS, BEARL LEE, auditor; b. Hastings, W.Va., May 16, 1920; s. Ora Lee and Carrie Mae (Le Masters) P.; diploma Mountain State Coll., 1942; student Prince George Coll., 1975-77; m. Iantha Ingram, June 28, 1969. Supr., Libby Owens Ford Glass Co., 1942-55; pub. accountant in pvt. practice, 1955-61; sr. auditor Def. Contract Audit Agency, Hyattsville, Md., 1966—. Baptist. Club: Masons. Home: 4910 42d Pl Hyattsville MD 20781 Office: 5510 Calvart Rd College Park MD 20782

PHILLIPS, DAVID GUY, psychoanalyst; b. Chgo., Apr. 6, 1935; s. Benjamin Guy and Dorothy Helen (Bloom) P.; B.A., U. Chgo., 1955; M.S.S., Adelphi U., 1962; certificate psychoanalysis Postgrad. Center for Mental Health, N.Y.C., 1971; m. Mary Anne DeGillio, Jan. 24, 1970. Clin. social worker VA Hosp., Northport, N.Y., 1962-65, Jewish Family Service, Bklyn., 1965-67; social work fellow Postgrad. Center for Mental Health, N.Y.C., 1967-71, dir. social work, 1971—, sr. supr., mem. faculty, 1972—; pvt. practice psychoanalysis, N.Y.C., 1969—. Served with AUS, 1956-59. Fellow Soc. Clin. Social Workers; mem. Nat. Assn. Social Workers, Am. Acad. Marriage and Family Counselors. Home: 400 E 89th St New York City NY 10028 Office: 124 E 28th St New York City NY 10016

PHILLIPS, DORIS HOLT, club woman, educator; b. Hartford, Conn., Aug. 14, 1911; d. Sidney E. and Olive (Holt) Phillips; A.A., Colby-Sawyer Coll. N.H., 1931; grad. Pratt Inst., 1934; student N.Y. U., 1933; student extension course, Columbia, 1945; student U. Guadalajara (Mex.), summer 1945 Tchr. Coll. of Conn., 1950, summer 1952, Hillyer Coll., 1955. Tchr. arts and crafts Orange (N.J.) High Sch., 1934-37; technician New London (N.H.) Players, 1934; tchr. arts and crafts Hall High Sch., West Hartford, Conn., 1937-57, Conard High Sch., West Hartford, Conn., 1957-58. Mem. New London Budget Com., 1963-65. Mem. New London Hist. Soc. (dir. 1961-65), Colby-Sawyer Coll. N.H. Alumni Assn. (sec. 1952-55, dir. 1958-62), New London Hosp. Ladies Aid (pres. 1961-62), N.H. Federated Garden Clubs (dist. dir. 1964-66), Dog Writers Assn. of Am. (award 1966, 76), Norwegian Elkhound Assn. of Am. (sec. 1964-73, bd. dirs. 1974-76), Hist. Soc. of Early Am. Decoration, League of Women Voters, Elkins Ladies Benevolent Soc., N.H. Hist. Soc., Dog Orgn. Granite State v.p. 1976—), Am. Dog Owners Assn. (bd. dirs. 1976—), Norwegian Elkhound Minutemen Assn. (sec. 1975—). Clubs: New London Garden (dir. 1961-72), Colby-Sawyer Coll. (alumnae council 1957-72, 74—), Appalachian Mountain, Lakes Region Kennel (dir. 1960-63, 65-68, 73—, v.p. 1969, pres. 1970-71, chmn. scholarship com. 1971—, del. to Am. Kennel Club 1976—). Editor: Pawprint, 1964-73; chmn. New Hampshire Dog Breeders Directory, 1971—; editor N.H. Barks in N.H. Sunday News, 1974—. Home: Elkins NH 03233

PHILLIPS, FRANCES ISABELLE, ednl. adminstr.; b. Newark, Feb. 5, 1912; d. William Webster and Susan Isabelle (Snyder) P.; diploma Newark State Coll., 1933; B.Ed., Rutgers U., 1938, M.Ed., 1949. Tchr., N.J. Elementary schs., 1933-48; tchr. of deaf, Newark, 1948-59; chmn. dept. edn. Gallaudet Coll., Washington, 1959-65; dir. spl. edn. West Essex Area Schs., Essex County, N.J., 1965-67; asso. prof. Paterson State Coll., 1967-68; coordinator programs for deaf and hearing impaired, Hackensack, N.J., 1968-73, Bergen County Spl. Services Sch. Dist., 1973-74; mem. Gov.s' Ad Hoc Com. on Deaf Edn., 1968-74; adv. bd. N.J. Assn. Children with Hearing Impairment. Recipient Outstanding Alumni award Kean Coll., 1970. Mem. AAUW, Conf. Execs. Am. Schs. for Deaf, Council for Exceptional Children, N.J. State Fedn. for Exceptional Children (newsletter editor 1965-73), Kappa Delta Pi. Mem. Order of Eastern Star. Club: Montclair (N.J.) College Womens. Home: 97 Haddon Pl Upper Montclair NJ 07043

PHILLIPS, JACKSON ROBERT EDWARD, investment co. exec.; b. Sherman, Tex., Jan. 2, 1921; s. Robert Sidney and Kathryn Ola (Kelly) P.; B.A., U. Tex., 1942; Ph.D., Columbia, 1957; m. Mary Martha Howard, June 3, 1946; children—Pamela Howard, Tenley Lind. Instr., U. Tex., Austin, 1946-48, Lehigh U., Bethlehem, Pa., 1950-51; research asso. N.Y.C. Mayor's Com. Mgmt. Survey, 1951-53; municipal analyst, dir. municipal research Dun & Bradstreet, Inc., N.Y.C., 1953-71; v.p., dir. municipal research Moody's Investors Service, N.Y.C., 1971—; adj. prof. fin. N.Y. U., 1960-70, Baruch Coll., City U. N.Y., 1960—. Served to capt. AUS, 1942-46. Mem. Am. Econ. Assn., Nat. Tax Assn., Soc. Municipal Analysts, Municipal Forum N.Y. Democrat. Episcopalian. Contbg. editor Nat. Municipal Rev., 1956-60, Duns Rev. & Modern Industry, 1960-67, Am. Ency. Ann., 1965—. Office: 99 Church St New York City NY 10007

PHILLIPS, JAMES DAVIS, abrasive grain co. exec.; b. Queens, N.Y., Nov. 6, 1935; s. Austin Stevenson and Elizabeth Dean (Bennett) P.; B.S., Davis-Elkins Coll., 1957; M.B.A., Fairleigh Dickinson U., 1961; m. Helen Ann Haggerty, July 16, 1960; children—William, Kathleen, Ann. With Lederle Labs. Div. Am. Cyanamid, Pearl River, N.Y., 1957-66, mgr. accounting, 1967-69, controller pigments div., 1969-71; v.p. finance Gen. Abrasive Co., Inc., Niagara Falls, N.Y., 1971, exec. v.p., 1973-75; v.p., plant mgr. Gen. Abrasive Ltd., Niagara Falls, Ont., Can., 1972, dir., 1971—, chief exec. officer, chmn. bd., 1975—. Vice-chmn. admission and allocations com. Rockland County (N.Y.) United Fund, 1965-69; treas. Parents Assn., Pompton Plains, N.J., 1970-71; mgr. local Little League Baseball, 1959-71; finance chmn. Rockland County (N.Y.) council Boy Scouts Am., 1964-65; pres. Youngstown Homeowners Assn.; mem. bus. curriculum adv. com. Rockland Community Coll., 1965-67; mem. Niagara U. Council, 1975—, Niagara Falls Area Industry-Edn. Council, Niagara County Health Adv. Bd., 1976—. Mem. Abrasive Grain Assn. (dir., chmn. bd. 1978—), Nat. Assn. Accountants, Niagara Falls C. of C. (dir.), Recreational Golf Assn. (pres. 1959-60), Alpha Sigma Phi, Beta Alpha Beta. Club: Niagara Falls (N.Y.) Country. Home: 432 Dansworth Dr Youngstown NY 14174 Office: 2000 College Ave Niagara Falls NY 14305

PHILLIPS, JEWELL KATHLEEN, vocat. guidance counselor; b. Aurora, Mo.; d. John Wesley and Bertha Allen (Briner) P.; student Drury Coll., 1929-31, 32-34; M.A., Wash. State U., 1944; student Geneva Sch. Internat. Studies, 1934. Tchr., Jenkins (Mo.) Sch., 1931-32, Sch. of the Ozarks, 1934-36, Nixa, Mo., 1936-37; asst. dean of women Wash. State U., Pullman, 1937-43; personal counselor Western Electric Co., Kearney, N.J., 1943-49; personnel and guidance dir. Goodwill Industries of N.Y., 1949-53, asst. dir., 1967-71, dir. personnel and community relations, 1972-76; asst. dir., then dir. dept. handicapped Bklyn. Bur. Community Services, 1953-66; mem. bd. Comprehensive Health Planning Agy. City N.Y., 1974-76; community rep. Community Council Greater N.Y., 1950-62. Mem. Am. Personnel and Guidance Assn., Am. Personnel Mgmt. Assn., Mortar Bd. Home: One University Pl New York City NY 10003

PHILLIPS, JOSEPH DANIEL, oceanographer; b. Woodbury, N.J., Sept. 11, 1938; s. Joseph F. and Katherine C. (Browne) P.; B.A., Rutgers U., 1961; M.S.E., Princeton, 1963, M.A., 1964, Ph.D., 1966; m. Gwendolyn Williams, July 11, 1961; children—Julia, Stephanie, Joseph. With Woods Hole (Mass.) Oceanographic Inst., 1965-77, Mass. Inst. Tech., 1977-79; prof. U. Tex., Austin, 1979—; lectr. geophysics, joint edn. program with Woods Hole, 1969—; vis. prof. U. Cambridge (Eng.), 1974-75; cons. Princeton Applied Research Corp. (N.J.), 1965—, Mobil Oil Corp., 1969, Bell Telephone Labs., 1977-78, Exxon Corp., 1977; chmn. paleomagnetism adv. panel Joint Oceanographic Instns. Deep Earth Sampling Program, 1968—. Mem. Am. Geophys. Union, Soc. Exploration Geophysicists, Phi Beta Kappa, Sigma Xi, Chi Phi. Contbr. articles to profl. jours. Ency. Brit. Office: Mass Inst Tech Cambridge MA 02142

PHILLIPS, KANELLA THEODORA, med. adminstr.; b. Norwich, Conn., May 1, 1920; d. Theodore Nicholas and Joanna (Micos) P.; R.N., William W. Backus Hosp., Norwich, 1941; student N.Y. Postgrad. Med. Sch. and Hosp., 1945; B.S., Fairleigh Dickinson U., 1959. Staff nurse operating room William M. Backus Hosp., 1941-44; asst. supr. operating room Mountainside Hosp., Montclair, N.J., 1945, supr., clin. instr., 1945-67; supr. operating room and recovery room St. Barnabas Med. Center, Livingston, N.J., 1968-78, asst. dir. nursing, operating room and recovery room, 1978—; cons. in field. Mem. Assn. Operating Room Nurses (pres. N.J. chpt. 1974-76), Am., N.J. (chmn. econ. security program; chmn. operating room sect. 1951—, dir. 1951) nurses assns., Operating Room Suprs. and Clin. Instrs. (pres. N.J. 1969—). Greek Orthodox. Contbg. author book. Home: 27 N Mountain Ave Montclair NJ 07042 Office: St Barnabas Med Center Old Short Hills Rd Livingston NJ 07039

PHILLIPS, M.C., editor, author; b. Clifton, N.J., Apr. 25, 1903; d. Ozro Bertsal and Sylvia (Cox) P. B.A., Wellesley Coll., 1924; m. Frederick John Schlink, 1932. Editor, Consumers' Digest, Washington, N.J., 1938-41; editor Consumers' Research Mag., Washington, 1941—, Warren Hosp. Messenger, 1959-70; vice chmn. pub. relations com. Warren Hosp., Phillipsburg, N.J., 1966-76; chmn. editorial com. Warren County Health Survey, 1956. Mem. Am. Mktg. Assn., Am. Soc. Quality Control, Consumer Council (alt.), Am. Nat. Standards Inst., N.J. Hist. Soc., N.J. Fedn. Republican Women. Congregationalist. Author: Skin Deep, 1934; More Than Skin Deep, 1948; (with F.J. Schlink) Discovering Consumers, 1934, Meat Three Times a Day, 1946; Don't You Believe It, 1966; contbr. articles to mags. Home: RD 4 Box 209 Washington NJ 07882 Office: Bowerstown Rd Washington NJ 07882

PHILLIPS, MARCELLA LINDEMAN (MRS. JAMES F. PHILLIPS), physicist; b. Cumberland, Iowa, Jan. 15, 1901; d. Frank and Marie (Marley) Lindeman; grad. Highland Park Coll., 1917; B.A., State U. Iowa, 1921, M.S., 1922; m. James F. Phillips, June 27, 1927; children—Laura Marley, Frederica Lindeman Phillips Weil. Asst. physicist State U. Iowa, 1919-22; instr. Hunter Coll., N.Y.C., 1924-25; physicist Gen. Electric Co., Nela Park Lab., Cleve., 1925-27, Thomas and Hochwait Lab., Dayton, Ohio, 1930-31; prof. physics Adamson U., Manila, 1937-39; physicist Carnegie Inst., 1940-42, Nat. Bur. Standards, Washington, 1942-51, Mass. Inst. Tech., 1951-53, cons. physicist, 1953—, also cons. including Am. Car & Foundry Industries, Electro-Physics Lab., Columbia, Md., ITT, Comité Consultativ Internat.-Radio, Union Radio Sci. Internat., 1953—. Mem. Am. Phys. Soc., Am. Geophys. Union, Washington Philos. Soc., Acoustical Soc. Am., Washington Acad. Sci., IEEE (chmn. wave propagation com. 1956-62), Sigma Xi. Contrb. articles to profl. publs. Address: 2510 Virginia Ave NW Washington DC 20037

PHILLIPS, MARY-ANN MONAHAN, counselor, educator; b. N.Y.C., Dec. 29, 1951; d. Francis Joseph and Maria Dolores (Broderick) Monahan; B.A., Fordham U., 1973; M.S., Kans. State U., 1975; m. Richard Lyle Phillips, Dec. 8, 1974. Apprentice tchr. Pub. Sch. 208, N.Y.C., 1972-73; tchr. St. Thomas Sch., Cornwall-on-Hudson, N.Y., 1973-74, Parsippany (N.J.) Adult Sch., 1974; developmental specialist, Homeward bound program coordinator Big Lakes Devel. Center, Manhattan, Kans., 1975-76; ednl. counselor Army Edn. Center, Friedberg, Germany, 1977—; pvt. music tchr., 1974—. Vol. probation officer, Manhattan, 1975-76. Homebound Program grantee, 1976-77. Mem. Assn. Humanistic Psychology, Am. Personnel and Guidance Assn., Phi Delta Kappa. Roman Catholic. Home: 5 Frankenstrasse Bad Hauheim Frankenstrasse Bade Neuheim Federal Republic of Germany also 4 Maplewood Dr Parsippany NJ 07054 Office: Army Edn Center Ray Barracks APO New York City NY 09074

PHILLIPS, MICHAEL, bus. exec.; b. N.Y.C., May 31, 1936; s. Harry and Anne (Kramer) Phillips; B.Mech. Engring., Cooper Union Sch. Engring., 1957; M.S., Mass. Inst. Tech., 1959; m. Carol Susan Zimmerman, May 31, 1958. Group leader Cutler-Hammer, Melville, N.Y., 1959-62; econ. engr. Am. Can Co., N.Y.C., 1962-63; mgmt. cons. Dunlap & Assos., N.Y.C., 1963-64; mgmt. scientist Am.-Standard, Inc., N.Y.C., 1964-67; asst. v.p. First Nat. City Bank, N.Y.C., 1967-71; asst. v.p. Security Nat. Bank, Melville, N.Y., 1971-74, v.p., 1974-75; dir. planning and mgmt. sci. Am. Express Inc., N.Y.C., 1975—. Mem. Inst. Mgmt. Sci., Ops. Research Soc. Am. Club: Mass. Inst. Tech. Bankers. Home: North Shore Towers 271-29D Grand Central Pkwy Floral Park NY 11005 Office: 125 Broad St New York City NY 10004

PHILLIPS, PRISCILLA MOULTON, educator; b. Lewiston, Maine, Nov. 6, 1918; d. Clement Richmond and Myrtle (Marston) Moulton; B.S., Boston U., 1947, M.S., 1948, certificate of advanced grad. study, 1962, Ed.D., 1965; m. Warren Davis Phillips, June 20, 1964. Tchr. bus. Edward Little High Sch., Auburn, Maine, 1942-47; prof. bus. edn. Bryant Coll. Bus. Adminstrn., Smithfield, R.I., 1948—, chmn. bus. edn. dept., dir. student teaching, 1968—. Mem. vestry St. Stephens Ch., Providence, 1976—, pres. Epis. Ch. Women, 1978—; mem. corp. St. Elizabeth Home, Providence, St. Mary's Home for Children, North Providence, R.I., 1978—; pres. Travelers Aid Soc. R.I., 1975-78; trustee Nashotah House, Episcopal Sem., Nashotah, Wis., 1974—. Mem. New Eng. Bus. Educators Assn. (pres. 1977-78), Eastern (state membership chmn.), R.I. (Outstanding Bus. Educator of Year award 1975) bus. edn. assns., Eastern States Assn. for Tchr. Edn. (pres. 1966-67), Colonial Dames R.I., Pi Lambda Theta, Delta Pi Epsilon. Republican. Clubs: Pottery and Porcelain (pres. Providence 1977—), Providence Art, Providence Garden; Handicraft; Agawam Hunt. Contbg. editor, Bus. Edn. World, 1962-64, 1969-74. Home: 72 Prospect St Providence RI 02906 Office: Bryant Coll Smithfield RI 02917

PHILLIPS, SAMUEL JOSEPH, mfg. co. exec.; b. North Vandergrift, Pa., Sept. 17, 1931; s. Samuel and Margaret (Solomon) P.; B.S., U. Md., 1953; M.B.A., Xavier U., 1960; m. Matina Fidanis, Jan. 28, 1953; children—Diana M., Samuel T., Candice A., Tracy L., Daniel J. With Procter & Gamble Co., Cin., 1956-67, mgr. cost accounting dept., food products div., 1964-65, controller, chief financial officer Folger Coffee Co. div., Kansas City, Mo., 1965-67; controller film div. Polaroid Corp., Waltham, Mass., 1967-69; group controller, Cambridge, Mass., 1969-70; v.p. operations Healthcare Corp., Boston, 1970; pres. advance surfaces div. and v.p. finance Parkwood Laminates, Lowell, Mass., 1971-72, pres., 1972-74, also dir.; now pres., chmn. Acton Corp. (Mass.); dir. Phillips Corp., College Park, Md. Active United Fund, Cin. Trustee Cin. Summer Opera, 1964-65, Phillips Found., Annapolis. Served to lst lt. Arty., AUS, 1953-56. Recipient Kansas City Boy Scout award for community service, 1966. Mem. Fin. Exec. Inst. Office: 411 Massachusetts Ave Acton MA 01720

PHILLIPS, THOMAS L., elec. mfg. co. exec.; b. May 2, 1924; B.S., Va. Poly. Inst., 1947, M.S., 1948; hon. doctorates Stonehill Coll., Northeastern U., Lowell Technol. Inst., Gordon Coll., Boston Coll. With Raytheon Co., Lexington, Mass., 1948—, exec. v.p., 1961-64, pres., chief operating officer, 1964-75, chief exec. officer, 1968—, chmn. bd., 1975—; dir. Nat. Shawmut Bank, Boston, John Hancock Life Ins. Co., State St. Investment Trust. Mem. industry adv. council office sec. def. Trustee Gordon Coll., Northeastern U., Joslin Diabetes Found. Recipient Meritorious Punb. Service award for work in Sparrow III missile system, U.S. Navy. Mem. Nat. Acad. Engring., Com. Econ. Devel., Pilgrims of U.S. Clubs: Algonquin, Comml. (Boston); Weston Golf. Home: 60 Black Oak Rd Weston MA 02193 Office: Raytheon Co Lexington MA 02173

PHILLIPS, WALTER MILLS, III, clin. psychologist; b. N.Y.C., Sept. 29, 1947; s. Walter Mills and Grace Mary (Mullen) P.; B.S., Fordham U., 1970; M.A., U. S.D., 1973, Ph.D., 1975; m. Anne Marie Boyle, July 3, 1971. Adolescent resident counselor Hawthorne (N.Y.) Cedar Knolls Sch., 1969-71; NIMH tng. fellow, 1971-75; clin. psychology intern Inst. of Living, Hartford, Conn., 1974-75, clin. staff psychologist, 1975—; pvt. practice psychotherapy, Hartford, 1976—. Licensed clin. psychologist, Conn. Mem. Am., Conn. (hosp. liaison com.). psychol. assns., Assn. for Humanistic Psychology, AAAS, Sigma Xi. Democrat. Contbr. articles to profl. jours. Home: 82 Cider Brook Rd Avon CT 06001 Office: 400 Washington St Hartford CT 06106

PHILLIPS, WARREN HENRY, newspaperman; b. June 28, 1926; s. Abraham and Juliette (Rosenberg) P.; A.B., Queens Coll., 1947; J.D., U. Portland, 1973; m. Barbara Anne Thomas, June 16, 1951; children—Lisa, Leslie, Nina. Copyreader Wall Street Jour., 1947-48, fgn. corr., Germany, 1949-50, chief London Bur., 1950-51, fgn. editor, 1952-53, news editor, 1953-54, mng. editor Midwest edit., 1954-57, mng. editor Wall Street Jour., 1957-65; exec. editor Dow Jones & Co. Publs. Wall St. Jour., 1965-70, v.p., gen. mgr. 1970-72, exec. v.p., 1972, pres., dir., 1972—, chmn., 1978—, also editorial dir., 1971—; dir. Richard D. Irwin Co.; copyreader The Stars & Stripes European edit., 1949. Trustee Bklyn. Inst. Arts and Scis., Freedom of Info. Found. Served with U.S. Army, 1943-45. Named 1 of 10 Outstanding Young Men Nation, U.S. Jr. C. of C., 1958. Mem. Am. Soc. Newspaper Editors (v.p., dir.), Am. Council on Edn. for Journalism (pres. 1971-73). Author: China: Behind the Mask, 1973. Office: 30 Broad St New York City NY 10004

PHILLIPS, WILLIAM EUGENE, advt. exec.; b. Chgo., Jan. 7, 1930; s. William E. and Alice P.; B.S., Cornell U., 1951; M.B.A., Northwestern Grad. Sch. Commerce, 1955; m. Elizabeth Earl, Aug. 13, 1971; children by previous marriage—Michael, Tom, Sarah. Brand mgr. Procter & Gamble, Cin., 1955-59; with Ogilvy & Mather, Inc., N.Y.C., 1959—, sr. exec. v.p., 1973-75, pres., 1975—, chmn., pres., 1978—; partner Snowbird Ski Area; dir. Gen. Housewares Corp. Mem. council Cornell U.; trustee Wells Coll.; bd. dirs. Police Athletic League. Served to lt. (j.g.) USNR, 1951-54; Korea. Home: Beekman Pl New York City NY 10022 Office: 2 E 48th St New York City NY 10017

PHILLIPS, WINFRED MARSHALL, educator; b. Richmond, Va., Oct. 7, 1940; s. Claude Marshall and Gladys Marion (Barden) P.; B.S. in Mech. Engring., Va. Poly. Inst., 1963; M. Aero. Engring., U. Va., 1966, D.Sc., 1968; m. Lynda Ann Bartlett, July 23, 1961; children—Stephen Marshall, Sean Mark. Mech. engr. U.S. Naval Weapons Lab., Dahlgren, Va., 1963; NSF trainee U. Va., 1965-67, research scientist, 1967-68; asst. prof. aerospace engring. Pa. State U., University Park, 1968-74, asso. prof., 1974-78, prof., 1978—, dir. engring. studies artificial heart and bypass. Bd. dirs. Central Pa. chpt. Am. Heart Assn. Recipient Dow award as outstanding young faculty mem. Pa. State U., 1971; Career Devel. award for hemodynamics NIH, 1975-80. Asso. fellow Am. Inst. Aero. and Astronautics; mem. Am. Soc. Engring. Edn., Am. Phys. Soc., AAAS, ASME, Applied Mechanics Revs., Am. Soc. Artificial Internal Organs, Biomed. Engring. Soc. Contbr. articles to publs. in field. Home: 924 W Fairmount Ave State College PA 16801 Office: 233 Hammond Bldg University Park PA 16802

PHILP, FRANCIS HIGGINSON, banker; b. N.Y.C., Aug. 21, 1930; s. Leonard Jerome and Louise Genevieve (Fellows) P.; A.B. cum laude, Princeton, 1952; postgrad. Harvard Law Sch., 1952-54, 56-58. Asso. law firm Dunnington, Bartholow & Miller, 1958-59, Dominick & Dominick, 1960-63 (both N.Y.C.); asst. treas. Empire Trust Co. (merged into Bank N.Y. 1967), N.Y.C., 1963-66, asst. v.p., 1968-72; v.p. Fiduciary Trust Co. N.Y., N.Y.C., 1972—. Trustee N.Y. Infirmary, Fund for Blind, Big Bros. N.Y., Clarion Music Soc., Council Arts Westchester, Clear Pool Camp, Carmel, N.Y., Princeton Library, N.Y.C. Mem. N.Y. Soc. Security Analysts, SAR, SR, Soc. Colonial Wars. Republican. Episcopalian. Clubs: Union, Brook, Down Town Assn. (N.Y.C.); Larchmont (N.Y.) Yacht. Home: 25 Rocky Rd Larchmont NY 10538 Office: Fiduciary Trust Co New York 94th Floor 2 World Trade Center New York City NY 10048

PHILP, RICHARD NILSON, author, editor; b. Plainfield, N.J., July 7, 1943; s. Lester Perry and Gladys Emma Linea (Nilson) P.; B.A. in English and Theatre cum laude, U. N.C., Chapel Hill, 1965; M.F.A. in Theater Lit. and Playwriting, Yale U., 1968. Author 8 plays, produced 1963-72; author: To Move, To Learn, 1977; Danseur: The Male in Ballet, 1977; also numerous articles; mng. editor Dance mag., 1970—; asso. editor After Dark, 1970-74; lectr. in field, appearances on radio and TV. Recipient spl. citation Soc. Illustrators, 1974. Mem. Citizens to Preserve Hudson Valley, Greene County Hist. Soc., Dance Critics Assn., Am. Rose Soc. Democrat. Episcopalian. Home: 551 Pacific St Brooklyn NY 11217 also RD 3 Box 46 Route 385 Catskill NY 12414 Office: DANAD Publns Suite 1455 10 Columbus Circle New York City NY 10019

PHINNEY, EDWARD E., artist; b. Boston, Mar. 3, 1934; s. Arnold and Beatrice (Cheney) P.; B.F.A., Boston U., 1956, M.F.A., 1958; m. Joyce Rodgers, Jan. 29, 1957; children—Edward E., Michelle René, Christopher David. One man shows: Met. Mus. Art, N.Y.C., 1965, 69, 75, 77, Corcoran Gallery Art, Washington, 1972, 75, 76, 78; group shows include: Addison Gallery Am. Art, Andover, Mass., 1975, Fogg Art Gallery, Cambridge, Mass., 1975; represented in permanent and pvt. collections; lectr. numerous colls. and univs. Active fund raising drives Am. Cancer Soc., Am. Heart Assn., Cystic Fibrosis Found. Served with U.S. Army 1958-60. Recipient Distinguished Alumnus award Boston U., 1973. Mem. NAD, Am. Fedn. Arts. Democrat. Methodist. Address: 63 Myrtle St Boston MA 02114

PHINNEY, WILLIAM FLAGG, ednl. adminstr.; b. Boston, May 5, 1928; s. Arthur Osgood and Lucile (Flagg) P.; A.B., Harvard, 1950; m. Perry Wynn Flynt, June 16, 1954; children—Robert Flynt, Lucile Flagg, Nathaniel Snow. Tchr., Dexter Sch., Brookline, Mass., 1954-57, asst. headmaster, 1957-64, headmaster, 1964—; pres. Beach Pub. Co., Southfield, Mich., Gosnold Arms, Inc. Chmn. ind. schs. sect. Mass. Bay United Fund, 1968-71. Trustee Dexter Sch., Faulkner Hosp.; corporator Winsor Sch., Camp O-At-Ka Inc. Served with AUS, 1951-54. Mem. Mass. Assn. Non-Profit Schs. and Colls. (exec. com. 1967—), Nat. Assn. Ind. Schs. (elementary schs. com. 1969-76). Address: 20 Newton St Brookline MA 02146

PHOCAS, GEORGE JOHN, lawyer, bus. exec.; b. N.Y.C., Dec. 1, 1927; A.B., U. Chgo., 1950, J.D., 1953; student U. Paris, France, U. Madrid, Spain; m. Katrin Gorny, Feb. 26, 1966; 1 son, Alexander. Admitted to N.Y. State bar, 1955, U.S. Supreme Ct. bar, 1962; asso. firm Sullivan & Cromwell, N.Y.C., 1953-56; counsel to Creole Petroleum Corp., subsidiary Standard Oil Co. N.J., Caracas, Venezuela, 1956-60, internat. negotiator Standard Oil Co. N.J., N.Y.C., 1960-63; sr. partner Casey, Lane & Mittendorf, London, Eng., 1963—, of counsel, 1973—; exec. v.p. Occidental Petroleum, 1973-75; advisor to U.S. delegation UN ECAFE Teheran, 1963. Served as capt. AUS, 1945-47. Mem. Law Soc. London, Brit. Inst. Comparative Law, Am. Soc. Internat. Law, Assn. Bar City N.Y., Am. Bar Assn., Nat. Aero Assn., Psi Upsilon. Home: 5020 Goodridge Ave Riverdale NY 10471 also 28 Aubrey Walk London W 8 England

PHOON, WAI WOR, physician; b. Hong Kong, Apr. 23, 1934; s. Seck Quai and Koon Sheung (Ng)P.; came to U.S., 1968, naturalized, 1973; M.B.B.S., U. Hong Kong, 1958; Diploma in Phys. Medicine, Royal Coll. Physicans, London, 1964; m. Alice Suk-Men Tang, Oct. 20, 1962; children—Colin, Kelvin. Intern, Grantham Hosp., Tsan-Yuk Hosp. (both Hong Kong), 1959; resident in orthopedics Hong Kong Govt. Hosp., 1960-62, in phys. medicine N.Y. U., N.Y.C., 1962-63, in phys. medicine and rehumatology Central Middlesex Hosp., London, 1963-64; med. dir. Med. Rehab. Center, Hong Kong, 1966-68; asst. prof. phys. medicine Case Western Res. U., Cleve., 1968-69, Temple U., Phila., 1969-70; asso. prof. phys. medicine Hahnemann Med. Coll., Phila., 1970-71; practice medicine specializing in phys. medicine and rehab., Wilmington, Del., 1971—; mem. staffs Wilmington Med. Center, St. Francis Hosp., A.I. DuPont Inst. (all Wilmington), Riddle Meml. Hosp., Media, Pa. Bd. dirs. Del. chpt. Arthritis Found. Am. President Lines fellow, 1962. Fellow Am. Acad. Phys. Medicine and Rehab.; mem. AMA, Am. Rheumatology Assn., Am. Congress Rehab. Medicine, Brit. Med. Assn., Brit. Assn. for Rehab. and Rheumatology, New Castle County Med. Soc. Republican. Home: 312 Earle's Ln Newtown Square PA 19073 Office: 3506 Kennett Pike Wilmington DE 19807

PIACITELLI, JOHN JOSEPH, pediatrician; b. Providence, Sept. 1, 1936; s. Joseph Albert and Erzilia M. P.; B.S., U. R.I., 1958; M.A., State U. N.Y., Buffalo, 1963; M.D., Creighton U., 1964; m. Carol Ann Keirn, Aug. 19, 1961; 1 son, James Hewitt. Intern, Buffalo Gen. Hosp., 1964-65; resident in pediatrics Buffalo Children's Hosp., 1965-67; practice medicine specializing in pediatrics, N. Babylon, N.Y., 1969—; mem. staff Syosset Hosp., Nassau County Med. Center; asst. clin. instr. pediatrics State U. N.Y., Buffalo, 1965-67; instr. clin. pediatrics Nassau County Med. Center, State U. N.Y., Stony Brook. Served to maj. U.S. Army, 1967-69. Diplomate Am. Bd. Pediatrics, Fellow Am. Acad. Pediatrics, Internat. Coll. Pediatrics, Suffolk Acad. Medicine; Mem. AMA, Med. Soc. State N.Y., Suffolk County Med. Soc. Contbr. articles on molecular biology to sci. jours. Home: 25 Beech Rd Islip NY 11751 Office: 300 Bay Shore Rd North Babylon NY 11703

PIAKER, PHILIP MARTIN, accountant, educator; b. N.Y.C., Oct. 26, 1921; s. Jacob and Sarah (Schloss) P.; B.A., City Coll. N.Y., 1943, M.B.A., 1949; m. Pauline Strum, Sept. 22, 1946; children—Susan, Alan, Matthew. Lectr. City Coll. N.Y., N.Y.C., 1949-52; asst. profl. accountancy State U. N.Y. Binghamton, 1952-57, asso. prof., 1957-62, prof., 1962—, chmn. dept. accounting, 1970-76; cons. in field; adv. dir. Endicott Bank N.Y.; mem. N.Y. State Bd. Pub. Accountancy, 1973—. Bd. dirs. Broome chpt. Am. Cancer Soc., 1974—; trustee Temple Israel, Binghamton, N.Y., 1978-79. State U. N.Y. SWANA fellow Jerusalem, 1966, Am. Prof. Peace in Middle East fellow Jerusalem, summer 1974; recipient Chancellors award teaching excellence, 1975. Mem. N.Y. State Soc. C.P.A.'s (pres. Binghamton chpt. 1963-65), Am. Inst. C.P.A.'s. Am. Accounting Assn., Accounting Research Assn., Nat. Assn. Accountants. Editorial bd. Binghamton Reporter, 1975—. Home: 301 Manchester Rd Binghamton NY 13903

PIAN, CHARLES HSUEH-CHIEN, research chemist; b. Tientsin, China, June 21, 1921; s. Chao-hsin and Chih-jian (Yen) P.; came to U.S., 1958, naturalized, 1964; B.S. in Chemistry, Fu Jen U., China, 1944; M.S., Northeastern U., 1964; Ph.D., State U. N.Y., 1969; m. Juliette Fan, Mar. 31, 1945; children—Carlson, Josie (Mrs. Douglas Breeden), May. Asst. engr. Ta-shin Paper & Pulp Factory, Peking, China, 1945-46; chief engr., plant dir. Shinei Pharm. Factory, Taiwan, 1946-51; specialist Bd. of Trustees for Rehab. Affairs, Taiwan, 1951-52; specialist Joint Comm. for Rural Reconstrn., Taiwan, 1952-54; group leader Joint Com. for Med. Supplies, Taiwan, 1954-56; instr. Nuclear Sci. Inst., Tsing Hua U., Taiwan, 1956-58; chemist Lexington Research Labs., Itek Corp., Lexington, Mass., 1959-62, sr. chemist, 1964-65, project leader, 1968-70; sr. chemist, project leader Nashua Corp. (N.H.), 1970—. Recipient Spl. award Gen. Electric Co., 1966. Mem. Am. Chem. Soc., Soc. Photog. Sci. and Engring., Rho Psi. Patentee in field. Home: 64 Fifer Ln Lexington MA 02173 Office: 44 Franklin St Nashua NH 03060

PIATIGORSKY, JORAM PAUL, biologist; b. Elizabethtown, N.Y., Feb. 4, 1940; s. Gregor and Jacqueline Rebecca (de Rothschild) P.; B.A., Harvard, 1962; Ph.D., Cal. Inst. Tech., 1967; m. Lona Anne Shepley, Aug. 24, 1969; children—Auran Paul, Anton Jacob. Head sect. cellular differentiation Lab. Molecular Genetics, Nat. Inst. Child Health and Human Devel., Bethesda, Md., 1969-72, research biologist, 1973—. Served with USPHS, 1967-69. Mem. AAAS, Am. Soc. Cell Biology, Am. Soc. Zoologists, Internat. Soc. Developmental Biologists, Soc. for Developmental Biology, N.Y. Acad. Scis., Sigma Xi. Contbr. articles to profl. jours. Home: 8435 Persimmon Tree Rd Bethesda MD 20034 Office: NIH Bldg 6 Bethesda MD 20014

PIATT, JACK BOYD, mfg. co. exec.; b. Washington, Pa., Jan. 8, 1928; s. Harold Boyd and Marie Violet (Amos) P.; grad. high sch.; m. Kathleen M. Shattuck, May 3, 1975; children—Jack Boyd II, Rodney L., Rebecca S., Regina M., Lucas Boyd, Marcus Miller. Owner Piatt Heating Co., Washington, Pa., 1948-52; gen. mgr. Piatt Machine Co., Washington, Pa., 1952-58; founder, chmn. Millcraft Industries, Inc., also 11 subsidiaries, Washington, Pa., 1958—, chmn., chief exec. officer, 1971—; chmn. bd. dirs. Jetcraft, Inc., Washington, 1968—; gen. partner Millcraft Center Ltd. Partnership, 1973—, Landmark Ltd. Partnership, 1975—. Co-chmn. Am. Cancer Crusade, Washington County, 1967, Pa. Radio Free Europe Dr., 1970; chmn. Am. Cancer Soc., 1968; div. chmn. United Fund, 1964-65. Bd. dirs. Pa. Assn. for Blind, 1969; bd. fellows U. Tampa (Fla.), 1970-75; trustee Robert Morris Coll., Pitts. Served with AUS, 1945-48. Mem. Young Pres.'s Orgn., Eastern States Blast Furnace and Coke Oven Assn., Assn. Iron and Steel Engrs., Smaller Mfrs. Council., Washington County C. of C. Clubs: Duquesne, Pittsburgh Athletic Assn., Pittsburgh Press, St. Clair Country (Pitts.); Coral Ridge Country (Ft. Lauderdale, Fla.); Bay Hill (Orlando Fla.). Home: PO Box 396 Meadow Lands PA 15347 Office: Millcraft Center 90 W Chestnut St Washington PA 15301

PIATT, RICHARD OWEN, ins. agt.; b. Easton, Pa., Apr. 18, 1932; s. Ira Adam and Alta May (Stackhouse) P.; student pub. schs., Wilson Borough, Easton, Pa.; m. Mary Edith Keiper, Oct. 6, 1951; children—Cynthia, Cylvia, Diana, Lori, Beth. Store mgr. George V. Seiple & Son, Easton, Pa., 1950-60; dist. agt. Prudential Ins. Co. Am., Easton, 1960—. Dist. chmn. Republican Party, 1969-74; asst. sec.-treas. Bushkill Lower Lehigh Joint Sewer Authority, 1972-76, sec., 1976—. Mem. Ins. Workers Internat. Union (past pres. local 151, sec.-treas. 1974—), Palmer Twp., Northampton County hist. socs., Wyckoff House and Assn., Geneal. Socs. Pa., N.J. Lutheran. Clubs: Blue Ridge Cherry Valley Rod and Gun. Home: 211 Old Orchard Dr Easton PA 18042 Office: 2100 Ferry St Easton PA 18042

PICARD, ALYRE JOSEPH, dermatologist; b. Drummond, N.B., Can. Oct. 7, 1942; s. Joseph Edmond and Arthimise (LaForst) P.; B.A., U. Moncton, 1962; M.D., U. Laval, 1967; m. Lucille Bedard, June 29, 1968; children—Lucie, Judith, Anne, Pierre, Agathe. Intern, Jeffrey Hale's Hosp., Que., 1967-68; resident in dermatology Hotel-Dieu de Quebec, 1968-72; practice medicine specializing in dermatology, Hotel-Dieu Alma, Alma P.Q., 1972—. Fellow Royal Coll. Physicians (Can.); mem. Can. Dermatological Assn., Am. Acad. Dermatology, Quebec Profl. Corp. Physicans, Assn. de Medicine de Langue Francaise, Royal Coll. Physicians & Surgeons Can., Canadian Dermatologic Found., Canadian Med. Assn. Roman Catholic. Home: 322 Pente Douce Alma PQ Canada Office: 535 Collard Alma PQ Canada

PICARD, RAYMOND JEAN, chem. co. exec.; b. Paris, Apr. 2, 1914; s. Jean Louis and Marcelle (Meunier) P.; came to U.S., 1945, naturalized, 1954; B.S., Ecole Superieure de Commerce de Paris, 1932; m. Lucette Annereau, June 10, 1972; children—Patrick, Bertrand. Founder, chmn., chief exec. officer Rhone-Poulenc Inc., N.Y.C., 1948—; pres. Merieux Inst., Inc., Poulenc Ltd., May and Baker (Can.) Ltd.; dir. Hosp. Med. Corp., Polychrome Corp., European Am. Bank, United Fire and Gen Ins., Urbaine Assurance Co., Neville Synthese Organics, Inc. Bd. dirs. Nat. Energy Found., France-Am. Found.; trustee French Inst., Maison Francaise of N.Y. U.; pres. Found. Advancement Internat. Research in Microbiology. Served with French Air Force, 1935-36. Decorated Legion of Honor (France). Mem. French-Am. C. of C., Am. Soc. French Legion of Honor (v.p.). Club: Links. Home: 130 East End Ave New York City NY 10028 Office: 600 Madison Ave New York City NY 10022

PICCOLI, LEONARD RALPH, hosp. adminstr.; b. Bronx, N.Y., June 21, 1933; s. Leonard John and Angela Marie (Altieri) P.; B.S., Fordham U. Coll. Pharmacy, 1955; M.S., Columbia U., 1957; m. Ruth Dorothy Damon, July 2, 1966; children—Anthony, Therese, Peter, Robert, James, Stephen. Adminstrv. asst. Montefiore Hosp., N.Y.C., 1958-59; asst. adminstr. Misericordia Hosp., Bronx, 1959-65; adminstr. Fordham Hosp., Bronx, 1965-67; exec. dir. Bird S. Coler Meml. Hosp. and Home, Roosevelt Island, N.Y., 1967-72; exec. dir. Bronx Municipal Hosp. Center, 1972—; mem. faculty Columbia U. Sch. Pub. Health, N.Y. U., Baruch Coll., Albert Einstein Coll. Medicine. Chmn. Now Yonkers Unites, 1971-72. Served with U.S. Army, 1955-63. Recipient Service to Youth award Bronx YMCA, 1974; Martin Luther King, Jr. Special Service award JFK Library for Minorities, 1975. Diplomate Am. Bd. Pharmacy. Mem. Am. Coll. Hosp. Adminstrs., Am. Pub. Health Assn., Am. Hosp. Assn. Home: 120 DeHaven Dr Yonkers NY 10703 Office: Bronx Municipal Hosp Center Pelham Pkwy S and Eastchester Rd Bronx NY 10461

PICKEN, HARRY BELFRAGE, aero. engr.; b. Grimsby, Ont., Can., Jan. 8, 1916; s. John Belfrage and Leila Lucinda (Jarvis) P.; B.Sc., U. Mich., 1940; m. Florence Elizabeth Runciman, July 7, 1945; children—Roger Belfrage, Donald William, Wendy Elizabeth, Chief engr. White Can. Aircraft Ltd., Hamilton, Ont., 1940-45, Weston Aircraft Ltd., Oshawa, Ont., 1946, Field Aviation Ltd., Oshawa, 1947-51; pres., chief engr. Genaire Ltd., Toronto and St. Catharines, Ont., 1951—; tech. dir. Avionics Ltd., Niagara-on-Lake, Ont., 1954-72; v.p. Ardrox Ltd., Niagara-on-Lake, 1968-75, Amasar, St. Catharine's, 1961—; design approval rep. Aeronautical, Can. Dept. Transport, 1948—. Chmn. Niagara (Ont.) Planning Bd., 1963-65; vice-chmn. bd. govs. Niagara Coll. Applied Arts and Tech., 1975—; vice-chmn. bd. dirs. Niagara Found., 1975—. Recipient Citizen of Yr. award for outstanding pub. service Town of Niagara, 1968. Registered profl. engr., Ont. Fellow Can. Aeros. and Space Inst. (asso.); mem. Am. Inst. Aeros. and Astronautics, Am. Helicopter Soc., Can. Soc. Nondestructive Testing, Am. Fedn. Musicians, Broadcast Music Inst. Can., Niagara Town and Twp. C. of C. (pres. 1961-62). Liberal Party. Presbyterian. Editor: Early Architecture Town and Township of Niagara, 1968; recorded album From Studio 1, 1971. Home: 26 Front St Niagara on the Lake ON L0S 1J0 Canada Office: Niagara Dist Airport PO Box 84 Saint Catharines ON L2R 6R4 Canada

PICKERING, TED WARRINGTON, photographer, editor; b. Providence, Nov. 12, 1922; grad. high sch.; m. Jennie Biello, Sept. 28, 1946; children—Thomas, Allan, Kenneth. Foundry insp. B-I-F unit Gen. Signal Corp., West Warwick, R.I., 1941-60, photographer, editor Parts Lists, 1960—; owner photography studio, Warwick, 1946—. Served in USAAF, 1943-46. Mem. profl. photographers assns. R.I. (award 1972), New Eng., Am. Roman Catholic. Home: 12 Middlefield Dr Warwick RI 02889 Office: 455 W Shore Rd Warwick RI 02889

PICKERT, ALTON EADES, hosp. adminstr.; b. Middleville, N.Y., July 9, 1922; s. Alton Custer and Rebecca Amelia (Peters) P.; m. Anne M. Corrigan, Apr. 8, 1961; 1 son, Richard Leon. Staff nurse Bklyn. State Hosp., 1943-44, head nurse, 1944-47; supr., clin. instr. psychiat. nursing Grasslands Hosp., Valhalla, N.Y., 1947-51, supr. nursing adminstrn., 1951-52; adminstrv. resident Greenwich Hosp. Assn. (Conn.), 1953-54; night adminstr. Jackson Meml. Hosp., Miami, Fla., 1954-56; hosp. adminstr. Dade County Civil Def. Council, Miami, 1956; asst. dir. U. Md. Hosp., Balt., 1956-67; dir. Baltimore County Gen. Hosp., Randallstown, Md., 1967-70, exec. v.p., 1970—; dir. Md. Blue Cross, Baltimore County Gen. Hosp. Found.; mem. exec. com. Md. Blue Cross; preceptor for grad. programs in health care adminstrn. George Washington U.; mem. adv. coms. Community Coll. Balt.; mem. vestry St. Barnabas Ch., Sykesville, Md. Fellow Am. Coll. Hosp. Adminstrs. (gov. dist. 2), Royal Soc. Health (life); mem. Hosp. Execs. Assn. (chmn.), Am. Hosp. Assn., Am. Heart Assn. (chmn. Md. affiliate), Hosp. Mgmt. Systems Soc., Am. Mgmt. Assn., Baltimore County C. of C. Episcopalian. Clubs: Advertising (Balt.); Masons (Newport, N.Y.); Wilson Point Men's (Balt.). Home: 5411 Emerald Dr Sykesville MD 21784 Office: 5401 Old Court Rd Randallstown MD 21133

PICKETT, DOYLE C., book wholesaling co. exec.; b. Greencastle, Ind., July 15, 1930; s. Joseph V. and Lora (Phillips) P.; A.B., Wabash Coll., 1952; M.B.A., Ind. U., 1953; m. Dorothy McGinnis; children—Brian Doyle, Marsha Ann. Grad. asst. dept. mgmt. Ind. U. Sch. of Bus., 1952-53; exec. trainee L.S. Ayres & Co., Indpls., 1953-56, employment interviewer, 1956-58, staff asst. to gen. mdse. mgr., 1958-60, office mgr., 1960-62, asst. store mgr., Lafayette, Ind., 1962-64; mgmt. analyst Cummins Engine Co., Inc., Columbus, Ind., 1964-67; adminstrv. asst. to pres. Baker & Taylor Co. div. W.R. Grace & Co., Momence, Ill., 1967-71, mgr. spl. projects, 1971-72, mgr. approval program, Somerville, N.J., 1972-74, mgr. acad. sales N.Am., N.Y.C., 1974-76, dir. program services, Somerville, 1976—. Class agt. Wabash Coll. Served with AUS, 1953-55. Recipient God and Country award Boy Scouts Am. Mem. Indpls. Zool. Soc. (charter), Nat. Trust for Historic Preservation, Am. Forestry Assn., ALA, Tex. Library Assn., Indiana Soc. N.Y., Greater Wabash Found., Nat. Assn. Wabash Men, Ind. U. Alumni Assn., Delta Tau Delta, Alpha Phi Omega, Pi

Delta Epsilon, Blue Key. Mem. Christian Ch. Mason, Kiwanian (charter pres. 1958-60). Co-author: Approval Plans and Academic Libraries, 1977. Home: 240 Great Hills Rd Bridgewater NJ 08807 Office: 6 Kirby Ave Somerville NJ 08876

PICKETT, LAWRENCE KIMBALL, med. adminstr., pediatric surgeon; b. Balt., Nov. 10, 1919; s. Herbert Elmer and Emily (Ames) P.; B.A., Yale U., 1941, M.D., 1944; m. Pauline Ferguson, Dec. 17, 1943; children—Lawrence Kimball, Nancy Pickett Thomas, Paul Stephen. Intern in surgery Children's Hosp., Boston, 1944-45, asst. resident, 1947-49, chief resident, 1949-50; intern in surgery Peter Bent Brigham Hosp., Boston, 1945-46, asst. resident, 1946-47; asso. surgeon Syracuse (N.Y.) Meml. Hosp. and Univ. Hosp., 1950-64; clin. asso. prof. surgery and pediatrics Yale U., 1964—, chief sect. pediatric surgery dept. surgery, 1964-73, asso. dean clin. affairs Sch. Medicine, 1973—; chief staff Yale-New Haven Hosp., 1973—, v.p. med. affairs, 1977—; cons. to community hosps.; chmn. Conn. Med. Exam. Bd. Served as capt. M.C., U.S. Army, 1951-53. Diplomate Am. Bd. Surgery. Fellow A.C.S., Am. Acad. Pediatrics (surg.); mem. AMA, New Haven County Med. Assn., Conn. Med. Soc., Brit. Assn. Pediatric Surgeons, Am. Pediatric Surg. Assn., Am. Surg. Assn., New Eng. Surg. Soc. Home: 205 Blake Rd Hamden CT 06517 Office: Yale-New Haven Hosp 789 Howard Ave New Haven CT 06504*

PICOWER, JEFFRY MARTIN, lawyer, accountant; b. N.Y.C., May 5, 1942; s. Abraham and Gertrude (Phillips) P.; B.S., Pa. State U., 1963; J.D., Bklyn. Law Sch., 1967; M.B.A., Columbia, 1966; LL.M., N.Y. U., 1968; m. Barbara Rubin, Nov. 17, 1968; 1 dau., Gabrielle. Accountant, tax mgr. Homes & Davis, N.Y.C., 1965-70; admitted to N.Y. State bar, 1967; tax mgr. Laventhol and Horwath, N.Y.C., 1970-72; pres. Jeffry M. Picower P.C., N.Y.C., 1972—; pres., dir. Decisions Inc.; lectr. Columbia, 1964—; dir. Capital Growth Co., Favorite Fund, Picson Mgmt. Co., J.F.M. Investment Co., DKD Inc. Mem. Am., N.Y. State bar assns., Am. Inst. C.P.A.'s, N.Y. State Soc. C.P.A.'s. Republican. Jewish religion Club: Atrium. Author: Tax Accounting Techniques to Save Taxes, 1970. Contbg. author, contbr. articles to profl. pubis. Home: 207 Gravel Hill Rd Kinnelon NJ 07405 Office: Jeffry M Picower PC 150 E 58th St New York City NY 10022

PIDGEON, JOHN ANDERSON, headmaster; b. Lawrence, Mass., Dec. 20, 1924; s. Alfred H. and Nora (Regan) P.; grad. Hebron Acad., 1943; B.A., Bowdoin Coll., 1949; D.Ed., Bethany Coll., 1973; m. Judith Shepard, Aug. 4, 1951; children—John Anderson, Regan Shepard, Kelly Charles. Instr. Latin, then adminstrv. asst. to headmaster Deerfield Acad., 1949-57; headmaster Kiskiminetas Springs Sch., Saltsburg, Pa., 1957—; dir. Indiana Savs. & Trust. Served as ensign USNR, 1943-46. Mem. Headmasters Assn., Delta Upsilon. Home: Kiskiminetas Springs Sch Saltsburg PA 15681

PIEHLER, GLENN RAYMOND, biologist; b. Elizabeth, N.J., Mar. 15, 1943; s. George Leonard and Ruth Elizabeth (Pries) P.; B.S. cum laude, Bloomfield Coll., 1965; M.S., Mich. State U., 1967; Ph.D., U. Mass., 1972; m. Karen Sue Foster, June 10, 1967; children—Geoffrey, Bruce. Teaching and lab. asst. Bloomfield Coll., 1964-65; research asst. Mich. State U., 1965-67, U. Mass., 1967-71; research asso. Normandeau Assos., Inc., Bedford, N.H., 1971-73, projects mgr., 1973-74; sr. scientist Ebasco Services Inc., N.Y.C., 1974-75; group leader, prin. scientist Envirosphere Co. div. Ebasco Services Inc., N.Y.C., 1975-77, supr. aquatic ecology Envirosphere Co. div., 1977—. Active Cub Scouts, Little League, 1977—. Mem. Am. Inst. Fishery Research Biologists, Am. Fisheries Soc. (certified fisheries scientist), Nat. Audubon Soc., Nat. Wildlife Fedn., Sigma Xi. Home: 101 Church St Fair Haven NJ 07701 Office: 19 Rector St New York City NY 10006

PIEL, GERARD, editor, publisher; b. Woodmere, L.I., N.Y., Mar. 1, 1915; s. William F.J. and Loretto (Scott) P.; grad. Phillips Acad., Andover, Mass., 1933; A.B. magna cum laude, Harvard U., 1937; D.Sc., Lawrence Coll., 1956, Colby Coll., 1960, U. B.C., Brandeis U., 1965; Litt.D., Rutgers U., 1961, Bates Coll., 1974; L.H.D., Columbia U., 1962, Williams Coll., 1966; LL.D., Tuskegee Inst., 1963, U. Bridgeport, 1964, Bklyn. Poly. Inst., 1965, Carnegie-Mellon U., 1968; m. Mary Tapp Bird, Feb. 4, 1938; children—Jonathan Bird. Samuel Bird (dec.); m. 2d, Eleanor Virden Jackson, June 24, 1955; dau., Eleanor Jackson. Sci. editor Life mag., 1938-44; asst. to pres. Henry J. Kaiser Co. (and asso. cos.), 1945-46; organizer (with Dennis Flanagan, Donald H. Miller, Jr.), Pres. Sci. Am., Inc., 1946—; pub. mag. Sci. Am., 1947—. Chmn., Commn. Delivery Personal Health Services City N.Y., 1967-68. Trustee Am. Mus. Nat. History, Radcliffe Coll., Phillips Acad., N.Y. Bot. Garden, N.Y. U., Henry J. Kaiser Family Found., Mayo Found., Found. for Child Devel.; bd. overseers Harvard U., 1966-68, 73—. Recipient George K. Polk award, 1961, Kalinga prize, 1962, Bradford Washburn award, 1966, Arches of Sci. award, 1969, Rosenberger medal U. Chgo., 1973. Fellow Am. Acad. Arts and Scis.; mem. Council Fgn. Relations, Am. Philos. Soc., Nat. Acad. Scis. Inst. Medicine, Phi Beta Kappa, Sigma Xi. Clubs: Harvard, Century, Coffee House (N.Y.C.); Cosmos (Washington); Somerset (Boston); Duquesne (Pitts.). Author: Science in the Cause of Man, 1961; The Acceleration of History, 1972. Home: 320 Central Park W New York City NY 10025 Office: 415 Madison Ave New York City NY 10017

PIEMONTE, ROBERT VICTOR, assn. exec.; b. N.Y.C., July 28, 1934; s. Rosario and Carmela (Santora) P.; B.S., L.I. U., 1967; M.A., Columbia U., 1968, M.Ed., 1970, Ed.D., 1976. Dir. dept. nursing services Am. Nurses Assn., N.Y.C., 1971-72; sr. mgmt. cons. N.Y.C. Health and Hosps. Corp., 1972-76; asso. prof. Tchrs. Coll., Columbia U., 1976-78; exec. dir. N.J. State Nurses Assn., Montclair, 1978—; adj. asso. prof. Columbia U. Served with Nurses Corps, U.S. Army Res., 1974—. Mem. Am. Nurses Assn., Am. Public Health Assn., Nat. League Nursing, Res. Officers Assn., Assn. Mil. Surgeons U.S., Nurses Coalition for Polit. Action, Phi Delta Kappa. Democrat. Roman Catholic. Contbr. articles to profl. jours. Home: 435 W 57th St New York NY 10019 Office: 60 S Fullerton Ave Montclair NJ 07042

PIER, JEROME ROLAND, railroad supply exec.; b. Mt. Jewett, Pa., June 25, 1926; s. Jerome Warner and Gladys LeJune (Eshbaugh) P.; B.S.M.E., Pa. State U., 1950; m. Betty Ann Simpson, Nov. 7, 1953; children—Bruce, Donald, Clifford, LeJune. Engr. WABCO, Wilmerding, Pa., 1950-64, mass transit engring. mgr., 1964-69, propulsion systems sales mgr., 1969-73; mgr. spl. projects Rohr Industries, Chula Vista, Calif., 1973, program mgr., turboliner div., 1974-76, engring. mgr. rail div., 1976-77; mgr. passenger/transit mktg. Westinghouse Air Brake, Wilmerding, 1977—; transp. cons. Sec., Sch. Bldg. Authority, Trafford, Pa., 1961-66. Served with U.S. Army, 1944-46. Mem. ASME, IEEE (land transp. com. 1973-76), R.R. Progress Inst. (steering com.), Am. Pub. Transit Assn. Republican. Presbyterian. Clubs: Pitts. Athletic Assn., Masons, Shriners. Contbr. articles to profl. jours.; patentee in pneumatic and elec. fields. Home: 259 Mt Vernon Ave Franklin Estates Export PA 15632 Office: Westinghouse Air Brake Div Wilmerding PA 15148

PIERCE, DONALD SHELTON, physician; b. Castine, Maine, May 21, 1930; s. Frederick Ernest and Jeannie (Emmet) P.; A.B. cum laude, Harvard U., 1953, M.D., 1957; m. Janet Ten Broeck, Dec. 29, 1956; children—Donald Shelton, Stanton Ten Broeck, Frederick Ernest, Jennifer Emmet. Intern, U. Hosp., Cleve., 1957-58, resident, 1958-62; research asso. Biomechanics Lab., U. Calif. at San Francisco, 1962-64; practice medicine, specializing in orthopedic surgery, San Francisco, 1962-64; instr. orthopedic surgery U. Calif. Med. Sch., San Francisco, 1962-64, Harvard Med. Sch., 1964-66; clin. and research asso. J.P. Kennedy Jr. Meml. Hosp., Brighton, Mass., 1964-66; clin. asso. in orthopedics Harvard Med. Sch., 1966—; chief dept. rehab. medicine Mass. Gen. Hosp., Boston, 1965-72, asso. orthopedic surgeon, 1969—; lectr. dept. mech. engring. Mass. Inst. Tech., 1970-72. Pres., Wellesley (Mass.) Friendly Aid Assn., 1965-67, dir., 1967-70; dir. Family Service Counseling Region West, Wellesley, 1965-67; exec. com., task force chmn., adv. bd. Mass. State Rehab. Planning Commn., 1966-68. Served with USAF, 1951-52. Fellow A.C.S., Am. Acad. Orthopedic Surgeons, Royal Soc. Health, Pan Am. Med. Assn., Société Internat. Chirurgerie, Ortopaedie et Traumatologie; mem. Orthopedic Research Soc., NRC (musculosbeletal com.). Co-author: Amputees and Their Prostheses, 1971; author: The Total Care of Spinal Cord Injuries, 1977; contbr. articles in field to profl. jours. Home: 170 Sargent Rd Brookline MA 02146 Office: 275 Charles St Boston MA 02146

PIERCE, ELIZABETH GAY (MRS. WILLIAM CURTIS PIERCE), civic worker; b. N.Y.C., Mar. 26, 1907; d. Martin and Julia (Stone) Gay; A.B., Barnard Coll., 1929; m. William Curtis Pierce, June 19, 1929; children—Martin Gay, Elizabeth Gay (Mrs. Joseph S. Stout, Jr.), Josiah. Vol. worker Boston City Hosp., 1929-30, Community Service Soc., N.Y.C., 1931-32; mem. dependent children's sect. Welfare Council, N.Y.C., 1939-40; chmn. house com. North Shore Holiday House, Huntington, L.I., 1944, pres., 1945; co-chmn. thrift shop com. Knickerbocker Hosp., N.Y.C., 1957-64; mem. exec. com. of women's com. Legal Air Soc., N.Y.C., 1958-59; mem. Women's Aux. Knickerbocker Hosp. (mem. exec. com. 1960-64). Mem. Soc. Colonial Dames in State N.Y. (bd. mgrs., 1962-67, corr. sec. N.Y. 1965-67, pres. 1967-70), Nat. Soc. Colonial Dames Am. (pres. 1972-76), Soc. for Preservation New Eng. Antiquities (Maine council), Nat. Grange. Episcopalian. Club: Colony. Home: 1088 Park Ave New York City NY 10028

PIERCE, ETHEL TAYLOR (MRS. EDWARD A. PIERCE), pharmacist; b. Grayling, Mich., July 27, 1910; d. Floyd L. and Elizabeth V. (Bunting) Taylor; B.S., Ferris State Coll., 1938, Ph.G., 1932, Sc.D., 1975; M.Pharmacy (hon.), Mass. Coll. Pharmacy, 1973; m. Edward A. Pierce, Apr. 29, 1939. Pharmacist, Central Drug Store, Grayling, 1934-35, L.F. Hamlin, Inc., Binghamton, N.Y., 1935-36, 1937-41, Nichols Meml. Hosp., Battle Creek, Mich., 1936-37, People's Drug Stores, Washington, 1945-46, Liggett Drug Co., Pittsfield, Mass., 1946-48; chemist Office Censorship, Cristobal, C.Z., 1941-44, Washington, 1944-45; chief pharmacist South Shore Hosp., South Weymouth, Mass., 1948-76; commr. Bd. Registration in Pharmacy, 1972-77. Mem. Abington exec. council Girl Scouts U.S.A., 1947-49; mem. Abington Bd. Health, 1954—, chmn., 1955-57, 72-76; mem. corp., hon. alumni mem. Mass. Coll. Pharmacy. Mem. Abington Republican Town Com., 1949-74. Recipient Distinguished Alumnus award Ferris State Coll., 1970. Mem. D.A.R. (mem. Am. Indian Com. chpt. 1950—; regent 1960-62, 63-65), Am. Pharm. Assn. (del. Pan Am. congresses 1951, 54, 57, 72, alt. del. 1960), Internat. Fedn. Pharmacy (del. 1962, 66, 68), Mass. Soc. Hosp. Pharmacists (pres. 1953; chmn. legis. com. 1957-67, mem. exec. com. 1958-67), Acad. Gen. Practice in Pharmacy, S. Shore Pharm. Assn. (v.p. 1966-67, pres. 1967-68, 69-70), Ferris State Coll. Alumni Assn. (dir. 1971—), Am. Soc. Hosp. Pharmacists, Mass. Pharm. Assn. (rec. sec. 1967-76, acting exec. sec. 1977-78, Pharmacist of Year award 1972), Nat., Mass. assns. sanitarians, Southeastern Mass. Assn. Bds. Health, Internat. Fedn. Pharmacy (asso.), New Eng. Historic Geneal. Soc. Boston, Royal Soc. Health, Am. Coll. Apothecaries, Conn. Soc. Genealogists. Clubs: Abington Women's; Order Eastern Star, Trinity Shrine, White Shrine Jerusalem (high priestess 1952-53, 1954-55, 68-69). Home: 19 Pearl St North Abington MA 02351

PIERCE, FRANCIS CASIMIR, cons. engr. co. exec.; b. Warren, R.I., May 19, 1924; s. Frank J. and Eva (Soltys) Pierce; student U. Conn., 1943-44; B.S., U. R.I., 1948; M.S., Harvard, 1950; postgrad. Northeastern U., 1951-52; m. Helen Lynette Steinouer, Apr. 24, 1954; children—Paul F., Kenneth J., Nancy L., Karen H., Charles E. Instr. civil engring. U. R.I., Kingston, 1948-49, U. Conn., Storrs, 1950-51; design engr. Praeger-Maguire & Ole Singstad, Boston, 1951-52; chief found. engr. C.A. Maguire & Assos., Providence, 1952-59, asso., 1959-69, v.p., 1969-72; sr. v.p. C.E. Maguire, Inc., 1972-76, officer-in-charge Honolulu office, 1976-77, corp. dir. ops., 1978—; lectr. found. engring. U. R.I., 1968-69; mem. U.S. com. Internat. Commn. on Large Dams. Vice chmn. Planning Bd. East Providence, R.I., 1960—. Served with AUS, 1942-46. Mem. ASCE (chpt. past pres., dir.), R.I. Soc. Profl. Engrs. (nat. dir., engr. of year award 1973), Am. Soc. Engring. Edn., Soc. Am. Mil. Engrs., ASTM, Am. Soc. Planning Ofcls., Harvard Soc. Engrs., Scientists, Providence Engrs. Soc., R.I. Soc. Planning Agys. (past pres.). Contbr. articles to profl. jours. Home: 156 Barney St Rumford RI 02916 Office: 31 Canal St Providence RI 02903

PIERCE, FREDERICK S., broadcasting exec.; grad. Baruch Sch. Bus. Adminstrn., Coll. City N.Y.; m. Marion Pierce; children—Richard, Keith, Linda. With ABC, 1956—, supr. audience measurements TV network research dept., 1957, mgr. audience measurements, 1958-61, dir. research, 1961, dir. research and sales devel., 1962, dir. sales planning and sales devel., 1962-64, v.p., nat. dir. sales for TV network, 1964-68, v.p. planning, 1968-70, v.p. charge planning, asst. to pres. TV network, 1970-72, v.p. charge TV planning and devel., 1972-74, sr. v.p. ABC-TV, 1974, pres., 1974-78, pres. Am. Broadcasting Cos., Inc., N.Y.C., 1978—, also dir. Served with Combat Engrs., U.S. Army; Korea. Office: care Am Broadcasting Cos Inc 1330 Ave of Americas New York NY 10019*

PIERCE, HORACE GREELEY, trade assn. exec.; b. Rochester, N.Y., July 12, 1928; s. Louis S. and Elizabeth (Baybutt) P.; B.A., U. Rochester, 1949, M.S., 1950; m. Phyllis Altman, May 7, 1955; children—Martha Ellen, Mark Evan. With Northeastern Retail Lumbermens Assn., Rochester, 1950—, adminstrv. asst., 1952-56, mng. dir., 1956-60, exec. v.p., 1960—; exec. trustee Northeastern Retail Lumbermens Assn. Group Ins. Trust Fund, 1960—; exec. v.p. Retail Lumber Dealers Found., 1968—. Fund drive chmn. West Webster Fire Dept., 1955-68. Served with AUS, 1950-52. Mem. Am. Soc. Assn. Execs., Nat. Retail Mchts. Assn., Rochester C. of C., Rochester Ad Club, West Webster Vol. Firmens Assn., Nat. Lumber and Bldg. Material Dealers Assn. (dir., chmn. supervisory com. for legislative and govt. agy. affairs 1974), Bldg. Material Execs. Assn., Am. Mgmt. Assn., Am. Soc. Tng. and Devel., Internat. Concatenated Order Hoo Hoo, Webster Grange, Sierra Club, Psi Upsilon. Republican. Episcopalian. Clubs: University, Oak Hill Country. Editor: Lumber Co-Operator, 1960—. Home: 413 Lake Rd Webster NY 14580 Office: 339 East Ave Rochester NY 14604

PIERCE, JOHN MICHAEL, interior design cons.; b. Elizabeth, N.J., Apr. 28, 1941; s. John Graham and Dorothea Adrienne P.; grad. (Nat. Soc. Interior Design N.J. chpt. scholar 1961), Newark Sch. Fine and Indsl. Arts, 1962; B.S., N.Y. U., 1965. Interior designer Zimmerman Design Assos., Hoboken, N.J., 1962-66, Franklyn Jacoty Indsl. Design, N.Y.C., 1966-67, Raymond Lowey/William Snaith, Inc., N.Y.C., 1967-69, First Nat. City Bank, N.Y.C., 1969; dir. design Citicorp Realty Consultants, N.Y.C., 1969-71, v.p. Environ. Research and Devel., Inc., N.Y.C., 1973; pvt. practice interior design cons., Elizabeth, N.J., 1971-73, 73—; guest lectr. U. Louisville, 1978. Pres. Elmore Assn., Elizabeth, 1974-77; mem. community relations council Kean Coll., Union, N.J., 1974, mem. continuing edn. adv. bd., 1975—; chmn. Mayor's Adv. Com. on Community Devel., City of Elizabeth, 1976. Recipient exec. office design award Modern Office Procedures, 1977. Mem. Soc. Archtl. Historians, Victorian Soc. Am., Nat. Trust Historic Preservation. Roman Catholic. Home and Office: 242 Parmelee Pl Elizabeth NJ 07208

PIERCE, LAWRENCE WARREN, judge; b. Phila., Dec. 31, 1924; s. Harold Ernest and Leora (Bellinger) P.; B.S. Bus. Adminstrn., St. Joseph's Coll., 1948, D.H.L., 1967; J.D., Fordham U., 1951; LL.D., Fairfield U., 1972; m. Wilma V. Taylor, Sept. 11, 1948; children—Warren Wood, Michael Lawrence, Mark Taylor. Admitted to N.Y. bar, 1951, U.S. Supreme Ct., 1968; staff atty. Legal Aid Soc., 1952-54; gen. law practice, N.Y.C., 1955-61; asst. dist. atty., Kings County, N.Y., 1954-61; dep. police commr., N.Y.C., 1961-63; dir. N.Y. State Div. for Youth, Albany, 1963-66; chmn. N.Y. State Narcotic Addiction Control Commn., 1966-70; vis. prof. Sch. Criminal Justice, State U. N.Y. at Albany, 1970-71; U.S. dist. judge So. Dist. N.Y., 1971—. Mem. State Crime Control Bd., 1968-71; mem. adv. panel to corrections task force Pres.'s Com. on Law Enforcement and Adminstrn. Justice; cons. Sec. Army, 1969-70; mem. Pres.'s Task Force Rehab. of Offenders, 1969-70; mem. U.S. delegation UN Conf. on Prevention Crime, Japan, 1970; mem. planning com. 2d Circuit Jud. Conf. Bd. mgrs. Lincoln Hall for Boys; founding mem. Supreme Ct. Hist. Soc. Served with AUS, 1943-46, MTO. Mem. Urban League of Albany, Osborne Assn. (dir.), NAACP, Am. Bar Assn. (commn. on correctional services and facilities 1970—, mem. com. on jud. adminstrn.), Assn. Bar City N.Y., SAR. Roman Catholic. Home: Canaan NY 12060

PIERCE, MILTON, lithography co. exec.; b. Providence, Aug. 26, 1928; s. Max and Gussie (Parness) P.; B.S., U. R.I., 1950; m. Betty Ann Bernstein, Aug. 30, 1953; children—Mindy Jill, Larry Edward. Owner, mgr., pres. Lafayette Studios, Providence, 1951-54, Commercial Photo Print Services, Providence, 1954—, Colorlith Corp., Providence, 1964—; dir. Chinaware Industries; pres. Prime Realty Inc.; owner Larwin Realty. Home: 26 Wildrose Ct Warwick RI 02888 Office: 777 Hartford Ave Johnston RI 02919

PIERCE, PATRICIA JOBE, art historian, art dealer; b. Seattle, May 18, 1943; d. Leonard Carl and Ruth Hazeltine (Baten) Jobe; student U. Conn., summers, 1963, 64; B.F.A., Boston U., 1965; m. Norman Brayton Pierce, June 26, 1965; children—Christine Ruth, Matthew Jobe. Actress, Southbury (Conn.) Playhouse, Conn. Playmakers, Greenwich, Glendale (Calif.) Centre Theatre, Shubert Theater, Boston, Boston U. Playhouse, 1957-65; mktg. dir. Kelly Services, Boston, 1965-67; tghr. English-drama, high sch., Wareham, Mass., 1967-68; pres. Pierce Galleries, Inc., North Abington and Hingham, Mass., 1968—; agt. for various artists. Fund raising chmn. Elma Lewis Afro-Am. Center, Roxbury, Mass., 1973-74; Chmn. stewardship Meth. Ch., East Bridgewater, Mass., 1974. Boston U. acting scholar, 1963-65. Mem. Appraisers Assn. Am., Boston Athenaeum, Boston Museum Fine Arts, Brockton Art Center, Frick Art Reference Library, Smithsonian Instn., Archives Am. Art (adv. council), Nat. Arts Club, Internat. Acad. Poets, Victorian Soc. Am. Author: John Joseph Enneking, American Impressionist Painter, 1972. Author: Living Painters Trained in Boston, 1975; The Ten (American Painters), 1976; Edmund C. Tarbell and the Boston School, 1978; author art catalogue raisonnes. Contbr. articles to profl. jours. Home: 721 Main St Route 228 Hingham MA 02043 Office: 721 Main St Hingham MA 02043

PIERCE, PAUL ARTHUR BRYON, psychologist; b. Oneonta, N.Y., Jan. 28, 1941; s. Paul Reynolds and Elizabeth (Tallmadge) P.; B.A., Hartwick Coll., 1963; M.Ed., Springfield (Mass.) Coll., 1968; Ed.D., U. Mass., 1970; m. Patricia Ann Marie Feeney, Nov. 2, 1963; children—Michelle, Sean, Darren, Nicole. Tchr. high sch. English, Whitney Point (N.Y.) Central Sch., 1963-64; tchr., dept. chmn. high sch. English, Worcester (N.Y.) Central Sch., 1965-66; asst. to registrar Springfield Coll., 1966-68; clin. psychologist dept. psychiatry Springfield Hosp. Med. Center (now Baystate Med. Center), 1970-75; individual practice clin. psychology, Amherst, Mass., 1970—; clin. supr. dept. psychology U. Mass. at Amherst, 1972-75; cons. in field. Alumni bd. dirs. Hartwick Coll., Oneonta, N.Y.; bd. dirs. Bur. for Exceptional Children, Holyoke, Mass., Little Red Schoolhouse Amherst Coll.; corporator Our Lady of Providence Children's Center, Inc., West Springfield, Mass. Recipient Outstanding Grad. Year award Hartwick Coll. Alumni Assn., 1963. Mem. Am., Mass. psychol. assns., Am. Fedn. Musicians, Cursillo Movement, Delta Sigma Phi. Democrat. Roman Catholic. Home: 45 Ward St Amherst MA 01002 Office: 20 Gatehouse Rd Amherst MA 01002

PIERCE, PHILIP SARGENT, psychologist; b. Medford, Mass., Aug. 25, 1941; s. Elmer Grandville and Pauline (Dudley) P.; B.A., U. Maine, 1963; M.A., U. N.H., 1965; Ph.D., U. S.C., 1971; m. Rae Foster, Oct. 10, 1967; children—Jennifer Pauline, Jessica Lillian, John Foster. Psychology asst. Pineland Hosp. and Tng. Center, Pownal, Maine, 1965-66, psychologist, asst. dir. dept. psychology, 1966-67, psychologist III, 1971, acting dir. psychology dept., 1971-72, chief psychologist Children's Psychiat. Hosp., 1972-73, dir. crisis intervention and prevention team, 1973-75, psychologist Child/Youth unit, 1975-76, dir. dept. psychology, 1976-77; clin. psychologist Togus (Maine) VA Center, 1977—; psychology intern U. Ala. Med. Sch., Birmingham, 1970-71; instr. lab. sects. statistics and perception, physiol. psychology U. S.C., Columbia, 1968-69; research asst. Inst. Study of Underprivileged and Disadvantaged, Columbia, 1969-70; research cons. Birmingham (Ala.) Police Dept., 1970-71; vis. prof. U. Maine, Portland, 1971-72; instr. St. Joseph's Coll., North Windham, Maine, 1972-73, asst. prof. psychology, 1973-77; asst. prof. psychology U. Maine, Augusta, 1977—. Served with AUS, 1966-71. Diplomate Am. Bd. Profl. Psychology. Mem. Maine Psychol. Assn. (pres. 1975—), Am. Psychol. Assn. (council of reps. 1977-78), AAAS, Assn. for Advancement Psychology, Am. Psychology-Law Soc., Me. State Employees Assn. (chpt. pres. 1973-74, area councillor 1973-77, dir. 1975-77), Sigma Mu Sigma, Psi Chi. Contbr. articles to profl. jours. Home: 79 Waites Landing Rd Falmouth Foreside ME 04105 Office: Togus VA Center Psychology Dept Togus ME 04330

PIERCE, RAYMOND KENNETH, educator; b. Lancaster, Pa., July 13, 1924; s. Raymond Reynolds and Anna (Wenger) P.; A.B., Franklin and Marshall Coll., 1948; M.Ed., Temple U., 1955; m. Sandra June Bair, Feb. 28, 1945 (dec. May 1969); children—Carol Pierce Furniss, Michael Kenneth, Robert Neal, Jerome David; m. 2d, Frances Ruth Friedman, July 2, 1969. Tchr., Solanco Jr.-Sr. High Sch., Quarryville, Pa., 1948-51, East Lampeter High Sch., Lancaster, Pa., 1951-53, Council Rock Jr. High Sch., Newtown, Pa., 1953-55; instr. secondary edn. Temple U., Phila., 1955-58; prin. jr. high sch., sr. high sch. Bristol (Pa.) Twp. Schs., 1958-65; dir. neighborhood youth corps, dir. youth study services Bucks County Supt. Schs. Office, Doylestown, Pa., 1965-69; high sch. prin. North Penn Schs., Lansdale, Pa., 1969-76; asso. dir. Commn. on Secondary Schs., Middle States Assn. Colls. and Schs., 1976—. Pres., Bucks County Human Relations Com., 1965-67;

mem. Bucks County Adv. Child Welfare Bd., 1966-70, chmn., 1969-70. Served with USMC, 1942-45. Recipient Minute of Year award Delaware Valley Friends Service Com., 1965, Chapel of Four Chaplains award, 1966. Mem. Pa. Assn. Secondary Sch. Prins. (exec. bd. 1974-77), Montgomery County Prins. Assn. (pres. 1973-74). Author: Observation of Student at Specific Learning Task, 1967. Home: Valley Stream Apts Route 463 and Line St Lansdale PA 19446 Office: 3624 Market St Philadelphia PA 19104

PIERCE, ROBERT RAYMOND, chem. engr.; b. Helena, Mont., Feb. 17, 1914; s. Raymond Everett and Daisy Mae (Brown) P.; student Benhke Walker Bus. Coll., 1933; B.S. in Chem. Engring., Oreg. State U., 1937; m. Stella Florence Kankos, June 12, 1938; children—Keith R., Patricia Pierce Wetzel, Diana Pierce Winters. Grain chemist State Oreg., Portland, 1937-38; flour mill chemist Terminal Flour Mills, Portland, 1938; grain chemist Peter B. Kerr Co., Portland, 1938-39; indsl. engr. Portland Gen. Electric, 1939-41; with Pennwalt Corp., various locations, 1941—, sr. tech. cons., Phila., 1965—. Bd. dirs. Phila. Air Pollution Control Bd., 1970—, vice chmn., 1973—, ad hoc chmn., 1976; mem. Penjerdel (Interstate Environ. Com.), 1977—. Mem. Am. Inst. Chem. Engrs. (co-founder materials scis. engring. div. 1967-68, world chmn. intersoc. corrosion com. 1961), Nat. Assn. Corrosion Engrs. (nat. dir. 1955-58), Internat. Com. Indsl. Chimneys, Air Pollution Control Assn., Pi Kappa Phi. Club: Rotary. Contbr. articles to profl. jours. Patentee in field. Home: 250 S 13th St Philadelphia PA 19107 Office: 3 Parkway Philadelphia PA 19102

PIERCE, SAMUEL RILEY, JR., lawyer; b. Glen Cove, N.Y., Sept. 8, 1922; s. Samuel R. and Hettie E. (Armstrong) P.; A.B. with honors, Cornell U., 1947, J.D., 1949; LL.M. in Taxation, N.Y. U., 1952, LL.D., 1972; postgrad. (Ford Found. fellow) Yale Law Sch., 1957; m. Barbara P. Wright, Apr. 1, 1948; 1 dau., Victoria Wright. Admitted to N.Y. bar, 1949; asst. dist. atty. County of N.Y., 1949-53; asst. U.S. atty. for So. Dist. N.Y., 1953-55; asst. to under sec. of labor, Washington, 1955-56; asso. counsel and counsel Judiciary Subcom. on Antitrust, U.S. Ho. of Reps., 1956-57; pvt. practice law, N.Y.C., 1957-58, 61-70, 73—; judge Ct. Gen. Sessions, N.Y.C., 1959-60; lectr. law N.Y. U., 1958-69, adj. prof. law Sch. Law, 1969—; gen. counsel U.S. Treasury, 1970-73; exec. dir., gen. counsel Emergency Loan Guarantee Bd., 1971-72; cons. bd. govs. Fed. Res. System, 1969-70; mem. adv. group Commr. IRS, 1974-75; mem. nat. adv. com. Comptroller Currency, 1975—; guest speaker colls. and univs.; dir. Prudential Ins. Co., U.S. Industries, First Nat. Boston Corp., Internat. Paper Co., Gen. Electric Co., Internat. Basic Economy Corp.; cons. Fund Internat. Social and Econ. Edn., 1961-67; bd. govs. Am. Stock Exchange, 1977—; U.S. del. Conf. on Coops., Georgetown, Brit. Guiana, 1956; mem. panel symposium Mil.-Indsl. Conf. on Atomic Energy, Chgo., 1956; mem. panel arbitrators Am. Arbitration Assn. and Fed. Mediation and Conciliation Service, 1957—; mem. Mayor's Com. Judiciary, 1965-70. Mem. N.Y.C. Bd. Edn., 1961-62; dir. YMCA Greater N.Y., 1960-70, sec. 1961-67, mem. nat. council, 1967-70, v.p., 1968-70; trustee Inst. Internat. Edn., 1967—, Fund for Peace, 1969-70; nat. exec. bd. Boy Scouts Am., 1969-75, bd. dirs. Police Athletic League N.Y.C., 1960-63, Sheltering Arms Children's Service, Inc., 1954-55, Louis T. Wright Meml. Fund, Inc.; trustee Cornell U., Hampton Inst., Mt. Holyoke Coll., 1965-75, Howard U.; overseers' vis. Com. Harvard U., 1969-75; mem. N.Y. State Republican Campaign Hdqrs. Staff, 1952; gov. N.Y. Young Rep. Club, 1952-53; campaign speaker Rep. Nat. Com., 1956. Served with AUS, 1943-46, as 1st lt. JAGC Res., 1950-52. Mem. Cornell Assn. Class Sec., Telluride Assn. Alumni, Cornell U. Alumni Assn. N.Y.C. (gov.), Am. Judicature Soc., Am. Bar Assn., Assn. Bar N.Y.C., N.Y. County Lawyers Assn., C.I.D. Agts. Assn. (gov.), Cornell Law Assn. (exec. com. 1962-65), Phi Beta Kappa, Phi Kappa Phi, Alpha Phi Alpha, Alpha Phi Omega. Methodist (commn. on interjurisdictional relations). Contbr. to profl. jours. Home: 16 W 77th St New York City NY 10024 Office: 280 Park Ave New York City NY 10017

PIERCE, SIDNEY KENDRICK, JR., educator, physiologist; b. Holyoke, Mass., Sept. 19, 1944; s. Sidney Kendrick and Mary Elizabeth (Streeter) P.; B.Ed., U. Miami (Fla.), 1966; Ph.D., Fla. State U., 1970. Mem. faculty U. Md., College Park, 1970—, prof. physiology, 1978—; Mem. corp. Marine Biol. Lab., Woods Hole, Mass., 1972—, instr. exptl. invertebrate zoology, 1973—. NSF grantee, 1972—; NIH grantee, 1977. Mem. Am. Soc. Zoology, AAAS, Tallahassee, Sopchoppy and Gulf Coast Marine Biol. Assn. (dir.). Home: 7974 Lakecrest Dr Greenbelt MD 20770 Office: Dept Zoology Univ Md College Park MD 20742

PIERPONT, GRACE ELIZABETH SCHMIDT (MRS. ROSS ZIMMERMAN PIERPONT), club woman; b. nr. Owings Mills, Md.; d. Hugo L.A. and Bessie (Moser) Schmidt; R.N., Md. Gen. Hosp., 1940; student U. Ia., 1945; m. Ross Zimmerman Pierpont, Feb. 21, 1942; 1 dau., Christine Celeste (Baroness Lippold von Klencke). Mem. exec. bd. Md. Gen. Hosp., 1958-61. Bd. Mem. Republican State Central Com.; chmn. 3d congl. dist. Md. dirs. Balt. Civic Opera. Mem. Womens Aux. Md. Gen. Hosp. (pres. 1958-60), Womens Aux. Southeastern Surg. Soc. (pres. 1962-63), Womens Golf Assn. Md., Golfers Charitable Assn., Womens Assn. Balt. Symphony Orch., Womans Aux. Balt. City Med. Soc., Balt. Civic Opera Guild, Womens Aux. AMA. Clubs: Baltimore Country, Three Arts, Roland Park Womans, Baltimore Music, Womens Civic League. Home: 5602 Enderly Rd Baltimore MD 21212

PIERSON-TISCH, MARJORIE, guidance counselor; b. Orange, N.J., Aug. 7, 1926; d. Frederick Raymond and Lillian Juliana (Danielson) Pierson; A.B., Upsala Coll., 1945; M.A., Kean Coll., 1972; postgrad. Fairleigh Dickinson U., 1969-70, Drew U., 1959-60; children—Deborah Tisch Edwards, Richard, Carolee Tisch Frye. Family caseworker, nat. ARC, Hackensack, N.J., 1945-46; tchr. elementary sch., New Providence, N.J., 1959-68, tchr. English, middle sch., 1968-74, tchr. English, guidance counselor, high sch., 1974-75, guidance counselor, career specialist, high sch., 1974—; co-adjutant Rutgers U., 1977—; cons., career, ednl., personal counseling, Spring Lake Heights, N.J., 1977—; N.J. coordinator Nat. Coll. Fair, N.Y.C., 1977; speaker Stockton State Coll., 1977; panelist recreation, careers, Kean Coll., 1975; mem. Adele Lynch Allied Health Scholarship Com., 1976—; presenter Tng. Inst. for Sex Desegregation, 1977—; mem. Affirmative Action Com., New Providence, 1977—, Career Edn. Com., 1977—. Mem. Summit C. of C., 1975—. Mem. Am. Personnel and Guidance Assn., Nat., N.J. (editor Intercom, 1976-77) Assns. Coll. Admissions Counselors, NEA, AAUW, Nat. Profl. Educators Assn., Nat. Sch. Counselors Assn., Nat. Vocat. and Guidance Assn. Club: Summit Coll. Author: New Providence Profile, 1974; contbr. articles to publs. Home and office: 58 Walnut Dr Spring Lake Heights NJ Office: New Providence High School New Providence NJ 07974

PIERSTORFF, BUCKLEY CHARLES, tech. co. exec.; b. Phila., Apr. 30, 1927; s. Arthur Lewis and Marion Louise (Paddock) P.; B.S., Ohio State U., 1951; m. Bette Smith, July 25, 1948; children—Lyle Ann, Scott Lewis. Research engr. servomechanisms Honeywell Corp., Phila., 1951-56; leader tech. staff RCA, Burlington, Mass., 1956-62; pres. Indatacon Corp., Newton, Mass., 1962-64; tech. staff Calspan Corp., Buffalo, 1964—, asst. head systems evaluation dept., 1967—; lectr. in field. Mem. safety bd. Village East Aurora (N.Y.) 1974—, planning bd., 1975—. Served with USAAF, 1944-47. Registered profl. engr. Pa., Mass. Mem. IEEE (sr.), Am. Inst. Aeros. and Astronautics, Assn. Old Crows, Soc. Computer Simulation, Aircraft Owners and Pilots Assn., Nat. Rifle Assn., Sigma Xi. Republican. Home: 479 Girard Ave East Aurora NY 14052 Office: 4455 Genesee St Buffalo NY 14221

PIERZ, JOSEPH FRANCIS, architect; b. Newark, June 13, 1941; s. Francis John and Barbara (Zegar) P.; B.Arch., Pratt Inst., 1964; b. Beverly Ann Field, June 20, 1964; children—Alison Maria, Kristan Ann. Project architect various firms, 1963-70; dir. bldg. systems Omniform, Inc.; v.p. M.N. Crabtree Asso., Inc., 1970-73; pvt. practice architecture and interior design, Wethersfield, Conn., 1973—; guest lectr. Pratt Inst., Yale. Alt. mem. Bd. Bldg. Appeals, Wethersfield, 1972-75, mem. Wethersfield Democratic Town Comm., 1973—, clk. Wethersfield Zoning Bd. Appeals, 1975-78; mem. Wethersfield Adv. Com. for Handicapped, 1976—. Recipient citation Conn. Bldg. Congress for excellence in archtl. design, 1969. Mem. AIA (nat. com. on architecture for health 1977—), Conn. Soc. Architects. Research and planning coordinator for 100 acre Comprehensive Health Care Comm., Conn. Home and Office: 115 Garden St Wethersfield CT 06109

PIES, HARVEY ELLIOT, lawyer, govt. ofcl.; b. Rochester, N.Y., July 30, 1943; s. Jacob and Frances (Shieldkret) P.; A.B., Cornell U., 1965; J.D., Harvard U., 1968, M.P.H. (Sch. scholar), 1975; postgrad. U. Mo. Sch. Medicine, 1968-69; m. Rena Joy Shiller, Apr. 25, 1971. Admitted to Mass. bar, 1969, D.C. bar, 1976, U.S. Supreme Ct. bar, 1973; asso. firm Friedman & Atherton, Boston, 1969-74; cons. in health law HEW, Washington, 1974-75; asst. minority counsel Ways and Means Com., U.S. Ho. of Reps., Washington, 1975—. Mem. Am. Bar Assn., Am. Public Health Assn., Am. Soc. Law and Medicine, Am. Soc. Hosp. Attys., Phi Beta Kappa, Phi Eta Sigma. Club: B'nai B'rith. Founding editor Am. Jour. Law and Medicine, 1974—; editor Medicolegal News, 1974. Office: 1105 Longworth House Office Bldg Washington DC 20515

PIETRAFESA, RICHARD CUSHING, clothing mfg. co. exec.; b. Syracuse, N.Y., Sept. 7, 1925; s. Anthony J. and Louise (Delmonico) P.; B.S., Syracuse U., 1950; m. Sarah Lombardi, Sept. 27, 1953; children—Anthony, Richard, Joseph, Sarah. With Joseph J. Pietrafesa Co., Inc., Syracuse, 1950—, v.p., 1956-70, exec. v.p., 1970-75, pres., 1975—; exec. v.p. Learbury Clothes, Inc., 1970-75, pres., 1975—; dir. First Fed. Savs. & Loan Assn. Syracuse, First Nat. Bank Rochester; chmn. bd. St. Mary's Hosp., 1966—. Mem. SSS, Syracuse, 1967—; bd. dirs. v.p. Syracuse Govtl. Research Bur.; past chmn. bd. dirs. Syracuse Symphony Orch.; trustee Everson Mus. Art, Onondaga County Pub. Library, Syracuse Library System; chmn. bd. St. Mary's Hosp., 1966—; bd. dirs., vice chmn. Community Gen. Hosp.; mem. N.Y. Republican State Com. 118th Dist. Served with USNR, 1944-46; PTO. Mem. Syracuse C. of C. (dir.), Syracuse Power Squadrons, Delta Kappa Epsilon (past pres. Central N.Y. Assn.). Roman Catholic. Clubs: Old Port Yacht (Palm Beach, Fla.); Lake Shore Yacht and Country (commodore) (Cicero, N.Y.). Home: 104 Wendell Terr Syracuse NY 13203 Office: 101 Salt St Syracuse NY 13201

PIETROWITZ, RICHARD GEORGE, real estate appraiser; b. Orange, N.J., Dec. 21, 1937; s. Clarence and Mable Elizabeth (Morschberger) P.; student Lodi (N.J.) pub. schs., 1951-55; m. Mary Ann LoBue, Jan. 6, 1962; children—Robyn Ann, Richard, Antoinette, John. Field appraiser Asso. Surveys, Passaic, N.J., 1958-60; owner, chief appraiser R.C.I. Appraisers, Inc., Passaic, 1960-62; v.p., chief appraiser Alexander Summer Co., Teaneck, N.J., 1962—; instr. extension div. Rutgers U., 1975—; instr. Career Inst., Parsippany, N.J. Pres., St. Leo's Home Sch. Assn., 1971-72, treas., 1970-71; trustee Alpine Assn., Lake Mohawk, 1977—. Mem. Soc. Real Estate Appraisers (instr., pres. met. chpt. 1975, vice-gov. dist. #16), Am. Soc. Appraisers, Am. Right of Way Assn., Nat. Assn. Real Estate Appraisers, Nat. Assn. Review Appraisers, Elmwood Park Jaycees (pres. 1968, v.p. 1967, dir. 1965-66). Home: 197 Alpine Trail Sparta NJ 07871 Office: c/o Alexander Summer Co 222 Cedar Ln Teaneck NJ 07666

PIKE, GEORGE BERTRAM, banker; b. Arlington, Mass., Jan. 14, 1931; s. George B. and A. Gertrude (Pike) P.; grad. certificate Am. Inst. Banking, 1965, Rugers Grad. Sch. Banking, 1968; m. Dorothy R. Ripley, May 28, 1950; children—Betsy, David, Alan, Sheryl. Teller Harvard Trust Co., Cambridge, Mass., 1948-54, mgr. 1958-68; v.p. Liberty Bank & Trust Co., Boston, 1968-69; sr. v.p. Collidge Bank & Trust Co., Watertown, Mass., 1969-70; exec. v.p. Tanners Nat. Bank, Woburn, Mass., 1970—; dir. Q.S.C. Industries, Inc., Billirica, Mass., Visidyne, Inc., Burlington, Mass. Lectr. SBA, Boston, 1968-69. Treas. Salvation Army, 1958—, dir. Belmont Family Service, 1958-68, Aux. Police Officer, Belmont, Mass., 1959—, Belmont Planning Bd., 1965, mem. Belmont Town Meeting, 1960—. Mason (Master 1965, sec. 1969-76), Rotarian (dir. 1968-70), Kiwanian. Home: 67 Lorimer Rd Belmont MA 02178 Office: Tanners Nat Bank Woburn MA 01801

PIKE, JOHN NAZARIAN, physicist; b. Boston, Feb. 13, 1929; s. Arthur Thorndike and Sarah Lucy (Nazarian) P.; A.B., Princeton U., 1951; Ph.D. in Physics and Optics, U. Rochester, 1958; m. Margaretta May Horner, Dec. 28, 1957; children—Sally Katharine, Susan Horner. Staff scientist Union Carbide Corp., Parma (Ohio) Research Center, 1956-63, sr. scientist Tarrytown (N.Y.) Tech. Center, 1963—; mem. physics faculty Baldwin-Wallace Coll., Berea, Ohio, 1961-63. Gen. campaign chmn. United Way No. Westchester, N.Y., 1971, pres., 1972-73, bd. dirs., 1970-76; bd. dirs. United Way Westchester, 1976—. Mem. Optical Soc. Am., Soc. Photog. Scientists and Engrs., Phi Beta Kappa, Sigma Xi. Republican. Home: 71 Cedar Ave Pleasantville NY 10570 Office: Union Carbide Corp Tarrytown NY 10591

PIKE, JOHN RAYMOND, osteo. physician; b. Utica, N.Y., Oct. 4, 1903; s. George N. and Jennie E. (Ferguson) P.; D.O., Chgo. Coll. Osteo. Medicine, 1925; m. Laura E. Craft, Nov. 16, 1926 (dec. Oct. 1942); children—John R., Nelson C., Robert E.; m. 2d, Virginia R. Cowell, Dec. 10, 1943; 1 son, Howard C. Intern, Chgo. Osteo. Hosp., 1926; pvt. practice osteo. medicine, Albany, 1926—; mem. N.Y. State Bd. Med. Examiners, 1953-63; mem. vol. N.Y. State Med. Adv. Com. to SSS, 1967—. Mem. Albany County Adv. Com., Year-round Head Start, 1966-72; bd. dirs. Albany Boys Club, 1940-64, Clinton Square Neighborhood Assn.; bd. dirs. Albany Inter-racial Council, Inc., 1969-76; trustee N.Y. State Coll. Devel. Found., 1974—; bd. govs. N.Y. Coll. Osteo. Medicine, 1975—. Mem. Am., N.Y. State (dir. 1947-58, v.p. 1966-67, pres. elect 1967-68, pres. 1968-69) osteo. assns., Hudson River North Osteo. Soc., Phi Sigma Gamma (pres. grand chpt. 1948-50). Presbyterian. Clubs: Masons, Kiwanis (past pres.), Torch (past pres.). Home: 12 Douglas Rd Delmar NY 12054 Office: 17 Morningside Dr Delmar NY 12054

PIKE, RALPH FORWARD, orthopaedic surgeon; b. Cranston, R.I., Mar. 19, 1924; s. Arthur Simpson and Mary Ernestine (Forward) P.; B.S., Providence Coll., 1945; M.D., N.Y. Med. Coll., 1949; m. Elizabeth Carmelengo, Aug. 9, 1950; children—Mark Forward, Troy Gilbert. Intern, Charity Hosp. of La., New Orleans, 1949-50, resident in orthopaedic surgery, 1950-53; practice medicine specializing in orthopaedic surgery, Providence, 1955—; chief orthopaedic surgery Our Lady of Providence Unit, Our Lady of Fatima Unit St. Joseph's Hosp., R.I. Hosp.; staff Roger William's Gen. Hosp., S. County Hosp.; instr. orthopaedic surgery Tulane U. Chmn. Gov.'s Advisory Com. on Workmen's Compensation; impartial examiner Workmen's Compensation Commn., 1958-77. Served to capt. U.S. Army, 1953-55. Diplomate Am. Bd. Orthopaedic Surgery. Fellow A.C.S., Boston Orthopaedic Club, Am. Acad. Compensation Medicine; m. Am. Acad. Orthopaedic Surgeons, Eastern, New England, R.I. orthopaedic socs., Internat. Coll. Surgeons, Pan-Pacific Surg. Assn., Latin-Am. Soc. Orthopaedics and Traumatology, Am., Providence med. assns., R.I. Med. Soc., Am. Profl. Practice Assn., Orthopaedic Research and Edn. Found. (life mem.), Internat. Arthroscopy Assn., Thomistic Guild, Providence Coll. Alumni Assn., Am. Holly Soc., Am. Beekeepers Assn., Mass. Archeol. Soc., Alpha Kappa Kappa. Clubs: Mal Brown Territorial, Masons, Shriners. Contbr. articles in field to Jour. Bone and Joint Surgery. Home: Congdon Hill Rd Saunderstown RI 02874 Office: 655 Broad St Providence RI 02907

PIKE, TERESA MARIA DE HOSPODAR (MRS. NATHAN R. PIKE), lectr., artist; b. Nagy Mihaly, Austria; d. John and Mary (Tasko) de Hospodar; student NAD, 1923-24, Drake Bus. Coll., 1925-26; m. Nathan R. Pike, Aug. 18, 1937. Came to U.S., 1912, naturalized, 1944. One-man shows, including Art Center, N.Y.C.; exhibited in group shows, including Am. Artists Profl. League, Nat. Arts Club, Salmagundi Club, Nat. League Pen Women; represented in pvt. collections. Lectr. on hist. antiquities, glass, primitive, ancient and Early Am. lighting; appraiser, cataloguer fine arts for mus. acquisitions, also collections. Chmn. fund raising Westchester Mental Hygiene Assn., 1953-57; mem. Friends of Greenwich Library, Glenville Community League. Recipient various prizes for paintings. Mem. Nat. League Am. Pen Women (Conn. publicity chmn., New Eng. regional editor Pen Woman 1962-64, Conn. art chmn. 1958-60, 66—, nat. archivist and scrapbook chmn. 1964-66, Conn. art and publicity chmn. 1966-72, nat. chmn. pre-teenage stories 1968-70, Conn. pres. 1969-70, 72-74, nat. com. commemorative endowment fund 1974-76), Am. Artists Profl. League (1st v.p. N.Y. State chpt. 1962-64). Clubs: College (Boston); Greenwich Woman's. Author: Fairy Lamps and How to Make Them, 1955; Collecting Early American Glass, 1965; Ballet in Porclain, 1969. Contbr. articles to Conn. and N.Y. newspapers. Address: Twas a Farm Soundview Ridge 7 Woods Ave Glenville CT 06830

PIKULSKI, JOHN JOSEPH, educator; b. Scranton, Pa., Aug. 3, 1940; s. John Joseph and Helen (Hnott) P.; B.A., Wilkes Coll., 1963; M.A., Temple U., 1965, Ph.D., 1969; m. Edna Jane Cooke, Aug. 30, 1969; 1 dau., Beth. Asst. supt. diagnosis, instr. psychology Temple U., Phila., 1965-69; supr. diagnosis Reading Study Center, U. Del., Newark, 1969—, asst. prof. edn., 1969-73, asso. prof., 1973—, dir. Reading Study Center, 1976—, pres. faculty senate, 1976; psychol. and reading cons., agencies and sch. dists. Mem. Internat., Diamond State (pres. 1972-73), Coll. (chmn. clin. div. 1976—) reading assns., Am. Psychol. Assn., Nat. Council Tchrs. English. Contbr. to profl. jours. Home: 227 Cheltenham Rd Newark DE 19711 Office: Reading Study Center Coll Edn U Del Newark DE 19711

PIKUS, JOSEPH DAVID, educator; b. N.Y.C., Feb. 6, 1916; s. David and Esther (Solomon) P.; B.S., N.J. State Tchrs. Coll., 1937; M.S., Columbia U., 1947, Ed.D., 1965; grad. exec. tng. seminar in mental retardation U. Wis., 1972; student ins. on health planning U. Chgo. Tchr. social studies, jr. high sch., Newark, 1937-39; instr. psychology jr. coll., Essex County, N.J., 1937-39; caseworker, Newark, 1939-41; psychiat. social worker VA, 1947-52; staff asst. Greater N.Y. Fund, 1952; div. mgr. United Appeals-Red Cross, Welfare Fedn. Newark, West Hudson and Irvington, 1952-54; sec. div. health and hosps. Newark Council Social Agys., 1953-59; exec. sec. Greater Newark Med. Center, 1955-59; exec. dir. Hosp. and Health Council Newark and Vicinity, 1959-67; acting exec. dir. Hosp. and Health Council Met. N.J., Newark and vicinity, 1967, 69, dir. program planning and devel., 1967-69, 69-70; asso. prof. health care adminstrn. Ithaca Coll., 1970-71; exec. dir. Essex unit N.J. Assn. Retarded Children, 1971-73; asso. prof. health sci. Jersey City State Coll., 1973—; mem. N.J. Nursing Home Adminstrs. Licensing Bd., 1974—; field instr. for univs., 1949-70; lectr. Colls. Pharmacy and Nursing, and mem. co-adj. staff Rutgers U., 1970-73; mem. adj. staff Montclair State Coll., 1976—. Served to maj. AUS, World War II. Mem. Acad. Cert. Social Workers, Am. Hosp. Assn., Nat. Assn. Social Workers, N.J. Hosp. Assn., N.J. League Nursing, N.J. Welfare Council, Am. Public Health Assn., Am. Coll. Nursing Home Adminstrs., N.J. Public Health Assn. (1st v.p. 1960-71, chmn. mental health-mental retardation com. 1971-73, mem. exec. com.), Kappa Delta Pi, Phi Delta Kappa. Jewish. Contbr. articles to profl. jours. Home: 38 Beverly Rd Cedar Grove NJ 07009

PILARSKI, LEONARD JACOB, ins. co. exec.; b. Pitts., Nov. 3, 1920; s. Jacob L. and Selma (Schroeder) P.; student U. Pitts., 1948, Pa. State U., 1950-51; ins. courses Duquesne U., 1955, Purdue U., 1963-64; m. Irene Operchal, Nov. 11, 1943; children—Dennis L., Donald L., Daria L., Douglas L., Dean L. With Prudential Ins. Co., Pitts., 1948-63; mgr. Gt. West Life Ins. Co., Pitts., 1963-68; pres. Golden Triangle Assos., Pitts., 1965-68; brokerage cons. Union Central Life Ins. Co., Pitts., 1968-70, mgr., 1970—. Life Ins. chmn., bd. dirs. Western Pa. Heart Assn., 1974—. Served with U.S. Army, 1942-45. Deocrated Bronze Star, Purple Heart. Mem. Nat., Pa. assns. life underwriters, Nat., Pitts. gen. agents and mgrs. assns., Pitts. Life Underwriters Assn., Estate Planning Council Greater Pitts., Ind. Ins. Agents Pitts., Ins. Club of Pitts., Am. Legion. Democrat. Roman Catholic. Clubs: Mt. Lebanon Golf. Home: 529 Clemson Dr Mount Lebanon PA 15243 Office: Suite 1413 301 Fifth Ave Pittsburgh PA 15222

PILAT, OLIVER, newspaperman; b. N.Y.C., Aug. 7, 1903; s. Oliver I. and Emma (Ramsay) P.; student N.Y. U., 1924; B.A., Amherst Coll., 1926; m. Avice Riddle, Apr. 11, 1930; children—Carl Jeffrey, Betsy. With Bklyn. Eagle, 1926-36; European corr., 1930-34; with N.Y. Post, 1936-65, Washington corr., 1943-49, polit. reporter, N.Y.C., 1949-65; asst. to Mayor Lindsay, N.Y., 1966-67; asst. to council Pres. Garelik, N.Y., 1970-71; writer in residence New Sch. Social Research, N.Y.C., 1974—. Vice chmn. N.Y. State Liberal Party. Mem. Authors Guild, Inner Circle, N.Y. Newspaper Guild (pres. 1965), Silurians (pres. 1972), Phi Beta Kappa, Phi Gamma Delta. Author: Sea-Mary, 1936; The Mate Takes Her Home, 1939; (with Jo Ranson) Sodom by the Sea, 1942; The Atom Spies, 1952; Revolt in the Mafia, 1962; Pegler: Angry Man of the Press, 1963; Lindsay's Campaign, 1968; Drew Pearson: An Unauthorized Biography, 1973. Home and Office: 24 Fifth Ave New York City NY 10011

PILCHER, JAMES OTTO, II, mech. engr.; b. Columbus, Ohio, Nov. 16, 1934; s. James Otto and Maxine Elizabeth (Williams) P.; student Ariz. State U., 1953-55; B.S. in Mech. Engring., N.Mex. State U., 1959; m. Mary Ridgely Willard, June 17, 1961; children—James Roger, William Frederick, Sarah Elizabeth, Rachel Jane. Student trainee, mech. engr. U.S. Army Ballistic Research Labs., White Sands Missile Range, N.Mex., 1956-58, mech. engr. Army Ballistic Research Lab., Aberdeen Proving Ground, Md., 1959—, team leader electro-mechanics team, mechanics and structures br., propulsion div., 1976—; mem. fuze adv. bd. Army Munitions Command,

1970-73, Army Armament Command, 1973-75; mem. U.S. Army Fuze/Munitions Environment Steering Com., 1975—, Army Steering Com. Precision Gun Dynamics, 1977—. Served to lt. U.S. Amry, 1959-62. Mem. Am. Def. Preparedness Assn. Democrat. Presbyterian (ruling elder). Patentee in field. Home: 1321 Charlestown Dr Edgewood MD 21040 Office: US Army Ballistic Research Lab DRDAR-BLP Aberdeen Proving Ground MD 21005

PILCHIK, RONALD, mgmt. cons.; b. Bklyn., Oct. 28, 1940; s. Irving and Sadie (Eichner) P.; B.S., Bklyn. Coll., 1962; M.S., Fairleigh Dickinson U., 1970, M.B.A., 1974; m. Rochelle Phyllis Turkel, Nov. 4, 1962; children—Evan, Robert, Nancy. Clin. chemist Bellevue Hosp., N.Y.C., 1962-64; supr. Gen. Diagnostics div. Warner Lambert Co., Morris Plains, N.J., 1964-69; sec. head Roche Diagnostics div. Hoffman-La Roche, Nutley, N.J., 1969-74; mgr. Gen. Diagnostics internat. div. Warner Lambert Co., Morris Plains and Dublin, Ireland, 1974-75; v.p. Harleco div. Am. Hosp. Supply Co., Gibbstown, N.J., 1975-78; pres. RPServices, Cherry Hills, N.J., 1978—; asst. prof. Fairleigh Dickinson U. dept. chemistry, 1968-70, grad. sch. bus., 1974—. Certified clin. chemist Nat. Registry in Clin. Chemistry. Mem. Am. Chem. Soc., Am. Assn. for Clin. Chemistry, Health Industries Mfrs. Assn. (chmn. metrication com.), Am. Nat. Metric Council (med. device sector com.). Home: 1816 Lark Ln Cherry Hill NJ 08003 Office: RP Services 1864 E Marlton Pike Cherry Hill NJ 08003

PILGRIM, SIDNEY ALFRED LESLIE, soil scientist; b. Berlin, N.H., Dec. 24, 1933; s. Sidney Alfred and Vivian Gertrude (Larocque) P.; B.S. in Agriculture, U. N.H., 1955; m. Faith Patricia Martin, June 9, 1956; children—Paul Garret, Kelly Lynn. With soil conservation service U.S. Dept. Agr., 1955—, soil scientist, Concord and Woodsville, N.H., 1955-61, Plymouth, INd., 1961-64, state soil scientist, Durham, N.H., 1964—; instr. soils and community planning courses U. N.H., 1973—. Coach Nordic Ski team Oyster River Sch. Dist., 1968-72. Served with AUS, 1956-58. Recipient certificates of merit U.S. Dept. Agr., 1960, 68. Registered soil scientist, Maine. Mem. Soil Sci. Socs. Am., No. New Eng. (pres. 1975-76), Soil Conservation Soc. Am. Roman Catholic. Club: Salmon Falls River. Beagle. Author, contbr. to numerous soil surveys. Home: 87 Mill Rd Durham NH 03824 Office: 3 Madbury Rd Durham NH 03824

PILLAI, BALA HARI, physician; b. Kuala Kangsar, Malaysia, May 27, 1946; s. Bala Krishna and Kamalakshi Bala P.; came to U.S., 1971, naturalized, 1978; M.B.B.S., Kasturba Med. Coll., 1969; m. Lathika Menon, Dec. 28, 1972; 1 son, Siddartha H. Intern, A.C. Logan Meml. Hosp., N.Y.C., 1971-72; resident Bronx-Lebanon Hosp., N.Y.C., 1972-74; fellow Sch. Medicine, State U. N.Y., Stony Brook, 1974-76; dir. dept. pulmonology Central Suffolk Hosp., Riverhead, N.Y., 1976—; instr. medicine State U. N.Y., Stony Brook. Mem. Am., Nassau-Suffolk (dir.) lung assns., Am. Coll. Chest Physicians, ACP, N.Y. Trudeau Soc., AMA. Home: 11 Private Ln Brookhaven NY 11719 Office: 43 Main St Westhampton Beach NY 11978

PILLAY, SIVASANKARA K.K., nuclear chemist; b. Puliyoor, India, Jan. 28, 1935; s. Raman T.N. and Janaki K. (Amma) P.; B.Sc. with honors, U. Mysore (India), 1955, M.Sc. (Govt. India scholar), 1956; Ph.D., Pa. State U., 1965; came to U.S., 1960, naturalized, 1974; m. Revathi Krishnamurthy, Mar. 22, 1964; 1 son, Gautam. Lectr. U. Mysore, 1956-60; teaching asst. Pa. State U., 1960-65; resident research asso. Argonne Nat. Lab., 1965-66; sr. research scientist Western N.Y. Nuclear Research Center, Inc., Buffalo, 1966-71; research asso. Brezeale nuclear reactor Pa. State U., University Park, 1971-74, asst. prof. nuclear engring., 1974-77, asso. prof., 1977—; cons. nuclear applications in health scis., chem. aspects of nuclear engring., environ. studies, and criminal investigations. Warden, Silver Jubilee Orphanage, 1958-60; treas. pack Boy Scouts Am., 1975-77. Kopper Chem. fellow, 1962-63. Fellow Am. Inst. Chemists; mem. Am. Chem. Soc., Am. Nuclear Soc., N.Y. Acad. Scis., AAAS, Sigma Xi. Contbr. articles to profl. jours., chpts. in books. Home: 496 Galen Dr State College PA 16801 Office: Breazeale Nuclear Reactor Pa State U University Park PA 16802

PILLOR, MARK HARLEN, physician; b. Barron, Wis., July 11, 1931; s. Frazier Harvey and Kristine (Odegar) P.; B.A., Pacific Union Coll., 1959; M.D., Loma Linda U., 1963; m. Sheila Rose Engleberg, Apr. 7, 1957; children—Harvey, Dalton, Daniel, William. Intern, Washington Adventist Hosp., Takoma Park, Md., 1963-64; dir. emergency unit Prince Georges Gen. Hosp., Cheverly, Md., 1964-65; asso. in family practice Lowery Meml. Med. Center, District Heights, Md., 1965-72; founder, dir. Oxon Hill (Md.) Family Med. Group, 1972—; mem. faculty George Washington U. Med. Sch., Washington, 1977—. Served with U.S. Army, 1952-54. Diplomate Am. Bd. Family Practice. Fellow Am. Acad. Family Practice; mem. AMA, Md. Med. Assn., D.C. Med. Soc. Republican. Adventist. Office: 6188 Oxon Hill Rd Oxon Hill MD 20021

PILNICK, SAUL, mgmt. and behavioral sci. cons.; b. N.Y.C., Aug. 14, 1931; s. Robert and Rose P.; B.A., Bklyn. Coll., 1953; M.S., Columbia U., 1955; Ph.D., N.Y. U., 1964; children—Michael, David. Caseworker, Jewish Family Service, N.Y.C., 1956-60; therapist Bklyn. State Hosp. and Assn. for Help Retarded Children, 1956-60; program dir. Fountain House Found., N.Y.C., 1956-60; prof. edn. Newark State Coll., Union, N.J., 1956-60; exec. dir. Essexfields Group Rehab. Center, Newark, 1961-65; project dir. Collegefields Group Ednl. Center, 1965-67; prof. edn. Newark State Coll., 1965-67; pres. Sci. Resources, Inc., mgmt. cons., 1967-69; pres. Human Systems Inst., New Vernon, N.J., 1969—. Bd. dirs. Willis Sch. Neurologically Impaired Children. Mem. Nat. Assn. Social Workers, Am., N.J. psychol. assns., Am. Sociol. Assn., Nat. Council on Crime and Delinquency, Am. Group Psychotherapy Assn., Acad. Polit. Sci., AAAS, Am. Mgmt. Assn., N.Am. Research Group on Mgmt. Author publs. in field. Home: 41 Skyline Dr Morristown NJ 07960 Office: Village Rd New Vernon NJ 07976

PIMENTAL, ANTHONY M., III, govt. ofcl.; b. New London, Conn., Jan. 25, 1947; s. Anthony Manuel and Antoinette E. (Pont) P.; B.S., Providence Coll., 1968; m. Andrea Boucher, Nov. 13, 1977. Fed. coordinator adminstrn. fed. and state grants Town of West Warwick (R.I.), 1971—, v.p. Electronic Implementation, Inc.; pres., dir. Engineered Safety Products, Inc. Mem. Vocat. Edn. Adv. Com., 1977—; mem. parish council St. Anthony's Ch., 1972, mem. Bicentennial Commn., 1975. Served with U.S. Army, 1968-70. Recipient certificate of award R.I. Intern and Vol. Consortium, 1977. Mem. Am. Mgmt. Assn. Patentee safety device. Home: 29 Sunset Ave West Warwick RI 02893 Office: 1170 Main St West Warwick RI 02893

PIMPINELLA, RONALD JOSEPH, surgeon; b. Utica, N.Y., Sept. 27, 1935; s. Joseph and Josephine (Paine) P.; B.S. magna cum laude, Syracuse U., 1956; M.D., U. Rochester, 1960; m. Margaret Krantz, June 29, 1961; children—Andrea, Giancarlo. Intern, Albany (N.Y.) Med. Center, 1960-61; resident in ear-nose-throat Columbia Presbyn. Med. Center, 1962-65; practice medicine specializing in otolaryngology, Torrington, Conn., 1967—; mem. Litchfield Hills Med. center, Torrington; v.p. Hearing Improvement Center; chief otolaryngology Charlotte Hungerford Hosp. Served with U.S. Army, 1965-67. Mem. Am. Assn. Ophthalmology and Otolaryngology, AMA, A.C.S., Conn. Med. Soc. (sec. treas. otolaryngology sect.). Roman Catholic. Contbr. articles to med. jours. Home: Milton Rd Litchfield CT 06759

PIMSLER, ALVIN J., artist; b. N.Y.C., May 17, 1918; s. Adolph and Jennie (Freedman) P.; student Pratt Inst. Sch. Fine and Applied Art, 1935-38, Art Students League, 1939-40; m. Norma Moran, Aug. 3, 1947; children—Meade, Paul S. Free lance illustrator; fashion artist; portrait painter; one man show Soc. Illustrators Gallery, 1972; exhibited in group shows Art Students League, 1958, Art Dirs. Exhbn., 1956, Soc. Illustrators fashion illustration exhbn., 1964, portrait painting, 1967, Portraits, Inc., 1968, 74, 11th and 12th Ann. Exhbns.-Illustration, 1969, 70, 73, 74, C.C. Price Gallery, 1970; Smithsonian Instn., 1973, Salmagundi Club, N.Y.C., 1973; tchr. Fashion Illustration, Sch. Visual Arts, 1966-67, Parsons Sch. Design, 1971—, Fashion Inst. Tech., 1975—. Served to capt. AUS, 1941-46; ETO. Decorated Combat Inf. Badge. Recipient William Collins award Hudson Valley Art Assn., 1971. Mem. Soc. Illustrators (pres. 1974), Artists Fellowship (trustee). Club: Lake Success Golf (pres. 1967-68). Address: 101 Central Park W New York City NY 10023

PINCUS, LIONEL I., investment banker; b. Phila., Mar. 2, 1931; s. Henry and Theresa Celia (Levit) P.; student (Internat. Schoolboy fellow) Wellington Coll., Eng., 1948-49; B.A., U. Pa., 1953; M.B.A. in Fin. and Managerial Econs., Columbia U., 1956. Asso., Ladenburg, Thalmann & Co., N.Y.C., 1955-60, gen. partner, 1960-63; pres., dir. Lionel I. Pincus & Co., Inc., N.Y.C., 1964-66; pres., chief exec. officer E.M. Warburg & Co., Inc., N.Y.C., 1966—, E.M. Warburg, Pincus & Co., Inc., 1970—; chmn., chief exec. officer EMW Ventures Inc., 1971; dir. Warner Co., Widener Pl. Fund. Trustee, exec. vice chmn. Montefiore Hosp.; pres., trustee Lionel I. Pincus Found, N.Y.C., Town Sch. Mem. Council Fgn. Relations, Nat. Golf Links Am. Address: 277 Park Ave New York City NY 10017

PINCUS, RALPH A., physician; b. N.Y.C., Oct. 4, 1933; s. Jacob and Mildred (Ginsberg) P.; student Bklyn. Coll., 1950-54; M.D., Columbia U., Coll. of Physicians and Surgeons, 1958; m. Ruth Pincus, Dec. 25, 1956; children—Jonathan, Andrea, Joshua. Intern, Jewish Hosp., Bklyn., 1958-59, asst. resident in medicine, 1959-60; asso. resident in medicine Strong Meml. Hosp., Rochester, N.Y., 1962-63, clin. asst. prof. medicine and exptl. radiology 1971—, clin. instr. medicine, 1965-71; practice medicine specializing in internal medicine, Rochester. Served to capt. U.S. Army, 1960-62. Diplomate Am. Bd. Internal Medicine. Fellow A.C.P.; mem. Monroe County Med. Soc., Am. Diabetes Assn., Phi Beta Kappa, Sigma Xi. Home: 321 Council Rock Ave Rochester NY 14610 Office: 200 White Spruce Blvd Rochester NY 14623

PINE, VANDERLYN RUSSELL, educator; b. Kingston, N.Y., Nov. 23, 1937; s. Gordon D. and Marion K. (Russell) P.; A.B., Dartmouth Coll., 1967, A.M. (Dartmouth Gen. fellow), 1969; Ph.D. (Univ. Scholar and USPHS Pre-Doctoral Research fellow), N.Y. U., 1971; m. Patricia Palmer Hannaford, Aug. 9, 1974; children—Gordon, Brian, Daniel; stepchildren—Paula Hannaford, Brenda Hannaford. Funeral dir. N.Y., N.H., 1957-67; instr. sociology Am. Acad. McAllister Inst., N.Y.C., 1967-68; teaching asst. sociology Dartmouth Coll., Hanover, N.H., 1968-69; asst. prof. sociology State U. N.Y. at New Paltz, 1971-73, asso. prof., 1973—, chmn. dept., 1977—; cons. Nat. Funeral Dirs. Assn., 1971—; nat. adv. bd. Center Death Edn. and Research, U. Minn., 1971—; profl. adv. bd. Found. Thanatology, Columbia U., 1972—; mem. internat. adv. council Nat. Inst. for Seriously Ill and Dying, Phila., 1976—; mem. internat. adv. bd. Forum for Death Edn. and Counseling, Arlington, Va., 1977—; bd. dirs. Internat. Work Group on Death, Dying and Bereavement, Phila., 1978—. Formerly active fund raising Heart Fund, Am. Cancer Soc. Served with U.S. Army, 1957-58. Recipient Chancellor's award for excellance in teaching State Univ. N.Y., 1974. Mem. Am. Sociol. Assn. (mem. council, undergrad. edn. sect. 1977—), Eastern Sociol. Soc., Am. Acad. Polit. and Social Sci. Clubs: Paltz, Rotary. Author: Caretaker of the Dead: The American Funeral Director, 1975; Introduction to Social Statistics, 1977. Editor: A Statistical Abstract of Funeral Service Facts and Figures of the United States, 1972, 73, 74, 75, 76, 77; Responding to Disaster, 1974; (with others) How to Evaluate Your Funeral Home, 1976; sr. editor Acute Grief and the Funeral, 1976. Contbr. articles to Practical Anthropology, Am. Funeral Dir., Director, Social Problems, N.Y. U. Sociologist, Contemporary Sociology, Sociology Rev. New Books, Jour. Thanatology, Death Edn.; author numerous research studies, papers, presentations for profl. socs. Home: 18 Plattekill Ave New Paltz NY 12561 Office: 128 Main St New Paltz NY 12561

PINEDA, LOURDES CASTRO, child psychiatrist; b. San Fernando, Pampanga, Philippines, Jan. 2, 1943; s. Isidoro Dizon and Obdulia Mercado (Castro) P.; came to U.S., 1968; M.D., U. Philippines, 1967. Rotating intern U. Philippines-Philippine Gen. Hosp. Med. Center, Manila, 1966-67, Luth. Med. Center, Cleve., 1968-69; practice family medicine, San Fernando, Pampanga, Philippines, 1967-68; resident in internal medicine Luth.-Cleve. Met. Gen. Hosp., Cleve., 1969-70; resident in gen. psychiatry Univ. Hosps. of Cleve., Tng. Hosp. of Case Western Res. U., Cleve., 1970-72; fellow in child psychiatry Washington U. Sch. Medicine, St. Louis, also career resident in child psychiatry Malcom Bliss Mental Health Center, St. Louis, 1972-74; instr. dept. psychiatry Sch. Medicine, Washington U., St. Louis, 1974-76; psychiatrist Kingsboro Psychiat. Center, Bklyn., 1976—; clin. instr. dept. child and adolescent psychiatry Downstate Med. Center, Coll. Medicine, State U. N.Y., Bklyn., 1976—; practice medicine specializing in child and adolescent psychiatry, Bklyn., 1977—. Diplomate Am. Bd. Psychiatry and Neurology. Mem. Am. Psychiat. Assn. Roman Catholic. Home: 681 Clarkson Ave Brooklyn NY 11203

PINES, ARIEL LEON, psychologist, educator; b. Butawayo, South Rhodesia, Dec. 29, 1947; s. Michael and Neima (Ratner) P.; B.Sc., Hebrew U., Jerusalem, 1973, M.Sc., 1974; Ph.D., Cornell U., 1977; m. Mary-Lynne Mormann, Sept. 2, 1977. Supr. audio tutorial elementary sci. project Cornell U., Ithaca, N.Y., 1974-76, researcher, 1976-77; asst. prof. developmental psychology U. Maine, Farmington, 1977—. Served with Israeli Tank Corps, 1967-70. Decorated Sinai-Canal decoration, Yom Kippur war decoration; recipient award for outstanding contbns. to edn. Israeli Def. Forces, 1969. Mem. Am. Psychol. Assn., Am. Ednl. Research Assn., Assn. for Supervision and Curriculum Devel., Nat. Assn. Research in Sci. Teaching, Nat. Sci. Tchrs. Assn., Am. Soc. Curriculum Devel., Am. Inst. Biol. Sci. Contbr. articles to profl. publs. Home: General Delivery Temple AZ 04984 Office: U Maine Farmington ME 04938

PINES, BEVERLY IRENE, psychologist; b. Bklyn., Nov. 11, 1925; d. Solomon and Jeannette (Radin) Grobstein; B.A., Bklyn. Coll., 1944, M.A., 1948; postgrad. N.Y. U.; m. Matthew Pines, Jan. 29, 1949; children—Elyse Pines Rosenstein, Elliot. Student psychologist Kings County (N.Y.) Hosp., 1945-47; med. asst. to physicians, 1942-49; instr., lectr. Bklyn. Coll., 1946-50, student guidance counselor, 1946-50, group therapist, 1948-50; pvt. practice psychol. and psychotherapist marriage counseling, Bklyn., 1948—; participating psychologist G.H.I. Nat. Register Health Service Providers in Psychology. Certified psychologist, N.Y. Mem. Am., N.Y. State, Bklyn. psychol. assns., Am. Soc. Clin. Hypnosis, Edn. and Research Found. Jewish. Address: 637 E 8th St Brooklyn NY 11218

PINES, WAYNE LLOYD, govt. ofcl.; b. Washington, Dec. 31, 1943; s. Jerome Martin and Ethel (Schnall) P.; B.A., Rutgers U., 1965; postgrad. George Washington U., 1969-71; m. Nancy Freitag, Apr. 16, 1966; children—Noah Morris, Jesse Mireth. Reporter, city editor Middletown (N.Y.) Times Herald-Record, 1965-68; copy editor Reuters News, 1968-69; asso. editor FDC Reports, Washington, 1969-72; chief Consumer Edn. and Info., FDA, also editor FDA Consumer, 1972-74; exec. editor Product Safety Letter and Devices and Diagnostics Letter, Washington, 1974-75; dep. asst. commr. for pub. affairs, chief press relations FDA, Rockville, Md., 1975-78, dep. asso. commr. pub. affairs, 1978—; Contbr. numerous articles in field to profl. jours. Home: 5821 Nevada Ave NW Washington DC 20015 Office: 5600 Fishers Ln Rockville MD 20857

PINKERT, DOROTHY MINNA, chemist; b. N.Y.C., June 2, 1921; d. Harry and Frieda Dorothy (Pinkert) Klein; A.B., Bklyn. Coll., 1944; M.S., Bklyn. Poly. Inst., 1952. Creep lab. techinican Am. Brakeshoe Co., Mahwah, N.J., 1942-44; research and quality control chemist Reed and Carnrick, Jersey City, 1944-48; chief quality control chemist Gold Leaf Pharmacal Co., New Rochelle, N.Y., 1948-56; research chemist Internat. Salt Co., Watkins Glen, N.Y. and N.Y.C., 1957-61; sr. asso. drug regulatory affairs Hoffmann-LaRoche Inc., Nutley, N.J., 1962—. Mem. Poly. Inst. N.Y. Alumni Assn. (life dir., mem. exec. com.), Am. Chem. Soc., AAAS, Am. Soc. Quality Control. Republican. Office: 340 Kingsland St Nutley NJ 07110

PINKETT, HAROLD THOMAS, archivist; b. Salisbury, Md., Apr. 7, 1914; s. Levin Wilson and Leah Catherine (Richardson) P.; A.B., Morgan Coll., Balt., 1935; A.M., U. Pa., 1938; Ph.D., Am. U., 1953; m. Lucille Cannady, Apr. 24, 1943. High sch. tchr., Balt., 1936-37; prof. history Livingston Coll., Salisbury, N.C., 1938-39, 41-42; archivist, then supervisory archivist Nat. Archives, Washington, 1942-71, chief legis. and natural resources br., 1971—; lectr. Howard U., 1970-76, Am. U., 1976-77. Served with U.S. Army, World War II. Fellow council Library Resources, 1972; recipient Commendable Service award Nat. Archives, 1964, 70. Fellow Soc. Am. Archivists (editor jour. 1968-71), Forest History Soc. (pres. 1976-78); mem. U.S. Capitol Hist. Soc. (trustee), Am. Hist. Assn., Orgn. Am. Historians, Agrl. History Soc., Assn. Study Afro-Am. Life and History, So. Hist. Assn., Am. Soc. Environ. History, Omega Psi Phi. Democrat. Methodist. Club: Cosmos. Author: Gifford Pinchot, Private and Public Forester, 1970; also articles. Co-editor: Research in the Administration of Public Policy, 1975; editorial bd. Jour. Negro History, Agrl. History; D.C. Hist. Records Adv. Bd., 1978—. Home: 5741 27th St NW Washington DC 20015 Office: National Archives Bldg Washington DC 20408

PINKUS, THEODORE FRANCIS, JR., pharmacist; b. Worcester, Mass., Oct. 10, 1942; s. Theodore Francis and Rita Eleanor (Thompson) P.; B.S., Mass. Coll. Pharmacy, 1965; D.Pharmacy, U. Cin., 1972; m. JoAnne Christine Jensen, Nov. 12, 1977; children—Elizabeth Ann, Christine Mary, Theodore Francis III. Staff pharmacist Meml. Hosp., Worcester, 1966-69; resident in hosp. pharmacy VA Hosp., Cin., 1969-71; dir. clin. services, asst. dir. pharmacy services R.I. Hosp., Providence, 1971—. Served with USAF, 1965-66. Recipient Ciba-Geigy Leadership award, 1977. Mem. Am., R.I. socs. hosp. pharmacists, Am. Pharm. Assn., Parenteral Drug Assn., Am. Soc. Parenteral and Enteral Nutrition, AAAS, Am. Assn. IV Therapy, New Eng. Council Hosp. Pharmacists (pres. 1976-77), Mass. Coll. Pharmacy Alumni Assn., Kappa Psi, Rho Chi. Author: Quality Control: An Essential Tool in Particulate Matter, 1972, Part II, 1974; A Continuing Problem—Particulate Matter, 1978. Home: 21 Glenwood Ave Pawtucket RI 02860 Office: 593 Eddy St Providence RI 02902

PINNEY, EDWARD LOWELL, JR., physician; b. Gauley Bridge, W.Va., Nov. 11, 1925; s. Edward Lowell and May (Vencill) P.; A.B., Princeton U., 1949; B.S., W.Va. Med. Sch., 1947; M.D., Washington U., St. Louis, 1949; m. Arline Claire Caldwell, Aug. 2, 1957; children—David Edward, Diane Arlene, Michael Leslie. Intern, St. Louis City Hosp., 1949-50; resident Bklyn. State Hosp., 1952-54, sr. psychiatrist, 1954-55; practice medicine, specializing in psychiatry, Bklyn., 1955-68; mem. staff St. John's Episcopal Hosp., 1956-68, Meth. Hosp., 1956-67, Bklyn. Cumberland, Gracie Square hosps., Beekman Downtown Hosp., N.Y.C.; partner, med. dir. Bklyn. Med. Assos. Psychiatry and Neurology, 1958-64; psychiat. cons., dir. Mental Hygiene Clin. Cumberland Hosp. div., Bklyn.-Cumberland Med. Center, 1964-68, attending psychiatrist, 1968-76, psychiat. cons., 1976—; psychiat. cons. Bklyn. Eye and Ear Hosp., 1967-76; attending psychiatrist Manhattan Eye, Ear and Throat Hosp., 1976—; clin. instr. State U. N.Y., Down State Med. Center, 1958-68; clin. asst. prof. psychiatry Cornell U. Med. Coll., 1968-71, clin. asso. prof., 1971-78; clin. asso. prof. N.Y. U., 1978—; physician health service L.I. U., 1962—; psychiat. cons. Bd. Edn., N.Y.C. Served as lt. M.C., USNR, 1950-52. Fellow Am. Psychiat. Assn., Am. Soc. Psychoanalytic Physicians (pres. 1973-74), Am. Group Psychotherapy Assn.; mem. Schilder Soc., AMA, Kings County, N.Y. County med. socs., N.Y. Soc. Clin. Psychiatry, Asso. Physicians L.I., Pan Am. Med. Assn., Assn. Mil. Surgeons U.S., Med. Soc. N.Y. State (chmn. sect. psychiatry 1976-77, alternate del. 1978), Eastern Psychiat. Research Assn., Assn. Research Nervous and Mental Diseases (sec.-treas.), AAAS, N.Y. State Hosps. Med. Alumni Assn. (pres. 1968-72), Phi Beta Pi. Club: N.Y. Athletic. Author: A First Group Psychotherapy Book, 1970; contbr. articles to profl. jours.; asso. editor The Bull. Area II dist. brs. Am. Psychiat. Assn. Home: 85 East End Ave New York NY 10028 Office: 150 Broadway New York City 10038 also Atlantic Ave Amagansett NY 11930

PINO, EDWARD HANS, educator; b. Quito, Equador, Jan. 1, 1950; s. Ernst and Hendrina (Arnold) P.; came to U.S., 1953, naturalized, 1959; B.S., N.Y. Inst. Tech., 1972; M.S., Nova U., 1973; postgrad. C. W. Post Coll., 1974-75. Fair trade investigator mgr. Gilbert E. Miller Sales Corp., Jericho, N.Y., 1971-74; student counselor, advisor N.Y. Inst. Tech. to N.Y.C. Police Dept., 1973-74; floor psychologist Boerum Hill Rehab. Residence, Bklyn., 1974-76, supr., 1976-77; adj. prof. N.Y. Inst. Tech., Behavioral Sci. Dept., 1973—; asst. dir. P.R.I.C.E. (Prevention, Referrae, Info., Counseling, Edn.) Center, Farmingdale, N.Y., 1977—; pres. bd. Broadhollow Counseling Center, 1977—; cons. in field. Mem. regional planning council Nassau County Dept. Drug and Alcohol, 1971-72: asst. scoutmaster Boy Scouts Am., Queens, N.Y., 1968—, advisor to Order of the Arrow, 1969—. Recipient Certificate of Appreciation and Recognition, PRICE Counseling Center, 1977; Estelle Aumount award, 1972. Mem. N.Y. Personnel and Guidance assn., Am. Personnel and Guidance Assn., Assn. to Advanced Ethical Hypnosis, Am. Rehab. Counseling Assn., Assn. for Specialist in Group work. Democrat. Jewish. Clubs: Nat. Camping Assn., Holland Sporting. Contbr. articles to profl. jours. Home: 144 3568th Dr Flushing NY 11367 Office: 399 Conklin St Farmingdale NY 11735

PINSKER, WALTER, allergist; b. Bay Shore, N.Y., Mar. 27, 1933; s. Albert H. and Irene (Kuchlick) P.; B.A., U. Rochester, 1954; M.D., Chgo. Med. Sch., 1958; m. Tillene Giller, June 15, 1958; children—Neil, Andrew, Susann. Intern, L.I. Jewish Hosp., 1958-59;

resident in internal medicine Bklyn. VA Hosp., 1959-60; resident in internal medicine Long Beach (Calif.) VA Hosp., 1960-61, resident in allergy, immunology, 1961-62; practice medicine specializing in allergy, Bay Shore, N.Y., 1964—; pres. Bay Shore Allergy Group, P.C., 1971—; attending physician Southside Hosp., Bay Shore, Good Samaratin Hosp., W. Islip, N.Y., Central Islip State Hosp.; bd. visitors Pilgrim State Hosp., 1974-77; asst. prof. clin. medicine State U. N.Y. Med. Sch., Stony Brook, 1972—; cons. in field. Pres. Suffolk Assn. Children with Learning Disabilities, 1972-74, exec. v.p., 1975—; trustee Leeway Sch., 1974-75, Bay Shore Jewish Center, 1974—, com. for handicapped W. Islip Sch. Dist. Served to capt. M.C., AUS, 1962-64. Recipient Physicians Recognition award AMA, 1969-72, 73-76, 77-79. Diplomate Am. Bd. Allergy and Immunology. Fellow Am. Assn. Certified Allergists, Am. Acad. Allergy, Am. Coll. Allergy, Am. Assn. Allergy and Clin. Immunology, Suffolk Acad. Medicine; mem. Internat. Assn. Aerobiology, N.Y. Acad. Scis., Am. Assn. Study Headache, Nassau-Suffolk Allergy Soc. (sec. 1974-77, dir. 1970—, v.p. 1977-78). Republican. Jewish. Clubs: U.S. Power Squadron; B'nai B'rith. Contbr. articles to med. publns. Office: 649 Montauk Hwy Bay Shore NY 11706

PINSKY, BYRON LLOYD, psychotherapist, marriage and family counselor; b. Bklyn., Oct. 13, 1935; s. Morris Nissan and Fay (Goldstein) P.; B.A., Bklyn. Coll., 1956; M.S.W., Tulane U., 1958, postgrad., 1962-70; m. Harriet Levitz, Dec. 30, 1956; children—Brian David, Sherri Diane. Intern counseling and psychotherapy program Merrill-Palmer Inst., Detroit, 1958-59; psychiat. social worker Kings County Hosp., Bklyn., 1958; chief Lee County Mental Health Center, Keokuk, Iowa, 1959-60, Newark Beth Israel Hosp., 1960-62; instr. Tulane U. Sch. Social Work, New Orleans, 1963-64, 65-66, asst. prof., 1966-70; exec. dir. Jewish Family Service of Greater Mercer County (N.J.), 1970-73, 76—; dist. dir. Jewish Family Service of Phila., 1974-76; psychotherapist New Hope Guild Guidance Center, Bklyn., 1962; sch.-community coordinator Project Head Start, New Orleans, summer 1965; project dir., tng. manual devel. La. Dept. Pub. Welfare, summer 1966; cons. S.E. La. State Hosp., 1967-68; pvt. practice marriage counseling, New Orleans, 1966-70; tng. cons. N.J. Dept. Pub. Welfare, 1971-72; pvt. practice psychotherapy and marriage and family counseling, Fairless Hills and Feasterville, Pa., 1970—. Bd. dirs. Tulane-Newcomb Hillel Found., New Orleans, 1968-70. Merrill-Palmer grantee, 1958-59; HEW grantee, 1966. Fellow Pa. Soc. Clin. Social Work (founding mem., exec. bd.); mem. Nat. Alliance Family Life (clin. and founding mem.), Am. Assn. Marriage and Family Counselors (supr.), Acad. Certified Social Workers, Mercer County Social Welfare Assn. (v.p. 1972-73), Nat. Assn. Social Workers (vice chmn. psychiat. social work sect. of chpt. 1961-62, exec. bd. chpt. 1967-70), Pa. Assn. Marriage and Family Counselors. Address: 712 Warwick Rd Fairless Hills PA 19030

PINSON, NANCY MACEDWARDS, ednl. adminstr., author; b. Newton, Mass. Dec. 17, 1926; d. John J. and Barbara (Chalmers) Fitzpatrick; B.S., Fla. State U., 1947; Ed.M., U. Md., 1970, Ph.D., 1977; m. David C. Pinson, June 8, 1952 (div. 1970); children—Mark, Douglas, Lori. Tchr., Nat. Cathedral Sch., Washington, 1947-51: researcher Govt. Printing Office, Washington, 1962-63; tchr. and dir. Kindergarten, Landover, Md., 1963-65; tchr. elementary schs. Riverdale and Hyattsville, Md., 1966-68. grad. asst. counseling U. Md., College Park, 1969-70; coordinator vocat. guidance and project basic liaison for research and devel. Md. Dept. of Edn., Balt., 1970—; cons. in career edn., 1970—; Lectr. in field. Mem. Assn. for Curriculum and Supervision, Nat., Md. (legis. chmn. 1975—) vocat. guidance assns., Am. Vocat. Guidance Assn. (trustee), Am., Md. (Outstanding Service award 1977) personnel and guidance assns., Assn. for Counselor Edn. and Supervision (editorial bd., accreditation officer). Author: (with others) Career Education, 1972; (with K.B. Hoyt) Career Education and the Elementary School Teacher (Pi Lambda Theta award), 1973; (with D. Jesser) A Priority of the Chief State School Officers, 1975: contbr. numerous articles on leadership development, education and counseling to profl. jours. Home: 5807 Swarthmore Dr College Park MD 20740 Office: Maryland State Dept of Education PO Box 8717 Baltimore Washington Airport Baltimore MD 21240

PINTON, GIORGIO ALBERTO, multilingual educator; b. Vicenza, Italy, Apr. 4, 1930; s. Amadio Mario and Constantina (Giacometti) P.; came to U.S., 1965, naturalized, 1970; B.A., Aloisianum, Gallarate, 1955; B.D., Hartford Sem. Found., 1968, Ph.D., 1972; M.Ed., U. Hartford, 1978; m. Margaret B. Diehl, June 21, 1960; children—Michel, Phillip, Sarah, Daniel, Cristina. Asst. dir. Istituto Toniolo, Treviso, Italy, 1956-58; sec. ecumenical team World Council Chs., Italy, 1960-65; mem. faculties U. Conn., Trinity Coll., U. Hartford, 1968-76; dir. bilingual program New Haven Correctional Center, 1976—. Bd. dirs. Group Homes Inc. teenage centers, Ethel Walker Sch.; mem. Canton Bd. Edn., 1975—; sec. Canton Democratic Town Com.; bd. dirs. Capitol Region Edn. Center. Recipient 1st Richard Weingart award for research Hartford Sem. Found., 1968. Mem. Am. Assn. Tchrs. Italian, Tchrs. English to Speakers Other Langs., Conn. Soc. Religion and Health (exec. sec.), Unity in Neighborliness Integrity, Charity and Opportunity (UNICO). Club: Royal Soccer Acad. Author: Philosophies and Philosophers: A Sourcebook, 1975. Transl. Vico's Metaphysics, 1976. Home: 70 Bunker Hill Rd Collinsville CT 06022 Office: 340 Capitol Ave Hartford CT

PIOTROWSKI, ZBIGNIEW ANTHONY (TONY), metallographer; b. Torun, Poland, Dec. 16, 1929; s. Anthony and Anthonina (Zalenska) P.; student Newark Coll., Engring., 1960; m. Teofila Rita, Dec. 29, 1951; children—Richard, Henry, Rita. Technician, metallographer in microwave and thermo-electric labs. RCA, Harrison, N.J., 1955-64; metallographer, sr. metallographer, metallography lab. supr., technologes metallography and photography, research and devel. Engelhard Minerals and Chems. Corp., Edison, N.J., 1964—. Served with U.S. Army, 1951-53. Recipient 2d place Internat. Metallographic Soc. Exhbn., 1970, hon. mention, 1971, Buehler Tech. Paper merit award, 1977. Mem. Am. Soc. for Metals, Internat. Metallographic Soc. Roman Catholic. Contbr. articles to profl. jours. Home: 19 Alanon St Whippany NJ 07981 Office: Menlo Park NJ 08817

PIPA, ANDREW MICHAEL, JR., lawyer; b. Marion Heights, Pa., Jan. 1, 1927; s. Andrew M. and Estelle (Binkoski) P.; A.B., Pa. State U., 1948; LL.B., Dickinson Sch. Law, 1951; m. Mary Rea Millard, Oct. 22, 1955; children—Gwen, Andrew, Michael, David, Anthony, Kurt, Anne. Admitted to Pa. bar, 1952; individual practice law, Shamokin, 1952—; sr. partner firm Andrew M. Pipa, Jr., P.C.; pres. Andrew M. Pipa, Jr., Inc.; partner Heritage Apts.; developer Hillcrest Manor; partner Host Hills Assos. Asst. dist. atty. Northumberland County (Pa.), 1956-57; solicitor Coal Twp. Commrs., 1960-67, Ralpho Twp. Suprs., 1965-67, Northumberland County Airport Authority, Northumberland County Housing Authority, Northumberland County Sheriff's Office; dir., chmn. exec. com. solicitor Central Pa. Savs. Assn., Shamokin, 1965-78; mem. hearing com. Disciplinary Bd., Supreme Ct. Pa. Law Seminar lectr. Mem. Am., Pa. (mem. medico-legal com.), Northumberland County (pres. 1978) bar assns., Am., Pa. (legislative com. 1969-70, gov. 1971-73) trial lawyers assns., Am. Judicature Soc., Shamokin C. of C. (dir. 1974), Phi Kappa Sigma. Democrat. Roman Catholic. Elk. Clubs: Sons of Poland (Mt. Carmel), Shamokin Valley Country (pres. 1976-78). Home: Hillcrest Dr Elysburg PA 17824 Office: Commerce at Market St Shamokin PA 17872

PIPER, COLIN BREWSTER, govt. ofcl.; b. Bridgeport, Conn., May 15, 1939; s. Colin Emerson and Mildred (Reed) P.; B.S. in Mech. Engring., Newark Coll., 1965, postgrad., 1966; postgrad. Stevens Inst. Tech., 1966-69, Bklyn. Poly. Inst., 1971; m. Frances L. Juliano, June 3, 1961; children—Cheryl L., Colin E. Data processing technician Chubb & Son, Milburn, N.J., 1957-59, Resistoflex Corp., Roseland, N.J., 1959-61; with Picatinny Arsenal, 1965—, gen. engr. U.S. Army Research and Devel. Command, Dover, N.J., 1977—. Mem. Am. Def. Preparedness Assn. Clubs: Lakeside Tennis, Algonquin Racquet. Home: 59 Foxtrail Rd Sparta NJ 07871 Office: Bldg 3305 MTD ARRADCOM Dover NJ 07801

PIPER, GEORGE EARLE, retailing design and services co. exec.; b. Greenfield, Mass., Jan. 31, 1932; s. George B. and Elizabeth J. (Jones) P.; B.E., Keene State Coll., 1959, postgrad., 1959-60; postgrad. U. Mass., 1959-60, Boston U., 1960-61; m. Elizabeth Ann Mancini, Oct. 17, 1970; children—Sherri, Terri, Luanne, Mark. Dir. aux. services Keene (N.H.) State Coll., 1959-61; dir. purchasing and aux. enterprises U. Vt., Burlington, 1961-64; dir. state univ. store system U. Maine, Orono, 1964-68; pres. Store Ops. Services, Inc. and Coll. Mgmt. Assos., Franklin, Mass., 1968—; pres. Retailing Design & Services, Inc., Lutherville, Md., 1977—; dir. Picini Realty Trust, Franklin; tchr. U. Maine, Orono, 1966-67; chmn. various profl. workshops, 1965-72; mem. various nat. merchandising coms. 1959-61, 69-71. Mem. sch. bd. Winchester, N.H., 1959-61. Served with AC, USN, 1951-55. Recipient 4 nat. merchandising awards, 1961-66, service awards Nat. Assn. Coll. Stores, 1969-70, Nat. Assn. Coll. Aux. Services, 1974-75; 2 week nat. tour award Nat. Assn. Aux. Enterprises, 1976. Mem. Nat. Assn. Coll. Aux. Services, Nat. Assn. Coll. Stores, Coll. Stores of New Eng. (pres. 1967-69), Mid-Atlantic Coll. Stores, Mass. Businessmen's Assn., Kappa Delta Phi. Clubs: Masons, Shriners, Sons of Italy. Designer over 275 coll univ. aux. service areas of stores; presented papers various profl. groups; contbr. articles profl. jours. Home: 12 Pleasant St Franklin MA 02038 Office: PO Box G Franklin MA 02038

PIPEROPOULOS, GEORGIOS P., psychologist, sociologist; b. Greece, Apr. 21, 1942; B.A. in Sociology and Psychology with hons. certification in social sci. (Fulbright, J.F. Kennedy, Goldman, Tremaine and Scuer scholar), City Coll. City U. N.Y., 1964; M.A. in Sociology (teaching fellow), U. Mass., Amherst, 1967; Ph.D. in Psychology and Sociology Laudabilem, U. Salzburg (Austria), 1972; came to U.S., 1960, naturalized, 1976; m. Angeligque Ladas; 1 dau., Natasha. Instr. sociology, asst. chmn. dept. Providence Coll., 1966-67; lectr. sociology U. Md. European div., Ger., 1967-69; dir. planning and research Progress for Providence, Inc., 1969-70; asst. prof. psychology and sociology Bryant Coll., Smithfield, R.I., 1969; dir. N.E. Greece br. Nat. Centre Social Research, Salonica, 1973-74; spl. adviser Greek Ministry Planning, Econ. Coordination and Govt. Policy, 1973-74, Ministry Social Services, 1974-75; exec. dir. Spectrum House, Inc., therapeutic community, N. Grafton, Mass., 1975—; cons. in field, dir. seminars. Mem. Am., Mass. psychol. assns., Am., Mass. sociol. assns., Internat. Assn. Applied Psychology, Tau Kappa Epsilon. Author: The German Experience: Migrant Greek Workers in West Germany, 1972; Sociological Themes: Essays and Applied Research, 1973; Koinoniologica Themata, 1974; Introduction to Sociology, 1975; also articles, monographs. Editor: Perspectives in the Psychology of Abnormal Behavior, 1971; The Challenge of Adjustment, 1972. Originator, editor Therapeutic Communities of Am., quar. newsletter, 1976—. Address: 211 Westboro Rd North Grafton MA 01536

PIPITONE, ANTHONY JOHN, pharm. co. exec.; b. Jersey City, July 2, 1937; s. Paul Frank and Mary Nicole (LaRosa) P.; A.A., Fairleigh Dickinson U., 1957; B.S., 1959, M.B.A., 1960; m. Ann J. Lobello, June 6, 1959; children—Paul, David. Sales promotion supr. Becton Dickinson & Co., 1960-66; advt. product mgr. Ayerst Labs., Am. Home Products, 1966-70; v.p. sales Physicians Book Compendium, 1970-71; sr. product mgr. Block Drug Co., Jersey City, 1971-74; sr. brand mgr. Schmid Products Co., Little Falls, N.J., from 1974; now mktg. mgr. DePree and Health-Gard divs. Chattem Labs. Served to 1st lt. U.S. Army, 1960-66. Mem. Pharm. Advt. Club N.Y., Fairleigh Dickinson Alumni Assn., U.S. Power Squadron. Roman Catholic. Home: 20 Kisling Rd Lake Hopatcong NJ 07843 Office: 1715 W 38th St Chattanooga TN 37409

PIPPIN, PAUL WHEATLEY TOMLINSON, architect; b. Chestertown, Md., Nov. 12, 1912; s. Walter Tomlinson and Anna (Cosden) P.; B.A., Washington Coll., 1934; M.Arch., Columbia U., 1942; postgrad. Cranbrook Acad. Arts, Bloomfield Hills, Mich., 1946, Ill. Inst. Tech., 1947; m. Elizabeth Louise Wood, Mar. 20, 1952; children—Elizabeth Durland, Curtis Comegys. With various archtl. offices, including Harrison & Abramovitz, N.Y.C., 1947-51; architect Skidmore, Owings & Merrill, N.Y.C., 1951—, asso. partner, 1963-78; cons. archtl. and engring. offices, 1978—; asst. headmaster Norfolk (Va.) Acad., 1936; vis. lectr. Sch. Architecture Yale U., New Haven. Bd. dirs. Columbia Archtl. Sch., 1965. Served to lt. USNR, 1942-46. Recipient Washington Coll. Alumni award, 1962. Mem. AIA. Democrat. Episcopalian. Clubs: Rocky Point (Old Greenwich, Conn.); Univ. (N.Y.C.). Important works include IBM Corporate Hdqrs., Armonk, N.Y., Scholastic Mag. Office Bldg., Englewood Cliffs, N.J., U. N.H. Sch. Bus. Adminstrn. and Social Sci. Bldg., State U. N.Y. at Oswego Master Plan and Bldg., Shell Oil Data Processing Center, Tulsa, Cornell U. Social Sci. Bldg., Ithaca, N.Y., Procter and Gamble Co. Projects, Cin., Syracuse U. Newhouse Communication Bldg., Gen. Electric Hdqrs. Bldg., Fairfield, Conn., Texaco Co. Hdqrs., Harrison, N.Y., So. Bell Tel. & Tel. Co. Hdqrs., Atlanta. Home: 21 Shore Acre Dr Old Greenwich CT 06870 Office: 400 Park Ave New York City NY 10022

PIRAINO, ANTHONY JOSEPH, clin. pharmacologist; b. Phila., Feb. 6, 1949; s. Joseph Thomas and Josephine Rose (Trinacria) P.; B.S. in Biology, St. Joseph's Coll., 1971; M.S. in Pharmacology, Hahnemann Med. Coll., 1973, Ph.D., 1976; m. Mary Ellen Staudinger, Aug. 24, 1974. Grad. instr. dept. pharmacology Hahnemann Med. Coll., Phila., 1972-76, postdoctoral fellow in clin. pharmacology, 1976-77, sr. instr. pharmacology, 1977-78, clin. lectr. pharmacology 1976-78; clin. pharmacologist Dialysis Inc., Lansdowne, Pa., 1977—; freelance lectr. pharmacology, 1976—; lectr. on drug abuse to schs. and social groups, 1972—. Mem. AAAS, Hahnemann Med. Coll., St. Joseph's Coll. alumni assns. Roman Catholic. Contbr. articles to sci. jours. Home: 83 3d Ave Broomall PA 19003 Office: Dialysis Inc Lansdowne PA 19050

PIRANEO, FRANK PETER, psychologist; b. Bklyn., July 30, 1951; s. Frank Philip and Josephine P.; B.A. in Psychology, N.Y. U., 1973; M.S. in Edn., Pace U., 1977; m. Marie Iovino, Apr. 13, 1975. Houseparent, Bronx (N.Y.) Group Home—St. Michael's Services for Children, 1973-74; ednl. counselor St. Michael's Services for Children, S.I., N.Y., 1974-76; psychometrician, staff psychologist Diocesan Diagnostic and Learning Center, Bklyn., 1976-77; intern N.Y.C. Bd. Edn. Bur. Child Guidance, 1976-77, South Huntington (N.Y.) Schs., 1976-77; sch. psychologist Greenwich (Conn.) pub. schs., 1977—. Certified sch. psychologist, N.Y., N.J., Conn. Mem. N.Y. State Psychol. Assn., Nat., Conn. (exec. bd.) assns. sch. psychologists, Kappa Sigma, Psi Chi. Roman Catholic. Author career edn., value clarification curriculum for emotionally disturbed high sch. students. Home: 25 Benedict Ct Norwalk CT 06850 Office: Greenwich Bd Edn Havemeyer Bldg Greenwich CT 06830

PIRICH, JOHN FRANCIS, pump co. exec.; b. Verplanck, N.Y., Sept. 5, 1936; s. Michael and Mary Ann (Karsko) P.; B.S. in Bus. Adminstrn., Bryant Coll., 1959; postgrad. Harvard U., 1976-77; m. Patty Lou Wagner, May 27, 1961; children—Michele Anne, Johnny Francis. With Owens-Corning Fiberglas, Newark, Ohio, 1959-63, Barrington, N.J., 1963-69; mgr. purchasing Ingersoll Rand Co., Allentown, Pa., 1970-72, mgr. materials, 1973-74; group purchasing agt. Worthington Pump Corp., Mountainside, N.J., 1975—. Mgr., Westfield Sports Assn., 1977-78. Served with USMC, 1953-54. Certified purchasing mgr. Mem. Nat. Purchasing Mgrs. Assn., Nat., Lehigh Valley purchasing assns., Mgmt. Assn. for Materials Control. Roman Catholic. Home: 621 Glen Ave Westfield NJ 07090 Office: Worthington Pump Corp (USA) 270 Sheffield St Mountainside NJ 07092

PIRICH, RONALD GARY, physicist; b. Johnson City, N.Y., May 13, 1947; s. Andrew and Hilda (Toman) P.; B.A. (N.Y. State Regents scholar), State U. N.Y., Binghamton, 1970, M.A., 1976, Ph.D. in Physics, 1976. Engr. IBM, Endicott, N.Y., 1966-70; teaching asst. in physics State U. N.Y., Binghamton, 1970-76, research asst., 1972-74, instr. physics Sch. Gen. Studies, 1975; postdoctoral fellow U. Cin., 1977; research scientist Grumman Corp., Bethpage, N.Y., 1977—. Grantee N.Y. State sect. Am. Phys. Soc., 1975; State U. N.Y. at Binghamton Alumni Assn. travel grantee, 1975-76. Mem. Am. Assn. Physics Tchrs., AAUP, Am. Phys. Soc., Nat. Honor Soc. Secondary Schs., Soc. Physics Students, Grad. Physics Club, Sigma Xi, Sigma Pi Sigma. Republican. Home: 114 Fox Hollow Rd Woodbury NY 11797 Office: Research Dept Grumman Aerospace Corp Bethpage NY 11714

PIRNIE, MALCOLM, JR., cons. engr.; b. Mount Vernon, N.Y., Mar. 15, 1917; s. Malcolm and Gertrude (Knowlton) P.; A.B., Harvard, 1939, S.M., 1941; m. Jane Purse, Nov. 7, 1942; children—Malcolm III, Pamela. WIth Malcolm Pirnie Engrs., 1946—, asso., 1948-51, partner, 1952-70; chmn. bd. Malcolm Pirnie, Inc., 1970—. Pres. Berkeley Assn., Scarsdale, 1954; mem. non-partisan com., Scarsdale, N.Y., 1954-57. Bd. dirs. White Plains YMCA, 1967-70, Westchester County Assn., 1978—; rep. Hoover Medal Com., 1978—. Served from lt. (j.g.) to lt. comdr. USPHS, 1941-45, now in Res. Diplomate Am. Acad. Environ. Engrs. Fellow ASCE (dir. Met. sect. 1956-57, v.p., 1960-62, pres., 1962-63, nat. dir. 1967-70), Am. Cons. Engrs. Council (v.p. 1973-75); mem. Am. Inst. Cons. Engrs. (councilor 1964-66, v.p. 1965-66, 71-72), Inter-Am. Assn. San. Engrs., Am. Shore and Beach Preservation Assn., Fla. Engring. Soc., Water Resources Congress (projects com.), Harvard Engring. Soc. (v.p. 1955), Engrs. Joint Council (planning com. 1955-58; mem. engring. manpower commn. 1965-70), Am. Water Works Assn. (chmn. planning com. 1966), Engrs. Council for Profl. Devel. (guidance com. 1953-58), N.Y. Assn. Cons. Engrs. (dir. 1971-75). Clubs: Harvard (N.Y.C.); Town (Scarsdale, N.Y.); Scarsdale Golf. Home: 15 Windsor Ln Scarsdale NY 10583 Office: 2 Corporate Park Dr White Plains NY 10602

PIRONTI, PASCAL ANTHONY, urologist; b. Newark, Feb. 2, 1934; s. Louis and Rose P.: B.A., Johns Hopkins U., 1955; M.D., Hahnemann Med. Coll., 1959; m. June 29, 1963; children—Louis, Carolyn. Intern, Hahnemann Hosp., Phila., 1959-60, resident in gen. surgery, 1960-61, resident in urology, 1961-64; individual practice medicine specializing in urology, Summit, N.J., 1964—; attending urologist Overlook Hosp., Summit, 1970—, Children's Specialized Hosp., Mountainside, N.J., 1970—; staff VA Hosp., Lyons, N.J.: asso. urology Columbia U., N.Y.C., 1975—; cons. in field. Sec.-treas. Overlook Hosp., 1977—. Served with M.C., U.S. Army, 1967-68; Vietnam. Decorated Army Commendation medal. Diplomate Am.Bd. Urology. Fellow A.C.S., Acad. Medicine N.J.; mem. Union County (v.p. 1977-78), N.J. (del. 1975—) med. socs., AMA, Am. Urol. Assn., Am. Assn. Clin. Urologists, Am. Fertility Soc. Roman Catholic. Clubs: Plainfield Country, Clover Hill Swim. Home: 124 Stoneridge Rd Murray Hill NJ 07974 Office: 475 Springfield Ave Summit NJ 07901

PISANI, LAWRENCE FRANK, sociologist; b. New Haven, Mar. 13, 1921; s. Anthony Vincent and Dora (Ciccarelli) P.; B.A., Yale U., 1942, M.A., 1944, Ph.D., 1951. Instr. sociology U. Mass., 1946-48; asst. prof. sociology N.Y. State U., Binghamton, 1948-55; asso. prof. sociology Cedar Crest Coll., Allentown, Pa., 1955-61; prof., chmn. dept. sociology So. Conn. State Coll., New Haven, 1961—. Active Boy Scouts Am. Recipient Silver Beaver medal Boy Scouts Am., 1954, St. George award, 1956. Mem. Am. Sociol. Assn., Eastern Sociol. Soc. AAUP. Roman Catholic. Author: The Italian in America, 1957. Home: 44 Belmont St Hamden CT 06517 Office: So Conn State Coll 501 Crescent St New Haven CT 06515

PISANO, ALAN DAVID, elec. engr., educator; b. Chelsea, Mass., Aug. 29, 1946; s. George John and Margaret Irene (Allen) P.; B.S. in Elec. Engring. summa cum laude, Tufts U., 1968; M.S. in Elec. Engring., Northeastern U., 1971, Ph.D., 1974; m. Kathleen Isabel Duggan, Apr. 18, 1976; 1 son, Alan. With Gen. Electric Co., 1968—, engr. medium steam turbine dept., 1968-76, engr., advanced control systems aircraft engine group, 1976-78, supr. advanced engring. program, 1978—; adj. asst. prof. systems engring. Boston U. Registered profl. engr., Mass. Mem IEEE, Control System Soc., Tau Beta Pi, Phi Kappa Phi, Eta Kappa Nu. Club: Boston Tufts (exec. bd. 1975—). Patentee in field. Home: 50 Kimball Rd Chelsea MA 02150 Office: 1000 Western Ave Lynn MA 01910

PISCITELLI, R. AMELIA, phys. chemist; b. Oneonta, N.Y., Feb. 10, 1940; d. Joseph and Mary A. P.; B.A. (Saxton fellow 1959), Hartwick Coll., 1961; postgrad. U. Rochester (N.Y.); M.A., State U. N.Y. at Oneonta, 1978. Jr. chemist Elec. Components div. Bendix Corp., Sidney, N.Y., 1966-68, chemist, 1969-74, sr. engr., 1974—. NSF fellow Syracuse U., 1960. Mem. Am. Phys. Soc., Chem. Soc./Royal Inst. Chemistry (Eng.), Soc. Applied Spectroscopy, Electrochem. Soc., Am. Soc. Metals, Sidney Engrs.' Club (past pres.), Sidney Bendix Mgmt. Club. Author: (with others) Metal-Slag-Gas Reactions and Processes, 1975; also articles in profl. jours. Office: Bendix Corp Sherman Ave Sidney NY 13838

PISETSKY, MYRON MATTHEW, psychiatrist; b. Hartford, Conn., July 12, 1935; s. Isador and Gussie (Langer) P.; B.S., Trinity Coll., 1957; M.D., Tufts U., 1961; m. Rita Baker, Aug. 28, 1960; 1 dau., Helena. Intern, St. Francis Hosp., Hartford, 1961-62; resident psychiatry Inst. Living, Hartford, 1962-65, dir. group psychotherapy tng. program, 1967—, asst. chief of sect., 1967—; practice medicine specializing in psychiatry, Hartford, 1967—; clin. asso. dept. psychiatry Health Center Sch. Medicine, U. Conn., Storrs, 1967-73, asst. clin. prof., 1973—. Served to capt. M.C., AUS, 1965-67. Diplomate Am. Bd. Psychiatry and Neurology. Fellow Am. Psychiat. Assn.; mem. AMA, Conn., Hartford, Hartford County med. assns., Conn. Psychiat. Soc., Am., Conn. group psychotherapy assns., Phi

Beta Kappa. Republican. Jewish. Home: 173 W Ridge Dr West Hartford CT 06117 Office: 400 Washington St Hartford CT 06106

PITASSY, CAESAR LEOPOLD, lawyer; b. N.Y.C., Dec. 26, 1914; s. Julius F. and Julia F. (DiSalle) P.; A.B., N.Y. U., 1937; LL.B., Fordham U., 1941; m. Margaret C. Cotter, June 30, 1942; 1 son, Richard N. Admitted to N.Y. State bar, 1941, D.C. bar, 1961, U.S. Supreme Ct. bar, 1971; asso. firm Rogers & Wells, and predecessors, N.Y.C., 1942-51, mem. firm, 1951—; dir. Gerli & Co., Inc., Mason, Nixon & Kennedy, Inc., Ramsona Fabrics, Ltd.; lectr. law Fordham U. Sch. Law, 1943-45. Mem. Am., N.Y., Westchester County bar assns., N.Y. County Lawyers Assn. (dir. 1975-78, chmn. judiciary com. 1975-78), Assn. Bar City N.Y., N.Y. Law Inst., Fordham U. Law Alumni Assn. (pres. 1959-64, dir. 1965—, medal of achievement 1972). Club: Winged Foot Golf (Mamaroneck, N.Y.). Editor-in-chief Fordham Law Rev., 1940-41. Home: 11 Hidden Green Ln Larchmont NY 10538 Office: 200 Park Ave New York City NY 10017 also 1666 K St NW Washington DC 20006

PITCHUMONI, CAPECOMORIN SANKAR, physician; b. Madura, India, Jan. 20, 1938; s. Sankara and Jaya (Lekshmi) Iyer; student St. Xavier Coll., India; M.B. B.S., Trivandrum (India) Med. Coll., 1959, M.D., 1965; m. Prema Iyer, Nov. 11, 1964; children—Sheila, Shoba, Suresh. Intern, Med. Coll., Trivandrum, India, 1961-63: resident in gastroenterology Yale U.; practice medicine specializing in gastroenterology, N.Y.C., 1972—; asst. prof. medicine Kottayam (India) Med. Coll., 1967; asst. prof. medicine N.Y. Med. Coll., 1972-75, asso. prof., 1975—; asso. preventive and social medicine, 1977; chief sect. gastroenterology Met. Hosp. Center N.Y., 1975—. Recipient Om Prakash award Indian Soc. Gasstrenterology, 1976. Fellow Royal Coll. Physicians and Surgeons Can., A.C.P., Am. Coll. Gastroenterology; Mem. Assn. Physicians India, Am. Gastroenterol. Assn., India Soc. Gastroenterology (life), Am. Inst. Nutrition, N.Y. Gastroenterol, Assn., Kerala Samajam (pres. 1977-78). Hindu. Contbg. author med. textbooks. Contbr. articles to med. jours. Home: 178 Fairmount Ave Glenrock NJ 07452 Office: 1901 1st Ave New York City NY 10029

PITKIN, FRANK IVAN, physician; b. Montpelier, Vt., Apr. 28, 1921; s. Perley Peabody and Sylvia (Sherman) P.; student Norwich U., 1943-44, Amherst Coll., 1944-45; M.D., U. Vt., 1949; postgrad. U. Pa., 1954-55; children—Karen, Dawn, Holly. Intern and med. resident Mary Fletcher Hosp., Burlington, Vt., 1949-51, 53-54; asst. med. dir. New Eng. Mut. Life. Ins. Co., Boston, 1955-64, asso. med. dir., 1964-70, sr. asso. med. dir., 1970-76, 2d v.p., med. dir., 1976—; asst. in medicine Peter Bent Brigham Hosp., Boston, 1956-73; chmn. subcom. on risk factor screening Greater Boston chpt. Mass. Heart Assn., 1968, com. on heart info. services, 1968, 69, chmn. pub. relations com., 1970-71, mem. program com., 1963-67. Served with AUS, 1942-46, to 1st lt. M.C., 1951-52. Diplomate Bd. Life Ins. Medicine. Fellow Am. Coll. Cardiology, Am. Coll. Chest Physicians (past mem. com. electrocardiography and vectorcardiography); mem. AMA, Mass. State Med. Soc., Suffolk Dist. Med. Soc. (past chmn. diabetes detection program), Assn. Life Ins. Med. Dirs. Am. (chmn. bd. life ins. medicine, 1975-76). Contbr. articles in field to profl. jours. Home: 7 Louisburg Sq Boston MA 02108 Office: 501 Boylston St Boston MA 02117

PITTA KIRK, PATRICIA JOYCE, psychologist; b. N.Y.C., July 3, 1947; d. John Joseph and Mildred (Giosa) Pitta; B.A., Queens Coll., 1968; M.S., Hunter Coll., 1973; Ph.D. (fellow), Fordham U., 1975; m. Eric E. Kirk, June 26, 1976. Ednl. and recreational therapist Roosevelt Hosp., N.Y.C., 1968-72, intern clin. psychology, 1972-73; therapist, evaluator N.Y.C. Bd. Edn., 1973-74; staff and cons. psychologist Bellevue Hosp., N.Y.C., 1974-77; cons. psychologist St. Johns Episcopal Hosp., Smithtown, N.Y. 1977—, N. Shore Univ. Hosp., 1977—; clin. instr. N.Y. U. Med. Sch., N.Y.C., 1974—; radio lectr. obesity control; dir. cognitive stimulus control program for obesity. Mem. Am., Nassau County (N.Y.) psychol. assns. Home and Office: 41 Fairway Ln Manhasset NY 11030

PITTMAN, CHARLES VERNON, banker; b. Balt., Jan. 22, 1948; s. Charlie James and Jean (Rogers) P.; B.S., Pa. State U., 1970; M.B.A., Gannon Coll., 1976; m. Maurese B. Thomas, June 27, 1970; children—Charles Anthony, Kira Michelle. Profl. football player St. Louis Cardinals, 1970-71, Balt. Colts, 1971-73, charge card officer Marine Bank, Erie, Pa., 1974-77, v.p., mgr. consumer credit, 1978—. Bd. dirs. YMCA, Erie Civic Center Assn., Boy Scouts Am., Erie United Way, Stairways, Inc.; v.p. Booker T. Washington Center, Erie. Named All Am. Football Player, Pa. State U., 1969. Mem. Black Assos. of Erie, Am. Inst. Banking. Home: 4704 Lawndale Dr Erie PA 16506 Office: 901 State St Erie PA 16501

PITTMAN, WALTER RUSSELL, ct. reporter; b. Warren, Pa., July 27, 1935; s. Paul Hollister and Evelyn Florence (Johnson) P.; student Jamestown Community Coll., 1958-59; m. Sandra Evelyn Berglund, Feb. 2, 1957; children—Deirdre Evelyn, Elizabeth Mary, Jane Margaret. Clk., Pa. R.R., Warren, Pa. and Olean, N.Y., 1953-70; reporter for motor vehicle hearings AJN Reporters, Albany, N.Y., 1970-72; freelance ct. reporter, Ithaca, N.Y., 1972-74; ct. reporter Chemung County, Elmira, N.Y., 1974—. Served with USN, 1954-58. Registered profl. reporter. Mem. Nat. N.Y. State shorthand reporters assns. Clubs: Chemung County Rod and Gun, Masons, Shriners. Home: 14845

PITTS, ALBERT S., investment firm exec.; b. Phila., Jan. 5, 1933; s. James R. and Christine (Dodds) P.; certificate N.Y. Inst. Fin., 1963; certificate Coll. Fin. Planning, 1973; m. Marian C. Szymanski, Apr. 18, 1953; children—James Albert, Thomas Morton, Christine, Kenneth Daniel. Apprentice typesetter, journeyman printing industry, Phila., 1950-60, typographic salesman, 1960-62; mut. fund salesman, part-time 1959-62; v.p., dir. pension and profit sharing dept. Robinson & Co., Inc., Phila., 1963-70; v.p. Mid-Atlantic states Putnam Fund Distbrs., Phila., 1970-74, v.p. Mid Atlantic States Shareholders Securities Corp., Los Angeles, 1974-75; pres., treas., exec. Design Investments, Inc., 1975—. Advisory com. Invest in Am. Nat. Council; advisory bd. Villanova U. Mem. Internat. Assn. Fin. Planners, Inst. Certified Fin. Planners Council, Del. Valley Assn. Fin. Planners (pres.). Republican. Roman Catholic. Kiwanian (dir.). Home: 124 E Glenolden Ave Glenolden PA 19036 Office: Suite 5 415 E Baltimore Ave Media PA 19063

PITTS, FRED, cons. elec. engr., artist; b. Alexander City, Ala., Sept. 19, 1934; s. Mathew Otis and Irene (Tate) P.; B.E.E., U. Fla., 1958; postgrad. Corcoran Sch. Art, 1963-69; m. Marjorie Elizabeth McInnis, Nov. 6, 1965; 1 dau., Samantha. Asso. engr. Westinghouse Electric Corp., Pitts., also Balt., 1958-62; sr. asso. Booz, Allen & Hamilton, Inc., cons.'s, Bethesda, Md., 1962-69, 72—; pvt. cons. collaborations in art and tech., Washington, 1969-72; mem. faculty Corcoran Sch. Art, Washington, 1972-77; Smithsonian Instn., Washington, 1973—, exhbns. cons., 1970—; executed with Juan Downey, electronic scupture, Tel Aviv Museum; collaborations in exhbns. for Bklyn. Mus., Corcoran Gallery, Everson Mus., Smithsonian Instn. and comml. galleries, solar photography Kitt Peak Nat. Obs., Ariz.; exhibited as Mus. History and Tech. of Smithsonian Instn., 1975-76. Mem. Neighborhood Arts Council, D.C. Commn. on Arts, 1972-73; adv. neighborhood commr., Washington, 1976—. Served with U.S. Army, 1954-56. Registered profl. engr., D.C. Research and devel. in heliography and photo-engraving. Patentee microwave radar devices. Home: 2636 Woodley Pl NW Washington DC 20008 Office: 4330 East-West Hwy Bethesda MD 20014

PIZZI, RAYMOND JAMES, electronic engr.; b. Newark, Jan. 2, 1933; s. James Raymond and Mary (Cifrodella) P.; B.S.E.E., N.J. Inst. Tech., 1957, M.S.E.E., 1972; m. Gladys Ann Miller, Apr. 4, 1965; 1 son, James. Elec. engr. IT&T, Nutley, N.J., 1957-68, Hewlett Packard, Berkeley Heights, N.J., 1968-75; measurement specialist Dept. Def., Fort Monmouth, Tinton Falls, N.J., 1975—. Bd. dirs. Ocean County council Boy Scouts Am., 1970-72. Recipient certificate of Accomplishment, Hewlett Packard, 1970; certificate of Achievement, Dept. Def., 1976. Mem. Am. Def. Preparedness Assn. (bd. dirs. 1972-75), Inst. Environ. Scientists, IEEE. Club: Kiwanis. Contbr. articles to profl. jours. Patentee in field of measurement and calibration. Home: 225 18th Ave Bricktown NJ 08723 Office: DAVAA-A Fort Monmouth NJ 07703

PIZZURRO, JOSEPH PATRICK, orthopedic surgeon; b. Bronx, N.Y., Sept. 10, 1937; s. Andrew Joseph and Rose Ann (Daddino) P.; B.S., St. Peter's Coll., 1959; M.D., St. Louis U., 1963; m. Linda Ann Abrams, Oct. 27, 1962; children—Joseph Patrick, Andrew William, Mark Marion. Intern, St. Louis U. Group Hosps., 1963-64; resident gen. surgery Bronx VA Hosp., N.Y.C., 1966-68; resident orthopedic surgery N.Y. U.-Bellevue, N.Y.C., 1968-71; individual practice medicine, specializing in orthopedic surgery, Ridgewood, N.J., 1971—; attending Valley Hosp., Ridgewood, 1971—, rep.-at-large to med. bd., also trustee, 1976-77; cons. in field; dir. United Jersey Bank N., Ridgewood. Served with M.C., U.S. Army, 1964-66; Vietnam. Decorated Army Commendation Medal with oak leaf cluster. Recipient K.C. Humanitarian award, 1977. Diplomate Am. Bd. Orthopedic Surgeons. Fellow Am. Acad. Orthopedic Surgeons, A.C.S.; mem. AMA (Physicians Recognition award 1969, 72, 75), Ridgewood, N.J., Bergen County (trustee 1977—) med. socs., N.J., Eastern orthopedic socs., Phi Rho Sigma. Roman Catholic. Clubs: Ridgewood Country, Darlington Racquet. Office: 10 Wilsey Sq Ridgewood NJ 07450

PLAKOGIANNIS, FOTIOS MICHAELIS, educator; b. Epitalion, Greece, June 6, 1934; s. Michael F. and Rodoula (Hiliou) P.; Pharm.Dipl., U. Athens, Greece, 1958; M.S., Ohio State U., 1964; Ph.D., U. So. Calif., 1967; m. Iro Athanasoulia, Dec. 27, 1971; children—Michael, Roda. Came to U.S., 1961, naturalized, 1968. Pharmacist, Athens, 1958-61; teaching asst. Ohio State U., Columbus, 1961-63; teaching asst., research fellow U. So. Calif., Los Angeles, 1963-67; prof. phys. pharmacy and biopharmaceutics Bklyn. Coll. Pharmacy, 1967—. Cons. to pharm. industry, 1969. Mem. N.Y. Acad. Sci., Acad. Basic Pharmaceutics, Assn. Coll. Pharmacy, Am. Pharm. Assn. Club: Hellenic University (N.Y.C.). Author: Contemporary Biopharmaceutics, 1973; Self-Assessment of Current Knowledge in Pharmacy, 1976; Basic Concepts in Biopharmaceutics: An Introduction, 1977; contbr. articles to profl. jours. Office: 75 DeKalb Ave Brooklyn NY 11201

PLANAS, ROBERTO FUENTES, author, judo instr.; b. Miami, Fla., Dec. 4, 1934; s. Roberto Fuentes and Margot Planas (Vasquez) Duani; B.S.L., Vedado Inst., 1952; student law U. Havana, 1956-60; m. Nurmi Diaz, Aug. 1, 1962; 1 son, Roberto Fuentes; m. 2d, Grace Planas, Aug. 5, 1970 (div.). Asst. judo tchr. Cranford (N.J.) Judo and Karate Center, 1970—; statis. typist Carter, Ledyard & Milburn, N.Y.C., 1969—; writer novels including Kiai, 1973; Mistress of Death, 1974; The Bamboo Bloodbath, 1974; Ninja's Revenge, 1975; Amazon Slaughter, 1976; contbr. short sci. fiction stories to Vertex Mag.; book reviewer, writer tech. articles Judo Times; mem. editorial bd. Am. Judoman, 1975—; asst. editor Am. Judo Mag. Mem. Sci. Fiction Writers Am., U.S. Judo Fedn., U.S. Judo Assn., Capital Judo Black Belt Assn., Mensa. Roman Catholic. Club: Spanish (Havana). 3d degree Black Belt in Judo; twice Grand Champion of Cuba in Judo; Met. Masters Judo champion, N.Y.C., 1974, 75, 76, also grand champion, 1976; Cuba freedom fighter. Home: 470 Jefferson Ave Apt 5A Elizabeth NJ 07201 Office: 2 Wall St New York City NY 10005

PLASTRIK, EUGENE ANGUS, financial and health care exec.; b. N.Y. State, Oct. 9, 1930; s. Harry and Sarah P.; B.A., City U. N.Y., 1959, M.A., 1967; m. DiAnne; children—Jonathan, Gillis. Asst. v.p. Look mag., 1962; dir. research Gardner Advt., 1963; exec. dir. Comprehensive Health Planning Council Central Mass., 1974; fin., accounting and mgmt. Nat. Health Care Mgmt. Devel. Group, Walden, N.Y., 1967—, now exec. v.p., dir.; gen. mgr. Plastrik Cons. & Fin. Services; dir. Technolloyds Modular & Bldg. Corp., Stonehenge Lloyds Corp., Gallapagas Electronics Co.; asst. prof. bus. and mktg. State U. N.Y., Genesee, 1967-70, Clarkson Coll., Potsdam, N.Y., 1971. Bd. dirs. Gillis Jonathan Center Research. Mem. Am. Acad. Med. Adminstrs. Author book, papers, reports in field. Office: Box 590A Walden NY 12586

PLATEK, STANLEY FRANK, cleaning fluid co. exec.; b. Newark, Mar. 21, 1920; s. Stanley and Caroline (Golba) P.; grad. Casy Jones Sch. Aeros., Newark, 1940; m. Grace Pennucci, Oct. 1942 (div. 1944); m. 2d, Barbara Kuchek, May 8, 1965. Civilian instr. aircraft repair U.S. Army, Middletown, Pa., 1942, Casey Jones Sch. Aeros., Newark, 1942; owner Magicleaner Co., Newark, 1948—. Served to sgt. USMCR, 1942-45. Recipient Gold medal 5th world selection Household Cleaning Products, Brussels, 1968. Patentee cleaning apparatus. Home: 739 Chancellor Ave Irvington NJ 07111 Office: Magicleaner Co 778 Chancellor Ave Irvington NJ 07111

PLATT, DAVID SANFORD, pathologist; b. Elmira, N.Y., May 26, 1930; s. Harold and Esther Hattie (Kahn) P.; B.S., Union Coll., 1952; M.D., U. Rochester, 1957; m. Marilyn L. Stutsky, Oct. 3, 1971. Intern, Strong Meml. Hosp., Rochester, N.Y., 1957-58, asst. resident in pathology, 1958-59, resident, 1959-60, resident fellow in pathology, 1960-61; instr. pathology U. Rochester, 1959-61, clin. asst. prof. pathology, 1966—; asso. pathologist Highland Hosp., Rochester, 1963-66, dir. dept. anatomic pathology, 1966—. Served to capt., M.C., USAF, 1961-63. Diplomate Am. Bd. Pathology, Nat. Bd. Med. Examiners. Mem. Internat. Acad. Pathology, N.Y. Assn. Pub. Health Labs., N.Y. Soc. Pathologists, Rochester Area Assn. Pathologists. Contbr. articles in field to med. jours. Home: 11 Danbury Circle N Rochester NY 14618 Office: Highland Hosp Rochester NY 14620

PLATT, LEE FREW, realtor; b. Gunnison, Colo., Nov. 15, 1914; d. James Ellis and Elsie Helen (Rau) Frew. Owner, operator Lee Frew Platt, Realtors, Bethesda, Md., 1953—; mem. Edn. Adv. Com. Real Estate Commn. Md.; cons. Ednl. Testing Service, Princeton, N.J.; dir. Montgomery County Bd. Realtors Fed. Credit Union; dir. St. Luke's House, Inc., 1972; instr. U. Md., Montgomery Coll. Mem. Nat., Md. assns. realtors, Montgomery County Bd. Realtors (past pres.), Realtors Nat. Mktg. Inst., Grad. Realtors Inst., Omega Tau Rho. Democrat. Author: The Real Estate Examination Study Guide, 1974, List Aides, 1971; Columnist: Real Problems. Home: Silver Spring MD 20902 Office: 4419 E-W Hwy Bethesda MD 20014

PLATT, MARTIN HAROLD, pediatrician; b. St. Louis, May 9, 1938; s. Abe and Laura (Kinberg) P.; B.A., Washington U., St. Louis, 1960, M.D., 1964; m. Judith Perlstein, Mar. 28, 1965; children—Reina Lauren, Thomas Andrew, Alec Bennett. Intern, Maimonides Hosp., Bklyn., 1964-65, resident in pediatrics, 1965, 66, 68; instr. pediatrics Albert Einstein Coll. Medicine; fellow gastroenterology Bronx Lebanon Hosp., 1969-70; practice medicine, specializing in pediatrics, Yorktown Heights, N.Y., 1970—; asst. attending staff No. Westchester Hosp., Mt. Kisco, N.Y., 1970—. Served to lt. M.C., USN, 1966-68. Recipient Research award, Maimonides Hosp., 1966. Fellow Am. Acad. Pediatrics; mem. Westchester Acad. Medicine. Jewish. Club: B'nai B'rith. Home: Crow Hill Rd Mount Kisco NY 10549 Office: 1940 Commerce St Yorktown Heights NY 10598

PLATTEN, DONALD CAMPBELL, banker; b. N.Y.C., Sept. 19, 1918; s. John Homer and Katherine Campbell (Viele) P.; B.A., Princeton U., 1940; grad. Advanced Mgmt. Program, Harvard U., 1966; m. Margaret Leslie Wyckoff, June 24, 1940; children—Kathlerine L. (Mrs. Randolph S. Naylor), Peter W., Alison C. (Mrs. Alfred G. Vanderbilt, Jr.). With Chem. Bank N.Y.C., 1940—, sr. v.p., 1964-67, exec. v.p., 1967-70, 1st v.p., 1970-72, pres., 1972-73, chmn. bd., 1973—; chmn. bd. Chem. N.Y. Corp., 1973—; dir. CPC Internat., Inc., Am. Chain & Cable Co., Otis Elevator Co., Thomson Newspapers, Inc. Mem. adv. council Pace Coll. Chmn. bd. dirs. Goodwill Industries Greater N.Y.; bd. dirs. United Fund Greater N.Y., Econ. Devel. Council N.Y., Spencer Found., Chgo., Nat. Fgn. Trade Council; trustee Collegiate Sch., N.Y.C., Am. U. Beirut, United Student Aid Funds; charter trustee Princeton. Served to 1st lt. AUS, 1944-46. Mem. Japan Soc., Council on Fgn. Relations, Internat. C. of C. (trustee U.S. council), Res. City Bankers Assn. Clubs: University, Blind Brook, Links, Downtown Assn., Presidents, Bond (N.Y.C.), Economic (N.Y.); Laurel Valley Golf (Ligonier, Pa.). Home: 9 Pasture Ln Darien CT 06820 also 200 E 66th St New York City NY 10021 Office: 20 Pine St New York City NY 10015

PLATTHY, JENO, editor, assn. exec.; b. Dunapataj, Hungary, Aug. 13, 1920; s. Joseph K. and Maria (Dobor) P.; came to U.S., naturalized, 1963; tchr.'s diploma Peter Pazmany U., 1942; Ph.D., Ferencz J. Univ., 1944; M.S., Catholic U. Am., 1965; D.Letters (hon.), Academica Sinica, 1975; Ph.D. (hon.), Yangmingshan U., 1975; D.Litt. (hon.), U. Libre Asie, 1977; m. Carol Louise Abell, Sept. 25, 1976. Lectr. various univs., Japan, China, Korea, Philippines, South Vietnam, 1956-59; with Internat. Inst. of Boston, 1959-62; sec. Trustees for Harvard U., Washington, 1962—; editor-in-chief Monumenta Classica Perennia, N.Y.C., 1967—; exec. dir. Fedn. Internat. Poetry Assns., 1976—; pres. 3d Internat. Congress Poets, 1976. Recipient Confucius award Chinese Poetry Soc., 1974. Fellow Internat. Poetry Soc.; mem. PEN, Internat. Platform Assn., Internat. Soc. Lit., Die Literarische Union, N.Y. Poetry Forum, Melbourne Shakespeare Soc., Poets Internat. Orgn., World Poetry Soc., Intercontinental, Accademia di Leonardo da Vinci, Translation Fund (trustee), United Poets Laureate Internat., New Eng. Poetry Club. Author: Tavasz, 1948; Sie wollten nur die Freiheit, 1957; From Budapest to Tokyo, 1957; Summer Flowers, 1960; Autumn Dances, 1963; Sources on the Earliest Greek Libraries with the Testimonia, 1968; Winter Tunes, 1975; Ch'u Yuan, His Life and Works, 1975; Springtide, 1976; (opera in 3 acts) Bamboo, 1976 (written 1965). Office: PO Box 39072 Washington DC 20016

PLATZ, JOSEPH, physician; b. Cologne, Ger., Apr. 11, 1905; s. Jacob and Rosa (Rosenthal) P.; came to U.S., 1933, naturalized, 1940; student U. Munich, 1928-29; M.D., U. Cologne, 1931; m. Esther L. Semenoff, Oct. 3, 1940; 1 son, James B. Intern, Fordham Hosp., N.Y.C., 1933-34, clin. asst., 1934-52; resident in surgery City Hosp., Offenburg, Germany, 1932-33; gen. practice medicine, N.Y.C., 1934-52, East Hartford, Conn., 1952—; mem. staff Mt. Sinai, E. Hartford, Manchester hosps.; chief staff East Hartford Hosp., 1958-63. Named master emeritus U.S. Chess Fedn., 1975; recipient numerous chess awards. Mem. Manchester, Hartford County, Conn. med. socs., AMA, Am. Assn. Family Physicians, U.S. Chess Fedn. Club: Hartford Chess. Columnist chess column Hartford Times, 1960-62; contbr. articles to profl. jours., popular mags. Home: 6 Bates Rd Manchester CT 06040

PLAUT, MARTIN EDWARD, physician; b. Leipzig, Germany, Feb. 19, 1937; s. Otto L. and Hannah (Lowenstein) P.; came to U.S., 1939, naturalized, 1946; A.B., Brown U., 1958; M.D., Tufts U., 1962; m. Sharon Evert, Sept. 10, 1965; children—Benjamin Bogart, Anne, Susan. Intern, Buffalo Gen. Hosp., 1962-63; resident Buffalo Gen. Hosp. and New Eng. Med. Center, Boston; fellow infectious diseases New Eng. Med. Center, 1964-67; practice medicine, specializing in infectious diseases; asst. prof. medicine State U. N.Y., Buffalo, 1967-72, asso. prof. medicine, 1972—; chief infectious diseases Buffalo Gen. Hosp., 1969—. Fellow ACP; mem. Am. Soc. Microbiology. Club: Ft. Erie (Ont.) Turf. Contbr. articles to profl. jours.; author novels (pseudonymn Paul Marttin) Heartsblood, 1970, Cocoa Blades. Address: 100 High St Buffalo NY 14203

PLAWSKY, BERNARD MORRIS, assn. exec.; b. N.Y.C., Sept. 9, 1926; s. Abraham and Sara (Lipman) P.; B.Social Sci., Coll. City N.Y., 1949; M.S.W., Pa. Sch. Social Work, 1962; m. Jean Plotkin, May 25, 1952; children—Joel, Cheryl. Dir. Neighborhood Centre, Phila., 1961-67, N.E. Health and Welfare Council, Phila., 1967-72; exec. dir. Human Services Planning Council, Flint, Mich., 1972-76; instr., guest lectr. Rutgers U., 1971-72, Community Coll. Phila., 1969-72. Mem. adv. com. Jewish Family Service, 1969-72; mem. exec. bd. NAACP, 1971-72; bd. dirs. Counseling Or Referral Assistance, B'nai B'rith Youth Orgn. Recipient Profl. Service award Neighborhood Centre, 1964; Legion of Honor, Chapel of Four Chaplains, 1972. Mem. Am. Soc. Pub. Adminstrn. Home: 4480 Nantucket Rd Harrisburg PA 17112 Office: 2 Shore Dr Office Center 2001 N Front St Harrisburg PA 17102

PLESKOW, ERIC ROY, film co. exec.; b. Vienna, Austria, Apr. 24, 1924; s. Joseph and Therese (Weisbartel) P.; came to U.S. 1939, naturalized, 1943; student engring., Coll. City N.Y., 1942-43; m. Barbara Black, Apr. 2, 1954; children—Michelle Sandy, Anthony Marcus. Asst. mgr. MPEA, Germany, 1948-50; with Sol Lesser Prodns., Germany, 1950-51; mng. dir. United Artists Corp. (SA) (Pty) Ltd., Johannesburg, South Africa, 1952; gen. mgr. United Artists GmbH, Germany, 1953-58; exec. asst. to continental mgr. UNARTISCO, Paris, 1958-60, continental mgr., 1960-62, v.p. and fgn. officer, N.Y.C., 1962-73, exec. v.p., 1973, pres., chief exec. officer, mem. exec. com., dir., 1973-78; president, chief exec. officer Orion Pictures Corp., N.Y.C., 1978—. Served with AUS, 1943-48. Decorated comdr. Order Al Merito Della Repubblica Italiana (Italy); recipient Golden Medal of Honor, City of Vienna, 1970. Mem. Anti Defamation League, Found. Child Mental Welfare. Clubs: Harmonie, Friars (N.Y.C.). Home: 710 Park Ave New York NY 10021 Office: 75 Rockefeller Plaza New York NY 10019

PLIMPTON, STEPHEN WARDWELL, photographer; b. Brookline, Mass., Aug. 23, 1923; s. Theodore Barnet and Irene (Snow) P.; student St. George's Sch., 1939-43, Brown U., 1944-46. Prodn. staff World Wide Broadcasting Found., Sta. WRUL, Boston, 1947-48; copywriter Batten, Barton, Durstine & Osborn, Inc., Boston, 1950-51; TV critic The Boston Herald, 1951; owner Stephen W. Plimpton, Comml. Photography, Boston, 1953—; v.p., dir. D.F. Farrington Co., Inc., Boston, 1964-75; asso. Boston Biomed. Research Inst., 1973—.

Mem. exec. com. Brit. Charitable Soc., Boston. Vol. Am. Field Service, N.Africa, Italy, 1943-44. Mem. Soc. Colonial Wars (dep. sec. Mass. 1969-77), Mass. Soc. Mayflower Descs. (dep. gov. Mass. 1976-77), Alpha Delta Phi. Republican. Episcopalian. Clubs: Brit. Officers Club of N.E. (trustee 1976-78) (Boston); Army and Navy (Washington).

PLONSKY, SEYMOUR, mfg. co. exec.; b. N.Y.C., June 21, 1924; s. Adam and Ida (Winkler) P.; B.E.E., City U. N.Y., 1947; postgrad Columbia U., 1948-50; m. Vera Lisbeth Kaufman, June 13, 1953; children—Leslie David, Richard Daniel. Test engr. Elec. Testing Labs., N.Y.C., 1947-49; devel. engr. Mergenthaler Linotype Co., N.Y.C., 1952-53; project mgr. Celanese Corp., Newark, 1950-51, 53-57; group leader process control and instrumentation Hoffmann-LaRoche, Inc., Nutley, N.J., 1957—. Chmn. com. Eagle Rock council Boy Scouts Am., 1966-67. Served with U.S. Mcht. Marine, 1944-46. Registered profl. engr., N.J. Mem. Instrument Soc. Am., Sigma Xi, Nat., N.J. woodcarvers assns. Home: 2 Marquette Rd Montclair NJ 07043 Office: Kingsland Rd Nutley NJ 07110

PLOSCOWE, STEPHEN ALLEN, lawyer; b. N.Y.C., Jan. 30, 1941; s. Samuel Stuart and Molly Florence (Slutsky) P.; B.S., Cornell U., 1962, LL.B., 1965; m. Wendie Sue Malkin, Sept. 5, 1964; children—Jon Brian, Lauren Beth. Admitted to N.J. bar, 1965; asso. atty. firm Cole, Berman & Garth, Paterson, N.J., 1965-69; partner firm Cole, Berman & Belsky, Paterson and Rochelle Park, N.J., 1970—; atty., Borough of N. Caldwell (N.J.), 1973—; instr. N.J. Inst. Continuing Legal Edn.; vis. lectr. Cornell U. Sch. Indsl. Labor Relations. Bd. govs. Daughters Israel Pleasant Valley Home; trustee Jewish Community Fedn. Met. N.J. Mem. Am., N.J. (chmn. com. housing and urban affairs 1976-78), Passaic County (N.J.) bar assns., Indsl. Relations Research Assn., Urban Land Inst. Republican. Jewish. Home: 76 Brookside Terr North Caldwell NJ 07006 Office: 365 W Passaic St Rochelle Park NJ 07662

PLOTKIN, IRVING H(ERMAN), cons. economist; b. Bklyn., July 19, 1941; s. Samuel H. and Dorothy (Falick) P.; B.S. in Econs., Wharton Sch., U. Pa., 1963; Ph.D. in Math. Econs., Mass. Inst. Tech., 1968; m. Janet V. Bufe, July 26, 1969; children—Aaron Jacob, Joshua Benjamin. Corporate planning analyst Mobil Oil Co., N.Y.C., 1962-63, Mobil Oil Italiana, Genoa, Italy, 1965; ind. cons. econs. and ops. research to banks, mut. funds, ins. cos. govt. agys., Cambridge, Mass., 1965-68; sr. economist Arthur D. Little, Inc., Cambridge, 1968—, dir. regulation and econs., 1974—. Instr. fin. and computer scis. Mass. Inst. Tech., 1965-68; lectr. maj. univ. U.S. and abroad; expert witness U.S. Senate coms., U.S. Ct. Claims, I.C.C., FTC, Fed. Maritime Commn., other fed. and state govt. agys., 1967—. NASA fellow, 1963-66, NSF fellow, 1967, Am. Bankers Assn. fellow, 1968. Mem. Am. Econ. Assn. Econometric Soc., Am. Fin. Assn., Beta Gamma Sigma, Pi Gamma Mu, Tau Delta Phi (chpt. pres. 1962-63). Editorial reviewer Jour. Am. Statist. Assn., 1968, Jour. Indsl. Econs., 1968—. Author: Prices and Profits in the Property and Liability Insurance Industry, 1967; The Consequences of Industrial Regulation on Profitability, Risk Taking, and Innovation, 1969; National Policy, Technology, and Economic Forces Affecting the Industrial Organization of Marine Transportation, 1970; Government Regulation of the Air Freight Industry, 1971; The Private Mortgage Insurance Industry, 1975; On the Theory and Practice of Rate Review and Profit Measurement in Title Insurance, 1978; Torrens in the United States, 1978; also numerous articles and papers in profl. jours. Home: 55 Baskin Rd Lexington MA 02173 Office: 35 Acorn Park Cambridge MA 02140

PLOTZKER, RICHARD IVAN, gastroenterologist; b. N.Y.C., Aug. 22, 1941; s. Jack and Bertie P.; B.S., U. Pitts., 1962; M.S., Fairleigh Dickinson U., 1965; postgrad. U. Rome, 1965-70; m. Maria Supko Ross, Dec. 30, 1972; children—Sofia Rachel, Michael Anton. Intern, Med. Coll. Pa., Phila., 1971, resident in internal medicine, 1973-74, chief resident, 1974, fellow gastroenterology, 1974-76, lab. supr. microbiology dept., 1962-63, instr. medicine at coll., 1975-76, clin. instr., 1976—; acting chief gastrointestinal dept., Phila. VA Hosp., 1976-77; chief internal medicine and gastroenterology service Coatesville (Pa.) Hosp.; courtesy staff Chester County and Riddle Meml. hosps., So. Chester County Med. Center. Diplomate Am. Bd. Internal Medicine. Mem. A.C.P., Am., Delaware Valley Socs. gastrointestinal endoscopy, Pa., Chester County med. socs. Home: 323 McKenzie Dr West Chester PA 19380 Office: 10th Ave and Olive St Coatesville PA 19320

PLOURDE, JOSEPH AURELE, clergyman; b. St. Francois, N.B., Jan. 12, 1915; s. Antoine and Suzanne (Albert) P.; student St. Joseph's Coll., 1935-39, Halifax Maj. Sem., 1939-44, Inst. Catholique de Paris, 1947-49, Ottawa U., 1949-51, La Gregorienne, Rome, 1959-60; Ph.D. in Edn. (hon.), Moncton, 1969. Ordained priest Roman Catholic Ch., 1944; consecrated aux. bishop, 1964; served as asst. pastor, pastor, prof. philosophy, retreat master, Army Chaplain; bishop, Alexandria, Ont., 1964-67; archbishop Ottawa, Ont., 1967—. Named Knight of Malta; Knight of Holy Sepulchre. Office: 256 King Edward Ave Ottawa ON Canada

PLOURDE, MICHEL, univ. dean; b. New Glasgow, Que., Can., May 3, 1931; s. Leonard Edmond and Annonciade (Lafresniere) P.; B.S., Coll. Joliette, Que., 1950; Lic. Theol., U. Ottawa, 1954; Lic. ès Lettres, U. Paris, 1959; Doct. és Lett., U. Laval, 1966; m. Monique Mus, Feb. 18, 1967; children—Nicolas, Sebastien. Tchr. French lit. College d'Amos, Amos, Que., 1954-57, 60-62, dean studies, 1962-64; lectr. U. Laval (Que.), 1961-66; dir. student teaching Faculty Edn., U. Montreal (Que.), 1966-69, asso. prof., 1968, vice dean, 1969, dean, 1970—, prof., 1974—. Mem. Govt. Que. Com. Tchr. Tng., 1968-71; mem. higher edn. commn. Que. Superior Council Edn., 1975—; mem. Can. Studies Found., 1975—; pres. Inter-Univ. Com. Tchrs. Tng., 1975—. Recipient grants Govt. Que., 1965-66, Can. Council, 1959-60. Mem. Canadian Assn. Amateur Theatre (v.p., 1961), Theatre Universitaire Canadien (dir. 1962), Assn. Que. Univ. Profs. Edn. (pres., 1968-70), Canadian Soc. Higher Edn., Soc. Paul Claudel, Assn. Quebecoise des professeurs de français, and others. Author: Paul Claudel, une musique du silence, 1970. Editor, founder Rev. Canadian Edn. Assn. French Lang., 1971—; founder, pres. Revue des sciences de l'éducation Can., 1975—. Home: 12397 rue Notre-Dame-des-Anges Montreal PQ H4J 2C3 Canada Office: Faculty Education Univ Montreal Montreal PQ Canada

PLOWMAN, HERBERT LAVERNE, JR., chemist; b. Hammond, Ind., Sept. 13, 1929; s. Herbert LaVerne and Edith Louise (Andrew) P.; A.B. in Chemistry, Blackburn U., 1953; m. Carole Rae Goin, Feb. 14, 1959; children—Robert Dean. Supr. quality control and lab. Gary-Hobart Water Corp., Gary, Ind., 1955-69; dir. utilities City of Grand Junction (Colo.), 1969-71; asst. supr. treatment Phila. Suburban Water Co., Bryn Mawr, Pa., 1971-73, supt. of treatment, 1973—. Chmn. United Fund city employees, City of Grand Junction, 1970-71; chmn. United Way, Phila. Suburban Water Co., 1977. Served with U.S. Army, 1953-55. Certified water utility operator, State of Pa. Mem. Am. Chem. Soc., Am. Water Works Assn., Am. Pub. Health Assn. Republican. Presbyterian. Club: Rotary. Contbr. articles in field to profl. jours. Home: 9 Riddlewood Dr Media PA 19063 Office: 762 Lancaster Ave Bryn Mawr PA 19010

PLUMMER, DAVIS WARD, JR., govt. ofcl.; b. Buffalo, May 8, 1947; s. Davis Ward and Olive Jane (Rogers) P.; B.B.A. (Price Waterhouse & Co. scholar), Susquehanna U., 1970. Staff accountant Price Waterhouse & Co., Buffalo, 1970-71; sr. accountant Eichhorn & Weinreber, Buffalo 1971-73; sr. med. facilities auditor N.Y. State Dept. Health, Bur. Audit and Investigation, Buffalo, 1973-74, asso. med. facilities auditor, 1974-76, prin. med. facilities auditor, 1976—. Mem. fin. com. Hickory Hill Homeowners Assn. C.P.A., N.Y. Mem. Am. Inst. C.P.A.s, N.Y. State Soc. C.P.A.s, Theta Chi. Home: 94 Hickory Hill Rd Williamsville NY 14221 Office: Dept Health 584 Delaware Ave Buffalo NY 14202

PLUMMER, PHILIP FRANK, govt. ofcl.; b. Tyrone, Pa.; s. Arthur Frank and Naomi Harriet (Mitchell) P.; student Susquehanna U., 1940-42; B.S., U.S. Naval Acad., 1945; m. Kathleen Lea Neal, Apr. 27, 1962; 1 dau., Kimberly. Commd. ensign U.S. Navy, 1945, advanced through grades to comdr., 1961, ret., 1969; engring. officer U.S.S. San Jacinto, 1945-46; commd. officer U.S.S. Midway, 1946-47; personnel officer, attack carrier squadron pilot, 1948-50; flight instr., Pensacola, Fla., 1950-52; ops. officer, attack carrier squadron, 1952-53; exec. asst., aide to chief of staff Supreme Allied Commander Atlantic, 1953-55; adminstrv. officer Naval Air Sta., Corpus Christi, Tex., 1955-59; flag sec. to comdr. carrier div. 4, 1959-61; personnel dir. personnel planning Joint Chiefs of Staff, Washington, 1961-64; logistics movement officer Comdr. in Chief U.S. Pacific Fleet, Pearl Harbor, 1964-67; asst. coordinator budget justification Office Chief Naval Ops. for Research and Devel., Navy Dept., Washington, 1967-69; comptroller Navy Regional Data Automation Center, Washington, 1969—. Mem. U.S. Naval Acad. Alumni Assn., Ret. Officers Assn., U.S. Naval Acad. Athletic Assn., Am. Legion. Methodist. Club: Army-Navy Country. Home: 4027 N 27th Rd Arlington VA 22207 Office: Automatic Data Processing Devel Activity Navy Yard Washington DC 20374

PLYMYER, DAVID ALAN, lawyer; b. Reading, Pa., May 6, 1949; s. Edward Jay and Edith Evelyn (Mengel) P.; B.A., Dickinson Coll., 1971; M.S.W., U. Pitts., 1973; J.D., U. Balt., 1978. Admitted to Md. bar, 1978; asst. state's atty. for Anne Arundel County, Md., Annapolis, 1978—; individual practice law, Annapolis, 1978—; instr. Cath. U. Am., Washington, 1975—, U. Md., 1976-78. Mem. Anne Arundel County Adv. Com. on Child Abuse, 1975—. Served with U.S. Army, 1971-77. Decorated Army Commendation medal; NIMH fellow, 1973. Mem. Am. Bar Assn., Md. State Bar Assn., Am. Hosp. Assn., Nat. Assn. Social Workers, Child Welfare League, ACLU. Democrat. Lutheran. Contbr. articles to profl. jours. Home: 19 Silverwood Circle Annapolis MD 21403 Office: Office of State's Atty Church Circle Annapolis MD 21401

PLYTER, NORMAN VINCENT, coll. ofcl.; b. Newark, N.Y., Sept. 16, 1938; s. Vincent Howard and Phyllis (Salatino) P.; B.A., U. Rochester, 1960, M.S., 1962. Lectr., sr. programmer Computing Center U. Rochester (N.Y.), 1960-66; dir. Computing Center, State U. N.Y. at Brockport, 1967—, chmn. computer sci., 1968-77. Recipient Chancellor's award State U. N.Y. at Brockport, 1974. IBM Systems Research Inst. fellow, 1966. Mem. Assn. for Computing Machinery, State U. N.Y. Computing Officers Assn. (exec. council). Home: 27 Maxon St Brockport NY 14420

PNIAKOWSKI, ANDREW FRANK, structural engr.; b. Grodno, Poland, Aug. 18, 1930; s. Josef Leon and Janina (Kodzynski) P.; Diploma Engr., Politechnika Warszawska, 1952; m. Margaret M. Czajkowski, Aug. 15, 1957; 1 dau., Mary. Bridge design and field engr. Govt. of Poland, Ministry of R.R., Warsaw, 1952-57; bridge design engr. Dept. Hwys., of Ont. (Can.), Toronto, 1958-66; sr. structural engr. Sverdrup & Parcel Assos. Inc., Boston, 1967-71; prin. structural engr. Louis Berger & Assos. Inc., Wellesley, Mass., 1972—; cons. engr. in transp., pub. bldgs., others. Registered profl. engr., Ont., Mass., Maine, N.H. Mem. Assn. Profl. Engrs. of Province Ont., Nat. Soc. Profl. Engrs. Roman Catholic. Office: 20 William St Wellesley MA 02181

POBINER, HARVEY, can co. exec.; b. Bklyn., Mar. 2, 1927; s. Joseph and Gussie (Seidman) P.; B.A. cum laude, Bklyn. Coll., 1948, M.A., 1956; postgrad. Bklyn. Poly. Inst., 1949-50; m. Amelia Deutsch, July 11, 1954; children—Joseph Andrew, Bonnie Fay. Chemist, Sperry Gyroscope, Great Neck, N.Y., 1948-54; group head Gen. Aniline & Film Corp., Linden, N.J., 1954-57; chemist Esso Research & Engring. Co., Linden, 1957-63; staff scientist Gen. Precision Co., Little Falls, N.J., 1963-64; supr. analytical chemistry Am. Can Co., Princeton, N.J., 1964-74, mgr. organic and analytical chemistry, 1974-77, mgr. analytical research and services, 1977—. Served with AUS, 1951-53; ETO. Mem. Am. Chem. Soc., Propylea Honor Soc. Patentee rare earth recoveries. Contbr. articles to profl. jours. Home: 29 Taylor Rd RD 4 Princeton NJ 08540 Office: 469 N Harrison St PO Box 50 Princeton NJ 08540

POCH, HERBERT EDWARD, physician; b. Elizabeth, N.J., Sept. 4, 1927; s. William and Min (Herman) P.; A.B., Columbia U., 1949, M.D., 1953; m. Leila Kosberg, Aug. 27, 1952; children—Bruce Jeffrey, Andrea Susan, Lesley Grace. Intern, Kings County Hosp. Center, Bklyn., 1953-54; resident Babies Hosp., Columbia-Presbyn. Med. Center, N.Y.C., 1954-56; practice medicine specializing in pediatrics, Union, N.J., 1956—; attending pediatrician Elizabeth Gen. Hosp., also chmn. dept. pediatrics; attending pediatrician St. Elizabeth Hosp.; mem. staff St. Barnabas Hosp.; instr. pediatrics Columbia U., 1956-72, asst. clin. prof. pediatrics, 1972—. Served with AUS, 1945-46. Diplomate Am. Bd. Pediatrics. Fellow Am. Acad. Pediatrics (dist. councillor N.J. chpt.); mem. N.J. Med. Soc. Address: 381 Chestnut St Union NJ 07083

POCHEDLY, CARL EUGENE, physician; b. Freedom, Ohio, Aug. 23, 1931; s. Martin Randolph and Mary (Marek) P.; A.B., Hiram Coll., 1952; M.D., Case Western Res. U., 1956; M.Med.Sci. (Univ. fellow), Ohio State U., 1959; m. Mable Philipp, June 20, 1953; children—Neal, Pamela. Intern, Akron (Ohio) Gen. Hosp., 1956-57; resident in pediatrics Children's Hosp. D.C., 1961-63; fellow in epidemiology and microbiology Harvard Sch. Pub. Health, 1957-58, in pediatric hematology N.Y. Med. Coll., 1965-67; practice medicine specializing in pediatrics, East Meadow, N.Y., 1963—; asso prof. pediatrics State U. N.Y., Stony Brook, 1973—; mem. staff Nassau County (N.Y.) Med. Center, 1963—, dir. pediatric hematology, 1967—; mem. staffs Central Nassau Med. Group, Nassau Hosp., Mineola, N.Y., Mid-Island Hosp., Bethpage, N.Y., Brunswick Hosp. Center, Amityville, N.Y., Mercy Hosp., Rockville Centre, N.Y.; mem. cons. staffs Huntington Hosp., Franklin Gen. Hosp.; chmn. med. adv. bd. L.I. chpt. Leukemia Soc. Am. Served to capt. M.C., U.S. Army, 1959-61. Diplomate Am. Bd. Pediatrics. Mem. AMA, Am. Assn. Cancer Research, Am. Acad. Pediatrics, Am. Soc. Hematology, Am. Soc. Clin. Oncology, Soc. Study of Blood. Congregationalist. Author: The Child with Leukemia, 1973; Clinical Management of Cancer in Children, 1975; Neuroblastoma, 1976; editor: (with T. Necheles) Major Problems in Childhood Cancer, 1973; Acute Childhood Leukemia, 1975; (with D. Miller) Wilms' Tumor, 1976, Hemophilia, vol. 1 ann. series Progress in Pediatric Hematology/Oncology, 1976; editor Seminars in Pediatric Hematology/Oncology, Am. Jour. Pediatric Hematology/Oncology; contbr. numerous articles to prof. jours. Home: 77 Mulberry Ave Garden City NY 11530 Office: Dept Pediatrics Nassau County Med Center 2201 Hempstead Turnpike East Meadow NY 11554

POCOCK, PHILIP F., archbishop; b. St. Thomas, Ont., Can., July 2, 1906; s. Stephen Bernard and Sarah-May (McCarthy) P.; student Assumption Coll., 1922-23; A.B., U. Western Ont., 1926; grad. St. Peter's Sem., 1930; student Cath. U. Am., 1931-32; J.C.D., Angelicum, Rome, 1934. Ordained priest Roman Catholic Ch., 1930; prof. moral theology and canon law St. Peter's Sem., 1934-44; consecrated bishop, June 29, 1944; installed as bishop of Saskatoon, Sask., Can., 1944; named apostolic adminstr. archdiocese of Winnipeg, 1951; titular archbishop Apro and coadjutor archbishop of Winnipeg, 1951, succeeded to see, 1952; titular archbishop of Isauropoli and coadutor archbishop of Toronto, 1961, succeeded to see, 1971. Address: 55 Gould St Toronto ON M5B 1G1 Canada

PODGWAITE, JOHN DAVID, microbiologist; b. New Haven, Nov. 16, 1940; s. John and Katherine May (Soule) P.; B.S., U. Conn., 1962, M.S., 1965, Ph.D., 1973; m. Nancy Elaine Gardiner, June 13, 1964; children—Linda Ann, Kurt Ian. Bacteriologist, U.S. Dept. Agr. Forest Insect and Disease Lab., Hamden, Conn., 1965-66, microbiologist, 1966—; lectr. on insect pathology and microbial control various local univs. Mem. Am. Soc. Microbiology, Soc. Invertebrate Pathology, Internat. Orgn. Biol. Control of Noxious Animals and Plants, Jr. C. of C., Gamma Sigma Delta, Sigma Xi. Home: 908 Peck Ln Cheshire CT 06410 Office: 151 Sanford St Hamden CT 06514

PODOLSKY, LEON, elec. engr.; b. Phila., Nov. 3, 1910; s. Nathan and Fannie (Haim) P.; E.E., Drexel Inst. Tech., 1934; D.Sc., 1965; postgrad. Temple U., 1935-37; m. Elynore Bernstein, Mar. 3, 1933; 1 son, Richard B. Pell. Radio engr. RCA Victor Co., Camden, N.J., 1929-31; research, cons. engr., 1931-38; research, devel. engr. Sprague Electric Co., Sprague Products Co., North Adams, Mass., 1938-46, mgr. field engring. dept., 1946-52, tech. asst. to pres., 1952-58, cons., 1959—; pres. Greylock Broadcasting Co., WBRK & WMGT, Pittsfield, Mass., 1947-58; v.p., dir. Sun Printing Corp., 1946-61; dir. Metro Audio Visual Co., Inc., Miami, Fla., Theta Electronics Corp., Pittsfield; pres. U.S. nat. com. Internat. Electrotech. Commn., 1974—, internat. v.p., 1975—, del. to Scheveningen, Netherlands, 1952, Optija, Yugoslavia, 1953, Phila., 1954, London, 1955, Munich, Germany, 1956, 73, Zurich, Switzerland, 1957, 71, New Delhi, 1960, Aix Les Bains, France, 1962, Tokyo, 1965, Tel Aviv, 1966, Washington, 1970, 1971, Athens, 1972, Bucharest, 1974, The Hague, 1975, Nice, France, 1976, Moscow, 1977; chmn. com. on components, mem. AGREE Task Force 5, Dept. Def.; chmn. Nat. Acad. Sci. Adv. Panel 425, cons. Nat. Bur. Standards, 1960-71, U.S. Dept. Commerce, 1974; mem. Tech. Experts for GATT; mem., co. mem. conf., vice chmn. internat. standards council Am. Nat. Standards Inst. Recipient Navy Commendation Ribbon, 1947, Gold Plaque IRE-Radio-Electronics-TV Mfrs. Assn., 1956. Contbn. award IRE, 1962, Leo B. Moore Gold medal Standards Engrs. Soc., 1967. Fellow IEEE (life; cons., recipient outstanding contbn. award profl. group on reliability 1972), Standards Engring. Soc.; mem. Nat. Acad. Engring. (com. engring. biology and medicine 1970-75), Electronic Industries Assn. (chmn. internat. standards com., award for outstanding accomplishment 1972, Distinguished Service medal 1974), Nat. Soc. Profl. Engrs., AAAS, Armed Forces Communications Assn., Am. Def. Preparedness Assn., Engrs. Club N.Y. Club: Univ. (Washington). Patentee in field. Home: 18 Lexington Pkwy Pittsfield MA 01201 Office: 77 Wendell Ave Pittsfield MA 01201

PODOS, STEVEN MAURICE, physician; b. N.Y.C., Nov. 7, 1937; s. Mark A. and Sophia L. (Landress) P.; A.B., Princeton U., 1958; M.D., Harvard U., 1962; m. Salle Garber, June 20, 1959; children—Richard Lance, Lisa Beth. Intern, U. Utah Affiliated Hosps., Salt Lake City, 1962-63; resident Washington U., St. Louis, 1963-67; practice medicine specializing in ophthalmology, N.Y.C., 1975—: clin. asso. ophthalmology NIH, Bethesda, Md., 1967-69; asst. prof. Washington U. Sch. Medicine, St. Louis, 1969, asso. prof., 1972, prof. ophthalmology, 1974-75; prof., chmn. Dept. Ophthalmology, Mt. Sinai Sch. Medicine and ophthalmologist in chief, Mt. Sinai Hosp., N.Y.C., 1975—. Mem. sci. adv. bd. Fight for Sight, 1975—; bd. dirs. Nat. Soc. for Prevention of Blindness, 1977—; trustees Assn. for Research in Vision and Ophthalmology, 1977-81. Served with USPHS, 1967-69. Recipient Award of Merit, Am. Acad. Ophthalmology and Otolaryngology; USPHS grantee, 1975—. Diplomate Am. Bd. Ophthalmology. Mem. Am. Acad. Ophthalmology and Otolaryngology, A.C.S., Am. Ophthalmological Soc., AAAS, N.Y. Acad. Medicine, Assn. for Research in Vision and Ophthalmology. Jewish. Club: Princeton. Contbr. articles in field to profl. jours.; editorial bd. Survey of Ophthalmology, 1972—; Investigative Ophthalmology, 1973—; Am. Jour. Ophthalmology, 1974—. Home: 950 Park Ave New York City NY 10028 Office: Mt Sinai Med Center 1 Gustave Levy Pl New York City NY 10029

POESNECKER, GERALD EUGENE, naturopathic physician; b. Seattle, May 15, 1930; s. Lloyd Eugene and Bertha Mary (Dargan) P.; student Reed Coll., 1953; Naturopathic Dr., Dr. Chiropractic, Western States Coll., 1956; postgrad. Highline Community Coll., 1968-69; m. Gloria Lorraine Patterson, June 18, 1948; children—Leyardia P. Black, Dian P. Bailey, Randolph, Jocelyn, Devon. Practice naturopathic medicine, Seattle, 1957-69; dir. Clymer Health Clinic, Quakertown, Pa., 1969—; clinic dir. Nat. Coll. Naturopathic Medicine, Seattle, 1960-64. Mem. Humanitarian Soc., Am. Soc. Natura Physicians (founder), Am. Chiropractic Assn., Pa. Chiropractic Soc., Am. Naturopathic Assn., Quakertown Cantata Singers. Author: It's Only Natural, 1975; Creative Sex, 1976. Home: RD 3 Axe Handle Rd Quakertown PA 18951 Office: RD 3 Clymer Rd Quakertown PA 18951

POETKER, JOEL SMITH, educator; b. Jackson, Ohio, Oct. 1, 1934; s. Norman Oakly and Lola Wanda (Smith) P.; student Ohio Wesleyan U., 1952-54; A.B., Muskingum Coll., 1958; M.A., Miami U., Oxford, Ohio, 1961; Ph.D., Ohio State U., 1971; m. Mabel Marie Riegel, Sept. 12, 1954; children—Susan, Ann, Samuel. Tchr., Middletown (Ohio) Sr. High Sch., 1958-61, Bexley (Ohio) High Sch., 1961-68; teaching asso. edn. Ohio State U., Columbus, 1968-70; asso. v.p. academic affairs, prof. history and social studies edn. State U. N.Y. Coll. at Buffalo, 1970—, chmn. dept., 1972-76. Recreation dir. City of Bexley, 1965-67. Served with U.S. Army, 1954-56. John Hay humanities fellow Williams Coll., 1963; Gen. Electric econs. fellow Purdue U., 1964. Mem. Am. Hist. Assn., Nat. Council Social Studies, N.Y. State Council Social Studies, Can. Assn. Social Studies, Phi Delta Kappa, Phi Alpha Theta, Phi Gamma Delta. Presbyterian. Author: The Fourteen Points, 1969; The Monore Doctrine, 1968. Contbr. articles to profl. publs. Home: 6 Willow Green Dr Tonawanda NY 14150 Office: 519 Grover Cleveland Hall State U NY Coll Elmwood Ave Buffalo NY 14222

POGANY, ANDRAS HENRIK, lawyer, librarian; b. Budapest, Hungary, June 26, 1919; s. Pal Antal and Gizella Katalin (Hoffmann) P.; came to U.S., naturalized, 1962; Dr. jur., Pazmany U., Budapest, 1942, Dr. pol., 1946; M.L.S., Conn. State Coll., 1960; m. Hortenzia Ida Lers, June 20, 1942; children—Aniko DePierro, Ildiko Deangelis, Andrew, Antal-Csaba, Orsolya, Balazs. Registered law clk., Budapest, 1942-46; mem. Budapest bar, 1946-56; asst. bibliographer Yale U.

Library, New Haven, 1959-60; asst. chief reference librarian Seton Hall U., South Orange, N.J., 1960-63, asso. dir. univ. library, 1963—, prof., 1970—; admitted to N.J. bar, 1975; mem. spl. adv. com. U.S. Dept. State, 1970-73; Hungarian-Am. adviser Rep. Nat. Com., 1969-73; neutral observer presdl. elections, South Vietnam, 1971. Pres. World Fedn. Hungarian Freedom Fighters, 1973—; commr. Bicentennial Commn. N.J., 1973—. Named hon. col. N.J. State Militia, 1977. Mem. Hungarian Freedom Fighters Fedn. U.S.A., (nat. chmn. 1966-73), Am. Council for Emigrees in Professions (dir. 1967-73), Fedn. Free Hungarian Jurists (dir. 1965—), Polish-Hungarian Fedn. (dir. 1971—). Author: Political Science and International Relations: a recommended list of books, 1967; City in Darkness, 1966; columnist various Am.-Hungarian newspapers. Home: 201 Raymond Ave South Orange NJ 07079

POGGE, HORST, distbn. co. exec.; b. Klingendorf, Ger., Mar. 6, 1926; s. Karl Wilhelm and Gertrude (Poel) P.; came to U.S., 1952, naturalized, 1957; grad. in Agr., Agrl. Coll. (Ger.), 1947; m. Irena B. Kant, Sept. 14, 1948; children—Hans-Juergen, Karin, Kirk-Horst. Store mgr. Albany (N.Y.) Pub. Markets, 1955-62; pres., gen. mgr. Grassland Equipment & Irrigation, Latham, N.Y., 1962—. Adv. consul 14 County Extension (coop.) N.Y. State. Recipient Million Dollar Sales award The Toro Co., 19—. Mem. N.Y. State Nurseryman Assn., U.S., Colonie (chmn. small bus. council) chambers commerce, Am., Northeastern, Vt., Hudson Valley golf course supt. assns. Clubs: Valhalla Country, Hudson River; Schuyler Meadows Country (Loudonville). Home: 892-898 Troy Schenectady Rd Latham NY 12110

POGGIO, GIAN FRANCO, educator; b. Genoa, Italy, Sept. 21, 1927; s. Alberto and Angela (Castagnino) P.; M.D., U. Genoa, 1951; came to U.S., 1954, naturalized, 1970. Faculty dept. neurology U. Genoa Sch. Medicine, 1951-54; fellow neurol. surgery Johns Hopkins Hosp., 1954-56, asso. prof. physiology Johns Hopkins Med. Sch., 1957-76, prof. physiology, 1976—. Home: 2 Elmhurst Rd Baltimore MD 21210

POGO, ANGEL OSCAR, molecular biologist; b. Buenos Aires, Argentina, Aug. 28, 1927; s. Bernard and Sara (Braverman) P.; came to U.S., 1964, naturalized, 1976; B.S., M. Moreno, Argentina, 1945; M.D., Buenos Aires U., 1953, D.M. Sci. summa cum laude, 1959; m. Beatriz Teresa Garcia-Tunon, Jan. 13, 1956; children—Gustave, Gabriela. Research asso. Inst. Anatomy and Embryology, Buenos Aires U., 1955-59; asst. prof. Inst. Cell Biology, Cordoba U., 1961-64; research asso. Rockefeller U., N.Y.C., 1964-66, asst. prof., 1966-74; investigator and head Lab. Cell Biology, N.Y. Blood Center, 1967-74, sr. investigator, head, 1974—; adviser John Simon Guggenheim Meml. Found. Nat. Cancer Inst. grantee, 1971-74, 75-78; Guggenheim fellow, 1959-60, 60-61; Nat. Heart and Lung Inst. grantee, 1967—; recipient Career Devel. award NIH, 1966. Mem. Argentine Soc. Biology, Am. Soc. Biol. Chemistry, Am. Chem. Soc., AAAS, Am. Soc. Cell Biology. Contbr. articles in field to profl. texts. Home: 237 Nyac Ave Pelham NY 10803 Office: 310 E 67th St New York City NY 10021

POGO, BEATRIZ, cell biologist and virologist; b. Buenos Aires, Argentina, Dec. 24, 1932; d. Dario and Maria Teresa (Vergnory) Garcia-Tunon; came to U.S., 1964; naturalized, 1976; B.S., Lycee No. 1, Buenos Aires, 1950; M.D., Sch. Medicine, Buenos Aires, 1956; D.M.Sci., 1961; m. Angel Oscar Pogo, Jan. 13, 1956; children—Gustav, Gabriela. Asst. prof. cell biology Inst. Cell Biology, Cordoba (Argentina) U., 1962-64; research asso. Rockefeller U., N.Y.C., 1964-67; asst. Pub. Health Research Inst., N.Y.C., 1967-69, asso., 1969-73, asso. mem., 1973—; prof. exptl. cell biology and microbiology Mt. Sinai Sch. Medicine, City U. N.Y., 1978—. Damon Runyon Fund fellow, 1964-65; Am. Cancer Soc. grantee, 1970-73; NIH grantee, 1975—. Mem. Am. Assn. for Cancer Research, Am. Soc. for Cell Biology, Harvey Soc., Assn. for Women in Sci., Am. Microbiol. Soc. Contbr. articles to profl. jours. Home: 237 Nyac Ave Pelham NY 10803 Office: Pub Health Research Inst 455 1st Ave New York City NY 10016

POGUE, GERALD ALBERT, educator; b. Toronto, Ont., Can., Nov. 28, 1937; s. Samuel Gerald and Bertha Winnifred (Corbett) P.; B.S., U. Toronto, 1960; M.B.A., U. Western Ont., 1964; M.S. (Ford Found. fellow), Carnegie-Mellon U., 1966, Ph.D., 1967; m. Mai Tuyet Nguyen, Feb. 12, 1972; children—Jacqueline, Gerald Albert. Sr. analyst Burroughs Corp., Toronto, 1960-62; asst. prof. Sloan Sch., Mass. Inst. Tech., Cambridge, 1967-71, asso. prof., 1971-73; prof. econs. and fin. Baruch Coll. City U. N.Y., 1973—, chmn. dept. econs. and fin., 1977—; sr. economist instnl. investor study SEC, Washington, 1969-71; pres. Planning & Decision Systems, Greenwich, Conn., 1971—; sr. partner G.A. Pogue & Assos., Greenwich, 1977—; cons. U.S., European corps., agys. including SEC, EPA, Communications Satellite Corp., Paine Weber, Investment Co. Inst., Eurofinance, Paris, Sincro, Paris. Served with RCAF, 1956-60. Mem. Am. Econ. Assn., Am. Statis. Assn., Inst. Mgmt. Scis., Ops. Research Soc. Am., Am. Fin. Assn., Zeta Psi. Club: Les Amis du Vin (Washington). Contbr. articles to profl. publs. Home: 60 Patterson Ave Greenwich CT 06830 Office: Baruch Coll 46 E 26th St New York City NY 10010

POGUE, MARY ELLEN (MRS. L. WELCH POGUE), youth and community worker; b. Fremont, Nebr., Oct. 27, 1904; d. Frank E. and Mary (Coe) Edgerton; B.F.A., U. Nebr., 1926; studied violin with Harrison Keller, Boston, 1926-28, Kemp Stillings Master Class, N.Y.C., 1939-40; m. L. Welch Pogue, Sept. 8, 1926; children—Richard Welch, William Lloyd, John Marshall. Mem. Potomac String Ensemble, 1948—. Historian, Gov. William Bradford Compact, 1966—; vice chmn. Montgomery County (Md.) Victory Garden Center, 1946-47; pres. Bethesda Community Garden Club, 1946-48; bd. dirs. Montgomery County YWCA, 1946-50, 52-55. Mem. Mayflower Soc. (dir. D. C. 1950-78), LWV, P.E.O. (pres. 1957-59), Mortar Bd. Alumnae (pres. 1965-67), Columbia Hist. Soc., Nat. Geneal. Soc., Welcome to Washington Internat. Club, Ind. Agy. Wives (asso.), Delta Omicron Music. Democrat. Methodist. Club: Capital Speakers. Editor: Favorite Recipes of Mary Edgerton of Aurora, Nebraska, 1963; compiler, editor Edgerton Coe History, 1965. Home: 5204 Kenwood Ave Chevy Chase MD 20015

POHORYLES, MANFRED, metal products mfg. co. exec.; b. Jaroslaw, Poland, Oct. 9, 1919; s. Joseph and Ida (Reich) P.; B.M.E., Queen's U., No. Ireland, 1942; m. Thea Jagermann, Nov. 7, 1943; 1 dau., Vivian. Came to Can., 1949, naturalized, 1971. With dept. project engring. Brit. European Airways, London, 1946-49; sr. lectr. McGill U., Montreal, Que., Can., 1949-50; engr. Air Conditioning Co. Ltd., Montreal, 1950-52; pres. Triplex Engring. Co. Ltd., Pointe Claire, Que., 1952—; pres. Triplex Inter Control Ltd.; pres. Triplex Industries Inc.; dir. Altronic Ltd. Bd. dirs. Criq Que. Govt. Research Inst. Served to flight lt. RAF, 1942-46. Asso. fellow Royal Aero. Soc. (Gt. Britain); mem. Profl. Engrs. Que., Charter Engrs. Gt. Britain. Home: 176 Wexford Crescent Hampstead PQ Canada Office: 181 Oneida Dr Pointe Claire PQ H9R 1A9 Canada

POIAN, EDWARD LICIUS DEBORBONE, union ofcl.; b. Trieste, Italy, June 10, 1945; s. Angelo DelPiccolo and Zaira Commelli (de Borbone) P.; student U.S. Govt. Inst., Washington, 1963-65; A.S., Columbia, 1967; student Mercy Coll., 1975-76; came to U.S., 1954, naturalized, 1960; m. Maria del Carmen Lopez-Cintron, Nov. 22, 1969; children—Jeanne-Marie, Nicole-Anna. Chief exec. Budget Fin. Plan div. Budget Industries, Pittsfield, Mass., 1968-70; pres., chief exec. Nat. Assn. Letter Carriers AFL-CIO, Chappaqua, N.Y., local 4674, 1971—. Mem. legis. assembly com. under Anthony Mercorella N.Y., 1967—; mem. Siwanoy Democratic Club, 1967-69. Served with USCG, 1963-67; Vietnam. Home: 29 Davenport suite 1C New Rochelle NY 10805 Office: 30 N Greeley Ave Chappaqua NY 10514

POINDEXTER, EMMETT WILLIAMSON, lawyer; b. Greelee, Va., Oct. 2, 1899; s. George F. and Susie (Williamson) P.; A.B., Washington and Lee U., 1920, M.A., 1923, LL.B., 1923; m. Wingfield Hardy, Aug. 19, 1926;children—Emmett Williamson, Robert Wingfield. Instr. econs., Washington and Lee U., 1920-23; head dept. history and social sci. Danville (Va.) High Sch., 1923-25; admitted to Va. bar, 1923, N.Y. bar, 1927; asso. Iselin, Riggs, Ferris & Mygatt, 1925-46; mem. Riggs, Ferris and Geer, N.Y.C., 1946-63, Poindexter & Boland, N.Y.C., 1963-67, 70—, Poindexter, Boland & Hart, 1967-70; dir. Bol-Inca Mining Corp. Mem. Bar Assn. City N.Y., N.Y. So. Soc., Sons Confederate Vets. (N.Y. camp comdr. 1934-36), The Virginians, Am., N.Y. State bar assns., N.Y. Law Inst., Am. Judicature Soc., Phi Beta Kappa Assos. (life), Phi Beta Kappa (pres. N.Y. 1953-54), Omicron Delta Kappa, Delta Upsilon (nat. trustee, nat. dir.), Phi Alpha Delta, Delta Sigma Rho. Presbyterian. Clubs: Columbia University, Lawyers (N.Y.C.). Home: 475 Stuyvesant Ave Rutherford NJ 07070 also (summer) RFD 3 Putnam Valley NY 10579 Office: 74 Trinity Pl New York City NY 10006

POINTEK, ALBERT JOSEPH, govt. ofcl.; b. Swoyersville, Pa., May 28, 1932; s. Albert W. and Anna M. (Chorba) P.; B.S. in Accounting, King's Coll., 1954; m. Patricia Ann George, June 3, 1961; children—Mary Ann, John. Auditor, U.S. Air Force, Binghamton, N.Y., 1962-64, contract price analyst, 1964-65; contract adminstr. Def. Logistics Agy., Binghamton, 1965-67, adminstrv. contracting officer, 1967-77, contract price analyst, 1977-78, supervisory adminstrv. contracting officer, 1978—. Bd. dirs. Binghamton U.S. Employees Fed. Credit Union, chmn. supervisory com., 1965—; treas. Kopernik Soc. Broome County, Binghamton, 1975—, also bd. dirs. Mem. Nat. Assn. of Accountants, Nat. Contract Mgmt. Assn. (certified). Home: 4171 Felters Rd Binghamton NY 13903 Office: 600 Main St Johnson City NY 13790

POIRIER, CHARLES CARROLL, III, paper co. exec.; b. Pitts., Oct. 28, 1936; s. William Harvey and Ida B. (Wallace) P.; B.S., Carnegie-Mellon U., 1958; M.B.A., U. Pitts., 1966; m. Carol Jeanne Betts, Dec. 13, 1972; 1 son, Craig Charles; children by previous marriage—Cheryl Ann, Charles, Christopher, Cynthia; step-children—Tracy, Megan. Chief engr. F.J. Kress Box Co., Pitts., 1958-59; asst. to prodn. mgr. St. Regis Paper Co., Container Div., Pitts., 1960-68, asst. gen. prodn. mgr., 1969-72, dir. mfg., 1972-77, dir. mktg., 1978—; faculty Allegheny Community Coll., Pitts., 1972—. Vice-chmn. Robinson Twp. Civic League, 1971-72; mem. Robinson Twp. PTA, 1966-72. Mem. TAPPI (chmn. prodn. com. 1972-73, chmn. container div. 1976, editorial staff TAPPI mag. 1971-73), Fibre Box Assn. (prodn. com.), Ops. Research Soc. Am. (asso. mem.), Assn. M.B.A. Execs., Am. Contract Bridge League, Mensa, Beta Gamma Sigma. Contbr. articles to profl. jours. Home: 1752 Taper Dr Pittsburgh PA 15241 Office: 875 Greentree Rd Pittsburgh PA 15220

POITRAS, JEAN-MAURICE, physician; b. Montreal, Que., Can., Nov. 27, 1916; s. Paul Eugene and Berthe (Mallette) P.; B.A., Columbia Coll., 1940; M.D., L.I. Coll. Medicine, 1947; m. Helen Murray, Dec. 7, 1940; children—Diane, Denis, Micheline, Michael, Jean-Maurice. Intern U.S. Naval Hosp., St. Albans, L.I., N.Y., 1947-48; resident in pediatrics U.S. Naval Hosp., Chelsea, Mass., 1953-55; gen. practice medicine, Antwerp, Ohio, 1949-50; chief sch. health services Anne Arundel County Health Dept., Annapolis, Md., 1968-69; chief pediatrics Meml. Hosp. Easton, Md., 1969-70; emergency room physician Arundel Gen. Hosp., Annapolis, Md., 1970-71, N. Arundel Hosp., Glen Burnie, Md., 1971—. Served with USNR, 1943-45, 47-61, USPHS, 1961-68. Diplomate Am. Bd. Pediatrics; licensed physician, Md. Fellow Am. Acad. Pediatrics; mem. Am. Heart Assn., Heart Assn. Md., Med. and Chirurg. Faculty Md., Am. Assn. History Medicine, Am. Coll. Emergency Physicians. Home: 107 Edgerton Rd Towson MD 21204 Office: North Arundel Hosp Glen Burnie MD 21204

POLACH, JAROSLAV GEORGE (JAY), economist, govt. ofcl.; b. Ostrava, Czechoslovakia, Apr. 20, 1914; s. Francis and Marie (Pachova) P.; came to U.S., 1952, naturalized, 1957; A.B., Masaryk U. (Czechoslovakia), 1934, Dr. of Law, 1938; M.A., Am. U., 1958; Ph.D., 1962, M.Compar. Law, George Washington U., 1959; m. Eva Bozena Mocek, Feb. 8, 1943. Internat. analyst. editor U.S. Govt., 1948-60; staff economist, research asso. Resources for the Future Inc., Washington, 1960-70; sr. indsl. economist IRS, 1970-75; sr. internat. economist, sr. adviser in energy U.S. Treasury, 1975—; lectr. indsl. econs. U. Md., 1970—; cons. Applied Research and Tech., Annapolis, 1967-69. Mem. exec. com. Am. Sokol, 1975—. Served with RAF, Czechoslovakian Forces in the West, 1939-45. Decorated Bravery medal, medal of Merit, Mil. Cross (Czechoslovakia); recipient certificate of achievement IRS, 1973. Mem. Am. Soc. Internat. Law (com. nuclear power and world order 1967-74), Czechoslovak Soc. Arts and Scis. Am. (exec. com. 1961-71, 76—), Am. Econ. Assn., Am. Statis. Soc., Phi Delta Phi. Co-author: Energy in the World Economy, 1972; editor Czechoslovak Soc. of Arts and Sciences in Am. (chmn. editorial bd.); contbr. articles to profl. jours. Home: 225 Panorama Dr Oxon Hill MD 20021 Office: U S Treasury Room 4120 15th & Pennsylvania Ave NW DC 20220

POLANSKY, GERALD ARTHUR, accountant; b. Wisconsin Rapids, Wis., Apr. 10, 1935; s. Arthur Henry and Olga Lillian (Buerger) P.; B.B.A., U. Wis., 1957; postgrad. Harvard; m. Elizabeth Arlene Iverson, June 29, 1957; children—Anne, Thomas, Barbara. With Touche Ross & Co., 1957—, Detroit, 1957-60, D.C., 1960—, partner, 1966—, partner in charge, 1968-78, regional partner, 1977—; dir. D.C. Service Center, pres. Touche Ross Found., 1972-78, also bd. dirs., 1975—. Bd. dirs., treas. Jr. Achievement of Met. Washington; pres. Lutheran Ch. of St. Andrew; pres. Manor Estates Community Assn. C.P.A., Mich., D.C., La. Mem. Beta Gamma Sigma, Beta Alpha Psi. Clubs: Manor Country (chmn. admissions com.), Internat., University. Home: 4002 Manor Park Ct Rockville MD 20853 Office: 1900 M St NW Washington DC 20036

POLAYES, IRVING MARVIN, plastic surgeon; b. New Haven, Sept. 2, 1927; s. Abraham Noah and Ida (Stern) P.; B.A., Duke U., 1948; D.D.S., Columbia U., 1953; M.D., Albany Med. Coll., 1959; m. Marcia Kresel, July 1, 1951; children—Roy Peter, Amy Lynn. Intern, Albany (N.Y.) Med. Center, 1959-60, resident gen. surgery, 1960-63, fellow plastic surgery, 1963-65; practice medicine specializing in plastic and reconstructive surgery, New Haven, 1965—; attending plastic surgeon Yale New Haven Med. Center, 1965—, asso. chief plastic surgery, 1969—; attending plastic surgeon St. Raphael's Hosp., New Haven; cons. plastic surgeon West Haven (Conn.) VA Hosp., Gaylord Hosp., Wallingford; asso. clin. prof. plastic and reconstructive surgery Yale Med. Sch., 1970-77. Concertmaster, violinist New Haven Civic Symphony Orch., 1970—; v.p. New Haven Symphony Orch., 1977—. Served to lt. comdr. USNR, 1954-56. Diplomate Am. Bd. Plastic Surgery. Fellow A.C.S.; mem. Am. Assn. Plastic Surgeons, Am. Soc. Plastic and Reconstructive Surgeons, Am. Trauma Soc., Am., New Eng. socs. plastic and reconstructive surgery, Am. Soc. Maxillofacial Surgery, Soc. Head and Neck Surgeons, Am. Soc. Aesthetic Plastic Surgery, Conn., New Haven County med socs., Alpha Omega Alpha. Co-author: Diseases of the Salivary Glands, 1976. Home: 49 N Racebrook Rd Woodbridge CT 06525 Office: 60 Temple St New Haven CT 06510

POLAYES, MAURICE BENJAMIN, electronic and indsl. test equipment distbg. co. exec.; b. New Haven, May 9, 1923; s. Abraham N. and Ida (Stern) P.; student Colo. U., 1941-43, Boston U., 1952; spl. degree Harvard U. Grad. Sch. Bus. Adminstrn., 1971; m. Adele Toby Oren, Apr. 22, 1963; children—Andrew, Gregory. Staff engr. Sta. WELI, New Haven, 1943-44, Sta. WSTC, Stamford, Conn., 1944; sr. engr. Sta. WLAW, ABC, Boston, 1944-54; engr. in charge radio Andover Police Dept., 1946-51; sales mgr. N.E. area Philips Indsl. Instrumentation Dealer, 1954-59; pres. Addelco Corp., Needham, Mass., since 1959—; dir. Astro Communications Co.; mgmt. cons., 1955—; adviser on disaster communications, 1954—. Active Boy Scouts Am. Registered profl. engr., Mass. Fellow Am. Soc. for Nondestructive Testing (past chmn. Boston sect.); mem. IEEE, Nat. Soc. Profl. Engrs., Am. Inst. Aeros. and Astronautics, Soc. for Exptl. Stress Analysis, Instrument Soc. Am. Clubs: Harvard (Boston), Harvard Faculty, Rotary. Contbr. articles on nondestructive testing, instrumentation and applications, phys. measurement applications, automated electronic testing procedures to profl. pubs. Home: 82 Pine Grove St Needham MA 02194 Office: 56 Pickering St Needham MA 02192

POLER, MICHAEL AVERY, chem. cellulose and woodpulp co. exec.; b. Huntington, N.Y., Sept. 23, 1935; s. Emmonds Edson and Helen Mills (Saylor) P.; B.S.B.A., Babson Coll., 1957; m. Petrea Doty Sweeny, Jan. 7, 1978; children—Christine, Theodore, Kimberly, Timothy. With Caltex Oil Co., N.Y.C., 1957-58; with ITT Rayonier, Inc., N.Y.C., 1958—, mfg. asst., 1958-61, exec. sales, 1961-78, gen. mgr. pulp sales, 1978—. Trustee Kent Sch., 1973-78. Mem. Newcomen Soc. N. Am., Sales Execs. Club N.Y., Paper Industry Mgmt. Assn., Camp Dudley Assn. (exec. com. 1972-74). Republican. United Ch. (deacon 1972-76). Club: Union League. Home: 325 Rowayton Ave Rowayton CT 06853 Office: ITT Rayonier 1177 Summer St Stamford CT 06902

POLERI, WILLIAM FRANK, newspaper editor; b. Hazleton, Pa., Feb. 24, 1934; s. Vito C. and Rose Rachel (Ranieri) P.; student Pa. State U., 1952-53, 57-59, City Coll., Syracuse, N.Y., 1956-57; B.S. in Journalism, Suffolk U., 1962; postgrad. U. Mass., 1969; m. Carolyn Ann Johnson, Jan. 25, 1958; children—Valerie, Frank, Steven, Linda. Lab. technician Roth Smelting Co., Syracuse, 1956-57; quality control insp. Boston Wire Co., Boston, 1960-61; reporter Springfield (Mass.) Daily News, 1962-63, copy editor, 1963-65, makeup editor, 1965—, theatre-fine arts editor, 1969—. Theater dir. Wilbraham (Mass.) Community Theater; Westfield (Mass.) Theater Group, Enfield (Conn.) Stage Co.; Somers (Conn.) Village Players; past pres., co-founder, playwright Readers and Playwrights Theater, 1972—; theater task force leader Greater Springfield Bicentennial Arts Festival, 1975-77; asso. bd. dirs. Arts Resources Council, 1971—; mem. artistic com. Stage West, Springfield Theatre Arts, 1977. Recipient Membership award Playhouse Acad., 1974-75; Rose Kamberg award Mass. div. Am. Nat. Theatre and Playhouse Acad., 1976. Served with AUS, 1954-56. Mem. Community Theater Assn. (co-founder, 1st pres., Directing award 1977). Home: 38 Virginia St Springfield MA 01108 Office: 1860 Main St Springfield MA 01101

POLESKIE, STEPHEN FRANCIS, artist; b. Pringle, Pa., June 3, 1938; s. Stephen Francis and Antoinette Elizabeth (Chluyzinski) P.; B.S., Wilkes Coll., 1959; postgrad. New Sch. for Social Research, 1961. Owner Chiron Press, N.Y.C., 1961-68; instr. Sch. Visual Arts, N.Y.C., 1968; prof. art Cornell U., Ithaca, N.Y., 1969—, chmn. dept., 1978—; vis. critic Pratt Graphic Arts Center, N.Y.C., 1965-68; vis. artist Colgate U., Hamilton, N.Y., 1973, Everhart Mus., Scranton, Pa., 1973, U. S.D., Brookings, 1973, Kutztown (Pa.) Coll., 1978—, others; vis. prof. U. Calif. at Berkeley, 1976; one man exhbn.: Louis K. Meisel Gallery, N.Y.C., 1978; represented in permanent collections: Met. Mus., N.Y.C., Mus. Modern Art, N.Y.C., Whitney Mus., N.Y.C., Walker Art Center, Mpls., Fort Worth Art Center, others. Am. Fedn. Arts grantee, 1965; Carnegie Found. grantee, 1967; Nat. Endowment for Arts grantee, 1973; N.Y. State Council on Arts grantee, 1973; Creative Artists Public Service grantee, 1978. Mem. Exptl. Aircraft Assn., Aircraft Owners and Pilots Assn., Internat. Aerobatic Club. Work reproduced in The Art of the Print; Images of an Era: The American Poster, 1945-75. Home: 306 Stone Quarry Rd Ithaca NY 14850

POLETTI, ROGER A., electronics co. exec.; b. N.Y.C., May 6, 1932; s. Louis A. and Agnes C. (Larkin) P.; B.S., State U. N.Y., 1955; postgrad. Hofstra U., 1962-64; m. Mildred J. Mann, Nov. 12, 1955; children—Roger A., Louis, Terence, Kenneth, Christopher. With Hazeltine Corp., Greenlawn, N.Y., 1959—, employee relations mgr., 1966-69, personnel dir., 1969-73, v.p. personnel and adminstrn., 1973—. Bd. dirs. L.I. sect. Jr. Achievement, 1973—; pres., mem. bd. Nassau Center for Emotionally Disturbed, 1971—; mem. adv. bd. L.I. sect. Nat. Alliance of Businessmen, 1975—. Served to lt. USNR, 1955-59. Mem. Am. Soc. Personnel Adminstrn., Personnel Dirs. Council L.I. Home: Westbury NY 11590 Office: Hazeltine Corp Cuba Hill Rd Greenlawn NY 11740

POLISNER, STUART BARRY, surgeon; b. Buffalo, Mar. 28, 1938; s. Sidney Herbert and Mary Beatrice (Kaplan) P.; B.A., Case Western Res. U., 1959; M.D., State U. N.Y., 1963; m. Marilyn Kahn, May 2, 1962; children—Paige Dana, Gae Hillary. Intern, Greenwich (Conn.) Hosp., 1963-64, resident in gen. surgery, 1964-65; resident in orthopedics U. Rochester, 1965-66, in hand surgery Nassau County Med. Center, 1968, in children's orthopedics St. Charles Hosp., Port Jefferson, N.Y., 1969; practice medicine specializing in pediatric orthopaedic surgery, Commack, N.Y., 1970—; mem. staff, mem. exec. com. St. John's Smithtown Hosp.; asst. prof. pediatric orthopedic and hand surgery State U. N.Y. at Stonybrook and Nassau County Med. Center, 1977—. Served to capt. M.C., AUS, 1966-68. Decorated Bronze Star. Diplomate Am. Bd. Orthopaedic Surgery. Fellow A.C.S., Am. Acad. Orthopaedic Surgeons, Am. Acad. Pediatrics, Internat. Coll. Surgeons; mem. Pediatric Orthopaedic Study Group, Suffolk County (del. 1975—), N.Y. med. socs., Suffolk County Bar Assn. (chmn. med.-legal com. 1975-76). Office: 160 Commack Rd Commack NY 11725

POLISZCZUK, GEORGE, banker; b. Lida, Poland, Oct. 9, 1932; s. Wolodymyr and Anna (Zwarycz) P.; came to U.S., 1971; student U. Heidelberg (Ger.), 1949; B.Commerce, McGill U., Montreal, Que., Can., 1957; m. Olga Mary Bentkowski, July 15, 1961; 1 dau., Alexandra Olga. Asso. treas. Sun Life Assurance Co. Can., Montreal, 1957-71; mng. dir. Harris & Partners Inc., N.Y.C., 1971-73; v.p. Mellon Bank, N.A., Pitts., 1973—. Served to lt. Canadian Navy, 1957-62. Mem. N.Y. State Soc. Security Analysts. Mem. Ukrainian Orthodox Ch. Clubs: Met., Canadian, Recess (N.Y.C.); Chartiers

(Pitts.). Home: 2 Couch Farm Rd Pittsburgh PA 15243 Office: Mellon Bank NA Mellon Sq Pittsburgh PA 15230

POLITO, ANTHONY JOHN, lawyer; b. Altoona, Pa., Mar. 1, 1938; s. Michael John and Emma (DeLeo) P.; B.A. with honors, St. Vincent Coll., 1959; LL.B. with honors, U. Buffalo, 1962; m. Margaret Louise Hammill, June 24, 1961; children—Michael, Anthony, Anne, Diane, Elizabeth. Admitted to Pa. bar, 1963; asso. firm Rose, Schmidt, Dixon, Haslen, Whyte and Hardesty, Pitts., 1962—, partner, 1967—. Mem. Am., Pa., Allegheny County bar assns., Pa. Defense Inst. Roman Catholic. Editor-in-chief Buffalo Law Rev., 1961-62. Home: 2952 Kings Mill Rd Bethel Park PA 15102 Office: Ninth Floor Oliver Bldg Pittsburgh PA 15222

POLIVCHAK, PHILIP MICHAEL, trade assn. exec.; b. Mpls., Dec. 22, 1933; s. Michael and Ilona (Berta) P.; student U. Minn., 1952-54, 57-59. Nat. sales rep. Maico Electronics, Mpls., 1959-63; nat. sales dir. Electronic Devel. Co., Mpls., 1963-66; sales/service engr. Indsl. Mktg. div. ESB, Mpls., 1966-67; dir. dept. manpower devel. and tng. Nat. Assn. Home Builders, Washington, 1967—. Participant White House Conf. on Corrections, 1971; mem. Pres.'s Com. for Prisoners of War, 1973. Served with U.S. Army, 1955-57. Mem. Nat. Assn. Trade and Indsl. Edn. (v.p. 1975), Am. Vocat. Assn., Am. Soc. Tng. and Devel. Contbg. editor: Builder, 1967—; producer film: Build a Better Life, 1977. Home: 1721 P St NW Washington DC 20036 Office: 15th St and M Sts NW Washington DC 20005

POLIVKA, JOHN MICHAEL, pub. relations exec.; b. Coaldale, Pa., Mar. 18, 1953; s. John and Anne T. (York) P.; A.A., Harrisburg Area (Pa.) Community Coll., 1973; B.S. in Pub. Communications, Syracuse (N.Y.) U., 1975; m. Mary M. Cavallo, July 17, 1976. Pub. relations account exec. Communication Services Inc., Mechanicsburg, Pa., 1975-76; mgr. communications Harrisburg Area YMCA, 1976-77; pub. relations account exec. Edward C. Michener Assos., Harrisburg, 1977—; vol. announcer Sta. WMSP-FM, Harrisburg. Mem. Pub. Relations Soc. Am. (asso.), Internat. Assn. Bus. Communicators, Pa. Pub. Relations Soc. Democrat. Roman Catholic. Home: 2914 George St Harrisburg PA 17109 Office: 1007 N Front St Harrisburg PA 17102

POLK, IRWIN JACOB, physician; b. Perth Amboy, N.J., Dec. 3, 1925; s. Henry and Nell (Rosenfeld) Polkowitz; B.S., Rutgers U., 1949; M.D., U. Pa., 1953; M.P.H., Columbia U., 1961; m. Elaine Reisfield, Dec. 18, 1955; children—Hollis, Page. Intern Phila. Gen. Hosp., 1953-54; resident, Sarah Welt fellow Mt. Sinai Hosp., N.Y.C., 1954-56; practice medicine, specializing in allergy, 1955-60, 63—; dir. ambulatory care Lutheran Med. Center, Bklyn., 1961-63; asst. prof. pediatrics Columbia U., 1972—; cons. Monmouth Med. Center, Long Branch, N.J., 1972—; producer, moderator weekly broadcast Medi-Call, Sta. WJLK, Asbury Park, N.J. Served with AUS, 1943-46. Fellow Am. Acad. Pediatrics, Am. Coll. Allergists, Am. Pub. Health Assn., Am. Coll. Chest Physicians; mem. Am. Med. Writers Assn., AAAS, Phi Beta Kappa. Med. columnist Man and Medicine, Copley News Service, San Diego, 1969-75, Family Weekly, 1976—; author: (with Peter Dunfield) Ice Skating for Everyone, 1978; contbr. articles to med. jours. Home: 19 Page Dr Red Bank NJ 07701 Office: 300 Half Mile Rd Red Bank NJ 07701

POLL, ROBERT EUGENE, JR., investment banker; b. Urbana, Ill., Apr. 16, 1948; s. Robert Eugene and Dorothy (Baker) P.; A.B., Kenyon Coll., 1970; M.B.A., Ind. U., 1972; postgrad. Pub. Fin. Inst., U. Mich., 1976; m. Leslie Boutwell Tompkins, Aug. 8, 1970. Asst. treas., portfolio investment banking div. Chase Manhattan Bank, N.Y.C., 1974-76, 2d v.p. treasury div., 1976-77, v.p. treasury div., 1977-78; investment banker Lazard Freres & Co., N.Y.C., 1978—. Adviser, Ind. Small Bus. Assistance Program, 1970; adv. bd. U. Mich. Pub. Fin. Inst. Mem. Am. Mgmt. Assn., Am. Mktg. Assn., Nat. Trust Historic Preservation, Met. Museum Art, Smithsonian Instn., Cooper Hewitt Mus., Ind. U., Kenyon Coll. alumni assns., Westchester Arts Council, Delta Tau Delta. Republican. Episcopalian. Clubs: Rockaway Hunt, Lawrence Beach, Cedarhurst Yacht, Union League, Wharton Bus. (N.Y.C.). Home: 351 E 84th St #3E New York City NY 10028 Office: 1 Rockefeller Plaza New York City NY 10020

POLLACK, HENRY CLINTON, JR., stock broker; b. Cambridge, Mass., Mar. 26, 1941; s. Henry Clinton and Sylvia (Holman) P.; A.B., Brown U., 1963; children—Alexa Carlin, Henry Clinton. Sr. market analyst J. Walter Thompson Co., N.Y.C., 1963-65; group v.p. Lippincott & Margulies, Inc., 1965-70; pres. Solutions Group, Inc., N.Y.C., 1970—; chmn. bd. Wall St. Discount Corp., 1978—; guest lectr. mktg. N.Y. U. Grad. Sch. Bus.; asso. mem. N.Y. Stock Exchange (asso.). Republican. Presbyterian. Clubs: Greenwich Country; Brown U. Home: 103 Husted Ln Greenwich CT 06830 also 333 W 76th St New York City NY 10023 Office: 100 Wall St New York City NY 10005

POLLACK, JEROME MARVIN, univ. pres.; b. Chgo., Apr. 16, 1926; s. David and Sylvia (Marcus) P.; B.S., U. Okla., 1949, M.S., 1951, Ph.D., 1959; m. Ruth Mary Stephens, Aug. 2, 1952; children—Eric, Cassy, Nancy, Michael. Geologist, Humble Oil & Refining Co., 1951-55; instr. geology U. Okla., 1955-58; asst. prof. Oklahoma City U., 1958-59, Harpur Coll., Binghamton, N.Y., 1959-61; asso. prof. geology, chmn. dept. geology and geography U. N.H., 1961-65; dean Coll. Arts and Scis., prof. geology U. R.I., Kingston, 1965-68, v.p. for acad. affairs, 1968-69, dean Coll. Arts and Scis., 1969-71; v.p. acad. affairs Fairleigh Dickinson U., 1971-73, exec. and acad. v.p., 1973-74, acting pres., 1974, pres., 1974—. Mem. Geol. Soc. Am., Am. Assn. Petroleum Geologists, Soc. Econ. Mineralogists and Paleontologists, AAUP, AAS, Sigma Xi. Home: PO Box 900 Teaneck NJ 07666 Office: Fairleigh Dickinson U Rutherford NJ 07070

POLLAK, GEORGE A., consumer assn. adminstr.; b. N.Y.C., June 22, 1925; s. William B. and Ellen (Schwartz) P.; B.S., in Chemistry, Coll. City N.Y., 1948; m. Lorraine Silverstein, Nov. 30, 1952; children—Melissa, Audrey, Kevin. Chemist, Standard Brands, Inc., Peekskill, N.Y., 1948-49; phys. research chemist Picatinny Arsenal, Dover, N.J., 1950; devel. chemist Clark Babbitt Industries, West Hanover, Mass., 1951; head of food, equipment research and devel U.S. Naval Supply Research & Devel. Facility, Bayonne, N.J., 1952-66; head of cost research group Office of Comptroller, U.S. Dept. of Navy, Pentagon, Washington, 1966-68; head of foods div. Consumers Union of U.S., Inc., Mt. Vernon, N.Y., 1968—; mem. adv. com. on mil. food service systems Nat. Acad. Sci./NRC, 1968-75. Served with AUS, 1943-46. Recipient Meritorious Civilian Service award U.S. Dept. Navy, 1964, Merit award, 1966. Fellow Royal Soc. Health; mem. Inst. Food Technologists, Am. Chem. Soc., Am. Inst. Chemists, AAAS, Washington Ops. Research Council. Contbr. numerous articles in field to profl. jours. Patentee in field. Home: 537 Salem Rd Union NJ 07083 Office: 256 Washington St Mt Vernon NY 10550

POLLAK, MARTIN MARSHALL, patent licensing exec.; b. N.Y.C., July 31, 1927; s. Edward and Jennie (Horwitt) P.; A.B., Syracuse U., 1950; LL.B., St. John's U., 1953; m. Ellen R. Spiegel, Nov. 23, 1950; children—David, Richard, Barbara. Admitted to N.Y. State bar, 1953, U.S. Supreme Ct. bar, 1959; partner Feldman & Pollak, N.Y.C., 1953-59; exec. v.p., treas., dir. Nat. Patent Devel. Corp., N.Y.C., 1959—; chmn. bd., dir. Hydron Pacific, Ltd., N.Y.C., 1968—; treas., dir. Hydromed Sci., Inc., N.Y.C., 1971—, also Hydron Europe, Inc., N.Y.C. Trustee Worcester Found. for Exptl. Biology, Shrewsbury, Mass. Served with USNR, 1945-46. Mem. Czechoslovak-U.S. C. of C. (vice-chmn.). Office: 375 Park Ave New York City NY 10022

POLLAN, STEPHEN MICHAEL, investment co. exec.; b. N.Y.C., May 19, 1929; s. Robert David and Harriet (Morganstern) P.; student L.I. U., 1947-49, Coll. City N.Y., 1949-51; LL.B., Bklyn. Law Sch., 1951; m. Corinne Staller, July 18, 1954; children—Michael, Lori, Traci, Dana. Admitted to N.Y. bar, 1951; founder law firm Pollan, Zimmer, Fishbach & Hertan, N.Y.C. and Melville, L.I., N.Y., 1953—; founder, pres. Country Capital Corp., small bus. investment corp., N.Y.C., 1960-70; pres. Royal Bus. Funds Corp. (Amex), 1970-76; sr. real estate cons. Nat. Bank N. Am., 1976-78; pres. Stephen M. Pollan & Assos., Ltd., 1978—; dir. Electrosound Corp., Holmes Protection, Bell TV; panelist, author, lectr. venture capital industry; mem. Small Bus. Investment Co. adv. council SBA. Vice chmn. UN Com. for UN Day, 1971-72; advisor Pres.'s Commn. Small Bus., 1974; bd. dirs. Nassau County (N.Y.) Cerebral Palsy Assn.; founder Gay Head Taxpayer's Assn., Martha's Vineyard, Mass.; pres. Gay Head Community Council, 1975. Mem. Nat. Assn. Small Bus. Investment Cos. (region pres. 1975, bd. govs., certificate of appreciation). Co-author: The Best on Martha's Vineyard. Home: 1095 Park Ave New York City NY 10028 also Gay Head Martha's Vineyard MA 02535 Office: 919 3d Ave New York City NY 10017

POLLARD, JACQUELINE, coll. admnstr.; b. Phila., May 17, 1945; d. Leroy Augustus, Sr. and Emma Lou (Harris) P., A.B., U. Pa., 1977. Purchasing supr. Ins. Co. N.Am., Phila., 1962-66; exec. sec., dept. head, lectr. Spring Garden Coll., Chestnut Hill, Pa., 1966-71; cons. ITEL Corp., Phila., 1971; asst. to exec. dir. personnel and labor relations U. Pa., Phila., 1972-77; dir. personnel Wellesley (Mass.) Coll., 1977—; cons. edn. and employment J&G Asso., Phila., 1976-77. Vice pres. bd. dirs. New Horizons Ednl. Research Inst., Phila., 1976-77; chmn. Eastern region Pa. Black Conf. on Higher Edn., Phila., 1976—; mem. PUSH, Phila., 1976—, Phila. Urban League 1975—; bd. dirs. Phila. office Nat. Scholarship Service for Negro Students, 1976—. Recipient service award Pa. Black Conf. on Higher Edn., 1977. Mem. Internat. Assn. for Personnel Women (pres. 1976-77), Am. Personnel and Guidance Assn., Assn. for Non-White Concerns, Coll. and U. Personnel Assn., Am. Assn. Higher Edn., Nat. Assn. Coll. and U. Bus. Officers. Democrat. Baptist. Office: 144 Green Hall Wellesley Coll Wellesley MA 02181

POLLARD, STEWART MACLAINE LAURENS, assn. exec.; b. Lyman, Maine, May 31, 1922; s. Ralph John and Millwee (Westmoreland) P.; student Bowdoin Coll., 1945-46; m. Margret Russell, Dec. 8, 1946; children—Carol Le, Bruce Edward. Enlisted U.S. Army, 1939, advanced through grades to capt., 1959; ret., 1970; mem. Nat. Sojourners, Alexandria, Va., 1956—, nat. sec.-treas., 1970-75, also editor. Mem. Waldoborough (Maine) Hist. Soc., 1971—; state chmn. Medal of Honor Grove, Freedoms Found., Valley Forge, Pa., 1972-75. Decorated Silver Star, Purple Heart; recipient Honor medal Freedoms Found., 1973-74. Mem. Nat. Assn. Uniformed Forces (life), SAR, Knox Meml. Assn. (life), Pearl Harbor Survivors Assn. (life), Res. Officers Assn. (life), Heroes of 76 (nat. adj. 1970-75), Va. Craftsman (hon.), Matrons and Patrons Assn. Germany (life), Philalethes Soc. Republican. Presbyterian. Clubs: Masons (33 deg.), K.T. Author: Tied to Masonic Apron Strings, 1968; Proudly Serving The Cause of Patriotism, 1973. Home: 10202 Bradley Ln Columbia MD 21044

POLLARD, WILLIAM EDWARD, physician; b. Lovington, Ill., Sept. 29, 1906; s. Wyde Claude and Mathilde (Shirey) P.; B.S., U. Ill., 1929; M.D., Columbia U., 1935; m. Margaret Sutherland Simpson, Oct. 6, 1942; children—Susan Sutherland, Kirsty Mackenzie. Jazz trumpeter with Red Nichols, Ben Pollack, Milt Shaw, others, N.Y.C., 1929-31; intern Orange Meml. Hosp., 1935-37; resident Sloane Hosp., N.Y.C., 1937-42, attending staff, 1942-52; pvt. practice, Princeton, N.J., 1946—; instr. Coll. Phys. and Surg., Columbia, 1942-52; chmn. dept. obstetrics and gynecology Princeton Hosp., 1949—; cons. Hunterdon Med. Center, Carrier Clinic, N.J. Neuropsychiat. Inst., 1950—. Served from capt. to maj. M.C., AUS, 1942-45, ETO. Diplomate Am. Bd. Obstetrics and Gynecology. Fellow A.C.S., Am. Coll. Obstetrics and Gynecology; mem. Soc. Surgeons N.J. Home: Province Line Rd RD 3 Princeton NJ 08540 Office: Med Arts Bldg Princeton NJ 08540

POLLIN, ABE, basketball exec.; b. Phila., Dec. 3, 1923; s. Morris and Jennie (Sack) P.; B.A., George Washington U., 1945; student U. Md., 1941-44; m. Irene S. Kerchek, May 27, 1945; children—Robert Norman, James Edward. Engaged in home bldg. bus., 1945—; pres. Abe Pollin, Inc., Balt., 1962—; pres. Balt. Bullets Basketball Club, Inc. (name now Capitol Bullets), 1964—; dir. County Fed. Savs. & Loan Assn., Rockville, Md. Bd. dirs. United Jewish Appeal, Nat. Jewish Hosp., Jewish Community Center; bd. dirs., adv. com. John F. Kennedy Cultural Center. Mem. Nat. Assn. Home: Builders, Asso. Builders and Contractors Md., Washington Bd. Trade. Jewish. Home: 2 Goldsboro Ct Bethesda MD 20034 Office: 6101 16th St Washington DC 20011

POLLNER, MARTIN ROBERT, lawyer; b. N.Y.C., Dec. 17, 1934; s. Andrew and Rose (Buchsbaum) P.; B.A., City Coll. N.Y., 1957; J.D., Bklyn. Law Sch., 1960; m. Mildred Brenner, Mar. 30, 1958; children—Daniel Mitchell, Richard Lawrence. Admitted to N.Y. bar, 1960, D.C. bar, 1972; atty. Office of Dep. Atty. Gen., U.S. Justice Dept., Washington, 1960-62, asst. U.S. atty. Eastern Dist. N.Y., 1963-66; asso. firm Mudge, Rose, Guthrie & Alexander, N.Y.C., 1966-70; dir., officer law enforcement U.S. Treasury Dept., Washington, 1970-72, dep. asst. sec. treasury, 1972-73; U.S. rep. UN Internat. Narcotics Control Bd., 1973, 74—; partner firm Amen, Weisman & Butler, N.Y.C., 1973-78, Pollner, Mezan & Stolzberg, N.Y.C., 1978—. Mem. White House Conf. Food, Nutrition and Health, co-chmn. consumer fraud sect., 1969-70. Named an Outstanding Young Man of Am., 1968, 70. Mem. Am. Bar Assn., Assn. Bar City N.Y., Nat., N.Y. State dist. attys assns. Home: 18 E 81st St New York City NY 10028 Office: Pollner Mezan & Stolzberg 277 Park Ave New York City NY 10017

POLLOCK, JOSEPH JORDAN, physician; b. Punxsutawney, Pa., Jan. 19, 1932; s. Robert James and Flora Beatrice (Jordan) P.; B.S., Grove City Coll., 1954; M.D., George Washington U., 1958; m. Nancy Jean Freeland, June 12, 1954; children—Amy Jean, Robert Joseph. Commd. 2d. lt. U.S. Air Force, 1956, advanced through grades to col., 1974; intern George Washington U. Hosp., Washington, 1958-59; resident Mary Hitchcock Meml. Hosp., Hanover, N.H., 1962-64, cardiopulmonary fellow, 1964-65; pulmonary fellow Wilford Hall Med. Center, Lackland AFB, Tex., 1968-69; gen. practice medicine, Stewart AFB, N.Y., 1959-62; practice internal medicine USAF Hosp., Elmendorf AFB, Alaska, 1965-68, chief pulmonary diseases, 1972-76, chief profl. services, 1973-75, chief dept. medicine, 1975-76; chief pulmonary diseases Malcolm Grow Med. Center, Andrews AFB, Md., 1969-72, dep. dir. profl. edn., 1971-72; ret., 1976; practice medicine, specializing in internal medicine and lung disease Internal Medicine Assos., Anchorage, 1976-77, State College, Pa., 1977—. Decorated Legion of Merit. Fellow A.C.P.; mem. Am. Thoracic Soc., Am. Coll. Chest Physicians, Pa., Centre County med. socs., Central Pa. Lung and Health Services Assn., Alaska Lung Assn. (chmn. med. advisory com., pres. 1978—). Republican. Presbyterian. Home: 18 Hampton Ct State College PA 16801 Office: 232 S Burrowes St State College PA 16801

POLLOCK, JOSEPH LEONARD, sch. adminstr.; b. Phila., Mar. 7, 1922; s. Samuel George and Rose (Madison-Cohen) P.; B.S., State Coll., West Chester, Pa., 1947; M.S., U. Pa., 1949; letter of eligibility for supt. schs., 1950; postgrad. Lehigh U., 1969-72; m. Mae Porter, Oct. 10, 1948 (dec. 1976); 1 son, Stephen George. Social studies tchr. Shoemaker and Sayre Jr. High Schs., 1947-54; U.S. history tchr. Sta. WHYY-TV, 1954-55; vice prin. Sayre Jr. High Sch., 1955-59; prin. Landreth Sch., 1959-61; adminstrv. asst. to pres. Phila. Sch. Bd., 1961-63; dir. info. service Phila. Schs., 1963-67; supt. schs., Scranton, Pa., 1967-68; prin. Beeber Jr. High Sch., 1968-72, Greenberg Sch., 1972-77, Germantown Sr. High Sch., Phila., 1977-78, Franklin Learning Center, Phila., 1978—; exec. dir. Citizens for City Coll., 1950. Served with U.S. Army, 1944-46. Decorated Bronze Star; recipient Distinguished Service award Phila. Home and Sch. Council, 1968. Mem. W. Phila. High Sch. Alumni Assn. (past pres.), Assn. Supervision and Curriculum Devel., Am. Assn. Sch. Adminstrs., Nat. Assn. Secondary School Prins., Phi Delta Kappa, (chpt. pres. 1955-56). Clubs: Masons, B'nai B'rith. Office: 15th and Mount Vernon St Philadelphia PA 19130

POLLOCK, WILLIAM BEATTY, veterinarian; b. Biddeford, Maine, May 16, 1942; s. Ernest Butler and Norma Arlene (Beatty) P.; B.A., Colby Coll., 1964; B.S. in Biology, Kans. State U., 1968, D.V.M., 1970; m. Jeanne Susan Anderson, Feb. 1, 1964; children—William Quinn, Anne Wendell. Sr. product engr. Electra Mfg. Co., 1965-66; pvt. practice small animal medicine and surgery, Beverly Farms, Mass., 1972—; vis. lectr. physics Manchester (Mass.) High Sch., 1974—. Served to capt. Vet. Corps, AUS, 1970-72. Recipient Upjohn award, 1970, Bogue Meml. award, 1970, Kans. State U. med. award, 1970. Mem. Am. Acad. Veterinary Cardiology, Am. Animal Hosp. Assn., AVMA, Mass., Maine, North Shore veterinary assns. Democrat. Contbr. articles to profl. jours. Home: 82 Pleasant St Manchester MA 01944 Office: 642 Hale St Beverly Farms MA 01915

POLON, JAMES ALLEN, chemist; b. South River, N.J., June 3, 1931; s. Albert Charles and Anna (Kuchka) P.; B.S., Rutgers U., 1955; J.D., Seton Hall U., 1977; m. Elaine Theresa Rittman, June 11, 1955; children—Mark James, Richard John, David Allen, Joanne Elaine; m. 2d, M. Joy Mikrut, June 4, 1972. Jr. chemist analytical dept. Chem. Constrn. Co., Linden, N.J., 1953-54, research chemist fundamental dept., Stamford, Conn., 1954-56; research chemist analytical dept. Engelhard Minerals & Chem. Corp., Menlo Park, Edison, N.J., 1956, research chemist applications dept., 1956-61, research supr. applications, 1961-70, group leader indsl. products research, 1970-72; product engring. mgr. Alpha Metals, Inc., 1972-75; product mgr. Electro-Sci. Labs., Pennsauken, N.J., 1975—; admitted to N.J. bar, 1978, Pa. bar, 1978. Pres., dir. M & C Credit Union. Fellow Am. Inst. Chemists; mem. Am. Bar Assn., Am. Chem. Soc., N.J. Pesticide Assn., Am. Musicians Union N.J. (corr. sec. 1970), N.J. Patent Law Soc., Assn. Trial Lawyers Am. Club: K.C. Contbr. articles to profl. jours. Patentee in field. Home: 10 Cambridge Rd Freehold NJ 07728 Office: 2211 Sherman Ave Pennsauken NJ 08110

POLOW, NANCY BETH GROSS, speech pathologist; b. N.Y.C., Feb. 11, 1946; d. Jack and Shirlee (Hirshleifer) Gross; B.S., N.Y. U., 1967; M.A., Seton Hall U., 1968; Ph.D., Fordham U., 1974; m. Peter Maurice Polow, Sr., May 16, 1970; children—Peter Maurice Jr., Candace Paige. Speech therapist Cerebral Palsy Rehab. Inst. of N.J. Orthopedic Hosp., Orange, 1967-68; instr. Miami-Dade Jr. Coll., 1968-70; speech therapist Title I Program, 1970, Millburn and Short Hills, N.J., elementary schs., 1970-71, Child Devel. Services Nursery Sch., Chatham, N.J., 1972-73, summer sch., West Caldwell and Caldwell, N.J., 1972; pvt. practice speech therapy, 1971-73; instr. William Paterson Coll., 1974-78; guest lectr. N.J. Sch. Systems; prof. Seton Hall U., 1978—; speech rep. N.J. Health Careers Workshop. Certified speech pathologist. Mem. Am. (chmn. state career info. 1974-75, ERA state rep., book reviewer jour.), N.J. (program chmn.) speech and hearing assns., Myofunctional Therapy Assn., Sigma Alpha Eta, Kappa Gamma Chi, Phi Delta Kappa. Author: An Articulation Curriculum for the S Sound, 1975; A Stuttering Manual for the Speech Therapist, 1975; Symptomatic Voice Therapy, 1978. Home: 667 Brentwood Dr South Orange NJ 07079

POLSKY, LOUIS SANFORD, obstetrician, gynecologist; b. Longview, Tex., July 20, 1932; s. Sam and Ruth P.; B.A., U. Tex., Austin, 1954; M.D., U. Tex., Galveston, 1958; m. Joyce Misthal, Jan. 22, 1961; children—Gary, Jay, Jeffrey. Intern, Phila. Gen. Hosp., 1958-59, resident in obstetrics, gynecology, 1961-64; practice medicine specializing in obstetrics, gynecology, Hackensack, N.J., 1964—; attending physician Hackensack Hosp., Bergen Women's Med. Center. Served with USN, 1959-61. Diplomate Am. Bd. Obstetrics and Gynecology. Fellow A.C.S., Am. Coll. Obstetrics and Gynecology, Am. Infertility Soc., Am. Assn. Laparoscopists, Am. Colposcopists; mem. Bergen County Med. Soc., AMA (Physicians Recognition award 1976). Jewish. Office: 90 Prospect Ave Hackensack NJ 07601

POLT, GEORGE DEWEY, JR., real estate broker and appraiser; b. Hunterdon County, N.J., July 9, 1926; s. George Dewey and Anna Janet (Schafer) P.; ed. pub. schs., Teterboro (N.J.) Sch. Aeros.; m. Margaret Carolyn Coleman, Mar. 15, 1952; children—Cynthia Ann, Terry Jane, Charles Herbert, George Woodward. Salesman, Gen. Baking Co., Easton, Pa., 1952; repair and maintenance supr. Polt Bus Co., Glen Gardner, N.J., 1952-68; registered rep., securities broker Investment Services, Belvidere, N.J., 1968-71; real estate broker George D. Polt, Jr., Washington, N.J., 1970—. Charter mem. Lebanon Twp. Fire Co.; mem. Lebanon Twp. Bd. Adjustments, 1971, Lebanon Twp. Governing Body, 1972-74; mayor Lebanon Twp., 1974. Served with USAAF, 1944-46. Mem. Warren County (pres., 1977, dir.), Nat., N.J. (dir. 1977) bds. realtors, Soc. Real Estate Appraisers (asso.). Home: 424 Hollow Rd Glen Gardner NJ 08826 Office: 111 W Washington Ave Washington NJ 07882

POLTORATZKY, NIKOLAI PETROVICH, educator; b. Istanbul, Turkey, Feb. 16, 1921; s. Peter F. and Barbara R. (Kapustian) P.; came to U.S., 1955, naturalized, 1961; student U. Sofia (Bulgaria), 1938-42; Philosophisch-Theologische Hochschule, Regensburg, Germany, 1946-47; Ph.D., U. Paris, Sorbonne, 1954; m. Tamara Diatlenco, May 24, 1954; 1 son, Vladimir. Instr. in Russian, U.S. Army Lang. Sch., Monterey, Calif., 1955; research asso., Russian area Inwood Project on Intercultural Communication, Bklyn. Coll., 1956-58; asst. prof. Russian lang. and lit. Mich. State U., E. Lansing, 1958-60, asso. prof., 1960-64, prof., 1964-67, dir. Russian program, 1962-64; prof. Slavic lang. and lit. U. Pitts., 1967—, chmn. Slavic dept., 1967-74; mem. faculty, asst. to dir. Inst. Soviet Studies, Middlebury Coll., summers 1958-65; vis. lectr. U. Calif. at Berkeley, summer 1966. Recipient research grants Am. Philos. Soc., 1960, Internat. Communication Inst., Mich. State U., 1964-65, Internat. Programs, U. Pitts., 1967-68, faculty research, U. Pitts., 1971-72. Mem. Am. Assn. Advancement of Slavic Studies, Am. Assn. Tchrs. of Slavic and E. European Langs.,

Modern Lang. Assn., Assn. Russian-Am. Scholars in USA. Greek Orthodox. Author: Berdiaev and Russia, 1967; I.A. Iljin and the Polemics Concerning His Ideas on Resistance to Evil by Force, 1975; editor: The World War Two, 1939-45, 1946; On Themes Russian and General, 1965; Russian Emigre Literature, 1972; I.A. Iljin: Russian Writers, Literature, and Art, 1973; Russian Religious-Philosophical Thought of the 20th Century, 1975; Russian Language Press and Radio Outside Russia, 1937-56; contbr. articles to profl. jours. Home: 800 Penn Center Blvd Pittsburgh PA 15235 Office: Slavic Dept L F 120 U Pitts Pittsburgh PA 15260

POLYDOROFF, THEODORE, lawyer; b. London, June 4, 1934 (parents Am. citizens); s. Wladimir John and Alexandra (Tulina) P.; B.A., U. Md., 1956; J.D., Washington Coll., Am. U., 1958; m. Susan Wills, June 13, 1964; children—Christopher Theodore, Stephen Herbert, Elise Alexandra, Michael Jackson. Admitted to Va. bar, 1958, D.C. bar, 1961, U.S. Supreme Ct., 1961; practiced in Arlington, Va., 1958-60, Washington, 1965-77, McLean, Va., 1977—; mem. firm Rea, Cross, Knebel, 1965-68, Morgan, Lewis and Bockius, 1968-70, Ephraim & Polydoroff, 1972-77; trial atty. ICC, Washington, 1960-65; asso. professorial lectr. George Washington U., 1958-75; guest lectr. Transp. Law Inst., Denver U. Law Sch., 1973; v.p., gen. counsel Nat. Capital Underwater Photog. Soc. Ltd., Washington, 1966—; gen. counsel Underwater Soc. Am., Phila., 1966-72; gen. counsel, dir. Wheaton Holding Corp., 1971—, Scan Tex Systems, Inc., 1975—; gen. counsel, sec. Gemini Assos., Inc., 1972—. Trustee Underwater Soc. Am. Found., 1969—. Mem. Am., Va., D.C. bar assns., Motor Carrier Lawyers Assn., Alpha Tau Omega, Delta Theta Phi. Club: Masons. Home: 4904 Morning Glory Ct Rockville MD 20853 Office: 1307 Dolley Madison Blvd McLean VA 22101

POMARA, VINCENT LAWRENCE, electronics ofcl.; b. Bronx, N.Y., Aug. 10, 1941; s. Louis Joseph and Vivian (Sica) P.; A.A.S., Suffolk Community Coll., 1969; student electronics State U. N.Y., Farmingdale, 1977—; m. Gail Vocht, Oct. 5, 1969; children—Stephanie Ann, Vincent Lawrence. Chief gage insp. Hazeltine Electronics Corp., Greenlawn, N.Y., 1962-68; quality assurance asso. engr. Maxson Electronics Corp., Great River, N.Y., 1968-69; configuration mgr. Telephonics div. Instrument Systems Corp., Huntington, N.Y., 1969-74; mgr. quality assurance Lambda Electronics, Melville, N.Y., 1974—. Served with USAR, 1963-69. Democrat. Roman Catholic. Home: 7 Beach Ave Port Jefferson Station NY 11776 Office: 515 Broad Hollow Rd Melville NY 11746

POMERANTZ, ALLEN, educator; b. N.Y.C., May 7, 1932; s. Joseph and Alice (Williams) P.; B.A., Bklyn. Coll., 1954; M.A., U. Wis., 1957; postgrad. Columbia, 1961-63, Pace U., 1963, N.Y. U., 1969—, U. Valladolid (Spain), 1966; m. Judith Ruth Burg, Apr. 3, 1960; 1 dau., Alison. Tchr. Spanish, high schs. N.Y., 1957-72; tchr. Spanish, Bronx (N.Y.) Community Coll., 1960-72, adj. lectr., 1962-70, adj. asst. prof. Spanish, 1970-72, asst. prof., 1972—, coordinator modern lang. workshop, 1973—; spl. examiner in Spanish, N.Y.C. Dept. Personnel, 1974—. Served with AUS, 1954-56. NDEA grantee, 1965; Fulbright-Hays travel grantee, Spain, 1966; Nat. Endowment for Humanities grantee, 1976. Mem. Modern Lang. Assn., Am. Council Tchrs. of Fgn. Langs., Council for Edn. Communications and Tech. Author: Spanish Now!, 1975, rev. edit., 1976, 77. Home: 640 West End Ave New York City NY 10024 Office: Bronx Community Coll Bronx NY 10453

POMERENE, JAMES HERBERT, elec. engr.; b. Yonkers, N.Y., June 22, 1920; s. Joel and Elsie (Bower) P.; B.E.E., Northwestern U., 1942; postgrad. Princeton U., 1950; m. Edythe R. Schwenn, Dec. 1, 1944; children—James Bennett, Katherine Ellen, Andrew Thomas Stewart. Elec. engr. Hazeltine Corp., Little Neck, N.Y., 1942-46; staff mem. electronic computer project Inst. Advanced Study, Princeton, N.J., 1946-51, chief engr., 1951-56; sr. engr. IBM, Poughkeepsie, N.Y., 1956-67, sr. staff mem., Armonk, N.Y., 1967—, IBM fellow, 1976; cons. in field. Fellow IEEE; mem. Sigma Xi (asso.), Tau Beta Pi. Home: 403 N Bedford Rd Chappaqua NY 10514 Office: Old Orchard Rd Armonk NY 10504

POMEROY, LEON RALPH, psychologist; b. Westfield, Mass.; s. L. Ralph and Rachel (Harlow) P.; B.A., U. Mass., 1959, M.A. in Biology, 1961; diploma Brain Research Inst., Mexico City, Mexico, 1965; Ph.D. in Psychology, U. Tex. at Austin, 1967. Research asst. Clayton Found. Biochem. Inst. U. Tex., Austin, 1962-65; fellow Inst. Advanced Study in Rational-Emotive Psychotherapy, N.Y.C. 1969-73. Asst. prof. dept. psychology L.I. U., Bklyn., 1967-70, asso. prof., 1971-72; asso. prof. psychology N.J. State Coll. at Union, 1972; clin. psychologist VA, N.Y.C., 1973—; chief, biofeedback and stress control unit Psychology Service; vis. prof. Queens Coll. City U. N.Y., 1969-73; adj. asso. prof. N.Y. U., N.Y.C., 1973—, New Sch. Social Research, 1978—; individual practice clin. psychology, N.Y.C., 1973—. Founding fellow Internat. Acad. Preventive Medicine (editor-in-chief acad. jour. 1972—, pres. 1975-76, chmn. research com. 1972—); mem. Am., Eastern psychol. assns. Editor: New Dynamics of Preventive Medicine series, 1973—; asso. editor: (with Benjamin Wolman) Handbook of General Psychology, 1973. Home: 1619-19 3d Ave New York City NY 10028 Office: care PO Box 394 Lenox Hill Sta New York City NY 10021

POMEROY, ROBERT WATSON, III, fin. co. ofcl.; b. N.Y.C., May 22, 1935; s. Robert W. and Estelle C. (Bassett) P.; B.A., Stanford U., 1958; postgrad. Am. U. of Beirut, 1958-59; m. Jane Graham Adams Ramsey, Feb. 11, 1960; children—Janet Fraser, Seth Bassett. Sales mgr. Fin. Services, Overseas Brokerage Services, Beirut, Lebanon, 1958-60; exec. asst. to gen. mgr. Internat. Basic Economy Corp., Brazil, 1961-64; dir. Arbor Acres, S.A., Indusquima S.A., Sao Paulo, Brazil, 1961-64; fin. analyst Inter-Am. Devel. Bank, Washington, 1965-73; dept. adviser Inter-Am. Devel. Bank, Washington, 1973—; chmn. Washington area Bus. Resource Group, Nat. Coordinating Com. for Promotion History, 1977—. Served with Signal Corps, U.S. Army, 1954-56. Mem. Am. Hist. Assn., Newcomen Soc. N.Am. Club: Internat. of Washington. Home: 3914 Harrison St NW Washington DC 20015 Office: 808 17th St NW Washington DC 20577

POMPIAN, RICHARD OWEN, communications co. exec.; b. Chgo., July 17, 1935; s. Bertram Edwin and Molly Mavis (Pumpian) P.; A.B., certificate in Journalism, U. Mich., 1958, Intern certificate in Advt., 1961; M.B.A. in Mktg. with distinction, N.Y. U., 1965, certificate in Pub. and Graphics, 1966, certificate in TV, 1967, certificate in Computer Systems, 1970; m. Rita Lillian Beyers, Dec. 20, 1970. Copywriter, Dancer-Fitzgerald-Sample, Inc., N.Y.C., 1960-68; self-employed advt. cons., N.Y.C., 1968-69; advt. agt., prin. ProSell Communications Co. (now Pompian Advt., Inc.), N.Y.C., 1970-74, pres., 1974—; editor Northeast Gazette, 1976—; partner Rita Pompian Tng. Consultants, 1977—; dir. Pompian Pools, Inc., Detroit, 1965-76; lectr. advanced writing course Pace U., N.Y.C., 1974-75. Served to 1st lt. arty. AUS, 1958-60. Mem. Nat. Acad. TV Arts and Scis., AAAS, U. Mich. Alumni Assn., N.Y. U. Alumni Assn., Sigma Delta Chi, Delta Sigma Phi. Club: U. Mich. (N.Y.C.). Author: Advertising: A First Book, 1970. Editor: The Rhythm Book (Peter Phillips), 1971. Home and Office: 300 Riverside Dr New York City NY 10025

POND, THOMAS TEMPLE, JR., learning disabilities therapist; b. Boston, Mar. 9, 1927; s. Thomas Temple and Virginia Kettering (Deacon) P.; B.A., Harvard U., 1951; M.Ed., Keene State Coll., 1972; m. Barbara Ann Koons, Jan. 25, 1958 (dec. Dec. 1976); 1 son, Francis Temple. Cons., Internat. Econ. Services, N.Y.C., 1963-65; registrar, instr. export traffic Acad. Advanced Traffic, N.Y.C., 1965-70, learning disabilities therapist Pub. Elementary Schs., Brattleboro, Vt., 1972-74, Hillsboro, N.H., 1975-76. Pres. Monadnock Assn. for Retarded Citizens, N.H. Assn. Retarded Citizens; bd. dirs. Monadnock Workshop, Peterboro, N.H. Mem. Am. Soc. Traffic and Transp. Clubs: Masons, Bostonian Soc., Boston Athenaeum. Home: Whitcomb House Main St Hancock NH 03449

PONS, LUIS ORLANDO, community agency exec.; b. Guantanamo, Cuba, May 6, 1930; s. Eduardo and Marina (Megret) P.; came to U.S., 1960, naturalized, 1966; student Havana U, 1950-53; m. Herminia Cubrie, Feb. 16, 1970; 1 dau., Lucia. Labor rep. to Guantanamo Twp., Cuba, 1950; asst. to Sec. Gen. of Cuban Workers Edn., 1951-55; adminstrv. dir. Fedn. Sugar Workers, Havana, Cuba, 1956-59; instr. Isnt. Labor Relations, U. P.R., 1960-62; staff Lower West Side Community Corp., N.Y.C., 1966—, exec. dir., 1970—; mem. adv. com. United Ams. Bank, N.Y.C., 1975—; v.p. Lower West Side Household Workers Corp., 1974. AFL/CIO-U.S. Govt. scholar, France, Italy, Germany, Brussels, Greece, London, 1964-65. Columnist, Azucar Mag., 1956-58, Mundo Americano, 1965-66. Home: 349 W 71st St New York City NY 10023 Office: 759 10th Ave New York City NY 10019

PONTIUS, ANNELIESE ALMA, psychiatrist; b. Chemnitz, Germany, May 19, 1921; d. Karl and Clara (Otto) Muller; M.D., Johann-Wolfgang Goethe U., Frankfurt, Germany, 1950; grad. Analytic Inst., Munich, 1953; m. Dieter Johann Jakob Pontius, July 7, 1951. Intern, Univ. Hosp., Frankfurt/Main, Ger., 1950-51; resident in psychiatry McGill U., Montreal, Que., Can., 1955-57; research asso. child psychiatry Lenox Hill Hosp., N.Y.C., 1962-64; practice medicine, specializing in psychiatry, N.Y.C., 1962—; med. advisor HEW, 1968—; vis. scientist NIMH, 1971-72; vis. neuropsychiatrist, dept. forenic psychiatry N.Y. U. Med. Center, 1969-73, clin. asst. prof., 1971-76; asst. psychiatrist McLean Hosp. Inst. Law and Psychiatry, Belmont, Mass., 1977—; lectr. psychiatry Harvard Med. Sch., 1977—. Diplomate Am. Bd. Psychiatry and Neurology. Mem. Am. Psychiat. Assn., AAAS, N.Y. Acad. Scis., Internat. Assn. Analytical Psychology. Contbr. articles to profl. jours. Office: 165 E 60th St New York City NY 10022

PONZILLO, STEPHEN JOSEPH, III, ednl. adminstr.; b. Balt., Jan. 16, 1947; s. Stephen Joseph and Patricia Rosemary (Harrison) P.; B.S., Towson State U., 1969, M.Ed., 1972; postgrad. Loyola Coll. Balt., 1973, Morgan State U., 1974-75, Johns Hopkins U., 1974, U. Md., 1975—; m. Marie Ione Petts, Apr. 7, 1974. Tchr. social studies Sparrow Point High Sch., Baltimore County (Md.) Bd. Edn., 1969-77, Dundalk Sr. High Sch., 1977—, asst. prin., 1977—. Mem. Heritage Com. Sparrows Point, 1974-77; active fundraising Am. Cancer Soc. Named an outstanding young educator Dundalk (Md.) Jaycees, 1973. Mem. Tchrs. Assn. Baltimore County, Md. Tchrs. Assn. NEA, Nat., Md. assns. secondary sch. prins., Md. Assn. Supervision and Curriculum Devel., Secondary Sch. Adminstrs. Assn. Baltimore County, Nat. Hist. Soc., Am. Hist. Assn. Democrat. Methodist. Clubs: Masons, Shriners. Home: Marsteph Hall 4 Norgate Ct Cockeysville MD 21030 Office: Dundalk Sr High Sch 1901 Delvale Ave Dundalk MD 21222

POOR, FREDERIC HEDGE, JR., lawyer; b. Yonkers, N.Y., Sept. 28, 1912; s. Frederic Hedge and Elizabeth (Hubbard) P.; A.B., Harvard U., 1934, LL.B., 1937; m. Elizabeth Louise Hart, May 6, 1943; 1 son, Frederic Hedge. Admitted to bar, 1937; asso. Montgomery, Peabody, Grace & Derby, N.Y.C., 1937-40, Montgomery, Grace & Derby, 1946, partner, 1947-49; partner Derby, French, Leigh & Poor, 1950-51, McKenzie, Hyde, Wilson, French & Poor, 1952-63, Browne, Hyde & Dickerson, 1963-71, Peck, Sprague & Poor, 1972—. Served from 1st lt. to lt. col. AUS, 1940-46. Decorated Bronze Star (U.S.), Order of Cloud and Banner (Nationalist China). Mem. Am. Bar Assn. Clubs: Harvard (N.Y.C.); Seawanhaka Corinthian Yacht (Oyster Bay, N.Y.). Home: 218 Piping Rock Rd Locust Valley NY 11560 Office: 34 Audrey Ave Oyster Bay NY 11771

POOR, THOMAS MARTIN, securities analyst; b. Greenfield, Mass., July 14, 1943; s. Henry Benjamin and Catherine Hartshorne (Ross) P.; B.A., Amherst Coll., 1965; m. Nancy Merrill Bradshaw, Aug. 31, 1968; 1 son, Morgan Ross. Tchr. math. Episcopal Acad., Phila., 1965-69, St. George's Sch., Newport, R.I., 1965-69; trainee Smith, Barney & Co., N.Y.C., 1969-70; corporate bond analyst Scudder, Stevens & Clark, Boston, 1970—, v.p. bonds, 1976—. Chartered fin. analyst, chartered investment counselor. Mem. Boston Soc. Security Analysts, U.S. Squash Racquets Assn. (asst. treas. 1973-75), Mass. Squash Racquets Assn. (treas. 1974-78, pres. 1978—), Tennis Racquet Club Boston (pres. 1976-77). Home: 243 Brigantine Circle Norwell MA 02061 Office: Scudder Stevens Clark 175 Federal St Boston MA 02110

POPE, (JOHN) JOSEPH, banker; b. Gistoux, Belgium, July 27, 1921 (parents Canadian citizens); s. Maurice Arthur and Simonne Marie (du Monceau de Bergendal) P.; student U. Ottawa (Can.), 1939; m. Claudine de Lannoy, June 8, 1953; children—Sybil, Francis, Allan, Lois, Nora, Julian, Michael. With Bank of Montreal, Ottawa, Ont., Can., 1940, Hull, Que., Can., 1941-47, Montreal, Que., 1947-54; dir. Burns Bros. & Denton Ltd., Toronto, Ont., 1954-62; propr. Pope & Co., Toronto, 1962—; pres., dir. Chaumont Securities Ltd., 1966—, Kamm, Garland & Co., Ltd., 1977—, also Marina Lodge. Served to lt., arty. Canadian Army, 1942-46. Fellow Inst. Canadian Bankers; mem. Investment Dealers Assn., Boston (asso.), Phila. (asso.), Montreal stock exchanges, Winnipeg Commodity Exchange. Mem. Liberal party Can. Roman Catholic. Clubs: Nat., Badminton and Racquet (Toronto). Home: 61 Cluny Dr Toronto ON M4W 2R1 Canada Office: 15 Duncan St Toronto ON M5H 3P9 Canada

POPE, LEAVITT JOSEPH, broadcasting co. exec.; b. Boston, Apr. 2, 1924; s. Joseph and Charlotte (Leavitt) P.; B.S., Mass. Inst. Tech., 1947; m. Martha Pascale, Nov. 20, 1948; children—Joseph, Daniel, Patricia, Elizabeth, Nancy, Maria, Joan, Christopher, Virginia, Matthew, Charles. Adminstrv. asst. N.Y. Daily News, N.Y.C., 1947-51; asst. to lgen. mgr. Sta. WPIX-TV, N.Y.C., 1951-56; v.p. ops. Sta. WPIX, WPIX-FM, N.Y.C., 1956-72; sec., dir. WPIX, Inc., N.Y.C., 1958-74, exec. v.p., 1972-74, pres., chief exec. officer, 1975—; exec. v.p., dir. Conn. Broadcasting Co., Bridgeport, 1967-74, pres., chief exec. officer, 1975—; dir. N.Y. Daily News, 1975—, Tribune Co., 1977—. Mem. N.Y. State Regents Ednl. TV Adv. Council, 1958; bd. govs. Daytop Village; trustee Cath. Communications Found., St. Thomas Aquinas Coll. Served with Signal Corps, AUS, 1942-46. Mem. ASME, Internat. Radio and TV Soc., Assn. Ind. TV Stas. (treas., chmn. 1974—), N.Y. State Broadcasters Assn. (dir. 1970-74, pres. 1975—), Sigma Nu. Club: Knights of Malta. Home: 173 Dorchester Rd Scarsdale NY 10583 Office: 220 E 42d St New York City NY 10017

POPE, RICHARD LOUIS, wholesale glass co. exec.; b. N.J., Sept. 19, 1939; s. William B. and Dorothy W. (Ulrich) P.; B.S. in Ceramics (State scholar), B.S. in Chemistry (State scholar), Rutgers U., 1962; M.S. in Indsl. Adminstrn., Purdue U., 1963; m. Jacqueline Ann Colacecchi, Oct. 3, 1964; children—Jennifer, Melissa, Brian. Product specialist Corning Glass Works (N.Y.), 1963-64, market specialist, 1965; pres., founder Vesta Glass Inc., Corning, 1965—, The Glass Menagerie, Corning, 1978—; adv. bd. Monroe Savs. Bank, 1978—. Mem. planning bd. Town of Corning, 1975—; bd. dirs. Three Rivers Devel. Found., Inc., 1978—; bd. dirs., v.p. Spencer Crest Nature Center, 1975—; mem. planning bd. SE Steuben County, 1976—. Mem. Greater Corning Area C. of C. (dir. 1977—), Tau Kappa Epsilon. Republican. Club: Rotary. Home: Overlook Dr Corning NY 14830 Office: PO Box 1426 Corning NY 14830

POPHAM, LEWIS CHARLES, III, educator; b. N.Y.C., Sept. 18, 1928; s. Lewis Charles and Harriet (Andreas) P.; student State Coll., E. Stroudsburg, Pa., 1946-48; B.S., Am. U., 1950; A.M., Harvard U., 1951. Lectr., asst. to dir. bus. affairs Am. U., Washington, 1951-54; asst. to pres. So. Conn. State Coll., New Haven, 1954-60; asst. to v.p. Central Mich. U., Mt. Pleasant, 1960-61; dir. gen. studies Dakota State Coll., Madison, S.D., 1961-63; chmn. div. social scis. Prince George's Community Coll., Largo, Md., 1963-64, acting pres., 1964-65; dean continuing edn. Orange County Community Coll., State U. N.Y., Middletown, 1965-73, dean continuing edn. State U. N.Y., Oswego, 1973—; dir. Sky Top Lodges, Inc., Pocono Hotels Corp.; producer, historian TV series Explorations: The World and its Peoples, WNHC-TV, New Haven, 1956; host radio series The College Speaks, KJAM, Madison, S.D., 1962-63. Chmn. Conn. br. Am. Ch. Union, 1958-60, nat. v.p., 1972-73. Fletcher scholar. Mem. New Eng. Tchr. Preparation Assn. (sec. 1957-60), Orgn. Am. Historians, Am., N.Y. state hist. assns., Western History Assn., Broadcast Edn. Assn., Assn. Higher Edn., Am. Assn. Sch. Adminstrs., Assn. Continuing Higher Edn. (dir., pres. 1978), Assn. Univ. Evening Colls. (former chmn. jr. coll. com.), Continuing Edn. Assn. State U. N.Y. (past pres.), Nat. Univ. Extension Assn. (former regional chmn.), Omicron Delta Kappa, Alpha Sigma Phi. Republican. Episcopalian (past mem. council N.Y. diocese). Clubs: Kiwanis (past club pres.); Skytop (bd. govs.), Squadron A. Home: 9 W 6th St Oswego NY 13126 Office: State U Coll Oswego NY 13126

POPHAM, RICHARD ROBERT, cons. engr.; b. Chgo., Feb. 21, 1917; s. Audrey Joseph and Lida Eugenia (Colborn) P.; B.S., Purdue U., 1940; M.M.E., Bklyn. Poly. Inst., 1947; m. Dorothy A. Hennig, June 7, 1947. Mech. and constrn. engr. Solvay Process div. Allied Chem. & Dye Corp., Hopewell, Va., 1940-41, United Engrs. & Constructors, Phila., 1941-42, Ebasco Services, Inc., N.Y.C., 1942-43, M.W. Kellogg Corp., Baton Rouge and Elizabeth, N.J., 1943-45, H.K. Ferguson Co., N.Y.C., 1945-46; chief mech. engr. Lockwood Greene Engrs., N.Y.C., 1946-47, Allied Process Engrs., N.Y.C., 1948-49; pres. Laramore, Douglass and Popham of N.Y., Inc. (formerly R.R. Popham Engrs.) 1949—, Laramore, Douglass and Popham, Inc., Chgo., 1963—. Registered profl. engr., N.Y., N.J., Pa., Ill., Fla., Calif., D.C., Md., Ind., N.D., Ariz., Mass. Mem. ASME, ASTM, N.Y. Geneal. and Biog. Soc., U.S. Com. on Large Dams, Delta Upsilon. Home: 60 Hanson Rd Darien CT 06820 Office: 260 Madison Ave New York City NY 10016 also 332 S Michigan Ave Chicago IL 60604

POPLER, KENNETH, psychologist; b. Bklyn., Nov. 7, 1945; s. Irving and Mildred (Wolkenfeld) P.; B.A., Bklyn. Coll., 1967; M.A., New Sch. for Social Research, 1969, Ph.D., 1974; m. Lois Lynne Cohen, Aug. 31, 1969. Trainee, Bklyn. Psychiat. Centers, Inc., 1970-72; project psychol. adviser Martin Van Buren High Sch., N.Y.C., 1972-73; psychometrician Hillside div. L.I. Jewish-Hillside Med. Center, Queens, N.Y., 1972-73; sr. psychologist, dir. psychol. services N.Y.C. Health and Hosp. Corp., Gouverneur Hosp., N.Y.C., 1973-78; cneter dir. St. Mary Community Mental Health Center, Hoboken, N.J., 1978—; individual practice psychol. counseling, 1976—; instr. Bklyn. Coll., 1972-73; vol. researcher Manhattan Sch. for Seriously Disturbed Children, N.Y.C., 1972-73; psychologist Mid-Nassau Community Guidance Center, Inc., Hicksville, N.Y., 1973-77. Mem. Consumers Union, 1970—. Mem. Am., Eastern, N.Y. State psychol. assns., Assn. Advancement Behavior Therapy, Bklyn. Coll. Alumni Assn., New Sch. Alumni Assn. Home: 301 E 22d St Apt 7D New York City NY 10010

POPMA, EUGENE JOHN, telephone co. exec.; b. Jackson, Mich., July 12, 1923; s. Nicholas John and Mary Agnes (Andrews) P.; B.S. in Indsl. Mgmt., U. Detroit, 1948; M.S. in Indsl. Mgmt., Mass. Inst. Tech., 1958; postgrad. Dartmouth, 1964; m. Maxine Guinon, June 3, 1946; children—Jeffrey John, Valerie Marie. Accountant Pacific Telephone Co., Los Angeles, 1948-53; accountant Am. Tel. & Tel. Co., N.Y.C., 1953-55; asst. comptroller Ind. Bell Telephone Co., Indpls., 1955-61, gen. traffic mgr., 1961-73, asst. v.p. pub. relations, 1973-75, dir. adminstrv. services, 1975—; dir. Channel 20 Pub. Broadcasting Sta., Wesley-Otterbein Ins. Corp.; arbitrator Central Ind. Better Bus. Bur. Inc., Indpls., 1974. Mem. Sch. bd. St. Luke Sch., Indpls., 1969-70; v.p. Boy Scouts Am., 1970-73; pres. Dad's Club and mem. Pres's. Council Brebeuf Preparatory Sch., Indpls., 1973; vice chmn., co-founder Life Today House for Drug Addicts, Indpls., 1971-73. Bd. dirs. Martin Center Inst. for Black Culture. Served with AC, USNR, 1943-46. Sloan fellow, 1957-58. Mem. Ind. Assn. Amateur Athletic Union of U.S. (pres. 1974-75), Amateur Athletic Union of U.S. (exec. com. 1974), Devon Civic League (v.p., 1956-57), Pub. Relations Soc. Am. (accredited). Roman Catholic. Clubs: Country of Indpls., Indpls. Athletic, Riveria. Home: 16 Glenmere Dr Chatham NJ 07928 Office: 295 N Maple Ave Room 7248 M Basking Ridge NJ 07920

POPOFF, EDNA SPIELER, ednl. psychologist; b. N.Y.C., Jan. 17, 1924; d. Isidor and Rose Spieler; A.B., Hunter Coll., 1945; M.A., Columbia U., 1947; m. William Popoff, Apr. 12, 1946; children—Joshua Julian, Leslie Ellen. Psychologist, VA, Bklyn. Poly. Inst., Vocat. Guidance Center, Bklyn., 1946-48; tchr. emotionally handicapped children, Bd. Edn., N.Y.C., 1960-68; sch. psychologist, Bur. Child Guidance, 1969—, dist. sch. psychologist, 1969-73, sch. psychologist with spl. edn. program for emotionally handicapped children, Bur. Child Guidance, 1974—; cons. Assn. for Advancement of Blind and Retarded, Inc., Jamaica, N.Y.; cons. as resource and vocat. psychologist to reps. of community agencies; lectr. in field PTA groups. Mem. Am. Psychol. Assn., Nat., N.Y.C. assns. sch. psychologists. Clubs: Am. Jewish Congress, B'nai B'rith. Home: 19 Brook Bridge Rd Great Neck NY 11021 Office: Bur Child Guidance 280 Broadway New York City NY 10007

POPOVIC, DEYAN HONEYMAN, investment counsel; b. Morristown, N.J., May 11, 1943; s. Milan Dusan and Fairlie (Honeyman) P.; B.S., Boston U., 1966. Analyst, portfolio mgr. N.Y. Hanseatic, N.Y.C., 1969-70; v.p. investment adv. div. G.H. Walker, Laird, N.Y.C., 1970-74; investment counselor, v.p. White, Weld & Co., Inc., N.Y.C., 1974-77; pres. Individual Investors, Inc., N.Y.C., 1977—. Trustee Cape Br. Found. Served to 1st lt. U.S. Army, 1966-69. Mem. N.Y. Soc. Security Analysts. Home: 70 W 87th St New York City NY 10024 Office: 115 Broadway Suite 203 New York City NY 10006

POPOVICH, CHARLES JAMES, librarian; b. Johnstown, Pa., June 22, 1940; s. Charles Peter and Helen (Pavlich) P.; B.S. cum laude, Youngstown State U., 1968; M.B.A., Xavier U., 1972; M.L.S., U. Ky., 1972; m. Marjorie Louise Phillips, June 14, 1975; 1 son, Charles Kristopher. Sales rep. Nat. Cash Register Co., Johnstown, Pa., 1968-70; reference librarian State U. N.Y., Buffalo, 1972-73, bus. bibliographer, 1973-75, bus./econs. librarian, 1975—. Mem. Spl. Libraries Assn. (editor newsletter bus. and fin. div. 1974-77, treas. div. 1977-78), ALA (chmn. bus. and reference services com. 1976-78). Home: 6309 Town Line Rd North Tonawanda NY 14120 Office: State U NY Lockwood Reference Buffalo NY 14260

POPPEL, SETH RAPHAEL, mgmt. cons.; b. Bklyn., Mar. 17, 1944; s. Frank M. and Fritzi R. (Axenzow) P.; B.S. magna cum laude, L.I. U., 1965; M.B.A., Columbia U., 1967; 1 son (by previous marriage), Jared; m. Danine Vokt, Jan. 5, 1974; children—Clarysa, Stacy. Asst. prof. L.I. U., Greenvale, N.Y., 1967-68; v.p. Synergistic Systems Corp., N.Y.C., 1968-77; v.p. corp. planning Chase Manhattan Corp., N.Y.C., 1977—; owner harness horses Seth Poppel and Lou Enos Stables, 1974—. E.I. DuPont fellow, 1965-67, Downie Muir fellow, 1965-66; recipient Claire F. Adler award in math., 1964-65. Mem. Am. Statis. Assn., Ops. Research Soc. Am., Inst. Mgmt. Sci., U.S. Trotting Assn., Beta Gamma Sigma, Psi Chi, Omega Epsilon. Home: 38 Range Dr Merrick NY 11566 Office: 1 Chase Manhattan Plaza New York City NY 10015

POPPER, ARTHUR N., neurobiologist; b. N.Y.C., May 9, 1943; s. Martin and Evelyn P.; B.A., N.Y. U., 1964; Ph.D., City U. N.Y., 1969; m. Helen Apfel, Nov. 30, 1968; 1 dau., Michelle. Asst. prof. zoology U. Hawaii, Honolulu, 1969-72, asso. prof., 1972-78, asso. zoologist Lab. Sensory Scis., 1972-78; asso. prof. anatomy Georgetown U. Sch. Medicine and Dentistry, Washington, D.C., 1978—. Recipient NIH Research Career Devel. award, 1978—. Mem. Am. Soc. Zoologists, Acoustical Soc. Am., Assn. for Research in Otolaryngology, Animal Behavior Soc., Soc. Neurosci., Sigma Xi. Office: Dept Anatomy Georgetown U 3900 Reservoir Rd NW Washington DC 20007*

POPPITI, JAMES ANTHONY, chemist; b. Wilmington, Del., Nov. 18, 1949; s. James John and Concetta Marie (Pomilio) P.; student U. Del., 1971; m. Victoria Lynn Bailey, May 15, 1976. Applications chemist, Sci. Research Corp., Balt., 1975, Finnigan Corp., Sunnyvale, Calif., 1975-77; chemist FDA, Washington, 1977—. Mem. Am. Soc. Mass Spectrometry. Contbr. papers to sci. confs., publs. Home: 9115 Grant Ave Laurel MD 20810 Office: FDA HFF 425 200 C St SW Washington DC 20204

PORCARI, SERAFINO, librarian; b. Carpineto Romano, Italy, Oct. 20, 1941; s. Beniamino and Teresa Annunziata (Battisti) P.; came to U.S., 1955, naturalized, 1962; B.A. in History and Philosophy, Le Moyne Coll., 1965; M.A. in History, State U. N.Y., Buffalo, 1968; m. Fabiola Verlezza, Sept. 7, 1968; children—Benjamin R., Richard J. Grad. and teaching asst. State U. N.Y., Buffalo, 1965-68, research fellow, 1969, asst. librarian serials dept., 1969-71; instr. history Rosary Hill Coll., Buffalo, 1970-71; instr. history, chmn. social scis. div. Trocaire Coll., Buffalo, 1971-74; successively reference libarian and adminstrv. asst., then tech. specialist central tech. services State U. N.Y. at Buffalo Libraries, 1975—. Mem. Am. Hist. Assn., Soc. for Study History, ALA, Internat. Inst. Buffalo, Italian-Am. Found. Roman Catholic. Author: (with John P. Halstead) Modern European Imperialism: A Bibliography of Books and Articles, 1815-172, 2 vols., 1974. Home: 13 Eley Pl Buffalo NY 14214 Office: Cataloging Dept Lockwood Library State U NY Buffalo NY 14260

PORIER, OMER ADELARDE, physician; b. Massena, N.Y., July 16, 1931; s. Omer and Frances (Lamendola) P.; B.S., Syracuse U., 1953; M.D., State U. N.Y., Syracuse, 1957; m. Isabella Foster, July 19, 1957; children—Omer G., Douglas, Suzanne. Intern, St. Jospeh's Hosp., Syracuse, 1957-58; practice gen. medicine, Massena, 1960—; staff Massena Meml. Hosp., 1968—, program chmn. edn., 1969—; tchr. Edward J. Nobel Found. Med. Students. Bd. dirs. Am. Cancer Soc.; mem. Massena Bd. Health. Served to capt. U.S. Army, 1958-60. Diplomate Am. Acad. Family Practice. Fellow Am. Acad. Family Physicians; mem. AMA (Physicians recognition award), Med. Soc. State N.Y., N.Y. State, St. Lawrence County acads. family practice, Pan Am. Med. Assn., Am. Geriatric Soc. Home: 11 Windsor Rd Massena NY 13662 Office: 173 E Orvis St Massena NY 13662

PORRECO, LOUIS JOHN, automobile dealer; b. Erie, Pa., Sept. 18, 1936; s. Ralph Anthony and Clara (Deltino) P.; student Gannon Coll., Erie, 1954-55; m. Katherine A. Simanowski, Sept. 6, 1958; children—Christina, Mary, Louis. Dist. exec. Boy Scouts Am., Erie, 1960-62; staff exec. Erie C. of C., 1962-63; pres. Canadian Holiday Lines, 1963-64; v.p. Mrs. Am. Prodns., Inc., N.Y.C., 1964-65; owner Quality Motors, Erie, 1966-70; pres. Porreco Motors Inc., Erie, 1968—, Erie Internat. Airport Authority, 68—, Erie Metro Taxi Co., 1978—. Bd. incorporators Gannon Coll., 1974—; chmn. fin. com. Erie County Democratic Com., 1969-70. Recipient Eagle Scout award Boy Scouts Am., 1950. Mem. Nat., Pa., Erie County (pres. 1970-76) automobile dealers assns., Nat. Thoroughbred Trainers Alliance, World Boxing Assn., Pa. Pub. Authorities Assn., Pa. Horse Breeders Assn., Miracle Mile Assn. Democrat. Roman Catholic. Clubs: Eric Yacht; Kahkwa, Univ. Home: 6214 Lake Shore Dr Erie PA 16505 Office: 5305 Peach St Erie PA 16509

PORT, YALE IRWIN, psychologist; b. N.Y.C., Sept. 26, 1932; s. Philip and Evelyn (Schulberg) P.; B.A., Yeshiva Coll., 1953; M.S., Coll. City N.Y., 1954; Ph.D., Yeshiva U., 1959, rabbi, 1956; m. Marlene Bachman, June 30, 1957; children—Evelyn, Jeffrey, Cynthia. Intern, N.Y. U.-Bellevue Med. Center, 1957-58; sr. clin. psychologist Central Islip State Hosp., L.I., 1958-59; sch. psychologist pub. schs., Bethpage, L.I., 1959-62; pvt. practice clin. psychology, Bklyn., 1961—; psychotherapist Bleuler Psychotherapy Clinic, Queens, 1962-63; psychol. cons. Yeshivah of Flatbush, Bklyn., 1960-70, Kingsway Acad., 1965-71, Ezra Acad., 1966-71. Bd. dirs. Yeshivah of Flatbush, 1969—, mem. Bd. Edn., 1963—. Recipient Honor award Fedn. Jewish Philanthropies, 1969; intern fellow Northside Center for Child Devel., 1956-57. Mem. Bklyn. Psychol. Assn. (dir. 1969-71). Club: B'nai B'rith. Office: 2022 Ave M Ave Brooklyn NY 11210

PORTER, BERNARD HARDEN, cons. physicist; b. Porter Settlement, Maine, Feb. 14, 1911; s. Lewis Harden and Etta Flora (Rogers) P.; B.S., Colby Coll., 1932; M.S., Brown U., 1933; D.Sc. (hon.), Inst. Advanced Thinking, Calais, Maine, 1959; m. Helen Elaine Hendron, July 15, 1946 (div. Aug. 1947); m. 2d, Margaret Eudine Preston, Aug. 27, 1955 (dec. Apr. 17, 1975); m. 3d, Lula Mae Blom, Sept. 9, 1976. Physicist, Acheson Colloids Corp., Port Huron, Mich., 1935-40; research physicist Manhattan Dist. Engrs., Princeton, N.J., Berkeley, Calif. and Oak Ridge, 1940-45; cons. physicist, San Francisco and Pasadena, Calif., Waldwick, N.J., Rockland, Belfast, 1945—; chmn. bd. Bern Porter, Inc., Pasadena, Rockland, Belfast, 1945—; pres. Bern Porter Books, Pasadena, Rockland, Belfast, 1929—, Bern Porter Internat., Belfast, 1974—; cons. Internat. Exec. Service Corps, 1968, SBA, 1968—. Republican candidate for gov. Maine, 1969; bd. dirs. Inst. Advanced Thinking, Belfast, chmn. bd., 1959—. Recipient awards P.E.N., 1975, 76, 77, Authors League, 1977; Carnegie author, 1975; diploma merit Centro Studi E Scambi Internazionale, Rome. Fellow Am. Astronautical Soc., Tech. Pub. Soc., Am. Rocket Soc. (asso.), Soc. Tech. Writers and Pubs. (asso.), Internat. Acad. Poets (London) (founding); mem. Am. Phys. Soc., Soc. Internat. Devel., Nat. Soc. Programmed Instrn., Phi Beta Kappa, Sigma Xi, Kappa Phi Kappa, Chi Gamma Sigma. Methodist. Clubs: Fenway (Boston); Algonquin, St. Andrews (N.B., Can.). Author: The 14th of February, 1971; I've Left, 1971; Founds, 1972; Hand Coated Chocolates, 1972; Contemporary Italian Painters, 1973; Trattoria Due Forni, 1973; The Book of Do's, 1974; The Manhattan Telephone Book, 1975; Run-On, 1975; Where, 1975; Selected Founds, 1975; Gee-Whizzles, 1976; also numerous articles, essays, monographs, 1928—; illustrator various books, mags., maps. Address: 22 Salmond Rd Belfast ME 04915

PORTER, C. RAY, JR., transp. co. exec.; b. N.Y.C., May 20, 1921; s. Chauncey R. and Edna R. (Rousseau) P.; B.A., Lafayette Coll., 1947; m. Margaret Wren, Mar. 12, 1973; children—Jay Kimball, Leigh Michelle, Tracey Rae. Asst. dean of students Lafayette Coll., 1947-50; mgr. research adminstrn. Philco Corp., 1953-56; owner, sr. v.p. Nat. Inst. Indsl. Research, Inc., Princeton, N.J., 1956-77; dir. adminstrn. Fruit Growers Express Co., Washington, 1977—. Served to lt. comdr. USNR, 1942-46, 50-53. Decorated Air medal. Mem. Am. Inst. Indsl. Engrs. (sr.), Am. Mgmt. Assn., R.R. Personnel Assn., Am. Trucking Assn. Republican. Presbyterian. Home: 10-7 Silverwood Circle Annapolis MD 21403 Office: 1101 Vermont Ave NW Washington DC 20005

PORTER, DARWIN FRED, writer; b. Greensboro, N.C., Sept. 13, 1937; s. Numie Rowan and Hazel Lee (Phillips) P.; B.A., U. Miami, Coral Gables, Fla., 1959. Bur. chief Miami Herald, 1959-60; v.p. Haggart Assos., N.Y.C., 1961-64; editor/author Arthur Frommer Inc., N.Y.C., 1964-67, Frommer/Pasmantier Pub. Corp., N.Y.C., 1967—. Recipient Silver award Internat. Film and TV Festival N.Y., 1977. Mem. Soc. Am. Travel Writers, Smithsonian Assn., Sigma Delta Chi. Democrat. Author: Frommer Travel Guides Eng., 1964, Spain, 1966, Scandinavia, 1967, Los Angeles, 1969, London, 1970, Lisbon/Madrid, 1972, Paris, 1972, Morocco, 1974, Rome, 1974, Frommer/Pasmantier Travel Guides Portugal, 1968, Eng., 1969, Italy, 1969, Germany, 1970, France, 1970; (novels) Butterflies in Heat, 1976; Marika, 1977. Home: 75 Saint Marks Pl Staten Island NY 10301

PORTER, FRANK THOMAS HENDERSON, physician, ins. co. exec.; b. Dundalk, Ont., Can., Sept. 14, 1929; s. Stuart Henderson and Edna Winnifred (Mason) P.; student Jarvis Collegiate Inst., Toronto, 1946; M.D., U. Toronto, 1952; m. Olive Doreen Acheson, Sept. 4, 1954; children—Susan Doreen, Shirley Aileen, Donna Lynn, Barbara Louise. Gen. intern Toronto E. Gen. Hosp., 1952-53; gen. practice medicine, Unionville, Ont., 1953-54; adminstrv. med. officer Physicians Services Inc. (Blue Shield Health Care Plan), Toronto, 1954-63; asst. sec. Ont. Med. Assn., Toronto, 1964-72, dep. gen. sec., 1972-73, gen. sec., 1973-77; asso. med. dir. Imperial Life Assurance Co. Can., Toronto, 1978—. Recipient Priory award St. John Ambulance Assn., 1966. Mem. Can., Ont., Que. (hon.) med. assns., Toronto Acad. Medicine. Mem. United Ch. Can. Club: Bd. Trade Toronto. Home: 5 Pinevale Rd Thornhill ON L3T 1J5 Canada Office: 195 St Clair Ave W Toronto ON M4V 1N7 Canada

PORTER, JACK NUSAN, sociologist, religious activist; b. Russia, Dec. 2, 1944; s. Irving S. and Faye (Merin) P.; came to U.S., 1947, naturalized, 1958; B.A., U. Wis., 1967; M.A., Northwestern U., 1969, Ph.D., 1971; m. Miriam Almuly, Sept. 18, 1977. Lectr., Northwestern U., 1970-71; ast. prof. sociology State U. N.Y., Cortland, 1971-72; lectr. theology Boston Coll., 1973-74, Pine Manor Coll., 1974-76; lectr. Jewish history Emerson Coll., Boston, 1976-77; lectr. sociology of Jewry, Boston Center Adult Edn., 1977-78. Atherton scholar Breadloaf Writers Conf., 1976; research fellow World Jewish Congress, 1970-71. Mem. Am., Eastern, Mass. sociol. assns., Soc. Study of Social Problems, Assn. Jewish Studies, Assn. Humanist Sociology, Ams. for Progressive Israel, Assn. Profs. for Peace in the Middle East, Habonim Labor Zionist Youth Movement, Jewish Student Movement, Breira, Student Zionist Orgn., Word Guild. Author or co-editor: The Study of Society, 1974; Student Protest and the Technocratic Society, 1973; Jewish Partisans, 1978; Jewish Radicalism, 1973; The Sociology of Jewry, 1978. Editor Jour. History of Sociology, 1977—; contbg. editor Ency. of Sociology, 1974; editorial bd. Dialogue, 1976-78, Qualitative Sociology, 1977—, Humanity and Society, 1977—; Genesis 2, 1973-76, Davka, 1974-78. Home: 28 Stanton Rd Brookline MA 02146

PORTER, JAMES REED, mortgage banker; b. Washington, Oct. 13, 1947; student Fla. State U., 1966, Md. U., 1967-69; B.A. in Bus. Adminstrn., Georgetown U., 1970. Asst. v.p. Md. Mortgage Co., 1972-73; v.p. United Mortgage Co., Washington, 1974-77, pres., 1977—, also dir.; dir. Mozel Devel. Corp.; guest lectr. Am. U.; cons. to lending instns. Served with USAF, 1966-69. Decorated Bronze Star medal. Republican. Clubs: U.S. Yacht Racing Union; Jockey, Marina Bay (Miami); Flag Harbour Yacht (dir.). Author: Understanding and Underwriting the Single Family Loan, 1977. Office: 1430 K St NW Suite 602 Washington DC 20005

PORTER, JAY ELIHU, educator; b. Boston, Mar. 28, 1941; s. Morris George and Sylvia (Richmond) P.; student Northeastern U., 1958-60; B.A., Boston Coll., 1965, postgrad., 1975—; postgrad. Boston State Coll., 1965, Keene State Coll., 1965-67; Ed.M., Salem State Coll., 1970; m. Gay Diana Sokolov, Aug. 9, 1964; children—Morris George, Todd Adam, Harris Nathaniel. Tchr., Keene (N.H.) Sch. Dist., 1965-67, Peabody (Mass.) Sch. Dept., 1967-78; edn. dir. Temple Beth Shalom, Peabody, 1971-75; chmn. Peabody Dept. Continuing Edn.; staff rep. Mass. Fedn. Tchrs., AFL-CIO, 1978—. Mem. Peabody Ins. Adv. Commn., 1971—, Peabody Community Service Com., 1973—; active Boy Scouts Am., 1965—; adviser Danvers (Mass.) DeMolay, 1970-72; mem. advisory com. P.A.C.E., Peabody. Trustee North Shore Labor Council, Cerebral Palsy Council North Shore, 1976—. Recipient Leadership award Boy Scouts Am., 1969, certificate merit United Cerebral Palsy Council N. Shore, 1977, 78. Ford Found grantee for tchr. leadership tng., 1972. Mem. Am. (mem. steering com.), Mass. (v.p. 1974, exec. bd.), Peabody (pres. 1972—) fedns. tchrs., Mass., North Shore labor councils, Prescription Parents. Jewish. Club: Masons. Home: 3 Quarry Terrace Peabody MA 01960

PORTER, JIMMY ANN (JAN), mgmt. cons. firm exec.; b. Porterdale, Ga., July 6, 1943; d. Frank Holt and Lucylle A. (Calvert) Langdon; ed. Oglethorpe U., 1961-62, Ga. State U., 1962-64, 1 dau., Delia Rae. Sr. conversion specialist Nat. Billing Systems, Atlanta, Ga., 1971; sr. systems liaison So. Co. Services, Inc., Atlanta, 1971-73; sr. systems analyst Blue Cross and Blue Shield of Atlanta, 1973-77; pres. Jan Porter and Assos., Atlanta, 1976—. Mem. Assn. of Records Mgrs. and Adminstrs., Inc., Nat. Entrepeneur's Assn., Nat. Micrographics Assn., Assn. of Systems Mgrs.

PORTER, JOHN WESTON, career guidance counselor; b. Fostoria, Ohio, Dec. 26, 1939; s. William Thomas and Ida Elizabeth (Carter) P.; student U. Cin., 1958; B.A., Heidelberg Coll., 1961; M.A. in Community Psychology, U. D.C., 1973, M.A. in Counseling, 1975; post grad. Antioch Coll., 1974, Frostburg (Md.) State Coll., 1970, George Washington U., 1968; Claims rep. Social Security Admnstrn., Cleve. and Akron, Ohio, 1961-62; office mgr. Phoenix Cos., Washington and Los Angeles, 1966-70; researcher Frostburg State Coll., U. D.C., 1970-73; edn. specialist career guidance D.C. Pub. Schs., 1973—. Vice chmn. Advisory Council, Group Health Assn., Washington 1977—. Served with USN, 1962-66. Recipient awards Ohio Acad. of Sci., 1954-57, Cleve. Plain Dealer Operation Demonstrate, 1956, service award Heidelberg Coll. Publs., 1961, recognition certificates Nat. Capital Personnel and Guidance Assn., 1975, 1976. Mem. Nat. Capital Personnel and Guidance Assn. (secy. 1977—, treas. 1975-77, exec. bd., 1975-78, pres.-elect 1978; certificate 1975, 76), Am. Personnel and Guidance Assn., Nat. Vocat. Guidance Assn., Dist. of Columbia Sch. Counselors Assn., The Retired Officers Assn., Washington Met. Council on Alcoholism and Drug Abuse, Group Health Assn. (advisory council). Episcopalian. Contbr. to program manual, presentation and article in field. Home: 1700 Harvard St NW Washington DC 20009 Office: 35th and R Sts NW Washington DC 20007

PORTER, SYDNEY WYNNE, JR., health physicist; b. Balt., June 27, 1932; s. Sydney Wynne and Ernestine (Temple) P.; B.A., St. Johns Coll., 1954; postgrad. in phys. chemistry Johns Hopkins U., 1956; m. Lynn Kony, Sept. 23, 1961; 1 dau., Dawn. Nuclear chemist Martin Co., Balt., 1956-57; health physics coordinator electric boat div. Gen. Dynamics Co., Groton, Conn., 1958-63; head radiation safety Armed Forces Radiobiology Research Inst., Bethesda, Md., 1963-69; cons. Phila. Electric Co., 1968; v.p. Radiation Mgmt. Corp., Phila., 1969-74; pres. Porter-Gertz Cons., Inc., Ardmore, Pa., 1974—; cons. U. Pa., Dept. Navy, Tullurometer, Inc.; mem. Army Insp. Gen.'s Reactor Inspection Team. Served with USCG, 1957. Recipient Outstanding Service award Health Physics Soc., 1968; certified in health physics Am. Bd. Health Physics. Mem. Am. Assn. Physicists in Medicine, Am. Chem. Soc., Am. Indsl. Hygiene Assn., Am. Nuclear Soc., Health Physics Soc. (pres. Balt.-Washington chpt. 1967-68), Del. Valley Soc. Radiation Protection (pres. 1972-74), English Speaking Union. Episcopalian. Club: Univ. Contbr. articles on environ. impact, nuclear reactors, health physics, radiol. environ. areas to tech. jours. Home: 620 Loves Ln Wynnewood PA 19096 Office: 76 Rittenhouse Pl Ardmore PA 19003

PORTER, WARREN ELLSWORTH, neurologist; b. Yonkers, N.Y., June 4, 1923; s. Alexander Murray and Lena Mary (Sibley) P.; A.B., Amherst Coll., 1945; M.D., U. Rochester, 1947; m. Edith Estella Searles, May 23, 1948; children—Frank Albert, Rolfe Sibley, Alexander Murray. Intern Balt. City Hosp., 1947-48, resident in neurology, 1948-49; resident in neurology Johns Hopkins Hosp., 1949-50, Boston City Hosp., 1950, Walter Reed Gen. Hosp., 1952-54; commd. 2d lt. M.C., U.S. Army, 1949, advanced through grades to col., 1966; ret., 1969; chief neurology service Clifton Springs (N.Y.) Hosp. and Clinic, 1969-75; chief neurology service Canandaigua (N.Y.) VA Hosp., 1975—; cons. F.F. Thompson Hosp.; clin. asst. prof. U. Rochester. Decorated Legion of Merit. Mem. AMA, Am. Acad. Neurology, Canandaigua Sci. Assn. Republican. Methodist. Home: Box 221 Gorham NY 14461

PORTER, WILLIAM CLAYTON, JR., physician; b. St. Petersburg, Fla., Apr. 29, 1926; s. William Clayton and Margaret Henderson P.; student Columbia U., 1943-44, Princeton U., 1944-46; M.D., Cornell U., 1950; m. Julie Porter, Aug. 24, 1953; children—Kathleen Downing, William Clayton. Intern, SUNY Downstate Med. Center, Bklyn., 1950-51, resident in surgery, 1951-52, resident in urology, 1952-53, 55-56, chief resident in urology, 1956-57; practice medicine specializing in urology, Huntington, N.Y., 1957—; attending physician in surgery sect. urology Huntington Hosp., 1959—; clin. asst. surgery SUNY, 1957-68; asso. attending surgery urology Stony Brook Med. Sch., 1970—; cons. dept. surgery Northport VA Hosp., 1965—; sr. attending Nassau County Med. Center, East Meadow, N.Y. Bd. dirs. Blue Shield, N.Y., 1966-75, Suffolk County (N.Y.) Am. Cancer Soc., Huntington YMCA, 1960-70; polit. chmn. Huntington Conservative Party, 1960-74. Served with USNR, 1943-45; served to capt. USAF, 1953-55. Diplomate Am. Bd. Urology. Fellow Am. Fertility Soc., A.C.S.; mem. N.Y. State Med. Soc., Suffolk County Acad. Medicine, Am. Urol. Assn. Episcopalian. Home: 66 Lawrence Hill Rd Huntington NY 11743 Office: 157 E Main St Huntington NY 11743

PORTER, WILLIAM JOSEPH, arborist; b. Bklyn. Nov. 21, 1924; s. Thomas John and Estelle (Herrman) P.; student pub. schs., Asbury Park, N.J.; children—Karen, Michael, Bruce, Thomas. Partner, Porter's Tree Service, Rumson, N.J., 1958—; mem. Bur. Tree Experts, N.J. Dept. Environ. Protection; owner, operator hort. cons. firm. Treas. Monmouth County Ecology Center. Served with USNR, 1943-46. Recipient Arborist of Year award Soc. Certified Tree Experts, 1972, Arborists Assn., 1964. Mem. Am. Soc. Cons. Arborists, Arborists Assn. (past pres.), N.J. Soc. Certified Tree Experts (past pres.), N.J. Fedn. Shade Tree Commn. (past pres.). Home: 28 Laurel Dr Highlands NJ 07732 Office: 95 Ave of Two Rivers Rumson NJ 07760

PORTER, WILLIAM MIDDLETON, energy program exec., educator; b. Long Beach, Calif., Dec. 25, 1936; s. William Baxter and Mary Margaret (Middleton) P.; A.B. in Internat. Relations and Polit. Sci., U. of N.C. at Chapel Hill 1960: M.S.A. in Internat. Business, George Wash. U. 1970; m. Mary-Carlin Boyle, June 8, 1968; children—Carlin Middleton, William Boyle. Enlisted U.S. Navy Res., 1953; commd. ensign U.S. Navy, 1960; various duties between 1960-70 including: ordnance officer U.S.S. Valley Forge; asst. ops. officer U.S.S. E.A. Greene; aide, flag lt. comcrudesflot 10 (U.S.S. Boston); chief engr. U.S.S. Stickell; dir. adminstrn. David Taylor Naval Ship R & D Center, Carderock, Md.; mgmt. cons. The Crystal Inst., McLean, Va. 1970-71; special asst. to dir. U.S. Bureau of Mines, Washington, 1971-72, to Asst. Secy. of Interior for Energy and Minerals, Washington, 1973-74; program mgr. energy conservation U.S. Fed. Energy Admnstrn., Washington, 1974-75; exec. asst. to. Asst. Admnstr. of Energy Conservation, U.S. Energy Research and Development Admnstrn., Washington, 1975-76, chief tech. and info. transfer Bldgs. and Industry Energy Conservation, 1976-77; chief in-country-programs Developing Countries Energy Program Office, U.S. Dept. Energy, Washington, 1977—; dir. pilot study NATO-CCMS Energy Conservation, 1973-77; rep. from U.S. to OECD-IEA organizing com. on energy conservation, Paris, 1974; mem. U.S.-Japan Working Group on Energy Research and Development, Tokyo, 1974; dir. U.S.-Peru Cooperative Energy Assessment Program, Lima, Peru, 1978; advisor Internat. Solar Commercialization Working Group, Washington, 1978; mem. faculty Wash. Internat. Coll., Washington D.C. 1976—. Mem. goals com. Fairfax County, Va. 1972, 5-yr. plan review com. 1972, park authority advisory com. 1972—; mem. advisory com. on natural and environmental resources N.Va. Planning Dist. Commn. 1972-75; v.p. Naval Reserve Assn., Wash. Chpt. 1976—; bd. dirs. Radii Found., Washington D.C. 1977—; chmn. World Hunger Com., Truro Ch., Fairfax, Va. 1977—. Recipient full NROTC scholarship U. of N.C. 1956-60; special achievement award Energy Research and Development Admnstrn. 1976. Mem. George Wash. U. Alumni Assn. (bd. governors 1973—, v.p. 1976-78, pres. 1978—), Naval Reserve Assn., George Washington U. Sch. Govt. and Bus. Alumni Assn. (founder, pres. 1977-78), Toastmasters Internat., Aircraft Owners and Pilots Assn. Episcopalian. Clubs: Army-Navy Country of Arlington,

Va.; Army-Navy of Washington. Contbr., sponsored devel. of numerous govt. reports on energy, 1973—. Home: 3103 Northwood Rd Fairfax VA 22031 Office: US Dept Energy Forrestal Bldg 1000 Independence Ave SW Washington DC 20585

PORTERFIELD, LOUIS EDWARD, publishing co. exec.; b. St. Louis, Feb. 10, 1928; s. Robert Edgar and Anna (Schmidt) P.; B.A., Lake Forest Coll., 1951; m. Barbara Jane MacArthur, June 16, 1951; children—Amy, John, Molly. With Hearst Advt. Service, Chgo., 1951-53, Haywood Pub. Co., Chgo., 1954-56; asso. Midwest mgr. Parents' mag., Chgo., 1956-65; with Downe Pub. Inc., pubs. Ladies Home Jour. mag., 1965—, Midwest mgr., Chgo., 1968, Western sales mgr., 1969-72, nat. advt. dir., N.Y.C., 1972—, v.p., 1973—, pub., 1974—. Mem. Dist. Sch. Bd., Crystal Lake, Ill., 1961-70. Served with U.S. Army, 1945-47. Mem. Phi Delta Theta. Republican. Congregationalist. Clubs: Univ., Mid-Am. (Chgo.); Woodway (Conn.) Country; Sky (N.Y.C.). Home: 54 St George Ln New Canaan CT 06840 Office: 641 Lexington Ave New York City NY 10022

PORTFOLIO, ALMERINDO GERARD, ophthalmologist; b. Union City, N.J., May 10, 1923; s. Pasquale and Angela (Falasca) P.; B.A., St. Peters Coll., 1943; M.D., N.Y. U., 1947, M.S., 1954; m. Claire Enright, Nov. 22, 1947; children—Deidre, Almerindo, Drew, Maura, Melissa. Intern, Kings County Hosp., 1947-49; resident in pathology Cleve. City Hosp., 1949-50; resident in ophthalmology Bellevue Hosp., 1951-53, now attending surgeon; practice medicine specializing in ophthalmology, Ridgewood, N.J., 1956—; attending Valley Hosp., Ridgewood, N.J.; asso. attending Univ. Hosp., N.Y.C.; clin. prof. ophthalmology N.Y. U. Med. Center. Served with U.S. Army, 1954-56. Diplomate Am. Bd. Ophthalmology and Otolaryngology. Fellow A.C.S.; mem. AMA, N.J., Begen County med. socs., N.J. Assn. Ophthalmology. Roman Catholic. Club: Indian Trail. Home: 330 Algonquin Rd Franklin Lakes NJ 07417 Office: 20 Wilsey Sq Ridgewood NJ 07450

PORTMAN, SHARON DEE, county adminstr.; b. Atlantic City, Apr. 27, 1941; d. Jack and Betty (Shilling) Gottlieb; B.S. in Edn., Temple U., 1963; M.S. in Student Personnel Service, Monmouth Coll., 1975; m. David Portman, June 23, 1963; children—Howard Neil, William Joel. Tchr. English, pub. schs., Bloomfield, N.J., 1963-64, Neptune (N.J.) High Sch., 1964-65; tchr. English and psychology Tech. Inst., Monmouth County (N.J.) Vocat. Sch., 1966-68, 71-73; Monmouth County career/vocat. coordinator N.J. Dept. Edn. Div. Vocat. Edn., 1976—; dir. Med. Edn. Dynamics; guest speaker for career days at schs., parents groups. Municipal vice chmn. Ocean Twp. (N.J.) Democratic Orgn., 1972-75; pres. Sisterhood Temple Beth Torah, Wanamassa, N.J. Mem. Am. Vocat. Assn., Vocat. Edn. Assn. N.J., Am. Personnel and Guidance Assn., N.J. Vocat. Guidance Assn., Jewish Community Center, Ocean Twp. Dem. Club, Phi Delta Kappa. Home: 14 Pal Dr Wayside NJ 07712 Office: NJ Dept Edn Div Vocat Edn Route 9 and Campbell Ct Freehold NJ 07728

PORTNOY, IRVING LEO, chemist; b. Bklyn., Oct. 4, 1925; s. Jacob and Lille (Weinstein) P.; B.S., Coll. City N.Y., 1948; M.A., Columbia U., 1953; m. Kyla Einstein (dec. 1964); children—Valerie, Edward; m. 2d, Judith Glass, Aug. 14, 1966. Chemist, Liquid Conditioning Corp., Linden, N.J., 1948-49; chief chemist Water Service Labs., Inc., N.Y.C., 1950-69; chief chemist Olin Water Service Labs., N.Y.C., 1970—, dist. mgr., 1972-74, bus. mgr., 1974—. Served with AUS 1944-46. Decorated Bronze Star medal; registered profl. engr., Calif. Mem. Am. Chem. Soc., Am. Soc. Heating, Refrigeration, Air Conditioning Engrs., N.Y. Water Pollution Control Assn., Nat. Assn. Corrosion Engrs. Home: 344 Beverly Rd Douglas Manor NY 11363 Office: 615 W 131st St New York City NY 10027

PORZIO, RALPH, lawyer; b. Bklyn., Aug. 27, 1914; A.B., Drew U., 1938; J.D., Harvard U., 1942. Admitted to N.J. bar, 1943, also U.S. Supreme Ct.; sr. partner firm Porzio & Bromberg, Morristown, 1962—; counsel bd. trustees Internat. Coll. Angiology; internat. nat. and local lectr., London, Copenhagen, Dublin, Rome, San Juan, Lisbon, Geneva, Montreal and U.S. Mem. Boonton Charter Commn., 1952-53, Bd. Edn., 1953-56; trustee Drew U., N.J. Conservation Found., Holmes Library, Boonton. Recipient Freedoms Found. citation for writings advancing Am. Way of life, 1951, Outstanding Achievements award in arts Drew U., 1956. Fellow Internat. Soc. Barristers, Internat. Acad. Law and Sci. (pres., bd. regents); mem. Am., N.J., Morris County (pres. 1970-71), Fed. bar assns., Am. Judicature Soc., N.Y. State N.J. plaintiffs trial lawyers assns., Law-Sci. Acad. Am., Am. Coll. Legal Medicine, Am. Soc. Law and Medicine, Trial Attys. N.J. (charter), Assn. Trial Lawyers Am., N.J. Assn. Sch. Attys. Club: Optimist (pres.) (Morristown). Author: The Transplant Age——Reflections on the Legal and Moral Aspects of Organ Transplants, 1969: editor-in-chief Lex et Scientia, Internat. Jour. Law and Sci., asso. editor, 1969-75; contbr. articles to profl. jours. Home: 123 Glover St Boonton NJ 07005 Office: 163 Madison Ave Morristown NJ 07960

POSAMENTIER, ALFRED STEVEN, educator; b. N.Y.C., Oct. 18, 1942; s. Ernest and Alice (Pisk) P.; A.B., Hunter Coll., 1964; M.A., Coll. City N.Y., 1966; postgrad. Yeshiva U., N.Y.C., 1967-69; Ph.D., Fordham U., 1973; m. Noreen Renee Woller, Sept. 17, 1967; 1 dau., Lisa Joan. Tchr. math. Theodore Roosevelt High Sch., Bronx, 1964-70; asst. prof. math. edn. Coll. City N.Y., 1970-76, asso. prof., 1977—; dep. chmn. dept. secondary and continuing edn., 1974—; supr. math. and sci. Mamaroneck (N.Y.) High Sch., 1976—; project dir. Math. Proficiency Workshop, Ossining, N.Y., 1976—, NSF Math. Devel. Program for Secondary Sch. Tchrs. Math., 1978—, N.Y.C. Profl. Preparation of Math. and Sci. Tchrs., 1978—; cons. Inst. Ednl. Devel., N.Y.C., 1970-73, Croft Ednl. Services, New London, 1971, Coop. Ednl. Resources and Tng. Center, N.Y.C., 1973, Design and Evaluation, 1973, Wiltwyk Sch. for Boys, Bklyn., 1973, N.Y.C. Bd. Edn., 1973-75, N.Y.C. Bd. Edn. Office of Evaluation, 1974—, Ossining Bd. Edn., 1975—; lectr. in field. Mem. Math. Assn. Am., Sch. Sci. and Math. Assn., Nat. Council Tchrs. Math., Assn. Tchrs. Math. N.Y.C. (exec. bd., 1966-67). Author: Geometric Constructions, 1973; Geometry, Its Elements and Structure, 1972, rev. edit., 1977; Challenging Problems in Geometry, 2 vols., 1970; Challenging Problems in Algebra, 2 vols., 1970; A Study Guide for the Scholastic Aptitude Test in Math., 1969, rev. edit., 1975; Excursions Into Advanced Euclidean Geometry, 1980; others; contbr. numerous articles to Sch. Sci. and Math., Models for Teaching, other profl. jours. Home: 32 Drury Ln Demarest NJ 07627 Office: Room K 114 City Coll New York City NY 10031

POSCH, ANTHONY G., civil engr.; b. N.Y.C., Jan. 2, 1939; s. Anton and Pauline (Ruzicka) P.; B.C.E., Manhattan Coll., 1960; postgrad. Columbia U., 1960-61; m. Eileen C. Maloney, June 3, 1961; children—Christopher, Elizabeth, Michael, Kathryn. Structural engr. Vollmer Assos., engrs. and architects, N.Y.C., 1960-64; project engr. Fredric R. Harris, Inc., cons. engrs., N.Y.C., 1964-68; v.p., project mgr. Van Houten Assos., Inc., cons. engrs., N.Y.C., 1968-74; sr. v.p. Frederic R. Harris Inc., cons. engrs., Lake Success, N.Y., 1974—. Registered profl. engr., N.Y., N.J. Mem. ASCE, Am. Inst. Steel Constrn., Am. Ry. Engrs. Assn., Nat. Soc. Profl. Engrs., Chi Epsilon. Home: 9 Birch Dr Plainview NY 11803 Office: 3003 New Hyde Park Rd Lake Success NY 11040

POSNAK, ROBERT LINCOLN, accountant; b. Northampton, Mass., Apr. 19, 1938; s. David Louis and Dorothy Davis (Lincoln) P.; student (Alfred P. Sloan Nat. scholar 1956-59) Dartmouth Coll., 1956-60; A.B., Calif. State U., 1962, M.B.A., 1971; m. Diane Dunkley, July 4, 1967. Controller, Calif. Oxygen Co., San Francisco, 1961-63; staff accountant Ernst & Ernst, San Francisco, 1963-64, in-charge accountant, 1965, sr. accountant, 1966, supr., 1967-69, mgr., 1969-72, partner, N.Y.C., 1972—. C.P.A. Mem. Calif., N.Y. State socs. C.P.A.'s, Am. Inst. C.P.A.'s, Ins. Accounting and Statis. Assn., Newcomen Soc. N.Am. Clubs: San Francisco Olympic; Vanderbilt Athletic N.Y., Atrium. Author books, contbr. articles to profl. publs. Home: 25 Sutton Pl S New York City NY 10022 Office: Ernst & Ernst Citicorp Center New York City NY 10022

POSNER, BARRY INNIS, physician; b. Winnipeg, Man., Can., Nov. 7, 1937; s. Solomon Dalton and Rebecca (Markovitz) P.; M.D., U. Man., 1961; m. Beatrice May Melmed, June 17, 1962; children—Ari, Rebecca, Daniel. Spl. student in biology Mass. Inst. Tech., 1963-64; research fellow and asso. New Eng. Med. Center, Boston, 1964-68; research asso. NIH, USPHS, Bethesda, Md., 1968-70; asst. prof. McGill U. Clinic/Royal Victoria Hosp., Montreal, Que., 1970-75, asso. prof., 1975—. Can. Med. Research Council scholar, 1971-76. Fellow Royal Coll. Medicine; mem. Can., Am. socs. clin. investigation, Can. Soc. Endocrinology and Metabolism, AAAS, Am. Diabetes Assn., Am. Endocrine Soc., N.Y. Acad. Sci. Jewish. Office: Royal Victoria Hosp Montreal PQ Canada

POSNER, JON, real estate broker; b. N.Y.C., Sept. 20, 1943; s. Hyman and Rosaline (Weiner) P.; B.A., Princeton U., 1964; M.B.A., N.Y. U., 1966; m. Jo-Anna Franks, Mar. 29, 1969. With Travelers Ins. Co., N.Y.C., 1968-70, Seidman & Seidman, N.Y.C., 1970-72; exec. v.p. Chester Beck Assoc., Inc.; N.Y.C., 1972—; cons. in field. Mem. Internat. Council Shopping Centers, Mortgage Bankers Assn. Democrat. Club: Univ. Home: 989 E Broadway Woodmere NY 11598 Office: 405 Park Ave New York City NY 10022

POSNER, ROBERT LUDWIG, mfg. co. exec.; b. Pforzheim, Germany, Apr. 4, 1909; s. Rudolf and Toni (Eber) P.; came to U.S., 1939, naturalized, 1944; student U. Geneva (Switzerland), 1927; m. Lotte H. Hirschhorn, Jan. 26, 1936; 1 son, Ralph Otto. Mgr., A-Z Chain Co., Providence, 1939-47; founder, pres. Rolo Mfg. Co., jewelry, Providence, 1947—. Active United Fund, Jewish Fedn. R.I., Nat. Jewish Hosp., Denver. Named Jewish Man of Year, N.Y. Fedn. Jewish Philanthropies, 1972. Mem. R.I. C. of C., Better Bus. Bur. Jewish. Home: 14 Brookway Rd Providence RI 02906 Office: 274 Pine St Providence RI 02903

POSNER, ROY EDWARD, fin., hotel, theatre and ins. exec., tobacco mfg. co. exec.; b. Chgo., Aug. 24, 1933; s. Lew and Julia (Cvetan) P.; student U. Ill., 1951-53; student Internat. Accountants Soc. Inc., Chgo., 1956-59, Loyola U., 1959; grad. Advanced Mgmt. Program, Harvard U., 1976; m. Donna Lea Williams, June 9, 1956; children—Karen Lee, Sheryl Lynn. C.P.A., Frank W. Dibble & Co., Chgo., 1956-61; C.P.A., supr. Harris Kerr Forster & Co., Chgo., 1961-66; with Loews Corp., N.Y.C., 1966—, v.p. fin. services, chief fin. officer, 1973—. Served with AUS, 1953-55. C.P.A., Ill. Mem. Am. Inst. C.P.A.'s, Ill., N.Y. State socs. C.P.A.'s, Fin. Execs. Inst., Ins. Accounting Statis. Assn., Internat. Hospitality Accountants Assn., Delta Tau Delta. Mem. com. 7th edit. Uniform System of Accounting for Hotels. Home: 273 Whitman St Haworth NJ 07641 Office: 666 5th Ave New York City NY 10019

POSS, ROBERT, orthopedic surgeon; b. N.Y.C., Oct. 26, 1936; s. Alex E. and Ada (Avis) P.; A.B., Ruters U., 1958; M.D. cum laude, State U. N.Y., Syracuse, 1962; m. Anita M. Osthoff, Sept. 17, 1966; children—Kirtland G., James A. Intern, Univ. Hosps., Cleve., 1962-63; resident in orthopedics Harvard Med. Sch., 1967-70; fellow in biology Mass. Inst. Tech., 1970-74; practice medicine specializing in orthopedic surgery, Boston, 1971—; orthopedic surgeon Robert B. Brigham Hosp.-Harvard Med. Sch., 1974—; research asso. in biology, dept. biology Mass. Inst. Tech., 1975—; mem. staffs Peter Bent Brigham, Robert B. Brigham hosps. Served with USNR, 1964-66. NIH fellow, 1972-74; Health Sci. Fund of Harvard and Mass. Inst. Tech. awardee, 1977-78. Diplomate Am. Bd. Orthopedic Surgery. Mem. Am. Acad. Orthopedic Surgery, Am. Rheumatism Assn., Orthopedic Research Soc., Am. Soc. Cell Biology, Alpha Omega Alpha. Office: 125 Parker Hill Ave Boston MA 02120

POSS, STANLEY MARIAN, chem. engr.; b. Nanticoke, Pa., July 10, 1929; s. Stanley and Celia Louise (Wempa) Pospieszynski; B.S., St. Bonaventure U., 1951; M.B.A., Syracuse U., 1973; m. Martha Ann Novinski, July 9, 1955; children—Andrew, Michael, Christopher. With G.T.E. Sylvania, Towanda, Pa., 1956—, project engr. spl. projects, 1966-71, project engr. environ. quality control, 1971-74, project engr. environ. quality control and plant services, div. energy coordinator, 1974—. Vol. ambulance driver, 1966-69; mem. sch. bd. St. Agnes Sch., 1966-70, sec., 1968-69. Served to 1st lt. USAF, 1952-56. Mem. Am. Inst. Chem. Engrs., Am. Chem. Soc. (alt. councilor 1968-70). Patentee in field. Home: 302 Wilmot Dr Towanda PA 18848 Office: Hawes St Towanda PA 18848

POST, NICHOLAS BERTRAM, copier mfg. co. exec.; b. Paterson, N.J., July 18, 1925; s. William J. and Margaret C. P.; student U. Pa., 1950-52; B.S., N.Y. U., 1955-62; postgrad. Cornell U., 1962; m. Jacqueline Shorrock, Feb. 11, 1945; children—Robert, James, Kathleen, William, Thomas. Sales, service rep. Pyrometer Service Co., North Arlington, N.J., 1944-49; supt. maintenance constrn. and repair Am. Cyanamid Co., Pearl River, N.Y., 1949-72; mgr. plant engring., maintenance Xerox Corp., Rochester, N.Y., 1972—. Active Boy Scouts Am., 1953-54. Named Mr. Industry, 1971. Registered profl. engr., Mass. Mem. Am. Inst. Plant Engrs. (pres. 1970-71), Upstate N.Y. Constrn. Users Council, Indsl. Mgmt. Club Rochester. Club: Ontario Country. Contbr. author handbooks. Home: 325 Brooksboro Dr Webster NY 14580 Office: 800 Phillips Rd Webster NY 14580

POST, SEYMOUR CYRUS, psychiatrist; b. Bklyn., Sept. 11, 1924; s. Isidore and Ida (Schwartz) Post; M.D., N.Y. U., 1947; m. Judith Cornman, May 30, 1947; children—Michael, Deborah, Nancy, Susan. Intern, N.Y. Beth Israel Hosp., 1947-48; resident in psychiatry Bellvue Hosp. Med. Center, N.Y. U., 1948-50, N.Y. State Psychiat. Inst., Columbia U., 1950-52; trainee N.Y. Med. Coll. Psychoanalytic Inst., 1948-51; practice medicine specializing in psychiatry and psychoanalysis, N.Y.C.; asso. clin. prof. psychiatry Columbia U. Coll. Physicians and Surgeons, 1950—; asso. attending psychiatrist Presbyn. Hosp.; cons. in field to U.S. AEC, State of N.Y. Served with U.S. Army, 1944-47, USPHS, 1953-55. Fellow Am. Acad. Psychoanalysis, Am. Psychiat. Assn., AAAS; mem. AMA, N.Y. Soc. Liaison Psychiatry, N.Y. Soc. Adolescent Psychiatry, Soc. Med. Psychoanalysts (pres. 1968-70), Phi Beta Kappa, Beta Lambda Sigma. Clubs: 7th Regiment Tennis (N.Y.C.); Provincetown (Mass.) Tennis, Pamet Harbor Tennis (Truro, Mass.). Editor: Moral Values and the Super-Ego Concept in Psychoanalysis, 1974. Home: 120 East End Ave New York City NY 10028 Office: 120 Central Park S New York City NY 10019

POSTEL, ROBERT IRA, city ofcl.; b. N.Y.C., June 9, 1939; s. Herman and Theresa (Lerner) P.; A.B. cum laude (Class of 1926 fellow, Sr. fellow, Rufus Choate scholar), Dartmouth, 1960; LL.B., Harvard, 1967; m. Joan Lana Schwartzberg, Oct. 5, 1969; 1 son, Darren Robert. Admitted to N.Y. State bar, 1967; asso. atty. Liebowitt, Milberg, Weiss & Fox, N.Y.C., 1967-69; individual practice law, N.Y.C., 1969-75; partner firm Brasich, Finley and Postel, Esq., 1975-76, Beck, Postel and Saiger, 1976—; mem. N.Y.C. Council, 1969—, councilman-at-large rep. Borough of Manhattan, 1970—; lectr. housing profl. meetings and seminars; faculty N.Y. U. Real Estate Inst., 1974—. Mem. Manhattan Borough Improvement Bd., 1970—; founder, mem. N.Y.C. Community Bd. Crime Council, 1971—; adv. bd. Organized Crime Intelligence Corps Inc. Democratic county committeeman from Manhattan, 1969, 71. Bd. dirs. Soc. for Prevention Cruelty to Children, Richmond County, N.Y., Pleasant Av. Day Care Center, Manhattan, Cosmopolitan Young People's Symphony Orch.; exec. bd. B'nai B'rith Anti Defamation League; counsel, dir. N.Y. Fraternal Order Police. Recipient Man of Year Humanitarian award Bronx County Soc. for Prevention Cruelty to Children, 1971, Our Town mag. Man of Year award, 1971, N.Y. Times Man in the News award, 1971. Mem. Am., N.Y. State (com. on landlord and tenant) bar assns., N.Y. County Lawyers Assn., Fed. Bar Council, NAACP. Mason. Club: City (N.Y.C.). Contbr. articles to publs. Home: 200 East End Ave New York City NY 10028 Office: 10 E 40th St New York City NY 10017

POSVAR, WESLEY WENTZ, univ. pres.; b. Topeka, Sept. 14, 1925; s. Vladimir L. and Marie (Wentz) P.; B.S., U.S. Mil. Acad., 1946; B.A. (Rhodes scholar), Oxford (Eng.) U., 1951, M.A., 1954; M.P.A., Ph.D. (Littauer fellow), Harvard U., 1964; LL.D., L.H.D.; research asso. Center Internat. Studies, Mass. Inst. Tech., 1963-64; m. Mildred Miller, Apr. 30, 1950; children—Wesley William, Margot Marina, Lisa Christina. Officer USAAF, later USAF, 1946-67; fighter test pilot Air Proving Ground Fla., 1946-48; pilot Berlin airlift, 1949; command pilot, 1949-51; asst. prof. social scis. U.S. Mil. Acad., 1951-54; mem. long range strategic planning group, Hdqrs. USAF, 1954-57; prof. polit. sci., head dept. USAF Acad., 1957-67, chmn. div. social scis., 1960-62, 66-67; chancellor (pres.), prof. political sci. U. Pitts., 1967—; dir. Eastern Air Lines, Inc., Federated Investors, Inc.; cons. various fed. agencies. Trustee Carnegie Endowment Internat. Peace, Presbyn.-Univ. Hosp., Rand Corp., Pitts. Symphony Soc., U. Health Center, numerous civic orgns.; former mem. vis. com. Harvard U., Mass. Inst. Tech.; exec. com. Allegheny Conf. Community Devel. Named one of ten outstanding young men U.S. Jr. C. of C., 1959. Mem. Pa. Assn. Colls. and Univs. (pres. 1971-72), Am. Polit. Sci. Assn., Am. Assn. Rhodes Scholars, Internat. Studies Assn. (pres. 1961-62), Internat. Inst. Strategic Studies, Council Fgn. Relations, Arms Control Assn. Clubs: Cosmos, Duquesne; University (N.Y.C.). Contbr. articles, editor books and publs. on mgmt. planning, fgn. affairs and higher edn. Address: U Pitts Pittsburgh PA 15260

POSY, CARL JEFFREY, educator; b. Bklyn., Oct. 15, 1944; s. Manuel and Frances (Hendel) P.; B.A., Yale Coll., 1966; student Hebrew U. Jerusalem, 1966-67; Ph.D., Yale, 1971; m. Phyllis Malka Butler, Oct. 29, 1972; children—Kenneth Bezalel, Michelle Tmima. Asst. prof. philosophy U. Pitts., 1971—; lectr. Internat. Philosophy Conf., N.Y., 1976. Recipient Nat. Endowment for Humanities Summer Stipend, 1973, fellow, 1975-76; Zionist Orgn. Am. fellow, 1966-67. Mem. Am. Philos. Assn., Assn. Symbolic Logic, Philosophy of Sci. Assn. Club: Elihu. Contbr. articles to profl. jours.; referee profl. jours. Office: Dept Philosophy U Pitts Pittsburgh PA 15260

POTAMKIN, MEYER, mortgage banker; b. Phila., Nov. 11, 1909; s. Jacob and Ida (Soloman) P.; Ph.B., Dickinson Coll., 1932, D.F.A., 1972; M.Ed., Temple U., 1941; m. Vivian Orleans, July 27, 1940; children—Macy Ann Potamkin Lasky, Marshall F. Social worker, dir. agy. Crime Prevention Assn., Phila., 1935-40; partner Orleans Constrn. Co., Phila., 1940-54; pres. Blvd. Mortgage Co., Phila., 1954—. Pres., Phila. council Boys Clubs Am., 1966-76; chmn. Camp William Penn, 1965—; bd. dirs. Glen Mills Sch. for Delinquent Boys, Phila. Art Commn., Gov.'s Justice Commn., Robin Hood Dell Concerts, Jewish Y's Center, Crime Prevention Assn. (pres.), Phi Epsilon Pi Frat. Found., Phila. Coll. Art; bd. dirs., co-founder Sarah Allen Nursing Home for Blacks; mem. adv. council to bd. trustees Dickinson Coll., 1977. Recipient Silver Keystone award Boys Clubs Am., 1977. Mem. Home Builders Assn., Mortgage Bankers Assn. Am., Middle States Assn. Accreditation of Colls. and Secondary Schs. (trustee), Zeta Beta Tau (grand council, v.p. 1978). Clubs: Locust, Bala Golf, Squires Golf. Home: The Barclay Rittenhouse Sq Philadelphia PA 19103 Office: 2608 Cottman Ave Philadelphia PA 19149

POTASH, CHARLES, lawyer; b. Phila., May 31, 1932; s. Morris and Betty (Yohlin) P.; B.A., U. Pa., 1953; J.D., Temple U., 1959; m. Jane Levy, Jan. 21, 1962; children—Andrew Samuel, Dorothy Frances. Admitted to Pa. bar, 1960; law clk. Justice Benjamin R. Jones, Pa. Supreme Ct., 1959-60; mem. firm Wisler, Pearlstine, Talone, Craig & Garrity, Norristown, Pa., 1960—, partner, 1967—; solicitor Methacton Sch. Dist., Methacton Sch. Dist. Authority, Sch. Dist. Cheltenham Twp., Cheltenham Sch. Authority, Lower Merion Sch. Dist., Sch. Dist. Springfield Twp., Upper Perkiomen Sch. Authority, Upper Dublin Sch. Dist., North Penn Sch. Authority, Lower Providence Twp. Sewer Authority. Served as 1st lt., arty., U.S. Army, 1953-56; Korea. Mem. Am., Pa., Phila., Montgomery County (dir. 1971-75) bar assns., Montgomery County Jr. Bar (chmn. 1962). Research editor Temple Law Quar., 1958-59. Home: 712 Custis Rd Glenside PA 19038 Office: 515 Swede St Norristown PA 19401

POTE, DORIS R., lawyer; b. Mass.; d. Guy S. and Margaret E. (Lyons) P.; A.B. cum laude, Radcliffe Coll.; J.D., Suffolk U., 1967; postgrad. Harvard Law Sch., 1972. Treas., Conant Littleton Co., Littleton, Mass., 1950-62; asst. to v.p. 1st Realty Co., Boston, 1962-67; admitted to Mass. bar, 1967; registrar, asso. prof. law Suffolk U. Law Sch., Boston, 1967—. Trustee Consumer Affairs Found., Inc., Boston, 1972—; chmn. Mass. Consumers' Council, 1975—; mem. Spl. Legis. Commn. Auto Ins., 1975-76, Spl. Legis. Commn. Blue Laws, 1976. Mem. Am., Mass. (chmn. consumer affairs subcom. 1972—, mem. nominating com. 1977-78) bar assns., Mass. Assn. Women Lawyers (pres. 1972-73), Phi Beta Kappa. Author: The Cemetery Industry in the United States, 1972; The Consumer Movement and the Mobile Home, 1973. Home: 46 Clinton Rd Brookline MA 02146 Office: 41 Temple St Boston MA 02114

POTH, HARRY AUGUSTUS, JR., lawyer; b. Phila., Nov. 5, 1911; s. Harry A. and Mary (Patton) P.; B.S., U. Pa., 1933, LL.B., 1936; m. Eleanor H. Sheils, Apr. 19, 1947; children—Christopher A., Jeremy D. Admitted to N.Y. bar, 1938, D.C. bar, 1948; asso. Reid & Priest, N.Y.C., 1937-48, partner, 1949—, mng. partner Washington office, 1949-58; dir. Am. Utility Shares, Inc.; adviser on electric pub. utility matters govts. Greece, 1953-54, Pakistan, 1962-63. Served to maj. USAAF, 1942-45. Decorated Bronze Star (U.S.); Cross Merit, Ordine Militario di Malta. Mem. Fgn. Policy Assn. (nat. council), Internat., Fed., Fed. Energy, N.Y., Am. (chmn. com. on taxation and accounting of pub. utility law sect.) bar assns., Edison Electric Inst., Zeta Psi. Clubs: Wall St., Stanwich, Indian Harbor Yacht (Greenwich, Conn.); Chevy Chase, Met. (Washington); Farmington Country (Charlottesville, Va.). Asso. editor U. Pa. Law Rev., 1935-36; contbr.

articles to profl. jours. Home: Winding Ln Greenwich CT 06830 Office: 40 Wall St New York City NY 10005

POTNICK, CARL DAVID, theatrical producer; b. Phila., Aug. 2, 1941; s. Henry and Phoebe Ann (Jacobs) P.; B.A., Temple U., 1965; student Temple U. Sch. Law, 1965-67; m. Christine Sasse, Dec. 24, 1970; m. 2d, Dale A. Lazowick, Oct. 26, 1973. Theatrical mgr., producer, pres. Carl D. Potnick Performing Arts Enterprises, music pub., Phila., 1967-77, N.Y.C., 1977—; pres. Potnick Productions-Internat., Celeen Records, Celeen Music, Potnick Music Cellen Industries. Communications officer Falls Twp. (Pa.) Civil Def., 1957—. Democrat. Jewish. Office: 1540 Broadway Suite 300 New York City NY 10036

POTOKER, EDWARD MARTIN, educator, author; b. Newark, June 13, 1931; s. Benjamin and Bessie (Linn) P.; A.B., Dartmouth, 1953; M.A., Columbia, 1955, Ph.D. (Pres.'s fellow 1962-63), 1964; postgrad. (Fulbright scholar) U. Munich (Germany), 1955-56; m. Berit Maria Arneberg, Sept. 3, 1958 (div. 1975); 1 son, Eric Benjamin. Mem. editorial staff New Yorker Mag., 1957-58; instr. English, U. Rochester, 1958-59; lectr. English, Hunter Coll, 1960; mem. faculty Coll. City N.Y., 1960—, asst. prof. English, 1966—; asst. prof. English, Bernard M. Baruch Coll., N.Y.C., 1968-72, asso. prof., 1972—, chmn. dept. English, 1971, 76—, faculty mem. coll. senate, also Baruch Sch. Edn. Mem. AAUP, Modern Lang. Assn., Internat. Platform Assn., Phi Beta Kappa. Club: Andiron (beadle 1965-75) (N.Y.C.). Author: The Corn Grain, 1956; Ronald Firbank, 1969; John Brain, 1978; contbr. to Ency. World Lit. in the 20th Century, Groliers Ency. Internat., The Dartmouth Alumni mag., Ramparts. Book reviewer Saturday Rev., 1965—, N.Y. Times Book Rev., 1962—; editor: The Ronald Firbank-Carl Van Vechten Correspondence; A Tragedy in Green and When Widows Love: Two stories by Ronald Firbank, 1978; founding mem. The Jour. Critical Analysis, 1969. Home: 186 Riverside Dr New York City NY 10024 Office: 17 Lexington Ave New York City NY 10010

POTOSNAK, ARTHUR ROBERT, utility co. exec.; b. Harrisburg, Pa., Oct. 7, 1935; s. Arthur James and Virginia Mary (Tonkin) P.; B.S., Moravian Coll., 1958; M.B.A. (scholar) Lehigh U., 1961; m. Alice Anne Farnschlader, Oct. 28, 1961; children—Arthur Robert, Linda, Karen, Christine. With Pa. Power & Light Co., Allentown, 1961—, adminstrv. coordinator employee benefits, 1969-75, employee services adminstr., 1975-78, employee services mgr., 1978—. Mem. adv. con. on learning disabilities Parkland Sch. Dist., 1974—; bd. dirs. ARC., Hosp. Central Services, Inc., Bethlehem, Pa., chmn. blood donor com. ARC., 1976—, vice chmn. bd. dirs. Lehigh County chpt., chmn., 1978; mem. Bethlehem (Pa.) Blood Center; mem. exec. com. Lehigh County United Way, 1978; chmn. operating com., recruitment and usage com. Miller Meml. Blood Center, 1974-78. Served with U.S. Army, 1958-60. Mem. Edison Electric Inst., Tau Kappa Epsilon. Roman Catholic. Club: K.C. Home: 3945 Longfellow St Allentown PA 18104 Office: 2 N 9th St Allentown PA 18101

POTSIC, WILLIAM PAUL, physician; b. Berwyn, Ill., May 22, 1943; s. Andrew and Estella (Buschak) P.; B.S., U. Ill., 1965; M.D. cum laude, Emory U., 1969; m. Roberta Ilene Kite, Aug. 6, 1967; children—Amie, Jordan. Surg. intern U. Chgo., 1969-70, resident in otolaryngology, 1970-74; practice medicine specializing in otolaryngology, Phila., 1974—; mem. staff Children's Hosp., VA Hosp. of Phila., Hosp. of U. Pa., Presbyn. Hosp., Pa. Hosp., Children's Seashore House, Atlantic City; asst. prof. dept. otorhinolaryngology and human communication U. Pa., Phila., 1974—. Diplomate Am. Bd. Otolaryngology. Mem. Internat. Acad. Cosmetic Surgery, Am. Acad. Ophthalmology and Otolaryngology (1st Prize award for clin. research 1977), AMA, Am. Acad. Pediatrics, Am. Council Otolaryngology, Pa., Philadelphia County med. socs., Phila. Coll. Physicians, Phila. Laryngol. Soc., Phila. Pediatric Soc., Phila. Soc. Facial Plastic Surgeons, Soc. Ear, Nose and Throat Advances in Children, Soc. Univ. Otolaryngologists, Politzer Soc., Alpha Omega Alpha, Phi Chi. Contbr. articles to profl. jours. Office: 34th and Civic Center Blvd Philadelphia PA 19104

POTTER, BARRETT GEORGE, historian; b. Cortland, N.Y., Oct. 28, 1929; s. Leo Barrett and Charlotte May (Hazen) P.; B.A., Hobart Coll., 1952, M.S. in Edn., 1955; M.A., Cornell U. 1959; Ph.D. in History, State U. N.Y., Buffalo, 1973; postgrad. State U. N.Y., Cortland, 1952, Syracuse U., 1962; m. Beverly Ann Platts, Aug. 6, 1961; children—Barrett George, Heather Gaye. Instr., Hobart Coll., Geneva, N.Y., 1952-54; lectr. State U. N.Y. Coll., New Paltz, 1955-57, summer 1960; high sch. tchr., Bayport, N.Y., 1957-58; asst. mgr. 1000 Acres Ranch Resort, Stony Creek, N.Y., 1958-59; asst. prof. history State U. N.Y. Tech. Coll., Alfred, 1959-64, prof., 1965—, chmn. dept., 1965-71; teaching asst. State U. N.Y., Buffalo, 1964-65. Mem. Alfred-Almond Central Sch. Bd. Edn., 1971-74, pres., 1973; bd. trustees Alfred Rural Cemetery Assn., 1973—, Alfred Hist. Soc., 1974-76, Union U. Ch., Alfred, 1977—. Coe Found. fellow in Am. Studies, 1961. Mem. Am. Hist. Assn., Orgn. Am. Historians, Am. Studies Assn., Popular Culture Assn., Forest History Soc., Am. Forestry Assn., Am. Fedn. Musicians, Phi Beta Kappa. Republican. Episcopalian. Clubs: Lions, Elks, Masons, Foster Lake (exec. com. 1972-74). Contbr. articles to profl. jours. Home: 76 S Main St Alfred NY 14802 Office: Social Science Dept State U NY Alfred NY 14802

POTTER, MILES MILTON, civil engr.; b. Gainesville, Ga., Sept. 5, 1945; s. Miles B. and Helen Rose (Bocci) P.; student U. Md., Heidelberg, Germany, 1966-67; B.C.E., Villanova U., 1972; certificate bus. mgmt. U. Maine, 1976; m. Martha Maurise Wines, Aug. 30, 1969. With Howard, Needles, Tammen and Bergendorf, Haverford, Pa., 1968-71, Catania Engring. Assos., Chester, Pa., 1971-73, Pennoni Assos. Inc., Phila., 1973-74; chief civil engr. Wright-Pierce-Barnes-Wyman, Topsham, Maine, 1974-76; prin. Miles Potter Assos., Cape Elizabeth, Maine, 1976—; pres. Minar Enterprises; rep. Maine Soc. Profl. Engrs. to Profl. Devel. Council Maine, 1975—, dir. Western Maine chpt., 1976—, v.p., 1977, pres., 1978. Regional dir. Ages of New Eng., Portland, Maine, 1977—. Served with USAF, 1963-67. Registered profl. engr., Maine, N.H., Pa. Mem. Nat. Soc. Profl. Engrs., Am. Cons. Engrs. Council, Am. Concrete Inst. Republican. Methodist. Home and Office: 22 Longfellow Dr Cape Elizabeth ME 04107

POTTERTON, JOHN PAUL, store mgr.; b. Wantagh, N.Y., June 12, 1951; s. James Edward and Marie Dolores (Sheridan) P.; B.A. in Sociology (N.Y. Regents scholar), Fairfield U., 1973; m. Dolores Bopp, June 5, 1976. Clerk Gt. Eastern Store, Hampstead Pike, East Meadow, N.Y., 1968-69; psychiat. technician St. Vincent's Hosp., Harrison, N.Y., 1970-73; mgr. The Appalachian House, a non-profit store, Fairfield, Conn., 1973—; dir. Appalachian Vols. Inc.; guest speaker on Appalachian culture, 1974—; dir. Experience Appalachia, an American Cultural Festival, 1975, 76, 77. Active vol. for Glenmary Home Missioners; active in campaign to re-elect Congressman Stewart B. McKinney, 1974; bd. dirs. Fairfield U. Alumni Assn. Mem. Missions in Focus. Roman Catholic. Home: 131 Village Ln Southport CT 06490 Office: 1591 Post Rd Fairfield CT 06430

POTTINGER, PAUL STEPHEN, assn. adminstr.; b. Dayton, Ohio, June 21, 1942; s. John Paul and Eleanor Louise (Zeller) P.; B.S., Denison U., 1965; Ph.D., U. N.C., 1971. Asst. prof. Coll. William and Mary, Williamsburg, Va., 1971; sr. research asso. Nat. Inst. Edn., HEW, Washington, 1972-74; dir. assessment systems McBer & Co., Boston, 1974-77; exec. dir. Nat. Center for Study of Professions, Washington, 1977—; dir. Diversified Concepts, Ltd., Washington. Mem. Am. Psychol. Assn. Home: 2439 P St NW Washington DC 20007 Office: 1725 DeSales St NW Washington DC 20036

POTTS, DOROTHY RUTH (PATTI) (MRS. ROBERT C. POTTS), theatre exec.; b. Orrville, Ohio, Apr. 7, 1917; d. James Daniel and Mildred Irene (Bainbridge) Counahan; B.A. magna cum laude, U. Del., 1938; m. Robert C. Potts., Mar. 23, 1940; children—David M., Sarah Potts Voll, Robert L., Deborah A. Potts Norgorodoff. Field dir. Girl Scouts U.S.A., Indpls., 1938-39; vol. staff, exec. sec. Children's Theatre Assn. Balt., 1950-68, dir., 1968-69, pres. bd., 1957-60, 71-74, 77—, treas., 1974-77, tchr. creative drama, 1958-60. Mem. pub. relations com. Girl Scouts U.S.A., 1948-49; treas. Md. Council for Ednl. TV, 1966-67; sec. Greater Balt. Arts Council, 1969-71; mem. Balt. Bicentennial Com., 1973-76, Balt. Mus. Art, 1972—. Mem. Phi Kappa Phi. Republican. Roman Catholic. Club: Towson Women's. Home: 415 Chestnut Ave Baltimore MD 21204 Office: 225 W 25th St Baltimore MD 21211

POTTS, RINEHART SKEEN, educator; b. Phila., July 13, 1927; s. Joseph Harrison and Jean Clayton (Chapman) P.; A.B., Temple U., 1953; M.L.S., Rutgers U., 1964; m. Grace Louise Moore, Dec. 11, 1954; children—Elizabeth Ann, Kenneth Chapman. Asst. prodn. control mgr., asst. to sales v.p., Aero Service Corp., Phila., 1953-58, chief librarian, 1958-64; dir. curriculum lab., govt. publs. dept. Glassboro (N.J.) State Coll., 1964-68, coordinator fed. grants and spl. projects, 1968-71, adminstrv. asst. to head library, 1971-72, asst. prof., 1972—; chmn. Gloucester County Library Commn., 1977—; sec., bd. trustees Willingboro Pub. Library, 1960-64; pres. bd. trustees Glassboro Pub. Library, 1973-75; sec. Camden-Gloucester Area Library Service Council, 1972-75. Pres. Citizens Assn. for Glassboro Schs., 1973—; v.p. Glassboro Bd. Edn., 1972-73; mem. Willingboro Bd. Edn., 1965-66; mem. exec. com. Human Services Coalition of Gloucester County, 1977—. Served with USAF, 1945-49. Mem. ALA, N.J. Library Assn. (pub. relations com.), Nat. Collegiate Honors Council, Am. Soc. Info. Sci., Am. Fedn. Tchrs., Spl. Libraries Assn., AAUP, Classification Soc., Gloucester County Library Assn. (pres. 1976—), Libraries Unltd. (sec. 1975—), Phi Delta Kappa. Democrat. Unitarian-Universalist. Editor, Gloucester County Newsletter, 1976—, Center for Instructional Research and Resources, 1977—. Home: 1223 Glen Terr Glassboro NJ 08028 Office: Library Edn Dept Glassboro State Coll Glassboro NJ 08028

POULSON, RICHARD JASPER METCALFE, lawyer; b. Elizabeth City, N.C., Sept. 4, 1938; s. Richard Jasper and Dorothy Martha (Morse) P.; B.A., U. Va., 1960; J.D., Am. U., 1968; LL.M., Georgetown U., 1970. Trust officer Am. Security & Trust Co., Washington, 1968-70; admitted to D.C. bar, 1968; mem. firm Hogan & Hartson, Washington, 1970—; adj. prof. real estate fin. Georgetown U. Law Center, Washington, 1971—. Pres. Mary and Daniel Loughran Found. Inc., 1968-70, v.p., dir., gen. counsel, 1970—; bd. dirs. Eastern Rugby Union Am., 1968-70, treas., 1969-70. Served to 1st lt. U.S. Army, 1961-63. Mem. Am., Va., D.C. bar assns., Barristers. Episcopalian. Clubs: Met., Univ., Columbia Country, City Tavern. Home: 3321 R St NW Washington DC 20007 Office: 815 Connecticut Ave NW Washington DC 20006

POUPARD, JAMES ARTHUR, microbiologist; b. Phila., Jan. 23, 1943; s. Arthur Richard and Alice Frances (Bradley) P.; certificate med. tech. Franklin Sch. Sci. and Arts Phila., 1961; student U. Pa., 1962-66; B.A., Temple U., 1972; M.S., Thomas Jefferson Med. Coll., 1974; postgrad., Bryn Mawr Coll., 1975—; m. Barbara A. Dehm, May 5, 1962; children—James, Nannette, Jacqueline. Virology technologist Wistar Inst. Anatomy and Biology, Phila., 1961-62, Smith Kline & French Labs., Phila., 1962-67; jr. toxicologist Nat. Drug Co., Phila., 1967-68; chief technologist microbiology div. Hosp. U. Pa., Phila., 1968-74; head microbiology div. Bryn Mawr (Pa.) Hosp., 1974—; cons. med. tech. Ednl. Communications, Inc., Wayne, Pa., 1972—, in microbiology Biomed. Labs., Phila., 1972-73, Penndel Labs., Ardmore, Pa., 1975—. Recipient grant Am. Philos. Soc., 1973. Mem. Am. Med. Technologists, Am. Soc. Microbiology, Am. Acad. Microbiology, Conf. Pub. Health Lab. Dirs., Leidy Micros. Soc., History Sci. Soc. Contbr. to profl. jours. Home: 3612 Earlham St Philadelphia PA 19129 Office: Bryn Mawr Hosp Bryn Mawr PA 19010

POUPKO, GARY GABRIEL, anesthesiologist; b. Phila., July 14, 1944; s. Reuben and Felice (Schuster) P.; student Rabbi Isaac Elchanor Theol. Sem., 1960-64; B.A., Yeshiva U., 1964; M.D., Thomas Jefferson U., 1969; m. Joy Brickman; children—Ruben, Jeremy, Rebecca. Intern, Thomas Jefferson U., Phila., 1969-70, resident in anesthesiology, 1970-72; attending anesthesiologist Waterbury (Conn.) Hosp., 1972-78, St. Mary's Hosp., Waterbury, 1972-78; mem. claims rev. panel for Conn. State Med. Soc. Chmn. curriculum com. Waterbury Community Religious Sch. of Jewish Studies; trustee B'nai Sholom Synagogue; bd. dirs. Hebrew Free Loan Assn. Waterbury. Recipient Swisher Meml. award Thomas Jefferson U., 1969. Diplomate Am. Bd. Anesthesiology. Fellow Am. Coll. Anesthesiology; mem. Conn. State, New Haven County med. socs., Am., New Eng., Conn. State socs. anesthesiology, Soc. Obstetric Anesthesia and Perinatology. Home: 34 Collins St Waterbury CT 06704 Office: 1389 W Main St Waterbury CT 06708

POUSADA, MANUEL, educator, biochemist; b. Mt. Kisco, N.Y., Jan. 28, 1930; s. Candido and Maria Isabel (Covelo) P.; student Cornell U., 1948-51; B.S., CCNY, 1965, postgrad., 1966—; m. M. Nieves Mejuto, July 15, 1953; children—Alicia, Lidia, Elena. With Stauffer Chem. Co., Chauncey, N.Y., 1953; research technician Collett-Week Corp., Ossining, N.Y., 1954-56, chief research chemist, 1956-60, dir. research, 1960-63; research biochemist L.I. Jewish Hosp., New Hyde Park, N.Y., 1963-66; research asst. CC NY, 1966—, instr. chemistry, 1970—. Mem. Am. Chem. Soc., AAAS. Contbr. articles to profl. jours. Home: 18 Orchard St Montrose NY 10548 Office: City Coll Chemistry Dept Convent Ave and 137 St New York NY 10031

POUSHTER, DAVID LEON, physician; b. Syracuse, N.Y., Jan. 14, 1925; s. Julius and Libby (Sacks) P.; A.B., Syracuse U., 1945, M.D., 1947; m. Phyllis Margaret Freeman, June 23, 1946; children—Linda, Susan, Karen. Intern, Harper Hosp., Detroit, 1947-48, asst. resident, 1948-49, asso. resident, 1949-50, resident, 1950-51; asst. resident otolaryngology City Detroit Hosp., 1949; resident in otolaryngology Children's Hosp., Detroit, 1950-51; clin. instr. otolaryngology State U. N.Y., Syracuse, 1953-56, clin. asst. prof., 1956-64, clin. prof., 1977—; practice medicine, specializing in otolaryngology, Syracuse, N.Y., 19—; pres. staff Crouse Irving Hosp., Syracuse, 1963, chief ear, nose and throat, 1965-68; chief ear nose and throat Crouse Irving Meml. Hosp., 1968-74. Bd. dirs. Am. Cancer Soc., 1960-66; pres., Temple Adath Yeshurun, Syracuse, 1973-75; pres. Jewish Family Service Bur., 1968-69; Served with USAF, 1951-53. Mem. Am. Med. Assn., N.Y. Med. Soc., Onondaga County Med. Soc. (pres. 1977-78), Central N.Y. Eye, Ear, Nose and Throat Soc., Am. Triological Soc., Jacobson-Eisner Med. Soc. (pres. 1965), Pan Am. Otolaryngological and Bronchoesophagological Soc. Club: Lafayette Country. Contbr. articles in field to profl. jours. Home: 219 Bradford Pkwy Syracuse NY 13224 Office: 406 University Ave Syracuse NY 13210

POVEY, THOMAS GEORGE, office systems co. exec.; b. Norristown, Pa., Dec. 27, 1920; s. Thomas and Blanche (Groff) P.; B.S., Temple U., 1948; m. Bettina O. Houghton, June 2, 1945; children—Bettina C., Denise E. With Sperry Remington div. Sperry Rand Corp., Phila., also Newark, N.Y.C., 1948—, eastern regional gen. sales mgr., 1960-63, nat. gen. sales mgr., N.Y.C., 1966-67, dir. mktg., Marietta, Ohio, 1968-71, v.p. mktg. 1972-73, v.p. fed. govt. mktg., Washington, 1973-76; pres. Remco Bus. Systems, Inc., Washington, 1976—; lectr. Newark High Sch., 1954-56, Belleville (N.J.) High Sch., 1956-58, Fairleigh Dickinson Coll., Paterson, N.J., 1957-58, Pace Coll., N.Y.C., 1965—, Georgetown U., 1974, ednl. TV, N.Y.C., 1965—; pres. Office Systems Equipment Coop., 1978—. Bd. dirs. Community Fund, Essex Fells, N.J., 1967. Served as 1st lt. with USAF, 1942-45. Decorated Air medal; named Remington Dartnell Salesman of Year, 1950. Mem. Internat. Systems Dealers Assn. (dir. 1977-78), Internat. Platform Assn., Assn. U.S. Army, Smithsonian Assos., Met. Washington Bd. Trade, Pi Delta Epsilon (pres. 1948). Republican. Methodist. Home: 227 Cape St John Rd Annapolis MD 21401 Office: 2233 Wisconsin Ave NW Suite 240 Washington DC 20007

POVICH, DAVID, lawyer; b. Washington, June 8, 1935; s. Shirley Lewis and Ethyl(Friedman) P.; B.A., Yale U., 1958; J.D., Columbia U., 1962; m. Constance Enid Tobriner, June 14, 1959; children—Douglas, Johanna, Judy, Andrew. Admitted to D.C. bar, 1962; clk. to Hon. Thomas D. Quinn, D.C. Ct. Appeals, 1962-63; mem. firm Williams & Connolly, Washington, 1963—. Home: 3306 Rittenhouse NW Washington DC 20015 Office: 1000 Hill Bldg Washington DC 20006

POWASNICK, JAMES RICHARD, indsl. engr.; b. Bayonne, N.J., June 7, 1946; s. Edward Andrew and Norma Lee (Butler) P.; B.S. in Indsl. Engring., N.J. Inst. Tech., 1970; m. Virginia Malone, Sept. 20, 1970. Indsl. engr., product line mgr. Gen. Cable Corp., Monticello, Ill., 1970-71; mgr. plan performance dept. Hosp. Service Plan N.J., Newark, 1971—, coordinator nat. performance standards. Mem. Nat. Blue Cross-Blue Shield Work Mgmt. Assn., MODAPTS Assn. Home: 278 Fulton Ave Jersey City NJ 07305 Office: 33 Washington St Newark NJ 07102

POWELL, ALFRED RICHARD, cons. chem. engr.; b. Athens, O., Feb. 1, 1891; s. William Alfred and Marie (Montzheimer) P.; B.S., U. Kans., 1914; A.M., U. Nebr., 1915; Ph.D., U. Ill., 1918; m. Maribelle Skinner, Sept. 4, 1919; children—Norma Powell Kolesar, Virginia Powell Francis, Maribelle Powell Denslow. Chemist, U.S. Bur. Mines, Pitts., 1919-23; chief chem. engr. Koppers Co., Pitts., 1923-55, asso. dir. research, 1955-56; pvt. cons. chem. engr., Pitts., 1956—. Served as 2d lt. U.S. Army, 1918-19. Mem. Am. Chem. Soc. (Pitts. award 1957), Engrs. Club, Sigma Xi, Alpha Chi Sigma, Gamma Alpha, Phi Lambda Upsilon. Club: Masons. Contbr. to profl. jours. Patentee in field. Presbyterian (elder). Address: 611 Naysmith Rd North Versailles PA 15137

POWELL, CHARLES PORTER, ins. co. exec.; b. Chula, Va., Sept. 20, 1923; s. Charles Porter and Marie (Scott) P.; M.D., Howard U., 1948; m. Margaret M. Dunn, Sept. 1, 1950 (dec.); children—Patricia M., Leslie Amy, Sylvia L. Intern, Harlem Hosp., N.Y.C., 1948-49; resident New Britain (Conn.) Gen. Hosp., 1953-54; practice medicine specializing in internal medicine and adminstrv. medicine, Hartford, Conn., 1975—; med. dir. Hartford Ins. Group, 1975—. Served to capt. M.C., USAF, 1951-53. Diplomate Am. Bd. Med. Examiners. Fellow A.C.P.; mem. AMA, Conn., Hartford County med. socs., Assn. Life Ins. Med. Dirs. Am. Contbr. articles to profl. jours. Office: Hartford Insurance Group Hartford Plaza Hartford CT 06115

POWELL, DONALD GEORGE, mfg. co. exec.; b. Stourport, Eng., Nov. 18, 1932; s. Samuel and Charity Hilda (Oliver) P.; came to U.S., 1968, naturalized, 1978; B.Sc. in Chemistry with honors, U. London, 1955; m. Pauline Mary Goodwin, Sept. 25, 1957; children—Anthony Donald, Timothy Malcolm, Ian Andrew. Ceramic engr. Steatite & Porcelain Products, Eng., 1957-66; works mgr. Worcester Porcelain Co., Jamaica, W.I., 1966-68; dir. engring. Lapp div. Interpace Corp., LeRoy, N.Y., 1968-75; gen. mgr. Pinco div. Joslyn Mfg. Co., Lima, N.Y., 1975—; pres. Joslyn Industries (Can.) Ltd., Newmarket, Ont., Can., 1978—. Served as flying officer RAF, 1955-57. Fellow Inst. Ceramics; mem. Am., Brit. ceramic socs., IEEE (sr.), Nat. Inst. Ceramic Engrs., Conference Internationale des Grands Reseauy Electriques a Havte Tension. Club: Lions (Avon, N.Y.). Patentee semi-conducting glazes. Home: 275 Linden St Avon NY 14414 Office: 7574 E Main St Lima NY 14485

POWELL, DOUGLAS SPENCER, county ofcl.; b. New Haven, Jan. 7, 1925; s. Adelbert Thompson and Beulah (Spencer) P.; B. Engring., Yale U., 1947; M.City Planning, Mass. Inst. Tech., 1950. Planning engr. McHugh & McCrosky, N.Y.C., 1949-50; resident planner Adams, Howard & Greeley, Cambridge, Mass., 1950-54; asso. editor Am. City mag., N.Y.C., 1954-58; planning dir. Regional Plan Assn., N.Y.C., 1958-61; dir. county planning Middlesex County Planning Bd., New Brunswick, N.J., 1961—. Bd. dirs. United Community Services Central Jersey, 1965-77, 1st v.p. 1965-67; mem. Thomas Edison council Boy Scouts Am., 1964—; mem. Middlesex County Criminal Justice Planning Com., 1973—, Middlesex County Solid Waste Adv. Council, 1972—; mem. comprehensive planning com. Middlesex-Somerset-Mercer Regional Devel. Council, 1967—. Served with U.S. Army, 1944-46. Recipient Outstanding Achievement award United Fund, New Brunswick, 1970; Spl. Area Community award Raritan Valley Regional C. of C., New Brunswick, 1978. Mem. Am. Inst. Planners (pres. N.Y. chpt. 1960-61, pres. N.J. chpt. 1962-66, certificate of merit N.Y. chpt. 1971), Am. Soc. Planning Ofcls., Interprofl. Com. on Environ. Design, Nat. Assn. Counties (dir. 1965-67), Nat. Assn. County Planning dirs. (dir. 1965-72), N.J. Fedn. Planning Ofcls. (asso. dir. 1963-68, 72). Home: 1340 Watchung Ave Plainfield NJ 07060 Office: 40 Livingston Ave New Brunswick NJ 08901

POWELL, EDWARD ALLEN, finance devel. cons.; b. Johnstown, Pa., Apr. 26, 1915; s. Leyburn Glenwood and Maude (Menoher) P.; A.B., Lebanon Valley Coll., 1940; m. Martha Searle, Nov. 29, 1947; children—Barbara, Jean, Marilyn, Robert. Dist. scout exec. DuBois and Johnstown (Pa.) councils Boy Scouts Am., 1941-49, asst. scout exec., Washington, 1950-58, Wilmington, Del., 1963-67, scout exec., Lewistown, Pa., 1958-63; gen. mgr. Printing div. Opportunity Center Inc., Wilmington, 1971-75; dir. fin. devel. Freedom Valley council Girl Scouts U.S., Valley Forge, Pa., 1975-78; freelance cons. fin. devel., Newark, Del., 1978—. Chmn. Com. Support Chs. in Their Aims, 1973—. Served to sgt. maj. U.S. Army, 1943-46. Mem. Nat. Soc. Fund Raising Execs., Alpha Phi Omega. Republican. Presbyterian. Club: Kiwanis. Author: How to Raise Capital Funds from Wealthy Individuals and Foundations, 1973. Home and office: 202F Village of Prestbury Newark DE 19713

POWELL, GAYLORD ELLIS, mfg. co. exec.; b. Gloversville, N.Y., June 29, 1928; s. Gaylord Cliffton and Alida Martha (Little) P.; B.A., St. Lawrence U., 1950; M.B.A., Syracuse U., 1952; m. Sande Grace

Field, Sept. 8, 1951 (div. 1976); children—Deniese Alida, Stephen Clifford, Cynthia Grace; m. 2d, Norma Lee Blackledge, Apr. 16, 1977. Mem. purchasing staff Sylvania Electric Products, Buffalo and Batavia, N.Y., 1951-55, Gen. Electric Co., Brockport, N.Y., 1955-60; with Xerox Corp., various locations, 1960—, corp. dir. procurement and distbn., Stamford, Conn., 1969-72, corp. dir. bus. devel., 1970-71, corp. dir. materials, 1973—; dir. Fighton Mfg. Co., Rochester, 1968-69. Mem. purchasing survey com. Monroe County, N.Y., 1965. Mem. Purchasing and Distbn. Council, AMA, Nat. Assn. Purchasing Mgmt. Presbyterian. Clubs: Masons, Oronogue Country (Stratford, Conn.). Home: 115B Chasta Ln Stratford CT 06497 Office: Xerox Corp Stamford CT 06904

POWELL, JIMMIE LEE, chemist; b. Liberty, Miss., May 16, 1945; s. Allen and Bernice (Floyd) P.; B.S. in Chemistry, Alcorn State U., 1965; m. Ora Dean Marshall, June 1, 1969; 1 dau., Yolanda A. Instr. chemistry lab. Alcorn State U., Lorman, Miss., 1966-69; with IBM E. Fishkill Facility, Hopewell Junction, N.Y., 1969—, staff engr., 1976—. Active Young Democrats. Recipient first invention achievement award IBM, 1975. Mem. Am. Chem. Soc., NAACP, Jaycees, Phi Beta Sigma. Baptist. Patentee area of solder glass tech.; contbr. articles to tech. publs. Office: IBM Corp D/249 B/300-090 East Fishkill Route 52 Hopewell Junction NY 12533

POWELL, JOHN MARCUS, JR., architect, artist; b. Little Rock, May 2, 1929; s. John Marcus and Jessica Beatrice (Myhand) P.; B.A., U. Ark., 1952; M.F.A., Princeton U., 1959; m. Susan Murray Via, Sept. 18, 1973; children by previous marriage—Marcus Carter, Jeffrey Thomas. Draftsman, Office of Victor Olgyay, Princeton, 1957, research asst. Princeton U., 1957-58, asst. to dir. research Sch. Architecture, 1957-58; with Office of Victor Olgyay, 1959, Ginocchio Cromwell Assos., Little Rock, 1959-60, Erhart, Eichenbaum, Rauch & Blass, Little Rock, 1960-61; asso. for design Pan Am. Design, Inc., San Juan, P.R., 1961-62; archtl. designer Curtis & Davis, New Orleans, 1963-64; pres. Lafayette Interiors, Inc. (La.), 1968-70; pres. Interior Planning Assos., Inc., New Orleans, 1970-73; exhibited paintings in one-man shows: U. Ark., Little Rock, 1959, 62, 7th St Gallery, Little Rock, 1960, Libra Gallery, Lafayette, 1967, U. Southwestern La. Gallery Fine Arts, 1968, Phila. Art Alliance, 1977, Western Electric World Hdqrs., 1977; exhibited in group shows: at U. Ark., 1950-51, 61, Delta Art Show, 1960, 61, Gallery Don Roberto, San Juan, 1961, Glade Gallery, New Orleans, 1967, Circle Gallery, New Orleans, 1971, Princeton Gallery Fine Art, 1973, Nabisco World Hdqrs., 1977; represented in permanent collections: Union Carbide of P.R., New Orleans, Johnson & Johnson, New Brunswick, N.J., Calif. Poly. U. Found.; tchr. oil painting Ark. Art Center, Little Rock, 1959-60; vis. asst. prof. design, dept. architecture Tulane U., 1962-64, lectr. interior design, 1963-64; vis. lectr. Sch. Architecture, Calif. State Poly. U., San Luis Obispo, 1964-66, summer 1968, vis. speaker, 1970, vis. lectr., 1970-71; prof., chmn. applied arts Sch. Art and Architecture, U. Southwestern La., Lafayette, 1966-70. Served to 1st lt. USAF, 1951-56. Address: 41 Ferry St New Hope PA 18938

POWELL, LARSON MERRILL, investment advisory service exec.; b. Pittsfield, Mass., Mar. 8, 1932; s. Harry LeRoy and Elsie Madeline (Larson) P.; A.B., Harvard U., 1954; student Columbia U. Law Sch., 1957-59; m. Anne C. Millett, Dec. 8, 1956; children—Larson Merrill, Anne Coleman, Miles Sloan. News editor, reporter Boston Daily Globe, 1954, 56-57; security analyst Moody's Investors Service, N.Y.C., 1959-62, regional mgr., 1964-67, v.p., 1967-68; pres. instl. investment mgmt. div. Anchor Corp., Elizabeth, N.J., 1968-70; pres. Res. Research, Ltd., N.Y.C., 1971—. Bd. mgrs. W.Side br. YMCA of Greater N.Y., 1970—, mem.-at-large citywide bd., 1976—; chmn. men's com. Am. Mus. Natural History, 1970-72; mem. Boro of Manhattan Community Planning Bd. 7, 1966-69; bd. dirs. Episcopal Camp and Conf. Center, 1978—. Served with AUS, 1954-56. Fellow Fin. Analysts Fedn.; mem. N.Y. Soc. Security Analysts, N.Y. Newsletter Pubs. Assn. Episcopalian. Clubs: India House, Harvard (N.Y.C.); Cumberland (Portland, Maine). Editor, pub. Powell Monetary Analyst, 1971—, Powell Gold Industry Guide, 1972—, Internat. Mining Analyst, 1976—. Office: 63 Wall St New York City NY 10005

POWELL, LENORE SARAH, psychotherapist, gerontologist; b. Bklyn., Aug. 17, 1938; d. Israel and Dora (Moniak) P.; B.A. cum laude in Psychology, CU NY, 1962; M.A. in Psychology (Ednl. Found. scholar), Columbia U., 1964, Ed.D. in Gerontology-Psychology (Adminstrn. on Aging, HEW fellow), 1978. Clin. intern Elmhurst Hosp./Mt. Sinai Hosp., Elmhurst, N.Y., 1967-68; psychotherapist Jewish Child Care Assn., N.Y.C., 1968-69, Jewish Family Service, Bklyn., 1969-75; pvt. practice psychotherapy and psychoanalysis, Bklyn., 1975—; cons., tchr. psychology Inst. for Study of Older Adults, N.Y.C. Community Coll., 1974—. Bd. dirs. Bklyn. Philharm. Chorus, Bklyn. Acad. Mus., 1975—. Recipient Joseph W. Beatman award Jewish Family Service, Inc., 1974; cert. sch. psychologist N.Y. State. Bklyn. Psycohol. Assn. (v.p. 1979—). Contbr. chpt. to Aging and Isolation. Office: 110 Ocean Pkwy Brooklyn NY 11218

POWELL, LEWIS FRANKLIN, JR., asso. justice U.S. Supreme Ct.; b. Suffolk, Va., Sept. 19, 1907; s. Lewis Franklin and Mary Lewis (Gwathmey) P.; B.S., Washington and Lee U., 1929, LL.B., 1931, LL.D., 1960; LL.M., Harvard U., 1932; LL.D., Hampden Sydney Coll., 1959, Coll. William and Mary, 1965, U. Fla., 1965, U. Richmond, 1970, U. S.C., 1972, Wake Forest U., 1975, Brigham Young U., 1975, Yeshiva U., 1976; m. Josephine Rucker, May 2, 1936; children—Josephine Powell Smith, Ann Pendleton Powell Carmody, Mary Lewis Gwathmey Powell Summer, Lewis Franklin, III. Admitted to Va. bar, 1931. U.S. Supreme Ct. bar, 1937; practiced law in Richmond, 1932-71; mem. firm Hunton, Williams, Gay, Powell and Gibson 1937-71; asso. justice U.S. Supreme Ct., 1972—. Chmn. bd. trustees Colonial Williamsburg Found.; chmn. spl. Charter Commn. for City of Richmond (prepared new city charter, approved in spl. election Nov. 1947); mem. Nat. Commn. on Law Enforcement and Adminstrn. Justice, 1965-67; mem. Blue Ribbon Def. Panel to study Def. Dept., 1969-70. Chmn. Richmond Pub. Schs. Bd., 1952-61; mem. Va. Bd. Edn., 1962-69, pres., 1968-69; mem. Va. Library Bd., 1954-64. Trustee Hollins Coll., 1956-68, Washington and Lee U., 1964—; hon. bencher Lincoln's Inn. Served from lt. to col. USAAF, 1942-46, 33 months overseas. Decorated Legion of Merit, Bronze Star (U.S.); Croix de Guerre with palms (France). Fellow Am. Bar Found. (pres. 1969-71), Am. Coll. Trial Lawyers (pres. 1969-70); mem. Am. (gov., pres. 1964-65), Va., Richmond (pres. 1947-48) bar assns., Bar Assn. City N.Y., Nat. Legal Aid and Defender Assn. (v.p. 1964-65), Am. Law Inst., Soc. Cincinnati, Sons Colonial Wars, Phi Beta Kappa, Phi Delta Phi, Omicron Delta Kappa, Phi Kappa Sigma. Presbyterian. Clubs: Alfalfa. Country of Va., Commonwealth; Century, Univ. (N.Y.C.). Office: US Supreme Ct Washington DC 20543

POWELL, LOUISE HILL CONKEY, historian, researcher, editor; b. Kansas City, Mo.; d. George Lissant and Louise Eugenia (Hill) Conkey; student spl. courses U. Grenoble (France), 1935-36; A.A., George Washington U., 1941, B.A., 1943, M.A., 1946; postgrad. Wilson Tchrs. Coll., 1944; m. W. Royce Powell, Mar. 24, 1934 (dec. Apr. 1961); children—Lissante Hill Powell Botsho, Julienne Powell Johnson, Katharine Evelyn Powell Crawley. Various positions, 1930-36; research asst. dept. physiology George Washington U. Med. Sch., 1939-53, asst. to chmn. physiology dept., 1953-55; research and adminstrv. asst. to various physicians George Washington U. Med. Sch. and Columbia U., N.Y.C., 1953-65; adminstrv. asst. dept. pharmacology Georgetown U. Med. Sch., Washington, 1966-67; asst. to editor Navy mag. of Navy League U.S., Washington, 1966—, nat. bldg. com., 1973—, historian D.C. council, 1975—. Publicity chmn. Georgetown Hosp. Ladies Bd., 1963-65, 68—; chmn. Republican Precinct Com., 1952; rec. sec. D.C. League Rep. Women, 1961-63; adminstrv. asst. to chmn. Inaugural Concert Com., Rep. Party, Washington, 1969, rep. vol. White House Spl. Projects, 1969-70. Mem. Magna Charta Dames, Nat. Trust Hist. Preservation, Smithsonian Assos., Colonial Dames Am., Colonial Dames Md., Daus. Brit. Empire in U.S.A., U.S. Naval Inst., Navy League U.S. (historian D.C. council 1974-76), World Affairs Forum, Preservation of Hist. Georgetown Found., Kenmore Assn., Descs. Lords of Md. Manors, Md. Hist. Soc., Prince Georges' County Hist. Soc., Pilgrims St. Mary's, Washington Club Jamestowne Soc., Sigma Xi. Clubs: Nat. Travel, Washington, Diplomatic and Counselor Officers Ret., Nat. Press, Am. Newspaper Women's. Home: Volta House 3434 Volta Pl NW Washington DC 20007 Office: Navy League of US 818 18th St Washington DC 20006

POWELL, MARGARET MILLER, interior designer; b. Lock Haven, Pa., Oct. 3, 1940; s. Kenneth Byron and Rosella Mary (Gallagher) Miller; B.A., Pa. State U., 1962; m. John Edward Powell, Oct. 9, 1971; 1 dau., Jennifer Erinn. Jr. designer, then sr. designer Woodward & Lothrop, dept. store, Washington, 1962-67; sr. designer, then v.p. Don McAfee Assos., Washington, 1969-72; owner, partner Irelan-Miller Assos., Washington, 1972—; owner Margaret M. Miller, Inc., Washington, 1978—; profl. liaison Internat. Inst. Interior Design, Washington. Mem. adv. com. Mt. Vernon Coll., Washington. Mem. Am. Soc. Interior Designers. Clubs: Chevy Chase, Gibson Island. Home: 13840 Esworthy Rd Germantown MD 20767 Office: 1621 Connecticut Ave NW Washington DC 20009

POWELL, RICHARD ANTHONY, dentist, educator; b. Buffalo, Apr. 11, 1917; s. Anthony C. and Stephanie M. (Urbanski) Pawlowski; A.B., Syracuse U., 1939; D.D.S., U. Buffalo, 1949; m. Juliet Ferreira, Aug. 15, 1943; children—Richard Anthony, Susan, Charles, Jonathan, Julieanne. Sales rep. Remington Rand Inc., Buffalo, 1939-40; mem. faculty of operative dentistry SUNY, Buffalo 1949—, asso. dean, 1966—, dir. clinics, 1971—. Served with USMC, 1940-46. Decorated Bronze Star, Purple Heart; recipient Disting. Alumnus award SUNY, Buffalo, 1977. Fellow Internat. Coll. Dentists, Am. Coll. Dentists; mem. ADA, Dental Soc. State of N.Y., 8th Dist. Dental Soc. (Achievement award 1963), Erie County Dental Soc., Am. Assn. Dental Schs. (chmn. sect. on dental sch. admissions officers 1979—, chmn. adv. com. application service 1979—, chmn. sect. on clin. adminstrn. 1974-75), N.Y. Acad. Dentistry (certificate of appreciation 1977). Republican. Roman Catholic. Clubs: Brookfield Country (Clarence, N.Y.); Buffalo Dist. Golf Assn. (pres. 1968-70, bd. dirs. 1965-75). Bd. editors Jour. Dental Edn., 1970-75; abstract writer N.Y. State Dental Jour., 1962-69. Home: 161 Southwood Dr Kenmore NY 14223 Office: 194 Farber Hall SUNY Buffalo Buffalo NY 14214

POWELL, WILLIAM JOHN, JR., physician; b. Pitts., Sept. 18, 1935; s. William John and Geraldine Baker (West) P.; grad. St. Paul's Sch., Concord, N.H., 1953; A.B. cum laude, Harvard, 1957, M.D., Columbia Coll. Phys. and Surg., 1961; m. Nancy Wilson Atkinson, Dec. 28, 1960 (div. 1975); children—William John III, Cynthia Atkinson. Intern, asst. resident, then fellow internal medicine Yale, 1961-64; investigator Lab. Cardiovascular Physiology Nat. Heart Inst., Bethesda, Md., 1964-66; sr. resident in medicine Mass. Gen. Hosp., 1966-67, asst. in medicine, 1969-73, asst. physician, 1973-78, asso. physician, 1978—; clin. and teaching fellow cardiology Mass. Gen. Hosp.-Harvard Med. Sch., 1967-69; instr. Harvard Med. Sch., 1969-71, asst. prof., 1971-74, asso. prof., 1974—; mem. research allocations com. Mass. affiliate Am. Heart Assn., Boston, 1973—, chmn., 1976-78, dir., mem. exec. com., 1976—, chmn. research rev. com., 1978—. Served as surgeon USPHS, 1964-66. Recipient Young Investigator's award Am. Coll. Cardiology, 1966. Diplomate Am. Bd. Internal Medicine. Fellow A.C.P., Am. Coll. Cardiology, Am. Heart Assn.; mem. Am. Soc. Clin. Investigation, Am. Physiol. Soc., Mass. Med. Soc., Paul Dudley White Soc. Unitarian. Clubs: Harvard, Tennis and Racquet (Boston); D.U., Hasty Pudding (Harvard). Contbg. author textbooks; contbr. numerous articles to profl. jours. Home: 58 Beacon St Boston MA 02108 Office: Cardiac Unit Mass Gen Hosp Fruit St Boston MA 02114

POWER, WILLIAM EDWARD, bishop; b. Montreal, Que., Can., Sept. 27, 1915; s. Nicholas Walter and Bridget Elizabeth (Callaghan) P.; B.A., Montreal Coll., 1937; student Grand Sem., Montreal. Ordained priest Roman Catholic Ch., 1941; parish asst., Montreal, 1941-47; vice-chancellor Diocese Montreal, 1947-50; diocesan chaplain Young Christian Workers and Christian Family Movement, 1950-53; nat. chaplain Young Christian Workers, 1953-59; chaplain, mgr. Cath. Men's Hostel, Montreal, 1957-59; pastor St. Barbara's Ch., Lasalle, Que., 1959-60; bishop of Antigonish, N.S., 1960—; chancellor St. Francis Xavier U., 1960—. Pres. Canadian Catholic Conf. of Bishops, 1971-73, bd. dirs., 1975—. Address: 155 Main St Box 1330 Antigonish NS B2G 2L7 Canada

POWERS, EDWIN MALVIN, chem. engr.; b. Denver, July 20, 1915; s. Emmett and Bertha Malvina (Guido) P.; B.S. in Chem. Engring., U. Denver, 1939, M.S., 1940; m. Dorothy Lavane Debler, Jan. 18, 1941; children—Dennis M., Kenneth E., James M., Steven R. Prodn. supr. Nat. Aniline Div., Buffalo, 1940-45; engr., project supr. Merck & Co., Rahway, N.J., 1945-72, purchasing engr., 1972—. Registered profl. engr., N.J., Colo. Mem. Am. Chem. Soc., Nat. Soc. Profl. Engrs., Am. Inst. Chem. Engrs. (treas. N.J. 1960, exec. com. 1961-63). Home: 13 Oneida Dr Westfield NJ 07090 Office: Merck & Co Inc 126 E Lincoln Ave Rahway NJ 07065

POWERS, ERNEST FREDERICK, govt. ofcl.; b. Kansas City, Kans., Nov. 6, 1934; s. Franklin E. and Ida J. (Hirons) P.; A.B., Baker U., 1956; M.S., Cornell U., 1972, Ph.D. (fellow), 1974; m. Suzanne W. Sowers, 1958; children—Patti Suzanne, Laurie Beth, Drew Martin. Tchr. pub. schs., Wyandotte County, Kans., 1956-57; research asso., edn. specialist U.S. Army Signal Sch., Ft. Monmouth, N.J.; with RCA Co., Cherry Hill, N.J., 1959-60; mgr. Tech. Control Center for meteorol. satellite, Greenbelt, Md., 1960-61; project coordinator for meteorol. satellites Goddard Space Flight Center, Greenbelt, Md., 1961-65, head ops. support office, 1965-67; mem. hdqrs. staff OEO, Community Action Program, Washington, 1967-68, chief spl. ops. staff, 1968-69; mem. staff Coll. of Human Ecology, Cornell U., Ithaca, N.Y., 1970-72, spl. asst. to dean, 1970-72, also mem. dept. community service edn., 1970-72; chief of utilization OEO, Washington, 1972-73; sr. social sci. analyst in policy research OEO, Exec. Office of the President, Washington, 1973; sr. social scientist Office of the President's Sci. Adviser, NSF, Washington, 1973-76, policy analyst, 1977—; exec. Cons. Office of Sec., HEW, 1978—; U.S. rep. on Intergovtl. Working Group on Social Sci. Policy, Orgn. Econ. Cooperation and Devel., Paris, 1973—; cons. N.Y. State Dept. Edn., 1972. Treas. Cayuga Heights (N.Y.) PTA, 1971-72; pres. Jr. High Sch. PTA, Greenbelt, 1972—; cons. to bishop of Washington area United Meth. Ch., 1968-69; chmn. of stewardship First United Meth. Ch., Hyattsville, Md., 1968-70, chmn. social concerns, 1963-69, pastor-parish relations, 1966-69, 76—; pres. Lay Advisory Council for Wesley Theol. Sem., Washington, 1972—; bd. dirs. YMCA, Ithaca, N.Y., Prince Georges County (Md.) Mental Health Assn., 1964-76, United Way, Prince Georges County, Md., 1972—. Served with U.S. Army, 1957-59. Recipient NASA Achievement award, 1965, Outstanding Performance award OEO, 1969, 72, Outstanding Performance award NSF, 1976; named One of Outstanding Young Men in Am., U.S. Jr. C. of C., 1965. Mem. Am. Sociol. Assn., Am. Acad. Polit. and Social Sci., AAAS, Zeta Chi, Council for Applied Social Research. Clubs: Rotary. Contbr. articles on pub. policy to profl. publs. Home: 7409 Radcliffe Dr College Park MD 20740 Office: 1800 G St NW Washington DC 20550

POWERS, JANE BIDDLE, librarian; b. Ann Arbor, Mich., July 11, 1915; d. Thomas Israel and Clemma Lydia (Mills) Biddle; A.B., U. Mich., 1936, B.S. in L.S., 1937; m. Wilbur Emmett Powers, June 18, 1939 (dec. June 1967); children—Carol Ann Powers Wood, Robert Emmett. Asst. librarian River Rouge (Mich.) Pub. Library, 1938-39; sr. librarian Hamilton Twp. Pub. Library, Trenton, N.J. 1959-64, dir., 1964—. Mem. Hamilton Twp. League Women Voters, 1968—. Mem. ALA, N.J. Library Assn., AAUW, Hamilton Twp. Hist. Soc. Office: Apt 1 1780 Klockner Rd Trenton NJ 08619

POWERS, KIRK MCDEARMON, data processing exec.; b. Pitts., Mar. 31, 1934; s. Frank B. and Margurite (McDearmon) P.; B.A., Wabash Coll., 1959; m. Alice Barbara Tauby, May 27, 1961; children—Kirk McDearmon, Patricia Lynn. Indsl. engr. Raytheon Mfg. Co., N. Dighton, Mass., 1959-62; indsl. engr., systems cons. Bruce Payne & Assos., N.Y.C., Europe, 1962-63; systems and data processing cons. Peat Marwick Mitchell & Co., N.Y.C., 1964-67; corporate data processor, systems mgr. Hopeman Bros., Inc., N.Y.C., 1967-72; dir. mgmt. info. systems Del Labs., Inc., Farmingdale, N.Y., 1972-75, Beker Industries Corp., Greenwich, Conn., 1975-78, Hilti Inc., Stamford, Conn., 1970—. Served with USMC, 1952-56. Mem. Data Processing Mgmt. Assn. (chpt. pres. 1970-71, dir. 1973-74), Assn. Systems Mgmt. Republican. Lutheran. Club: Elk. Home: 249 Tokeneke Rd Darien CT 06820 Office: 124 W Putnam Ave Greenwich CT 06830

POWERS, L. LINDLEY, educator; b. Albany, N.Y., Aug. 19, 1926; d. William Tibbits and Winifred Lispenard (Robb) Powers; A.B., Smith Coll., 1948; M.A., M.F.A., U. Wis., 1963, Ph.D. (E.B. Fred fellow), 1968; postgrad. Episcopal Theol. Sch., 1972-74, Weston Coll. Sch. Theology, 1974-75; m. Davis Spencer, Mar. 5, 1949 (div. Oct. 1961); children—Eleanor Tibbits (Mrs. Robert R. Tupper, Jr.), Joseph Allen Powers (dec.); m. 2d, Gerald E. Fosbroke, Dec. 17, 1976. Children's librarian N.Y. Pub. Library, N.Y.C., 1949-50; tchr. art and English composition Racine (Wis.) High Sch., 1959-61; dir. Wis. 4-H Drama Program, Madison, 1961-65, research asst., 1961-63, instr., 1963-65; teaching asst. U. Wis. Sch. Music, Madison, 1965-66, instr. speech U. Wis., 1966-67; asst. prof. drama Bridgewater (Mass.) State Coll., 1968-69; asso. prof. theatre edn., dir. grad. study Emerson Coll., Boston, 1969-72, asso. prof. fine arts, 1972-76, prof. fine arts, 1976—; mem. Boston Chorus Pro Musica, 1949-51; asso. Iona Community, Argyll, Scotland. Bd. dirs. Boston Ch. Home Soc.; trustee, sec. Iona Community New World Found. U.S.A.; mem. vicar's adv. council Episcopal Ch. St. John the Evangelist, Boston. Mem. AAUP, Speech Communication Assn., Appalachian Mountain Club, Phi Beta. Club: Shakespeare (Boston). Author: Masks in Theatre, also drama handbooks. Home: Lewis Wharf 538 Boston MA 02110

POWERS, MARY RITA, mathematician; b. Norwich, Conn., Aug. 4, 1920; d. George Shea and Ellen Regina (Foley) Powers; B.A., Conn. Coll., 1942; M.A. in Math., U. Calif. at Los Angeles, 1955. Mathematician, U.S. Army Aberdeen (Md.) Proving Ground, 1942-46, digital computing div. USN Underwater Systems Center, New London (Conn.) Lab, 1946—. Mem. Assn. for Computing Machinery, Fed. Profl. Assn., Conn. Coll. Alumni Assn. (mem. fin. com. 1971-74, pres. New London chpt. 1964-66), Council Catholic Women (pres. Norwich dist. 1962-64, treas. 1957-59, treas. Norwich Diocesan Council 1964-66). Contbr. articles on underwater acoustics to profl. jours. Home: 7 Cliff Pl Norwich CT 06360 Office: Fort Trumbull New London CT 06320

POWNALL, KENNETH FRANKLYN, coll. adminstr.; b. Toronto, Ont., Can., Aug. 3, 1924; s. George Franklin and Elizabeth Georgina (Steele) P.; D.D.S., U. Toronto, 1951; m. Nora Jean Cumberland, June 9, 1951; children—John, Janet, Keith. With Canadian Jr. Red Cross Dental Project, Nfld., 1951-52; gen. practice dentistry, Toronto, 1952-65; staff dentist Hosp. for Sick Children, Toronto, 1953-63; asst. prof. ethics and jurisprudence U. Toronto, 1965—; registrar Royal Coll. Dental Surgeons of Ont., 1965—. Exec., Ont. div. Canadian Red Cross, 1959-64; warden/chmn. adv. bd. Christ Ch. Mimico, Toronto, 1961—. Served with Canadian Army, 1943-46. Fellow Internat., Am. colls. dentists; mem. Canadian, Ont. dental assns., Fedn. Dentaire Internationale, Pierre Fauchard Acad., Acad. Dentistry (hon.), Medico-Legal Soc. Ont., Canadian Soc. Forensic Sci. Club: Masons. Writer of Ken's Comments, Jour. Ont. Dental Assn., 1969—. Home: 2591 Lakeshore Blvd W Toronto ON M8V 1G5 Canada Office: 230 St George St Toronto ON M5R 2N5 Canada

POWNING, MAYNARD WALKER, elec. mfg. co. exec.; b. Boston, Sept. 21, 1931; s. Kimball Colby and Carolyn (Walker) P.; A.B. in Social Relations, Harvard U., 1953. With Koehler Mfg. Co., Marlboro, Mass., 1957—, purchasing agt., 1961-64, pres., dir., 1964—. Served to 1st lt. USAF, 1954-56; Korea. Mem. Smaller Bus. Assn. New Eng., The Newcomen Soc., Young Pres.'s Orgn. Clubs: Somerset, Harvard (Boston). Home: 780 Boylston St Boston MA 02199 Office: 123 Felton St Marlboro MA 01752

POZZA, NICHOLAS JOHN, surgeon; b. Phila., Apr. 18, 1928; s. Peter and Nina Pozza; B.A., Central High Sch., Phila., 1945; B.S., Villanova U., 1949; M.D., Temple U., 1955; m. Clara Rose Primoli, July 11, 1953; children—Steven, John, Jacqueline, David. Intern, Meth.-Episc. Hosp., Phila., 1955-56; resident in surgery Jefferson Med. Coll., Phila., 1956-60; practice medicine specializing in surgery, Oil City, Pa., 1960—; surg. staff Oil City Hosp., 1960—, chief surgery, 1975—; affiliate instr. U. Pitts. Sch. Medicine, 1970—. Served with U.S. Army, 1950-51. Diplomate Am. Bd. Surgery. Fellow A.C.S., Internat. Coll. Surgeons, Am. Soc. Abdominal Surgeons; mem. AMA. Republican. Roman Catholic. Home: 29 Oakwood Dr Oil City PA 16301 Office: 9 Glenview Ave Oil City PA 16301

PRABHU, VASANT KRISHNA, elec. engr.; b. Kumta, India, May 13, 1939; s. Krishna Padmanabh and Rukmini (Krishna) P.; came to U.S., 1961, naturalized, 1973; B.Sc. with honors, Karnatak U., India, 1958; B.E., Indian Inst. Sci., 1962; S.M., Mass. Inst. Tech., 1963, Sc.D., 1966; m. Barbara Frances Williams, Dec. 10, 1966; 1 son, Jayant. Communications scientist Bell Labs., Holmdel, N.J., 1966—. Vice pres. Assn. Indians in Am., N.Y.C., 1972-73. Grassman fellow, 1962-65. Recipient Alfred Hay Gold medal Indian Inst. Sci., 1961. Mem. IEEE (chmn. 1973-74), Internat. Sci. Radio Union, Sigma Xi, Tau Beta Pi, Eta Kappa Nu. Home: 138 Crawfords Corner Rd Holmdel NJ 07733 Office: Bell Labs Holmdel NJ 07733

PRABHUDESAI, MUKUND MADHAV, pathologist; b. Goa, India, Mar. 17, 1942; s. Madhav R. and Kusum M. P.; came to U.S., 1967, naturalized, 1976; M.B.B.S., G.S. Med. Coll., Bombay, India, 1966; m. Usha Mujumdar, Feb. 4, 1972; 1 child, Nitin Prabhudesai. Intern, St. Joseph Hosp., Lorain, Ohio, 1968; resident in pathology Albert Einstein Coll. Medicine, Bronx, N.Y., 1968-72, clin. asst. prof. lab. medicine, 1976—; asst. pathologist Fordham Hosp., Bronx, 1973-74, asso. pathologist, 1974-76; asso. dir. clin. pathology Lincoln Hosp., Bronx, 1976, dep. dir. pathology, 1977—; clin. asst. prof. pathology N.Y. Med. Coll., Valhalla, 1978—. Diplomate Am. Bd. Pathology. Fellow Coll. Am. Pathologists, Am. Soc. Clin. Pathology; mem. India Assn. L.I. (founding). Home: PO Box 181 Station H Central Islip NY 11722 Office: Lincoln Hosp Bronx NY 10451

PRAEGER, DONALD LEWIS, ophthalmologist; b. Poughkeepsie, N.Y., Aug. 25, 1933; s. M. Fred and Isabel (Abramsky) P.; B.S., Union Coll., 1955; M.D., N.Y. Med. Coll., 1959; postgrad. U. Pa., 1960; m. Helene C. Schechtman, Apr. 15, 1976; 1 son, Denton Cooley; children by previous marriage—Jennifer, Frederick. Intern, Albany (N.Y.) Med. Center, 1959-60; resident in ophthalmic surgery Wills Eye Hosp., Pa., 1961-63; practice medicine specializing in ophthalmology, Poughkeepsie, 1964—; attending ophthalmic surgeon St. Francis Hosp., Poughkeepsie, 1970—; dir. cataract surg. service N.Y. Med. Coll.-Westchester County Med. Center, Valhalla, N.Y., 1970—, clin. prof. ophthalmology, 1978—; dir. cataract surg. service, Flower and Fifth Ave. Hosp., N.Y.C., 1977—; cons. in field; surgeon dir. N.Y. Intraocular Lens Seminar Inc., 1974—; mem. adv. com. ophthalmology Catholic Charities N.Y., 1975—. Diplomate Nat. Bd. Med. Examiners, Am. Bd. Ophthalmology (asso. examiner 1974—). Fellow Am. Soc. Geriatrics, Mil. Soc. Ophthalmologists, Am. Acad. Ophthalmology and Otolaryngology, Ophthalmic Sox. U.K., Ophthalmic Soc. Republic France, Am. Acad. Facial and Reconstructive Plastic Surgery, A.C.S., Barraquer Inst., Coll. Physicians Phila., Westchester Acad. Medicine; mem. Internat. Coll. Surgeons (splty. chmn. ophthalmology 1970-74), Pan-Am. Assn. Ophthalmology, Contact Lens Soc. Am., U. Pa. Alumni Ophthalmologic Assn., Internat. Intraocular Implant Soc., Am. Intra-Ocular Implant Soc., Internat. Phaco-Emulsification Cataract Methodology Soc. (dir. 1975), N.Y. State Ophthalmologic Soc., N.Y. Soc. Clin. Ophthalmology. Contbr. chpts. to texts, articles to profl. jours. Home: 41 Yates Blvd Poughkeepsie NY 12601 Office: 9 Fulton Ave Poughkeepsie NY 12603 also 630 Park Ave New York City NY 10021

PRAGAY, DESIDER ALEX, educator, clin. scientist; b. Clausenburg, Transylvania, Aug. 12, 1921; s. Joseph and Lenke (Barabas) P.; B.S., Agric Coll. (Clausenburg), 1945; M.S., U. Budapest, 1950, Ph.D., 1956; m. Eva Bakay, July 20, 1956. Came to U.S., 1960, naturalized, 1965. Instr., U. Budapest (Hungary), 1950-53, asst. prof. biochemistry, 1953-56; asst. prof. biochemistry State U. Utrecht (Netherlands), 1956-60; research asso. U. Buffalo, 1960-64; Am. Heart Assn. advanced research fellow Mass. Gen. Hosp. and Retina Found., Boston, 1964-66; clin. asst. prof. State U. N.Y., Buffalo, 1966-70, asso. prof. biochemistry, 1970—, asst. dir. Erie County clin. chemistry lab. Meyer Hosp., 1966-70, dir. clin. chemistry lab., 1970—, clin. asso. prof. pathology, 1977—; cons. Buffalo Columbus Hosp. labs., 1968—. Bd. dirs. Diabetes Detection Service of Erie County Dept. Health. Served with Hungarian Army, 1944-45. Recipient numerous teaching citations; Bausch and Lomb awardee; NIH fellow, 1962-63, asst. dir. NIH Gen. Med. Scis. tng. grant, 1969—. Fellow Am. Inst. Chemists, Nat. Acad. Clin. Chemists; mem. AAUP, Am. Chem. Soc., Am. Assn. Clin. Chemists (chpt. chmn. 1970, chmn. com. on history 1971-72, chmn. com. labor safety 1973—, sec. nat. congress, Buffalo, 1970), Acad. Clin. Lab. Physicians and Scientists, N.Y. Acad. Scis., Sigma Xi. Patentee in field. Author: (with others) Experiments in Chemistry, 1954; Experiments in Biochemistry, 1955. Contbr. articles to profl. jours. Office: care Meyer Hosp 462 Grider St Buffalo NY 14215

PRAGER, ALICE HEINECKE, music exec.; b. N.Y.C., Aug. 2, 1930; d. Paul and Ruth (Collin) Heinecke; grad. Russell Sage Coll., 1951; postgrad. N.Y. U.; m. George L. Drescher. With SESAC, Inc., N.Y.C., 1946—, former exec. v.p., mng. dir., pres., now chmn. Trustee Hampton Hosp. and Med. Center; chmn. bd. Duke Ellington Cancer Center. Named hon. citizen, Tenn., Fla., hon. Ky. col. Mem. Internat. Radio and TV Soc., Am. Women in Radio and TV, AIM, Broadcast Pioneers, Nat. Acad. Rec. Arts and Scis., Advt. Women N.Y., Women's Forum, The Bedside Network; life mem. Country Music Assn., Gospel Music Assn. Home: 300 Central Park W New York City NY 10024 Office: The Coliseum Tower 10 Columbus Circle New York City NY 10019

PRAGLIN, JULIUS, med. instrumentation exec.; b. Boston, June 12, 1927; s. Aaron and Helen (Rosenberg) P.; A.B., Clark U., 1948; M.S., U. Ill., 1950, Ph.D., 1952; m. Rosabelle Wolfson, June 12, 1949; children—Judith Ellen, Laura Jane, Martha Dale. Instr. physiology Western Res. U., Cleve., 1952-55; research engr. Keithley Instruments, Inc., Cleve., 1955-57, v.p. engring., 1957-68, dir., 1964-68; chief elec. engr. Instrumentation Lab., Lexington, Mass., 1968-70; mgr. instrumentation Pfizer Diagnostics div. Pfizer, Inc., Groton, Conn., 1970-73, dir. research and devel., 1973—. Served with USNR, 1947-48. Mem. IEEE, Assn. Advancement of Med. Instrumentation, Sigma Xi. Home: 6 Ferro Ct East Lyme CT 06333 Office: Pfizer Inc Eastern Point Rd Groton CT 06340

PRAMER, DAVID, microbiologist; b. Mt. Vernon, N.Y., Mar. 25, 1923; s. Coleman and Ethel (Toback) P.; student St. John's U., 1940-41, Tex. A. and M. Coll., 1941; B.Sc., Rutgers U., 1948, Ph.D., 1952; m. Rhoda Lifschutz, Sept. 6, 1950; children—Andrew, Stacey. Vis. investigator Butterwick Research Labs., Imperial Chems., Ltd., Eng., 1952-54; asst. prof. microbiology Rutgers U., New Brunswick, 1954-57, asso. prof., 1957-60, prof., 1960—, chmn. dept. biochemistry and microbiology, 1965-69, dir. biol. scis., 1969-73, dir. univ. research, 1973-75, asso. v.p. for research, 1975—; dir. New Brunswick Sci. Co.; Am. del. Internat. Commn. on Microbial Ecology, 1970-73; dep. mem. UNESCO Panel on Microbiology, 1973; chmn. life scis. adv. com. Council for Internat. Exchange Scholars. Committeeman, Democratic party, Highland Park, N.J., 1960-65. Served with USAAF, 1943-46. Recipient Fulbright awards, 1969, 72. Fellow Am. Acad. Microbiology; mem. Internat. Assn. Ecology, Am. Soc. Microbiology, AAAS, Phi Beta Kappa, Sigma Xi, Alpha Zeta. Author: (with E.L. Schmidt) Experimental Soil Microbiology, 1964; Life in the Soil, 1965; (with H.A. Lechevalier) The Microbes, 1971. Home: 37 Grant Ave Highland Park NJ 08904 Office: 116 College Ave New Brunswick NJ 08903

PRASAD, RAJENDRA (GUPTA), physician; b. Mathura, U.P., India, May 19, 1948; s. Ramji Dass and Somvati (Devi) Gupta; came to U.S., 1975; B.Sc., Agra U., India, 1964; M.B., B.S., Rajasthan U., Jaipur, India, 1969, M.D., 1973; m. Vinod Kumari, Dec. 14, 1974; children—Vanita, Amit. Intern, R.N.T. Med. Coll., Udaipur, India, 1969-70, registrar internal medicine, 1971-72, Govt. India fellow, 1973; cons. physician Seema Nursing Home, Udaipur, 1973; registrar internal medicine Maidenhead Hosp., Eng., 1975; resident St. Francis Med. Center, Trenton, N.J., 1975-77; practice medicine, specializing in internal medicine and gastroenterology; fellow in gastroenterology and clin. instr. N.J. Coll. Medicine and Dentistry, Newark, 1977-79; emergency room physician Mercer Med. Center, Trenton, 1977—; asso. attending physician Runnells Hosp., Buckley Heights, N.J., 1977—. Recipient Best Thesis award R.N.T. Med. Coll., 1972. Mem. A.C.P., Brit. Med. Assn. Home: 56 Coventry Circle Piscataway NJ 08854

PRASSAS, MILTON JOHN, architect, engr.; b. Pitts., Jan. 4, 1917; s. John K. and Anna (Clausnitzer) P.; student Art Inst. Chgo., 1933-35; B.S. in Archtl. Engring., Purdue U., 1939; postgrad. Armour Inst. Tech., 1940-41, George Washington U., 1956; m. Viola Snider Rutz, Aug. 6, 1943; 1 dau., Marilyn (Mrs. Franklin Peterson). Constrn. engr. Permanent Constrn. Co., Chgo., 1937; asst. instr. Purdue U., 1938-39; architect-engr. Holabird & Root, Architects, Chgo., 1939-41; pvt. practice architecture and engring., Washington, 1945-56; prin. Milton J. Prassas & Assos., Architects and Engrs., Bethesda, Md., 1956-74; prin. Milton J. Prassas, Architect and Profl. Engr., Bethesda, 1974—; lectr. Montgomery Coll., Md., 1974-75; profl. cons. Lutheran Hosp. and Homes Soc., Fargo, N.D., 1975—, Internat. Brotherhood Elec. Workers, 1968—. Mem. Luth. Laymen's Fellowship, 1955—, pres., 1957-58; mem. High Point Citizens Assn. Md., 1952—, 1st v.p., 1954-60; mem. bldg. and zoning adv. com. Montgomery County Council, 1966-68; bd. dirs. Glen Echo Fire Dept., 1954—, 20 year citation for pub. service, 1975; chmn. bd. trustees Fellowship Sq. Found., 1960-62; hon. mem. John A. Middleton Found., Atlanta, 1975—. Served with USNR, 1941-43, Civil Engr. Corps, USN, 1943-45. Recipient Luth. of Year award Nat. Fedn. Luth. Clubs, 1958; registered architect, Md., D.C., Va., Ga., Fla., Ind.; registered profl. engr., Md., D.C. Fellow ASCE; mem. AIA (citation for Excellence in Community Architecture 1966, nat. com. on ins. 1967, 69-73, nat. com. on housing 1973—, nat. com. on housing steering com. 1978—, cons. nat. design-build task force 1975—, chmn. HUD/AID joint liaison task force 1977—, cons. nat. documents rev. bd. 1976—, vice chmn. nat. com. housing 1979), Purdue Alumni Assn. (life), Tau Beta Pi (life), Chi Epsilon. Clubs: Lauderdale Yacht (Ft. Lauderdale, Fla.); Kenwood Golf and Country (Bethesda). Prin. archtl. works include Middleton Towers Dormitory, Morris Brown Coll., Fellowship House, Reston, Va., Friendship House, W. Lafayette, Ind., Spingarn Stadium, Washington, St. Matthews Luth. Ch., Washington, Pilgrim Luth. Ch., Bethesda, Christ Ch. (Full Gospel), Washington, 4600 Apts., Washington, Circle Apts., Arlington, Va., Allen Temple Apts., Atlanta, Bethel Ch. Homes Apts., Athens, Ga., Crown Point Apts., Virginia Beach, Va., William Tyler Page Elementary Sch., Montgomery County, Md., Eugene Clark Elementary Sch., Washington. Contbr. articles to profl. jours. Address: 5915 Massachusetts Ave Bethesda MD 20016

PRATER, CHARLES DWIGHT, research co. exec.; b. Sylacauga, Ala., Jan. 2, 1917; s. Ruben Walter and Mary Hunt (Corley) P.; B.S. in Chemistry, Auburn U., 1940; postgrad. U. Chgo., 1940-41; Ph.D. in Biophysics, U. Pa., 1951; m. Willie Lee Miller, May 28, 1938; children—Anne Marie (Mrs. Michael Richard Heath), Linda Lee. Physicist, Bartol Research Found., Swarthmore, Pa., 1942-46; research asso. biophysics Johnson Found., U. Pa., Phila., 1946-51; sr. research physicist Mobil Research and Devel. Corp., Paulsboro, N.J., 1951-57, research asso., 1957-62, sr. research asso., 1962-67, mgr. process research and devel., 1967-77, sr. scientist, 1977—. Mem. AAAS, Am. Chem. Soc., Am. Inst. Chem. Engrs. (Alpha Chi Sigma award in chem. engring. research 1972), Nat. Acad. Engring. Home: 112 Monroe Ave Pitman NJ 08071 Office: Mobil Research and Devel Corp Paulsboro Lab Paulsboro NJ 08066

PRATT, GEORGE ORAMEL, ret. soc. ofcl.; b. Kansas City, Mo., Oct. 5, 1903; s. Oramel Whittlesey and Bertha Ellen (Pepper) P.; B.A., Yale, 1925, LL.B., 1927; m. Elizabeth Sherwood Lambertson, Sept. 30, 1925; children—George Oramel, Sherwood Lambertson. Admitted to Mo. bar, 1927; lawyer Lathrop, Crane, Reynolds, Sawyer & Mersereau, Kansas City, Mo., 1927-34; regional dir. NLRB, Kansas City, 1934-37, chief trial examiner, Washington, 1937-42; chief div. intelligence procurement OSS, London, Eng., 1942-45; asst. regional dir. Bur. Reclamation, Billings, Mont., 1946-50, Washington, 1950-53; with Kuljian Corp., Phila., 1953-65, v.p., 1954-65, ret., 1965. Mem. U.S. Com. Internat. Commn. on Irrigation and Drainage (dir. 1953-59). Home: 640B Heritage Village Southbury CT 06488

PRATT, GERALD HILLARY, surgeon, educator; b. Montello, Wis., Dec. 15, 1906; s. Martin Henry and Margaret Anne (Farr) P.; B.S., U. Minn., 1924; M.D., U. Iowa, 1928; hon. degrees U. Bordeaux (France), U. Madrid (Spain), U. Barcelona (Spain); m. Mae Dolores Gargin, Mar. 19, 1936 (dec. Apr. 1954); children—Margaret Anne (Mrs. Thomas Taylor), Judith Mae Kingsley, Gerald Hillary; m. 2d, Nancy Hildegarde Brown, Mar. 22, 1956; children—Dennis Gerald, James Martin. Intern, resident L.I. Coll. Med. Sch. and Hosp. (Bklyn.), 1928-30; chief resident U. Louisville Med. Sch. and Hosp., 1930-31; fellow, instr. Temple U. Med. Sch. and Hosp., Phila., 1931-35; practice medicine specializing in gen. and cardiovascular surgery, N.Y.C., 1935—; mem. staff St. Vincent's Hosp. and Med. Center, St. Clare's Hosp. and Health Center, Doctors Hosp., 1955—; mem. faculty Columbia, 1935-48; asst. clin. prof. surgery, 1938-48; asso. clin. prof. surgery N.Y. U. Sch. Medicine, 1948—; lectr. surgery N.J. Coll. Medicine and Dentistry, 1935—; founder, chief cardiovascular clinic St. Vincent's Hosp., 1948, N.Y. Post Grad. Med. Sch. and Hosp., Columbia U., 1935; cons. med. adv. bd., council on circulation Am. Heart Assn., 1936—; cons. to surgeon gen. U.S. Navy, 1945—, U.S. Naval Hosp., St. Albans, L.I., 1941—, St. Joseph's Hosp., Morristown, N.J., 1936—, Meadowbrook Hosp., 1935—, All Souls Hosp., Morristown, 1948—, Armed Forces Soc., 1960—; surg. com. Armed Forces Cons., 1978. Served to maj. M.C., AUS, 1938-41; from lt. comdr. to capt. M.C. USNR, 1942-45. Decorated Order Don X (Spain); recipient Service citation N.Y. U., 1973. Diplomate Am. Bd. Surgery. Fellow A.C.S., Am. Heart Assn., N.Y. Acad. Medicine, Am. Coll. Chest Physicians, Am. Geriatrics Soc., Pan Am. Med. Assn. (v.p. 1940—), Internat. Coll. Surgeons, Internat. Soc. Surgery; mem. AMA, N.Y. County, N.Y. State (certificate recognition 50 years pub. service), Queens County med. socs., N.Y. Heart Assn. (dir. 1936), N.Y. Diabetes Assn. (dir.), N.Y. Acad. Scis., N.Y. Surg. Soc., N.Y. Cardiovascular Surg. Soc. (founding), West Side Clin. Soc. N.Y., Am. Cardiovascular Soc. (founding), Am. Therapeutic Soc. (v.p. 1954-55, pres. 1956-57), Am. Soc. Clin. Pharmacology and Therapeutics (hon. dir. 1978—), Am. Acad. Compensation Medicine (founding), Babcock Surg. Soc. Phila., Assn. Mil. Surgeons U.S., surg. socs. Marseilles (France), U. Barcelona (Spain), Madrid (Spain), Cuba, Venezuela, Nu Sigma Nu, Phi Gamma Delta, Tau Upsilon Kappa. Club: Century. Author: Surgical Management of Vascular Diseases, 1948; Spanish edit., 1952; Cardiovascular Surgery, 1954; Vascular Surgery: Guide and Handbook, 1976; Saga of a Surgeon, 1976; also chpts. in other books. Co-editor Angiology, 1951-60; cons. editor Jour. Gen. Practice, Jour. AMA, Surg. Gynecology and Obstetrics, Mil. Medicine; contbr. articles and book revs. to profl. jours. Home: 211 Ocean Ave Sea Girt NJ 08750 Office: Dept Surgery St Clares Hospital 415 W 51st St New York City NY 10019

PRATT, JAMES LELAND, JR., electronics co. exec.; b. Colesville, N.Y., Dec. 17, 1933; s. James Leland and Agnes Carrie (Allen) P.; B.A., Hartwick Coll., 1958; M.S. (Gen. Aniline & Film grantee), Broome Coll., 1962; m. Judith Ann Esposito, June 21, 1974. Mgr., Gen. Aniline & Film, Binghamton, N.Y., 1957-65; prodn. mgr. N.Am. Phillips, Saugerties, N.Y., 1965-67; systems mgr. Control Data Corp., Rockville, Md., 1969-71; mktg. devel. mgr. Bunker Ramo Corp., Chgo., 1971-75; telecommunications mktg. dir. Gulf & Western Elco Corp., Willow Grove, Pa., 1975-77; dir. mktg. GTE Sylvania, Titusville, Pa., 1977—. Bd. dirs. Binghamton Recreation Comm., bd. dirs., pres. Alpha Delta Omega, Phi Sigma Kappa Alumni. Mem. Mil. Electronics and Communications Assn., Soc. Photog. Sci. Engrs., Soc. Phometric Instrumentation Engrs., Internal Electronic Elec. Engrs., U.S. Ind. Telephone Assn.; Electronic Connector Study Group. Patentee in field. Home: 3700 Kinter Hall Rd Edinboro PA 16412 Office: RD 2 Titusville PA 16354

PRATT, RICHARD DEAN, musician; b. Kansas City, Kans., Mar. 11, 1944; s. John Henry and Willa (Beachum) P.; student U. Kans., 1962-66. Football player N.Y. Giants, 1967-70; performer with Am. Symphony, Alvin Ailey, Joffrey Ballet, Ain't Suppose to Die, Dude, Raisin; performed with many jazz and rock groups including N.Y. Jazz Quartet, Della Reese, Nancy Wilson, Aretha Franklin, Temptations, 1972—. Mem. Phi Mu Alpha. Composer: 87th Street. Home and Office: 7 W 87th St Apt 3F New York City NY 10024

PRATT, ROBERT ARMSTRONG, educator, medievalist; b. Rockingham, Vt., July 22, 1907; s. Arthur Peabody and Helen (Armstrong) P.; A.B., Yale U., 1929, Ph.D., 1933; m. Nathalie May Rodgers, Dec. 21, 1936; children—Deborah Macy (Mrs. Michael Frederick William Borst), Susan Huntington, (Mrs. Edward Gibson Lanpher), James Rodgers. Instr. English, U. Rochester (N.Y.), 1933-36, asst. prof., 1936-38; instr. Queens Coll., Flushing, N.Y., 1938-41, asst. prof., 1941-48, asso. prof., 1948-51; prof. U. N.C. Chapel Hill, 1951-57; mem. Inst. for Advanced Study, Princeton, N.J., 1955, 57-58; prof. U. Ill., 1958-61; prof. English U. Pa., Phila., 1961-75, emeritus prof., 1975—; John S. Guggenheim Meml. fellow, 1946-47, 54-55; vis. research fellow Merton Coll., Oxford U., 1976. Fellow Mediaeval Acad. Am. (councillor 1957-60); mem. Acad. Literary Studies, Modern Lang. Assn. Am. (chmn. Chaucer library com. 1969—), Am. Philol. Assn., Dante Soc., Loyal Legion, Colonial Soc. Pa., Phila. Art Alliance. Clubs: Franklin Inn, Penn, Philobiblon (Phila.). Author: (with others) Sources and Analogues of Chaucer's Canterbury Tales, 1941, Studies in Medieval Literature, 1961. Editor: The Tales of Canterbury by Geoffrey Chaucer, 1974. Mem. Bd. govs. U. N.C. Press, 1952-57; editorial bd. Studies in Philology, 1955-57, PMLA, 1954-66, Chaucer Rev., 1966—; mem. adv. bd. Speculum, 1966-69. Contbr. articles on Chaucer to profl. jours. Home: 537 New Gulph Rd Haverford PA 19041

PRATTER, MARIANNE BUNZL (MRS. PAUL J. PRATTER), chem. co. exec.; b. Vienna, Austria, Dec. 21, 1938; d. Izidor and Cerest (Bleier) Bunzl; came to U.S., 1960, naturalized, 1967; B.S. in Chemistry, Budapest U. (Hungary), 1957; M.S. in Chemistry, U. Calif. at Los Angeles, 1962; m. Paul J. Pratter, Dec. 13, 1962; children—Joshua E., Adam S. Inorganic chemist Eastern div. Research Organic/Inorganic Chems. Corp., Belleville, N.J., 1963-65, adminstrv. dir., 1965-68, pres., 1968—; pres. Western div. Research Organic/Inorganic Chems. Corp., Sun Valley, Calif., 1968—. Mem. Am. Chem. Soc. Home: 50 Rock Spring Rd West Orange NJ 07052 Office: 507-519 Main St Belleville NJ 07109

PRAUSNITZ, FREDERIK W., conductor; b. Cologne, Germany, Aug. 26, 1920; s. Fred F. and Maria (Moritz) P; came to U.S., 1937, naturalized, 1944; m. Margaret Britten Grenfell, Oct. 21, 1961; children—Sebastian, Margaret Maja. Profl. debut as conductor Detroit Symphony, 1944; guest conductor B.B.C., London Symphony Orch., various others, 1957—; asso. dir. pub. activities Juilliard Sch. Music, 1947-49, asst. dean, 1949-61, dir. choral music, asso. condr. Juilliard Orch., 1956-61, condr. New Eng. Conservatory Symphony Orch., Boston, 1961-69; music dir., condr. Syracuse (N.Y.) Symphony Orch., 1971-75; chief condr. Peabody Conservatory Orch., Balt., music dir. Peabody Opera Theatre, 1976—; cons. Dmitri Mitropoulos Competition, 1961, Lincoln Center for Performing Arts, 1963; lectr. on music Harvard U.; various conducting tours, Europe, Mex., C.Am. Recipient Gustav Mahler medal Am. Bruckner Soc., 1974; Rockefeller Found. grant, 1966. Hon. fellow U. Sussex, Eng., 1970; cons., spl. asst. to provost Oakland (Mich.) U., 1970—. Mem. Internat. Soc. Contemporary Music (dir. 1960-62), Am. Symphony Orch. League. Club: Savage (London). Recordings for Columbia, Emi, Epic, Angel, Phillips, Argo. Address: care Peabody Inst Baltimore MD 21202

PRAVDA, MILTON FRANK, research co. exec.; b. N.Y.C., Dec. 25, 1923; s. Frank and Nellie (Preplata) P.; student Tex. A. and M. U., 1943-44; B.S. in Elec. Engring., Newark Coll. Engring., 1947. Mgr. reactor design Knolls Atomic Power Labs., Schenectady, 1950-60; dir. engring. and research Martin Co., Balt., 1960-68; founder Dynatherm Corp., Cockeysville, Md., 1968, pres., 1968—, chmn. bd., 1971—; chmn. bd. Bossalina Machine Co., Inc. Served with AUS, 1943-46; ETO. Mem. AAAS, IEEE (sr.), Am. Nuclear Soc., Tau Beta Pi. Contbr. articles to profl. jours. Home: 7708 Greenview Terrace Towson MD 21204 Office: 1 Industry Lane Cockeysville MD 21030

PREM, F. HERBERT, JR., lawyer; b. N.Y.C., Jan. 14, 1932; s. F. Herbert and Sybil (Nichols) P.; A.B., Yale U., 1953; J.D., Harvard U., 1959; m. Patricia Ryan, Nov. 18, 1978; children—Julia N., F. Herbert III. Admitted to N.Y. bar, 1960; asso. Whitman & Ransom, N.Y.C., 1959-66, partner, 1967—; dir. Fuji Foto Film U.S.A. Inc., Micro Display Systems, Inc., Micro Power Systems, Inc., Noritake Co. Inc., Seiko Instruments, Inc., Shimano Am. Corp. Bd. dirs., treas. Community Action for Legal Services, Inc., N.Y.C., 1967-70; bd. dirs. Legal Aid Soc., N.Y.C., 1969-73. Served to lt. (j.g.), USNR, 1953-56. Mem. Assn. Bar City N.Y. (sec. 1967-69), Am., N.Y. State bar assns., Am. Law Inst., Zeta Psi. Episcopalian. Clubs: Yale, Univ. (N.Y.C.). Home: 325 E 72d St New York City NY 10021 Office: 522 Fifth Ave New York City NY 10036

PREMINGER, ALEXANDER SALO, educator, librarian; b. Berlin, Germany, July 29, 1915; s. Saly and Lea (Sprechman) P.; came to U.S., 1940, naturalized, 1943; B.A. cum laude, N.Y. U., 1950; M.S. cum laude, Columbia, 1952; m. Augusta Friedman, Aug. 7, 1960. With Bklyn. Coll. Library, City Univ. N.Y., Bklyn., 1952—, asst. prof., chief humanities div., 1965-68, asso. prof., 1969-77; asso. prof. Hofstra U. Library, 1978—; edit. cons. Frederick Ungar Publs., N.Y.C., 1965—; hon. cons. aesthetics and lit. criticism Folger Shakespeare Library, Washington, 1971—; mem. adv. bd. Ency. World Lit. in 20th Century, 1967-71; chmn. Flushing (N.Y.) Affiliates Ednl. Broadcasting Corp., 1963-66. Served with AUS, 1942-45. Bollingen Found. fellow, 1962-63. Mem. Columbia Sch. L.S. Alumni Assn. (dir. 1964-67), ALA, Modern Lang. Assn., Internat., Am. comparative lit. assns., N.Y. Library Club, Phi Beta Kappa, Beta Phi Mu. Editor: Princeton Ency. Poetry and Poetics, 1965; Harry D. Gideonse, Against the Running Tide, 1967; (with others) Classical and Medieval Literary Criticism, 1974. Author: (with A. Ciolli, L. Lester) The Urban Educator, 1970. Editor: Princeton Ency. of Poetry and Poetics, enlarged edit., 1975; mem. internat. adv. bd. Jour. for Descriptive Poetics and Theory of Lit., 1976—. Contbr. articles to profl. jours. Home: 1311 Decker St Valley Stream NY 11580 Office: Hofstra U Library Hempstead NY 11550

PREMO, PATRICK MERVYN, educator; b. Potsdam, N.Y., June 7, 1942; s. Mervyn Alexander and Marion Edna (Perry) P.; B.S., Ithaca Coll., 1964; M.S., St. Bonaventure U., 1973; m. Kathleen Marie Boser, June 3, 1972; children—Maureen Noelle, Eileen Catherine. Staff accountant Haskins & Sells, Rochester, N.Y., 1964-66, sr. accountant, 1968-70; asso. prof. accounting St. Bonaventure (N.Y.) U., 1970—. Vol. ARC, 1970, Community Chest, 1971. Served with AUS, 1966-68. C.P.A., N.Y. Mem. Am. Inst. C.P.A.'s, N.Y. State Soc. C.P.A.'s, Nat. Assn. Accountants (dir. 1973—), Am. Accounting Assn. Inventor game: They're Off, 1977; columnist Table Top Sports, Avalon Hill's All-Star Replay. Home: RD 1 1240 Chipmonk Rd Allegany NY 14706 Office: PO Box 75 St Bonaventure Univ St Bonaventure NY 14778

PREMPAS, LOUIS NICHOLAS, educator; b. Springfield, Mass., Aug. 24, 1928; s. Nicholas Helias and Mary Nicholas (Scourletos) P.; B.A. cum laude, Am. Internat. Coll., 1950; M.A., Central Conn. State Coll., 1961; 6th yr. degree U. Conn., 1963, postgrad., 1964-68. Employed in retail business, Springfield, 1950; beater engr. Premoid Products Co., West Springfield, Mass., 1953-57; tchr. pub. schs., Stafford Springs, Conn., 1958-78; prin. Borough Sch., Stafford Springs, 1960-63. Mem. NEA, Conn., Stafford edn. assns., Horseman's Benevolent Protection Assn., Alpha Chi. Greek Orthodox.

PREMPREE, AMPORN LOHSUVANA, cardiologist; b. Prajinburi, Thailand, June 25, 1935; d. Boonmee and Charoon Lohusuvana; M.D., Siriraj Hosp., U. Med. Scis., Bangkok, Thailand, 1958; m. Thongbliew Prempree, Mar. 29, 1963. Resident in internal medicine Sinai Hosp., Balt., 1961-63; fellow in pediatric cardiology Johns Hopkins U. Hosp., Balt., 1963-67; cardiologist Sinai Hosp., Balt., 1967-69; instr. cardiology Ramathibodi Med. Sch., Bangkok, Thailand, 1969-70; dir. cardiac graphic lab. cardiology North Charles Gen. Hosp., Balt. 1972—. Mem. Am. Heart Assn., Am. Soc. Echocardiography, Balt. City Med. Soc. Home: 9321 Dunloggin Rd Ellicott City MD 21043 Office: 2724 N Charles St Baltimore MD 21218

PREMPREE, THONGBLIEW, physician; b. Rajburi, Thailand, Feb. 1, 1935; s. Korn and Kam (Thongloima) P.; came to U.S., 1961, naturalized, 1978; M.D., Siriraj Med. Sch. (Thailand), 1958; Ph.D., Johns Hopkins U., 1968; m. Ampron Lohsuvana, Apr. 30, 1963. Intern, Siriraj Med. Sch., 1958-59; resident U. Md., 1961-63; dir. radiobiology div. dept. therapeutic radiology Tuft U. Hosp., Boston, 1970-71; asst. prof. dept. radiology Johns Hopkins U., Balt., 1971-74; asso. prof. dept. radiology U. Md. Hosp., Balt., 1974-77, asso. chmn., asso. prof. dept. radiation therapy, 1978—; radiotherapist cons. St. Agnes Hosp., Balt., 1976—, Dorchester Gen. Hosp., Cambridge, Md., 1975—. Mem. human vol. research com. U. Md. Hosp., 1976—, mem. human use subcom. radiation control, 1977—. Diplomate Am. Bd. Radiology. Mem. Am. Soc. Therapeutic Radiologists, Am. Coll. Radiology, AAAS, Radiation Research Soc., Fedn. Am. Scientists, Radiol. Soc. N. Am. Buddhist. Contbr. articles to med. jours. Home: 9321 Dunloggin Rd Ellicott City MD 21043 Office: 22 S Greene St Baltimore MD 21201

PRENDERGAST, WILLIAM EDWARD, JR., psychologist; b. Bridgeport, Conn., Apr. 2, 1932; s. William Edward and Helen Irene (Galla) P.; A.B., Fairfield U., 1950; M.A. (fellow), U. Detroit, 1961; Ph.D., Walden U., 1979; m. Mildred Pauline Colletto, June 18, 1966; 1 son, Shawn. Psychol. intern State Home for Boys, Jamesburg, N.J., 1960-61; staff clin. psychologist N.J. State Diagnostic Center, Menlo Park, N.J., 1961-67; dir. Rahway (N.J.) Treatment Unit for Sex Offenders, 1967-76; dir. profl. services Adult-Diagnostic and Treatment Center, Avenel, N.J., 1976—. Certified sex therapist. Mem. Soc. Sci. Study Sex (v.p. Eastern region, nat. dir.), Am. Correction Assn., Am., N.J. psychol. assns., Sex Info. and Edn. Council U.S., Am. Assn. Sex Educators, Counselors and Therapists, Navy League U.S. Roman Catholic. Office: 8 Production Way PO Box 190 Avenel NJ 07001

PRENTICE, COLGATE SELDEN, govt. ofcl.; b. Newport News, Va., Jan. 10, 1924; s. Bryant Hawk and Susan Selden (Dimmock) P.; B.A., Swarthmore Coll., 1949; M.P.A., Princeton U., 1951; m. Pamela Davis, Sept. 2, 1950; children—Christine, Stephen, Selden. Budget examiner U.S. Bur. Budget, 1951-52; legis. asst. to U.S. Sen. H. Alexander Smith, 1952-53; adminstrv. asst. to Rep. Peter Frelinghuysen (N.J.), 1953-59; exec. asst. to Vice Pres. Richard M. Nixon, 1959-61; adminstrv. asst. to U.S. Sen. John Sherman Cooper, 1961-63; internat. relations officer Dept. State, 1963-69, dep. asst. sec. state for congressional relations, 1969-73, spl. asst. Bur. Pub. Affairs, 1973—. Bd. dirs. Bryant and Stratton Schs., Buffalo. Served with USAAF, 1943-45. Decorated Air medal with 2 oak leaf clusters. Episcopalian. Club: Federal City (Washington). Home: 213 Woodland Terr Alexandria VA 22302

PRESBY, J. THOMAS, mgmt. cons.; b. Newark, Feb. 15, 1940; s. George and Shirley (Kandel) P.; B.S. in Elec. Engring., Rutgers U., 1961; M.S. in Indsl. Adminstrn. (grad. scholar), Carnegie Mellon U., 1963; m. Elaine Merle Smith, Aug. 19, 1961; children—Philip, Terry, Mona. Cons. Touche Ross & Co., C.P.A.'s, Dayton, O. and N.Y.C., 1963-69, partner, N.Y.C., 1972-76, European regional partner, Paris, 1976—; v.p. Shareholders Capital Corp., London, Eng., 1969-71; sr. v.p. Toga Group, Inc., N.Y.C., 1971-72; mem. internat. com. Discover Am. Travel Orgn., 1973—. C.P.A.; certified mgmt. cons. Mem. Am. Inst. C.P.A.'s (task force forecasting standards), N.Y. State, Ohio socs. C.P.A.'s. Contbr. articles to profl. jours. Office: care Touche Ross & Co 1633 Broadway New York City NY 10019 also 6 rue de Berri Paris 75008 France

PRESCOTT, PATRICIA ROEHS, civic worker, counselor; b. Richmond, Va., May 19, 1941; d. Frederick Joseph and Mary Catherine (McNulty) Roehs; R.N. diploma Petersburg (Va.) Gen. Hosp. Sch. Nursing, 1963; B.Applied Sci. in Nursing Edn., Methodist Coll. N.C., 1975; M.S. in Counseling and Human Devel., Troy State U., 1978; m. Daniel J. Prescott, Apr. 26, 1963; children—Deborah, Raymond, Patrick, Danielle. Dir. nursing service Lee Nursing Home, Petersburg, 1963; dir. vols., first aid instr. ARC Field Office, Zweibrucken, Germany, 1965-68, vol. community counselor, 1976—; staff nurse intensive care Petersburg Gen. Hosp., 1968-70; developer, coordinator health edn. program, adult edn. div. Fayetteville (N.C.) Tech. Inst., 1970-75; counselor, tchr. cardio-pulmonary resuscitation; vol. blood pressure screening and counseling, health edn. counseling for teens; vol. health counselor hypertension screening. Mem. Am. Personnel and Guidance Assn., Am. Nurses Assn., NOW. Methodist. Club: Officers Wives. Address: care Maj Daniel J Prescott USA CSC SGE APO NY 09052

PRESNELL, WALTER MADISON, psychiatrist; b. Knoxville, Sept. 23, 1925; s. James Henry and Cloteal Lillian (Hardy) P.; B.S., U. Mich., 1949; M.D., Meharry Med. Coll., 1954; m. Clarice Clotilde Davis, Aug. 30, 1957; children—Craig Madison, Ricardo Davis. Intern, San Francisco County Hosp., 1954-55; resident in psychiatry Stanford, 1955-56, Harvard, 1956-58; practice medicine, specializing in psychiatry Lynn, Mass., 1968—; staff, chief of unit, Hawaii State Hosp., Honolulu, 1963-65; chief profl. services, supt. Undercliff Hosp., Meriden, Conn., 1965-68. Mem. Town of Marblehead (Mass.) Bd. Health, 1974-75. Served with USAAF, 1943-46. Mem. Am. Psychiat. Assn. Author: Handbook on Psychiatry 1970. Contbr. articles to profl. publs. Home: 4 Longfellow Pl Boston MA 02114 Office: 41 Nahant St Lynn MA 01902

PRESSLER, MARION JOAN, librarian; b. Hollidaysburg, Pa., June 24, 1925; d. Howard Delo and Alice Elizabeth (Buehler) Pressler; B.S., State Tchrs. Coll., Slippery Rock, Pa., 1946; M.L.S., Carnegie Inst. Tech., 1959; certificate of advanced study U. Chgo., 1969. Tchr. high sch., Sandy Lake, Pa., 1946-47; librarian high sch., Phillipsburg, Pa., 1947-49; staff mem. Altoona Mirror, newspaper, 1950-53; tchr. high sch., East Berlin, Pa., 1953-55, Hollidaysburg, 1955-58; librarian Mt. Lebanon Sch. Dist., Pitts., 1959—, chmn. library services, 1971-74. Gen. chmn. Council Sch. Librarians, Pitts., 1967-68. Bd. dirs. Hollidaysburg Library. Frick Found. scholar, 1960-63. Mem. Nat., Pa. edn. assns., Mt. Lebanon Edn. Assn., Am., Pa. library assns., Blair County Hist. Soc., Friends of the Library, Altoona Community Theater, Altoona Music League, Sigma Tau Delta, Beta Phi Mu, Pi Lambda Theta, Alpha Psi Omega. Clubs; Blair County Women's, Hollidaysburg Women's. Contbr. articles to profl. jours. Home: Chatham Center Pittsburgh PA 15219 Office: Mount Lebanon School District Moffett St Pittsburgh PA 15243

PRESSMAN, EDMUND NORMAN, educator; b. Phila., May 31, 1935; s. Edward and Bernice (Roubert) P.; B.A., U. Pa., 1956, M.D. 1960; m. Lois Fisher, Sept. 10, 1960; children—John, Alison. Intern, Presbyn. Hosp., Phila., 1960-61, resident, 1961-63; anesthesiologist N. Pa. Hosp., Lonsdale, Pa., 1965-66; asst. prof. anesthesiology Jefferson Med. Coll., Phila., 1966-69; chief anesthesiology Phoenixville (Pa.) Hosp., 1969—, Taylor (Pa.) Meml. Hosp., 1975—, West Park Hosp., Phila., 1975—; prof. anesthesiology, asso. chmn. dept. Med. Coll. Pa., Phila., 1972-76, asst. prof. emergency medicine, 1976—; pres., Edmund N. Pressman M.D. Assos., Bala, Pa., 1971—; mem. staff Jefferson Med. Coll. Hosp., Hosp. Med. Coll. Pa., Phoenixville Hosp. Served with USNR, 1963-65. Diplomate Am. Bd. Anesthesiology. Fellow Am. Coll. Anesthesia. Club: Varsity Univ. Pa. Home: 1256 Lakemont Rd Villanova PA 19085 Office: 315 GSB Bldg 1 Belmont Ave Bala-Cynwyd PA 19004

PRESTIA, MICHAEL ANTHONY, accounting exec.; b. S.I., N.Y., Oct. 6, 1931; s. Anthony and Antoinette (Folino) P.; M.B.A., N.Y. U., 1956; B.A., 1953; m. Nancy Ferrandino, July 4, 1959 (div. May 1970); 1 son, Anthony. Sr. accountant Gluckman & Schacht, C.P.A.'s, N.Y.C., 1953-60; chief fin. officer Franklin Broadcasting Co., N.Y.C., 1960-63; chief accountant asst. to bus. officer, sec. The Cooper Union for Advancement Sci. and Art, N.Y.C., 1963-66; bus. officer Inst. Pub. Adminstrn., N.Y.C., 1966-71, controller, 1971-78, treas., 1978—; cons. taxation and tax planning, govt. contract accounting and adminstrn., 1959—. Served with AUS, 1953-55. C.P.A., N.Y. Mem. Am. Inst. C.P.A.'s, N.Y. State Soc. C.P.A.'s. Home: 53-06 Francis Lewis Blvd Bayside NY 11364 Office: 55 W 44th St New York City NY 10036

PRESTON, KENDALL, JR., electro-optical engr.; b. Boston, Oct. 22, 1927; s. Kendall and Dorothy Fletcher (Allen) P.; grad. Milton Acad., 1945; B.A. cum laude, Harvard, 1950, M.S., 1952; m. Sarah Malcolm Stewart, Aug. 23, 1952; 1 dau., Louise. Mem. tech. staff Bell Tel. Labs., Murray Hill, N.J., 1952-60, sect. head scanning and data processing, 1960, mgr. new product devel., 1961; sr. staff scientist Perkin-Elmer Corp., Norwalk, Conn., 1961-74; prof. engring. and bioengring. Carnegie-Mellon U., Pitts., 1974—; prof. radiation health Grad. Sch. Public Health, U. Pitts., 1977—; chmn. Internat. Optical Computing Conf., Zurich, Switzerland, 1974; U.S. chmn. U.S.-Japan Seminar on Digital Processing of Biomed. Images, Pasadena, Calif., 1975; faculty NATO Advanced Study Inst. on Digital Image Processing and Analysis, Bonas, France, 1976; mem. Tech. Audit Bd., Inc., N.Y.C., 1976—. Chmn. Ecclesia, YMCA, Summit, N.J., 1958-60; chmn. conf. automatic cytology Engring. Found. N.Y.C., 1971-72, chmn. conf. coherent radiation systems, 1973, chmn. conf. on comparative productivity of non-invasive techniques for med. diagnosis, 1976; chmn. health services industry com. Automation Research Council, Am. Automatic Control Council, N.J., 1973-76; mem. NSF Fact Finding Team on Egyptian Scientific Instrumentation, 1974-75. Served with arty., AUS, 1946-47. Fellow IEEE (chmn. Conn. PTGEC 1966-67); mem. AAAS, Biol. Engring. Soc. Gt. Britain, Biomed. Engring. Soc. (charter), Harvard Engrs. and Scientists (pres. students 1952), N.Y. Acad. Sci., Cum Laude Soc. Clubs: D.U., Hasty Pudding Inst. 1770; Harvard of Western Pa.; Country (Brookline, Mass.); Lake (Dublin, N.H.); Hillsboro (Pompano Beach, Fla.); Lawn (New Haven, Conn.); Capitol Hill (Washington). Author: Coherent Optical Computers, 1972; editor: (with Dr. Onoe) Digital Processing of Biomedical Images, 1976; (with Drs. Ayer, Johnson and Taylor) Medical Imaging Techniques: A Comparison, 1979. Patentee blood smear spinning, laser location of chomosomes on microscope slide, acoustic holography, others. Asso. editor Pattern Recognition; editorial adviser Biocharacterist. Contbr. numerous articles to profl. jours. Office: Dept Elec Engring Schenley Park Pittsburgh PA 15213

PRESTON, NATHANIEL STONE, educator; b. Boston, Mar. 1, 1928; s. Jerome and Iva (Stone) P.; A.B., Boston U., 1950; M.A., U. Pa., 1951; Ph.D., Princeton, 1960; m. Ravida Duryee Kennedy, Nov. 22, 1958; children—Emily Duryee, Andrew Greeley, Sarah Ells. Instr., W.Va., U., 1953-55; lectr. Boston Coll., 1957; lectr. Tufts U., 1957-58; instr. Trinity Coll., Hartford, Conn., 1959-61; asst. prof. Am. U., Washington, 1961-63, asso. prof., 1963-66, prof., 1966—, dir. Washington semester program, 1962-73, v.p. acad. affairs, 1973-76. Corp. mem. Squam Lakes Sci. Center, Holderness, N.H., 1971—; dir., officer Squam Lakes Assn., 1972-78; bd. dirs. Iona House, Washington, 1976—, v.p., 1977-78, pres., 1978—; trustee Potomac Sch., 1978—. Mem. Am., D.C. (past mem. council) polit. sci. assns., Collegium Distinguished Alumni Coll. Liberal Arts Boston U., Phi Beta Kappa, Omicron Delta Kappa, Pi Sigma Alpha. Republican. Episcopalian. Clubs: Cosmos (Washington); Chevy Chase (Md.). Author: Politics, Economics and Power, 1967; Public Authorities, 1971; Special Districts in American Local Government, 1977. Editor: The Senate Institution, 1969. Home: 5212 Partridge Ln Washington DC 20016 Office: Am Univ Washington DC 20016

PRETSCH, PAUL GEORGE, health planner; b. Jamaica, N.Y., Nov. 24, 1940; s. Paul and Chrystal (Leanhart) P.; B.A., Wittenberg U., 1962; m. Catherine Alice Psolla, Aug. 11, 1962; children—Stephen, Kristen, David. Asst. editor, prodn. mgr. Indsl. Pub. Co., Cleve., 1962-65; sr. editor, feature writer, mng. editor Ames Pub. Co., Phila., 1965-67; dir. pub. realtions Emery Advtg. Co., Balt., 1967-70; dir. pub. relations and community devel. Md. Gen. Hosp., Balt., 1970-76, dir. community health planning, 1976—; dir. mktg., dir. community health planning Md. Health Care Systems, Inc., 1978—. Pres. Cool Spring Civic Assn., 1975-76; bd. dirs. Vol. Action Center of Md., Inc. Mem. Md. Hosp. Pub. Relations Soc. (pres. 1972-73), Md.-D.C.-Del.-Va. Hosp. Assn. (pub. relations chmn. 1974), Am. Soc. Hosp. Pub. Relations Dirs., Pub. Relations. Soc. Am. Lutheran. Home: 2014 Gumtree Terr Bel Air MD 21014 Office: 827 Linden Ave Baltimore MD 21201

PRETTYMAN, DANIEL TRAVERS, judge; b. Taylors Island, Md., June 27, 1919; s. Daniel Bagwell and Elizabeth (Travers) P.; A.B., U. Md., 1939, J.D., 1948; m. Jean English Burbage, June 7, 1941; children—Daniel Travers II, Anne Elizabeth. Admitted to Md. bar, 1948; practiced in Berlin, Md., 1948-64; partner firm Sanford & Prettyman, Berlin, Md., 1948-49; states atty. Worcester County, 1955-64; asso. judge 1st Jud. Circuit Md., 1964-75, chief jduge, 1975—; mem. Gov.'s Commn. Criminal Law. Pres. Worcester County Mental Health Assn 1962-63; dir. Heart Assn. Lower Eastern Shore, 1960-65; mem. Worcester County com. Md. Hist. Trust, 1969—. Served from pvt. to maj. AUS, 1942-47. Mem. Am., Md. (exec. council 1963-64), Worcester County (pres. 1958-59) bar assns., Eastern Shore Police Assn. (pres. 1963-64), Worcester County Hist. Soc. (pres. 1962-63), Berlin C. of C. (pres. 1956-57), Am. Judicature Soc., Nat. Conf. State Trial Judges, Nat. Conf. Juvenile Ct. Judges, Am. Judges Assn., Am. Legion, Pi Sigma Alpha, Alpha Psi Omega, Alpha Tau Omega. Democrat. Methodist. Mason (Shriner, master 1958-59), Elk; mem. Order DeMolay (chmn. adv. bd. Berlin 1959-60), Order Eastern Star (patron 1955-56). Lion (pres. Berlin club 1957-58). Club: Nassawango Country (Snow Hill, Md.). Home: 3 Vine St Berlin MD 21811 Office: Ct House Snow Hill MD 21863

PREVEN, DAVID W., physician, educator; b. Scranton, Pa., May 19, 1937; s. Sam and Reva (Weinberg) P.; A.B., summa cum laude, Harvard, 1959, M.D., cum laude, 1963; m. Ruth Levinson, June 21, 1959; children—Eric Samuel, Anne, Joshua S. Intern, Univ. Hosp., Mpls., 1963-64; resident psychiatry Albert Einstein Coll. Medicine, Bronx, N.Y., 1964-67, NIMH fellow, 1969-70; dir. psychiat. liaison div. Bronx Municipal Hosp. Center, 1970-73; asst. prof. psychiatry Albert Einstein Coll. Medicine, 1970-76, asso. prof., 1976—, dir. student edn. psychiatry, 1973—. Served to maj. M.C., AUS, 1967-69. Diplomate Am. Bd. Psychiatry and Neurology. Fellow Am. Psychiat. Assn.; mem. AAUP, Am. Psychomatic Soc., Assn. for Academic Psychiatry (treas. 1976—), Eastern Assn. Sex Therapists, Assn. Dirs. Student Teaching Psychiatry. Office: Albert Einstein College of Medicine Dept Psychiatry 1300 Morris Park Ave Bronx NY 10461

PREVIN, ANDRE, composer, condr.; b. Berlin, Germany, Apr. 6, 1929; s. Jack and Charlotte (Epstein) P.; came to U.S., 1938, naturalized, 1943; student Berlin Conservatory, Paris Conservatory, privately with Pierre Monteux, Mario Castelmuovo-Todesco; m. Mia Farrow, Sept. 10, 1970 (div.); children—Matthew and Sascha (twins), Fletcher, Lark Song, Summer, Soon-Yi. Rec. artist classical music, 1946—; composer chamber music, cello concerto, guitar concerto, piano music, music for strings, serenades for violin, brass quintet, wind quintet, also song cycle on poems by Philip Larkin, Every Good Boy Deserves Favour, others; composer film scores Metro-Goldwyn-Mayer, 1950-59; guest condr. most maj. symphony orchs., U.S. Europe; rec. artist for RCA, EMI, English Decca; condr.-in-chief Houston Symphony, 1967-69; prin. condr. London Symphony Orch., 1968—; music dir. South Bank Music Festival, London, 1972-74, Pitts. Symphony, 1976—; guest condr. Covent Garden Opera, festivals in Salzburg, Edinburgh, Flanders, Vienna, Osaka, Prague; mem. faculty Guildhall Sch., London, Royal Acad. Music. Served with AUS, 1950-51. Recipient 4 Acad, awards, awards Nat. Grammophone Soc. Mem. Acad. Motion Picture Arts and Scis., Dramatists Guild, Brit. Composers Guild, Nat. Composers and Condrs. League. Club: Garrick. Author: Music Face to Face, 1971. Office: care Harrison/Parrott Ltd 22 Hillgate St London W8 England also care Pittsburgh Symphony Orch 600 Penn Ave Pittsburgh PA 15222

PREVOZNIK, STEPHEN JOSEPH, anesthesiologist; b. McAdoo, Pa., June 21, 1929; s. John George and Mary Margaret (Ficek) P.; R.N., St. Joseph Hosp. Sch. Nursing, Phila., 1951; B.S., U. Notre Dame, 1955; M.D., U. Pa., 1959; m. Rita Agnes Kellett, Aug. 20, 1955; children—Mary Therese, Stephen Joseph, John Cyril, Michael Edward, Margaret Anne, Rita Marie, Thomas William, Jean Marie. Intern Fitzgerald Mercy Hosp., Darby, Pa., 1959-60; resident anesthesia U. Pa., Phila., 1960-62; practice medicine, specializing in anesthesiology, Phila., 1962—; mem. staff U. Pa. Hosp., 1962—; prof. anesthesia, dir. clin. activities U. Pa., 1971—. Mem. Upper Darby (Pa.) Health Adv. Bd., 1972-74. Mem. Am., Pa., Phila. (pres.) socs. anesthesiologists, Internat. Anesthesia Research Soc. Contbr. to textbooks on anesthesiology. Home: 474 Fairfax Rd Drexel Hill PA 19026 Office: Dept Anesthesia Hosp U Pa Philadelphia PA 19104

PREWITT, JUDITH MARTHA SHIMANSKY, mathematician; b. Bklyn., Oct. 16, 1935; d. Charles Theodore and Rebecca (Sanders) Shimansky; student Harvard U., 1954; B.A. with high honors, Swarthmore Coll., 1957; M.A. in Math., U. Pa., 1959, postgrad., 1959-62, 65-66, Uppsala (Sweden) U., 1978; m. Richard Hickman Prewitt III, July 2, 1956 (div. 1971); 1 son, David Joshua. Asst. devel. engr. Burroughs Corp., Paoli, Pa., 1956-57, mathematician, 1958; mathematician, analyst programmer Auerbach Corp., Phila., 1961-62; asst. instr. dept. math. U. Pa., Phila., 1960-62, research asst., 1962, research mathematician, instr. dept. radiology Sch. Medicine, 1962-71; mathematician div. computer research and tech. NIH, Bethesda, Md., 1971—; vis. scientist dept. computer sci. and numerical analysis Uppsala U.; cons. Community Mental Health Center, Hahnemann Med. Coll.; cons. div. radiotherapy, dept. radiology and William J. Pepper Hematology Lab., Hosp. U. Pa. Mem. com. for cytology automation, diagnostic radiology advisory com., breast cancer diagnosis advisory com. Nat. Cancer Inst.; mem. automation research council Am. Assn. for Automatic Control; mem. com. on ultrasonic tissue characterization NSF; del. to numerous internat. confs; adviser NIH, Nat. Cancer Inst., NIMH, EPA, numerous others. Recipient award for sustained high quality work performance HEW/USPHS/NIH, 1973. Mem. Math. Assn. Am., Am. Assn. Women in Math., Am. Math. Soc., Cell Kinetics Soc., Classification Soc., Soc. Indsl. and Applied Math. (former chmn. Delaware Valley sect., mem. nat. com. on sects., writer career booklet), Classification Soc., Assn. Computing Machinery, Biomed. Engring. Soc. (charter mem.), Soc. for Analytical Cytology, Internat. Acad. Cytology, IEEE (sr. mem., mem. bd. automation research council, transactions reviewer), Mortar Board, Internat. Platform Assn., AAAS, Phi Beta Kappa, Sigma Xi. Editor: Image Pressing and Computer Graphics. Research applied math., pattern recognition and machine inteligence; decision-making in biomedicine; automatic analysis of biomed. images; nav. computers; math. modelling of tumor growth and cancer radiotherapy and chemotherapy optimization; computer models for investment portfolios; computer curricula in med. tng. Contbr. numerous articles to profl. jour. and books; reviewer. Home: 8008 Aberdeen Rd Bethesda MD 20014 Office: Div Computer Research and Technology NIH Bethesda MD 20014

PREZELSKI, FRANK JOSEPH, investment analyst; b. N.Y.C., Mar. 15, 1941; s. Anthony John and Juliette Florence (Arapin) P.; student W.Va. U., 1958-60; B.S. in Econs., Columbia U., 1968; postgrad. N.Y. U. Grad. Sch. Bus., 1968-70; m. Susan Lee Merril, Jan. 11, 1970; children—Benjamin M., Kate M. Investment analyst Coll. Retirement Equities Fund, N.Y.C., 1968-70, Ford Found., N.Y.C., 1970-73; v.p., investment analyst Chase Investors Mgmt. Corp., N.Y.C., 1973-77, Citibank, N.Y.C., 1977—. Dist. leader Democratic party, 1975-77; treas. Cortlandt (N.Y.) Dem. Com., 1976-77. Served with Intelligence Corps, U.S. Army, 1962-65. Chartered fin. analyst. Mem. Machinery Analysts N.Y. (pres. 1978-79), Elec. Products Group N.Y. (pres. 1975-76), N.Y. Soc. Securities Analysts, Fin. Analysts Fedn., Inst. Chartered Fin. Analysts, N.Y. Zool. Soc. Home:

340 Grand St Croton-on-Hudson NY 10520 Office: 153 E 53d St New York NY 10043

PRIBOR, HUGO CASIMER, physician, scientist, pathologist; b. Detroit, June 12, 1928; s. Benjamin H. and Wanda (Mioskowski) Pribors ky; B.S., St. Mary's Coll., Winona, Minn., 1949; M.S., St. Louis U., 1951, Ph.D., 1954, M.D., 1955; m. Judith Elinor Smith, Dec. 22, 1955; children—Jeffrey D., Elizabeth, Kathryn. Research asso. dept. pathology St. Louis U. Sch. Medicine, 1954-55; intern Providence Hosp., Detroit, 1955-56; resident pathology, Clin. Center, NIH, Bethesda, Md., 1956-59; sr. asst. surgeon USPHS, 1956-60; instr. pathology Bowman Gray Sch. Medicine, Winston-Salem, N.C., 1956-60; asso. pathologist Bon Secours Hosp., Grosse Pointe, Mich., 1960-63; dir. labs. Anderson Meml. Hosp., Mt. Clemens, Mich., 1963-64; chief pathologist, dir. dept. labs. Perth Amboy Gen. Hosp., 1964-73; pres., chmn. bd. Center for Lab. Medicine, Inc., Metuchen, N.J., 1973-78; exec. med. dir. MDS Health Group Inc., Highlands, N.J., 1978—; instr. pathology Wayne State U., 1962-64; asso. prof. chemistry Detroit U., 1960-64; clin. asso. prof. dept. pathology Med. Sch., Rutgers, The State U., 1966-68; vis. prof. biomed. sci. Rutgers U., 1971-76. Chmn. bd. St. Mary's Coll., Winona, Minn., 1972-73. Mem. A.M.A., Am. Soc. Clin. Pathologists, Coll. Am. Pathologists, Internat. Acad. Pathology, AAAS, Am. Fedn. Clin. Research, Am. Soc. Exptl. Pathology, N.J. Acad. Medicine (chmn. clin. pathology sect. 1965-66), N.J. Med. Soc. (chmn. blood commn. 1965-66), N.J. Pathology Soc. (chmn. blood commn. 1965-66) N.J. Soc. Pathologists (exec. com. 1965—), Sigma Xi. Clubs: N.Y. Yacht (N.Y.C.); Detroit Yacht. Contbr. articles to med. jours. Home: Monmouth Hills Highlands NJ 07732 Office: 7 Monmouth Hills Highlands NJ 07732

PRICE, ELY, dermatologist; b. N.Y.C., Aug. 9, 1932; s. Jacob and Mary (Flattau) P.; B.S. cum laude, City Coll., City U. N.Y., 1953; M.A., Ind. U., 1956; M.D., U. Lausanne (Switzerland), 1964; m. Harriet Shapiro, Mar. 30, 1969; children—Jeremy, Andrew. Intern, Brookdale Med. Center, Bklyn., 1964-65, asst. resident, 1965-66; resident in dermatology Kings County Hosp., Bklyn., 1966-68; chief resident in dermatology State U.-Kings County Med. Center, Bklyn., 1968-69; asst. attending Maimonides Med. Center, Bklyn., 1969-71, asso. attending, 1971-75, attending, 1975—; practice medicine specializing in dermatology, Bklyn., 1969—; asst. attending Luth. Med. Center, Bklyn., 1970, attending, 1973; attending dermatologist Kings County Hosp. Center, Bklyn., 1974—; clin. asst. prof. dermatology Downstate Med. Center, State U. N.Y., Bklyn., 1975—. Diplomate Am. Bd. Dermatology. Fellow A.C.P., N.Y. Acad. Medicine; mem. Bklyn. Dermatologic Soc. (pres. 1977-78), Am. Acad. Dermatology, AMA, N.Y. Med. Soc., N.Y. Dermatologic Soc., Kings County Med. Soc., Contbr. articles in field to med. jours. Home: 48 Kent St Staten Island NY 10306 Office: 7502 Ridge Blvd Brooklyn NY 11209

PRICE, FLOYD MILTON, educator; b. Dayton, Tenn., July 2, 1928; s. Manuel and Sue (Caudle) P.; B.S., Middle Tenn. State Coll., Murfreesboro, 1954; postgrad. U. Wis., summers 1962, 63, 65, 66, U. Tenn., summers 1969-71, Interam. U., Mex., summers 1960-61. Tchr. Spanish and history North East (Md.) High Sch., 1954—. Travel grantee Wye Inst., 1967. Mem. Assn. Am. Geographers, Pan Am. Inst. Geography and History, Conf. Latin Am. Geographers, Am. Assn. Tchrs. Spanish and Portuguese, Nat. Trust Historic Preservation, Nat. Council Social Studies, Cecil County Classroom Tchrs. Assn., Md. Tchrs. Assn., NEA, Md. Fgn. Lang. Assn., Am. Council on Teaching Fgn. Langs., History Tchrs. Assn. Md., Orgn. Am. Historians, Soc. of History Edn., Am. Assn. for State and Local History, Rhea County Hist. Soc. Editor: History of North East, Maryland, 1966. Home: Route 1 North East MD 21901

PRICE, GERALD LOUIS, educator; b. Alexandria, Va., Dec. 14, 1944; s. Martin Jess and Madge Miller (Snoddy) P.; B.A., Columbia Union Coll., 1967; M.A., Cath. U. Am., 1972; m. Elaine Priscilla Alden, Aug. 23, 1965; children—Richard Edwin, Helen Michele. Tchr., Lynchburg (Va.) Elementary Sch., 1967-68, Beltsville (Md.) Elementary Sch., 1968-69; instr. to asso. prof. English, Columbia Union Coll., 1969—. Mem. Modern Lang. Assn., Nat. Council Tchrs. of English, Shakespeare Assn. Am. Seventh-day Adventist. Research on structuralist literary theory as related to Shakespearean dramatic systems. Home: 7637 Carroll Ave Takoma Park MD 20012 Office: Columbia Union Coll Takoma Park MD 20012

PRICE, KENNETH E(LBERT), research adminstr.; b. Cumberland, Md., Aug. 12, 1926; B.S., U. Md., 1950, M.S., 1952, Ph.D. in Bacteriology, 1954. Head dept. bacteriology, agrl. research and devel. center Charles Pfizer & Co., Inc., 1954-60; coordinator cancer research program, then asst. dir. microbiol. research Bristol Labs., Syracuse, N.Y., 1965-70, dir. microbiol. research, 1970-77, asso. dir. research and devel., 1977—; chmn. med. chem. sect. Gordon Research Conf., 1977. Served with USN, 1944-46. Mem. AAAS, Am. Soc. Microbiology, N.Y. Acad. Scis., Am. Chem. Soc. Editorial bd. Antimicrob. Agts. and Chemotherapy. Address: Bristol Labs Thompson Rd Syracuse NY 13201

PRICE, RALPH MORTON, physician; b. Montreal, Can., Nov. 25, 1939; s. Clarence Cecil and Laurene Beatrice (Walker) P.; B.A., McMaster U., Hamilton, Ont., 1961; M.D., U. Toronto, 1965; m. M. Patricia Hoare, Jan. 31, 1962; children—Kimberley Ann, Matthew John Galen, Taylor David. Jr. intern Toronto Western Hosp., 1965-66; physician Bklyn. Med. Centre, Brooklin, Ont., 1966-68, Med. Assos. of Port Perry (Ont.), 1968—; chief med. staff Community Hosp., Port Perry, 1975—. Mem. Ont. Med. Assn., Coll. Physicians and Surgeons Ont. Conservative. Anglican. Antiquarian, folk art authority. Office: Paxton St Port Perry ON L0B 1N0 Canada

PRICE, RICHARD CARR, engring. and mfg. co. exec.; b. Chicago Heights, Ill., Nov. 12, 1926; s. Franklin Carr and Galene (Neher) P.; B.S. with high honors, U. Ill., 1950, M.S., 1951; m. Margaret May Phelps, July 26, 1975; children by previous marriage—Karen, Barbara, Sandra, David, Robert, Carol; stepchildren—John R. and Carolyn Howard. Engr., Sta. WILL, Urbana, Ill., 1947-48; researcher radar weather Ill. State Water Survey, Urbana, 1948-49; faculty elec. engring. U. Ill., Urbana, 1950-51; engr. Sperry Gyroscope Co., Great Neck, N.Y., 1951-57, engring. supr., 1957-64, engr. mgr. Sperry Systems Mgmt. div. Sperry Rand Corp., Reston, Va., also N.Y. and W.Ger., 1964—. Chmn. fin. com. Westbury United Methodist Ch., N.Y., 1967-69, chmn. adminstrv. bd., 1969. Served with USNR, 1944-46. Mem. IEEE (chmn. L.I. sec. 1965-66), Assn. Old Crows, Am. Def. Preparedness Assn. Republican. Methodist. Patentee in field. Home: 3711 Munsey St Wheaton MD 20906 Office: 11517 Sunset Hills Rd Reston VA 22090

PRICE, RICHARD LEE, lawyer; b. N.Y.C., Sept. 19, 1940; s. Saul and Claire (Bernstein) P.; B.A., Roanoke Coll., 1957; J.D., N.Y. Law Sch., 1964; m. Carolyn Small, Oct. 7, 1965; children—Lisa, Howard. Legal asst. N.Y. State Dept. Law, 1962-64, Arnold D. Roseman, N.Y.C., 1965; admitted to N.Y. bar, 1965; atty. Zoloto, Karger & Zurkow, N.Y.C., 1965-67, Harry H. Lipsig, N.Y.C., 1967-69; law sec. to judge Civil Ct., N.Y.C., 1969-76, chief law asst. charge law dept., 1976—. Pres. Arbitrators Assn. Small Claims Ct.; bd. dirs. N.Y. Consumers Assembly, Grand St. Consumer Soc., Fedn. Coops.; mem. N.Y. State Bd. Certified Shorthand Reporting, 1978-81. Chmn., Manhattan Pub. Safety Com., 1972-77; lt. N.Y.C. Aux. Police; mem. citizens advisory council to Pres. N.Y.C. Council, 1969; chmn. East River House Com.; active United Jewish Appeal, Fedn. Jewish Philanthropies; vice chmn. N.Y.C. Community Sch. Bd., 1972; mem. Manhattan Borough Pres.'s Planning Bd., 1969-77. Pres., Lower East Side Democratic Assn.; county committeeman Dem. party. Mem. Civil Ct. Law Secs. (pres.), Am. Judges Assn., Am., N.Y. State, Customs bar assns., N.Y. County Lawyers Assn., Assn. Bar City N.Y., Assn. Trial Lawyers Am., N.Y. State Assn. Trial Lawyers, Ednl. Alliance Alumni Assn. (v.p.), Pi Lambda Phi, Phi Delta Phi. Jewish (dir. synagogue). K.P.; mem. B'nai B'rith. Clubs: Executive Gun (N.Y.C.), Lions. Home: 577 Grand St New York City NY 10002 Office: 111 Centre St New York City NY 10013

PRICE, ROBERT EDMUNDS, civil engr.; b. Lyndhurst, N.J., Jan. 8, 1926; s. William Evans and Charlotte Ann (Dyson) P.; B.S. in Civil Engring., Dartmouth Coll., 1946; M.S., Princeton, 1947; m. Margaret Akerman Menard, June 28, 1947; children—Robert Edmunds, Alexander Menard. Mgr., P&S Standard Vacuum Oil Co., N.Y., London and Sumatra, 1947-55; project engr. Metcalf & Eddy, Cons. Engrs., Boston, 1956-59; structural engr. Lummis Co., Cons. Engrs., Newark, 1960-61; mgr. engring. materials Interpace Corp., Wharton, N.J., 1961—; cons. cement and concrete design and constrn. Mem. Denville (N.J.) Bd. Health, 1963-66, chmn., 1966; mem. Denville Bd. Adjustment, 1966-69. Served with USNR, 1943-46. Registered profl. engr., N.J. Fellow Am. Concrete Inst.; mem. ASTM (chmn. subcom. spl. cements 1976—). Episcopalian. Home: Lake Openaka Openaki Rd Danville NJ 07834 Office: 150 N Main St Wharton NJ 07885

PRICE, STEPHEN JR., III, social worker; b. Birmingham, Ala., Feb. 23, 1935; s. Stephen B. and Mary E. (Wright) P.; A.A., S.I. Community Coll., 1975; B.A., Richmond Coll., 1976; m. Lillian Bell Waters, Jan. 4, 1956; children—Stephen L., Ingrid, Jason R., Monique Y., Eric. Dir. Youth Econ. Devel. Program, S.I., 1970-72; bd. dirs. N.Y.C. Addiction Service Agy. Summer Playstreet Projects, 1973-74; counselor Richmond Coll., 1976-77; cons. S.I. Community Corp., 1968—, Youth Programs, 1973-76; laborer CETA, N.Y.C. Environ. Protection Adminstrn., 1977—. Committeeman Richmond County, 1974—. Served with U.S. Army, 1955-57. Mem. Am. Personnel and Guidance Assn., So. Christian Leadership Conf. (pres. S.I. chpt. 1972-73), Am. Legion. Clubs: Elks, Masons. Home: 77 Hill St Staten Island NY 10304 Office: 648 Bay St Staten Island NY 10304

PRICE, WALLACE WALTER, bus. cons.; b. East St. Louis, Ill., Mar. 10, 1921; s. Sam P. and Pennie (Johnson) P.; B.Ed., So. Ill. U., 1942; postgrad. Mt. Vernon Sch. Law, 1947-48, U. Md., 1948-49; M.S., Va. State Coll., 1953; postgrad. U. Pa., 1959, Sch. of Law Seton Hall U., Newark, 1977-79; m. Hortense M. McWoods, Dec. 1, 1944; children—Sandra D., Wallace Walter II, Catherine A. Inducted as pvt., Q.M.C., U.S. Army, 1943, advanced through grades to lt. col., 1963; major assignments include chief of logistics U.S. Army Security Agy., Europe, 1960-63; Far Eastern commd., Japan, 1949-51, Korea, 1950-51; dir. tng., asso. prof. mil. sci. tactics dept., Comdt of Cadets Va. State Coll., Petersburg, 1951-53; plans officer U.S. Army Gen. Depot, 1954-57, others; ret., 1964; mgr. of procedures and grant of operating authority, Olin Corp., Stamford, Conn., 1964-71; asst. v.p. of personnel Seatrain Shipbuilding Corp., Bklyn. Navy Yard, 1972; pres. Adminstrv. Mgmt., Teaneck, N.J., 1972-73; dir. Urban Affairs and Equal Opportunity, Pan Am. World Airways, N.Y.C. 1972-75; pres., co-founder The Edges Group, Inc., N.Y.C., 1969-77; corporate mgr. Affirmative Action Programs Becton Dickinson & Co., Rutherford, N.J., 1976-77, cons., 1976—; spl. cons. Gov. of V.I. Planning Group, 1974; dir. First Nat. City Bank Capital Corp., N.Y.C., 1972-74. Mem. Advisory Bd. for Community Relations, Teaneck, N.J., 1965-76; pres. Urban League for Bergen County (N.J.), 1968-70; council man, Teaneck, 1977-78; chmn. affirmative action com. Bd. Edn., Teaneck, N.J. 1976—; v.p. European Congress of Am. Parents and Tchrs., 1962-63; bd. dirs. Bergen County United Fund, 1972—, Community Chest, 1970—; mem. affirmative action com. N.J. Sports and Expn. Authority, 1974. Decorated Air medal: recipient One of 10 Great Men of Bergen County (N.J.) award, 1970; Outstanding Achievement award Urban League of Bergen County, 1972. Mem. Nat. Market Developers Assn. (treas. 1965-67), Ret. Officers Assn., Parents of West Point Cadets Assn., Defense Logistical Assn., Bus. and Profl. Men's Orgn. (pres. 1968-70), NAACP (life), Alpha Phi Alpha (Ann. Merit award eastern region 1960), Mu Tau Pi. Democrat. Methodist. Club: Masons. Author: (poems) Sweet and Low, 1955; editor: Atomic Observer, 1946; asso. editor So. Ill. U. newspaper, 1940-42. Home: 585 W Englewood Ave Teaneck NJ 07666 Office: 91 S Harrison St East Orange NJ 07018

PRICE, WARREN ALEXANDER, assn. exec.; b. Wilmington, N.C., Apr. 16, 1942; s. Warren Kimball and Katie Teresa P.; ed. high sch.; m. Linda Jane Vander Veen, June 10, 1974. Salesman, Standard Electronics Co., Dover, Del., 1959-64; owner, operator Diamond Motor Sports Co., Camden, Del., 1964—; mng. gen. agt. Internat. Underwriters Ins. Co., Camden, 1972—; owner, operator Insura Cycle Co., splty. ins. agency, Camden, 1972—; pres. Del. Motorcycle Dealers Assn., 1972—; promoter Am. Motorcycle Assn. Grand Nat. Championship, 1975, Engine Specialties Inc. Mem. Del. Gov.'s Task Force on Off-road vehicles, 1974—. Served with USNR, 1963-64. Mem. Motorcycle Industry Council, Del. Ins. Agts. Republican. Baptist. Home: 1990 Mitten St Dover DE 19901 Office: PO Box 13 Route 13 Camden DE 19934

PRICKETT, WILLIAM FRANKLIN, computer scientist; b. Pine Bluff, Ark., July 21, 1941; s. Percy Edward and Hazel Elizabeth (Parnell) P.; came to Can., 1968; B.A. magna cum laude with honors, Vanderbilt U., 1963; M.S., Ind. U., 1965, Ph.D., 1968; m. Dorothy Osborne Holt, June 8, 1968; children—Robert Percy, Catherine Hazel. Physicist, Naval Research Lab., Washington, 1963; NASA trainee Ind. U., Bloomington, 1963-66; postdoctoral fellow U. Man. (Can.), Winnipeg, 1968-70; systems analyst Revenue Can., Ottawa, Ont., 1970-74, sect. head taxation computer systems, 1974—. Mem. Am. Phys. Soc., Canadian Assn. Physicists, Data Processing Inst., Canadian Aviation Hist. Soc., Civil Service Recreational Assn., Sigma Xi (asso.). Designer computer benchmark system, 1973; initiator Revenue Can. computer hardware monitoring program, 1973-74; developed Revenue Can. taxation, quality assurance for IBM systems, 1974-75, head online data entry project for remote taxation centers, 1977-78. Home: 671 Mayer St Gatineau PQ J8R 1H5 Canada Office: Revenue Can Taxation 875 Heron Rd Ottawa ON K1A 0L8 Canada

PRIEST, DORMAN EATON, optical engr.; b. Canton, N.Y., Mar. 2, 1915; s. Ward Curtiss and Barbara (Cramer) P.; B.S. in Physics with honors, St. Lawrence U., 1937; postgrad. U. Mich., 1937-39; m. Katherine Luella Mawhinney, July 1, 1944; children—Ward Curtiss, Barbara Cramer, Terri Coburn; m. 2d, Miriam Ida Marshall, Nov. 11, 1978. Research asso. Harvard, Cambridge, Mass., 1944-45; v.p., chief engr. Calidyne Co. div. LTV Corp., Winchester, Mass., 1955-62; tech. dir. Research & Control Instruments Co., Westwood, Mass., 1962-69; v.p. advanced devel. Spectrametrics, Inc., Burlington, Mass., 1969-70; prin. engr. Polaroid Corp., Waltham, Mass., 1971—. Mem. Inst. Environmental Sci. (nat. dir. 1960), Soc. Applied Spectroscopy, Optical Soc. Am., Acoustical Soc. Am., Beta Theta Pi, Sigma Pi Sigma. Republican. Universalist-Unitarian. Patentee in field. Home: 19 Diana Ln Lexington MA 02173 Office: 565 Technology Sq Boston MA 02139

PRIEST, EVA LOUISE, pub. service assn. exec.; b. Indpls., May 16, 1935; d. Jesse Lynn and Laura Mae (Reed) P.; student Ind. U., 1962-66; B.S., Ind. State U., 1976; postgrad. George Mason U., 1977-78; 1 son, David Lee Fisher. Aquatic dir. Central YMCA, Indpls., 1962-66; dir. safety services ARC, Evansville, Ind., 1966-72, water safety specialist, Washington, 1973-77, asst. nat. dir. water safety, 1977—; cons. Canadian Red Cross Soc., 1974—, govts. of Alta., Can., 1975—, Dept. of Edn. of Alaska, 1976—, Dept. HEW, 1973—; guest lectr. Pa. State U., 1975—. Robert Kipputh scholar, 1971-72. Mem. Council of Nat. Cooperation in Aquatics (treas. of bd. 1976-78), Nat. Consortium on Phys. Edn. and Recreation for Handicapped, Alpha Chi, Psi Chi. Author: Adapted Aquatics, 1977; Focus on Ability (film), 1974; editor: Fun in Aquatics, 1978. Home: 10338 Layton Hall Fairfax VA 22030 Office: 17th and D Sts NW Washington DC 20006

PRIEST, JEROME, computer corp. exec.; b. Providence, Oct. 16, 1931; s. Ira Marcus and Mildred Edna P.; A.B., Yale U., 1953; M.B.A., Columbia U., 1957; m. Christine Lynn, Dec. 16, 1961; children—Julia Marie, Alexander Raphael. In sales mgmt., gen. mgmt. IBM, White Plains, N.Y., 1957-67; pres. Computer Resources Corp., Darien, Conn., 1967—; pres. Graphicenter E. Ltd., Darien, 1975—; vis. prof. Norwalk Community Coll.; dir. 630 Holding Co., Product Design Corp. Bd. dirs. Nat. Multiple Sclerosis Soc. So. Fairfield County; bd. dirs. Alumni Assn. Bus. Sch. Columbia, Opera New Eng., Norwalk Hist. Soc. Served with C.E., U.S. Army, 1953-55. Contbr. articles to mags. Office: 1171 Post Rd Darien CT 06820

PRIESTLEY, ELDON BRUCE, chem. physicist; b. Trochu, Alta., Can., Sept. 25, 1943; s. Samuel and Alberta Pearl (Gay) P.; came to U.S., 1965; B.Sc., U. Alta., 1965; Ph.D., Calif. Inst. Tech., 1969; m. Fern Joyce Sharp, Sept. 1, 1961; children—Eldon Scott, Brian Matthew. Research fellow div. engring. and applied physics Harvard, 1969-71; mem. tech. staff David Sarnoff Research Center, RCA Labs., Princeton, N.J., 1971-77; staff chemist, group head corporate research labs. Exxon Research and Engring. Co., Linden, N.J., 1977—. Recipient Outstanding Achievement award RCA Labs., 1975. Mem. AAAS, Am. Phys. Soc., Am. Vacuum Soc. Author: (with Peter J. Wojtowicz and Ping Sheng) Introduction to Liquid Crystals, 1975; contbr. articles to profl. jours. Home: 83 Oak Creek Rd East Windsor NJ 08520 Office: Exxon Research Engring Co PO Box 45 Linden NJ 07036

PRINCE, ELMER WOODWARD, JR., educator; b. Morgantown, W.Va., Nov. 15, 1930; s. Elmer Woodward and Rosetta (Reed) P.; B.S. in Civil Engring., W.Va. U., 1952, M.A. in Psychology, 1965; M.S. in Civil Engring., N.C. State U., 1954; m. Mildred Helen (Bimi) Atwater, Dec. 19, 1970; 1 dau., Susan. Design engr. firm Lockwood, Kessler & Bartlett, Syosset, N.Y., 1957-61; engring. psychologist McDonnell Aircraft Co., St. Louis, 1963-66; asst. prof. dept. psychology Western Md. Coll., Westminster, 1966-70; asso. prof. behavioral scis. Berkshire Community Coll., Pittsfield, Mass., 1972—, chmn. dept., 1973-75, 77; cons., psychologist Carroll County Mental Health Clinic, Westminster, 1969-70; singer, musician, part-time 1962-64, 71-72. Capt., pilot Civil Air Patrol, 1968—, Berkshire County Civil Def., 1978—. Served to capt. USAF, 1952-57. Mem. Am. Psychol. Assn., Assn. Mormon Counsellors Psychotherapists, Phi Delta Kappa, Chi Epsilon, Tau Beta Pi, Psi Chi, Phi Delta Theta (province pres.). Mem. Ch. Jesus Christ Latter-day Saints (elder, br. pres., missionary). Office: Berkshire Community Coll Pittsfield MA 01201

PRINCE, HERBERT NORMAN, exptl. biologist; b. N.Y.C., Aug. 8, 1929; s. Edward and Lillian G. (Fenenbock) P.; A.B., N.Y. U., 1950; Ph.D., U. Conn., 1956; m. Leah F. Berman, Jan. 30, 1955; children—Daniel, Richard, Robert. Bacteriologist, N.Y.C. Health Dept., 1950; NIH Pub. Health Research fellow U. Conn., 1953-56; research biologist Wallace & Tiernan, Inc., Belleville, N.J., 1956-60; virologist, asst. dir. chemotherapy Hoffmann-La Roche, Inc., Nutley, N.J., 1960-70; pres. Gibraltar Biol. Labs., Inc., Fairfield, N.J., 1970—, also dir. Adj. prof. biology Fairleigh Dickinson U., 1957-71, Seton Hall U., 1970-71; cons. microbiology, infectious diseases St. Michael's Med. Center, Newark, 1972—; adj. prof. microbiology Rutgers U., 1979—. Served with M.C., AUS, 1950-52. Fellow Am. Acad. Microbiology, N.J. Acad. Medicine; mem. Am. Soc. for Microbiology (exec. com. N.J. br. 1977—), N.Y. Acad. Scis., Soc. Exptl. Biology and Medicine, Sigma Xi. Jewish (sec. congregation, dir. 1969-71). Contbr. articles to profl. jours. Co-discoverer Procarbazine for treatment Hodgkins Disease, 1960-67. Office: 23 Just Rd Fairfield NJ 07006

PRINCE, JOSEPH JOHN, interior designer; b. Trenton, N.J., Dec. 10, 1949; s. John Edward and Mary Agnes (Moran) P.; B.A., Monmouth Coll., 1972. Asst. decorator Levitz Furniture Corp., Cherry Hill br., 1973, mgr. accessory dept. King of Prussia (Pa.) br., 1974, metro accessory coordinator visual merchandising, 1975—; tchr. art, Asbury Park, N.J., 1972. Mem. Monmouth Coll. Alumni Assn. Democrat. Roman Catholic. Home: Church Rd Titusville NJ 08560 Office: 201 Allendale Rd King of Prussia PA 19040

PRINCE, LEON MAXIMILIAN, chemist; b. N.Y.C., Jan. 8, 1911; s. Leon and Clara Pearl (Tanenbaum) P.; A.B., Columbia, 1931, M.A., 1933; Mech. Engr., Mass. Inst. Tech., 1931; m. Adelaide Roslyn Wald, May 24, 1942; children—Judith (Mrs. John McDonald Delehanty), Alice (Mrs. B Smith Hopkins III). Chemist, Am. Home Products Corp., Jersey City, 1938-40; engr. Chem. Warfare Service, Edgewood Arsenal, Md., 1942-43; chemist, group leader Manhattan Project, Columbia, 1943-46; owner Emulsion Chem. Co., S.I., N.Y., 1946-54; mgr. emulsion devel. Reichhold Chems., Elizabeth, N.J., 1955-61; research scientist Lever Bros. Co., Edgewater, N.J., 1961-76; cons. surface chemist, 1976—. Mem. Recreation Commn., Town Westfield, N.J., 1963-72. Mem. Am. Chem. Soc., Research Soc. Am., Am. Inst. Chemists (former fellow), Beta Sigma Rho. Editor: Microemulsions, Theory and Practice (author 4 chpts.), 1977; co-editor Biological Horizons in Surface Science (author chpt. on emulsions), 1973. Home: 7 Plymouth Rd Westfield NJ 07090

PRINCE, ROY WEBSTER, JR., printing cons.; b. Washington, Aug. 4, 1916; s. Roy Webster and Jeannette Cunningham (Harrison) P.; B.S., Coll. William and Mary, 1937; S.B., Mass. Inst. Tech., 1940; m. Mary Palmer Wilson, July 31, 1940; children—Alan, Douglas. Instr. physics dept. Mass. Inst. Tech., Cambridge, 1939-41, mem. staff office sci. research and devel., 1941-45; engr. Bell Telephone Labs., 1945-48; with Am. Newspaper Pubs. Assn. Research Inst., Easton, Pa., 1948-64, dir. research, 1954-64; dir. research graphic arts products W.R. Grace & Co., Cambridge, 1964-74, cons., 1974-75; cons. Diebold Group, 1964; cons. printing, South Sutton, N.H., 1975—. Bd. dirs. Easton Hosp., 1961-64; mem. Easton Area Sch. Com., 1959-64, v.p., 1961-63; pres. Riegelsville (Pa.) Bd. Edn., 1956-63; selectman Town of Sutton (N.H.), 1977—. Recipient Army and Navy award for research and devel., 1947. Mem. Soc. Printing Tech. (London, hon.), IEEE, Am. Phys. Soc., Tech. Assn. for Graphic Arts (pres. 1969), Sigma Xi, Sigma Pi Sigma. Republican.

Congregationalist. Patentee in field. Home: Box 3 South Sutton NH 03273

PRINCEVALLE, ROBERT, elec. engr.; b. San Jose, Calif., Apr. 15, 1922; s. Anthony and Ada (Rossi) P.; B.S. in Elec. Engring., Calif. State Poly. Coll., 1952; M.M.A., U. R.I., 1970; m. Jacqueline M. Owens, Mar. 6, 1957; children—Mark Owen, Phillip Ryan, Heidi Erin. With Electric Boat div. General Dynamics Corp., Groton, Conn., 1953—, various engring. positions in design and constr. of submarines, until 1965, in deep submergence devel. 1965—, project engr., 1965-70, engring. mgr. Mark II Deep Diving System for Sea Lab. III Operations, 1970; engring. mgr. Tracor Inc., Rockville, Md., 1975—; v.p. U.F.O. Inc., Lakeville, Conn., 1970-75; flight instr. Served with submarine force USN, 1941-47. Mem. Marine Tech. Soc. (past chmn. So. New Eng. chpt.). Designer, builder urethane foam houses. Home: 28 Laurel Hill Dr Niantic CT 06350

PRINGLE, STUART HOUGHTON, JR., lawyer; b. Greenwich, Conn., June 3, 1937; s. Stuart Houghton and Elizabeth Pierson (Child) P.; B.A., Yale, 1959; J.D., U. Mich., 1967; LL.M., N.Y. U., 1971. Admitted to N.Y. State bar, 1968, since practiced in N.Y.C.; asso. atty. firm Thacher, Proffitt & Wood, 1967-71, partner, 1971—. Served to lt. USNR, 1959-65. Mem. Am., N.Y. State bar assns., Assn. Bar City N.Y. Clubs: University (N.Y.C.). Home: 225 E 36th St New York City NY 10016 Office: 40 Wall St New York City NY 10005

PRISCH, ROBERT ALLERTON, investment co. exec.; b. Warsaw, N.Y., May 7, 1920; s. Raymond Todd and Ruth Marie (Rice) P.; B.M.E., Cornell U., 1943; m. Betty Brooks Coit, May 27, 1946; children—Stephanie Brooks, Cary Perkins. Pres., Allerton Chem. Co., Inc., Rochester, N.Y., 1949-65, Brooks Research, Inc., Rochester, 1957-65; partner G.D.B. Bonbright & Co., Rochester, 1970-74; chmn. bd. Quality Measurement Systems, Inc., Rochester, 1976—; dir. LSB Corp., Inc., Rochester, Erdle Preforating Co., Inc., J. Nelson Pruitt Co. Chmn. chem. engring. adv. com. U. Rochester, 1959-63; fin. chmn. Rochester Republican city council campaign, 1976. Mem. Soc. Fin. Analysts. Clubs: Council (Rochester); Genesee Valley, Cornell. Address: 1170 East Ave Rochester NY 14607

PRISCO, NICHOLAS ALLEN, hosp. adminstr.; b. Englewood, N.J., Aug. 4, 1943; s. Nicholas and Ruth Esther (Allen) P.; A.A., Mt. San Antonio Coll., 1965; B.A., U. Calif. at Riverside, 1967; M.Hosp. and Health Services Adminstrn., Cornell U., Ithaca, N.Y., 1973; m. Sarah Jane Watson, Aug. 16, 1969; children—Kimberly Ann, Ginger Marie, Nicholas Edwin. Asst. admistr. Tompkins County Hosp., Ithaca, 1973-75; adminstr. Little Falls (N.Y.) Hosp., 1975—; mem. exec. bd. Regional Perinatal Program, Upstate Med. Center, Syracuse, N.Y., 1976—; mem. Herkimer County (N.Y.) Pub. Health Council, 1975—; internship preceptor, health adminstrn. program Ithaca Coll., 1973-75; residency preceptor, health adminstrn. program State U. N.Y. at Utica, 1976—. Served to Capt. M.S.C., U.S. Army, 1967-71; Vietnam. Decorated Bronze Star. Mem. Am. Coll. Hosp. Adminstrs., Am., N.Y. State, Central N.Y. (dir. 1977—) hosp. assns. Clubs: Little Falls Rotary, Civic. Home: 25 Top Notch Rd Little Falls NY 13365 Office: 140 Burwell St Little Falls NY 13365

PRITCHARD, HIRAM BERT, III, plastics specifications cons.; b. Elmira, N.Y., Oct. 17, 1927; s. Hiram Bert and Ethel Marie (Hanna) P.; A.S., St. Lawrence U., Canton, N.Y., 1950; postgrad. U. Rochester (N.Y.), Rochester Inst. Tech.; m. Sally Noonan, Feb. 14, 1953; children—Hiram Bert, James E., David G., Dianne E. Color lab. technician Eastman Kodak Co., Rochester, 1953-56; indsl. sales engr. Chamberlin Rubber Co., Rochester, 1956-67, sales mgr., 1967-70; engaged in sales and mktg. Celanese Piping Systems, Inc., Louisville, 1970-75, indsl. thermoplastics cons., 1975—; project mgr. reconstrn. Lady Chapel, Episcopal Cathedral Ch. of Christ, 1978—; dir. Scott Pump Co., 1961-64. Regional coordinator blood program ARC, 1973-74; rector's warden St. Marys Episcopal Ch., Phila., 1977—; bd. dirs. Finger Lakes Conf., Inc., 1974—; mem. bldg. com. Cathedral Village Retirement Community, Phila., 1977—; mem. standing com. Episc. Diocese of Rochester, 1973-75. Served with USN, 1944-48, USMCR, 1950-52; Korea. Music scholar Eastman Sch. Music, Rochester, 1939-41; Art scholar Meml. Art Gallery, Rochester, 1937-38; recipient Distinguished Service award Rochester Jaycees, 1959; mem. LaCrosse Found., Johns Hopkins U., 1976—. Mem. Constrn. Specifications Inst., Welsh Soc. Phila. Republican. Club: Masons. Home: 2303 N Gilinger Rd Lafayette Hill PA 19444 Office: PO Box Cornwells Heights PA 19020

PRITCHARD, NORMAN HENRY, II, poet; b. N.Y.C., Oct. 22, 1939; s. Norman Henry and Winnie Ursula (Ramsey) P.; A.B., N.Y. U., 1961, postgrad. Inst. Fine Arts, 1961-63; postgrad. Columbia, 1962. Author: The Matrix: Poems, 1960-1970, 1970; EECCHOOEESS, 1971. Co-chmn. nat. standing com. on poetry Am. Festival Negro Arts, 1963-64; poet-in-residence Friends Sem., N.Y.C., 1968-75; instr. New Sch. for Social Research, N.Y.C., 1969-75; project coordinator Am. Mus. Natural History, N.Y.C., 1976—; asso. project dir. artists project Cultural Council Found., N.Y.C., 1977—. Recipient stipend Abraham Woursell Found., Austria, 1969-73; Carnegie Fund for Authors grantee, 1976-77. Mem. Asia Soc., Nat. Trust for Historic Preservation, St. George's Soc. N.Y. Home: 871 St Marks Ave Brooklyn NY 11213

PRITCHARD, WILBUR L., engr.; b. N.Y.C., May 31, 1923; s. Harmon and Jessie (Roth) P.; B.S., Coll. City N.Y., 1943; postgrad. Mass. Inst. Tech., 1948-52; m. Kathleen Hunton Moss, Apr. 24, 1949; children—Hugh Arthur, Sarah Margaret, and Ruth Wells. Br. mgr. microwave and transmitter br. Raytheon Co., 1950-58, dept. mgr. surface radar dept., 1958-59, mgr. engring. surface radar and navigation ops., 1959-60, dir. engring. Europe, 1960-62, group dir. communications satellite systems Aerospace Corp., El Segundo, Calif., 1962-67; v.p., dir. labs. Communications Satellite Corp., Washington, 1967-73; pres. Fairchild Space & Electronics Co., Fairchild Industries, Inc., 1973-74, Satellite Systems Engring., Inc., 1974—. Recipient USAF Systems Command award, 1967; Aerospace Communications award, 1972. Registered profl. engr., Mass., Md. Fellow IEEE, Am. Inst. Aeros. and Astronautics (dir.); mem. Eta Kappa Nu. Home: 9201 Laurel Oak Dr Bethesda MD 20034 Office: 7315 Wisconsin Ave Washington DC 20014

PRITCHETT, JOHN PERRY, historian, educator; b. Brooks, Calif., June 3, 1902; s. John Wesley and Derinda (Clark) P.; A.B., Stanford, 1921, A.M., 1922; grad. student U. Minn., 1922-23; M.Litt., Oxford U., 1927; Ph.D., Queen's Univ., Kingston, Can., 1928. Teaching fellow U. Minn., 1922-23; asst. prof. Macalester Coll., St. Paul, 1923-26; part time lectr. U. Minn., 1924-25; lectr. Queen's U., 1928-29; asst. prof. Russell Sage Coll., Troy, N.Y., 1929-30; asso. prof. U. N.D., 1930-35, Vassar, 1935-38; mem. faculty Queens Coll. City of N.Y., 1938-40, asst. prof., 1940-47, asso. prof. history, 1947-50, faculty grad. div. Bklyn. Coll., 1939-50; prof. history and social studies Trenton Jr. Coll. and Sch. Indsl. Arts, Trenton, 1953—, dean of students, 1954-63, pres., 1963-67; mem. summer faculty U. Wash., 1925, Queen's U., Can., intermittently, 1926-40; guest lectr. history Am. Coll. Paris and The Sorbonne, 1967-68, U. London, Oxford U., Cambridge U., 1970. Pres. Jr. Coll. Council Middle Atlantic States. Chmn. Trenton Tercentenary Com., 1962-63, 62-64. Spl. cons. Adj. Gen. Office: 1943. Recipient Fellowship in Econs., Found. Econs. Edn., 1955. Fellow Royal Hist. Soc., Internat. Inst. Arts and Letters; mem. Am., Can., Miss. Valley, Am. Cath. hist. assns., Minn., L.I., N.Y., U.S. Catholic (trustee 1949-55), Trenton hist. socs. (pres. 1964-66), Hudson Bay Record Soc., Greater Trenton C. of C., Phi Beta Kappa, Phi Alpha Theta, Alpha Phi Zeta, Pi Gamma Mu. Clubs: Rotary, Carteret (Trenton). Author: Canada and the Red River, 1928; Calhoun, His Defence of the South, 1937; The Red River Valley, 1942; Christianity and America, An American History (with John Meng and others), 1948; Catholic Pioneering in the Northwest, 1950; The Croasdale Painting of Lincoln, 1951; Black Robe and Buckskin, 1960; Interest and Principle in Literary Criticism, 1965. Contbr. to Acculturation in the Americas, 1951; Dictionary American History; Catholic Pioneering in the Northwest, 1950; Atrophy in Education, 1962; Red China—U.N. Member ?, 1962; also history revs. Asst. editor N.D. Hist. Quarterly, 1930-35; editorial dir. Kelsey Review. Research asso. The Christopher, 1951-52. Home: Standish House 455 W State St Trenton NJ 08618

PRIZGINT, EDNA. see Zdenek, Edna Prizgint

PROBBER, LLOYD, fin. cons.; b. Bklyn., Apr. 26, 1929; s. Joseph and Edna P.; ed. pub. schs.; children—Judith, Shelley, Helene, Mark. With Equitable Life Assurance Soc., N.Y.C., 1961-62, Conn. Mut. Life Ins. Co., Hartford, 1962; life underwriter New Eng. Life Ins. Co., N.Y.C.; pres. 666 Equities Corp., N.Y.C., 1970—. Served with U.S. Army, 1952-54. Mem. Nat. Assn. Life Underwriters, Million Dollar Round Table, Soc. Chartered Life Underwriters. Jewish. Home: 136 E 56th St New York City NY 10022 Office: 750 3d Ave New York City NY 10017

PROBST, DAVID ARTHUR, univ. adminstr.; b. Pitts., July 8, 1920; s. Arthur Greene and Izetta Anna (Benter) P.; B.S., U. Pitts., 1943, M.S., 1945; Ph.D., Northwestern U., 1953; m. Jeanne Edna Willoughby, June 3, 1943; children—Lynn Austin, Pamela (Mrs. Lincoln H. Lippincott III). Petroleum engr. Shell Oil Corp., Venezuela, 1953-57; investment adviser Standard Oil Co. N.J., N.Y.C., 1958-63; dir. corporate and fgn. govt. relations Princeton, 1964—, lectr. Sch. Engring. and Applied Sci., 1965—; exec. v.p., dir. Demat Corp.; exec. v.p., trustee Univ. Properties Holding Corp.; dir., v.p. Coll. Petroleum and Minerals Found., Dhahran, Saudi Arabia; dir. Internat. Schs. Services. Mem. Am. Assn. Petroleum Geologists, Geol. Soc. Am., Am. Mgmt. Assn., Am. Statis. Assn., Elijah Mitchell Honor Soc., Phi Beta Kappa, Sigma Xi, Sigma Tau, Sigma Gamma Epsilon. Clubs: Princeton (N.Y.C.); Echo Lake Country (Westfield, N.J.). Home: 304 Roanoke Rd Westfield NJ 07090 Office: PO Box 39 Princeton NJ 08540

PROCTOR, GEORGE NEWTON, investment adviser; b. Brookline, Mass., Nov. 10, 1909; s. George Newton and Emma Bartol (Bowden) P.; A.B., Dartmouth, 1931; m. Dorothy Lutz, Sept. 27, 1958; children—Natalie (Mrs. A. Elliot Gardiner), Roger C. Asso. with Proctor Cook & Co., Boston, 1932—, partner, 1936—, chmn. bd., 1970-73; partner Adams & Peck, N.Y.C., 1973-76, Tucker, Anthony & R.L. Day, Inc., 1976—; dir. Felters Co., Millbury, Mass., Arbeka Webbing Co., Pawtucket, R.I. Served to 1st lt. AUS, 1941-42. Mem. Theta Delta Chi. Home: 91 West St Beverly Farms MA 01915 Office: 1 Beacon Boston MA 02108

PROCTOR, JAMES FAUST, mech. engr.; b. Durham, N.C., July 21, 1934; s. Sidney Leroy and Thelma (Faust) P.; B.S. in M.E., Duke, 1956; M.S., U. Md., 1960; m. Maude Elizabeth Harris, June 16, 1956; children—James Faust, Kinion Harris. Research mech. engr. U.S. Naval Surface Weapons Center, Silver Spring, Md., 1956—, sr. scientist, 1969-75, head Explosion Dynamics br., 1975—. Cons. U.S. NRC, 1965—. Recipient Meritorious Civilian Service award Naval Surface Weapons Center, 1972. Registered profl. engr., Md. Mem. Soc. for Exptl. Stress Analysis (chpt. pres. 1968-69, papers com. 1970—), A.A.A.S., White Oak Athletic Assn. (coach 1970—), Phi Beta Kappa, Sigma Xi, Tau Beta Pi, Pi Tau Sigma, Pi Mu Epsilon. Methodist (chmn. ofcl. bd. 1966-67). Editor: Stresses and Strains, 1966-68. Home: 1133 Spotswood Dr Silver Spring MD 20904 Office: Naval Surface Weapons Center Silver Spring MD 20910

PROCTOR, WILLIAM GILBERT, JR., writer, editor; b. Atlanta, Oct. 11, 1941; s. William Gilbert and Maud (Moore) P.; B.A. magna cum laude in History, Harvard U., 1963, J.D., 1966; m. Priscilla Adrian Moore, June 17, 1967. Admitted to Tex. bar, 1966, N.Y. bar, 1976; reporter N.Y. Daily News, 1969-73; editor-in-chief Ch. Bus. Report, N.Y.C., 1976—; dir. Ch. Research Inc., Related Designs Inc.; free-lance writer, N.Y.C., 1973—; works include Survival on the Campus, 1972, Help Wanted: Faith Required, 1974. Jews for Jesus, 1974, The Art of Christian Promotion, 1975, The Commune Kidnapping, 1975, Women in the Pulpit, 1976, RX: The Christian Love Treatment, 1976, PDA-Personal Death Awareness, 1976, On the Trail of God, 1977. Lay leader Park Ave United Methodist Ch., N.Y.C., 1978—, trustee, 1976—. Served with USMC, 1966-69. Mem. Authors Guild, Tex. Bar, N.Y. City Bar Assn. Home: 7 Peter Cooper Rd New York City NY 10010 Office: PO Box 4025 Grand Central Station New York City NY 10017

PROKOPY, JOHN ALFRED, procurement analyst, cons.; b. Phila., May 23, 1926; s. John A. and Mary Genevieve (Frushour) P.; diploma Bentley Sch. Accounting and Fin. (now Bentley Coll.), 1950; B.B.A., Northeastern U., 1956; m. L. Maureen St. Pierre, July 10, 1948 (div. Mar. 1971); children—Cheryl, Dale, Scott, Kent, Keith. Chief accountant for several gen. contractors, Boston, 1950-56; controller Peters & Co., Inc., Boston, 1956-61; procurement analyst, cons. U.S. Dept. Def., Boston, 1961—, dir., past pres. fed. credit union, 1971—; lectr. profl. assns. Served with USN, 1944-46. Recipient Spl. Service award U.S. Dept. Def., 1975; certified profl. contract mgr., Mass.; certified program mgr., Mass.; notary pub., licensed real estate broker, Mass. Mem. Nat. Contract Mgmt. Assn., Am. Legion. Home: 34 Melbourne St Boston MA 02124 Office: DCASR Boston 666 Summer St Boston MA 02210

PROKOPY, JOHN VICTOR, Realtor; b. Danbury, Conn., Apr. 9, 1909; s. Paul and Maria (Loisch) P.; ed. high sch.; m. Marguerite Farwell, 1934 (dec. 1956); 1 son, Ronald John; m. 2d, Angela Lo Medico, 1963 (dec. 1976). With mortgage dept. Danbury Nat. Bank, 1928-40, Union Savs. Bank, 1940-44; pres. Prox Danbury, Prox New Milford, Durprox Realty, 1944-60; in comml. real estate, 1960-66; Realtor, owner John Prokopy Agency, Danbury, 1966—. Mem. Danbury Multiple Listing Service, Danbury Bd. Realtors, Am. Assn. Certified Appraisers, Nat. Assn. Realtors, Old Timers Assn. Lutheran. Home: 4 Possum Dr New Fairfield CT 06810 Office: PO Box 781 Danbury CT 06810

PROL, ELBERTUS JAMES, JR., curator; b. Paterson, N.J., Dec. 17, 1943; s. Elbertus James and Ruth Jeannette (Verblaauw) P.; B.A., King's Coll., Briarcliff Manor, N.Y., 1968; m. Cornelia Densel, Oct. 6, 1972. Curator, Ringwood State Park (N.J.), 1968—, also mem. citizens adv. com. Chmn. Ringwood Bicentennial Com., 1978—; chmn. Ringwood's UN Day, 1976; historian Borough of Ringwood; liaison officer between Ringwood, N.J., and Ringwood, Hampshire, Eng., 1976—; created Robert Erskine Ind. Co. of Foot Militia as a living museum, 1975—, adjutant, 1977—, comdr., 1978—, Distinguished Service award, 1976. Recipient Distinguished Service award Ringwood Jr. Womens Club, 1976. Mem. Am. Assn. Conservators and Restorers, Nat. Trust Historic Preservation, North Jersey Highland Hist. Soc. Home: 23 Winters St Oakland NJ 07436 Office: Ringwood Manor House Mus Sloatsburg RD PO Box 1304 Ringwood NJ 07456

PROLL, GEORGE SIMON, psychologist; b. Würzburg, Germany, June 30, 1931; s. Jack Ignatz and Irma (Kramer) P.; brought to U.S., 1936, naturalized, 1943; B.A., Yale, 1953; M.A., Boston U., 1958, Ph.D., 1962; m. Rita Rosina Rado, Aug. 9, 1954; children—Lauren, Douglas. Intern clin. psychology VA, Brockton, also Bedford, Lowell (all Mass.), 1958-62; dir. dept. psychology, psychologist mental health clinic Trenton (N.J.) Psychiat. Hosp., 1962-67, East Hosp., 1973-75; prin. clin. psychologist Ancora Psychiat. Hosp., 1975—; dir. profl. services Youth Reception, Correction Center, Yardville, N.J., 1967-73. Pvt. practice clin. psychology, Willingboro, N.J., 1969—. Mem. exec. bd. Psychol. Services Center, Trenton, 1965-66; mem. Drug Study Commn., Willingboro, 1971-72; mem. steering com. Community Mental Health Center, Princeton, N.J., 1973. Served with USN, 1955-57. Winner several chess competitions, including State N.H., 1957, State Mass., 1962, So. N.J., 1971, 74, N.J. Amateur Class A, 1972. Mem. Am., Eastern, N.J. (Burlington County rep. to legis. com. 1968-72), Burlington County psychol. assns. Clubs: Yale (Princeton); Moorestown (N.J.) Chess. Home: 48 Trebing Lane Twin Hill Park Willingboro NJ 08046 Office: Ancora Psy Hosp Outpatient Dept 4th St Camden NJ

PROSSER, JOSEPH LAWRENCE, heavy machinery mfg. co. exec.; b. Camden, N.J., May 3, 1923; s. Paul John and Nellie Loretta (Ross) P.; B.E., Johns Hopkins, 1947; m. Elizabeth Ann Hughes, June 26, 1948; children—Joseph Lawrence, James, Elizabeth, Patrick, Paul, Nancy. Chief engr. Baugh Cos., 1950-54; gen. mgr. A.J. Sackett Sons Co., 1954-60; pres. Prosser Co., Glen Arm, Md., 1960—, also dir.; dir. Glen Arm Leasing Co., Inc., Ray V. Watson Co., Inc., Prosser Fertilizer & Agrotec Co., Ltd. Served with C.E., AUS, 1943-46. Roman Catholic (chmn. parish council 1968-72). Patentee in field. Home: 4407 Meadowcliff Dr Glen Arm MD 21057 Office: Glen Arm Rd Glen Arm Md 21057

PROTHRO, GERALD DENNIS, computer co. exec.; b. Atlanta, Sept. 27, 1942; s. Charles Emery and Esther (Jones) P.; B.S., Howard U., 1966, M.S., 1969; postgrad. Harvard Grad. Sch. Bus. Adminstrn., 1975; m. Brenda Jean Bell, Feb. 14, 1976; 1 son, Gerald Dennis. Physicist, NASA, Goddard Space Flight Center, Green Belt, Md., 1965-69; asso. systems analyst, 1969-71, mgr. process line central engring. systems, 1971, mgr. process line central analysis systems, 1971-73, project mgr. systems facilities and support, 1973-74, mgr. info. systems strategy System Product div., White Plains, N.Y., 1974-75, dir. system assurance, data processing product group, 1975—. NDEA fellow, 1967-69; NASA grantee, 1965-69; recipient Black Achievers award YMCA Harlem, 1976. Mem. NAACP, Urban League, Am. Inst. Physics, AAAS, Automatic Computing Machines, Sigma Phi Sigma, Beta Kappa Ki. Presbyn. Club Harvard N.Y.C. Contbr. articles to profl. jours. Home: 83-10 Courtland Ave Stamford CT 06902 Office: 1000 Westchester Ave White Plains NY 10604

PROULX, ADOLPHE, clergyman; b. Hanmer, Ont., Can., Dec. 12, 1927; s. Augustin and Marie-Louise (Tremblay) P.; B.A., St. Augustine's Sem., Toronto, Ont.; postgrad. in canon law, Rome, Italy, 1958-60. Ordained priest Roman Catholic Ch., 1954; parish priest, North Bay and Sudbury, Ont., Can., 1954-57; chancellor Sault Ste. Marie (Ont.) Diocese, 1960-64, aux. bishop, 1965-67; bishop Alexandria (Ont.) Diocese, 1967-74; bishop Hull, Que., Canada, 1974—. Address: 119 Carillon Hull PQ Canada

PROULX, MARIE ANTOINETTE, clin. psychologist; b. Newark, Nov. 9, 1921; d. Anthony Paul and Lena Mary (Salerno) Iannarone; A.B., U. Cin., 1962, M.A., 1963; widow; 1 dau., Barbara Chandler. Co-owner indsl. electronics equipment co.; staff clin. psychologist Marlboro (N.J.) Psychiat. Hosp., 1968; part-time instr. Monmouth (N.J.) Coll., 1969, Brookdale Coll., 1970; expert on pre-retirement problems. N.J. State fellow psychology, 1967. Fellow N.J. Psychology Assn.; mem. Am., (asso.), Monmouth-Ocean County psychol. assns., Gerontol. Assn., Assn. N.J. Instl. Psychologists, Internat. Platform Assn. Mensa, Right to Life, Fish, Phi Beta Kappa. Home: 431 Spring St Red Bank NJ 07701 Office: Marlboro Psychiat Hosp Marlboro NJ 07746

PROUT, JAMES HAROLD, educator; b. Oak Park, Ill., Dec. 23, 1927; s. Harold Bertram and Elta Jewett (Lewis) P.; B.S., Purdue U., 1952; M.S., U. Mich., 1958; m. Leora Louisa Schmidt, Aug. 24, 1954; 1 son, David Eltan. Research asso. U. Mich. Willow Run Labs., Ann Arbor, 1953-61; asso. prof. engring. research Pa. State U. Applied Research Lab., University Park, 1961-71, asso. prof. Environ. Acoustics Lab., 1971—. Served with USN, 1945-48. Mem. Acoustical Soc. Am., Am. Audiology Soc., Inst. Noise Control Engring. (affiliate), Sigma Xi. Patentee in field. Home: 1169 S Garner St State College PA 16801 Office: 110 Moore Bldg Pa State U University Park PA 16802

PROUT, JOHN WILLIAM, surgeon; b. Pitts., Oct. 21, 1914; s. Thomas Edwin and Mary Dorothy (Good) P.; A.B., Allegheny Coll., 1937; M.D., Hahnemann Med. Coll., 1941; m. Dorothy Marie Baker, Mar. 16, 1946; 1 dau., Pamela Marie. Intern, Pottsville (Pa.) Hosp., 1941-42; resident gen. surgery U. Pitts., 1946-49; practice medicine specializing in surgery Niagara Falls, N.Y.; mem. staff St. Mary's Hosp., Lewiston, N.Y.; mem. staff Niagara Falls Meml. Hosp., chief surgery, 1956-66. Bd. dirs. ARC. Served to capt. M.C., AUS, 1942-46; ETO. Diplomate Am. Bd. Surgery. Fellow A.C.S.; mem. AMA, N.Y., Niagara County med. socs., Niagara Falls Acad. Medicine (pres. 1955-56), Niagara Falls C. of C. Republican. Clubs: Niagara, Niagara Falls Country. Home: 652 Mt View Dr Lewiston NY 14092 Office: 549 4th St Niagara Falls NY 14301

PROVENCHER, HENRY DAVID, state ofcl.; b. Dorchester, Mass., Mar. 1, 1921; s. Archille Joseph and Lucy Marie (Hasken) P.; ed. Lowell Tech. Inst., 1938-42, McIntosh Bus. Coll., 1946-49, Indsl. Tech. Sch., 1948-52, Lawrence Indsl. Sch., 1952-55; m. Veronica Mary King, Feb. 19, 1950; children—Paul, Mary, Samuel, Kathleen, Dorothy. With Commonwealth of Mass., Middleborough, 1951—, storekeeper, 1951-53, prin. storekeeper, 1953-78, adminstrv. storekeeper hwy. repair foreman, 1978—; adminstr. Danvers State Mental Hosp., Hawthorne, Mass., 1973-74; custodian Middleborough Sch. Dept., 1957-71. Served with AUS, 1942-45. Mem. D.A.V. (comdr. 1975-76, trustee 1968-75), Am. Legion, Am. Fedn. State County & Municipal Employees Assn., Mass. Storekeepers Assn., Internat. Aux. Police Assn., Am. Fedn. Trades Council, VFW, Am. Automobile Assn. Roman Catholic. Democrat. Clubs: Eagles, Elks, Country Pond Fish and Game. Home: 14 Courtland St Middleborough MA 02346 Office: 151 Pierce St Middleborough MA 02346

PROVENZANO, ANTHONY JOHN, acquisition research cons.; b. N.Y.C., Apr. 22, 1947; s. John Dominic and Ida Mary (Cappelletti) P.; B.S., Fordham U., 1968; M.B.A., N.Y. U., 1971; m. Phyllis Anne nunes, June 5, 1971; 1 dau., Lisa Nicole. Reporter, columnist S.I. (N.Y.) Advance, 1968-69; mil. intelligence analyst CIA, Washington,

1971-73, econ./cost analyst, 1973-75; fin. researcher/cons. Logistics Mgmt. Inst., Washington, 1975—; adviser to bd. Byway Corp. Mem. Assn. M.B.A. Execs. Roman Catholic. Clubs: Washington Canoe Cruiser Assn., Courts Royal Raquetball. Home: 2226 Loch Lomond Dr Vienna VA 22180 Office: 4701 Sangamore Rd Washington DC 20016

PROWELL, HAROLD RICHARD, lawyer; b. Steelton, Pa., Jan. 1, 1907; s. Tolbert and Helen (Brough) P.; student Harrisburg Acad., 1925; A.B. summa cum laude, Princeton, 1929; LL.B., U. Pa., 1932; m. Myra Vickery, Nov. 27, 1933; children—Tolbert V., Gilbert V., Myra M. Admitted to Pa. bar, 1932, since practiced in Harrisburg; mem. firm Prowell & Stoner, attys.; gen. counsel Pa. Motor Fed.-AAA, 1937-70; spl. counsel Commonwealth Pa., Dept. Transp. and Dept. Pub. Welfare; dir., counsel Commonwealth Nat. Bank; solicitor Harrisburg-Steelton-Highspire Tech. Sch., Steelton-Highspire Sch. Dist. Gen. counsel Pa. United Fund, Inc., past pres. Harrisburg Community Chest; Gov.'s Hosp. Study Commn., Susquehanna River Basin Assn. Pres., Dauphin County Bar Found. Mem. Am. (com. fed. income tax 1943—), Pa. (chmn. medico-legal com. 1952-53), Dauphin County (pres.) bar assns., Dickinson Law Sch. Forum (dir.), C. of C. (dir.), Pa. Soc., Phi Beta Kappa. Author articles on Motor Vehicle Law and Law of Sepulture. Legal editor: The Am. Cemetery N.Y.C. Home: 3000 Mayfred Ln Camp Hill PA 17011 Office: Dauphin Bldg Harrisburg PA 17101

PRUDDEN, JOHN FLETCHER, surgeon; b. Fostoria, Ohio, Feb. 4, 1920; s. Meryl Ashley and Sallie Wells (Gibson) P.; B.S. cum laude, Harvard U., 1942, M.D., 1945; Sc.D., Columbia Physicians and Surgeons, 1950; m. Ruth Carla Williamson, Jan. 22, 1955; children—Peter, Pamela, Elaine, John Fletcher, Sarah Milford, James Nelson. Intern, Bellevue Hosp., N.Y.C., 1945-46; resident Roosevelt Hosp., N.Y.C., 1947-49, Peter Bent Brigham Hosp., Boston, 1950-51, Pondville Cancer Hosp., Walpole, Mass., 1951-52; instr. Columbia Coll. Physicians and Surgeons, 1954-62, asst. prof., 1962-67, asso. prof. surgery, 1967-76; asso. atending surgeon Presbyn. Hosp., N.Y.C., 1967-76; attending surgeon Delafield Hosp., N.Y.C., 1966-76, Nyack (N.Y.) Hosp., Drs. Hosp., N.Y.C., 1976—, Roosevelt Hosp., N.Y.C., 1977—. Cons. surgery Harlem Hosp., N.Y.C., 1964-76, N.Y. Rehab. Hosp., Haverstraw, N.Y., 1967—. Dir. Lescarden, Ltd., Goshen, N.Y., Barinco, Inc., Blooming Grove, N.Y. Trustee Nyack (N.Y.) Hosp. Served to capt. AUS, 1952-54. Mem. A.C.S., N.Y. Surg. Soc., Soc. for Exptl. Biology and Medicine, Harvey Soc., Soc. for Alimentary Tract Surgery, N.Y. Acad. Scis., AAAS, AMA, Am. Geriatrics Assn., Am. Chem. Soc., N.Y. State, N.Y. County med. socs., Pan Pacific Surg. Assn., AAUP, Whipple Soc. Clubs: Mid-Ocean (Bermuda); Rockland Country (Sparkill, N.Y.); Nyack Field, Upper Nyack Tennis. Contbr. articles to profl. jours. Home: 409 N Broadway Upper Nyack NY 10960 Office: 51 E 73d St New York City NY 10021 also 310 N Broadway Upper Nyack NY 10960

PRUGH, THOMAS AUSTIN, engring. cons.; b. Dayton, Ohio, June 11, 1920; s. Thomas Kemp and Dorothy (Austin) P.; Elec. Engr., U. Cin., 1942; m. Mary Frances Burton, Dec. 18, 1945; 1 dau., Amy Jo. Elec. engr. Dept. Def., Washington, 1946-51; sect. chief Nat. Bur. Standards and Harry Diamond Labs., Washington, 1951-59; with Nat. Security Agy., Fort Meade, Md., 1959-75, comdt. Nat. Cryptologic Sch., 1973-75. Cons. com. on telecommunications NRC, 1976; cons. engr., 1977—. Served to capt. Signal Corps, AUS, 1943-46. Mem. IEEE (sr. mem.), Assn. Computing Machinery, Sigma Xi, Tau Beta Pi, Eta Kappa Nu. Patentee in field. Contbr. profl. jours. Home: 11705 Eden Rd Silver Spring MD 20904

PRUITT, DEAN GARNER, psychologist; b. Phila., Dec. 26, 1930; d. Dudley M. and Grace (Garner) P.; B.A., Oberlin Coll., 1952; M.S., Yale U., 1954, Ph.D., 1957; m. France Juliard, Dec. 27, 1959; children—Andre, Paul, Charles. Postdoctoral fellow dept. psychology U. Mich., 1957-59; research asso. internat. relations program Northwestern U., 1959-61; asst. prof. dept. psychology U. Del., 1961-65, asso. prof., 1965-66; asso. prof. psychology State U. N.Y., Buffalo, 1966-69, prof., 1969—; orgnl. cons. Hart, Shaffner and Marx, Inc. NIMH grantee, 1967-68; NSF grantee, 1969—; Guggenheim fellow, 1978-79. Fellow Am. Psychol. Assn., Soc. Psychol. Study Social Issues; mem. Internat. Studies Assn., Soc. Exptl. Social Psychology. Author: Theory and Research on the Causes of War, 1969; Problem Solving in the Department of State, 1964; Psychology of Integrative Bargaining, 1977. Home: 6305 Valley Rd Bethesda MD 20034 Office: Dept Psychology State U NY 4230 Ridge Lea Rd Buffalo NY 14226

PRUPAS, MELVERN IRVING, food co. exec.; b. Montreal, Que., Can., Dec. 16, 1926; s. Harry and Esther (Braunstein) P.; student Sir George Williams U., 1943-45, Montreal Tech. Inst., 1946, Mt. Allison U., 1967, N.Y. State Coll. Agr., Cornell U., 1971, U. Guelph, 1971-72; m. Sheila Ditkofsky, Mar. 21, 1948; children—Michael, Richard, Norman, David, Dianne. Salesman, Crescent Cheese Co., 1947-50, sales mgr., 1951-56, dir., v.p., 1956-72, dir., v.p., sec., 1972-77; v.p., dir. Maycrest Co. Ltd., 1960-77; sec.-treas., dir. Les Produits Laitiers Marieville (Que., Can.) Ltee., 1956-72, v.p., sec., dir., 1972-77; founder En Ville newspaper, 1962; pres., dir. Ambassador Foods Mfg. Ltd., 1964—; sec.-treas., dir. Proops Press Inc., 1967-70 (all Montreal); pres. Dadnaram Ltd. of Edmonton, 1973—. Bd. dirs. YM-YWHA of Montreal, 1954-72, gov., 1956-66, gov.-benefactor, 1967—, met. campaign chmn., 1966; cubmaster Boy Scouts of Can., Mount Royal, 1960-71; chmn. food div. Combined Jewish Appeal. Montreal, 1961-63, trade coordinator, 1964-65, vice chmn. trades, 1969-70, vice chmn. spl. names, 1972-73; bd. dirs. Jewish Nat. Fund Montreal, 1970-72; v.p. Algonquin Home and Sch. Assn., 1971-72. Recipient Scouters Warrant, Boy Scouts of Can. 1963; Chevalier Medal, Chaine des Rotisseurs, 1964; Ida Steinberg Meml. trophy Combined Jewish Appeal, 1969; Golden Gloves heavyweight boxing champion, 1941; mem. Can. Olympic basketball team, 1948. Mem. Province of Que. Food Brokers Assn. (dir. 1968-70), Food Service Execs., Assn., Can. Restaurant Assn., Chaine des Rotisseurs in Montreal Baillage, Confrerie Des Vignerons De St. Vincents, Guilde Fromagers Confrerie de Saint-Uguzon, Montreal Bd. of Trade, Can. C. of C., Comml. Travellers Assn. Can., Food Brokers Assn. Can., Can. Importers Assn., Can-Israel C. of C., Am. Mus. Natural History, Playwrights Workshop, Jewish Theol. Sem. Am., Canadian Council Christians and Jews, Mt. Royal Property Owners Assn. (dir. 1968-70). Jewish religion (dir. Congregation Beth El 1960—, v.p. 1964-65, sec. 1969-70, v.p. 1971-73, pres. 1973-75). Mem. B'nai B'rith. Clubs: Cedarbrooke Golf and Country (St. Sophie); Montreal Anglers and Hunters, Rotary, Canadian, Amici (pres. 1950-51, 65-66). Address: Bayside Towers Suite 707 80 Lakeshore Rd Pointe Claire PQ H9S 4H6 Canada

PRUSLIN, FRED HOWARD, microbiologist; b. N.Y.C., Oct. 24, 1951; s. Irving and Helene (Berliner) P.; student Queens Coll., 1969-71; B.A. summa cum laude, Yeshiva U., 1973; Ph.D. in Microbiology, Cornell U. Grad. Sch. Med. Scis., 1978. Microbiologist dept. microbiology Cornell U. Grad. Sch. Med. Scis., N.Y.C., 1973-78, teaching asst. microbiology, 1974-77; asst. research scientist dept. pharmacology N.Y. U., N.Y.C., 1978; postdoctoral fellow Rockefeller U., 1978—. N.Y. State Regents Coll. scholar, 1969-73. Mem. Am. Soc. Microbiology, AAAS, Soc. Gen. Microbiology, Soc. Israel Philatelists. Home: 70-25 Kissena Blvd Flushing NY 11367 Office: Rockefeller University New York NY 10021

PRUSSIN, JEFFREY ALAN, health care cons., writer; b. Bklyn., Aug. 11, 1943; s. Samuel and Shirley (Solomon) P.; A.B. in Polit. Sci., U. Calif., Los Angeles, 1965; M.A. (Paul McCoy prize polit. sci.), Johns Hopkins, 1967; m. Judith May, June 2, 1962; children—Aaron Justin, Leya Monique. Jr. instr. polit. sci. Johns Hopkins, 1966-67; adj. asst. prof. Portland (Oreg.) State U., 1969-70, Linfield (Oreg.) Coll., 1969-70; vis. asst. prof. Oreg. State U., 1970; asst. to dir. Health Services Research Center, Kaiser Found. Hosps., Oreg. region. 1969-70; dir. prepaid group practice sch. Kaiser-Permanente Med. Care Program, 1970-71; dir. dept. edn. and tng. Group Health Assn. Am., Inc., 1971-73; mgr. program devel., health systems div. Westinghouse Electric Corp., 1972-73; cons. on health care orgn., delivery and financing systems, Kensington, Md., 1971—; adv. com. health adminstrn. manpower needs Bur. Health Manpower Edn., NIH, 1971; editor-in-chief Washington Info. Nat. Health Ins., 1973-76; sr. v.p. planning and devel., dir. Health Maintenance Systems, Inc., 1974-75; dir. tech. affairs, dir. Inst. Comprehensive Med. Care, Inc., 1974-75; editor-in-chief HMO and Health Services Report, 1973—, Washington Monitor on Energy, 1975—; pres., chmn. bd. dirs. Washington News Services, Inc., 1974—; writer, cons. in field. NDEA Title IV fellow, 1965-68; grantee NIH, 1968. Mem. Am. Polit. Sci. Assn., Am. Acad. Polit. and Social Scis., Am. Pub. Health Assn., Am. Hosp. Assn., Group Health Assn. Am., Am. Acad. Health Adminstrs., Royal Soc. Health. Club: Nat. Press (Washington). Author: Health Maintenance Organization Legislation in 1973-74, 1974; Employee Health Benefits: HMO's and Mandatory Dual Choice; co-author Topics in Health Care Financing: Private Third Party Reimbursement, 1975. Contbr. articles to profl. publs. Address: PO Box 50 Kensington MD 20795

PRYOR, BARBARA LEONE, realtor; b. Boston, Oct. 8, 1931; d. Harold Austin and Christine (Mackenzie) Willoughby; student St. Louis U., 1954-58; Am. U., 1969-70; m. David Lee Pryor, Dec. 20, 1952; 1 son, David Victor Pryor. Vice pres. Julien J. Studley, Inc., Washington, 1966—. Served with USMC, 1950-53. Mem. Nat. Fedn. Bus. and Profl. Women (pres. Pendalum Club of D.C., fedn. 1973—), Nat. Assn. Realtors, Washington, N.Y. bds. realtors, Friends of the Nat. Zoo, Friends Kennedy Center. Home: 3901 Connecticut Ave NW Washington DC 20008 Office: 1900 M St NW Washington DC 20036 also 342 Madison Ave New York City NY 10017

PRYOR, ROGER WELTON, physicist; b. Worcester, Mass., May 21, 1939; s. Walter Eugene and Opal Margaret (Lukey) P.; B.S. in Physics, Worcester Poly. Inst., 1968; M.S. in Physics, Pa. State U., 1971, Ph.D., 1972; m. Beverly Ellen Clark, June 10, 1967. Mem. tech. staff Bell Labs., Whippany, N.J., 1972-76; sr. physicist Pitney Bowes, 1976—. Served with USN, 1958-62. Mem. AAAS, Am. Phys. Soc., IEEE, Sigma Xi. Contbr. papers on threshold switching bi-level printing to profl. jours.; patentee optical transducer and bi-level printing. Home: PO Box 272 Trumbull CT 06611 Office: Pitney Bowes Box 6050 Norwalk CT 06852

PSATY, MARTIN MELVILLE, lawyer, concrete restoration and waterproofing co. exec., state legislator; b. Bklyn., Dec. 3, 1917; s. Charles I. and Leah (Seham) P.; A.B. with honors in Econs., U. Calif. at Berkeley; J.D. (Law Rev. grad.), N.Y. Law Sch., 1960; m. Claire Ringelheim, Oct. 25, 1942; children—Beverly (Mrs. Pomerantz), Alan, Madelyn. Admitted to N.Y. bar, 1961; practiced law, N.Y.C., 1961—; pres. Psaty-Horn Corp., N.Y.C.; mem. N.Y. State Assembly, 1962—, mem. ways and means, codes coms. Adj. prof. econs. and mgmt. Grad. Sch. Bus., St. John's U., N.Y.C. Founder, pres. Queens Jewish Center, Forest Hills; trustee awards United Jewish Appeal, Bonds for Israel, Yeshiva U., Union Orthodox Congregations, Young Israel of Am., 1964. Served as 1st lt. Ordnance, AUS, World War II; chief price analyst Birmingham and N.Y. Ordnance Dist., Korean War. Mem. N.Y. State, Queens County bar assns., Assn. Bar City N.Y., Real Estate Bd. N.Y. (legis. com., municipal affairs com., city planning com.), Execs. Assn. N.Y., Am. Ordnance Assn. (dir. N.Y. post), Phi Delta Phi. Clubs: Real Estate Square (pres.) (N.Y.C); Glen Head Country (Glen Cove, N.Y.). Home: 64-29 110th St Forest Hills NY 11375 Office: 500 Fifth Ave New York City NY 10036

PUCCINELLI, ALFRED RICHARD, aircraft instrument mfg. co. exec.; b. Astoria, L.I., N.Y., June 7, 1920; s. Alfred Ralph and Marie Vinjencia (Ciafone) P.; student Queens Coll., 1937-39; B.Aero. Engring., N.Y. U., 1943; m. Frances Veronica Fischer, June 9, 1952; children—Richard Alfred, Claire Patricia, Joan Marie. Aero. engr., flight engr. Pan Am. World Airways, N.Y.C., 1943-50; aero. engr. advanced Navy research projects Edo Corp., N.Y.C., 1950; powerplant engr. Wright Aero. Corp., Woodridge, N.J., 1950-51; aero. design evaluation engr. FAA, Kennedy Internat. Airport, N.Y.C., 1951-59; electronic sales engr. to maj. def. contractors in N.Y.-N.J.-Conn. area, 1959-65; founder, pres., owner A.R.P. Industries Inc., Huntington, N.Y., 1965—; cons. in field, participant air shows. Served to lt. (j.g.) USNR, 1943-52. Designated engring. rep. FAA, licensed aircraft and engine mechanic FAA. Mem. Nat. Assn. Designated Engring. Reps. (charter), Aviation Council L.I., Bay Hills Property Owners Assn., Suffolk County CB REACT. Inventor, developer, patentee aircraft carburetor ice detector and icing rate meter. Contbr. articles on aviation safety to profl. publs. Address: 36 Bay Dr E Huntington NY 11743

PUGH, DAVID MARTIN, mgmt. cons.; b. Harrisburg, Pa., Sept. 24, 1942; s. Albert L. and June E. (Erdossy) P.; B.S. in Accounting, Elizabethtown (Pa.) Coll., 1970; m. Judith A. Hart, Nov. 14, 1964. Accounting supr. Commonwealth Pa., Harrisburg, 1960-62; audit supr. Ernst & Ernst, C.P.A.'s, Harrisburg, 1970-73; v.p., treas. Hay-Huggins Data Services, Inc., Phila., 1973—. Served with USMC, 1962-66. C.P.A., Pa. Mem. Am., Pa. insts. C.P.A.'s. Republican. Clubs: Tuesday, Rotary (Harrisburg); West Shore Racquet. Home: RD 3 Duncannon PA 17020 Office: 800 N 3d St Harrisburg PA 17102 also 1401 Walnut St Philadelphia PA 17105

PUGH, EMERSON MARTINDALE, educator, physicist; b. Ogden, Utah, July 19, 1896; s. William and Hattie (Martindale) P.; B.S., Carnegie Inst. Tech., 1918; M.S., U. Pitts., 1927; Ph.D., Calif. Inst. Tech., 1929; m. Ruth Hazel Edgin, Sept. 18, 1920; children—George Edgin, Emerson William. Instr. physics Carnegie Inst. Tech., Pitts., 1920-27, faculty, 1930—, prof. physics, 1948-65, asso. head dept., 1961-65, chmn. com. on coordinating teaching in all depts., 1937-41, prof. emeritus, 1965—; Am. Petroleum Inst. fellow Calif. Inst. Tech., Pasadena, 1927-29; dir. research projects U.S. Naval Research and Office Scientific Research and Devel., 1943-66; cons. to various industries, govt. agencies. Served as ensign, USN, 1918-19. NRC fellow, 1929-30. Mem. Soc. for Promotion of Engring. Edn., Sigma Xi, Tau Beta Pi, Pi Mu Epsilon, Phi Kappa Phi, Delta Tau Delta. Author: (with Emerson William Pugh) Principles of Electricity and Magnetism, 1960, 2nd edit. 1970; (with George H. Winslow) Analysis of Physical Measurements, 1966; Wyoming Scientist-Horses to Space Ships, 1976 (hist. autobiography); discoverer extraordinary hall effect in ferromagnetic materials, 1929-30; producer band theory for ordinary hall effects in ferromagnetic alloys, discovered why Bazooka's conical shaped charge was invented and how it destroys armored tanks. Home: 1427 Walnut St Pittsburgh PA 15218

PUGH, EMERSON WILLIAM, physicist; b. Pasadena, Calif., May 1, 1929; s. Emerson Martindale and Ruth Hazel (Edgin) P.; B.Sc., Carnegie-Mellon U., 1951, Ph.D., in Physics, 1956; m. Elizabeth Burnam, Mar. 1, 1958; children—William Russell, Sarah Elizabeth, David Emerson. Asst. prof. physics Carnegie-Mellon U., Pitts., 1957; research scientist IBM, Yorktown Heights, N.Y., 1958-62, mgr. memory devel., 1961-66, dir. planning, 1967-68, cons., 1968-73, mgr. exploratory magnetics Research div., 1976—. Fellow Am. Phys. Soc., AAAS, IEEE; mem. IEEE Magnetics Soc. (pres. 1972-73). Co-author: Principles of Electricity and Magnetism, 2d edit., 1970. Editor: Trans. on Magnetics, 1968-70. Home: Brandon Dr Mount Kisco NY 10549 Office: IBM PO Box 218 Yorktown Heights NY 10598

PUGKHEM, TRETORN, thoracic surgeon; b. Thailand, July 3, 1939; s. Geo and Fern P.; came to U.S., 1965; M.D., Siriraj Med. Sch., Bangkok, Thailand, 1964; m. Sumarn Donavanik, Sept. 6, 1969; children—Joyce, Julie. Intern, L.I. Coll. Hosp., Bklyn., 1965-66; resident Bellevue Hosp. Center and N.Y. U. Hosp., 1966-72; practice medicine specializing in thoracic and cardiovascular surgery, Flushing, N.Y., 1974—; mem. staff Booth Meml. Med. Center, Flushing, 1974—; clin. asst. prof. surgery N.Y. U.; cons. VA Hosp., N.Y.C. Diplomate Am. Bd. Surgery, Am. Bd. Thoracic Surgery. Mem. N.Y., New York County med. socs., Clin. Vascular Surgery Soc. Buddhist. Home: Soundview Ln Sands Point NY 11050 Office: 58-18 Main St Flushing NY 11355

PUGLIESE, ANTHONY CHARLES, hosp. adminstr.; b. West Pittston, Pa., July 1, 1939; s. Anthony Michael and Matilda Lucia P.; B.S. in Biology, Kings Coll., Pa., 1961; M.S. in Molecular Biology, Rutgers U., 1968, Ed.D., 1974; m. Mary Rita, Aug. 26, 1967; children—Rita, Anthony, Aileen. Adj. faculty mem. Kings Coll., Pa., 1960-61; faculty Metuchen (N.J.) High Sch., 1961-71; coordinator Ambulatory Induction Methadone Clinic, Roosevelt Hosp., Metuchen, 1971-72, program and research dir. Middlesex County Methadone Clinic, 1972-75, chief outpatient services Roosevelt Hosp., 1975—; cons. Fred Streit Research Assos., part-time 1973—; faculty State Dept. Health, Tng. and Edn. Center, 1975—, Rutgers U. Summer Sch. Alcohol and Drug Abuse Studies, 1977; adj. prof., dept. social rehab. Middlesex County Coll., 1977—. Mem. Metuchen Sch. Bd., 1975-78; bd. dirs. Metuchen-Edison br. YMCA; mem. Adv. Council Profl. Youth Services, Perth Amboy, N.J. Mem. Am. Hosp. Assn., Am. Social Health Assn., Middlesex County Tennis Assn. (pres.), Rutgers U. Grad. Sch. Edn. Alumni Assn., Kappa Delta Pi (chpt. pres. 1977—). Democrat. Roman Catholic. Clubs: Booster; Tennis. Reviewer Jour. Studies of Alcohol; contbr. articles to profl. jours. Home: 86 Blair Ave Metuchen NJ 08840 Office: Roosevelt Hosp PO Box 151 Metuchen NJ 08840

PUKITE, ALFRED S., med. technologist; b. Smiltene, Latvia, Feb. 8, 1923; s. Alexanders and Marija (Krastins) P.; came to U.S., 1950, naturalized, 1955; Cand. Med., Ulius Maximillian U. (Germany), 1949; Med. Tech., Hunter Coll., 1953; m. Irene Grauds, Jan. 29, 1949. With Meml. Hosp. for Cancer and Allied Diseases, N.Y.C., 1952—, supr., lab. mgr., 1957—; examiner for lab. personnel City of N.Y. Mem. Am. Coll. Med. Technologists (asso.), Am. Soc. for Med. Technologists, Clin. Lab. Mgmt. Assn., Latvian Welfare Assn. Daugavas Vanagi (pres. 1954-56), Am. Latvian Assn. (v.p. 1956-66), World Fedn. Free Latvians (dir. 1966-70). Republican. Lutheran. Home: 358 Tulip Ave Floral Park NY 11001 Office: 1275 York Ave New York City NY 10021

PUKLIN, JAMES EDWARD, ophthalmologist; b. Chgo., May 11, 1941; s. Marvin Morton and Lorraine Annette (Goldman) P.; A.B., Darmouth Coll., 1963; M.D., Chgo. Med. Sch., 1968; m. Diane Aileen Venezky, June 14, 1964; children—Barbara Elise, Eileen Andrea Charlotte. Intern in medicine U. Ill. Research and Ednl. Hosps., Chgo., 1968-69; resident ophthalmology Northwestern U., Chgo., 1971-74; fellow in diseases of retina and vitreous, dept. ophthalmology Univ. Ill. Eye and Ear Infirmary, Chgo., 1974-75; practice medicine specializing in opthalmology (vitreoretinal diseases); mem. staffs Yale New Haven Hosp., VA Hosp., West Haven Conn.; asst. prof. Yale U., New Haven, Conn., 1976—. Served to lt. M.C., USNR, 1969-71. Fellow A.C.S.; mem. Am. Acad. Opthalmology and Otolaryngology, New Eng. Ophthal. Soc., Conn. Med. Soc., Conn. Soc. Eye Physicians. Contbr. articles in field to profl. jours. Home: 241 Hunter's Trail Madison CT 06443 Office: 333 Cedar St New Haven CT 06510

PULLEN, DAVID JOHN, educator, nuclear physicist; b. London, Eng., June 28, 1936; s. Arthur Lester and Alexandria (Griffith) P.; B.Sc. 1st class, spl. honours physics, Kings Coll., U. London, 1958; D.Phil., Trinity Coll., Oxford U., 1963; m. Heather Morgan, Aug. 6, 1960; children—Katrina, Adrian, Lester, Andrew. Research asso., instr. Mass. Inst. Tech., 1963-65; asst. prof. physics U. Pa., 1965-70; asso. prof. physics Lowell (Mass.) Tech. Inst., 1970-74; prof. physics U. Lowell, 1974—. Sr. studentship Royal Commn. Exhbn. 1851, 1961-63. Mem. Am. Phys. Soc., Sigma Xi. Home: 2 Reeves Rd Bedford MA 01730 Office: U Lowell Lowell MA 01854

PULLEN, PHYLLIS KOUWENHOVEN, physician; b. Balt., Feb. 10, 1923; d. Frank Wolfert and Alice Witherell Kouwenhoven; A.B., Goucher Coll., 1944; M.D., U. Md., 1962; m. Keats A. Pullen, Jr., Jan 6, 1945; children—Peter K., Paul V., Keats A., Andrew W., Victoria F. Intern, U. Md., Balt., 1962-63, fellow in medicine and arthritis, 1963-64, asst. resident in dermatology, 1964-65; gen. practice medicine, Kingsville, Md., 1965—. Diplomate Am. Bd. Family Practice. Mem. AMA, Med. and Chirurg. Faculty Md., Hartford County Med. Soc., Phi Beta Kappa, Alpha Omega Alpha. Republican. Presbyterian. Club: Delta Gamma. Home and Office: 2807 Jerusalem Rd Kingsville MD 21087

PULLING, LISA CANBY, social service adminstr.; b. Wilmington, Del., Feb. 24, 1940; d. Henry M. and Elizabeth R. (Gawthrop) Canby; B.A., Smith Coll., 1961; M.A., Hunter Coll., 1968; children by previous marriage—Elizabeth R., Edward L. Tchr., chmn. humanities dept. St. Ann's Episcopal Sch., Bklyn., 1968-72; dir. devel. Spence Sch., N.Y.C., 1972-74; cons. for found., corp. and individual appeals Nat. Bd. of YWCA, N.Y.C., 1974-75; exec. dir. Fresh Air Fund, N.Y.C., 1975—; writer New York mag., 1974—; contbr. to YWCA Fin. Manual, 1975-76; editor Fund Raising Guide, 1974. Mem. devel. com. of YWCA, N.Y.C., 1975—. Mem. Nat. Soc. Colonial Dames, Nat. Soc. Fund Raisers (dir. N.Y. chpt. 1975—). Republican. Episcopalian. Home: 125 E 84th St New York City NY 10028 Office: 300 W 43d St New York City NY 10028

PULLING, THOMAS LEFFINGWELL, investment banking exec.; b. N.Y.C., May 1, 1939; s. Edward and Lucy (Leffingwell) P.; B.S. cum laude, Princeton U., 1961; m. Sheila Sonne, Mar. 12, 1970; children—Elizabeth, Edward, Victoria, Diana, Christopher. Asst. treas. Morgan Guaranty Trust Co., N.Y.C., 1962-68; asso. N.Y. Securities, Inc., N.Y.C., 1968-71; v.p., stockholder L.M. Rosenthal & Co., Inc., N.Y.C., 1971-76; v.p. Shearson Hayden Stone, Inc., N.Y.C., 1976—; dir. Mulford Securities Corp. Bd. dirs. NCCJ, Met. Opera, Houston Grand Opera, Opera Orch. N.Y.; trustee Woodlawn Cemetery, Episcopal Mission Soc. Served with USMCR, 1962. Mem. Bond Club N.Y. Republican. Episcopalian. Clubs: Met. Opera,

Pilgrims, Piping Rock, Racquet and Tennis, Doubles Ltd. Home: 1115 5th Ave New York City NY 10028 Office: 767 Fifth Ave New York City NY 10022

PULLMAN, DOUGLAS ROBERT, sociologist, educator; b. Edmonton, Alta., Can., Jan. 12, 1921; s. Carl Douglas and Edith Lillian (Stanton) P.; B.Ed., U. Alta., Edmonton, 1947; M.A., U. Toronto (Ont. Can.), 1949, Ph.D., 1960; m. Janet Chisholm Paterson, June 28, 1945; children—Robert James, Carolyn Jean Edith. Teaching fellow, instr. U. Toronto, 1949-51; asst. prof. sociology U. N.B. (Can.), Fredericton, 1951-59, asso. prof., 1959-66, prof., 1966—, head, chmn. dept. sociology and psychology, 1966-74, chmn. dept. sociology, 1974—; chmn. grievance rev. bd. N.B. Civil Service, 1966-70; mem. selection coms. Can. Council, 1968-75. Served with RCAF, 1941-45. Can. Council leave fellow, 1972, conf. grantee, 1969; Ont. Alcholism Found. grantee, 1951; Bickle Fund grantee, 1953; Atlantic Devel. Bd. grantee, 1967, Mem. Can. Polit. Sci. Assn. (exec. council 1960-62), Atlantic Assn. Sociologists and Anthropologists (pres. 1969), Am. Sociol. Assn., Can. Sociology and Anthropology Assn., Can. Assn. Univ. Tchrs. Mem. United Ch. Can. Club: U. N.B. Faculty. Author: (with Nels Anderson) The Sociology of Economic Development in the Atlantic Provinces, 1967. Contbr. articles to profl. publs. Home: 324 Albert St Fredericton NB E3B 2B6 Canada Office: Dept of Sociology U NB Fredericton NB E3B 5A3 Canada

PULVER, NORMAN, coll. adminstr.; b. N.Y.C., Feb. 26, 1930; s. Abraham and Molly (Fine) P.; B.S., Fairleigh Dickinson U., 1952, M.B.A., 1965; m. Arlene Gloria Schall, Sept. 19, 1954. Pres., mgr. Pulver's, Rutherford, N.J., 1955-70; dir. purchasing F. H. LaGuardia Community Coll., L.I., N.Y., 1970-76, Coll. Medicine and Dentistry N.J., Newark, 1976—. Pres., N.J. Gift Assn., Irvington, 1965-67. Served with U.S. Army, 1950-56. Certified purchasing mgr., Nat. Assn. Purchasing Mgmt. Mem. Rutherford C. of C. (pres. 1963-65), Nat. Assn. Purchasing Mgmt., Nat. Assn. Ednl. Buyers, Nat. Assn. Coll. and Univ. Bus. Officers, Am. Mgmt. Assn., N.Y., N.J. purchasing mgmt. assns. Jewish. Home: 88 Vanderburgh Ave Rutherford NJ 07070 Office: 100 Bergen St Newark NJ 07103

PUMPHREY, PRESTON VAN VORHEES, investment broker; b. N.Y.C., Feb. 25, 1935; s. Preston Hubbell and Ruth (Vorhees) P.; B.A., Dartmouth, 1956; m. Barbara Sauve, June 11, 1961; children—Kathleen, Lynne, Nancy. Registered rep. Bacon, Stevenson & Co., N.Y.C., 1958-62; underwriting mgr. William S. Morris & Co., N.Y.C., 1962-63; registered rep. Banco Credito, N.Y.C., 1963-64, A.G. Edwards & Sons, N.Y.C., 1964-66; pres. Preston Pumphrey & Co., Inc., Syosset, N.Y., 1966-74; br. mgr. James J. Duane & Co., 1974—; adj. asst. prof. fin. C.W. Post Coll. Served with AUS, 1956-58. Home: 11 Beatrice Ave Syosset NY 11791 Office: 75 Jackson Ave Syosset NY 11791

PURCELL, EDWARD MILLS, educator; b. Taylorville, Ill., Aug. 30, 1912; s. Edward A. and Mary Elizabeth (Mills) P.; B.S., Purdue U., 1933, D.Engring. (hon.), 1953; Internat. Exchange student Technische Hochschule, Karlsruhe, Germany, 1933-34; A.M., Harvard U., 1935, Ph.D., 1938; m. Beth C. Busser, Jan. 22, 1937; children—Dennis W., Frank B. Instr. physics Harvard U., 1938-40, asso. prof., 1946-49, prof. physics, 1949-58, Donner prof. sci., 1958-60, Gerhard Gade prof., 1960—; sr. fellow Soc. of Fellows, 1949-71; group leader Fundamental Devels. Group Radiation Lab., Mass. Inst. Tech., 1941-45. Mem. Pres.'s Sci. Advisory Com., 1957-60, 62—. Mem. sci. advisory bd. USAF, 1947, 48, 53-57. Co-winner Nobel prize in Physics, 1952. Mem. Am. Philos. Soc., Nat. Acad. Sci., Phys. Soc., Am. Acad. Arts and Scis. Contbg. author: Radiation Lab. series, 1949, 50. Contbr. sci. papers on nuclear magnetism, radioastronomy, astrophysics, biophysics. Home: 5 Wright St Cambridge MA 02138

PURCELL, FENTON PETER, cons. civil engr.; b. Paterson, N.J., Nov. 23, 1942; s. Lee Thomas and Dorothy (Charette) P.; B.C.E., Rensselaer Poly. Inst., 1965; m. Susan Duggan, Feb. 20, 1971; children—Aimee and Suzie (twins), Jacqueline. Engr., Lee T. Purcell Assos., cons. engrs., Paterson, 1965-66, partner, 1969—. Vice pres. Fenton Corp., Paterson, 1970—. Bd. dirs. Ramapo Valley chpt. ARC. Served to capt. AUS, 1966-69. Registered profl. engr., N.Y., N.J., Pa., Mass. Mem. Am. Water Works Assn., Water Pollution Control Fedn., N.J. Cons. Engrs. Council. Home: 4 Highview Terr Upper Saddle River NJ 07458 Office: 60 Hamilton St Paterson NJ 07505

PURCELL, FRANCIS EUGENE, bldg. materials co. exec.; b. Las Vegas, N.Mex., Apr. 6, 1931; s. Charles A. and Mary Florence (Elliott) P.; B.S., N.Mex. Highlands U., 1956, M.S., 1958; J.D.S., U. Balt., 1964; m. Carol Marie Burke, Sept. 4, 1961; children—Francis Eugene, Suzanne Burke, David Elliott. Research asso. Nat. Heart Inst., Bethesda, Md., 1958-59; asst. to v.p.-sales, mktg., advanced planning, pub. affairs, mgr. Washington office Martin-Marietta Corp., 1959-67; v.p. pub. affairs Portland Cement Assn., Washington, 1967-71; v.p. adminstrn. Lone Star Industries Inc., Greenwich, Conn., 1971-78, sr. v.p. public affairs, 1978—. Bd. dirs. Pub. Affairs Council, Conn. Pub. Expenditures Council. Mil. service, 1951-54; capt. USAF Res. Hon. col.-aide-de-camp Gov. N.Mex., 1966. Democrat. Roman Catholic. Clubs: Univ. (Washington); Bethesda Country; Aspetuck Valley Country (Ct.). Home: 561 Nod Hill Rd Wilton CT 06897 Office: One Greenwich Plaza Greenwich CT 06830

PURCELL, GERVAISE, personnel adminstr.; b. Washington, Jan. 26, 1940; s. Ganson and Catharine (Farnham) P.; student Kenyon Coll., 1958-60, U. Md., 1964-67; m. Mary Navarre Dansard, Apr. 8, 1961; children—Frances Mercer, Gervaise Hamilton. Personnel adminstr., United Parcel Service, Watertown, Mass., N.Y.C., Landover, Md., 1963-70; personnel mgr. Central Charger Service, Washington, 1970—; dir. Residential Manpower Center, 1970-71; mem. ad hoc com. to develop human resources curriculum, Masters degree program, Nat. Grad. U. Served with USMC, 1959-64. Mem. Washington Personnel Assn. (pres.), Am. Soc. Personnel Adminstrs., Washington Bd. Trade. Home: 3802 Williams Lane Chevy Chase MD 20015 Office: 1215 E St NW Washington DC 20004

PURCELL, LEO THOMAS, JR., sanitary engr.; b. Pompton Lakes, N.J., July 28, 1935; s. Leo Thomas and Dorthy (Charette) P.; student St. Lawrence U., 1953-55; B.C.E., Manhattan Coll., 1958; m. Rosemary E. Hewitt, Aug. 23, 1958; children—Leo Thomas III, Cynthia Anne. With Lee T. Purcell, Cons. Engr., Paterson, N.J., 1958, engr., 1962-64; engr. Interstate Sanitation Commn., N.Y.C., 1958-59; partner Lee T. Purcell Assos., Cons. Engrs., Paterson, 1965—; pres. Fenton Corp. Served to lt. Med. Service Corps., AUS, 1959-62. Registered profl. engr., N.J., N.Y., Pa., Fla., Conn.; registered profl. planner, N.J. Mem. Am. Acad. Environ. Engrs., ASCE, Water Pollution Control Fedn., N.J. Water Pollution Control Assn., N.J. Cons. Engrs. Council, Am. Water Works Assn., N.J. Inst. Bldg. and Constrn., Beta Theta Pi. Home: 7 Seminole Way Chatham NJ 07928 Office: 60 Hamilton St Paterson NJ 07505

PURCELL, THEODORE V., clergyman, educator; b. Evanston, Ill., June 6, 1911; s. Theodore Vincent and Anna Loretta (Wallace) P.; A.B., Dartmouth Coll., 1933; A.M. in Econs., Loyola U., Chgo., 1945, S.T.L., 1946; Ph.D. in Social and Indsl. Psychology (Wertheim fellow), Harvard, 1952. Mem. crew Borden-Field Mus. Alaska-Arctic Expdn., 1927; sales and merchandising man Commonwealth Edison Co., 1933-36; joined Soc. of Jesus, 1936, ordained priest Roman Catholic Ch., 1945, asst., psychology Loyola U., Chgo., 1952-54, asso. prof., 1954-58, prof., 1958-62, dir. Loyola-Danforth Mgmt. Ethics seminar, 1959-62; William Jewett Tucker lectr. Dartmouth Coll., 1960-61; dir. Inst. Social Order, St. Louis, 1962-65; dir. Cambridge (Mass.) Center Social Studies, 1965-68, research asso., 1965-71, fellow, 1971—; research prof. Jesuit Center Social Studies Georgetown U., 1971—; lectr. social psychology Harvard, 1966-67, Epis. Theol. Sch., 1967-68; vis. prof. Sloan Sch. Mgmt., 1970-71, U. Calif. at Berkeley, 1972, 74. Mem. Ill. Gov.'s Com. Unemployment, 1961-62; mem. Ill. Commn. Human Relations, 1962-63, Ill. adv. com. U.S. Commn. Civil Rights, 1962-65, Nat. Com. on Ethics, 1976—. Trustee Creighton U., Omaha, 1968-75. Recipient McKinsey Found. award, 1968. Mem. Indsl. Relations Research Assn., Am. Psychol. Assn., Internat. Assn. Applied Psychology, Psychologists Interested in Religious Issues, Assn. Social Econs., Acad. Mgmt. Author: The Worker Speaks His Mind on Company and Union, 1953; Blue Collar Man, 1960; Cases in Business Ethics, 1968; The Negro in the Electrical Industry, 1971; Blacks in the Industrial World, 1972. Contbr. numerous articles to profl. jours. Address: Jesuit Center Social Studies Georgetown U Washington DC 20057

PURDON, JOHN, valuation cons., appraiser; b. N.Y.C., Jan. 6, 1908; s. John and Marcia Latham (Richardson) P.; student N.Y. U., 1927, Columbia U., 1933-34; m. Virginia Rogers, Oct. 2, 1943. Property mgr. Wood Harmon Warranty Corp., N.Y.C., 1933-40; appraiser, property mgt. S. E. Kazdin, N.Y.C., 1940-48; valuation cons. Marsh & McLennan, Inc., Ins. Brokers, N.Y.C., 1948—. Mem. Westchester County Grand Jury Assn., 1972—. Served with AUS, 1942-46, 1950-52; lt. col. (ret.). Decorated Soldiers medal, Bronze Star. Fellow Am. Soc. Appraisers (pres. N.Y. chpt. 1963-64, treas. 1967-68, internat. v.p. 1968-71, pres. White Plains chpt. 1973-74); mem. Real Estate Bd. N.Y., Inc., Am. Contract Bridge League, N.Y. State Soc. Real Estate Appraisers, Res. Officers Assn., Nat. Assn. Realtors, Ret. Officers Assn. Episcopalian. Clubs: Siwanoy Country, Army-Navy of N.Y., Assn. Ex-Members of Squadron A. Home: 9 Tanglewylde Av Bronxville NY 10708 Office: 1221 Ave of the Americas New York City NY 10020

PURDON, ROGER ANTHONY, advt. exec.; b. Camden, N.J., Aug. 5, 1915; s. David and Mary Elizabeth (Duffy) P.; student N.Y. U., 1933-34, Pace Coll., 1934-38; m. Marie Tully, Dec. 1, 1939; children—Anne Marie, Roger Anthony, Liam Oliver. Vice pres., creative dir. Bryan Huston, Inc., N.Y.C., 1952-55, McCann-Erickson, N.Y.C., 1955-61; pres., creative dir. Kudner Agy., N.Y.C., 1961-65; v.p., creative dir. D'Arcy Agy., N.Y.C., 1965-67; v.p., creative dir. London Press Exchange-Leo Burnett, London, Eng., 1967-70; v.p. nat. advt. div. Nat. Advt. Rev. Bd., N.Y.C., 1971-74; v.p. Lefton Co., N.Y.C., 1974—; lectr. in field. Served with U.S. Mcht. Marines, 1942-46. Named Alumnus of Year, Pace U., 1963. Mem. Copy Research Council N.Y. Club: Recess (Detroit). Address: 215 Main St Cold Spring Harbor NY 11724

PURDY, SUSAN GOLD, author, illustrator; b. N.Y.C., May 17, 1939; d. Harold A. and Frances (Joslin) Gold; student Vassar Coll., 1957-59, Sorbonne and Ecole des Beaux Arts, Paris, France, 1959-60; B.S., N.Y. U. 1962; m. Geoffrey Hale Purdy, Sept. 29, 1963; 1 dau., Cassandra Heather. Textile designer Wamsutta Mills, N.Y.C., 1961-63; free-lance designer, 1963-64; co-founder, co-dir. Music and Art Day Camp, Wilton, Conn., 1964-66; author, illustrator, 1964—. Mem. Author's Guild and League of Am. Author and illustrator: My Little Cabbage, 1965, If you Have a Yellow Lion, 1966, Be My Valentine, 1966, Christmas Decorations For You To Make, 1965, Holiday Cards For You To Make, 1967, Festivals for You To Celebrate, 1969, Jewish Holidays, 1969; Costumes For You To Make, 1971; Books For You To Make, 1973; Let's Give A Party, 1976; Christmas Cookbook, 1976; Christmas Gifts For You To Make, 1976; Halloween Cookbook, 1977; illustrator: Suddenly a Witch; Developing Children's Perceptual Skills in Reading; contbr. articles to mags., including Good Housekeeping, Ladies Home Jour., Family Circle; tchr. cooking for young people CBS-TV, 1973—, demonstrator crafts various TV programs.

PURKAYASTHA, ARINDAM, surgeon; b. India, Apr. 1, 1940; s. Arabinda and Jyotsna (Datta) P.; came to U.S., 1967; M.B., B.S., U. Calcutta, 1963; M.S., U. Delhi, 1967; m. Deepa Choudhury, May 27, 1973; 1 dau., Tania. Intern, St. Joseph Hosp., Lorain, Ohio, 1968; resident Wilson Meml. Hosp., Johnson City, N.Y., 1960-70; resident, chief resident Sisters of Charity Hosp., Buffalo, 1971-72; practice medicine specializing in gen. surgery, Susquehanna, Pa., 1974—; gen. surgeon Barnes Kasson Hosp., Susquehanna, 1976—. Diplomate Am. Bd. Surgery. Mem. Susquehanna County Med. Soc. Home: Box 126A Route 2 Windsor NY 13865 Office: Barnes Kasson Hospital Sudquehanna PA 18847

PURNELL, DALLAS MICHAEL, pathologist; b. Tacoma, Wash., July 9, 1939; s. Dallas John and Lorna Barbara (Thompson) P.; B.S., U. Puget Sound, 1963; M.S., Idaho State U., 1965; Ph.D., U. Wash., 1971; m. Dolores Marian Rago, Mar. 11, 1972; children—Jamie Jennifer, Robert Michael. Fellow pathology Pa. State U., Hershey, 1971-72, instr., 1973-75, asst. prof. pathology, 1975-77; asst. prof. pathology dept. pathology Sch. Medicine U. Md., Balt., 1977—. USPHS grantee, 1976—. Mem. N.Y. Acad. Sci., Am. Soc. Microbiology, Internat. Soc. Human and Animal Mycology, Am. Assn. Pathologists, Am. Assn. Cancer Research, AAAS. Contbr. articles in pathology, anatomy, mycology and cancer to profl. jours. Home: 1401 Jordan St Baltimore MD 21217 Office: Dept Pathology School Medicine Univ Maryland Baltimore MD 21201

PURNELL, JAMES EDGAR, ophthalmologist; b. San Antonio, Sept. 9, 1918; s. Luther Cleveland and Laura Ramsay (Pixley) P.; B.S., U. Tex., 1941; M.D., U. Ark., 1945; postgrad. Harvard Med. Sch., 1948-49; m. Jean Mowry, Nov. 26, 1959; 1 son, James Edgar. Intern, Charity Hosp., New Orleans, 1945-46; resident Wills Hosp., Phila., 1949-52; practice medicine specializing in ophthalmology, N.Y.C., 1953—; mem. staff Manhattan Eye, Ear and Throat Hosp. Republican. Episcopalian. Clubs: Union (N.Y.C.); Field (Greenwich, Conn.). Home: 148 Hunt Dr Princeton NJ 08540 Office: 927 Park Ave New York City NY 10028

PURPLE, THOMAS CLAYTON, paper mfg. co. exec.; b. Greenfield, Mass., Sept. 8, 1947; s. Carl Richmond and Geniveve L. (Barber) P.; B.B.A. in Mktg., Nichols Coll., 1969; m. Leslie Lynne Bredimus, Jan. 10, 1976. With S.D. Warren div. Scott Paper Co., 1971—, asst. to mgr. print quality control, Westbrook, Maine, 1971-72, employment mgr., 1974-77, book pub. papers customer rep., Boston, 1972-73, field rep., Bala Cynwyd, Pa., 1977—. Served with Army N.G., 1969-75. Mem. Personnel Mgmt. Assn. Clubs: So. Maine Personnel Execs., Susquehana Litho (Lancaster, Pa.), Phila. Crickett. Office: SD Warren div Scott Paper Co 1 Bala Cynwyd Plaza Rm 210 Bala Cynwyd PA 19004

PURPURA, ANTHONY GRAHAM, physician; b. Bklyn., Apr. 28, 1939; s. John Anthony and Edith (Graham) P.; B.A., Colgate U., 1960; M.D., George Washington U., 1963; m. Julia Mae Bensle, Aug. 28, 1960; children—John Edward, Julia Ann. Intern, Meadowbrook Hosp., L.I., N.Y., 1963; practice family medicine, Bklyn., 1963—; mem. staffs Victory Hosp., Meml. Hosp., Flatbush Gen. Hosp. Bd. dirs. S.I. YMCA, 1971—, pres., 1974-75; bd. govs. S.I. Acad., 1971-75; active Cub Scouts; swim coach Notre Dame Acad. High Sch.; coach, v.p. S.I. Aquatic Assn.-AAU. Served to lt. S.G., USNR, 1964-66. Mem. Am. Acad. Family Practice, AMA, Bay Ridge, Ridge Borough med. socs. Lutheran. Club: Richmond County Country. Home: 3 Helena Rd Staten Island NY 10304 Office: 8684 15th Ave Brooklyn NY 11228

PURPURA, PETER ANGELO, psychologist-psychotherapist; b. Bklyn., Dec. 14, 1941; s. Peter Paul and Josephine (Caserta) P.; B.A., Queens Coll., 1963; M.A. (grad. asst.), Fordham U., 1970, Ph.D. in Clin. Psychology (Nat. Inst. Mental Health fellow), 1970; m. Angela Pisciotta, May 21, 1967; children—Cassandra, Cara. Sch. psychologist Lindenhurst (N.Y.) High Sch., 1968-70; supervising psychologist Rockaway Mental Health Center, Far Rockaway, N.Y., 1970-74; pvt. practice adult, child psychotherapy, Sea Cliff, N.Y., 1971—; faculty Washington Sq. Inst. Psychotherapy, 1977—; cons. in field. Mem. Am. Psychol. Assn., Sigma Psi, Psi Chi, Alpha Psi Omega. Address: 67 Glen Ave Sea Cliff NY 11579

PURRELLI, CHARLES JOHN, ins. co. exec.; b. Bklyn., Apr. 25, 1933; s. Charles and Ann (Cavaretta) P.; B.S., St. Peters Coll., 1956; M.B.A., Rutgers U., 1961; m. Dolores Helen Cummings, Dec. 1, 1956; children—Carol Anne, Rose Marie, John Cavaretta. Dir. mgmt. services Tenneco Corp., N.Y.C., 1963-69; corporate dir. Raytheon Corp., Lexington, Mass., 1969-71; v.p. Citicorp., N.Y.C., 1971-74; 1st sr. v.p. Commercial Union Assurance Cos., Boston, 1974—. Served to 1st lt. AUS, 1954-64. Roman Catholic. Home: Concord MA 01742 Office: 1 Beacon St Boston MA 02108

PURSLEY, ROBERT EDWIN, corporate exec., ret. air force officer; b. Muncie, Ind., Nov. 23, 1927; s. Wilbur F. and Ina Jennesse (Puckett) P.; student Ball State Tchrs. Coll., 1944-45; B.S., U.S. Mil. Acad., 1949; M.B.A., Harvard, 1957, postgrad., 1957-58; m. Phyllis L. Roberts, May 9, 1953; children—Mark E., Anne J., Elizabeth S., Kristin L., Carol R. Commd. 2d lt. U.S. Air Force, 1949, advanced through grades to lt. gen., 1972; operational assignments, Tex., Korea, 1949-55; asso. prof. econs. U.S. Air. Force Acad., 1958-63; systems analyst Office of Sec. Def., 1963-65; student, mem. faculty Air War Coll., 1965-66; mil. asst. to Sec. Def., 1966-72; comdr. U.S. Forces Japan, and 5th Air Force, Fuchu, Japan, 1972-74; ret., 1974; ops. v.p., exec. v.p. Insilico Corp., Meriden, Conn., 1974-77; partner J.H. Whitney & Co., 1977—. Decorated D.S.M. with 2 oak leaf clusters, Legion of Merit, D.F.C., Air medal with clusters; recipient Orval Anderson award Nat. Geog. Soc., 1966. Mem. Council on Fgn. Relations, Air Force Assn., Dadelian Soc., Japan Soc., Am. Acad. Polit. Social Sci., Am. Mgmt. Assn., Assn. Grads. U.S. Mil. Acad. Club: Home (Meriden). Home: 555 Haviland Rd Stamford CT 06903 Office: 630 5th Ave New York City NY 10020

PURTELL, WALTER CHARLES, law enforcement ofcl.; b. Syracuse, N.Y., Sept. 3, 1936; s. Walter Joseph and Dorotha Irene (Burke) P.; B.S. cum laude, LeMoyne Coll., 1958; grad. N.Y. State Sch. Police, 1960; M.S. in Edn., State U. N.Y., Geneseo, 1972; also numerous spl. courses and in-service seminars; m. Gloria E. Spezzano, Oct. 25, 1961; 1 stepdau., Gail E. MacCollam. With N.Y. State Police, 1959—, sgt., 1967-74, Troop A Traffic Supr., Batavia, 1974—, tech. sgt., 1974—; instr. criminal procedure, penal, vehicle and traffic law N.Y. State Police Acad.; former asst. prof. criminal justice Genesee Community Coll.; mem. Western N.Y. Traffic Safety Council. Chmn. liturgical com. tri-parish council St. Lucy's Ch., Retsof, N.Y.; treas. Genesee Valley Chs., Geneseo, N.Y. Served with USAF, 1961-62. Mem. Internat. Assn. Chiefs Police, Police Benevolent Assn. N.Y. State Police, LeMoyne Coll. Alumni Assn., Pi Gamma Mu. Roman Catholic. Club: A-ON-DO-WA-NUH Sportsman's (past dir.). Home: 2827 Genesee St Wadsworth NY 14565 Office: NY State Police Troop A Hdqrs W Saile Dr Batavia NY 14020

PURVIS, GEORGE PORTER, III, hosp. adminstr.; b. Bryn Mawr, Pa., Aug. 31, 1942; s. George Porter and Virginia Moore (Smith) P.; B.A., B.S., Pa. State U., 1969, M.B.A., 1971; m. Jacqueline M. Pavone, Sept. 21, 1974. Residence hall coordinator Pa. State U., University Park, 1969-71; ops. mgr. Western Electric Co., Phila., 1971-73; sr. mgmt. cons. MECCS, Princeton, N.J., 1973-76; asso. hosp. dir., dir. fin. M.S. Hershey Med. Center, Hershey, Pa., 1976-78, asso. hosp. dir., dir. profl. services, 1978—; instr. mgmt. and fin. Pa. State U., University Park, 1972-78. Served with USAF, 1962-66. Mem. Am. Coll. Hosp. Adminstrs., Hosp. Fin. Mgmt. Assn., Hosp. Mgmt. Systems Soc., Am. Inst. Indsl. Engrs., Alpha Pi Mu, Beta Gamma Sigma. Home: 3515 Schoolhouse Ln Harrisburg PA 17109 Office: M S Hershey Med Center 500 University Dr Hershey PA 17033

PUSAR, ARNOLD, psychoanalyst; b. Bklyn., May 16, 1928; s. Murry and Ray (Littman) P.; B.A., Syracuse U., 1948, M.A., 1950, Ph.D., 1954; m. Florence Unger, Mar. 18, 1951; children—Jeffrey, Susan. Clin. psychologist N. Shore Neuropsychiatric Center, Roslyn, N.Y. 1955-58; pvt. practice psychoanalyis, Rockville Center, N.Y., 1955—. Pres. Dads Club, Hewlett (N.Y.) High Sch., 1972-73. Chmn. bd. trustees Nassau Psychol. Services Inst., Hempstead, N.Y., 1970-73. Diplomate Am. Bd. Psychology. Fellow Soc. Psychoanalytic Study and Research (past pres.); mem. Nassau County (pres. 1968-69), N.Y. State (rep. clin. div.) psychol. assns., Sigma Xi, Psi Chi. Club: Shelter Rock Tennis (Manhasset, N.Y.). Home: 1078 Fordham Lane Woodmere NY 11598 Office: 165 N Village Av Rockville Centre NY 11570

PUSIN, MAX NATHANIEL, psychiatrist; b. Kiev, Russia, Sept. 22, 1917; s. Nathan and Rachel (Golberg) P.; B.S. with distinction, U. Minn., 1938, M.B., 1940; M.D., U. Minn., 1941; m. Mildred Monheit, May 30, 1947; children—Russett Sue, Nikki; m. Frieda Mowshowitz, June 11, 1964; came to U.S., 1923, naturalized, 1928. Intern, Med. Center, Jersey City, 1940-41; resident VA Hosp., Bronx, N.Y., 1949-50; chief neurology VA Hosp., Lyons, N.J., 1950-52, asst. chief psychiatry, 1952-58; chief mental hygiene clinic VA Regional Office, Newark, 1958; chief low-cost psychotherapy clinic Beth Israel Hosp., Newark, 1958-62; practice medicine specializing in psychiatry, Short Hills, N.J., 1958—; cons. psychiatry VA Hosp., East Orange, N.J., 1959-78, VA Hosp., Lyons, N.J., 1960-71, Kean Coll. N.J., Union, 1979—; clin. asst. prof. psychiatry N.J. Coll. Medicine, Newark, 1960—; asst. clin. prof. psychiatry of medicine Albert Einstein Coll. Medicine, Bronx, N.Y., 1969-74; cons. psychiatrist Sch. System, Montclair, N.J., 1959—. Served to capt., M.C., AUS, 1942-46. Diplomate Am. Bd. Internal Medicine, Am. Bd. Neurology and Psychiatry. Fellow Am. Psychiat. Assn.; mem. AMA, Israel-Am. Physician's Fellowship, N.J. Neuropsychiat. Assn., Essex County Med. Soc. Weizmann Inst. Israel (contbg.). Jewish. Club: B'nai B'rith. Author publs. in medicine and psychiatry. Office: 16 Holly Dr Short Hills NJ 07078

PUTNAM, CAROLINE JENKINS (MRS. ROGER LOWELL PUTNAM), civic worker; b. Glymont, Md., Nov. 16, 1892; d. Thomas Canfield and Eleanor (Compton) Jenkins; student Mt. St. Agnes Acad., 1905-07; LL.D., Newton Coll. Sacred Heart, 1967, St. Mary's Coll., 1959, Regis. Coll., 1952, St. Michael's Coll., 1956;

L.H.D., Am. Internat. Coll., 1950, Manhattanville Coll., 1959; L.H.D. (hon.), Duquesne U., 1969; m. Roger Lowell Putnam Oct. 9, 1919; children—Caroline Canfield, Roger Lowell, William Lowell, Anna Lowell (Mrs. Putnam Finnerty), Mary Compton (Mrs. Charles W. Chatfield), Michael Courtney Jenkins. Mem. Springfield (Mass.) Housing Authority, 1952-62; mem. advisory bd. Mass. Commn. Against Discrimination, Springfield, 1949—; mem. Comm. for Study of De Facto Segregation Pub. Schs. of Mass., 1964-65; mem. Mass. sub-com. under Nat. Commn. on Civil Rights, 1959-64; pres. Catholic Scholarships for Negroes, Inc., 1946—. Recipient Nat. Human Relations award NCCJ, 1976. Mem. Kappa Gamma Phi (hon.). Democrat. Roman Catholic. Home: 101 Mulberry St Springfield MA 01105

PUTNAM, LOTHAR FABER, advt. rep., horse breeder; b. Brownsville, Tex., Jan. 14, 1924; s. Brock and Margaret (Faber) P.; B.A., Amherst Coll., 1948; m. Barbara Elliott, May 3, 1975; children—Conrad, Geoffrey, Molly, Mark, Cecil. Trainee, Warwick & Legler, N.Y.C., 1948-49; account exec., treas. Osgood & Hazen, N.Y.C., 1949-52; advt. mgr. Eberhard Faber, Inc., Bklyn., 1952-56, Boating Mag., N.Y.C., 1956-64, Rudder Mag., N.Y.C., 1964-66; eastern advt. mgr. Golf Digest, N.Y.C., 1966-68, Motor Boating & Sailing Mag., N.Y.C., 1968-76; owner, mgr. Putnam Assos., Old Brookville, N.Y., 1976-78; partner Candlewick Farms, Brookville, N.Y., 1978—. Served to lt. U.S. Army, 1942-46. Decorated Bronze Star, Purple Heart with cluster. Mem. Marine Trades Assn., N.Y. Assn. Boat and Engine Mfrs. Republican. Episcopalian. Home and office: Hegemans Ln Old Brookville NY 11545

PUTNEY, RICHARD ANDREW, banker; b. Peterborough, N.H., Jan. 3, 1932; s. Andrew LeRoy and Charlotte Margaret (Thompson) P.; Asso. sci. Becker Jr. Coll., 1949-51; B.S., U. N.H., 1956; m. Kathleen Alexandra Taylor, Feb. 16, 1955; children—Andrew Taylor, Brock Richard, Kathleen Lisa, Daniel Willard. Bus. trainee Gen. Electric Co., Schenectady, 1951-53; office mgr. New Eng. Mut. Life Ins. Co., Boston, 1956-58, Cleve., 1958-60; sr. investment officer Harvard Trust Co., Cambridge, Mass., 1962-71; investment officer Boston Safe Deposit & Trust Co., 1971-74; v.p. investments Multibank Financial Corp., Quincy, Mass., 1974—; treas. Ednl. Exchange Greater Boston, 1966-71; cons. in field. Mem. finance com. Cambridge Vis. Nurse Assn., 1966-69. Chartered fin. analyst. Mem. Inst. Chartered Financial Analysts, Boston Security Analysts Soc., Alpha Omicron, Psi Epsilon. Episcopalian. Clubs: New Eng. Govt. Bond, Masons. Home: 178 Summer St Norwell MA 02061

PUTTLITZ, DONALD HERBERT, microbiologist; b. Kingston, N.Y., Apr. 21, 1938; s. Adalbert Siegfried and Elizabeth Agnes (Barthel) P.; B.S. with distinction, State U. N.Y. at New Paltz, 1959; M.S. State U. N.Y. at Albany, 1961; Ph.D. (NSF traineeship) Cornell U., 1965; m. Barbara Ann Dingman, July 19, 1969; children—Michelle Suzanne, Brian Robert. NIH traineeship in clin. microbiology Columbia Coll. Physicians and Surgeons, N.Y.C., 1965-67; clin. microbiologist Beth Israel Med. Center, N.Y.C., 1967—. Faculty Mt. Sinai Coll. Medicine, N.Y.C., 1968—. Diplomate Am. Bd. Med. Microbiology. Mem. Am. Soc. Microbiology, Am. Pub. Health Assn., Phi Kappa Phi. Home: 166-05 Highland Ave Jamaica NY 11432 Office: 10 Nathan D Perlman Pl New York City NY 10003

PYKE, CAROL JUNE, librarian; b. Miami, Fla., Mar. 20, 1944; d. Robert O. and June (Grim) Renville; B.A., George Washington U., 1966; M.S. in L.S., Catholic U. Am., 1968; M.A., George Washington U., 1973; m. Thomas N. Pyke, Jr., June 22, 1968; 1 son, Christopher Renville. Asst. librarian Mt. Vernon Coll., Washington, 1968-70; asst. dir., tech. services librarian Urban Inst. Library, Washington, 1970-78, dir., 1978—. Mem. Friends of the Zoo, Suncoast Seabird Sanctuary, Parent and Child, Smithsonian Assos., Spl. Library Assn., D.C. Library Assn., Beta Phi Mu. Episcopalian. Home: 4720 N 21st St Arlington VA 22207 Office: Urban Inst Library 2100 M St NW Washington DC 20037

PYKE, THOMAS NICHOLAS, JR., computer engring. exec.; b. Washington, July 16, 1942; s. Thomas Nicholas and Pauline Marie (Pingitore) P.; B.S. (Westinghouse scholar), Carnegie Inst. Tech., 1964; M.S. (Ford Found. fellow), U. Pa., 1965; m. Carol June Renville, June 22, 1968; 1 son, Christopher Renville. Student trainee Nat. Bur. Standards, Washington, 1960-64, electronic engr., 1964-69, chief computer systems sect., 1969-73, chief computer networking sect., acting div. chief, 1973-75, chief computer systems engring. div., 1975—; organizer, ofcl. several profl. computer confs., 1970—. Chmn. Carnegie Tech. Student Congress, 1963-64; bd. dirs. Glebe Commons Assn., 1976—, v.p., 1977—. Recipient Silver Medal award Dept. Commerce, 1973. Fellow Washington Acad. Sci. (Engring. Sci. award 1974); mem. IEEE (bd. govs. computer soc. 1971-73, 75-77), Am. Fedn. Info. Processing Socs. (dir. 1974-76), AAAS, Assn. Computing Machinery, Nat. Geog. Soc., Sigma Xi, Eta Kappa Nu, Omicron Delta Kappa, Pi Kappa Alpha. Episcopalian. Contbr. articles to profl. jours. Home: 4720 N 21st St Arlington VA 22207 Office: Nat Bur Standards Washington DC 20234

PYLE, HOWARD, III, tobacco co. exec.; b. Richmond, Va., Feb. 1, 1940; s. Wilfrid and Anne Woolston (Roller) P.; A.B., Princeton, 1962; LL.B., U. Va., 1967, J.D., 1970; m. Caroline Oglesby Smith, June 18, 1965; children—Elizabeth Roller, Howard. Career trainee CIA, Washington, 1967-69; adminstrv. asst. to Congressman Odin Langen, Washington, 1969-70, Congressman Hastings Keith, Washington, 1971; asst. to sec. Dept. Interior, Washington, 1971-73; Washington rep. Standard Oil Co. of Ind., Washington, 1973-77; mgr. fed. pub. affairs R.J. Reynolds Industries, Inc., Winston-Salem, N.C., 1977—. Served with USN, 1962-64. Mem. Am. Bar Assn., D.C., Va. bars, Nat. Rifle Assn. (life), Res. Officers Assn., SAR (life), Delta Theta Phi. Republican. Episcopalian. Clubs: Va. Country, Kenwood Golf and Country. Home: 4930 Quebec St NW Washington DC 20016 Office: 2550 M St NW Suite 770 Washington DC 20037

PYLE, LOUIS APGAR, JR., physician; b. Jersey City, Apr. 7, 1920; s. Louis Apgar and Elizabeth H. Pyle; A.B., Princeton U., 1941; M.D., Columbia U., 1950; m. Janet Hanson, June 25, 1949; children—Thomas, Sally, Elizabeth. Intern U. Oreg., 1951, resident in pediatrics, 1952-53; practice medicine specializing in pediatrics, Ridgewood, N.J., 1954-71; univ. physician, dir. clin. services Princeton U. Health Services, 1972-77, dir. athletic medicine, 1976-78, dir. univ. health services, acad. officer, 1977—; med. dir. Bergen County (N.J.) Narcotic Treatment Center, part-time, 1972—; clin. instr. Coll. Medicine and Dentistry N.J.-Rutgers Med. Sch., 1978—; mem. med. adv. bd. Planned Parenthood Mercer County (N.J.); trustee Hun Sch., Princeton, 1978—. Served with USNR, 1942-46; PTO. Diplomate Am. Bd. Pediatrics. Fellow Am. Acad. Pediatrics; mem. Am. Coll. Health Assn., Am. Coll. Sports Medicine, Alpha Omega Alpha. Episcopalian. Clubs: Tower; Princeton. Home: 107 McCosh Circle Princeton NJ 08540 Office: McCosh Health Center Princeton U Princeton NJ 08540

PYLES, THOMAS TERRILL, mktg. exec.; b. St. Louis, Aug. 11, 1942; s. Manuel Aaron and Mary Lucille P.; A.A.S., Syracuse U., 1968, A.A.S. (with honors), 1969; B.B.A.(with honors), U. Cincinnati, 1970; m. Louise Agnes Meyer, June 17, 1967. Pricing mgr. Gen. Cable Corp., N.Y.C., 1970-71; prod. mgr. major appliances, Westinghouse Internat., N.Y.C., 1971-74; corp. dir. mktg. Bro-Dart Industries, Williamsport, Pa., 1974-75; mgr. mktg. Gen. Cable Corp., Greenwich, Conn., 1975-77; v.p. mktg. ATI, Inc., 1977—; cons. in field, dir. Ken Woodburn, Inc. Awards judge Clio Internat. Adut. awards for excellence. Served with USAF, 1961-66. Recipient Best New Product Concept award N.J. Design Art Inst., 1976. Mem. Am. Mgmt. Assn. Am. Mktg. Assn., Beta Gamma Sigma (Phi Beta Kappa), U. Cincinnati Alumni Assn. Clubs: Halloween Yacht, Southport Racquet. Home: 26 Chesterfield Rd Stamford CT 06902 Office: PO Box 4 49 John St Southport CT 06490

PYNE, EBEN WRIGHT, banker; b. N.Y.C., June 14, 1917; s. Grafton H. and Leta Constance (Wright) P.; grad. Groton Sch., 1935; A.B., Princeton, 1939; m. Hilda Holloway, Dec. 16, 1941; children—Lillian Pyne-Corbin, Mary Alison. Clk., First Nat. City Trust Co. (formerly) City Bank Farmers Trust Co., 1939, v.p., asst. to pres., 1952-56, exec. v.p., 1956, pres., dir. 1957-61; asst. cashier Citibank, N.A., 1946-50, asst. v.p., 1950-52, v.p., 1952-53, sr. v.p., 1960—; dir. Phoenix Assurance Co. N.Y., U.S. Life Ins. Co. City of N.Y., City Home Corp., Gen. Devel. Corp., City Investing Co., L.I. Lighting Co., W.R. Grace and Co. Bd. dirs. Met. Transp. Authority, 1965-75, Triborough Bridge and Tunnel Authority, 1965-75, N.Y.C. Transit Authority, 1965-75, Manhattan and Bronx Surface Transit Operating Authority, 1965-75, Stewart Airport, 1965-75, S.I. Rapid Transit Operating Authority, 1965-75, Winifred Masterson Burke Relief Found., 1958-70, Downtown Bklyn. Devel. Assn., 1965-74; mem. adv. bd. Nassau County council Boy Scouts Am. Bd. dirs. Nassau Hosp., trustee St. Luke's Hosp., Grace Inst., Bklyn. Inst. Arts and Scis., Juilliard Sch., Dowling Coll., Hall of Sci. City N.Y., Inc., United Fund L.I., Groton Sch., 1957-62; governing com. Bklyn. Mus. Served as maj. AUS, 1940-46. Mem. Pilgrims of U.S. (exec. com.), N.Y. Zool. Soc. (trustee). Clubs: Piping Rock (Locust Valley, L.I.); Bond, Links (gov.), Racquet and Tennis, River (N.Y.C.); Ivy (Princeton, N.J.); Links Golf (North Hills, L.I.); Nat. Golf Links Am. (Southampton, L.I.). Home: Old Westbury NY 11568 Office: One Citicorp Center New York NY 10043

QUADLAND, MICHAEL CORNELIUS, counseling psychologist; b. Washington, Mar. 31, 1943; s. Marten Warren and Doris (Trudeau) Q.; B.A., Dartmouth Coll., 1965; M.P.H., Yale U., 1967; Ph.D. in Counseling Psychology, N.Y. U., 1978. Research asso. Harvard U. Med. Sch., 1969-71; health services researcher U. Vt., 1971-72; psychologist, marriage counselor, sex therapist, N.Y.C., 1975—; cons. program planning and implementation in human sexuality to colls. and med. sch. Served as commd. officer USPHS, 1967-69. Mem. Am. Assn. Marriage and Family Therapists, Am. Assn. Sex Educators, Counselors and Therapists, Nat. Council Family Relations, Am. Psychol. Assn., Eastern Assn. Sex Therapists, Soc. Sci. Study of Sex. Author: Human Reproduction and Family Planning, 1972. Research on cognitive correlates of secondary erectile dysfunction in men.

QUAILER, MARTIN LEONARD, ednl. adminstr.; b. N.Y.C., June 24, 1928; B.B.A. in Accounting, Coll. City N.Y., 1949, M.A. in Edn., Accounting, 1953. Fiscal Officer, Manpower Program Bd. of Edn., N.Y.C., 1964-68; comptroller Grove Press, Inc., 1968-70; asst. treas. UEC Inc., 1970-72; asst. dir. Bur. of Reimbursable Programs. N.Y.C. Bd. of Edn., 1972-77; asst. adminstr. Office Sch. Food Services, 1977—. Mem. N.Y. State Adminstrs. in Compensatory Edn., Council of Suprs. and Adminstrs., Comml. Edn. Assn., Nat. Assn. of Adminsrs. o State and Federally Assisted Edn. Programs (asst. adminstrative dir.). Home: 33-52 81st St Jackson Heights NY 11372 Office: 50-01 Northern Blvd Long Island City NY 11104

QUATTLEBAUM, OWEN MCDERMED, banker; b. Anniston, Ala., Dec. 26, 1935; s. Lester Nowell and Lucy (McDermed) Q.; A.B., U. Ga., 1957; M.A., Fletcher Sch. Law Diplomacy, 1959. Asst. sec. Bank N.Y., N.Y.C., 1966, investment officer, 1967-69, v.p., 1969—, v.p., dept. head, investment mgrs. service, 1970-77, mgr. investment counsel div., 1977—. Vice chmn. bd. mgrs. Bklyn. Central YMCA, recipient Man of Yr. award, 1973. Served with USCG, 1959-60. Mem. N.Y. Soc. Security Analysts, Inst. Chartered Financial Analysts, Am. Bankers Assn. (trust investment com.). Episcopalian Club: Heights Casino. Home: 198 Columbia Heights Brooklyn NY 11201 Office: 48 Wall St New York City NY 10015

QUATTRONE, PHILIP ANTHONY, tax accountant; b. Gallatin, Pa., Sept. 10, 1940; s. Nunzio Samuel and Marie Angela (Urso) Q.; studnet Duff's Bus. Coll., 1960-62; Calif. State Coll., 1958-59, 1963-64; m. Karen Lee Natali, Oct. 2, 1965; children—Ledea Marie, Philip Nunzio, Derrico Vincent. Tax accountant Chiurazzi & George, C.P.A.'s, Pitts., 1962-64; owner, operator Quattrone Accountants, Inc., New Eagle, Pa., 1964—. Served with AUS, 1962-68. Certified internal auditor, Pa. Mem. Nat., Pa. assn. tax cons., Assn. Enrolled Fed. Agts. Democrat. Roman Catholic. Clubs: Elks. Home: 115 Prosser Dr Monongahela PA 15063 Office: Chess and Maple Sts New Eagle PA 15067

QUEEN, EVANGELINE PALMER, psychologist, school dir.; b. Beaufort, S.C., May 15, 1905; d. Laurence Henry and Daisy Dean (Nix) Palmer; A.B. in Edn., Howard U., 1928; M.A. in Edn., Columbia U., 1933; Ph.D., N.Y. U., 1951; postgrad. U. Wis., 1935, Cath. U., 1940, Am. U., 1940; Montessori diploma, 1964; m. Edward Jerome Queen, Feb. 26, 1942; 1 dau., Evangeline Marie. Tchr. D.C. Pub. Sch.s., Washington, 1927-39, research asst., sch. psychologist, 1939-49, asst. sch. prin., 1949-64; founder, dir., pres. Avalon Montessori Children's House, Washington, 1964—; asso. prof. edn. and psychology D.C. Tchrs. Coll., 1972-75; pvt. practice psychology, Washington, 1973—. Recipient hon. diploma Tchrs. Coll. Columbia U., 1933. Mem. Am. (life), D.C. (life) psychol. assns., Am. Montessori Soc., Assn. Montessori Internationale, AAUW, Delta Pi Epsilon (life). Home: 1424 Girard St NE Washington DC 20017 Office: 2814 Franklin St NE Washington DC 20018

QUEEN, ROBERT ISAAC, pub. relations exec.; b. N.Y.C., Aug. 12, 1919; s. Joseph and Clara (Rodin) Q.; B.S., Coll. City N.Y., 1942; L.H.D., Am. Coll. Police Sci., Nat. Police Acad., 1968; m. Bella Arkin, Sept. 2, 1955; children—Alan N., Joseph W., Ann-Claire. Began career with U.S. Govt., 1942-55; owner, partner Robert I. Queen & Assos., pub. relations, N.Y.C., 1955—; N.Y.-N.J. mng. editor Press Wire Services, 1955—, Teaching cons. pub. relations Sch. Continuing Profl. Studies, Pratt Inst., 1963-65; pub. relations counsel N.Y.C. Transit Police PBA, 1967-69, N.Y. Housing Patrolmen's PBA, 1969; Council Higher Ednl. Instns., Voorhees Tech. Inst.; dir. pub. relations Bronx County Office Civil Defense; press cons. Congressman Alfred E. Santangelo, 1960-63, 65, 66; pub. relations counsel N.Y. State Senator John R. Dunne, 1969-70; legislative press aide to Hon. Thomas J. Manton, 1970-73; pub. affairs officer Meth. Hosp., Bklyn., 1973-75, pub. relations aide to chmn. edn. com., 1973-77; pub. relations counsel to chmn. finance minority com. U.S. Senate, 1977-79. Served with AUS, World War II. Recipient Nat. Short Story award Delta Sigma Lambda, 1951, Police Commendations, N.Y.C., 1966; Presdl. commendation, 1974; Gov.'s citation, 1974; Mayor's citation, 1974; also numerous awards for community service. Mem. Broadcast Pioneers (life), Nat. Writers Club, Newspaper Reporters Assn. N.Y.C., N.Y. Press Club, Newspaper Guild N.Y., Pub. Relations Soc. Am., Army-Navy Union (past N.Y. State pub. relations dir.), Am. Hosp. Assn. Soc. Pub. Relations Dirs., D.A.V. (past county comdr.), Silurians Sigma Delta Chi. Club: Overseas Press. Author books: Emigres in Wartime, 1940; Tabloid Tales, 1945; Guilty—They Said!, 1945; Handbook on Public Relations, 1957, rev., 1967; Creative Public Relations in Planning Special Events, 1965, 67. Writer TV series: Tabloid Tales, Million Dollar Showcase, Operation: Maverick, WABO-TV Nick Kenny Shows; Suspense, The Green Hornet, The Web, The Shadow; also cons. radio-TV script writer-editor, 1950—. Address: 144-45 35th Ave Flushing NY 11354

QUEENY, JAMES FRANCIS, educator; b. Quincy, Mass., Jan. 30, 1920; s. James Francis and Caroline Agnes (Donovan) I; B.A. in English Lit., Harvard, 1947; M.A. in 18th Century Lit., Trinity Coll., Dublin, Ireland, 1948; postgrad adminstrn. Harvard U.; married; 5 children. Tchr., Hingham (Mass.) pub. schs., 1950-51; tchr. Duxbury (Mass.) Intermediate Sch., 1953-68, head of guidance, 1968—. Trustee Duxbury Free Library, 1973—; chmn. Duxbury Bicentennial Com., 1975—; dir. adult edn. Town of Duxbury, 1970—; prin., dir. Meeting House Sch., 1953—. Certified guidance counselor, dir., tchr., prin. Mem. NEA, Mass., Duxbury tchrs. assns., South Shore Guidance Assn., Mass. Sch. Counselors Assn., Duxbury Frostbite Soc., Duxbury Wharf Rats, U.S., Mass. Bay yacht racing unions, U.S. Naval Inst. Clubs: Cohasset Yacht (sailing master 1955-65), Duxbury Yacht (sailing master 1972—). Home: 9 Beaverbrook Ln Duxbury MA 02332 Office: Intermediate Sch St George St Duxbury MA 02332

QUELLMALZ, HENRY, printing co. exec.; b. Balt., May 18, 1915; s. Frederick and Edith Margaret (Shaw) Q.; B.A., Princeton, 1937; m. Marion Agar Lynch, Aug. 2, 1940; children—Lynn Quellmalz Johnson, Susan Quellmalz Mastan, Jane. Dir. personnel, Macy's Men's Store, 1938-40; asst. mgr. Fowlers Dept. Store, Glens Falls, N.Y., 1940-41; personnel dir. U.S. Army postexchanges, Fort Meade, Md., 1941-44; with Boyd Printing Co., Albany, N.Y., 1944—, pres., 1952—; pres. Q Corp. U.S. Agt. for WHO publs., 1960—; dir. Bankers Trust Co. Albany. Campaign chmn. ARC, Albany, 1957; bd. dirs. Camelot Home for Boys; bd. govs. Doane Stewart Sch., Albany, 1977—, treas., 1977-78. Served with AUS, 1943. Recipient Pres.'s award Am. Assn. Mental Deficiency, 1976. Mem. Albany Area C. of C., Printing Industry Am., Princeton Club. N.Y. Democrat. Episcopalian. Clubs: Princeton, University, Fort Orange, Hudson River, Board Room. Home: 1 Park Hill Dr Menands NY 12204 Office: 49 Sheridan Ave Albany NY 12210

QUERIDO, ARTHUR JAMES, ednl. counselor; b. N.Y.C., Feb. 16, 1942; s. Antonio F. and Maria L. (Carneiro) Q.; B.S., Trinity Coll., 1964; M.Ed., U. Hartford, 1972. Sch. counselor, Hartford (Conn.) Pub. High Sch., 1968—. Active Human Relations Devel. Orgn., 1975—; trustee Jacob and Lewis Fox Found., 1978—. Served with USAF, 1964-68. Decorated Bronze Star. Mem. Am., Conn. personnel and guidance assns., Am., Conn. (pres. 1977-78) sch. counselors assns., Phi Delta Kappa. Democrat. Roman Catholic. Home: 210 Main St Manchester CT 06040 Office: 55 Forest St Hartford CT 06105

QUIGLEY, HERBERT GERALD, educator; b. Newark, Nov. 14, 1943; s. Herbert Edward and Anna Josephine (Cardillo) Q.; B.A., Rutgers U., 1965; M.B.A., 1967; D.Bus. Adminstrn., George Washington U., 1977; m. Behnaz Zolghadr, Aug. 24, 1974; 1 dau., Narda Roxanne. Accountant Legal Mimeographing Service, Newark, 1965-67; lectr. Upsala Coll., East Orange, N.J., 1967-68; instr. N.H. Coll., Manchester, 1968-69; asst. prof. Mt. Vernon Sq. campus Univ. D.C., Washington, 1969-76, asso. prof., 1976— (developed undergrad. statis. program); cons. HEW, Washington, 1973-75; faculty adviser Univ. D.C. Bus. Fin. Assn.; cons. exptl. programs Upward Mobility Coll. NIH, Bethesda, Md. Nat. teaching fellow, NFS, 1967-68. Mem. Acad. Mgmt., AIDS, Eastern Fin. Assn., Doctoral Assn. George Washington U. (acad. v.p.), Pi Delta Epsilon. Home: 13004 Turkey Branch Pkwy Rockville MD 20853 Office: 1331 H St NW Washington DC 20005

QUIGLEY, HUGH JOHN, real estate broker, educator; b. Newark, June 5, 1922; s. Michael Joseph and Lina Marie Q.; student George Washington U., 1945-46; LL.B., Blackstone Sch. Law, 1957; m. Mildred Schroth, June 14, 1947 (div. 1973); children—Mildred, Patricia, Joann, Michael, Susan, Kevin, Mary Elizabeth, Joseph. Real estate broker Morris and Monmouth County, N.J., 1953—; various positions in sales and mgmt., 1964-73; various positions Sterling Thompson & Assos., Middletown, N.J., 1973—, dir. edn., 1976—; dir. Sterling Thompson Sch. Real Estate. Served with USAAC, 1942-45. Decorated Air medal with 4 clusters. Mem. Nat. Assn. Realtors, Mensa. Club: Masons. Home: P-13 Avon Village East Windsor NJ 08520 Office: 239 Route 9 Howell NJ

QUIGLEY, JOHN HOWDEN, ophthalmologist, educator; b. Halifax, N.S., Can., Apr. 21, 1925; s. John Gordon and Sarah Eileen (Crowell) Q.; B.S., Dalhousie U., 1946, M.D., 1951; m. Gloria Lorraine Monseur, June 11, 1951; children—Michael Gordon, Robert Lawrence, Paula L. Intern, Victoria Gen. Hosp., Halifax, N.S., 1950-51; resident in internal medicine Sunnybrook Vets. Hosp., Toronto, Ont., Can., 1951-52; research in ophthalmology Banting Inst., Toronto, 1952-53; resident in ophthalmology U. Toronto Hosps., 1953-55; practice medicine specializing in ophthalmology, Toronto, 1955-56, Beverly Hills, Calif., 1957, Halifax, 1957—; mem. courtesy staff in ophthalmology and otolaryngology Victoria Gen. Hosp., 1956-59, active staff, 1959-62, asst. in ophthalmology, 1962-65, asso. ophthalmologist, 1970—; head dept. ophthalmology Halifax Infirmary, 1965—; mem. courtesy staff Halifax Children's Hosp., 1956-59, active staff, 1959-65; active staff Isaac Walton Killam Hosp. Children, 1970—; cons. ophthalmologist N.S. Rehab. Centre, 1959—; instr. dept. ophthalmology Dalhousie U., Halifax, 1959-61, lectr. in ophthalmology, 1961-66, asst. prof., 1966-69, asso. prof., 1970—, mem. faculty council, 1974-77; mem. Provincial Med. Bd., N.S., 1974-76, pres., 1976-78. Served as cadet Royal Navy, 1944-45. Diplomate Am. Bd. Ophthalmology. Fellow Royal Coll. Surgeons of Can.; mem. Soc. of Eye Surgeons, Assn. for Research in Ophthalmology, Halifax Med. Soc. (pres. 1972-73), Med. Soc. of N.S., Canadian Med. Assn., N.S. Soc. of Ophthalmology and Otolaryngology (pres. 1971-72), Canadian Ophthal. Soc. (pres. 1977-78), Contact Lens Assn. of Ophthalmologists Inc. Contbr. articles to profl. jours.; asso. editor N.S. Med. Bull., 1959-62; editorial bd. Canadian Jour. Ophthalmology, 1965—. Home: 1079 Belmont on the Arm Halifax NS B3H 1J2 Canada Office: 1674 Oxford St Halifax NS B3H 3Z4 Canada

QUILLEN, WILLIAM TATEM, state supreme ct. justice; b. Camden, N.J., Jan. 15, 1935; s. Robert J. and Gladys (Tatem) Q.; B.A., Williams Coll., 1956; LL.B., Harvard, 1959; m. Marcia Everhart Stirling, June 27, 1959; children—Carol Everhart, Tracey Tatem. Admitted to Del. bar, 1959; practiced in Wilmington, 1963-64, 66; adminstrv. asst. to Gov. Del., 1965; asso. judge Superior Ct. Del., 1966-73; chancellor Ct. of Chancery Del., 1973-76; sr. v.p. Wilmington Trust Co., 1976-78; justice Supreme Ct. Del., 1978—. Served to capt. USAF, 1959-62. Mem. Am., Del. bar assns., Phi Beta Kappa. Home: 30 The Strand New Castle DE 19720 Office: Public Bldg Wilmington DE 19801

QUIMBY, FREEMAN HENRY, physiologist; b. Battle Creek, Mich., June 11, 1915; s. Lyle Edward and Chloe (Eisenhood) Q.; B.A., Andrews U., 1938; M.S., Northwestern U., 1941; postgrad. Mich. State U., 1940; Ph.D., U. Md., 1947; m. Juanita Lenore Artress, Nov. 10, 1949; children—Kelvin, David, Carole. Mgr., Penny-a-Dish Cafeteria, Battle Creek, 1935-36; prof. biology Columbia Union Coll., 1941-48; head physiology br. Office Naval Research, Washington, 1948-56, chief scientist, San Francisco, 1956-59; chief research analysis Army Research Office, Arlington, Va., 1959-60; chief exobiology br. NASA, Washington, 1960-66; specialist life scis. Library of Congress, Washington, 1966-76; sr. scientist Tracor-Jitco, Rockville, Md., 1976—; cons. Ops. Research Office, U.S. Army, Mem. Fedn. Am. Soc. Exptl. Biology, AAAS, Am. Phys. Soc., Sigma Xi. Author: Search for Extraterrestrial Life, 1963; The Participation of Federal Agencies in International Scientific Programs, 1967; Medical Experimentation on Human Beings, 1968; The State of Technology in Nonlethal Guns, 1968; Chemical and Biological Weapons, 1969; Flouridation: A Modern Paradox in Science and Public Policy, 1970; The Politics of Global Health, 1971; Leading Causes of Death, 1972; Federal Regulations in Human Experimentation, 1975; contbr. articles to profl. jours. Home: 3926 Rickover Rd Silver Spring MD 20902

QUINN, CARROLL THOMAS, pharm. co. exec.; b. Brunswick, Ga., Nov. 14, 1946; s. Thomas Gregory, Jr. and Norma Lee (Allen) Q.; B.A. in Natural Sci., St. Anselm's Coll., Manchester, N.H., 1968; J.D., New Eng. Sch. Law, Boston, 1974; children—Todd Michael, Jeffrey Carroll. Sales rep. Parke Davis & Co., Lowell, Mass., 1964-75; admitted to Mass. bar, 1974; pvt. practice, Lowell, 1974-75; area sales mgr. Parke Davis & Co., Detroit, 1975-76; nat. sales mgr. Whitestone Products Co., Piscataway, N.J., 1976—; prof. bus. law Lowell U., 1974-75. Named Salesman of Year, Parke Davis & Co., 1969, 73. Mem. Am., Mass. bar assns. Home: 29 Park Ave Newton NJ 07860 Office: 40 Turner Pl Piscataway NJ 08854

QUINN, EDWARD JAMES, banker; b. N.Y.C., Apr. 2, 1911; s. Edward M. and Mary M. (Schneider) Q.; student Hofstra Coll., 1946-52; grad. Am. Inst. Banking, 1932-39, Grad. Sch. Banking at Rutgers, 1955-57; m. Marie A. Stafford, Apr. 22, 1939; children—Mary Ann (Mrs. Mary Ann Brown), James E., Patrick M., Sheila G. Messenger, J.S. Bache & Co., N.Y.C., 1926-27; bookkeeper Nassau-Suffolk Bond & Mortgage Guaranty Co., Mineola, N.Y., 1928. Chmn. investment com. United Fund L.I., 1968-71; treas. Nassau County Boy Scouts Am., 1936-39, Nassau County March Dimes, 1947-48, Nassau County Easter Seal Appeal, 1948-55, Suffolk County Cancer Soc., 1955-57, Union Free Sch. Dist. 22, Farmingdale, 1948-57; mem. U.S. Savs. Bond Com., Nassau County, 1952-65; bd. regents Royal Arcanum, 1938-39, grand committeeman, 1940-41. Mem. bd. appeals Village of Farmingdale, 1941-56. Served with Med. Detachment AUS, 1943-46. Mem. Municipal Forum N.Y., Municipal Finance Officers Assn. U.S., L.I. Bankers Assn. (chmn. check clearing com. 1955, legislative com. 1965-71), Nat. Assn. Accountants, Am. Legion. Rotarian, Clubs: Brentwood (N.Y.) Country; Gull Haven Golf (Central Islip, N.Y.); Harbor Hills Country (Belle Terre, N.Y.). Home: 383 West Hills Rd Huntington NY 11743 Office: 1727 Veterans Hwy Central Islip NY 11722

QUINN, GERALD JOSEPH, agrl. chem. co. exec.; b. Wilmington, Del., Sept. 14, 1947; s. James Michael and Dorothy Cecilia (Dagenais) Q.; B.S., U. Del., 1969, M.S., 1971; m. Jeanette Marie Ewonishon, June 20, 1970; children—Sean Michael, Matthew James. Product devel. rep. agrl. div. Rhodia, Inc., Cary, N.C., 1972-74, group leader, 1974-75, mgr. field devel., 1975—. U. Del. research fellow, 1970-71. Mem. Entomol. Soc. Am., Weed Sci. Soc. Am., Alpha Zeta, Chi Rho. Home: DeHart Dr Belle Mead NJ 08502 Office: PO Box 125 Monmouth Junction NJ 08852

QUINN, JOHN RAYMOND, artist, naturalist, author; b. Teaneck, N.J., July 17, 1938; s. Raymond M. and Mary Rose (Dempsey) Q.; B.A., Parsons Sch. Design, 1959; div.; children—Denise, Erika, Meredithe. Display artist, designer Ohrbach's, N.Y.C., 1959-61, Arnold Constable, N.Y.C., 1961-62, E.J. Korvette, N.Y.C., 1963-65; artist-preparator Acad. Natural Scis. of Phila., 1965-68; exhibits head Squam Lakes Sci. Center, Holderness, N.H., 1968-73; newswriter, columnist Laconia (N.H.) Evening Citizen, Plymouth (N.H.) Record-Citizen; exhibits cons. zoos and public aquaria. Recipient various awards for art. Mem. Soc. Animal Artists, Word Guild (sr.). Author: The Winter Woods, 1977; Nature's World Records, 1978; The Summer Woodlands, 1979. Home and Office: 3 Langdon St Plymouth NH 03264

QUINN, MICHAEL DESMOND, mortgage banker; b. Balt., Sept. 4, 1936; s. Michael Joseph and Gladys (Baldwin) Q.; B.A., U. Md., 1970; m. Mary Annette McHenry, Apr. 11, 1961; children—Cailin A., Maureen K., Patricia B., Marianne P. Regional mgr. trainee Household Finance Corp., Chgo., 1958-60; with Weaver Bros., Inc. of Md. (now Chesapeake Fin. Corp.), Balt., 1960-77, investment v.p., corp. dir. interim loan dept., 1968-77; chmn. bd., pres. Wye Mortgage Corp., 1977—; mem. faculty evening coll. Johns Hopkins U., 1967—; mem. faculty Essex Community Coll. Mem. gov.'s task force Md. Housing Ins. Fund; mem. Cath. Commn. on Aged; bd. dirs. Stella Maris Hospice Corp.; dist. advisory council U.S. Small Bus. Adminstrn. Served with USNR, 1956-58. Mem. Md. Mortgage Bankers Assn. (pres. bd. govs.), Real Estate Bd. Greater Balt. (dir.), Home Builders Assn. Md., Md. Bankers Assn., Ancient Order Hibernians, Balt. Jr. Assn. Commerce (Richard Troja Meml. award 1967, Outstanding Young Man of Balt. 1969), Citizens Planning and Housing Assn. Home: 8207 Robin Hood Ct Baltimore MD 21204 Office: 28 Allegheny Ave Towson MD 21204

QUINN, THOMAS HOWARD, banker; b. N.Y.C., Aug. 4, 1902; s. Thomas Charles and Frances (Quinn) Q.; LL.B., N.Y. U., 1927; m. Adele G. Pearl, Aug. 28, 1948 (dec.). Founder, pres. USLife Title Ins. Co. N.Y. (formerly Inter-County Title Ins. Co. N.Y.), 1937-74; founder, chmn. First Gen. Resources Co., 1962—; dir. West Side Fed. Savs. and Loan Assn., N.Y.C., Park Electro Chem. Co.; regional dir. Valley Bank N.Y., 1949—; regional dir. County Trust Co., White Plains, N.Y., 1954—. Bd. dirs. N.Y.C. Pub. Devel. Corp.; pres., bd. dirs. Caldwell B. Esselstyn Found.; trustee, pres. Columbia Meml. Hosp., Hudson, N.Y.; trustee Olana, Hudson. Mem. N.Y. State Land Title Assn. (dir.). Clubs: Old Chatham (N.Y.) Hund (dir.); Clover Beach Bath and Tennis (West Ghent, N.Y.); Columbia Golf and Country (Hudson, N.Y.); N.Y. Athletic (N.Y.C.). Home: The Alrae 37 E 64th St New York City NY 10021 Office: 505 Park Ave New York City NY 10022

QUINONES, MARK ANTHONY, health care adminstr.; b. N.Y.C., Jan. 13, 1931; s. Marcos A. and Josephine Maria (Martinez) Q.; B.A., Southeastern La. U., 1953; M.Health Adminstrn., Wayne State U., 1956; M.A., La. State U., 1955, Ph.D., 1971; M.P.H., Columbia, 1973; m. Marlene Emerson, Jan. 26, 1952; children—Roxane Marie Francioni, Karen Leigh. Health educator Tb League Pitts., 1956-57; cons. N.J. Tb Assn., 1957-62; exec. dir. Passaic County (N.J.) Heart Assn., 1962-64; mng. dir. NW Area N.J. Tb and Respiratory Disease Assn., 1964-68; asso. prof., dep. chmn. dept. preventive medicine, dir. div. social medicine N.J. Med. Sch., Newark, 1969—; mem. faculty Fairleigh Dickinson U., 1965-66; preceptor U. Mass., summers 1974-75; cons. Puerto Rican Congress N.J.; adv. bd. Soc. Prevention Drug Abuse, 1971-75; chmn. adv. com. Nat. Assn. P.R. Drug Abuse Programs, 1975—; mem. minority adv. com. Alcohol, Drug Abuse and Mental Health Adminstrn., HEW, 1978—; adv. bd. Nat. Drug Abuse Center Tng. and Resource Devel. Fellow Am. Pub. Health Assn., Soc. Pub. Health Adminstrs.; mem. Assn. Tchrs. Preventive Medicine, Assn. Schs. Allied Health Professions, Caribbean Studies Assn., Royal Soc. Health. Exec. co-editor Drug Forum, 1971-75; editorial bd. Jour. Allied Health, 1972—; contbr. articles to health, med. and sociol. jours. Home: 44 Dorothy Dr Morristown NJ 07960 Office: Dept Preventive Medicine Coll Medicine and Dentistry NJ Med Sch 100 Bergen St Newark NJ 07103

QUINT, ROBERT HAROLD, elec. engr.; b. Boston, Oct. 25, 1924; s. Edward and Bessie (Gordon) Q.; B.S. Mass. Inst. Tech., 1948; m. Ala Chackielewicz, Dec. 24, 1957; children—Alexander Norman, Erica Elizabeth, Frederick. Elec. engr. Naval Research Lab., Washington, 1948-52; research engr. Raytheon Mfg. Co., Waltham, Mass., 1952-54; chief elec. engr. Am. Cystoscope Makers. 1954-59; asso. dir. research and devel. Cavitron Ultrasonics, Long Island City, N.Y., 1959-61; dir. research and devel. Electromation Components Corp., Huntington Station, N.Y. 1961-62, now dir.; cons. Am. Cystoscope Makers, Pelham Manor, N.Y., 1962—. Cons. dept. neurosurgery N.Y. U. Postgrad. Med. Schs., Helene Curtis Industry. Served with USNR, 1943-45. Mem. Optical Soc. Am. Acoustical Soc. Am., Am. Inst. Physics, AAAS. Contbr. articles to profl. jours. Home: 85-02 Midland Pkwy Jamaica NY 11432 Office: 8 Pelham Pkwy Pelham Manor NY 10803

QUIRK, LAWRENCE JOSEPH, author, editor; b. Lynn, Mass., Sept. 9, 1923; s. Andrew Lawrence and Margaret Louise (Connery) Q.; B.A. with honors, Suffolk U., 1949; postgrad. Boston U., 1949-50. Author: Robert Francis Kennedy, 1968; The Films of Joan Crawford, 1968; The Films of Ingrid Bergman, 1970; The Films of Paul Newman, 1971; the Films of Fredric March, 1971; The Films of William Holden, 1973; The Great Romantic Films, 1974; The Films of Robert Taylor, 1975; (novel) Some Lovely Image, 1976; The Films of Ronald Colman, 1977; The Films of Warren Beatty, 1979; The Films of Myrna Loy, 1979; editor, pub. Quirk's Revs., 1972—; editor The Best of Quirk's Revs., 1979; free-lance contbr. to numerous mags., newspapers; writer foreword for anthology Photoplay; coll. guest lectr. on films. Originator, donor James R. Quirk awards. Served with AUS, 1950-53. Home: 74 Charles St New York City NY 10014

QUIROGA, GARY TRISTAN, cardiologist; b. Potosi, Bolivia, July 3, 1944; s. Juan Antonio and Nieves Susana (Ramos) Q.; came to U.S., 1971; M.D., San Simon U., 1970; m. Maria Esther Prada, Sept. 20, 1969; children—Alvaro, Rebecca. Intern and resident in internal medicine St. John Hosp., Detroit, 1971-74; fellow in cardiovascular diseases Cleve. Clinic Ednl. Found., 1974-76; practice medicine specializing in cardiology, Dover, Del.; cons. cardiologist Kent Gen. Hosp., Dover. Diplomate Am. Bd. Internal Medicine. Mem. Am. Soc. Internal Medicine, Del. Med. Soc. Office: 31 Gooden Ave Dover DE 19901

QUIS, HAROLD JOSEPH, JR., corp. exec.; b. Newark, May 6, 1929; s. Harold Joseph and Helen C. (Crealey) Q.; A.A., Union Jr. Coll., 1950; B.A., Fla. So. Coll., 1951; postgrad. Columbia U., 1953; m. Marguerite J. Schaul, July 2, 1955; children—Stephanie Anne, Daphne Dianne, Aimee Suzanne. Industry marketing specialist Market Planning Service, N.Y.C., 1954-56; asst. to dir. planning Celanese Chem. Co., N.Y.C., 1956-58, asst. to controller, supr. sales research and forecasting, 1958-60, mgr. mktg. analysis and forecasting, 1960-62, dir. mktg. planning, 1962-64, dir. marketing services, 1964-65; mgr. chem. industry services N.Y. Central System, 1965-66; mgr. chem. divs. planning Wallace & Tiernan, 1966-70; pres., chmn. bd. Jersey Industries, Inc., 1968-73; dir. corporate devel. Union Camp Corp., Wayne, N.J., 1970-72; pres., chief exec. officer X-Rail Systems Inc., 1972—. Pres. Young Men's Bd. Trade, N.Y.C., 1962-63, chmn. bd. dirs., 1963-64; dir. N.Y. Bd. Trade, 1963-64. Councilman, Borough of Bernardsville, N.J., 1971-78, pres. council, 1976-77; mem. Newark Transp. Council, 1976—. Served with USMCR, 1946, 51. Home: Anderson Hill Rd Bernardsville NJ 07924 Office: 60 Park Pl Newark NJ 07102

QURAISHI, HAMEED MOHAMMED ABDUL, microbiologist; b. Hyderabad, India, Aug. 7, 1939; s. Gafoor Mohammed and Faqrunisa Begam (Mahmood) Q.; B.Sc., Marathwada U., 1959; M.S., Liverpool U., 1965; Ph.D., Leeds U., 1971; m. Khurshid Sultana Qammeruddin, Dec. 15, 1960; children—Zahir Iqbal, Rafat Iqbal. Tchr. biology London Edn. Authority, Hillingdon, Middlesex, 1965-68; chief clin. microbiologist Nathen B. Van Etten Hosp., Bronx, N.Y., 1971—; asso. lab. medicine Albert Einstein Coll. Medicine, 1973-75, instr. microbiology, 1975—. Mem. Inst. Biology (London), Am. Soc. Microbiology. Contbr. articles to profl. jours. Home: 182 Larchmont Ave Larchmont NY 10538 Office: Van Etten Hosp Morris Park Ave Bronx NY 10461

RAAB, DAVID MICHAEL, mgmt. co. exec; b. Pitts., Nov. 16, 1953; s. Leonard Anthony and Marcella Grace R.; B.S., U. Pitts., 1975; m. Helen Susan Berish, Feb. 26, 1977; 1 son, Marc Aaron. Asst. mgr. Franchise Mgmt. Corp., Pitts., 1975-76; tng. adminstr., 1976-77, mgmt. tng. supr., 1977—. Mem. Am. Soc. Tng. and Devel., Phi Beta Kappa. Home: 319 Venture St Pittsburgh PA 15214 Office: 834 Ridge Ave Pittsburgh PA 15212

RAAB, KURT, physician; b. Vienna, Aug. 22, 1913; s. Simon and Henriette Raab; came to U.S., 1950, naturalized, 1955; M.D., U. Vienna, 1948; m. Stella Suchy, Aug. 29, 1948; children—Rita, Simone. Intern, Perth Amboy (N.J.) Gen. Hosp., 1950-51; resident in gen. practice Morristown (N.J.) Meml. Hosp., 1951-52; staff physician R.I. State Infirmary, Cranston, 1952-53; gen. practice medicine, Block Island, R.I., 1953-55; staff physician VA Hosp., Bath, N.Y., 1955-56; resident in rehab. medicine Bronx (N.Y.) VA Hosp., 1956-59; chief rehab. medicine service Vets. Hosp., Balt. and Ft. Howard, Md., 1959—; rehab. medicine asso. prof. U. Md. Diplomate Am. Bd. Phys. Medicine and Rehab. Mem. Am. Acad. Phys. Medicine and Rehab., Balt. Med. Soc., Am. Physicians Fellowship, Am. Paraplegic Soc. Jewish.

RAAB, RICHARD HAROLD, export cons.; b. Detroit, Dec. 21, 1920; s. Earl R. and Leah (Little) R.; B.S., Rose-Hulman Inst., 1943; m. Jean Evelyn Johnston, Feb. 14, 1943; 1 son, Philip Lane. Sales mgr. Anning-Johnson Co., Indpls., 1948-58; v.p. Roper Eastern, Columbia, Md., 1958-77; pres. Interface Assos. Inc., Washington, 1977—; mng. dir. Maes Holding B.V., Harderwijk, Holland, subs. Roper Corp., Kankakee, Ill., 1976. Served to lt. USNR, 1944-46. Mem. Nat. Soc. Profl. Engrs., SAR. Mason. Home: 174 Dividing Ct Arnold MD 21012 Office: 2243 Wisconsin Ave NW Washington DC 20007

RAB, KHANDKER SHAHIDUR, architect, health care facility specialist; b. Faridpur, Bangladesh, Dec. 9, 1944; s. Khandker Abdur and Hazera Begum R.; came to U.S., 1963; student Bangladesh U. Engring. and Tech., Dacca, 1961-63; B.Arch. with honors, Tex. A. and M. U., 1966, M.Arch., 1970; m. Wajeda Jafar, June 20, 1967. Lectr., Sch. Architecture, Bangladesh U. Engring. and Tech. and pvt. practice architecture, Dacca, 1966-69; grad. research asst. Tex. A. and M. U., 1969; cons. on design univ. hosp. U. Sri Lanka, 1970; partner M.S. Jafar Architects and Engrs., Dacca, 1970-71; dir. design Friesen Internat., Inc., Washington, 1971—; vis. lectr. Bangladesh U. Engring and Tech.; continuing edn. lectr. George Washington U.; cons. health care facility design. Bd. dirs. U.S.A.-Bangladesh Cultural Forum; pres. Bangladesh Assn. Am., Washington, 1975-77; exec. producer musical program Kennedy Center, Washington, 1977. Registered architect, Md. Mem. AIA, Inst. Architects Bangladesh, Acad. Health Care Cons., Tau Beta Pi, Phi Kappa Phi. Moslem. Author VA directional graphics man.; developed team patient care room design. Home: 4509 Westbrook Ln Kensington MD 20795 Office: 1055 Thomas Jefferson St Washington DC 20007

RABCHEVSKY, GEORGE ANTHONY, geologist; b. Bobruisk, Belorussia, Apr. 2, 1936; s. Mikhail Stepan and Raissa Peter (Rabchevsky) Soloviev; came to U.S., 1951, naturalized, 1957; B.S., Am. U., 1961; M.S., George Washington U., 1963, M.Phil., 1969, Ph.D., 1972; m. Olga Grigorovich-Barsky, June 20, 1965; children—Alexander, Natalie. Technician, translator U.S. Geol. Survey, Washington, 1959-63, cons., 1973—; geology lectr. George Washington U., 1965-69; sr. research geologist Allied Research Assos., Inc., Greenbelt, Md., 1969-73; geologist, dir. remote sensing Photo Sci., Inc., Gaithersburg, Md., from 1973; v.p./sec. Rainbow Systems, Inc., Alexandria, Va., 1970—; cons., NASA, 1972—. Instr. Pathfinders St. George council, 1972—. NSF fellow, 1967. Mem. Am. Soc. Phogrammetry, Remote Sensing and Interprestion Div., Geol. Soc. Am., Am. Assn. Profl. Geologists, AAUP, Contbr. articles to profl. jours. Home: 4013 Simms Dr Kensington MD 20795

RABI, ISIDOR ISAAC, physicist; b. Austria, July 29, 1898; s. David and Jennie (Teig) R.; brought to U.S. in infancy; B.Chem., Cornell U., 1919; Ph.D., Columbia U., 1927; grad. study in Munich, Copehagen, Hamburg, Leipzig, Zurich, 1927-29; hon. D. Sc.; Princeton, 1947, Harvard, 1955, Williams Coll., 1958, U. Birmingham, 1960, Clark U., 1962, Adelphi Coll., 1962, Technion, 1963, Franklin Marshall Coll., 1964, Brandeis U., 1965, U. Coimbra, Portugal, 1966, Hebrew U., Jerusalem, 1972; L.H.D., Hebrew Union Coll., Cin., 1958, Oklahoma City U., 1960; LL.D., Dropsie Coll., 1956; D.H.L., Yeshiva U., 1964; Litt. D., Jewish Theol. Sem., 1966; m. Helen Newmar, 1926; children—Nancy Elizabeth, Margaret Joella. Tutor in physics, Coll. City N.Y., 1924-27; lectr. Columbia, 1929-30, asst. prof., 1930-35, asso. prof., 1935-37, prof., 1937-64, Higgins prof., 1950-64, Univ. prof., 1964-67, Univ. prof. emeritus, 1967—, also exec. officer, dept. physics, 1945-49; Karl Taylor Compton vis. prof. physics, 1968-69; lectr. U. Mich., summer 1936, Stanford U., summer 1938; cons. sci. adv. com. Ballistic Research Lab., Aberdeen, 1939-65; mem. sci. bd. Itek Corp. Staff mem. and asso. dir., Radiation Lab., Mass. Inst. Tech., 1940-45; mem. gen. adv. com. AEC, 1946—, chmn., 1952-56, cons., 1956—; chmn. sci. adv. com. ODM, 1953-57; mem. Naval Research Adv. Com., 1952—, cons., sci. adv. com. v.p. Internat. Conf. on Peaceful Uses Atomic Energy, Geneva, 1955, 58, 64; v.p. UN Conf. on Peaceful Uses Atomic Energy, 1971—; mem. President's Sci. adv. Com. (chmn. 1957); mem. NATO Sci. Com., 1958; cons. Research and Devel. Bd., 1946-49; U.S. del. UNESCO Conf., Florence, Italy, 1950; mem. U.S. Nat. Commn. UNESCO, 1950-53, 58; mem. UN Sci. Com., 1954—; mem. IAEA Sci. Com., 1958-72; vis. prof. Rockefeller U. (formerly Inst.), 1957—; Shreve fellow Princeton, 1961-62; Karl Taylor Compton lectr. Mass. Inst. Tech., 1962; gen. adv. com. ACDA, 1962—. Served in S.A.T.C., 1918. Decorated Officer French Legion of Honor, 1956; comdr., 1968. Barnard fellow, 1927-28; Internat. Ednl. Bd. fellow, 1928-29; Ernest Kempton Adams fellow, 1935; Sigma Xi Semicentennial prize for physicial scis., 1936; $1,000 prize from A.A.A.S., for study of radio frequency spectra of atoms and molecules; Elliot Cresson medal of Franklin Inst., 1942; Nobel Prize in Physics, 1944; Barnard medal, 1960; Medal for Merit, 1948; King's Medal (British, 1948); Comdr., Order So. Cross, Brazil, 1952. Trustee Assoc. Univs., Inc., pres., 1961-62, chmn. bd., 1962-63. Priestley Meml. Award Dickenson Coll., 1964; Niels Bohr Internat. Gold Medal, 1967; co-recipient, Atoms for Peace award, 1967. Fellow Am. Phys. Soc. (pres. 1950-51); mem. council on Fgn. Relations, Am. Philos. Soc., Japanese Acad. (fgn. mem.), Sigma Xi. Clubs: Cosmos (Washington); Faculty (Columbia U.); Athenaeum (London). Author: My Life and Times as a Physicist, 1960. Asso. editor Physical Review, 1935-38, 1941-44. Contbr. to sci. jours. in field. Home: 450 Riverside Dr New York City NY 10027

RABIDEAU, RONALD EVEREST, constrn. exec.; b. Plattsburgh, N.Y., Dec. 29, 1943; s. Everest A. and Lillian (Venne) R.; A.A., Albany Bus. Coll., 1964; postgrad. Oswego State U., 1972-73, Syracuse U., 1974. Office engr. Slattery Constrn. Co., Maspeth, N.Y., 1964-66; sr. technician Seelye, Stevenson, Value & Knecht, N.Y.C., 1966-68; resident engr. King & Gavaris Co., N.Y.C., 1968-70, Konski Engrs. Co., Syracuse, N.Y., 1970-72, Calocerinos & Spina Co., Liverpool, N.Y., 1972—; cons. in field. Mem. Am. Concrete Inst. (v.p. Central N.Y. chpt.), N.Y. Airport Mgrs. Assn., ASTM, Illuminating Engring Soc. Club: Elks. Home: 7395 Liffey Ln Liverpool NY 13088 Office: 1020 7th N St Liverpool NY 13088

RABINOWITZ, ANN, assn. exec.; b. Manchester, Eng., Feb. 15, 1946; d. William Samuel and Fay Fanny (Fink) Rabinowitz; came to U.S., 1946, naturalized, 1954; A.A., Miami Dade Jr. Coll., 1966; B.A., Fla. State U., 1968, postgrad., 1969; postgrad. U. Md. Summer intern U.S. Dept. Transp., Tallahassee, 1969; environ. hwy. planner Ga. Dept. Transp., Atlanta, 1969-73; asso. planner Fairfax County, Va., 1973-74; community planner D.C. Recreation Dept., 1974-75; nat. program coordinator Nat. Urban Coalition, Washington, 1975-76; full time vol., mem. transition staff Carter-Mondale Campaign, Washington, 1976-77; asst. dir. Big Bros., Inc. of Prince Georges County, Md., 1977—; cons. Arthur D. Little, Inc.; field reader U.S. Office Edn., Office of Gifted and Talented, Ethnic Heritage Office. Mem. newspaper staff Roosevelt Democratic Club, 1976-78, mem. legis. com., 1976-78, mem. nominating com., 1977-78, membership com., 1976-77, program com., 1976-78; Dem. poll watcher Presdl. Primary and Gen. Election, 1976; mem. Md. Health Arbitration Program, 1976-78; adv. Md. Community Arbitration Program, 1978; mem. Bowie Human Resources Coalition, 1978, Coalition for Responsible Community Residential Care, Prince George's County, 1978; mem. social service needs assessment com., transp. needs subcom. United Way of Prince George's County, 1977-78; mem. speaker's bur. League Women Voters, 1974-78; mem. goals task force D.C. Commn. on Status of Women, 1975-76; mem. S.W. Washington Planning Adv. Com., 1974-75; mem. U. Md. Ethnic Studies Adv. Council, 1976—. John F. Kennedy scholar, 1964-66, Lion's Club scholar, 1964-66; Fla. State U. Grad. fellow, 1968-69. Mem. Am. Inst. Planners, Am. Soc. Pub. Adminstrn., Am. Soc. Planning Ofcls., Ga. Planning Assn., Am. Mgmt. Assn., Transp. Research Bd., Ga. Roadside Council, So. Govt. Economists, So. Econ. Assn., Women's Transp. Seminar. Democrat. Jewish. Home: PO Box 176 Greenbelt MD 20770 Office: 1424 16th St NW Washington DC 20036

RABINOWITZ, BARRY MARC, photographer; b. Phila., July 30, 1946; s. Arthur Jack and Fredda Miriam (Shore) R.; student So. Conn. State Coll., 1966-68, Brooks Inst., Santa Barbara, Calif., 1970-72; m. Claudia LaVallee, Sept. 6, 1969; 1 dau., Sara Kimberly. Freelance photographer for mags. and advt. agencies, 1972—; tchr. Jewish Community Center, Waterbury, Conn., 1973. Chmn. March of Dimes, Carpinteria, Calif., 1970. Served with USAF, 1968. Recipient award excellence AIA, 1975. Mem. Profl. Photographers Am. (2 awards of excellence 1974), Am. Soc. Mag. Photographers. Home: 515 Willow St Waterbury CT 06710 Office: PO Box 1574 Waterbury CT 06720

RABINOWITZ, JACOB MOSES, coll. dean; b. N.Y.C., June 1, 1926; s. I. Nathan and Rachel (Fenster) R.; B.A., Yeshiva Coll., 1946; postgrad. Rabbi Isaac Elchanan Theol. Sem., 1942-48; M.S., Poly. Inst. Bklyn., 1951; m. Toby Berger, Jan. 22, 1949; children—Fayge (Mrs. Eliyahu Safran), Baruch, Joseph, David, Esther. Rabbi, 1948; instr. Stern Coll. Women, 1959-64, asst. prof., dir. guidance, 1964-66; dean undergrad. students Yeshiva U., 1966-68, dean undergrad. Jewish studies, 1977—; dean Erna Michael Coll., N.Y.C., 1968—; ednl. dir. Camp Morasha, Lake Como, Pa., 1963—; mem. Shulamit Sch. Bd. Edn., 1968—; mem. exec. com. Nat. Council for Jewish Edn., 1974-77. Bd. dirs. Ohel Children's Home. Mem. Am. Chem. Soc., Educators Council Am. (v.p. 1976—), Sigma Xi, Phi Lambda Upsilon, Alpha Epsilon Delta. Contbr. articles to profl. jours. Home: 1752 45th St Brooklyn NY 11204 Office: 185th St and Amsterdam Ave New York City NY 10033

RABINOWITZ, RONALD, pediatric urologist; b. Pitts., Feb. 24, 1943; s. Mac and Anne (Morgan) R.; B.S. in Chemistry, U. Pitts., 1964, M.D., 1968; m. Sally Jean Miller, June 4, 1967; children—Marni Lynn, Tara Ann, Aaron Dov. Intern, Hosps. U. Health Center, U. Pitts., 1968-69, resident in surgery, 1969-70, resident in urol. surgery, 1972-75; resident, clin. fellow in pediatric urol. surgery Hosp. for Sick Children, Toronto, 1975-76; asst. prof. urol. surgery, asst. prof. pediatrics U. Rochester, 1976—; pediatric urologist U. Rochester Birth Defects Center; dir. urol. tng. Rochester Gen. Hosp.; attending urologist Strong Meml., Rochester Gen. hosps. Served to maj. USAF, 1970-72. Diplomate Am. Bd. Urology; recipient Physicians Recognition awards AMA, 1974—. Fellow A.C.S.; mem. Am. Urol. Assn. (essay prize 1976, 77), Am. Acad. Pediatrics, Rochester Acad. Medicine, Rochester Path. Soc., Rochester Spina Bifida Assn. (Gold award 1978). Contbr. articles to profl. jours., chpts. to books. Home: 40 Viennawood Dr Rochester NY 14618 Office: Div of Urology University of Rochester Medical Center 601 Elmwood Ave Rochester NY 14642

RABINOWITZ, WILBUR MELVIN, container co. exec.; b. Bklyn., Feb. 18, 1918; s. Harry A. and Caroline (Simmons) R.; Ph.B., Dickinson Coll., 1940; J.D., Harvard U., 1943; m. Audrey H. Perlmutter, Apr. 30, 1944; 1 son, Michael B. Vice pres., gen. mgr. J. Rabinowitz & Sons, Inc., Bklyn., 1945-67, pres., 1967—; pres. Met. Glass & Plastic Containers, 1967—; dir. Republic N.Y. Corp., Cromwell Products, Inc. Pres. Rabinowitz Found., Bklyn., 1967—; bd. advisers Dickinson Coll. Served with AUS, 1943-45; ETO. Mem. Nat. Assn. Container Distbrs. (past pres.), U.S. Power Squadrons (past comdr.). Clubs: Explorers, Sag Harbor Yacht, Desert Forest Golf. Home: 7002 Blvd East Guttenberg NJ 07093 Office: 1300 Metropolitan Ave Brooklyn NY 11237

RABSTEJNEK, GEORGE JOHN, JR., mgmt. cons.; b. Queens, N.Y., June 14, 1932; s. George John and Rose Anna (Krasa) R.; B.Indsl. Engring., Ga. Inst. Tech., 1954; postgrad. law U. Conn., 1969, bus. adminstrn. N.Y. U., 1965-69, Harvard Bus. Sch., 1975; m. Patsy Kidd, July 17, 1964; 1 dau., Marley Ann. Supr. purchasing Westinghouse Electric Corp., Bridgeport, Conn., 1957-61; project mgr. systems div. IBM, Poughkeepsie, N.Y., 1961-65; dir. material mgmt. services div. Harbridge House, Inc., mgmt. cons., Boston, 1965-69, v.p., group head, 1969-75, exec. v.p., 1975-76, pres., 1976—, also dir.; chmn. bd. Devel. Sci. Services, Inc., 1978—; dir. Target Industries, H. Golightly Internat., Gellman Research Assn. Mgr. Cohasset United Fund Com., 1974; mem. adv. bd. Town of Cohasset; bd. dirs. Old Colony Sch. Served to comdr. USNR, 1958-75. Mem. Navy League, Naval Res. Assn., Nat. Def. Preparedness Assn., Nat. Security Indsl. Assn., Am. Security Council, Pres.'s Club, Am. Inst. Indsl. Engrs., Aircraft Owners and Pilots Assn., Brit. Am. C. of C., Alpha Pi Mu, Phi Kappa Sigma. Unitarian. Clubs: Harvard (Boston); Union League (N.Y.C.); Cohasset Yacht, Cohasset Tennis and Squash; East India, Devonshire Sports and Public School (London). Contbr. articles to profl. jours. Home: 181 Border St Cohasset MA 02025 Office: 11 Arlington St Boston MA 02116

RABY, JOHN CORNELIUS, educator; b. N.Y.C., May 18, 1944; s. John Cornelius and Adele Joan (Lambrose) R.; B.A. in History, Stanford U., 1966; M.A., Columbia U., 1968; postgrad. N.Y. U., 1971-74; m. Betty Louise Hays, July 31, 1971; 1 son, John Hays. Tchr. social studies Mountain High Sch., West Orange, N.J., 1968-71, James Caldwell High Sch., West Caldwell, N.J., 1973—. Chmn. Caldwell-West Caldwell Pub. Schs. Bicentennial Com., 1974-76; mem. sch. adv. com. Global Edn. Assos., 1976—. Mem. NEA, N.J., Essex County, Caldwell-West Caldwell edn. assns., Nat. Council for Social Studies, Am. Hist. Assn., Orgn. Am. Historians, ACLU, Cousteau Soc., Fellowship of Reconciliation, Cath. Peace Fellowship. Roman Catholic. Home: 1472 Springfield Ave New Providence NJ 07974 Office: James Caldwell High Sch Westville Ave West Caldwell NJ 07974

RACE, IVA LAVERNE, artist, educator; b. Mohawk, N.Y., July 12, 1907; d. David George and Helen Greene (Mitchell) Brown; B.S., Cornell U., 1936; m. George A. Race, Sept. 1, 1925; 1 dau., Luella Mae Race Wheeling. Tchr., Munson Inst., Utica, N.Y., 1943-44; tchr.-artist, New Haven, 1944-46; instr., artist IvaCraft Studio, Attleboro, Mass., 1948—; adviser in field; exhibited one-man shows various galleries, Mass. and Pa., 1948—; represented in permanent collections. Recipient numerous awards and prizes. Bd. dirs. Mass. Regional Shows. Mem. Mass., Attleboro art assns., DAR. Club: Fedn. Women's (state art chmn. 1948—). Home and office: 18 Starkey Ave Attleboro MA 02703

RACEK, EDWARD WILLIAM, mfg. co. exec.; b. Bklyn., Jan. 30, 1922; s. Edward Lee and Anna (Slezak) R.; B.S. in Petroleum Engring., U. Tulsa, 1948, M.A. in Sch. Adminstrn.; m. Mary A. Hall, July 20, 1945; children—Edward L., Donald J., Richard W. Petroleum engr. Acme Well Supply Co., N.Y.C., 1948-68, sec.-treas., Piscataway, N.J., 1962—; cons., prin. St. Mary's Sch., Plainfield, N.J.; asst. sch. bus. adminstr. Middlesex County Vocat. and Tech. Sch., 1971-77. Served with USAAF, 1942-45. Decorated Air medal with three oak leaf clusters, Purple Heart. Mem. Am. Inst. Mining Metall. and Petroleum Engrs., Kappa Alpha. Roman Catholic. Home and office: 218 Old New Brunswick Rd Piscataway NJ 08854

RACHALS, RICHARD, mfg. co. exec.; b. Pitts., May 27, 1910; s. Walter Carl and Aimee (Gartland) R.; M.E., Stevens Inst. Tech., 1932, M.S., 1950; m. Marguerite Hubbard, Feb. 9, 1935; 1 son, Richard H. Tech. asst. to pres. Gibbs & Cox, Inc., N.Y.C., 1938-48; exec. engr. Edo Corp., College Point, N.Y., 1948-57; exec. v.p. Kollmorgen Corp., Hartford, Conn., 1957-63, pres., 1963-73, chmn. exec. com., 1973-75, now dir.; dir. Andersen Labs., Inc., Bloomfield, Conn., Edo Corp., College Point, N.Y., Kollmorgen Corp. Mem. Sigma Nu, Tau Beta Pi. Clubs: N.Y. Yacht, Cruising of Am. (N.Y.C.). Home: 100 Sheffield St Old Saybrook CT 06475 Office: 60 Washington St Hartford CT 06106

RACHAMALLA, KUMARA SWAMY, economist; b. Hyderabad, India, Oct. 9, 1936; s. Vishwanatham and Ramachandramma (Veerabomma) R.; came to Can., 1965, naturalized, 1971; B.Engring., Osmania U., India, 1960; M.Engring., U. Sheffield (U.K.), 1964; M.B.A., U. Toronto, 1969; m. Vijayanthi Grandhi Swamy, Feb. 1, 1967; children—Teja Tansy, Deepta Mayura. Sr. fin. analyst, advisor Instl. Investment Services, Toronto, 1969-73; policy analyst, advisor Govt. of Ont., Div. Natural Resources and Ont. Energy Corp., Toronto, 1973—; instr. in engring. mgmt. U. Toronto. Recipient Mgrs. certificate of Competency, Ministry of Power, U.K. Mem. Toronto Soc. Fin. Analysts, Assn. Profl. Engrs. (Ontario), Am. Inst. Mining, Metall. and Petroleum Engrs., Can. Inst. Mining and Metallurgy Engrs. Club Toronto. Contbr. articles in field to profl. jours. Home: 42 Marydon Crescent Agincourt ON M1S 2H1 Canada Office: 880 Bay St Toronto ON M5S 1Z8 Canada

RACHELSON, MORTON HERMAN, physician; b. Bklyn., Dec. 31, 1927; s. William and Ethel (Peltz) R.; A.B. magna cum laude, Syracuse U., 1946; M.D., Tulane U., 1950; m. Natalie Gutterman, May 25, 1952; children—Marjorie, Barbara. Intern, Queens Gen. Hosp., Jamaica, N.Y., 1950-51; resident Willard Parker Hosp., N.Y.C., 1951-52, Jewish Hosp., Bklyn., 1952, Childrens Med. Center, Boston, 1955; fellow pediatrics Babies Hosp., N.Y.C., 1955-56; practice medicine, specializing in pediatrics, Caldwell, N.J., 1956—; attending in pediatrics St. Barnabas Hosp., clin. asst. prof. Columbia U., 1956-78; clin. asst. prof. pediatrics CMDNJ-NJMS, 1978—. Served to capt. M.C., USAF, 1953-55. Mem. Am. Acad. Pediatrics, AMA, Am. Heart Assn., N.J. Acad. Medicine, AAAS, Am. Physicians Fellowship, Phi Lambda Kappa. Jewish. Club: B'nai B'rith. Contbr. articles to profl. jours. Office: 700 Passaic Ave West Caldwell NJ 07006

RACHLIN, HARVEY BRANT, author; b. Phila., June 23, 1951; s. Philip and Mazie Rachlin; B.A. in Biology, Hofstra U., Hempstead, N.Y., 1973. With music publishing companies, 1973—; owner Western Hemisphere Music Co., Manhasset Hills, N.Y., 1975—; faculty Five Towns Coll., Merrick, N.Y., 1978—; author: The Songwriter's Handbook, 1977; free-lance music journalist. Mem. Am. Guild Authors and Composers, L.I. Songwriters Workshop (dir.). Address: 252 Robby Ln Manhassett Hills NY 11040

RACHOW, LOUIS A(UGUST), librarian; b. Shickley, Nebr., Jan. 21, 1927; s. John Louis and Mable (Dondlinger) R.; B.S., York Coll., 1948; M.S. in L.S., Columbia U., 1959. Librarian York (Nebr.) Coll., 1949-54; instr. library asst. Queens Coll., N.Y.C., 1956-57; serials acquisition asst. Columbia U. Law library, N.Y.C., 1957-58; asst. librarian Univ. Club, N.Y.C., 1958-62; librarian Walter Hampden Meml. Library at The Players, N.Y.C., 1962—; cons. theatre sect. U. Calif., San Diego, new campuses program, 1964; mem. library adv. bd. Eugene O'Neill Meml. Theatre Center, 1966—. Mem. adv. bd. Am. Theatre Co., OKC Theatre Prodns. Served with AUS, 1954-56. Mem. Theatre Library Assn. (recording sec. 1966-67, pres. 1967-72, v.p. 1976—, editor Broadside 1973—), ALA, Spl. Libraries Assn. (sec.-treas. mus. group N.Y.C. chpt. 1964-66), Am. Ednl. Theatre Assn., ANTA, New Drama Forum Assn., Am. Soc. Theatre Research, N.Y. Tech. Services Librarians (sec. Kelcey Allen award com. 1968), Archons of Colophon, Episcopal Actors Guild Am. (dir. 1976—). Club: Players. Editor, compiler Guide to the Performing Arts, 1968; asso. editor Am. Notes and Queries, 1971-74; asst. editor: American Notes and Queries, 1967-71; mem. editorial adv. bd. Nat. Dir. for Performing Arts and Civic Centers; editor Performing Arts series Gale Info. Guide. Contbr. articles and rev. to profl. jours. Home: 528 W 114th St New York City NY 10025 Office: 16 Gramercy Park New York City NY 10003

RADACSY, JOHN JOSEPH, III, fin. cons.; b. Monessen, Pa., Aug. 18, 1947; s. John Joseph and Grace Patricia (Dibacco) R., Jr.; A.S. in Accounting and Systems, Point Park Coll., 1967; B.S. in Accounting, Duquesne U., 1969; postgrad. U. Pitts., 1978—; m. Adele Maria Romasco, June 3, 1972; children—John Joseph, IV, Kristin Marie. Staff accountant Price Waterhouse & Co., Pitts., 1969-70; comptroller Bidwell, Inc., Pitts., 1970—; cons. in field, Pitts. area. Served with USMC, 1969. C.P.A., Pa. Mem. Am. Mgmt. Assn., Nat. Assn. Accountants, Am., Pa. assns. C.P.A.'s. Republican. Roman Catholic. Home: 1498 King William Dr Pittsburgh PA 15237 Office: Suite 2010 2010 Kinvara Dr Pittsburgh PA 15237

RADCLIFFE, LYNN JAMES, clergyman, author; b. Cornwall, N.Y., Apr. 14, 1896; s. Harry Richardson and Mary E. (Ehlers) R.; B.A., Wesleyan U., 1919, D.D., 1962; M.Div., Boston U., 1924; D.D., Syracuse U., 1937; m. Verna Gorsuch, July 7, 1957; children (by previous marriage)—Lynn Edmund, Marie (Mrs. Paul S. Townsend). Ordained to ministry Meth. Ch., 1922; minister, Coll. Av. Meth. Ch., West Somerville, Mass., 1921-35, First Syracuse Meth. Ch., 1935-41, First Oak Park (Ill.) Meth. Ch., 1941-48, Hyde Park Community Meth. Ch., Cin., 1948-61; dir. prayer missions and spiritual life retreats in U.S. and fgn. countries; mem. Bd. Missions Meth. Ch., 1952-60, mem. coordinating council, 1960-64. Chmn., Crime Prevention Bur., Syracuse, N.Y., 1935-41; chmn. Race Relations Com., Chgo., 1941-48. Bd. dirs. N.E. Deaconess Hosp., Boston, 1928-35; organizing bd. dirs. Meth. Theol. Sch. Ohio, 1948-56; trustee Ohio Wesleyan U., 1950-61. Recipient medal of Year, Ohio Library Assn., 1953. Mem. Syracuse Council Chs. (pres. 1937-41), Phi Beta Kappa, Delta Sigma Rho, Sigma Nu. Republican. Mason, Rotarian. Author: Making Prayer Real, 1952; With Christ in the Garden, 1959; 7 Steps to Spiritual Progress, 1959; With Christ in the Upper Room, 1960. Home: 21 Ferndale Rd Madison NJ 07940

RADDING, PHILIP, orthopedic surgeon; b. Springfield, Mass., Aug. 3, 1924; s. Morris and Sarah Lily (Katz) R.; student Coll. William and Mary U. N.C.; M.D., Harvard, 1948; m. Marsha Weinberg, Dec. 23, 1945; children—Adrienne Barbara, Jeffrey Alan, Carolyn Beth. Intern U.S. Naval Hosp., St. Albans, N.Y., 1948-49, Buffalo Gen. Hosp., 1949-50; intermediate surg. resident VA Hosp., Newington, Conn., 1952-53; chief resident orthopedic surgery Grace-New Haven Hosp., 1953-55; instr. orthopedic surgery Yale Med. Sch., 1953-55; fellow Nat. Found. Infantile Paralysis, 1954-56; pvt. practice, Hartford, Conn., 1956—; resident orthopedic surgery Newington Hosp. Crippled Children, 1955-56, asst. orthopedic surgeon, 1956-70, asso. orthopedic surgeon, 1970—; asso. orthopedic surgeon Mt. Sinai Hosp., Hartford, 1961-65, attending orthopedic surgeon, 1965-70, chmn. div. surgery, 1970-71, dir. div. orthopedics, 1971—. Served to capt. M.C., AUS, 1950-52. Diplomate Am. Bd. Orthopedic Surgery, Orthopedic Sect. Pan Am. Med. Assn. Mem. A.M.A., Eastern Orthopedic Assn., N.Y. Acad. Sci. Contbr. articles to profl. jours. Home: 89 Lyman Rd West Hartford CT 06117 Office: 60 Gillett St Hartford CT 06105

RADER, MILLICENT CAROLYN, artist; b. Utica, N.Y., May 13, 1936; d. LeRoy Arthur and Irene Anna (Schwenk) R.; B.F.A., Wichita State U., 1958; M.F.A., Cath. U. Am., 1975; 1 dau., Heather Viola Harris. Sr. tech. illustrator Analytic Services, Inc., Falls Church, Va., 1959-67, cons., 1967-68; co-owner MRRH Studio Gallery, Fairfax, Va., 1970—; corr. Alexandria (Va.) Gazette, 1972; artist-in-residence, bd. dirs. Trident Found., Washington, 1974—; instr. art women's bur. D.C. Dept. Corrections, 1974—; tech. asst. Catholic U., 1974-75; installations/instr. Nat. Park Service Art Barn, 1976-79; artist in residence St. Ann's Catholic Ch., Washington, 1976—; art cons. Women's Nat. Bank, Washington, 1978—; dir. The Rainbow Place, studio/workshop, Washington, 1978—; dir. arts and humanities sch. St. Ann's, Washington; exhibited in group shows: Wichita (Kans.) Art Mus., 1957, 58, 59, Mulvane Art Inst., Topeka, 1958, Smithsonian Instn., Washington, 1962-63, Dept. Commerce, Washington, 1966, Deilger Art and Antique Gallery, Alexandria, Va. and Madison, N.Y., 1966—, Salt Palace, Salt Lake City, 1970, Goldman Fine Arts Gallery, Rockville, Md., 1971, 72, Arts Club, Washington, 1973, 74, 76, 77, Art Barn, Washington, 1973, 74, 76, 77, Cath. U. Am., Washington, 1973, 74, Fed. Dept. Interstate Commerce, 1974, 76, 77, Am. Spirit Gallery, Washington, 1974, Regis Coll., Boston, 1974, Salve Regina Gallery, Washington, 1974, Sculpture Garden at Firenze, Washington, 1974, Martin Luther King Library, Washington, 1976, others; represented in permanent collections: Holy Name Coll., Wichita State U. Area chmn. March of Dimes, 1970-74; adviser Arts Barn Assn.; campaign mgr. Congl. candidate, 1972. Exec. bd. No. Va. Conservation Council, 1973. Recipient best in show award, best portrait, state exhibit Nat. League Am. Pen Women, 1970, also 1st prize in nat. yearbook competition, 1971. Mem. Artists Equity Assn. (bd. mem., pub. relations 1974—), Washington Watercolor Assn. (pres. 1974-75, pres. 1976-77), Nat. League Am. Pen Women (br. v.p. 1972-74, state art chmn. 1972-74), D.C. Arts Congress (steering com. visual arts 1974—), Internat. Platform Assn., NOW, Va. Women's Polit. Caucus (state policy council 1972), Mt. St. Sepulchre Frat., 3d Order St. Francis, Mortar Bd., Kappa Pi, Delta Delta Delta. Roman Catholic. Home: 3511 Davenport St #309 Washington DC 20008 Office: 4001 Yuma St NW Washington DC 20016

RADFORD-BENNETT, WILLIAM, orch. condr., dir.; b. Durham, N.C., Feb. 1, 1941; s. Arthur Rollins and Nettie Daisy (Grissom) Bennett; A.B. (Kiwanis Club scholar), U. N.C., 1963; postgrad. Am. U., Washington, 1964-65. Asst. condr. Am. U. Orch., 1964-65; past condr. Washington Civic Symphony, Baroque Arts Orch., D.C. Community Orgn., music dir., prin. condr. Washington Festival Orch., 1966—. Guest condr. various orchs., including Washington Nat. Symphony. Mem. Nat. Music Critics Assn. Contbr. articles to profl. jours. Condr. first performances in Washington of many compositions of Am. and English composers, including Sir Arthur Bliss, Jackson Hill, Gwyneth Walker; arranger J.C. Penney gift to nation bicentennial mus. collection, 1975. Address: 5113 Wissioming Rd Glen Echo Heights MD 20016

RADIMER, KENNETH JOHN, research chemist; b. Clifton, N.J., Mar. 31, 1920; s. John and Emma Emelie (Lullwitz) R.; S.B., Mass. Inst. Tech., 1942, Ph.D., 1947. Chemist, Nat. Research Corp., Boston, 1942; research and teaching asst. Mass. Inst. Tech., Cambridge, 1943-44; chemist Kellex Corp., Jersey City, 1944-45, research chemist, 1951-54; research asst. Manhattan Project, SAM Lab., N.Y.C., 1945-46; instr. chemistry Lehigh U., Bethlehem, Pa., 1947-48; asst. prof. Ind. U., Bloomington, 1948-50; chemist Allied Chem. & Dye Corp., Long Island City, N.Y., 1950-51; research chemist M.W. Kellogg Co., Jersey City, 1954-57, 59-62, Minn. Mining & Mfg. Co., St. Paul, 1957-58; chief chemist CBS Labs., Stamford, Conn., 1958-59; mgr. metals applications, research asso. FMC Corp., Princeton, N.J., 1962—. Harshaw fellow, 1946-47. Fellow AAAS; mem. Electrochem. Soc., Nat. Assn. Corrosion Engrs., Research Soc. Am., Sigma Xi, Phi Lambda Upsilon. Congregationalist. Contbr. articles to tech. jours. Patentee in field. Home: 12 Martin Pl Little Falls NJ 07424 Office: FMC Corp Box 8 Princeton NJ 08540

RADINI, RICHARD ROLAND, civil engr.; b. Biwabyck, Minn., May 31, 1952; s. John Niclo and Maria Angela; B.E.C.E., Manhattan Coll., 1974, M.B.A., C.W. Post Coll., 1978. Civil engr. Burns & Roe, Woodbury, N.Y., 1974—; speaker 5th Internat. Conf. Structural Mechanics in Reactor Tech., Berlin, 1979. Mem. ASCE, Assn. M.B.A. Execs. Home: 28 Fairway Pl Cold Spring Harbor NY 11724 Office: 185 Crossways Park Dr Woodbury NY 11797

RADLER, LOUIS, chem. mfg. co. exec.; b. N.Y.C., July 29, 1931; s. Benjamin and Hattie (Eisenberg) R.; B.S., U. Bridgeport, 1953; postgrad. N.Y. U. Grad. Sch. Bus., 1953-55; m. Harriet Weisburg, Apr. 11, 1954 (dec. Feb. 1970); children—Lauren Beth, Jeffrey Alan, Allyson. Pres., Chem. Spl. Sales Corp., Fairfield, Conn., 1962—, Chessco Industries Inc., Fairfield, 1965—; gen. partner Recreation Ventures Inc., Bridgeport, Conn., 1968—. Mem. Easton (Conn.) Bd. Edn., 1966-71; trustee U. Bridgeport, 1974—; mem. Democratic Town Com. Easton, 1964-70. Served with AUS, 1953-55. Mem. Newcomen Soc., Young Pres.'s Orgn. Club: Rolling Hills Country (Wilton, Conn.). Home: Mills Ln Weston CT 06880 Office: 1960 Bronson Rd Fairfield CT 06430

RADNAY, PAUL ANDREW, physician; b. Szolnok, Hungary, Aug. 6, 1913; s. Ferenc and Ida (Varsa) R.; came to U.S., 1949, naturalized, 1954; M.D., U. Szeged, 1937; m. Eva Balazs, Aug. 6, 1939. Intern Univ. Clinics, Budapest and Szeged, 1936-37; chief head and neck surgery outpatient dept. Orszagos Tarsadaiom Biztosito Intezet, Budapest, 1945-49; asst. prof. Polyclinic Hosp., Budapest, 1945-49; resident in anesthesiology Queens Gen. Hosp., Jamaica, N.Y., 1953-54; dir. anesthesia sect. cardio-thoracic surgery Montefiore Hosp., Med. Center, N.Y.C., 1970—; asso. prof. anesthesiology Albert Einstein Coll. Medicine, Bronx, N.Y., 1975—. Vice chmn. bd. dirs. Am. Hungarian Found. Decorated Cross Knighthood Order of St. Martin (Austria), St. John of Jerusalem, Knights Malta. Served to capt., M.C., Hungarian Army, intermittantly 1934-45. Recipient Dr. Max Goldzieher award distinguished services Am.-Hungarian Med. Assn., 1974; Distinguished Service award Am. Hungarian Found., 1978. Diplomate Hungarian Bd. Surgery, Hungarian Bd. Dentistry, Am. Bd. Anesthesiology. Fellow Am. Coll. Anesthesiologists, N.Y. Acad. Medicine, N.Y. Cardiological Soc., Internat. Coll. Surgeons; mem. Am., N.Y. State socs. anesthesiologists, N.Y. County, N.Y. State med. socs., Am.-Hungarian Found. (vice-chmn. bd. dirs. 1974—), Am.-Hungarian Med. Assn. (pres. 1966-67). Contbr. chpt. in book, articles to profl. publs. Home and office: 969 Park Ave New York City NY 10028

RADNER, JOSEPH SYDNEY, counselor; b. Jersey City, May 23, 1938; s. Max and Gertrude Ruth Radner; student Panzer Sch., 1957-58; B.A., Montclair State U. (merger Panzer Sch. and Montclair State U. 1958), 1961, M.A., in Pupil Personnel Service, 1965. Tchr. health and phys. edn. pub. schs., Jersey City, 1961, 64-74, elem. sch. guidance counselor, 1974—, Accredited Evening High Sch., 1975-76; tchr., supr. YMCA. Certified in health, phys. edn., pupil personnel services, career edn., N.J. Mem. Montclair State Coll. Alumni, Parents' Council Jersey City, NEA, N.J., Jersey City edn. assns., Jersey City Personnel and Guidance Assn. (pres. 1978-79), Am. Sch. Counselor Assn., Nat., N.J., Jersey City, Hudson guidance assns., Automobile Club Am., Phi Delta Kappa. Home: 119 Graham St Jersey City NJ 07307 Office: Academic High Sch 168 Sip Ave Jersey City NJ 07306

RADTKE, RONALD ROSCOE, ins. co. exec.; b. N.Y.C., Dec. 1, 1931; s. John Arthur and Emma (Neu) R.; B.A., Queens Coll., 1953; postgrad. Coll. of Ins., 1963, 64; ins. seminar Nat. Assn. Ins. Commrs., 1970; m. Barbara Ann Donohue, Feb. 1, 1964; children—Reid, Heather Lynn, Holly Ann, Todd Donohue. With Reciprocal Mgrs.,

Inc., N.Y.C., 1963-66; fire rate and forms analyst Ins. Div., Vt. Dept. Banking and Ins., Montpelier, 1966-67, chief ins. services, 1967-74, dir. ins. regulation, 1974-77; now mgr. compliance services Met. Property and Liability Ins. Co., Warwick, R.I., 1977—. Mem. Montpelier Charter Revision Commn., 1972-73. Home: 77 Landmark Rd Warwick RI 02886 Office: 700 Quaker Ln Warwick RI 02887

RADZIMSKI, GERALD PAUL, chemist; b. Buffalo, July 20, 1927; s. Anthony Francis and Mary Celia (Dobinski) R.; B.A., U. Buffalo, 1955; postgrad. Ohio State U., 1956-57, Oak Ridge Inst. Nuclear Studies, 1960. Analytical chemist Hooker Electrochem. Corp., Niagara Falls, N.Y., 1955-56; teaching asst. Ohio State U., Columbus, 1956-57; cancer research scientist Roswell Park Meml. Inst., Buffalo, 1957—. Served with U.S. Army, 1951-52. Mem. Am. Chem. Soc., Phi Beta Kappa. Roman Catholic. Contbr. articles in field to profl. jours. Home: 98 Newburgh Ave Buffalo NY 14211 Office: 98 Newburgh Ave Buffalo NY 14211

RAEDER, ARTHUR O., orthodontist; b. Bklyn., Sept. 15, 1915; s. Rubin and Minnie (Lassman) R.; D.D.S., N.Y. U., 1937, postgrad. orthodontic certificate, 1941. Orthodontist, Bklyn., 1937—; instr. N.Y. U. Coll. Dentistry, 1945-55, coordinator dental research, 1950-53; dir. orthodontic clinic Unity Hosp., 1965-69; radiospeaker Oral Health Com. Greater N.Y. Mem. council judges to Ann. City-wide Sci. Fair N.Y.C. Recipient Congl. medal of merit, 1945; Presdl. citation, 1945; Wisdom award Honor, 1973. Diplomate Am. Bd. Orthodontics, Pan Am. Med. Assn. Fellow N.Y. Acad. Scis., Royal Soc. Health; mem. Am. Assn. Orthodontics, N.Y. U. Orthodontic Soc. (pres. 1952-53), ADA (state council on dental trade and lab. relations 1962-68), European Orthodontic Soc., Federation Dentaire Internat., Am. Bicentennial Research Inst., Alpha Omega. Mason (Shriner). Contbr. to N.Y. Jour. Dentistry, others. Co-producer movie Tongue Position Role. Invented cephalo-myolator for correction of muscular dysfunction asso. with malocclusions and speech defects and facial deformities; originated one-visit bonded bridge, modality for alveolar bone regeneration. Home: 615 Eastern Pkwy Brooklyn NY 11216

RAEMER, HAROLD ROY, elec. engr., educator; b. Chgo., Apr. 26, 1924; s. Leo and Fannie (Marx) R.; B.S., Northwestern U., 1948, M.S., 1949, Ph.D., 1959; m. Paulyne Barkin, Dec. 21, 1947; children—Daniel, Liane, Diane. Teaching asst. Northwestern U., 1950-52; physicist Bendix Research Labs., Detroit, 1952-55; staff engr. Cook Research Labs., Chgo., 1955-60; sr. engring. specialist Sylvania Applied Research Lab., Waltham, Mass., 1960-63; asso. prof. elec. engring. Northeastern U., Boston, 1963-65, prof., 1965—, chmn. dept., 1976-77; vis. lectr. Harvard U., 1962; cons. in field. Served with USAAF, 1943-46. Mem. IEEE, AAAS, Am. Phys. Soc., Am. Soc. Engring. Edn., Sigma Xi, Pi Mu Epsilon, Eta Kappa Nu, Tau Beta Pi. Author 1 book; contbr. articles to profl. jours. Home: 120 Noanett Rd Needham MA 02194 Office: Northeastern U Dept Elec Engring Boston MA 02115

RAEZER, SPENCER DORWORTH, physicist; b. Lancaster, Pa., May 5, 1926; s. Spencer Bear and Esther Elizabeth (Dorworth) R.; A.B., Franklin and Marshall Coll., 1949, B.S., 1951; M.S., Lehigh U., 1954; m. Marilyn Louise Clewell, Aug. 30, 1952; children—Cynthia, Evelyn, Charles, Patricia, George, Victoria, Dorothy, Paul, Mark, Bruce. Mem. sr. staff Johns Hopkins U. Applied Physics Lab., Silver Spring, Md., 1954-68; research engr. Greyrad Corp., Princeton, N.J., 1968-70; pres. Raezer Co., Taneytown, Md., 1970—. Bd. dirs. Carroll Players, 1978. Served with USNR, 1944-46. Mem. Air Pollution Control Assn., Taneytown C. of C., Sigma Xi. Club: Elks (Westminster, Md.). Contbr. articles to profl. jours. Patentee. Office: PO Box 282 Taneytown MD 21787

RAFFA, JAMES NICHOLAS, lawyer, business exec.; b. Astoria, N.Y., Dec. 21, 1945; s. James Joseph and Marie Nicolina (Musto) R.; B.A., U. N.H., 1967; J.D., Suffolk U., 1970; m. Barbara Janet Carr, Aug. 7, 1971. Commd. capt. U.S. Air Force, 1971; tech. photo intelligence officer Fgn. Tech. div. Wright-Patterson AFB, Dayton, Ohio, 1972-75; contracting officer, negotiator Electronic Systems div. Hanscom AFB, Mass., 1975-78; now inactive Res.; sr. contracts officer Merrimack br. Digital Equipment Corp., 1978—. mem. systems command jr. officers speakers bur., 1973-74. Mem. contract negotiation com. Stow (Mass.) Sch. Bd. Decorated Air Force Commendation Medal. Mem. Nat. Contract Mgmt. Assn. Home: 75 Lowell Dr Stow MA 01775

RAFFELSON, MICHAEL, paper co. exec.; b. Bklyn., Jan. 2, 1946; s. Leo and Fay Rebecca (Clumpus) R.; B.B.A., Coll. City N.Y., 1967; M.B.A., City U. N.Y., 1969; m. Eileen Judith Tauber, Mar. 23, 1975; 1 dau., Elyse Lauren. Accountant, Am. Metal Climax Inc., N.Y.C., 1967-69; financial analyst Anaconda Co., N.Y.C., 1971-74; sr. fin. analyst corp. staff Internat. Paper Co., N.Y.C., 1975-76, bus. analyst white papers group, 1976—, instr. fin. mgmt. edn. program, 1977; cons. Coin Concepts, Baldwin Harbor, N.Y. Served with AUS, 1969-71. Mem. Fin. Mgmt. Assn., Internat. Platform Assn., East Bayside Homeowners Assn., Zeta Beta Tau, Phi Epsilon Pi (pres. chpt. 1966). Home: 210-24 33d Ave Bayside NY 11361 Office: 220 E 42d St New York City NY 10017

RAGAN, EDWARD JOHN, physician; b. Toronto, Ont., Can., May 21, 1938; s. John Louis and Anna Maria Ragauskas; B.A., U. Western Ont., 1960, M.D., 1965; M.P.H., Johns Hopkins U., 1974; m. Judith Anne Romyn, Dec. 31, 1960; children—Elizabeth, Mitch ell. Med. officer dept. aborigines Gombak Aborigine Hosp., Gombak, Malaysia, 1966-68; med. dir. Can. U. Services Overseas, 1968-73; coordinator Health Services for the Elderly, Ottawa, Ont., 1974-76; sr. med. adviser Can. Health Survey, Ottawa, 1976-78; chief health services Bank of Can., Ottawa, 1975—; emergency physician Riverside Hosp. Bd. dirs. Centretown Community Resource Center; del. WHO/UNICEF Conf. on Primary Health Care, fellow Internat. Devel. and Research Centre, 1973-74. Mem. Can. Soc. Tropical Medicine and Internat. Health, Can. Med. Assn., Ont. Med. Assn. Can. Public Health Assn., Fedn. Gen. Practitioners of Quebec, Am. Public Health Assn., Am. Occupational Health Assn., Royal Soc. Tropical Medicine, Soc. Internat. Devel. Contbr. articles to profl. jours. Home: 150 Billings Ave Ottawa ON K1H 5K9 Canada Office: 245 Sparks St Ottawa ON K1A 0G9 Canada

RAGOT, HENRY WARREN, lawyer, state asst atty. gen.; b. Mt. Kisco, N.Y., June 30, 1921; s. Henry E. and Mabel P. (Mandeville) R.; A.B., Lafayette Coll., 1943; LL.B., U. Pa., 1946; m. Virginia F. Valentine, May 16, 1953; 1 dau., Kathleen E. Admitted to Pa. bar, 1950; individual practice law, Easton, Pa., 1947-60; asst. title officer Commonwealth Land Title Ins. Co., Lancaster, Pa., Phila., 1954-60, title officer City Title Ins. Co., Levittown, Pa., 1960-69; asst. atty. gen. Pa. Gen. State Authority, merged into Pa. Dept. Gen. Services 1975, Harrisburg, 1969—; dir. Consol. Realty Corp., Diversified Real Estate Trust; instr. realty courses. Sec. council St. Mark's Evangelical Luth. Ch., Harrisburg, Pa., 1970-75, del. Central Pa. Synod, 1978. Mem. Pa. Bar Assn. Home: 3103 Schoolhouse Ln Harrisburg PA 17109 Office: Pennsylvania Dept General Services 6th Floor North Office Bldg Harrisburg PA 17120

RAHENKAMP, JOHN EDWARD, planner/landscape architect; b. Montclair, N.J., Mar. 15, 1937; s. William Edward and Mildred (Swanson) R.; B.S., Mich. State U., 1959; M.Landscape Architecture, U. Pa., 1961; m. Suzanne Charles, June 29, 1957; 1 son, John Creigh. Pres. Rahenkamp, Sachs, Wells and Assos. Inc., Phila. and Denver, 1961—; guest columnist House & Home mag., 1971—; adj. prof. U. Pa., Drexel U.; dir. Fellowship Bank. Chmn. Mt. Laurel Twp. Planning Bd., 1967-70; chmn. Penjerdel Open Space Commn., 1972-73; bd. dirs. Del Valley Water Resources Assn., 1976—. Mem. Am. Soc. Landscape Architects (nat. award merit 1965-70), Am. Inst. Planners (award of merit Phila. regional chpt. 1972). Republican. Presbyterian. Contbr. articles to profl. publs. in land use planning and mgmt. Home: 166 E St Andrews Dr Moorestown NJ 08057 Office: 1717 Spring Garden St Philadelphia PA 19130 also 738 Pearl St Denver CO 80203

RAHMAN, ABDUL R., food technologist; b. Mosul, Iraq, Nov. 15, 1924; B.Sc., Cairo U., 1948; M.S., Utah State U., 1953; Ph.D., Ore. State U., 1956; m. Ethel E. Offerl, Dec. 15, 1956; children—Fred, Amira, Abib, Alda, Emir. Dir. agr. Mosul-Iraq, 1958-59; mem. faculty U. P.R., San Juan, 1959-64; food technologist U.S. Army Natick Labs. (Mass.), 1964-74, head research and devel. plant products, 1974—; pres. Am.-Islamic Foods, Inc., Natick. Mem. Inst. Food Technologists, Am. Chem. Soc., AAAS, Framingham Artists Guild (pres.), Internat. Platform Assn., Am. Def. Preparedness Assn. Sigma Xi, Phi Sigma, Gamma Sigma Delta. Clubs: Rotary (pres.). Patentee in field. Contbr. articles to profl. jours. Home: 38 Walnut Natick MA 01760

RAHN, RICHARD WILLIAM, economist; b. Rochester, N.Y., Jan. 9, 1942; s. William Fred and Evelyn Janet (Chapman) R.; B.A., U. So. Fla., 1963; M.B.A., Fla. State U., 1964; Ph.D., Columbia U., 1972; m. Ann Clarke Sherman, Jan. 30, 1971; 1 dau., Margie Lynn. Instr., Fla. State U., Tallahassee, 1964-66; instr. mgmt. Poly. Inst. N.Y., 1966, asst. prof., 1967-72, asso. prof., 1973, head. dept. mgmt., 1972-73; mng. dir. Ripon Soc., Cambridge, Mass., 1973-74; pres. Richard Rahn & Assos., Fairfax, Va., 1974-75; exec. dir., bd. dirs. Am. Council for Capital Formation, Washington, 1976—; lectr. George Mason U., 1974—. Mem. N.Y. County Republican Com., 1973; bd. dirs. Am. Council for Capital Formation, Center for Policy Research, 1977—. Mem. Nat. Econs. Club, Nat. Assn. Bus. Economists, Beta Gamma Sigma. Author: The Determination of Reasonable Royalty, 1973. Contbr. articles to profl. jours. and newspapers. Home: 2939 Rosemoor Ln Fairfax VA 22030 Office: 1425 K St NW Suite 1000 Washington DC 20005

RAIFMAN, IRVING, clin. psychologist; b. N.Y.C., Oct. 21, 1924; s. Samuel and Gussie (Feldberg) R.; B.S., Union Coll., 1947; M.A., Columbia U., 1949; Ph.D., N.Y. U., 1952; m. Grace Schacht, Sept. 18, 1948; children—Lawrence J., Alan M., Gregory R. Clin. psychologist VA Hosps., N.Y.C., Washington, 1947-53, chief psychol. services, Washington, 1953; tng. officer in psychology Naval Hosp., Bethesda, Md., 1953-63; dir. Consultation and Guidance Center, Silver Spring, Md., 1960—; cons. in field. Bd. dirs. Montgomery County Mental Health Assn., 1968-70; bd. dirs. Montgomery County Jewish Community Center, 1965-68; chmn. Bd. Examiners of Psychologists, State of Md., 1967-70. Served with USNR, 1942-46. Fellow Md. Psychol. Assn., Soc. Personality Assessment; mem. Montgomery-Prince George Counties Assn. Psychologists in Pvt. Practice (pres.), Am., D.C. psychol. assns. Home: 3102 Woodhollow Dr Chevy Chase MD 20015 Office: 1105 D Spring St Silver Spring MD 20910

RAIFORD, WILLIAM RUSSELL, investment exec.; b. Valdosta, Ga., May 21, 1930; s. William Franklin and Clara Ophelia (Shepherd) R.; B.S., U.S. Mil. Acad., 1952; m. Mary Chase Berger, Apr. 7, 1956; children—Richard Renz, David Shepherd, William Postell. Commd. 2d lt. U.S. Army, 1952, served with C.E., 1952-57, resigned, 1957; with IBM, N.Y., Wis., D.C., 1957-64, adminstrv. asst. to pres. Fed. Systems div., 1963-64; with Ferris & Co., Washington, 1964-70, mgr. investment adv. dept., 1968-70; investment counselor, partner Loomis-Sayles & Co., Inc., Washington, 1970—, v.p., 1974—; lectr., U. Md., 1965-69; dir. Am. Bank Md. Chmn., N.W. trades and industries Met. D.C. Cancer drive, 1965. Democratic precinct chmn. Montgomery County, Md., 1964-66; chmn. for safety Presdl. Inaugural Ball Com., 1965; chmn. bd. Washington Chamber Orch. Decorated Bronze Star medal. Mem. West Point Soc. D.C. (gov. 1962-67, 73-77, pres., past treas., sec.), N.C. Soc. Cin. (mem. standing com. 1967—), Soc. Cin. (sec. 1967-71, mem. finance com. 1968—, dir.), Washington Soc. Investment Analysts, Fin. Analysts Fedn., Mensa, Intertel. Clubs: Rotarian, Cosmos, Army and Navy, University (mem. house com. 1971—, bd. admissions 1973-77, gov. 1977—) (Washington). Author: West Point and Society of the Cincinnati, 1967. Composer: The Sesquicentennial March, 1967. Home: 12011 Old Bridge Rd Rockville MD 20852 Office: 888 17th St NW Washington DC 20006

RAILTON, WILLIAM SCOTT, lawyer; b. Newark, July 30, 1935; s. William Scott and Carolyn Elizabeth (Guiberson) R.; B.S. in Elec. Engring., U. Wash., 1962; J.D. with honors, George Washington U., 1965; children—William Scott III, Anne Greenwood. Admitted to Md., D.C. bars, 1966; asso. Kemon Palmer & Estabrook, Washington, 1965-68, partner, 1968-70; sr. trial atty. U.S. Dept. Labor, Washington, 1970-71, asst. counsel for trial litigation, 1971-72; chief counsel U.S. Occupational Safety and Health Rev. Commn., Washington, 1972-77, acting gen. counsel, 1975-77; Washington resident partner firm Reed, Smith, Shaw & McClay, Pitts., 1977—; mem. Occupational Safety and Health Act faculty George Washington U. Sch. Law, 1977—, Practicing Law Inst., 1976—. Pres., Montgomery Sq. Citizens Assn., Potomac, Md., 1970-71. Regional chmn. Republican party Montgomery County, Md., 1968-70. Served with USMC, 1953-58. Recipient Meritorious Achievement award U.S. Dept. Labor, 1972; Outstanding Service award U.S. Occupational Safety and Health Rev. Commn. Mem. Young Lawyers D.C. Bar (vice chmn. 1971, sec. 1970), Am., Md. bar assns., Bar Assn. D.C., I.E.E.E., Order of Coif, Sigma Phi Epsilon, Phi Delta Phi. Club: Oval of U. Wash. (Seattle). Episcopalian (vestryman 1968-70, lay reader 1968-71). Author: The Examination System and the Backlog, IDEA, 1965; The OSHA General Duty Clause, 1977; The OSHA Health Standards, 1977. Contbg. author Employee Relations Law Jour., 1978—. Home: 8216 Jeb Stuart Rd Potomac MD 20854 Office: 1150 Connecticut Ave NW Washington DC 20036

RAIMONDI, LOUIS ARNOLD, civil engr.; b. Paterson, N.J., Oct. 18, 1932; s. Mario and Virginia (Pepe) R.; B.S. in Civil Engring., Newark Coll. Engring., 1959, M.S. in C.E., 1964; m. Martha Gambuti, Jan. 30, 1955; children—Christopher, Michael, David, Laura. Asst. to profl. engr. and land surveyor Charles D. Geiger, Paterson, N.J., 1953-58; hwy. designer Parsons, Brinkerhoff, Hall & MacDonald, 1958; design engr., adminstrv. asst. Boswell Engring., Ridgefield Park, N.J., 1958-64; hydraulics engr. Bergen County Engring. Dept., Hackensack, N.J., 1964-65; v.p., asso. Canger Engring. Assos., Fairlawn, N.J., 1965-68; prin., Raimondi Assos., Monroe, N.Y., 1968—; sec., Ramapo Valley Testing Lab., 1971—. Com. chmn. Ridgewood-Glen Rock council Boy Scouts Am., 1971-73; area comdr. Community Chest, Ridgewood, Glen Rock, N.J., 1968. Served with USCGR, 1952-54. Registered profl. engr., N.J., N.Y., Pa., Conn., Fla. Fellow Am. Soc. C.E.; mem. Cons. Engrs. Council, Nat., Passaic County (pres. 1967) socs. profl. engrs., Chi Epsilon. Home: 329 Libby Ave Ridgewood NJ 07450 Office: 110 Stage Rd Monroe NY 10950

RAINEY, PATRICIA ANN, counselor; b. Dover, N.H., Oct. 14, 1937; d. Wilbur Robert and Helen Mary Rainey; B.A., U. N.H., 1960, M.Ed., 1967, certificate Counseling and Personnel Services, 1976. Grad. asst. Ford Found., U. N.H., 1960-61; tchr. social studies Colebrook (N.H.) Acad., 1961-65; counselor Exeter (N.H.) High Sch., 1966-68; asst. prof. psychology Cleveland (Tenn.) State Community Coll., 1968-72; lecture asst. dept. edn. U. N.H., 1973; lectr. Merrimack Valley br., 1974, lectr. Centrex Office, 1973—; counselor Renew Counseling Center, N. Hampton, N.H., 1977—. Mem. Am. Personnel and Guidance Assn. Author: Illusions: A Journey Into Perception, 1973; contbr. articles in field to Creative Teacher, Saturday Review, Today's Education. Home: 173 Mount Vernon St Dover NH 03820 Office: 4 North Rd North Hampton NH 03862

RAINIS, EUGENE CHARLES, banker; b. N.Y.C., Sept. 24, 1940; s. Charles William and Louise Theresa (Nold) R.; B.S., Fordham Coll., 1962; M.B.A., U. Pa., 1964; m. Jane Margaret Micucci, Nov. 28, 1964; children—Ellen, David, Mark. Security analyst trainee Merrill Lynch, Pierce, Fenner & Smith, 1963-65; short term investment specialist Brown Bros. Harriman & Co., 1965-67, asst. head bond dept., 1967-71, mgr., head bond dept., 1972-77, partner, 1977—. Served with USAR, 1964. Chartered fin. analyst. Mem. Inst. Chartered Fin. Analysts, N.Y. Soc. Security Analysts. Republican. Roman Catholic. Clubs: Municipal Bond, Downtown Assn. (N.Y.C.). Home: Mountainside Rd Mendham NJ 07945 Office: 59 Wall St New York City NY 10005

RAINWATER, JAMES, educator; b. Council, Idaho, Dec. 9, 1917; s. Leo J. and Edna E. (Teague) R.; B.S., Calif. Inst. Tech., 1939; Ph.D., Columbia, 1946; m. Emma Louise Smith, Mar. 7, 1942; children—James Carlton, Robert Stephen, Elizabeth (dec.), William George. Asst. physics Columbia, 1939-42, scientist OSRD and Manhattan dist., 1942-46, instr., 1946-47, asst. prof. physics, 1947-49, asso. prof. physics, 1949-52, prof. physics, 1952—; dir. Nevis Cyclotron Lab., 1951-53, 56-61, research scientist AEC and Office Naval Research projects, 1947—. Mem. adv. com. physics and electronuclear divs. Oak Ridge Nat. Lab., 1962-65; mem. physics rev. panel Argonne Nat. Lab., 1967-70. Recipient Ernest Orlando Laurence award AEC, 1963, Nobel prize in physics, 1975. Fellow AAAS, IEEE, Am. Phys. Soc., N.Y. Acad. Scis.; mem. Am. Inst. Physics, Am. Assn. Physics Tchrs., Optical Soc. Am., Nat. Acad. Scis. Contbr. articles to profl. jours. Home: 342 Mt Hope Blvd Hastings-on-Hudson NY 10706

RAISON, CHARLES WILLIAM, theatre arts exec.; b. Detroit, May 1, 1936; s. Oscar Everett and Lillian (Walker) R.; B.A., Mich. State U., 1959; M.F.A., Tulane U., 1961; m. Diane Millicent Deuvall, July 12, 1958; children—Jennifer Scott, Andrew Michael, Coleman Walker. Instr. theatre Lycoming Coll., Williamsport, Pa., 1961-63, asst. prof., 1963-68, asso. prof., 1968-69, chmn. dept. theatre, 1961-69; exec. dir. Am. Acad. Dramatic Arts, N.Y.C., 1969-74, dir., 1974-75; dir. mgmt. Studio Arena Theatre, Buffalo, 1975-76, asso. dir., 1976-77, dir. devel. and planning, 1977—; communication cons. Ins. N. Am., 1972-73, Hoffman-LaRoche, 1974, Allied Chem. Co., 1975-76, Stauffer Chem. Co., 1976-77; founder, producer, dir. Arena Theatre, Williamsport, 1961-69. Bd. dirs. Commonwealth Playhouse Found., Buffalo Theatre Dist. Assn.; adv. council for arts Daemon Coll., Canisius Coll., Buffalo High Sch. Visual and Performing Arts. Mem. Am. Theatre Assn., Nat. Collegiate Players, Theta Alpha Phi. Home: 121 Robin Hill Dr Williamsville NY 14221 Office: 710 Main St Buffalo NY 14202

RAISSLE, HELEN CATHERINE, nurse, hosp. adminstr.; b. South Bend, Ind., July 11, 1926; d. John Crist and Margaret Ann (Geist) R.; diploma Meml. Hosp. Sch. Nursing, South Bend, 1947; B.S. in Nursing Ind. U., 1955; M.S.Ed., Butler U., 1961. Asst. dir. nursing Indpls. Gen. Hosp., 1955-56; instr., VA Hosp., Indpls., 1957-59, then head nurse, supr.; asst. chief nursing service VA Hosp., Helena, Mont., 1964-67, Martinez, Calif., 1967-69; chief nursing service VA Hosp., Balt., 1971-73, VA Hosp. Research, Chgo., 1973-75, VA Hosp., Pitts., 1975—; mem. Mont. Gov's Rehab. Conf., 1963; clin. asst. prof. nursing service adminstrn. U. Pitts. Served with Nurse Corps USAF, 1949-50. Mem. Am. Nurses Assn. (dist. pres. 1963-64), Nat. League Nursing, Nat. Assn. Nursing Service Adminstrn., Ind., Butler univ. alumni assns., Sigma Theta Tau, Pi Lambda Theta. Republican. Episcopalian. Research on perception of communication by nursing chiefs with med. chief of staff, 1970. Home: 2406 Clearview Dr Glenshaw PA 15116 Office: VA Hosp University Dr C Pittsburgh PA 15240

RAITEN, SUSAN GAIL, psychoanalyst; b. N.Y.C., Apr. 27, 1949; d. Benjamin and Doris Bell (Demerer) Raiten; B.A., Bklyn. Coll., 1971; M.S., L.I. U., 1973; postgrad. Manhattan Center for Advanced Psychoanalytic Studies. Counselor Developmental Clinic, L.I. U., 1972-73; therapist Stanley S. Lamm Clinic, L.I. Coll. Hosp., 1975-76; therapist Manhattan Center for Advanced Psychoanalytic Studies Treatment Service, N.Y.C., 1976—; tchr. elementary edn., N.Y.C.; pvt. practice psychoanalysis, N.Y.C. Mem. Am. Personnel and Guidance Assn., Nat. Accreditation Assn. Psychoanalysis, N.Y. State United Tchrs., United Fedn. Tchrs. Office: 15 E 10th St New York City NY 10011

RAJ, RISHI SHARMA, aerospace engr.; b. Moga, India, Sept. 18, 1945; s. Thakur Dass and Krishna (Devi) Sharma; B.S. with honors, Punjab (India) U., 1964; M.S. with honors, People's Friendship U., Moscow, 1969; Ph.D., Pa. State U., 1974; came to U.S., 1970, naturalized, 1976; m. Swadesh Sharma, Sept. 12, 1970; children—Rashmi, Vishwa. Scientist, Nat. Aero. Lab., Bangalore, India, 1969-70; research asso., asst. dept. aerospace engring. and Garfield Thomas water tunnel ordnance research lab. Pa. State U., University Park, 1970-75; asst. prof. mech. engring. City Coll. N.Y., N.Y.C., 1975—; tech. cons. power systems Curtiss-Wright Corp., Wood-Ridge, N.J., 1976—. English-Russian interpreter, translator Nat. Acad. Scis./NRC fellow, 1975; NSF turbomachinery research grantee, 1976; City U. N.Y. grantee, 1977. Mem. ASME (vice-chmn. tech., fluid machinery components 1977, chmn. tech. turbulence in turbo machinery 1979), Am. Inst. Aeros. and Astronautics, Tensor Soc. Japan, Indian Sci. Congress, Sigma Xi. Researcher wakes, turbulence, erosion in turbomachinery. Home: 86 Wortendyke Ave Emerson NJ 07630 Office: T-15 City Coll NY 138th and Convent Ave New York City NY 10031

RAJAN, SUNDAR RAMAKRISHNAN, scientist; b. Madurai, India, July 10, 1946; s. Vasudevan and Laxmi R.; came to U.S., 1970; B.Sc. with honors, Poona U., 1964; Ph.D. in Physics, U. Calif., Berkeley, 1973; m. Uma Ayyar, Aug. 29, 1974; 1 son, Sanjeev. Research asso. Tata Inst. Fundamental Research, Bombay, 1965-70; research asst. dept. physics U. Calif., Berkeley, 1970-73; research fellow Calif. Inst. Tech., Pasadena, 1973-75; research fellow dept. terrestrial magnetism Carnegie Instn., Washington, 1975-77, staff mem., 1977—. Mem. Am. Phys. Soc., Am. Geophys. Union, Meteoritcal Soc., Sigma Xi. Democrat. Hindu. Contbr. numerous articles to profl. jours. Home: 9910 New Orchard Dr Upper Marlboro MD 20870 Office: 5241 Broad Branch Rd NW Washington DC 20015

RAJAPAKSA, TRIKANTE NALINI, physician; b. Sri Lanka, Oct. 5, 1945; d. Vernon Henry Gunasekera and Nalini (Tennekoon) DeAlwis; M.D., Med. Sch. U. Sri Lanka, 1970; m. Anura Rajapaksa, Dec. 3, 1970; 1 child, Roshini. Resident in internal medicine Coney Island Hosp., Bklyn., 1972-74; fellow in psychosomatic medicine Downstate Med. Center, State U. N.Y., Bklyn., 1974—, attending physician psychosomatic medicine, 1976—, asst. prof. clin. medicine, 1976—. Diplomate Am. Bd. Internal Medicine. Mem. A.C.P., N.Y. Soc. Liaison Psychiatrists, Am. Psychosomatic Soc. Co-author: Treatment of a Dying Patient - Advances in Thanatology. Contbr. articles to profl. jours. Home: 82 Palmer Ave Scarsdale NY 10583 Office: 450 Clarkson Ave Box 127 Brooklyn NY 11203

RAK, WOLODYMYR, banker; b. Jaroslawychi, Ukraine, Sept. 4, 1925; s. Dmytro and Ewdokia (Drapinsky) E.; B.A., Grad. Sch. Econs., Munich, Germany, 1949; postgrad. Columbia, 1951-52; M.B.A., N.Y. U., 1956; m. Anna Shkoruta, Mar. 18, 1950; children—Ihor, Andrew. Accountant, Chase Manhattan Bank, N.Y.C., 1956-70, asst. treas., 1970-72, 2d v.p., 1972-77, v.p., 1977—; pres., Plast Inc., N.Y.C., 1959-60, treas., 1961-64, dir., 1965-66, exec. v.p., 1967-69, dir., 1969—; pres. Shevchenko Sci. Soc., Inc., 1978—. Mem. Am. Accounting Assn., Bank Adminstrn. Inst., Tax Soc. N.Y. U., N.Y. U. Alumni Fedn. Home: 34-29 33d St Astoria NY 11106 Office: 1 Chase Manhattan Plaza New York City NY 10015

RAKOVAN, LAWRENCE FRANCIS, artist; b. Eleria, Ohio, Oct. 26, 1939; s. George Edward and Mary (Muir) R.; B.S., Wayne State U., 1967; M.A., R.I. Sch. Design, 1969; m. Jeana Dale Bearce, June 7, 1969; children—Barbara Emily, Luke, Francesca. Exhibited one-man shows Maine Art Gallery, 1969-70, Union Theol. Sem., Rotunta Gallery, N.Y.C., 1972, Bowdoin Coll., 1974, St. Peter's Center Gallery, N.Y.C., 1973, Gallery 2, U. Maine, 1970, 77, Treat Gallery, Bates Coll., 1976; represented in permanent collections Bklyn. Mus. Art, Bates, Colby, Bowdoin Mus. Art, Portland Mus. Art, U. Maine; instr. art and art history U. Maine, 1967-70, asst. prof., 1970-76; asso. prof. U. So. Maine, 1976—; guest lectr. Portland Mus. Art; art columnist Brunswick News; mem. Maine com. Skowhegan Sch. Painting and Sculpture. Bd. dirs. Maine Art Gallery. Served with USAF, 1963-67. U. Maine grant, 1973-74. Home: Mere Point Rd 5 Brunswick ME 04011

RAKSIN, IRVING JACOB, oral surgeon; b. Balt., Aug. 14, 1939; s. Bernard Phillip and Rose Miriam (Kramer) R.; B.S., U. Md., 1960, D.D.S., 1964; m. Barbara Merri Zimring, Apr. 20, 1968; children—Patricia Beth, David Adam, Jonathan Neal. Intern, Sinai Hosp., Balt., 1964-65; asst. resident in oral surgery N.Y. Hosp.-Cornell Med. Center, 1965-66, resident, 1966-67, chief resident, 1967-68; fellow in surgery Cornell Med. Sch., 1966-68; practice dentistry specializing in oral surgery, Balt., 1970—; head div. oral surgery Sinai Hosp., Balt.; mem. staff Baltimore County Gen. Hosp., Greater Balt. Med. Center. Served as capt. AUS, 1968-70. Diplomate Am. Bd. Oral Surgery. Mem. Md. Soc. Oral Surgery (chmn. health plans and ins. com., pres. 1977-78), Baltimore County, Balt. City (membership chmn. 1975) dental socs., Am. Soc. Oral Surgeons, ADA, Md. State Dental Assn., Baltimore County Dental Soc., U. Md. Dental Sch. Alumni, Alpha Omega (editor 1972-73). Democrat. Jewish. Home: 5705 Chilham Rd Baltimore MD 21209 Office: 6810 Park Heights Ave Baltimore MD 21215

RALPH, RICHARD GARRICK, investment co. exec.; b. Syracuse, N.Y., Nov. 17, 1935; s. Charles H. R. and Adeline C. (Garrick) R.; B.S., Syracuse U., 1957, postgrad., 1958-60; postgrad. U. Md., 1958, N.Y. Inst. Fin., 1958; m. Lynn C. Weegar, June 21, 1969; children—Brian, Christopher, Kevin. With Reynolds Securities Inc., Syracuse, 1958—, mgr. br., 1968-72, sr. mgr., 1972-73, v.p., 1973—, mem. pres's. council, 1974, 75, mem. chmn's. council, 1975-76; v.p. sales Loeb Rhoades, Hornblower & Co., 1977—; pres. Upstate N.Y. State Investors League; instr. adult edn. investing and econs. Treas., bd. dirs. Upstate chpt. Am. Heart Assn.; gov. Citizens' Found., Syracuse; bd. dirs. Leukemia Soc. Am., Austin Park Assn.; active United Way of Central N.Y. Recipient awards Muscular Dystrophy Assn., 1972, Am. Heart Assn., 1974, 75, others. Mem. Bond Club of Syracuse (pres. 1974-75, Appreciation Dinner recognition 1976), Nat. Assn. Security Dealers (prin.), Commodity Futures Trading Commn., N.Y. State Ins., Syracuse U. Alumni Assn., Phi Kappa Psi Alumni Assn. (dir.). Republican. Lutheran. Clubs: Skaneateles Country, Skaneateles Ski, Masons, Shriners, Royal Order Jesters, Syracuse Athletic, Kiwanis. Writer Investors Corner, newspaper column; writer, producer Investors Corner, daily radio program, 1964-68. Home: RD 3 East Lake Rd Skaneateles NY 13152 Office: 220 S Warren St Syracuse NY 13202

RALSTON, ALEXANDER HOYLE, JR., cons. engring. co. exec.; b. Upper Darby, Pa., Sept. 30, 1939; s. Alexander Hoyle and Marjorie Livingston (Brereton) R.; B.S. in Mech. Engring., Drexel U., 1963; m. Judith Ann Reynolds, Nov. 26, 1976; children by previous marriage—Pamela Lyn, Alexander Hoyle. Mech. contractor, project mgr. A.H. Ralston Co., Phila., 1963-66; archtl.-mech. design engr. Alexander Ewing & Assos., Phila., 1966-70; v.p., gen. mgr. Synergo Co., Phila., 1970-77; hosp. market mgr. Energy Mgmt. Services, Inc., Phila., 1977—. Registered profl. engr., Pa. Mem. Am. Soc. Heating, Refrigeration and Air Conditioning Engrs., Pa. Soc. Profl. Engrs. Republican. Presbyterian. Home: U 168 Woodstock Dr Villanova PA 19085 Office: 400 Market St E Philadelphia PA 19106

RALSTON, MRS. BYRON BROWN (LUCY VIRGINIA GORDON), club woman, pianist; b. San Antonio, Feb. 6, 1896; d. James Riely and Mary Lamar (Sprigg) Gordon; student Mlle. Veltin's Sch., N.Y.C., Mrs. Dow's Sch., Briarcliff Manor, N.Y., also pvt. schs. in Europe; m. Byron Brown Ralston, June 4, 1919; 1 dau., Lucy Virginia Gordon. Co-chmn. patron and patroness com. First Versailles (France) Debutante Ball, 1958; bd. dirs., rec. sec. Republican Com. One Hundred, Inc., N.Y.C., 1961-65. Mem. Daus. of the Cincinnati, Huguenot Soc. Am., Nat. Soc. Magna Charta Dames, Colonial Soc. Descs. Knights of Garter, Colonial Soc. Americans of Royal Descent, Colonial Soc. Order of Crown, Colonial Dames So. Md., Brit. Soc. Friends St. George and Descs. of Knights of Garter, DAR (def. chmn. Knapp chpt. 1940-46). Episcopalian. Clubs: Manor (v.p. French sect. 1936-46, emeritus 1968), Pelham Country (emeritus) (Pelham, N.Y.); Internat. Garden, Bartow-Pell Mansion Mus. (N.Y.C.). Home: 159 Corlies Ave Pelham Heights NY 10803

RALSTON, DAVID CORNELL, civil engr.; b. Beloit, Wis., May 6, 1930; s. Kenneth M. and Evelyn (Belden) R.; B.S., U. Ill., 1952, M.S., 1958; postgrad. Harvard U., 1963; m. Margaret L. Speer, June 16, 1956; children—Roger, David, Barbara, Andrew. Area engr. Soil Conservation Service, U.S. Dept. Agr., Urbana, Ill., 1954-58, design engr., Milw., 1958-64, asst. state engr., St. Paul, 1964-66, state engr., Morgantown, W.Va., 1966-71, regional design engr., Portland, Oreg., 1971-74, soil engr., Washington, 1975-76, chief Design br., 1977—. Mem. bd. zoning appeals, Morgantown, W.Va., 1970-71. Served with U.S. Army, 1952-54; CBI. Registered profl. engr., Ill., W.Va. Mem. Am. Soc. Agrl. Engrs. (state pres. 1970-71), ASCE, Nat. Soc. Profl. Engrs., Profl. Engrs. of Oreg. Presbyterian (elder 1969-71). Home: 4631 Tara Dr Fairfax VA 22030 Office: Room 5243 S Agr Bldg Washington DC 20250

RALSTON, LUCY VIRGINIA GORDON, artist; b. Washington, Sept. 9, 1926; d. Byron Brown and Lucy Virginia (Gordon) R.; grad. Finch Jr. Coll., 1942; pvt. art tng.; student Leon Kroll. One-woman show Pelham (N.Y.) Meml. High Sch., 1939; pvt. shows in Pelham home; group shows include: Manor Club, Pelham, 1945-48, Nat. Arts Club, N.Y.C., 1950-62, Westchester Fedn. Women's Clubs, Bronxville, N.Y., 1954, Mt. Vernon (N.Y.) Art Assn., 1955, Allied Artists Am. ann. exhbn., N.Y.C., 1955; represented in permanent collections Assn. Jr. Leagues Am., N.Y.C. and on tour U.S. and Can., John Jay and Eliza Jane Watson Found., Elizabeth, N.J.; mural called Gay Nineties in Westchester Restaurant, Mamaroneck, N.Y.; freelance artist Tiffany and Co., 1947-48; designer U.S.S. Constn. book plate used by Am. Bible Soc. and John Jay and Eliza Jane Watson Found. for presentation Bibles to grads. U.S. Naval Acad., C.G. Acad., Merchant Marine Acad., 1953—. Recipient Popular prize Manor Club exhibit, 1947, 48, 2d prize, 1958, 1st prize for graphic art, 1957; Popular prize Westchester Assn. Women's Clubs, 1951, Mt. Vernon Art Assn., 1954; 2d prize Met. Mus., Pelham, 1969. Mem. Jr. League Pelham, Internat. Garden Club, Bartow-Pell Mansion Mus., Nat. Arts Club, D.A.R. (registrar Knapp chpt. 1961-63), Daus. of the Cincinnati (registrar 1973—), Nat. Soc. Colonial Dames State N.Y., Colonial Soc. Ams. Royal Descent, Nat. Soc. Magna Charta Dames, Allied Artists Am. (asso.), Colonial Soc. Descs. Knights of Garter, Colonial Order of Crown, Huguenot Soc. Am. Club: Pelham Pelham Country. Commd. by pres. of Brit.-Am. Soc. to paint life-size portraits of Princess Anne and Prince Charles in his invsetiture robes as Prince of Wales, to be pub. in London in British-American Chronicle and exhibited at ann. reception of Daus. of the Cincinnati, N.Y.C., 1974. Home and Studio: 159 Corlies Ave Pelham Heights NY 10803

RAM, RAMASWAMY SATHASIVA, urologist; b. Parakkai, India, July 9, 1934; s. Ramaswamy and Avai (Ramaswamy) R.; immigrated to Can., 1972, naturalized, 1976; M.D., U. Trivandum (India), 1958; m. Shantha, Mar. 12, 1966; children—Ava, Kala. Gen. surg. tng., U.K., 1960; urol. tng., Can., 1966; practice medicine specializing in urology, New Glasgow, N.S., Can., 1973—; cons. urologist Aberdeen Hosp. Fellow royal colls. surgeons Eng., Edinburgh, Can., A.C.S.; mem. Canadian Med. Assn., Canadian Urol. Assn., Internat. Coll. Angiology, Am. Assn. Geriatrics, Assn. Surgeons India. Hindu. Home: 491 Martin Ave New Glasgow NS Canada Office: 20 Abercrombie Rd New Glasgow NS B24 1K1 Canada

RAMANATH, HASSAN KRISHNA, surgeon; b. India, May 8, 1943; s. N.C. and N.C. (Andalamma) KrishnaIyengar; came to U.S., 1966; M.B.,B.S., Govt. Med. Coll., Mysore, India, 1965; m. Usha Sitharam, July 14, 1971; children—Archana, Vijay. Intern, then resident in surgery U. Rochester (N.Y.), 1966-71, fellow in surgical onocology, asso. in surgery, 1971-72, clin. asst. prof. surgery, 1974—; practice medicine specializing in surgery, Rochester, N.Y., 1972—; mem. staffs Rochester Gen. Hosp., Park Ridge Hosp.; cons. Lakeside Meml. Hosp. Recipient Physicians Recognition award AMA, 1966-79. Diplomate Am. Bd. Surgery. Fellow A.C.S., Rochester Acad. Medicine; mem. Med. Soc. of N.Y. Home: 14 Esternay Ln Pittsford NY 14534 Office: 1400 Portland Ave Rochester NY 14621

RAMANATHER, SIRITHARA, physician; b. Sri-Lanka, Feb. 23, 1946; s. Ramanather Chellapah and Camalawathy; came to U.S., 1971, naturalized, 1973; M.B.B.S., U. Ceylon, Sri-Lanka, 1969; m. Anusha, July 13, 1977. Intern, S. Balt. Gen. Hosp., 1971-72, resident in internal medicine, 1971-74, resident in cardiology, 1974-75, staff cardiologist, 1977—; fellow in cardiology Albert Einstein Med. Center, Phila., 1975-77; lectr. and cons. in field. Diplomate Am. Bd. of Internal Medicine, also subsplty. in cardiology. Home: Apt 1A 8142 Harold Ct Glen Burnie MD 21061 Office: 3001 S Hanover St Baltimore MD 21230

RAMBAUSKE, WERNER ROBERT, engring. cons.; b. Breslau, Ger., Mar. 1911; s. Emanuel Julius and Minna Helene (Brodde) R.; came to U.S., 1947, naturalized 1957; grad. Humanistic Gymnasium, 1930; Dr. Rer. Nat. Universities Munich, Goettingen, Berlin, 1940; m. Hedy Maria Kropp, June 26, 1946; children—Alexander, Elizabeth, Mary Anne. Leader X-Ray Lab. J. Gollnow & Son, Stettin, Ger., 1938-40; leader electo-optics lab. Askania Ag, Berlin, Ger., 1940-45; staff physicist Wright Patterson AFB, Dayton, Ohio, 1947-55, cons., 1956-66; prof. physics U. Dayton, 1956-66, also research physicist; mem. staff System Devel. Corp., Dayton, 1967-68; cons. scientist, prin. engr. Raytheon Comp. Missile System Div., Bedford, Mass., 1968-76. Named outstanding prof. U. Dayton, 1960, Outstanding Inventor award USAF, 1961; recipient outstanding inventors award Raytheon Comp., Bedford, Mass., 1975. Mem. Am. Phys. Soc., Soc. Physics Tchrs., Optical Soc. Am., AAAS, N.Y. Acad. Sids., Roman Catholic. Patentee in field. Contbr. articles to profl. jours. Home: 170 Acton St Carlisle MA 01741

RAMBO, JOHN HENRY THOMAS, otologist; b. Menlo, Ga., Apr. 21, 1915; s. Gordon Martin and Martha Mae (Kennedy) R.; M.D., Emory U., 1940; postgrad. Harvard U. Med. Sch., 1945-46; m. Kathleen Frances Foreman, Dec. 31, 1949; children—Michael Robert, Tracy Lynn. Rotating intern Grady Meml. Hosp., Atlanta, 1940-41; resident Mass. Eye and Ear Infirmary, Boston, 1946-48; instr. otolaryngology Harvard Med. Sch., 1948; fellow Lempert Inst. Otology, N.Y.C., 1948-49; practice medicine specializing in otology, N.Y.C., 1950; mem. staff Lenox Hill Hosp.; cons. N.Y. Eye and Ear Infirmary. Served from 1st lt. to lt. col. M.C., AC, U.S. Army, 1941-46. Diplomate Am. Bd. Otolaryngology. Fellow Am. Acad. Ophthalmology and Otolaryngology; mem. Am. Otol. Soc., Am. Laryngological, Rhinological and Otological Soc., N.Y. Otol. Soc., N.Y. Acad. Medicine, AMA, N.Y. State, N.Y. County med. socs., New Eng. Otol. Soc., Sociedad Panamericana de Otolaryngologia, N.Y. Physicians Golfing Assn., N.Y. Geneal. and Biog. Soc. Home and Office: 150 E 77th St New York City NY 10021

RAMER, MARVIN MAXWELL, engring. and constrn. co. exec.; b. Phila., Aug. 11, 1919; s. Edward James and Julia (Hoffmann) R.; B.Chem. Engring., Rensselaer Poly. Inst., 1940; postgrad. Columbia, 1948-49; m. A. Stella Hornstein, May 20, 1945; children—Joan E., Karen J. (Mrs. Simon J. Sinnreich), Frances M. Project mgr. Allied Chem. Co., Camden, N.J., Buffalo, 1940-47; co-mgr. Arlin Chem. Co., Elizabeth, N.J., 1947-50; dist. sales mgr. Blaw Knox Co., Pitts., 1950-61; exec. v.p., dir. Lummus Co. subs. Combustion Engring. Inc., Bloomfield, N.J., 1961—, also pres., dir. Resource Devel. Services, Bloomfield, N.J. Registered profl. engr., N.J., Okla. Mem. Am. Inst. Chem. Engrs., Am. Inst. Mining, Metall. and Petroleum Engrs., Petroleum Engrs. Soc. Clubs: Crestmont Country (West Orange, N.J.); Marco Polo (N.Y.C.). Home: 24 Pine Rd Roseland NJ 07068 Office: C-E Lummus 1515 Broad St Bloomfield NJ 07003

RAMETTA, CONCETTO SAL, physician; b. Solarino, Italy, Oct. 5, 1945; s. Sebastian and Lucy R.; came to U.S., 1953, naturalized, 1955; A.B., Seton Hall U., 1967; M.D., Georgetown U., 1971; m. Mary Perrino, July 5, 1969; children—Thomas, Rachel, Benjamin, Robert. Intern, U.Va., Charlottesville, 1971-72, resident, 1972-74; chief Dept. of Clinics, Kimbrough Hosp., Fort Meade, Md., 1974-76; asst. attending, Horton Hosp., Middletown, N.Y., 1976—. Vice pres. Orange-Rockland-Sullivan Counties, Am. Heart Assn.; bd. dirs. Am. Cancer Soc. Orange County. Served to maj. M.C. U.S. Army, 1974-76. Fellow Am. Coll. Angiology, Internat. Coll. Angiology, Am. Coll. Utilization Review Physicians; mem. A.C.P., Am. Soc. Internal Medicine, Am. Soc. Geriatrics, Am. Occupational Med. Assn. Lodge: Elks. Office: 22 Grove St Middletown NY 10940

RAMEY, JAMES WENDELL, social worker; b. Donora, Pa., Nov. 8, 1925; s. Lee and Nannie Sue (Swanson) R.; B.S., Howard U., 1946; M.S.W., U. Pitts., 1957. County supr. Pa. Dept. Pub. Welfare, Washington, 1951-65; exec. dir. Hill House Assn., Pitts., 1965-67, Mon Valley United Health Services Inc., Charleroi, Pa., 1967-71; exec. dir. Mon Valley Health and Welfare Council Inc., Monessen, Pa., 1971—; asso. prof. California (Pa.) State Coll., 1975—. Mem. bd. visitors Grad. Sch. Public Health, U. Pitts., 1977—; mem. exec. com. Pa. Pub. Health Assn., 1977—; mem. exec. com. Statewide Health Coordinating Com., 1976—, Western Pa. Gerontology Center, 1977—; chmn. Family Planning Council of Western Pa., 1976—. Mem. Nat. Assn. Social Workers, Am. Public Health Assn., Pa. Mental Health Assn., Western Pa. Public Health Council, Nat. Council on Social Welfare. Republican. Baptist. Office: Mon Valley Health and Welfare Eastgate 8 Monessen PA 15062

RAMIREZ, ALBERTO, cardiologist; b. Cali, Colombia, July 30, 1939; s. Jaime and Aura (Carvajal) R.; arrived U.S., 1963, naturalized, 1977; B.S., Colegio San Luis Gonzaga, 1955; M.D., U. del Valle, 1963; m. Florencia Martinez, Sept. 6, 1969; children—Eduardo Alberto, Jaime Andres, Monica. Intern, Cambridge (Mass.) Hosp., 1970-71; resident in internal medicine Med. Coll. of Va., Richmond, 1963-65; research fellow in medicine Harvard Med. Sch., Boston, 1965-68; asst. prof. medicine Universidad Nacional de Colombia, Bogota, 1968-70, chief cardiology, 1968-70; instr. medicine Harvard Med. Sch., Boston, 1971-72, asst. prof., 1972-74, asst. clin. prof., 1974—; chief cardiology Cambridge Hosp., 1971-72; chief cardiology, asso. dir. medicine Faulkner Hosp., Boston, 1974—; advisor Pan Am. Health Orgn., Bogota, 1968-70, lectr. Tufts U., Boston, 1975—. Diplomate Am. Bd. Internal Medicine. Fellow A.C.P., Am. Coll. Cardiology, Mass. Med. Soc. Roman Catholic. Club: Wellesley Country. Contbr. articles in field to profl. jours. Home: 53 Garden Rd Wellesley Hills MA 02181

RAMM, JOHN ROBERT, aluminum co. exec.; b. Englewood, N.J., Apr. 5, 1951; s. Robert William and Jane Brown (Wilson) R.; B.A., Lafayette Coll., 1973; postgrad. George Washington U., 1977-78; m. Linda Joan Eagan, June 29, 1974. Trainee, Aluminum Co. Am., 1973; indsl. sales engr. aluminum mill products, Morris Plains, N.J., 1973-76, govt. mktg. rep., Washington, 1976—; also chmn. N.Y. dist. sales tng. com. Head boys' basketball coach St. Martin's Sch., 1977-78; active Montgomery County Young Republicans. Mem. Nat. Security Indsl. Assn., Am. Def. Preparedness Assn., Nat. Space Club, Smithsonian Assos., Lafayette Coll. Alumni Club, Theta Delta Chi. Republican. Roman Catholic. Home: 9219 Frostburg Way Gaithersburg MD 20760 Office: Alcoa 1200 Ring Bldg NW Washington DC 20036

RAMSBURG, HELEN HARRIS, microbiologist; b. Miami, Fla., Oct. 29, 1925; d. William Henry and Naomi Catharine (Shafer) Harris; A.B. in Biology, Hood Coll., 1947, postgrad., 1973—; postgrad. U. Md., 1956-60; m. Staley William Ramsburg, Sept. 7, 1946; children—Cassandra Ramsburg Duncan; foster child—Angela Halbrook Fry. Med. lab. technician Frederick (Md.) Meml. Hosp., 1947-48; biol. aid NIH, Bethesda, Md., 1949-50; bacteriology lab. technician U.S. Army Research Inst. Infectious Diseases, Frederick, Md., 1955-56, med. biology technician, 1957, research technician, 1958, bacteriologist, 1959-61, microbiologist, 1962—. Recipient Spl. Act and Service award Dept. Army, 1964. Lutheran. Contbr. articles to profl. jours. Home: 9201 Dublin Rd Walkersville MD 21793 Office: Virology Division USAMRIID Fort Detrick Frederick MD 21701

RAMSDELL, JOHN ALAN, surgeon; b. N.Y.C., Mar. 25, 1927; s. Edwin G. and Bessie (Sadler) R.; B.A. in Econs., Yale U., 1949; M.D., Columbia U., 1954; M.S. in Surgery, U. Minn., 1959; m. Barbara Greer, Apr. 23, 1955; children—Pamela Barclay, John Sadler, Peter Dickinson. Intern, Bellevue Hosp., N.Y.C., 1954-55; resident in surgery Mayo Clinic, Rochester, Minn., 1955-59, asst. staff mem., 1959-60; practice medicine specializing in surgery, White Plains, N.Y., 1960—; attending surgeon White Plains Hosp. Med. Center, 1960—, chief of staff, 1974—, bd. govs., 1970-72, 74—; attending surgeon Burke Rehab. Center, 1962—; attending surgeon St. Anges Hosp., 1973—; cons. surgery N.Y. Hosp., Westchester div., 1973—; mem. med. bd. City of White Plains, Bd. Health County of Westchester; chmn. med. adv. bd. Associated Vis. Nurse Services; bd. dirs., past pres. Am. Cancer Soc. Westchester div.; mem. adv. com. Bank of N.Y. County Trust Region. Pres., White Plains YMCA, 1969-71, White Plains United Fund, 1964; bd. dirs. United Fund of Westchester, 1965-70. Served to sfc. sgt. Fin. Corps, U.S. Army, 1945-47. Diplomate Am. Bd. Surgery. Fellow A.C.S.; mem. Westchester County Med. Soc. (pres. 1977-78, dir.), Med. Soc. State N.Y., AMA, Westchester Surg. Soc. (past pres.), Yale Westchester Alumni Assn. (bd. dirs., past treas.). Republican. Club: Rotary. Contbr. articles to med. jours. Home: 49 Hathaway Ln White Plains NY 10605 Office: Medical Centre 170 Maple Ave White Plains NY 10601

RAMSDEN, NEIL G., educator; b. Boston, Oct. 22, 1944; s. George Andrew and Elizabeth Catherine (O'Neil) R.; B.A., Merrimack Coll., 1966; M.Ed., Salem (Mass.) State Coll., 1969, postgrad., 1969-74. Tchr. English, Spaulding Jr. High Sch., Suitland, Md., 1966-67, Essex (Mass.) Elementary Sch., 1967—; mem. Sch. Needs Study Com., Essex, 1972-74. Mem. alumni council, bd. govs. Merrimack Coll., North Andover, Mass., 1973-76. Mem. NEA, Mass. (life), Essex (pres. 1971-74, sec. 1974-76) tchrs. assns. Home: Beach St Rockport MA 01966 Office: Story St Essex MA 01929

RAMSEUR, TRUMILLER BEATRICE WIMBERLEY, sch. ofcl.; b. Edgecombe County, N.C., Aug. 30, 1931; d. John Russell and Geneva Beatrice (Stith) Wimberley; B.S., Livingstone Coll., 1952; M.S., Hofstra U., 1971; postgrad. State U. N.Y., 1977—; m. James Edward Ramseur, July 8, 1953; children—Angela Floriska, James Edward. Asst. supr. statistics Nat. Indsl. Conf. Bd., N.Y.C., 1952-55; social investigator City of N.Y., 1959-61; claims examiner State of N.Y., 1962-65, employment counselor, 1965-70; guidance counselor Amityville L.I. Sch. Dist., N.Y.C., 1970—. Mem. Hempstead (N.Y.) Civic Orgn., 1970—. Mem. Western Suffolk, Am., N.Y. personnel and guidance assns., Nat. Vocat. Guidance Assn., Am. Sch. Counselor Assn., NEA, Black Counselor Assn., Delta Sigma Theta. Home: 148 Rhodes Ave Hempstead NY 11550

RAMSEY, COLLETTE NICKS (MRS. HOBART COLE RAMSEY), civic worker; b. Nashville, Aug. 31, 1918; d. Charles S. and Virginia (Christian) Nicks; m. Hobart Cole Ramsey, Sept. 30, 1936; children—Collette Christian Wynn, Janet Houston Conrad. Founder, pres. Deafness Research Found., N.Y.C., 1958-68, vol. adminstr., dir. programs, fund-raising, 1958-68, chmn. bd., 1968—, chmn. exec. com., 1969-72, founder, cons., 1972—, instrumental in establishing affiliated Centurion Club, 1963. Mem. President's Com. Employment of Handicapped, 1964—; adviser N.J. League for Hard of Hearing, Inc., 1967—; mem. Surgeon Gen.'s Council, Nat. Inst.

Neurol. Diseases and Blindness, 1964-67; mem. Nat. Com. Research in Neurol. Disorders, 1962—. Co-committeewoman Republican party, 1950's. Bd. dirs. Nat. Assn. Hearing and Speech Agys., N.J. Hist. Soc., Summit Speech Sch., Alexander Graham Bell Assn. for Deaf, Inc. (hon.); trustee St. Barnabas Med. Center, Livingston, N.J. Recipient Citizens award for Meritorious Service N.Y. Co. Med. Soc., 1962, Ann. citation Am. Triological Soc., 1963, Ann. Achievement award N.J. Acad. Ophthalmology and Otolaryngology, 1963, citation Am. Otological Soc., 1964, Honors citation Alexander Graham Bell Assn. for Deaf, 1965, Distinguished Service award Rotary Club N.Y., 1966, Eleanor Roosevelt award N.Y. League for Hard of Hearing, 1968, Citizen's Award medal Acad. Medicine N.J., 1968, merit award Am. Laryngol., Rhinol. and Otol. Soc., 1972, Recognition award Am. Acad. Opthalmology and Otolaryngology, 1972; named candidate for Great Living Ams. award Nat. C. of C., 1963, Outstanding Woman N.J. Fairleigh-Dickinson U., 1964. Congregationalist. Contbr. numerous articles, booklets in field of deafness. Office: 342 Madison Ave New York City NY 10017

RAMSEY, RICHARD LIVINGSTON, county ofcl.; b. Moline, Ill., Apr. 4, 1918; s. George Abner and Mary Ann (Livingston) R.; B.Chem. Engring., N.Y. U., 1944; postgrad. Rutgers U., 1972-73, Ocean County Coll., 1973; m. Janet Louise Scanland, Aug. 28, 1964. Devel. engr., process engr., pilot plant supr. CPC Internat., Argo, Ill., 1945-49; process engr., mgr. process engring. Pabst Brewing Co., Milw., 1949-57; from process engr. to chief engr. Revlon, Inc., Edison, N.J., 1957-65; cons. food processing, New Brunswick, N.J., 1965-66; project engr., vinyl fabrics Union Carbide Corp., Bound Brook, N.J., 1966-72; engr. Dept. Environmental Protection State of N.J., Trenton, 1972; sr. engr., prin. engr. Pub. Works Dept. Cape May County, N.J., 1972—. Registered profl. engr., Ill., N.J. Mem. AAAS, Am. Chem. Soc., Am. Inst. Chem. Engrs. Home: 1242 Ohio Ave Cape May NJ 08204 Office: Library-Office Bldg Cape May Court House NJ 08210

RAMSTAD, JAMES M., lawyer; b. Jamestown, N.D., May 6, 1946; s. Marvin Joseph and Della Mae (Fode) R.; B.A., U. Minn., 1968; J.D. with honors, George Washington U., 1973. Adminstrv. asst. to speaker L.L. Duxbury, Minn. Ho. Reps., 1969; research asst. U.S. Congressman Thomas S. Kleppe of N.D., 1970; admitted to N.D. bar, D.C. bar, 1973; practiced in Jamestown, 1973, Washington, 1974—; instr. Am. govt. Montgomery (Md.) Coll., 1974; adj. prof. Am. U., Washington, 1975—. Mem. sponsoring com. Hubert H. Humphrey Inst. Pub. Affairs. Served as 1st lt. U.S. Army, 1968-73. Mem. Am., Fed., D.C., N.D. bar assns., Nat. Assn. Criminal Def. Lawyers, Nat. Legal Aid and Defender Assn., Trial Lawyers Assn. D.C., George Washington Law Assn., Assn. Trial Lawyers Am., U. Minn. Alumni Assn. (nat. dir.), Phi Beta Kappa, Phi Delta Theta. Republican. Clubs: Nat. Lawyers, Mpls. Athletic, Nat. Press, Kenwood Country, U. Minn. Alumni (pres. Washington). Home: 1528 31st St NW Washington DC 20007 Office: 1523 L St NW Suite 310 Washington DC 20005

RANAWAT, CHITRANJAN SINGH, surgeon; b. Sarwaniya, India, Apr. 1, 1935; s. Bhairon S. and Udai K. (Rathore) R.; came to U.S., 1963, naturalized, 1969; B.Sc., Holkar Coll., India, 1953; M.B., B.S., Med. Coll. India, 1958; M.S., 1961; m. Gudrun J. Auer, July 1, 1967; children—Amar, Chet, Anil. Intern, Maharaja Yeshwanta-Rao Hosp., Inodre, India, 1958-59, St. Peter's Hosp., Albany, N.Y., 1963-64; resident in surgery M.Y. Hosp., Indore, 1959-63; resident gen. surgery Albany Med. Center, 1964-65; fellow Hosp. Spl. Surgery, N.Y.C., 1966-67, reconstructive surgery, 1967-69; practice medicine specializing in orthopaedic surgery, N.Y.C., 1969—; asso. attending orthopaedic surgeon Hosp. Spl. Surgery and N.Y. Hosp., N.Y.C., 1969—; attending physician in orthopaedic surgery VA Hosp., Bronx, N.Y., 1971—; asst. instr. in surgery Albany (N.Y.) Med. Coll., 1964-65, Cornell U. Med. Coll., N.Y.C., 1967-69, clin. asso. prof. surgery, 1970—. Diplomate Am. Bd. Orthopaedic Surgery. Mem. A.C.S., Am. Soc. Surgery of Hand, Am. Acad. Orthopaedic Surgeons, Hand Soc. N.Y.C., N.Y. Acad. Medicine, Med. Soc. County N.Y., Eastern Orthopaedic Assn., Royal Coll. Physicians and Surgeons Can., Assn. Surgeons India, AMA, Am. Rheumatism Assn., Trauma Soc., Royal Soc. Medicine. Contbr. articles on orthopedics and surgery to med. jours. Office: 535 E 70th St New York City NY 10021

RAND, ALONZO CUTTING, JR., mech. engr., environ. research co. exec.; b. Ipswich, Mass., Nov. 1, 1922; s. Alonzo C. and Amy Milton (Dickinson) R.; B.S. in Mech. Engring., Northeastern U., 1947; postgrad. Mass. Inst. Tech., 1947-49, N.Y. U., 1953-56; m. Margaret Chase Hubbard, Dec. 31, 1944; children—Alison Cutting, Elizabeth Rand Keys, Peter Dickinson, John Bradstreet. Mech. engr. exptl. equipment Brookhaven Nat. Lab., Upton, N.Y., 1949-1955; mgr. nuclear dept. Marsh & McLennan, Inc., N.Y.C., 1956-71, mgr. corporate loss prevention, 1970-71, mgr. M&M Protection Consultants, 1971-1976, sr. v.p., 1975—, also dir.; alternate dir. Marsh & McLennan (Bermuda), Ltd.; pres. Clayton Environ. Consultants, Inc., Southfield, Mich., 1975—; cons. So. Interstate Nuclear Bd., 1966. Bd. dirs. treas., fin. chmn., founding mem. Nat. Energy Found., 1976—; adviser on nuclear ins. Panel of Experts, Internat. Atomic Energy Agy., Vienna, 1969. Served with U.S. Army, 1943-46. Registered profl. engr., N.Y. Mem. ASME, Am. Nuclear Soc., Nat., N.Y. State socs. profl. engrs., Nat. Fire Protection Assn., Safety Execs. of N.Y. Episcopalian. Club: Hearth. Inventor system for unloading reactors. Home: 51 Munsell Rd East Patchogue NY 11772 Office: 1221 Ave of Americas New York City NY 10020

RAND, MELVIN AARON, psychologist; b. Long Branch, N.J., Oct. 9, 1934; s. Max and Sarah (Schein) R.; B.A., Monmouth Coll., 1961; M.S., L.I. U., 1962; Ph.D., Okla. U., 1967; postgrad. (clin. med. psychology postdoctoral fellow), N.J. Coll. Medicine, 1968; m. Daryl Harrison, Nov. 22, 1962; children—Jason, David. Sr. psychologist N.J. State Diagnostic Center, Menlo Park, N.J., 1968, chief psychologist, 1969; psychologist parole bd. Rahway (N.J.) State Prison, 1969; pvt. practice psychology, Union City, N.J., 1969—; adj. prof. Fairleigh Dickinson U., Teaneck N.J., 1970—; sch. psychologist North Bergen (N.J.) Pub. Schs., 1973—; cons. psychologist State of N.J. Served with U.S. Army, 1955-57. Mem. Am., N.J. psychol. assns., Am., N.J. socs. clin. hypnosis, Hudson County Mental Health Bd. Contbr. articles in field to profl. jours. Office: 1906 Kennedy Blvd Union City NJ 07087

RANDALL, CLIFFORD ELTON, electron microscopist; b. Sayre, Pa., Mar. 12, 1929; s. Charles Ebinezer and Myrtle Elnora (Scott) R.; B.S. cum laude, State U. N.Y., Oswego, 1955; certificate Syracuse U., 1959; m. Dorothy Belle Pirong, Sept. 11, 1954; children—Audrey Jean, James Clifford, John Charles, Michael Steven. Tchr. indsl. arts edn. Cattaraugus Central Sch., N.Y., 1955-59; supr. cadet tchr. State U. N.Y., Buffalo, 1959-60; tchr. indsl. arts edn. Arkport (N.Y.) Central Sch., 1960-62; electronics engring. technician N.Y. State Coll. Ceramics, 1962-64, electron microscopist, 1964—; transformer engr. Ontario Industries, Hornell, N.Y., 1960-63; tchr. electronics, adult evening extension Steuben County Bds. of Coop. Edn. Services, 1973—. Del., N.Y. State Tchrs. Retirement System, 1972—. Mem. univ. council Alfred (N.Y.) U., 1970-72. Served with USMC, 1946-51. Fulbright scholar, 1956-59; recipient awards for indsl. arts edn. Ford Found., 1956-59. Mem. Electron Miscroscopy Soc. Am., Am. Indsl. Arts Assn. (life), Kappa Delta Pi, Epsilon Pi Tau. Democrat. Seventh Day Adventist. Clubs: U.S. Power Squadron, DAV (life), Masons. Created display micrographs for Corning Glass Mus., Alfred U. Home: RD 1 Box 47 County Line Rd Arkport NY 14807 Office: Box 92 Alfred NY 14802

RANDALL, EUDORA PATRICIA, nurse; b. North Bridgeton, Maine, Jan. 23, 1930; d. Lewis Calvin and Emily Wilson (Sanborn) Randall; B.S. in Nursing, Boston U., 1960, M.S., 1965. Staff nurse Augusta (Maine) Gen. Hosp., 1951-52, VA Center, Togus, Maine, 1952-55; with Maine Dept. Health and Welfare, 1956-73, staff nurse, supv., also pub. health nursing cons., 1973—; dir. nursing Portland (Maine) Health Dept., 1973-78; sr. supr. Community Health Services, Inc., Portland, 1978—. Fellow Royal Soc. Health; mem. Am. Nurses Assn., Am. Pub. Health Assn., Am. Assn. Mental Deficiency, AAUW, Literacy Vols. Am., Nat. League Nursing, Altrusa Internat. Republican. Baptist. Home: 37 Forest Park Apt 2 Portland ME 04101 Office: 98 Chestnut St Portland ME 04111

RANDALL, GERALD ROBERT, music pub. and record co. exec.; b. Summitville, N.Y., May 27, 1936; s. Samuel Jay and Florence Katherine (Boyce) R.; student pub. schs., Ellenville, N.Y. Freelance writer, 1957—; lyricist and composer, 1965—; ind. record producer and personnel mgr. musical group, 1967—; pres. H & G Randall Pub. Co. and Randall Records, Syracuse, N.Y., 1972—; v.p. P.J. Reilly Funeral Homes, Inc., Middletown, N.Y. Served with AUS, 1959-61. Mem. ASCAP. Republican. Methodist. Home: 29 Elaine Rd Milford CT 06460 Office: 1900 W Genesee St Syracuse NY 13204

RANDALL, RICHARD STUART, polit. scientist, educator; b. N.Y.C., Mar. 3, 1935; s. Leslie Van and Dorothy Conradina (Ahrens) R.; B.A., Antioch Coll., Yellow Springs, Ohio, 1956; M.A., U. Wis., 1962, Ph.D., 1966. Asst. prof. U. Nebr., 1965-69; asso. prof. polit. sci. N.Y. U., 1969—, chmn. dept. politics, 1970—, asso. dean U. Coll., 1972-73; project dir. study self regulation in Am. film industry President's Commn. Obscenity and Pornography, 1969-70; cons. in field. Mem. Am. Polit. Sci. Assn. Author: Censorship of the Movies; The Social and Political Control of a Mass Medium (Broadcaster Preceptor award Broadcast Industry Conf. 1969), 1968; also monograph, articles. Home: 3 Washington Sq Village New York City NY 10012 Office: Dept Politics New York Univ Washington Sq New York City NY 10003*

RANDALL, RICHARD WILLIAM, optometrist; b. Jamestown, N.Y., Nov. 29, 1931; s. Harry William and Claudia (Thompson) R.; O.D., Ill. Coll. Optometry, 1963; m. Ruth Jeannette Roy, May 28, 1954; children—David, Deborah, Douglas, Dawne. Optician, House of Vision Inc., Chgo., 1960-63; pvt. practice optometry, Geneseo, N.Y., 1963—; chief optometry sect. No. Livingston Health Center, Geneseo, 1974—, Red Jacket Med. Center, Dansville, N.Y., 1975—; pres. Lad-Nar Realty, Inc.; pres., gen. mgr. Ladco Internat.; exec. dir. Ladco Rental Property, Geneseo Profl. Bldg. (all Geneseo); cons. in field. Exec. dir. Livingston County (N.Y.) Traffic Safety Bd., 1976—. Served with USAF, 1951-53; Korea. Recipient scholarship award Am. Bd. Opticianry, 1960, Clin. Optometry award Ill. Coll. Optometry, 1963. Fellow Am. Acad. Optometry; mem. Am., N.Y. State (chmn. master plan com. 1976—) optometric assns., Livingston Area Comprehensive Health Planning Com., Health Systems Agency, Optometric Center N.Y., Better Vision Inst., Am. Pub. Health Assn. Roman Catholic. Home: 48 Avon Rd Geneseo NY 14454 Office: 4384 Lakeville Rd Geneseo NY 14454

RANDALL, ROBERT GORDON, fund raising exec.; b. Eugene, Oreg., July 31, 1945; s. Gordon Henry and Emma Marie (Wetterstrom) R.; student Netherlands Inst. Fgn. Representation, 1965; B.S., U. Oreg., 1967; M.B.A., Columbia U., 1969; m. Terry Ratcliff, Aug. 31, 1974. Staff accountant Peat Marwick Mitchell & Co., C.P.A.'s, N.Y.C., 1968-70; asso. dir. Environ. Action Coalition, Inc., N.Y.C., 1970-74, trustee, 1975—; mgr. spl. gifts The Salvation Army, N.Y.C., 1975-76; dir. devel. United Student Aid Funds, Inc., N.Y.C., 1976-77; asso. dir. maj. gifts Yale U., New Haven, 1978—. Mem. Nat. Assn. Fund Raisers, Columbia Bus. Club. Home: UVW 80 Ivy Ln Englewood NJ 07631 Office: 155 Whitney Ave New Haven CT 06520

RANDALL, ROBERT L., bus. economist; b. Aberdeen, S.D., Dec. 28, 1936; s. Harry Eugene and Juanita Alice (Barstow) R.; S.M. in Phys. Chemistry, U. Chgo., 1960, M.B.A., 1963. Mem. staff chem. research and devel. lab. U.S. Army Chem. Corps, Edgewood, Md., 1960-62; market devel. chemist E.I. du Pont de Nemours & Co., Inc., Wilmington, Del., 1963-65; chem. economist Battelle Meml. Inst., Columbus, O., 1965-68; mgr. market and econ. research Kennecott Copper Corp., N.Y.C., 1968-74, staff economist, Lexington, Mass., 1974—. Mem. AAAS, Am. Econ. Assn., Am. Statis. Assn., Am. Inst. Mining Engrs., Am. Chem. Soc. Club: Chemists (N.Y.C.). Home: 808 Memorial Dr Cambridge MA 02139 Office: 128 Spring St Lexington MA 02173

RANDALL, ROLAND RODROCK, real estate counselor; b. Doylestown, Pa., Oct. 12, 1898; s. William Lacey and Anna Elizabeth (Rodrock) R.; B.S. in Economics, Wharton Sch., U. Pa., 1921; student case study course Am. Inst. Real Estate Appraisers, U. Pa., 1939; m. Marion Burnside Heist, Dec. 5, 1922 (dec. May 1977); children—Roland Rodrock, Sue Randall. Engaged as securities salesman, 1921-25; then real estate broker, cons., appraiser specializing in indsl., comml., instl., large scale housing and specialty types real estate, Phila., 1925-52; real estate counselor Phila., 1952—; faculty, lectr. real estate extension, evening sch. U. Pa., 1947—; treas., dir. N.E. Corner Walnut and Juniper Streets, Inc., bd. trustees will of Stephen Girard. Mem. adv. com. econ. devel. analysis for indsl. land facilities in Phila., Phila. Devel. Corp. Former chmn. bds. of view for acquisition of land by U.S. War Dept., also U.S. Signal Corps, World War II; cons. expert, mem. speakers bur. War Loan Drives, World War II. Active YMCA; chmn. real estate div. ARC, 1945; chmn. real estate com. March of Dimes, 1948; chmn. estate div. United Fund, 1951, vice chmn., real estate div., 1952—; dir., real estate counselor Jr. Achievement Phila. Met. Area, Inc., 1953-65; chmn., mem. Phila. Housing Authority, 1937-47; com. mem. Citizens Council on City Planning, 1954-55; dir. Nat. Com. on Housing, Inc., chmn. Greater Phila. Com. for Emergency Def. Plant Location, ODM, 1951—; chmn. Phila. County div., mem. exec. com. Greater Phila.-Del.-South Jersey Council; bd. govs. Delaware Valley Council, 1956—; adv. com. Phila. Eastwick Housing Market Analysis; real estate counselor Dept. of Commerce, Phila.; chmn. Pa. Real Estate Commn.; mem. Joint Exec. Com. for Improvement and Devel. Phila. Port Area; nat. treas., mem. exec. council Spiritual Frontiers Fellowship; mem. com. on finance and property. Episcopal Diocese Pa.; del. Episcopal Diocesan Conv. Mem. bd. corporators, exec. planning council Med. Coll. Pa. and Hosp.; v.p., bd. dirs, mem. exec. Mem. bd. com., chmn. nominating com. Nat. Council on Alcoholism Delaware Valley Area. Served as 2d lt. U.S. Army, World War I. Recipient Silver award U.S. Treasury Dept. War Financing Program, World War II; Phila. 21st Ward Community Council award, 1961; award for contbn. to revitalization Center City Phila., Girard Sq. Assn., 1966. Mem. Am. Soc. Real Estate Counselors (nat. pres. 1953-55), Soc. Indsl. Realtors (nat. pres. 1949), Am. Inst. Real Estate Appraisers (pres. Phila. 1947), Am. Inst. Real Estate Mgmt., Nat. Assn. Real Estate Bds. (dir. past officer), Pa. Realtor Assn. (pres. 1941), U.S. C. of C. (nat. councillor; pres. 1941), Phila. Real Estate Bd. (bd. govs., pres. 1938), Nat. Inst. Real Estate Brokers, Urban Land Inst. (indsl. council, community builders council), Nat. Assn. Housing and Redevel. Ofcls., Greater Phila. C. of C., Internat. Real Estate Fedn. Assessors Assn. Phila., Municipal Assessors Assn. Pa., Property Service, Inc., Saving Fund Soc. Germantown (bd. mgrs.), Pa. Soc. (adv. council), Naval Affairs City Phila., Bucks County Hist. Soc., Cruiser Olympia Assn. (dir.), Am. Legion, Am. Arbitration Assn. (nat. panel arbitrators), Underdown-Assembly Artisans, Order of St. Luke The Physician, Phi Gamma Delta, Lambda Alpha (charter mem. Phila. chpt.). Episcopalian (past sr. warden). Mason. Clubs: Philadelphia Country, Racquet (bd. govs.), Church, Alden Park Players (pres. 1948-49) (Phila.). Contbr. articles on real estate. Home: The Dorchester Rittenhouse Sq Philadelphia PA 19103 Office: Jackson-Cross Co 2000 Market St Philadelphia PA 19103

RANDALL, THELMA MAYE, educator; b. Malakoff, Tex., Dec. 6, 1936; d. Melvin and Clara (Thompson) Langley; B.S., Prairie View A. and M. U., 1956; M.A., Cath. U. Am., 1971; M.A.T., Trinity Coll., 1974; m. Ferrell Baysing Randall, Dec. 29, 1956; children—Roderick Daryl, Alan Wayne. Editorial clk. U.S. Dept. Agr., Forest Service, Washington, 1958-64; travel audit clk. Walter Reed Army Med. Center, Washington, summer 1966; curriculum writer Office of Supervising Dir., Bus. and Office Edn., Pub. Schs. of Washington, 1972; tchr. bus. and office edn. Pub. Schs. of D.C., Washington, 1964—, chmn. dept. bus. and office edn., 1970-73; coordinator Cooperative Office Edn. Program, Cardozo Sr. High Sch., 1970-74. Sec., Brightwood Civic Assn., 1968. Mgmt. of Ednl. Change program fellow, 1973-74. Mem. NEA, D.C. Edn. Assn., Am. Bus. Women's Assn., Eastern Bus. Tchrs. Assn., Nat. Bus. Edn. Assn., Am. Personnel and Guidance Assn., Nat. Vocational Guidance Assn., Nat. Council for Accreditation of Tchr. Edn., Prairie View A. and M. U. Alumni Club (Washington chpt.), Delta Sigma Theta. Democrat. Roman Catholic. Office: 13 and Clifton Sts NW Washington DC 20009

RANDALL, THOMAS DUDLEY, constrn. co. exec.; b. Johnstown, N.Y., July 9, 1913; s. George Waltham and Edna Morse (Ripley) R.; B.S. in Civil Engring., Union Coll., 1936; M.C.E., N.Y. U., 1939; postgrad. Columbia, 1939-42; m. Jean Bresee Grant, Jan. 27, 1945; 1 son, Grant Ripley. Instr. engring. N.Y. U., 1936-37; with Beech-Nut Packing Co., 1938-41; project mgr. Douglas McBean, Engrs., Rochester, N.Y., 1946-48; v.p. Geo. W. Randall Co., Inc., Johnstown, 1948-63, pres., 1963—; owner Thomas D. Randall Assos., Gloversville, N.Y., 1966—; chmn. regional bd. Nat. Comml. Bank. Mem. Gloversville Bd. Edn., 1953-68, pres., 1962-68; charter mem. Gloversville Indsl. Devel. Organ., 1950—; chmn. bd. trustees Dist. Council Carpenters Welfare and Pension Fund. Trustee Am. Inst. Econ. Research; mem. Com. for Monetary Research and Edn. Served with USAAF, 1942-46; now maj. Res., ret. Registered profl. engr., N.Y. Mem. Eastern N.Y. Constrn. Employers Assn., N.Y. Profl. Engr. Soc., Cons. Engrs. Council, Assn. Gen. Contractors, Am. Soc. C.E., Nat. Soc. Profl. Engrs., Gloversville C. of C. Episcopalian (vestryman, warden). Club: Eccentric (Gloversville). Home: 170 East Blvd Gloversville NY 12078 Office: POB 908 Gloversville NY 12078

RANDALL, WILLARD STERNE, historian; b. Phila., Mar. 13, 1942; s. Leslie Fairbanks and Joan (Shepherd) R.; student St. Joseph's Coll., Phila., 1960-65, 68-70, m. Mary Anne Hogan, Jan. 23, 1965; children—Christopher Fairbanks, Mary Anne, Alice Amanda. Reporter, Pottstown (Pa.) Mercury, 1960-61; legal writer, U.S. Corp. Co., 1961-65; reporter Mainland Jour., Pleasantville, N.J., 1966; bur. chief, editor, feature writer Phila. Evening and Sunday Bull., 1966-71; editorial dir., asso. editor, investigative reporter Phila. mag., 1971-72; corr. Time-Life News Service, Phila., 1972-73; freelance historian, editor, writer, Ocean City, N.J., 1973—; founder Ocean City (N.J.) Writers Workshop, 1973; v.p., dir. Ocean City Cultural Arts Center, 1976—. Mem., state del. Ocean City Bd. Edn., 1978—. Recipient Nat. Mag. award pub. service Columbia Grad. Sch. Journalism, 1972, Best Story of Year award Standard Gravure Assn., also Sidney Hillman Found. award, John Hancock award and Gerald Loeb award, 1976. Mem. Am. Soc. Journalists and Authors, N.Y. Acad. Sci., Pa., N.J. hist. socs. Club: Poor Richard (Phila.). Author: Journalist, 1975; (with others, also sr. editor) The Founding City, 1976; The Proprietary House in Amboy, 1976; (with others) Building 6, 1977; The Franklins. Contbg. author, contbr. articles to profl. pubis. Office: Ray Lincoln Lit Agency 4 Surrey Rd Melrose Park PA 19126

RANDELL, JOAN, vocat. rehab. specialist; b. Bklyn., June 26, 1946; d. Leonard Bertram and Isabel Maxine (Pross) Randell; B.A., Syracuse U., 1968; M.A., N.Y. U., 1970. Vocat. rehab. counselor Beth Israel Med. Center, N.Y.C., 1970-77, sr. vocat. rehab. counselor, 1972-76, acting dir. vocat. rehab., 1976-77, dir., 1977—; cons. Vera Inst. Justice, N.Y. Urban Coalition; tchr. N.Y. U., Columbia U.; speaker radio programs; co-chmn. Methadone Coalition for Equal Opportunity; participant Greater N.Y. Conf. Soviet Jewry. Bd. dirs. Central Bur. Jewish Aged and Solidandad Humana; Recipient Rehab. Counselors Assn. traineeship award, 1968-70. Mem. Am. Personnel and Guidance Assn., Rehab. Counselors Assn. Jewish. Contbr. articles to profl. jours. Home: 145 E 15th St New York City NY 10003 Office: 245 E 17th St New York City NY 10003

RANDOLPH, CHARLES CLIFFORD, III, publishing co. exec.; b. Point Pleasant, N.J., July 8, 1926; s. Charles Clifford Jr. and Mildred (Biddle) R.; A.B., Dartmouth, 1948; m. Joan Krayer, Feb. 12, 1947; children—Katherine, John. Classified advt. salesman McGraw-Hill Pub. Co., N.Y.C., 1948-49, dist. mgr. Food Engring., 1949-54, dist. mgr. Business Week, 1954-58, Eastern advt. sales mgr., 1958-60, advt. dir., 1960-63, pub., 1966—; pub. Electronics, 1963-66. Served with USN, 1943-46. Mem. Assn. Indsl. Advertisers, Econ. Club N.Y. Clubs: N.Y. Athletic; Winged Foot Golf (Mamoroneck, N.Y.); Aspetuck Valley Country (Weston). Home: Ladder Hill Rd Weston CT 06883 Office: 330 W 42d St New York City NY 10036

RANDOLPH, JUDITH HOWARD, tchr., counselor; b. Fort Defiance, Va., Dec. 22, 1937; d. George Washington and Ruth Irene Howard; B.S., Va. State Coll., 1960; postgrad. U. Md., 1967; M.S., Va. Polytech. Inst. and State U., 1977; m. Lynwood Parker Randolph, Aug. 27, 1960; children—Leslie Patrice, Lynwood Parker, Leonard Patrick, Lemuel Preston. Instr. Drew Sch., Arlington Va., 1962-64; spl. edn. Upper Marlboro (Md.) pub. schs., 1966-70; instr., counselor adult edn. Arlington pub. schs., 1970—. Mem. exec. com. DC Youth Orchestra, 1977—, treas., 1977—. Recipient Bausch and Lomb Sci. award, 1960. Mem. Am. Personnel and Guidance Assn., Nat. Vocat. Guidance Assn., Quest, Adult Edn. Assn. Va., Nat. Assn. U. Women. Democrat. Episcopalian. Club: Foxtrappe, Ocean Pines. Home: 3000 Fairhill Ct Silver Hill MD 20023 Office: 4854 Lee Hwy Arlington VA 22207

RANGANATHAN, NARASIMHAN, cardiologist; b. Rangoon, Burma, Jan. 10, 1939; s. Narasimha Chari and Jayalakshmi Ammal R.; came to U.S., 1963; M.B., B.S., U. Madras (India), 1961; m. Saroja, Dec. 1, 1966; children—Shyam, Yashoda. Intern, Balt. City Hosp., 1963-64; resident Buffalo Gen. Hosp., 1964-66; resident in cardiology Tulane Med. Sch., V.A. Hosp., New Orleans, 1966-68; research fellow cardiology Toronto (Ont., Can.) Gen. Hosp., 1968-70; staff cardiologist St. Michael's Hosp., Toronto, 1970—; instr. medicine

Tulane U., 1966-68; asso. in medicine U. Toronto, 1970-72, asst. prof., 1972-76, asso. prof., 1976. Diplomate Am. Bd. Internal Medicine. Fellow Royal Coll. Physicians and Surgeons Can., A.C.P., Royal Soc. Medicine; mem. Ont. Med. Assn., Canadian Cardiovascular Soc., Am. Coll. Cardiology, Am. Heart Assn. (council on clin. cardiology). Hindu religion. Contbr. articles to med. jours. Home: 32 Cobblestone Dr Willowdale ON M2J 2X7 Canada Office: Div Cardiology St Michaels Hosp 30 Bond St Toronto ON M5B 1W8 Canada

RANGEL, CHARLES B., congressman; b. N.Y.C., June 11, 1930; s. Ralph and Blanche (Wharton) R.; B.S., N.Y. U., 1957; LL.B., St. John's Law Sch., 1960, J.D., 1968; m. Alma Carter, July 26, 1964; children—Steven, Alicia. Admitted to N.Y. bar, 1960; asst. U.S. atty. N.Y. Dept. Justice, 1961; counsel to assembly speaker, N.Y. Assembly, Pres. Johnson's Draft Revision Com.; mem. N.Y. Assembly, 1966-70; mem. 92d-96th Congresses from 19th N.Y. Dist.; mem. ways and means com., chmn. health subcom. Borough pres., mem. adv. bd. Community Planning Bd., N.Y.C. Served to sgt. AUS, 1948-52. Decorated Purple Heart, Bronze Star. Mem. N.Y. State Bar Assn., 369th Vets. Assn., NAACP, Nat. Assn. State Legislators, Phi Alpha Delta, Alpha Phi Alpha. Address: 74 W 132d St New York City NY 10037

RANGELER, DWIGHT DWAIN, pub. co. exec.; b. Fostoria, Ohio, June 19, 1932; s. F. Troy and Hazel Clare (McKee) R.; B.A., Bowling Green State U., 1953, M.A., 1954; postgrad. Cornell U., 1954-56. TV copywriter Charles W. Hoyt Co., N.Y.C., 1956-58; pub. relations writer, editor Dodge Group News, F.W. Dodge Corp., N.Y.C., 1958-61; staff writer McGraw-Hill News, McGraw-Hill, Inc., N.Y.C., 1961-65, asst. dir. internal communications, 1965-68, editor McGraw-Hill News, 1968-74, dir. internal communications, 1974—; lectr. communications techniques Am. Mgmt. assn., Greater N.Y. Fund, N.Y. Assn. Commerce and Industry seminars. Mem. Indsl. Communication Council, N.Y. Bus. Communicators, Internat. Assn. Bus. Communicators, N.Y. Assn. Indsl. Communicators (past dir., v.p., exec. v.p.). Contbr. chpt. to Case Studies in Organizational Communication, 1975. Home: 240 E 35th St New York City NY 10016 Office: 1221 Ave of Americas New York City NY 10020

RANGOS, JOHN G., mfg. co. exec.; b. Steubenville, Ohio, July 27, 1929; s. Gust and Anna (Svokas) R.; student Houston Bus. Coll., 1949-50; children—John G., Alexander W. Pres., chmn. bd. U.S. Utilities Service Corp., Monroeville, Pa., U.S. Services Corp., Monroeville, Chambers Devel. Co., Inc., Monroeville, 1978—, So. Alleghenies Disposal Services, Hosopple, Pa., 1978—, William H. Martin Inc., Washington, Pa., 1978—, Tri Valley Municipal Supply, 1978—, Ran Sales Inc., 1978—, Security Bur., Inc., 1978—. Bd. dirs. Craig House-Technoma, 1974-75, treas., 1975-76; mem. nat. com. UN Assn., 1977—; chmn. fund raising UNICEF, Pitts., 1977; bd. dirs. Holy Cross Sem. Theology, Boston, 1962-63; mem. Clergy Laity Council N.Y.; bd. dirs. Greek Orthodox Ch. Presentation of Christ, Pitts., 1968-70. Served with U.S. Army, 1951-54; Korea. Democrat. Clubs: Nat. Football Hall of Fame, Press, Allegheny, Churchvill Valley Country, Masons, Shriners. Pioneer in sewage sludge disposal, disposal sites and resource recovery systems of complex wastes (methane energy). Home: 78 Locksley Dr Pittsburgh PA 15235 Office: 470 Mall Circle Dr Monroeville PA 15146

RANKIN, WILLIAM PARKMAN, publisher; b. Boston, Feb. 6, 1917; s. George William and Bertha W. (Clowe) R.; B.S., Syracuse U., 1941; M.B.A., N.Y.U., 1949; m. Ruth E. Gerard, Sept. 12, 1942; children—Douglas W., Joan W. Sales exec. Redbook mag., N.Y.C., 1945-49; sales executive This Week Mag., N.Y.C., 1949-55, adminstrv. exec., 1955-60, v.p. 1957-60, v.p., director advt., 1960-63, exec. v.p., dir., 1963-69; exec., newspaper div. Time Inc., N.Y.C., 1969-70; gen. mgr. Feature Service-Newsweek Inc., 1970-73, financial and ins. advt. mgr., 1974—; lectr. Syracuse U., N.Y.U., and Berkeley Sch.; mem. planning com. Advt. Research Found. Mem. advisory council Syracuse U. Sch. Journalism. Mem. Sigma Delta Chi, Alpha Delta Sigma. Clubs: Marco Polo, Dutch Treat, Met. Adv. Golf Assn., Winged Foot Golf. Author: Selling Retail Advt., 1944; The Technique of Selling Mag. Advertising, 1949. Home: 15 York Rd Larchmont NY 10538 also Bridge Rd Bomoseen VT 05732 Office: 444 Madison Ave Bldg New York City NY 10022

RANNELS, HERMAN WOLFE, physician; b. Rowenna, Pa., Nov. 6, 1909; s. Oscar Vaughn and Minnie May (Wolfe) R.; B.S., Dickinson Coll., 1934; M.D., U. Pa., 1938; m. Nancy J. Nixdorf, Sept. 2, 1953; children—Gail, Herman. Intern, Chestnut Hill Hosp., Phila.; resident Kensington Hosp. for Women, Phila., also N.Y. Post Grad. Med. Sch. and Hosp., N.Y.C., 1939-41; chief obstetrics and gynecology St. Joseph's Hosp., Lancaster, Pa., 1941-53; cons. gynecology Rossmere Sanitorium, 1941-53; cons. obstetrics Columbia (Pa.) Hosp., 1941-53; instr. obstetrics and gynecology Sch. Nursing, St. Joseph's Hosp., 1941-53; asst. prof. obstetrics and gynecology N.Y.C., 1953-60; dir. obstetrics and gynecology Hunterdon Med. Center, Felmington, N.J., 1953-60; chief clin. services, chief obstetrics and gynecology Miners Meml. Hosp. Assn., Inc., Man Meml. Hosp., W.Va., 1959-64; med. dir. Orange County Med. Center, 1964-72; clin. prof. obstetrics and gynecology U. Calif. at Irvine Coll. Medicine, 1967-70, clin. prof. community medicine, 1970-72, also asst. dean; dir. Community Mental Health Services, 1964-71; prof. community medicine U. Pa., 1972—; v.p., med. dir. Williamsport (Pa.) Hosp., 1972-77; field rep. dept. grad. med. edn. AMA, 1977—; cons. space and info. systems div. N.Am. Aviation, Inc.; pres. Calif. Conf. Local Mental Health Dirs. Served as lt. (s.g.) M.C. USN, 1944-46. Diplomate Am. Bd. Obstetrics and Gynecology. Fellow Am. Coll. Obstetrics and Gynecology (founding), A.C.S., Am. Pub. Health Assn., Royal Soc. Health; mem. AMA, Obstet. Soc. Phila. Clubs: Masons (32 deg.), Rotary (past pres.). Lutheran. Contbr. articles to profl. jours. Home: RD 1 Box 45A Marietta PA 17547

RANSOHOFF, PRISCILLA BURNETT, psychologist, govt. ofcl.; b. Pitts., June 16, 1912; d. Levi Herr and Clara (Brown) Burnett; B.S., U. Pitts., 1941; phys. therapist Hosp. for Spl. Surgery, 1945; M.A., Columbia U., 1952, Ed.D., 1954; m. Nicholas S. Ransohoff, Nov. 27, 1947; 1 dau. by previous marriage, Priscilla B. Johnston Fuller. Supr. rehab. Monmouth Med. Center, Long Branch, N.J., 1945-54; mem. coadj. staff Inst. Labor and Mgmt. Relations, Rutgers U., New Brunswick, N.J., 1945-57; pres. Cons. Assos. Corp., Long Branch, 1954-64; v.p. Dale Elliott Mgmt. Cons. Corp., N.Y.C., 1958-60; edn. adviser U.S. Army Electronics Command, Ft. Monmouth, N.J., 1964-74, staff asst. for edn., 1974—; cons. dept. edn. tech. Sch. Edn., Catholic U. Am., Washington, 1966-72; lectr. in sociology Monmouth Coll., West Long Branch, N.J., 1966-68; coadj. prof. psychology and sociology Ocean County Coll., Toms River, N.J., 1968-69, 72; coadj. instr. in psychology and sociology Brookdale Community Coll., Lincroft, N.J., 1969—; founder Monmouth Center for Vocat. Rehab., Red Bank, N.J., 1958, pres., 1958-60. Vice-chairperson N.J. del. Internat. Women's Year, Houston. Recipient Action award U.S. Army Materiel Command, 1973, Equal Employment Opportunity award Sec. Army, 1973. Mem. NEA (life), Federally Employed Women (past pres.; dir.), Women's Equity Action League, NOW. Episcopalian. Club: Toastmistress. Contbr. articles on mgmt. and edn. to various jours. Home: 13 River Ave Monmouth Beach NJ 07750 Office: US Army Communication Electronics and Materiel Readiness Command Fort Monmouth NJ 07703

RANSOM, DANIEL GORDON, dept. store exec.; b. Mt. Vernon, Ohio, May 26, 1929; s. Kenneth and Priscilla Pauline (Porterfield) R.; B.A., Ohio Wesleyan U., 1951; m. Betty J. Yeakle, Jan. 21, 1961; 1 dau., Melissa. Trainee buyer Lazarus Co., Columbus, Ohio, 1951-58; merchandise mgr. Stewart Dry Goods Co., Louisville, 1958-64, Baer & Fuller Co., St. Louis, 1964-66, Denver Dry Goods Co., Denver, 1966-68; exec. v.p., gen. merchandise mgr. William Hengerer Co., Buffalo, 1968-69, pres., 1969-78; sr. v.p., dir. mktg. Marine Midland Bank, Buffalo, 1978—; dir. Fed. Res. Bank, Marine Midland Bank Western. Chmn. Com. Fed. Action; mem. Greater Buffalo Devel. Found., United Way of Buffalo and Erie County. Served with AUS, 1953-55. Named Man of Year, Buffalo Evening News, 1975, Exec. of Yr., State U. Buffalo Sch. Mgmt., 1977. Mem. Retail Merchants Assn., Buffalo C. of C. (dir.). Clubs: The Buffalo, Orchard Park Country. Home: 7307 East Quaker Rd Orchard Park NY 14127 Office: 1 Marine Midland Center Buffalo NY 14240

RANSON, NANCY S., artist; b. N.Y.C., Sept. 13, 1905; d. Bernard and Ida (Jablonsky) Sussman; grad. Pratt Inst. Art Sch., 1926, B.F.A., 1974; student Art Students League, Bklyn. Mus. Art Sch.; m. Jo Ranson, Jan. 1927 (dec. July 1965); children—Justine Ranson Schachter, Ellen Toby Ranson Adams. Exhibited at Am. Water Color Soc., 1940, 42, 43, Nat. Assn. Women Artists, 1943—, Bklyn. Soc. Artists, 1941-62, Am. Soc. Contemporary Artists, 1963—, Tomorrow's Masterpieces, 1943, Artists for Victory, 1944, Critics Choice Show, Grand Central Galleries, 1947, Prize Winner's Show, 1947, Butler Inst. Am. Art, 1950, Bklyn. Artists Biennial, Bklyn. Mus., 1950, 54, 56, N.W. Printmakers Internat., 1952, 56, Boston, 1955, Silvermine Guild Ann., 1956, Nat. Mus. Art, Sydney, Australia, 1956, Nat. Exhbn. Contemporary Arts U.S., Pomona, Calif., 1956, N.Y. Soc. Women Artists, 1952—, Am. Color Print Soc., 1952—, Pa. Acad. Fine Art, 1957, Color Prints of The Americas, N.J. State Mus., 1970, other shows; one-woman shows: George Binet Gallery, N.Y., 1948, 50, Bklyn. Pub. Library Main Br., 1951, Mexican Govt. Tourist Commn., Radio City, N.Y., 1952, U. Me., 1964, 78; exhibited group shows museums and galleries U.S., India, Can., France, Switzerland, Japan, including Artists Equity, Whitney Mus., 1951, others; represented collections at Fogg Mus. Art, Mus. Art, Norfolk, Va., Brandeis U., U. Maine, Mexican Govt. Tourist Commn., Mus. City N.Y., Butler Instn. Am. Art, Youngstown, Ohio, Key West Art Hist. Soc., Reading Pub. Mus., Free Library, Phila., Arts and Crafts, Peking, China, 1976, also nat. mus., Jerusalem, New Delhi, Tokyo, Syndey, Smithsonian Instn. Archives Am. Art, Washington. Recipient hon. mention Bklyn. Mus., 1946; Nat. Assn. Women Artists Ann., 1952, Clendenin prize, 1953, medal of Honor in Graphics, 1956, Nat. Acad. Galleries, 1952; popular painting prize Critics Choice Show Grand Central Galleries, 1947; Grumbacher award Bklyn. Soc. Artists, 1954, 1st prize in graphics, 1955, 58; Presentation Print, Am. Color Print Soc., 1955, Bklyn. Soc. Artists, 1962; Joseph Torch award, 1955, Francesca Wood Award, 1955; 1st prize graphics Nat. Assn. Women Artists, 1958, print and drawing exhbn., 1962, Harold Kovner prize Audubon Artists Ann., 1958, award, 1961; Gramercy prize Nat. Soc. Painters in Casein, 1963; Andrew-Nelson-Whitehead award Am. Soc. Contemporary Artists, 1964, First prize in Graphics, 1970; MacDowell Found. fellowship, 1964, Kulicke award in Casein, 1975; Internat. Women's Year award for Cultural Contbns., 1975-76. Mem. N.Y. Soc. Women Artists (v.p. 1968-69), Nat. Assn. Women Artists (chmn. fgn. exhbns. 1964-67, admissions 1969-71, oil jury 1973-75, nominations 1975-77, mem. adv. bd. 1977—), Bklyn. Soc. Artists (corr. sec. 1948-53, pres. 1954-56), Am. Color Print Soc., Hunterdon County Art Center, Audubon Artists (chmn. awards com. 1958, dir. graphics 1970-73, 75-78), Nat. Soc. Painters in Casein and Acrylics, Am. Soc. Contemporary Artists (chmn. constitution 1963—, pres. 1969-71, permanent dir. 1971—), Internat. Assn. Art (del. U.S. com. 1963-77, rec. sec. 1977—). Lectures: Art and Archaeology Around the World; Indonesia-Exotic Trek; India-Affectionate Journey; Africa-Archaelogy to Wildlife. My 21 Days in China. Home and Studio: 1299 Ocean Ave Brooklyn NY 11230

RANT, WALTER FRANCIS, chem. co. exec.; b. N.Y.C., Aug. 4, 1925; s. Francis Walter and Anastazia (Kindrick) R.; B.S., U. Pitts., 1950, M.Litt. 1950; postgrad. N.Y.U., 1957-63; m. Evelyn M. Buddy, Oct. 7, 1950; children—Melinda, Nadine, Walter Francis II. Asst. mgr. investment research dept. Walston & Co., 1951-56; mgr. investment research dept. Cosgrove, Miller & Whitehead, 1956-57, Gregory & Sons, 1957-58; sr. security analyst Lionel D. Edie & Co., 1958-60, Goodbody & Co., 1960-65 (all N.Y.C.); v.p. Essex Chem. Corp., Clifton, N.J., 1965—. Served with USAAF, 1943-47; now maj. Res., ret. C.F.A. Mem. Am. Econ. Assn., Am. Inst. Banking, N.Y. Soc. Security Analysts. Contbr. articles to profl. jours. Home: 19 Beresford Rd Allendale NJ 07401 Office: 1401 Broad St Clifton NJ 07015

RANWEZ, JEAN-LOUIS FERNAND, engring. co. exec.; b. Montigny-sur Sambre, Belgium, Feb. 5, 1918; s. Fernand Edouard and Helene Urbina (Scheins) R.; came to U.S., 1945, naturalized, 1960; B.A., Sacred Heart Coll., Argentina, 1936; E.E., Institut Gramme, Liege, 1940; m. Jane Thatcher Moses, June 25, 1946; children—Helene Taylor, Francis, Corinne Clark. Student engr., Combustion Engring. Inc., 1945, field supr. France, 1946-56, supr. research and devel., N.Y.C., 1956-60, European rep., Paris, 1960-63, Madrid, 1963-65, Australian mgr., Sydney, New South Wales, 1965-69, project mgr. Windsor, Conn., 1969—. Served with Signal Corp, Belgian Army, attached to Brit. Army, 1940-45. Mem. ASME. Republican. Roman Catholic. Home: 184 Fern St West Hartford CT 06119 Office: Combustion Engring Inc 1000 Prospect Hill Rd Windsor CT 06095

RAO, KRISHNAPPA NAGARAJA, scientist; b. Bangalore, India, June 11, 1921; s. Subbanna Krishnappa and Savithramma R.; came to U.S., 1946, naturalized, 1959; B.S. in Phys. Chemistry with honors, U. Mysore (India), 1942, M.S., 1943, B.T., Maharaja's Coll., U. Mysore, 1945; M.S., Ill. Inst. Tech., 1948, Ph.D., 1950; m. T. Shankaramma, May 8, 1939; children—Harsha, Edward, Marguerite, Sheila. Lectr. in phys. chemistry, U. Mysore, India, 1943-44; ednl. officer, dept. pub. instrn., Govt. Mysore, 1944-45; teaching asst., dept. chem. engring., Ill. Inst. Tech., Chgo., 1946-50; research engr., Inst. Gas Tech., Chgo., 1950-51; cons. indsl. devel. Ministry of Econ. Affairs, Govt. Indonesia, 1951-53; asst. dir., coordinator internat. services div., Dunwoody Indsl. Inst., Mpls., 1953-65; program officer, Ford Found. Sci. Tech. and Edn., Latin Am. and Caribbean Program, 1965-74, cons. Sci. and Engring. Programs in Latin Am., 1974—; sr. research asso., Center for Policy Alternatives, and sr. lectr., Div. Study and Research in Edn., Mass. Inst. Tech., Cambridge, 1974—; quality control engr., Korean Tech. Inst., Seoul, 1950; cons. AID, U.S. Govt., World Bank, Interam. Devel. Bank, indsl. corps., sci. and engring. ednl. agencies, Sudan, Lebanon, Burma, Argentina, Chile, Brazil, Nigeria, Ghana; chmn. panel on research adminstrn. and tech. entrepreneurship, Nat. Acad. Scis., 1972-73. Bd. dirs. Nat. Assn. Fgn. Student Advisors, 1964-65, Minn. Internat. Center, 1960-65. Recipient gold medals, U. Mysore, 1943, 1942, Bhabha Meml. Award in Edn., 1944; Govt. India Overseas Fellow, 1946-49. Mem. Am. Inst. Chem. Engrs., and N.Y. Chpt., Am. Soc. Engring. Edn., AAAS, Sigma Xi, Tau Beta Pi, Phi Lambda Upsilon, Phi Delta Kappa. Unitarian. Club: Faculty Mass. Inst. Tech. Contbr. tech. papers on chem. engring., internat. devel., tech. edn., univ. planning, tech. policy to publs. and confs.

RAO, PAUL PETER, fed. judge; b. Prizzi, Italy, June 15, 1899; s. Vincenzo and Antonina (Fugarini) R.; came to U.S., 1904, naturalized, 1920; LL.B., Fordham U., 1923; H.H.D. (hon.), Philathea Coll., London, Ont., Can., 1958; LL.D. (hon.), Manhattan Coll., 1971, Pace Coll., 1972; m. Grace Malatino, June 22, 1922 (dec.); children—Nina Rao Cameron, Grayce Rao Visconti, Paul Peter; m. 2d, Catherine Marolla, Nov. 17, 1971. Admitted to N.Y. bar, 1924, U.S. Supreme Ct. bar; asst. dist. atty. New York County, 1925-27; asst. atty. gen. U.S. customs div., 1941-48; judge U.S. Customs Ct., 1948—, chief judge, 1965-71. Dir., Cardinal Spellman Servicemen's Club, Nat. Catholic Community Service, 1945-78; hon. mem. Cath. Ct. Attaches Guild, N.Y.C., 1941-78; gen. pres. Holy Name Socs., Archdiocese of N.Y., 1931-41; trustee Ch. of Our Lady of Peace. Served with USN, 1917-19. Decorated knight of Lateran, knight Order St. Hubert; recipient Star of Solidarity, Italian Govt., 1953, Star and Cross of Acad. honor Am. Internat. Acad. of U.S.A., 1958, grand cross Eloy Alfaro Internat. Found., Republic of Panama, 1959, Commemorative cross Royal Yugoslav Army, 1965, commendatore Order of Merit, Italian Republic, 1968, Charles A. Rapallo award, 1970, Antonio Rizzuto award Unico Nat., 1972, commendatore Republic of San Marino, 1973, Gold medal Nat. Acad. Sci., Rome, 1973, Pub. Service award Italian Hist. Soc. Am., 1974, Pub. Service award Polish Cultural Soc. Am., 1975, Italian Army medallion, 1976. Hon. fellow Truman Library Inst.; mem. Am., Fed., N.Y., N.J., Conn. bar assns., Am. Justinian Soc. of Jurists (founder, 1st pres.), Bklyn.-Manhattan Trial Counsel Assn. (hon.), New York County Press Assn. (hon.), Am. Legion, VFW (grand marshal Loyalty Day Parade 1960, hon. comdr. New York County council 1951-56, 57-62), DAV, Fordham Law Alumni Assn. (dir.), Fed. Bus. Assn. N.Y. (exec. com., chmn. nominating com. 1958-73), Phi Alpha Delta (Man of Year 1969). Democrat. Club: Tiro a Segno (hon.). Home: 210 E 61st St New York City NY 10021 Office: US Customs Ct One Federal Plaza New York City NY 10007

RAO, SREEPADA TUMKUR KRISHNA MURTHY RAO, internist, nephrologist; b. Kolar, India, June 4, 1944; s. T. K. Krishnamurthy and Nagamma K. (Murthy) R.; came to U.S., 1967, naturalized, 1972; P.U.C., Nat. Coll., Bangalore, India, 1960; M.B., B.S., Bangalore Med. Coll., 1966; m. Pushpa, Mar. 9, 1972; 1 son, Kiran. Rotating intern Bangalore Med. Coll., 1966-67; intern in medicine Newark City Hosp., 1967-68; resident in medicine N.J. Coll. Medicine, Newark and East Orange, 1968-70, chief resident in medicine, 1970-71; fellow in renal medicine State U. N.Y. Downstate Med. Center, 1971-73; asst. clin. instr. medicine, 1971-73, instr. in surgery, 1973-74, asst. prof. surgery, 1974-75, asst. prof. medicine, 1975—, dir. hemodialysis unit, 1976—; chief div. nephrology Wyckoff Heights Hosp., Bklyn., 1973—; cons. in nephrology Bklyn. VA Hosp., 1975—. Mem. exec. com. Kannada Koota of N.Y.C. Recipient 5 Gold medals with top honors Bangalore Med. Coll., 1966. Diplomate Am. Bd. Internal Medicine, Am. Bd. Nephrology. Fellow A.C.P.; mem. Internat. Transplantation Soc., Internat., Am. socs. nephrology, Internat. Soc. Artificial Organs, Am. Soc. Artificial Internal Organs, Nat. Kidney Found., Smithsonian Inst., Hindu Temple Soc. Contbr. numerous articles on kidney disease to med. publs.; research on heroin associated renal diseases; editorial bd. Internat. Jour. Artificial Organs, 1978—. Home: 525 Bunker Ct North Woodmere NY 11581 Office: 450 Clarkson Ave Brooklyn NY 11203

RAO, VATSALA V., obstetrician and gynecologyst; b. Bangalore, India; d. Venkat M. and Ratna (Tankasala) R.; came to U.S., 1963, naturalized, 1977; B.Sc., Maharanis Coll. for Women, 1956; M.D., Bangalore Med. Coll., 1963. Intern, St. Peter's Med. Center, New Brunswick, N.J., 1964; resident obstetrics and gynecology St. Clares Hosp., N.Y.C., 1965-69; practice medicine specializing in obstetrics and gynecology, New Brunswick, 1973—; med. dir. Planned Parenthood League of Middlesex County (N.J.), 1977—; clin. asst. prof. dept. obstetrics and gynecology Rutgers Med. Sch., Piscataway, N.Y., 1977—; mem. attending staff St. Peter's, Middlesex hosps. Diplomate Am. Coll. Obstetricians and Gynecologists. Fellow Am. Coll. Obstetricians and Gynecologists; mem. AMA (Physicians Recognition award), Middlesex County Med. Soc. Home: 11 Desmet Ave Milltown NJ 08850 Office: 61 Livingston Ave New Brunswick NJ 08901

RAO, YALAMANCHILI A. K., allergist, immunologist; b. Godavarru, India, Sept. 15, 1943; s. Subba Rao V. and Kamalamma Yalamanchili; M.D., Guntur (India) Med. Coll., 1969; M.S. in Human Nutrition, Columbia U., 1971; m. Sunkara Sujatha Kumari, Aug. 21, 1970; children—Haresh, Rajesh. Resident in internal medicine and pediatrics, fellow in allergy and immunology L.I. Coll. Hosp., Bklyn., 1971-77, attending physician in allergy and immunology, 1977—, S.I. Hosp., 1977—; practice medicine specializing in allergy and immunology, Bklyn., 1977—. Certified Am. Bd. Allergy and Immunology, Am. Bd. Internal Medicine and Pediatrics. Mem. Am. Acad. Allergy, A.C.P., Am. Acad. Pediatrics. Home: 151 Labau Ave Staten Island NY 10301 Office: 159 Clinton St Brooklyn NY 10301

RAPHAEL, CARL SAMUEL, pharm. co. exec.; b. Kew Gardens, N.Y., Apr. 23, 1943; s. Harold and Ruth R.; B.S., Dalhousie U., 1965; postgrad. Queens Coll., 1966; M.B.A., Fordham U., 1974; m. Ellen Gibson Muller, Jan. 15, 1966; children—Larissa, Heather. Pharm. rep. Hoffman LaRoche, Nutley, N.J., 1967-70, med. center rep., 1970-71, mktg. research asst., 1971-72, mktg. research analyst, 1972-73; sr. analyst, coordinator health econs. Health Application Systems, Inc., Saddle Brook, N.J., 1973-75, mktg. mgr., 1975-76; sr. mktg. analyst Merck, Sharp & Dohme, West Point, Pa., 1976-78; product research mgr. hosp. and diagnostic products, mgr. market devel. E.R. Squibb & Sons, Princeton, N.J., 1978—; cons. health care adminstrn. Committeeman Union County Consumer Affairs Adv. Com., 1974, vice chmn., 1975-76, chmn., 1976-77. Mem. Group Health Assn. Am., Assn. M.B.A. Execs., Pharm. Mfrs. Assn., Am. Mktg. Assn., Eastern Pharm. Mktg. Research Group, AAU, Warrington Ambulance Corps, Am. Philatelic Assn., Tau Epsilon Phi. Home: 1705 LaRue Ln Warrington PA 18976 Office: UVW ER Squibb & Sons PO Box 4000 Princeton NJ 08540

RAPHAEL, CHESTER MARTIN, physician; b. Rockaway Beach, N.Y., Oct. 7, 1912; s. Jack and Lena (Schoenfeld) R.; A.B. cum laude, U. Mich., 1933; M.D., U. Mich., 1937; m. Margaret Mary Hubbert, Aug. 15, 1943; children—Maura Ann, Barbara Lynn. Intern Monmouth Meml. Hosp., Long Branch, N.J., 1937-39; resident physician N.J. State Hosp., Marlboro, N.J., 1939-42, 46-48; practice medicine specializing in psychiatry and orgonomy, Forest Hills, N.Y., 1948—. Sec. Wilhelm Reich Found., 1949-54; co-dir. Orgone Energy Clinic, 1949-54. Bd. dirs. Guide Dog Found. for Blind, Friends of Wilhelm Reich Museum. Served with AUS, 1942-46. Fellow Am. Geriatric Soc., Acad. Psychosomatic Medicine; mem. Queens County Med. Soc., A.M.A., Am. Psychiat. Assn., Am. Assn. for Med. Orgonomy, AAAS, Wilhelm Reich Inst. for Orgonomic Studies (dir.), Assn. for Advancement Psychotherapy, Tau Delta Phi. Club: University of Michigan (N.Y.C.). Author: (with Helen E. MacDonald) Orgonomic Diagnosis of the Cancer Biopathy, 1952; Wilhelm Reich: Misconstrued-Miseteemed; Some Questions and Answers About Orgone Theory; asso. editor: Jour. of Orgonomic Medicine, 1955-56. Editor: (with Mary Higgins) Reich Speaks of Freud, The Cancer Biopathy (Wilhelm Reich); Early Writings (Wilhelm Reich); The Bion Experiments on The Origin of Life

(Wilhelm Reich). Home and office: 69-17 Fleet St Forest Hills NY 11375

RAPHAEL, HAROLD JAMES, ednl. adminstr.; b. North Bergen, N.J., Apr. 15, 1918; s. James V. and Theresa E. (Benz) R.; B.S., Mich. State U., 1942, Ph.D., 1954; M.S., Oreg. State U., 1950; m. Evelyn M. Huber, Feb. 5, 1943; children—Jane Roberta (Mrs. William A. Dittmore), James Henry, Peter George, Ann Theresa. Faculty, Mich. State U., 1953-70, prof. Sch. Packaging, 1966-70; mgr. research and devel. dept. Avon Products, Inc., Suffern, N.Y., 1970-73; dir. dept. packaging sci. Rochester (N.Y.) Inst. Tech., 1973—. Cons., lectr. in field. Trustee Packaging Found. Served to lt. USNR, 1942-45. Mem. ASTM, Packaging Inst., TAPPI, Sigma Xi, Xi Sigma Pi. Author: Package Production Management, 1976. Home: 125 Brentwood Ln Fairport NY 14450 Office: One Lomb Memorial Dr Rochester NY 14623

RAPP, CULLEN F., illustrators agt.; b. N.Y.C., Sept. 11, 1919; s. Morris and Lena (Cohen) Rappaport; student Parsons Sch. Design, N.Y.C., 1936-38; m. Anne Tannebaum, Nov. 26, 1942; children—Gerald, Ellen, Tina. Layout and lettering artist Warner Bros., N.Y.C., 1941-42; art dir. Al Paul Lefton Co., N.Y.C., 1942-44; pres. Cullen Rapp Studios, N.Y.C., 1944-58, Cullen Rapp Inc., N.Y.C., 1958-73, Gerald & Cullen Rapp, Inc., N.Y.C., 1973—; illustrators agt., 1944—; charter mem., treas. Soc. Photography and Artists Reps., 1963—; evening faculty Sch. Visual Arts, N.Y.C., 1977-79. Scholarship student Parsons Sch. Design, 1936, Vesper George Sch. Art, Boston, 1936; recipient medal merit Sch. Art League N.Y.C., 1936. Mem. Soc. Illustrators, Nat. Assn. Watch and Clock Collectors. Home: 2 Pool Dr Roslyn NY 11576 Office: 251 E 51st St New York City NY 10022

RAPP, DOUGLAS MARK, metals co. exec.; b. Bklyn., Aug. 8, 1945; s. Harry J. and Lydia M. (Zolotorofe) R.; B.A., U. Vt., 1967; M.A., Columbia U., 1972; m. Joan A. Kaufman, July 6, 1975. Tng. dir. East River Savs. Bank, N.Y.C., 1972-74; mgmt. devel. staff Chem. Bank, N.Y.C., 1974-75; controller Aluminum Alloys Corp., Central Islip, N.Y., 1975—. Mem. Am. Psychol. Assn. (asso.), Psi Chi. Office: 185 Oval Dr Central Islip NY 11722

RAPP, HARVEY MARVIN, clin. psychologist; b. Schenectady, June 1, 1940; s. Philip and Ruth (Levine) R.; B.A., U. Rochester, 1962; M.A., Hollins Coll., 1964; certificate in sch. psychology Hofstra U., 1966; Ph.D., U. Md., 1970; m. Susan Ellen Kliger, Apr. 11, 1965; 1 son, Howard Solomon. Psychologist, Fairfax-Falls Church Mental Health Center, Springfield, Va., 1968-70, Spring Grove Hosp. Center, Catonsville, Md., 1970-74; psychologist, sch. consultation program Howard County Bur. Mental Health, Columbia, Md., 1974-77, sr. staff psychologist outpatient program, 1977—; adj. asso. prof. psychology Loyola Coll., 1970—; co-dir. children's recreational devel. com. Lincoln U., 1976—; mem. health adv. com. Head Start, Howard County, Md., 1977—; mem. residential admissions, review com. Howard County Assn. Retarded Citizens, 1977—; mem. Md. Bd. Examiners Psychologists, 1977—. Mem. Am., Eastern, Md. (pres.-elect Div. II 1978—) psychol. assns., Am. Personnel and Guidance Assn., Am. Sch. Counselors Assn. Jewish. Home: 9213 Osprey Ct Columbia MD 21045

RAPP, RICHARD TILDEN, economist; b. Miami, Fla., Nov. 30, 1944; s. Melville B. and Rachel; B.A., Bklyn. Coll., 1965; M.A., U. Pa., 1966; Ph.D., 1970; m. Wilma J. Levin, Aug. 20, 1967; children—Ethan, Sandra. Asst. prof. SU NY, Stony Brook, 1970-75, asso. prof., 1976-77; sr. economist Nat. Economic Research Assos., Inc., N.Y.C., 1977—. Kent fellow, 1968-70; Fulbright scholar, Venice, Italy, 1968-69. Mem. Am. Econ. Assn., Econ. History Assn. Author: (with Shepard B. Clough) European Economic History, 1975; Industry and Economic Decline in Seventeenth-Century Venice, 1976. Home: Central Dr Glen Head NY 11545 Office: 80 Broad St New York NY 10004

RAPP, ROBERT CHARLES, law enforcement ofcl.; b. Bronx, N.Y., July 24, 1937; s. Robert H. and Ann (Lauber) R.; B.A., Hunter Coll., 1961; LL.B., Fordham U., 1966; m. Kathleen Hibson, June 7, 1958; children—Robert, John, Thomas. With N.Y.C. Police Dept., 1958-67; asst. dist. atty. Suffolk County, Riverhead, L.I., N.Y., 1967-73; dep. commr. Suffolk County Police Dept., Hauppauge, L.I., 1973-77; admitted to N.Y. bar, 1966; pvt. practice law, 1977—; adj. asst. prof. C.W. Post Coll., 1973—. Mem. Suffolk County Bar Assn., Internat., N.Y. State assns. chiefs of police. Home: 16 Seacliff Ln Miller Place NY 11764 Office: 803 Main St Port Jefferson NY 11777

RAPPAPORT, FLORENCE WARD, mgmt. cons.; b. Ft. Sam Houston, Tex., Oct. 6, 1928; d. Edward Joseph and Florence Emily (Bock) Ward; B.A., Our Lady of Lake U., San Antonio, 1949; postgrad. Trinity U., San Antonio, 1949-50; m. Sheldon R. Rappaport, Mar. 2, 1950 (div. July 1969); children—Bruce Ward, Lisa Lynn. Co-founder, asst. to pres. Pathway Sch., Norristown, Pa., 1961-68; adminstrv. dir. Neurosurg. Clinic for Children, Media, Pa., 1968-70; v.p. for devel. Vanguard Schs., Haverford, Pa., 1970-72; asst. to pres. Elwyn (Pa.) Inst., 1972-75; pvt. practice mgmt. cons., Media, 1976-78; cons. employee relations dept. E.I. DuPont de Nemours & Co., Inc., Wilmington, Del., 1978—. Pres. bd. dirs. Montgomery County Mental Health Clinics, 1965-68; bd. dirs. Phila. United Fund, 1969-72; bd. mgrs., sec. Garrett-Williamson Found., 1973—; bd. dirs. Mary Campbell Center, Wilmington, 1978. Mem. Pub. Relations Soc. Am., Jean Piaget Soc. (sec.-treas. 1976—). Editor: The Genetic Epistemologist, 1976—. Home: 2 Yarmouth Ln Media PA 19063 Office: Nemours Bldg 10th St and Market St Wilmington DE 19898

RAPPAPORT, GEORGE, electronics cons.; b. N.Y.C., Dec. 7, 1919; s. Joseph and Anna R.; B.E.E., Coll. City N.Y., 1941; M.Sc., Ohio State U., 1947, Ph.D., 1949; LL.D. (hon.), Parsons Coll., Fairfield, Iowa, 1964; m. Sonia B. Sharlin, Sept. 1968; children—Nolan W., Barbara D. Rappaport Brown, Lisa, Julie, Michael, Douglas. Chief scientist USAF, Wright Field, Ohio and Washington, 1941-56; v.p. Emerson Radio and Phonograph Corp., also Emerton, Inc., Silver Spring, Md., 1956-62; pres. Warnecke Electron Tubes, Inc., Des Plaines, Ill., 1962-64; v.p. Scope Electronics Inc., Reston, Va., 1964-70, Dewey Electronics Co., Paramus, N.J., 1970-71; pvt. corporate cons., Washington, 1971—; research prof. engring. George Washington U.; dir. Warnecke Electric Tubes, Inc. Bd. dirs. Kaufman Camp, Washington, 1974-76. Fellow IEEE; mem. Assn. Old Crows (Pioneer medal 1978). Address: 6244 Clearwood Rd Bethesda MD 20034

RAPPAPORT, IRWIN, physician; b. N.Y.C., Apr. 4, 1931; s. Philip and Ella (Elitzak) R.; B.S., Columbia U., 1953; M.D. (Avalon scholar), Med. Coll. Va., 1962; m. Barbara Radin, Feb. 14, 1954; children—Michael Keith, William James. Intern, Bellevue Hosp., N.Y.C., 1962-63; resident in pediatrics Cornell Med. Center, N.Y. Hosp., N.Y.C., 1963-65; fellow in pediatric allergy St. Vincent's Hosp. and Med. Center, N.Y.C., 1965-66; practice medicine specializing in pediatric allergies, N.Y.C., 1966—; asso. dir. pediatrics Polyclinic Hosp., N.Y.C., 1965-71; dir. pediatric allergy sect. of allergy and immunology N.Y. Hosp. (Cornell Med. Center), N.Y.C., 1971—. Served with U.S. Army, 1954-56. NIH grantee in pediatric allergy, 1965-66. Diplomate Am. Bd. Allergy and Immunology, Am. Bd. Pediatrics, subsplty. bd. pediatric allergy. Fellow Am. Acad. Allergy, Am. Coll. Allergists, Am. Acad. Pediatrics; mem. N.Y. Allergy Soc., N.Y. Acad. Sci., N.Y. State, N.Y. County med. socs., Cornell Allergy Club, Alpha Omega Alpha, Sigma Zeta. Office: 530 E 20th St New York City NY 10009 also 445 E 68 St New York City NY 10021 Home: 601 E 20th St New York City NY 10010

RAPPEPORT, ALFRED MAURICE, shipping co. exec.; b. N.Y.C., Feb. 6, 1922; s. Gustave and Lena (Spector) R.; B.A., Bklyn. Coll., 1947; postgrad., Institut Des Hautes Etudes Cinematographiques, 1947; m. Gloria Esther Hernandez, Jan. 31, 1953; children—Jeffrey, Betty, Susan, Ruth, Jerry, Rosalind, Letty Marie and Janet Marie (adopted). Photocopy clerk War Dept., N.Y.C., 1939-42; free lance photographer, Paris, 1948-51; pres. Interstate Auto Shippers, Inc., 1956—, Gen. Am. Shippers, Inc., 1961—. Served with USNR, 1942-45. Mem. Nat. Geographic Soc., Am. Legion, Nat. Customs Brokers Assn., N.Y. C. of C., Bklyn. Coll. Alumni Assn., Am. Soc. Travel Agts. Home: 2307 E 66th St Brooklyn NY 11234 Office: 225 W 34th St Suite 2001 New York City NY 10001

RAPPIN, ADRIAN, artist; b. N.Y.C., Jan. 20, 1934; student Acad. Fine Arts Rome, Italy, 1951-52; B.A., Brandeis U., 1955; student Art Acad. Cin., 1955-56, Art Students League N.Y.C., 1956-59; m., 1960; 1 dau. One man shows Barzansky Galleries, N.Y.C., 1964, 66, 69, Four Winds Gallery, 1970, Capricorn Gallery, 1975; exhibited in ann. group shows N.A.D. Galleries, 1960—, Fifty Am. Artists, N.Y.C., 1965-69, UNICEF Internat., Monaco, 1965-67; represented in permanent collection S.I. Mus., Randolph Macon Coll., Lynchburg, Va., Lincoln U., Oxford, Pa., Brandeis U., Kellogg Found., Battlecreek, Mich., Gibbes Gallery, Charleston (S.C.) Mus., others. Mem. Am. Artists Profl. League, Allied Artists Am., Fifty Am. Artists. Home: 14 W 68th St New York City NY 10023

RAPPLEYE, WILLARD COLE, JR., editor; b. New Haven, June 30, 1924; s. Willard C. and Elizabeth (Cunningham) R.; grad. Phillips Exeter Acad., 1941; B.A., Yale, 1945; m. Marita Crofton, May 1, 1962; children—Willard C. III, Charles McMillan, Thomas Armistead. Contbg. editor Time Mag., 1947-50, corr., S.W. bur. chief Dallas-Houston, 1952-57, nat. econ. corr., Washington, 1957-61, N.Y., 1962; PIO ECA Formosa 1951; editor Am. Banker N.Y.C., 1962-75; chmn. editorial bd. First Chgo. World Report, 1976; editor Financier Mag., 1977—. Served with USAAF, 1943-45; CBI. Club: Century Assn. (N.Y.C.). Home: 31 E 79th St New York City NY 10021 Office: 919 3d Ave New York City NY 10022

RAPPORT, MAURICE M., scientist, educator; b. N.Y.C., Sept. 23, 1919; B.S., Coll. City N.Y., 1940; Ph.D. in Organic Chemistry, Calif. Inst. Tech., 1946; married 1942; children—Erica, Ezra. Prof. biochemistry Coll. Physicians and Surgeons Columbia, N.Y.C., 1967—; chief dept. pharmacology N.Y. State Psychiat. Inst., N.Y.C., 1968-69, chief div. neurosci., 1969—; mem. research rev. panel Nat. Multiple Sclerosis Soc., 1961-74. Recipient Ketcham Prize in Econs., 1938; Fulbright scholar, 1952. Mem. Soc. Neurosci., Am. Soc. Neurochemistry (councillor 1975—), Am. Soc. Biol. Chemists. Mem. editorial bd. Jour. Lipid Research, 1962-65, 72—, asso. editor, 1969, editor, 1969-72; mem. editorial bd. Jour. Neurochemistry, 1965-73, Procs. Soc. Exptl. Biology and Medicine, 1976—. Home: 3967 F Sedgwick Ave New York City NY 10463 Office: NY State Psychiat Inst 722 W 168th St New York City NY 10032

RASBERRY, STANLEY DEXTER, physicist; b. Lubbock, Tex., July 23, 1941; s. Dayle Howard and Nova Vera (Hancock) R.; A.B. (Univ. scholar 1959-63), Johns Hopkins U., 1963; postgrad. George Washington U., 1964-66; m. Judith Ann Simpson, Nov. 24, 1961; children—Steven Dale, Cynthia Ann. With Nat. Bur. Standards, Washington, 1959—, exec. asst. in dir.'s office, 1975—. Bd. dirs. Gaithersburg (Md.) Presbyterian Ch., 1978—, also elder. Mem. Am. Phys. Soc., Va. Acad. Sci., Soc. for Applied Spectroscopy (past chmn.), Microbeam Analysis Soc., U.S. Power Squadron. Club: Selby Bay Yacht. Contbr. articles to profl. jours. Home: 818 Crystal Court Gaithersburg MD 20760 Office: National Bureau Standards 1123 Adminstration Bldg Washington DC 20234

RASELY, CHARLES WESLEY, JR., educator; b. Easton, Pa., Apr. 26, 1921; s. Charles Wesley and Ethel Dora (Jacobs) R.; diploma Juilliard Sch. Music, 1942; B.M. in Music Edn., Syracuse U., 1970; m. Margaret Jane Hawk, Dec. 8, 1946; children—Robert, Thomas, Dianne. Pvt. voice tchr., Easton, 1948-62; tchr., choral dir. Oneida (N.Y.) Pub. Schs., 1962—, chmn. dept. music, 1974—; dir. music Christ Ch., Sherrill, N.Y., 1962-71, 1st Presbyn. Ch., Oneida, 1971—; accompanist Oneida Area Civic Chorale, 1969—. Served with AUS, 1942-45. Mem. Nat., N.Y. State tchrs. assns., Madison County Music Tchrs. Assn. (pres. 1972—), N.Y. Sch. Music Assn., Oneida Little Theatre (pres. 1967-70). Composer choral compositions including Everybody Sings, Church's One Foundation, To See A World in A Grain of Sand, others. Home: 415 E Campbell Ave Sherrill NY 13461

RASHKIN, JAY ARTHUR, chemist; b. N.Y.C., Sept. 21, 1933; s. Abraham and Hilda (Ebenstein) R.; B.A. cum laude, N.Y. U., 1955; M.A., Princeton U., 1957, Ph.D. (McCay fellow 1957-58), 1961; m. Shirley Fruchtman, Mar. 13, 1960; children—Lauren, David. Research chemist Du Pont Co., Gibbstown, N.J., 1959-62; mem. tech. staff Space Tech. Labs., Redondo Beach, Calif., 1962-64; research specialist Monsanto Co., St. Louis, 1964-66; sr. research chemist Cities Service Co., Cranbury, N.J., 1966-76, Halcon Catalyst Industries, Little Ferry, N.J., 1976—. Mem. Am. Chem. Soc., Am. Phys. Soc., Catalysis Soc., ASTM, Materials Research Soc. Club: Catalysis of N.Y.C. Patentee in field. Home: 551 Hanson Ave Piscataway NJ 08854 Office: Halcon Catalyst Industries 49 Industrial Ave Little Ferry NJ 07643

RASHKIND, WILLIAM JACOBSON, pediatric cardiologist; b. Patterson, N.J., Feb. 12, 1922; s. Jacob Louis and Charlotte Florence (Jacobson) R.; A.B., U. Louisville, 1943, M.D., 1946; m. Rita Shirley Leisten, Dec. 17, 1949; children—Marilyn, Jean, Charles. Intern, Michael Reese Hosp., Chgo., 1946-47; resident in pediatrics U. Pa. Hosp., Phila., 1953-55; asst. prof. physiology U. Pa. Sch. Medicine, Phila., 1950-53, asst. prof. pediatrics, 1959-63, asso. prof., 1963-71, prof., 1971—; dir. cardiovascular labs. Children's Hosp. Phila., 1955—; mem. internat. com. coding congenital heart disease, 1969-72; mem. intersoc. commn. heart disease resources, 1971-74; mem. exec. com., congenital heart disease com. Am. Heart Assn., 1970-74. Served with USN, 1943-49. Nat. Heart and Lung Inst. fellow, 1949-50; NIH grantee, 1952—; diplomate Am. Bd. Pediatrics, Am. Bd. Pediatric Cardiology. Mem. Am. Pediatric Soc., Soc. Pediatric Research, Am. Physiol. Soc., Am. Acad. Pediatrics, Soc. Artificial Internal Organs, Assn. European Pediatric Cardiologists. Inventor balloon atrioseptostomy cardiac catheter, transatrial septal defect closure system; contbr. articles in field to med. jours. Home: 121 Merion Rd Merion PA 19066 Office: One Children's Center 34th St and Civic Center Blvd Philadelphia PA 19104

RASMANIS, EGONS, electronics co. exec.; b. Riga, Latvia, July 12, 1924; s. Janis Andrejs and Anna (Smemanis) R.; came to U.S., 1950, naturalized, 1955; B.Sc., Friedrich Alexander U., Erlangen, Germany, 1949; postgrad. Northeastern U., 1955; m. Vita Anita Skulte, June 30, 1956; children—Anita Ilze, Ingrid Inta, Linda Irene. Mgr. devel. engring. CBS Electronics, Lowell, Mass., 1956-60; project mgr., prin. engr. GT & E Sylvania, Waltham, Mass., 1960-64; mgr. microelectronics Amperex Co., Cranston, R.I., 1964-69, mgr. mfg., 1969-72; co-founder, v.p. sales Micro Components Corp., Cranston, 1972—. Pres. Latvian Acad. Soc. Fraternitas Metropolitana, Boston, 1957-59, 62-64, 75-77. Mem. Internat. Soc. Hybrid Micro[electronics. Lutheran. Patentee in field of semicondrs. and microelectronics. Home: 151 Westwood Dr East Greenwich RI 02818 Office: 99 Bald Hill Rd Cranston RI 02920

RATCHFORD, MICHAEL WILLIAM, food co. exec.; b. Archbald, Pa., June 12, 1933; s. William Aloysius and Margaret (Pickard) R.; B.S., U. Scranton, 1956; m. Joanne Marie Kelly, Nov. 9, 1957; children—Michael, Susan, Lynn, Kathleen, Christopher. Mgmt. trainee to accounting mgr. Standard Brands Inc., N.Y.C., 1957-61, mgr. adminstrn., asst. to v.p. sales, Wilkes-Barre, Pa., 1961-65, systems analyst, systems project leader, mgr. data processing, 1965-70, regional controller, asst. nat. controller systems design and planning, nat. dir. credit, 1971-78, dir. planning, 1978—; lectr. in field. Mem. Am. Mgmt. Assn., Credit Research Found., Ops. Research Soc. Am., N.Y. Credit and Fin. Assn., U. Scranton Alumni Assn. (pres. Lackawanna Valley chpt. 1964-65), Fife and Drum Hist. Soc. Roman Catholic. Home: 1801 N Washington Ave Scranton PA 18509 Office: 632 S Main St Wilkes-Barre PA 18701 also 460 Park Ave New York City NY 10022

RATCHFORD, WILLIAM RICHARD, congressman; b. Danbury, Conn., May 24, 1934; s. Harold and Susie (Klinzing) R.; A.B., U. Conn., 1956; postgrad. Georgetown U. Law Sch., 1956-59; m. Barbara Jean Carpenter, June 22, 1957; children—Shaun, Scott, Brian. Admitted to Conn. bar, 1959, since practiced in Danbury; mem. Conn. Ho. of Reps., 1963-78, asst. majority leader, 1967-68, house speaker, 1969-72, minority leader at large, 1972-78; mem. 96th Congress from 5th Dist. Conn., Washington, 1979—; instr. polit. sci. Western Conn. State Coll., 1976. Adviser Danbury Assn. to Advance Retarded; vice chmn. Regional Legal Aid Program; mem. clean air com. Conn. Tb Assn.; chmn. Community Action Com.; v.p. U. Conn. Alumni Council; chmn. Democratic State Conv., 1970-71, co-chmn. platform com., 1970, 72; pres. Nat. Legis. Conf., 1972-73; chmn. bd. dirs. Camp Fire Girls, 1963-64; mem. Presdl. Adv. Commn. on Intergovernmental Relations; chmn. Gov.'s Blue Ribbon Com. to Investigate Nursing Homes, 1976. Served with Conn. N.G., 1965. Recipient State Vocat. Edn. award, 1969; Outstanding Legis. Leadership award Nat. Citizens Conf., 1971, award for contbn. to vocat. edn., 1975. Mem. U. Conn. Nat. Alumni Assn. (past 1st v.p., mem. council), Phi Beta Kappa. Universalist Unitarian (past chmn. bd.). Home: 2 Johnson Dr Danbury CT 06810 Office: US Ho of Reps The Capitol Washington DC 20515

RATCLIFF, WALTER FULTON, bus. cons.; b. Busti, N.Y., July 20, 1918; s. Darius Mitteer and Ethel Lepine (Fulton) R.; student Houghton Coll., 1935-37; B.S., La. State U., 1939, M.S., 1946; m. Dorothy Mae Thigpen, Nov. 15, 1939; children—Margaret G., Charles C., Thomas D. Research chemist Exxon Corp., 1939-50, design engr., 1951-52, cost analyst, 1953-54, long range planner, 1955-69, econs. adviser, 1970-72; cons. bus. mgmt., Naples, N.Y., 1973—. Bd. dirs. Naples Mill Sch. Arts and Crafts. Chmn., Naples Village Zoning Bd. Appeals, 1973—; bd. mgrs. Am. Baptist Chs. in N.Y. State, 1975—. Mem. Am. Chem. Soc., Am. Inst. Chem. Engrs. Baptist (deacon 1973—). Rotarian. Patentee in field. Address: Route 1 Naples NY 14512

RATH, GEORGE EDWARD, bishop; b. Buffalo, Mar. 29, 1913; s. Edward F. and Eudora Pearl (Chadderdon) R.; A.B., Harvard, 1933; B.D., Union Theol. Sem., 1936; S.T.D., Gen. Theol. Sem., 1964; m. Margaret Webber, Apr. 7, 1934; children—Peter F. (dec. July 1968), Gail (Mrs. Richard M. Sherk). Ordained deacon Episcopal Ch., 1938, priest, 1939; asst. to chaplain Columbia, 1936-39, asst. chaplain, 1939-41; vicar All Saints' Ch., Millington, N.J., 1941-49, rector, 1949-64; suffragan bishop Episcopal Diocese Newark, 1964-70; bishop coadjutor, 1970-73, bishop, 1974—; archdeacon Morris County, 1959-64; chmn. bd. trustees Christ Hosp., Jersey City, 1966-79. Trustee Appalachian Trail Conf. Club: Sierra. Home: 2 Cedar Land Rd East Orleans MD 02643

RATH, JAMES ARTHUR, III, pub. relations exec.; b. Honolulu, Dec. 30, 1931; s. James Arthur and Ruth(Lyman) R.; B.A., Hamilton Coll., 1953; postgrad. Syracuse U., 1958-62; m. Jenaud Schwartz, Feb. 14, 1976; children (by previous marriage)—Lani, Scott, Luana, Koene, James Arthur. Advt. mgr. Ottaway Newspapers Radio, N.Y. and Pa., 1953-57; account exec. Spitz Advt., Syracuse, N.Y., 1957-60; v.p. L.M. Harvey, N.Y.C. and Syracuse, 1960-63; partner Rath-Johnston Co., Rochester, N.Y.C., and Syracuse, 1963-65; pres. The Rath Orgn., Syracuse, Rochester and N.Y.C., 1965—; adj. prof. Newhouse Sch. Communications, Syracuse U., 1973—; lectr. in field. Bd. dirs. Syracuse Ballet Theatre, 1975-76, Civic Morning Musicals, 1974-76, Planned Parenthood, 1966-68, Urban League, 1967-69, Priority One, 1969-75, Consolidated Industries, 1966-68, Salt City Playhouse, 1965-75. Recipient Silver Anvil, Pub. Relations Soc. Am., 1963, 65, 66, 68; Cold Coin, Bank Mktg. Assn., 1969; named Am. Mktg. Assn. Man of the Year, 1969; N.Y. Art Dirs. N.Y.C. award, 1977, others. Mem. Pub. Relation Soc. Am. (chpt. pres. 1966-68), Bank Mktg. Assn., Bus. and Indsl. Communications, Hawaiian Mission Soc. Contbr. articles in field to profl. jours.; author: History of Professional Photography; 1977; Marketing Professional Photography, 1978; columnist in field. Home: 17 Montgomery St Cherry Valley NY 11320 Office: Hills Bldg Syracuse NY 13202

RATH, THOMAS DAVID, state ofcl., lawyer; b. East Orange, N.J., June 1, 1945; s. Harvey E. and Helen (Feeley) R.; A.B., Dartmouth Coll., 1967; J.D., Georgetown U., 1971; m. Christine Casey, Dec. 18, 1971; children—Erin and Timothy (twins). Admitted to N.J. bar, 1971, N.H. bar, 1972, U.S. Supreme Ct. bar, 1978; law clk. to Hon. C. S. Fisher, judge Dist. N.J., 1971-72; atty. criminal div. Atty. Gen.'s Office, State of N.H., Concord, 1972-73, asst. atty. gen., Concord, 1973-76, dep. atty. gen., 1976-78, atty. gen., 1978—; mem. N.H. Gov.'s Commn. on Crime and Delinquency; mem. N.H. Supreme Ct. Com. on Character and Fitness; mem. Jud. Planning Com.; mem. Police Standards and Tng. Council. Mem. adv. council N.H. Sudden Infant Death Syndrome Project; bd. dirs. Friends Program, Concord. Mem. N.H. Bar Assn., Nat. Assn. Attys. Gen. Roman Catholic. Club: Merrimack County (N.H.) Dartmouth Alumni. Home: 120 Franklin St Concord NH 03301 Office: 25 Capitol St Concord NH 03301

RATLIFF, GERALD LEE, educator, lit. critic; b. Middletown, Ohio, Oct. 23, 1944; s. Frank Henry and Peggy Jane (Ratliff) Donisi; B.A. magna cum laude, Georgetown Coll., 1967; M.A., U. Cin., 1969; Ph.D., Bowling Green U., 1975. Instr. English and theatre Glenville (W.Va.) State Coll., 1970-72; lectr. theatre history Bowling Green State (Ohio) U., 1972-75; asst. prof. drama Montclair (N.J.) State Coll., 1975—. Recipient Poetry Congress Achievement award, 1968, Promethean Lamp prize El Camino Poets, 1965. Fellow Internat. Acad. Poets; mem. Speech and Theatre Assn. N.J. (sec.), Ohio Community (dir. 1972-73), Am. theatre assns., Speech Communication Assn. (state adv. council), W.Va. Assn. Speech (chmn. 1971-72), Am. Poetry Congress, Phi Kappa Phi, Alpha Psi Omega (v.p. 1965—), Alpha Phi Gamma (pres. 1966—), Pi Kappa

Delta, Sigma Tau Delta (La Plume prize 1967), Phi Alpha Theta. Club: Kiwanis. Feature writer of Lexington (Ky.) Herald-Leader, 1968-69; asst. editor W.Va. Speech Directory, 1969-70. Contbr. to New Voices in American Poetry, 1978. Home: 89 Clinton Ave Montclair NJ 07042 Office: Dept Speech/Theatre Montclair State Coll Montclair NJ 07043

RATNER, HAROLD, pediatrician; b. Bklyn., June 19, 1927; s. George and Bertha (Silverman) R.; B.S., Coll. City N.Y., 1948; M.D., Chgo. Med. Sch., 1952; m. Lillian Gross, Feb. 4, 1961; children—Sanford Miles, Marcia Ellen. Intern, Jewish Hosp., Med. Center Bklyn., 1952-53, resident in pediatrics, 1953-55; practice medicine specializing in pediatrics, Bklyn.; clin. instr. pediatrics State U. N.Y. Downstate Med. Center, N.Y.C., 1955-67, clin. asst. prof., 1967-69, clin. asso. prof., 1969—; chief of pediatrics Greenpoint Hosp., Bklyn., 1967—, pres. med. staff, 1970-71, 74-78; mem. adv. council to pres. N.Y.C. Health and Hosp. Corp., 1970-71, 74-76, sec., 1975, v.p., 1976-78; mem. med. bd., dir. Camp Sussex, camp for underprivileged children; bd. dirs. Kings County Health Care Rev. Orgn., Bklyn., 1976—, also co-chmn. hosp. rev. com., continuing med. edn., med. care evaluation com. Served with AUS, 1945-47. Diplomate Nat. Bd. Med. Examiners, Am. Bd. Pediatrics. Fellow Am., Bklyn. acads. pediatrics, Kings County Med. Soc. (pediatrics sect.), Royal Soc. Health; mem. AMA, N.Y. State, Kings County, Pan-Am. med. socs. Democrat. Jewish. Contbr. articles on pediatrics to med. jours. Home: 55 Bluebird Dr Great Neck NY 11023 Office: 300 Skillman Ave Brooklyn NY 11211

RATNER, LILLIAN GROSS (MRS. HAROLD RATNER), psychiatrist; b. N.Y.C., Aug. 18, 1932; d. Herman and Sarah (Widelitz) Gross; B.A., Barnard Coll., 1953; postgrad. U. Lausanne (Switzerland), 1954-56; M.D., Duke U., 1959; m. Harold Ratner, Feb. 4, 1961; children—Sanford Miles, Marcia Ellen. Intern, Kings County Hosp., Bklyn., 1959-60, resident, 1967-70, fellow in child psychiatry, 1969-70, psychiatrist devel. evaluation clinic, 1970-72; resident Jewish Hosp. Bklyn., 1960-62, fellow in pediatric psychiatry, 1962-63; physician in charge pediatric psychiatric clinic Greenpoint (N.Y.) Hosp., 1964-67; pvt. practice psychiatry, Great Neck, N.Y., 1970—. Clin. instr. psychiatry Downstate Med. Center, Bklyn., 1970-74, clin. asst. prof., 1974—; psychiatric cons. N.Y.C. Bd. Edn., 1972-75; psychiat. cons. Creedmore Hosp., 1975—; mem. med. bd. Camp Sussex, Sussex, N.J. 1963—. Diplomate Am. Bd. Pediatrics, Am. Bd. Psychiatry and Neurology, Am. Bd. Child Psychiatry. Fellow Am., Bklyn. acads. pediatrics, Am. Acad. Child Psychiatry; mem. Am., Nassau, Bklyn. psychiat. assns., Bklyn. Pediatric Soc. (sr. mem.), AMA, N.Y., Nassau County med. socs. Home and office: 55 Bluebird Dr Great Neck NY 11023

RAUCH, ARTHUR IRVING, investment analyst; b. N.Y.C., Sept. 18, 1933; s. David and Miriam (Frankel) R.; B.A. magna cum laude (Rufus Choate Scholar), Dartmouth, 1954, M.S., Amos Tuck Sch. Bus. Adminstrn., 1955; m. Roxane M. Spiller, Aug. 19, 1962 (div. Sept. 1977); children—David S., Janine B. Security analyst Lionel D. Edie & Co., N.Y.C., 1959-64; group dir. research Eastman Dillon, Union Securities & Co., N.Y.C., 1964-68; v.p., sr. analyst Laird, Inc., N.Y.C., 1968-69, dir. research, 1969-71, sr. v.p., dir., 1971-73; partner Oppenheimer & Co., N.Y.C., 1973-77; v.p. corp. devel. Rorer Group Inc., Ft. Washington, Pa., 1977—. Exec. com. Dartmouth Class of 1954, 1968—; bd. dirs. Schuster Fund, 1968-69. Served to lt. (j.g.), USNR, 1956-59. C.F.A. Mem. N.Y. Soc. Security Analysts, Fin. Analysts Fedn., Assn. Corporate Growth. Phi Beta Kappa. Home: 116 Cheshire Dr Penllyn PA 19422 Office: 500 Virginia Dr Fort Washington PA 19034

RAUCHER, HERMAN, novelist, screen writer; b. Bklyn., Apr. 13, 1928; s. Benjamin Brooks and Sophie (Weinshank) R.; B.S., N.Y. U., 1949; m. Mary Kathryn Martinet, Apr. 20, 1960; children—Jacqueline Leigh, Jennifer Brooke. Asst. trade ad mgr. 20th Century Fox Films, N.Y.C., 1950-54; copy dir. Walt Disney Studios, N.Y.C.; copy supr. Calkins & Holden Advt., N.Y.C., 1955-57; copy dir., v.p., dir. Reach McClinton Advt., N.Y.C., 1957-63; v.p., creative dir. Maxon Advt., N.Y.C., 1963-64; creative supr. Gardner Advt., N.Y.C., 1963-65; v.p. advt., cons. Benton & Bowles Advt., N.Y.C., 1965-67; author: Summer of 42 (novel and screenplay), Watermelon Man (novel and screenplay), Ode to Billy Joe (novel and screenplay), A Glimpse of Tiger (novel), Sweet November (screenplay), Class of 44 (screenplay), Hieronymus Merkin (screenplay), The Other Side of Midnight (screenplay), There Should Have Been Castles (novel and screenplay), 1978; writer of various dramas appearing on TV in Studio One, Alcoa Hour and Goodyear Playhouse; pres. Bearfilm Prodns., 1971—. Served with AUS, 1950-52. Mem. Writers Guild Am., Authors League Am., Dramatists Guild, Acad. of Motion Picture Arts and Scis.

RAUSCHER, NORMAN EARL, newspaper editor; b. Bklyn., Aug. 15, 1926; s. John J. and Ada Williams (Burns) R.; student Fairleigh Dickinson U., 1964-65; m. Hannah Buxenbaum, May 14, 1952. Reporter, Woodhaven (N.Y.) Leader Observer; editor Richmond Hill Record, Richmond Hill, N.Y., 1946-47, Saint Albans (N.Y.) Life, 1947-52; advt. dir. Forest Hills (N.Y.) Post, 1953-56; editor Summit (N.J.) Herald, 1956—; guest lectr. Summit High Sch., 1970; mem. adv. bd. Summit Fed. Savs. & Loan Assn., 1972—. Chmn. United Way of Summit, 1974-75; pres. Summit Camp Fund, 1959—; pres. bd. mgrs. John E. Runnells Hosp., 1975—; mem. adv. bd. Fair Oaks Hosp., 1976—; bd. dirs. Summit Civic Found., N.J. State Opera, Summit Com. on Drug Abuse, N.J. Arthritis Found. Recipient Americanism award B'nai B'rith, 1975, Service award Union County Bd. of Freeholders, 1975; Prentice Hall scholar, 1964. Mem. N.J. Press Assn., Sigma Delta Chi. Republican. Home: 5 Midland Terr Summit NJ 07901 Office: 22 Bank St Summit NJ 07901

RAUSEN, AARON REUBEN, pediatrician, hematologist; b. Jersey City, June 30, 1930; s. David and Ruth (Schwartz) R.; student Dartmouth, 1947-50; M.D., State U. N.Y., 1954; m. Emalou Watkins Apr. 7, 1968; children—David Jacob, Susan Dinah, Elisabeth Ann. Intern, Bellevue Med. Center, N.Y.C., 1954-55, asst. resident in pediatrics, 1955-56; chief resident in pediatrics Mt. Sinai Hosp., N.Y.C., 1958-59; fellow in pediat. hematology Children's Hosp., Center, Boston, 1959-61; clin. asst. in pediatrics Mt. Sinai Hosp., N.Y.C., 1961-62, attending pediatrician, 1971—; acting chief Greenpoint Hosp., Bklyn., 1962-63, chief pediatrician, 1963-64; chief pediatrician Elmhurst Hosp., Queens, N.Y., 1964-73; dir. pediatrics Beth Israel Med. Center, N.Y.C., 1973—; asso. prof. pediatrics Mt. Sinai Sch. Medicine, N.Y.C., 1966-72, prof., 1972—; cons. in pediatric hematology Beekman Downtown Hosp., N.Y.C., also USPHS Hosp., S. I., N.Y., Hackensack (N.J.) Hosp.; vis. physician Rockefeller U. Hosp. Served to capt. M.C., AUS, 1956-58. USPHS fellow in pediatric hematology, 1959-61. Diplomate Am. Bd. Pediatrics with subsplty. in pediatric hematology and oncology. Mem. Am. Pediat. Soc., Am. Hematology Soc., Am. Assn. Cancer Research, Am. Soc. Clin. Oncology, Am. Acad. Pediatrics, N.Y. Acad. Medicine, Harvey Soc. Jewish. Contbr. articles to profl. jours. Home: 1370 Pleasant Pl Hewlett Harbor NY 11557 Office: Dept Pediatrics Beth Israel Medical Center New York City NY 10003

RAUTH, DAVID ROBERT, elec. and nuclear engr.; b. Plainfield, N.J., Sept. 29, 1937; s. Edwin Henry and Ethel (Watson) R.; B.S. in Elec. Engring., Rutgers U., 1962; M.S. in Nuclear Engring., N.Y. U., 1966; m. Margaret Ann Vreeland, July 6, 1963; children—J. Theodore, D. Thomas, Nancy Jo. Research engr. Columbia U., N.Y.C., 1962-67; sr. scientist Bettis Atomic Power Lab., W. Mifflin, Pa., 1967-77; sr. engr. plant apparatus div. Westinghouse Electric Co., Pitts., 1977—; tchr. reliability theory and application; cons. reliability application. Served with USN, 1955-58. Mem. Am. Nuclear Soc. Republican. Methodist. Home: 1419 Highland Villa Dr Pittsburgh PA 15234 Office: 500 Penn Center Blvd Bldg 5 Pittsburgh PA 15235

RAVEN, RONALD JACOB, educator; b. San Francisco, Jan. 7, 1935; s. Jacob and Ella (O'Connor) R.; B.S. in Biology, U. San Francisco, 1956; M.A. in Biology, San Francisco State Coll., 1960; Ed.D., U. Calif. at Berkeley, 1965; m. Cynthia Opacinch, May 27, 1967; children—Michael, Julie Lynn. Mem. faculty State U. N.Y. at Buffalo, 1965—, prof. ednl. research; vis. prof. U. Calif. at Berkeley, 1968, U. Toronto, 1970, U. Iowa, 1973, Universidade Fed. de Minas Gerais, Brazil, 1976; cons. Nat. Assessment of Edn. Progress-Sci., 1967-72, Brazilian Ministry Edn., Ednl. Testing Service, NSF. Served to 1st lt. AUS, 1957-58. Fellow AAAS; mem. Am. Ednl. Research Assn., Nat. Assn. Research in Sci. Teaching (dir.), Assn. Edn. of Tchrs. of Sci. (dir.). Author: Raven Test of Logical Operations; Raven Content Comprehension Test; asso. editor Sci. Edn., 1972-75; contbr. articles to profl. jours.; editorial bd. Jour. Research in Sci. Teaching, 1968—. Home: 53 Wellingwood Dr Amherst NY 14051 Office: Faculty Ednl Studies State U NY Buffalo NY 14214

RAWDON, ALBERT HENRY, JR., mech. engr.; b. Worcester, Mass., Apr. 26, 1923; s. Albert Henry and Blanche Anna (Trahant) R.; B.M.E., Worcester Poly. Inst., 1947, M.M.E., 1961; m. Constance Y. Paul, Oct. 16, 1948; children—Sherrie Ann, Dana Paul. Machine designer U.S. Envelope Co., Worcester, 1947; design engr. Riley Stoker Corp., Worcester, 1948-60, dept. mgr., 1965-78, dir. research and devel., 1978—; sr. engr. Arthur D. Little, Cambridge, Mass., 1960-65. Edn. officer Worcester County Power Squadron, 1977. Served in USNR, 1942-46; PTO. Registered profl. engr., Mass. Mem. ASME (chpt. v.p. 1977), Worcester Engring. Soc. (chmn. awards 1975), Combustion Inst., Air Pollution Control Assn. Roman Catholic. Patentee in field (5). Contbr. chpt. to Energy, 1977. Home: 11 Park St W Shrewsbury MA 01545 Office: 9 Neponset St Worcester MA 01613

RAWLINGS, ROBERT LEE, JR., mental health specialist; b. Weldon, N.C., Mar. 3, 1938; s. Robert Lee and Rosa Lee (Williams) R.; B.S., N.C. A. and T. U., 1962; M.Ed., U. Md., 1972; m. Pecolia Ann Togans, July 5, 1962; children—Linda, Renee, Cynthia. Tchr. indsl. arts Otisville (N.Y.) State Tng. Sch., 1962; vocat. rehab. specialist D.C. Vocat. Rehab. Adminstrn., 1969-72; counselor Mental Health Adminstrn., 1972—. Served with U.S. Army, 1963-66. Mem. Nat. Rehab. Assn., Am. Personnel and Guidance Assn. Democrat. Baptist (deacon 1967—, Sunday sch. tchr.). Home: 2024 Colebrooke Dr Hillcrest Heights MD 20031

RAWLS, WALTON HENDRY, editor; b. Charleston, S.C., May 28, 1933; s. Lucian Russell and Mary Louise (Hendry) R.; B.A., Harvard, 1955; postgrad. U. S.C., 1955-56, N.Y. U. and New Sch. for Social Research, 1961-65; m. Mary Jane Harley, Feb. 14, 1965 (dec. Dec. 1970); 1 dau., Anna Harley. Editorial trainee Charles E. Tuttle Co., Tokyo, Japan, 1958, sales promotion mgr., Rutland, Vt., 1958-60; dir. advt. and promotion Twayne Pubs., N.Y.C., 1961-66; editor McGraw-Hill Book Co., N.Y.C., 1966-70, editor-in-chief Art And Illustrated Books, N.Y.C., 1970-73; pres. Rawls & Moskof, Inc., N.Y.C., 1974-77; sr. editor Harry N. Abrams Inc., N.Y.C., 1977—. Served with AUS, 1956-58. Club: Harvard (N.Y.C.). Editor: The Century Book L.I. Hist. Soc., 1964. Home: 176 8th Ave Brooklyn NY 11215 Office: 110 E 59th St New York City NY 10022

RAWLS, WENDELL LEE, JR., journalist; b. Goodlettsville, Tenn., Aug. 18, 1941; s. Wendell Lee and Madolyn (Murphy) P.; B.A., Vanderbilt U., 1970; m. Kathryn Coston Stark, June 19, 1971; children—Amanda Coston, Matthew Bradley. Reporter, Nashville Tennessean, 1967-72, Phila. Inquirer, 1972-77; investigative reporter N.Y. Times, Washington, 1977—. Served with U.S. Army, 1965. Recipient Pulitizer prize for reporting, 1977; Robert F. Kennedy Journalism award, 1977; Nat. Headliner award, 1977; Heywood Broun award, 1977; Clarion award, 1977; Keystone Press award, 1975; Thomas L. Stokes spl. citation, 1975; AP Mng. Editors award, 1977; Sigma Delta Chi Regional award, 1977; Pa. Prison Soc. award, 1977; Media award Nat. Mental Health Assn., 1977. Mem. Alpha Tau Omega. Methodist. Home: 3800 Mode St Fairfax VA 22031 Office: 1920 L St NW Washington DC 20036

RAWSON, ARLINE FRANCES, former dietitian; b. Framingham, Mass., Oct. 10, 1916; d. Samuel and Grace A. (Wiggin) Crown; B.S. in Edn., Framingham Tchrs. Coll., 1939; m. William Otis Rawson, Oct. 11, 1975. Dietician, Boston Young Men's Christian Union, summers 1937, 38, 39, 40, Portsmouth (N.H.) Hosp., 1941-52, 59-76, Huggins Hosp., Wolfeboro, N.H., 1952-59; tchr. home econs. and sewing evening div. Portsmouth High Sch., 1969-72. Mem. Am. Soc. for Hosp. Food Service Adminstrs., N.H. Deitetic Assn., Mass. Hosp. Food Service Dirs. Assn. Republican. Mem. Congregational Ch. Editor, Portsmouth Herald Cookbook, 1970-71. Address: 284 Grove Rd Rye NH 03870

RAY, AJIT KUMAR, educator; b. Calcutta, India, Feb. 1, 1925; s. Jyotish Chandra and Kiron (Moyee) R.; immigrated to Can., 1960, naturalized, 1968; B.Sc. with honors (Asutosh Meml. scholar 1943), Calcutta U., 1944, M.Sc. (Gold medal, Univ. prize 1947), 1947; D.Sc. in Math. (Alexander von Humboldt scholar 1953-54, Calcutta U. Spl. Fgn. scholar 1954), U. Göttingen (Ger.), 1955; m. Ratna Ray, Aug. 12, 1956; children—Arindam, Leena. Prof. applied math. Austosh Coll., Calcutta U., 1948-55; reader aero. engring. Indian Inst. Sci., Bangalore, 1956-60; asso. research officer Nat. Aero. Establishment/NRC Can., Ottawa, 1960-64; research scientist, math. adviser telecommunications div. Canadian Transp. Dept., 1964-65; asst. prof. Clarkson Coll. Tech., Potsdam, N.Y., 1965-66; mem. faculty U. Ottawa (Can.), 1966—, prof. applied math., dir. research, 1975—. Fellow U.K. Inst. Math. and Applications, AAAS, Royal Aero. Soc.; asso. fellow Am. Inst. Aeros. and Astronautics; mem. Soc. Indsl. and Applied Math., Am. Math. Soc., N.Y. Acad. Scis., Canadian Math. Congress; fgn. mem. Indian Sci. Congress (life). Contbr. articles to profl. jours. Address: #1601 Cross-Winds 641 Bathgate Dr Ottawa ON K1K 3Y3 Canada Office: 585 King Edward Ave Room 202 Ottawa ON K1N 9B5 Canada

RAY, GEORGE W(ASHINGTON), JR., lawyer; b. Cripple Creek, Colo., Mar. 23, 1898; s. George Washington and Esther Livona (Magee) R.; A.B. U. Tex., 1920; J.D., M.A., Columbia, 1922; LL.D., Piedmont, 1969; m. Belle Trimble, Sept. 18, 1923; children—George Carleton, Nancy Trimble; m. 2d Bonnie Dowd Van Dyk, Aug. 31, 1946; children—James Van Dyk, Bonnie Van Dyk. Admitted to N.Y. bar, 1923, U.S. Supreme Ct. bar, 1933, Conn. bar, 1963, Vt. bar, 1968; mem. legislative drafting research bur. Columbia, 1921-22; prosecuted claims by U.S. on behalf of Am. nationals against Germany, before Mixed Claims Commn., U.S. and Germany, 1922-24; counsel Tex. Co., 1922-42, gen. atty., 1942-47; gen. counsel Arabian Am. Oil Co., Trans Arabian Pipe Line Co., Aramco Overseas Co., 1947-61, internat. arbitration between Royal Govt. Saudi Arabia and Arabian Am. Oil Co., 1954-58. Chmn. adv. bd. and exec. com. Internat. Oil and Gas Ednl. Center, 1959-62, Southwestern Legal Found.; chmn. adv. bd. and exec. com. Internat. Comparative Law Center, 1962-66, mem. adv. bd., 1962—; counsel Black & Plante, White River Jct., 1968—. Served with Air Flying Corps, USNR, 1918-22. Mem. Assn. Bar N.Y.C., Am., Vt. bar assns., Acad. Polit. Sci., Am. Acad. Polit. and Social Sci., (dir. N.A.M. 1960-62, chmn. internat. econ. affairs com. 1960-61), Council on Fgn. Relations, Kappa Alpha, Phi Delta Phi. Republican. Conglist. Club: University (N.Y.C.). Author: The Law Governing Contracts between States and Foreign Nationals, 1960; Law and the Perfecting Process, 1964; numerous articles. Home: RD 1 East Thetford VT 05043 Office: 24 N Main St White River Junction VT 05001

RAY, GORDON THOMPSON, utility exec.; b. N.Y.C., Jan. 31, 1928; s. John Henry and Hama Thompson (Potter) R.; B.E.E., Rensselaer Poly. Inst., 1954; children—Stuart John. With The Bell System, various locations, 1954—; successively engr., chief engr. N.Y. Telephone, Albany, Utica, Jamaica, Bklyn., White Plains, now asst. v.p. planning; mem. tech. staff Bell Telephone Labs., N.Y.C., Murray Hill and Holmdel, N.J.; engr. AT&T, N.Y.C.: asst. v.p. long range planning N.Y. Telephone, N.Y.C., also dir. Bell System Computer Seminar, del. Body Planning Internat. Direct Distance Dialing. Chmn. bd. trustees N. Chatham (N.Y.) Methodist Ch. Served with U.S. Army, 1946-49. Mem. Nat. Soc. Profl. Engrs. (sr. mem.), IEEE (sr. mem.), Nat., Regional planning assns., Assn. Computer Machinery, N. Am. Soc. Corp. Planning, Armed Forces Communications and Electronics Assn., Am. Mgmt. Assn., AAAS. Office: 1250 Broadway 36th floor New York City NY 10001

RAY, WILLIAM F., banker; b. Cin., Sept. 17, 1915; s. William F. and Adele (Daller) R.; A.B., U. Cin., 1935; M.B.A., Harvard, 1937; m. Helen Payne, 1939; children—Katharine (Mrs. Robert Sturgis), Barbara (Mrs. Jerald Stevens), Mary (Mrs. Harvey Struthers, Jr.), Margaret (Mrs. Thomas Gilbert), Deborah, William F. III, Susan. With Brown Bros. Harriman & Co., 1937—, asst. mgr., 1944-49, mgr., Boston, 1950-67, partner N.Y.C., 1968—; trustee Atlantic Mut. Ins. Co., N.Y.C.; dir. Centennial Ins. Co., N.Y.C. Vice pres., bd. dirs. Robert Brunner Found.; bd. dirs. Downtown-Lower Manhattan Assn., Inc. Mem. Bankers Assn. for Fgn. Trade (pres. 1966-67), Harvard Bus. Sch. Assn. (pres. 1963-64, exec. council), Robert Morris Assos. (pres. N.E. 1962-63), Pan Am. Soc. U.S., Am. Australian Assn. (dir., v.p.), Pilgrims of U.S., Phi Beta Kappa. Republican. Clubs: Skating (pres. 1956-58) (Boston); Country (Brookline, Mass.); Harvard, Union, India House, Links Golf (N.Y.C.); Apawamis (Rye, N.Y.); Woods Hole Golf (Mass.); Ardsley (N.Y.) Curling. Home: 1 East End Ave New York City NY 10021 Office: 59 Wall St New York City NY 10005

RAYBURN, CAROLE ANN (MS. RONALD ALLEN RAYBURN), clin. psychologist; b. Washington, Feb. 14, 1938; d. Carl Frederick and Mary Helen (Milkie) Miller; B.A., Am. U., 1961; M.A., George Washington U., 1965; Ph.D., Catholic U. Am., 1969; m. Ronald Allen Rayburn, June 18, 1964 (dec.). Clin. psychology extern D.C. Gen. Hosp., 1962-63; clin. psychologist Spring Grove State Hosp., Catonsville, Md., 1966-68; research psychologist Regional Med. Services of Washington, also lectr. psychology Strayer Coll., Washington, 1969-70; clin. psychologist, instl. care services div. D.C. Children's Center, Laurel, Md., 1970-78. Cons. psychologist for community psychologists, Washington and Md., 1966—; psychotherapist, Silver Spring, Md., 1971—; cons. psychologist Julia Brown Montessori Sch., Laurel and Columbia, Md., 1970-76; lectr. psychology and assertiveness tng. Mem. Tamarack Triangle Civic Assn., Silver Spring, 1973—. Fellow Md. Psychol. Assn. (mem. ethics and profl. standards com. 1973-74, chmn. pub. info. 1974-75, co-chmn. liaison with other profl. groups 1974-75, editor newsletter 1975-76, liaison with Com. on Women in Psychology 1975-77, with Assn. Advancement Psychology 1976-78, mem.-at-large 1976-78; Recognition award 1978), Am. Orthopsychiat. Assn.; mem. Am. (chmn. com. on equal rights and affirmative action div. clin. psychology 1978—, membership chmn. div. child and youth services 1977-78), D.C. (community affairs com. 1971-72; Recognition award 1974) psychol. assns., Am., D.C. (mem. task forces on use of drugs, monitoring and evaluation of health programs, instl. care children and adults 1973-75) pub. health assns., Assn. for Advancement Psychologists, Montgomery County Mental Assn., AAAS, Council Advancement of Psychol. Professions and Scis. (state chmn., bd. govs., mem. fin. com. 1974-76), Balt. Assn. Cons. Psychologists (pres. 1976-78), Internat. Council Psychologists, Internat. Assn. Applied Psychology, Psi Chi. Seventh-Day Adventist (asst. chairperson community services 1973-74, health com. 1974-75, bd. counselors to youth 1974-75). Home: 1200 Morningside Dr Silver Spring MD 20904 Office: Institutional Care Services Div Laurel MD 20810

RAYBURN, JOHN WILLIAM, coll. dean; b. Eau Claire, Wis., May 19, 1928; s. J.A. and E.E. (Jaquish) R.; B.S., U. Wis., 1950; M.A., Columbia U., 1957, Ph.D., 1961. Dir. music, pub. schs., Wis., Mich., Mo., N.Y., 1950-65; concert accompanist for leading artists, 1957-75; condr. Gen. Motors Chorus of N.Y., 1973-76; mem. faculty Mercy Coll., Dobbs Ferry, N.Y., 1961—, dean dept. music and fine arts, 1961—; appearances as concert soloist or accompanist include: Town Hall, Avery Fisher Hall, Carnegie Hall, Old Met. Opera; dir. music St. Margaret's Ch., Riverdale, N.Y., 1968—, founder, condr. Riverdale Singers, 1970—. Recipient citations from various community and civic groups. Mem. Coll. Music Soc., Music Educator Nat. Conf., AAUP, Nat. Assn. for Lit. and Arts. Author: Gregorian Chant, A History of the Controversy Concerning Its Rhythm, 1964; Artistic Choral Singing, 1970. Home: 2390 Palisade Ave Riverdale NY 10463 Office: Mercy Coll 555 Broadway Dobbs Ferry NY 10522

RAYMAN, JACK RICHARD, psychologist; b. Elberon, Iowa, Sept. 19, 1944; s. Robert John and Harriet Norma (Olsen) R.; B.S., Iowa State U., 1967; Ph.D., U. Iowa, 1974; m. Barbara Kay Blakeslee, Aug. 20, 1967; 1 dau., Jamie Beth. Peace Corps vol., tutor Rajang Tchrs. Coll., Binatang, Sarawak, Malaysia, 1967-70; research asst. Am. Coll. Testing Program, Iowa City, 1971-73; career adviser, career planning and placement office U. Iowa, Iowa City, 1973-74; asst. prof. research, dir. coll. level devel. Project Discover, Western Md. Coll., Westminster, Md., 1974—. Sec.-treas., Discover Found. Inc., 1976—. Mem. Am. Psychol. Assn., Am. Personnel and Guidance Assn., Assn. Measurement and Evaluation in Guidance, Am. Coll. Personnel Assn. Author: (with F. Harcleroad and C.T. Molen) The Regional State Colleges and Universities Enter the 1970s, 1973. Contbr. articles to profl. publs. Home: 610 Gist Rd Westminster MD 21157

RAYMENT, WILLIAM FRANCIS, bus. exec.; b. Taunton, Mass., May 26, 1904; s. William Albert and Loraine (Campbell) R.; m. Kathrine M. Goggin, June 22, 1929; children—Donald W., Wilma M., Paul J., Susan K. Exec. v.p. New Eng. Brass Co., Taunton, Mass.; pres., dir. Weir Coop. Bank. Mem. Selective Service Adv. Bd., 1940-45. Mem. Taunton C. of C. (past v.p.). Clubs: Wlks, Masons. Home: 3 Monica St Taunton MA 02780

RAYMOND, BRUCE ALLEN, thoracic and cardiovascular surgeon; b. Aberdeen, S.D., Dec. 8, 1924; s. Samuel A. and Pearl Adele (Blackstone) R.; student Stanford U., 1943-44; B.S., U. S.D., 1946; M.D., Washington U., St. Louis, 1949; m. Virginia Stratmann, Apr. 2, 1948 (div.); children—Judith Ann Raymond Hultquist, Jacqueline Marie, Bruce Allen, Brian Andrew; m. 2d, Jane Molnar, Nov. 15, 1969; children—Douglas A., Andrew D. Intern, U. Oreg. Med. Schs. Hosp., 1949-50; commd. 1st lt. U.S. Army, 1949, advanced through grades to col., 1967; resident surgery Walter Reed Gen. Hosp., Washington, 1953-57, resident thoracic surgery, 1957-59, asst. chief thoracic surgery, 1959-60; chief thoracic surgery Letterman Gen. Hosp., San Francisco, 1960-64; chief thoracic surgery, asst. chief dept. surgery Fitzsimmons Gen. Hosp., Denver, 1967-69, chief dept. surgery, 1969-71; cons. thoracic surgery Surgeon, U.S. Army, Europe, 1964-67; chief surg. cons. U.S. Army, Vietnam, cons. thoracic surgery, Thailand, Japan, Okinawa, 1971-72; dir. div. profl. support services Am. Hosp. Assn., Chgo., 1973-74; asst. clin. prof. surgery U. Colo. Med. Sch., 1967-71; asso. clin. prof. surgery Northwestern U. Sch. Medicine, Chgo., 1973-75; practice medicine specializing in thoracic surgery, partner R.I. Cardiothoracic and Vascular Assos., Ltd., Warwick, 1975—; mem. staff Kent County Meml. Hosp., Warwick, Miriam Hosp., Providence, Roger Williams Gen. Hosp., Providence; mem. steering com. Inter-Soc. Commn. for Heart Disease Resources, 1973-74; mem. Nat. Commn. on Certification on Physicians' Assts., 1973-74; mem. Adv. Com. for Accreditation of Respiratory Therapists, 1973-74. Decorated Legion of Merit. Diplomate Am. Bd. Surgery, Am. Bd. Thoracic Surgery. Fellow A.C.S., Am. Coll. Cardiology, Am. Coll. Chest Physicians; mem. AMA, Soc. Thoracic Surgeons, Assn. Mil. Surgeons, Am. Assn. Med. Instrumentation, Phi Delta Theta, Nu Sigma Nu. Republican. Presbyterian. Contbr. articles to profl. jours.

RAYMOND, JUDITH ELLEN, advt. exec.; b. N.Y.C., Oct. 21, 1946; d. Ben and Katherine Rita Raymond; A.S., Fashion Inst. Tech., N.Y.C., 1967. Account exec. Eleanor Lambert Inc., N.Y.C., 1967-69; pub. relations exec. Essie Pinsker, Inc., N.Y.C., 1969-71; with Butterick Fashion Mktg. Co., N.Y.C., 1971-73, publicity coordinator, dir. advt. and promotion, 1973-75, v.p. advt., promotion and market services, 1975—. Recipient citation Art Dirs. Club, 1974, Copy Club, N.Y.C., 1974. Mem. Pub. Relations Soc. Am., Advt. Women N.Y., Publicity Club N.Y. Home: 411 Bronx River Rd Yonkers NY 10704 Office: 161 6th Ave New York City NY 10013

RAYMUNDO, SEVERINO ANTONIO, plant pathologist; b. Laoag, Philippines, Nov. 6, 1936; s. Antioco Daquioag and Maria (Antonio) R.; came to U.S., 1968; B.S., U. Philippines, Quezon City, 1959, M.S., 1967; Ph.D., Okla. State U., 1972; m. June 27, 1964; 1 son, Jose Rey. Tech. researcher Philippines Bur. Plant Industry, Manila, 1959-61; research asst. instr. to research instr. agr. U. Philippines, Laguna, 1960-68; asst. scientist plant pathology Internat. Inst. Tropical Agr., Rokupr, Sierra Leone, 1974—; research scholar Internat. Rice Research Inst., 1966-67. Mem. Am., Philippine phytopath. socs., Internat. Soc. Plant Pathologists, Sierra Leone Agrl. Soc., Sigma Xi, Phi Sigma. Roman Catholic. Contbr. articles to profl. jours. Home: 210 Oak St Toronto ON M5A 2C9 Canada Office: Internat Inst Tropical Agr Rice Research Sta Rokupr Sierra Leone

RAYNOR, WILFRED LOUIS, real estate broker; b. Warwick, N.Y., Feb. 25, 1897; s. Fred Cary and Lucy May (Smith) R.; student Cornell U., 1916, Rohs Inst. Real Estate Appraisal, 1951, Orange County Community Coll., 1952-53, Mich. State U., 1955; m. Dorothy Dunton Richards, June 19, 1919; 1 son, Wilfred Louis. With Raynor's Market, 1919-50; owner W.L. Raynor Inc., Warwick, N.Y., 1951—. Pres., Orange County Bd. Realtors, 1965. Founding mem. Warwick Humane Soc., 1955—; commr., treas. Orange County Airport, 1964—; mem. Orange County Farm Bur. and Extension Service, 1935—, Future Farmer Found., 1955—; mem. adv. bd. Warwick Valley Central Sch., 1965—. Pres., Republican Citizens Club Orange County, 1968-69. Named Outstanding Realtor of Year, Orange County Bd. Realtors, 1966; Nat. Farm and Land Broker, Nat. Inst. Farm and Land Brokers, 1967. Mem. Orange County Bd. Realtors (hon. life), Nat. Assn. Real Estate Bds., Orange County Soc. Real Estate Appraisers (pres. Mid-Hudson chpt. 1967), Warwick C. of C. (charter), Warwick Hist. Soc., Omega Tau Rho. Methodist. (trustee 1935-50). Mason, Rotarian. Club: Warwick Valley Country (Charter). Home: Hathorn Farm Hathorn Rd Warwick NY 10990 Office: 26 Main St Warwick NY 10990

RAZIN, ANDREW MICHAEL, clin. psychologist, psychiatrist; b. Boston, Aug. 10, 1945; s. Ishmael Wolf and Ann (Weingart) R.; A.B., Brown U., 1967; Ph.D. (USPHS fellow), Columbia U., 1972; M.D. (Rock Sleyster psychiatry scholar AMA), Albert Einstein Coll. Medicine, 1976; m. Hilary Jean Distler, Aug. 23, 1970. Postdoctoral fellow Yale U. Sch. Medicine, 1971-73; practice clin. psychology, Bronx, N.Y., 1973—; resident in dept. psychiatry Albert Einstein Coll. Medicine, Bronx, 1976-79, chief resident, 1978-79; tchr. psychology, psychiatry. Laughlin fellow Am. Coll. Psychiatrists, 1978; licensed clin. psychologist and physician, N.Y. Mem. Am. Psychol. Assn., Phi Beta Kappa, Sigma Xi. Author: Effective Psychotherapy, 1977; contbr. articles on psychotherapy and cardiology to profl. jours. Home: 1925 Eastchester Rd Bronx NY 10461

RAZON, BEN DAVID, med. center adminstr.; b. Pam Panga, Philippines, Feb. 19, 1937; s. Rafael Mesa and Segundina (David) R.; came to U.S., 1970, naturalized, 1976; B.B.A., U. of the East, Manila, 1958; m. Florferida A. Ancheta, June 6, 1965; children—Jonathan, JoAnne, Josephine. Fiscal accountant U.S. Naval Supply Depot, Subic Bay, Philippines, 1958-62; budget analyst, officer in charge of constrn. U.S. Naval Supply Depot, Subic Bay, 1962-65; accounting instr. Columbia Coll., Olongapo, Philippines, 1962-65; budget officer/mgr. cost and constrn. accounting Iligan Intergrated Steel Mills, Inc., Manila, 1965-70; accounting clk. Monsour Hosp. and Clinic, Jeannette, Pa., 1970-71, asst. to exec. v.p., 1971, v.p. fin., 1971-75, exec. v.p., 1975—; dir. Norwin Indsl. Devel. Corp., Irwin, Pa., 1977—. Bd. dirs. Westmoreland County Indsl. Devel. Authority, 1976—, Westmoreland Home Health Care Agy., 1977—. Mem. Hosp. Fin. Mgmt. Assn., Nat. Accountants Am., Hosp. Assn. Pa., C. of C. Roman Catholic. Club: Lions. Address: 7701 Kifer Ln North Huntington PA 15642

READ, GLORY MEEHAN (MRS. WILLIAM M. READ III), pub. relations exec.; b. Balt.; d. Michael Joseph and Margaret (Hill) Meehan; student Duke U., 1949; m. William M. Read III, Mar. 20, 1952; children—William M. IV, Philip Mark. Feature writer Herald-Sun Papers, Durham, N.C., 1949-51; writer, news bur. and pub. relations office Duke U., Durham, 1954-57; account exec. Pub. Relations Counsel, Inc., N.Y.C., 1958-63, v.p., 1963-67, pres., 1967—. Lectr. pub. relations at various univs.; newspaper columnist. Mem. Pub. Relations Soc. Am., Cosmetic Career Women. Author: New Hairstyle and Beauty Ideas, 1966. Home: 87 Anderson Dr Clifton NJ 08113 Office: 18 E 41st St New York City NY 10017

READER, GEORGE GORDON, physician; b. Bklyn., Feb. 8, 1919; s. Houston Parker and Marion (Payne) R.; B.A., Cornell U., 1940, M.D., 1943; m. Helen C. Brown, May 23, 1942; children—Jonathan, David, Mark, Peter. Intern medicine N.Y. Hosp., N.Y.C., 1944, research fellow medicine, 1946-47, asst. resident physician, 1948-49, dir. comprehensive care and teaching program, 1952-68, chief med. clinic, 1951-72, attending physician, 1962—; head div. ambulatory and community medicine N.Y. Hosp.-Cornell Med. Center, 1969-72; instr. medicine Cornell U., 1948-51, asst. prof., 1951-53, asso. prof., 1953-57, prof., 1957—, Livingston Farrand prof., chmn. dept. pub. health, 1972—. Chmn. human ecology study sect. NIH, 1961-65; chmn. med. adv. com. Union Family Med. Fund. of Hotel Industry of N.Y.C., 1964—; chmn. med. adv. com. Vis. Nurse Service N.Y., 1963—, bd. dirs. 1962—; trustee Cancer Care, 1957-76; mem. med. control bd. Health Ins. Plan of Greater N.Y., 1964—; bd. dirs. Winifred Masterson Burke Found., Westchester Community Health Plan, Miriam Osborn Home Assn., 1977—. Served as lt. USNR, 1944-46; PTO. Diplomate Am. Bd. Internal Medicine. Fellow A.C.P., Am. Pub. Health Assn. (governing council 1968-69, N.Y. Acad. Medicine (chmn. com. on med. edn. 1967-70, v.p. 1978), Am. Sociol. Assn., Am. Coll. Preventive Medicine; mem. AAAS, AMA, Assn. Am. Med. Colls., Harvey Soc., Internat. Sociol. Assn., N.Y. Acad. Scis., N.Y.C. Pub. Health Assn. (pres. 1956), Am. Geriatric Soc. (pres. 1969-70, chmn. bd. 1970-71), Internat. Epidemiol. Assn., Sigma Xi, Alpha Omega Alpha. Author: (with R. Merton and P. Kendall) The Student Physician, 1957; (with M.E.W. Goss) Comprehensive Medical Care and Teaching, 1967; (with M. Olendzki and C.H. Goodrich) Welfare Medical Care: An Experiment, 1969. Editor: Milbank Meml. Fund Quarterly, 1972-76; mem. editorial bd. Medical Care, 1967-70, Jour. Med. Edn., 1975—. Contbr. to publs. in field. Home: 155 Stuyvesant Ave Rye NY 10580 Office: 1300 York Ave New York City NY 10021

REAGAN, REGINALD LEE, biologist; b. Broadford, Pa., July 19, 1910; s. James Blaine and Helen (McLauquius) R.; Ph.D., U. Md., 1956; m. Marie Ann Johnson, Mar. 5, 1932; children—Nelda (Mrs. Dan Cullivan), Helen (Mrs. Bill Savage), Bill Olsen, Elsie (Mrs. Leo Sullivan). Joined U.S. Army, 1928, advanced through grades to maj., 1946; Rockefeller Found. Research asso. Rockefeller Inst., N.Y.C., 1936-40; faculty U. Md., College Park, 1946-61, asso. prof., 1948-52, prof. med. virology, 1952-61; chief virologist Jen-Son Lab., Kansas City, Mo., 1961-62; biologist Nat. Cancer Inst., Bethesda, Md., 1962—. Mem. N.Y. Acad. Sci., Soc. Exptl. Biology and Medicine, Electronmicroscopic Soc., Ret. Officers Assn., Soc. Clin. Pathologists, AAUP. Contbr. articles to profl. jours. Home: 8402 Piney Br Ct Silver Spring MD 20901 Office: Nat Cancer Inst NIH Bethesda MD 20901

REALS, JANICE LYNN, hosp. adminstr.; b. N.Y.C., May 14, 1946; d. Otto Peter and Ann Astolfi; B.B.A., U. Iowa, 1968; M.A., Rider Coll., 1978. Adminstrv., research asst. Internat. Dept. Shareholders Mgmt. Co., Boston, 1969-70; internal control supr. Equity Funding Corp., Los Angeles, 1970-71; dir. admissions Cooper Med. Center, Camden, N.J., 1971-73, dir. employee relations and personnel, 1973-77, v.p. for employee relations and personnel, 1977—; mem. Bur. Nat. Affairs Personnel Dirs. Forum, Washington. Mem. adv. council N.J. State Employment Service; mem. adv. council Camden County Adult Edn. Com. Mem. Am. Soc. Personnel Adminstrs., N.J. Soc. Hosp. Personnel Dirs. (pres. elect), Am. Soc. Hosp. Personnel Adminstrs. Home: 200 Locust St Philadelphia PA 19106 Office: Cooper Med Center 6th and Stevens Sts Camden NJ 08103

REARDON, DONALD THOMAS, fin. cons.; b. Irvington, N.J., Sept. 13, 1934; s. Paul and Marie Anne (Tears) R.; B.S. in Bus. Adminstrn., Seton Hall U., 1956; m. Marlene C. Golembeski, Feb. 8, 1958; children—Caryl Lynn, Donald Thomas, Suzanne, Patricia Anne, Jacqueline, Jennifer. Systems analyst Colonial Life Ins. Co., East Orange, N.J., 1958-61; dist. supr. systems reps. Burroughs Corp., N.Y.C., 1961-64; v.p. Bank N.Am., N.Y.C., 1964-67; v.p. Seamen's Bank for Savs., N.Y.C., 1967-72; exec. v.p. Carteret Savs. and Loan Assn., Newark, 1973-76; fin. cons., 1976-77; br. mgr. Datasaab Systems Inc. U.S., N.Y.C., 1977—. Served to lt. comdr. USCGR, 1956-57. Home: 5 Prince Rd East Brunswick NJ 08816 Office: 437 Madison Ave New York City NY 10022

REBALSKY, ROBERT SIDNEY, health facility adminstr.; b. Phila., Mar. 13, 1930; s. Frank and Rebecca R.; grad. Franklin Sch. of Sci. and Arts, 1949; student Temple U. Sch. Bus. and Public Adminstrn., 1953-54; m. Carolyn D'Ascanio, Sept. 30, 1967; children—Rebecca, Franklin, Emily, Gerard. Dir., Haverford Nursing & Rehab. Center, Havertown, Pa., 1967-71; exec. v.p. Leader Nursing Centers, Bryn Mawr, Pa., 1971-72; dir. communications Greater Del. Valley Regional Med. Program, Haverford, Pa., 1972-73; exec. dir. Saunders House, Phila., 1973—; instr. long term health care U. Del., 1978-79. Trustee Haverford State Hosp., 1975; alt. del. White House Conf. on Aging, Washington, 1971; chmn. State Govt. Service Program for Health, 1977; sr. committeemen 6th Ward Democrats, Radnor Twp., Delaware County, Pa., 1973; mem. exec. com. State Comprehensive Health Planning Agency, 1970-75. Served to 2d lt. CAP-Aux., USAF, 1953-56. Recipient Silver medal SAR, 1976; Freedoms Found. award, 1977. Fellow Royal Soc. Health (London), Am. Coll. Nursing Home Adminstrs.; mem. Am. Public Health Assn., Gerontol. Soc., Hist. Soc. Pa. Editor Elder Care, Jour. of Pa. Assn. Nursing & Convalescent Homes, 1969-71. Contbr. articles, book reviews to Jour. Am. Assn. Homes for the Aged, Jour. Long Term Care Adminstrn. Office: care Saunders House Lancaster and City Line Aves Philadelphia PA 19151

REBER, CARL ANTHONY, atmospheric physicist; b. Reading, Pa., Feb. 24, 1933; s. Carl Augustus and Anna Marie (Crist) R.; B.S., Pa. State U., 1955; Ph.D., U. Mich., 1973; m. Carol Marie Bauer, Aug. 25, 1972; children—Jan, Jill, Gregory, Stephen. Research asst. ionosphere research lab. Pa. State U., 1954-55; research and teaching asst. physics dept. U. Md., 1955-59; atmospheric physicist Goddard Space Flight Center, NASA, Greenbelt, Md., 1959—; mem. Com. Extension of U.S. Standard Atmosphere; mem. working group 4.A., upper atmosphere structure, com. space research Internat. Council Sci. Unions. NASA fellow, 1968-69; recipient Spl. Achievement award NASA/Goddard Space Flight Center, 1974, 77, 78. Mem. Am. Geophys. Union, Internat. Assn. Geomagnetism and Aeronomy, Smithsonian Assos., Sports Car Club Am., Porsche Club Am., Chi Phi, Alpha Nu. Contbr. articles to profl. jours. Home: 15400 Tindlay St Silver Spring MD 20904 Office: Stratosphere Physics and Chemistry Br Code 624 Goddard Space Flight Center Greenbelt MD 20771

REBUCK, ERNEST CHARLES, hydrologist; b. Klingerstown, Pa., Sept. 24, 1944; s. Ernest Guy and Rosie Merle (Dobson) R.; B.S. in Agrl. Engring., Pa. State U., 1966; M.S., 1967; Ph.D., U. Ariz., 1972; m. Carmella Brady Verdugo, Aug. 16, 1969; 1 dau., Estrella Cheverly. Research asst. U. Ariz., 1967-71; asst. prof. U. Md., 1971-74; hydrologist Md. Dept. of Water Resources Adminstrn., Annapolis, 1974—, chief water supply div., 1978—; vis. asst. prof. U. Md., 1974-77. Mem. council Town of Cheverly, 1975—. Recipient student honor award Am. Soc. Agrl. Engrs., 1966. Mem. Am. Soc. Agrl. Engrs., ASCE, Am. Geophys. Union, Soil Conservation Soc. Am., Sigma Xi, Alpha Zeta, Sigma Tau. Lutheran. Home: 5601 Lockwood Rd Cheverly MD 20785 Office: Tawes State Office Bldg Annapolis MD 21401

RECHCIGL, MILOSLAV, JR., govt. ofcl., research scientist, author, editor; b. Mlada Boleslav, Czechoslovakia, July 30, 1930; s. Miloslav and Marie (Rajtr) R.; B.S., Cornell U., 1954, M. Nutrition Sci., 1955, Ph.D., 1958; m. Eva Marie Edwards, Aug. 29, 1953; children—John Edward, Karen Marie. Came to U.S., 1950, naturalized, 1955. Teaching asst. Cornell U., 1953-57, grad. research asst., 1957-58, research asso., 1958; pub. health service research fellow Nat. Cancer Inst., 1958-60, chemist enzymes, metabolism sect., 1960-61, research biochemist, tumor host relations sect., 1962-64, sr. investigator, 1964-68, biosynthesis sect., 1968; USPHS grants asso. program, 1968-69; spl. asst. for nutrition and health to the dir. Regional Med. Programs Service, Health Services and Mental Health Adminstrn., HEW, 1969-70; nutrition adviser AID, Dept. State, 1970—, chief Research and Instnl. Grants div., 1970-73, asst. dir. Office Research and Instl. Grants, 1973-74, acting dir., 1974-75, dir. interregional research staff, 1975—. Exec. sec. nutrition program adv. com. H.S.M.H.A., 1969-70; exec. sec. research and instl. grants council AID, 1970-74, exec. sec. research adv. com., 1971—; AID rep. USC/FAR com., 1972—. Mem. council Nat. Cancer Inst. assembly scientists, 1963-65; del. White House Conf. on Food, Nutrition and Health, 1969; cons. Office of Sec. U.S. Dept. Agr., 1969-70, Dept. Treasury, 1973—. Fellow AAAS, Internat. Coll. Applied Nutrition, Washington Acad. Scis. (del. 1972—), Am. Inst. Chemists; mem. Am. Pub. Health Assn., Internat. Soc. for Research on Civilisation Diseases and Vital Substances, Am. Chem. Soc., Am. Inst. Biol. Scis., N.Y. Acad. Scis., Am. Soc. Animal Sci., Am. Assn. Cancer Research, Am. Inst. Nutrition, Soc. Exptl. Biology and Medicine, Soc. for Biol. Rhythm, History Sci. Soc., Soc. Research Adminstrs., Am. Assn. Advancement Slavic Studies, Soc. Internat. Devel., Soc. Geochemistry and Health, Soc. Devel. Biology, Internat. Platform Assn., Am. Soc. Biol. Chemists, Am. (councilor 1972-74), D.C. (pres. 1972-74, councilor 1974—) insts. chemists, Am., Internat. socs. for cell biology, Czechoslovak Soc. Arts and Scis. (councilor 1962—, v.p. 1968-74, dir. publs. 1962-68, 70-74, pres. 1974-78; hon.), Delta Tau Kappa (hon.). Phi Kappa Phi, Sigma Xi. Club: Cosmos (Washington). Author: Czechoslovakia and its Arts and Sciences: A Selective Bibliography in the Western European Languages, 1964; The Czechoslovak Contribution to World Culture, 1964; Ten Years of the Czechoslovak Society of Arts and Sciences in America, 1966; Czechoslovakia Past and Present, 1968; Essays on Arts and Sciences, 1968; Czechoslovakia in Bibliography: A Bibliography of Bibliographies, 1968; Studies in Czechoslovak Culture and Society; (with Z. Hruban) Microbodies and Related Particles, 1969; Enzyme Synthesis and Degradation in Mammalian Systems, 1971; Food, Nutrition and Health, 1973; Man, Food and Nutrition, 1973; World Food Problem: A Selective Bibliography of Reviews, 1975; Carbohydrates, Lipids and Accessory Growth Factors, 1976; Nutrient Elements and Toxicants, 1976; co-editor: Internat. Jour. Cycle Research, 1969-74, Jour. Applied Nutrition, 1970—; editor-in-chief: CRC Handbook of Nutrition and Food, 1977—; editorial bd. Nutrition Reports Internat., 1977—; translator and abstractor: Chemical Abstracts, 1959—; also articles in field. Home: 1703 Mark Ln Rockville MD 20852 Office: Interregional Research Staff DS/RES AID Dept State Washington DC 20523

RECKTENWALD, LESTER NICHOLAS, psychologist, educator; b. Hartford, Minn.; s. Peter Wendel and Katherine Ann (Delsing) R.; B.S. with honors, U. Minn., 1930, M.A., 1935; student St. Cloud State U., 1921-24, Marquette U., 1937-40, U. Wis., 1940-54, Columbia U., 1941-43; Ph.D., Sussex (Eng.) Coll. Tech., 1976; m. Hilda Gertrude Markert, Apr. 22, 1946 (dec. 1964); 1 son, John Francis. Tchr., prin., counselor, guidance dir. pub. schs., Minn., N.D., Wis., N.Y. and Tenn., 1920-43; counseling psychologist, counselor vets. units Coll. City N.Y., 1945-46, Marquette U., 1946-47, pvt. agency, N.Y.C., 1947-49; chmn. counseling unit Loyola U. of South, 1949-51; asst. prof. psychology, organizer dept. psychology Villanova U., 1951-59; asst. prof. counseling U. Scranton, 1960-61; asso. prof. edn. and psychology Pa. State Coll., West Chester, 1962-73, prof., 1974—; Recipient Hon. citation West Chester State Coll., 1973; Carnegie grantee, 1950. Fellow Internat. Inst. Arts and Letters (life); mem. Am. Personnel and Guidance Assn. (life; pres. Wis. br. 1940-41), Eastern Psychol. Assn. (life), West Chester State Coll. Assn. Higher Edn. (pres. local chpt. 1966-68), Internat. Council Psychologists (life), Internat. Assn. Applied Psychology, Internat. House (world), Archives of History Am. Psychology (life contbr.), Eugene Field Soc. (hon.), Internat. Mark Twain Soc. (hon.), Phi Delta Kappa (emeritus). Author books, including: Hail Tomorrow, 1944; Guidance and Counseling, 1953; The Psychology Inventory, 1956; monographs; contbr. articles to profl. jours. Home and Office: 480 Quigley Rd Wayne (Strafford) PA 19087

RECUPERO, JOHN, mech. engring. co. exec.; b. Schenectady, July 29, 1931; s. Salvatore and Antoinette (Martini) R.; B.B.A., Bryant Coll., 1952; m. Marie J. Lippiello, Aug. 18, 1956; children—Rose-Ann Marie, John Joseph. Pub. and tax accounting practice, Schenectady, 1950—; Specialist corp. gen. engring. lab. accounting services Gen. Electric Co., Schenectady, 1952-62, specialist corp. renegotiation accounting, 1962-65; treas., fin. officer Mechanical Technology, Inc., Latham, N.Y., 1965—; mgr. contract adminstrn., research and devel., 1974-77, bus. mgr. Research and Devel. div., 1977—; treas., dir. The Redford Corp., 1968-76, Boice Realty Inc., 1968-76, Avionics Communication Systems Inc., 1970-76, Aims Inc., 1970-76; treas. Datafile Systems Corp., 1969-77, Turbonetics Inc. 1970-76; cons. in govt. accounting and contract adminstrn., 1978—. Mem. Schenectady Symphony Orch., 1947-66; former guest lectr. Siena Coll., State U. N.Y. at Albany. Past officer, mem. Cub Scout com.; former welfare unit officer CD. Mem. Nat. Assn. Accountants. Republican. Roman Catholic. Clubs: Mohawk Valley Sportsmens. Home: 1381 Kingston Ave Schenectady NY 12308 Office: 968 Albany-Shaker Rd Latham NY 12110

REDD, RICHARD JAMES, artist, educator; b. Toledo, Oct. 22, 1931; s. Dale Shaw and Hazle Winifred (Sanders) R.; B.Ed., U. Toledo, 1953; M.F.A., U. Iowa, 1958; m. Marianna Hill, Sept. 7, 1957; children—Adrienne Dale, Rachel Barton, Coryon Shaw. Tchr. art pub. schs., Britton, Mich., 1953-54; instr. art Lehigh U., Bethlehem, Pa., 1958-61, asst. prof., 1961-64, asso. prof., 1964-71, prof., 1971—, chmn. dept. fine arts, 1970-77; one-man shows include: Allentown (Pa.) Art Mus., 1961, Kemerer Mus., Bethlehem, 1972, Lehigh U., 1959, 68, 73, Kutztown State Coll., 1968, Moravian Coll., 1971, Hazleton Art League, 1968; group shows include: Earth Art, Phila., 1973, Hunterdon (N.J.) Art Center, 1978, Pa. Printmakers, 1975, Reading (Pa.) Mus., 1972, Toledo Mus., 1960, 61, Everhart Mus., Scranton. Pres. Lehigh Art Alliance, 1976-78; bd. dirs. Kemerer Mus., Bethlehem, 1977—. Served with U.S. Army, 1954-56. Recipient Outstanding Tchr. award Lehigh U., 1966; Garth Howland award Lehigh Art Alliance, 1962, 75, Mellon grantee, 1978. Mem. AAUP, Artists Equity Assn., Coll. Art Assn., Omicron Delta Kappa, Kappa Delta Pi, Pi Kappa Alpha. Home: RD 3 Stonesthrow Rd Bethlehem PA 18015 Office: Bldg 17 Lehigh U Bethlehem PA 18015

REDD, RUDOLPH JAMES, chem. engr.; b. Charlottesville, Va., Mar. 25, 1924; s. Hampton J. and Leona Thomas R.; student Morgan State U., 1942-44, 46-48; B.S., U. Pa., 1950; postgrad U. Md., 1951-53, Johns Hopkins U., 1970-73; children from previous marriage—Rudolph James Jr., Tersa M. Chemist, Dept. Army, Aberdeen Proving Ground, Md., 1948-72, chief chemist, 1972-74, chief collective protection br., 1974—, U.S. data exchange scientist to W. Ger., 1974—; owner, pres. Redd's Sounds Unltd., Inc., electronic equipment installation, Balt., 1959—. Pres., Hernwood Heights Neighborhood Assn., Denison Rd Neighborhood Assn.; mem.

Baltimore County Charter Revision Commn., 1976—. Served with AUS, 1944-46. Reccipient EEO award Dept. Army, 1972. Mem. Am. Chem. Soc., Am. Inst. Chem. Engrs., Acad. Model Aeros., Am. Def. Prepardesness Assn., AAAS, Balt. Amateur Radio Club, Kappa Alpha Psi. Methodist. Home: 4 Reldas Ct Apt L Cockeysville MD 21030

REDD, VIVIAN CORTEZZA, labor union exec.; b. Harrisonburg, Va., Sept. 18, 1934; d. Minerva Mamie Dealla Redd; student LaSalle Extension U., 1968, LL.B., 1974. Co-organizer, founder U.S. Dept. Commerce Com. for Women, 1970, treas., 1971-73; equal employment opportunity counselor U.S. Patent and Trademark office, Washington, 1972-76; v.p. non-profls. Patent Office Employees Union, Local 2600, 1976-77, pres., 1977—; part-time nursery sch. instr., 1952-60; mem. nat. adv. bd. Am. Security Council, 1972—. Recipient certificate Social Service Adminstrn., 1972; certificate of appreciation White House Conf. on Indsl. World Ahead, 1972; founder's certificate Center for Internat. Security Studies, Am. Security Council Edn. Found., 1977. Democrat. Methodist. Home: 2301 S Jefferson Davis Hwy #1316 Arlington VA 22202 Office: US Patent and Trademark Office Washington DC 20231

REDDALL, H(ENRY) HASTINGS, ret. business exec.; b. Bloomfield, N.J., Nov. 8, 1893; s. John William and May Eloise (Smith) R.; B.S., Colgate U., 1918; postgrad. U.S. Naval War Coll., 1932, 33, Rutgers U., 1955; m. Janet Ewing, Oct. 15, 1925. Joined Western Electric Co., N.Y.C., 1913 (on leave, 1915-19), auditor assigned No. Electric Co., Montreal, Que., Can., 1919-22, asst. cashier Western Electric, 1922, asst. treas., 1922-31, 32-41, 46, treas. Nassau Smelting & Refining Co., Inc., Tottenville, N.Y. subsidiary Western Electric, 1931-32, chief corp. accountant Western Electric, 1941-43, chief factory auditor, 1943-45, chief field auditor, 1945-46, treas. 1946-58; treas. Weco Corp., 1946-58, dir., 1947-58. Chmn. finance com., treas. St. James Episcopal Ch., Brookhaven, N.Y.; del. diocesan convs.; Bishop's Cross Diocese L.I. 1971. pres. bd. trustees Brookhaven Free Library, now past pres.; trustee Dodge Fund Colgate U., 1950-60; bd. dirs. Colgate Alumni Corp., 1937-40, 43-46. Served to lt. (j.g.) USNR, 1917-36. Recipient alumni award for distinguished service to Colgate U., 1945. Mem. Mil. Order Fgn. Wars, S.R., Soc. Colonial Wars, Mil. Order Loyal Legion U.S., Bellport-Brookhaven Hist. Soc. (trustee 1966—, treas., chmn. bldg. com. 1966-71, trustee meml. fund). Soc. for Preservation L.I. Antiquities, Soc. Descs. Washington's Army at Valley Forge, South Country Antique Soc., U.S. Yacht Racing Union, Great South Bay Yacht Racing Assn., N.S. Hist. Soc., Stamford Geneal. Soc., Telephone Pioneers Am., Soc. for Preservation Book of Common Prayer, Vets. Corps Arty., Phi Beta Kappa, Phi Kappa Psi. Republican. Clubs: Bellport Bay (N.Y.) Yacht (comdr. 1946-47, 59-60, hon. trustee 1960—); Old Inlet; Key Largo Anglers; Quantuck Beach (West Hampton, N.Y.). Contbr. (under pseudonym A. Crosby Downs) crossword puzzles to N.Y. Times, Chgo. Tribune, others, 1958-78. Home: Bay Rd Brookhaven NY 11719

REDDEN, MARTHA ROSS, psychologist, ednl. adminstr.; b. Richmond, Ky., Sept. 4, 1932; d. Robert Lee and Virginia Eudelle (Hurst) Ross; A.B., Georgetown (Ky.) Coll., 1954; M.A., Murray State U., 1966, M.S., 1968; Ed.D., U. Ky., 1976; m. John D. Redden, Dec. 27, 1953 (dec. 1968); children—Mary, Patricia, Michael, Mark. Tchr., Jefferson County Schs. (Ky.), 1954-57, Campbellsburg, Ky., 1957-59, Columbus, Ky., 1963-64; instr. Murray State U., 1965-66; dir. psychol. services Paducah Pub. Schs., 1967-70; psychologist Louisville Pub. Schs., 1971-74; dir. project on handicapped in sci. AAAS, Washington, 1975—; coordinator project Heath Higher Edn. and the Handicapped, Am. Council Edn., Washington, 1977—; intern Univ. Council Edn. Adminstrn. Nat. Level, 1974-75; mem. nat. adv. group Closer Look, 1976-77; mem. Pres. Carter's Task Force on Handicapped Americans, 1976. Mem. Am. Psychol. Assn., AAAS, Council Exceptional Children, Nat. Sci. Tchrs. Assn., Sci. for Handicapped Assn. Author: The Effects of Stimulus Redundancy on Concept Formation, 1968; A Study of Mainstream Competencies in Regular Elementary Teachers, 1976; Barrier Free Meetings: A Guide to Professional Associations, 1976; Science Technology and the Handicapped, 1976. Home: 1718 Corcoran St NW Washington DC 20009 Office: 1776 Massachusetts Ave NW Washington DC 20036

REDEKOPP, ALEXANDER BENJAMIN, environ. engr.; b. Nikitovka, Ukraine, July 20, 1934; s. Benjamin B. and Antonia (Kusmenko) R.; came to Can., 1949, naturalized, 1955; B.Applied Sci., U. Toronto, 1959, M.Applied Sci., 1960; m. Marlene Rempel, July 14, 1962; 1 son, Bradley. Field engr. Ont. Water Resources Commn., Toronto, 1960-63, dist. engr., 1963-65, supr. water works, 1965-71, supr. tng. and licencing, 1971-72; chief tng. and tech. transfer Fed. Dept. Environment, Ottawa, Ont., 1972—; cons. WHO, Pan Am. Health Orgn. Recipient Silver medal Queen's Silver Jubilee, 1977. Mem. Am. Water Works Assn. (Ambassador award 1973, Man of Yr. award 1975), Water Pollution Control Fedn., Internat. Assn. Water Pollution Research, Internat. Water Supply Assn., Profl. Engrs. Ont. Home: 2020 Hollybrook Crescent Ottawa ON K1J 7Y6 Canada Office: 351 St Joseph Blvd Hull PQ K1A 1C8 Canada

REDING, PAUL FRANCIS, clergyman; b. Hamilton, Ont., Can., Feb. 14, 1925; s. Thomas Augustine and Florence (Fleming) R.; grad. St. Augustine's Sem., Toronto, Ont., 1943-50. Ordained priest Roman Catholic Ch.; now bishop, Hamilton, Ont., Can. Home: 722 King St W Hamilton ON L8P 1C7 Canada Office: 700 King St W Hamilton ON L8P 1C7 Canada

REDINGTON, THOMAS, communications exec.; b. White Plains, N.Y., Mar. 10, 1943; s. Edgar H. and Harriette P. (Phillips) R.; B.A. in Mktg., N.Y. U., 1968; student U. West Indies, 1962; m. Joan E. Kingsley, Dec. 9, 1972; 1 dau., Jessica. Account exec. Burson-Marsteller, N.Y.C., 1968-70; gen. mgr. Davi-Callahan Co., N.Y.C., 1970-71; pres. Thomas Redington Co., N.Y.C., 1971-76, Redington, Inc., Stamford, Conn., 1977—; chmn. Gourmet Galley, Inc.; dir. Internat. Food Mktg. Corp., 1976—. Chmn. pub. info. com. Nat. Council on Alcoholism, 1976-77, hon. dir., 1978—. Republican. Episcopalian. Clubs: Landmark (Stamford); Union League (N.Y.C.). Office: 15 Bank St Stamford CT 06901

REDMAN, JOHN DAVID, contract hardware co. exec.; b. Clarkson, N.Y., Jan. 14, 1921; s. Dorr Clark and Mabel (Yelland) R.; student State Tchrs. Coll. at Brockport, N.Y., 1940-41, 46; B.S., Springfield Coll., 1948, M.Edn., 1952; m. Bronia A. Surdyka, Feb. 18, 1950; children—Deborah, Anne, Richard, David, James. Program dir. Pa. R.R. Y.M.C.A., N.Y.C., 1950-51; salesman Sullivan Hardware Co., West Springfield, Mass., 1951-52; salesman Builders Specialty Hardware Corp., 1952-53, Hardware Specialties Inc., 1953-58, v.p., 1958-75, pres., 1975— (all West Springfield); v.p. Springfield (Mass.) Home Builders, 1957-58; instr. hardware inst. Ohio State U., Columbus, 1967, U. Chgo., 1972—; lectr. Western New Eng. Coll., 1969-75; dir. New Eng. area Door and Hardware Inst., 1977—. Chmn. Am. Cancer Drive, West Springfield, 1965; sec. finance com. of West Springfield, 1966-68; mem. Town Meeting, West Springfield, 1970—, West Springfield Sch. Com., 1972-75; sec.-treas. long-range planning program, W. Springfield, 1978—; bd. dirs. Jr. Achievement of Western Mass., Eastern States Expn., 1973—. Served with USCGR, 1942-45. Mem. Am. Soc. Archtl. Hardware Cons. (mem. edn. com. 1957—), New Eng. Builders Hardware Club (pres. 1961-63, chmn. edn. com. 1958—), Constrn. Industry Assn. Western Mass. (dir., clk. 1976-79, clk.-treas. 1979—), Sales and Mktg. Execs. (bd. dirs. Springfield chpt. 1966-70, pres. 1968-69), West Springfield C. of C. (pres. 1966-68, dir. 1978—), PTA, Westfield Watershed Assn. Conglist. Clubs: Rotarian (local pres. 1971-72), Pioneer Valley Sportsmen's (West Springfield). Home: 81 Paucatuck Rd West Springfield MA 01089 Office: 211 Union St West Springfield MA 01089

REDMOND, ANDREW J., banker, state senator; b. St. George, Que., Can., Dec. 21, 1920; s. John Stephen and Mary Jane (Grenier) R.; came to U.S., 1949, naturalized, 1955; student pub. schs., St. George; m. Normande Loubier, June 16, 1946; children—William, Lillian, Mark, Audrey, Pierre, Andrew. Lumberman and wood processor, Franklin City and Somerset City, Maine, 1949-58; founder A. Redmond, Inc., North Anson, Maine, 1958-72; founding mem. Border Trust Bank, Jackman, Maine, 1969-78, pres. Border Trust Co., 1973-78; mem. Maine Senate, 1977-78; dir. Maine Publicity Bur.; chmn. Maine's Woods Council; mem. North ustries Maine, Nat. Council State Legislators, Banking Inst. Am. Republican. Home: RFD 4 E Madison Rd Skowhegan ME 04976 Office: State House Augusta ME 04333

REDO, S(AVERIO) FRANK, surgeon; b. Bklyn., Dec. 28, 1920; s. Frank and Maria (Guida) R.; B.S., Queens Coll., 1942; M.D., Cornell U., 1950; m. Maria Lappano, June 27, 1948; children—Philip, Martha. Intern in surgery N.Y. Hosp., N.Y.C., 1950-51, asst. resident surgeon, 1951-56, resident surgeon, 1956-57, asst. attending surgeon, 1958-60, asso. attending surgeon, 1960-66, surgeon in charge pediatric surgery, 1960, attending surgeon, 1966—; practice medicine specializing in surgery; clin. asso. prof. surgery Cornell U. Med. Coll., 1963, prof., 1972—. Served to capt. USAAF, 1942-46. Diplomate Nat. Bd. Med. Examiners, Bd. Thoracic Surgery, Am. Bd. Surgery with certificate spl. competency in pediatric surgery, Pan Am. Med. Assn. Fellow ACS, Am. Coll. Chest Physicians; mem. Harvey Soc., Soc. U. Surgeons, Am. Acad. Pediatrics, Am. Fedn. for Clin. Research, Internat. Cardiovascular Soc., Am. Surg. Assn., Am. Assn. Thoracic Surgery, Soc. for Surgery Alimentary Tract, Am. Soc. Articicial Internal Organs, Am. Acad. Pediatrics, Assn. Advancement Med. Instrumentation, Soc. Thoracic Surgeons, Internat. Soc. Surgery, N.Y. Gastroent. Soc., N.Y. Acad. Sci., N.Y. Cardiovascular Soc., N.Y. Acad. Medicine, N.Y. Soc. Thoracic Surgery, N.Y. Pediatric Soc., Med. Soc. County N.Y., Queens Coll. Alumni Assn. (bd. govs. 1962—), Sigma Xi. Author: Surgery in the Ambulatory Child, 1961; Principles of Surgery in the First Six Months of Life, 1976; Atlas of Surgery in the First Six Months of Life, 1977. Contbr. articles to profl. jours. Patentee in field. Home: 435 E 70th St New York City NY 10021 Office: 525 E 68th St New York City NY 10021

REDSTONE, SUMNER MURRAY, theatre exec., lawyer; b. Boston, May 27, 1923; s. Michael and Belle (Ostrovsky) R.; B.A., Harvard, 1944, LL.B., 1947; m. Phyllis Gloria Raphael, July 6, 1947; children—Brent Dale, Shari Ellin. Admitted to Mass. bar, 1947, D.C. bar, 1951, also U.S. Supreme Ct.; law sec. U.S. Ct. Appeals for 9th Circuit, 1947-48; instr. U. San Francisco Law Sch. and Labor Mgmt. Sch., 1947; spl. asst. to U.S. atty. gen., 1948-51; partner firm Ford, Bergson, Adams, Borkland & Redstone, Washington, 1951-54; exec. v.p. N.E. Drive-In Theatre Corp., 1954-68; pres. N.E. Theatre Corp.; dir. ACE Prodns. Inc. Chmn. Jimmy Fund, Boston, 1960; met. div. N.E. Combined Jewish Philanthropies, 1963; sponsor Boston Mus. Sci. Trustee Children's Cancer Research Found., Art Lending Library; bd. dirs. Boston Arts Festival, Will Rogers Meml. Fund; bd. overseers Sidney Farber Cancer Inst.; mem. corp. New Eng. Med. Center. Served to 1st lt. AUS, 1943-45. Decorated Army Commendation medal; named one of ten outstanding young men Greater Boston C. of C., 1958; William J. German Human Relations award entertainment and communications div. Am. Jewish Com., 1977. Mem. Am. Cong. Exhibitors (exec. com. 1961—), Theatre Owners Am. (asst. pres. 1960-63, pres. 1964-65), Nat. Assn. Theatre Owners (chmn. bd. dirs. 1965-66). Mason. Clubs: University, Variety New Eng., Harvard, Boston. Home: 98 Baldpate Hill Rd Newton MA 02159 Office: 31 St James Ave Boston MA 02116

REED, EUNICE PADDIO (PAT), state ofcl.; b. Crowley, La., June 25, 1928; d. Henry Paddio and Cécile Atris (Cheslé) Paddio Williams; B.S., Grambling State U., 1949; M.A., U. Calif. at Los Angeles, 1960; postgrad. La. State U., U. Minn.; m. Clarence H. Reed, Sept. 11, 1949; children—Deidre Verne, Clarence H., Henry Paddio, Bertrand Johnathan, Cécile Atris. Tchr., St. Helena Parish, Greensburg, La., 1949-67, 71-72, counselor, 1968-71; dir. St. Helena Assistance Resource Establishment Inc., Greensburg, 1972-73; extension asso. N.Y. State Coop. Extension, Cornell U., Ithaca, N.Y., 1973-77, adminstr., 1977—. Mem. Sch. Bd. St. Helena Parish; mem. Ithaca Sch. Bd.; bd. dirs. Family and Childrens Service, NAACP, Planned Parenthood Tompkins County. Mem. Am. Personnel and Guidance Assn., Nat. Assn. Extension 4H Agts. Methodist. Clubs: Essence, Order Eastern Star. Home: 520 W Clinton St Ithaca NY 14850 Office: 212 Roberts Hall Cornell U Ithaca NY 14853

REED, GEORGE EDWARD, former pub. relations exec.; b. Harrisburg, Pa., Oct. 18, 1912; s. George L. and Helen (Moorhead) R.; A.B., Dickinson Coll., 1935. Reporter, Harrisburg (Pa.) Telegraph, 1935-41, asst. city editor, 1948; regional publicity dir. Nat. Assn. Mfrs., Pitts., 1951-53; mem. pub. affairs staff Am. Petroleum Inst., N.Y.C., 1953-59; dir. pub. information Asso. Petroleum Industries Pa., Harrisburg, 1959-77. Served to capt. USAAF, 1941-46, lt. col., USAF Res., ret. Mem. Pa. Soc. Pub. Relations Soc. Am. (past pres., dir. Central Pa. chpt. Mid-Atlantic dist. chmn. 1977), Keystonians Soc. (past pres.), Pa. Pub. Relations Soc. (pres. 1974), Petroleum Writers Assn., Air Force Assn., Res. Officers Assn., Ret. Officers Assn., Nat. Sojourners, Mil. Order World Wars, Phi Kappa Sigma. Republican. Presbyterian. Clubs: Harrisburg Rotary, Masons (Shriner). Home: 3513 Hillcrest Rd Harrisburg PA 17109

REED, HARRY WILLIAM, JR., aircraft co. exec.; b. Detroit, Feb. 26, 1919; s. Harry William and May (Hardy) R.; student Wayne U., 1936-37; B.S. in Engring., U. Mich., 1940, M.B.A., 1941; m. Nancy Elizabeth Sanders, Mar. 21, 1945; children—Robert Alexander, John Stevens, Margaret Elizabeth. Asst. supr. then supr. wage and salary adminstrn. Pratt & Whitney Aircraft, East Hartford, Conn., 1946-67; asst. to indsl. relations dir. United Aircraft Corp. (now United Techs. Corp.), East Hartford, 1968-71, dir. wage and salary programs, 1972—; chmn. Aerospace Industries Assn. Compensation Commn., 1973-74. Chmn. Planning and Zoning Com., Glastonbury, Conn., 1959-63; vice chmn. Glastonbury Bd. Edn., 1963-67; mem. Republican Town Com., 1959-77; mem. personnel com. Greater Hartford Red Cross and Community Blood Bank; mem. ins. advisory com. Town of Glastonbury. Served as lt. (j.g.) USNR, 1944-46. Mem. Am. Compensation Assn., Nat., Hartford Audubon socs., Nature Conservancy (chmn. Glastonbury subchpt. 1971-73), Nat. Trust Historic Preservation, Glastonbury Hist. Soc., Beta Gamma Sigma, Sigma Phi Epsilon. Conglist. (trustee ch. 1968-72, deacon 1956-64). Clubs: Appalachian Mountain; Orchard Hill (Glastonbury). Home: 163 Tall Timbers Rd Glastonbury CT 06033 Office: United Technologies Corp Hartford CT 06101

REED, JAMES ALEXANDER, JR., lawyer; b. Rochester, N.Y., Feb. 7, 1930; s. James Alexander and Rose Winifred (Nellist) R.; B.A. cum laude, Amherst Coll., 1952; LL.B., Harvard, 1955; m. Dora Anne de Vries, Feb. 17, 1972; children—John G. Walber, Jeffrey R. Walber, Penelope F., Geoffrey M., Diane E., Wende J. Walber. Admitted to N.Y. State bar, 1958; asso. firm Lines, Wilkens, Osborn & Beck, and predecessors, Rochester, 1958-63, partner, 1964—; dep. town atty. Pittsford (N.Y.), 1976-77, town atty., 1977—. Served to lt. (j.g.), USNR, 1955-58. Mem. Monroe County, N.Y. State, Am. bar assns., Am. Judicature Soc. Republican. Episcopalian. Clubs: University, Amherst (pres. 1963-64) (Rochester). Home: 21 Gladbrook Rd Pittsford NY 14534 Office: 47 S Fitzhugh St Rochester NY 14614

REED, JOHN CARRE, investment banker, co. exec.; b. Phila., Dec. 29, 1943; s. Frank Carre and Mary Frances (Stoughton) R.; B.A. in Econs., Boston U., 1967; M.B.A., Rutgers U., 1969; m. Marcia Ann Moore, Aug. 26, 1967; children—Amanda Elizabeth, Kristi Carre. Fin. analyst Bache & Co. (now Bache Halsey Stuart Shields), N.Y.C., 1969-73; asst. treas. Chase Manhattan Bank, N.Y.C., 1973-76; v.p. research John J. Ryan & Co., West Orange, N.J., 1976—. Republican. Club: Fayson Lakes Yacht (Capt. 1978). Home: 149 Boonton Ave Kinnelon NJ 07405 Office: 80 Main St West Orange NJ 07052

REED, JOHN HENRY, educator; b. Youngstown, Ohio, Apr. 15, 1937; s. W. Brooks and Kathryn (Beighley) R.; B.S. in Physics, U. N.C., 1959; postgrad. U.Mo., 1962-64; M.A., Am. U., 1968, Ph.D., 1972; m. Barbara J. Rockelman, June 7, 1964; children—William Randolph, Stephanie Jean, Kurtis Elvin. Commd. ensign U.S. Navy, 1959, advanced through grades to lt., 1964; served on U.S.S. Bordelon, 1959-62, U.S.S. Providence, 1964-66; resigned, 1969; prof. bus. adminstrn. Clarion (Pa.) State Coll., 1971—. Fellow AAAS; mem. Ops. Research Soc. Am., Inst. Mgmt. Scis., Am. Soc. for Pub. Aminstrn., Sigma Phi Epsilon, Delta Phi Alpha. Club: Masons, Shriners. Author: The Application of Operations Research to Court Delay, 1973; contbr. articles to profl. jours. Home: RD 3 Emlenton PA 16373 Office: Clarion State Coll Clarion PA 16214

REED, JOHN WILLIAM, standardization engr.; b. Bellows Falls, Vt., Aug. 23, 1934; s. Hugh Elmer and Katherine Mary (Richards) R.; student U. Vt., 1952-54; children—John Richard, Anne Marie. Standization engr. Raytheon Co., Andover, Mass., 1957—. Mem. industry adv. group Govt.-Industry Data Exchange Program, 1974—, chmn., 1978—. Served with U.S. Army, 1954-57. Republican. Mem. United Ch. of Christ. Club: Odd Fellows. Home: Derry NH 03038 Office: 350 Lowell St Andover MA 01810

REED, KATHRYN MERCER, savs. and loan assn. exec.; b. Frederick County, Md., Nov. 22, 1918; d. Ira Robert and Mary Othetta (Ramsburg) Mercer; student Frederick (Md.) Visitation Acad., 1936, Ben Franklin U., Washington, 1946, Frederick Community Coll., 1973; m. Robert John Reed, May 25, 1968; stepchildren—Christopher, Steven, Michael. With Potomac Electric Co., 1936-41; audit supr. Sears, Roebuck & Co., Frederic, 1941-49, 55-73; gen. office mgr. Hogan Bros. Lumber Co., Athens, Ga., 1950-55; asst. sec., then asso. and br. mgr. Frederick office Citizens Bldg. and Loan Assn., 1973—; participant workshops. Mem. Frederick Commn. Comprehensive Health Planning Council and Health Services, 1973—; mem. Frederick County Adv. Council Vocat. Tech., 1973—; organizer Golden Age Group, Mt. Pleasant, 1975; pres. Inter-Ch. Bowling League, 1969-70; asst. Girl Scout leader, 1961-66; active YMCA campaign; pres. United Methodist Women, 1958, Frederick County zone Meth. Chs., 1962; bd. dirs. United Way of Frederick County, 1977—; trustee Frederick dist. United Meth. Ch., 1969—, chmn. council ministries Mt. Pleasant chs., 1970—, mem. adminstrv. bd., 1958—, mem. women's div. nominating com., 1977—; certified lay speaker Meth. Ch.; bd. dirs. Frederick County Assn. Retarded Citizens, treas., 1978-79; co-chmn. fund drive YMCA, 1978. Recipient Outstanding Citizen award 1973. Mem. Met. Washington Savs. and Loan League, Bus. and Profl. Women's Club (pres. Frederick 1969-71, Md. 1972-73; named Md. Woman of Year 1973), Md. Vet. Aux. Assn. (pres. 1956-57), Frederick County Sq. Mchts. Assn. (treas. 1973—), Frederick County C. of C. (chmn. edn. com. 1973—, pres. 1977-78), Internat. Platform Assn. Democrat. Home: Route 10 Box 216 Frederick MD 21701 Office: 1003 W Patrick St Frederick MD 21701

REED, LEON SAMUEL, govt. ofcl.; b. Warren, Ohio, July 6, 1949; s. Walter Charles and Lois Avalene (Botroff) R.; B.A. in Economics and Journalism, Antioch Coll., 1971; m. Margaret Smith, Dec. 27, 1975. Project dir. Council on Economic Priorities, N.Y.C. and Washington, 1970-75; sr. mem. profl. staff Joint Com. on Def. Prodn., U.S. Congress, Washington, 1975-77; mem. profl. staff Com. on Banking, Housing and Urban Affairs, U.S. Senate, Washington, 1977—; bd. dirs. Council on Economic Priorities, 1971-73. Mem. exec. com., pres. Randolph Civic Assn. Mem. Disciples of Christ Ch. Co-author: Efficiency in Death, 1970, Guide to Corporations, 1973, Conflict of Interest and the Condor-Missile Program, 1976; author: Military Maneuvers, 1975; contbr. Unterwegs zum Frieden, 1972. Office: A-421 Senate Annex III Washington DC 20510

REED, ROLLAND MAURICE, heavy machinery co. exec.; b. LaCrosse, Wis., July 15, 1927; s. Christen Leiver and Norma Marie (Peterson) R.; B.S. in Econs., U. Wis., 1951; grad. Ind. U. Exec. Program, 1974; m. Irene Ann Sukup, June 16, 1951; children—Christen J., Mark O., Joseph P., John C., Ann C. Ty. mgr. Baker Mfg. Co., 1951-52; with Caterpillar Tractor Co., Peoria, Ill., 1953-69, asst. mgr. Western sales, 1966-69; distbr. sales mgr. Internat. Harvester Co., Melrose Park, Ill., 1969-73, mgr. distbr., dealer br. devel. and adminstrn., 1973-76; v.p. mktg. U.S.-Can., Grove Mfg. Co., Shady Grove, Pa., 1976-78; v.p. mktg., partner Long Machinery Co., Missoula, Mont., 1979—; mem. nat. industry roundtable Associated Equipment Distbrs. Chmn., instr. polit. action course U.S. C. of C.; adviser, grad. asst. Dale Carnegie Course; lectr. U. Ind. Mem. nat. council Boy Scouts Am., leader Norway World Scout Jamboree, recipient Silver Beaver; mem. exec. advisory bd. Ind. U. Served with USNR, 1945-47. Mem. Am. Mining Congress, Pacific Logging Congress, Am. Legion, Beavers. Clubs: Rogue Valley Country, K.C. Contbr. articles to forest industry publs., constrn. and conservation jours. Home: 233 Potomac Heights Ave Hagerstown MD 21740 Office: Long Machinery Co Missoula MT 59806

REED, THEODORE HAROLD, zool. park dir.; b. Washington, July 25, 1922; s. Ollie William and Mildred Marie (Body) R.; D.V.M., Kans. State Coll., 1945; m. Mary Elizabeth Crandall, Apr. 20, 1945; children—Mark Crandall, Mary Alyce. Practice veterinary medicine, Ceylon, Minn., also Caldewll, Idaho, Ashland and Portland, Oreg.; veterinarian Nat. Zool. Park, 1955-57, acting dir., 1956-58, dir., 1958—. Mem. Internat. Waterfowl Assn., Am. Assn. Zool. Parks and Aquariums, Internat. Union Dirs. Zool. Gardens, Kenya Wildlife Soc., Wildlife Disease Assn. Home: 5005 Baltimore Ave Washington DC 20016 Office: National Zoological Park Washington DC 20009

REED, THOMAS EVILLE, research and devel. exec.; b. Ft. Pierce, Fla., Feb. 21, 1929; s. William Henry and Mildred Marsh (Jackson) R.; B.E.E., Mass. Inst. Tech., 1958; m. Shirley Sapp, Dec. 12, 1952; children—Arthur Lee, William Walter, Debra Anne. Dep. asso. dir. Mass. Inst. Tech. Instrumentation Lab., Cambridge, 1972; div. leader

C.S. Draper Lab. Inc., Cambridge 1974—. Served with U.S. Army, 1950-52. Mem. Sigma Xi. Home: 57 New Bridge Rd Sudbury MA 01776 Office: 555 Technology Sq Cambridge MA 02139

REED, WILLIAM CARLISLE, environ. mgmt. co. exec.; b. Paterson, N.J., Mar. 4, 1943; s. George M. and Adah (Smith) R.; B.Arch., Syracuse U., 1966; M.Arch., Harvard U., 1968. Designer, Sasaki, Dawson & DeMay, Watertown, Mass., 1966-67, Sert Jackson & Assos., Cambridge, Mass., 1968-69; prin. partner Reed & D'Andrea, land and space planning, Franconia, N.H. and Cambridge, Mass., 1969-75; pres. Center for Natural Areas, Washington, Los Angeles and Gardiner, Maine, 1975—. Trustee, v.p. Maine Audubon Soc., 1977—; chmn. Gardiner Conservation Commn., 1976—; mem. Mayor's Round Table, 1977—; mem. ad hoc com. on environ. studies program reorgn. Bur. Land Mgmt., 1978—; mem. Nat. Resources Council Maine. Home: River Rd South Gardiner ME 04359 Office: PO Box 98 River Rd South Gardiner ME 04359

REED, WINSTON HARRISON, chem. engr., aerosol mfg. co. exec.; b. Fallon, Nev., Jan. 25, 1909; s. Murry Eugene and Gertrude Emeline (Hicks) R.; B.S. in Chem. Engring., Clarkson Coll. Tech., 1931; M.S. in Phys. Chemistry, Cornell U., 1933; Ph.D. in Chem. Engring., Va. Poly. Inst., 1951; postgrad. Western Res. U., U. Mich., U. Minn., Syracuse U.; m. Kathleen Phyllis Kaser, Feb. 10, 1940; children—Diane Kathleen, Winston Harrison. Chemist, Harshaw Chem. Co., Cleve., 1931-32, Racquette River Paper Co., Potsdam, N.Y., 1933-34; chem. engr. Nat. Carbon Co., Fremont, Ohio, 1934-36, Long Valley Ore Co., Lowville, N.Y., 1936-37; asst. prof. chem. engring. Lawrence Inst. Tech., Detroit, 1937-41; instr. chem. engring. U. Minn., Mpls., 1941-42, Syracuse (N.Y.) U., 1942-48; cons., research asst. Carrier Corp., Syracuse, 1944-48; Carrier fellow Va. Poly. Inst., Blacksburg, 1948-51; research chem. engr., asst. chief chemist Bridgeport (Conn.) Brass Co., 1951-55; chmn. chemistry Inter-Am. U., San German, P.R., 1963-65; dir. applied research Boyle Midway, Cranford, N.J., 1965-67; pres. Reed Research and Gen. Aerosols, Inc., Shelton, Conn., 1955-62, W. H. Reed Co., Shelton, 1967—. Active Shelton Bicentennial Commn., 1975-76. Mem. Am. Chem. Soc., Am. Inst. Chem. Engrs., Sigma Xi, Phi Lambda Upsilon, Alpha Chi Sigma. Republican. Patentee azeotropic refrigerants, propellents. Home and Office: 104 Mill St The Mill Shelton CT 06484

REEDER, FRANK FITZGERALD, marketing research co. exec.; b. Big Stone Gap, Va., Apr. 9, 1932; s. Andrew Horatio and Suzanne Fitzgerald (Bourdon) R.; B.S. in Econs., U. Va., 1954; postgrad. Columbia, 1955; m. Judith Ann Sands, Feb. 16, 1957; children—Diane Frances, Gail Sands. Asst. to pres. Advt. and Mktg. Cons., Inc., Princeton, N.J., 1954-57; gen. service exec. Gallup & Robinson, Inc., Princeton, 1957-60; research group head Colgate Palmolive Co., N.Y.C., 1960-63; account research mgr. J. Walter Thompson Co., N.Y.C., 1964-72; v.p. Research 100, Inc., Princeton, 1972-73; pres. Frank Reeder Mktg. Research Co., Princeton, 1973—. Recipient Wall St. Jour. award, 1954. Mem. Am. Mktg. Assn., U. Va. Alumni Assn. Republican. Episcopalian. Club: Pike Brook Country. Author: Big Is Bad-A Treatise on Individualism, 1977. Home: Herrontown Circle Princeton NJ 08540 Office: PO Box 532 Palmer Sq Princeton NJ 08540

REEDER, MARGENE VLIEGER, ednl. adminstr.; b. Sheldon, Iowa, Sept. 9, 1931; d. Tom and Jennie (Ruisch) Vlieger; b B.A. cum laude, Central Coll., Pella, Iowa, 1953; M.Ed., U. Md., 1968; certificate of advanced study in Edn. Loyola Coll., Balt., 1978; m. Ralph Charles Reeder, Nov. 24, 1957; children—Charles Matthew, Jane Luella. Tchr., Atlantic (Iowa) High Sch., 1953-55; recreation therapist ARC, Oakland, Calif., 1955-56; tchr., counselor Oakland Pub. Schs., 1956-60; counselor Prince Georges County (Md.) Schs., 1960-61, state aid specialist, 1969-73, asst. in spl. edn., 1973—; exec. dir. Prince Georges County Mental Health Assn., 1963-64, bd. dirs., 1965-68; mem. adv. bd. Mental Health Study Center, HEW, Adelphi, Md., 1975-76. Vice pres. Community Citizens Assn., College Park, Md., 1969-70, sec., Silver Spring, Md., 1977-78. Mem. Council Exceptional Children, Am. Personnel and Guidance Assn., Nat., Md. State, Prince Georges County edn. assns. Home: 10507 De Neane Rd Silver Spring MD 20903 Office: Office Spl Edn Prince George County Schs Upper Marlboro MD 20870

REES, THOMAS DEE, plastic surgeon; b. Nephi, Utah, Feb. 2, 1927; s. Don M. and Norma (Anderson) R.; B.A., U. Utah, 1946, M.D., 1948; m. Natalie Bowes, Mar. 25, 1949; children—Thomas, David, Elizabeth. Intern, Genesee Hosp., Rochester, N.Y., 1948-49, asst. resident, 1950-51; resident N.Y. Hosp., Cornell Med. Center, N.Y.C., 1949-50, 52-53; research fellow neurosurgery Yale U. Med. Sch., New Haven, 1951; resident plastic surgery VA Hosp., Bronx, 1953-55; practice medicine specializing in plastic surgery, 1958—; mem. staffs N.Y. U.-Bellevue Med. Center, U. Hosp., N.Y.C., chmn. dept. plastic surgery Manhattan Eye, Ear and Throat Hosp., N.Y.C., 1977—; attending plastic surgeon Doctors Hosp., N.Y.C., VA Hosps., Manhattan, N.Y.C.; cons. Southhampton (N.Y.) Hosp., U.S. Naval Hosp., St. Albans, N.Y.; clin. prof. surgery N.Y. U., 1977—. Served to lt. comdr. USNR, 1945, 57-58. Recipient Distinguished Service award Young Men's Bd. Trade, N.Y.C., 1961; Distinguished Service award and Young Man of Year, N.Y. State Jaycees, 1961; USPHS grantee, 1964—; NIH grantee, 1965-69. Diplomate Am. Bd. Plastic Surgery. Fellow A.C.S.; mem. Am. Assn. Plastic Surgeons, AMA, Med. Soc. County N.Y., Am. Soc. Plastic and Reconstructive Surgeons, Am. Soc. Cleft Palate Rehab., Soc. Rehab. of Facially Disfigured, Pan-Pacific Surg. Assn., Pan.-Am. Med. Assn., Am. Soc. Aesthetic Plastic Surgery, N.Y. Acad. Medicine, N.Y. Med. Soc., N.Y. Regional Soc. Plastic Surgery, Internat. Confedn. Plastic Surgeons. Mormon. Club: N.Y. Athletic. Author: Cosmetic Facial Surgery, 1972; Cancer of the Skin, 1976; contbr. articles to med. jours. Home: 176 E 72d St New York City NY 10021

REESE, EBER ORAM, metal mfg. exec.; b. Lancaster, Pa., June 10, 1915; s. Issachar Polk and Anna Mae (Greider) R.; B.S. in Metall. Engring., Drexel U., 1939; M.E., U. Pa., 1948; postgrad. in bus. edn. Drexel U., 1950-52, in metallurgy and materials U. Pa., 1969-70; m. Leonore Catherine Lentz, Oct. 2, 1936; children—L. Catherine, Cynthia L., Martha L., I. Philip, Nancy L. Chief engr. Reese Padlock Co., Lancaster, 1939-42, factory mgr., 1943-49, pres., 1949-61; spl. devel. engr. ammunition U.S. Rubber Co., Eau Claire, Wis., 1942-43; pres. Lancaster Plating, Lancaster, 1961-67; pres. IRC Corp., Lancaster, 1961—; pres. RMPC, Lancaster, 1951—, also treas., dir. Pres. Lancaster Opera Workshop, 1959-60. Mem. Am. Ordnance Assn., Am. Powder Metallurgy Inst., Am. Soc. Metals, ASME, NAM. Presbyterian. Club: Masons. Address: 1502 Hiemenz Rd Lancaster PA 17601

REESE, ROLLIN DAVID, business broker, organist; b. Kenbridge, Va., July 15, 1923; s. John and Blanche E. (Crowder) R.; student Bloomfield Coll., 1940-42, McAllister Coll., 1946-48; M.B.A., Rutgers U., 1952; m. Margaret Ellen Webb, Nov. 12, 1945; 1 son, Rollin David. Examiner, auditor IRS, 1953-56; internal auditor, exec. office Tappins Jewelers Chain Stores, Newark, 1956-60; adminstrv. asst. Engelhard Minerals and Chems. Corp., Menlo Park, N.J., 1965-74; owner, operator Rollin D. Reese & Assos. Agy., bus. brokers, Montclair, N.J., 1974—; organist, choir dir. Mt. Sinai Bapt. Ch., Newark, 1960—, St. Mark A.M.E. Ch., East Orange, 1976-78, Union Bapt. Ch., Passaic, N.J., 1977—. Active Montclair South End Civic Assn., Jr. Achievement, Explorer Scouts. Served with U.S. Army, 1942-46. Mem. Nat. Assn. Accountants (dir.), Am. Guild Organists, N.J. Oratorio Soc. Club: Masons. Home: 12 Grenada Pl Montclair NJ 07042

REESE, WILLIAM WILLIS, banker; b. N.Y.C., July 8, 1940; s. Willis Livingston Meiser and Frances Galletin (Stevens) R.; B.A., Trinity Coll., 1963; M.B.A., J.D., Columbia U., 1970. Admitted to N.Y. bar, 1972; research analyst Morgan Guaranty Trust Co., N.Y.C., 1971-73, investment research officer, 1973-77, asst. v.p., 1977—. Bd. dirs. N.Y.C. Ballet, 1975—, Counseling and Human Devel. Center, 1977—, 3d St. Music Sch. Settlement, 1976—; trustee Millbrook Sch., 1972—. Served with USAF, 1963-67. Mem. Am., Inter-Am., N.Y. State (sec. com. on internat. law 1973-76), Dutchess County bar assns., N.Y. Soc. Security Analysts, Certified Fin. Analysts, Assn. Bar City N.Y. Republican. Episcopalian. Clubs: Union, Racquet and Tennis, Rockaway Hunt, Mt. Holyoke Lodge. Home: Obercreek Farm New Hamburg NY 12560 Office: 9 W 57th St New York City NY 10019

REESIDE, ARTHUR GORDON, JR., nutritionist, hosp. adminstr.; b. Balt., Apr. 24, 1942; s. Arthur Gordon and Dorothy (Bridges) R.; B.A., Coll. William and Mary, 1963; m. Cheryl Lee Adams, Nov. 7, 1964; children—Michelle, Scott. Employment mgr. Blue Cross and Blue Shield Md., Balt., 1965-68; adminstrv. coordinator community medicine Sinai Hosp., Balt., 1968-69; various positions ARA Services Inc., Balt., 1969—, ops. analyst, 1973—, dist. mgr., 1974—, dir. food service, 1969—; resident dist. mgr., dir. nutrition Johns Hopkins Hosp., Balt., 1976—. Served with U.S. Army, 1963-65. Mem. Am. Soc. Hosp. Food Service Adminstrs. (pres.-elect Md chpt.). Democrat. Methodist. Home: Winterbottom Point Bozman MD 21612 Office: Johns Hopkins Hosp 601 N Broadway St Baltimore MD 21205

REESING, JOHN PALMER, JR., educator; b. Gatesville, Tex., Sept. 15, 1920; s. John Palmer and Anne (Baines) R.; B.A., Baylor U., 1941; M.A., Tulane U., 1942; Ph.D., Harvard U., 1954. Instr. in English, George Washington U., 1946-48, asst. prof. English, 1948-49, 54-57, asso. prof., 1957-62, prof., 1962—, chmn. dept. English, 1963-70, 75—, acting chmn. dept., 1972-73; instr. Oberlin Coll., 1953-54. Served to 1st lt. AUS, 1942-46. Mem. Modern Lang. Assn. Am., Modern Humanities Research Assn., Internat. Assn. Univ. Profs. English, Renaissance Soc. Am. Episcopalian. Club: Harvard of Washington. Author: Milton's Poetic Art, 1968. Office: Dept English George Washington U Washington DC 20052

REEVE, RALPH TICHENOR, engring. co. exec.; b. Newark, Apr. 18, 1899; s. William Edgar and Mamie (Tichenor) R.; student Wesleyan U., 1916-18; A.B., Cornell U., 1920; LL.D., Sch. Ozarks, 1978. With buying dept. Halsey Stuart Corp., N.Y.C., 1921-29; mgr. bond dept. J.R. Williston Co., N.Y.C., 1929-35; investments-pvt. underwriting Conn. Mut. Life Ins. Co., Hartford, Conn., 1935-41; cons., 1941-45; pres., treas., dir. Bowen Engring., Inc., North Branch, N.J., 1945-76, vice chmn. bd. dirs., 1976—; pres., treas., dir. Reeve Co., North Branch, 1949-74; dir. Derby Gas & Electric Co.; dir., mem. exec. com. Sigma Investment Shares. Trustee Somerset Hosp., 1957-75. Served with arty. U.S. Army, World War I. Mem. Am. Inst. Chem. Engrs., N.J. Hist. Soc., SAR, Corinthians. Clubs: Nassau (Princeton, N.J.); Richmond County Yacht (Great Kills, N.Y.); Somerville-Raritan Exchange (pres. 1962); Mason (Shriner). Home: Ridge to River Farm 361 Vanderveer Ave Somerville NJ 08876

REEVES, CAROLINE BUCK (MRS. WILLIAM HARVEY REEVES), author, civic worker; b. St. Louis; d. Philo Melvin and Aletheia (Hall) Buck, Jr.; A.B., Wellesley Coll., U. Wis., 1928; M.A., Columbia, 1934; m. William Harvey Reeves, Aug. 29, 1931 (dec. July 9, 1970); children—Aletheia Nevius, Harvey Van Kirk. Editorial department Henry Holt & Company, publishers, N.Y.C., 1928-31; indsl. economist U.S. Govt., Washington, 1942-45, Rockefeller U., N.Y.C., 1970—. Pres. bd. mgrs. Home for Old Men and Aged Couples, N.Y.C., 1955-58, mem. bd., 1951-69, sec. bd., 1960-62, trustee, 1969—; trustee Amsterdam Nursing Corp., N.Y.C., 1974—; mem. com. on aging Fedn. of Protestant Welfare Agys., N.Y.C., 1951-58; mem. hobby show com. Community Council of Greater N.Y., 1955-63; mem. bd. The Bargain Box; N.Y. com. Frontier Nursing Service, Inc. Mem. Colonial Dames Am., Delta Delta Delta. Clubs: Colony, Pequot Yacht. Author of books: Impact of War on Tri-City Area, 1917-19, 43; Impact of World War I on Hampton Roads Area, 1944; Disposition of Surplus Machine Tools by the War Department following World War I, 1944; also articles. Home: 273 Harbor Rd PO Box 214 Southport CT 06490

REEVES, LOVEJOY, cosmetic co. exec.; b. Bronxville, N.Y., May 7, 1944; d. Rosser and Elizabeth Lovejoy (Street) R.; B.A., St. John's Coll., 1967; m. William M. Duryea, Jr., Aug. 7, 1976; 1 son, Robert Atwell. Sr. copywriter Compton Advt. Co., N.Y.C., 1967-70; copywriter Avon Products Inc., N.Y.C., 1970-71, copychief, 1971-73, group-coordinator, 1973-74, mgr., 1974, creative mgr., 1975, project mgr., 1975-76, mgr. nat. rep. recruiting, 1976—. Founder N.Y. chpt. Achievement Rewards Scientists Found. Inc., 1972, dir. at large, 1974-76, dir., 1975-76, membership chmn., 1976-77, 1st v.p., 1978-79; active Jr. League N.Y., 1968-76. Recipient certificate of appreciation Avon Products Inc., 1978. Clubs: Fishers Island Country, Leash. Home: 1158 Fifth Ave New York City NY 10029 Office: 9 W 57th St New York City NY 10019

REEVES, SIDNEY ALEXANDER, constrn. co. exec.; b. Sydney, N.S., Can., Jan. 21, 1927; s. Sidney Ellison and Ella Marjorie (Fownes) R.; B.C.E., N.S. Tech. Coll., 1949; m. Mary Charlotte MacIntyre, July 15, 1950; children—Deborah Jane Reeves King, David Alexander, Susan Marjorie. Jr. engr. Ont. Hydro Electric Co. (Can.), 1949; head engring. dept. Superline Oils Ltd. & Asso. Cos., Halifax, N.S., 1950-52; chmn. bd. Maritime Builders Ltd., Sydney, Can., 1952—; pres. Reeves Bldg. Supplies Ltd., Sidella Enterprises Ltd., Fisher Electronics Ltd., Shaw and MacDonald Ltd., Seveer Realty Ltd., Reeves Modular Homes Ltd.; v.p. Midtown Mgmt. Ltd.; dir. Maritime Telephone & Telegraph Co. Ltd., Oland Breweries Ltd., Dominion Life Assurance Co., A.W. Allen Ltd.; chmn. N.S. Power Corp.; pres. Sydney Bd. of Trade, 1962-63; pres. Asso. Bds. of Trade of Cape Breton, 1963-64. Active Sydney YMCA, past pres.; gen. chmn. Sydney Centennial Commn., 1967; bd. regents Mt. Allison U. Mem. Cape Breton Island Constrn. Assn. (past pres.), Assn. Profl. Engrs., Engring. Inst. Can., Can. Constrn. Assn. Baptist. (past N.S. pres.). Club: Lingan Golf and Country (past pres.). Home: 68 St Peters Rd Sydney NS B1P 4P4 Canada Office: 333 Welton St Sydney NS B1P 6H1 Canada

REEVES, WILLIAM RAY, real estate devel. co. exec.; b. Corbin, Ky., Feb. 8, 1937; s. Leslie Joseph and Phoebe Mae (Hale) R.; B.Chem. Engring., U. Cin., 1959; postgrad. Harvard U., 1960-61; M.B.A., U. Va., 1964; m. Mary Agnes O'Rourke, Dec. 30, 1972; children—Katherine Margaret, David William Joseph, Robert Sean Hale. Cons., Fantus div. Dun & Bradstreet, N.Y.C., 1969-70; pres. Barnett Chem. Products, Inc., Phila., 1970-72; cons. Nat. Center for Resource Recovery, Washington, 1972-73; v.p. Interstate Gen. Corp., St. Charles, Md., San Juan, P.R., 1973—; dir. St. Charles Health Services, Inc., 1977—. Served as capt. U.S. Army, 1960-61. Registered profl. engr., Ohio, Md. Mem. Port Tobacco Restoration Soc. (pres., dir. 1976—), Charles County (Md.) Heart Assn. (chmn. 1976-77), Nat. Energy Resources Orgn., Met. Washington Bd. Trade, Harvard Bus. Sch. Club Washington. Club: Hawthorne Country. Patentee radio controlled fishing boat, 1968. Home: Sunnytop Farm Port Tobacco MD 20677 Office: 336 Post Office Rd St Charles MD 20601

REEVES, WILLIAM RAY, cons. civil engr.; b. Punxsutawney, Pa., Aug. 28, 1932; s. William Alexander and Dorothy Jeanette (Lockwood) R.; B.C.E., Pa. State U., 1954; m. Josephine Lorraine Makufka, June 1, 1957; children—Susan Marie, Timothy John, Kathleen Ann. Survey party chief Simpson & Madison, DuBois, Pa., 1952-54, asst. office mgr., design engr., 1954-55, office mgr., design engr., 1956-58; chief engr. civil div. Yost Assos., Inc., DuBois, 1958-70; airport dept. head L. Robert Kimball, Ebensburg, Pa., 1970—, v.p., 1973—. Lector, commentator St. Michael Ch., DuBois, Pa., 1966-70, pres. Holy Name Soc., 1969; treas. Crestwood Community Assn., 1975-76; mem. exec. bd. Penns Wood council Boy Scouts Am., 1975—, chmn. north dist., 1976—; mem. Cambria County Transit Authority, 1977—. Served with U.S. Army, 1955-56. Registered profl. engr., 14 states. Mem. ASCE, Am. Cons. Engrs. Council, Nat. Assn. State Aviation Ofcls., Am. Assn. Airport Execs., Am., Pa. socs. profl. engrs., Aviation Council Pa., Chi Epsilon, Sigma Tau. Republican. Roman Catholic. Home: RD 3 Box 382 Crestwood Ebensburg PA 15931 Office: 615 W Highland Ave Ebensburg PA 15931

REGAN, FREDERIC DENNIS, physician; b. Newburyport, Mass., Aug. 21, 1921; s. Dennis and Catherine R. (Haley) R.; student Syracuse U., 1940-42; M.D., U. Buffalo, 1945; m. Marilyn, June 24, 1945; children—Denise, Frederic, Michael. Intern, USPHS Hosp., Staten Island, N.Y., 1945-46, research fellow in cardiology, 1947, resident medicine, dep. chief medicine, chief cardiac clinic, 1950-52; practice medicine specializing in cardiology and internal medicine; mem. staffs USPHS Hosp., Seaview Hosp. Diplomate Am. Bd. Internal Medicine. Fellow A.C.P., Am. Coll. Cardiology, N.Y. Cardiology Soc.; mem. Richmond County Med. Soc. (pres. 1961-62). Office: 347 Edison St Staten Island NY 10306

REGAN, GERALD AUGUSTINE, fgn. govt. ofcl.; b. Windsor, N.S., Can., Feb. 13, 1929; s. Walter Edward and Rose M. (Greene) R.; ed. St. Mary's Coll., Dalhousie U.; m. Carole Harrison; children—Gerald, Geoffrey, Miriam, Nancy, David, Laura. Mem. Parliament, 1963-65, N.S. Legislature, 1967—; premier N.S., pres. exec. council, 1970—; now leader of opposition Province of N.S.; chmn. N.S. Power Corp., 1970-76. Chmn. exec. com. Commonwealth Parliament Assn., 1973-76. Leader N.S. Liberal party, 1965—. Roman Catholic. Address: Province House Halifax NS Canada

REGAN, JAMES RAYMOND, psychologist, ednl. adminstr.; b. Poughkeepsie, N.Y., Aug. 6, 1947; s. Vincent C. and Anne E. (Jackson) Regan; B.S., Loyola U., Chgo., 1969; M.A. in Clin. Psychology, St. John's U., 1971, postgrad., 1971—; m. Carol Antalek, Aug. 23, 1969; children—Shawn Vincent, Erin Stephanie. Staff psychologist Suffolk Psychiat. Center, Central Islip, N.Y., 1970-73; staff psychologist Harlem Valley Psychiat. Center, Wingdale, N.Y., 1973-74, chief of serivce, 1974-75, chief of service Alcoholism Service, 1975-76, dir. edn. and tng., 1976-78, asso. dir. Center, 1978—. dir. alcoholism service Bio-Psych. Center, Inc., White Plains, N.Y., 1977—; cons. to South Forty Corp., Poughkeepsie, N.Y., 1975—; adj. instr. grad. dept. psychology Marist Coll., Poughkeepsie, 1975—, Dutchess Community Coll., Poughkeepsie, 1973—. Bd. dirs. Valley Edn. Corp. Recipient U.S. Jaycee award, 1976. Mem. N.Y. State Fedn. Profl. Health Educators, Alpha Delta Gamma, Psi Chi. Home: RD 3 Lauer Rd Poughkeepsie NY 12603 Office: Harlem Valley Psychiatric Center Wingdale NY 12594

REGAN, JOHN FRANCIS, telephone co. exec.; b. Forsyth, Mont., Aug. 18, 1918; s. Thomas Joseph and Mary Elizabeth (Hurley) R.; B.S., Harvard U., 1939; M.B.A., George Washington U., 1962, D.Bus. Adminstrn., 1968; m. Martha B. Moore, Jan. 22, 1943; children—Katharyn H., Martha M. Szczur. Various managerial assignments C&P Telephone, Washington, 1939-43, dist. mgr., 1954-59, staff assignments, 1959-70, staff supr., personnel research and devel., 1973—; engr. AT&T, N.Y.C., 1952-54, project mgr. human resources research, 1971-72; adj. prof. mgmt. sci. George Washington U., 1963—. Served with USNR, 1943-46. Mem. Am., D.C. psychol. assns., Acad. Mgmt., Soc. Gen. Systems Research, Telephone Pioneers Am. (chpt. pres. 1968-69). Club: Cosmos. Home: 6001 Osceola Rd Bethesda MD 20016 Office: 1710 H St NW Washington DC 20006

REGGIO, ROBERT BRUCE, biologist; b. Bklyn., Oct. 19, 1934; s. Carl Anthony and Catherine Gertrude (Rodi) R.; B.A., N.Y. U., 1956; M.S., St. John's U., 1964, Ph.D., 1973; m. Carol Marie Coppola, June 20, 1959; children—Nina, James, John, Carolyn. Research asst. Boyce Thompson Inst., Yonkers, N.Y., 1959-63, Geigy Chem. Co., Ardsley, N.Y., 1963-64; asso. prof. biology Coll. of New Rochelle (N.Y.), 1964—, chmn. dept., biology, 1970-76. Served with U.S. Army, 1956-58. NSF grantee, 1969-70; Sigma Xi grantee, 1968-69; Faculty Fund for Scholarly Research grantee, 1975-76. Mem. AAAS, Inst. of Society, Ethics and Life Scis. Contbr. articles to profl. jours. Home: 40-26 202 St Bayside NY 11361 Office: Dept Biology College of New Rochelle New Rochelle NY 10801

REGNIER, LOUIS A., property mgr., real estate developer; b. Cranston, R.I., June 27, 1927; s. Louis A. and Delia (MacPhail) R.; student U. Denver, 1951-52, San Francisco State U., 1974-76; C.P.M., Inst. Real Estate Mgmt.; m. Carol Jean Hall, Aug. 25, 1951; children—Stephen Dean, Lynn Ann, Christine Ann. Salesman, U.S. Radiator, Chto., 1947-48, Clark-Babbitt Industries, Boston, 1948; founder Contractors' Insulation Co., Providence, 1948-51; founder, treas. Regnier-Laurienzo & Co., Inc., 1953-63; pres. Exec. House, Providence, 1961—, Louis A. Regnier Asso., Inc., 1963—, Lynn Investment Corp., 1962—; treas. Reservoir Investment Corp., 1961—; pres. Doki Corp., 1973—; chmn. bd. D.D.K. Jewelry Inc., Bel-Air Industries; dir. Eastern Pollution Corp.; real estate investment cons. Served with USN, 1945-46, USAF, 1952. Mem. Inst. Real Estate Mgmt., Nat. Assn. Realtors, Nat. Assn. Home Builders, Apt. Owners Assn. R.I. (chmn.), Continental Varnums, Providence C. of C., Aircraft Owners and Pilots Assn., Urban Land Inst., Apt. Owners and Mgmt. Assn. (nat. dir.), Am. Hereford Assn., Houston Apt. Assn., Builders Assn. Houston. Clubs: Greenwich, R.I. Yacht. Home: Fletcher Rd North Kingston RI 02852 Office: Suite 1620 One Hospital Trust Plaza Providence RI 02903

REGNIER, RAYMOND COBINGTON, JR., cons. engr.; b. Balt., July 10, 1915; s. Raymond Charles and Anna (Zimmerman) R.; B.Engring., Johns Hopkins U., 1935; m. Frances Goodwin Lockwood, Sept. 28, 1940; children—Robert L., Joanna J. (Mrs. J.M. Moore), Elizabeth E. (Mrs. M. E. Beil). Designer, engr. Whitman, Requardt & Smith, 1936-42; with Whitman, Requardt & Asso., 1946-77, successively engr. on water supply, sewerage and storm drainage projects, asso. engr., 1946-56, partner, 1957-77; ret., 1977. Served from 1st lt. to maj., C.W.S., 1942-46. Fellow ASCE, Am. Cons. Engrs.

Council, Royal Soc. Health; mem. Am. Water Works Assn., Nat. Soc. Profl. Engrs., Water Pollution Control Fedn., Am. Pub. Works Assn., Nat. Rifle Assn., Kappa Sigma. Diplomate Environmental Engring. Intersoc. Bd. Club: Engineers (Balt.). Home: 102 Cross Keys Rd Baltimore MD 21210

REGOLI, VERA PAULA, office machine mfg. co. exec.; b. Trenton, N.J., Oct. 28, 1952; d. Anthony and Ester (Angeletti) R.; A.A.S. with honors, Mercer County (N.J.) Community Coll., 1972. Programmer, then programmer/analyst Olivetti Corp. Am., 1972-78, software mgr., Phila., 1978—. Address: 23 City Line Ave Bala Cynwyd PA 19004

REGUEIRO, JOSE MIGUEL, educator; b. Cordoba, Argentina, Dec. 20, 1938; s. Gumersindo and Casimira (Martinez) R.; came to U.S., 1961, naturalized, 1968; student U. Nacional de Cordoba, 1961; Ph.D. (fellow), U. Pa., 1972; m. Judith Eleanor Anderson Hale, June 14, 1964; children—Miguel Duclos, Richard Anderson. Tchr., Binat. Center, Cordoba, Argentina, 1957-60, Am. Sch., Cordoba, 1960-61, The Episcopal Acad., Merion Station, Pa., 1962-65, The Hill Sch., Pottstown, Pa., 1965-67; mng. editor Hispanic Rev., 1972—; asst. prof. romance langs. U. Pa., Phila., 1972-78, asso. prof., 1978—. Am. Philos. Soc. grantee, 1974. Mem. Modern Lang. Assn. Am., Renaissance Soc. Am., Am. Assn. Tchrs. of Spanish and Portuguese. Author: Spanish Drama of the Golden Age, 1971; co-author: Dramatic Manuscripts in the Hispanic Society of America, 1978; contbr. revs. and articles to lit. publs. Office: 521 Williams Hall Univ of Pennsylvania Philadelphia PA 19104

REHBERGER, GUSTAV, artist; b. Riedlingsdorf, Austria, Oct. 20, 1910; s. Joseph and Elizabeth (Piff) R.; brought to U.S., 1923, naturalized, 1928; student Art Inst. Chgo., 1924-34, Art Instrn. Schs., Mpls., 1926-28. Fine arts painter, also former illustrator for nat. mags., motion picture promotion, book; designer, illustrator nat. advt. campaigns; one-man shows at Library, North Canton, Ohio, 1940, Stevens-Gross Gallery, Chgo., 1950, Soc. Illustrators, N.Y. City, 1957, 65, Nat. Arts Club, Montreal, 1967, Wyoming Valley Art League, Wilkes-Barre, Pa., 1967, Wickersham Gallery, N.Y.C., 1971, Jacques Seligmann Gallery, N.Y.C., 1977; exhibited in group shows N.A.D., Audubon Artists, Allied Artists Am., Painters in Casein, Internat. Water Color Show at Chgo. Art Inst., Nat. Galleries, London, Nat. Gallery, Washington, Am. Water Color Soc., N.Y.C., Nat. Drawing Exhbn., Oklahoma City; represented in permanent collections Lyman Allyn Mus., New London, Conn., St. Johns U., Sports Hall, Peking, China, also pvt. collections U.S., Can., Europe, China, Saudi Arabia; tchr., lectr. composition, anatomy, drawing and painting the figure Art Students League N.Y., 1972—; lectr., painting and drawing demonstrator The Spirit of Form and Movement. Recipient award for creative painting 7th Ann. Audubon Artists Exhbn.; Art Dirs. Show award, N.Y.C., 1954, 55; Soc. Typographic Arts award, Chgo.; Minnie R. Stern award 24th Ann. Audubon Artists Exhbn., 1966; Paul Puzinas Meml. award Allied Artists Am., 1974; Tiro A. Segno Found. award Pastel Soc. Am., 1976. Mem. Allied Artists Am., Pastel Soc. Am., Audubon Artists. Pioneer in use expressionism in Am. illustration and design. Address: Carnegie Hall Studio 1206 New York City NY 10019

REHBERGER, JOHN MARTIN, physician-surgeon; b. Sweetair, Md., June 21, 1916; s. George Edward and Lena Ellen (Martin) R.; B.S., Loyola Coll., 1940; M.D., N.Y. Med. Coll., 1947; postgrad. in otolaryngology U. Pa. Sch. Medicine, 1948-49; 1 son, John M. Intern, Union Meml. Hosp., Balt., 1947; resident Hosp. U. Pa., 1949-51; practice otolaryngology, Balt., 1951—; mem. staff Woman's Hosp., Presbyn. EENT Hosp., Franklin Sq. Hosp., Mercy Hosp., Md. Gen. Hosp., Union Meml. Hosp., Greater Balt. Med. Center. Served to capt. AUS, 1943-46, 52-54. Diplomate Am. Bd. Otolaryngology. Fellow Am. Acad. Ophthalmology and Otolaryngology, A.C.S.; mem. Balt. County Med. Soc. AMA, Med.-Chirurg. Faculty Md., Am. Acad. Otolaryngology. Roman Catholic. Club: Green Spring, Penn. Office: 6301 N Charles St Baltimore MD 21212

REHL, MARGARET ANN, librarian; b. Cresco, Iowa, Mar. 7, 1936; d. David J. and Eva (Lanning) Robbins; B.A. with high honors, State U. Iowa, 1956; M.L.S. (Lydia Roberts fellowship), Columbia U., 1957; m. John M. Rehl, Jan. 25, 1957; children—Mark, John. Library asst. edn. library Queens (N.Y.) Coll., 1957; librarian Escola Graduada de Sao, Paulo, Brasil, 1959-62, John Jay High Sch., HopeWell Junction, N.Y., 1970—. Mem. Sch. Librarians S.E. N.Y., Phi Beta Kappa, Alpha Lambda Delta. Methodist. Home: 5 Plum Ct Wappingers Falls NY 12590 Office: John Jay High School #52 Hopewell Junction NY 12590

REHMAN, FREDERICK MAX, optical co. exec.; b. Pottsville, Pa., Dec. 26, 1931; s. Bernard Herman and Emma Katrinka (Schnell) R.; student U. Pa., 1949-52; m. Donis Louise Horning, Jan. 8, 1960; children—Mark Edward, Timothy Paul. Controller, Kawecki Chem. Co., Boyertown, Pa., 1966-69; regional controller Ogden Foods, Miami Springs, Fla., 1969-70; asst. treas. Kawecki Berylco Industries, Reading, Pa., 1970-73; acctg. mgr. Retail Optical Group, Dentsply Internat., York, Pa., 1973—. Bd. dirs., treas. Mason Dixon Library. Served with U.S. Army, 1952-55. C.P.A., Pa. Lutheran. Club: Masons. Home: RD 1 Box 266 Stewartstown PA 17363 Office: 570 W College Ave York PA 17404

REHNQUIST, WILLIAM HUBBS, Supreme Ct. justice; b. Milw., Oct. 1, 1924; s. William Benjamin and Margery (Peck) R.; B.A., M.A., Stanford, 1948, LL.B., 1952; M.A., Harvard, 1949; m. Natalie Cornell, Aug. 29, 1953; children—James, Janet, Nancy. Admitted to Ariz. bar; law clk. to former justice Robert H. Jackson, U.S. Supreme Ct., 1952-53; with firm Evans, Kitchel & Jenckes, Phoenix, 1953-55; mem. firm Ragan & Rehnquist, Phoenix, 1956-57; partner firm Cunningham, Carson & Messenger, Phoenix, 1957-60; partner firm Powers & Rehnquist, Phoenix, 1960-69; asst. atty.-gen. office of legal counsel Dept. of Justice, Washington, 1969-71; asso. justice U.S. Supreme Ct., 1971—. Mem. Nat. Conf. Commrs. Uniform State Laws, 1963-69. Served with USAAF, 1943-46. Mem. Fed., Am. Maricopa (Ariz.) County bar assns., State Bar Ariz., Nat. Conf. Lawyers and Realtors Order of Coif, Phi Beta Kappa, Phi Delta Phi Lutheran. Contbr. articles to law jours. nat. mags. Office: Supreme Ct US Washington DC 20543

REICH, STEPHEN, psychologist, lawyer; b. Bklyn., May 24, 1939; s. Arnold and Helen P. (Rosen) R.; B.A., Columbia Coll., 1960, J.D., 1963, M.B.A., 1963; M.A., Fordham U., 1970, Ph.D., 1972. Admitted to N.Y. State bar, 1964; asso. firm Herman Odell, N.Y.C., 1964-65; asst. atty. gen., State of N.Y., N.Y.C., 1965-68; instr. psychology Cornell U. Med. Coll., N.Y.C., 1972-73, asst. prof., 1973—; pvt. practice psychology, N.Y.C., 1974—; cons. psychologist Consol. Edison Co., N.Y.C., 1977—; asst. attending psychologist N.Y. Hosp., 1972—. USPHS fellow, 1968-71. Mem. Am. Psychol. Soc., N.Y. Acad. Scis., Am. Psychol.-Law Soc., Soc. Contbr. articles to profl. jours. Office: 57 W 57th St New York NY 10019

REICH, THEOBALD, surgeon; b. Svidnik, Czechoslovakia, Jan. 1, 1927; s. David J. and Susan (Ritter) R.; came to U.S., 1939, naturalized, 1953; B.A., N.Y. U., 1948; M.D., St. Louis U., 1951; m. Ida E. Westerman, May 21, 1961; children—David J., A.H. Jonathan. Intern, Bellevue Hosp., N.Y.C., 1951-52; research biochemist, div. labs. and research N.Y. State Dept. Health, N.Y.C., 1952-53; asst. to chief resident Bellevue Hosp., 1955-59; fellow in surgery N.Y.U. Sch. Medicine, N.Y.C., 1959-61; instr. in surgery, 1960-67; attending surgeon and research project dir. Miseracordia Hosp., N.Y.C., 1961-65; asst. prof. surgery Mt. Sinai Sch. Medicine Hosp., N.Y.C., 1965-67; asso. prof. surgery N.Y.U. Sch. Medicine, 1967-73, prof. surg. research, 1973—; surgeon N.Y.C. Police Dept., 1970—; Dept. Def. grantee, 1967; NSF grantee, 1974; NIH grantee, 1961; Rippel Found. grantee, 1974; Engring. Found. grantee, 1974. Served with U.S. Army, 1953-55. Diplomate Am. Bd. Med. Examiners, Am. Bd. Surgery. Fellow A.C.S.; mem. N.Y. Acad. Medicine, Am. Physiol. Soc., Biomed. Engring. Soc., N.Y. Surg. Soc., N.Y. Soc. Cardiovascular Surgery, Am. Heart Assn., AMA, N.Y. Police Dept. Superior Officers' Council. Contbr. articles to profl. jours. Patentee in field (3). Home: 100 Bleeker St New York City NY 10012 Office: Inst Rehab Medicine NY Univ Med Center 400 E 34th St New York City NY 10016

REICHART, BESSIE MAY CRISWELL, ret. educator, librarian; b. Emlenton, Pa., May 16, 1907; d. Fleming Byers and Hattie Catharine (May) Criswell; diploma Clarion State Normal Sch., 1926; B.S. in Edn., Clarion State Tchrs. Coll., 1941; M.A. in Edn. and L.S., 1954; postgrad. U. Pitts., 1941-43; m. Joseph Lyle Reichart, July 14, 1944; 1 foster dau., Martha Diane Stewart. Tchr., Richland Twp., Venango County, Pa., 1926-28, Emlenton (Pa.) Pub. Schs., 1928-56; head librarian Fox Chapel (Pa.) Sr. High Sch., 1956-66; former mem. evaluation coms. Am. Council on Edn. Librarian, Emlenton United Presbyterian Ch., 1967—. Mem. ALA, Pa. Library Assn., Pitts. Suburban Council Sch. Librarians, Nat., Pa., Allegheny County ret. tchrs. assns. (life), AAUW. Republican. Clubs: Emlenton Civic, Order Eastern Star, Rebekah. Home: PO Box 331 Hill St Emlenton PA 16373

REICHLE, FREDERICK ADOLPH, surgeon; b. Neshaminy, Pa., Apr. 20, 1935; s. Albert and Ernestine R.; B.A. summa cum laude, Temple U., 1957, M.D., 1961, M.S. in Biochemistry, 1961, M.S. in Surgery, 1966. Intern, Abington Meml. Hosp., 1962; resident Temple U. Hosp., Phila., 1966, surgeon, 1966—; practice medicine specializing in surgery, Phila., 1966—; asso. attending surgeon Episcopal Hosp., St. Marys Hosp., St. Christophers Hosp. for Children; cons. VA Hosp., Wilkes Barre, Pa.; prof. surgery, chief peripheral vascular sect., dept. surgery Temple U. Sch. Medicine, 1976—. Recipient Surg. Residents Research Paper awards Phila. Acad. Surgery, 1964, 66, Gross Essay prize Phila. Acad. Surgery, 1972. Am. Heart Assn. grantee, 1973. Diplomate Am. Bd. Surgery. Fellow A.C.S.; mem. Am. Surg. Assn., Soc. U. Surgeons, AMA, Pa. Med. Soc., Assn. Acad. Surgery, N.Y. Acad. Sci., AAAS, Am. Fedn. Clin. Research, Nat. Assn. Professions, Am. Gastroent. Assn., Am. Assn. Cancer Research, Am. Heart Assn., Phila. Acad. Surgery, Heart Assn. Southeastern Pa., Internat. Soc. on Thrombosis and Haemostasis, Nat. Kidney Found., Soc. for Surgery Alimentary Tract, Soc. Vascular Surgery, Colleguim Internationale Chirurgie Digestivae, Am. Soc. Pharmacology and Exptl. Therapeutics, Soc. Internationale de Chirurgie, Am. Soc. Abdominal Surgeons, Surg. Hist. Soc., Am. Aging Assn., Am. Geriatrics Soc., Gerontol. Soc., Am. Diabetes Assn., Surg. Biology Club, Alpha Omega Alpha, Sigma Xi, Phi Tho Sigma. Contbr. articles to profl. jours. Home: 771 Easton Rd Warrington PA 18976 Office: 3400 N Broad St Philadelphia PA 19140

REID, ALEXANDER DARRELL GORDON, securities co. exec.; b. Vancouver, B.C., Can., July 8, 1937; s. Alexander Kissam Gordon and Margaret Lillie (McLaren) R.; student pub. schs.; m. Marcia Eleanor Thomas, June 15, 1956; (div. Nov. 1978); children—Alexander Richard, Michael Bruce, Susan Margaret. Resident dir. D.D. Creighton & Co., Ltd., Toronto, Ont., 1963-66; v.p., dir. Brawley Cathers, Ltd., Toronto, 1966-70; head internat. sales, dir. F.H. Deacon & Co., Ltd., Toronto, 1970-74; dir. Martens, Ball, Albrecht Securities Ltd., 1975-76; pres. A.D.G. Reid Corp., Ltd., Toronto, 1976—; V.P., dir. Brawley Cathers Ltd., 1977—; chmn. bd. Grimm's Foods, Ltd.; v.p., dir. RMW Corp. Ltd., Armagh Investments, Ltd. Mem. Toronto Soc. Fin. Analysts, Toronto Men's Press Club. Progressive Conservative. Clubs: Albany, Celebrity, Toronto Lawn Tennis, Shaughnessy Heights Golf, Cambridge (Toronto); Adelaide, Genesis, Caledon Ski, Royal Canadian Yacht. Contbr. articles to periodicals including Investors Digest of Can.; author weekly column Financial Post, 1962—, Toronto Sun, 1978—; editor Financial Post Investors Handbook, 1976. Home: 487 Oriole Pkwy Toronto ON Canada Office: Suite 1501 11 King St W Toronto ON Canada

REID, CHARLES FREDERICK, JR., educator; b. Leechburg, Pa., Apr. 25, 1898; s. Charles Frederick and Nellie (Arnold) R.; A.B., Colgate U., 1923; A.M., Columbia, 1929, Ph.D., 1940; m. Dorothy Sarah Leader, Aug. 14, 1936; 1 son, Charles Frederick III; m. 2d, Amelia Alfandre Hacker, Aug. 6, 1972; 1 son, Sander Hacker. Supervising prin. Victor (N.Y.) High Sch., 1925-29; asst. to pres. Carnegie Found. for Advancement Teaching, 1929-31; faculty Sch. Edn. City Coll. City U. N.Y., 1931-68, now prof. emeritus; staff mem. Ednl. Survey, Holyoke, Mass., 1929, Panama Canal Zone, 1930; research asst. The Nat. Adv. Com. Edn., 1930, sr. specialist, 1937; vis. prof. Summer Session U. P.R., 1941, Worcester (Mass.) State Tchrs. Coll., 1948, Ore. State Bd. Higher Edn., 1949; profl. lectr. U. Philippines, 1953-55. Trustee Hastings-on-Hudson, N.Y., 1948-52, mayor, 1957-59. Served with U.S. Army, World War I, World War II, with USAF, Korean War. Recipient Gold medal U. Philippines; 1955. Fellow AAAS; mem. Am. Assn. Sch. Adminstrs., Alpha Tau Omega, Phi Delta Kappa. Presbyterian. Author: Education in the Territories and Outlying Possessions of the United States, 1941; Overseas America, Headline Book No. 35, 1942. Editor: Bibliography of the Island of Guam, 1939; Bibliography of the Virgin Islands of the United States, 1941. Home: 4407 NW 49th Dr Tamarac Fort Lauderdale FL 33319 also 350 1st Ave New York NY 10010

REID, H(ENRY) TERRY, educator; b. Washington, Ga., Jan. 13, 1939; s. Terry and Bessie (Hayes) R.; A.A., St. Peters Coll., Jersey City, 1974, B.S., 1976; M.B.A. summa cum laude, Fairleigh Dickinson U., 1978; children—Bernice, Mark, Terrance, Duane, Tanzy. Mgr. Bayonne Wholesale Food Co. (N.J.), 1957-60; mgr. warehousing Hartfield/Zody's, Inc., N.Y.C., 1960-69; registrar, computer instr. Sigma Bus. Coll., Newark, 1969-74; computer programming instr., systems analyst Newark Manpower Tng. Skill Center, div. vocat. edn. N.J. Dept. Edn., 1974-79; prof. computer sci. St. Peters Coll., Jersey City, 1979—. Sec. The Profls., Inc., Jersey City, 1974—. Served with U.S. Army, 1962-64, Res., 1964-68. Roman Catholic. Home: 53 Grand Ave Newark NJ 07106 Office: 2641 Kennedy Blvd Jersey City NJ 07306

REID, JEAN D. CHANG, banker; b. Kingston, Jamaica, Jan. 24, 1935; d. Chang King Pow and Isaline M. (Rattray); came to U.S., 1958, naturalized, 1963; diploma West Indies Coll., 1952; certificate bus. adminstrn., Radcliffe Coll., 1963; M.B.A. (Margaret Earhardt Smith award 1963), Harvard U., 1964; m. Bernard Francis Heiler, Sept. 7, 1974; 1 son, Jerome Reid, Jr. Investment analyst State St. Bank & Trust Co., Boston, 1965-72; investment coordinator, charge investment research Fiduciary Trust Co., Boston, 1972—; vis. lectr. Simmons Coll., Boston, 1974-75. Mem. com. to select sch. prins., Watertown, Mass., 1974-75; religious edn. com. Unitarian Ch., Cambridge, Mass., 1970—. Certified fin. analyst. Mem. Boston Security Analysts Soc., Harvard Bus. Sch. Assn. Boston, Boston Mus. Fine Arts, New Eng. Aquarium. Republican. Clubs: Univ., Radcliffe (Boston); Women's Republican (Watertown). Home: 141 Common St Watertown MA 02172 Office: PO Box 1647 Boston MA 02105

REID, JOHN WALLING, psychologist, educator; b. Binghamton, N.Y., Nov. 8, 1917; s. Joseph and Edna Eliza (Cooke) R.; B.A., Swarthmore Coll., 1940; M.A., U. Pa., 1947; Ed.D., Columbia U., 1961; m. Carol Alice Jurgens, June 12, 1947; 1 son, Warren Benjamin. Cost accountant Autocar Co., 1940-42; master English The Haverford Sch., 1947; instr. psychology, 1947-48; asst. prof. Westminster Coll., New Wilmington, Pa., 1948-50; acting dir. psychol. services Albright Coll., Reading, Pa., 1950-51; asst. prof. psychology Kans. State Coll., 1952-54; counseling psychologist VA, Syracuse, N.Y., 1954-57, Wilkes-Barre, Pa., 1957-59, Newark Coll. Engring., 1959-61, Howard U., summer 1965; chmn. dept. psychology Cedar Crest Coll., Allentown, Pa., 1961-62; asso. prof. psychology Indiana U. of Pa., 1962-69, prof., 1970—, counseling psychologist, 1970—, dir. psychol. clinic, 1962-65; postdoctoral fellow Mental Health Service U. Fla., 1972-73. Served with inf., U.S. Army, 1942-46. Decorated Purple Heart, Bronze Star, Belgian Fourragère; USPHS grantee, 1972-73. Fellow Pa. Psychol. Assn.; mem. Nat. Vocat. Guidance Assn. (profl.), Am. Personnel and Guidance Assn. (life). Republican. Contbr. articles in field to profl. jours. Home: 621 S 6th St Indiana PA 15701 Office: 102 Pratt Hall Indiana U of Pa Indiana PA 15705

REID, ROSS, lawyer, bus. exec.; b. Spokane, Wash., Mar. 9, 1917; s. William George and Margaret (Gamble) R.; A.B., Whitman Coll., 1938; student law U. Wash., 1938-40; J.D., Northwestern U., 1942; m. Sara Falknor, Dec. 31, 1940 (div.); 1 dau., Heather (Mrs. Edmund A. Schaffzin); m. 2d, Marney Sick Meeker, Jan. 19, 1966. Admitted to Ill. Bar, 1941, N.Y. bar, 1943, D.C. bar, 1960; asso. firm Root, Clark, Buckner & Ballantine, N.Y.C., 1942-53; mem. firm Dewey, Ballantine, Bushby, Palmer & Wood and predecessors, N.Y.C., 1954-62; v.p., dir., gen. counsel Beechnut Life Savers, Inc., 1962-68; sr. v.p., dir., gen. counsel, exec. com. Squibb Corp., N.Y.C., 1968—; dir. Allegheny Power Systems; trustee Prudential Savs. Bank. Mem. N.Y. State Lawyers Com. to Support Ct. Reorgn., 1958-60. Dir., exec. com., chmn. bd., Am. Heart Assn., 1972-74, chmn. fin. com., Gold Heart award, 1970; dir., exec. com., chmn. N.Y. Heart Assn., 1964-72; bd. dirs., 1st v.p. Internat. Soc. and Fedn. Cardiology, 1978—; bd. dirs. Internat. Cardiology Found. trustee Whitman Coll., Robert A. Taft Inst. Served with USAAF, 1945. Fellow Am. Bar Found.; mem. Am., N.Y., N.Y. County bar assns., Assn. Bar City N.Y. (exec. com. 1962-66), Jud. Conf. 2d Circuit (exec. sec. planning com. 1962-64), Am. Judicature Soc., Order of Coif, Beta Theta Pi, Delta Sigma Rho, Delta Theta Phi. Clubs: Univ., West Side Tennis (N.Y.C.), Coral Beach and Tennis (Bermuda); Seattle Tennis. Home: 142 E 71st St New York City NY 10021 Office: 40 W 57th St New York City NY 10019

REIDY, JOHN SHERBURNE, investment analysis exec.; b. Boston, Feb. 25, 1938; s. John A. and Alice (Sherburne) R.; A.B. cum laude, Harvard, 1960, M.B.A., 1963. Securities analyst Loeb, Rhoades & Co., N.Y.C., 1963-69; partner, securities analyst Auerbach Pollak & Richardson, N.Y.C., 1969-71; v.p., investment analyst William D. Witter, Inc., N.Y.C., 1971-76; v.p. research, investment analyst Drexel Burnham Lambert Inc., N.Y.C., 1976—. Head N.Y. fund raising for Congressman Timothy Wirth. Served with U.S. Army Res., 1961. Named Instl. Investor All-Star Analyst, 1972-78; chartered fin. analyst. Fellow Fin. Analysts Fedn.; mem. Entertainment Analysts Group, Printing and Pub. Analysts Assn., N.Y. Soc. Security Analysts (vice chmn. programming). Home: 72 E 79th St New York City NY 10021 Office: 60 Broad St New York City NY 10004

REIFF, DOVIE KATE, architect, urban planner; b. Birmingham, Ala., Nov. 5, 1931; d. Roy Humes and Lou Ada (Erwin) Petty; B.Arch., U. Pa., 1954, M. City Planning, 1969, postgrad., 1974-76; m. Donald Allen Reiff, Dec. 25, 1956 (div. Dec. 1977); children—Donna Lynn, Benjamin Lyle, Johanna Carol. Archtl. draftsman, designer Oskar Stonorov, architect, Phila., 1954-57; pvt. practice architecture, Phila., 1958-64; research asst. Inst. Environ. Studies, U. Pa., 1967-68; sr. planner Montgomery County Planning Commn., Norristown, Pa., 1969-71; urban planner Wallace McHarg Roberts & Todd, Phila., 1971-74; research analyst Del. Valley Regional Planning Commn., Phila., 1974, 75-76; planner Heritage Conservation and Recreation Service, N.E. Regional Office, Dept. Interior, Phila., 1977-78; pvt. practice as urban planner, Phila., 1969—. Mem. Pres.'s Com. on Employment of Handicapped, 1975-78. Theophilus Chandler fellow, 1954. Mem. AIA (Arnold Brunner scholar 1974; exec. com. Phila. chpt. 1978), Am. Inst. Planners (rep. to Center for Planning Design and councillor Phila. regional chpt. 1970-75), Am. Inst. Planning Ofcls., Am. Acad. Polit. and Social Sci., Nat. Center Barrier Free Environment, Pa. Planning Assns., World Affairs Council, Tau Sigma Delta. Republican. Research on space and mobility needs of the disabled. Home: 8 Yeakel Ave Philadelphia PA 19118

REIFSNYDER, CHARLES FRANK, lawyer; b. Ottumwa, Iowa, Sept. 6, 1920; s. Charles L. and Lena (Emery) R.; A.B., George Washington U., 1944, LL.B., 1946; m. Sally Ann Evans, Dec. 27, 1948; children—Daniel Alan, Jeremy Evans; m. 2d, Nancy Lee Laws, Mar. 4, 1960; 1 son, Frank Laws. Admitted to D.C. bar, 1945; sec. to Judge T. Alan Goldsborough, U.S. Dist. Ct., Washington, 1945; law clk. Chief Judge Bolitha J. Laws, U.S. Dist. Ct., 1946-47; asst. U.S. atty., Washington, 1947-51; spl. asst. to Atty. Gen. U.S., 1950-51; asso. firm Hogan & Hartson, Washington, 1951-58, partner, 1959—. Chmn. personnel security rev. bd. ERDA (formerly AEC); trustee Legal Aid Agy. (now Pub. Defender Service), Washington, 1960-67; bd. dirs. Nat. Coll. State Judiciary, Reno, 1968-70. Fellow Inst. Jud. Adminstrn., N.Y.C., 1967-68. Fellow Internat. Soc. Barristers, Am. Bar Found.; mem. Am. (chmn. spl. com. on coordination jud. improvements 1971-74, mem. spl. com. on atomic energy law 1969-73, chmn. sect. jud. adminstrn. 1967-68, del. 1968-69), Fed., Fed. Energy (mem. exec. com.; chmn. natural gas 1967-68), D.C. (dir. 1955-56) bar assns., Am. Arbitration Assn., (nat. panel arbitrators), Am. Judicature Soc. (dir. 1972-76), Phi Delta Phi, Sigma Nu. Episcopalian. Clubs: Metropolitan, Nat. Lawyers, Barristers, Lawyers (Washington); Gibson Island (Md.) Yacht Squadron; Annapolis (Md.) Yacht, Farmington Country (Charlottesville, Va.). Home: Gibson Island MD 21056 Office: 815 Connecticut Ave Washington DC 20006

REIFSNYDER, WILLIAM EDWARD, meteorologist; b. Ridgway, Pa., Mar. 29, 1924; s. Howard William and Madolin (Boyer) R.; B.S. in Meteorology, N.Y. U., 1944; M.F., U. Calif., Berkeley, 1949; Ph.D., Yale U., 1954; m. Marylou Bishop, Dec. 19, 1954; children—Rite, Cheryl, Gawain. Meteorologist, Pacific S.W. Forest and Range Expt. Sta., 1952-55; mem. faculty Yale U., 1965—, prof. Meteorology, 1967—; cons. World Meteorol. Orgn. Bd. dirs. Am. Youth Hostels. Served with USAAF, 1943-47. Fellow AAAS; mem. Am. Meteorol. Soc., Soc. Am. Foresters, Internat. Soc. Biometeorology. Author: Hut Hopping in the Austrian Alps; Footloose in the Swiss Alps; regional editor for Americas, Agrl. Meteorology, 1977—. Address: Stantack Rd Middletown CT 06457

REIGLE, MARGARET ANN, diversified fin. co. exec.; b. Balt., May 3, 1944; d. Ellsworth Bosley and Mary Louise (Willis) R.; B.S. magna cum laude, U. Md., 1966. Audit mgr. Arthur Young & Co., C.P.A.'s, N.Y.C., 1966-75; treas., chief fin. officer Kenai Drilling Ltd., N.Y.C., 1975-77; asst. corp. controller Am. Express Co., N.Y.C., 1977—, v.p. Mgmt. Info. Card div., 1978—. Pres. 2 Beekman Pl. Coop. Corp., 1978—. C.P.A., N.Y. State. Mem. Am. Inst. C.P.A.'s, N.Y. State, Md. socs. C.P.A.'s, Fin. Execs. Inst., Nat. Assn. Accountants, Fin. Women's Assn. Methodist. Home: 2 Beekman Pl New York NY 10022 Office: Am Express Plaza New York NY 10004

REIHER, JOHN FREDERICK, ednl. adminstr.; b. Newark, Jan. 14, 1937; s. John Joseph and Alberta Florence (Kirk) R.; B.S.Edn., St. Edward's U., 1961; M.Ed. in Sci. Edn., U. Md., 1970; certificate in curriculum, U. Del., 1976; Ed.D. in Sch. Adminstrn., Nova U., 1977. Tchr. sci. St. Edmond's Acad., Wilmington, Dec., 1961-63; instr. in sci. St. Augustine's Coll., Butitti, Uganda, 1963-65; asst. supt. Diocese of Wilmington, 1965-69, dir. religious edn. pre-sch. through adult, 1976—; state supr. sci./environ. edn. Del. Bd. Edn., Dover, 1970-76; Del. dir. Sci. and Humanities Symposium, 1972-76, State Sci. Fair, 1969-74; Del. recruiter Youth Conservation Corps, 1974-77; mem. exec. bd. Delmarva Ecumenical Agy. Mem. Phi Delta Kappa. Author: You And Your Body 5-8, 1973; You And Your Environment 1-8, 1973; author evaluation packet Nat. Sci. Tchrs. Assn. Home: PO Box 395 Dover DE 19901 Office: 1626 N Union St Wilmington DE 19806

REILEY, THOMAS PHILLIP, electronics co. exec.; b. Ft. Lewis, Wash., May 5, 1950; s. Thomas Phillip and Anne Marie (Russick) R.; B.Sc. in Biophysics, Pa. State U., 1973; postgrad. in Bus. Adminstrn., Rutgers U. Inventory supr. Leland Tube Co., S. Plainfield, N.J., 1973-76; prodn. inventory control supr. Bomar Crystal Co., Middlesex, N.J., 1976—. Mem. Am. Inventory and Prodn. Control Soc. (chmn. ednl. com. Raritan Valley chpt.). Republican. Home: 56 Carlton Club Dr Piscataway NJ 08854 Office: 201 Blackford Ave Middlesex NJ 08846

REILLY, DANIEL PATRICK, clergyman; b. Providence, May 12, 1928; s. Francis E. and Mary (Burns) R.; student Our Lady of Providence Sem., Warwick, R.I., 1943-48, Grand Seminaire, St. Brieuc, France, 1948-53, Harvard Grad. Sch. Bus. Adminstrn., 1954-55, Boston Coll. Sch. Bus. Adminstrn., 1955-56. Ordained priest Roman Catholic Ch., 1953, became monsignor, 1965; asst. pastor Cathedral Saints Peter and Paul, Providence, 1953-54; asst. chancellor Diocese Providence, 1954-56, sec. to bishop, 1956-64, chancellor diocese, 1964-72, adminstr. diocese, 1971-72, vicar gen., 1972-76; bishop, Norwich, Conn., 1976—; state chaplain K.C., 1964—; Episcopal moderator Nat. Cath. Cemetery Corp., 1977—; bd. dirs. Christian Conf. Conn., 1977, Dirs. Conn. Interfaith Housing, 1977, New Eng. Conf. Cath. Hosp. Assn., 1978. Trustee St. Joseph's Hosp., Providence, 1964—, Providence Coll., 1969—, Our Lady of Providence Sem. Coll., Warwick, 1969—; bd. dirs. United Way Southeastern Conn., 1976, Conn. State Drug and Advisory Council, 1978—. Recipient Ann. award NCCJ, 1972. Club: Rotary. Home: 274 Broadway Norwich CT 06360

REILLY, EDWARD PATRICK, brokerage co. exec.; b. N.Y.C., Apr. 4, 1936; s. Hugh I. and Elizabeth (O'Hara) R.; B.B.A., Iona Coll., 1958; M.B.A., N.Y. U., 1960; m. Roseann Dolan, Sept. 21, 1963; children—Edward Patrick, Patricia Ann, Kevin Séan. With Home Ins. Co., N.Y.C., 1962-64, Clark Dodge, N.Y.C., 1964-68; oil and gas analyst E.F. Hutton, N.Y.C., 1968-72; with Loeb Rhoades, N.Y.C., 1972-76; oil analyst, v.p. Prescott Ball & Turben, N.Y.C., 1976-78; oil analyst, v.p. Fahnestock & Co., N.Y.C., 1978—. Mem. N.Y. Soc. Security Analysts, Nat. Inst. Petroleum Investment Analysts, Ind. Assn. Petroleum Analysts Am. Republican. Roman Catholic. Home: 31 Eileen Way Edison NJ 08817 Office: 110 Wall St New York City NY 10005

REILLY, EUGENE LEO, III, behavioral and mktg. research co. exec.; b. N.Y.C., Oct. 6, 1924; s. Eugene Leo and Dorothy Helen (Dunphy) R.; B.A., Amherst Coll., 1945; m. Isabelle T. Connelly, Aug. 28, 1947; children—Kathleen, Kevin, Megan, Sheila, Carey, Eugene, Ellen. Instr. Tabor Acad., Marion, Mass., 1947-50; chmn. dept. English, Canterbury Sch., New Milford, Conn., 1950-57; dir. sales, v.p. Trendex, Inc., N.Y.C., 1957-61; founder, pres. E.L. Reilly Co., Inc., N.Y.C., 1961-70; founder, pres., chief exec. officer Gene Reilly Group, Darien, Conn., 1970—. Vol. summer poverty worker, Va., W.Va., Ky., 1968-76. Served with AUS, 1942-46; ETO. Mem. Am. Mktg. Assn. Democrat. Roman Catholic. Founder, chmn. The Child, Inc.; contbr. articles to profl. jours. Home: Morehouse Ln Darien CT 06820 Office: 1574 Post Rd Darien CT 06820

REILLY, JOHN FRANCIS, ins. co. exec.; b. Mt. vernon, N.Y., Sept. 29, 1929; s. Harry Lawrence and Mary Margaret R.; B.A. Iona Coll., 1953; M.B.A., N.Y. U., 1959; m. Mary Patricia Mullarkey, Oct. 5, 1957; children—Mary Euphemia, Colleen Margaret, Kathleen Deborah, Michael Patrick. Various positions Continental Ins. Co., White Plains, N.Y., 1955-63; v.p. sec. Miller, Schwartzman & Reilly Inc., ins. co., Pelham, N.Y., 1963—; adj. asst. prof. Coll. Ins., N.Y.C., 1972—; adj. prof. Westchester Community Coll., 1975—. Mem. town com. Conservative Party Westchester, N.Y., 1968—. Served to sgt., Paratroopers, U.S. Army, 1953-55. Mem. Am. Risk and Ins. Assn., Ind. Ins. Agts. N.Y. State, Westchester County Assn. Ins. Agts. (pres. 1978—), Mt. Vernon Assn. Ins. Agts. (pres. 1968—). Roman Catholic. Club: Larchmont Shore. Home: 56 Woodbine Ave Larchmont NY 10538 Office: 118 5th Ave PO Box X Pelham NY 10803

REILLY, JOSEPH JOHN, JR., energy, chem. and metal products mfg. co. exec.; b. N.Y.C., Apr. 24, 1931; s. Joseph John and Anna Mae (Walsh) R.; A.B., Coll. Holy Cross, 1955; M.A., Emmanuel Coll., 1970; m. Elinor M. Flynn, Aug. 20, 1955; children—Anne, Joseph, Kathleen, Brendan, Terence, Gael, Timothy. Employment interviewer Filene's Boston, 1955-58; supr. personnel Sylvania, Woburn, Mass., 1958-62; asst. personnel mgr. ITT, N.Y.C., 1962-64; indsl. relations mgr. Standard Pressed Steel, Jenkintown, Pa., 1964-66; v.p. indsl. relations Transitron, Wakefield, Mass., 1966-70; dir. indsl. relations Fairchild Camera & Instrument, Mountain View, Calif., 1970-71; exec. dir. Mass. Catholic Conf., Boston, 1971-74; group dir. employee relations Gen. Instrument, N.Y.C., 1974-77; v.p. human resources Cabot Corp., Boston, 1977—. Mem. Mass. Legis. Commn. on Correction Reform, 1972-74, Mass. Commn. on Christian Unity, 1972-74; chmn. bd. dirs. Mass. Citizens for Life; trustee North Conway Inst. Recipient God and Youth medal, 1962, Pius X medal, 1971. Mem. Nat. Alliance Businessmen (Boston met. chmn. 1978-79), Am. Soc. Personnel Adminstrn., Personnel Mgmt. Council, Electronic Industries Personnel Assn., Am. Mgmt. Assn., Holy Cross Alumni Assn., Ancient Order Hibernians. Democrat. Roman Catholic. Club: Holy Cross of Boston. Home: 6 Olympia Way Andover MA 01810 Office: 125 High St Boston MA 02110

REILLY, RICHARD MENTON, assn. exec.; b. Bklyn., Oct. 1, 1945; s. James Joseph and Kathleen Claire (Stapleton) R.; B.A., Fordham U., 1967; M.A., St. Johns U., 1972; M.B.A., Pace U., 1979; m. Valerie B. Reilly, May 27, 1972. Tchr. pub. schs., Phila., 1968-69; tribunal adminstr. Am. Arbitration Assn., N.Y.C., 1970-72, ednl. program dir., 1972-75, regional dir., Boston, 1975—. Mem. Labor Guild Boston. Served with U.S. Army, 1969. Mem. Indsl. Relations Research Assn., Soc. Profl. Dispute Resolution, Am. Soc. Tng. and Devel. Democrat. Roman Catholic. Office: 294 Washington St Boston MA 02108

REIMAN, DONALD HENRY, educator; b. Erie, Pa., May 17, 1934; s. Henry Ward and Mildred Abbie (Pearce) R.; A.B., Coll. of Wooster, 1956; M.A., U. Ill., 1957, Ph.D., 1960; m. Mary Warner, 1958 (div. 1974); 1 dau., Laurel Elizabeth; m. 2d, Hélène Liberman Dworzan, Oct. 3, 1975. Instr. English, Duke, 1960-62, asst. prof., 1962-64; asso. prof. U. Wis., Milw., 1964-65; adj. asso. prof. grad. program in English, City U.N.Y., 1967-68; adj. prof. English, Columbia, 1969-70, sr. research asso. in English, 1970-73; vis. prof. St. John's U., Jamaica, N.Y., 1974-75; editor Shelley and His Circle, Carl H. Pforzheimer Library, N.Y.C., 1965—; vis. lectr. U. Ill., 1963; cons. Harvard U. Press., Yale U. Press, Johns Hopkins U. Press, others, cons. Garland Pub. Inc., Macmillan & Co. Active ACLU, Common Cause. Am. Council Learned Socs. study fellow, 1963-64, Wesleyan Center for Advance Studies fellow, 1963-64. Mem. Modern Humanities Research Assn. (life), Modern Lang. Assn. Am. (life), Wordsworth-Coleridge Assn. Am. (founder), Byron Soc. (Am. com., 1973—), Keats-Shelley Assn. Am. (dir. treas. 1973—), AAUP. Democrat. Presbyterian. Author: Shelley's The Triumph of Life, A Critical Study, 1965; Percy Bysshe Shelley, 1969, 2d edit., 1974; (with D.D. Fischer) Byron on the Continent, 1974. Editor: Shelley and His Circle, 1973, The Romantics Reviewed: Contemporary Reviews of English Romantic Writers, 9 vols., 1972; (with S.B. Powers) Shelley's Poetry and Prose: A Norton Critical Edition, 1977; The Romantic Context: Poetry, 128 vols., 1976—; (with M.C. Jaye and B.T. Bennett) The Evidence of the Imagination, 1978; mem. editorial com. adv. bd. Publs. of Modern Lang. Assn., 1969-70; mem. editorial bd. Keats-Shelley Jour., 1968-73; mem. adv. bd. Milton and the Romantics, 1975—, Studies in Romanticism, 1977—; contbr. articles to books and profl. jours. Home: 6495 Broadway Bronx NY 10471 Office: 41 E 42d St Room 815 New York City NY 10017

REIMAN, RALPH JOHN, pub. relations exec.; b. Buffalo, May 28, 1913; s. Walter John and Laura Louise (Fisher) R.; A.B., Princeton, 1935; J.D., Harvard, 1939; m. Mary Ellen Reeder, May 5, 1945; children—Ralph John, Joanne (Mrs. Peter A. Santoriello), Barbara (Mrs. George J. Byrnes III). With Gen. Accident Assurance Co., Ltd., Phila., 1946-51; employment mgr. radio and TV div. Philco Corp., Phila., 1951-53; personnel mgr. John Wood Co., Conshohocken, Pa., 1953-56, Congoleum-Nairn Corp., Wilmington, Del., 1957; sec., dir. pub. relations Matthey Bishop, Inc., Malvern, Pa., 1958-78. Served with AUS, 1942-46. Recipient 6 Freedoms Found. awards, 1961-72. Mem. Pub. Relations Soc. Am. (accredited), Chem. Communications Assn. (dir.), Mfg. Assn. Del. Valley, Risk Ins. Mgmt. Soc., NAM. Republican. Episcopalian. Clubs: Union League (Phila.); Nassau, Tower (Princeton). Editor in chief: The Chessboard, 1958—. Home: 1227 Blythe Ave Drexel Hill PA 19026 Office: 4 Malin Rd Malvern PA 19355

REIN, JOHN MICHAEL, advt. co. exec.; b. Mpls., Dec. 18, 1942; s. Raymond W. and Frances C. (Mason) R.; A.S., U. Minn., 1962. Divisional mgr. Walter Reade Orgn., Oakhurst, N.J., 1966-72; exec. dir. N.J. Jaycees, Hightstown, N.J., 1972-73; gen. mgr. Land Acquisitions Inc., Belmar, N.J., 1973-75; gen. sales mgr. Campers of Am. Inc., Neptune, N.J., 1975-77; pres. John Michael & Assos., Scotch Plains, N.J., 1977—. Mem. Nat. Com. for Prevention of Child Abuse, 1977—; trustee Assn. for Children of N.J., 1978—, Little Silver Community Appeal, 1977—. Mem. Am. Soc. Notaries, Direct Mail/Mktg. Assn. Republican. Roman Catholic. Home: 459 Prospect Ave Little Silver NJ 07739 Office: 514 Martin Place Scotch Plains NJ 07076

REINDOLLAR, ROBERT MASON, JR., civil engr.; b. Easton, Md., June 6, 1918; s. Robert Mason and Elizabeth (Swank) R.; C.E., Cornell U., 1946; m. Valaska L. Yazel, Nov. 7, 1942; children—Elizabeth Ann, Nancy L., Valerie L. Engr., Whitman, Requardt & Assos., Balt., 1938-41; airport planning engr. Trans World Airlines, N.Y.C., 1946-47; field engr. Portland Cement Assn. Pa., Phila., 1947-51, dist. engr., Pa., Md., Del., 1951-56; asso. Rummel, Klepper & Kahl, Balt., 1957-59, partner, 1959-77; county engr. Talbot County, Easton, Md., 1978—. Bd. dirs. Automobile Club Md. Served to capt. USAAF, 1941-46; ETO. Decorated Air medal with three oak leaf clusters, D.F.C. Registered profl. engr., Pa., Md., D.C. Mem. Cons. Engrs. Council Md. (past pres., dir.), Md. Assn. Engrs. (past pres.) Soc. Am. Mil. Engrs. (past pres. Balt.), ASCE, Nat. Soc. Profl. Engrs., Engrs. Club Balt., Pennsylvania Assn. Cons. Engrs. (past pres.), Phi Kappa Phi, Tau Beta Pi, Chi Epsilon, Delta Tau Delta. Clubs: Rotary, Center (Balt.). Home: Route 1 Box 208 Miles River Rd Easton MD 21601 Office: Court House Easton MD 21601

REINER, LEOPOLD, pathologist; b. Leipzig, Germany, Jan. 22, 1911; s. Joel and Golda Rivka (Michlewitsch) R.; came to U.S., 1939, naturalized, 1945; student U. Freiburg, 1930, U. Leipzig, 1930-33; M.D., U. Vienna, 1936; m. Lillian Irene Myers, Sept. 22, 1946. Intern, N.J. Hosp., Camden, 1939-40, resident, 1940-46; resident pathology Beth Israel Hosp., Boston, 1946-48, asst. pathologist, 1948-52, asso. pathologist, 1952-55, acting pathologist, 1955-56; dir. dept. pathology Bronx-Lebanon Hosp. Center (N.Y.), 1956—; instr., asso. pathology Harvard Med. Sch., 1950-56; vis. asso. prof. pathology, 1956-72; prof. pathology Albert Einstein Coll. Medicine, 1972—; vis. scientist Tel Hashomer Hosp., Israel, 1965. Diplomate Am. Bd. Pathology. Fellow N.Y. Acad. Medicine; mem. Am. Assn. Pathologists, Internat. Acad. Pathology, Histochem. Soc., Harvey Soc., AMA, Am. Soc. Clin. Pathologists, N.Y. Pathology Soc., N.Y. Pathologists Club. Contbr. articles on cardiovascular pathology to profl. jours. Home: 277 Old Colony Rd Hartsdale NY 10530 Office: 1276 Fulton Ave Btonx NY 10456

REINER, THOMAS FRANCIS, instrument co. exec.; b. Farkasgyepu, Hungary, Sept. 9, 1945; s. Paul and Elizabeth (Mayer) R.; B.S., Fairleigh Dickinson U., 1971, M.B.A., 1975; m. Linda Eileen Godden, Mar. 4, 1967; children—Lisa, Tommy, Krissy. Purchasing and traffic mgr. Jersey Dyeing Corp., Paterson, N.J., 1967-74; with Sparta Instrument Corp., div. Cooper Labs., Fairfield, N.J., 1974—, now dir. purchasing and ops. Head coach Youth Basketball Assn., 1975-77. Recipient Traffic Club award, 1972; named Employee of the Year, Jersey Dyeing Corp., 1970. Mem. North Jersey Purchasing Assn., Am. Mgmt. Assn., North Jersey Purchasing Mgmt. Assn. Clubs: North Jersey Traffic; Newman. Home: 302 Andrew Pl Bloomingdale NJ 07403 Office: 305 Fairfield Ave Fairfield NJ 07006

REINGOLD, ALFRED MULLER, electron microscopist; b. Phila., July 18, 1923; s. Irving and Esther (Muller) R.; B.S. Chemistry, Franklin and Marshall Coll., 1950; M.A., Temple U., 1958; m. Dolores Portnoy, July 4, 1952 (div. Mar. 1975); children—Leonard Jay, Sherry Lynn. Asst. chief clin. chemist Samson Labs., Phila., 1950-54; analytical research chemist Atlantic Refining Co., Phila., 1954-56, research chemist applications research, 1956-60, research chemist electron microscopy, 1960-62; sr. electron microscopist TRW, Inc., Phila., 1962-69; supr. anatomy dept. electron microscopy labs. U. Pa. Med. Sch., Phila., 1969—; lectr. in electron microscopy. Asst. scoutmaster, Boy Scouts Am., Broomall, Pa., 1970-73, scoutmaster, 1968-70, mem. instl. com., 1967-68. Served with USAAF, 1943-45. Mem. Electron Microscopy Soc. Am., Phila. Electron Microscopy Soc. (chmn. 1971-72), Smithsonian Assos., Sigma Xi. Jewish. Club: Myo-Bio. Contbr. articles to profl. jours. Home: 517 Philmar Ct Apt D Springfield PA 19064

REINHARD, ROBERT ANDREW, soft drink co. exec.; b. Cumberland, Md., July 29, 1921; s. John Joseph and Ada Marion (Gleason) R.; student Villanova Coll., 1939-40; m. Katherine Lee Rudd, June 20, 1939; children—Robert Rudd, George Douglas, Joseph Lynn, Sarah Katherine. Office clk. Pepsi-Cola Bottling Co., Cumberland, 1940-46, officer mgr., 1946-55, sec.-treas., gen. mgr., 1955—; pres. Laurel Packaging, Inc., Johnstown, Pa., 1968—; dir. Cumberland Savs. Bank. Sec.-treas. Allegany County (Md.) San. Commn., 1960-70. Served with C.E., AUS, 1943-46; PTO. Mem. Pepsi Cola Bottlers Assn. (mgmt. edn. com. 1969—), Md. Soft Drink Assn. (pres. 1962-66), Mid-Atlantic Pepsi Cola Bottlers Assn. (pres. 1969). K.C. Club: Cumberland Country. Home: 844 Camden Ave Cumberland MD 21502 Office: Paca and Chase Sts Cumberland MD 21502

REINHERZ, HELEN ZARSKY, educator, ednl. adminstr.; b. Boston, Aug. 4, 1923; d. Zachary and Anna (Cohen) Zarsky; A.B. magna cum laude, Wheaton Coll., 1944; M.S., Simmons Coll., 1946; S.M., Harvard U., 1963, Sc.D., 1965; m. Samuel E. Reinherz, Aug. 29, 1943; 1 son, Ellis. Social worker Newton (Mass.) Family Service, 1946-49, Mass. Gen. Hosp., Boston, 1949-51; supr. psychiat. social work State Hosp., Waltham, Mass., 1958-61; prof. methods research Simmons Coll., Boston, 1965—, dir. research Sch. Social Work, 1968—; prin. investigator Identifying Children at Risk, 1976—. Research cons. Dept. Mental Health, 1970—; lectr. Social Work continuing edn. Boston U., 1974-75; prin. investigator study of adolescent drug abuse, 1971-73. Chmn. Gov.'s Adv. Council Mental Health and Retardation, 1972. Bd. dirs. Family Soc. Malden, 1950-65. Recipient Maida H. Solomon award Simmons Coll. Alumni, 1961; NIH tng. fellow, 1961-65; Grant Found. grantee, 1963, Med. Found. grantee, 1967-69; NIMH grantee, 1975—. Fellow Am. Orthopsychiat. Assn.; mem. Acad. Certified Social Workers, Am. Pub. Health Assn., Council Social Work Edn., League Women Voters (dir. 1951-59), Malden Mental Health Assn. (v.p. 1966-68), Harvard Sch. Pub. Health Alumni Assn. (sec. treas. 1965-68), Phi Beta Kappa, Delta Omega. Author: (with H. Wechsler and D. Dobbin) Social Work Research in the Human Services, 1976; (with M. Heywood and P. Camp) A Community Response to Drug Abuse, 1976. Cons. editor Community Mental Health Jour., 1968—. Contbr. articles on mental health to profl. publs. Home: 17 Corey Rd Malden MA 02148 Office: Simmons College School of Social Work 51 Commonwealth Ave Boston MA 02116

REINKE, MARVIN ERNEST, assn. exec.; b. Tawes City, Mich., Mar. 5, 1941; s. Martin T. and Ernestine May (Cecil) R.; B.S. in Social Group Work and Adminstrn., George Williams Coll., Chgo., 1963; m. Linda Jeanette Grabill, June 22, 1963. Program dir. Cudahy br. Milw. YMCA, 1963-66; asso. exec. dir. Sioux City (Iowa) YMCA, 1968-71; exec. dir. Fairfax County br. YMCA, Fairfax, Va., 1971-76; asso. gen. dir. Met. Washington YMCA, 1976—, also mgr. communications, mem. exec. staff cabinet; mem. devel. tng. team Nat. YMCA. Bd. dirs., treas. Fairfax County Community Action Adminstrn., 1974-76, Central Services for Retarded Persons, 1972-74. Served with U.S. Army, 1966-68. Recipient Diamond Jubilee Testimonial award George Williams Coll., 1968. Mem. Assn. Profl. YMCA Dirs., Am. Radio Relay League, Fairfax County C. of C. Office: 1711 Rhode Island Ave Washington DC 20006

REINL, HARRY CHARLES, economist; b. Muttersdorf, Germany, Nov. 13, 1932 (parents Am. citizens); s. Carl and Angela (Plass) R.; B.S., Fordham U., 1953; certificate U.S. Dept. Agr. Grad. Sch., 1966; A.M., George Washington U., 1968; student spl. program, applied urban econs. Mass. Inst. Tech., 1972. Jr. observer Sperry Rand Corp., N.Y.C., 1958-62; labor economist Office Manpower Adminstr., U.S. Dept. Labor, Washington, 1962-68; labor economist CSC, 1968—; mgr. N.Y. br. Willmark Service System, 1971. Asso. Nat. Archives, 1976—; mem. nat. bd. sponsors Inst. Am. Strategy, 1972-76; founder Center for Internat. Security Studies of Am. Security Council Edn. Found., 1977; sustaining mem. Republican Nat. Com., 1975—. Served to 1st lt. AUS, 1953-55. Mem. Am. Econ. Assn., Am. Security Council (nat. adv. bd. 1972), George Washington U. Gen. Alumni Assn., Am. Police Hall of Fame, Smithsonian Instn. (nat. asso.). Clubs: Capitol Hill, Officers Service (Washington). Home: 1111 Arlington Blvd M-521 Arlington VA 22209 Office: US Dept Labor Washington DC 20025

REIS, DONALD JEFFERY, educator, neurologist; b. N.Y.C., Sept. 9, 1931; s. Samuel H. and Alice (Kiesler) R.; A.B., Cornell, 1953, M.D., 1956. Intern, N.Y. Hosp., N.Y.C., 1956; resident neurology Boston City Hosp., Harvard Med. Sch., 1957-59; Fulbright fellow, United Cerebral Palsy Found. fellow, London, Eng., Stockholm, Sweden, 1959-60; research asso. Nat. Inst. Mental Health, Bethesda, Md., 1960-62; spl. fellow NIH, Nobel Neurophysiology Inst., Stockholm, 1962-63; asst. prof. neurology Cornell U. Med. Sch., N.Y.C., 1963-67, asso. prof. neurology and psychiatry, 1967-71; prof., 1971—. Mem. Am. Physiol. Soc., Am. Neurol. Assn., Am. Pharmacological Soc., Am. Acad. Neurology, Harvey Soc., Telluride Assn., Am. Soc. Clin. Investigation, Phi Beta Kappa, Sigma Xi, Alpha Omega Alpha. Contbr. articles to profl. jours.; mem. editorial bd. numerous profl. jours. Home: 190 E 72d St New York City NY 10021 Office: 1300 York Ave New York City NY 10021

REISA, JAMES JOSEPH, JR., ecologist; b. Oak Park, Ill., Dec. 13, 1941; s. James Joseph and Blanche Helen (Zavoral) R.; student Mass. Inst. Tech., 1959-61, U.S. Mcht. Marine Acad., 1962-64; B.S., Loyola U. Chgo., 1966; M.S. (NSF, NDEA fellow), Northwestern U., 1968, Ph.D., 1971. EPA postdoctoral fellow, Northwestern U., 1971-72; vis. asst. prof. biology Mundelein Coll., Chgo., 1971-72; staff biologist Argonne Nat. Lab. (Ill.), 1972-74; staff mem. Pres. Council on Environ. Quality, Washington, 1974-77, sr. staff mem., 1977-78; dir. environ. rev. div. Office Toxic Substances EPA, 1978—; chmn. Pres.'s Task Force on Environ. Data and Monitoring, 1977-78; chmn. Fed. Task Force on Air Quality Indicators, 1975-76. Mem. Ecol. Soc. Am. (vice chmn. applied ecology sect. 1975-77), AAAS, Am. Inst. Biol. Scis., Am. Fisheries Soc. (certified fisheries scientist), Am. Soc. Limnology and Oceanography, Fed. Water Quality Assn., Sigma Xi. Home: 4638 S 36th St Arlington VA 22206 Office: Environ Rev Div (TS-792) Office Toxic Substances US EPA 401 M St SW Washington DC 20460

REISFIELD, DONALD RICHARD, obstetrician, gynecologist; b. New Brunswick, N.J., Feb. 3, 1926; s. Alexander and Hannah (Brody) R.; B.S., Rutgers U., 1948, M.S., 1949; M.D., Columbia U., 1954; m. Gray Gustafson, Sept. 4, 1955; children—Scott, Lian Gray, Derek, Craig. Intern, Yale-New Haven Hosp., 1954-55; resident Sloan Hosp. for Women, Columbia Presbyn. Med. Center, 1955-58; asst. in obstetrics and gynecology Columbia Coll. Physicians and Surgeons, 1960-72; asst. clin. prof. obstetrics and gynecology Rutgers Med. Sch., 1972—; asso. dir. dept. obstetrics and gynecology Middlesex Hosp., New Burnswick, 1975—. Served with U.S. Army, 1945-46. Amos Tucker Traveling fellow Columbia U., 1958-59. Diplomate Am. Bd. Obstetrics and Gynecology. Mem. AMA, N.J. Obstet. and Gynecol. Soc., Alpha Omega Alpha. Contbr. articles on med. complication of pregnancy and gynecologic cancer to profl. publs. Office: 650 Easton Ave Somerset NJ 08873

REISINGER, ROBERT ROLAND, design engr.; b. York, Pa., Apr. 21, 1935; s. Russell Eugene and Lottie Marie (Walker) R.; A.A., Pa. State U., 1960; m. Maryllyn May Bentzel, Mar. 3, 1956; children—Randall Robert, Jane Madellyn. With hoist and crane div. Am. Chain and Cable Co., York, 1960—, designer, 1960-65, sr. designer, 1965-68, design engr., 1968-69, project engr., 1969-71, customer relations mgr., 1972-74, chief engr., 1974—. Advisor Jr. Achievement, York, 1969-70; dean, elder United Ch. Christ, York, 1965-70. Served with USAF, 1954-58. Registered profl. engr., Pa., N.J. Mem. ASME, Am. Soc. Metals, Nat. Soc. Profl. Engrs., Hoist Mfrs. Inst., Crane Mfrs. Assn. Am., Am. Nat. Standards Inst. (com. mem.). Democrat. Contbr. articles to profl. jours. Home: 2515 Midpine Dr York PA 17404 Office: 1110 E Princess St York PA 17403

REISNER, DAVID JOHNSON, physician; b. N.Y.C., Mar. 5, 1919; s. Edward Hartman and Elizabeth (Johnson) R.; B.A., Wesleyan U. 1940; M.D., Columbia, 1950; m. Muriel Evans, Aug. 9, 1947; children—David Evans, Austin Dale, Allison. Intern, St. Luke's Hosp., N.Y.C., 1950-51, resident internal medicine, 1951-54; practice medicine specializing in internal medicine, Morristown, N.J., 1954—; attending physician Morristown Meml. Hosp. Organizer, Dismal-Harmony Brooks Natural Area Com., Mendham Twp.; trustee N.J. Conservation Found., 1970—, pres., 1973-75. Served with AUS, 1941-45. Decorated Bronze Star medal. Mem. ACP, Med. Soc. N.J., Morris County Med. Soc., Audubon Soc., Alpha Delta Phi. Presbyterian. Clubs: Adirondack Mountain, Adirondack Forty-sixers, Sierra. Home: Stony Hill Rd Brookside NJ 07926 Office: 45 Franklin St Morristown NJ 07960

REISS, HARRY E., ednl. adminstr.; b. N.Y.C., Mar. 4, 1929; B.S. in Social Scis., City Coll. N.Y.C., 1950. M.A. Edn., 1955; Candidate Ed.D. in Teaching Social Studies, Columbia; m. Marion Halpern, May 30, 1956; children—Linda, Wendy, Jonathan. Asst. prin. Jr. High Sch. 1967, Bronx, N.Y., 1969-73, prin. Pub. Sch. Ill., 1973-74, dir. spl. programs Sch. Dist. 11, 1974—; lectr., cons. Holocaust studies; adj. faculty Rockland Community Coll., Suffern, N.Y. Certified prin., Supt. secondary edn. Mem. Council Suprs., Adminstrs., Assn. Suprs. Social Studies N.Y.C. Author publs. in field. Home: 27 Smolley Dr Monsey NY 10952 Office: 3016 Yates Ave Bronx NY 10469

REITAN, PAUL HARTMAN, educator; b. Kanawha, Iowa, Aug. 18, 1928; s. John Olsen and Anna (Meldahl) R.; A.B., U. Chgo., 1953; Ph.D., U. Oslo, 1959; m. Reidun Engebretsen, Sept. 28, 1962; children—Kirsten Berit, Eric Hartmann. Geologist, U.S. Geol. Survey, 1953-56; instr. U. Ill., Chgo., 1954-55; state geologist Geol. Survey of Norway, Oslo, 1956-60; asst. prof. mineralogy Stanford (Calif.) U., 1960-66; asso. prof. State U. N.Y., Buffalo, 1966-69, prof., 1969—, acting provost Faculty Nat. Sci. and Math., 1975-76, provost, 1976—. Served with M.C., AUS, 1946-49. Salisbury fellow, 1953-55; Fulbright fellow, 1955-56; Nato sr. fellow, 1972; G. Unger Vetlesen fellow, Oslo, 1973. Fellow Geol. Soc. Am., Mineral. Soc. Am.; mem. Am. Geophys. Union, Geochem. Soc., Internat. Assn. Geochemistry and Cosmochemistry, Nat. Assn. Geology Tchrs., Norsk Geol. Forening AAAS, Sigma Xi. Contbr. articles to profl. jours. Home: 120 Walton Dr Buffalo NY 14226 Office: State U New York Buffalo NY 14260

REITBOECK, HERBERT J.P., biophysicist; b. Ried, Austria, June 22, 1933; s. Johann N. and Rosa L. (Poringer) R.; B.S., Tech. U. Vienna, 1955, M.S., 1958, Ph.D., 1964; Ph.D., U. Frankfurt, 1963. Staff scientist Max Planck Inst. fuer Biophysik, Frankfurt, Germany, 1959-66; adv. scientist Westinghouse Research Labs., Pitts., 1966—; prof. biophysics Philipps U., Marburg, Germany, 1978—; cons. expert Internat. Atomic Energy Agy., Vienna, 1965-66, 68-69. Mem. AAAS, Deutsche Biophysikalische Gesellschaft, Deutsche Gesellschaft fuer Medizin u Biolog. Elektronik. Office: Westinghouse Research and Devel Center Pittsburgh PA 15235

REITER, WILLIAM MARTIN, chem. co. exec.; b. Phila., Sept. 23, 1925; s. William Henry and Marie Catherine (Farrell) R.; B.Sc. in Chem. Engring., Drexel U., 1949; m. Helen C. Fuchs, May 31, 1947; children—William L., Ann C. Chem. engr. Allied Chem. Co., Claymont, Del., 1949-52; process design engr. Catalytic Constrn. Co., Phila., 1952-53; engring. group leader Allied Chem. Co., Phila., 1953-65; mgr. research and devel., vinyl products Allied Chem. Co., Painesville, O., 1965-72, asst. corp. dir. air and water pollution control, Morristown, N.J., 1972-77, corp. dir. pollution control, 1977—; adj. asst. prof. chem. engring. Drexel U., Phila., 1960-65; pres. Springview Farms (Pa.), 1963-65. Served with AUS, 1943-46. Registered profl. engr., Pa., N.J. Mem. Am. Inst. Chem. Engrs., Water Pollution Control Fedn., Air Pollution Control Assn. (dir. sect. 1962-65, dir. Mid-Atlantic States sect.), Tau Beta Pi, Phi Kappa Phi. Contbr. articles to profl. jours. Home: 7 Mansfield Ct Mendham NJ 07945 Office: Box 1057R Morristown NJ 07960

REITERS, LUDVIGS OSVALDS, chem. engr.; b. Lubana, Lativa, May 28, 1910; s. Emils Augusts and Alvina (Kazoks) R.; came to U.S., 1957, naturalized, 1963; B.Sc., U. Latvia, 1939; postgrad., U. London, (Eng.), 1948-52; m. Austra Dikmanis, Oct. 22, 1949; children—Janis Eric, Dace. Chief chem. asst. Fortiphone Ltd., London, 1951-55; chem. Ardente Acoustic Lab., Ltd., London, 1955-57; devel. engr. C.B.S. Hytron, Inc., Lowell, Mass., 1957-60; sr. devel. engr. BLH Elecs., Inc., Waltham, Mass., 1960-76; engr. cons. Hottinger Baldwin Messtechnik G.m.b.H., W. Ger. Registered profl. engr., Mass. Mem. Am. Chem. Soc., Electrochem. Soc., Inc., Am. Assn. for Crystal Growth, Assn. Latvian Engrs. Lutheran. Co-author monographs for profl. jours.; holder of 3 patents. Home: 9 Ridge Ave Natick MA 01760

REITZ, JULIA KRAUS, assn. exec.; b. Brookville, Pa., Aug. 30, 1935; d. Alexander B. and Bernadine C. (Lyle) Kraus; R.N., St. Vincents Med. Center, 1956; student, Pa. State U., 1969-70, U. Pitts., 1975-79; m. Richard F. Reitz, Nov. 23, 1957 (dec. 1974); children—Elizabeth, Steven, Susan, Gregory. Nurse, Brookville (Pa.) Hosp., 1956-57; asst. dir. nursing Port Allegany Community Hosp. (Pa.), 1965-77; nursing dir. McKean County Visiting Nurse Assn., Bradford, Pa., 1977—. Mem. Nat. League Nursing, Regional Edn. Cons. on Nursing. Roman Catholic. Home: 308 Mill St Port Allegany PA 16743

REITZEL, HILDA MARIE, librarian; b. Pitts., May 9, 1921; d. Harry A. and Mary (Senn) Reitzel; A.B., U. Pitts., 1943, M.A., 1952; B.S. in L.S., Carnegie Inst. Tech., 1945. Asst. med. librarian U. Pitts., 1943-45, asst. reference dept., 1945-52, research librarian, 1952; librarian Mine Safety Appliances Co., 1952-54; head reference dept. U. Pitts., 1954-56; librarian Mine Safety Appliances Co., 1956—. Recipient Pitts. Female Coll. Assn. award, 1942. Mem. Spl. Libraries Assn. (pres. 1958-59), Pa. Library Assn. (editor bull. 1961-72, certificate of merit 1967), Phi Delta Gamma. Club: Library pres. 1950-51) (Pitts.). Home: Bigelow Apts Pittsburgh PA 15219 Office: 600 Penn Center Blvd Pittsburgh PA 15235

REIZES, LESLIE NOEL, lawyer; b. N.Y.C., Nov. 27, 1949; s. Kurt N. and Sonia S. R.; B.A., Boston U., 1970; J.D., Suffolk U., 1975; m. Margaret Burns, Sept. 5, 1976. Vice-pres. ops. Credit Corp. Am., Medford, Mass., 1970-73; asso. Alan J. Friedlander Esq., Waverly, N.Y., 1975-77; admitted to Fla. bar, 1975, Mass. bar, 1975, N.Y. State bar, 1976; partner Friedlander, Friedlander & Reizes, Waverly and Ft. Lauderdale, Fla., 1977—; judge Philip C. Jessup internat. moot ct. competition, 1977, 78. Bd. dirs. Valley Econ. Devel. Assn., Waverly, 1976—, pres., 1978—. Mem. Waverly Indsl. and Profl. Men's Assn. (dir. 1978—), Am., Mass., N.Y. State, Boston bar assns., Am. Soc. Internat. Law, Assn. Trial Lawyers Am., Fla. Bar. Home: 750 S Main St Athens PA 18810 Office: 427 Park Ave Waverly NY 14892

REJEBIAN, GEORGE PETER, orthodontist; b. Binghamton, N.Y., Aug. 30, 1929; s. Peter Arakel and Dicranouhi (Zopabourian) R.; B.A., State U.N.Y., 1951; D.D.S., Georgetown U., 1955; certificate in orthodontics Columbia U., 1961; m. Marion Ekizian, Apr. 13, 1957; children—Gary Peter, Vivian Angele. Practice dentistry specializing in orthodontics, Binghamton, N.Y. and Endwell, N.Y., 1961—; courtesy staff Our Lady of Lourdes Hosp., Binghamton, 1970—; orthodontic cons. N.Y. State Dept. Health, 1971—. Dir. WSKG Public TV, 1971—. Served to lt. Dental Corps, USN, 1956-59. Diplomate Am. Bd. Orthodontics. Mem. ADA, Am. Assn. Orthodontists, N.Y., 6th Dist. (pres. 1976-77), Broome County (pres. 1969-70) dental socs., Northeastern Soc. Orthodontists, Tweed Found. for Orthodontic Research, Pierre Fauchard Acad. Mem. Armenian Orthodox Ch. (vice chmn. parish council 1976-78). Editor: N.Y. State Dental Jour., 1975-76, Sixth Dist. Dental Soc. Newsletter, 1975-76. Home: 30 Larchmont Rd Binghamton NY 13903 Office: 107 Oak St Binghamton NY 13905

RELIS, ROCHELLE R., actress, singer, painter; b. Lwow, Poland, June 21, 1914; s. Ozjasz and Chaja (Lichtenblum) Relis; came to U.S., 1953, naturalized. 1958; M.F.A., U. East Fla., 1971; m. Bernard Bardach, Apr. 19, 1935; 1 son, Artur (dec.). Profl. actress and singer in Poland and other countries, 1930—; participated in concert tours to displaced persons camps in W.Ger., Austria, 1946-47; appeared at Republic-Theater, Paris, Music Hall Alhambra, Paris, also in Brussells and London, 1947-53; appeared in theaters, concerts, radio and TV broadcasts in U.S. and Can., 1953—; exhibited paintings in U.S., 1953—; Several one-woman and juried exhbns., several awards and medals, represented in permanent collections L.B.J. Meml. Library, Bertrand Russell House (Eng.), many pvt. collections, U.S., Europe and Israel. Mem. AFTRA, AGVA, Nat. Acad. Television Arts and Scis., Nat. Soc. Lit. and Arts, Internat. Platform Assn., Smithsonian Assos. Democrat. Jewish. Home: 484 W 43d St Apt 18-A New York City NY 10036

RELYEA, BARRY DONALD, realtor; b. Schenectady, Feb. 23, 1944; s. Donald Frederick and Gladys Ada (Elmendorf) R.; B.A. in Psychology, Gordon Coll., 1966; m. Yetta Jean Pennington, Aug. 28, 1965; children—Tania Lynne, Keira Leigh. Sales asso. Blake Realty, Inc., Schenectady, 1972, br. sales mgr., 1973-75, div. sales mgr., 1976—, v.p., 1977—. Bd. dirs. Schenectady Christian Schs. Served to capt. USAF, 1967-71. Mem. Realtors Nat. Mktg. Inst., N.Y. State Assn. Realtors, Schenectady Bd. Realtors (bd. govs.). Presbyterian. Club: Kiwanis. Home: 42 Witbeck Dr Scotia NY 12302 Office: 200 State St Schenectady NY 12305

REMBSKI, STANISLAV, artist, portrait painter; b. Sochaczew, Poland; s. Ludwik and Magdalena (Liechtenstein) R.; came to U.S., 1922, naturalized, 1929; student Technol. Inst. Warsaw, Ecole des Beaux Arts, Royal Acad. Fine Arts (Berlin); m. Isabelle Walton Everett, Dec. 24, 1927. Prin. works include Nude, Newark Mus.; portraits of notable pub. figures, educators, and clergyman in ednl., pub. and pvt. collections, among more recent being: Adm. William S. Pye, Naval War Coll., Newport; Adm. of the Fleet, William D. Leahy, Washington; Pres. Woodrow Wilson, Woodrow Wilson Nat. Shrine, Washington; Pres. Franklin D. Roosevelt, F.D.R. Meml. Library, Hyde Park, N.Y.; Comdr. Joshua Barney, Naval Mus., Washington; Dr. Maurice J. Pincoffs, Dr. Eduard Uhlenhuth (U. Md. Med. Sch.); Dr. Hubert McNeill Poteat (Wake Forest Coll.); Dr. John B. Zinn (Gettysburg Coll.); Col. William Baxter, Dr. Thomas G. Pullen, Senator George L. Radcliffe, J. Harold Grady (mayor Balt.), Gov. J. Millard Tawes of Md., Maj. Gen. William Purnell, Howard MacCarthy, Jr., Lawrence Cardinal Shehan, Commodore Thomas Truxton, USN, Frigate Constellation, Balt., Thomas Jefferson and Md. Signers of Declaration of Independence (for the Constellation), others; murals: Triptych, 19x22 feet, St. Bernard of Clairvaux at St. Bernard's Sch. for Boys, Gladstone, N.J.; I Am the Life, Meml. Ch., Episcopal, Balt.; wives 5 Md. govs. for Govt. House, Annapolis. Lectr., vis. critic Md. Inst. Art, 1952-55. Mem. Allied Artists Am., Nat. Soc. Mural Painters, Am. Artists Profl. League. Clubs: Univ., Charcoal (Balt.), Churchman's; Paint and Powder; Salmagundi (N.Y.C.). Home and Office: 1404 Park Ave Baltimore MD 21217

REMICK, ROBERT MERRICK, fin. services co. exec.; b. Newton, Mass., May 8, 1924; s. Robert Merrick and Mary Lombard (Moore) R.; B.S., N.Y.U., 1952; children—Lee, Scot, Lynn. Jr. security analyst Moody's Co., N.Y.C., 1947; asst. to pres. Investors Counsel, Inc., N.Y.C., 1947-50; sales supr. New Eng. Life Ins. Co., N.Y.C., 1950-54; ednl. dir. Conn. Mut. Life Ins. Co., N.Y.C., 1954-57; founder, pres. Income Planning Assos., Ltd., N.Y.C., 1957—; gen. agt. Conn. Mut. Life Ins. Co., N.Y.C., 1957-73, regular agt., 1974—; chmn. bd. dirs. Computer Income Planning Corp., N.Y.C., 1967—; instr. econs. and fin. Coll. Ins., N.Y.C., 1967-72. Served with USNR, 1942-45. C.L.U., enrolled actuary. Mem. Million Dollar Round Table (life), Am. Soc. C.L.U.'s, N.Y. Soc. Security Analysts, Nat. Assn. Security Dealers, Am. Acad. Actuaries, Am. Soc. Pension Actuaries, Am. Pension Conf., Nat. Assn. Life Underwriters. Home: 116 Central Park S New York City NY 10019 Office: 342 Madison Ave New York City NY 10017

REMLAND, MARJORIE ELLEN, health care products co. exec.; b. Bklyn., Sept. 13, 1943; d. Murray and Ann Rae (Weisman) Block; B.S., Coll. City N.Y., 1964; M.B.A., Fairleigh Dickinson U., 1978; m. Keith Remland, Mar. 5, 1967. Researcher, asso. producer CBS News, N.Y.C., 1964-67; pub. relations asso. Am. Lung Assn., N.Y.C., 1968-73; pub. relations asso. Warner-Lambert Co., Morris Plains, N.J., 1973-77; editor Morris Plains News and Warner Lambert World; mgr. employee communications Schering-Plough Corp., Kenilworth, N.J., 1977—, also editor Schering-Plough World; pub. relations cons. Am. Occupational Therapy Assn., 1968-71, Assn. Children with Learning Disabilities, 1973. Mem. Lincoln Park (N.J.) Environ Control Com., 1970-73. Mem. Internat. Assn. Bus. Communicators, N.J. Bus. Communicators Assn. Club: Ramapo Kennel (trustee). Home: 8 Brightwood Rd Lincoln Park NJ 07035 Office: Galloping Hill Rd Kenilworth NJ 07033

REMMERS, KURT WILLIAM, educator; b. Mineola, N.Y., Dec. 13, 1944; s. Herbert Kort and Irene Mary (Kelly) R.; B.A., Westminster Coll., 1966, M.Ed., 1967; M.A., N.Y. U., 1971; m. Deborah Marie Winter, Aug. 20, 1966; children—Kirsten, Megan. Grad. asst., asst. dir. media center Westminster Coll., New Wilmington, Pa., 1967; tchr. history and econs. Fair Lawn (N.J.) High Sch., 1967-69; asst. dir. Center for Ednl. Tech., Jersey City State Coll., 1969-70; dir. Media Resource Center, Drew U., Madison, N.J., 1970—; producer, dir. series ednl. TV programs Ednl. Consortium fdr Cable, Summit, N.J., 1978—. Mem. exec. com. Higher Edn. Assn. for TV, Channel 13, WNET-TV, N.Y.C., 1971-72; founder N.J. Ednl. Media Consortium, 1973, bd. dirs., 1975. Served with U.S. Army, 1967. Mem. Assn. Ednl. Communications and Tech., Nat. Ednl. Assn. Broadcasting, N.J. Assn. Ednl. Communications and Tech. Democrat. Lutheran. Home: Townhouse 28 Drew U Madison NJ 07940 Office: Media Resource Center Drew U Madison NJ 07940

REMSON, NORMAN, ednl. adminstr.; b. N.Y.C., Jan. 3, 1926; B.S. in Edn. and English, Coll. City N.Y., 1949; M.A. in Elementary and Secondary Edn., Columbia U., 1949 Ed.D. in Curriculum and Adminstrn., 1956; m. Barbara Remson; 2 children. Dir. Curriculum Fair Lawn (N.J.) pub. schs., 1963-68; asst. supt. schs. Nanuet (N.Y.) pub. schs., 1968-71; supt. schs. Old Tappan (N.J.) pub. schs., 1972-74; asst. supt. schs. Roxbury Twp. pub. schs. Succasunna, N.J., 1974—. Mem. Am. Assn. Sch. Adminstrs., Assn. for Supervision and Curriculum Devel., NEA, AAUP, Kappa Delta Pi. Author: A Practical Guide to Teaching, 1960. Certified sch. dist. adminstr., N.Y. N.J. Home: 21 Lawrence Ct Old Tappan NJ 07675 Office: 25 Meeker St Succasunna NJ 07876

RENCK, ROBERT LEO, JR., security analyst; b. N.Y.C., Apr. 18, 1948; s. Robert Leo and Agnes E. (Fives) R.; B.S., St. John's U., 1968; M.B.A., 1971; m. Diane P. Elder, Nov. 22, 1969 (div. May 1978); children—Susan Lynn, Robert Leo III. Asst. v.p. Bache & Co., N.Y.C., 1968-72; v.p. Laird, Inc. and successor G. H. Walker, Laird, Inc., N.Y.C., 1972-74; v.p. Cyrus J. Lawrence Inc., N.Y.C., 1974—. Served with U.S. Army, 1969-75. Mem. Fin. Analysts Fedn., Soc. Photog. Scientists and Engrs., Nat. Micrographics Assn., N.Y. Soc. Security Analysts. Roman Catholic. Author: Photo Notes. Home: 70 Erickson Dr Stamford CT 60903 Office: 155 E 73d St New York City NY 10006

RENKIS, ALAN ILMARS, plastics formulating co. exec.; b. Preili, Latvia, Apr. 16, 1938; s. Joseph and Malvine (Sturitis) R.; came to U.S., 1950, naturalized, 1956; B.S. in Chem. Engring., Pa. State U., 1960; m. Inara Balodis, July 15, 1961; children—Martin Alan, Laura Alise. With product devel. and tech. service div. Diamond Alkali Co., Painesville, Ohio, 1960-63; tech. dir. G.S. Plastics Co., Cleve., 1963; founder, pres. Thermoclad Co., Erie, Pa., 1963—, also Norwalk, Calif., 1972—. Mem. Young Pres.'s Orgn., Soc. Plastics Engrs., Sigma Pi, Fraternitas Metropolitana (Latvian Student frat.). Clubs: Univ., Erie, Maennerchor, Kahkwa (Erie). Developer comml. PVC resins for formulating fluidized bed coating powders; formulations and compounding techniques. Home: 5109 Watson Rd Erie PA 16505 Office: 4690 Iroquois Ave Erie PA 16511

RENO, BOB, record mfr.; b. Jersey City, Oct. 20, 1937; s. Casper and Dorothy (DeSena) Amorino; grad. high sch.; m. Lauren Corini, Jan. 22, 1972; 1 dau., Amanda. Promotion mgr. Coed Records, N.Y.C., 1962-64; prof. mgr. Mills Music, Inc., N.Y.C., 1965-67; v.p. popular product Mercury Records, N.Y.C., 1967-69; dir. popular product Vanguard Records, N.Y.C., 1969-70; v.p. Buddah Records, N.Y.C., 1970-73; pres. Midland Internat. Records, N.Y.C., 1973—. Mem. Nat. Acad. Rec. Arts and Scis. Clubs: Friars, New Rochelle Shore. Address: Midland Internat Records 1650 Broadway New York City NY 10019

RENOFF, PAUL VERNON, ret. elec. mfrs. rep.; b. Balt., July 17, 1911; s. Henry John and Mary E. (Snyder) R.; B.E.E., Johns Hopkins, 1932; m. Margaret Hamilton Houghton, June 18, 1937; children—Ronald Hamilton, Lois Ellen (Mrs. Henry Ward Brockett), Cynthia Houghton (Mrs. George A. Taler). Engr., H.R. Houghton, 1933-36; partner Houghton & Renoff, 1936-45, Paul V. Renoff Co., 1945-66; pres. Renoff Assos., Inc., 1966-76; former dir. Sken-A-Matic Corp., United Co. Pres., Roland Ct. Maintenance Corp.; former pres. Arundel Beach Improvement Assn.; mem. Magothy River Assn.; dir. Roland Park Civic League. Registered profl. engr., Md. Mem. Amigas de Calle del Cristo 255, Engrs. Club, IEEE, U.S. Power Squadron, Md. Hist. Soc., Md. Acad. Scis. Democrat. Clubs: Johns Hopkins, Chartwell Golf & Country (Severna Park, Md.). Home: 4326 Roland Ct Baltimore MD 21210 also PO Box 1 Sugar Loaf Shores FL 33044 also Route 454 Arundel Beach Rd Severna Park MD 21146

RENOUD, DOROTHY OWEN, publishing co. exec.; b. Far Rockaway, N.Y., Aug. 11, 1933; d. Herbert William and Elizabeth (Fischer) Owen; ed. pub. schs., bus. courses; m. David F. Renoud, Jan. 18, 1958; children—David, Douglas. File clk. Reinhold Pub. Co., N.Y.C., 1951-59, sales adminstrv. mgr., 1959-61; asst. to circulation mgr. United Tech. Pub. Co., Garden City, N.Y., 1961-63, circulation dir., 1963—. Mem. Subscription Fulfillment Mgrs. Assn., Nat. Bus. Circulation Council Long Beach Fire Dept. Ladies Aux. Home: 527 West Chester St Long Beach NY 11561 Office: 645 Stewart Ave Garden City NY 11530

RENSTROM, ARTHUR GEORGE, librarian; b. Willmar, Minn., Oct. 30, 1905; s. Peter Olof and Amanda (Lofgren) R.; B.A., U. Minn., 1927; B.S., U. Ill., 1928; M.S., Columbia, 1930; m. Mary Agnes Long, Sept. 21, 1932. Librarian, St. Paul Pub. Library, 1922-28, librarian Battle Creek (Mich.) Coll. Library, 1928-29; sr. asst. librarian aero. div. Library of Congress, Washington, 1935-45, asst. chief aero. div., 1946-53, bibliographer tech. info. div., 1954, curator sci. room, 1954-62, head reference sec. sci., tech. div., 1962-63, sr. sci. reference librarian, biblog. specialist, 1963-65, head aero. sec., aero. project, 1965-75, cons. aviation history, 1975—; librarian CAA, Washington, 1945-46. Mem. D.C. Library Assn., Spl. Libraries Assn. Author: United States Aviation Policy, 1947; Aeropolitics, 1948; Aeronatical and Space Serials, A World List, 1962; Bibliographical Note on the History of Rocket Technology, 1964; Wilbur and Orville Wright, A Bibliography Commemorating the Hundredth Anniversary of the Birth of Wilbur Wright, 1968; Wilbur and Orville Wright, A Chronology Commemorating the Hundredth Anniversary of the Birth of Orville Wright, 1975; Charles A. Lindbergh, A Selective Bibliography Commemorating the Golden Anniversary of Lindbergh's Solo Flight to Paris, 1977. Contbr. articles to profl. jours. Home: 5306 N Washington Blvd Arlington VA 22205 Office: Sci Tech Div Library of Congress Washington DC 20540

RENTSCHLER, GEORGE ADAM, JR., steamship co. exec.; b. N.Y.C., Dec. 2, 1937; s. George Adam and Rita Rend (Mitchell) R.; A.B. with honors, Princeton U., 1960; postgrad. in Mgmt. Devel., Harvard Bus. Sch., 1970; m. Frederica Price Schlaff, Nov. 11, 1972. Truckers billing clk. Pier 11, U.S. Lines, Balt., 1964, asst. pier supt., N.Y.C., 1964-65, asst. dist. mgr., Kansai, Japan, 1965-66, asst. mgr. Far East and Hawaiian Service, N.Y.C., 1966-69; mgr. planning Trinidad Corp., N.Y.C., 1969-73, v.p., 1973-77; v.p. Barber Oil Corp., 1971-78, now dir.; mgr. ops. Norton, Lilly & Co., N.Y.C., 1978—. Served with AUS, 1960-63. Mem. Soc. Naval Architects and Marine Engrs. (asso.). Republican. Roman Catholic. Clubs: Whitehall, Links, Leash. Office: 90 West St New York City NY 10006

REPETTI, ANDREW JOSEPH, educator; b. Passaic, N.J., Apr. 7, 1950; s. Guido Victor and Concetta Rose (DeBello) R.; A.A., Bergen Community Coll., 1972; B.A., William Paterson Coll., 1974, M.A., 1976, M.Ed., 1977; m. Laura Lee Spinelli, July 9, 1977. Tchr. Am. history and Am. govt. Lodi (N.J.) High Sch., 1974—. Mem. Bergen

County Democratic Com., 1970-77; municipal chmn. Lodi Dem. Com., 1976-77; mem. Bergen County polit. edn. com. N.J. Dem. Com., 1977-78; merit badge counselor Boy Scouts Am.; advisor Catholic Youth Orgn.; mem. adv. bd. Bergen County Historic Sites; assembly aide N.J. assemblymen Paul Contillo and Robert Burns. Tchr. certification Social Studies, N.J.; adminstr. certification, N.J. Mem. AAUP, Am. Soc. Planning Ofcls., Nat. Council for Social Studies, Am. Acad. Polit. and Social Sci., Am. Soc. for Pub. Adminstrn., Acad. Polit. Sci., U.S. Capitol Hist. Soc., Am. Soc. Notaries, NEA, N.J. Edn. Assn., Bergen County Edn. Assn., Cath. War Vets. Served with USAF, 1968-69. Office: care Lodi High Sch Putnum St Lodi NJ 07644

REPPETTO, THOMAS ANTHONY, educator; b. Chgo., Aug. 17, 1931; s. George Franklin and Hazel June (Blakely) R.; B.A., Roosevelt U., 1965; M. Pub. Adminstrn., Ill. Inst. Tech., 1967; D. Pub. Adminstrn. (Littauer fellow), Harvard U., 1970; m. Christa L. Carnegie, Jan. 31, 1975; 1 dau. by previous marriage—Martha R. Patrolman, Chgo. Police Dept., 1952-60, sgt., 1960-61, lt., 1961-63, capt., 1963-66, comdr. detectives, 1966-70; researcher Mass. Inst. Tech.-Harvard Joint Center Urban Studies, 1970-71; prof. criminal justice John Jay Coll. Criminal Justice, City N.Y., 1971—, dean grad. studies, 1976—, v.p., 1978—; cons. in field. Named to Law Enforcement Task Force, U.S. Commn. on Productivity, 1973-74. Served in USAR, 1948-61. Mem. Am. Soc. Pub. Adminstrn. (chmn. sect. criminal justice 1977-78), Am. Soc. Criminology, Internat. Assn. Chiefs of Police. Roman Catholic. Author: Residential Crime, 1974; The Blue Parade, 1978; contbr. articles to profl. jours. Home: 51 Hillside Terr Irvington NY 10533 Office: 444 W 56th St New York City NY 10019

REPS, DAVID NATHAN, mgmt. cons.; b. N.Y.C., July 30, 1926; s. Samuel and Fay (Ginsberg) R.; B.S. in Elec. Engring., Columbia, 1948; M.S. in Elec. Engring., U. Pitts., 1953; Ph.D. in Mgmt. and Econs., 1966; m. Helen Marilyn Shifrin, Aug. 10, 1958; children—Tamara, Aaron, Steven, Jennifer. Elec. engr. Ford, Bacon & Davis, Inc., N.Y.C., 1948-50; electric power systems engr. Westinghouse Electric Corp., Pitts., 1950-63; corporate cons. managerial econs., 1963-66; dir. mgmt. services div. S.D. Leidesdorf & Co., N.Y.C., 1967-70, prin., dir., 1970-75; dir. group mktg. Med. Data Systems, Inc., 1976-77; cons. long-range systems planning Mt. Sinai Hosp., N.Y.C., L.I. Jewish Med. Center, New Hyde Park, N.Y.; adj. asso. prof. in bus. adminstrn. L.I. U. Sch. Bus. Adminstrn., 1973-77, prof., 1977—, chmn. dept. fin., bus. econs. and pub. policy, 1977—; cons. bus. planning Harrigan Med. Products, Inc., 1977—; program chmn. health care and hosps. Info 75, 76. Trustee, treas. Jewish Community Center, White Plains, 1971-74. Served with USNR, 1944-46. Mem. IEEE (sr.), Nat. Assn. Bus. Economists, Econometric Soc., Am. Econ. Assn., Inst. Mgmt. Scis., Nat. Economists Club, Met. Econs. Assn., AAAS, Soc. for Computer Medicine. Republican. Jewish. Author: Electric Power Distribution Systems Reference Book, 1957; Planning and Control Models for Large Diversified Companies, 1966; Current State of Art in Hospital Information Systems, 1972; Can Your Corporate Plan Achieve its Goals?, 1973; also articles in field. Home: 98 Soundview Ave White Plains NY 10606 Office: LI U Sch Bus Brooklyn NY 11201

RESCHKE, MORRIS MEIER, physician; b. Berlin, Germany, Nov. 21, 1899; s. Solomon and Marianne (Schwarz) R.; came to U.S., 1935, naturalized, 1940; M.D., Friedrich Wilhelm U., Berlin, 1926; m. Selma Metzger, Jan. 17, 1937; 1 son, Stephen. Intern, Berlin Met. Hosp., 1926-27, resident in dermatology, 1930-31; asst. vis. dermatologist Bellevue Med. Sch., N.Y. U., 1938-52, instr. clin. dermatology, 1946-52; cons. N.Y. State Ins. Fund, 1946, Patrolmen's Benevolent Assn., 1947; cons., contbr. to Ars Medici (Switzerland), 1938-73; writer, essayist, encyclopedist, poet; contbr. to Lexikon de Judentums, Germany, 1976; contbr. articles to Am. and Swiss med. jours.; author English, German and Hebrew poetry and essays. Diplomate Am. Bd. Dermatology. Fellow Israel Med. Assn.; mem. Nat. Soc. Published Poets, AMA, N.Y. State (citation for 50 years service 1977), N.Y. County med. socs., N.Y. State Soc. Dermatology, Zionist Orgn. Am. Home: 505 West End Ave New York NY 10024

RESNICK, ARTHUR, dentist; b. N.Y.C., May 22, 1918; s. David and Fannie (Post) R.; Ph.G., Ph.C., St. Johns U., 1939, B.S. in Pharmacy, 1940; D.D.S., U. Pa., 1943; m. Vicki Trop, Dec. 24, 1942; 1 dau., Jill Ronnie (Mrs. Morris Gindi). Pvt. practice dentistry, N.Y.C., 1947—; lectr. St. Johns U. Coll. Pharmacy, 1948-64. Hon. dep. sheriff, Sullivan County, 1958—; co-founder, past pres. N.Y. U. Oral Rehab. Soc.; trustee Ocean Pkwy. Jewish Center, Bklyn. Served with Dental Corps, AUS 1943-46; PTO. Fellow Am., Internat. colls. dentists, Acad. Gen. Dentistry, N.Y. Acad. Dentistry, Royal Soc. Health; mem. Am. Dental Assn., N.Y. State, 2d Dist. (trustee) dental socs., Assn. Mil. Surgeons U.S.A., Fedn. Dentaire Internat. (life), Am. Acad. Oral Medicine, Internat. Narcotic Officers Assn., Police Chiefs Assn. N.Y., St. Johns Coll. Pharmacy Alumni Assn. (pres. 1966). Clubs: Masons; B'nai B'rith. Home: 455 Ocean Pkwy Brooklyn NY 11218 Office: 1440 Broadway New York City NY 10018

RESNICK, EDWARD J., orthopedic surgeon; b. Phila., June 17, 1925; s. Morris and Rose (Greenberg) R.; student Temple U., 1943-44, M.D., 1951; m. Irene Barbara Max, Oct. 23, 1960; children—Bernard Max, Jane Elizabeth. Intern, Phila. Gen. Hosp., 1951-52; resident Temple U. Hosp., Phila., 1952-55; prof. orthopaedic surgery Sch. Medicine, Temple U., Phila., 1970-78, dir. pain control center, 1975—. Bd. dirs. Phila. Lyric Opera Co., 1965-74, Care-Medico-Eastern Pa., 1974—. Served with M.C. U.S. Army, 1943-46. Mem. A.C.S., Am. Acad. Orthopaedic Surgeons, Eastern Orthopaedic Assn., AMA, Pa., Phila. County (sec., 1973-78) med. socs., Phila. Orthopaedic Soc. (pres., 1977-78), La Société Internationale de Chirurgie Ortho pedique et de Traumatologie. Contbr. writings in field to med. publs. Home: 357 Hidden River Rd Penn Valley PA 19072 Office: Dept Orthopaedic Surgery Temple Univ Hosp 3401 N Broad St Philadelphia PA 19140

RESNIK, SOL LEON, mfg. co. exec.; b. Providence, May 16, 1930; s. Nathan and Fanny (Priest) R.; B.S., U. R.I., 1953; M.B.A., U. Pa., 1954; m. Esther Petersohn, June 20, 1954; children—David, Marcia, Linda. Founder, exec., pres. Emblem & Badge Inc., Providence, 1954—; partner Village Park Realty, 1970—; pres. 859 Realty Co., Providence, 1960-74; partner Diplomat Assos., Providence, 1970—, Eleven-Eleven Assos., Providence, 1974-75; chmn. bd. dirs. Promotion Corp. Am., Providence, 1970-76. Bd. dirs. Providence Hebrew Day Sch., 1960-73; bd. dirs. R.I. Broadway Theatre League, 1965-73, R.I. Jewish Community Center, 1974—, Jewish Fedn. R.I., 1973-79, Narragansett Bay Devel. Soc., 1974—, Temple Emanu-El, 1978-79. Mem. Mfg. Jewelers and Silversmiths Am. Mason (Shriner, 32 deg.). Home: 41 Westford Rd Providence RI 02906 Office: 859 N Main St Providence RI 02940

RESSEGUIE, FRANKLIN BRUNDAGE, lawyer; b. South Gibson, Pa., May 28, 1921; s. Frank Fitch and Grace (Brundage) R.; B.A., Harper Coll., 1949; LL.B., Cornell U., 1952; m. Ruth Mildred Kaminski, May 31, 1947; children—John Franklin, Elizabeth DeAnne. Admitted to N.Y. bar, 1954; asso. Pearis, Resseguie & Stone, Binghamton, 1952-54; practiced in Binghamton, 1954—; founder, sr. partner law firm Resseguie, Powers & Richards, Binghamton, 1962, then Resseguie & Richards; now engaged in individual practice; owner and developer Highland Oaks, Hiawatha Island; pres. Locator Map, Inc., Highland Oaks Devel. Corp., Hiawatha Island Corp.; former dir. Whitney Point Sand and Gravel Corp.; past dir. Log-Line Corp., Tioga Heritage Corp. Pres. Broome County Young Republican Club, 1960; Rep. primary candidate for Congress, 27th Dist. N.Y., 1974. Served to capt. USAAF, 1942-47, lt. col. Res., ret. Mem. Am. Judicature Soc., Am., N.Y. State, Broome County (civil rights com.) bar assns., Internat. Platform Assn., Phi Delta Phi. Clubs: Masons (32 deg.), Sertoma (pres. 1964-65), Highland Racquet and Riding. Author: (poems) Eagle Feathers. Home: 23 Oakridge Dr Binghamton NY 13903 Office: 600 O'Neil Bldg Binghamton NY 13901

RESSLER, CHARLES, physician; b. N.Y.C., Feb. 14, 1914; s. Joseph and Bertha (Rosenberg) R.; B.S. summa cum laude, Lafayette Coll., 1934; M.D., Cornell U., 1938; m. Eleanor Boyar, June 14, 1942; children—Donna, Howard David. Intern, Cornell Div. Bellevue Hosp., N.Y.C., 1938-40; resident in medicine Mt. Sinai Hosp., N.Y.C., 1940-41, also asst. attending physician; practice medicine specializing in internal medicine, N.Y.C., 1941—; dir. dept. medicine Italian Hosp., N.Y.C., 1950-70; cons. physician Cabrini Health Center, 1972-76; asst. attending physician Cornell-N.Y. Hosp., chief med. service Manhattan Eye, Ear and Throat Hosp.; instr. in medicine Cornell Med. Coll.; asst. prof. clin. medicine Mt. Sinai Hosp. Served to capt. M.C., U.S. Army, World Ward II. Decorated as cavallieri, also commendatore (Italy); diplomate Am. Bd. Internal Medicine. Fellow A.C.P.; mem. AMA, Pan-Am. Med. Soc., Am. (chmn. membership com. 1974-77), Internat., N.Y. State (pres. 1977-78), N.Y. County (pres. 1967) socs. internal medicine, Phi Beta Kappa, Alpha Omega Alpha. Democrat. Jewish. Clubs: Harmonie (N.Y.C.), Griffis Faculty (Cornell). Contbr. articles on liver diseases, metabolism and obesity to med. publs. Home and Office: 625 Park Ave New York City NY 10021

RESTIANO, RICHARD ANGELO, photographer; b. S.I., N.Y., May 9, 1948; s. Angelo and Michelina (Giannetti) R.; B.S. in Edn., Fordham U., 1970; m. Vincenza Faustini, Aug. 16, 1970; children—Alessandra Michele, Richard Angelo, Claudio Terese. Tchr. N.Y.C. pub. schs., 1970-71; photog. cons. Am. Yearbook Co., 1971-73; founder, owner N.Y. Photo Graphic, Inc., Mt. Vernon, N.Y., 1973—. Mem. Westchester Profl. Photographers Assn., Mt. Vernon C. of C., Westchester Better Bus. Bur., Am. Assn. Yearbook Photographers, Profl. Photographers Am. Club: Mt. Vernon Lions. Home: 10 Merriam Pl Bronxville NY 10708 Office: 113 Gramatan Ave Mount Vernon NY 10550

REUBEN, ALLAN H., lawyer; b. Pitts., June 24, 1931; s. Monte M. and Miriam (Barthfeld) R.; B.A. summa cum laude, U. Pitts., 1953; LL.B. magna cum laude, Harvard, 1956; m. Gladys Winkler, May 25, 1956; children—John David, Patricia Anne, Catherine Ellen. Admitted to Pa. bar, 1957; law clk. to Judge U.S. Ct. of Appeals for 3d Circuit, 1956-57; asso. law firm Wolf, Block, Schorr & Solis-Cohen, Phila., 1957-65, partner, 1965—; lectr. Banking Law Inst., 1969; trustee Lawyers Com. for Civil Rights under Law, 1976—. Mem. bd. commrs. Cheltenham Twp. (Pa.), 1972—; chmn., mem. governing bd. Employment Discrimination Referral Project of Phila. Bar Assn. and Lawyers Com. for Civil Rights Under Law, 1971-75; mem. exec. com. bd. dirs. Pub. Interest Law Center Phila.; mem. Southeast Regional Planning Council-Gov.'s. Justice Commn.-Pa., 1973—, mem. exec. com., 1974—; bd. dirs. Phila. Am. Jewish Com., 1965—, v.p., 1973—; mem. Jewish Community Relations Council, Phila., 1965—, bd. dirs., 1973—, chmn. civil rights com., 1975—; trustee Community Legal Services Phila. 1971; bd. dirs. Pa. Legal Services Center, 1978—; bd. govs. Renal Youth Rehab. Program, 1976—. Mem. Am. Judicature Soc., Am., Fed., Pa., Phila. (co-chmn. subcom. riots in N. Phila. 1965, chmn. subcom. invasion of privacy by electronic means 1966-70, 72—; law day speakers chmn. 1966, pub. relations com. 1966—, chmn. speakers bur. 1967, vice chmn. civil rights com. 1969-70, chmn. 1971, mem. sect. of corp., banking and bus. law 1965—, exec. com. 1969-70, 72, sec. 1973, chmn. com. on fin. 1966-67, editor Phila. Lawyer 1969-74, co-chmn. editorial bd. 1974—) bar assns., Phi Beta Kappa. Home: 7914 Ivy Ln Elkins Park PA 19117 Office: Packard Bldg Philadelphia PA 19102

REUBEN, GARY M., automobile co. exec.; b. Pitts., Sept. 20, 1942; s. George and Eva (Martin) R.; B.S. in Labor Relations, U. Akron, 1965; grad. program for mgmt. devel. Harvard U., 1973; m. Mara Ruth Goldstein, June 19, 1966; children—Traci, Gregg. Corp. dir. indsl. relations Levinson Steel Co., 1969-72; exec. v.p., chief operating officer Levco Automotive Products Co., Pitts., 1972-77; v.p. sales and mktg. Safeguard Automotive Co., Pitts., 1977—; mem. faculty Advanced Mgmt. Research Inc., 1977-78; tchr. Am. Mgmt. Assn., Robert Moriss Coll. Mem. Am. Soc. Personnel Adminstrn., Harvard Bus. Sch. Assn. Pitts., Automotive Parts Rebuilder Assn. (dir. 1975-78), S. Side Pitts. C. of C. (past v.p.), Pitts. Personnel Assn. (dir., past pres.). Home: 1227 Bellerock St Pittsburgh PA 15227 Office: 1100 Park Bldg Pittsburgh PA 15222

REUBEN-LOCKERMAN, GENEVA LORENE, counselor; b. Silverstreet, S.C., Nov. 4, 1928; d. James and Matilda (Stewart) Reuben; B.A., Benedict Coll., 1949; M.A., Columbia U., 1950; postgrad. N.Y. U., 1951, 59; m. Joseph Howard Lockerman, June 10, 1953; 1 son, Joseph Howard. Freshman counselor Fla. A & M U., Tallahassee, 1951-53; service rep. N.Y. Tel. Co., 1954-55; tchr. Jersey City Bd. Edn., 1958-64; edn. specialist Jersey City Can Do, 1965-68; asso. dir. students Jersey City State Coll., 1968-71, psychologist-counselor, 1971-75, counselor I, 1975—; lectr. Dartmouth Coll., Hanover, N.H., 1971-74, supr. counselors Dartmouth Edn. Center, 1975-76. Bd. dirs. NAACP, Jersey City Ednl. Center, YWCA, Jersey City; mem. Jersey City Bd. Personnel Practices. Mem. Am. Personnel and Guidance Assn., NEA, Nat. Vocat. Guidance Assn., Jersey City State Coll. Faculty Assn. (sec. 1977-78), Assn. Counselor Edn. and Supervision, Assn. Non White Concerns in Personnel and Guidance. Democrat. Baptist. Home: 144 Bayview Ave Jersey City NJ 07305 Office: 2039 Kennedy Blvd Jersey City NJ 07305

REUBENS, EDWIN PIERCE, educator; b. N.Y.C., Mar. 27, 1914; s. Max Hirsch and Sylvia (Brager) R.; A.B., City Coll. N.Y., 1935; M.A., Columbia, 1939, Ph.D., 1952; m. Beatrice Gomberg, Feb. 26, 1943; 1 dau., Margot. With U.S. War Prodn. Bd., Washington, 1942-43, 46-47; asst. prof. Cornell U., Ithaca, N.Y., 1947-52; prof. econs. City Coll. N.Y., 1952—, chmn. Ph.D. program in econs., 1963-69; vis. prof. Columbia, 1954, 55, 64, New Sch., 1960, 62, 64; sr. research fellow, U. West Indies, 1960-61; cons. project dir. UN, 1952-53, 65-66, 71-72, 72-74; cons. U.S. AID, 1967, 71. Mem. commn. urban affairs, Am. Jewish Congress, 1971-72; co-founder Assn. Asian Studies, Omicron Delta Epsilon. Served to lt. USN, 1943-46. Social Sci. Research Council research grantee, 1961-62; Ralph Bunche Inst. on UN, research grantee, 1975; City U. Research Found. grantee, 1975-78. Mem. Am. Economic Assn., Phi Beta Kappa, Lock and Key. Author monographs, contbr. chpts. to books, articles to profl. jours. Home: 60 Riverside Dr New York City NY 10024 Office: Dept Econs City Coll NY Convent Ave New York City NY 10031

REUSCHE, FRANK LOUIS, ceramic decorating supply co. exec.; b. Bklyn., Feb. 17, 1925; s. Frank Louis and Marjorie Theresa (Ryan) R.; grad. Fordham Prep. Sch., 1941; B.S., Bethany Coll., 1944; postgrad. Ohio State U., 1945, Rutgers U., 1947-48; m. Amelia V. Ozimek, Sept. 18, 1949 (dec. Oct. 1972); children—Frank Louis III, Thomas R., Marjorie A., Mary T., Madeline C.; m. Jane Fabian Verney, Dec. 28, 1975; stepchildren—Bruce S. Verney, Kim K. Verney, Kerry J. Verney, Alison E. Verney. Grad. chemist So. Acid & Sulfur Co., Columbus, O., 1945; chemist research and devel. L. Reusche & Co., Newark, 1947-51, v.p., 1951-66, pres., 1966—. Served with USAAF, 1945-47. Mem. Am., N.J. ceramic socs., Sigma Nu. Patentee in field. Home: 164 Canoe Brook Pkwy Summit NJ 07901 Office: 2-6 Lister Ave Newark NJ 07105

REUSCHEL, JAMES PHILIP, health services adminstr.; b. Burlington, Vt., July 17, 1942; s. Carl J. and Leona I. (Hammond) R.; B.A., U. Vt., 1965; postgrad. (Kellog fellow) in Health Adminstrn., U. Calif., Los Angeles, 1970-71; doctoral candidate in pub. adminstrn. Nova U., 1977—; m. Bernadette M. Barewicz, July 25, 1964; children—Lori Ann, Curtis James, Nicole Ann. Bank examiner FDIC, Washington, 1965-68; adminstr. Surg. Assos. Found., Inc., Burlington, 1968-73; dir. ops. Univ. Health Center, Inc., Burlington, 1973-75, adminstrv. dir., 1975—; instr. Concord Coll., Burlington, 1972-73; cons. in health adminstrn., 1974—. Mem. Am. Hosp. Assn., Am. Coll. Med. Group Adminstrs., Am. Mgmt. Assn., Am. Profl. Practice Assn., Group Health Assn. Am., Burlington C. of C., Med. Group Mgmt. Assn. Clubs: Rotary, Ethan Allen, K.C. Home: 25 Buckingham Dr Colchester VT 05446 Office: 1 S Prospect St Burlington VT 05401

REVESZ, PETER THEODORE, elec. engr.; b. Budapest, Hungary, Apr. 24, 1929; came to U.S., 1948, naturalized, 1954; B.S., U. Denver, 1953, M.S., 1958; m. Jane M. Witter, July 13, 1956; children—Sandra Elizabeth, Michael Bela. Designer microwave radio systems Mountain States Telephone, 1955-58, project engr., Denver, 1962-66; mem. tech. staff Bell Telephone Labs., Whippany, N.J., 1959-61; with Mountain Bell Telephone Co., Arvada, Colo., 1966—, gen. planning coordinator, 1965-76; asst. engring. mgr. Am. Tel. & Tel. Co., Basking Ridge, N.J., 1976—. Mem. Citizens' Adv. Com. Jefferson County Schs. Registered profl. engr., Colo. Mem. Nat. Soc. Profl. Engrs. Home: Rural Route 1 Box D-70 Brook Dr Chester NJ 07930 Office: 295 N Maple Ave Basking Ridge NJ 07920

REVZIN, STANLEY ALEXANDER, mfg. co. exec.; b. N.Y.C., Jan. 13, 1924; s. Boris and Fannie (Ellinoff) R.; B.E.E., Coll. City N.Y., 1948; postgrad. Poly. Inst. Bklyn., 1951-53; m. Marcia Korsun, Sept. 3, 1950; children—Marc Warren, Bruce David. Electronic engr. U.S. Army Signal Corps Engring. Labs., Fort Monmouth, N.J., 1948-54; mgr. engring. Lewyt Mfg. Corp., N.Y.C., 1954-60; with Bristol Electronics Inc., New Bedford, Mass., 1960—, v.p., 1961-69, pres., 1969—; dir. Transdyne Corp., New Bedford; pres., Bristol Industries, Inc., New Bedford, 1967—, Bristol Electronics Internat., New Bedford, 1972—. Mem. Town Meeting, Dartmouth, Mass., 1970—. Bd. dirs. Moby Dick council Boy Scouts Am., 1964—, Jewish Welfare Fedn., 1970—. Served to 1st lt. AUS, 1942-46; ETO. Decorated Combat Infantryman Badge, Bronze Star medal. Mem. IEEE, SBA of New Eng., Sigma Kappa Tau, Mason. Home: 47 Evelyn St North Dartmouth MA 02747 Office: 651 Orchard St New Bedford MA 02744

REX, KENNETH JOHN, solar heating co. exec.; b. Kingston, Pa., Dec. 8, 1952; s. Alexander John and Albina Marie (Rusetski) R.; B.S. in Commerce and Fin., Wilkes Coll., Wilkes-Barre, Pa., 1976. Journeyman plumber Rex Plumbing & Heating Co., Kingston, 1968-71, master plumbing and heating contractor, 1971-76, mgr. solar heat div., 1976—; instr. Luzerne County Coll.; cons. in field. Mgr., coach Kingston League Baseball, 1970-76; commr. Kingston Baseball Inc., 1974-76. Served with USNR, 1972. Mem. Nat. Home Builders Assn., Solar Energy Industries Assn., Internat. Solar Energy Soc., ASTM (chmn. subcom. writing standards solar energy swimming pools), Pa. Solar Energy Industries Soc. (dir.), Omicron Delta Epsilon. Roman Catholic. Clubs: Wyo. Valley Ski, Offshore Sailing. Home: 194-C Zerby Ave Kingston PA 18704 Office: 192 Zerby Ave Kingston PA 18704

REYES, SERGIO JOSE, clergyman; b. San Antonio, Philippines, Dec. 14, 1916; s. Benito Mercado and Julia Alcantara (Jose) R.; B.Theology, Union Theol. Sem., Philippines, 1947; B.A., Philippines Christian Coll., 1949; B.D., Oberlin Coll., 1954; M.S.T., Boston U., 1959; m. Susana Tuazon Santos, Oct. 28, 1947; 1 dau., Ruby Ann. Ordained deacon, United Methodist Ch., 1947, ordained to ministry as elder, 1949; minister chs., Philippines, 1944-69; chaplain Mary Johnston Hosp., 1960-67, dist. supt., 1967-69; interim pastor Seneca United Meth. Ch., Buffalo, 1970-71, Riverview United Meth. Ch., Buffalo, 1971-72; chaplain supr. Drug and Alcohol Addiction Center, Washingtonian Hosp., Boston, 1971-72; chaplain Clinton Correctional Facility, Dannemora, N.Y., 1972—, sr. chaplain for Clinton Correction Facility, 1975—. Mem. Am. Coll. Chaplains, Am. Correctional Chaplains Assn. (regional v.p.), Am. Protestant Correctional Chaplains Assn., N.Y. State Chaplains Assn. Republican. Club: Lions (past pres.). Home: PO Box 345 Dannemora NY 12929

REYES-DOLLETE, FE TAVERNERO, pediatrician; b. Manila, Philippines, Sept. 15, 1941; d. Escolastico Villaneuva and Rosa (Tavernero) Reyes; came to U.S., 1966; M.D., Far Eastern U., Manila, 1965; m. Rodolfo Dollete, Aug. 9, 1969; 1 dau., Melissa Ann Dollete. Rotating intern Waltham (Mass.) Hosp., 1966-67; resident in pediatrics Boston City Hosp., 1967-70; instr. in pediatrics Johns Hopkins U., 1973—, pediatrician Johns Hopkins U. Hosp., 1973—. Home: 1108 Temfield Rd Towson MD 21204 Office: Johns Hopkins Hosp Baltimore MD 21205

REYES-GUERRA, ANTONIO, dental surgeon; b. San Salvador, El Salvador, Aug. 4, 1919; s. Antonio and Linda Elizabeth (Hardesty) R.-G.; came to U.S., 1945, naturalized, 1950; B.S., B.A., U. El Salvador, 1943, D.D.S., 1943; D.D.S., U. Pa., 1947; m. Olive Isabella Scott, Nov. 27, 1954; children—Richard Bruce, Alan Scott. Intern, Rosales Hosp., El Salvador, 1943-44, resident oral surgery, anesthesia, 1944-45; asst. attending oral surgeon Lincoln 7 Polyclinic Hosp., N.Y.C., 1956-66; dir. dept. dentistry and oral surgery Lawrence Hosp., Bronxville, N.Y., 1970—. Served to capt. Dental Corps, USAF, 1952-55. Diplomate N.Y. Bd. Oral Surgery. Fellow Am. Coll. Dentistry, Am. Soc. Advancement Anesthesia in Dentistry (pres. 1969-71, exec. sec. 1971—); mem. Eastchester (pres. 1975—), Am., 9th. Dist. N.Y. State dental socs., Am. Acad. Gen. Practice, Acad. Oral Pathology. Republican. Episcopalian. Clubs: St. Andrews (Hastings on the Hudson, N.Y.); Masons, Shriners, Lions (pres. Tuckahoe Eastchester 1975). Author: Treatment of Fractures of the Mandible, Maxilla and Zigoma, 1969; Modern Anesthesia in Dentistry, 1977. Contbr. articles oral surgery, dental anesthesia to dental jours. Home: 50 Winter Hill Rd Tuckahoe NY 10707 Office: 475 White Plains Rd Eastchester NY 10707

REYMAN, MARIA LANDOLFI, educator; b. Utica, N.Y., Nov. 4, 1917; d. Thomas and Frances (Turchetti) Landolfi; B.A., Keuka Coll., 1940; M.A., Syracuse U., 1950; postgrad. Mohawk Valley

Community Coll., Utica Coll.; m. Vernon Reyman, June 23, 1951 (div. May 1972). With N.Y. State Tax and Finance Dept., 1940-43; tchr. Westmoreland (N.Y.) High Sch., 1943-44, Lyons Falls (N.Y.) High Sch., 1944-46, Proctor High Sch., Utica, 1946-47; tchr. English, Utica Free Acad., 1947—. Tchr. Italian, adult evening classes Hamilton Coll., 1966; co-dir. sch. for gifted, Londonderry, Vt., summers 1956-58. Del. White House Conf. Edn., 1955. Bd. dirs. United Way Agy., Utica. Recipient Bronze medal for studies in Italian, Columbia, 1935; Keuka Coll. awards music, 1940, Alumnae award for profl. achievement, 1971. Mem. NEA, AAUW, N.Y. State United, Utica (sec. 1972-73) tchrs. assns., Utica Free Acad. Tchrs. Assn. (pres. 1952, sec. 1970-72), UN Assn. U.S.A., Am. Security Council (mem. nat. adv. bd. 1972—), Dante Lit. Soc. of Harvard, Robert Browning Soc. Boston, Internat. Platform Assn., Syracuse U., Keuka alumnae clubs. Clubs: Order of Eastern Star (past matron), White Shrine of Jerusalem (past high priestess); New Century (pres. 1976—). Exhibitor, lectr. rare books, rare fabrics; pioneer teamteaching. Home: 4 Hughes Ln New Hartford NY 13413 Office: Utica Free Acad Kemble St Utica NY 13501

REYNDERS, CHARLTON, JR., investment banker; b. N.Y.C., Dec. 1, 1937; s. Charlton and Eliza Ellen (Lemon) R.; A.B., Princeton U., 1959; m. Knowlton Ames, Sept. 23, 1961; children—John V.W. III, Charlton III, Alys Ames. With Harris, Upham & Co., Inc., N.Y.C., 1963-76, v.p., 1968-73, 1st v.p., 1973-76, also dir., mem. exec. com., 1st v.p., dir. Smith, Barney, Harris Upham & Co., Inc., N.Y.C., 1976—; ofcl. Am. Stock Exchange, 1974-78. Served to lt. (j.g.) USNR, 1959-62. Mem. Wall St. Planning Group. Republican. Episcopalian. Clubs: Racquet and Tennis (N.Y.C.); Bedford Golf and Tennis. Home: McLain St Mount Kisco NY 10549 Office: 1345 Ave of Americas New York City NY 10019

REYNOLDS, BENEDICT MICHAEL, surgeon; b. N.Y.C., Sept. 12, 1925; s. Benedict and Delia (Coan) R.; student Columbia U., 1942-43, U. Rochester, 1943-44; M.D., N.Y. U., 1944-48; m. Alice Marie Hodnett, May 3, 1952; children—Benedict, John, Ann Marie, Mary Alice, Daniel. Intern, Bellevue Med. Center, N.Y.C., 1948-49, surg. resident, 1951-55; asst. in surgery N.Y. U., N.Y.C., 1953-55; instr. surgery Albert Einstein Coll. Medicine, Bklyn., 1955-56, asst. prof. surgery, 1956-58, clin. asst. prof., 1958-71, vis. prof. surgery, 1977; prof. surgery N.Y. Med. Coll., N.Y.C., 1971—; practice medicine specializing in surgery, Bronx, 1955—; dir. surgery Misericordia Hosp. Med. Center, Bronx, 1962—; dir. surgery Fordham Hosp., 1964-76; chmn. Dept. Surgery Lincoln Hosp., Bronx, 1976—; attending surgeon Flower and Fifth Ave. Hosps., N.Y.C., 1972—; attending surgeon Met. Hosp., N.Y.C., 1972—; cons. Community Gen. Hosp. of Sullivan County, 1972—. Served with USN, 1943-45, 49-51. Diplomate Am. Bd. Surgery, Pan Am. Med. Assn. Fellow N.Y. Acad. Medicine, ACS; mem. Am. Med. Assn., N.Y. State Med. Soc., N.Y. Acad. Sci., Soc. Surgery of the Alimentary Tract, N.Y. and Bklyn./Regional Chpt. on Trauma, Internat. Soc. Lymphology, N.Y. Surg. Soc., Am. Gastroenterological Assn. Roman Catholic. Contbr. articles in field to med. jours. Home: 150 Overhill Rd Bronxville NY 10708 Office: 600 E 233d St Bronx NY 10466

REYNOLDS, CHARLES VAUGHN, JR., educator; b. Boston, Mar. 27, 1929; s. Charles V. and Eileen E. (Kennally) R.; B.S., Holy Cross Coll., 1950; M.A., Boston Coll., 1967; Ph.D., Boston U., 1978; m. Jean M. Sullivan, Oct. 24, 1953; children—Marianne, Ellen, Elizabeth, Alicia, Jean, Charles Vaughn III. With Reynolds Bros. Inc., Canton, Mass., 1955-60; treas. Ponkapoag Realty Corp., Canton, 1960-78; prof. history Boston State Coll., 1967-78; dir. Canton Cooperative Bank, 1962-78. Town meeting mem., Wellesley, Mass., 1972-78. Served to lt. (j.g.), USNR, 1951-54. Mem. Am. Hist. Assn., Orgn. Am. Historians, Naval Records Soc. (London), Morgan Horse Club, Carriage Assn., Tenn. Walking Horse Breeders Assn. Democrat. Roman Catholic. Club: Wellesley Country. Author: Why Not Admit Red China to the United Nations?, 1970. Home: 61 Kenilworth Rd Wellesley MA 02181 Office: PO Box 266 Canton MA 02021

REYNOLDS, EDWIN WILFRED, JR., ednl. adminstr.; b. Englewood, N.J., Mar. 23, 1937; s. Edwin W. and Ellen H. (Heuber) R.; B.A. cum laude, Fairleigh Dickinson U., 1961, M.A. Teaching magna cum laude, 1966; postgrad. N.Y. U., 1964-65, Seton Hall U., 1970-71, Montclair State Coll., 1972-73, Pace Coll., 1954-55; m. Zitta Wiese, Aug. 19, 1961. Installation supr. Western Electric Co., N.Y.C., 1961-65; tchr. social studies Teaneck (N.J.) High Sch., 1965—, dept. chmn., 1968-71; supr. social studies Teaneck Secondary Schs., 1971—; coordinator M.A.T. program Fairleigh Dickinson U., 1969-71; mem. planning com. N.E. Regional Social Studies Conf. Elder Presbyterian Ch., U.S.A. Served with USN, 1955-57. Certified social studies tchr., supr., tchr. psychology, N.J. Mem. Nat., Middle States, Bergen County (N.J.) (pres.), N.J. (v.p.) councils for social studies, Social Studies Suprs. Assn. (dir.), Assn. Ednl. Suprs. (pres.), Assn. Supervision and Curriculum Devel., Am. Hist. Assn., United Teaching Profession, Phi Delta Kappa, Phi Omega Epsilon. Author curriculum devel and learning guides, 1973—; cons. in world history Scott Foresman Pub. Co. Home: 107 Ralph Ave Hillsdale NJ 07642 Office: care Teaneck High Sch 100 Elizabeth Ave Teaneck NJ 07666

REYNOLDS, JAMES, mgmt. cons.; b. Detroit, Mar. 22, 1941; s. Richard James and Esther (Nikander) R.; B.A. in Econs., N.Y. U., 1965, postgrad., 1965-66. Cons. to pres. Rothrock, Reynolds & Reynolds Inc., N.Y.C., 1966-70; v.p. Booz, Allen & Hamilton, health, med. div., N.Y.C., 1970—; dir. Booz, Allen & Hamilton, Inc., Health Center Mgmt. Inst.; faculty mem. to United Hosp. Fund of N.Y. Mem. Shared Services Com. of Regional Med. Program, N.Y.C.; bd. Salvation Army Children's Day Center, N.Y.C., 1967-70, Salvation Army Women's Lodge, N.Y.C., 1969-70. Recipient N.Y. U. Founders award, 1965. Mem. Am. Pub. Health Assn., Am. Mgmt. Assn., Assn. Am. Med. Colls., Am. Hosp. Assn., Hosp. Mgmt. Systems Soc., Hosp. Fin. Mgmt. Assn., Phi Beta Kappa. Episcopalian. Clubs: Mus. Modern Art, Met. Mus. Art, Met. Opera Guild (N.Y.C.). Developer regional health system for No. Ala., 1970; integrated mgmt. system for academic health centers, 1977. Home: 45 Sutton Pl S New York City NY 10022 Office: 245 Park Ave New York City NY 10017

REYNOLDS, MARTHA LOUISE, librarian; b. Indpls., Apr. 20, 1928; d. Richard Theodore and Gertrude (Ayers) R.; A.B., Hanover Coll., 1950; M.L.S., Ind. U., 1956. Br. asst. Indpls. Pub. Library, 1950-54; head adult services Vigo County Pub. Library, Terre Haute, Ind., 1955-63; asst. coordinator adult services Montgomery County (Md.) Pub. Libraries, Bethesda, 1963-65, asst. chief pub. services, 1965-67; dir. Frederick County (Md.) Pub. Libraries, Frederick, 1967—; trainer library adult edn. project bur. studies in adult edn. Ind. U. and Purdue U., Bloomington, 1956-63. Bd. dirs. Lung Assn. Mid-Md., 1976-77. Mem. AAUW, Frederick Hist. Soc., ALA (notable books council 1964-66, 74-77, chmn., 1965, bd. mem. staff orgns. round table 1962-63, guidelines and standards com. 1976-78), Ind. Library Assn. (chmn. in-service edn. com. 1957-59, mem. library certification com. 1959-61, editor Focus on Ind. Libraries 1961-63), Md. Pub. Library Adminstrs. (pres. 1970-72), Alpha Beta Alpha, Beta Phi Mu. Club: Frederick Woman's Civic. Home: 575 East St Frederick MD 21701 Office: 520 N Market St Frederick MD 21701

REYNOLDS, SISTER MARY CONSILII, educator; b. Providence, Aug. 14, 1922; d. Henry A. and Mary Ellen (Hopkins) R.; B.Ed., Catholic Tchrs. Coll., 1953; B.A., Salve Regina Coll., 1957; M.A., Boston Coll., 1964. Elementary tchr. Cathedral Sch., Fall River, Mass., 1943-55; high sch. tchr. Holy Family High Sch., New Bedford, Mass., 1956-64; prin. Mt. St. Mary High Sch., Fall River, 1964-67; asst. prof. history The Newport Coll.-Salve Regina, Newport, R.I., 1967—; tchr. homebound students and program unwed mothers Newport Sch. Dept., 1962—. Mem. Nat. Council for Social Studies, Am. Cath. Hist. Assn., Am. Hist. Assn., Berkeley Soc. Home: The Newport Coll-Salve Regina Ochre Point Ave Newport RI 02840

REYNOLDS, MARY TRACKETT, polit. scientist; b. Milw., Jan. 11, 1914; d. James P. and Mary (Nachtwey) Trackett; B.A., U. Wis., 1935; M.A., 1935; postgrad. (Rebecca Green fellow) Radcliffe Coll., 1935-36; Ph.D. (U. fellow, Barnard fellow), Columbia U., 1939; m. Lloyd G. Reynolds, June 12, 1937; children—Anne Reynolds Skinner, Priscilla Reynolds Roosevelt, Bruce. Research asst. Littauer Sch., Harvard U., 1938-39; instr. Queens Coll., 1939-40, Hunter Coll., 1941-42, lectr., 1945-47; asso. in polit. sci. Johns Hopkins U., 1942-43; lectr. Conn. Coll, 1947-48, asst. prof., 1948-50; asst. prof. U. Bridgeport, 1950-51; research asso. in econs. Yale U., 1961-67; vis. lectr. in English, Yale U., 1973—. Research asst. Pres.'s Com. Adminstrn. Mgmt., 1936; sr. economist Nat. Econ. Com., 1940; adminstrn. asst. Glenn L. Martin Aircraft Co., Balt., 1942-43; editorial asst. pub. adminstrn. com. Social Sci. Research Council, 1944-45; cons. Nat. Def. Adv. Commn., 1949, Nat. Municipal Assn., 1956, Orgn. Econ. Cooperation and Devel., Paris, 1964, U.S. State Dept.-AID 1965. Active Women's Civic League. Mem. Am. Polit. Sci. Assn., Dante Soc. Am. AAUP, Am. Soc. Pub. Adminstrn., League Women Voters, New Haven Hosp. Aux (bd. dirs.), Phi Beta Kappa. Clubs: Lawn (New Haven); Appalachian Mountain. Author: Interpartmental Committees in the National Administration, 1940; Joyce and Nora, 1964; Source Documents in Economic Development, 1966; Joyce's Debt to Dante, 1968; Two Essays on James Joyce, 1970; Joyce and Dante, 1974; Joyce and D'Annunzio, 1976. Contbr. articles to profl. jours. Home: 75 Old Hartford Turnpike Hamden CT 06517

REYNOLDS, NANCY BRADFORD DUPONT (MRS. WILLIAM GLASGOW REYNOLDS), artist; b. Greenville, Del., Dec. 28, 1919; d. Eugene Eleuthere and Catherine Dulcinea (Moxham) duPont; student Goldey-Beacom Coll., Wilmington, Del., 1938; m. William Glasgow Reynolds, May 18, 1940; children—Kathrine Glasgow Reynolds Sturgis, William Bradford, Mary Parminter (Mrs. John Schofield Savage), Cynthia duPont (Mrs. Kemit Farris). Exhibited in one-man show at Rehoboth (Del.) Art League, 1963, J.E. Caldwell Co., Wilmington, Del., 1968, Del. Art Mus., 1976; exhibited in group shows at Corcoran Gallery, Washington, 1943, Soc. Fine Arts, Wilmington, 1937, 38, 40, 41, 48, 50, 62, 65, NAD, N.Y.C., 1964 Pa. Mil. Coll., Chester, 1966, Met. Mus. Art, N.Y.C., 1977, Goldsbrough Gallery, Goldbranch, N.C., 1977; represented in permanent collections at Wilmington Trust Co., I.E. duPont de Nemours & Co., Children's Home, Inc., Claymont, Del. Goldbrough Bldg., Wilmington; bronze statue at Children's Bur. of Del., carving in lucite and copper Stevenson Center of Nat. Scis. Vanderbilt U., lucite carvings Brandywine Bldg., Wilmington, Del., carving for meditation room Luth. Towers, Wilmington, fountain Longwood Gardens, Kennett Sq., Pa.; mem. guild and research staff Henry Francis DuPont Winterthur Mus., 1955-63. Organizer vol. service Del. chpt. A.R.C., 1938-39; chmn. Com. For Revision Del. Child Adoption Law, 1950-52. Pres., bd. dirs. Children Bur. Del.; past pres., trustee Childrens Home, Inc. Recipient Confrerie des Chevaliers du Tastevin Clos de Vougeot-Bourgogne France, 1960, Hort. award Garden Club Am., 1964, Westover Alumni award Westover Sch., Middlebury, Conn., 1974, medal of merit Garden Club of Wilmington, 1976. Mem. Nat. League Am. Pen Women, Pa. Hort. Soc., Wilmington Art Mus., Brit. Embroidery Guild, English-Speaking Union, Burr Artists, Mayflower Descs., Del. Hist. Soc., Nat. Trust For Hist. Preservation, Colonial Dames. Episcopalian. Clubs: Catherine Lorillard Wolf Art, Burr Artists (N.Y.C.), Garden of Wilmington (past pres.), Garden of America (past asst. zone 4 chmn.), Vicmead Hunt, Greenville Country, Chevy Chase (Washington). Address: Foxwood Old Kennett Rd Greenville DE 19807

REYNOLDS, RICHARD LEE, mg. co. exec.; b. Pleasant Ridge, Mich., Mar. 13, 1933; s. Gordon A. and Anna M. (Schovan) R.; grad. Gen. Motors Inst., 1957; m. Barbara Elizabeth Hancock, Jan. 18, 1969; children—Charles, Steven, Lisa, Thomas. With Gen. Motor Corp. Detroit and Flint, Mich., 1954-68; engr. Ill. Tool Works, Elgin, 1968-72; with Litton Fastening Systems, Lakewood, Calif., 1972-76; v.p. products devel. and mktg. Amerace Co., Union, N.J., 1976-77; with Rexnord, Inc., Paramus, N.J., 1977—, v.p. sales and mktg., 1977—. Served with U.S. Army, 1953-54. Mem. Soc. Automotive Engrs., Soc. Mfg. Engrs., Am. Defense Preparedness Assn. Republican. Roman Catholic. Patentee in field. Home: 6 Stratford Ln Ho-Ho-Kus NJ 07423 Office: Rexnord Inc 22 Spring Valley Rd Paramus NJ 07652

REYNOLDS, ROBERT GREGORY, toxicologist; b. Chgo., July 29, 1952; s. Robert G. and Loys Delle (Kever) R.; B.S., Mass. Inst. Tech., 1973, postgrad. in genetic toxicology, 1973—, Sloan Sch. Mgmt., 1977-78. NSF research fellow Mass. Inst. Tech., 1973, founder, mng. editor Grad. mag., 1975-78; toxicological cons. Energy Resources Co., Inc., Cambridge, Mass., 1976-77; v.p. Internat. Contact Bur., Ft. Lauderdale, Fla., 1977—; staff toxicologist, asst. to v.p. for mktg. Enviro Control, Inc., Rockville, Md., 1978—. Mem. AAAS, Am. Acad. Clin. Toxicology. Episcopalian. Contbr. chpts. to text and lab. manual. Office: Enviro Control Inc One Central Plaza 11300 Rockville Pike Rockville MD 20852

REYNOLDS, RUSSELL SEAMAN, JR., exec. recruiting cons.; b. Greenwich, Conn., Dec. 14, 1931; s. Russell Seaman and Virginia Dare (Carter) R.; B.A., Yale, 1954; postgrad. N.Y. U., 1958-61; m. Deborah Ann Toll, July 21, 1956; children—Russell Seaman, III, Jeffrey Toll, Deborah Chase. Asst. v.p. nat. div. Morgan Guaranty Trust Co. of N.Y., 1957-66; partner William H. Clark Assos., Inc., 1966-69; pres. Russell Reynolds Assos., Inc., N.Y.C., 1969-71, chmn., 1971—. Chmn., Campaign for Yale for Greenwich Area, 1976—; bd. dirs. Bruce Mus. Assos., Inc., Greenwich Hist. Soc.; trustee Hurricane Island Outward Bound Sch.; adv. bd. Salvation Army Greater N.Y.; trustee The Hotchkiss Sch. Served as 1st lt., SAC, USAF, 1954-57. Mem. Assn. Exec. Recruiting Consultants. Clubs: Round Hill; Indian Harbor Yacht; Links; Recess; Yale; Amateur Ski (treas.); Econ., N.Y. Yacht (N.Y.C.); Mill Reef; Calif. Home: 39 Clapboard Ridge Rd Greenwich CT 06830 Office: 245 Park Ave New York City NY 10017

REYNOLDS, WILLIAM GLASGOW, lawyer; b. Dover, Tenn., July 15, 1911; s. John Lacey and Harriett Edwina (Glasgow) R.; A.B., Vanderbilt U., 1932, J.D., 1935; m. Nancy Bradford duPont, May 18, 1940; children—Katherine Glasgow Reynolds Sturges, William Bradford, Mary Parminter Reynolds Savage, Cynthia duPont Reynolds Farris. Admitted to Tenn. bar, 1935, D.C. bar, 1964, U.S. Supreme Ct., 1945; practiced in Nashville, 1935; with legal dept. E.I. duPont de Nemours & Co., Wilmington, 1935-40, trade marks counsel, 1946-53, chief counsel advt., pub. relations and research depts., 1954-71; trademark and patent counsel Morris, Nichols, Arsht & Tunnell, Wilmington, Del., 1971—; resident counsel Remington Arms Co., Bridgeport, 1940-41; atty. Office Gen. Counsel, Navy Dept., 1942-43, Exec. Office Sec. Navy, 1944-45; dir. Del. Trust Co., 1974—, mem. exec. and trust coms., 1976—; chem. industry del. Internat. Conf. Indsl. and Municipal Air Pollution, Washington, 1949, U.S. water resources policy com., 1950; permanent mem. Ann. Conf. Fed. Judges, 3d Jud. Circuit, 1955—; mem. U.S. Patent Commrs. adv. com., 1954; chmn. Nat. Assay Commn. for assay Denver, Phila. mints, 1958; mem. Com. Experts on Internat. Trademark Treaties, Geneva, 1969-71; legal counsel U.S. diplomatic mission to World Intellectual Property Congress, Hapsburg Palace, Vienna, Austria, 1973. Bd. dirs. United Fund No. Del., 1948-53, exec. com., 1949-51; trustee Children's Home, Inc., Claymont and Wilmington, Del., 1946-47, pres., 1947-51; trustee St. Mary's-in-the-Mountains Sch. for Girls, Littleton, N.H., 1959-63, mem. exec. com., 1961-63; mem. U. Del. Research Found.; dir., sec. Rencourt Found.; chmn. law sch. visitation council Vanderbilt U., 1968, chmn. univ. devel. council, 1969-70, mem. chancellor's adv. com., 1971—; Del. alt. del. Republican Nat. Conv., 1956; mem. Rep. Nat. Com. Assos., 1956-65. Recipient citations USN, 1943, 45; Founders medal Vanderbilt U. Law Sch., 1935. Mem. U.S. Trade-Mark Assn. (dir. 1960—, pres., chmn. bd. 1964-65, hon. chmn. 1965-66), Vanderbilt U. Alumni Assn. (dir. 1961-64), Am. Hort. Soc., Am., Pa. Bonsai socs., Fed., Am., Del., Nashville bar assns., Del., Tenn. trial lawyers assns., Assn. Internat. pour Protection de Propriété Industrielle, Navy League U.S., Am. Judicature Soc., Mfg. Chemists Assn. (lawyers adv. com. 1946-53, chmn. 1954), Wilmington Soc. Fine Arts (dir.), Order of Coif, Phi Kappa Psi. Episcopalian. Clubs: Aurora Gun, Vicmead Hunt, Greenville Country; (Wilmington, Del.); Chevy Chase (Md.) Country; Confrerie des Chevaliers du Tastevin (commandeur Wilmington 1967—, grand officer 1972, mem. grand Am. consuel 1973, grand intendant for Eastern U.S. 1975—, delegé-gen. 1976, grand pilier gen. U.S. 1977, N.Am. 1978); Del. Lincoln (dir. 1969-70). Author: The Law of Water and Water Rights in the Tennessee River Valley, 1934; Local Restrictions on the Pollution of Inland Waters, 1948; (with Stewart W. Richards) Trademark Management—A Guide for Businessmen, 1955; Operational Rules in Advertising, 1957; Contemporary Problems in Trademark Licensing, 1959; Legal Curbs on Advertising, 1959; Trademark Selection, 1960, The Chemical Engineer and Public Liability Law, 1962; A Brief for Corporate Counsel, 1964; Legal Servicing of Industrial Publicity, 1967; Planning a Bonsai Collection, 1968; Reynolds History Annotated, 1978. Home: Old Kennett Rd Greenville DE 19807 Office: 1702 American Internat Bldg Wilmington DE 19801

REZNICK, JEROME, health assn. exec.; b. Pitts., July 24, 1918; s. Myer and Pauline (Eisenstein) R.; B.S., U. Pitts., 1941; M.S. in Social Work, U. Pa., 1948; m. Adelaide Weinstein, Feb. 28, 1952. Casework, Assn. Jewish Children, Phila., 1948-52; field and casework supr. Crime Prevention Assn., Phila., 1952-56; asst. exec. dir. Phila. Youth Bd., 1956-58; exec. dir. Phila. Assn. Retarded Children, 1958-62; exec. dir. Rehab. Programs, Inc., Poughkeepsie, N.Y., 1962-78; asso. bus. mgr. Cancer Care Inc. of Nat. Cancer Found., Inc., N.Y.C., 1978—; instr., field placement supr. eve. dir. Russell Sage Coll., Poughkeepsie, 1968-78. Co-chmn. regional com. Gov.'s Vocational Rehab. Statewide Survey, Unit. Served with AUS, 1942-45; PTO. Fellow Royal Soc. for Health; mem. Inernat. Assn. Rehab. Facilities, Nat. Assn. Social Workers. Mem. Athelston Lodge (Phila.). Home: 6600 Blvd East The Versailles 8-H West New York NJ 07093 Office: 1 Park Ave 12th Floor Suite New York City NY 10016

REZNIK, NEIL DAVID, educator; b. Ellenville, N.Y., Oct. 6, 1931; s. Max and Ida (Levy) R.; B.S. magna cum laude, N.Y. U., 1956; M.A., U. Pa., 1958, postgrad. 1958-62; C.L.U., Am. Coll. Life Underwriters, 1960; m. Pearl Diana Wexler, Nov. 26, 1953; children—Mindy Suzan, Deborah Ruth. Instr., Wharton Sch. U. Pa., Phila., 1956-61; lectr. City U. N.Y., 1962-64; asso. prof. State U. N.Y., Agrl. and Tech. Coll., Canton, 1964-66; asso. prof. econs. Community Coll. Phila., 1966—, chmn. dept. econs. and accounting, 1968-71, 76—; cons. bus., indsl., ins. firms; bd. graders Am. C.L.U., 1958—, Am. Inst. for Property and Liability Underwriters, 1975—. Served with AUS, 1948-52. C.L.U., C.P.C.U. Fellow S.S. Huebner Found. for Ins. Edn., 1961, Am. Risk and Ins. Assn., 1957, 58, 65. Mem. Am. Risk and Ins. Assn., Am. Econ. Assn., AAUP, Am. Soc. C.L.U.'s, Soc. C.P.C.U.'s. Club: Edgmont (Pa.) Country. Home: 532 Portland Dr Broomall PA 19008 Office: 34 S 11th St Philadelphia PA 19107

REZNIKOFF, LEON, psychiatrist; b. Feodosia, Russia, July 19, 1900; s. Naftoli and Vera (Fronshtein) R.; came to U.S., 1923, naturalized, 1929; M.D., U. Berne (Switzerland), 1931; m. Belle Schulman, June 5, 1936; 1 dau., Vera. Intern, Newark Meml. Hosp., 1931-32; resident psychiatrist Hudson County Mental Hosp., 1932-37, clin. dir., 1937-60, chief psychiatrist, dir. psychiat. edn., 1960-65; pvt. practice cons. in psychiatry, Clifton, N.J., 1957—; cons. psychiatrist N. Hudson Hosp., Weehawken, N.J. Bd. dirs. Clifton Mental Health Center, 1960-66. Served to maj. M.C., U.S. Army, 1944-46. Diplomate Am. Bd. Psychiatry and Neurology. Fellow Am. Psychiat. Assn. (life), Assn. Advancement of Psychotherapy, Acad. Psychosomatic Medicine; mem. N. Jersey Psychiat. Soc. (past pres.). Contbr. articles to psychiat. jours. Home and Office: 42 Robinston Terr Clifton NJ 07013

RHEE, PETER CHANG-HEE, metallurgist; b. Kimchun, Korea, May 8, 1935; s. Chong-Yeon and Hi-Yeon (Park) R.; came to Can., 1969, naturalized, 1974; B.Sc. in Engring., Seoul (Korea) Nat. U., 1957; Dipl.-Eng., Technische Hochschule, Aachen, Germany, 1964, Dr.-Eng., 1967; m. Catherine Myong-Ye Lee, June 1, 1963; 1 dau., Jacqueline. Research mem. Sci. Research Inst., Ministry of Nat. Def., Seoul, 1957-61; postdoctoral research in metallurgy Technische Hochschule, Aachen, Germany, 1967-69; research asso., staff specialist Steel Co. of Can., Ltd., Hamilton, Ont., 1969—. Served with Republic of Korea Army, 1957-60. Recipient scholarship award Deutscher Akademischer Austausch Dienst, 1961. Mem. Assn. Profl. Engrs. of Ont., Can. Inst. Mining and Metallurgy, Verein Deutscher EisenHüttenleute, Am. Inst. Metal. Engring., Korean Scientists and Engrs. Assn. Home: 796 Forest Glen Ave Burlington ON Canada Office: 100 King St W Hamilton ON Canada

RHEINGOLD, IRA H., pharmacist; b. Albany, N.Y., Feb. 12, 1937; s. Jacob J. and Jeannette (Salit) R.; B.S. in Pharmacy, Albany Coll. Pharmacy, Union U., 1960; M.Ed., U. Mass., 1975, postgrad., 1975—; m. Judith Geller, Nov. 11, 1962; children—Heidi Lara, Chad Howard. Pharmacist, Rheingold's Pharmacy, Albany, 1960-66, owner, pharmacist, 1966-72; sr. pharmacist Oswald D. Heck Devel. Center, Schenectady, 1972—; cons. clin. pharmacy Mass. Dept. Mental Health, 1975; adv. bd. Homemakers Upjohn, 1977—; health adv. council Schenectady County Coordinated Community Child Care Program (Head Start), 1978—; tech. adv. com. Office Health Services, N.Y. State Office Mental Retardation, 1978—. Served with N.Y. Army N.G., 1961-64. Mem. Am. Pub. Health Assn., Fedn. Internat. Pharmaceutique, Albany County Pharm. Soc. Home: 15 W Bayberry Rd Glenmont NY 12077 Office: O D Heck Devel Center Balltown and Consaul Rds Schenectady NY 12304

RHIEW, FRANCIS CHANGNAM, radiologist; b. Korea, Dec. 3, 1938; s. Byung Kyun and In Sil (Lee) R.; came to U.S., 1967, naturalized, 1977; B.S., Seoul Nat. U., 1960, M.D., 1964; m. Kay

Kyungja Chang, June 11, 1967; children—Richard C., Elizabeth. Intern, St. Mary's Hosp., Waterbury, Conn., 1967-68; resident in radiology and nuclear medicine L.I.U.-Queens Hosp. Center, N.Y., 1968-71; instr. radiology W. Va. U. Sch. Medicine, Morgantown, 1971-73; mem. staff Mercy Hosp. and Moses Taylor Hosp., Scranton, Pa., 1973—, also dir. nuclear medicine. Served with M.C., Korean Army, 1964-67. Recipient Minister of Health and Welfare award, 1963; certified Am. Bd. Nuclear Medicine. Mem. Soc. Nuclear Medicine, N.Am. Radiol. Soc., Am. Coll. Radiology, Am. Inst. Ultra Sound, AMA. Clubs: Glen Oak Country, Pres.'s U. Scranton, Elks. Home: 101 Belmont Ave Clarks Summit PA 18411 Office: 746 Jefferson Ave Scranton PA 18501

RHOADES, JOHN H., ret. investment banker; b. N.Y.C., Aug. 11, 1911; s. Lyman and Carol Beardsley (Nye) R.; grad. Hotchkiss Sch., 1929; student U. Ariz., 1929-30; A.B., Williams Coll., 1930-34; m. Patricia Wilson, June 28, 1941; (dec. Mar. 1968); children—Lyman, John, Barbara; m. 2d, Alice M. Bird, Aug. 21, 1969; 1 son, James C. With Guaranty Trust Co. of N.Y., 1934-41, Chgo. corr., 1940-41; with Goldman, Sachs & Co., 1946-76, partner, 1963-68, ltd. partner, cons., 1969-76; vol. exec. projects in Colombia, Thailand, Philippines, Internat. Exec. Service Corps, 1974—. Hon. trustee Amsterdam House, N.Y.C., Cancer Research Inst. Commd. ensign USNR, 1941; with fin. div. Bur. Ordnance, 1941-43, indsl. readjustment br., 1944-45; econ. div. Office Mil. Govt. U.S. Zone, 1945; on inactive duty as lt. comdr., 1945—. Mem. Delta Psi. Episcopalian. Clubs: Bedens Brook (Princeton); Lake Placid. Home: 186 Russell Rd Princeton NJ 08540

RHOADS, JAMES BERTON, archivist; b. Sioux City, Iowa, Sept. 17, 1928; s. James Harrison and Mary (Keenan) R.; student Southwestern Jr. Coll., Tex., 1946-47, Union Coll., Lincoln, Nebr., 1947-48; B.A., U. Calif., Berkeley, 1950, M.A., 1952; Ph.D., Am. U., 1965; m. S. Angela Handy, Aug. 12, 1947; children—Cynthia Patrice Rhoads Neven, James Berton, Marcia Marie. With Nat. Archives and Records Service, GSA, Washington, 1952—, asst. archivist for civil archives, 1965, dep. archivist of U.S., 1966-68, archivist of U.S., 1968—; chmn. Nat. Archives Trust Fund Bd.; chmn. adminstrv. com. Fed. Register; chmn. Nat. Hist. Publs. and Records Commn.; mem. Fed. Council on Arts and Humanities. Trustee, Woodrow Wilson Internat. Center for Scholars. Recipient Meritorious award GSA, 1966, Distinguished Service award, 1968, 79. Fellow Soc. Am. Archivists (pres. 1974-75); mem. Am. Hist. Assn., Internat. Council Archives (pres. 1976), Am. Antiquarian Soc., Orgn. Am. Historians, Mass. Hist. Soc. (corr.), Phi Alpha Theta, Phi Kappa Phi. Club: Cosmos. Office: Nat Archives Bldg Washington DC 20408

RHOADS, JOSEPH, lawyer; b. Wilmington, Del., July 7, 1910; s. Joseph Edgar and Edith (Chambers) R.; B.A., Haverford Coll., 1932; LL.B., U. Pa., 1936; m. Elia Brill, Apr. 4, 1953; 1 son, Joseph. Admitted to Pa. bar, 1936, Del. bar, 1941; asso. MacCoy, Brittain, Evans & Lewis, Phila., 1936-40; with Wilmington Trust Co., 1940-75, asst. sec., asst. trust officer, asst. v.p., 1940-53, v.p., 1953-75; v.p., dir. Jeflion Investment Co., Wilmington, 1974-78; dir. Dolphin Del. Corp., Dolphin Tanker Corp., Dover Tanker Corp. Bd. dirs. Family Service, Inc. of No. Del., 1943-69; bd. mgrs. Wilmington Friends Sch., 1942-51. Mem. Am., Del. (sec. 1948-50) bar assns., S.A.R., Phi Beta Kappa. Club: Wilmington Country. Home: 2401 Pennsylvania Ave Wilmington DE 19806

RHOADS, LORNA CRARY, trade assn. exec.; b. San Francisco, June 29, 1945; d. Ralph Ward and Marjory Helen (Learned) Crary; student Pa. State U., 1963-66; B.S., U. Md., 1978. Editorial asst. Nat. Assn. Wholesalers, Washington, 1967-70; editor Nat. Assn. Securities Dealers, Washington, 1971-74; prodn. mgr. Nat. Consumer Fin. Assn., Washington, 1975-76; editorial and prodn. mgr. Cosmetic, Toiletry and Fragrance Assn., Washington, 1976-77, dir. pub. info., 1977—. Mem. Am. Soc. Assn. Execs., Pub. Relations Soc. Am., Am. Women in Radio and TV, Am. Newspaper Women's Club, Alpha Delta Pi. Office: 1133 15th St NW Washington DC 20005

RHODE, ALFRED SHIMON, bus. cons.; b. Vienna, Austria, July 31, 1928; s. Aron and Olga (Schwarz) Rothkirch; came to U.S., 1940, naturalized, 1949; B.C.E., City U. N.Y., 1950; M.E.A., George Washington U., 1959; Ph.D., Am. U., 1973; m. Phyllis Mazur, Dec. 28, 1959; children—Yael, Tamar, Yvette, Liane. Engr., Bur. of Reclamation, Sacramento, 1950-52; various engring. positions U.S. Govt., 1954-63; head logistics research Navy Supply Systems Command, Washington, 1963-68; head support forces, manpower and logistics br. Navy Program Planning Office, Washington, 1968-75; v.p. Info. Spectrum, Inc., Arlington, Va., 1976—; professorial lectr. George Washington U., 1969-75. Served to capt. USAF, 1952-54. Congl. fellow, 1962. Registered profl. engr., Md., D.C. Mem. ASCE, Mil. Ops. Research Soc. (1st v.p., dir.), Operations Research Soc. Am., Washington Operations Research Council. Contbr. articles to profl. jours. Home: 8305 Fox Run Potomac MD 20854 Office: 1745 S Jefferson Davis Hwy Suite 401 Arlington VA 22202

RHODEN, RICHARD ALLAN, pharmacologist; b. Coatesville, Pa., May 8, 1930; s. Irving and Dorothy R.; A.B. cum laude, Lincoln U., 1951; M.S., Drexel U., 1967, Ph.D. (USPHS fellow), 1971; m. Kathryn Vernice Coursey, Sept. 20, 1969; 1 son, Richard Allan. Analytical chemist U.S. Dept. Def., Phila., 1951-56, organic chemist, 1956-62, research chemist, Warminster, Pa., 1962-72; environ. scientist EPA, Washington, 1972-75; pharmacologist Nat. Inst. Occupational Safety and Health, Rockville, Md., 1975—; lectr. biol. scis. Phila. Coll. Art, 1971, Fed. City Coll., Washington, 1973-74. Fellow Am. Inst. Chemists, AAAS; mem. Am. Chem. Soc., Am. Indsl. Hygiene Assn., Soc. Occupational and Environ. Health, Am. Conf. Govt. Indsl. Hygienists, N.Y. Acad. Scis. Contbr. papers to sci. jours. and meetings. Home: 12 Vallingby Circle Rockville MD 20850 Office: 5600 Fishers Ln Rockville MD 20857

RHODES, BODE OROBIYI, accountant; b. Lagos, Nigeria, West Africa, June 25, 1925; s. Kwao O. and Mary K. (D'Almeida) R.; B.A. in Accounting, Howard U., 1953; M.B.A., N.Y.U., 1954; m. Antoinette Green, Mar. 31, 1962; children—Laura Ayodele, Bode O. Accountant, Mobil Oil Co., N.Y.C., and Lagos, 1955-57; asst. chief accountant Esso West Africa Inc., Lagos, 1958-60; chief accountant Mesurado Corp., Monrovia, Liberia, 1960-62; accountant UN Secretariat, N.Y.C., 1962—, chief accountant, 1974—; lectr. Nigerian Centre Higher Studies, 1958-60. Mem. Am. Accounting Assn., Am. Inst. C.P.A.'s, Nat. Assn. Accountants, Am. Acad. Polit. and Social Sci. Methodist. Home: 86-88 Pinto St Holliswood NY 11423 Office: UN Secretariat New York City NY 10017

RHODES, FRANK HAROLD TREVOR, geologist, univ. pres.; b. Warwickshire, Eng., Oct. 29, 1926; s. Harold Cecil and Gladys (Ford) R.; B.Sc., U. Birmingham, 1948, Ph.D., 1950, D.Sc., 1963; m. Rosa Carlson, Aug. 16, 1952; children—Jennifer, Catherine, Penelope, Deborah. Came to U.S., 1968. Post-doctoral fellow, Fulbright scholar, vis. lectr. geology U. Ill., summers 1951-52; lectr. geology U. Durham, 1951-54, asst. prof., 1954-55, asso. prof., 1955-56; dir. U. Ill. Field Sta., Wyo., 1956, prof. geology, head geology dept., 1956-68, dean faculty of sci., 1967-68; prof. geology and mineralogy Coll. Lit., Sci. and Arts, U. Mich., 1968-77, dean, 1971-74, v.p. for acad. affairs, 1974-77; pres. Cornell U., Ithaca, N.Y., 1977—. Gurley lectr. Cornell U., 1960; Brownnocker lectr. Ohio State U., 1966. Trustee Carnegie Found. for Advancement of Teaching, 1978—; bd. dirs. NSF, Am. Geol. Inst.; mem. Australian vice-chancellors' visitor to Australian univs., 1964. Recipient Bigsby medal, 1967; NSF sr. vis. research fellow, 1965-66. Mem. Geol. Soc. London (council 1963-66), Palaeontol. Assn. (v.p. 1963-68), Brit. Assn. Advancement Sci., Geol. Soc. Am., Am. Assn. Petroleum Geologists, Soc. Econ. Paleontologists and Mineralogists, Phi Beta Kappa (hon.). Author: The Evolution of Life, 1962; Fossils, 1963; Geology, 1972; The Paleobiology of Conodonts, 1973; Evolution, 1974. Contbr. articles to sci. jours. Office: Office of Pres Cornell U Ithaca NY 14850

RHODES, GILBERT ALFRED, JR., mech. engr.; b. Alexandria, La., June 3, 1922; s. Gilbert Alfred and Alleen Elizabeth (Parker) R.; student in aero. engring. U. Ala., 1943, indsl. mgmt., 1947; m. Anna Ruth Roorda, June 16, 1953; children—Ann Elizabeth Rhodes Conley, Barbara Joan, Thomas Marion, Robert John. Mech. engr. Goslin-Birmingham Mfg. Co., 1947-49, Birmingham Ornamental Iron Co., 1949-50, Va. Steel Co., 1950; gen. engr. U.S. Army Mobility Equipment Research and Devel. Command, Ft. Belvoir, Va., 1969—. Cubmaster, Boy Scouts Am., 1968-74, scoutmaster, 1973—; chmn. adminstrv. bd. Bells United Methodist Ch., 1965-67, chmn. council ministries, 1968-71, lay del. to Balt. ann. conf., 1975—. Served with USAAF, 1943-46, USAF, 1951-68. Recipient Dist. award merit Boy Scouts Am., 1977. Mem. Air Force Assn., Am. Def. Preparedness Assn., Am. Inst. Aeros. and Astronautics, Sci. Research Soc. Am., Ret. Officers Assn., Res. Officers Assn., Appalachian Trail Conf., Smithsonian Resident Assos. Republican. Methodist. Club: Masons. Home: 7801 Pinewood Dr Clinton MD 20735 Office: US Army Mobility Equipment Research and Devel Command Fort Belvoir VA 22060

RHODES, WILLIAM OLIVER, educator; b. Marblehead, Mass., Sept. 7, 1914; s. Harry Story and Gladys Marion (Oliver) R.; certified dental technician Boston Sch. Mech. Dentistry, 1954; m. Theresia Schilcher, Feb. 28, 1948; children—Harry Gregory, Karin Theresia. Dental technician Smith Porcelain Dental Lab., Boston, 1953-60, Boston div. Park-Davis Co., Cambridge, Mass., 1960-63; owner, operator Rhodes Dental Lab., Marblehead, 1963-65; instr. dental technicians Sch. Dental Medicine, Tufts U., 1965—. Served with U.S. Army, 1942-46. Decorated Bronze Stars (3); certified dental technician. Mem. Nat. Bd. for Certification in Mass. Home: 25 Humphrey Marblehead MA 01945 Office: 1 Kneeland St Boston MA 02111

RHUDE, BETH ESTHER, psychologist, clergyman; b. Quincy, Mass., July 1, 1935; d. Clarel P. and Mary E. (MacKenzie) Rhude; student Oberlin Coll., 1954-55; B.A. magna cum laude, Boston U., 1957; B.D., Harvard U., 1960; Ed.D. (Pres.'s scholar), Columbia U., 1967; postgrad. Union Theol. Sem., 1960, Mich. State U., 1968; postdoctoral psychoanalytic tng. N.Y. U., 1974; m. Richard Morse Colgate, Aug. 3, 1974; 1 dau., Cara Marie-Jean Colgate. Ordained to ministry United Ch. of Christ, 1964; asst. chaplain Mt. Holyoke Coll., South Hadley, Mass., 1960-63; grad. fellow Danforth Found., St. Louis, 1963-64; chaplain, asst. prof. U. Seven Seas, Orange, Calif., 1964-65; campus minister Riverside Ch., N.Y.C., 1965-66; lectr. psychology, counselor Queensboro Community Coll., N.Y.C., 1966-67; dean of women, lectr. religion Dickinson Coll., Carlisle, Pa., 1967-68; psychotherapist in pvt. practice, N.Y.C., 1968—; lectr. N.Y. Theol. Sem., 1971-72, 77—; asst. dir. Ecumenical Found. Higher Edn. and Religion, N.Y.C., 1968-71; supr. doctoral program N.Y. U.; asst. prof. Sch. Theology, supr. doctoral candidates Boston U., 1977—; Payne Whitney Family Therapy Clinic of N.Y. Med. Sch., 1973-76. Bd. dirs. bd. homeland ministries United Ch. Christ, 1978—. Billings scholar, 1954-57; Ford Travel grantee, 1962; NDEA grantee, 1965, 67, 68; Danforth grantee, 1963; others. Mem. Nat. Assn. Coll. and Univ. Chaplains, Am. Psychol. Assn., NAACP, AAUP, AAUW, Am. Assn. Personnel and Guidance Counselors, Am. Assn. Marriage and Family Counselors (treas. N.Y. chpt. 1973-75), Am. Acad. Psychotherapists, Ortho Psychiatry Assn., Eastern Group Psychotherapy Assn., Am. Humanist Psychology Assn., Am. Assn. for Higher Edn., Common Cause, Phi Beta Kappa. Contbr. articles and revs. to various publs. Home: PO Box 76 South Stratford VT 05070 Office: care Danielson Center 745 Commonwealth Ave Boston U Boston MA 02215

RHUDE, HENRY BURTON, lawyer; b. Halifax, N.S., Can., Nov. 11, 1923; s. Samuel Burton and Laura Gertrude (Latter) R.; LL.B., Dalhousie U., 1950; m. Elsie Foster, Dec. 21, 1946; children—David Burton, John Peter, Michael Henry. Admitted to N.S. bar, 1951; apptd. Queen's counsel, 1966; asso. mem. firm Stewart, MacKeen & Covert, Halifax, 1951-57, partner, 1957—; dir. Halifax, Halifax Devels. Ltd., Nat. Sea Products Ltd., Halifax Sobeys Stores Ltd., Stellarton Empire Co. Ltd., Stellarton Atlantic Shopping Centres Ltd., Stellarton United Fin. Mgmt. Ltd., Northumberland Gen. Ins. Co., Toronto, Ivanhoe Ins. Mgmt. Ltd., Toronto, Reins. & Excess Mgrs. Ltd., Vancouver, Commonwealth Ins. Co., Vancouver; chmn., chief exec. officer, dir. Central & Eastern Trust Co., Halifax, 1978—; chmn., dir. Nat. Sea Products Ltd., Halifax, 1978—; pres., dir. Sobey Leased Properties Ltd., Stellarton, 1967—. Served with RCAF, 1941-45. Decorated D.F.C. Mem. Can. Bar Assn., N.S. Barristers Soc., Can. Tax Found. Liberal party. Mem. United Ch. Canada. Club: Halifax. Home: 28 Rockwood St Halifax NS Canada Office: 1583 Hollis St Halifax NS Canada

RHULAND, FRED ANGUS, former shipbldg. co. exec.; b. Lunenburg, N.S., Can., Nov. 11, 1910; s. George Alfred and Florence Sophia (Zinck) R.; B.Commerce, Dalhousie U., Can., 1934; B.S., Mt. Allison U., Can., 1932; m. Margaret Keyes, Oct. 12, 1937 (dec. Sept. 1964); children—George Frederick, Margaret Melissa (Mrs. Douglas Snyder); m. 2d, Gabrielle P.W. Dowding, Jan. 8, 1972. Statistician, Atlantic & Pacific Tea Co. Ltd., Toronto, Ont., Can., 1934-42; head of statistics Foods Adminstrn.-Wartime Prices and Trade Bd., Ottawa, Ont., 1942-44; pres., mgr., dir. Smith & Rhuland Ltd., Lunenburg, 1944-78, also Rhuland Marina Ltd.; dir. Lunenburg Marine Ry. Co. Ltd. Pres. Bd. Trade, Lunenburg, 1958-60; mem. planning com. Hosp. Plan, Province of N.S., 1958-77; dep. mayor, councillor Town of Lunenburg, 1952-60; bd. dirs. Fisherman's Meml. Hosp., 1950—, chmn., 1954-68, mem. fin. com., 1954—; bd. dirs. Citizens Home, Harbourview Haven, 1969—. Clubs: Masons (32 deg.); Yacht (commodore 1958-60), Curling (Lunenburg). Home and Office: Martin's Brook NS Canada

RHYDWEN, DAVID A., librarian; b. Scarborough, Ont., Can., June 14, 1918; s. Caradog and Jessie (Tiffin) R.; student Scarboro Collegiate Inst., 1932-37; certificate Shaw Bus. Sch., 1938. Chief librarian The Globe and Mail, Toronto, Ont., Can., 1944—. Chmn. Com. of Adjustment, Town of Markham (Ont.), 1956—. Recipient Burness award for outstanding contribution to newspaper librarianship, 1966. Mem. Am. Soc. for Info. Specialists, Spl. Libraries Assn., Canadian Library Assn. Home: 260 Wellington St W Markham ON L3P 1B9 Canada Office: 444 Front St W Toronto ON M5V 2S9 Canada

RIBAS, JORGE LUIS, educator, veterinarian; b. Guayaquil, Ecuador, Jan. 19, 1942; s. Ramon Francisco and Marta Leonor (Vera) R.; came to U.S., 1963, naturalized, 1973; A.A., SW Baptist Coll., 1966; B.S., SW Mo. State U., 1968; D.V.M., U. Mo., 1971; m. Sharon Lee Fristoe, July 8, 1967; children—John Michael, Tamara Michele. Postdoctoral fellow U. Rochester, 1971-72; research veterinarian dept. neurophysiology Walter Reed Army Inst. Research, Washington, 1972-75; research veterinarian dept. neurochemistry Armed Forces Radiobiol. Research Inst., Bethesda, Md., 1975-77; guest worker dept. neuropathology Armed Forces Inst. Pathology, Washington, 1972-75; guest worker lab. clin. pharmacology NIMH, Bethesda, 1975-76; asso. prof. anatomy Sch. Medicine, Uniformed Services U. Health Scis., Bethesda, 1976—. Served with AUS, 1972-77. Mem. Soc. Neurosci., Tissue Culture Assn., Electron Microscopy Soc., AAAS, AVMA, World Assn. Vet. Anatomists, Am. Assn. Vet. Anatomists (historian 1974—), Am. Assn. Neuropathology, Am. Physiol. Soc., Am. Assn. Anatomists. Contbr. articles to profl. jours. Home: Silver Spring MD Office: Dept Anatomy Sch Medicine Uniformed Services U Health Scis Bethesda MD 20014

RIBICOFF, ABRAHAM A., U.S. senator; b. New Britain, Conn., Apr. 9, 1910; s. Samuel and Rose (Sable) R.; LL.B. cum laude, U. Chgo., 1933; hon. degrees Trinity, Hillyer, Hebrew Union, Amherst, Am. Internat., Dropsie, Coe, Boston, Bard, Bryant colls., Wesleyan, Yeshiva, Fairfield, DePaul, N.Y. univs., U. Cal., Albany Med. Coll., Rockhurst Coll., Jewish Theol. Sem., Hartt Coll., Union Coll., U. Bridgeport, Kenyon Coll.; m. Ruth Siegel, June 28, 1931 (dec.); children—Peter, Jane; m. 2d, Lois Mathes, Aug. 4, 1972. Admitted to Conn. bar, 1933; judge Hartford Municipal Ct., 1941-43, 45-47, chmn. Conn. Assembly Municipal Ct. 45-47, chmn. Conn. Assembly Municipal Ct. Judges, 1941-42; mem. 81st, 82d Congresses, 1st Conn. Dist., mem. com. fgn. affairs; governor Conn., 1955-61; secretary of health, education and welfare, 1961-62; U.S. senator from Conn., 1963—, chmn. governmental affairs com. Mem. Conn. Legislature, 1938-42; mem. exec. com. Nat. Govs. Conf. Democrat. Author: (with Jon O. Newman) Politics: The American Way, 1967; America Can Make It, The American Medical Machine, 1972. Home: Hartford CT 06105 Office: Russell Senate Office Bldg Washington DC 20510

RIBICOFF, IRVING S., lawyer; b. New Britain, Conn., Apr. 16, 1915; s. Samuel and Rose (Sable) R.; B.A. summa cum laude, Williams Coll., 1936; LL.B., Yale U., 1939; m. Belle Krasne, June 27, 1955; children—Dara K., Sarai K. Admitted to Conn. bar, 1939, since practiced in Hartford; instr. in pub. speaking Williams Coll., 1934-36; atty. reorgn. div. SEC, 1939-41; chief price atty. for Conn., OPA, 1942-44; partner firm Ribicoff & Kotkin, and predecessors, 1941-78, firm Schatz & Schatz, Ribicoff & Kotkin, 1978—. Mem. Hartford County Grievance Com., 1957-61, chmn., 1960-61; bd. dirs. Law Sch. Fund of Yale U., Hartford Festival Music, Hartford Jewish Fedn.; trustee Greater Hartford YMCA; bus. adv. com. N.E. Colls. Fund. Mem. Am., Fed. (Conn. pres. 1964-75), Conn. (chmn. fed. bar-bench relations com. 1967-69, chmn. specialization com. 1969-74), Hartford County bar assns., N.E. Law Inst. (adv. council), Symphony Soc. Greater Hartford (dir.), Yale Law Sch. Grad. Bd., Yale Law Sch. Assn. (exec. com.), Order of Coif, Phi Beta Kappa. Home: 56 Scarborough St Hartford CT 06105 Office: One Financial Plaza Hartford CT 06103

RICARDS, JOHN DAY, internat. trade and shipping co. exec.; b. St. Louis, Feb. 2, 1915; s. John Boggs and Ora (Day) R.; student pub. schs. South Pasadena, Calif.; m. Margaret Smyth, Dec. 22, 1946. Asst. mgr. Grace Line/Gen. S.S. Corp., Los Angeles, 1935-38; mgr. Dodwell & Co., Los Angeles, 1938-43, Manila, Philippines, 1946-49; v.p. Wm H. Muller & Co., N.Y.C., 1950-55, exec. v.p., dir., 1955-68, pres., 1968-72; pres., dir., Caemi Internat., Inc., N.Y.C., 1972—. Pres., Republican Club, North Stamford, Conn., 1960-66. Served to lt. Seabees, USNR, 1943-46. Mem. Am. Inst. Mining and Metall. Engrs., Brazilian Am. C. of C. (dir. 1976). Episcopalian. Clubs: Duquesne (Pitts.); Pinnacle (N.Y.C.). Home: 18 Sherry Ln Darien CT 06820 Office: 122 E 42d St New York City NY 10017

RICCARDI, NICHOLAS BRUCE, microbiologist; b. N.Y.C., May 6, 1949; s. Anthony Louis and Elsie Theresa (Torino) R.; B.S., St. John's U., 1969, M.S., 1971; Ph.D., Fordham U., 1977. Lectr. microbiology Queensborough Community Coll., Bayside, N.Y., 1971-77, N.Y. Inst. Tech., N.Y.C., 1972-73; epidemiologist, researcher, bur. venereal disease control N.Y. City Dept. Health, 1977—. Mem. Am. Soc. Microbiology, Am. Venereal Disease Assn. (membership com. 1977, publs. com. 1978), Sigma Xi, Pi Delta Epsilon. Home: 86 27 103d Ave Ozone Park NY 11417

RICCI, ROBERT CHARLES, elec. engr., govt. adminstr.; b. Boston, June 13, 1936; s. Steven Anthony and Marie G. (Croatti) R.; B.E.E. (Inst. scholar), Mass. Inst. Tech., 1959, M.E.E., 1959, M.S. in Mgmt. (Alfred P. Sloan fellow), 1976; m. Elizabeth M. Grieder, June 13, 1964; children—Linda, Anne, Diana. Mem. tech. staff David Sarnoff Research Center, RCA, Princeton, N.J., 1959-64, Astro-Electronics div., Hightstown, N.J., 1964-66; chief br. flight computer NASA Electronics Research Center, Cambridge, Mass., 1966-70; engring. mgr. transp. systems center U.S. Dept. Transp., Cambridge, 1970—. Registered profl. engr., Mass. Mem. IEEE. Roman Catholic. Contbr. articles to profl. jours. Home: 54 Meadowbrook Rd Bedford MA 01730 Office: US Dept Transp Transp Systems Center Kendall Square Cambridge MA 02142

RICCIARDI, ANTONIO, dentist; b. Jersey City, June 5, 1922; s. Frank and Eugenia (Izzo) R.; student Upsala Coll., 1941-42, B.A. in Chemistry, 1951; D.D.S., Temple U., 1958; m. Lucy DePalma, June 18, 1945; children—Eugenia, Lynda. Purchasing agt. Dade Bros., Newark, Airport, 1951-52; asst. work mgr. Cooper Alloy Steel Co., Hillside, N.J., 1954; chemist White's Pharm. Co., Union, N.J., 1954; practice gen. dentistry, Westfield, N.J., 1958—; dentist Westfield Pub. Schs., 1958-60; mem. staff Mountainside Hosp., Montclair, N.J., St. Elizabeth's Hosp., Elizabeth, N.J.; implant staff John F. Kennedy Hosp., Edison, N.J.; clin. chmn. implant study Columbia U. Sch. Oral Surgery and Dentistry; implant cons. Columbia Presbyn. Sch. Oral Surgery and Dentistry, N.Y.C.; cons. Implants Internat., N.Y.C., 1971—. Pres. Nat. Gymnastics Clinic, Sarasota, Fla., 1968—; v.p. rebound tumbling center Welmarick Inc., Plainfield, 1958—. Gymnastics ofcl. Eastern Coll. Conf., 1954—. Served to lt. col. USMCR, 1942-48, 52-54; Korea. Fellow Acad. Gen. Dentistry, Royal Soc. Health (Eng.), Internat. Coll. Oral Implantology (founding mem.), Am. Acad. Gen. Dentistry; mem. Am. Acad. Implant Dentistry (program chmn. nat. conv. 1974, sec. 1976, pres. sect. 1978), Inst. Endosseous Implants, Inst. for Advance Dental Research, ADA, Union County and Plainfield Dental Soc., German, Italian dental implant socs. (hon.), Nat. Gymnastics Judges Assn. (pres. Eastern div.; named to Hall of Fame 1978), Delta Sigma Delta. Writer, lectr. on implantology. Address: 200 E Dudley Ave Westfield NJ 07090

RICE, ARGYLL PRYOR, educator; b. Va.; d. Theodorick Pryor and Argyll (Campbell) R.; B.A., Smith Coll., 1952; M.A., Yale U., 1956, Ph.D., 1961. Instr. Spanish, Yale U., New Haven, 1959-60, 61-63; asst. prof. Conn. Coll., New London, 1964-67, asso. prof., 1967-72, prof., 1972—, chmn. dept., 1971-74, 77—. Mem. Modern Lang. Assn. Am., Am. Assn. Tchrs. Spanish and Portuguese, Am. Council on Teaching Fgn. Langs., AAUP, Phi Beta Kappa. Author: Emilio Ballagas: poeta o poesía, 1967. Office: Connecticut College New London CT 06320

RICE, ARNOLD SANFORD, historian; b. Albany, N.Y., May 9, 1928; s. David and Rose (Levitt) R.; B.A., State U. N.Y. at Albany, 1950; M.A., Columbia U., 1951; Ph.D., Ind. U., 1959; m. Marcia Joy Griff, June 27, 1954; 1 son, Noah Bruce. Tchr., East Greenbush (N.Y.) Central Sch., 1953-54; teaching asst. Ind. U., 1955-56; tchr. Wallkill (N.Y.) Central Sch., 1956-58; adj. prof. Rutgers U., New Brunswick, N.J., 1959-63; Fulbright exchange prof. St. Montfort Coll., Rotterdam, Netherlands, 1964-65; instr. dept. history Kean Coll. of N.J., Union, 1958-61, asst. prof., 1961-64, asso. prof., 1964-67, prof., 1967—, chairperson, 1971-77; cons. on minority history and culture, sch. dists. N.J. Served with U.S. N.G., 1948-50. Recipient Risley Meml. History award State U.N.Y. at Albany, 1950; Faculty Research award Kean Coll. of N.J., 1967; Fulbright grantee, HEW, 1964-65, N.J. Hist. Commn. grantee, 1971-72. Mem. Am. Hist. Assn., Orgn. Am. Historians, Signum Laudis, Pi Gamma Mu, Phi Alpha Theta, Alpha Sigma Lambda. Author: The Ku Klux Klan in American Politics, 1962; Herbert Hoover, 1971; Newark, 1666-1970, 1977; (with John A. Krout) U.S. Since 1865, 1977; contbr. articles to profl. jours. Home: 191 Lorraine Dr Berkeley Heights NJ 07922 Office: Dept of History Kean College NJ Union NJ 07083

RICE, ARTHUR MAE, dietitian, hosp. adminstr.; b. Salisbury, N.C., Aug. 28, 1940; d. Arthur L. and Novella (Currence) Winford; student A. and T. State U., B.S., 1963; m. James Oliver Rice, Apr. 17, 1960; children—Anthony George, Michael Christopher. Food service supr., dietitian Delaware State Hosp., Farnhurst, 1963-65; asst. food service mgr. U. Del., Newark, 1965-67; dietetic cons. Foulk Manor Retirement Home, Inc., Wilmington, Del., 1966-67; dir. food services Rush Hosp., Malvern, Pa., 1967-70; dietary coordinator Am. Medicorp, Inc., 1970-71; dir. dietetics Tri-County Hosp., Springfield, Pa., 1971—, adminstrv. asst., 1975-77; dietetics lectr. dietetics, 1971—; appeared on TV program Sta. 6, Phila., 1975. Recipient Profl. Achievement award Downingtown Motor Inn, 1975, Pres. award Bus. and Profl. Women's Club, 1977; Sojourner Truth award, 1978; certificate Gov. Pa., 1978. Mem. Am., Phila. dietetic assns., Hosp. Food Dir. Assn. (dir. 1963—), Am. Soc. Hosp. Food Service Adminstrs. of Am. Hosp Assn., Middle Atlantic Soc. Hosp. Dietary Dirs. (pres.'s award 1976), Am. Home Econs. Assn., NAACP, West Chester Bus. and Profl. Women's Club (pres. 1976-77), Jack and Jill Am., Alpha Kappa Alpha, Iota Tau Omega. Republican. Co-author: Efficiency of Vegetarian Diets as a Source of Protein. Home: 500 N Five Points Rd West Chester PA 19380 Office: Tri County Med Center Sproul and Thomson Rds Springfield PA 19064

RICE, BLAINE MILLARD, commercial banker; b. Nazareth, Pa., Jan. 22, 1934; s. Lester Charles and Helen M. (Repsher) R.; bus. diploma, Churchman Bus. Coll., 1956; student in banking, U. Wis., 1976. Teller 1st Stroudsburg Nat. Bank (Pa.), 1959-67, br. mgr., 1967-70, auditor, 1970-71; asst. auditor 1st Eastern Bank of N.Am., Stroudsburg, 1971-77, ops. and security officer for 7 brs., 1977, asst. cashier, 1977—. Pres., organizer Monroe County (Pa.) Ch. Softball League, 1968-73; fin. sec. 1st United Methodist Ch. of Stroudsburg, 1971, mem. pastoral relations com., 1975; treas. Monroe chpt., Am. Cancer Soc., 1959; treas. Stroud Twp. Vol. Fire Dept. and Relief Assn., 1975—; treas. Eastern Inter-County Fed. of Firemen, 1978—. Served with U.S. Army, 1956-59. Mem. Am. Inst. Banking (pres. 1976-77, bd. dirs. and pres. Pocono chpt. 1975-78), Pa. State Fire Police Assn., Pa. State Firemen's Assn., Monroe County Fire Police Assn. (pres., founder, 1975—), Four County Firemen's Assn. (sec. 1968—). Democrat. Methodist. Clubs: Lions (organizer, treas. 1968—), Lake Manzaneta Rod and Gun Club (treas. 1975—), Order of DeMoley (advisor). Home: 1942 Pocono Park Dr Stroudsburg PA 18360 Office: 639 Main St Stroudsburg PA 18360

RICE, DOROTHEA MCKIM (MRS. LEON RICE), tech. librarian; b. Worcester, Mass.; d. Paul and Katherine E. (McKim) Coine; A.B., Boston U., 1935, postgrad., 1937-38; postgrad. Columbia U., 1945-46, 52-53; m. Leon Rice, Apr. 20, 1946. Librarian, Boston Pub. Library, 1936-45; reference asst. 1st Nat. City Bank, N.Y.C., 1945-46; librarian Vick Chem. Co., N.Y.C., 1946-48; spl. project cataloger Port of N.Y. Authority, 1949; asst. librarian Nat. Indsl. Conf. Bd., 1949-51; tech. librarian Am. Metal Climax, Inc. (formerly Am. Metal Co., Ltd.), 1951—. Vol. work various N.Y. hosps. Mem. Spl. Libraries Assn. (editor metals div. News; chmn. auditing com. 1956-58, chmn. nominating com. metals div. 1962-64, tech. div. 1966-67, chmn. pub. relations com. 1964, chmn. goals com. metals div. 1966-67, nat. chmn. non-serials publs. com. 1966-67, chmn. metals div. 1970, exec. bd. of tech.-sci. div. 1971), Am. Soc. Metals, Mus. Modern Art, Wilderness Soc., Delta Delta Delta. Unitarian. Home: 5 Peter Cooper Rd New York City NY 10010 Office: AMAX Center Greenwich CT 06830

RICE, EMERY VAN DAELL, financial planning exec.; b. Boston, Feb. 13, 1937; s. Thomas Emerson Proctor and Margaret (van Daell) R.; grad. Phillips Andover Acad., 1955; B.S., Haverford Coll., 1959; M.A., Bryn Mawr Coll., 1960; LL.B., U. Minn., 1965; children—Margaret, Jonathan. Admitted to Mass. bar, 1966; mem. sr. tax staff Ernst & Ernst, Boston, 1966-69; asst. tax officer Boston Safe Deposit & Trust, Boston, 1969-72; asst. v.p. Boston Co. Fin. Strategies, Inc., 1972-77, v.p., 1977—; dir. N.W. Rice Co., Boston. Mem. Am. (taxation and real property sects.), Mass., Boston bar assns., Boston Estate Planning Council, Bank Cashiers Assn. Boston, Phi Alpha Delta. Home: 126 Myrtle St Boston MA 02114 Office: 1 Boston Pl Boston MA 02106

RICE, HENRY HART, real estate exec.; b. N.Y.C., Mar. 2, 1911; s. Sidney Henry and Maude (Jacobs) R.; student Townsend Harris Prep. Sch., 1924-26, N.Y.U., 1927; m. Grace Hecker, Aug. 9, 1936 (dec.); children—Edward Hart, Eve Hart; m. 2d, Margaret Goldfarb, Apr. 9, 1976. Real estate broker Hanford and Henderson, Inc., 1932-36, Butler & Baldwin, 1936-41; asst. adminstr. rent dept. OPA, tech. adviser Nat. Housing Agy., chief conversion mgmt. div., chief sales div. Fed. Pub. Housing Adminstrn., Washington, 1942-46; chief appraiser N.Y.C. regional office Fed. Pub. Housing Adminstrn., 1947; v.p. J. Clarence Davies Realty Co., Inc., N.Y.C., 1947-53; v.p. James Felt & Co., N.Y.C. 1953-70, sr. v.p., 1970-73; exec. v.p. James Felt-Huberth & Huberth, Inc., 1973-75; chmn. bd. James Felt Realty Services, Inc., 1975—; v.p., dir. 480 Park Ave Corp.; asso. prof. Sch. Continuing Edn. and Extension Services, N.Y. U.; mem. adv. bd. N.Y. U. Real Estate Inst. Former chmn., Sales Brokers Com. Real Estate Bd. of N.Y.; dir. Realty Found. N.Y.; former gov. Real Estate Bd.; former trustee North Castle Free Library; mem. N.Y.C. Pub. Devel. Corp. Recipient Most Ingenious Realtor award, 1957-69. Mem. N.Y.C. Real Estate Bd. (gov., dir. brokerage div.), Am. Soc. Real Estate Counselors. Columnist Real Estate Weekly. Editorial bd. Real Estate Review. Home: 210 Hook Rd Katonah NY 10536 also 480 Park Ave New York City NY 10022 Office: 488 Madison Ave New York City NY 10022

RICE, JOHN CARTER, lawyer; b. Clinton, Iowa, Mar. 17, 1936; s. John Clark and Irene A. (Carter) R.; A.B., State U. N.Y., Albany, 1957; LL.B., Albany Law Sch., 1960; m. Shirley A. Johnson, Feb. 12, 1955; children—John Carter, Bradley F. Admitted to N.Y. bar, 1960; asso. Bliss & Bouck, Albany, N.Y., 1960-61; asso. DeGraff, Foy, Conway and Holt-Harris, Albany, 1962-65, partner, 1965—. Mem. Am., N.Y. State, Albany County bar assns., Justinian Soc. Episcopalian. Clubs: Fort Orange, Schuyler Meadows. Editor-in-chief Albany Law Rev., 1959-60. Home: One Loudon Heights N Loudonville NY 12211 Office: 90 State St Albany NY 12207

RICE, JOSEPH ALBERT, banker; b. Cranford, N.J., Oct. 11, 1924; s. Louis A. and Elizabeth J. (Michael) R.; B.Aero. Engring., Rensselaer Poly. Inst., 1948; M.Indsl. Engring., N.Y. U., 1952, M.A., 1968; m. Katharine Wolfe, Sept. 11, 1948; children—Walter, Carol, Philip, Alan. With Grumman Aircraft Engring. Corp., 1948-53; with IBM, N.Y.C., 1953-65, mgr. ops., real estate, constrn. divs., 1963-65; dep. group exec. N.Am. Comml. telecommunications group, pres. telecommunications div. ITT Corp., N.Y.C., 1965-67; sr. v.p. Irving Trust Co., N.Y.C., 1967-69, exec. v.p., 1969-72, sr. exec. v.p., 1972-73, vice chmn., 1973-74, pres., 1974;, also dir.; exec. v.p. Charter N.Y. Corp., 1971-74, vice chmn., 1974-75, pres., 1975—, also dir.; dir. Depository Trust Co. Dir., treas. Greater N.Y. Fund; trustee Rensselaer Poly. Inst. Served to 1st lt. C.E., AUS, 1943-46. Mem. Assn. Bank Holding Cos. (dir. 1978). Clubs: Univ. (N.Y.C.); Sleepy Hollow Country (Scarborough, N.Y.). Home: 15 Rose Ln Chappaqua NY 10514 Office: 1 Wall St New York City NY 10015

RICE, LAWRENCE ROGER, investment co. exec.; b. N.Y.C., July 20, 1946; s. Lewis Henry and Gloria Virginia (Hoffman) R.; B.A. in Econs., U. Calif., Los Angeles, 1967; M.B.A. in Finance, Columbia, 1969. Analyst Dupont Walston, Inc., N.Y.C., 1969-74, E. F. Hutton & Co., Inc., 1974; v.p., dir. Bree, Rice & Co., Inc., 1975-76; v.p. Rosenkrantz, Ehrenkrantz, Lyon & Ross, Inc., 1977—. Served in N.Y. Nat. Guard, 1969-74. Mem. N.Y. Soc. Security Analysts, Entertainment Analysts Group, U. Calif. at Los Angeles Alumni Assn. Club: Columbia Bus. Sch. Office: 6 E 43d St New York City NY 10017

RICE, MICHAEL STEPHEN, broadcasting co. exec.; b. Madison, Minn., Nov. 3, 1941; s. Edward William and Gertrude (Schonberg) R.; A.B. magna cum laude, Harvard U., 1963; B.A. (Rhodes scholar), Oxford U., 1965. With Sta. WGBH Ednl. Found. (Sta. WGBH-TV, WGBX-TV, WGBH Radio), Boston, 1965—, successively TV program mgr., 1967-73, v.p., gen. mgr., 1973—. Sec. Mass. Rhodes Scholar Selection Com., 1975—; bd. dirs. Jobs for Youth Boston, Inc., 1977—; mem. Harvard vis. com. Office Info. Tech., 1974—. Clubs: St. Botolph, Harvard Music. Editorial bd. Pub. Telecommunications Rev., 1974—. Home: 44 Chestnut St Boston MA 02108 Office: 125 Western Ave Boston MA 02134

RICE, WILLIAM THOMAS, radiologist; b. Steward, Ohio, Nov. 19, 1905; s. William Byron and Mary Margaret (McGraw) R.; M.D., Jefferson Med. Coll., 1932; m. Iva M. Mayberry, Aug. 10, 1938; children—Susan, Sara, Sharon. Intern, Geisinger Med. Center, Danville, Pa., 1932; staff physician Molly Stark Sanatorium, Canton, Ohio, 1935-37; chief resident Jameson Meml. Hosp., New Castle, Pa., 1937-39; resident in radiology Roper Hosp., Charleston, S.C., 1939-42; radiologist Rochester (Pa.) Gen. Hosp. and Beaver Valley Gen. Hosp., New Brighton, Pa., 1942-66; practice medicine specializing in radiology, Rochester, 1942—; instr. radiology Roper Hosp., 1939-42; staff radiologist Beaver County Geriatric Center, 1960-78. Fellow Am. Coll. Radiologists; mem. Am. Med. Assn., Pa. Med. Soc., Beaver County Med. Soc., Radiol. Soc. N. Am., Pa. Radiol. Soc. (pres. 1955-56), Pitts. Roentgen Soc. (pres. 1952-53), Beaver County Cancer Soc. (pres. 1954-55). Republican. Club: Elks. Home: 149 Windy Ghoul Beaver PA 15009 Office: 262 Connecticut Ave Rochester PA 15074

RICERETO, JAMES, III, engring. exec.; b. Jersey City, Jan. 14, 1947; s. James and Helen (Mastropolo) R.; B.S., Rutgers U., 1968; M.S. in Engring. (Ford Found. fellow), U. Pa., 1969; Cert. in City Planning, U. Calif., Berkeley, 1975; m. JoAnn Lucibello, Aug. 23, 1969. Structural engr. Port Authority of N.Y. and N.J., N.Y.C., 1969; civil/structural engr. Modjeski & Masters, Phila., 1970; project mgr. Tudor Engring. Co., San Francisco, 1972-78; dep. mgr. bus. devel. Parsons Brinkerhoff Quade & Douglas, N.Y.C., 1978—. Served as lt. C.E., U.S. Army, 1970-72; Vietnam. Decorated Bronze Star; registered profl. engr., Calif., N.J. Mem. Soc. Am. Mil. Engrs. (nat. com. new initiatives 1976-77, bd. dirs. San Francisco post 1975-76), ASCE (acting sec. San Francisco sect. 1976, editor newsletter 1976-78), Nat. Soc. Profl. Engrs., San Francisco Bay Area Engring. Council (career guidance com. 1974-75), Am. Inst. Cert. Planners, Am. Planning Assn. Home: 531 Main St New York NY 10044 Office: 250 W 34th St New York NY 10001

RICH, AVERY EDMUND, plant pathologist, educator; b. Charleston, Maine, Apr. 9, 1915; s. Nathan Harold and Myrtle (Schermerhorn) R.; B.S., U. Maine, 1937, M.S., 1939; Ph.D., Wash. State U., 1950; m. Erma Pauline Littlefield, June 15, 1938; children—Alice Ann Rich Fowler, Donna Rich Moody. Asst. agronomist R.I. State Coll., Kingston, 1943-47; instr. plant pathology Wash. State U., Pullman, 1947-50, asst. prof., 1950-51; asso. prof. plant pathology U. N.H., Durham, 1951-57, prof., 1957—, asso. dean life scis. and agr., 1972—. Mem. Am. Phytopath. Soc., Sigma Xi. Mem. United Ch. of Christ. Home: 13 Burnham Ave Durham NH 03824 Office: 201 Taylor Hall U NH Durham NH 03824

RICH, ELIZABETH MARGARET ANN (MRS. WILLIAM NICOLO PROVENZANO), pub. relations exec.; b. N.Y.C.; d. Louis Anthony and Margaret Ann (Gilchrist) Rich; B.A., LL.B., St. John's U.; postgrad. Columbia U.; m. William Nicolo Provenzano, July 1, 1966. Reporter, editor Chgo. Tribune Press Service, N.Y.C., 1947-59; account exec. Rowland Co., pub. relations, N.Y.C., 1959-61; account exec. A.A. Schechter Assos., Inc., N.Y.C., 1961-62, v.p., 1967-73, sr. v.p., 1973—; account exec. Hill & Knowlton, Inc., pub. relations, N.Y.C., 1962-67; lectr. journalism Dominican Coll. for Women, Blauvelt, N.Y., Mem. Am. Bar Assn., Nat. Assn. Women Lawyers. Club: Overseas Press (N.Y.C.). Contbr. articles to various mags. Home: 59 Kings Hwy Tappan NY 10983 Office: 633 3d Ave New York City NY 10017

RICH, ERIC, sales exec.; b. Znojmo, Czechoslovakia, Oct. 1, 1921; s. Sandor and Alice (Schifferes) Reich; came to U.S., 1955, naturalized, 1962; ed. U. Coll. Wales, Bangor, U.K.; m. Ilse L. B. Renard, Nov. 14, 1959; children—Susan Frances, Sally Dora, Charles Anthony. Export sales mgr. Pilot Radio, Ltd., London, Eng., 1945-49; dir. Derwent Exports, Ltd., London, 1949-55; export sales mgr. Am. Molding Powder & Chem. Corp., N.Y.C., 1956-58; with Gering Plastics Co. dept. Monsanto Chem. Co., Kenilworth, N.J., 1958-67; v.p., gen. mgr. Goldmark Plastics Internat., Inc., New Hyde Park, N.Y., 1967—. Served with RAF, 1941-45. Decorated Gallantry medal, 1939-43 Star, Atlantic Star. Home: 111 7th St Garden City NY 11530 Office: Nassau Terminal Rd New Hyde Park NY 11040

RICH, GILES SUTHERLAND, judge; b. Rochester, N.Y., May 30, 1904; s. Giles Willard and Sarah Thompson (Sutherland) R.; B.S., Harvard U., 1926; LL.B., Columbia U., 1929; m. Gertrude Verity Braun, Jan. 10, 1931 (dec.); 1 dau., Verity Sutherland Rich Grinnell; m. 2d, Helen Gill Field, Oct. 10, 1953. Admitted to N.Y. bar, 1929; registered to practice U.S. Patent Office, 1934; practice law, N.Y.C., 1929-56, specializing patent and trademark law; partner firm Williams, Rich & Morse, 1937-52, Churchill, Rich, Weymouth & Engel, 1952-56; asso. judge U.S. Ct. Customs and Patent Appeals, 1956—; lectr. patent law Columbia U., 1942-56, N.Y. Law Sch., 1952; adj. prof. Georgetown U. Law Sch., 1963-69. Recipient Jefferson medal N.J. Patent Law Assn., 1955, Kettering award Patent Trademark and Copyright Inst., George Washington U., 1963, Founders Day award for distinguished govt. service, 1970, Freedman Found. award Am. Inst. Chemists, 1967, Eli Whitney award Conn. Patent Law Assn., 1972. Mem. Assn. Bar City N.Y., Am. Bar Assn., Am., N.Y. (pres. 1950-51), Rochester (hon. life), Los Angeles (hon.) patent law assns., Nat. Lawyers Club (hon.). Clubs: Harvard, Cosmos (Washington). Author articles in field. Home: 4949 Linnean Ave NW Washington DC 20008 Office: US Ct Customs and Patent Appeals 717 Madison Pl NW Washington DC 20439

RICH, NEIL IAN, dentist; b. N.Y.C., Dec. 19, 1934; s. Harry and Rose (Schechtman) R.; student City Coll. N.Y., 1952-54; B.A., U. Vt., 1956; D.D.S., Fairleigh Dickinson Sch. Dentistry, 1960; student N.Y. U., 1962-63; m. Nina I. Berlad, June 26, 1960; m. 2d, Carole E. Cooper, Jan. 9, 1977; children—Andrew Robert, Jennifer Lynn, Gary Alan, Robert Marc. Practice dentistry, N.Y.C., 1961-63, specializing in periodontia and oral medicine, Plainview, N.Y., 1963—, Aquebogue, N.Y., 1978—; cons. Boro Dental Group; attending dentist Boys Club N.Y. Mem. ADA, Am. Acad. Peridontology, Am. Acad. Oral Medicine, Nassau-Suffolk Acad. Dentistry, N.E., L.I. socs. peridontists, Alpha Epsilon Pi. Home: 4 Cherokee Ln Commack NY 11725 Office: 1070 Old Country Rd Plainview NY 11803 also Aquebogue Sq PO Box 656 Main Rd Aquebogue NY 11931

RICH, ROBERT ELWOOD, physician; b. Newark, Apr. 26, 1920; s. Charles and Martha (Moore) R.; A.B., Amherst Coll., 1941; M.D., Jefferson Med. Coll., 1944; postgrad. N.Y.U. Med. Sch., 1948-49; m. Kathlene Pasco, Sept. 1, 1945; children—Roberta Ellen Rich Hart, Barbara Jean Rich Danckwerth. Intern, Newark City Hosp. 1944-45, resident, 1949-52; gen. practice medicine, Newark, 1947-48; chief resident surgery Newark City Hosp., 1949-52; practice medicine specializing in surgery, Newark 1952-63; Belleville, N.J., 1963—; pres. med. staff Clara Maass Meml. Hosp., Belleville, 1970-71, trustee, 1973—, dir. surgery, 1974—; preceptor surg. anatomy, Coll. Medicine and Dentistry of N.J., 1974—. Served with M.C., U.S. Army, 1945-47, 53. Diplomate Am. Bd. Surgery. Fellow A.C.S., Royal Soc. Health; mem. AMA, N.J. Soc. Surgeons, Pan Am., Pan Pacific surg. assns., Am. Soc. Colon and Rectal Surgeons, Phi Chi, Phi Delta Theta. Republican. Presbyterian. Clubs: Practitioners of Newark, Essex Fells Country. Home: 88 Devon Rd Essex Fells NJ 07021 Office: 50 Newark Ave Belleville NJ 07109

RICHARD, ST. CLAIR SMITH (MRS. GEORGE CHARLES RICHARD, 2D), pub. relations exec.; b. Newton, Iowa, Nov. 16, 1910; d. William Walter and Nelle Grace (Van Dusseldorp) Smith; student U. Iowa, 1930, Barnard Coll., 1931; B.S., Columbia Sch. Journalism, 1933; m. George Charles Richard, 2d, Dec. 4, 1933; children—Thomas Lane, Randall St. Clair, Deborah Nell duChane. Mng. partner Halo House, Larchmont, N.Y., 1946—. Instr., Good Counsel Coll., White Plains, N.Y., 1961-64. Promotions asst. Westchester County Recreation Commn., 1960-61; asst. to mayor Mt. Vernon, N.Y., 1962-63; pub. relations dir. Westchester Library System, Mt. Vernon, 1966-71; pub. info. officer Westchester County Med. Center, 1974-76. Mem. pub. relations com. N.Y. State Recreation Soc., 1971—; mem. advisory bd. St. Paul's Eastchester, Mt. Vernon, 1971—; council adminstr. Larchmont Tng. Center, 1971. Press sec. vice-chmn. Republican State Com., 1964; pub. relations Westchester Democratic com., 1972—. Bd. dirs. UN Assn. U.S., Mt. Vernon chpt., Afro-Am. Cultural Found., White Plains; vice chmn. bd. Nat. Shrine/Bill of Rights. Mem. Am. Assn. Improvement Boxing (mem. bd., chmn. publicity), Westchester County Assn., Westchester Park & Recreation Soc., Delta Gamma. Editor: Women in Public Service, 1964, Straight Talk, 1964, Women in the News, 1956-60, Men of the Pulpit, 1958-62, Scribblings, 1966-71, Newberry Award Newsletter, 1971-72, Westchester Ind. Herald, 1965-66, The Voice, 1977—. Home: 60 The Boulevard New Rochelle NY 10801 Office: Box 85 Larchmont NY 10539

RICHARDS, CHARLES FLEMING, JR., lawyer; b. Phila., Nov. 11, 1937; s. Charles Fleming and Helen (Scovill) R.; A.B., Princeton U., 1959; LL.B., Yale U., 1962; m. Pamela S. Millikin, Aug. 26, 1961; children—Heather, Bettina, Charles Fleming. Admitted to Del. bar, 1963; prof. law U. E. Africa, Dar es Salaam, Tanzania, 1962-63; dep. atty. gen. State of Del., 1963-64; partner firm Richards, Layton & Finger, Wilmington, Del., 1967—. Pres., chief exec. officer Del. League for Planned Parenthood, 1970-71, chmn. bd., 1971-73; sec., trustee Tower Hill Sch., 1967—; gen. counsel Republican party State of Del., mem. Rep. State Com. Mem. Del., Am. bar assns. Episcopalian. Clubs: Wilmington, Wilmington Country. Home: 2204 N Grant Ave Wilmington DE 19806 Office: 4072 DuPont Bldg Wilmington DE 19899

RICHARDS, CHRISTINE-LOUISE, artist; b. Radnor, Pa., Jan. 11, 1910; d. Joseph Ernest and Katherine (Fletcher) Richards; student pvt. schs.; art schs. N.Y.C., Munich, Germany. One-woman shows Stockbridge, Mass., 1947, 48, 52, 53, Oneonta, N.Y., 1960, 61; exhibited in group shows Stockbridge Art Assn., 1931-32; represented in collections, Cal., Mass., N.Y.; founder, owner Blue Star Music Pub. Co., Pittsfield, Mass., 1946-55; now owner, pres. Blue Star Music Pub. Co., New Berlin and Morris, N.Y. Mem. Nat. Assn. Composers U.S.A., Phila. Art Alliance, Am. Fedn. Musicians, Nightingale-Bamford Alumni Assn., Met. Mus. Art, Audubon Soc., Emergency Aid of Pa., Pa. Acad. Fine Arts, Internat. Platform Assn., Marquis Library Soc., Intercontinental Biog. Assn., others. Club: Peale (Phila.). Author: The Blue Star Fairy Book of Stories for Children. Author, illustrator: The Blue Star Fairy Book of More Stories for Children. Composer (song) What Makes Me Dream of You, 1950, numerous other songs. Contbr. to Artists U.S.A. Home: Springslea Morris NY 13808 Office: POB 185 Morris NY 13808

RICHARDS, (ALBERT) DEWEY, physician, educator; b. Industry, Maine, Mar. 4, 1927; s. Albert Dodge and Nellie (Booker) R.; B.A. with distinction, U. Maine, 1956; M.D., Tufts U., 1960; m. Emily Gamage, Mar. 18, 1950; children—Susan Joy Finch, Michael, Donna Hansen, Catherine, Daniel, John. Farmer, Farmington, Maine, 1950-52; salesman pharms., Worcester, Mass., 1952-54; intern Maine Med. Center, Portland, 1961; gen. practice medicine Bridgton, Maine, 1961-68, family practice, 1968-75; faculty Tufts U. Sch. Medicine, Boston, 1973—, chmn. div. family medicine, 1978—; chief family practice service Eastern Maine Med. Center, Bangor, 1975—. Adv. com. U. Maine Med. Sch., 1975; chmn. profl. adv. com. Home Health Service Bangor, 1975-77; mem. Maine Gov.'s Task Force on Post Grad. Tng., 1975-76; mem. Medicare Adv. Com. Maine, pres., 1975-76. Served with Airborne Corps, U.S. Army, 1946-48; ATO. Diplomate Am. Bd. Family Practice (charter). Fellow Am. Acad. Family Physicians (charter; del. 1976—); mem. Maine Acad. Family Physicians (pres. 1967-68, exec. sec. 1977-78), AMA, Penobscot County Med. Soc., Soc. Tchrs. Family Medicine. Republican. Clubs: Bangor Med., Masons, Shriners, K.T. Home: 180 Main St Orono ME 04473 Office: 417 State St Bangor ME 04401

RICHARDS, JAMES WARD, geol. engr.; b. Ft. Morgan, Colo., Sept. 8, 1933; s. Winston Lowell and Opal (Plumb) R.; B.A., U. Colo., 1955; student U. Utah, 1958; m. Betty Darlene Jones, Apr. 6, 1962 (dec. Mar. 1975); children—Barbara Ann, Patricia Lynn. Party mgr., geophysicist Continental Geophys. Co., Midland, Tex., 1958-59, party mgr., 1962-63; party mgr., geophysicist Namco Internat., Tripoli, Libya, 1959-62; geol. engr. Santa Barbara County, Santa Barbara, Calif., 1963-67; geophysicist, geol. engr. Pa. Transp. Dept., Harrisburg, 1967-76; pres., geol. engr. Branthoover & Richards, Harrisburg, 1976—. Served with USMC, 1956-58. Registered profl. engr., Pa., Colo., Ky.; registered geologist, Calif. Mem. Soc. Exploration Geophysicists, Assn. Engring. Geologists, European Assn. Exploration Geophysicists, Harrisburg Geol. Soc., Internat. Soc. Rock Mechanics, ASCE, Nat. Soc. Profl. Engrs., Phi Beta Kappa, Sigma Gamma Epsilon. Home: PO Box 6074 Harrisburg PA 17112 Office: 2449 N 2d St Harrisburg PA 17110

RICHARDS, JOHN BENJAMIN, mgmt. cons.; b. Rochester, N.Y., Sept. 21, 1948; s. Thomas Beddoe and Mary Sofia (Savidge) R.; B.A., Bucknell U., 1970; M.B.A., U. Pa., 1976. Sales mgmt. staff Procter & Gamble Co., Balt. and Cin., 1970-74; engagement mgr. McKinsey & Co., Inc., Washington, 1978—; cons. to Nat. Symphony Orch., Washington, 1978—. Advisor Jr. Achievement, Balt., 1972-74. Wharton Sch. pub. policy fellow to Consumer Product Safety Commn., 1975; Wharton-Honeywell common market fellow, Brussels, Belgium, 1975-76. Mem. Am. Mktg. Assn., Common Cause, Bucknell Alumni Assn. (v.p. Balt. chpt. 1972). Baptist. Contbr. research for Consumer Product Safety Commn. Address: 1700 Pennsylvania Ave NW Washington DC 20006

RICHARDS, JOHN JOSEPH, assn. exec.; b. Albany, N.Y., July 2, 1925; s. John Henry and Marion Margaret (Clark) R.; B.A., Siena Coll., 1950; m. Jane Sheridan, Nov. 15, 1947; children—Barbara (Mrs. Gary Maggio), Ellen, Susan, John, Patricia, Carol. Asst. sec. Bldg. Industry Employers N.Y. State, Albany, 1950-53; exec. dir. Builders Exchange of Rochester, 1953—; mem. adv. bd. Rochester Inst. Tech. Center for Employer-Employee Relations; trustee many union welfare, pension funds. Served with USNR, 1943-46. Mem. Am. Soc. Assn. Execs., Internat. Builders Exchange Execs., Constrn. Specifications Inst., Labor Relations Research Assn. Republican. Roman Catholic. Home: 353 Imperial Circle Rochester NY 14617 Office: 65 College Ave Rochester NY 14607

RICHARDS, LAWRENCE MARION, chem. processing co. exec.; b. Moorpark, Calif., June 8, 1916; s. Raymond W. and Anna Magdalena (Socin) R.; B.A. in Chemistry magna cum laude, UCLA, 1937, M.A. in Organic Chemistry, 1938; Ph.D., U. Wis., 1941; m. Martha Elizabeth Phillips, July 11, 1942; children—Lawrence Marion, Nicholas J., Nancy G. Teaching asst. UCLA, 1937-38; research chemist Shell Devel., Emeryville, Calif., 1938-39; research chemist central chem. dept. E.I. duPont de Nemours & Co., Wilmington, Del., 1941-47; sr. organic chemist Stanford Research Inst., Menlo Park, Calif., 1947-48, head organic chemistry sect., 1948-49, acting chmn. dept. chemistry and chem. engring., 1950-51, chmn., 1951-54, asst. dir. research phys. and biol. scis., 1954-55; asst. mgr. research and devel. Anaheim (Calif.) Research Center, Richfield Oil Corp., 1955-58, mgr., 1958-66; v.p. research and devel. Anaheim Research Center ARCO Chem. Co., Atlantic Richfield Co., Phila., 1966-67; pres. Atlantic Richfield Hanford Co. (subsidiary ARCO Chem. Co.), Richland, Wash., 1967-73; coordinator Nuclear devel. Atlantic Richfield, Los Angeles, 1973-79, v.p. Arco Chem. div. Atlantic Richfield, 1979—. Mem. econ. adv. com. State of Wash., 1970—. Mem. Am. Chem. Soc., Am. Petroleum Inst., AAAS, Sci. Research Soc. Am., Sigma Xi, Alpha Chi Sigma, Phi Lambda Upsilon. Numerous patents, publs. in field. Home: 219 Sugartown Rd Wayne PA 19087 Office: 1500 Market St Philadelphia PA 19101

RICHARDS, MCDONALD ARNOLD, chem. systems cons.; b. Trinidad, B.W.I., May 9, 1945; s. Frederick Alexander and Erma Natalie (McDonald) R.; came to U.S. 1946; B.S., Poly. Inst. Bklyn., 1967; M.S. (Martin Luther King fellow 1968-70), Northeastern U., 1970; Ph.D. (Univ. fellow 1973-74), 1974. Research chemist Forsythe Dental Center, Boston, 1970; research asso. Northeastern U., Boston, 1970-74; sr. staff mem. Arthur D. Little Inc., Cambridge, Mass., 1975—. Sr. cons. long range planning to Pres. of Roxbury Community Coll., 1977-78. Am. Chem. Soc. Petroleum Research Fund scholar, 1966-67. Mem. Am. Chem. Soc., AAAS, Am. Mgmt. Assn., Sigma Xi. Presbyterian. Home: 210 Lake Shore Rd Brighton MA 02135 Office: 25 Acorn Park Cambridge MA 02140

RICHARDS, ROBERT BARTSON, sugar processing co. exec.; b. Paterson, N.J., Mar. 6, 1944; s. Robert W. and Dorothy B. (Bartson) R.; grad. N.Y. Inst. Photography, 1963; A.S. in Bus. Adminstrn., Dean Jr. Coll., 1964; B.S., Denver U., 1966, M.B.A., 1968; postgrad. Fairleigh Dickinson U., 1976—; m. Lynne M. Roberts, Mar. 18, 1967; children—Laura Lynne, David Bartson. Dir. mktg. Bartson Fabrics Inc., N.J., 1973-76; tng. dir. Retention Systems, N.J., 1976-77; indsl. tng. exec. Am. Sugar div. Amstar Corp., Bklyn., 1977—. Served with USAF, 1968-72. Mem. Am. Soc. Tng. and Devel., Internat. Mgmt. Council, Am. Mgmt. Assn., Assn. M.B.A. Execs., Am. Ordnance Assn. Episcopalian. Club: Toastmasters. Home: 104 Brookside Ave Ridgewood NJ 07450 Office: 49 S 2d St Brooklyn NY 11211

RICHARDS, ROBERT LEROY, assn. exec.; b. Harrisburg, Pa., May 14, 1920; s. Lester Lewis and Marie Emma (Ripper) R.; A.B., Gettysburg Coll., 1943; postgrad. Biarritz (France) U.; m. Suzanne C. Baptisti, Aug. 31, 1943; children—Lynn Susan Richards Browne, Marcia Ann Richards Allen. Asst. dir. Pa. Med. Soc., Harrisburg, 1947-58; exec. dir. Am. Soc. Internal Medicine, San Francisco, 1958-60; exec. adminstr. Ill. State Med. Soc., Chgo., 1960-67; pres. Nat. Confectioners Assn., Chgo., 1967-69; gen. mgr. Am. Hotel and Motel Assn., N.Y.C., 1969-73, exec. v.p., 1974—; instr., chmn. bd. regents Inst. for Orgn. Mgmt. sponsored by U.S. C. of C., 1969-70. Served with paratroopers U.S. Army, 1943-46. Decorated Silver Star, Purple Heart; recipient citation of outstanding contbn. to Am. Assn. Med. Soc. Execs., 1967; certificate of appreciation U.S. C. of C., 1967. Mem. Am. Soc. Assn. Execs. (trustee), Med. Soc. Exec. Assn., Chgo., N.Y. (pres.) socs. assn. execs., U.S. C. of C. (chmn. assn. com.). Republican. Lutheran. Clubs: Kiwanis, Nassau Country, Athletic Assn. Ill. Home: 10 Summit Dr Manhasset NY 11030 Office: Am Hotel and Motel Assn 888 Seventh Ave New York City NY 10019

RICHARDS, ROGER THOMAS, acoustical scientist; b. Akron, Ohio, June 19, 1942; s. Clyde Irvin and Thelma Josephine (Whitaker) R.; B.S. in Physics, Westminster Coll., New Wilmington, Pa., 1964; M.S. in Physics, Ohio U., 1968; postgrad. in Acoustics (NASA fellow), Pa. State U., 1971—. Grad. asst. in physics Ohio U., 1965-67, research asst. in acoustics, 1967-68; asso. engr. transducer lab. Gen. Dynamics/Electronics Co., Rochester, N.Y., 1968-69, engr. acoustics dept., 1969-71; NASA trainee Pa. State U., 1971-74, grad. asst. in acoustics, 1974—; staff asso. Applied Research Lab., State College, Pa., 1976—. Mem. Acoustical Soc. Am., Am. Instr. Aeros. and Astronautics, Nat. Speleological Soc. (vice chmn. Nittany Grotto 1975-76), Am. Cryptographic Assn., AAAS, U.S. Chess Fedn. (capt. Pa. State U. team 1973), Am. Go Assn., Am. Contract Bridge League (pres. local club 1970-71), Pa. State U. Alumni Assn. (alumni council and exec. bd. 1973-74), Kappa Mu Epsilon, Sigma Pi Sigma (nat. del. 1967). Contbr. articles to profl. jours.; research in acoustic propagation and scattering, sonar transducer and array design. Home: 718 E Foster Ave State College PA 16801 Office: Applied Research Lab PO Box 30 State College PA 16801

RICHARDS, RONALD FRANCIS, mech. engr.; b. Evanston, Ill., Sept. 29, 1943; s. Robert Bernard and Virginia Katherine R.; B.M.E., Northwestern U., 1965; M.M.E., U. Conn., 1973; m. Nancy Carol Peters, Mar. 11, 1963; children—Bryan, Christopher. Engr., Pratt and Whitney Aircraft Co., East Hartford, Conn., 1965-67; engr. Conn. Power and Light Co., Montville, 1968-75, ops. supr., 1975—. Mem. Bd. Fin. Andover (Conn.), 1969-75; pres. Young Republicans, Andover, 1968-70. Mem. ASME, Am. Radio Relay League. Republican. Office: PO Box 345 Uncasville CT 06382

RICHARDSON, ALFONSO AUSTIN, hosp exec.; b. Aruba, Dutch West Indies, Feb. 29, 1932; s. Ashley A. and Elvia H. (Richardson) R.; came to U.S., 1951; B.S., L.I. U., 1959; m. Florence C. St. Hilaire, Sept. 7, 1957; children—Paula, Kathy, Peter, Steven, Edward, Vernon. Sr. accountant Phillip Kaplan & Co., N.Y.C., 1959-64; auditing supr. Western Electric Co. Inc., Kearny, N.J., 1964-68; sr. mgmt. analysts, CBS, N.Y.C., 1968-69; controller Node 4 Assos., Inc., Bklyn., 1969-71; asst. controller Kings County Hosp. Center, Bklyn., 1971-74, controller, 1975—; controller Cumberland Hosp., Bklyn., 1974-75; owner Richardson Mgmt. Assos., cons.; dir. Orgen Industries Ltd., Bklyn. Served with U.S. Army, 1952-55. Mem. Am. Mgmt. Assn., Hosp. Fin. Mgmt. Assn., Am. Accounting Assn., Nat. Assn. Accountants (dir., sec.), Bklyn. Fed. Credit Union. Home: 704 Empire Blvd Brooklyn NY 11213 Office: 451 Clarkson Ave Brooklyn NY 11203

RICHARDSON, ARLEIGH DYGERT, III, ednl. adminstr.; b. Columbus, Ohio, Apr. 28, 1922; s. Arleigh Dygert, Jr. and Elizabeth (Wheeler) R.; A.B., Yale, 1944, M.A., 1948, Ph.D., 1953; m. Joan Vivian Shearman, Aug. 29, 1953; children—Elizabeth Sarah, Marjorie Anne, Peter Dygert. Instr. in English, Yale, New Haven, 1946-50, asst. dean, 1950-56; headmaster Columbus (Ohio) Sch. for Girls, 1956-65; exec. officer Social Studies Curriculum Program, Edn. Devel. Center, Cambridge, Mass., 1965-68; dir. Nat. Humanities Faculty, Concord, Mass., 1968-76; tchr. The Lawrence Acad., Groton, Mass., 1977—; chmn. Concord Adult Edn. Com.; mem. Braitmayer Found. Selection Com.; alumni trustee Phillips Acad., Andover, 1969-70; bd. govs. Concord Antiquarian Soc.; mem. devel. com. Lawrence Acad.; trustee Abbot Acad. Assn., St. Mark's Sch.; mem. hist. commn. Town of Concord, Met. Council for Ednl. Opportunity; mem. visitors com. Boston Mus. Fine Arts; bd. advisors Concord Art Assn. Served to lt. USN, 1943-46. Decorated Purple Heart. Folger Shakespeare Library fellow, lectr., 1967; recipient Nat. Council Tchrs. of English award, 1971; MAHE award, 1972. Mem. Nat. Council Tchrs. of English, Modern Language Assn., Nat. Assn. for Humanities Edn. Democrat. Editor: The Merchant of Venice, Yale Shakespeare, 1960; gen. editor Nat. Humanities Faculty: Why Series, 1973. Home: 78 Shirley St Pepperell MA 01437 Office: The Lawrence Acad Groton MA 01450

RICHARDSON, ARTEMAS PARTRIDGE, landscape architect; b. Phila., May 24, 1918; s. E. Stanley and Jessica (Ripple) R.; B.A., Williams Coll., 1940; B.S., Iowa State Coll., 1947; student Pa. State Coll., 1940-42; m. Frederica McAfee, Sept. 2, 1945; children—Steven, David, Ann, Vida, Stanley. Gen. landscape architect asst. McCloud & Scatchard, Lititz, Pa., 1947-48; gen. landscape architect asst. Olmsted Brothers, Brookline, Mass., 1949-50, partner, landscape architect, 1950-61; partner, landscape architect Olmsted Assos., Brookline, Mass., 1961-64, pres., treas., 1964—; lectr. landscape architecture Harvard, 1961; mem. Mass. Bd. Registration Landscape Architects, 1968-77, chmn. bd., 1968-73. Chmn. Sagamore dist. Boy Scouts Am., 1968-71, mem. exec. bd. Boston council, 1962-70, 71-72, mem. nat. council, 1967-70; trustee, Trustees of Reservations, Milton, Mass., 1963—. Served to lt. USNR, 1942-46. Fellow Am. Soc. Landscape Architects, Boston Soc. Landscape Architects (pres. 1952-56); mem. Scarab, Delta Phi, Tau Sigma Delta, Pi Gamma Alpha. Club: Rotary (club pres. 1965-66, dist. trustee 1968-69, dist. gov. 1970-71, dir. R.I. 1978—). Home: 101 Warren St Brookline MA 02146 Office: 99 Warren St Brookline MA 02146

RICHARDSON, CARLTON DUQUESNE, financial exec.; b. West Brookfield, Mass., Oct. 5, 1935; s. Milton C. and Charlotte R. (Brooks) R.; B.B.A., U. Mass., 1957; m. Lois Luke, Dec. 23, 1970; children—Christine Dorothy, Carla Duquesne; children by previous marriage—Linda Ann, Craig David. Sr. auditor Arthur Andersen & Co., C.P.A.'s, N.Y.C., 1957-64; audit mgr. Manual Cole & Co., C.P.A.'s, Hartford, Conn., 1964-66; audit supr. C.E., Inc., Windsor, Conn., 1966-67, controller, Chattanooga div., 1967-73; v.p. finance C.E. Bldg. Products div., Miami, Fla., 1973-76; v.p. finance and adminstrn. C.E. Glass div., Pennsauken, N.J., 1976—. Served with Ordnance Corps, AUS, 1961-63. C.P.A., N.J., Tenn. Mem. Am. Inst. C.P.A.'s, N.J., Conn. socs. C.P.A.'s, Financial Execs. Inst. (sec.-treas. 1972-73). Author: How To Increase Profits with Cost Management, 1978. Home: 209 Douglas Ct Moorestown NJ 08057 Office: 825 Hylton Rd Pennsauken NJ 08110

RICHARDSON, ELLIOT LEE, govt. ofcl.; b. Boston, July 20, 1920; s. Edward P. and Clara (Shattuck) R.; A.B. cum laude, Harvard, 1941, LL.B. cum laude, 1947, then LL.D.; LL.D., U. N.H., Emerson Coll., Springfield Coll., Lowell Tech. Inst., U. Pitts., Yeshiva U., Ohio State U., Lincoln U., Temple U., Mich. State U., Gallaudet Coll.; L.H.D., Mass. Coll. Optometry, Brandeis U., Whittier Coll.; m. Anne Francis Hazard, Aug. 2, 1952; children—Henry Shattuck, Anne Hazard, Michael Elliot. Admitted to Mass. bar, 1949; law clk. judge Learned Hand, 1947-48, justice Felix Frankfurter, 1948-49; asso. firm Ropes, Gray, Best, Coolidge & Rugg, Boston, 1949-53, 54-56; lectr. law Harvard, 1952; asst. to Senator Leverett Saltonstall, 1953-54; asst. sec. for legislation HEW, 1957-59; U.S. atty. Mass., 1959-61; spl. asst. to atty. gen. of U.S., 1961; partner firm Ropes & Gray, Boston, 1961-64; lt. gov. State of Mass., 1965-67, atty. gen., 1967-69; under sec. of state Dept. State, Washington, 1969-70; sec. HEW, 1970-73; sec. def., Jan.-May 1973; atty. gen. U.S., May-Oct. 1973; practice in Washington, 1974-75; ambassador to Ct. St. James's, U.K., London, Eng., 1975; sec. Dept. Commerce, 1976-77, ambassador-at-large, spl. rep. of Pres. to Law of Sea Conf., 1977—. Past v.p., dir. Mass. Bay United Fund; mem. adv. council Trustees of Reservations; bd. govs. A.R.C.; past pres., dir. World Affairs Council Boston; past dir. Salzburg Seminar in Am. Studies, United Community Services of Met. Boston; past chmn. Greater Boston United Fund Campaign; past trustee Mass. Gen. Hosp., Radcliffe Coll., Cambridge Drama Festival, Brookline (Mass.) Pub. Library; past mem. bd. overseers Harvard Coll.; past chmn., mem. overseers com. to visit Harvard John F. Kennedy Sch. Govt., past mem. overseers coms. to visit Harvard U. Press, Dept. Govt., Law Sch., Med. and Dental Schs. Served to 1st lt., 4th Inf. Div., AUS, 1942-45. Decorated Bronze Star medal, Purple Heart with oak leaf cluster. Fellow Woodrow Wilson Internat. Center for Scholars, 1974-75. Fellow Am. Acad. Arts and Scis., Am. Bar Found.; mem. Am., Mass., Boston bar assns., Harvard Alumni Assn. (past dir.), Council on fgn. Relations (gov.), D.A.V., V.F.W., Am. Legion. Home: 1100 Crest Lane McLean VA 22101 Office: care Dept State Washington DC 20520

RICHARDSON, FREDERICK DOUGLASS, editor; b. Bklyn., Oct. 17, 1942; s. Lionel and Elise C. (Rollock) R.; student L.I. U., 1960-61, Berklee Music Sch., 1961, N.Y. Inst. Photography, 1961, N.Y. U., 1962, N.Y. Coll. Music, 1962-63, New Sch. for Social Research, 1964, 65, Medgar Evers Coll., 1974, L.I. U.; m. Maira Rivera, Mar. 11, 1978; children—Taji Hekima, Elizabeth Betsabell. Mgr., owner Richardson's Afro-Am. Bookstore, Bklyn., 1964-69; editor-in-chief Negro News, Queens, N.Y., 1969; sports editor, asst. editor The Adafi, Bklyn., 1974-75; editor-in-chief Atumpan Yearbook, Medgar Evers Coll., Bklyn., 1975-77; founder, pub., editor-in-chief Soul Singer: Jour. of Poetry and Touch, Vibrations of Poetry, Bklyn., 1975-76. Mem. Assn. Black Journalists and Publishers (founder, pres. 1976-77). Home: 898 Sterling Pl Brooklyn NY 11216

RICHARDSON, GORDON, engring. cons.; b. Walla Walla, Wash., Apr. 9, 1942; s. Norman Egbert and Ann Pendleton (Gordon) R.; A.B., Amherst Coll., 1964; postgrad. U. R.I., 1967-70; m. Susan Virginia Merrill, June 12, 1965; children—E. Derek, Robin G. Tech. mgr., v.p. engring. Storm Wave Dynamics, Inc., Fort Lauderdale, Fla., 1970-73; chief engr. Eastman Whipstock, Inc., Houston, 1973-77; sr. mem. profl. staff electronic systems sect. Arthur D. Little, Inc., Cambridge, Mass., 1977—. Dir. Broward Citizens for Environ. Preservation, 1972-73; mem. exec. com., dir. Southgate Civic Assn., 1974-76. Mem. IEEE, ASME. Congregationalist. Home: 9 Everett Ave Winchester MA 01890

RICHARDSON, HENRY HOWE, entomologist; b. Millis, Mass., Feb. 22, 1906; s. Evan Fussell and Geneive Frances (Howe) R.; B.S., U. Mass., 1926; M.S., Iowa State U., 1929, Ph.D., 1931; M.P.H., U. N.C., 1969; m. Sylvia Hodgson, Nov. 27, 1931; children—Donald Carleton, Brian Henry. Jr. to asso. antomologist U.S. Dept. Agr. Research Service, Washington, 1926-28, 31-43, project to investigations leader, Hoboken, N.J., 1946-66, spl. research leader, Bahamas, 1947, Argentina, 1949, Netherlands and W. Ger., 1950, P.R. 1952, 56, Cuba, 1956, 59; cons. to U.S. Dept. Agr. on Australian and other plant quarantine treatments, 1970—. Active Chatham (N.J.) Shade Tree Commn., 1956-67. Served to maj. M.C., U.S. Army, 1943-46. Fulbright research scholar, Australia, 1969-70; Air Pollution Control fellow, U. So. Calif., 1967. Mem. N.Y. Acad. Scis., Entomol. Soc., Am. Air Pollution Control Assn., S.A.R., Sigma Xi, Phi Kappa Phi. Developer chem. and phys. plant quarantine treatments; contbr. articles to sci. jours. Home: Rural Route 3 Box 115 Milford NJ 08848

RICHARDSON, MADISON FRANKLIN, otolaryngologist; b. Prairie View, Tex., Dec. 26, 1943; s. William Agustus and Vivian Richardson (Perry) R.; B.S., Howard U., 1965, M.D., 1969; m. Constance Moore, July 31, 1965; children—Kelly, Kimberly, Karen. Commd. lt. U.S. Army, 1968, advanced through grades to lt. col., 1976; intern Walter Reed Med. Center, Washington, 1969-70, resident, 1970-74, fellow, 1974-75; practice medicine specializing in orolaryngology and head and neck surgery; chief head and neck surgery Walter Reed Med. Center, 1977—; asst. prof. surgery Uniformed Services U. Health Scis., Bethesda, Md., 1977—. Mem. AMA, A.C.S., Nat. Med. Assn., Soc. Head and Neck Surgeons, Am. Acad. Facial Plastic and Reconstructive Surgery, Alpha Omega Alpha, Kappa Alpha Psi. Contbr. articles to med. jours. Home: 4717 Falcon St Rockville MD 20853

RICHARDSON, MARIE SMITH (MRS. ELVA RICHARDSON), engring. co. librarian; b. Decaturville, Tenn., Sept. 2, 1924; d. Myron Cortell and Narcia (Ellison) Smith; student U. Tenn., 1943-46; B.S., U. Chattanooga, 1960; postgrad. So. Conn. State Coll., 1962; m. Elva Richardson, Oct. 18, 1946; children—Priscilla Ann (Mrs. F.M. Fuhrken), Stephen Fred. Dir. consumer research and testing Chicopee Mfg. Co., Milltown, N.J., 1956-57; chief librarian Combustion Engring., Inc., Chattanooga, 1957-60, chief librarian engring. research library, Windsor. Conn., 1961-63, departmental mgr. corporate library system, 1963—; tchr. pub. schs., Chattanooga, 1960-61; cons. Dixie Mercerizing Co., Chattanooga, 1960, Bowaters So. Paper Corp., Calhoun, Tenn., 1960; John Cotton Dana lectr. La. State U., 1967; mem. spl. adv. com. devel. and cooperation Conn. State Library. Mem. Tenn., Southeastern, Conn. (mem. com. on library tech. asst. tng. program 1968—) library assns., Spl. Libraries Assn. (pres. Conn. Valley chpt. 1966-67, cons. com. 1967-69, sec.-treas. engring. div. 1972-74, 74-78). Author articles profl. jours. Home: 1111 North St Suffield CT 06078 Office: 1000 Prospect Hill Rd Windsor CT 06095

RICHARDSON, PAUL ARTHUR, hosp. exec.; b. Glendale, Calif., Mar. 14, 1946; s. Raymond and Gertude R.; B.S. in Bus. Adminstrn., U. R.I., 1972; M.S., Rensselaer Poly. Inst., 1978; m. Susan Reardon, Apr. 21, 1974. Mgr. central sterile supply St. Raphael Hosp., New Haven, Conn., 1974-77; mgr. central sterile supply Mt. Sinai Hosp., N.Y.C., 1977-78; dir. material mgmt. Clara Maass Meml. Hosp., Belleville, N.J., 1978—. Served with USAF, 1964-68. Mem. Am. Hosp. Assn. Central Service Soc., N.J. Central Service Assn., N.J. Purchasing Mgrs. Assn. Roman Catholic. Home: 7002 Blvd East #10A Guttenberg NJ 07093 Office: 1 Franklin Ave Belleville NJ 07109

RICHARDSON, RONALD JOHN, chem. co. exec.; b. London, England, Oct. 12, 1930; s. John Henry and Violet Anne (Grout) R.; came to U.S., 1960; B.S., U. Manchester, 1952; D.Sc., U. London, 1976; m. Pamela Mary Harris, Dec. 29, 1956; children—Rhoda Anne, Philip Karl. With info. office U.K. Atomic Energy Authority, Harwell, England, 1952-57; chemist Atomic Energy Can., Ottawa, 1957-60; info. specialist Monsanto Textiles Co., Decatur, Ala., 1960-62; mgr. product tech. info. Allied Chemical Corp., Hopewell, Va., 1962-69, mgr. mktg. systems, N.Y.C., 1969—. Fellow Am. Inst. Chemists; mem. Am. Chem. Soc., Chem. Inst. Can., Am. Assn. Textile Tech., Can. Inst. Textile Sci., Am. Assn. Textiles Chemists & Colorists. Anglican. Club: Internat. Textile. Contbr. Encyclopedia Polymer Sci., Kirk-Othmer Encyclopedia. Home: 48 Green Mountain Dr Freehold NJ 07728 Office: 1411 Broadway New York NY 10018

RICHARDSON, SCOVEL, fed. judge; b. Nashville, Feb. 4, 1912; s. M. Scovel and Capitola W. (Taylor) R.; A.B., U. Ill., 1934, A.M., 1936; J.D., Howard U., 1937; LL.D. (hon.), Lincoln U., 1973; m. Inez Williston, July 3, 1937; children—Elaine Richardson Harrisingh, Alice Inez, Mary Louise Richardson Johnson, Marjorie Linda Richardson Forsythe. Admitted to Ill. bar, 1938, U.S. Supreme Ct. bar, 1943, Mo. bar, 1945; individual practice law, Chgo., 1938-39; asso. prof. law Lincoln U., St. Louis, 1939-43, prof., dean Sch. Law, 1944-53; sr. atty. OPA, Washington, 1943-44; mem. U.S. Bd. Parole, Dept. Justice, 1953, chmn., 1954-57; judge U.S. Customs Ct., N.Y.C., 1957—. Trustee, Colgate U., Howard U., Nat. Council Crime and Delinquency; sec. bd. govs. New Rochelle (N.Y.) Hosp.; mem. adv. bd. Urban League of Westchester County (N.Y.). Recipient Selective Service medal, 1946, Alumni award Howard U. Bd. Trustees, 1958, Wisdom award of Honor, 1970, Internat. Trade Service award Wall St. Synagogue, 1973, Lincoln U. Law Sch. Grads. citation, 1976. Mem. Am., Fed., Nat. (sec. 1947-51, pres. 1951-53, C. Francis Stradford award 1967), Mo., St. Louis, N.Y. bar assns., Am. Law Inst., Kappa Alpha Psi, Sigma Pi Phi. Presbyterian. Contbr. articles to law jours. Office: US Customs Ct One Federal Plaza New York City NY 10007

RICHARDSON, WINONA BELLE, dormitory supr., poet; b. Northwood, N.H., Jan. 9; d. John Hodgdon and Katharyne Eva (O'Connor) R.; B.E., Keene State Coll., 1935; postgrad. Bob Jones U., 1961-62. Tchr. English, N.H. high schs., 1935-43; office positions various state depts. in N.H., 1948-56; sec. to mag. editor; asst. dir. tchr. certification N.H. Edn. Dept., 1968-69; dormitory supr., Concord, N.H., 1969—; columnist Voice of N.H. Poets, poetry editor Concord Shoppers News, 1971—; mem. Nat. Poetry Day Com., Inc., 1969; organizer, dir. N.H. Poetry Week, 1969—, Ann. N.H. Student Poetry Contest, 1971-74, Ann. Capitol City Student Poetry Contest, Concord, 1973-75, N.H. Hosp. Poetry Club, 1970-72. Recipient Freedoms Found. award in poetry, 1968, also various other poetry awards. Mem. Poetry Soc. N.H., N.H. Animal Rights League (founder, chmn.), Concord Soc. Prevention Cruelty to Animals, Humane Soc. U.S., New Eng. Anti-Vivisection Soc. Baptist. Home: 24 Center St Concord NH 03301

RICHART, DOUGLAS STEPHEN, research and devel. chemist; b. Harrisburg, Pa., June 6, 1931; s. Howard Winans and Muriel Matilda (Long) R.; student Pa. State U., 1950-51; B.S., Franklin and Marshall Coll., 1954; m. Avis A. Sholley, June 23, 1953 (dec. 1973); children—Deborah, Sandra, Stephen, Catherine; m. 2d Josephine H. Sargen, Dec. 24, 1973. Coatings research Union Carbide Corp., 1954-60; mgr. powder coating research and devel. Polymer Corp., Reading, Pa., 1960—. Mem. Am. Chem. Soc., Soc. Plastics Engrs. Episcopalian. Contbr. articles to tcach. jours. and books. Patentee in field. Home: 8 Upland Rd Reading PA 19609 Office: 2120 Fairmont Ave Reading PA 19603

RICHETTE, LAWRENCE JARVIS, lawyer; b. Phila., Jan. 9, 1919; s. Anthony John and Philomena (Aquilino) R.; B.S., Temple U., 1940, LL.B., 1948; m. Lisa C. Aversa, Apr. 12, 1958 (div. June 1971); 1 son, Lawrence Anthony II. Instr. Sch. Bus., Temple U., 1946-47; asst. prof. bus. adminstrn. Pa. Mil. Coll., Chester, Pa., 1948; partner Meehan, Neil & Richette, Phila., 1950-60; now pvt. practice; Dir. Phila. Lyric Opera Co. Mem. Republican com. Phila., 1948-58. Served from pvt. to s.sgt. USAF, 1942-45. Mem. Am., Pa., Phila. bar assns., Justinian Soc. (gov., past chancellor), St. Thomas More Soc., Am. Judicature Soc., Am.-Italy Soc. of Phila., Pa. Soc. of N.Y. Republican. Roman Catholic. Clubs: Lawyers, Peale, Phila. City Business (dir., past chmn. bd.) (Phila.). Home: 336 S 2d St Philadelphia PA 19106 Office: 1420 Walnut St Philadelphia PA 19102

RICHMAN, ALAN, mag. pub. and editor; b. Bronx, N.Y., Nov. 12, 1939; s. Louis and Sonia (Carity) R.; B.A., Hunter Coll., 1960; m. Kelli Shor, June 21, 1964; children—Lincoln Seth Shor, Matthew Mackenzie Shor. Reporter, Leader-Observer, weekly newspaper, N.Y.C., 1960-61; asst. editor Modern Tire Dealer, publ., N.Y.C., 1962-64; asso. editor ASTA Travel News, N.Y.C., 1964-65; pub. relations rep. M.J. Jacobs, Inc., advt. agy., N.Y.C., 1965-66; mng. editor Modern Floor Coverings, N.Y.C., 1966-68; editor Bank Systems & Equipment, N.Y.C., 1968—, asso. pub., 1969-71, co-pub., 1971-73, pub., 1973-76; pub., Bank Systems & Equipment Internat., 1976-77; editorial cons. Health Care Product News, N.Y.C., 1976—. Served with AUS, 1961-62. Recipient Jesse H. Neal certificate merit Am. Bus. Press, 1973. Mem. N.Y. Bus. Press Editors Assn. Author: Czechoslovakia in Pictures, 1969; A Book on the Chair, 1968. Home: 5 Clayton Rd Morganville NJ 07751 Office: 1515 Broadway New York City NY 10036

RICHMAN, DANIEL SEYMOUR, food service cons. co. exec.; b. Detroit, Dec. 26, 1939; s. Max and Beatrice Richman; B.S.B.A., Mich. State U., 1966; m. Marjorie Biggerstaff, June 10, 1967; children—Joel, Michael. Dir. personnel Howard Johnson Co., 1966-69; mgr. Red Coach Grill div. Howard Johnson Co., 1969-72, supr., 1972-73; owner, operator Daniel Webster Inn, Sandwich, Mass., 1973, Bert's Restaurants, Hingham and Plymouth, Mass., 1975—; owner, pres. Richman/Fortun Assn. Inc., Plymouth, Mass., 1975—. Pres. Race New Eng., 1978—. Served with U.S. Army, 1961-64. Mem. Nat., Mass. restaurant assns., Plymouth C. of C. (dir.). Democrat. Office: 85 Samoset St Plymouth MA 02360

RICHMAN, JOHN ALFRED, JR., chemist; b. Richmond, Va., Jan. 15, 1930; s. John Alfred and Margaret Virginia (Bowman) R.; B.S., U. Richmond, 1956, M.S., 1968; postgrad. Mass. Inst. Tech., 1966-67, Georgetown U., 1971-72, Va. State Coll., 1968-69; Ph.D., U. Pacific, 1977; m. Susan Elizabeth Capps, Dec. 28, 1967; children—Christopher Steven, Lisa Faye. Asst. elec. engr. Va. Electric & Power, Richmond, 1955-56; mng. chemist control lab. Hercules Powder Co., Hopewell, Va., 1956-58; research chemist A. H. Robins Pharm. Co., Richmond, 1958-68; chemistry instr. Va. Commonwealth U., Richmond, 1965-66; chemist, group leader in research Firestone Co., Hopewell, 1968-69; sr. reviewing chemist Bur. Drugs, FDA, Rockville, Md., 1969—, chmn. info. retrieval com., 1975—. Bd. dirs. Fed. Credit Union, 1976-77. Served with USN, 1950-54. Recipient Merit Achievement award FDA, 1975. Mem. Am. Inst. Chemists, Am. Assn. Analytical Chemists, Sigma Xi, Theta Tau. Episcopalian. Clubs: Sailing of Parklawn, Olympic. Author: A Qualitative Study of the Bohlmann Band, 1967; Novel Psychopharmacologic Drugs, 1977; patentee in field. Home: 12212 Millstream Dr Bowie MD 20715 Office: 5600 Fishers Ln Rockville MD 20857

RICHMAN, PETER, cons. electronics engr., electronics mfg. co. exec.; b. N.Y.C., Nov. 7, 1927; s. Emil H. and Janet (Seidler) R.; B.S., Mass. Inst. Tech., 1946; M.S., N.Y. U., 1953; m. Vivian Hoffman, July 29, 1951; children—Meredith, Jeremy. Asst. chief engr. Reeves Instrument Corp., Garden City, N.Y., 1948-58; chief engr. Epsco, Inc., Cambridge, Mass., 1959-60; v.p., co-founder Rotek Instrument Corp., Watertown, Mass., 1960-64; v.p. Weston-Rotek, Lexington, Mass., 1964-67; cons. electronics engr., Lexington, 1967—; founder, pres. KeyTek Instrument Corp., 1976—; mem. NRC/Nat. Acad. Scis./Nat. Acad. Engring. Evaluation Panel for electricity div. Nat. Bur. Standards; mem. sci. adv. groups for several indsl. and sci. orgns. Fellow IEEE; mem. Instrument Soc. Am. (sr.), Sigma Xi, Tau Beta Pi. Patentee in precision electronic instrumentation; pioneer in precision dc and audio-frequency measurements, surge generation and measurements. Contbr. articles to profl. jours. Address: Lexington MA 02173

RICHMAN, SEYMOUR, pub. relations exec.; b. N.Y.C., Sept. 21, 1930; s. Morris and Ida (Topor) R.; B.S.S. in Social Psychology, Coll. City N.Y., 1952; postgrad. N.Y. U., 1952-53; m. Marjorie Levy, Aug. 23, 1953; children—Charles Jay, Ann Debra. Account exec. Myron Jonas Co. Inc., 1952-53; exec. v.p. Lee-Stockman Inc., 1953-54; advt. mgr. Auth Electric Co., Inc., 1955-56; asst. to pres. Greer Hydraulics, Inc., N.Y.C., 1956-58; pres. Dunwoodie Assos., Inc., N.Y.C., 1958-71, Dunwoodie Consultants, Inc., Garden City, N.Y., 1965-71, Dunwoodie Communications Inc., 1971—; chmn., treas. Schacher-Greentree & Co., Inc., 1977—. Bd. dirs. Greater Flushing YM and YWHA, 1966—, treas., 1970-71, v.p., 1972-73, pres., 1974-77. Club: Sales Executives (N.Y.). Home: 35-20 165th St Flushing NY 11358 Office: 211 E 43d St New York City NY 10017

RICHMOND, ERNEST LEON, mech. engr.; b. Catskill, N.Y., Sept. 11, 1914; s. Leon J. and Beulah B. R.; student Casey Jones Sch. Aeros., 1934-35, Antioch Coll., 1936-39; B.M.E. cum laude, Clarkson Coll. Tech., 1942; postgrad. N.J. Inst. Tech., 1959-61, Rutgers U., 1961-64; m. Constance Vroom, Oct. 9, 1943. Test engr. Mack Trucks Co., Plainfield, N.J., 1936-45; with Plainfield works Worthington Corp., 1945-58, asst. chief engr., 1952-56, chief engr., 1956-58; research engr. Ethicon, Inc. div. Johnson & Johnson, Somerville, N.J., 1958-75, ret., 1975; cons. Logos Internat., Plainfield, 1975—; mem. speakers' bur. Worthington Corp., 1950-58. Basketball coach YMCA, Plainfield, Church League, Plainfield. Licensed profl. engr., N.J. Mem. ASME (life), Nat., N.J., Union County (N.J.) socs. profl. engrs., Am. Electroplaters' Soc., Tau Beta Pi (life). Republican. Presbyterian. Contbr. articles on engring. analysis to profl. jours. Patentee electropolishing method, apparatus. Home: 1275 Rock Ave Apt F-1 North Plainfield NJ 07060 Office: PO Box 314 Dunellen NJ 08812

RICHMOND, FREDERICK WILLIAM, congressman, industrialist; b. Boston, Nov. 15, 1923; s. George and Frances (Rosen) R.; student Harvard, 1942-43; A.B., Boston U., 1945; LL.D., Pratt Inst.; 1 son, William McNeir. Engaged in import-export bus., 1945-49; chmn. bd. Brubaker Tool Corp., Millersburg, Pa., 1950-57; chmn. exec. com., dir. Nat. Valve & Mfg. Co., Pitts., 1955—, Landers, Frary & Clark, New Britain, Conn., 1958-60; chmn. bd. Houston Oil Field Material Co., Inc., 1958-62, Pub. Service Radio Network, Inc., N.Y.C., 1961—; pres. F. W. Richmond & Co., Inc., East Island Devel. Corp., N.Y.C., and subsidiaries, Carthage Machine Co., N.Y., Fed. Drop Forge Co., Lansing, Mich., Lansing Drop Forge Co., Lansing, Gen. Industries, Elyria, O., Capitol Machine Co., Columbus, O., Mitts & Merrill Inc., Saginaw, Mich., Nat. Casket Co., Boston; chmn. bd. Walco-Linck Corp., Clifton, N.J., 1961—; mem. 94th and 95th Congresses from 14th N.Y. dist., mem. Agr. com., Welfare Reform subcom. Mem. City Council, City of N.Y., 1973-75. Chmn. emeritus Gov.'s Com. on Sch. Achievement; mem. N.Y.C. Commn. on Human Rights, 1962-67; pres. Community Improvement Corp. of Manhattan, Neighborhood Study Clubs, Inc.; chmn. N.Y.C. Businessmen's Com. for Employment Ex-offenders; pres. Frederick W. Richmond Found.; hon. chmn. Young Audiences, Inc. Chmn. bd. Carnegie Hall Corp., N.Y.C.; dir. N.Y. World's Fair 1964 Corp.; trustee Citizens Union, Citizens Budget Commn.; mem. N.Y. Council Arts. Served with USNR, 1943-45. Recipient Outstanding Young Man award Jr. C. of C., N.Y.C., 1955. Mem. Urban League Greater N.Y. (hon. pres.), Americans for Democratic Action (v.p. 1977—). Democrat. Author: The Need for Businessmen to Become Active in Politics: Corporate Integration. Home: 43 Pierrepont St Brooklyn NY 11201 Office: 743 Fifth Ave New York City NY 10022 also 147 Montague St Brooklyn NY 11201

RICHMOND, ROBERT PRICE, author; b. Jersey City, Dec. 14, 1914; s. Ralph P. and Rebecca (Holtz) R.; student pub. schs.; m. Frances M. Chaffee, Sept. 21, 1940 (dec. Feb. 1971); children—Robert C., Carol Stone, Marion Dwyer; m. 2d, Evelyn L. Blake, Feb. 12, 1973. Payroll supr. VA, White River Junction, Vt., 1947-72; author: Escape on Ice Skates, 1963; Day the Indians Came, 1966; Powder for Bunker Hill, 1968; Powder Alarm—1774, 1971; John Stark—Freedom Fighter, 1976. Served with AUS, 1943-46. Mem. N.H. Hist. Soc. Contbr. articles to mags., hist. publs. Home: 51 Springdale Ave Waterbury CT 06708

RICHMOND, WALTER ELLIOTT, educator; b. Bklyn., June 30, 1921; s. Madison Elliott and Mable (Hunt) R.; A.B., Syracuse U., 1942, M.A., 1947, M.S., 1963; m. Janis Arlene King, Aug. 17, 1947; children—Gregg, Janine. Tchr. math. Oxford (N.Y.) Acad. and Central Sch., 1947-50, head dept. math., 1950-58; tchr. sci. and math. Campus Sch., State U. N.Y. at Oswego, 1958-65, chmn. jr. high, 1961-65, asso. prof. math. edn., 1965—, undergrad. advisement coordinator, 1968—. Active YMCA, Boy Scouts Am. Served with AUS, 1942-46. NSF research grantee, 1959; NSF summer fellow, 1960-63. Mem. N.Y. State Tchrs. Assn. (ho. of dels. 1961), N.E.A., Phi Delta Kappa, Sigma Pi Sigma, Pi Mu Epsilon, Kappa Phi Kappa. Methodist. Mason. Home: 158 E Utica St Oswego NY 13126

RICHTER, HOWARD S., physician; b. Paterson, N.J., Apr. 8, 1932; s. Irving and Helen (Grossman) R.; B.S. in Physics, Rutgers U., 1953; M.D., Jefferson Med. Coll., 1957; m. Linda Notkin, Dec. 27, 1955; children—Michael, Ronni. Intern, Pa. Hosp., Phila., 1960-61; resident in medicine Tufts-New Eng. Med. Center and Harvard-Beth Israel Hosp., Boston, 1960-63; practice medicine specializing in internal medicine, Woburn, Mass., 1963—; chmn. dept. internal medicine Choate Meml. Hosp., Woburn, 1976—. Served with M.C., USAF, 1958-60. Diplomate Am. Bd. Internal Medicine. Fellow A.C.P.; mem. Mass., Middlesex East Dist. med. socs., Am., Mass. socs. internal medicine. Jewish. Home: 26 Suzanne Rd Lexington MA 02173 Office: 53 Pleasant St Woburn MA 01801

RICHTER, VIRGIL JOHN, chemist; b. St. Cloud, Minn., Sept. 5, 1925; s. Arthur H. and Gertrude (Welle) R.; B.A., Whitman Coll., 1948; M.S., Ohio State U., 1950; m. Eloise S. Sipley, June 26, 1948; children—John, Patricia, Frederick, Marilyn, Lisa. With Colgate Palmolive Co., Piscataway, N.J., 1950—, research chemist, 1950-55, group leader exploratory oral products, 1955-60, sect. head household products, 1960—. Served to lt. USNR, 1943-46. Mem. Am. Chem. Soc., Am. Oil Chem. Soc., Sigma Xi. Roman Catholic. Patents and publs. in field. Office: 909 River Rd Piscataway NJ 08854

RICKELS, KARL, physician, educator; b. Wilhelmshaven, Germany, Aug. 17, 1924; s. Karl E. and Stephanie (Roehrhoff) R.; M.D., U. Muenster, 1951; m. Rosalind Wilson, June 27, 1964; children—Laurence Arthur, Stephen W., Michael R. Came to U.S., 1954, naturalized, 1960. Intern, Dortmund (Germany) Hosp., 1951-52; postgrad. tng. U. Erlangen, U. Frankfurt, City Hosp. Kassel, 1952-54; resident in psychiatry Mental Health Inst., Cherokee, Iowa, 1954-55; resident in psychiatry Hosp. U. Pa., Phila., 1955-57; instr. U. Pa., Phila., 1957-59, asso., 1959-60, asst. prof., 1960-64, asso. prof., 1964-69, prof. psychiatry, 1969—, prof. pharmacology 1973—, Stuart and Emily B.H. Mudd prof. human behavior and reprodn., 1977—, dir. psychopharmacology research unit, 1964—, attending physician, dir. psychopharmacology research unit, 1964—; chief psychiatry Phila. Gen. Hosp., 1975-77. Fellow Am. Coll. Neuropsychopharmacology (charter), Acad. Psychosomatic Medicine, Am. Psychiat. Assn., Royal Soc. Medicine; mem. A.M.A., Am. Soc. for Clin. Pharmacology and Therapeutics, Soc. for Pharmacology and Exptl. Therapeutics, Am. Psychosomatic Soc., Collegium International Neuro-Psychopharmacologicum. Contbr. numerous articles to profl. publs. Home: 1518 Sweetbriar Rd Gladwyne PA 19035 Office: 203 Piersol Bldg Hosp of U Pa 3400 Spruce St Philadelphia PA 19104

RICKETSON, ROBERT BRADFORD, silverware co. exec.; b. Taunton, Sept. 17, 1930; s. Ralph Lewis and Janet Beatrice (Hunter) R.; student Lehigh U., Brown U.; m. Carol Gretchen Schmidt, Dec. 27, 1950; children—Robert Bradford Jr., Jon C., Keith H., Mark P. Mgr. order control Raytheon Co., N. Dighton, Mass., 1958-60; prodn. mgr. Poole Silver Co., Taunton, 1960-66; prodn. control mgr., new goods mgr. Reed & Barton Co., Taunton, 1966—. Bd. dirs. United Way; chmn. trustees Taunton State Hosp.; pres. Prep. Rehab. for Individual Devel. and Employment Community Workshop; chmn. Cub Scouts; mem. Republican City Com. Served with USAF, 1948-52. Recipient Merit certificate Mass. Dept. Mental Health. Mem. Taunton C. of C., Am. Prodn. and Inventory Control Soc., Taunton Mgmt. Club. Episcoplaian. Club: Masons. Home: 6 Edwards Ave Taunton MA 02780 Office: 144 Britannnia St W Taunton MA 02780

RIDDICK, FLOYD MILLARD, parliamentarian; b. Trotville, N.C., July 13, 1908; s. John Bembry and Helen (Blanchard) R.; B.A., Duke, 1931, Ph.D., 1935; M.A., Vanderbilt U., 1932; m. Marguerite Louise Faerber, Feb. 24, 1940; children—Johanne Marjorie (Mrs. Riddick-Betsch), John Lindsay, Carol Dianne (Mrs. Panos Spiliotakos). Statis. analyst Fed. Govt., 1935-36; instr. polit. sci. Am. U., 1936-39; asso. Congl. Intelligence, Inc., Washington, 1939-43; legislative research dept. law and govt. Columbia, 1942-43; legislative analyst U.S. C. of C., 1943-47; editor Senate sec. Daily Digest of Congl. Record, 1947-51; asst. parliamentarian U.S. Senate, Washington, 1951-64, parliamentarian, 1965-74, ret., 1974, parliamentarian emeritus, cons. to Senate Com. on Rules and Adminstrn., 1974—; instr., professorial lectr. George Washington U., 1944-70. Spl. research project and study U. Berlin, Germany, 1937-38. Decorated officer's cross Order of Merit Fed. Republic Germany, 1975. Club: Cosmos (Distinguished Service citation 1975) (Washington). Author: Congressional Procedure, 1941; (with George H. E. Smith) Congress in Action, 1948 49, 53; U.S. Congress: Organization and Procedure, 1949; (with Charles L. Watkins) Senate Procedure, 1958, 64; Senate Procedure, 1974. Contbr. articles to profl. jours. Office: Senate Office Bldg Room 305 Washington DC 20510

RIDDLE, ROBERT LEWIS, electronics co. exec.; b. Smithland, Iowa, Oct. 28, 1922; s. Ingersoll J and Emma Isabel (Foster) R.; B.S. in Elec. Engring., State U. Iowa, 1949, M.S. in Elec. Engring., 1951, postgrad., 1954-55; m. Margaret Jane Stover, Apr. 15, 1954; children—Deborah Ann, Patricia Jean. Asst. prof. elec. engring. Pa. State U., State College, 1951-56; with HRB Singer Inc., State Coll., 1956-68, v.p. electronic systems, 1964-68; pres. Locus Inc., State College, 1968—; cons. Collins Radio, Cedar Rapids, Iowa, 1954-55. Served with AUS, 1943-46, USAF, 1950-51. Mem. Air Force Assn., Sigma Xi, Eta Kappa Nu, Tau Beta Pi. Democrat. Methodist. Author: (with M.P. Ristenbatt) Transistor Physics and Circuits, 1958. Home: 201 Twigs Ln State College PA 16801 Office: 1012 E Boal Ave Boalsburg PA 16827

RIDEOUT, BLANCHARD LIVINGSTONE, univ. ofcl.; b. Johannesburg, South Africa, Apr. 28, 1906 (parents Am. citizens); A.B., Harvard U., 1927, A.M., 1930; Ph.D., Cornell U., 1936; m. 1937; 2 children. Instr. in French and Spanish, U. Vt., 1927-28; instr. in Romance langs., tutor div. modern lang. Harvard U., 1928-30, tutor Radcliffe Coll., 1929-30; instr. in French, U. Rochester, 1930-33; asst. prof. Romance langs. and lit. Cornell U., 1937-42, asso. prof., 1942-52, prof., 1952-71, emeritus prof. Romance studies, 1971—, in charge admissions Coll. Arts and Sci., 1940-52, dir. Navy program, 1943-45, asst. dean, 1946-52, dir. div. unclassified students, 1952-65, project dir. Peace Corps Tng. program, Peru, summers 1962, 64, 65, Sierra Leone, summer 1963, univ. marshal, 1951—, sec. univ., 1966-71; prof. in charge jr. yr. in France, Sweet Briar Coll., 1949-50, 56-57; tng. officer, cons. Peace Corps, Washington, 1964-65; dir. Middlebury Coll. Grad. Sch. French, France, 1965-66; escort, interpreter in French, Dept. State, Washington, 1971—; lectr. cruises S.S. France, 1972-74. Mem. Modern Lang. Assn., AAUP. Author: (with Wilson Micks) Témoins d'une époque, 1947. Home: 110 Midway Rd Ithaca NY 14850

RIDEOUT, DAVID FRANK, radiologist; b. Bedford, Eng., Feb. 21, 1931; s. Sidney and Hilda Rose (Davis) R.; came to Can., 1968, naturalized, 1974; M.B., U. Coll. Med. Sch., (London), 1954, B.S., 1954, D.M.R.D., 1961; m. Grizel Margaret Patrick, June 23, 1955; children—Sarah Jane, Susan Fiona, Miles David, Guy Michael. Intern, U. Coll. Hosp., London, 1954; resident in Internal medicine New End Hosp., London, 1958-60; resident in radiology Middlesex Hosp., London, 1960-64; radiologist in charge Princess Alexandra Hosp., Essex, Eng., 1965-68; dir. diagnostic radiology Princess Margaret Hosp. and Ont. (Can.) Cancer Inst., Toronto, 1968—; prof. U. Toronto, 1968—. Served to capt. Royal Army Med. Corps., 1955-57. Recipient Liston Gold Medal for surgery, 1953. Fellow Royal Coll. Radiology (Eng.), Royal Coll. Physicians and Surgeons (Can.), Acad. Medicine Toronto; mem. Am. Coll. Radiology, Am. Thermographic Soc., Canadian Thermographic Assn. (pres. 1977), Canadian Oncology Soc. (dir.), Paleeopathology Soc. Baptist. Club: Joseph Lister. Home: 160 Forest Hill Rd Toronto ON M5P 2M9 Canada Office: 500 Sherbourne St Toronto ON M4X 1K9 Canada

RIDER, ALLEN BURR, JR., pub. co. exec.; b. Brookline, Mass., May 29, 1913; s. Allen Burr and Mable (Whitcomb) R.; A.B., Harvard, 1935; M.B.A., Boston U., 1960; m. Mima Borland Robertson, Feb. 17, 1940; children—Linda (Mrs. William A. Royall, Jr.), Gillian (Mrs. Howard Stone Perkins), Allen Burr III. Mgr. Frontier Press Co., Boston, 1935-47, owner, 1947—; exec. v.p., dir. Frontier Press Co., Columbus, Ohio, 1959—. Bd. dirs. Animal Rescue League, Boston; trustee Eliot Sch., Boston. Served with USNR, 1944-46. Decorated Bronze Star. Mem. Profl. Bookmen Am. (sec. 1953-67). Episcopalian. Rotarian. Clubs: Harvard (Boston); Brookline (Mass.) Thursday. Home: 131 Dunster Rd Boston MA 02130 Office: 25 Huntington Ave Boston MA 02116

RIDER, KENNETH LLOYD, mgmt. cons.; b. N.Y.C., July 8, 1943; s. Frederick Cregier and Mildred Elaine (Cohen) R.; A.B., Columbia, 1965; Ph.D., Yale, 1970; research asso. dept. physics City Coll. N.Y., 1970-72; mgmt. systems analyst N.Y.C.-Rand Inst., 1972-74, project leader fire protection studies, 1974-75; spl. asst. to state spl. dep. comptroller for N.Y.C., dir. spl. services, 1975-78; sr. cons. Deloitte Haskins & Sells, 1978—. Trustee, Nat. Task Force for Disability and the Arts, Inc. NSF fellow, 1965-67; Nat. Merit scholar. Mem. Am. Economic Assn., Inst. Mgmt. Scis., Ops. Research Soc., IEEE, Assn. for Computing Machinery, Nat. Fire Protection Assn. (com. on fire reporting), Sigma Xi. Club: Yale of N.Y.C. Asso. editor Mgmt. Sci.; contbr. articles on pub. policy and mgmt. sci. to profl. jours. Home: 60 E 8th St New York City NY 10003 Office: Deloitte Haskins & Sells 2 Broadway New York City NY 10004

RIDER, WILLIAM DECKER, banker; b. Bridgeport, Conn., Apr. 21, 1924; s. Ernest Walters and Irene (Decker) R.; B.A., Yale, 1947; M.B.A., Columbia, 1960; student Grad. Sch. Savs. Banking, Brown U., 1966; m. Virginia Gregory Walters, June 27, 1953; children—Ann Sherwood, Debra Walters, Carolyn Decker. With People's Savs. Bank, Bridgeport, 1947-70, auditor, 1956-66, v.p., investment officer, 1967-70; exec. v.p. Derby Savs. Bank (Conn.), 1970-71; sr. v.p. Middletown Savs. Bank (N.Y.), 1971-74; pres. Citizens Savs. Bank Stamford (Conn.), 1974—. Asst. treas. Pomperaug council Boy Scouts Am., 1957-70, dir. Fairfield County Council, 1976—; chmn. organizing com. Conn. Sch. Savs. Banking, Hartford and Bridgeport, 1962-64; bd. dirs. Orange County Adv. Com. on Housing, 1973-74, Stamford-Darien Homemakers Service, 1974-78, Voluntary Action Center Southwestern Fairfield County, Rehab. Center Southwestern Conn. Served with AUS, 1943-45, USAAF, 1945-46. Mem. Savs. Banks Assn. Conn. (chmn. Group III exec. com., mem. assn. exec. com.), Bank Adminstrn. Inst. (New Haven pres. 1960-61, Conn. dir. 1962-64), Am. Inst. Banking (instr. 1961-70), Inst. Chartered Financial Analysts, N.Y. Soc. Security Analysts, Newcomen Soc. N. Am., Mid-Orange County C. of C. (dir. 1972-74), Stamford Area Commerce and Industry Assn. (dir. 1975, v.p., sec. 1976, vice chmn. 1978—). Congregationalist. Clubs: Midtown (Stamford); Woodway Country (Darien); Rotary. Home: 634 Silvermine Rd New Canaan CT 06840 Office: 65 Bank St Stamford CT 06904

RIDGELY, HENRY JOHNSON, lawyer; b. Camden, Del., Nov. 17, 1913; s. Charles duPont and Helene Marjorie (Rudolph) R.; A.B., U. Del., 1935; J.D., George Washington U., 1939; m. Mary Lillie Berry, Dec. 3, 1938 (dec.); children—Nicholas, Henry duPont; m. 2d, Gloria Jailler, Sept. 9, 1967 (div.); 1 son, John Henry; m. 3d, Sandra M. Maybee, Mar. 16, 1974. Admitted to D.C. bar, 1939, Del. bar, 1940, U.S. Supreme Ct. bar, 1943; practiced in Dover, 1940—; sr. partner firm Ridgely & Ridgely; dep. atty. gen. of Del. for Kent County, 1943, 47-54; atty. Kent County Levy Court, 1947-49; revised Code Commn., 1949-53; dir. Legislative Reference Bur. (Chief counsel to gov. and Gen. Assembly), 1957-61; dir. Del. R.R. Co., div. Penn Central R.R., 1966-78. Del. commn. Shell Fish, 1943, commn. for Feebleminded, 1955-56; vice chmn. econ. devel. com. Gov. Del. Tomorrow Project, 1974-77; mem. Del. Code Revision Commn., 1957-61, Del. Rep. Nat. Conv., 1952, 56; bd. dirs. Del. Humane Soc., Kent County Arts Council; 1st chmn. Del. Bd. Pension Trustees, 1970-74; bd. dirs. Del. State Ballet. Served as lt. USNR, 1943-46. Mem. Inter-Am., Am., Del. (v.p. 1962-64), Fed., Kent County (pres. 1967-68) bar assns., Am. Judicature Soc., Hist. Soc. Del., Hist. Soc. Md., Hist. Soc. Pa., Am. Trial Lawyers Assn., Nat. Assn. Railroad Trial Counsel, Chesapeake Bay Yacht Racing Assn., Air Force Assn., SAR, Magna Charter Barons, Sigma Nu. Episcopalian. Republican. Clubs: Mason (32 deg., K.T., Shriner); Blue and Gold (U. Del.); Church of Del. (pres. 1961-63); Tred Avon Yacht, Amateur Radio. Home: Spruce Haven RD2 Box 194A Camden DE 19934 Office: 307 S State St PO D C Dover DE 19901

RIDGELY, JOSEPHINE JONES, nurse; b. Clairton, Pa., Jan. 19, 1920; d. Joseph William and Rosa Elanor (Manigault) J.; R.N., Harlem Hosp. Sch. of Nursing, 1941; B.S. in Nursing Edn., N.Y. U., 1948; M.Litt., U. Pitts., 1955; m. Paul Cromwell Ridgely, Aug. 19, 1961. Staff nurse Harlem Hosp., N.Y.C., 1942-50; clin. instr. St. Francis Hosp., Pitts., 1950-51; staff nurse, clin. instr. Montefiore Hosp., Pitts., 1951-61; operating room supr. Brownsville (Pa.) Hosp., 1961-66; adminstrv. supr. Uniontown (Pa.) Hosp., 1966—. Registered nurse, Pa., N.Y. Mem. Am. Nurses Assn., Assn. Operating Room Nurses (pres. Pa. and W.Va. 1963-67), NAACP, Nat. Council Negro Women (life), Mental Health Assn. Mem. African Methodist Episcopal Ch. Home: Howell St Dawson PA 15428

RIDKER, CAROL MAY, ceramist; b. Newark, Dec. 4, 1934; d. Arthur and Frances R. (Cohen) Eisner; student U. Wis., 1952-55; B.A., Washington U., St. Louis, 1957; postgrad. Syracuse U., 1964-65, Corcoran Sch., Art, 1965-67; m. Ronald Ridker, Sept. 6, 1955; children—Anne, Paul. One-woman exhbns.: New Delhi, India, 1968, Woodbridge, N.J., 1971, Richmond, Va., 1972, St. Louis, 1973, Washington, 1970-78; numerous regional and nat. group shows, including: Knoll Internat., Washington, 1974, Phila. Art Alliance, 1973, Marietta Nat., 1974; represented in permanent collections: Mus. Fine Arts, Salt Lake City, Phila. Mus.; instr. Corcoran Sch. Art, 1967; adj. prof. dept. art Am. U., Washington, 1976—; cons. All India Handicraft Bd., 1967-69, 73. Recipient 1st prize Creative Crafts Biennial, Washington, 1970, Ceramics prize Md. Craft Council, 1976. Mem. Am. Crafts Council, Washington Kiln Club (1st prize 1971, 2d prize 1972). Travels, lectures, demonstrations in Japan, 1967, 73, India, 1967-69, 73, 78, Thailand, 1967, Indonesia, 1972, Spain, 1974, 75, Colombia, 1975, 76, Mexico, 1975, Peru, 1976. Home and Office: 9121 Burdette Rd Bethesda MD 20034

RIDOLFI, SIDO LOUIS, state senator, lawyer; b. Trenton, N.J., Sept. 28, 1913; s. Joseph and Silvia (Ceccarelli) R.; A.B., Princeton, 1936; LL.B., Harvard, 1939; postgrad. math., navigation N.Y. U., 1944, Seamen's Ch. Inst., N.Y.C., U.S. Coast Guard Acad., 1944; m. Beatrice Agabiti, June 19, 1946; children—Robert, Jane, Susan. Admitted to N.J. bar, 1940, since practiced in Trenton; sheriff Mercer County (N.J.), 1947-50; commr. City Trenton, 1951-57; mem. N.J. Senate, 1953-72, minority leader, 1955-66, majority leader, 1966, pres., 1967. Mem. schs. and scholarships com. Princeton U. Bds. dirs. Trenton Vis. Nurses Assn., Trenton Am. Cancer Soc., Multiple Sclerosis Soc., Boys Club Trenton, Mercer County Cerebral Palsy Assn. Served with USCGR, 1942-46. Mem. Mercer County Bar Assn. (pres. 1952), N.J. Assn. for Retarded Children (dir.). Home: River Rd Titusville NJ 08560 Office: 3131 Princeton Pike Lawrenceville NJ 08648

RIECK, JONN PAUL, chemist, educator; b. Millville, N.J., Dec. 15, 1943; s. Leonard Harry and Eleanor Ida (Reeves) R.; B.S., Glassboro State Coll., 1966; postgrad. Beaver Coll., Glenside, Pa., 1968, Bowdoin Coll., 1971; postgrad. Fla. Inst. Tech., Melbourne, 1975—; m. Joyce Marie Hand, Oct. 14, 1967; 1 dau., Lisa Marie. Passenger trainman, freight brakeman Pa.-Reading Seashore Lines R.R., Camden, N.J., 1962-66; tchr. chemistry Millville (N.J.) Sr. High Sch., 1966-70; mgmt. trainee Wheaton Glass Co., Millville, 1970-71; tchr. chemistry Vineland (N.J.) Sr. High Sch., 1971—, head sci. dept., 1974—. Sec., Downe Twp. Planning Bd., Newport, N.J., 1976-78, sec.-treas., 1978—. N.J. Dept. Edn. grantee, 1972. Mem. AAAS, Am. Chem. Soc., N.J., Nat., Vineland edn. assns., N.J. Assn. Secondary Sch. Prins. and Suprs., Nat. Sci. Tchrs. Assn., Notaries Pub. N.J., Am. Soc. Notaries, Model Train Collectors Assn. Home: PO Box 433 Newport NJ 08345 Office: Sci Dept Vineland Sr High Sch 2880 E Chestnut Ave Vineland NJ 08360

RIEDL, JOHN ORTH, educator; b. Milw., June 10, 1905; s. Lucas Henry and Olive (Orth) R.; A.B., Marquette U., 1927, A.M., 1928, Ph.D., 1930; postgrad. U. Wis., 1930-32, U. Toronto, 1930, 37, Columbia U., 1934, 36, U. Breslau, Germany, 1938-39; m. Clare Carmelita Quirk, Aug. 17, 1932; children—Annelore, John Orth, Joseph, Paul, Rose Virginie, William. Mem. faculty dept. philosophy Marquette U., 1930-46, 54-66, asso. prof., 1944-46, named prof., 1954-66, dean Grad. Sch., 1954-60; dean faculty, prof. philosophy Queensborough Community Coll., City U. N.Y., Bayside, 1966-75, prof. emeritus, 1975—, dean-in-charge, 1966-67; chief of Catholic affairs, Office Mil. Govt. for Germany, 1946-48, chief edn. br., 1948-49, chief edn. br. Office U.S. High Commr. for Germany, 1949-52, pub. affairs officer Pub. Affairs Field Center, Freiburg, Germany, 1952-53; research writer, N.Y.C., 1953-54; staff, faculty Naval Res. Officers Sch., Milw., 1957-58; staff U.S. Naval War Coll., Newport, R.I., 1962. Cons. mgmt. research, Gen. Electric Co., 1960. Adv. bd. Wis. Conf. Christians and Jews, 1956-66; mem. citizen consultation com. U.S. Nat. Commn. for UNESCO, 1957-61; mem. Bd. Fgn. Scholarships 1958-63. Served from lt. (j.g.) to lt. comdr., USNR, 1942-45. Mem. Religious Edn. Assn. U.S. and Can., Metaphys. Soc. Am., Am. Philos. Assn., Charles S. Pierce Soc., Hegel Soc. Am., Am. Cath. Philos. Assn. (pres. 1935), Midwest Conf. on Grad. Study and Research (chmn. 1958), Nat. Conf. Christians and Jews (commn. on ednl. orgns. 1957-61), Das Delphische Institut, Mainz, Germany (hon. com. 1953—), Am. Assn. for Higher Edn., Cath. Commn. on Intellectual and Cultural Affairs, Societe Thomiste Belgium, Alpha Sigma Nu. Author: Exercises in Logic: A Catalogue of Renaissance Philosophers; The University in Process, 1965. Translator: Giles of Rome, Errores Philosophorum. Home: 42-19 219 St Bayside NY 11361 Office: Queensborough Community Coll Bayside NY 11364

RIEGER, HENRY VICTOR, JR., banker; b. Balt., Feb. 14, 1938; s. Henry Victor and Albertina Florence (DuVall) R.; B.S., Johns Hopkins, 1965; grad. Rutgers U. Stonier Sch. Banking, 1972; m. Anne Marie Orr, June 6, 1959; children—Suzanne Joy, Stephen Victor. With Union Trust Co. Md., Balt., 1959—, loan officer, asst. v.p., 1967-73, comml. unit head, v.p., 1973-75, head loan adminstrn., sr. loan officer, 1975—, head div. credit policy and adminstrn., 1978—; adviser Md. Composition Co., Inc., 1971—; credit com. Union Tidewater Leasing Co., 1975—. Mem. adv. bd. Balt. dist. SBA, 1975—; mem. Johns Hopkins Task Force, 1976; team capt., adviser Hopkins 100's, 1975. Served with Army N.G., 1961. Mem. Robert Morris Assos. (pres. Chesapeake chpt. 1978), Nat. Assn. Credit Mgmt., Am. Inst. Banking, Balt. Jr. C. of C. (Key Man award 1969, Outstanding Jaycee Grad. award 1974, v.p. 1970, Senator), Johns Hopkins U., Kappa Alpha alumni assns. Roman Catholic. Clubs: Hopkins, Center, Greenspring Racquet, Nativity Men's, Roland Run. Home: 221 E Timonium Rd Timonium MD 21093 Office: Baltimore and St Paul Sts Baltimore MD 21203

RIEGER, ROBERT ALLEN, optical products exec.; b. N.Y.C., Oct. 26, 1950; s. Andrew and Edna May (Armstrong) R.; B. Ceramic Engring., Ga. Inst. Tech., 1972, M.S. in Ceramic Engring., 1973; M.B.A., Syracuse U., 1977; m. Susan Patricia Kunze, July 29, 1972; children—Diane Karen, Robert James. Research engr. melting tech. Corning Glass Works (N.Y.), 1973-74, sr. research engr., 1974, sr. process control engr. Erwin Automotive plant, 1974-76, sr. engr. phys. properties optical engring. dept., 1976-77, now supr. tech. mktg. optical products. Dist. commr. Big High Horse dist. Boy Scouts Am., 1975; pres., elder Redeemer Luth. Ch., Corning, 1975—. Mem. Am. Ceramic Soc., Nat. Inst. Ceramic Engrs., Nat. Eagle Scout Assn., Mensa, Keramos, Sigma Xi. Home: 3547 Park Terr Horseheads NY 14845 Office: Corning Glass Works Corning NY 14830

RIEGGER, WILLIAM JOSEPH, SR., naval electronics engring. adminstr.; b. Balt., Sept. 30, 1920; s. William George and Marie Elizabeth (Stock) R.; A.B. in Physics, Allegheny Coll., 1942; postgrad. George Washington U., 1942-44, 57-59, U. Md., 1950-53; m. Nena Sasuta, Nov. 14, 1947; children—Catherine Marie, William Joseph. Electronic scientist Naval Research Lab., Washington, 1942-44, 45-51; br. head, electronics engr., Bur. Ships, 1951-66; capt. U.S. Navy, 1966; br. head, electronics engr., Naval Electronic Systems Command, Washington, 1966-75, tech. dir., test and evaluation coordination office Naval Electronic Systems Command, Washington, 1975—; mem. elec. electronic standards mgmt. bd. Am. Nat. Standards Inst.; mem. adv. group electron devices Dept. Def., 1951—. Served with USNR, 1944-45. Recipient commendation Commandant 5th Naval Dist., Norfolk, Va., 1959; citation Research Engring., Dir. Def., 1966. Mem. Am. Phys. Soc., Inst. Radio Engrs., Am. Soc. Naval Engrs., Profl. Assn. Naval Engrs. and Scientists. Russian Orthodox. Contbr. articles to profl. jours. Home: 9920 Indian Queen Point Rd Oxon Hill MD 20022 Office: Naval Electronic Systems Command ELEX 05E Washington DC 20360

RIENDEAU, LEONARD JOSEPH, educator; b. Holyoke, Mass., Aug. 13, 1936; s. Leo Joseph and Linda Caroline (Molino) R.; B.S., Emerson Coll., 1964, M.S., 1965. Actor, stage mgr. Somers (Conn.) Playhouse, 1954-60; asst. mgr. Court Sq. Theater, Springfield, Mass., 1961, Arcade Theater, Springfield, 1962-63; producer The Beautiful Jailer, Actor's Playhouse, N.Y.C., 1963; prof., dir. secondary sch. drama Emerson Coll., 1965—; v.p. New Eng. Theatre Conf., 1970-71. Mem. AAUP, Speech Communication Assn., Theatre Hist. Soc. Am. Author: Public Reaction Toward the Actor After the Assassination of Abraham Lincoln, 1965. Home: 85 Charles St Boston MA 02114 Office: Emerson Coll 148 Beacon St Boston MA 02116

RIENDEAU, ROBERT, charitable assn. exec.; b. Montreal, Que., Can., May 6, 1922; s. Rene and Hortense (Prieur) R.; B.A., Jesuits' Coll., 1944; postgrad. in theology Montreal U., 1944-48; M.A., Montreal Sch. Social Work, U. Montreal, 1954. Dir., Community Welfare Council Diocese of Montreal, 1954-64; dir. Office of Social Affairs Archdiocese of Montreal, nat. dir. Health and Welfare Office of Can. Cath. Conf., 1965-71; gen. adminstr. Caritas Internationalis, Rome, 1971-72; exec. dir. Cardinal Leger and his Endeavours, Montreal, 1972—; v.p. Can. Council Human Rights, 1966-71; pres. Psycho-Edn. Centre Que., 1976—; bd. dirs. Ste-Justine's Hosp., 1966-71, Villa Notre-Dame-de-Grace, 1970-72. Home: 1450 St Joseph Blvd E Montreal PQ H2J 1M5 Canada Office: 2065 Sherbrooke St W Montreal PQ H3H 1G6 Canada

RIEPE, DALE MARURICE, educator; b. Tacoma, June 22, 1918; s. Roland and Martha (Johnson) R.; B.A., U. Wash., 1944; M.A., U. Mich., 1946, Ph.D., 1954; postgrad. U. Hawaii, 1949, Madras U., 1952, Banaras Hindu U., 1951, Waseda U., 1957-58; m. Olave Patricia Hoyle Sheppard, Sept. 23, 1938; children—Katharine Leigh Riepe Herschlag, Dorothy Lorraine; m. 2d, Charleine Harriet Williams, May 24, 1948. With No. Pacific Ry., 1937-42; marine electrician Asso. Shipbuilders Corp., 1942-45; faculty U. Mich., 1945-48, Carleton Coll., 1948-51, U. S.D., 1952-54, U. N.D., 1954-62, C.W. Post Coll., 1962-63; prof. philosophy State U. N.Y., Buffalo, 1963—, asso. dean Grad. Sch., 1964-65; editorial cons. various univ. presses, 1964—; cons. N.Y. State Dept. Edn., 1971—, Centre for Sci. and Indsl. Research, Govt. of India, 1978-79. Rockefeller grantee, 1949, John Hancock fellow, 1956, Fulbright grantee, 1951-52, 57-58, Carnegie Found. grantee, 1960-61, Penrose grantee Am. Philos. Soc. 1963-64, Am. Inst. for Indian Studies grantee, 1966-67, London Sch. Oriental and African Studies grantee, 1971, Bul-Bulgarian Acad. Sci. grantee, 1975, Zaheer Sci. Found. grantee, 1978. Mem. AAAS, Am. Math. Assn., Am. Philos. Assn., Archaeol. Inst. Am., Asiatic Soc. Calcutta, Eastern Inst., Inter-Univ. Program on East-West Thought, Japanese Assn. for Philosophy of Sci., Royal Asiatic Soc., Soc. for Asian and Comaparative Philosophy, Soc. for Creative Ethics, Soc. for Philos. Study of Marxism, Soc. for Study Social Issues, Internat. Neo-Platonist Soc., United Univ. Professions (v.p. 1977-78), Buffalo Acad. Fine Arts, Buffalo Meml. Soc., Buffalo Zool. Soc., Niagara-Ontario Japan Assos., Western N.Y. Archaeol. Soc. Clubs: Buffalo, Four Seasons Tennis, Forest Acres Swimming. Author: The Naturalistic Tradition in Indian Thought, 1961; Phenomenology and Natural Existence, 1973; Indian Philosophy since Independence, vol. 1, 1978. Co-editor; Structure of Philosphy, 1966, Radical Currents in Contemporary Philosophy, 1971, Essays in East-West Dialogue, 1973, Explorations in Philosophy and Sociology, 1978; editorial bd. Chinese Studies in History, 1968—, Chinese Studies in Philosophy, 1968—, Revolutionary World, 1972—, Philosophical Currents, 1972—. Home: 48 Capen Blvd Buffalo NY 14214 Office: 605 Baldy Hall State U NY Amherst NY 14260

RIFE, DAVID HOWARD, geol. engr.; b. Miles City, Mont., Jan. 9, 1933; s. Samuel Perry and Nellie Mae (Edwards) R.; B.S. in Geol. Engring., Mont. Sch. Mines, 1964. Jr. geophys. engr. Geophys. Service, Inc., New Orleans, 1964-65, asst. party chief, 1965-67; engr. Columbia Gas Transmission Corp., Cumberland, Md., 1967-75, sr. prodn. and storage well engr., 1975—. Served with USAF, 1952-56. Mem. AIME, Am. Inst. Mining, Metall. and Petroleum Engrs., Soc. Exploration Geophysicists, Wine Appreciation Soc. (past v.p.). Republican. Club: Elks. Home: 12916 N Cresap St SW Apt 5 Cumberland MD 21502 Office: PO Box 1440 Cumberland MD 21502

RIFELJ, CAROL DE DOBAY, educator; b. Milw., Dec. 29, 1946; d. Raymond and Gerturde Helene (Niefer) de Dobay; student U. Aix-Marseille (France), 1966-67; B.A., U. Wis., Milw., 1968, M.A., Madison, 1969, Ph.D., 1972; m. Anton Rifelj, June 28, 1969. Asst. prof. French, Middlebury Coll., 1972-79, asso. prof., 1979—, chmn. dept. French, 1977—; cons. Nat. Endowment Humanities, 1978, 79, guest lectr. summer seminar, 1979. Nat. Endowment for Humanities fellow, 1976-77. Mem. Modern Lang. Assn., Northeastern Modern Lang. Assn. (chairperson Women's Caucus Program), Am. Assn. Tchrs. French. Contbr. articles, revs. to profl. jours. Office: French Dept Middlebury Coll Middlebury VT 05753

RIFKIN, FRANK RAY, mfg. exec.; b. Phila., Apr. 4, 1914; s. William and Rose (Zamsky) R.; student Tucker Inst., 1931-35; m. Jacqueline Edelman, Oct. 25, 1942; 1 son, Andrew Ray. Partner Velrose Mfg. Co., 1932—; writer Peerless Publns., 1934—; pub. Nutrition Health Rev. Trustee Edmund Bergler Psychiatric Found. Served from pvt. to tech. sgt. AUS, 1943-45. Home: Tunbridge Rd Haverford PA 19041 Office: 143 Madison Ave New York City NY 10016

RIFKIN, IRWIN ARNOLD, accountant; b. Bklyn., Jan. 20, 1934; s. Reuben and Evelyn (Saltzman) R.; B.B.A., Coll. City N.Y., 1955; J.D., Bklyn. Law Sch., 1959; m. Bernice Albinder, Dec. 26, 1954; children—Mark, Jeffrey, Bruce. Accountant, Louis A. Rifkin & Co., N.Y.C., 1953-57; accountant Oscar Lindner, N.Y.C., 1957-70, partner, 1976—; partner Hirsch & Rifkin, N.Y.C., 1969-70; pres. Delton Formal Wear, Inc., N.Y.C., 1970-75; admitted to N.Y. bar, 1960; asso. Malone & Dorfman, Attys., 1963-70. Trustee Rosedale Jewish Center; officer, trustee Deborah Hosp. Found. C.P.A., N.Y. Mem. Beta Gamma Sigma, Alpha Beta Psi. Home: 37 N Wood Ln Woodmere NY 11598 Office: 198 Broadway New York City NY 10038

RIFKIND, MARILYN ARLENE, educator; b. Tarrytown, N.Y., Apr. 11, 1949; d. Estelle F. Rifkind; B.Music Edn., Jacksonville U., 1971; M.S. in Edn., U. Bridgeport, 1975. Tchr., Lakeland Middle Sch., Peekskill, N.Y., 1971-72; tchr. vocal music Pleasantville (N.Y.) Middle Sch., 1972—. Mem. Music Educators Nat. Conf., Harrison High Sch. Chorus Alumni Assn. (chmn. 1977-78), Tchrs. Assn. Pleasantville. Home: 11 Lake St Apt 6-T White Plains NY 10603 Office: Pleasantville Middle Sch Romer Ave Pleasantville NY 10570

RIGG, RUTH DEHAVEN, nursing adminstr.; b. Glenshaw, Pa., Mar. 15, 1926; d. William and Irma B. (Simpson) DeHaven; student Westminster Coll., 1943-45; B.S., Pa. Coll. for Women, 1947; R.N., Allegheny Gen. Hosp. Sch. of Nursing, 1951; M.N.Ed., U. Pitts., 1964; 1 dau., Kimberly DeHaven. Research asst. animal toxicology Mellon Inst., Pitts., 1947-48; staff. nurse, instr. Allegheny Valley Hosp., Tarentum, Pa., 1951-56; office nurse, Tarentum, 1956-59; asst. to and acting dir. inservice, instr., supr. Allegheny Gen. Hosp., Pitts., 1959-63; research asst. and research asso. in med. and hosp. adminstr. Grad. Sch. Pub. Health, U. Pitts., 1963-71; asst. prof. nursing Pa. State U., State Coll., asso. chief nursing service for edn. VA Hosp., Pitts., 1971—; cons. nursing adminstrn.; reviewer Choice, Mag. of Books for Coll. Libraries. Hosp. Chairperson United Fund, also women's program coordinator; active Girl Scouts USA. Lic. real estate salesperson, Pa. Mem. Exec. Women's Council of Greater Pitts., Nurse Adminstrs. of Western Pa., Am. Pub. Health Assn., Pa. Assn. of Notaries, Sigma Theta Tau, Mu Sigma, Beta Sigma Omicron. Contbr. articles on med. care research to profl. jours. Home: 112 Eade Ave Glenshaw PA 15116 Office: VA Hospital Highland Dr Pittsburgh PA 15206

RIGGIO, THOMAS PASQUALE, educator; b. N.Y.C., Jan. 28, 1943; s. Anthony and Anna R. (Cappola) R.; B.A., Fordham U., 1964; M.A. (Woodrow Wilson fellow, Harvard fellow), Harvard U., 1967; Ph.D., 1972; m. Milla Cozart, June 21, 1969; children—Anna Maria, Thomas P. II. Asst. prof. English, U. Conn., Storrs, 1972—. Mem. Bicentennial Parade Com., Manchester, Conn., 1976. Mem. Modern Lang. Assn., Phi Beta Kappa. Democrat. Club: Italian-Am. (Manchester). Cons., reviewer Choice; reader/cons. Am. Quar.; contbr. articles in field to profl. jours. and books; editorial staff Complete Works of Theodore Dreiser. Home: 114 Chestnut St Manchester CT 06040 Office: U-25 U Conn Storrs CT 06286

RIGSBY, RADFORD BARLOW, mgmt. co. exec.; b. El Paso, Tex., Feb. 19, 1942; s. Robert Leslie and Jane Margaret (Barlow) R.; student Colgate U., 1960-62; B.A. cum laude in Economics, Am. U., 1966; M.Sc. in Economics, London Sch. Economics, 1968; M.B.A. in Finance, Harvard, 1971. Economic researcher IBRD, Washington, 1965-66; financial researcher OECD, Paris, 1968-69; investment researcher, portfolio mgr., Standish Ayer & Wood, Boston, 1971-74; portfoilo mgr. Harvard Mgmt. Co., Boston, 1974—. Bd. dirs. Big Brother Assn. Boston; sponsor Boston Symphony Orch. Served to 1st lt. U.S. Army, 1962-64. Fulbright scholar, Argentina, 1966-67; Hon. Woodrow Wilson fellow, 1967. Mem. Boston Soc. Security Analysts, Inst. Chartered Financial Analysts, Bond Protolio Mgrs. Assn., Am. Economic Assn., Soc. Protection Animals. Presbyterian. Home: 44 Concord Ave Cambridge MA 02138 Office: 70 Federal St Boston MA 02110

RIINA, JOHN ROY, lit. agent; b. N.Y.C., Oct. 10, 1927; s. Charles and Catherine (Piazza) R.; B.S., N.Y. U., 1952; m. Lorraine B. Dionne, Apr. 12, 1947 (dec. June 1976); children—Patricia Riina Brynes, William John, John Charles; m. 2d, Agnes G. Donohue O'Connor, Jan. 8, 1977. Asst. v.p., exec. editor Prentice-Hall Inc., Englewood Cliffs, N.J., 1954-72; dir. admissions and fin. aid Johns Hopkins U., 1972-74; mgr. audio-visual div. Johns Hopkins U. Press, 1974-76; propr. John R. Riina, Balt., 1977—; mem. adv. panel comml. publs. AEC, 1969-72; cons. editor Reston Pub. Co. Inc., 1977—; pres. Personnel Assessment and Selection Service Inc.; pub. cons. Marine Biol. Lab., Woods Hole, Mass., 1978. Trustee Park Ridge (N.J.) Bd. Edn., 1967-70, v.p., 1969-70; bd. dirs. Ethel E. Smith Scholarship Fund, 1967-70, pres., 1968-69; asso. mem. Marine Biol. Lab., Woods Hole. Served with USMCR, 1945-47. Mem. Washington Book Pubs. Assn., Ericson Chesapeake Sailing Assn. Club: Nyack (N.Y.) Boat. Address: 5905 Meadowood Rd Baltimore MD 21212

RIKE, PAUL MILLER, physician; b. Duquesne, Pa., Feb. 6, 1913; s. J. A. Garfield and Emma (Miller) R.; B.S., U. Pitts. 1936, M.D., 1938; D.Sc., Thiel Coll., 1970; m. Hazel Snyder, Oct. 13, 1945. Intern, Western Pa. Hosp., 1938-39; clin. asst. prof. medicine U. Pitts., 1947—; active staff Magee-Women's Hosp., Presbyn. U. Hosp.; cons. internist Western Psychiatric Inst. and Clinic, 1945—. Diplomate Am. Bd. Internal Medicine. Fellow A.C.P., Am. Coll. Cardiology, Am. Coll. Angiology; mem. Am. Soc. Internal Medicine, Am., World med. assns. Home: 4625 Fifth Ave Pittsburgh PA 15213 Office: Forbes and Halket Sts Pittsburgh PA 15213

RILES, WARREN HOUSTON, funeral dir.; b. Canonsburg, Pa., Dec. 4, 1940; s. James A. and Florence E. (Houston) R.; diploma, Pitts. Inst. Mortuary Sci., 1967-68. Owner, operator Riles Funeral Home, Forestville, N.Y., 1970—; v.p., treas. Jaquay Funeral Home Inc., South Dayton, N.Y., 1977—. Youth recreation dir. City of Forestville; coroner Chatauqua County, N.Y., 1974-78; sr. warden St. Peter's Episcopalian Ch., Forestville, 1975—. Mem. N.Y. State Coroners and Med. Examiners Assn. (dir. 1974—), Nat., N.Y. State, Chautauqua County (sec.-treas. 1971—) funeral dirs. assns. Clubs: Masons, Shriners, Silver Creek Moose (sec. 1976-77). Address: Riles Funeral Home 39 Main St Forestville NY 14062

ROSENBERG, ROBERT ALLEN, optometrist, educator; b. Phila., July 31, 1935; s. Theodore Samuel and Dorothy (Bailes) R.; B.A., Temple U., 1957, M.A., 1964; B.S., Pa. Coll. Optometry, 1960, O.D., 1961; certificate Gesell Inst. Child Devel., New Haven, 1977; m. Geraldine Bella Tishler, Sept. 3, 1961; children—Lawrence David, Ronald Joseph. Instr., then asst. prof. Pa. Coll. Optometry, Phila., 1962-67; pvt. practice optometry, Roslyn, Pa., 1965—; asst. prof. psychology Community Coll. Phila., 1967-76, asso. prof., 1976—. Fellow Am. Acad. Optometry; mem. Am., Pa., Bucks-Montgomery County optometric assns., AAUP, Roslyn Jaycees, Alumni Assn. Pa. Coll. Optometry. Republican. Jewish. Club: Lions. Contbr. artlcies to profl. jours. Home: 1151 Easton Rd Roslyn PA 19001

ROSENBERG, ROBERT CHARLES, housing corp. exec.; b. Bronx, N.Y., Oct. 21, 1934; s. Bernard L. and Flora (Popiel) R.; B.S., N.Y. U., 1955; LL.B., Columbia, 1958; m. Diane Stricof, Jan. 28, 1962 (dec.); children—Andrew, Scott; m. 2d, Frances Kaufman, Sept. 11, 1976; stepchildren—Michael Kaufman, Benjamin Kaufman. bar, 1959; adminstrv. asst. N.Y. State Dept. Law, N.Y.C., 1957-58; asso. firm Barron Rice & Rochmore, N.Y.C., 1959-62, Carro Spanbock & Londin, N.Y.C., 1962-68; first dep. commr. for devel. dept., N.Y.C. Housing and Devel. Adminstrn., 1968-73; v.p. Starrett Housing Corp., N.Y.C., 1973—; gen. mgr. Starrett City; lectr. Practicing Law Inst. Candidate for N.Y. State Assembly, 1958, 65; sec. N.Y. State Assn. Young Republican Clubs, 1959-61. Served with USAF, 1958. Mem. Am., N.Y. State, Bronx bar assns., N.Y. County Lawyers Assn., Citizens Housing and Planning Council, Nahro. Democrat. Club: Free Sons of Israel. Author N.Y. acts for residential constrn., rent. Home: 326 W 246th St New York City NY 10471 Office: 909 3d Ave New York City NY 10022

ROSENBERG, RUDY, chem. co. exec.; b. Charleroi, Belgium, Feb. 26, 1930; s. Hilaire and Frieda (Friedemann) R.; came to U.S., 1949, naturalized, 1954; grad. in classical studies Atheneum Leon Lepage, Brussels, Belgium, 1946; m. Rose H. Wauters, Nov. 7, 1953; 1 son, Rudy. Buyer, Lever Bros., Brussels, 1946-49; head Biochem. div. Mann Research Labs., N.Y.C., 1954-61, Gallard-Schlesinger, Carle Pl., N.Y., 1961-75; pres. Accurate Chem. & Sci. Corp., Hicksville, N.Y., 1975—. Served with U.S. Army, 1951-53. Mem. Reticuloendothelial Soc. Internat. Democrat. Clubs: Antique Automobile, Rolls Royce, Puppetry Guild Greater N.Y., Great Neck Acting Theater Group. Home: 68 Custer Ave Williston Park NY 11596 Office: 28 Tec St Hicksville NY 11801

ROSENBERG, SEYMOUR, psychologist, educator; b. Newark, Sept. 7, 1926; s. Morris and Celia (Weiss) R.; B.S., The Citadel, 1948; M.A., Ind. U., 1951, Ph.D., 1952; children—Harold Stanley, Michael Seth. Research psychologist USAF, San Antonio, 1952-58, U. Kans., Lawrence, 1958-59, Bell Telephone Labs., Murray Hill, N.J., 1959-65; vis. prof. psychology Columbia, N.Y.C., 1965-66; prof. psychology Rutgers U., New Brunswick, N.J., 1966—, adj. prof. Rutgers U. Med. Sch., 1974—; panel mem. NSF, 1970-72. Served with USN, 1945-46. NSF grantee, 1965—, Nat. Inst. Mental Health fellow, 1966-68, Social Sci. Research Council fellow, 1973-74. Fellow Am. Psychol. Assn.; mem. Psychonomic Soc., Psychometric Soc., Classification Soc., N.Y. Acad. Sci., Eastern Psychol. Assn. Cons. editor Jours. Personality and Social Psychology, 1968-69, asso. editor, 1970-73; contbr. articles in field to profl. jours. Home: Box 385 RFD 3 Canal Rd Somerset NJ 08873 Office: Dept Psychology Livingston Coll Rutgers Univ New Brunswick NJ 08903

ROSENBERG, THOMAS JOHN, pub. relations counselor; b. N.Y.C., July 16, 1920; s. Julius and Ann (Lederer) R.; A.B., U. Wis., 1942; 1 son, Thomas P.J. Asst. to pres. United World Films, 1946-48; partner Anna M. Rosenberg Assos., N.Y.C., 1948—; lectr. pub. relations New Sch. Mem. fgn. affairs com. Am. Jewish Congress, 1968—; mem. Nat. Mental Health Com., 1959-68; mem. N.Y.C. Citizens Moblzn. Bd., 1975-76. Served to capt. Signal Corps, AUS, 1938-42. Mem. Pub. Relations Soc. Am., Acad. Hosp. Pub. Relations, Am. Soc. Hosp. Pub. Relations. Home: 1136 Fifth Ave New York City NY 10028 Office: 444 Madison Ave New York City NY 10022

ROSENBERG, VICTOR I., plastic surgeon; b. N.Y.C., Nov. 15, 1936; s. Leonard C. and Sarah G. (Berger) R.; A.B., N.Y. U., 1957; M.D., Chgo. Med. Sch., 1961; m. Deborah Iskoe, Jan. 2, 1966; children—Spencer, Ria. Intern, Beth Israel Hosp., N.Y.C., 1961-62, resident, 1962-63, 64-66; resident Beekman Downtown Hosp., 1963-64, Bronx Municipal Hosp., 1966-67, Mt. Sinai Hosp., N.Y.C., 1967-68; practice medicine specializing in plastic surgery, N.Y.C., 1968—; asst. attending surgeon Beth Isreal Hosp., 1968—; asst. attending surgeon Beekman Downtown Hosp., 1968—, chief plastic surgery, 1976—; sr. clin. asst. Mt. Sinai Hosp., N.Y.C., 1968—; asso. dept. plastic surgery City U. N.Y., N.Y.C. Served to comdr. USN, 1968-70. Diplomate Am. Bd. Plastic Surgery. Fellow A.C.S., Internat. Coll. Surgeons; mem. Am., N.Y. Regional socs. plastic and reconstructive surgeons, Am. Soc. Aesthetic Plastic Surgery, AMA, Am. Cleft Palate Assn., N.Y. Acad. Medicine, N.Y. State, N.Y. County Med. Socs., Pan Am. Med. Assn. (diplomate sect. plastic surgery). Club: Friars. Office: 4 Sutton Pl New York City NY 10022

ROSENBERGER, HOMER TOPE, historian, personnel tng. cons.; b. Lansdale, Pa., Mar. 23, 1908; s. Daniel Hendricks and Jennie Kulp (Markley) R.; grad. Albright Coll., 1929, LL.D., 1955; M.A., Cornell U., 1930, Ph.D., 1932; m. Gertrude Pauline Richards, July 14, 1934 (dec. June 1975); children—Arley Jane (Mrs. Harry C. Furminger), Lucretia Hazel (Mrs. Patrick Robert Myers); m. 2d, Jean Hershey Richards, Apr. 12, 1977. Tchr. history Tidioute (Pa.) High Sch., 1930-31; prof. history and govt. Susquehanna U., summer 1933; tchr. Adult Night Sch., Lock Haven, Pa., 1933-35; ednl. research and adminstrn. U.S., Office Edn., 1935-42; supr. tng. U.S. Bur. Prisons, 1942-57; chief tng. Bur. Pub. Rds., U.S. Dept. Commerce, 1957-65; mem. steering com. Tng. Officers Conf., U.S. Govt., 1947-67, chmn., 1949-50, 55-57, chmn. com. preparation Tng. Specialists' Directory, 1948-49, exhibits com., 1947, 49; mem. com. on tng., mem. subcom. tng. policy and legislation Fed. Personnel Council, 1949-51; trustee Nat. Inst. for Reading Improvement, 1953-54; vice chmn. Pa. Bd. Pvt. Corr. Schs., 1968-71, chmn., 1972-73. Mem. adv. com. on career counseling U.S. Dept. Agr. Grad. Sch., 1965-66; cons. mgmt. Inst. Pub. Adminstrn., N.Y.C., 1963-64; cons. personnel mgmt. United Hosps., Newark, N.J., 1960-69, Pa. Dept. Hwys., Pa. Civil Service Commn., State N.Y. Dept. Civil Service. Organizer, moderator Rose Hill Seminars, 1963—; study tour govtl. mgmt. recommendations Western Nigeria, Africa, 1963-64. Mem. Pa. Com. on Correctional Staff Tng., 1955-57; mem. exec. com. corrections sect. United Community Services Washington, 1954-55; dir. Bur. Rehab. Nat. Capital Area, 1951—, pres., 1958-61, mem. exec. com., 1967-71, mem. personnel com., 1975—; mem. U.S. Civilian Conservation Corps Safety Council, 1938-42; organizer Pa. Hist. Junto, 1942, pres. 1942-46, 54-56, exec. com., 1942—, chmn. program com., 1946-49; mem. Pa. Hist. and Mus. Commn., 1972—; editorial bd. Social Studies Tchrs. Adminstrs., 1949-59. Mem. Pa. Hist. Assn. (mem. governing body 1945—, chmn. membership com., 1943-45, chmn. pubs. com., 1946-48, 51-67, chmn. program com., 1947, pres. 1967-69), Pa. German Soc. (dir. 1949—, v.p. 1952-57, chmn. citation com. 1954-56, pres. 1957-69, chmn. nominating com. 1976—), Pa. Prison Soc. (exec. com. 1949-66, chmn. awards com. 1952-64), Howard League Penal Reform (London), Columbia Hist. Soc. Washington (bd. mgrs. 1953—, 1st v.p. 1959-68, chmn. program com. 1959-68, chmn. exec. com. 1963-68, pres. 1968-76), Am. Peace Soc. (dir. 1960—, exec. com. 1961-64, chmn. com. publ. monographs 1963-65), Phi Alpha Theta, Alpha Pi Omega, Phi Delta Kappa, Pi Gamma Mu. United Methodist. Club: Cosmos (hist. com., awards com.) (Washington). Author: Testing Occupational Training and Experience, 1948; What Should We Expect of Education, 1956; Manuals for Executives, 1956, 58; Techniques for Getting Things Done, 7th edit., 1964; Letters from Africa, 1965; The Pennsylvania Germans, 1891-1965, 1966; Adventures and Philosophy of a Pennsylvannia Dutchman, 1971; The Philadelphia and Erie Railroad: Its Place in American Economic History, 1975; Mountain Folks: Fragments of Central Pennsylvania Lore, 1974; (3 vol. trilogy Horizons of the Humanities) Man and Modern Society: Philosophical Essays, 1972, Grassroots Philosophy for the Modern Mind, 1976, Vignettes of Philosophy: Thirty Five Vital Subjects, 1977; The Enigma: How Shall History Be Written?, 1979. Editor: Pennsylvania's Contributions to the Professions, 1964; Intimate Glimpses of the Pennsylvania Germans, 1965; Pennsylvania's Contributions to Art, 1967; contbg. editor Pa. History mag., 1943-75, mem. editorial bd., 1975—; mem. editorial bd. Pa. Heritage, 1974—. Contbr. articles to profl. jours. and mags. Author visual edn. and vocational guidance materials, employee tng. courses and occupational tests. Home: 2121 Massachusetts Ave NW Washington DC 20008 also Rose Hill Rural Route 4 Waynesboro PA 17268 Office: 1307 New Hampshire Ave NW Washington DC 20036

ROSENBERGER, PETER BIRNIE-BYE, pediatric neurologist; b. Youngstown, Ohio, Feb. 11, 1934; s. Ross Dewey and Jane Ruth (Bown) R.; B.A., Haverford Coll., 1955; M.A., Columbia, 1956; M.D., Western Res. U., 1960; m. Amy Constance Coldsnow, Dec. 21, 1958; children—Chandler, Margareta, Seth, Kurt. Intern, Children's Hosp., Boston, 1960-61, resident in pediatrics, 1961-62; resident in neurology Mass. Gen. Hosp., Boston, 1962-65, asso. neurologist, pediatrician, 1969-75, asso. neurologist, pediatrician, 1975—, also dir. research Fernald State Sch., Waltham, Mass. Asst. prof. neurology Harvard Med. Sch., 1969—. Served to maj. M.C., AUS, 1966-69. Diplomate Am. Bd. Pediatrics, Am. Bd. Psychiatry and Neurology. Mem. Am. Acad. Neurology, Child Neurology Soc., Eastern Psychol. Assn., Acad. Aphasia (sec. 1975—), Phi Beta Kappa, Alpha Omega Alpha. Contbr. articles to profl. jours. Home: 49 Cabot St Winchester MA 01890 Office: Mass Gen Hosp Boston MA 02114

ROSENBLATT, ARTHUR ISAAC, museum exec., architect; b. Bronx, N.Y., Aug. 31, 1931; s. Harry and Helen (Satz) R.; diploma Cooper Union, 1952, B.Arch., Carnegie-Mellon U., 1956; postgrad. Mass. Inst. Tech., 1966; m. Ruth Ann Turteltaub, Aug. 6, 1956; children—Paul Mark, Judith Alice. Architect, designer Katzman Assos., 1956-57, Isadore and Zachary Rosenfield, architects, 1957-60, Max Abramowitz, Simon Breines, Robert Cutler, 1960-61, Pomerance & Brienes, 1961-63, Irwin S. Chanin, 1963-65; 1st dep. adminstr. N.Y.C. dept. parks, 1966-68 (all N.Y.C.); v.p. Met. Mus. Art, 1971—; adminstr. for architecture and planning Met. Mus. Art, N.Y.C., 1968-71, Bklyn. Mus., 1968. Mem. teaching faculty Sarah Lawrence Coll., Bronxville, N.Y., 1966-68; adv. council Cooper Union Sch. Architecture, N.Y.C., 1967—. Vice chmn. Community Planning Bd. N.Y.C., 1964-66; mem. Citizens Housing and Planning Council, 1963—, adv. bd. Council for Parks and Playgrounds, 1964-68; bd. dirs. Archtl. League N.Y., 1967-71, pres., 1970-72 (all N.Y.C.). Served with AUS, 1953-55. Recipient Thesis prize Carnegie Inst. Tech., 1956; citation for profl. achievement Cooper Union, 1967. Mem. AIA (exec. com. N.Y. chpt. 1967-68), Cooper Union Alumni Assn. (pres.). Contbr. articles to profl. jours. Home: 1158 Fifth Ave New York City NY 10029 Office: Met Mus Art New York City NY 10028

ROSENFELD, DONALD ALAN, bus. exec.; b. Cambridge, Mass., Apr. 20, 1944; s. Jerome M. and Elaine L. (Ackerson) R.; grad. Cheshire Acad. (Conn.), 1962; student Bryant and Stratton, 1964. Research asst. radar meteorology Mass. Inst. Tech., Cambridge, 1965-67; meteorologist radio stas. WREB, WBCN and WERS, Holyoke; Boston, 1965-68; pres. New Eng. News & Photo Co., Boston, 1968—, New Eng. Service Co., Boston, 1969—, Investment Co. of New Eng., Boston, 1970—, New Eng. Electronics Co., 1971—; dir. Jerome Press, Inc., Boston; chief photographer N.E. Legal Photography Co., Boston, 1970—; Mass. Registry of Motor Vehicles, 1974—. Mem. Nat. Press Photographers Assn., Am. Meteorology Soc. (sec., treas. Boston chpt. 1964-67), Evidence Photographers Internat. Council, Internat. Assn. Identification, New Eng. Police Photographers Assn. Address: PO Box 10 Brookline MA 02146

ROSENFELD, JOSEPH, concrete co. exec.; b. Medway, Mass., Dec. 3, 1907; s. Abraham and Annie (Candleman) R.; student pub. schs., Milford, Mass. Mgr. Abraham Rosenfeld Sand & Gravel Co., Milford, Mass., 1925-32; owner, operator Rosenfeld Washed Sand & Stone Co., Hopedale, Dedham, Ashland, Walpole and Plainville, Mass., 1932—; dir., v.p. Home Nat. Bank, Milford, Milford Water Co. Mem. Milford Indsl. Com., 1955-58; pres. Milford Combined Charities, 1958-59, chmn., 1958-59; mem. gifts com. Milford Hosp., 1961; mem. Town Meeting, 1935-76; chmn. Milford High Sch. Centennial, 1950; sponsor Milford Little League, Babe Ruth League, Greater Boston Assn. Retarded Children, Inc., Nat. Jewish Hosp.; mem. adv. bd. Algonquin council Boy Scouts Am., hon. chmn. Milford Heart Fund, 1964. Trustee, mem. mng. bd. Milford Hosp. Chmn. Milford Indsl. Devel. Com., 1966—; mem. Jewish Meml. Hosp. Men's Assos.; chmn. Milford area Mass. Assn. for Mental Health; mem. Milford Sch. Bldg. Planning Com.; hon. chmn. Milford Heart Fund, 1964-70, Milford Area March of Dimes campaign, 1970. Recipient citation United Jewish Appeal, 1953, citation Milford Kiwanis Club, 1960, Community Service award V.F.W. Post 9373, 1961, citation Milford Heart Fund, 1963, Xaverian Missionary Fathers, 1963, Crusade award Greater Boston Assn. Retarded Children, Inc.; citation Mass. Assn. Mental Health, 1968; citation Nat. Found. March of Dimes, 1970, Distinguished Service award Greater Milford C. of C., 1976, others. Mem. Home Builders Assn. Greater Boston, Nat. Assn. Home Builders U.S., Mass. Motor Truck Assn. Inc., Mass. Concrete Inst. (dir.), Milford Hebrew Assn. (citation 1958, trustee), Asso. Gen. Contractors Am., Mass. Bldg. Congress, Utility Contractors New Eng., Portuguese De Instrucao E Recreio Inc. (hon. life mem.). Am. Inst. Mgmt. (mem. pres.'s council 1966), Milford (dir., indsl. com.), Greater Boston chambers commerce, Republican. Jewish religion. Lion (charter Milford, pres. 1956-57), Elk; mem. B'nai B'rith (25 year silver honor certificate for humanitarian programs 1961). Clubs: Milford Sons of Italy Dramatic and Sportsman's (hon.); Bungay Brook Sporting (hon.); Hopedale Country (life); Century. Home: 34 Cedar St Milford MA 01757 Office: 75 Plain St Hopedale MA 01747

ROSENFELD, REBA, educator; b. Balt.; d. Max and R. Clara (Shorr) Rosenfeld; student Goucher Coll., Johns Hopkins, 1954-56, postgrad., 1961, 66-67, summer 1965; B.F.A., Md. Inst. Coll. Art, 1956; M.Ed. in Guidance and Personnel, U. Md., 1962. Social worker Dept. Pub. Welfare, Balt., 1944-45, ARC, 1945-46; tchr. pub. schs., Balt., 1946-54, 56-59, counselor, 1959—. Former med. field agt. SSS. Mem. Am., Md. personnel and guidance assns., Am. Sch. Counselors Assn., Nat. Vocat. Guidance Assn., Md. Tchrs. Assn., Pub. Sch. Tchrs. Assn. Home: 3422 Barry Paul Rd Randallstown MD 21133

ROSENFELD, RONALD MARVIN, advt. agy. exec.; b. Balt., July 13, 1932; s. Bernard and Bessie (Feinglass) R.; student Balt. City Coll., 1946-49; children—Bonnie, Ned. Copywriter, Applestein, Levinstein & Golnick, Balt., 1955-57; v.p., co-copy chief Doyle Dane Bernbach, N.Y.C., 1957-68; sr. v.p., creative mgmt. supr. J. Walter Thompson, N.Y.C., 1968-69; prin., exec. v.p., co-creative dir. Rosenfeld, Sirowitz & Lawson, Inc., N.Y.C., 1970—. Bd. dirs. Daytop Village, drug program, N.Y.C., 1974-76, Hope for Diabetics Found. Served with U.S. Army, 1953-55. Named to Copywriters Hall of Fame, 1971; recipient numerous awards, including Copy Club N.Y., Art Dirs. Club, Clio awards. Mem. One Show (co-chmn.). Home: 300 Central Park W New York City NY 10024 Office: 1370 Ave of Americas New York City NY 10019

ROSENKRANTZ, JACOB ALVIN, physician, hosp. adminstr.; b. N.Y.C., Feb. 12, 1914; s. Philip and Liza R.; B.S., Coll. City N.Y., 1933; M.A., Columbia U., 1934, M.D., 1938; m. Sadie Harzoff, July 25, 1936; children—Judith Ann, Jonathan Earl, Lorna Carrie, Melinda Gale. Intern, N.Y. Postgrad. Hosp., N.Y.C., 1939-41, fellow 1941-42, 46, research asst. dept. medicine, 1941-46; chief out-patient clinic, asst. chief of staff Bronx VA Hosp., 1946-52; chief of staff VA Hosp., E. Orange, N.J., 1952-56, chief outpatient clinic, 1971—; adminstr. So. div. Albert Einstein Med. Center, Phila., 1956-59; exec. dir. Newark Beth Israel Med. Center, 1959-68; exec. dir., asso. dean., clin. asso. prof. dept. community and preventive medicine N.Y. Med. Coll.-Flower and Fifth Ave Hosps., N.Y.C., 1968-71; instr. clin. medicine Univ. Hosp., N.Y. U., 1954-56; Presdl. appointee, vol. exam. physician SSS, N.Y.C., 1942; mem. U.S. Civil Service Examiners, VA Hosp., Bronx, N.Y., 1951; com. Newark Community Survey, Welfare Fedn. Newark, 1960-61; health planning com. Council Jewish Fedn. and Welfare Funds, 1960-63; trustee Newark Beth Israel Hosp. Research Found., 1959-68; adv. research panel, Livingston, N.J., 1974. Served to maj., M.C., U.S. Army, 1942-46. Fellow A.C.P., Am. Coll. Hosp. Adminstrs., Am. Coll. Preventive Medicine, Am. Pub. Health Assn., Am. Geriatrics Soc., Royal Soc. Health (London), N.Y., N.J. acads. medicine; mem. Am. Diabetes Assn., Assn. Am. Med. Colls., Am. Hosp. Assn., Am. Soc. Tropical Medicine and Hygiene, Assn. Mil. Surgeons U.S., Internat. Soc. Internal Medicine, N.Y. Acad. Scis., N.Y., N.J. pub. health assns., N.J. Hosp. Assn. (chmn. ins. fund safety program 1966-68, chmn. ins. com. 1967-68, trustee 1967-68), Social Welfare Research Found. Jewish. Clubs: Alumni Assns. Coll. Physicians and Surgeons, Columbia U., Grad. Faculties, Columbia U., N.Y. Postgrad. and Univ. Hosps., Coll. City N.Y. Editorial bd. Newark Beth Israel Hosp. Med. Jour., 1961-68; condr. seminar on alcoholism and drug addiction Fed. Exec. Bd., Met. No. N.J., 1971. Home: 192 E Mount Pleasant Ave Livingston NJ 07039 Office: 20 Washington Pl Newark NJ 07102

ROSENLOF, CARL CORNELIUS, design engr.; b. Hartford, Conn., Aug. 17, 1918; s. Joel Cornelius and Blenda Victoria (Swanson) R.; B.S. with honors, Trinity Coll., 1946-50; m. Theodora Zafranis, Sept. 17, 1955; children—Robert, Barbara. Successively project engr., town engr., chief design engr. Town of West Hartford (Conn.), 1950-78; ret., 1978. Served with AUS, 1944-46. Registered profl. engr. Conn., N.Y. Mem. ASCE, Nat. Soc. Profl. Engrs., Am. Pub. Works Assn., Phi Beta Kappa. Lutheran. Home: 79 Crestwood Rd West Hartford CT 06107

ROSENQUIT, BERNARD, artist; b. Hotin, Roumania, Dec. 26, 1923, (parents Am. citizens); s. Eli and Ida (Schotkin) R.; student (Monitor scholar) Art Students League, N.Y.C., 1947-50, (Mrs. John D. Rockefeller III scholar) Atelier 17, N.Y.C., 1954-55, (Monitor scholar) Bklyn. Mus. Sch. Fine Art, N.Y.C., 1955-56, Fontainebleau Sch. Fine Arts, France (Fulbright grantee), 1947, Inst. Art and Archaeology, Paris, France, 1958-59. Instr. painting, drawing Riverdale Neighborhood and Library Assn., Fieldston Sch. Arts Center (both Riverdale, N.Y.), 1962-64, Five-Towns Music and Art Found., Cedarhurst, N.Y., also Bronx House Community Center, N.Y.C., 1961-62; exhibited in one-man shows Roko Gallery, N.Y.C., 1951, 53, 58, 61, 62, 66, 71, Student Union Gallery, U. Mass. at Amherst, 1976; exhibited in group shows Honolulu Acad. Fine Arts, Boston Mus. Fine Art, Bklyn. Mus. Fine Art, Newark Mus. Art, Toronto Mus. Fine Arts, Oakland (Calif.) Art Mus., U.S. Nat. Mus. Washington, Seattle Mus. Fine Arts, Mus. Modern Art, N.Y.C., New Sch. Social Research, U. So. Ill., and others; represented in permanent collections Met. Mus. Art, Bklyn. Mus. Fine Art, Victoria and Albert Mus. (London), Smithsonian Instn., Bryn Mawr Coll., U. Kans. Mus., Dallas Art Assn., Peabody Coll. Mus., N.Y. Pub. Library; works reproduced in book rev. sect. N.Y. Times. Louis Comfort Tiffany Found. grantee, 1959. Mem. Artists Equity Assn., Art Students' League N.Y.C., Phila. Print Club. Home: 87 Barrow St New York City NY 10014

ROSENSAFT, MELVIN, chem. co. exec., mgmt. cons., educator; b. N.Y.C., Jan. 28, 1919; s. Nathan and Yetta (Applebaum) R.; certificate State Tchrs. Coll., Paterson, N.J., 1938-40; B.S. cum laude, Rider Coll., 1942; M.B.A., Suffolk U., 1978; m. Beatrice Golombeck, June 27, 1954; children—David Norman, Lester Jay, Emily Susan. Field dep. IRS, Newark, 1942-43; office mgr. Gt. Am. Plastics, 1944-46, comptroller, 1946-47, works mgr., 1947-48; pres. Artefactos Plasticos, Mexico City, 1948-49, Irwin Products, Toronto, Ont., Can., 1949-50; asst. to pres. Gt. Am. Plastics, 1950-52, v.p. mfg., 1956-62, exec. v.p., gen. mgr., 1962-71; mgr. plastics div. Ideal Plastics Co., Hollis, N.Y., 1953-55; exec. v.p., gen. mgr. Gt. Am. Chem. Corp., Fitchburg, Mass., 1962-71, dir., 1969-77, pres., 1971-76; mgmt. cons., 1976—; exec. v.p., gen. mgr. Irwin Corp., N.Y.C., also Fitchburg Realty Corp., Factory St. Realty Corp., Nashua, N.H., 1962-71; dir. Lastomerex, Inc., Jefferson, Mass., 1978—; mem. Fitchburg Indsl. Devel. Commn.; advisor economic and indsl. devel. City of Leominster (Mass.); faculty Suffolk U. Grad. Sch. Bus. Adminstrn., Boston, Fitchburg State Coll., Mt. Wachusett Community Coll., Gardner, Mass. Pres., trustee, bd. dirs. Fitchburg-Leominster Community Center; v.p., bd. dirs. F.I.A. Credit Union; mem. adv. com. Leominster Urban Renewal, Mass. Regional Vocational Tech. Sch.; chmn. troop com. Boy Scouts Am.; bd. dirs. Fitchburg Gen. Hosp. Community Center; examiner ARC. Served with AUS, 1943-44. Fellow Benjamin Franklin Assos. of U. Pa., Scheie Eye Inst. of Presbyn. Hosp.; mem. Soc. Plastics Engrs., Chem. Soc. Gt. Britain, Soc. Plastics Industry (vinyl chloride and polyvinyl chloride producers com.), Am. Mgmt. Assn., Delta Mu Delta, C. of C. Home: 59 Crescent Rd Leominster MA 01453 Office: 59 Crescent Rd Leominster MA 01453

ROSENSAFT, MENACHEM ZWI, author, lectr.; b. Bergen-Belsen, Germany, May 1, 1948; s. Josef and Hadassah (Bimko) R. came to U.S., 1958, naturalized, 1962; B.A., M.A., Johns Hopkins, 1971; M.A., Columbia U., 1975, J.D., 1979; m. Jean Bloch, Jan. 13, 1974; 1 dau., Joana Deborah. Adj. lectr. dept. Jewish studies City Coll. N.Y., 1972-74, professorial fellow, 1974-75; research fellow Am. Law Inst., 1977-78. Author: Moshe Sharett, Statesman of Israel, 1966; Fragments, Past and Future (poetry), 1968; Not Backward to Belligerency, 1970; editor Bergen Belsen Youth Mag., N.Y.C., 1965; editorial adv. bd. Jewish Quar., London, Eng., 1971-72; law clk. to Judge U.S. Dist. Ct. N.Y., 1979-81; contbr. to various publs. including Columbia Human Rights Law Rev., Jewish Social Studies, Midstream, Leo Baeck Inst. Year Book XXI, Jewish Chronicle, Yediot Aharonot, Tel Aviv, Letzte Nayes, Tel Aviv, Asahi Evening News, Tokyo,

Jewish Spectator, Jerusalem Post; appeared various radio and TV programs. Harlan Fiske Stone scholar. Mem. Phi Beta Kappa. Ind. Democrat. Jewish. Address: 179 E 70th St New York City NY 10021

ROSENSTEIN, ALAN HERBERT, phys. sci. adminstr.; b. Balt., July 4, 1936; s. Harry and Gertrude (Grabush) R.; B.S. in Metall. Engring., Drexel Inst. Tech., 1959; M.A. in Personnel Mgmt., George Washington U., 1963; M.S. in Metall. Engring., Colo. Sch. Mines, 1965, D.Sc., 1966; m. Diane Carol Harrison, Jan. 15, 1961; children—Gary Foster, Jamie Sue. Phys. metallurgist Naval Ship Research and Devel. Center, Annapolis, Md., 1959-68, head ferrous metallurgy br., 1968-71; program mgr. for structural materials Air Force Office Sci. Research, Washington, 1971—; faculty Colo. Sch. Mines, 1964-65, Am. Soc. Metals, 1966-67, George Washington U., 1967. Registered profl. engr., Colo., Md. Mem. Am. Soc. Metals (chmn. D.C. chpt. 1972-73, exec. com. D.C. 1966-74), Am. Welding Soc., ASTM, Severn Tech. Soc., Sigma Xi (hon.). Jewish. Contbr. articles to profl. jours. Home: 12217 Wynmore Ln Bowie MD 20715 Office: Air Force Office Sci Research Bolling AFB Washington DC 20332

ROSENSTEIN, ROBERT, pharmacologist; b. N.Y.C., Aug. 7, 1933; s. David and Tillie (Yashun) R.; B.S., Columbia U., 1955, M.S., 1957; Ph.D., U. Utah, 1962; m. Oma Jaunice Chapman, Apr. 25, 1964; children—Gerald Allan, Darrell Douglas, Lori Kim. From instr. to asst. prof. research pharmacology U. Okla. Coll. Medicine, 1962-65; mem. faculty Dartmouth Coll. Med. Sch., 1968—, asso. prof. pharmacology, 1977—; research pharmacologist FAA, Oklahoma City, 1962-65; pharmacologist VA, White RiverJunction, Vt., 1965—. NIH fellow, 1958-61. Mem. Am. Soc. Pharmacology and Exptl. Therapeutics, Am. Physiol. Soc., Soc. Neurosci., AAAS, Sigma Xi. Jewish. Club: B'nai B'rith. Contbr. to profl. jours. Home: PO Box 64 Norwich VT 05055 Office: VA Center White River Junction VT 05001

ROSENSTOCK, ROBERT, lawyer; b. N.Y.C., Mar. 1, 1935; s. Jesse Metzger and Edith (Baruch) R.; A.B., Cornell U., 1957; LL.B., Columbia U., 1961; m. Gerda Michorl, Aug. 21, 1970; children—Elisabeth, Thomas. Admitted to N.Y. State bar, 1961, since practiced in N.Y.C.; asso. firm Havens, Wandless, Stitt & Tighe, 1961-64; adviser legal affairs U.S. mission to UN, 1964—; mem. U.S. delegations 19th-31st sessions UN Gen. Assembly; alternate U.S. rep. to legal com. 24th-31st sessions UN Gen. Assembly; alternate U.S. rep. UN Spl. Com. Principles Internat. Law; U.S. rep. UN Spl. Com. Definition of Aggression; Legal Com. Drafting Caribbean Devel. Bank Charter; mem. U.S. delegation Conf. Law of Treaties, UN Commn. Internat. Trade Law, Stockholm Conf. Human Environment. Mem. adv. council U.S. Inst. Human Rights. Recipient Meritorious Service award Dept. State, 1972, Superior Honor award, 1974. Mem. Am. Bar Assn. (chmn. com. UN activities 1969-73), Am. Soc. Internat. Law (mem. panels law of treaties, Internat. Ct. Justice, protection of diplomats). Contbr. articles to profl. jours. Home: 208 Highbrook Ave Pelham NY 10803 Office: 799 UN Plaza New York City NY 10017

ROSENTHAL, BENJAMIN STANLEY, congressman, lawyer; b. N.Y.C., June 8, 1923; s. Joseph and Ceil (Fischer) R.; student L.I. U., Coll. City N.Y.; LL.B., Bklyn. Law Sch., 1949; LL.M., N.Y. U., 1952; m. Lila Moskowitz, Dec. 23, 1951; children—Debra, Edward. Admitted to N.Y. bar, 1949, U.S. Supreme Ct. bar, 1954; practiced in N.Y.C., 1949-70; mem. 87th-96th Congresses from 8th N.Y. Dist.; mem. Fgn. Affairs Com., Europe subcom., Inter-Am. affairs subcom.; mem. Govt. Ops. Com., chmn. commerce, consumer and monetary affairs subcom. Served with AUS, 1943-46. Mem. Am., N.Y. State, Queens County bar assns. Democrat. Home: 88-12 Elmhurst Ave Elmhurst NY 11373 Office: Ho of Reps Washington DC 20515 also 41-65 Main St Flushing NY 11351

ROSENTHAL, DAVID STANLEY, internist, hematologist; b. Boston, July 2, 1938; s. Edward I. and Sara G. (Rosenfield) R.; B.A., Harvard U., 1959; M.D., Tufts U., 1963; m. Judith Biller, June 19, 1960; 1 dau., Laura Nancy. Intern, Tufts Med. Service, Boston City Hosp., 1963-64, jr. asst. resident, 1964-65; sr. asst. resident Beth Israel Hosp., 1965-66; teaching fellow medicine Harvard Med. Sch., Boston, 1965-66, research fellow in medicine, 1968, instr. medicine, 1970-71, asso. prof. medicine, 1977—; hematology fellow Tufts Hematology Lab., Boston City Hosp., 1966-67, research fellow, 1966-67; asst. in medicine Peter Bent Brigham Hosp., Boston, 1967-68, jr. asso. medicine, 1970-72, asst. prof. medicine, 1971-77, asso. medicine, 1972-74, sr. asso. medicine, 1974, clin. dir. hematology div., 1976—; hematology cons. First Army, Ft. Devens, Mass., 1970. Trustee, Temple Israel, Boston, 1973—; bd. govs. Wightman Tennis Center, 1972-75. Served to maj. M.C., USAF, 1968-70. Fellow ACP; mem. Am. Fedn. Clin. Research, Am. Physicians Fellowship, Soc. Air Force Physicians, Am. Soc. Hematology, Mass. Med. Soc., AAAS, Am. Cancer Soc. (bd. dirs. 1976), Internat. Soc. Hematology, Am. Soc. Clin. Oncology, Soc. Exptl. Biology and Medicine. Jewish. Club: Boston Blood (pres. 1973-74). Contbr. articles to med. jours. Home: 30 Haynes Rd Newton Center MA 02159 Office: 721 Huntington Ave Boston MA 02115

ROSENTHAL, HERBERT MARTIN, psychiatrist; b. Giessen, Germany, Jan. 22, 1913; s. Siegfried and Sophie (Mayer) R.; student Geneva U., 1932, Frankfurt U., 1933; Ph.D., Naples U., 1936; diploma London Imperial Coll. Sci., 1937; Ph.G., U. Basel (Switzerland), 1939, M.D., 1946; grad. Am. Inst. Psychoanalysis, 1963; m. Irmgard Helen Busenhart, Feb. 7, 1946; 1 dau., Victoria Anne. Came to U.S., 1946, naturalized, 1954. Research biochemistry Basel U., 1939-46; rotating intern Jewish Meml. Hosp., N.Y.C., 1946-47; resident Crownsville (Md.) State Hosp., 1947, Croton Manor Sanitarium, Cronton-on-Hudson, N.Y., 1948, Central Islip (N.Y.) State Hosp., 1948-52; supervising psychiatrist Manhattan State Hosp., N.Y.C., 1952-54; asso. psychiatrist U. Consultation and Treatment Center, Bronx, 1952-56; adj. psychoanalyst Karen Horney Clinic, N.Y.C., 1954-58; asso. med. dir. Jamaica Center Psychotherapy, N.Y.C., 1956-75; dir. Woodstock Center Psychotherapy, 1961-69; asso. attending adolescent and children's div. Roosevelt Hosp., 1967-74, attending child and adolescent psychiatry out-patient dept., 1974—, also dean faculty Advanced Inst. for Analytic Psychotherapy; mem. faculty Am. Inst. Psychoanalysis, 1975—. Pres. Fedn. Mental Health Centers, Inc., 1960—; cons. psychiatrist Gateway Industries, Kingston, N.Y., 1965-69. Fellow Assn. Med. Group Psychoanalysts; mem. AMA, Am. Psychiat. Assn., N.Y. County Psychiat. Assn., Am. Assn. Ind. Psychology, World Fedn. Mental Health, Am. Acad. Psychoanalysis, Assn. Advancement Psychoanalysis. Jr. editor Ars Medici, 1940-45. Home: Stuyvesant NY 12173 Office: 30 W 60th St New York City NY 10023 also Stuyvesant NY 12173 also Red Barn Elwyn Ln Woodstock NY 12498

ROSENTHAL, LAURENCE, lawyer; b. N.Y.C., Sept. 1, 1911; s. Sig and Alpha (Korn) R.; B.A. with honor, Yale, 1933; LL.B., Harvard, 1936; m. Clara Steinhardt, Apr. 18, 1940; children—Ellen (Mrs. Lawrence Sosnow), Joan (Mrs. Melvin Sokotch). Admitted to N.Y. bar, 1937; partner Elvin Edwards, Mineola, N.Y., 1938-41; partner firm Fried, Frank, Harris, Shriver & Jacobson, N.Y.C., 1948—. Chmn., Nassau County San. Dist. 1, 1950-70; pres. Five Towns Community Chest, 1958-59, Five Towns Community House, 1955-60. Trustee Adelphi U., Hewlett-Woodmere Pub. Library; hon. trustee Five Towns United Fund. Served with USNR, 1943-46. Mem. Am., Fed., N.Y. State, Nassau County (chmn. com. on estates and trusts 1971-74) bar assns., Assn. Bar City N.Y. Clubs: Woodmere (N.Y.) Country (pres. 1969-70); Bankers, Lawyers (N.Y.C.). Home: 130 Harold Rd Woodmere NY 11598 Office: 120 Broadway New York City NY 10005

ROSENTHAL, LILLIAN MANDELL, educator; b. Chgo.; d. Morris and Eudice Mandell; B.A. in Psychology, Roosevelt U., Chgo., 1947; M.S. in Edn., Queens Coll., Flushing, N.Y., 1968; m. Erich Rosenthal; children—Barbara Herta, Theodore Marcus. Reading tchr. Great Neck (N.Y.) Pub. Schs., 1958—; workshop coordinator North Shore Sc. Mus., 1965—. Mem. Internat. Reading Assn., Nassau Reading Council, Orton Soc. Author: A-E-I-O-U and Sometimes Y, 1977. Contbr. articles to profl. jours.; developed game Two Is A Pair, an aid for decoding and reinforcing selected phonic elements. Home: 15 Longview Pl Great Neck NY 11021 Office: Great Neck Schs Great Neck NY 11020

ROSENTHAL, MILTON FREDERICK, corp. exec.; b. N.Y.C., Nov. 24, 1913; s. Jacob C. and Louise (Berger) R.; B.A., City Coll. N.Y., 1932; LL.B., Columbia, 1935; m. Frieda Bojar, Feb. 28, 1943; 1 dau., Anne Janine. Admitted to N.Y. bar, 1935; research asst. N.Y. State Law Revision Commn. 1935-37; law sec. Fed. Judge William Bondy, 1937-40; asso. atty. Leve, Hecht & Hadfield, 1940-42; sec., treas. Hugo Stinnes Corp., 1946-48, exec. v.p., treas., 1948-49, pres., dir., 1949-64; pres., dir. Minerals and Chems. Philipp Corp., N.Y.C., 1964-67; pres., dir. Engelhard Minerals & Chems. Corp., N.Y.C., 1967-77, chmn., chief exec. officer, 1977—; dir. European-Am. Banking Corp., European-Am. Bank & Trust Co., Ferro Corp., Midlantic Banks Inc., Schering-Plough Corp. Dir. Nat. Council U.S.-China Trade, U.S.-USSR Trade and Econ. Council, Inc.; chmn. U.S. sect. Romanian-U.S. Econ. Council. Bd. dirs. Mt. Sinai Med. Center; trustee Mt. Sinai Hosp. Served to 1st lt., JAG U.S. Army, 1942-45. Mem. Assn. Bar City N.Y., Chgo. Bar Assn., Columbia Law Sch. Alumni Assn., Judge Adv. Assn., Fgn. Policy Assn. (dir.), Phi Beta Kappa. Home: Woodlands Rd Harrison NY 10528 Office: 1221 Ave of Americas New York City NY 10017

ROSENTHAL, MYRON MARTIN, electronics engr.; b. Bklyn., Nov. 5, 1930; s. Murray Morris and Selma Locke (Belsky) R.; B.E.E., Coll. City N.Y., 1953; M.S., Adelphi U., 1957; m. Dolores Elaine Winard, June 21, 1953; children—Lynn, Debbie, Richard. Sr. engr. Republic Aviation Corp., Farmingdale, L.I., 1955-61; pres. Myron M. Rosenthal & Staff, 1957-61; program mgr. Loral Electronics, Bronx, N.Y., 1962-64; engring. mgr. Singer-Kearfott div. The Singer Co., Wayne, N.J., 1964—; adj. prof. Poly. Inst. N.Y., Bklyn., 1954—; chmn. bd. Electronics and Aerospace Conv., 1974; bd. dirs. Nat. Aerospace and Electronics Conf., 1972-75; notary pub., N.J. Founder Randal Carter PTA cultural workshop, Wayne, 1965; lighting commr. Wayne, 1956. Recipient Picatinny Arsenal U.S. Army Engring. and Leadership commendations, 1969, 71, 73; Poly. Inst. N.Y. faculty award, 1975; Nat. Aerospace and Electronics Conf. award, 1968, 75, 76; Electronics and Aerospace Conv. award, 1974; registered profl. engr., N.J.; licensed pub. accountant, N.J. Mem. IEEE (sr. mem.; award 1972, 74), Nat. Soc. Profl. Engrs., Am. Inst. Aeros. and Astronautics, ASME, ASCE, Illuminating Engring. Soc., Am. Assn. Clin. Chemistry, Am. Inst. Indsl. Engrs., Assn. U.S. Army, Navy League, Marine Corps Assn., Am. Def. Preparedness Assn., Air Force Assn., ASTM, Aerospace Systems Soc. (bd. govs. 1968-74, v.p. 1972), Armed Forces Communications and Electronics Assn., AAUP, Am. Assn. Physics Tchrs., Am. Physics Soc., Am. Soc. Safety Engrs. (profl. mem.), Constrn. Specifications Inst., Am. Soc. Pub. Adminstrn., Am. Pub. Works Assn., Am. Assn. Cost Engrs., Am. Ceramic Soc., Nat. Mgmt. Assn. (certified), Nat. Council Tchrs. Math., Am. Radio Relay League, Nat. Assn. Accountants, Nat. Soc. Pub. Accountants, ALA, Soc. Automotive Engrs., Am. Craft Council, Nat. Soc. Architechs, Am. Soc. Interior Design, Nat. Sci. Tchrs. Assn., Soc. Plastics Engrs. Audio Engring. Soc., Internat. Assn. Assessing Officers, Am. Hist. Assn., Am. Philos. Assn., Modern Lang. Assn., Inst. Nav. (program com. 1978), Am. Judicature Soc., Aircraft Owners and Pilots Assn., Refrigeration Service Engrs. Soc., Am. Motorcycle Assn., AAAS, Boat Owners Assn., Jewish Tchrs. Assn., Am. Assn. Higher Edn., Nat. Aeros. Assn., Nat. Assn. Social Workers, Nat. Council Young Israel, Am. Rose Soc., Nat. Assn. of Deaf, Nat. Eye Research Found., Am. Council for Blind, Nat. Rehab. Assn., Am. Jewish Council, Workmen's Circle, Sigma Xi. Republican. Jewish. Clubs: B'nai B'rith (trustee 1966-77), Toastmasters (pres. 1969, area gov. 1970, best speaker of the year 1968, 69, 75). Patentee inflatable antenna, cylindrical flat plate 35 GHz antenna, rotating lens antenna seeker-head. Amateur radio operator. Home: 48 Tall Oaks Dr Wayne NJ 07470 Office: 150 Totowa Rd Wayne NJ 07470

ROSENTHAL, ROBERT KENNETH, orthopedic surgeon; b. Boston, Dec. 27, 1936; s. Louis and Dorothy (Hamel) R.; A.B., Boston U., 1958; M.D., Tufts U., 1962; m. Esther Lowell Zamore, Sept. 3, 1960; children—Geoffrey, Emily, Jocelyn. Intern, Tufts-New Eng. Med. Center, Boston, 1962-63, resident, 1965-66; resident Met. Hosp., N.Y.C., 1966-67, St. Joseph's Hosp., Paterson, N.J., 1967-69; clin. fellow orthopaedic surgery The Hosp. Spl. Surgery, N.Y.C., 1969-71; instr. orthopaedic surgery Cornell U., 1969-71; instr. Harvard U., 1971-78, asst. clin. prof., 1979—; asso. in orthopaedic surgery Children's Hosp. Med. Center, Boston, 1971—; jr. asso. Peter Bent Brigham Hosp., Boston, 1971—; chief orthopaedic cerebral palsy clinic Children's Hosp. Med. Center. Served with USAF, 1963-65. Diplomate Am. Bd. Orthopaedic Surgery. Fellow Am. Coll. Surgeons; mem. Am. Acad. Orthopaedic Surgeons, Am. Acad. Pediatrics, Am. Acad. Cerebral Palsy. Jewish. Club: Newton Squash and Tennis. Contbr. articles in field to profl. jours. Home: 66 Hartman Rd Newton Centre MA 02159 Office: 300 Longwood Ave Boston MA 02115

ROSENWALD, ALBERT JOHN, microbiologist; b. McKees Rocks, Pa., Dec. 4, 1927; s. Albert Harold and Margaret Matilda (Hartz) R.; student Muhlenberg Coll., 1946; B.S., Mt. St. Mary's Coll., 1950; postgrad. U. Md., 1955-60, George Washington U., 1961, NIH, 1962; m. Julia Teresa Arnold, June 20, 1953; children—John M., James T., Jeffrey A., Joseph M., Julie Ann. Bacteriologist, U.S. Army Biol. Center, Frederick, Md., 1951-68; biologist Naval Intelligence Support Center, Washington, 1968—. Sec.-treas. Lewistown (Md.) Citizens Assn., 1963-66; v.p. Lewistown PTA, 1968-69, pres., 1969-70. Served with USNR, 1945-46. Recipient Quality award U.S. Army Biol. Center, 1966, Outstanding Performance award, 1967. Mem. Sci. Research Soc. Am. Club: Thurmont (Md.) Sportsmen and Conservation. Contbr. papers to sci. publs. Home: 7627 Utica Rd Thurmont MD 21788 Office: 4301 Suitland Rd Washington DC 20390

ROSKO, MILTON, JR., beer mfr.; b. Newark, July 19, 1930; s. Milton and Anne (Curlik) R.; student pub. schs., Newark; m. June Helen Whitmeyer, Nov. 1, 1953; children—Linda June Rosko Basilio, Robert Milton. With Anheuser-Busch, Inc., Newark, 1948—, adminstv. mgr. Newark beer br., 1963—; outdoor photojournalist, lectr. Asst. scoutmaster Boy Scout Troop 32, Watchung, N.J., 1973—, committeeman, 1973; mem. Ch. Council Zion Evang. Lutheran Ch., 1971-78. Served with USMC, 1951-53. Recipient Old Salt award N.J. Travel and Resort Assn., 1966. Mem. Outdoor Writers Assn. Am. (Wheels Afield award 1965, past dir.), Rod and Gun Editors Assn. Met. N.Y. (past pres.), N.J. Brewers Assn., N.J. Outdoor Writers Assn. Republican. Author: Fishing From Boats, 1968; Secrets of Striped Bass Fishing, 1966; (with others) Spinfishing, the System That Does It All, 1973. Contbr. articles to mags. Home: 268 High Tor Dr Watchung NJ 07060 Office: 200 US Hwy 1 Newark NJ 07101

ROSNAGLE, ROBERT SHIELDS, otolaryngologist; b. Columbus, Ohio, Dec. 9, 1931; s. Francis Ernest and Mary Belle R.; B.A., Coll. Wooster, 1953; M.D., Case-Western Res. U., 1957; m. Barbara Letitia Mortensen, Aug. 8, 1954; children—Elisabeth Ann, Mary Susan, Diane Margaret. Intern, Univ. Hosp., Cleve., 1957-58; resident otolaryngology U. Ill. Research and Ednl. Hosps., Chgo., 1960-63; asst. prof. surgery Yale U., New Haven, 1963-66, asso. clin. prof. medicine, 1966—; individual practice medicine, specializing in otolaryngology, New Haven, 1966—. Mem. Guilford (Conn.) Bd. Edn., 1973-77, Guilford Health Council, 1976. Mem. Am. Acad. Ophthalmology and Otolaryngology, Am. Triological Soc., Am. Acad. Facial, Plastic and Reconstructive Surgery, New Eng. Otolaryngologic Soc., Conn. Ear, Nose and Throat Soc. (pres. 1975-77). Republican. Home: 140 Deer Ln Guilford CT 06437 Office: 98 York St New Haven CT 06511

ROSNER, IRVING STANLEY, audio-visual communications systems co. exec.; b. N.Y.C., Apr. 23, 1926; s. David and Esther (Lesser) R.; B.E.E., Cooper Union Coll., 1949; M.S. in Indsl. Engring., Columbia U., 1954; m. Risha Fraiberg, Feb. 10, 1963; children—Amy, David. Television engr. CBS, N.Y.C., 1949-59; TV systems engr. RCA, Camden, N.J., 1959-60; founder Rosner Television Systems, Inc., N.Y.C., 1960, pres., 1960—. Served with USNR, 1944-46. Fellow Soc. Motion Picture and Television Engrs.; mem. Audio Engring. Soc., IEEE. Contbr. articles to profl. jours. Home: 17 Mitchell Dr Kings Point NY 11024 Office: 250 W 57th St New York City NY 10019

ROSOF, PATRICIA JANE FREEMAN, historian; b. N.Y.C., May 19, 1949; d. Sylvan D. and Charlotte (Fischer) Freeman; A.B., N.Y. U., 1970, M.A., 1971, Ph.D., 1978; m. Alan H. Rosof, Sept. 13, 1970; children—Jeremy Sage, Simon Jay. Tutor in history Empire State Coll., Old Westbury, N.Y., 1975; guest lectr. State U. N.Y., Old Westbury, 1977; adj. lectr. history Baruch Coll., N.Y.C., 1977; instr. Iona Coll., New Rochelle, N.Y., 1978—. Mem. Institute for Research in History, Coordinating Com. for Women in the Hist. Profession, Phi Beta Kappa. Contbr. poem, articles to publs. Office: Iona Coll New Rochelle NY 10801

ROSOW, MICHAEL PHILIP, psychologist; b. Phila., Nov. 7, 1945; s. Jerome Morris and Rosalyn (Levin) R.; B.A., Windham Coll., 1969; M.A. in Psychology, Hofstra U., 1971, Ph.D. in Psychology, 1974; m. Rayna Feldman, June 30, 1968; children—Lori Beth, Alison Jill. Research asso. Daniel Yankelovich, Inc., N.Y.C., 1972-73, Stamford, Conn., 1973-75; sr. project dir., nat. analysts div. Booz-Allen & Hamilton, N.Y.C., 1975, acting mgr. N.Y. region, 1975-76; sr. research asso. Work In Am. Inst., Scarsdale, N.Y., 1976—; cons. productivity and quality of working life U. Ill., Sawmill Internat., Inc. Rehab. research fellow Social and Rehab. Service, HEW, 1971-75. Mem. Am. Soc. Personnel Adminstrn., Am. Mktg. Assn., Am. Soc. Info. Sci. Club: Claiborne Athletic (pres. 1968). Author: The Conditioning of Attitudes Toward the Physically Disabled, 1974; supr. research and writing: Mid-Career Perspectives...,Productivity and the Quality of Working Life, Trends in Product Quality and Worker Attitude, Managerial Productivity, Worker Alienation, Human Resource Accounting. Home: 10 Heritage Ln Stamford CT 06903 Office: 700 White Plains Rd Scarsdale NY 10583

ROSS, ADRIAN E., diamond drilling co. exec.; b. Clintonville, N.Y., Mar. 6, 1912; s. James A. and Bertha (Beardsley) R.; B.S. in Elec. Engring., Mass. Inst. Tech., 1934, M.S. in Elec. Engring., 1935; m. Ruth T. Hill, Mar. 2, 1934; children—James A., Daniel R. Materials engr. USN, 1935-37; devel. engr. Electrolux Corp., 1937-41; chief engr. and asst. to pres. Sprague & Henwood, Inc., Scranton, Pa., 1946-53, dir., 1951—, pres., 1953-75, chmn. bd., 1963—; chmn. bd. Hands-Eng. Drilling Ltd., 1968, Sprague & Henwood de Venezuela, 1969—; dir. Scranton Lackawanna Indsl. Building Co., N.E. Pa. Bank & Trust Co., Wesel Corp., profl. engrs. Trustee, former chmn. bd. trustees Keystone Jr. Coll.; pres., bd. dirs. James A. Ross Found.; pres., dir. Sprague & Henwood Found.; chmn. bd. trustees Johnson Sch. Tech. Served from lt. to lt. col. Air Communications. USAAF, 1941-46. Profl. engr., Pa. Mem. Diamond Core Drill Mfrs. Assn. (past pres.), Am. Inst. Mining Engrs., Am. Soc. C.E., Moles, Soc. Profl. Engrs., U.S. Nat. Council Soil Mechanics, Indsl. Diamond Assn. Am. (past pres.). Presbyterian. Clubs: Mining (N.Y.C.); Scranton, Mass. Institute Technology (Scranton, Pa. and N.Y.C.). Contbr. articles to Mining Congress Jour., Mining Engring., Engring. and Mining Jour., Diamond Drill Handbook. Home: 5 Overlook Rd Clarks Green PA 18411 Office: 221 W Olive St Scranton PA 18502

ROSS, ALAN O(TTO), psychologist; b. Frankfurt am Main, Germany, Dec. 7, 1921; s. Walter M. and Elizabeth L. (Keller) R.; B. Social Sci., Coll. City N.Y., 1949; M.S., Yale U., 1950, Ph.D., 1953; came to U.S., 1940, naturalized, 1943; m. Ilse Wallis, Sept. 2, 1950; children—Judith, Pamela. Chief psychologist C. Beers Guidance Clinic, New Haven, 1956-59, Pitts. Child Guidance Center, 1959-67; prof. psychology State U. N.Y., Stony Brook, 1967—; cons. VA, 1967—. Mem. Planning Bd., Village of Poquott, 1970—. Served with U.S. Army, 1943-46, 51-56. Certified psychologist, N.Y. Diplomate Am. Bd. Profl. Psychology. Fellow Am. Psychol. Assn. (pres. div. clin. psychology 1969-70); mem. Assn. for Advancement of Behavior Therapy, Soc. for Research in Child Devel. Author: The Practice of Clin. Child Psychology, 1959; The Exceptional Child in the Family, 1964; Psychological Disorders of Children, 1974; Psychological Aspects of Learning Disabilities, 1976; Learning Disability, 1977. Office: Dept Psychology State U NY Stony Brook NY 11794

ROSS, ALEXANDER SEYMOUR, corporate exec.; b. Bklyn., May 25, 1929; s. Davis and Rose (Marcus) Rosenzweig; B.B.A., Coll. City N.Y., 1954; postgrad. N.Y. U., 1958; m. Marilyn Kopp, June 12, 1955; children—Michelle, Ruth, Deborah. Circulation mgr. Ind. News Co., N.Y.C., 1949-51, Pines Pubs., N.Y.C., 1951-55; with Berkey Photo, Inc., N.Y.C., 1956-78, v.p. purchasing, 1964-71, pres. Berkey Tech. (mfg. group), 1971-75, corporate v.p., 1974-78, pres. Keystone div., 1975-76, pres. Willoughby retail div., 1976-77; pres. Sir Max Industries, Inc., 1978—; pres. Clearview Products, Inc., 1978—; exec. v.p. Holmes Amb. Corp., 1978—. Served with AUS, 1953-54; ETO. Mem. Purchasing Mgmt. Assn., Graphic Arts Mgmt. Assn., Am. Mgmt. Assn. Mem. B'nai B'rith. Home: 20 Bayport Ln Great Neck NY 11023 Office: 1327 2d Ave New Hyde Park NY 11040 also 495 Flatbush Ave Brooklyn NY 11225

ROSS, DAN CONNOR, cable TV and engring. co. exec.; b. Indpls., Apr. 20, 1923; s. Connor Dan and Anna (Dennison) R.; student Amherst Coll., 1943-44; B.S., Purdue U., 1946, M.S., 1949; postgrad. Columbia U., 1952-53, 59; Dr. Engring., Johns Hopkins U., 1964; m. Deen Dunn, Oct. 12, 1945; children—Douglas, Keith, Kenneth, Alan, Glen, Elizabeth. Instr. elec. engring. Purdue U., 1946-51; instr. U.S. Mil. Acad., 1951-53; engr., exec. Fed. Systems div. IBM, Kingston, N.Y., also Gaithersburg, Md., 1953-69; pres. Ross

Telecommunications Engring. Corp., Washington, 1969—; pres. CATV Gen. Corp., Washington, 1971-75, dir., 1971—; instr. Johns Hopkins U., 1960-61, 1964-66, cons. engring. faculty, 1966—. Served with U.S. Army, 1943-46, 51-53. Mem. IEEE, AAAS, Soc. Gen. Systems Research Clubs: Johns Hopkins (Balt.); Army and Navy (Washington). Contbr. articles to tech. jours.; patentee computer input-output systems; computer data transmission systems; air traffic control and nav. systems. Home: 6308 Maiden Ln Bethesda MD 20034 Office: 2814 Pennsylvania Ave NW Washington DC 20007

ROSS, DANIEL PAUL, nuclear engr.; b. N.Y.C., Feb. 24, 1930; s. Meyer and Gertrude (Levine) R.; B.E.E. magna cum laude, Coll. City N.Y., 1952; M.S., Columbia, 1952; Ph.D., U. Pa., 1965; m. Rita Bianca Schmelkes, Aug. 1, 1963; children—Joseph Allen, Steven Warren, Anne Terri, Kenneth Marc, David Jan. Teaching asst. Columbia U., 1952-53, trainee Oak Ridge Sch. Reactor Tech., 1953-54; sr. engring. specialist TRW, Cleve., 1954-61; spl. lectr. nuclear engring. Case Inst., 1956-58; with Gen. Electric Co., Phila., 1961—, cons. engr. advanced energy and ocean systems, 1964-72, project engr., staff scientist advanced systems effectiveness analysis, 1973—. Recipient certificate achievement, Gen. Electric Co., 1974. Registered profl. engr., Ohio. Mem. Am. Inst. Aeros. and Astronautics (com. marine sci. and tech.), Nat. Acad. Engring. (working group). Contbr. articles to profl. jours., chpts. to books. Home: 1220 Drayton Ln Philadelphia PA 19151 Office: 3198 Chestnut St Philadelphia PA 19101

ROSS, DAVID HARVEY, physician; b. N.Y.C., Aug. 15, 1911; s. Morris and Rebeca (Müller) R.; B.Sc. summa cum laude, N.Y. U., 1932, M.D., 1936; M.P.H., Harvard U., 1941; m. Pearl Frandesen, Nov. 9, 1946 (dec.); 1 son, Randolph E. Intern, house surgeon Fordham Hosp., N.Y.C., 1936-38, resident in pathology, 1938; resident in medicine, Seaview Hosp., 1939; epidemiologist N.Y. State Dept. Health, 1940-41; asst. dir. Mt. Sinai Hosp., N.Y.C., 1941-47; exec. dir. Jewish Hosp. of Cin., 1947-68; exec. dir. Hosp. for Joint Diseases, N.Y.C., 1968-70; med. dir. Nassau County Dept. Health, Mineola, N.Y., 1970-79; practice medicine, cons. in field, Mineola, 1979—; asst. prof. dept. preventive medicine Coll. Medicine, U. Cin., 1951-68; vis. lectr. Sch. Public Health, Columbia U., 1955-60; asso. prof. hosp. adminstrn. Mt. Sinai Coll. Medicine, 1968-70; chmn. bd. Ohio State Bd. Health, 1967-68; pres. Greater Cin. Hosp. Council, 1963-64. Recipient Samuel Sussman Meml. gold medal, N.Y. U., 1930. Fellow N.Y. Acad. Medicine, Am. Coll. Hosp. Adminstrs., Royal Soc. Health (London); mem. Am. Hosp. Assn., Harvard Sch. Public Health Alumni Assn., Mt. Sinai Hosp. Alumni Assn., Ohio Hosp. Assn. (pres. SW dist., bd. trustees 1958-60), Am. Public Health Assn., Phi Beta Kappa (pres. N.Y. U. chpt. 1932). Club: Harvard (N.Y.C). Contbr. articles to profl. jours. Home: 338 Cold Spring Rd Syosset NY 11791 Office: 240 Old Country Rd Mineola NY 11501

ROSS, DONALD JOSEPH, JR., property assessor; b. Bridgeport, Conn., Dec. 18, 1953; s. Donald Joseph and Christine Dorothea (Laforet) R.; A.B., Fairfield U., 1975; m. Arlene Teresa Richter, Oct. 9, 1976. Apprentice assessor, Fairfield, Conn., 1975-76, personal property assessor, 1976—; mem. profl. writing program Fairfield U. Mem. Internat., Conn. assns. assessing officers. Roman Catholic. Club: Fairfield U. Alumni Assn. Home: 295 Country Rd Fairfield CT 06430 Office: Town Hall 611 Old Post Rd Fairfield CT 06430

ROSS, DORIS G., civic worker; b. Thompsonville, Conn.; d. Philip A. and Eva (Saffir) Sisitzky; student Barnard Coll., Max Reinhardt Drama Workshop, N.Y. U. Radio Workshop, Lee Strasberg Theatre Inst., Royal Acad. Dramatic Arts; m. Lewis H. Ross, Jan. 4, 1942; children—Phyllis, Allyne. Dir. New Eng. Zionist Youth Com., 1943-45; dir. theatre arts Manchester Inst, Arts and Scis., 1947-48; pres. Manchester Girls Club, 1950-51, dir., 1949-53, 54-58, 59-69, mem. exec. com., 1955—, chmn. nat. adv. bd., 1955-57, v.p., 1956-57, pres., 1957-59, first acting chmn. past pres. com., 1974, 1st pres. past pres. club, 1975-77, chmn. silver jubilee com., 1969-70, chmn. directions and social concerns com., 1978—; bd. dirs. Girls Clubs Am., 1955—, exec. com., 1955-60, 78—; exec. com. Girls Clubs N.Y., 1970-73, bd. dirs., 1970-73, sustaining dir., 1973—, co-chmn. long range planning com., 1970-71; 1st pres. Theatre Art Players, Temple Emanuel, N.Y.C., 1970-71; dir. Manchester Settlement Assn., 1951-54, Manchester Vis. Nurses Assn., 1955-61; del. Nat. Soc. Welfare Assembly, 1957-59, White House Conf. on Children and Youth, 1960, voting del. nat. council state coms., 1960, mem. N.H. state exec. com., 1960, N.H. state sub-com. on Leisure Times Activites chmn., 1960; charter colleague Nat. Assembly Nat. Voluntary Health and Welfare Orgns., Inc., 1976—, mem. Nat. Juvenile Justice Program Collaboration, Mem. Pres.'s Citizens Adv. Com. on Fitness of Am. Youth, 1958-60; mem. exec. com. Gov.'s Com. on Children and Youth, 1961-63; gov.'s rep. to Pres.'s Conf. on Youth Fitness, 1962; pres. Manchester Garden Club, 1963-64; dir. Opera League New Hampshire, Inc., 1964-69; trustee Actors Studio. Mem. Hadassah (pres. Manchester chpt. 1943-44, dir. Manchester chpt. 1942-49, New Eng. regional v.p. 1944-46). Address: 985 Fifth Ave New York City NY 10021

ROSS, DOUGLAS CARROLL, hist. preservationist; b. Hackensack, N.J., Apr. 4, 1930; s. Douglas Carroll and Elsa Louise (Gysel) R.; A.B., Harvard, 1952; student USCG Acad., 1953, Dartmouth Med. Sch., 1973—; m. (Alice) Elizabeth Sherburne, Sept. 28, 1963. Asst. to mgr. CALTEX, Paris and Abidjan (Ivory Coast) burs., 1954-55; salesman, editor, mng. editor ednl., med. and sci. book div. Oxford U. Press, Inc., N.Y.C., 1955-62; mgr. Chgo. office Pergamon Press, 1962-63; v.p. Tontine Corp., Barnard, Vt., 1963-65; pres. Elm St. Assos., Inc., Woodstock, Vt., 1964-66, Upland Assos., Inc., Woodstock, 1965—; cons. Eva Gebhard-Gourgaud Found., Paris and N.Y.C. Chmn. history and hist. sites Ottauquechee Regional Planning and Devel. Commn.; sec. Woodstock Nat. Hist. Dist.; v.p., sec.-treas. Vt. Found. for Hist. Preservation, Middlebury; Vt. coordinator N.H.-Vt. Bicentennial Ednl. Resources. Trustee Vt. Assn. Crippled, 1968-70, Calvin Coolidge Meml. Found., 1965—; chmn. Coolidge Centennial, 1974; founding trustee Hist. Windsor, Inc., 1971-74. Served as navigator USCG, 1952-54. Mem. Nat. Trust for Hist. Preservation (patron), Am. Mus. Natural History, Asia Soc., Vt. Inst. Natural Scis., S.R., Soc. Colonial Wars, St. Andrews Soc., St. Nicholas Soc. Democrat. Episcopalian (vestryman). Clubs: Hajji Baba (N.Y.C. and Washington); Harvard (N.Y.C. and Vt.); Hartland (Vt.) Nature, Woodstock Country. Has reference collection of over 15,000 transparencies in preservation law (European, Egyptian), history of art and architecture, Americana in conjunction with Dartmouth Art Library. Home: Vantage Church Hill Woodstock VT 05091 also 480 Park Ave New York City NY Office: 5 The Green Woodstock VT 05091 also Wilson Hall Dartmouth Coll Hanover NH 03755

ROSS, ESSYE BUCH (MRS. LEONARD ROSS), lawyer; b. N.Y.C., Nov. 9, 1920; d. Samuel Montgomery and Rebecca (Harris) Buch; B.A., Hunter Coll., 1940; J.D., N.Y. U., 1945; m. Leonard Ross, June 3, 1943; children—Richard K., Robert S. Admitted to N.Y. bar, 1946, U.S. Supreme Ct. bar, 1966; mem. firm Ross & Ross, Hempstead, N.Y., 1951—. Law guardian Family Ct. Nassau County, 1964-70; adv. counsel Nat. Orgn. for Women, L.I., 1969-74; alternate rep. of Internat. Fedn. Women Lawyers to UN, 1970. Organizer, chmn. com. to aid in bldg. of Hofstra U. Law Sch., 1970; v.p. Central Nassau unit Am. Cancer Soc., 1968-69. Recipient Woman of Yr. award Bus. and Profl. Women's Club Nassau County, 1972. Mem. Am., Nassau County bar assns., Nat. Assn. Women Lawyers, Internat. Fedn. Women Lawyers (regional chmn. Mid-East br. 1970-73), Nassau-Suffolk Women's Bar Assn. (pres. 1965-66), Bus. and Profl. Women's Club Nassau County, East Meadow C. of C. (dir. 1968-76). Home: 510 Poplar Ln East Meadow NY 11554 Office: 91 N Franklin St Hempstead NY 11550

ROSS, FRANZ ERNEST, computer co. exec.; b. Munich, Germany, Oct. 4, 1918; s. Hugo and Martha (Braun) Rosenbaum; came to U.S., 1947, naturalized, 1952; student London U., 1943; B.A. with high distinction, U. Ky., 1949; M.A., U. N.C., 1952; m. Margaret Louise Belcher, Oct. 21, 1950; children—Karen Elizabeth, Victoria Bassel, Franz Hugo, Fredericka Louise. Farmer, Middle East, 1935-37; with Brit. Colonial Police, 1938-40; auditor, rate regulation specialist Ky. Dept. Motor Transp., 1950-51; sr. accountant Lybrand, Ross Bros. & Montgomery, Louisville and Phila., 1951-55; pvt. rate cons. to City of Louisville, 1955; with IBM and subs., 1955—, mgr. data security, North Tarrytown, N.Y., 1977—. Trustee Long Ridge Fire Co., 1974—. Served with Brit. Army, 1940-47. C.P.A., Pa.; named Ky. col. Mem. Am., Pa. insts. C.P.A.'s, Pound Ridge Hist. Soc., Phi Beta Kappa, Pi Mu Epsilon. Home: RFD 1 Box 200 Pound Ridge NY 10576 Office: IBM Ams/Far East Corp Town of Mt Pleasant Route 9 North Tarrytown NY 10591

ROSS, GEOFFREY SINCLAIR, venture devel. co. exec.; b. New Haven, Conn., Sept. 22, 1952; s. Edmund Thomas and Barbara Elaine (Sinclair) R.; student George Washington U., 1970-72, Fairfield U., 1973. Founder and partner, then pres. BMSA Entertainment, Wilton, Conn., 1970-75; pres. The Producers, Inc., Wallingford, Conn., 1975-76; cons. media-entertainment corps., Wallingford, 1975-76; founder, pres., chief exec. 20 Nova 7 System, Ltd., Norwalk, Conn., 1976—; dir. Aviation Internat. Resources Corp., Scotch Whiskey Blenders Corp. Past mem. Wilton Republican Campaign com.; mem. Wilton Rep. town com. Mem. C. of C. Clubs: AMORC. Pub., The Eagle, 1976—. Home: 5 Old Forge Rd Wilton CT 06897 Office: 83 Wall St Norwalk CT 06850

ROSS, HAROLD LEROY, JR., advt. exec.; b. Trenton, N.J., July 5, 1934; s. Harold Leroy and Lucy Fortch (Zeller) R.; B.S. in Econs., Rutgers U., 1955; m. Robina Margaret Mould, July 3, 1964; children—Peter Stuart, Brian Alexander, Jennifer Karen. With Gallup & Robinson Co., Princeton, N.J., 1955-72, v.p., dir., 1965-72; founder Mapes and Ross, Inc., Princeton, 1972, chmn. bd., 1972—; also dir.; dir. Montgomery Nat. Bank. Served with AUS, 1957-59. Mem. Am. Mktg. Assn. Author studies advt. effectiveness; created syndicated TV and mag. test systems. Home: Cherrybrook Dr Princeton NJ 08540 Office: 1101 State Rd Princeton NJ 08540

ROSS, JEFFREY STUART, pathologist, educator; b. Fort Monroe, Va., Sept. 30, 1945; s. Maxwell Shrager and Roslyn (Fassberg) R.; B.A., Oberlin Coll., 1966; M.D., SUNY, Buffalo, 1970; m. Karen Elizabeth Coy, Feb. 16, 1979; children—Mary Martin, Merrill Stuart, Michael Shrager. Intern, Mass. Gen. Hosp. Boston, 1970, resident in pathology, 1971-74; teaching fellow Harvard Med. Sch.; instr. Albany Med. Coll., 1976—; asst. prof. U. Mass. Med. Center, 1976—; cons. exptl. surgery Mass. Gen. Hosp. and Harvard Med. Sch., 1974—; asso. pathologist Berkshire Med. Center, Pittsfield, Mass., 1976; asso. med. examiner Berkshire County, Mass. 1976—. Served as major M.C., USAR, 1974-76. Mem. Am. Soc. Clin. Pathologists, Coll. Am. Pathology, Internat. Acad. Pathology, Am. Soc. Cytology, Nat. Assn. Med. Examiners, Mass. Med. Soc., N.E. Pathology Soc., Mass. Soc. Pathologists, Mass. Soc. Cytologists, Mass. Mediolegal Soc., Berkshire Med. Soc. Contbr. articles to numerous sci. periodicals. Office: Berkshire Med Center Pittsfield MA 01201

ROSS, JOHN, architect; b. Houston, Mar. 4, 1944; s. Sampson and Edna (Goodie) R.; B.Arch., Howard U., 1967; M.City Planning, Yale U., 1970; m. Sylvia Ann Ravenell, Aug. 24, 1974; 1 son, Marcus Ravenell. Architect, Daniel, Mann, Johnson & Mendenhall, Washington, 1967-69; architect, planning cons. Mitchell-Ross-Worthy, Washington, 1972—; asso. prof. urban planning U. D.C., Washington, 1970—. Bd. dirs., sec. Washington Devel. Assos., Inc., 1972-78. Recipient Community Devel. award D.C. Housing Corp., 1977. Mem. Am. Inst. Planners, Am. Soc. Planning Ofcls., Nat. Tech. Assn., Nat. Orgn. Minority Architects. Democrat. Roman Catholic. Home: 1732 Irving St NW Washington DC 20010 Office: 6406 Georgia Ave NW Washington DC 20012

ROSS, JOHN ALLEN, demographer, sociol. research adminstr.; b. Paola, Kans., Dec. 24, 1934; s. Smiley Allen and Daisy Juanita (Miller) R.; B.A., Ottawa (Kans.) U., 1956; M.A. (fellow), Yale U., 1957, Ph.D., 1961; postgrad. U. Chgo., summer 1964, U. Mich., 1964-65; m. Harriet Elizabeth Shelton, June 7, 1958; children—David Shelton, Allen Douglas. Research sociologist with heart disease control program, USPHS, Washington, 1960-61; asst. prof. sociology Albion (Mich.) Coll., 1961-64; research demographer Population Council, N.Y.C., 1965-66, Council's rep. to Korea, 1968-70, adviser to Korean Ministry of Health and Social Affairs, 1967-70, asso. dir. tech. assistance div., N.Y.C., 1970-75; asso. prof. Sch. Pub. Health, Center for Population and Family Health, Columbia U., N.Y.C., 1975—. Fellow Am. Sociol. Assn.; mem. Population Assn. Am., Internat. Union for Sci. Study Population. Author: (with T.I. Kim and G.C. Worth) The Korean National Family Planning Program, 1972; contbr. articles on family planning and population studies to profl. jours. Home: 15 Rogers Ave Hartsdale NY 10530 Office: 60 Haven Ave New York City NY 10032

ROSS, JOHN JOSEPH, lawyer; b. St. Johns, N.Y., Apr. 6, 1929; s. John J. and Anna Marie (Heatherton) R.; B.S., Va. Mil. Inst., 1951; LL.B., Georgetown U., 1956; m. Marie B. Katch, July 5, 1954; children—Terence P., Brendan S., Maura A., Kara A. Admitted to D.C. bar, 1956; asso. firm Hogan & Hartson, Washington, 1956-64, partner, 1964—. Dir. Jewell Ridge Coal Sales Co., Tazewell, Va., 1965-66. Chmn. P.L.I. Equal Employment Compliance Programs, 1972-77; chmn. P.L.I. Affirmative Action Workshop, 1973. Served to maj. USMCR, 1951-54. Decorated Navy Cross, Silver Star. Mem. Am., Fed., D.C. bar assns., Am. Judicature Soc., Am. Acad. Polit. Sci., Newcomen Soc. Clubs: Army-Navy, Belle Haven Country, Metropolitan. Author: Special Problems in the Protection of Trade Secrets in Dealing with the Government, 1966. Home: 7021 Marian Dr Alexandria VA 22307 Office: 815 Connecticut Ave NW Washington DC 20006

ROSS, JOSEPH MURPHY, govt. ofcl., community planner; b. Newport News, Va., Mar. 10, 1928; s. Joseph Gerhart and Annie (Murphy) R.; B.C.E., Ga. Inst. Tech., 1953; m. Evelyn Marie Williford, Feb. 26, 1949. Asso. partner, Harland Bartholomew and Assos., Atlanta, 1955-74; asst. exec. dir. Newport News Redevel. and Housing Authority, 1974-76; dir. devel. City of Newport News, 1976-78; community planner U.S. Dept. Commerce, Washington, 1978—; cons. urban planning. Served with USMCR, 1946-48, 50-51. Mem. ASCE, Nat. Assn. Housing and Redevel. Ofcls. Roman Catholic. Author city plans Charlottesville, Va., 1958, Harrisonburg, Va., 1962, Hopewell, Va., 1964, Anderson, S.C., 1965, Greenwood, S.C., 1967. Home: 250 S Van Dorn St Apt N-404 Alexandria VA 22304 Office: US Dept Commerce 14th St and E St NW Room 7830-A Washington DC 20230

ROSS, LUISA M., personnel exec.; b. Wasserburg, Germany, May 27, 1927; d. Alois and Katherine (Simon) Reile; came to U.S., 1947, naturalized, 1953; B.A. in German and Personnel Mgmt. magna cum laude, State U. N.Y., Buffalo, 1975; m. Christopher T.W. Ross, June 11, 1952; children—Mark Alexander, Katherine Luise, Sonya Christine (dec.). Apprentice in organizational adminstrn. Ministry of Economics, Germany, 1942-44; interpreter U.S. Mil. Govt., Germany, 1945-46; office mgr. law offices, Buffalo, 1961-69; asst. personnel mgr., indsl. relations dept. Arcata Graphics, Depew, N.Y., 1971—. Founding mem., bd. dirs. St. Josephs Hosp. Guild, 1967-68. Mem. Am. Soc. Personnel Adminstrn., Adminstrv. Mgmt. Soc., Alpha Sigma Lambda (sec. 1975-76). Clubs: Buffalo Athletic (bd. women's activity, founder, capt. women's ski club, women's swimming team, 1968-71), Erie County Bar Assn. Women's Aux. (v.p. dir. 1968-70). Home: 296 Forbes Ave Tonawanda NY 14150

ROSS, MARY COWELL (MRS. JOHN O. ROSS), lawyer; b. Oklahoma City, Oct. 1, 1910; d. Sears F. and Elizabeth (Van Zwaluwenburg) Riepma; A.B., Vassar Coll., 1932; LL.B. cum laude, So. Law U. (now part of Memphis State U.), 1938; LL.D., U. Nebr., 1973; m. Richard N. Cowell, Mar. 1, 1946 (dec. Jan. 1953); m. 2d, John O. Ross, Mar. 31, 1962 (dec. June 1966). Admitted to Tenn. bar, 1938, D.C. bar, 1944, N.Y. bar, 1947; atty. U.S. Govt., Washington, 1940-44; pvt. practice Cromelin & Townsend, Washington, 1944-46, Royall, Koegel & Rogers, N.Y.C., 1946-61; pvt. law practice, N.Y.C., 1961—; treas., dir. 39 E. 79th St. Corp., 1966-73; dir. 795 Fifth Ave. Corp., 1977—. Adv. com. N.Y. Commn. Estates, 1965-67. Trustee, bd. dirs. U. Nebr. Found.; trustee Nebr. Art Assn.; dir. Cunningham Dance Found., Inc., 1969-72, Silver Cross Day Nursery, 1963-70, Central Park Community Fund, 1977—. Mem. Am. Bar Assn., D.C. Bar, N.Y. Women's Bar Assn. (pres. 1955-57, dir. 1957-63, 74—, adv. council 1963—), Bar Assn. City N.Y., (library com. 1965—), Nat. Assn. Women Lawyers (state del. 1958-61, corr. sec. 1961-62, assembly del. 1962-64, 73-74, membership trophy 1959, 63; UN observer 1965-67, v.p. 1967, Distinguished Service award 1973), Vassar College Alumnae Assn., Phi Alpha Delta, Delta Gamma. Clubs: Metropolitan, Regency, Vassar (N.Y.C.). Address: 2 E 61st St New York City NY 10021

ROSS, ROBERT DONALD, librarian; b. N.Y.C., Mar. 28, 1931; s. William and Ceceile (Cross) Rosenfeld; B.A., Coll. City N.Y., 1954; student N.Y. U., 1956-64; M.L.S., Rutgers U., 1966; Post M.L.S., Columbia U., 1968; m. Madeleine Ladner, May 28, 1961; children—Jeffrey Laurence, Jodie Dianne. Reference librarian Bklyn. Pub. Library, 1965; reader services librarian Suffolk County (N.Y.) Community Coll., 1966-69; dir. S. Brunswick (N.J.) Pub. Library, 1969-73, Ridgewood (N.J.) Pub. Library, 1973—; adj. prof. Middlesex County (N.J.) Community Coll., 1973-76; mem. adv. com. Nat. Project Center for Film and the Humanities, 1971-75, chmn. Libraries of S. Middlesex, 1970-73; chmn. dirs. council N. Bergen Fedn. Libraries, 1975. Mem. exec. bd. S. Brunswick Community Council, 1970-73; mem. Ridgewood (N.J.) Bicentennial Commn., 1975—. Certified profl. librarian, N.J. Mem. ALA, N.J. Library Assn. Club: Kiwanis. Home: 351 Walthery Ave Ridgewood NJ 07450 Office: 125 N Maple Ave Ridgewood NJ 07450

ROSS, RODERIC HENRY, ins. co. exec.; b. Jamestown, N.Y., July 14, 1930; s. Edwin A. and Mary Elizabeth (Dornberger) R.; A.B., Hobart Coll., 1952; C.L.U., Am. Coll., Bryn Mawr, Pa., 1960; m. Patricia Johnson, Aug. 6, 1955; children—Timothy, Amy, Jane, Christopher. With pub. relations dept. Phila. Life Ins. Co., 1954-55, group ins. dept., 1955-57, field rep., 1957-70, exec. asst. to chmn. of co., 1970-72, sr. v.p. mktg., 1972-73, pres., 1973—; dir. Phila. Life Ins. Co., Provident Bank, Phila. Vestryman St. David's Ch., Radnor, Pa., 1972—; bd. dirs. Better Break '76, 1974—, Upper Main Line YMCA, 1967-74, Old Phila. Devel. Corp., 1976—; trustee Hobart Coll., 1972—, vice chmn. bd., 1978—. Served with U.S. Army, 1952-54. Mem. Nat., Phila. assns. life underwriters, Million Dollar Round Table (life), Am. Soc. C.L.U.'s, Ins. Fedn. Pa. (vice-chmn. 1978—). Episcopalian. Clubs: Pine Valley Golf (Clementon, N.J.); St. David's (Pa.) Golf; Racquet, Union League, Orpheus (Phila.). Home: 770 Pugh Rd Wayne PA 19087 Office: 111 N Broad St Philadelphia PA 19107

ROSS, SIGMUND LANCE, mining engr.; b. Tarrytown, N.Y., Apr. 23, 1921; B.S. in E.M., 1940. Quarry supt. Morrison Knudson Co., Middle East. and Greece, 1947-49; v.p., drilling supt. Geomantle Oil Co., 1958-73; cons. Combustion Equipment Assn., Inc., 1973—; engr. Am. Electric Power Service Corp., 1975—; cons. in field. Dep. dir. info. and tng. City of N.Y. Office Civil Def., 1950. Served to 1st sgt. U.S. Army, 1940-46. Mem. Am. Def. Preparedness Assn., Arctic Inst. N. Am., Nat. Rifle Assn., Internat. Assn. Drilling Contractors, Am. Security Council (adv. bd.). Republican. Patentee in field. Home: 1280 E 53d St Brooklyn NY 11234

ROSS, THOMAS MCCALLUM, assn. exec.; b. Hamilton, Ont., Can., May 5, 1931; s. Laverne Robinson and Della Louise (McCallum) R.; B.S. in Pharmacy, U. Toronto, 1955, M.B.A., 1961; m. Marguerite Hilda Ross, Aug. 14, 1954; children—Thomas Wayne, Gregory (dec.), Karyn. Mgr., Sutherland Pharmacy, Hamilton, 1955-60; asso. sec. Canadian Pharm. Assn., Toronto, Ont., 1960-63; mem. research staff Royal Commn. Health Services Govt. Can., Ottawa, Ont., 1963-64; exec. dir. Canadian Retail Hardware Assn., Toronto, 1964—; dir. Raymond Bros., London. Bd. dirs. Lords Day Alliance Can., Toronto. Founding fellow Hardware Mgmt. Inst.; mem. Canadian Wholesale Hardware Assn. (chief adminstrv. office 1970—), Internat. Fedn. Ironmongers Assns. (council 1970—), Inst. Assn. Execs. (chmn. ins. trustees 1968), Canadian C. of C., Am. Soc. Assn. Execs. Home: 59 Walby Dr Oakville ON Canada Office: 290 Merton St Toronto ON Canada

ROSS, WILBUR LOUIS, JR., investment banker; b. Weehawken, N.J., Nov. 28, 1937; s. Wilbur Louis and Agnes Hope (O'Neill) R.; A.B., Yale U., 1959; M.B.A. with distinction, Harvard U., 1961; m. Judith Nodine, 1969; children—Jessica, Amanda. Asso., Wood, Struthers & Winthrop, N.Y.C., 1963-64; v.p. de Vegh Internat. Corp., N.Y.C., 1963-64; gen. partner Faulkner, Dawkins & Sullivan, N.Y.C., 1964—, pres., dir., 1971—; dir. exec. com. Peabody Internat. Corp., Inc., Texstar Corp.; dir. Aileen, Inc., Armada Corp., Land Resources Corp., Mid-Central Properties, Ltd., Hoskins Mfg. Co., Ryan Fin. Services, Inc., New Ct. Securities Corp., Sheldon Petroleum Corp., Investors Ins. Holding Co., New Court Leasing, Inc. Mem. Joint Legis. Commn. on Energy Policy for State N.Y. Treas. N.Y. State Democratic Com.; gov., mem. exec. com. Bklyn. Mus.; trustee Bklyn. Inst. Arts and Scis. Served as 1st lt. AUS, 1961-63. Chartered financial analyst. Author: (with others) Teaching Machines, 1962; (with others) Applied Programed Instruction, 1962. Home: 1 W 72d St New York City NY 10023 Office: 1 Rockefeller Plaza York City NY 10020

ROSS, WILLIAM DANIEL, chemist; b. Elmira, N.Y., Nov. 22, 1917; s. Walter P. and Mary (Daly) R.; B.A., Columbia, 1938; B.S., Columbia Engring. Sch., 1939; m. Sophie Gebert, 1961; 1 dau., Celia M. Chemist pigments dept. E.I. Du Pont de Nemours & Co., 1939—, research fellow, 1968—. Mem. Am. Chem. Soc., A.A.A.S., Am. Inst. Chem. Engrs., N.Y. Acad. Scis., Optical Soc. Am., Phila. Soc. Coatings Tech., Phi Beta Kappa. Phi Lambda Upsilon. Contbr. articles to profl. jours. Patentee in calcination. Home: 36 Ridgewood Circle

Wilmington DE 19809 Office: DuPont Co Pigments Dept Exptl Sta Wilmington DE 19898

ROSS, WINSTON ALTON, social service adminstr.; b. St. Kitts, W.I., Dec. 2, 1941; s. Reginald and Ruby K. (Swanston) R.; A.A.S., N.Y.C. Community Coll., 1961; B.S. in Edn., N.Y. U., 1963; M.S., Columbia U., 1971; m. Rosalind Golden, Aug. 16, 1969. Caseworker, N.Y.C. Dept. Social Services, 1966-72; unit supr. preventive services Bur. Child Welfare N.Y.C., 1972-73; exec. supr. group home program St. Dominic's Home, 1973-75; social work supr. Graham Home for Children, 1976-77; unit dir. Wiltwyck Sch., 1977-78; coordinator energy programs Westchester Community Opportunity Program, Inc., Elmsford, N.Y., 1978—. Pres. Yonkers (N.Y.) br. NAACP, 1971-78, regional dir. Westchester region N.Y. State Conf. NAACP Brs., 1978—; sponsor Ann. Whitney M. Young, Jr. Meml. Conf. on Racism and Delivery Human Services. Served with U.S. Army, 1963-66; ETO. Recipient Freedom Fighter award Yonkers br. NAACP, 1978. Mem. Nat. Assn. Social Workers (pres.-elect Westchester div. 1978—, co-chmn. Westchester anti-racims com., Assn. Black Social Workers, Am. Public Welfare Assn., Nat. Conf. Social Welfare. Democrat. Mem. African Methodist Episcopal Ch. Club: Rotary (Yonkers). Home: 53 Hunt Ave Yonkers NY 10710 Office: Westchester Co-Op Inc 33 W Main St Elmsford HY 10523

ROSSELLI, CHARLES ANTHONY, environ. engr.; b. Medford, Mass., Sept. 13, 1944; s. Anthony C. and Eleanor (Gaumond) R.; B.S. in Engring., Northeastern U., 1969, M.S., 1974; m. Marsha Read, July 19, 1969. Lab. technician LeMessurier Assos., Boston, 1965-69; field engr. Golder-Gass Assos., Boston, 1969-70; asso. prof. Wentworth Inst. Tech., Boston, 1969—; cons. in civil engring., 1974—. NSF grantee, 1974, 76; HEW grantee, 1978; licensed Class A-F Builders. Mem. ASCE, Boston Soc. Civil Engrs., Soc. Am. Mil. Engrs., Am. Soc. Engring. Edn. (Outstanding Young Faculty award 1974), Am. Assn. Bioengrs. Home: 69 Mt Vernon St Somerville MA 02145 Office: 550 Huntington Ave Boston MA 02115

ROSSELOT, MAX B., univ. adminstr.; b. West Elkton, Ohio, June 30, 1913; s. Harvey L. and Gertrude (Vance) R.; A.B., Denison U., 1935; A.M., Miami U., Oxford, Ohio, 1950; postgrad. Ind. U., 1953-54, summer 1960; m. Lillian Anna Draut, Oct. 5, 1940; children—Deborah Rosselot Bramiage, Michael T., Keith V. (dec.), Bruce E., Pamela H. Sales corr. Armco Internat. Corp., Middletown, Ohio, 1936-43; asst. to pres. E.B. Thirkield & Sons, Franklin, Ohio, 1943-46; pres. M.B. Rosselot Sales Co., Middletown, 1946-47; asst. prin., tchr. Monroe (Ohio) High Sch., 1947-49; mem. faculty Miami U., Oxford, 1949-68, asso. registrar, asst. prof. office skills and mgmt. 1956-60, registrar and asso. prof., 1960-68; dir. univ. records and studies State U. N.Y. at Stony Brook, 1968—, dean for student adminstrv. services, 1971—; cons. U. Ibadan (Nigeria), 1966-67, vis. registrar, cons. in the registry, 1972-74; cons. N.Y. State Edn. Dept. Bd. dirs. Hamilton County council Boy Scouts Am. Grantee State U. N.Y., Rockefeller Found.; recipient Citation U. Ibadan. Mem. Am. Assn. Higher Edn., NEA, Am. Council on Edn., Nat. Office Mgmt. Assn. (dir. Butler County chpt. sec. 1958-60), Am. (chmn. research in admissions ann. meeting 1970, chmn. nat. standing com. 1970-72), Ohio (past sec., treas., pres. elect) assns. collegiate registrars and admissions officers, State U. N.Y. Registrars Assn. (v.p. 1974-75), AAUP (sec. Miami U. chpt. 1954-55), Common Cause, Am. Acad. Polit. and Social Scis., Nat. Assn. Student Personnel Adminstrs., Am. Acad. Arts and Scis., Assn. Community and Univ. Cooperation (v.p. 1975—), Am. Mgmt. Assn., L.I. Coll. Student Personnel Assn. (pres. 1978-79), N.Y. Zool. Soc., Am. Mus. Natural History, ACLU, Theta Chi, Delta Pi Epsilon, Phi Delta Kappa. Episcopalian. Clubs: Masons, Rotary, Old Field (gov.). Home: 96 Christian Ave Stony Brook NY 11790 Office: State U NY Stony Brook NY 11790

ROSSI, JOSEPH O., artist; b. Paterson, N.J.; s. Pasquale and Marion (Stampone) R.; student Newark Sch. Fine and Indsl. Art, Grand Central Sch., Columbia; pvt. art study with John R. Grabach, Harven Dunn; m. Joan O'Mara; children—Robert J., Donald J., Sharon M., Carolyn J. Tchr., Newark Sch. Fine and Indsl. Art, Art Students League, N.Y.C.; pvt. art instr.; exhibited in group shows at Am. Watercolor Soc. Ann., Allied Artists Ann. N.Y.C., Audubon Artists Ann. N.Y.C., N.A.D., N.Y.C., Watercolor U.S.A., Md., Rockport (Mass.) Art Assn., Northshore Art Assn., Gloucester, Mass.; represented in permanent collections at Salmagundi Club Collection, Norfolk Mus., Bergen Mall Collection, Newark Hosp. Collection, Valley Hosp. Collection Ridgewood, N.J., also pvt. collections. Recipient various art awards. Mem. Am. (dinner chmn.), N.J. (past v.p.) watercolor socs., Allied Artists Am. (past work chmn.), Audubon Artists, Soc. Illustrators. Clubs: Salmagundi (past art chmn.), Phila. Watercolor. Address: 45 Lockwood Dr Clifton NJ 07013

ROSSI, ROBERT, ret. criminal investigator; b. Union City, N.J., May 9, 1928; s. Guerino and Antionetta (Fochesato) R.; B.B.A. in Acctg., Rutgers U., 1951, M.B.A., 1956; student Pace U., 1978; m. Romana Gaioni, Aug. 27, 1955; children—Mary Ellen, Roberta Lita, Mark Warren. Clk., accounts payable Met. Life Ins. Co., N.Y.C., 1953-54; accountant Philip Flaxman & Co., Union City, 1954-56; agt., criminal investigator Intelligence div. IRS, Dept. of Treasury, Newark, 1956—; spl. assignments Dept. Customs, U.S. State Dept. and Dept. of Justice. Mem. Ams. for Effective Law Enforcement, 1975—, N.Y.C. Police Reserve, 1977—. Served to cpl. U.S. Army, 1951-53. Mem. Nat. Treasury Employee Union, Fed. Criminal Investigators Assn. (nat. chmn. pub. relations, pres. Newark chpt. 1973, 76, 78), Internat. Assn. Chiefs of Police, Internat. Assn. Credit Card Investigators (speakers com. 1976—), Am. Legion; hon. mem. N.Y.C. Police Honor Legion. Clubs: DAV, Lions, AAU. Home: 100 Linden Ave Emerson NJ 07630

ROSSIGNOL, JOYCE HALL, editor; b. Smyrna Mills, Maine, May 7, 1929; d. Joseph Dell-Sawyer and Florence Lillian (Barker) Hall; student U. Hartford, 1953-56; m. Gilman Rossignol, May 10, 1947; children—Mary, James, Harry, Sarah. Women's editor East Hartford (Conn.) Gazette, 1956-62; asso. editor Conn. Life, West Hartford, 1962-69; editor Wethersfield (Conn.) Post, 1971—. Recipient 1st prize New Eng. Press Assn., 1957, 70, 73. Mem. Wethersfield C. of C. (sec.-treas. 1976—), Conn. Editorial Assn. (v.p. 1975—), New Eng. Press Assn., Wethersfield Hist. Soc. Democrat. Roman Catholic. Clubs: Wethersfield Women's, Businessmen's and Civic Assn. Address: 369 Goff Rd Wethersfield CT 06109

ROSSMAN, HOWARD SAMUEL, chem. engring. personnel cons.; b. N.Y.C., July 17, 1939; s. Abraham and Lillian (Lazarow) R.; B.Chem. Engring., McGill U. (Can.), 1961; M.B.A. cum laude, Fairleigh Dickinson U., 1965; m. Carol Kondell, Mar. 22, 1964; children—Matthew, Jordan, Mark, Judd. Chmn. engr., prodn. supt., project engr. E.I. duPont de Nemours & Co., Inc., Parlin, N.J., 1961-68; owner Engring. Employment Agy. Consultants, Inc., Westfield, N.J., 1968—. Guest speaker on job hunting techniques for engrs. Mem. Am. Inst. Chem. Engrs. (chmn. N.J. sect. 1973-74), Air Pollution Control Assn., Water Pollution Control Fedn. Contbr. articles to profl. jours. Home: 1441 Kearney Dr North Brunswick NJ 08902 Office: 189 Elm St Westfield NJ 07090

ROSSMAN, NEWELL WILLIAM, JR., ednl. adminstr.; b. Kingston, Pa., Sept. 4, 1916; s. Newell William and Mildred (Pake) R.; B.A., Syracuse U., 1939; LL.D., Parsons Coll., 1963; m. Kathleen M. Walker, Sept. 26, 1942; 1 dau., Muriel Jeanne Rossman Dustin. Asst., dean men's office, instr. polit. sci. Syracuse U., 1939-41, field sec., dir. alumni fund Alumni Assn., 1945-56, dir. devel., 1956, v.p. univ., 1956-68, vice chancellor univ. relations, 1968-74, vice-chancellor, spl. asst. to chancellor, 1974—; personnel asst., div. personnel supervision and mgmt. Panama Canal, 1941, chief research and service bur., 1944-45; dir. Am. Gen. Life Ins. Co. N.Y., Inc. Mem. Republican Bd., 1959—, Citizens Found.; bd. dirs. Blue Cross Central N.Y., YMCA, Aid to Edn. of Methodist Ch.; trustee Syracuse Savs. Bank and Canal Mus. Mem. Empire State C. of C. (dir., mem. edn. com.), Am. Coll. Pub. Relations Assn., Alpha Chi Rho, Tau Theta Upsilon. Clubs: N.Y. Athletic; Onondaga Golf and Country (Fayetteville, N.Y.); Cazenovia (N.Y.) Golf; Century, Press (Syracuse); Cazenovia. Home: 123 Lincklaen St Cazenovia NY 13035

ROSSMAN, ROBERT HARRIS, value and cost engr.; b. Phila., Jan. 27, 1932; s. Benjamin Bernard and Vivian (Silnutzer) R.; B.S., U.S. Mcht. Marine Acad., 1953; M.S. with honors in Mech. Engring., U.S. Naval Postgrad. Sch., 1963; children—Rodger Samuel, Robbi Jennifer, Ronni Esther. Commd. ensign U.S. Navy, 1953, advanced through grades to comdr., 1968; planning and design adviser, Vietnam, 1967-68, chief prodn. engring. Def. Contract Adminstrn. Services, 1968-70; dir. cost reduction, 1970-73; design mgr. (ships), 1973, ret., 1973; partner Kempter-Rossman Internat., Washington, 1974—; staff lectr., course coordinator various univs. Pres. PTA, 1969; pres. local civic assn., 1970-71; v.p. Assn. of Civic Assns., Fairfax County, 1972; bd. dirs. Value Found., Washington. Decorated Navy Commendation medal with oak leaf cluster. Mem. Soc. Am. Value Engrs. (certified value specialist), Am. Soc. Performance Improvement (certified profl. mgr. human resources), Am. Soc. Naval Engrs., Soc. Naval Architects and Marine Engrs., Ret. Officers Assn., Sigma Xi. Republican. Jewish. Club: Kings Point (Washington). Asso. editor Performance mag., 1970-76; contbr. articles in cost field to various mags. Home: 4927 Americana Dr Annandale VA 22003 Office: 700 National Press Bldg Washington DC 20045

ROSSOFF, SHELDON T., guidance counselor; b. Bklyn., May 26, 1935; s. Philip W. and Elsie Rossoff; B.A., N.Y. U., 1956; M.A., Bklyn. Coll., 1957; postgrad. Bklyn. Coll., C.W. Post Coll., Hofstra U., 1958—; m. Barbara J. Stern, Dec. 25, 1963; children—Risa Michele, Julie Beth. Tchr. sci. Akiba Acad., 1956; tchr. sci. Bellmore Merrick Central High Sch. Dist., 1957-60, guidance counselor, 1962-70, guidance chairperson, 1971-78, guidance grant coordinator, 1978—; guidance counselor East Meadow Sch. Dist., 1961. Mem. exec. bd. Mens Club Temple Emanuel. Served with U.S. Army, 1957. Mem. N.Y. State, Bellmore Merrick united tchrs. assns., Am., N.Y. State, L.I. personnel and guidance assns., Am. Camping Assn. Home: 660 Garner Pl East Meadow NY 11554

ROSTROPOVICH, MSTISLAV, cellist; b. Baku, USSR, Aug. 12, 1927; ed. Moscow Conservatory; s. Leopold and Sofia (Fedotova) R.; m. Galina Vishnevskaya; children—Olga, Yelena. Debut as violoncellist, 1935; soloist Moscow Philharmonic Orch., 1946, performer world concert tours; became faculty mem. Moscow Conservatory, 1953, became prof., 1960, also head cello and double-bass dept.; formerly prof. Leningrad Conservatory; hon. prof. Cuban Nat. Conservatory, 1960—; mem. trio with Emil Gilels, Leonid Kogan. Recipient many awards, including Stalin prize, 1951, 53, Lenin prize, 1964. Hon. mem. Brit. Royal Acad. Music. Address: care Tchiakovsky Conservatory Music 13 Gertzen St Moscow USSR*

ROTBERG, ROBERT I., historian, polit. scientist; b. Newark, Apr. 11, 1935; s. Louis and Mildred Rotberg; A.B., Oberlin Coll., 1955; M.P.A., Princeton U., 1957; D.Phil. (Rhodes scholar), Oxford U., 1960; m. Joanna Henshaw, June 17, 1961; children—Rebecca, Nicola, Fiona. Asst. prof. Harvard U., 1961-68; research dir. Twentieth Century Fund, N.Y.C., 1968-71; prof. polit. sci. and history Mass. Inst. Tech., Cambridge, 1968—; cons. U.S. Dept. State. Mem. Lexington (Mass.) Sch. Com., 1974-77; v.p. Cambridge Civic Assn., 1969-72; chmn. Middlesex County (Mass.) Govtl. Review Task Force, 1972-73. Guggenheim fellow, 1971; Hazen fellow, 1976-77. Mem. Social Sci. History Assn., Am. Hist. Assn. (chmn. nominating com. 1978), Council on Fgn. Relations, Royal Geog. Soc., African Studies Assn. Author: Black Heart: Gore-Browne and the Politics of Multiracial Zambia, 1978, the Black Homelands of South Africa, 1977, 14 other books. Editor Jour. Interdisciplinary History, 1970—. Home: 14 Barberry Rd Lexington MA 02173 Office: 14N-323 MIT Cambridge MA 02139

ROTENBERG, RONALD HYMAN, educator; b. Montreal, Que., Can., Nov. 4, 1941; s. Phil and Celia (Teaman) R.; B. Commerce, Sir George Williams U., 1964; M.B.A., McMaster U., 1966; Ph.D., Pa. State U., 1974; m. Vivien Pollak, June 13, 1965; children—Amy, Andrew, Cara. With mktg. and sales promotion Bernal Labs., Montreal, 1961-65; faculty Concordia U., Montreal, 1966-77, asso. prof. mktg. 1974-77; asso. prof. Sch. Adminstrn. Studies, Brock U., St. Catherines, Ont., Can., 1977—; mktg. cons. Ronald Rotenberg & Asso. Can. Ltd., 1974—. Mem. Am. Mktg. Assn., Canadian Assn. Adminstrv. Scis. Author: (with V.H. Kirpalani) Cases and Readings in Marketing, 1974; Le Marketing au Canada, 1975; contbr. articles to profl. jours. Home: 17 Lochinvar Dr St Catherines ON Canada Office: Brock University St Catherines ON Canada

ROTGIN, PHILIP NORMAN, lawyer; b. Long Beach, N.Y., Mar. 29, 1942; s. Louis and Rheba Rotgin; B.S. in Econs., Wharton Sch. of Fin., 1963; LL.B., Columbia U., 1966; m. Rochelle M. Schneeweis, July 3, 1965; children—Karen Ann, Michael Alan. Admitted to N.Y. State bar, 1967; atty. Home Life Ins. Co., N.Y.C., 1966-70; individual practice law, N.Y.C., 1970—; pres. Philip N. Rotgin, P.C., N.Y.C., 1972—; mem. faculty L.I. U., Am. Paralegal Inst., N.Y.C., 1977—. Recipient Delaware Valley Risk Mgmt. award, 1963. Mem. Assn. of Bar of City of N.Y., N.Y. State Bar Assn., Profl. Planners Forum, Estate Planning Council of N.Y. Jewish. Editorial bd. Estate Planners Quarterly, 1974—. Home: 2277 Halyard Dr Merrick NY 11566 Office: 622 3rd Ave New York City NY 10017

ROTH, CARL, financial exec.; b. Frydlandt, Czechoslovakia, Dec. 15, 1946; s. Samuel and Elizabeth (Ehrlich) R.; came to U.S., 1949, naturalized, 1956; B.S., Fairleigh Dickinson U., 1969; m. Geraldine Miller, 1977. Sr. accountant Price Waterhouse & Co., Newark, 1969-72, mgr. internal audit, 1972-73; dir. fin. planning Bonwit Teller, N.Y.C., 1973-74; asst. corp. controller The Duplan Corp., N.Y.C., 1974-77; group controller M. Lowenstein & Sons, Inc., N.Y.C., 1977-78; dir. internal audit Bonwit Teller, N.Y.C., 1978—. Mem. community tax aid program, N.Y.C. C.P.A., N.J., N.Y. Mem. Am. Inst. C.P.A.'s, Inst. Internal Auditors, Nat. Assn. Accountants, N.J., N.Y. socs. C.P.A.'s. Home: 235 Prospect Ave Hackensack NJ 07601 Office: 721 Fifth Ave New York City NY 10022

ROTH, DAVID MORRIS, historian, educator; b. Phila., Aug. 22, 1935; s. Irwin E. and Delia A. (Gannon) R.; B.A. cum laude in History, Bklyn. Coll., 1957; M.A. in History, Clark U., 1958, Ph.D. in History, 1971; m. Sandra L. Kushner, Dec. 25, 1957; 1 dau., Deborah Anne. Lectr. in history, evening div. Clark U., Worcester, Mass., 1959-60, Bklyn. Coll., 1960-62; instr. in history Eastern Conn. Coll., Willimantic, 1962-65, asst. prof. history, 1965-69, asso. prof., 1969-76, prof., 1976—, dir. Center for Conn. Studies, 1970—; historian of the Am. Revolution Bicentennial Commn. of Windham (Conn.), 1974—, spl. cons. on prodn. of Bicentennial films, 1974-75; hist. cons. to WCBS-TV, N.Y.C., 1975. Recipient President's award for Distinguished Scholarship, Eastern Conn. State Coll., 1973. Mem. Am., New Eng. hist. assns., Am. Assn. for State and Local History, Assn. for Study of Conn. History (dir. 1969-71, pres. 1973-75), AAUP (pres. Eastern Conn. State Coll. chpt. 1965-66), Conn. Hist. Soc., Orgn. Am. Historians, Kappa Delta Pi. Author: (with Freeman Meyer) From Revolution to Constitution: Connecticut, 1763-1818, 1975; Connecticut's War Governor: Jonathan Trumbull, 1974; contbr. articles on Am. history to scholary jours.; series editor: Center for Conn. Studies Series in Conn. History, 5 vols., 1975; editor: Connecticut History, 1969-75. Home: 178 Foster Dr Willimantic CT 06226 Office: Eastern Conn State Coll Willimantic CT 06226

ROTH, SISTER E. SUE, social work adminstr.; b. Cleve.; d. Walter and Adele M. (Schlueter) Roth; Ph.B., Mt. Mary Coll., 1944; M.A., U. Minn., 1949. Supr. case work Mpls. Soc. for Blind, 1946-48, Lutheran Children's Bur., Phila., 1950-52; registrar Luth. Deaconess Sch. Ch. Workers, 1952-58, dir. clin. tng., 1952-58; cons. Services to Blind and Partially Sighted with Luth. Synod Eastern Pa., Bd. Social Ministry, Phila., 1958-68, Luth. Synod. Southeastern Pa., Com. on Social Ministry, 1968-70; dir. social service Center for the Blind, Phila., 1970-74; pvt. clin. practice, 1974—; dir. social service Center City Hosp., Phila., 1977—. Diaconate Luth. Ch. Am.; mem. tech. adv. com. Nat. Aid to Visually Handicapped, 1968-72; lectr. Scheie Eye Inst., Phila. Recipient Madonna medal for profl. achievement Mt. Mary Coll., Milw., 1966; Community Service award Pa. Acad. Ophthalmology and Otolaryngology, 1970. Mem. Acad. Certified Social Workers, Nat. Assn. Social Workers, Nat. Assn. Workers for Blind, Nat. Luth. Social Welfare Conf. Home: 1810 Rittenhouse Sq Philadelphia PA 19103

ROTH, HAROLD, architect; b. St. Louis, June 30, 1934; s. Samuel and Dorothy (Yawitz) R.; student Washington U. at St. Louis, 1951-55; B.Arch., Yale, 1957; m. Dvora Feigon, Dec. 6, 1959; children—Elizabeth, David. Designer, Warner, Burns, Toan & Lunde, N.Y.C., 1957; sr. designer Eero Saarinen & Assos., Birmingham, Mich., 1959-65; partner Harold Roth-Edward Saad, 1965-72, partner Roth Saad Moore, Architects, 1972, sr. partner Roth and Moore, Architects, 1973—. Design critic Yale, 1964-67, 72—; cons. to pres. U. Mass., 1972-76. Bd. dirs. Long Wharf Theatre, New Haven; mem. standards com. New Haven Preservation Trust. Served with AUS, 1957-59. Recipient Honor award New Eng. region A.I.A., 1968, Nat. Council Religious Architecture, 1970, Conn. Soc. Architects/A.I.A., 1974, 78, New Haven Preservation Trust, 1978. Fellow, Pierson Coll., Yale U. Mem. A.I.A., Am. Arbitration Assn. (nat. panel), Assn. Yale Alumni (mem. assembly). Clubs: Elihu, New Haven Lawn. Works include: Mack House, Cheshire, Conn., 1966; Am. Field Service Hdqrs., N.Y.C., 1966; Surf Club West, Milford, Conn., 1967; Trinity Ch. Nazarene, Orange, Conn., 1967; West Rock Nature Center, New Haven, 1968; YMCA, Hamden, Conn., 1968; Ridge Hill Sch., Hamden, 1970; Etkind & Solcoff Distbn. Center, Hamden, 1972; staff housing Ausable Club, St. Huberts, N.Y.; 1973; Oak Lane Country Club, Woodbridge, Conn., 1973; Phys. Edn. Center Dundee Sch., Greenwich, Conn., 1974; Dundee Sch., Greenwich, 1974, Ch. of Redeemer, New Haven, 1976; VanLeeuwen Advt., N.Y.C., 1976, Long Wharf Theater, New Haven, 1977; Bullard's, New Haven, 1977; Fitzwilly's, New Haven, 1978; Zuckerman House, Woodbridge, 1978. Home: 37 Autumn St New Haven CT 06511 Office: 99 Ives Pl New Haven CT 06511

ROTH, JOHN KENNETH, hosp. adminstr.; b. Camden, N.J., Apr. 10, 1929; s. Earl L. and Anna M. (Hawley) R.; B.S. in Accounting, Villanova U. and LaSalle Coll., 1953; postgrad. Temple U., 1955-56; m. Joan E. Davis, Aug. 25, 1956; children—J. Gregory, Donna A., Timothy P. Asst. to dir. accounting Campbell Soup Co., Camden, N.J., 1956-62; installation mgr. Alexander Proudfoot Co., Chgo., 1962-66; sr. cons. Main LeFrentz and Co., C.P.A.'s, Phila., 1967-73; prin. cons. Cole Warren and Long Inc., Phila., 1973-76; asst. dir. Perth Amboy (N.J.) Gen. Hosp., 1976—; partner Cole Warren and Long Inc., cons., 1973-76. Bd. dirs. Assn. Children with Learning Disabilities, 1970-74, Haddonfield Civic Assn., 1956-63, Centennial Pines Club, 1974-78. Served with U.S. Army, 1953-55. Mem. Nat. Assn. Accountants (asst. dir. 1970), Assn. Systems Mgmt. (pres. Central N.J. chpt. 1975, div. dir. 1974-75), Hosp. Mgmt. Systems Soc., N.J. Hosp. Assn. Roman Catholic. Clubs: K.C., Men's St. Mary's Ch. Author: Computer Security Handbook, 1975. Home: West Centennial Dr Centennial Lake Marlton NJ 08053 Office: 530 New Brunswick Ave Perth Amboy NJ 08861

ROTH, JUDITH MARIE BLACKFELD, occupational health nurse; b. Passaic, N.J., Aug. 25, 1946; d. Harold and Elizabeth (Lazur) Blackfeld; R.N., Hackensack (N.J.) Hosp., 1967; postgrad. N.Y. U., 1977; m. Bruce Alvin Roth, Oct. 27, 1967. Mem. nursing staff Valley Hosp., Ridgewood, N.J., 1967-68; occupational health nurse S. Klein's Dept. Store, Wayne, N.J., 1969; occupational health nurse, safety dir. Abex Corp. Research Center, Mahwah, N.J., 1969—; co-chmn. pub. edn. com., mem. exec. com., co-chmn. indsl. edn. com. Bergen County unit Am. Cancer Soc., 1977-78, bd. mgrs., 1978—; CPR instr. Am. Heart Assn.; 1st aid instr. A.R.C. Mem. Am., N.J. (dir. 1972-76, editor jour. 1974—), Palisade (pres. 1972-76, rec. sec. 1976—) assns. occupational health nurses, Hackensack Hosp. Sch. Nursing Alumnae Assn., Ninety Nines (chpt. chmn. 1978-79). Home: 13 Pine St Midland Park NJ 07432 Office: 65 Valley Rd Mahwah NJ 07430

ROTH, JUNE DORIS SPEIWAK, author; b. Haverstraw, N.Y., Feb. 16, 1926; d. Harry I. and Ida (Glazer) Spiewak; student Pa. State U., 1942-44; grad. Tobe-Coburn Sch. for Fashion Careers, 1945; m. Frederick Roth, July 7, 1945; children—Nancy, Robert. Vice pres. evening group Teaneck (N.J.) br. Nat. Council Jewish Women, 1954, pres., 1955, v.p. day group, 1956. Mem. Authors League Am., Tobe-Coburn Alumni Assn., Internat. Platform Assn., Town and Gown Soc. Fairleigh-Dickinson U., Am. Soc. Journalists and Authors, Nat. Fedn. Press Women. Club: Nat. Press (Washington). Author: The Freeze and Please Homefreezer Cookbook, 1963; The Rich and Delicious Low-Calorie Figure Slimming Cookbook, 1964; Thousand Calorie Cookbook, 1967; How to Use Sugar to Lose Weight, 1969; Fast and Fancy Cookbook, 1969; How to Cook like a Jewish Mother, 1969; The Take Good Care of My Son Cookbook for Brides, 1969; The Indoor-Outdoor Barbecue Book, 1970; The Pick of the Pantry Cookbook, 1970; Let's Have a Brunch Cookbook, 1971; Edith Bunker's All in the Family Cookbook, 1972; The On-Your-Own Cookbook, 1972; Healthier Jewish Cookery: The Unsaturated Fat Way, 1972; Elegant Desserts, 1973; Old-Fashioned Candy Making, 1974; Salt-Free Cooking with Herbs and Spices, 1975; The Troubled Tummy Cookbook, 1976; Cooking For Your Hyperactive Child, 1977; The Galley Cookbook, 1977; The Food/Depression Connection, 1978; syndicated newspaper column Special Diets. Address: 1057 Oakland Ct Teaneck NJ 07666

ROTH, LAURENCE GEORGE, physician; b. Stafford, N.Y., Nov. 1, 1920; s. Frank Louis and Marcia Frances (Buckland) R.; B.A. cum laude, Hobart Coll., 1941; M.D., Yale U., 1944; m. Catherine

Kirchner, June 19, 1943; children—Marcia Frances, Laurence George, James Tyler. Intern and resident, 1946-50; practice medicine specializing in obstetrics and gynecology, Batavia, N.Y., 1954-76, practice ltd. to gynecology, 1976—; mem. staff Genesee Meml. Hosp., Batavia, also mem. exec. com., bd. dirs.; from instr. to asst. prof. obstetrics and gynecology State U. N.Y. at Buffalo Sch. Medicine, 1974—, instr. U. Rochester Sch. Medicine, 1954—. Bd. govs. Empire Polit. Action Com., 1974; active Boy Scouts Am., recipient Silver Beaver, 1975; mem. exec. bd. Genesee Symphony. Served with USN, 1943-46, 50-54. Recipient numerous awards. Diplomate Am. Bd. Obstetrics and Gynecology, Nat. Bd. Med. Examiners. Fellow Am. Coll. Obstetricians and Gynecologists (com. on pub. edn., sec. dist. II), A.C.S.; mem. AMA, Med. Soc. State of N.Y., Genesee County Med. Soc., Buffalo Gynecol. and Obstet. Soc., Genesee County Fish and Game Protective Assn., Order of the Arrow, Phi Beta Kappa, Kappa Sigma, Nu Sigma Nu. Republican. Presbyterian. Clubs: Kiwanis, Batavia. Author: (with others) Understanding Natural Childbirth, 1950; contbr. articles to profl. jours. Home: 255 East Ave Batavia NY 14020 Office: 207 Summit St Batavia NY 14201

ROTH, MICHAEL, lawyer; b. N.Y.C., July 22, 1931; s. Philip A. and Mollie F. (Breitenbach) R.; B.A., Yale, 1953; J.D., Columbia, 1956, M.Internat. Affairs, 1964; m. Jeanny Macoir, Nov. 24, 1957; children—Micheline Beth, Jeffrey Marc, Catherine Irene. Admitted to N.Y. bar, 1956, practiced law in N.Y.C.; sr. partner Roth, Carlson & Spengler, 1964-74; chmn. N.Y. State Liquor Authority, N.Y.C., 1974-77; asst. to dir. Internat. Cooperation Adminstrn., 1956-57. Treas. Westchester County Rep. Com., 1969-72; alt. del. Rep. Nat. Conv., 1968; Rep. candidate N.Y. State Atty. Gen., 1978. Bd. govs. Hebrew Union Coll., Jewish Inst. Religion; former chmn. com. on legislation, bd. dirs. Louise Wise Services, N.Y.C.; trustee United Hosp., Rye, N.Y. Jewish. Club: Sunningdale Country (Scarsdale). Home: Rye NY 10580

ROTH, NORMAN GEORGE, hosp. adminstr.; b. Nyack, N.Y., June 16, 1952; s. Norman Walter and Grace Rose (Chiapperino) R.; B.A., Am. U., 1974; M.A., George Washington U., 1977. Adminstrv. asst., methods analyst Prentice Hall Pubs., Inc., Englewood Cliffs, N.J., 1974-75; instr., research asso. Quinnipiac Coll., Hamden, Conn., 1977—; adminstrv. reisdent VA Hosp., W. Haven, Conn., 1976-77, adminstrv. asst. to asso. chief of staff for ambulatory care, 1977—. Bd. dirs. Hill Health Center, Inc., New Haven, 1976—. Mem. Am. Hosp. Assn., Am. Coll. Hosp. Adminstrs. Author: Safety, Sanitation and Infection Control. Home: 32 Terrace Ave Nanuet NY 10954 Office: VA Hosp West Spring St West Haven CT 06516

ROTH, ROBERT GEORGE, physician; b. N.Y.C., Aug. 26, 1932; s. Emil and Bertha (Rosta) R.; B.A. (state scholar), N.Y. U., 1953; M.D., N.Y. Med. Coll., 1957; m. Patricia Cahill, Jan. 9, 1959; children—Patrick, Katherine, Megan. Intern, Michael Reese Hosp., Chgo., 1957-58, NSF fellow, 1958-59; research physician perinatal br. Nat. Inst. Neurol. Diseases and Blindness, NIH, Bethesda, Md., 1958-59; resident neurology Bronx Municipal Hosp. Center, Albert Einstein Coll. Medicine, Bronx, N.Y., 1961-64; practice medicine specializing in neurology, Port Jefferson, N.Y., 1965—; asst. attending physician Bronx Municipal Hosp., 1965-67, Albert Einstein Coll. Medicine Hosp., 1966-67; mem. staffs St. Charles, Mather Meml. hosps., Port Jefferson, 1967—. Instr. neurology Albert Einstein Coll. Medicine, 1965-67; clin. instr. neurology State U. N.Y., Stony Brook, 1972—. Served with USPHS, 1959-61. Diplomate Nat. Bd. Med. Examiners. Me. Am. Bd. Psychiatry and Neurology, Phi Beta Kappa. Contbr. articles to med. jours. Office: 120 N Country Rd Port Jefferson NY 11777

ROTH, ROBERT MERLE, stock broker; b. Milw., Mar. 6, 1930; s. Stanley and Elsie (Erman) R.; B.A., Colby Coll., 1951; m. Helen Harper Palen, Apr. 16, 1955; children—Mark, Karen, Jeffrey. Vice pres. Waddell & Reed, Inc., Miami, Fla., 1955-57, Wilmington, Del., 1957-63, Hartford, Conn., 1963-66; pres. Mark Securities, Inc., West Hartford, Conn., 1966—. Mem. West Hartford Bd. Edn., 1973-77. Served to lt. (j.g.) USNR, 1951-55. Mem. Internat. Assn. Fin. Planners (dir.), West Hartford C. of C. Club: Conn. Traditional Jazz (dir.). Home: 96 Van Buren Ave West Hartford CT 06107 Office: 1007 Farmington Ave West Hartford CT 06107

ROTH, SOL, clergyman; b. Poland, Mar. 8, 1927; s. Joseph and Miriam (Lamm) R.; came to U.S., 1934, naturalized, 1939; B.A., Yeshiva Coll., 1948, grad. Theol. Seminary of Yeshiva U., 1950; M.A., Columbia, 1953, Ph.D., 1966; D.D. (hon.), Yeshiva U., 1977; m. Debra H. Stitskin, Nov. 26, 1957; children—Steven D., Michael J., Sharon J. Ordained rabbi, 1950; rabbi Temple Ashkenaz, Cambridge, Mass., 1951-52, Jewish Center of Atlantic Beach, N.Y., 1956—; asst. prof. philosophy Yeshiva Coll., N.Y.C.; dean chaplaincy sch. N.Y. Bd. Rabbis, pres. bd., 1974-76. Served with U.S. Army, 1952-54. Recipient award synagogue adv. council United Jewish Appeal, 1975; citation N.Y. Bd. Rabbis, 1976. Mem. Am. Philos. Assn., Philosophy of Science Assn. Rabbinical Council Am. (v.p. 1974). Author: The Jewish Idea of Community, 1977. Mem. editorial bd. Tradition. Home: 99 Tioga Ave Atlantic Beach NY 11509 Office: 100 Nassau Ave Atlantic Beach NY 11509

ROTH, STEPHEN IRA, environ. engr.; b. N.Y.C., Mar. 25, 1945; s. Aaron Lieb and Gussie (Hochman) R.; student Queens Coll., 1961-63; B.S. in Mech. Engring., Coll. City N.Y., 1967; m. Sandra Cheryl Snyder, Nov. 22, 1969; children—Jason, Jeffrey. Estimator, asst. supt. Heyward-Robinson Co., N.Y.C., 1964-67; maintenance engr. Allied Chem. Co., Elizabeth, N.J., 1967-68; plant engr. Alcoa Co., New Kensington, Pa., 1968-71, environ. engr., Pitts., 1971—. Mem. Acoustical Soc. Am., ASME (asso.), Inst. Noise Control Engrs. (asso.), Am. Indsl. Hygiene Assn., Am. Inst. Physics. Contbr. articles to profl. jours. Home: 2352 Norton Rd Pittsburgh PA 15241 Office: Aluminum Company of America Alcoa Bldg Pittsburgh PA 15219

ROTH, THEODORE WILLIAM, probate investigator; b. Bklyn., Feb. 2, 1916; s. Theodore and Pauline C. (Smith) R.; grad. Bolan Acad. Investigation, Detection and Criminology, 1948; m. Helen Barbara Wildelska, Feb. 20, 1946. Established in locating missing heirs, 1935—; dir. Missing Heirs Internat. Major Asso. Spl. Investigators Internat., Inc. Pres. Floral Park Republican Club, 1935-40; hon. trustee Internat. Police Hall Fame; mem. police crime prevention council Internat. Police Hall Fame Found. Served with USAAF, 1942-46. Recipient seven citations criminal investigation div. AUS, Italy, 1946-47. Fellow Am. Assn. Criminology; mem. VFW, Am. Fedn. Police, Nat. Rifle Assn., Air Force Assn., Am. Detective Assn., Catholic War Vets., CID Agts. Assn., Inc., Sheriffs' Assn. Tex., Legion Mexicana (hon.), N.J. State Assn. Chiefs Police (hon.), Assn. Fed. Investigators, Internat. Assn. Aux. Police, N.Y. Vets. Assn., Am. Law Enforcement Officers Assn. Clubs: Playboy (charter), Airways. Author: Is Their a Fortune Waiting For You?, 1974. Contbr. stories to mags. and newspapers. Engaged in spl. geneal. research. Office: 19 W 44th St New York City NY 10036

ROTH, WILLIAM V., JR., U.S. senator; b. Great Falls, Mont., July 22, 1921; B.A., U. Ore.; M.B.A., LL.B., Harvard; m. Jane K. Richards; children—William V. III, Katherine Kelland. Admitted to Del. bar, Cal. bar, U.S. Supreme Ct.; mem. 90th-91st congresses at large from Del.; U.S. senator from Del., 1971—. Chmn. Del. Republican State Com., 1961-64; mem. Rep. Nat. Com., 1961-64. Served to capt. AUS, 1943-46. Decorated Bronze Star medal. Mem. Am., Del. bar assns. Republican. Episcopalian. Home: 3327 Reservoir Rd NW Washington DC 20007 Office: Dirksen Senate Office Bldg Washington DC 20510

ROTHBELL, EARLE NORRIS, physician; b. Bklyn., Feb. 2, 1927; s. Michael and Pearl (Bookbinder) R.; student Cornell U., 1946-49; M.D., Harvard U., 1953; m. Joan Spitzer, Nov. 10, 1970; children—David, Judith, Laurie, Jill. Intern, Charles S. Wilson Meml. Hosp., Johnson City, N.Y., 1953-54; resident State U. N.Y. Upstate Med. Center, Syracuse, 1954-57, instr., 1956-57; practice medicine specializing in internal medicine, Colonia, N.J., 1957—; attending physician Rahway (N.J.) Hosp., 1957—, chmn. dept. medicine, 1975-76; asst. prof. medicine Rutgers U. Med. Sch., Newark, 1972—. Interviewer, Harvard U., Radcliffe Coll.; officer Gifted Students PTA. Served to petty officer USN, 1945-46. Diplomate Am. Bd. Internal Medicine. Mem. A.C.P., Am. Soc. Internal Medicine, Am. Coll. Allergists, Am. Soc. Geriatrics. Democrat. Jewish. Club: Shackamaxon Golf and Country. Home: 350 New Dover Rd Colonia NJ 07067 Office: 689 Inman Ave Colonia NJ 07067

ROTHBERG, SIDNEY, commodity and stock trader; b. Phila., Dec. 17, 1924; s. Harry and Sarah (Rosenberg) R.; B.S., U. Pa., 1949; divorced; children—Michael, Saranne. Vice pres. Nat. Banner Corp., Phila., 1960-64; fin. cons., Phila., N.Y.C., Atlantic City, 1964-73; commodity trader, Phila., N.Y.C., 1965—; pres. Securities and Options Traders, Inc., Phila., 1974—; lectr. seminars. Served with AUS, 1943-45. Mem. Commodity Exchange, Inc., N.Y.C. Mercantile Exchange, N.Y. Cotton Exchange, PBW Stock Exchange. Home: N 1406 Park Towne Pl Philadelphia PA 19130

ROTHBLATT, HENRY BARNETT, lawyer; b. N.Y.C., Aug. 13, 1916; s. Barnet and Florence (Shinderman) R.; student Coll. City N.Y., 1933-35; LL.B., Bklyn. Law Sch. St. Lawrence U., 1938, LL.M., 1939; 1 dau., Henrietta (Mrs. Bergino Santo). Admitted to N.Y. bar, 1939, Calif. bar, 1949, D.C. bar, 1972, Fla. bar, 1973; partner firm Hammer & Rothblatt, N.Y.C., 1942-63; individual practice, N.Y.C., 1963-66; partner firm Rothblatt & Rothblatt, N.Y.C., 1966-71, firm Rothblatt, Rothblatt, Seijas & Peskin, 1971—. Adj. prof. law N.Y. Law Sch., 1973—; faculty lectr. Am. Trial Lawyers Assn., 1967—, Practising Law Inst., 1967—; faculty Backster Sch. Lie Detection, N.Y.C., 1969—; pres. Darrow Investigative Service, Inc., N.Y.C., 1970—, Inst. Research Rheumatic Diseases, 1975—. Chmn. liaison, fgn. lang. groups UN Com. N.Y.C., 1951-63; counsel Consular Corps Com. N.Y.C., 1959-63; chmn. lawyer's com. N.Y.C.-Tokyo Sister City Affiliation, 1961-63. Mem. Am. (chmn. penal reform com. 1973—, Leadership award 1971, chmn. criminal law sect. 1970-72), N.Y. State (chmn. criminal law sect., 1964-65) trial lawyers assns., Am. Bar Assn., Am. Acad. Forensic Scis. Author: Handbook of Evidence for Criminal Trials, 1965; Criminal Law of New York: The Criminal Procedure, 1971; Criminal Law of New York: The Revised Penal Law, 1971; (with F. Lee Bailey) Defending Business and White Collar Crime, 1969, Investigation and Preparation of Criminal Cases, 1970, Successful Techniques for Criminal Trials, 1971, Handling Narcotic and Drug Cases, 1972, Crimes of Violence: Homicide and Assault, 1973; Crimes of Violence: Rape and Other Sex Crimes, 1973; Fundamentals of Criminal Advocacy, 1974; Handling Misdemeanor Cases, 1976; Cross Examination in Criminal and Civil Cases, 1978; (novel, with Robin Moore) Court Martial, 1971; (novel, with Robert L. Fish) A Handy Death, 1973. Editor-in-chief Jour. Nat. Assn. Def. Lawyers in Criminal Cases, 1961-65. Contbr. articles to profl. jours. Address: 232 West End Ave New York City NY 10023

ROTHENBECK, CHARLES FREDERICK, plastics co. exec.; b. Phillipsburg, N.J., Sept. 7, 1942; s. Harry H. and Cecilia B. (Philhower) R.; A.A., Rider Coll., 1962, B.S., 1965; certificate Bowdoin Coll., 1974; m. Margaret A. Vincent, Dec. 1, 1970; 1 son, Charles Frederick III. Prosthetics coordinator Johnson & Johnson, Somerville, N.J., 1968-70; infrared spectroscopist Nat. Starch & Chem. Corp., Bridgewater, N.J., 1970-76; mgr./group leader quality assurance/analytical services Tenneco Chems. Inc., Flemington, N.J., 1976—; cons. in field. Served with U.S. Army, 1965-68. Mem. Am. Mgmt. Assn., Am. Chem. Soc. Patentee in field. Home: 8 Starglo Dr Hampton NJ 08827 Office: Tenneco Chems Inc River Rd Flemington NJ 08822

ROTHENBERG, ALBERT, psychiatrist; b. N.Y.C., June 2, 1930; s. Gabriel and Rose (Goldberg) R.; A.B., Harvard U., 1952; M.D., Tufts U., 1956; m. Julia C. Johnson, June 28, 1970; children—Michael, Mora, Rina. Intern, Pa. Hosp., Phila., 1956-57; resident in psychiatry Yale U., West Haven (Conn.) VA Hosp., 1957-58, Grace-New Haven Hosp., 1958-59, Yale Psychiat. Inst., New Haven, 1959-60; practice medicine specializing in psychiatry New Haven, 1960-61, 63-75, San Juan, P.R., 1961-63, Farmington, Conn., 1975—; asst. dir. Yale Psychiat. Inst., 1963-64, mem. sr. staff, 1964-75; mem. staff Yale-New Haven Med. Center, 1964—, VA Hosp., West Haven, 1967—, U. Conn. Health Center, Farmington, 1975—; cons. to Cath. Family Service, 1964-69, Susan Sheridan Middle Sch., 1964-69, various jours. in psychiatry, 1964—; asst. prof. dept. psychiatry Yale U. Sch. of Medicine, 1964-68, asso. prof., 1968-74, clin. prof., 1974—; prof. psychiatry U. Conn. Sch. Medicine, Farmington, 1975—, dir. residency tng., 1976-78, dir. clin. services, 1975-78; prin. investigator Studies in the Creative Process, 1963—; vis. prof. Pa. State U., 1971, adj. prof., 1971—. Served with M.C., U.S. Army, 1961-63. Recipient Tufts Med. Alumni award, 1956, Research Scientist Career Devel. award NIMH, 1964, 69; Guggenheim Meml. fellow, 1974-75; diplomate Am. Bd. Psychiatry and Neurology. Fellow Am. Psychiat. Assn., Royal Soc. Health; mem. Conn., New Haven-Middlesex psychiat. socs., Am. Soc. Aesthetics, Soc. Phenomenology and Existentialism, Pan Am. Med. Assn., Sigma Xi. Democrat. Jewish. Author: (with C.R. Hausman) The Creativity Question, 1976; contbr. numerous articles on the creative process, schizophrenia and psychotherapy to profl. jours.; research on creativity in the arts and sciences. Home: 139 Webb Circle Monroe CT 06468 Office: U Conn Health Center Farmington CT 06032

ROTHENBERG, PETER JOHN, clin. psychologist; b. N.Y.C., Nov. 26, 1941; s. Benjamin Jack and Emma (Rubin) R.; B.A., Lehigh U., 1963; Ph.D., Washington U., 1967; postdoctoral fellow Yale, 1970-72; children—Karen Lynne, Sara Beth. Clin. dir. Shoreline Mental Health Service, Clinton, Conn., 1972—, also psychotherapist Psychotherapy Assos., New Haven, 1972—; tchr. N.C. State U., 1968-69, So. Conn. State Coll., 1970-73, Middlesex Community Coll., Middletown, Conn., 1974. Served with M.S.C., U.S. Army, 1968-70. USPHS trainee, 1963-67; NIMH fellow, 1970-72. Mem. Conn., Am. psychol. assns., Nat. Council Grad. Edn. in Psychology. Contbr. articles profl. jours. Home: Lanes Pond Northford CT 06472 Office: 210 Prospect St New Haven CT 06511 also 4 Canterbury Ln Clinton CT 06413

ROTHERMEL, JOEL EDWARD, orthopedic surgeon; b. Covington, Ohio, Aug. 30, 1940; s. Edward Miles and Eleanor Adele (Coppock) R.; B.A., Kenyon Coll., 1962; M.D., U. N.C., 1967; m. Constance Lee Davis, Dec. 9, 1967; 1 son, Stephen Miles. Intern, Roosevelt Hosp., N.Y.C., 1967-68, resident gen. surgery, 1968-69; resident orthopedic surgery, N.Y. Orthopedic Hosp., Columbia-Presbyn. Med. Center, N.Y.C., 1969-72; asst. attending surgeon Roosevelt Hosp., 1974—; asso. orthopedic surgery Columbia U., N.Y.C., 1974—, researcher orthopedic surgery, 1974—; indivdual practice medicine, specializing in orthopedic surgery, N.Y.C., 1974—. Hon. surgeon N.Y.C. Police Dept., 1975—. Served with USNR, 1972-74. Carl Berg traveling fellow orthopedics, 1973. Mem. Am. Acad. Orthopedic Surgeons, AMA, Eastern Orthopedic Assn., N.Y. Acad. Sci., N.Y. Acad. Medicine, Alpha Omega Alpha. Republican. Episcopalian. Home: 55 Central Park W New York City NY 10023 Office: 343 W 58th St New York City NY 10019

ROTHFELD, GLORIA KARMEN, interior designer; b. N.Y.C., Feb. 4, 1928; s. Isidore David and Rose Karmen; A.B., Bklyn. Coll., U. City N.Y., 1949; children—Robin Rothfeld, Laurie Rothfield, Isidore David. Former stylist Lord & Taylor; owner Interiors by Gloria K. Rothfeld, Great Neck, N.Y., 1967—. Mem. Allied Bd. Trade. Home and Office: 4 Maple Dr Great Neck NY 11021

ROTHHOLZ, PETER LUTZ, pub. relations exec.; b. Berlin, Germany, June 23, 1929; s. Alfred and Bertha (Isner) R.; came to U.S., 1945, naturalized, 1947; B.A., Queens Coll., 1950; postgrad. N.Y. U., 1956-60; certificates, U. London, 1949, McGill U., 1950; m. Paula Trachtman, Sept. 16, 1951; 1 dau., Amy Elisabeth; m. 2d, Barbara Peters Margules, July 4, 1971; stepchildren—David, Thomas. With Lissone-Lindeman U.S., Inc., N.Y.C., 1953-56, KLM Royal Dutch Airlines, 1956-61; exec. v.p. Simmons Tours, Inc., N.Y.C., 1961-62; pres. Peter Rothholz Assos., Inc., N.Y.C., 1962—. Mem. faculty div. bus. mgmt. Sch. Continuing Edn., N.Y. U., 1969-70, 77. Pres., Queens Museum, 1977—. Served with AUS, 1951-52. Fellow Inst. Certified Travel Agts; mem. Pub. Relations Soc. Am., Soc. Am. Travel Writers, Alumni Assn. Queens Coll. Inc. (pres. 1973-75), Phi Alpha Theta. Clubs: Publicity of New York, Inc. (past v.p., dir.); New York University (bd. govs.). Contbr. articles to publs. Home: 100-17 67th Dr Forest Hills NY 11375 Office: 380 Lexington Ave New York NY 10017

ROTHMAN, ESTHER POMERANZ, educator-psychologist; b. N.Y.C.; d. Max and Annie (Reiner) Pomeranz; B.A., Hunter Coll., 1942; M.A., Columbia, 1946; M.A., Coll. City N.Y., 1951; Ph.D., N.Y. U., 1957; m. Arthur Rothman, Apr. 13, 1946; 1 dau., Amy. Tchr., N.Y.C. schs., 1942-49, Bellevue Psychiat. Hosp., N.Y.C., 1949-55, tchr.-therapist, 1957-58; psychologist Univ. Hosp., 1956-57; research supr. Shield of David, 1958-62; prin. Livingston Sch. for Girls, 1959—; staff psychologist Girls Service League, 1959-62; guest lectr. Queens Coll., N.Y. U., Hunter Coll.; adj. prof. Fordham U., 1973-74. Cons., Center for Urban Edn., 1967-71; project dir. Crisis Intervention by Use of Telephone Therapy, 1972-74, Tchrs. Hot Line, 1976—; mem. Citizens Com. for Children. Recipient Am. Educators Medal award Freedoms Found. Valley Forge; elected to Hunter Coll. Hall of Fame. Fellow Am. Orthopsychiat. Assn.; mem. Am., N.Y. State psychol. assns., Council Exceptional Children (chpt. pres.), Pi Lambda Theta, Kappa Delta Pi. Author: (with Pearl Berkowitz) Disturbed Child, 1958; Buttons: Projective Test of Personality, 1963; (with Pearl Berkowitz), Education for Disturbed Children in N.Y.C., 1966; Angel Inside Went Sour, 1971; Troubled Teachers, 1977. Contbr. numerous articles to profl. jours. Home: 200 E 16th St New York City NY 10003 Office: 29 King St New York City NY 10014

ROTHMAN, FRANK, mktg. exec.; b. N.Y.C., May 24, 1930; s. Harry and Rose (Greenman) R.; B.A., Bklyn. Coll., 1952; M.B.A., Coll. City N.Y., 1958; postgrad. N.Y. U., 1958-62; m. Sheila E. Handshoe, Sept. 2, 1956; children—Andrew Steven, Richard Robert. Mgr. advt. budgets and adminstrn. Trans World Airlines, Inc., N.Y.C., 1952-58; research dir. Forbes Mktg. Research, Inc. subs. Forbes, Inc., N.Y.C., 1958-62; asst. research dir. Young & Rubicam, Inc., N.Y.C., 1962-68; mktg. research dir. Hartford Ins. Group subs. IT&T, Conn., 1968-71; mgr. surveys and communication research Gen. Electric Co., Bridgeport, Conn., 1971—; lectr. City U. N.Y., 1958-68; asst. prof. Quinnipiac Coll., Hamden, Conn., 1971—. Dir. pub. opinion polling Conn. senatorial campaign J. Duffey, 1970. Mem. Am. Mktg. Assn. Democrat. Home: 38 Oak St Westport CT 06880 Office: Gen Electric Corp 1285 Boston Ave Bridgeport CT 06602

ROTHMAN, HERBERT DAVID, communications co. exec.; b. Bklyn., Apr. 2, 1946; s. Julius and Sara (Spiegel) R.; B.B.A., Baruch Sch. Bus., City Coll. N.Y., 1968; M.B.A., 1972; m. Harriet Freedman, June 3, 1972. Asst. to v.p. Gilbert Flexivan Corp., Secaucus, N.J., 1966-69; founder, editor, pub. Gramercy Herald Newspaper, N.Y.C., 1970—; pres. Herald Communications Corp., N.Y.C., 1970; dir. Community Consumers Cons. Corp., Corp. Advt. Agency, Community Media Found., Herco Typesetting Corp.; cons. Borough pres. of Manhattan. Served with USAF, 1964-69. Named Outstanding Citizen, N.Y. TASK. Mem. N.Y. Press Assn. (Journalism award, dir.), Third Ave. Merchants Assn. (dir.), Stuyvesant Park Neighborhood Assn. (dir.), Phi Beta Kappa. Home: 242 E 19 St New York City NY 10003 Office: 110 E 23 St New York City NY 10010

ROTHMAN, JOHN, info. scientist; b. Berlin, Germany, Apr. 21, 1924; s. Max and Henny (Marcuse) R.; came to U.S., 1939, naturalized, 1943; B.A. summa cum laude, Queens Coll., 1946; M.A., N.Y. U., 1949; Ph.D., Columbia U., 1956; m. Gertrude Phyllis Ullmann, June 23, 1946; children—Vivien Rothman Tartter, Andrew James. Indexer, N.Y. Times Index, 1946-50, asst. editor, 1950-64, editor, 1964-67, dir. info. services, 1967-75, dir. research and info. tech., 1975—; dir. Microfilming Corp. Am., N.Y. Times Info. Services Inc.; lectr. Pratt Inst. Grad. Sch. Library and Info. Sci.; mem. advisory com. Copyright Clearance Center; mem. U.S. Nat. Com. ICSU/AB. Served with M.I., U.S. Army, 1943-45. Mem. Info. Industry Assn. (dir.), Am. Soc. Info. Sci., Met. Reference and Research Library Agy. (trustee). Author: Dramatic Criticism on The New York Times, 1949. Originator, developer N.Y. Times Info. Bank, 1965-74, created, edited N.Y. Times Thesaurus, 1968, 71, 73. Contbr. to encys., profl. jours. Home: 101 Highland Rd Glen Cove NY 11542 Office: 229 W 43d St New York City NY 10036

ROTHROCK, HENRY SHIRLEY, chemist; b. Bloomington, Ind., Sept. 17, 1906; s. David Andrew and Helena Grace (Shirley) R.; A.B., Ind. U., 1926; M.S., Purdue U., 1928; student Northwestern U., 1929; Ph.D., Pa. State U., 1931; m. Roberta Pacetti, Sept. 17, 1932; 1 dau., Gail Chardon Rothrock Trozzo. Research chemist E.I. du Pont de Nemours & Co., Wilmington, Del., 1930-37, research supr., 1937-60, liaison mgr., 1960-71; cons. Tech. Services div. U. Del., 1971—. Mem. Am. Chem. Soc., Ind. Acad. Sci., Sigma Xi, Phi Beta Kappa, Phi Kappa Psi. Republican. Episcopalian. Club: Wilmington Country. Patentee in field. Home: Boxwood 3 Red Oak Rd Wilmington DE 19806

ROTHSCHILD, RICHARD CHARLES, writer, lectr.; b. Chgo., Mar. 24, 1895; s. Charles E. and Justine (Sonnenberg) R.; A.B., Yale, 1916; m. Bessie Newburger, May 17, 1920; children—Barbara, Richard S. Engaged in business until 1935; lectr. philosophy New Sch. for Social Research, 1935-38; dir. Parents Mag. 1928-46; active Am. Jewish Com., 1938—, chmn. survey com., 1939, planner and dir. campaign against anti-Semitism in U.S., 1938-50; mem. exec. com., Gen. Jewish Council, 1939-40; propaganda adviser to Nelson Rockefeller, Coordinator of Inter-Am. Affairs, 1941-44. Served as ensign. U.S. Naval Aviation, on active duty in anti-submarine service,

1918, World War I. Jewish. Club: Yale (N.Y.C.). Author: Paradoxy, the Destiny of Modern Thought, 1931; Reality and Illusion, a New Framework of Values, 1934; Three Gods Give an Evening to Politics, 1936. Home: 1165 Park Ave New York City NY 10028

ROTHSTEIN, PAUL FREDERICK, lawyer, educator; b. Chgo., June 6, 1938; s. Alexander and Lillian Alice (Spitler) R.; B.S., Northwestern U., 1958, LL.B., 1961; postgrad. (Fulbright scholar) Oxford (Eng.) U., 1961; m. Thelma Ann McDermott, July 30, 1963; children—Vanessa Jane, Christopher Paul. Admitted to Ill. bar, 1961, D.C. bar, 1967, U.S. Supreme Ct. bar, 1975; instr. Law Sch., U. Mich., Ann Arbor, 1963; asso. prof. law U. Tex., Austin, 1963-67; atty. firm Surrey, Karasik & Morse, Washington, 1967-71; prof. law Georgetown U., Washington, 1971—; reporter, cons. Nat. Conf. Commrs. on Uniform State Laws; cons. to govt. agys. and coms.; chmn. continuing legal edn. and law revision projects. Recipient law award U. Iowa, 1974. Mem. Assn. Am. Law Schs. (chmn. evidence sect. 1977), Am., Fed. (dir.) bar assns., Internat. (officer), Nat. assns. of crime victims compensation bds., Order of Coif. Author: Evidence in a Nutshell, 1970; Understanding the Federal Rules of Evidence, 1973, rev. edit., 1975; The Federal Rules of Evidence, 1974, rev. edit., 1978. Mem. bd. editor Washington Legal Times and Criminal Law Bull., 1978—. Contbr. articles to legal periodicals. Office: Georgetown U Law Center 600 New Jersey Ave NW Washington DC 20001

ROTHSTEIN, SIDNEY DAVID, film co. exec.; b. Phila., Aug. 18, 1921; s. Edward E. and Mary E. (Moss) R.; B.A., U. Del., 1942; M.B.A., Temple U., 1947; Ph.D., U. Md., 1973; m. Selma Hilda Rosenfeld, Sept. 19, 1942; children—Fredell Donner, Mark Alan. Mgr. advt. and sales promotion Porcelite Paint Co., Phila., 1946-57; pres. Admark Assos., Phila., 1957-69; exec. v.p. J.J. Dugan Co., Jenkintown, Pa., 1969-72; v.p. Film Corp. Am., Phila., 1972—; instr. mktg. Wharton Sch., U. Pa.; lectr. LaSalle U., Temple U., Pa. State U.; mem. faculty Charles Morris Price Sch. Advt. Journalism; prof. mktg. Beaver Coll. Mem. Jewish Family Service Council, Phila. Fellow Acad. Mktg. Scis. Author: Retail Advertising, 1970; Concise Course in Copywriting, 1971; Special Aspects of Marketing, 1978; contbr. articles to profl. jours. Office: Film Corporation America Caroline and Charter Rds Philadelphia PA 19176

ROTHWARF, ALLEN, physicist, univ. adminstr.; b. Phila., Oct. 1, 1935; s. Max and Bessie R.; A.B. in Physics, Temple U., 1957; M.S., U. Pa., 1960, Ph.D. in Physics, 1964; m. Bernice Cecelia Golansky, June 16, 1957; children—Richard, Jeanne, David. Instr., Rutgers, The State U., Camden, N.J., 1960-62; mem. tech. staff RCA Labs., Princeton, N.J., 1964-72; postdoctoral fellow U. Pa., 1972-73; mgr. solar cell test and analysis Inst. Energy Conversion, U. Del., 1973—. Mem. Am. Phys. Soc., Am. Vacuum Soc., Electrochem. Soc. Contbr. numerous articles on physics of supercondrs., metals and photovoltaic solar cells to profl. jours. Home: 1206 Tyson Ave Philadelphia PA 19111 Office: 1 Pike Creek Center Wilmington DE 19808

ROTHWEILER, PAUL ROGER, ins. agt., author; b. Woodbridge, N.J., Apr. 18, 1931; s. George F. and Doris E. R.; m. Verna J. Slutter, Aug. 30, 1952 (div. 1978); children—Paul Roger, Dona Rothweiler Maynard, Judith Rothweiler Cheslock, Edith A. Reporter, Courier-News, Plainfield, N.J., 1948-57; spl. agt. Prudential Ins. Co., 1957-68, brokerage mgr., 1971-76, spl. agt., N.J., 1976—; supr. Peoples Life, Washington, 1968-71. Served with USAF, 1951-55. Mem. Am. Soc. Chartered Life Underwriters (pres. Central N.J. chpt. 1968-69, ednl. v.p. 1969—), Authors League, Guild Am. Author: The Sensuous Southpaw, 1976, Japanese edit., 1977; The Sophomore Jinx, Japanese edit., 1979; The New Olympians, 1979. Address: RD 1 Stewartsville NJ 08886

ROTKO, BERNARD BENJAMIN, physician, educator; b. Rovno, Poland, May 23, 1908; s. Benjamin and Rose (Tabachnick) R.; came to U.S., 1921, naturalized, 1925; B.S., Villanova Coll., 1931; M.D., Jefferson Med. Coll., 1935; m. Bessie Goldberg, Sept. 4, 1933; children—Michael, Judith. Intern St. Joseph's Hosp., Phila., 1936-37; pvt. practice internal medicine, Phila., 1937—; med. dir. Rolling Hill Hosp., Elkins Park, Pa., 1953—; pres. Rolling Hill Hosp., Inc., 1953—; chmn. bd. R.H. Med. Services, 1969—; chmn. bd. dirs. Hosp. Mortgage Advisers; chmn. bd. trustees, chief exec. officer Hosp. Mortgage Group. Mem. Cheltenham Twp. Bd. Health, Pa., 1959—. Served to lt. comdr. War Shipping Adminstrn., USN, 1943-46. Mem. AMA, Pa. State, Phila. County med. socs. Office: Rolling Hill Hosp 60 E Township Line Elkins Park PA 19117

ROTMAN, BERTRAM THEODORE, psychologist; b. Boston, July 7, 1935; s. Harry and Janet (Sherman) R.; M.S., L.I. U., 1961; Ph.D., U. Ottawa (Ont., Can.), 1964; m. Eleanor Lea Katz, June 12, 1960; 1 son, Scott Randall. Psychologist, Aloholism and Drug Addiction Research Found., Ottawa, 1961-64, Bedford (Mass.) VA Hosp., 1964-65, Hanover and West Essex Pub. Schs., 1970-73, Pequannock Valley Mental Health Center, Pompton Plains, N.J., 1968-70; pvt. practice psychology, Wayne, N.J., 1966—; staff cons. Chilton and Paterson hosps.; psychol. cons. Bur. Youth Services Morris County. Bd. dirs. Temple Beth Tikvah, 1972—. Mem. Am., N.J., Essex County psychol. assns. Address: 701 Valley Rd Wayne NJ 07470

ROTMAN, ELEANOR LEA (MRS. BERTRAM T. ROTMAN), psychologist; b. N.Y.C., Apr. 7, 1938; d. Isidore and Dora (Lapchinsky) Katz; B.S., Hofstra U., 1959; M.S., L.I. U., 1962; postgrad. U. Ottawa, 1962-63, Newark State Coll., 1966-68, Paterson State Coll., 1968-69, Montclair State Coll., 1969-71; m. Bertram T. Rotman, June 12, 1960; 1 son, Scott. Psychologist, Alcoholism and Drug Addiction Clinic, Ottawa, Ont., Can., 1961-64; psychologist Met. State Hosp., Waltham, Mass., Mass., 1964-66; cons. psychologist to pvt. and pub. schs., 1969—; cons. Lincoln Sch. for Adaptive Edn. Licensed dog show judge Am. Kennel Club. Mem. Am., N.J. psychol. assns., Nat., N.J. assns. sch. psychologists, Psi Chi. Clubs: Watchung Mount Poodle (pres. 1972-74, sec. 1975-77, treas. 1977—), K-9 Obedience Training (sec. 1967-73). Home and office: 701 Valley Rd Wayne NJ 07470

ROTMAN, JESSE LOUIS, pub. relations cons.; b. Chgo., Oct. 28, 1947; s. Morris B. and Sylvia (Sugar) R.; B.S. in Journalism, Ohio U., 1969; m. Diana Lee Yegelwel, Nov. 27, 1977. Reporter, anchorman Sta. KBAK-TV, Bakersfield, Calif., 1969-71; stringer corr. CBS-TV, Los Angeles, 1970-71; sr. v.p., group supr. Harshe-Rotman & Druck, Inc., Chgo. and N.Y.C., 1971—. Mem. men's council Mus. Contemporary Art, Chgo., 1971-72; bd. dirs. Ackerman Inst. Family Therapy, N.Y.C. Mem. Pub. Relations Soc. Am. (recipient Silver Anvil), Soc. Profl. Journalists-Sigma Delta Chi, Chgo. Headline Club, N.Y. Publicity Club. Jewish. Club: New York Health. Home: 200 E 33d St New York City NY 10016 Office: 300 E 44th St New York City NY 10017

ROTONDO, VINCENT JOHN, city ofcl.; b. Bridgport, Conn., July 1, 1928; s. John Baptiste and Florence (Santillo) R.; grad. with honors Norwalk Community Coll., 1969; m. Louise Carmela Nappa, Oct. 13, 1951; children—Vincent John, John Anthony. Dir. water pollution control Town of Westport (Conn.), 1960-70, 71-72, dir. dept pub. works, 1972-75; dir. edn. water pollution control Conn. State Dept. Edn., 1970-71; commr. pub. works City of Stamford (Conn.), 1975-78; exec. mgr. Oronoque Village Owners Corp., Stratford, Conn., 1978—; bd. dirs. Conn. Pollution Abatement Assn., 1969-73. Third Selectman Town of Westport, 1975—. Served with USAF, 1950-53. Recipient E. Sherman Chase award, 1967. Mem. New Eng. Water Pollution Control Assn., Am. Pub. Works Assn. Republican. Roman Catholic. Club: Minute Man Yacht (Westport). Contbr. articles in field to profl. jours. Home: 15 Mansfield Pl Westport CT 06880 Office: North Community House North Trail Stamford CT 06901

ROTTER, PAUL TALBOTT, life ins. exec.; b. Parsons, Kans., Feb. 21, 1918; s. J. and LaNora (Talbott) R.; B.S. summa cum laude, Harvard U., 1937; m. Virginia Sutherlin Barksdale, July 17, 1943; children—Carolyn Sutherlin, Diane Talbott. Asst. mathematician Prudential Ins. Co. Am., Newark, 1938-46; with Mut. Benefit Life Ins. Co., 1946—, successively asst. mathematician, asso. mathematician, mathematician, 1946-59, v.p., 1959-69, exec. v.p., 1969—. Mem. Madison Bd. Edn., 1958-64, pres., 1959-64; trustee, mem. budget com. United Campaign of Madison, 1951-55; mem. bd., chmn. advancement com. Robert Treat council Boy Scouts, 1959-64. Fellow Soc. Actuaries (gen. chmn. edn. and exam. com. 1963-66, bd. govs. 1965-68, chmn. adv. com. edn. and exams. 1969-72); mem. Am. Acad. Actuaries (dir., chmn. edn. and exam. com. 1965-66, chmn. rev. and evaluation com. 1968-74, v.p. 1968-70), Brit. Inst. Actuaries (asso.), N.Y. Actuaries Club (pres. 1967-68), Asso. Harvard Alumni (regional dir. 1965-69), Harvard Alumni Assn. (v.p. 1964-66), Phi Beta Kappa, Phi Beta Kappa Assos. Clubs: Harvard of N.J. (pres. 1956-57); Harvard of N.Y.; Morris County Golf. Office: 520 Broad St Newark NJ 07102

ROTTERDAM, HEIDRUN Z., pathologist; b. Germany, Mar. 21, 1943; d. Walter Ludwig and Ruth Margarete (Barner) Vogelberg; came to U.S., 1968; student U. Kiel, U. Marburg, U. Berlin, U. Munich, Germany, U. Innsbruck, U. Vienna, Austria, 1962-68; M.D., U. Munich, 1968; m. Paul Rotterdam, Apr. 11, 1968; 1 dau., Charlotte. Intern, Evangelisches Krankenhaus Monchengladbach, Germany, 1968, Cambridge (Mass.) City Hosp., 1969, Evangelisches Krankenhaus, Koln, Germany, 1970; resident in pathology Peter Bent Brigham Hosp., Boston, 1970-73; chief resident in pathology Lenox Hill Hosp., N.Y.C., 1973-74, asst. adj. pathologist, 1975-76, adj. pathologist, 1976—; trainee surg. pathology Columbia Presbyn. Med. Center, N.Y.C., 1974-75; asso. in clin. pathology Columbia U. Diplomate Am. Bd. Pathology. Fellow Am. Cancer Soc. Contbr. articles to med. jours. Home: 115 W Broadway New York NY 10013 Office: 100 E 77th St New York NY 10021

ROTTERDAM, Z. PAUL, artist; b. Wiener Neustadt, Austria, Feb. 12, 1939; s. Peter and Emilie Zwietnig-Rotterdam; came to U.S., 1968, naturalized, 1978; student U. Vienna, 1960-65; m. Heidrun Vogelberg, Apr. 10, 1968; 1 dau., Charlotte. Numerous one-man shows, 1961—, including DeCordova Mus., Lincoln, Mass., 1970; Mus. Joanneum, Graz, Austria, 1970; Nielsen Gallery, Boston, 1973; Susan Caldwell Gallery, N.Y.C., 1975; Musée de Nice (France), 1976; Birmingham (Ala.) Mus. Art, 1977; exhibited in numerous group shows, 1961—, including Whitney Biennial of Am. Art, Whitney Mus., N.Y.C., 1975; Artist Immigrants of Am.: 1875-1975, Hirshhorn Mus., Washington, 1975; Guggenheim Mus., N.Y.C., 1975; Eight Abstract Painters, Phila. Art Inst., 1978; represented in permanent collections at Albertina, Vienna; Birmingham Mus. Art; Centre National d'Art et de Culture Georges Pompidou, Paris; Guggenheim Mus.; U. Sydney (Australia); lectr. visual studies Harvard U., 1968—. Mem. Internat. Platform Assn. Home and studio: 115 W Broadway New York NY 10013

ROUBIK, ROBERT ANDREW, nurse anesthetist; b. Chgo., May 20, 1939; s. Andrew Anton and Jeannette Irene (Olsen) R.; diploma Mpls. Sch. Anesthesia, 1962, Hennepin County Gen. Hosp. Sch. Nursing 1960; B.S. in Respiratory Therapy, U. Chgo., 1971; M.S., George Washington U., 1978-79; m. Elaine A. Hoveland, Aug. 24, 1962; children—A. Geoffrey, Andrea Karin. Pvt. practice as anesthetist, Newport, Toledo, Lincoln City, Oreg., 1967-73; chief nurse anesthetist George Washington U. Med. Center, Washington, 1976—; dir. devel., bd. mem. Pulmonary Cons. Ltd., Washington, 1977—. Served with USAF, 1962-65, 73-76; to maj. Res. George Washington U. research grantee, 1978. Mem. Internat. Anesthesia Research Soc., Am. Hosp. Assn., Am. Soc. Regional Anesthesia, Am. Assn. Respiratory Therapy, Am., D.C. (v.p. 1978-79) assns. nurses anesthetists, Air Force Assn. Nurse Anesthetists, Res. Officers Assn., Oreg. Thoracic Soc. Republican. Lutheran. Club: Masons. Home: 9813 Muirfield Dr Upper Marlboro MD 20870 Office: Dept Anesthesiology George Washington U Med Center Washington DC 20037

ROUFA, ARNOLD, physician; b. St. Louis, Oct. 30, 1938; s. Maurice I. and Bee (Hoffman) R.; B.S., Tulane U., 1959; M.D., La. State U., 1963; m. Myrna March, July 29, 1973. Intern, Kings County Hosp. Center, Bklyn., 1964; resident in obstetrics and gynecology Woman's Hosp., St. Lukes Hosp. Center, N.Y.C., 1966-70, asst. attending, 1970-77, chief pregnancy counseling service, 1970-77; med. dir. Planned Parenthood N.Y.C., Boro Hall Center, 1974—; practice medicine, specializing in obstetrics and gynecology, N.Y.C. Served with U.S. Army, 1963-65. Diplomate Am. Bd. Obstetrics and Gynecology. Mem. Am. Coll. Obstetrics and Gynecology, N.Y. County Med. Soc., Phi Delta Epsilon. Home: 400 E 56 St New York City NY 10022 Office: 59 E 54th St New York City NY 10027

ROUNDS, JOHN SCOVILLE, trust co. exec.; b. Boston, Sept. 8, 1927; s. Ezra Pike and Melvina Em-May (Scoville) R.; A.B., Swarthmore Coll., 1951; postgrad. Temple U. Law Sch., 1952-53, Nat. Grad. Trust Sch. Am. Bankers Assn., Northwestern U., 1968-70; m. Anne Harvey Dight, June 17, 1967; children—John Scoville, Harold B., Christopher P. Trust and estate adminstr. Provident Tradesmen's Bank and Trust Co., Phila., 1951-62; peace edn. sec. Middle Atlantic region Am. Friends Service Com., Phila., 1963-66; asst. trust officer Washington Trust Co., Westerly, R.I., 1967-73, trust officer, 1974, v.p. and trust officer, 1975—; cons. to Edfac Pub. Co., Pekin, Ill. Active Friends Peace Com., Phila., 1957-67, Am. Friends Service Com., Nat. Peace Edn. Com., Phila., 1961-62, R.I. Area Com., Providence, 1973-77; gen. com. Friends Com. on Nat. Legis., Washington, 1962-67, 74—, mem. policy com., 1977—; mem. bd. mgrs. investments and permanent funds New Eng. Yearly Meeting of Friends, 1976—; dir. Del. County (Pa.) chpt. Single Parents Soc., 1966-67. Served with U.S. Mcht. Marine, 1945-47. Mem. R.I. Bankers Assn. (chmn. trust com. 1978—), R.I. Estate Planning Council, Southeastern Conn. Estate and Tax Planning Council. Club: Phila. Trail. Author: Decedents' Estates in Rhode Island - Administrative Problems and Procedures, 1971. Home: 4 Spruce St Westerly RI 02891 Office: Washington Trust Co Westerly RI 02891

ROUSLIN, MARC ALAN, food service dir.; b. Brookline, Mass., May 24, 1948; s. Richard Bruce and June Marjorie (Grossman) R.; B.S., U. R.I., 1970; m. Diane Altruda, June 26, 1976. Asst. food service dir. ARA Food Services, Phila., 1970-72; food service dir. State of R.I. Dept. Mental Health Retardation and Hosps., Div. Rehab. Services, Cranston, R.I., 1972—. Served with U.S. Army, 1970. Mem. Am. Soc. Hosp. Food Service Adminstrs., Hosp. Assn. R.I. Home: 9 Michigan Ave Providence RI 02905 Office: Box 8269 RIMC Gen Hosp Cranston RI 02920

ROWAN, ARBE JAMES, neurologist; b. Los Angeles, Apr. 3, 1937; s. Rosslyn Beauford and Geraldine Lucile (Shaw) R.; B.S., Mass. Inst. Tech., 1957; M.D., Stanford U., 1961. Intern, Mt. Sinai Hosp., N.Y.C., 1961-62; resident in internal medicine Boston VA Hosp., 1962-63; resident in neurology Neurol. Inst. Columbia-Presbyn. Hosp., 1963-66; sr. registrar neurology and electroencephalography The London Hosp., 1968-70; instr. neurology Columbia U. Coll. Physicians and Surgeons, N.Y.C., 1970-71, asst. prof., 1971; asst. prof. neurology Albert Einstein Coll. Medicine, N.Y.C., 1971-75, asso. prof., 1975—; dir. electroencephalography dept. Montefiore Hosp. Med. Center, N.Y.C., 1971—; cons. in neurology and EEG Instituut voor Epilepsie bestrijding, Heemstede, Netherlands, 1976—. Served with USAF, 1966-68. Diplomate Am. Bd. Psychiatry and Neurology. Mem. Am. EEG Soc., Am. Epilepsy Soc., Eastern Assn. Electroencephalographers, Am. Acad. Neurology. Research in field. Home: 320 Central Park W New York City NY 10025 Office: 111 E 210th St Bronx NY 10467

ROWAN, RICHARD LAMAR, educator; b. Guntersville, Ala., July 10, 1931; s. Leon Virgle and Mae (Williamson) R.; A.B., Birmingham-So. Coll., 1953; postgrad. Auburn U., 1956-57; Ph.D., U. N.C., 1961; m. Marilyn Walker, Aug. 3, 1963; children—John Richard, Jennifer Walker. Instr. Auburn (Ala.) U., 1956-57, U. N.C., Chapel Hill, 1958-59, 60-61; lectr. U. Pa., Phila., 1961-62, asst. prof., 1962-66, asso. prof. industry, 1966-73, prof. industry, 1973—, co-dir. indsl. research unit; visitor to faculty econs. and politics Cambridge U. (Eng.), 1972. Mem. personnel com. Del. Valley Settlement Alliance, 1966-68. Served with Transp. Corps, AUS, 1953-56. Mem. Indsl. Relations Research Assn. (sec. Phila. 1964-65), Am. Econ. Assn., So. Econs. Assn. Democrat. Episcopalian. Author: (with H.R. Northrup) The Negro and Employment Opportunity, 1965, Readings in Labor Economics and Labor Relations, 1976; The Negro in the Steel Industry, 1969; The Negro in the Textile Industry, 1970; Negro Employment in Basic Industry, Vol. I, Negro Employment in Southern Industry, Vol. IV, Studies of Negro Employment, 1970; Educating the Employed Disadvantaged for Upgrading, 1972; Collective Bargaining: Survival in the 1970's, 1972; Opening the Skilled Construction Trades to Blacks, 1972; Multinational Bargaining in Food and Allied Industries, 1974; Multinational Collective Bargaining Activity: The Factual Record in Chemicals, Glass and Rubber Tires, 1974; Multinational Bargaining in Metals and Electrical Industries, 1975; (with others) The Impact of Government Manpower Programs, 1975; Multinational Bargaining Approaches in the Western European Flat Glass Industry, 1976; Multinational Union Activity in the 1976 U.S. Rubber Tire Strike, 1977; Multinational Union-Management Consultation: The European Experience, 1977; International Enforcement of Union Standards in Ocean Transport, 1977. Home: 113 Blackthorn Rd Wallingford PA 19086 Office: Wharton School U Pa Philadelphia PA 19174

ROWAND, ROBERT ELLWOOD, physician; b. Lafayette, Ind., May 21, 1921; s. Ellwood M. and Ruth (Bowker) R.; student Swarthmore Coll., 1938-40; A.B., Lehigh U., 1942; M.D., Jefferson Med. Coll., 1945; postgrad. U. Pa. Grad. Sch. Medicine, 1956-57; m. Frances Faber Noyes, Jan. 21, 1950; children—Patricia Faber, Janet Lee. Intern U.S. Naval Hosp., Memphis, 1945-46; resident internal medicine U.S. Naval Hosp., Phila., 1948-51; commd. ensign U.S. Navy, 1942, advanced through grades to comdr., 1954; sr. med. officer naval sta., Key West, Fla., 1947-48; cons. logistics div. Bur. Medicine, Bklyn., 1953-56; asst. chief medicine U.S. Naval Hosp., Phila., 1957-59; sr. med. officer Navy Sta. Hosp., Bermuda, 1959-62; exec. officer U.S. Naval Amphibious Base Dispensary, Little Creek, Norfolk, Va., 1962-63, ret., 1963; asso. med. dir. Lederle Labs, div. Am. Cyanamid Co., Pearl River, N.Y., 1963-67; med. mgr. pharms. div. DuPont Co., Wilmington, Del., 1967-70; asso. dir. clin. devel. Ciba-Geigy Pharms., Summit, N.J., 1970—. Mem. A.M.A., A.C.P., Internat. Platform Assn., Navy League, U.S. Naval Inst., Assn. Med. Dirs., Pharm. Mfrs. Assn., Am. Acad. Clin. Toxicology, Indsl. Med. Assn., Lambda Chi Alpha, Alpha Kappa Kappa. Unitarian. Home: 17 Club Dr Summit NJ 07901 Office: Ciba-Geigy Pharms Summit NJ 07901

ROWDEN, GEOFFREY, cell biologist; b. Burnham-on-Sea, Somerset, Eng., Sept. 28, 1940; s. Leonard Percival and Gwendolin Mabel (Facey) R.; immigrated to Can., 1971; B.Sc. in Zoology with honors (Zoology prize 1962), Exter U., 1962; M.Sc. in Radiation Biology and Physics, London U., 1962-64, Ph.D. in Sci., 1970; m. Ann Daw, Nov. 20, 1966; children—Louise, Sarah. Jr. research fellow Royal Free Hosp. Med. Sch., London, 1964-65, asst. lectr., then lectr. cellular radiology, 1965-71; lectr. cell sci. Meml. U., Nfld., Can., 1971-73; mem. faculty McGill U. Med. Sch., Montreal 1973-77, asso. prof. pathology, 1976-77, mem. sr. staff cancer research unit, 1973-77, asso. prof. pathology Georgetown U., Washington, 1977—. Grantee Wellcome Found., 1966, Sci. Research Council U.K., 1967, Nat. Cancer Inst. Can., 1973-77. Fellow Royal Micros. Soc.; mem. Soc. Investigative Dermatology, Histochem. Soc., Electron Microscopy Soc. Am., Canadian Soc. Cell Biology, Canadian Microscopy Soc. (editor sect. in bull.), Royal Coll. Pathologists. Clubs: Pointe Claire Soccer; Highbridge Piscatorials. Author papers, abstracts, chpts. in books. Home: 4503 Dalton Rd Chevy Chase MD 20015 Office: Dept Pathology Georgetown U Washington DC 20007

ROWE, BENJAMIN ACKLEY, realtor; b. Syracuse, N.Y., July 27, 1913; s. Benjamin Ackley and Mary Edna (Alexander) R.; B.S., Rollins Coll., 1935; m. Marjorie Murphy, June 21, 1951; children—Jillian, Allison, Abigail, Wendy. Ins. broker Johnson & Higgins, N.Y.C., 1932-39; sales mgr. H.B. Smith Co., N.Y.C., 1950-60; v.p., chmn. bd. Preferred Properties Inc., Stamford, Conn., 1960—; cons. real estate. Served to capt., U.S. Army, 1940-49. Mem. Greenwich, Stamford, New Canaan, Darien and Westport bds. realtors, N.Y. Bd. Realtors, Inter-City Relocation Service (nat. dir. 1974—), Conn. Assn. Real Estate Bds., Nat. Assn. Real Estate Appraisers, Stamford Area Commerce and Industry Assn. Republican. Conglist. Clubs: Greenwich Country, N.Y. Athletic, Palm Springs Racquet, Mason (Shriner). Home: 23 Rockridge Ave Greenwich CT 06830 Office: 175 W Putnam Ave Greenwich CT 06830

ROWE, CHARLES ALFRED, painter, designer, educator; b. Gt. Falls, Mont., Feb. 7, 1934; s. Alfred Lewis and Alice Lillian (Ledbetter) R.; student Mont. State U., 1952-53, So. Meth. U., 1956-57, U. Chgo., 1959-60; B.F.A., Sch. Art Inst. Chgo., 1960; M.F.A., Tyler Sch. Art, 1968; m. Eugenia Dean, July 5, 1958; children—Allison Rene, Jon Garner, Dorian Leigh. Prin., Charles Rowe Advt., Chgo., 1957-60; graphic designer Am. Can Co., Bellwood, Ill., 1960-62, Abrams-Bannister Engraving, Inc., Greenville, S.C., 1962-64; instr. art U. Del., 1964-68, asst. prof., 1968-70, asso. prof., 1970-75, prof., 1975—; one-man shows include: C.M. Russell Museum, Gt. Falls, 1973, Mickelson Gallery, Washington, 1974, Pleiades Gallery, N.Y.C., 1977; numerous group shows include: Ball State U., 1974, C.M. Russell Mus., 1974, 76, 78, Am. Painters in Paris, 1976, MONAC Western Art Exhibit, Spokane, Wash., 1977-78; represented in permanent collections: U. Del., Gt. Falls Pub. Schs.; fabrics designer Galleon Fabrics, Inc., N.Y.C., Jones of N.Y.C., Ship 'n Shore, Saks Fifth Ave., J.C. Penney Co.; designed graphics Mont. State Arts Council. Served with inf. U.S. Army, 1954-56. U. Del. grantee-in-aid, 1964-78; Nat. Endowment for Arts and Humanities grantee, 1972-73; U. Del. Bicentennial grantee 33, 1976. Mem. AAUP, Pleiades Gallery. Home: 133 Aronimink Dr Chapel Hill Newark DE 19711 Office: Dept Art U Del Newark DE 19711

ROWE, CHARLES WRIGHT, advt. exec.; b. Ossining, N.Y., Sept. 8, 1948; s. Edward Bird and Marjorie Eileen (Wright) R.; A.A. in Bus. Mktg., Westchester Community Coll., 1972; B.B.A. cum laude, Mercy Coll., 1977; 1 dau., Ashley Allison. Asst. store mgr. Calico Corners Inc., East Hanover, N.J., 1972-73, Mamaroneck, N.Y., 1973-74; advt. account exec. Tarrytown (N.Y.) Daily News, 1974; advt. account exec. Ossining Citizen Register, Ossining, 1974, White Plains (N.Y.) Reporter Dispatch, 1975-76, asst. advt. mgr., 1976-77; advt. dir. no. zone Westchester Rockland Newspapers Inc., White Plains, 1978—; mktg. cons. Advt. Directions Inc., Yonkers, N.Y., 1976—. Served with USMC, 1966-69; Vietnam. Mem. Internat. Advt. Execs. Assn., Sales Execs. of Westchester, Advt. Club of Westchester, Yorktown, Ossining, Mt. Kisco, White Plains, Putnum County chambers commerce. Home: Holly Stream Condominiums Brewster NY 10509 Office: One Gannett Dr White Plains NY 10604

ROWELL, HARRY BROWN, JR., corp. exec.; b. Roberta, Ga., Sept. 21, 1941; s. Harry B. and Essie J. Rowell; B.B.A., U. Ga., 1965, cum laude, M.A. with high honors, 1966; m. Mary Jeanette Hancock, Sept. 17, 1961; children—Harry Brown III, Timothy Scott. Dir., Computer Software Mgmt. Info. Center, U. Ga., Athens, 1964-70; dir. ops. div. Carnegie-Mellon U., Pitts., 1970-74; v.p., treas. U. Bridgeport (Conn.), 1974-78; v.p. corp. devel. and planning Harvey Hubbell Corp., Orange, Conn., 1978—; dir. City Savs. Bank, Bridgeport. Bd. dirs. Greater Bridgeport YMCA, 1975—, Goodwill Industries SW Conn., 1976—. Mem. Nat. Assn. Coll. and U. Bus. Officers, Fin. Execs. Inst., Bridgeport C. of C. (dir. 1976—), Am. Mgmt. Assn. Clubs: Algonquin; Brooklawn Country. Home: 535 Stonehouse Rd Trumbull CT 06611

ROWELL, MARGARET KENNY, ret. librarian; b. Fall River, Mass., June 11, 1906; d. Bernard Francis and Catherine (Connell) Kenny; A.B., Brown U., 1927; M.Ed., Boston U., 1932; B.S. in L.S. with high honors, Columbia, 1937; m. Gordon Allen Rowell, Nov. 20, 1948; 1 dau., Mary Rowell Mony. Tchr. English, librarian St. Regis Falls (N.Y.) High Sch., 1929-31; tchr. English, librarian Central Square (N.Y.) High Sch., 1933-36; cataloger Hunter Coll. Library, N.Y.C., 1937-42; chief catalog librarian Bklyn. Coll. Library, 1942-64; chief librarian Grad. Sch. Library, City U. N.Y., 1965-76, ret., 1976. Mem. Am. Soc. Info. Sci., N.Y. Tech. Service Librarians, Beta Phi Mu. Club: N.Y. Library, Brown U. (N.Y.C.). Editor library catalogs. Home: 67-38 108th St Forest Hills NY 11375

ROWEN, RUTH HALLE (MRS. SEYMOUR M. ROWEN), musicologist; b. N.Y.C., Apr. 5, 1918; d. Louis and Ethel (Fried) Halle; B.A., Barnard Coll., 1939; M.A., Columbia U., 1941, Ph.D., 1948; m. Seymour M. Rowen, Oct. 13, 1940; children—Mary Helen (Mrs. David Obelkevich), Louis Halle Rowen. Mgt. ednl. dept. Carl Fischer, Inc., music pub., N.Y.C., 1954-63; asso. prof. music Coll. City N.Y., 1967-72, prof., 1972—; mem. doctoral faculty in musicology City U. N.Y., 1967—. Mem. ASCAP, Am. Musicological Soc., Music Library Assn., Coll. Music Soc., Nat. Fedn. Music Clubs (nat. musicianship chmn. 1962, nat. young artists auditions com. 1964), Phi Beta Kappa. Author: Early Chamber Music, 1948, 74; (with Adele T. Katz) Hearing—Gateway to Music, 1959; (with William Simon) Jolly Come Sing and Play, 1956; Music Through Sources and Documents, 1979. Home: 115 Central Park W New York City NY 10023

ROWLAND, CLIFFORD VANCE, labor relations exec.; b. New Castle, Pa., Apr. 6, 1930; s. Faunt Mitchell and Mary Elizabeth (Lour) R.; B.S., Cornell U., 1953; m. Jeanette Jane Smith, Aug. 29, 1952; children—Theresa Gayle, Michell Vance. Fin. analyst W.R. Grace & Co., N.Y.C., 1953-55; asst. v.p. fin. Grace Line Inc., 1955-61, asst. v.p. ops., 1961-67, asst v.p. labor relations, 1967-69, v.p. indsl. relations, N.Y.C., 1969-71; asst. regional postmaster gen. for employee and labor relations N.E. Region, U.S. Postal Service, N.Y.C. and Washington, 1971-75, nat. bargaining labor relations exec., 1971-75, labor relations exec. North Jersey dist., 1976—. Served with USNR, 1948-55. Mem. Nat., N.Y. indsl. relations research assns. Presbyterian. Clubs: Lions, Kiwanis. Home: 122 Southern Blvd Chatham NJ 07928 Office: US Post Office Fed Sq Newark NJ 07102

ROWLEY, ELMER CLIFFORD, assn. exec.; b. nr. Emigrant Gap, Calif., May 27, 1913; s. Henry Parson and Grace Alta (Price) R.; student U. Calif. at Berkeley, 1931-35; m. Thelma Brown, Dec. 6, 1936; children—Lee Raymond, Clifford Robert. Vice pres. Collett Week Corp., Ossining, N.Y., 1946-55; pres. Barlow Chem. Corp., Ossining, 1955-62; v.p., dir. Electro-Nite Co., Phila., 1962-68; v.p. 1st Investment Annuity Co., Phila., 1968-73; pres. N.J. Audubon Soc., 1973-74. Pres., Burlington County (N.J.) Natural Scis. Club, 1967-68; active Boy Scouts Am., United Fund; mem. Medford Twp. (N.J.) Environ. Commn., 1974-77, chmn., 1976-77; chmn. Water Bd. Croton-on-Hudson, N.Y., 1962-63; chmn. advisory com. Burlington County Pinelands Conservation Easement, 1977—. Served with USMC, 1935-36, 40-46; col. ret. Mem. Marine Corps Res. Officer Assn., Marine Corps Assn., Pine Barrens Conservationists, Phila. Acad. Natural Sci., Zool. Soc. Phila., Delaware Valley Ornithol. Club, Nat., N.J. Audubon socs., Sierra Club, N.J. Conservation Found., Phi Beta Kappa. Club: Rotary (past pres. Ossining and N. Phila. clubs). Home: Centennial Lake Marlton NJ 08053

ROY, CONCETTA CONSTANCE CORNELIA CORNACCHIA (MRS. LEO J. ROY), ednl. adminstr.; b. Bklyn, Dec. 7, 1906; d. John and Pasqualina (Saggese) Cornacchia; B.S., N.Y.U., 1931; M.A., Columbia, 1932; M.S., Queens Coll., 1958; m. Leo J. Roy, July 2, 1938. Sec. Litty & McElroy, 1924-26, W.T. Grant, 1926-28, Boyd, Weir & Sewell, 1942-43; office and credit mgr. Joseph J. Carlin, N.Y.C., 1928-36; tchr. secretarial studies Bushwick High Sch., Bklyn., 1936-38, Washington Irving Evening High Sch., 1936-38, John Jay High Sch., 1938-42; tchr. secretarial studies Flushing (N.Y.) High Sch., 1942-56, chmn. dept., asst. prin. 1956-70, acting prin., 1968, 70. Sec., liaison P.T.A., Flushing, (N.Y.) High Sch., 1944-72. Mem. U. Women Am., Am. Personnel and Guidance Assn., High Sch. Tchrs. Assn. (sec., exec. bd. 1946-59, pres. 1955-57), High Sch. Asst. Prins. Assn. (sec. exec. bd. 1957-69, pres. 1966-68), Council Supervisory Assn. (sec. exec. bd. 1965-69), N.Y. State Guidance Assn., AAUW, Nat. Council Adminstrv. Women in Edn., N.Y. Acad. Pub. Edn., Retired Sch. Suprs. Adminstrs. (treas. 1971—), Delta Pi Epsilon (life), Delta Kappa Gamma. Address: 209-01 82d Ave Queens Village NY 11427

ROY, JOY BENJAMIN, psychologist; b. N.Y.C., May 13, 1924; d. Harry V. and Ethel (Holzman) Schechter; B.A., Hunter Coll., 1950; M.S., City Coll. N.Y., 1952; Ph.D., N.Y. U., 1957; m. Murray I. Kofkin, Dec. 5, 1958; children—Glen, Amanda, Jennifer. Pvt. practice psychology, N.Y.C., 1957—; instr. Harlem Hosp. Sch. Nursing, 1954-65, Finch Coll., 1959-60; cons. in field. Certified psychologist, N.Y. Mem. Am. Psychol. Assn., N.Y. Soc. Clin. Psychologists. Democrat. Jewish. Children's drawings exhibited Met. Mus. Art, United Nations, Smithsonian Inst., 1958. Home and Office: 106 E 85th St New York City NY 10028

ROY, MAURICE, Cardinal; b. Quebec City, Que., Can., Jan. 25, 1905; s. Ferdinand and Mariette (Legendre) R.; B.A., Petit Seminarie, Quebec, 1923; D.Th. (D.D.), Laval U., 1927; D.Ph., Institutum Angelicum, 1929; postgrad. Institut Catholique and Sorbonne, Paris, 1929-30. Ordained priest Roman Catholic Ch., 1927; prof. theology Laval U., 1930-46; rector Grand Sem., Laval U., 1956; bishop Trois-Rivieres, Que., 1946-47; bishop ordinary to Canadian Armed Forces, 1946—; archbishop of Quebec City, 1947—, cardinal, 1965—; named chmn. Council of Lay Apostolate and Pontifical Commn. Justice and Peace, 1967. Served as chaplain (hon. col.) Canadian Army Overseas, 1939-45. Decorated Order Brit. Empire; chevalier Legion of Honor; comdr. Order of Orange Nassau (Netherlands); Primate of Can., 1956. Club: Quebec Garrison. Address: Archbishop's Residence CP 459 Quebec City PQ G1R 4R6 Canada

ROY, PAUL NORMAN, diversified mfg. co. exec.; b. Fitchburg, Mass., Nov. 25, 1934; s. Joseph and Della (Lavoie) R.; B.S., Boston Coll., 1956; M.B.A., Babson Inst., 1967; m. Mary Elizabeth Duggan, May 30, 1959; children—Mary E., Ann E., Kathleen T., Michele A., Ellen M., Paul N. Staff, Gen. Electric Co., Pittsfield, Mass., 1956-62, Arthur Andersen & Co., Boston, 1962-65; with Barry Wright Corp., Watertown, Mass., 1965—, treas., 1970-73, v.p. fin., 1973-75, v.p. fin. and adminstrn., 1975-76, exec. v.p. fin. and adminstrn., 1976—, also dir. Chmn. fund-raising drs. United Fund, 1960-65, Archbishop Cushing Jubilee Fund, 1965-68, Waltham Hosp., 1978; trustee, chmn. fin. com., chmn. acad. and fiscal priorities com. Emmanuel Coll., 1976—; trustee Newton-Wellesley Hosp., 1978—. Served to 1st lt. U.S. Army, 1956-58, C.P.A. Mem. NAM (mem. coms.), Am. Mgmt. Assn., Watertown C. of C. (dir. 1975—), Fin. Execs. Inst. (v.p. Boston 1974-78, pres. 1978—, dir. 1972—), Machinery and Allied Products Inst. (fin. council), Am. Inst. C.P.A.'s, Mass. Soc. C.P.A.'s. Republican. Roman Catholic. Club: Brae Burn Country (Newton, Mass.). Home: 11 Beech Rd Weston MA 02193 Office: 680 Pleasant St Watertown MA 02172

ROYCROFT, HOWARD FRANCIS, lawyer; b. Balt., Sept. 9, 1930; s. Howard F. and Bessie (Weaver) R.; B.A., U. Md., 1953; LL.B., Georgetown U., 1958; m. Barbara Lee Seal, Mar. 20, 1954; children—Suzanne Carol, Nancy Lee. Admitted to D.C. bar, 1958, since practiced in Washington; mem. firm Hogan & Hartson, 1958, partner, mem. exec. com., 1970-73; lectr. Howard U. Sch. Law, 1973-74. Mem. Met. Washington Bd. Trade. Bd. dirs. YMCA Met. Washington, 1974-76. Served to 1st lt. USMC, 1953-55. Mem. Am., Va. State, Fed. Communications bar assns., Bar Assn. D.C., Nat. Broadcasters Club, Barristers, Aircraft Owners and Pilots Assn., Nat. Acad. TV Arts and Scis., Broadcast Pioneers, Kappa Alpha, Beta Kappa, Delta Theta Phi. Republican. Methodist. Clubs: Bryce Mountain Ski and Country (dir., pres. 1974); Washington Tennis Patrons, Internat. Home: 8703 Eaglebrook Ct Alexandria VA 22308 also Racoon Rd Bryce Mountain Bayse VA Office: 815 Connecticut Ave Washington DC 20006

ROYDEN, ERNEST JEROME, stockbroker; b. N.Y.C., July 7, 1944; s. Thomas Jerome and Catherine Mary (Toosey) R.; student Trinity Coll. Sch., Port Hope, Ont., Can., 1957-63, McGill U., Montreal, Que., Can., 1963-65; m. Suzanne Vivienne Adams, Aug. 31, 1974. Accountsman, Marsh & McLennan, Montreal, 1965-67; analyst Baker Weeks of Can., Montreal, 1967-72; stockbroker instl. sales R.A. Daly & Co., Ltd., Montreal, 1972—. Mem. Montreal Bd. Trade. Clubs: Royal and Ancient Golf, Royal Montreal Golf, Montreal Badminton and Squash. Home: 121 Cameron Hudson PQ J0P 1H0 Canada Office: 1220 Capitol Centre 1200 McGill College Ave Montreal PQ H3B 4G7 Canada

ROZEL, SAMUEL JOSEPH, mfg. co. exec.; b. Louisville, Apr. 22, 1935; s. Sam and Anna (Sessmer) R.; B.S., U. Louisville, 1955, LL.B., 1957; m. Jeanne Frances Foulkes, July 3, 1965; children—Brooke Jane, John Samuel. Admitted to Ind. bar, 1970, Ky. bar, 1958, D.C. bar, 1962. Minn. bar, 1968; staff atty. FTC, Washington, 1962-67; sr. atty., antitrust counsel Honeywell, Inc., Mpls., 1967-69; counsel, consumer electronics group Magnavox Co., N.Y.C., 1969-71, v.p., gen., sec., 1973-76; sr. v.p. U.S. Philips Corp., 1976—; asso. gen. counsel N.Am. Philips Corp., 1976—; sec. governing com. U.S. Philips Trust. Served to capt. Judge Adv. Gen. Corps, AUS, 1958-62. Mem. Am. Fed., Ind., Ky. bar assns. Clubs: Union League (N.Y.C.); Lawyers (Washington). Home: 245 S Bald Hill Rd New Canaan CT 06840 Office: 100 E 42d St New York City NY 10017

ROZENE, JACK IRVING, advt. agy. exec.; b. Belfast, Ireland, Oct. 18, 1904; s. Saul and Rose (Leah) R.; came to U.S., 1908; student U. Bridgeport (Conn.), 1943, Columbia U.; m. Florence Hanewitz, May 31, 1931; 1 dau., Beverly Hershatter. Account exec. Bridgeport Post Telegram, 1925-31, 33-35; advt. mgr. retail store Bridgeport, 1931-33; pres. Rozene Advt. Agy., Inc., Bridgeport, 1935—. Instr., U. Bridgeport, 1952. Mem. Stratford (Conn.) Community Concert Band, Jewish Community Center, Bridgeport; mem. Rodeph Sholom Synagogue, Bridgeport. Recipient Legion of Honor, Order DeMolay, 1968; named Alumni Man of Yr., Univ. Sch., Bridgeport. Mem. Advt. Club Bridgeport (Man of Yr., past pres.), Mill River C. of C. Mason (Shriner) (Pierpont Edward medal of honor, past master); mem. Order Golden Chain (past grand patron), Order Girls of Golden Ct. (founder, supreme adv. councilor, past dad adviser). Club: Probus (past pres.) (Bridgeport). Home: 43 Eaton St Bridgeport CT 06604 also The Fountains 4070 Tivoli Ct Lake Worth FL 33463 Office: 571 Fairfield Ave Bridgeport CT 06604

ROZNER, ALEXANDER GEORGE, metallurgist; b. Krakow, Poland, June 11, 1929; s. Leopold and Klara Maria (Schenker) R.; came to U.S., 1957, naturalized, 1963; M.Sc., Tech. U., Krakow, Poland, 1952; Ph.D. (Office Naval Research fellow), U. Notre Dame, 1961; m. Solvejg Berg, Sept. 29, 1966. Project engr. Biprostal, Krakow, 1953-57; research fellow U. Notre Dame (Ind.), 1958-61; research metallurgist DuPont Exptl. Sta., Wilmington, Del., 1961-64; metallurgist U.S. Naval Surface Weapons Center, White Oak, Md., 1964—. Recipient Outstanding Performance awards U.S. Navy, 1971, 74, 77. Fellow Am. Inst. Chemists, AAAS; mem. Am. Inst. M.E., Am. Soc. for Metals, Sigma Xi. Contbr. articles in field to profl. jours. Patentee in field. Home: 9441 Holbrook Ln Potomac MD 20854 Office: US Naval Surface Weapons Center White Oak MD 20910

RUARK, RICHARD WILLIAM, comml. artist; b. Columbus, Ohio, July 16, 1951; s. Robert Edwin and Kathryn Harriet (Cartus) Geis; ed. pub. schs.; m. Carrie Mae Fannon, Apr. 9, 1977; children by previous marriage—Jamie, Aaron. With Lord Corp., Erie, Pa., 1969; bindery technician Gen. Electric Co., Erie, 1970, comml. artist and interactive graphics computer operator, 1971—; free-lance jewelery and furnishings designer. Lutheran. Patentee in field. Home: 213 Baer Dr Erie PA 16505 Office: 2901 E Lake Rd Erie PA 16531

RUBEL, MARTIN, physician; b. Bklyn., Feb. 6, 1934; s. Harry and Dorothy (Wilk) R.; B.A. cum laude, Lehigh U., 1954; M.D., Jefferson Med. Coll., 1959; m. Rena Esther Osterneck, Aug. 15, 1959; children—Joanne, Jonathan, Elizabeth. Intern, Jefferson Hosp., Phila., 1959-60; resident Temple Hosp., Phila., 1960-62, NIMH; clin. asso. Bethesda, Md., 1963-64; clin. dir. Phila. Psychiat. Center, 1964-70; dir. outpatient dept. Northwestern Inst. Psychiatry, Phila., 1970-72; clin. asst. prof. psychiatry Temple U. Med. Coll., Phila., 1972—; dir. adolescent treatment program Inst. Pa. Hosp., 1977—; faculty Phila. Psychoanalytic Inst., 1977—. Mem. Am. Psychiat. Assn., Phila. Psychoanalytic Soc. Home: 1123 Penhurst Ln Narberth PA 19072 Office: Inst Pa Hosp 111 N 49th St Philadelphia PA 19139

RUBEN, ALBERT, artist; b. New Orleans, Dec. 4, 1918; s. Alex and Rachel (Hurwitz) R.; B.A. in Art with honors, U. Cal. at Los Angeles, 1941; student Art Students League N.Y., 1943-47; m. Mildred Licata, Apr. 30, 1956. Exhibited in one-man shows at Regina Gallery, N.Y.C., 1955, Studio Gallery Workshop, N.Y.C., 1959, Doll and Richards Gallery, Boston, 1961, Brielle Art Gallery (N.J.), 1969; instr. art Pels Sch. Art, N.Y.C., 1965-66, Montserrat Sch. Art, Beverly, Mass., 1973-75. Elizabeth Greenshields Found. grantee, 1969. Recipient Meml. Gold medal Am. Vet. Art Soc., 1957; N.Y.C. Summer Festival award, 1964. Mem. Allied Artists Am., Art Students League N.Y., Copley Art Soc., Salmagundi, Nat. art clubs, N. Shore (Meml. prize 1971), Rockport (Mass., Gold medal 1968) art assns. Address: Bearskin Neck Rockport MA 01966

RUBEN, BRENT DAVID, communication cons., educator; b. Cedar Rapids, Iowa, Oct. 17, 1944; s. Nate and Ruth E. (Subotnik) R.; B.A., U. Iowa, 1966, M.A., 1968, Ph.D., 1970; m. Jann Mayberry, Oct. 3, 1967; children—Robbi Lynn, Marc David. Instr., research asst. U. Iowa, Iowa City, 1966-70, asst. prof. mass communication, 1970-71; asst. prof. communication Rutgers U., New Brunswick, N.J., 1971-74, asso. prof., 1974—, dir. Inst. Communication Studies, 1971—; cons. Canadian Internat. Devel. Agy., N.Y. Times, AID, Nat. Assn. TV and Radio announcers; v.p. Newstatements Communication and Devel. Cons., Inc. Mem. Human Relations Commn., Franklin Twp., N.J. Nat. Assn. Broadcasters grantee, 1969-70. Mem. Internat. Communications Assn., Speech Communication Assn., Soc. Gen. Systems Research, Internat. Inst. Gen. Semantics. Author-editor: Human Communication Handbook: Simulations and Games, 1975, vol. 2, 1978; Approaches to Human Communication, 1972; (with R. Budd) Beyond Media, 1978; Interact, 1973; Interact II, 1977; (with J. Kim) Human Communication and General Systems Theory, 1975; editor Communication Yearbook. Home: 2 Regina Dr Belle Mead NJ 08502 Office: Inst for Communication Studies Van Dyck Hall Rutgers Univ New Brunswick NJ 08903

RUBEN, ROBERT JOEL, physician, educator; b. N.Y.C., Aug. 2, 1933; s. Julian Carl and Sadie (Weiss) R.; A.B., Princeton, 1955; M.D., Johns Hopkins, 1959; children—Ann, Emily, Arthur. Intern, Johns Hopkins Hosp., Balt., 1959-60, resident, 1960-64, dir. neurophysiology lab., div. otolaryngology, 1958-64; practice medicine specializing in otorhinolaryngology, N.Y.C., 1964—; mem. staffs Bronx Municipal Hosp. Center, Hosp. Albert Einstein Coll. Medicine, hosps. Montefiore, Lincoln, Morrisania Hosp.; asst. prof. otorhinolaryngology N.Y. U. Sch. Medicine, 1966-68; asso. prof., chmn. dept. otolaryngology Albert Einstein Coll. Medicine, N.Y.C., 1968-70, prof., 1970—, chmn. dept. otorhinolaryngology, 1970—. Mem. Head Start med. adv. com., human resources adminstrn. Community Devel. Agy., 1969. Bd. dirs. N.Y. League Hard of Hearing. Served to surgeon USPHS, 1964-66. Recipient Research award Am. Acad. Ophthalmology and Otolaryngology, 1962. Fellow A.C.S., N.Y. Acad. Medicine; mem. Am. Assn. Anatomists, Audiology Study Group N.Y. (pres. 1968-69), Acoustical Soc. Am., AMA, Am. Acad. Ophthalmology and Otolaryngology, Soc. U. Otolaryngologists, Assn. Acad. Surgery, Triological Soc. (Edmund Prince Fowler award 1973), Soc. for Ear, Nose and Throat Advances in Children, (pres. 1973). Office: 1300 Morris Park Ave New York City NY 10461

RUBENFELD, STANLEY IRWIN, lawyer; b. N.Y.C., Dec. 7, 1930; s. George and Mildred (Rose) R.; B.A., Columbia U., 1952, J.D. (Stone scholar), 1956; m. Caryl P. Ellner, June 8, 1952; children—Leslie Ann, Lise Susan, Kenneth Michael. Admitted to N.Y. bar, 1956; practiced in N.Y.C., 1956-65, 68—, Paris, 1965-68; asso. firm Shearman & Sterling, N.Y.C., 1956-65, partner, Paris, 1965-68, N.Y.C., 1968—; dir. Eleda Corp., Orbisphere Corp. Chmn. Port Washington (N.Y.) Community Chest Fund Drive, 1973-74; chmn. placement com. Columbia Law Sch., 1973—. Bd. dirs. Port Washington (N.Y.) Community Chest, Residents for a More Beautiful Port Washington. Served to lt. (j.g.) USNR, 1952-54. Grantee Rockefeller Found., 1955. Mem. Am., N.Y. State, N.Y.C. (tax com.) bar assns., Tax Discussion Group, Columbia Law Sch. (dir. 1974—), Columbia Coll. (constn. and by-laws com.) alumni assns., Tax Club, Phi Delta Phi, Tau Epsilon Phi. Clubs: Downtown Assn., Princeton, Broad St. (N.Y.C.). Editor-in-chief Columbia Law Rev., 1955-56; contbr. articles to profl. jours. Home: 41 Longview Rd Port Washington NY 11050 Office: 53 Wall St New York City NY 10005

RUBENS, MERTON, securities exec.; b. Rochester, N.Y., Dec. 29, 1929; s. Barney and Katherine (Fitelson) R.; student Syracuse U., 1949, U. Miami, 1953; m. Sherry Horowitz, June 30, 1957; children—Jeffrey, Jill, Laurie, Adam, Cynthia. Pres., Regent Industries, Inc., Rochester, 1961-68; v.p. Monroe Securities, Inc., Rochester, 1968-73, 77—, pres., 1968-73; sec. dir. 3C Gen. Corp.; fin. cons. to various cos., 1973—. Mem. Rochester Soc. Security Analysts, Bond Club Rochester. Office: 1122 First Fed Plaza Rochester NY 14620

RUBENSTEIN, ABRAHAM DANIEL, physician, hosp. adminstr.; b. Lynn, Mass., Nov. 19, 1907; s. Max and Dora (Mamber) R.; A.B., Harvard U., 1928; M.D., Boston U., 1933; M.P.H., Harvard U., 1940; m. Delilah Riemer, Dec. 26, 1937; children—Joel J., David H., Susan S. Intern, Brockton (Mass.) Hosp., 1933-35; house officer in internal medicine Boston City Hosp., 1936-38; dep. commr., dir. bur. of hosps. Mass. Dept. Pub. Health, 1948-69, hosp. cons., 1969—; asso. prof. epidemiology Sch. Pub. Health, Harvard U., 1950-61; sr. lectr., vis. prof. epidemiology Mass. Inst. Tech., 1963-72; adminstr. Mt. Pleasant Hosp., Inc., Lynn, Mass., 1972—; cons. preventive medicine Beth Israel Hosp., Jewish Meml. Hosp., Boston; pres. Mass. Health Council, 1955, New Eng. Sinai Hosp., Bos 1953-70. Trustee St. Margaret's Hosp., Dorchester, Mass.; mem. adv. bd. Mass. Soc. Prevention of Blindness. A. Daniel Rubenstein lectureship in geriatrics established at Boston Coll. Sch. Nursing, 1965. Diplomate Am. Bd. Preventive Medicine. Fellow Royal Soc. Health; mem. AMA, Am. Pub. Health Assn., Mass. Med. Soc., Am., Mass. (award of Merit 1963) hosp. assns., Am. Assn. Hosp. Planning (pres. 1963), Phi Delta Epsilon. Contbr. articles in field to profl. jours. Home: 164 Ward St Newton Centre MA 02159 Office: 60 Granite St Lynn MA 02104

RUBENSTEIN, ALLAN EARL, neurologist; b. Buffalo, Dec. 8, 1944; s. Theodore and Sara Rubenstein; B.A., Cornell U., 1966; postgrad. U. Rochester, 1966-68; M.D., Tufts U., 1970; m. Paula Herman, Dec. 7, 1970; children—Hillary Dana, Emily Caitlin. Intern, Harlem Hosp., N.Y.C., 1970-71; resident in neurology Columbia Presbyn. Hosp., N.Y.C., 1971-74; instr. neurology Mt. Sinai Sch. Medicine, N.Y.C., 1974-77, asst. prof., 1977—; examiner Am. Bd. Psychiatry and Neurology, 1977—. Chmn. med. adv. bd. Nat. Neurofibromatosis Found. Mem. Am. Acad. Neurology, Assn. Research Nervous and Mental Disease. Contbr. articles to profl. jours. Office: 1200 Fifth Ave New York City NY 10029

RUBENSTEIN, HOWARD, educator; b. Bklyn., Jan. 26, 1937; s. Maurice Solomon and Sarah Belle (Seiden) R.; B.S., Davis and Elkins Coll., 1956; postgrad. in edn. Hofstra U., 1975; m. Deborah Spevack, Mar. 28, 1959; children—Paula, Douglas, Stephen. Tchr. chemistry W.C. Bryant High Sch., Bd. Edn. City N.Y., 1958, Gen. George Wingate High Sch., 1959, F. K. Lane High Sch., 1959-61, M. Van Buren High Sch., 1961, A. Lincoln High Sch., 1962-65; tchr. chemistry Queens Vocat. High Sch., 1965—, also dir. programming, 1971-73, asst. prin., 1973-74; instr. Sch. Respiratory Therapy, Peninsula Hosp. Centre, Far Rockaway, N.Y., 1969-73. Sec., Rockville Centre (N.Y.) Soccer Club, 1977, Rockville Centre Little League, 1975; v.p. So. N.Y. State Youth Soccer Assn. Certified as sch. adminstr. and supr., sch. dist. adminstr., N.Y. Mem. Am. Assn. Respiratory Therapy, Nat. Hist. Soc., Am. Chem. Soc., AAAS; fellow Am. Inst. Chemists. Jewish. Home: 340 Hempsted Ave Rockville Centre NY 11570 Office: 37-02 47th Ave Long Island City NY 11101

RUBENSTEIN, LEONARD, engring. corp. exec.; b. Bklyn., June 18, 1931; s. William and Sylvia (Jaffe) R.; B.S., Bklyn. Poly. Inst., 1963; m. Geraldine Marylyn Porper, Aug. 15, 1965; children—Alan, Elaine, Philip, Ruth Jennie. Support engr. Western Electric Co., N.Y.C., 1956-63; job engr. Bechtel Assos., N.Y.C., 1963-65; elec., project engr. Pope, Evans & Robbins, N.Y.C., 1965-67; elec. engr. Gibbs & Hill, N.Y.C., 1967-69; chief engr. Kliegl Bros., N.Y.C., 1969-71; power plant design, constrn. project engr. Stone & Webster Engring. Corp., N.Y.C., 1971—, Va. Electric & Power Co., 1973-74, Power Authority State N.Y., 1974-76, Savannah Electric & Power Co., 1976—. Served with AUS, 1951-53. Registered profl. engr., N.Y., Ga. Mem. IEEE (sr.), League Tech. Profls. (pres. 1977—), Dynamion Soc. (pres. 1975-76). Democrat. Home: 450 West End Ave New York City NY 10024 Office: PO Box 1350 1 Penn Plaza New York City NY 10001

RUBENSTEIN, SIDNEY, optometrist; b. Phila., Nov. 16, 1916; s. Joseph and Hattie (Abrahams) R.; O.D., Pa. Coll. Optometry, 1940; m. Myrel Sisman, June 20, 1942; children—Lyn, Eileen, Hope, Jan. Pvt. practice optometry, Harrisburg, Pa., 1950—; mem. Pa. Bd. Optometric Examiners, 1972; cons. Pa. Dept. Welfare, 1973—. Democratic candidate for Pa. Legislature, 1966; pres. Harrisburg Jewish Community Center, 1965. Served with USNR, 1942-45. Mem. Am., Pa., Central optometric assns. Clubs: Elks (pres. 1960), B'nai B'rith (regional pres. 1975) (Harrisburg). Home: 2209 N 2d St Harrisburg PA 17110 Office: 508 N 2d St Harrisburg PA 17101

RUBENSTEIN, STANLEY ELLIS, pub. relations exec.; b. Balt., July 25, 1930; s. Albert B. and Lee (Goodman) R.; B.A., U. Md., 1953; m. Ruth Anne Zinder, Feb. 8, 1953; children—Deborah Carol, Steven Mark, Michael Lee, Kenneth Jay, Andrew Lewis. Writer, researcher Bozell & Jacobs, N.Y.C., 1953; fin. writer N.Y. Jour. Commerce, N.Y.C., 1954-55; writer, account exec. Ruder & Finn, Inc., N.Y.C., 1955-59; founder Rubenstein, Wolfson & Co., Inc., N.Y.C., 1959, prin., 1959—; cons. pub. relations, 1955—. Mem. Great Neck (N.Y.) Bd. Edn., 1968-74, pres., 1970-73. Served with USNR, 1948-49. Mem. N.Y. Fin. Writers Assn., Pub. Relations Soc. Am. Home: 51 Colgate Rd Great Neck NY 11023 Office: 230 Park Ave New York City NY 10017

RUBIN, ARNOLD PERRY, journalist; b. Richmond, Va., Nov. 21, 1946; s. David and Lillian (Rogolsky) R.; B.A., Hunter Coll., 1969; M.S.J., Northwestern U., 1971. Tchr., N.Y.C. public schs., 1969-70; writer, editor Scholastic Mags., N.Y.C., 1971—; freelance writer, author, lectr.; books include: The Evil That Men Do: the Story of the Nazis, 1977; The Youngest Outlaws; Runaways in America, 1976; author weekly newspaper column The Scholastic Youth Poll, distbd. by N.Y. Times Syndicate; coordinator Nat. Inst. Student Opinion, Scholastic Mags., Inc., 1976—. Recipient award for newswriting Ednl. Press Assn. Am., 1974. Mem. Soc. Profl. Journalists, Forum of Writers for Young People, Authors Guild. Club: Deadline.

RUBIN, ARTHUR HERMAN, ednl. adminstr.; b. N.Y.C., Aug. 14, 1927; s. Samuel and Bessie (Moritt) R.; B.S., N.Y. U., 1950, M.A., 1951; m. Janice Levy, Apr. 9, 1950 (div. 1965); children—Renee Ellen, Linda Joy; m. 2d, Audrey M. Schmidt, July 1, 1973. Adminstrv. asst., office asst. to asst. dean Sch. Edn., N.Y. U., 1947-54, lab. asst. bus. edn. dept., 1950-54, instr., 1954-56, program dir. grad. students orgn., 1954-63, dir. tours, 1955-58, co-ordinator summer sessions activities, 1959-64, dir. Bur. Pub. Occasions, 1963-74, dir. Bur. Conf. Facilities, 1968-69, officer of adminstrn., 1973-75, asst. v.p. pub. occasions, 1974-75, dir. extramural affairs Coll. Dentistry, 1976, asso. dean adminstrn., 1976—, adj. asst. prof. behavioral scis. and community health, 1976—; tchr. Patrick Henry Jr. High Sch., N.Y.C., 1949-58; acting asst. prin. Robert F. Wagner Jr. High Sch., N.Y.C., 1958-63; cons. in field. Trustee Agnew Found., 1967—. Recipient N.Y. U. Presdl. citation, 1971, Ernest O. Melby award Sch. Edn. Alumni Assn., 1976; citation Bus. Edn. Assn. Met. N.Y., 1976. Mem. Eastern Bus. Tchrs. Assn. (chmn. exhibits 1953-74, exec. bd. 1969-71, pres. 1972-73, award 1974), Bus. Edn. Assn. of Met. N.Y. (mem. exec. bd. 1962—), Bus. Edn. Securities Club, Inc (pres. 1963-66, v.p. ops. 1967-68), Arch Securities Club, Inc. (pres. 1963-66, v.p. ops. 1967-68), Nat. Bus. Edn. Assn. (mem. exec. bd. 1972-74, conv. mgr. 1974—), N.Y. Acad. Pub. Edn., Educators Securities Club, Inc. (v.p. ops. 1966-68), N.Y. U. Edn. Alumni Assn. (v.p. 1961-62, 64-67), Delta Pi Epsilon (Service award Alpha chpt. 1971), Kappa Phi Kappa, Alpha Delta Pi Securities Club, Inc. (pres. 1963-66, v.p. ops. 1967-68). Club: N.Y. University (bd. govs. 1972-78). Home: 110 Bleecker St New York City NY 10012 Office: NYU Dental Center 421 1st Ave New York City NY 10010

RUBIN, DONALD S., constrn. co. exec.; b. Albany, N.Y., June 5, 1922; s. Louis and Bessie (Lutsky) R.; B.C.E., Rensselaer Poly. Inst., 1943, B.Arch., 1947; m. Bernice B. Coplin, Dec. 21, 1947; children—Lynn Dee, David Mark. Instr. dept. architecture Rensselaer Poly. Inst., 1947-48; chief engr., estimator Sano-Rubin Constrn. Co., Albany, 1948-65, pres., 1965—. Trustee Siena Coll.; mem. adv. council dept. architecture Rensselaer Poly. Inst. Served with USNR, 1944-46. Registered profl. engr., N.Y. Mem. Am. Arbitration Assn., N.Y. State Soc. Profl. Engrs. (past pres. Albany chpt.). Mem. Sigma Xi, Chi Epsilon. Elk. Home: 15 Chestnut Hill S Loudonville NY 12211 Office: 624 Delaware Ave Albany NY 12209

RUBIN, GABRIEL KEVI, psychiatrist; b. Bklyn., Feb. 9, 1927; s. Samuel and Augusta (Katz) R.; B.A., N.Y. U., 1946; M.D., Hahnemann Med. Coll., 1950. Intern, Lincoln Hosp., Bronx, N.Y., 1950-51; resident Bellevue Hosp., N.Y.C., 1953-54, Pilgrim State Hosp., West Brentwood, L.I., 1954-56; practice medicine specializing in psychiatry, Forest Hills, N.Y., 1956—; med. dir., dir. psychiatry Fifth Ave. Center for Counseling and Psychotherapy, 1961-76; cons. psychiatrist Terrace Heights Hosp., Parkway Hosp., Hillcrest Gen. Hosp., Whitestone Gen. Hosp., Parsons Hosp., Deepdale Gen. Hosp., Physician's Hosp., Blvd. Hosp., Astoria Gen. Hosp.; adj. psychiatrist Beth Israel Hosp., Grand Central Hosp., N.Y.C.; asst. attending psychiatrist Roosevelt Hosp.; sr. instr. in psychiatry Mt. Sinai Med. Sch. chmn. faculty Met. Inst. Psychoanalytic Studies, 1964-76. Served as 1st lt. M.C., USAF, 1951-53. Diplomate Am. Bd. Psychiatry and Neurology. Mem. Am., L.I., Queens County psychiat. assns., Am. Group Psychotherapy Assn., N.Y. Acad. Medicine, N.Y. Acad. Scis., N.Y. Soc. for Clin. Psychiatry, Queens County Med. Soc., N.Y. County Health Services Review Orgn., Bronx Med. Services Found., Queens County Services Peer Review Orgn. Home: 200 E 71st St New York City NY 10021 Office: 98-30 67th Ave Forest Hills NY 11374

RUBIN, HAROLD SYDNEY, rheumatologist; b. Boston, Nov. 13, 1920; s. Benjamin and Marion (Perlinsky) R.; B.S. magna cum laude, Tufts U., 1942, M.D., 1945; m. Jean Levin, Aug. 15, 1946; children—Marcy Beth, Mark Howard. Intern, Worcester (Mass.) City Hosp., 1945-46, resident in internal medicine, 1949-50; grad. student internal medicine Tufts U. Med. Sch., Boston, 1948-49; resident in internal medicine and rheumatology Hosp. Spl. Surgery, N.Y.C., 1950-51; research fellow in cardiology and rheumatic fever House of Good Samaritan, Children's Med. Center, Boston, 1951-52; clin. fellow Arthritis Found., New Eng. Med. Center, Boston, 1952-54; practice medicine specializing in rheumatology, Swampscott, Mass., 1952—; mem. staff Lynn and Union hosps., Lynn, Mass., Salem (Mass.) Hosp.; dir. arthritis clinic Lynn Hosp., 1960—; sr. clin. instr. medicine Tufts U. Med. Sch., 1978—; trustee, exec. com. Mass. Arthritis Found., 1978—. Served as capt. M.C., AUS, 1946-48. Diplomate Am. Bd. Internal Medicine. Mem. AMA, Am. Rheumatism Assn., Am., Lynn (pres. 1962-64) heart assns., New Eng. Rheumatism Soc., Mass. Med. Soc. Jewish. Contbr. to med. jours. Office: 519 Humphrey St Swampscott MA 01907

RUBIN, HOWARD, educator; b. Middletown, N.Y., Sept. 14, 1934; B.A. in History, Coll. City N.Y., 1956; M.A. in Social Studies, Bklyn. Coll., 1963; married; 4 children. Tchr. jr. high schs., Bklyn., 1956-68, acting asst. prin., 1962-65; asst. prin. Blind Brook-Rye Union Free Sch. Dist., Rye Town, N.Y., 1968—; prin. Kneses Tiferoth Israel Religious Sch. Certified sch. dist. adminstr., secondary sch. prin. Mem. Am. Assn. Sch. Adminstrs., N.Y. State Ednl. Communications Assn., Phi Delta Kappa. Developed individualized scheduling of middle schs. Home: 9 Meadowlark Rd Port Chester NY 10573 Office: Ridge Street School N Ridge St Port Chester NY 10573

RUBIN, HOWARD MYRON, advt. exec., cons., mfrs. rep.; b. Bklyn., Jan. 21, 1923; s. Harry and Anna Pearl (Rosenbaum) R.; student pub. schs.; m. Norma Isabel Sorrels, July 18, 1964; children—Renee Marlin Analovitch, Faye Lottie Nietto. Traffic mgr. Curtis Partition Corp., Kearny, N.J., 1946-71, Stance Industries, Inc., Bklyn., 1971-75; pres. HMR Assos., Bklyn., 1975—. Served in U.S. Army, 1942-45. Recipient Inaugural Ball medal Johnson-Humphrey Adminstrn., 2 personally inscribed books from Pres. Johnson. Mem. N.Y. Jewish, Bklyn.-Queens, N.Y. traffic clubs, Met. Traffic Assn., Postal Customer Council, Nat. Indsl. Traffic League, Traffic Assn. Am., Nat. Small Shippers Conf. Club: Pres.'s (Washington). Office: Box CCC Flatbush Sta Brooklyn NY 11226

RUBIN, KENNETH ALLEN, lawyer; b. Rockville Centre, N.Y., Nov. 24, 1947; s. Albert Alton and Marion (Osterweis) R.; B.S., Cornell U., 1969, M.S., 1971, J.D., 1973. With EPA, 1972; admitted to D.C. bar, 1974; with U.S. Justice Dept., 1973-74; asso. firm Morgan, Lewis & Bockius, Washington, 1974—; prof. environ. law Antioch Law Sch. and Open U., Washington, 1976—, U.S. Dept. Agr., 1978—; spl. lectr. on environ., energy and solar law at indsl. confs. and univs.; chmn. Nat. Conf. on Solar Energy Law, Policy and Financing, 1978. NSF grantee, 1964. Mem. Am. Bar Assn. (chmn. solar law com.). Club: Cornell (Washington). Home: 1001 26th St NW Washington DC 20037 Office: 1800 M St NW Washington DC 20036

RUBIN, MICHELE BARRIE, psychologist; b. Far Rockaway, N.Y., Dec. 29, 1944; d. Robert Lee and Blanche Rose (Rosen) Hirsch; B.A. in Psychology, Syracuse U., 1966; M.A. in Tchrs. Coll., Columbia U., 1968, profl. diploma in sch. psychology, 1968; D.Ed. in Counseling, Lehigh U., 1974; m. Saul S. Rubin, Mar. 3, 1968; children—Rachel, Sarah, Jessica, Beth. Dir. child study team, sch. psychologist Warren Twp. (N.J.) Pub. Schs., 1968-70; staff psychologist Somerset County Community Mental Health Center, Somerville, N.J., 1975—. Mem. Am., N.J. psychol. assns., N.J. Assn. Sch. Psychologists. Home: Box 6450 Bridgewater NJ 08807 Office: 22 N Bridge St Somerville NJ 08876

RUBIN, SAMUEL SOLOMON, psychologist, educator; b. N.Y.C., Apr. 21, 1931; s. George and Matilda R.; B.S. magna cum laude, Columbia U., 1953, M.A., 1956, Ph.D., 1962; grad. Advanced Inst. Analytic Psychotherapy, 1973. Adj. prof. psychology Queens Coll. City U. N.Y., 1965-75; supervising psychologist Advanced Center Psychotherapy, Forest Hills, N.Y., 1967—; faculty Advanced Inst. Analytic Psychotherapy, N.Y.C., 1971—; asso. dept. human behavior Columbia U. Dental Sch., 1977-78; dir. N.Y. Workshop Living Learning, 1977—. Certified psychologist, N.Y. Mem. Nat. Accreditation Assn. Psychoanalysis (certified), Council Nat. Register Health Service Providers Psychology (certified), N.Y. Soc. Clin. Psychologists, Am., Eastern psychol. assns., Phi Beta Kappa. Jewish. Contbr. articles to psychol. jours. Home: 300 Winston Dr Cliffside Park NJ 07010 Office: 109 33 71st Rd Forest Hills NY 11375

RUBIN, WILLIAM HANNIBAL, psychiatrist; b. N.Y.C., Feb. 7, 1927; s. Maurice and Rose (Marness) R.; B.A., N.Y. U., 1945; M.D., Chgo. Med. Sch., 1949. Practice medicine specializing in psychiatry, Bklyn.; mem. faculty State. U. N.Y. Downstate Med. Sch., N.Y.C. Served with M.C., U.S. Army, 1951-53. Diplomate Am. Bd. Psychiatry and Neurology. Mem. Am. Psychiat. Assn. Research, publs. on psychiat. study juvenile offenders; research on psychosomatic illness. Office: 9 Prospect Park W Brooklyn NY 11215

RUBINI, DENNIS ANTHONY, historian, educator; b. Southampton, N.Y., July 2, 1939; s. Earl Paul and Mary Patton (William) R.; B.A., Yale U., 1961; D.Phil., Christ Ch. Oxford (Eng.) U., 1966. Asst. lectr., lectr. dept. history U. Exeter, Devonshire, Eng., 1965-69; asso. prof. history Temple U., Phila., 1969—. Cons., Pa. Gov's. Council for Sexual Minorities, chmn. Interdisciplinary Com. Human Sexuality. Fellow Royal Hist. Soc.; mem. Am. Hist. Assn., Orgn. Am. Historians, Italian Am. Hist. Assn. Democrat. Author: Court and Country, 1968; editor: Wykeham-Martin Papers, 1969; Shrewsbury Papers, 1978; contbr. articles to hist. jours. Home: 1301 Spruce St Philadelphia PA 19107 Office: Temple Univ History Dept Philadelphia PA 19122

RUBINSTEIN, LOUIS BARUCH, lawyer, editor; b. Providence, Dec. 5, 1908; s. Israel Sessel and Fannie Rebecca (Rubin) R.; B.A., Yale, 1931, LL.D., J.D., 1934; m. Lillian Berger; children—Louis Henry, Michael Laurence. Admitted to D.C. bar, 1936, R.I. bar, 1938; atty., cons. internat. law Mexican claims arbitration State Dept., 1934-39; pvt. practice, Providence, 1939—; counsel to firm Zietz, Sonkin & Radin, 1948—; chief Temporary Disability Ins. Div. R.I., 1967-72; chief legal officer R.I. Dept. Employment Security, from 1972; now editor-in-chief R.I. bar jour.; labor-mgmt. arbitrator Mem. legal com. interstate conf. Employment Security Agys., 1973—; chmn. 18 States Legal Affairs Conf., 1973; speaker Internat. Assn. Indsl. Accidents Bds. and Commns., 1968, Nat. Ins. Inst. Israel, Jerusalem, 1969; mem. legal com. Providence Charter Commn., 1939. Sec. Jewish Fedn. R.I., 1970—; hon. pres. R.I. council Jewish Nat. Fund, 1976—, v.p. N.E. region, 1971. Hon. mem. bd. dirs. Jewish Community Center R.I.; bd. dirs. N.E. region Anti-Defamation League, Jewish Fedn. R.I., 1976—. Served with USAAF, 1942-45. Mem. R.I. Bar Assn. (exec. com., award of merit 1976), Jewish War Vets. (past nat. asso. judge adv., Am. Arbitration Assn. (panel). Jewish (sec. temple 1968-76, hon. life trustee). Mason (past master, chaplain emeritus; Shriner). Club: Yale of R.I.; Kirkbrae Country (Lincoln, R.I.). Contbr. to legal jours. Home: 9 Lincoln Ave Providence RI 02906 Office: 131 Wayland Ave Providence RI 02906

RUBINSTEIN, MAX G., educator; b. N.Y.C., June 13, 1907; s. Harry and Sarah (Golub) R.; B.S., City Coll. N.Y., 1928; M.A., N.Y. U., 1930; m. Sadie Kaplan, June 21, 1928; children—Robert J., Daniel. Tchr., prin. in elementary and jr. high schs., N.Y.C. and Bronx, 1944-61; asst. supt., jr. high sch. div., N.Y.C., 1961-65, dist. and community supt., Queens, 1965-74; adj. prof. York Coll., Fordham U., Pace U., 1974—; lectr. Conn. U., R.I. U., 1962-63; asst. prof. City Coll. N.Y., 1963. Dir. Queens NCCJ, 1970-74, active City of Hope; pres. Jewish Tchrs. Community Chest, 1964-68. Title III grantee for studies in non-western culture, 1967; named to City Coll. N.Y. Hall of Fame (basketball), 1969; recipient Educator of Year plaque Jr. High Sch. Prins. Assn., 1977. Mem. N.Y. Acad. Pub. Edn., Assn. Asst. Supts., Assn. Adminstrs. and Supts., Assn. Jr. High Sch. Prins. (life), Emile Fraternity. Jewish. Author articles, texts. Home and Office: 165 West End Ave New York City NY 10023

RUBOY, JORDAN SUMNER, pediatrician; b. Taunton, Mass., Nov. 22, 1927; s. Samuel and Jean (Krasnow) R.; B.S., George Washington U., 1950, M.A., Boston U., 1951, M.D., 1955. Intern, Boston City Hosp., 1955-56; resident in pediatrics Mass. Gen. Hosp., Boston, 1958-60, teaching fellow, 1959-60, asst. pediatrician, 1974—; practice medicine specializing in pediatrics, Concord, Mass., 1960—; chief pediatrics Emerson Hosp., Concord, 1976—; mem. staff Mass. Gen. Hosp., Boston Hosp. for Women; clin. instr. pediatrics Harvard U., Tufts U.; corporator Eliot Guidance Center, Concord. Served as capt. M.C., U.S. Army, 1956-58. Mem. Am. Acad. Pediatrics, New Eng. Pediatric Soc., New Eng. Med. Soc. Club: Harvard. Community organizer in child abuse prevention. Home: 531 Monument St Concord MA 01742 Office: Hillside Med Park Baker Ave Concord MA 01742

RUBULOTTA, JOSEPH ANTHONY, mfg. co. exec.; b. Newark, Jan. 12, 1935; s. Anthony and Josephine (Manno) R.; student St. Johns U., 1974, Fordham U., 1968, Newark Coll. Engring., 1960-64; m. Ethel Reynolds Rockefeller, May 14, 1960; children—Diane Marie, Joseph Anthony. Apprentice tool and machine designer Singer Engring. Co., 1953-57; mfg. mgr. REDM Corp., Wayne, N.J., 1963-67; v.p. Instrument & Fuze Corp., Newark, 1967-69; project mgr. Airspec div. Tyco Labs., Fairfield, N.J., 1969-71; gen. mgr. Electro-Mech. div. REDM Corp., Fairfield, N.J., 1971—. Served with U.S. Army, 1957. Mem. Soc. Tool and Mfg. Engrs., Def. Preparedness Assn. Home: 170 College Pl South Orange NJ 07079 Office: 8 Audrey Pl Fairfield NJ 07006

RUBY, JOHN ROBERT, pub. sch. psychologist; b. McKeesport, Pa., Sept. 8, 1929; s. Paul and Julia (Nemeth) R.; B.S. in Indsl. Arts, California (Pa.) State Coll., 1956; postgrad. in psychol. testing Duquesne U., 1960-61; M.Ed. in Guidance, Counseling, Indiana U. of Pa., 1962; Ph.D. in Spl. Edn., Rehab., U. Pitts., 1975; m. Lillian Jordanhazy, Apr. 10, 1950; children—Toni Lynn, John Robert, Jeffrey, James (dec.), Tammy. Substitute tchr. McKeesport Area Sch. Dist., 1954-56; tchr. of indsl. arts, guidance counselor Norwin Sch. Dist., Irwin, Pa., 1957-65, pub. sch. psychologist, 1962-65; pub. sch. psychologist Charleroi (Pa.) Area Sch. Dist., 1965-66; pub. sch. psychologist Duquesne (Pa.) Sch. Dist., 1966—; child care attendant Allegheny County (Pa.) Juvenile Ct. Detention Home, 1963-64; mem. admissions com. Mon-Yough Adult Retarded Center, McKeesport, Pa., 1965; psychologist Western State Sch. and Hosp., Cannonburg, Pa., 1965; psychologist Bur. Vocat. Rehab., Allegheny County, Pa., 1966—, Allegheny County Behavior Clinic, Criminal Div., Pitts., 1971—; adj. prof. Union Grad. Sch., Cin., 1976—. Certified as supr. of spl. edn., Pa. Mem. Am., Pa., Greater Pitts. psychol. assns., Phi Delta Kappa. Author: The Right to Education—An Analysis of the Hearing Process, 1975. Home: 1212 Fawcett Ave McKeesport PA 15131 Office: John F Kennedy Sch Crawford and Hill Duquesne PA 15110

RUDAVSKY, AMIEL ZACHARY, physician; b. Bklyn., Mar. 16, 1933; s. David and Sarah (Sameth) R.; A.B., Columbia U., 1954; M.S., N.Y. U., 1956; postgrad. Chgo. Med. Sch., 1956-58; M.D., N.Y. U., 1960; m. Susan Kaplan, May 29, 1960; 1 dau., Shari. Sect. chief Harlem Hosp., N.Y.C., 1965-66; instr. Med. Faculty, Columbia U., N.Y.C., 1965-66; intern Montefiore Hosp., Bronx, 1960-61, resident in internal medicine, 1961-63; trainee in endocrinology Mt. Sinai Hosp., N.Y.C., 1963-65; dir. scanning div., asst. attending physician, also asst. prof. biophysics Mt. Sinai Hosp. and Med. Sch., N.Y.C., 1966-72; asst. attending physician Montefiore Hosp. and Med. Center, Bronx, N.Y., 1966-78, adj. attending physician, 1978—; head nuclear medicine lab., Morrisania Hosp., Montefiore affiliation, Bronx, 1972-76; asso. clin. prof. medicine and radiology Albert Einstein Coll. Medicine, Bronx, 1974—; individual practice medicine, specializing in endocrinology, nuclear medicine, internal medicine, N.Y.C., 1972—; head nuclear medicine lab., attending physician N. Central Bronx Hosp., Montefiore affiliation, Bronx, 1976—. Mem. Sch. Bd. Riverdale Temple, Bronx, 1974—; bd. dirs. Learning Tree Nursery Sch., Christ Ch., Bronx, 1976—. Diplomate Am. Bd. Nuclear Medicine. Fellow Am. Coll. Nuclear Medicine, A.C.P.; mem. AMA, N.Y. County, N.Y. State med. socs., N.Y. Thyroid Club, Soc. Nuclear Medicine, Am. Coll. Nuclear Physicians, Clin. Radioassay Soc. Jewish. Contbr. articles to profl. jours. nuclear medicine, radiation protection, radiation therapy, endocrinology. Home: 10 Rivercrest Rd Bronx NY 10471 Office: 1020 Park Ave New York City NY 10028

RUDD, DAVID WILLIAM, engr.; b. Floral Park, N.Y., Dec. 31, 1931; s. Edward Lynn and Joanna (McSorley) R.; B.A., Colby Coll., 1953; M.S., Northeastern U., 1962; m. Harriet Fay Sart, Aug. 8, 1953; children—Rebecca, Rachel. Research chemist Monsanto Chem. Co., Everett, Mass., 1956-58, Kendall Co., Walpole, Mass., 1958-60, Metal Hydrides, Beverly, Mass., 1960-62; sr. staff engr. Western Electric Co., N. Andover, Mass., 1969-78, mem. research staff Engring. Research Center, Princeton, N.J., 1978—; co-founder, dir. Solardynamics, Kingston, N.H., 1975—. Served with U.S. Army, 1953-55. Recipient Western Electric Co. Engring. Excellence award, 1969, C.B. Sawyer Meml. award, 1974. Mem. Electronic Industries Assn., Am. Assn. Crystal Growth. Research in surface chemistry, permeability of metals to hydrogen, rocket propellant synthesis infrared method of Q evaluation synthetic quartz, crystal growth, printed circuit tech., metal joining. Home: Lakeview Dr Lambertville NJ 08530

RUDD, IRENE TAKACS, pharmacist; b. McKeesport, Pa., May 17, 1923; d. John and Emma W. (Racsko) Takacs; B.S., U. Pitts., 1944, postgrad., 1945-48; m. John Harold Rudd, July 1, 1955; 1 son, John Robert. Chief pharmacist McKeesport Hosp., 1944-48, dir. dept. pharmacy, inpatient services, 1963—; owner, operator Takacs Pharmacy, McKeesport, 1949-53; mgr. Bridges Pharmacy, McKeesport, 1960-63; adj. instr. pharmacy Duquesne U., 1976—. Mem. product adv. com. Hosp. Council Western Pa., 1977—. Mem. Western Pa., Pa., Am. socs. hosp. pharmacists. Republican.

Presbyterian. Club: Coll. Office: 1500 Fifth Ave McKeesport PA 15132

RUDEL, THOMAS RYDER, machine tool exec.; b. Montreal, Que., Can., Apr. 20, 1905 (parents U.S. citizens); s. Clarence Merrill and Anna (Ryder) R.; A.B., Princeton, 1929; m. Doris Taylor, July 3, 1934; (dec. Feb. 1970); 1 dau., Barbara Susan (Mrs. John K. Wendt); m. 2d, Margaret Murchison, Apr. 3, 1971. With Eberhard Faber Pencil Co., 1932-52, pres., chmn. bd., 1949-52; with Rudel Machinery Co., Ltd., 1938-60, chmn. bd., 1944-60; founder, chmn. bd. Rudel Machinery Co., Inc., 1941—; founder, chmn. bd., dir. Am. SIP Corp., 1950—; chmn. bd. V & O Press Co., Inc.; dir. AMT Consortium Inc., Lynch Corp., Baker Bros., Inc.; trustee Lincoln Savs. Bank. Asst. dir. machine tool div. NPA, Washington, 1951-52. Trustee Ethel Walker Sch., Lawrenceville Sch., Goucher Coll. Mem. Acad. Polit. Sci. (life), Newcomen Soc., Am. Machine Tool Distbrs. Assn. (dir.), U.S. Trade Mark Assn. (dir. 1940-52), Am. Soc. Tool Engrs., Am. Arbitration Assn. (mem. panel arbitrators), Nat. Machine Tool Builders Assn. (treas. 1969-72, dir. 1969-77, chmn. 1977-78). Episcopalian. Home: 2 Sutton Pl S New York City NY 10022 Office: 100 E 42d St New York City NY 10017

RUDGE, PETER DAVID, theatrical prodn. co. exec.; b. Wolverhampton, Eng., Mar. 6, 1946; s. Daniel Thomas and Katherine Jean (Bartlett) R.; came to U.S., 1974; B.A. in History, Fitzwilliam Coll., Cambridge, 1968; m. Frances Wright, Apr. 5, 1969; children—Joseph Daniel Dougan, Charlotte. Dir., Track Records, London, Eng., 1972; chmn. Five-One Prodns., London, 1972-74; pres. Sir Prodns., Inc., N.Y.C., 1974—. Mem. Ch. of England. Clubs: Friars (N.Y.C.); Marks (London). Office: Sir Prodns Inc 5 W 86th St New York NY 10024

RUDHART, ALEXANDER HUGO, historian; b. Vienna, Austria, May 24, 1930; s. Hugo Alexander and Leopoldine (Gruener) R.; Doctor Juris Utriusque, U. Vienna, 1952, Ph.D., 1962; postgrad. Columbia U., 1960-61; m. Kate Blake Considine, Aug. 17, 1963; 1 son, Alexander Joseph. Mem. faculty dept. history Villanova (Pa.) U., 1954—, prof. history, 1969—. Mem. Am. Hist. Assn., AAUP, Am. Com. History Second World War. Author: Twentieth Century Europe, 1975. Office: Dept History Villanova U Villanova PA 19085

RUDICH, GERALD ALLAN, transp. co. exec.; b. Bronx, N.Y., Nov. 23, 1942; s. Marvin and Laura (Duckor) R.; B.A., L.I. U., 1964; M.B.A., City U.N.Y., 1969; m. Lois Sheila Lacov, July 2, 1966; 1 son, Mitchell Brian. Employment interviewer N.Y. State Labor Dept., 1964-67; service personnel supr. Volkswagen of Am., Inc., Englewood, Cliffs, N.J., 1967-72; personnel mgr. Maher Terminals, Inc., Jersey City, 1972-73; mgr. personnel and purchasing Tension Envelope Corp., South Hackensack, N.J., 1973-78; dir. personnel and indsl. relations Purolator Security Inc., Piscataway, N.J., 1978—. Served with U.S. Army, 1965. Mem. Am. Soc. Personnel Adminstrn., Nat. Assn. Purchasing Mgt., Nat. Safety Council. Club: Mid-Bergen Rotary. Home: 6 Roxbury Ct Spring Valley NY 10977 Office: 255 Old New Brunswick Rd Piscataway NJ 08854

RUDIN, ARNOLD JAMES, rabbi; b. Pitts., Oct. 7, 1934; s. Philip Gordon and Beatrice (Rosenbloom) R.; B.A., George Washington U., 1955; M.A., Hebrew Union Coll., 1960; postgrad. U. Ill., 1965-68; m. Marcia Ruth Kaplan, July 27, 1969; children—Eve Sandra, Jennifer Anne. Ordained rabbi, 1960; asst. rabbi Congregation B'nai Jehudah, Kansas City, Mo., 1962-64; rabbi Sinai Temple, Champaign, Ill., 1964-68; asst. nat. dir. inter-religious affairs Am. Jewish Com., N.Y.C., 1968—; panelist weekly program Religion on the Line, WMCA, N.Y.C., 1970-73; guest Today Show, NBC-TV; coordinator Catholic-Jewish-Protestant Convocation, Seton Hall U., Jewish-So. Baptist meetings in Louisville and Cin., Conf. on Civil Religion, Wake Forest, N.C., Jewish-United Presbyn. Consultations, Princeton, N.J., Greenwich, Conn., Jewish-Methodist Colloquium, Dayton, Ohio, Jewish-Greek Orthodox meeting, N.Y.C., Black-Jewish Nat. Consultation, Nashville, Evang.-Jewish Conf., N.Y.C., 1968—; cons. Nat. Council Chs; mem. Am. Bapt. Chs. Task Force on Middle East; ofcl. Jewish observer World Meth. Conf., Denver, 1971; exec. chmn. Nat. Interreligious Task Force on Soviet Jewry; leader interreligious del. to Lebanon, Jordan and Israel, 1974; leader Interreligious Task Force del. to Belgrade Conf. on European Security and to Vatican, 1977. Nat. coordinator Am. Jewish Emergency Effort for Biafran Relief, 1968-69. Served with USAF, 1960-62. Recipient Joshua Evans award George Washington U., 1955, Nelson and Helen Glueck prize, 1957. Mem. Religious Edn. Assn. (program chmn. nat. conv. 1975), Central Conf. Am. Rabbis (commn. interfaith activities), Am. Jewish Hist. Soc. (exec. council). Co-editor: Evangelicals and Jews in Conversations, 1978; contbr. articles to profl. publs. Home: 129 E 82d St New York City NY 10028 Office: 165 E 56th St New York City NY 10022

RUDISILL, RICHARD ALLEN, ednl. adminstr.; b. Riegelsville, Pa., Nov. 16, 1922; s. Jacob Emmanuel and Martha Mehring (Hartman) R.; B.A., Gettysburg Coll., 1947; M.S., U. Pa., 1949, Ed.D., 1962; m. Lorna Jeanne Boland, May 16, 1944; children—Richard Boland, Vincent Boland. Dir. reading clinic Valley Forge Mil. Acad., Wayne, Pa., 1947-51; remedial reading tchr. Milton Hershey Sch., Hershey, Pa., 1951-52, dean of boys, 1952-55, dir. sr. homelife, 1955-58, asst. supt., 1958-63, headmaster, 1963—, v.p., 1974—. Chmn. bd. trustees Patton Sch., Elizabethtown, Pa.; mem. steering com. Ednl. Devel. Center, Millersville (Pa.) State Coll.; mem. program com. Pub. TV for S. Central Pa.; bd. dirs. Americans for Competitive Enterprise System. Served to lt. U.S. Army, 1943-46. Mem. Pa., Am. assns. sch. adminstrs., Boarding Sch. Headmasters of Middle States, Pa. Sch. Counselors Assn., Nat. Assn. Secondary Principals, Am. Personnel Guidance Assn., Pa. Assn. Private Academic Schs., Coll. Entrance Examination Bd., Phi Delta Kappa. Lutheran. Clubs: Hershey Rotary, Masons (past dist. dep. grand master), Shriners. Home: 725 Homestead Ln Hershey PA 17033 Office: Founders Hall Hershey PA 17033

RUDMAN, JOAN ELEANOR, artist, educator; b. Owensburg, Ind., Oct. 7, 1927; d. William Hobart and Elizabeth Joaquin (Edington) Combs; B.A., Mich. State U., 1949, M.A., 1951; student of E.A. Whitney, Greenwich, Conn., 1966-78; m. William Rudman, June 9, 1951; children—Mary Beth, Pamela Ann. Tchr. art Arlington High Sch., Poughkeepsie, N.Y., 1951-57; tchr. art classes Ryle Elementary Sch., Stamford, Conn., 1967-69, Franklin Elementary Sch., 1967-69, Dolan Jr. High Sch., 1967-69; tchr. watercolor classes in adult edn., Stamford, 1966—; tchr. watercolor painting Round Hill Community Guild, Greenwich, Conn., 1974—, King Sch., Stamford, 1974-77, Darien (Conn.) Community Assn., 1976; artist-in-residence North Br. Club, Mt. Snow, West Dover, Vt., 1974-76, So. Vt. Art Center, Manchester, 1978—; dir. watercolor workshops, Greenwich, 1974—; one woman shows include: Leon G. Gallery, East Lansing, Mich., 1969, Town and Country Club, Hartford, Conn., 1975, Wiley Gallery, Hartford, 1975 Hour Glass Gallery, Kent, Conn., 1977-78; group shows include: Nat. Art Club, 1968-77, Lord and Taylor Gallery, 1971, Am. Watercolor Soc. Exhbn., 1974, 77, Hudson Valley Art Assn. Award Winning Mems. Exhbn., 1975, Miniature Painters, Sculptors and Gravers Soc. Show, 1976, Whiskey Painters Am., Akron, Ohio, Am. Artists Prof. League, 1978, Salmagundi Club Show, 1978, Wadsworth Atheneum, Hartford, New Britain (Conn.) Mus. Am. Art, numerous others; represented in permanent collections. Mem. Conn. Watercolor Soc. (Nelson White award 1970), Hudson Valley Art Assn. (dir. 1969—, corr. sec. 1968—, Herbert Bohnert award 1970), Nat. League of Am. Pen Women (pres. pioneer br. 1972-74), Conn. Women Artists, Catherine Lorillard Wolfe Art Club (Anco award 1978), D.A.R. (historian 1969-71), Hoosier Salon (Purchase award 1975), Pen and Brush Club (2d prize 1976). Republican. Congregationalist. Contbr. articles to various newspapers. Address: 274 Quarry Rd Stamford CT 06903

RUDOLF, DONALD I., oral and maxillofacial surgeon; b. Phila., May 29, 1939; s. Frank M. and Pauline (Mellitz) R.; D.D.S., Temple U., 1963; postgrad. Grad. Sch. Medicine, U. Pa., 1964-65; m. Meryl B. Devins, June 6, 1962; children—Jonathan, Gregory, Steven. Resident Episcopal Hosp., 1965-67, practice oral surgery, Doylestown, Pa., 1967—; mem. staff Doylestown, Grand View, Warminster Gen., Kensington hosps. Mem. Am. Soc. Oral Surgeons, Pa., Delaware Valley socs. oral surgeons, Philadelphia County Dental Soc., ADA, John Kolmer Med. Honor Soc., Frederic James Honor Soc., Clin. Pathology, Oral Surgery Soc. Grad. Sch. Medicine U. Pa., Montgomery Bucks Dental Soc., Doylestown C. of C. Club: Philmont Country. Office: Landmark Bldg Clinton and W Court St Doylestown PA 18901 also Pennridge Med Arts Bldg Sellersville PA 18960 also 1930 Keith Rd Abington PA 19001

RUDOLFER, GEORGE, indsl. engr.; b. Vienna, Austria, Oct. 29, 1930; s. Fred and Paula (Zeilinger) R.; came to U.S., 1939, naturalized, 1945; B.S., Columbia U., 1957, M.S. in Indsl. Engring., 1958; m. Jacqueline Lemort; children—Job, Stefan, Peter. Gen. mgr. Greeting Service Corp., Webster, Mass., 1962-67; mgr. mfg. systems Rogers Corp. (Conn.), 1967-72; sr. cons. Hurdman & Cranston, N.Y.C., 1972-76; cons. G.E.R.A., Closter, N.J., 1976—. Served with U.S. Army, 1951-53. Mem. Internat. Material Mgmt. Soc., Prodn. and Inventory Control Soc. Contbr. articles to profl. jours. Home: 44 Smith St Closter NJ 07624

RUDOLPH, MALCOLM ROME, investment banker; b. Balt., Sept. 22, 1924; s. Louis and Sara E. (Rome) R.; A.B., Harvard U., 1947; postgrad. U. Grenoble, U. Paris (France), 1948, Hayden Stone Mgmt. Sch., 1965; m. Zita Herzmark, July 1, 1956; children—Malcolm R. II, Margot R. With div. internat. confs. State Dept., Paris, 1949; registered rep. trainee Orvis Bros. & Co., N.Y.C., 1949, registered rep., asst. mgr., acting mgr., 1950-64; mgr. Hayden Stone, Inc., Washington, 1964-68, partner, 1968-69; chmn. bd. Donatelli, Rudolph & Schoen, Inc., Washington, 1970-74, Multi-Nat. Fin. Group, Inc., Washington, 1974—, Multi-Nat. Precious Metals Corp., Washington, 1974—, Multi-Nat. Money Mgmt. Co., Inc., Washington, 1974—. Rudolph & Schoen Inc., Washington, 1975—; sr. v.p., dir. Laidlaw-Coggeshall, Inc., 1975—; pres. Laidlaw Resources, Inc., 1976—, Sutton Energy, Inc., 1976—, Laidlaw Investment Services, Inc., v.p., dir. Option Writer's Fund, Inc., 1977—; dir. Jack Hoag & Assos., Inc.; gen. partner Indsl. Gas Assos., 1975—. Vice pres. Tulip Hill Citizens Assn., 1964; treas. benefit com. Washington Performing Arts Soc., 1968, men's com., 1973-74; mem. presdl. Inaugural Com., 1960, 64. Served with USNR, 1943-46. Mem. Assn. Investment Brokers Met. Washington (v.p. 1965-66, pres. 1967), Bond Club Washington, Washington Met. Bd. Trade. Clubs: Internat., Harvard (asst. treas. 1957-60, treas. 1960-64, chmn. investment com. 1958-59, exec. com. 1957-67), Nat. Aviation (Washington). Home: 1200 N Nash St Arlington VA 22209 Office: 1775 K St NW Washington DC 20006

RU DUSKY, BASIL MICHAEL, physician; b. Wilkes-Barre, Pa., July 27, 1933; s. Michael and Anne RuD.; B.A., Va. Mil. Inst., 1955; M.D., U. Pitts., 1959; m. Bernadine RuDusky, 1957; children—Daryl, Bryan. Intern, Martin Army Hosp., Ft. Benning, Ga., 1959-60; resident Youngstown (Ohio) Hosp. Assn., 1962-63, Temple U. Hosp., 1963-66; practice medicine specializing in internal medicine, Wilkes-Barre, Pa., 1966—; mem. staff Mercy Hosp., 1966—, chief of medicine, 1966-70, dir. intensive and coronary care units, 1966-70, dir. phonocardiography lab., 1966-70; mem. staff Wilkes-Barre Gen. Hosp.; cons. cardiology Armed Forces Examining Service; sr. cons. Social Security Adminstrn., HEW; sr. cons. physician Met. Ins. Co. Am.; cons. internal medicine and cardiology Retreat State Hosp.; clin. instr. medicine Temple U., 1966-70. Served to capt. M.C., U.S. Army, 1959-62. Diplomate Am. Bd. Internal Medicine. Fellow A.C.P., Am. Coll. Angiology, Am. Coll. Chest Physicians, Am. Coll. Cardiology; mem. Am. Soc. Internal Medicine, AMA, Nat. Rehab. Assn., Am. Geriatrics Soc., Assn. Mil. Surgeons U.S., Ferrari Club Am., Maserati Owners Club, Lamborghini Owners Club, Amateur Fencers League Am. Home: 7 Pinetree Rd Mountaintop PA 18707 Office: Bicentennial Bldg 15 Public Square Wilkes-Barre PA 18701

RUDY, DOROTHY LUCILLE, poet, educator; b. Hamilton, Ohio, June 27, 1924; d. William Herman and Marjorie Delma (Rammel) Richardson; A.B., Queens Coll., 1945; A.M., Columbia U., 1948; postgrad. Radcliffe Coll., 1949-50; m. Willis Rudy, Jan. 31, 1948; children—Dorothy Elizabeth, Willis Philip, Willa Catherine. Tchr. English and creative writing in various schs., L.I., N.Y., Mass., N.Y. State, 1945-61; tchr. English, Worcester (Mass.) Jr. Coll., 1961-63, Tenafly (N.J.) High Sch., 1963-64; prof. English, Rutgers Evening Div., Newark, 1963-64; prof. English and creative writing Montclair State Coll., Upper Montclair, N.J., 1964—, also coordinator ind. study; lectr. N.Y. Poetry Forum, 1975-78; reader original poetry Clifton Pub. Library, 1975, N.Y. Poetry Forum, Danbury State Coll., also N.J. Council Tchrs. English, New Eng. Small Press Assn., various N.Y. and N.J. locations; speaker N.Y. Press Women's Lit. Day, 1977, 78; judge various poetry contests. Am. Poets Fellowship Soc. grantee, 1970. Mem. New Eng. Small Press Assn., New York Poetry Forum, N.J. Council Tchrs. English, Am. Pen Women, Centro Studi e Scambi Internazionali. Club: Radcliffe Alumnae. Author: (poems) Quality of Small, 1971; Psyche Afoot and Other Poems, 1978. Editor: Americana Anthology, 1976. Contbr. poems to various publs. Home: 161 W Clinton Ave Tenafly NJ 07670 Office: Montclair State Coll Upper Montclair NJ 07043

RUDY, WILLIS, historian; b. N.Y.C., Jan. 25, 1920; s. Philip and Rose (Handman) R.; B.S.S., Coll. City N.Y., 1939; M.A., Columbia U., 1940, Ph.D., 1948; m. Dorothy L. Richardson, Jan. 31, 1948; children—Dee Dee, Willa. Instr. Coll. City N.Y., 1939-49; instr., lectr. Harvard U., 1949-52, 53, 57, 58; prof. Mass. State Coll., Worcester, 1953-63; prof. history Fairleigh Dickinson U., Teaneck, N.J., 1963—, editorial bd. Fairleigh Dickinson U. Press, 1966-77. Mem. Am. Hist. Assn., Orgn. Am. Historians, Phi Beta Kappa. Author: The College of the City of New York, A History, 1847-1947, 1949; 1976; The American Liberal Arts College Curriculum, 1960; Higher Education in Transition, 1958, 68, 76; Schools in an Age of Mass Culture, 1965. Home: 161 W Clinton Ave Tenafly NJ 07670 Office: Dept History Fairleigh Dickinson U Teaneck NJ 07666

RUE, WILLIAM JAMES, chem. co. exec.; b. Belle Haven, Va., Aug. 11, 1914; s. Healy Parker Bagwell and Edna Louise (Willis) R.; B.S., Hampden-Sydney Coll., 1936; m. Lucie Ellen Mapp, Oct. 5, 1946; children—Jennie Rue Virgin, William James. With Hercules, Inc., 1940—, mgr., Kenvil, N.J., 1976—; cons. Dept. Def. to European rocket industry; dir. First Nat. Bank & Trust Co. of W.Md., 1970-75. Vestryman, Emanual Episcopal Ch., 1973-76; pres. Potomac council Boy Scouts Am., 1973-74; bd. dirs. Welkind Neurol. Hosp.; mem. adv. bd. Sacred Heart Hosp., 1970-75. Recipient Silver Beaver award Boy Scouts Am., 1973. Mem. Am. Chem. Soc., Am. Inst. Chem. Engrs., Am. Inst. Aeros. and Astronautics, Md. Ornithol. Soc., Lambda Chi Alpha. Republican. Clubs: Masons, Shriners, K.T., Rotary, Cumberland Country, Eastern Shore Yacht and Country. Home: 51 Hercules Rd Kenvil NJ 07847 Office: Howard Blvd Kenvil NJ 07847

RUEBEL, ARMIN ALFREDLUDWIG, urologist; b. Scheinfeld, Bavaria, Germany, Apr. 22, 1938; s. Armin Alfred Friedrich and Anna Ernestine Gerda (Stiller) R.; came to U.S., 1965, naturalized, 1971; M.D., U. Würzburg, 1963; m. Catherine Carmel Mary D'Amico, Aug. 8, 1970; children—April Lea, Heather Ernestine. Rotating intern, Germany, 1964-65; intern, U. Würzburg Hosp., 1965-66; resident surgery Sinai Hosp., Balt., 1967; resident urology Hosp. of U. Pa., Phila., 1968-71, chief resident, 1970-71; practice medicine specializing in urology, Doylestown, Pa., 1971—; mem. staff Doylestown Hosp., Warminster Gen. Hosp. Diplomate Am. Bd. Urology. Mem. AMA, Pa., Bucks County med. socs., Urol. Assn. Pa., Aircraft Owners and Pilots Assn. Lutheran. Home: RD 1 Gordon Rd Doylestown PA 18901 Office: 76 W Court St Doylestown PA 18901

RUEPPEL, MERRILL CLEMENT, art cons.; b. Haddonfield, N.J., May 7, 1925; s. George H. and Nellie (Lester) R.; B.A., Beloit Coll., 1949; M.A., U. Wis., 1951, Ph.D., 1955; m. Joan Marie Storberg, Sept. 15, 1956; children—Philip Cameron, Sarah Githens. Research asst. Mpls. Inst. Arts, 1956-57, asst. to dir., 1957-59, asst. dir., 1959-63; asst. dir. City Art Mus., St. Louis, 1961-64; dir. Dallas Mus. Fine Arts, 1964-73, Mus. Fine Arts, Boston, 1973-75; asso. prof. art and archaeology Washington U., St. Louis, 1963; cons. mus. curatorial tng. program Ford Found., 1963-66. Served with AUS, 1943-46; ETO. Mem. Assn. Art Mus. Dirs. (sec.-treas. 1967-68), Am. Assn. Museums, Archaeol. Inst. Am., Phi Beta Kappa. Clubs: Somerset; Odd Volumes (Boston). Author numerous exhbn. catalogues. Home: 766 Chestnut St Needham MA 02192

RUETH, MARION URSULA, librarian; b. Washington; d. George A. and Belle (Skinner) Rueth; student Ursuline Coll., Santa Rosa, Calif., Georgetown Visitation Jr. Coll., Trinity Coll.; M. Mus., Cath. U. Am., 1946; M.A. in L.S., Fla. State U., 1962. Dir. Silver Studio Music, Silver Spring, Md., 1944-50; library asst. St. Petersburg (Fla.) Pub. Library, 1953-58; music specialist and cataloger Fla. State U. Library, Tallahassee, 1958-62; asst. head acquisitions McKeldin Library, U. Md., 1962-66; dir. library Hood Coll., Frederick, Md., 1966-78. Mem. ALA, Md. Library Assn., Music Library Assn., Beta Phi Mu, Pi Kappa Lambda. Roman Catholic. Author: The Tallahassee Years of Ernst von Dohnanyi, 1962. Home: Willowbrook Old Middletown Rd Jefferson MD 21755 also 8228-25th Ave North St Petersburg FL 33710

RUFEH, FIROOZ, nuclear engr.; b. Persia, Feb. 14, 1937; s. Eberhim and Marian R.; came to U.S., 1955, naturalized, 1972; B.S. in Chemistry Cornell U., 1959; M.S. in Nuclear Engring., U. Calif. at Berkeley, 1963; m. Heide-Marie Haseruck, June 12, 1965; children—Bejan-Renard, Jiela-Marian. Jr. scientist Lawrence Radiation Lab., Berkeley, Calif., 1960-63; research scientist Thermo Electron Corp., Waltham, Mass., 1963-67, mgr. research dept., 1967-75, dir. energy conservation and research, 1975—. Mem. Am. Phys. Soc. Republican. Presbyterian. Contbr. articles in field to profl. jours. Home: 185 Hunters Ridge Rd Concord MA 01742 Office: Thermo Electron Corp 101 1st Ave Waltham MA 02154

RUFF, ALONZO WILLIAM, refrigeration engr.; b. Esperence, N.Y., Mar. 24, 1902; s. William Alonzo and Matie (Bell) R.; Refrigeration Engring., Mass. Inst. Tech., 1921-26; m. Pauline Zercher, June 24, 1930; children—Anita, Josephine, Susan, Kathlene, William; m. 2d, Beatrice Maye Clock, July 9, 1977. Asst. to mgr. Harding Mfg. Co., Cobbskill, N.Y., 1921-22; head equipment devel. York Corp., York, Pa., 1926-37, mgr. devel., 1937-45; v.p. engring. and devel. York-Shipley, Inc., York, 1939-46; v.p., sec. Patterson & Assos., York, 1945-55; engr., chmn. bd. St. Onge, Ruff & Assos., York, 1955-74; pres., engr. Expertise Assistance, Inc., York, 1976—; cons. refrigerator design, food processing. Active vol. with various community groups including YMCA, Boy Scouts of Am., and Community Improvement Com. Served with Engring. Corps, USAR, 1924-26. Registered mech. engr., Pa., Md., Nova Scotia; named York Engr. of Yr., 1968. Life mem. ASME, Am. Soc. Heating Refrigeration and Air Conditioning Engrs., Inst. Food Tech., Oil Heat Inst., Inst. Internat. Ammonia Refrigeration; mem. Inst. Am. Refrigerated Warehouses, Pa. Soc. Profl. Engrs., Internat. Inst. Refrigeration. Republican. Baptist. Club: York Country. Holder over 70 patents in fields including air conditioning, evaporation, compression, automatic machinery and controls, dry ice, combustion equipment, refrigerated structures and cyrogenics. Address: 101 S Yale St York PA 17406

RUFFALO, SIBYL WINIFRED MASQUELIER, mgmt. cons.; b. Canonsburg, Pa., July 8, 1946; d. David Jules Grace (Strickland) Masquelier; A.B., U. Pitts., 1967; M.Ed., U. Miami, 1969; 1 dau., Phaedra Danielle. Teaching asst. U. Miami, Coral Gables, Fla., 1967-69; personnel mgr. Div. Family Services, State of Fla., Miami, 1970-73; employment mgr. Miami Herald, Knight Ridder Newspapers, 1974-76; labor relations search cons. Gordon Wahls Co., Media, Pa., 1976—. Active March of Dimes, Assn. for Learning Disabled Children. Mem. Am. Soc. Personnel Adminstrn. (accredited specialist). Republican. Episcoplian. Home: 445 S Jackson Media PA 19063 Office: 610 E Baltimore Pike Media PA 19063

RUFFOLO, ROBERT EUGENE, II, antique book dealer; b. Dec. 21, 1951; s. Robert Eugene and Elizabeth Ann (Wagoner) R.; student N.C. State U., 1970-73; B.S. in Bus. Adminstrn., Stockton (N.J.) State Coll., 1978. Book dealer 1970—; owner, antique dealer Princeton Antiques, Atlantic City, N.J., from 1973; owner, operator Princeton Antiques Galleries, Atlantic City, from 1973; pres. Princeton Antiques Bookservice, Inc., Atlantic City, 1974—. Named Outstanding Jaycee of the Year, Greater Atlantic City Jaycees, 1974. Mem. Am. Soc. Appraisers (asso.), Future Farmers Am. (pres. Northeast Guilford City (N.C.) chpt. 1970), Atlantic City Jaycees, Alpha Phi Omega (2d v.p. Iota Lambda chpt. of N.C. State U. 1973). Home: 2915-17 Atlantic Ave Apt 1 Atlantic City NJ 08401 Office: 2915-17-31 Atlantic Ave Atlantic City NJ 08401

RUGANI, ALEXANDER E., lawyer; b. N.Y.C., Apr. 15, 1925; s. Lambert H. and Carolina (Lolla) R.; student Coll. City N.Y., 1942-45, N.Y. U., 1945-46; LL.B., Fordham U., 1950; m. Irene H. Scarsi, Apr. 20, 1952. Admitted to N.Y. bar, 1951, U.S. Supreme Ct. bar, 1970; practiced in N.Y.C., 1951—; asso. firm Kirlin, Campbell & Keating, 1951-63, jr. partner, 1964-69, sr. partner, 1970—. Served with AUS, 1946-47. Mem. Am. Bar Assn., Maritime Law Assn. U.S., Assn. Bar City N.Y., N.Y. Law Inst., Gen. Average Adjusters Assn. U.S., Assn. Average Adjusters London, Soc. Naval Architects and Marine Engrs. Clubs: Whitehall Lunch; Bankers of Am. Asso. editor American Maritime Cases. Home: 241 Ave of Americas New York City NY 10014 Office: 120 Broadway New York City NY 10005

RUGARI, JOSEPH FRANK, accountant; b. Utica, N.Y., July 10, 1948; s. Louis and Maria (Labbozzetta) R.; B.S., Utica Coll., Syracuse U., 1970; m. Maria R. Pedulla, June 29, 1974; children—Joseph,

Marianne. Staff accountant Price Waterhouse & Co., N.Y.C., 1970-73; internal auditor Chgo. Pneumatic Tool Co., N.Y.C., 1973, accounts recivable mgr., Utica, 1973-75, sr. fin. analyst, 1975-76, mgr. accounting systems, 1976—. Mem. Am. Inst. C.P.A.'s, N.Y. State Soc. C.P.A.'s. Democrat. Home: 7 Beaton Dr Utica NY 13502 Office: 2200 Bleecker St Utica NY 13503

RUGGIERI, NICHOLAS TINO, artist; b. Vieste, Italy, June 15, 1908; s. Carl S. and Victoria (Cirillo) R.; came to U.S., 1920, naturalized, 1937; student N.Y. Art Student League, 1935-37, Italian Nat. Acad., Florence, 1939; m. Rose Rezzo, Sept. 6, 1937; 1 dau., Rosemary Ruggieri Baer. Artist, Harrisburg (Pa.) Telegraph, 1939-41; art dir. Harrisburg Patriot-News Co., 1941—; tchr. Harrisburg Art Assn.; Earl Wright lectr. Shippensburg (Pa.) State Coll., 1976. Recipient Grumbacher award, 1964; Silver Medal award Pa. Advt. Fedn., 1973; Art Achievement citations Pa. Senate, Ho. of Reps., 1975; George Washington Honor Medal award. Fellow Royal Soc. Arts London; mem. Art Assn. Harrisburg (past pres.), Balt. Watercolor Soc., Kappa Pi. Roman Catholic. Clubs: Exchange Club Harrisburg (pres.), Harrisburg Camera. Author: Pennsylvania: A Commemorative Portrait, 1975; Pennsylvania Sketchbook, 1976. Home: 621 Harding St New Cumberland PA 17070 Office: Patriot-News 814 Market St Harrisburg PA 17105

RUGGIERI, PAULINE PAPPAS, mfg. co. exec.; b. Pawtucket, R.I., June 15, 1930; d. Nicholas Zessimos and Julia (Kacharo) Pappas; student Am. Inst. Banking, 1948-52, Brown U. Extension Div., 1954-57, R.I. Sch. Design Evening Div., 1977; m. John Michael Ruggieri, June 2, 1956; children—Nicole Johanna, Kristin Paula. With Indsl. Nat. Bank, Pawtucket, R.I., 1948-57, head fgn. exchange dept., 1954-57; exec. v.p., sec. C.P.I. Controls, Inc., Pawtucket, 1973—. Greek Orthodox. Home: 4 Albert St Pawtucket RI 02861

RUGGIERO, RICHARD SALVADOR, liquor co. exec., educator; b. Utica, N.Y., Sept. 20, 1944; s. Thomas Joseph and Theresa (Passalacqua) R.; B.A. (N.Y. State Regents scholar), Niagara U., 1966; postgrad. Syracuse U., Colgate U., State U. N.Y. Coll. Tech., Elmira Coll.; m. Janis E. Ziolkowski, July 2, 1966. Tchr. English, Utica City Sch. Dist., 1966—; v.p., treas. T.J. Liberty Liquors, Inc., Utica, 1969—, chmn. bd., 1974—; partner Glacier Ice Cream Co., Utica, 1971-73. Mem. Utica City Council, 1978—; mem. exec. bd. City of Utica Democratic Com.; commr. of deeds City of Utica; bd. dirs. Sr. Day Center of Utica; mem. devel. council St. Elizabeth Hosp.; mem. Ridgewood Neighbors Assn.; pres. parish council Ch. Our Lady of Lourdes. Certified in secondary English, State N.Y. Mem. Am. Fedn. Tchrs., N.Y. State United Tchrs., Utica Tchrs. Assn., Internat. Reading Assn., N.Y. State Assn. City Councils, Niagara U. Alumni Assn., Friendly Sons St. Patrick, Mohawk Valley Package Stores Assn., Sons Italy in Am., Police Conf. N.Y., Phi Delta Kappa. Clubs: K.C., Night Stick, Engine 11, Comity (v.p.), Kiwanis (Utica). Home: 131 Westminster Pl Utica NY 13501 Office: 138 Liberty St Utica NY 13502

RUGGIERO, THOMAS WILLIAM, psychotherapist; b. Bklyn., Nov. 19, 1942; s. Joseph and Louise (Luperelli-Albion) R.; B.A., St. John's U., 1964; M.S.W., Adelphi U., 1969; 1 dau., Maia Jo. Supr., N.Y.C. Dept. Social Services, 1969-72; psychiat. social worker Luth. Med. Center, Bklyn., 1972—; staff psychotherapist, supr. Washington Sq. Inst. Psychotherapy and Mental Health, N.Y.C., 1969—; pvt. practice psychoanalytic psychotherapy, N.Y.C., 1972—. Mem. Soc. Clin. Social Work Psychotherapists (mem. edn. com.), Nat. Assn. Social Workers, Acad. Certified Social Workers, Nat. Assn. Advancement Psychoanalysis. Office: 35 W 9th St New York NY 10011

RUIZ, TOMAS, pathologist; b. Cuenca, Spain, Aug. 24, 1936 s. Tomas and Maria (Lopez) R.; came to Can., 1963, naturalized, 1969; M.D., Zaragoza U., Spain, 1960; M.P.H., U. Madrid, 1962; m. Mariette Fortin, Dec. 5, 1964; children—Anik, Mary-Eve. Intern, Zaragoza M.I. Hosp., 1961-62; resident in pathology Notre Dame Hosp., 1964-69, Sainte Justine Hosp., 1968-69; practice medicine specializing in pathology, Cowansville, Que., 1969—; asst. prof. histology U. Zaragoza, 1960-61; asst. prof. pathology U. Montreal, 1964-68, 72—; dir. labs. BMP Hosp., Cowansville, 1970-75, chmn. dept. pathology, 1976—. pres. med. council, 1974-75, bd. dirs., 1974-75. Served with 20th Regt. Arty., Spanish Army, 1961-62. Mem. Que. Assn. Pathologists, Can. Soc. Cytology, Internat. Acad. Pathology, Can. Assn. Pathologists, Med. Assn. Montreal. Home: 19 Maple St Sutton PQ J0E 2K0 Canada Office: BMP Hosp Cowansville PQ J2K 1K3 Canada

RUMA, STEVEN JAMES, psychologist; b. Boston, Sept. 29, 1936; s. Charles Dominic and Helen Virginia (Koury) R.; B.S., Columbia U., 1961; postgrad. U. Vienna (Austria), 1959, 62; M.A., Boston U., 1963; Ph.D., Ohio State U., 1966. Asst. prof. pediatrics and psychology Ohio State U., Columbus, 1967-70; asst. prof. (vis.) pub. health and epidemiology Yale U., New Haven, 1970-71; adj. asso. prof. social psychology Tchrs. Coll., Columbia U., N.Y.C., 1972-73; pres. Internat. Assn. Applied Social Scientists, Washington, 1971-73; pres. Better Homes & Orgns., E. Boothbay, Maine and N.Y.C.; cons. Harvard Med. Sch., Boston, U. Chgo. Med. Center, N.Y. U. Med. Center, UN Devel. Program, Mobil Oil Corp., Digital Equip. Corp. Served with U.S. Army, 1954-57. USPHS fellow, 1963-64. Mem. Am. Psychol. Assn., Internat. Assn. Applied Social Scientists. Roman Catholic. Contbr. articles in field to profl. jours. Address: PO Box 139 East Boothbay ME 04544

RUMER, RALPH RAYMOND, JR., educator; b. Ocean City, N.J., June 22, 1931; s. Ralph Raymond and Anna (Hibbard) R.; B.S. in Civil Engring., Duke U., 1953; M.S., Rutgers U., 1959; Sc.D. (ASCE research fellow), Mass. Inst. of Tech., 1962; m. Shirley Louise Haynes, Nov. 30, 1953; children—Sherri, Sue, Sandra, Sarah. With Lukens Steel Co., Coatsville, Pa., 1953-54; instr. dept. civil engring. Rutgers U., New Brunswick, N.J., 1956-59; civil engr. U.S. Dept. Agr., New Brunswick, summer 1957-59; research asst. Hydrodynamics Lab., Mass. Inst. Tech., Boston, 1961-62; asst. prof. dept. civil engring. Mass. Inst. Tech., 1962-63; asso. prof. dept. civil engring. State U. of N.Y. at Buffalo, 1963-69, acting head, 1966-67, chmn., 1967-73, prof., 1969-76, 78—, dir. Center for Inland Water Resources, 1972-74, acting provost engring. and applied scis., 1974-75; prof., chmn. dept. civil engring. U. Del., Newark, 1976-78; com. mem. Erie County Sewerage and Drainage Agency, N.Y.; mem. Environ. Conservation Advisory Com., Amherst, N.Y.; participant Can.-U.S. Univ. Seminar on Instl. Arrangements for the Integrated Mgmt. of the Water and Land Resources of the Eastern Great Lakes; tech. cons. to govt. and industry in hydraulics, water resources, and environ. engring. Served with U.S. Army, 1954-56. Ford fellow, 1962-63, sr. research fellow Calif. Inst. of Tech., 1970-71; licensed profl. engr., N.Y. Mem. ASCE (bd. dirs. Buffalo sect.), Am. Water Resources Assn., Internat. Assn. Hydraulic Research, Am. Geophys. Union, Am. Soc. Engring. Edn., Internat. Assn. Great Lakes Research, Internat. Assn. Theoretical and Applied Limnology, Sigma Xi, Chi Epsilon. Contbr. research articles in field to profl. jours. Home: 821 Eggert Rd Buffalo NY 14226

RUMMLER, JOSEPH CHADWICK, realtor; b. Phila., May 14, 1919; s. Joseph H. and Edna (Sprecher) R.; grad. high sch.; m. Dorothy Patricia Peters, Oct. 25, 1945; children—Craig J., Rand C., Eric G., Brett C., Marc A. Owner, Seashore Improvement Co., Port Republic, N.J., 1950-65, Blueberry Hill Campgrounds, Port Republic, 1960-70, Campers Equipment & Rental Co., Port Republic, 1960-70, J.C. Rummler Realty, Galloway Twp., N.J., 1968—, Arrowhead Tavern, Pomona, 1972—; v.p. Atlantic County Enterprises, Inc., 1972—; mng. broker Alconver, Inc., 1976—. Pres., City Council, Port Republic, 1949-65, mayor, 1965-67, councilman, 1967-70, city clk., 1970-72. Bd. dirs. Atlantic Mainland Indsl. Com. Atlantic County, 1963. Served with AUS, 1942-46. Mem. Navy League, Am. Soc. Notaries, Am. Legion (past post comdr.) Atlantic City, Atlantic County, Nat. bds. realtors, Galloway Twp. C. of C. (pres., 1973), Atlantic County Businessmans Assn. (pres. 1966), Atlantic County Tavern Owners (pres. 1975-76). Kiwanian. Home: Cologne Port Rd Port Republic NJ 08241 Office: Cologne Port Rd Galloway Twp NJ 08241

RUMSTEIN, REGINA, psychologist; b. Vienna, Austria, Feb. 26, 1922; d. Michael and Pearl (Malter) Geber; came to U.S., 1938, naturalized, 1943; B.A. cum laude, Hunter Coll. City U. N.Y., 1960; M.A., Columbia U., 1963, Ed.D., 1970; m. David Rumstein, 1942 (dec. 1972). Lectr. in psychology H. H. Lehman Coll. City U. N.Y., 1970-72, asst. prof. psychology, 1972-74; adj. asso. prof. Pace U., 1974—. Mem. Westchester (N.Y.), Am. psychol. assns., N.Y. Acad. Scis., Kappa Delta Pi, Pi Lambda Theta, Psi Chi, Phi Beta Kappa. Contbr. articles on ednl. psychology to profl. jours.

RUNDEN, CHARITY EVA WILLIAMS, educator; b. Lake City, Minn., Oct. 1, 1910; d. Harley Albert and Edith (Burchard) Williams; A.B., Ball State U., 1933, M.A., 1940; M.S. in Pub. Health (USPHS fellow), U. N.C., 1944; Ph.D., Ind. U., 1951; m. John Paul Runden, Aug. 23, 1944; children—John Paul, Ingrid Eve. Tchr. high schs., Ind., 1937-43; health educator, N.C. and Ind., 1944-46; faculty Ind. U., 1950-52, U. Ky., 1952-54; instr. Western Ill. U., Macomb, 1954-57, acting dean grad. div., 1957-59; asst. prof. psychology and edn. Montclair State Coll., Upper Montclair, N.J., 1959-63, dean of women, 1963-65, asso. chmn. grad. studies, 1965-67, prof. psychology and edn., 1966—, exec. dir. Ednl. Found. for Human Sexuality, 1967—. Fellow Am. Pub. Health Assn.; mem. Modern Lang. Assn., N.J. Health Edn. Council, N.J. Assn. Health, Phys. Edn. and Recreation, Nat. Council on Family Relations, Am. Assn. Sex Educators and Counselors, Sex Info. and Ednl. Council U.S. (asso.). Author: Twentieth Century Educators, 1965; Selected Readings in Sex Education, 1968. Contbr. articles to profl. jours. Home: Glen Rock Rd Little Falls NJ 07424 Office: Montclair State College Valley and Normal Aves Upper Montclair NJ 07043

RUNNION, NORMAN RAY, newspaper editor; b. Kansas City, Mo., Oct. 14, 1929; s. Ray and Winifred (Hoover) R.; B.S. in Journalism, Northwestern U., 1951; m. Marjorie Bruce, June 22, 1952; 1 son, David Bruce. With City News Bur. of Chgo., 1951, Chgo. Sun-Times, 1951-52, UPI, N.Y.C., Washington, London and Paris, 1953-66; dir. devel. Windham Coll., 1966-67; mng. editor Brattleboro (Vt.) Reformer, 1969—. Corporator, Brattleboro Meml. Hosp., 1974—. Mem. Vt. Press Assn. (pres. 1977-78), Vt. Hist. Soc. (trustee), Brattleboro C. of C. (dir. 1966-68, 73-75). Democrat. Episcopalian. Author: Gemini, 1966; Up the Ivy Ladder, 1969. Contbr. to World Book Ency. Home: 2 Allerton Ave Brattleboro VT 05301 Office: 71 Main St Brattleboro VT 05301

RUNSTEIN, ROBERT E., meat co. exec., author; b. Winthrop, Mass., Feb. 23, 1947; s. Abraham and Gertrude (Belson) R.; B.A., Cornell U., 1969; postgrad. Cleve. Inst. Electronics, 1972; m. JoAnne Aline Adler, May 23, 1973. Chief engr., tech. dir. Intermedia Sound, Boston, 1970-72; chief engr. N. Country Prodns., Brighton, Mass., 1972-74; chief engr., tech. dir., studio mgr. Great No. Recording Studio Ltd., Maynard, Mass., 1974-75; salesman Morrison & Schiff Inc., Brighton, Mass., 1975-76, office mgr., 1976-78, treas., 1978—, also dir. Mem. Audio Engring. Soc. Recipient gold record for single hit Sunshine, 1971. Author: Modern Recording Techniques, 1974. Contbr. articles in field to various trade mags. Home: 1105 Massachusetts Ave Apt 4E Cambridge MA 02138 Office: 35 Hichborn St Brighton MA 02135

RUNYON, HOWARD LEROY, law enforcement ofcl.; b. Clinton, N.J., May 28, 1938; s. Arthur N. and Myrtle C. (Hummer) R.; A.A., County Coll. Morris, 1973; student Drakes Coll., 1958, Ariz. State Coll., 1956; m. Lauretta Vargo, Apr. 9, 1976; children—Howard L., Sharon, Debbie, Christopher Padula, Laurie Padula. Salesman, Sealtest Co., Plainfield, N.J., 1958-59, Schmalz Dairy, Warren Twp., N.J., 1959-62; patrolman Twp. of Harding (N.J.), 1962-63; patrolman Twp. of Passaic, Stirling, N.J., 1963-66, chief of police, 1966—; cons. Internat. Assn. Chiefs of Police, 1971—; commr. N.J. Police Tng. Commn., 1977-78; dir. tng. Morris County Fire Fighters and Police Acad., 1967—, chmn. bd. dirs. 1974—; cons. Gen. Learning Corp., 1972-73, Morris County Drug Abuse Council, 1973-74. Chmn. civil disturbance com. Morris County, 1968-75; adviser Morris County Coll. Police Sci., 1969—, com. chmn., 1976—; adviser Morris County Juvenile Officers Assn., 1970—; co-chmn. Morris County Mut. Aid, 1969—; mem. Internat. Com. on Drug Abuse, 1974—; regional coordinator police found. Internat. Assn. Chiefs of Police, 1973; founder, pres. Passaic Twp. Youth Center, 1968-71; dir. Passaic Twp. Communications Network, 1967—; mem. Millington Fire Co., 1962—, First Aid Squad, 1962—; mem. N.J. First Aid Commn., 1964—; pres. bd. trustees Passaic Twp. Youth Center Assn., 1968-71. Recipient Distinguished Service award Passaic Twp. Jr. C. of C., 1965; Meritorious Service award Passaic Twp. Grange, 1969; Leadership award Passaic Twp. Youth Center Assn., 1970; named Police Officer of Year, Twp. of Passaic, Am. Legion, 1976-77. Mem. Nat. Rifle Assn., Morris County Police Chiefs Assn. (pres. 1972-73), N.J. (exec. bd. 1970-76, 6th v.p.), Internat. (exec. com. 1977—) assns. chiefs of police, N.J. Narcotic Assn., Fed. Narcotic Officers Assn., Fed. Bur. Narcotic Alumni Assn., Internat. Juvenile Officer Assn., Internat. Conf. Police Assn., N.J. Wrestling Ofcls. Assn., FBI Nat. Acad. Assn. Club: Northfield Rod and Gun (v.p. 1962-69). Contbr. articles in field to profl. jours. Home: 20 Fairview Dr S Basking Ridge NJ 07920 Office: 264 Mercer St Stirling NJ 07980

RUNYON, JOHN HAROLD, twp. ofcl.; b. Reading, Pa., June 30, 1945; s. James Hilliard and Ruth Emma (Kantner) R.; B.A. (Rose Meml. honor scholar), Drew U., 1967; student London City Coll., 1965; postgrad. Union Theol. Sem., 1967-68; M.A., Rutgers U., 1969; m. Sally Sutphen, July 8, 1967; 1 dau., Erica Lyn. Rockefeller Found. fellow Union Theol. Sem., 1967-68; asst. dir. Center for State Legislative Research and Service, Eagleton Inst. Politics, Rutgers U., 1969-71, asst. to pres., 1971-73; adminstr. Twp. of East Brunswick, N.J., 1973—; cons. ABC Election News Coverage N.J., 1970, 72, 74, 76, 78, N.J. Pub. Broadcasting System, 1971; tabulation coordinator News Election Service, 1970. Trustee Drew U., Madison, N.J., 1971-76; chmn. Middlesex County 208 Water Quality Mgmt. Planning Program; mem. East Brunswick Planning Bd., 1974—. Mem. Am. Polit. Sci. Assn., Internat. City Mgmt. Assn., N.J.-East Brunswick Hist. Soc. Author: (with others) Source Book of American Presidential Campaign and Election Statistics, 1972. Home: 36 South Dr East Brunswick NJ 08816 Office: 1 Jean Walling Civic Center East Brunswick NJ 08816

RUOF, RICHARD ALAN, clergyman; b. Lancaster, Pa., Oct. 11, 1932; s. Robert Jacob and Geneva May (Devers) R.; A.B., Franklin and Marshall Coll., 1954; M.Div., Lancaster Theol. Sem. and Union Theol. Sem. Va., 1960; S.T.M. Luth. Theol. Sem., Gettysburg, Pa., 1974; postgrad. doctoral program McCormick Theol. Sem., 1977—; m. Anne Margaret Demos; children—Mark Alan Demos Ruof, Anne Tracy Demos Ruof, Richard James Demos Ruof. Ordained in ministry United Ch. Christ, 1960; pastor Harrisville (Va.) Charge of United Ch. Christ, 1959-62, Thurmont (Md.) Charge, 1962-67, First Congl. Ch., Cortland, N.Y., 1967-77, St. Paul's United Ch. Christ of Hamlin, Fredericksburg, Pa., 1977—. Registrar-treas. Susquehanna Assn., N.Y. Conf., United Ch. Christ, 1968-74. Served with USNR, 1954-56. Club: Lions. Home: RD 1 Box 410 A Fredericksburg PA 17026

RUPERT, MARYBETH KIMBERLY, info. mgmt. specialist; b. St. Petersburg, Fla., Oct. 14, 1948; d. Claude Kimberly and Sara Elizabeth (Somers) R.; S.B., Mass. Inst. Tech., 1970; M.T.S., Gordon-Conwell Theol. Sem., 1971; M.A., Georgetown U., 1972; M.Phil., Ph.D., Yale U., 1974. Lab. asst. Melpar, Inc., Falls Church, Va., summers, 1966-67; research asst., info. specialist, sci. writer Tracor Jitco, Inc., Rockville, Md., 1968-75, research asso. social and policy studies 1976-77; asst. prof. religion Central Mich. U., Mt. Pleasant, 1974-76; prin. lit. scientist Franklin Inst. Research Labs., Rockville, 1977—. Served to lt. (j.g.) USNR-R. Mem. Am. Acad. Religion, Am. Studies Assn., Am. Hist. Assn., Am. Soc. Ch. History, Soc. Sci. Study of Religion, Am. Acad. Polit. and Social Sci., Naval Res. Assn. Quaker. Clubs: Yale (N.Y.C.); Sailing (Washington). Office: 11611 Old Georgetown Rd Rockville MD 20852

RUPERT, RICHARD EUGENE, lab. exec.; b. Maryville, Mo., June 11, 1935; s. Charles L. and W. June (Boyer) R.; student Iowa State Coll., Ames, 1953-55; B.S. in Mech. Engring., U. So. Calif., Los Angeles, 1961; m. Barbara Gesine Mueller, June 25, 1965; children—Jeffrey Michael, Nicole Babette. Project engr. for qualification of aerospace equipment Wyle Labs., El Segundo, Calif., 1956-63, dir. mktg. for Eastern ops., Huntsville, Ala., 1963-67, dir. govt. mktg., Washington, 1967-70, v.p. program devel. Sci. Systems and Services Group, Silver Spring, Md., 1970—. Registered profl. engr., Ala. Mem. Nat. Soc. Profl. Engrs., ASME, Soc. Automotive Engrs., Am. Inst. Aeros. and Astronautics, Inst. Environ. Sci., Nat. Contracts Mgmt. Assn., Assn. U.S. Army. Republican. Lutheran. Home: 12220 Seven Locks Rd Potomac MD 20854 Office: 2361 Jefferson Davis Hwy Arlington VA 22202

RUPOLO, JOHN GEORGE, chiropractor; b. Bklyn., Oct. 30, 1947; s. Joseph and Mary Ada (Commisso) R.; B.A., Lehman Coll., Bronx, N.Y., 1969; grad. cum laude Nat. Coll. of Chiropractic, 1972. Tchr., Massapequa (N.Y.) Pub. Schs., 1969-70; instr. physiology Lincoln Coll. of Chiropractic, Indpls., 1971; asst. clinic intern Nat. Coll. Chiropractic, Lombard, Ill., 1972; gen. practice of chiropractic, Floral Park, N.Y., 1972—; mem. staff N.Y. Chiropractic Coll., Westbury, N.Y., 1975—. Licensed as chiropractor, N.Y. Bd. Higher Edn. Mem. Am. (mem. council on roentgenology 1972—, council on physiotherapy 1971-73, council on neurology 1972-78, council on nutrition 1973-78), N.Y. State (chmn. ins. com. 1975-76, mem. indsl. relations com. 1975-78) chiropractic assns. Roman Catholic. Club: Floral Park Lions (bull. editor 1975-78). Home: 1615 Putney Rd Valley Stream NY 11580 Office: 148 Tulip Ave Floral Park NY 11001

RUPPERT, ROBERT WILLIAM, engring. co. exec.; b. Kenilworth, N.J., May 16, 1926; s. Emile and Kathryn (Chiovarou) R.; B.S., N.J. Inst. Tech., 1951, M.S., 1956; m. Sept. 13, 1947; children—Robert Todd, William Tait. Research and devel. engr. Pulverizing Machinery Co., Summit, N.J., 1953-56; project engr. Fred S. Carver, Inc., Summit, 1956-69; mgr. spl. projects McKiernan-Terry Corp., Dover, N.J., 1959-64; pres. Emro Engring. Co., Inc., Summit, 1964—; dir. Carver Greenfield Corp., Hanover, N.J., 1969-71; cons. engr., corporate dir.; spl. lectr. N.J. Inst. Tech., 1966-70. Served with Army AC, 1944-45. Registered profl. engr., N.J. Fellow Am. Inst. Aeros. and Astronautics; mem. Aerospace Med. Assn., ASTM, Nat. Soc. Profl. Engrs., Nat. Pilots Assn., Am. Soaring Soc. Patentee and inventor in field. Office: PO Box 536 Summit NJ 07901

RUSH, JOHN PATRICK, coll. adminstr.; b. Pitts., Aug. 23, 1946; s. Harry Dudley and Mary Catherine (Mulvey) R.; B.S.Ed., Memphis State U., 1969, M.Ed., 1971; postgrad. in higher edn. U. Pitts., 1975—; m. Carol Ann McCabe, Aug. 3, 1974; 1 dau., Jennifer Ann. Tchr. safety edn. Memphis Bd. Edn., 1969-76; grad. asst. Inst. Higher Edn., U. Pitts., 1976-77, teaching asst. higher edn. program, 1977-78; asst. dir. fin. aid Robert Morris Coll., 1978; asst. dir. fin. aid Duquesne U., 1978—. Mem. Am. Assn. Higher Edn., Nat. Assn. Student Personnel Adminstrs., Am. Coll. and Personnel Assn., Eastern Assn. Student Fin. Aid Adminstrs., Am. Ednl. Research Assn., Kappa Delta Pi. Roman Catholic. Home: 7204 Thomas Blvd Pittsburgh PA 15208

RUSHER, WILLIAM ALLEN, publisher; b. Chgo., July 19, 1923; s. Evan Singleton and Verna (Self) R.; A.B., Princeton U., 1943; J.D., Harvard U., 1948; D.Litt. (hon.), Nathanial Hawthorne Coll., 1973. Admitted to N.Y. bar, 1949; asso. firm Shearman & Sterling & Wright, N.Y.C., 1948-56; spl. counsel fin. com. N.Y. Senate, 1955; asso. counsel internal security com. U.S. Senate, 1956-57; pub. Nat. Review mag., N.Y.C., 1957—; dir., v.p. Nat. Review, Inc.; advocate TV program The Advocates, 1970-73; mem. Adv. Task Force on Civil Disorders, 1972. Bd. dirs. Chinese Cultural Center, N.Y.C.; past vice chmn. Am. Conservative Union. Served from 2d lt. to capt., USAAF, 1943-46. Recipient Distinguished Citizen award N.Y. U. Law Sch. Mem. Am. Bar Assn., Nat. News Council, Am.-African Affairs Assn. (past co.-chmn., now dir.). Anglican. Clubs: Univ. (N.Y.C.); Met. (Washington). Author: Special Counsel, 1968; (with Mark Hatfield and Arlie Schardt) Amnesty? 1973; The Making of the New Majority Party, 1975; columnist Universal Press Syndicate, 1973—. Home: 30 E 37th St New York City NY 10016 Office: 150 E 35th St New York City NY 10016

RUSINOW, DENNISON I., assn. exec.; b. Newark, Oct. 29, 1930; s. Sydney I. and Eulalie Barnes (Menuez) R.; B.A., Duke U., 1952; B.A. (Rhodes scholar 1952), New Coll., Oxford (Eng.) U., 1954, M.A., 1959, D.Phil., 1963; m. Mary Worthington, June 19, 1965; children—Alison Lucy, Tamara Craig. Extramural lectr. New Coll., 1960-62; Balkan asso. Am. Univs. Field Staff, Belgrade/Vienna, 1963—, asso. dir., 1973-76; vis. lectr. Mich. State U., 1965, Calif. Inst. Tech., 1970; adj. prof. Dartmouth Coll., 1976. Served to lt. (j.g.) USNR, 1955-58. Fellow Inst. Current World Affairs, 1958-63. Author: Italy's Austrian Heritage, 1969; The Yugoslav Experiment, 1977; also articles. Home: 91 Baumgartenstrasse Vienna A-1140 Austria Office: PO Box 150 Hanover NH 03755

RUSIS, ARMINS, legal specialist; b. Bulduri, Latvia, July 1, 1907; s. Heinrichs Fricis and Elizabeth Vilhelmine (Feldmans) R.; tchr.'s certificate Tchrs. Inst. English, Riga, Latvia, 1928; M. Juris, U. Latvia, 1929, M. Juris Habilis, 1937; certificate Acad. Internat. Law, 1931; D. Juris cum laude, UNRRA U., Munich, W.Ger., 1947; LL.B., LaSalle Extension U., Chgo., 1955; postgrad. George Washington U., 1955; m. Margarete Schortmann, Dec. 12, 1931; children—Robert H., Armins I. Librarian-indexer-digester European Law div. Library of Congress, Washington, 1952; librarian-legal analyst, 1952-60, librarian, reference law, 1960-63, librarian reference law, 1963-68, sr. legal specialist, 1968-72, 1972—; admitted to Latvian bar, 1929, practiced in Latvia, 1929-44; admitted to D.C. bar, 1956, since practiced in Washington; asst. prof. internat. law, legal adviser UNRRA U., Munich, 1946-47; legal and adminstrv. officer U.S. Zone Hdqrs., Munich, Lutheran World Fedn. Service to Refugees, 1949-51. Vice-pres. Fedn. Latvian Evang. Luth. Chs. Am., also v.p. exec. council Latvian Evang. Ch. in Exile, 1957—. Mem. Am. Assn. Law Libraries, Am. (vice-chmn. internat. criminal law com. 1974—), Fed. bar assns., Am. Soc. Internat. Law, Fraternity Lettonia (pres. Washington chpt. 1975-76). Co-author: Legal Sources and Bibliography of the Baltic States, 1963; The Soviet (Socialist) Theory of International Law, 1963; (with others) Guide to Laws and Regulations on Federal Libraries, 1968; contbg. author: Sovereignty within the Law, 1965. Co-editor Res Baltica, 1968. Home: 4202 54th St Bladensburg MD 20710 Office: Library of Congress Washington DC 20540

RUSK, DANIEL MCDONALD, JR., aviation co. exec.; b. Paterson, N.J., May 14, 1922; s. Daniel M. and Mary (McKiernan) R.; student pub. schs.; m. Monica Ida Steger, Feb. 1, 1964; children—Daniel M. III, Jon Todd, John C.M., Donna M., Barbara M., Matthew C.M. Commd. ensign USN, 1942, advanced through grades to comdr., 1960; ret., 1963; with Atlantic Aviation Corp., Wilmington, Del., 1963—, gen. mgr., 1970—, v.p., 1978—; dir. Chesapeake Isle Corp. Mem. Am. Inst. Aeros. and Astronautics. Episcopalian. Home: 2523 Eaton Rd Wilmington DE 19810 Office: Wilmington Airport Wilmington DE 19899

RUSKIN, ARTHUR SANFORD, securities trader; b. Bklyn., Dec. 13, 1934; s. Edward and Violet (Levine) R.; student Rensselaer Poly. Inst., 1952-53; B.S., N.Y. U., 1956; m. Honey Jane Siegel, Dec. 10, 1960; children—Les Scott, Andrew David, Brian Seth. Trader, Singer, Bean & Mackie, Inc., 1955-63, Mitchell & Co., 1963-67; sr. trader Brukenfeld Mitchell, N.Y.C., 1967-72; partner Josephthal & Co., N.Y.C., 1972-74; dir. Shoenberg Hieber, Inc., N.Y.C., 1975-76; chmn. bd., pres. LABCO Brokerage Inc. (formerly Arthur Ruskin Assos.), N.Y.C., 1976—; mem. Am. Stock Exchange, Amex Commodities Exchange, Inc. Treas. PTA, Livingston, N.J., 1973-74; chmn. Cub Scout pack North Mountain council Boy Scouts Am., 1969-71, 73—; mem. Twp. of Livingston Police Aux. Served with AUS, 1957-59. Mem. Security Traders N.Y. K.P. Home: 6 Downing Pl Livingston NJ 07039 Office: 86 Trinity Pl New York City NY 10006

RUSSAKOFF, DON, health orgn. exec.; b. N.Y.C., June 12, 1944; s. Leonard and Helen (Edelstein) R.; B.A. in Psychology, Queens Coll., 1969; M.B.A., Baruch Coll., 1973; m. Judith Janis, Sept. 14, 1968; children—Adam, Kim. Research adminstrv. asso. Met. Life Ins. Co., Inc., N.Y.C., 1969-71; dir. adminstrn. and research Samaritan Halfway Soc., Richmond Hill, N.Y., 1971-73, asso. exec. dir., Forest Hills, N.Y., 1974—; dist. dir. Queens/Staten Island Dist. Office, Ozone Park, N.Y., 1973; asst. commr. dir. ops. Addiction Services Agency, N.Y.C., 1973-74. Chmn., Therapeutic Communities Am., N.Y.C., 1978—; bd. dirs. Health Services Agy., 1977—; treas. Queens Treatment Coalition, 1977—; mem. Jewish Bd. Guardians Task Force on N.Y.C. Crisis, 1978—. Served with U.S. Army, 1966-68. Grantee Narcotic Addiction Control Commn., 1972-73, Addiction Services Agency, 1972-73, Nat. Inst. Drug Abuse, 1973-74. Mem. Am. Mgmt. Assn., Am. Psychol. Assn. Home: 15 Millbury Ln South Setauket NY 11720 Office: Samaritan Halfway Soc 118-21 Queens Blvd Forest Hills NY 11375

RUSSANO, ROBERT OLIVER, dentist; b. Bklyn., Aug. 18, 1941; s. George Vincent and Helen (DeGiuseppe) R.; B.A., Washington Sq. Coll. N.Y. U., 1961, D.D.S., 1965; m. Louise Pagliughi, Aug. 3, 1963; children—Cristina, Gregory. Pvt. practice dentistry, N.Y.C., 1967-73, Paterson, N.J., 1970—. Vice pres. Profl. Practices, Ltd., Princeton, N.J., 1970-74; treas. Physiodata Inc., 1975—; instr. N.Y. U. Coll. Dentistry, 1967-70, lectr., 1969—. Served with AUS, 1965-67. Recipient Student Council Outstanding Tchr. award N.Y. U. Coll. Dentistry, 1970. Mem. 1st Dist., Italian dental socs., Am., N.J. (council on dental care), Passaic County (trustee) dental assns., Am. Pedodontic Soc., Am. Soc. Preventive Dentistry, Xi Psi Phi. Roman Catholic. Republican. Home: 30 Manor Ln Morris Plains NJ 07950 Office: 100 Main St Paterson NJ 07505

RUSSELL, ALFRED MICHEL, dentist; b. N.Y.C., June 28, 1913; s. Max L. and Emma (Fabian) R.; student U. of Bishop's Coll., Que., Can., 1930-32, N.Y. U., 1933; D.D.S., N.Y. U., 1938; m. Isabelle Lowe Gokay, Aug. 16, 1960. Gen. practice dentistry, Bklyn., 1938-43, N.Y.C., 1943—; supt. dental clinic N.Y.C. Dept. Welfare, 1951-53; attending dentist, asso. dir. dental service Cumberland Hosp., Bklyn., Bklyn. Cumberland Med. Center; attending dentist Bklyn. Hosp.; clinician Greater N.Y. Dental Meeting. Fellow Am. Coll. Dentists, N.Y. Acad. Dentistry, Acad. Gen. Dentistry; mem. Am. Acad. Periodontology (asso.), Fedn. Dentaire Internat., Am. Assn. Hosp. Dentists, Am. Dental Assn., N.Y. State, 2d Dist. dental socs., N.Y. U. Alumni Assn. Mason (Shriner). Club: New York Univ. (N.Y.C.). Home: 107-40 Queens Blvd Forest Hills NY 11375 Office: 52 Vanderbilt Ave New York City NY 10017

RUSSELL, ALLISON KAPLAN, assn. exec.; b. N.Y.C., Nov. 24, 1951; d. George Michael and Eleanor May (Warshauer) Kaplan; B.A. in Journalism, Ohio State U., 1972; m. Mark Russell, Dec. 17, 1978. Pub. relations asst. Paul Werth Assos., Columbus, Ohio, 1972; pub. affairs and continuity dir. Sta. WMNI, Columbus, 1973; news editor Sta. WCOL, Columbus, 1973-74; media specialist Am. Trucking Assns., Washington, 1974-78; asst. Mark Russell Comedy Spls., Pub. Broadcasting Service, 1975—; mgr. advt. and promotion Sta. WKYS, Washington, 1978—; guest lectr. George Washington U.; freelance publicist. Named Outstanding Grad., Ohio State U., 1970. Mem. Pub. Relations Soc. Am., Advt. Club Met. Washington. Office: 4001 Nebraska Ave NW Washington DC 20016

RUSSELL, ARGENTINA EUGENIA, educator; b. New Britain, Conn., Sept. 4, 1922; B.S.Ed. in Spl. Edn., Westfield State Coll., 1972, also postgrad.; widow; 1 child. Tchr. Easthampton (Mass.) Sch. system, 1972—. Office: Maple Elementary Sch 7 Chapel St Easthampton MA 01027

RUSSELL, BARRETT BEARD, 3D, chem. co. exec.; b. Brockton, Mass., Nov. 27, 1920; s. Barrett Beard and Beulah Marie (Flickinger) R.; student Taft Sch., 1937-39; B.S. in Chem. Engring., Mass. Inst. Tech., 1943; m. Eileen Herrick, Aug. 12, 1944; children—Barrett Beard 4th, Dennis C.; m. 2d, Estelle Elizabeth Gardner, Nov. 24, 1972. Engr., Standard Oil Devel. Co., Linden, N.J., 1943-50; marketing mgr. additives, DuPont de Nemours & Co., Inc., Wilmington, Del., 1962-69, marketing mgr. antiknocks, 1969-71, mgr. new bus. devel., organic chems. dept., 1971-75, eastern regional mgr., 1975—. Mem. Soc. Automotive Engrs., Am. Inst. Chem. Engrs., Am. Petroleum Inst. (25 Year Club), Am. Chem. Soc., Mayflower Soc. (sec. 1965-72, gov. 1976—), Alpha Tau Omega. Club: Radley Run Country (West Chester). Patentee in field. Home: 1406 Carroll Brown Way Westtown Twp West Chester PA 19380 Office: DuPont Co 308 E Lancaster Ave Wynnewood PA 19096

RUSSELL, C. ANDREW, investment co. exec., former profl. football player; b. Detroit, Oct. 29, 1941; s. William R. and Esther (Blackinton) R.; M.B.A., U. Mo., 1967; m. Nancy Tussey, Aug. 11, 1962; children—Andrew Keith, Amy Esther. Linebacker, Pitts. Steeler Football Club, 1963-76; with Oliver Tyrone Corp., 1967-70; pres. Russell Investments, Inc., tax shelter syndications, Pitts., 1970—. Served to capt. Armed Forces. Named to All Rookie Team, Nat. Football League, 1963; named Most Valuable Player, Pitts. Steeler Football League, 1970; recipient Whizzer White Humanitarian award, 1973. Republican. Unitarian. Home: 2531 Lindenwood Dr Pittsburgh PA 15241 Office: 460 Manor Oak One 1910 Cochran Rd Pittsburgh PA 15220*

RUSSELL, EDWARD THOMAS, banker; b. Stamford, Conn., June 15, 1941; s. Thomas B. and Margaret L. (Mead) R.; A.S., Quinnipiac Coll., 1962, B.S. in Accounting, 1964; student Stonier Grad. Sch. Banking, 1977; m. Beverly J. Richards, June 17, 1967; children—David R. and Deborah L. (twins), Kevin G. With Fidelity Trust Co., Stamford, 1964—, asst. v.p. treasurer's dept., 1972-74, v.p., 1974—. Cubmaster, Cub Scout Pack 46, Stamford, 1976-78; coach little league baseball, youth soccer league, youth basketball; bd. dirs. Stamford Youth Soccer League, 1978-79; treas., jr. warden Emmanuel Episcopal Ch., 1978-79. Mem. Am. Inst. Banking (dir. Stamford chpt. 1977-79), Bank Adminstrn. Inst. (dir. treas. Western Conn. chpt. 1977-78, v.p. 1978-79). Club: Hubbard Heights Men's (gov., pres. 1976-79). Home: 73 Maple Tree Ave Stamford CT 06906 Office: 129 Atlantic St Stamford CT 06904

RUSSELL, ELBERT, electronic co. exec., city ofcl.; b. Orange, N.J., Aug. 9, 1929; s. Elbert and Effie D. (Anderson) R.; B.S. in Mech. Engring., W.Va. State Coll., 1952; postgrad. Newark Coll. Engring., 1958; m. Anna Draughon, July 3, 1958 (div.); children—Byron, Alan, Elaine, Arlene; m. 2d, Sandra G. Ellington, Sept. 21, 1976; stepchildren—Arnold, Valarie. Engr., Airtron Corp., Linden, N.J., 1954-55; sr. engr. Emerson Radio & TV Co., Jersey City, 1955-67; prin. engr. Lockheed Electronics Co., Plainfield, N.J., 1967—. Mem. Plainfield City Council, 1973-75. Served to 1st lt. AUS, 1952-54. Mem. Kappa Alpha Psi. Baptist (chmn. bd. trustees). Home: 362 Elmwood Ave Maplewood NJ 07040 Office: Hwy 22 Plainfield NJ 07060

RUSSELL, GARY CHARLES, festivals and spl. events cons.; b. Halifax, N.S., Can., Jan. 12, 1946; s. Basil St. Clare and Lois Winnifred (Glavin) R.; diploma in pub. relations U. King Coll., 1968; student in bus. adminstrn. St. Marys U., 1971; Bookmobile librarian, County of Halifax (N.S.), 1966-68; asst. film librarian, 1968-70, film editor, 1970-76, film librarian, 1976—, film researcher, 1977-78; dir., co-chmn. program com. Canadian Folk Arts Council, 1969-76, vice chmn., dir., 1970-76, 78, 79, coordinator Can Week activities for N.S., 1977, 78, 79; instr., lectr. N.S. Drama League, 1972-74; treas. Halifax Ind. Theatre, 1978-79; N.S. coordinator XI Commonwealth Games Cultural Program, 1978; producer Canada Is, 1978; N.S. del. to Can. Multicultural Conf., 1975, 76; mem. Festival N.S. Com.; exec. dir. Joseph Howe Festival, 1976, bd. dirs., 1978-79. Bd. dirs. Theatre Can., 1975-78, Multicultural Assn. N.S., 1978-79, Sea Chest on Wharf Ltd., 1978-79. Recipient N.S. Folk Arts Achievement award, 1967, Metro award Metro Toronto Internat. Caravan, 1976; Queen's Silver Jubilee medal, 1977; recognition awards Joseph Howe Festival, 1976, 77, 78; award of recognition N.S. Dept. Recreation, 1978; Festival Can. award, 1978; grantee cultural tour Sec. State, 1970, cultural festival, 1974. Mem. N.S. Designer Craftsmen, N.S. Drama League, Theatre Canada-Dominion Drama Festival, Multi-Cultural Council N.S., N.S. Folk Arts Council (pres. 1970-76, 78, 79), Canadian Polish Soc. (hon. life), Dance N.S., Recreation Assn. N.S., Theatre Arts Guild, Heritage Trust, Halifax Jaycees (project chmn. 1978-79). Conservative. Anglican. Clubs, Opimian Soc., Masons. Editor: Callboard, 1968-75; contbr. articles and revs. to theatrical jours. and multicultural newsletter Share. Home and Office: PO Box 3292 Halifax South Halifax NS B3J 3H5 Canada

RUSSELL, HARRIET VIRGINIA HEIT, mental health adminstr.; b. Ossining, N.Y., Dec. 31, 1936; d. George and Ruth Virginia (Miller) Heit; student Barnard Coll., 1954-55; B.S. Edn., Ohio U., 1958; M.A., U. Mich., 1959; postgrad. State U. N.Y. at New Paltz, 1969-75; m. J. Thomas Russell, Oct. 24, 1959 (separated 1978); children—Elizabeth, Margaret, Gregory. Tchr., Parry McCluer Sch., Buena Vista, Va., 1959-61; counselor Newburgh (N.Y.) City Sch. Dist., 1967-70, dir. guidance, 1970-74; dir. profl. services Family Conseling Service Orange County Inc., Newburgh, 1974-75, exec. dir., 1975—; lectr. in field. Mem. Planning Bd. Village of Cornwall (N.Y.), 1972—, chairperson, 1977; sec. Orange County Joint Mental Health Contract Agencies, 1978—; mem. mental health com. Hudson Valley Health Systems Agy., 1977—; mem. sub-area adv. council Orange County Health Systems Agy., 1978—, chmn. project rev. com.; chairperson pub. relations Orange Area United Way, 1977—; treas. N.Y. State Assn. Family Service Agencies, 1977—; pres. Greater Newburgh Council Community Agencies, 1976-77. Mem. Eastern Orange County C. of C. (edn. com.), Kappa Delta. Author: Career Education Area Resource Guide, 1974. Home: Wilson Rd Cornwall-on-Hudson NY 12520 Office: 21 Grand St Newburgh NY 12550

RUSSELL, LEONARD HOWLAND, mfg. co. exec.; b. Ware, Mass., Apr. 28, 1927; s. Leonard H. and Beryl (Barbier) R.; student St. Lawrence U., 1949-51, Boston U., 1951-52; m. Joan Bernardo, Mar. 6, 1977; children—William, Lisa, Susan, Martha, Lynda, Christina, Joan, Desiree, Chris. Mfg. rep. Russell Assos., Sudbury, Mass., 1950-68; exec. v.p. Pactron Corp., Westfield, N.J., 1968-69; v.p. Corrofab, Franklin, Mass., 1968—; pres. Foamfab Inc., Mansfield, Mass., 1970—. Served with USMCR, 1944-46. Mem. Soc. Packaging and Handling Engrs. (pres. New Eng. 1967-68, v.p. Eastern region 1970-71), Nat. Indsl. Security Assn. (instr. 1967—). Clubs: Masons (32 deg.), Shriners. Office: 411 Oakland St Mansfield MA 02048

RUSSELL, OLIVE RUTH, psychologist and educator; b. Delta, Ont., Canada, July 9, 1897; d. W.A. and Alice A. (Henderson) Russell; B.A., U. Toronto, 1931; (honors course in psychology); Ph.D., U. Edinburgh (Scotland), 1935; postgrad. student under Adler, Buhler and Dengler, Vienna, summer 1932, Columbia U., summer, 1941. Came to U.S., 1947. Tchr. math. and sci. Albert Coll., Belleville, Ont., 1920-22; prin. elementary and secondary sch., Delta, Ont., 1922-28; psychol. interne Ontario Hosp. for mentally deficient, summer 1931; attended world conf. on edn. in France, and conf. on internat. affairs, Geneva, summer 1932; research asst. dept. ednl. research U. Toronto (Ont.), 1933-35; head math. dept., psychologist and dir. ednl. and vocat. guidance Moulten College, Toronto, 1935-42; lectr. psychology for tchrs., Ont., summer sch. 1939; exec. asst. dept. of vet. affairs, Ottawa, Ont., 1945-47; govt. cons. to nat. adv. council of service clubs in Can., 1945-47; asso. prof. psychology Winthrop Coll., Rock Hill, S.C. 1947-49; prof. psychology and head of psychology dept. Western Md. Coll., Westminster, 1949-62; tchr. psychology, Johns Hopkins U., summer 1956. Mem. gen. council, U. Edinburgh. Served as capt., personnel selection ofcr. Dept. Nat. Def., Canadian Women's Army Corps, 1942-45. Fellow Am. Psychol. Assn., Internat. Council Psychologists, Ont. Vocat. Guidance Assn. (chmn. bull. com., exec. com. 1940), Am. Acad. Polit. and Social Sci., AAUW, AAUP, U.N. Assn., Nat. Councils of Women (Canadian del. to intercontinental conf., N.Y. 1946), Pi Lambda Theta, Pi Gamma Mu. Fraternal del. from World Fed. of U.N. Assn. to conf. Internat. Fed. Univ. Women, 1947. Author: Freedom to Die, 1975. Contbr. articles to profl. jours. Home: 3305 Shepherd St Chevy Chase MD 20015

RUSSELL, PAUL GEORGE, lawyer; b. Akron, Ohio, Feb. 23, 1929; s. Paul George and Fern (Winter) R.; A.B. with honors in Polit. Sci., Kenyon Coll., 1950; postgrad. in Bus., Western Res. U., 1956; LL.B., Harvard, 1957. Admitted to N.Y. bar, 1958; asso. firm Dewey, Ballantine, Bushby, Palmer & Wood, N.Y.C., 1957-60; asst. to mng. partner E.F. Hutton & Co., then sec. E.F. Hutton & Co., Inc., N.Y.C., 1960-63; asso. LeBoeuf, Lamb, Leiby & MacRae, N.Y.C., 1963-67, partner, 1967-78; partner firm Morgan, Lewis & Bockins, N.Y.C., 1978—. Served to lt. USNR, 1951-54. Mem. Am. (chmn. utility financing com., mem. council pub. utility law sect. 1976—), N.Y. State, Fed. Power bar assns., Assn. Bar City N.Y., Beta Theta Pi, Tau Kappa Alpha. Episcopalian. Clubs: Racquet and Tennis, Down Town Assn. (N.Y.C.); Piping Rock (Locust Valley, N.Y.). Home: 3 E 77th St New York City NY 10021 Office: 9 W 57 St New York City NY 10005

RUSSELL, PAUL HENRY, JR., environ. engr.; b. Williamson, N.Y., June 7, 1938; s. Paul Henry and Lulu Elsie (Hender[son) R.; B.S., St. Lawrence U., 1961; B.C.E., Rensselaer Poly. Inst., 1961; postgrad. Syracuse U., 1964, 65; m. Adriana Giancursio, July 6, 1963; project engr./mgr. Stearns & Wheler, Cazenovia, N.Y., 1963-67; engring. partner Harnish & Lookup, Assoc., Newark, N.Y., 1967—; environ. engring. cons. Nat. Kraut Packers Assn., Nat. Canners Assn. Mem. Am. Water Works Assn., Water Pollution Control Fedn., ASCE, N.Y. Water Pollution Control Assn., Am. Acad. Environ. Engrs. (diplomate). Republican. Episcoplian. Club: Rotary. Contbr. articles in field to profl. jours. Home: 567 Filkins Rd Newark NY 14513 Office: 615 Mason St Newark NY 14513

RUSSELL, PHEBE GALE (MRS. FRANK M. RUSSELL), broadcasting, TV exec.; b. N.Y.C., Dec. 23, 1910; d. George H. and Marian (Hyde) Gale; grad. high sch.; m. Frank M. Russell, Sept. 25, 1940; children—Gale, Morgan N. Publicity dir. NBC, Washington, 1929-39; v.p. radio sta. WICO, Salisbury, Md., 1958-62; pres. Ellensburg (Wash.) TV Corp., 1961-68, PGR Enterprises, 1962-70; owner TV Cable Cos., Appalachia, Norton, and Big Stone Gap, Va., 1962-78; dir. Delmarva Broadcasting Co., 1958-62. Mem. women's bd. George Washington U. Hosp. Mem. D.A.R., Mayflower Soc. Huguenot Soc., Internat. Platform Assn., Nepal Soc. U.S., Md. Golf Assn., Daus. of Cincinnati. Clubs: Congessional Country (Washington) Kenwood Garden (pres. 1962-64). Address 5101 River Rd Apt 918 Washington DC 20016

RUSSELL, SANFORD EUGENE, fin. exec.; b. N.Y.C., May 26, 1930; s. Abraham and Anna (Green) Rosenthal; B.A., U. Okla., 1958; M.P.A., Syracuse U., 1959; m. Joan Brooke Sussman, Aug. 3, 1963; children—Noel, Gregory, Brooke. Program asst. Office of Gov., N.Y. State, Albany, 1959-62; research analyst N.Y. State Assembly, Albany, 1962-64; internal auditor N.Y. State Dept. Transp., Albany, 1964-66; budget analyst Senate Finance Com., Albany, 1966-70, 71-72; asst. adminstr. for mgmt. Municipal Services Adminstrn., N.Y.C., 1970-71; dir. budget studies N.Y. State Senate Finance Com., Albany, 1972—. Pres. PTA, Division St. Sch., Saratoga, N.Y., 1975—; pres. PTA Council, Saratoga, 1976-77; research dir. Upstate N.Y., mem. gubernatorial campaign Nelson Rockefeller, 1962. Served with Signal Corps, U.S. Army, 1953-55; ETO. Woodrow Wilson fellow, 1958. Mem. Am. Soc. Pub. Adminstrn., Inst. Internal Auditors (chpt. v.p. 1970-71), Am. Polit. Sci. Acad., Phi Alpha Theta, Pi Sigma Alpha. Republican. Jewish Religion. Clubs: Mason. Home: 22 Fredrick Dr Saratoga Springs NY 12866 Office: 18th Floor Agency Bldg 4 Empire State Plaza Albany NY 12223

RUSSELL, WARREN EDWARD, portrait and landscape painter; b. Syracuse, N.Y., Dec. 21, 1924; s. Edward Henry and Ada Mae (Mosher) R.; student Art Students League, 1947-51; m. Rosa Mae Orsak, July 16, 1946; 1 son, Rodney R. One-man show Barbizon Galleries, N.Y.C., 1952, James Graham Gallery, 1959, 63, exhibited in group shows N.A.D., 1953, 55, 59, Allied Artists Am., 1954, Conn. Acad. Artists, 1954, 55, 57, Audubon Artists, 1956, 57, Everson Mus., Syracuse, 1956, 57, 58, others. Served as navigator, USAAF, 1943-46. Recipient honorable mention Conn. Acad., 1954; Julius Halgarten prize N.A.D., 1958; popular vote award Everson Mus., Syracuse, 1957, 60, 61, 62; Am. Acad. Arts and Letters purchase prize, 1958; Julius Halgarten prize, 1958, S. J. Wallace Truman Prize N.A.D., 1959; Best in Show award Munson-Williams-Proctor Inst., Utica, N.Y., 1960, 63. Mem. Conn. Acad. Fine Art, Art Students League, Acad. Artists Assn., Springfield. Home: 35 Parkwood Ave Rochester NY 14620

RUSSELL, WILBERT COLEMAN, city ofcl.; b. Long Branch, N.J., Feb. 1, 1935; s. Nathaniel P. and Edna S. (Shreaves) R.; B.S. in Accounting, Monmouth Coll., West Long Branch, N.Y., 1965, M.B.A., 1973; m. Yvonne Jackson, May 5, 1968; children—Steven, Tanya, Todd. Mgmt. analyst Dept. Def., 1955-65; dir. Small Bus. Devel. Center, 1965-67; dep. dir. M.C.A.P., 1967-71; exec. dir. Anti-Poverty Program, Long Branch, 1971—; chmn. Nat. Community Action Agys. Legis. Com., 1973—; trustee Nat. Center for Community Action, 1974—; chmn. Nat. Community Action Trust Fund, 1974—; mem. adv. bd. SBA, 1968-70. Active Monmouth County United Fund; exec. council Monmouth council Boy Scouts Am., 1969-70; pres. Long Branch City Council, 1968-70; commr. Long Branch Housing Authority, 1967—; mem. Community Services Council; Served with AUS, 1956-58. Recipient Outstanding Young Man Am. award Monmouth Coll., 1969. Mem. Nat. Assn. Community Devel. (dir.), Nat. Assn. Community Action Agys. (dir.), Am. Mgmt. Assn. (adv. bd. 1970—), Nat. Community Action Agy. Exec. Dirs. Assn. (pres. 1975—), Nat. Masters Bus. Adminstrn. Assn. Home: 280 Florence Ave Long Branch NJ 07740 Office: 279 Broadway Long Branch NJ 07740

RUSSO, JOSEPH ALOYSIUS, JR., mgmt. cons.; b. Bklyn., Oct. 2, 1942; s. Joseph Aloysius and Mary (Giaquinto) R.; B.B.A., Pace U., 1965, M.B.A., 1969; m. Marie Troiano, Sept. 4, 1965; children—Karen, Eileen. Adj. asso. prof. accounting, finance, mgmt. Pace U., N.Y.C., 1967—; v.p. Hornblower & Weeks, Hemphill-Noyes, Inc., N.Y.C., 1972-75; prin. Joseph A. Russo, Jr., C.P.A., P.C., N.Y.C., 1975-77; tchr. edn. programs Am. Mgmt. Assn., 1975—, Nat. Assn. Accountants, 1971—. C.P.A. Mem. Am. Inst. C.P.A.'s, N.Y. Soc. C.P.A.'s, Nat. Assn. Accountants. Home: 94 Fern Ave Staten Island NY 10308 Office: 20 Exchange Pl New York City NY 10005

RUSSO, PETER FRANCIS, fin. co. exec.; b. Brockton, Mass., May 24, 1932; s. Francis George and Mary Alice (Maxwell) R.; B.S., Bryant Coll., 1957; m. Joan Theresa Dolfuss, June 6, 1959; children—Frank John, Paul Robert, Laura Jean. Corporate auditor Am. Standard, Inc., N.Y.C., 1957-59; supr. Spark, Mann & Co., C.P.A.'s, Boston, 1959-66; asst. treas. Stevens Linen Assos., Webster, Mass., 1966-67; dir. corporate accounting and fin. Rustcraft Greeting Cards, Inc., Dedham, Mass., 1967-70; v.p. fin., treas. Multibank Fin. Corp., Boston, 1970—; dir. Multibank Computer Corp., Multibank Internat. Mem. bd. dirs. Battleship Mass., 1974—, Old Colony Council, Catholic Charities, 1974—. Served with USN, 1950-54. C.P.A., Mass. Mem. Nat. Assn. Accountants, Am. Inst. C.P.A., Mass.

Soc. C.P.A.'s, Tax Exec. Inst., Bank Adminstrn. Inst., Nat. Assn. Controllers. Home: 86 Tilton Ave Brockton MA 02401 Office: 1400 Hancock St Quincy MA 02169

RUSSO, VINCENT JOSEPH, surgeon; b. Phila., Apr. 15, 1939; s. Joseph Vincent and Yolanda Italia (D'Ambrosio) R.; A.B., Columbia U., 1960; M.D., Boston U., 1964; m. Sheila Kay Roos, June 8, 1963; children—Teresa, Joseph, Katrina, Anita. Chief resident in surgery Boston City Hosp., 1968-69; practice medicine specializing in cancer surgery, Newburyport, Mass., 1971—; chief surgery Anna Jaques Hosp., Newburyport, Mass., 1977—; chief surgery Amesbury (Mass.) Hosp., 1972-77, chief staff, 1976-77; clin. instr. surgery Boston U. Sch. Medicine, 1968-69; corporator Newburyport Five Cent Savs. Bank. Bd. dirs. ARC, Newburyport chpt.; v.p. Am. Cancer Soc., Essex N. chpt. Served to lt. comdr. M.C. USNR, 1969-71. Diplomate Am. Bd. Surgery. Fellow A.C.S.; mem. Mass. Med. Soc. (councillor), Pentucket Assn. Physicians. Roman Catholic. Club: Rotary. Home: 2 Toppans Ln Newburyport MA 01950 Office: 21 Highland Ave Newburyport MA 01950

RUSSO, WILLIAM RICHARD, chem. co. exec.; b. Naples, Italy, July 27, 1940; s. Umberto Claudio and Helen (Vinti) R.; came to U.S., 1948, naturalized, 1949; B.S. in Zoology, U. R.I., 1962, Ph.D. in Chemistry (NSF fellow), 1968; m. Jeannette Lockwood, Mar. 21, 1963; children—Mark, Claudia, John. Chemist, Nat. Lead Co., Perth Amboy, N.J., 1962-63, sr. chemist, 1963-64; research asso. Uniroyal Inc., Naugatuck, Conn., 1968, sr. group leader, 1968-76; adj. prof. chemistry U. New Haven, 1971-77; v.p. RFR Corp., Hope, R.I., 1976—. Bd. dirs. Cheshire (Conn.) Bd. Health, 1975, United Italian Ams., Inc., 1977—. NSF grantee, 1965-68. Mem. Am. Chem. Soc., AAAS. Home: 3 Jodie Beth Dr East Greenwich RI 02818 Office: 1 Main St Hope RI 02831

RUST, LAURENCE DEWITT, educator; b. Chgo., Nov. 9, 1933; s. Rolynn Reid and Florence (Goddard) R.; student Los Angeles City Coll., 1951-53; A.B., U. Calif. at Santa Barbara, 1959; M.A., McGill U., 1960; Ph.S., State U. N.Y. at Buffalo, 1965; m. E. Arlene Crossman, Sept. 12, 1964; children—Kevin Lee, David Laurence, Krista Lynn. Explt. psychology trainee (Buffalo) VA Hosp., 1961-64; asst. prof. psychology Skidmore Coll., Saratoga Springs, N.Y., 1964-66, asso. prof. State U. N.Y., Potsdam, 1966—. Served with AUS, 1953-57. Mem. Eastern Psychol. Assn., N.Y. State Coaches and Swimming Ofcls. Assn. (chpt. pres. 1973-75). Contbr. articles to profl. jours.; coordinating producer TV series Probe, Pub. Broadcasting System. Home: 15 Castle Dr Potsdam NY 13676 Office: 141 Morey Hall State U NY Potsdam NY 13676

RUST, META MILDRED LIBBY, nurse; b. South Portland, Maine, Jan. 7, 1923; d. Carl Clarence and Lillian Marie (Nielsen) Libby; R.N., Maine Gen. Hosp. Sch. Nursing, 1944; m. Myron Davis Rust, Feb. 25, 1945; children—Libby Karen, John Davis. Staff nurse Maine Gen. Hosp., Portland, Maine, 1944-46, 48-49; staff nurse Mass. Gen. Hosp., Boston, 1946-47; supr. York (Maine) Hosp., 1959-78, supr. operating room, post anesthesia recovery, infection surveillance Central Services, 1976—, supr. CSR, infection control practitioner, 1978—. Mem. York Republican Com., 1960-67. Mem. Am., Maine State, Western Dist. nurses assns., Assn. Practitioners in Infection Control. Republican. Club: Order Eastern Star (worthy matron 1964). Home: Yorkholme York ME 03909 Office: 15 Hospital Dr Yorke ME 03909

RUST, MYRON DAVIS, lawyer; b. Boston, Nov. 12, 1923; s. Harrison Davis and Julia Elizabeth (Mooney) R.; student U. Maine, 1941-42, 46; grad. Maine Maritime Acad., 1943; J.D., Northeastern U., 1949; m. Meta M. Libby, Feb. 25, 1945; children—Libby Karen, John Davis. Admitted to Maine bar, 1949, N.H. bar, 1957; practiced in York and Kittery, Maine, and Portsmouth, N.H., 1949—; mem. firm. Rust & Rust, York, 1949-53, Henry M. Fuller, Portsmouth, 1955-57; mem. Maine Ho. of Reps., 1961-65. Fin. chmn. York County Pine Tree council Boy Scouts Am., 1963-64, dist. chmn., 1964-65, exec. com. 1965-70; mem. Selective Service Bd.; chmn. 1st Congressional Dist. Com., York Republican Town Com., 1959-64; trustee Harbor Hosp., 1956-67; bd. dirs. Seacoast United Fund, 1965-69; rep. bd. trustees Shriners Hosp. Crippled Children, Springfield, Mass., 1975-76. Mem. Am. Trial Lawyers Assn., York County (exec. com. 1976-78), Portsmouth City, Rockingham County, Maine, N.H. bar assns., Maine Maritime Acad. Alumni Assn. (exec. bd. 1957-68), York C. of C. (dir. 1960-65). Clubs: Masons, Shriners, Jesters (past master, past potentate, past grand steward), Lions (past 1st v.p. Portsmouth, past pres. York); Order Eastern Star (past patron). Home: Yorkholme Ridge Rd York ME 03909 Office: Profl Bldg 161 State Rd Kittery ME 03904

RUST, VELMA IRENE MILLER (MRS. RONALD STUART RUST), Canadian govt. ofcl.; b. Edmonton, Alta., Can., May 22, 1914; d. Cecil Johnstone and Lillie (Runions) Miller; B.Sc., U. Alta., 1934, tchrs. diploma, 1935, B.Ed., 1944, M.Ed., 1947; Ph.D., U. Ill., 1959; m. Ronald Stuart Rust, Apr. 9, 1955. Tchr., 1936-42, 43-44; insp. Inspection Bd. U.K. and Can., Montreal, 1942-43; mem. staff, faculty U. Alta., 1944-56, asst. prof. edn., 1955-56; grad asst. U. Ill., 1956-59; researcher in directorate of personnel planning RCAF Hdqrs., 1960-62; chief staff tng., inspection services Dept. Nat. Def., Ottawa, 1962-65; statistician Aviation Statistics, Fed. Govt., 1965-67; supr. Can. pension plan statistics Health and Welfare Dept. Can., Ottawa, 1967-71, supr. math. research and analysis dept., 1971-74, sr. policy analyst, 1974—. Mem. Canadian Edn. Assn., Am. Econ. Assn., Am. Statis. Assn., Am. Soc. Quality Control, U. Alta. Alumni Assn. (br. sec. 1967-68, br. v.p. 1968-69, pres. 1969-70), Ont., English, Irish geneal. socs., Kappa Delta Pi. Mem. United Ch. of Can. (mem. session 1966—). Clubs: University Women's (Ottawa), Ottawa Women's Canadian. Home: 811 Adams Ave Ottawa ON K1G 2Y1 Canada Office: Health and Welfare Canada Tunney's Pasture Ottawa ON Canada

RUST, WILLIAM ANTHONY, JR., educator; b. Bloomington, Ill., Apr. 12, 1933; s. William Anthony and Alice (Ryan) R.; A.B., Bradley U., 1958; M.A., Boston U., 1960; Ph.D., Columbia U., 1970; m. Marie Rosalie Gagliardi, May 26, 1963. Instr. polit. sci., Rutgers Coll., Rutgers U., New Brunswick, N.J., 1963-65, Coll. of the Holy Cross, Worcester, Mass., 1965-70; asso. prof. politics, Framingham (Mass.) State Coll., 1971—; book reviewer for Choice, 1967-73. Served with AUS, 1954-56. Mem. AAUP, NEA, Am. Polit. Sci. Assn., Am. Soc. Internat. Law, Worcester Assn. Model Railroaders. Democrat. Home: 14 Deerfield Rd Shrewsbury MA 01545 Office: Dept Politics Framingham State Coll Framingham MA 01701

RUSTON, HENRY, elec. engr.; b. Lodz, Poland, July 23, 1929; s. Edward and Rose (Anklewitz) R.; student Munich Inst. Tech., 1948-49; B.S.E., U. Mich., 1952, Ph.D., 1960; M.S., Columbia, 1955; m. Janet Ruth Margulies, Aug. 15, 1959; children—Anne Sherri, Lillian Sue, Eileen Fran. Intermediate test engr. Curtiss-Wright Corp., Woodridge, N.J., 1955; elec. engr. Reeves Instrument Co., Mineola, N.Y., 1955-56; asso. research engr. U. Mich. Research Inst., 1956-60; asst. prof. elec. engr. U. Pa., 1960-64; asso. prof. elec. engrng. Poly. Inst. of N.Y., 1964—; engrng. cons., 1960—; lectr. U. Pa., 1964. Served with AUS, 1952-54. Mem. I.E.E.E. (sr.), Sigma Xi, Eta Kappa Nu, Tau Beta Pi. Co-author: Electric Networks: Functions, Filters, Analysis, 1966; author Programming with PL/I, 1978. Contbr. articles to profl. jours. Home: 222 Exeter St Brooklyn NY 11235 Office: 333 Jay St Brooklyn NY 11201

RUTENBER, CLEMINETTE DOWNING, educator; b. Augusta, Ga., Oct. 17, 1908; d. George Edward and Clemmie Nette (Gunn) Downing; A.B., Agnes Scott Coll., 1930; m. Ralph Dudley Rutenber, Jr., Dec. 29, 1932; children—Anne (Mrs. Roger L. Clifton), John Downing. Tchr. Grant Park Elementary Sch., Atlanta, 1930-32; asso. head MacDuffie Sch. for Girls, Springfield, Mass., 1941-72. Active Belchertown (Mass.) State Sch. Friends Assn., 1968—. Bd. dirs. Children's Study Home, Springfield, 1956-70; trustee, sec., asst. treas. MacDuffie Sch. for Girls, Springfield, 1941-72, hon. trustee, 1972—; corporator Springfield Hosp. Med. Center, 1944—, Wesson Meml. Hosp., Springfield, 1946—, Girls' Club, Springfield, 1948-50. Recipient (with husband) citation for services to young people Bd. of Springfield Coll., 1972. Mem. Headmistresses' Assn. East, AAUW, Cum Laude Soc. Clubs: Women's (dir. 1964-66, corr. sec. 1964-66, pres. 1978—) (Springfield); College (dir. 1943-46, corr. sec. 1943-46) Century, Colony (Springfield). Home: 334 Maple St Springfield MA 01105

RUTENBER, RALPH DUDLEY, JR., educator; b. Bardonia, N.Y., Aug. 3, 1905; s. Ralph Dudley and Margaret Jane (Gerow) R.; A.B., Princeton U., 1926; M.A., Columbia U., 1940; D.Litt., Am. Internat. Coll., 1959; postgrad. Cornell U., 1930; m. Cleminette Downing, Dec. 29, 1932; children—Anne Downing Rutenber Clifton, John Downing. Master in Latin, Choate Sch., Wallingford, Conn., 1926-28; head English dept. Wooster Sch., Danbury, Conn., 1928-33, sr. master, 1933-41; headmaster MacDuffie Sch. for Girls, Springfield, Mass., 1941-72, pres., 1975-79; ednl. cons. Trustee MacDuffie Sch., 1941-72, 75—, Springfield Library and Mus. Assn., 1967-74; bd. dirs. Mental Health and Retardation Area Bd. Springfield, 1970-76, Hampden Dist. Mental Health Clinic, 1964-70. Recipient Outstanding Servant of Public award WWLP Channel 22, 1973. Mem. Nat. Assn. Prins. Schs. for Girls (pres. 1971-73), Ind. Schs. Found. Mass., Ind. Sch. Assn. Mass. (dir. 1966-68), Headmasters Assn., Phi Beta Kappa. Episcopalian. Clubs: Colony, The Club, Century, Gladden. Author: How to Bring Up 2,000 Teenagers, 1979; contbr. articles to profl. jours. Address: 334 Maple St Springfield MA 01105

RUTGERS, KATHARINE PHILLIPS (MRS. FREDERIK LODEWIJK RUTGERS), dancer; b. Butler, Pa., Sept. 2, 1910; d. Thomas Wharton and Alma (Sherman) Phillips; diploma Briarcliff Coll., 1928; student L'Hermiage, Versailles, France, 1929-30; pupil ballet Vera Trefilova, Paris, Carl Raimund, Vienna, Varga Troyanoff, Budapest; pupil modern dance with Iris Barbura, Bucharest Ballet, Vincenzo Celli, N.Y.C., Igor Schwezoff, N.Y.C., Jean Yazvinsky, N.Y.C.; m. Frederik Lodewijk Rutgers, Feb. 2, 1942; children—Alma, Corinne (Mrs. James Tolles). Performed dance concerts Bucharest, 1937-40, U.S., 1941—; repertoire includes patriotic, dramatic, poetical dances, religious interpretations; dance therapist St. Barnabas Hosp., N.Y.C., 1965-70. Chmn. ethnol. dance dept. Bruce Museum Assos., Greenwich, Conn., 1970—. Bd. dirs. Bruce Museum. Recipient citation for promoting culture with dance programs Nat. Fedn. Music Clubs, 1973. Mem. Conn. Fedn. Music Clubs (chmn. dance dept. 1965-66), Nat. League Am. Pen Women (local v.p. 1973-78), Alliance Francaise, Mayflower Soc., Colonial Dames Am., D.A.R., Federated Music Club N.Y.C. (dir.). Clubs: Marion Farm and Garden (dir.) (N.Y.C.), Indian Harbor (Greenwich, Conn.). Author numerous pamphlets on the dance, also verses for choreographies. Home: La Cova Pecks Land Rd Greenwich CT 06830 Studio: 211 W 58th St New York City NY 10023

RUTH, THOMAS GRISWOLD, educator; b. Benton Harbor, Mich., Nov. 7, 1940; s. John Griswold and Ruth Margery (Hopkins) R.; B.A., U. Mich., 1963; M.A., U. Tex., 1968. Tchr., Escuela Americana-Nicaragense, Managua, Nicaragua, C.A., 1965-67; instr. history The Hill Sch., Pottstown, Pa., 1968—. Mem. Orgn. Am. Historians, Am., Nat. hist. assns. Home and Office: The Hill Sch Pottstown PA 19464

RUTH, VINCENT WISMER, veterinarian; b. Franconia, Pa., Dec. 17, 1911; s. Abram Moyer and Ella (Wismer) R.; D.V.M., U. Toronto (Ont., Can.), 1938; m. Mary Wallace, Dec. 9, 1939. Veterinarian in gen. practice, Charleston, W.Va., 1938-39; owner, operator, veterinarian Ruth Vet. Hosp., Lansdale, Pa., 1940—; practice vet. medicine, specializing in internal medicine, surgery of dogs and cats. Mem. Am., Pa., Keystone (pres. 1944-46), Bucks-Montgomery County (Pa.) (sec. 1950-53, pres. 1947-48) vet. med. assns., Am. Animal Hosp. Assn., Montgomery County Gurnsey Assn., Ont. Vet. Coll. Alumni Assn. (adv. council 1960—). Republican. Lutheran. Clubs: Century of U. of Gulph (Can.) (founding mem.). Home: 1003 Columbia Ave Lansdale PA 19446 Office: 1200 W Main St Lansdale PA 19446

RUTHERFORD, JOHN LOFTUS, mfg. co. exec.; b. Phila., Mar. 6, 1924; s. Robert John and Mary Ellen (Loftus) R.; B.A., U. Pa., 1952, M.S., 1962, Ph.D., 1963; m. Sara Mary Richards, Aug. 30, 1947; children—David, Peter. Lab. technician Sharples Corp., Phila., 1945-52; physicist Franklin Inst. Labs., Phila., 1952-60; research mgr. Kearfott div. Singer Co., Little Falls, N.J., 1963—, prin. staff scientist, 1966—. Bd. dirs. Found. for Religion and Mental Health N.Y. and N.J. Served with USAAF, 1942-45. Decorated Air medal with 8 oak leaf clusters, Purple Heart; Croix de Guerre (Belgium). Mem. Am. Soc. Metals., Am. Inst. Metall. Engrs., Am. Inst. Aeros. and Astronautics, Sigma Xi. Democrat. Lutheran. Contbr. articles on metallurgy and materials sci. to profl. publs. Home: 161 Pershing Ave Ridgewood NJ 07450 Office: Singer Co Kearfott Div 1150 McBride Ave Little Falls NJ 07424

RUTIMANN, HANS, assn. exec.; b. Zurich, Switzerland, Mar. 4, 1939; s. Adolf and Anna (Mock) R.; came to U.S., 1965, naturalized, 1975; diploma Handelsschule, Zurich, 1958; student Sorbonne U., 1959, U. Amsterdam, 1960, U. Zurich, 1961-63; m. Marjorie Lebow, Jan. 29, 1971; 1 dau., Sophie. Conv. coordinator Tourist Office, Zurich, 1955-58; sales agt. Swiss Nat. Tourist Office, Paris, Amsterdam, 1959-60; documentary credit specialist Union Bank Switzerland, Zurich, 1962-64; research asst. Modern Lang. Assn. Am., N.Y.C., 1965-66, research asst. statis. research, 1966-67, asst. dir. Statis. research, 1967-70, dir. computer services, 1970-75, dep. exec. dir., 1975—; instr. English, Am. Council for Emigres in Professions; mem. nat. advisory bd. Center for the Book Library of Congress, 1979—. Served to 1st lt. Swiss Army, 1958-65. Nat. Endowment for Humanities grantee, 1976—; Mem. Modern Lang. Assn. Am., Am. Council on Teaching Fgn. Langs., Am. Soc. Info. Sci. Contbr. articles to profl. jours. Home: 110 Bleecker St New York NY 10012 Office: 62 Fifth Ave New York NY 10011

RUTKA, HOWARD JOSEPH, telecommunications co. exec.; b. Wilkinsburg, Pa., Jan. 26, 1947; s. Alexander G. and Josephine A. (Gorzelnik) R.; B.S. in Civil Engring., U. Ky., 1969; M.B.A., Youngstown U., 1976; m. Cynthia Fammartino, Oct. 6, 1973; children—Jason, Jamie. Sales engr. Westinghouse Electric, Sharon, Pa., 1969-73; design engr. Wean United, Warren, Ohio, 1973-76; dist. sales mgt. ITT Telecommunications, Raleigh, N.C., 1976—. Mgr. sr. div. Little League Baseball, Sharon, 1973-77. Registered profl. engr., Ohio, Pa. Mem. Assn. M.B.A. Execs. Home: 802 Thornton St Sharon PA 16146 Office: 2912 Wake Forest Rd Raleigh NC 27611

RUTKOWSKI, CONRAD PHILEMON, educator; b. Detroit, Apr. 20, 1939; s. Stanley A. and Helen (Klakulak) R.; A.B., U. Detroit, 1962; M.A., Fordham U., 1964, Ph.D., 1971; m. Susan Leigh Kerr, Dec. 30, 1967; 1 dau., Alice Imogen. Teaching fellow Fordham U., N.Y.C., 1966-67, instr., 1967-70, exec. asst. to pres., 1978—; vis. asst. prof. Hunter Coll., City U., N.Y., 1970-71; vis. asso. prof., MacMurray Coll., Jacksonville, Ill., 1972-73; asso. prof. polit. sci. Sangamon State U., Springfield, Ill., 1972—, program asso. Center Comparative Study of Middle-Sized Cities, 1973—; project coordinator nat. program devel. strategies for juvenile delinquency prevention HEW, 1971-72; dep. exec. dir. N.Y. Constl. Conv. internship program Ford Found., 1967; research asso. Temporary State Commn. Constl. Conv. N.Y., 1966-67; exec. dir. advisory council reapportionment N.Y. State Legislature, 1965-66; chief exec. officer NAACP, Wayne County. Mich., 1960-62, state v.p. NAACP Youth Conf., 1960-62. Am. Polit. Sci. Assn. Congl. fellow, 1966-67; Ford Found. grantee, N.Y. Senate Intern, 1964-65. Mem. AAUP, ACLU, Am., Midwest polit. sci. assns., NAACP, Pi Sigma Alpha. Fgn. corr., Der Volksbote, Innsbruck, Austria, 1965-66. Contbr. to various publs. on govtl. activities. Home: 82 Gordon St Yonkers NY 10701 Office: Fordham University New York City NY 10458

RUTLEDGE, PEARL BLACK, counselor; b. N.Y.C., Oct. 14, 1927; d. John Scribner and Harriette Althea (Bedell) Black; B.S., Western Ky. U., 1953; M.A., Murray State U., 1963; Ph.D., U. Ky., 1974; m. Edward Rutledge, Nov. 11, 1945; children—Richard, Rebecca. Tchr., U. Ky. Tng. Sch., Lexington, 1956; dir. women's recreation City of Paducah (Ky.), 1960; dir. Balt. Ecumenical Sch., 1965-70; co-dir. Lab. Trainers and Cons.'s Akron, Ohio, 1973-77; asst. prof. psychology Centre Coll., Danville, Ky., 1970-74; asst. prof. psychology Pace U., Pleasantville, N.Y., 1975—; exec. dir. Gestalt Tng. Network, Silver Spring, Md., 1977—; cons./trainer Am. Mgmt. Assn. Mem. Assn. Humanistic Psychology, Am. Personnel and Guidance Assn., Assn. Specialists in Group Work, Assn. Mental Health Counselors, Assn. Creative Change in Religious and Other Social Systems. Democrat. Presbyterian. Contbr. articles to profl. jours. Home: 19 George St Bloomfield NJ 07003 Office: Dept Psychology Pace U Pleasantville NY 10570

RUTSKY, LESTER, garment supplies co. exec.; b. N.Y.C., May 23, 1924; s. Samuel and Bess (Millman) R.; student pub. schs., Seward Park; m. Elaine Selesnik, Aug. 30, 1959. Mgr., Arc Mills, N.Y.C., 1965—; free lance writer, 1963—. Active March of Dimes, ARC, Blanche Shuldiner Sr. Citizens Center, Dept. Social Services City N.Y., 1978. Mem. Am. Poetry League, Mich. (Paul Elliot Meml. award), Ky., Ind., Fla. poetry socs., Poets Study Club of Terre Haute, Acad. Am. Poets. Contbr. poems to mags. Home: 2930 W 5th St New York City NY 11224 Office: 225 W 37th St New York City NY 10018

RUZICKA, MARY FRANCES, counselor; b. Balt., Dec. 4, 1943; d. Francis Frederick and Margaret Mary (Kernan) Ruzicka; B.A. cum laude, Georgian Ct. Coll., 1966; M.A., Seton Hall U., 1971; Ph.D., Fordham U., 1975. Tchr. St. Matthews Sch., Edison, N.J., 1966-68, St. Mary Sch., South Amboy, N.J., 1968-71; guidance counselor Sayreville (N.J.) High Sch., 1971-73; asso. prof. edn. Seton Hall U., South Orange, N.J., 1973—; counselor VA Center, 1973—; pvt. practice psychol. counseling, marriage counseling mgmt. tng. Mem. Am. Personnel and Guidance Assn., Am. Psychol. Assn. AAUP, N.Y. Acad. Scis. Contbr. articles to profl. jours. Home: 12 Northview Terr Maplewood NJ 07040 Office: Seton Hall Dept Counseling and Spl Services South Orange NJ 07079 also 55 Morris Ave Suite 202 Springfield NJ 07081

RYAN, ALAN RICHARD, food co. exec.; b. South Bend, Ind., Dec. 14, 1924; s. Elmer Charles and Irma (Young) R.; student Western Mich. U., 1943-44; B.S., Northwestern U., 1948; advanced mgmt. program Harvard U., 1973; m. Carolyn Hawk, June 30, 1951; children—Mary Roblen, Mark Young, Constance Lynn. Sales promotion mgr. Hekman Biscuit div. Keebler Co., Grand Rapids, Mich., 1951-57, mktg. mgr., 1957-62, dir. mktg. parent co., Elmhurst, Ill., 1962-67, dir. mktg. services, 1967-68; group product mgr., food service div. Quaker Oats Co., Chgo., 1968-69, dir. mktg. Burry div., 1969-70, gen. mgr., 1970-72, v.p., 1972-75, pres., 1975—. Chmn. pub. info. United Community Fund, Grand Rapids, 1959; mem. Assos. Council, Devel. Council Aquinas Coll., 1960-62; mem. pub. relations com. DuPage Area council Boy Scouts Am., 1966-68; pres. Catholic Sch. Bd., Glen Ellyn, Ill., 1966-70; vice chmn. Village of Glen Ellyn Plan Commn., 1969-74; mem. lay bd. Bellarmine Hall, Barrington, Ill., 1969-73; mem. exec. com., devel. council Central DuPage Hosp., Winfield, Ill., 1971-74; trustee Alexian Bros. Hosp., Elizabeth, N.J., 1975—, co-chmn., 1978—; bd. dirs. United Way of Union County, Elizabeth, 1976—, gen. campaign chmn., 1976. Served to lt. (j.g.) USNR, 1943-46. Mem. Biscuit and Cracker Mfrs. Assn. (pres. 1974-76, dir. 1971—), Eastern Union County C. of C. (dir. 1974-78), Am. Mktg. Assn., Am. Mgmt. Assn., Alpha Delta Phi. Club: Merchants and Manufacturers (Chgo.); Canoe Brook Country (Summit, N.J.); Suburban Golf (Union, N.J.). Home: 5 Wickham Way Chatham NJ 07928 Office: 1265 Durant St Elizabeth NJ 07202

RYAN, CHARLES EDWARD, JR., lawyer; b. Boston, Mar. 2, 1914; s. Charles Edward and Anna Vivian (Farrell) R.; A.B., Harvard, 1935; LL.B., Boston Coll., 1939; m. Mary Theresa Hampl, Oct. 10, 1942; children—Charles Edward, Patricia K., Judith M. Admitted to Vt. bar, 1942; with Boston & Me. R.R., 1942-46; atty. New Eng. Motor Rate Bur., Burlington, Mass., 1946—. Instr., Traffic Mgrs. Inst., Boston, 1954-63. Mem. Am. Soc. Traffic and Transp., ICC Practitioners Assn., Transp. Club New Eng. (pres. 1964), Delta Nu Alpha. Moose. Home: 15 Sheridan Rd Stoneham MA 02180 Office: 14 New Eng Exec Park Burlington MA 01803

RYAN, CLAUDE, newspaperman; b. Montreal, Que., Can., Jan. 26, 1925; s. Henri-Albert and Blandine (Dorion) R.; student Coll. St.-Croix, Montreal, 1937-44, Sch. Social Service, U. Montreal, 1944-46, Pontificial Gregorian U., Rome, Italy, 1951-52; m. Madeleine Guay, July 21, 1958; children—Paul, Monique, Therese, Patrice, Andre. Gen. sec. L'Action Catholique Canadienne, 1945-62; with Le Devoir, daily newspaper, Montreal, Que., 1962-78, pub., 1964-78; mng. dir. Imprimerie Populaire Ltd., 1964-78; leader Liberal party of Que., 1978—. Pres., Inst. Canadian Edn. des Adults 1955-61; Leonard Brockington visitor Queen's U., Kingston, Ont., 1976. Recipient Human Relations award Canadian Council Christians and Jews, 1966; named to Canadian News Hall of Fame, 1968. Roman Catholic. Office: Liberal Party Canada (Quebec) 1440 St Catherine St W Montreal PQ H3G 1R3 Canada*

RYAN, EUGENE ANTHONY, supt. schs.; b. Camden, N.J., May 26, 1926; s. Joseph J. and Mary A. (Duffner) R.; B.S. in Edn., Glassboro (N.J.) State Coll., 1950; M.S. in Ednl. Adminstrn., U. Pa., Phila., 1960; m. Ruth E. Ryan; children—Robert Hughes, William Hughes, Merry Ryan Collins. Adminstrv. prin. Pine Hill (N.J.) Pub. Schs., 1961-62; prin. Oak Valley Elementary Sch., Deptford, N.J., 1962-65, Monongahela Jr. High Sch., Deptford. 1965-69; supt. schs. Winslow Twp. (N.J.) Pub. Schs., 1969—. Sec. S. Jersey Schoolmen's Club, 1975—, Community Club, Inc., 1972—. Recipient Presdl. Ednl.

Pacesetter award, Nat. Validation award in ednl. devel. Mem. Am., N.J. assns. sch. adminstrs., NEA (life), Camden County Chief Sch. Adminstrs. (pres. roundtable). Home: 428 Green Tree Rd Turnersville NJ 08012 Office: 213 Central Ave Blue Anchor NJ 08037

RYAN, EUGENE JOSEPH, state ofcl.; b. Brownsville, Tex., Aug. 28, 1932; s. Richard Sylvester and Stella Loyolla (Carpenter) R.; A.B., Harvard, 1954. Staff, UN Internat. Refugee Orgn., Europe, 1948-49; with U.S. Fed. Govt., Europe, 1949-51, City of Boston, 1957-67; dir. Office for Med. Instns., Nursing Homes, Med. Assistance and Mental Health, Mass. Dept. Pub. Welfare, Boston, 1967—; now propr. Boston Athenaeum. Bd. dirs. John Alden Carpenter Meml., Marsalin Psychiat. Inst. Mem. Pub. Welfare Adminstrs. Assn. (dir.), Nat. Assn. Govt. Employees (pres. Mass. chpt.). Roman Catholic. Clubs: Harvard Faculty, Algonquin, Bay (Boston); Beacon Soc. Home: 151 Tremont St Boston MA 02111 Office: 41 Hawkins St Boston MA 02114

RYAN, FRANK JAMES, investment co. exec.; b. Boston, May 22, 1934; s. James Francis and Edna Anna (Schnaufer) R.; B.Sc., Cornell U., 1955, M.B.A., 1959, M.A., 1959; postgrad. N.Y. U. Sch. Law, 1961-62; m. Catherine Joyce Fujiwara, July 15, 1966; children—Nicole Melia, Todd Thomas, Scott James. With fgn. investment dept. Goodbody & Co., N.Y.C., 1959-61; asst. v.p. fgn. investment Am. Fgn. Ins. Assn., N.Y.C., 1962-66; asst. treas. fgn. investment Am. Life Ins. Co., Bermuda, 1966-69; v.p. fgn. investment C.V. Starr & Co., N.Y.C., 1969-78; v.p. InterSec Research Corp., N.Y.C., 1978—. Served with AUS, 1955, 58-59. Mem. Acad. Polit. Sci., Am. Acad. Polit. and Social Sci., Am. Soc. Internat. Law, Cornell Soc. Engrs., Cornell Soc. Hotelmen, Internat. Studies Assn., N.Y. Soc. Security Analysts, Fgn. Analysts Fedn. Club: N.Y. Athletic. Home: 27 Minute Man Hill Westport CT 06880 Office: 122 E 42 St New York City NY 10017

RYAN, GAIL MARGARET, physician; b. N.Y.C., July 14, 1936; d. James W. and Margaret (Egan) R.; B.A., U. Calif., Los Angeles, 1956; M.D., U. So. Calif., Los Angeles, 1960; 1 son, James C. Brown. Intern, Roosevelt Hosp., N.Y.C., 1960-61; resident in anesthesiology St. Luke's Hosp., N.Y.C., 1961-63; resident in anesthesiology Columbia Presbyn. Hosp., N.Y.C., 1963-64; practice medicine specializing in anesthesiology, N.Y.C., 1964-74; clin. asst. anesthesiologist Meml. Hosp., 1964-66, asst. attending anesthesiologist, 1966-69, attending anesthesiologist, 1972—; asst. attending anesthesiologist N.Y. Hosp., N.Y.C., 1970-71, attending anesthesiologist, 1972-74; clin. instr. anesthesiology Cornell U. Med. Coll., N.Y.C., 1968-70, asst. prof., 1970-74; asso. med. dir. Pfizer Labs. Div., N.Y.C., 1974-77, group product physician Pfizer Internat., 1977—. Diplomate Am. Bd. Anesthesiology. Mem. Am. Coll. of Anesthesiologists, Internat. Anesthesia Research Soc., N.Y. State Soc. of Anesthesiologists, AMA, Soc. of Critical Care Medicine, N.Y. County Med. Soc., N.Y. Acad. Sci., Nat. Fire Protection Assn. Contbr. articles in field to med. jours. Home: 112 Imperial Ave Westport CT 06880 Office: 235 E 42d St New York City NY 10017

RYAN, JAMES DANIEL, educator; b. Buffalo, Nov. 29, 1938; s. James Daniel and Antoinette M. (Lateer) R.; B.A. cum laude, St. Bonaventure U., 1960; M.S. in Edn., Canisius Coll., 1962; Ph.D., N.Y. U., 1973; m. Jeanne Anne O'Grady, Apr. 15, 1963; children—James Daniel, Julia Regina, Matthew George. With City U. N.Y., Bronx, 1966-67, Seton Hall U., S. Orange, N.J., 1967-69, St. Lawrence U., Canton, N.Y., 1969, L.I. U., 1969-70; asso. prof. history City U. N.Y., Bronx, 1970—. N.Y. Regent's Teaching fellow, 1962, 63, 64; N.Y. Regents fellow for advanced studies in arts and scis., 1965. Mem. Am. Hist. Assn., Mediaeval Acad. Am., Cath. Hist. Assn., Soc. for History of Technology, Am. Assn. Polit. and Social Sci. Democrat. Roman Catholic. Author: The Interrelation of the Mission and Crusade Activities of the Papacy Under Nicholas IV, 1973. Office: Univ Ave and 181st St Bronx NY 10453

RYAN, JOHN WILLIAM, assn. exec.; b. Manchester, N.H., Sept. 16, 1937; s. William C. and Mary Anna (Marcoux) R.; B.A., St. Anselm's Coll., 1959; M.A., Niagara U., 1960; Ph.D., St. John's U., Jamaica, N.Y., 1965; m. Carol J. Battaglia, Sept. 17, 1960; children—James, Kathleen, John, Michael. Asst. prof. history Gannon Coll., 1965-66; grad. edn. specialist U.S. Office Edn., Washington, 1966-68, regional coordinator for grad. acad. programs, 1968-70; dir. coll., univ. programs Univ. Assos., Inc., Washington, 1970-72; asst. to pres. Council Grad. Schs. in U.S., Washington, 1972—. First v.p. Fairfax County (Va.) Council PTA's, 1976-78. Mem. Am. Assn. Higher Edn., Washington Higher Edn. Group (sec. 1970-71). Editor: Proc. Council of Graduate Schools, 1972. Home: 6321 Capella Ave Burke VA 22015 Office: 1 Dupont Circle NW Washington DC 20036

RYAN, LEONARD EAMES, lawyer, pub. affairs cons.; b. Albion, N.Y., July 8, 1930; s. Bernard and Harriet Earle (Fitts) R.; A.B., U. Pa., 1954; J.D., N.Y. U., 1962; m. Ann Allen, June 18, 1973; 1 son, Thomas Eames Allen. Admitted to D.C., N.Y. bars, 1963, U.S. Supreme Ct. bar, 1967; reporter Upper Darby (Pa.) News, 1954; newsman AP, Pitts., Phila., Harrisburg, Pa. and N.Y.C., 1955-62; reporter, spl. writer on law N.Y. Times, 1962-63; info. adviser corporate hdqrs. IBM, N.Y.C., 1963; atty. firm Perrell, Nielsen & Stephens, N.Y.C., 1964-66; trial atty. civil rights div. Dept. Justice, Washington, 1966-68; asst. to dir. bus. affairs CBS News, N.Y.C., 1968; program officer Office Govt. and Law, Ford Found., N.Y.C., 1968-74; individual practice law and pub. affairs cons., N.Y.C., 1974—; v.p., sec. W. P. Carey & Co., Inc., N.Y.C., 1976—; hearing examiner N.Y. State Div. Human Rights, 1976—; spl. impartial hearing officer Office for Handicapped, N.Y.C. Bd. Edn., 1976—; mem. panel of attys. under Criminal Justice Act of 1964, U.S. Dist. Ct. So. Dist. N.Y., 1975-77; mem. nat. gas transmission and distbn. adv. com. U.S. Dept. Energy, Washington, 1976—, mem. spl. ad hoc com. on winter planning, 1978; mem. indigent defendants legal panel Supreme Ct., N.Y. County. Bd. dirs. Community Action for Legal Services, Inc., N.Y.C., 1971-77, vice-chmn., 1975-77; co-chmn. Citizens Com. to Save Legal Services, N.Y.C., 1975-76; bd. dirs. Lower East Side Service Center, N.Y.C., 1978—. Mem. Am. Arbitration Assn. (panel), Group for Advancement Corrections, Am. Judicature Soc., Nat. Legal Aid and Defender Assn., Assn. Bar City N.Y. (com. profl. responsibility 1977-78), N.Y. County Lawyers Assn. (com. on supreme ct. 1978—), N.Y. State Bar Assn., Delta Phi Found. (pres.). Democrat. Club: St. Elmo (Phila.). Author: (with B. Ryan, Jr.) So You Want to Go into Journalism, 1963; contbr. articles to profl. jours. Home: 32 Orange St Brooklyn NY 11201 Office: 67 Wall St New York NY 10005

RYAN, MARY KATHRYN, counselor; b. Brockton, Mass., Oct. 23; d. John T. and Martha (O'Malley) Ryan; B.S.Ed., State Coll. Mass., Bridgewater; Ed.M., Boston U.; postgrad. Boston State Coll., Tufts U., Bridgewater State Coll. Tchr., pub. schs., Brockton, Mass., 1946-60, counselor West Jr. High Sch., 1960-69, guidance coordinator, 1969—. Bd. dirs. Old Colony Mental Health Assn. Mem. Am. (v.p. 1971-75), Mass. (sec. 1975-78; award 1977), sch. counselors assns., Am. (chmn. awards and credentials coms. 1978-79), Mass. (sec. 1972-74) personnel and guidance assns., South Shore Guidance Assn. (past pres.), Brockton Edn. Assn. (past v.p., sec.), Mass. Tchrs. Assn., NEA. Column author, editor: Elementary Guidance and Counseling Jour., 1972-75; contbr. articles to profl. jours. Home: 127 Manomet St Brockton MA 02401 Office: West Jr High Sch West St Brockton MA 02401

RYAN, MILES FRANCIS, JR., govt. ofcl.; b. Cleve., Jan. 28, 1919; s. Miles Francis and Lola Veronica (Wagner) R.; B.A. magna cum laude, Western Res. U., 1940, J.D., 1948; m. Vernance Dolores Beste, Aug. 18, 1962; children—Miles Francis III, Patrick Andrew. Research asst. Bur. Pub. Adminstrn., U. S.C., Columbia, 1946; chief status of equipment unit, specifications div. USAF Material Command, Wright Field, Ohio, 1941; admitted to Ohio bar, 1948, U.S. Supreme Ct. bar, 1964; atty. antitrust div. Justice Dept., Cleve., 1948-60, Washington, 1960—, atty.-adviser, 1970-77, trial atty., 1978—; instr. polit. sci. and econs. Western Res. U., Cleve., 1946-51; cons. on patents, tech. data, copyrights Com. on Govt. Procurement, 1971. Served with AUS, 1941-45. Deocrated Bronze Star. Mem. Phi Beta Kappa, Delta Kappa Epsilon. Roman Catholic. Recipient U.S. Atty. Gen.'s Sustained Superior Performance award, 1967. Author publs. on pub. adminstrn. Home: 12502 Two Farm Dr Silver Spring MD 20904 Office: Antitrust Div Justice Dept Washington DC 20530

RYAN, ROBERT S., bank exec.; b. Morristown, N.J., July 20, 1924; s. Francis J. and Ida May (Keefe) R.; B.S., U. Tulsa, 1952; postgrad. Stanford Sch. Credit, Finan. Mgmt., 1963-66; m. Margie Riehl, Oct. 17, 1953; children—Mary Beth, Robert S., Joseph A., Kate K. Petroleum engr. Pan Am. Petroleum Corp., Tulsa, 1952-59; petroleum engr. Citibank Nat. Assn., N.Y.C., 1959-62, asst. v.p., 1962-69, v.p. metals, mining dept., 1969-76, v.p., head of global project finance dept., 1976—. Mem. spl. gifts com. United Fund, Madison, N.J., 1969. Served with USN, 1942-48; PTO. Decorated Purple Heart, 7 Asia-PTO stars; registered profl. petroleum engr., Okla. Mem. Am. Inst. Mining Engrs. (dir., v.p. finance, 1972-75, Krumb Fund investment com. 1972-75, Hoover medal bd. award 1977—), Soc. Petroleum Engrs., Soc. Mining Engrs., Am. Mining Congress. Office: 399 Park Ave New York City NY 10022

RYAN, VINCENT FRANCIS, JR., electronics engr.; b. Phila., June 19, 1929; s. Vincent Francis and Amelia (Steelman) R.; B.E.E., Villanova U., 1951; M.S. in Engring., Moore Sch., U. Pa., 1963; m. Mary Agnes Teresa Hegarty, Feb. 4, 1956 (dec. May 1969); children—Vincent F.M., Mary E., Patricia A., Teresa A.; m. 2d, Mary Margret Martin Saboe, June 3, 1978. Engr., Philco Corp., Phila., 1951-55, engring. specialist, Willow Grove, Pa., 1960-62; engr. RCA, Moorestown, N.J., 1955-57, Camden, N.J., 1957-60; control engr. on loan to C-Stellerator Assos., Princeton, N.J., 1959; sr. engr. Burroughs Corp., Paoli, Pa., 1962-65; mgr. dir. Ke Gen. Corp., 1965; project engr. Borders Electronics, Pennsauken, N.J., 1965-67; sr. systems engr. Trevose (Pa.) ops. United Aircraft Corp., 1967-68; dir. engring. and ops. Logic Corp., 1968-69; tech. dir. Lew Malnak Assos. DTI Inc., Cherry Hill, N.J., 1969-77; engr. RCA, Camden, N.J., 1977-78, Moorestown, N.J., 1978—; dir. Dynamic Tech. Internat., Inc., Cheyroh Gen. Systems; ins. salesman John Hancock, 1965, Intercontinental Life, 1965-71. Mem. Haddonleigh Civic Assn., 1956—. Mem. IEEE, Am. Soc. Cybernetics, Internat. Platform Assn., Armed Forces Communications and Electronics Assn., Smithsonian Assos., Soc. Gen. Systems Research, Artorgd Assn. Roman Catholic. Club: K.C. Home: 596 Coles Mill Rd Haddonfield NJ 08033

RYAN, WILLIAM HOWARD, mfg. co. exec., archtl. historian, inventor; b. Rochester, N.Y., Mar. 18, 1914; s. Willis James and Amelia Mary (Ginter) R.; student Ill. Inst. Tech., 1938-39; B.S., Boston U., 1955; postgrad. Harvard, 1965-66; m. Mary Elizabeth Black, Aug. 9, 1941. Equipment engr. Automatic Electric Co., Chgo., 1937-39; research scientist Polaroid Corp., Cambridge, Mass., 1939-65; pres. Polyphor Corp., indsl. coatings, Framingham, Mass., 1970—, New Eng. Pressed Steel Co., Natick, Mass., 1970—. Research cons., Polaroid Corp., Cambridge, 1965-71. Trustee Colonial Restorations Trust, Lexington, Mass., 1960—, Mary B. and William H. Ryan Found., Framingham, 1968—. Mem. Soc. Motion Picture and TV Engrs. (del. intersoc. color council 1946-71), Soc. Photog. Scientists and Engrs., Royal Photog. Soc. Gt. Britain, History of Sci. Soc., Soc. Archtl. Historians Gt. Britain, Soc. Archtl. Historians. Patentee in three dimensional photography, instant-photography, light polarizers. Author: (with H.T. Kalmus, Jack Warner and others) New Screen Techniques, 1952; (with Desmond Guinness) Irish Houses and Castles, 1971. Office: 89 Washington Ave Natick MA 01760

RYBECK, JAMES PETER, fin. co. exec.; b. Hartford, Conn., Nov. 29, 1929; s. William Howard and Beatrice Ellen (Mell) R.; B.S., U. Conn., 1951; M.B.A., U. Pa., 1956; m. Barbara Duryea, Aug. 20, 1955; children—Betsy, Dean, Jennifer. With William H. Rybeck & Co., Inc., Meriden, Conn., 1955—, pres. 1969—; dir. UMC Electronics Co., Nat. Indsl. Bank. Sec., treas. Walnut Grove Cemetery, 1969—; pres. Meriden Bd. Edn., 1959-65; alderman City of Meriden, 1967-71. Served to 1st lt. AUS, 1951-54. Decorated Purple Heart. Mem. Conn. Investment Bankers Assn. (pres. 1976—), Conn. Security Traders Assn. (pres. 1972-73), Boston Stock Exchange (gov. 1970-73, 77—), Nat. Assn. Securities Dealers (dist. vice-chmn.). Republican. Clubs: Rotary, Home, Farms Country. Home: 281 Wall St Meriden CT 06450 Office: 31 Pratt St Meriden CT 06450

RYBURN, SAMUEL MCCHESNEY, investment co. exec.; b. Morristown, Tenn., Oct. 25, 1914; s. Samuel M. and Mary (Whittaker) R.; B.S., U. Ala., 1936; postgrad. U. Vienna, 1937-38; M.B.A., Boston Coll., 1962; m. Beverley Huse, June 5, 1943; children—John Huse, Marie Du Plessis. Pres., Textron Adv. Group Inc., Providence; past dir. Miller and Fink Inc., Darien, Conn., Glasrock Products, Inc. Atlanta, Millmaster Onyx Chem. Corp., N.Y.C., Context Corp., Burlington, Mass., Memory Tech., Inc., Sudbury, Mass., Summagraphics, Inc., Fairfield, Conn., Voc Hyd, Inc., Detroit, Telephonax Inc., Portland, Anacon Inc., Ashland, Mass., Oreg. Hill Electronics, Mechanicsburg, Pa., Aluminum Silicates, Inc. Washington, Ga., Producers Transport, Inc., Akron, Microtek Engring. Corp., Baton Rouge, Electronic Metals and Alloys, Attleboro, Ga. CATV, Inc., Atlanta, R & D Mfg. Co., New Bedford, Mass., Creative Studies Inc., Boston, James River Paper Corp., Richmond, Auckland Woolcrafters Ltd., Boston, MicroDynamics, Inc., Boston, Space Ordnance Systems Inc., Encenita, Cal., Totel Systems Inc., Bridgeport, Conn., Novatronics, Inc., Pompano Beach, Cal., Telefile Computer Systems Inc., Boston, Telecontrol Corp., Greenwich, Conn., Photics, Inc., Montgomeryville, Pa. Editor, The Clarendon Press 1959-63. Trustee Hale Reservation; v.p. Dover Found. Pres. bd. trustees Charles River Sch., 1960-63. Served as lt. comdr. USNR. World War II, 1941-45. Recipient Gamma Sigma Epsilon award, Internat. Scholarship award. Mem. Am. Chem. Soc., Phi Gamma Delta, Gamma Sigma Epsilon. Club: Dedham Country and Polo. Home: Wilsondale St Dover MA 02030 Office: 40 Westminster St Providence RI 02903

RYCHLIK, FRANK FELIX, educator; b. Boston, May 30, 1945; s. Frank John and Viola Mary (Pawlowski) R.; B.A., State U. N.Y. Coll. at Geneseo, 1972, M.S., 1975; m. Kathy Ann Patton, July 13, 1973. Tchr., Victor (N.Y.) Central Sch., 1972. Adviser, Victor Internat. Youth Club, 1973—, Model UN Club, Victor, 1973, Boston (N.Y.) Fire Co., 1963-72; mem. N.Y. Conservation Council, Boston, 1969-72; mem. Parish council Neuman Found., Geneseo, 1964-65, 69-72. Served with USMC, 1966-69. Mem. Nat. Assn. Geography (Acad. Achievement award 1972), N.Y. Council Social Studies, Am. Assn. Geographers, Finger Lakes Social Studies Orgn., Nat. Council Geog. Edn., Am. Fedn. Tchrs. and N.Y. Tchrs. Assn. Club: Geneseo Veterans. Democrat. Roman Catholic. Author: Cartographer: 52 Peaceful Societies (Matthew Melko), 1973. Home: 162 Park St Canandaigua NY 14424 Office: Social Sci Dept Victor Sr High Sch Victor NY 14564

RYD, BEVERLY JEAN, librarian; b. Boston, Aug. 3, 1935; d. Eric Albert and Vinita (Blake) Ryd; B.S. in Library Sci., Simmons Coll., 1957; M.S.L.S., Columbia U., 1959. Law librarian Conn. Gen. Ins. Corp., Hartford, Conn., 1957-58; reference librarian Grad. Sch. Bus., Pub. Adminstrn. Cornell U., 1959-64; asst. cataloger Fed. Res. Bank N.Y., N.Y.C., 1964-65; librarian First Boston Corp., N.Y.C., 1965—, asst. v.p., 1976—; mem. pres.'s com. N.Y. State Gov.'s Conf. on Libraries, 1977-78. Mem. Spl. Libraries Assn. (sec. N.Y. chpt. 1975-76, v.p. chpt. 1976-77, pres. chpt. 1977-78). Club: N.Y. Library. Home: 345 E 52d St New York City NY 10022 Office: 20 Exchange Pl New York City NY 10005

RYDER, KENNETH GILMORE, univ. pres.; b. Brockton, Mass., Apr. 30, 1924; s. Russell Gilmore and Etta Coffin (Carr) R.; A.B. (Augustus Howe Buck fellow 1941-46), Boston U., 1946; A.M. (A.H. Buck fellow 1946-48), Harvard, 1947; L.H.D., Nasson Coll., 1972; m. Virginia Patricia Gagnon, June 29, 1944 (div. July 1975); children—Anne, Jeanne, Bruce. Instr. history Cambridge Jr. Coll., 1948; instr. history and govt. Northeastern U., 1949-53, asst. prof., 1953-57, asso. prof. history, 1957—, dean of adminstrn., 1958-67, v.p., dean of univ. adminstrn., 1967-71, exec. v.p., 1971-75, pres., 1975—. Past pres. Friends of the Library of Boston U.; trustee Cambridge Jr. Coll., Forsyth Dental Center; adv. council Mass. Gen. Hosp. Sch. Nursing; mem. Adv. Council Vocat. Tech. Edn., Citywide Coordinating Council Boston Sch. Desegregation. Served to lt. (j.g.) USNR, World War II. Mem. NEA, Am. Hist. Assn., Am. Soc. Engring. Edn., New Eng. Assn. Schs. and Colls., Boston U. Alumni Assn., Boston U. Coll. Liberal Arts Alumni Soc. (past pres.), PTA (local pres. 1962-63), Phi Beta Kappa, Phi Alpha Theta, Phi Kappa Phi, Kappa Delta Pi, Beta Gamma Sigma. Episcopalian (vestryman). Contbg. author Handbook of College and University Adminstration, 1970. Office: Office of Pres Northeastern Univ 360 Huntington Ave Boston MA 02115*

RYDER, ROBERT GUY, educator, univ. dean; b. Newark, July 22, 1934; s. Guy Monsalve and Helen Wrigley (Grimes) R.; B.A. cum laude, Rutgers U., 1957; M.A., U. Mich., 1958, Ph.D., 1961; m. Mary Alice Scheider, Aug. 24, 1957; children—Steven, Rebecca. Research psychologist Family Devel. sect. Nat. Inst. Mental Health, Bethesda, Md., 1961-64, chief family devel. sect., 1964-75, pvt. practice, Washington, 1964-75; prof., head dept. child devel. and family relations U. Conn. at Storrs, 1975, dean Sch. Home Econs. and Family Studies, 1976—; instr. family and community devel. U. Md., 1973-74. Bd. dirs. Groves Conf. on Marriage and the Family, 1973-76, pres., 1978—. Mem. Am. Assn. Marriage and Family Counselors, Am. Assn. Sex Educators and Counselors, Am. Psychol. Assn., Nat. Council Family Relations, Sigma Xi. Contbr. articles to profl. jours. Home: 28 C Anton Rd Storrs CT 06268

RYEA, JOHN LAWRENCE, JR., indsl. hygiene technician; b. Aberdeen, Md., Mar. 28, 1949; s. John Lawrence and Rolande Marie (Roy) R.; student Harford Community Coll., 1969-71. Indsl. hygiene instrumentation repairman U.S. Army Environ. Hygiene Agy., Aberdeen Proving Grounds, Md., 1967-72, engring. technician, 1972-75, indsl. hygiene technician, 1975—; lectr. indsl. hygiene courses. Recipient Outstanding Performance awards Dept. Army, 1970, 73, 74, 75, 77; certified engring. technician. Mem. Am. Conf. Govtl. Indsl. Hygienists, Am. Indsl. Hygiene Assn. Democrat. Roman Catholic. Clubs: West Shore Tennis, Gunpowder Neck Boat. Home: PO Box 914 Edgewood MD 21040 Office: USAEHA-IHD Aberdeen Proving Gounds MD 21010

RYGELIS, JOSEPH, mech. engr.; b. Lithuania, Aug. 12, 1920; s. Antanas and Veronica (Puodziukynas) R.; came to U.S., 1949, naturalized, 1955; ed. Vytautas The Gt. U. (Lithuania), 1942-44; grad. Tech. U. Darmstadt (W. Ger.), 1949; m. Aldona Tercijonas, Apr. 16, 1950; children—Aldona, Anthony, Vincent, Regina, Vita. Design engr. Honolulu Iron Works, N.Y.C., 1950-51, Greer Hydraulics, Bklyn., 1951-53; chief design engr. Gorn Electric Co., 1953-54; project engr. Singer Research and Devel., Bridgeport, Conn., 1954-57; chief engr. analytical methods Avco-Lycoming, Stratford, Conn., 1957-70; staff engr., tech. cons. dynamics, heat transfer and stress Singer-Kearfott, Wayne, N.J., 1970—. Pres., Am. Lithuanian Community, Bridgeport, 1960-70; dir. youth activities Lithuanian Cath. Assn., 1959-63. Mem. ASME (chmn. Bergen-Passaic subsect. 1977), Lithuanian Engrs. and Architects Assn. in U.S.A., Am. Def. Preparedness Assn., Lithuanian Cath. Sci. Acad. Republican. Roman Catholic. Clubs: Toastmaster Internat. Home: 5 Edgemere Trail Kennelon NJ 07405 Office: 150 Totawa Rd Wayne NJ 07470

RYKERT, JOHN CHARLES, investment fund exec.; b. London, Eng., Mar. 19, 1930; s. Harold Edmund and Aimee (Gundy) R.; came to Can., 1931; degree bus. adminstrn. with honors, U. Western Ont. (London, Can.), 1953; m. Carol S. Hudson, Aug. 27, 1955; children—Serena, Elizabeth, Pamela, John Charles. With Wood Gundy Ltd., Toronto, Ont., Can., 1954-69, security analyst, 1959-64, registered rep., 1964-69; individual practice as fin. cons., Toronto, 1969-71; treas., dir. Canadian Gen. Investments Ltd., Toronto, 1971—; treas., dir. 3d Canadian Gen. Investment Trust, Toronto, 1971—; dir. Foodex Systems Ltd., Toronto, Bd. dirs. Bishop Strachan Sch., Toronto; trustee Upper Can. Coll. Found. Clubs: Toronto, York, Badminton and Racquet (all Toronto). Home: 103 Poplar Plains Rd Toronto ON M4V 2N1 Canada Office: 110 Yonge St Suite 1702 Toronto ON M5C 1T4 Canada

RYLANDER, DAVID JOHN, shipbuilding co. exec.; b. Bklyn., Aug. 12, 1935; s. Clarence Bernard and Frances (Smith) R.; B.S., Webb Inst. Naval Architecture, 1957; M.B.A., Harvard, 1959; m. Patricia Anne Deming, Oct. 21, 1961; children—David John II, Brian Ashley, Kimberley Rumel, Andrea Frances. Mgr. electric boat div. Gen. Dynamics Co., Groton, Conn., 1959-68, sr. staff asst., 1972-74; ind. mgmt. cons., Lyme, Conn., 1968-69, 74-76, 78—; controller, dir. mgmt. info. Litton Ship Systems div. Litton Industries, Pascagoula, Miss., 1969-72; dir. fin. planning Todd Shipyards Corp., N.Y.C., 1976-78. Registered profl. engr., Conn. Mem. Soc. Naval Architects and Marine Engrs. Republican. Home: Becket Hill Lyme CT 06371

RYNDES, LEONARD JAMES, assn. exec.; b. Oneonta, N.Y., Oct. 1, 1912; s. Herbert and Lena (Leal) R.; student Hartwich Coll., 1932-33, 50-51; m. Dorothy Genevieve Goodwin, June 24, 1936. Owner, prin. Ryndes Market, Oneonta, 1936-51; quality analyst elec. components div. Bendix Corp., Sidney, N.Y., 1951-68; exec. dir. Upper Catskills Community Council Arts, 1970—. Co-chmn. Festival Arts, State U. N.Y. at Oneonta, 1970—; mem. citizens bd. Hartwich Coll., 1974; bd. dirs. Catskill Festival Opera Co.; 1st v.p., bd. dirs. Old Mill Museum, East Meridith, N.Y.; mem. Bicentennial Commn. City of Oneonta. Mem. Phi Sigma Kappa. Club: Oneonta Country. Home:

49 Union St Oneonta NY 13820 Office: Old Milne Library SUCO Oneonta NY 13820

RYSER, HUGUES JEAN-PAUL, educator; b. Chaux-de-Fonds, Switzerland, June 11, 1926; s. Ernest Jacob and Marthe Alice (Zimmermann) R.; came to U.S., 1958, naturalized, 1972; M.D., U. Berne Med. Sch. (Switzerland), 1953, Dr. Med., 1955; m. Carol Leigh Pierson, June 10, 1961; children—Marc Alain, Jeannine, Eve. Instr. pharmacology Harvard Med. Sch., 1960-62, asso. in pharmacology, 1962-64, asst. prof. pharmacology, 1964-69; asso. prof. cell biology and pharmacology U. Md. Med. Sch., 1969-70, prof., 1970-72; prof. pathology and pharmacology Boston U. Sch. Medicine, 1972—; cons. ZYMA-CIBA, Switzerland, 1969-72; cons. biology dept. Dynapol Corp., Palo Alto, Cal., 1972—. Recipient Lederle Med. Faculty award, 1964-67; Nat. Cancer Inst., Research Career Devel. award, 1968-69; NIH Research Grant, 1961-69; Nat. Cancer Inst. grantee, 1972—. Mem. Am. Histochem. Soc., Am. Assn. Cancer Research, Am. Soc. Cell Biology, Am. Soc. Gen. Physiology, AAAS, Am. Soc. Exptl. Pharmacology and Therapeutics. Contbr. numerous articles to sci. jours. Home: 503 Annursnac Hill Rd Concord MA 01742 Office: 80 E Concord St Boston MA 02118

RYTTEN, JACK EDWARD, criminologist, investigator; b. Port Chester, N.Y., Sept. 23, 1914; s. Charles and Anita (Lazarone) R.; student pub. and pvt. schs.; m. Patti Dize, Feb. 25, 1950; 1 dau., Barbara Ann. Asst. credit mgr. Blums Dept. Store, Balt., 1938-42; credit mgr., comptroller Ann Lewis Shops, Balt., 1942-44; investigative cons., Balt., 1944—; spl. cons. police-community relations, 1963—; police sci. lectr., N.Y.C., Pa., Fla., 1954-58; feature writer The Police Chief, 1955-60; vis. lectr. Balt. chpt. Am. Inst. Banking, 1965, Balt. chpt. Nat. Assn. Bank Audit and Control, 1968, Mt. St. Agnes Coll., 1968, Balt. Grand Jurors Assn., 1968, Balt. County Dental Aux., 1969, Engring. Soc. Balt., 1969; vis. commentator Sta. WCBM, Balt., 1965; spl. cons. consumer credit fraud investigations Equitable Trust Co., Balt., 1971-72; spl. internal security cons. First Nat. Bank Md., 1975—. Co-founder Profl. Forum, pres., 1965-68; mem. nat. adv. bd. Am. Security Council. Chmn. com. on juvenile delinquency Baltimore County Council PTA's 1957-59; chmn. sub-com. law enforcement Rep. State Central Com. Md., 1962-64; bd. sponsors Nat. Right to Work Legal Found., 1973—. Recipient Liberty award Congress of Freedom, Inc., 1969. Mem. Engring. Soc. Balt. (press liaison and community relations com. 1977-78), Internat. Assn. Identification, Am. Soc. Criminology, Mil. Police Assn., Pa. Chiefs of Police Assn., AAAS, Am. Conservative Union, Md. Hist. Soc., Police-Law Soc. Chgo. Republican. Methodist. Author: Basic Laws on the Admissibility of Confessions, 1961; Judicial Oversights and Punishment, 1965; (with Thomas N. Clifford) Examination of Private Investigators in Deposition Proceedings, 1968; Re-Affirming Our Role as Professionals, 1969; An Investigator's View of Crime and Punishment, 1973; An Investigator's View of the Liberal Press, 1974; Socialized Misery, 1975; Public vs. Private Education, 1975; Public Relations and the Engineering Profession, 1975; Pre-Trial Accident Investigation, 1976; The Age of Illiteracy, 1977; The Assault on Competence, 1978; contbg. writer Assn. Am. Physicians and Surgeons, 1969; editor Police Rev., 1958-61; contbg. feature writer Daily Record, Balt., 1970—; feature writer Balt. Engr., 1978—; author syndicated column The Investigator's Notebook, Delmarva Press, 1977—; contbr. articles to profl. jours. Home: 8415 Bellona Ln Baltimore MD 21204 Office: 315 Ruxton Towers Baltimore MD 21204

RZEPECKI, RAYMOND MICHAEL, JR., semi-conductive films mfg. co. exec.; b. Pawtucket, R.I., Sept. 24, 1946; s. Raymond Michael and Mary Wanda (Golombiewski) R.; B.S., U. R.I., 1968; m. Lynne Helen Stewart, Sept. 2, 1967; children—Raymond Robert, Robyn Lynne. Process control chemist Uniroyal Co., Woonsocket, R.I., 1968, Port Clinton, Ohio, 1969, research chemist, Providence, R.I., 1970-71; process control mgr. Pervel Ind. Inc., Plainfield, Conn., 1972-73, product mgr., 1974—. Mem. bd. deacons Phillips Meml. Bapt. Ch., Cranston, R.I., 1975-78. Mem. Am. Chem. Soc., Am. Assn. Textile Chemists and Colorists. Republican. Home: RFD 1 Box 9AA Rockland Rd North Scituate RI 02857 Office: Pervel Ind Inc Community Ave Plainfield CT 06374

SAAD, EDWARD THEODORE, architect; b. Jerusalem, Palestine, Jan. 25, 1923; s. Theodore and Kafa (Ghandour) S.; came to U.S., 1947, naturalized, 1954; B.A. in Archtl. Engring., U. Nebr., 1953; m. Alice Ruth Harms, May 24, 1954; children—Roxana, Theodore, Lydia, Mark. Project mgr. Eero Saarinen & Assos., Bloomfield Hills, Mich., 1955-65; partner Harold Roth & Edward Saad, Hamden, Conn., 1965-72; prin. Edward Saad & Assos. Architects, Cheshire, Conn., 1973—. Cons. Upjohn Co., North Haven, Conn., 1966-67. Mem. AIA (corporate mem., Honor award New Eng. chpt. 1968, Honor award nat. council religious architecture div. 1970). Rotarian (bd. dirs. Hamden, pres. 1972-73). Important archtl. works include Mack House, Cheshire, 1966; Am. Field Service Hdqrs., N.Y.C., 1966; Surf Club West, Milford, Conn., 1967; Trinity Ch., Orange, Conn., 1967; No. Br. YMCA, Hamden, 1968; West Rock Nature Center, New Haven, 1968; Ridge Hill Sch., Hamden, 1970; Ernestine Stodelle Dance Studio, Cheshire, 1973; Cheshire Pub. Library, 1974; Cheshire Acad. Place Profl. Centre, 1976. Address: 608 S Brooksvale Rd Cheshire CT 06410

SAALBACH, RAYMOND CURRIER, univ. adminstr.; b. Coatesville, Pa., Jan. 10, 1919; s. Carl J. and Mildred (Currier) S.; B.S., West Chester (Pa.), State Coll., 1940; M.A. in English, U. Pa., 1949, M.S. in Guidance, 1950, Ed.D., 1952; m. Elaine Anderson, Mar. 1943, div. 1951. instr. English, U. Pa., Phila., 1947-48, chief recruiter undergrad. admissions, 1949-60; dir. admissions Wharton Grad. Sch., 1960-67, editor faculty-staff handbook, 1967-69, dir. devel. office meml. programs, 1969—. Pres. Collingdale (Pa.) Sch. Bd., 1958-71; mem. Collingdale Planning Commn., 1972—; Collingdale Library Bd., 1965—, (pres. 1974—). Served with USN, 1942-45. Republican. Contbr. articles in field to profl. jours. Home: 1124 MacDade Blvd Collingdale PA 19023 Office: 417 Franklin Bldg U of Pa Philadelphia PA 19174

SABIA, VINCENT NICHOLAS, mktg. co. exec.; b. Riverside, Conn., July 2, 1949; s. Vincent Nicholas and Mary Catherine (Perna) S.; B.S. in Life Scis., N.Y. Inst. Tech., 1972; postgrad. C.W. Post Coll., L.I. U., 1972-73; m. Dolores Loretta, May 26, 1973; 1 son, Christopher Vincent. Instr., technologist N.Y. Inst. Tech., 1970-72; chemistry technologist Cornell U. Med. Center, North Shore Univ. Hosp., 1972-73; sales rep. Met. Life Ins. Co., Prudential Ins. Co., Garden City, N.Y., 1973-75; account mgr. Hallmark Mktg. Corp., Wickford, R.I., 1975—. Named Mktg. Profl. of Year, Hartford dist. Hallmark Cards, 1977. Mem. N.Y. Acad. Scis., Soc. Biomedical Scis. (pres. 1970-71), R.I. Pharmacy Assn. Traveling Mens Aux., Alumni Assn. N.Y. Inst. Tech. Roman Catholic. Home: 157 Lantern Ln E Wickford RI 02852

SABLATASH, MIKE, communications research scientist; b. Bienfiat, Sask., Can., Sept. 30, 1935; s. Fred and Katryna (Rawlinko) S.; B.Sc.Eng., U. Man., 1957, M.Sc., 1964; Ph.D., U. Wis., 1968; m. Sophie Dmyterko, Aug. 5, 1961; children—Tania Deirdre, Loren Dante Michael, Lisa Genevieve. Mem. sci. staff No. Electric Co., Ottawa, Ont., Can., 1961-65; asst. prof. elec. engring. U. Toronto (Ont.), 1968-72; statistician Nat. Energy Bd. Can., Ottawa, 1972-76; research scientist dept. communications Govt. of Can., Ottawa, 1976—; cons. Aladdin Electronics, 1967, Consociates Ltd., U. Toronto, 1968-72. NRC Canada grantee, 1968-72; Ford Found. fellow, 1965-68. Mem. AAAS, IEEE, Assn. Profl. Engrs. Ont., N.Y. Acad. Scis., Sigma Xi. Liberal. Unitarian. Contbr. articles to profl. jours. Home: 16 Bradgate Dr Ottawa ON K2G 0R6 Canada Office: Data Systems and Networks Dept Communications Communications Research Centre PO Box N 11490 Postal Sta H Ottawa ON K2H 8S2 Canada

SABO, JACK CHARLES, thoracic surgeon; b. Bklyn., Sept. 26, 1936; s. Solomon and Nettie S.; B.A., Rutgers U., 1957; M.D., Jefferson Med. Coll., 1961; m. Marilyn Elaine Padgursky, June 21, 1959; children—Stephen, Robert, Elizabeth. Intern, Kings County Hosp., Bklyn., 1961-62, resident in gen. and thoracic surgery 1962-66, 68-70; USPHS fellow Downstate Med. Center, Bklyn., 1963-64; practice medicine specializing in surgery and thoracic surgery, Lakewood, N.J., 1970—; mem. staff Paul Kimball Hosp., Community Meml. Hosp. Adviser Med. Explorers Post 4, 1974—; mem. council Boy Scouts Am., 1975—; trustee Temple Beth Am, 1973—, v.p., 1976-77, pres., 1978-79. Served as capt. M.C., U.S. Army, 1966-68. Diplomate Am. Bd. Surgery, Am. Bd. Thoracic Surgery. Fellow A.C.S., Am. Coll. Chest Physicians, Acad. Medicine N.J.; mem. AMA, Ocean County Med. Soc., Alpha Omega Alpha, Phi Beta Kappa. Clubs: Rotary (dir. 1978) (Lakewood); Woodlake Country (dir. 1976—). Office: 5 Prospect St Lakewood NJ 08701

SABOKBAR, NASSER, pediatric allergist; b. Teheran, Iran, June 18, 1927; s. Shamsedin and Ghamar S.; M.D., U. Geneva (Switzerland), 1956; m. M. Ann Wallis, Aug. 1, 1959; children—Julie M., Karen L. House physician St. Peters Hosp., Chertsey, Eng., 1956-57; sr. house officer Childrens Hosp., Nottingham, Eng., 1957-58, Childrens Hosp., Derby, Eng., 1958-59; resident in pediatrics Strong Meml. Hosp., Rochester, N.Y., 1961-62; practice medicine specializing in pediatrics, Lansdale, Pa., 1962-66, specializing in pediatric allergy, Sellersville, Pa., 1967—; fellow in pediatric allergy St. Christophers Hosp., Phila., 1966-67. Diplomate Am. Bd. Pediatrics, Am. Bd. Allergy and Immunology. Fellow Am. Coll. Allergy, Am. Acad. Pediatrics, Am. Acad. Allergy, Am. Coll. Chest Physicians; mem. AMA, Brit. Med. Assn., Phila., Pa. allergy socs. Clu Rotary. Home: 127 Holly Dr Lansdale PA 19446 Office: 711 Lawn Ave Sellersville PA 18960

SABOTTKE, HELEN LOUISE AHLBERG, educator; b. Middletown, Conn., Dec. 7, 1926; B.S. in Bus. Edn., Central Conn., State Coll., New Britain, 1949; M.S. in Elementary Edn., So. Conn. State Coll., New Haven, 1967, diploma in reading, 1971; certificate in adminstrn., U. Bridgeport, Conn., 1974; children—Craig, Mark. Tchr., Trumbull (Conn.) Bd. Edn.; 1963-70, cons., reading, 1970-74, coordinator, reading and lang. arts, 1974—; also dir. right-to-read program. Certified elementary edn., reading cons.; Title IV grantee. Mem. Internat. Reading Assn., NEA, Conn. Edn. Edn. Assn., Conn. Assn. Right-to-Read, Nat. Assn. Tchrs. English, Smithsonia Assos., Kappa Delta Pi, Delta Kappa Gamma (pres. chpt.). Home: 17 Old Orchard Ln Trumbull CT 06611 Office: Trumbull High Sch Strobel Rd Trumbull CT 06611

SACCO, ANTHONY CARMINE, accountant; b. N.Y.C., May 6, 1921; s. John and Maria (Bruno) S.; B.B.A., St. John's U., 1948; m. Angelina Pellegrino, June 24, 1951; children—John M., Marie, Michael. Accountant, Gaynor News Co., Mt. Vernon, N.Y., 1948-52, Murray G. Levine, N.Y.C., 1953-55, Consol. Retail Stores, Inc., N.Y.C., 1956-57, Colonial Trust Co., N.Y.C., 1958-60; accountant Joel E. Mitchell & Co., N.Y.C., 1961—, gen. partner, 1969-76; with Matthews, Panariello Profl. Corp., N.Y.C. and Fiduciary Spl. Services, Inc., 1978—. Served with AUS, 1942-45. C.P.A., N.Y. Mem. Am. Inst. C.P.A.'s, N.Y. State Soc. C.P.A.'s. Home: 1 Parr Rd Valhalla NY 10595 Office: 2 World Trade Center New York City NY 10048

SACCOCCIO, ANTHONY ROBERT, former real estate co. exec., jewelry findings mfg. co. exec.; b. Cranston, R.I., Jan. 20, 1910; s. Luigi and Maddalina (DeMeo) S.; grad. pub. schs., Cranston; m. Katherine DeLellis, June, 1931, (dec. Feb. 1938); children—Louis A., Madeline A. (Mrs. Robert F. Montaquila). Toolmaker, T. & R. Jewelry Co., Providence, 1926-32, Albert Mfg. Co., Providence, 1933-35; pres. Aro-Sac Inc., Providence, 1935-72, chmn. bd., 1972-78; pres., treas. A.R. Saccoccio Co., Inc., Providence, 1941-78; chmn. bd. Cas-Ora Ltd., Providence, 1973-78. Mem. Jewelry Bd. Trade, Providence C. of C., St. Mary's Feast Soc. (hon.). Roman Catholic. Elk. Clubs: City Hall Athletic (pres. 1943-45), Alpine Country (Cranston). Patentee in jewelry field. Home: 39 Hamden Rd Cranston RI 02920 Office: 350 Washington St Providence RI 02903

SACCONE, ANTHONY DANIEL, educator; b. Foggia, Italy, Jan. 10, 1922; s. Nicola and Maria (Albano) S.; permanent cert. SUNY, Oswego, 1966; B.A., Empire State Coll., 1973; naturalized, 1928; m. May 22, 1948; children—Anthony and Daniel (twins). Offset pressman Greenwood Co., Albany, N.Y., 1940-42; owner Artistic Press, Albany, 1946-48; compositor Brate Printing Office, 1948-51, Knickerbocker News, 1951-58; tchr. Albany Occupational Center, 1958-78; coordinator Urban Center, Albany, 1968; pub., editor Salem Hills Lamp Post, 1968-70; chief negotiator Albany Pub. Sch. Tchrs. Assn., 1970-71. Pres. Salem Hills Park Assn., 1967-68, Salem Hills Owners Trust, 1968-70; exec. officer Glenmont Devel. Corp., 1967-68. Served with U.S. Army, 1942-46. Mem. Internat. Typographical Union, N.Y. State United Tchrs., Albany Pub. Sch. Tchrs. Assn. Roman Catholic. Club: K.C. Home: 18 Par Circle Albany NY 12208 Office: 99 Kent St Albany NY 12206

SACEWICZ, MARTIN ROBERT, pharmacist; b. N.Y.C., Aug. 21, 1933; s. Matthew Philip and Anna (Lashkow) S.; B.S., Fordham U., 1954; M.S., Bklyn. Coll. Pharmacy, 1973; m. Linda Vivian Nelin, May 4, 1963; children—Lisa Nicole, Laura Natalie. Pharmacist, C. & R. Timmermann Pharmacy, N.Y.C., 1954-56, mgr., 1956-58; staff pharmacist Dept. Hosps., N.Y.C., 1958-62; chief pharmacist for operations The New York Hosp., N.Y.C., 1962-72; staff pharmacist St. Elizabeth's Hosp., N.Y.C., 1973-75; dir. of pharmacy Jewish Meml. Hosp., N.Y.C., 1975—; purchasing dir. pharms. and hosp. supplies Interglobal Distbn. Ltd., N.Y.C.; adj. prof. Arnold and Marie Schwartz Coll. Pharmacy. Mem. Am. Soc. Hosp. Pharmacists, N.Y. State Council Hosp. Pharmacists, Am. Pharm Assn., N.Y. Botan. Garden, N.Y. Zool. Soc. Republican. Ukranian Orthodox. Home: 2425 Hering Ave Bronx New York City NY 10469 Office: Jewish Meml Hosp Broadway and 196th St New York City NY 10040

SACHAR, HOWARD MORLEY, historian; b. St. Louis, Feb. 10, 1928; s. Abram Leon and Thelma (Horwitz) S.; B.A., Swarthmore Coll., 1947; M.A., Harvard U., 1950, Ph.D., 1953; m. Eliana Steimatzky, July 23, 1964; children—Sharon, Michele, Daniel. Instr. history U. Mass., 1953-54; dir. Hillel Found., U. Calif., Los Angeles, 1954-57; dir. Hillel Found., Stanford U., 1959-61; dir. Hiatt Inst. in Israel, 1961-64; asso. prof. history George Washington U., Washington, 1964-66, prof. history, 1966—. Charles Brown fellow, 1957-58, Nat. Endowment for Humanities fellow, 1970-71. Mem. Am. Hist. Assn., Am. Jewish Hist. Soc. Democrat. Jewish. Author: The Course of Modern Jewish History, 1958; Aliyah, 1961; From the Ends of the Earth, 1964; The Emergence of the Middle East, 1969; Europe Leaves the Middle East, 1972; A History of Israel, 1976. Home: 9807 Hillridge Dr Kensington MD 20795 Office: Dept History George Washington U Washington DC 20052

SACHAR, THOMAS VINCENT, chem. engr.; b. Yonkers, N.Y., June 3, 1942; s. Vincent Joseph and Casimira Regina Sachar; B.Chem.Engring., Manhattan Coll., 1964; M.B.A., Fairleigh Dickinson U., 1979; m. Rozalie Stram, Oct. 15, 1966; children—Barbara, Kenneth, Steven, Tina. Quality Control supr. U.S. Gypsum Co., Stony Point, N.Y., 1964-66; research engr. propellants and explosives Picatinny Arsenal, Dept. Army, Dover, N.J., 1966-69; project engr. explosives facilities modernization Hdqrs. U.S. Army Munitions Command, Dover, 1969-73; tech. mgr. munitions prodn. base modernization U.S. Army Devel. and Readiness Command, Dover, 1973—. Foreman, Warren County (N.J.) Grand Jury, 1976. Recipient Outstanding Performance award Dept. Army, 1971, 72, 77. Mem. Am. Def. Preparedness Assn., Am. Mgmt. Assn., Am. Inst. Chem. Engrs., Holy Name Soc. (pres. 1977-78). Roman Catholic. Home: 5 Somerset Dr Belvidere NJ 07823 Office: US Army Devel and Readiness Command Picatinny Arsenal Bldg 171 Dover NJ 07801

SACHS, JULIUS JOHNSON, physician; b. Waterbury, Conn., Apr. 8, 1915; s. Henry M. and Gertrude (Johnson) S.; B.A., Yale U., 1936; M.D., N.Y. U., 1940; m. Sylvia Sandra Glassman, June 25, 1944; children—Rhoda Sachs Zahler, Carolyn Faye, Harriet Sachs Sessa, Joseph Alan. Intern, Bellevue Hosp., N.Y.C., 1940-42, asst. resident, 1946; asst. in medicine, N.Y. U., N.Y.C., 1948-50, clin. instr. internal medicine, 1950-51; practice medicine specializing in internal medicine, Hartford, Conn., 1951—; attending staff Mt. Sinai Hosp., also trustee, 1977—. Served to maj. M.C., USAAF, 1942-46. Decorated Bronze Stars. Diplomate Am. Bd. Internal Medicine. Fellow A.C.P.; mem. Alpha Omega Alpha. Contbr. articles in field to profl. jours. Office: 60 Gillett St Hartford CT 06105

SACHS, LEE ALLEN, psychologist; b. N.Y.C., June 5, 1945; s. Erwin and Berta (Linker) S.; B.S. in English and Edn., Belknap Coll., 1968; M.S. in Guidance, L.I. U., 1970; postgrad. St. John's U., 1970-72; Ed.D. in Counseling Psychology, U. S.D., 1973. Intern in family therapy St. John's U., Jamaica, N.Y., 1971; supr. internship in psychol. testing and group therapy Yankton (S.D.) State Hosp., 1972; tchr. N.Y.C. Bd. Edn., 1970-72; dir. human relations workshops Sheldon (Iowa) Sch. Systems, 1972-73; dir. of youth and family counseling YMCA of L.I., 1975-76; pvt. practice counseling, Kings Park, N.Y., 1976—; instr. adult edn. Commack (N.Y.) High Sch., 1978; coordinator Indian Awareness Workshops, U. S.D., Vermillion, 1974-75. Mem. Am. Personnel and Guidance Assn. Democrat. Jewish. Author: Rape Intervention Resource Manual, 1977. Home and office: 86 Rosewood Rd Kings Park NY 11754

SACHS, WALTER, JR., planning cons., educator; b. Phila., May 13, 1930; s. Walter and Virginia (Metzgar) S.; B.A., Pa. State U., 1953; M.Arch., U. Pa., 1966, M. City Planning, 1970; m. Sally Binford, Aug. 18, 1950; children—Sandra Sachs Graves, Suzanne Sachs Haslett, Steven, Scott. Vice pres. Walter S. Sachs & Co., Inc., investments, Phila., 1954-62; treas. Rahenkamp Sachs Wells & Assos. Inc., planners, Phila., 1965-76; pres. First Phila. Group, Inc., real estate and cons., 1976—; adj. prof. city planning U. Pa., Phila., 1973—. Constable, local election poll, 1971-74. Named Planner of Year with John Rahenkamp, House and Home Mag., 1969. Mem. Am. Inst. Planners, Swedish Colonial Soc., Lambda Alpha. Clubs: Faculty, Racquet. Contbr. articles to profl. jours. Home: 83 Merbrook Ln Merion PA 19066 Office: PO Box 249 King of Prussia PA 19406

SACHS-STERN, LISBETH JOSEPHINE, psychiatrist; b. Grandenz, Germany; d. Sally and Johanna (Leiser) Samulon; B.S., U. Wurzburg, 1930; M.D., U. Berlin, 1934; M.D., U. Berne, 1938; m. 2d, Bernard Herbert Stern. Intern Berlin (Germany) Jewish Hosp., 1935-36, resident 1936-38; resident in pathology Lincoln Hosp., Bronx, N.Y.C., 1941-42, Queens Gen. Hosp., N.Y.C., 1942-44; asst. pathologist Greenpoint Hosp., 1944-46; resident psychiatrist Hillside Hosp., 1952-54; pvt. practice, N.Y.C., 1951—; resident psychiatrist Kings County Hosp. Center, 1954-55, chief psychiatrist Children's and Adolescent Services and Child Guidance Clinic, 1955-58; attending psychiatrist Gracie Sq. Hosp., N.Y.C., 1962—; asso. attending psychiatrist Flower and Fifth Av. hosps., N.Y.C., 1966—, Brookdale Hosp. Center; cons. psychiatrist Jewish Bd. Guardians, Madeleine Borg Child Guidance Inst., 1962-63; asst. prof. psychiatry State U. N.Y. Med. Coll. at Downstate Med. Center, 1957-66, N.Y. Sch. Psychiatry, N.Y.C., 1958-60; asso. clin. prof. N.Y. Med. Coll., 1966—; asso. clin. prof. psychiatry N.Y. U. med. center, 1970—. Mem. profl. adv. com. Childville, Inc. State U. N.Y. Research Found. grantee, 1958-66. Mem. A.M.A., Research Soc. N.Y. State Med. Center, N.Y. Council Child Psychiatry, Bklyn. Assn. Mental Health, N.Y. State U. Research Soc., Kings County Med. Soc., N.Y. Path. Soc., Am., Bklyn. psychiat. assns., Am. Orthopsychiat. Assn., Hillside Hosp. Alumni Assn., N.Y. Acad. Scis., A.A.A.S., Internat. Platform Assn., Am. Acad. Child Psychiatry, Am. Soc. Adolescent Psychiatry, Royal Soc. Health. Mem. Hadassah. Author articles in med. jours., books in field. Home: 750 Kappock St Riverdale NY 10463 Office: 10 Plaza St Brooklyn NY 11238 also 750 Kappock St Riverdale NY 10463

SACKLOW, STEWART IRWIN, advt. exec.; b. Albany, N.Y., July 29, 1942; s. Jacob David and Freda Ruth (Pearlman) S.; A.A.S., N.Y.C. Community Coll., 1962; B.S., Western Mich. U., 1965; m. Harriette Lynn Cooperman, July 2, 1967; 1 son, Ian Marc. Asst. dist. office Humble Oil & Refining Co., Inc., Albany, 1963-65; dir. advt. and sales promotion Albany Pub. Markets div. Weiss Foods, 1965-68; v.p. advt. and sales promotion Golub Corp., Schenectady, 1968-78; pres., creative dir. Wolkcas Advt., Inc., 1978—. Mem. Dist. Atty.'s readiness team; active Albany County Cerebral Palsy Telethons, 1966-68; mem. fund drive com. WMHT-TV ednl. TV, 1967-74; bd. dirs. Video Spirit, Upstate Leukemia Assn.; mem. bd. Gov. Clinton council Boy Scouts Am. Recipient certificate merit Nat. Research Bur., 1966, Freedoms Found., 1966, Amsterdam Recorder, 1968, Retail Advt. Conf., 1969, 70, Woman's Day Mag., 1971, 72, 73, 74, 75, 76; Grand Nat. award Am. Dairy Assn., 1969, Hunt Wesson Foods, 1970; recipient 4 1st place awards Am. Advt. Fedn., 1972, Crystal Prism award, 1973; Effie award Am. Mgmt. Assn., 1972; Silver medal award Am. Advt. Fed., 1973, Addy award, 1973, 74, 75; award excellence Retail Advt. Conf., 1971; Best 15 Internat. Ads award Internat. Newspaper Advt. Execs., 1972. Mem. Ad Club N.Y. (dir., 1974—, pres., 1976—; Am. Advt. Fedn. (bd. govs. 1975). Profl. Pub. Relations Council. Mem. B'nai B'rith. Clubs: Albany Yacht, Schenectady Racquet. Home: 162 Fairfield Ct Voorheesville NY 12186 Office: 8 Wade Rd Latham NY 12110

SADA, RUDOLPH MUNTU, physician; b. Indonesia, Oct. 3, 1946; s. Joseph Hadisuyono and Lucy Sada; M.D., U. Indonesia, 1971; came to U.S., 1972, naturalized, 1978; m. Tien Sulistini Sudira, Oct. 3, 1970; children—Abraham Gene, Cynthia Natalie. Resident in internal medicine U. Indonesia Hosp., 1971-72; intern Beekman Hosp., N.Y.C., 1972-73, resident, 1973-74; resident in nuclear medicine State U. N.Y. at Buffalo Med. Sch. Hosps., 1974-76, clin. asso. in nuclear medicine, 1974—; fellow in nuclear medicine Roswell Park Meml. Inst., Buffalo, 1976; dir. nuclear medicine Lockport (N.Y.)

Meml. Hosp., 1976—. Diplomate Am. Bd. Nuclear Medicine. Mem. Soc. Nuclear Medicine, ACP, AMA, Med. Soc. Niagara County, State Med. Soc. N.Y. Home: 7076 Academy Ln Lockport NY 14094 Office: Lockport Meml Hosp 521 East Ave Lockport NY 14094

SADEGHI-NEJAD, ABDOLLAH, physician; b. Meshed, Iran, Apr. 29, 1938; s. Abdolhossein and Azizeh (Djabbari) S.-N.; came to U.S., 1958, naturalized, 1970; B.A., Beloit Coll., 1960; M.S., M.D., U. Chgo., 1964; m. Marion M. Marquardt, Jan. 26, 1974; 1 son, Nathan Reza. Intern, U. Chgo. Hosps., 1964-65, resident in pediatrics, 1965-67; fellow in pediatric endocrinology and metabolism Tufts New Eng. Med. Center, 1967-69; fellow in pediatric endocrinology U. Calif., San Francisco, 1969-70; asso. prof. pediatrics Tufts U. Sch. Medicine, Boston, 1970—; pediatric endocrinologist New Eng. Med. Center, Boston, 1970—. Recipient Sheard-Sanford award Am. Soc. Clin. Pathologists, 1964. Nat. Endowment Humanities fellow, summer 1974; diplomate Am. Bd. Pediatrics. Mem. AAAS, N.Y. Acad. Sci., Am. Acad. Pediatrics, Endocrine Soc., Am. Diabetes Assn., Mass. Med. Soc., Inst. Society, Ethics and Life Scis., Lawson Wilkins Pediatric Endocrine Soc., Soc. Pediatric Research. Contbr. articles in pediatric endocrinology to med. jours. Home: 125 Arlington Rd Chestnut Hill MA 02167 Office: 171 Harrison Ave Boston MA 02111

SADETSKY, HARRIET JANET, guidance counselor; b. Queens, N.Y., May 4, 1934; d. Abe and Fay (Stampler) Wolfman; student Nassau Community Coll., 1960-63; A.B., Empire State Coll., State U. N.Y., 1974; M.S. C. W. Post Coll., L.I. U., 1975, P.D. (scholar), 1977; m. Irwin S. Sadetsky, June 22, 1952; 2 sons, Steven Mark, Richard Errol. Traffic safety project asst. Nassau Bd. Coop. Ednl. Services, 1969-74; attendance tchr., Levittown (N.Y.) Pub. Schs., 1974-75; guidance counselor Islip (N.Y.) Jr. High Sch., 1976—. Campaign coordinator, Dorfman for dist. atty. Nassau County, 1968; pres. S. Nassau Unitarian Ch., Freeport, N.Y., 1971-72; pres. Civil Service Employees Assn., Nassau Boces, 1972. Mem. Am., N.Y. State, Western Suffolk personnel and guidance assns., N.Y. State Sch. Counselors Assn., Vocat. Guidance Assn., Phi Delta Kappa. Democrat. Home: 205 Lincoln Ave Port Jefferson NY 11777 Office: Islip Junior High School 211 Main St Islip NY 11751

SADLON, ERROL MICHAEL, rehab. counselor; b. Butler, Pa., Aug. 24, 1946; s. Gustav Earl and Virginia (Bartsch) S.; B.S., W.Va. Wesleyan U., 1968; M.Edn. in Counselor Edn., Slippery Rock (Pa.) State Coll., 1975; postgrad. Pa. State U., 1977-78; m. Joyce Dresch, Apr. 11, 1972; 1 son, Michael Jonathan. Environmentalist, Butler County, Butler, 1971-73; rehab. counselor Pa. Bur. Vocat. Rehab., New Castle, 1973-77; dir. client services Butler Sheltered Workshop, 1977—. Served with U.S. Army, 1969-71. Am. Field Service student, Finland, 1963. Mem. Am. Personnel and Guidance Assn., Nat. Vocat. Guidance Assn., Am. Rehab. Counseling Assn. Democrat. Lutheran. Home: 106 Fairway Dr Butler PA 16001 Office: 100 N Washington St Butler PA 16001

SADOWSKI, EDWARD PETER, metallurgist; b. Bayonne, N.J., July 16, 1922; s. Adam and Florence (Domurat) S.; B.S. in Metallurgy, U. Notre Dame, 1950; postgrad. Stevens Inst. Tech., 1953-54, William Paterson Coll., 1977-78; m. Charlotte Trudelle, Sept. 3, 1949; children—Peter, Richard, Anne, Edith, Mary. Staff metallurgist M.W. Kellogg Co., Jersey City, 1950-53; sr. metallurgist Crucible Steel Co. Am., Harrison, N.J., 1953-55; sr. project engr. Internat. Nickel Co., Inc., Bayonne, N.J. and Suffern, N.Y., 1955—. Served with USAAF, 1943-46. Recipient IR 100 award Indsl. Research mag., 1963. Mem. Am. Soc. Metals, Am. Welding Soc., N.Y. Acad. Sci., Sigma Xi (past br. pres.). Clubs: K.C. (past diocese chmn.); Marian Columbia Assn. (pres. 1977-78) (Pompton Lakes, N.J.). Author, patentee in field. Home: 57 Walker Dr Ringwood NJ 07456 Office: Internat Nickel Co Inc Sterling Forest Suffern NY 10901

SADRUDDIN, MOE, constrn. co. exec.; b. Hyderabad, India, Mar. 3, 1943; s. Mohammed and Izzath Unnisa (Begum) Jamaluddin; came to U.S., 1964, naturalized, 1974; B.S., Osmania U., 1964; M.S., N.Y. U., 1966; I.E., Columbia U., 1969, M.B.A., 1970; m. Aug. 25, 1964; children—Irfan, Rubaina. Engr., Ford Bacon & Davis, N.Y.C., 1966; staff engr. J.C. Penney Co., N.Y.C., 1966-68; sr. cons. Drake Sheahan Stewart Dougall, N.Y.C., 1968-70, Beech-Nut, Inc., N.Y.C., 1970-72; pres., founder Azmath Constrn. Corp., Englewood, N.J., 1972—. Grad. fellow Calif. Inst. Tech., 1964. Home and Office: Kenwood St Englewood NJ 07631

SADTLER, BARBARA ANN KOLTES, mktg. exec.; b. Hutchinson, Kans., Mar. 1, 1940; d. Edwin Michael and Rose (Meyers) Koltes; B.A., U. Minn., 1961. With fashion dept. Dayton's in Mpls., 1956-61; fgn. affairs analyst Dept. of Def., Washington, 1961-63; fashion coordinator Jordan Marsh, Boston, 1963-65; fashion editor, columnist Newhouse Nat. News Service, 1965-72; corporate v.p. advt. and promotion Leslie Fay, Inc., N.Y.C., 1972-77; dir. mktg. Helena Rubenstein Inc., N.Y.C., 1977—. Mem. Fashion Group, AAUW, Delta Gamma. Home: 213 Riverside Ave Riverside CT 06878 also 400 E 56th St New York City NY 10022 Office: 300 Park Ave New York City NY 10018

SADWIN, ARNOLD, neurologist, psychiatrist, psychoanalyst; b. Woonsocket, R.I., Nov. 12, 1926; s. Louis Eli and Edythe F. (Finstein) S.; B.A., Boston U., 1948; postgrad. spl. student Brown U., 1948-49; postgrad. in dentistry Northwestern U., 1951-52; M.D., Chgo. Med. Sch., 1956; grad. Phila. Psychoanalytic Inst., 1969; m. Sue Matney, Nov. 24, 1955; children—Donna Liane, Stuart Glenn, Lori Sheryl. Cancer researcher R.I. Hosp., 1949-50; intern, Jackson Meml. Hosp., Miami, Fla., 1956-57; resident in psychiatry Lafayette Clinic, Detroit, 1957-60; practice medicine specializing in neurology and psychiatry, Phila., 1960—, also specializing in psychoanalysis, 1969—; psychoanalytic cons. Presbyterian Neighborhood Counseling Center; cons. pastoral counseling ednl. tng. Presbyn. U. of Pa. Hosp., Phila., 1968-75; med. dir., v.p. Multiple Sclerosis Assn. So. N.J. Served with USNR, 1945-46. Recipient Humanitarian of Yr. award Multiple Sclerosis Assn. So. N.J., 1975; Amateur Radio Operator of Yr. award Dayton Hamfest, 1977. Fellow Am. Acad. Psychosomatic Medicine; mem. AMA (Physicians Recognition award), Am., South Jersey psychiat. assns., Am. Acad. Psychosomatic Medicine, Phila. Med. Soc., Pa. Med. Assn., Four Chaplains Legion of Honor. Clubs: Phil Mont Mobile Radio (pres.), Delaware Valley amateur radio assns., South Jersey Radio Assn., Camden County (N.J.) Auto Patch Repeater Assn. Contbr. articles to profl. publs. Home: 1205 Heartwood Dr Cherry Hill NJ 08003 Office: 275 S 19th St Philadelphia PA 19103

SADWITH, HOWARD MARVIN, mfg. co. exec.; b. N.Y.C., Dec. 23, 1916; s. Ryan and Rosalind (Shack) S.; M.E., Stevens Inst. Tech., 1938; m. Elizabeth Glasser, June 24, 1941; children—Geoffrey, Barbara, John, James. Sales engr. Indsl. Washing Machine Corp., Matawan, N.J., 1938-43, v.p., 1943-50, pres., chmn. bd., 1950—. Registered profl. engr., N.J. Mem. ASME (chmn. fin. com.), Matawan C. of C. (dir. 1970, now pres.). Club: Optimist. Home: 16 Fairway E Colts Neck NJ 07722 Office: 32 Main St Matawan NJ 07747

SAFE, KENNETH SHAW, JR., profl. trustee co. exec.; b. Providence, Oct. 13, 1929; s. Kenneth Shaw and Louise (King) S.; A.B., Harvard, 1951; m. Elizabeth Kelley, Dec. 20, 1952; children—Hope, Elizabeth; Kenneth, Thorn and Edith (triplets). Intelligence officer CIA, Washington, 1954-56; with trust dept. Old Colony Trust Co., Boston, 1956-59; registered rep. Tucker Anthony & R.L. Day, Boston, 1959-68; partner Welch & Forbes, Boston, 1968—; trustee Adams Fiduciary Bond Fund, Boston; dir. Abnaki Resources Corp., Boston. Trustee, asst. treas. Woods Hole (Mass.) Oceanographic Instn.; bd. dirs., past pres. Travelers Aid Soc. of Boston, Inc.; bd. dirs., past pres. Community Workshops, Inc., Boston; corporator New Eng. Deaconess Hosp., Boston; bd. dirs., asst. treas. Boston Port and Seaman's Aid Soc.; bd. dirs., treas. Boys and Girls Camps, Inc., Boston. Served with U.S. Army, 1952-54. Mem. Boston Security Analysts Soc. Republican. Episcopalian. Clubs: Somerset, Country, Duxbury Yacht, Marshall St. Hist., Mason. Home: 207 King Caesar Rd Duxbury MA 02332 Office: 73 Tremont St Boston MA 02108

SAFFORD, ROBERT OWEN, ins. co. exec.; b. Meadville, Pa., Aug. 3, 1934; s. Owen S.; B.S., Cornell U., Ithaca, N.Y., 1956; m. Patricia Hofheins, Dec. 18, 1956; children—Robert Owen, Susan Diane, Thomas Hofheins, Ann Elizabeth. Nat. sales trainer Easterling Co., Chgo., 1958-62; regional dir. Land of Lincoln Life Ins. Co., Springfield, Ill., 1962-63; co-founder, dir., exec. v.p. Alexander Hamilton Life Ins. Co., Farmington, Mich., 1963-71; dir. Nat. Liberty Corp., Valley Forge, Pa., 1972-75; exec. v.p., chief operating officer Nat. Home Life Assurance Co., Malvern, Pa., 1973—. Active Campus Crusade for Christ, Voice of Christian Youth, Christian Businessmen's Com. Served to 1st lt. USMC, 1956-58. Mem. Sales/Mktg. Execs., Internat. Platform Assn., Nat. Assn. Life Cos. (v.p.), Fellowship of Christian Athletes, Delta Upsilon. Republican. Clubs: Cornell, Orchard Lake Country, Waynesborough Country; Detroit Athletic (Detroit). Home: 403 Margo Ln Berwyn PA 19312 Office: Nat Home Life Assurance Co Liberty Park Malvern PA 19355

SAFIRE, WILLIAM, journalist, author; b. N.Y.C., Dec. 19, 1929; s. Oliver C. and Ida (Panish) S.; student Syracuse U., 1947-49; m. Helene Belmar Julius, Dec. 16, 1962; children—Mark Lindsey, Annabel Victoria. Reporter, N.Y. Herald Tribune Syndicate, 1949-51; corr. WNBC-WNBT, Europe and Middle East, 1951; radio-TV producer WNBC, N.Y.C., 1954-55; v.p. Tex McCrary, Inc., 1955-60; pres. Safire Pub. Relations, Inc., 1960-68; spl. asst. to Pres., Washington, 1969-73; columnist N.Y. Times, Washington, 1973—. Served with U.S. Army, 1952-54. Recipient Pulitzer Prize, 1978. Republican. Author: The Relations Explosion, 1963; Plunging into Politics, 1964; The New Language of Politics, 1968, rev. edit., 1972; Before the Fall, 1975; Full Disclosure, 1977; Safire's Political Dictionary, 1978. Address: NY Times 1000 Connecticut Ave NW Washington DC 20036

SAFRO, PAUL, accountant; b. Warsaw, Poland, May 29, 1912; s. Meyer and Fannie (Zelaznick) S.; came to U.S., 1932, naturalized, 1938; student Baruch Sch., Coll. City N.Y., 1933-40; m. Rose Roth; children—Julia Safro Edelman, Marti Safro Kutnik, Naomi Safro Kolbrenner, Adele Safro Rosen. Owner, Paul Safro, C.P.A., N.Y.C., 1939-64; sr. partner Safro, Gould & Rudolph, C.P.A.'s, N.Y.C., 1964-71, Westheimer, Fine, Berger & Co., C.P.A.'s, N.Y.C., 1971—, Elmer Fox, Westheimer & Co., C.P.A.'s, 1975—; past dir. Flushing (N.Y.) Nat. Bank. Past pres. Kfar Masada, Inc., Youth summer camp; chmn. Israel Bonds, 1953-65; mem. World Zionist Action Com., 1971—, mem. Jewish Agy. Assembly, 1973—; bd. dirs. United Jewish Appeal, 1973—, Rabbi Herzog World Acad., Jerusalem, 1965—; trustee Am. Friends of Tel Aviv U., 1972—; pres. Bnai Zion, 1978; v.p. Am.-Israel Friendship League, 1977. C.P.A., N.Y. Mem. N.Y. Soc. C.P.A.'s, Am. Inst. C.P.A.'s. Clubs: Masons, Odd Fellows, B'nai B'rith, Lawrence Golf. Author: Pay-As-You-Go-Tax Explained; Your Tax Guide. Home: 360 Central Ave Lawrence NY 11559 Office: 1211 Ave of Americas New York City NY 10036

SAGALL, ELLIOT LAWRENCE, physician; b. Chelsea, Mass., July 6, 1918; s. Barnard and Rose (Ansel) S.; A.B. magna cum laude, Harvard, 1939, M.D. cum laude, 1943; m. Annette Yvonne Turn, June 16, 1944; children—Richard Joel, Ronald David. Intern Beth Israel Hosp., Boston, 1943, resident, 1944-45; practice medicine specializing in cardiology, Boston, 1948—; mem. staff Beth Israel Hosp., Boston, Brookline Hosp., Boston; clin. instr. medicine Harvard Med. Sch., 1948-76, asst. clin. prof., 1976—; instr. legal medicine Boston Coll. Law Sch., 1970—; lectr. law and medicine Boston U. Sch. Law, 1969-71. Bd. dirs. Mass. Heart Assn., 1969-76, mem. exec. com., 1973-75. Served with M.C., AUS, 1945-47. Diplomate Nat. Bd. Med. Examiners, Am. Bd. Internal Medicine. Fellow Am. Coll. Cardiology, Am. Acad. Compensation Medicine (gov. 1967—), Council Clin. Cardiology; mem. Am. Soc. Law and Medicine (pres. 1973—), Mass. Soc. Law and Medicine (pres. 1972-73), Am. Heart Assn. (founding mem. com. stress, strain and heart disease 1969—), Phi Beta Kappa, Alpha Omega Alpha. Author: (with J.E.F. Riseman) Electrocardiogram Clinics, 1958, Cardiac Arrhythmias, 1963; (with B.C. Reed) The Heart and the Law, 1968, The Law and Clinical Medicine, 1970; Medicine in the Courtroom, 1971; editor: (with I. Lucas) Malpractice Hazards in Cardiology, 1973; exec. editor: Am. Jour. Law Medicine, 1976, Medicolegal News, 1975—. Home: 178 Old Farm Rd Newton Center MA 02159 Office: 454 Brookline Ave Boston MA 02215

SAGAN, CARL EDWARD, astronomer, educator; b. N.Y.C., Nov. 9, 1934; s. Samuel and Rachel (Gruber) S.; A.B., U. Chgo., 1954, B.S., 1955, M.S., 1956, Ph.D., 1960; D.Sc., Rensselaer Poly. Inst., Denison U., Clarkson Coll. Tech., 1977, U. Wyo., 1978, Clark U., 1978; D.H.L., Skidmore Coll., 1976. Miller research fellow U. Calif. at Berkeley, 1960-62; vis. asst. prof. genetics Stanford U. Med. Sch., 1962-63; astrophysicist Smithsonian Astrophys. Obs., Cambridge, Mass., 1962-68; lectr., asst. prof. astronomy Harvard, 1962-68; asso. prof, astronomy Cornell U., Ithaca, N.Y., 1968-70, prof., 1970—, now David Duncan prof. astronomy; dir. Lab. Planetary Studies, 1968—. NSF-Am. Astron. Soc. vis. prof. various colls., 1963-67; mem. various adv. groups to NASA and Nat. Acad. Scis., 1960—; mem. adv. council Smithsonian Instn., 1975—; Condon lectr. State of Oreg., 1967-68; vis. asso. Calif. Inst. Tech., 1971-72; Vanuxem lectr. Princeton, 1973; Smith lectr. Dartmouth, 1974; Tobias Wagner lectr. U. Pa., 1975; Jacob Bronowski lectr. U. Toronto, 1975; Royal Instn. lectr., London, 1977; Danz lectr., vis. prof. U. Wash., Seattle, 1976, Damon lectr. NSTA, 1978; Dixon Johnson lectr. Pa. State U., 1978; vice chmn. working group on moon and planets com. on space research Internat. Council Sci. Unions, 1968-74. Chmn. U.S. delegation Joint Nat. Acad. Scis.-Soviet Acad. Sci. Conf. Communication with Extraterrestrial Intelligence, Armenia, 1971. NSF fellow, 1955-60; Alfred Sloan Research fellow, 1963-67; recipient NASA Apollo Achievement Award, 1970, Medal for Exceptional Sci. Achievement, NASA, 1972; Prix Galabert (Internat. Astrons. Prize), Paris, 1973; John W. Campbell Meml. award, 1974; Klumpke-Roberts prize Astron. Soc. Pacific, 1974; Joseph Priestley medal, 1975; NASA medal for disting. pub. service, 1977; Pulitzer prize, 1978. Fellow AAAS (chmn. astronomy sect. 1975-76), AIAA, Am. Astronautical Soc., Am. Geophys. Union; mem. Am. Astronom. Soc. (councillor 1969-72, chmn. div. planetary studies 1975), Am. Phys. Soc., Soc. for Study Evolution, Genetics Soc., Am., Internat. Astronom. Union, Internat. Acad. Astronautics, Sigma Xi. Editor: Icarus: Internat. Jour. Solar System Studies, 1968—; Planetary Atmospheres, 1971; Space Research XI, 1971; UFO's: A Scientific Debate, 1972; Communication with Extraterrestrial Intelligence, 1973. Research on physics and chemistry of planetary atmospheres and surfaces, space vehicle exploration of planets, exobiology. Author: Atmospheres of Mars and Venus, 1961; Planets, 1966; Intelligent Life in the Universe, 1966; Planetary Exploration, 1970; The Cosmic Connection, 1973 (Campbell Meml. award); Mars and the Mind of Man, 1973; Other Worlds, 1975; Dragons of Eden (Pulitzer prize, Book-of-Month Club selection). Office: Lab Planetary Studies Cornell U Ithaca NY 14850

SAGAR, VIDYA VETTIYATTIL, physician; b. Irinjalakuda, Kerala, India, Mar. 31, 1942; s. Kunju Chelakkat and Kunchi Kutty (Vettiyattil) Menon; came to U.S., 1967, naturalized, 1974; B.S., Christ Coll. Kerala, 1961; M.B., B.S., Calicut Med. Coll., India, 1967; M.S., State U.N.Y. at Buffalo, 1972; m. Marsha Bania, June 5, 1970; children—Anita Maya, Jina Priya, Jay Vidya. Med. officer Govt. Kerala, 1967; intern Luth. Med. Center, Bklyn., 1967-68; resident in medicine N.J. Coll. Medicine, Newark, 1968-70; resident in nuclear medicine State U.N.Y. at Buffalo, 1970-72; dir. nuclear medicine dept. VA Hosp., Wilmington, Del., 1972—; asst. prof. nuclear medicine Temple U., Phila., 1973—; instr. medicine Jefferson Med. Coll., Phila., 1973—. Fellow A.C.P.; mem. Am. Coll. Nuclear Physicians (charter), Soc. Nuclear Medicine, Del. Acad. Medicine. Unitarian. Research on mechanism bone blood flow. Home: 2204 Clearview Ave Wilmington DE 19810 Office: 1601 Kirkwood Hwy Wilmington DE 19805

SAGE, ROBERT, hotel exec.; b. Boston, June 11, 1926; s. Harry and Mollie (Goodsnyder) Sagansky; A.B., Colby Coll., 1949, M.A., 1974; m. Phyllis Sara Caplan, June 5, 1949; children—Marjorie, William, Jane. Mgr., Phillips Drug Co., Boston, 1949-50; treas. Coronet Sales Co., Boston, 1950-58; pres. Fenway Motor Hotels, Boston, 1958—; dir. Garden City Trust Co. Chmn., Colby Coll. Alumni Fund, 1968-71; pres. Parker Hill Med. Center, 1968-74; bd. dirs. Jewish Meml. Hosp.; trustee Colby Coll., 1974—, chmn. devel. com., 1975—; v.p. Hebrew Rehab. Center for Aged, 1978—; vice chmn. Greater Boston Conv. and Tourist Bur., 1978—. Served with AUS, 1945-47. Recipient Hotel Hall of Fame award Hospitality mag., 1970, Hotelman of Year award New Eng. Hotel Sales Mgmt. Assn., 1965. Mem. Mass. Hotel-Motel Assn. (pres. 1968-70), Am. Hotel and Motel Assn. (dir. 1974-78), Hotel Sales Mgmt. Assn. (chpt. past pres. 1965), New Eng. Inn Keepers Assn. (pres. 1976-78), Greater Boston Hotel and Motel Inn Assn. (pres. 1971-72), Mass. Restaurant Assn. (dir. 1971-77), Colby Coll. Alumni Assn. (pres. 1972-74), Wightman Tennis Center, Tau Delta Phi. Mason. Home: 6 Cynthia Rd Newton MA 02159 Office: 475 Commonwealth Ave Boston MA 02215

SAGE, ROBERT EPHRAM, psychotherapist; b. N.Y.C., Oct. 1, 1945; s. Aaron and Sylvia (Buiar) S.; B.A., Queens Coll., 1967; Ph.D., St. Johns U., 1976; m. Elaine Zahnstecher, Aug. 17, 1968; children—Holly, Jeremy. Tchr., Pub. Sch. 297, Bklyn., 1968-73; psychol. counselor, dir. peer counseling services Bklyn. Coll., 1973-76; clinic dir. methadone maintenance treatment program Jamaica (N.Y.) Hosp., 1976-77; mental health cons., coordinator mental health services Addiction Research and Treatment Corp., Bklyn., 1977—; clinic dir. Plaza Consultation Center, Flushing, N.Y., 1976—, bd. dirs., 1977—; bd. dirs. Family Consultation Center. Mem. Am. Psychol. Assn., Am. Personnel and Guidance Assn., Assn. Counselor Educators and Suprs., Biofeedback Soc. Am., Biofeedback Soc. N.Y. Home: 214-11 Richland Ave Bayside NY 11364 Office: 937 Fulton St Brooklyn NY 11216 also 140-15 Sanford Ave Flushing NY 11355

SAGER, CLIFFORD JULIUS, psychiatrist; b. N.Y.C., Sept. 28, 1916; s. Max and Lena (Lipman) S.; B.S., Pa. State U., 1937; M.D., N.Y. U., 1941; certificate in psychoanalysis N.Y. Med. Coll., 1949; children—Barbara L., Philip T., Rebecca J., Anthony F. Rotating intern Montefiore Hosp., N.Y.C., 1941-42; resident Bellevue Hosp., N.Y.C., 1942, 46-48; practice medicine specializing in psychiatry, N.Y.C., 1946—; attending psychiatrist Bird S. Colar Hosp., 1960-71; dir. therapeutic services, asso. dean Postgrad. Center Mental Health, 1948-60; vis. psychiatrist, med. bd. Flower and Fifth Ave. Hosp., 1960-71, Met. Hosp., 1960-71, dir. psychiat. tng. and edn. N.Y. Med. Coll., 1960-61, clin. dir., 1960-63, asso. prof. psychiatry, 1960-65, prof., 1966-71, dir. partial hosp. programs and family treatment and study unit, 1964-71; clin. prof. psychiatry Mt. Sinai Sch. Medicine, 1971—; attending psychiatrist Mt. Sinai Hosp., 1971—; chief Behavioral Scis. Gouverneur Hosp.; chief family treatment unit Beth Israel Med. Center, 1970-71, asso. dir. family and group therapy, 1971-74; psychiat. dir. Jewish Family Service, 1974—, also Jewish Bd. Family and Children's Services. Served to capt. M.C., AUS, 1942-46. Diplomate Am. Bd. Neurology and Psychiatry (asso. examiner 1949). Fellow Am. Psychiat. Assn. (life), Am. Orthopsychiat. Assn. (life), Acad. Psychoanalysis, Am. Group Psychotherapy Assn. (pres. 1968-70, dir. 1962—), Soc. Med. Psychoanalysts; mem. AMA, Soc. Med. Psychoanalysts (pres. 1960-61, dir. 1958-62), Am. Soc. Advancement Psychotherapy (dir. 1954-60), N.Y. Soc. Clin. Psychiatry, Eastern Assn. Sex Therapy (pres. 1976-77). Mem. editorial bd. Am. Jour. Orthopsychiatry, 1960-69; Internat. Jour. Group Psychotherapy, 1968—; Family Process, 1969—; Divorce, 1977—, Comprehensive Rev. Jour. Family and Marriage, 1978—; cons. Sexual Medicine, 1974—; editor: Progress in Group and Family Therapy, 1972; co-editor Jour. Sex and Marital Therapy, 1974—, Jour. Marriage and Family Counseling, 1977—, Internat. Jour. Family Counseling, 1977—; author: Marriage Contracts and Couple Therapy, 1976. Contbr. numerous articles to profl. jours. and book Black Ghetto Family in Therapy, 1970. Office: 65 E 76th St New York City NY 10021

SAGER, MARVIN MILES, obstetrician, gynecologist; b. Balt., Aug. 15, 1929; s. Harry H. and Anne (Levin) S.; B.A., U. Va., 1953, M.D., 1957; m. Beverly Rosenberg, June 27, 1954; children—Michael, Wendy. Intern, Ind. U., Indpls., 1957-58; resident Sinai Hosp., Balt., 1958-62; practice medicine specializing in obstetrics and gynecology, Balt., 1962—; mem. staffs Sinai Hosp., Franklin Sq. Hosp., Balt. County Gen. Hosp. Trustee Temple Oheb Shalom, Balt., 1970-73, 2d v.p., 1973-75, 1st v.p., 1975-77, pres., 1977—; mem. med. advisory bd. Save a Heart Found., Planned Parenthood Assn. Pres., Council Synagogue Presidents, 1978-79. Served with USMC, 1950-52. Diplomate Am. Bd. Obstetricians and Gynecology. Fellow Am. Coll. Obstetrics and Gynecology; mem. Balt. City Med. Soc., Md. Soc. Obstetrics and Gynecology. Jewish. Office: 3655 Old Ct Rd Baltimore MD 21208

SAGER, THOMAS BRINKER, plastics engr.; b. Phila., Sept. 17, 1933; s. Aubrey Palmer and Margaret (Brinker) S.; student Embry Riddle Aero. Inst., 1956-58; m. Nancy Dressler, Nov. 4, 1961; children—Tanya, Jonathan. Mgr. applications engring. Ultra Sonic Seal, Broomall, Pa., 1960-75; mgr. plastics applications Sonobond Corp., West Chester, Pa., 1975-76; application devel. engr. Branson Sonic Power Co., Danbury, Conn., 1977—; cons. thermoplastic films and fabrics. Served with U.S. Army, 1953-55; Korea. Mem. Soc. Plastics Engrs. Patentee in field. Home: 127 Sugar St Newton CT 06470

SAGGESE, ANTHONY JAMES, JR., lawyer; b. New Canaan, Conn., Jan. 8, 1949; s. Anthony James and Marie Louise (Schutte) S.; B.S., So. Conn. State Coll., 1971; J.D. magna cum laude, Western New Eng. Coll., 1974; LL.M., N.Y. U., 1977; m. Nancy L. Iversen, May 22, 1976. Admitted to Mass. bar, 1974, Conn. bar, 1977, N.Y. bar, 1975, U.S. Tax Ct. bar, 1978; tax specialist Alexander Grant & Co., N.Y.C., 1975-76; corp. tax atty. Sperry Rand Corp., N.Y.C., 1976-78; corp. tax atty., exec. hdqrs. Texaco Inc., White Plains, N.Y., 1978—. Mem. Am., Conn., Mass., N.Y. State bar assns., Assn. Bar City N.Y. Republican. Roman Catholic. Club: N.Y. U. Contbr. articles to legal and tax jours. Home: 34 Oak Ledge Ln Wilton CT 06897 Office: 2000 Westchester Ave White Plains NY 10650

SAHAI, DUSHYANT BASANTKUMAR, surgeon; b. Allahabad, India, Apr. 21, 1935; s. George Sylvester and Lois (Tika) S.; came to Can., 1963, naturalized, 1970; student Lucknow Christian Coll., 1952; grad. Christian Med. Coll., 1959; m. Sylvia Vasantha Kanagaraj, Dec. 28, 1962; children—Anand, Michelle. Intern, Reddy Meml. Hosp., 1963-64; resident in gen. surgery Montreal Gen. Hosp., 1964-67, 68-69, Jewish Gen. Hosp., Montreal, 1967-68; teaching fellow in surgery Montreal Gen. Hosp., 1969-70; cons. surgeon Santa Cabrini Hosp., Montreal, 1971—. Fellow Royal Coll. Surgeons; mem. Assn. Gen. Surgeons Que. Club: Montreal Country. Contbr. articles in field to profl. jours. Home: 51 Northridge Rd Ile Bizard PQ H9E 1A8 Canada Office: 5601 Belanger St Montreal PQ 410 Canada

SAHANEK, TATANA, librarian, editor; b. Prague, Czechoslovakia, Nov. 2, 1922; d. Emanuel and Frances (Blovsky) Sahanek; naturalized, 1969; JUDr., Masaryk U., Brno, Czechoslovakia, 1947; B.L.S., U. Toronto, Ont., Can., 1953; Ph.D. (Higher Edn. Act fellow), U. Tex., Austin, 1973. Cataloger, Toronto Pub. Library, 1953-55; law librarian, gen. reference librarian Ont. Legis. Library, Toronto, 1956-61; head catalog and classification div. Harvard Law Sch. Library, 1962-65; head catalog dept. Law Library, U. Mich., Ann Arbor, 1965-66; translator, interpreter Dow Chem. Internat., Midland, Mich., 1967-68; librarian-translator Dow Chem. Co., Tex. div., Freeport, 1968-70; asst. librarian Antioch Sch. Law, Washington, 1972-74; editor Index to Legal Priodicals, H.W. Wilson Co., Bronx, N.Y., 1974—. Recipient award U. Tex. Grad. Sch. Subvention Fund, 1972. Mem. Assn. Am. Law Libraries, Spl. Libraries Assn., ALA, Canadian, Ont. library assns., Czechoslovak Soc. Arts and Scis. Clubs: Worldwide Sportsmen's; New York Library. Author: Entries for Provincial Publications, Province of Ontario, 1867-1960, 1960. Editor Index to Legal Periodicals, 1973—. Home: 1590 Anderson Ave 12F Fort Lee NJ 07024 Office: 950 University Ave Bronx NY 10452

SAHLIN, MONTE CARL, clergyman; b. St. Joseph, Mo., May 17, 1948; s. Carl William and June Janice (Wilson) S.; B.A., Loma Linda U., 1970; postgrad., U. Calif. at Riverside, 1972, Pitts. Theol. Sem., 1977; m. Norma Jean Seal, Oct. 20, 1974. Asso. dir. pub. relations Voice of Prophecy Evangelistic Assn., Los Angeles, 1970-71; dir. A.C.T. House, San Bernadino, Calif., 1971; planning dir. Econ. Opportunity Commn., Imperial, Calif., 1972; asst. to pres. Columbia Union Coll., Washington, 1972-73; dir. Boston Urban Ministries, 1974-77; licensed to ministry Seventh-day Adventist ch., 1970; pastor ch., Pitts., 1977—; instr. Kettering Coll., Dayton, Ohio; cons. Urban Tng. Assos., Pitts. Bd. dirs. Riverside (Calif.) Voluntary Action Center, 1971-72, S.E. Calif. Health Systems Agy., El Centro, 1972, Shadyside Action Coalition, Pitts., 1977-78. Mem. Am. Mgmt. Assn., Nat. Soc. Fund Raisers, Nat. Community Devel. Assn., Evangs. for Social Action. Jr. C. of C. Democrat. Author: Student Power in Christian Action, 1972; Handbook for Community Ministry, 1974; editor Jour. Urban Ministry, 1975—. Home and office: 150 Penn St Washington PA 15301

SAID, ABDUL AZIZ, educator; b. Amouda, Syria, Sept. 1, 1930; s. I. Ishak S.; came to U.S., 1950, naturalized, 1962; B.S., Am. U., 1954, M.A., 1955, Ph.D., 1957; m. Elizabeth Miller, Aug. 8, 1964; children—Riyad Michael, Jamil Walter. Prof., Sch. Internat. Service, Am. U., Washington, 1957—; lectr. Fgn. Service Inst., Dept. State, 1962—. Pres., Center for Mediterranean Studies. Recipient Faculty Excellence award Am. U., 1969; Outstanding Faculty award Mortar Bd., 1977; Ann. Coll. award Am. U. Coll. Pub. Affairs, 1978, Univ. Faculty award, 1978. Mem. Internat. Studies Assn. Author: (with Charles O. Lerche, Jr.) Concepts of International Politics, 1963; (with Daniel Collier) Revolutionism, 1968; The African Phenomenon, 1968; Theory of International Relations: The Crisis of Relevance, 1968; America's World Role in the '70's, 1970; Protagonist of Change: Subcultures in Development and Revolution, 1971; (with L.R. Simmons) The New Sovereigns: multinational Corporations as World Powers, 1974, Drugs Politics and Diplomacy, 1974, Ethnicity in an International Context, 1976, Ethnicity and U.S. Foreign Policy, 1977; Human Rights and World Order, 1978; asso. editor Society mag., 1970—. Home: 5045 Garfield St NW Washington DC 20016

SAIDI, AHMAD, export co. exec.; b. Khoy, Iran, Jan. 28, 1904; s. Abol Hassan and Khanombozorg (Abolghassemi) S.; came to U.S., 1931; B.A., U. Okla., 1935; M.A., George Washington U., 1937; m. Elizabeth Gettner, Feb. 12, 1954; 1 son, Ali Emerson. Asst. to pres. M. Dilmaghani & Co., Scarsdale, N.Y., 1938-41; instr. Persian Inst., 1942; chief Persian Desk, OWI, N.Y.C., 1942-43; chief Persian sect. Dept. Def., N.Y.C., 1943-45; exec. sec. Iran Am. C. of C., N.Y.C., 1945-75; pres. Gen. Fgn. Sales Corp., Scarsdale, N.Y., 1946-68, chmn. bd. 1968—; pres. Iran Trading Corp., Scarsdale, 1949-68; chmn. bd. Export Promotion Center Iran, 1967-68. Mem. high coordinating econ. com., Tehran, Iran, 1967-68. Mem. nat. gift com. NCCJ, 1964; mem. lay council Internat. Cardiology Found. Decorated Order of Homayoon, Shah of Iran, 1962. Mem. Am. Soc. Internat. Law, Am. Hist. Assn., Nat. Geog. Soc., Am. Security Council, Am. Platform Assn., Pi Sigma Alpha. Editor: Iran Am. Monthly Newsletter, Iran Am. Rev., 1945-75.

SAIGER, GEORGE LEWIS, physician, educator, med. research cons.; b. Burlington, Vt., Dec. 5, 1922; s. Simeon Hillel and Sophie (Snider) S.; certificate Stanford U., 1944; B.S., U. Vt., 1945, M.D., 1948; M.P.H., Columbia U., 1951, Dr.P.H., 1955; m. Faye Toby Diamond, Nov. 4, 1948. Intern, U.S. Marine Hosp., Cleve., 1948-49; asst. county health officer chronic disease div. USPHS, Prince Georges County, Md., 1949-50; instr. biostatistics Columbia U., 1951-52, prof., 1956-59, prof. epidemiology, 1959-64, also cons. med. research and biometrics; med. cons., bur. medicine FDA, Washington, 1963, dir. div. research and reference and FDA info. center on adverse reactions and hazards, 1963-64; cons. in med. research, Palisade and Ft. Lee, N.J., 1964-67; owner-dir. George L. Saiger & Assos., Cons. in Med. Research, Palisade, Ft. Lee, 1967-72, Englewood Cliffs, N.J., 1972—; land acquisition and devel., 1969—; vis. lectr. State U. N.Y. at Bklyn., 1952; asst. prof. preventive medicine La. State U., 1955; med. research cons. and part time pvt. practice, Ft. Lee, 1952-53; cons. to med. jours., 1952—; med. research cons. Rand Corp., 1955-57; med. research cons., chief biometrician, asst. to dir. Army Med. Research Lab., Ft. Knox, Ky., 1953-55; Rockefeller Found. fellow U. Aberdeen (Scotland), 1959; mem. thesis examining com. and mental, cardiovascular, radiation research coms. Columbia U. and Argonne Nat. Lab., 1956-63; mem. adv. com. model prescription rec. system study Sch. Pharmacy U. Pitts., 1963-64; guest speaker spl. conf. on drug info. services Am. Soc. Hosp. Pharmacists, 1964, med. Sect. Pharm. Mfrs. Assn. 1964; expert witness Com. on Commerce U.S. Senate, 1965, Com. on Interstate and Fgn. Commerce Ho. of Reps., 1965, 69. Served with AUS, 1943-46; capt. M.C., 1953-55; asst. surgeon (R) USPHS, 1948-53. Recipient Nat. Found. Infantile Paralysis fellowship award, 1951; Social Sci. Research Council Internat. Conf. Travel grant, 1961. Fellow Am. Pub. Health Assn., Am. Geriatrics Soc., AAAS, N.J. Acad. Sci.; mem. World Med. Assn. (U.S. com.), Internat. Platform Assn., Am. Statis. Assn., Biometric Soc., Assn. Alumni Columbia Sch. Pub. Health and Adminstrv. Medicine, Assn. Tchrs. Preventive Medicine, U. Vt. Med. Alumni Assn., Assn. Alumni Columbia. Author: Tables of the Normal, t, F and Chi-Square Distributions, 1953; A Laboratory Manual of Biometry, 1953, 54; Techniques in Multivariate Analysis as Applied to Medical Data, 1955; Medical Biometry, A Course Outline for Medical Students, 1958; Fundamentals of Epidemiology, 1961; Chemical and Biological Effects of Chemosol, a Tobacco Additive, 1976; contbr. articles to profl. jours. Address: 28 John St Englewood Cliffs NJ 07632

SAILER, JOHN RUDOLPH, lawyer; b. Elizabeth, N.J., Sept. 8, 1918; s. Rudolph John and Alice (Norris) S.; student Rutgers U., 1935-39, J.D., 1948; m. Katharine Wright Grove, Feb. 2, 1952; children—John Hampton Norris, Katharine de Courcy Wright. Admitted to N.J. bar, 1949; atty. at law, Elizabeth, 1949-52; dep. atty. Gen. Pub. Utility Commn., 1952-54; counsellor at law, Elizabeth, 1954-74; counsel Nat. Utilities & Industries Corp., Elizabethtown Gas Co., 1954-72; asst. v.p., gen. counsel Elizabethtown Water Co., Mt. Holly Water Co.; utility law reporter Nat. Water Co. Conf., 1958-67; counsel Am. Water Works Assn., 1961-64. Pres. Young Republicans of Elizabeth, 1951; councilman City of Summit (N.J.), 1961; trustee Summit Art Assn., 1958-63. Served from 2d lt. to maj., inf., AUS, 1940-46. Recipient Loyal Sons of Rutgers award, 1964. Mem. Am., N.J. (chmn. pub. utility law sect. 1970), Fed. Energy, Union bar assns., Newcomen Soc. N.Am., U.S. (law officer dist. 4, 1972-74), Watchung (law officer 1969-76) power squadrons Episcopalian. Club: Mantoloking (N.J.) Yacht. Author: New Jersey Gun Laws, 1966. Home: 141 Hobart St Summit NJ 07901 Office: 47 W Grand St Elizabeth NJ 07202

ST. AMAND, GLENDA WEAVER, ednl. adminstr.; b. Akron, Ohio, Apr. 17, 1923; d. Christian and Selma E. (Johnson) Weaver; B.A., Houghton Coll., 1945; M.S.W., Columbia U., 1947; postgrad. Rider Coll., Mary Wood Coll; m. Leonard St. Amand, Mar. 24, 1951; children—Janet, David. Social worker Family Service Bur., Bklyn.; med.-psychiat. social worker Roosevelt Hosp., N.Y.C., also dir. social service; sch. social worker Neshominy Sch. Dist., Langhorne, Pa. Active Republican party Bucks County, Pa. Salvation Army fellow. Mem. NEA, Nat. Assn. Social Workers, Am. Personel and Guidance Assn. Presbyterian. Club: Lower Makefield Women's. Home: 20 Oakdale Blvd Morrisville PA 19067 Office: Neshominy Sch Dist Langhorne PA 19047

ST. AMAND, JOSEPH, systems analyst; b. New Orleans, May 1, 1940; s. Victor Joseph and Gertrude Millie (Coleman) St. A.; B.S. (Ford Found. scholar), Morehouse Coll., 1959; Sc.M. (fellow), Howard U., 1961; Ph.D., Boston Coll., 1975. Research physicist Nat. Bur. Standards, Washington, 1960-61; prof. physics and chemistry Fla. A. and M. U., Tallahassee, 1962-66, Southeastern Mass. U., North Dartmouth, Mass., 1974-75, Simmons Coll., Boston, 1976; aerospace engr. C.S. Draper Lab., Cambridge, Mass., 1969-74; research asso. Boston Coll., Chestnut Hills, Mass., 1975—; systems analyst Mitre Corp., Bedford, Mass., 1977—. NSF grantee, 1966. Mem. Am. Phys. Soc., Inst. Nav., Nat. Tech. Assn., ACLU, Common Cause, Sierra Club, Sigma Xi. Contbr. articles to profl. jours. Home: 993 Massachusetts Ave Arlington MA 02174 Office: Mitre Corp Box 208 Bedford MA 01730

ST. ANGELO, MILO JESSE, sch. psychologist; b. Providence, Mar. 3, 1937; s. Frank E. and Louise (Narducci) St. A.; A.B. magna cum laude, Providence Coll., 1958; M.A. in Teaching, Brown U., 1960; C.A.E.S., Boston Coll., 1970. With Providence Sch. Dept., 1959—, tchr. Latin, French, English, 1959-65, counselor, 1965-71, head guidance dept., 1971-78, sch. psychologist, 1978—; cons. mental health assns. and clinics; mem. bd. govs. Mental Health Services of Northwestern R.I., Inc. Active Providence Tchrs. Credit Union. Fulbright scholar. Mem. Am. Personnel and Guidance Assn., R.I. Guidance Assn., Classical Assn. New Eng., Tchrs. of Classics in New Eng., Providence Coll., Brown U., Boston Coll. alumni assns., Delta Epsilon Sigma. Roman Catholic. Clubs: Barnard of R.I.; Boston Coll. of R.I. Home: 7 Sherwood Ln Greenville RI 02828 Office: 150 Washington St Providence RI 02903

ST CLAIR, GUY LEWIS, librarian, art curator; b. Montgomery County, Va., July 21, 1940; s. Frank Lee and Mildred (Austin) St.C.; A.B., U. Va., 1963; M.S., U. Ill., 1965; children—Guy Gaillard, George Austin. Library asst. Library of Congress, Washington, 1960-61; reference asst. Alderman Library, U. Va., Charlottesville, 1962-64; reference librarian Richmond (Va.) Pub. Library, 1965-67; circulation librarian U. Richmond (Va.), 1967-68; librarian Univ. Coll., 1968-69; librarian, art curator Union League Club, N.Y.C., 1969-77, dir. cultural programs, 1978—. Mem. Spl. Libraries Assn. (chmn. museums, arts and humanities div., 1975-77, mem. edn. com. 1977—). Episcopalian. Home: 175 W 73d St Apt 6-G New York City NY 10023 Office: Union League Club 38 E 37th St New York City NY 10016

ST. FLORIAN, FRIEDRICH GARTLER, architect, educator; b. Graz, Austria, Dec. 21, 1932; s. Friedrich and Anna Maria (Prassl) G.; came to U.S., 1967, naturalized, 1973; diploma in architecture U. Graz, 1958; M.S. in Architecture, Columbia U., 1962; m. Livia Campanella, Jan. 12, 1967; children—Alisia, Ilaria. Instr. architecture Columbia U., N.Y.C., 1962-63; asst. prof. R.I. Sch. Design, Providence, 1963-70, asso. prof., 1974-77, chmn. div. archtl. studies, 1977-78, dean of architecture, 1978—; vis. asso. prof. M.I.T., Cambridge, 1970-71, 74-75; prin. St. Florian/Howes Assos., Architects, Providence, 1978—. Recipient Nat. Endowment for the Arts award, 1972-73, 76-77, 79; 26th ann. Progressive Architecture Mag. award, 1979; Center for Advanced Visual Studies fellow M.I.T., 1970-77. Mem. AIA. Works exhibited: Nat. Inst. Architects, Rome, 1967, 14th Triennale, Milan, Italy, 1968, Moderna Museet, Stockholm, 1969, Hayden Gallery, M.I.T., 1973, Mus. Modern Art, N.Y.C., 1975, Drawing Center, N.Y.C., 1979. Office: 231 S Main St Providence RI 02903

ST. GEORGE, GEORGE H., hosp. adminstr.; b. N.Y.C., July 23, 1948; s. Harold Joseph and Roxanna Louise (Breedlove) St. G.; B.S. in Bus. Adminstrn., State U. N.Y., Buffalo, 1970, M.B.A., 1971; M. Hosp. Adminstrn., Med. Coll. Va.-Va. Commonwealth U., 1974; m. Janice Ruth Judd, Aug. 22, 1970; children—Brian Christopher, Jeffrey Judd. Mgmt. cons., 1972-73; adminstrv. resident and asst. Med. Center Hosps., Norfolk, Va., 1973-74; asst. adminstr. St. Luke's Hosp., Bethlehem, Pa., 1974—; mem. ad hoc com. to assist in resolution of health facility needs of med. underserved area Pa. Sec. Health; adj. mem. Center Health Policy and Mgmt. Studies, Lehigh U.; mem. exec. com. and chmn. personnel com., bd. dirs. Eastern Pa. Med. Services Council; bd. dirs. Homemaker-Health Aide of Bethlehem, Sub-Area Adv. Council of Health Systems Council Eastern Pa. Mem. Freedom Train com. YMCA Membership Dr., Bethlelhem. Recipient Student Achievement award Wall St. Jour., 1970, citation for contbrn. to Pa. U.S. bicentennial activities, 1976. Mem. Am. Coll. Hosp. Adminstrs., Am., Pa. hosp. assns., Greater Phila. Health Assembly. Club: Rotary (Bethlehem). Home: 1590 Harmor Ln Bethlehem PA 18017 Office: Saint Luke's Hosp 801 Ostrum St Bethlehem PA 18015

ST. GERMAIN, DOLPHUS JOSEPH, investment, banker; b. Ellenburg, N.Y., July 27, 1893; s. Dolphus and Adeline (Rivers) St. G.; student N.Y. U., 1917-18, Columbia, 1933-35; D.C.S. (hon.), Western New Eng. Coll., 1964; H.H.D. (hon.), Assumption Coll., Worcester, Mass., 1977; m. Dorothy Mae Himmelmann, Sept. 17, 1919; children—Marjorie St. Germain Haunton, Marion St. Germain Williams, J. Gordon, Dorothy St. Germain Maxson, Nancy St. Germain Sanders, J. Brewster, Mildred St. Germain Gale. Driver-salesman Armour & Co., Springfield, Mass., 1912-19; mgr. Gen. Mortgage & Loan Corp., Springfield, 1919-23; founder, owner, operator D.J. St. Germain & Co., investments, Springfield, 1924—, Spring Lake Farm, Monson, Mass., 1936—; organized 1st Springfield Trust Co., 1922—. Del. Republican Nat. Conv., 1940, 48, 56; chmn. city com. Springfield, 1942-44, 46-48; pres. Rep. Club. Mass., 1944-45; trustee Western New Eng. Coll., 1962—. Served with 2d Regt., 104th Inf., U.S. Army, 1916. Recipient spl. award merit Citizens Com. for Hoover Report, 1952, spl. tree farm award Am. Forest Product Industries, 1958. Mem. Herbert Hoover Presdl. Library Assn. (perpetual hon. asso. mem.), Springfield C. of C. (dir. 1943-46), Am. Forestry Assn., Am. Legion. Conglist. Clubs: Colony, State Mass. Elks. Home: Spring Lake Farm Bradway Rd Monson MA 01057 Office: 1500 Main St Springfield MA 01115

ST. GERMAIN, FERNAND JOSEPH, congressman; b. Blackstone, Mass.; s. Andrew Joseph and Pearl (Talaby) St. G.; Ph.B. in Social Sci., Providence Coll., 1948, LL.D., 1965; LL.B., Boston U., 1955; J.S.D. (hon.), Suffolk U., 1976; m. Rachel O'Neill, Aug. 20, 1953; children—Bonnie Laurene, Lisette. Admitted R.I. bar, 1956; mem. R.I. Ho. of Reps., 1952-60; mem. 87th to 96th Congresses from 1st Dist. R.I., mem. com. steering and policy, banking, fin. and urban affairs, govt. ops., coms. Mem. Young Democrats R.I. Served with AUS, 1949-52. Mem. Am., R.I., Woonsocket, Fed. bar assns., alumni assns., Our Lady of Providence Sem., Providence Coll., Boston U. Law Sch., Am. Legion. Club: Elks. Home: 121 Woodland Rd Woonsocket RI 02895 Office: House Office Bldg Washington DC 20515

ST. GERMAIN, JEAN MARY, med. physicist; b. N.Y.C.; d. Herbert and Mary J. (Newman) S.; B.S., Marymount Manhattan Coll., 1966; M.S., Rutgers U., 1967. Fellow radiol. health USPHS, Rutgers U., New Brunswick, N.J., 1967; fellow dept. med. physics Meml. Hosp., N.Y.C., Cornell U. Med. Coll., 1967-68, asst. physicist, 1968-71, instr. radiology (physics), 1971-78, clin. asst. prof., 1978—; asst. attending physicist Meml. Sloan-Kettering Cancer Center; cons. in field. Diplomate Am. Bd. Health Physics. Mem. Health Physics Soc., Am. Assn. Physicists in Medicine (dir.), Soc. Nuclear Medicine, Radiol. Soc. N. Am., N.Y. Acad. Sci., Radicl. and Med. Physics Soc. N.Y. (past pres.). Author: The Nurse and Radiotherapy, 1978; contbr. articles, chpts. to med. jours., texts. Office: 1275 York Ave New York City NY 10021

SAINT-PIERRE, JACQUES, coll. adminstr.; b. Trois Rivières, Que., Canada, Aug. 30, 1920; s. Oscar and Lucie (Landreville) St.P.; B.S., U. Montreal, 1948, M.S., 1951; Ph.D., U. N.C., 1954; m. Marguerite Lachaine, July 15, 1947; children—Marc, Guy, Andre, Louis, François, Mireille. Mem. faculty U. Montreal, 1947—, prof. statistics, 1960—, dir. computing center, 1964-71, v.p. planning, 1971—; cons. statistician, 1954—. Mem. Inst. Math. Statistics, Am. Statis. Assn., Biometric Soc., Canadian Ops. Research Soc., Canadian Math. Congress, Canadian Assn. Univ. Tchrs. (pres. 1965-66). Contbr. articles to profl. jours. Home: 1795 Croissant Sauve Duvernay Laval PQ Canada Office: Univ Montreal Box 6128 Montreal H3C 3J7 PQ Canada

ST PIERRE, PAUL EMILE, mech. engr.; b. Montreal, Que., Can., Dec. 26, 1924; s. Hector Jules and Marie Rose (LaPierre) St.P.; came to U.S., 1964, naturalized, 1970; higher nat. certificate Royal Naval Acad., 1942; LL.B., N.Y.U., 1970; m. Yvette Dion, Aug. 28, 1950; children—Francine, Henry, Johanne. Sr. resident inspecting engr. E.I. Du Pont de Nemours & Co. Inc., St. Louis, 1964-69; mgr. project program Gilbert Assos. Inc., Reading, Pa., 1969-73; supervising engr. Pa. Power & Light Co., Allentown, 1973-77; cons. codes and standards. Served to lt. comdr. Royal Navy, 1939-50; PTO. Registered profl. engr., Calif.; commd. boiler and pressure vessel insp.; 2d class steam and diesel marine engr. Bd. Trade. Mem. ASME, Corp. Power Engrs., Am. Nuclear Soc., Am. Soc. Nondestructive Testing. Republican. Roman Catholic. Home: 124 S Chestnut Fleetwood PA 19522

SAJJADI, PETER S., engring. co. exec.; b. Tehran, Iran, July 18, 1934; s. Mohamad S. and Fakhri S.; came to U.S., 1954, naturalized, 1964; B.S. in Polit. Sci., U. Houston, 1958, B.S. in Inddsl. Psychology, 1962, M.B.A. in Indsl. Mgmt., 1965; m. Delores Patricia Klipphahn, July 17, 1957; children—Steven, Pierre, Russell. Quality control supr. Gen. Elec. Co., Houston, 1958-65; dir. personnel Hills-McCanna Co., Iowa, 1965-67; personnel mgr. Hastings Industries (Nebr.), 1967-72; tng. mgr. Dravo Corp., Pitts., 1972-74, dir. personnel devel. and internat. personnel, 1974—; leader mgmt. seminars; cons. univs. Dir. CD, 1967-72; mem. edn. com. YMCA, 1977-8; mem. adv. com. Tech. Coll., 1965-72; mem. Civil Service Adv. Com., 1969-70; mem. curriculum com. M.B.A. program U. Pitts., 1977-78; first aid instr. ARC, 1967-72. Mem. Am. Soc. Tng. and Devel. (outstanding contbr. to chpt. 1976), Am. Soc. Safety Engrs. (certified), Am. Soc. Personnel Adminstrn., Inter Am. Soc., Am. Econs. Assn., Am. Assn. Polit. and Social Sci., Orgn. Devel. Network, Internat. Indsl. Relations Assn., World Affairs Council. Republican. Home: 258 Rutledge Dr Bridgeville PA 15017 Office: 1 Oliver Plaza Pittsburgh PA 15222

SAJKOVIC, VLADIMIR, educator; b. Pavlovsk, Russia, Jan. 25, 1912; s. Ivan S. and Lidia I. (Shishkin) S.; B.A., Russkoe Realnoe Uchilische, Terjoki, Finland, 1927-32; postgrad. Ceska Visoka Skola Technicka, Brno, Czechoslovakia, 1932-35, U. Helsinki (Finland), 1935-37; M.A., U. Pa., 1949, Ph.D., 1953; m. Miriam Dorcas Taylor, Nov. 22, 1956; children—Tomislav, Marko, Aleksey. Came to U.S., 1946; permanent resident. Instr. Pendle Hill Sch., Wallingford, Pa., 1946-47, U. Pa., 1949-51, U. Kans., 1951-52; from instr. to asso. in Russian, U. Pa., 1953-59; instr. Bryn Mawr Coll., 1954-57; asst. prof. to prof. Mt. Holyoke Coll., 1959-77, chmn. dept. Russian lang. and lit., 1959-70, prof. emeritus, 1977—; translator, interpreter Immigration and Naturalization Service, Phila., 1948-49; vis. prof. Middlebury Coll., summer 1960, U. Pa., summer 1966. Served with Yugoslav Army, 1940-46 (prisoner of war in Germany 1941-45). Mem. Am. Assn. Tchrs. Slavic and East European Langs., Am. Assn. Advancement Slavic Studies, Soc. Sci. Study Religion, Modern Lang. Assn., Assn. Russian-Am. Scholars U.S.A., Internat. Dostoevsky Soc., AAUP. Home: 101 College St South Hadley MA 01075

SAKELL, ACHILLES NICHOLAS, fgn. service officer; b. Greece, Jan. 27, 1906; s. Nicholas and Matenia (Economides) Sakellarides; came to U.S., 1923, naturalized, 1938; diplome Nat. Sch. Langs. and Commerce, Istanbul, Turkey, 1923; M.Sc., Lehigh U., 1936; M.A., Princeton U., 1939, Ph.D. in Polit. Sci. and Internat. Law, 1941; m. Alexandra Calbos, Feb. 28, 1945; 1 dau., Matenia. Chief, Near Eastern sect. news bur. OWI, 1941-43; rep. to UNRRA Conf., Atlantic City, 1943, chief fgn. lang. press and radio div., 1944-45; sec., mem. bd. Allied Mission to Observe Greek Elections, 1946; editor report on Greece, FAO, 1947; lectr. internat. law George Washington U., 1948-50; vis. lectr. internat. law Nat. War Coll. and Fgn. Service Inst., Dept. State, 1953-56; chief fgn. langs. publs. br. Dept. State, 1950-53, fgn. affairs info. officer, 1955, dir. Pub. Services div., 1969-74, insp. fgn. econ. and mil. assistance, 1975-76; lectr. internat. law Fgn. Service Inst., Dept. State, Nat. War Coll. Mem. supreme adminstrv. council Greek Orthodox Ch. N. and S. Am., 1977. Decorated Archon Chartophylax (Prime Minister) of Greek Orthodox Ch.; Grand Golden cross St. Andrew and companion gold Star Ecumenical Patriarchate of Constantinople; recipient Superior Achievement award Dept. State, 1974. Mem. Am. Soc. Internat. Law, Am. Polit. Sci. Assn., Am. Acad. Polit. and Social Scis., Pan-Macedonian Assn. Am., Inst. Homeric Studies (hon.), Fgn. Corrs. Greece, Acad. Balkan Studies. Clubs: Nat. Press, Princeton (Washington). Author: Careers in the Foreign Service, 1962; Our Southern Partners, 1956; You and the United Nations, 1956; Communist Infiltration in Latin America, 1955; contbr. articles to State Dept. publs. Home: 203 S Yoakum Pkwy Alexandria VA 22304

SAKELLAROPOULOS, GEORGE PANAYOTIS, chem. engr.; b. Kalamata, Greece, Apr. 10, 1944; s. Panayotis and Eudokia (Renieris) S.; came to U.S., 1970; diploma in Chem. Engring., Nat. Tech. U. Athens, 1966; Ph.D. in Chem. Engring., U. Wis., 1974. Instr., Greek Naval Acad., Pireaus, 1966-69; process engr. Gen. Cement Co., Volos, Greece, 1969-70; vis. prof. and lectr. chem. engring. U. Wis., Madison, 1975; asst. prof. chem. engring. Rensselaer Poly. Inst., Troy, N.Y., 1976—; cons. Gen. Electric Co., 1976—; reviewer of various jours. in chem. engring., 1975—. Registered profl. engr., Greece. Mem. Am. Chem. Soc., Am. Inst. Chem. Engrs., Electrochem. Soc., Chem. Engrs. Soc. Greece, Sigma Xi, Phi Kappa Phi, Phi Lambda Upsilon. Mem. Christian Orthodox Ch. Contbr. articles on electrochem. processes to profl. jours. Home: Rose Garden Ct 7-6 Latham NY 12110 Office: Dept Chem Engring Rensselaer Poly Inst Troy NY 12181

SAKOUTIS, STEPHEN PANAYOTIS, transp. exec.; b. N.Y.C., Aug. 28, 1930; s. Michael John and Calliope (Sakoutis) S.; B.S., Pace Coll., 1956; postgrad. N.Y. U., 1965; m. Stella Mecalianos, Aug. 23, 1953; children—Michael, Thalia. Traffic mgr. Shoe Factory Supply Co., Bklyn., 1960-62; traffic mgr. Embassy Industries, Inc., Farmingdale, N.Y., 1962-67, gen. traffic mgr., 1967—, corporate transp. consul to parent co., P & F Industries, Gt. Neck, from 1968—, now also gen. mgr. distbn. and traffic services Bilnor Corp. div.; traffic cons.; transp. cons. Utility Mfg. Co., Westbury, N.Y. Served with AUS, 1951-53. Mem. L.I. Assn. Commerce and Industry (chmn. L.I. shippers council 1965-68), German Am. Jr. Soccer League (gen. sec. 1967—), L.I. Soccer Football League (sec. 1971), Nat. Council Phys. Distbn. Mgmt., Delta Nu Alpha. Clubs: Blue Star Sport (v.p. 1968-70), Everest (pres.) (N.Y.C.) Home: 167-05 12th Ave Beechurst NY 11357 Office: 350 Smith St Farmingdale NY 11735

SALA, RAUL PEREZ, physician; b. Cebu City, Philippines, Aug. 18, 1940; s. Severino and Lourdes (Perez) S.; came to U.S., 1968, naturalized, 1974; A.A., U. San Carlos (Philippines), 1961; M.D., Cebu Inst. Tech., 1966; m. Marietta Corderosala, Jan. 6, 1968; children—John, Mark, Raul Perez, Michael. Intern, St. Peter's Hosp., Albany, 1968-69; resident N.Y. U.-Bellevue Hosp., N.Y.C., 1970-71, Downstate Med. Center, Bklyn., 1971-72; asst. dir. Roosevelt Hosp., N.Y.C., 1972-73; instr. State U. N.Y. Coll. Medicine, 1973-76; practice medicine specializing in phys. medicine and rehab., Bklyn., 1973-76, N.Y.C., 1976—; mem. staff Beth Israel Med. Center, N.Y.C., 1976—; asso. Mt. Sinai Sch. Medicine, N.Y.C., 1976—. Served to maj. M.C., USAR, 1976-78. Diplomate Am. Bd. Phys. Medicine and Rehab. Fellow Am. Acad. Phys. Medicine, N.Y. Acad. Medicine; mem. AMA (Continuing Med. Edn. award 1972), State N.Y., Kings County (N.Y.) med. socs., Am. Congress Rehab. Medicine, N.Y. Soc. Phys. Medicine and Rehab., Am. Geriatric Soc. Democrat. Roman Catholic. Home: 36 Emerson Ct Staten Island NY 10304 Office: 10 Nathan Perlman Pl New York City NY 10003 also 11 Ralph Pl Staten Island NY 10304

SALADINO, JOHN LEONARD, elec. mfg. co. exec.; b. Phila., May 5, 1946; s. John Louis and Mary Theresa (Pomilio) S.; B.S. in Engring., Princeton U., 1968; m. Monika Weiss, Aug. 24, 1968; 1 son, John David. Tchr. math. Princeton (N.J.) Day Sch., 1968-72; alternative sch. dir. Rutland (Vt.) High Sch., 1972-73; instr. philosophy Castleton (Vt.) State Coll., 1974; mfg. engring. planner Gen. Electric Co., Rutland, 1974-76, mgr. methods and processes, 1976—, math. instr. in co. apprentice program, 1974—. Recipient managerial award for tech. excellence Gen. Electric Co., 1976, Kenneth N. Bush award for technol. achievement, 1977; certified tchr., Vt. Mem. Engrs. Club Rutland County. Gen. Electric Co. Mgmt. Assn. Roman Catholic. Home: RD 1 Sugarwood Hill Rutland VT 05701 Office: 210 Columbian Ave Rutland VT 05701

SALANT, MARILYN MOFFAT (MRS. ROBERT S. SALANT), educator; b. N.Y.C., Nov. 14, 1937; d. Daniel and Georgina Ellen (Thomson) Moffat; B.S., Queens Coll., 1962; M.A., N.Y. U., 1964, Ph.D., 1973; m. Robert S. Salant, Sept. 12, 1970. Staff phys. therapist Inst. Rehab. Medicine, N.Y. U. Med. Center, 1963-64, sr. phys. therapist, 1964-65, unit supr. pediatric phys. therapy service, 1965, unit supr. pulmonary rehab. service, 1965-67, unit supr. spl. projects, 1967—, dir. symposium chest rehab. for phys. therapists, 1968, participant chest rehab. symposium, 1970, 71; instr. dept. health and phys. edn. Queens Coll., 1967; instr. N.Y. U., 1967-72, asst. prof., 1972-75, asso. prof., 1975—; inservice program instr. St. Vincent's Hosp., N.Y.C., 1969, North Shore Hosp., Manhasset, N.Y., 1972; lectr. pulmonary physiology Skidmore Sch. Nursing, 1972; vis. faculty U. Pitts., 1971, U. Del., 1974-78, Albany Med. Coll., 1975, 76; co-dir. Inst. Devel. Human Resource and Potential, Queens Coll., 1967; mem. panel Chest Rehab. Discussion, N.Y.C. Phys. Therapy Dist., 1968; asst. dir. N.Y. State grant-supported Critical Health Issues Program, 1968-71; tech. adviser Fed. Programmed Anatomy Project, 1968-71; tech adviser, script writer phys. therapy ednl. films Vocational Rehab. Adminstrn., 1965-71. Recipient Service award United Cerebral Palsy. Mem. Am. Phys. Therapy Assn. (dist. dir. N.Y.C. 1976-78, editor jour. 1968-70, editor Phys. Rehab. Edn. 1974-78, pres. N.Y. chpt. 1978-80), Am. Med. Writers Assn., Am. Assn. Schs. Allied Health Professions, Pi Lambda Theta, Kappa Delta Pi. Mem. Order Eastern Star. Contbr. articles to profl. jours., monographs. Home: Ludlam Ln Locust Valley NY 11560 Office: Dept Phys Therapy New York Univ 333 E 30th St New York City NY 10016

SALAS, HENRY JOSEPH, environ. engr.; b. N.Y.C., Jan. 30, 1947; s. Alberto and Orestes (Martinez) S.; B.C.E., Manhattan Coll., 1969, M.S. in Environ. Engring. (Fed. fellow), 1970; m. Jeanette Ann Morais, Aug. 23, 1970. Engr., Hydrosci., Inc., Westwood, N.J., 1970-72, project mgr., 1972—; cons. Pan Am. Health Orgn., Peru, 1976, Cuba, 1977, Argentina, 1978. Registered profl. engr., N.Y. Mem. ASCE, Water Pollution Control Fedn. Roman Catholic. Home: 15 Broadway Terr New York City NY 10040 Office: 363 Old Hook Rd Westwood NJ 07675

SALCMAN, MICHAEL, neurosurgeon, neurophysiologist, educator; b. Pilsen, Czechoslovakia, Nov. 4, 1946; s. Arthur and Edith (Atlas) S.; came to U.S., 1948, naturalized, 1953; B.A. in Med. Sci. magna cum laude, M.D. magna cum laude, Boston U., 1969; m. Ilene Rebarber, July 27, 1969; 1 son, Joshua. Intern in surgery U. Hosp. Boston U. Med. Center, 1969-70; research asso. in neurophysiology lab. neural control Nat. Inst. Neurol. Diseases and Stroke NIH, Bethesda, Md., 1970-72; resident in neurosurgery Neurol. Inst. N.Y., Columbia-Presbyn. Med. Center, N.Y.C., 1972-76; asst. prof. neurosurgery organizer neuro-oncology service, U. Md., 1976—, 1978; lectr. univs. Served with USPHS, 1970-72. Recipient Lange Med. Pub. award in biochemistry Lange Pub. Co., 1966, Meml. award Boston U. Class 1930, 1967, Boston U. Alumni award, 1968; Nat. Eye Inst. grantee, 1974—; Am. Cancer Soc. grantee, 1978—. Mem. AMA, Am. Physiol. Soc., Soc. Neurosci., AAAS, IEEE, Neuroelectric Soc., Congress Neurol. Surgeons, Assn. Brain Tumor Research, Am. Heart Assn. (stroke council), Assn. Advancement Med. Instrumentation, Soc. Neurol. Edn., Assn. Acad. Surgery, N.Y. Acad. Scis., Begg Soc., Phi Beta Kappa, Alpha Omega Alpha. Contbr. articles on physiology of brain, spinal cord, clin. neurosurgery and biomed. engring. to profl. jours.; contbr. numerous poems to lits. jours., anthologies; patentee electrode device to provide brain stimulation in program to provide sight for blind; developer microwave treatment for brain tumors. Home: 5401 Springlake Way Baltimore MD 21212 Office: U Md Hosp 22 S Green St Baltimore MD 21201

SALEEBA, GEORGE JOSEPH, photographer; b. New Haven, Oct. 3, 1910; s. John Joseph and Martha Marie (Zemke) S.; grad. high sch.; m. Vera Evelyn Cahoon, Apr. 21, 1951; children—Laura (Mrs. Ray Dobbs), Thomas, Cynthia, Kenneth, George, John. Photographer U.S. Color Lab., New Haven, 1923-45, chief photographer, 1949-60; chief photographer Conn. Telephone & Electric, Army Field Telephones, Meriden, Conn., 1945-49; staff photographer Channel 8, New Haven, 1960-65, Milford (Conn.) Citizen, 1965—. Faculty Bridgeport (Conn.) U., 1972. Mem. Conn. News Photographers Assn. Home: 659 3d Ave West Haven CT 06516 Office: 117 Broad St Milford CT 06460

SALEM, HARRY, pharmacologist, toxicologist; b. Windsor, Ont., Can., Mar. 21, 1929; s. Oscar and Bessie (Pierce) S.; B.A., U. Western Ont., 1950; B.S. in Pharmacy, U. Mich., 1953; M.A., U. Toronto (Ont.), 1955, Ph.D., 1958; m. Florence Rosenbaum, June 30, 1957; 1 son, Jerry. Came to U.S., 1959, naturalized, 1965. Research asst. U. Toronto, 1958-59; pharmacologist Air Shields, Inc., Hatboro, Pa., 1959-62; sr. pharmacologist Smith, Kline & French Labs., 1962-65; dir. respiratory research labs. Nat. Drug Co., Phila., 1965-70; dir. pharmacology and toxicology Smith, Miller & Patch, Inc., New Brunswick, N.J., 1970-72; dir. pharmacology Cooper Labs., Cedar Knolls, N.J., 1972-77; pres., chief toxicologist Cannon Labs. Inc., Reading, Pa., 1977—; asst. prof. U. Pa., 1968-75, asso. prof., 1975—; adj. prof. environ. health Temple U., 1968—; cons. in field. Fellow N.Y. Acad. Scis.; mem. Am. Acad. Clin. Toxicology, Am. Chem. Soc., AAAS, Am. Pharm. Assn., Am. Soc. Pharmacology and Exptl. Therapeutics, Drug Information Assn., Internat. Inflammation Club, Internat. Soc. Biochem. Pharmacology, Pharm. Soc. Can., Physiol. Soc. Phila., Soc. Comparative Ophthalmology, Soc. Toxicology, Am. Coll. Clin. Pharmacology, Am. Soc. Clin. Pharmacology and Therapeutics, Am. Coll. Toxicology. Author, editor 3 vols. Internat. Ency. Pharmacology and Therapeutics, 1970. Contbr. articles to profl. jours., chpts. to books. Home: 918 Rock Ln Elkins Park PA 19117 Office: Cannon Labs PO Box 3627 Reading PA 19605

SALENSKY, GEORGE, chem. engr.; b. N.Y.C., July 2, 1925; s. Isaac and Anna (Matuszonek) S.; B.Chem.Engring., Poly. Inst. Bklyn., 1945, M.Chem.Engring., 1947; m. Rita C. Velten, Sept. 22, 1951; children—Marianne, Kathryn. Chem. engr. Keystone Varnish, Bklyn., 1945-48, Philip A. Hunt Co., Palisades Park, N.J., 1948-54; tech. dir., v.p. Gusmer Coatings, Inc., Woodbridge, N.J., 1954-63; with Union Carbide Corp., Bound Brook, N.J., 1963—, sr. devel. scientist, 1975—. Mem. Am. Chem. Soc., Sigma Xi, Tau Beta Pi, Phi Lambda Upsilon. Patentee in field with expertise in polymers for elec. insulation, coatings and corrosion control. Home: RD 3 Scrabbletown Rd Whitehouse Sta NJ 08889 Office: 1 River Rd PO Box 670 Bound Brook NJ 08805

SALES, FRANK, constrn. co. exec.; b. Windsor Locks, Conn., Mar. 5, 1928; s. Dominick and Maria (Corocio) S.; student pub. schs.; m. Joan Felice Gallus, Oct. 7, 1950; children—Susan, Rebecca, Samuel, Frank. Pres., Sales Constrn. Co., Windsor Locks, 1947—; owner Airport Indsl. City, Windsor Locks, 1965—, Barkwin Co., Barkhamsted, 1969—. Mem. Conn. Gov.'s Task Force on Pub. Works, 1975—, Conn. Housing Authority, 1976—. Address: 10 Woodland Hollow Windsor Locks CT 06096

SALGO, MICHAEL NICHOLAS, engring. co. adminstr.; b. Oradea, Romania, Jan. 17, 1914; s. Louis and Celia (Kain) S.; came to U.S., 1914, naturalized, 1923; B.S. in Engring., Northwestern U., 1937; M.S. in Civil Engring., Va. Poly. Inst., 1938; m. Ruth Farkas, Aug. 20, 1944; children—Peter L., Jeffrey B. Commd. lt. Civil Engrs. Corps, U.S. Navy, 1949, advanced through grades to comdr.; sr. structural engr., 1940-46, prin. maintenance engr. for naval superintending civil engr., 1946-48, asst. to dist. civil engr. 3rd Naval Dist. Hdqrs., 1948-57; dir. facilities engring. CBS, Inc., N.Y.C., 1957-74; mgr. systems, transp., also N.Y. engring. L. K. Comstock & Co., Inc., N.Y.C., 1974-77; asso. Ammann & Whitney, 1977—; research fellow in civil engring. Va. Poly. Inst., 1937-38; teaching asst. Ill. Inst. Tech., 1938, instr., 1939. Fellow ASCE (pres. met. sec., nat. dir., nat. v.p., treas., chmn. research council on performance of structures); mem. Nat. Soc. Profl. Engrs., Soc. Am. Mil. Engrs. Club: N.Y. R.R. Contbr. articles to profl. jours. Home: 137-32 76th Ave Flushing NY 11367 Office: 2 World Trade Center 17th Floor New York NY 10048

SALINE, LINDON EDGAR, indsl. co. exec.; b. Mpls., Mar. 16, 1924; s. Emil and Anna (Hinz) S.; B.E.E., Marquette U., 1945; M.S. in Elec. Engring., U. Wis., 1948, Ph.D. in Elec. Engring., 1950, Sc.D. (hon.), 1973; m. Jane Sprenger, Oct. 14, 1950; children—Sandra, Susan, Jeffrey, Bradley. With Cutler-Hammer, Milw., 1946-47; with Gen. Electric Co., Croton-on-Hudson, N.Y., 1948—, tech. and mgmt. positions in power systems, computers, aerospace and def. corp. staff, mgr. profl. devel. operation GE Mgmt. Devel. Inst., 1975—; advisory com. on sci. edn. NSF. Leader nat. minority engring. effort; chmn. State of Conn. Task Force on Mgmt. Human Resources, 1977-78. Served with USN, 1942-46. Recipient distinguished service citation U. Wis., 1973; registered profl. engr., N.Y. Mem. IEEE, ASME, Am. Soc. Tng. and Devel., Nat. Soc. Profl. Engrs., Am. Soc. Engring. Edn., Sigma Xi, Tau Beta Pi, Eta Kappa Nu, Pi Mu Epsilon. Republican. Congregationalist. Club: No. Rippowan Yacht and Tennis. Lectr. in field; contbr. tech. papers and articles to profl. publs. Home: 141 Pinney Rd New Canaan CT 06840 Office: PO Box 368 Croton-on-Hudson NY 10520

SALISBURY, ROBERT ELMORE, financier, industrialist; b. N.Y.C., Apr. 15, 1922; s. Zoll Elmore and Margaret B. (Cameron-Boveda) S.; student N.Y. U., 1940-41; m. Nancy Hoadley Kirkland, Aug. 18, 1972; children by previous marriage—Robert Cameron, Joyce Ellen, Elizabeth Anne, Nancy Jane. Chief operating officer Citibank N.A., Rio de Janeiro, Brazil, 1946-52; dir. Latin Am. pub., Time-Life internat., N.Y.C., 1952-62; dep. dir. Regional Office Central Am., AID, Guatemala City, 1962-63; pres. Internat. Capital Devel. Ltd., Basel, Switzerland, 1963-67; v.p. Coenen & Co., Inc., N.Y.C., 1968-69; pres. Cameron, Stuart & Co., N.Y.C., 1970—, Cam Stuart Petroleum Group Ltd., N.Y.C., 1973—. Treas. Am. Sch., Rio de Janeiro, 1948-56; dir., vice chmn. Com. on Fund Distbn., The Greater New York Fund, N.Y.C., 1976—; chmn. bd. trustee French & Polyclinic Med. Sch., N.Y.C., 1975—; bd. dirs. Girls Club of N.Y., 1977—; trustee Child Study Willmet Assn., 1976-78; bd. dirs. Children of Bellevue, 1977. Served with USAAF, 1941-45. Mem. Ind. Petroleum Assn. Am. (regional dir. 1974-78), Nat. Inst. Social Scis. (v.p., dir. 1978—), Am. Benevolent Soc. (Mexico City) (v.p. 1956-59), Young Republicans of Fla. (nat. com. 1960-61), Am. C. of C. in Rio de Janeiro (dir. 1952-56). Episcopalian. Clubs: Metropolitan, Doubles (N.Y.C.); Bellport (N.Y.) Bay Yacht; Nat. Golf Links Am. (Southampton, N.Y.). Home: 945 Fifth Ave New York City NY 10021 also 36 Thornhedge Rd Bellport NY 11713 Office: 501 Madison Ave New York City NY 10022

SALKIND, MICHAEL JAY, engr., govt. engr.; b. N.Y.C., Oct. 1, 1938; s. Milton and Esther (Jaffe) S.; B.Metall. Engring., Rensselaer Polytech. Inst., 1959, Ph.D. (Allegheny Ludlum fellow), 1962; m. Miriam E. Schwartz, Aug. 16, 1959; children—Michael Jay, Elizabeth Jane, Jonathan Hillson, Joshua Isaac. With United Aircraft Research Labs., East Hartford, Conn., 1964-68, chief, advanced metallurgy, 1967-68; chief structures and materials Sikorsky Aircraft div. United Aircraft Corp., 1968-75; dir., product devel. Avco Systems div., 1975-76; mgr. structures and dynamics NASA, 1976—. Lectr. metallurgy Trinity Coll., Hartford, Conn., 1968-69. Mem. Town Com. Republican party, Glastonbury, Conn., 1966-69. Mem. bd. suprs. Fairfield County Conservation Dist., 1970-75; chmn., 1973-75; mem. waste disposal adv. com. Danbury Area Council Chambers Commerce; bd. dirs. Housatonic Valley Assn., 1973-75; chmn. tech. adv. group Conn. Dept Environ Protection, 1973-75. Served to capt. AUS, 1962-64. Mem. Am. Soc. Testing and Materials (chmn. com. D-30 on high modulus fibers and their composites 1968-74). Am. Inst. Aeros. and Astronautics, Am. Helicopter Soc., Am. Inst. Mining, Metall. and Petroleum Engrs., Am. Soc. Metals, Brit. Inst. Metals, Research Soc. Am., Plansee Soc., Sigma Xi, Alpha Sigma Mu. Cons. editor Internat. Jour. Fibre Sci. and Tech.; editor Applications Composite Materials, 1973; contbr. articles to jours. textbooks. Home: 3712 N Woodrow St Arlington VA 22207 Office: NASA RWS-3 Washington DC 20546

SALLARD, BENJAMIN WILMORE, mfg. cons.; b. Phila., Apr. 19, 1929; s. Eugene H. and Lucy (Wilmore) S.; B.S., Drexel U., 1967; M.B.A., U. New Haven, 1978; m. Catherine Stephenson, Nov. 27, 1958; children—Benjamin W., Susan, Michael, David. Various positions, Phila., 1954-61; mgr. mfg. proposals Gen. Electric Co., Phila., 1961-68, mgr. prodn. control, 1968; gen. mgr. Progress Aerospace Enterprises, Inc., Phila., 1968-70; gen. mgr. Indsl. div. Nat. Progress Assn. for Econ. Devel., 1970-72; gen. mgr. parts fabrication div. Electronic Assos., Inc., Long Branch, N.J., 1972-74; with Corp. Cons. Services, Gen. Electric Co., Bridgeport, Conn., 1974—. Past chmn. Yorktown Community Orgn., mem. exec. com., 1964-68; bd. dirs. Phila. Council Internat. Visitors, Goodwill Industries, Health and Welfare Council Phila.; mem. steering com. Phila. Crime Commn. Served to 1st lt. AUS, 1951-54. Mem. Am. Mgmt. Assn. Club: Masons. Home: 106 Hilltop Dr Nichols CT 06611 Office: 1285 Boston Ave Bridgeport CT 06602

SALLEY, GEORGE PADDOCK, landscape architect; b. Salley, S.C., Jan. 20, 1929; s. Henry Briggs and Margaret Key (Sawyer) S.; B.S., Clemson U., 1951; B.Landscape Architecture, U. Ga., 1958. Designer, Darling & Webel, N.Y.C., 1962-63; project mgr. Vollmer Assos., N.Y.C., 1968-72; landscape architect Zion & Breen Assos., Imlaystown, N.J., 1963-72; landscape architect N.Y.C. Housing Authority, 1973—. Mem. Brooklyn Heights Assn., 1968—. Served with USNR, 1951-53. Mem. Am. Soc. Landscape Architects (Merit award certificate 1958), Phi Kappa Phi. Democrat. Episcopalian. Landscape architect: Boca Raton (Fla.) Yacht and Country Club, 1960; Damrosch Park, Lincoln Center, 1963; Performing Arts Center, Lewiston, N.Y., 1972. Home: 74 Hicks St Brooklyn NY 11201 Office: 250 Broadway New York City NY 10007

SALLICK, RICHARD MARSHALL, psychiatrist; b. N.Y.C., Sept. 3, 1936; s. Myron A. and Marion (Marshall) S.; A.B., Harvard, 1958; M.D., Cornell U., 1962; m. Lucy Ellen Riley, June 25, 1960; children—Hilary, Margaret, John. Intern, Vanderbilt U. Hosp., Nashville, 1962-63; resident in psychiatry N.Y. Hosp., 1963-66; fellow in psychiatry Cornell U. Med. Coll., 1964-66; dep. dir. div. spl. mental health programs NIMH, Bethesda, Md., 1966-68; asst. prof. psychiatry Cornell, 1968-72; dir. outpatient dept. Payne Whitney Clinic, N.Y.C., 1968-72; chmn. psychiatry dept. Norwalk Hosp., (Conn.), 1972—; asst. prof. Yale, 1972—; asso. clin. prof. N.Y. Med. Coll., 1977—. Served with USPHS, 1966-68. Fellow Am. Psychiat. Assn.; mem. Conn. Psychiat. Soc., Fairfield County Med. Soc. Home: 77 Long Lots Rd Westport CT 06880 Office: Norwalk Hospital Norwalk CT 06856

SALLIE, ARNETHA, accountant; b. Monongahela, Pa., June 15, 1924; d. Robert E. and Lucinda Lee; LL.B., LaSalle U., 1977; m. James Edward Sallie, Oct. 25, 1947; children—James Edward, Carol Ann Sallie Lawrence, Reginald and Ronald (twins). With World War II Def. Plant, N.Y.C., 1942-43, Casey Jones Aero. Sch., Rome, N.Y., 1943-44; with Westinghouse Electric Co., Trenton, N.J., 1944-48; with Fashion Frocks, Inc., Cin., 1961-71; pvt. practice accounting, McKeesport, Pa., 1977—. Recipient merit award SBA. C.P.A., Pa. Mem. Am. Inst. C.P.A.'s. Baptist. Clubs: LaSalle Alumnae, McKeesport Tigers Mothers. Address: 2002 Flagler St McKeesport PA 15132

SALLUSTIO, ANTHONY THOMAS, educator; b. Flushing, N.Y., June 26, 1936; s. Santo and Josephine (Badamo) S.; B.A. (French award), Iona Coll., 1958; M.A., St. John's U., 1960; Ph.D., Fordham U., 1973; m. Loretta Fasolino, June 25, 1960. Instr. modern lang. Iona Coll., 1960-63; asst. prof. fgn. lang. Pace U., N.Y.C., 1963-73, asso. prof., 1973—, asst. chmn. dept. fgn. lang., 1966-68, chmn., 1968—, instr., asst. dir. NDEA Inst., 1961-62; lectr. Bronx Community Coll., 1962-63; lang. examiner N.Y.C. Dept. Personnel. Mem. Modern Lang. Assn., Am. Assn. Tchrs. French, N.Y. State Assn. Fgn. Lang. Tchrs. Roman Catholic. Home: 4 Lloyd Ln Nesconset NY 11767 Office: Pace U Pace Plaza New York City NY 10038

SALMON, JAMES HENRY, neurosurgeon; b. Centerville, Pa., Feb. 25, 1932; s. Ray J. and Ruth (Humes) S.; B.S., Pa. State U., 1953; M.D., Hahnemann Med. Coll., 1957; m. Louisa Potts, Oct. 14, 1967; children—Rebecca, James Thomas. Intern, Charity Hosp. La., New Orleans, 1957-58; resident gen. surgery Hahnemann Hosp., Phila., 1960-61; resident neurosurgery Yale-New Haven Hosp., 1961-65, Hartford (Conn.) Hosp., 1964-65; Knight fellow neuropathology Yale U., New Haven, 1962-63, instr. neurol. surgery, 1964-65; postgrad. fellow Inst. Neurology Queen Sq., London, 1965; instr. neurosurgery U. Cin., 1966-67, asst. prof., 1967-69, asso. prof., 1969-72; chief neurosurgery Cin. VA Hosp., 1966-72; asst. dir. neurosurgery Children's Hosp. Cin., 1970-72; prof., chmn. div. neurosurgery So. Ill. U. Sch. Medicine, 1972-77; asst. clin. prof. U. Pitts., 1977—; individual practice medicine, specializing in neurosurgery, Erie, Pa., 1977—; attending St. Vincent, Hamot med. centers, Erie, 1977—; lectr. in field. Served with USNR, 1958-60. Mem. Central Neurosurg. Soc. (pres. 1977-78), Ill. Neurosurg. Soc. (dir. 1975-77), Central Ill. Pediatric Soc., Assn. Acad. Surgeons, A.C.S., Am. Assn. Neurosurgeons, Soc. Neurosci., others. Republican. Methodist. Contbr. articles to profl. publs. Designer shunt to control hydrocephalus. Home: 220 Anderson Dr Erie PA 16509 Office: 225 W 25th St Erie PA 16502

SALOMON, FRANK ERNEST, musical adminstr.; b. N.Y.C., Apr. 2, 1936; s. Albert and Anna Theresa (Lobbenberg) S.; student N.Y. U., 1953-58; m. Martha Laredo, June 1, 1961; children—Lisa Ana,

Yana Elena. Adminstrv. dir. Alexander Schneider's New Sch. Concerts series, N.Y.C., 1959—; co-adminstr. Rudolf Serkin's Marlboro (Vt.) Music Festival 1960—, coordinator Music from Marlboro, touring program, 1965—; founder Christmas String Seminar/N.Y. String Orch., ann. program with Carnegie Hall, 1969—; rep. musicians including Peter Serkin, 1964—, Murray Perahia, 1969—, Tashi, 1973—, Alexander Schneider, Juliana Markova, Richard Stoltzman, Kalichstein-Laredo-Robinson Trio; founder Brandenburg Ensemble Orch., 1972; mgr. People's Symphony Concerts series, N.Y.C., 1972—. Served with U.S. N.G. 1958. Mem. Assn. Coll., Univ. and Community Arts Adminstrs., Internat. Soc. Performing Arts Adminstrs. Office: 201 W 54th St New York City NY 10019

SALOMON, LUCY, psychiatrist; b. Zagreb, Yugoslavia, Jan. 25, 1925; s. Kornel and Yolanda (Schlesinger) Tarjan; came to U.S., 1950, naturalized, 1955; B.S., Beloit Coll., 1962; M.D., U. Wis., 1968; m. Salomon M. Salomon, Feb. 4, 1950; children—Ronald M., Gary D., Melinda. Intern, Madison (Wis.) Gen. Hosp., 1968-69; resident in psychiatry McLean Hosp., Belmont, Mass., 1969-71, Beth Israel Hosp., Boston, 1971-72; pvt. practice psychiatry, Brookline, Mass., 1972—; asst. attending psychiatrist McLean Hosp., Belmont, Mass., 1972—; asst. psychiatrist Beth Israel Hosp., Boston, 1972—; instr. Harvard Med. Sch., 1972—. Diplomate Am. Bd. Psychiatry and Neurology. Mem. AMA, AAAS, Am. Assn. Psychotherapy, Am. Psychiat. Assn. Contbr. articles to profl. jours. Address: 219 Buckminster Rd Brookline MA 02146

SALOMON, ROBERT JESS, real estate co. exec.; b. Bklyn., Apr. 19, 1925; s. Gilbert H. and Hilda D. (Seiderman) S.; student Pa. State U., 1942-44; B.S., U.S. Naval Acad., 1949; m. D. Gloria Green, Dec. 6, 1952; children—Elizabeth, James, Alice, Bruce, Richard. Commd. ensign U.S. Navy, 1949, advanced through grades to lt.; comdg. officer U.S.S. Courser, ret., 1954; with various real estate firms, 1954-65; asst. v.p., asst. rental mgr. Rockefeller Center, Inc., N.Y.C., 1965-72; v.p. Warner Communications Inc., N.Y.C., 1972—. Trustee YMHA. Mem. Nat. Assn. Real Estate Execs. (pres. N.Y. chpt.), Naval Acad. Alumni, Athletic Assns. Home: 756 Bowne Rd Ocean NJ 07712 Office: 75 Rockefeller Plaza New York City NY 10019

SALOMON, ROBERT VAL, electronics co. exec.; b. Auburn, N.Y., Aug. 29, 1944; s. Robert Fred and Rhea (King) S.; B.S., Union Coll., 1972; M.S., Syracuse U., 1976; m. Joanne Bishop, Aug. 17, 1968; children—Heather Suzzane, Brian Douglas. With Randtech. Corp., Amsterdam, N.Y., 1972-73; sr. project mgr. Welch Allyn Inc., Skaneateles Falls, N.Y., 1973-77; mgr. prodn. engring. Skanamatic Inc., Elbridge, N.Y., 1977—. Served with USN, 1962-71. Mem. IEEE, Inst. Engring. Educators, Instrument Soc. Am. Home: 4864 Pembridge Circle Syracuse NY 13215 Office: Skanamatic Inc Rt 5 W Elbridge NY 13060

SALOMON, SUZANNE EVAN, bus. planner; b. Chgo., Mar. 15, 1947; d. Joseph Klee and Jane Evonne (Rovee) S.; B.A. cum laude (Durant scholar), Wellesley Coll., 1969; M.P.A. (Woodrow Wilson Sch. fellow), Princeton U., 1971; certificate lit. Oxford (U.K.) U., 1967. Asso. econ. cons., Gladstone Assos., Washington, 1971-74; pres. Susal Assos., econ. cons., Washington, 1974-76; market analyst Internat. Paper Co., N.Y.C., 1976-77, mgr. strategic planning, 1977-78; v.p. corporate devel. div. Chase Manhattan Bank, N.Y.C., 1978—; lectr. in field. Bd. dirs. N.Y. chpt. Am. Jewish Com. Mem. Fin. Women's Assn., Am. Inst. Planners. Home: 320 E 57th St New York City NY 10022 Office: Chase Manhattan Bank 1 Chase Manhattan Plaza 28th Floor New York City NY 10015

SALOMONSON, VINCENT VICTOR, research meteorologist; b. Longmont, Colo., July 19, 1937; s. Victor Philip and Eunice (Cole) S.; B.S., Colo. State U., 1959, Ph.D., 1968; B.S., U. Utah, 1960; M.S., Cornell U., 1964; m. Peggy Lucille Swanner, June 8, 1963; children—Scott Houston, Aaron Phillip, Sarah, Karla. Grad. asst. Cornell U., 1962-64; grad. research asst. Colo. State U., 1964-68; research hydrologist Lab. for Atmospheric Scis., Applications Directorate, Goddard Space Flight Center, NASA, Greenbelt, Md., 1968-72, sr. research scientist, 1972—, head br., 1973—. Mem. remote sensing in hydrology working group Nat. Acad. Sci./Internat. Hydrological Decade; chmn. water resources discipline Earth Resources Survey Program, NASA, 1972-77, Landsat-D project scientist, 1977—. Served to 1st lt. weather officer USAF, 1959-62. Recipient awards for exceptional performance ofcl. duties NASA, 1974-77, medal for exceptional sci. achievement, 1976; Honor engr. Colo. State U., 1959. Mem. Am. Meteorol. Soc., Am. Geophys. Union, Sigma Xi, Phi Kappa Phi. Mem. Ch. of Jesus Christ of Latter-day Saints (high priest 1977—). Contbr. articles to profl. jours. Home: 2812 Spindle Ln Bowie MD 20715 Office: Code 913 Goddard Space Flight Center Greenbelt MD 20771

SALOP, ARNOLD, physician; b. N.Y.C., Oct. 19, 1923; s. Alexander and Anna (Lefrak) S.; A.B., Oberlin Coll., 1943; B.M., Northwestern U., 1949, M.D., 1950; m. Lynne Gusikoff, Sept. 24, 1950; children—Andrea, Holly, Evan Arnold. Intern, resident in internal medicine Beth Israel Hosp., 1949-52; resident in internal medicine Goldwater Meml. Hosp., 1950-51, Kingsbridge VA Hosp., 1952-53; practice medicine specializing in internal medicine Ossining, N.Y., 1957—; physician IBM, Westchester County, 1957—; cons. Stony Lodge Sanatorium; dir. ECG dept.; dir. medicine Phelps Meml. Hosp., N. Tarrytown, N.Y.; asso. attending physician Montefiore Hosp., Bronx; asst. clin. prof. medicine Albert Einstein Coll. Medicine. Served from pvt. to pfc. AUS, 1943-45, 1st lt. USAF, 1953-54. Fellow A.C.P., Am. Coll. Cardiology; mem. Am. Heart Assn., Am. Geriatrics Assn., Am. Rheumatism Assn., Alpha Omega Alpha. Office: 43 S Highland Ave Ossining NY 10562

SALPETER, BURTON FOCH, physician; b. Bklyn., Sept. 8, 1918; s. Samuel H. and Leah K. (Kahan) S.; B.S., U. Va., 1939; M.D., Georgetown U., 1943; m. Lucy Lasser, Sept. 19, 1948; children—Ann Miriam, Steven Lee. Intern, Jewish Hosp. of Bklyn., 1943; resident Bristol (Conn.) Hosp., 1946; practice medicine specializing in family practice, Rockaway Park, N.Y., 1946—; dir. family practice Peninsula Hosp. Center, Far Rockaway, N.Y., 1971—. Served with M.C., AUS, 1943-46. Decorated Bronze Star medal with oak leaf cluster. Diplomate Am. Bd. Family Practicce. Mem. AMA, Queens County Med. Soc., Rockaway Med. Soc., Am. Acad. Family Practice, Am. Legion, D.A.V., V.F.W., C. of C., Alpha Epsilon Pi. Jewish. Club: Rotary (pres. 1956-57). Office: 119-15 Rockaway Beach Blvd Rockaway Park NY 11694

SALSALI, MORTEZA, thoracic surgeon; b. Teheran, Iran, Mar. 15, 1930; s. Mehdi and Azizeh (Sadri) S.; came to U.S., 1956, naturalized, 1976; M.D., Teheran U., 1955. Intern, St. Agnes Hosp., White Plains, N.Y., 1956-57; resident in thoracic surgery U. Hosp., Balt., 1965-66; thoracic surgeon Pack Med. Group, N.Y.C., 1968-69; practice medicine specializing in thoracic surgery and surg. oncology, N.Y.C., 1970—. Recipient Arthur Purdy Stout award N.Y. Cancer Soc., 1965. Fellow A.C.S., Am. Coll. Angiology, N.Y. Acad. Medicine; mem. N.Y. County Med. Soc., N.Y. Cancer Soc. Moslem. Contbr. articles in field to med. jours. Home: 137 E 36th St New York City NY 10016 Office: 137 E 36th St New York City NY 10016

SALTEN, DAVID GEORGE, technol. inst. adminstr.; b. N.Y.C., Aug. 23, 1913; s. Max E. and Gertrude (Brauer) S.; Sc.B., Washington Square Coll., 1933; A.M., Columbia, 1939; Ph.D., N.Y. U., 1944; m. Frances Claire Brown; children—Phoebe (Mrs. Merrill Weingrod), Cynthia (Mrs. James L. Ackerman), Melissa. Chemist, Almay Pharm. Corp., N.Y.C., 1934; chemist City of N.Y., 1938-40; tchr. N.Y.C. Bd. Edn., 1940-43, sci. dept. chmn., 1943-48, prin., 1948-50; asso. prof., lectr. grad. program Hunter Coll., 1947-63; city supt. schs., Long Beach, N.Y., 1950-62; lectr. Yeshiva U., N.Y.C., 1953, 59; lectr. ednl. adminstrn., N.Y. U., 1959-61; city supt. schs., New Rochelle, N.Y., 1962-65; exec. dir. Fedn. Jewish Philanthropies, N.Y.C., 1965, exec. v.p., 1966-69; provost N.Y. Inst. Tech., 1969—, exec. v.p., 1974—; cons. mayor's com. on mgmt. survey of schs. and colls. of City of N.Y., 1951. Pres. Nassau County Mental Health Assn., 1953, N.Y. State Citizen's Council, 1957; mem. White House Conf. Edn., 1955, White House Conf. on Youth, 1960; vice chmn. N.Y. Mental Hygiene Council, 1968-76; U.S. resource person on edn. World Mental Health Congress, Paris, 1961; mem. Gov. Rockefeller's Com. on Children and Youth, 1963; mem. bd. edn. Hawthorne Cedar Knolls, N.Y., 1963-65; cons. ednl. tech. U.S. Office Edn., 1964-65; chmn. adv. council to select com. higher edn. N.Y. State Legislature, 1971—; pres. Nat. Council on Aging, 1972-74. Bd. dirs. NAACP Legal Defense Fund, 1964-74; trustee N.Y. Inst. Tech., 1965-71; chmn. adv. council N.Y. U. Sch. Edn., 1963-65; adv. council Columbia Sch. Social Work, 1967—. Recipient citation USNR, 1947. Fellow AAAS; mem. N.E.A., Am. Assn. Sch. Adminstrs., Am. Ednl. Research Assn., Am. Psychol. Assn., Council Sch. Supts. Author: (with others) Mathematics, A Basic Course, 1957. Home: 41 Park Ave New York City NY 10016

SALTER, THOMAS LOWELL, comml. sch. pres.; b. Worcester, Mass., Oct. 2, 1916; s. Harold and Dorothy (Lowell) S.; B.A., Clark U., 1940; m. Constance Davis Smith, Nov. 8, 1941; children—Robin (Mrs. David Chevalier), Christopher L. Instr. Salter Sch., Worcester, 1946-50; asst. to purchasing dir. Norton Co., Worcester, 1950-60; v.p. Salter Secretarial Sch., 1960-68, pres., treas., 1968—. Mem. Bd. Assessors West Boylston, Mass., 1968-73, chmn., 1972—. Mem. adv. com. Wachusett Meadows Wildlife Sanctuary Mass. Audubon Soc., 1965—; mem. adv. com. bus. schs. Mass. Dept. Edn., 1972—. Served to lt. comdr. USNR, 1942-46. Mem. Adminstrv. Mgmt. Soc. (pres. 1967-68), Mass. Assn. Bus. Schs. (pres., 1966-68), New Eng. Bus. Coll. Assn. (pres. 1964-66), Assn. Ind. Schs. and Colls. (commr. 1972-74). Mason. Home: 92 Pierce St West Boylston MA 01583 Office: 45 Cedar St Worcester MA 01609

SALTZER, PAUL, chem. co. exec.; b. N.Y.C., June 12, 1916; s. Zoltan and Margaret (Rosenfeld) S.; m. Mildred Wurman, Oct. 29, 1943; children—Susan Sophia, Sandra Zena. B.B.A., Bernard Baruch sch. Bus. City Coll. N.Y., 1939. Sr. accountant S.D. Leidesdorf & Co., C.P.A.'s, N.Y.C., 1939-54; controller Sonneborn Chem. and Refining Co., N.Y.C., 1954-60; asst. controller Witco Chem. Corp., N.Y.C., 1960-71, sec., 1971-77, v.p. personnel, 1977—. CPA, N.Y. State. Mem. Am. Inst. C.P.A.s, N.Y. State Soc. C.P.A.s. Home: 50 Ridgeland Rd Yonkers NY 10710 Office: 277 Park Ave New York NY 10710

SALUTER, PHILIP ARTHUR, II, mgmt. exec.; b. Malden, Mass., May 26, 1941; s. Philip Arthur and Eleanor Maynes (Young) S.; B.B.A. in Mktg. cum laude, U. Mass.; m. Connie Loraine Tate, Aug. 26, 1973. Mktg. dir., asst. gen. mgr. Berkshire E. Ski Area, Charlemont, Mass., 1974-75; dir. mktg. Mount Snow (Vt.) Resort Complex, 1975-76, v.p., gen. mgr., 1976-78; regional mktg. dir. Region III Holiday Inns, Inc., Hartford, Conn., 1978—; founder, pres. Arthur Alan Douglas & Assos. Served to capt. C.E., U.S. Army, 1965-73; Vietnam. Decorated Bronze Star. Mem. Am. Mgmt. Assn., Am. Mktg. Assn., Eastern Ski Writer's Assn., Deerfield Valley C. of C. Home: 157 Reed Rd Tolland CT 06084 Office: Suite 313 Holiday Inn 50 Morgan St Hartford CT 06120

SALVA, NIEVA DUQUE, obstetrician and gynecologist; b. Dagupan City, Philippines, Apr. 5, 1944; d. Francisco Quimson and Florencia Maglanoc (Tiongson) Duque; came to U.S., 1969; M.D., U. St. Tomas (Philippines), 1967; m. James B. Salva, May 30, 1969; children—Francisco, Catherine Rose, Anthony James. Intern, Delaware County Meml. Hosp., Lansdowne, Pa., 1968; resident in obstetrics and gynecology Albert Einstein Med. Center, Phila., 1969-72; house physician Wilmington (Del.) Med. Center, 1972-73, asst. to dir. dept. obstetrics and gynecology, 1973—; cons. New Castle County Family Planning Centers, 1973—; mem. adv. bd. Del. League for Planned Parenthood, 1977—; clin. instr. Jefferson Med. Coll., Phila., 1973—. Diplomate Am. Bd. Obstetrics and Gynecology. Fellow Am. Coll. Obstetricians and Gynecologists; mem. New Castle County Med. Soc., Del. Obstet. Soc., AMA. Roman Catholic. Home: 1 Perth Dr Wilmington DE 19803 Office: 2018 Naamans Rd Wilmington DE 19810 also Gen Div Wilmington Med Center South Brook St Wilmington DE 19805

SALVAGE, LYNN DIANE, bank exec.; b. N.Y.C., June 6, 1946; d. Edward and Rita (Hofman) S.; B.A. in Germanics cum laude, U. Pa., 1968, M.A., 1968; M.B.A., Harvard U., 1970; postgrad. in internat. fin. N.Y. U., 1973—. Mgr. internat. investment div., v.p. Bankers Trust Co., N.Y.C., 1970-77; on leave as spl. asst. for internat. affairs Pres.'s Exec. Interchange Program, U.S. Treasury Dept., Washington, 1976-77; pres. First Women's Bank of N.Y., 1977—; dir. N.Y. Bd. Trade; mem. N.Y. Dist. Export Council; past mem. Mayor's Task Force on N.Y.C. Fin. Regional rep. Internat. Women's Yr.; past bd. dirs. YWCA of New York. Recipient N.Y.C. Jaycees Pub. Service award, Mem. Nat. Assn. Bank Women, Fin. Women's Assn., Money Marketeers, Harvard Businesswomen N.Y.C. (past chmn.), Women's Action Alliance (dir.). Clubs: Harvard, Harvard Bus. Sch., Atrium. Office: First Womens Bank 111 E 57th St New York City NY 10022

SALVARY, STANLEY CECIL WINSTON, accountant; b. Trinidad, West Indies, Nov. 21, 1937; came to U.S., 1958, naturalized, 1963; A.A.S., Bklyn. Coll., 1962, B.S. cum laude, 1965; M.B.A., L.I. U., 1969; Ph.D., N.Y. U., 1977; m. Veronica Rodriguez, June 29, 1958; children—Sharlene Susan, Lisa, Roxanne, Keisha. Auditor, Henry Brout & Co., N.Y.C., 1962-66; audit accountant Lever Bros., 1966-67; credit mgr., divisional accountant, systems analyst Glamorene Products Co., 1967; spl. project adminstr. mgr. Francis I. DuPont Co., N.Y.C., 1967-70; pres. Salvary & Daniels, N.Y.C., 1970; cons. C.P.A., Bklyn., 1970—; part-time lectr. accountancy Baruch Coll., N.Y.C., 1970, full time, 1970-76, asst. prof., 1976; asso. prof. accountancy Concordia U., 1978—. Recipient Richard Littlefield Meml. award Bklyn. Coll., 1962. C.P.A., N.Y. Mem. Am. Inst. C.P.A.'s, N.Y. State Soc. C.P.A.'s, Am. Accounting Assn., Accounting Research Assn., Fin. Mgmt. Assn., C.W. Post Tax. Inst., Am. Econ. Assn., Alpha Sigma Lambda. Home: 6555 Kildare Rd #302 Cote St Luc PQ H4W 2X4 Canada Office: 1455 De Maisonneuve Blvd W Montreal PQ H3G 1M8 Canada

SALVATI, EUGENE PHILIP, surgeon; b. Pursglove, W.Va., Sept. 7, 1923; s. Nicholas Peter and Mary Angela (Pellegrin) S.; A.B., W.Va. U., 1944, B.S., 1945; M.D., U. Md., 1947; m. Laura Dawson, June 17, 1950; children—Barbara Jeanne, Maribeth, Laura Lynn, Carol Ann, Douglas Eugene, Roger Leo, Catherine Robb, Georgianna. Intern and resident Muhlenberg Hosp., Plainfield, N.J., 1947-49; resident in surgery St. Vincent's Hosp., Indpls., 1949-50, VA Hosp., Indpls., 1950-51, Ind. U. Med. Center, Indpls., 1953-54; resident in colon and rectal surgery Allentown (Pa.) Gen. Hosp., 1954-56; sr. attending surgeon Muhlenberg Hosp., Plainfield, 1956—, chief div. colon and rectal surgery, dir. residency tng. program, 1970—; sr. attending surgeon Raritan Valley Hosp., Greenbrook N.J., 1966—; attending surgeon John Fitzgerald Kennedy Hosp., Edison, N.J., 1976—; clin. asst. prof. surgery Med. and Dental Sch. N.J., Rutgers Med. Sch., Piscataway, N.J., 1971—. Served with U.S. Army, 1943-45, 51-53. Decorated Bronze Star. Fellow A.C.S.; mem. Am., N.Y., N.J., Pa. socs. colon and rectal surgeons, Royal Soc. Medicine, AMA, Southeastern Surg. Soc., N.J., Union County med. socs. Republican. Roman Catholic. Club: Country (Plainfield). Home: 1040 Hillside Ave Plainfield NJ 07060 Office: 1010 Park Ave Plainfield NJ 07060

SALVATIERRA, RICHARD DEAN, mgmt. and govtl. cons., internat. mktg. co. exec.; b. Temple, Tex., May 3, 1944; s. Richard Caballero and Clara Celeste (Roseboro) S.; B.A., U. Ariz., 1967; M.P.A., U. Md., 1973; M.B.A., George Washington U., 1979; m. Patricia Anne Holton, Aug. 9, 1969; children—Richard Dean, Christopher Neil. Program officer Devel. Assos., Inc., Washington, 1972-74; asst. nat. dir. Nat. Edn. Service Center, Washington, 1974-76; pres. Nat. Econ. Devel. Assn., Washington, 1976-78, Triton Corp., Washington, 1978—. Participant, White House Conf. Balanced Nat. Growth and Econ. Devel., 1978; mem. steering com. Nat. Pub. Radio, 1976. Served with USNR, 1968-72. Mem. Nat. Soc. Assn. Execs., Am. Polit. Sci. Assn., Am. Soc. Pub. Adminstrn. Republican. Roman Catholic. Home: 3613 Shepherd St Chevy Chase MD 20015 Office: 1730 K St NW Washington DC 20006

SALVATORE, FRANCIS PAUL, SR., gynecologist; b. Wildwood, N.J., July 30, 1923; s. Gennaro and Kathairne (Ricco) S.; A.A., U. Fla., 1943; B.S., U. Miami, 1944; M.D., Hahnemann Med. Coll., Phila., 1948; postgrad. Columbia U., 1968-78, New Sch., 1970-78, N.Y. U., 1970; m. Deborah Elizabeth Deck, July 25, 1973. Intern, Jersey City Med. Center, 1948-49, Margaret Hague Maternity Hosp., 1949, Woman's Hosp., N.Y.C., 1952-53; gen. practice medicine, Jersey City, 1949-50; resident Woman's Hosp., N.Y.C., 1952-56; practice medicine specializing in obstetrics-gynecology, Englewood, N.J., 1956—; sr. attending obstetrics-gynecology Englewood (N.J.) Hosp., 1956-78, Bergen Pines Hosp., Paramus, N.J., 1956-75. Served with U.S. Army, 1942-43, USNR, 1943-49, USAF, 1949-56. Recipient Service award Englewood Hosp., 1977. Diplomate Am. Bd. Obstetrics and Gynecology. Mem. A.C.S., Am. Coll. Obstetrics and Gynecology, AMA, N.J. State Med. Soc., N.J. Obstetrics and Gynecology Soc., Bergen County Med. Soc. Roman Catholic. Clubs: Knickerbocker Country (Tenafly, N.J.), N.Y. Athletic. Contbr. articles in field to profl. jours. Home: 555 North Ave Apt 22S Fort Lee NJ 07026 Office: 200 Engle St Englewood NJ 07631

SALWIN, LESTER NATHAN, lawyer, govt. ofcl.; b. Kansas City, Mo., Nov., 1911; s. Earl R. and Minnie (Wolf) S.; student Jr. Coll. Kansas City, 1927-29; A.B. cum laude, U. Ill., 1931, LL.B. cum laude, 1933; m. Lillian Levinson, Jan. 13, 1932; 1 dau., Marjorie Beth. Admitted to Ill. bar, 1933, Mo. bar; practiced in Chgo., 1933-39; adjudicator Social Security Adminstrn., Washington, 1940-42; with OPA, 1942-43; asst. to gen. counsel Smaller War Plants Corp., 1943-44; with ct. rev., research and opinion div. OPA, 1944-45; alien property custodian Office of Gen. Counsel, 1945-46; chief trade laws and spl. asst. for legal affairs Econ. and Sci. Sect., SCAP, 1945-52; chief Japan mission U.S. Dept. Justice, Am. Embassy, Tokyo, Japan, 1952-60; with legislative div. U.S. Civil Adminstrn., of Ryuku Islands, 1960-61; spl. asst. Legal Investment div. Office Gen. Counsel, Small Bus. Adminstrn., 1961—; spl. counsel on adminstrv. procedures Nelsen Commn., 1971—. Recipient meritorious service award Dept. Def. Mem. Atlantic Council of U.S. Mem. Fed., Mo., Ill. bar assns., Acad. Polit. Sci., Acad. Polit. and Social Scis., Nat. Lawyers Club, Nat. Council on Crime and Delinquency, Phi Beta Kappa, Order of Coif. Author articles in field; drafted Japanese anti-monopoly, trade assn., corp. laws Comml. Code, Book II. Home: 3812 N Nelson St Arlington VA 22207 Office: Imperial Bldg 1441 L St NW Washington DC 20416

SALZBURG, JOSEPH SHELDON, govt. ofcl.; b. Mayfield, Pa., July 13, 1926; s. Samuel and Anna (Eber) S.; student U. So. Calif., 1945-46; A.B. in Clin. Psychology, U. Miami (Fla.), 1951; postgrad. U. Pitts. Grad. Sch. Pub. and Internat. Affairs, 1968; m. Carmen A. Albaladejo, Apr. 16, 1978. Field dir. ARC, various locations, 1951-63, exec. dir., Jersey City, 1963-67; fgn. service res. officer U.S. Dept. State/AID, 1967—, project mgr. rural devel., Mali, 1978—. Shelter mgr. Office of CD, Jersey City, 1964-67. Served with U.S. Army, 1947-48. Decorated Purple Heart, Bronze Star; recipient Presdl. Medal of Freedom, 1954. Mem. Am. Fgn. Service Assn., Am. Numis. Assn., Smithsonian Assos., Am. Film. Inst. Author: (short stories) A Child of Unknown Parents, 1954, The Little Things, 1956; Tales of Aragon, 1960; (essays) Moments of Inspiration, 1961; (poetry) The Joys of Living, 1963; (fiction) The Dividing Lines, 1965; (short stories) Of Power and Faith, 1967; (novel) Evil Be My Good, 1970; (poetry) A Thousand Delights, 1970; (novels) No Place of Her Own, 1971, The Dream-Seeker, 1972, The Right Time, The Right Place, 1978; (non-fiction) Vietnam: Beyond the War, 1975; also tech. articles. Home: care Schiff 830 S Greenbrier St Arlington VA 22204 Office: US Dept State Washington DC 20523

SALZMAN, HERBERT, ambassador; b. N.Y.C., May 2, 1916; s. William S. and Minnie (Reich) S.; B.A., cum laude with honors Yale, 1938; postgrad. Columbia Grad. Sch. Bus., 1956; m. Rita Friedman, May 26, 1947; children—Anthony David, Jeffrey Jonathan. Formerly v.p. sales Standard Bag Corp., v.p. prodn., pres., 1959-66; asst. adminstr. for devel. finance and pvt. enterprise AID, Washington, 1966-67, asst. adminstr. for pvt. resources, 1967-71; exec. v.p. Overseas Pvt. Investment Corp., 1971-73, dir., 1973-77; U.S. ambassador to OECD, Paris, 1977—. Bd. dirs. Kennedy Center Prodns., Inc., Studio Theatre, John F. Kennedy Center for Performing Arts; mem. vis. com. Harvard U. Center for Internat. Affairs. Served from ensign to lt. comdr. USNR, 1941-46. Mem. Council on Fgn. Relations. Clubs: Federal City, International (Washington); Yale, Harmonie (N.Y.C.); Cedar Point Yacht (Westport, Conn.).

SAM, CHUNG LAM, chem. co. scientist; b. Amoy, China, Mar. 2, 1944; s. Hsi Mei and Mu Cheng (Wang) Shen; came to U.S., 1967; B.Sc., U. Hong Kong, 1966; M.S., Brown U., 1973, Ph.D., 1974; m. Mary Ho, Aug. 22, 1970; 1 dau., Sylvia. Staff physicist Philips Labs., Briarcliff Manor, N.Y., 1974-76; staff laser physicist Allied Chem. Corp., Morristown, N.J., 1977—. Mem. IEEE. Home: 44 Center Grove Rd Randolph NJ 07801 Office: PO Box 1021R Morristown NJ 07960

SAMAAN, SELIM TAWFICK, surgeon; b. Alexandria, Egypt, Jan. 23, 1932; s. Tawfick Elias and Eva Nichola (Hamoui) S.; came to U.S., 1960, naturalized, 1971; M.B.B.Ch., Alexandria U., 1951, M.D., 1958; m. Judith Lane Watson, Dec. 29, 1962; children—Eva, Peter, Andrew, Catherine. Intern, Harlem Hosp., N.Y.C., 1960-61, resident surgery Union Meml. Hosp., Balt., 1961-63, chief resident in surgery, 1964-65; resident in colon and rectal surgery Lahey Clinic, Boston, 1965-66, asst. staff, 1966-67; practice medicine specializing in colon and rectal surgery, Garden City, N.Y., 1967—; chief colon and rectal surgery Mercy Hosp., 1975—; asst. clin. prof. State U. N.Y. Bd. dirs. L.I. div. Am. Cancer Soc. Diplomate Am. Bd. Surgery, Am. Bd. Colon and Rectal Surgery. Fellow A.C.S., AMA, Am. Soc. Colon and Rectal Surgery; mem. N.Y., Nassau County med. socs., N.Y. Soc. Surgeons, N.Y., Pa. socs. colon and rectal surgery. Republican. Greek Orthodox. Club: Cherry Valley. Office: 520 Franklin Ave Garden City NY 11530

SAMENT, SIDNEY, neurologist; b. Lithuania, Apr. 25, 1928; s. Bernard and Mina Liebe (Liebson) S.; M.B., B.Ch., Witwatersrand U., South Africa, 1952, postgrad., 1960-64; postgrad. Harvard Med. Sch., 1967-69; m. Linda Tamara Lurie, Aug. 3, 1960; children—Hilary, Brian, David. Came to U.S., 1964, naturalized, 1973. Intern, Baragwanath Hosp., Johannesburg, 1953-54; resident in neurology Jersey City Med. Center, 1964-65, New Eng. Med. Center, 1965-67; fellow Harvard Med. Sch., Boston, 1967-69; asst. prof. neurology Hahnemann Hosp., Phila., 1970-73; practice medicine specializing in neurology and electroencepalography, Easton, Pa., 1973—. Recipient Spl. award for continuing postgrad. edn. A.M.A., 1970-73. Diplomate Am. Bd. Electroencephalography. Mem. A.M.A., Am. Acad. Neurology, Phila. Neurol. Soc., Am., Eastern EEG socs. Contbr. articles to profl. publs. Research, 1st describer non-ketotic diabetic coma. Home: 3515 Southwood Dr Easton PA 18042 Office: 2040 Lehigh St Easton PA 18042

SAMET, CHARLES MERLE, physician; b. Mpls., May 27, 1928; s. Joseph and Rela (Greenberg) S.; B.A. magna cum laude, U. Minn., 1948, B.S., 1950, M.B., 1952, M.D., 1953; m. Rochelle Renee Rosenberg, June 19, 1955; children—Rhonda Claire, Jeffrey Allen. Intern, Boston City Hosp., 1952-53, resident in internal medicine, 1953-54; resident in internal medicine Boston VA Hosp., 1956-57; fellow in infectious disease Tufts U.-New Eng. Center Hosp., Boston, 1957-59; practice medicine specializing in internal medicine and infectious diseases, Manhasset, N.Y., 1959—; asso. prof. clin. medicine State U.N.Y., Stony Brook; clin. asst. prof. medicine Cornell U., Ithaca, N.Y.; cons. medico-legal aspects of infectious disease; mem. med. advisory com. Vis. Nurse Assn. L.I. Served with M.C., USAF, 1954-56. Fellow A.C.P.; mem. infectious Diseases Soc. Am., Am. Fedn. Clin. Research, N.Y. Acad. Sci., Alpha Omega Alpha. Jewish. Contbr. articles on infectious diseases to med. jours. Home: 22 Olive St Lake Success NY 11020 Office: 535 Plandome Rd Manhasset NY 11030

SAMORAJCZYK, JOHN FRANK, psychologist; b. Bridgeport, Conn., Mar. 4, 1932; s. John Frank and Sophia Ladislaus (Zysk) S.; A.B. in Psychology, Calif. State Coll., 1959, M.A., 1961; Ph.D., U. Md., 1968; m. Ruth Ziehm, Aug. 13, 1966; children—Lisa, John Frank. Intern, Spring Grove State Hosp., Balt., 1968, 69, clin. psychologist, 1969-70; psychol. cons., Pediatric Clinic, Greater Balt. Med. Center, 1970-71; dir. Hamilton Children's Center, Hyattsville, Md., 1970—; clin. psychologist, Asso. Life Scis., Inc., Landover, Md., 1972—; child, cons. psychologist, Prince George's Gen. Hosp., Cheverly, Md.; mem. adv. bd., NIMH Study Center; dir. therapy program, vocat. rehab. unit Spring Grove State Hosp.; supr. vol. tutors and psychometrists; dir. fgn. exchange program, Whittier, Calif. Asst. chmn. edn. commn. Grace United Methodist Ch., Gaithersburg, Md., 1976. Served with AUS, 1952-54. Mem. Am., D.C., Md. psychol. assns., Psi Chi. Republican. Contbr. articles to profl. jours. Home: 19205 Seneca Ridge Ct Gaithersburg MD 20760 Office: 4112 Hamilton St Hyattsville MD 20781

SAMPIETRO, PIERLUIGI, pub. relations cons.; b. Candia, Italy, Jan. 30, 1928; s. Carlo and Maria (Scarabello) S.; came to U.S., 1954, naturalized, 1964; Ph.D. in Philosophy, Rome U., 1949; Ph.D. in Econs., Salzburg U., 1950; Ph.D. in Music, Mozarteum, Salzburg, 1950; m. Elena Giurdanella, June 22, 1957; 1 dau., Maria Lucia. Internat. pub. relations cons. to fgn. govts., govt. agencies and pvt. cos.; founder, pres. Sampietro Internat. Inc., Harrison, N.Y., 1973—; cons. fgn. countries, real estate investment. Mem. Internat. Diplomatic Corps. Author: Sampietro Report, 1961; Sampietro International Business Forum, 1978; Sampietro Real Estate Investments, 1977; piano records: Sampietro Plays Your Favorite Songs, 1977. Address: care Joseph Vassallo 185 Halstead Ave Harrison NY 10528

SAMPSON, ARTHUR FRANCIS, coal co. exec.; b. Warren, R.I., Oct. 8, 1926; s. Arthur Francis and Dora (Couturier) S.; B.S., U. R.I., 1951; m. Blanche Bouffard, Sept. 20, 1947; children—Arthur Francis III, Phillip R., Jason E., Matthew S. Accountant, Gen. Electric Co., Erie, Pa., 1951-62; dep. sec. procurement State of Pa., 1963-66, sec. adminstrn. and budget, 1967-68, sec. Pa. Gov.'s cabinet, 1968-72; commr. fed. supply service Gen. Services Adminstrn., also commr. pub. bldgs. service, dep. adminstr. for spl. projects, 1969-72, adminstr., 1972-75; pres. San-vel Concrete Corp., Littleton, Mass., 1976-77, Serec, Inc., Fairfield, Ala., 1978—. Served with USAAF, 1944-47. Recipient Presdl. citation Soc. Am. Value Engrs. Republican. K.C. Home: 19 Oak Ave Camp Hill PA 17011 Office: 319 44th St Fairfield AL 35064

SAMS, NED HOUSTON, cons. engr. co. exec.; b. Asheville, N.C., Aug. 20, 1920; s. Sylvester V. and Ina (Wood) S.; A.B., Maryville Coll., 1941; M.S., U. Tenn., 1952; m. Marthena Densberger, Mar. 21, 1943; children—M. Randolph, Nedine E., Janis E., Rodney W. Co-mgr. book store U. Tenn., Knoxville, 1951, mgr. Carolyn P. Brown Meml. Univ. Center, 1953-54; mgr. Ind. Chem. div. Sanfax Corp., Harrisburg, Pa., 1955-62; sales mgr. Hoch Co., Harrisburg, 1962-71; bus. devel., pub. relations mgr. firm Gannett Fleming Corddry & Carpenter, Inc., Harrisburg, 1971—; active Water Pollution Control Assn. Pa., 1963—, editor ofcl. mag., 1967-71, pres. central sect., 1970, mem. exec. bd., 1967—, 2d v.p., 1974—, mem. aims and objectives com., 1974—, pres., 1976-77; mem. publs. com. Water Pollution Control Fedn., 1972—. Served to 1st lt. AUS, 1943-46. Decorated Army Commendation medal; recipient Top Hat award Water Pollution Control Assn. Pa., 1966, also C. Eber Wengert award Eastern sect., 1968, Central sect., 1973. Mem. Am. Water Works Assn., Nat. Assn. Mfrs. (environ. quality com.), Pa. C. of C. (pollution abatement com.), Am. Pub. Works Assn. (chpt. pub. relations chmn. 1977-78), Pa. Municipal Authorities Assn. (membership com.), Pa. Boroughs Assn. (conf. com.), Am. Mktg. Assn., Delta Sigma Pi. Episcopalian. Clubs: Masons, Shriners; Nat. Sojourner. Home: 69 W Caracas Ave Hershey PA 17033 Office: PO Box 1963 Harrisburg PA 17105

SAMSELL, LEWIS PATRICK, auditor; b. Morgantown, W.Va., Feb. 20, 1943; s. Lewis Hildreth and Harriet Elizabeth (Gidley) S.; B.S. with honors in bus. adminstrn., W.Va. U., 1970; M.B.A., George Washington U., 1975; m. Linda Joyce Hewitt, July 19, 1967. Supervisory auditor U.S. Gen. Accounting Office, Washington, 1971—; instr. in bus. Prince George's Community Coll., Largo, Md., 1974-77. Mem. resident camping com. Potomac Area Council Camp Fire Girls; bd. dirs. Applewalk Condominium, Laurel, Md. Served with USN, 1964-67. Certified Mgmt. Accountant. Mem. Nat. Assn. Accountants (bd. dirs. Washington and Montgomery-Prince Georges), Assn. Govt. Accountants, Municipal Fin. Officers Assn., Am. Accounting Assn., Inst. Mgmt. Accounting, Am. Mgmt. Assn., Soc. for Advancement Mgmt., W.Va. Soc. of Washington, Episcopalian. Home: 11354 Laurelwalk Dr Laurel MD 20811 Office: 441 G St NW Washington DC 20548

SAMUEL, ERIC RUDOLF, watchmaker; b. Cologne, Germany, Oct. 22, 1906; s. William and Paula (Dreyfuss) S.; came to U.S., 1947, naturalized, 1952; certified master watchmaker, Watchmakers Sch., Cologne, 1926; master certified watchmaker Watchmakers Coll., Hamburg, 1929; m. Thekla Bamberger, Nov. 13, 1938; children—Lydia, Ellen, Jeannette. Asst. mgr. Karstadt Dept. Store, Bremen, Germany, 1931-33; pvt. practice watchmaking Amsterdam, Netherlands, 1933-35, Elizabethville, Belgian Congo, 1935-47; watchmaker Gubelin Watch Co., N.Y.C., 1947-48, Eterna Watch Co., N.Y.C., 1948-49; watchmaker, Rochester, N.Y., 1949-69; dir. Am. Watchmaker Inst., Cin., 1975—; conv. chmn. N.Y. State Watchmakers Assn., 1955—, Watchmaker of Year, 1977, pres. 1972-74. Mem. Rochester Watchmakers Guild (pres. 1962—), Fla. Watchmakers Assn. Jewish. Clubs: Masons, Shriners. Home: 59 Avondale Park Rochester NY 14620

SAMUELS, HAROLD, art dealer, antiquarian book dealer; b. Bklyn., July 9, 1917; s. Michael and Frieda S.; B.A., Ohio U., 1937, M.A., 1938; LL.B., Harvard U., 1941; student Art Students League, 1945; m. Peggy Bardsley, Apr. 30, 1948; children—Peter, Amy, Matthew, Joan. Co-prin. Peggy and Harold Samuels, dealers in Am. art, antiquarian books on Am. art, Locust Valley, N.Y., 1961—; lectr. on buying Western paintings for investment, restoring paintings. Mem. U.S. Horse Cavalry Assn. Author: (with Peggy Samuels) Illustrated Biographical Encyclopedia of Artists of the American West, 1976; Collected Writings of Frederic Remington, 1979. Home and office: PO Box 465 Locust Valley NY 11560

SAMUELS, PEGGY BARDSLEY, art dealer, antiquarian book dealer; b. Bklyn., Nov. 27, 1922; d. James and Anna Bardsley; B.S., N.Y. U., 1944; m. Harold Samuels, Apr. 30, 1948; children—Peter, Amy, Matthew, Joan. Editor, Woman's Day mag., 1945-48; co-prin. Peggy and Harold Samuels, dealers in Am. art, antiquarian books on Am. art, Locust Valley, N.Y., 1961—; lectr. on buying Western paintings for investment, restoring paintings. Mem. U.S. Horse Cavalry Assn. Author: (with Harold Samuels) Illustrated Biographical Encyclopedia of Artists of the American West, 1976; Collected Writings of Frederic Remington, 1979. Home and Office: PO Box 465 Locust Valley NY 11560

SAMUELS, RICHARD MEL, psychologist; b. Bklyn., Mar. 22, 1943; s. Murrsy and Rose S.; Asso. Applied Sci., State U. N.Y., 1961; B.A., Hofstra U., 1965, M.A., 1967; Ph.D., City U. N.Y., 1973; m. Harriet A. Schwartz, July 30, 1966; children—Lisa, David. Adj. asso. prof. City U. N.Y., 1970-73; sr. clin. psychologist N.J. Med. Sch., Newark, 1973-74, sr. clin. prof. human sexuality program, dept. obstetrics and gynecology, also adj. asst. prof. dept. psychiatry, 1974-76, dir. gender dysphoria clinic, 1974-76; clin. psychologist, dir. Center for Sexual and Relationship Enrichment, Teaneck, N.J., 1976—; mem. clin. faculty Sch., Applied and Profl. Psychology, Rutgers U. Grad. Sch.; cons. Teaneck Group Home for Girls. Cons. Bergen County Explorers Orgn. Recipient Albert J. Harris award City U. N.Y., 1967. N.J. Med. Sch. fellow, 1973-74. Fellow Behavior Therapy and Research Soc., Eastern Assn. Sex Therapists (charter); mem. Am. Psychol. Assn., AAAS, Assn. Advancement of Behavior Therapy, N.Y. Acad. Sci. Author: Sex During Pregnancy and the Postpartum Period, 1976; A Gender Dysphoria Clinic in New Jersey, 1977; cons. editor Behavior Therapy, 1973—; editor Pvt. Practitioner, 1976—. Home: 89 Meadowbrook Rd Randolph NJ 07801 Office: 175 Cedar Ln Teaneck NJ 07666

SAMUELSON, EDWIN ARTHUR, chiropractor; b. Richmond Hill, N.Y., Apr. 24, 1939; s. Edwin Arthur and Violet Emma (Schmitt) S.; D.C., Chiropractic Inst. N.Y., 1965; postgrad. in roentgenology Nat. Coll. Chiropractic, 1972-75. Extern Chiropractic Inst., 1964-65; gen. practice chiropractic, N.Y.C., 1966—; advisor Yorkville Alliance for Comprehensive Health Care, 1972-73; postgrad. in chiropractic orthopaedics, 1975-78. Mem. N.Y. State Chiropractic Assn., Nat. Coll. Chiropractic Alumni Assn. Republican. Episcopalian. Home: 446 E 76th St New York City NY 10022 Office: 133 E 58th St New York City NY 10022

SAMUELSON, PAUL ANTHONY, economist; b. Gary, Ind., May 15, 1915; s. Frank and Ella (Lipton) S.; B.A., U. Chgo., 1935, LL.D., 1961; M.A., Harvard U., 1936, Ph.D. (David A. Wells prize 1941), 1941; LL.D., U. Chgo., Oberlin Coll., 1961, Boston Coll., 1964, Ind. U., 1966, U. Mich., 1967, Claremont Grad. Sch., 1970, U. N.H., 1971, Keio U., 1971, D.Sc., East Anglia U., Norwich, Eng., 1966; D.Litt. (hon.), Ripon Coll., 1962, No. Mich. U., 1973; L.H.D., Seton Hall Coll., 1971, Williams Coll., 1971; D.Sc., U. Mass., 1972, U. R.I., 1972; LL.D. (hon.), Harvard U., 1976, 1972, Gustavus Adolphus Coll., 1974, U. So. Calif., 1975, U. Pa., 1976, U. Rochester (N.Y.), 1976, Cath. U. Louvain, 1976, Emmanuel Coll., 1977; m. Marion Crawford, July 2, 1938; children—Jane Kendall, Margaret Wray, William Frank, Robert James, John Crawford, Paul Reid. Prof. econs. Mass. Inst. Tech., 1940—, inst. prof., 1966; cons. Nat. Resources Planning Bd., 1941-43, WPB, 1945, U.S. Treasury, 1945-52, 61—, RAND Corp., 1948—, Fed. Res. Bd., 1965—; Stamp Meml. lectr., London, 1961; Wicksell lectr., Stockholm, 1962; Franklin lectr., Detroit, 1962; Hoyt vis. fellow Calhoun Coll., Yale, 1962; Carnegie Found. reflective yr., 1965-66; John von Neumann lectr. U. Wis., 1971; Sultzbacher Meml. lectr. Columbia Law Sch., N.Y.C., 1974. chmn. Pres.'s Task Force Maintaining Am. Prosperity. Guggenheim fellow, 1948-49; Ford Found. research fellow, 1958-59; recipient John Bates Clark medal Am. Econ. Assn., 1947; Alfred Nobel Meml. prize in econs. sci., 1970. Fellow Brit. Acad. (corr.), Am. Philos. Soc., Am. Econ. Assn. (hon.; pres. 1961); mem. Com. Econ. Devel. (research advisory bd. 1960), Am. Acad. Arts and Scis., Internat. Econ. Assn. (pres. 1966-68, hon. pres.), Nat. Acad. Scis., Econometric Soc. (pres. 1951), Phi Beta Kappa. Author: Foundations of Economic Analysis, 1947; Economics, 1948-76; Readings in Economics, 1955; (with R. Dorfman and R.M. Solow) Linear Programming and Economic Analysis, 1958; Collected Scientific Papers 4 vols., 1966, 72, 77; co-author other books; contbr. articles to profl. jours. Columnist for Newsweek. Home: 75 Clairemont Rd Belmont MA 02178

SANANMAN, MICHAEL LAWRENCE, neurologist; b. Bklyn., Oct. 11, 1939; s. Jack and Sarey (Bykofsky) S.; A.B., Swarthmore Coll., 1960; M.D., Columbia U., 1964; m. Elisa Joan Freeman, Apr. 12, 1964; children—Amy, Peter. Intern, Univ. Hosp., San Francisco, 1964-65; resident in neurology N.Y. Neurol. Inst., N.Y.C., 1966-69; practice medicine specializing in neurology, Elizabeth, N.J., 1972—; cons. neurologist St. Elizabeth's Hosp., Elizabeth Gen. Hosp., Alexian Bros. Hosp., Rahway (N.J.) Hosp.; instr. neurology Columbia U., N.Y.C., 1971-75; asso. clin. prof. neurology N.J. Coll. Medicine and Dentistry, Newark, 1975—; mem. advisory council N.J. chpt. Multiple Sclerosis Soc. Served to lt. comdr. M.C., USNR, 1969-71. Diplomate Am. Bd. Psychiatry and Neurology. Mem. Am. Acad. Neurology, AMA, Am. Epilepsy Soc. (advisory council N.J. chpt.), N.J. Acad. Medicine, Am., Eastern EEG socs. Office: 700 N Broad St Elizabeth NJ 07208

SANBORN, DONALD EDWARD, III, therapist; b. Concord, N.H., Nov. 28, 1942; s. Donald Edward and Lena (Cross) S.; B.A., New Eng. Coll., 1965; M.Ed., Plymouth State Coll., 1971; M.Ed., U. N.H., 1973; postgrad. Mass. Sch. Profl. Psychology, 1977—. Research analyst dept. community medicine Dartmouth Med. Sch., 1972-74, edn. dir., 1974-75, psychotherapist dept. psychiatry, 1975-77, behavioral therapist unit behavioral medicine Brattleboro (Vt.) Retreat, 1977—. Mem. Am. Assn. Suicidology, Am. Personnel and Guidance Assn., Nat. Council Family Relations. Contbr. articles to profl. publs. Home: RFD 3 Box 183B Putney VT 05346 Office: Behavioral Medicine Unit Dartmouth Med Sch Brattleboro Retreat Brattleboro VT 05301

SANBORN, EVERETT CLARENCE, librarian; b. Troy, Maine, June 21, 1937; s. Clarence Irvin and Adele Louise (Bennett) S.; B.A., U. Maine, 1959; M.S., Columbia, 1962; certificate U. Bridgeport, 1972. Asst. librarian Math. Library, Columbia U., 1959-60; trainee West Farms br. N.Y. Pub. Library, 1960-62; librarian young adult sect. New Canaan (Conn.) Pub. Library, 1962-64; librarian Broadview Jr. High Sch., Danbury, Conn., 1964—. Mem. adv. com. to supt. Danbury Pub. Schs., 1973—. Mem. NEA (sec. Danbury), Conn., Danbury edn. assns., New Eng., Conn. sch. librarians assns., Conn., New Eng. library assns., Wilton Hist. Soc., Phi Delta Kappa. Home: 228 Catalpa Rd Wilton CT 06897 Office: Hospital Ave Danbury CT 06810

SANBORN, RALPH DURELL, mgmt. cons.; b. Palmer, Mass., May 10, 1917; s. Harry Brackett and Mabelle Malinda (Durell) S.; B.S. in Mech. Engring., U. Maine, 1939; m. Edith Louise Thomas, June 28, 1940. Tool designer Moore Drop Forging Co., Springfield, Mass., 1939; tech. apprentice Am. Steel & Wire Co., Donora, Pa., 1939-41; design analyst, exptl. engr. Brown & Sharpe Mfg. Co., Providence, 1941-46; mech. devel. engr., devel. project mgr. Arthur D. Little Inc., Cambridge, Mass., 1946-73; cons. devel. project mgmt., 1974—. Registered profl. engr., Mass. Mem. Am. Def. Preparedness Assn., Tau Beta Pi. Home and Office: Star Route 1 Wolfeboro NH 03894

SANDBERG, IRWIN WALTER, research mathematician; b. N.Y.C., Jan. 23, 1934; s. Ben and Estelle (Hornick) S.; student CCNY, 1951-53; B.E.E., Poly. Inst. Bklyn., 1955, M.E.E. (Westinghouse fellow), 1956, D.E.E., (Bell Telephone Labs. fellow), 1958; m. Barbara A. Zimmerman, June 15, 1958; 1 dau., Heidi L. Tech. aid Bell Telephone Labs., Inc., Murray Hill, N.J., summer 1954, mem. tech. staff, 1958-67, head systems theory research dept., 1967-72, mem. math. and stats. research center, 1972—; engr. Wheeler Labs., Great Neck, N.Y., summer 1955; vis. prof. U. Calif., Berkeley, 1965. U.S. del. Union Radio Scientifique Internationale, Munich, Fed. Republic Germany, 1966; U.S. nat. inst. rep. Advanced Study Inst. on Network and Signal Theory, NATO, Bournemouth, Eng., 1972; invited lectr. study insts. NATO, Knokke, Belgium, 1966, Copenhagen, Denmark, 1970; distinguished invited speaker Asilomar Conf., 1973, 74. Recipient Best Paper award Asilomar Conf., 1970. Fellow IEEE (adminstrv. com. group circuit theory 1969-70, vice chmn. group circuit theory 1971-72); mem. AAAS, Eta Kappa Nu, Sigma Xi, Tau Beta Pi. Patentee in field. Home: 100 Lenape Ln Berkeley Heights NJ 07922 Office: Mountain Ave Murray Hill NJ 07974

SANDE, RHODA, art gallery exec.; b. N.Y.C., Mar. 12, 1928; d. Herman and Ruth (Unger) Herman; student Parsons Sch. Design, Pratt Inst., 1950. Radio actress, 1938-43; tchr. jewelry design Dennison Corp., 1945-46; jewelry designer Hattie Carengie and own bus., 1947-50; styling cons. Iroquois China Co., 1952; columnist Town and Village newspaper, 1950-51; free lance interior designer, 1949-53; owner, designer, dir. Rhoda Sande Gallery, N.Y.C., 1954—. Active, Mus. Modern Art, Met. Mus., Am. Pl. Theater, Cooper-Hewett Mus. Mem. Am. Soc. Interior Designer, East Mid-Manhattan C. of C. (dir.). Work shown in numerous mags. Gallery: 61 E 57th St New York City NY 10022

SANDEEN, MARY REED (MRS. RUSSELL G. SANDEEN), ret. educator; b. Ernest, Pa., Dec. 22, 1903; d. William and Sarah (Anderson) Reed; B.S., U. Pa., Indiana, Pa., 1930; M.A., Columbia U., 1952; m. Russell G. Sandeen, June 30, 1945. Tchr., Indiana County (Pa.) Schs., 1922-28, Bradford Area Schs., McKean County, Pa., 1930-69, Smethport Area Schs., 1969-70. Treas., McKean County Sch. Employees Credit Union, 1942-70, Bradford Twp. Sch. Employees Service League, 1956-58. Mem. Pa., Nat. edn. assns., Elementary Prins. Assn., AAUW, McKean County Sch. Employees Ret. Tchrs. Assn. (treas.), Delta Kappa Gamma (state budget and fin. chmn. 1955-67, state treas. 1953-55; conv. treas. 1960, 62, treas. Alpha Epsilon chpt. 1951-58, 70-76). Methodist. Club: Order Eastern Star (organist 1969—). Address: 205 Congress St Bradford PA 16701

SANDER, HANS K., architect; b. Berlin, Oct. 17, 1925; s. Ernst and Martha (Laewen) S.; B.A., Columbia, 1947; M.F.A., Princeton, 1955; m. Cintra Carter Sander, 1969; children—Cintra H., Richard M., Leslie H., Whitney F., Casilda C. Job capt. Vincent G. Kling, Phila., 1955-59; owner H.K. Sander, Princeton, N.J., 1959-64; partner, Walker, Sander, Ford & Kerr, Princeton, 1965-71; sec.-treas., dir. Walker, Sander, Ford & Kerr, Princeton, 1971-73, pres., dir., 1973-74; pres. Hellmuth, Obata & Kassabaum, Princeton, 1975—. Chmn., Princeton Twp. Planning Bd., 1966-69, Princeton Regional Planning Bd., 1970-76. Fellow AIA (mem. design com. 1969-73, chmn. subcom. design rev. bds. of com. on design 1969-73); mem. N.J. Soc. Architects (state dir. 1966-73, chpt. pres. 1967, 70, chmn. environ. design ordinance com. 1968-73). Clubs: Pretty Brook, Nassau (Princeton); Devon Yacht (East Hampton, N.Y.). Home: 213 Constitution Dr Princeton NJ 08540 Office: 18 Nassau St Princeton NJ 08540

SANDERS, CHARLES ADDISON, hosp. adminstr., physician; b. Dallas, Feb. 10, 1932; s. Harold Barefoot and May Elizabeth (Forrester) S.; M.D., U. Tex., 1955; m. Elizabeth Ann Chipman, Mar. 6, 1956; children—Elizabeth, Charles Addison, Carlyn, Christopher. Intern, asst. resident Boston City Hosp., 1955-57, chief resident, 1957-58; clin. and research fellow in medicine Mass. Gen. Hosp., Boston, 1958-60, chief cardiac catheterization lab., 1962-72, gen. dir., 1972—, physician, 1973—, program dir. myocardial infarction research unit, 1967-72, program dir. MEDLAB systems, 1969-72. Asso. prof. medicine Harvard U., 1969—; lectr., mem. vis. com. for sponsored research Mass. Inst. Tech., 1973—. Mem. vis. com. Sch. Medicine, U. Miami, 1973—. Bd. dirs. United Way of Mass. Bay, Mass. Citizens Com. for Dental Health; bd. govs. Mass. Sci. and Tech. Found.; mem. corp. Charles Stark Draper Lab., Cambridge, Mass. Served to capt. M.C., USAF, 1960-62. Mem. Am. Fedn. for Clin. Research, Am., Mass. (dir.) heart assns., Mass. Med. Soc., A.C.P., Am. Physiol. Soc., Am. Clin. and Climatol. Soc., Am. Coll. Cardiology, Am. Soc. for Clin. Investigation, Soc. Hosp. Adminstrs. Unitarian. Club: Harvard. Mem. editorial bd. New Eng. Jour. Medicine, 1969-72. Home: 171 Concord St Wayland MA 01778 Office: Mass Gen Hosp Boston MA 02114

SANDERS, CLIFFORD CHARLES, educator; b. Kittanning, Pa., Nov. 30, 1934; s. Charles Ray and Veronica Jane (McCafferty) S.; B.S., Frostburg State Coll., 1963, M.Ed., 1967; postgrad. U. Md., Pa. State U.; m. Wanda Kaye Tate, Nov. 23, 1960; 1 dau., Kelly Ann. Broadcaster, asst. mgr., program dir. Sta. WCUM, Cumberland, Md., 1962-65; program dir. Sta. WTBO, Cumberland, 1965-66; tchr. Hereford Jr.-Sr. High Sch., Parkton, Baltimore County, Md., 1967-76; chmn. dept. English, Pikesville (Md.) Jr. High Sch., 1976-78, Kenwood Sr. High Sch., Baltimore County, Md., 1978—; lectr., reader of poetry in colls. and various civic groups. Served with AUS,

1957-59. Mem. Md. Council Tchrs. English (tchr. of Yr. award 1975-76), Poetry Soc. Am., Pa. Poetry Soc., Tchrs. Assn. Balt. County, Md. Tchrs. Assn., NEA. Episcopalian. Club: Rotary. Author: DP 163 and Other Poems, 1976. Home: Holly Hill Rd 2 New Freedom PA 17349 Office: Kenwood Sr High School Baltimore MD 21221

SANDERS, FRANK, bus. exec.; b. Tarboro, N.C., July 30, 1919; grad. Armstrong Jr. Coll., Savannah, Ga., 1938; J.D., George Washington U., 1953; M.A. in Govt. and Politics, U. Md., 1972. Mem. staff Com. on Appropriations, U.S. Ho. of Reps., 1948-69; asst. sec. Navy, 1969-72, under sec., 1972-73; pres. Logistics Mgmt. Inst., Washington, 1973-74; v.p. Signal Cos., Potomac, Md., 1974—; v.p. Burmah Oil & Gas Co. subs. Burmah Oil, Ltd., 1974-77, Flying Tigers Lines, 1977—. Elder, trustee Fourth Presbyn. Ch., Bethesda, Md.; asso. mem. Inst. Strategic Studies, London; mem. Govt. Procurement Commn., 1969-72; trustee Washington Bible Coll. Served to capt. U.S. Army, 1941-45. Decorated Bronze Star. Mem. Pi Sigma Alpha. Address: 12413 Over Ridge Rd Potomac MD 20854

SANDERS, GWENDOLYN W., community coll. adminstr.; b. St. Louis, Dec. 17, 1937; d. Adolph and Burnett Fisher; student St. Louis U., 1953-55; B.S., Hams Tchrs. Coll., 1962; M.A., St. Louis U., 1968; Ed.D., Nova U., 1976; m. Gordon Burell Sanders, Aug. 13, 1954; children—Darrell F., Romona R., Jocelyn M. Tchr., St. Louis Pub. Schs., 1962-66; Head Start dir. Lincoln (Nebr.) Pub. Schs., 1966-68; dir., tchr. health program St. Peter's Cathedral, Wilmington, Del., 1969-70; edn. planner City of Wilmington, 1970-72; facility planner Del. Tech. and Community Coll., Wilmington, 1972-73, dean of student services, 1973—; cons. Dept. Justice, Ednl. Testing Services, Urban Edn., community orgns.; tchr. U. Del. Continuing Edn.; workshop leader and trainer. Allocations and membership coms. United Way; mem. Latin Am. Community Center, 1972-75, edn. task force Model Cities, NAACP, Del. Human Relations Commn., Cityside, Inc., intergovtl. manpower service Comprehensive Employment Tng. Act. Recipient merit award Title I Parent Adv. Bd., 1973. Mem. Am. Personnel and Guidance Assn., AAUP, Nat. Assn. Student Personnel Adminstrs., Nat. Vocat. Guidance Assn., Eastern Assn. Coll. Deans, Am. Coll. Personnel Assn., Delta Sigma Theta. Republican. Roman Catholic. Home: 44 E Salisbury Dr Wilmington DE 19809 Office: 333 Shipley St Wilmington DE 19801

SANDERS, JAMES JOSEPH, accountant; b. Emmitsburg, Md., Sept. 7, 1920; s. James Clarence and Mary (Rider) S.; B.C.S., Benjamin Franklin U., 1941, M.C.S. 1948; m. R. Pearl Cantrell, Aug. 25, 1951; 1 stepson, James G. Accounting FHA, 1938-42; partner O'Connell & Co., C.P.A.'s, 1951-56; partner Townsend & Sanders, 1956-61; practice accounting, Bethesda, Md., 1961-72; partner firm Sanders & Howard, 1972-73; individual practice, 1973-76; partner firm Stoy Malone & Co. C.P.A.'s, 1976—. Served with AUS, 1942-46. C.P.A., Md. Mem. Am. Inst. C.P.A.'s Chevy-Chase C. of C. (dir.), Md. Assn. C.P.A.'s (pres., founder Montgomery-Prince George chpt.; dir. 1967—), U.S. Power Squadrons. Clubs: Reciprocity (past treas.) (Bethesda); Columbia Country (Chevy Chase, Md.). Home: 7107 Radnor Rd Bethesda MD 20034 Office: Air Rights Bldg East 7315 Wisconsin Ave Bethesda MD 20014

SANDERS, JOHN DAVID, investment banker; b. Louisville, Aug. 2, 1938; s. Wallace Wolfred, Sr., and Mary Jane (Brownfield) S.; B.E.E., U. Louisville, 1961, M.Eng., 1973; M.S., Carnegie-Mellon U., 1962, Ph.D., 1965; m. Carole Claudia Ewing, Aug. 19, 1967; children—Elaine, Paul. Devel. engr. Gen. Elec. Co., Owensboro, Ky., 1962; teaching asst. Carnegie-Mellon U., Pitts., 1962-64; research scientist C.I.A., Washington, 1965-68; v.p. Wachtel & Co., Inc., Washington, 1968—; dir. Design Specs, Inc., Alexandria, Va., Temporaries, Inc., Washington, Indsl. Tng. Corp., Rockville, Md., Policyholder Service Corp., Falls Church, Va. NSF fellow, 1962. Mem. IEEE, Washington Soc. Investment Analysts, Nat. Soc. Profl. Engrs. Home: 4600 N 26th St Arlington VA 22207 Office: 1000 Vermont Ave NW Washington DC 20005

SANDERS, REUBEN AUGUSTUS, accountant; b. Smithfield, N.C., Feb. 16, 1913; s. Malcolm Lemay and Mary Taylor (Sanders) S.; LL.B., Nat. U., 1937; B.C.S., Benjamin Franklin U., 1948; J.D., George Washington U., 1968; m. Marjorie Poole, July 17, 1937; children—Robert Allen, Patricia Anne. Office mgr. Baraca Philathea Union, 1933-39; navy auditor Potomac River Naval Command, 1939-44; chief accountant Air Force Aid Soc., Inc., Washington, 1946-64, asst. sec., 1964-74, sec., 1974—. Budget chmn. Md. P.T.A., 1958-58, rules and proceedings chmn., 1961-63; treas. Montgomery County (Md.) P.T.A. Council, 1958, pres., 1959-60; mem. Montgomery County Tchrs. Career Recognition Com., 1960; sub chmn. Montgomery County Curriculum Study Commn., 1960-61; trustee Montgomery County Scholarship Fund, 1965; Democratic precinct chmn., 1964-74. Served with USNR, 1944-46. C.P.A., Md. Mem. Am. Inst. C.P.A.'s, Md. Assn. C.P.A.'s. Democrat. Methodist. Clubs: K.P., Dramatic Order Knights of Kohrassans. Home: 11402 Gainsborough Rd Potomac MD 20854 Office: Air Force Aid Society Inc 1117 N 19th St Arlington VA 22209

SANDERS, ROBERT MARTIN, commodity trader; b. Amsterdam, Netherlands, Feb. 8, 1928; s. Hugo Benjamin and Jean (van der Linden) S.; came to U.S., 1941, naturalized, 1949; B.A., Queens Coll., 1948, M.S., Columbia, 1950; postgrad. New Sch. Social Research, 1953-61; m. Ingrid Vera Borchardt, Apr. 12, 1959; children—Mark Robert, Steven George. Research asst. Netherlands Govt., 1948-50; with fgn. accounting dept. Colgate-Palmolive-Peet, 1950; with A.C. Israel Commodity Co., Inc., N.Y.C., 1952-71, asst. mgr. rubber dept., 1963-67, mgr. rubber dept., 1967-71, v.p., 1967-70, v.p., 1970-71, v.p. ACLI Internat., Inc., 1971—; pres. A.C. Israel Rubber Co. div., 1971-76, ACLI Rubber Co., 1976—; v.p. ACLI Commodity Services, Inc., 1975—; dir. ACLI (Malaysia) Sdn. Berhad, Kuala Lumpur; mem. N.Y. Cocoa Exchange, 1975-78. Served with AUS, 1950-52. Mem. Internat. Rubber Assn. (pro-tem com. 1970-71, mgmt. com. 1971—, dep. chmn. 1974-77), Am.-Indonesian C. of C. (dir. 1974—), Am. Importers Assn. (dir. 1975-77), Rubber Trade Assn. N.Y. Inc. (dir. 1970-74, 76—, v.p. 1971-72, 73-74, pres. 1972, 78—). Home: 310 Clinton Ave Dobbs Ferry NY 10522 Office: 717 Westchester Ave White Plains NY 10604

SANDERSON, HOWARD MARTIN, engring. and constrn. exec.; b. Milw., Jan. 16, 1927; s. Howard Tennyson and Norma Marion (Bear) S.; B.S. in Mech. Engring., U. Wis., 1952; m. Barbara Marion Enkosk, June 12, 1948; children—Kristen, James, Daniel, Julie, Peter. Vice pres. Commonwealth Assos., cons. engrs., Jackson, Mich., 1965-71, dir., 1969-71; v.p., dir. Hoad Engrs., cons. engrs., Ypsilanti, Mich., 1971-74; sr. v.p. Morrison Constrn. Co., Hammond Ind., 1974-76; mgr. Stone & Webster Engring. Corp., Cherry Hill, N.J., 1976—. Chmn. adv. com. Napoleon (Mich.) Sch. Bd., 1967-71. Served with USN, 1945-47. Recipient 1st prize paper award Wis. Electric Tech. Assn., 1959, 60; registered profl. eng. Mem. ASME (past chmn. process industries profl. div. Chgo. sect.), Am. Mgmt. Assn., Nat. Soc. Profl. Engrs. Presbyn. Club: Woodmar Country. Home: 30 E Centennial Dr Marlton NJ 08053 Office: 3 Executive Plaza Cherry Hill NJ 08034

SANDLER, BERNICE, women's rights advocate; b. N.Y.C., Mar. 3, 1928; d. Abraham Hyman and Ivy (Ernst) Resnick; B.A., Bklyn. Coll., 1948; M.A., Coll. City N.Y., 1950; Ed.D., U. Md., 1969; LL.D. (hon.), Bloomfield (N.J.) Coll., 1973, Hood Coll., Md., 1974; L.H.D. (hon.), Grand Valley State Coll., Mich., 1974; children—Deborah Jo, Emily Maud. Research fellow Coll. City N.Y., 1951-52; lectr., instr., research asst. U. Md., 1964-69; instr. Mt. Vernon Coll., Washington, 1968-69; ednl. specialist Spl. Subcom. on Edn., U.S. Ho. of Reps., 1970; dep. dir. Women's Action Program, HEW, 1971; dir. Project on Status and Edn. Women, Assn. Am. Colls., Washington, 1971—. Mem. coordinating com. Coalition for Women in Appointments, 1977-78; del. from Md. to Houston, Internat. Women's Year Conf., 1977; bd. dirs. Center for Women's Policy Studies, Inst. for Studies in Equality; trustee Women's Equity Action League, 1970-77, WEAL Ednl. and Legal Fund, 1975—; chmn. adv. com. Inst. Ednl. Leadership; mem. adv. bd. Wellesley Center for Study Women in Higher Edn. and Professions, Project on Equal Edn. Rights, Women's Hdqrs.; mem. nat. panel Am. Council on Edn., Nat. Identification Program; mem. adv. group Women's Work Force, Wider Opportunities for Women; mem. adv. com. Women's Legal Def. Fund; mem. adv. panel Am. Jewish Com. Recipient Athena award Intercollegiate Assn. Women Students, 1974, Elizabeth Boyer award Women's Equity Action League, 1976, Rockefeller Pub. Service award, 1976. Mem. Am. Psychol. Assn., Am. Personnel and Guidance Assn. Jewish. Mem. adv. bd. Jour. Reprints of Documents Affecting Women, 1976—, Women's Rights Law Reporter, 1971—, Spokeswoman, 1971—; contbr. articles on sex discrimination to profl. jours. Office: 1818 R St NW Washington DC 20009

SANDLER, LESLIE NEAL, psychologist; b. Phila., July 28, 1946; s. Sidney and Marilyn (Rothstein) S.; B.S., Temple U., 1968, Ed.M., 1970, Ed.D., 1979; m. Karen F. Dressler, Dec. 7, 1974; children—Shari Ruth, Eva Simcha. Counselor, Pa. Bur. Corrections, 1968; research asst. Head Start Research and Evaluation Center, Phila., 1969; clin. psychol. intern Phila. Gen. Hosp., 1970; staff psychologist N.E. Community Mental Health Center Phila., 1970-73; chief psychologist Temple U. Hosp. Community Mental Health Center, Phila., 1971-72; dir. rehab. A.I.D., Inc., Phila., 1972-76, Mantua Halfway House, Phila., 1976; pres. Lansdale Counseling Assos., Ltd. (Pa.), 1976—; cons. to industry, schs. Mem. Internat. Assn. Applied Psychology, Am., Pa. psychol. assns., Pa. Rifle and Pistol Assn. (life), Souderton-Harleysville Game, Fish and Forestry Assn., Gt. Swamp Fish, Game and Forestry Assn. Jewish. Clubs: Masons, Lehigh Valley. Home and Office: 1327 Lansdale Ave Lansdale PA 19446

SANDONATO, PATRICK DANIEL, adminstrv. social worker; b. Port Chester, N.Y., July 19, 1946; s. Patrick Michael and Rose Lucy (Polese) S.; B.A. in Sociology, Gannon Coll., 1968; M.S.W., Washington U., St. Louis, 1970; m. Claudia Ellen Bourgin, Oct. 23, 1972; children—Steven Alessio, Aaron Michael. Researcher, Harborcreek (Pa.) Sch. for Boys, 1969, dir. intermediate unit, 1970-73, dir. intensive treatment program, 1973—; mem. social work program adv. bd. Edinboro State Coll.; field work supr. various area colls.; planner Bridge Community Drug Center, Erie, Pa. Mem. Assn. Advancement Behavior Therapy, Acad. Cert. Social Workers, Nat. Assn. Social Workers. Follow-up/recidivism rate study of residents of Harborcreek Sch. for Boys, 1960-68. Home: 4396 W Sturbridge St Erie PA 16509 Office: 5712 Iroquois Ave Harborcreek PA 16421

SANDOR, THOMAS, biochemist; b. Budapest, Hungary, Nov. 3, 1924; s. Miksa and Iren (Forstner) S.; Dipl. Chem., U. Budapest, 1948; Ph.D., U. Toronto, 1960; m. Vera Varkonyi, July 5, 1949; 1 dau., Catherine-Susanne. Research fellow Inst. A. Fournier, Paris, France, 1949-50, Hosp. for Sick Children, U. Toronto (Ont., Can.), 1951-56; research biochemist Hotel Dieu Hosp., Montreal, Que., Can., 1956-59; sr. research asso. Hosp. Notre Dame, Montreal, 1959—; research asst. prof. medicine U. Montreal, 1961-67, research asso. prof., 1967-70, research prof., 1970—; prof. (hon.) McGill U., Montreal, 1969—; asso. Med. Research Council of Can., 1962—; vis. prof. U. Sheffield (Eng.) 1970-71, U. Buenos Aires, 1974; co-prin. Thomas Assos., sci. cons., Montreal, 1969—. Mem. Can. Biochem. Soc., Can. Soc. for Clin. Investigation, Royal Soc. Medicine (Gt. Britain), N.Y. Acad. Sci., Endocrine Soc., Biochem. Soc. (Gt. Britain), Soc. for Endocrinology (Gt. Britain), Am. Soc. Zoologists, European Soc. Comparative Endocrinologists, Am. Fedn. Clin. Research, Order Chemists of Que., Que. Hosp. Biochemists Assn. Corr. editor Jour. Steroid Biochemistry; mem. editorial bd. Gen. and Comparative Endocrinology. Contbr. chpts. on steroid biochemistry to books, numerous articles to profl. jours. Home: 4140 Cote St Catherine Montreal PQ H3T 1E3 Canada Office: 1560 Sherbrooke St E Montreal PQ H2L 4M1 Canada

SANDS, JOHN ELIOT, lawyer, educator; b. Bklyn., Jan. 14, 1941; s. Abraham M. and Edith Sylvia (Abeloff) S.; A.B., Princeton U., 1962; J.D., Yale U., 1965; m. Linda H. Lamel, July 31, 1977. Admitted to N.Y. bar, 1965; partner firm Schulman, Abarbanel, Perkel & McEvoy, N.Y.C., 1965-70; gen. counsel Mayor's Office Labor Relations, N.Y.C., 1970-73; prof. law Albany (N.Y.) Law Sch., Union U., 1973—; arbitrator, mediator labor relations disputes, 1972—; mem. Capital Dist. Bds. Advisers, Cornell U. Sch. Indsl. and Labor Relations and Nat. Center for Dispute Settlement. Mem. Nat. Acad. Arbitrators, Indsl. Relations Research Assn. (pres. Capital Dist. chpt. 1978—), Assn. Am. Law Schs. (chmn. labor law sect. 1977), Am., N.Y. State (sec. labor law sect. 1977-78, chmn. continuing legal edn. com. 1978—), Albany County, N.Y.C. bar assns., Am. Arbitration Assn. (upstate bd. advisers), Soc. Profls. in Dispute Resolution, Princeton Alumni Assn. No. N.Y. (pres.). Contbr. articles on labor, arbitration and ins. law to profl. jours. Home: 2324 Rosendale Rd Schenectady NY 12309 Office: 80 New Scotland Ave Albany NY 12208

SANDS, JOHN KEATING, banker; b. Morristown, N.J., Mar. 1, 1922; s. William Franklin and Edith (Keating) S.; A.B. in Econs., U. N.C., 1948; postgrad. N.Y. U., 1955-58; m. Patricia Pulling, Aug. 29, 1959; children—Elizabeth Douglass, Catherine Hilda, John Keating, Margaret Mercer. With U.S. Rubber Co., 1948-51, McKinsey & Co., 1953-55, Dillon, Read & Co., 1956-59; asso. buying dept. W. C. Langley & Co., investment bankers, N.Y.C., 1959, gen. partner, 1960-65; v.p. Morgan Guaranty Trust Co., 1965—; dir. Sigma Instrument Co., Morgan Guaranty Internat. Fin. Corp. Served with USNR, 1943-46, to lt., 1951-53, Republican. Roman Catholic. Clubs: Shinnecock Hills Golf, Cold Spring Harbor (N.Y.) Beach; Edgartown Yacht; Brook, Links, Down Town Assn. (N.Y.C.); Met. (Washington). Home: Yellowcote Rd Oyster Bay NY 11771 Office: 23 Wall St New York City NY 10015

SAN FELICE, GIACAMO (JACK), law enforcement ofcl.; b. New Castle, Pa., June 6, 1939; s. Anthony J. and Laura (Acquaviva) San F.; student Geneva Coll., 1957, 60-63; certificate in adminstrn. of justice Am. U., 1970, Asso. Sci. in Law Enforcement, 1970, B.S. in Law Enforcement, 1971, M.S., 1974; m. Wynne F. McNerney, Apr. 25, 1964; children—Anthony John, Russell James, Cheri Lynne. Mem. Met. Police Dept., Washington, 1963-66; various patrol and staff assignments Prince George's County (Md.) Police Dept., 1966-73, tactical squad sgt., 1974-75, lt., 1975—; instr. Prince George's Community Coll., U. Md., 1971-75; asso. instr. Prince George's County Police Acad., 1969-76. Served with U.S. Army, 1958-60, 61-62. Recipient Chief's award Prince George's County Police Dept., 1973. Mem. Internat. Assn. Chiefs of Police, Fraternal Order of Police, Pi Alpha Alpha. Democrat. Presbyterian. Home: Huntington MD 20639 Office: 3415 N Forestedge Rd Forestville MD 20028

SANFORD, CARL FREDERICK, county ofcl.; b. Jamestown, N.Y., Jan. 23, 1912; s. Charles W. and Mary (Anderson) S.; student U. Ala., 1931-32, Traffic Inst. Northwestern U., 1942-43; m. Adaline C. Caccamise, Oct. 3, 1933; children—Dianne Sanford Washburg, James C., Bonnie K. Sanford Gilmartin, Riley T., Mark Q., Rachel M. Engr., Jamestown Mut. Ins. Co., 1946-53; mayor City of Jamestown, 1956-61; city mgr. City of Elmira (N.Y.), 1962-68; mgr. County of Schenectady, 1968-77; ret., 1977. Pres. Jamestown City Council, 1951-53. Mem. Internat. City Mgmt. Assn., Mgmt. Assn. N.Y. State, County Execs. Assn. N.Y. State. Mem. Reformed Ch. Clubs: Mohawk (Schenectady); Town (Jamestown); Masons, Shriners. Home: 150 Hazeltine Ave Jamestown NY 14701

SANFORD, LEDA, publisher, editor; b. Tuscany, Italy, Oct. 11, 1933; d. Fausto and Josephine (Lazzuri) Giovannetti; A.A.S., Fashion Inst. Tech.; children by previous marriage—Robert Wayne, Scott Howard. Editor Teens & Boys Mag., N.Y.C., 1971-72, Men's Wear Mag., Fairchild publ., N.Y.C., 1973-75; pres., pub., editor-in-chief Am. Home mag., N.Y.C., 1975-77; pub., pres. Chief Exec. mag., N.Y.C., 1978—. Presbyterian. Home: 160 E 65th St New York City NY 10021 Office: 645 Fifth Ave New York City NY 10021

SANFT, LOUIS, hair stylist, cosmetologist; b. Fall River, Mass., Aug. 1, 1939; s. Israel and Celia (Cohen) S.; diploma Fall River Acad. Beauty Culture, 1962. Instr. advanced styling Fall River, New Bedford and Taunton (Mass.) beauty acads., 1965—; styling dir. Mr. Louis Hairstyling Salon, Fall River, 1966—. Served with USNR, 1959-61. World record holder hairdressing marathon, 1976; recipient Prestige de Paris Cup, 1976; coupe de Paris award, Paris, 1977. Mem. Hair Fashion Com., Mass. Cosmetologists Assn., Nat. Hairdresses and Cosmetologists Assn., Asso. Master Barbers and Beauticians Am. Home: 1772 S Main St Fall River MA 02724

SANGER, JOAN OYAAS, editor; b. Eau Claire, Wis., Aug. 3, 1924; d. John and Martha M. (Arnsdorf) Oyaas; B.A. with honors, U. Wis., 1946; M.A., N.Y. U., 1970; m. Frank de Wolfe Sanger, Mar. 18, 1961. Feature writer Eau Claire Leader Telegram, 1944-46; activities editor Rhinelander (Wis.) Daily News, 1946-49; asst. dir. sch.-coll. activities, St. Paul chpt. ARC, 1950-53; prodn. editor Frat. Press, St. Paul, 1953-57; editor Personal Efficiency, dir. publs. LaSalle Extension U., Chgo., 1957-59; asso. editor Nat. Assn. Social Workers, N.Y.C., 1960-61; mng. editor Phys. Therapy N.Y.C., 1962-69; free lance writer, copy editor Nursing Research, N.Y.C., 1971-78, mng. editor, 1978—. Nat. chmn. Hospitalized Vets. Writing Project, 1972-77. Treas. Community Chest, Douglaston, N.Y., 1973-77; mem. Douglaston (N.Y.) Civic Assn., sec., 1965-69. Mem. U. Wis. Alumni Club N.Y. (dir. 1966—, pres. 1970-72), Wis. Alumni Assn. (Spark Plug award 1972, dir. 1972-78), Women in Communications, Kappa Delta. Home: 73 Poplar St Douglaston NY 11363 Office: 10 Columbus Circle New York City NY 10019

SANO, JULIAN HAJIME, mech. engr.; b. N.Y.C., Mar. 1, 1918; s. Julian Kiokichi and Angela (Albus) S.; B.M.E., Bklyn., Poly. Inst., 1950; m. Gladys E. Richardson, Sept. 16, 1946. With G.M. Giannini Co., Springfield, N.J., 1950-52; v.p., chief engr. Colvin Labs., East Orange, N.J., 1952-59, owner, cons. engr. Princeton Machine & Devel. Co., Inc., Princeton Junction, N.J., 1959—. Mem. Inst. Aero. and Astronautics. Home: 29 Washington Rd Princeton Junction NJ 08550 Office: PO Box 187 Princeton Junction NJ 08550

SANO, RICHARD MITSUTO, med. instrumentation co. exec.; b. Chgo., Apr. 9, 1940; s. Clifford Minoru and Lillian Yuri (Matsukawa) S.; student U. Chgo., 1956-59, U. Miami (Fla.), 1959-61; m. Marjorie Hersh Rosenblum, Oct. 9, 1966; children—Leslie Marer, Laura Davey, Lanie Veith. Research asso. neurology and med. instrumentation U. Miami Med. Sch., 1962-68; corp. sec. Phys. Instruments, Inc., Coral Gables, Fla., 1961-64; cons. Nuclear Data Co., 1963, N. Am. Aviation Co., 1963-64, Hewlett Packard Co., 1965-67; mgr. tech. resources, clin. diagnostic systems Picker Corp., Northford, Conn., 1967—; U.S. indsl. rep. Internat. Electrotech. Commn.; cons. Soc. Nuclear Medicine, 1977—. Mem. Nat. Elec. Mfrs. Assn., Sci. Apparatus Makers Assn. Author papers in field. Home: 153 Sanford Ln Stamford CT 06905 Office: 12 Clintonville Rd Northford CT 06472

SANOIAN, CORIGAN, indsl. cons.; b. Niagara Falls, N.Y., July 22, 1929; s. Jack and Helen (Sarkissian) S.; B.S. in M.E., U. Buffalo, 1954; postgrad. U. Heidelburg (Germany), 1956; m. Lollie Ann Gamboian, Aug. 18, 1962; children—Jeffrey Jack, Brett Samuel, Holly Joy. Project mgr. J. Frucht Van Assos., Niagara Falls, 1958-74; with C. Sanoian & Assoc., Niagara Falls, 1974-76; with Indsl. Cons., Inc., Niagara Falls, N.Y., 1976—, pres., 1978—; pres. Quid Logistics, Energy Scanners, Inc.; with Indsl. Engring., Inc., Niagra Falls, 1976-78. Active Amateur Athletic Union, 1947-49. Served to maj. U.S. Army, 1947-49. Registered profl. engr., N.Y. Fellow Am. Inst. Chemists; mem. Nat. Soc. Profl. Engrs., Am. Soc. Heating, Refrigerating and Air Conditioning Engrs., Internat. Assn. Shell Structure, Am. Soc. Plumbing Engrs., Am. Soc. Gas Engrs. Episcopalian. Home: 696 Orchard Pkwy Niagara Falls NY 14301 Office: 3909 Witmer Rd Niagara Falls NY 14305

SANSCHAGRIN, ALBERT, bishop; b. St-Tite, Que., Can., Aug. 5, 1911; s. Henri and Leontine (Chevron) S.; student arts, U. Ottawa, 1930; oblate scholasticate, Richelieu, Que., 1931, Sainte Agathe des Monts, 1934. Ordained priest Roman Catholic Ch., 1936; tchr. oblates scholasticate, 1937-39; asst. gen. chaplain Young Christian Workers, Montreal, 1939-47; founder world wide Preparation for Marriage Course, 1941; missionary to Chile, 1947-53; superior provincial Oblates of M.I., 1953-57; bishop of Amos, Que., 1957-67, of St. Hyacinthe, 1967—. Pres. Joint Commn. Bishop-Religious, 1968—. Address: 1900 Girouard St-Hyacinthe PQ J2S 3A3 Canada

SANSLONE, WILLIAM ROBERT, educator, research exec.; b. Vineland, N.J., Feb. 16, 1931; s. Fortunato and Rose (Pelli) S.; B.S., Rutgers U., 1953, Ph.D., 1961; M.S., U. N.H., 1955; m. Alice E. Koury, June 25, 1960; 1 dau., Catherine. Biochemistry research asst. U. Conn. at Storrs, 1955-56; instr. biochemistry State U. N.Y. Downstate Med. Center, Bklyn., 1961-64, asst. prof. biochemistry, 1964-70, asso. prof., 1970-71; project scientist NIH, Bethesda, Md., 1971-72, sr. project scientist, 1972-73, exec. sec. biochemistry study sect., 1973-74, program dir. rev., 1974—; vis. asso. prof. physiology and biophysics Med. Coll. Pa., Phila., 1970. Served to 1st lt. USAF, 1956-58. Mem. A.A.A.S., Harvey Soc., Biophys. Soc., Am. Inst. Nutrition, Soc. Exptl. Biology and Medicine, Sigma Xi, Alpha Gamma Rho (chpt. treas. 1968-70). Contbr. articles to profl. jours. Home: 6835 Old Stage Rd Rockville MD 20852 Office: 805 Westwood Bldg NIH Bethesda MD 20014

SANSONE, THOMAS, accountant; b. Yonkers, N.Y., July 11, 1956; s. Carmine and Christina M. (Ricca) S.; B.S., Seton Hall U., 1978. With Adler, Lowengrub & Ampno, Union, N.J., 1974-78, Deloitte, Haskins & Sells, Morristown, N.J., 1978; staff accountant Coopers & Lybrand, Newark, 1978—. Bd. dirs. N. Ward Ednl. and Cultural Center, Newark, 1978—. Registered pub. accountant. Mem. Nat. Assn. Accountants, Nat. Soc. Pub. Accountants, N.J. Soc. Pub. Accountants, Am. Soc. Notaries. Roman Catholic. Office: 520 Broad St Newark NJ 07102

STO. DOMINGO, JOSE EUSTAQUIO, neonatologist; b. Philippines, Oct. 26, 1944; s. Braulio G. and Bonifacia (Eustaquio) Santo D.; M.D., U. Santo Tomas, Philippines, 1968; m. Iluminada de Guzman, Aug. 4, 1967; children—Joel, James. Intern, Perth Amboy Gen. Hosp., 1970-71; resident in pediatrics Maimonides Med. Center, N.Y.C., 1971-73, fellow in neonatology, 1973-74; fellow in neonatology Brookdale Hosp. Med. Center, Bklyn., 1974-75; practice medicine specializing in neonatology, Livingston, N.J., 1975—; chief neonatology sect. St. Barnabas Med. Center, Livingston, 1975—, asst. dir. pediatrics, 1975—. Diplomate Am. Bd. Pediatrics. Fellow Am. Acad. Pediatrics; mem. Essex County, N.J. med. socs. Office: St Barnabas Med Center Livingston NJ 07039

SANTOPIETRO, RICHARD FRANK, solar energy scientist; b. Providence, Apr. 15, 1940; s. Frank Ralph and Victoria (Marzilli) S.; Sc.B. in Engring. with honors, Brown U., 1962, Sc.M. in Elec. Engring., 1964; Ph.D. in Engring., U. Pa., 1973; m. Mary-Charles Smith, May 23, 1970. Research engr. Naval Underwater Systems Center, Newport, R.I., 1966-74, biomed. research scientist, 1971-74, data processing cons., 1974-76, solar energy scientist New London (Conn.) Lab., 1976—; guest lectr. New London Ind. High Sch., 1976; acoustics cons. Waterford Conservation Commn., 1976. Recipient Naval Underwater Systems Center spl. achievement awards, 1969, 71, 73, 75, 77. Mem. Internat. Solar Energy Soc., Acoustical Soc. Am., IEEE, Assn. Engrs. and Scientists New London Lab. Office: New London Lab Naval Underwater Systems Center New London CT 06320

SANTORO, SAMUEL, JR., psychologist, educator; b. New Haven, July 25, 1936; s. Samuel and Antoinette (DeCerbo) S.; B.S., So. Conn. State Coll., 1958; M.Ed., Springfield Coll., 1959; Ph.D., U. Pitts., 1971, hypnosis certificate, 1973; m. Ann Denise Heaphy, July 4, 1960; children—Pamela Ann, Steven Samuel. Dir. Kennedy Center, Bridgeport, Conn., 1959-63; project dir. Community Progress, New Haven, 1963-67; dir. fed. programs Pitts. Bd. Edn., 1967-71; supt. Long Lane Sch., Middletown, Conn., 1971-73; asso. prof. juvenile delinquency, adminstrn justice div. U. Pitts., 1973—; dep. dir. research and evaluation div. Pitts. Dept. Planning and Devel., 1974-76; pvt. practice psychology, 1974—; asso. prof. So. Conn. State Coll., 1964-67, Yale, 1964-67, 71-73; cons. juvenile delinquency; mem. various task forces on adolescence and edn., 1959—. Chmn., Comprehensive Area Manpower Planning System for Western Pa., 1969-71. Bd. dirs. Freedom House, Neighborhood Alliance, Pitts. Mem. Am., Pa., Greater Pitts. psychol. assns., Am. Soc. Clin. Hypnosis, Internat. Platform Assn. Rotarian. Club: Italian Sons and Daughters of Am. Contbr. articles to profl. jours. Home: 1125 Windermere Dr Pittsburgh PA 15218 Office: Bellefield Bldg 160 N Craig St Suite 111 Pittsburgh PA 15213

SANTOS, ROBERT FREDERICK, mfg. exec.; b. Cambridge, Mass., Sept. 15, 1934; s. John Jerome and Anna Gertrude (Silva) S.; B.S.E.E., Mass. Inst. Tech., 1956; m. Elaine Constance Gagnon, Sept. 10, 1960; children—Robert Frederick, Anne Marie, William, Steven. Engr., New Eng. Tel. & Tel., Boston, 1956-59, project engr., 1959-61, data systems engr., Boston, 1963, planning supr., 1964-68, gen. planning supr., 1968, dir. planning, 1968-70, asst. v.p. computer systems, 1970-73; mem. tech. staff Bell Tel. Lab., Murray Hill, N.J., 1961-62; dir. data systems AT&T, N.Y.C., 1973-78; asst. v.p. Data Systems, 1978—. Mem. town com. of Lynnfield, Mass., 1968-73; active Boy Scouts Am., 1968—. Registered profl. engr., Mass. Mem. Mgmt. Systems Council-Am. Mgmt. Assn., Subcom. Officers Conf. Group. Roman Catholic. Club: K.C. Home: Lowery Ln Mendham NJ 07945 Office: 30 Knightsbridge Rd Piscataway NJ 08854

SANTOS, SERGIO ESTEBAN, accountant; b. San Juan, P.R., Dec. 26, 1896; s. Hilario and Aurelia (Villaroel) S.; B.C.S., N.Y.U., 1919; student spl. courses Cornell U.; m. Catharine Tyler Slater, Dec. 31, 1918 (dec. Jan. 1970); children—Gregory S. Slater, Craig S. Slater, Stephanie S. Slater (Mrs. James T. Clark). Accountant, N.Y.C., 1922-32; auditor N.Y. State Electric & Gas Corp., Ithaca, N.Y., 1932-62, self-employed accountant, Ithaca, 1962—; spl. lectr. Ithaca Coll., 1952-54. C.P.A., N.Y. State. Mem. Nat. Security Council, Am. Inst. C.P.A.'s, N.Y. State Soc. C.P.A.'s, Spanish Inst. Inc. Address: 709 Triphammer Rd Ithaca NY 14850

SANTRY, ARTHUR JOSEPH, JR., engring. co. exec.; b. Brookline, Mass., Aug. 1, 1918; s. Arthur Joseph and Suzanne (Cawley) S.; B.A., Williams Coll., 1941; LL.B., Harvard, 1948; m. Julia Timmins, June 4, 1955; children—Arthur Joseph III, Suzanne, Peter, Charles, Robert. Admitted to Mass. bar, 1948; partner firm Putnam Bell Santry & Ray, Boston, 1948-56; sec. Combustion Engring., Inc., Stamford, Conn., 1956-57, v.p., 1957, vice chmn., 1957, pres., chief exec. officer, vice chmn. exec. com., 1963—, also dir.; dir. Bristol-Myers Co., N.Y.C., AMAX, Inc., Greenwich, Conn., Jenney Oil Co., Inc., Newton, Mass., N. Am. Reins. Corp., N.Y.C., N. Am. Reassurance Co., N.Y.C., Putnam Trust Co. of Greenwich (Conn.), Singer Co., N.Y.C. Served to lt. (s.g.) USN, 1942-46. Mem. Soc. Naval Architects and Marine Engrs., Navy League U.S., Newcomen Soc. N. Am., Econ. Club N.Y. Clubs: Board Room, Links, N.Y. Yacht (N.Y.C.); Seawanhaka Corinthian Yacht (Oyster Bay, N.Y.); Storm Trysail (Larchmont, N.Y.); Country (Brookline, Mass.); Eastern Yacht (Marblehead, Mass.); Indian Harbor Yacht, Field, Round Hill (Greenwich); Lyford Cay (Nassau, Bahamas); Royal Bermuda Yacht (Hamilton, Bermuda); Royal Ocean Racing (London). Home: 62 Vineyard Ln Greenwich CT 06830 Office: 900 Long Ridge Rd Stamford CT 06902

SANTUCCI, ARTHUR ANTHONY, psychologist, educator; b. Orange, N.J., Nov. 24, 1932; s. Attilio Thomas and Concetta (Italiano) S.; A.B., Seton Hall U., 1955, M.A., 1967; Ed.D., Lehigh U., 1972; m. Anita Imperatrice, Nov. 28, 1964. Counselor, N.J. Employment Service, Dover, 1960-62; probation caseworker Essex County (N.J.) Probation Dept., Newark, 1962-67; asso. prof. counseling and spl. services Seton Hall U., 1968—; dir. counseling West Orange (N.J.) Family-Youth Service, 1971-75, chmn. bd. trustees, 1975-76; gen. practice psychology, marriage counseling, West Orange, 1972—; program devel. and tng. cons. Bd. govs. N.J. Law Enforcement Planning Agy., Trenton. Served with U.S. Army, 1956-58. Recipient Pub. Service Appreciation award Office of Mayor Town of West Orange, 1972; licensed psychology, N.J., Pa.; licensed marriage counselor, N.J. Mem. Am., N.J. psychol. assns., Am. Assn. Marriage and Family Counselors Unico Nat., Seton Hall, Lehigh U. alumni assns. Democrat. Roman Catholic. Home: 17 Gregory Ave West Orange NJ 07052 Office: 470 Prospect Ave West Orange NJ 07052

SANTUCCI, GARY JOSEPH, counselor; b. E. Rochester, N.Y., May 10, 1948; s. Dominick and Florence (DeMare) S.; B.S., St. John Fisher Coll., 1972; M.Ed., State U. N.Y., 1974, Ed.S., 1974; m. Pamela Shepard, July 9, 1972. Career counselor Rensselaer/Columbia Boces, Troy, N.Y., 1974-76; community educator Planned Parenthood, Albany, N.Y., 1976-77; career counselor for autistic adolescents Parsons Child and Family Center, Albany, 1977—; marriage and family counselor, Schenedctady, 1976—; lectr. in field. Mem. joint com. on guidance services for mentally handicapped, Albany; mem. S. Colonie Sch. Dist. Bd. Edn., Albany, 1978. Served with USAR, 1968-74. Mem. Am. Personnel and Guidance Assn., Am. Assn. Sex Educators. Democrat. Roman Catholic. Home: 35A Commodore Albany NY 12205 Office: 3010 Troy Rd Schenectady NY 12309

SAPAROFF, GERALD ROBIN, ophthalmologist; b. Boston, Apr. 23, 1945; s. Michael and Delphine Barbara (Campbell) S.; B.S., Harvard Coll., 1967; M.D., Tufts U., 1971; m. Linda Wilkins, June 17, 1967; children—Nicholas, Katherine. Intern, Mt. Auburn Hosp., Cambridge, Mass., 1971-72; resident ophthalmology U. Iowa, Iowa City, 1972-76; individual practice medicine, specializing in ophthalmology, Newport, Vt., 1976—; mem. staff N. Country Hosp., Newport. Diplomate Am. Bd. Ophthalmology. Mem. Am. Acad. Ophthalmology, Vt. Ophthalmol. Soc., Vt. Med. Assn., Orleans County Med. Soc. Home: Barton Mountain Rd Barton VT 05822 Office: Prouty Dr Med Arts Bldg Newport VT 05855

SAPERSTON, HOWARD TRUMAN, JR., indsl. relator; b. Buffalo, Oct. 4, 1939; s. Howard Truman and Nan Lucille (Basch) S.; B.A., Franklin Marshall Coll., 1963; m. Mary Barnard Franklin, Sept. 9, 1967; children—Howard Truman III, William Scott. Vice pres. Saperston Real Estate Assos., Inc., Buffalo, 1963—. Pres., Buffalo Boys' Club, 1973-75; trustee Nichols Sch., 1975—; bd. dirs. Salvation Army, 1967—; mem. adv. bd. Children's Hosp., 1973-78; bd. dirs. Buffalo Sabre Hockey Team, YMCA, Jr. Achievement, 1969-78, Multiple Sclerosis Soc., 1968-70, Planned Parenthood Assn., 1966-69; chmn. Buffalo area U.S. Olympic Com. Mem. Soc. Indsl. Realtors, Greatei Buffalo Bd. Realtors (dir.), Buffalo Area C. of C. (chmn. real estate council). Republican. Jewish. Club: Buffalo. Home: 100 Morris Ave Buffalo NY 14214 Office: Saperston Real Estate Assos Inc 560 Delaware Ave Buffalo NY 14202

SAPIN, ROBERT, pediatrician; b. Bklyn., Feb. 21, 1931; s. Samuel and Sadie (Kirschbaum) S.; B.S., Bklyn. Coll., 1952; M.D., U. Geneva, 1957; m. Gertrude Fine, Mar. 28, 1953; children—Joyce, Deborah, Francine. Intern, L.I. Coll. Hosp., Bklyn., 1958; resident Kings County Hosp., Bklyn., 1959-60; practice medicine specializing in pediatrics, Bklyn., 1961-62, Woodcliff Lake, N.J., 1963-75; med. dir. Newark Comprehensive Health Services Plan, 1976-77, United Cerebral Palsy Assn. N.Y. State, 1977—; instr. pediatrics Downstate Med. Sch., 1962. Mem. AMA, Am. Pub. Health Assn., Am. Acad. Pediatrics. Home: 22 Terkuile Rd Montvale NJ 07645 Office: 2800 Victory Blvd Staten Island NY 10314

SAPOFF, MEYER, electronics component co. exec.; b. N.Y.C., June 2, 1927; s. Benjamin and Mary (Charney) S.; student Mohawk Coll., 1946-48, Poly. Inst. Bklyn., 1948-50, 52-53; B.S. in Elec. Engring. magna cum laude, Poly. Inst. Bklyn., 1950; postgrad. Mass. Inst. Tech., 1951, U. Pa., 1951-52, Poly. Inst. Bklyn., 1952-53; M.S. in Elec. Engring., Drexel Inst. Tech., 1952; m. Janet Flack, Dec. 24, 1953; children—Robert Jay, Judith Beryl. Research engr. Franklin Inst. Labs., Phila., 1950-52; research fellow sr. grade Poly. Inst. Bklyn., 1952-53; dir. research Victory Engring. Corp., Springfield, N.J., 1953-57, dir. engring., 1957-63, v.p., 1963-69; cons., sr. staff scientist Keystone Carbon Co., St. Mary's, Pa., 1969-70; pres. Thermometrics, Inc., Edison, N.J., 1970—, dir., 19—; cons. in field. Active Citizens League W. Orange, 1962-75, W. Orange PTA, 1960-76. Served with USN, 1945-46. Recipient Indsl. Research IR-100 award, 1974. State of N.Y. U. scholar, 1948-50; Poly. Inst. Bklyn. fellow, 1973. Mem. Mfrs. Assn. of Union, N.J. Mfrs. Assn., Poly. Inst. Bklyn. Alumni Assn., IEEE, Am. Ceramic Soc., ASTM, Internat. Orgn. for Legal Metrology, Am. Nat. Standards Inst., Am. Vacuum Soc., Tau Beta Pi, Eta Kappa Nu. Jewish. Club: K.P. Contbr. articles in field to profl. jours.; patentee in field. Home: 83 Crystal Ave West Orange NJ 07052 Office: 808 US Hwy 1 Edison NJ 08817

SARAFIDIS, HELEN GIRASSIS, interior designer; b. Salonica, Greece, Aug. 11, 1939; d. Xenophon and Thomais (Bayou) Girassis; came to U.S., 1965, naturalized, 1978; student Poly. Sch. Fine Arts, Athens, Greece, 1958-61, Studio Fine Arts, Athens, 1961-63, Md. Inst., Balt., 1969-70; 1 dau., Cynthia-Theodora. Interior designer E.B.M.E. Tsaousoglou, Athens, 1964-65, Koch Office Supply Co., Balt., 1969-71, Price-Modern Inc., Balt., 1971-77, Md. Casualty Co., Balt., 1977—. Tchr., Balt. Greek Community Sch. Mem. Am. Soc. Interior Designers (asso.), Smithsonian Instn. Greek Orthodox. Club: Hellenic Univ. Home: 1401 Weldon Pl S Baltimore MD 21211 Office: 3900 Keswick Rd Baltimore MD 21211

SARASIN, RONALD ARTHUR, congressman; b. Fall River, Mass., Dec. 31, 1934; s. Joseph Arthur and Mary Dorothy (Pereira) S.; B.S. in Bus. Adminstrn., U. Conn., 1960, J.D., 1963. Admitted to Conn. bar, 1963, U.S. Supreme Ct. bar, 1964; atty. Bracken & Zoarski, New Haven, 1963-65; atty. Perelmutter, Sarasin & Cohen, Seymour, Conn., 1965-72; mem. Conn. Ho. of Reps., 1969-72, asst. minority leader, 1971-72; mem. 93d-95th Congresses from 5th Dist. Conn.; asst. prof. law U. New Haven, 1963-66. Mem. Republican State Platform Com., 1968-70. Served with USNR, 1952-56. Recipient Distinguished Service award Lions Club of Beacon Falls, 1969. Mem. Am., Conn. bar assns., Am. Trial Lawyers Assn., Am. Arbitration Assn. Lion. Home: 155 Munson Rd Beacon Falls CT 06403 Office: Cannon House Office Bldg Washington DC 20515

SARBANES, PAUL SPYROS, senator; b. Salisbury, Md., Feb. 3, 1933; s. Spyros P. and Matina (Tsigounis) S.; A.B., Princeton, 1954; B.A., Oxford U. (Eng.), 1957; LL.B., Harvard, 1960; m. Christine Dunbar, June 11, 1960; children—John Peter, Michael, Janet. Asso. law firm Venable, Baetjer and Howard, Balt., 1965-70; asst. to chmn. Council Econ. Advisers, Washington, 1962-63; exec. dir. City Charter Revision Commn., Balt., 1963-64; exec. dir. Md. Citizens for Johnson-Humphrey, 1964; state coordinator Md. Kennedy for Pres. Com., 1968; mem. Md. Ho. of Dels., 1966-70; mem. 92d-94th Congresses from 3d Md. Dist.; senator from Md., 1977—. Home: 320 Suffolk Rd Baltimore MD 21218*

SARGENT, JOHN TURNER, publisher; b. Lawrence, N.Y., June 26, 1924; s. Charles and Dagmar (Wetmore) S.; m. Neltje Doubleday, May 16, 1953 (div.); children—Ellen, John Turner. Editor Doubleday & Co., Inc., N.Y.C., 1946-49, v.p., 1960-61, pres., 1961-78, chmn. bd., 1978—, also dir.; trustee East River Savs. Bank. Trustee N.Y. Zool. Soc., Kips Bay Boys Club, N.Y. Pub. Library. Home: Halsey Ln Watermill NY 11976 Office: 245 Park Ave New York City NY 10017

SARIBEYOGLU, SAFA ISMAIL, psychiatrist; b. Turkey, Aug. 12, 1931; s. Rifat and Ayse S.; came to U.S., 1959; M.D., U. Istanbul (Turkey), 1958; m. Erdinc Sermin, Jan. 15, 1960. Intern, St. Anthony Hosp., Louisville, 1959-60; resident Louisville Gen. Hosp., 1960, Utica (N.Y.) State Hosp., 1961-63, Rockland State Hosp., Orangeburg, N.Y., 1963-64; cons. psychiatrist Community Health Center, 1967-74; asst. chief children's unit Rockland Psychiat. Center, 1967-71; practice medicine specializing in psychiatry, Spring Valley, N.Y., 1971—; chief inpatient service Children's Psychiat. Center, Orangeburg, N.Y., 1971-73, chief community service, 1973-74, dir. center, 1974—; mem. staff Good Samaritan Hosp., Suffern, N.Y., 1973—; preceptor George Washington U.; faculty N.Y. Med. Coll., 1977. Served with mil., 1964-66. Fellow Am. Psychiat. Assn. (pres. W. Hudson dist.); mem. Turkish Am. Psychiat. Assn. (pres.), Execs. Info. Guild (asso.). Home: 134 Blaisdell Rd Orangeburg NY 10962 Office: 200 W Clarkstown Profl Bldg Spring Valley NY 10977

SARINO, EDGARDO FORMANTES, physician; b. Laoag City, Ilocos Norte, Philippines, Nov. 6, 1940; s. Epafrodito Cruz and Esperanza Raval Formantes S.; came to U.S., 1965; M.D., Univ. of the East, 1964; m. Milagros Felix Ona, Dec. 6, 1965; children—Edith Melanie, Edgar Michael, Edenn Michele. Rotating intern St. Clare's Hosp., N.Y.C., 1965-66; resident in anatomical pathology Coney Island Hosp., N.Y.C., 1966; resident in gen. surgery Manhattan VA Hosp., N.Y.C., 1966-67, N.Y. U.-Bellevue Med. Center, N.Y.C., 1967-68; resident in radiology Manhattan VA Hosp., N.Y.C., 1968-71, fellow in diagnostic radiology, 1971-73; staff radiologist Mercer Med. Center, Trenton, N.J., 1973—; teaching asst. in gen. surgery N.Y. U.-Bellevue Med. Center, N.Y.C., 1967-68. Recipient Certificate of Merit, Mallinkrodt Pharm., 1969. Diplomate Am. Bd. Radiology. Mem. Am. Med. Assn., Am. Coll. Radiology, Radiol. Soc. N. Am., Mercer County Med. Soc., N.J. Med. Soc., N.J. Radiol. Soc., Philippine Am. Med. Soc. of N.J. Contbr. articles to med. jours. Home: 131 Brookstone Dr Princeton NJ 08540 Office: 446 Bellevue Ave Trenton NJ 08607

SARNO, RONALD ANTHONY, author; b. Jersey City, Sept. 26, 1941; s. Anthony and Philomena Maria (Pilla) S.; student Bellarmine Coll., 1959-63, Weston Coll., 1963-65; A.B., Boston Coll., 1965, M.A., 1966; M.Div., Woodstock Coll., 1972; postgrad. N.Y. U., 1975—; m. Una McGinley, 1975. Tchr. Xavier High Sch., N.Y.C., 1966-69; asso. editor Sacred Heart Messenger, N.Y.C., 1967; asst. program dir. Sacred Heart Radio TV Program, St. Louis, 1969; retreat dir. St. Ignatius House, Manhasset, N.Y., 1972-75; nat. coll. moderator Nat. Fedn. Christian Life Communities, 1970-75, East region rep., 1975—. Mem. N.Y. Archdiocesan Fedn. Sodalities (pres. moderators 1968-70), Manhasset Interfaith Council (chmn. publicity com. 1973-75), Internat. Platform Assn., Loyola Christian Life Community. Author: Achieving Sexual Maturity, 1969; Let Us Proclaim the Mystery of Faith, 1970; The Story of Hope, 1972; Prayers for Modern Urban Uptight Man, 1973; The Cruel Caesars, 1977; librettist David and Bathsheba, 1977. Editor: Liturgical Booklet for CLC's, 1974. Office: Pediatric Grants St Joseph's Hosp and Med Center Paterson NJ 07503

SARNOFF, EDWARD, mfg. exec.; b. N.Y.C., Jan. 9, 1921; s. David and Lizette (Hermant) S.; grad. Phillips Acad., 1938; B.S., Brown U., 1942; m. Jean Brown, Jan. 26, 1947; children—James David, Russell Edward, John Clifford. Spl. events supr. news, spl. events dept. ABC, N.Y.C., 1946-47; advt., sales promotion mgr. Radio & Appliance Distbrs. Inc., East Hartford, Conn., 1947-49, exec. v.p., gen. sales mgr., 1949-54, dir., 1947-54; founder, pres., dir. Edco Distbg. Co., Fresno, Calif., 1954-58; pres., dir. Silver Secretarial Service, 1958-59; exec. v.p. Fleet Messenger Service, Inc., 1958-59, dir., 1958-64; became pres., owner Fleet Services Inc., N.Y.C., 1959, chmn., chief exec. officer, 1969—, dir., 1964—; pres., owner Fleet Messenger Service Inc., Fleet Motor Delivery Services, Inc., Fleet Manpower Service, Inc., Fleet Courier Service, Inc.; chmn. Collier Photo Engraving, Inc., 1969-71. Bd. dirs. Fresno chpt. ARC, 1955-58, St. Agnes Hosp., Fresno, 1955-58, Jr. Achievement Soc., Fresno, 1957-58, Julius Hartt Musical Found. Served as capt. AUS, 1945-46; capt. U.S. Signal Corps Res., 1946—. Mem. IEEE, Am. Inst. Mil. Engrs., Brown U. Engring. Soc. Clubs: Hemisphere (N.Y.C.); Brown University; Century Country (Purchase, N.Y.); City Athletic. Home: 435 E 52d St New York City NY 10022 Office: Fleet Services Inc Sperry Rand Bldg 1290 Ave of Americas New York City NY 10019

SARNOFF, LILI-CHARLOTTE DREYFUS (MRS. STANLEY J. SARNOFF), artist, ret. business exec.; b. Frankfurt, Germany, Jan. 9, 1916; d. Willy and Martha (Koch von Hirsch) Dreyfus; grad. Reimann Art Sch. (Germany), 1934, U. Berlin, 1935; student U. Florence (Italy), 1936-37; m. Stanley Jay Sarnoff, Sept. 11, 1948; children—Daniela Martha Sarnoff Bargezi, Robert L. Came to U.S., 1941, naturalized, 1944. Research asst. Harvard Sch. Pub. Health, 1948-54; research asso. cardiac physiology Nat. Heart Inst., Bethesda, Md., 1954-59; pres. Rodana Research Corp., Bethesda, 1958-61; v.p. Catrix Corp., Bethesda, 1958-61; inventor, pres. Flolite Light Sculptures, 1968—; one-woman shows (under name Lolo Sarnoff): Agra Gallery Washington, 1969, Corning Glass Center Mus., Corning, N.Y., 1969, Franz Bader Gallery, Washington, 1976; group shows include: Air and Space Mus., Washington, The Art Barn, Washington, Gallery K, Washington; represented in collections Corning Glass Center Mus., Anthony Vischer, Basel, Switzerland, David Lloyd Kreeger Collection, Washington, U.S. embassy New Delhi, Kennedy Center, Washington, others. Bd. dirs. Fgn. Student Service Council, Washington Performing Arts Soc., Mem. Women's Com. Corcoran Gallery of Art. Club: City Tavern (Washington). Democrat. Co-inventor electrophrenic respirator; inventor flowmeter. Home: 7507 Hampden Ln Bethesda MD 20014

SARRIS, NICHOLAS, legal educator; b. Newburyport, Mass., Oct. 20, 1934; s. George S. and Penelope (Demesthihas) S.; B.S., U. N.H., 1953; M.A., Fairfield (Conn.), U., 1960, certificate of advanced study, 1961; J.D., Boston Coll., 1975; postdoctoral certificate Boston U., 1978; m. Patricia Williams, Oct. 3, 1953; 1 dau., Jo Ann. Tchr. bus. high schs. in Conn. and Mass., 1958-60; prof. bus. law and real estate No. Essex Community Coll., Haverhill, Mass., 1961—, chmn. div. bus. adminstrn., 1961-68; dir. Merrimac Valley Consumer Protection Center, Haverhill, Essex Consumer Affairs; moderator TV series; cons. in field. Served with USN, 1947-49. Grantee Kellogg Found., 1964, Boston Coll. Law Sch., 1972; recipient various certificates of appreciation. Mem. Am. Bar Assn., Boston Bar Assn., New Eng. Bus. Law Assn., NEA, Mass. Tchrs. Assn., Mass. Assn. Realtors, Internat. Coll. Evaluation Scis. (Can.). Democrat. Mem. Hellenic Orthodox Ch. Club: Shriners. Author manual, articles, TV scripts. Home: 192 Storey Ave Newburyport MA 01952 Office: Northern Essex Community Coll Haverhill MA 01830

SARVET, WALTER MORTON, mfg. co. exec.; b. Coatesville, Pa., Aug. 15, 1928; s. Benjamin P. and Betty (Batt) S.; B.S., Temple U., 1953; m. Ruth M. Marcus, Dec. 22, 1957; children—Nancy, Barry. Revenue examiner City of Phila., 1954-56; pub. accountant Ralph M. Fratkin & Co., C.P.A., Phila., 1956-57; accountant J.K. Lasser & Co., N.Y.C., 1957-62; 1st v.p., tax dir. Shearson, Hammil & Co., Inc., N.Y.C., 1962-75; tax mgr. Matsushita Electric Corp. Am., Secaucus, N.J., 1976—. Served with AUS, 1946-49. C.P.A., N.Y. Mem. Am. Inst. C.P.A.'s, N.Y. State Soc. C.P.A.'s, Tax Execs. Inst. (mem. com. of brokers and dealers on taxation 1967—), Wall St. Tax Assn., Am. Accounting Assn. Home: 108 Kings Walk Massapequa Park NY 11762 Office: One Panasonic Way Secaucus NJ 07094

SARWER-FONER, GERALD, psychiatrist, psychoanalyst; b. Volkovsk, Poland, Dec. 6, 1924; s. Michael and Ronia (Caplan) S.; B.A., U. Montreal, 1945; M.D., 1950; Dr. Psychiatry, McGill U., 1955; m. Ethel Sheinfeld, May 28, 1950; children—Michael, Gladys, Janice, Henry, Brian. Cons. in psychiatry, dir. psychiat. research Queen Mary Vet. Hosp., Montreal, Que., 1955-60; dir. clin. investigation unit, dir. psychiat. research Jewish Gen. Hosp., Montreal, 1955-66; cons. psychiatry Notre Dame Hosp., Montreal, 1965-70; dir. dept. psychiatry, psychiatrist-in-chief Queen Elizabeth Hosp., Montreal, Can., 1966-70; dir. dept. psychiatry, psychiatrist-in-chief Ottawa Gen. Hosp., 1971—; lectr. psychiatry U. Montreal, 1953-55; clin. instr. McGill U. Faculty Medicine, Montreal, 1955-58, lectr., 1955-58, asst. prof., 1958-62, asso. prof. psychiatry, 1962-70; prof. U. Ottawa Faculty Medicine, 1971—, chmn. dept. psychiatry, 1974—; vis. prof. psychiatry Laval U. Faculty Medicine, Que., 1964—, Chgo. Med. Sch., 1968-78; tng. and supervising analyst Canadian Inst. Psychoanalysis, 1969—. Mem. advisory panel Psychiat. Def. Research Bd. Can., 1958-62; adv. com. health City Westmount, 1969-74. Gov. Queen Elizabeth Hosp. of Montreal. Served as lt. col. RCAMC, CA (M). Fellow Royal Coll. Phys. and Surg. (Can.), Am. Psychiat. Assn. (pres. Que. dist. br. 1960-61, 65-66, chmn. com. psychiatry and law 1974-77), chmn. Scient. Prog. Comm. VI World Congress, chmn. Model Commitment Code Task Force, 76-78.) AAAS, Am. Orthopsychiat. Assn., Am. Coll. Psychopharmacology, Internat. Coll. Psychosomatic Medicine, Royal, Am. colls. psychiatrists (bd. regents 1978-80), Am. Coll. Psychoanalysts; (chmn. arrangements com. 1977, bd. regents 1978-80); mem. Am. Acad. Psychiat and Law (pres. 1975-77), Canadian Inst. Psychoanalysis, Can. Psychoanalysis Soc. (pres. 1978-80), Can. Psychiat. Assn. (council, dir. 1958-62; founder, 1st chmn. sect. psychotherapy), Can. Med. Assn., Internat. Psychoanalysis Assn., Soc. Biol. Psychiatry, Collegium Internat. Neuropsycho. Pharm., Gwan Psychiat. Research Soc. (founder), Que. Psychiat. Assn. (pres. 1966-68). Editor: The Dynamics of Psychiatric Drug Therapy, 1960; Research Conference on the Depressive Group of Illnesses, 1966; Psychiatric Crossroads-The Seventies-Research Aspects, 1972. Address: 197 Cumberland St Ottawa ON K1N 7H4 Canada

SASS, NEIL LESLIE, toxicologist; b. Balt., Oct. 24, 1944; s. Samuel and Blanche (Radoon) S.; B.S. in Biology, Wake Forest Coll., 1966; M.S. in Physiology, W.Va. U., 1969, Ph.D., in Biochemistry, 1971; m. Diane F. Moats, Aug. 3, 1969; children—Krista Lynn, Brian Scott. Commd. 2d lt. U.S. Army, 1971, advanced through grades to capt., 1971; research biochemist toxicology div. Biomed. Labs, U.S. Army, Edgewood Arsenal, Md., 1971-74; chief Med. Research and Devel. Service, William Beaumont Army Med. Center, El Paso, Tex., 1974-77; comdr. (sr. scientist) USPHS, Washington D.C., 1977—; toxicologist div. toxicology Bur. Foods, FDA, HEW, Washington, 1977—; faculty perinatal obstetrics W. Beaumont Army Med. Center, El Paso, 1975-77; asst. prof. nursing U. Tex., El Paso, 1976-77. Mem. Am. Chem. Soc., Soc. Armed Forces Med. Lab. Scientists, Soc. for Applied Spectroscopy, Sigma Xi. Jewish. Contbr. numerous articles to profl. jours. Address: 5710 Old Buggy Ct Columbia MD 21045

SASSO, LOUIS ANTHONY, civil engr., planner; b. Providence, Aug. 6, 1934; s. Lewis Joseph and Rose (Carlone) S.; B.S., Widener Coll., 1956; postgrad. Rensselaer Poly. Inst., 1965; m. Eleanor Catherine Ashworth, Sept. 14, 1957; children—Ellen Marie, Ann Marie, Robert Lewis. Constrn. engr. S.M. Constrn. Co., Providence, 1958-63; faculty Roger Williams Coll., Providence, 1963—, chmn. engring. dept., 1965-70, asst. dean, dir. coop. edn., 1967-74; pres. Bay Enterprises Inc., Cranston, R.I., 1963-72, dir., 1963-72; treas., sr. partner H-S & Assos. Photogrammetrists Inc., East Providence, R.I., 1972—; pres., dir. Co-op Credit Union, Premium Fin. Inc. Served with C.E., U.S. Army, 1956-58. Mem. Dist. Nurses Assn. (dir. 1977), Traffic Safety Council, Citizens for Better Schs., ASCE, Am. Congress Mappers and Surveyors, Am. Soc. Engring. Edn., Coop. Edn. Assn., Ret. Officers Assn. Clubs: Kiwanis, East Greenwich Yacht, (dir. 1976—). Home: 60 Glenmere Dr Cranston RI 02920 Office: 1021 Waterman Ave East Providence RI 02914

SASSO, RUTH MARYANN, educator; b. Bridgeport, Conn., Dec. 9, 1928; d. Angelo Nicholas and Mildred Rita (Hayes) Sasso; B.S. in Edn., St. Joseph Coll., 1957, M.A., 1968. Tchr., Catholic Schs. of Conn., 1950-68; founder, dir. Berkeley Primary Sch., Waterbury, Conn., 1969-71; assoc. prof. early childhood edn., coordinator child care program Mattatuck Community Coll., Waterbury, 1971—, dir. early childhood edn., coordinator child care program, 1971—, dir. early childhood edn. lab. sch., 1976—; mem. adv. council on early childhood edn. Conn. Dept. Edn.; cons. in field. Bd. dirs. Child Care Center Abused Children, Waterbury, 1971—. Recipient Service award Head Start Policy Com., Danbury, Conn., 1973. Mem. Nat. Assn. Edn. Young Children, Soc. Nutrition Edn., Action Children's TV, Nat. Council Campus Child Care Centers, Day Care and Child Devel. Council Am. Democrat. Roman Catholic. Author: Field Placement Manual for Student Teachers, 1971. Home: 86C Falls Terr Oakville CT 06779 Office: Mattatuck Community Coll 750 Chase Pkwy Waterbury CT 06708

SASSOVER, NATHAN, electronics co. exec.; b. Deggendorf, Germany, July 27, 1948; s. Adolf and Anna Sassover; came to U.S., 1949, naturalized, 1955; B.A. in Music, U. Wis., 1969; student (Scholar) Berklee Coll. Music, 1964, 65. Ind. composer and producer of film and TV music, 1969-72; prin. Motion Picture Music, Inc., N.Y.C., 1970-72; founder, pres., chmn. TMX, Inc. (became subs. Rusco Industries, Inc. 1978), N.Y.C., 1972-77, gen. mgr., 1978—; cons. to microelectronic and consumer products cos. Mem. Am. Fedn. Musicians. Patentee vehicle security system. Office: care Michael S Toorock 65 E 55th St New York City NY 10022

SATALINE, LEE ROY, physician, educator; b. New Britain, Conn., Oct. 31, 1929; s. Andrew James and Irene (Mongillo) S.; B.A., Georgetown U., 1950; M.S., Wesleyan U., 1951; M.D., Bologna U., 1956; m. Therese Jane Reckmack, Aug. 2, 1956; children—Laura, Suzanne. Intern and resdient St. Raphael Hosp., New Haven, 1956-60; fellow Ohio State U., Columbus, 1960-62, instr., 1961-64; med. dir. Lakewood-Toledo (Ohio) Hosps., 1964-67; asst. prof. medicine Case Western Res. U., Cleve., 1964-67; chief medicine St. Luke's Hosp., Bethlehem, Pa., 1967-72; asso. prof. clin. medicine Jefferson Med. Coll., Phila., 1967-72; practice medicine, specializing in gastroenterology, Cheshire, Conn., 1972—; dir. gastroenterology Bradley Meml. Hosp., Southington, Conn. and Waterbury (Conn.) Hosp., 1972—; asst. clin. prof. medicine U. Conn., 1972—. Recipient VA Research award, 1961. Fellow A.C.P.; mem. Am. Gastroenterol. Assn., Am. Soc. Gastrointestinal Endoscopy, Am. Fedn. Clin. Research, Am. Soc. Law and Medicine, Conn. Med. Soc. Contbr. articles in field to profl. jours. Home: 505 Squire Hill Cheshire CT 06410 Office: 366 S Main St Cheshire CT 06410

SATCHELL, LOU EDWIN, accountant; b. Easton, Md., Jan. 15, 1945; s. Oliver and C. Clotilda (Slaughter) S.; A.A., Goldey-Beacom Jr. Coll., 1966; B.S. in Bus. Adminstrn., East Carolina U., 1968; m. Lenette Carol Dayton, Aug. 12, 1967; children—L. Stephen, Kimberley W. Staff accountant Granger, Faw & Co., Easton, 1968-72; partner Beatty, Satchell & Co., Easton, 1972—; dir. 2d Nat. Bldg. & Loan, Inc. Bd. dirs. Easton br. Talbot County United Fund, 1969—, mem. bus. and industry com., profl. com.; bd. dirs., treas. Talbot County YMCA, 1975—. C.P.A., Md. Mem. Am. Inst. C.P.A.'s, Md. Assn. C.P.A.'s (cooperation with bar com., ins. com.), Am. Accounting Assn., Nat. Assn. Accountants, Delmarva Estate Planning Council, Talbot County C. of C., Ducks Unltd. Methodist. Clubs: Talbot Country, Rotary, Elks. Home: Route 4 Box 304 Easton MD 21601 Office: PO Box 1187 Easton MD 21601

SATIN, LAWRENCE Z., cardiologist; b. Conn., Jan. 30, 1938; s. Nathan H. and Betty P. S.; B.A., U. Conn., 1959; M.D., Chgo. Med. Sch., 1963; m. Karen Weiss, Sept. 11, 1961; children—Wendy, Scott, Kim. Med. intern Mt. Sinai Hosp., Chgo., 1963-64; med. resident Mt. Sinai Hosp., N.Y.C., 1964-66; cardiology resident Washington VA Hosp., 1968-69; sr. attending cardiologist Prince George's Gen. Hosp., Cheverly, Md., 1969—, chief dept. cardiology, 1978; chief dept. cardiology Greater Laurel-Beltsville Hosp., Laurel, Md., 1978; mem. retirement med. rev. com. Prince George's County, 1977-78. Served to capt. USAF, 1964-66. Diplomate Nat. Bd. Med. Examiners, Am. Bd. Internal Medicine. Fellow Am. Coll. Cardiology, Council Clin. Cardiology of Am. Heart Assn.; mem. Am. Heart Assn., AMA, Md., Prince George's County med. assns. Jewish. Office: 5711 Sarvis Ave Suite 300 Riverdale MD 20740

SATTERFIELD, JOHN, coll. adminstr.; b. Danville, Va., Dec. 4, 1921; s. John Roberts and Sarah Elise (Council) S.; B.A., Mus.M., U. N.C., 1950, M.A., 1955, Ph.D., 1962; m. Carolyn Keith Talley, Dec. 18, 1948; children—John Roberts III, Kenneth Scott, Keith Charles, Jean Council. Asst. prof. music Davidson (N.C.) Coll., 1953-60; faculty Fla. Presbyn. Coll., St. Petersburg, Fla., 1960-68, prof. music, 1963-67, prof. humanities and music, 1967-68; v.p. for acad. affairs Elmira (N.Y.) Coll., 1968-70; asst. dir., acad. programs specialist N.C. State Bd. Higher Edn., Raleigh, 1970-72; asst. v.p. acad. affairs U. N.C. Gen. Adminstrn., Chapel Hill., 1972; provost, exec. v.p., prof. humanities Kalamazoo Coll., 1972-75; pres. Wagner Coll. S.I., N.Y., 1975—; vis. prof. U. Tex., 1966, U. Ky., 1964. Cons., Fla. State Dept. Edn., U.S. Office Edn., N.Y. State Dept. Edn., N.Y. State Dept. Civil Service, numerous colls. Founding dir. N.C. Center for Continuing Renewal of Higher Edn., N.C. Inst. for Undergrad. Curricular Reform. Served to capt. USAAF, 1942-45. Decorated Bronze Star; Belgian Fourragère; recipient Composer's award N.C. Symphony Soc., 1951; Harbison award Danforth Found., 1965; Research grantee Davidson Coll., 1956-57, U. N.C., 1957-58, Presbyn. Ch. in the U.S., 1960-61, Fla. Presbyn. Coll., 1960-61, Danforth Found., 1965-66. Mem. Melville Soc. Author: Private Higher Education in North Carolina: Conditions and Prospects, 1971; also music articles, short stories, revs. Editor: (Christopher Tye) The Latin Church Music, 2 vols., 1972. Translator: The Technique of My Musical Language, 2 vols., (Olivier Messlaen), 1956. Home: 193 Longview Rd Staten Island NY 10301 Office: Wagner Coll Staten Island NY 10301

SATZ, ARTHUR KING, coll. pres.; b. N.Y.C., Mar. 22, 1929; s. Sol M. and Rose S.; B.A., U. Rochester, 1951; M.A., U. So. Calif., 1953; M.F.A., Princeton U., 1957. Faculty, Vassar Coll., Poughkeepsie, N.Y., 1957-61, Yale U., 1961-63; asst. dir. N.Y. Sch. Interior Design, N.Y.C., 1963-72, dir., pres., 1972—. Fulbright scholar, Munich, W.Ger., 1953-55. Mem. Am. Soc. Interior Designers, Interior Design Educators Council, Archtl. League N.Y., Interior Design Soc. (adv. bd. 1977—), Phi Beta Kappa. Club: Princeton N.Y. Editor: 4th edit. Interior Design and Decoration (by Sherrill Whiton), 1974. Home: 333 E 68th St New York City NY 10021 Office: NY Sch Interior Design 155 E 56th St New York City NY 10022

SATZ, MARTIN ALLEN, psychologist; b. Mpls.; s. Samuel and Bertha (Shulman) S.; B.A., U. Minn., 1936, M.A., 1938; Ph.D. (Univ. fellow), U. Wash., 1952; m. Miriam Faye Lerner, June 20, 1948; children—Ronald Wayne, Barry Albert, Stephanie Teri, Madelyn Rachel. Dir. student affairs, prof. psychology Southwestern State Coll., Weatherford, Okla., 1952-58; asso. prof. Bloomsburg State Coll., 1958-62, prof., 1962—, chmn. dept. psychology, 1969-73; psychol. cons. Sch. of Hope, Danville State Hosp. and Geisinger Med. Center; psychol. examiner Social Security Disability. Pres. Columbia County (Pa.) Mental Health Assn., 1962-64, dir., 1964-69; trustee, chmn. sch. com. Jaques Weber Found., N.Y.C., 1969—. Served to capt. USAAF, 1941-46; Alaska-Aleutian Theater. Decorated Bronze Star; licensed psychologist, Pa. Mem. Am., Eastern, Pa. psychol. assns., Biofeedback Soc. Am., N.Y. Acad. Scis. Club: Internat. Torch (pres. 1972-73). Research on prediction of acad. success, biofeedback techniques in clin. psychology. Home: 185 Nottingham Rd Sherwood Vill Bloomsburg PA 17815 Office: Bloomsburg State Coll Bloomsburg PA 17815

SAUER, JOHN W., health care services exec.; b. San Francisco, Dec. 26, 1929; s. Leonard W. and Esther G. (Wright) S.; student Northwestern U., 1948-50; B.B.A., U. Oreg., 1952; m. Denise B. Warne, Jan. 19, 1973; children—Scott, Mark. Project mgr., systems cons. Stanford Research Inst., Menlo Park, Calif., 1966-70; gen. mgr. Advanced Mgmt. Systems, Brussels, Belgium, 1970-73; v.p. Case & Co., Mgmt. Cons., San Francsico, 1973-75; v.p. Nat. Assn. Blue Shield, Chgo., 1975-77, Blue Shield/Blue Cross Del., Wilmington, 1977—. Home: 1327 Richards Alley Wilmington DE 19806

SAUER, LAWRENCE MICHAEL, govt. exec.; b. Milw., May 22, 1940; s. Francis Edward and Josephine Marie (Farley) S.; B.S., U. Wis., 1964, M.S., 1965; postgrad. George Washington U., 1965-67; m. Sherrie Huberman, May 29, 1969; 1 son, John David. Mgmt. intern HEW, Washington, 1965-66, spl. asst. to asst. sec. for legis., 1967-68, dir. office legis. Health Services Adminstrn., Rockville, Md., 1975—; agy. liaison rep. Am. Optometric Assn., Washington, 1969-70; cons., Washington, 1970-72; dir. legis. Am. Hosp. Assn., Washington, 1973-75. Served with USN, 1958-60. Recipient Sustained High Quality Performance award Health Services Adminstrn., 1975. Mem. Am. Public Health Assn., Am. Hosp. Assn. Roman Catholic. Office: 5600 Fishers Ln Rockville MD 20857

SAUERWALD, JOHN PAUL, instrument co. ofcl.; b. Phila., May 9, 1938; s. John and Dorothy (Wenhold) S.; student pub. schs., Hatfield, Pa.; m. Dolores Ann Lapinski, Oct. 28, 1972; children—Brian Joseph, Matthew John. With Philco Corp., Lansdale, Pa., 1961-64, Asso. Valve Co., North Wales, Pa., 1964-67, Trailmobile Co., West Point, Pa., 1968-71; quality control insp., then quality control supr. Brooks Instrument Co. div. Emerson Electric Co., Hatfield, Pa., 1966—. Served with USN, 1955-59. Mem. Am. Soc. Nondestructive Testing. Home: 29 Hillcrest Rd Quakertown PA 18951 Office: 407 W Vine St Hatfield PA 19440

SAUNDERS, ALBERT HENRY, mfg. co. exec.; b. Logan, Iowa, Feb. 11, 1902; s. Arthur Lumb and Sarah (Hix) S.; grad. high sch.; m. Edith Rhodes, June 7, 1925 (dec. Dec. 1968); 1 son, Joseph Arthur. Operator family ranch, Creston, Mont., 1928; with Remington Rand Typewriter Co., 1928-37, br. mgr., Youngstown, Ohio, 1933-36, spl. rep., 1936-38; eastern sales rep. Acoustor Co., Youngstown, 1938-40; salesman Royal Typewriter Co., supplied div., Maine, N.H., Vt., Portland, Maine, 1942-46; founder, chmn. bd. Saunders Mfg. Co., Inc., Winthrop, Maine, 1946—. Home: RD 2 Winthrop ME 04364 Office: Box 243 Winthrop ME 04364

SAUNDERS, AMOS CHARLES, judge; b. Paterson, N.J., Mar. 9, 1934; s. Amos Joseph and Gertrude (Hollar) S.; B.A., Hampden-Sydney Coll., 1955; LL.B., Columbia, 1958; m. Janet Lee Botbyl, Aug. 20, 1955; children—Amos Charles, Richard Peter, Pamela Jane. Admitted to N.J. bar, 1959, U.S. Supreme Ct. bar, 1963; partner firm Dobrin, Muscarella, Saunders & Bochet, Fair Lawn, N.J., 1962-77; judge N.J. Superior Ct., Paterson, N.J., 1977—; municipal prosecutor Borough of Totowa (N.J.), 1962, atty. Zoning Bd. Ajustment, 1963-68; atty. Bd. Health, 1963-65, atty. Bd. Edn., 1965-69; judge Municipal Ct. Borough of Totowa, 1969-70; municipal atty. Borough of Totowa, 1970-77; adminstrv. judge Waterfront Commn. N.Y. Harbor, 1971-77. Chmn. March Dimes, 1960. Trustee, Totowa Borough Vol. Ambulance Corps 1963—. Mem. Am., N.J., Bergen County, Passaic County (trustee 1974-76, sec. 1976—) bar assns., Lambda Chi Alpha, Pi Delta Epsilon, Sigma Upsilon. Mem. The Church in Radburn, Fair Lawn (trustee 1966-68, pres. 1968—). Clubs: Mason, Rotary. Home: 115 Winifred Dr Totowa Borough NJ 07512 Office: Passaic County Court House Paterson NJ 07501

SAUNDERS, BEATRICE NAIR, editor, assn. exec.; b. New Britain, Conn., Dec. 26, 1915; d. Frank and Sophie (Adler) Nair; B.A., Smith Coll., 1936; m. Dero Ames Saunders, May 23, 1936; children—David Nair, Richard Ames. Tchr. pub. schs., New Britain, 1936; editorial asst. Cordon Co., N.Y.C., 1937-39, Family Welfare Assn. Am., N.Y.C., 1939-42; supr. editorial div. publs. div. A.R.C., Washington, 1943-46; free-lance editor various publs. N.Y.C., 1946-50; editor-in-chief, publs. dept. Girl Scouts U.S.A., N.Y.C., 1950-55; dir. publs. dept., editor Social Work, Nat. Assn. Social Workers, N.Y.C., 1955—; staff editor-in-chief Ency. of Social Work, 1971 edit., 1977 edit. Vol., A.R.C., Freeport, L.I., 1946-47, Child Care Center, Freeport, 1946-47; chmn. parents assn. Downtown Community Sch., 1948-50; chmn. 22d-21st St. Community Council, 1954-58, 62-63; chmn. com. on existing housing Chelsea Community Council, 1957-60; vice chmn. Chelsea Com. for Neighborhood Devel., 1960-63, chmn., 1963-65. Clubs: Advt., Heights Casino. Home: 446 W 22d St New York City NY 10011 Office: Nat Assn Social Workers 2 Park Ave New York City NY 10016

SAUNDERS, BETTY HUEY (MRS. AULUS WARD SAUNDERS), writer; b. St. Louis, July 11, 1909; d. Leslie and Kathryn Artimissia (Hyer) Huey; A.A., Stephens Coll., 1929; B.J., U. Mo., 1931; m. Aulus Ward Saunders, June 12, 1931; children—Alan Ward, Susan Beth (Mrs. William Harry Cook). Staff writer, corr., columnist, advt. salesman News-Champion, St. Louis County, Mo., 1937; playwright, one-act plays and radio plays, 1930—; free-lance writer with works pub. in newspapers and mags. including Reader's Digest, New Yorker, St. Louis Post-Dispatch, Wall St. Jour., People, numerous others. Pub. relations chmn., playwright, v.p. Oswego (N.Y.) Players, 1941-69; cons. pub. relations to N.Y. community theatres, 1949-69; lit. critic Nat. Writers Club, 1964—; playwrighting cons. Oswego (N.Y.) Chancel Theatre Group, 1973-77. Formerly mem. exec. bd., chmn. pub. relations Oswego County chpt. A.R.C., also Community Chest. Recipient poetry and short story writing prizes Nat. Writers Club Contests, 1959, 64; prize N.Y. State Drummond One-Act Playwrighting Contest, 1956. Mem. Bus. and Profl. Women's Club. Conglist. Editor The Grail, weekly religious mag., 1928-30. Editor-agt.-collaborator (with Dan Saunders) non-fiction books and articles on Alaska. Address: 165 E 3d St Oswego NY 13126

SAUNDERS, JOHN RICHARD, dentist; b. Stanislav, Poland, May 19, 1925; D.M.D. cum laude, U. Erlangen, Germany, 1949; D.M.D., Tufts U., 1952; m. Annalie Deborah Bean, Sept. 6, 1959; children—Lesley Pauline, Andrea Elizabeth. Research dept. Tufts Dental Sch., Boston, 1952; dentist Univ. Health Services, Harvard, 1955-56; supervising dentist, U. Bridgeport Sch. Dental Hygiene; practice dentistry, Boston, dentist Harvard U., 1956-64; instr. prosthodontics grad. div. Tufts U. Dental Medicine, 1964-65; Sponsor Hardy Prosthetic Conf.; lectr. dental meetings. Served from 1st lt. to capt. USAF, 1952-55. Fellow Royal Soc. Health, Acad. Gen. Dentistry, Internat. Coll. Dentists; mem. Am., Mass., Met. dental socs., Fed. Dentaire Internationale, Tufts U. Dental Alumni Assn., Acad. Gen. Dentistry, Am. Prosthodontic Soc., New Eng., Greater Boston, Boston In Town, Northeastern dental socs. Research in viscosity of dental alloys. Home: 23 Woodridge Circle Weston MA 02193 Office: 10 Post Office Square Boston MA 02109

SAUNDERS, JOSEPH ARTHUR, corp. exec.; b. Creston, Mont., July 9, 1926; s. Albert Henry and Edith Margaret (Rhodes) S.; student schs., Youngstown, Ohio, and Winthrop, Maine; m. Lois Evelyn White, June 19, 1948; children—Albert Henry II, Margaret Jean. With Saunders Mfg. Co., Inc., Winthrop, Maine, 1947—, pres., 1977—; dir. Forms Mfg. Equipment, Inc., Orlando, Fla.; co-founder, sec., dir. Dirigo Bank and Trust Co., Augusta, Maine. Bd. dirs. Maine State C. of C.; trustee Augusta Gen. Hosp. Served with U.S. Army, 1945-47. Mem. Internat. Bus. Forms Industries (Assos. chmn. 1976-77), Nat. Bus. Forms Assn., Printing Industries Am., Assn. Systems Mgmt., Binding Industries Am., Soc. Mfg. Engrs. (certified new products engr.), Am. Mgmt. Assn., Am. Legion. Clubs: Masons, (Readfield, Maine); Shriners (Lewiston, Maine). Patentee in field. Home: Touisset Point Readfield ME 04355 Office: Box 243 Winthrop ME 04364

SAUNDERS, MARY FRANCES, mathematician; b. Medford, Mass., July 30, 1927; d. Albert William F.J. and Mary Dolores (Kennedy) S.; student New Eng. Conservatory of Music, 1943-45; B.A. Emmanuel Coll., 1949; postgrad. Boston U., 1949-50, 63, George Washington U., 1952-53; student U.S. Naval Sch. of Mil. Justice, 1951, U.S. Navy Sonar Sch., 1953, U.S. Navy Antisubmarine Warfare Tactical Sch., 1962. Actuarial student John Hancock Ins. Co., Boston, 1949-50; mathematician electronic counter-countermeasures group Sanders Assos., Nashua, N.H., 1959-62; adminstrv. engr. to dir. photocondr. div. Electronics Corp. Am., Cambridge, Mass., 1962-64; research scientist Thomas Co., Westwood, Mass., 1964-66; aerospace mathematician Electronic Research Center, NASA, Cambridge, 1966-70; founder, propr. M.F. Saunders & Co., Boston, 1970—, pres., 1970—; participant research and devel. of prototype antisubmarine warfare firecontrol systems, 1951-54; participant Microprocessor Data Base Study, 1975, Air Traffic Control Study, 1972-73. Sec. New Boston Com., 1949-50. Served with USN, 1950-58. Mem. Am. Math. Soc. Optical Soc. Am., Accoustical Soc. Am., Assn. for Computing Machinery, Am. Mgmt. Assn., Naval Res. Assn., Res. Officers Assn., World Affairs Council. Republican. Roman Catholic. Originated the U.S. Navy Weapons' Systems Concept; developer computer program info. retrieval system. Home: 144 Washington St Arlington MA 02174 Office: 15 School St Boston MA 02108

SAUNDERS, ROBERT HARRIS, criminalist; b. Gary, Ind., Sept. 27, 1914; s. George Douglas and Dorothy (Harris) S.; A.B., U. Ill., 1937, M.S., Ill. Inst. Tech., 1941, Ph.D., 1944; m. Ruth Alberta Zweig, Jan. 2, 1943; children—Nancy Saunders Williams, George Douglas, Robert Withers. Research supr. Hercules Powder Co., Wilmington, Del., 1944-70; asso. prof. chemistry and physics West Chester (Pa.) State Coll., 1970-75; explosives and arson technologist Delaware-Chester Counties Crime Lab., Lima, Pa., 1975—. Mem. Am. Chem. Soc., Am. Soc. Microbiology, Sigma Xi, Alpha Chi Sigma, Zeta Psi. Contbr. articles in field to profl. jours. Patentee in field. Home: RD 2 Box 81 Chaddsford PA 19317 Office: 300 N Middletown Rd Lima PA 19037

SAUNDERS, STANLEY, univ. music dir., orchestral conductor; b. Newport, Gt. Brit., May 3, 1927; s. Albert and Beatrice S.; diploma music U. Wales (Gt. Brit.), 1951; Mus.M., U. Oreg., Eugene, 1967, D.Mus.Arts (Can. Council doctoral fellow), 1970; m. Barbara Elaine Davies, Oct. 31, 1950. Music specialist Glamorgan Edn. Authorities, S. Wales, Gt. Brit., 1951-58; lectr. extra-mural classes U. Wales, 1951-58; performer, instrumentalist, conductor BBC Radio and TV, 1951-58; lectr., asst. prof., asso. prof. music, Mt. Allison U., Sackville, N.B., Can., 1958-74; founder, conductor Provincial N.B. Youth Orch., 1958-74; performer, instrumentalist, conductor, CBC Radio and TV, 1958—; mem. guest faculty U. Oreg., Eugene, 1964-70; dir. music, cultural affairs U. Guelph (Ont., Can.), 1974—; condr. U. Guelph Civic Orch. and Brantford (Ont.) Symphony Orch., 1974—;

v.p. Canadian Conf. Arts, 1968-74; exec. mem. Nat. Youth Orch., 1976—. Recipient Fgn. Student Acad. award U. Oreg., 1969-70; Canadian Silver Jubilee medal Queen Elizabeth II, 1978. Contbr. articles and book revs. to music jours. and ency. Office: Director Music College Arts Univ Guelph Guelph ON Canada

SAUNDERS, WILLIAM BEVERLY, adminstrv. librarian; b. Smithers, W.Va., Oct. 3, 1927; s. William S. and Lillie G. (Mosby) S.; B.S. in Secondary Edn., Bluefield (W.Va.) State Coll., 1947; M.A. in Edn., U. W.Va., 1948; M.S. in Library Sci., U. Pitts., 1957; m. Lucretia R. Heyward, June 15, 1957; children—Robinlu, William. Tchr., social studies and English, pub. high sch., Denton, Md., 1948-51; librarian Free Library Phila., 1957-59; jr. bus. librarian Temple U., Phila., 1959-63, edn. librarian, 1970-72; head, Mktg. Sci. Inst. Library, Phila., 1963-67; head librarian Inst. Advancement Bio-Med. Communication, Phila., 1967-69; curriculum librarian, audio-visual librarian Cheyney (Pa.) State Coll., 1969-70; dir. Antioch U. Library, Phila., 1972—, instr. grad. studies, 1973, 74. Mem. U.S. Pres.'s Com. Employment of Handicapped, 1975—; mem. Fair Housing Council, Landsdowne, Pa., 1963-66; bd. dirs. Fair Housing Council Delaware Valley (Pa.), 1965-67; co-founder Edn. Librarians of Delaware Valley, 1974—. Mem. Pa. Abolition Soc., Friends of N.W. Regional Library, Free Library Phila. Roman Catholic. Contbr. articles to library and Black history jours. Home: 337 W Mount Airy Ave Philadelphia PA 19119

SAUNDERS, WILLIAM FRANCIS, lawyer; b. Jersey City, N.J., Dec. 31, 1915; s. Richard Loesch and Cassie Alice (Betts) S.; B.S., Washington & Lee U., 1938, LL.B., 1940; m. Ann Sutherland Price, Oct. 5, 1940; 1 dau., Mary (Mrs. Richard H. Turner). Admitted to Va. bar, 1939, N.Y. bar, 1941; asso. mem. firm Dunnington, Bartholow & Miller, N.Y.C., 1940-47, partner, 1948—. Chmn. residential donations Community Chest, East Ridgewood, N.J., 1959—. Trustee Ridgewood Independence Day Assn., 1952-70, The Valley Hosp., Ridgewood, 1967—. Served to lt. comdr. USNR, 1942-46; ETO, PTO. Mem. U.S. Naval Inst., Naval War Coll. Found., Order of Coif, Phi Beta Kappa, Beta Gamma Sigma, Omicron Delta Kappa, Delta Upsilon. Episcopalian. Clubs: Brook, Union League (N.Y.C.). Home: 520 Fairway Rd Ridgewood NJ 07450 Office: 161 E 42d St New York City NY 10017

SAUSE, EDWIN FRANCIS, psychologist; b. S.I., N.Y., June 14, 1942; s. Edwin Francis and Helen Frances (Bay) S.; A.B., St. Joseph's Coll., 1964; M.S. Wagner Coll., 1966; profl. diploma Fordham U., 1969, Ph.D., 1970; m. Rosemary A. Quinn, Nov. 21, 1971; 1 dau., Siobhan. Research asso. Edn. Research Council Am., Cleve., 1969-71; asst. prof. St. John's U., Jamaica, N.Y., 1971-76; evaluator State U. N.Y., Stony Brook, 1976; instr. N.Y. Inst. Tech., Old Westbury, 1976-78; staff psychologist St. John's Residence and Sch., Rockaway Park, N.Y., 1977—; adj. prof. St. Joseph's Coll., Brentwood, N.Y.; cons. to pub. and pvt. schs. Bd. dirs. Warrensville Heights Civic Assn., 1970-71; mem. Richmond County Health Planning Council, 1971-73. U.S. Office Edn. fellow, 1966-69. Mem. Am., Suffolk County psychol. assns., Phi Delta Kappa. Club: K.C. Contbr. articles in field to psychol. and ednl. jours. Home: 143 Waterside Ave Northport NY 11768 Office: 144 Beach 111th St Rockaway Park NY 11694

SAUTER, LAURENCE JAMES, indsl. engr.; b. Cin., Feb. 27, 1924; s. William Andrew and Edna Lucy (Jones) S.; B.S., Chase Coll., 1952; M.B.A., Southeastern U., 1978; m. Grace Christine Miles, Mar. 7, 1964; children—Laurence J., Laura Jean. Mgr. devel. engring. Air Force Systems Command, Andrews AFB, Md., 1963-66; chief quality and reliability engr. Def. Logistics Agy., Alexandria, Va., 1966-67; dir. value engring. office Naval Air Systems Command, Washington, 1967-73, dir. joint logistics office, 1973—. Served with USMCR, 1942-45. Fellow Soc. Am. Value Engrs., Am. Inst. Aeros. and Astronautics, Am. Inst. Indsl. Engrs., Am. Soc. Quality Control; mem. Soc. Logistics Engrs., Am. Soc. Pub. Adminstrn., Nat. Soc. Profl. Engrs. Republican. Baptist. Clubs: Ft. Leslie McNair Officers, Masons, Shriners. Home: 6600 Temole Hill Rd Camp Springs MD 20031

SAUTER, MICHAEL OTTMAR, physician; b. Jamacia, N.Y., May 9, 1946; s. Ottmar Emil and Frances Rita (Schneider) S.; B.S. in Biology cum laude, Siena Coll., 1967; M.D., Loyola U., Ill., 1971; m. Laurnel Marie Henry, Oct. 25, 1969; children—Matthew, Michelle. Intern, Nassau County Med. Center, East Meadow, N.Y., 1971-72, resident medicine, 1972-74, resident neurology, 1974-77; practice medicine, specializing in neurology, Port Jefferson, N.Y., 1977—; mem. staff St. Charles Hosp., Mather Meml. Hosp.; instr. medicine State U. N.Y. at Stoneybrook, 1976—. Mem. Am. Acad. Neurology, Suffolk County Med. Soc., Alpha Omega Alpha. Roman Catholic. Club: K.C. Office: 120 N Country Rd Port Jefferson NY 11777

SAUVAYRE, GEORGES THEOPHILE, govt. ofcl.; b. Maraussan, France, Apr. 30, 1923; s. Xavier and Isabelle (Loubet) S.; came to U.S., 1966; grad. Superior Inst. Tourism, Paris, 1951; m. Marie-Therese Delcambre-Couedel, Apr. 22, 1954; children—Pascal, François. Lectr. sightseeing dept. Thos. Cook and Son, Paris, 1950-57; dep. dir. French Govt. Tourist Office, Zurich, Switzerland, 1957-60, London, 1960-66, regional mgr. Middle West-Chgo., U.S., 1969-72, dir. gen. U.S., N.Y.C., 1972—. Served in French Resistance and First French Army, 1942-46; decorated Mil. Cross with silver star (France). Mem. Am. Soc. Assn. Execs., European Travel Commn., Am. Soc. Travel Agts., Soc. Am. Travel Writers. Roman Catholic. Clubs: Sales Exec., Paris Am. Home: 250 E 87th St New York City NY 10028 Office: 610 Fifth Ave New York City NY 10020

SAVAGE, HENRY LYTTLETON, educator; b. Phila., Sept. 13, 1892; s. Charles Chauncey and Ann (King) S.; A.B., Princeton U., 1915; student U. Pa., 1915-17; Ph.D. (fellow in English), Yale U., 1924; m. Mary Radclyffe Furness, June 24, 1932; children—Caroline Savage Langan, Charles, Henry. Instr., U. Pa., 1916-17; instr. English, Princeton U., 1923-26, asst. prof. English, 1926-29, asso. prof., 1929, archivist Univ. Library, 1944-58, keeper of Princetoniana, 1958-62. Air raid warden Mercer County, N.J.; trustee Pub. Library Borough of Princeton, 1953-59, chmn. bd., 1959. Served from 2d lt. to 1st lt., 7th Div., AEF, 1917-18. Mem. Soc. Colonial Wars (historian N.J.), Modern Lang. Assn. Am., Phila. Shakespere Soc., Soc. for Study Medieval Langs. and Lit. (Oxford, Eng.), Hist. Soc. Princeton (asst. sec.), Phi Beta Kappa. Republican. Presbyn. Clubs: Princeton (Phila. and N.Y.C.); Franklin Inn (Phila.); Mory's Assn. (New Haven); Grolier (N.Y.C.). Author: The Gawain-Poet, 1956; Life of Dr. Witherspoon, 1972; editor: St. Erkenwald, 1926; Nassau Hall, 1956; The Art of Angling, 1958. Home: 210 Prospect St Princeton NJ 08540

SAVAGE, JOHN ADDISON, librarian; b. Utica, N.Y., Jan. 15, 1921; s. John Orville and Cora (Rossiter) S.; A.B., U. Mich., 1950, M.A. in L.S., 1951; m. Victoria Peterson, Aug. 1, 1947; children—Susan, Janet, Robert. Reference asst. Cornell U. Libraries, Ithaca, N.Y., 1951-55; asst. librarian Hicksville (N.Y.) Pub. Library, 1956-58; high sch. librarian Levittown (N.Y.), Pub. Schs., 1958-65; library dir. North Babylon (N.Y.) Pub. Library, 1965—. Served with USAAF, 1943-46. Mem. A.L.A., N.Y., Suffolk County library assns., Hist. Soc. Pa. Home: 4 Tomkins Ct Commack NY 11725 Office: 815 Deer Park Ave North Babylon NY 11703

SAVAGE, WARREN HOWARD, hosp. exec.; b. Princess Anne, Md., Feb. 23, 1940; s. Walter Theodore and Hattie Jane (Henderson) S.; grad. high sch. Pianist, Great Oak Lodge, Chestertown, Md., 1958-67; purchasing asst. Leland Meml. Hosp., Riverdale, Md., 1967-70, purchasing dir., 1970—. Mem. Md. Hosp. Assn., Hosp. Council of Washington, Am. Purchasing Soc. Democrat. Methodist. Home: 3902 Oliver St Hyattsville Hills MD 20782 Office: 4408 Queensbury Rd Riverdale MD 20840

SAVAGE, WILLIAM MICHAEL, social work adminstr.; b. Syracuse, N.Y., Oct. 9, 1939; s. William Francis and Marguerite Mary (Relihan) S.; M.S.W., Syracuse U., 1966; m. Ann Mary Sheehe, Sept. 30, 1967; 1 dau., Elizabeth Ann. Psychiat. social worker Crouse Irving Meml. Hosp., Syracuse, 1966-70; project dir. Family Counseling Service, Geneva, N.Y., 1970-72; dir. dept. social work St. Joseph's Hosp., Elmira, 1972—, adminstrv. dir. sourtherntier alcoholism rehab. services, 1973—; pvt. practice psychotherapy. Chmn. Regional Mental Health Council, 1978—. Served with N.Y. State Air NG. 1963-69. Mem. Acad. Certified Social Workers, Nat. Assn. Social Workers, Cert. Social Workers N.Y. State Nat. Soc. Hosp. Social Work (dir. chpt.), N.Y. State Soc. Clin. Social Work Psychotherapists, Nat. Registry Health Care Providers in Clin. Social Work, Am. Polit. Items Collectors. Home: 110 Fairmont Rd Elmira NY 14905

SAVAS, EMANUEL S., educator; b. N.Y.C., June 8, 1931; s. John and Olga (Limbos) S.; B.A., U. Chgo., 1951, B.S., 1953; M.A., Columbia, 1956, Ph.D., 1960; m. Helen Andrew, Dec. 25, 1955; children—Jonathan, Stephen. Control systems cons. IBM, Yorktown Heights, and White Plains N.Y., 1959-65; urban systems mgr., N.Y.C., 1966-67; 1st dep. city adminstr. Office Mayor, N.Y.C., 1967-72, chmn. Mayor's Urban Action Task Force, 1969-72; prof. Columbia, 1972—, dir. Center for Govt. Studies, 1973—, asso. dir. Center for Policy Research, 1973—. Cons., NSF, 1973—; mem. U.S.-USSR Joint Working Group on Computers in Mgmt., 1972—; mem. evaluation panel Nat. Bur. Standards, NRC, 1973-75; mem. voting bd. Blue Cross and Blue Shield Greater N.Y., 1976—; advisor panel Nat. Acad. Engring., 1972; cons. HUD, 1976. Cons., State Charter Revision Com. for N.Y.C., 1973-75; advisor Com. Econ. Devel., Work in Am. Inst.; bd. dirs. Central Park Community Fund, 1976—. Served with AUS, 1953-54; Korea. Recipient Systems Sci. and Cybernetics award IEEE, 1968, Louis Brownlow award Internat. City Mgmt. Assn., 1970. Mem. Adminstr. and Mgmt. Research Assn. N.Y.C. (bd. dirs., 1969-76), AAAS, Assn. Computing Machinery (chmn. urban conf., 1967, vice chmn. joint computer conf. 1972), Inst. Mgmt. Scis. (v.p. coll. local govt., 1969-74), rep. to AAAS 1977—), Urban and Regional Information Systems Assn., Sigma Xi, Psi Upsilon. Democrat. Greek Orthodox. Club: City of N.Y. (trustee 1974-77). Author: Computer Control of Industrial Processes, 1965; Organization and Efficiency of Solid Waste Collection, 1977. Asso. editor Mgmt. Sci.; editor Alternatives for Delivering Public Services, 1977. Office: Columbia U New York City NY 10027

SAVEL, LEWIS EUGENE, obstetrician, gynecologist; b. N.Y.C., Nov. 9, 1911; s. Morris J. and Rose (Siegel) S.; B.S., N.Y. U., 1932; M.D., N.Y. Med. Coll., 1936; m. Grace Salenger, Jan. 7, 1973; 1 dau., Susan H. Intern Beth Israel Hosp., Newark, 1936-38; resident in obstetrics and gynecology Margaret Hague Maternity Hosp., Jersey City, 1944-46; practice medicine specializing in gynecology obstetrics, South Orange, N.J., 1938—; attending in obstetrics and gynecology Martland Hosp., Newark; chief obstetrics and gynecology Beth Israel Med. Center, Newark, 1958—, pres. med. staff, 1968, 69, 70; asso. clin. prof. obstetrics and gynecology N.J. Coll. Medicine and Dentistry, Newark, 1967—; chmn. med. adv. com. Planned Parenthood Essex County, N.J., 1955—; chmn. med. adv. com. Community Nursing Service, Newark, 1964-67, 72—. Served with AUS, 1942-43. Diplomate Am. Bd. Obstetrics and Gynecology. Fellow Am. Coll. Obstetricians and Gynecologists, A.C.S., I.C.S. Editor Jour. Beth Israel Hosp., Newark, 1965-67. Contbr. articles to profl. jours. Home: 51 Sherwood Rd Springfield NJ 07081 Office: 468 Irvington Ave South Orange NJ 07079

SAVITSKY, LINDA REBECCA, city ofcl.; b. New Haven, Dec. 26, 1948; d. Martin and Rosalind Simon (Schaefer) S.; B.A., Clark U., 1970; postgrad. U. Bridgeport, 1975-76, U. N.H., 1976-77. Resident adviser, dir. student activities Assumption Coll., Worcester, Mass., 1970-71; asst. to comptroller Home Fed. Savs. & Loan Assn., Worcester, 1971-73; Tax collector City of Shelton (Conn.), 1974—, dir. fin., 1978—. Bd. dirs. Shelton League Women Voters, 1975-77; treas. Valley Arts Council, 1976-78; mem. Long Wharf Theatre Assos., 1976—; admissions rep. Clark U. Alumni, 1975—. Mem. Tax Collectors Assn. Conn., Fairfield County Tax Collectors Assn. (treas.-sec. 1975-78), Municipal Fin. Officers Conn., Municipal Fin. Officers Am., Clark U. Alumni Assn. (v.p. 1976-78). Jewish. Home: 56 Wakelee Ave Extension 60 Shelton CT 06484

SAVITT, ARNOLD JAY, electronics co. exec.; b. Thomasville, Ga., Mar. 12, 1926; s. Samuel and Rose (Silverbrand) S.; B.B.A., Coll. City N.Y., 1949; postgrad. Bklyn. Poly. Inst., 1962-63; M.S.A., L.I. U., 1975; m. Thelma Manheim, Aug. 3, 1952; children—Daniel Lawrence, Samuel Jeffrey, Howard Adam. Prodn. engr. Panoramic Radio Corp., 1943-44; div. head mfg. Hazeltine Corp., Greenlawn, N.Y., 1949-57, exec. asst. v.p. ops., 1957-69, dir. ops., 1969-76; dir. mfg. GTE Sylvania, Needham Heights, Mass., 1976—; cons. to electronic mfrs. Active Strathmore Civic Assn., Gt. Neck, N.Y., Waban Improvement Assn., Newton, Mass. Registered profl. engr., Calif.; certified mfg. engr. Mem. Am. Inst. Indsl. Engrs., Am. Prodn. and Inventory Control Soc. (dir.), Internat. Assn. Quality Circles, Am. Mgmt. Assn., Nat. Security Indsl. Assn., Electronics Industry Assn. Clubs: U.S. Power Squadron, Ednl. Alliance, Baruch Coll. Alumni, Mass. Audubon Soc., Smithsonian Assos. Patentee printed circuit device. Home: 36 Bonnybrook Rd Waban MA 02168 Office: 77 A St Needham Heights MA 02194

SAVITT, SAM, artist, author; b. Wilkes-Barre, Pa.; s. Hyman and Rose (Eskowitz) S.; grad. Sch. Illustration, Pratt Inst., 1939-41; student Art Students League, 1950-51; m. Bette Joan Orkin, Mar. 28, 1946; children—Darah Vickery, Roger Scott. One man shows: Aqueduct Art Gallery, Jamaica, N.Y., 1966, Concourse Gallery, Boston, 1969, Piccolo Mondo, Palm Beach, Fla., 1974, Internat. Sports Core, Oak Brook, Ill., 1975; group shows include: Crossroads of Sport, N.Y.C., 1964, 66, The Crest, Aiken, S.C., 1972, Ackerman Gallery, N.Y.C., 1972, 76; represented in permanent collections: Old Time Galleries, San Diego, pvt. collections; ofcl. artist U.S. Equestrian Team, 1956—; designer comml. items, including Sam Savitt Horse Charts; illustrator 106 books; author-illustrator: Step-A-Bit, 1956, Midnight, Champion Bucking Horse, 1957, There Was a Horse, 1961, Around the World with Horses, 1962, Rodeo: Cowboys, Bulls and Broncos, 1963, Vicki and the Black Horse, 1964, A Day at the LBJ Ranch, 1965, America's Horses, 1966, Equestrian Olympic Sketchbook, 1968, Sam Savitt's True Horse Stories, 1970, Wild Horse Running, 1973, Vicki and the Brown Mare, 1976, The Dingle Ridge Fox and Other Stories, 1978; co-author: Ups and Downs, 1973, How To Take Care of Your Horse Until the Vet Comes, 1975, Great Horses of the United States Esquestrian Team, 1977. Served to 1st lt., AUS, 1942-46. Recipient Boys' Clubs Am. Jr. Book award for Midnight, 1958. Address: One Horse Farm North Salem NY 10560

SAWHILL, JOHN, economist, educator, univ. pres.; b. Cleve., June 12, 1936; s. James Mumford and Mary Munroe (Gipe) S.; A.B., Princeton, 1958; Ph.D., N.Y. U., 1963; m. Isabel Van Devanter, Sept. 13, 1958; 1 son, James W. With Merrill, Lynch, Pierce, Fenner & Smith, Washington, 1958-60; asst. dean, prof. N.Y.U. Sch. Bus. Adminstrn., 1960-63; dir. credit research and planning Comml. Credit Co., Balt., 1964-66, sr. v.p., 1968-73; sr. asso. McKinsey & Co., Washington, 1966-68; asso. dir. for natural resources Office Mgmt. and Budget, Washington, 1973-74; adminstr. Fed. Energy Adminstrn., Washington, 1973-75; now pres. N.Y. U., Washington Sq.; dir. Am. Internat. Group, Inc., Automatic Data Processing, Inc., Crane Co., Gen. Am. Investors Co., Inc., ICI Americas, Inc., N.Am. Coal Corp., Philip Morris Inc., RCA; trustee Consol. Edison, Inc. Trustee Md. Inst. Coll. Art, Commn. on Ind. Colls. and Univs., World Peace Found., Com. for Econ. Devel., Common Cause; bd. dirs. Whitehead Med. Research Inst.; mem., dir. Trilateral Commn.; chmn. Mayor's Long Range Planning Com. on Future N.Y.C. Mem. AAAS (dir.). Clubs: Metropolitan (Washington); Chevy Chase (Md.); Maryland (Balt.). Office: NYU 70 Washington Sq S New York City NY 10012

SAWITSKY, HELEN MARYANN, nursing adminstr.; b. Peabody, Mass., Jan. 13, 1922; d. Metislaw and Mary Anne (Mageski) S.; B.S. in Nursing Edn., Boston U., 1953, M.S., 1959. Staff, Beth Israel Hosp., Boston, 1943-62, asst. dir. nursing, 1960-62; faculty Boston U. Sch. Nursing, 1963-66; asst. dir. in charge of in-service Salem (Mass.) Hosp., 1966-69, asso. dir. nursing, 1969—. Mem. Am. Nursing Assn., Am. Hosp. Assn., N.E. Regional Council of Dirs. Nursing, LWV. Home: 17 Kirkland Rd Peabody MA 01960 Office: 81 Highland Ave Salem MA 01970

SAWYER, RICHARD GEORGE, chemist; b. Rochester, N.Y., Aug. 28, 1944; s. Ralph Albert and Mina (Coffee) S.; student Rochester Inst. Tech., 1963-64; B.S., Otterbein Coll., 1967; postgrad. (NDEA fellow) Syracuse U., 1967-69; m. Jacqueline Rita Michaud, Nov. 29, 1969; children—James Richard, Robert George. Research scientist Syracuse U. Research Corp., 1967-73, cons., 1973-78; prodn. chemist Welch Allyn Inc., Skaneateles Falls, N.Y., 1973—. Asst. scoutmaster Hiawatha council Boy Scouts Am., 1967-71, scoutmaster, 1971-77, chmn. troop com., 1977—. Certified san. plant operator, N.Y. Mem. Am. Chem. Soc., Transp. Research Bd., Am. Concrete Inst., Soc. Am. Mil. Engrs., Am. Electroplaters Soc. (v.p.). Republican. Methodist. Contbr. articles to profl. jours.; patentee chem. communition, mining coal; research in innovation illumination sources, med. instruments. Home: 339 Scott Ave Syracuse NY 13224 Office: Welch Allyn Inc Skaneateles Falls NY 13153

SAWYER, THOMAS KNOWLTON, marine biologist; b. Phoenix, May 11, 1929; s. Francis Lucas and Grace Christine (Schaeffer) S.; B.S., Am. U., 1953; M.S., George Washington U., 1960; Ph.D., U. Md., 1973; postgrad. Army Command and Gen. Staff Coll., 1978; m. Dorothy May Lee, June 1, 1951; children—Patricia Lee, Robert Knowlton, Barbara Lynn. Biologist, USPHS, Dept. Agr., Walter Reed Army Inst. Research, 1953-64; fishery biologist Dept. Commerce, Oxford, Md., 1964—; adj. researcher coll. marine studies U. Del., 1976—; guest lectr. U. Md., 1973—, Georgetown U., 1976—; cons. Armed Forces Inst. Pathology, Washington. Served with U.S. Army, 1946-47, to maj. Res., 1956—. Mem. Am. Soc. Parasitologists (editorial bd.), Am. Micros. Soc. (v.p. 1978, program chmn. Centennial Meeting 1978), Am. Soc. Protozoologists, Helminthological Soc. Washington (pres. 1973), Sigma Xi, Phi Sigma. Presbyterian. Clubs: Kiwanis of Easton (v.p. 1970); Isaac Walton League. Co-author: Key to Marine Amoebae of N.E. United States, 1978; contbr. articles to profl. jours. Home: Route 5 Box 425 Easton MD 21601 Office: US Dept Commerce NOAA Nat Marine Fisheries NE Fisheries Center Oxford Lab Oxford MD 21654

SAXE, ELIZABETH LEE, historian; b. N.Y.C., June 10, 1934; d. Hugo and Katherine Knowles (McMunn) Steiner; A.B. magna cum laude, Radcliffe Coll., 1955; M.A., Richmond Coll. U. City N.Y., 1972; M.A., Yale U., 1972, M.Phil., 1974, postgrad., 1974—; m. John Brooke Saxe, Feb. 25, 1956 (dec. Mar. 1970); children—John Matthew, Charles Calvin, Andrew Frederick. Research asso. S.I. Inst. Arts and Scis., 1967-68; adj. instr. Coll. New Rochelle, 1978; lectr. in history Yale U., 1978. Mem. S.I. Community Planning Bd., 1966-69. Recipient Oliver-Dabney History prize Radcliffe Coll., 1955, award of merit Office Pres. Borough Richmond, N.Y.C., 1968; Yale U. fellow, 1971-74; Yale Council Fgn. Relations travel grantee, 1974. Mem. Am. Hist. Assn., Medieval Acad. Am. Lutheran. Club: Yale of N.Y. A subject of film: By Themselves, 1975. Home: 47 Carmalt Rd Hamden CT 06517

SAXE, THEODORE LANGDON, urologist; b. Passaic, N.J., May 31, 1918; s. Solomon M. and Sophie Reba (Jaffe) S.; A.B., U. Mich., 1940, M.D., 1943; m. Marjorie Mina Mayers, May 3, 1946; children—Leonard Roy, Carol Saxe Buda. Intern, Beth Israel Hosp., Boston, 1943, resident in urology, 1944; dir. urology Christ Hosp., Jersey City, 1969—; bd. govs. Palisade Gen. Hosp., North Bergen, N.J. Served as capt. M.C., U.S. Army, 1944-46. Diplomate Am. Bd. Urology. Fellow A.C.S.; mem. Am. Urol. Assn., Soc. Surgeons N.J. Office: 2777 Kennedy Blvd Jersey City NJ 07306

SAXON, GEORGE EDWARD, mfg. co. exec.; b. Pitts., July 17, 1932; s. George and Julia S.; B.S.M.E., U. Pitts., 1955; m. Frances Jane Bartosiewicz, June 30, 1956; children—Regina, Edward, George, Gregory. Mfg. engr. Gen. Electric Co., various locations, 1955-63; purchasing engr. Westinghouse Electric Co., Cheswick, Pa., 1963-66; purchasing mgr. tubular products div. Babcock Wilcox Co., Beaver Falls, Pa., 1967-70; gen. mgr. Universal Lubricating Systems, Inc., Oakmont, Pa., 1970-71; pres., chmn. Condenser Cleaners Mfg. Co., Inc., Verona, Pa., 1971—; dir., sec. Smaller Mfrs. Council, 1976; cons. in field. Served with U.S. Army, 1955-57. Mem. ASME, Am. Iron and Steel Engrs., Soc. Am. Value Engrs. Republican. Roman Catholic. Clubs: U. Pitts Century, N. Park Sportsman's, Elks. Contbr. articles in field to profl. jours. Home: 665 9th St Oakmont PA 15139 Office: 135 Sylvan St Verona PA 15147

SAXTON, GERALD O., hosp. inst. adminstr.; b. Montreal, Que., Can., Mar. 5, 1926; s. Bertram and Adorella S.; B.Commerce, Sir George Williams U., 1966; m. Doreen, Oct. 8, 1949 (separated Nov. 1976), 1 dau., Cynthia Dawn. Exec. dir. Can. Arthritis and Rheumatism Soc., 1963-68, United Red Feather Services, Montreal, 1968-71; nat. dir. Boys' and Girls' Clubs Can., Montreal, 1971-75; exec. dir. Montreal Joint Hosp. Inst., 1975—; lectr. Laval U., 1965-68, U. Montreal, 1965-68, Sir George Williams U., 1977. Mem. Can. Coll. Health Service Execs., Inst. Assn. Execs., Corp. Chartered Adminstrs., Am. Hosp. Assn. (council shared service orgns.). Contbr. articles to profl. jours. Office: 1110 Pine Ave W Montreal PQ H3A 1A3 Canada

SAYLOR, ROBERT HOMER, counselor educator; b. Roaring Spring, Pa., Nov. 7, 1922; s. Clarence Edgar and Ruie Mae (Stuckey) S.; B.S. Juniata Coll., 1949; M.Ed., Pa. State U., 1952, Ed.D., 1959; m. Margaret Rose Seybert, Feb. 23, 1952; children—Linford Thomas, Elizabeth Jane, Joan Patton. Tchr. secondary schs., Hustontown, Pa., 1949-51; dir. guidance Bloomsburg (Pa.) Pub. Schs., 1954-56; instr. edn. and psychology Wittenberg U., Springfield, Ohio, 1956-58; asst.

prof. psychology and edn. Va. Mil. Inst., Lexington, 1959-60; asso. dean student affairs, also asst. prof. edn. Pa. State U., 1960-61; prof. counselor edn. Indiana U. Pa., 1961—, pres.'s adv. council, 1962-70; cons. in field. Bd. edn. Indiana Area Sch. Dist., 1969-75, 77; mem. Indiana Borough Sch. Authority, 1978—. Served from pvt. to col., U.S. Army, 1942-47, 52-53. Pa. State U. fellow, 1958-59; Danforth Asso., 1964—. Mem. Am., Pa. personnel and guidance assns., Assn. Counselor Edn. and Supervision, Pa. Assn. Counselor Edn. and Supervision, VFW, Res. Officers Assn., Ret. Officers Assn., Phi Delta Kappa, Iota Alpha Delta. Club: Masons. Home: 543 S 6th St Indiana PA 15701

SAYONG, SALVADOR ACALA, accountant; b. Burauen, Leyte, Philippines, Apr. 25, 1932; s. Epifanio Ola Sayong and Emelia Salarda Acala S.; came to U.S., 1970, naturalized, 1975; B.S. in Bus. Adminstrn., U. Philippines, 1955; m. Alita B. Aniano, May 25, 1970; children—Marian, Salvador, Joshua, Manolito, Epifanio, Edwin. Mem. audit staff Price Waterhouse & Co., Manila, 1955-61; fin. officer operation brotherhood USAID, Laos, 1961-63; office mgr., chief accountant Rohm & Haas Co., Manila, 1964-67; asst. region controller Coca-Cola Export Corp., Manila, Philippines, 1967-70; accountant Pinkerton's Inc., N.Y.C., 1970-72; accountant AEI/Wings & Wheels of N.Y., N.Y.C., 1972-73; internal auditor, supr. Flintkote Co., Stamford, Conn., 1973—. C.P.A. Mem. Inst. Internal Auditors, Philippine Inst. C.P.A.'s, Philippine Mgmt. Assn. Democrat. Roman Catholic. Home: 40 Union Ave Rutherford NJ 07070 Office: 1351 Washington Blvd Stamford CT 06902

SAYRE, ANNE, author; b. Wis., Apr. 10, 1924; d. Edward St. Clair and Claudia Middleton (deVinny) Colquhoun; B.A., Radcliffe Coll., 1943; J.D., N.Y. U., 1978; vis. scholar Lucy Cavendish Coll. Cambridge (Eng.) U., 1970-75; m. David Sayre, Dec. 26, 1947. Works include: The Charm, 1959, All in the Family, 1961; Fear No Evil, 1962; Never Call Retreat, 1957; Rosalind Franklin and DNA, 1975; also many short stories. Episcopalian. Club: Cosmopolitan. Home: The Shore House Harbor Rd St James NY 11780

SAZER, GARY NEIL, lawyer; b. Chgo., July 14, 1946; s. David and Eleanor (Miller) S.; B.A., N.Y. U., 1971; J.D., Hofstra Law Sch., 1974; m. Lois Gail Kolen, Aug. 21, 1971; children—Eric Scott, Jonathan Adam. Acquisitions cons. Empress Internat., Ltd., N.Y.C., 1970-72; admitted to N.Y. State bar, also U.S. dist. cts.; asso. firm Windels & Marx, N.Y.C., 1972-76; partner firm Rubinstein & Sazer, N.Y.C., 1976—; lectr. comml. law Nassau Bar Assn. Exec. asst. to mayor Great Neck Plaza, N.Y.C., 1971-73. Mem. Internat., Am., N.Y. State bar assns., Assn. of Bar of City of N.Y., N.Y. County Lawyers Assn., Am. Horse Council. Republican. Jewish. Contbr. articles to legal jours. Home: 28 Woodland Pl Great Neck NY 11021 Office: 845 3d Ave New York City NY 10022

SCALA, SINCLAIRE MAXIMILIAN, cons. aerospace scientist, mech. engr.; b. Charleston, S.C., June 27, 1929; s. George and Goldie (Bocker) S.; B.S. cum laude in Mech. Engring., Coll. City N.Y., 1950; postgrad. Columbia U., 1950, N.Y. U., 1950-51; M.M.E., U. Del., 1953; M.A. (Guggenheim fellow), Princeton U., 1955, Ph.D., (Bakhmeteff fellow), 1957; M.B.A., U. Pa., 1978; m. Enid Joan Perlin, Mar. 25, 1951; children—Howard Alexander, Richard Perlin, Susanna Linda. Advanced devel. engr. Westinghouse Electric Corp., Lester, Pa., 1951-53; research fellow Princeton U., James Forrestal Research Center, N.J., 1953-56; research engr. Gen. Electric Co., Phila., 1956-58, cons. high altitude gas dynamics, 1958-59, mgr. of high altitude aerodynamics, 1959-64, mgr. theoretical fluid physics, 1964-68, mgr. fluid physics projects, 1968-69, mgr. environ. scis., lab., 1969-73, chief scientist, 1973-74, sr. cons. scientist, 1974—, tech. dir. ind. research and devel. program, 1974—; guest lectr. Mass. Inst. Tech., Cambridge, 1964-66; lectr. physics dept. Temple U., Phila., 1960-61; colloquium lectr. at various univs., 1953—. Pres., Wyncote-West Elkins Park Community Council, 1963-65; v.p. Cheltenham Council Civic Assns., 1964-65; bd. dirs. Parents Assn. Syracuse (N.Y.) U., 1969-73. Recipient Alumni award Coll. City N.Y., 1950; registered profl. engr., N.Y. Fellow Am. Inst. Aeros and Astronautics; mem. Am. Phys. Soc., Am. Soc. Engring. Edn., AAAS, N.Y. Acad. Scis., Pa. Assn. Adult Edn., Sigma Xi, Tau Beta Pi, Sigma Phi Omega, Pi Tau Sigma. Contbr. numerous articles on aerodynamics, heat transfer and ablation of reentry vehicles to tech. jours.; inventor jet engine thrust reverser. Home: 7812 Knox Rd Laverock PA 19118 Office: 3198 Chestnut St Philadelphia PA 19101

SCALERA, NICHOLAS ROBERT, state ofcl.; b. Newark, Dec. 28, 1941; s. Vincent Alexander and Lillian Dolores (deCicco) S.; B.A., Seton Hall U., 1963; M.S. cum laude (Benjamin Franklin scholar, Columbian Found. scholar), Columbia, 1964; certificate achievement British politics U. Edinburgh (Scotland), 1964. Corr., Evening News, Newark, 1964-65, AP, Phila., 1966; pub. information asst. N.J. OEO, Trenton, 1966-67; chief Office Pub. Information, N.J. Dept. Community Affairs, Trenton, 1967-72; research cons. Center for Analysis of Pub. Issues, Princeton, 1972; asst. dir. N.J. Div. Youth and Family Services, Trenton, 1972—; free-lance writer with contbns. to Cath. Layman, Houston Chronicle, Shreveport Sunday Times, others. Founder, treas., pres. Larry Williams Scholarship Fund, 1968-73. Commr. Newark, Zoning Bd. Adjustment, 1970-72; mem. N.J. Study Commn. on Adolescent Edn., 1976-77. Mem. Am. Soc. Pub. Adminstrn., Phi Kappa Theta (editor quar. mag., trustee, v.p. 1965-73), Soc. Profl. Journalists-Sigma Delta Chi. Home: 961 Broad St Bloomfield NJ 07003 Office: 1 S Montgomery St Trenton NJ 08625

SCALFAROTTO, ROBERT EMIL, chemist, chem. co. exec.; b. Alexandria, Egypt, June 4, 1920; came to U.S. 1957, naturalized 1962; s. Gino P. and Rita (Zagni) S.; D.Sc. in Indsl. Chemistry U. Genoa, 1948; postgrad. U. Modena (Italy), 1949-51; m. Ella Lechner, Feb. 23, 1946; 1 son, Henry G. Chemist, tech. dir. pigments Lechner & Muratori Co., Genoa, Italy, 1946-56; tech. mgr. gen. chems. Merc. Devel., Inc., N.Y.C., 1956-58; application research chemist Am. Cyanamid Co., Bound Brook, N.J., 1958-63; asst. mgr. pigments div. CIBA Chem. & Dye Co., Fair Lawn, N.J., 1963-69, promotion coordinator, 1969-70; tech. devel. mgr. pigments dept. CIBA-GEIGY Co., Ardsley, N.Y., 1970-76; mgr. internat. indsl. chems. research and devel. Am. Cyanamid Co., Wayne, N.J., 1976-78, mgr. new products testing, Stamford, Conn., 1978—; cons. Shell Italiana (Genoa) Chem. Service, 1950-54, Societa Italiana Materie Chimiche, Turin, Italy, 1953, Chimica Internazionale, Milan, 1951-53, Societa Italiana Celluloide Castiglione Olona, 1954. Agt. world com. YMCA Aid to Displaced Persons and Prisoners of War, Geneva, Switzerland, 1945-46. Mem. Am. Chem. Soc., Am. Assn. Textile Chemists and Colorists, N.Y. Soc. Paint Tech. Club: N.Y. Pigment. Contbr. articles in field. Home: 1 Conrad Ct PO Box 378 Montvale NJ 07645 Office: Berdan Ave Wayne NJ 07470

SCALLON, FRANK JOHN, louver co. exec.; b. Brewster, N.Y., Aug. 29, 1899; s. Francis John and Johanna (Moriarty) S.; student pub. schs., Ridgefield, Conn.; m. Florence Matilda Miller, May 18, 1933. Started as bellhop Lake Waccabuc Inn, South Salem, N.Y.; from clk. to asst. radio engr. Marconi Wireless Co., N.Y.C.; later with Hayden-Stone brokerage, N.Y.C.; herdsman on estate of A.B. Barnes, Wilton, Conn., 2 yrs.; insp. Norwalk Tire & Rubber Co., until 1929; ins. agt. John Hancock Co., 1929-36; founder, owner Scallon Roofing Co., 1936-48; founder, pres. Midget Louver Co., Norwalk, Conn., 1948—. Roman Catholic. Elk. Patentee midget louvers; contbr. numerous articles on ventilation to various publs. Home: 255 West Rocks Rd Norwalk CT 06852 Office: 800 Main Ave Norwalk CT 06852

SCALORA, FRANK SALVATORE, data processing exec.; b. N.Y.C., June 16, 1927; s. Salvatore F. and Cesaria (Silluzio) S.; A.B., Harvard, 1949; A.M., U. Ill. at Urbana, 1951, Ph.D., 1958. Teaching asst. U. Ill. at Urbana, 1949-54; mathematician Republic Aviation Corp., Farmingdale, L.I., N.Y., 1955, mathematician IBM Corp., N.Y.C., 1956—, sr. operations research analyst, 1963-66, information planning mgr., 1966-67, data mgmt. mgr., 1967—, applications specialist, 1961-62, adv. mathematician, 1962-63, sr. industry devel. analyst data processing div., 1974-78, market adviser, 1978—; project leader-ops. analysis IBM World Trade Corp., 1965-71, sr. analyst, 1971-74; adj. prof. Poly. Inst. Bklyn., 1961-62, N.Y.U., 1962—. Mem. Am. Math. Soc., Inst. Math. Statistics. Club: Harvard of New York City. Home: 225 E 57th St New York City NY 10022 Office: IBM Corporate Litigation 153 E 53d St New York City NY

SCANLON, EDWARD CHARLES, clin. psychologist; b. Bradford, Pa., Dec. 3, 1931; s. Edward John and Martha Karlous (Charles) S.; A.B. cum laude, U. Buffalo, 1954; Ed.B. (Thayer scholar), Harvard U., 1961, Ed.M., 1968; m. Constance Reese Morgan, May 19, 1962 (div. Jan. 1976); 1 dau., Heather Marie. Adj. prof., acting dir. Home and Sch. Visitor Project, Wilkes Coll., Wilkes Barre, Pa., 1969-71; clin. psychologist Schuylkill County (Pa.) Mental Health and Mental Retardation, 1971-72; clin. psychologist Northampton County Mental Health and Mental Retardation, Bethlehem, Pa., 1972—. Served to capt. USAFR, 1954-57. Certified sch. psychologist, Pa.; licensed psychologist, Pa. Mem. Am. Assn. Higher Edn., Am. Personnel and Guidance Assn., Am. Psychol. Assn., Res. Officers Assn. Democrat. Episcopalian. Clubs: Harvard (Phila.), Masons. Home: Bridle Path Woods D-2 Bethlehem PA 18017 Office: BSU482 2604 Schoerersville Rd Bethlehem PA 18017 also BSUV481 2009 Lehigh St Easton PA 18042

SCANLON, JOHN WILLIAM, physician; b. Yonkers, N.Y., Sept. 28, 1939; s. John W. and Mary D. (Drohan) S.; A.B., Columbia U., 1961; M.D., Boston U., 1965. Intern, Mass. Gen. Hosp., Boston, 1965-66, asst. resident, 1966-68, Wyeth pediatric fellow, 1966-68; fellow in medicine Children's Hosp. Med. Center, Boston, 1970-72; clin. fellow in pediatrics Harvard Med. Sch., Boston, 1970-72; research fellow in neonatology Boston Hosp. for Women, 1970-73; practice medicine specializing in neonatal pediatrics, Boston, 1970-75, Washington, 1975—; clin. asso. in pediatrics Mass. Gen. Hosp., Boston, 1970-75; asst. pediatrician Boston Hosp. for Women, 1970-73, pediatrician, 1973-75; staff pediatrician and cons. in neonatology South End Community Health Center, Boston, 1971-74; dir. of neonatology Columbia Hosp. for Women, Washington, 1975—; physician-in-charge Beth Israel Hosp., Newborn Nurseries, Boston, 1974-75; asst. prof. pediatrics Georgetown U., Washington, 1975-78, asso. prof. pediatrics, 1978—, program coordinator for research, neonatal div., 1976—; vis. prof. dept. anesthesia U. Calif., San Francisco, 1976, dept. obstetrics, U. N.D., Grand Forks, 1976, 77, U. Tenn., Memphis, 1977, dept. pediatrics Loyola U. Sch. Medicine, Chgo., 1973; lectr. Sch. Nursing, Catholic U., Washington, 1978; cons. EPA, 1977; mem. profl. advisory council Parent and Child, Inc., Washington, 1976—; adj. prof. Union Grad. Sch., Yellow Springs, Ohio, 1977. Served with USPHS, 1968-70. Diplomate Am. Bd. Pediatrics, subsplty. neonatal-perinatal medicine. Fellow Am. Acad. Pediatrics (chmn. com. on environ. hazards Mass. chpt. 1971-73), Royal Soc. Health; mem. Mass. Med. Soc., So. Perinatal Soc. (mem. regional adv. bd. 1976—), Soc. for Research in Child Devel., So. Soc. for Pediatric Research, AAAS, Alpha Omega Alpha. Contbr. articles on neonatology to med. jours.; editor Neonatology, 1976—.

SCARBOROUGH, CHARLES BISHOP, III, newscaster; b. Pitts., Nov. 4, 1943; s. Charles Bishop, Jr., and Esther Francis (Campbell) S.; B.S., U. So. Miss., 1969; m. Linda Anne Gross, Dec. 9, 1972. Prodn. mgr. Sta. WLOX-TV, Biloxi, Miss., 1966-68; reporter Sta. WDAM-TV, Hattiesburg, Miss., 1968-69; asst. news dir./newscaster Sta. WAGA-TV, Atlanta, 1969-72; newscaster Sta. WNAC-TV, Boston, 1972-74; news corr. NBC News, N.Y.C., 1974—. Served with USAF, 1961-65. Recipient 6 AP awards and 4 Emmy awards for various reporting skills, 1969-75, Aviation and Space Writers award. Mem. Phi Kappa Phi. Author: Stryker, 1978; contbr. to Boston mag. Office: 30 Rockefeller Plaza New York City NY 10019

SCARLATA, PAUL ANTHONY, dentist; b. McKeesport, Pa., Apr. 3, 1935; s. Joseph Mario and Josephine Gloria (Battaglia) S.; B.S., U. Pitts., 1957, D.D.S., D.M.D., 1961; m. Mary Jane Parks, June 15, 1963; children—Stephanie, Anthony, Christopher, Matthew, Sarah. Resident oral surgery Western Pa. Hosp., Pitts., 1962-63, St. Luke's Hosp., N.Y.C., 1963-64; practice dentistry specializing in oral surgery, Chambersburg, Pa., 1967—; chief dental service Chambersburg Hosp., 1974-76; mem. dental staff Waynesboro (Pa.) Hosp., Fulton County Med. Center, Annie Warner Hosp., Gettysburg, Pa. Treas., Franklin County (Pa.) Heritage, 1971—, pres., 1977—. Served with AUS, 1964-67. Mem. ADA, Pa., Western Pa., Gt. Lakes socs. oral surgeons, N.Y. Soc. Clin. Oral Pathologists, Am. Dental Soc. of Anesthetists. Clubs: Chambersburg, South Penn Chess, Cumberland Valley Railroad Enthusiasts (Chambersburg); Lions. Home: 809 Philadelphia Ave Chambersburg PA 17201 Office: 1479 Lincoln Way E Chambersburg PA 17201

SCERNO, J. BENEDICT, employee relations exec.; b. Bklyn., Dec. 25, 1936; s. Benedict Joseph and Mary Laura (DeMartini) S.; B.S. in Indsl. Relations, N.Y. U., 1962; M.A. in Counseling, Marywood Coll., 1977; m. Patricia Ann Bucci, June 11, 1960; children—Joseph Benedict III, George Patrick. Vice pres., gen. mgr., personnel dir. Express Haulage Corp., N.Y.C., 1960-64; asst. dir. indsl. relations Tech. Materiel Corp., Mamaroneck, N.Y., 1964-66; dir. indsl. relations Circle F Industries, Trenton, N.J., 1966-67; personnel mgr. Swivelier Co., Inc., Nanuet, N.Y., 1967-68; dir. indsl. relations Sel-Rex Co. div. Occidental Petroleum Corp., Nutley, N.J., 1968-72; dir. personnel Hosp. for Joint Diseases and Med. Center, N.Y.C., 1972-74; dir. employee and community relations INTEXT-ICS, Scranton, Pa., 1974—; personnel cons. City of Scranton, 1975—; mem. Urban League, Essex County, N.J., 1969—. Bd. dirs. Prospect House, East Orange, N.J. Served with USAF, 1954-57. Accredited exec. in personnel. Mem. Am. Soc. Personnel Adminstrn. (pres. North Jersey chpt. 1969-71), Internat. Mgmt. Assn. (v.p. Newark chpt. 1969-72), Am. Acad. Polit. Social Sci., Am. Soc. Tng. and Devel., Am. Compensation Assn., Am. Soc. Hosp. Personnel Adminstrn., Westchester Personnel Mgmt. Assn., Am. Mgmt. Assn., Arbitration Soc., Scranton C. of C., Internat. Personnel Assn., Scranton Personnel Assn., Tri-County Personnel Assn., Mensa (chpt. publicity dir. 1970-77), Pa. Soc., Mu Gamma Tau, Pi Sigma Epsilon, Zeta Beta Tau. Clubs: Elks, Palm Coast Yacht, Golf. Home: 206 Appletree Ln Clarks Summit PA 18411 Office: Oak and Pawnee Sts Scranton PA 18515

SCHACH, WILLIAM O., investment co. exec.; b. Balt., Sept. 25, 1924; s. William and Anne (Luers) S.; B.S. U.S. Coast Guard Acad., 1946; M.S., Sloan Sch. Mass. Inst. Tech., 1950; m. Harriet Frances Sawtelle Ratchford, Oct. 16, 1954; children—Carey Coeburn, Ann Tracy. With Merill Lynch, Pierce, Fenner & Smith, Inc., Pitts., 1951—, resident v.p., 1970—. Trustee, Arthritis Found., Ellis Sch., Shadyside Hosp., Jr. Achievement; past trustee Balt. Civic Opera; bd. dirs. NCCJ. Served with USCG, 1942-48, PTO. Standard Oil Calif. fellow, 1949-50. Mem. Bond Club (past pres.). Home: 1085 Devon Rd Pittsburgh PA 15213 Office: 2 Gateway Center Pittsburgh PA 15222

SCHACKNOW, PAUL NEIL, psychologist; b. Bklyn., June 1, 1948; s. Max J. and Evelyn (Ruditsky) S.; B.S. with honors in Psychology, Bklyn. Coll., 1970; Ph.D. in Exptl. Psychology, City U. N.Y., 1976. Research asst. dept. psychology Bklyn. Coll., 1970-74, instr. (part-time), 1970-74; lectr. in psychology State U. N.Y., Purchase, 1974-76, asst. prof. psychology, 1976—; pres. Regency Measuring Corp., 1969—. Bd. dirs. Student Service Corp., Bklyn. Coll., 1972-73. Mem. Am. Psychol. Assn., Acoustical Soc. Am., N.Y. Acad. Scis., AAAS, Psi Chi. Contbr. numerous articles on hearing sci. to profl. jours. Home: Rural Route 4 PO Box 173 Scofield Rd Pound Ridge NY 10576 Office: Div of Natural Sciences State Univ of New York Purchase NY 10577

SCHADE, ROBERT RICHARD, physician; b. Rockville Center, N.Y., Jan. 5, 1948; s. Robert Richard and Loretta Katherine (McGovern) S.; B.A., Colgate U., 1969; M.D., George Washington U., 1973; m. Rosann Foster, Oct. 14, 1972; 1 dau., Danielle Nicole. Intern internal medicine Rush-Presbyn. St. Luke's Med. Center, Chgo., 1973-74, resident, 1974-76; fellow hepatology Yale U., New Haven, 1976-78, postdoctoral research fellow gastroenterology, 1978—. Recipient Nat. Research Service award NIH, 1978—. Diplomate Am. Bd. Med. Examiners, Am. Bd. Internal Medicine. Mem. AAAS, A.C.P. Home: 42 Hesse Rd Hamden CT 06517 Office: West Haven VA Hospital Spring St West Haven CT 06516

SCHAEFER, CHARLES JAMES, III, advt. agy. exec.; b. Orange, N.J., Dec. 17, 1926; s. Charles James and Adelaide Josephine (Conklin) S.; A.B., Dartmouth Coll., 1948, M.Comml. Sci., Amos Tuck Sch. Bus. Adminstrn., 1949; m. Eleanor Anne Montville, Apr. 8, 1961; 1 son, Charles James. Mgr. foods promotion dept. Beech-Nut Packing Co., Canajoharie, N.Y., 1949-52; v.p. Dickie-Raymond, Inc., N.Y.C., 1952-66; sr. v.p., regional mgr. Metromail Creative Mktg. Services, Metromedia, Inc., N.Y.C., 1967-69; exec. v.p., treas. DR Group, Inc., N.Y.C., 1969-76, pres., 1976—, dir., 1969—. Bd. govs. Dartmouth Alumni Assn. N.Y., 1963-73, pres., 1968-70. Served with USNR, 1945-46. Mem. Direct Mail/Mktg. Assn. (chmn. awards com. 1971-76, chmn. Hall of Fame Com. 1978—), Mktg. Communications Execs. Assn. Clubs: 100 Million, Dartmouth, Lotos (N.Y.C.); Canoe Brook Country (Summit, N.J.). Home: 307 Hobart Ave Short Hills NJ 07078 Office: 342 Madison Ave New York City NY 10017

SCHAEFER, KARL ERNST, physiologist; b. Bad-Nauheim, Germany, Apr. 19, 1912; s. Ernst and Christine (Grunewald) S.; student U. Frankfurt, 1930, U. Marburg, 1931, U. Innsbruck, 1932; M.D., U. Kiel, 1935; m. Ursula M. Kolbe, Nov. 26, 1938; children—Michael, Christoph, Barbara Maria Schaefer Quinn, Ernst John. Intern, resident U. Clinics Hamburg and Frankfurt, 1936-37; research asst. dept. physiology U. Heidelberg, 1937-39; docent physiologist, Heidelberg, 1946-49, acting chmn. dept., 1948-49; physiologist U.S. Naval Med. Research Lab., New London, Conn., 1949-51, head physiology br., 1951-76; adj. prof. environ. biology U. R.I., 1965-70; vis. prof. U. Mainz, 1971; vis. prof. environ. physiology and medicine Brown U., 1971—; dir. biomed. scis. dept. U.S. Naval Submarine Med. Center, 1976-78; lectr. Yale U., 1959-67, fellow J.B. Pierce Found., 1970; mem. Gov.'s Com. on Environ. Policy for Conn., 1970. Served as med. officer, German Navy, World War II. Mem. Armed Forces Nat. Res. Council Com.; bio-astronaut, 1958-61; mem. panel closed Ecol. Systems Space Sci. Bd., 1961-62; mem. com. adv. NASA Office Biotech. and Human Research, 1962-64; mem. NRC-Nat. Acad. Sci. Com. Underwater Physiology and Medicine, 1971-73. Fellow Am. Coll. Cardiology, AAAS; mem. Aerospace Med. Assn., Am. Physiol. Soc., Internat. Soc. Biometeorology, Internat. Soc. Study Biol. Rhythms, N.Y. Acad. Scis. Editor: Man's Dependence on the Earthly Atmosphere, 1962; Environmental Effects on Consciousness, 1962; Bioastronautics, 1964; Topics on Environmental Physiology and Medicine; co-editor CO2 and Metabolic Regulations, 1972; contbr. articles to profl. jours. Home: Neck Rd Old Lyme CT 06371 Office: US Naval Med Research Lab New London CT 06320

SCHAEFER, MARYANN BILELLO, psychotherapist; b. N.Y.C., Mar. 24, 1947; d. Sylvester Frank and Jacqueline Marie (Giardelli) Bilello; B.A., Queens Coll., 1968; M.S., St. Johns' U., 1973, P.D., 1976, A.B.D., 1977; m. Edward C. Schaefer, Jr., Dec. 21, 1968; children—Kristin Danelle, Darren Thomas. Acad. aide Coll. Discovery and Devel. Program, Jamaica, N.Y., 1966-68, Project Upward Bound, Flushing, N.Y., 1967-68; bus. analyst Dun & Bradstreet, N.Y.C., 1968-70; tchr. English Floral Park (N.Y.) Meml. High Sch., 1970-71; substitute techr. Sewanhaka Central High Sch. Dist., Franklin Square, N.Y., 1971-73; psychotherapy intern Archbishop Molloy High Sch., Jamaica, N.Y., 1973-74, Our Lady of Lourdes Sch., Queens Village, N.Y., 1974-75; grad. asst. St. John's U., Jamaica, 1974-75; career edn. cons. Lavelle Sch. for the Blind, Bronx, N.Y., 1975-76; process observer Found. for Community Creativity, Washington, 1977-78, also adj. instr. Adelphi U., Garden City, N.Y., 1977—; psychotherapist, N.Y.C., 1976—. Mem. Am. Personnel and Guidance Assn., Am. Psychol. Assn., Assn. Specialists in Group Work, Council Ednl. Freedom in Am., Doctorate Assn. N.Y. Educators, Soc. Gifted and Talented Children, Phi Delta Kappa. Research on androgyny in creative female adolescents and their parents. Home: 89 37 208th St Queens Village NY 11427

SCHAEFER, ROBERT ANTHONY, physician; b. N.Y.C., Mar. 1, 1939; s. George J. and Regina M. (Farrell) S.; A.B., Yale U., 1959; M.D., Columbia U., 1963; m. Mary Jeanne Kreek, Jan. 24, 1970; children—Robert Anthony, Esperance Anne. Intern Vanderbilt U. Hosp., Nashville, 1963-64, resident, 1964-65; resident Med. Center Hosp. Vt., 1967-69; fellow in gastroenterology N.Y. Hosp., 1969-71; instr. medicine Cornell U., N.Y.C., 1971-72, asst. prof., 1972-77, clin. asso. prof., 1977—; asso. attending physician N.Y. Hosp., 1977—. Served with U.S. Navy, 1965-67. Mem. A.C.P., Am. Gastroent. Assn., Am. Assn. for Study of Liver Disease, Am. Fedn. for Clin. Research, Am. Soc. Gastrointestinal Endoscopy. Office: 525 E 68th St New York City NY 10021

SCHAEFER, WILLIAM DONALD, mayor Balt.; b. Balt., Nov. 2, 1921; s. William Henry and Tululu Irene (Skipper) S.; student City Coll., 1939; LL.B., U. Balt., 1943, LL.M., 1952, LL.D. (hon.), 1976; J.D. (hon.), Loyola Coll., 1976. Admitted to Md. bar; practiced in Balt., 1945—; mayor Balt., 1971—. Mem. City Council, Balt., 1955-67, pres., 1967-71. Served to capt., AUS, 1942-45. Recipient 1st Ann. Civic Statesmanship award Citizens Planning and Housing Assn., Alumni of Year award U. Balt.; J. Jefferson Miller Ann. award for Civic Accomplishment; certificate of appreciation HUD; named Man of Yr. NCCJ, 1976. Mem. Nat. League Cities (dir.). Democrat. Episcopalian. Home: 620 Edgewood St Baltimore MD 21229 Office: City Hall Baltimore MD 21202

SCHAEFFER, FREDERICK ROBERT, sporting goods co. exec.; b. Chgo., May 9, 1941; s. Bertram Frederick and Evelyn Pearl (Benson) S.; B.A., U. Ill., 1964; M.B.A., Northwestern U., 1965; m. Carol Eleanor Witte, Feb. 9, 1964; children—Frederick, Kysa. Asst. brand mgr. Procter & Gamble, Inc., Cin., 1965-68; direct mktg. mgr., subs. v.p. Polaroid Corp., Cambridge, Mass., 1968-70; founder, treas., pres., chief exec. officer, dir. Salomon/N.Am., Inc., Peabody, Mass., 1970-77; founder, treas., chief exec. officer, dir. Salomon Sports Can., Ltd., Montreal, Que., 1975-77; treas., chief exec. officer Schaeffer & Co., Inc., Boston, 1977—. Youth leader Hyde Park Episcopal Ch., 1966-68; profl. campaign coordinator Com. to Re-elect Sargeant, 1968; tax reduction adviser Com. to Elect E.J. King for Gov., 1978; mem. Com. to Retain N. Shore Community Coll., 1978; mem. Bd. Edn. First Bapt. Ch., Beverly, Mass., 1978—. Recipient Ruth Hahn award for achievement in mktg. U. Ill., 1964, Top Ten Srs. award, 1964, Men's Assn. Outstanding Sr. award, 1964. Mem. Ski Industries Am. (dir., v.p., mktg. chmn.), Am. Soc. Testing Materials (chmn. ednl. com.), Young Pres.'s Orgn., Nat. Sporting Goods Assn., Profl. Assn. Diving Instrs., Nat. Assn. Underwater Industries, New Eng. Divers, Beta Gamma Sigma. Baptist. Home: 3 Wilson Ave Beverly MA 01915 Office: 137 Newbury St Boston MA 02116

SCHAEFFER, FREDERICK STEVEN, ornithologist; b. Nijmegen, The Netherlands, Aug. 28, 1940; s. Anton Augustus and Nelly (Imbach) S.; came to U.S., 1954, naturalized, 1960; student Cornell, 1975; Teletype operator Eastman Dillon Union Securities, N.Y.C., 1960-69; operator KLM Royal Dutch Airlines, N.Y.C., 1969-71; teleticketing agt. SAS-Scandinavian Airlines, Jamaica, N.Y., 1971-74, group agent, 1974—. Licensed Bird Banding cooperator to U.S. Dept. Interior, Fish and Wildlife Service, 1964—. Mem. British Ornithol. Union, Am. Ornithologists Union, Wilson Ornithol. Soc., Northeastern Bird Banding Assn., Eastern Bird Banding Assn. (dir. 1969—, membership chmn. 1978—), Gateway Bird Banding Group (pres. 1977—). Editor emeritus Eastern Bird Banding Assn. Office: 138-02 Queens Blvd Jamaica NY 11435

SCHAEFFER, KLAUS HEYMANN, operations analyst; b. Charlottenburg, Germany, Feb. 28, 1921; came to U.S. 1939, naturalized 1951; s. Ernst Johann Heymann and Olga Elisabet (Kurnik) S.; B.A., Oberlin Coll., 1943; postgrad. Yale, 1943-44, U. Mich., 1949-51; B.D., Luth. Theol. Sem., Gettysburg, Pa., 1946; M.A., U. Nebr., 1947; m. Eunice Eileen Barth, Jan. 26, 1945; children—Mark H. (dec.), Frank H. Instr. German, Gettysburg Coll., 1945-46; instr. philosophy Coll. William and Mary, 1947-48; asst. prof. philosophy and psychology Alma Coll., 1948-50, prof., 1950-51; research staff and mgmt. positions U. Mich., 1951-58, Stanford Research Inst., Menlo Park, Calif., 1958-63, Mitre Corp., Bedford, Mass., 1963-69, Analytical Systems Corp., Burlington, Mass., 1969-70, Transp. Systems Center, U.S. Dept. Transp., Cambridge, Mass., 1970—. Mem. Ops. Research Soc. Am., Philosophy Sci. Assn. Author: (with Elliott Sclar) Access for All-Transportation and Urban Growth, 1975. Home: 3 Acacia St Cambridge MA 02138 Office: 55 Broadway Cambridge MA 02142

SCHAEVITZ, ABRAHAM ROBERT, diversified co. exec.; b. N.Y.C., Dec. 11, 1923; s. Harry Gerson and Anna (Finkle) S.; grad. pub. schs.; m. Estelle Malerman, Oct. 21, 1944; children—Susan Elaine, Frances Rosanne, Lester Paul. Vice pres., treas. Super Tire Engrng. Co., Pennsauken, N.J., 1941-65, chmn. bd., pres., 1966—; v.p., treas. Supercap Corp., 1956-65, chmn. bd., pres., 1966—; Active Mus. Assos., 1973—, Assos. Commn., 1975—(both Phila. Mus. Art), The Benjamin Franklin Assos. of U. Pa., 1969—, Franklin Inst., Phila., 1975—, Phila. Orch. Assn., 1975—. Served with AUS, 1943-44. Fellow Scheie Eye Inst.; mem. Nat. Tire Dealers and Retreaders Assn., Am. Retreaders Assn., N.J. (dir.), Pa., N.Y. motor truck assns., Rolls Royce Enthusiasts (Eng.), Classic Car Club Am., Rolls Royce Owners, Del. Valley Tire Dealers Assn. (dir.), Antiquarian Horological Soc. (Eng.). Clubs: Marco Polo, Atrium, Curzon Holbe (London), Le Cercle (London), Vesper Club (Phila.), Variety Club Internat. Patentee tire with undertread probe. Home: Indian Creek Rd Wynnewood PA 19151 Office: 7255 Crescent Blvd Pennsauken NJ 08110

SCHAFER, DON FRANCIS, marine officer; b. San Francisco, Oct. 27, 1943; s. Don Francis and Laura Mae (Conners) S.; B.S., San Jose State Coll., 1965; M.B.A., So. Ill. U., 1977; m. Mary Cathryn Meenan, Sept. 25, 1965; children—Elizabeth Marie, Julie Ann. Commd. 2d lt. U.S. Marine Corps., 1965, advanced through grades to maj.; served in Calif., Viet Nam, Va., N.C. and Ga.; rep. to Program Joint Interoperability of Tactical Command and Control Systems, Washington, 1976—. Bd. dirs. United Givers Fund, Jacksonville, N.C., 1975-76. Recipient Combined Fed. Campaign award, 1976. Mem. Marine Corps Assn. Republican. Methodist. Clubs: Jaycees. Home: 4230 Woodside Dr Fredericksburg VA 22401 Office: Joint Plans Group HDQA-DAAC JI Washington DC 20310

SCHAFFER, DAVID EDWIN, retail exec.; b. N.Y.C., Nov. 3, 1929; s. Karl and Jeanette (Gotthelf) S.; student Wharton Sch. of U. Pa., 1948-49; B.A., New Sch. for Social Research, 1959; m. Ariel Williams Sullivan, May 3, 1951; stepchildren—Adrienne Sullivan Smith, James W. Sullivan. Spl. edn. tchr. of emotionally disturbed children, various schs. and hosps., 1954-65; br. mgr. First Westchester Nat. Bank, New Rochelle, N.Y., 1965-66; v.p. Longines-Symphonette Inc., spl. asst. to chmn. bd. Longines Wittnauer Inc., Larchmont, N.Y., 1966-72; pvt. practice mgmt. cons., Franconia, N.H., 1973-77; v.p., dir. ops. Carroll Reed Ski Shops, Inc., 1978—; instr. econs. Am. Inst. Banking, 1965-66. Moderator, Town of Franconia, 1973—, co-chmn. Frost Pl. com.; bd. dirs. White Mountain Community Services, 1973-77; bd. dirs., pres. No. N.H. Mental Health Services, 1975-77. Served with Signal Corps, AUS, 1951-53. Mem. Direct Mail Credit Assn. Am. (founding mem.), Asso. Retail Credit Men of N.Y.C., Direct Mail Assn. Am. (past chmn. subcom. on consumer affairs and regulator agys.). Republican. Episcopalian. Club: Profile (treas., dir.) (Franconia). Producer numerous record albums. Home: River Rd Franconia NH 03580

SCHAFFER, JOAN LOTHROP, civic worker; b. Chevy Chase, Md., Nov. 23, 1920; d. Samuel Kirkland and Rachel (Warren) Lothrop; B.A., Barnard Coll., 1943; M.A., Columbia U. Tchrs. Coll., 1959, postgrad. in math., 1964-66; m. George H. Schaffer, June 29, 1968; children—Janina M. Jagel, Chandra Mukerji. Tchr. pub. schs., N.Y., Mass., 1959-67; asso. editor math. textbooks MacMillan Co., N.Y.C., 1967-69; chmn. Westchester (N.Y.) Recycling Conf., 1973-76; chmn. seminars on solid waste, environ. studies and energy League Women Voters, Bronxville, N.Y., 1975-77, dir., 1964-78, pres., 1977-79; bd. dirs. Bronxville Recreation Commn., Tuckahoe (N.Y.) Library, Eastchester Family Consultation Service; speaker on environ. topics, especially energy, solid waste, food additives. Chmn. Democratic Com., Bronxville, 1952-59; candidate for village trustee Town of Eastchester (N.Y.), 1954, 56, Dem. campaign chmn., 1957; founder Polit. Discussion Club, Bronxville, 1953; v.p., dir. N.Y. Choral Soc., 1965-67; pres. Westchester Chorale, 1975-76; concert singer, concert halls, radio, TV; pres. Canticum Novum Singers. Home: 85 Hunter Ave New Rochelle NY 10801

SCHAFFHOUSER, ARTHUR, labor union ofcl.; b. Franklin, N.J., Mar. 5, 1931; s. Stephen and Mary Elizabeth (Shuppon) S.; student pub. schs., Franklin, N.J. Vice pres. United Rubber Workers Local 584 AFL-CIO, Franklin, 1959-61, pres., 1961—. Served with USMCR, 1952-54. Mem. Am. Legion. Roman Catholic. Club: K.C. Home and office: 43 Butler St Franklin NJ 07416

SCHAIBLE, MICHAEL DUANE, interior designer; b. Oakley, Kans., Apr. 29, 1940; s. Carl Tracy and Myrtle Maude (Sellers) S.; B.F.A., U. Colo., 1964; student Universita di Firenza, Florence, Italy, 1961, Parson's Sch. of Design, 1964-65. Designer Saphier, Lerner & Schindler, N.Y.C., 1965-67, Ford & Earl Design Assn., N.Y.C., 1967-69; pres., designer Bray & Schaible Design, Inc., N.Y.C., 1969—; adv. bd. Parson's Sch. of Design, N.Y.C., 1977—. Recipient Young Designer of Year award Burlington Industries, 1972. Democrat. Author: High-Tech; The Bed and Bath Book; The New York Times Book of Interior Design and Decoration; contbr. numerous articles and designs to profl. mags. Office: 80 W 40th St New York City NY 10018

SCHALLER, ELMER OTTO, educator; b. Chippewa Falls, Wis., Mar. 29, 1907; s. August and Amelia (Muckenhausen) S.; A.B., U. Wis., 1928; M.S., N.Y. U., 1929, D.C.S., 1936; student Columbia U., Harvard U. With N.Y. U., 1929—, successively instr. sch. retailing, asst. prof., asso. prof., 1929-47, prof., 1947-72, prof. emeritus, 1972—, asst. dean, 1953-58, asso. dean, 1958-71, acting dir. Inst. Retail Mgmt., 1971-72; lectr. U. Fla., 1932-36; vis. prof. retailing U. N.C., 1946; cons. on merchandising. Sr. economist, head econ. research unit textile and apparel br. OPA, 1942-43, prin. bus. economist, head reports and surveys sect. consumer goods price div., 1943-45. Mem. Am. Mktg. Assn., Eta Mu Pi, Iota Lambda Sigma, Sigma Pi Epsilon, Beta Gamma Sigma. Author: Techniques of Retail Merchandising (with John W. Wingate), 1956; (with John W. Wingate and Irving Goldenthal) Problems in Retail Merchandising, 1961; Workbook for Retailing Buying and Marketing, 1954; Solutions to Problems in Retail Merchandising, 1961; (with John W. Wingate and F. Leonard Miller) Retail Merchandise Management, 1972, French edit., 1973; (with John W. Wingate and Robert Bell) Problems in Retail Merchandising, 1973; Solution Manual-Problems in Retail Merchandising, 1974. Home: Apt 11L 3 Washington Sq Village New York City NY 10012

SCHANBERG, SYDNEY HILLEL, journalist; b. Clinton, Mass., Jan. 17, 1934; s. Louis and Freda (Feinberg) S.; B.A., Harvard U., 1955; m. Janice Leah Sakofsky, Oct. 22, 1967; children—Jessica, Rebecca. Joined N.Y. Times, 1959, became reporter, 1960, bur. chief, Albany, N.Y., 1967-69, chief bur., New Delhi, India, 1969-73, S.E. Asia corr., Singapore, 1973-75, met. editor, 1977—. Served with AUS, 1956-58. Recipient Page One award for fgn. reporting Newspaper Guild N.Y., 1972; George Polk Meml. award for fgn. reporting, 1972, spl. award for coverage fall of Phnom Penh, 1975; Overseas Press Club award for fgn. reporting, 1972, for fgn. photography, 1974; Front Page award Newspaper Guild, 1975; Sigma Delta Chi award for disting. service in journalism, 1975; Pulitzer prize Internat. Reporting, 1976. Address: care NY Times 229 W 43d St New York City NY 10036

SCHANDLER, HERBERT YALE, assn. exec.; b. Asheville, N.C., Jan. 2, 1928; s. David Sigmond and Sara (Salem) S.; B.S., U.S. Mil. Acad., 1952; M.P.A., Harvard U., 1956, Ph.D., 1974; m. Sharron Ann Britten, June 4, 1977; children—Mary Ann, Karen Rebecca. Commd. 2d lt. U.S. Army, 1952, advanced through grades to col., 1973, ret., 1975; specialist in nat. def. Congressional Research Service, Library of Congress, Washington, 1975-78; v.p. Am. League for Exports and Security Assistance, Inc., Washington, 1978—; asst. prof. dept. social scis. U.S. Mil. Acad., 1957-60; mem. faculty Nat. War Coll., 1972-73. Decorated Legion of Merit with 3 oak leaf clusters, Bronze Star with 2 oak leaf clusters and others. Author: The Unmaking of a President: Lyndon Johnson and Vietnam, 1977; author reports on nat. security and fgn. policy. Home: 8455 Brook Rd McLean VA 22101 Office: 475 L'Enfant Plaza SW Suite 4400 Washington DC 20023

SCHANTZ, CATHERINE HALLECK, constrn. co. exec.; b. N.Y.C., Oct. 17, 1910; d. John Joseph and Catherine Mansfield (Hurley) Halleck; B.S., Syracuse U., 1931; M.Ed., U. Rochester, 1950; m. Frank Joseph Schantz, Apr. 2, 1932; children—Francis Timothy, John Joseph, Catherine Dolores, Veronica Ann. Substitute tchr. Rochester (N.Y.) Pub. Schs., 1936-42; sec.-treas., prin. Schantz Homes Inc., Rochester, 1944—. Mem. AAUW, Women's Ednl. and Indsl. Union, Syracuse U. Alumni Assn. (nat. award 1975), Syracuse U. Alumnae Club of Rochester (Service award, 1960), Fedn. of Women's Clubs (Achievement award 1976), Susan B. Anthony Republican Club, Catholic Women's Club (Distinguished Service award 1977), Rosary Soc. St. Thomas Ch. Republican. Roman Catholic. Club: Oak Hill Country (women's assn.). Home and Office: 4029 St Paul Blvd Rochester NY 14617

SCHAPIRA, HANS ERWIN, urologist; b. Vienna, Austria, Aug. 1, 1925; s. Paul and Felicitas (Mayer) S.; M.D. cum laude, U. Rome, 1955; came to U.S., 1956, naturalized, 1960; m. Ruth Jelinek, Aug. 31, 1957; children—Ralph Mark, Paul Victor. Intern, The Bronx Hosp., N.Y.C., 1957-58; resident in gen. surgery Beth Israel Hosp., N.Y.C., 1958-59; resident urology Mt. Sinai Hosp., N.Y.C., 1959-62, clin. asst. urology, 1962-64, asst. prof. urology, 1965-71, asso. prof., 1971—; practice medicine specializing in urology, N.Y.C., 1962—; mem. staffs Mt. Sinai Med. Center. Diplomate Am. Bd. Urology. Fellow A.C.S.; mem. Am. Fertility Soc., N.Y. Acad. Medicine, Am. Urol. Assn. Jewish. Contbr. articles in field to profl. jours. Home: 335 W 246th St Bronx NY 10471 Office: 47 E 77th St New York City NY 10021

SCHAPIRO, JEROME BENTLEY, chem. mfg. co. exec.; b. N.Y.C., Feb. 7, 1930; s. Sol and Claire (Rose) S.; B.Chem. Engring., Syracuse U., 1951; postgrad. Columbia, 1951-52; m. Edith Irene Kravet, Dec. 27, 1953; children—Lois, Robert, Kenneth. Project engr. propellents br. U.S. Naval Air Rocket Test Sta., Lake Denmark, N.J., 1951-52; with Dixo Co., Inc., Rochelle Park, N.J., 1954—, pres., 1966—. Lectr. detergent standards, drycleaning, care labeling, consumers standards, orgns., U.S., 1968—; U.S. del. spokesman drycleaning Internat. Standards Orgn., Newton, Mass., 1971, Brussels, Belgium, 1972, U.S. del. consumer affairs meeting, Geneva, 1973, mem. U.S. del. care labeling of textiles meeting, The Hague, 1973, Paris, 1976, mem. internat. standards steering com. for consumer affairs, Geneva, 1978-80; U.S. spokesman dimensional stability of textiles meeting, Paris, 1974, Ottawa, 1977; chief U.S. del. consumer affairs meeting, Geneva, 1974, 75, to ISO Council Com. on Consumer Policy, Geneva, 1977. Mem. Montclair (N.J.) Sch. Study Com., 1968-69. Served as 2d lt. USAF, 1952-53. Fellow ASTM (award of merit 1970, chmn. com. detergents 1974—); mem. Am. Inst. Chem. Engrs., Am. Nat. Standard Inst. (vice chmn. consumers council 1975, chmn. 1976, dir. 1976), Internat. Standards Council, Execs. Standards Council (chmn. internat. consumer policy advisory com.), N.J Acad. Sci., Am. Assn. Textile Chemists and Colorists (mem. exec. com. research, internat. test methods com., chmn. drycleaning com.), Am. Chem. Soc., Standards Engrng. Soc., Montclair Soc. Engrs. Jewish (v.p., treas. temple). Mason. Home: 197 N Mountain Ave Montclair NJ 07042 Office: 158 Central Ave Rochelle Park NJ 07662

SCHAPIRO, RUTH GOLDMAN (MRS. DONALD SCHAPIRO), lawyer; b. N.Y.C., Oct. 31, 1926; d. Louis Albert and Sarah (Shapiro) Goldman; A.B., Wellesley Coll., 1947; LL.B., Columbia, 1950; m. Donald Schapiro, June 29, 1952; children—Jane Goldman, Robert Andrew. Admitted to N.Y. bar, 1950; asst. to reporters Am. Law Inst. Fed. Income Tax Statute, N.Y.C., 1950-51; asso., then mem. firm Proskauer, Rose, Goetz & Mendelsohn, 1955—; mem. adv. com. N.Y. U. Inst. on Fed. Taxation, 1972—; mem. U.S. Tax Ct. Nominating Commn., 1978—. Mem. Am., N.Y. State (chmn. com. on incentives, tax sect. 1977-78, mem. exec. com. tax sect. 1974—, sec. tax sect. 1978-79, 2d vice chmn. tax sect. 1979-80) bar assns., Assn. Bar City N.Y. (mem. com. on taxation 1972-75, 78—), N.Y. County Lawyers Assn., Am. Judicature Soc. Jewish. Clubs: N.Y. Wellesley (N.Y.C.). Editor: Tax Shelters After Tax Reform, 1977; notes editor Columbia Law Rev., 1949-50. Contbr. articles to legal jours. Home: 1035 Fifth Ave New York City NY 10028 Office: 300 Park Ave New York City NY 10022

SCHARY, DORE, motion picture producer, play-wright; b. Newark, Aug. 31, 1905; s. Herman Hugo and Belle (Drachler) S.; ed. Central High Sch., Newark; L.H.D. (hon.), Coll. Pacific, 1951; Wilberforce U.; D.F.A. (hon.), Lincoln Coll., 1960; m. Miriam Svet, Mar. 5, 1932; children—Jill, Joy, Jeb. Dir. Little Theatre; actor, playwright publicity and newspaper work, 1926-32; with Columbia, Paramount, Warners as writer of 35 screen plays, 1933-37; writer Metro-Goldwyn-Mayer studios; 1938-41; exec. producer, 1941-43; producer David O. Selznick, 1943-46; exec. v.p. in charge prodn. RKO Studios, 1947-48; exec. v.p. in charge prodn. and studio operations, M-G-M Studios, Culver City, Calif., 1948-57, became head; ind. producer, 1957—; pres., chief exec. officer TheatreVision, Inc., N.Y.C., 1972—. Mem. Citizens Crusade Against Poverty, Pres.'s Com.-Nat. Citizens Commn., Nat. adv. Com. Farm Labor, Nat. Com. Immigration; commr. cultural affairs City N.Y. Fellow, trustee Eleanor Roosevelt Meml. Found. Acad. Award winner Story of Boys Town; Antoinette Perry award for Sunrise at Campobello, 1958. Mem. Author's League, Screen Writers, Producers Guilds, Acad. Motion Picture Arts and Scis., Dramatists Guild Fund (pres.), Anti Defamation League (nat. chmn. 1963-69, now hon. chmn.). Democrat. Mem. B'nai B'rith. Author: Boys Town, Edison the Man, Young Tom Edison; Case History of A Movie; For Special Occasions, 1962; (with Sinclair Lewis) Storm in the West, 1963; Brightower, 1969. Exec. producer of Joe Smith, American, Journey for Margaret. Bataan, Lassie Come Home, Lost Angel. Producer of Spiral Staircase, I'll Be Seeing You, The Farmer's Daughter, The Bachelor and the Bobby-Soxer, Till the End of Time, Battleground, The Next Voice You Hear, Go For Broke, Plymouth Adventure, Dream Wife, Take the High Ground, Bad Day at Black Rock, The Last Hunt, also, Designing Woman; writer, co-producer Sunrise at Campobella, 1958; co-producer, dir. A. Majority of One, 1959; writer-dir.-co-producer The Highest Tree. 1959, The Devils Advocate, 1960; writer-producer motion picture Sunrise at Campobello, 1960, Israel—The Right To Be, 1975, Herzl, 1976; co-producer, dir. The Unsinkable Molly Brown, 1960, Something About a Soldier, 1962, The Zulu and The Zayda, 1965; producer, dir., writer motion picture Act One, 1963; producer One By One, 1964; writer F.D.R., 1977. Home: 50 Sutton Pl South New York City NY 10022

SCHATZ, CECIL RUSKAY (MRS. ARTHUR H. SCHATZ), social worker, civic worker; b. Far Rockaway, N.Y., Jan. 9, 1923; d. Cecil Benjamin and Sophie (Liebovitz) Ruskay; A.B., Cornell U., 1943; M.S. in Social Work, Columbia, 1945; m. Arthur H. Schatz, Feb. 11, 1945; children—Ellen L., Robert F., Daniel N. Placement worker specializing in handicapped children Children's Services Conn., Hartford, 1946-51, 62—; counselor Sr. Citizens Job Bank West Hartford, 1973—; chmn. older adult program planning Hartford Jewish Community Center, 1974—; vol. aide Conn. Citizens Action Group, Greater Hartford. Life mem. women's div. Am. Soc. Technion, N.Y.C., 1961—, bd. dirs., 1970-74; life mem. women's div. Brandeis U., Waltham, Mass., 1960—, bd. dirs. women's com., 1970-74; bd. dirs. Hartford Jewish Community Center, 1974—; life mem. Hadassah, 1961—; bd. dirs. Hartford div. Nat. Council Jewish Women, 1958—, v.p., 1966, pres., 1968-72, del. 2d summit conf., Israel, 1974, mem. nat. subcom. on aging, 1975—, mem. nat. com. on internat. affairs, 1975—; mem. bd. Beth El Temple Sisterhood; co-chmn. Beth El Art Show, Hartford, 1964-66; chmn. Artists in Residences Program West Hartford, 1968-73; mem. Jewish Theol. Sem. Am. Mem. Planned Parenthood Assn. Conn. (bd. dir. Hartford sect. 1977), Am. Assn. Social Workers, Alumni Assn. Columbia Sch. Social Work, Alumni Assn. Conn. Citizens Research Group, Conn. Child Welfare Assn., Sigma Delta Tau. Clubs: Cliffside Country (Simsbury, Conn.); Bloomfield (Conn.) Indoor Tennis. Author: Placement of Handicapped Children, 1945. Donor, Celia Pessin Scholarship Technion, Haifa, Israel, 1962. Home: 33 Juniper Rd Bloomfield CT 06002

SCHECTER, ARNOLD JOEL, coll. adminstr., physician; b. Chgo., Dec. 1, 1934; s. Benjamin and Leonore Natalie (Lyon) S.; student Shimer Coll., 1949-51; B.A., U. Chgo., 1954, B.S., 1957; M.D., Howard U., 1962; M.P.H., Columbia U., 1976; m. Martha Jean Berenson, Feb. 14, 1964; children—Benjamin Seth, David Anton, Anna Beth. Intern, Beth Israel Hosp., Boston, 1966; instr. medicine Harvard U. Med. Sch., 1963-65; dir. OEO Center, Floyd County, Ky., 1970-71; dir. drug abuse program Coney Island Hosp., 1972-73; dir. research drug abuse Downstate Med. Center, Kings County Hosp., Bklyn., 1972-74; asso. dir., office primary health care, office dean N.J. Med. Sch., Newark, 1975—. Served with U.S. Army, 1967-69. Diplomate Am. Bd. Preventive Medicine. Fellow Am. Coll. Preventive Medicine, A.C.P., Am. Pub. Health Assn. Democrat. Jewish. Co-founder Am. Jour. Drug and Alcohol Abuse; editor: Rehabilitation Aspects of Drug Dependence and Treatment Aspects of Drug Dependence, 1978; Procs. Nat. Drug Abuse Confs., 1975, 76, 78. Pioneer in use of naltrexone in opiate rehab. Address: 1633 Marine Pky Brooklyn NY 11234

SCHEELE, CHRISTINA MARIE, virologist; b. Washington, June 18, 1940; d. Andrew Fredrick and Mary Christine (Scanlon) Scheele; A.B., Randolph-Macon Woman's Coll., 1962; student U. Edinburgh (Scotland), 1960-61; Ph.D., Harvard U., 1970; m. Dean C. Rohrer, Dec. 20, 1969; children—Jonathan W., Mary K., Jay A. Biol. research asst. NIH, Bethesda, Md., 1962-65; postdoctoral fellow Pub. Health Research Inst. City N.Y., 1970-73. Chmn. bd. dirs. Pound Ridge Community Ch. Play Sch., 1975-78. Nat. Inst. Gen. Med. Scis. fellow, 1965-70; Damon Runyon Cancer Research fellow, 1970-72; Leukemia Soc. Am. spl. fellow, 1972-73. Mem. Am. Soc. Microbiology, AAAS. Contbr. articles to profl. jours. Home: Woodland Rd Pound Ridge NY 10576

SCHEELE, GEORGE AUGUSTUS, III, physician, cell biologist; b. Washington, Sept. 28, 1939; s. George Augustus and Margaret (Burgess) S.; A.B., Princeton U., 1961; M.D., Johns Hopkins U., 1965. Intern, med. resident Johns Hopkins Hosp., 1965-69; resident U. Calif., San Francisco, 1969-70; NIH fellow dept. cell biology Rockefeller U., N.Y.C., 1970-72, research asso., NIH grantee, 1973-74, asst. prof. dept. cell biology, 1974—; mem. Nat. Study Group for Pancreatic Cancer. Served with USPHS, 1968-69. Mem. Am. Soc. Cell Biology. Clubs: N.Y. Explorers. Home: 430 E 63d St

New York City NY 10021 Office: 66th and York Aves New York City NY 10021

SCHEER, CARL WESTON, radiologist; b. Berkeley, Calif., June 27, 1931; s. George B. and Ruth (Weston) S.; A.B., Stanford U., 1953, M.D., 1956; m. Helen Colosimo; children—William, Lisa, Bradley, Suzanne. Intern, Kings County Hosp., Bklyn., 1956-57; resident State U. N.Y., Bklyn., 1957-60; practice medicine specializing in radiology, 1960—; mem. staff Permanente Med. Group, San Francisco, 1960-65; asst. attending radiologist Mt. Sinai Hosp., N.Y.C., 1965-66; sr. attending radiologist Meriden (Conn.)-Wallingford Hosp., 1966—. Mem. AMA, Conn., New Haven County (bd. govs.) med. socs., New Eng. Roentgen Ray Soc., Am. Coll. Radiology, Radiol. Soc. Conn. (pres.), Meriden Wallingford Med. Soc. (pres.), Am. Inst. Ultrasound in Medicine. Presbyterian. Home: 100 State St Apt 152 North Haven CT 06473 Office: 335 Cook Ave Meriden CT 06450

SCHEERS, SUSAN ADAMS, counselor; b. Providence, Feb. 16, 1946; s. Leon Robert and Ethel Louise (Gould) A.; B.A., Oakland U., 1968; M.Ed., U. Del., 1974; 1 son, John Adam; m. Gilbert Scheers, Dec. 23, 1978. Tchr. social studies Perryville (Md.) High Sch., 1968-72; guidance counselor Ogletown Middle Sch., Newark, Del., 1973—. Vol., Cystic Fibrosis Campaign. Mem. Am., Del. personnel and guidance assns., Am., New Castle County sch. counselors assns., NEA, Del., New Castle County edn. assns. Home: 711A Village Circle Newark DE 19713 Office: Ogletown Middle St Brennen Dr Newark DE 19713

SCHEFFER, RICHARD HERBERT, hosp. adminstr.; b. N.Y.C., July 28, 1938; s. I. Herbert and Marjorie Elizabeth (Dickinson) S.; B.S., U. R.I., 1959; M.Pub. Adminstrn., Cornell U., 1961; m. Rosalind M. Matheson. Aug. 27, 1960; children—Susan E., Mark M., Robert M. Adminstrv. planning cons. Mercy Hosp., Springfield, Mass., 1967-69; asst. dir. Valley Hosp., Ridgewood, N.J., 1969-71; exec. v.p., adminstr. Harrington Meml. Hosp., Southbridge, Mass., 1971-77; pres. Chestnut Hill Hosp., Phila., 1977—; preceptor Sloan Inst. Hosp. Adminstrn., Cornell U., 1972—. Mem. grad. studies adv. com. Holy Cross Coll., 1974-77; mem. sch. com. Tantasqua Regional Sch., 1973-76; bd. dirs. United Way Southbridge, 1973; trustee Central Mass. Health Care Found. Served to capt., USAF, 1961-67. Recipient Better Life award, 1974. Mem. Southbridge C. of C. (dir. 1972-75), Am. Coll. Hosp. Adminstrs., Central Mass. Hosp. Council (pres. 1975-76), Mass. Hosp. Assn. (trustee 1975-77). Episcopalian. Home: 350 Crestview Dr Fort Washington PA 19034 Office: 8835 Germantown Ave Philadelphia PA 19118

SCHEIB, GARY LAMAR, optometrist; b. Danville, Pa., June 19, 1944; s. Irvin Paul and Christobel Pauline (Reed) S.; A.B., Susquehanna U., 1966; B.S., Pa. Coll. Optometry, 1967, O.D., 1970; postgrad. Gesell Inst. Child Devel., New Haven, 1976-77; m. Joanne Evelyn Brink, July 15, 1967; 1 son, Jeffrey Lamar. Pvt. practice optometry, Pottsville, Pa., also Lykens, Pa., 1970—; optometric visual perception cons. Tri Valley Sch. Dist., 1974-77. Mem. Am., Pa. optometric assns., Anthracite Optometric Soc., Optometric Ext. Program, Coll. Optometrists in Vision Devel., Am. Optometric Found. Republican. Lutheran. Clubs: Masons, Rotary (pres. 1976-77). Home: 25 Overlook Dr Pottsville PA 17901 Office: 307 Mahantongo St Pottsville PA 17901 also 559 W Main St Lykens PA 17048

SCHEIBNER, RUTH MARTIN, educator, psychologist; b. Phila., Aug. 24, 1921; d. James Frederick and Rebecca Bamford (Carmen) Martin; A.B., Temple U., 1960, M.A., 1962, Ph.D., 1969; m. Lawrence Frederick Scheibner, Jr., May 27, 1950; 1 dau., Judith (Mrs. John Joseph Massaro). Psychology intern VA Hosp., Coatesville, Pa., 1961-62, VA Hosp., Phila., 1962-63; instr., counseling psychologist, acad. adviser Temple U., 1963-69; sch. psychologist, Marlton, N.J., 1966-67; lectr. Thomas Jefferson U., 1968-69; asst. prof. Phila. Coll. Pharmacy and Sci., 1968-70, asso. prof., 1971-76, prof. psychology, 1976—. Individual practice psychotherapy, 1968—; counsellor family relations com. Phila. Soc. Friends, 1969—. Bd. dirs. Phila. br. human engring. lab. Johnson O'Connor Research Found., 1954-56, Human Services Center, 1976—. Recipient award for excellence in psychology Psi Chi, 1962. Mem. Am., Eastern, Pa. psychol. assns., AAUP, AAAS, Phila. Soc. Clin. Psychologists (chmn. continuing edn. com. 1977—), Kappa Epsilon. Home: Orchard Dr MR 2 Ambler PA 19002 Office: Phila Coll of Pharmacy and Sci 43d St and Woodland Ave Philadelphia PA 19104

SCHEID, ETHEL CHARLLEEN EDWARDS, counselor; b. Phila., Nov. 30, 1913; d. Edward Burke and Lidie Ethel (Roper) Edwards; B.S., Beaver Coll., 1936; postgrad. U. Pa., 1937-40; M.Ed. in Guidance and Counseling, Lehigh U., 1967; m. Robert Tyson Scheid, May 24, 1941; children—Barbara Charlleen Scheid Frack, Deborah Louise Scheid Hodge, Robert Tyson. Tchr. third grade Schwenksville (Pa.) Consol. Sch. Dist., 1936-43; substitute tchr. Lansdale (Pa.) Pub. Schs., 1946-49, Bethlehem (Pa.) Area Sch. Dist., 1955-60; homebound tchr. Bethlehem Schs., 1960-67, elementary sch. counselor, 1967—, Title I counselor, 1967-70, 77-79; home-sch. coordinator summer enrichment program, 1969; participating counselor Pa. State Dept. Edn. Workshop, P.R., summer 1969. Active PTA; leader parent edn. groups; pres. Wesley United Methodist Ch. Women's Soc. of Christian Service, Bethlehem, 1958-60, v.p., 1961-63; com. chmn. Bethlehem YWCA. Mem. Bethlehem Edn. Assn. (com. chmn.), Lehigh Valley Mental Health Assn., Pa. State Edn. Assn., NEA, Pa. Dept. Pupil Personnel Services, Am. Personnel and Guidance Assn., Am., Pa. sch. counselors, United Meth. Women, Delta Kappa Gamma. Independent Republican. Club: Bethlehem Bus. and Profl. Women's (pres. 1970-72, dist. 9 Parliamentarian 1977-79). Home: 1203 Maple St Bethlehem PA 18018

SCHEID, JOHN EDGAR, surgeon; b. Tarentum, Pa., Apr. 3, 1923; s. John Edgar and Charlotte Irene (Wolfe) S.; M.D., Duke U., 1946; m. Jean Schorr; children—Jennifer Scheid Williams, Jeff, Laurie. Intern, Western Pa. Hosp., Pitts., 1946-47; resident in surgery Cleve. Clinic, Bellvue Hosp., N.Y.C., 1949-52, Mountain Home (Tenn.) VA Hosp., 1952-54; practice medicine specializing in surgery, Natrona Heights, Pa., 1954—; chief med. staff Allegheny Valley Hosp., Natrona Heights, 1954—; mem. staff Citizens Gen. Hosp., New Kensington, Pa. Served with NSN, 1947-49. Diplomate Am. Bd. Surgery. Fellow A.C.S.; mem. Royal Soc. Medicine (Eng.), Pitts. Surg. Soc., AMA, Westmoreland County Med. Soc. (exec. com.). Clubs: Masons, Shriners. Home: 132 Claremont Dr Lower Burrell PA 15068 Office: Med Arts Bldg Natrona Heights PA 15065

SCHEID, PAUL, organist, choirmaster, educator; b. Plattsburg, N.Y., Jan. 13, 1938; s. Charles William and Frances Elizabeth (Pond) S.; B.A., Mich. State U., 1960; M.Music Edn., Rutgers U., 1966; profl. diploma Tchrs' Coll. Columbia, 1972; m. Winifred Elizabeth Potts, Dec. 29, 1963; 1 son, Jonathan Paul. Minister of music Clinton Ave. Baptist Church, Trenton N.J., 1963-65; organist, choirmaster Immanuel Lutheran Church, New Brunswick, N.J., 1965-66; tchr., gen., vocal music Upper Regional Schs., Allentown, N.J., 1965-67; organist, choirmaster Christ Church, Bordentown, N.J., 1966—; asso. prof. choral music, organ, voice, music appreciation Mercer County (N.J.) Coll., 1967—; lectr. church music; condr. choir festivals, choral workshops; music cons. subcom. music N.J. Masterplan for Edn. Served to lt. U.S. Army, 1961-63. Nat. Endowment for Humanities fellow Princeton U., 1977. Mem. Am. Guild Organists (past dean central N.J. chpt.), Music Educators' Nat. Conf., Royal Sch. Church Music, Coll. Music Soc., Internat. Soc. Music Educators, Assn. Anglican Musicians. Episcopalian. Editor newsletter Music Commn. Diocese, N.J., 1975—. Home: 10 Pershing Ave Trenton NJ 068168 Office: Mercer County Community Coll 1200 Old Trenton Rd Trenton NJ 06890

SCHEID, WALTER EVANS, educator; b. Pitts., May 7, 1937; s. John Edgar and Charlotte Irene (Evans) S.; A.B., Grove City Coll., 1959; M.Ed., Pa. State U., 1964; Ph.D., Ohio U., 1974; m. Karen Joyce Vorlage, June 18, 1960; children—Eric Matthew, Jody Charlotte. Tchr. speech Grove City (Pa.) High Sch., 1960-65; instr. speech and theatre Westminster Coll., New Wilmington, Pa., 1965-70, asst. prof., 1970-75, asso. prof., 1975—, chmn. dept., 1974—. Vice-chmn. Mercer County (Pa.) Young Republicans, 1969. J.S. Mack Found. grantee, 1967, 72. Mem. Debating Assn. Pa. Colls. (pres. 1976-77), Am., Pa. speech communication assns. Clubs: New Castle (Pa.) Coin (pres. 1975), Masons. Home: RD 3 New Wilmington PA 16142

SCHEIGE, FORTUNA FAYE GORELICK, rehab. counselor; b. Havana, Cuba, July 9, 1950; d. Samuel and Susana (Nardea) Gorelick; B.A. in Psychology, Rutgers U., 1972; M.Counseling, U. Md., 1978; student Manhattan Sch. Music, summer 1972; m. Steven Schiege, July 8, 1973. Piano tchr. Newark Community Center of Arts and De Belli's Music Studio, Newark, 1971-72; teaching asst. English for speakers of other langs. Montgomery County (Md.) Pub. Schs., Silver Spring, 1972-73; sr. escrow analyst Pennamco, Washington, 1973-75; rehab. counselor, div. vocat. rehab. Md. Dept. Edn., Rockville, 1977—; mem. Pres.'s Com. on Employment of Handicapped, 1977, White House Conf. Handicapped Individuals, 1977. Mem. Am., Md. (dir., jour. editor) rehab. counseling assns., Am. Personnel and Guidance Assn., Am. Psychol. Assn., Nat., Md. rehab. assns. Office: 6110 Executive Blvd Rockville MD 20852

SCHEIN, BERNARD, former library dir.; b. N.Y.C., Nov. 16, 1911; s. Louis and Ida (Cohen) S.; A.B., Rutgers U., 1939; B.L.S., Pratt Inst., 1942; M.A., Columbia, 1946; m. Beatrice Weiss, Oct. 15, 1939. Br. librarian Newark Pub. Library, 1942-52, chief librarian acquisitions and processing, 1953, asst. dir., 1954-58, dep. dir., 1958-72, dir., 1972-77, ret., 1977; faculty Grad. Library Sch. Rutgers, 1962—, Drexel Inst. Library Sch., 1964—. Pres., Family Service Bur., Newark and West Hudson, 1973—. Mem. N.J. Library Assn. (pres. 1959-60), Municipal Careermen of Newark (pres. 1961). Lion (pres. Newark). Home: 405 Highland Ave Newark NJ 07104

SCHEIN, PHILIP SAMUEL, physician; b. Asbury Park, N.J., May 10, 1939; s. Irving and Henrietta (Setzer) S.; A.B., Rutgers U., 1961; M.D., Upstate Med. Center, Syracruse, N.Y., 1965; m. Dorothy Rosenfeld, May 28, 1967; children—Deborah, Andrew. Intern Beth Israel Hosp., Boston, 1966-68, resident, 1968-69, 70-71; sr. house officer Radcliffe Infirmary, Oxford, Eng., 1969-70; instr. in medicine Harvard, 1970-71; sr. investigator Nat. Cancer Inst., Bethesda, Md., 1971-74; head clin. pharm. sect. Nat. Cancer Inst., 1973-74; chief div. med. oncology Georgetown U. Hosp. and Cancer Center, 1974—; cons. oncology Walter Reed Gen. Hosp., Washington, 1971—, Clin. Center, NIH, 1971—; asso. prof. medicine and pharmacology Georgetown U., 1974-77, prof., 1977—; adviser FDA, 1974—. Diplomate Am. Bd. Internal Medicine. Fellow Royal Soc. Medicine, A.C.P.; mem. Royal Coll. Physicians London, Am. Soc. Clin. Oncology, Am. Assn. Cancer Research, Am. Soc. Hematology, Alpha Omega Alpha. Research on mechanism of action of cancer chemotherapy drugs, prediction and prevention drug toxicity, treatment malignant and hematologic diseases. Home: 6212 Robinwood Rd Bethesda MD 20034 Office: Div Med Oncology Georgetown U Hosp Washington DC 20007

SCHEINBERG, LABE CHARLES, physician; b. Memphis, Dec. 11, 1923; s. Jacob and Ardie (Cohen) S.; student Southwestern U. at Memphis, 1943-44; A.B., U. N.C., 1945; M.D., U. Tenn., 1948; m. Louise Goldman, Jan. 6, 1952; children—Susan, David, Ellen, Amy. Intern, Wesley Meml. Hosp., Chgo., 1948-49; resident Elgin (Ill.) State Hosp., 1949-50, Neurol. Inst. N.Y., N.Y.C., 1952-56; asst. in neurology Columbia U., N.Y.C., 1955-56; instr. medicine Albert Einstein Coll., N.Y.C., 1956-57, asst. prof. medicine, 1957-61, asso. prof. neurology, 1961-64, dean Coll. of Medicine, 1970-72, prof. neurology, 1964—; dir. neurology St. Barnabas Hosp., Bronx, N.Y., 1974—, Multiple Sclerosis Treatment Center, Bronx, 1975—. Served with USN, 1944-45, to capt. M.C., USAF, 1951-52. Diplomate Am. Bd. Psychiatry and Neurology. Mem. Am. Soc. Exptl. Pathology, Am. Neurol. Assn., Soc. Clin. Neurologists. Contbr. chpt. to Textbook of Medicine, 1978; researcher in multiple sclerosis and brain tumors for profl. assn. Home: 9 Oak Ln Scarsdale NY 10583 Office: 4422 3d Ave Bronx NY 10457

SCHEINER, ELLEN, physician; b. Bklyn., Jan. 27, 1932; d. Morris and Pauline (Harber) Scheiner; A.B. cum laude, Bklyn. Coll., 1952; M.D., U. Lausanne, 1960. Intern, Kings County Hosp., Bklyn., 1960-61; resident N.Y. Infirmary, 1961-62; resident Meml. Hosp., N.Y.C., 1962-64, sr. pub. health renal trainee, 1964-66, asst. attending medicine, clin. physiology and renal service, 1970-75, asso. attending physician, 1975—; cons. med. audit, 1973—; asso. clinician Sloan-Kettering Inst., N.Y.C., 1970-76, clinician, 1976—; asst. prof. medicine Cornell U. Med. Coll., N.Y.C., 1970-76, clin. asso. prof., 1976—; co-dir. biomed. data sect. div. med. systems Meml. Sloan-Kettering Cancer Center, N.Y.C., 1974-75. Ellse L'Esperance fellow, 1962-63. Diplomate Am. Bd. Internal Medicine. Fellow A.C.P.; mem. N.Y. Acad. Scis., AAAS, N.Y. Nephrology Soc., Am. Soc. Nephrology, Thanatology Soc. (profl. advisory bd.). Home: 77 Seaview Ave New Rochelle NY 10801 Office: 1275 York Ave New York City NY 10021

SCHELL, NORMAN BARNETT, pub. health exec.; b. N.Y.C., May 25, 1925; s. Jack and Sylvia Ada (Rosen) S.; B.A., N.Y.U., 1946, M.D., 1950; M.P.H., Harvard, 1971; m. Lila Barbara Mendelsohn, Aug. 27, 1950; children—Martin, Judith, Steven. Intern, Beth Israel Hosp., N.Y.C., 1950-51; resident Mt. Sinai Hosp., N.Y.C., 1951-52, N.Y. Hosp.-Cornell, N.Y.C., 1952; practice medicine specializing in pediatrics, Jericho and Hicksville, N.Y., 1956-69; pub. health physician Nassau County (N.Y.) Dept. Health, Mineola, 1969-70, med. dir., 1971-75, dep. commr. health, 1976—; asso. prof. clin. community medicine State U. N.Y., Stony Brook, 1974—, adj. prof. health care adminstrn. C.W. Post Coll., L.I. U., 1974—; lectr. sch. health Yale U. Sch. Medicine, 1978—; cons. in pediatrics Nassau County Med. Center, 1976—. Served with M.C., USN, 1953-55. Recipient Physicians Recognition award AMA, 1970; NIH grantee, 1961-63; diplomate Am. Bd. Pediatrics, Am. Bd. Preventive Medicine. Fellow Am. Acad. Pediatrics (nat. com. on sch. health 1971-77), Am. Coll. Preventive Medicine, Am. Pub. Health Assn., Am. Sch. Health Assn., Royal Soc. Health, Nassau Acad. Medicine; mem. N.Y. State (chmn. sch. health com.), Nassau County med. socs., Am. Assn. Pub. Health Physicians, N.Y. State Pub. Health Assn., Phi Beta Kappa. Club: Harvard (N.Y.C.). Editor sch. health sect. N.Y. State Jour. Medicine; contbr. articles to profl. jours. Home: 63 Birchwood Park Dr Jericho NY 11753 Office: 240 Old Country Rd Mineola NY 11501

SCHELLENGER, JAMES KNOX POLK, investment co. exec.; b. Cape May, N.J., Sept. 14, 1919; s. Henry E. and Edythe (Dellett) S.; B.S. in Econs., U. Pa., 1941, J.D., 1947; m. Ann H. Fussell, Dec. 11, 1948; children—Suzanne F. (Mrs. James G. Williamson), James Knox Polk III, Elizabeth Dellett, Henry Ewen, Georgeann Dock. Admitted to Pa. bar, 1948; practiced in Phila., 1948-53; with Delaware Fund, Inc., Phila., 1954—, exec. v.p., 1965-71, pres., 1971-76, chmn. bd., 1977—, also dir.; with Decatur Income Fund, Inc., Phila., 1956—, exec. v.p., 1965-71, pres., 1971-76, chmn. bd., 1977—, also dir.; with Del Mgmt. Co., Inc., Phila., 1955—, exec. v.p., 1965-71, pres., 1971-76, also dir.; exec. v.p Delta Trend Fund, Inc., Phila., 1968-71, pres., 1971-76, chmn. bd., 1977—; also dir.; exec. v.p. Delchester Bond Fund, Inc., Phila., 1970-71, pres., 1971-76, chmn. bd., 1977—, also dir.; chmn. Del. Investment Advisers, Inc., Phila., 1972—, also dir.; chmn. bd., dir. DMC Tax-Free Income Trust-Pa., 1977—; partner Del. Co., Phila., 1954—; chmn. bd., dir. Del. Cash Res., 1978—. Served to lt. USNR, 1942-46. Mem. Am., Phila. bar assns., Phila. Fin. Analysts Club, U. Pa. Alumni Assn., Navy League, Investment Co. Inst., Nat. Assn. Security Dealers. Clubs: Lawyers, Racquet, Union League (Phila.); Varsity (U. Pa.); Waynesboro Country (Paoli, Pa.). Home: 421 Timber Ln Devon PA 19333 Office: 7 Penn Center Plaza Philadelphia PA 19103

SCHENCK, HARRY PAUL, otolaryngologist; b. Phila., Jan. 6, 1894; s. James Buchanan and Savilla Ettinger (Fries) S.; B.S., Haverford Coll., 1918; M.D., U. Pa., 1923; m. Edna Manvillier Leinbach, Dec. 1924. Staff U. Pa. Hosp., 1923-25, 38—; curator Mutter Mus., Coll. Physicians of Phila., 1925-37; staff U. Pa., 1927-37, Evans Inst., 1932-59, head dept. otolaryngology U. Pa., 1938-59, prof. otolaryngology grad. sch. medicine, 1939-59, prof. emeritus, 1959—; asso. otolaryngologist Lankenau Hosp., Phila., 1949-59; research cons. New York E E Infirmary, 1956-66. Cons. in otolaryngology VA. Trustee research fund Central Bur. Research. Served as pvt. M.C., AEF, World War I; capt. M.C., USNR, World War II. Recipient Casselberry award Am. Laryngol. Assn., 1929; Newcomb award Am. Laryngological Assn., 1959. Diplomate Am. Bd. Otolaryngology (bd. dirs.). Fellow Coll. Physicians of Phila., A.C.S. (bd. govs. 1956-66); mem. AMA, Collegium Oto-Rhino-Laryngolicum Amicitae Sacrum, Am. (pres. 1967-68), Phila. (past pres.) laryngol. assns., Phila. Allergy Soc. (past pres), N.Y. Acad. Scis., Am. Otol. Soc., Am. Acad. Allergy, Coll. Allergists, Am. Laryngol. Rhinol. and Otol. Assn., Am. Acad. Ophthalmology and Otolaryngology, Assn. Mil. Surgeons U.S., Soc. Med. Cons. to Armed Forces. Republican. Lutheran. Clubs: University, Phila. Country, Philobiblon, Contemporary, Union League (Phila.) Editor-in-chief Cyclopedia of Diseases of the Ear, Nose and Throat. Contbr. articles to profl. jours. Home: 1235 Wyngate Rd Wynnewood PA 19096 Office: 3400 Spruce St Philadelphia PA 19104

SCHENKEL, SUSI, psychologist; b. Poland, Apr. 21, 1946; d. Leon and Siddi Schenkel; came to U.S., 1949, naturalized, 1953; B.A., U. Wis., 1967; Ph.D., SUNY, Buffalo, 1973. Staff psychologist Fitchburg (Mass.) State Coll. Counseling Center, 1972-75; staff psychologist div. alcoholism Boston City Hosp., 1975-76; chief psychologist Cambridge (Mass.) Ct. Clinic, 1976—; instr. psychology dept. psychiatry Harvard Med. Sch., 1976—; lectr. U. Mass., Boston, 1978. Mem. Harvard Neighbors, 1976—. Mem. Am. Psychol. Assn. Home: 146A Huron Ave Cambridge MA 02138

SCHENKELBACH, LEON, ret. air force officer, safety mgmt. cons.; b. N.Y.C., Sept. 1, 1917; s. Max and Gussie (Weiner) S.; student Coll. City N.Y., 1935, Cooper Union Inst., 1938; grad. Command and Staff Coll. Air U. Maxwell AFB, Ala., 1962; m. Lucille Ross, Oct. 6, 1946. Commd. 2d lt. U.S. Army, 1942, advanced through grades to lt. col., 1961; dir. safety Bklyn. Army Terminal, 1962-66, Mil. Ocean Terminal, Bayonne, N.J., 1963-66; dist. safety mgr. Def. Contracts Adminstrn. Services, Hartford, Conn., 1966-69; mgr. weapons systems safety U.S. Army Weapons Command, Rock Island, Ill., 1969-73; worldwide responsibility for safety of armor, arty., aircraft weapons, and small arms weapons systems; ret., 1973; ind. safety mgmt. cons., Cromwell, Conn., 1974—; guest faculty Hartford Grad. Center, U. New Haven, U. Hartford; exec. bd. Hartford Indsl. Health and Safety Inst., 1974—. Dir. Quad-Cities World Affairs Conf., Davenport, Iowa, 1970-73. Mem. Am. Soc. Safety Engrs. (certified, chpt. pres.-elect), Conn. Safety Soc. (pres.), Am. Def. Preparedness Assn. (dir. chpt. 1978—). Author: The Safety Management Primer, 1975. Home: 7 Great Oak Ct Cromwell CT 06416

SCHENKER, IRWIN WILLIAM, ins. co. hosp. exec.; b. N.Y.C., Dec. 29, 1929; s. Bernard and Clara S.; B.A., N.Y. U., 1951, M.A., 1956; m. Carole Cohen, Mar. 6, 1955; children—Marcia Jill, Wendy Anne, Michael Bruce, Stacy Beth. Asst. adminstr. Meth. Hosp., Bklyn., 1956-67; exec. dir. Hillcrest Gen. Hops., Flushing, N.Y., 1967—; v.p. Group Health Inc., Flushing, 1967—. Chmn. labor relations com. Assn. Pvt. Hosps., 1970—; trustee, bd. dirs. N.Y. State Assn. Pvt. Hosps., 1970-74; pres. Temple Beth Sholom, Smithtown, N.Y., 1974-76; mem. Smithtown Med. Ethics Com., 1977—. Served with U.S. Army, 1951-53; Korea. Mem. Am. Hosp. Assn., Am. Coll. Hosp. Adminstrs., Am., Greater N.Y. hosp. assns. Home: 83 Wichard Blvd Commack NY 11725 Office: 158-40 79th Ave Flushing NY 11366

SCHENKERMAN, STANLEY, educator; b. N.Y.C., Apr. 19, 1930; s. Joseph and Edna Rhoda (Merrin) S.; B.E.E., City Coll. N.Y., 1952; M.E.E., N.Y. U., 1954, M.S. in Indsl. Mgmt., 1964; Ph.D. in Ops. Research, Poly. Inst. N.Y., 1972; m. Elaine Susan Mitteldorf, June 28, 1952; children—Jodine Lee, Rona Dale. Sr. engr., then prin. engr. Ford Instrument Co. div. Sperry Rand Corp., L.I. City, N.Y., 1956-60; sect. head product engring. Budd Electronics Co., L.I. City, 1960-62; successively project engr., dep. program mgr., mgr. optical instruments, dir. product assurance, dir. new products Perkin-Elmer Corp., Norwalk, Conn., 1962-72; asso. prof. Coll. Bus. Adminstrn., U. Bridgeport (Conn.), 1972—; adj. instr. Poly. Inst. N.Y., 1959-61; cons. in field. Served with U.S. Army, 1954-56. Registered profl. engr., N.Y. Mem. IEEE, Am. Inst. Decision Sci., Beta Gamma Sigma, Alpha Iota Delta. Club: Masons. Contbr. articles in field to profl. jours.; patentee in field; referee Decision Sci., 1975—. Home: 953 W Boston Post Rd Mamaroneck NY 10543 Office: Coll Bus Adminstrn Univ Bridgeport Bridgeport CT 06602

SCHER, JILL DIENER, vocat. rehab. counselor; b. N.Y.C., Dec. 5, 1944; d. Harry and Dorothy (Edelstein) Diener; B.A., U. Miami, 1966; M.A., Seton Hall U., 1975; 1 son, Matthew Douglas. Rehab. counselor N.J. Div. Vocat. Rehab. Services, East Orange, 1966-68, supervising counselor, Newark, 1968-69; youth leader YM-YWHA, West Orange, 1969-72; vocat. counselor South Orange/Maplewood Sch. Dist., N.J., 1975—; vocat. counselor dept. spl. edn. Career Edn. Inst., Columbia U., N.Y.C., 1976-77; pvt. practice vocat. rehab. counseling. Mem. pub. edn. com. Cancer Care, Inc., YWCA, Orange, 1969-79. Certified vocat. rehab. counselor. Mem. Nat. Vocat. Guidance Assn., Am. Rehab. Counseling Assn. of N.J., Am. Personnel and Guidance Assn., Nat. Rehab. Assn., U. Miami Alumni Assn. Home: 47A Lawrence Ave West Orange NJ 07052 Office: 59 Scotland Rd South Orange NJ 07079

SCHER, ROBERT SANDER, mech. engr.; b. Cin., May 24, 1934; s. Stanford Samuel and Eva (Ordan) S.; S.B., Mass. Inst. Tech., 1956, S.M., 1958, Mech. Engr., 1960, Sc.D., 1963; m. Audrey Erna Gordon, Oct. 21, 1961; children—Sarah Elizabeth, Alexander Benjamin, Aaron Zalmen. Research and teaching asst. Mass. Inst. Tech., 1957-62; control systems engr. Astro Electronics div. RCA, 1963-65; engring. mgr. Sequential Info. Systems, Elmsford, N.Y., 1965-71, tech. dir., 1971-77; v.p. engring. Teledyne Gurley, Troy, N.Y., 1977—. Bd. dirs. Lake George Opera Festival. Mem. ASME, Optical Soc. Am. (pres. Hudson-Mohawk chpt. 1977-78), Sigma Xi, Pi Tau Sigma, Tau Beta Pi. Home: 2 Laurel Oak Ln Clifton Park NY 12065 Office: 514 Fulton St Troy NY 12181

SCHEREMETA, WILLIAM WALTER, physician; b. N.Y.C., Aug. 11, 1911; s. Henry and Mary (Synovic) S.; student Coll. City N.Y., 1929-32; A.B., N.Y. U., 1935; M.D., St. Louis U., 1939; m. Nelda Lorraine Ninotti, Feb. 19, 1944; children—Corliss Sue, Lois Jane, William Henry Scheremeta. Intern, N.Y.C. Hosp., 1939-41; pvt. practice, N.Y.C., 1946-75; asst. attending physician N.Y. Infirmary, 1968-76, asst. attending physician emeritus, 1976—; aviation med. examiner, aircraft accident investigator FAA, 1961. Served to lt. col. M.C., AUS, 1941-46. Mem. N.Y. State, N.Y. County med. socs., AMA, Aerospace Med. Assn., Nat. Bd. Med. Examiners, Aircraft Owners and Pilots Assn., Alpha Omega Alpha. Home: Holiday Point Rd Sherman CT 06784

SCHERER, DONALD RICHARD, computer scientist; b. Jersey City, Aug. 14, 1939; s. Henry and Rose S.; M.E., Stevens Inst. Tech., 1961; M.A., Seton Hall U., 1971; Ph.D., Cath. U. Am., 1974. Engr. prodn. and devel. Western Electric/Bell Telephone Labs., Kearny/Murray Hill, N.J., 1961-64; engr. research and devel. Abex Corp. Research Center,Mahwah, N.J., 1964-67; research engr. Seton Hall U., S. Orange, N.J., 1968-74, prof. computer sci., 1974—; systems cons. Cath. U. Am., Washington, 1975—; ordained priest Roman Catholic Ch., 1967. NSF computer sci. grantee, 1970, sci. grantee, 1968; NASA orbital mechanics grantee, 1969. Mem. N.J. Assn. Ednl. Data Systems (dir.), Internat. Assn. Ednl. Data Systems, Assn. for Computing Machinery, IEEE, Internat. Mission Radio Assn. Author: Intrinsic Motivation in Programmed Learning, 1974; The Technico 9900 Microcomputer Handbook, 1978; contbr. tech. articles to profl. publs., paper to sci. conf. Home: 400 S Orange Ave South Orange NJ 07079 Office: Mail Station #73 Seton Hall Univ South Orange NJ 07079

SCHERR, MARVIN GERALD, psychologist; b. Balt., June 21, 1940; s. Harry and Fannie (Glazer) S.; B.A. cum laude (William Deiches scholar, Central Scholarship Bur. grantee 1961-62, (univ. scholar), U. Md., 1962; M.A. in Organizational Psychology, George Washington U., 1972, M. Philosophy in Psychology, 1975. Research psychologist Social Security Adminstrn., HEW, Balt., 1967-72, policy specialist supplemental security income, 1972-74, exec. fellow, 1975-76. Vice chmn. Columbia (Md.) Tennis Com., 1974; mem. budget com. Wilde Lake Village Bd., Columbia, 1975, Pro Cantare Chorus, 1977-78. Mem. Am. Psychol. Assn., AAAS, Washington Statis. Soc., Assn. for Advancement Psychology, Psi Chi. Home: 10387 Barcan Circle Columbia MD 21044 Office: 1875 Connecticut Ave NW Washington DC 20009

SCHETLIN, ELEANOR M., univ. ofcl.; b. N.Y.C., July 15, 1920; d. Henry Frank and Elsie (Chew) Schetlin; B.A., Hunter Coll., 1940; M.A., Tchrs. Coll., Columbia, 1942, Ed.D., 1967. Playground dir. Dept. of Parks, N.Y.C., 1940-42; librarian Met. Hosp. Sch. Nursing, N.Y.C., 1943-44, dir. recreation, 1944-48, dir. recreation and guidance, 1948-59; coordinator student activities State U. N.Y., Plattsburgh, 1959-63, asst. dean students, 1963-64; asst. prof., coordinator student personnel services City U. N.Y., Hunter Coll., 1967-68; asst. dir. student personnel Columbia U., Coll. Pharm. Scis., N.Y.C., 1968-69, dir. student personnel, 1969-71; asso. dean for students Health Scis. Center, State U. N.Y. at Stony Brook, 1971-73, asst. v.p. for student services, 1973-74, asso. dean for students, dir. student services, 1974—. Mem. So. N.Y. League Nursing (dir. 1954-56, 64-66), Student Nurse Assn. N.Y. State (adviser 1955-59), NEA, Am. Assn. Higher Edn., Am. Personnel and Guidance Assn., Nat. Assn. Women Deans, Adminstrs. and Counselors, Am. Coll. Personnel Assn. Contbr. articles to profl. jours. Home: 20 Barberry Ln Sea Cliff NY 11579 Office: Health Scis Center State U NY at Stony Brook Stony Brook NY 11794

SCHEUER, JAMES H(AAS), congressman; b. N.Y.C. Feb. 6, 1920; s. S(imon) H. and Helen (Rose) S.; A.B., Swarthmore Coll., 1942; L.A., Harvard, 1943; LL.B., Columbia, 1948; m. Emily Malino, Mar. 21, 1948; children—Laura Lee, Elizabeth Helen, James H(aas), John William. Admitted to N.Y. State bar, 1949; economist FEA, 1942; mem. legal staff OPA, 1951-52; chmn. housing adv. council N.Y. State Commn. Against Discrimination, 1955-64; mem. N.Y. State Task Force Middle Income Housing; cons. Pres. Kennedy and White House staff on housing and human rights problems, 1960-64; pres. Renewal and Devel. Corp.; lectr. in field, 1950—; mem. 89th to 92d congresses from 22d N.Y. dist., mem. 94th-96th Congresses from 11th N.Y. dist. Del. UN Conf. Housing, Human Rights, City Planning and Urban Renewal in Europe and Far East, 1958, 60, 61, 62; pres. Citizens Housing and Planning Council N.Y.C., 1958-61; mem. exec. bd. Citizens Union N.Y.C., 1950-64. Pres. N.Y. chpt. Am. Jewish Com., 1960; chmn. exec. com. Met. council Am. Jewish Congress, 1964. Bd. dirs. Nat. Housing Conf., Bronx Boys Club, Bronx chpt. NCCJ. Served with USAAF, 1943-45. Recipient 1st Walter White Meml. award Nat. Com. Against Discrimination in Housing, 1956, 1st Human Relations award Urban League Greater N.Y., 1962. Mem. Bar Assn. City N.Y., Am. Arbitration Assn. (panel arbitrators), Civil Rights Leadership Conf. Democrat. Contbr. articles to profl. jours. Office: US Ho of Reps Washington DC 20515

SCHIAVINA, LAURA MARGARET, librarian, artist; b. Springfield, Mass., Nov. 27, 1917; d. Joseph A. and Egidia (Bernini) Schiavina; student Traphagen Sch. of Fashion, 1944-46, U. R.I., 1967, Cornell U., 1968, Art Students League, 1973-74. With Eastern States Farmers Exchange, Springfield, 1935-44; with Marsh & McLennan, 1944-75, adminstrv. asst., 1971-75; librarian Wm. M. Mercer, Inc., N.Y.C., 1975—; exhibited in one-man shows at Little Gallery, Barbizon Hotel, N.Y.C., 1968, Galerie Internat., N.Y.C., 1969; exhibited in group shows at Westfield (Mass.) Coll., 1968, Nat. Acad., N.Y.C, 1969; Lever House, N.Y.C., 1973, 74, also various exhbns. with Wall St. Art Assn., Nat. Art. League and Jackson Heights Art Club; represented in pvt. collections. Recipient numerous prizes, awards. Mem. Spl. Libraries Assn., Wall St. Art Assn. (v.p. 1972-77), Am. Artist Profl. League, Nat. Art League. Club: Jackson Heights Art (pres. 1970-71), Salmagundi (N.Y.C.). Home: 35-25 78th St Jackson Heights NY 11372 Office: 1211 Ave of the Americas New York City NY 10036

SCHICK, CONSTANCE JOYCE, educator; b. Abilene, Tex., Apr. 11, 1939; d. Marshall F. and Velma Joyce (Hawes) Wilson; student McMurry Coll., 1957-58, 60; B.B.A., Angelo State U., 1969; Ph.D., Tex. Tech U., 1973; m. William Brewster Schick, July 8, 1972; 1 dau., Jana Kaye. Mgr., co-owner Hamrick Photog. Studio, Graham, Tex., 1958-60; treas. Concho Camera Corp., San Angelo, Tex., 1961-63; research asst. dept. psychology Tex. Tech U., Lubbock, 1970-72, teaching asst., 1972-73; asst. prof. psychology Bloomsburg (Pa.) State Coll., 1973-78, asso. prof., 1978—, mem. affirmation action commn., 1973—. Mem. Soc. Advancement Social Psychology, World Future Soc., AAUP, Am., Eastern, Southwestern, Rocky Mountain psychol. assns., Alpha Chi, Psi Chi, Phi Kappa Phi (pres. chpt. 1977-78). Democrat. Episcopalian. Home: 827 Light St Rd Bloomsburg PA 17815 Office: Dept Psychology Bloomsburg State Coll Bloomsburg PA 17815

SCHICK, IRVIN HENRY, educator; b. Wilkes-Barre, Pa., Aug. 10, 1924; s. Irvin and Elizabeth (Valentine) S.; diploma Bliss Elec. Sch., 1947; B.E.E., George Washington U., 1958; M.S. in Elec. Engring. (NSF fellow), U. Md., 1961; m. Marilyn Freeman, July 17, 1954 (dec. Aug. 1961); m. 2d, Marjorie Bletch Beach, Dec. 23, 1967; 1 dau., Carolyn Patricia. Engring. asst. Jeddo-Highland Coal Co. (Pa.), 1942-43; instr. Bliss Elec. Sch., Washington, 1947-50; prof. math. and elec. engring., dept. head Montgomery Coll., Rockville, Md., 1950-65, dir. extension, 1965-67, dean adminstrn., 1967-75, adminstrv. v.p., 1975—. Tchr., tutor, cons. indsl. cos. 1949—. Served with USAAF, 1943-46. Mem. Am. Assn. U. Profs., Montgomery County Edn. Assn., Md. State Tchrs. Assn., I.E.E.E., Am. Assn. Sch. Adminstrs., Internat. Platform Assn., Bliss Elec. Soc. (bd. govs.), Theta Tau, Sigma Tau, Sigma Pi Sigma, Tau Beta Pi. Home: 105 Fleetwood Terr Silver Spring MD 20910

SCHICK, PAUL KENNETH, educator; b. Bruno, Czechoslovakia, Oct. 12, 1932; s. Oskar T. and Vilma (Ross) S.; came to U.S., 1939, naturalized, 1944; student Tufts U., 1951-53; D.D.S., Balt. Coll. Dental Surgery, 1957; M.D., Boston U., 1961; m. Barbara Gail Pinsley, June 30, 1962; children—Darryl Richard, Jessica Ellen. Intern, Kings County Hosp., Bklyn., 1961-62, med. resident, 1962-63; med. resident N.Y. Med. Coll., 1963-65; pvt. practice internal medicine, Manchester, Conn., 1965-69; hematology fellow Montefiore Hosp., Bronx, 1969-71; asst. prof. medicine Med. Coll. Pa., Phila., 1971-76, asso. prof. medicine and asst. prof. biochemistry, 1976—; chief hematology sect. VA Hosp. Service of Med. Coll. Pa., 1976—. Merit badge counsellor in photography Boy Scouts Am., Phila., 1974-76. Recipient Best Research Paper of 1974 award Montefiore Hosp. Alumni and Staff; diplomate Nat. Bd. Med. Examiners, Am. Bd. Internal Medicine. Fellow ACP; mem. Am. Soc. Hematology, AAAS, Internat. Soc. Thrombosis and Haemostasis, Am. Fedn. Clin. Research, Sigma Xi. Contbr. articles in field to profl. jours. Office: Med Coll Pa 3300 Henry Ave Philadelphia PA 19129

SCHIDDEL, EDMUND, author; b. Chgo., Jan. 27, 1909; s. Karl W. and Maria Louisa (Müller) S.; student Colo. Coll., 1929-30; B.A. with honors in English Lit., Coll. William and Mary, 1933. Statistician, U.S. Dept. Labor, N.Y.C., 1933-35; radio scriptwriter, producer J. Walter Thompson, CBS, 1935-39; author: Scratch the Surface, 1939; The Other Side of the Night, 1954; Break-Up, 1954; The Girl With the Golden Yo-Yo, 1955; Safari to Dishonor, 1956; Love in a Hot Climate, 1957; A Bucks County Trilogy: The Devil in Bucks County, 1959; Scandal's Child, 1963; The Good and Bad Weather, 1965; Good Time Coming, 1969; The Swing, 1975. Decorated Chevalier du Mérite Culturel et Artistique Francais. Contbr. articles to various mags. Office: care Simon and Schuster Inc 1230 Ave of Americas New York City NY 10020

SCHIEFFELIN, GEORGE RICHARD, ednl. cons.; b. N.Y.C., July 3, 1930; s. George McKay and Louise (Winterbotham) S.; B.A., Hobart Coll., 1953. Ednl. cons., Denver, 1956-62, New Haven, 1962—; dir. Charles Scribner's Sons, N.Y.C., Scribner Book Stores, N.Y.C., Pubs. Realty Co., N.Y.C., Macro Communications, N.Y.C.; asst. to lt. gov. of Colo., 1958-61. Trustee Hobart and William Smith Colls., 1969-78. Served with AUS, 1953-55. Clubs: Morristown Field; University (Denver); Princeton (N.Y.). Address: 239 Bradley St New Haven CT 06511

SCHIEFFER, BOB LLOYD, journalist; b. Austin, Tex., Feb. 25, 1937; s. John and Gladys (Payne) S.; B.A., Tex. Christian U., 1959; m. Patricia Neville Penrose, Apr. 15, 1967; children—Susan Neville, Sharon Penrose. News reporter Sta. KXOL, Ft. Worth, 1957-59; reporter Ft. Worth Star-Telegram, 1962-66; news anchorman Sta. WBAP-TV, Ft. Worth, 1966-68; corr. CBS, Washington, 1969—, Pentagon corr., 1970-74, White House corr., 1974—. Served to capt. USAF, 1959-62. Recipient Emmy awards, 1972, 74. Mem. Sigma Delta Chi. Office: 2020 M St Washington DC 20036*

SCHIFF, IRWIN ALLEN, ins. exec., publisher, economist; b. New Haven, Feb. 23, 1928; s. Jacob and Anna S.; B.S. in Econs. and Accounting, U. Conn., 1950; children by previous marriage—Peter David, Andrew Jay. Pres. Irwin A. Schiff, Inc., Hamden, Conn., 1960—, Group Insurers, Inc., Hamden, Conn., 1960—; testified in opposition to removal of gold backing from U.S. currency Senate Com. on Banking and Currency, 1968. Served with U.S. Army, 1950-52. Mem. Libertarian Party. Jewish. Author: The Tax Rebel's Guide to the U.S. Constitution and Declaration of Independence, 1978; The Biggest Con: How the Government is Fleecing You, 1976; active in opposition to present U.S. income taxes and irredeemable paper currency. Home and Office: 2405 Whitney Ave Hamden CT 06518

SCHIFFMAN, ALAN THEODORE, accounting firm exec.; b. N.Y.C., Feb. 18, 1942; s. Herbert and Lenore Dorothy (Dick) S.; B.S., Lehigh U., 1963; m. Sedra Gail Snapperman, June 30, 1963; children—Marc David, Lauren Beth. Staff accountant Touche Ross & Co., Phila., 1965-67; supr., mgr. Main Lafrentz & Co., Phila., 1967-71; partner Laventhol & Horwath, C.P.A.'s, Phila., 1972—, also nat. dir. practice rev.; instr. Montgomery County Community Coll., 1973-77. Chmn., adminstrv. bd., fin. dir. Nat. Tay Sachs and Allied Diseases Assn. Served with U.S. Army, 1963-65. Mem. Am., Pa. insts. C.P.A.'s, Nat. Assn. Accountants. Clubs: Meadowlands Country, Upper Dublin Racquet, Whitemarsh Tennis, Golden Slipper. Home: 107 E Mill Rd Flourtown PA 19031 Office: 1845 Walnut St Philadelphia PA 19103

SCHIFFMAN, LOUIS F., chemist; b. Poland, July 15, 1927; s. Harry and Bertha (Fleder) S.; B. Chem. Engring., N.Y. U., 1948, M.S., 1952, Ph.D., 1955; m. Mina Rose Hankin, Dec. 28, 1963; children—Howard Laurence, Laura Lea. Engr., Pa. Grade Crude Oil Assn., Bradford, 1948-50; teaching fellow chemistry dept. N.Y. U., 1950-54; research chemist E. I. du Pont Co., Wilmington, Del., 1954-56, Atlantic Refining Co., Phila., 1956-59; project leader, group leader, head, corrosion sect. Amchem Products Inc., Ambler, Pa., 1959-70; pres. Techni. Research Assos., Inc., Willow Grove, Pa., 1968—; pub., editor Patent Licensing Gazette, 1968—; mem. adv. oversight com. NSF, 1975; participant, workshop moderator Energy Conf., ERDA, Washington, 1976, Las Vegas, 1977; indsl. and mgmt. cons. Recipient Founder's Day award N.Y. U., 1956. Fellow Am. Inst. Chemists; mem. N.Y. Acad. Scis., Am. Chem. Soc., Nat. Assn. Corrosion Engrs., Am. Electroplaters Soc., Licensing Execs. Soc., Am. Assn. Small Research Cos. (editorial contbr. Newsletter), Sigma Xi, Phi Lambda Upsilon. Contbr. articles to encys. and profl. jours. Patentee in field. Home: 1837 Merritt Rd Abington PA 19001 Office: Profl Center Bldg Willow Grove PA 19090

SCHIFFMAN, NANCY ELIZABETH, transp. planner; b. Everett, Mass., May 6, 1937; d. Joseph Coelho and Helen (Buchanan) Perry; B.A. cum laude, Boston U., 1973, M.S. in Urban Affairs, 1976; m. Yale M. Schiffman, June 23, 1974; children—David, Steven. Planning cons. Assos. for Community Resources, Sudbury, Mass., 1973-77; community relations specialist YWCA, Natick, Mass., 1975-76; regional transp. planner Central Mass. Regional Planning Commn., Worcester, 1977—. Mem. women's and minority com. Area Manpower Planning Bd., Marlboro, Mass., 1976; mem. subcom. Sudbury Housing Authority, 1977. Mem. Am. Inst. Planners (asso.), Met. Assn. Urban Designers and Planners. Contbr. articles to profl. jours. Home: 5105 12th Rd S Arlington VA 22204 Office: 71 Elm St Worcester MA 01609

SCHIFFRIN, MILTON JULIUS, physiologist; b. Rochester, N.Y., Mar. 23, 1914; s. William and Lillian (Harris) S.; A.B., U. Rochester, 1937, M.S., 1939; Ph.D. cum laude, McGill U., 1941; m. Dorothy Euphemia Wharry, Oct. 10, 1942; children—David Wharry, Hilary Ann. Instr. physiology Northwestern U. Med. Sch., 1941-45; lectr. pharmacology U. Ill. Med. Sch., 1947-57, clin. asst. prof. anesthesiology, 1957-61; with Hoffmann-La Roche, Inc., Nutley, N.J., 1946—, dir. drug regulatory affairs, 1964-71, asst. v.p., 1971—. Served from 2d lt. to capt. USAAF, 1942-46. Mem. Am. Med. Writers Assn. (dir. 1967—; pres. N.Y. chpt. 1967-68; pres. 1972-73), Am. Physiol. Soc., Internat. Coll. Surgeons, Am. Therapeutic Soc., Coll. Clin. Pharmacology and Therapeutics, Am. Chem. Soc. Author: (with E.G. Gross) Clinical Analgetics, 1955. Editor: Management of Pain in Cancer, 1957. Home: 13 Hathaway Ln Essex Fells NJ 07021 Office: Hoffmann-La Roche Inc Nutley NJ 07110

SCHILL, GERALD FRANCIS, photographer; b. Oil City, Pa., Mar. 21, 1948; s. Bernard Francis and Margaret Elizabeth (Guth) S.; certificates in photography (2) Winona Sch. Profl. Photography, 1972; m. Pamela Geraldine Ochs, Oct. 12, 1968; children—Andrew Loren, Amy Elizabeth, Sarah Ann. Electrician, plumber Bendix Homes, Inc., Clarion, Pa., 1970-74; owner, operator Bride's Dream, Marble, Pa., 1971-76, Cranberry, Pa., 1976—; pvt. practice photography, Marble, 1974—; asst. dist. mgr. and bus. rep. nation's bus. dept. U.S. C. of C., Washington, 1978—; exhibited in one-man shows: Sawmill Center for Arts, Cook Forest, Pa., 1976; group shows include Knox (Pa.) Centennial Art Show, 1976. Vol. ambulance driver, Leeper, Pa.; coach Jr. Legion Baseball, Leeper. Served with USAF, 1966-70; Vietnam. Recipient ribbons Autumn Leaf Festival Art Show, Clarion, 1974, 75, 76, Laurel Festival Art Show, Brookville, Pa., 1976, Pennbank Art Show (2), 1977, Kennerdell Art Festival, 1977. Mem. Bi-County Artists Assn. (pres. 1976), St. Mary's Holy Name Soc. (pres. 1973-75, treas. 1975-77), Oil City C. of C., Nat. Fedn. Ind. Businessmen. Republican. Roman Catholic. Home: 405 E 4th St Oil City PA 16301

SCHILLER, MARVIN, mgmt. cons.; b. N.Y.C., May 25, 1933; s. Morris and Jessie (Wechsler) S.; B.A., Queens Coll., 1956; M.A., Mich. State U., 1958, Ph.D., 1959; m. Nancy C. Klayf, Dec. 14, 1957; children—Lori Jo, Mark L., Steven C. Asso. A.T. Kearney Inc., mgmt. consultants, Chgo., 1959-65, prin., Los Angeles, 1965-69, v.p., 1969-70, v.p., N.Y.C., 1970—, also dir.; dir. Istel Fund. Pres. Am. Soc. Prevention Cruelty Animals, 1976—. Served with U.S. Army, 1952-55. Diplomate Am. Bd. Profl. Psychology. Mem. Am. Psychol. Assn., Inst. Mgmt. Consultants (dir.). Clubs: Quaker Ridge Golf, Marco Polo. Office: A T Kearney Inc 437 Madison Ave New York City NY 10022

SCHINNERER, VICTOR OSCAR, ins. cons.; b. Wyncote, Pa., Feb. 13, 1906; s. Frederick D. and Sarah (Field) S.; A.B., Pa. State U., 1928; m. Muriel Reid Johnson, Sept. 8, 1934; children—Sally Schinnerer Fant, William Reid, Sandra Schinnerer Younger. Underwriter, spl. agt., ins. analyst Aetna Casualty & Surety Co., Phila., 1928-37, supt. agts., Washington, 1937-38; formed own firm in 1938, which inc. in 1947 as Victor O. Schinnerer & Co., Inc. (became subs. Marsh & McLennon Inc.), ret. as chmn., 1974; sr. v.p., Marsh & McLennon, Inc., 1970-74; dir. Nat. Sav. & Trust Co., Washington, Schinnerer & Younger, Inc. Adv. council Boy Scouts Am., 1963—; pres. D.C. Soc. for Crippled Children, 1962-64; trustee Fed. City Council, 1970—; bd. assos. Gettysburg Coll., 1965—; bd. dirs. Met. Washington Bd. Trade, 1954-67, pres., 1958-59, mem. sr. council, 1959—; chmn. Washington Conv. and Visitors Bur., 1962-65, mem. exec. com., 1965-75; bd. dirs. Washington Heart Assn., 1960-61. Mem. D.C. (past pres.), Nat. (past dir.) assns. ins. agts., Newcomen Soc. (mem. Washington com.), Phi Kappa Psi. Clubs: Kiwanis (Washington); Columbia Country, Congressional Country, Seaview Country; Royal Palm Yacht and Country, Key Largo Anglers. Home: Martingham St Michaels MD 21663 Office: 4340 Connecticut Ave Suite 400 NW Washington DC 20008

SCHIRMANN, PETER JUDE, chemist; b. Buffalo, Mar. 26, 1946; s. Charles William and Margaret (Foisset) S.; B.S., Canisius Coll., 1968; Ph.D., Syracuse U., 1973; m. Sharon Mary Schooley, Apr. 4, 1970. Sr. research scientist Am. Cyanamid Co., Stamford, Conn., 1974—, chmn. academic interaction com., 1976—. Chmn. Fairfield Spl. Olympics Program, 1978, 79. Served to capt. U.S. Army Res. Mem. Fairfield Jaycees (Jaycee of Year 1977; dir. 1977-78, v.p. 1978-79), Am. Chem. Soc., CYCO Athletic and Social Orgn. (dir. 1977-78, v.p. 1978-79, pres. 1979—), Investment Club STAC (sec. 1978, v.p. 1979), Alpha Chi Sigma. Republican. Roman Catholic. Home: 89 Eunice Ave Fairfield CT 06430 Office: 1937 W Main St Stamford CT 06902

SCHIRMEISTER, BARBARA FREDERICKS, interior designer; b. Dover, N.J., May 23, 1931; s. Arthur Joy and Sara Augusta (Lawrence) Fredericks; student St. Lawrence U., Ohio State U.; grad. Parsons Sch. Design, 1956; postgrad. N.Y. U., Seton Hall U.; m. Charles F. Schirmeister; children—Pamela Joy, Charles Bradford. Designer, Hilton Hotels Corp., N.Y.C., 1956-60; adj. prof. Parsons Sch. Design, N.Y.C., 1959-61, Fashion Inst. Tech., N.Y.C., 1961-64, 71-72, Kean Coll. N.J., 1977; design cons. Mitsubishi Internat. Corp., N.Y.C., Tokyo, Pacific House Textiles, Tokyo, Bobst Champlain, N.J., Suburban Propane, N.J.; prin. Barbara Schirmeister Interiors, N.Y.C.; mem. U.S. del. of designers to China, 1977. Mem. Am. Soc. Interior Designers (dir.), Decorators Club N.Y. (dir.), Internat. Inst. Interior Designers, Inter-Soc. Color Council (del. chmn. 1978), D.A.R., Pan Pacific and Southeast Asia Womens Assn., Delta Delta Delta. Republican. Presbyterian. Design cons., coordinator restoration Union Congl. Ch., Montclair, N.J., 1976-77. Home: 15 Beechcroft Rd Short Hills NJ 07078 Office: 118 E 60th St New York City NY 10022

SCHIRMER, NORBERT ERICH, elec. engr.; b. Chgo., Mar. 2, 1929; s. Walter Karl and Martha Schirmer; B.S. in Indsl. Mgmt., U. Balt., 1961; m. Grace Anderson Kemler, May 4, 1968; children—David Allen, Bruce Bennett, Stephanie Ann. Customer engr. IBM Corp., Balt., 1953-61; elec. engr. Bethlehem Steel Co. plant, Sparrows Point, Md., 1961-75, asst. gen. foreman elec. maintenance, 1975—; tchr. in field. Served with USNR, 1947-50, USCGR, 1950-53. Mem. Am. Assn. Iron and Steel. Democrat. Lutheran. Club: Sparrows Point Engineers. Address: Coke Oven Elec Maintenance Sparrows Point MD 21219

SCHKEEPER, PETER ALEXANDER, cons. co. exec.; b. New Brunswick, N.J., Aug. 27, 1923; s. Alexander and Leokadia (Surdacki) S.; diploma in piano pedagogy Trenton Conservatory Music, 1950; postgrad. in mech. engring., bus. adminstrn. and psychology various colls., univs.; m. Marguerite Elizabeth Ann Leibner, Sept. 9, 1943; children—Peter A., William E., Catherine A. Schkeeper England, Susan M. Schkeeper Maronpot. Plant mgr., asst. to pres. N.J. Meter

Co., Plainfield, 1946-57; asst. plant supt., liaison engr. Komline-Sanderson Engring. Corp., mfrs. vacuum filtration machinery and equipment, Peapack, N.J., 1957-61; pres., founder Marpet Cons., Inc., counselors to small bus. and mgmt., Somerville, N.J., 1961—; mem. Active Corps of Execs./SBA; dir. Far Hills Constrn. Co. Chmn. Republican Com., Peapack-Gladstone, 1962-63; mem. planning bd., Peapack-Gladstone, 1963-75, chmn., 1964-72; founding trustee, treas. Somerset Hills Montessori Sch., Peapack, N.J., 1978—. Served with USCG, 1942-45; NATOUSA, ETO. Registered pub. accountant, N.J. Mem. Inst. Mgmt. Cons., Am. Arbitration Assn., Inst. Environ. Scis. Club: Plainfield Engrs. Home: 1 Tainter St Peapack NJ 07977 Office: 2 Bell Ave Somerville NJ 08876

SCHLAGER, MAYNARD M., psychologist; b. Winthrop, Mass., Apr. 3, 1928; s. Saul and Rose S.; student Mesivta Chaim, Berlin, Ger., Jewish Theol. Sem., Hebrew Union Coll.-Jewish Inst. Religion; B.A., L.I. U., 1949; M.A., Assumption Coll., 1976; D.Ministry, Andover Newton Theol. Sem., 1978; m. Nathalie Lewin Dec. 30, 1967; children—Mason, Diane, David, Michael. Ordained rabbi, 1956; rabbi Temple Shalom, Needham, Mass., 1956-57, Temple Beth Torah, West Roxbury, 1957-58; clin. intern Danvers State Hosp., Tewksbury State Hosp., Melrose-Wakefield Hosp.; pvt. practice psychol., marriage and family counseling, Malden, Mass. Served with USAF, 1950-54. Mem. Am. Assn. Marriage and Family Counselors (clin.), Am. Psychol. Assn. Soc. Family Therapy and Research, Am. Assn. Sex Educators, Counselors and Therapists, Jewish War Veterans, Am. Legion. Club: B'nai Brith (past pres. Swampscott Marblehead, Mass.). Office: PO Box 40 Malden MA 02148

SCHLAGER, THOMAS PAUL, correctional adminstr.; b. Lancaster, Pa., Aug. 15, 1947; s. Joseph Edward and Genevieve Elizabeth (Ganse) S.; student Millersville State Coll., 1965-66; B.S., Pa. State U., 1972, postgrad.; m. Barbara Ann Bartush, Aug. 23, 1969; one son, Christopher. Probation, parole officer Cumberland County Probation Dept., Carlisle, Pa., 1972-73; warden Cumberland County Prison, Carlisle, 1973-76, Lancaster County Prison, Lancaster, 1976—; vis. instr. basic tng. acad. Pa. Bur. Correction, 1974—; del. Pa. Standards and Goals Criminal Justice System, 1975; bd. dirs. Opportunities Industrialization Center, Carlisle, 1975-76. Served with U.S. Army, 1966-69. Certified Pa. Bur. Corrections, Am. Arbitration Assn. Mem. Pa. Interscholastic Athletic Assn., Am. Correctional Assn. (del. standards accreditation team 1978), Am. Assn. Wardens and Supts., Pa. State U. Alumni Assn., Pa. Wardens Assn., Pa. Assn. Probation, Parole and Corrections, Phi Kappa Phi, Lambda Alpha Epsilon. Republican. Roman Catholic. Home: 434 Philmont Dr Lancaster PA 17601 Office: 625 E King St Lancaster PA 17602

SCHLAIFER, ALAN NORRIS, lawyer; b. Newark, Mar. 23, 1943; s. Norman Sam and Ruth (Blum) S.; B.S. cum laude, U. Pa., 1965; J.D., Harvard U., 1968; m. Jane Pasachoff, Sept. 24, 1972. Admitted to Md. bar, 1969, D.C. bar, 1970, U.S. Supreme Ct. bar, 1973; asso. firm Frank, Bernstein, Conaway & Goldman, Balt., 1968-69, Howrey & Simon, Washington, 1969-71; trial atty., civil div., frauds sect. U.S. Dept. Justice, Washington, 1971-73; trial atty. FTC, Washington, 1973-74, sr. trial atty., 1974—, program adviser, 1978—. Vol. atty. Legal Aid Soc. Washington, 1974—. Mem. Harvard Law Sch. Assn., Fed. Bar Assn. Club: Harvard. Home: 7204 Denton Rd Bethesda MD 20014 Office: FTC Consumer Protection Bur Washington DC 20580

SCHLAIFER, CHARLES, advt. exec.; b. Omaha, July 1, 1909; s. Abraham S.; privately ed.; Litt.D. (hon.), John F. Kennedy Coll., 1969; m. Evelyn Chaikin, June 10, 1934; children—Arlene Lois Schlaifer Silk, Roberta Sandra Schlaifer Semer. Newspaper reporter, Omaha, 1926-29; advt. dir. Publix Tri-States Theatres, Nebr., Iowa, 1929-37; mng. dir. United Artists Theatres, San Francisco, 1937-42; nat. advt. cons. United Artists Producers, 1937-42; nat. advt. mgr. 20th Century-Fox Film Corp., N.Y.C., 1942-45, v.p. charge advt. and pub. relations, 1945-49; pres. Charles Schlaifer & Co., Inc., N.Y.C., Los Angeles, 1949—. Vis. prof. New Sch. Social Research; expert witness U.S. Congl. and Senatorial coms. on mental health, 1949—. Mem. Pres.'s Com. Employment Handicapped, 1960—; founder, co-chmn. Nat. Mental Health Com., 1949-57; mem. nat. mental health adv. council Surgeon Gen. U.S., 1950-54; sec.-treas. Joint Commn. Mental Illness and Health, 1955-62; vice chmn. Found. Child Mental Welfare, 1963; mem. Gov.'s Youth Council State N.Y. Chmn. N.Y. State Mental Hygiene Facilities Improvement Corp., 1965—, White House Conf. Children, 1970; chmn. N.Y. State Facilities Devel. Corp., 1973—; sec.-treas., bd. dirs. Joint Commn. Mental Health Children; bd. dirs. Hillside Hosp., League Sch. For Seriously Disturbed Children, Menninger Found.; mem. adv. council NIMH, 1976—. Recipient Karen Horney Clinic Social Conscience award, 1972. Hon. fellow Postgraduate Center for Mental Health. Fellow Am. Psychiat. Assn. (hon.), Brit. Royal Soc. Health (hon.), Am. Orthopsychiat. Assn. (hon.). Co-author: Action for Mental Health, 1961; also articles in psychiat. jours. Home: 150 E 69th St New York City NY 10021 Office: 150 E 58th St New York City NY 10022 also 6430 Sunset Blvd Los Angeles CA 90028

SCHLAIN, DAVID, chem. engr.; b. Phila., July 21, 1910; s. Joseph and Anna (Klotka) S.; B.S. in Chem. Engring., U. Pa., 1932, M.S. in Edn., 1937; Ph.D. in Chem. Engring., U. Md., 1951. Chemist, U.S. Geol. Survey, 1937; with U.S. Bur. Mines, 1937—, electrochemist, supervisory chem. engr., College Park, Md., 1948-73, research chem. engr., 1974—. Registered profl. engr., Md. Fellow Am. Inst. Chemists; Washington Acad. Scis.; mem. Electrochem. Soc. (past chmn. Nat. Capital area sect.), Am. Inst. Chem. Engrs., Am. Inst. Mining and Metall. Engrs., Electroplaters Soc., Am. Chem. Soc., Nat. Assn. Corrosion Engrs. (corrosion specialist), Am. Soc. for Metals, Sigma Xi. Contbr. articles to profl. jours. Home: 2A Gardenway Greenbelt MD 20770 Office: US Bur Mines Avondale MD 20782

SCHLAM, MARK HOWARD, marine co. exec.; b. Bklyn., Sept. 24, 1951; s. Murray J. and Sophia (Bonis) S.; B.S. in Elec. Engring. (N.Y. State Regents scholar), Poly. Inst. Bklyn., 1972, M.S., 1973. Sales asso. F.W. Madigan Real Estate Co., Flushing, N.Y., 1973-74; sales engr. Dayton T. Brown Inc., Bohemia, N.Y., 1975-77; sr. mktg. rep. Sperry Marine Systems, Gt. Neck, N.Y., 1977—; asso. editor Poly. Press, Bklyn., 1969-76. Mem. Audio Engring. Soc., Acoustical Soc. Am., Am. Inst. Aeros. and Astronautics, Am. Soc. Nondestructive Testing, Assn. Old Crows, IEEE, Nat. Contract Mgmt. Assn., Soc. for Tech. Communication, Soc. Automotive Engrs., AAAS, Nat. Pilots Assn., Nat. Soc. Profl. Engrs., Realtors Nat. Mktg. Inst., Poly. Inst. N.Y. Alumni Assn. (asso. dir. 1973—), Tau Delta Phi. Club: Masons. Asst. editor: Computer Processing in Communications, 1970, Submillimeter Waves, 1971; asso. editor Computers and Automata, 1971, Computer-Communications Networks and Teletraffic, 1972, Optical and Acoustical Micro-Electronics, 1975; Computer Software Engineering, 1976. Home: 25 Chateau Dr Melville NY 11746 Office: Sperry Marine Systems Worldwide Hdqrs Marcus Ave Great Neck NY 11020

SCHLEGEL, HARLAN EDGAR, sch. adminstr.; b. Hegins, Pa., Mar. 14, 1916; s. Francis Irvin and Alice Mary (Savidge) S.; B.S., Kutztown State Coll., 1946; M.S., U. Fla., 1964; M.S., Bucknell U., 1960; m. Elizabeth Kukla Beiler, June 18, 1938; 1 child—Lanier Harold. Tchr. Lykens Twp. Sch., Gratz, Pa., 1937-41, E. Brunswick Twp. Schs., McKeansburg, Pa., 1941-43, Cressona-Auburn (Pa.) High Schs., 1943-46; tchr. Tri-Valley High Sch., Valley View, Pa., 1946-59, prin., 1959-61, guidance counselor, tchr., 1961-67; dir. pupil services Schuylkill County Area Vocat. Tech. Sch., Pottsville, Pa., 1967—. Leader 4-H Club, Hegins, 1955-60, community chmn. Salvation Army, Hegins, 1959-61, Boy Scouts Am., Hegins and Valley View, 1959-62. Recipient Keystone Farmers degree Pa. Future Farmers, 1973; selected to attend annual guidance inst. U. Fla., Gainesville, 1962-63, spl. program on counselor effectiveness, Pa. State U., State College, 1967. Mem. Pa. Future Farmers Assn., Hegins, Pa., Am. edn. assns., Hegins, Pa., Am. guidance assns., Am. Personnel and Guidance Assn., Pa., Am. vocat. assns. Democrat. Methodist. Home: RD 1 Hegins PA 17938 Office: Mar Lin PA 17951

SCHLEGELMILCH, REUBEN ORVILLE, elec. engr.; b. Green Bay, Wis., Mar. 8, 1916; s. Raymond Adolph and Emma J. (Schley) S.; B.S., U. Wis., 1938; M.S. in Engring., Rutgers U., 1940; postgrad. Cornell U., 1941, U. Ill., 1942, Poly. Inst. Bklyn., 1951; M.S., in Indsl. Mgmt., Mass. Inst. Tech., 1955; Ph.D. in Elec. Engring., Syracuse U., 1959; m. Margaret E. Roberts, Aug. 22, 1943; children—Janet R., Raymond J., Joan C., Margaret Ann. Instr. engring. Rutgers U., New Brunswick, N.J., 1938-40; research engr. U. Ill., 1941-42; br. chief, chief engr. Radar Lab., Air Material Command, Watson Labs., Eatontown, N.J., 1942-51; chief Radar Lab., Rome Air Devel. Center, USAF Command, Rome, N.Y., 1951-55, dir. research and devel., 1955-59; tech. dir. def. group Westinghouse Electric Co., Washington, 1959-63; mgr. advanced tech. and missile guidance program IBM, Owego, N.Y., 1963-68; gen. mgr., pres. Schilling Industries, Galesville, Wis., 1969-71; mgr. preliminary systems engring. design directorate U.S. Army Advanced Concepts Agy., Alexandria, Va., 1971-74; mgr. Gun Fire Control Systems Devel., Naval Sea Systems Command, Washington, 1974—; instr. engring. Cornell U., 1940-41; cons. Guided Missile and Space Council, Washington, 1959-63. Registered profl. engr., N.J.; Alfred P. Sloan fellow, 1954-55. Mem. IEEE, Nat. Soc. Profl. Engrs., AAAS, Soc. Sloan Fellows, Assn. U.S. Army, Philos. Soc. Washington, Am. Preparedness Assn., N.Y. Acad. Scis. Republican. Methodist. Clubs: Rotary, Masons (32 deg.), Shriners. Contbr. articles in field to profl. jours. Home: 8415 Frost Way Annandale VA 22003 Office: Naval Sea Systems Command Code 65321 Washington DC 20361

SCHLEIN, STEPHEN P., clin. psychologist; b. N.Y.C., Nov. 24, 1939; s. Irving and Ann (Seigal) S.; B.S., U. Ill., 1962; M.A., Columbia U., 1965; Ph.D., Pa. State U., 1971; m. Toby Goldstein, Sept. 7, 1969; children—Karen Elizabeth, Sarah Kate. Therapist, Blueberry Day Treatment Center, N.Y.C., 1963-64; tchr.-therapist Pride of Judea Children's Services, N.Y.C., 1964-65; psychologist Assn. for Help of Retarded Children, N.Y.C., 1965-67; psychologist Queens Child Guidance Center, N.Y.C., 1967-69, Bklyn. Center for Psychotherapy, 1967-69; psychotherapist Pa. State U., 1969-71; postdoctoral fellow in clin. psychology Austen Riggs Center, Stockbridge, Mass., 1971-73; psychologist McLean Hosp., Belmont, Mass., 1973-74; sr. supervising clin. psychologist Youth Guidance Center Framingham (Mass.), 1974—; practice psychotherapy, Lexington, Mass., 1971—. Mem. Am., Mass. psychol. assns. Home: 4 Longfellow Rd Lexington MA 02173

SCHLESINGER, IRWIN D., neurologist; b. Bklyn., Sept. 13, 1935; s. Edward and Eva (Parkoff) S.; B.A., Bklyn. Coll., 1956; M.D., State U. N.Y., 1961; m. Marcia Rubinstein, Jan. 29, 1967; 1 dau., Lisa. Intern, asst. residence medicine Cornell Med. div. Bellevue Hosp., N.Y.C., 1961-63; resident neurology Bronx (N.Y.) Municipal Hosp. Center, 1965-68; practice medicine specializing in neurology, Great Neck, N.Y., 1968—; attending physician North Shore Univ. Hosp., Manhasset, N.Y., 1968—; mem. staff L.I. Jewish Med. Center; chief dept. neurology Deepdale Gen. Hosp., Little Neck, N.Y., 1970—; asst. clin. prof. neurology Cornell U. Med. Coll., N.Y.C., 1971-78, asso. prof. neurology, 1978—. Bd. advisers Myasthenia Gravis Found., L.I., N.Y., 1973—. Served to capt. USAF, 1963-65. Mem. Am. Acad. Neurology, A.M.A., Pan Am. Med. Assn., Am. Soc. Law and Medicine, A.C.P., Weimaraner Club Am., Physicians Martial Arts Assn., Alpha Omega Alpha, Phi Delta Epsilon. Home: 55 Foxhunt Crescent Oyster Bay Cove NY 11791 Office: 29 Barstow Rd Great Neck NY 11021

SCHLESINGER, JAMES RODNEY, sec. energy U.S.; b. N.Y.C., Feb. 15, 1929; s. Julius and Rhea (Rogen) S.; A.B. summa cum laude, Harvard U., 1950, A.M., 1952, Ph.D., 1956; m. Rachel Mellinger, June 19, 1954; children—Cora K., Charles L., Ann R., William F., Emily, Thomas S., Clara, James Rodney. Asst. prof., then asso. prof. U. Va., 1955-63; sr. staff mem. RAND Corp., 1963-67, dir. strategic studies, 1967-69; asst. dir. Bur. of Budget, 1969, acting dep. dir., 1969-70, asst. dir. Office Mgmt. and Budget, 1970-71; chmn. AEC, 1971-73; dir. CIA, Feb.-July 1973; U.S. sec. def., 1973-75, asst. to pres., 1976-77, sec. energy, 1977—; vis. scholar Sch. Advanced Internat. Studies, Johns Hopkins; cons. in field. Mem. bd. assos. Fgn. Policy Research Inst., U. Pa., 1962-63. Frederick Sheldon prize fellow Harvard U., 1950-51. Mem. Am. Econ. Assn., Phi Beta Kappa. Republican. Lutheran. Author: The Political Economy of National Security, 1960; co-author: Issues in Defense Economics, 1967; asso. editor Jour. Finance, 1964-65. Home: 3601 N 26th St Arlington VA 22207 Office: Dept Energy 1000 Independence Ave SW Washington DC 20585

SCHLESINGER, LOUIS BARRY, clin. psychologist; b. Perth Amboy, N.J., Aug. 19, 1949; s. Melvin S. and Nettie (Polonsky) S.; B.A., Rider Coll., 1971; Ph.D., New Sch. Social Research, 1975; m. Elizabeth Walsh, Nov. 18, 1973. Psychology intern Menlo Park Diagnostic Center, 1973-74, Trenton (N.J.) Prison, 1974; clin. psychologist J.F.K. Med. Center, Edison, N.J., 1975-76; coordinator violence clinic VA Hosp., East Orange, N.J., 1976—; clin. asst. prof. N.J. Coll. Medicine and Dentistry, Newark, 1977—; cons. Fair Oaks Hosp., Summit, N.J., 1976—; pvt. practice clin. psychology, Maplewood, N.J., 1976—. N.J. fellow in clin. psychology, 1973-74. Mem. Am. Orthopsychiat. Assn., Acad. Psychosomatic Medicine, Am., N.J. psychol. assns., Tau Kappa Epsilon. Home and Office: 12 Tower Dr Maplewood NJ 07040

SCHLESINGER, RICHARD B., real estate broker; b. N.Y.C., Apr. 13, 1939; s. Al and Lillian (Gitelson) S.; B.A., Lafayette Coll., 1960; postgrad. Columbia Law Sch., 1960-61; m. Sheila Epstein, Feb. 5, 1970; children—A. Lauren, John-Christophe, Katherine Ann. Mktg. supr. Joseph E. Seagram & Sons, N.Y.C., 1963-66; v.p. Liberty Tile & Marble Co., N.Y.C., 1966; real estate broker Brown, Harris, Stevens Inc., N.Y.C., 1967-69; pres. R.B. Schlesinger & Co., real estate brokers, N.Y.C., 1970—; pres. Eastern Brokerage Services Corp., N.Y.C., 1972—; cons. comml. real estate leasing. Bd. dirs. Pound Ridge Assn., Ad Hoc Com. for Better Downtown N.Y.C. Served with U.S. Army, 1962-63. Mem. Nat. Assn. Real Estate Bds., Real Estate Bd. N.Y. Club: Pound Ridge Tennis. Contbr. articles to trade publs. Home: West Ln Pound Ridge NY 10576 Office: R B Schlesinger & Co Inc 230 Park Ave New York City NY 10017

SCHLESINGER, ROBERT LEE, fin. cons.; b. N.Y.C., Nov. 12, 1918; s. Edwin James and Lucile Helen (Wolff) S.; B.A., N.Y. U., 1939, M.B.A., 1942. Security analyst Edwin J. Schlesinger, Investment Counsel, N.Y.C., 1939-42; v.p. fin. services Ebasco Bus. Cons. Co., N.Y.C., 1946—. Served to capt. U.S. Army, 1942-46. Mem. N.Y. Soc. Security Analysts, Chartered Fin. Analysts Soc., Nat. Soc. Rate of Return Analysts, Soc. Internat. Devel. Contbr. articles to profl. jours. Expert witness on fin. matters. Home: 400 E 57th St New York City NY 10022 Office: 100 Church St New York City NY 10007

SCHLESS, GUY LACY, physician; b. Phila., May 22, 1929; s. Robert Avrom (M.D.) and Bena S.; B.A., Stanford U., 1951; M.D., Jefferson Med. Coll., Phila., 1955; m. Nancy Esther Halverson, July 19, 1952; children—Karina Halverson, Laurits Halverson. Intern, Meth. Hosp., Phila., 1955-56; resident and research fellow in metabolism Pa. Hosp., Phila., 1956-58, asst. physician, 1959-68, asso. physician, 1968-71, physician, 1971—, chief med. clinics, 1965-67, sr. Mellon fellow in medicine, 1962-63; vis. fellow, hon. sr. registrar medicine Guy's Hosp., U. London, 1958-59, vis. research fellow in medicine Med. Sch., 1963-71, hon. cons., 1971—; instr. medicine U. Pa., 1962-64, asso., 1964-68, asst. prof. medicine, 1968—; fellow in medicine Am. Philos. Soc.; cons. in medicine 5th naval dist. U.S. Navy, 1965—; cons. in medicine U.S. Naval Regional Med. Center, Portsmouth, Va., 1965—; participant White House Conf. Food, Nutrition and Health, 1969. Served as 1t. comdr. M.C., USNR, 1960-62. Fellow Royal Soc. Medicine (London), Phila. Coll. Physicians, Royal Soc. Health (London), Royal Soc. Arts (London); mem. A.C.P., Pa., Phila. County med. socs., Am. Diabetes Assn., European Assn. Study Diabetes, Athenaeum of Phila., Victorian Soc. in Am. (dir., v.p. 1977), Soc. Archtl. Historians, Nu Sigma Nu. Republican. Contbr. articles on metabolism to profl. jours. Home: 3926 Henry Ave Philadelphia PA 19129 Office: Franklin Med Bldg Pa Hosp 829 Spruce St Philadelphia PA 19107

SCHLIMM, GERARD HENRY, structural and civil engr.; b. Balt., May 26, 1929; s. August Frederick and Anna Elizabeth (Schmidt) S.; B.C.E., U. Md., 1957; M.S., N.J. Inst. Tech., 1960; Ph.D., U. Md., 1970; m. Janice Marion Althouse, June 10, 1956; children—Frederick Bruce, Karl August, Paul Gerard. Mech. equipment engr. Esso Research & Engring. Co., Florham Park, N.J., 1957-60; instr. civil engring. U. Md., 1960-62; asst. prof. mech. engring. U.S. Naval Acad., 1962-66; dir. div. engring. and phys. sci. evening coll. Johns Hopkins U., 1966—; cons. engr. Trident Engring. Asso., Cadcom, Ellicott City Engring. Co. Mem. Mayor's Manpower Com., 1973-76; chmn. Civic Design Commn. Balt., 1974-77; mem. Md. Gov.'s Sci. Adv. Council, 1975-78. Served with U.S. Army, 1951-53. Ford Found. fellow, 1964-66; registered profl. engr., Md. Mem. ASCE (pres. Md. sect. 1973-74), Am. Soc. Engring. Edn., Engrs. Council Md., Engring. Soc. Balt. (pres. 1975-76), Nat. Soc. Profl. Engrs., Sigma Xi, Tau Beta Pi, Phi Eta Sigma, Chi Epsilon, Omicron Delta Kappa, Phi Kappa Phi. Home: 125 Croydon Rd Baltimore MD 21212 Office: Johns Hopkins U 3400 N Charles St Baltimore MD 21218

SCHLOSS, WALTER JEROME, investment co. exec.; b. N.Y.C., Aug. 28, 1916; s. Jerome Henry and Evelyn (Gomprecht) S.; certificate N.Y. Stock Exchange Inst., 1940; m. Louise Edith Filer, July 26, 1946; children—Edwin W., Stephanie. Asst. cashier Carl M. Loeb-Rhoades & Co., N.Y.C., 1934-41; asst. sec. Graham-Newman Corp., N.Y.C., 1946-55; gen. partner Walter J. Schloss Assos., N.Y.C., 1955—. Served to 2d lt S.C. AUS, 1941-45; ETO. Mem. Inst. Chartered Financial Analysts, N.Y. Soc. Security Analysts. Club: City (N.Y.C.). Contbr. articles in field to profl. jours. Home: 863 Park Ave New York City NY 10021 Office: 67 Wall St New York City NY 10005

SCHLOSSBERG, HARVEY, police psychologist; b. Bklyn., Jan. 27, 1936; s. Harry and Sally (Frankel) S.; B.S., Bklyn. Coll., 1958; M.S., L.I. U., 1960; Ph.D., Yeshiva U., 1970; m. Cynthia Marks, Sept. 5, 1964; children—Mark Anthony, Alexander, James, Steven. With N.Y.C. Police Dept., 1958—, police cons., adviser hostage negotiation and antiterrorism, 1973—; pvt. practice psychotherapy, N.Y.C., 1973—; adj. prof. psychology John Jay Coll. Criminal Justice, 1974—; adj. asso. prof. psychology L.I. U., 1975—. Mem. Am. Psychol. Assn., Soc. Personality Assessment, N.Y. Acad. Scis., Acad. Police Sci., Nat. Council Crime and Delinquency, Council for Nat. Register of Health Services. Author: Psychologist With A Gun, 1974. Contbr. articles to profl. jours. Developer psychol. tactics for hostage negotiations. Office: 67-39 108th St Forest Hills NY 11375

SCHLUSSEL, SEYMOUR, obstetrician, gynecologist; b. N.Y.C., Mar. 22, 1928; s. Albert and Lillian (Schreiber) S.; B.A., Johns Hopkins U., 1946; M.D., N.Y. Med. Coll., 1951; m. Aug. 19, 1951; 1 son, Ralph Michael. Intern, Flower & Fifth Ave. Hosps., N.Y.C., 1951-52; resident Flower & Fifth Ave. Hosps., Mt. Sinai Hosp., N.Y.C., 1952-56; mem. faculty N.Y. Med. Coll., N.Y.C., 1956—, prof. obstetrics and gynecology, 1975—; mem. staffs Mt. Sinai, Lenox Hill, Met., Doctors hosps. (all N.Y.C.). Served with M.C., U.S. Army, 1953-55; Korea. Diplomate Am. Bd. Obstetrics and Gynecology. Fellow A.C.S., Am. Coll. Obstetricians and Gynecologists, Internat. Coll. Surgeons. Office: 992 Fifth Ave New York City NY 10028

SCHLUTER, PETER MUELLER, electronics co. exec.; b. Greenwich, Conn., May 24, 1933; s. Fredric Edward and Charlotte (Mueller) S.; B.M.E., Cornell U., 1956; m. Jaquelin Ambler Lamond, Apr. 18, 1970; children—Jane Randolph, Charlotte Mueller, Anne Ambler. Sr. engr. Thiokol Chem. Corp., Brigham City, Utah, 1958-59; asso. Porter Internat. Co., Washington, 1960-65, v.p., 1965-66, pres., treas., dir., 1966-70; pres., treas. dir. Zito Co., Derry, N.H., 1970-72; internat. bus. cons., Washington, 1972-74; v.p. Buck Engring. Co. Inc., Farmingdale, N.J., 1975, pres., chief exec. officer, dir., 1975—; dir. Keystone Forging Co., Northumberland, Pa. Mem. Republican Inaugural Book and Program Com., 1969; mem. community adv. bd. Monmouth council Girl Scouts U.S. Mem. Pi Tau Sigma. Club: Met. (Washington). Home: 3 N Cherry Ln Rumson NJ 07760 Office: PO Box 686 Farmingdale NJ 07727

SCHMAUS, SIEGFRIED H. A., research engr.; b. Muelheim/Ruhr, W. Ger., Dec. 23, 1915; s. Wilhelm Friedrich and Hedwig (Flader) S.; student Staatliche Ingenieur Schule, Duisburg, W. Ger., 1940-41, Esslingen, W. Ger., 1945-46; m. A. Babette Schmid, Aug. 17, 1946. Apprentice-designer Demag A.G., Duisburg, 1930-36; designer/supr. Meissner, Cologne, W. Ger., 1936-38; designer aircraft engines Daimler-Benz A.G., Stuttart, W. Ger., 1943-45; designer Fischer & Porter, Warminster, Pa., 1948-53, Ametek Inc., Sellersville, Pa., 1954-65; staff research engr. Fischer & Porter, Warminster, 1966—; pres. Sensor Devel. Inc., Broomall, Pa., 1977—. Sec. Humboldt Circle, 1955—. Served with German Luftwaffe, 1938-42. Recipient Hess Ingenuity award, 1962. Mem. Franklin Inst., Instrument Soc. Am., Am. Soc. Mfg. Engrs. Republican. Lutheran. Club: Masons. Patentee in field. Home: 806 Powder Mill Ln Penfield Downs Philadelphia PA 19151 Office: Fischer & Porter E County Line Rd Warminster PA 18974

SCHMAUSS, DAVID C., med. center exec.; b. St. Paul, Mar. 21, 1931; s. John Henry and Catherine Ann (Caulfield) S.; B.A., U. Minn., 1955, M. Hosp. Adminstrn., 1962; m. Judy Ann Buckbee, Oct. 8, 1955; children—Mark, Edward, Jennifer. Adminstr., Sister Elizabeth Kenny Rehab. Inst., Mpls., 1963-66; exec. sec. Cath. Hosp. Assn. Service Bur., Washington, 1966-68; adminstr. Appalachian Regional Hosp., Beckley, W.Va., 1968-74; asst. v.p. Appalachian Regional Hosps., Lexington, Ky., 1973-74; v.p., gen. dir. No. div. Albert

Einstein Med. Center, Phila., 1974-78, bd. dirs., 1976—; bd. dirs. Internat. Assn. Rehab. Facilities; preceptor Xavier U.; mem. field faculty Meharry Med. Coll.; chmn. Raleigh County (W.Va.) Health Council. Bd. mgrs. Mpls. YMCA, 1966-68; area vice chmn. Mpls. United Fund, 1967. Served with USMCR, 1948-58. Fellow Am. Pub. Health Assn., Am. Coll. Hosp. Adminstrs.; mem. Assn. Am. Med. Colls., Nat. League Nursing. Home: 428 Dartmouth Ct Cornwells Heights PA 19020 Office: Albert Einstein Med Center Philadelphia PA 19141

SCHMEICHEL, NEILL RICHARD, accountant; b. Detroit, Aug. 7, 1931; s. Fred E. and Pearl L. S.; B.B.A., U. Mich., 1956, M.B.A., 1957; m. Joan Marie Pierce, Aug. 11, 1951; children—Cynthia Joanne, Scott Frederick, Susan Irene, Karen Lee, Kristen Perie. Mgr., Ernst & Ernst, Detroit, 1965-68, partner, Jackson, Mich., 1968-74, partner-in-charge, Phila., 1974—. Trustee, Baldwin Sch., 1975—. Served to capt. USAF, 1950-52. Named Man of Year, Jackson, 1973. Mem. Nat. Assn. Accountants (nat. dir. 1973-74), Greater Jackson (pres. 1972-73), Phila. (dir. 1975—) chambers of commerce, Am., Pa. insts. C.P.A.'s, Mich. Assn. C.P.A.'s, Alpha Tau Omega, Alpha Kappa Psi, Beta Alpha Psi. Republican. Clubs: Phila. Country, Merion Golf, Union League, Pine Valley Golf. Home: 640 Carlsbrooke Rd Bryn Mawr PA 19010 Office: Ernst & Ernst 2900 Centre Sq Philadelphia PA 19102

SCHMELKIN, BENJAMIN, accountant; b. N.Y.C., Sept. 1, 1910; s. Joseph and Lucy (White) S.; B.S., Coll. City N.Y., 1930; postgrad. Baruch Sch. Bus.; m. Selma Landsman, June 18, 1944; children—Alan, Kenneth, Mark. Tchr. accounting high sch., N.Y.C., 1932-36; partner Schmelkin & Schmelkin, C.P.A.'s 1932—; accountant Am. Acad. Dental Medicine. Mem. Muscular Dystrophy Com., 1956—; leader fund drive Bronx div., Boy Scouts Am., 1951-52; mem. Israel Bond Drive Com., Bronx and Westchester, 1955—; chmn. Lyric Cemetery, Bethel, N.J., 1956—; past patron Mt. Vernon Y.M. Assn. Bd. dirs. Menninger Found. Served with AUS, 1942-43. C.P.A. Mem. Am. Inst. C.P.A.'S, C.P.A. Soc. N.Y. Alumnus Coll. City N.Y., Zionist Orgn. Am. (mem. exec. bd.), Internat. Platform Assn., Am. Security Council, Jewish War Vets., Smithsonian Instn., Anti-Defamation League, Am.-Israeli Pub. Affairs Com. Odd Fellow (past dist. dep., past rep. convs.). Clubs: Men's (past pres.) Emanuel (Mt. Vernon, N.Y.). Home: 12 Marion Pl Mount Vernon NY 10552 also Stephentown NY 12168 Office: 54 W Broad St Mount Vernon NY 10552

SCHMELKIN, CHARLES LAZAR, lawyer; b. N.Y.C., Dec. 1, 1925; s. Joseph and Lucy (White) S.; B.A., Coll. City N.Y., 1945; LL.B., N.Y. U., 1948, J.D., 1968; m. Elaine Gale Robbins, June 1, 1958; children—Joel, Ira J., Neil B., Alan E., Martin L., Steven H. Admitted to N.Y. State bar, 1948; individual practice law, N.Y.C., 1948—; legal cons. to law firm F. Lee Bailey & Aaron J. Broder, N.Y.C., 1968—. Served with AUS, 1944-45. Mem. N.Y. State Bar Assn., N.Y. State Trial Lawyers Assn., N.Y. U. Law Alumni Assn. Jewish (trustee temple 1968-71, chmn. religious com. 1967-68, trustee Men's Club). Club: Odd Fellows (past noble grand). Home: 6 Surrey Rd Great Neck NY 11020 also 45 Cranston Hill Rd Stephentown NY 12168 Office: 54 W Broad St Mount Vernon NY 10552

SCHMICK, WILLIAM FREDERICK, JR., newspaper exec.; b. Balt., Dec. 3, 1913; s. William Frederick and Nancy M. (Reindollar) S.; A.B., Princeton U., 1936; m. Mary E. Novak, Apr. 17, 1939; children—Elizabeth A., William Frederick III, Mary J., John E. With A. S. Abell Co., publishers Balt. Sun papers and owners sta. WMAR-TV, Balt., 1938—, exec. v.p., 1953-60, pres., 1960—. Clubs: Maryland, Elkridge (Balt.). Home: 315 Overhill Rd Baltimore MD 21210 Office: Calvert and Centre Sts Baltimore MD 21202

SCHMID, JAMES FRANCIS, engr.; b. Longbranch, N.J., Aug. 21, 1922; s. Emil and Anna (Lhota) S.; grad. U.S. Mcht. Marine Acad., 1944; B.S. in Mech. Engring., Poly. Inst. Bklyn., 1972; m. Mary Wohlpart, Jan. 22, 1944; 1 son, James J. Engring. instr. U.S. Mcht. Marine Acad., Kings Point, N.Y., 1944-46; engring. officer U.S. Lines at Sea, 1946-49; maintenance engr. N.Y. Eye and Ear Infirmary, N.Y.C., 1949-51; engr. Hotel New Yorker, N.Y.C., 1951-53; bldg. supt. Chrysler N.Y. Co. div. Chrysler Corp., N.Y.C., 1953-56; chief engr. Nassau Hosp., Mineola, N.Y., 1956-63; dir. engring. Bklyn. (N.Y.) Hosp., 1963-78; plant engr. Bush Terminal Assos., Bklyn., 1978—; cons. in field. Mem. Am. Nat. Standards Inst., Nat. Assn. Power Engrs. (nat. pres. 1975-76), ASME, Am. Soc. Hosp. Engrs., Nat. Fire Protection Assn., Hosp. Exec. Engrs. Assn. Greater N.Y., Greater N.Y. Hosp. Assn. (engrs. adv. com. com.), Air Pollution Control Assn. (TS2.2 com.), Nat. Inst. for Uniform Licensing of Power Engrs. (nat. dir.), U.S. Mcht. Marine Acad. Alumni Assn. (life). Roman Catholic. Home: 52 Galewood Dr Matawan NJ 07747 also 63 Mark Dr Manahawkin NJ 08050 Office: 269 37th St Brooklyn NY 11232

SCHMID, WALTER ERNST, engring. co. exec.; b. Zurich, Switzerland, June 27, 1932; s. Otto and Klara (Sachsenmeier) S.; came to U.S., 1962, naturalized, 1968; B.E.E., Juventus Inst. Tech., Zurich, 1956; m. Margaret Zingg, Sept. 19, 1958; children—Ursula Marilyn, Heidi Sylvia. Head elec. dept. Sun Shipbldg. and Dry Dock Co., Chester, Pa., 1962-68; mgr., dir. elec. engring. Litton Ship Systems, Culver City, Calif., 1968-72; mgr., v.p. Washington office George G. Sharp, Inc., Hyattsville, Md., 1972-78, dir., N.Y.C., 1974-78; pres., dir. NKF Engring. Assos., Inc., Silver Spring, Md., 1978—. Served with Swiss Armed Forces, 1951-58. Registered profl. engr., Pa., Va. Mem. Soc. Naval Architects and Marine Engrs., Am. Soc. Naval Engrs., IEEE, Am. Def. Preparedness Assn. Republican. Presbyterian. Author: (with others) Mountain Railroads of Switzerland, 1959. Home: 12913 Two Farm Dr Silver Spring MD 20904 Office: 8720 Georgia Ave Silver Spring MD 20910

SCHMIDT, GERHARD JOHANN, economist, educator; b. Berlin, Germany, June 25, 1902; s. Salli and Johanna (Lebenheim) S.; student U. Berlin, 1920-25; U. Freiburg, U. Munich; Dr. rer. pol.; postgrad. N.Y. U. With Nat. Bur. Statistics, Berlin, 1926-27; partner Isr. Schmidt Söhne, Berlin-Frankfurt, 1928-38; instr. Bergen Jr. Coll., Teaneck, N.J., 1946-54; asst. prof. Fairleigh Dickinson U., 1954-66, asso. prof., 1966-70, prof., 1970-75, prof. emeritus, 1975—; prof. Dowling Coll., Oakdale, L.I., N.Y., 1975-76, New Sch. Social Research, 1976—. Mem. Inst. Mediterranean Affairs, Am. Council Emigres in Professions, Accademia Tiberina (Rome). Author: Der Konstante Geldwert von Oresmius bis Knapp, 1925; An Introduction into the History, Theory and Administration of Money, 1970; also articles in field. Home: Hotel Greystone Broadway at 91st St New York City NY 10024

SCHMIDT, HAROLD ROBERT, lawyer; b. Braddock, Pa., Sept. 4, 1913; s. Abraham I. and Gustella (Frankle) S.; A.B., U. Mich., 1934; LL.B., U. Pitts., 1937; m. Bernice V. Williams, June 24, 1941; children—Barbara N. Schmidt Wickwire, Edward C., Gordon W. Admitted to Pa. bar, 1937, since practiced in Pitts.; sr. partner charge litigation Rose Schmidt Hasley Whyte Dixon & Hardesty, and predecessors, 1946—; asso. gen. counsel Joy Mfg. Co. Chmn. Com. to Modernize Jury Selection Procedures; co-chmn. Lawyers Non-partisan Com. to Secure 5 Judges; chmn. Com. to Revise 2d Class Jury Selection Statute; mem. grievance com. U.S. Dist. Ct. for Western Pa.; permanent mem. Jud. Conf. 3d Jud. Circuit U.S.; panel participant U. Rome; lectr. London Med. Coll., Pitts. Inst. Legal Medicine; former govt. appeal agt., local bd. 19, SSS, Pitts.; lectr. Hastings Center Trial and Appellate Advocacy Hastings Coll. Law and conv.-seminar Internat. Acad. Trial Lawyers, San Francisco, 1978; Bd. dirs. Ft. Pitt Museum Assos.; chmn. exec. com. Pitts. chpt. Am. Jewish Com.; mem. ann. giving fund bd. U. Pitts.; bd. visitors U. Pitts. Sch. Law, 1978—. Served from pvt. to capt. AUS, World War II. Fellow Internat. Acad. Trial Lawyers (dir. 1970-76); mem. Am. (vice chmn. civil practice and procedure com. of antitrust law sect.), Pa., Allegheny County bar assns., Internat. Soc. Barristers (bd. govs.), World Assn. Lawyers (founder, life mem.), Supreme Ct. Hist. Soc., Nat. Assn. R.R. Trial Counsel, Judge Adv. Gen. Assn., Acad. Trial Lawyers Allegheny County (pres. 1962-63), Am. Law Inst., Def. Research Inst., Pa. Def. Inst., World Peace Through Law Center, Res. Officers Assn. U.S., U. Pitts. Law Sch. Alumni Assn. (past pres), Pa. Soc., Order of Coif, Phi Beta Kappa. Jewish. Clubs: Masons; U. Mich. (past pres.), Downtown (past pres.), Concordia, Lawyers (Pitts.). Author: Handbook and Guide to the Federal Coal Mine Health and Safety Act of 1969 and Related State Statutes, 1970; editor-in-chief U. Pitts. Law Rev., 1936-37. Home: 5419 Northumberland St Pittsburgh PA 15217 Office: Oliver Bldg Pittsburgh PA 15222

SCHMIDT, JAMES LEE, physician, clin. pharmacologist; b. Clarksburg, W. Va., July 26, 1935; s. Edmund Charles and Lois (Coffman) S.; A.B., W.Va. U., 1958, M.S. in Pharmacology, 1961, Ph.D. in Pharmacology, 1962, M.D., 1964; m. Eleanor Jane White, Aug. 18, 1957; children—Eleanor Jane, James L. II; m. 2d., Fredericka Ann Singer, May 16, 1970. Research asst. dept. pharmacology W.Va. U. Med. Center, summer 1962, grad. asst., med. pharmacology lab., 1960-62, instr. pharmacology Sch. Medicine, 1962-64, lectr., 1961-63, 63-64; intern Meml. Hosp., Charleston, W.Va., 1964-65; resident in pediatrics, 1965; sr. instr. Sch. Submarine Medicine, Naval Submarine Base, Groton, Conn., 1967; dir. health, North Stonington, Conn., 1968—; sch. physician Burrough of Stonington, 1968—; cons. physician Mystic Manor Convalescent Hosp. (Conn.), 1967-69, chief of staff, 1969—; mem. profl. adv. group Stonington Vis. Nurses Assn., 1967—; attending physician Westerly (R.I.) Hosp., 1968—; referral staff Lawrence and Meml. Hosps., New London, Conn., 1968—; med. dir. marine youth programs Marine Hist. Soc., 1969—, Edward Weck, Inc., 1971—, Cerro Wire & Cable Corp., Mystic, 1972—; dir. health Town of Groton, 1969—; Town of Stonington, 1972—; individual practice family medicine, Mystic, 1967—. Pres., PTA Noank Elementary Sch., Conn., 1968-69. Bd. dirs., incorporator Mystic River Homes, Groton Vis. Nurses Assn. USPHS fellow, 1960-61, 61-62. Served with USNR, 1965-68. Fellow Royal Soc. Health; mem. AMA, AAAS, Indsl. Med. Assn., Conn. Indsl. Med. Assn., Am. Pub. Health Assn., Am. Acad. Clin. Toxicology, East African Wild Life Soc. (sponsor), Theta Chi, Alpha Phi Omega, Phi Beta Pi (sec. 1958-61, pres. 1961-62), Sigma Xi. Rotarian (dir Mystic, Conn. 1969-72), Mason (K.T. Shriner, 32 deg.), Elk. Contbr. articles to profl. jours. Home: Pequot Trail Stonington CT 06378 Office: Box 38 Mystic CT 06355

SCHMIDT, JANET ANNE, market specialist; b. Bklyn., July 31, 1945; d. Arthur and Rita Beatrice (Belden) Leary; A.A., S.I. Community Coll., 1968; B.A., Pace U., 1972; m. Richard Arthur Schmidt, Feb. 14, 1976. Librarian, Morgan Guaranty Trust Co., N.Y.C., 1965-67; chief librarian Mktg. Library, Joseph E. Seagram & Son Ltd., N.Y.C., 1967-69; chief librarian Mktg. Library, Olin Corp., Stamford, Conn., 1969-71; chief librarian corp. bus. library Am. Can Co., Greenwich, Conn., 1971-77; market specialist Disclosure Inc., N.Y.C., 1978, Environ. Info. Center, N.Y.C., 1978—. Apptd. mem. Conn. Target 76 Com. Mem. TAPPI, Spl. Library Assn. (pres. Hudson Valley chpt.), Southwestern Conn. Library Group (pres. 1973-74), Am. Soc. Info. Sci., ALA, Nat. Microfilm Assn., Am. Dog Owners Assn., St. Bernard Club Am. Club: Midday. Editor On-Line Systems Jour. Home: Oak Hill Bridgewater CT 06752 Office: Environ Info Center 292 Madison Ave New York City NY 10007

SCHMIDT, PAUL RUDOLF, mining engr.; b. Glogau, Germany; s. Paul and Mary (Kuegaloth) S.; came to Can., 1951; B.Sc., Sir George Williams U., 1967; m. Joan Leslie McMannis; children—Karen, Mark, Donald. Research technician Imperial Tobacco Co. Ltd., Montreal, Que., Can., 1959-64; successively asso. scientist, project engr., pilot plant supr., group leader Noranda Mines Ltd., Montreal and Noranda, Que., 1965-70; tech. asst. to dir. process tech. Internat. Nickel Co. Can. Ltd., Toronto, 1970-75; project engr. Rio Algom Ltd., Uranium Mining, Toronto, 1975—. Registered profl. engr., Ont. Mem. Am. Inst. Mining, Metall. and Petroleum Engrs., Canadian Inst. Mining and Metallurgy. Author, patentee in field. Home: 1205 Stavebank Rd Mississauga ON L5G 2V1 Canada Office: 120 Adelaide St W Toronto ON Canada

SCHMIDT, RAYMOND PAUL, historian; b. Western, Nebr., Sept. 14, 1937; s. Reuben Edward and Angeline Agnes (Kudlik) S.; B.A., U. Nebr., 1958; M.A., U. Wis., 1966; postgrad. U. Md., 1960-62, Am. U., 1975—; m. Roberta Ruth Schrom, June 11, 1961; 1 son, Douglas Craig. Instr. history, Madison, 1966-68; historian, archivist, records mgr., security mgr. Naval Security Group Command, 1968—. Mem. com., merit badge counselor Boy Scouts Am., 1974—. Served with USN, 1959-64. Mem. Am. Hist. Assn., Acad. Polit. Sci., U.S. Commn. Mil. History, Soc. Am. Archivists, U.S. Naval Inst., Nat. Classification Mgmt. Soc., Nat. Council Social Studies, Res. Officers Assn., Naval Res. Assn., U. Nebr. Alumni Assn., Nat. Trust Historic Preservation. Office: 3801 Nebraska Ave NW Washington DC 20390

SCHMIDT, RICHARD PENROSE, physician, health services facility exec.; b. Akron, Ohio, July 27, 1921; s. Richard Homer and Frances Angeline (Speakman) S.; studen Miami U., Oxford, Ohio, 1939-40; M.D., U. Louisville, 1945; B.S., Kent State U., 1953; m. Betty Corrine Heminger, June 5, 1943; children—Victoria Frances, Richard Penrose. Asst. prof. U. Wash., 1953-58; asso. prof. U. Fla., 1958-60, prof., 1960-70, head div. neurology, 1958-61, chmn. dept. medicine, 1961-65, asso. dean, 1965-70; dean, v.p. for acad. affairs SUNY Upstate Med. Center, Syracuse, 1970-75, acting pres., 1974-75, pres., 1975—; mem. council Am. Epilepsy Soc., 1956-69, sec., 1960-63, pres., 1964; chmn. Nat. Com. for Research in Neurol. and Communicative Disorders, 1975-76, chmn. emeritus, 1976—; chmn. med. adv. bd. Nat. Multiple Sclerosis Soc., 1977-78; bd. dirs. Plaza Nursing Home, Research Found. SUNY. Served as capt. M.C., U.S. Army, 1946-48. Diplomate Am. Bd. Psychiatry and Neurology. Mem. Am. Electroencephalographic Soc., AMA, Am. Neurol. Assn., Assn. Research in Nervous and Mental Disease, A.C.P., Internat. Fedn. Multiple Sclerosis Socs., Middle States Assn. Colls. and Secondary Schs., N.Y. State Health Research Council, N.Y. State Health Systems Agy., Onondaga County (N.Y.) Med. Soc., Am. Acad. Neurology (trustee 1961-71, pres. 1967-69), Sigma Xi, Alpha Omega Alpha. Author: (with B.J. Wilder) Epilepsy, 1968; contbr. numerous articles to med. jours. Home: 6282 Quintard Rd Jamesville NY 13078 Office: 750 E Adams St Syracuse NY 13210*

SCHMIDT, THOMAS CARSON, state ofcl.; b. York, Pa., Oct. 15, 1930; s. George Small and Josephine Foot (Reifsnider) S.; A.B., Princeton, 1952; M.Div., Va. Sem., 1955; Ph.D. in Policy Scis., State U. N.Y., 1971; m. Lucy Carter Searby, Aug. 21, 1954; children—Peter, Lucy, Thomas. Ordained to ministry Episcopalian Ch., 1955; rector St. Alban's Ch., Bogotá, Colombia, 1955-58; asst. St. James', New London, Conn., 1958-61; rector St. Andrew's, Longmeadow, Mass., 1961-68, on leave serving Diocese Zululand-Swaziland, South Africa, 1965-68; mgmt. cons., 1968-71; asst. commr. edn. State of R.I., Providence, 1971-73; spl. asst. to R.I. Gov. for Policy and and Program Rev., 1973-74; commr. edn., R.I., 1975—. Mgmt. cons. to nat. and fgn. firms. Mem. priorities com., steering com. Ednl. Commn. States; vice chmn. legislative com. Chief State Sch. Officers. Mem. State Higher Edn. Exec. Officers Assn., Internat. Assn. Applied Social Scientists. Home: 28 Benefit St Providence RI 02904 Office: Office of Commr Suite 200 Dept Edn 199 Promenade St Providence RI 02903

SCHMIDT, WILLIAM MAX, paper co. exec.; b. Danville, Pa., Nov. 23, 1947; s. Frank Wilhelm and Doris Savilla (Maurer) S.; B.S., U. Pa., 1969; M.B.A., Northwestern U., 1971. Mktg. specialist Moody's Investors Service, N.Y.C., 1971-72; dir. mktg. research, 1972-73; asso. cons. William E. Hill & Co., Inc., N.Y.C., 1973-75; mgr. mktg. analysis, white papers group Internat. Paper Co., N.Y.C., 1975-77, product supr. carbonizing tissue, white papers group, 1977—. Adviser, Jr. Achievement; mem. Knickerbocker Republican Club. Mem. U. Pa. Assn. N.Y.C. (dir.), Wharton Bus. Sch. Club N.Y., Am. Paper Inst., N. Am. Soc. Corp. Planning, Am. Mktg. Assn., Am. Forestry Assn., S.R. Mem. United Ch. Christ. Clubs: St. Bartholomew Community, Univ. Glee N.Y., Miramar Ski, University. Home: 147 E 82d St New York City NY 10028 Office: 220 E 42d St New York City NY 10017

SCHMITT, ABRAHAM, educator, marriage counselor, therapist; b. Sask., Can., Aug. 7, 1927 (came to U.S. 1951, naturalized 1960); s. Jacob and Maria (Friesen) S.; B.A., Goshen Coll. and Bibl. Sem., 1953, B.E. and B.D., 1955; M.S.W., U. Pa., 1958, certificate marriage counseling, 1961, advanced curriculum certificate, 1962, D.Social Work, 1966; m. Dorothy Stover, Aug. 14, 1954; children—Mary Lou, Ruth Ann, David Dean, Lois Lynn. Dir. mental health worker tng. Phila. State Hosp., 1963-68; asst. prof. social work in psychiatry, dept. psychiatry and Grad. Sch. Social Work, U. Pa., 1968-74, tng. supr. The Marriage Council, 1968-74; supr. clin. services Pastoral Inst. Lehigh Valley, Allentown, Pa., 1968—; adj. prof. Marywood Coll., 1974—; lectr. Mainland Inst., 1974—; cons. Bethanna Home for Boys and Girls, 1972—. Mem. Nat. Assn. Social Work, Acad. Certified Social Workers, Am. Assn. Marriage and Family Counselors (supr.). Mem. Mennonite Ch. Author: Dialogue with Death, The Art of Listening with Love. Home: 165 S 4th St Souderton PA 18964

SCHMITT, ROGER MICHAEL LAWRENCE, ins. broker; b. N.Y.C., Oct. 21, 1952. Ins. broker Johnson & Higgins, N.Y.C.; with Coll. of Ins., N.Y.C.; instr. Center for the Blind. Mem. St. George's Soc. N.Y., English Speaking Union, Am. Flag Inst., New Eng. Soc., Royal Oak Found., Hist. Register U.S. Army, St. Andrews Soc., Am. Scottish Found., Mil. Soc. War 1812, Order Stars and Bars, SAR, St. Nicholas Soc., Soc. Mayflower Descs., Downtown Assn., Order Founders and Patriots Am., Order Crown Charlemagne, Baronial Order Magna Charta, Soc. Descs. Signers Declaration Independence, Huguenot Soc., Mil. Order Loyal Legion, Soc. Colonial Wars, Mil. Order Fgn. Wars, Order Colonial Lords Manors, Soc. Calif. Pioneers, U.S. Polo Assn., U.S. Ct. Tennis Assn. Phi Beta Kappa. Republican. Clubs: Sandanona Hare, Hounds (Millbrook); Winter Wheezers (Oyster Bay); Piping Rock (Locust Valley); Theodore Roosevelt Sanctuary; Am. Fox Hound; N.Y. Croquet. Author: Anthology of 1000 Poems, 1970. Home: Woodbine House Muttontown Rd Muttontown PO Syosset NY 11791 Office: Johnson and Higgins 95 Wall St New York City NY 10005

SCHMITZ, KAREN LEE, mfg. co. exec.; b. Warwick, N.Y., Dec. 6, 1946; d. Willard Franklin and May Bernyce (Maconeghy) Schmitz; B.S. magna cum laude, Western Carolina U., 1968. Gen. accountant Gen. Telephone Co. S.E., Durham, N.C., 1968, tax accountant, 1968-69, revenue accounting supr., 1969-70, internal auditor, 1970-71, disbursements supr., 1971-72, supr. div. revenue, 1972-73, mgr. revenues and earnings, 1973-77; adminstr. revenue requirements GTE Service Corp., Stamford, Conn., 1977—; lectr. in field Named Career Woman, City Durham, 1974. Mem. Nat. Assn. Accountants (chpt. pres. 1972-73, nat. dir. 1975—), Western Carolina Univ. Alumni Assn., Bus. and Profl. Womens Club, Beta Sigma Phi (v.p. chpt. 1972). Democrat. Roman Catholic. Club: Toastmasters. Office: Dept Regulatory Matters GTE Service Corp One Stamford Forum Stamford CT 06904

SCHMOKE, SARAH LEE LINNETTE, counselor handicapped students; b. Norfolk, Va., June 30, 1912; d. Samuel and Susie Etta Linnette; certificate Norfolk unit Va. Union U., 1942; B.S., Shaw U., 1944; M.Ed., Pa. State U., 1952; m. Harold Louis Schmoke, Mar. 5, 1951; 1 dau., Harriette Parham. Tchr. home econs. New Hope High Sch., Rutherfordton, N.C., 1944-47; asst. dietician Shaw U., Raleigh, N.C., 1947-52; tchr. home econs. Rockingham (N.C.) High Sch., 1952-53, Bell Alton (Md.), 1953-66, Indianhead (Md.) High Sch., 1966-67, Banneker Jr. High Sch., Washington, 1967-68; counselor Sharpe Health Sch., handicapped students, Washington, 1968—. Sec. Shiloh Mut. Aid Soc., Shiloh Bapt. Ch., 1968—; treas. 45th. Pl. Block Club, 1974. Mem. Am., Nat Capitol personnel and guidance assns., D.C., Am. sch. counselors assns., Washington Tchrs. Union, Women's Bus. and Profl. Orgn., Delta Sigma Theta. Baptist. Home: 1100 45th Pl St Washington DC 20019

SCHMUCKLER, STANLEY LLOYD, mgmt. services co. exec.; b. New Rochelle, N.Y., Mar. 25, 1925; s. Joseph and Ida S.; B.B.A., Iona Coll., 1949; M.B.A., N.Y. U., 1955; m. Margaret E. Joyce, Oct. 3, 1959; children—Joseph Redmond, Joyce Ann, Frances Catherine, John David. Asst. to dir. indsl. relations Am. Cable & Radio Corp., N.Y.C., 1950-55; mgr. tng. Farnsworth Electronics Corp., Fort Wayne, Ind., 1956-57; personnel mgr. Fed. Electric Corp., Paramus, N.J., 1957-65; dir. personnel ITT Data Services, Paramus, 1966-69; dir. personnel, sr. v.p. personnel and manpower planning div. Seattle First Nat. Bank, 1969-75; prin. Mgmt. Services Co., 1975—; dir. exec. resources Sun Co., Inc., Radnor, Pa., 1976—. Instr. mgmt. Purdue U. extension, Fort Wayne, 1956-57; vice chmn. Advisory Council on State Govt. Productivity. Served with USNR, 1943-45. Mem. Am. (employee relations com.), Wash. bankers assns., Bank Adminstrn. Inst., Pacific N.Y. Mgmt. Assn., Am. Soc. Personnel Adminstrn., Assn. Wash. Bus. Western Pension Conf., Am. Mgmt. Assn. Republican. Roman Catholic. Home: 3214 Saw Mill Rd Newton Sq PA 19073 Office: care Sun Company Inc Matsonford Rd Radnor PA 19087

SCHMUKLER, ANITA GLORIA, physician; b. Phila., Mar. 9, 1941; d. Martin Edward and Rose (Schwartz) S.; B.A., Temple U., 1964; D.O., Coll. Osteo. Medicine and Surgery, Phila., 1970. Intern, Cherry Hill (N.J.) Med. Center, 1970-71; resident in psychiatry Phila. Psychiat. Center, 1971-74; practice medicine, specializing in pschiatry, Phila., 1974—; clin. instr. psychiatry U. Pa. Med. Sch., Phila., 1978—; unit dir. Phila. Psychiat. Center, 1976-77, staff psychiatrist, 1977—. Diplomate Am. Bd. Psychiatry and Neurology. Mem. Pa., Philadelphia County med. socs., Am. Psychiat. Assn., Am. Psychoanalytic Assn. (affiliate). Office: D-119 Presidential Apts Philadelphia PA 19131

SCHMUT, RUDOLF, cons. on pollution control and paper sci.; b. Graz, Austria, Apr. 10, 1930; s. Hubert and Johanna Maria (Roeder) S.; B.S., Inst. Tech., Graz, 1951, B.Engring., 1954, M.Engring., 1955, D.Sc., 1957; A.B., Western Mich. U., 1952. Came to U.S., 1957, naturalized, 1965. Sr. research chemist Westvaco, Charleston, S.C., 1957-66; mgr. devel. Texon, South Hadley, Mass., 1966-67, spl. cons. to pres., sr. research asso., 1968-70; cons. pollution control, pulp and paper mgmt., Indian Orchard, Mass., 1967—; mgr. research and devel. Spaulding Fibre Co., Rochester, N.Y., 1968; pres. Capital Laundry Co., Indian Orchard, 1972, Eco Systems, Inc., Indian Orchard, 1972; paper scientist Scott Paper Co., Phila., 1974; mng. chemist Folienwalzwerke Teich, St. Pölten, Austria, 1975; project mgr. engring. and equipment div. Vöestalpine, Linz, Austria, 1976—. State commr. Boy Scouts, Graz, 1954-57. Recipient Fulbright grants, 1951-52, 55. Registered profl. engr., Mass., N.H. Mem. N.Y., S.C. acads. scis., Am. Acad. Polit. and Social Scis., Acad. Polit. Sci., T.A.P.P.I. (dir.), Am. Soc. Testing and Materials, A.A.A.S., Paper Industry Mgmt. Assn., Am. Mgmt. Assn., Vols. for Internat. Tech. Assistance, Am. Inst. Chem. engrs., Nat. Soc. Profl. Engrs., Engrs. Club N.Y., Acad. Papermakers Soc., Alpha Phi Omega. Clubs: Charleston Yacht; Austrian Alpine (Graz); Chemists (N.Y.); Homestead (Hot Springs, Va.). Contbr. articles to profl. jours. Patentee in field. Home: Chemists Club 52 E 41st St New York City NY 10017 Office: Harterfeldstrasse 9/144 A 4060 Leonding Austria

SCHMUTZHART, SLAITHONG CHENGTRAKUL, sculptor, educator; b. Bangkok, Thailand, Jan. 1, 1934; d. Kemp and Sunee Chengtrakul; B.A. in Fine Arts, Corcoran Sch. Art, 1970; postgrad. U. D.C., 1972-77; m. Berthold Schmutzhart, Aug. 25, 1962. Asst. lectr. sculpture Office of Econ. Opportunity, 1965; instr. art Kingsbury Center Lab. Sch., Washington, 1968-71; lectr. sculpture Mt. Vernon Coll., Washington, 1979—; one-woman exhibitions include: Franz Bader Gallery, Washington, 1977, U. D.C., 1977, Mt. Vernon Coll., 1979; group exhibitions include: Nat. Collection Fine Arts, Washington, 1964, Fredericksburg (Va.) Gallery Modern Art, 1967, 73, Corcoran Gallery Art, 1972, Textile Mus., Washington, 1973, Internat. Monetary Fund, Washington, 1976; represented in permanent collections: City of Inkster (Mich.). Ford Found. fellow, 1966. Mem. Artists Equity Assn. Buddhist. Address: 1011 E Capitol St Washington DC 20003

SCHNABEL, WILHELM JOSEPH, chemist; b. Berlin, Germany, July 9, 1915; came to U.S., 1955, naturalized, 1960; M.S., U. Goettingen, 1947; Ph.D., U. Berlin, 1949; m. Marguerite Engel, Apr. 26, 1958; children—Joachim, Robert, Johannes. Instr. chemistry U. Berlin (Germany), 1948-50; research chemist Riedel de Haen AG, Berlin, 1950-55; research chemist Olin Corp., 1955—, sr. research asso., 1965—. Mem. Am. Chem. Soc., Sigma Xi. Contbr. articles to sci. jours. Patentee chem. products and processes. Home: 28 Sunset Hill Dr Pine Orchard CT 06405 Office: Olin Corp 275 Winchester Ave New Haven CT 06504

SCHNALL, EDITH LEA (MRS. HERBERT SCHNALL), educator; b. N.Y.C., Apr. 11, 1922; d. Irving and Sadie (Raab) Spitzer; A.B., Hunter Coll., 1942; A.M., Columbia U., 1947, Ph.D., 1967; m. Herbert Schnall, Aug. 21, 1949; children—Neil David, Carolyn Beth. Clin. pathologist Roosevelt Hosp., N.Y.C., 1942-44; instr. Adelphi Coll., Garden City, N.Y., 1944-46; asst. med. mycologist Columbia Coll. Physicians and Surgeons, N.Y.C., 1946-47, 49-50; instr. Bklyn. Coll., 1947; faculty Sarah Lawrence Coll., Bronxville, N.Y., 1947-48; lectr. Hunter Coll., N.Y.C., 1947-67; adj. asso. prof. Lehman Coll., City U. N.Y., 1968; asst. prof. Queensborough Community Coll., City U. N.Y., 1967, asso. prof. microbiology, 1968-75, prof., 1975—; vis. prof. Coll. Physicians and Surgeons, Columbia U., N.Y.C., 1974; advanced biology examiner U. London, 1970—. Mem. Alley Restoration Com., N.Y.C., 1971—; mem. legis. adv. com. Assembly State of N.Y., 1972; mem. Community Planning Bd. #11, Queens, N.Y., 1974—; pub. dir. of bd. dirs. Inst. Continuing Dental Edn. of 11th dist. Dental Soc. State of N.Y. and ADA, 1973—. Research fellow NIH, 1948-49; Faculty Research fellow, grantee-in-aid Research Found. State U. N.Y., 1968-70; Faculty research grant Research Found. City U. N.Y., 1971-74. Mem. Internat. Soc. Human and Animal Mycology, AAAS, Am. Soc. Microbiology, Med. Mycology Soc. N.Y. (sec.-treas. 1967-68, v.p. 1968-69, 78-79, pres. 1969-70), Bot. Soc. Am., Med. Mycology Soc. Americas, Mycology Soc. Am., N.Y. Acad. Scis., Sigma Xi, Phi Sigma. Clubs: Torrey Bot. (N.Y. State); Queensborough Community Coll. Women's (pres. 1971-73) (N.Y.C.). Editor newsletter Med. Mycology Soc. N.Y., 1969—; founder, editor Female Perspective newsletter of Queensborough Community Coll. Women's Club, 1971-73. Home: 214-06 29th Ave Bayside NY 11360

SCHNECKENBURGER, ROGER CARL, architect; b. Warsaw, N.Y., Aug. 4, 1932; s. Carl John and Ruby Mae (Mead) S.; B.S. in Landscape Arch., Mich. State Coll., 1955; m. Grace Redfield Tennant, Aug. 8, 1959; children—Laurel Ann, Amy Lynn, Jill Karen. Landscape mgr. Four Winds Nursery, Inc., Getzville, N.Y., 1958-66; landscape architect Kideney, Smith & Fitzgerald, Buffalo, 1966-71; pvt. practice landscape architecture, site planner, Glenwood, N.Y., 1971—. Cons. Village of Lancaster (N.Y.), 1973—, Town of Colden (N.Y.), 1973—, Town of Brant (N.Y.), 1973—, Western N.Y. Nurserymen's Assn., 1962—, Fed. Hist. Renovation Ansley Wilcox Mansion, Buffalo, 1973—. Bd. dirs. Maude Gordon Holmes Arboretum, Buffalo, 1971—, v.p., 1973—. Served to 1st lt. AUS, 1955-58. Mem. Buffalo C. of C., Am. Soc. Landscape Architects, Western N.Y. Nurserymen's Assn. Presbyterian (elder 1973—). Rotarian. Archtl. works include Mirror Lake, Buffalo, Greenlake, Orchard Park, N.Y., Cherry Street Pedestrian Mall, Jamestown, N.Y., Lancaster (N.Y.) Urban Core, Ransom Oaks Planned Unit Devel., Amherst, N.Y. Address: Hardwood Ct Glenwood NY 14069

SCHNEIDER, BERNARD ARNOLD, govt. ofcl.; b. Washington, June 8, 1944; s. Samuel Louis and Beatrice (Yuter) S.; B.S., U. Md., 1966, M.S. (Alpha Zeta scholar), 1968, Ph.D., 1971; m. Barbara Beth Adelman, June 22, 1968; children—Eileen Harriet, Deborah Faye. Research aide, agronomy dept. U. Md., 1963; lab. technician, mycology investigations U.S. Dept. Agr., Beltsville, Md., 1964-66; grad. asst. agronomy dept. U. Md., College Park, 1966-71; plant physiologist EPA, Beltsville, Md., 1972—. Chmn. Plant Biology Seminars, 1972—. Recipient certificate of scholarships, U. Md., 1964-66, Outstanding award for outstanding grad. student in biol. scis. Phi Sigma, 1971, letter of commendation Outstanding Reregistration Task Force. Mem. Am. Soc. Agronomy (outstanding sr. award 1966), Weed Sci. Soc. Am., Plant Growth Regulator Working Group (chmn. nomenclature com.), Northeastern Weed Sci. Soc., ASTM, Agronomy Grad. Student Orgn. (vice chmn. 1970), Nat. Wildlife Soc., Sigma Xi, Alpha Zeta (censor 1966), Phi Kappa Phi, Phi Sigma. Co-author manual on field crops. Contbr. articles to profl. jours. Home: 9517 Farewell Rd Columbia MD 21045 Office: Plant Biology Lab EPA Agr Research Center-E Bldg 402 Beltsville MD 20705

SCHNEIDER, BEVERLY ANN, nursing adminstr.; b. Phillipsburg, N.J., July 10, 1948; d. Richard and Mildred G. Crouse; B.S. in Nursing, Hartwick Coll., 1970; m. William Stanley, Sept. 6, 1975; 1 dau., Stacie Leigh. Nurse, Warren County (N.J.) Pub. Health Service, 1970-73; dir. staff devel., now dir. patient edn. Hackettstown (N.J.) Community Hosp., 1972—. Bd. mgrs. Am. Cancer Soc.; med. adv. bd. Keltating chpt. Juvenile Diabetic Assn. Mem. Am. Diabetes Assn., Am. Heart Assn., Am. Nurses Assn. Home: Box 99 Pierson Ln Buttzville NJ 07829 Office: Hackettstown Community Hosp Hackettstown NJ 07840

SCHNEIDER, CARL STANLEY, physicist, educator; b. Balt., Dec. 20, 1942; s. Stanley Samuel and Viola Jeannette (Sayles) S.; B.A., Johns Hopkins U., 1963; S.M., Mass. Inst. Tech., 1965, Ph.D., 1968; m. Carole Anne Bottom, Dec. 24, 1971; children—Kathleen Suzanne, James Andrew. Asso. prof. physics U.S. Naval Acad., Annapolis, Md., 1968—; guest physicist Nat. Bur. Standards, 1968-76; guest physicist Naval Ship Research and Devel. Center, Annapolis, 1976—, cons., 1976—. Cape St. Claire (Md.) rep. Broadneck Fedn. Md., 1973; bd. govs. Cape St. Claire, 1978—; pres. Lower Broadneck Fedn., 1974-76. NSF grantee, 1974-76. Mem. Broadneck Jaycees (v.p. 1976-77), Am. Phys. Soc., Phi Beta Kappa, Sigma Xi. Republican. Methodist. Contbr. articles to profl. jours. Home: 1047 Little Magothy View Annapolis MD 21401

SCHNEIDER, CARL WILLIAM, lawyer; b. Phila., Apr. 27, 1932; s. Nathan J. and Eleanor (Milgram) S.; B.A., Cornell U., 1953; LL.M. magna cum laude, U. Pa., 1956; m. Mary Ellen Baylinson, Mar. 3, 1957; children—Eric M., Mark A., Adam D., Cara L. Admitted to Pa. bar, 1957; law clk. U.S. Ct. Appeals for Third Circuit, Phila., 1956-57; sr. law clk. U.S. Supreme Ct., 1957-58; mem. firm Wolf, Block, Schorr & Solis-Cohen, Phila., 1958—, partner, 1965—; spl. adviser div. corp. fin. SEC, Washington, 1964; lectr. securities law U. Pa. Law Sch., 1968-70, vis. asso. prof., 1978-80, acting dir. Center for Study of Fin. Instns., 1978-79; mem. adv. bd. N.Y. U. Sch. Law Securities Inst.; bd. editors, advisors Rev. of Securities Regulation. Mem. Am., Fed., Pa., Phila. (co-chmn. com. on secrities regulation 1967-70) bar assns. Author: SEC Consequences of Corporate Acquisitions, 1971; editorial advisory bd. Securities Regulation Law Jour.; contbr. articles in field to profl. jours. Office: 12th floor Packard Bldg Philadelphia PA 19102

SCHNEIDER, ERICH, cardiologist; b. Porto Alegre, Brazil, Apr. 12, 1937; s. Alfred and Sybil (Lautert) S.; naturalized, 1974; B.S., Fed. U. R.G. Sul, Brazil, 1958, M.D., 1964; m. Marilynne M. Theis, Sept. 19, 1970; 1 son, Erich Alfred. Intern, Univ. Hosps., Fed. U. R.G. Sul, Brazil, 1965; asst. prof. medicine Catholic Med. Sch., Porto Alegre, Brazil, 1967-68; fellow in cardiology St. Vincent Charity Hosp., Cleve., 1968-70; resident in medicine Case Western Res. U., 1971-73, resident in cardiology, 1973-75; attending physician Lourdes Hosp., Binghamton, N.Y., 1975—, Wilson Hosp., Johnson Cit, N.Y., 1975—, Gen. Hosp., Binghamton, 1975—; clin. instr. State U. N.Y. Diplomate Am. Bd. Cardiovascular Disease, Am. Bd. Internal Medicine. Fellow Am. Coll. Cardiology, Council on Clin. Cardiology of Am. Heart Assn.; mem. AMA, N.Y. State, Broome County med. socs., Am. Heart Assn. (dir. 1977-79, chmn. physician edn. Broome County chpt.). Republican. Home: 616 Stonehedge Dr Vestal NY 13850 Office: 3 Park Ave Binghamton NY 13903

SCHNEIDER, JULIUS, ophthalmologist; b. N.Y.C., June 6, 1912; s. Morris and Frieda (Hacker) S.; B.S., N.Y. U., 1933, M.D., 1937; m. Beatrice Spring, Dec. 22, 1940; children—Richard and Lawrence (twins). Intern, Beth Israel and Lincoln hosps., N.Y.C., 1937-40; asst. fellow in pathology Mt. Sinai Hosp., N.Y.C., 1940; resident in ophthalmology N.Y.C. VA Hosp., 1940-44; practice medicine specializing in ophthalmology, N.Y.C., 1947—; mem. staffs Manhattan Eye and Ear and N.Y. hosps.; cons. N.Y.C. Dept. Health. Served to maj. M.C., AUS, 1944-46. Diplomate Am. Bd. Ophthalmology. Fellow A.C.S., Am. Acad. Ophthalmology and Otolaryngology; mem. AMA, AAAS, Assn. Research in Ophthalmology. Jewish. Contbr. articles to profl. jours. Home: 105 Hanson Ln New Rochelle NY 10804 Office: 903 Lexington Ave New York City NY 10021

SCHNEIDER, ROBERT WILLIAM, metal co. exec.; b. S.I., N.Y., Dec. 30, 1925; s. Otto William and Anna Viola (Androvette) S.; B.S. (Merck fellow) Lehigh U., 1948, M.S. (Merck fellow), 1949; m. Phyllis Mae Rantz, Dec. 24, 1946; children—Craig Robert, Dean Alan, David William. Asst. design and metall. engr. Linde Air Products Co., Tonawanda, N.Y., 1949-54; head code fabrication shop inspection dept. Travelers Indemnity Co., Hartford, Conn., 1954-60; asst. supt. engring. dept. Oak Ridge Nat. Lab., 1960-68; v.p. engring. Bonney Forge div. Gulf & Western Industries, Inc., Allentown, Pa., 1968—, also cons. other divs. of corp. Mem. Springhouse Farms Civic Assn. Served to ensign USNR, 1943-46. Registered profl. engr., Ont., Can., Pa. Mem. ASME (chmn. subgroup design rules, subgroup on openings, mem. petroleum refinery code), Welding Research Council (vice chmn. design div. pressure vessel research com., mem. subgroup on bolted flanged connections). Presbyn. Contbr. tech. papers to profl. publs. Home: 3918 Lincoln Pkwy W Allentown PA 18104 Office: Cedar and Meadow Sts Allentown PA 18105

SCHNELLER, EUGENE STEWART, educator, sociologist; b. Cornwall, N.Y., Apr. 9, 1943; s. Michael Nicholas and Anne Ruth (Gruner) S.; B.A. in Sociology, C.W. Post Coll., 1967; Ph.D., N.Y. U., 1973; m. Ellen Ann Stauber, Mar. 24, 1968; 1 son, Andrew Jon. Research asst. sociology N.Y. U., 1968-70; project dir. Montefiore Hosp. and Med. Center, N.Y.C., 1970-72; asst. prof. community health scis. and sociology Duke U., 1972-75; asso. prof., chmn. dept. sociology Union Coll., Schenectady, 1975—, dir. Health Studies Center, 1978—; dir. health adminstrn. program Albany Coll. Pharmacy/Ohio Coll., 1978—. Recipient Founders Day award N.Y. U., 1973. Mem. Am., Internat. sociol. assns., Soc. Study of Social Problems, N.Y. State Health Research Council, Health Systems Agy. Author: A Comprehensive Bibliography on Physician's Assistants, 1974; Interprofessional Legal Practitioners: The Case of the M.D.-LL.B., 1975; The Design and Evolution of the Physician's Assistant, 1976; The Physician's Assistant, 1978. Home: 2513 Hilltop Rd Schenectady NY 12309 Office: Dept Sociology Social Scis Bldg Union Coll Schenectady NY 12308

SCHNURMANN, ERIKA, librarian; b. Paterson, N.J.; d. Karl and Martha (Buegen) S.; A.B., Pembroke Coll., 1937; postgrad. Simmons Coll., 1938; M.L.S., Columbia U., 1947. Head pub. relations and order dept. Paterson Pub. Library, 1942-66; dir. Hawthorne (N.J.) Pub. Library, 1966-68, Little Falls (N.J.) Pub. Library, 1968-69, Kearny (N.J.) Pub. Library, 1969—; librarians-cons. Wayne (N.J.) Pub. Library, 1960-64, West Paterson Pub. Library, 1961-62, Nursing Edn. Library, Paterson Gen. Hosp., 1963; pub. relations cons. Morris County Library, 1967; asso. book reviewer Paterson Morning Call, 1955-57. Sec. program chmn. Council Service Clubs, 1960-62; sec. Hudson County Revolutionary Bicentennial Com., 1973-76; active various civic affairs. Mem. AAUW, N.J. Press Women's Club, Nat. League Am. Pen Women (pres. North Jersey chpt. 1974-76), N.J. Library Assn., Bergen-Passaic County Library Club (past pres.), North Jersey Libraries Round Table (past chmn.), Hudson County Library Assn. (pres. 1972-74), South Bergen-West Hudson C. of C., Kearny Safety Council, Library Pub. Relations Council of N.Y., Passaic County Health, Edn. and Welfare Assn. (past pres.), Chaucer Guild. Contbr. articles to profl. jours. and newspapers. Home: 335 Sylvan St Rutherford NJ 07070 Office: 318 Kearny Ave Kearny NJ 07032

SCHOCK, WILLIAM WALLACE, physician; b. Huntingdon, Pa., Aug. 15, 1923; s. Clarence and Mabel (Decker) S.; student Juniata Coll., 1941-43; M.D., Temple U., 1947; m. Doris Ann Wilson, July 1, 1944; 1 son, William Wallace. Intern Conemaugh Meml. Hosp., Johnstown, Pa., 1946-48; gen. practice medicine, Huntingdon, 1948-50; pediatrician Warren AFB Hosp., 1951-52; chief outpatient service USAF, Cheyenne, Wyo., 1951-52; practice medicine, specializing in pediatrics, Huntingdon, 1952—; pediatrician J. C. Blair Meml. Hosp.; local pub. health pediatrician. Pres. Huntingdon chpt. Am. Cancer Soc., 1955-57. Bd. dirs. local chpt. Am. Heart Assn., 1955-62. Served with AUS, 1942-45, USAF, 1950-52. Recipient Wisdom award, 1970. Fellow Royal Soc. Health; mem. Pa., Huntingdon County (past pres.) med. socs., Med. Alumni Assn. Temple U., Pa., Huntingdon pediatric socs., Am. Assn. Mil. Surgeons U.S., Am. Acad. Gen. Practice (past pres. Huntingdon), Am. Acad. Pediatrics (asso.), A.M.A., Internat. Platform Assn., Phi Rho Sigma. Republican. Presbyn. Rotarian. Clubs: Huntingdon Country, Hiedelburg Country (Altoona, Pa.). Home: RD 2 Huntingdon PA 16652 Office: 213 Standing Stone Ave Huntingdon PA 16652

SCHOEN, DONALD ROBERT, med. equipment mfg. exec.; b. Mt. Vernon, N.Y., Apr. 25, 1920; s. Charles John and Elizabeth (Dietz) S.; B.A., Lehigh U., 1941; M.B.A., Harvard U., 1948; m. Barbara M. Taylor, Nov. 9, 1946; children—Robert, John, Claire, Susan. Mem. tech. staff Bell Telephone Labs., N.Y.C., 1941-46; research asst. Harvard Bus. Sch., 1948-49, instr., 1949-52, asst. prof., 1952-55; v.p. mfg., exec. v.p., dir. Hays Corp., Michigan City, Ind., 1955-57; asst. to pres., regional mgr., v.p. mktg., v.p. and gen. mgr. Picker X-Ray Corp., White Plains, N.Y., 1958-68; sr. asso., prin., v.p. Cresap, McCormick Paget Inc., N.Y.C., 1968-76; sr. v.p. Philips Med. Systems, Inc., Shelton, Conn., 1976-77, pres., 1977—; spl. cons. to Sec. Army, 1951-52; mem. adv. bd. Inst. Mgmt. Cons.'s, 1977—. Chmn. planning commn. Village of Bronxville (N.Y.), 1973-74, trustee, 1974-75, mayor, 1975-78. Served to capt., Signal Corps, AUS, 1943-45. Mem. Phi Beta Kappa. Republican. Mem. Dutch Reformed Ch. Contbr. articles on gen. mgmt. to Harvard Bus. Rev. Home: 101 Park Ave Bronxville NY 10708 Office: Philips Med Systems Inc Shelton CT

SCHOEN, LESTER ARTHUR, optometrist; b. N.Y.C., Jan. 23, 1919; s. Jacob Paul and Pauline (Brendinger) S.; B.S., Columbia U., 1950, O.D., 1951; m. Esther Schoen, June 9, 1946; children—Debra Lynn, Pamela Marcia. Practice optometry, Bay Shore, L.I., N.Y., 1953—; lectr. adult edn., 1958—. Served with U.S. Army, 1940-44. Mem. N.Y. State, Am. optometric socs., Nat. Health Fedn. Jewish. Club: Lions. Contbr. articles to profl. publs. Home: 615 Montauk Hwy West Islip LI NY 11795 Office: 1 E Main St Bay Shore LI NY 11706

SCHOEN, REM, bus. exec.; b. N.Y.C.; d. Harry L. and Rita (Connors) S.; B.S., Trinity Coll., Burlington, Vt., 1951. Registered rep. Bache & Co., N.Y.C., 1956-61; instl. sales Gruntal & Co., 1961-65; v.p., partner, dir. instl. sales Pressman, Frohlich & Frost, Inc., N.Y.C., 1965-74; allied mem. N.Y. Stock Exchange; with Bernard Herold & Co., Inc., N.Y.C., 1974-77, Hamershlag, Kempner & Marks, N.Y.C., 1978—; fin. adviser to banks in Paris, Milan, Geneva. Vol., Lighthouse, N.Y. Assn. for Blind; fund chmn. ex-officio Trinity Coll., also trustee. Author: Childhood Poems, 1972. Home: 225 E 70th St New York City NY 10021 Office: 40 Wall St New York City NY 10005

SCHOENEMAN, CHARLES WILSON, lawyer; b. Washington, Sept. 22, 1931; s. Charles Ralph and Anna Louisa (Wilson) S.; A.B. cum laude, Bowdoin Coll., 1953; LL.B., Harvard U., 1958; m. Dorothy Spalding, Aug. 25, 1962; children—Charlotte Ann, George James, Charles Andrew. Admitted to D.C. bar, 1958, Va. bar, 1972; clk. U.S. Tax Ct., Washington, 1958-59; asso. firm Hogan and Hartson, Washington, 1959-60; asso. frim Silverstein and Mullens, Washington, 1961-65, partner, 1965-72; partner firm Schoeneman and Ralston, Reston, Va., 1973-75; individual pratice law, Reston, 1976—; asso. prof. Law Sch., George Washington U., 1967-70; arbitrator Am. Arbitration Assn. Served with U.S. Army, 1954-55. Mem. Am., Va., D.C. bar assns. Democrat. Episcopalian. Clubs: Nat. Democratic, Nat. Lawyers. Home: 1564 Westmoreland St McLean VA Office: 1819 H St NW Washington DC 20006

SCHOENER, JAMES FRANKLIN, lawyer; b. Piqua, O., Dec. 10, 1923; s. George M. and Faith F. (Stein) S.; B.A., Mich. State Coll., 1948; J.D., U. Mich., 1950; m. Frances Capdarest, Feb. 11, 1949; children—Mary Frances, James Morris. Admitted to Mich. bar, 1950, D.C. bar, 1974; practiced in Muskegon, Mich., 1950-71; circuit judge, 1971-74; minority counsel U.S. senate rules com., 1974-78. Mem. Mich. Codification Election Laws Com., 1955; chmn. drug abuse Com. Nat. Conf. Trial Judges, 1973-76. Chmn., Mich. Fedn. Young Republicans, 1954-55; campaign mgr. Griffin for Senator, 1966. Former chmn. Mich. Bd. Canvassers. Served to 1st lt. USAAF, 1944-46. Mem. Muskegon County (pres.), Am. (criminal law sect. drug com.), D.C., Fed. bar assns., Nat. Lawyers Club, Am. Judicature Soc. Club: Capitol Hill. Home: 203 Yoakum Pkwy #323 Alexandria VA 22304 Office: 2033 M St NW Suite 504 Washington DC 20036

SCHOENFELD, CY, scientist, educator; b. Bklyn., Nov. 13, 1939; s. Joseph and Etta (Kupferberg) S.; B.S., Bklyn. Coll., 1962; M.S., Long Island U., 1965; Ph.D., N.Y. U., 1972; m. Eunice Fleishman, Dec. 29, 1976; children—Linda, Stacey Alicia. Technician, Margaret Sanger Research Bus., N.Y.C., 1962-63; lab. supr. Infertility Clinic Bellevue Hosp., N.Y.C., 1963-72; sr. research technician dept. pathology N.Y. U., 1963-64, sr. research technician dept. preventive medicine, 1964-66, asst. research scientist, 1966-70, asso. research scientist, 1970-72, teaching asst., 1972-73, instr. research urology, 1973-75, research asst. prof., 1975—; dir. research, supr. lab. Fertility Lab., Inc., N.Y.C., 1972—; cons. Universal Diagnostic Lab., Bklyn., Arnel Products Co., Bklyn. Mem. Am. Soc. Microbiology, Royal, Am. socs. tropical medicine and hygiene, Am. Fertility Soc., Am. Soc. Andrology, Soc. Study of Reproduction, Sigma Xi. Contbr. articles in field to profl. jours. Home: 156 Oxford St Brooklyn NY 11235 Office: 137 E 36th St New York City NY 10016

SCHOENFELD, MICHAEL P., lawyer; b. Bronx, N.Y., Oct. 17, 1935; s. Jack and Anne S.; B.S. in Accounting, N.Y.U., 1955; LL.B., LL.D., Fordham U., 1958; m. Helen Schorr, Apr. 3, 1960; children—Daniel, Steven, Tracy. Admitted to N.Y. bar, 1959; atty. Am. Home Assurance Co., N.Y.C., 1958-62; partner firm Schoenfeld & Schoenfeld, Melville, 1959—; v.p. Interstate Brokerage Corp., 1965—; partner Melville Realty Co., 1977—; legal adviser various bus. orgns. Vice pres., trustee Temple Beth David, Commack, N.Y., 1972-75; chmn. Community Action Com. of Dix Hills and Commack, 1970-72, Dix Hills Planning Bd., 1972-74; treas. Dix Hills Republican Club, 1976—. Recipient United Jerusalem award Israel Bond Drive, 1977. Mem. N.Y. State Bar Assn. Home: 14 Clayton Dr Dix Hills NY 11746 Office: 60 Broad Hollow Rd Melville NY 11746

SCHOENFELD, THEODORE MARK, indsl. engr.; b. N.Y.C., July 10, 1907; s. Emil and Serena (Kertesz) S.; B.S., Coll. City N.Y., 1930; grad. certificate in pub. adminstrn. N.Y.U., 1938; grad. certificate in indsl. engring. Stevens Inst. Tech., 1945; m. Lila Pesses, Sept. 1, 1946; 1 son, Edward Lawrence. With Daily News Record, Christian Sci. Monitor and Sci. Service, 1930-33; asst. dir. methods and systems

City of N.Y., 1934-41; adminstrv. officer U.S. Dept. State, N.Y.C., 1943-45; chief indsl. engr. M.G.M. Internat. Films Corp., N.Y.C., 1945-48; mgmt. and indsl. engring. cons., N.Y.C. and Park Ridge, Ill., 1949-73; pres. T.M. Schoenfeld Service, N.Y.C., 1974—; v.p. Ramco Mfg. Co., Roselle Park, N.J., 1974—; lectr. indsl. subjects. Dir. U.S. Peace Corps Aux. for N.Y.C. and L.I., 1968-69; chmn. pub. affairs com. Bklyn. Soc. for Ethical Culture, 1965-70; mem. nat. pub. affairs com. Am. Ethical Union, 1965-70; pres. Bklyn. Soc. for Ethical Culture, 1978—. Recipient Nat. John C. Vaaler Chem. Processing award, 1978; registered profl. engr., Calif. Mem. Am. Inst. Indsl. Engrs. (chmn. various coms. 1960—, nat. divisional dir. 1974-75), Soc. Plastic Engrs. Democrat. Contbr. articles to profl. jours. Co-developer Ramco Spra-Gard safety shield. Home: 140 Cadman Plaza W Brooklyn NY 11201 Office: 540 Westfield Ave W Roselle Park NJ 07204

SCHOENWALD, MAURICE L., lawyer; b. N.Y.C., Mar. 30, 1920; s. Jacob and Gertrude (Maier) S.; B.A., Washington Square Coll., 1943; J.D., Western Res. U., 1946; m. Susan Zysman, Nov. 24, 1943; children—David, Beth Cindy, Robin Maude. Admitted to N.Y. State bar, 1947, Fla. bar, 1978; practiced in N.Y.C., 1947—; lectr. Acad. Aeros., LaGuardia Field, 1949-50; adminstr. Boro Med. Group, also Midland Med. Group, 1955-75; pres. Accrued Equities, Inc., N.Y.C., 1954—; lectr. Hofstra U., 1967-68, Great Neck Village Sch., 1971; gen. counsel Opengate Sch. for Spl. Children, 1969-71. Cooperating atty. Nassau County Civil Liberties Union, 1967. Served to lt. j.g. USNR, 1943-46. Fellow Acad. Matrimonial Lawyers; mem. Nassau County Bar Assn. (matrimonial and family law com.). Clubs: Steppingstones Yacht, L.I. Sound Yacht Racing Assn., Midget Ocean Racing (sec. 1966-67). Contbg. author: Handbook of Wealth Management, 1977; contbr., mem. adv. editorial panel Profl. Investing mag., until 1974. Home: 8 Nirvana Ave Great Neck NY 11023 Office: 295 Northern Blvd Great Neck NY 11021

SCHOFER, HARRY STANLEY, information systems specialist; b. Washington, Sept. 24, 1936; s. Arthur Julius and Gertrude Anne (Feldman) S.; B.S., U. Md., 1959; postgrad. George Washington U., 1960-61, Am. U., 1968-69; m. Paulette S. Brodsky, Aug. 3, 1964; children—Gail Lisa, Gregory Steven. Physicist, Nat. Bur. Standards, Washington, 1959-63; sr. analyst Def. Documentation Center, Def. Supply Agency Alexandria, Va., 1963-69; info. systems analyst Nat. Acad. Scis., Washington, 1969-73, mgr. systems devel. and ops., 1973—. Mem. Am. Soc. Info. Sci., Spl. Libraries Assn., Internat. Fedn. Documentation (subcom. universal decimal classification 1970—). Jewish. Office: Transp Research Bd 2101 Constitution Ave Washington DC 20418

SCHOFIELD, WILLIAM GREENOUGH, author; b. Providence, June 13, 1909; s. Harry L. and Elizabeth (Smallman) S.; student Brown U., 1927-31; m. Blanche Hughes, Nov. 21, 1934; children—Elinor, Michael, Peter. Feature writer Boston Traveler, 1940-55, chief editorial writer, 1955-67; mgr. editorial services Raytheon Co., Lexington, Mass., 1967-70; asso. dir. pub. information Boston U., 1970-74. Founder, Freedom Trail, Boston; mem. Freedom Trail Commn. Served with USNR, 1942-45; with Navy Dept., Washington, 1945; capt. Res. Mem. Navy League, Ret. Officers Assn., Nat. Soc. Lit. and Arts, Am. Newspaper Guild, Boston Press Club, Alpha Tau Omega. Club: Brown (Boston). Author: Ashes in the Wilderness, 1940; The Cat in the Convoy, 1946; Payoff in Black, 1947; The Deer Cry, 1948; Seek for a Hero, 1956; Sidewalk Statesman, 1958; Destroyers 60 Years, 1962; Treason Trail, 1964; Eastward the Convoys, 1966; Freedom by the Bay, 1974. Home: 16 Hunnewell Circle Newton MA 02158 Office: 19 Deerfield St Boston MA 02215

SCHOLL, CHARLES ELMER, ednl. testing service exec.; b. Clio, Mich., Nov. 28, 1918; s. Charles Elmer and Josephine Emma (Jackson) S.; B.A., Wayne State U., 1940; M.A., 1947; Ph.D. (Burke Aaron Hinsdale scholar 1956-57), U. Mich., 1957; m. Loleta May Kellam, Mar. 12, 1943; 1 dau., Susan. Asst. employment mgr. Parke, Davis & Co., Detroit, 1946-48; research asso., instr. mgmt. Wayne State U., Detroit, 1948-51; account exec. Roger Bellows & Assos., Detroit, 1951-54; dir. indsl. relations Burroughs Corp., Detroit, 1954-67; v.p., dir. spl. projects ETS, Princeton, N.J., 1967—. Campaign chmn. United Fund Princeton, 1972; twp. committeeman East Amwell Twp. (N.J.), 1975—; mem. Hunterdon County Manpower Planning Com., 1975, Hunterdon County Title XX Coalition. Served with USAF, 1941-46. Certified cons. psychologist, Mich. Mem. Am. Psychol. Assn., Nat. Vocat. Guidance Assn. (profl.), Am. Personnel and Guidance Assn., Psi Chi, Phi Kappa Phi, Phi Delta Kappa, Delta Sigma Pi. Club: Hillsborough Country. Contbr. articles to profl. publs. Home: PO Box 118 RD 2 Ringoes NJ 08551 Office: Rosedale and Carter Rds Princeton NJ 08540

SCHOLZ, CATHERINE HAMMERSLEY, artist; b. N.Y.C.; d. Frederick and Mary (Hammersley) Scholz; grad. (scholar) N.Y. Sch. Fine and Applied Art, 1935. Free-lance fashion illustrator Harpers Bazaar, McCalls, Lentheric, Mademoiselle, 1935—, House Beautiful, Good Housekeeping, Ladies Home Jour., Seagrams, Am. Druggist, Family Circle, packaging for Richard Hudnut, William R. Warner, 1940—, Pantene, 1965-66, book jackets for Julian Messner and Young Readers Press. Mem. Women's Nat. Book Assn., Berkshire Garden Center. Republican. Episcopalian. Illustrator over 25 books, 1949—, including: Understanding Why, 1951, Its Fun To Cook, 1952, Christmas in Song and Story, 1953, Before I Go To Sleep, 1953, Sewing Is Fun, 1958, Ballet for You, 1959, Lords of the Blue Pacific, 1962, Shari Lewis Book of Fairy Tales, 1961, Adventure at Riverton Zoo, 1966; Play a Part (one act plays); Instant Macrame, 1971; Instant Money, 1971; The Instant Art of Needlepoint, 1972-73; The Quilt Book, 1975-76; The Puff Quilt Book, 1975-76; The New Pillow, 1975-76; The Envelope Quilt Book, 1977; also textbooks, readers. Address: 39-24 215 Pl Bayside NY 11361

SCHOMP, ARTHUR HERBERT, fin. services co. exec.; b. Newark, Apr. 15, 1924; s. John Herbert and Mildred Wilhelmina (Hirth) S.; B.A. cum laude, Drew U., 1945, M. Div. cum laude, 1947; M.A., U. Minn., 1951; M.B.A., U. Chgo., 1959; m. Lois Ann White, June 14, 1949; 1 dau., Katherine Ann. Clin. psychologist Minn. State Hosp., Moose Lake, 1949-51; zone mgr. Investors Diversified Services, Inc., Bemidji, Minn., 1951-52; with exec. devel. program No. Trust Co., Chgo., 1952-54; account exec., asst. to exec. v.p. Julien Collins & Co., Chgo., 1954-57; account exec. Merrill Lynch, Pierce, Fenner & Smith, Inc., Chgo., 1957-68, retail sales mgr., 1968-71, asst. br. office mgr., 1971-72, resident v.p., mgr. Morristown, Short Hills and Westfield (N.J.) offices, 1972—. Trustee, N.J. Shakespeare Festival; mem. corp. United Way of Morris County; chmn. parent ann. giving Kent Place Sch., Summit, N.J. Served with Chaplains Corps, USN, 1943-46. Mem. Am. Psychol. Assn., Bond Club Chgo., Bond Club N.J. Republican. Clubs: Canoe Brook Country (Summit); Economic, Executives, Union League (Chgo.); Masons. Home: 10 Mohawk Rd Short Hills NJ 07078 Office: 159 South St Morristown NJ 07960

SCHONBERG, JACKSON RICHARD, univ. adminstr., spl. edn. cons.; b. Plainfield, N.J., July 13, 1939; s. Jackson Roy and Eleanor N. (Cooper) S.; B.A., Fairleigh Dickinson U., 1962; M.S., Purdue U., 1964; Ed.D. (Office of Edn. fellow), Columbia, 1971; children—Dawn Elizabeth, Karen Michelle. Dir. pupil services Bloomfield (Conn.) Pub. Schs., 1970-73; asso. prof. Sch. Psychology, Spl. Edn. and Adminstrn., U. Hartford, W. Hartford, Conn., 1973—, co-dir. div. human resources Coll. Edn., 1973-77, dir. div. human resource devel., 1977—; project chief, supr., spl. edn. sch. for emotionally disturbed and socially maladjusted Capitol Region Edn. Council, Bloomfield, 1973—; cons., program evaluator State of Conn.; chmn. edn. council spl. sch. dist. Conn. Dept. Mental Retardation; chairperson, supts. adv. planning council N. Central Regional Center, Bloomfield, 1973—. Republican. Congregationalist. Office: Coll Edn U Hartford 200 Bloomfield Ave West Hartford CT 06117

SCHONHOLTZ, JOAN SONDRA HIRSCH, banker, civic worker; b. N.Y.C., Sept. 8, 1933; d. Joseph G. and Mildred (Klebanoff) Hirsch; student Vassar Coll., 1950-52; B.A., Barnard Coll., 1954; postgrad. Am. U., 1963; m. George J. Schonholtz, Aug. 21, 1951; children—Margot Beth, Steven Robert, Barbara Ellen. Chmn. bd. dirs., founding mem. 1st Women's Bank of Md., 1976—. Pres. Ft. Benning (Ga.) Med. Wives, 1962-63; sec. Montgomery County (Md.) Women's Med. Aux., 1968; sec. Service Guild of Washington, 1969-70, bd. dirs., 1968—, pres., 1975—; mem. Washington Adv. Council on Deaf-Blind Children, 1972—; bd. dirs. Pilot Sch. for Blind Multiple Handicapped Children, Washington, 1968—; spl. gifts chmn. Cancer Soc., Montgomery County, Md., 1968, 69 pres. Service Guild of Washington, 1975-77, recipient Outstanding Service award, 1969. Republican. Jewish. Clubs: Vassar, Barnard. Home: 11310 Old Club Rd Rockville MD 20852

SCHOOLEY, DOLORES (MRS. CHARLES E. SCHOOLEY), artist mgr.; b. Nora Springs, Iowa, May 2, 1905; d. Amil A. and Elizabeth (Sefert) Zemke; B.E., B.A., U. Colo., 1927; M.A., Northwestern U., 1931; m. Leslie J. Harter, June 5, 1934 (dec. Oct. 1963); m. 2d. Charles E. Schooley, Apr. 1, 1966. Tchr. high schs., Johnston, Colo., 1927-28, Byers, Colo., 1928-29, Clayton, Mo., 1931-34; instr. theatrical make-up dramatic clubs N.J. Theatre League; lectr., demonstrator theatrical make-up, dramatic and women's clubs, high schs., N.J. and N.Y. area; dir. projects Phi Beta, 1951-60, nat. officer, mem. nat. council, 1956-60, dir. community relations Wingspread Summer Theatre, Colon, Mich., 1955; co-chmn. Valley-Shore Community Concerts, 1958-61; artist mgr., 1959—. Trustee Sharon Creative Arts Found., 1970-73; hon. trustee Bar Harbor Festival, 1968—; bd. dirs. Music Mountain, Falls Village, Conn., 1975—; chmn. Sharon Hosp. Benefit Ball, 1970; pres. Wingspread Found., 1977—. Mem. Berkshire Hills Music and Dance Assn. (founder, pres. 1970—). Phi Beta (originator, cons. radio program 1961-65). Alpha Omicron Pi. Conglist. Clubs: Montclair Dramatic (chmn. make-up, instr. make-up); Rehearsal (program chmn.); Women's (dir. plays, chmn. drama dept.) (Glen Ridge, N.J.); Sharon Country, Sharon Womens. Address: Wingspread PO Box 36 Sharon CT 06069

SCHOONMAKER, ALBERT VOORHIS, composer; b. Grandforks, N.D., May 1, 1919; s. Albert V. and Laura Cooper (Nichols) S.; B.S. in Music Theory, MacPhail Coll. Music, Mpls., 1949, M.S. in Composition, 1950. Free-lance musician, 1935—; tchr. composition and theory Chgo., 1951-53; cons. music prodn., N.Y.C., 1954—; composer numerous works including String Quartet No. 3, 1959, Opera in Two Acts, 1963, Symphony No. 2, 1970, Saxaphone Quartet, 1976, Symphony No. 3, 1978, Brass Quintet, 1978; works performed by N.Y. Saxaphone Quartet, N.Y. Brass Quintet and other groups. Served with U.S. Army, 1942-45. Mem. Am. Fedn. Musicians, Acad. Recording Arts and Scis., Am. Soc. Music Arrangers, Am. Soc. Music Copyists, Am. Composers Alliance, Am. Music Center, Sons of Desert. Address: 252 W 47th St New York City NY 10036

SCHOONMAKER, HERBERT GARRETTSON, historian; b. N.Y.C., Oct. 14, 1921; s. Herbert Sage and Antoinette (Taylor) S.; B.S., U.S. Naval Acad., 1945; M.A., U. Ga., 1971, Ph.D., 1977; m. JoAnn Teeple, Aug. 29, 1959; children—Mark G., Christopher C. Commd. ensign U.S. Navy, 1945, advanced through grades to comdr., 1965; exec. Destroyer Escort, 1953-55, Atlantic Fleet, naval gunfire liaison officer 2d Marine Div., Camp Lejeune, N.C.; ret., 1958; ednl. specialist Bur. Personnel, Navy Dept., Washington, 1959-62; intelligence research analyst CIA, Washington, 1962-69; teaching asst. U. Ga., 1969-74; historian U.S. Air Force Tactical Air Command, Langley AFB, Va., 1974-76; command historian U.S. Army Hdqrs. 21st Support Command, 1976—. Mem. U.S. Naval Inst., Am., So. hist. assns., Holland Soc., Social Sci. History Assn. Episcopalian. Office: Hdqrs 21st Support Command APO New York City NY 09325

SCHOOR, HOWARD M., cons. engr.; b. S.I., N.Y., Jan. 13, 1939; s. Samuel Edward and Sadie Diana (Garelick) S.; B.C.E., Lafayette Coll., 1961; postgrad. N.Y.U., 1962-63; m. Frances A. Loscoe, Dec. 14, 1973; children—Barbara, Debra. Field engr. N.Y. State Dept. Pub. Works, 1961-63; project mgr. Aurnhammer Assos., Inc., Summit, N.J., 1963-68; pres. Schoor Engring., Inc., cons. engrs., Matawan, N.J., 1968—; muniicpal engr., boroughs of Sayreville, Keyport, Spotswood, Roosevelt, Matawan, Sea Bright, Red Bank, East Rutherford, twps. of Millstone, Hazlet, Shrewsbury, Barnegat, Little Egg Harbor. Mem. nat. fin. council Dem. Nat. Com. Mem. ASCE, Am. Water Works Assn., Nat., N.J. Monmouth County socs. profl. engrs., N.J. Soc. Profl. Planners, N.J. Shore Builders Assn., N.J. Builders Assn., Nat. Assn. Home Builders, N.J. Soc. Municipal Engrs., Fedn. Planning Ofcls., Am. Congress Mapping and Surveying, Water Pollution Control Fedn. Clubs: Woodlake Country (Lakewood, N.J.); Aventura Country (North Miami Beach, Fla.); Masons. Home: 22 Mill Rd Matawan NJ 07747 Office: 356 Main St Matawan NJ 07747

SCHOPLER, ERNEST HUGO, law writer; b. Fuerth, Bavaria, Germany, Sept. 5, 1895; s. Nathan Heinrich and Frieda (Bing) Schopflocher; came to U.S., 1938, naturalized, 1944; J.U.D. summa cum laude, U. Erlangen-Nuernberg, 1920; LL.B. (Salmon W. Dahlberg scholar), U. Wis., 1940; S.J.D., Harvard U., 1942; m. Erna Oppenheimer, June 6, 1923; children—Irene Solomon, Eric, John. Partner law firm, Fuerth, 1922-38; instr. U. Wis. Law Sch., 1940-41; editor, mng. editor Lawyers Coop. Pub. Co., Rochester, N.Y., 1941-70; legal adviser, chief German law sect., chief legislation br. Office Mil. Govt., Berlin, 1945-48; cons. law firm Nixon, Hargrave, Devans & Doyle, Rochester, 1970-73; law writer, 1973—; participant confs. Am. Law Inst., 1940-41; lectr. constl. law U.S. Zone in Germany, Dept. War, 1949, Dept. State, 1950. Recipient Joseph H. Beale prize Harvard Law Sch., 1941. Mem. Order of Coif (hon.), Epsilon Tau Rho. Republican. Contbr. articles to legal jours. Home: 120 Highland Pkwy Rochester NY 14620

SCHOR, WILLIAM THEODORE, mortgage banker; b. New Brunswick, N.J., Dec. 23, 1938; s. Jacob and Rose Ruth (Friedburg) S.; B.S., Rider Coll., 1962; postgrad. in mortgage law Sch. Mortgage Banking, 1975; children from previous marriage—Jeffrey, Debra, Irving, Robert. Regional sales mgr. J.I. Kislak Mortgage Corp., Newark, 1962-65; asst. v.p. sales mgr. South Jersey Mortgage Co., Camden, N.J., 1965-67; owner, mgr. Dynamic Mortgage Securities Assos., Cherry Hill, N.J., 1967-69; pres. Bond and Mortgage Co. N.J., Cherry Hill, 1969-75; exec. v.p., dir. Bankers Bond & Mortgage Guarantee Co. Am., Phila., 1974-76; founder, pres., chmn. bd. Mortgage Services of Am., Cherry Hill, 1976—. Recipient Century Club award YMCA, 1973, United Fund award, 1974. Mem. Cherry Hill C. of C., Mortgage Bankers Assn. Am., Mortgage Bankers Assn. N.J., Phila. Mortgage Bankers Assn., Soc. Savs. and Loan Mortgage Officers, Nat. Assn. Realtors, Nat. Assn. Home Builders, N.J. Assn. Realtors, N.J. Builders Assn., Home Builders League South Jersey, Camden County Bd. Realtors. Home: 342 Kings Croft Cherry Hill NJ 08034 Office: 1 Cherry Hill Suite 104 Cherry Hill NJ 08034

SCHOSHEIM, PEARL ESTELLE (MRS. ARNOLD M. SCHOSHEIM), ednl. adminstr.; b. Bklyn, Aug. 3, 1922; d. George Bernard and Tillie (Levy) Sugarman; B.A., N.Y. U., 1942; M.A., Columbia, 1943; m. Arnold M. Schosheim, Dec. 22, 1946; children—John Paul, Peter Mark. Tchr. English, Rhodes Prep. Sch., N.Y.C., 1943-45; tchr. speech improvement N.Y.C. Bd. of Edn., 1945-66; lectr. speech edn. Queen's Coll., Flushing, N.Y., 1966-68; acting supr. Speech Improvement and Coordinator Title I, Non-pub. Sch. Speech Program, N.Y.C., 1970; supr. Speech Improvement Trchs., N.Y.C., Bd. of Edn., 1970-77. Mem. Community Chest Drive Com., 1960-65. Mem. N.Y. State, L.I. speech and hearing assns., N.Y. State, Eastern States speech assns., Speech Communication Assn., Council for Exceptional Children (hospitality chmn. 1974), Am. Jewish Congress, Hadassah, Alpha Epsilon Phi. Home: 250 Clent Rd Great Neck NY 11021 Office: 110 Livingston St Brooklyn NY 11201

SCHOTT, JOHN R., educator, govt. ofcl.; b. Rochester, N.Y., Jan. 30, 1936; s. John and Ellen (Waite) S.; B.A. magna cum laude, Haverford Coll., 1957; Ph.D., Harvard, 1964; m. Diane Elizabeth Dempsey, June 19, 1963; children—Elizabeth Ann (dec.), Jennifer, Jared Reed, George Kermit Alexander. Resident tutor in govt. Eliot House, Harvard Coll., 1960-64; instr. polit. sci. Wellesley (Mass.) Coll., 1964-66; chief Title IX div. AID, Washington, 1966-68, policy planning specialist, 1969-70; vis. prof. polit. devel. Fletcher Sch. Law and Diplomacy, Medford, Mass., 1968-69; sr. v.p. Thunderbird Grad. Sch., Phoenix, 1970-71; cons. in internat. affairs, 1971—. Mem. S.E. Asia Devel. Adv. Group, 1967-69; ofcl. U.S. del. World Assembly Internat. Secretariat for Vol. Service, New Delhi, 1967. Mem. bd. adjustment Town of Francestown, N.H., 1968-69, mem. planning bd., 1969-70, sec., 1970-75, chmn. bicentennial com., 1968-72, mem. bd. selectmen, 1975-78, chmn., 1977; v.p. Village Improvement Soc., Francestown, 1968-69, pres. 1969-71. Trustee Spaulding Youth Center, Tilton, N.H., 1972-73, v.p., 1973-74, pres., 1974-77. Rotary Found. fellow, 1957-58; Coslett Found. fellow, 1958-59; Harvard Arts and Scis. fellow, 1960-61; Fulbright fellow 1962-63. Fellow African Studies Assn.; mem. Internat. Studies Assn., Am. Polit. Sci. Assn. Club: Harvard (Boston). Author: Kenya Tragedy: European Colonization in East Africa, 1964; Frances' Town: A History of Francestown, N.H., 1972. Contbr. articles to profl. jours. and regional mags. Home: Main St Francestown NH 03043 Office: Schott & Assos Inc Francestown NH 03043

SCHRACK, VIVIAN BUNNELL, educator; b. Scio, N.Y., Mar. 13, 1913; d. Eldyn Lorenzo and Mary Beatrice (Palmer) Bunnell; A.B., Houghton Coll., 1932; M.A., Alfred U., 1953; Ph.D., Pa. State U., 1968; m. Stewart Miller Schrack, June 30, 1938 (dec.). Tchr. pub. schs., Scio, 1932-33, Richburg (N.Y.) Central Sch., 1933-39, York Central Sch., Retsof, N.Y., 1941-46, 48-63; tchr. West Irondequoit Central Sch., Rochester, N.Y., 1963-78, head dept. history and social scis., 1966-78. Mem. Nat., N.Y. State councils social studies, Am. Hist. Assn., N.Y. State United Tchrs., Rochester Assn. for UN, Civic Music Assn., Irondequoit Friends of Library, Irondequoit Hist. Soc., Rochester Landmark Soc., Ednl. TV Soc., Phi Alpha Theta, Delta Kappa Gamma. Democrat. Methodist.

SCHRADE, ROBERT WARREN, musician; b. Walden, N.Y., Dec. 2, 1924; s. Louis J. and Elizabeth M. (Eitner) S.; student Oberlin Coll. and Conservatory, 1941-43, Manhattan Sch. Music, 1946-47, 47-48, Mus.B., 1948, M.Mus., 1948; m. Rolande Maxwell Young, Dec. 21, 1949; children—Robelyn, Rhonda Lee, Rolisa, Randolph, Rorianne. Debut as concert pianist Columbia U., 1933; piano soloist Nat. Orchestral Assn., Carnegie Hall, N.Y.C., 1965, Town Hall, N.Y.C., 1949, 51, 53; solo piano concerts, Carnegie Hall, N.Y.C., 1954, 57, 60, Nat. Gallery, Washington, 1956, Constitution Hall, Washington, 1969, Alice Tully Hall, 1977; concert tours in Europe, 1958, 60, N.Am., 1959-64; piano soloist N.Y. World's Fair, 1964; tchr. piano Manhattan Sch. Music, 1948-53, 68—, Chapin Sch., N.Y.C., 1948—, Brearley Sch., 1948-52; dir. music Allen-Stevenson Sch., N.Y.C., 1967-68; founder, music dir. Sevenars Concerts, Inc., Worthington, Mass., 1975—; pres. Sevenars Music House, Inc. Trustee Historic Landmark Ch., South Worthington, Mass. Served with USAAC, 1943-46. Recipient Hour of Music award Cosmopolitan Club, 1947; Schepp Found. award, 1958. Mem. Nat. Soc. Lit. and the Arts, ASCAP, Worthington Hist. Assn. Address: 30 East End Ave New York City NY 10028

SCHRADER, JANE MARIE JACQUELINE, librarian; b. Passaic, N.J., June 17, 1945; d. Andrew Dennis and Phyllis Marie (Sudol) Waller; B.A., Caldwell Coll., 1967; M.A. magna cum laude, Fairleigh Dickinson U., 1970; m. Stephen P. Schrader, July 4, 1969. Cataloguer N.J. room spl. collection Fairleigh Dickinson U., Rutherford, 1967-70, reference librarian, 1970-73; head librarian Silver Burdett Editorial Library, Morristown, N.J., 1973—. Mem. League Women Voters, Spl. Libraries Assn. (bull. editor), N.J. Library Assn., Am. Acad. Polit. Scientists. Club: Jr. Women's. Republican. Home: 9 Fenwick Rd Whippany NJ 07981 Office: 250 James St Morristown NJ 07960

SCHRECENGOST, HARRY ALLEN, JR., govt. adminstr.; b. New Kensington, Pa., June 17, 1924; s. Harry A. and Susanne (Lavery) S.; B.A., Kings Coll., Wilkes Barre, Pa., 1950; postgrad. Am. U., 1967-69; m. Margaret A. McGroarty, Aug. 13, 1949; children—Harry A., III, Eric P., Marc J., Maura A., John G., Hugh E. Tchr. high sch., Swoyerville, Pa., 1950-51; buyer, dept. mgr. Lazarus Dept. Store, Wilkes Barre, 1951-57, Globe Dept. Store, Scranton, Pa., 1957-61; gen. mgr. GEM Stores, Washington, 1961-64; br. chief Dept. Commerce Nat. Tech. Info. Service, Springfield, Va., 1964-68; research and devel. liaison officer Def. Supply Agy., Alexandria, Va., 1968-72; div. chief micrographic processing officer Def. Documentation Center, Alexandria, Va., 1972—; mem. staff U.S. Army Personnel Mgmt. for Execs. Course. Pres. The Blackthorn Stick Sch. Irish Music and Dance, Riverdale, Md.; owner, mgr. Blackthorn Ceili Band, Washington, D.C. Served with USAAF, 1943-46. Certified tchr., Pa. Mem. Nat. Micrographics Assn. (prin. Def. Logistics Agy./Def. Documentation Center mem.), Fed. Govt. Micrographics Council (mem. panel and steering com.). Democrat. Roman Catholic. Clubs: Am. Legion, K.C. Home: 6504 Inlet St New Carrollton MD 20784 OFfice: Def Documentation Center (DDC-TCA-1) Cameron Sta Alexandria VA 22314

SCHRECK, RICHARD THOMAS, accountant; b. Waterloo, N.Y., Apr. 27, 1930; s. George L. and Isabella (Cowan) S.; B.S. in Music Edn., Ithaca Coll., 1953; postgrad. Syracuse U., part time 1956-63, m. Barbara Ann Walsh, June 25, 1960; children—Michael J., James E., Mary Ann. Accountant, G.L. Schreck accounting firm, Waterloo, N.Y., 1955-56; pvt. practice accounting, Waterloo, 1956—. Mem. 7th Army Symphony Orch., 1955; trustee, Village Waterloo, 1964-77, Waterloo Library and Hist. Soc., 1965—; research chmn. Waterloo Meml. Day Centennial Com., 1965-66; heritage co-chmn. Seneca

County Bicentennial Com., 1975-77; treas. Waterloo Meml. Day Com., 1966—; co-founder, trustee Waterloo Meml. Day Mus., 1966—; historian St. Marys Ch., 1966—. Served with U.S. Army, 1953-55. Mem. C. of C. (pres. 1967-68), Nat. Soc. Pub. Accountants. Democrat. Roman Catholic. Author: (with John S. Genung) The History and Origin of Memorial Day in Waterloo, 1966. Home and office: 75 Washington St Waterloo NY 13165

SCHREIBER, CHARLES ERIC, cemeterian; b. Bklyn., Sept. 19, 1934; s. Edward George and Anna Christina (Lobinger) S.; grad. Am. Acad. of Funeral Services, 1959; children—Eric, Tara. Mgr., Werson Funeral Home, Linden, N.J., 1959-72; propr., pres. Rosedale Cemetery, Linden, 1972—, Rosehill Cemetery, Linden, N.J., 1977—. Pres., Magician Roundtable, 1978-79; bd. dirs. Police Athletic League, 1978—. Served with USN, 1952-56; Korea. Mem. Soc. of Am. Magicians, Internat. Soc. Magicians. Club: Lions. Home: 1625 Lenape Rd Linden NJ 07036 Office: PO Box 161-750 Linden NJ 07036

SCHREIBER, EILEEN SHER, artist; b. Denver; d. Michael Herschel and Sarah Deborah (Tannenbaum) Sher; student U. Utah, 1942-45, N.Y. U. extension, 1966-68, Montclair (N.J.) State Coll., 1975—; also pvt. art study; m. Jonas Schreiber, Mar. 27, 1945; children—Jeffrey, Barbara, Michael. Exhibited Morris Mus. Arts and Scis., Morristown, N.J., 1965-73, N.J. State Mus., 1969, Lever House, N.Y.C., 1971, Paramus (N.J.) Mus., 1973, Am. Water Color Soc., Audubon Artists, N.A.D. Gallery, N.Y.C., Pallazzo Vecchio Florence (Italy); represented in permanent collections Morris Mus., Seton Hall U., Bloomfield (N.J.) Coll., Lanza Industries, N.J., Morris County State Coll., Broad Nat. Bank, Newark, Park B. Smith Inc., Am. Telephone Co., RCA, IBM Corp., Barclay Bank of Eng., Johnson & Johnson, others; also pvt. collections. Recipient awards N.J. Watercolor Soc., 1969, 72, Nat. Assn. Women Artists, 1970; 1st award in watercolor Hunterdon Art Center, 1972, Best in Show award Short Hills State Show, 1976, purchase award Somerset Coll., 1977, numerous others. Mem. Nat. Assn. Women Artists (chmn. watercolor jury), N.J. Artists Equity, Nat. Painter and Sculptors Assn., Hunterdon Art Center. Home: 22 Powell Dr West Orange NJ 07052 Office: care Lillian Kornbluth Gallery 7-21 Fair Lawn Ave Fair Lawn NJ 07410 also Reece Galleries 39 W 32d St New York City NY 10001 also 30 W 57th St New York City NY 10019

SCHREIBER, FLORA RHETA, theatre arts and speech specialist, author, educator; b. N.Y.C., Apr. 24, 1918; d. William and Esther (Aaronson) S.; B.S., Columbia U., 1938, M.A., 1939; certificate Central Sch. Speech Tng. and Dramatic Art, U. London, 1937, N.Y. U. Radio Workshop, 1942. Instr., speech and dramatic art dept. Bklyn. Coll., 1944-46; creator-producer Bklyn. Coll. Radio Forum on WNYC, N.Y.C., 1944-46; drama critic Players mag., 1941-46; instr. Exeter Coll., U. Southwest, Eng., 1937; asst. prof. speech and dramatic arts dept. Adelphi Coll., Garden City, L.I., 1947-53, dir radio-TV div. Center Creative Arts, 1948-51; lectr. New Sch. Social Research, U. City N.Y., 1952—, now prof. English and speech, dir. publs., asst. to pres. John Jay Coll. Criminal Justice; numerous appearances on radio and TV, U.S., Can., Eng., 1973—; numerous lectures, 1976—. Recipient award for distinguished service in med. book writing Am. Med. Writers Assn., 1976; Cornelia Otis Skinner scholar, 1937. Mem. AAUW, AAUP, Speech Assn. Am., ANTA, Speech Assn. Eastern States, Am. Soc. Journalists and Authors (v.p. 1974-76), Authors League Am., P.E.N., Overseas Press Club. Author: William Schuman (biography), 1954; Your Child's Speech, 1956; Jobs With a Future in Law Enforcement, 1970; Sybil, 1973 (also fgn. edits.); also short stories, plays, opera libreti and art songs; contbr. to nat. mags. including Cosmopolitan, Reader's Digest, Good Housekeeping, The Freeman, Redbook, Mademoiselle, Am. Mercury, N.Y. Times, Quar. Film, Radio, and TV, Family Weekly, Today's Health, Woman's Day, others; formerly monthly columnist Sci. Digest. Producer radio forum on Community Theater for NBC, 1949; other radio and TV appearances; feature writer N.Y. Times Spl. Features, United Features. Home: 32 Gramercy Park S New York City NY 10003

SCHREIBER, HARRY, JR., mgmt. cons.; b. Columbus, O., Apr. 1, 1934; s. C. Harry and Audrey (Sard) S.; B.S., Mass. Inst. Tech., 1955; M.B.A., Boston U., 1958; m. Margaret Ruth Heinzman, June 12, 1955; children—Margaret Elizabeth, Thomas Edward, Amy Katherine. Accountant truck and coach div. Gen. Motors Corp., Pontiac, Mich., 1955; instr. Mass. Inst. Tech., 1958-62; pres. Data-Service, Inc., Boston, 1961-65; pres. Harry Schreiber Assos., Wellesley, Mass., 1965; mgr., nat. dir. merchandising Peat, Marwick, Mitchell & Co., N.Y.C., 1966-70, partner, Chgo., 1970-75; chmn. Close, Martin, Schreiber & Co., Washington, 1975—; dir. Redeemer Housing Corp. Staff, Work Simplification Conf. Lake Placid, N.Y., 1960-61. Served to 1st lt. AUS, 1956-58. Mem. Am. Inst. Indsl. Engrs. (chmn. data-processing div. 1964-66, chpt. v.p. 1961, 65, chmn. retail div. 1976), Com. Internat. Congress Transp. Confs., Assn. for Computing Machinery, Assn. for Systems Mgmt., Inst. Mgmt. Scis., Retail Research Soc., Controllers Congress, Nat. Retail Mchts. Assn. (retail systems specifications com.), Food Distbn. Research Soc. (dir. 1972, pres. 1974), Internat. Trade Club, Japan-Am. Soc. Chgo., Washington Bd. Trade. Republican. Methodist. Clubs: MIT of New York; Skokie Country; Reston Golf and Country; Army-Navy (Washington); Plaza (Chgo.). Home: 12137 Stirrup Rd Reston VA 22091 Office: 1629 K St NW Washington DC 20006

SCHREIBER, JOEL S., linen rental co. exec.; b. Far Rockaway, N.Y., Dec. 24, 1941; s. Samuel and Adele S.; B.S., N.Y. U., 1966; m. Susan Kimmel, Dec. 22, 1962; children—Brian, Nancy. Pres., Environ. Linen Systems, Inc., Corona, N.Y., 1973—, Corona Laundry Service, Inc., Corona, 1975—, Active Linen Service Co., Corona, 1967—. Jewish. Home: 1303 Auerbach Ave Hewlett Harbor NY 11557 Office: 104-35 44th Ave Corona NY 11368

SCHREIBER, PATTI JEANNE, interior designer; b. Buffalo, Apr. 10, 1936; d. Samuel N. and Rose (Getsler) Valenti; A.A., Bryant Stratton Bus. Inst., 1972; m. Henry Schreiber, Feb. 22, 1954; children—Douglas, Wendi. Free-lance interior designer, 1972—; owner, operator Patti Interiors, Amherst, N.Y., 1972—. Mem. Am. Soc. Interior Designers. Jewish. Clubs: B'nai Brith, Pythians.

SCHREINER, SAMUEL AGNEW, JR., author; b. Mt. Lebanon, Pa., June 6, 1921; s. Samuel Agnew and Mary (Cort) S.; A.B., Princeton U., 1942; m. Doris Ann Moon, Sept. 22, 1945; children—Beverly Ann Schreiner Carroll, Carolyn Cort Schreiner. Reporter Pitts. Sun-Telegraph, 1946-51; asst. mng. editor Parade magazine, N.Y.C., 1951-54; sr. editor Reader's Digest, Pleasantville, N.Y., 1954-73; author: Thine Is The Glory, 1975, Pleasant Places, 1977, The Condensed World of the Reader's Digest, 1977, Angelica, 1978. Sec. Darien (Conn.) Library Bd., 1963-68; chmn. Darien Youth Adv. Commn., 1972-73. Served with OSS, 1942-45. Decorated Bronze Star. Presbyterian. Club: Overseas Press (N.Y.C.). Address: 111 Old Kings Hwy S Darien CT 06820

SCHRIEFFER, JOHN ROBERT, physicist; b. Oak Park, Ill., May 31, 1931; s. John H. and Louise (Anderson) S.; B.S., Mass. Inst. Tech., 1953; M.S., U. Ill., 1954, Ph.D., 1957, Sc.D. (hon.), 1974; Sc.D. (hon.), U. Geneva (Switzerland), 1968, U. Pa., 1973, U. Cin., 1977; D.Natural Sci., Die Technische Hochschule, Munich, Germany, 1968; m. Anne Grete Thomsen, Dec. 26, 1960; children—Anne Bolette, Paul Karsten, Anna Regina. NSF fellow U. Birmingham (Eng.) and U. Copenhagen (Denmark), 1957-58; asst. prof. physics U. Chgo., 1958-59; asst. prof. U. Ill., 1959-61, asso. prof., 1961-62; prof. U. Pa., Phila., 1962—, Mary Amanda Wood prof. physics, 1964—; Andrew D. White prof. Cornell U., 1969-75. Guggenheim fellow U. Copenhagen, (Denmark), 1966-67. Recipient Comstock prize Nat. Acad. Sci., 1968; Oliver E. Buckley Solid State prize Am. Phys. Soc., 1968; Nobel prize in physics, 1972; John Ericsson medal Am. Soc. Swedish Engrs., 1976. Mem. Am. Acad. Arts and Scis., Am. Philos. Soc. Nat. Acad. Sci. Author: Theory of Superconductivity, 1965. Home: 1303 Club House Rd Gladwyne PA 17935 Office: Dept of Physics U Pa Philadelphia PA 19104

SCHRIESHEIM, ALAN, research exec.; b. N.Y.C., Mar. 8, 1930; s. Morton and Frances (Greenberg) S.; B.S. in Chemistry, Poly. Inst. Bklyn, 1951; Ph.D. in Phys. Organic Chemistry, Pa. State U., 1954; m. Beatrice D. Brand, June 28, 1953; children—Laura Lynn, Robert Alan. Chemist, Nat. Bur. Standards, 1954-56; with Exxon Research & Engring. Co., 1956—, lab. dir. corp. research, chem. scis. lab., 1968-75, dir. corp. research labs., 1975—; mem. adv. bd. Stanford Inst. for Energy Studies; mem. com. on chem. scis. NRC; mem. pure and applied chem. del. to People's Republic of China, 1978. Mem. corp. vis. com. chemistry dept. Mass. Inst. Tech. Fellow N.Y. Acad. Scis.; mem. Am. Chem. Soc. (exec. com. petroleum div., chmn. 1976, councillor, 1977—; Petroleum Chemistry award 1969), Am. Inst. Chemists, AAAS, Phi Lambda Upsilon, Author, patentee in field. Mem. editorial bd. Chemtech. Home: 69 Druid Hill Rd Summit NJ 07901 Office: POB 45 Linden NJ 07036

SCHRIFTGIESSER, KARL (JOHN), author; b. Boston, Nov. 12, 1903; s. Berthold and Hetty (Row) S.; ed. Roxbury Latin Sch., Boston; m. Ruth Mansfield, Aug. 5, 1928; 1 dau., Karla E. (Mrs. Peter Irvine). Mem. editorial staff Boston Post, 1920-24, Boston Evening Transcript, 1924-34, Washington Post, 1934-36, N.Y. Times, 1937-44; asso. dir. information Com. Econ. Devel., 1956-68. Mem. Londonderry Hist. Soc. (pres. 1972—). Clubs: Coffee House, Overseas Press (N.Y.C.); National Press (Washington). Author: Families, 1940; Amazing Roosevelt Family, 1942; Gentleman from Massachusetts, 1944; This Was Normalcy, 1947; The Lobbyists, 1951; Business Comes of Age, 1960; Business and Public Policy, 1967; CMC: An Adventure in Policy Making, 1974. Address: Mansfield Ln Londonderry VT 05148

SCHROCK, ROBERT D., JR., orthopedic surgeon; b. Omaha, Aug. 6, 1938; s. Robert D. and Elizabeth (Wetherbee) S.; B.A., Princeton U., 1960; M.D., Cornell U., 1964; m. Carolyn Jane Gorthy, May 30, 1964; children—Robert D. III, Suzanne Bartlett. Intern, U. Wash. Affiliated Hosps., Seattle, 1964-65, resident in orthopedic surgery, 1965-70; group practice in orthopedic surgery, Rochester, N.Y., 1972—; clin. asst. prof. orthopedics U. Rochester, 1972—; v.p. Monroe Plan for Med. Care Inc., Rochester, 1975—; attending surgeon Strong Meml., Genesee hosps., Rochester; courtesy staff Rochester Gen., Highland hosps.; cons. United Cerebral Palsy Center, Rochester. Served to maj. M.C., U.S. Army, 1970-72. Seattle Prosthetics Research Study fellow, 1968-69. Diplomate Am. Bd. Orthopedic Surgery. Mem. AMA, Monroe County Med. Soc., Am. Acad. Orthopedic Surgeons, A.C.S. Am. Acad. Cerebral Palsy and Developmental Medicine. Republican. Presbyterian. Clubs: Tennis Club (Rochester), Ski Valley. Office: 220 Alexander St Rochester NY 14607

SCHROEDER, AARON HAROLD, pub. co. exec.; b. Bklyn., Sept. 7, 1926; s. Max and Pearl (Miller) S.; student pub. schs., N.Y.C.; m. Abby Steinberg, Oct. 31, 1967; 1 dau., Rachel Amy. Contact man Warner Bros. Music, Mills Music; profl. mgr. Charley Barnett, N.Y.C.; owner A. Schroeder Internat., Ltd. (and subsidiary cos.), N.Y.C., 1960—; pres. Musicor Records, N.Y.C., 1960-65; judge Am. Song Festival competition, 1976. Mem. ASCAP, Nat. Assn. Rec. Arts and Scis. (bd. govs. 1962). Composer: It's Now or Never, 1960, Good Luck Charm, 1961, I Got Stung, 1958, Stuck On You, 1959, Mandolins in the Moonlight, 1958, Not as a Stranger, 1954, Twixt Twelve and Twenty, 1959, Fools Hall of Fame, 1959, Because They're Young, 1959, Today's Teardrops, 1960, French Foreign Legion, 1959, Time and the River, 1959, I'm Gonna Knock on Your Door, 1959, Rubber Ball, 1960, Once She Was Mine (theme film Four Musketeers), 1974, Play Our Love's Theme, 1974, many others. Office: 25 W 56th St New York City NY 10019

SCHROEDER, CHARLES WILLIAM HENRY, bus. exec.; b. Bronx, N.Y., May 12, 1920; s. Karl Christian Johann and Martha Magdaline (Huerstel) S.; m. Jeanne Stagg, Jan. 14, 1944; children—Charles Fredric, Kim Dorothy. Salesman, Kipe Offset Lithography, N.Y.C., 1946-47; fireman N.Y.C. Fire Dept., 1947-64; salesman Austin Nichols, liquor distbr., 1964-66; with Pleasant Valley Wine Co., Hammondsport, N.Y., 1966—, Pa. state mgr., asst. control states mgr., 1975—. Served with USAF, 1943-72; lt. col. Res. ret. Mem. Air Force Assn. (past pres. Pitts. chpt.), AAU (pres. Allegheny Mountain assn.). Republican. Clubs: N.Y. Athletic, Woodland Hills Swim. Home: 1781 Lenape Rd West Chester PA 19380

SCHROEDER, JAMES LOUIS, JR., mech. engr.; b. York, Pa., Oct. 13, 1921; s. James Louis and Verna Grace (Zarfoss) S.; student Pa. State U., 1940-42; B.S. in Mech. Engring., George Washington U., 1945; m. Frances Irene Litsinger, Oct. 11, 1942; children—James Louis III, George K. Product designer Am. Chain & Cable Co., York, Pa., 1948-52; program mgr. Bowen-McLaughlin-York Co., York, Pa., 1952-57, chief engr., 1972—; engring. mgr. Cole Steel Equipment Co., York, Pa., 1957-72. Served with USNR, 1943-46. Registered profl. engr., Pa.; certified mfg. engr. Mem. Soc. Automotive Engrs., Soc. Mfg. Engrs., Am. Soc. for Metals, Am. Def. Preparedness Assn. Republican. Lutheran. Clubs: Masons, Shriners. Home: 1302 Green Briar Rd York PA 17404 Office: PO Box 1512 York PA 17405

SCHROEDER, JANET GREGG WALLACE (MRS. HENRY A. SCHROEDER), sculptor; b. St. Louis, May 4, 1902; d. Cecil Dudley and Jessie Marian (Howard) Gregg; student Bryn Mawr Coll., 1920-21, Washington U. Sch. Art, 1929-30; m. Asa Brookings Wallace, 1922 (dec. 1942); children—Marian (Mrs. M. W. Ney), Janet, (Mrs. Andrew B. Jones), Eugenie (Mrs. Marius S. Darrow, Jr.); m. 2d, Henry Alfred Schroeder, May 20, 1949 (dec. Apr. 1975). Tchr. sculpture John Burroughs Sch., St. Louis, 1937-38, Hickory Ridge Sch., Putney, Vt., 1946-47; exhibited Feragils, British Am. Gallery, St. Louis Art Mus., Julius Polk, Inc., St. Louis, Manchester (Vt.) Art Gallery, Book Cellar Gallery, Brattleboro, Vt., 1959, Black Starr, Gorham (N.Y.C.), 1948-49; portraits in bronze in permanent collections Robert S. Brookings, Dr. Arthur H. Compton, Rt. Rev. Father Alphonse Schwitalla, Rev. Mother Concordia, Pierre Laclede; exhibited permanent collections two portraits Nat. Portrait Gallery, Smithsonian Instn., Washington; portrait Marlboro (Vt.) Coll.; works include bronze portrait Ambassador Ellsworth Bunker, 1974, Walter Muir Whitknell, 1977. Home: 56 Todd Pond Rd Lincoln MA 01773

SCHROEDER, THEODORE CONRAD, elec. engr., mktg. exec.; b. Pitts., Feb. 11, 1922; s. Eugene A. and Hazel G. (Steimer) S.; B.S.E.E., U. Pitts., 1943, postgrad., 1948-50, 62, 67; m. Alice M. Workman, Feb. 7, 1944; 1 son, Theodore Conrad. Elec. engr. Fodor Research Labs., Pitts., 1942-43; project engr. R.J. Cummings, Jr. & Associates, Pitts., 1946-48; devel. engr. Bacharach Indsl. Instrument Co., Pitts., 1948-51; project engr. M.S. Jacobs & Assos., Pitts., 1952-53; design engr. Union Switch & Signal div. Westinghouse Airbrake Co., Pitts., 1953-69, mktg. mgr. aerospace dept., 1967-69; v.p. mktg. Babcock Electronics Co., Costa Mesa, Calif., 1969—; lectr. elec. engring. U. Pitts., 1947-51; partner Busse & Schroeder, elec. engring. cons., 1950-52. Served to 1st. lt., inf., U.S. Army, 1942-46, capt. Signal Corps., 1952-53. Decorated Bronze Star with V device and oak leaf cluster, Purple Heart; registered profl. engr., Pa. Mem. Instrument Soc. Am. (dir. trans. div. 1958-61), Gideons Internat., Eta Kappa Nu (pres. Pitts. alumni chpt. 1959), Sigma Tau. Republican. Presbyterian (elder). Club: Masons. Patentee in field. Home: 2 Forest Dr Pittsburgh PA 15220 also 21551 Brookhurst Huntington Beach CA 92646

SCHROTH, THOMAS ANTHONY, surgeon; b. Newark, Apr. 7, 1918; s. Frederick Felix and Catherine S.; A.B., Temple U., 1940; M.D., Hahnemann Med. Coll., 1943; m. Margaret Susan Schilling, Apr. 4, 1942; children—Susan Catherine, Thomas Frederick. Intern, St. Luke's and Children's Med. Center, Phila., 1943-44; resident U. Pa. Grad Sch., Phila., 1947-48, Hahnemann Med. Coll. and Hosp., Phila., 1948-51, Children's Hosp., Boston, 1951-52; practice medicine specializing in surgery, Chester, Pa., 1953—; staff surgeon Crozer-Chester Med. Center, 1953-68, vice-chief surgery, 1963-68, v.p. med. affairs, 1970—, CORE Teaching coordinator, 1970-77; chief surgery Sacred Heart Hosp., Chester, 1960-61; asso. prof. surgery Hahnemann Med. Coll., 1970—. Asst. scoutmaster Valley Forge council Boy Scouts Am., 1954-56. Served to capt. U.S. Army, 1945-47, USAF, 1953. Diplomate Am. Bd. Surgery. Fellow A.C.S., Am. Coll. Utilization Rev. Physicians; mem. AMA., Pa., Delaware County med. socs., Am. Bd. Quality Assurance and Utilization Rev. Physicians, Am. Trauma Soc. Republican. Lutheran. Club: Springhaven. Condr. Hahnemann Symphony Orch., Phila., 1943, concertmeister, 1940-42. Home: 205 Martroy Ln Wallingford PA 19086 Office: Crozer-Chester Med Center Chester PA 19013

SCHRUBEN, JOHANNA STENZEL, mathematician; b. Flushing, N.Y.; d. Wolfram G. and Janet (Lazewski) Stenzel; B.S., magna cum laude, Queens Coll., 1964; M.A., U. Mich., 1966, Ph.D., 1968; m. Dale L. Schruben, July 5, 1969. Instr., U. Minn., 1968-69; sr. scientist Westinghouse Research Labs., Pitts., 1969—. Mem.-at-large Internat. Commn. on Illumination, 1976-78. NSF fellow, 1965-67. Mem. Am. Math. Soc., Soc. Indsl. and Applied Math., Optical Soc. Am., Illuminating Engring. Soc. (chmn. veiling reflections subcom. 1974-78), Phi Beta Kappa. Contbr. articles to profl. publs. Office: Westinghouse Research Labs Pittsburgh PA 15235

SCHUCHMAN, HERBERT, dentist; b. Bklyn., Apr. 6, 1935; s. Irving and Evelyn (Bender) S.; B.A., N.Y. U., 1956, D.D.S., 1960; m. Marian C. Jacobs, Aug. 29, 1959; children—Ilene, Donna. Pvt. practice dentistry, Wantagh, L.I., 1963-66, N.Y.C., 1966—. Lectr., Midtown Dental Soc. Served to capt. USAF, 1961-63. Mem. Am. Acad. Implant Dentistry, Am. Dental Assn. (lectr.), Acad. Gen. Dentistry, 10th Dist. Dental Soc. Home: 3176 Ann St Baldwin NY 11510 Office: 10 W 15th St New York City NY 10011

SCHUCK, VICTORIA, coll. pres.; b. Oklahoma City, Mar. 16, 1909; d. Anthony B. and Anna (Priebe) Schuck; A.B. with great distinction, Stanford, 1930, M.A., 1931, Ph.D., 1937. Univ. fellow Stanford, 1931-33, teaching asst., 1934-35, acting instr., 1935-36, instr., 1936-37; asst. prof. Fla. State Coll. Women, 1937-40; mem. faculty Mt. Holyoke Coll., 1940—, prof. polit. sci., 1950-75; pres. Mt. Vernon Coll., Washington, 1977—; vis. lectr. Smith Coll., 1948-49; vis. prof. Stanford, summer 1952; guest scholar The Brookings Instn., Washington, 1967-68, summers 1968, 70. Principal program analyst, planning for local bds. OPA, 1942-44; cons. Office Temporary Controls, 1945-47; mem. internat. secretariat UN Conf., San Francisco, 1945; mem. Mass. Commn. Interstate Coop., 1957-60; mem. U. Mass. Bldg. Authority, 1960-68; Mass. adv. com. U.S. Commn. Civil Rights, 1962—; mem. President's Commn. Registration and Voting Participation, 1963; mem. Berkshire Community Coll. Planning Com., 1964-68, Greenfield Community Coll. Planning Com., 1965-67; mem. Town of South Hadley Planning Bd., 1959-67, chmn., 1961-67; mem. Mass. Bd. Higher Edn., 1976-77; trustee U. Mass., 1958-65. Haynes Found. grantee, 1951-52, Asia Soc. grantee, 1971-72. Mem. Internat., Am. (sec. 1959-60 v.p. 1970-71), New Eng. (pres. 1950-51), Northeastern (v.p. 1971-72, pres. 1972-73) polit. sci. assns., Assn. Asian Studies, AAUW (pres. Mass. 1946-50, nat. chmn. legis. program com., bd. dirs. 1965-69), Am. Assn. Polit. Cons., Am. Soc. Pub. Adminstrn., AAUP (pres. Mt. Holyoke 1962-64), Phi Beta Kappa, Chi Omega, Mortar Bd. (hon.). Club: Cosmopolitan (N.Y.C.). Contbr. profl. jours. Regional editor Ency. Brit., 1958-61. Office: Mt Vernon Coll Washington DC 20007

SCHUCMAN, HELEN COHN (MRS. LOUIS SCHUCMAN), psychologist, educator; b. N.Y.C.; d. Sigmund and Rosa (Black) Cohn; B.A., N.Y. U., 1936, M.A., 1953, Ph.D., 1957. Asso. research scientist N.Y. U., 1958-59; chief research psychologist child devel. program Columbia Coll. Physicians and Surgeons, 1959-68, research asso. dept. psychiatry, 1962-63, asst. prof. med. psychology, 1963-71, asso. prof. med. psychology, 1971-75, spl. lectr., 1975-78; chief psychologist Neurol. Inst., Columbia-Presbyn. Med. Center, 1963-75; practice psychology, 1975—; research cons. Inst. Retarded Children of Shield of David, 1958—, Study Program Human Ecology, Cornell U. Med. Coll., 1961-68. Fellow Internat. Council Psychologists, Am. Assn. Mental Deficiency; mem. AAAS, Am., N.Y. State psychol. assns., Psychometric Soc., Psi Chi, Pi Lambda Theta, Kappa Delta Pi. Contbr. articles to profl. jours. Home: 200 E 16th St New York City NY 10003 Office: 200 E 16 St New York City NY 10003

SCHULENBERG, DONALD WARREN, educator; b. Fargo, N.D., Nov. 4, 1926; s. Walter William and Gilma (Shirley) S.; B.E., Moorhead U., 1956; M.A., Syracuse U., 1959; m. Olga C. Chester, June 20, 1959; 1 dau., Elizabeth Ann. Tchr., New York Mills, Minn., 1957; resident advisor Syracuse U., 1958-59; tchr. Onondaga Valley Acad., 196 -61; chmn. social studies dept. Clary Jr. High Sch., 1962-63; tchr. Henninger Sr. High Sch., 1964-66, Nottingham Sr. High Sch., Fayetteville, N.Y., 1966—; tchr., counsellor Boys' State Minn., 1954-56; mem. Cornell Law Inst. for Social Studies Tchrs., 1973-74; participant Law, Youth and Citizenship Conf., 1974, Teaching About Law and Values, 1975, Project LEGAL, 1976. Sec. Young Republicans, 1952-53; treas. Swarthout Grove Assn., Auburn, N.Y., 1969. Served with AUS, 1944-46, 47-53; PTO. Asia Soc. scholar, 1959-60, fellow, 1961. Mem. Am. Sociol. Assn., Syracuse Tchrs. Assn., N.Y. State Edn. Assn., NEA, DAV, Vets. Caucus N.Y., Nat. Pilots Assn., Kappa Delta Phi. Lutheran. Club: Optimist. Home: 7135 E Genesee St Fayetteville NY 13066

SCHULER, MATHIAS JOHN, III, chem. co. exec.; b. N.Y.C., Apr. 29, 1918; s. Mathias John and Anna Theresa (Hobbs) S.; B.A., Bklyn. Coll., 1938; m. Marion Randall Brandner, Apr. 4, 1942; children—Marion Janet, Robert Craig, Betty Jean, Susan Pamela. Research asst. Meml. Hosp. Research Labs., N.Y.C., 1938-39; analytical chemist Continental Baking Co., N.Y.C., 1939-40, Ansbacher-Siegle Corp., N.Y.C., 1940-41; tchr. Bd. Edn., N.Y.C., 1941-44; supr. Kellex Corp., N.Y.C., 1944-45; with E.I. duPont de

Nemours & Co., Inc., Wilmington, Del., 1945—, sr. research chemist, 1959-64, research asso., 1964-69, supr., 1969-70, div. head, dye application research, 1970-75, head supporting services div., 1975—. Mem. adv. com. Glassboro (N.J.) State Coll., 1958-61; mem. sci. adv. com. Gloucester County Coll., Sewell, N.J., 1967-69. Mem. Bd. Edn., Pitman, N.J., 1958-64, 70-74, pres., 1972-73. Mem. Am. Chem. Soc., Am. Assn. Textile Chemists and Colorists. Contbr. articles to profl. jours. Patentee in field. Office: EI duPont De Nemours & Co Wilmington DE 19898

SCHULER, WILLIAM GRANVILLE, ins. co. exec.; b. Finland, Pa., Nov. 11, 1921; s. William C. and Florence N. (Gerhart) S.; grad. Am. Tech. Soc., 1942; student U. Miss., 1942-43, U. Biarritz (France), 1945, Ursinus Coll., 1964-65; m. Elizabeth B. Bosler, Feb. 8, 1947; children—Jeffrey, Gary, Rodney. Div. claim supr. Harleysville (Pa.) Ins. Cos., 1956-62, div. claim mgr., 1962-63, dir. sales, 1963-68, v.p. sales, 1968-76, sr. v.p. ops., 1976—. Served with USAAF, 1942-45; ETO. Mason. Office: 355 Maple Ave Harleysville PA 19438

SCHULLER, DIANE ETHEL, pediatric allergist and immunologist; b. Bklyn., Nov. 27, 1943; d. Charles William and Dorothy (McWilliams) Schuller; A.B. cum laude with honors in Biology, Bryn Mawr Coll., 1965; M.D., State U. N.Y., Downstate Med. Sch., 1970. Intern, then resident in pediatrics Roosevelt Hosp., N.Y.C., 1970-72, resident in allergy Cooke Inst. Allergy, 1972-74; asso. in pediatrics Geisinger Med. Center, Danville, Pa., 1974—, dir. dept. pediatric cardio-respiratory and allergic diseases, 1978—; asst. clin. prof. pediatrics Hershey Med. Coll., Pa. State U., 1974—; mem. Columbia-Montour Home Health Services Adv. Group of Profl. Personnel, 1975—. Mem. scholarship com. Bryn Mawr Club, N.Y., 1970-75. Diplomate Am. Bd. Allergy and Immunology; recipient Physicians Recognition award AMA, 1973-76, 74-76, 75-78. Diplomate Am. Bd. Pediatrics, Nat. Bd. Med. Examiners. Fellow Am. Acad. Pediatrics, Am. Coll. Allergists, Am. Assn. Clin. Immunology and Allergy; mem. Am. Acad. Allergy, Pa., N.Y. State allergy socs., N.Y. State, N.Y. County med. socs. Home: Box 50 Heather Hills Dr RD 4 Danville PA 17821 Office: Geisinger Med Center Danville PA 17821

SCHULMAN, BRIAN MARTIN, psychiatrist; b. N.Y.C., Aug. 15, 1946; s. Leon and Gertrude Schulman; B.A. with distinction, George Washington U., 1968, M.D., 1971; m. Marie Janet Levine, Feb. 24, 1973; children—Beth, Lisa. Intern, Met. Hosp., N.Y.C., 1971-72; resident in psychiatry Payne Whitney Clinic, Cornell Med. Center, N.Y.C., 1972-75; practice medicine specializing in psychiatry, Bethesda, Md., 1977—; asst. prof. psychiatry Georgetown U. Sch. Medicine, Washington, 1975—; cons. psychiatry Nat. Naval Med. Center, Bethesda, 1977—. Served to lt. comdr. USN, 1975-77. Mem. Am. Psychol. Assn., Washington Psychiat. Soc. Home: 1403 Stratton Dr Potomac MD 20854 Office: 4400 East-West Hwy Bethesda MD 20014

SCHULMAN, CAROL BRIMBERG, physician; b. Washington, Dec. 17, 1944; d. Murry M. and Mary (Epstein) Brimberg; A.B. cum laude, Radcliffe Coll., 1966; student Harvard Med. Sch., 1966-68; M.D., Georgetown U., 1970; m. Joseph Daniel Schulman, June 14, 1964; children—Erica Nancy, Julie Katherine. Intern, resident in pediatrics N.Y. Hosp.-Cornell Med. Center, 1970-73; clin. asso. NIH, Bethesda, Md., 1975-76; pediatrician Group Health Assn., Washington, 1976—; attending physician Children's Hosp., Nat. Med. Center; asst. clin. prof. George Washington U. Med. Sch. Diplomate Am. Bd. Pediatrics. Fellow Am. Acad. Pediatrics; mem. D.C. Med. Soc. Home: 9207 Aldershot Dr Bethesda MD 20034 Office: 2121 Pennsylvania Ave Washington DC 20037

SCHULMAN, HERBERT, safety engr.; b. Bklyn., July 6, 1932; s. Philip and Mary (Pakula) S.; diploma in machine design Mondell Inst., 1956; B.S. in Physics, Bklyn. Coll., 1965; m. Barbara Schiff, Mar. 10, 1956; children—Susan Jayne, Mitchell Jay. Draftsman, E. J. Seiber Engring. Co., N.Y.C., 1955-56; designer Gibbs & Cox, N.Y.C., 1956-65; design engr. Brookhaven Nat. Lab., Upton, N.Y., 1965-71, hazards engr., 1971—. Mgr., Little League Baseball Team, Port Jefferson Station, N.Y., 1969-74. Served with U.S. Army, 1953-54; Germany. Mem. Am. Soc. Safety Engrs. (profl.). Patentee dental light reflector and visual-audio analgesic assembly. Home: 24 Clematis St Port Jefferson Sta NY 11776 Office: Bldg 535 Brookhaven Nat Lab Upton NY 11973

SCHULMAN, JOSEPH DANIEL, physician; b. Bklyn., Dec. 20, 1941; s. Max and Miriam (Grossman) S.; B.A., Bklyn. Coll., 1961; M.D., Harvard U., 1966; m. Carol Ann Brimberg, June 14, 1964; children—Erica N., Julie K. Intern, resident in pediatrics Mass. Gen. Hosp., Boston, 1966-68; clin. asso. Nat. Inst. Arthritis and Metabolic Diseases, 1968-70; resident in obstetrics and fellow in pediatrics N.Y. Hosp., Cornell Med. Center, 1970-73; Gilbert and Nat. Found. fellow Cambridge U. (Eng.), 1973-74; head sect. human biochem. genetics Nat. Inst. Child Health and Human Devel., NIH, Bethesda, Md., 1974—; prof. obstetrics and pediatrics George Washington U., 1975—. Served with USPHS, 1968-70. Diplomate Am. Bd. Pediatrics, Am. Bd. Obstetrics and Gynecology. Fellow Am. Coll. Obstetrics and Gynecology; mem. Soc. Pediatric Research (council), Soc. Gynecologic Investigation, Am. Soc. Human Genetics, Phi Beta Kappa, Sigma Xi. Jewish. Clubs: Harvard, Cosmos. Author 2 books; contbr. articles to med. jours. Home: 9207 Aldershot Dr Bethesda MD 20034 Office: Rm 13N 260 Bldg 10 NIH Bethesda MD 20014

SCHULTHEIS, EDWIN MILFORD, educator; b. N.Y.C., Apr. 15, 1928; s. Milford Theodore and Lillian May (Hill) S.; B.S., Hofstra Coll., 1950; M.B.A., N.Y. U. Grad. Sch. Bus. Adminstrn., 1958, Ed.D., Sch. Edn., 1972; m. Joan Edna Bruckner, June 23, 1956. Officer mgr., sales rep. Topton Rug Mfg. Co., N.Y.C., 1950-54; area mgr., trainer Mobil Oil Co., N.Y.C., 1954-62; coordinator distributive edn. North Babylon (N.Y.) Pub. Schs., 1962—; prof. bus. adminstrn. State U. N.Y., Farmingdale, 1970—; asst. prof. edn. N.Y. U., 1973—; dir. edn. Syracuse (N.Y.) U., 1973—; test writer, cons. N.Y. State Dept. Edn., Albany, 1965—; textbook reviewer McGraw-Hill Book Co., N.Y.C., 1967-69; cons. Cornell U., 1975; dist. adviser Distributive Edn. Clubs N.Y., 1970, bd. govs., 1967-68, trustee, 1975—; mem. curriculum adv. council Suffolk County (N.Y.) Distributive Edn. Assn., 1967—. Named N.Y. State Tchr. of Yr., 1976; recipient Outstanding Service award Distributive Edn. Clubs. N.Y., Suffolk County Distributive Edn. Assn. Mem. Acad. Mgmt., Am. Petroleum Inst., Am. Security Council, Suffolk County Assn. Distributive Edn. Tchrs. (mem. exec. bd. 1962-74), N.Y. State (pres. 1975—), L.I. (exec. bd. 1972—) distributive edn. assns., N.Y. State Occupational Edn. Assn. (v.p. 1975—), Distributive Edn. Clubs Am. (regional leader 1972-75), Phi Delta Kappa, Sigma Alpha Lambda. Presbyn. Club: Bellport (N.Y.) Golf. Author: Modern Petroleum Marketing, 1971. Home: 10 Brendan Ave Massapequa Park NY 11762 Office: North Babylon Pub Schs North Babylon NY 11703

SCHULTZ, ALLAN JOSEPH, cons. engr.; b. Trenton, N.J., May 1, 1925; s. Sol E. and Mildred (Levy) S.; B.S. in Elec. Engring., Ore. State U., 1948; m. Helene Von Transehe, Oct. 27, 1974; 1 dau., Adonica. Analytical engr. Gen. Elec. Co., Schenectady, 1948-59; prin. engr. H. Zinder & Assos., N.Y.C., 1959-68; owner Allan J. Schultz, cons. engr., N.Y.C., 1968—. Served with AUS, 1943-46. Decorated Purple Heart; recipient 1st prize for tech. paper AIEE, 1956. Mem. Nat. Soc. Profl. Engrs., IEEE, Am. Nuclear Soc., N.Y. Acad. Scis., Am. Cons. Engrs. Council, Am. Water Works Assn., Eta Kappa Nu, Sigma Tau. Jewish. Home: 332 W Mt Airy Rd Croton-on-Hudson NY 10520 Office: 440 Park Ave S New York City NY 10016

SCHULTZ, GEORGE JOSEPH, advt. and pub. relations cons.; b. Milw., Apr. 27, 1932; s. George Frank and Kathryn Marguerite (Peters) S.; B.A., St. Norbert Coll., 1954; postgrad. Sch. Advanced Internat. Studies, Johns Hopkins, 1966-67; m. Sophia Vera Beryk, Nov. 20, 1965; children—George Anthony, John Gregory, Marianna. News reporter Radio Sta. WBAY, Green Bay, Wis., 1952, Sta. WDUZ, Green Bay, 1952-54, Green Bay Press-Gazette, 1956-61; legis. asst. Rep. Gracie Pfost of Idaho, Washington, 1961; press officer AID, Washington, 1962-67, U.S. Dept. Commerce, Washington, 1967-69, N.Y.C., 1969-74; founder Schultz/Princeton Assos., Princeton, N.J., 1974—, AdRep Services, 1977—; chmn. pub. relations com. N.Y.-N.J. World Trade Week, 1971, 73. Community ambassador of Green Bay to St. Etienne, France, 1953; organizer, 1st mng. dir. Ars Nova Chamber Orch., Mercer County, N.J., 1970-71. Served to 1st lt., AUS, 1954-56. Mem. Nat. Press Club, World Trade Writers Assn. (v.p. 1978), Acad. Internat. Bus. Author: The Foreign Trade Market Place, 1977. Home: 325 Oak Ln Hightstown NJ 08S20 Office: 37 Station Dr Princeton Junction NJ 08550

SCHULTZ, HERBERT FERDINAND, sch. adminstr.; b. Newark, Feb. 18, 1916; s. Frederick A. and Carolyn (Seiber) S.; student N.Y. U., 1949-50, U. Pa., 1950-51, Glassboro State Coll., 1953-54; B.S., Rutgers U., 1956, M.Ed., 1958; m. Mildred S. Chamberlin, May 28, 1938; children—Carol Lyn, Susan Schultz Monks, Holly Ann. Pub. personnel adminstr. N.J. Civil Service Dept., Trenton, 1936-49; asst. supt. Vineland (N.J.) State Sch., 1949-61, chief exec. officer, 1965—; supt. Woodbine (N.J.) State Sch., 1961-65; dir. div. community and profl. services N.J. Dept. Instns. and Agys., 1966. Fellow Am. Assn. Mental Deficiency, Civil Service Assn., Assn. Retarded Children, N.J. Edn. Assn., Pub. Personnel Assn., Nat. Assn. Supts. Pub. Residential Facilities. Clubs: Kiwanis, Rotary. Address: 1676 E Landis Ave Vineland NJ 08361

SCHULTZ, LESLIE EDWARD, chem. mfg. co. exec.; b. Palm Beach, Fla., Nov. 16, 1925; s. Leslie Edward and Adele Angelina (Malerba) S.; B.S. in Psychology, Manhattan Coll., 1953; m. Nancy Mary Migliorato, Mar. 28, 1948; children—Jeanne, Leslie Edward, Renald, Edward. Biologist, Am. Cyanamid Co., Lederle Labs., Pearl River, N.Y., 1953-57, personnel analyst, salary adminstr., 1957-66, agrl. div., Princeton, N.J., 1966-70, personnel mgr., 1970—; job study cons. Boy Scouts Am., Good Samaritan Hosp., Nyack Hosp. Dir. Rockland County Civil Def., 1956-66. Served with USN, 1944-46. Recipient Lederle Top Thinker Golden award, 1957; N.Y. State Pub. Service commendation, 1967; Adminstrv. Mgmt. Soc. award of merit, 1976. Mem. Am. Soc. Compensation Analysts, Del. Valley, Princeton (past pres.) personnel assns., Adminstrv. Mgmt. Soc. (past pres.), Urban League Met. Trenton, Nat. Alliance Businessmen, Tuskegee Inst. Bus.-Industry Cluster. Republican. Roman Catholic. Clubs: Reaville Sportsmen's Assn., Fairfield Aeroclub, K.C. Home: Route 8 Madison Ave Flemington NJ 08822 Office: Box 400 Quakerbridge Rd Princeton NJ 08540

SCHULTZ, ROBERT KENNETH, architect, engr.; b. Emmaus, Pa., Jan. 8, 1938; s. Howard Robert and Dorothea Mae (Kehm) S.; B.Archtl. Engring., Pa. State U., 1961; m. Carol Ann Peacock, Oct. 29, 1960; children—Cynthia Ann, Cheryl Ann, Robert K. Apprentice architect Wolf and Hahn, Architects, Allentown, Pa., 1961-63; project architect Coston-Frankfurt-Short, Architects and Engrs., Bethlehem, Pa., 1963-65; architect Jack Williams, AIA, Allentown, 1965-69; partner Williams & Schultz, Architects, Engrs. and Planners, Allentown, 1969—; tchr. archtl. tech. Northampton Community Coll., 1975. Mem. Emmaus Planning Commn., 1971—. Registered profl. engr., Pa.; registered architect, Pa., N.J. Mem. AIA, Pa. Soc. Architects. Home: 29 N 8th Emmaus PA 18049 Office: 4210 Tilghman Allentown PA 18104

SCHULTZE, CHARLES LOUIS, educator, govt. ofcl.; b. Alexandria, Va., Dec. 12, 1924; s. Richard Lee and Nora Woolls (Baggett) S.; A.B., Georgetown U., 1948, M.A., 1950; Ph.D., U. Md., 1960; m. Rita Irene Hertzog, Sept. 6, 1947; children—Karen M., Kevin C., Helen L., Kathleen, Carol, Mary. Mem. staff Pres.'s Council Econ. Advisers, 1952-58, chmn., 1977—; asso. prof. econs. Ind. U., 1959-61; prof. econs. U. Md., 1961; asst. dir. U.S. Bur. of Budget, 1962-65, dir., 1965-67; sr. fellow Brookings Instn., 1968—. Served with AUS, 1943-46; ETO. Decorated Purple Heart, Bronze Star medal. Mem. Am. Econ. Assn., Royal Econ. Soc. Author: Recent Inflation in the United States, 1959; The Politics and Economics of Public Spending, 1969; (with others) Setting National Priorities: The 1974 Budget. Home: 5826 Nevada Ave NW Washington DC 20015 Office: Exec Office of Pres 1600 Pennsylvania Ave Washington DC 20500

SCHULTZE, DIETRICH FRANZ, photog. co. exec.; b. Dortmund, Germany, July 30, 1934; s. Werner Friedrich and Magdalena J. (Starck) S.; came to U.S., 1958; Arbitur, U. Mannheim, 1953; Physics, Heidelberg U., 1955; Ph.D., U. Munich, 1958; postgrad. (univ. fellow) Northwestern U., 1958-59; m. Celia Y. Ancona, July 6, 1960; children—Christina, Katia, Karin, Axel, Ingrid, Dietrich, Peter, Joachim. Research and devel. fellow Mellon Inst., Pitts., 1959-61; chemist Agfa AG, Leverkusen, W. Ger., 1961-63, tech. dir. Agfa Gevaert Inc., Teterboro, N.J., 1964—. Fulbright scholar, 1958; Mellon fellow, 1960. Mem. Soc. Photog. Scientists and Engrs. (sr.), Soc. Photo Optical Instrumentation Engrs. Contbr. articles to profl. publs. photog. sci. and processes. Patentee in field. Office: Agfa Gevaert Inc 275 North St Teterboro NJ 07608

SCHULZ, FRANK CARL, JR., educator; b. Bklyn., Sept. 6, 1945; s. Frank Carl and Margaret Ethel (Conway) S.; B.S., Tex. A. and I. U., 1968; diploma Cornell U., 1969. Instr., Tex. A. and I. U., Corpus Christi, 1968-69, N.Y. Mil. Acad., Cornwall, 1969-72; tchr. Lakeland (N.Y.) Sch. Dist., 1972-77; v.p. Cooper Hill Farms, Katonah, N.Y., 1976—; dir. Muscoot Farm for County of Westchester (N.Y.), 1976—; cons. Readers Digest Book Co., 1977—, Borden Co., 1972—. Served with USAF, 1968-69. Mem. Internat. Oceanographic Soc., AAAS, Am. Ordnance Soc., Am. Mil. Engrs., Nat. Parks and Recreation Assn., Am. Beef Cattle Assn. Democrat. Roman Catholic. Club: Bedford Farmers. Home: 3579 Sagamore Ave Mohegan Lake NY 10547 Office: Muscoot Farm Route 100 Katonah NY 10536

SCHULZ, MILFORD DAVID, radiotherapist; b. Sister Bay, Wis., Dec. 12, 1909; s. William George and Anna Fredericka Wilhelmina (Lucht) S.; B.A., North Central Coll., 1931; M.B., Northwestern U., 1935, M.D., 1936; m. E(sther) Marie Brandt, July 3, 1937; 1 dau., M(ary) Catherine. Intern, West Suburban Hosp., Oak Park, Ill., 1935-36; resident in radiology Northwestern U. Med. Sch., Chgo., 1936-37; radiation therapist Collis B. Huntington Meml. Hosp., 1940-41; radiation therapist Mass. Gen. Hosp., Boston, 1941-76, sr. cons. in radiation therapy, 1976—; mem. faculty Harvard Med. Sch., 1942-76, prof. radiation therapy, 1970-76, prof. emeritus, 1976—; cons. Mass. Eye and Ear Infirmary, 1942—, Mass. Div. Pub. Health, 1950—. Mem. AMA, Mass. Med. Soc., Am. Roentgen Ray Soc., Radiol. Soc. N.Am., Am. Radium Soc. (past pres., Gold medal 1974), Am. Soc. Therapeutic Radiologists (past pres.), Am. (past pres. Mass. div., Bronze medal 1969), New Eng. (past pres.) cancer socs., Am. Coll. Radiology (past chancellor), Am. Soc. Clin. Oncology, Assn. U. Radiologists. Contbr. chpts. to books, articles to profl. jours. Home: 50 Bow Rd Belmont MA 02178 Office: Mass Gen Hosp Boston MA 02114

SCHULZ, RICHARD BURKART, scientific cons.; b. Phila., May 21, 1920; s. Herman and Laura (Burkart) S.; B.S.E.E., U. Pa., 1942, M.S., 1951, postgrad., 1951-53; m. Jeannette Charlotte Vollmer, Nov. 22, 1958; 1 son, Steven Edward. Radio engr. Hazeltine Service Corp., Little Neck, N.Y., 1942; research asso. U. Pa., Phila., 1942-45; partner firm Schulz and Weisbecker Co., Williamstown, N.J., 1945-47; owner Electro-Search, Phila., 1947-55; program devel. coor. Armour Research Found., Chgo., 1955-61; chief electro-interference sect. United Control Corp., Redmond, Wash., 1961-62; chief electrocompatibility The Boeing Co., Seattle, 1962-70; staff engr. S.W. Research Inst., San Antonio, 1970-74; scientific adv. IIT Research Inst., Annapolis, Md., 1974—. Registered profl. engr., Pa. Fellow IEEE (editor Trans. on Electromagnetic Compatibility); mem. Am. Contract Bridge League (life master). Republican. Lutheran. Contbr. articles to profl. jours. Patentee in field. Home: 840 Meadow Heights Ln Arnold MD 21012 Office: IIT Research Inst N Severn Annapolis MD 21402

SCHULZE, RICHARD TAYLOR, congressman; b. Phila., Aug. 7, 1929; s. John L. and Grace (Taylor) S.; student U. Houston, 1948, 50, Villanova U., 1952, Temple U., 1968; m. Nancy Lockwood, May 14, 1955; children—Karen, Richard Taylor, Michael, Linda. Propr., Home Appliance Center, Paoli, Pa., 1950—; register of wills, clk. Orphans Ct., Chester County, 1967-69; mem. Pa. Ho. of Reps. from 157th Dist., 1969-74, sec. ways and means com., 1973-74, sec. bus. and commerce com., 1973-74; mem. 94th-96th Congresses from 5th Pa. dist. Pres. Upper Main Line Jr. C. of C., 1956; scoutmaster local Boy Scouts Am., 1954, chmn. Chester County council Philmont com., 1956, chmn. advancement com. Conestoga 1957; chmn. Paoli Meml. Hosp. Day, 1970. Chmn. Tredyffrin Twp. Republican Com., 1966; pres. Upper Main Line Young Rep. Club, 1963, Chester County Fedn. Rep. Clubs, 1965; mem. Pa. Young Reps., 1965; chmn. nominating com. Pa. Young Rep. Biennial Conv., 1966; exec. com. Rep. County Com. Chester County, 1965, campaign chmn., 1964, 66, 69, 70; chmn. Richard M. Nixon Day, 1968. Served with AUS, 1951-53. Recipient Scoutmaster Key award Boy Scouts Am., 1957, Dist. Merit award, 1958, Retail Promotion of Year award Nat. Elec. Mfrs. Assn., 1965, Distinguished Mcht. award Gen. Electric Co., 1967, 68; named Outstanding Jaycee of Year, Upper Main Line chpt. Jr. C. of C., 1955. Mem. Paoli Bus. Assn. (past v.p. dir.), Hillside Sch. P.T.A. (charter), Great Valley Jr. C. of C., Archaeol. Inst. Am., Great Valley Assn., Register of Wills Assn. Pa., Am. Legion, Circus Saints and Sinners, Green Valleys Assn. Presbyterian. Mason. Clubs: Maxwell Football (Phila.); Conestoga High School Gridiron (Berwyn, Pa.) Pa.). Home: Swedesford Rd Box 512 1 Malvern PA 19355 Office: 95 E Lancaster Ave Paoli PA 19301 also US Ho of Reps Washington DC 20515

SCHUMAN, ISADORE, drug co. exec.; b. Phila., May 7, 1928; s. Louis and Sarah (Brenner) S.; B.S., Phila. Coll. Pharmacy and Sci., 1951; children—Michael Howard, Robin Ellyn, Kerry Scott. With Sun Ray Drug Co., 1944-55; owner, operator Dellicker Pharmacy, North Wales, Pa., 1955-61, Schuman Discount Drugs, Lansdale, Pa., 1961—; pres. Medicare Wholesale Drugs Inc., Lansdale, 1968—; cons. major pharm. cos.; dir. Sonex Corp., Computer Entry Corp., Model Vending Co., Bell Consumer Corp. Bd. dirs., campaign chmn. Montgomery County March of Dimes, 1974-77. Mem. Nat. Assn. Retail Drugs, Nat. Assn. Chain Drug Stores, Nor Gwyn (Pa.) C. of C. (pres. 1954-55), Smithsonian Instn. Asso. Club: Lions. Home: 606 Gillinder St Lansdale PA 19446 Office: 214 N Broad St Lansdale PA 19446

SCHUMANN, OTHO DOUGLAS, cons. firm exec.; b. New Orleans, Sept. 10, 1924; s. Otho Charles and Eunice Grace (Douglas) S.; B.B.A., Tulane U., 1947; M.B.A., N.Y. U., 1953; m. Mary Elizabeth Coughlin, July 19, 1952. Indsl. engr. Lane Cotton Mills, New Orleans, 1947-48; cost accountant Pomona Mfg. Co., Greensboro, N.C., 1948; indsl. engr. Morgan Cotton Mills, Laurinburg, N.C., 1949-50; cost estimator, salesman product devel. U.S. Rubber Co., N.Y.C., 1950-55; mgr. market devel. Am. Enka, N.Y.C., 1955-60; indsl. sales mgr. Air Reduction Co., N.Y.C., 1960; asst. to v.p. sales Aberfoyle Mfg. Co., N.Y.C., 1961; group mgr. mktg. research Deering Milliken Corp., N.Y.C., 1962-71; pres. Yorkfab Ltd., N.Y.C., 1972, Schumann Intergroup Inc., Manhasset Hills, N.Y., 1972—. Served to capt. USNR, 1942-46, 61-62. Recipient Distinguished Service award Cath. War Vets., 1975. Mem. Am. Assn. Textile Tech. (bd. govs. 1969-74), Am. Assn. Textile Chemists and Colorists, Am. Arbitration Assn. (nat. panel arbitrators 1965-76), Res. Officers Assn., Naval Res. Assn. (adv. bd.), N.Y. Mil. Assn., Navy League (dir. 1970-78, v.p. 1977-78). Contbg. editor Modern Textiles mag., Modern Knitting Mgmt. mag.; pub. Textile News & Notes. Home: 18 Monterey Dr Manhasset Hills NY 11040

SCHUMYLOWYCH, TARAS, artist, archtl. designer; b. Javoriw, Ukraine, Nov. 22, 1916; s. Wasyl and Olena (SasJaworska) S.; came to U.S., 1950, naturalized, 1956; student Meisterschule for Graphic und Buchgeverbe, Berlin, 1942-44, Berlin U., 1944-45, Columbia U., 1954-55; grad. in arch. Mechanics Inst., N.Y., 1960, postgrad. in comml. art, 1961-62; postgrad. interior design Sachs Inst., N.Y.C., 1973; m. Iryna Gribkoff, May 31, 1945; children—Marianna, Olena, Vera, Wasyl. Archtl. designer Fellgheimer & Wagner, N.Y.C., 1956-57, Wm. Boegel, Architect, 1957, LaPierre, Litchfield & Partners, N.Y.C., 1957-58, 59-61, Guy B. Panero, Cons. Engrs., N.Y.C., 1958, Paul L. Wood & Lee Borrero Asso. Architects, N.Y.C., 1961-67, John A. Pruyn & Assos., N.Y.C., 1968-77, Realistic Designs, N.Y.C., 1977—; over 28 one-man shows including N.Y. Pub. Library, Ottendorfer Br., 1967, Yonkers (N.Y.) Pub. Library, 1967, World Trade Center, N.Y.C., 1974, Ukranian Sports Club Gallery, N.Y.C., 1977, Haines Falls (N.Y.) Library, 1977, Nippon Mus., N.Y.C., 1978; numerous group shows including Tannersville (N.Y.) Show (1st prize), 1971, Composers, Authors and Artists Am. Show (1st prize graphics), 1975, Hempstead (N.Y.) Show (1st prize graphics), 1976; represented in permanent collections Ukrainian museums, N.Y.C., N.J., Rome. Mem. ch. choir Met. Andrey Sheptycky, N.Y.C., 1960—, Ukrainian Chorus Dumka, N.Y.C., 1950—, Ukrainian Opera Ensemble, N.Y.C., 1970—. Recipient Gold medal, George Hoe prize Mechanics Inst., 1960. Mem. Mechanics Inst. Alumni Assn., Ukrainian Artists Assn. U.S.A., Am. Artists Profl. League, Composers, Authors and Artists Am. (pres. N.Y. State 1971-73, art chmn. 1975, 78-79). Columnist Murray Hill News, N.Y.C., 1971—. Writer numerous articles about artists to mags. and newspapers. Address: 92 2d Ave New York City NY 10003

SCHUR, WALTER ROBERT, physician; b. Webster, Mass., June 17, 1914; s. Robert O. and Alma L. (Gatzke) S.; student Valparaiso U., 1931-34; M.D., Middlesex U., Waltham, Mass., 1940; m. Delta Jean Newman, June 17, 1944; children—Paul, David, Jonathan, Ruth, Timothy, Peter, Stephen, Mary, Joel, Daniel, Rhoda. Resident, Milford (Del.) Meml. Hosp., 1940-41, Grace Hosp. Cleve., 1942-43;

intern Lutheran Hosp., Cleve., 1941-42; pvt. practice, Oxford, Mass., 1944—; bd. dirs., pres. Doctors Hosp., Worcester, Mass. Bd. dirs. Atlantic dist. Luth. Ch.-Mo. Synod, 1960—, mem., sec. edn. com., missions com., 1960—, mem. stewardship com., youth com., edn. com., 1951-57, chmn. edn. com. Atlantic dist., 1954-57, mem. commn. on mission and ministry in ch., named Dist. Layman of Year, 1966, chmn. com. on ministry Atlantic dist., 1970; bd. dirs. Luth. Assn. Works of Mercy; pres., scholarship chmn. N.E. dist. Luth. Laymen's League, 1946-57; nat. bd. govs. Nat. Luth. Laymen's League, 1957; vice chmn. Luth. Hour Operating Com., 1958; New Eng. bd. dirs. Assn. Evang. Luth. Chs., 1977—, trustee East Coast Synod, 1977—; mem. Oxford Sch. Com., 1961—. Mem. Mass. Commn. on Christian Unity. Bd. dirs. Valparaiso U. Recipient Award of Merit, Internat. Luth. Laymen's League, 1963. Fellow Am. Acad. Gen. Practice; mem. AMA, Mass., Worcester Dist. med. socs., Am. Geriatrics Assn., New Eng. Obstet. and Gynecol. Soc., Valparaiso U. Alumni Assn. (past pres.), Luth. Acad. for Scholarship (dir. 1977—), Concordia Hist. Inst., Internat. Platform Assn. Rotarian (pres.). Home: Charlton Rd Oxford MA 01540 Office: 367 Main St Oxford MA 01540

SCHURE, ALEXANDER, coll. pres.; b. Can., Aug. 4, 1921; s. Harry Joshua and Bessie (Ginsberg) S.; A.S.T. in Elec. Engring., Pratt Inst., 1943; B.S., Coll. City N.Y., 1947; M.A., N.Y. U., 1948, Ph.D., 1950, Ed.D., 1953; D.Engring. Sci., Nova U., N.Y. Inst. Tech., 1976; LL.D., Boca Raton Coll., 1975; m. Dorothy Rubin, Dec. 8, 1943; children—Barbara, Matthew, Louis, Jonathan. Asst. dir. Melville Radio Insts., N.Y.C., 1945-46; pres. Crescent Sch. Radio and Television, Bklyn., 1946-53, Crescent Electronics Corp., N.Y.C., 1952-55, N.Y. Tech. Inst., Bklyn., 1953-55, N.Y. Inst. Tech., 1955—; chancellor Nova U.; dir. Seversky Electronatom Corp., N.Y.C. Cons. N.Y. State Dept. Edn., U.S. Office Edn.; mem. Regents Regional Coordinating Council for Post-Secondary Edn. in N.Y.C., 1973—, Nassau County Consortia on Higher Edn., L.I., 1971—, Alfred P. Sloan Found. adv. com. for expanding minority opportunities in engring., 1974; rep. to Nat. Assn. State Adv. Council, 1975—; mem. steering com. L.I. Regional Adv. Council, 1974— Pres. bd. dirs. L.I. Ednl. TV Council, Garden City; bd. dirs. Council Higher Ednl. Instns., N.Y.C., 1973-74. Served with Signal Corps, AUS, 1942-45. Mem. I.E.E.E., N.Y. Acad. Sci., Am. Inst. Engring. Edn., N.E.A., Electronic Industries Assn. (chmn. task force curriculum devel.), Phi Delta Kappa, Delta Mu Delta. Author and-or editor textbooks. Film producer. Designer automatic teaching machine. Patentee in field. Home: 268 Wheatley Rd Old Westbury NY 11568 Office: NY Inst Tech Old Westbury Campus Wheatley Rd Old Westbury NY 11568

SCHUSLER, MARIAN LUCILLE MARTIN (MRS. HERBERT HENRY SCHUSLER), educator; b. Woodcliff, N.J., Oct. 14, 1926; d. Theodore and Marian (Rover) Martin; B.S., Bucknell U., 1946; M.Litt., U. Pitts., 1950, Ph.D., 1964; m. Herbert Henry Schusler, Mar. 3, 1955; 1 dau., Dawn Lucille, Tchr., Reno Sr. High Sch., 1953-55; analytical statistician Census Bur., Washington, 1951-52, Navy Dept., Washington, 1952-53; tchr., chmn. dept. math. Wilkinsburg (Pa.) Sr. High Sch., 1955-66; lectr. U. Pitts., 1964-66; asso. prof. math. Slippery Rock (Pa.) State Coll., 1966-70; tchr. Shady Side Acad., Fox Chapel, Pa., 1970—. Vol. worker Children's Hosp., Pitts.; mem. Am. Host Program, Vol. Internat. Tech. Assistance. Recipient NSF award, summer 1961. Mem. Am. Ednl. Research Assn., Nat., Pa. councils tchrs. math., Math. Council Western Pa., Pa. Assn. Pvt. Sch. Tchrs., Mensa, Pi Mu Epsilon, Kappa Delta Epsilon. Presbyterian. Contbr. articles to profl. jours. Home: RD 1 Box 362 Saxonburg PA 16056 Office: Shady Side Academy Fox Chapel PA 15238

SCHUSTER, FREDERICK LEE, educator; b. Bklyn., Jan. 23, 1934; s. Jacob and Esther (Ox) S.; B.S., Bklyn. Coll., 1956; M.A., U. Calif. at Berkeley, 1958, Ph.D., 1962; m. Jean Wendy Glickman, Apr. 23, 1960; children—Deborah Susan, Michael Thomas. Research specialist Langley Porter Neuropsychiat. Inst., San Francisco, 1962-63; research asso. Argonne Nat. Lab., 1963-66; prof. dept. biology Bklyn. Coll., 1966—. Mem. Am. Soc. Cell Biology, Am. Soc. Zoologists, Soc. Protozoologists, N.Y. Soc. Electron Microscopists, AAAS, Sigma Xi. Home: 154 Beach 133d St Belle Harbor NY 11694 Office: Dept Biology Bklyn Coll Brooklyn NY 11210

SCHWAB, FRANK, JR., mgmt. cons.; b. Brookline, Mass., Dec. 19, 1931; s. Frank and Phyllis (Robinson) S.; B.A. in History, Rutgers U., 1952; M.B.A., Harvard, 1956; Exec. trainee Federated Dept. Stores, Dallas, 1956; internal auditor, staff accountant, mgmt. engr. Champion Paper and Fibre Co. (name changed to Champion Internat.), Hamilton, Ohio, and Houston, 1956-58; gen. mgmt. cons. Booz, Allen and Hamilton, N.Y.C., 1958-65; dir. transp. cons. dept. Planning Research Co., Los Angeles, 1965; founder, mgtm. cons. F.R. Schwab & Assos., Inc., N.Y.C., 1965—. Served with U.S. Army, 1952-54. Mem. Inst. Mgmt. Cons. (founding mem.), Am. Arbitration mgmt. (panel mem.). Clubs: Maidstone (E. Hampton, Long Island); Seventh Regiment Tennis (N.Y.C); West Side Tennis Forest Hills (N.Y.). Office: 645 Madison Ave New York City NY 10022

SCHWAB, GEORGE DAVID, educator, author; b. Nov. 25, 1931; s. Arkady and Klara (Jacobson) S.; B.A., City Coll. N.Y., 1954; M.A., Columbia, 1955, Ph.D., 1968; m. Eleonora Storch, Feb. 27, 1965; children—Clarence Boris, Claude Arkady, Solan Bernhard. Lectr., Columbia Coll., N.Y.C., 1959; lectr. City U. N.Y., 1960-68, asst. prof. history, 1968-72, asso. prof. history, 1973—. Mem. Columbia U. Seminar on Legal and Polit. Thought; chmn. Conf. History and Politics, City U. N.Y. Bd. dirs., mem. exec. com. Nat. Com. Am. Fgn. Policy. Mem. Am. Hist. Assn., Am. Polit. Sci. Assn., Authors Guild, Conf. for Study Polit. Thought, Internat. Com. for History 2d World War, Internat. Platform Assn. Author: Beyond Abstract Art, 1967; Enemy oder Foe, 1968; Switzerland's Tactical Nuclear Weapons Policy, 1969; The Challenge of the Exception: An Introduction to the Political Ideas of Carl Schmitt, 1970; Appeasement and Detente, 1975; Carl Schmitt: Political Opportunist?, 1975. Translator: The Concept of the Political with Comments by Leo Strauss (Carl Schmitt), 1976; Legality and Illegality as Instruments of Revolutionaries in their Quest for Power: Remarks Occasioned by the Outlook of Herbert Marcuse, 1978; The German State in Historical Perspective, 1978; Ideology: Reality or Rhetoric?, 1978; Ideology and Foreign Policy, 1978; The Decision: Is the American Sovereign at Bay?, 1978. Home: 140 Riverside Dr New York City NY 10024 Office: City U NY New York City NY 10036

SCHWAB, HAROLD LEE, lawyer; b. Bklyn., Feb. 5, 1932; s. Harold Walter and Beatrice (Braverman) S.; B.A., Harvard, 1953; LL.B., Boston Coll., 1956; m. Rowena Vivian Strauss, June 12, 1953; children—Andrew Laurence, Lisa Carey, James Harold. Admitted to N.Y. bar, 1957, U.S. Supreme Ct. bar, 1967; v.p. H.W. Schwab Textile Corp., N.Y.C., 1959-60; asso. firm Emile Z Berman and A. Harold Frost, N.Y.C., 1960-67, partner, 1967-74; sr. partner firm Lester Schwab Katz & Dwyer, N.Y.C., 1975—. Mem. nat. panel arbitrators Am. Arbitration Assn., 1969—; referee small claims div. Civil Ct. N.Y.C., 1972—. Bd. dirs. Rockaway Music and Arts Council, Inc., 1956—. Served to 1st lt. USAF, 1956-58. Mem. N.Y. State Bar Assn. (sec. trial lawyers sect. 1978—, com. on certification and specialization 1978—), Assn. Bar City N.Y., Fedn. Ins. Counsel, Def. Assn. N.Y., N.Y. County Lawyers Assn., ASTM. Club: Masons. Mem. bd. Jour. Products Liability, 1976—. Contbr. articles to profl. jours. Home: 205 Beach 142 St Neponsit NY 11694 Office: 77 Water St New York City NY 10005

SCHWADRON, MITCHELL CARL, lock mfg. co. exec.; b. Bklyn., Dec. 4, 1948; s. Leslie Samuel and Rita (Zara) S.; student Queens Coll., 1968-70, N.Y. U., 1972-73, John Jay Coll. Criminal Justice, 1975-76. Locksmith, N.Y.C., 1968—; owner Schwadron Locksmiths, Flushing, N.Y., 1976—, also Alarmsmiths and Gatesmiths div., 1979—; dir., gen. mgr. Strategic Systems Inc., 1977—; dir. bur. engring. John Jay Coll. Criminal Justice. Mem. ad-hoc mchts. com., Flushing; mem. aux. police program, N.Y.C.; asst. dist. commr. Queens council Boy Scouts Am., chmn. health and safety com., 1973—. Mem. Am. Soc. Indsl. Security, Associated Locksmiths Am., Nat. Locksmiths Assn. Home: 26 25 141st St Flushing NY 11354 Office: 135 53 Northern Blvd Flushing NY 11354

SCHWAGER, EDITH COHEN, editor; b. Trenton, N.J., Dec. 16, 1916; d. Michael and Clara (Panitch) Cohen; children—Michael J., Karen S. Exec. editor, adj. lectr. Hahnemann Med. Coll. and Hosp., Phila., adminstrv. dir. Alcoholism Clinic, 1966-75; med. editor Dorland & Sweeney Inc., Phila.; tchr. English usage and abusage workshops. Fellow Am. Med. Writers Assn. (pres. Delaware Valley chpt. 1974-77, nat. chmn. editors sect. 1977, mem. nat. bd.; editor Med. Communications; guest editor Fishbein Festschrift). Editor: Gastrointestinal Emergencies, 1976; Endocrinology and Diabetes, 1975; Hemodialysis in the Home, 1975; others. Home: 4404 Sherwood Rd Philadelphia PA 19131

SCHWAID, BENJAMIN NATHAN, dentist; b. N.Y.C., July 17, 1913; s. Josiah Jerome and Rose Anne (Nathanson) S.; B.S., Coll. City N.Y., 1937; D.D.S., N.Y. U., 1941; m. Madeline Hadassah Chavkin, June 7, 1941; children—Theodora Schwaid Rubin, Stephen William. Gen. practice dentistry, specializing in gen. anesthesia, New Hyde Park, N.Y., 1946—; asst. prof. dental anesthesiology Albert Einstein Coll. Medicine, Bronx, N.Y., 1965—; full attending dentist Kingsbrook Jewish Med. Center, Bklyn., 1953—. Served to capt. AUS, 1943-46. Fellow Am. Coll. Dentists, Am. Dental Soc. Anesthesiology (asso. editor jour. 1959-61); mem. Am. Dental Assn., N.Y. State Dental Soc. Anesthesiology (pres. 1963, dir. 1964—), Fedn. Dentaire Internationale. Club: Investment (treas. 1960—) (Nassau County, N.Y.). Contbr. articles to profl. jours. Home: 661 Bellmore Ave East Meadow NY 11554 Office: 11 Pilgrim St New Hyde Park NY 11040

SCHWAID, MADELINE CHAVKIN, educator; b. N.Y.C., Apr. 20, 1917; d. Solomon and Elizabeth (Ornstein) Chavkin; B.A., Hunter Coll., 1938; M.N., Yale U., 1941; M.A., N.Y. U., 1961, Ph.D., 1976; m. Benjamin Schwaid, June 7, 1941; children—Theodora, Stephen. Staff nurse French Hosp., N.Y.C., 1941-42; instr. sci. Manhattan State Hosp., 1942-43; instr. nursing Creedmore State Hosp., N.Y.C., 1946-47, Queens Hosp. Center (N.Y.C.), 1956-58; asst. prof. dept. nursing Adelphi U., Garden City, N.Y., 1961-68, asso. prof., 1968-75, prof., 1976—. Mem. Am. Nurses Assn., Nat. League Nursing, AAUP. Home: 661 Bellmore Ave East Meadow NY 11554 Office: Dept Nursing Adelphi U South Ave Garden City NY 11530

SCHWANER, ANNIE MAE GINN, state legislator; b. Carnesville, Ga., Apr. 24, 1912; d. Charles Holman and Mary Elizabeth (Terrell) Ginn; m. Nelson Marshall Schwaner (dec. 1967); children—Gordon Wesley, Audrey Mae, Susan Anne, Marsha Mae, Nelson Marshall II. Sec., Tubize Corp., Hopewell, Va., 1934-35; former reporter Hopewell News; former columnist Progress Index, Petersburg, Va.; mem. N.H. Ho. of Reps., 1963—, mem. municipal and county govt. com., 1963, constl. conv., 1964, resources, recreation, and devel. com. Mem. State Security Task Force, also Price Stablzn. Bd., 1964—; founder, 1st pres. Plaistow (N.H.) Civic Orgn., 1959-60; chmn. vols. Greater Haverhill (Mass.) chpt. ARC, 1954-57, nat. del., 1955, exec. bd., 1954-57; com. chmn. P.T.A. council, Worcester, 1947-48; exec. bd. Sea Coast Regional Plan, 1965-67; v.p. Seacoast Regional Devel. Assn.; mem. Diocesan Sch. Bd., 1965-71; chmn. various fund-raising drs.; mem. nat. fund raising and adv. bd. Am. Heart Assn.; mem. Rockingham County Selective System Draft Bd. Pres., Plaistow Women's Republican Club, 1964-66. Bd. dirs. N.H. Heart Assn., state heart fund chmn., 1973; bd. dirs. N.H. Commn. on Status of Women, 1975—, So. N.H. Mental Health Assn., 1975—. Recipient Bronze medal N.H. Heart Assn., 1959, certificate of merit Am. Mothers Com., 1960, certificate of honor N.H. D.A.V., 1965. Mem. Cath. Daus. Am., Cath. Women's Guild (past pres.), Am. Judicature Soc., N.H. Council on World Affairs, N.H. Council for Better Schs., Nat. Order Women Legislators (state pres. 1973). Roman Catholic (ch. adv. bd.). Home: Elm St Plaistow NH 03865

SCHWANHAUSSER, ROBERT ROWLAND, engring. co. exec.; b. Buffalo, Sept. 15, 1930; s. Edwin Julius and Helen Putnam (Rowland) S.; B.S., Mass. Inst. Tech., 1952; m. Mary Lea Hunter, Oct. 17, 1953 (div. 1978); children—Robert Hunter, Mark Putnam. Project engr. Continental Aviation & Engring. Co., Detroit, 1954; field service rep. Ryan Aero. Co., San Diego, 1954-56, project engr., 1956-59, program mgr., 1959-62, chief engr., 1962-64, v.p. aerospace, 1966-72, exec. v.p. programs, 1972-75, exec. v.p. internat., 1973-74; pres. Condur Engring. Corp., San Diego, 1974-77, Condur Aerospace Corp., El Paso, Tex., 1976-77; v.p. bus. devel. All Am. Engring. Co., Wilmington, Del., 1977—. Bd. dirs. Cornerstone Found. Served to 1st lt. USAF, 1952-54. Asso. fellow Am. Inst. Aeros. and Astronautics; mem. Am. Def. Preparedness Assn., Navy League, Nat. Rifle Assn., Calif. Rifle and Pistol Assn., Nat. Assn. Remotely Piloted Vehicles (hon. trustee 1972—), Greenhead Hunting Club (founder), Theta Delta Chi. Home: 2512 Society Dr Claymont DE 19703 Office: PO Box 1247 801 S Madison St Wilmington DE 19899

SCHWANINGER, JAMES CRAIG, SR., retail chain exec.; b. St. Louis, Aug. 30, 1942; s. Robert Henry and Marjorie Faye (Faber) S.; student S.E. Mo. State U., 1963-65; B.J., U. Mo., 1967; m. Marilyn Faye Grojean, July 3, 1965; children—James Craig, Jeffrey Carl, Joseph Christopher. News dir. Mo. Press Assn., Columbia, 1965-70; dir. pub. relations Columbia Coll., 1970-72; regional pub. relations rep. J.C. Penney Co., Rolling Meadows, Ill., 1972-74, mgr. product info., N.Y.C., 1974-78, asst. dir. corp. responsibity, 1978—. Bd. dirs. Columbia United Way, 1970-72, Columbia chpt. A.R.C., 1971-72; active Boy Scouts Am., 1976—; chmn. bd. advisers Our Own of Ocean, Inc., 1977—. Served with USMC, 1959-63. Recipient outstanding community service award City of Columbia, 1972; community service award J.C. Penney Co., 1977; service award U.S. Treasury Dept., 1977. Mem. Pub. Relations Soc. Am., U. Mo. Alumni Assn., USMC Combat Corrs. Assn., Columbia Jaycees (dir. 1970-72), Sigma Tau Gamma (dist. gov. 1970-71), Alpha Delta Sigma. Democrat. Roman Catholic. Author: Tooting Your Own Horn, 1978. Home: 10 Buckingham Dr Jackson NJ 08527 Office: 1301 Ave of Americas New York City NY 10019

SCHWARTING, ARTHUR ERNEST, pharmacognosist, univ. dean; b. Waubay, S.D., June 8, 1917; s. John E. and Johanna M. (Boelte) S.; B.S., S.D. State U., 1940; Ph.D., Ohio State U., 1943; m. Roberta L. Mitchell, June 14, 1941; children—J. Michael, Stephen A. (dec.), Gerald A. Instr. pharmacognosy U. Nebr., Lincoln, 1943-45, asso. prof., 1945-49; asso. prof. pharmacognosy U. Conn., Storrs, 1949-53, prof., 1953—, dean Sch. Pharmacy, 1970—; cons., div. physician manpower HEW, 1966-70, FDA, 1975—; vis. prof. U. Munich (Germany), 1968-69; dir. Am. Found. Pharm. Edn., 1974—; cons. Bur. Drugs, FDA. Mem. Mansfield (Conn.) Bd. Edn., 1967-70. Recipient Alumni Assn. award U. Conn., 1965; Centennial Achievement award Ohio State U., 1970. Fellow Acad. Pharm. Scis., AAAS; mem. Am. Pharm. Assn. (Research Achievement award 1964), Am. Soc. Pharmacognosy, Am. Assn. Colls. Pharmacy (pres. 1971-72, chmn. council deans 1977-78), Sigma Xi, Rho Chi, Phi Kappa Phi, Phi Lambda Upsilon. Republican. Author: (with V.E. Tyler) Experimental Pharmacognosy, 1955; (with J.M. Bobbitt and R.J. Gritter) Introduction to Chromatography, 1968; editor: Lloydia, Jour. Natural Products, 1960-76; author book chpts. Home: 18 Ledgewood Dr Storrs CT 06268 Office: Univ Connecticut Storrs CT 06268

SCHWARTZ, ADOLPH FRANZ, cons. actuary; b. Brighton, Eng., Jan. 7, 1896; s. Adolph George and Antonia (Held) S.; came to U.S., 1919, naturalized, 1926; B.Sc., U. London (Eng.), 1921; m. Dorothy L. Chestnut, Sept. 5, 1925; children—Dorothy Mary, Robert George. With Brit. Civil Service, 1911-21; actuary exec. Penn Mut. Life Ins. Co., Phila., 1921-61; cons. actuary, 1961-67; actuary Pa. State Ins. Dept., Phila., 1967; cons. actuary, Swarthmore, Pa., part-time, 1967—. Served with Brit. Army, 1916-19. Fellow Soc. Actuaries; charter mem. Am. Acad. Actuaries. Republican. Methodist. Club: Delaware County Coll. Mens (pres. 1952). Home: 1104 Muhlenberg Ave Swarthmore PA 19081

SCHWARTZ, ALBERT AARON, orthopedic surgeon; b. N.Y.C., Feb. 11, 1913; s. Benjamin and Freida (Manaker) S.; B.S., N.Y.U., 1934; M.D., Dalhausie U., 1940; m. Suzanne Roberts, July 1, 1956; children—Jeffrey Lewis, Mark Philip. Intern Coney Island City Hosp., Bklyn., 1940-42; resident Sea View Hosp., S.I., N.Y., 1946-47, Permanente Found. Hosp., Oakland, Calif., 1947-49; practice medicine specializing in orthopedic surgery, Perth Amboy, N.J., 1949—; dir. orthopedic surgery Perth Amboy Gen. Hosp., 1968—, v.p. med. staff, 1972-75, pres. med. staff, 1975-78; dir. orthopedic surgery John F. Kennedy Community Hosp., Edison, N.J., 1968-71; co-chief orthopedic service Roosevelt Hosp., 1971—. Trustee Rutgers Prep. Sch., Somerset, N.J. Served with AUS, 1942-46. Decorated Bronze star with 2 oak leaf clusters. Diplomate Am. Bd. Orthopedic Surgery. Fellow Am. Acad. Orthopedic Surgeons, A.C.S., Internat. Coll. Surgeons, Am. Fracture Assn.; charter mem. Eastern Orthopedic Assn. Contbr. articles to profl. jours. Home: 8 Moraine Rd Edison NJ 08817 Office: 280 Hobart St Perth Amboy NJ 08861

SCHWARTZ, ALLAN BRADLEY, chem. engr.; b. Bklyn., Aug. 8, 1935; s. Adolph and Rachel Kate (Dunn) S.; B.S. Chem. Engring., Poly. Inst. N.Y., 1957, M.S., 1963; m. Nancy Claire Fisher, May 24, 1970; children—Rosalee, Richard, Robert, Roy. Chem. engr., aerospace med. div. Wright Patterson AFB, Dayton, Ohio, 1958-60; chem. engr. Uniroyal, Naugatuck, Conn., 1963-64; sr. exptl. engr. Hamilton Standard div. United Technology, Windsor Locks, Conn., 1964-67; sr. project engr., cryogenics cons. Naval Ship Engring. Center, Phila., 1967—. Contbr. articles to profl. jours. Home: 910 Chelten Pkwy Cherry Hill NJ 08034 Office: Naval Ship Engineering Center Philadelphia PA 19112

SCHWARTZ, DAVID, judge; b. N.Y.C., July 7, 1916; s. Hyman and Nettie (Strauss) S.; A.B. cum laude, N.Y. U., 1936; LL.B. magna cum laude, Harvard U., 1939; m. Louisa Van Wezel, June 15, 1968; children by previous marriage—Jonathan, Joanna M. Admitted to N.Y. bar, 1940, D.C. bar, 1965, U.S. Supreme Ct. bar, 1946, Ct. of Claims bar, 1954; practice law, Washington, 1940-56, N.Y.C., 1956-68; law clk. Mr. Justice Stanley F. Reed, 1942-43; spl. asst. to atty. gen. Justice Dept., Washington, 1941-42, chief trial atty. antitrust and enemy property divs., 1945-56; legal adviser Greece and Balkan missions UNRRA and predecessor Dept. State, 1943-45; counsel Devel. & Resources Corp., N.Y.C., 1956-57; partner Stroock & Stroock & Lavan, N.Y.C., 1957-68; trial judge U.S. Ct. Claims, Washington, 1968—; adj. prof. Georgetown Law Center, 1954-55; adj. asso. prof. N.Y. U. Law Sch., 1957-69; vis. prof. U. Wis. Law Sch., summers 1976, 78, U. San Diego, 1977, 79. Recipient John D. Rockefeller III Pub. Service award, 1955. Mem. Am., D.C., Fed. bar assns., Assn. Bar City N.Y. Democrat. Jewish. Author: (with S.B. Jacoby) Government Litigation-Cases and Notes, 1963; Litigation with the Federal Government, 1970. Home: 1417 33d St NW Washington DC 20007 Office: US Ct of Claims 717 Madison Pl NW Washington DC 20005

SCHWARTZ, DAVID LOUIS, lawyer; b. N.Y.C., Dec. 22, 1936; s. Abraham and Anne (Wasserman) S.; A.B., Columbia, 1957; LL.B., U. Va., 1960; m. Nancy Ruth Schnitzer, Sept. 21, 1963; children—Sally Jean, Anne Judith, Daniel Adam. Admitted to Va. bar, 1960, N.Y. bar, 1961; asso. firm Cravath Swaine & Moore, N.Y.C., 1960-68, partner, 1969—. Served with AUS, 1960-61. Mem. Assn. Bar City N.Y., Am., N.Y. State, Va. bar assns. Home: 1021 Park Ave New York City NY 10028 Office: 1 Chase Manhattan Plaza New York City NY 10005

SCHWARTZ, GARY EDWARD, psychologist; b. Mineola, N.Y., June 4, 1944; s. Howard and Shirley Sara Schwartz; A.B., Cornell U., 1966; M.A., Harvard U., 1969, Ph.D., 1971; m. Jeanne Iris Gross, June 13, 1965. Asst. prof. psychology Harvard U., 1971-75; vis. asso. prof. psychology U. B.C., 1975-76; vis. asso. prof. psychiatry U. Calif. Med. Sch., San Francisco, 1976; asso. prof. psychology and psychiatry Yale U., 1976—; cons. in field. Grantee NIMH, NSF. Mem. Biofeedback Soc. Am. (pres. 1973-74), Soc. Psychophysiol. Research (dir. 1975-78), Am. Psychol. Assn. (Young Psychologist award 1972, Early Career award 1978), AAAS, Acad. Behavioral Medicine Research, Claude Bernard Club, Phi Beta Kappa, Sigma Xi, Psi Chi, Alpha Epsilon Pi. Co-editor: Consciousness and Self-Regulation, Vol. 1, 1976, Vol. 2, 1978; Biofeedback: Theory and Research, 1977. Home: 326 Colonial Rd Guilford CT 06437 Office: Yale Univ 2 Hillhouse Ave New Haven CT 06520

SCHWARTZ, GORDON FRANCIS, surgeon, educator; b. Plainfield, N.J., Apr. 29, 1935; s. Samuel H. and Mary (Adelman) S.; A.B., Princeton U., 1956; M.D., Harvard U., 1960; m. Rochelle Gail Krantz, Sept. 5, 1959; children—Amory Blair, Susan Leslie. Intern, N.Y. Hosp.-Cornell Med. Center, N.Y.C., 1960-61; resident in surgery Columbia-Presbyn. Med. Center, N.Y.C., 1963-68; instr. surgery Columbia U., N.Y.C., 1966-68; asso. in surgery U. Pa., Phila., 1963-70; asst. prof. surgery Jefferson Med. Coll., Phila., 1970-71, asso. prof., 1971-78, prof. surgery, 1978—, dir. clin. services, Breast Diagnostic Center, 1973—; practice medicine, specializing in surgery, Phila., 1968—; dir., chmn. Breast Health Found., 1977—. Mem., Princeton Alumni Schs. Com., 1975—; mem. Pa. Gov.'s Task Force on Cancer, 1976—; mem. breast cancer task force Phila. chpt. Am. Cancer Soc., 1976—. Served to capt. AUS, 1961-63. NIH Cancer Control fellow, 1968-69. Mem. ACS, Assn. for Acad. Surgery, Allen O. Whipple Surg. Assn., Internat. Cardiovascular Soc., Soc. for Surgery Alimentary Tract, Am. Soc. Clin. Oncology, Gynecol. Soc. for Study of Breast Diseases, AMA, Phila. County Med. Soc., Pa. Med. Soc., Am. Soc. Transplant Surgeons, N.Y. Acad. Scis., AAUP, Am. Soc. Artificial Internal Organs, Internat. Coll. Surgeons, Société Internationale Senologie, Sigma Xi, Phi Beta Kappa, Alpha Omega Alpha, Nu Sigma Nu. Republican. Jewish. Clubs: Princeton (Phila.,

N.Y.C.); Harvard (Phila.); Princeton Terrace. Author: The Breast Book, 1979; editor Cancer Therapy Abstracts, 1976—; contbr. articles in field to med. jours. Home: 425 Mulberry Ln Haverford PA 19041 Office: 1025 Walnut St Philadelphia PA 19107 also 888 Glenbrook Ave Bryn Mawr PA 19010

SCHWARTZ, HAROLD F. X., ednl. adminstr.; b. N.Y.C., Mar. 21, 1916; s. John S. and Kathryn A. (Carroll) S.; student St. Francis Xavier Coll., N.Y.C., 1934; A.B., Mt. St. Marys Coll., Emmitsburg, Md., 1939; m. Margaret Faye Miller, Apr. 21, 1961; children—Peter, Paul, Mary, Kathryn, John, Michael, James. Research analyst, dept. transp. U.S. Army, Washington, 1946-63; with Def. Intelligence Agy., Dept. Def., Washington, 1963-77, chief of transp., India, 1970-77; dir. coll. resources and alumni affairs Mt. St. Mary's Coll., Emmitsburg, Md., 1978—. Served with USNR, 1942-46. Decorated Bronze Star medal, Purple Heart. Mem. Mt. St. Marys Coll. Alumni Assn. (nat. pres. 1966-71). Republican. Roman Catholic. Home: RD 6 Country Club Rd Waynesboro PA 17268

SCHWARTZ, HELEN FRENCH (MRS. HARRY MARVIN SCHWARTZ), librarian; b. Scranton, Pa., Nov. 29, 1924; d. Myron Everett and Dorothy Lillian (Jones) French; B.A. magna cum laude, Waynesburg Coll., 1948; postgrad. (Stipend scholar), Pa. State U., 1949-50; M.L.S., Drexel U., 1968; postgrad. Millersville State Coll., 1972, Coll. of Misericordia, 1976; m. Harry Marvin Schwartz, Mar. 23, 1952; children—Myron Eliot, Judith Rose. Instr. English, Waynesburg (Pa.) Coll., 1948-49; mgr. bookstore Rutgers U., Camden, N.J., 1950-52; library asst. Farrell Sch., Phila., 1966-67; librarian Conwell Middle Magnet Sch., Phila., 1967-68; cataloger Free Library of Phila., 1968-71, asst. head central children's dept., 1971-72; librarian Frederick Douglass Instructional Materials Center, Phila., 1972—. Library Resource person for Child Advocacy Program, Frederick Douglass Sch., 1973-74. Mem. Am., Pa. library assns., Assn. for Ednl. and Communications Tech., Pa. Sch. Librarians Assn., Assn. Phila. Sch. Librarians, Library Pub. Relations Assn. Greater Phila., Booksellers Assn., Beta Phi Mu, Phi Alpha Theta. Home: 1458 Higbee St Philadelphia PA 19149 Office: 22d and Norris St Philadelphia PA 19121

SCHWARTZ, HILDA G., judge; b. N.Y.C.; d. Solomon and Anna Leah (Rubin) Ginsburg; B.S., Washington Sq. Coll. of N.Y. U.; LL.B., N.Y. U., 1929; m. Herman N. Schwartz, Feb. 21, 1930; 1 son, John Michael. Admitted to N.Y. bar, 1930; pvt. practice law, 1930-46; sec., bur. head, trial commr. Bd. Estimate, 1946-51; city magistrate, N.Y.C., 1951-58; treas., head dept. finance City of N.Y., 1958-62, dir. finance, 1962-65; judge N.Y.C. Civil Ct., 1965-71; justice N.Y. State Supreme Ct., 1972—. Chmn. law com. Bd. Magistrates, 1953-58; chmn. home term panel judges, 1954-56; judge Adolescent Ct., 1952-58; mem. welfare adv. bd. N.Y. Jr. League, 1953-56; bd. mgrs. Greenwich House, 1946-48; bd. dirs. Washington Sq. Outdoor Art Exhibit, 1950-58; bd. dirs. Washington Sq. Coll., merit achievement award 1968; pres. Women's Nat. Democratic Club, 1942-44; v.p. Young Dem. Club, 1935-37. Mem. N.Y. Women's Bar Assn. (past pres., distinguished service award 1977), Nat. Assn. Women Lawyers (past v.p.), Assn. Bar City N.Y., N.Y. County Lawyers Assn., Am., N.Y. State bar assns., Trial Lawyers Assn., Assn. Supreme Ct. Judges City N.Y. (dir.). Office: 60 Centre St New York City NY 10007

SCHWARTZ, IRVING, container mfg. co. exec.; b. N.Y.C., July 20, 1915; s. Nathan and Ida (Estrich) S.; B.S. in Econs., Tufts U., 1937; m. Hannah E. Carlin, June 4, 1939; children—Alan M., Harold W., Susan L. Pres., Allied Container Corp., Dedham, Mass., 1937—, also dir. Bd. dirs. Asso. Industries Mass., Mass. Higher Edn. Assistance Corp.; trustee Newton-Wellesley Hosp., Hebrew Rehab. Center Aged, Combined Jewish Philanthropies Greater Boston; bd. dirs. Jewish Meml. Hosp.; bd. overseers Jewish Theol. Sem. Recipient Community Service award Jewish Theol. Sem. Am., 1963, 80th Ann. medal, 1966. Mem. Fibre Box Assn. (dir.). Jewish (dir. temple). Clubs: Masons; Pinebrook Country (Weston, Mass.); Tufts (Boston). Home: 85 East India Row Boston MA 02110 Office: 1 Allied Dr Dedham MA 02026

SCHWARTZ, JACK JAMES, pediatrician; b. Newark, Dec. 9, 1922; s. Walter S. and Julia (Bodnar) S.; B.A., Cornell U., 1943; M.D., Med. Coll. Va., 1946; m. Lillian Feldman, Dec. 22, 1946; children—Jeffrey Hugh, Laurens Robert. Intern, Cin. Gen. Hosp., 1946-47; resident pediatrics St. Louis Children's Hosp., 1947-48, 50-51, Med. Coll. Va. Hosp., Richmond, 1948; individual practice medicine, specializing in pediatrics, Millburn, N.J., 1951—; dir. med. edn. Newark Children's Hosp., 1966-70; clin. asso. prof. pediatrics N.J. Coll. Medicine and Dentistry, Newark, 1976—. Served with M.C., U.S. Army, 1948-50. NIH postdoctoral research fellow, 1948. Fellow Am. Acad. Pediatrics; mem. N.Y. Acad. Scis., Am. Soc. Nephrology, Am. Soc. Pediatric Nephrology, Phi Beta Kappa, Alpha Omega Alpha. Research and publs. in field. Home: 524 Ridge Rd Watchung NJ 07060 Office: 120 Millburn Ave Millburn NJ 07041

SCHWARTZ, JAMES PETER, real estate broker; b. Bridgeport, Conn., Oct. 30 1919; s. Joseph and Fannie (Tischler) S.; student Coll. Commerce New Haven, 1939-40; m. Natalie Postol, Mar. 12, 1944; 1 son, Joseph William. Reporter, Bridgeport Times-Star, 1940-41; reporter, photographer Bridgeport Post, 1942-43, 45-49; pres. Jay James Inc., Fairfield, Conn., 1949-70; owner James P. Schwartz & Assos., Fairfield, 1970—; dir. Lafayette Bank & Trust Co. Pres. Barnum Festival Soc., 1975-76; justice of peace, 1970—; mem. Easton (Conn.) Zoning Bd. Appeals, 1971-76; police commr. Easton, 1976—; bd. assos. U. Bridgeport, 1962—; bd. dirs. Am. Cancer Soc., 1976—. Served with AUS, 1943-45. Named Man of Year dept. sociology U. Bridgeport 1962. Mem. Greater Bridgeport (pres. 1979), Fairfield bds. realtors, Conn., Nat. assns. realtors. Club: Masons. Contbg. editor Photog. Trade News, 1960-70. Home: 78 Blanchard Rd Easton CT 06612 Office: 161 Kings Hwy Fairfield CT 06430

SCHWARTZ, JEROME, obstetrician, gynecologist; b. N.Y.C., Oct. 23, 1915; s. Louis and Sarah (Lieberman) S.; B.S., N.Y.U., 1937, M.D., 1941; m. Ellen Irma Rubin, Aug. 2, 1942; children—Seth, Elwin, Lyle. Intern, Morrisania Hosp., Bronx, N.Y., 1942-43; resident in obstetrics and gynecology Fordham Hosp., Bronx, 1946-50; practice medicine specializing in obstetrics and gynecology, Lynbrook, N.Y., 1950—; mem. staff South Nassau Communities Hosp., Oceanside, N.Y., 1950—, Nassau County Med. Center, East Meadow, N.Y., 1950—; chief obstetrics and gynecology Hempstead (N.Y.) Gen. Hosp., 1952-74, Franklin Gen. Hops., Valley Stream, N.Y., 1963—. Served with M.C., U.S. Army, 1943-46. Diplomate Am. Bd. Obstetrics and Gynecology. Fellow A.C.S., Am. Coll. Obstetrics and Gynecology, Internat. Coll. Surgeons, Am. Soc. Abdominal Surgeons, Am. Coll. Gynecologic Laparoscopy, Am. Coll. Nuclear Physicians; mem. N.Y. Soc. Surgeons, N.Y. Acad. Scis. Contbr. articles to profl. publs.; also surg. inventions. Home: 1321 Club Dr Hewlett Harbor NY 11557 Office: 144 Hempstead Ave Lynbrook NY 11563

SCHWARTZ, JOHN FREDERICK, optometrist; b. Beaver Falls, Pa., Jan. 24, 1928; s. Frederick Keller and Laura Vernie (Alexander) S.; B.A., Gettysburg Coll., 1950; O.D., Pa. Coll. Optometry, 1954; m. Mary Louise Spangler, Jan. 2, 1955; 1 son, Karl David. Gen. practice optometry, Lemoyne, Pa., 1955—. Chmn., E. Berlin (Pa.) Planning Com., 1963-65, E. Berlin Bicentennial Program; pres. Adams County Pub. Library, 1972; pres. council Lutheran Ch. 1973, 75. Served with USN, 1945-46. Certified in develop. vision Optometry Extension Program, 1968. Fellow, Am. Acad Optometry; mem. Central Pa. (Local Man of Year, 1975), Pa., Am. Optometry assns., Vistion Conservation Inst., Better Vision Inst., Am. Optometry Found., Vision Welfare League, Pa. Optometric Polit. Action Com., Beta Sigma Kappa, VFW, Am. Legion. Republican. Clubs: Rotary, Torch, Civil War Round Table. Home: 261 Baltimore St Gettysburg PA 17325 Office: 833 Market St Lemoyne PA 17043

SCHWARTZ, JOSEPH WILLIAM, banker; b. Bridgeport, Conn., Dec. 22, 1950; s. James Peter and Natalie (Postol) S.; B.A., Union Coll., Schenectady, 1972. Planning intern Capital Dist. Regional Planning Agy., Albany, N.Y., 1973; real estate broker, mgr. James P. Schwartz & Assos., Fairfield, Conn., 1973—; adj. faculty Sacred Heart U., Bridgeport, 1975-77; corporate banking rep. Conn. Nat. Bank, Bridgeport, 1977—. Justice of peace; Easton, Conn., 1973-75; mem. town com. Democratic party Easton, 1973—; mem. Conn. State Senate, also chmn. elections com., 1975-77; bd. selectmen Town of Easton, 1977—; bd. dirs. Woodfield Family Services, 1978—; chmn. Heart Fund Easton, 1976—. Recipient 3d. Ann. Legis. award Caucus Conn. Dems., 1976. Jewish. Club: Lions. Home: 21 Dogwood Dr Easton CT 06612 Office: 888 Main St Bridgeport CT 06604

SCHWARTZ, LAWRENCE, hosp. adminstr.; b. Bridgeport, Conn., Aug. 6, 1941; s. Alvadore and Marion (Deutsch) S.; B.A., Mich. State U., 1963; M.Pub. Adminstrn., City U. N.Y., 1966; postgrad. Pace U., 1976; m. Emilia Salanga, Sept. 3, 1968. Intern, N.Y. State Dept. Mental Hygiene, N.Y.C., 1967-68; asst. adminstr. Gracie Sq. Hosp., N.Y.C., 1968-71, adminstr., 1971—; asst. prof., program adviser Manhattan Coll., 1976. Mem. Am. Coll. Hosp. Adminstrs., Assn. Mental Health Adminstrs. Address: Gracie Sq Hosp 420 E 76th St New York City NY 10021

SCHWARTZ, MARTIN WEBER, lawyer; b. N.Y.C., Sept. 30, 1944; s. Robert and Rose (Weber) S.; B.A., N.Y. U., 1965; J.D., Bklyn. Law Sch., 1968. Police officer City of Yonkers (N.Y.) Police Dept., 1967-69; spl. agt. customs agy. service U.S. Treasury Dept., N.Y.C., 1970-71, internal security div., 1973-76; admitted to N.Y. State bar, 1971, U.S. Supreme Ct. bar, 1975; asst. dist. atty., chief welfare frauds unit Bronx County (N.Y.), 1971-73; mem. firm Jack B. Solerwitz, Mineola, N.Y., 1976-77. Recipient awards Canadian govt., 1971, U.S. Dept. Treasury, 1976. Mem. Am., N.Y. bar assns., Assn. Bar City N.Y., Fed. Criminal Investigators Assn., Bklyn. Law Sch. Alumni Assn. Home: Scarsdale NY 10583 Office: 23 Centuck Station Yonkers NY 10710

SCHWARTZ, MARVIN W., artist; b. N.Y.C., Aug. 8, 1937; s. Harry M. and Bella (Weiss) S.; 1 dau., Rachel. One-man shows Whitney Mus. Am. Art, Inst. Culture P.R.; group shows include Am. Fedn. Arts, Nat. Collection Fine Arts, Pensacola (Fla.) Mus., 3d World Exhbn. Photography, U. P.R.; represented in permanent collections Whitney Mus. Am. Art, The Hirshorn Mus., Smithsonian Instn., Washington, Library of Congress; tchr. U. P.R., 1965. Served with USN, 1955-57. Named Press Photographer of Year, P.R. Press Assn., 1960, 65, 66. Author: Puerto Rico, 1969; The Artist's Adressbook, 1973; Calder's Circus, 1972; The Burgher's of Calais, 1976; Huellas-Traces of Taino Indians of Puerto Rico, 1976. Home and office: 223 W 10th St New York City NY 10014

SCHWARTZ, MORTIMER LEONARD, physician, educator; b. Orange, N.J., Jan. 12, 1915; s. Herman and Rose (Nussbaum) S.; student Wesleyan U., 1931-34; M.D., Eclectic Med. Coll., Cin., 1938; m. Rene Kanengiser, Mar. 25, 1941; children—Gary Stephen, Jessica Lynn, Alison Jane. Intern Irvington Gen. Hosp., N.J., 1938-39, Alexian Bros. Hosp., Elizabeth, N.J., 1939-40; resident internal medicine Jersey City Med. Center, 1947-48; pvt. practice internal medicine and cardiovascular diseases, Irvington and Maplewood, N.J., 1940-42, 46-47, 48-60; attending physician medicine and dir. Cardiac Clinic, Jersey City Med. Center, 1954-67; asso. prof. medicine New Jersey Coll. Medicine, also dir. course phys. diagnosis, 1960-72, prof. medicine, 1966-72, also dir. clin. cardiology; prof. medicine Albert Einstein Coll. Medicine, 1972-77; dir. med. service Martland Med. Center; dir. medicine Irvington Gen. Hosp., 1952-76; chief cardiovascular sect. Bronx-Lebanon Hosp. Center, 1972-77; dir. medicine Mountainside Hosp., Montclair, N.J., 1977—; chmn. Nat. Com. for Emergency Coronary Care, 1969-73. Served to maj. AUS, 1942-46. Recipient Harry Gold award, 1974. Diplomate Am. Bd. Internal Medicine. Fellow A.C.P., Am. Coll. Cardiology, Am. Coll. Clin. Pharmacology, Am. Heart Assn. (council clin. cardiology) Am. Coll. Chest Physicians, N.Y. Cardiol. Soc.; mem. Essex Co. Heart Assn. (trustee 1957-72). Research in cardiology. Home: 49 Sommer Ave Maplewood NJ 07040 Office: 51 Sommer Ave Maplewood NJ 07040

SCHWARTZ, NORMAN A., Realtor; b. N.Y.C., Jan. 29, 1922; s. Max David and Rose (Ginenthal) S.; student Bklyn. Coll., 1938-41; m. Jeanette Zloth, Dec. 15, 1946; children—Ronni Lynn, David Bennett. Founder, Pioneer Home Furnishings, Rochester, N.Y., 1947-57; real estate salesman 1st Realty Co., Rochester, 1957-62; pres. Realtor, Appraiser Norman A. Schwartz, Inc., Realtors & Assos., Rochester, 1962—. Served with USAAF, 1943-46. Recipient Civic Pride award Jewish Community Center, 1968. Mem. Real Estate Bd. Rochester, N.Y. State Realtors Assn., Soc. Residential Appraisers, Jewish War Vets. Democrat. Jewish. Clubs: K.P., B'nai B'rith. Home: 65 Towpath Ln Rochester NY 14618 Office: 1664 Monroe Ave Rochester NY 14618

SCHWARTZ, NORMAN LARRY, elec. engr.; b. Bklyn., May 17, 1932; s. Abe and Anna (Oliver) S.; B.E.E., Coll. City N.Y., 1960; M.E.E., Poly. Inst. Bklyn., 1965; m. Annette Rochelle Raphael, Aug. 6, 1960; children—Eric Bruce, Alissa Beth. Elec. engr. Maspeth Telephone & Radio, N.Y.C., 1950-52, Am. Bosh Arma, Garden City, N.Y., 1960-61, Janus Products, Syosset, N.Y., 1961-63, EDO Corp., N.Y.C., 1963-66, Telesignal Corp., Woodbury, N.Y., 1966-67; v.p. Multiplex Communications, Hauppauge, N.Y., 1967—; pres. NLS Consultants, Stony Brook, N.Y., 1977—. Served with USAF, 1952-56. Mem. Armed Forces Communications and Electronics Assn. Patentee in field. Home: 12 Manchester Ln Stony Brook NY 11790 Office: 123 Marcus BlVd Hauppauge NY 11787

SCHWARTZ, RALPH MONROE, physician; b. Bklyn., Mar. 6, 1914; s. Leo Samson and Ada (Schapiro) S.; A.B., Cornell U., Ithaca, N.Y., 1934; M.D., State U. N.Y. at Bklyn., 1938; m. Frances Cohen, Mar. 19, 1942; children—Stephen, Richard, Leo, Elsa Ann. Intern, Jewish Hosp. Bklyn., 1938-40, L.I. Coll. Hosp., Bklyn., 1940-41; resident Kings County Hosp., Bklyn., 1941-44; practice medicine, specializing in obstetrics and gynecology, Bklyn., 1946-48; chief dept. obstetrics and gynecology Greenpoint Hosp., Bklyn., 1970-78; asst. clin. prof. obstetrics and gynecology State U. N.Y., 1974—; dir. Med. Liability Mut. Ins. Co. N.Y.; chmn. N.Y. State Bd. Medicine, 1976-77. Served with M.C., AUS, 1944-46. Diplomate Am. Bd. Obstetrics and Gynecology. Fellow A.C.S., Am. Coll. Obstetricians and Gynecologists, Bklyn. Gynecol. Soc. (pres. 1970-71); mem. Kings County (N.Y.) Med. Soc. (pres. 1971-72, trustee 1972—), Med. Soc. State N.Y. (del. to AMA 1975—), AMA. Jewish. Club: Cornell of N.Y.

SCHWARTZ, ROBERT NASH, pub. relations exec.; b. Chgo., Mar. 6, 1917; s. Jacob and Sarah (Nerush) S.; B.A. cum laude, U. Ill., 1940; m. Judith Goldman, June 3, 1940; children—Frances, James. Reporter, Champaign (Ill.) News-Gazette, 1941-42; reporter, editor St. Louis Post-Dispatch, 1942-43; writer, editor N.Y. Times Sunday dept., 1943-46; editorial writer Chgo. Sun, 1946; bur. mgr., sci. editor Internat. News Service, Chgo., 1947-51; with Manning, Selvage & Lee, N.Y.C., 1957—, sr. v.p., 1967-71, vice chmn. bd., 1971-73, pres., 1973—, chief exec. officer, 1978—. Mem. Pub. Relations Soc. Am., Nat. Assn. Sci. Writers, Phi Beta Kappa. Clubs: Univ., Chemists (N.Y.C.). Home: 33 W 93d St New York City NY 10025 also Truro MA 02666 Office: 99 Park Ave New York City NY 10016

SCHWARTZ, SANFORD ALAN, psychologist; b. Bklyn., Mar. 15, 1949; s. Alex and Bertha S.; B.A. magna cum laude, Bklyn. Coll., 1971; M.S. in Ednl. Psychology, Yeshiva U., 1972; profl. diploma in urban sch. psychology Fordham U., 1976, now postgrad. in urban sch. psychology; m. Marsha Nicha Henenberg, June 16, 1975; 1 dau., Rebecca Gayle. Intern in psychology Burke Rehab. Center, White Plains, N.Y., 1973-74; staff psychologist Mental Retardation Inst., N.Y. Med. Coll., N.Y.C., 1974-75, Valhalla, N.Y., 1975-76; psychologist Bernard Fineson Developmental Center, N.Y. State Dept. Mental Hygiene, Corona, 1976—, Howard Beach (N.Y.) Child Guidance and Family Counseling Center, 1978—. Certified sch. psychologist, N.Y. Mem. Am. Psychol. Assn., Am. Assn. on Mental Deficiency, Assn. for Supervision and Curriculum Devel., Phi Beta Kappa, Alpha Sigma Lambda. Democrat. Home: 65-36 99th St Apt 3K Rego Park NY 11374

SCHWARTZ, SHELDON DAVID, mfg. co. exec.; b. Bklyn., Apr. 21, 1934; s. Issie H. and Hattie S.; B.S. mktg., N.Y. Univ., 1965; m. Rochelle B. Feingold, Sept. 4, 1961; children—Lauren, Jessica. Asst. product mgr. Merck Sharp and Dohme Internat., N.Y.C., 1954-68; mgr. promotion services Am. Home N.Y.C., 1968-72; pres. The LORJES Internat. Corp., S.I., 1972—. Served with U.S. Army, 1954-56. Mem. Am. Mktg. Assn. Author: The Chicken and the Egg, 1967. Inventor energy saving adapters. Office: GPO Box 507 Staten Island NY 10314

SCHWARTZ, TILLIE, pediatrician; b. Winnipeg, Man., Can.; d. Leon and Sophie (Idell) S.; came to U.S., 1950, naturalized, 1959; B.A., U. Man., Winnipeg, 1936, M.D., 1950. Accountant various cos., Winnipeg, 1936-44; intern St. Boniface Hosp., Winnipeg, 1949-50; resident pediatrics Met. Hosp., N.Y.C., 1951-52, Univ. Hosp., N.Y.C., 1952-53; med. resident Gouverneur Hosp., N.Y.C., 1950-51; individual practice medicine, specializing in pediatrics, pediatric allergy, Kew Gardens, N.Y., 1953—; asst. pediatrics Booth Meml. Med. Center, 1957—, chief pediatric allergy Clinic, 1958—; asst. pediatrics Flushing Hosp. Med. Center (N.Y.), 1960—; asst. prof. clin. pediatrics N.Y. U.-Bellevue Med. Center, N.Y.C., 1975—. Mem. AMA, N.Y. State, Queens County med. socs., Am., N.Y. State, N.Y.C. Women's med. assns., Queens Pediatric Soc., N.Y. Allergy Soc., Am. Acad. Pediatrics, Am. Acad. Allergy, Am. Jewish Congress. Club: B'nai B'rith. Office: 83-62 Main St Kew Gardens NY 11435

SCHWARTZBERG, ALLAN ZELIG, psychiatrist, educator; b. Cleve., Dec. 5, 1930; s. Joseph and Jeannette E. Schwartzberg; B.S. cum laude, Case Western Res. U., 1951; M.D., Ohio State U., 1955; m. Katherine Weiss, June 19, 1955; children—Susan Irene, Robert Michael. Intern, Johns Hopkins Hosp., Balt., 1955-56, resident in psychiatry, 1956-59; practice medicine specializing in psychiatry, Washington, 1964—; asst. prof. psychiatry Georgetown U. Sch. Medicine, Washington, 1964-66, asst. clin. prof., 1966—; cons. NIMH, 1970-73; with Washington Psychoanalytic Inst., 1964-66; mem. vis. faculty seminar community psychiatry Harvard U. Med. Sch., 1965-67; chief psychiatry Suburban Hosp., Bethesda, Md., 1974-75. Mem. Am. Soc. Adolescent Psychiatry (chpt. pres. 1975-76), Am. Soc. Physician Analysts (exec. bd. 1977—), Phi Beta Kappa. Contbr. articles in mental Health and adolescent psychiatry to profl. jours. and books. Home: 6616 Kenhill Rd Bethesda MD 20034 Office: 7910 Woodmont Ave Bethesda MD 20014

SCHWARTZMAN, LOIS PAULA, guidance counselor; b. N.Y.C., Feb. 6, 1937; d. Solomon and Sadie (Goldstein) Shapiro; B.A., Hunter Coll., 1958; M.S., 1972; postgrad. Yeshiva U., 1978—; m. Allan Jules Schwartzman, Sept. 15, 1957; children—Linda, Charles (dec.), Eric. Tchr., N.Y.C., and Rockland County (N.Y.), 1958-60, 67-70; guidance counselor, N.Y.C., 1971-75; vocat. counselor, co-founder, dir. Options Unltd., Inc., N.Y.C., 1974-76. Co-founder, v.p. Pediatric Cancer Research Found.; co-chmn. cultural arts com. Greenburgh Sch. Dist., 1971. Mem. Am. Personnel and Guidance Assn., Fort Hill Players.

SCHWARZ, ALFRED WILLIAM, pathologist; b. Vienna, Austria, Feb. 1, 1909; s. Ernest and Olga (Stern) S.; M.D., U. Vienna, 1932; came to U.S., 1938, naturalized, 1944; m. Hilda Feingold, Jan. 9, 1939; children—Ellen Olivia, Steven Michael. Intern, Vienna Gen. Hosp., 1933-35; resident Univ. Hosp. Vienna, 1935-38; resident in pathology Jewish Meml. Hosp., N.Y.C., 1938-42, asst. pathologist, 1943-48, asso. pathologist, 1949-54, pathologist, dir. labs., 1954—; trainee in cytology McGill U., Montreal, Que., Can., 1949; faculty Albert Einstein Coll. Medicine, N.Y.C., 1954—; clin. prof. pathology N.Y. Med. Coll., 1977—; pathologist Physicians Hosp., N.Y.C., 1954—; cons. pathologist St. Clare's Med. Center, N.Y.C., 1954—; chmn. Bd. Examiners, Commr. Health N.Y., 1972-77, mem. adv. council on clin. labs., 1972-77. Mem. Citizens Com. for Improvement Pub. Schs., Yonkers, N.Y., 1960-63. Diplomate Am. Bd. Pathology. Mem. AAAS, AMA, Am. Assn. Blood Banks, Assn. Am. Med. Colls., Assn. Clin. Scientists, Am., N.Y. (past pres.) socs. clin. pathologists, Coll. Am. Pathologists (N.Y. State commr. for inspection, accreditation clin. labs. 1965), Internat. Acad. Pathology, N.Y. Acad. Medicine, N.Y. State Blood Banks Assn., N.Y. State Assn. Pub. Health Labs. (v.p. 1977-78, pres. 1978-79). Democrat. Jewish. Club: Pathologists of N.Y. (past pres.). Contbr. chpts. to books, numerous articles to profl. jours. Editor-in-chief Jewish Meml. Hosp. Bull., 1954-72. Home: 121 Chittenden Ave Crestwood-Yonkers NY 10707 Office: 196th St and Broadway New York City NY 10040

SCHWARZ, ERNEST ISAAC, automotive co. exec.; b. Vienna, Austria, Feb. 29, 1896; s. Karl and Rosa (Plaschkes) S.; came to U.S., 1910, naturalized, 1919; ed. pub. sch. Vienna; m. Theresa R. Schwarz, Aug. 31, 1919; children—Maurice L., Bernard M., Myrna A. With Barney's Auto Parts, N.Y.C., 1916-25; Schwarz Sales Co., N.Y.C., 1926-28; owner, operator Schwarz Auto Parts, N.Y.C., 1929-48, EIS Mfg. Co., N.Y.C., 1932-41; with EIS Automotive Corp., Middletown, Conn., 1942—, pres., 1942-67, chmn. bd., 1967—. Pres. EIS Found. Inc., 1960—; trustee YMCA Middletown. Paul Harris fellow, 1975; Hillel Found. fellow, 1962. Mem. Motor Equipment Mfg. Assn., Automotive Service Assn., Mfrs. Assn. Conn. Jewish. Rotary. Mem. B'nai B'rith. Patentee automotive field. Home: 404 Ball Fall St Middletown CT 06457 Office: N Main and High St Middletown CT 06457

SCHWARZ, SIDNEY MAY, real estate exec.; b. Orange, N.J., Dec. 15, 1912; s. Harry L. and Marbelle E. (May) S.; B.S. in Bus., Lehigh U., 1935; postgrad. U. Chgo., 1935, 38; U. Pa., 1939; m. Ethel Furstman, Apr. 6, 1941; children—Claudia Robert, Donald. Instr. real estate appraisal Newark Bd. Realtors' Appraisal Sch., 1939-41, Fairleigh Dickinson U., Madison, N.J., 1962-63; asso. firm Harry L. Schwarz & Co., Dover, N.J., 1935—, pres., 1966—; bd. mgrs. Morris County Savs. Bank. Trustee Dover Gen. Hosp., 1961—. Licensed real estate broker, N.J. Mem. Dover C. of C. (pres. 1953-54), Morris County Bd. Realtors (past pres.), Am. Inst. Real Estate Appraisers (past pres. N.J. chpt.), Soc. Real Estate Appraisers, Inst. Real Estate Mgmt., Am. Right of Way Assn. Contbr. articles to profl. jours. Office: 28-30 N Sussex St Dover NJ 07801

SCHWARZ, WOLFGANG, psychologist; b. Stuttgart, Germany, Oct. 30, 1926; s. Mole and Edith (Gutstein) S.; brought to U.S., 1934, naturalized, 1940; A.B., N.Y. U., 1948, A.M., 1949, Ph.D., 1956; m. Cynthia Mae Johnson, Sept. 12, 1949 (div.); children—Amy Maria, Casey Andrew, Darcy Lynn, Priscilla Anne, Lydia Beth, Emily Jane; m. 2d, Susan Decker, 1976; 1 son Jaime Bartholomew. Intern, Bellevue Med. Center, N.Y., 1949-51; chief psychology Rip Van Winkle Med. Found., Hudson, N.Y., 1951-53; dir. psychology Hillcrest Med. Center, Tulsa, 1953-56, Hollywood Presbyn. Hosp., Los Angeles, 1956-58; cons. psychology Cedars Lebanon Hosp., Los Angeles, 1956-58; spl. cons. to D.C. Govt., 1959-61, NIH, Bethesda, Md., 1962-64; dir. psychol. research Mass. Dept. Mental Health, Boston and Malden, 1965-68; individual practice clin. psychology, Tulsa, 1953-56, Beverly Hills, Calif., 1956-59, Washington, 1959-63, Concord and Malden, Mass., 1965-73, Mt. Kisco, N.Y., 1973—; lectr. U. Tulsa, 1953-54, Hillcrest Med. Center, Tulsa, 1953-56, Los Angeles State Coll., 1956-57; asst. prof. Howard U., 1961; asso. prof. George Washington U., 1961-62; vis. research asst. Harvard Psychiatry, Lab., 1966-68; prof. Malden Hosp., 1968-71; cons. No. Westchester Hosp., 1974—, United Hosp., 1975—, Four Winds Hosp., 1975—; cons. psychology Peace Corps, Mass., 1969—. Mem. exec. com. Mayor's Model City Program, Malden, 1967-68. Served with USNR, 1945-46. Recipient Founder's Day award N.Y. U., 1956, Individual award USPHS/NIH, 1960-64. Diplomate Am. Bd. Profl. Psychology. Mem. Am., N.Y., Mass. psychol. assns., Washington Soc. History of Medicine (exec. com. 1963-64), N.Y. Acad. Scis., Psi Chi, Beta Lambda Sigma. Author: A Survey of the Mental Health Facilities in the District of Columbia, 1961; also articles. Home: 220 Mill River Rd Chappaqua NY 10514 Office: 295 Main St Mount Kisco NY 10549

SCHWARZER, OTTO OSCAR, instrument co. exec.; b. Gersau, Switzerland, Aug. 25, 1930; s. Otto and Adelheid (Baggenstos) S.; B.S., equivalent, Tech. Sch., Neuhausen, Switzerland, 1950; postgrad. Sch. Commerce, Schaffhausen, Switzerland, 1954-55; m. Anice V. Peterson, Oct. 25, 1959; children—Trenton Otto, Travis Eldon. Came to U.S., 1956, naturalized, 1963. Research and design, plastics div. Georg Fischer & Co. Ltd., Schaffhausen, 1951-56; project engr. N.Mex. Hwy Dept., Farmington, 1956-61; engring. and design W.C. Powell & Assos., Santa Fe and Farmington, N.Mex., 1961-66; cons. engr. Fish Engring. Co., Farmington, 1967-68; with Kern Instruments, Inc., subsidiaries Kern & Co. Ltd. of Aarau, Switzerland, Brewster, N.Y., 1968—, v.p., 1969—. Mem. Farmington Civic Improvement Com., 1967-68. Seventh-day Adventist (treas. deacon). Home: Beekman Rd Box 455 RD 1 Hopewell Junction NY 12533 Office: Terravest Corporate Park Geneva Rd Brewster NY 10509

SCHWEBEL, RENATA MANASSE (MRS. JACK P. SCHWEBEL), sculptor; b. Zwickau, Germany, Mar. 6, 1930; d. George and Anne Marie (Simon) Manasse; brought to U.S., 1940, naturalized, 1946; B.A., Antioch Coll., 1953; M.F.A., Columbia U., 1961; m. Jack P. Schwebel, May 10, 1955; children—Judi, Barbara, Diane. Cartographer, Ecostat, Inc., Ridgewood, N.J., 1949; display artist Silvestri, Inc., Chgo., 1950-51; asst. Mazzolini Art Found., 1952; student asst. art dept. Antioch Coll., Yellow Springs, Ohio, 1952-53; exhibited one-woman shows: Sculpture Center, Columbia U., Greenwich Art Barn; exhibited group shows: Wadsworth Atheneum, Hudson River Mus., New Britain Mus. Am. Art, Stamford Mus., Silvermine Guild, Bergen County Mus., Sculpture Center, others; represented in permanent collections: Columbia U., Colt Industries, also pvt. collections. Bd. dirs. Antioch Coll. Assn., 1971-77; del. Fine Arts Fedn. N.Y. Recipient Purchase award Columbia U., 1961; awards Westchester Art Soc., 1969—, Nat. Assn. Women Artists. Mem. Sculptors Guild (dir., exec. bd., v.p.), Audubon Artists, Artists Equity N.Y., Nat. Assn. Women Artists, Conn. Acad. Fine Arts, others. Home: 36 Silver Birch Dr New Rochelle NY 10804 Studio: 170 Webster Ave New Rochelle NY 10801

SCHWEICH, LEO, dermatologist; b. Trier, Germany, Sept. 26, 1894; s. Herman and Augusta (Mayers) S.; student U. Kiel, 1914, U. Strassburg, 1915, U. Bonn, 1916; M.D., U. Cologne, 1920; m. Dorothea Valeska Mendelsohn, Dec. 2, 1938. Dermatologist, Dept. Dermatology, U. Cologne, also Municipal Hosp., Elberfeld, 1921-26; mem. staff Columbia-Presbyn. Med. Center, N.Y.C., 1934-72; mem. staff Lenox Hill Hosp., 1934—, attending dermatologist emeritus, 1961—; attending dermatologist Vanderbilt Clinic, 1944-72; pvt. practice dermatology. Mem. U.S. com. World Med. Assn. Fellow Am. Acad. Dermatology, N.Y. Acad. Medicine; mem. AMA, Soc. for Investigative Dermatology, German Dermatol. Soc., Assn. Dermatologists Rhenish-Westphalia, Dermatol. Soc. Venezuela (corr.), Societas Internat. Dermatologiae Tropicae, Assn. Am. Med. Colls. Home and Office: 137 E 38th St New York City NY 10016

SCHWEIKER, RICHARD SCHULTZ, U.S. senator; b. Norristown, Pa., June 1, 1926; s. Malcolm Alderfer and Blanche (Schultz) S.; B.A., Pa. State U., 1950; LL.D. (hon.), Ursinus Coll., 1963, Pa. Med. Coll., 1972, Dickinson Coll., 1972, LaSalle Coll., 1973, Albright Coll., 1973; Dr.Pub. Service, Temple U., 1970; L.H.D., Pa. Coll. Podiatric Medicine, 1973; D.C.L., Widener Coll., 1973; m. Claire Joan Coleman, Sept. 10, 1955; children—Malcolm C., Lani L., Kyle Claire, Richard Schultz, Lara Kristi. Exec. in sales and mfg. field, 10 yrs., mem. 87th to 90th congresses from 13th Congressional Dist. Pa.; U.S. senator from Pa., mem. senate appropriations com., human resources com., ranking mem. health subcom., fgn. ops. subcom. Hon. mem. nat. council Boy Scouts Am.; bd. dirs. Schwenkfelder Library; alt. del. Republican Nat. Conv., 1952, 56, del., 1972. Served with USN, World War II. Named Outstanding Young Man Jr. C. of C., Pa., 1961; recipient Liberty Bell award Pa. Jr. Bar Assn., 1965; K.C. award, 1966; Distinguished Alumnus award Pa. State U., 1970; Bringer of Light award Jewish Nat. Fund, 1971; Samuel H. Daroff Humanitarian award Anti-Defamation League, B'nai B'rith, 1971; Charles H. Best award Am. Diabetes Assn., 1974; Nat. Soc. for Prevention Blindness award, 1974; Humanitarian award Juvenile Diabetes Found., 1974; Nat. Assn. Mental Health award, 1974; Israel Prime Minister's medal, 1974; Jobs for Spanish Speaking Constituency award, 1974; Key award Opportunities Industrialization Centers, 1974. Mem. Navy League, SAR, Am. Legion, VFW (life), Amvets (life), Pa. Soc., Anthrasilicosis League Pa. (hon.), Phi Beta Kappa. Clubs: Lions, Kiwanis (hon.), Rotary (hon.); Slumbering Groundhogs (hon.) (Quarryville). Office: Senate Office Bldg Washington DC 20510 also Fed Office Bldg 600 Arch St Philadelphia PA 19106 also Fed Office Bldg 1000 Liberty Ave Pittsburgh PA 15222 also POB 65 Fed Sq Sta Harrisburg PA 17108

SCHWEITZER, THOMAS FRED, educator, writer; b. Queens, N.Y., Dec. 10; s. T. Robert and Bertha Helen (Mathesie) S.; A.B., Columbia, 1959; A.M., N.Y. U. (N.Y. State Regents War Service scholar), 1962. Sci. tchr. Great Neck (L.I.) South Jr. High Sch., 1967—; founder, chmn. NATURE (East Queens Ad Hoc Com. for a Natural Attitude toward Urban Recreational Environment), 1970—; columnist Queens County Times, 1969-75, Glen Oaks News, 1975-76. Served with U.S. Army, 1952-55. NSF grantee, 1965; decorated Conspicuous Service Cross, N.Y. State, 1955. Mem. Nat. Sci. Tchrs. Assn., N.Y., Queens (v.p. 1969-75, trustee 1969-75, Slocum Meml. com. chmn. 1973—) hist. socs., Japan Soc., (activities com. 1960-61), Torrey Bot. Club (environ. preservation com. 1970-71), Internat. Postcard Collectors Assn. (elected to Hall of Fame 1972), Brit. Anti-Slavery Soc., Thoreau Fellowship, Alpha Phi Omega. Author: (with others) Ideas and Techniques for Seventh Grade Science: A Guide for Teachers, 1964; asst. editor Am. Biology Tchr., 1966-69, editorial staff, 1966-75. Home: 89-19 218th St Queens Village Long Island NY 11427

SCHWENN, LEE WILLIAM, hop hosp. adminstr.; b. Morrisonville, Wis., Dec. 23, 1925; s. LeRoy William and Vivian Mae (Kramer) S.; B.S., U. Wis., 1948; M.P.H., U. N.C., 1956; m. Glenna Edith Mehne, Jan. 16, 1947; 1 son, William Lee. Tchr. Pub. Schs. Appleton (Wis.), 1948-52; teaching cons. Wis. Dept. Health, 1952-53; adminstrv. asst. Madison (Wis.) Health Dept., 1953-57; adminstrv. cons. Atlanta regional office U.S. Children's Bur., 1957-58; adminstr. USPHS, Washington, 1958-66; asso. dir. D.C. Dept. Health, 1966-70, D.C. Dept. Human Resources, 1970-71; exec. v.p. Maimonides Med. Center, Bklyn., 1971—. Recipient Distinguished Public Service award D.C. Govt., 1970. Mem. Am. Public Health Assn., Am. Acad. Health Adminstrs. Office: 4802 10th Ave Brooklyn NY 11219

SCHWER, ROBERT THOMAS, accountant; b. Munhall, Pa., July 29, 1932; s. Thomas William and Anne Marie (Perhach) S.; B.S., Duquesne U., 1954; m. Joyce Elise DeRosier, June 22, 1957; children—Thomas J., Karen L., Gary R., Douglas A. Accountant, partner Colley, Trumbower & Howell, C.P.A.'s, Orlando, Fla., 1956-63; tax mgr., prin. J.K. Lasser & Co., Pitts., 1963-67; pres. R.T. Schwer & Assos., C.P.A.'s, Pitts., 1967—; instr. Allegheny County Community Coll., 1968-69. Served with USAF, 1954-56. Mem. Am. Inst. C.P.A.'s, Pa. Inst. C.P.A.'s. Republican. Roman Catholic. Club: Highland Country. Home: 109 Snowden Dr Pittsburgh PA 15229 Office: Union Trust Bldg Pittsburgh PA 15219

SCHWERDTLE, DIANA CARLISLE, educator; b. Phila., May 9, 1935; d. Edgar Grafton and Lilian (Baker) Carlisle; B.A., Middlebury Coll., 1957; M.A., Fairfield U., 1975; m. Edward Sterling Schwerdtle, Apr. 26, 1958; children—Elizabeth, Susan, Amy Hart. Elementary tchr. Fairfield (Conn.) Pub. Schs., 1957-59; employment mgr. Schwerdtle Stamp Co., Bridgeport, Conn., 1976; project dir. career and vocat. internship program Masuk High Sch., Monroe, Conn., 1976—. Mem. Newtown (Conn.) Charter Revision Commn., 1971-72; bd. dirs. Community Action Newtown, 1971-73; 2d selectman Newtown Bd. Selectmen, 1972-73; co-chmn. Monroe Career and Vocat. Edn. Plan of Action Com., 1977—, Monroe Citizens Adv. Com. for Career and Vocat. Edn., 1977—. Mem. Am. Personnel and Guidance Assn., Nat. Vocat. Guidance Assn., LWV (pres. Newtown 1969-71). Democrat. Congregationalist. Editor: Newtown Past and Present, 1975. Home: 5 Longview Heights Rd Newtown CT 06470 Office: Masuk High Sch Monroe Turnpike Monroe CT 06468

SCHWERSENZ, JACK WOLF, cons. accountant; b. Berlin, Feb. 1, 1930; s. Arthur and Grete (Jacob) S.; came to U.S., 1941, naturalized, 1946; A.B., N.Y. U., 1954, M.B.A., 1959; m. Roslyn S. Levene, Nov. 23, 1958; children—Nanette A., Audrey H. Employee, accounting and systems functions N.Y.C. div. IBM, 1959-60; reviewer, tech. cons. Aronson & Oresman, C.P.A.'s, N.Y.C., 1960-70; prin. Aronson & Oresman-Clarence Rainess & Co. C.P.A.'s., N.Y.C., 1970-73; dir., auditing standards, finance and practice mgmt. Am. Inst. C.P.A.'s, N.Y.C., 1973-75; pres. Building Blocks C.P.A. Firms, N.Y.C., 1975—; asst. prof. accounting Coll. Bus. Adminstrn., U. Bridgeport, 1966-70; adj. prof. accounting Roth Grad. Sch. Bus. Adminstrn., L.I. U., 1971-76; asso. prof. accounting Pace U., 1977—. Bd. dirs. Kissena Park Coop. Inc., 1958-59; cons. Headstart programs Morningside and other community centers, 1966. Served with U.S. Army, 1954-56. C.P.A., N.Y. Mem. Am. Inst. C.P.A.'s, N.Y. Soc. C.P.A.'s. Contbr. articles to accounting and bus. jours. Home and office: 44-59 Kissena Blvd Flushing NY 11355

SCHWIMMER, STEVE, exterminating co. exec.; b. Jamaica, N.Y., Mar. 5, 1940; s. Chester and Florence (Cohn) S.; m. Marilyn Beaman, June 26, 1965; children—Scott, David, Eric. With Fumex Sanitation, Inc., New Hyde Park, N.Y., 1960—, pres., 1973—; mem. structural pest control adv. com. N.Y. State Dept. Environ. Conservation. Leader cub pack Boy Scouts Am., 1975—; bd. dirs. Queens Speech and Hearing Service Center, 1976—, L.I. Better Bus. Bur., 1978—; mem. S. Woodbury Taxpayers Assn., 1976—. Mem. L.I. Pest Control Assn. (pres. 1970-74, dir.), Entomol. Soc. Am., Nat. Pest Control Assn. (dir. 1975—, regional v.p. 1978), Profl. Exterminators Assn., Empire State Pest Control Assn. Jewish. Clubs: Masons (master 1972-73), Rotary (pres. 1970-71). Home: Woodbury NY 11797 Office: 131 Herricks Rd New Hyde Park NY 11040

SCIVERES, ANTHONY, data processing exec.; b. Paterson, N.J., Dec. 26, 1928; s. Vincent and Josephine (Uculano) S.; A.A.S. in Accounting, Bergen Community Coll., 1975; B.A. in Accounting, William Paterson Coll., 1978; m. Marion Naples, July 3, 1952; 1 dau., Stephanie. Data processing mgr. Swivelier Co., Nanuet, N.Y., 1967-69, U.S. Pipe Co., East Orange, N.J., 1969-72, Kem Mfg. Co., Fairlawn, N.J., 1972—. Served with U.S. Army, 1951. Mem. Northern Valley Organist Guild. Home: 303 James Way Wyckoff NJ 07481 Office: River Rd and Maple Ave Fair Lawn NJ 07410

SCOFIELD, RODERICK ARTHUR, satellite meteorologist; b. Louisville, Dec. 3, 1942; s. Edward Harold and Alice Hortense (Gillespie) S.; B.S. in Physics, U. Louisville, 1964; M. Meteorology, St. Louis U., 1969, Ph.D. in Meteorology, 1973; m. Eileen Joyce Wiedmar, Aug. 22, 1964; children—Michelle Eileen, Matthew Roderick, Brett Edward. Lectr. weather and climatology So. Ill. U., Edwardsville, 1969-71; research meteorologist, trajectory modelling Nat. Weather Service, Silver Spring, Md., 1972-73, research meteorologist, hurricane modelling, Camp Springs, Md., 1973-74; satellite meteorologist Nat. Environ. Satellite Service, Camp Springs, 1974—; part-time faculty Charles County Community Coll. Vestryman, adult edn. chmn., high sch. Sunday sch. tchr., dir. youth group Episcopal Ch., Mem. Am. Meteorol. Soc., Am. Geophys. Union, Sigma Xi, Pi Delta Epsilon. Republican. Contbr. articles to profl. jours.; developer operational technique for using satellite data in detection of flash floods. Home: 1207 Adams Ct Waldorf MD 20601 Office: Nat Environ Satellite Service Applications Div World Weather Bldg Room 806 Washington DC 20233

SCOLES, PETER SERAFINO, physician; b. N.Y.C., June 21, 1908; s. Joseph Albert and Angeline (Lovisco) S.; B.S., U. Md., 1932; D.P.H., U. Kansas City, 1937; M.D., U. Lausanne (Switzerland), 1947; postgrad. McGill U., Montreal, Que., Can., 1963; M.P.H., U. N.C., 1964; m. Julia Mary Barry, Feb. 6, 1949; children—Peter, Marianne, Michael. Intern, Commonwealth Ave. Hosp., Boston, 1934-35; house physician Park East Hosp., N.Y.C., 1935-36, 42-43; instr. anatomy U. Kansas City (Mo.), 1936-37; asst. to Dr. A.V. Cash, Abilene, Tex., 1937-39; asst. camp physician to Dr. Frank Clark, Abilene, 1939-42; house physician Royal Hosp., N.Y.C., 1943-44, Hunts Point Hosp., N.Y.C., 1944-45; house officer Monmouth Meml. Hosp., Long Branch, N.J., 1947-49; commd. 1st lt. U.S. Army, 1949, advanced through grades to col., 1964; bn. and regtl. surgeon 7th Cav. Regt., Korea, 1950-51; chief ops. Med. Div., Mil. Adv. Group, Greece, 1952-53; div. surgeon, med. br. comdr. 43d Inf., Germany, 1953-55; comdg. officer 16th Surg. Hosp., chief obstetrics-gynecology U.S. Army Hosp., Ft. Devens, Mass., 1955; brigade and regional surgeon 1st Region Air Def. Command, N.Y., 1955-58; Med. Group comdr. 54th Med., Ft. Benning, Ga., 1958-59; chief Med. Div., Combat Devel. Experimentation Center, Ft. Ord, Calif., 1959-61; dep. comdr. Army Med. Service Combat Devels., Ft. Sam Houston, Tex., 1961-63; comdg. officer 55th Med. Group, Ft. Bragg, N.C., 1964-65, Kimbrough Army Hosp., Ft. George G. Meade, Md., 1965; ret., 1968; gen. practice medicine, Sea Girt, N.J., 1968—; med. dir. Tower Lodge Nursing Home, 1969; mem. staff Monmouth Med. Center. Mem. nat. adv. bd. Am. Security Council. Decorated Legion of Merit, Silver Star, Bronze Star with oak leaf cluster, Purple Heart with oak leaf cluster, Commendation medal with oak leaf cluster, Combat Med. badge; recipient medal of Merit, OAS, 1965, UN medal, 1951. Fellow Internat. Acad. Law and Sci., Am. Pub. Health Assn., Acad. Medicine N.J.; mem. Civil Aviation Med. Assn., AMA, Aerospace Med. Assn., Am. Coll. Hosp. Adminstrs., Royal Soc. Health (Eng.), Am. Acad. Family Physicians, Profl. Health Officers Soc. N.J., Balt. City (asso.), N.J., Monmouth County med. socs., Medico-Chirurg. Soc. Md., Société de Vaud (Switzerland), N.J. Assn. Nursing Home Adminstrs. Republican. Roman Catholic. Home: 1311 W Chicago Blvd Sea Girt NJ 08750 Office: Laurel Ave Sea Girt NJ 08750

SCOTT, BERTHA DIXON, govt. ofcl.; b. Littleton, N.C., Sept. 9, 1926; d. John Wesley and Emma (Shelton) Dixon; student Shaw U., 1945-49, Morgan State Coll., 1959, 61, 66, Towson State Coll., 1976-77, U. N.Y. Regents External Degree Program, 1977-78; m. Augustus Scott, Nov. 24, 1951. Clk., VA, Washington, 1951-52. Dept. Army, Ft. Meade, Md., 1952-59; with div. personnel and tng., Social Security Adminstrn., HEW, Balt., 1959-63, disability claims examiner, employee devel. specialist, 1963—; cons. to upper mgmt. Sec., Mondawmin Neighborhood Assn., 1962-66; mem. Social Security Adminstrn. Vol. Services Group; mem. Johns Hopkins Fellows Program on Community and Orgn. Devel. Recipient Suggestion award for work improvement, 1965. Mem. NAACP, Am. Soc. Tng. Dirs., Federally Employed Women (co-organizer Greater Balt. chpt., past sec., treas.). Democrat. Club: Internat. Toastmistress (pres. Woodlawn unit 1971). Home: 10113 Darlington Rd Ellicott City MD 21044 Office: Dept HEW Social Security Adminstrn 6401 Security Blvd Baltimore MD 21235

SCOTT, BLAINE WAHAB, III, ins. co. exec.; b. Phila., Apr. 22, 1927; s. Blaine W., Jr., and Dorothy (Fox) S.; ed. Friends' Central Sch.; m. Mary L. Howe, Nov. 14, 1964; children—M. Kathleen, Bruce K., Sharon L., Linda, Blaine W., Carol, Robert. Pres., dir. World Life & Health Ins. Co., also Worlco, Inc. (Del.); chmn. bd., dir. World Mut. Health & Accident Ins. Co. Pa., WorlCo Travel, Inc., Keystone Mgmt. Services, Inc., White Whale Restaurants, Harrisburg, Pa., Lafayette Mgmt. Co., N.Am. Med. Centers, Worlco Data Systems, Inc.; chmn. World Fire & Casualty Assos., Ltd.; pres., treas., dir. Upper Merion Investment Corp.; v.p., dir. Peacock Inns, Inc.; sec., dir. Bank of King of Prussia; treas. dir. Valley Forge Holiday Inn; dir. Allied-Augusta Mut. Ins. Co., Portland, Maine, Middle Atlantic Gen. Investment Co., Royal Oak Life Ins. Co.; dir. Gen. Devices, Inc. Mem. Upper Merion Bd. Suprs., 1960-66, chmn., 1961-66. Trustee Temple U., 1969-72, Valley Forge Mil. Acad., 1978—; mem. Villanova U. Devel. Council, 1975—. Served with AUS, World War II, Korea. Named One of 5 Outstanding Young Men of Commonwealth, Pa. Jr. C. of C., 1962. Mem. Ins. Fedn. Pa. (dir.), Greater Valley Forge C. of C. (dir.), VFW, S.R., Pa. SR, Fraternal Order Police Montgomery County. Clubs: Union League (Phila.); Ocean City (N.J.) Yacht; Seaview Country. Home: 480 General Washington Rd Wayne PA 19087 Office: 550 W DeKalb Pike King of Prussia PA 19406

SCOTT, CARMALITA FOSTER BENSON, educator; b. Madison, Wis.; d. Robert Henry Reese and Mary Carmalita (Lewis) Benson; B.A., U. Calif., 1952; M.Ed., Springfield Coll., 1973, C.A.S., 1975; m. Walter Hilton Scott, Mar. 22, 1955; children—Aurélia C., Hilary S. Profl. actress, 1954-69; parent coordinator Headstart, Pittsfield, Mass., 1970; columnist Berkshire Eagle, Pittsfield, 1970; spl. edn. group cons. Pittsfield Alternate Sch., 1973-74, spl. edn. tchr., 1974-78; guidance counselor Pittsfield Sch. System, 1978—. Pres. Berkshire Mental Health Assn., 1975-78; area bd. dirs. Mass. Dept. Mental Health, 1975—; mem. task force on career edn. Mass. Dept. Edn., 1977—; mem. parent nominating com., bd. dirs. Berkshire Country Day Sch., Lenox, Mass. Named Best Actress, Williamstown Theatre, Williams Coll., 1968. Mem. Mass. Assn. Sch. Psychologists, Am. Personnel and Guidance Assn., Council Exceptional Children, Nat. Assn. Sch. Psychologists. Actors Equity (sr.). Club: English-Speaking Union (Boston). Home: Old Rectory Stockbridge MA 01262 Office: Crosby Sch Pittsfield Sch Dept Pittsfield MA 01201

SCOTT, DAVID BYTOVETZSKI, dentist, govt. ofcl.; b. Providence, May 8, 1919; A.B., Brown U., 1939; D.D.S., U. Md., 1943; M.S., U. Rochester, 1944; married; 3 children. Staff, Nat. Inst. Dental Research, NIH, HEW, Bethesda, Md., 1944-56, chief lab. histology and pathology, 1956-65, dir. inst., 1976—; Thomas J. Hill Distinguished prof. phys. biology, prof. anatomy Sch. Medicine, Case Western Res. U., 1965-76, dean Sch. Dentistry, 1969-76. Recipient Arthur S. Flemming award, 1955; award for research in mineralization Internat. Assn. Dental Research, 1968; Research Achievement award Mass. Dental Soc., 1978; Spenadel Dental Research medal Columbia U., 1978. Mem. ADA, Am. Acad. Forensic Sci., Electron Micros. Soc. Am., Internat., Am. colls. dentists, Internat. Assn. Dental Research, Royal Soc. Medicine (hon.). Office: Nat Inst Dental Research NIH HEW 9000 Rockville Pike Bethesda MD 20014

SCOTT, DAVID HENRY, ophthalmologist; b. Arcadia, Fla., Aug. 18, 1916; s. David Henry and Edith Barbara (Baird) S.; B.S., U. Fla., 1937; M.D., Harvard U., 1941; m. Joanne Marion Waite, June 27, 1942; children—Edith J., David W., Marion B., Janna Ruth, Mercia C., Meredith S., Raymond B., Laura C., Douglas R. Intern, Charity Hosp. New Orleans, 1941-42; recipient in ophthalmology Mass. Eye and Ear Infirmary, Boston, 1947-49; practice medicine specializing in ophthalmology, Beverly, Mass., 1949—; mem. staff Beverly Hosp., Salem (Mass.) Hosp., Hunt Hosp., Danvers, Mass., Cable Hosp., Ipswich, Mass., Mary A. Alley Hosp., Marblehead, Mass., Mass. Gen. Hosp., Boston; sr. cons. surgeon Mass. Eye, Ear Infirmary; cons. ophthalmologist to hosps.; instr. in opthalmology Harvard U.; mem. North Shore Health Planning Council. Served with U.S. Army, 1942-46. Mem. Mass. Med. Soc., AMA, Mass. Soc. Eye Physicians, Surgeons, New Eng. Ophthalmol. Soc., Am. Acad. Ophthalmology, Am. Assn. Ophthalmology, Assn. Am. Physicians and Surgeons. Baptist. Home: 208 Main St Wenham MA 01984 Office: 7 Thorndike St Beverly MA 01915

SCOTT, DONALD HUNT, assn. exec.; b. Bloomfield, N.J., Oct. 22, 1916; s. Benjamin and Janet (McAlpine) S.; B.S., Rutgers U., 1948; LL.D., Bloomfield Coll., 1969; m. Ruth M. Keating, Dec. 13, 1942;

children—Donald Hunt, Dale Heather. Various adminstrv. positions AT&T, N.Y.C., 1935-46; entrepreneur, Bloomfield, 1946-59; mgr. pub. affairs Am. Cyanamid Co., Wayne, N.J., 1959-71; pres. N.J. C. of C., Newark, 1971—. Councilman, Bloomfield, 1948-49, mayor, 1950-60. Trustee Bloomfield Coll., chmn., 1960-74. Served from pvt. to maj., USAAF, 1942-46. Home: 59 Winding Ln Bloomfield NJ 07003 Office: 5 Commerce St Newark NJ 07102

SCOTT, DUNCAN NICHOLAS, JR., writer, editor; b. LaPorte, Tex., Aug. 3, 1909; s. Duncan Nicholas and Mary Ophelia (Fitzgerald) S.; A.B., magna cum laude, Sul Ross State Coll., Alpine, Tex., 1928; B.J., U. Mo., 1929; M.A., U. Tex., 1932; m. Sally Atwood Wilson, Aug. 1, 1951; children—Patricia (Mrs. Roger Wertheimer), Sandra (Mrs. John D'Emilio), Susan (Mrs. James Hogan), David Wilson. Journalist, Des Moines Register, 1929-31; prin. Marathon Tex. High Sch., 1932-35; prof. English, journalism N.M. State U., Bowling Green (Ohio) State U., Miami U., 1935-39, 47-49; info. specialist U.S. Dept. Agr., Washington, 1940-41, 45-47, 49-51; fgn. service officer USIA, Washington, Karachi, Tokyo, London, Calcutta, 1951-72; writer-editor Nat. Retired Tchrs. Assn., Am. Assn. Retired Persons, Washington, 1973—. Served with USNR, 1943-45. Recipient Superior Service award USIA, 1961. Mem. Am. Foreign Service Assn., Diplomatic and Consular Officers Retired. Home: 11336 Orchard Ln Reston VA 22090 Office: 1909 K St NW Washington DC 20049

SCOTT, EDWARD WALTER, clergyman; b. Edmonton, Alta., Can., Apr. 30, 1919; B.A., U. B.C.; L.Th., Theol. Coll., Vancouver, 1942; m. Isabel Florence Brannan; children—Maureen Scott Harris, Patricia Anne Scott Robinson, Douglas, Elizabeth Jean. Ordained to ministry Anglican Ch. Can.; rector St. Peters, Seal Cove, Prince Rupert, B.C., 1942-45; gen. sec. Student Christian Movement U. Man., 1945-49; also part-time lectr. St. Johns Coll.; rector Ch. of St. John the Baptist, Fort Garry, 1949-55, St. Jude's, Winnipeg, 1955-60; named dir. social service and priest-dir. Indian work Diocese of Ruperts Land, 1960; helped establish first Indian-Metis Friendship Center; joined staff Ch.'s nat. hdqrs., Toronto, 1964; consecrated bishop of Kootenay, 1966; primate Anglican Ch. of Can., 1971—; moderator central com. World Council Chs., 1975—. Address: 600 Jarvis St Toronto ON M4Y 2J6 Canada

SCOTT, JOHN AINSWORTH, JR., counselor, educator; b. Albany, N.Y., Apr. 10, 1939; s. John Ainsworth and Clara Belle (Shutts) S.; student Albany Acad., 1952-57, Lafayette Coll., 1958-61; B.A., U. Mass., 1965, M.A., 1970; m. Susan Elizabeth Nims, Nov. 19, 1966; children—Barbara Beach, John Ainsworth III. Salesman, Scott Paper Co., 1965-66; tchr., coll. guidance dir. Worcester (Mass.) Acad., 1966-70; dean acads. and guidance Northwood Sch., Lake Placid, N.Y., 1970-73; dir. guidance and counseling, tchr. English, film and photography Peddie Sch., Hightstown, N.J., 1973—; cons. Conn. Assn. Ind. Schs.; photographer. Scoutmaster, tng. chmn., fund-raiser, com. chmn. Mohigan, Adirondack, George Washington councils Boy Scouts Am., 1966—; mem. edn. bd. Holden (Mass.) Congregational Ch.; mem. adminstrv. bd. Lake Placid Community Ch.; vol. Big Bros., Worcester and Hightstown, 1969—. Served with USMC, 1957-58, 61-62. Recipient Tng. award Boy Scouts Am., 1970, Scouter's Key and Wood Badge, 1973. Mem. Am., N.J., Mercer County (N.J.) personnel and guidance assns., Nat. Assn. Coll. Admissions Counselors, N.J. Inst. Film Arts, Photog. Soc. Am., All Am. Karate Fedn. Presbyterian. Home: 128 Etra Rd Hightstown NJ 08520 Office: The Peddie Sch Hightstown NJ 08520

SCOTT, JOHN BROOKS, electronics engr., research exec.; b. Morenci, Ariz., Aug. 8, 1931; s. Brooks and Lucile (Slagle) S.; B.S. in Math., U. Ariz., 1957, M.A. in Math., 1959; children—Janice, Steven, Sarah. Asst. prof. systems engring. U. Ariz., 1959-60; mgr. data processing Bell Aerosystems Co., Tucson, 1961-62; dep. dir. tech. ops electromagnetic compatibility analysis center IIT Research Inst., Annapolis, Md., 1963—. Served with USAF, 1951-55. Mem. IEEE (sr.). Republican. Lutheran. Club: Naval Acad. Sailing Squadron. Home: 407 Halsey Rd Annapolis MD 21401 Office: PO Box 1711 Annapolis MD 21404

SCOTT, JOHN RAYMOND, JR., counselor; b. Morgantown, W.Va., Feb. 2, 1923; s. John Raymond and Joanna Jeanette (Dye) S.; B.S., W.Va. U., 1947, M.S., 1948; m. Evan Virginia Arrington, Sept. 16, 1950; 1 son, Michael James. Chmn. sci. dept. High Point High Sch., Beltsville, Md., 1954-59; chmn., resource tchr. sci. Northwood High Sch., Silver Spring, Md., 1959-69; chmn., resource tchr. sci., Sligo Jr. High, 1969-70; counselor Pyle Jr. High Sch., Bethesda, Md., 1970—. Served with U.S. Army, 1943-46, 50-52. NSF grantee, 1958, 59, 60; grantee George Washington U., 1962. Mem. Am. Personnel and Guidance Assn., Home: 14107 Heathfield Ct Rockville MD 20853 Office: 6311 Wilson Ln Bethesda MD 20034

SCOTT, JONATHAN LAVON, grocery chain exec.; b. Nampa, Idaho, Feb. 2, 1930; s. Buell Bonnie and Jewel Pearl (Horn) S.; B.A. magna cum laude, Coll. Idaho, 1951; grad. Advanced Mgmt. Program, Harvard U.; m. Barbara Jean Albertson, May 28, 1952 (div. Mar. 1962); children—Joseph Buell, Anthony Robert (dec.); m. 2d, Dolores Hormechea, Dec. 21, 1963; children—Richard Teles, Daniel. With Western Enterprises, Inc., 1952-53; with Albertson's Inc., Boise, Idaho, 1953-75, vice chmn. bd., chief exec. officer, 1972-75; vice chmn. bd. Gt. Atlantic & Pacific Tea Co., Inc., Montvale, N.J., 1975, chmn. bd., chief exec. officer, 1975—; dir. Morrison-Knudsen Co., Bendix Corp. Trustee, Com. Econ. Devel.; bd. dirs. Boys' Clubs Am., United Way Tri-State Area; chmn. retail foods industry com. U.S. Indls. Payroll Savs. campaign, 1978; trustee Com. Econ. Devel., Coll. Idaho. Served to 1st lt. USAF, 1953-54. Mem. Young Pres.'s Orgn. Clubs: Economics, Harvard, Sky, Arid (N.Y.C.). Office: Gt Atlantic & Pacific Tea Co Inc 2 Paragon Dr Montval NJ 07645

SCOTT, LESTER RAYMOND, JR., educator; b. Nazareth, Pa., Apr. 19, 1928; s. Lester Raymond and Esther Mary (Oswald) S.; student Internat. Corr. Schs., 1946-49, Temple U., 1969-72, Pa. State U., 1970-73, Northampton Community Coll., 1971-75; m. Marguerite Ellen Remel, June 11, 1949; children—Bryan Douglas, Curtis Lee, Melanie Ann. With Bethlehem Steel Co. (Pa.), 1944, Green Acres Alfalfa Farm, Nazareth, Pa., 1945-46; apprentice Frank Abel Painting & Decorating, Nazareth, 1945-48; painter, decorator, sign painter Binney & Smith Inc., Easton, Pa., 1948-69; tchr. Vocat. Tech. Sch. of Eastern Northampton County, Easton, 1969—; cons. for Pa. painting and decorating course, 1973—; mayor Borough of Tatamy (Pa.), 1970-78. Scoutmaster troop 22 Boy Scouts Am., 1949-52; pres. Tatamy Sch. Bd., 1957-59; mem. Nazareth Sch. Bd., 1959-67; deacon St. Peters United Ch. of Christ, Tatamy, 1960-68; chmn. Tatamy Planning Commn., 1968-70; adviser Vocat. Clubs Am., 1973-76. Served with USAF, 1952-56; Korea. Mem. Am., Pa. vocat. assns., NEA, Pa. Edn. Assn., Vocat. Tech. Sch. Eastern Northampton County Educators Assn. (chmn. steering com.), Nat. Wood Carvers Assn., Tatamy Fire Co. Clubs: Masons, Paint Box Art. Home: 436 Broad St Tatamy PA 18085 Office: Vocat Tech Sch of Eastern Northampton County Easton PA 18042

SCOTT, OSBORNE ERNEST, educator; b. Gloucester, Va., Feb. 5, 1916; s. Ernest Lee and Elizabeth (Evans) S.; B.S., Hampton Inst., 1938; B.D., Oberlin Grad. Sch. Theology, 1941; M.A., Columbia U., 1951; m. Jean Bernice Sampson, Dec. 29, 1947; children—Osborne Ernest, Michael D. Commd. 2d lt. U.S. Army, 1941, advanced through grades to lt. col., 1964; asst. div. chaplain 2d Inf. Div., Korea, 1953, div. chaplain 8th Inf. Div., Europe, 1960-63, mem. staff, faculty U.S. Army Chaplain Sch., 1950-53, 56-59; ret., 1964; exec. v.p. Am. Leprosy Mission, Inc., N.Y.C., 1964-69; prof. chmn. dept. urban and ethnic studies Coll. City N.Y., 1969-71, prof. dept. Black studies, 1972—, mem. exec. com. faculty senate; sr. asso. Leadership Resources Inc., Washington; pastor Trinity Baptist Ch., Bklyn. Bd. dirs. Council for Econ. Devel. and Empowerment Black People, Ch. World Service; mem. N.Y. State Welfare Assn. Decorated Bronze Star. Mem. African Acad. Arts and Research (co-chmn.), African Heritage Assn., Assn. Study Afro-Am. Life and History. Home: 323 Egmont Ave Mount Vernon NY 10553 Office: 138th St and Convent Ave New York City NY 10031

SCOTT, R(USSELL) STEPHEN, govt. ofcl., writer; b. Atlanta, May 29, 1945; s. Clayton R. and Mary E. (Daniels) S.; B.A. cum laude, Allegheny Coll., 1967; M.A. (fellow), Case Western Res. U., 1969; postgrad. (fellow) U. Pitts., 1969-70; m. Jean M. Adams, Dec. 27, 1969; 1 son, Jeffrey R. Asst. dir. forensics U. Pitts., 1969-70; pub. affairs officer, AEC, Washington, 1970-74; asst. to dir. adminstrn., U.S. Nuclear Regulatory Comm., Washington, 1974—; adj. prof. speech, Montgomery Coll., 1970—; cons. in field. Served to lt., USAF, 1967-69. Rotary scholar, 1963. Mem. Nat. Assn. Govt. Communicators, Fed. Editors Assn. (past pres.), Speech Communications Assn., DAV, Mensa, Foster Parents Assn. of Montgomery County. Baptist. Editor: Nuclear Newsfeatures, 1971-74, Jour. Pub. Communications, 1976—; author: The U.S. Atomic Energy Commission, 1973. Home: 5 Winder Ct Rockville MD 20850 Office: Nuclear Regulatory Commission Washington DC 20555

SCOTT, RICHARD THURSTON, pub. co. exec.; b. Glens Falls, N.Y., Apr. 28, 1936; s. R. Thurston and Yvonne M. (Roulier) S.; B.A., Colgate U., 1958; M.S. in Edn., Coll. St. Rose, 1968; m. Jeanne M. DeFilippo, Sept. 27, 1959; children—Kimberly Anne, Debra Lynn. Tchr., Tulare (Calif.) City Schs., 1958-59; credit investigator Dun & Bradstreet, N.Y.C., Albany, N.Y., 1959-62; tchr. Glens Falls City Schs., 1962-66; reading coordinator Kingston (N.Y.) City Schs., 1966-68; asso. editor ednl. div. Reader's Digest, Pleasantville, N.Y., 1968-72, sr. editor ednl. div., 1972-75, dir. and gen. mgr. ednl. div., 1975—. Trustee Mahopac (N.Y.) Pub. Library, 1971-77, pres. bd. trustees, 1975-77. Mem. Assn. Am. Publs., Internat. Reading Assn., Assn. of Media Producers. Home: 26 Geymer Dr Mahopac NY 10541 Office: Reader's Digest Pleasantville NY 10570

SCOTT, ROBERT STEVEN, engineer; b. North Tonawanda, N.Y., Apr. 28, 1916; s. William Henry and Angela (Lavarello) S.; B.S. in Mech. Engring., Stevens Inst. Tech., 1937, M.S., 1950; postgrad. Syracuse U., 1960-65; m. Marie Teresa Rettagliata, Nov. 11, 1951; children—William Steven, Peter Downing, Michael Alan. Design engr. O.C. Michaelis Inc., N.Y.C., 1937-38, Bur. Ordnance, Dept. Navy, Washinqton, 1938-42, Devenco Inc., N.Y.C., 1948-51; product safety engr. IBM, Poughkeepsie, N.Y., 1951—. Served to capt. U.S. Army, 1942-48. Licensed profl. safety engr., Calif. Mem. ASME, Am. Ordnance Assn. (life). Patentee in field of semicondr. fabrication. Home: 13 Pleasant Ln Wappingers Falls NY 12590 Office: IBM Corp SPD Dept 348 Bldg 224 PO Box 390 Poughkeepsie NY 12602

SCOTT, ROBERT WILLARD, dermatologist; b. N.Y.C., July 9, 1940; s. Willard Phillip and Lucille Holly (Westrom) S.; B.S., Ohio State U., 1963; M.D., Cornell U., 1967; m. Barbara Joan Wepler, Sept. 5, 1970; children—Jennifer Joan, Jill Christine. Intern, Jefferson Med. Coll. Hosp., 1967-68; resident in dermatology Hosp. U. Pa., 1968-69, 71-73; practice medicine specializing in dermatology, Jamestown, N.Y., 1967—; mem. staff, cons. dermatology Buffalo Gen. Hosp., W.C.A. Hosp., Jamestown; clin. asst. prof. dermatology State U. N.Y., Buffalo. Bd. dirs. Lutheran Social Services of Western N.Y., 1974—, Chautauqua Lake Assn., 1975—; chmn. Lakewood Citizens Police Com., 1977; chmn. Gustavus Adolphus Children's Home, 1975—; mem. Busti Republican Com., 1977—; trustee Village Bd., Lakewood, N.Y., 1978—. Served to lt. comdr. M.C., USNR, 1969-71. Diplomate Am. Bd. Dermatology, Nat. Bd. Med. Examiners. Fellow Am. Acad. Dermatology; mem. Soc. for Investigative Dermatology, AMA, N.Y. State Soc. Dermatology, Buffalo-Rochester Dermatological Soc., Ind. Order of Vikings, Pi Mu Epsilon, Alpha Epsilon Delta, Delta Upsion, Nu Sigma Nu. Republican. Presbyterian. Clubs: Moonbrook Country, Chautauqua Lake Yacht, Norden. Contbr. articles to med. jours. Home: 51 E Terrace Ave Lakewood NY 14750 Office: 320 Prather Ave Jamestown NY 14701

SCOTT, WALTER NEIL, ophthalmologist, educator; b. Evansville, Ind., Mar. 2, 1935; s. Paul Kruger and Pauline Virginia (Kimbley) S.; B.S., Western Ky. State Coll., 1956; M.D., U. Louisville, 1960; m. Margaret Ann Simon, Nov. 21, 1959; 1 son, Walter David Kimbley. Intern, New Eng. Center Hosp., Boston, 1960-61, resident, 1961-62; NIH fellow medicine Mass. Meml. Hosps., Boston, 1962-63; USPHS fellow biophys. lab. Harvard Med. Sch., Brookline, Mass., 1963-65; spl. NIH fellow biochemistry Mass. Inst. Tech., Cambridge, 1965-66; biochemist Sch. Aerospace Medicine, San Antonio, 1966-68, acting chief biochem. pharmacology div., 1967-68; asst. prof. Mt. Sinai Grad. Sch., N.Y.C., 1968-71; mem. grad. faculty City U. N.Y., N.Y.C., 1968—; asst. prof. ophthalmology Mt. Sinai Med. Sch., N.Y.C., 1971-74, asso. prof. ophthalmology, 1974—, asso. prof. physiology, 1974—, asst. dean research, 1976—; mem. Nat. Eye Inst. Cornea Task Force, 1972, Vision Research Program Com., 1975—; cons. metabolic biology program NSF, 1976—; established investigator Am. Heart Assn., 1971-76; Molly Berns sr. investigator N.Y. Heart Assn., 1976—; chmn. Gordon Conf. Biology and Chemistry of Peptides, 1978; mem. organizing com. 3d Gordon Conf. on Peptides, 6th Am. Peptide Symposium. Served to capt. USAF, 1966-68. Fellow N.Y. Acad. Scis. (gov. 1978—, vice-chmn. conf. organizing com. 1979—); mem. Am. Physiol. Soc., Biophys. Soc., Soc. Exptl. Biology and Medicine, Am. Heart Assn., AAAS, Am. Chem. Soc., Am. Soc. Nephrology, Endocrine Soc., Soc. Cell Biology, Sigma Xi, Alpha Omega Alpha. Contbr. articles to sci. publs. Home: 1095 Park Ave New York City NY 10028 also Calhoun KY 42327 Office: Mt Sinai Sch Medicine 100th St and Fifth Ave New York City NY 10029

SCOTT, WILLIAM GREGORY, educator; b. White Plains, N.Y., Mar. 10, 1934; s. Percy James and Malissa Belle (Dunn) S.; B.S., State U. N.Y., Fredonia, 1959; M.S., U. Buffalo, 1969; m. Ruth Elaine Holland, Aug. 19, 1961; children—Gregory Earl, June Alicia, Crystal Elaine. Dir. vocal music Delevan-Machias (N.Y.) Central Schs., 1959-69, James Madison High Sch., Rochester, N.Y., 1969—; asst. dir., program dir. Fresh Air Assn. of St. John, Inc., Tomkins Cove, N.Y., 1952-72 (summer camp); adjudicator for vocal solo choir N.Y. State Sch. Music Assn., 1972—; cons. Cattaraugus County Bd. Coop. Ednl. Services, 1962-64. Chmn. com. mgmt. Arnett br. YMCA, 1972-75, bd. dirs., 1974-75; chmn. youth com. 19th ward, Rochester, N.Y. Community Assn., 1974—; Dem. county committeeman, 1972—; bd. dirs. Rochester Philharmonic Orch., 1972—; Mem. new city hall com. Rochester, 1977-78; chmn. performing arts Subcom. City Com., Rochester, 1978—. Served with AUS, 1954-57. Recipient award of Appreciation, Arnett br. YMCA of Rochester and Monroe County, 1975. Mem. Cattaraugus County Music Assn. (pres. 1965-66), N.Y. State Tchrs. Assn., N.Y. State Sch. Music Assn., Music Educators Nat. Conf., Monroe County Music Educators Assn. (pres. 1976-78), N.Y. State Sch. Music Assn. (chmn. 1974—), NEA, N.Y. State United Tchrs., Rochester Tchrs. Assn., Nat. Neighbors, Inc. Club: Kiwanis (pres. 1967-68). Home: 30 Arvine Heights Rochester NY 14611 Office: 101 Epworth St Rochester NY 14611

SCRIBNER, LLOYD HOLMES, orthopedic surgeon; b. Peekskill, N.Y., Aug. 16, 1934; s. Lloyd Holmes and Florence Viola (Yost) S.; B.A. with honors, Atlantic Union Coll., 1955; M.D., Loma Linda U., 1959; m. Marjorie Howes, June 12, 1955; children—Brenda, Greg, Keith, Kelvin, Robson. Rotating intern State U. N.Y. Upstate Med. Center Hosps., Syracuse, 1959-60; resident gen. surgery Buffalo Gen. and VA Hosps., 1960-61; resident orthopedic surgery Buffalo Mercy, Gen., Children's, VA hosps., 1961-65, chief resident, 1964-65; physician McGinnis Indsl. Med. Center, Los Angeles, 1957-59; med. examiner Aetna, N.Y. Life, Paul Revere, Travelers life ins. cos., 1960-65 (Buffalo); attending physician Surburban, Holy Cross, Washington Adventist, Montgomery Gen., Leland Meml. hosps., Takoma Park, Md., 1965—; chief orthopedics Leland Hosp., 1966—; asso. chief surgery Washington Adventist Hosp., 1969-71; lectr. in field. R.G. Pulvertaft fellow orthopedic surgery, Eng., 1965. Diplomate Nat. Bd. Med. Examiners, Am. Bd. Orthopedic Surgeons; licensed physician Calif., N.Y. State, Md., D.C. Fellow A.C.S., Internat. Coll. Surgeons, Am. Acad. Orthopedic Surgedns; mem. Pan Am. Med. Assn., Montgomery County Med. Soc., Med. and Chirurg. Faculty Md. Seventh-day Adventist. Mason. Address: 7717 Carroll Ave Takoma Park MD 20012

SCRIVAN, MICHEL ANDREW, mech. engr.; b. Chorzow, Poland, Apr. 5, 1931; s. Michael Skrzywan and Maria A. (Kornecka) S.; naturalized, 1967; B.M.E., Warsaw Poly. Inst., 1953; M.M.E., Columbia, 1968; m. Millicent Anne Cross, Sept. 12, 1970; children—Katherine Anne, Michael Andrew. Project engr. Qualiqua, Paris, 1960-62; Syska & Hennessy, Inc., N.Y.C., 1962-65; cons. engr. Ford, Bacon and Davis, Inc., 1965-68; v.p. engring. Systems Simulation, Inc., 1968-71; dir. facilities maintenance Sky Chefs subs. Am. Airlines, N.Y.C., 1971—. Mem. Am. Soc. Heating, Refrigerating and Air Conditioning Engrs., U.S. Power Squadrons. Clubs: Riverside Yacht, Flying Scot Sailing Assn. Home: 6 Saint Claire Ave Old Greenwich CT 06870 Office: 605 3rd Ave New York City NY 10016

SCRIVO, JERRY VANCE, rubber co. exec.; b. Highland Park, Mich., Aug. 18, 1941; s. John R. and Martha A. (Woodcox) S.; B.S.M.E., Mich. Tech. U., 1963; M.B.A., Wayne State U., 1966; m. Carol Ann Lillstrang, June 20, 1964; children—Michelle Marie, Robert John. Devel. engr. Truck and Coach div. Gen. Motors Corp., Pontiac, Mich., 1963-66; supr. exptl engring. and vehicle test Teledyne Continental Motors, Muskegon, Mich., 1967-72; mgr. application devel. engring. Davidson Rubber Co., Inc., Dover, N.H., 1972—. Mem. Engring. Soc. Detroit, Soc. Automotive Engrs., Soc. Plastics Engrs., Am. Mgmt. Assn., Beta Sigma Psi (N.E. regional v.p. 1967-71, pres. Detroit alumni 1963-67). Republican. Methodist. Contbr. articles to profl. jours. Home: 17 Lisa Beth Circle Dover NH 03820 Office: Industrial Park Dover NH 03820

SCUDDER, PHILMORE MAJOR, JR., chemist; b. Princeton, N.J., Oct. 10, 1943; s. Philmore Major and Cordelia Janet (Wells) S.; A.S., Trenton Jr. Coll., 1964; B.A., Cheyney State Coll., 1967; M.S., St. Joseph's Coll., 1978; m. Sandra Roosa, Aug. 10, 1968; 1 dau., Tara R. Chemist, Sun Oil Co., Marcus Hook, Pa., 1968-72, Hercules Inc., Wilmington, Del., 1972-78, Nat. Foam Co., Lionville, Pa., 1978—. Mem. Am. Chem. Soc. Office: Union and Adams Sts West Chester PA 19830

SCULLY, JOHN THOMAS, obstetrician, gynecologist; b. N.Y.C., Mar. 11, 1931; s. John Thomas and Mildred Frances (Dunstrop) S.; B.S., Georgetown U., 1952; M.D., U. Mexico Sch. Medicine, 1959; m. Donna Eckardt, July 29, 1977; children—John, Helen Mary, Thomas, Nora, James, Sara, Jason Bishop. Intern, Nassau Hosp., 1959-60, resident, 1960-63; practice medicine specializing in obstetrics and gynecology, 1963—; dir. dept. obstetrics and gynecology St. Peter's Med. Center, 1971-76; clin. prof. obstetrics and gynecology Rutgers U. Med. Sch., 1971—. Diplomate Am. Bd. Obstetrics and Gynecology. Fellow A.C.S., Am. Coll. Obstetrics and Gynecology; mem. N.J., Middlesex County med. socs., N.J. Obstetrics and Gynecology Soc., N.J. Right to Life (charter). Republican. Roman Catholic. Office: 23 Duke St New Brunswick NJ 08901

SCURLOCK, REAGAN ANDREW, assn. exec.; b. LaRue, Tex., Apr. 14, 1916; s. Joseph Gordon and Olive E. (Butler) S.; B.S., Sul Ross Coll., 1939; postgrad. So. Meth. U., 1947-48; J.D., U. Tex., 1950; m. Mary Caroline Daniels, May 9, 1943; children—Peggy Scurlock Johnson, Jan Scurlock O'Hara. Commd. 2d lt. USAAF, 1941, advanced through grades to col. USAF, 1958, ret., 1968; asst. to asst. sec. def., 1958-61, chief Procurement and Prodn. Electronic Systems Command, 1961-65, chmn. Armed Services Procurement Com., 1965-68, dir. research adminstrn., asso. comptroller U. Pa., Phila., 1968-76; exec. dir. com. on govtl. relations Nat. Assn. Coll. and Univ. Bus. Officers, Washington, 1976—. Decorated Legion of Merit with oak leaf cluster, Silver Star, D.F.C., Air medal with oak leaf cluster. Mem. State Bar Tex., Nat. Assn. Coll. and Univ. Bus. Officers, Com. Govtl. Relations (chmn. subcom. grant and contract policies and procedures 1971-75), Nat. Council Univ. Research Adminstrs., Eastern Assn. Coll. and Bus. Officers, Phi Alpha Delta. Author: Principal Investigator's Handbook, 1973; Government Contracts and Grants for Research, 1975. Home: 7313 Idylbrook Ct Falls Church VA 22043 Office: One Dupont Circle Washington DC 20036

SCUTT, DER, architect; b. Reading, Pa., Oct. 17, 1934; s. George W. and Hazel (Smith) S.; student Wyomissing Poly. Inst., 1952-54, Pa. State U., 1956-58; B.Arch. (Winchester Wirt travel fellow), M.Arch., Yale, 1961; m. Leena Liukkonen, Feb. 18, 1967; children—Hagen, Kristi Karina. Partner Poor, Swanke, Hayden & Connell, architects, N.Y.C., 1975—; tchr. architecture Barlow Sch., Amenia, N.Y., 1964-66; numerous radio and TV appearances on energy conservation, also other subjects. Bd. govs. N.Y. Bldg. Congress. Recipient medal AIA, 1961. Rotary Internat. fellow, 1955-56. Mem. AIA (sec. N.Y. chpt. 1970-72, fin. com. 1974-78, Brunner scholarship com. 1975-76), Archtl. League N.Y. (chmn. scholarships and award com. 1970-72, exec. com. 1970—, v.p. for architecture 1972-73 chmn. Brunner scholarship com. 1976-77), U.S. Inst. Theatre Tech. (dir. 1970-72), Illuminating Engrs. Soc. (bd. mgrs. N.Y. sect. 1971-72, 74-75, v.p. 1972-73, pres. 1973-74, Distinguished Service award 1976). Methodist. Contbr. articles to profl. jours.; lectr. Contbg. editor Lighting Design and Applicaton, 1972—. Project designer prin. works include library Barlow Sch., Amenia, N.Y., 1964, Crossroads Office Bldg., Rochester, N.Y., 1969, One Astor Plaza and Minskoff Theatre, N.Y.C., 1973, Western Union office bldg., Upper Saddle River, N.J., 1973, Equitable Life Assurance Data Center, Easton, Pa., 1973, Creative Perfumery Center, Roure Bertrand DuPont, Teaneck, N.J., 1973, Hercules, Inc. Computer Center, Wilmington, Del., 1974. Office: 400 Park Ave New York City NY 10022

SEABROOK, VICTOR MELVILLE, lawyer; b. Ottawa, Ont., Can., June 25, 1928; s. Richard Melville and Marjorie Edith (Crawford) S.; B.A., U. Toronto (Ont.), 1951; postgrad. Osgoode Hall Law Sch.,

1951-55; m. Ruth Isobel Cameron, Dec. 27, 1955; children—Richard Melville, Peter Cameron, Timothy Victor. Called to Ont. bar, 1955, practiced in Toronto; partner firm Wright & McTaggart, 1958-68, MacKinnon & McTaggart, Toronto, 1968-75, Seabrook, Outerbridge, McElwain & Burk, Toronto, 1975-76, Seabrook, McElwain, Burk & Elliott, 1976-77, Seabrook & Assos., 1977—; dir. Barclays Can. Ltd., Granada TV Rental Ltd., Velcro Can. Ltd., F.G. Bradley Co. Ltd., Internat. Balfour Resources Ltd., Robbins & Myers Co. Can., Ltd. Mem. Canadian Bar Assn., Canadian Tax Found., County York Law Assn. Clubs: Canadian (N.Y.C.); Granite, Albany, Golf (Toronto). Home: 126 Forest Hill Rd Toronto ON M4P 2L9 Canada Office: Suite 3300 First Canadian Pl Toronto ON M5X 1A9 Canada

SEADLER, STEPHEN EDWARD, mgmt. cons., social scientist; b. N.Y.C.; s. Silas and Deborah (Gelbin) S.; A.B. in Physics, Columbia U., 1947; postgrad. George Washington U., 1948-50; m. Ingrid Linnea Adolfsson, Aug. 7, 1954; children—Einar Austin, Anna Carin. Legal research asst., editor AEC, Washington, 1947-51; electronic engr. Cushing & Newell, Warner, Inc., N.Y.C., 1951-54; seminar leader, leader trainer Am. Found. for Continuing Edn., N.Y.C., 1955-57; exec. dir. Medimetric Inst., 1957-59; mem. long-range planning com., chmn. corporate forecasting com., mktg. research mgr. W. A. Sheaffer Pen Co., Ft. Madison, Iowa, 1959-65; founder Internat. Dynamics Corp., Ft. Madison, 1965, pres., 1965-71. Founder Ideological Def. Center, Ft. Madison and N.Y.C., 1968, pres., 1968—; pres. UNICONSULT, computer-based mgmt. scis., N.Y.C., 1973—; instr. polit. sci. Iowa State Penitentiary, 1959-62; originator new social sci. of ideologics. Served with AUS, 1944-46. Mem. Am. Phys. Soc., Am. Statis. Assn., Acad. Polit. Sci., IEEE, Am. Mgmt. Assn., Am. Sociol. Assn. Clubs: Princeton (N.Y.C.); Masons (32 deg.), Shriners. Unitarian. Contbr. articles to profl. jours. Office: 521 Fifth Ave New York City NY 10017

SEAGER, RICHARD HUGH, educator; b. Dalton, N.Y., Jan. 21, 1934; s. Hugh Chandler and Evelyn Margaret (Downs) S.; B.S., State U. N.Y., Geneseo, 1957; M.S., State U. N.Y., Brockport, 1962; M.A., Ariz. State U., 1969, Ed.S., 1979; m. Ursula R. Buhrer, June 22, 1957; children—Timothy Richard, Philip Hugh. Elementary tchr. City Sch. Dist., Rochester, N.Y., 1957-64, secondary social studies tchr., 1964-68, guidance counselor grades 7 to 12, 1969—; faculty Roberts Wesleyan Coll., North Chili, N.Y. Vol. fireman, med. emergency technician Scottsville (N.Y.) Vol. Fire Dept., 1961-75. NDEA fellow, 1968-69. Mem. Am., Genesee Valley personnel and guidance assns., Am. Sch. Counselors Assn., Rochester Counselors Assn., N.Y. State United Tchrs., Rochester Tchrs. Assn., SAR. Republican.

SEAL, WILLIAM CONOR, lime co. exec.; b. Indpls., Sept. 13, 1931; s. Justin F. and Nellie (O'Connor) S.; B.S., Ind. U., 1955; M.B.A., U. Detroit, 1962; postgrad. U. Del., 1970-72; m. Margaret Louise Sullivan, Aug. 22, 1953; children—Elizabeth Seal Burkhard, Barbara, Liam, Brian, Catherine, Mary. With Great Lakes Steel Co., Detroit, 1958-62; sales service engr. Phoenix Steel Co., Claymont, Del., 1962-64; sales mgr. Eastern region Warner Co., Devault, Pa., 1964—. Pres., Holiday Hills Civic Assn., 1968, treas., 1976; rep. New Castle County Council Civic Assns., 1966-68. Served with U.S. Army, 1955-57. Mem. Am. Inst. Metall. Engrs., Am. Soc. Metals, Water Pollution Control Fedn. Democrat. Roman Catholic. Home: 2203 Riviera Ln Wilmington DE 19810 Office: Warner Co Devault PA 19432

SEALEY, LEONARD GEORGE WILLIAM, ednl. cons., author; b. London, May 7, 1923; s. George William and Gertrude Mary (Holmes) S.; came to U.S., 1967; student Loughborough Coll. Advanced Tech., 1942-44; tchr.'s certificate Peterborough Tng. Coll., 1948; Dip. Ed., M.Ed., U. Leicester, 1964; m. Joan Mary Hearn, Mar. 11, 1944 (dec.); children—Richard, Andrew, Nicholas, Edward; m. 2d, Nancy Marie Verre, Aug. 29, 1972; 1 son, Christopher. Tchr., prin. sch., Leicestershire, Eng., 1948-55; adviser to elementary schs., Leicestershire, 1956-65; prin. North Bucks (Eng.) Coll. Edn., 1965-67; dir. regional ednl. lab. program Ednl. Devel. Center, Newton, Mass., 1967-68; cons. to various govt. depts., found., pvt. cos., other orgns., 1968—; painter, sculptor, 1950—; exhibited in internat. group shows, since 1953—. Served with Royal Navy, 1942-46. Fellow Royal Soc. Arts; mem. Phi Delta Kappa. Author numerous books on elementary math., lang. arts and reading, 1960—, latest being Open Education: A Study of Selected American Elementary Schools, 1978; co-author: Children's Writing, 1979. Home and office: 11 Chilton St Plymouth MA 02360

SEAMAN, ALFRED J(ARVIS), advt. exec.; b. Hempstead, L.I., N.Y., Sept. 17, 1912; s. Alfred J. and Ellen (Delaney) S.; B.S., Columbia U., 1935; m. Mary M. Schill, Sept. 26, 1937 (dec. June 1975); children—Marilyn (Mrs. John Olen Pickett, Jr.), Susan, Barry, Deborah; m. 2d, Honor S. Mellor, July 16, 1977. Account exec. Fuller & Smith & Ross, Inc., N.Y.C., 1937-41; partner Knight & Gilbert, Inc., Boston, 1941-43; with Compton Advt., Inc., N.Y.C., 1946-59, exec. v.p., creative dir., dir., 1954-59; vice chmn. bd., chmn. exec. com. SSC&B, Inc. (formerly Sullivan, Stauffer, Colwell & Bayles, Inc.), 1959-67, pres., 1960—; chmn. ops. com. SSC&B-Lintas Internat., 1970—. Trustee, Village of Upper Brookville, L.I., 1958—, chmn. planning com., 1962—, mayor, 1966; trustee Hofstra U., 1972—; mem. exec. com. Samuel Waxman Cancer Research Fund, 1975—. Served to lt. USNR, 1943-45. Mem. Am. Assn. Advt. Agys. (mem. advisory council 1969, pres. ednl. found. 1977—), Advt. Council (dir.), Nat. Outdoor Advt. Bur. Clubs: The Creek (pres. 1975), Beaver Dam (Locust Valley, (L.I.); Racquet and Tennis, The Links (N.Y.C.); Piping Rock (Locust Valley, N.Y.); Mid-Ocean (Bermuda); Nat. Golf Links Am. (Southampton, N.Y.); Jupiter Island (Fla.). Home: Wolver Hollow Rd Upper Brookville Oyster Bay NY 11771 Office: One Dag Hammarskjold Plaza New York NY 10017

SEAR, ALAN MARTIN, research methodologist; b. Chattanooga, Jan. 25, 1944; s. Louis and Rose Ella (Rosenthal) S.; B.S., U. Tenn., 1965, M.A., 1967; Ph.D., Purdue U., 1971; m. Nancy Adele Kinsey, Oct. 10, 1964; children—Celeste, Jacqueline. Asst. prof. Tenn. Technol. U., 1969-70; research asso., asst. prof. Tulane U., 1970-74; dir. population studies unit Inst. for Health Services Research, 1973-74; chief research design and analysis unit Internat. Inst. for Study of Human Reprodn., Columbia, 1974—, research asso., asst. prof., 1974—; cons., program in community medicine Universidad del Valle, Cali, Colombia, Autonomous U. of Mex., Toluca; cons. Ministry of Health, Quito, Ecuador. Campaign coordinator for Eugene McCarthy, Clinton County, Ind., 1968. Adminstrv. dir. regional perinatal care network, Columbia. Purdue Research Found. fellow, 1967-69. Mem. Am. Sociol. Assn., Population Assn. Am., So. Regional Demographic Group, AAAS, Alpha Kappa Delta. Democrat. Contbr. articles to profl. jours. Office: 630 W 168th St New York City NY 10032

SEARS, ROBERT ALLEN, internist, endocrinologist; b. Torrington, Conn., June 20, 1928; s. James Andrew and Doris (Denison) S.; B.S., Tufts U., 1950, M.D., 1954; m. Norma W. Sample, Aug. 22, 1953; children—Robert Allen, James Andrew, II, Stuart D., Martha W., David D. Intern, Cambridge (Mass.) City Hosp., 1954-55; asst. resident New Eng. Center Hosp., Boston, 1957-58, fellow in rheumatic disease, 1960-61; resident New Eng. Deaconess Hosp., Boston, 1958-59; sr. resident Tufts med. service Boston City Hosp., 1959-60; practice medicine specializing in internal medicine and endocrinology, Springfield, Mass., 1961—; mem. staff Baystate Med. Center, Springfield, Mary Lane Hosp., Ware, Mass.; pres., dir. Colony Med. Assos. Inc., 1974—; vis. physician, endocrinologist Baystate Med. Center, 1961—; fellow in diabetes Joslin Clinic, Boston, 1958-59; sr. clin. instr. medicine Tufts U. Sch. Medicine, Boston, 1975—; dir. Health Care Found. Western Mass., West Springfield, 1970—, sec., 1977—; dir. Western Mass. Profl. Standards Rev. Orgn., West Springfield, 1972—, chmn. utilization rev. com., 1975—; trustee Pioneer Valley Multiple Sclerosis Soc., Srpingfield, 1962-70; chmn. Health Fair '69, Springfield. Mem. Cub Pack com. King Phillip council Boy Scouts Am., 1967-70; trustee, mem. exec. com. Genesis II, Inc., Sprinfield, 1970-74. Served to lt. comdr. USPHS, 1955-57. Recipient award for outstanding service Hampden Dist. Med. Soc., 1969; diplomate Am. Bd. Internal Medicine. Mem. A.C.P. (life), Am., New Eng., Pioneer Valley (dir. 1975—) diabetes assns., Am., Mass. (council) socs. internal medicine, AMA, Mass. Med. Soc., Tufts Alumni Assn. Republican. Episcopalian. Club: Field of Longmeadow (Mass.). Home: 263 Concord Rd Longmeadow MA 01106 Office: 130 Maple St Springfield MA 01103

SEATON, DOUGLAS GRAHAM, home for aged adminstr.; b. Toronto, Ont., Can., June 3, 1917; s. Thomas and Annie Allen (Graham) S.; grad. Dominion Bus. Coll., Toronto, 1941; student U. Toronto, 1944; diploma Knox Theol. Coll., 1947, B.D., 1951; m. Ruth Virginia McDowell Rocha, Dec. 19, 1968; 1 son, Douglas Graham. Missionary, Presbyn. Student Mission Fields, Ont., N.S., Alta., B.C., Can., 1942-47; ordained to ministry Presbyterian Ch., 1947; pastor St. Andrew's Presbyn. Ch., Sackville, N.B., Can., 1947-49, Paterson Meml. Presbyn. Ch., Sarnia, Ont., 1949-56, Leaside Presbyn. Ch., Toronto, 1956-66; adminstr. Adult Cerebral Palsy Inst., Toronto, 1966-74, Toronto Aged Men's and Women's Homes, Belmont House, 1974—; mem. exec. bd. of adminstrv. council Presbyn. Ch. Can., sec. orgn. and planning com., 1957-63; pres. Leaside Sr. Citizens Council; exec. mem. North Toronto area Toronto Social Planning Council; founding exec. mem. Ont. Fedn. Physically Handicapped; exec. mem. Ont. Fedn. Cerebral Palsied. Mem. Ont. Assn. Homes for Aged, Toronto Social Planning Council, Knox Coll. Alumni Assn. (pres.). Club: Rotary. Home: 88 Bloor St E No 3110 Toronto ON M4W 3G9 Canada Office: 55 Belmont St Toronto ON M5R 1R1 Canada

SEAWELL, DONALD RAY, publisher, lawyer, theatrical producer; b. Jonesboro, N.C., Aug. 1, 1912; s. Ashley A.F. and Bertha (Smith) S.; A.B., U. N.C., 1933, J.D., 1936; L.H.D., U. No. Colo., 1978; m. Eugenia Rawls, Apr. 5, 1941; children—Brook (Mrs. Joseph Speidel), Donald Brockman. Admitted to N.C. bar, 1936, N.Y. bar, 1947; with SEC, 1937-41, 45-47, U.S. Dept. Justice, 1942-43; partner Bernstein, Seawell, Kaplan & Block, N.Y.C., 1947-75; partner Bernstein, Seawell & Kove, N.Y.C., 1975—; pres., pub., chmn. bd., dir. Denver Post, Inc., 1966—, Gravure West, Los Angeles, 1968—; partner Bonfils-Seawell Enterprises, N.Y.C., 1960—; dir. Swan Prodns., London, Eng. Chmn. bd. Bonfils Theatre; mem. theatre panel Nat. Council for Arts, 1970-74; chmn. bd. ANTA, 1965—; trustee Am. Acad. Dramatic Arts, N.Y.C., 1967—; pres. Helen G. Bonfils Found., Frederick G. Bonfils Found., Denver, Denver Opera Found.; chmn. bd. Denver Center for Performing Arts; trustee Denver Symphony, Central City Opera Assn.; chmn., pres. Civilian Mil. Inst.; bd. dirs. Nat. Inst. Outdoor Drama; chmn. exec. com. Air Force Acad. Found., Newspaper Advt. Bur., Hammond Mus., North Salem, N.Y.; mem. Bus. Com. for Arts, Conf. Bd. Served with AUS, 1942-45. Clubs: Players, Dutch Treat (N.Y.C.), Bucks (London); Denver Country, Cherry Hills Country, Denver, Mile High (Denver); Garden of Gods (Colorado Springs). Office: 295 Madison Ave New York City NY 10017 also Denver Post 650 15th St Denver CO 80202

SEBASTIANELLI, MARIO JOSEPH, nephrologist; b. Jessup, Pa., Sept. 14, 1935; s. Carlo and Antoinette (Antonelli) S.; B.S., U. Scranton (Pa.), 1958; M.D., Jefferson Med. Coll., 1962; postgrad. U. N.Mex., 1967-68, U. Miami (Fla.), 1968-69, St. Joseph's Coll., 1970-71; m. Prisca A. Palermo, Jan. 15, 1970 (dec.). Intern, Phila. Gen. Hosp., 1962-63, resident, 1963, 65-67; resident U. N.Mex., Albuquerque, 1967-68; nephrology fellow U. Miami, 1968-69; practice medicine specializing in nephrology, 1969—; sr. instr. medicine Hehnemann Med. Coll., 1969-70, asst. prof., 1970-71, staff physician, 1969—, vis. asst. prof., 1971-77, clin. asso. prof., 1977—; asst. attending physician Phila. Gen. Hosp., 69-70, attending physician, 1970-71; lectr. Hershey (Pa.) Med. Center, 1975—; prof. nephrology Kings Coll., Wilkes-Barre, Pa., 1976—; dir. hemodialysis unit Moses Taylor Hosp., Scranton, Pa., 1972-76; staff physician Mercy Hosp., Scranton, Scratnon State Hosp., Scranton Community Med. Center, Mid-Valley Hosp., Peckville, Pa., St. Joseph's Hosp., Carbondale, Pa.; mem. Pa. Gov.'s Renal Disease Adv. Co., 1973-76; dir. Scranton-Lackawanna Human Devel. Agency, Inc., 1977—; mem. tech. rev. com. Greater Del. Valley Regional Med. Program, 1973; nephrologist coordinator Kidney Doner Program, Scranton, 1977—. Bd. dirs. Lackawanna unit Am. Cancer Soc., 1976-77. Served to lt. USN, 1963-65. Diplomate Am. Bd. Internal Medicine. Fellow A.C.P., Am. Coll. Angiology; mem. Pa. Soc. Internal Medicine (pres. n. central region 1974—), Pa. Med. Soc., AMA, Hemodialysis Patients Assn. Northeastern PO, Vis. Nurses Assn., Home Health Maintenance Orgn., Am., Internat. socs. nephrology, Alpha Omega Alpha. Republican. Roman Catholic. Clubs: K.C., Elks. Contbr. articles in field to med. jours. Home: 176 Constitution Ave Jessup PA 18343 Office: 1416 Monroe Ave Dunmore PA 18512

SEBEKOS, THOMAS GEORGE, utility exec.; b. N.Y.C., June 12, 1919; s. George Peter and Mary (Lepach) S.; student N.Y. U., 1947-49, Internat. Corr. Schs., 1950-53, Bristol Instrument and Telemetry Sch., 1952, Quindar Electronic Sch., 1954, N.Y. Inst. Tech., 1971; m. Catherine Hock, Oct. 5, 1946; children—George Richard, Nancy Ruth, Marianne. With Jamaica (N.Y.) Water Supply Co., 1946—, chief ops., 1953-69, v.p. operations, 1969-78, sr. v.p. ops., dir., 1978—; v.p. ops. Sea Cliff Water Co. (N.Y.), 1969—; asst. instr. indsl. engring. Columbia U., 1949-50; instr. Nassau and Suffolk Counties Water Treatment Plant Operators Sch., 1956. Served to capt., inf., AUS, 1940-46. Mem. Am. Water Works Assn., L.I. Water Conf., Am. Inst. Plant Engrs. Home: 3782 Charles Ct Seaford NY 11783 Office: 410 Lakeville Rd Lake Success NY 11040

SEBES, JOSEPH SCHOBERT, educator; b. Nagypall, Baranya M. Hungary, Aug. 18, 1915; s. Joseph and Catherine (Kungl) Schobert; came to U.S., 1950, naturalized, 1956; grad. Pius X Gymnasium, Pecs, Hungary, 1934; licentiate Gregorian U. Rome., 1947; Ph.D., Harvard U., 1958; Ph.D. (hon.), Georgetown U., 1976. Joined Society of Jesus, 1934; asst. prof. Asian history Georgetown U., Washington, 1958-65, regent Edmund A. Walsh Sch. Fgn. Service and Bus. Adminstrn., 1961-64, dean Sch. Bus., 1964-66, dean Sch. Fgn. Service, 1966-68; prof. Asian history, 1968—. Fellow Woodrow Wilson Internat. Center for Scholars, 1976-77. Mem. Nat. Com. for U.S.-China Relations, Am. Fgn. Service Assn., Toho Gakkai (Inst. Eastern Cultures) Tokyo, Am. Hist. Assn., Assn. Asian Studies, Am. Oriental Soc. Roman Catholic. Author: The Jesuits and the Sino-Russian Treaty of Nerchinsk 1689, 1961; The Diary of Thomas Pereira, S.J., 1962. Home: Jesuit Community Georgetown Univ Washington DC 20057 Office: Dept History Georgetown Univ Washington DC 20057

SEBOK, LOUIS STEPHEN, electronics co. exec.; b. Budapest, Hungary, June 28, 1927; s. Lajos and Helen (Baky) S.; came to U.S., 1957, naturalized, 1963; M.S. in Mech. Engring., Tech. U. Budapest, 1949, Candidate of Scis., 1954; m. Anna B. Szekacs, Dec. 1, 1956; children—Veronica H., Thomas L. Asso. prof. Tech. U., Budapest, 1949-56; application engr. IBM, London, 1956-57; div. mgr. LFE Inc., Boston, 1958-68; div. mgr. Polaroid Corp., Boston, 1968-73; v.p., gen. mgr. Gould Allied Control, Plainville, Conn., 1974-76; pres. Chloride Pyrotector, Hingham, Mass., 1977—. Named Man of Year, Soc. Photog. Equipment Tech., 1973; registered profl. engr., Mass. Mem. IEEE (v.p. nuclear group), Soc. Exptl. Stress Analysis, Am. Vacuum Soc. Congregationalist. Clubs: Falmount Yacht, Charles River Tennis. Author books, articles in field of accoustics, vibrations, nuclear instrumentation. Home: 16 June Lane Newton MA 02159 Office: 333 Lincoln St Hingham MA 02043

SECOR, JOHN RALPH, bookselling co. exec.; b. Malden, Mass., Apr. 22, 1939; s. Ralph William and Emilie Mary (Glynn) S.; student Boston Coll., 1957-61; m. Sally Ann Bayley, Nov. 28, 1959; children—Glenn, Heidi Jo, Traci. Dir. sales tng., devel. Prentice-Hall, Inc., Englewood Cliffs, N.J., 1965-71; pres. Yankee Book Peddler, Inc., Contoocook, N.H., 1971—, Select Press Book Service, Inc., Milford, N.H., 1975—, Small Press Exhibit Service, Milford, 1976—; exec. v.p. The Country Scholar, Inc., Contoocook, 1975—. Mem. New Eng., Mass. library assns., Mass. (state v.p. 1966), Groveland (charter pres. 1965) jaycees, U.S. Jr. C. of C. (nat. dir. 1967). Home: Pleasant St Westford MA 01886 Office: Yankee Book Peddler Inc Maple St Contoocook NH 03229

SEDER, LAWRENCE RICHARD, equipment leasing and comml. finance co. exec.; b. Worcester, Mass., Mar. 2, 1935; s. David Jerome and Sylvia (Beizer) S.; B.B.A., U. Mich., 1957, M.B.A., 1958; m. Lesley Crossman, July 20, 1969; children—Lynn, Robin. Vice-pres. Gen. Discount Corp., Boston, from 1958, now pres.; pres. CBT Leasing Corp., Boston. Instr. finance Boston U., 1959-61. Served with USAF, 1961-62. Mem. Pi Lambda Phi. Jewish. Club: Belmont Country. Home: 135 Willard Rd Brookline MA 02146 Office: 100 State St Boston MA 02109

SEDGLEY, ALFREDA JULIA, hosp. adminstr.; b. Essen, Ger., Dec. 25, 1916; came to U.S., 1929, naturalized, 1933; d. Michael Julius and Frieda Christina (Siege) Schneider; student Trenton State Coll., 1969-71; m. Chester Arthur Sedgley, May 4, 1940; children—Richard Arthur, Ronald Michael, Christine Anne. Operating room nurse Eye and Ear Infirmary, 1940-41, Irvington (N.J.) Gen. Hosp., 1938-40; head nurse Office Dependency Benefits, 1941-45. nurse East Orange (N.J.) Gen. Hosp. and Hosp. of the Oranges, 1954-60; head nurse, obstetrics West Essex (N.J.) Gen. Hosp., 1960-68, asst. dir. nursing, 1967-69, dir. nursing, 1969; nursing cons., 1971-73, purchasing agt., 1971—, acting adminstr., 1973-74, asst. adminstr., purchasing agt., 1974—, sec. bd. trustees, 1977—. Mem. Am. Osteo. Assn., Asst. Hosp. Dirs. Assn., N.J. Hosp. Purchasing Mgmts. Assn., Essex County Disaster Council, Martland Med. Center Aluni Assn. Episcopalian. Home: 19 Sturgis Rd West Point Island Lavallette NJ 08735 Office: 204 Hillside Ave Livingston NJ 07039

SEDLAK, EMERY PAUL, assn. exec.; b. Homestead, Pa., July 11, 1918; s. Emery Henry and Annie (Ehnot) S.; B.S. in Pub. Adminstrn., U. So. Calif., 1947; m. Ellen Boyd, July 28, 1947; children—Emery H., William C., Elizabeth, Annie. Research asso. Mercer County br. Pa. Economy League, Inc., 1949-53, asst. dir., dir. research, 1953-72, dir. Western div., Pitts., 1973—; v.p., sec., treas. Aviation Research Corp. Sec., Greater Pitts. Airport Adv. Com., 1960—. Served to maj. AUS, 1942-47. Named Man of Year, Shenango Valley Jr. C. of C., 1953. Mem. Govtl. Research Assn. (awards), Municipal Fin. Officers Assn., Am. Planning Ofcls. Assn., Am. Assn. Airport Execs., World Affairs Council Pitts. Clubs: Aero (Pitts.); Nemacolin Country, Duquesne. Home: 727 Pinetree Rd Pittsburgh PA 15243 Office: 2 Gateway Center Pittsburgh PA 15222

SEEDMAN, GEORGE JAMES, retail co. exec.; b. N.Y.C., Dec. 4, 1896; s. James and Bertha (Karmel) S.; student Browne Bus. Coll., Jamaica, N.Y., 1913-14; m. Barbara Wilcox, Apr. 29, 1967; children—Richard Jay, Charles Stedwell, Wendy, William Doremus. Reporter, Fairchild News, 1915-16; self-employed in automotive chain stores and wholesale distbn., 1918—; pres., now chmn. bd. Seedman Co., Times Sq. Stores Corp., Union Cycle Co., Ltd., Gotham Products Corp., Wilcox Internat. Corp.; chmn. bd. Martins Fashion Shops, Inc., Royce Union Co. Chmn., pres. Am. Bus. Congress, 1940-48. Bd. dirs. United Jewish Appeal, Fedn. Jewish Philanthropies. Served with USNRS, 1918-19. Named Man of Year, B'nai B'rith, 1971; Mdse. Man of Year, Adelphi U., 1974; recipient Ann. Humanitarian award March of Dimes, 1975. Home: Centre Island Rd Centre Island Oyster Bay NY 11771 Office: 104-01 Foster Ave Brooklyn NY 11236

SEEL, MARTIN ANTHONY, banker; b. Jersey City, Mar. 3, 1933; s. Martin and Mildred (Dileo) S.; B.S., Bucknell U., 1955; M.B.A., N.Y. U., 1961; m. Marilyn Kaye Schwartz, Sept. 25, 1955; children—Martin A., Robin Ann, Ellen Mildred, Catherine Elizabeth. Asst. v.p., mgr. Wall St. office Bank Leumi Trust Co., N.Y.C., 1964-71; v.p., mgr. domestic credit dept. Republic Nat. Bank N.Y., N.Y.C., 1971—; tchr. Am. Inst. Banking, Clifton, N.J., 1962-72. Chmn. stewardship com. Christ Ch., Bloomfield/Glen Ridge, N.J., 1978—, dir. usher guild, 1977—, vestryman, 1978—; pres. Glen Ridge Music Parents Assn., Inc., 1977—. Mem. Robert Morris Assos., Nat. Assn. Credit Mgmt., Credit Men's Frat., Bank Credit Assos. N.Y. (bd. govs. 1978—). Home: 19 Woodland Ave Glen Ridge NJ 07028 Office: 452 Fifth Ave New York City NY 10018

SEELBACH, CHARLES WILLIAM, chemist; b. Buffalo, Dec. 13, 1923; s. Charles George and Marcia (Grimes) S.; A.B., Cornell U., 1948; M.S., Western Res. U., 1952; Ph.D., Purdue U., 1955; m. Patricia C. O'Reilly, July 6, 1946; children—Janet K., Jeanne L., Paul W. Research chemist Standard Oil (Ohio), Cleve., 1948-52; project leader Esso Research, Linden, N.J., 1955-56, sect. head, 1957-61; asst. sect. head Esso Standard Oil Co., Baton Rouge, 1956-57; chem. coordinator Esso Internat., N.Y.C., 1961-63; mgr. project devel. Polymers div. Esso. Chem. Co., 1963-66, mgr. new investments and planning Elastomers div., 1966-67; dir. indsl. chems. devel. USS Chems. div. U.S. Steel, 1968-69, dir. hydrocarbon raw material devel., 1969-70, mgr. comml. devel. plastics, 1970-76, mgr. comml. devel. indsl. chemistry, 1976-77, mgr. comml. devel. petrochem. devel., 1977—. Served with USMC, 1942-45. Fellow Am. Inst. Chemistry; mem. N.Y. Acad. Sci., Am. Chem. Soc., AAAS, Comml. Devel. Assn., Sigma Xi, Phi Lambda Upsilon. Patentee in field. Home: 1405 Parkview Dr Allison Park PA 15101 Office: USS Chemicals US Steel Bldg Pittsburgh PA 15230

SEELEY, CLINTON BARNUM, radiologist; b. N.Y.C., Aug. 28, 1927; s. Nathaniel S. and Louise (Talbot) S.; B.S., Mass. Inst. Tech., 1951; M.D., U. Rochester, 1955; m. Gail Ruth Robyn, Sept. 8, 1956; children—Laura, David, Paul, Kathryn. Rotating intern Strong Meml. Hosp., U. Rochester (N.Y.), 1955-57; resident in radiology Mass. Gen. Hosp., Boston, 1957-60, staff radiologist, 1960-65; practice medicine specializing in radiology, Andover, Mass., 1961—; mem. staff Lawrence (Mass.) Gen. Hosp.; mem. staff Melrose-Wakefield

Hosp., Melrose, Mass., 1961—, pres. med. staff, 1977; pres. L & M Radiology, Inc. Served with U.S. Army, 1945-47. Diplomate Am. Bd. Radiology. Fellow Am. Coll. Radiology; mem. AMA, Mass. (council), Middlesex East Dist. (pres. 1977-78) med. socs., Radiol. Soc. N. Am., Am. Coll. Radiology (council), Mass. Radiol. Soc. (exec. com.). Office: 358 N Main St Andover MA 01810

SEELY, JOHN CONOR, JR., agrl. co. exec.; b. Pittsfield, Mass., May 6, 1939; s. John Conor and Clarice Virginia (Fredenburg) S.; student U. Vt., 1959-62; B.A., U. Mass., 1964, M.B.A., 1965; m. Pamela Marie Blewitt, Aug. 24, 1968. Faculty U. Mass., Amherst, 1965-66; mktg. specialist Gen. Electric Co., N.Y.C., 1966-67; pres. Consumer Cons. Corp., Pittsfield, Mass., 1967-69; chmn. bd. Lawn Medic, Inc., Rochester, N.Y., 1969—; chmn. bd. Real Estate Time Sharing Inc., Rochester, 1975—; dir. Pre-Germ Seeding Corp., Bergen, N.Y., F.M. Mills Co., Inc., Bergen, Creative Prospects, Inc., Rochester; cons. to numerous corps. and instns. Trustee Real Estate Equity Diversification Trust. U. Mass. faculty fellow, 1963-64. Mem. Am. Mktg. Assn., C. of C., Beta Gamma Sigma. Clubs: Burdy Hollow Ski (Rochester); Brighton (N.Y.) Tennis. Home: 188 Pitts Colony Dr Rochester NY 14623 Office: 1024 Sibley Tower 25 North St Rochester NY 14604

SEELY, ROBERT DANIEL, physician; b. Woodmere, N.Y., Nov. 4, 1923; s. Harry and Ethel (Weil) S.; B.S., N.Y. U., 1943; M.D., Columbia U., 1946; m. Marcia Ann Wells, June 19, 1953; children—Ellen Wells, Anne Wells. Intern, Mt. Sinai Hosp., N.Y.C., 1946-47, asst. resident in medicine, 1950-51, resident in pathology, 1951-52, chief resident medicine, 1952-53; Sara Welt fellow in cardiovascular research Presbyn. Hosp., N.Y.C., 1953-54; instr. dept. physiology, cardiovascular research Western Res. U. Med. Sch., Cleve., 1947-48; chief rheumatic heart disease clinic Mt. Sinai Hosp., N.Y.C., 1961-70, attending physician medicine and cardiology, 1978—; asso. clin. prof. medicine, asso. clin. prof. cardiology Mt. Sinai Hosp. Sch. Medicine, 1970—; practice medicine, specializing in internal medicine (cardiovascular disease), N.Y.C., 1953—. Served as capt. M.C., AUS, 1948-50. Recipient Solomon Berson Meml. award Mt. Sinai Hosp., 1977; Wortis award in biol. scis., 1946, N.Y. U. Fellow Am. Coll. Cardiology, A.C.P.; mem. N.Y. Heart Assn., AMA, N.Y. County Med. Soc., Soc. Certified Internists of N.Y., Phi Beta Kappa, Alpha Omega Alpha, Beta Lambda Sigma. Contbr. articles on cardiovascular research to Am. Jour. Physiology, Circulation, Am. Jour. Medicine, Annals of Internal Medicine. Home: 49 E 96th St New York City NY 10028 Office: 994 Fifth Ave New York City NY 10028

SEEMAN, BERNARD, editor, author; b. N.Y.C., Oct. 19, 1911; s. William J. and Lena (Kerner) S.; student pub. schs.; m. Geraldine Adele Micallef, Jan. 19, 1933. Free lance writer Ken mag., 1938-39; mil. writer, Far East specialist Friday mag., 1939-40; Latin Am. corr. Click mag., 1940-41; war corr. Far East Theatre, 1945 for Readers Scope, Internat. Digest; asso. editor Mag. Digest, Hillman Publs., 1946-54, med. and sci. editor, 1954-61; editor Internist Observer, Inc., 1962-75; exec. v.p. Sci. and Medicine Pub. Co. Spl. cons. on Japan OWI, 1944. Mem. Acad. Polit. Sci., Fedn. Am. Scientists, Astron. Soc. Pacific, L.B.S. Leakey Found., Nat. Acad. Rec. Arts and Scis., AAAS, Nat. Assn. Sci. Writers, Authors League, Authors Guild, Am. Mus. Natural History, Museum Modern Art. Author: Enemy Japan, 1945; The River of Life, 1961 (winner Howard W. Blakeslee award Am. Heart Assn.); Man Against Pain, 1962; The Story of Electricity and Magnetism, 1962; Your Sight; Folklore, Fact and Common Sense, 1968; co-author (with Lawrence Salisbury) Cross-Currents in the Philippines, Inst. of Pacific Relations, 1946; (with Dr. Henry Dolger) How to Live with Diabetes, 1958, rev. edit., 1965, 3d edit., 1972, 4th edit., 1977. Address: Moonwalk Obtuse Rocks Rd Brookfield Center CT 06805 also 372 Central Park West New York City NY 10025

SEEMAN, MANFRED, furniture mfr.; b. Vienna, Austria, Mar. 7, 1924; s. Max and Yetta (Fruchtman) S.; B.B.A., Coll. City of N.Y., 1947; M.B.A. with distinction, Harvard, 1949; m. Carol E. Misch, May 6, 1951; children—Charles Alan, William Henry. Came to U.S., 1938; naturalized, 1944. Sales rep. Jens Risom Design, Inc., 1952-58; v.p. Isabel Scott Fabrics, 1958-59; pres. Helikon Furniture Co., Inc., 1959—, Helikon of Conn., Inc., 1969—. Served with inf. AUS, 1943-45. Decorated Bronze Star medal, Purple Heart; named Conn. Man of Year, SBA, 1975. Mem. Am. Soc. Interior Designers (co-chmn. nat. com. industry found.), Designers Saturday (chmn.). Jewish (pres. and dir. temple). Club: Harvard Bus. Sch. (N.Y.C.). Home: 211 Harland Rd Norwich CT 06360 Office: 607 Norwich Ave Taftville CT 06380

SEGAL, BARRY MAYER, physician; b. Bklyn., Dec. 26, 1934; s. O. Saul and Doris Segal; B.A., Syracuse U., 1956; M.D., State U.N.Y., Syracuse, 1959; m. Susan Grossman, June 17, 1961; children—Jeffrey Howard, Helaine Beth. Intern, resident Cornell div. Bellevue Hosp., Meml. Hosp. Center, N.Y.C., 1959-61; resident in medicine N.Y. Med. Coll., 1962-63; ivs. fellow Columbia Presbyn. Med. Center, 1963-65; practice medicine specializing in endocrinology, Briarcliff, Mt. Kisco, N.Y., 1965—; clin. asso. prof. medicine N.Y. Med. Coll.; asst. chief endocrinology Westchester County Med. Center. Served to capt. USAF, 1961-62. Diplomate Am. Bd. Internal Medicine, Am. Bd. Nuclear Medicine. Fellow Am. Coll. Nuclear Physicians, A.C.P.; mem. Endocrine Soc., Am. Thyroid Assn., Fedn. Clin. Research, Am. Diabetes Assn., Soc. Nuclear Medicine, AMA, N.Y. State, Westchester County med. socs. Jewish. Contbr. Articles to med. jours. Home: 520 Sleepy Hollow Rd Briarcliff Manor NY 10510 Office: 316 Chappaqua Rd Briarcliff Manor NY 10570 also 439 Main St Mount Kisco NY

SEGAL, BERNARD, rabbi, religious assn. ofcl.; b. Lipno Poland, Nov. 15, 1907; s. Eli Icek and Gittel (Zucker) S.; student Hebrew Theol. Coll., Chgo., 1923-28; B.S., Columbia U., 1931; student Jewish Theol. Sem. Am., 1929-33, M.H.L., Rabbi, 1933, D.H.L., 1950, D.D., 1964; m. Hattie Clark, Nov. 25, 1934; children—Gita Leah Segal Rotenberg, David Mordecai. Came to U.S., 1922, naturalized, 1927. Rabbi, Patchogue (L.I.) Jewish Center, 1933-34, Queens Jewish Center, Queens Village, L.I., 1934-40; exec. v.p. Rabbinical Assembly Am., 1946-49; asst. to pres. Jewish Theol. Sem., 1949-51, exec. v.p., 1951-53; exec. dir. United Synagogue of Am., N.Y.C., 1953-70, exec. v.p., 1970—. Mem. Mayor's Com. on Housing, N.Y.C., 1954-57; scholarship bd. Utility Workers Union Am., 1955-72; bd. judges Jewish Conciliation Bd. Am., 1967—. Served as chaplain U.S. Army, 1940-46. PTO. Mem. Nat. Ramah Commn., Res. Officers Assn., Mil. Chaplains Assn. (nat. v.p. 1947-49), Assn. Jewish Chaplains Army and Navy U.S. (pres. 1946-48). Contbr. articles to profl. publs. Home: 110-21-73d Rd Forest Hills NY 11375 Office: 3080 Broadway New York City NY 10027

SEGAL, DONALD HENRY GILBERT, city ofcl.; b. Phila., Mar. 29, 1928; s. A. Louis and Harriet B. S.; B.S. in Econs., U. Pa., 1950; m. Jane Sporkin, June 24, 1951; children—Susan, John. Vice pres. Sandee Constrn. Co., Brookhaven, Pa., 1951-59; pres. Segal Constrn. Co., Cinnamonson, N.J., 1959-76; pres. Donald Segal Assos., Inc., Bellmaur, N.J., 1976—; commr. Lower Merion Twp., Pa., 1972—, pres. bd. commrs., 1974—. Mem. Mid Atlantic Chpt. Community Assns. Inst. (dir.). Republican. Jewish. Home: 928 Bryn Mawr Ave Narberth PA 19072 Office: City Hall Lower Merion PA 19003

SEGAL, IRVING RANDALL, lawyer; b. Allentown, Pa., Oct. 15, 1914; s. Samuel I. and Rose (Kantor) S.; B.A., U. Pa., 1935; LL.B., 1938; m. Eleanor F. Smolens, Dec. 26, 1943; children—Betsy A., Kathy J., Robert J. Admitted to Pa. bar 1938; instr. polit. sci. U. Pa., 1938-42; law clk. Ct. Common Pleas No. 4, Philadelphia County, 1938-39; asso., then partner firm Schnader, Harrison, Segal & Lewis, Phila., 1939-42. 46—. Permanent mem. Jud. Conf. 3d Circuit U.S. Ct. Appeals; regional rationing atty. OPA, 1942; v.p. Nat. Kidney Disease Found., 1954-59, hon. lifetime del., 1959-64; pres. Nephrosis Found., Phila., 1953-56; bd. mgrs. Woman's Hosp. Phila., 1957-64, v.p., 1962-63; bd. Jewish Edn. Phila., 1948-72; trustee YM and YWHA Phila., 1954-58. Served from pvt. to capt., Judge Adv. Gen. Dept., AUS, 1942-46. Decorated Mil. Commendation medal. Fellow Am. Coll. Trial Lawyers (chmn. or mem. Pa. state com. 1967-68, 70-71, bd. regents 1976—); mem. Am. Bar Found., Am. Law Inst., Am. Judicature Soc., Phila. Socialegal Club, World Peace Through Law, Internat. Law and Social Legislation, Am. Acad. Polit. and Social Sci., Fed. (chmn. transp. 1963), Internat., Am. (com. on correctional facilities and services), Pa., Phila. (chmn. civil judicial procedure com. 1963, law day seminar com. 1966) bar assns., Phi Beta Kappa, Order of Colf., Pi Gamma Mu, Delta Sigma Rho. Jewish religion (dir., v.p. temple). Clubs: Midday, Philadelphia Lawyers, Art Alliance, Peale, Philobiblon, Locust. Home: 250 S 17th St Philadelphia PA 19103 Office: Packard Bldg Philadelphia PA 19102

SEGEL, ARNOLD LESTER, surgeon; b. Cambridge, Mass., May 6, 1911; s. Sydney and Celia (Kramer) S.; A.B., Harvard U., 1932, M.D., 1936; m. Ruth Cohn, Mar. 9, 1948; children—William D., Margaret W., James W., Arthur I., Ann E. Intern, Beth Israel Hosp., Boston, 1936-38, resident, 1938-41, vis. surgeon, 1946-74, cons. surgeon, 1974—; pvt. practice medicine specializing in surgery, Boston, 1946-74; instr. in surgery Harvard U., 1946-77, instr. emeritus, 1977—; surgeon ambulatory care sect. Boston VA Hosp., 1974—. Served with M.C., U.S. Army, 1941-46. Decorated Bronze Star, Navy Bar and Star (U.S.); Croix de Guerre with palm (France); recipient 25 Years Teaching award Harvard U. Med. Sch., 1971; USPHS grantee, 1955-60. Mem. Mass., Norfolk County med. socs., AMA, A.C.S., Boston Surg. Soc. Democrat. Jewish. Club: Masons. Contbr. articles on anticoagulants, intestinal antibiotics, biliary tract surgery to med. jours. Home: 129 Clinton Rd Brookline MA 02146 Office: 150 S Huntington Ave Boston MA 01050

SEGEL, J. NORMAN, garment exec.; b. Toledo, Aug. 1, 1939; s. Sam S. and Dorothy (Gross) S.; B.B.A., Western Res. U., 1961; m. Sheila Benkovitz, Jan. 14, 1961; children—Scott Jonathan, David Seth, Hope Deborah. Accountant, Bobbie Brooks, Cleve., 1961-62; controller Stacy Ames, Long Island City, N.Y., 1962-65, dir. fin., 1965-66, sec.-treas., 1966-70, exec. asst. to pres., 1968-70; v.p. fin. Fairfield-Noble Inc., N.Y.C., 1970-77; treas. Levin & Hecht, Inc., N.Y.C., 1977—. Mem. alumni admission bd. Case Western Res. U. Bd. dirs. Hewlett-East Rockaway Jewish Center, 1972—. Mem. Adminstrn. Mgmt. Soc., Am. Arbitration Assn., Am. Apparel Mfrs. Assn., Am. Assn. Corporate Controllers, Delta Sigma Pi, Sigma Alpha Mu, Alpha Phi Gamma. Home: 3447 5th St Oceanside NY 11572 Office: 350 Fifth Ave New York City NY 10001

SEGGERMAN, ANNE CRELLIN, bio-med. research adminstr.; b. Los Angeles, May 13, 1931; d. Curtin Vergil and Yvonne Madeleine (LaGrave) Crellin; student Sch. of Decorative Arts, Paris, France, 1949-50; student of piano with Albert Levesque, 1948-50, l'Ecole du Louvre, Paris, 1949-50; student Albertus Magnus Coll., Conn., 1949-51; m. Harry G.A. Seggerman, Apr. 14, 1951; children—Patricia, Henry, Marianne, Yvonne, Suzanne, John. Tchr. French, Beverly Hills, Calif., 1958-60; ofcl. translator for Los Angeles World Affairs Council, 1958-60; founder, pres. Fairfield County chpt. Huxley Inst. for Bio-Social Research, Westport, Conn., 1972—, trustee, 1971—; founder, pres. Fourth World Found. for Interfaith Media Action, 1977. Mem. Westport com. Am. Shakespeare Festival, Stratford, Conn., 1972; mem. Fairfield County Organic Gardeners; founding mem. West Side Sch. for Gifted Children, Beverly Hills, 1958-60; precinct chpt. Republican Com., West Los Angeles, 1960. Mem. Nat. Health Fedn., Am. Soc. for Psychical Research, Am. Fedn. of Homemakers, New Eng. Inst., Natural Food Assn. Roman Catholic. Clubs: Fairfield County Hunt, York. Home: 5060 Congress St Fairfield CT 06430 Office: The Huxley Institute Greens Farms CT 06436

SEGGEV, MEIR, radiologist; b. Bulgaria, Jan. 23, 1939; s. Bouco and Helen Salomon; came to U.S., 1969, naturalized, 1976; M.D., Hebrew U. and Hadassah Med. Sch., 1966. Intern, George Washington U.-D.C. Gen. Hosp., 1969-70; resident in radiology Beth Israel Hosp., Boston, 1970-73; attending radiologist Peter Bent Brigham Hosp., Boston, 1973-74; chmn. dept. radiology Hale Hosp., Haverhill, Mass., 1977—; instr. radiology Harvard U., 1973—. Clin. fellow in radiology Harvard U., 1971-73; diplomate Am. Bd. Radiology. Mem. Am. Inst. Ultrasound in Medicine, New Eng. Soc. Ultrasound, New Eng. Roentgen Ray Soc., Am. Coll. Radiology, Radiol. Soc. N.Am., AMA, Mass. Med. Soc., Harvard Med. Alumni Assn. Club: Harvard. Home: 35 Morton St Andover MA 01810 Office: 44 Mill St Haverhill MA 01830

SEHAM, MARTIN CHARLES, lawyer; b. Jersey City, June 30, 1932; s. Samuel and Libbie (Siegel) S.; B.A. summa cum laude, Amherst Coll., 1954; LL.B. magna cum laude, Harvard U., 1957; m. Phoebe Williams, Apr. 18, 1955; children—Amy, Jenny, Lee, Lucy. Admitted to N.Y. State bar, 1957, D.C. bar, 1970, U.S. Supreme Ct. bar, 1963; asso. firm Chadbourne, Parke, Whiteside and Wolff, N.Y.C., 1957-60, firm Poletti, Freidin, Prashker, Feldman & Gartner, N.Y.C., 1960-63; partner firm Kopple & Seham, N.Y.C., 1963-68, Surrey, Karasik, Morse & Seham, N.Y.C., 1963—; counsel Owners Com. on Electric Rates, Inc., Allied Pilots Assn. Staff asst. Senator Hubert H. Humphrey, 1954; legal asst. Sub-Com. Constl. Rights U.S. Senate Judiciary Com., 1955. Mem. Bergen County Democratic County Com., 1965—; chmn. Bergen County Citizens for Hubert H. Humphrey, 1968; bd. dirs. Bergen County Urban League, 1965-74, v.p. housing and devel. corp., 1978; bd. dirs. Citizens Ednl. Council, 1974. Mem. Am. Bar Assn. (chmn. internat. labor law com. 1976—), Assn. Bar City of N.Y., Am. Arbitration Assn., Phi Beta Kappa. Club: Harvard (N.Y.). Author: Federal Wage and Hour Laws, 1962. Home: 19 Creston Ave Tenafly NJ 07670 Office: 485 Madison Ave New York City NY 10022

SEHGAL, ROBERT, govt. ofcl.; b. Pakistan, Dec. 25, 1927; s. Shivdas and Mimi S.; came to U.S., 1948, naturalized, 1956; B.S., Punjab U., 1947; B.S., U. Mich., 1951; M.S., N.Y. U., 1952; m. Ellen Blementhal, June 19, 1955; children—Evan David, Jeffrey Bruce. Project engr. Reaction Motors Inc., Denville, N.J., 1952-55; dep. rocket research div. Aerojet Gen. Corp., Sacramento, 1955-57; sr. research specialist missiles and space systems Calif. Inst. Tech. Jet Propulsion Lab., Pasadena, 1957-65; cons. space systems NASA, Washington, 1965-69; tech. adviser U.S. Army Materiel Command, Washington, 1969-73, tech. adv. U.S. Army Operational Test and Evaluation Agy., Falls Church, Va., 1973—. Fellow Am. Inst. Aeros. and Astronautics (asso., tech. com. on missile systems); mem. Inst. Aero. Scis., Sigma Xi. Contbr. articles to profl. jours. Home: 3505 Leland St Chevy Chase MD 20015 Office: 5600 Columbia Pike Falls Church VA 22041

SEIBERT, DONALD VINCENT, retail chain exec.; b. Hamilton, Ohio, Aug. 17, 1923; s. Carl F. and Minnie L. (Wells) S.; student U. Cin., 1942, D.C.S. (hon.), 1975; LL.D. (hon.), Nyack Coll., 1974; m. Verna S. Stone, Aug. 24, 1945; children—Donna Jeanne, Diane Loree Seibert Goodbar, Robert Donald. Mgmt. trainee J.C. Penney Co., Inc., N.Y.C., 1947-56; store mgr., 1957-58, dist. mgr., 1959-62, corporate exec., 1963-73, chmn., chief exec. officer, 1974—; dir. Continental Can Co., Inc. Trustee Nyack Coll.; mem. East Coast adv. bd. U. Cin. Served with USAAF, 1943-46. Mem. Nat. Retail Mchts. Assn. (exec. com). Mem. Christian and Missionary Alliance. Office: 1301 Ave of Americas New York City NY 10019

SEIBERT, JANET LOOS, nursing adminstr.; b. DuBois, Pa., Aug. 22, 1932; d. Harold and Ida Black (Hammond) Loos; B.S. in Nursing Edn., Chatham Coll., 1955; m. William Armin Seibert, June 21, 1958 (dec.); children—Laura, Kathryn Eileen, Janet Gay. Chief nurse New Eng. Les Chalets Francais, Deer Isle, Maine, summers, 1968, 75; instrn. LPN Sch. Nursing, Indiana, Pa., 1969-70; asst. dir. nursing Lancaster (Pa.) Gen. Hosp., 1970-73; dir. nursing Alfred I. DuPont Inst., Wilmington, Del., 1975—; lectr. U. Del., 1977—. Mem. Assn. for Care Children in Hosps., Am. Hosp. Assn., Am. Mgmt. Assn., Am. Soc. Hosp. Nursing Service Adminstrs. Republican. Episcopalian. Home: 220 Stone Crop Rd Wilmington DE 19810 Office: PO Box 269 Wilmington DE 19899

SEIBOLD, HERMAN RUDOLPH, veterinarian, educator; b. Phila., Aug. 30, 1908; s. Frederick Leonard and Auguste Louise (Meyer) S.; V.M.D., U. Pa., 1931; m. Clara Bond Taylor, Oct. 20, 1934; children—John Rudolph, Robert William, Jean Marie Seibold Brough, Edward Albert, James Richard. Research fellow Henry Phipps Inst., U. Pa., 1931-32; meat insp. Meat Inspection div. Bur. Animal Industry, Dept. Agr., Cleve. and N.Y.C., 1932-34, pathologist trainee Br. Lab., Pathol. Div., Chgo., 1934-39, pathologist, 1939-51, head gen. pathology sect., Washington, 1948-51, research veterinarian Plum Island Animal Disease Lab., 1956-62, chief research veterinarian, 1963-67; prof. dept. pathology and parasitology Auburn U. Veterinary Sch., 1951-56, prof., head dept., 1963; head pathology dept. Delta Regional Primate Research Center, Tulane U., 1967-72; asst. dir. Diagnostic and Investigational Lab., U. Ga., Tifton, 1973-75; pathologist Litton Bionetics, Kensington, Md., 1975—. Mem. faculty discussants Davis Found., 1975—. Chmn. dist. com. Boy Scouts Am., Auburn, Ala., 1954-55. Served with cav. U.S. Army, 1927-28. Recipient Jeanette Blair prize for work in small animal clinic, 1931, Leonard Pearson award for prospective contbn. to vet. sci., 1931. Mem. AVMA (pres. student chpt.), N.Y. Acad. Scis., Am. Assn. Lab. Animal Sci., Am. Assn. Swine Practitioners, Conf. Research Workers in Animal Diseases N.Am., Am. Coll. Veterinary Pathologists (pres.), Internat. Primatol. Soc., Tissue Culture Assn., Am. Soc. Microbiology, Am. Soc. Cell Biology, AAAS, Washington Soc. Pathologists (pres.), Sigma Xi, Phi Zeta. Presbyterian. Bd. reviewers Am. Jour. Veterinary Research, 1965-77; contbr. articles to profl. jours. Home: 504 Castleford St Rockville MD 20851 Office: Litton Bionetics 5516 Nicholson Ln Kensington MD 20795

SEIDEL, CARL WILLIAM, chemist; b. Hempstead, N.Y., Aug. 18, 1938; s. Charles Francis and Wilhelmina Marie (Coppola) S.; B.S., U. Wis., 1959; M.S., U. Notre Dame, 1962; m. Suzanne Winslow Dana, June 29, 1963; children—Lisa Marie, Michael Dana, Rebecca Suzanne, Elaine Marie. Chemist, Nuclear Sci. and Engring. Corp., Pitts., 1962-69; tech. mktg. staff New Eng. Nuclear Corp., 1966-69, product mgr., Boston, 1969-72, asst. div. mgr., North Billerica, Mass., 1973—; com. chmn. Am. Nat. Standards Inst. Pres., Whitehall (Pa.) Young Republicans, 1965. Mem. Am. Chem. Soc., Friends of Sturbridge Village, Mass. Audubon Assn. Republican. Roman Catholic. Clubs: Chelmsford Colonial Minutemen, Russell Mill Swim and Tennis, (v.p. and treas. 1976-77). Editor: The Mössbauer Effect and its Application in Chemistry, 1967; editor: (with Irwin Gruverman) Mössbauer Effect Methodology, vols. 8, 9, 10, 1973, 74, 76; mem. editorial adv. bd. Mössbauer Effect Reference and Data Jour., 1978—. Office: 601 Treble Cove Rd North Billerica MA 01862

SEIDEL, JANET CONRAD, ednl. psychologist; b. Pitts., June 29, 1926; d. Kenneth Russell and Susan Elizabeth Conrad; B.S., Drexel U., 1947; M.Ed., West Chester State Coll., 1969; Ed.D., Temple U., 1972; children—Suzanne E., Cynthia R., Robert C. With Anderson Assos., West Chester, Pa., 1977—; chmn. criminal justice dept. West Chester State Coll., 1976—; pvt. practice psychol. counseling, 1976—. Mem. Am., Pa. psychol. assns., Am. Personnel and Guidance Assn., NEA, Assn. Pa. State Coll. and Univ. Faculties. Home: 326 W Union St West Chester PA 19380

SEIDEN, HENRY, advt. agy. exec.; b. Bklyn., Sept. 6, 1928; s. Jack S. and Shirley (Berkowitz) S.; B.A., Bklyn. Coll., 1949; M.B.A., Coll. City N.Y., 1951-54; m. Helena Ruth Zaldin, Sept. 10, 1949; children—Laurie Ann, Matthew Ian. Trainee, Ben Sackheim Advt. Agy., 1949-51; nat. promotion mgr. N.Y. Post Corp., 1951-53; promotion mgr. Crowell-Collier Pub. Co., Inc., N.Y.C., 1953-54; copy group head Batten, Barton, Durstine & Osborn, Inc., N.Y.C., 1954-60; v.p., creative dir. Keyes, Madden & Jones, N.Y.C., 1960-61; v.p., asso. creative dir. McCann-Marschalk, Inc., N.Y.C., 1961-64; sr. v.p., creative dir. The Marschalk Co., Inc., 1964-65 pres., partner, sr. v.p., creative dir. Hicks & Greist, N.Y.C., 1966-73, exec. v.p., 1974—; guest lectr. Bernard M. Baruch Sch. Bus. and Pub. Adminstrn. Coll. City N.Y., 1962—; guest columnist, also contbg. editor for Madison Avenue mag.; guest columnist N.Y. Times; cons. pub. relations and communications to mayor of New Rochelle, 1959—; communications adviser to pres. City Council, N.Y.C., 1972-73, to police commr. City N.Y., 1973; cons. mktg. dept. Ohio State U.; spl. cons. to postmaster gen. U.S.; guest lectr. New Sch. Social Scis., Barbizon Sch. Vice pres. Little League and Albert Leonard League New Rochelle. Bd. dirs. Police Res. Assn. City N.Y., 1973—; bd. dirs., exec. v.p. N.Y.'s Finest Found., 1975. Recipient award 1960, promotion award Editor and Pub., 1955; Am. TV Commls. Festival award, 1963, 69; Four Freedoms Found. award, 1959; Printers Ink award, 1960; awards Advt. Club of N.Y., 1964, 1965; Effie awards (2) Am. Marketing Assn., 1969; Man of Yr. award Graphic Arts lodge B'nai B'rith, N.Y., 1971. Mem. A.I.M. (asso.), Advt. Writers Assn. N.Y. (gold key award for best newspaper advt. of yr. 1962, also for best trade advertisement of yr. 1964; dir., awards chmn. 1965-66), Nat. Acad. TV Arts and Scis., Alpha Phi Omega. Clubs: Copy (awards com.); Advertising N.Y. (exec. judge Andy awards). Author: Advertising Pure and Simple, 1976. Home: 12 Winchcombe Way Scarsdale NY 10583 Office: 522 Fifth Ave New York City NY 10036

SEIDEN, MANFRED, C.P.A.; b. Bochum, Ger., Dec. 6, 1932; s. Julius and Klare (Fruchter) S.; (parents Am. citizens); A.B., Brown U., 1954; M.B.A., Dartmouth, 1956; m. Beverly Ruth Broomfield, June 17, 1956; children—Jeffrey Steven, Mark Lawrence. C.P.A., Arthur Andersen & Co., N.Y.C., Boston and Hamburg, Ger., 1956-68, audit mgr., Boston, 1969; audit partner Laventhol & Horwath, Providence, R.I., 1969-71, partner in charge, 1972, N.Y.C., 1973—, mem. nat. council, 1974—. Mem. corp. Miriam Hosp. Served in U.S. Army, 1956-59. C.P.A., Mass., R.I., La., N.C., Va., Mich. Mem. Am. Inst. C.P.A.'s, Mass., R.I., N.Y. State socs. C.P.A.'s, Am. Hosp. Assn., Hosp. Fin. Mgmt. Assn., Westchester County Assn., Am. Accounting Assn. Jewish. Club: Mason (Ger.). Home: 7 Hilltop Rd Larchmont NY 10538 Office: 919 Third Ave New York NY 10022

SEIDENSTEIN, JEAN TRAGER, interior designer; b. Cin., July 21, 1941; d. Newton Junior and Louise (Goldsmith) Trager; student U. Miami (Ohio), 1959-60, U. Cin., 1960-63, Internat. Inst. Interior Design, 1974-76; m. Louis W. Seidenstein, Mar. 10, 1962; children—Ellen Louise, Richard Neal, Steven Alva. Free lance interior designer, Rockville, Md., 1973—; asso. Potomac Designs, Rockville and Bethesda, 1973—. Bd. dirs. Layhill Rd. Civic Assn., 1965-66, Saddlebrooke Elementary Sch. PTA, 1966-69, Citizens Com. for Reading, 1972-74; active Democratic presdl. campaigns, 1964-72. Mem. Nat. Urban League, Nat. League Women Voters, NOW. Office: 11300 Rockville Pike Rockville MD 20852

SEIDL, JEAN ELAINE (MRS. RICHARD H. HAMILTON), physician; b. N.Y.C., Sept. 26, 1927; d. Frank Norbert and Jennie (Vavra) Seidl; B.A., Barnard Coll., 1946; M.D., N.Y. U., 1950; m. Richard H. Hamilton, Oct. 31, 1957; children—Elizabeth, Minard, Gordon. Intern Bellevue Hosp., N.Y.C., 1952-54, resident internal medicine, 1954-57; fellow in endocrinology N.Y. U. Coll. Medicine, 1957-58; practice medicine specializing in internal medicine, N.Y.C., 1958—; asst. univ. physician N.Y. U. Student Health Service, Washington Square, N.Y., 1960-72; asst. prof. clin. medicine N.Y. U. Hosp. and Coll. Medicine, N.Y.C., 1958—. Diplomate Am. Bd. Internal Medicine. Mem. A.M.A., N.Y. State, New York County med. socs. Presbyn. Home: 63 E 66th St New York City NY 10021 Office: 120 E 34th St New York City NY 10016

SEIDMAN, ARTHUR H., elec. engr.; b. N.Y.C., Jan. 7, 1923; s. Jack and Frances (Sieser) S.; B.E.E., Coll. City N.Y., 1951; M.A. in Physics, Hofstra U., 1958; m. Lenore Cohn, Jan. 30, 1948; children—Benjamin, Rebecca. Engr., Electro-Marine Corp., 1951-54; sr. engr. Sperry Gyroscope Co., 1954-59; mem. faculty, dept. elec. engring. Coll. City N.Y., 1959-63; mem. faculty Sch. Engring., Pratt Inst., Bklyn., 1963—, prof. elec. engring., 1971—, acting dean, 1975-78; cons. electronics. NSF grantee, 1964, 65, 72, 73. Mem. IEEE (sr.), Am. Soc. Engring. Edn., AAAS, Tau Beta Pi, Eta Kappa Nu, Sigma Pi Sigma. Author: (with C. Ghaznavi) Electronic Circuit Analysis, 1972; (with J. Waintraub) Electronics, Devices, Discrete and Integrated Circuits, 1977; (with M. Kaufman) Handbook for Electronic Technicians and Engineers, 1976. Office: Sch of Engring Pratt Inst Brooklyn NY 11205

SEIDNER, GILBERT, oral surgeon; b. Bklyn., Feb. 9, 1941; s. Sidney and Ruth (Mazur) S.; B.A., Adelphi U., 1962; D.D.S., Columbia, 1966; m. Alane Goodman, Feb. 22, 1970; children—Robin, Syndee. Intern, resident oral surgery Mt. Sinai Hosp., N.Y.C., 1966-69; oral surgeon, Oceanside, N.Y., 1969—; mem. staff Mt. Sinai Hosp., South Nassau Communities Hosp., Oceanside, Long Beach (N.Y.) Meml. Hosp., L.I. Jewish Med. Center. Faculty, Mt. Sinai Sch. Medicine, 1969—. Diplomate Am. Bd. Oral Surgery. Mem. Am., N.Y. State socs. oral surgeons, Am. Dental Assn. Home: 1467 Stevenson Rd Hewlett NY 11557 Office: 2940 Lincoln Ave Oceanside NY 11572

SEIDNER, STANLEY SAMUEL, educator; b. N.Y.C., June 26, 1945; s. Jack W. and Ann Seidner; B.A., Bklyn. Coll., 1968; M.A., St. Johns U., 1970, Ph.D. with highest honors, 1975; 6th year degree City U. N.Y., 1976; postgrad. Columbia U., 1978; m. Elise Margaret Gordon, Sept. 1, 1968. Tchr., adminstr. N.Y.C. Bd. Edn., 1968-75; adj. prof. bilingual edn. and ethnic studies Glassboro State Coll., N.J., 1977—; sr. research asso. Inst. for Urban and Minority Edn., Tchrs. Coll., Columbia U., 1976—. Dir. 1st Nat. Ethnic Heritage Studies Conf. Mem. Nat. Doctoral Assn. (trustee), Polish Inst. Arts and Scis., Czechoslovak Soc. Arts and Scis., Am. Hist. Assn., Am. Acad. Polit. and Social Sci., Doctoral Assn. N.Y. Educators, Phi Delta Kappa. Contbr. articles to profl. jours.; designer 1st bilingual programs for Soviet Jews. Home: 1368 E 89th St Brooklyn NY 11236 Office: Tchrs Coll Columbia U Box 11 New York City NY 10027

SEIFERT, RALPH HAMMOND, ins. co. exec.; b. Balt., Mar. 27, 1928; s. Ralph Edwin and Ferole (Hammond) S.; B.A., Brown U., 1950; m. Cynthia Ruder, June 14, 1950 (div. 1978); children—Mitchel Grant, Susan Leslie, Arthur Bradford, Melissa Louise. Salesman, Liberty Mut. Ins. Co., Phila., 1950-51, S.B. Goodard & Son Co., Woburn, Mass., 1951-54; sales mgr. W.S. Attridge Co., Boston, 1954-57; partner Herbert E. King Agy., Mansfield, Mass., 1957-70; pres. New Eng. Security Ins. Agy., Inc., Mansfield, 1970—, Fin. Security Corp., Mansfield, 1970—; trustee Attleboro Savs. Bank (Mass.). Chmn. Mansfield Indsl. Devel. Commn., 1970—; moderator Town of Mansfield, 1970-73; mem. Downtown Devel. Com., 1975—; chmn. bldg. com. Orthodox Congregational Ch., Mansfield, 1968-70; trustee Citizens' Scholarship Found. Am., 1960—, pres. Mass. chpt., 1959-66, Mansfield chpt., 1963-64. Served to lt. comdr. USNR, 1950-70. Mem. Ind. Ins. Agts. Mass., Ind. Mut. Agts. New Eng. (past pres.), Mansfield Assn. Ins. Agts (past pres.), Bristol Norfolk Ind. Ins. Agts. (past pres.), Rumford Hist. Assn. (pres. 1966-69, treas. 1969—), Mansfield Jaycees (pres. 1960-61). Clubs: Rotary (pres. 1962-63), Masons, Shriners. Contbr. articles to trade jours. Home: Old Maple St Mansfield MA 02048 Office: PO Box 260 100 N Main St Mansfield MA 02048

SEIFFER, DAVID A., educator; b. N.Y.C., Sept. 8, 1943; s. Joseph and Rose (Meyer) S.; A.B., Hunter Coll., N.Y.C., 1965; M.A. (Sam Shubert Playwriting fellow), N.Y. U., 1970; postgrad. Tufts U., U. Mass.; m. Susan Maas, Nov. 25, 1965; children—Jonathan Adam, Todd Alexander. Programmer, ABC, 1965; publicity dir. Corning (N.Y.) Summer Theatre, 1966, 67, 72, Cape Cod Melody Tent, 1973; tchr. N.Y.C. Pub. Schs., 1966-70; mem. faculty Worcester (Mass.) State Coll., 1970—, asst. prof. theatre and media, 1978—, founder, producing dir. summer theatre, 1977—. co-founder/co-dir. A.M. Performing Artists Mgmt., Worcester, 1977—; adjudicator Am. Coll. Theatre Festival, 1975, 76. NDEA fellow, 1971-72; recipient Four Winds Press Playwriting award, 1969, PerSe Playwriting award, 1972. Mem. Am. Theatre Assn., New Eng. Theatre Conf. (publicity chmn. 1973-74), Dramatists Guild, Alpha Psi Omega. Author: (plays) The Compromise, 1965, Dramatika, 1965, If I Ruled the World, 1971; (handbook) On Stage, 1972. Office: 486 Chandler St Worcester MA 01602

SEIGLE, NATALIE R., educator; b. Providence, Apr. 4, 1920; d. Samuel and Gertrude J. (Woolf) Rosen; student Brown U., 1937-38; B.S. in Bus. Adminstrn., Simmons Coll., 1941; certificate in library sci. U. R.I., 1963, M.A. in English, 1968; m. Saul Seigle, Dec. 27, 1942; children—David, Richard, Betty D. Elias. English instr. U. R.I., Providence, 1968-69; spl. lectr. English, Providence Coll., 1969-70, instr. bus. communications, 1970—; career cons. Simmons Coll., 1974—. Pres. Ladies Assn. Jewish Home for Aged R.I., 1958-60; mem. Temple Emanuel Providence, Hadassah Med. Orgn., Brandeis U. Nat. Women's, Com. Mem. Am. Bus. Communications Assn., Am. Collegiate Retailing Assn., Speech Communications Assn., AAUW (2d v.p. R.I. div., membership chmn. 1976—), Nat. Council Adminstrv. Women in Edn. Jewish. Club: Ledgemont Country. Contbr. articles in field to profl. jours. Home: 21 Bedford Rd Pawtucket RI 02860 Office: Providence College Eaton St and River Ave Providence RI 02918

SEIGWORTH, GILBERT RONALD, obstetrician and gynecologist; b. Warren, Pa., May 1, 1932; s. Gilbert Herr and Mabel Loretta (Walters) S.; B.S., Pa. State U., 1954; M.D., U. Pa., 1958; m. Ora Lillian Dieffenderfer, Aug. 26, 1956; children—David Gilbert, Jeffrey Warren. Intern, Robert Packer Hosp., Sayre, Pa., 1958-59; asst. resident in obstetrics and gynecology Hosp. Women Md., Balt., 1963-64; fellow, asst. resident dept. obstetrics and gynecology Johns Hopkins Hosp., Balt., 1964-65; asst. resident Greater Balt. Med. Center, 1965-66, resident, 1966-67; practice medicine, specializing in obstetrics and gynecology, Endicott and Binghamton, N.Y., 1967—; v.p. Obstetric and Gynecologic Assos. of the So. Tier, 1976—; chmn. dept. obstetrics and gynecology Ideal Hosp. Endicott, 1973-77, pres. med. staff, 1974-76; asst. chmn. dept. obstetrics and gynecology Wilson Meml. Hosp., 1976—, exec. com., 1976-78; clin. instr. Upstate Med. Center Clin. Campus at State U. N.Y., Binghamton. Adminstrv. bd. Vestal United Meth. Ch., Vestal, N.Y., 1972-74, chmn. adult and family ministry, 1972-74; panelist WNBF-TV, Binghamton, 1976; med. adv. bd. Broome County Com. Planned Parenthood, 1968—. Served with USAF, 1956-63. Diplomate Am. Bd. Obstetrics and Gynecology. Mem. Am. Coll. Obstetricians and Gynecologists, A.C.S., N.Y., Broome County med. socs., John E. Savage Obstetrical Soc., Allan Barnes Obstetrical and Gynecol. Soc., Tioga County Hist. Soc., Internat. Corr. Soc. Obstetricians and Gynecologists. Republican. Club: Vestal Central High Sch. Athletic. Contbr. articles in field to profl. jours. Home: 405 Clarkson Dr Vestal NY 13850 Office: 24 Madison Ave Endicott NY 13760

SEILER, JOHN PHILIP, govt. ofcl.; b. Pitts., Mar. 3, 1949; s. Milton Ray and Edith Dee (Wardrip) S.; student, Pa. State U., 1967-69, 71; m. Chris Harbodin, Apr. 28, 1973; children—Danielle Joy, Bonnie Clair. With U.S. Bur. Mines, 1971-73, U.S. Dept. Interior, Pitts., 1973—. Registered profl. engr. Mem. Nat. Soc. Profl. Engrs., Inst. Noise Control Engring., Accoustical Soc. Am., Pa. Soc. Profl. Engrs. Democrat. Home: 4634 Interboro Ave Pittsubrgh PA 15207 Office: U S Dept of Interior 4800 Forbes Ave Pittsburgh PA 15213

SEILER, KARL, III, economist; b. Phila., Aug. 21, 1921; s. Karl and Marguerite Barbara (Auer) S.; B.S., U. Pa., 1948, postgrad., 1960-62; M.B.A., Temple U., 1967; m. Mary Louise Ashcraft, Oct. 2, 1948; 1 dau., Mary Beth. Mgr. ops. research Lockheed Corp., Plainfield, N.J., 1967-68; bus. systems cons. Bell Telphone Labs., Piscataway, N.J., 1969-70; chief research and methodology Office of Comptroller of the Army, Washington, 1971-76; mgr. ops. research FAA, Washington, 1976—; adj. prof. Temple U. Grad. Sch. Bus., 1969-70. Served with USN, 1943-46. Mem. Econometric Soc., Ops. Research Soc. Presbyterian. Club: Tuckahoe Athletic. Home: 1229 Old Stable Rd McLean VA 22102 Office: 800 Independence Ave SW Washington DC 20591

SEILER, KATHARINE LOUISE, nurse; b. Balt., Aug. 21, 1926; d. Henry A. and Myrle L.M. (Wack) Seiler; diploma Hosp. for Women of Md., 1949; B.S., Johns Hopkins U., 1969, M.S., 1975. Nurse, Woman's Hosp., Balt., 1949-64, Union Meml. Hosp., Balt., 1964-66; dir. nursing, asst. adminstr. Balt. County Gen. Hosp., 1966-73; nursing and continuing edn. cons., 1973-76, part-time, 1976—; asst. adminstr. nursing service Washington County Hosp., Hagerstown, Md., 1976—; tchr. in continuing edn. at nursing homes and community colls. Registered nurse, Md. Mem. Am., Md. nurses assns., Am. Soc. for Health Manpower Edn. and Tng. (pres. Md. chpt.), Am. Soc. for Nursing Service Adminstrs., Phi Delta Gamma. Republican. Lutheran. Club: Johns Hopkins. Home and office: 1837 Meadowood Dr Hagerstown MD 21740

SEILHEIMER, CHARLES HENRY, JR., real estate exec.; b. Buffalo, Jan. 4, 1942; s. Charles Henry and Erma Claire (Kreinheder) S.; B.A., Middlebury Coll., 1963; LL.B., J.D., George Washington Law Sch., 1966; m. Mary Louise Morton, Sept. 24, 1966; children—Anne Randolph, Charles Henry. With Berger & Co., 1967-69; v.p., dir. Potomac Equities Corp., Washington, 1969-74; v.p. Previews Inc., Greenwich, Conn., 1974-76; pres., dir. Sotheby Parke Bernet Internat. Realty Corp., N.Y.C., 1976—. Chmn., Fauquier County Parks and Recreation Bd., 1973-76; bd. dirs. Va. Arthritis Found., 1974—, Mid-Fauquier Assn., 1971—. Republican. Episcopalian. Clubs: Met. (Washington); City Tavern (Georgetown, D.C.); Fauquier Springs Country, Fauquier, Chestnut Forks Tennis (Warrenton, Va.); Farmington Country (Charlottesville, Va.). Home: Leeton Forest Warrenton VA 22186 Office: 980 Madison Ave New York NY 10021

SEINIGER, DAVID HALLAMORE, SR., soap co. exec.; b. Los Angeles, June 9, 1929; s. Charles William and Pretoria (Hallamore) S.; student Trinity Coll., 1947-49; B.A., Columbia U., 1951; m. Sandy W. Seiniger, Oct. 31, 1963; children—Kimberley, Pretoria, David Hallamone. Staff, McCann-Erickson Co., N.Y.C., 1951-54; pres. Empire Imports Inc., N.Y.C., 1954-71, Marisa Christina Inc., N.Y.C., 1971-76, Marisa Christina, C.B.A. div., Colgate-Palmolive Co., N.Y.C., 1976—; dir. Peconic Industries Co. Served with U.S. Army, 1948-51. Republican. Episcopalian. Clubs: Westhampton Country, Westhampton Yacht Squadron, Westhampton Mallet. Home: 55 Beach Ln Westhampton Beach NY 11978 Office: Marisa Christina CBA div Colgate-Palmolive Co 1410 Broadway New York City NY 10018

SEITELMAN, LEON HAROLD, mathematician; b. N.Y.C., May 27, 1940; s. Solomon and Yetta (Greenberg) S.; B.E.E. (N.Y. State Scholar), Cooper Union, 1960; S.M., U. Chgo., 1963; Ph.D. in Applied Math. (Univ. fellow), Brown U., 1967; m. Brenda Auerbach, Sept. 1, 1962; children—David Jeffrey, Ellen Rachel. Tech. supr. Pratt & Whitney Aircraft Co., East Hartford, Conn., 1967—, asst. project engr., 1967-71, asso. research scientist, 1971-73, sr. applied mathematician, 1973—. Mem. Town of Glastonbury Ad Hoc Com. on Computing, 1977-78. Mem. Am. Math. Soc., Soc. for Indsl. and Applied Math., AAAS, Sigma Xi, Tau Beta Pi. Quiz Kid, 1951. Office: 400 Main St (EB-1K) East Hartford CT 06108

SEITTELMAN, ELIZABETH EDITH, educator; b. N.Y.C., Dec. 22, 1922; s. Isidore A. and Jennie (Schorr) S.; A.B. cum laude, Hunter Coll., N.Y.C., 1943; A.M., Fordham U., 1944, Ph.D. (Hugh Grant grad. asst.), 1952. Tchr., Acad. Mt. St. Ursula, N.Y.C., 1947-49, James Monroe High Sch., N.Y.C., 1949-50, Nathan Hale Sch., N.Y.C., 1950-59; asst. prin., then acting prin. Simon Baruch Jr. High Sch., N.Y.C., 1959-69; adj. lectr. English, Bronx Community Coll., 1961-68; adj. lectr. classical and comparative langs. Bklyn. Coll., 1967-69; prof. classical langs. York Coll., City U. N.Y., 1969—, chmn. dept. tchr. preparation, 1972—; resource cons. Airlie House Conf., 1964; ednl. evaluator for accreditation commn. Nat. Assn. Trade and Tech. Schs. Recipient Earle prize Hunter Coll., 1943, Builder of Brotherhood award Queens chpt. NCCJ, 1973. Mem. Am. Ednl. Research Assn., Medieval Acad. Am., Am. Philol Assn., Classical Assn. Atlantic States, Am. Classical League (chmn. com. study of classical humanities in elementary schs. 1977—), N.Y. Classical Club, Phi Beta Kappa, Kappa Delta Pi. Author numerous articles in field. Editor-in-chief Epitome, 1972—, Dicta, 1973—; audio visual editor Classical World, 1961—. Office: York Coll 150-14 Jamaica Ave Jamaica NY 11451

SEITTELMAN, ESTELLE, educator; b. N.Y.C.; d. Isidore A. and Jennie (Schorr) Seittelman; B.A. cum laude, Hunter Coll., 1947; M.A., Columbia, 1955. Tchr. various pub. schs., 1948-59; asst. and acting prin. Pub. Sch. 59, Bronx, N.Y.C., 1959-68; prin. Alfred E. Smith Sch., 1968—; instr. Bronx Community Coll., 1963-67; sometimes lectr.; adj. asst. prof. instructional internship program Fordham Sch. Edn., 1970, 72, mem. adv. policy and planning com. of apprentice tchr. program, 1973—. Mem. N.Y. State English Council, N.Y.C. Elementary Sch. Prins. Assn. (exec. bd. 1973—), Nat. Assn. Elementary Prins., Council Supervisory Assns., Phi Beta Kappa, Sigma Tau Delta. Office: 163 W 97th St New York City NY 10025

SEITZ, COLLINS JACQUES, judge; b. Wilmington, Del., June 20, 1914; s. George Hilary and Margaret Jane (Collins) S.; A.B., U. Del., 1937, LL.D., 1962; LL.B., U. Va., 1940; LL.D., Widener Coll., 1975; m. Virginia Anne Day; children—Virginia Ann, Collins Jacques, Mark, Stephen. Admitted to Del. bar, 1940; vice chancellor Del., 1946, chancellor, 1951-66; judge U.S. Ct. Appeals, 3d Circuit, 1966—, chief judge, 1971—. Recipient James J. Hoey award, 1954; award NCCJ, 1957; Pro Ecclesia et Pontifice (papal award), 1965. Mem. Am., Del. bar assns. Democrat. Roman Catholic. Club: Wilmington. Home: 410 Stafford Rd Wilmington DE 19803 Office: Federal Bldg 844 King St Wilmington DE 19801

SEITZ, FREDERICK, former univ. pres.; b. San Francisco, July 4, 1911; s. Frederick and Emily Charlotte (Hofman) S.; A.B., Leland Stanford Jr. U., 1932; Ph.D., Princeton, 1934; Doctorate Hon. Causa, U. Ghent, 1957; D.Sc., U. Reading, 1960, Rensselear Poly. Inst., 1961, Marquette U., 1963, Carnegie Inst. Tech., 1963, Case Inst. Tech., 1964, Princeton, 1964, Northwestern U., 1965, U. Del., 1966, Poly. Inst. Bklyn., 1967, U. Mich., 1967, U. Utah, 1968, Brown U., 1968, Duquesne U., 1968, St. Louis U., 1969, Nebr. Wesleyan U., 1970, U. Ill., 1972; LL.D., Lehigh U., 1966, U. Notre Dame, 1962, Mich. State U., 1965, Ill. Inst. Tech., 1968, N.Y. U., 1969; L.H.D., Davis and Elkins Coll., 1970; m. Elizabeth K. Marshall, May 18, 1935. Instr. physics U. Rochester, 1935-36, asst. prof., 1936-37; physicist research labs. Gen. Electric Co., 1937-39; asst. prof. Randal Morgan Lab. Physics, U. Pa., 1939-41, asso. prof., 1941-42; prof. physics, head dept. Carnegie Inst. Tech., Pitts., 1942-49; prof. physics U. Ill., 1949-57, head dept., 1957-64, dir. control systems lab., 1951-52, dean Grad. Coll., v.p. research, 1964-65; exec. pres. Nat. Acad. Scis., 1962-69; pres. Rockefeller U., N.Y.C., 1968-78; dir. tng. program Clinton Labs., Oak Ridge, 1946-47; chmn. Naval Research Adv. Com., 1960-62; vice chmn. Def. Sci. Bd., 1961-62, chmn., 1964-68; sci. adviser NATO, 1959-60; dir. Akzona Inc., Tex. Instruments Inc.; affiliated Ogden Corp., 1977—. Trustee Rockefeller Found., 1964-77, Princeton, 1968-72, Lehigh U., 1970—, Research Corp., 1966—, Inst. Internat. Edn., 1971—, Woodrow Wilson Nat. Fellowship Found., 1972—, Internat. Commn. Nutrition, 1973—, John Simon Guggenheim Meml. Found., 1973—. Recipient Franklin medal Franklin Inst. Phila., 1965; Nat. Medal of Sci., 1973. Fellow Am. Phys. Soc. (pres. 1961); mem. Nat. Acad. Scis. (pres. 1962-69), Am. Acad. Arts and Scis. Am. Inst. Mining, Metall. and Petroleum Engrs., Am. Philos. Soc., Am. Inst. Physics (chmn. governing bd. 1954-59), Inst. for Def. Analysis, Belgian Am. Ednl. Found., Finnish Acad. Sci. and Letters (fgn. mem.). Author: Modern Theory of Solids, 1940; The Physics of Metals, 1943; Solid State Physics, 1955. Address: Rockefeller U 66th St and York Ave New York City NY 10021

SEITZER, ROBERT H., govt. ofcl.; b. Hepburnville, Pa., Feb. 21, 1916; s. Grover C. and Ruth Ellen (Shafer) S.; B.S., Lock Haven State Coll., 1941; M.A., Bucknell U., 1951; m. Marjorie Sprankle, June 12, 1942; 1 dau., Rebecca Rae (Mrs. John J. Tafaro). Tchr., Williamsport, Pa., 1937-42, South Williamsport, 1946-51; prin., South Williamsport, 1952-54, Glen Rock, N.J., 1954-58, East Orange, N.J., 1958-59; supt. schs., East Orange, 1959-68; asst. commr. edn. N.J. Dept. Edn., Trenton, 1968-71; regional commr. edn. HEW, N.Y.C., 1971-76; exec. spl. asst. Officer Commr. Edn., Washington, 1976—. Tchr., Paterson (N.J.) State Coll., 1955-58, Newark State Coll., 1959-60; lectr. Columbia, 1965-67; vis. prof. Fordham U., 1976—. Cons. edn. parks, Seattle, Miami, others. Dir. Civil Def., Lycoming County, Pa., 1950-54; mem. West Branch (Pa.) council Boy Scouts of Am., 1948-53, Orange council, 1962-68; mem. exec. com. Essex County (N.J.) Mental Health Assn., 1962-64; mem. curriculum adv. com. Channel 13, N.Y.C., 1968-73. Bd. dirs. nursing sch. East Orange Gen. Hosp. Served with inf. AUS, 1942-46; ETO. Mem. Am. Legion (post comdr. 1953-54), Lycoming County Tchrs. Assn. (pres. 1948-49), N.J. Edn. Assn., Am., N.J. assns. sch. adminstrs., N.J. Schoolmasters Assn., N.Y. Acad. Edn. Clubs: 744 (Newark); Merchants (N.Y.C.). Home: 21 Boulevard Glen Rock NJ 07452

SEITZMAN, LAWRENCE ALAN, obstetrician, gynecologist; b. Paterson, N.J., July 13, 1936; s. Max Robert and Anne L. (Levy) S.; B.A. in Chemistry, Vanderbilt U., 1958; M.D., Chgo. Med. Sch., 1962; children—Michael A., Robin L. Rotating intern Newark Beth Israel Med. Center, 1962-63, resident in obstetrics and gynecology, 1963-66; practice medicine specializing in obstetrics and gynecology, Edison, N.J., 1968—; dir. dept. obstetrics and gynecology J.F.K. Med. Center, Edison, 1978—. Served to capt. M.C., U.S. Army, 1966-68. Diplomate Am. Bd. Obstetrics and Gynecology. Fellow Am. Coll. Obstetrics and Gynecology; mem. Am. Physicians Fellowship, AMA, N.J., Union County med. socs., Am. Soc. Gynecol. Laparoscopists.

SEIXAS, FRANK ARCHIBALD, physician; b. N.Y.C., Oct. 5, 1919; s. Archibald Sousa and Ethel Miriam (Isaacs) S.; B.A., Cornell U., 1939; M.A., Columbia U., 1940, M.D., 1951; postgrad. Rutgers U., 1966, A.C.P., 1970; m. Judith Sartorius, Sept. 29, 1946; children—Peter, Abigail Seixas Horowitz), Noah. Intern, Montefiore Hosp., Bronx, N.Y., 1951-52; resident Roosevelt Hosp., N.Y.C., 1952-54; fellow in psychiatry Mt. Sinai Hosp., 1954-55; practice medicine specializing in internal medicine, N.Y.C., 1955—; mem. staff N.Y. Cardiac Center, Yonkers, 1956-65, Roosevelt and N.Y. hosps., 1955—; clin. asst. prof. medicine Cornell U. Med. Coll., 1966-75; med. dir. Nat. Council on Alcoholism, 1968-78; adminstr. Support Program for Alcoholism Research-NCA; med. dir. ACCEPT, 1965-70; rep. to UN and Pan-Am. Health Orgn. for ICAA, 1966—. Chmn. bd. Shipping Digest; bd. dirs. N.Y. Assn. for New Ams., Lower East Side Service Center, Westchester Council on Alcoholism; mem. adv. council on alcoholism Dept. Mental Health and Mental Retardation Services of N.Y.C. Served to lt. comdr. USNR, 1940-45. Diplomate Am. Bd. Internal Medicine. Fellow A.C.P., Hastings Inst.; mem. Pan Am. Med. Assn. (v.p. alcoholism div. Western Hemisphere), S.A.R. Club: Princeton U., Cornell U. Med. Faculty. Editor-in-chief Physicians Alcohol Newsletter of AMA, 1965—; editor Annals of N.Y. Acad. Scis., Vols. 178, 197, 215, 233, 252, 1968—, Alcoholism Clin. and Exptl. Research, 1977—, Currents in Alcoholism, Vols. 1-4, 1977-78. Home: 2 Summit Dr Hastings-on-Hudson NY 10706

SEKERAK, RICHARD JOHN, otolaryngologist; b. Bridgeport, Conn., May 30, 1909; s. Joseph R. and Frances A. (Ledvak) S.; grad. Villanova U., 1931; M.D., U. Md., 1934; m. Eileen M. Lavery, Feb. 7, 1942; children—Eileen, Judith, Dianne, Karen. Richard. Intern, Mercy Hosp., Balt., 1934-35; resident in otolaryngology Bklyn. Eye and Ear Hosp., 1935-37; practice medicine specializing in otolaryngology, Bridgeport, Conn., 1950—; attending otolaryngologist St. Vincent's Hosp., Bridgeport, 1950-74, cons.,

1974—, pres. staff, 1955-57; asst. clin. prof. Yale Sch. Medicine, 1951-59. Diplomate Am. Bd. Ophthalmology and Otolaryngology. Fellow Am. Acad. Otolaryngology; mem. Bridgeport, Conn., Fairfield County med. socs., AMA. Club: Mill River Country. Home: 26 Waverly Pl Bridgeport CT 06608 Office: 1400 E Main St Bridgeport CT 06610

SELDEN, ELLEN JACOBI, artist; b. Cin., Mar. 30, 1921; d. Lester E. and Helen (Rothschild) Jacobi; A.B., Wilson Coll., 1943; m. Walter Selden, Aug. 12, 1944 (div. 1949); children—Peter W. (dec.), William Lester. One-man show Crespi Gallery, 1963, Berkshire Playhouse, Stockbridge, 1949, Compass Gallery, Nantucket, Mass., 1969, Pocker & Son, 1970, Main St. Gallery, Nantucket, 1971, 72, Little Gallery, Nantucket, 1975, 79; one-man sculpture show Roko, 1967; exhibited in group shows Kenneth Taylor Gallery, Nantucket, 1950, 68—, Contemporary Arts Gallery, N.Y.C., 1949, 54, 61, 62, Art U.S.A., 1958, Positano Art Workshop, Italy, Ahda Ardst Gallery, N.Y.C., 1960, Allied Artists Am., 1959, Nat. Assn. Women Artists, 1960—, Bertuch Gallery, N.Y.C., 1962, Roko Gallery, 1966, Lobster Pot Gallery, 1968, Munson Gallery, Nantucket, Compass Gallery, Allied Artists, Audubon Artists, Winetraub Gallery, Emil Walters, Lever House, Pisces Gallery, Nantucket, Bannon Gallery; represented in permanent collections Galleria Schneider, Rome, Italy, Butler Art Inst., Wilson Coll., Dartmouth, Venice Artists Workshop; also pvt. collections; pvt. tchr. art, 1958—; founder Nantucket Artists Workshops, 1974. Vol. occupational therapy art tchr. Montefiore Hosp., 1959-62; vol. Mt. Sinai Hosp., 1950-55; ambulance driver, ARC, 1942-44; chmn. art com. Montefiore Hosp., 1962—; mem. com. for Positano Art Workshop. Recipient prize Nat. Assn. Women Artists, 1970, Amelia Peabody award, 1973. Mem. Nantucket Artists Assn. (bd. dirs. 1972-77). Home: 12 Milk St Nantucket MA 02554

SELDIN, S(TEWARD) DANIEL, oral surgeon; b. N.Y.C., July 15, 1909; s. Max Rubin and Bertha Elka (Arsch) S.; student N.Y. U., 1927-29, State U. Iowa Coll. Dentistry, 1929-31; D.D.S., U. Ill., 1933; m. Sybil H. Rosenman, June 30, 1946; children—Barbara (Mrs. Edward H. Bray, Jr.), Margaret J. Intern, Kings County Hosp., Bklyn., 1933-34, resident in oral surgery, 1934-35; practice dentistry specializing in oral surgery, N.Y.C., 1935—; cons. oral surgeon, trustee Community Hosp., Peekskill, N.Y.; cons. oral surgeon Harlem Hosp., N.Y.C.; cons. Med. Arts Center, Norwalk Gen., St. Francis hosps., N.Y. Infirmary; instr. anesthesia and oral surgery 1st Dist. Dental Soc., 1937-49. Vice pres. Putnam Valley Sch. Bd., 1962-65, Putnam County Sch. Bds., 1964, Putnam County Bd. Health, 1967—; v.p. Putnam Valley Library, 1965-75, hon. trustee, 1975—. Served to maj. AUS, 1942-46. Diplomate Am. Bd. Oral Surgery. Fellow Internat. Congress Anesthetists, Internat. Coll. Dentistry, AAAS, Internat. Assn. Oral Surgeons; mem. ADA, Am. Assn. Oral and Maxillofacial Surgery (life), 1st Dist., Cuban (hon.) dental socs., Am., N.Y. State (past pres.) socs. oral surgeons, Am. Soc. Dental Medicine, Am. Soc. Dental Anesthesiology, Jewish War Vets., 2d Aux. Surg. Group, Omicron Kappa Upsilon (hon.), Alpha Omega (past pres. N.Y. alumni). Democrat. Jewish (v.p. temple). Club: Illinois Dental Alumni of N.Y. (past pres.). Contbr. numerous articles to dental jours. Home and office: Box 169 Mill St Putnam Valley NY 10579

SELDNER, ABRAHAM, chemist; b. Weehawken, N.J., Sept. 22, 1920; s. Henry and Rose (Finkelstein) S.; B.A., Columbia, 1940, postgrad., 1940; m. Esther Wachtel, Feb. 14, 1942; children—David, Michael, Joseph. With various aroma mfg. cos., 1940-65; tech. dir. Lanvin-Charles of the Ritz, Holmdel, N.J., 1965-69; mgr. spltys. products devel. Personal Products Co. div. Johnson & Johnson, Milltown, N.J., 1969-74; v.p. research and devel. Vanda Beauty Counselor div. Dart Industries, St. Louis, 1974-77; dir. tech. services Amerchol Corp. div. CPC Internat., Edison, N.J., 1977—; guest lectr. on fragrance U. So. Calif. Sch. Pharmacy; cons. Calif. State Essential Oil Project. Secondary sch. rep. Columbia, 1960-70; county chmn. Ams. for Democratic Action, Essex County, N.J., 1954-56; campaign mgr. Princeton Dem. Party, 1963-66. Mem. Am. Chem. Soc., Soc. Cosmetic Chemists, Am. Soc. Perfumers, Am. Inst. Chemists, Inst. Food Technologists. Democrat. Jewish. Author articles on essential oils, odor problems, cosmetics, new aromatic chems. Patentee abatement of fluid and vapor stream pollution. Home: 188 Grover Ave Princeton NJ 08540 Office: Talmadge Rd Edison NJ 08817

SELIG, J. DANIEL, museum exec.; b. Phila., Apr. 12, 1938; s. Milton and Mildred S.; B.A. with hons., U. Pa., 1959; A.M. (Faculty of Arts and Scis. fellow 1959, Nat. Trust fellow 1960), Harvard U., 1960; M.A. (Univ. fellow), Yale U., 1962. Archtl. historian Boston Redevel. Authority, 1963-65; lectr. Boston Coll., 1966-69; asst. prof. dept. architecture U. Notre Dame, 1969-71; vis. lectr. U. Ill., Chgo. Circle, 1971-72; curator, asst. to dir. Wichita (Kans.) Art Museum, 1972-73; dir. Reading (Pa.) Public Mus., 1973-76, Trenton City Mus., 1977—; mem. fine arts commn. Albright Coll., 1974-76. Nat. Endowment for Arts grantee, 1973; N.J. Hist. Commn. grantee, 1978. Mem. Am. Assn. Mus. (certificates in mus. adminstrn.), N.E. Museum's Conf. (chmn. com. small museums 1974-77), Victorian Soc. Am., Charlestown (Mass.) Hist. Soc. (life), Berks (Pa.) Art Alliance (life), Phi Beta Kappa, Alpha Epsilon Delta. Author mans., catalogues on Am. painting, architecture, decorative arts, mus. adminstrn.; contbr. articles, revs. to newspapers, jours., books. Home: 386 Sunset Rd West Reading PA 19611 Office: 10 Capitol St Trenton NJ 08608

SELIGMAN, BERNARD, physician; b. N.Y.C., Aug. 25, 1898; s. Jacob and Esther (Levy) S.; M.D., N.Y. U., 1920; m. Edith Duberstein, June 28, 1928; 1 son, Stephen J. Intern, Jewish Hosp., 1920-23; resident Montefiore Hosp., 1926-28; practice medicine specializing in internal medicine, Bklyn., 1929—; cons. Jewish, Kings County hosps.; mem. faculty L.I. Med. Coll., 1935-39, Downstate Med. Coll., 1948-69; cons. N.Y.C. Dept. Health. Bd. dirs. Prospect Park Jewish Center, Prospect Park Nursing Home; vice chmn. advancement Boy Scouts Am. Served with U.S. Army, World War I. Recipient art awards, N.Y., Am. physicians Chautauqua art assns. Fellow A.C.P., Royal Soc. Health; mem. N.Y. U. Med. Coll. Alumni Soc. (v.p.), Kings County Med. Soc. (adviser diabetic com.; trustee 1974—), Am. Heart Assn., AMA, Am. Pub. Health Assn., Am. Endocrine Soc., N.Y. Acad. Sci., Internat. Coll. Medicine, Am. Physicians Art Assn. (v.p.), Drs. Club Bklyn. (pres.). Contbr. articles to profl. jours. Home: 1818 Newkirk Ave Brooklyn NY 11226

SELIGSON, LINDA WEINER, journalist; b. Pottsville, Pa., Nov. 30, 1946; d. E. Gerald and Mary L. (Stern) Weiner; m. Stephen L. Seligson, Nov. 21, 1971; 1 dau., Lauren Jill. Copywriter York (Pa.) Gazette and Daily, 1968, reporter-photographer, 1968-70, editor biweekly youth supplement, 1970-71; editor family sect. York Daily Record, 1971-76, city editor, 1976—. Bd. dirs. York Council Community Edn., 1969-71, Community Progress Council Com. on Alcoholism, 1970, Humane Action for Pets, 1971-72, Women's Occupational Resource Com., 1974, Planned Parenthood York County; mem. community adv. com. LWV, 1975. Recipient Keystone Press award Pa. Newspaper Pubs. Assn., 1975. Mem. Pa. Women's Press Assn., Pa. Soc. Newspaper Editors, Newspaper Guild (unit treas), Ohev Sholom Sisterhood (dir.), Hadassah, Temple Beth Israel and Sisterhood (dir.). Democrat. Home: 428 Allegheny Dr York PA 17402 Office: 1750 Industrial Hwy York PA 17402

SELL, LEO LEWIS, psychiatrist; b. Yonkers, N.Y., Apr. 8, 1927; s. John and Elizabeth (Wicht) S.; student N.Y.U., 1944; B.S. magna cum laude, Wheaton Coll., 1951; M.D., Temple U., 1955; m. Laura Marie Blasko, Aug. 5, 1950; children—Laura Lee, John Daniel, David Andrew, Rebecca, Deborah. Intern, Albert Einstein Med. Center, Phila., 1955-56; resident Coatesville (Pa.) Hosp., 1956-57; resident in psychiatry. Ancora Psychiat. Hosp., Hammonton, N.J., 1959-62, dir. tng., 1968-74, acting hosp. dir., 1969-70, asst. med. dir., 1961-68; practice gen. medicine, Coatesville, 1957-59; practice medicine, specializing in psychiatry, Haddonfield, N.J., 1964—; staff West Jersey Hosp., Our Lady of Lourdes Hosp.; asst. dir. community mental health services Divs. of Mental Health and Hosps., State of N.J., 1974-75. Served with AUS, 1945-46. Diplomate Am. Bd. Psychiatry and Neurology. Mem. Christian Med. Soc. (past sec.-v.p. psychiat. sect.), AMA, N.J. State, Camden County med. socs., Am. Psychiat. Assn., N.J. Neuropsychiat. Assn., A.C.P., Acad. Medicine N.J., Phila. Psychiat. Soc. Methodist. Home: 118 Pine Valley Dr Medford NJ 08055 Office: 250 Kings Hwy E Haddonfield NJ 08033

SELLNER, GERALD PAUL, civil engr.; b. Trenton, N.J., Oct. 3, 1945; s. Herman Paul and Helen Louise (Yard) S.; B.Civil Engring., Manhattan Coll., 1967; M.Civil Engring., Cornell U., 1968; M.B.A., Rider Coll., Trenton, 1976; m. Marguerite Ann Montana, May 10, 1969; children—Jason Alois, Jeffrey Paul. With N.J. Dept. Transp., Trenton, 1967—, engr. structures, plans and specifications, 1975-77, project engr. structures, 1977—. Bd. dirs. Ewing (N.J.) Jaycees, 1970-71; ticket consignment chmn. N.J. Jaycees Football Classic, 1970. Recipient Spoke award N.J. Jaycees, 1969. Registered profl. engr., N.J. Mem. ASCE, Mensa, U.S. Chess Fedn., Arnold Air Soc., Chi Epsilon. Roman Catholic. Home: 132 Washington Crossing Pennington Rd Titusville NJ 08560 Office: 1035 Parkway Ave Trenton NJ 08625

SELMECZI, JOSEPH GABOR, geol. engr.; b. Banhida, Hungary, Apr. 12, 1930; s. Jozsef and Paula (Szkokan) S.; came to U.S., 1956; Dipl. Eng. summa cum laude, Sopron (Hungary) Tech. U., 1953; m. Ilona Fekete, June 22, 1954; children—Gabor Joseph, Gary Barna. Asst. prof. Tech. U., Sopron, Hungary, 1953; asst. chief geologist Tatabanya Coal Mining Trust, Hungary, 1953-56; laborer Haweg Corp., C.W. Lauman Co., Wilmington, Del., 1957, hydrogeologist, water analyst, Bethpage, N.Y., 1957; chief chem. engr. Radiant Utilities Corp., Bklyn., 1959-60; gen. mgr. Crystal Research Labs., Hartford, Conn., 1960-64; tech. dir. Gen. Ionics Corp., Birdgeville, Pa., 1964-68; lab. supr. Dravo Corp., Pitts., 1968-70, mgr. labs., 1970-71, mgr. process devel., 1971-72, mgr. research, 1972-74, mgr. supporting tech. devel., 1976—; mgr. research and devel. Dravo Lime Co., Pitts., 1975-76, v.p. research, 1976. Served with Hungarian Army, 1953. Mem. Am. Chem. Soc., Am. Inst. Chem. Engrs., Soc. Mining Engrs., Water Pollution Control Fedn., Air Pollution Control Assn., AAAS, Pa. Water Pollution Control Assn., Internat. Zeolite Assn., N.Y. Acad. Scis., Republican. United Presbyterian. Home: 513 Clemson Dr Pittsburgh PA 15243 Office: 3600 Neville Rd Pittsburgh PA 15225

SELMORE, JOSEPH WAYMOND, clin. psychologist; b. St. Augustine, Fla., Nov. 11, 1933; s. Guy and Queen Victoria (Thomas) S.; student Xavier U., 1951-52; B.S., Fla. Meml. Coll., 1955; M.A., Howard U., 1968; postgrad. U. Fla., 1972-75. Psychologist, Receiving Home for Children, Washington, 1966-67; tchr., coach, county adminstr. West Palm Beach (Fla.) Bd. Edn., 1958-68; dean students Edward Waters Coll., 1968-71; counselor Federal City Coll., 1971-72; intern VA Hosp., Gainesville, Fla., 1974-75; dir. Community Coll. St. Augustine, 1975-76; intern Area C, Community Mental Health Center, D.C. Gen. Hosp., Washington, 1977—. NIMH fellow, 1966-68, Woodrow Wilson Nat. Fellowship Found. fellow, 1972-75. Mem. Assn. Black Psychologists, Am. Psychol. Assn., Am. Personnel and Guidance Assn., Assn. for Non-White Concerns in Personnel and Guidance, Am. Fedn. Tchrs., Alpha Phi Alpha. Club: Big Brothers Am. Contbr. articles to profl. jours. Home: 136 Rhode Island Ave NW Washington DC 20001 Office: 1905 E St SE Washington DC 20003

SELTZER, EMILY RUTH, designer; b. Providence, Jan. 6, 1947; d. Arthur M. and Naomi (Jolson) Grueneberg; B.F.A., R.I. Sch. Design, 1968; M.S., Pratt Inst., 1971; postgrad. St. John's U., 1972, N.Y. U., 1975, R.I. Coll., 1977; m. Arthur Jay Seltzer, June 15, 1968; 1 son, Daniel Micah. Free-lance illustrator, painter, Forest Hills, N.Y., 1968-73; founder Cards by Emily, 1976-78; pres., designer Cards by Emily, Ltd., N.Y.C., 1978—; tchr. Summit Sch., Forest Hills, 1969-76; tchr. coordinator life skills pre-vocational program, 1976-78, coordinator guidance and vocat. service, 1978—. Jewish. Home: 10 Holder Pl Forest Hills NY 11375 Office: 27 W 24th St New York City NY 10010

SELTZER, IRVING, communications co. exec.; b. Phila., June 7, 1929; s. Frank M. and Yetta (Applebaum) S.; B.S., Temple U., 1951, M.A. Equivalency in Econs. and Statistics, 1953; m. Joan M. Faber, Oct. 28, 1951; children—Steven, Michael, Alison, Alex. Pres., Modern Communications Corp., Altoona, Pa., 1961—, Manpower, Inc., 1965—; instr. bus. Pa. State U., Altoona, part time. Served to col. USAR, 1951—. Named Jaycee of Year, Altoona, 1964, outstanding state Americanism and govt. affairs chmn. Pa., 1964. Mem. Am. Econ. Assn., Pa. Assn. Radio Common Carriers (v.p.), Pa. Asso. Telephone Answering Services (past pres.), Mid-East Telephone Answering Services (past pres.). Jewish. Clubs: B'nai B'rith (past pres. Altoona), Rotary (past pres. Altoona, dist. gov. 1977—). Office: 1215 16th St Altoona PA 16601

SELTZER, MURRAY HAROLD, surgeon; b. Newark, Apr. 29, 1939; s. Martin and Bess (Perlman) S.; A.B., Franklin Marshall Coll., 1961; M.D., U. Pa., 1965; m. Marilyn Susan Mellitz, June 18, 1961; children—David, Michael, Melissa. Intern in surgery U. Pa. Hosp., Phila., 1965-66, resident in surgery, 1966-71, Am. Cancer Soc. clin. fellow in breast cancer research, Harrison dept. surg. research, 1968-69, asst. instr. surgery Sch. Medicine, 1966-70, instr. surgery, 1970-71; practice medicine, specializing in gen. and vascular surgery, Livingston, N.J., 1973—; asso. attending in surgery, St. Barnabas Med. Center, Livingston; clin. asst. prof. surgery N.J. Coll. Medicine Dentistry. Served to maj. M.C., U.S. Army, 1971-73. Recipient Hon. Lifetime Silver memebrship N.J. Policemans Benevolent Assn., 1975; diplomate Am. Bd. Surgery. Fellow A.C.S.; mem. AMA, Am. Soc. Parenteral Enteral Nutrition (treas.), Med. Soc. N.J., Essex County Med. Soc., N.J. Acad. Medicine, N.J. Gastroent. Soc. Republican. Jewish. Contbr. articles to med. jours.; researcher biochem. aspects breast cancer; patentee self-lubricating surg. glove. Home: 72 Westview Rd Short Hills NJ 07078 Office: 201 S Livingston Ave Livingston NJ 07039

SELTZER, (HERBERT) RICHARD, telecommunications co. exec.; b. Phila., Feb. 7, 1925; s. Henry Louis and Rose (Rolan) S.; student Leeds (Eng.) U., 1945-46; B.S., Pa. State U., 1951, M.S. in Elec. Engring., 1952, M.S. in Bus. Adminstrn., 1958; m. Adeline Marie Wilwers, May 24, 1944; children—Nadine Dorothy, Carole-Anne. Project mgr. RCA, Moorestown and Camden, N.J., 1953-69, corp. staff cons., Cherry Hill, N.J., 1969-73; mgr. transmission systems planning ITT World Communications, Inc., N.Y.C., 1973-76, v.p., dir. plans and programs ITT Domestic Transmissions Systems, Inc., 1976—; guest lectr. LaSalle Coll., Phila., part-time 1956-70, grad. student adviser, 1967-70. Bd. dirs. Rolling Greens (N.J.) Civic Assn., 1958-61, Nat. Rare Blood Assn., 1958—. Served to 1st lt. AUS, 1943-47; ETO. Recipient Cross Keys award LaSalle Coll., 1970, Tech. Excellence award RCA, 1972. Mem. IEEE, Am. Mgmt. Assn., Armed Forces Communications and Electronics Assn., Internat. Radio Consultative Com., L'Alliance Franciase (dir.), Eta Kappa Nu, Phi Eta Sigma. Clubs: Engrs. of Phila., Penn Athletic of Phila. Patentee nuclear radiation level counter and calibrator, airborne surveillance camera, remote LF antenna. Home: 10 Wedgewood Dr Riverton NJ 08077

SELTZER, RICHARD WARREN, b. Washington, June 5, 1923; A.B. in History, U. Md., 1948, Ed.D. in Ednl. Adminstrn., 1957; M.S. in Social Sci., U. Pa., 1951; postgrad. Army War Coll.; married; 2 children. Dean Plymouth (N.H.) State Coll., 1959-63; supt. Bristol (Pa.) Borough Schs., 1963-64, Lower Moreland, Huntingdon Valley, Pa., 1964-74, Columbia (Pa.) Borough Schs., 1974—; post doctoral work in anthropology. Fellow IDEA; mem. Pa., Am. Assns. Sch. Adminstrs., Assn. Supervision and Curriculum Devel., Suburban Sch. Study Council, Am. Council Econ. Edn. (dir.), Columbia C. of C. (chmn. ednl. com. 1975—), Phi Delta Kappa. Club: Rotary (pres. 1978-79). Participant NDEA Inst. early childhood edn. Home: 825 Hallowell Dr Huntingdon Valley PA 19006

SELVERNE, LEE J., publ. co. exec.; b. N.Y.C., July 15, 1932; s. Harry and Nettie (Schwart) S.; B.S., L.I. U., 1958; M.S., N.Y. U., 1960; m. Linda Nancy Himel, May 26, 1972; 1 son, Michael. Jr. statistician L. Sonneborne & Sons, N.Y.C., 1958-59; research dir. bus. publs. Hearst Corp., N.Y.C., 1959-60; mem. exec. staff Publ. Distbg. Co., N.Y.C., 1960-65; chmn. bd., dir. Worldwide Media Service, N.Y.C., 1968—; v.p. circulation, cons. Harvey Publs., Inc.; pres. Worldwide Spanex Corp. Served with U.S. Army, 1950-52. Recipient Small Bus. Mgmt. award L.I. U., 1958. Mem. Internat. Newsstands Circulation Execs. Assn. Club: Alpine (N.J.) Country. Home: 200 E 64th St New York City NY 10021 Office: Worldwide Media Service 386 Park Ave S New York City NY 10016

SELWYN, DONALD, handicapped rehab. researcher; b. N.Y.C., Jan. 31, 1936; s. Gerald Selwyn and Ethel (Waxman) Selwyn Moss; A.A., B.A., Thomas Edison State Coll.; B.S. in Elec. Engring. and Ph.D. (hon.), Dallas State Coll., 1972; m. Delia Nemec, Mar. 11, 1956; children—Laurie, Gerald, Marcia. Service engr. Bendix Aviation, Teterboro, N.J., 1956-59; service mgr. Bogue Electric Mfg. Co., Paterson, N.J., 1959; proposal engr. advanced design group Curtiss-Wright Corp., East Paterson, N.J., 1960-64; ind. bio-engr., rehab. engring. cons., N.Y.C., 1964-67; pres. bd. trustees, exec. tech. dir. Nat. Inst. for Rehab. Engring., Pompton Lakes, N.J., 1967—. Cons., N.Y. State Office Vocat. Rehab., 1964—, Pres.'s Com. on Employment of Handicapped, 1966—, also numerous state rehab. agys., health depts., vol. groups; tchr., lectr. on rehab. Trustee Nat. Inst. for Rehab. Engring. Rehab. Research Center Trust. Recipient Humanitarian award U.S. Ho. of Reps., 1972. Mem. Am. Acad. Consultants, IEEE (sr. mem.; past chmn. engring. mgmt. group N.Y. Met. chpt.), Soc. Tech. Writers and Pubs. (sr.), Nat. Rehab. Assn., N.Y. Acad. Scis., Mensa. Elk, Knight Malta. Contbr. articles on amateur radio, rehab. of severely and totally disabled to profl. and gen. mags. Home: 238 Poplar Ave Pompton Lakes NJ 07442 Office: Nat Inst for Rehab Engring 97 Decker Rd Butler NJ 07405

SEMAAN, KHALIL IBRAHIM HANNA, educator; b. Safita, Syria, Mar. 6, 1920; s. Ibrahim Hanna and Martha Elias (Khoury) S.; came to U.S. 1950, naturalized 1960; B.S.L., Georgetown U., 1954; M.A., Columbia U., 1955, Ph.D., 1959; m. Aline Elofson, May 6, 1960; children—Jan Jeffery, Johan Nicholas, Ingrid Emily Theresa. Asso. in Arabic, Georgetown U., 1951-54; lectr. Semitics, N.Y. U., 1956; lectr. Arabic, Columbia U., 1957; research historian, acting asst. prof. Oriental langs. U. Calif., Los Angeles, 1957-59; bibliographer, reference librarian Library of Congress, 1960-61; research in Sweden, Finland, Norway, Iraq, Jordan, and Syria; dir. Afro-Asian Research Inst., Stockholm, Sweden, 1962-64; vis. scholar Columbia U. Tchrs. Coll., 1964-65; mem. faculty State U. N.Y., Binghamton, 1965—, prof. Arabic, 1970—, dir. Arabic Studies, 1965-1975; dir. Mediterranean studies Royal U. Malta, 1975-76. Served with French and Free French Armies, 1939-45; with Syrian Army, 1945-50. Mem. Am. Oriental Soc., Middle East Study Assn. N.Am., Am. Assn. Tchrs. of Arabic (founding) Arab-Am. U. Grads., Georgetown Arabic Club, State U. N.Y. Binghamton Arabic Circle. Author: Ash-Shafi'i's Risalah, 1962; Ibn Sina's Risalah, 1963; Linguistics in the Middle Ages, 1967; translator: Murder in Baghdad, 1972. Home: 713 Country Club Rd Binghamton NY 13903 Office: Classical/Near Eastern Studies State U NY Binghamton NY 13901

SEMANCHUK, PETER PAUL, transport refrigeration cons.; b. Buffalo, June 8, 1933; s. Roman and Anastasia (Herman) S.; A.A.S., Erie (Pa.) Community Coll., 1953; B.S., Gen. Motors Inst., 1956; M.S., SUNY at Buffalo, 1970; m. Raissa Zolin, Aug. 10, 1963; children—Alexis Ann, Larissa. Chief engr. Bell Aerospace Co., Niagara Falls, N.Y., 1958-72; co-owner Seatre Inc., Buffalo, 1972—; mem. faculty Erie Community Coll., Buffalo, 1961—, prof. mech. engring., 1972—; dir. Seatre Inc., M & S Enterprises. Served with U.S. Army, 1958. Recipient award Erie Community Coll. Alumni Assn., 1977; project Sure-Fire award, 1970; registered profl. engr., N.Y. Mem. Soc. Mfg. Engrs. (sr., dir. chpt. 10 1960—, merit recognition award 1977), Instrument Soc. Am. (sr.), Fluid Power Soc., Confedn. Alumni Assns. SUNY (pres. 1976-77), Phi Delta Kappa. Eastern Orthodox. Office: Erie Community Coll Youngs Rd and Main St Williamsville NY 14221

SEMANOFF, LEON, apparel mfg. co. exec.; b. Allentown, Pa., Aug. 28, 1921; s. Meyer and Sarah (Gorochov) S.; B.S., Pa. State Coll., 1942; postgrad. U. Del., 1942, Muhlenberg Coll., 1946-47; m. Sylvia Milgram, Jan. 30, 1949; children—Ira, Harold, Steven. Pres., Tru-Cut Garment Co., Charlotte, N.C., 1960-63; mgr. Rowan Mfg. Corp., Salisbury, N.C., 1964-66; sr. v.p. Philtex Mfg. Co., Phila., 1966-75; v.p., dir. mfg. Robert Bruce, Inc., 1976—. Served with USAAF, 1942-46. Mem. Knitted Outerwear Mfrs. Assn. Pa. (v.p.), Jewish War Vets., Kappa Delta Pi. Author: Guideposts to Good Supervision, 1967. Address: 332 Sinkler Rd Wyncote PA 19095

SEMERJIAN, MADELLE LYONS HEGELER, art broker; b. Danville, Ill.; d. Edward C. and Madelle (Lyons) Hegeler; student Northwestern U., 1948; B.A., Vassar Coll., 1952; M.A., Sorbonne, Paris, France, 1954; postgrad. Ecole du Louvre, Paris, 1955; m. Luigi A. Grassi, Nov. 29, 1962 (div. Oct. 1969); children—Cornelia Maria, Giovanna Camilla; m. 2d, George G. Semerjian, Feb. 19, 1977. Dir. pub. relations, saleswoman French & Co., N.Y.C., 1956-58, fgn. rep., 1959-60; self-employed art broker, Paris, 1960—; pres. Meadowmere Interiors and Gallery, Southampton, N.Y. Bd. dirs. Stony Brook (N.Y.) Found. Mem. Delta Delta Delta. Republican. Episcopalian. Home: Brigadune Gin Ln Southampton NY 11968 Office: 25 Main St Southampton NY 11968

SEMINARA, ELEANOR FRANCES, librarian; b. Bklyn., Mar. 14, 1931; d. Louis and Vincenzia (DeStafano) Seminara; B.S., U. Montevallo, 1952; M.S., Columbia U., 1957; postgrad. in doctoral program So. Ill. U., 1977. Chemist, Fisher Sci., N.Y.C., 1952-54; chemist Stein, Hall & Co., Long Island City, N.Y., 1954, lit. chemist,

1957; tech. librarian Olin Mathieson Chem. Corp., Niagara Falls, N.Y., 1957, head tech. librarian, to 1960; head librarian Thiokol Chem. Corp., Huntsville, Ala., 1960-61; curriculum librarian Bd. Edn., Niagara Falls, N.Y., 1961-63; dir. Library Learning Center, Niagara County Community Coll., Sanborn, N.Y., 1963—. HEW grantee 1968, 68-69, 71; Delta Kappa Gamma fellow, 1976. Mem. ALA, Nat. Assn. Ednl. Broadcasters, Assn. Ednl. Communications Tech., N.Y. State Ednl. Communications Assn., Western N.Y. Library Resources Council (trustee), Western N.Y. Ednl. Communications Council (pres. higher edn. affiliate 1975-77), Delta Kappa Gamma, Pi Lambda Theta, Phi Delta Kappa. Club: Quota (pres. 1975) (Niagara Falls, N.Y.). Hdme: 5105 Dana Dr Lewiston NY 14092

SEMMEL, BERNARD, educator; b. N.Y.C., July 23, 1928; s. Samuel and Tillie (Beer) S.; B.A., Coll. City N.Y., 1947; M.A., Columbia U., 1951, Ph.D., 1955; postgrad. London Sch. Economics, 1959-60; m. Maxine Loraine Guse, Mar. 19, 1955; 1 son, Stuart Mill. With Nat. Citizens Commn. for Pub. Schs. and Council for Fin. Aid to Edn., N.Y.C., 1951-55; asst. prof. history Park Coll., Parkville, Mo., 1956-60; mem. faculty State U. N.Y., Stony Brook, 1960—, prof. history, 1964—, chmn. dept., 1966-69; vis. prof. Columbia U., 1966-67, asso., seminar in social and polit. thought, 1968—; fellow Lehrman Inst., 1974-76. Rockefeller Found. fellow, 1959-60, Am. Council Learned Socs. fellow, 1964-65, Guggenheim fellow, 1967-68, 74-75. Fellow Royal Hist. Soc.; mem. Am. Hist. Assn., Economic History Soc., Conf. Brit. Studies, U.S. Strategic Inst. Editor, Jour. Brit. Studies, 1969-74. Home: Box 1162 6 Woodbine Ave Stony Brook NY 11790 Office: Dept History State U New York Stony Brook NY 11794

SEMPLE, CECIL SNOWDON, mfg. co. exec.; b. Assam, India, Aug. 12, 1917; s. Fordyce B. and Anne (Munro) S.; brought to U.S., 1927, naturalized, 1948; B.A., Colgate U., 1939. Buyer, div. supt. R. H. Macy & Co., 1939-48; buyer Montgomery Ward, 1948-50; v.p. Nachman Corp., Chgo., 1950-55; gen. mgr. radio receiver dept. sales Gen. Electric Co., Bridgeport, Conn., 1955-60, marketing cons., merchandising, N.Y.C., 1966-67, gen. mgr. audio products dept., 1967-68, dep. div. gen. mgr. housewares div., 1968-69, gen. mgr. housewares div., 1969, v.p., 1969-71, comml. v.p., 1971—; v.p. Rich's, Inc., Atlanta, 1960-62, sr. v.p., 1962-66, also dir.; dir. Electric Mut. Liability Ins. Co., Lynn, Mass., Electric Ins. Co., Lynn; trustee Peoples Savs. Bank, Bridgeport. Mem. adv. com. Emory U. Sch. Bus.; mem. exec. com., gen. chmn. Atlanta United Appeal campaign, 1965. Chmn. bd. Jr. Achievement Greater Atlanta, 1962-66; bd. dirs., Bridgeport Area Found., Bridgeport Hosp., Ga. Soc. Crippled Children and Adults; mem. exec. com. Ga. State Coll. Found., 1963-66; trustee Colgate U. Served to maj. USAAF, 1942-46. Mem. Assn. Home Appliance Mfrs. (dir.), Soc. Advancement Mgmt. (pres. Ga. chpt.), Am. Mgmt. Assn., Atlanta Retail Mchts., Assn. (pres. 1964-66), U.S. C. of C. (mfr.-domestic distbn. com.), Atlanta C. of C. (dir.), Bridgeport C. of C., Better Bus. Bur. (v.p. 1964-66), Atlanta Conv. Bur. (dir.), St. Andrews Soc. State N.Y. (chmn. bd. mgrs.), Lenox Square Mchts. Assn. (pres.), Colgate U. Alumni Assn. (pres.), Delta Kappa Epsilon. Clubs: Brooklawn Country (Fairfield, Conn.); Country of Fairfield (Conn.). Home: 25 Cartright St Bridgeport CT 06604 Office: Fairfield CT 06431

SEMPREVIVO, PHILIP CARMINE, computer service co. exec.; b. Amsterdam, N.Y., Apr. 14, 1941; s. Peter Felice and Emily Carmela (Principe) S.; B.A. in Psychology, U. N.H., 1964; M.S. in Ednl. Adminstrn., State U. N.Y. at Albany, 1974; postgrad. Columbia, 1975—; m. Margaret Helen Cook, Jan. 25, 1964; children—Stephanie, Stephen, Philip. Adminstrv. trainee N.Y. State Dept. Civil Services, Albany, 1964-65; sr. systems analyst, asst. to dir. EDP, N.Y. State Dept. Transp., Albany, 1965-68; sr. systems analyst Mohasco Industries, Amsterdam, 1968-70; dir. computer services State U. N.Y. at Cobleskill, 1970-73, asst. prof., chmn. dept. data processing, 1973-74; dir. computer services State U. N.Y. at New Paltz, 1974-76, also instr. systems analysis; mgr. adminstrv. systems devel. State U. N.Y. at Albany, 1976—. Team mgr. Schenectady Little League Assn.; cons. N.Y. State Assn. for Retarded Children. Mem. Ednl. Communications Assn. (instl. rep.), Coll. and Univ. Systems Exchange, State U. N.Y. Computing Officers Assn. (exec. council). Author: Systems Analysis, Definition, Process and Design, 1976. Contbr. articles in field to profl. jours. Home: 950 Pearse Rd Niskayuna NY 12309 Office: State U NY Computer Center 1400 Washington Ave Albany NY 12222

SEN, TAPAS KUMAR, research mgr.; b. Calcutta, India, Mar. 1, 1933; s. Pulin B. and Parul B. (Gupta) S.; came to U.S., 1959, naturalized, 1976; B.S., Calcutta U., 1951, M.S., 1954; Ph.D. (Pre-doctoral fellow 1959), John Hopkins U., 1963; m. Sondra Lee Kotzin, July 3, 1966; children—Rajorshi, Monisha. Research scholar Indian Statis. Inst., Calcutta, 1955-59; asso. psychologist Applied Physics Lab., John Hopkins U., 1960-63; mem. tech. staff Bell Telephone Lab., Holmdel, N.J., 1963-72; project mgr. human resources planning AT & T, Basking Ridge, N.J., 1972-77, supr. corporate planning, 1978—; chmn. council tech. groups Human Factors Soc., 1972-77. Recipient Outstanding Area Gov. of Year award Toastmaster Internat., 1970. Mem. Am. Psychol. Assn., AAAS, Population Assn. Am., Psychometric Soc. Club: Assn. Indians in Am., Inc. (founding chmn.). Contbr. articles to Bell System Tech. Jour., Jr. Optical Soc. Am., IEE Transactions on Audio and ElectroAcoustics, Psychologia. Home: 29 Arden Rd Mountain Lakes NJ 07046 Office: 295 N Maple Ave Room 6155G3 Basking Ridge NJ 07920

SENAY, TERENCE PATRICK, computer processing adminstr.; b. Grove City, Pa., May 10, 1948; s. Andrew Bernard and Ann Dolores (Sabolcik) S.; B.S. in Computer Sci., Point Park Coll., 1975. Applications programmer Mgmt. Sci. Assos., Inc., Pitts., 1975-77, sr. programmer, 1978—; applications analyst Control Data Corp., Rochester, N.Y., 1977-78; instr. computer sci. dept. Point Park Coll., Pitts., 1978—. Served with USN, 1970-72. Democrat. Home: 462 S Aiken Ave Apt 4 Pittsburgh PA 15232 Office: Management Science Associates 5100 Centre Ave Pittsburgh PA 15232

SENDAX, VICTOR IRVEN, dentist; b. N.Y.C., Sept. 14, 1930; s. Maurice and Molly (Rubin) Sendacz; B.A., Washington Sq. Coll., 1951; D.D.S., N.Y. U., 1955; postgrad. Harvard Sch. Dental Medicine, 1969-72; m. Deborah DeLand Cobb, Dec. 17, 1969; 1 dau., Jennifer Reiland. Extern, Lebanon Hosp., N.Y.C., 1955; practice dentistry encompassing oral rehab. and implantology, N.Y.C., 1957—; cons. mem. Vocal Dynamics Lab. Dept. Otolaryngology Lenox Hill Hosp., N.Y.C.; cons. Juilliard Sch. Music, N.Y.C.; acting asst. attending in oral implantology St. Lukes Hosp., N.Y.C.; dir. implant prosthodontics research and tng. program Columbia Sch. Dental and Oral Surgery, also adj. asst. clin. prof. div. prosthodontics; commr. N.Y. State Dental Service Corp., 1969-73; tchr. Post-Grad. Sch. of 1st Dist. Dental Soc. N.Y., 1959-69; pres. Bio-Dental Research Found., Inc. Mem. Mayor's com. for N.Y. Shakespeare Festival; mem. Mayor's Com. for N.Y.-Tokyo Sister Cities Affiliation, 1963-67; spl. projects co-chmn. Friends of City Center Music and Drama, 1961-69; bd. dirs. City Center of Music and Drama (Lincoln Center for Performing Arts), 1966-75; trustee N.Y. chpt. Leukemia Soc. Am., 1967. Served to capt. Dental Corps, USAF, 1955-57. Fellow Am., Coll. Internat. colls. dentists, Am. Acad. Implant Dentistry (v.p.; chmn. com. oral implant edn. and teaching standards; pres. N.E. dist.; mem. ADA (ho. of dels. 1969), Eastern Dental Soc. N.Y. (pres. 1969), 1st Dist. Dental Soc. N.Y. (dir. 1967), Dental Soc. State N.Y., Federation Dentaire Internationale, Am. Prosthodontic Soc., Fedn. Prosthodontic Orgns., Am. Equilibration Soc., Am. Analgesia Soc., Am., Internat. assns. dental research, Am. Acad. Periodontology (asso.), Am. Soc. Preventive Dentistry, N.Y. Acad. Scis., Northeastern Gnathological Soc., Royal Soc. Medicine (Eng.) (fgn. affiliate), Asso. Council Arts, Soc. Am. Magicians, Internat. Brotherhood Magicians (Order Merlin), London Magic Circle, Amagansett Hist. Assn. (adv. bd.), Japan Soc. (membership and activities com. 1965-67), Soc. Asian Music (dir.), Sigma Epsilon Delta. Club: Players. Contbg. author: Dental Clinics of North America; asso. editor Jour. Oral Implantology; author: Dental Implants and You. Co-developer oral anti-calculus system. Home: 70 E 77th St New York City NY 10021 Office: 30 Central Park S New York City NY 10019

SENG, MINNIE ANNA, librarian, editor; b. Muskegon, Mich., Nov. 30, 1909; d. Edward and Ella Barbara (Pattie) S.; student Muskegon Community Coll., 1927-29; A.B., U. Mich., 1932, A.B. in Library Sci., 1935, M.A. in Library Sci., 1943. Asst. med. librarian U. Iowa, 1935-39; cataloger Bay City (Mich.) Pub. Library, 1939-40; order librarian Mich. Technol. U., Houghton, 1940-42; continuations cataloger U. Ark., 1943-44; head cataloger Fresno (Calif.) State U., 1944-59; editor Edn. Index, H.W. Wilson Co., Pubs., Bronx, N.Y., 1959-66; head cataloger St. Ambrose Coll., Davenport, Iowa, 1967-72; periodicals librarian Frostburg (Md.) State Coll., 1972-74; ret., 1974. Mem. Am. Hort. Soc., N.Y. Library Club, AAUW, Smithsonian Assos. Republican. Mem. Christian Ch. Home: 110 S Broadway Apt Q Frostburg MD 21532

SENGSTAKEN, ROBERT WILLIAM, physician; b. Bklyn., Sept. 17, 1923; s. John Henry and Ruth (Kannofsky) S.; student Columbia, 1940-43, M.D., 1946; m. Ruth Quimby Gifford, Mar. 26, 1946 (div. Aug. 1956); children—Elizabeth Anne, Robert William, John Robert, David Edward, Michael William; m. 2d, Geraldine Boyce Neary, Aug. 23, 1956. Intern Columbia-Presbyn. Med. Center, N.Y.C., 1946-47; resident neurology and neurosurgery Neurol Inst. N.Y., 1947-53; practice medicine, specializing in neurol. surgery, Huntington, N.Y., 1953-78; asso. prof. clin. surgery (neurosurgery) State U. N.Y. at Stony Brook; chief Spina Bifida Treatment Center of St. Charles Hosp., Port Jefferson, N.Y.; mem. staff Community Hosp. Glen Cove, St. Charles Hosp., Huntington Hosp., Nassau Hosp., Meadowbrook Hosp., Mather Meml. Hosp.; cons. various hosps. Mem. com. on ministry Episcopal Diocese of L.I. Diplomate Am. Bd. Neurol. Surgery. Fellow A.C.S., Nassau Acad. Medicine; mem. Am. Assn. Neurol. Surgeons, AMA, Congress Neurol. Surgeons, N.Y. Neurosurg. Soc., Suffolk County Med. Soc., Nassau Surg. Soc., Neurol. Inst. N.Y. Alumni Assn., Nassau Acad. Medicine, Nassau-Suffolk Neurosurg. Soc., Nassau-Suffolk Physicians Guild, Assn. for Research in Nervous and Mental Disorders, Sigma Xi. Author publs. Invented Sengstaken esophageal ballon. Home: 1 The Rise Woodbury NY 11797 Office: 166 E Main St Huntington NY 11743 also 635 Belle Terre Rd Port Jefferson NY 11777 Died Jan. 8, 1978.

SENITT, JOSEPH A., retail trade co. exec.; b. N.Y.C., Sept. 25, 1918; s. Charles and Bella (Leffel) S.; grad. high sch.; m. Violet Mass, Mar. 3, 1957; 1 dau., Carla. With Waldbaum Inc., Central Islip, N.Y., 1935—, grocery buyer, 1942-65, v.p. grocery purchasing, 1965—. Mem. Food Industry Alliance (dir.). Mem. B'nai B'rith. Home: 100 Highwood Circle Oyster Bay NY 11771 Office: Hemlock St Central Islip NY 11722

SENSENIG, DAVID MARTIN, surgeon; b. Gladwyne, Pa., May 4, 1921; s. Wayne and Elizabeth Long (Crawford) S.; B.S., Haverford Coll., 1942; postgrad. Sch. Medicine, U. Pa., 1942-43; M.D., Harvard U., 1945; m. Constance Campbell, June 6, 1947; children—Philip Campbell, David Martin, Andrew Wilson, Thomas O'Brien; m. 2d, Bernice Evans, Dec. 20, 1975. Rotating intern Allentown (Pa.) Hosp., 1945-46; surg. house officer, jr. asst. resident Peter Bent Brigham Hosp., Boston, 1948-50; sr. asst. resident, resident surgeon New Eng. Center Hosp., Boston, 1950-52; surg. resident Westfield (Mass.) State Sanatorium, 1952-53; asst. chief surg. service, dir. surg. research lab. VA Med. Teaching Group Hosp., Memphis, 1953-55; asst. chief surg. service VA Hosp., Albany, N.Y., 1955-57; resident in thoracic and cardiac surgery Univ Hosp., State U. Iowa, Iowa City, 1957-59, instr. in surgery, 1957-58, asso. in surgery, 1958-59, asst. prof., asso. prof. surgery, 1960-62; chief thoracic surgery sect. VA Hosp., Phila., 1959-60, asst. chief surg. service, 1963-66; cardiothoracic surgeon Pa. Hosp., Phila., 1962-63; asst. prof. surgery U. Pa., Phila., 1962-66, supr. Animal Research Lab., 1963-66; practice medicine specializing in surgery, Bangor, Maine, 1966—; attending surgeon Eastern Maine Med. Center, Bangor, 1966—; attending surgeon St. Joseph Hosp., Bangor, 1966-74, chief surg. service, 1974—. Served to capt. M.C., U.S. Army, 1943-48. Diplomate Am. Bd. Surgery, Am. Bd. Thoracic Surgery. Mem. AMA, A.C.S., Pa. Assn. Thoracic Surgery, Penobscot County Med. Soc. (pres. 1974), Maine, Am. thoracic socs., AAAS, Internat. Cardiovascular Soc., Am. Geriatric Soc., Iowa, Phila. acads. surgery, Am. Coll. Chest Physicians, Bangor Med. Club (pres. 1970), Maine Vascular Soc. (pres.), New Eng. Surg. Soc., N.Y. Acad. Scis., New Eng. Soc. Vascular Surgery. Republican. Episcopalian. Contbr. articles to sci. publs. Home: 436 State St Bangor ME 04401 Office: 431 State St Bangor ME 04401

SENTER, ROGER CAMPBELL, hotel co. exec.; b. Manchester, N.H., Apr. 21, 1932; s. Kenneth Lee and Beatrice (Campbell) S.; B.A., Boston U., 1954, LL.B., 1956. Grad. student tng. program Westinghouse, Pitts., 1956-59; asst. mgr. recruiting Semi-Condr. div. Raytheon, Boston, 1959-61; founder McGovern, Senter & Assos., Boston, 1961, v.p., 1961-65; dir. recruiting ITT World Hdqrs., N.Y.C., 1965-70; sr. v.p., dir. personnel Sheraton Corp., Boston, 1970—, sr. v.p., 1976—. Bd. dirs. Mass. Mental Health Assn. Mem. Am. Hotel and Motel Assn., Hotel Sales Mgmt. Assn. (pres.). Club: Corinthian Yacht (Marblehead, Mass.). Home: Roundy's Hill Marblehead MA 01945 Office: 60 State St Boston MA 02210

SENTNER, PHILLIP JOHN, educator; b. Driftwood, Pa., May 14, 1928; s. Andrew Bridge and Catherene (Getty) S.; B.S., Villanova U., 1950; postgrad. Pa. State U., 1954-55; M.S., Drexel Inst. Tech., 1958; postgrad. Bryn Mawr Coll., 1958—; m. Ragnhild Irene Johnson, Sept. 23, 1950; children—Phillip John, Mary V., David A. Engr. gen. engring. dept. Sylvania Elec. Products, Emporium, Pa., 1950-55; asst. prof. physics Villanova (Pa.) U., 1955-72, asso. prof., 1972—, acting chmn. physics dept., 1976-77, nuclear radiation safety officer, 1976—; cons. Applied Pschol. Services, Wayne, Pa., 1963—. Mem. Am. Assn. Physics Tchrs., Sigma Xi. Democrat. K.C. Home: 218 E Conestoga Rd Devon PA 19333 Office: Dept Physics Villanova U Villanova PA 19085

SEREMETIS, MICHAEL GEORGE, surgeon; b. Thessaloniki, Greece, Nov. 8, 1925; s. George Demetrius and Poppi (Tatti) S.; M.D., U. Thessaloniki, 1951; m. Anastasia Nedelcos, Dec. 22, 1956; children—George, Constantine, Paola, Christine. Research asso. Cornell Med. Center, N.Y.C., 1957-59; chief surgeon U.S. Army Hosp., Paris, 1962-67, chief thoracic surgeon Beaumont Hosp., El Paso, 1967-68; asst. prof. surgery Downstate Med. Center, Bklyn., 1968-69; asst. prof. thoracic surgery Georgetown Med. Sch., Washington, 1969—; sr. attending surgeon Washington Hosp. Center, Greater South East Community Hosp., Doctors Hosp., Washington, So. Md. Hosp. Center; practice medicine specializing in thoracic/cardiovascular surgery, N.Y.C., 1968-69, Washington, 1969—; research at Georgetown Med. Sch. Served to lt. col. M.C., AUS, 1962-68. Diplomate Am. Bd. Surgery, Am. Bd. Thoracic Surgery. Mem. AMA, A.C.S., Am. Coll. Chest Physicians, Am. Coll. Cardiology, Soc. Thoracic Surgeons, D.C. Med. Soc. Contbr. articles to profl. jours. Home: 4737 36th St NW Washington DC 20008 Office: 3301 New Mexico Ave NW Washington DC 20016

SERENSEN, WILLIAM, JR., hosp. exec.; b. New Brunswick, N.J., Apr. 3, 1914; s. William and Carrie (Peterson) S.; student pub. schs., N.J.; m. Antoinette Malone, Nov. 20, 1941; children—Bonnie Lee, Barbara Ann. With Dept. Def., 1940-71, engr. Picatinny Arsenal, N.J., 1961-71; auditor Weber, Borrelli & Malone, C.P.A.'s, Highland Park, N.J., 1971-75; purchasing officer Roosevelt Hosp., Menlo Park, N.J., 1975—; chmn., asso. dir. Brunswick Bank and Trust; pres. Anwil, Inc. Elder, Reformed Ch. of North Brunswick. Served with USCGR, 1945. Address: 1006 Kearney Dr North Brunswick NJ 08902

SERENYI, ISTVAN VITEZ, retail store salesman; b. Trencsenteplic, Hungary, Dec. 13, 1917; s. Istvan and Josephin (Zimmermann) S.; student Coll. Phys. Edn., Budapest, 1941; m. Elizabeth Nicolini, Dec. 26, 1953. Came to U.S., 1956, naturalized, 1964. Ofcl., City of Veszprem (Hungary), 1938-41; various newspaper positions, Hungary, 1941-45, 47-48; circulation mgr. Stars and Stripes U.S. Army newspaper, Salzburg, Austria, 1949-55; optical technician Am. Optical Co., Innwood, N.Y., 1958-71; now salesman Saks Fifth Ave., N.Y.C. Art dealer, N.Y.C., 1973—. Chmn. world wide crusade Freedom for Hungary, Freedom for All. Recipient Hungarian Freedom awards; Gold Key to N.Y.C., 1962. Club: Republica Congressional (Washington). Made Hungarian Commemorative Run from N.Y. to Washington in 8 days with scroll of captive nations, 1960, 3200 mile walk from San Francisco to N.Y. in 74 days in name of freedom-seeking peoples, 1962. Home: 10-33 115th St Flushing NY 11356 Office: 611 Fifth Ave New York City NY 10022

SERENYI, PETER, art historian; b. Budapest, Hungary, Jan. 13, 1931; s. Nicholas and Emma (Josika) S.; came to U.S., 1950, naturalized, 1954; A.B. cum laude, Dartmouth Coll., 1957; M.A., Yale U., 1958; Ph.D., Washington U., St. Louis, 1968; m. Agnes Kertesz, Aug. 28, 1969; children—Peter, Denis. Part-time instr. art and archaeology Washington U., 1959-61; instr. fine arts Amherst Coll., 1961-64; vis. lectr. Smith Coll., 1962-63, U. Pa., 1964-66, Boston U., 1966-68; mem. faculty Northeastern U., Boston, 1968—, asso. prof. art history, 1973-79, prof., 1979—. Served with AUS, 1953-55. Grantee Nat. Endowment Humanities, summer 1970, Am. Philos Soc., 1970, Graham Found. Advanced Studies Fine Arts, 1974-75; Fulbright scholar, 1974-75. Mem. Soc. Archtl. Historians (pres. New Eng. chpt. 1978—), Victorian Soc. Am., Soc. Preservation New Eng. Antiquities, City Conservation League. Democrat. Roman Catholic. Editor, contbr.: Le Corbusier in Perspective, 1975. Contbr. articles to profl. jours. Address: 79 Greenough St Brookline MA 02146

SERFASS, ROBERT WILLIAM, chem. engr.; b. Wadsworth, Ohio, Oct. 26, 1925; s. Carl Victor and Eva Mae (Dutt) S.; B.S., U. Mo., 1950; M.S., Ohio State U., 1955; m. Gloria Elaine Dean, Sept. 5, 1948; children—Rosalind E., Suzanne M. (Mrs. Ronald W. Freund), Thomas D. Project mgr. Nestle Co., White Plains, N.Y., 1955-60; engring. mgr. Cowles Chem., Skaneateles Falls, N.Y., 1960-65; chief engr. Hatcodiv. W.R. Grace, Fords, N.J., 1965-67; process engring. mgr. Engrs., Inc., Newark, 1967-69; dir. engring. Ciba Geigy, Ardsley, N.Y., 1969-73; pvt. cons. chem. engr., Chappaqua, N.Y., 1973-74; exec. v.p. Bowen Engr., Inc., Somerville, N.J., 1974-75, pres., 1976-77; pres. Serfass Assos., Lebanon, N.J., 1977—; instr. chem. engring. Ohio State U., 1952-55. Served with USNR, 1943-45. Registered profl. engr., N.J. Mem. Am. Inst. Chem. Engrs., Nat., N.J. (v.p. 1969-70) socs. profl. engrs., Engrs. Club U. Mo., Alpha Chi Sigma, Pi Mu Epsilon, Phi Lambda Upsilon. Research on thermodynamic properties of fluorinated hydrocarbons. Home: RD 2 Box 183A Lebanon NJ 08833 Office: POB 898 Somerville NJ 08876

SERNAK, JOSEPH LAWRENCE, ednl. adminstr.; b. Hazelton, Pa., July 16, 1943; s. Joseph L. and Veronica D. S.; student Kings Coll., Wilkes-Barre, Pa., 1961-63; B.S., Campbell Coll., Buies Creek, N.C., 1967; M.A., Cath. U., Washington, 1975. English instr., athletic coach Carolina Mil. Acad., Maxton, N.C., 1967-68; claims adjuster-in-charge Crawford & Co. Ins. Adjusters, Inc., Phila., St. Croix, V.I., 1968-71; tchr. health and phys. edn. Sion Farm Elementary Sch., dir. phys. edn. dept., coach football St. Croix Central High Sch., Govt. U.S. V.I. Dept. Edn., 1971-72; resident counselor, group home dir. Boy's and Girls Home Montgomery County, Rockville, Md., 1972-75; coordinator jr. high alternative edn. program, area II Montgomery County Pub. Schs., Silver Spring, Md., 1975—. Chmn. youth services com. YMCA, 1977-78, chmn. affirmative action com., 1977-79; mem. bd. mgmt. Silver Spring YMCA, 1976-80, chmn. Partner with Youth fundraising campaign, 1977, 79; mem. Montgomery County Youth Employment Council, 1977—, Montgomery County Employment Devel. Commn., mem. citizens adv. com. Montgomery Coll. Mental Health Program, 1977-79; mem. adv. bd. Montgomery County Project 70001, 1977-79; vol. Bethesda Help, 1975—. Recipient Adult Leader of Yr. award Silver Spring YMCA, 1979. Mem. Am. Rehab. Counseling Assn., NEA, Am., Md. personnel and guidance assns., Montgomery County Ednl. Assn., Inst. Rational Living, Md. State Tchrs. Assn., Greater Washington Inst. Transactional Analysis.

SERPE, SALVATORE JOHN, physician; b. Bklyn., Oct. 16, 1928; s. Raymond and Letezia (Feltrinelli) S.; B.S., Fordham U., 1950; M.D., U. Bologna (Italy), 1955; m. Dorothy Ann Hughes, Jan. 4, 1958; children—John, Edward, Richard, Valerie, Drew, Sean. Intern, St. Vincent's Hosp., N.Y.C., 1955-56, resident, 1956-59; practice internal medicine, Massapequa, N.Y., 1961—; mem. staff St. Vincent's Hosp., N.Y.C., Brunswick Gen. Hosp., Amityville, N.Y. Served to capt. U.S. Army, 1959-61. Diplomate Am. Bd. Internal Medicine. Fellow A.C.P.; mem. AMA, Med. Soc. State N.Y., Nassau County Med. Soc. Republican. Roman Catholic. Office: 113 Clark Ave Massapequa NY 11758

SERRA, ROBERT FRANKLIN, hosp. food services adminstr.; b. Westerly, R.I., Dec. 21, 1933; s. Sylvester Charles and Anna Rita Serra; student U. R.I., 1953-55; m. Doris K. Serra, Nov. 11, 1955; children—Andrew M., Melanie L. Owner restaurant, Westerly, R.I., 1960-69; asst. dir. food services Seiler Corp., Waltham, Mass., 1970-72; dir. food services Westerly Hosp., 1972-74; dir. food services Kent County Meml. Hosp., Warwick, R.I., 1974—; food service cons. hosps., nursing homes, colls., restaurants and hotels. Mem. Am. Soc. Hosp. Food Services Adminstrs., N.E. Hosp. Assembly, Hosp. Assn. R.I. Democrat. Roman Catholic. Home: 60 Sherwood Hills Westerly RI 02891 Office: Kent County Meml Hosp Warwick RI

SERVISS, ANN EARL, educator; b. Jamestown, N.Y., Jan 14, 1919; d. Thomas K. and Marjorie (Bradt) Earl; B.S. in Edn., State U. N.Y., Buffalo, 1941; m. George H. Serviss; children—Georia Serviss Mushow, Thomas H. Tchr. 5th grade Union Free Sch. Dist., Kenmore, N.Y., 1941-44; tchr. Ithaca (N.Y.) City Sch. Dist., 1961-67, reading tchr., 1967—, now also dir. library learning center. Vice pres. Young Women's Hosp. Aid, 1960-63; mem. Ithaca Sch. Bd. Nominating Com., 1964-67, sec., 1966-67. Mem. NEA, N.Y. Educators Assn., Ithaca Tchrs. Assn., N.Y. State Reading Assn., Delta Kappa Gamma. Developed reading program designated as 1 of 5 exemplary reading programs in state N.Y. State Edn. Dept., 1975; dir. Cayuga Heights Sch. library-learning center. Certified in common br. teaching, N.Y. State; specialist in individualized diagnostic-prescriptive reading program. Home: 114 Winston Dr Ithaca NY 14850 Office: 110 E Upland Rd Ithaca NY 14850

SERWER-BERNSTEIN, BLANCHE LURIA, psychologist, educator; b. N.Y.C., July 13, 1910; d. Philip and Rebecca (Isaacson) Luria; B.A., Barnard Coll., 1931; B.H.L., Jewish Theol. Sem. Am., 1931; M.A., Columbia U., 1933; M.S., City Coll. N.Y., 1960; Ph.D., N.Y. U., 1966; postgrad. Boston Family Inst., 1969-71, Am. Inst. Sociotherapy, 1974—; m. Nahum A. Bernstein, Dec. 29, 1974; children by previous marriage—Philip Serwer, Daniel Paul Serwer, Jeremy Richard Serwer. Psychologist, Queens Coll. Speech and Hearing Center, Queens, N.Y., 1960-64; counseling psychologist, instr. City Coll. N.Y., N.Y.C., 1960-64; coordinator research City U. N.Y., 1964-66; vis. lectr., research asso. Harvard U., Cambridge, Mass., 1966-69; prof. edn. Boston U., 1969-75, co-dir. Psycho-Ednl. Clinic, 1969-73; vis. clin. prof. psychology in psychiatry Payne Whitney Psychiat. Clinic, N.Y.C., 1977—; tng. supr. family therapy Day Hosp. of Payne Whitney, N.Y.C., 1977—; cons. in field. Recreation commr. New Rochelle (N.Y.), 1957-61; adv. com. on kindergarten Commonwealth of Mass., 1969-71; advisor Mass. Assn. Children with Learning Disabilities, 1969-75; chmn. Com. for Integrated Schs. in New Rochelle, 1955-65; bd. dirs. New Rochelle Child Guidance Clinic, 1961-66. State of Mass. research grantee, 1969-71; certified psychologist, N.Y., Mass. Mem. Am., Mass. (bd. profl. affairs 1970-73) psychol. assns., Acad. Psychologists in Marital and Family Therapy, Am. Orthopsychiat. Assn., Am. Soc. Group Psychotherapy and Psychodrama, Inter-Am. Soc. for Psychology, Am. Assn. for Humanistic Psychology, AAUP, Assn. for Children with Learning Disabilities. Clubs: Old Oaks Country, Excelsior. Author: Experimental Model School Program for Children with Specific Learning Disabilities, 1970; Let's Steal the Moon (juvenile), 1970; (with A.J. Harris) Comparison of Reading Approaches in First Grade Teaching with Disadvantaged Children, 1966. Contbr. articles to profl. jours. Address: 340 E 64th St New York City NY 10021

SESSIONS, JUDITH ANN, librarian; b. Lubbock, Tex., Dec. 16, 1947; d. Earl Alva and Anna Mary (Mayer) S.; B.A. cume laude, Fla. Tech. U., 1970; M.S., Fla. State U., 1971. Asst. librarian in charge of pub. services U. S.C., Spartanburg, 1971-74; head librarian U. S.C. Salkachatchie campus, Allendale, 1974-77; dir. library and learning resources center Mt. Vernon Coll., Washington, 1977—. Rep., Coll. Library Council, Washington Met. Council of Govts., 1978—. Mem. ALA, Southeastern, S.C., D.C. library assns., Beta Phi Mu. Home: 4597 MacArthur Blvd #6 Washington DC 20007 Office: 2100 Foxhall Rd NW Washington DC 20007

SESSOMS, ALLEN LEE, physicist, educator; b. N.Y.C., Nov. 17, 1946; s. Albert Earl and Lottie Beatrice (Leff) S.; B.S., Union Coll., 1968; M.S., U. Wash., 1969; M.Phil., Yale U., 1971, Ph.D., 1972; m. Susan Beatrice Mayer, Sept. 14, 1968. Sci. asso. European Center for Nuclear Research, Geneva, 1973-75; asst. prof. physics Harvard U., 1975— (on leave); phys. sci. officer ACDA, Washington, 1978—. Ford Found. grantee, 1973-75; Alfred P. Sloan Found. fellow, 1977-79. Mem. Am. Phys. Soc., Fedn. Am. Scientists, AAAS, Sigma Xi. Contbr. articles to profl. jours. Home: 5601 Seminary Rd Apt 2105N Falls Church VA 22041 Office: ACDA 320 21st St NW Washington DC 20451

SESTITO, JOSEPH F.J., cons. engr.; b. Malden, Mass., Dec. 13, 1922; s. Vito and Maria (Obid) S.; A.M.E., Lincoln div. Northeastern U., 1952; m. Catherine T. D'Agosta, Dec. 9, 1945; children—Karen M., Jane M. Designer, Edward C. Brown Co., Boston, 1946-54; design engr. R.G. Vanderwell Co., Boston, 1954-56; chief mech. engr. Boston office Lockwood Greene A-E, 1956-63; owner Sestito & Assos., Cons. Engrs., Melrose, Mass., 1963—. Served with U.S. Army, 1943-45; ETO. Registered profl. engr., Mass., R.I., N.H., Conn. Mem. Nat. Soc. Profl. Engrs., Am. Soc. Heating, Refrigeration and Air Conditioning Engrs., Profl. Engrs. in Pvt. Practice, Am. Soc. Plumbing Engrs., Nat. Fire Protection Assn., Illuminating Engring. Soc. Democrat. Roman Catholic. Club: Moose. Home and office: 28 Shadow Rd Melrose MA 02176

SETCHELL, JOHN STANFORD, JR., physicist; b. Bklyn., Dec. 4, 1942; s. John Stanford and Elisa (Muenzfeld) S.; B.S. in Physics, Rensselaer Poly. Inst., 1963; M.S., U. Ill., 1969; postgrad. in statistics and reliability Rochester Inst. Tech., 1977—; m. Cynthia Florence Andreasen, Feb. 27, 1965. Research project physicist Eastman Kodak Co., Rochester, N.Y., 1969—. Served with USN, 1963-67. Mem. ASTM, Am. Sci. Presbyterian. Home: 376 English Rd Rochester NY 14616 Office: 901 Elmgrove Rd Rochester NY 14650

SETH, ANAND KUMAR, mech. engr.; b. Nashipur, India, Oct. 16, 1945; s. Girdhar Das and Pratibha (Devi) Seth; came to U.S., 1967, naturalized, 1977; B.Sc., Gorakhpur (India) U., 1962, U. Allahabad (India); postgrad. U. Maine; m. Cherrie Nadeau, Feb. 27, 1972. Grad. asst. U. Maine, 1967-69; teaching asst. Okla. State U., 1969-70; project engr. Balco, Inc., Boston, 1970-74; mech. engr. Harvard U., 1974—; mem. faculty Franklin Inst., Boston; cons. in energy conservation. Registered profl. engr., Mass. Mem. ASME, Nat., Mass. (chmn. scholarship com. Met. chpt. 1978) socs. profl. engrs., ASHRAE (chmn. research promotion Boston chpt. 1977—). Club: Masons. Home: 17 Gordon Rd North Reading MA 01864 Office: 175 N Harvard St Allston MA 02134

SETON, CHARLES B., lawyer; b. Bridgeport, Conn., Oct. 1, 1910; s. Charles Hillison and Stella (Rosen) Shapiro; B.A., Yale, 1931, LL.B., 1934; m. Suzanne Alexia Maimin, Mar. 7, 1948; children—Pam Elinor Lorenzo, Charles B. Admitted to N.Y. bar, 1934; practiced in N.Y.C., 1934—; asso. firm Rosenman, Goldmark, Colin & Kaye and predecessor firms, 1935-51; partner Rosen & Seton, 1955-58, Rosen, Seton & Sarbin, 1958-74, Rosen & Seton, 1974—; sec. Ziff-Davis Pub. Co., 1974-77, gen. counsel, 1958—; sec. Ziff Corp., 1976-77; guest lectr. Advanced Copyright Seminar, N.Y. U. Law Sch., 1953-76, Practicing Law Inst., 1955-74. Co-chmn. Copyright Luncheon Circle, 1952—. Founding dir., v.p. Arthur Judson Found., 1959—, Music for Westchester, Inc., 1962-75; founding trustee Copyright Soc. U.S., 1953-77, past v.p. Served to lt. comdr. USNR, 1942-45. Mem. Fed. Bar Council, Internat. Fgn. Law Assn., Inter Am., Am. bar assns., Consular Law Soc., Assn. Bar City N.Y. Club: Yale. Participating author: The Business and Law of Music, 1965, International Music Industry Conference, 1969. Contb. articles to profl. jours. Home: 16 Ervilla Dr Larchmont NY 10538 Office: 1889 Palmer Ave Larchmont NY 10538

SETON, FENMORE ROGER, mfg. co. exec.; b. Bridgeport, Conn., Nov. 27, 1917; B.A., Yale U., 1938, M.A. in Edn., 1956; m. Phyllis W. Zimmerman, Apr. 5, 1942; 1 dau., Diana Seton Adams. Pres., Seton Name Plate Corp., New Haven, 1956—. Mem. Pres.'s Com. Employment Handicapped, 1973—; bd. dirs. New Haven Scholarship Fund, 1962-70, Nat. Industries Severely Handicapped, Inc., Washington, 1974-76; pres. Conn. Easter Seal Soc., 1972-75, Easter Seal Goodwill Rehab. Center, New Haven, 1971-73; dir. Rehab. Internat. (RIUSA), 1973—, v.p., 1974—; mem. exec. council Internat. Soc. Rehab. Disabled, 1974—, treas., 1976—; bd. dirs. People-to-People Program, 1975—, New Haven Symphony Orch., 1975—. Served to 1st lt. AUS, 1941-45; to maj. USAF, 1952-56. Decorated Belgian Fourragère. Mem. Nat. Assn. Metal Name Plate Mfrs. (pres. 1968-69), Internat. Marking Device Assn. (pres. 1973-74), Screen Printers Assn. (dir. 1976—), NAM (edn. com.), Direct Mail Advt. Assn., Am. Soc. Heating, Refrigeration and Air Conditioning Engrs., Union Interalliée, Assn. des Graveurs Européens (Amsterdam), Instrument Soc. Am., New Haven C. of C. (dir. mfrs. div. 1966—, pres. div. 1974—), AAUP, Assn. European Engravers, Mory's Assn., Grad. Club Assn. New Haven. Clubs: Yale (N.Y.C., New Haven); Yale Faculty; Union Interalliee (Paris, France); Kiwanis, New Haven Lawn. Home: 2 Old Orchard Rd North Haven CT 06473 Office: Seton Name Plate Corp 592 Blvd New Haven CT 06505

SEVEGIAN, ARAM HAIG, chemist; b. Mattapan, Mass., May 10, 1932; s. Haig Ohanes and Surpoohy Terzian Tarbassian S.; student Northeastern U., 1949-54; B.S. with honors, Suffolk U., 1960, M.A. in Edn. (fellow), 1962; postgrad. (NSF grantee) Trinity U., San Antonio, 1968. With E & F King Corp., Norwood, Mass., 1952-53; indsl. diamond dust researcher Raytheon Mfg. Co., Waltham, Mass., 1953-54; chem. analyst Petrochem. div. Nat. Research Corp., Cambridge, Mass., 1957-58; instr. chemistry and physics lab. Suffolk U., Boston, 1959-60, instr. grad. chemistry lab., 1960-62, lectr. chemistry, 1962-66; tchr. chemistry and physics Westwood (Mass.) High Sch., 1960-63, Braintree (Mass.) High Sch., 1963—; cons. on drug identification and chemistry coordinator, 1972—. Served with U.S. Army, 1955-57. Life mem. NEA, Mass. Tchrs. Assn., AAAS, U.S. Chess Fedn., Mass. Chess Assn., Nat. Rilfe Assn., Mass. Rifle and Pistol Assn., GOAL, Am. Def. Preparedness Assn., Internat. Benchrest Shooters, Nat. Bench Rest Assn.; mem. Am. Chem. Soc. (div. chem. educators), Am. Inst. Physics, Am. Assn. Physics Tchrs., Braintree Edn. Assn., Norfolk County Tchrs. Assn., Mass. Assn. Sci. Tchrs., N.E. Assn. Chemistry Tchrs. Mem. Armenian Apostolic Ch. Clubs: Braintree Rifle and Pistol (dir. jrs. 1974—), Masons. Office: Braintree High Sch 128 Town St Braintree MA 02184

SEVIER, JOHN CHARLES, educator; b. Bklyn., Feb. 23, 1922; s. Charles E. and Lillian (Owen) S.; student Coll. City N.Y., 1936-42; B.S. cum laude, Temple U., 1952; M.A., U. Pa., 1954, postgrad., 1952-64; L.H.D., Combs Coll. Music, 1976; m. Grace Mary Rogers, May 17, 1947. Asst. prof. econs. Pa. Mil. Coll., Chester, 1954-56; asst. prof. mgmt. Temple U. Sch. Bus. Adminstrn., Phila., 1956-65; asst. prof. econs. and mgmt., head mgmt. dept PMC Colls. (now Widener Coll.), Chester, Pa., after 1965, now asso. prof. mgmt., staff statistician Joint Center for Urban Affairs, 1965—; project dir. Research Bur., Temple U., 1956-65. Mem. Del. County council Girl Scouts U.S.A., 1958—; staff mem. ann. drs. United Fund, Delaware County, Pa. 1956—; chmn. finance com., adv. bd. Salvation Army Citadel, Chester. Bd. dirs. Concord Day Care Center, Chester. Served with AUS, 1942-48. Recipient Legion of Honor Chapel of the Four Chaplains, 1973, Distinguished Service award Kiwanis, 1973, Gen. E.E. MacMoreland award civic service, 1973; Outstanding Service award Valley Forge council Boy Scouts Am., 1973, Order of Merit, Explorer div., 1975, 78, Silver Beaver award, 1978, Woods Sch. award for service to handicapped, 1978; Distinguished faculty award Widener Coll. Alumni Assn., 1973; Share Your Life award Pa. dist. Kiwanis Internat., 1974, Touch a Life award, 1975, bronze medal Chester club, 1975. Fellow Internat. Inst. for Community Service (founding; bronze medal 1975); mem. Am. Inst. Property and Casualty Underwriters (bd. examiners 1957—), Nat. Soc. Pershing Rifles (nat. adv. bd. 1969—), Cross Keys, Beta Alpha Psi, Beta Gamma Sigma, Phi Alpha Theta, Pi Gamma Mu, Omicron Delta Epsilon, Psi Chi, Alpha Chi, Delta Sigma Pi. Home: 401 Southcroft Rd Springfield PA 19064 Office: Widener Coll Chester PA 19013

SEXTON, BARBARA ROYSTER, urban transp. cons.; b. Lafayette, Ind., Feb. 9, 1923; d. Paul F. and Nina E. (Pease) Royster; student Purdue U., 1940-41, Ind. U., 1942-45; m. Burton H. Sexton, Sept. 3, 1946; children—Paul R., Ann Sexton Larson, Mary A. Ind. cons. pub. transp., 1952, 75—; partner Sexton & Sexton Assos., 1952-73; asso. Wilbur Smith & Assos., 1973-75. Mem. Chi Omega. Address: 7028 Heather Hill Rd Washington DC 20034

SEYMOUR, WHITNEY NORTH, lawyer; b. Chgo., Jan. 4, 1901; s. Charles Walton and Margaret (Rugg) S.; A.B., U. Wis., 1920, LL.D., 1962; LL.B., Columbia U., 1923, LL.D., 1960; LL.D., Dartmouth Coll., 1960, Duke U., 1961, U. Akron, 1961, U. Man. (Can.), 1961, Trinity Coll., 1964; D.C.L., N.Y. U., 1971; m. Lola V. Vickers, June 17, 1922 (dec.); children—Whitney North, Thaddeus. Admitted to N.Y. bar, 1924; asso. firm Simpson, Thacher & Bartlett, N.Y.C., 1923-29, partner, 1929-31, 33—; instr. law sch. N.Y. U., 1925-31; asst. solicitor gen. U.S., 1931-33; lectr. Law Sch., Yale, 1935-45. Mem. N.Y. Temporary Commn. on Cts., 1953-58; mem. Atty. Gen. Com. on Anti-trust Laws; spl. asst. atty. gen. N.Y., waterfront controversey, 1954. Pres. Legal Aid Soc., N.Y., 1945-50, chmn. bd. sponsors; emeritus trustee Practicing Law Inst.; chmn. bd. Freedom House, 1954-59, 64, now hon. chmn.; distbn. com. N.Y. Community Trust; chmn. bd. trustees Carnegie Endowment, 1958-70; chmn. Council on Library Resources; chmn. William Nelson Cromwell Found.; pres. Joint Conf. Legal Edn.; chmn. Council for Legal Edn. in Profl. Responsibility. Decorated Knight Order St. John of Jerusalem; recipient Bard Coll. Episcopal Layman of Year award, 1976; Pres.'s medal Municipal Art Soc., 1976. Fellow Am. Bar Found. (pres. 1960-64), Am. Coll. Trial Lawyers (pres. 1963-64), Bar Assn. City N.Y. (pres. 1950-52), Am. (pres. 1960-61, Gold medal 1971), Fed. (hon.), Minn. (hon.), Wis. (hon.), N.H. (hon.), Tenn. (hon.), Miss. (hon.), Ga. (hon.), Hawaii (hon.), Canadian (hon.), N.Y. State bar assns., Law Soc. Eng. (hon.), Am. Arbitration Assn. (pres. 1953-55, chmn. bd. 1955-57), Inst. Jud. Adminstrn. (past pres.), Lincoln's Inn (hon. bencher), St. Nicholas. Soc. (historian), Order Coif, Phi Gamma Delta. Republican. Episcopalian (sr. warden). Clubs: Century, Players, Downtown, Merchants, Church, Salmagundi, Recess (N.Y.C.); Nat. Lawyers, Metropolitan (Washington); Pilgrims. Home: 40 Fifth Ave New York City NY 10011 Office: Battery Park Plaza New York City NY 10004

SGAMBATO, JOSEPH JOHN, indsl. engr.; b. Providence, Apr. 9, 1949; s. John and Josephine (Santopietro) S.; student R.I. Jr. Coll., 1969; A.S. in M.E., Roger Williams Coll., 1971, B.S., 1973. Draftsman, G.W. Dahl Co., Bristol, R.I., 1970; design engr. fire protection div. ITT Grinnell, Providence, 1974; applications engr. Masoneilan Internat., Norwood, Mass., 1978, asst. mgr. sales engring., 1978—. Mem. Instrument Soc. Am., Assn. Iron and Steel Engrs. Club: Norfolk Tennis. Home: 70 Barrows St North Attleboro MA 02760 Office: 63 Nahatan St Norwood MA 02062

SHAEVEL, MORTON LEONARD, food co. exec.; b. Boston, June 7, 1936; s. Louis and Lee Shaevel; B.S. in Food Tech., U. Mass., 1958; postgrad. Fairleigh Dickinson U., 1962-64; m. Elinor H. Michelson, June 17, 1961; children—Andrew Jeffrey, Karen Judith. Food technologist B. Manischewitz Co., Newark, 1958-62; food technologist Nabisco, Inc., Fairlawn, N.J., 1962-65, sr. research chemist, 1965-66, head dept. frozen food devel., 1966-68, head dept. food systems devel., 1968-69, mgr. new product devel., 1969-72, dir. new product devel., 1972-73; v.p. research and devel. Freezer Queen Foods, Inc., Buffalo, 1973—. Pres. Farmstead Civic Assn., Parsippany, N.J., 1968-69. Mem. Inst. Food Technologists (Man of Yr. in N.Y. 1973), Am. Frozen Food Inst. (chmn. prepared foods 1972-73, chmn. research council 1974-76, Meritorious Service award 1977), Am. Mgt. Assn. Home: 246 Ranch Trail W Williamsville NY 14221 Office: 2544 Clinton St Buffalo NY 14224

SHAFER, BARBARA GRACE, social worker; b. Easton, Pa., Jan. 11, 1944; d. Fredrick William and Grace Evelyn Shafer; B.A. in Sociology and Elementary Edn., Cedar Crest Coll., 1965; M.A. in Guidance and Counselling, Villanova U., 1969; postgrad. Marywood (Md.) Inst., 1975-78. Kindergarten tchr., first grade tchr. Lansdowne Aldan Sch. Dist., 1965-69, sch. social worker, 1969-70; sch. social worker Wm. Penn Sch. Dist., Lansdowne, Yeadon and Darby, Pa., 1971, Upper Darby (Pa.) Sch. Dist., 1972-77, also parent edn. group leader. Active, Community Y of Eastern Delaware County; mem. adv. council Cross County Sch.; mem. Multidisciplinary Team Approach for Child Care Service. Recipient Optimists award, 1958. Mem. Am. Personnel and Guidance Assn., NEA, Pa., Upper Darby edn. assns., Pace. Republican. Mem. United Ch. of Christ. Club: Springton Lake Racquet. Home: Chetwynd 327 Rosemont PA 19010 Office: Beverly Hills Jr High Sch Sherbrook and Garrett Rds Upper Darby PA 19082

SHAFER, STEPHEN QUENTIN, physician; b. Barrytown, N.Y., Dec. 18, 1944; s. Frederick Quentin and Margaret Mary (Creal) S.; B.A., Harvard U., 1966; M.D., Columbia U., 1970, M.P.H., 1977, M.A., 1979; m. Elizabeth Jay Stillman, July 2, 1966; children—Theodora Marigot, David Jay Creal. Intern Harlem Hosp. Center, N.Y.C., 1970-71, resident in medicine, 1971-72, clin. fellow in neurology, 1972-74, mem. staff, 1975-78; Robert Wood Johnson clin. scholar Columbia U., 1976-78, asst. prof. pub. health and neurology Sergievsky Center, Columbia U., 1978—. Vice pres. Friends of Earth Found.; trustee Environ. Def. Fund. Mem. Am. Pub. Health Assn., Soc. for Epidemiologic Research, Am. Fedn. for Clin. Research, Assn. Am. Geographers. Democrat. Episcopalian. Clubs: Sierra, Central Park Track. Home: 285 Riverside Dr New York City NY 10025 Office: 630 W 168th St New York City NY 10032

SHAFFER, ELLA LOUISE (ELOISE), mfg. co. exec.; b. Hagerstown, Md., Feb. 1, 1926; d. H. Mason and A. Florence (Leatherman) Troupe; student pub. schs., Hagerstown, Md.; m. Edward Franklin Shaffer, Jr., Nov. 21, 1951 (dec. Jan. 1975). With Fairchild Industries, Germantown, Md., 1944—, exec. asst. to chmn. bd., chief exec. officer, 1961—. Mem. Am. Defense Preparedness Assn., Nat. Assn. Exec. Secs. Club: Shannondale Bath Ltd. Home: PO Box 2043 Hagerstown MD 21740 also Route 2 Shannondale Harpers Ferry WV 25425 Office: Fairchild Industries Germantown MD 20767

SHAFFER, HELEN SNYDER, county ofcl.; b. Coatesville, Pa., July 9, 1924; d. William P. and Helen T. (Doran) Snyder; student Pa. State U., 1970, Villanova U., 1976; m. J. Irwin Shaffer Jr., Aug. 12, 1944; children—Helenann, John III, Gail, Beth, Robert, Andrea. Dep. controller County of Chester, West Chester, Pa., 1948—. Home: 1432 Boot Rd West Chester PA 19380 Office: Controller's Office Room 511 Courthouse West Chester PA 19380

SHAFFER, JOHN WHITCOMB, research scientist; b. Harrisburg, Pa., Jan. 6, 1932; s. William Andrew and Annie Martha (Lauffer) S.; B.S., Pa. State U., 1953, M.S., 1954, Ph.D., 1957; m. Sandra Miriam Slifkin, Jan. 30, 1953; children—Jeffrey Brian, Clifford Alan. Instr. to asso. prof. med. psychology Johns Hopkins U. Sch. Medicine, Balt., 1957—; cons. in Balt., Friends Med. Sci. Research Center, Inc., 1960—, Social Security Adminstrn., 1965—, Md. Dept. Mental Hygiene, 1967—; pvt. practice research cons., Balt.; mem., chmn. Md. Bd. Examiners of Psychologists, 1968-71; investigator, co-investigator govt. and pvt. behavioral and med. scis. research. Lic. psychologist, Md., D.C. Mem. Am. Statis. Assn., Am., Md., D.C. psychol. assns. Presbyterian. Author, co-author sci. articles in books, nat., internat. sci. and profl. jours. Home and Office: 406 Crosby Rd Baltimore MD 21228

SHAFFER, MARGARET THOMPSON, research exec.; b. Cumberland, Md., Mar. 28, 1938; d. Robert Finley and Elizabeth (Brengle) Thompson; B.Mus., U. Rochester, 1960; M.S. (USPHS fellow), U. So. Ill., 1964; children—Ian Montgomery, Marc Christopher. Dir. planning research Century Research Corp., Arlington, Va., 1964-66; asst. mgr. human factors Tracor, Inc., Rockville, Md., 1966-69; v.p. Urban Scis. Corp., Bethesda, Md., 1969-70; pres., cons. Urban Studies Assn., Potomac, Md., 1970-76; pres., chmn. bd. PARADIGM, Inc., Potomac, 1976—; seminar lectr. SBA. Mem. Am. Inst. Planners, Am. Psychol. Assn., Internat. Ergonomics Assn., Am. Soc. Polit. and Social Scis., Nat. Assn. Women Bus. Owners, Transp. Research Bd. Contbr. numerous articles to profl. jours.

SHAH, BIPIN CHANDRA, banker; b. Patan, India, July 23, 1938; s. Manilal Mohanlal and Kashar (Bhandari) S.; came to U.S., 1958, naturalized, 1967; B.A., Baldwin-Wallace Coll., 1962; M.A., U. Pa., 1965; m. Fay Janet Goldie, Aug. 18, 1962; children—Neile; 1 step-son—Kyle Ober. Info. retrieval specialist Xerox Corp., Rochester, N.Y., 1966; mgr. systems Gen. Electric Co., Valley Forge, Pa., 1966-68; dir. info. div. Mauchley Assos., Phila., 1969-70; pres. Vertex Systems, Inc., King of Prussia, Pa., 1970-74, dir., 1973-74; v.p., sr. officer Fed. Res. Bank of Phila., 1974—; lectr. Wharton Sch. Bus., U. Pa., Phila., 1967-68. Recipient Am. Mgmt. Assn. award, 1967. Mem. Am. Mgmt. Assn., Nat. Hon. Philos. Soc. (pres. 1961-62). Democrat. Author: Information Retrieval: State-of-the Art, 1966. Home: 143 Woodside Rd Ardmore PA 19003 Office: 100 N 6th St Philadelphia PA 19106

SHAH, HASMUKH SANKALCHAND, truck mfg. co. exec.; b. Baroda, India, Jan. 12, 1944; s. Sankalchand Harivallabhdas and Girjaben Gokaldas (Patel) S.; came to U.S., 1968; B.S. in E.E., U. Baroda (India), 1963; M.S. in Indsl. Engring., W.Va. U., 1969, M.B.A., 1972; m. Kokila Naginlal Gandhi, Aug. 6, 1968; children—Ketan, Amy and Samir (twins). Product engr. Mahindra and Mahindra, Ltd., Bombay, 1964-67; chief insp. Batliboi Machine Tools, Surat, India, 1967-68; plant indsl. engr. Morgan Shirt Co., Morgantown, W.Va., 1969-72; successively indsl. engr., sr. indsl. engr., supervising indsl. engr., sect. mgr., mgr. material handling Mack Trucks, Inc., Allentown, Pa., 1972-77, dir. ops. planning, 1977—; tchr., cons., systems analyst. Recipient Prof. Subbarao Meml. prize, 1963. Mem. Am. Mgmt. Assn., Am. Inst. Indsl. Engrs., Am. Prodn. and Inventory Control Soc. Hindu. Home: Box 352A RD 3 Tupelo Rd Allentown PA 18104 Office: PO Box M 2100 Mack Blvd Allentown PA 18105

SHAH, SUDHIR ASHALAL, civil engr.; b. Bareja, India, Feb. 15, 1942; s. Ashalal Motilal and Savita (Ashalal) S.; came to U.S., 1966, naturalized, 1975; B.S., Gujarat U. (India), 1963; M.S., Worcester Poly. Inst., 1967; m. Jyotsna Rasiklal, Jan. 15, 1966; children—Julie Sudhir, Rupal Sudhir, Manisha Sudhir. Civil engr. M/S K.B. Mehta, Ahmedabad, India, 1963-64, Fadia Dalal & Co., Ahmedabad, 1964-65; v.p. Purcell Assos., Glastonbury, Conn., 1967—. Registered profl. engr., Conn. Mem. ASCE, Nat., Conn. socs. profl. engrs., Am. Concrete Inst., India Assn. Greater Hartford (sec. 1969-70). Democrat. Jainist. Designer bridge over Housatonic River, 1977. Home: 20 Nuthatch Knob Glastonbury CT 06033 Office: 90 National Dr Glastonbury CT 06033

SHAHINIAN, SIROON PASHALIAN, bus. exec.; b. N.Y.C., June 28, 1926; d. Leon and Margret (Mardirosian) Pashalian; B.A. in Math., Hunter Coll., 1946; M.A., N.Y. U., 1949, Ph.D. in Indsl. Psychology, 1957; m. Zareh Shahinian, Dec. 5, 1960; 1 son, John Zareh. Research asso. Fordham U., N.Y.C., 1951-53; research specialist Community Service Soc., N.Y.C., 1955-58; asst. personnel mgr. N.W. Moody Corp., N.Y.C., 1958-59; staff asso. Herrold Assos., N.Y.C., 1959-60; research psychologist N.Y. State Dept. Mental Hygiene, Queens Village, N.Y., 1961-68; research asso. Hillside Hosp., Glen Oaks, N.Y., 1965-69; asst. to dir. profl. exam. service Am. Pub. Health Assn., 1970; placement counselor Alpha Employment Agy., Great Neck, N.Y., 1971-72; adminstrv. asst. N.Y. State Psychol. Assn., N.Y.C., 1972; tchr. placement counselor York Coll., City U. N.Y., Jamaica, 1972-76; v.p. Avid Enterprises, Inc., 1976—; asst. prof. mgmt. St. John's U., Jamaica, N.Y., 1977—; lectr. in psychology Queens Coll., N.Y.C., 1951-55. Sec., also dir. Armenian Welfare Assn., N.Y.C., 1968-72. Bd. dirs., also exec. dir. Hye Bardez Nursery Sch., Bayside, N.Y., 1968-69, 71-72; mem. Armenian Profl. Adv. Council, 1976—. Office Naval Research grantee, 1951-53; NIMH grantee, 1965-69. Mem. Am., Eastern, N.Y. State, Nassau County psychol. assns., Psychometric Soc., Gerontol. Soc., Met. N.Y. Assn. Applied Psychologists, Am. Personnel and Guidance Assn., Psi Chi. Contbr. articles to profl. jours. Home: 1 Sussex Rd Great Neck NY 11020

SHAIKH, BAHU SULTAN, physician; b. Karachi, Pakistan, Aug. 31, 1945; s. Noor Mohammad and Shahkhatoon (Channa) S.; came to U.S., 1969; grad. St. Patrick's Coll., Karachi, 1961-63; M.B., B.S., Dow Med. Coll., U. Karachi, 1968; m. Yasmeen Khamisani, Mar. 25, 1972; children—Maheen, Sasha. Intern, Ellis Hosp., Schenectady, 1969-70; resident Thomas Jefferson U. Hosp., Phila., Methodist Hosp., Phila., Phila. Gen. Hosp., Landis State Hosp. for Chest Diseases, 1970-72; Cardeza clin. research fellow Thomas Jefferson U., Phila., 1972-74; practice medicine specializing in internal medicine, hematology and oncology, Hershey, Pa., 1974—; attending physician Milton S. Hershey Med. Center, Hershey, 1974—; cons. hematologist and oncologist U.S. Army Health Clinic, Carlisle, Pa., 1974—, Lebanon (Pa.) VA Hosp., 1974—; asst. prof. medicine hematology div. Milton S. Hershey Med. Center, Pa. State U., Hershey, 1974—. Merit scholar, 1963-68; Dr. M.A. Mistri Gold medal, Pfizer Gold medal, Habib Bank Gold medal U. Karachi, 1968. Diplomate Am. Bd. Internal Medicine. Mem. A.C.P., Am. Soc. Hematology, Am. Soc. Clin. Oncology, Dauphin County Med. Soc., Pa. Assn. Blood Banks, Am. Fedn. Clin. Research, Pakistan Med. Assn., Phila. Hematology Soc., AMA (Physicians Recognition award 1976). Home: 6433 Darlington Ave Harrisburg PA 17111 Office: 500 University Dr Hershey PA 17033

SHAIKH, ZAHIR AHMAD, educator; b. Jullundur, India, Mar. 31, 1945; s. Zafer Ahmad and Mehmooda Begum (Chohan) S.; came to U.S., 1972; B.Sc., U. Karachi (Pakistan), 1965, M.Sc., 1967; Ph.D., Dalhousie U. (Can.), 1972; m. Mary Butterfield, Aug. 23, 1975; 1 child, Faraz. Research asso. environ. health U. Okla., Oklahoma City, 1972-73; sr. postdoctoral fellow in pharmacology and toxicology U. Rochester (N.Y.), 1973-75, asst. prof. pharmacology and toxicology, 1975—. NIH fellow, 1974-76; NIH grantee, 1976-79. Mem. Soc. Toxicology, AAAS. Contbr. articles in field to profl. jours. Home: 114 Snowberry Crescent Rochester NY 14606 Office: 601 Elmwood Ave Rochester NY 14642

SHAIN, RICHARD ARTHUR, psychologist; b. Miami Beach, Fla., Mar. 18, 1948; s. Arthur M. and Betty Jane (Hess) S.; B.A., Queens Coll., Flushing, N.Y., 1969; M.A., Temple U., 1972, Ph.D., 1976. Dir. work study div. Lymelight, Inc., S. Fallsburg, N.Y., 1969-70; tchr.-coordinator spl. edn. Mt. Vernon (N.Y.) Pub. Schs., 1970; research asst. Temple U., 1971-73, lectr. psychology, 1973-75; mem. early childhood consortium Edn. Commn. States, 1975-76; dir. grants mgmt., research and evaluation Millville (N.J.) Bd. Edn., 1977—; lectr. Grad. Sch. Edn., U. Pa., 1976; cons. in field. NSF fellow, 1974; Temple U. summer fellow, 1973; recipient Boulton Fund award, 1975, Magna Cum Laude World Poet award, 1970; certified sch. psychologist, N.J. Mem. Am. Psychol. Assn., Psychometric Soc., Soc. Research Childhood Devel., Jean Piaget Soc., Council Exceptional Children, World Poetry Soc. Internat., Assn. Supervision and Curriculum Devel., Phi Delta Kappa, Psi Chi. Author research publs., poems in newspapers, mags. and anthologies. Home: 505 Cherrywood Apts Clementon NJ 08021 Office: Millville Bd Edn Millville NJ 08332

SHAKE, J(AMES) CURTIS, musician; b. Princeton, Ind., Mar. 27, 1918; s. Clarence Arthur and Clara Josephine (Yunker) S.; B.Mus., DePauw U., Greencastle, Ind., 1940; M.Mus., Eastman Sch. Music, Rochester, N.Y., 1941; Ph.D., Syracuse U., 1957; m. Cornelia Mcpherson Hughes, May 8, 1943; children—James Curtis, Thomas Hughes. Mem. faculty Jordan Conservatory, Indpls., 1941-42, W.Va. Wesleyan Coll., 1942-45; mem. faculty Syracuse U. Sch. Music, 1945—, acting dean, 1971-72, faculty adminstrv. asst., 1977—; organist, choir dir. St. Alban's Episcopal Ch., Syracuse; composer: A Christmas Carol, 1954; The Three Marys, 1956. Mem. Am. Guild Organists (dean 1974-76), Nat. Soc. Lit. and Arts, Nat. Hist. Soc., Nat. Trust Historic Preservation, Victorian Soc. in Am., Phi Mu Alpha (province gov. 1962-70), Pi Kappa Lambda. Episcopalian. Author: Primer for Piano Students, 1958; co-author: Basic Piano. Home: 1029 Westcott St Syracuse NY 13210 Office: 212 Crouse Coll Syracuse Univ Syracuse NY 13210

SHAKOUR, GABRIEL MITCHELL, publisher; b. Worcester, Mass., Aug. 24, 1917; s. Mitchell G. and Adele (Kefrouni) C.; student Northeastern U., 1941; m. Barbara Handy, Jan. 10, 1949 (dec. Apr. 1972); children—Peter, Mitchell G.; m. 2d, Marie Handy, Nov. 10, 1973. Owner, operator Keene (N.H.) Drive-In Theatre, 1953—, Northfield (Mass.) Drive-In Theatre; founder, pub. Keene Shopper, 1959—; pub. Keene Shopper News; incorporator Cheshire County Savs. Bank, 1973. Mem. exec. bd. Daniel Webster council Boy Scouts Am., chmn. Cheshire County area explorers; mem. council St. Bernard's Ch., 1971—, chmn. fin. com., 1974—. Served with armoured inf. AUS, 1941-45; ETO. Decorated Purple Heart. Mem. Am. Legion, VFW. K.C. Home: 20 W Diane Dr Keene NH 03431 Office: 445 West St Keene NH 03431

SHALIT, BERNARD LAWRENCE, dentist; b. Quincy, Mass., Feb. 17, 1920; s. L. Melville and Mildred (Kolb) S.; D.M.D., Tufts U., 1944; m. Helen L. Shoener, Oct. 11, 1951; children—Barbara L., William L. Pvt. practice dentistry, Quincy. Dir. Quincy Taxpayers Assn. Served from lt. (j.g.) to lt. Dental Corps. USNR, 1944-46. Life fellow seminars on Hypnosis Found.; mem. Mass. Dental Soc., Am. Dental Assn., Am., New Eng. socs. clin. hypnosis, Nat. Rifle Assn. (life), St. Stephen's Royal Arch Chpt. Mason. Home: 94 Crabtree Rd North Quincy MA 02171 Office: 14 Walker St North Quincy MA 02171

SHALITA, ALAN REMI, dermatologist; b. Bklyn., Mar. 22, 1936; s. Harry and Celia; A.B., Brown U., 1957; B.S., U. Brussels, 1960; M.D., Bowman Gray Sch. Medicine, 1964; m. Simone Lea Baum, Sept. 4, 1960; children—Judith and Deborah (twins). Intern, Beth Israel Hosp., N.Y.C., 1964-65; resident dept. dermatology N.Y. U. Med. Center, 1967-68, NIH tng. grant fellow dept. dermatology, 1968-70, instr. dermatology, 1970-71, asst. prof., 1971-73; asst. prof. dermatology Columbia U. Coll. Physicans and Surgeons, 1973-75; asso. prof. medicine, head div. dermatology State U. N.Y. Downstate Med. Center, Bklyn., 1975—; asst. attending in dermatology Univ. Hosp., N.Y.C., 1970-73, Bellevue Hosp. Center, 1970-73, Manhattan VA Hosp., 1972-74, Presbyn. Hosp., 1973-75; dir. dermatology service State Univ. Hosp., Bklyn., 1975—, Kings County Hosp. Center, 1975—; cons. dermatology Bklyn. VA Hosp., 1975—; chief dermatology Brookdale Med. Center, 1977—. Served to lt. M.C., USNR, 1965-67. Recipient Surg. and Pediatric awards Beth Israel Hosp., N.Y.C., 1965; Spl. fellow NIH, 1970-73. Mem. Am. Acad. Dermatology, Soc. Investigative Dermatology, Dermatology Found. (trustee), AMA, N.Y. Acad. Scis., A.C.P., Nat. Program Dermatology, Am. Soc. Dermatol. Surgery (past dir.), AAAS, Internat. Soc. Tropical Dermatology, N.Y. State Med. Soc., Soc. Cosmetic Chemists, N.Y. Acad. Medicine, Dermatol. Soc. Greater N.Y., N.Y. State Dermatology Soc. (dir.). Republican. Jewish. Contbr. articles in field to med. jours. Home: 70 E 77th St New York City NY 10021 Office: 450 Clarkson Ave Brooklyn NY 11203

SHALITA, PAUL ROY, pressure sensitive tape mfg. co. exec.; b. N.Y.C., Dec. 10, 1921; s. Martin and Rose (Hoffman) S.; B.S., Coll. City N.Y., 1943; M.S., Poly. Inst. Bklyn., 1946; m. Eileen Gasner, July 3, 1962; children—Ronald, Carol, Nan, Amy. Tech. dir. Cofax Corp., Lynbrook, L.I., N.Y., 1942-47; v.p., tech. dir. Tech. Tape Corp., New Rochelle, N.Y., 1947-61; tech. dir. Facile div. Sun Chem. Corp., Paterson, N.J., 1962-71; pres. Shalita Assos., Roslyn Heights, N.Y., 1971—; v.p. Finite Industries, Carlstadt, N.J. Mem. Am. Chem. Soc., Soc. Plastic Engrs., Pressure Sensitive Tape Council. Home: 130 Westwood Circle Roslyn Heights NY 11577

SHAMES, WILLIAM HENRY, holding co. exec.; b. N.Y.C., Mar. 28, 1931; s. Samuel and Frances (Label) S.; B.B.A. magna cum laude, U. Okla., 1952; m. Sybil Zeligson, June 23, 1953 (div. 1973); children—Jeffrey Alan, Erica Leslie, Jonathan Adam; m. 2d, Diane Dohoney, Mar. 2, 1974 (div. 1975). Jr. exec. Gimbel's Dept. Store, N.Y.C., 1953-54; v.p mktg. C.C.I. Corp., Tulsa, 1954-61; founder, pres. Sibany Mfg. Corp., Riverside, Conn., 1961-72; founder, chmn. Risers Venture Mgmt. Co., Inc., N.Y.C., 1972—; founder Risers' Fitness Schs., 1977; pres. Identimation Corp. Northvale, N.J., 1969-72; chmn. bd. Metrodyne Corp., Riverside, Conn., 1969-72; pres. Mile Ahead Industries Inc., Greenwich, Conn., 1975-76; dir. Internat. Oceanographic Corp., Greenwich, 1965-72; pub. The Marketplace: New Ventures in Better Health, 1975—; lectr. women as entrepreneurs, 1977—. Vice pres. Shames Found., 1969-72. Recipient Inventor's Show Distinction award Internat. Inventors Exhbn., 1965, Mem. Author's Guild, Internat. Platform Assn., U. Okla. Assn. Author: Venture Management. Home and office: 5 Tudor City Pl New York City NY 10017

SHAMOUN, EDWARD, physician; b. Baghdad, Iraq, May 14, 1927; s. Simon H. Ben Shimon and Zelda Z. Bahar; came to U.S., 1956, naturalized, 1962; M.D., U. Paris, 1956. Intern, Yonkers (N.Y.) Gen. Hosp., 1957; resident in obstetrics and gynecology Mt. Vernon (N.Y.) Hosp., practice medicine specializing in obstetrics and gynecology, Forest Hills, N.Y., 1965—; chief dept. gynecology Kew Gardens Hosp., 1975—; mem. staff North Shore, Jamaica, Hillcrest hosps., N.Y. Infirmary. Diplomate Am. Bd. Obstetrics and Gynecology. Fellow A.C.S., Am. Coll. Obstetricians and Gynecologists; mem. N.Y. State, Queens County med. socs., Westchester Acad. Medicine. Club: Mason. Office: 102-40 67th Dr Forest Hills NY 11375

SHANAHAN, SHEILA ANN, pediatrician; b. N.Y.C., July 1, 1943; d. James Patrick and Eleanor Margaret (Breslin) S.; B.A., Trinity Coll., Washington, 1960-63; M.D., cum laude, Med. Coll. Pa., 1969; m. Justin L. Cashman, Jr., Sept. 14, 1968; children—Justin III, Gillis. Intern straight pediatrics Presbyn. Hosp., N.Y.C., 1969-70, resident in pediatrics, 1970-72; pvt. practice medicine specializing in pediatrics, Greenwich, Conn., 1972—; asst. attending Greenwich Hosp., 1972-73, asso. attending, 1973—; asst. in clin. pediatrics Presbyn. Hosp., N.Y.C., 1972-75, asso., 1975—; instr. Columbia, 1972-75, asso. clin. pediatrics, 1975—. Recipient Honorable Mention citation for scholastic achievement Am. Med. Women's Assn., 1969; diplomate Am. Bd. Pediatrics. Mem. Greenwich Med. Soc., Fairfield County, Conn. State med. socs., Am. Acad. Pediatrics. Office: 42 Sherwood Pl Greenwich CT 06830

SHANKER, ALBERT, union ofcl.; b. N.Y.C., Sept. 14, 1928; s. Morris and Mamie (Burko) S.; B.A. in Philosophy with honors, U. Ill. at Urbana; M.A., Columbia, postgrad. in Philosophy and Mathematics, Columbia; m. 2d, Edith Gerber, Mar. 11, 1960; children—Carl (by previous marriage), Adam, Jennie, Michael. Tchr. math., pub. schs., N.Y.C., 1952-59; del. N.Y. Tchrs. Guild, late 1950's; organizer Am. Fedn. Tchrs., 1959-60, with United Fedn. Teachers, 1960—, sec. Local 2, subsequently editor United Tchr., orgn.'s ofcl. newspaper, chief asst. to pres., union pres., 1964—; exec. v.p. N.Y. State United Tchrs., 1972-78; v.p. AFL-CIO; pres. Am. Fedn. Tchrs., 1974—; v.p. N.Y.C. City Central Labor Council, N.Y. State AFL-CIO; asso. univ. seminar of labor Columbia; mem. exec. com Workers Def. League; dir. League for Indsl. Democracy. Mem. bldg. and devel. fund Wiltwyck Sch. for Boys; sec. Jewish Labor Com.. Bd. dirs. United Housing Found., N.Y.C. Council Econ. Edn., Internat. Rescue Com., United Way Tri-State; bd. sponsors Legal Aid Soc.; mem. N.Y.C. Manpower Planning Council; trustee Center for Urban Edn. Office: 260 Park Ave S New York City NY 10010

SHANLEY, BERNARD M(ICHAEL), lawyer, Republican nat. committeeman; b. Newark, 1903; s. Bernard Michael and Regina (Ryan) S.; student Columbia U., 1925, Fordham U. Law Sch., 1928; m. Maureen Virginia Smith, Aug. 1, 1936; children—Maureen Shanley Kirk, Seton, Kevin, Brigid, Brendan. Admitted to N.J. bar, 1929, D.C. bar, 1969; sr. partner Shanley & Fisher, Newark, 1945—; on leave of absence from firm to act as dep. chief staff, spl. counsel to Pres., 1953-55, sec. to Pres. U.S., 1955-57. Mem. exec. com. N.J. Republican Com.; mem. Rep. Nat. Com. from N.J., 1960-64, 68—, vice chmn. N.E. region, 1973—; adviser on Gen. Eisenhower's personal staff, 1952 campaign; trustee Victoria Found., Am. Inst. Mental Studies, N.J. Research Assn. Mental Hygiene, Inc., Allocca Found.; vice chmn. United Hosps. Newark; chmn. St. Benedict's Adv. Bd. Newark; exec. com. Archbishop's Com. of Laity, Newark. Served with U.S. Army, 1942-45. Recipient War Dept. citation. Fellow Am. Bar Found.; mem. Am., N.J., Essex County, Somerset County bar assns. Clubs: 200 of Essex and Somerset Counties, Met., Capitol Hill (Washington); Nat. Golf Links (Southampton); Roxiticus Golf (pres. 1967—) (Mendham, N.J.). Home: Bernardsville NJ 07924 Office: 550 Broad St Newark NJ 07102

SHANNAHAN, JOHN WILLIAM, state ofcl.; b. Cambridge, Mass., Oct. 2, 1940; s. John Percy and Edith (Gronblom) S.; B.S. in Bus. Adminstrn., Northeastern U., 1963; m. Suzanne Mucci, Oct. 16, 1965; children—Jonathan, Antonia. Spl. asst. Conn. Hist. Commn., Hartford, 1969-73, supt. hist. sites, 1973-74, commn. dir., 1974—, dir. Am. Revolution Bicentennial Commn. of Conn., 1974—, state hist. preservation officer, 1974—; founder, 1st pres. Tobacco Valley Regional Tourist Bur., Inc., 1973-75; adv. bd. State Hist. Records. Bd. dirs. East Granby (Conn.) Land Conservation Trust, 1975—, pres., 1977—; mem. Gov.'s Vacation Travel Council, 1977—. Served to capt. USAF, 1963-69. Decorated Air medal; recipient Outstanding Sr. award Phi Sigma Kappa, 1963. Mem. Am. Assn. State and Local History, Conn. Hist. Soc., Old State House Assn., East Granby Jaycees (1 of 12 Outstanding Jaycees for Conn. 1973, pres. 1973-74). Home: 105 Newgate Rd East Granby CT 06026 Office: 59 S Prospect St Hartford CT 06106

SHANNON, ELEANOR THELMA, govt. ofcl.; b. Honolulu, Oct. 20, 1927; d. Victor Manuel and Elizabeth Jo Ann (Medeiros) Pereira; diploma Margaret Dietz Comml. Coll., 1947; m. Adolphine Mendez, Jan. 8, 1951; children—Marleen Marie, Marccelle Ann, Rudy Ramon, Anita Dolores; m. 2d, Richard T. Shannon, Dec. 10, 1963; 1 son, Kevin Patrick. Dancer, 1943-65; salesperson Pyramid Properties, Hawaii, 1971-72; personnel mgmt. specialist Commerce Dept., 1972-74; equal opportunity specialist Fed. Women's Program, DOT, Washington, 1974-76; specialist personnel staffing Fed. Women's Program, IRS, Washington, 1976—. Personnel work various depts. U.S. govt., 1947-72. Active in support of Equal Rights Amendment; DOT rep. to Internat. Women's Year, 1975-76. Recipient numerous govt. commendations and awards. Mem. Women's Equity Action League (chmn. publicity Honolulu chpt), Federally Employed Women. Home: 412 Girard St Apt 304 Gaithersburg MD 20760 Office: 1111 Constitution Ave NW Washington DC 22024

SHANNON, JAMES MICHAEL, congressman; b. Methuen, Mass., Apr. 4, 1952; s. Martin Joseph and Mary Jane (Sullivan) S.; B.A., Johns Hopkins U., 1973; J.D., George Washington U., 1975; m. Silvia de Araujo Castro, Dec. 29, 1973. Admitted to Mass. bar, D.C. bar; practice law, 1976-78; mem. 96th Congress from 5th Dist. Mass. Trustee Johns Hopkins U., 1973-77. Mem. Mass. Bar Assn., D.C. Bar Assn. Democrat. Roman Catholic. Home: 142 E Haverhill St Lawrence MA 01841 Office: US House of Representatives Washington DC 20515

SHANNON, MARGARET RITA, educator; b. Cambridge, Mass., May 20, 1915; d. James J. and Catherine M. (McDonough) Shannon; B.S., Mass. State Coll., 1936; M.Ed., Harvard, 1947, Ed.D., 1959. Tchr. pub. schs., Cambridge, 1936-51; asst. prof. Mass. State Coll., 1951-59, asso. prof., 1959-65, prof., 1965—, chmn. dept. edn., 1969-74; dean Coll. Edn. U. Lowell (Mass.), 1974—. Mem. Am. Ednl. Research Assn., Internat. Reading Assn., Nat. Council Tchrs. English, Delta Kappa Gamma, Pi Lambda Theta (chpt. pres. 1958-61). Author textbooks. Contbr. articles to profl. jours. Home: 374 Park Ave Arlington MA 02174 Office: Coll of Education University of Lowell South Campus Lowell MA 01854

SHAPER, RUTH STAFFORD, health program evaluation cons.; b. Brasov, Romania, Jan. 2, 1925; d. James and Irma (Weigl) Stafford; student Smith Coll., 1941-42; B.S., Columbia U., 1946, M.A., 1947, postgrad, 1947-49; m. Daniel J. Shaper, Aug. 2, 1958; children—Alan James, Florence Daphne. Teaching asst. Columbia U., 1946-49; clin. psychologist dept. mental hygiene State of N.Y., Jamestown, 1955-56; psychometrician Profl. Examination Service, Am. Pub. Health Assn., N.Y.C., 1950-51, asst. dir., 1958-63, asso. dir., 1963-70; dir. Health Program Reporting System, Assn. State and Territorial Health Ofcls., Washington, 1970-73; pvt. practice health program evaluation consulting, Walpole, Maine, 1973—. Mem. Am. Pub. Health Assn., Am. Acad. Health Adminstrs. Home and Office: Ridge Rd Walpole ME 04573

SHAPIRO, A. GERALD, physician; b. Schenectady, Sept. 19, 1929; B.S., Union Coll., Schenectady, 1951; M.D., New York Med. Coll., 1956; married; 2 children. Rotating intern Ellis Hosp., Schenectady, 1956-57, asst. resident, 1957-58; chief resident Flower-Fifth Ave. Hosps., N.Y.C., 1958-59, asst. pulmonary disease, 1960-61, asst. anesthesiologist, 1959-63; practice medicine, specializing in anesthesiology and pulmonary care, N.Y.C.; asst. exec. dir. for med. affairs Knickerbocker Hosp., N.Y.C., 1970; asst. vis. anesthesiologist Met. Hosp., N.Y.C., 1960-63; attending in medicine, instr. med. edn. pulmonary care dept., dir. pulmonary care unit Sch. Inhalation Therapy Emphysema Clinic, Bergen Pines County Hosp., Paramus, N.J., 1967-70; med. dir. dept. inhalation therapy New York Polyclinic Med. Sch. and Hosp., 1968-70, lectr., asst. attending anesthesiologist, 1968—; cons. anesthesiology St. Barnabas Hosp., N.Y.C., 1963—; asst. attending anesthesiologist Bronx Eye and Ear Infirmary, 1963-72; asso. dir. Joint Commn. on Accreditation of Hosps., Chgo., 1973-75; attending anesthesiologist, dir. dept. anesthesiology and pulmonary care unit Arthur C. Logan Meml. Hosp., N.Y.C., 1963-75, chmn. med. staff, 1975, dir. anesthesiology, trustee, treas., 1978—; asst. attending in medicine, dir. respiratory therapy and pulmonary lab. Valley Hosp., Ridgewood, N.J., 1968-74; attending in respiratory therapy Fairlawn (N.J.) Meml. Hosp., 1971—; med. dir. Emerson Convalescent Center, 1975-76; surveyor Joint Rev. Com. on Respiratory Therapy Edn., 1969—; examiner Am. Registry Respiratory Therapists, 1966—; trustee Nat. Bd. Respiratory Therapy, 1976—; chmn. dept. anesthesiology, operating rooms, intensive care units Jersey City Med. Center, 1975-78, med. dir. respiratory therapy, acting med. dir. clin. services, 1976-77, attending in anesthesiology and respiratory care, 1978—; attending anesthesiologist, cons. pulmonary medicine Jewish Hosp. Rehab. Center N.J., Jersey City, 1977—; dir. med. edn. St. Charles Hosp., Mather Hosp., Port Jefferson, N.Y., 1978—; instr. dept. biology Union Coll., 1952; clin. instr. anesthesiology New York Med. Coll., 1959-63; prof., chmn. dept. respiratory therapy Alphonsus Coll., Woodcliff Lake, N.J., 1970-73; mem. advisory com. Sch. Respiratory Therapy, Bergen Community Coll., Paramus, N.J., 1972-74, Sch. Respiratory Therapy, Union (N.J.) Tech. Inst., 1975—; med. dir., adj. prof. respiratory therapy Sch. Respiratory Therapy, Hudson County Community Coll., 1975-77; clin. prof. anesthesiology Coll. Medicine Dentistry, Newark, 1977—; co-chmn., coordinator St. Barnabas Med.-Surg. Symposium, 1965, 67; chmn. Symposium on Cardiac and Respiratory Therapy, Polyclinic Hosp. and Med. Sch., N.Y.C., 1968; dir. Respiratory Seminar, New York Hosp. Cornell Med. Center, 1970; police surgeon Borough of Haworth, N.J., 1968—; cons. on pulmonary disease Nat. Inst. for Rehab. Engring., Pompton Lakes, N.J., 1969—. Diplomate Am. Bd. Anesthesiology. Fellow Am. Coll. Anesthesiologists, Am. Coll. Cardiology (asso.), Am. Coll. Chest Physicians, N.J. (chmn. sect. anesthesiology), N.Y. acads. medicine, Am. Coll. Sports Medicine; mem. AMA, N.Y. State, New York County med. socs., Am., N.J. (asso. editor Newsletter 1976—), N.Y. State (asso. editor Jour. Bull. 1967-71) socs. anesthesiologists, Am. Assn. for Respiratory Therapy (med. adviser N.J. chpt. 1968—, pres.'s award N.J. chpt. 1973, chpt. award 1976), Internat. Anesthesia Research Soc., Soc. Med. Jurisprudence, AAAS, New York, Bergen

County (N.J.) heart assns., Am. Thoracic Soc., Soc. Critical Care Medicine, Sommlier Soc., Am. Inst. Parliamentarians, Delphic Soc., Cor et Manus, La Chaine Des Rotisseurs (chevalier). Co-editor: Rheumatic and Coronary Heart Disease, 1967; Therapeutic Advances in the Practice of Cardiology, 1970. Contbr. articles to med. jours. Home: 585 Beech St Haworth NJ 07641 Office: St Charles Hospital Port Jefferson NY

SHAPIRO, ABRAHAM, chiropractor; b. N.Y.C., Jan. 29, 1922; s. William and Pearl S.; student N.Y. U., 1939-40; Dr. Chiropractic, Columbia Inst. Chiropractic, 1947, Dr. Chiropractic Philosophy, 1952; m. Dorothy Gromet, Mar. 28, 1948; children—Sherry Lynn, Barry David. Instr., Columbia Inst. Chiropractice, 1948-54, dean, 1955-59; asst. dir. chiropractic div. Medicaid, N.Y.C. Health Dept., 1975-76, dir. chiropractice div. Medicaid, 1976—. Served with M.C., U.S. Army, 1942-46; PTO. Fellow Am. Coll. Chiropractic; mem. Am., N.Y. State, Fla. chiropractic assns., Am. Pub. Health Assn., N.Y. Acad. Scis. Office: 220 Cortelyou Rd Brooklyn NY 11218

SHAPIRO, E. DONALD, lawyer, ednl. adminstr.; b. York, Pa., Nov. 1, 1931; s. Samuel Milton and Sarah (Levetan) S.; student Sorbonne, Paris, France, 1952; A.B. summa cum laude, Dickinson Coll., 1953, LL.D. (hon.), 1975; J.D., Harvard, 1956; LL.D., N.Y. U., 1973; m. Merle Judith Mandell, Aug. 12, 1956; children—Felicia, Rachel, Carol, Richard. Publicity dir. Cape Cod (Mass.) Melody Tent, 1954-55; drama critic sta. WSBA-TV, York, 1955; admitted to Pa. bar, 1957, D.C. bar, 1957, Mich. bar, 1967; with firm Freedman, Landy & Lorry, Phila., 1956-57; instr. Boston U. Law Sch., 1957-59; prof. law Detroit Coll. Law, 1959-60; dir. Inst. Continuing Legal Edn., U. Mich. Law Sch.-Wayne State U. Law Sch., also mem. faculty U. Mich. Law Sch., 1960-68; asso. dean state-wide edn. for continuing legal edn. U. Mich., 1965-68; lectr. U. Mich. Sch. Social Work, 1961-66, prof. social welfare law, 1966-68; adj. prof. law N.Y. U. Sch. Law, 1968-74, adj. prof. legal medicine Sch. Medicine, 1974—; dean and prof. law N.Y. Law Sch., 1973—; dean, 1973—; adj. prof. social work Sch. Social Work, Fordham U., 1968-73; vis. prof. Anglo-Am. Studies Inst. U. Padua, 1970—; fellow Inst. Jud. Adminstrn., N.Y.C., 1969—; dir. Practicing Law Inst., 1968-71; chmn. bd. Struthers Sci. & Internat., Inc., 1971-72; pres. ABC Industries, 1971-72, vice chmn. bd. editors N.Y. Law Jour., 1972—; gen. partner Andresen & Co., 1972-73. Cons. continuing legal edn. com. Nat. Jr. Bar Conf., 1960-62; cons., joint com. on continuing legal edn. Am. Law Inst. and Am. Bar Assn., 1962-64; chmn. com. on continuing legal edn. Am. Law Inst. and Am. Bar Assn., 1962-64; chmn. com. on continuing legal edn. Am. Assn. Law Schs., 1966-68; dir. tng. Juvenile Court Hearing Officer Tng. Project, 1963-65; project dir. Tng. Ct. Officers, 1964-65; cons. Practicing Law Inst., 1960-67, Jud. Conf. Mich. 1962-67, Am. Trial Lawyers Assn., 1965-67; adv. com. Fed. Jud. Center, 1968-70, co-chmn. jud. edn. subcom., 1968-70. Mem. nat. planning com. 2d World Meeting on Med. Law, Washington, 1970—; dir. tng. USAID-Central Bank Brazil Capital Markets Program, 1969-70. Trustee Dickinson Coll., Milton Helpern Library Legal Medicine, N.Y.C., Nat. Center for Automated Info. Retrieval, N.Y.C., 1969—. Practicing Law Inst. Found., 1969-72, exec. v.p. 1970-71, N.Y. U. Law Sch.; trustee, nat. bd. dirs. Odyssey House, N.Y.C. Recipient United States Nat. Extemporaneous Speaking award, 1952; nat. achievement award Phi Epsilon Pi, 1967. Hon. fellow Am. Coll. Legal Medicine; mem. Am. Law Inst., Practicing Law Inst. (trustee, 1968-72), Bar Assn. City N.Y., Am. Bar Assn., AAUP, Harvard Law Assn. Mich., State Bar Assn. Mich. (com. on criminal code revision 1964—), Fed. Bar Council, NAACP (life), Phi Beta Kappa, Omicron Delta Kappa, Tau Kappa Alpha, Phi Epsilon Pi (Nat. Undergrad. of Year award, 1953, Nat. Achievement award 1967). Jewish religion. Clubs: Lawyers (bd. govs. 1971—), Harvard (N.Y.C.). Editor: Michigan Basic Practice Series, 1960, 3d edit., 1965. Co-editor: Mich. Basic Practice Handbooks, 8 vols., 1962-67; Mich. Splty. Handbook Series, 25 vols., 1962-67; Mich. Course Handbooks, 30 vols., 1961-67; Personal Injury Library, 6 vols., 1965-67; various other legal publs. Home: 1 Princeton Terr Short Hills NJ 07078 Office: 57 Worth St New York City NY 10013

SHAPIRO, GEORGE M., lawyer; b. N.Y.C., Dec. 7, 1919; s. Samuel N. and Sarah (Milstein) S.; B.S. cum laude, L.I. U., 1939; LL.B. (Kent scholar), Columbia, 1942; m. Rita V. Lubin, Mar. 29, 1942; children—Karen, Sanford. Admitted to N.Y. bar, 1942; mem. staff gov. N.Y., 1945-51; counsel to gov. N.Y., 1951-54; partner firm Proskauer Rose Goetz & Mendelsohn, 1955—; pres. Edmond de Rothschild Found., 1964—; dir. Bank of Calif.; counsel, majority leader N.Y. Senate, 1955-59; Counsel N.Y. Constl. Revision Commn., 1960-61. Mem. Gov.'s Com. Reapportionment, 1964, Mayor's Com. Jud. Selection, 1966-69. Chmn. council State U. Coll. Medicine, 1955-71; chmn. Park Avenue Synagogue, 1973—. Served with USAAF, 1943-45. Recipient Alumnus of Year award L.I. U., 1954; medal Port of N.Y. Authority, 1973; Learned Hand award Am. Jewish Com., 1976. Mem. Council on Fgn. Relations. Clubs: Harmonie, Metropolis. Home: 1160 Park Ave New York City NY 10028 Office: 300 Park Ave New York City NY 10022

SHAPIRO, IRVING SAUL, chem. co. exec.; b. Mpls., July 15, 1916; s. Sam I. and Freda (Lane) S.; B.S., U. Minn., 1939, LL.B., 1941; m. Charlotte Farsht, Mar. 1, 1942; children—Stuart Lane, Elizabeth Irene. Admitted to Minn. bar, 1941, Del. bar, 1958; atty. criminal div. Dept. Justice, 1943-51; with E.I. du Pont de Nemours & Co., Inc., 1951—, v.p., 1970-73, vice chmn. bd., 1973, chmn., chief exec. officer, 1974—; also dir., chmn. exec. com., chmn. pub. affairs com.; dir. Bank of Del., Citicorp., CitiBank, IBM, Continental Am. Ins. Co. Mem. Adv. Council on Japan-U.S. Econ. Relations, U.S.-USSR Trade and Econ. Council, Bus. Council, Bus. Roundtable. Bd. dirs. Greater Wilmington Devel. Council; trustee Ford Found. Urban Inst., Conference Bd., U. Del. Mem. Nat. Center for State Cts. (bus. and profl. friends com.). Clubs: Wilmington; Bidermann Country; Greenville Country; Alfalfa. Office: 9000 du Pont Bldg Wilmington DE 19898

SHAPIRO, JOHN MARTIN, exec.; b. Cambridge, Mass., Apr. 9, 1940; s. George Israel and Lucille (Gorin) S.; A.B. cum laude, Harvard, 1962; M.B.A., Stanford, 1965; m. Luana Lee Burke, June 29, 1965; children—Kurt, Krista, Kier. Coordinator, Office Civil Def., San Mateo County, Calif., 1963; cons. Gardiner Shoe Co., Inc., Lewiston, Maine, 1968-69, exec. v.p., 1969-70, pres., chmn. bd., chief exec. officer, 1970-75; gen. mgr. Barker-Chadsey Co., Johnson, R.I., 1975—. Served to lt. USAF, 1965-68. Mem. AIM (pres.'s council), Stanford Bus. Sch. Assn. Clubs: 100 of R.I., Harvard of R.I., Cobbosseecontee Yacht (sec.-treas.). Home: Highland Dr Jamestown RI 02835 Office: 27 Mill St Johnston RI 02919

SHAPIRO, MANHEIM SIMEON, sociologist; b. Bklyn., Sept. 5, 1913; s. Solomon M. and Bella (Yanowitz) S.; B.A., Bklyn. Coll., 1934; student U. Mich., 1943-45, New Sch. for Social Research, 1950-56; m. Esther Merlin Binder, Mar. 21, 1935 (dec. Jan. 1968); 1 son, Ezra Shapiro; m. 2d, Gloria L. Gaston, June 3, 1977. Tchr., Benjamin Franklin High Sch., N.Y.C., 1935-38; social worker Welfare Dept., N.Y.C., 1938-43; dir. program and publs. B'nai B'rith Youth Orgn., Washington, 1946-49; dir. Jewish Communal Affairs Dept., Am. Jewish Com., N.Y.C., 1949-66; exec. dir. Bur. for Careers in Jewish Service, 1968-69; adj. prof. Coll. City N.Y., 1972; cons.-dir. Insight Devel. Services, 1969—. Cons. Nat. Jewish Welfare Bd., 1966-69, 71, Nat. Council of Jewish Women, 1966-67, U.S. State Dept., 1949, Council Jewish Fedns. and Welfare Funds, 1965-69, 71, Stanlinco, Ltd., 1969—, Riegel Paper Corp., 1969-70, B'nai B'rith, 1970. Conf. leader Kells Dental Research Group, 1969-70, Soc. Oral Physiology and Occlusion, 1970, 1st Dist. Dental Soc. N.Y., 1970, Chgo. Dental Soc., 1971, Am. Acad. Occlusodontia, 1971, So. New Eng. Practice Acad., 1972, Phila. Dental Study Group, 1972. Served with AUS, 1943-46. Fellow Am. Sociol. Assn.; mem. Nat. Assn. Social Workers, Nat. Assn. Intergroup Relations Ofcls., Soc. for Sci. Study of Religion, Nat. Conf. Jewish Communal Service, Assn. Jewish Community Relations Workers, Acad. Certified Social Workers, Nat. Assn. Jewish Center Workers, Adult Edn. Assn., Am. Soc. Tng. and Devel., Soc. Profl. Mgmt. Cons. Contbr. numerous articles in field to profl. jours. Home: 5 Ridgeview Ave West Orange NJ 07052

SHAPIRO, MILTON STANLEY, lawyer; b. N.Y.C., May 9, 1922; s. Philip and Lena (Cohen) S.; B.A., Bklyn. Coll., 1942; LL.B. cum laude, N.Y. U., 1948; m. Beatrice Leibowitz, June 9, 1946; children—Susan Shapiro Levkoff, Philip J. Admitted to N.Y. bar, 1948, U.S. Supreme Ct. bar, 1961; asso. firm Bernheimer & Zucker, N.Y.C., 1948-55; individual practice law, N.Y.C., 1955-65; partner firm Zucker, Weiden & Shapiro, N.Y.C., 1965-73, Shapiro, Weiden & Mortman, 1973-75, Kun, Shapiro, Goldman, Cooperman & Levitt, N.Y.C., 1975-78, Shapiro, Mortman & Schwartz, 1978—; dir. Chelsea Town Co., Nutrient Ltd., Petrocelli Clothes, Inc., Mayflower Studios, Ltd., Amanuensis Ltd., Eagle Shirt Co., Ohio Match Co., others. Pres., Nirvana Gardens Civic Assn., Great Neck, N.Y., 1962-65; vice chmn. 29th-30th St Community Council, 1964—; bd. dirs. Vocal Arts Found., N.Y.C. Served with USAAF, 1942-45. Ky. col. Mem. Assn. Bar City N.Y., Am. Bar Assn., Smithsonian Assos., ACLU. Jewish. Clubs: K.P.; Muttowntown Golf and Country (East Norwich, N.Y.); Banyan Golf (Palm Beach, Fla.). Mem. law rev. N.Y. U., 1947-48. Home: 2 N Clover Dr Great Neck NY 11021 Office: 800 3d Ave New York City NY 10022

SHAPIRO, MORRIS ARNOLD, physician; b. Glens Falls, N.Y., Aug. 13, 1909; s. David and Dora (Schulberg) S.; A.B., Union Coll., 1932; M.D., Albany Med. Coll., 1936; postgrad. Mt. Sinai Hosp., 1939-40, Mass. Gen. Hosp., 1946; m. Hester M. Blatt, Dec. 21, 1941; children—Susan, William A. Intern, Ellis Hosp., Schenectady, 1936-37, resident, 1937-40, attending physician medicine, attending cardiologist, chief staff, 1963-65; practice medicine specializing in cardiology, Schenectady, 1947—; attending physician medicine, cardiologist St. Clare's Hosp., Schenectady, chief staff, 1965-67, now chief cardiology; cons. cardiology Northeastern Orthopedic Hosp., chenectady Hosp., Schenectady, 1951—, Community Hosp., Cobleskill, N.Y., 1956—, Daus. of Sarah Jewish Home, Troy, N.Y., 1958—; asso. medicine Albany Med. Coll., 1948-65, clin. instr., 1965—; mem. N.Y. State Com. on Cardiovascular Diseases. Chmn. Schenectady Heart Fund dr., 1958-62; bd. dirs. Schenectady Mus., Schenectady Recreational Adv. Commn. Served to maj. M.C., AUS, 1941-46. Decorated Silver Star with oak leaf cluster, Purple Heart. Diplomate Am. Bd. Internal Medicine. Fellow Am. Coll. Cardiology (gov. Upstate N.Y. 1964-67), A.C.P., Am. Coll. Chest Physicians (pres. N.Y. State chpt.), Am. Soc. Internal Medicine; mem. Schenectady Med. Soc. (pres. 1964), Med. Soc. State N.Y. (chmn. sect. on chest diseases), Schenectady Health Assn. (dir.). Club: Shaker Ridge Country. Contbr. articles to profl. jours. Home: 2009 Lexington Pkwy Schenectady NY 12309 Office: 1603 Union St Schenectady NY 12309

SHAPIRO, PHYLLIS (MRS. ABRAHAM SHAPIRO), hotel adminstr.; b. Montreal, Que., Can., Mar. 12, 1922; d. Isadore and Sadie (Novack) Hochmitz; student Sullivan Bus. Coll., Montreal, 1939-41; m. Abraham Shapiro, Aug. 22, 1961. Asst. mgr. Nat. Food Store Ltd., Montreal, 1942-45; office comptroller Dixon Watch Importing Co., 1945-48, adminstr. Bernard Schaeffer & Sons, importing agy., 1948-51; exec. sec. William Rosenberg, architect, 1951-57; exec. sec. Eugene Meth Assos., Financier, 1957-61; adminstr., conv. mgr. Twin City Motel, Brewer, Maine, 1968—; pres. The Carriage Inn, Pittsfield, Maine, 1979—. Jewish. Clubs: B'nai B'rith, Hadassah. Home: 58 Broadway Bangor ME 04401 Office: 453 Wilson St Brewer ME 04412

SHAPIRO, ROBYN DEBRA, psychotherapist; b. Bklyn., Jan. 15, 1953; d. Arnold Morton and Beatrice S.; B.A. cum laude, Bklyn. Coll., 1974; M.S., C.W. Post Coll., 1975; m. Steven E. Meierfeld, Dec. 11, 1976. Psychotherapist, L.I. Family Consultation Center, Roslyn, 1975-76, Para-Med. Thermo Labs. Inc. breast cancer detection, Bklyn., 1975-76; cons. death and bereavement counseling N.Y.C. Ombudsman's Office, 1976-77; pvt. practice psychotherapy, N.Y.C., since 19—; creator course, lectr. death and bereavement Marymount Manhattan Coll., N.Y.C., 1976—; creator workshops. Mem. Am. Personnel and Guidance Assn., C.W. Post Mental Health Workers Assn., Am. Coll. Personnel Assn., South Nassau Community Hosp. Thanatology Soc. Office: 221 71st St E New York NY 10021

SHAPIRO, SOLOMON BERNARD, clergyman; b. Rumania, Mar. 29, 1922; s. Mordecai and Molly (Rabinowitz) S.; grad. Mesivta Talmudaical Sem., 1943; B.A., Bklyn. Coll., 1943; D.D., Phila. Coll., 1962; m. Mildred Sodden, June 11, 1946; children—Mordecai, Brocha, Miriam, Mala. Rabbi, 1943; June 11, 1946; children—Mordecai, Brocha, Miriam, Mala. Rabbi, 1943; prin. Beth Rivkah Sch. for Girls, 1943-45; exec. dir. Mesifta Rabbi Chaim Berlin, 1946-48; rabbi Congl. Anshei Ozaritz, Bklyn., 1945-47; rabbi B'nai Abraham of East Flatbush, 1947—, Degal Mordecai of Bklyn., 1947—; rabbi and chaplain Kingsbrook Jewish Med. Center, 1944—; chaplain Kings County Hosp. Center, 1950—; religious adviser Downstate Med. U. Chmn. Rabbinical Bd. of East Flatbush, Rabbinical Alliance of Am., 1957-59; mem. bd. of trustees Union of Orthodox Rabbis, U.S. and Canada; mem. exec. bd. Rabbincal Council of Am.; mem. Rabbinical Bd. of Greater N.Y.; pres. Rabbinical Alumni Mesivta Torah Vodaath; chmn. bd. dirs. Rugby-East Flatbush United Jewish Community Council. Bd. dirs. Bklyn. Assn. for Mental Health, Bklyn. Jewish Community Council. Mem. Free Sons of Israel, Mizrachi Orgn. Am., Nonparil Social Club, Am. Correctional Assn., Am. Sociol. Assn., Acad. Religion and Mental Health. Author articles in field. Home: 831 Linden Blvd Brooklyn NY 11203 Office: 407 E 53d St Brooklyn NY 11203

SHAPIRO, STEPHEN DANIEL, elec. engr., educator; b. N.Y.C., Feb. 18, 1941; s. Harold S. and Dorothy (Medoff) S.; B.S., Columbia U. Sch. Engring. and Applied Sci., 1963, M.S., 1964, Ph.D. (NDEA fellow), 1967; m. Terry Colen, Oct. 12, 1969; 1 son, Aaron. Mem. tech. staff Bell Telephone Labs., N.J., 1967-71; cons. on computers, communications and mktg. to indsl. firms, 1971—; asso. prof. dept. elec. engring. Stevens Inst. Tech., Hoboken, N.J., 1974-78, prof., 1978—; mem. Egleston Associates, Columbia U. Sch. Engring. and Applied Sci., 1976—; cons. dir. computer sci. edn. program for high level tech. staff Bell Telephone Labs., 1976—. Bd. dirs. Riverdale YM-YWHA, 1972—. NSF research grantee, 1976—. Mem. IEEE (sr.), IEEE Computer Soc. (machine intelligence and pattern analysis tech. com., exec. com. 1969—, co-editor newsletter 1975—, vice chmn. tech. interest council software and applications 1978—), Assn. for Computing Machinery, Sigma Xi. Contbr. numerous articles on software aspects of computer sci. to tech. jours. Office: Dept of Elec Engineering Stevens Inst of Technology Hoboken NJ 07030

SHAPIRO, SUSAN HOLLY, interior designer; b. Bklyn., Aug. 27, 1943; s. Murray and Roslyn (Benjamin) Chalkin; B.A., Syracuse U., 1964; M.Ed., N.Y. U., 1965; postgrad. fine arts Harvard U., 1962; m. Leon Shapiro, Dec. 3, 1969; 1 son, Christopher Morrow. Pres., Trio Designs Inc., Huntington and Roslyn, N.Y., 1975—, Apricot Designs Inc., Huntington; nat. field sec. Alpha Epsilon Phi, Pttis., 1964-65; tchr. pub. schs., N.Y.C., 1965-67; designer Bagatelle Assos., N.Y.C., 1971-73, Wallpaper Place Unltd., Roslyn, N.Y., 1974-75. Vice pres. fundraising Roslyn Hadassah, 1976, League Women Voters, Roslyn. 1975; adv. budget dir. Roslyn Pub. Schs., 1974; v.p. Norgate Civic Assn., 1974. Named Woman of Year, Hadassah, 1975. Mem. Assn. Environ. Designers, Allied Bd. Trade. Home: 40 Wickham Rd East Hills NY 11577 Office: 345 Main St Huntington NY 11743 also 20 Lumber Rd Roslyn NY 11576

SHARBAUGH, AMANDUS HARRY, elec. co. exec.; b. Richmond, Va., Mar. 28, 1919; s. Amandus Harry and Jacqueline (Harrison) S.; A.B., Case Western Res. U., 1940; Ph.D., Brown U., 1943; postdoctoral Union U., 1945-55; m. Doris Eitle, Sept. 23, 1940; children—Amandus Harry, Durell Dean. With Gen. Electric Co., Schenectady, 1942—, mgr. plasma physics br., 1973—. Mem. IEEE, Nat. Acad. Scis. Conf. Dielectric Phenomena. Democrat. Methodist. Contbr. numerous articles in field to profl. jours. Patentee in field (6). Holder world record for high frequency radio communication. Mem. Phi Beta Kappa, Sigma Xi. Home: 28 Hemlock Dr Clifton Park NY 12065 Office: 1 River Rd Schenectady NY 12345

SHARE, ROBERT WILLIAM, mfg. co. exec.; b. Columbus, Ohio, May 8, 1920; s. Marshall Irving and Edna May (Strader) S.; student Auburn Community Coll., 1965, Cornell U., 1969; m. Ellen Elaine Ely, Jan. 13, 1946; children—Stephanie (Mrs. Thomas John Conger), Robyn (Mrs. Dominick Puzo). With SCM Corp., N.Y.C., Toronto, Orangeburg, S.C., Singapore, Groton and Cortland, N.Y., 1939—, dir. Smith Corona group mfg. resources, 1973—. Mem. mech. tech. adv. com. Tompkins-Cortland Community Coll., Groton, 1972-75. Mem. exec. bd. Boy Scout council, Cortland County, N.Y., 1971-73, v.p., 1973; mem. exec. bd. Cortland County United Fund, 1971-73; mem. Cortland County Planning Bd., 1971-73. Trustee Groton Village Bd., 1964-68. Served with USAAF, 1941-45. Mem. Am. Mgmt. Assn., Am. Legion, VFW. Rotarian. Home: 7 Colony Dr Cortland NY 13045 Office: Route 13 South Cortland NY 13045

SHARIFY, NASSER, librarian, educator, author; b. Tehran, Iran, Sept. 23, 1925; s. Ebrahim and Eshrat (Saghafy) S.; came to U.S. 1963, naturalized, 1972; Licencié es Lettres, U. Tehran, 1947; M.S., Columbia U., 1954, Dr. L.S., 1958; m. Homayoun Taslimy, June 14, 1950 (div. 1978); children—Sharareh, Shahab. Translator, announcer All India Radio, 1948-49, librarian, dep. dir. Library of Parliament of Iran, Tehran, 1949-53; cataloger Library of Congress, 1954-55; program asst. libraries devel. sect. UNESCO, Paris, 1959-61, acting chief servicing sect. Dept. Edn., 1962-63; dir. gen. Ministry Edn., Tehran, 1961-62; asst. prof. library and info. scis. and internat. edn. U. Pitts., 1963-66, founder, dir. Internat. Library Info. Center, 1964-66; vis. lectr. Sch. Library Sci., State U. N.Y., Albany, summer 1966; dir. internat. librarianship and documentation internat. studies and world affairs State U. N.Y. at Oyster Bay, 1966-68; dean, prof. Grad. Sch. Library and Info. Sci., Pratt Inst., Bklyn., 1968—, chmn. Research Council, 1971—; dir. Grad. Library Tng. Program, UNESCO Mission, Nat. Tchrs. Coll., Tehran, 1960, cons. campus planning, 1972-73; Iran's ofcl. del. to UNESCO Conf. Ednl. Pubs., Geneva, 1961, S.E. Asia Edn. Secs. Conf., Murree, Pakistan, 1961, Internation Conf. on Cataloging Prins., Paris, 1961, CENTO Library Devel. Conf., Ankara, Turkey, 1962; chmn. standing com. for preparation of reading materials for new literates UNESCO, Tehran, 1961-62; dir. Conf. on Internat. Responsibility Coll. and Univ. Librarians, Oyster Bay, N.Y., 1967; U.S. del. to 33d Conf. and Internat. Congress on Documentation, Tokyo, 1967; ALA del. UN Conf. Non-Govtl. Orgns., 1969; lectr. Inst. Internationalism in Curriculum of Library Edn., Sch. Library Sci., U. Okla., 1969; cons. U.S. AID, Conf. on Book Devel., 1967; mem. advisory bd. Ency. Library and Info. Scis., 1969—; chmn. Pre-Am. Library Assn. Conf. Inst. Orgn. Internat. Library Manpower, Edn. and Placement in N.Am., Detroit, 1970; trustee Bklyn. Pub. Library, 1970—; chmn. bd. cons. Pahlavi Nat. Library of Iran, 1975—; bldg. cons. Learning Resources Center, Tchrs. Tng. Coll., Iran, 1972-73; chmn. bd. cons. for campus planning Nat. U. Iran, 1973-74; UNESCO cons. to Morocco for Nat. Sch. Info. Sci., 1973-74. Mem. Am. (chmn. com. equivalencies and reciprocity 1965-71, mem. UNESCO panel 1966-70, mem. com. on internat. library sch. 1968-71, nominating com. 1972, com. on internat. library edn. 1972—, chmn. Pakistan and Middle East Resource panels), N.Y. (dir. library edn. sect. 1969-72) library assns., Internat. Fedn. Library Assns. (advisory group com. on library edn., v.p. library schs. sect. 1973—), Am. Assn. Library Schs., Am. Soc. Info. Scientists, Spl. Librarian Assn., Assn. des Bibliothecaire Français. Author: Cataloging of Persian Works, Including Rules for Transliteration Entry and Description, 1959; Book Production, Importation and Distribution in Iran, Pakistan and Turkey, 1966; The Pahlavi National Library of the Future, 1976. Contbr. to Ency. of Library and Info. Sci., 1969, also to profl. publs. Former co-editor jours., Teheran, Iran. Home: PO Box 287 East Norwich NY 11732 Office: 215 Ryerson St Brooklyn NY 11205

SHARMAN, RICHARD LEE, bus. machines co. exec.; b. Warren, Pa., Oct. 23, 1932; s. Scott Albert and Viola (Kittner) S.; B.S., U. Toledo, 1959; M.S., Cornell U., 1961; m. Diane Van Patten, Nov. 3, 1973; 1 child, Daria Lee; children from previous marriage—Suzanne Annette, Cynthia Lee. With Gen. Electric Co., Ithaca and Syracuse, N.Y., 1959-68, program mgr., 1965-66, mgr. infrared instrumentation, 1966-67, mgr. optical and infrared techs. 1967-68; dir. tech. ops. Librascope Optical Tech. Center, Rockville, Md., 1968-69; mgr. industry mktg. info. service dept. Gen. Electric Co., 1969-70, mgr. data communications terminals, 1970-71, market mgr. info. network Info. Services Bus. Div., 1971-73; mgr. comml. analysis Xerox Corp., Rochester, N.Y., 1973-76, product planning mgr., 1976—; teaching asst. Toledo U., 1958-59. Served with USCG, 1951-54. Mem. Optical Soc. Am., IEEE, Cornell Engrs. Soc., Tau Beta Pi, Pi Kappa Phi. Republican. Episcopalian. Home: 3 Mile Post Ln Pittsford NY 14534 Office: Xerox Sq Rochester NY 14644

SHARON, JOHN HURFORD, lawyer; b. Oakland, Calif., Mar. 5, 1927; s. Hurford C. and Evelyn (Reyland) S.; A.B., Princeton U., 1949; J.D., George Washington U., 1958; m. Frances Virgin, June 29, 1968; children—Lisa, Laura, John Hurford, Barclay, William (dec.), Edward. Admitted to D.C. bar, 1959; legis. asst. U.S. Ho. of Reps., Washington, 1949-51; spl. asst. to Under Sec. of Army, Washington, 1951-52; law clk. firm Cleary, Gottlieb, Steen & Hamilton, Washington, 1953-55, 56-58, asso., 1958-61; adminstrv. asst. Hon. Adlai Stevenson, Chgo., 1955-56; partner firm Clifford & Miller, Washington, 1961-68, Sharon, Glass, McIlwaine & Finney, Washington, 1968-69, Sharon, Pierson, Semmes, Crolius & Finley, Washington, 1969-76; counsel firm Shaw, Pittman, Potts & Trowbridge, Washington, 1977—; chmn. bd. Ad-Wear, Inc., 1977—. Pres., Rollingwood Citizens Assn., 1950-52; spl. advisor Pres. John F. Kennedy, 1960-63, Pres. Lyndon B. Johnson, 1964-65; vestryman, warden All Souls Meml. Episcopal Ch., Washington, 1954-74; licensed lay reader Epsicopal Ch., Diocese of Washington, 1960—; convenor Convocation III, 1966-68; bd. dirs. Children's Hosp. Nat.

Med. Center, 1966—, v.p., 1971-74, pres., chmn. bd. dirs., 1974—. Named Man of Yr., Cosmopolitan Club of Washington, 1976; recipient Distinguished Community Service award Princeton Club of Washington, 1976. Mem. Fed., Am., D.C. bar assns., Am. Hosp. Assn., Am. Judicature Soc., Princeton Alumni Council. Democrat. Clubs: Princeton (bd. dirs. 1960-64), Met., Chevy Chase. Home: 45 W Lenox St Chevy Chase MD 20015 Office: 1800 M St NW Washington DC 20036

SHARP, DANIEL ASHER, lawyer, corporate exec.; b. San Francisco, Mar. 29, 1932; s. Joseph C. and Miriam (Asher) S.; B.A., U. Calif. at Berkeley, 1954; J.D., Harvard, 1959; m. Jacqueline Borda, Feb. 24, 1967 (div. Feb. 1975); 1 son, Benjamin Daniel. Admitted to Calif. bar, 1959; dep. atty. gen. State of Calif., San Francisco, 1959-61; asst. dir. div. internat. programs U.S. Peace Corps, Washington, 1961-62, asso. dir., Cuzco, Peru, 1962-64, acting dir., La Paz, Bolivia, 1964, creator, dir. Staff Tng. Center, Washington, 1965-68, dir. div. edn. resources, 1966; dir. edn. and Latin Am. programs and asst. dir. Adlai Stevenson Inst., U. Chgo., 1968-70; dir. tng. IT&T, Latin Am., 1970-72, mgr. mgmt. devel. corporate hdqrs., N.Y.C., 1973; dir. human resources devel. Xerox Latin Am. Group, 1973-75, chmn. overhead value analysis, 1975-76, dir. ops. support, 1976-77, dir. Inter-Am. affairs, 1977—; cons. Dept. State, fgn. govts., pvt. corps.; mem. U.S. del. to UN Econ. and Social Council, Geneva, 1961; U.S. rep. Internat. Conf. on Vol. Programs, The Hague, Netherlands, 1961; chmn. advisory bd. Council of Americas. Trustee Latin Am. Scholarship Program of Am. Univs., 1971-74; trustee, vice chmn. bd. dirs. African Student Aid Fund; bd. dirs. Fund for Multinat. Mgmt. Edn.; adv. council Partners of Americas. Served with AUS, 1954-55; capt. Res. Recipient Medalla de Oro y Diploma de Honor del Concejo Provincial del Cuzco, 1963. Mem. State Bar Calif., San Francisco Bar Assn., Council on Fgn. Relations of N.Y.C., Chgo. Council Fgn. Relations (trustee 1969), Pickwick Soc. (dir.). Club: Harvard (N.Y.C.). Editor: United States Foreign Policy and Peru, 1972. Home: 50 Glenbrook Rd Stamford CT 06902 Office: Xerox Latin Am Group 3 Pickwick Plaza Greenwich CT 06830

SHARP, HENRY FRANKLIN, investments co. exec.; b. York, Pa., June 21, 1919; s. Charles Claude and Elsie May (Reel) S.; student Inst. Drugless Therapy, 1953; D.A., Okla. Coll. Audiometry, 1955; m. Doris Ethel Klinger, Oct. 4, 1941; 1 son, Henry Franklin. Entertainer clubs and theatres, 1938-41; sales service mgr., personnel mgr. Ga. Pacific Corp., Reading, Pa., 1945-61; zone mgr. I.D.S. Corp., Pa., 1961-63; divisional mgr. Channing Corp., Reading, 1963-69; div. mgr. CNA Investors, Pa., 1969-70; pres., chmn. bd. Century Investments, Inc., Camp Hill, Pa., 1970—; dir. ins. plans and services Consumers Life Ins. Co., Camp Hill; mem. ednl. council Lincoln Coll. Naturopathic Physicians Surgeons. Certified fin. planner. Mem. Nat. Assn. Securities Dealers, Assn. Fin. Planners, Am. Writers Assn., Nat. Assn. Personnel Mgrs. Mormon. Author articles on sales techniques and personnel mgmt. Home: 104 Greenwood Dr Temple PA 19560 Office: 1004 Fernwood Dr Camp Hill PA 17011

SHARP, J(AMES) FRANKLIN, bus. exec.; b. Johnson County, Ill., Sept. 29, 1938; s. James Albert and Edna Mae (Slack) S.; student So. Ill. U., 1954-56; B.S., U. Ill., 1959; M.S., Purdue U., 1961, Ph.D., 1966. Asst. prof. engring. and econs. Rutgers U., New Brunswick, N.J., 1964-67; asst. prof. bus. N.Y. U. Grad. Sch. Bus., 1967-71, asso. prof., 1971-74; supr. bus. research Am. Tel. & Tel., 1974-77, supr. corporate planning, 1977—; prof. fin. and accounting Grad. Sch. Bus. Pace U., 1975—; speaker, moderator meetings; cons. sharp math. models. Mem. N.Am. Soc. for Corporate Planning (treas. 1976-77, chpt. dir. 1975—, dir. at large 1977-78), Inst. Mgmt. Sci. (chpt. v.p.-acad. 1973-74, chpt. v.p.-program 1974-75, chpt. v.p. membership 1975-76, chpt. pres. 1976-77), Ops. Research Soc. Am. (pres. corporate planning group 1976—), Theta Xi. Republican. Fin. editor Planning Rev., 1975-78; corr. Interfaces, 1975-78. Contbr. articles to numerous publs. Home: 315 E 86th St New York City NY 10028

SHARP, MARTIN WILLIAM, JR., educator; b. Vineland, N.J., July 12, 1941; s. Martin William and Catherine (Casazza) S.; B.A., Glassboro State Coll., 1963, M.A., 1966; D.Ed., Pa. State U., 1973. Tchr., Oakcrest High Sch., 1963-68; instr. Am. history Glassboro State Coll., 1966-68; instr. Pa. State U., 1969-72, asst. prof. edn., asso. mem. Grad. Sch., 1973—. Cons. N.J. Dept. Edn.; mem. vis. com. Middle States Assn., 1966—. Adviser, Boy Scouts Am., 1973; mem. Delaware County Intermediate Bd., 1973—. Named Outstanding Young Educator of N.J., N.J. Jr. C. of C., 1966. NDEA grantee, 1966; Ford Found. grantee, 1973; scholar, diplomat grantee Dept. State, 1976. Mem. NEA, Am. Hist. Assn., Nat. Council Social Studies, Assn. Student Teaching, Am. Assn. Higher Edn., Assn. Supervision and Curriculum Devel., Phi Delta Kappa. Co-author: Teaching-Content and Discontent, 1970. Office: 25 Yearsley Mill Rd Media PA 19063

SHARP, MITCHELL WILLIAM, Canadian govt. ofcl.; b. Winnipeg, Man., Can., May 11, 1911; s. Thomas and Elizabeth (Little) S.; B.A., U. Man., 1934; postgrad. London Sch. Econs., 1937-38; LL.D., U. Man., 1965; D.Sc.Soc., U. Ottawa, 1970; LL.D., U. Western Ont., 1977; m. Daisy Boyd, Apr. 23, 1938 (dec.); 1 son, Noel; m. 2d, Jeannette Dugal, Apr. 14, 1976. Statistician, Sanford Evans Statis. Service, 1926-36; economist James Richardson Sons, Ltd., 1937-42; officer Can. Dept. Fin., Ottawa, 1942-51; dir. econ. policy div., 1947-51; asso. dep. minister Canadian Dept. Trade and Commerce, 1951-57, dep. minister, 1957-58, elected to Parliament, 1963, minister trade and commerce, 1963-65, minister fin. and receiver gen., 1965-68; sec. state for external affairs, 1968-74; pres. Privy Council, 1974-76; commr. No. Pipeline Agy., Ottawa, 1978—; v.p. Brazilian Traction, Toronto, Ont., Can., 1958-62. Address: 140 Wellington St Ottawa ON K1P 5A2 Canada

SHARPE, J. C. TIMOTHY, advt. exec.; b. Balt., Jan. 31, 1933; s. John Charles and Lillian Laselle (Fisher) S.; A.B., Stanford, 1955; m. Joan Heppiner, 1959; children—Jason, Amory. Unit mgr. NBC, Inc., N.Y.C., 1957-60; account exec. McCann-Erickson, Inc., N.Y.C., 1960-64, Grey Advt. Inc., N.Y.C. 1964-65, Wunderman, Ricotta & Kline, Inc., 1965-70; N.Y. bd. dirs., v.p., gen. mgr. TLK Direct Marketing div. Tatham-Larid & Kudner, Inc., 1970-76; dir. mktg. services Schwab/Beatty Co., N.Y.C., 1976-78; exec. v.p. Response Industries, Inc., N.Y.C., 1978—; lectr. N.Y.U. Served with AUS, 1955-57. Mem. Assn. Direct Marketing Agys. (exec. com.), Am. Assn. Advt. Agys. (direct mail com.), Direct Mail Marketing Assn. Contbr. articles to Reporter Direct Marketing Mag. Home: 434 E 52d St New York City NY 10022 Office: 485 Lexington Ave New York City NY 10017

SHARPLESS, JOSEPH BENJAMIN, county ofcl.; b. Takoma Park, Md., Feb. 4, 1933; s. William R. and Julia (Rouse) S.; B.A. in Health, Phys. Edn. and Recreation, Earlham Coll., 1955; M.S. in Parks and Recreation Adminstrn., Pa. State U., 1960; m. Nancy Kathleen Steffen, July 28, 1962; 1 dau., Carole Marie. Recreation instr. Dept. Recreation Montgomery County (Md.), 1957-58; program supr. Recreation and Parks Dept. Livingston (N.J.), 1959-63, dir., 1963-70; chief recreational services Md.-Nat. Capital Park and Planning Commn., Riverdale, 1970-77, supt. parks and recreation, 1977—; chmn. numerous major athletic events including: Nat. AAU Volleyball Championships, 1966-69, N.J. Playground Olympics, 1962, 65, 68, N.J. Swimming Jr. Olympics, 1969, 70, Am. Legion Dist. Baseball Championships, 1966-70; coordinator Volleyball Internat. Tour, U.S.-East vs. West German women, 1974; mem. Track and Field Games Com., U.S. Olympics; cons. Livingston (N.J.) Adult Sch. Pres. Livingston Municipal Employees Bowling League; mem. Livingston Fourth of July Celebration Com.; trustee Livingston Athletic Found., Livingston Baseball, Inc. Served with U.S. Army, 1955-57. Recipient Merit award Am. Legion, 1964, 70, Citizenship award Livingston Kiwanis Club, 1967, Man of Year award Sch. and Coll. Ofcls. Assn., 1969, Proclamation of Recognition, Prince George's County Council, 1975, Spl. Achievement award U.S. Air Force, 1976, Distinguished Citizen award U.S. Air Force, 1977. Mem. U.S. Volleyball Assn. (nat. commr. 1976—, v.p. 1972-76, 78—, dir. 1971—, Emil Breitkreutz Nat. Volleyball Leadership award 1972), U.S. AAU (Pub. Recreation Man of Year 1976, bd. govs.), Potomac AAU (mem. bd. govs. 19—, del. to nat. conv. 19—), N.J. AAU (pres. 1968-70, bd. govs. 1960-70), Nat. Recreation and Park Assn. (rep. to U.S. Volleyball Assn. Bd. Govs., chmn. track and field subcom.), Md. Recreation and Park Assn. (pres. 1977-78, exec. bd. 1971—), N.J. Recreation and Park Assn. (pres. 1967, exec. bd. 1963-70) Livingston Hist. Soc. (trustee), Livingston Council for Arts, Livingston Mcpl. Employment Bowling League, Phi Epsilon Kappa. Quaker. Contbr. articles on recreation and phys. edn. to profl. jours. Home: 8754 Oxwell Ln Laurel MD 20811 Office: 6600 Kenilworth Ave Riverdale MD 20840

SHATTO, PAUL FREDERICK, chem. engr.; b. Reger, Mo., Jan. 7, 1921; s. Fred Harmon and Vera Maude (Spangler) S.; B.S. in Chem. Engring., Mo. Sch. Mines and Metallurgy, 1948; M.S., U. Md., 1970; m. Dell Napier, Jan. 13, 1944; children—Barbara (Mrs. Peter Helmut Zipfel), Sue (Mrs. Tom Luther Browning), Nancy (Mrs. Michael Francis Stull), Rebecca, John. Project engr. Freeport Sulfur Co. (Tex.), 1944-47, So. Alkali Co., Lake Charles, La., 1948; sr. project engr. Mut. Chem. Co., Balt., 1948-54; br. chief U.S. Army Biol. Labs., Frederick, Md., 1954-70; chem. engr. FDA, Rockville, Md., 1970—. Served to 2d lt. C.E., AUS, 1942-44. Registered profl. engr., Mo. Mem. Am. Inst. Chem. Engrs., Research Soc. Am., Mo. Soc. Profl. Engrs., Sigma Xi, Alpha Chi Sigma. Republican. Home: 401 Fairview Ave Frederick MD 21701 Office: FDA HFD-530 5600 Fishers Ln Rockville MD 20857

SHATTUCK, JOSEPH BOARDMAN, JR., ins. co. exec.; b. Damariscotta, Maine, Aug. 2, 1925; s. Joseph Boardman and Marcia Vivian (Parker) S.; B.A., U. Maine, 1949; children—Henry, June, Pamela, Patricia, William. With Liberty Mut. Ins. Co., 1949—, insp., N.Y.C., 1949-51, engr., Phila., 1951-52, dist. engr., Buffalo, 1953-55, div. engr., Newcastle, Pa., 1955-57, sect. engr., Boston, 1957-62, mgr., 1962-69, div. service mgr. fire protection, 1969-77, tech. dir., 1977—. Mem. Salisbury (Mass.) Fin. Bd., 1964-65, Salisbury Planning Bd., 1965-71. Served with USAAF, 1943-45. Registered profl. engr., Mass.; certified safety profl., hazard control mgr. Mem. Greater Newcastle C. of C., Soc. Fire Protection Engrs., Am. Soc. Safety Engrs., Assn. Mut. Ins. Engrs. (pres.), Am. Legion. Republican. Baptist. Clubs: Masons, Shriners. Home: 109 Folly Mill Rd Salisbury MA 01950 Office: 13 Riverside Rd Weston MA 02193

SHAUGHNESSY, GEORGE ALBERT, educator; b. Westminster, Vt., July 7, 1926; s. George Cornelius and Annie (Foster) S.; A.B., St. Michael's Coll., 1951; M.Ed., Bridgewater State Coll., 1965; m. Elizabeth Cecelia Vantran, Dec. 28, 1957; children—Maryann Cecelia, Brian Michael, Maureen Christina, Colleen, Michael Vantran. Tchr. pub. schs., Walden, N.Y., 1955-57, Syosset, N.Y., 1957-61; tchr. Rockland (Mass.) High Sch., 1961—, also head dept. social studies, 1964-67. Chmn. edn. com. Hastings Keith for Ho. of Reps. 1970-72; educator's coordinator Gerry Studds for Congress campaign 12th Dist., 1972. Chmn. bd. Syosset High Sch. Scholarship Found., 1959-60. Served with AUS, 1944-46; PTO. Recipient Philosophy Club award St. Michael's Coll., 1951, Student Govt. Philosophy Medal award, 1951; distinguished service award Rockland Tchrs. Assn., 1964, 65, 68, Plymouth County Edn. Assn., 1969; named Educator of Year, Syosset Kiwanis Club, 1957. Mem. Rockland (past pres.), Plymouth County (past pres.), Mass. (field rep., dir.) tchrs. assns. K.C. (4 deg.). Club: Bennington (Vt.).

SHAUGHNESSY, JOHN WILLIAM, JR., labor union exec.; b. East Hartford, Conn., May 1, 1925; s. John William and Catherine (Fitzgerald) S.; student spl. univ. courses in labor laws, union rights and responsibilities, job evaluation, and collective bargaining; m. Elizabeth J. Heffron, May 15, 1948; children—Michael, Brian. Pres., Conn. Union of Telephone Workers, 1959—, Telecommunications Internat. Union, Hamden, Conn., 1962—; v.p. Nat. Ind. Union Council, 1960-63; exec. v.p. Nat. Fedn. Ind. Unions, 1963-78, chmn. legis. com., 1968-78. Mem. town council, East Hartford, 1954-59, chmn. bldg. commn., 1954-59, mayor, 1965-67; pres. East Hartford Democratic Town Club, 1967-70; active Human Relations Council, Cath. Interracial Council, Sch. System Work Study Commn., U. Conn. Labor Edn. Adv. Commn.; bd. dirs. United Way, 1978; del. White House Conf. on Aging, 1960, White House Conf. on Indsl. World Ahead, 1972; mem. Pres. Commn. Dept. Labor 50th Anniversary; trustee East Cath. Found.; regional v.p. Nat. Kidney Found. Served with USAAF, 1944-46. Named Outstanding Ind. Union Officer, 1961, 71; recipient Outstanding Service award Kidney Found. Conn., 1974, Vol. Service award, 1975. Home: 287 Oak St East Hartford CT 06118 Office: 3055 Dixwell Ave Hamden CT 06518*

SHAULIS, NELSON JACOB, viticulturist, educator; b. Somerset, Pa., Sept. 10, 1913; s. Guy Stanley and Minnie (Stufft) S.; B.S., Pa. State U., 1935, M.S., 1937; Ph.D., Cornell U., 1941; m. Lillian Hedwig Huep, Aug. 16, 1941; children—Catherine Luise Shaulis Osterhout, Margaret Ann Shaulis Harty. Instr. pomology Pa. State Coll., 1938-44; asst. soil conservationist Soil Conservation Service, Arendtsville, Pa., 1938-44; asst. prof. pomology N.Y. State Agrl. Expt. Sta., Cornell U., Geneva, 1944-47, asso. prof. 1947-48, prof., 1948-67, prof. viticulture, 1967—. Mem. bd. edn. Geneva City Sch. Dist., 1964-67, v.p., 1966-67. Fulbright sr. research scholar, Australia, 1967-68. Fellow Am. Soc. Hort. Sci.; mem. Am. Soc. Enologists, Am. Soc. Agronomy, Soil Sci. Soc. Am., Crop Sci. Soc. Am., Sigma Xi, Phi Kappa Phi. Republican. Lutheran. Club: Torch. Contbr. chpts. to books, articles to profl. jours. Home: 505 W North St Geneva NY 14456 Office: Dept Pomology and Viticulture NY State Agr Expt Sta Geneva NY 14456

SHAVEL, MIKE H., med. research co. exec.; b. N.Y.C., Sept. 25, 1931; s. Louis B. and Ida (Shapiro) S.; student Bklyn. Coll., 1948-50, Nat. Coll., Chgo., 1950-54; m. Marjorie Rothstein, Oct. 12, 1958; children—Michael J., James A. Sales tng. mgr. Gen. Diagnostics div. Warner Lambert, Morris Plains, N.J., 1962-68; group product mgr. biology Fisher Sci. Co., Fair Lawn, N.J., 1968-70; diagnostic products sales mgr. Roche Diagnostics div. Hoffmann-La Roche, Nutley, N.J., 1970-72; v.p. marketing Princeton Biomedix, Inc., Princeton, N.J., 1972-75; dir. mktg. Diagnostic div. Sclavo Inc., Wayne, N.J., 1975-78; v.p. Norwood Sci. Assos., Norwood, N.J., 1978—. Pres., Cromwell Hills Civic Assn., Convent Station, N.J., 1971-72; active Boy Scouts Am., 1969—. Served with AUS, 1954-56. Mem. Am. Assn. Clin. Chemists, Biomed. Mktg. Assn. (chmn. com. on regents 1973-74), Am. Philatelic Soc., USCG Aux. Sr. editor Guide to Clinical Diagnostic Kits, 1972. Home: 66 Chimney Ridge Dr Convent Station NJ 07961 Office: PO Box 12 Norwood NJ 07648

SHAW, ARTHUR JACK, product mktg. co. exec.; b. N.Y.C., June 22, 1926; s. Herman and Henrietta S.; B.A., City Coll. N.Y.; m. Roslyn Scoufield, 1948; children—Linda, Elyse. Pres., Shaw-Shon Inc., N.Y.C., 1946-56, OGI Enterprises Inc., N.Y.C., 1956—; producer TV Marketplace. cons. in field. Served with Air Force, USN, 1944-46. Mem. Advt. League. Producer tape on mail order of diamond jewelry; pioneer new approach in mail order and retail mktg. Office: 114 E 32d St OGI Enterprises New York City NY 10016

SHAW, CHARLES ERNEST, educator; b. Bridgeport, Conn., July 26, 1926; s. Ernest Charles and Helen Florence (Grogan) S.; B.A., St. Mary U., Balt., 1947, S.T.B., 1950; M.A., Fairfield U., 1961; M.S., Central Conn. State Coll., 1972; PH.D., U. Conn., 1976. Prin., St. Francis Sch., Naugatuck, Conn., 1951-56, Immaculate Conception Sch., Hartford, Conn., 1956-59; asst. supt. schs. Archdiocese Hartford, 1960-61; prin. E. Cath. High Sch., Manchester, Conn., 1961-70; counselor St. Joseph Coll., West Hartford, 1970-72, acad. dean, 1972-76; dir. guidance dept. St. Thomas High Sch., New Britain, Conn., 1977—; mem. Conn. Bd. Higher Edn., also Joint Conn. Com. Tchr. Edn., 1977—. IDEA fellow Kettering Found., 1966; predoctoral fellow U. Conn., 1975. Mem. Am., Conn. personnel and guidance assns., Am. Assn. Higher Edn., Phi Delta Kappa, Phi Kappa Phi. Address: St Paul Rectory 2577 Main St Glastonbury CT 06033

SHAW, FREDERICK, city ofcl.; b. N.Y.C., Sept. 24, 1912; s. Theodore and Hermina (Farkas) S.; B.A., Coll. City N.Y., 1932; M.A., Columbia U., 1933, Ph.D., 1950; postgrad. Oxford U., 1937, New Sch. Social Research, 1939-40, N.Y. U., 1939-40, 54-56, Cornell U., 1961; m. Daisy I. Katz, Nov. 20, 1940; children—Richard, Ellen. Social studies tchr., N.Y., 1935-43, 46-53; chmn. social studies dept. Washington Irving Even High Sch., N.Y.C., 1942-43; research asso. Bur. Adminstrv. and Budgetary Research, N.Y.C., 1953-64, 66-67; vis. prof. polit. sci. City U. N.Y., 1964-66; coordinator federally funded projects for handicapped N.Y.C. Bd. Edn., 1967, dir. Bur. Ednl. Program Research and Statistics, Bklyn., 1967-75, dir. research Office Bilingual Edn., 1975-78; ednl. cons., 1976—; mem. Retirement and Life Planning Inst., 1978—; instr., condr. thesis seminars, adj. asst. prof. Baruch Coll., Coll. City N.Y., 1958-72; spl. examiner N.Y.C. Dept. Personnel, 1965; research cons. for legis. fin. unit City Council N.Y., 1966; cons. N.Y. State Charter Revision Commn. N.Y.C., 1973; mem. constl. conv. com., charter revision and implementation, city council coms. Citizens Union N.Y., 1966-67, 73—. Trustee Payne Ednl. Sociology Found., N.Y. U.; planning com. N.Y.C. Council Econ. Edn., 1970-76; adv. com. City U. N.Y. Grad. Center Gerontol. Studies. Served with AUS, 1943-46. Named Distinguished Educator by Mayor N.Y.C., 1976; recipient Educator of Year award Doctorate Assn. N.Y. Educators, 1974; ann. award for service to edn. Council Suprs. and Adminstrs., 1975; Outstanding Service and Leadership award Council of Dirs., 1976. Mem. Acad. Polit. Sci., Am. Acad. Polit. and Social Sci. (book reviewer Annals), Am. Assn. Sch. Adminstrs., Am. Ednl. Research Assn., Am. Polit. Sci. Assn., Doctorate Assn. N.Y. Educators (past pres.), Nat. Assn. Bilingual Edn., Nat. Municipal League, N.Y. Acad. Pub. Edn., Phi Delta Kappa (past pres. N.Y. U. chpt.). Clubs: City N.Y. (chmn. edn. com.), Schoolmasters (bd. govs.). Author: The American City, 1953; History of the New York City Legislature, 1954, 65; Urban Affairs, 1962; Economics in a Free Society, 1962; Using Economics, 1975, 78; contbr. chpts. to Book of Knowledge, Cowles Comprehensive Ency., Bibliography for Governing New York City, The Schools and the Urban Crisis, Urban Social and Educational Issues, Bilingual Education; contbr. book revs. and articles to profl. jours. Home: 41 Henry St Brooklyn NY 11201

SHAW, GRACE GOODFRIEND (MRS. HERBERT FRANKLIN SHAW), editor; b. N.Y.C., Dec. 27, 1920; d. Henry Bernheim and Jane Elizabeth (Stone) Goodfriend; student Bennington Coll., 1938-39; B.A., Fordham U., 1976; m. Herbert Franklin Shaw, Dec. 7, 1943; 1 son, Brandon Hibbs. Reporter, Port Chester (N.Y.) Daily Item, 1942-45; editorial coordinator World Scope Ency., N.Y.C., 1946-50; asso. editor Clarence L. Barnhart, Inc., Bronxville, N.Y., 1950; free-lance writer for reference books, 1951-61; sr. editor, coll. dept. Bobbs-Merrill, N.Y.C., 1961-62, mng., editor, 1963-65; editing supr. World Pub. Co., N.Y.C., 1965-68, mng. editor, 1968-69, sr. editor, 1969; mng. editor Peter H. Wyden Co., N.Y.C., 1969-70; asso. editor Dial Press N.Y.C., 1971-72, sr. editor, 1972; sr. editor David McKay Co., N.Y.C., 1972-75; sr. editor Grosset & Dunlap, 1975-77, chief editor Today Press, 1977—; gen. editor Ams. All series Garrard Press, 1970. Mem. Overseas Press Club. Home: 85 Lee Rd Scarsdale NY 10583 Office: 51 Madison Ave New York City NY 10010

SHAW, HENRY, oil co. exec., chem. engr.; b. Paris, Oct. 25, 1934; s. Joseph and Sadie (Milstein) S.; came to U.S., 1947, naturalized, 1955; B.Chem.Engring., Coll. City N.Y., 1957; M.S. in Chem. Engring., N.J. Inst. Tech., 1962; Ph.D. (Allied Chem. fellow), Rutgers U., 1967, M.B.A., 1976; m. Evelyn Goodman, Aug. 11, 1963; children—Laura, David, Jessica. Chem. engr. energy div. Babcock and Wilcox, Lynchburg, Va., 1957-61; research engr. central research div. Mobil Oil Co., Princeton, N.J., 1961-65; research asso. govt. research labs. Exxon Research and Engring. Co., Linden, N.J., 1967-76, mgr. environ. and energy conservation area, 1976—; adj. prof. physics and math. Trenton Jr. Coll., 1962-63; instr. radiation sci. Rutgers U., 1965-66; organizer, chmn. symposia in field. Served to capt. C.E., U.S. Army, 1958. Mem. Am. Inst. Chem. Engrs. (chmn. sub-com. energy research), ASME, Air Pollution Control Assn., N.Y. Acad. Scis., Combustion Inst., Phi Lambda Epsilon. Club: Elks (Lynchburg). Contbr. numerous articles to profl. jours.; patentee in field. Home: 2 Gary Ct Scotch Plains NJ 07076 Office: PO Box 8 Linden NJ 07036

SHAW, JACK ALLEN, communications co. exec.; b. Auburn, Ind., Jan. 1, 1939; s. Marvin Dale and Vera Lucille (Harter) S.; B.S. in Elec. Engring., Purdue U., 1962; m. Martha Sue Collins, Aug. 24, 1963; 1 son, Mark Allen. Project engr. space systems div. Hughes Aircraft Co., El Segundo, Calif., 1962-69; dir. programs ITT Space Communications, Inc., Ramsey, N.J., 1969-74; v.p., sec., dir. corporate devel., dir. Digital Communications Corp., Gaithersburg, Md., 1974—. Mem. IEEE. Republican. Clubs: Argyle Country, All Seasons Racquet. Home: 15005 Wellwood Rd Silver Spring MD 20904

SHAW, JAMES WOODLAND, cons. engr.; b. N.Y.C., Mar. 22, 1921; s. James Woodland and Madeline (Willing) S.; B.C.E., Cornell U., 1942; M.A., Bklyn. Poly. Inst., 1945; m. Joan Elizabeth Roy, Oct. 14, 1948; children—Jacquelyn Shaw-Loughlin, Sandra Shaw-Lewis. Civil engr. War Dept. USED, Syracuse, 1942-43; design engr. York Research Corp., N.Y.C., 1944-45, Curtiss Wright Devel. Div., Bloomfield, N.J., 1945-46; structural engr. Voorhees, Walker, Foley & Smith, N.Y.C., 1946-48; project engr. Kellex Corp., N.Y.C., 1948-49; dir. contracts N.Y.C. Dept. Traffic, 1949-54; v.p. Ramp Bldgs. Corp., N.Y.C., 1954-56; mgr., dir. Inter Ramp Co., A.G.: v.p. Ramp Cons. Service, Inc., N.Y.C.: partner Ramp Engring. Assos.; dir. Park of Edgewater, Inc., N.Y.C., Ramp Engr., Nederlands, N.V., Amsterdam, Roi-Shaw A.G. Mem. Pres. Johnson's Com. Safety,

1964; active Scarsdale United Fund, 1968-69. Served with AUS, 1943-44. Fellow Inst. Traffic Engrs.; mem. Nat. Soc. Profl. Engrs., Cornell Soc. Engrs., N.Y. State Soc. Profs., Fedn. Internat. de la Prescontrainte, AAAS, Internat. Municipal Parking Congress bd. dirs. Delta Chi. Episcopalian. Mason. Home: 95 Carthage Rd Scarsdale NY 10583 Office: Ramp Inc 1615 Northern Blvd Manhasset NY 11030

SHAW, JOHN EUGENE, holding co. exec.; b. Balt., July 22, 1935; s. Joseph Robert and Mary Grace (McCummings) S.; B.S., Loyola Coll. (Md.), 1957; m. Sylvia Dawn Feltner, Nov. 3, 1973; 1 son, David; children by previous marriage—Shawn, Colleen, Karla, Michael, Kelly. Electronic data processing dir. Kronheim Co., Balt., 1964-67; systems analyst Crown Central Petroleum, Balt., 1967-70; info. services dir. ELT Corp., Balt., 1970—; tchr. Litton Industries Programming and Systems, 1965-69. Pres. PTA, Glen Burnie, Md., 1965; pres. Balt Paint Fed. Credit Union, 1974-75. Served with USAF, 1957-61. Mem. Data Processing Mgmt. Assn., Assn. Systems Mgmt., Am. Univac Users Assn. Roman Catholic. Clubs: Elk, Moose. Home: 2333 Maytime Dr Gambrills MD 21054 Office: 2 E Chase St Baltimore MD 21202

SHAW, JOHN HODGDON, surgeon; b. Tilton, N.H., July 15, 1929; s. John Albert and Florence Mabel (Hodgdon) S.; B.S., U. N.H., 1951; M.D., Tufts U., 1955; m. Jane Hancock, Sept. 25, 1954; children—Hillary, John Hodgdon. Intern, Maine Med. Center, Portland, resident in gen. surgery, 1955-60; attending surgeon Gardiner (Maine) Gen., Augusta (Maine) Gen. and State hosps., 1962—; chief surgeon Augusta Gen. Hosp., 1968-70, chief staff, 1971-76; pres. M.A.S.H, multisurg. group, 1962—. Mem. Natural Resources Council, 1968—. Served with USN, 1960-62. Diplomate Am. Bd. Surgery. Fellow A.C.S. (pres. Maine chpt. 1975-77), New Eng. Surg. Soc.; mem. AMA, Maine Med. Assn. (ho. of dels. 1970—), Internat. Atlantic Salmon Assn. Republican. Methodist. Clubs: Masons, Shriners, Fishing Club of Am. Home: Pond Rd Manchester ME 04351 Office: 89 Hospital St Augusta ME 04330

SHAW, JON ANGUS, army officer, psychiatrist; b. Portland, Oreg., Oct. 14, 1937; s. Leland B. and Vena (Catskill) S.; B.A., U. Oreg., 1959, M.S., 1964, M.D., 1964; m. Diane A. Hamlin, June 24, 1962; children—Deborah, Daniel, David. Commd. officer U.S. Army, advanced through grades to col., 1978; intern Letterman Gen. Hosp., San Francisco, 1964-65; resident in gen. psychiatry Walter Reed Gen. Hosp., Washington, 1965-67, resident in child psychiatry, 1967-69, fellow in clin. psychiatry research, 1972-73; chief dept. psychiatry Heidelbert, Germany, 1969-72; asst. chief child psychiatry, tng. dir. child psychiatry service Walter Reed Army Med. Center, Washington, 1973-75, chief adult psychiatry outpatient clinic, 1975-76, chief child and adolscent psychiatry dept. psychiatry and neurology, 1976—. Recipient 1st J. Franklin Robinson M.D. award, 1970; Lewis B. Hill award, 1977. Mem. Am. Psychiat. Assn., Am. Acad. Child Psychiatry, Am. Soc. Adolescent Psychiatry, Am. Psychoanalytic Assn., Phi Beta Kappa, Alpha Omega Alpha. Contbr. articles in field to profl. jours. Home: 3621 Littledale Rd Kensington MD 20795

SHAW, LEE NELSON, banker; b. New Rochelle, N.Y., Feb. 28, 1930; s. Leo Nelson and Marie (Heffernan) S.; B.A., Amherst Coll., 1951; m. Corinne de St. Aubin. With J.P. Morgan & Co., N.Y.C., 1951, asst. sec., 1959-62 (name changed to Morgan Guaranty Trust Co.), asst. v.p., 1962-66, v.p., 1966-73; v.p., mgr. Nat. Bank Commerce of Seattle, 1973-75; sr. agt. Banque Canadienne Nationale, 1976—; dir. Banque Canadienne Nationale (Bahamas) Ltd. Mem. Bankers Assn. Fgn. Trade, Inst. Fgn. Bankers, Forex Club Am., Internat. Forex Club. Clubs: Westchester Country (Rye, N.Y.), Owasco Country (Auburn, N.Y.). Home: 1036 Old White Plains Rd Mamaroneck NY 10543 Office: 450 Park Ave New York City NY 10015

SHAWN, WILLIAM HENRY, lawyer; b. Montgomery, Ala., Oct. 27, 1947; s. Robert A. and Emily (Mason) S.; B.A., George Washington U., 1970, J.D., 1973; m. Glenna C. Delp, June 3, 1972; children—Kristen Sanderson-Hope, Hamilton. Admitted to Pa. bar, 1973, D.C. bar, 1974; examiner ICC, 1973-74; asso. firm Grove, Jaskiewicz, Gilliam & Cobert, Washington, 1974-78, partner, 1978—; pres. The Anshaw Corp., 1977—; vice chmn. Com. on Liaison Canadian and Am. Transp., 1977; gen. counsel Canadian-Am. Motor Carriers Assn., 1978. Mem. Am., Fed. Energy, Pa., D.C. bar assns., Motor Carriers Lawyers Assn., ICC Practitioners Assn. Republican. Episcopalian. Club: Univ. Office: 1730 M St NW Washington DC 20036

SHEA, GEORGE MATTHEW, social worker; b. N.Y.C., Apr. 10, 1926; s. George M. and Della Katherine (Noonan) S.; M.S. in Social Work, Fordham U., 1951; m. Susan E. Johnson, Mar. 31, 1951; children—Barbara, George, Michael. Commd. 2d lt. U.S. Army, 1951, advanced through grades to lt. col., 1966; ret., 1973; supr. social work staff Trenton (N.J.) Psychiat. Hosp., 1973-78; dir. social work Evergreen Park Psychiat. Hosp., New Lisbon, N.J., 1978—; cons. Buttonwood Hall, New Lisbon, 1978—, Gamboa Penitentiary, Panama Canal Zone, 1967-70. Mem. Nat. Assn. Social Workers, Acad. Certified Social Workers. Roman Catholic. Home: 4792 Split Rock Rd Browns Mills NJ 08015 Office: Evergreen Park Psychiat Hosp New Lisbon NJ 08064

SHEA, MICHAEL JAMES, property disposal specialist; b. Manchester, N.H., Sept. 3, 1936; s. Jeremiah Gerard and Barbara Teresa (Padden) S.; student St. Thomas Jr. Coll., 1957-58, St. Anselms Coll., 1963-64; m. Phan Ngoc Diep, May 18, 1971; children—Duncan James, Moira Doreen. Inventory mgmt. asst., Ft. Devens, Mass., 1966-68; inventory mgmt. specialist U.S. Army Inventory Control Center, Vietnam, 1968-72; property mktg. specialist Property Disposal Office, Ft. Devens, 1972-73, property disposal officer, Newport, R.I., 1973-74; residency group leader Def. Property Disposal Residency, Newport, 1974-78; property disposal officer Property Disposal Office, Chambersburg, Pa., 1978—. Served with U.S. Army, 1960-63. Mem. Am. Def. Preparedness Assn., Assn. U.S. Army, Nat. Rifle Assn., 1st Logistics Command Assn. Roman Catholic. Home: 4095 Ricklyn Dr Chambersburg PA 17201 Office: Def Property Disposal Office Letterkenny Army Depot Chambersburg PA 17201

SHEA, PETER JOHN, mfg. co. exec.; b. Hackensack, N.J., May 5, 1946; s. John Francis and Vincenza Theresa (Coaloa) S.; B.S. in Bus. Mgmt., Fairleigh Dickinson U., Rutherford, N.J., 1970; M.B.A., Fordham U., 1975; m. Geralyn Henry, Oct. 18, 1975; children—Peter J., Kathleen Mary, John Francis. With Xerox Corp., 1966—, mgr. adminstrv. processing systems Northeast regional office, Greenwich, Conn., 1976, fin. project leader manpower/expense planning and analysis, 1978—. Mem. exec. bd. St. Teresa Roman Catholic Youth Council, Trumbull, Conn., 1977—. Mem. Stamford Area Commerce and Industry Assn., Internat. Word Processing Assn. Address: 10 Ascolese Rd Trumbull CT 06611

SHEA, STEPHEN MICHAEL, physician, educator; b. Galway, Ireland, Apr. 25, 1926; s. Stephen and Margaret Mary (Cooke) S.; came to U.S., 1956, naturalized, 1966; B.Sc. in Anatomy and Pathology, Univ. Coll., Galway Nat. U. Ireland, 1948, M.B., B.Ch. in Medicine, 1950, M.Sc. in Pathology, 1951, M.D., 1959. Intern, St. Vincent's Hosp., Dublin, Ireland, 1950-51; Dr. Keenan travelling scholar dept. physiology Univ. Coll., London, 1951-53; asst. lectr. pharmacology Univ. Coll., Dublin, 1953-56; resident in pathology Mallory Inst. Pathology, Boston City Hosp., 1956-59, chief resident, 1958-59; asst. prof. pathology U. Toronto (Ont., Can.), 1959-61; instr. Harvard Med. Sch., 1961-63, instr. math. biology, 1963-65, asso. in pathology, 1965-67, asst. prof. pathology, 1967-70, asso. prof., 1970-73; asso. pathologist Mass. Gen. Hosp. and Shriners Burns Inst., both Boston, 1972-73; prof. pathology Coll. Medicine and Dentistry, N.J.-Rutgers Med. Sch., 1973—. Diplomate Am. Bd. Pathology. Fellow Royal Coll. Pathologists (U.K.), Royal Coll. Physicians (Can.); mem. Am. Assn. Pathologists, Internat. Acad. Pathology, Am. Soc. Cell Biology, Biophys. Soc., Soc. Math. Biology, Microcirculatory/Soc. Roman Catholic. Clubs: Harvard Travellers', Harvard of Boston. Contbr. articles to profl. publs. Home: 1050 George St Apt 12L New Brunswick NJ 08901 Office: Rutgers Med Sch Piscataway NJ 08854

SHEA, THOMAS WEST, assn. exec.; b. Canton, Ohio, Sept. 21, 1942; s. L. West and Helen Kathryn (Mills) S.; student U. Pitts., 1965-67; m. Gerda Marie Koerber, Sept. 23, 1964; children—Christian Thomas, Steven West, Kathryn Marie. With Shea Mgmt. Inc., Pitts., 1965—, pres., 1965—; mng. dir. Rack Mfrs. Inst., Pitts., 1974—; sec.-treas. Material Handling Inst. Inc., Pitts., 1969—; asst. exec. dir. Safety Equipment Distbrs. Assn., Pitts., 1975—; mng. dir. Metal Bldg. Component Mfrs. Assn., 1976—. Served with U.S. Army, 1961-65. Mem. SAM, Am. Mgmt. Assn., Inst. Assn. Mgmt. Cos. (dir.), Nat. Assn. Exposition Mgrs., Am. Mgmt. Assn., Am. Soc. Assn. Execs. Republican. Presbyterian. Office: 1326 Freeport Rd Pittsburgh PA 15238

SHEALEY, GLENN ELLIOTT, lawyer; b. Brockton, Mass., Feb. 16, 1947; s. Francis and Mary (Hopkins) S.; student Goethe Inst., Munich, W. Ger., 1967; B.A., Williams Coll., 1969; M.A., Harvard U., 1970, J.D., 1977; postgrad. N.Y. U. Law Sch.; m. Anne C. Ritchie, May 28, 1978. Teaching fellow hist. Harvard U., Cambridge, Mass., 1970-74, asst. to dean, 1972-74, sr. tutor Dunster Ho., 1974-75; with corp. trust dept. Irving Trust Co., N.Y.C., 1976; admitted to Mass. bar, 1977; atty. Legal Adviser's Office Dept. State, Washington, 1978; asso. Palmer & Dodge, Boston, 1978—. Trustee Soc. Arts & Crafts, Boston; asso. class agent Williams Coll. Mem. Am. Bar Assn., Mass. Bar Assn., Boston Bar Assn., Internat. Law Soc. (Am. br.), Am. Soc. Internat. Law, Soc. for Historians of Am. Fgn. Relations, Am. Hist. Assn. Clubs: Harvard, Williams. Home: 16 Gray Gardens E Cambridge MA 02138

SHEAN, TIMOTHY JOSEPH, engr.; b. Norfolk, Va., Sept. 19, 1945; s. Hobart Philip and Rita Regina (Perez) S.; B.S. in Mech. Engring., U. Notre Dame, 1967; m. Adriana Bergo, July 12, 1970; children—Jonathan Michael, Arianne Marie. Sales engr. Shean Equipment Co., Syracuse, N.Y., 1967-69; application engr. customer service Gen. Electric Co., Schenectady, 1970-71, prodn. control supr., 1972-75, process devel. engr., 1975-78, project mgr., 1978—; treas., dir. W. Hill Devel. Inc., Rotterdam, N.Y., 1977—. Sr. patroller Nat. Ski Patrol, Wilmington, Vt., 1970—; instr./trainer first aid Red Cross, Schenectady, 1975-78; vice-chmn. Red Cross Disaster Services, Schenectady, 1976-77. Roman Catholic. Home: 347 Terrace Rd Schenectady NY 12306 Office: 1 Campbell Rd Schenectady NY 12345

SHEAR, THEODORE LESLIE, JR., educator, archaeologist; b. Athens, Greece, May 1, 1938; s. Theodore Leslie and Josephine (Platner) S.; A.B. summa cum laude, Princeton, 1959, M.A., 1963, Ph.D., 1966; student Am. Sch. Classical Studies at Athens, 1959-60; m. Ione Doris Mylonas, June 24, 1959; children—Julia Louise, Alexandra. Instr. Greek and Latin, Bryn Mawr Coll., 1964-66, asst. prof., 1966-67; asst. prof. art and archaeology Princeton U., 1967-70, asso. prof. art and archaeology, 1970—, chmn. program in classical archaeology, 1970—, asso. chmn. dept. art and archaeology, 1976—; mem. mng. com. Am. Sch. Classical Studies, Athens, 1972—; mem. archaeol. expdns. Greece and Italy, including Mycenae, 1953-54, 58, 62-63, 65-66, Eleusis, 1956, Perati (Attica), 1956, Corinth, 1960, Morgantina (Sicily), 1962; mem. archaeol. expdns. Ancient Agora of Athens, 1955, 67, field dir., 1968—. Mem. Archaeol. Inst. Am., Am. Philol. Assn. Republican. Episcopalian. Clubs: Nassau (Princeton, N.J.); Princeton (Phila.); Hellenic Yacht (Piraeus, Greece). Contbr. to profl. jours. Home: 87 Library Pl Princeton NJ 08540

SHEARER, FRANCIS ALLEN, clergyman; b. Etters, Pa., Feb. 8, 1904; s. John Edmund and Meda (Loucks) S.; B.A., Gettysburg Coll., 1924, L.H.D., 1955; M.Div., Phila. Luth. Sem., 1927; A.M., U. Pa., 1947; m. Emma Sipe, June 15, 1927; children—Cynthia (Mrs. Edwin Johnson), Mary Ann (Mrs. Douglas Craver). Ordained minister Lutheran Ch., 1927; pastor, Clarks Summit, Pa., 1927-31, Jim Thorpe, Pa., 1931-42; asst. exec. sec. bd. inner missions Luth. Ministerium Pa., Phila., 1942-45; sec. for inner missions, bd. social missions United Luth. Ch. Am., N.Y.C., 1945-56; exec. sec. bd. social ministry Eastern Pa. Synod, Luth. Ch. Am., Phila., 1957-69; sec. asst. to pres. Luth. Synod Southeastern Pa., 1969-71; exec. dir. Pa. Assn. Non-Profit Homes for the Aging, 1971-75, cons., 1975—. Del. to White House Conf. on Children and Youth, 1950, 60, Nat. Conf. on Aging, 1951; mem. Pa. Assn. Non-Profit Homes for Aging; mem. Phila. Commn. on Services to the Aging, chmn., 1976—. Pres. bd. dirs. Houston Found.; bd. dirs. Am. Assn. Homes for Aging, 1965-68, Homemaker-Home Health Aide Services Met. Phila.; pres. Older Philadelphians Legal Service Plan; pres. Northwest Center for older Adults, Cathedral Village. Bd. govs. Council for Clin. Tng., 1952-58, Nat. Council on Aging, 1951-55, Pa. Prison Soc., 1943-49. Fellow Gerontological Soc.; mem. Am. Correctional Assn., Nat. Council on Aging, SAR. Lutheran. Contbr. to Ency. Lutheran Ch. Home: 3436 W Coulter St Philadelphia PA 19129

SHEARER, JANE KELLY, educator; b. Wise, Va., Oct. 23, 1914; d. Emerson Wyntoun and Dorcas Elizabeth (Lewis) K.; B.S., U. Tenn., 1940, M.S., 1950; Ph.D. (Riatt fellow 1958-59), Fla. State U., 1960; m. Ralph Durward Shearer, May 11, 1940; children—John Jackson, Barbara Jane, Ellen. Faculty, Va. Intermount Coll., Bristol, 1935-39; with Knoxville (Tenn.) Adult Edn. program, 1940-42, 49-52; interior design cons. Parks Furniture, Knoxville, 1950-51; faculty Fla. State U., Tallahassee, 1952-65; faculty, chmn. dept. housing and applied design U. Md., College Park, 1965-72, 73-77, coordinator interior design, 1977—; interior design cons. Mem. Am. Assn. Housing Educators, AAUP, Am. Home Econs. Assn., Am. Soc. Interior Designers, Interior Design Educators Council, Omicron Nu. Presbyterian. Editor, Home Econs. Research Abstracts, 1967, 68. Office: Bldg FF Univ of Md College Park MD 20742

SHEDD, MARK REDANS, state ofcl.; b. Quincy, Mass., June 1, 1926; s. Guy Vaughn and Sarah Kathryn (Redans) S.; A.B., U. Maine, 1950, M.Ed., 1954, LL.D., 1969; Ed.D., Harvard U., 1960; LL.D., Coll. Wooster, 1970, Bates Coll., 1971; Litt.D., Drexel U., 1970; m. Shirley Greene, Oct. 18, 1968; children—Lynne Shedd Simonds, Mark Daniel, Dale Shedd Whitesell, Nancy Shedd Scott, Kim, Andrew Christopher. Tchr., prin., then supr. pub. schs., Bangor, Caribou and Auburn, Maine, 1950-60; rural dist. supt. Conn. Dept. Edn., 1960-62; supt. schs. City of Englewood (N.J.), 1962-67, City of Phila., 1967-71; vis. prof. edn. Harvard Grad. Sch. Edn., Cambridge, Mass., 1972-74; commr. edn. State of Conn., 1974—; trustee Hazen Found., U. Conn.; trustee, mem. exec. com. Conn. Pub. TV Corp.; mem. Conn. State Tchrs. Retirement Bd., Conn. State Library Bd.; cons. Instn. for Social and Policy Studies, Yale U., 1972-74; mem. Edn. Commn. of States from N.J. Served with USN, 1944-46. Recipient A. Philip Randolph award Negro Trade Union Leadership Council Phila., 1968; Man of Yr. award Ednl. Equality League Phila., 1971; Distinguished Service award Phila. Urban Coalition, 1972. Mem. Council Chief State Sch. Officers, Am. Assn. Sch. Adminstrs., Nat. Urban Coalition, NAACP, Harvard Grad. Sch. Edn. Alumni Council, Phi Delta Kappa. Democrat. Contbr. articles to profl. jours. Home: 19 Foxridge Rd West Hartford CT 06107 Office: PO Box 2219 Hartford CT 06115

SHEEHAN, JOHN JOSEPH, med. co. exec.; b. N.Y.C., Feb. 19, 1919; s. John Joseph and Margaret Veronica (Healy) S.; B.B.A., Manhattan Coll., 1946; postgrad. in gen. mgmt. Wharton Sch. Bus., U. Pa., 1969; postgrad. in planning and fin. control Columbia U., 1972; m. Margaret Mary Egan, Aug. 30, 1947; children—Ellen, John, James, Steven, Carol, Nancy, Daniel. Salesman, Procter and Gamble, Chgo., 1947-50; salesman, sales trainer Ethicon Inc., Chgo., 1950-55, sales tng. dir., New Brunswick, N.J., 1955-57, div. mgr., Boston/N.Y., 1957-60, regional sales mgr., asst. to v.p. sales, nat. sales mgr., Somerville, N.J., 1960-65; v.p. mktg. Codman and Schurtleff, Boston, 1965-70; pres. dental div. Howmedica, Inc., Chgo., 1970-75, v.p., gen. mgr. orthopedic div., Rutherford, N.J., 1975-77, corp. v.p. mktg. devel. worldwide, N.Y.C., 1977—, corp. dir., 1970—. Served to capt. U.S. Army, 1941-46. Mem. Am. Mgmt. Assn., Am. Mktg. Assn. Clubs: Upper Montclair Golf, Woods Hole Golf. Home: 37 Salt Pond Rd Falmouth MA 02540 Office: 235 E 42nd St New York City NY 10017

SHEEHAN, JUNE MULVEY, govt. ofcl.; b. Washington, June 7, 1923; d. Gerald Kevin and Adele A. (Norton) Mulvey; student Southeastern U., Washington, 1945-46, George Washington U., 1942-43, Bookings Instn., 1962; m. John J. Sheehan, Jr., June 30, 1946; 1 dau., Kristie Lynn (Mrs. William A. Merryman). Chief manuals and forms sect. Fed. Pub. Housing Authority, Washington, 1945-52; mgmt. analyst Pub. Housing Adminstrn., 1952-68; chief orgn. and mgmt. surveys sect. HUD, 1968-72, dir. mgmt. sers. div., 1972-76, dep. dir. Office of Mgmt., 1976-77, dir. Mgmt. Div., 1977—. Past pres. HUD Credit Union, now v.p.; mem. Michigan Park Civic Assn., Cath. Sodality, St. Vincent DePaul Soc. Recipient certificate spl. achievement HUD, 1970, Superior Performance awards, 1969-71, 73, 75, 78, certificate of merit, 1973. Mem. Am. Legion Aux., VFW Aux., Nat. Assn. Housing and Redevel. Ofcls., Hibernians, Friends of Kennedy Center for Performing Arts, Nat. Symphony, Wolftrap Performing Arts. Home: 5057 Sargent Rd NE Washington DC 20017 Office: HUD 7th and D Sts SW Washington DC 20413

SHEEHAN, MARILYN ROSE, psychologist; b. Asbury Park, N.J., Dec. 5, 1932; d. Joseph Raymond and Anne Frances (Fiorillo) S.; B.A., Monmouth Coll., Long Branch, N.J., 1962; M.A., Columbia U., 1967; postgrad. Kean Coll., Union, N.J., 1972; Ph.D., U. Sarasota (Fla.), 1975. Tchr. Asbury Park Elementary Schs., 1962-64, Hazlet Twp. (N.J.) Elemntary Schs., 1964-67, Middletown (N.J.) High Sch., 1967-68; asst. prof. psychology Brookdale Community Coll., N.Y.C., 1969-70; instr. psychology Monmouth (N.J.) Coll., 1968-71; intern sch. psychology Ocean County (N.J.) Mental Health Clinic and Bayville (N.J.) Sch. System, 1971-72; sch. psychologist Newark Bd. Edn., 1972—. Served with USMC, 1950-53; Korea. Certified tchr., psychologist, N.J. Mem. Am., N.J., Eastern, Monmouth-Ocean County psychol. assns., N.J. Assn. Sch. Psychologists, AAAS, Monmouth Coll., Columbia U. alumnae assns., N.J. Edn. Assn. Home: Stoney Hill Apt 213B Eatontown NJ 07724

SHEEHAN, ROBERT JAMES, assn. exec.; b. Pitts., May 13, 1937; s. Regis James and Helen (O'Leary) S.; B.S. in Econs., U. Pitts., 1966, M.A. in Econs., 1970; m. Marie Elizabeth Yoskovich, Apr. 24, 1965; children—Stephanie Ann, Robert James III. Engaged as a research analyst with ACTION-Housing, Inc., Pitts., 1960-62; adminstrv. asst. Dept. City Planning, Pitts., 1962; project rep. Urban Redevel. Authority Pitts., 1963-65, devel. coordinator, 1965-67, dir. rehab., after 1968; now dir. econs. Nat. Assn. Homebuilders, Washington. Treas., Kent Garden Sch. PTA, 1974-75, pres., 1975—; treas. Kent Garden Recreation Club, 1978-79. Mem. Am. Econ. Assn., Regional Sci. Assn., Nat. Economists Club, Nat. Assn. Bus. Economists, Am. Real Estate and Urban Econs. Assn., Pi Kappa Alpha. Roman Catholic. Club: K.C. (fin. sec. 1962-65). Contbr. articles to profl. jours. Home: 1606 Wrightson Dr McLean VA 22101 Office: Nat Assn Homebuilders 15th and M Sts NW Washington DC 20005

SHEEHAN, THOMAS EDWARD, banker; b. N.Y.C., Apr. 15, 1932; s. John Joseph and Anne (Kenny) S.; B.S., Villanova U., 1954; m. Mary Fagan Anderson, Nov. 25, 1961; children—Mark Anderson, David Nichols. Salesman, Internat. Paper Co., N.Y.C., Pitts., Boston, 1958-64; security analyst Singer, Deane & Scribner, Pitts., 1964-67, dir. research, 1967-69, research partner, 1969-73; instl. sales partner Butcher & Singer, Pitts., 1973-77; instl. sales E. F. Hutton & Co., Pitts., 1977-78; asst. v.p. investments Union Nat. Bank, Pitts., 1978—. Mem. exec. com. Western Pa. chpt. Arthritis Found., 1971—, treas., 1975-78, exec. v.p., 1978—; chmn. fund-raising Three Rivers Art Festival, 1978—. Served with CIC, AUS, 1954-57. Mem. Inst. Chartered Fin. Analysts. Clubs: Bond (Pitts.); Pitts. Golf. Home: 499 Locust St Pittsburgh PA 15218 Office: Union Nat Bank Pittsburgh PA 15230

SHEEHY, MARTIN JAMES, physician; b. Bklyn., Mar. 10, 1941; s. Martin James and Jane Helen (Gutzeit) S.; B.S., Coll. of Holy Cross, Worcester, Mass., 1962; M.D., Boston U., 1966; m. Patricia Anne Rafferty, Oct. 14, 1967; children—Susan Mary, Christina Michelle, Melissa Jane. Intern and med. resident Phila. Gen. Hosp., 1966-69; fellow in pulmonary disease U. Pa., Phila., 1969-70; practice medicine, Westfield, N.J., 1972-76; chief respiratory therapy and asst. dir. family practice residency program John F. Kennedy Med. Center, Edison, N.J., 1976—. Mem. Joint Civic Com., Westfield, 1977. Served to maj. M.C., USAF, 1970-72. Fellow Coll. Chest Physicians; mem. AMA, N.J. Union County Med. Soc., Am., N.J. thoracic socs. Democrat. Roman Catholic. Clubs: Jaycees (Westfield), K.C. Asst. editor J.F.K. Med. Center Family Practice Jour. Home: 441 Lenox Ave Westfield NJ 07090 Office: John F Kennedy Medical Center Edison NJ 08817

SHEERAN, JAMES JENNINGS, mktg. exec., author, editor; b. Chgo., Nov. 16, 1932; s. Kieran F. and Evelynne (Walsh) S.; B.S., Ph.B., Marquette U., 1953; M.A., Columbia, 1957; m. Kathryn Ann Leuver, June 13, 1953; children—Suzanne, Kathryn, Leslie, Mary Elizabeth. Brand mgr. Helene Curtis Industries, Inc., Chgo., 1955-60; account supr. B.B.D. & O. Advt., Inc., Chgo., 1960-64; advt. and promotion dir. Pepsi-Cola Co., N.Y.C., 1964-67; pres. Creative Mktg. Mgmt. div. Litton Industries, N.Y.C., 1967-72; pres. Sheeran Corp., N.Y.C., 1972—; mktg. editor Travel Trade, Discover Am., Beverage World mags. Instr. De Paul U., 1957-60, Columbia, 1958-64. Served as capt. USMCR, 1953-55. Named one of Nation's Ten Outstanding Young Men, 1963. Mem. Am. Mktg. Assn., Am. Soc. Travel Writers, N.Y. Criminal Ct. Bar Assn., Authors Guild. Clubs: Merchandising

Executives of Chicago (dir.), Economic (Chgo.); Atrium, New York Athletic, Sales Promotion Executives of New York (dir.). Author: Five-Figure Income, 1964; The Opportunist, 1972; The Businessman's Handbook, 1976. Office: 118 E 61st St New York City NY 10021

SHEETS, NORMAN L., univ. ofcl.; b. Cass, W.Va., June 25, 1928; s. Charles N. and Cora O. Sheets; A.B., Glenville State Coll., 1949; M.S., W.Va. U., Ed.D., 1958; m. Verna Dean Ellis, Aug. 19, 1949; children—Deana Kay, Stephanie Jan. Tchr., Howard County (Md.) Pub. Sch., 1949-50; asst. prin. Highland County (Va.) Pub. Sch., 1950-52; grad. asst. W.Va. U., 1954-56; chmn. dept. health, phys. edn. and recreation Davis and Elkins Coll., Elkins, W.Va., 1956-60, dean students, 1957-60; asso. chmn. dept. health, phys. edn. and recreation Temple U., Phila., 1960-67; dean Sch. Health and Phys. Edn., West Chester (Pa.) State Coll., 1967-69; dean div. applied scis. Towson State U., Balt., 1969—. Served with USCG, 1952-54. Fellow Am. Sch. Health Assn.; mem. Am., Md. pub. health assns., Am. Assn. Higher Edn., Nat. Coll. Phys. Edn. Assn. for Men, Am., Md. assns. health, phys. edn. and recreation, Am. Heart Assn., Assn. Allied Health Personnel Adminstrs., Phi Delta Kappa. Baptist. Contbr. to books, articles on health and phys. edn. to profl. publs. Home: 2317 Killoran Rd Timonium MD 21093*

SHEETZ, HARRY JOHN, III, systems engr.; b. Phila., Nov. 20, 1931; s. Harry John and Ethel May (Heinrich) S.; diploma in Mech. Engring., Drexel U., 1959, B.S., 1961; m. Barbara Jane Mieicke, Aug. 8, 1970; children—Deborah Ann, Harry Kevin, Robert George Applegate. Designer def. and comml. systems RCA, Camden, N.J., 1950-61, astro-elec. div. program mgr., Princeton, N.J., 1961-71; program mgr. Fairchild Space and Electronics Co., Germantown, Md., 1971-73; mgr. spacecraft implementation Am. Satellite Corp., Germantown, 1972-73; mgr. earth radiation program Mitre Corp., McLean, Va., 1973—; instr. electronics Naval Air Res., Lakehurst, N.J., 1955-58; exec. v.p., dir. Hahn Motor Co., Hamburg, Pa., 1960-69. Pres. Lawrence Twp. Sch. PTA; mem. Lawrence Twp. Adv. Com. Mem. Am. Inst. Aeros. and Astronautics (chmn. joint energy com., chmn. community action com. Washington chpt.), ASME. Patentee in field. Home: 15801 Norman Dr Gaithersburg MD 20760 Office: Mitre Corp Westgate Research Park McLean VA 22101

SHEFF, MADELON, educator; b. N.Y.C., Mar 26, 1936; A.B. in Polit. Sci. and Econs., Hunter Coll., 1952; M.A. in Edn. and Reading Splty., Manhattan Coll., 1974; m. Aaron Sheff; children. Tchr., Pub. Sch. 41, Bronx, N.Y., 1959-61, 69-73, early identification of learning disabilities tchr., 1973—. Mem. Internat. Reading Assn. Research on handwriting, pupil promotion policy, bilingual edn. Certified as reading specialist, adminstr. Ill. Test of Psycholinguistic Abilities, N.Y.C. Home: 13 Vista Pl Hartsdale NY 10530 Office: 3352 Olinville Ave Bronx NY 10467

SHEFFLER, M. ANDREW, pension fund admnstr.; b. DuBois, Pa., May 25, 1940; s. Jack C. and Eugenia G. (Groves) S.; B.A. in Econs., Allegheny Coll., 1962; m. Gaye Allyson Wolcott, Apr. 22, 1967. Chief spl. projects Pa. Dept. Commerce, Harrisburg, 1967-68, dist. coordinator Appalachia program, 1968-70,asst. dir. bus. services, 1970; asst. exec. dir. Pa. Pub. Sch. Retirement System, Harrisburg, 1970-77, acting exec. dir., 1977, exec. dir., 1977—. Mem. bd. West Shore chpt. Order of Demolay, Camp Hill, Pa., 1976-78. Served with U.S. Army, 1963-65. Mem. Pa. Assn. Sch. Bus. Ofcls., Nat. Council on Tchr. Retirement, Nat. Conf. on Pub. Employee Retirement Systems (exec. com.), Phi Delta Theta. Lutheran. Clubs: West Shore Country, Masons. Home: 501 Skyport Rd Mechanicsburg PA 17055 Office: 301 Chestnut St Harrisburg PA 17101

SHEFT, LEONARD ALVIN, lawyer; b. N.Y.C., Aug. 8, 1931; s. Benjamin H. and Gertrude L. (Goldberg) S.; B.A., N.Y. U., 1951; J.D., Yale, 1954; m. Monique Eisinger, July 3, 1952; children—Peter Ian, Danielle Anne. Admitted to N.Y. bar, 1956; practiced in N.Y.C., 1956—; partner Emile Z. Berman and A. Harold Frost, 1956-68; sec. Tekni-Plex, Inc.; dir. Spotless Stores, Inc. Served to capt. USAF, 1954-56. Mem. N.Y. State, Nassau County bar assns., N.Y. County Lawyers Assn., Assn. Bar City N.Y. (com. on ins. law 1967—), Met. Trial Lawyers Assn., Am. Arbitration Assn., Bklyn-Manhattan Trial Lawyers Assn., Excess and Surplus Lines Assn. Clubs: Yale (N.Y.C.); Plandome Country (Manhasset, N.Y.); Eastepointe Golf (Palm Beach, Fla.). Home: 132 Brookville Rd Muttontown NY 11545 also 5380 N Ocean Dr Singer Island FL 33404 Office: 111 Broadway New York City NY 10006

SHEFTEL, ROGER TERRY, investment banking co. exec.; b. Denver, Sept. 10, 1941; s. Edward and Dorothy (Barnett) S.; B.S. in Econs., U. Pa., 1963; m. Phoebe A. Sherman, Sept. 7, 1968; children—Tisha B., Ryan B. Comml. lending officer Provident Nat. Bank, Phila., 1963-65; asst. to pres. Continental Finance Corp., Denver, 1965-68; v.p. Eastern Indsl. Leasing Corp., Phila., 1968-71, exec. v.p., dir. 1971-73; pres., dir. Zebley & Strouse, Inc., Phila., 1973-75; prin. Trivest, Phila., 1973—, Oakland Assos., Oak Tree Village Assos., Ltd., 1974—, Riveredge Partnership, 1974—, Timberfalls Assos., Ltd., 1974—, Ashton Assos., Ltd., 1974—, Westchester Pike Assos., Ltd., 1974—, Braewood Assos., Ltd., 1974—, CVS Assos., Ltd., 1974—. Mem. bd. organized classes, exec. com. U. Pa. Mem. Archaeol. Inst. Am., Kite and Key Soc. Club: Friars. Home: 414 Barclay Rd Rosemont PA 19010 Office: PO Box 219 Haverford PA 19041

SHEFTON, JOHN HERBERT, banker; b. Phila., Jan. 8, 1948; s. Herbert E. and Ethel L. (Drew) S.; B.S., St. Josephs Coll., 1969; M.B.A., U. Pa., 1975; m. Marcia Y. Hamilton, Nov. 12, 1977. Mgmt. trainee, 1st Pa. Bank, Phila., 1968-69; data preparation mgr. Phila. Nat. Bank, 1972-76, mgr. quality control, 1976—. Pres., Phila. Fin. Basketball League. Served with AUS, 1969-72. Mem. Am. Soc. Quality Control (vice chmn. banking com.). Democrat. Episcopalian. Home: 395 Hillside Rd King of Prussia PA 19406 Office: 1 N 5th St Philadelphia PA 19106

SHEHAN, CARDINAL LAWRENCE JOSEPH, archbishop; b. Balt., Mar. 18, 1898; s. Thomas Patrick and Anastasia (Schofield) S.; student St. Charles Coll., Md., 1911-17; A.B., St. Mary Sem., Balt., 1919, A.M., 1920; S.T.D., N. Am. Coll., Rome, Italy, 1923. Ordained priest Roman Catholic Ch., 1922; asst. St. Patrick Ch., Washington, 1923-41, pastor, 1941-45; pastor Saints Philip and James' Ch., Balt., 1945; named titular bishop of Lydda and aux. bishop of Balt. and Washington, 1945, aux. bishop, Balt., 1948, 1st bishop of Bridgeport, Conn., 1953, co-adjutor archbishop of Balt., 1961, archbishop, 1961-74; cardinal, 1965—. Home: 408 N Charles St Baltimore MD 21201 Office: Cath Center 320 Cathedral St Baltimore MD 21201

SHEINKMAN, JACOB, labor union exec.; b. N.Y.C., Dec. 6, 1926; s. Shaia and Bertha (Rosenkrantz) S.; student Coll. City N.Y., 1943-44; B.S., Cornell U., 1948, LL.B., 1952; certificate in econs. Oxford (Eng.) U., 1949; m. Betty F. Johnson, May 30, 1954; children—Michael Adair, Joshua Louis, Mark Robert. Admitted to N.Y. bar, 1952; atty., adviser NLRB, 1952-53; atty., gen. counsel Amalgamated Clothing Workers Am. (AFL-CIO), N.Y.C., 1953-72, v.p., 1968-72, sec.-treas., Amalgamated Clothing and Textile Workers Union, 1972—. Guest lectr. N.Y. State Sch. Indsl. and Labor Relations Extension Service, Cornell U.; lectr. Practising Law Inst.; employee mem. Minimum Wage Bd., U.S. Dept. Labor, P.R., 1959, 63; mem. N.Y. U. Ann. Conf. on Labor; acting sec. N.Y. State Full Employment Council; mem. adv. com. Pension and Welfare Plans U.S. Dept. Labor, 1969—; v.p. indsl. union dept AFL-CIO; vice chmn. N.Y. Econ. Devel. Bd.; bd. dirs. Community Services, Inc., Workers Def. League, Internat. Rescue Com., Inc., Am. Arbitration Assn.; pres. Jewish Labor Com.; trustee, sec. Amalgamated Cotton Garment and Allied Industries Fund. Mem. Telluride Assn., UN Assn. (economic policy council, Brit. N.Am. com.); trustee Cornell U. Served with USNR, 1944-46. Mem. Phi Kappa Phi. Contbr. to various legal publs. Home: 639 West End Ave New York City NY 10024 Office: 15 Union Sq New York City NY 10003

SHELDON, ROGER ALPHA, mag. editor; b. Baton Rouge, May 12, 1922; s. William Hannaman and Arta (Sims) S.; B.A., La. State U., 1942, postgrad., 1946; m. Suzanne R. Eaton, Jan. 30, 1972; children by previous marriage—Mark, Elizabeth (Mrs. Alan Danneman), Bonnie (Mrs. Craig Eaton), Paul, David, Patricia; 1 stepson, Thomas Eaton. Dep. info. officer Houston regional office War Assets Adminstrn., 1946-47; account exec. George Kirksey & Assos., Houston, 1947-49; pub. relations counsel Tex. div., Am. Cancer Soc., Houston, 1949-51; editor-writer Merkle Press, Inc., Washington, 1951-61, v.p., editorial dir., 1962-71, v.p. spl. projects, 1971-76; asso. editor The Carpenter, Washington, 1977—; info. officer Pres.'s Commn. on Status of Women, Washington, 1962. Troop committeeman Nat. Capitol Area council Boy Scouts Am., 1968-74; community relations chmn. Allied Civic Group, Montgomery County, Md., 1955-56; Democratic precinct chmn., Montgomery County, 1968-70. Served with USAAF, World War II. Decorated Air medal; recipient Service certificate Boy Scouts Am., 1960. Mem. Washington Newspaper Guild (mem. bd. 1959-60). Unitarian. Club: Nat. Press. Author: Opportunities in Carpentry Careers; Vocational Biographies; This Is Your Washington. Home: 6113 Massachusetts Ave Bethesda MD 20016 Office: 101 Constitution Ave NW Washington DC 20001

SHELLEY, EDWIN FREEMAN, engr.; b. N.Y.C., Feb. 19, 1921; s. Robert and Jessie (Sinick) S.; A.B., Columbia Coll., 1940, B.S., 1941; m. Florence Dubroff, Aug. 29, 1941; children—William, Carolyn. Project engr. charge Vibration Test Unit, Propeller div. Curtiss-Wright Corp., Caldwell, N.J., 1941-47; cons. electronics Wilson Mech. Instrument Co., N.Y.C., 1945-47, Bridgeport, Conn., 1945-47; pres., chief engr. Am. Chronoscope Corp., Mt. Vernon, N.Y., 1948-50; spl. cons. Mercury Totalizator Co., Inc., N.Y.C., 1949-50; chief engr. Bulova Research & Devel. Labs., Inc., Flushing, N.Y., 1951-55, v.p., gen. mgr., 1955-57; dir. advanced programs U.S. Industries, Inc., N.Y.C., 1957-60, v.p., 1960-64, pres. Robodyne div., 1958-60; pres., dir., chief exec. officer E.F. Shelley & Co., Inc., N.Y.C., 1965-72, chmn., 1972-75; dir. Center for Energy Policy and Research, N.Y. Inst. Tech., Old Westbury, 1975—. Past pres. Nat. Council Aging; mem. adv. com. OEO. Trustee N.Y. Inst. Tech., Nova U.; bd. dirs. Center for Community Change. Mem. IEEE (sr.), Am. Phys. Soc., Am. Inst. Aeros. and Astronautics, Newcomen Soc. N.Am., AAAS. Patentee in field. Home: 339 Oxford Rd New Rochelle NY 10804 Office: NY Inst Tech Old Westbury NY 11568

SHELP, RONALD KENT, ins. holding co. exec.; b. Cartersville, Ga., Sept. 29, 1941; s. Clarence Harrison and Willie Marion (Puckett) Mulkey; A.B. cum laude, U. Ga., 1964; M.A. (Crown-Zellerbach fellow 1964-65, Francis Bolton fellow 1965-66), Johns Hopkins Sch. Advanced Internat. Studies, 1966. Sr. asso. C. of C. of U.S.A., Washington, 1966-73; exec. sec. Assn. Am. Chambers Commerce in Latin Am., 1969-73; exec. sec. Internat. Ins. Adv. Council, trade assn. U.S. ins. cos. operating overseas, Washington, 1966-73; v.p. Am. Internat. Group, Inc., 1973—; v.p., dir. Am. Internat. Underwriters; v.p. other cos.; dir. Am. Internat. Ins. Co. Ireland, Ltd.; exec. v.p., also partner Art Enterprises Internat., 1971-72; U.S. expert del. Bus. Adv. Council OAS, Caracas, Venezuela, 1970; co-chmn. pvt. sector adv. group to Dept. State on UN Conf. Sci. and Tech. for Devel.; U.S. expert selected for Trade Policy Research Centre Studies on Internat. Trade and Investment in Services; U.S. rep. Commn. on Ins., ICC, Paris, 1974—, chmn. working party non-tariff measures in ins., 1976—; adv. bd. Council of Ams., 1976—; exec. com. Internat. Ins. Adv. Council, 1974—; alt., adviser to vice chmn. Polish-U.S. Econ. Council, 1974—; guest lectr. London Sch. Econs.; participant radio series. Mem. Pres.'s Peru Earthquake Vol. Assistance Group, rep., del. OECD, 1975—; co-chmn. Young Execs. for Humphrey-Muskie, Greater Washington area, 1968; trustee Pan Am. Devel. Found., 1978—. Served with AUS, 1966-72. Mem. Peruvian-Am. Assn. (dir. 1975—), Internat. C. of C. (fgn. investment com. U.S. council), Center for Inter-Am. Relations, Fgn. Policy Assn. (asso.), Council Fgn. Relations, U.S. Can. Com. Blue Key, Phi Beta Kappa, Phi Kappa Phi, Phi Eta Sigma, Pi Sigma Alpha, Omicron Delta Kappa. Democrat. Clubs: Internat., India House, Downtown Athletic (Washington). Author: The Post Industrial Society: Services in the World Economy in the 1980's, 1978; (with J. Peno and N. Truitt) Transfer of Technology in Service Industries: Its Role in Economic Development, 1979; contbr. articles to internat. jours. Home: 32 Washington Sq W Apt 16E New York City NY 10011 Office: 102 Maiden Ln New York City NY 10005

SHEN, CHIN CHIU, elec. engr.; b. Nanking, China, Dec. 22, 1947; s. K.C. and T.C. (Han) S.; came to U.S., 1970; B.S. in Elec. Engring., Nat. Taiwan U., Taipei, 1969; M.S., State U. N.Y., Stony Brook, 1971; Ph.D. in Elec. Engring., Stanford U., 1976; m. Nancy Liu, June 22, 1974; 1 dau., Emily L. Engring. asst. Philco Ford Co., Taiwan, 1966; lectr. Army Signal Sch., Chungli, Taiwan, 1969-70; teaching asst. State U. N.Y., Stony Brook, 1970-71; research asst. solid-state electronics lab. Stanford U. (Calif.), 1972-76; mem. tech. staff applied physics group Lincoln Lab., Mass. Inst. Tech., Lexington, 1976-78, staff scientist Laser Diode Lab., Metuchen, 1978—. Mem. IEEE, Am. Phys. Soc.

SHENFELD, MARVIN, retail co. exec.; b. N.Y.C., Dec. 6, 1930; s. Solomon and Rose (Kohn) S.; B.S., Tufts Coll., 1952, M.A., 1956; m. Sheila Greenblatt, Mar. 30, 1958; children—Steven, Robert, David. Systems engr. IBM, N.Y.C., 1956-60; mgmt. cons., N.Y.C., 1960-67; v.p. S. Kleins Dept. Stores, N.Y.C., 1967-72; v.p. Alexander Dept. Stores, N.Y.C., 1972—; instr. N.Y. U. Sch. Advanced Studies. Served with U.S. Army, 1952-54. Mem. Am. Mktg. Assn., Assn. Computing Machinery, Met. Controllers Congress. Home: 1 Arthur Dr E Rockaway NY 11518 Office: 31 W 34th St New York City NY 10001

SHENKMAN, MARK RONALD, mut. fund exec.; b. Providence, Aug. 17, 1943; s. George and Florence (Littman) S.; B.A., U. Conn., 1965; M.B.A., George Washington U., 1967; m. Gloria J. Abrams, May 26, 1974; 1 son, Andrew Harris. Security analyst New Eng. Mchts. Nat. Bank, Boston, 1969-71; financial analyst Stone & Webster Securities Co., Boston, 1971-73; portfolio analyst Fidelity Mgmt. & Research Co., Boston, 1973-76; portfolio mgr. Fidelity Aggressive Income Fund, 1977—. Trustee Wilbraham and Monson Acad., Wilbraham, Mass., 1970—. Served to 1st lt. Q.M.C., U.S. Army, 1967-69. Mem. Boston Security Analysts Soc., Bond Analysts Soc. Boston, Fin. Analysts Fedn. Home: 18 Minebrook Rd Sudbury MA 01776 Office: 82 Devonshire St Boston MA 02109

SHEPARD, ELEANOR STORM, dietitian; b. Nashua, N.H., Jan. 31, 1924; d. Stephen George and Marion Katherine (Barnes) Storm; B.S., U. N.H., 1944; postgrad. Mich. State U., 1948-49, 53-54; m. Frederick Ward Shepard, Mar. 21, 1959. Staff dietitian Boston City Hosp., 1944-45; head dietitian Cushing VA Hosp., Framingham, Mass., 1949-50; adminstrv. dietitian VA Hosp., Northampton, Mass., 1955-72, chief dietetic service, 1972—. Mem. Pelham (Mass.) Council on Aging, 1973—; bd. dirs. Highland Valley Elder Service Center, Northampton, 1974—; mem. Hampshire County Housing Authority, 1978. Served with Women's Med. Specialist Corps, U.S. Army, 1946-48, 51-52. Mem. Am., Mass. dietetic assns. Zonta (pres. Northampton chpt. 1978—). Home: Arnold Rd Pelham MA 01002 Office: VA Hosp Northampton MA 01060

SHEPARD, GEORGE, JR., obstetrician, gynecologist; b. Raleigh, N.C., Feb. 27, 1923; s. George and Beatrice S.; B.S., Howard U., 1946, M.D., 1950; m. Evelyn Dolores, June 27, 1946; children—Peggy, Nina, Ana Shelley, George, Gregory. Intern, Freedmen's Hosp., Washington, 1950-51, resident, 1951-55; chief obstetrics and gynecology Mercer Med. Center, Trenton, 1970-73, attending obstetrician and gynecologist, 1974-76, chief obstetrics and gynecology, dept. chmn., 1976—; asst. dir. clin. research Abbott Labs., North Chicago, Ill., 1973-74; med. dir. Planned Parenthood, Mercer County, 1976—; chief obstetrics and gynecology Mercer Regional Med. Group, 1976—; attending obstetrician, Henry J. Austin Health Center, 1974—. Served with U.S. Army, 1944-46. Recipient award for profl. service to pub. Community Health Center, 1977. Diplomate Am. Bd. Obstetrics and Gynecology. Fellow Am. Coll. Obstetricians and Gynecologists; mem. AMA, Nat. Med. Assn., N.J. Med. Soc. and Mercer Component. Methodist. Club: Alpha Phi Alpha. Home: 12 Shadowstone St Lawrenceville NJ 08648 Office: 433 Bellevue Ave Trenton NJ 08618

SHEPARD, JEAN HECK HASTINGS, author; b. N.Y.C., Feb. 2, 1930; d. Chester Reed and Anna S. (Charig) Heck; B.A., Barnard Coll., 1950; m. Lawrence V. Hatings, Mar. 29, 1950; 1 son, Lance; m. 2d, Daniel A. Shepard, July 26, 1954; 1 son, Bradley Reed. With sch. and library dept. Viking Press, N.Y.C., 1956-57; asst. dir. sch. and library promotion E.P. Dutton Co., N.Y.C., 1957-58; dir. publicity, advt. and promotion Thomas Y. Crowell Co., N.Y.C., 1958-62; dir. advt. Charles Scribner's Sons, N.Y.C., 1962-67; cons. Stephen Greene Press, Brattleboro, Vt., 1970-72; author: Simple Family Favorites, 1971; Herb and Spice Cooking, 1972; The Harvest Home Steak Cookbook, 1974; Earth Watch: Notes on a Restless Planet, 1974; Cook with Wine!, 1973; The Fresh Fruits and Vegetables Cookbook, 1975; A Survival Handbook for Women, 1978. Mem. Authors Guild, Authors League Am. Methodist. Address: 69 Deerfield Dr Greenwich CT 06830

SHEPARD, JOAN HAYDEN, actress, theatrical producer; b. N.Y.C., Jan. 7, 1933; d. Hayden Carlos and Sylvia Delane (Wasson) Shepard; student Hunter Coll., 1950-51, Royal Acad. Dramatic Art, London, 1951-52; m. Evan Thompson, Dec. 13, 1959; children—Owen Harlan Thompson, Jennifer Sylvia Thompson. Appeared in Broadway plays: Romeo and Juliet, 1940, Sunny River, 1941, The Strings Are False, 1942, This Rock, 1943, Tomorrow the World, 1943-44, Foolish Notion, 1945-46, A Young Man's Fancy, 1946, 47, 48, My Romance, 1948-49, The Member of the Wedding, 1950-51; appeared in Off-Broadway plays: Othello, 1953-54, The Prince and The Pauper, 1963-64, others; appeared in title roles at Madison Sq. Garden: Alice Through The Looking Glass, 1969, Pinocchio, 1969; exec. producer, leading player Fanfare Theatre Ensemble, N.Y.C., 1971—. Treas. Fourth St. Block Assn., N.Y.C. Mem. Actors' Equity Assn., Screen Actors Guild, AFTRA. Club: N.Y. Health and Racquet. Co-author musical plays for children, including: The Pied Piper of Hamelin, 1966 (shown on Nat. Ednl. TV, 1967, 68-69; recipient spl. award WITF-TV, Hershey, Pa.). Home: 102 E 4th St New York City NY 10003 Office: 100 E 4th St New York City NY 10003

SHEPARD, ROBERT DANIEL, clin. psychologist; b. Bklyn., Dec. 18, 1944; s. Albert Morton and Esther (Salzman) S.; B.S., U. Mich., 1967; Ph.D., Cath. U., 1974; m. Jane Blair, Jan. 20, 1979; 1 dau., Lisa Suzanne. Faculty cons., research psychologist John Hopkins U., Balt., 1973-74; research psychologist Nat. Inst. Occupational Safety and Health, Cin., 1974-75; clin. psychologist VA Hosp., Hampton, Va., 1975-76, acting dir. Mental Hygiene Clinic, 1976, coordinator alcoholism services, 1976-77; v.p. Motivation Dynamics, Inc., Yorktown Heights, N.Y.; adj. instr. various colls. and univs.; cons. in field. USPHS grantee, 1974-75. Mem. Am. Psychol. Assn., Va. Assn. Alcoholism Counselors, Council on Alcoholism (dir. Newport News, Va. chpt.). Democrat. Unitarian. Co-editor: Shiftwork and Health, 1976. Contbr. articles on alcoholism to profl. jours. Home: 93 Paulding Ln Crompond NY 10517

SHEPARD, THOMAS R., JR., publishing cons.; b. N.Y.C., Aug. 22, 1918; s. Thomas R. and Marie (Dickinson) S.; B.A., Amherst Coll., 1940; m. Nancy Kruidenier, Sept. 20, 1941; children—Sue Shepard Mould, Molly Shepard Lunkenhelmer, Amy K., Thomas R. With Look mag., 1946-71, mgr. West Coast, 1947-49, asst. to pub., promotion dir., 1955, mgr. N.Y.C., 1956, asst. advt. mgr., 1957, advt. sales mgr., 1961-64, advt. dir., 1964-67, pub., 1967-71; v.p. Cowles Communications, Inc., 1958-71, also dir., cons., 1972-76; cons. Outdoor Advt. Assn. Am., 1972-74; pres. Inst. Outdoor Advt., 1974-77; dir. Advt. Council. Pres., Greenwich Community Chest, 1965-66; chmn. Taft Inst. Govt. Served to lt. comdr. USNR, 1941-45. Recipient George Washington medal Freedoms Found., 1970, 73. Co-author: The Disaster Lobby. Home: 44 Lismore Ln Greenwich CT 06830

SHEPHERD, DONALD, ins. cons.; b. Gloucester, Mass., Apr. 24, 1908; s. George C. and Blanche (Poole) S.; student Northeastern U. Sch. Bus. Adminstrn., 1927; m. Catherine L. Lee, Oct. 28, 1933; 1 dau., Jean Lee Shepherd Sears. Ins. cons., Boston, 1930—; dir. Electro Switch Corp., Weymouth, Mass., Scituate Savs. and Loan. Bd. dirs., trustee South Shore Hosp., Weymouth, pres., 1961-63; pres. Million Dollar Round Table Found., 1971-72. Named Man of Year, John Hancock Life Ins. Co., 1974. Mem. Boston Life Underwriters Assn. (pres. 1963), Nat. Assn. Life Underwriters (exec. com. Million Dollar Round Table 1962-67, pres. 1966, mem. polit. action com. 1966—), NCCJ (dinner com.), Boston C. of C. Episcopalian. Republican. Clubs: Rotary; Bay (Boston); Scituate (Mass.) Country. Home: 104 Edward Foster Rd Scituate MA 02066 Office: One Winthrop Sq Boston MA 02110

SHEPHERD, RICHARD MONTGOMERY, chem. engr.; b. Phila., June 25, 1919; s. Richard and Florence (Regester) S.; B.S., Lehigh U., 1941; m. Margaret Veeder, May 15, 1943; children—Joan R., Margot M., Sandra G., David M. Engr., devel. supr., 1945-56, tech. supt., mfg. supt., 1957-63, plant mgr., 1966-71, tech. mgr., 1971-72, environ. cons., 1973—. Served with AUS, 1941-45: ETO. Decorated Bronze Star medal. Mem. Am. Inst. Chem. Engrs., Am. Def. Preparedness Assn., Alpha Sigma Phi. Republican. Protestant Episcopalian. Patentee hydrogen cyanide process. Home: 8 School Rd Wilmington DE 19803 Office: DuPont Bldg Wilmington DE 19898

SHEPPARD, JACK CORNELL, JR., social worker; b. Woodbury, N.J., Jan. 31, 1953; s. Jack Cornell and Helen Mae S.; B.A., W.Va. Wesleyan Coll., 1975; M.A., W.Va. U., 1976. Case mgr. Cornell & Co., Woodbury, N.J., 1976; social worker, counselor N.J. Div. Mental Retardation, Wenonah, 1977—. Bd. dirs. Robins Nest Group Home, Glassboro Child Devel. Center, 1977-78; baseball coach Pony League, Wenonah, summers 1976, 77. Mem. Am. Personnel and Guidance Assn., Theta Chi. Home: Box 258 US 322 Williamstown NJ 08094 Office: 730 White Horse Pike Hammonton NJ

SHEPPARD, POSY (MRS. JOHN WADE SHEPPARD), social worker; b. New Haven, Aug. 23, 1916; d. John Day and Rose Marie (Herrick) Jackson; student Vassar Coll., 1938; m. John W. Sheppard, May 16, 1936; children—Sandra (Mrs. Allan Rodgers), Gail G. (Mrs. J. Truman Bidwell, Jr.), Lynn S. (Mrs. William Muir Manger), John W. Vol. field cons. Conn. A.R.C., 1955-61; mem. bd. govs. Am. Nat. Red Cross, 1960-66, vice chmn. 1962-66; rep. League Red Cross Socs. to UN, 1957—; rep. Am. Nat. Red Cross to com. internat. social welfare Nat. Social Welfare Assembly, 1957-61; chmn. non-govtl. orgns. com. UNICEF, 1962-64, 71-73; chmn. non-govtl. orgns. exec. com. Office Pub. Info., UN, 1963-66; pres conf. non-govtl. orgns. in consultative status with ECOSOC, 1966-69; mem. Internat. Yr. of Child Com. Mem. Nat. Inst. Social Scis. (v.p.), Nat. Soc. Colonial Dames, Jr. League Greenwich, Am. Soc. Polit. and Social Sci., Soc. Internat. Devel. Club: Cosmopolitan. Home: 535 Lake Ave Greenwich CT 06830

SHEPPARD, WALTER LEE, JR., cons.; b. Phila., June 23, 1911; s. Walter Lee and Martha Houston (Evans) S.; B.Chem., Cornell U., 1932; M.S., U. Pa., 1933; m. Dorothy Virginia Cosby Vanderslice, Oct. 11, 1942 (div. Mar. 1947); m. 2d, Boudinot Atterbury Oberge Kendall, Mar. 24, 1953; stepchildren—Charles H. Kendall Jr., John Atterbury Kendall. Control chemist various cos., 1933-35; advt. writer N.W. Ayer & Son, 1936-37; asst. to editor The Houghton Line, 1937-38; salesman Atlas Mineral Products, 1938-47; plant mgr., cons. engr. Tanks & Linings, Ltd., Droitwich, Eng., 1948-49; sales engr., dist. mgr. ElectroChem. Engring. & Mfg., and successor cos., 1949-68; field sales mgr. Corrosion Engring. div. Pennwalt Corp., Phila., 1968-76; pres. C.C.R.M., Inc.; cons. on chemically resistant masonry, 1976—; profl. genealogist, 1936—; ordained deacon Liberal Catholic Ch., 1954, priest, 1955. Dir. displaced persons camps UNRRA, also staff Chief of Mission, Vienna, Austria, 1945-46. Founding trustee Bd. Certification Genealogists, 1965—, pres., 1969-78, chmn., 1978—. Served to maj. U.S. Army, 1941-45; lt. col. Res. (ret.). Registered profl. engr., Del., Calif. Diplomate Am. Acad. Environ. Engrs. Fellow Am. Soc. Genealogists (sec. 1958-61, 66-67, v.p. 1967-70, pres. 1970-73), Nat., Pa. geneal. socs.; mem. Welcome Soc. (pres. 1966-76), Illegitimate Sons and Daus. of Kings and Queens of Britain (founder, sec. 1950-68, pres. 1968—), Flagon and Trencher Soc. (founder, pres. 1967-73), Nat. Assn. Corrosion Engrs. (certificate competence in corrosion engring.; chmn. Phila. sect. 1959), Nat. Soc. Profl. Engrs., ASTM, Assn. Cons. Chemists and Chem. Engrs., Colonial Soc. Pa. (council 1975—), New Eng. Historic Geneal. Soc., Nat. Geneal. Soc. (contbg. editor quar.), Soc. Genealogists (London), Yorkshire Archeol. Soc., Savoy Co., Gilbert and Sullivan Soc. (founder, Eng. pres. Phila. br. 1957-63), Phi Kappa Psi (nat. v.p. 1964-68, pres. 1968-70), Sovereign Order St. John of Jerusalem, Mil. Order Fgn. Wars, Mayflower Descs., Order of Three Crusades, Alpha Chi Sigma. Author: Handbook of Chemically Resistant Masonry, 1977; Ancestors of Edward Carleton and Ellen Newton, His Wife, 1977; editor: Ships and Passengers; Ancestral Roots of 60 New England Colonists, 6th edit.; contbg. editor Am. Genealogist; mem. publs. com. Pa. Geneal. Mag., 1960-76; contbr. articles on corrosion resistant masonry constrn. to profl. jours. Home and Office: 923 Old Manoa Rd Havertown PA 19083

SHERBURNE, ALBERT LOVERING, optometrist; b. Somerville, Mass., Oct. 12, 1947; s. Gordon R.and Mildred E. (Lovering) S.; B.A., Boston U., 1969; O.D., Mass. Coll. Optometry, 1973; m. Barbara C. Robson, May 29, 1971; children—Melissa B., Carole E. Practice optometry, Lexington, Mass., 1975—; clin. asso. Optometric Extension Program; chmn. N.E. Congress Optometry. Served with USAF, 1973-75, Mass. Air N.G., 1975—. Mem. Mass. Soc. Optometrists (chmn. Middlesex dist.), Am. Optometric Assn., Mass. Pub. Health Assn. Democratic. Evangelical Protestant. Club: Lexington Lions. Home: 88 Waverley St Arlington MA 02174 Office: 120 School St Lexington MA 02173

SHERER, JOSEPH FOREST, JR., genito-urinary surgeon; b. Worcester, Mass., Oct. 17, 1918; s. Joseph Forest and Marion (Osborn) S.; A.B., Harvard U., 1941; M.D., Tufts U., 1945; M.Sc., U. Pa., 1951; m. Mary Frances Mackintosh, Dec. 27, 1943; children—Adelaide Orie Sherer Bennet, Joseph Forest. Intern, Boston City Hosp., 1945-46; resident in urology U. Pa. and Lankenau Hosp., 1948-51; practice medicine specializing in urology, Worcester, Mass., 1951—; chief urology Meml. Hosp., Worcester, 1965—; staff U. Mass. Med. Center, St. Vincent's Hosp.; asso. prof. urology U. Mass. Med. Sch., Worcester, 1974—. Mem. Brooks Sch. Council, N. Andover, 1965-75; trustee Worcester Sci. Mus., 1972—; trustee, pres. Bancroft Sch., 1961-73. Served to capt. M.C., U.S. Army, 1942-48. Diplomate Am. Bd. Urology. Fellow A.C.S.; mem. Am. Urol. Assn. (exec. com. 1975—), Worcester Dist., Mass. med. socs., New Eng. Cancer Soc., New Eng. Urol. Soc., Worcester Fire Soc. Baptist. Clubs: Tatnuck Country, Yellow Label, Laurel Brook, Seaconnet Golf, Black Brook Salmon, Anglers, Sr. Golf Assn. Contbr. articles in field to med. jours. Office: 25 Oak Ave Worcester MA 01605

SHERIDAN, AMELIA PANZARELLA, restaurant exec.; b. N.Y.C., Jan. 27, 1949; d. Stanley and Laura (Culmone) Panzarella; B.A., Adelphi U., 1970; M.A., Hofstra U., 1971; m. Robert J. Sheridan, June 13, 1971. Speech pathologist, London and N.Y.C., 1971-75; Field analyst Ky. Fried Chicken of South Queens, 1975-78; corp. sec. Rebel Five Rib House, Rosedale, N.Y., 1977-78; mgr. catering sales Ky. Fried Chicken and Rebel Five Rib House, 1978—; coordinator farmers flea market, Rosedale, 1978—. Cert. of clin. competence in speech pathology Am. Speech and Hearing Assn.; lic. in speech pathology N.Y. State. Mem. Am., N.Y. State speech and hearing assns., Sigma Alpha Eta. Co-founder, editor, pub. (with Robin Hirshon) Living In Paradise mag. Home: 153 Beech St Valley Stream NY 11580 Office: 241-08 140th Ave Rosedale NY 11422

SHERIDAN, PATRICK MICHAEL, ins. co. exec.; b. Grosse Pointe, Mich., Apr. 13, 1940; s. Paul Phillip and Frances Mary (Rohan) S.; B.B.A., U. Notre Dame, 1962; M.B.A., U. Detroit, 1975; m. Jane Louise Hansinger, May 30, 1962; children—Mary, Patrick, Kelly, Kevin, James. C.P.A., Peat, Marwick, Mitchell & Co., Detroit, 1962-72, audit mgr., 1969-72; exec. v.p. finance Alexander Hamilton Life Ins. Co., Farmington, Mich., 1973-76; sr. v.p. ops. Sun Life Ins. Co. Am., Balt., 1976-78, exec. v.p., 1978—; pres. Sun Ins. Services, Inc., 1979—. Republican candidate for U.S. Congress, 1972. Trustee Met. Fund; bd. dirs. Regional Citizens. Served to capt. AUS, 1963-65. Recipient various Jaycee awards. Mem. Am. Inst. C.P.A.'s, Mich. Assn. C.P.A.'s (ins. com.), Md. Assn. C.P.A.'s, U.S. (treas. 1973-74), Mich. (pres. 1971-72), Detroit (pres. 1968-69) jaycees. Home: 175 Spalding Mill Dr Atlanta GA 30338 Office: Sun Life Bldg Baltimore MD 21201

SHERIDAN, VINCENT GEORGE, ecologist, land planner, real estate cons.; b. N.Y.C., Apr. 15, 1921; s. Vincent Justus and Julia Martha (Rohde) S.; student Stevens Inst. Tech., 1938-40, 47, N.Y. U., 1942, Mohawk Coll., 1946, Russell Sage Coll.; B.S. in Civil Engring., U. Colo., 1951, B.S. in Bus., 1951; postgrad. Union Coll., 1956, 67, Cornell U., 1962, Am. Savs. and Loan Inst., 1962-63, Russell Sage Coll., U. Conn., U. Md., Fairleigh Dickinson U., 1977-78; others; D.Religious Humanities. Expediter, Western Electric Co.; indsl. engr. DeLaval Separator Co.; asst. engr. N.Y. State Dept. Pub. Works; civil engr. Savin Constrn. Co., McDonald Engring. Co.; asst. supt. Beacon Constrn. Co.; elec., mech. engr. Gen. Electric Co.; valuation engr. Bur. Claims, Bd. Water Supply, N.Y.C.; cons. open space planning and design, rural planning and devel., appraising, real estate, engring., land surveying, sanitation, bldg. and hwy. design and constrn., water supply, econs., drainage and flood control, Eastern N.Y. State, 1957—; pres. Tri-State Planners & Developers, Inc.; chmn. Fed. Appraisal and Devel., Inc.; prin. Dailey-Sheridan Assos., Estate and Tax Cons., Andes; chmn. Ecol. Corp. Am.; prin. Buck-Sheridan Assos., Sheridan and Gally Realtors, Kingston. Condemnation commr. urban renewal Catskill, N.Y.; mem. faculty Ulster Co. Community Coll., Delhi Agr. and Tech. Coll., Bus. Planning Inst. Chmn. Greene County Planning Com., 1961-62; sec. Vol. Fire Co., Leeds, N.Y., 1954-57, pres., 1961—. Pres. Young Republicans Club, Greene County, 1960-61; 3d jud. dist. chmn. N.Y. State Young Rep. Clubs 1959-61, mem. exec. com. 1960-61; vice chmn. Conservative party, Greene County, 1966-68. Served with USNR, 1942-46; ETO, PTO. Registered profl. engr., N.Y., Pa. Fellow Am. Congress Surveying and Mapping, Royal Soc. Health, N.Y. State Recreation and Park Soc.; mem. Am. Soc. Appraisers, Am. Water Works Assn., Am. Right of Way Assn., ASCE, Am. Water Resources Assn., Am. Arbitration Assn., Am. Soc. Planning Ofcls., Am. Soc. Agrl. Engrs., Am. Acad. Polit. and Social Sci., Community Planning Assn. Can., Am. Inst. Urban and Regional Affairs, Am. Ordnance Assn., Ground Water Resources Inst., N.Y. State Assn. Professions, Nat. Conf. State Parks, N.Y. State Fedn. Ofcl. Planning Orgns., Water Resources Assn. Del. River Basin, Soc. Am. Mil. Engrs., Soc. Internat. Devel., Bldg. Research Inst., NRC, Am. Forestry Assn., N.Y. State Soc. Real Estate Appraisers, Nat. Farm and Land Inst., Nat. Fencing Coaches Assn. Am., Nat. Soc. Profl. Engrs., Am. Coll. Real Estate Cons., Nat. Fire Protection Assn., Am. Soc. Bus. and Mgmt. Cons., Am. Real Estate and Urban Econs. Assn., Appraisal Inst. Can., Am. Cons. Engring. Council, Ecol. Soc. Am., Fin. Mgmt. Assn., Human Ecol. Soc., Nat. Assn. Fire Underwriters, Nat. Assn. Real Estate Appraisers, Nat. Assn. Environ. Profls., Nat. Assn. Review Appraisers, Nat. Assn. Realtors, Nat. Assn. Tax Consulators, Nat. Planning Assn., Nat. Recreation and Park Assn., Nat. Soc. Park Resources, Urban Land Inst., Sigma Tau, Chi Epsilon, Tau Beta Pi, numerous other socs. and assns. Mason (32 deg.), Kiwanian. Home: RD 2 Vedder Rd Catskill NY 12414 Office: Boze's Ln Kingston NY 12401

SHERLOCK, DULCIE-ANN STEINHARDT, civic worker; b. N.Y.C., Nov. 1, 1925; d. Laurence A. and Dulcie (Hofmann) S.; student Am. Women's Coll., Istanbul, Turkey, 1941-43; m. Allan Arthur Sherlock, Oct. 7, 1950 (dec. Mar. 1971); children—Laurene-Ann, Victor Allan. Social sec. to U.S. ambassador, Ankara, Turkey, 1943-45, Prague, Czechoslovakia, 1945-48, Ottawa, Ont., Can., 1948-50; ceremonial officer Dept. State, Washington, 1974-76. Pres. Home and Sch. Assn., Morin Heights, P.Q., Can., 1956; sec. Maret Sch. Parent's Assn., Washington, 1964; chmn. fund-raisings Sidwell Friends Sch., 1968, 70; sec. Parent's Assn., Sheridan Sch., Washington, 1969; vestryman All Saint's Ch., Chevy Chase, Md., 1971-76, pres. Women's Bd., 1969; pres. women's bd. Episcopal Ch. Home, Washington, 1972-74; mem. and v.p. bd. govs. Episcopal Ch. Home and Friendship Terrace Inc., Washington, 1972-74. Clubs: Columbia Country (Chevy Chase, Md.); Coral Beach and Tennis (Paget, Bermuda); Georgetown (Washington); Cap Estate (St. Lucia, W.I.). Home: 5808 Connecticut Ave Chevy Chase MD 20015

SHERLOCK, PAUL, physician; b. N.Y.C., Oct. 7, 1928; s. Joseph and Estelle (Salzman) (dec.) S.; B.S., Queens Coll., 1950; M.D., Cornell U. Med. Coll., 1954; m. Marcia Regina Rohr, Mar. 29, 1952; children—Diane, Susan, Nancy. Intern Bellevue Hosp., N.Y.C., 1954-55; resident Bellevue Hosp.-Meml. Sloan-Kettering Cancer Center, 1957-60; Nat. Cancer Inst. trainee, 1959-60; Am. Cancer Soc. postdoctoral research fellow, 1960-62; head gastrointestinal physiology sect. Sloan Kettering Inst. for Cancer Research, N.Y.C., 1978—; chief gastroenterology service Meml. Sloan-Kettering Cancer Center, 1970-78, asso. chmn. dept. medicine, 1976-77, acting chmn., 1977-78, chmn., 1978—; cons. med. staff North Shore U. Hosp., 1978—; vis. physician Rockefeller U. Hosp., 1978—; practice medicine specializing in gastroenterology and internal medicine, N.Y.C., 1962—; attending physician N.Y. Hosp., N.Y.C., 1975—; prof. medicine Cornell U. Med. Coll., N.Y.C., 1975—; med. dir. Moore McCormack Lines, Inc., N.Y.C., 1967—; working cadre, co-chmn. early diagnosis prevention and human genetics of nat. large bowel cancer project Nat. Cancer Inst., Bethesda, Md., 1973-77, mem. diagnostic radiology com., 1974-76; mem. nat. comm. digestive diseases NIH, 1977-78. Trustee Lenox Sch., N.Y.C., Alumni Assn. Queens Coll., Flushing, N.Y. Served to lt. comdr. USNR, 1955-57. Recipient Gold medal VIII Internat. Congress Gastroenterology, 1968. Diplomate Am. Bd. Internal Medicine (asso. mem. bd. govs. 1975—, also certified and mem. subsplty. bd. gastroenterology). Fellow A.C.P., Am. Coll. Gastroenterology, N.Y. Acad. Gastroenterology, N.Y. Acad. Scis.; mem. Am. Soc. Internal Medicine, AMA, Am. Fedn. Clin. Research, Soc. Surg. Oncology (exec. council 1976—), Am. Soc. Gastrointestinal Endoscopy (chmn. membership com. 1972-75, governing bd. 1974—, sec. 1976-77, pres. elect 1977-78, pres. 1978—), Am. Soc. Clin. Oncology, Am. (chmn. council on cancer 1975-78, liaison mem. nat. cancer adv. bd. 1975—), N.Y. (pres. 1973-74) gastroent. assns., Harvey Soc., Am. Cancer Soc. (task force on colon and rectal cancer 1974—), N.Y. Cancer Soc., Nat. Found. Ileitis and Colitis (sci. adv. com. 1977—), Am. Assn. Study Liver Diseases. Asso. editor Am. Jour. Digestive Diseases, 1973-77, editorial bd., 1977—; editorial staff Gastroenterology, 1973-76. Contbr. articles to profl. jours. Home: 345 E 68th St New York City NY 10021 Office: 425 E 67th St New York City NY 10021

SHERMAN, CONSTANCE DENISE, educator; b. Oberlin, Ohio, Sept. 6, 1909; d. Philip Darrell and Amanda Pearl (Thirkield) Sherman; student Oberlin Coll., 1926-30; A.B., Smith Coll., 1932; A.M., Sorbonne 1933; Diplome d'aptitude pour l'enseignement, U. Grenoble; postgrad U. Munich, U. Mex., Middlebury Coll.; Cours d'ete, U. Laval; Litt.D., Keuka Coll., 1961. Instr. Edgewood Park, Briarcliff Manor, N.Y., 1933-38; asst. prof. Coker Coll., Hartsville, S.C., 1938-43; translator Cross Cultural Survey, Yale, 1943-44; fgn. lang. sec. Am. Mus. Natural History, N.Y.C., 1945-61; prof. modern lang. Queensborough Community Coll., City U. N.Y., Bayside, N.Y.; lectr. Wagner Coll. S.I., N.Y., 1952-59. Trustee fellowship Smith Coll., 1931-32. Recipient faculty research fellowship State U. N.Y., 1970. Mem. P.E.N., Soc. Woman Geographers (chmn. N.Y. group 1969-72; nat. v.p. 1969-72, sec. N.Y. Council 1972—), Nat. Soc. Colonial Dames, Daus. Founders and Patriots (N.Y. State registrar 1976), N.Y., R.I., hist. socs., N.Y. Geneal. and Biog. Soc., Phi Beta Kappa. Republican. Episcopalian. Author and translator. Home: 21 Iowa Rd Great Neck NY 11020 Office: Queensborough Community Coll Bayside NY 11364

SHERMAN, GERALD HOWARD, lawyer; b. N.Y.C., Aug. 29, 1932; s. Abraham and Jean (Rose) S.; B.B.A., Coll. City N.Y., 1953; LL.B., Harvard U., 1958; m. Lola Barbara Kay, Mar. 19, 1961; children—Jonathan, Ann. Admitted to N.Y. bar, 1959, D.C. bar, 1960; practiced in Washington, 1958—; mem. firm Cooper & Silverstein, 1958-61, partner Silverstein & Mullens, 1961—; adj. prof. Georgetown U. Law Center, 1974—, also mem. Adv. Bd. Tax Mgmt., 1960—, BNA Pension Reporter. Mem. Am. Bar Assn., Bar Assn. D.C. Home: 11112 Whisperwood Ln Rockville MD 20852 Office: 1776 K St NW Washington DC 20006

SHERMAN, JONATHAN GOODHUE, clergyman; b. St. Louis, June 13, 1907; s. Stephen Fish and Marion Louise (Goodhue) S.; A.B., Yale U., 1929; S.T.B., Gen. Theol. Sem., 1936, S.T.D., 1949; D.C.L., Nashotah House, 1971; m. Frances Le Baron Casady, Jan. 1, 1938; children-Thomas Oakley, Sallie Goodhue, Marilyn Nancy, Jonathan Goodhue. Fellow and tutor Gen. Theol. Sem., 1933-35; ordained priest Episcopal Ch., 1934; priest in charge St. Thomas's Ch., Farmingdale, L.I., 1935-38; rector St. Thomas Ch., Bellerose, L.I., 1939-49; suffragan bishop, L.I., 1949-66, bishop, L.I., 1966-77; instr. Holy Scripture George Mercer Jr. Meml. Sch. Theology, 1956—; Protestant chaplain Creedmoor State Hosp., 1940-49; sec. Trustees of Estate Belonging to Diocese of L.I., 1945-48; mem. nat. council Episc. Service for Youth, 1945-56, pres., 1952-56; pres. Ch. Mission of Help, Diocese L.I., 1944-51; pres. Am. Church Bldg. Fund Commn., 1955-73; pres. Episc. Ch. Bldg. Fund, 1973—; chmn. joint commn. Ch. Architecture and Allied Arts, 1956-65; mem. com. Pastoral Devel., 1958-74; mem. Standing Liturgical Commn., 1965-70; mem. Anglican-Orthodox Consultation, 1968-77; mem. Joint Commn. Ecumenical Relations, 1973-77; chmn. Council Relations with the Eastern Chs., 1972-77; mem. Dept. Christian Edn., 1937-44, dir., 1956-60; dean Diocesan Leaders' Conf., 1938, 1945, 1946; trustee Gen. Theol. Sem., 1961-76; visitor The Poor Clares, 1967—; mem. exec. council C.W. Post Coll., 1964-70; trustee House of the Redeemer, 1949—, v.p., 1966—. Mem. Anglican Soc. (pres. 1953-62), Pi Alpha. Club: Union League (N.Y.C.). Author: The Christian Faith, 1935; The Spirit of Knowledge, 1961; editor Tidings, 1943-45. Home: 120 Cherry Valley Rd Garden City NY 11530 Office: 36 Cathedral Ave Garden City NY 11530

SHERMAN, JOSEPH VINCENT, cons. economist, writer; b. Beacon, N.Y., Dec. 18, 1905; s. Joseph Francis and Catherine Adele (Killeen) S.; A.B., Columbia, 1928; m. Viola Signe Maria Lidfeldt, Nov. 18, 1944. Mgr. investment dept. Nat. Newark & Essex Banking Co., Newark, 1929-36; statistician Case, Pomeroy & Co., N.Y.C., 1936-38; v.p. Econ. Analysts, Inc., N.Y., 1938-42; asso. Herbert R. Simonds, cons. engr., 1943-45. Served with AUS, 1942-43. Mem. AAAS, Am. Econ. Assn., Am. Statis. Assn. Author: Research as a Growth Factor in Industry, 1940; The New Plastics, 1945; Plastics Business, 1946; The New Fibers, 1946. Contbr. to Barron's Nat. Bus. and Financial Weekly and various other pubs., 1939—. Home: 160 Columbia Heights Brooklyn NY 11201 Office: 280 Broadway New York City NY 10007

SHERMAN, JULIUS, mailing list co. exec.; b. Chgo., Oct. 28, 1917; s. Harry and Rose (Gliberman) S.; B.S., Coll. City N.Y., 1946; m. Florence Klein, Dec. 8, 1944; children—Rita, Ray. Dir. research Lewis Kleid Co., N.Y.C., 1950-52; with Walter Drey Inc., N.Y.C., 1952-64; with Dependable Mailing Lists Inc., N.Y.C., 1964—, dir. mail research, 1964—. Served with USAAF, 1942-45. Mem. Am. Mktg. Assn., Direct Mktg. Advt. Assn., Mailing List Brokers Profl. Assn., N.Y. Jazz Mus., Jazz Interactions. Home: 3360 21st St Long Island City NY 11106 Office: 257 Park Ave S New York City NY 10010

SHERMAN, LAWRENCE WILLIAM, sociologist; b. Schenectady, Oct. 25, 1949; s. Donald Lester and Margaret Louise (Heckman) S.; B.A., Denison U., 1970; M.A. (Univ. fellow), Chgo. U., 1970; diploma in criminology Cambridge (Eng.) U., 1973; M.A., Yale U., 1974, Ph.D., 1976; m. Eva Fass, Oct. 7, 1973. Urban fellow Office of Mayor, N.Y.C., 1970-71; projects dir. N.Y.C. Office of Police Commr., 1971-72; asso. in research Yale U., 1974-76; asst. prof. Sch. Criminal Justice, State U. N.Y., Albany, 1976—; exec. dir. Nat. Adv. Commn. on Higher Edn. for Police Officers, 1976—; cons. to police depts., founds., pubs., jours.; lectr. in field. Ford Found. travel and study grantee, 1972-73. Mem. Am. Sociol. Assn., Acad. Criminal Justice Scis., Phi Beta Kappa, Pi Sigma Alpha. Democrat. Quaker. Club: Yale (N.Y.C.). Author: (with C. Milton and T. Kelley) Team Policing, 1973; Scandal and Reform, 1978; The Quality of Police Education, 1978; editor: Police Corruption, 1974; contbg. editor Criminal Law Bull., 1977—. Home: 220 Lancaster St Albany NY 12210 Office: Sch Criminal Justice State U NY 1400 Washington Ave Albany NY 12222

SHERMAN, MARK MELVIN, cardiothoracic surgeon; b. Providence, Aug. 3, 1940; s. David Harold and Mollie Helen (Jaffe) S.; B.A., Clark U., 1962; M.D., Cornell U., 1966; m. Jane Lea Kotzer, Jan. 16, 1977. Intern, N.Y. Hosp., N.Y.C., 1966-67, gen. surgery resident, 1967-68, 70-73; resident in thoracic and cardiovascular surgery Boston U. Med. Center, 1974-76; practice medicine, specializing in cardiothoracic and vascular surgery Cardio-Thoracic and Vascular Surgery, Inc., Springfield, Mass., 1976—; clin. instr. surgery Tufts U. Med. Sch., Boston, 1977—; mem. staff Baystate Med. Center, Mercy Hosp. (both Springfield), Holyoke, Providence hosps. (both Holyoke, Mass.), Noble Hosp., Westfield, Mass. Served with USNR, 1968-70. Recipient Physicians Recognition award AMA, 1976; diplomate Am. Bd. Surgery, Am. Bd. Thoracic Surgery. Mem. Am. Coll. Chest Physicians, Mass., Hampden Dist. med. socs. Jewish. Contbr. articles to profl. jours. Home: 8 Greenwood Rd Wilbraham MA 01095 Office: 125 Liberty St Springfield MA 01103

SHERMAN, OTTO MARTIN, ins. co. exec.; b. N.Y.C., Apr. 7, 1910; s. Martin and Eva (Roth) S.; student N.Y. U., 1930; LL.B., Bklyn. Law Sch., 1931; m. Edna Rosen, May 29, 1936; children—Gail (Mrs. David Banker), James Paul. Admitted to N.Y. State bar, 1931; regional atty. OPA, N.Y. regional office, 1944-45; practiced law, 1945-49; with Equitable Life Ins. U.S., 1949—, asst. mgr., 1951-52; gen. agt. U.S. Life Ins. Co., 1952-59, pres. chmn. bd. Constn. Agy., Inc., 1952—; asso. dir. agys. Eastern Life Ins. Co. N.Y., 1959-60; exec. v.p., dir. Employers Planning Corp., 1960-63; v.p., dir. agys. Standard Security Life Ins. Co., 1960-62; pres., chmn. bd., chmn. exec. com. Pension Life Ins. Co. Am., 1963-66; pres., chmn. bd. Ben Franklin Life Ins. Co., 1964-74; chmn. bd. Am. Commonwealth Corp., 1964; pres., chmn. bd. Duo-Fund Plan Corp., 1969—; adv. bd. U.S. Trust Fund; mem. arbitration panel N.Y. Civil Ct., Am. Arbitration Assn. Mem. Internat. Assn. Health Underwriters (v.p., dir. N.Y. chpt.), Nat. Assn. Life Underwriters, Assn. Advanced Life Underwriters, Passaic-Bergen Life Underwriters Assn. (past pres.), Am. Acad. Polit. and Social Sci., Am., Eastern pension confs., Am. Soc. Pension Actuaries, Am. Risk and Ins. Assn., Am. Mus. Natural History Assn. Home: 1275 15th St Fort Lee NJ 07024 Office: 2083 Center Ave Fort Lee NJ 07024

SHERMAN, RALPH W(ILLIAM), entomol. cons., govt. ofcl.; b. Burlington, N.J., Oct. 16, 1897; s. William Conover and Mary (Morton) S.; B.S., Kans. State U., 1924; student N.Y. U., 1942-43, U.S. Dept. Agr. Grad. Sch., 1947-50, Control Data Corp. Inst., 1968;

m. Mary Eldridge Sholl, June 6, 1929; children—Emilie B., Ralph William, Roger W. With U.S. Dept. Labor, Washington, 1918-20; with bur. entomology and plant quarantine U.S. Dept. Agr., 1924-27, jr. to sr. plant quarantine officer, N.J., Conn., Pa., N.Y., asst. to chief of bur., Washington, 1947-53, staff asst. to chief of plant quarantine and plant pest control divs., 1954-59, chief regulatory services, plant quarantine div. Agrl. Research Service, 1959-67; dir. communications project Entomol. Soc. Am., 1968-69; entomol. cons., 1969—; dir. U.S. Dept. Agr. Welfare Assn., 1951-67, pres., 1958-59. Mem.-at-large Nat. Capital Area council Boy Scouts Am., 1963—; pres. Woodside Forest Citizens Assn., 1964-68; chmn. zoning, planning com. Allied Civic Group, Inc., 1963-66, 72, 74, corr. sec., 1967, pres., 1968-70, recipient outstanding civic service award, 1975; mem. Met. Congress Citizens, 1971—, treas., 1972, 76—, pres., 1973-74; vice-chmn. Montgomery County Bd. Edn. Adv. Com. Family Life, 1972-76, chmn., 1977-78; mem. Montgomery Coll. Adv. Com. Community Services, 1972-75; chmn. pub. safety citizen's adv. com. Met. Washington Council Govts., 1976-78; trustee Kans. State U. Endowment Assn., 1963—; bd. dirs. Silver Spring (Md.) Devel. Council, 1976—. Recipient citation U.S. Treasury Dept., 1945, U.S. Dept. Agr., 1957; Distinguished Service award Kans. State U., 1967. Registered Am. Registry Profl. Entomologists (governing council 1977-78). Mem. Orgn. Profl. Employees U.S. Dept. Agr. (v.p. pub. service 1966-69, recipient honor award 1967), AAAS, Entomol. Soc. Am. (governing bd. 1959-62, 71-73; program chmn. 1960; fin. com. 1962-67, 72, chmn. 1964-67; chmn. sect. E soc. 1967; chmn. Eastern br. 1968; editorial bd. Jour. Econ. Entomology 1969-74), Entomol. Soc. Washington (sec. 1950-51), Kans. Entomol. Soc., Insecticide Soc. Washington (pres. 1954-55), N.Y.C. Alumni Assn. Kans. State Coll. (pres. 1935-37, 39-41), Washington Alumni Assn. Kans. State Coll. (pres. 1951-53), Am. Coll. Quill Club, Sigma Xi, Phi Kappa Phi, Alpha Zeta (Distinguished Service award 1978), Gamma Sigma Delta, Pi Kappa Delta. Methodist (chmn. stewardship 1961-62, 73—). Club: Rotary (dir. 1957-59, 66-68, program chmn. 1959-60; chmn. Internat. Youth Commn. 1972-76). Co-author: History of Entomology in World War II, 1957; editor Plant Quarantine Service and Regulatory Announcements, 1947-57; contbr. articles to profl. jours., encys. and nat. mags. Home and Office: 1713 Luzenne Ave Silver Spring MD 20910

SHERMAN, ROBERT EDWAY, designer, mktg. cons.; b. Toledo, Sept. 15, 1924; s. Franklin Leonard and Janet Marjorie (Cogley) S.; student, Art Soc. St. Louis, 1938-40, U. Toledo, 1940-41, Art Center Sch. Los Angeles, 1943-44, Cranbrook Acad. Art and Architecture, 1944-45; m. Julianne Diehl Tiegel, Nov. 22, 1956; children—Deborah, Jan. Mfrs. rep. Scholtz Homes, Toledo, 1952-53; v.p. homebldg. activities System Built Homes, Norfolk, Va., 1954-56; dir. research and planning Crawford Homes, Baton Rouge, 1956-60; founder, partner, designer, mktg. cons. Sherman Assos., 1960—; cons. numerous mags., corps., over 160 major home builders, Nat. Assn. Homebuilders, numerous city planning groups, Home Mfrs. Assn., and Md. Handicap Programs. Served with USAAF, 1942. Recipient 1st place prize Best Interior Contest, Good Housekeeping mag. and Nat. Assn. Homebuilders, 1977. Mem. Nat. Assn. Homebuilders, Home Mfrs. Assn., Nat. Home Fashions League, Nat. Platform Assn., Nat. Soc. Interior Designers. Republican. Quaker. Club: Wash. Press. Designer, builder Quaker Meeting House, Virginia Beach, Va., 1956; inventor computer programs applicable to interior and archtl. design, 1978; contbr. over 100 articles to profl. magazines, newspapers. Home: 4620 North Park St Chevy Chase MD 20015 Office: 4901 Fairmont Ave Bethesda MD 20014

SHERMAN, ROBERT LEE, psychiatrist; b. N.Y.C., Mar. 3, 1929; s. Lee Daniel and Winnie (Borne) S.; student Cornell U., 1946-48; A.B., Washington U., St. Louis, 1950; M.S. in Medicine, Hahnemann Med. Coll., 1955; M.D., U. Geneva, 1960; m. Claudine Martin-de Lorme, June 21, 1974; children—Vicki Lee, Frank Scott. Intern in family practice Nassau County Med. Center, E. Meadow, N.Y., 1960-62; resident in psychiatry Kings Park (N.Y.) State Hosp., 1967-70; practice family medicine, Huntington, N.Y., 1963-68; dir. girls' adolescent unit N.E. Nassau Psychiat. Center, Kings Park, 1969-74, dir. med. edn., 1972-74; dir. psychiat. services Suffolk Developmental Center, Melville, N.Y., 1975-76, chief of service, adolescent and developmentally disabled units, 1976-77; chief med. officer Pilgrim Psychiat. Center, W. Brentwood, N.Y., 1978—; faculty Adelphi U., 1975-76, State U. N.Y. at Stony Brook, 1976-78. Chmn., United Fund Huntington Twp., 1964; mem. Suffolk County Adv. Bd., 1975-77; mem. N.Y. State Task Force on Autistic Children, 1973-75, L.I. Regional Task Force on Children and Youth, 1976-78. Recipient Community Service award Huntington Twp., 1964. Diplomate Am. Bd. Psychiatry and Neurology. Mem. Am. Psychiat. Assn., Am. Soc. Adolescent Psychiatrists, Am. Acad. Clin. Psychiatry, Royal Soc. Health. Club: Cercle Francais de Huntingtn. Contbr. articles to profl. jours. Office: Pilgrim Psychiat Center West Brentwood NY 11717 also 3003 Cardinal Dr Vero Beach FL 32960

SHERMAN, ROBERT MYLES, pharm. co. exec.; b. N.Y.C., Feb. 24, 1915; s. Jacob J. and Jeanette Sherman; student Bklyn. Poly. Inst., 1933-34, Cooper Union Inst., 1934-35, Baruch Sch. Bus., Coll. City N.Y., 1950-52; m. Gloria-Lee Jacobs, Oct. 27, 1949; children—Jeffrey, Bruce, Judi. Pres., Consol. Housing, Inc., 1959—, Martex Realty Corp., 1959—, Ultrex Realty Corp., 1958—, Butterfield Realty Corp., 1960—, Deltex Realty Corp., 1961—, owner Spl. Preparations Co., 1955—, Clin. Formulations, 1977— (all N.Y.C.). Served with USAAF, World War II. Decorated D.F.C., Air medal with 5 clusters. Office: 313 E 84th St New York City NY 10028

SHERMETA, DENNIS WILLIAM, pediatric surgeon; b. Hinsdale, Ill., Oct. 17, 1939; s. Peter Samuel and Stella Olga (Harris) S.; B.S., U. Mich., 1961, M.D., 1965; m. Margo Mensing, Aug. 2, 1963; children—Nicholas Harris, Benjamin James. Intern, U. Mich., Ann Arbor, 1965-66, r esident in surgery, 1966-67, Johns Hopkins Hosp., Balt., 1967-68; Robert Garrett fellow in pediatric surgery Johns Hopkins U. Sch. Medicine, 1968-69; resident in surgery dept. surgery U. Mich., 1969-71; chief resident div. pediatric surgery Johns Hopkins Hosp., 1973-74; asst. prof. surgery and pediatric surgery Sch. Medicine, Johns Hopkins U., Balt., 1974-77, asso. prof., 1977—; asst. prof. surgery and pediatric surgery U. Md. Sch. Medicine, Balt., 1974-76, asso. prof., 1976—; chief div. pediatric surgery U. Md. Hosp., 1974—; cons. div. pediatric surgery Union Meml. Hosp., Balt., 1975-76, Mercy Hosp., Balt., 1975—; vis. surgeon Balt. City Hosps., 1976—; cons. Pediatric Oncology Clinic, Johns Hopkins Hosp. and Birth Defects Treatment Center, John Hopkins Hosp., 1976—. Served to maj. M.C., USAF, 1971-73. Diplomate Am. Bd. Surgery. Recipient Frederick A. Coller award Mich. chpt. A.C.S., 1971. Mem. Balt. City Med. Soc., U. Md., Am. pediatric surg. socs., Assn. Academic Surgery, So. Soc. Pediatric Research, Soc. Surgery of Alimentary Tract, So. Perinatal Soc., A.C.S., Am. Acad. Pediatrics, Nu Sigma Nu. Republican. Contbr. articles in field to med. jours. Home: 7 Elmhurst Rd Baltimore MD 21210 Office: 600 N Broadway Baltimore MD 21205

SHERO, FRED ALEXANDER, profl. hockey coach; b. Winnipeg, Man., Can., Oct. 23, 1925. Profl. hockey player, 1943-57; defenseman N.Y. Rangers Nat. Hockey League team, then coach N.Y. Rangers farm clubs, 1957-58; coach Am. Hockey League team, Buffalo, 1968-70. Omaha Central Hockey League team, 1970-71, Phila. Flyers Nat. Hockey League team, 1971—. Address: care Philadelphia Flyers The Spectrum Pattison Pl Philadelphia PA 19148

SHERR, ABRAHAM I., glove mfg. co. exec.; b. N.Y.C., July 4, 1920; s. Ivens and Ethel (Kurlan) S.; B.A., N.Y. U., 1930; M.B.A., Harvard U., 1932; m. Jean Frank, Apr. 23, 1944; children—Rita Marion, Barbara Jean, Alan I. With Fownes Bros. & Co. Inc., N.Y.C., 1936—, pres., 1965—. Served with USCGR, 1942-45. Jewish (temple trustee, pres.). Clubs: Beach Point (Mamaroneck, N.Y.); Harmonie (N.Y.C.). Home: 700 Park Ave New York City NY 10021 Office: 411 Fifth Ave New York City NY 10016

SHERR, MERRILL FREDERICK, librarian; b. N.Y.C., Oct. 5, 1941; s. Max and Lillian (Baron) S.; B.A. cum laude, Queens Coll., 1963; M.A. in History, Columbia U., 1964, M.S. in L.S., 1972; Ph.D. in History (univ. fellow), N.Y. U., 1969. Lectr. history City Coll. N.Y., 1966-70, Queensborough Community Coll., Bayside, N.Y., 1969-72; asst. librarian State U. N.Y. at Buffalo, 1972-76; head library N.Y. Post, N.Y.C., 1976—. Mem. Am. Hist. Assn., Conf. on Brit. Studies, Spl. Libraries Assn., N.Y. Newspaper Guild. Contbr. articles to profl. jours. Home: 182-41 80th Rd Jamaica NY 11432 Office: 210 South St New York City NY 10002

SHERROD, ROBERT LEE, writer; b. Thomas County, Ga., Feb. 8, 1909; s. Joseph Arnold and Victoria Ellen (Evers) S.; A.B., U. Ga., 1929; m. Elizabeth Hudson, Oct. 8, 1936 (dec. Dec. 1958); children—John Hudson, Robert Lee; m. 2d, Margaret Carson Ruff, May 5, 1961 (div. 1972); m. 3d, Mary Gay Labrot Leonhardt, Aug. 26, 1972 (dec. July 1978). Reporter Atlanta Constitution, Palm Beach (Fla.) Daily News, others, 1929-35; with Time and Life mags. as Washington corr., asso. editor, war and Far East corr., 1935-52; Far East corr. Sat. Eve. Post, 1952-55, mng. editor, 1955-62, editor, 1962, and editor-at-large, 1963-64; v.p., editorial coordinator Curtis Pub. Co., 1965-66; writing on fgn. affairs and history, 1966—; contract writer Life mag., N.Y.C., 1966-68. Mem. U. Ga. Pres.'s Adv. Council, 1975—; mem. USMC History Adv. Com., 1973-76. Trustee Corrs. Fund. Commended by U.S. Navy Dept., Battle of Attu, May 1943, Battle of Tarawa, Nov. 1943; recipient Headliners Club award, for war reporting, 1944; Benjamin Franklin award U. Ill., 1954; Overseas Press Club certificate, 1955. Mem. Mil. Order of Carabao. Episcopalian. Clubs: Federal City, National Press (Washington); Century, Overseas Press (N.Y.C.). Author: Tarawa, the Story of a Battle, 1944, new edit., 1973; On to Westward, 1945; History of Marine Corps Aviation in World War II, 1952; also of text for Life's Picture History of World War II, 1950 and Kobunsha's Picture History of the Pacific war (in Japanese), 1952. Contbr. to Apollo Expdns. to the Moon, 1975. Home: 4000 Massachusetts Av NW Washington DC 20016 Office: 4000 Cathedral Ave NW Washington DC 20016

SHERRY, CATHERINE THERESE, biologist; b. N.Y.C.; d. Felix Gerard and Mary Frances (McDonough) Sherry; B.S., Coll. Mt. St. Vincent, 1947; M.S., N.Y. U., 1961, postgrad. Joined Sisters of Charity, 1951; chemist Fleischman Labs., Standard Brands, N.Y., 1947-51; supr. labs. St. Vincent's Hosp. and Med. Center, N.Y.C., 1954-58, asst. to dir. labs., 1958-71, asso. dir. labs., 1971—; adj. asst. prof. St. John's U., N.Y.C., 1976—; med. lab. cons. Profl. Exam. Service, N.Y.C., 1973—; mem. adv. com. med. tech. program N.Y.C. Community Coll., City U. N.Y., 1966—; mem. adv. com. med. technician curriculum Elizabeth Seton Coll., N.Y.C., 1976—. Mem. Am. Assn. Med. Tech., Am. Assn. Blood Banks, Am. Chem. Soc., Am. Assn. Clin. Chemistry, Am. Soc. Microbiology, Am. Soc. Clin. Pathology, N.Y. Acad. Scis., Empire State Assn. Med. Tech. (chmn. adminstrn. sect.), Blood Banks Assn. N.Y. State (dir. 1972-78), Kappa Gamma Pi. Republican. Roman Catholic. Office: 153 W 11th St New York City NY 10011

SHERRY, GERALD JOSEPH, refrigeration co. exec.; b. Spangler, Pa., Sept. 15, 1939; s. Vincent Gerald and Mary Grace (Farabaugh) S.; student refrigeration Gen. Gateway Tech., 1967-68; m. Sylvia Anne Kaufman, Apr. 28, 1962; children—Dawn Ann, Deborah Sue, Deanna Marie. With Quaker Store, Barnesboro, Pa., 1957-58; store mgr. Johns Bargain Stores, Cleve., 1964-65; radar tech. Fairview Park Nike Site, Cleve., 1965-66; with Grossman's Music Co., Cleve., 1966-67; service mgr. Allegheny Refrigeration, Carrolltown, Pa., 1968—. Served with AUS, 1958-63. Mem. Refrigeration Service Engrs. Soc., Cambria Heights Jr. C. of C. (pres. 1971-72, dir. 1973-74), Pa. Jr. C. of C. (state chmn. 1972-73), U.S. Jr. C. of C. (dir. 1973-74). Home: PO Box 318 Carrolltown PA 15722 Office: PO Box 310 Carrolltown PA 15722

SHERRY, HOWARD SAMUEL, chemist, chem. engr.; b. N.Y.C., Nov. 18, 1930; s. Irving and Rose (Beckenstein) Shevitz; B.S. in Chem. Engring., N.Y. U., 1955; M.A. in Chemistry, State U. N.Y. at Buffalo, 1962, Ph.D., 1963; m. Rhoda Horowitz, June 6, 1955; children—Alan, Jonathan, Deborah, David. Research chem. engr. Union Carbide Corp., Niagara Falls, N.Y., 1957-59; research asso. State U. N.Y. at Buffalo, 1959-62; group leader, research asso. Mobil Research and Devel. Corp., Paulsboro, N.J., 1962-77; tech. mgr. research and devel. Phila. Quartz Co., Lafayette Hill, Pa., 1977—; vis. lectr. U. Colo., Boulder, 1965-66. Served with U.S. Army, 1951-54. Union Carbide Corp. fellow, 1960-61. Mem. Am. Chem. Soc., Am. Inst. Chem. Engrs., Mineralogical Soc. Am., Catalysis Club of Phila., Research Mgmt. Group of Phila., Internat. Zeolite Assn., ASTM, Nat. Acad. Sci. (panel on rare earths 1967), Delaware Valley Earth Sci. Soc. Contbr. articles to profl. jours. and books; patentee in field. Address: 416 S Cranford Rd Cherry Hill NJ 08003

SHERRY, PATRICIA ANN, counselor; b. Balt., Nov. 25, 1952; d. Ernest Robert and Anna Marie (Kutz) S.; B.S. in Psychology and Communication Scis., Towson State U., 1976; grad. certificate in mgmt. U. Balt., 1978; postgrad. in counseling psychology Loyola Coll., Balt., 1977—. Statistician-mgr. Koppers Co., Inc., 1971-78; speech pathologist Balt. Assn. for Retarded Citizens and Towson (Md.) State Speech and Hearing Clinic, 1974-76; counselor Balt. Center for Counseling Services, 1976—, chmn. tng., 1977—, asst. dir., 1978—; counselor, librarian, mem. tng. com. Howard County Rape Crisis Center, 1977—; pvt. practice psychotherapy, 1977—; youth task force mem. Howard County Assn. Community Services. Mem. Am. Personnel and Guidance Assn., Assn. for Counselor Edn. and Supervision, Nat. Employment Counselors Assn., Inst. Natural History, Sigma Alpha Eta. Democrat. Roman Catholic. Research on visual memory, birth order and cultural attitudes. Home: 3637 Valley Rd Ellicott City MD 21043 Office: 3697 Park Ave Ellicott City MD 21043

SHERWIN, OSCAR, former educator, writer; b. N.Y.C., July 6, 1902; s. Nathan and Lee Sherwin; A.B. cum laude, Columbia, 1922, M.A., 1928; Ph.D., N.Y. U., 1940; m. Stella Zins, Apr. 14, 1929; children—James Terry, Nancy. Faculty, Coll. City N.Y., 1934-67, prof. English, 1958-67, emeritus prof., 1967—; author: Mr. Gay, 1929; Benedict Arnold, Patriot and Traitor, 1931; Prophet of Liberty: Wendell Phillips, 1958; Uncorking Old Sherry, 1960; Goldy: Oliver Goldsmith, 1961; Friend of the People: John Wesley, 1961; A Man of Wit and Fashion: George Selwyn, 1963. Mem. Modern Lang. Assn., Am. Hist. Assn., AAUP, Assn. Study Negro Life and History, Phi Beta Kappa. Unitarian. Contbg. editor Phylon, 1948-52; editorial bd. Am. Jour. Econs. and Sociology. Contbr. articles to profl. jours. Home: 207 W 106th St New York City NY 10025

SHERWIN, RICHARD JACK, indsl. psychologist; b. Cleve., Aug. 8, 1928; s. James Eugene and Leona (Droome) S.; B.S., U. Ga., 1962, M. Ed., 1964, Ed.D., 1966; m. Margaret Ann Morris, Nov. 5, 1960; 1 dau., Heather Courtney. Staff psychologist, Rohrer, Hibler & Replogle, Mpls., 1966-70, partner, Boston, 1970-73; pvt. practice, indsl. psychol. cons., Boston, 1973—. Served with USMC, 1950-53. Certified, licensed psychologist, Mass.; licensed, Minn. Mem. Am., Mass. psychol. assns., Phi Delta Kappa, Kappa Delta Pi. Republican. Clubs: Wazata Country, Mpls. Athletic. Home and Office: 14 Larnis Rd Framingham MA 01701

SHERWOOD, HUBERT JAMES, sch. supt.; b. Waterford, Pa., Jan. 31, 1915; s. Willis Winton and Minnie Minten (Duncan) S.; B.E., Edinboro State Tchrs. Coll., 1936; M.A., Columbia, 1949; m. Mary Sophrona Fuller, Nov. 18, 1936; children—Richard Floyd, Mary Sherwood Wise, Sarah Sherwood Scott. Tchr./coach Edinboro (Pa.) High Sch., 1937-49; tchr. Lawrence Park High Sch., Erie, Pa., 1949-52; high sch. prin. Brokenstraw Valley Schs., Youngsville, Pa., 1952-54, supervising prin., 1954-65; supt. Wilmington Area Sch. Dist., New Wilmington, Pa., 1965—. Mem. Am., Pa. assns. sch. adminstrs., Pa. Sch. Bds. Assn., Phi Delta Kappa. Republican. Methodist. Clubs: Kiwanis (past pres.) (Youngsville); Masons (Coudersport, Pa.). Home: RFD 1 New Wilmington PA 16142 Office: 350 Wood St New Wilmington PA 16142

SHERWOOD, RICHARD CURRY, physicist; b. Worcester, Mass., June 19, 1929; s. Harold Clements and Doris Sophia (Nordmark) S.; student Franklin Tech. Inst., 1950-52, Newark Coll. Engring., 1953-54; m. Hope Grace Hedley, Sept. 17, 1955; children—John Hedley, Peter Richard. Mem. tech. staff Bell Telephone Labs., Murray Hill, N.J., 1952—. Served with U.S. Army, 1947-49. Mem. Am. Phys. Soc. Contbr. numerous articles on magnetism and magnetic materials to profl. jours.; patentee in field. Home: 8 Vista Ln New Providence NJ 07974 Office: 600 Mountain Ave Murray Hill NJ 07974

SHETLER, FREDERICK CHARLES, sci. co. exec.; b. Indiana, Pa., Mar. 8, 1943; s. Frederick Clarence and Goldie May (Kunkle) S.; grad. Grantham Sch. Electronics, 1965. Asst. to chief engr. stas. WDAD, WQMU, Indiana, 1964—; insp. Fisher Sci. Co., Indiana, 1968—; repeater officer VHF-FM communications State of Pa., Ind., 1974—. Served with U.S. Army, 1965-67. Mem. Laurel Mt. VHF Soc. (v.p. 1976—), Nitnany Amateur Radio Club. Republican. Odd Fellow. Home: 977 Oak St Indiana PA 15701 Office: Sta WOAO/WQMV Indiana PA 15701

SHETTERLY, HENRY TITUS, ednl. adminstr.; b. Denver, Nov. 27, 1926; s. Charles Russell and Mildred (Leake) S.; B.A., Washington Coll., 1950; M.Ed., U. Md., 1953; Ed.D., U. Denver, 1970; m. Nancy Lee Smith, Mar. 26, 1951; children—Jancy Lee, Andrew Hunter. Tchr. secondary and elementary sch. Montgomery County (Md.) Pub. Schs., 1950-56, pupil personnel staff, 1956-65, area supr. pupil services, 1965-73, dir. pupil services, 1973-77, area dir. for continuum edn., 1977—; adj. prof. Va. Poly. U. Grad. Center, Reston, 1973-75. Mem. Council on Adolescents, Montgomery County, 1973—; mem. Emergency Med. Adv. Com., Montgomery County, 1975-77; mem. vestry Ch. of the Ascension, Silver Spring, Md., 1957-59. Served with USN, 1944-46; PTO. Mem. Am. Personnel and Guidance Assn., NEA, Md., Montgomery County edn. assns., Phi Delta Kappa, Lambda Chi Alpha. Episcopalian. Club: Kenwood Golf and Country. Contbr. articles to profl. jours. Home: 4707 Broad Brook Dr Bethesda MD 20014 Office: 7921 Lynnbrook Dr Bethesda MD 20014

SHEVECK, JOSEPH JEROME, systems analyst; b. New Kensington, Pa., June 29, 1939; s. Joseph Stanley and Mary Cecilia (Garbinski) S.; B.A., Columbia U., 1961, B.S., 1962, M.S., 1965, I.E., 1969; m. Dorinda Dee Dubetsky, Feb. 4, 1967; children—Jay Jerome, Joel Jerome. Coll. recruited Colgate-Palmolive Co., N.J., 1962-65; asso. engr., IBM, East Fishkill, N.Y., 1965-68, sr. asso. engr., 1968-70, staff engr., 1970-74, adv. systems analyst, 1974—, Hopewell Junction, N.Y., 1962—. Mem. Am. Inst. Indsl. Engrs., ASME. Home: 37 Weston Ave Fishkill NY 12524 Office: Dept 77J Bldg 333-71A IBM Route 52 Hopewell Junction NY 12533

SHIEH, WEI TONG, metall. engr.; b. Keelung, Taiwan, Jan. 22, 1934; s. Kuo Sian and Wu Mou (Lin) S.; came to U.S., 1961, naturalized, 1973; B.Applied Sci., U. Toronto, 1961; M.S., U. Ill., 1963, Ph.D., 1968; m. Mai Wei, Dec. 30, 1961; children—Karl, Karen, Denise. Production mining engr. Taiwan Gold and Copper Mining Bur., Chinkuashu, 1957-59; research asst. U. Ill., Urbana, 1961-68; research metallurgist Timken Co., Canton, Ohio, 1968-72, research specialist, 1972-77; sr. engr. Gen. Electric Co., Utica, N.Y., 1977—. Profl. engr., Taiwan. Mem. Am. Soc. for Metals, ASTM (tech. coms.), Am. Phys. Soc., Nat. Assn. Corrosion Engrs., Am. Welding Soc. (tech. coms.), Metals Soc. Contbr. articles to profl. jours.; developer Compressive maximum shear crack speciman, 1976. Home: 47A Upper Woods Rd New Hartford NY 13413 Office: 901 Broad St Utica NY 13503

SHIELDS, BRUCE MACLEAN, steel co. exec.; b. Wilkinsburg, Pa., Sept. 27, 1922; s. Edwin Bruce and Edith Barbara (Kennedy) S.; B.S., Carnegie-Mellon U., 1944; M.S., Mass. Inst. Tech., 1952; m. Nancy Garwood Adams, June 2, 1951; children—Duncan Maclean, Gordon Adams. With U.S. Steel Corp., 1942—, chief metallurgist Duquesne Works, 1957-60, chief metallurgist South Chicago Works, 1960-65, mgr. process metallurgy, 1965-68, mgr. tubular products metallurgy, 1968-72, gen. mgr. process metallurgy, 1972-76, gen. mgr. customer tech. services, Pitts., 1976-78, dir. metall. engring., 1978—. Dist. chmn., bd. dirs. Allegheny Trails council Boy Scouts Am., 1975—, recipient Silver Beaver award. Served with C.E., AUS, 1943-46. Fellow Am. Soc. Metals; mem. Am. Iron and Steel Inst., Metals Soc. (Brit.), Am. Inst. Mining and Metall. Engrs., ASTM, Am. Petroleum Inst., Am. Def. Preparedness Assn. Republican. Presbyterian (elder, trustee). Clubs: Chartiers Country, Duquesne. Patentee in field. Home: 104 Altadena Dr Pittsburgh PA 15228 Office: 600 Grant St Pittsburgh PA 15230

SHIELDS, CORNELIUS, author, former brokerage co. exec.; b. St. Paul, Apr. 7, 1905; s. Cornelius and Theresa (McMogh) S.; student Loyola Coll., Montreal, Que., Can.; m. Jan. 22, 1922; 2 children. With Merrill Lynch, 1921-23; partner Shield Co., N.Y.C., 1923—; with Bache Halsey Stuart Shields (merger Shields and Bache Halsey Stuart), N.Y.C., to 1977, hon. dir., 1977—; author: Cornelius Shields on Sailing, 1964, Cornelius Shields and The Masters, 1973. Served with USN, 1917-20. Clubs: Larchmont (N.Y.) Yacht, Cruising of Am.; N.Y. Yacht (N.Y.C.); Winged Foot Golf (Mamaroneck, N.Y.); Everglades (Palm Beach, Fla.). Home: 62 Larchmont Ave Larchmont NY 10538 Office: Bache Halsey Stuart Shields New York City NY 10038

SHIELDS, GERALD ROBERT, librarian, educator; b. Waukegan, Ill., Nov. 24, 1925; s. Louis and Viola (Coop) S.; B.S. in Speech, U. Wis., Milw., 1960; M.L.S., U. Wis., 1961; m. Joyce Farley, Oct. 18, 1958; 1 dau., Maureen Ryanna. Personnel supr. Inland Steel Products, Milw., 1956-59; adult edn. coordinator Central YMCA, Milw.,

1959-60; reference librarian Marquette U., Milw., 1961-63; head social sci. Dayton and Montgomery County Pub. Library, 1964-67; editor Ohio Library Assn. Bull., 1964-67, Am. Libraries, ALA, Chgo., 1968-73; asst. prof. State U. N.Y., Buffalo, 1973-75, asst. dean, 1976—; councilor-at-large ALA, 1974—, columnist for Library Jour., 1974-76; alt. del. White House Conf. on Libraries, 1979. Served with AUS, 1941-45, USAF, 1950-55. Recipient award for best library periodical H.W. Wilson, 1967, award for best editorial Ednl. Press, 1971, 72. Mem. N.Y. Library Assn. (chmn. intellectual freedom com. 1976-78). Co-editor: Budgeting for Accountability in Libraries, 1974; Children's Library Service: School or Public?, 1974. Home: 546 College Ave Niagara Falls NY 14305 Office: Sch Info and Library Studies State U NY Amherst NY 14260

SHIELDS, JOHN EDGAR, editor; b. Camden, N.J., May 8, 1924; s. Emmett Paxton and Marion Amy (Kilheffer) S.; B.A., U. Md., 1950; m. Louisa Yonsei Room, Mar. 24, 1951; children—David Sanford, Richard Paxton, Diane Karen. Producer, dir. CBS, Washington, 1946-49; sec. to Ambassador William C. Bullitt, 1950; with CIA, 1950-52; exec. Asia Found., various Far Eastern countries, 1952-55; fgn. corr., author, editor various media, 1952-60; with Nat. Geog. Soc., 1960-62; asso. editor Congl. Digest, Washington, 1962-68, editor, 1968—; dir. mining corps. Served with USNR, 1942-45. Mem. S.A.R., Mensa, Phi Kappa Phi, Alpha Phi Omega, Sigma Alpha Epsilon. Methodist. Clubs: Nat. Press. Author books on local history, genealogy, including A History of the Shields Family, 1968; East Tennessee Migrations; Factors and Families, 1969; The Scotch-Irish in Augusta County, Virginia, 1971; Narratives of Westward Movement, 1973; Irish Origins of the Shields Family, 1975. Home: 19128 Roman Way Gaithersburg MD 20760 Office: 3231 P St NW Washington DC 20007

SHIELDS, LAWRENCE THORNTON, orthopedic surgeon; b. Boston, Oct. 2, 1935; s. George Leo and Catherine Elizabeth (Thornton) S.; A.B., Harvard U., 1957; M.D., Johns Hopkins U., 1961; m. Karen S. Kraus, Sept. 21, 1968; children—Elizabeth Coulter, Laura Thornton, Sarah Daly, Michael Lawrence. Intern, Barnes Hosp., Washington U., St. Louis, 1961-62, resident, 1962-63; resident orthopedic surgeon Children's Hosp. Med. Center, Boston, 1966-67, Mass. Gen. Hosp., Boston, 1967-68, Peter Bent Brigham, Robert Breck Brigham hosps., Boston, 1968-69; resident orthopedic surgeon Harvard Med. Sch., Boston, 1965-69, instr., 1969—; orthopedic surgeon Peter Bent Brigham, Children's hosps., 1969—; orthopedic surgeon Waltham (Mass.) Hosp., 1969—, also chief orthopedic surgery, pres. med. staff; mem. Waltham-Weston Orthopedic Assos.; mem. staffs Hahnemann Hosp., Boston, Newton-Wellesley (Mass.) hosps.; cons. orthopedic surgeon VA Hosp., Boston; mem. faculty Harvard Med. Sch.; pres. Massachusetts Bay Investment Trust. Bd. dirs. Mass. Acad. Emergency Med. Technicians, Waltham Boys' Club; trustee, exec. com. Waltham Hosp. Served to lt. M.C., USNR, 1963-65. Diplomate Am. Bd. Orthopedic Surgery. Fellow Am. Acad. Orthopedic Surgeons, A.C.S.; mem. New Eng., Boston orthopedic clubs, Charles River Dist. (treas., exec. com.), Mass. (councillor) med. socs. Clubs: Harvard (Boston); Pi Eta (Harvard); Rotary. Contbr. articles to med. jours. Home: 9 Beverly Rd Newton MA 02161 Office: 721 Huntington Ave Boston MA 02115 also 20 Hope Ave Suite 314 Waltham MA 02154

SHIELDS, RICHARD, bus. exec., tax cons.; A.B., Bklyn. Coll., 1937; LL.B., N.Y. U., 1940, J.D., 1940; M.B.A., Harvard U., 1942; m. Frances Augenstein; 1 dau., Eileen. Admitted to N.Y. bar, 1940; corp. practice law, 1940-60; sec., treas. Forbes Realty Corp., 1960-70; exec. v.p. Forbes Industries, Ltd., 1965-70; exec. v.p. Am. Diversified Industries Corp., 1964-66, pres., chmn. bd., 1966-76; exec. v.p. Daily Mirror, Sunday Mirror, N.Y.C.; chmn., chief exec. officer, dir. TTC Industries, also subs. Armstrong Glass Mfg. Corp., Erwin, Tenn., 1970—; pres., dir. Euro Industries, Ltd., and dir. subs. Town Formal Wear, subs. Lady B. Fashions, 1971-73; pres., chief exec. officer, dir. Dairene Industries, Ltd., 1971—; tax cons. Franklin Cons., Ltd., Great Neck, N.Y., 1974—; dir. Blue Ribbon Mktg. Corp.; govt. appeal agt. U.S. Selective Service; mem. N.Y. State Commn. on Human Rights; referee, arbitrator Civil Ct., N.Y.C. Served to maj. USAAF, 1942-46; CBI. Decorated Commendation medal, Legion of Merit. Mem. Am. Inst. Mgmt., Nat. Assn. Accountants, Nat. Tax Assn., Tax Inst. Am., Assn. Bar City N.Y. Club: Harvard. Home: Great Neck NY 11021 Office: 98 Cutter Mill Rd Great Neck NY 11021

SHIELDS, RICHARD TYNER, investor; b. Kansas City, Mo., Feb. 22, 1908; s. Edwin Willis and Martha (Deardorff) S.; Ph.B., Yale, 1929; M.B.A., Harvard, 1931; m. Jean Koehler, Mar. 5, 1949 (div. 1954); m. 2d, Elizabeth Bayne de Vegh, May 21, 1964. With Bankers Trust Co., N.Y.C., 1931-63, asst. trust officer, 1939-44, asst. v.p., 1944-50, v.p. investment research, 1950-63; adviser to Gen. Electric Pension Fund, 1955-63; v.p., dir., mem. exec. com. One William St. Fund, Inc., 1963-65, dir., mem. exec. com., 1965-71; dir. Partners Fund, Inc., N.Y.C., 1975—. Trustee, mem. fin. com. Boys Club N.Y., 1964—; mem. Yale Devel. Bd., 1967—. With War Prodn. Bd., 1942-43, Office Lend Lease, 1943-44, Fgn. Econ. Adminstrn., 1944. Clubs: River, Univ. (N.Y.C.); Pauma Valley Country (Calif.). Home: 812 Fifth Ave New York City NY 10021 Office: 30 Rockefeller Plaza New York City NY 10020

SHIFRIN, BRUCE CARL, elec. engr.; b. Balt., June 14, 1947; s. Joseph Lewis and Sylvia (Spuntoff) S.; B.S.E.E., Poly. Inst. Bklyn., 1968; M.S.E.E., Northeastern U., 1972, M.S.E.M., 1976; m. Caryn Barbara Nadler, June 29, 1969; children—Jason Adam, Ian Todd. Engr., equipment devel. labs. Raytheon Co., Wayland, Mass., 1968-72, 73-77, sr. staff engr. spl. programs office, 1977, systems engring. mgr. editorial systems, Sudbury, Mass., 1977—; staff engr. C.S. Draper Lab., Mass. Inst. Tech., Cambridge, 1972-73. Mem. IEEE Computer Soc. (chmn. Central New Eng. chpt. 1978-79). Democrat. Jewish. Home: 631 Edgebrook Dr Boylston MA 01505 Office: 528 Boston Post Rd Sudbury MA 01776

SHIFRIN, DAVID LAWRENCE, physician; b. Pitts., Jan. 10, 1942; s. Victor and Julia (Browarsky) S.; A.B., Washington and Jefferson Coll., 1963; M.D., W.Va. U., 1967; m. Sylvia Perer, June 12, 1966; children—Michael, Joshua. Intern, St. Francis Hosp., Pitts., 1967-68, resident, 1968-69, Hartford (Conn.) Hosp., 1971-74; practice medicine specializing in obstetrics and gynecology, Springfield, Mass., 1974—; asso. Hampden County Obstetrics and Gynecology, Inc.; staff mem. Cooley-Dickinson Hosp., Northampton, Baystate Med. Center, Springfield; cons. Planned Parenthood Western Mass.; med. lectr. Western New Eng. Law Sch.; faculty U. Mass. Med. Sch., Tufts U. Med. Sch. Mem. Springfield Jewish Fedn.; bd. dirs. Western Mass. March of Dimes; mem. exec. com. Heritage Acad. Served as lt. comdr. M.C., USNR, 1969-71. Research fellow dept. psychiatry Western Va. U. Med. Sch., 1964, Harvard U. Student Health Center, Cambridge, Mass., 1966. Diplomate Am. Bd. Obstetrics and Gynecology. Fellow Am. Coll. Obstetrics and Gynecology; mem. Mass., Hampden Dist., Maimonides med. socs. Contbr. to Harvard Student Health Study, 1966, Pharm. Clin. Research, 1975—. Home: 213 Tanglewood Dr Longmeadow MA 01106 Office: 110 Maple St Springfield MA 01103

SHIM, KUN IL, radiologist; b. Kyunggido, Korea, Nov. 2, 1942; s. Chung Sup and Bo Kyung (Oh) S.; came to U.S., 1970, naturalized, 1975; M.D., Yonsie U., Korea, 1967; m. Seung Jin Yu, Oct. 7, 1967; 1 dau., Michelle. Intern, Mt. St. Mary's Hosp., Lewiston, N.Y., 1970-71; resident Millard Fillmore Hosp., Bufflao, 1971-74; radiologist Salamanca (N.Y.) Dist. Hosp., 1974—. Mem. Am. Coll. Radiology, Radiol. Soc. N.Am. Office: 150 Parkway Dr Salamanca NY 14779

SHIM, NAK KWANG, orthopaedic surgeon; b. Seoul, Korea, Feb. 7, 1936; s. Young Soon and Kui Dong (Park) S.; came to U.S., 1964, naturalized, 1977; M.D., Yonsei U., 1960; m. So Ok, June 20, 1961; children—John, Steven, Joon, Louise. Intern, Yonsei U. Med. Center, Seoul, 1960-61, resident, 1961-64; resident N.Y. U. Med. Center, 1964-70, instr. anatomy and cell biology, 1961-64; mem. staff Auburn (N.Y.) Meml. Hosp.; clin. instr. dept. orthopaedic surgery Upstate Med. Center, Syracuse, N.Y. Bd. dirs. Cayuga County United Fund, 1974-77. Fellow A.C.S., Am. Acad. Orthopaedic Surgeons; mem. Am., N.Y. State, Cayuga County (treas. 1976-77) med. assns., N.Y. State Orthopaedic Assn. Club: Skaneateles Country. Home: West Lake Rd Skaneateles NY 13152 Office: One Lincoln St Auburn NY 13021

SHIMIZU, ARTHUR GEORGE, nephrologist, educator; b. Vancouver, B.C., Can., Feb. 28, 1929; s. James Motoji Shimizu; B.Sc., McGill U., 1952; certificate in pub. health, U. Toronto, 1955; M.D., Ottawa U., 1959; m. Audrey Norrington, Sept. 5, 1959; children—Francine, Frederika. Intern, Montreal (Que., Can.) Gen. Hosp., 1959-60; resident Queen Mary Vets. Hosp., Montreal, 1960-61, Belfast (No. Ireland) City Hosp., 1961-62, Toronto (Ont., Can.) Western Hosp., 1963-64, Montreal Gen. Hosp., 1964-65, Cleve. Clinic, 1966; practice medicine specializing in nephrology, Hamilton Ont., 1967—; dir. dialysis St. Joseph's Hosp., Hamilton, 1967—; asst. prof. medicine McMaster U. Med. Sch., Hamilton, 1969-72, asso. prof., 1972—. Co-ordinator Hypertensive Program, Ont. br. Kidney Found., 1975—; examiner Can. Soc. Perfusionists, 1975—; chmn. Can. Renal Failure Registry, 1976; chmn. Hamilton, Kitchener-Waterloo St. Catherine's Chronic Renal Failure Program. Fellow Royal Coll. Physicians, A.C.P.; mem. Can., Brit. med. assns., Can., Internat. Am. socs. nephrology, Am. Soc. Artificial Internal Organs, Royal Soc. Medicine (London), Eng.), Kidney Found. Can. Home: 175 Hess St S Hamilton ON L8P 3P1 Canada Office: St Joseph's Hosp Charlton Av E Hamilton ON L8N 1Y6 Canada

SHINKLE, ROBERT FRANKLIN, telephone mfg. equipment engr.; b. Trenton, N.J., Jan. 6, 1933; s. Amos Raymond and Caroline (Bailey) S.; m. Joann Kauffmann, Oct. 19, 1957; children—Patti Sue (dec.), Jeffrey Douglas. Acrobat and diver, performed various TV programs, 1947-54; propr. Bob's Electronics, Trenton, N.J., 1954-55; with IBM Co., Endicott, N.Y., also Trenton, 1955-58; electronic technician Forrestal Research Center, Princeton U., 1960-61; engr., combining lasers and computers into prodn. line equipment Western Electric Co., Princeton, N.J., 1961—. Bd. dirs. Trenton chpt. ARC, 1965—, chmn. disaster service, instr. first aid water safety, 1958—. Home: 174 Park Ave Trenton NJ 08690 Office: PO Box 900 Carter Rd Princeton NJ 08540

SHINN, RICHARD RANDOLPH, life ins. co. exec.; b. Lakewood, N.J., Jan. 7, 1918; s. Clayton Randolph and Carrie (McGravey) S.; B.S., Rider Coll., 1938; m. Mary Helen Shea, Nov. 8, 1941; children—Kathleen, Patricia, John. With Met. Life Ins. Co., 1939—, 2d v.p., 1959-63, v.p., 1963-64, sr. v.p., 1964-66, exec. v.p., 1966-68, sr. exec. v.p., 1968-69, pres., dir., 1969—, chief exec. officer, 1973—; dir. Allied Chem. Corp., Norton Simon, Inc., Sperry Rand Corp., Chase Bank, May Dept. Stores Co. C.L.U.. Clubs: The Blind Brook, (Port Chester, N.Y.); The Stanwich (Old Greenwich, Conn.); Riverside Yacht; Union League (N.Y.C.). Home: 31 Lindsay Dr Greenwich CT 06830 Office: 1 Madison Av New York City NY 10010

SHINOZUKA, MASANOBU, civil engr., educator; b. Tokyo, Dec. 23, 1930; s. Akira and Kiyo S.; came to U.S., 1957, naturalized, 1971; B.S., Kyoto (Japan) U., 1953, M.S., 1955; Ph.D., Columbia U., 1960; m. Fujiko Sakamoto, Oct. 25, 1954; children—Rei, Naomi, Megumi. Research asst. civil engring. Columbia U., 1958-61, asst. prof., 1961-65, asso. prof., 1965-69, prof., 1969-77, Renwick prof., 1977—; vis. scholar N.C. State U., Raleigh, 1967-68; pres. Modern Analysis Inc., Ridgewood, N.J., 1972—; cons. in field. NSF grantee, 1968—. Mem. Nat. Acad. Engring., ASCE (Walter L. Huber prize 1972, State-of-the-Art Civil Engring. award 1973, Alfred M. Freudenthal medal 1978), ASME, Am. Inst. Aeros. and Astronautics, ASTM, Japan Soc. Civil Engrs., Sigma Xi. Editor: Reliability Approach in Structural Engineering, 1975. Home: 229 Oak St Ridgewood NJ 07450 Office: 610 Mudd Columbia U New York City NY 10027

SHIP, IRWIN, dental educator; b. N.Y.C., July 11, 1932; s. Max and Lillian (Gootnick) S.; student Columbia U., 1949-52; D.M.D., Harvard U., 1956; M.S. in Epidemiology and Preventive Medicine, U. Pa., 1965; m. Gabriella Wolfsohn, June 24, 1956; children—Jonathan Avram, Sara Ann, Jordan Robert. Intern in oral surgery and oral medicine Mass. Gen. Hosp., Boston, 1956-57; prin. investigator clin. br. NIH, Bethesda, Md., 1957-60, clin. asso., cons. oral medicine, 1962—; asst. chief dental research Phila. Gen. Hosp., 1960-62, research com., 1962—, chief dental research, 1962—, sr. attending dentist, 1973-74; attending dentist Children's Hosp. Phila., 1962—; asst. prof. oral medicine U. Pa. Sch. Dental Medicine, Phila., 1960-63, asso. prof., 1963-66, prof., 1966—, dir. hosp. edn., 1963—, chmn. dept. oral medicine, 1973-78, prof. dept. otorhinolaryngology, 1974—, dir. Clin. Research Center, 1978—; mem. staff Hosp. U. Pa., 1973—, Presbyn. U. Hosp., 1976—; vis. prof. oral medicine Hebrew U., Jerusalem, 1968, 69-70, 72, dir. affiliated program, 1975—; vis. prof., Japan, 1976; dir. Robert Wood Johnson Found. Rural Dental Health Program, U. Pa., 1975—. Chmn. adult edn. Temple Beth Hillel, 1964-69, bd. dirs., 1965-70, exec. com., 1966-70, fin. sec., 1966-69. Served with USPHS, 1957-60. Recipient Grace Milliken award Harvard U., 1956, Myrle Wreath award Phila. chpt. Hadassah, 1973; spl. citation Am. Friends Hebrew U., 1978. Mem. ADA, Am. Pub. Health Assn., Am. Acad. Oral Medicine (Samual Charles Miller award 1978), Am. Soc. Hosp. Dentists, Am. Bd. Oral Medicine (bd. examiners 1977—), Am. Soc. Dentistry for Handicapped, Internat. Assn. Dental Research (sec.-treas. 1963-66, pres. Phila. sect. 1965-67, counsellor 1967-68, chmn. emblem com. 1968-69, chmn. pub. relations 1972-73), Coll. Physicians (Phila.). Cons. to editorial bds, reviewer for med., dental jours.; contbr. chpts. to books, articles to profl. publs. Home: 340 Haverford Rd Wynnewood PA 19096 Office: Univ Pa Sch Dental Medicine Philadelphia PA 19174

SHIPLEY, GERRY STEWART, real estate devel. exec.; b. Balt., Feb. 9, 1945; s. John Stewart and Reta Belle Shipley; B.A., San Francisco State U., 1971; M.A., Pa. State U., 1979; m. Susan Jane Straub, Aug. 12, 1967; children—Jessica Straub, Todd Stewart. Dir. market research Land Growth Investments, Camp Hill, Pa., 1973-74; dir. mortgage servicing Pa. Housing Fin. Agy., Harrisburg, 1974-79; v.p. Nat. Devel. Enterprises, Harrisburg, 1979—. Served with USAF, 1963-67. Office: 3713 Woodridge Dr Harrisburg PA 17110

SHIPMAN, MARK SAMUEL, lawyer; b. Hartford, Conn., Apr. 16, 1937; s. Paul David and Reeva (Joseph) S.; B.A., U. Conn., 1959, J.D., 1962; m. Sonia Sosensky, Aug. 28, 1960; children—Paul D., Lawrence S., William H. Admitted to Conn. bar, 1962, U.S. Supreme Ct. bar; asso. firm Schatz & Schatz, Hartford, 1962-64; partner firm Iosco & Shipman, Newington, Conn., 1964-66; prosecutor 15th Circuit Ct. State of Conn., 1964-66; partner firm Schatz & Schatz, Ribicoff & Kotkin, 1967—; atty. Town of Newington, 1975-78; dir. adv. bd. New Britain Bank & Trust Co. Councilman, Town of Newington, 1966-67, 73-74; chmn. charter revision com. Town of Newington, 1969, 72, 75; vice-chmn. Greater Hartford Transit Dist., 1973—. Fellow Am. Acad. Forensic Scis. (sec. jurisprudence sect. 1974, chmn. 1975); mem. Am., Conn., Hartford County bar assns., Am., Conn. trial lawyers assns. Democrat. Jewish. Clubs: Lions (sec.-treas. Newington 1971), Indian Hill Country (v.p. 1968-70), Tumblebrook Country, Masons, B'nai B'rith (sec. lodge 1972). Home: 221 Cedarwood Ln Newington CT 06111 Office: One Financial Plaza Hartford CT 06103

SHIPPS, HAMMELL PIERCE, physician; b. Delanco, N.J., Sept. 13, 1900; s. Charles Carpenter and Clara Elizabeth (Fenimore) S.; B.S., Temple U., 1922; M.D., Jefferson Med. Coll., 1926; Sc.D. (hon.), Asbury Coll., 1957; m. Flora Bell Collings, June 28, 1928; children—Charles Collings, Elizabeth Pembrooke Crouse, Gordon Thomas; m. 2d, Anne E. Snyder, June 13, 1968. Intern Cooper Hosp., Camden, N.J., 1926-27, resident, 1927-28, mem. staff, 1928—, chief of staff, 1941-61, emeritus mem. staff, 1970—; gen. practice medicine, Delanco, 1928-34; practice medicine specializing in gynecology and obstetrics, Camden, 1934-71, Cinnaminson, N.J., 1971-76; ret., 1976; asst. prof. gynecology and obstetrics Jefferson Med. Coll., 1946-65. Lay speaker United Meth. Ch., 1918—; del. World Meth. Conf., 1976; trustee Zurbrugg Meml. Hosp. Diplomate Am. Bd. Obstetrics and Gynecology. Fellow A.C.S., Am. Coll. Obstetricians and Gynecologists, N.J. Obstet. and Gynecol. Soc. (past pres.); mem. Phila. Obstet. Soc. Republican. Home: 1602 Second St Delanco NJ 08075

SHIREY, SAMUEL MARTIN, accounting exec.; b. North East, Pa., Oct. 21, 1928; s. Samuel and Elsie Pearl (Phanco) S.; B.S.C., Ohio, U. 1952; m. Helen Myra Suter, Sept. 21, 1956; children—Paul Martin, Elizabeth Anne, Samuel, Linda Kitsell. Sr. accountant Ernst & Ernst, Youngstown, Ohio, 1952-56; with, Hill, Barth & King, Youngstown, Ohio, New Castle, Pa., 1956—, partner, 1962—. Served with AUS, 1946-47. C.P.A. Mem. Am., Pa. insts. C.P.A.'s, Ohio Soc. C.P.A. Republican. Presbyterian. Home: 2966 Melvin Dr New Castle PA 16105 Office: 632 1st National Bank Bldg New Castle PA 16101

SHIVE, ROY ALLEN, chem. cons.; b. York, Pa., Feb. 6, 1901; s. Jacob Allen and Lizzie (Conley) S.; B.S., Pa. State U., 1921; M.S., U. Ill., 1922, Ph.D., 1924; m. Mary Elizabeth Thompson, Sept. 19, 1925 (dec. 1973); children—Roy Allen, Richard Byron. Research chemist Liberty Yeast Corp., Peking, Ill., 1923-24, U.S. Rubber Co., N.Y.C., 1924-26, E.I. duPont de Nemours & Co., Inc., Wilmington, Del., 1926-32; mgr. devel. and prodn. Arco Co., Cleve., 1932-34; mgr. pigment devel. Am. Cyanamid Co., Bound Brook, N.J., 1932-56; cons. to chem. industry, 1956—. Head chem. manufacture for synthetic rubber war-time program U.S. Govt., 1942-45. Recipient Modern Pioneer award, Nat. Assn. Mfrs., 1940. Mem. Am. Chem. Soc. Am. Inst. Chemists, Comml. Chem. Devel. Assn., Sigma Xi, Phi Lambda Upsilon. Club: Chemists (N.Y.C.). Address: 1782 Middlebrook Rd Bound Brook NJ 08805

SHIVELY, GLENN ALAN, bus. services co. exec.; b. Phila., May 19, 1946; s. Howard Gordon and Dorothy (Schmid) S.; B.S., U. Pa., 1968, M.B.A., 1973. Cons., Coopers & Lybrand, Phila., 1973-76, mgr., 1976-78, dir. health care cons., 1978—; career counselor Wharton Grad. Sch., U. Pa., 1976—. Served to lt. (j.g.), USNR, 1969-72. Decorated Navy Achievement medal. Mem. Hosp. Fin. Mgmt. Assn. Club: Wharton Grad. Home: 916 Bannockburn Ave Ambler PA 19002 Office: 1900 Three Girard Plaza Philadelphia PA 19102

SHMUKLER, STANFORD, lawyer; b. Phila., June 16, 1930; s. Samuel and Tessye (Dounne) S.; B.S. in Econs., U. Pa., 1951, J.D., 1954; m. Anita Golove, Mar. 21, 1951; children—Jodie Lynne, Joel Mark, Steven David. Admitted to Pa. bar, 1954; atty. U.S. Bur. Pub. Rds., 1954-55; individual practice law, Phila., 1955—; lectr. Temple U. Law Sch.; sec., exec. dir., mem. criminal procedural rules com. Pa. Supreme Ct., 1971—; bd. dirs. Ecumenical Halfway House, Phila. Council Narcotics, Drug Abuse, 1967-71; mem. lawyer's adv. com. Ct. Appeals 3d Circuit; del. Govs. Conv. Criminal Justice Standards and Goals, 1975. Served to col. JAGC, USAR, 1955—. Mem. Am., Pa., Phila. (chmn. criminal law com. 1968-69, bd. govs. 1970-73, award for distinguished service to criminal justice system criminal law sect. 1977), bar assns., Nat. Assn. Criminal Def. Lawyers, Am. Judicature Soc., Pa., Phila. trial lawyers assns., Phila. Lawyers Club. Democrat. Jewish. Contbr. articles to profl. jours. Home: 1400 Melrose Ave Melrose Park PA 19126 Office: 12th Floor 1314 Chestnut St Philadelphia PA 19107

SHOCK, MANVERN FLOYD, sch. adminstr.; b. Anmoore, W.Va., July 27, 1923; s. Victor Ahva and Vergie Daye (Kesling) S.; B.S., Salem Coll., 1949; postgrad. Ohio U., 1950, 64, U. Wyo., 1954, 1964; m. Roberta Marie O'Brist Klein, June 15, 1962; children—Kenneth Floyd, Sandra Lynn. Credit mgr. Firestone Store, Shinton, W.Va., 1950; tchr. bus. edn. Sciotoville, Ohio, 1951; football and track coach, tchr. pub. schs., Rock Springs, Wyo., 1954-58; track coach, trainer, tchr. bus. edn. pub. schs., Crestline, Ohio 1958-61; football coach, tchr. bus. edn. DuVal Sr. High Sch., Prince Georges County, Md., 1961-73, adminstrv. asst., 1973—; owner, operator Belair-Clinton Bookkeeping & Tax Service, New Carrollton, Md., 1962—; sec., treas. WAM Corp., Pecos, Tex., 1974—. Served with USAAF, 1941-42. Mem. Nat. Soc. Pub. Accountants, Nat., Md., Prince Georges tchrs. assns., Am. Legion. Democrat. Club: Elk. Home: 5801 Rittenhouse St Riverdale MD 20840

SHOEMAKER, THOMAS EARP, II, physician; b. Elkins Park, Pa., Mar. 5, 1921; s. Robert and Helen M. (Kruger) S.; A.B., U. Pa., 1944, M.D., 1947; m. Constance M. Bennett, June 11, 1956; children—Alexandra B., Deborah. Psychiat. fellow Inst. of the Pa. Hosp., Phila., 1948-51; analytic tng. Psychosomatic Inst., Heidelberg (Germany) U., 1954-55; practice medicine specializing in psychiatry, 1951—; instr. psychiatry med. sch. U. Pa., Phila., 1951-52; staff psychiatrist Del. Hosp., Wilmington, 1951-52, Abington (Pa.) Hosp., 1951-52; clin. dir. Carrier Clinic, Belle Mead, N.J., 1956—; cons. psychiatry Somerset Hosp., Somerville, N.J., 1956—, research div. N.J. Neuropsychiat. Inst., Princeton, N.J., 1960—. Served to capt. M.C., AUS, 1952-56. Diplomate Am. Bd. Psychiatry and Neurology. Fellow Am. Psychiat. Assn.; mem. Eastern Assn. Electroencephalographers, Royal Coll. Psychiatry London. Club: Union League (Phila.). Home: 4 Greenholm St Princeton NJ 08540 Office: Carrier Clinic Belle Mead NJ 08502

SHOESMITH, MILTON HENRY, accountant; b. Providence, R.I., June 23, 1921; s. William and Annie Gilcrist (Brown) S.; B.B.A., Bryant Coll., 1948; s. m. Shirley Virginia Hopkins, Apr. 14, 1943; children—Virginia, Thomas Francis Ryan, Barbara, Gregory Laux, Steven Milton. Salesman, R.L. Greene Paper Co., 1945-51, pres., 1951-57; sales mgr. J.C. Campbell Paper Co., Pawtucket, R.I., 1957-70; sales mgr. indsl. papers Lyons & Morrison Paper Co., Pawtucket, 1971—; dir., sec. James H. Russell Transp. Inc.; dir. Providence Springfield Dispatch Inc. Trustee, treas. Peoples Bapt. Ch., Cranston, R.I.; treas. Baptist Home R.I. Served with USAAF,

1942-45. Decorated D.F.C., Air medal, Purple Heart. Mem. Nat. Soc. Pub. Accountants. Home: 117 Hopkins Johnston RI 02919 Office: 304 Cottage Pawtucket RI 02860

SHOLL, CALVIN KENNETH, mgmt. cons.; b. Phila., June 5, 1924; s. John Gurney and Helen (Hare) S.; A.B., Bucknell U., 1946; M.B.A., Syracuse U., 1955; m. Nancy Carolyn Ireland, Mar. 3, 1945; children—Lawrence Edward, John Leslie, Gwen Sholl Aquadro, Christine Beth. Asst. dir. personnel Bristol Labs., Inc., Syracuse, N.Y., 1946-56; dir. indsl. relations Fitchburg (Mass.) Paper Co., 1956-62; pres. Parker, Eldridge and Sholl, mgmt. cons., Waltham, Mass., 1962—; instr. Boston U. Met. Coll., 1964-74. Moderator Town of Lunenburg, 1968—, mem. finance com., 1958-64, chmn. personnel com., 1964-68. Served to lt., USNR, 1944-46. Certified mgmt. cons. Mem. Inst. Mgmt. Cons. (sec. 1970—, dir. 1973—), Assn. Mgmt. Cons. (pres. 1974-75, trustee 1976—), Am. Soc. Tng. and Devel., Am. Soc. Personnel Adminstrn. Home: 10 Whiting St Lunenburg MA 01462 Office: Parker Eldridge and Sholl 440 Totten Pond Rd Waltham MA 02154

SHOOK, THEODORE ALBERT, tech. co. exec.; b. New Haven, Conn., Apr. 24, 1926; s. Clarence Albert and Camille Frances (Northrup) S.; B.S., Lehigh U., 1948, M.S., 1950; m. Constance Rose Reithaar, Apr. 18, 1953; children—Karen, Paul, Elaine. With Westinghouse Elec. Corp., Lester, Pa., 1950-62, Univac div. Sperry Rand Co., Blue Bell, Pa., 1963-64; prin. engr. Reentry Systems Div., Gen. Electric Co., Phila., 1964-68, sr. engr. Switchgear Div., 1968-75; research, devel. engr. Fischer & Porter Co., Warminster, Pa., 1975—; lectr. physics Moravian Coll., 1948-50; adj. asso. prof. physics Drexel U., 1957—. Treas., v.p. Bowling Green Civic Assn., 1968—. Served with U.S. Army, 1945-47. Mem. Internat. Assn. Hydraulic Research, ASME. Republican. Lutheran. Composer march and several short pieces for flute/piano accompaniment. Patentee electromagnetic pumping device, researcher semi-condr. cooling. Home: 50 Shady Grove Circle Doylestown PA 18901 Office: Fischer & Porter Co Dept 269 Warminster PA 18974

SHOOSHAN, DANIEL MARTIN, labor negotiator; b. Worcester, Mass., Dec. 18, 1941; s. Martin Daniel and Claire Corrine (Bousquet) S.; B.S., Norwich U., 1964; postgrad. Western New Eng. Coll. Sch. Law, 1973; postgrad. in arbitration and collective bargaining U. Conn., 1976; m. Sandra Ann Bellucci, July 22, 1972. Engaged in labor relations Spalding div. Questor Co., Chicopee, Mass., 1972-73, Veeder-Root div. Western Pacific Industries, Hartford, Conn., 1973-76, structural foam machinery div. Hoover Universal Co., Springfield, Mass., 1976—; guest lectr. Am. Internat. Coll., Springfield. Served to capt. USAF, 1964-72; Vietnam. Decorated D.F.C., Air medal eight oak leaf clusters. Mem. Am. Soc. Personnel Adminstrn., Western Mass. Indsl. Relations Assn. (exec. bd.). Home: 194 E Longmeadow Rd Hampden MA 01036 Office: 600 Berkshire Ave Springfield MA 01109

SHOPEY, ROBERT JOHN, mfg. co. exec.; b. Bristol, Conn., June 8, 1939; s. Dennis and Jennie (Sarajak) S.; student Gilbert Sch., 1953-56; children—Robert John II, Linda M. With Pratt & Whitney Aircraft Co., E. Hartford, Conn., 1960-69; shop supt. William Tell Corp., Thomaston, Conn., 1969-71; quality control mgr. Egan Machine Corp., Bristol, Conn., 1971—. Vice pres. Winsted Safety Council, 1960—; chmn., commr. Winchester Housing Authority, 1973—; commr. Econ. Devel. Commn., 1974—; mem. Winsted Fire Dept., 1969—; commr. Housing Bd. Code of Appeals, 1973—; mem. Republican Town com., 1977—; mem. bd. Christian edn. 1st Ch. of Winsted; mem. Community Devel. Action Plan, 1970-71, Public Safety Task Force, 1970-71. Served with USAF, 1956-60. Recipient award Nat. Vehicle Safety Check, 1968; award for distinction State of Conn., 1976. Mem. Conn. Assn. Municipal Devel., Conn. Orgn. for Econ. Devel., Indsl. Mgmt. Club. Clubs: Redmens, Masons, Elks. Office: 135 Center St Bristol CT 06098

SHOPSIN, BARON, psychiatrist; b. N.Y.C., Aug. 7, 1935; s. Emanuel and Charlotte Shopsin; B.A., Bklyn. Coll., 1957; M.D. cum laude, U. Louvain, Belgium, 1963; m. Barbro Loxdal, July 21, 1966; children—Brett, Bo. Rotating intern U. Hosps., Louvain, 1962-63, L.I. Jewish Hosp., N.Y., 1964; resident in psychiatry Creedmoor State Hosp., Queens, N.Y., 1964, Payne Whitney Psychiat. Clinic N.Y. Hosp.-Cornell Med. Center, N.Y.C., 1965, N.Y. U. Med. Center, 1968-69; practice medicine specializing in psychiatry with subsplty. in neuropsychopharmacology; attending psychiatrist Gracie Sq. Hosp., N.Y.C., 1970—, Bellevue Hosp., N.Y.C., 1970—; asso. attending psychiatrist U. Hosp., N.Y.C., 1970—; research psychiatrist N.Y. U. Bellevue Med. Center, 1970—, chief of unit for study and treatment of affective disorders, 1972—; clin. asst. prof. psychiatry N.Y. U. Sch. Medicine, N.Y.C., 1972-74, asso. clin. prof., 1974-77, asso. prof. psychiatry, 1977—; chmn. rev. panel Drug Interaction Evaluation Program Am. Pharm. Assn., 1975—; cons. to FDA, 1973—; mem. sci. advisory bd. Bernard W. Schlesinger Found., 1977—; lectr. in field. Served to lt., M.C., USN, 1965-67. NIMH grantee, 1975—; Cancer Research Inst. grantee, 1977; diplomate Am. Bd. Psychiatry and Neurology. Mem. Am. Psychiat. Assn., Congress Internat. Neuropsychopharmacologium, Am. Psychopathol. Assn., Soc. Biol. Psychiatry, Am. Soc. Clin. Pharmacology and Therapeutics, Assn. for Research in Nervous and Mental Diseases, Internat. Soc. Psychoneuroendocrinology, Am. Coll. of Neuropsychopharmacology, AMA, N.Y. Acad. Scis. Author: (with S. Gershon) Lithium: Its Role in Psychiatric Research and Treatment, 1973; editorial advisory bd. various med. jours., 1977—; contbr. more than 100 articles on neuropsychopharmacology and therapeutics to profl. jours. Office: Dept Psychiatry New York Univ Med Center 550 First Ave New York City NY 10016

SHORE, BENJAMIN, plastic surgeon; b. Montreal, Que., Can., Apr. 13, 1940; s. Isaac and Molly (Mandel) S.; B.Sc., McGill U., 1961; M.D., 1965; m. Merelyn Ann Jones, Feb. 4, 1971; children—Michael David, Timothy John. Intern, Montreal Gen. Hosp., 1965-66, resident, 1966-67; resident Ottawa (Ont., Can.) Civic Hosp., 1967-68, Toronto (Ont.) Sick Children's Hosp., 1969-70; practice medicine, specializing in plastic and hand surgery; cons. plastic surgery Peel Meml. Hosp., Brampton, Ont., Cosmetic Inst., Woodridge, Ont.; cons. Maxillo-Facial Clinic Crippled Children's Center, Toronto, 1974; lectr. Sheridan Coll. Nursing, Mississalga, Ont. Bd. dirs. Peel Regional YMCA, 1974; nat. med. adv. Can. Ski Patrol System, 1972. Fellow Royal Coll. Surgeons Can.; mem. Canadian, Ont. (chmn. plastic surg. sect. 1976) med. assns., Canadian Soc. Plastic Surgery, Am. Soc. Plastic and Reconstructive Surgery, Internat. Assn. Plastic and Reconstructive Surgery. Contbr. articles to profl. jours. Home: 105 Main St S Brampton ON L6Y 1N1 Canada Office: 178 John St Suite 202 Brampton ON L6W 2A4 Canada

SHORE, MILTON PAUL, judge HEW; b. McKeesport, Pa., Oct. 26, 1909; s. Abraham and Bessie (Kimelman) S.; B.A., U. Pitts., 1932, J.D., 1935; spl. postgrad. course in bus. adminstrn., Harvard U., 1971; m. Shirley Elizabeth Nayhouse, July 25, 1937; 1 son, Alan J. Admitted to Pa. bar, 1935, U.S. Supreme Ct., 1966; practice law, Pitts., 1935-41, 46-63; asst. exec. v.p. M.B. Speer & Co., Pitts., 1941-46; atty. Office Gen. Counsel, Commerce Dept., Washington, 1963-66; sr. trial atty. Office Gen. Council, SBA, 1966-71; atty. in Exec. Office of Pres., 1971; adminstrv. law judge Bur. Hearings and Appeals, Social Security Adminstrn., HEW, Detroit, 1971-76, Pitts., 1976—. Recipient certificate of achievement SBA, 1971; letter of commendation Office Emergency Preparedness, 1971. Mem. Fed. Bar Assn., Allegheny County Bar Assn., Am. Judicature Soc., Zeta Beta Tau. Club: Masons. Co-inventor therapeutic table. Home: 6315 Forbes Ave Apt 201 Pittsburgh PA 15217 Office: 5th Floor Park Bldg 355 5th Ave Pittsburgh PA 15222

SHORR, EDWARD JEFFREY, paper co. exec.; b. Providence, Mar. 23, 1942; s. Albert A. and Beatrice (Namerow) S.; B.S., Boston U., 1963; m. Ellen Seligman, Dec. 30, 1967; children—Eric Mark, Jennifer Beth, Daniel Seligman. With Albert A. Shorr Co., Woonsocket, R.I., 1963-69; pres. Riverside Industries, Inc., Woonsocket, 1969—. Bd. dirs. Congregation B'nai Israel, 1st v.p., 1978—. Mem. C. of C., Fraternal Order Police. Clubs: B'nai B'rith (Woonsocket chpt. pres. 1974-76), Highridge Swim & Tennis (Lincoln, R.I.). Home: 173 Gaskill St Woonsocket RI 02895 Office: 159 Singleton St Woonsocket RI 02895

SHORR, NORMAN, mil. engr.; b. Pitts., Mar. 25, 1917; s. Benjamin and Ida S.; Ph.D., Calif. Western U., 1977; m. Pearle V. Gawlowski, Feb. 13, 1943. Sr. devel. engr. Goodyear Aircraft Corp., Akron, Ohio, 1953-55; sr. engring. asso. PPG Industries Inc., Pitts., 1955-76; cons. mil. engr., Mt. Lebanon, Pa., 1976—. Served with USNR, 1940. Registered profl. engr., Pa., Ohio, W.Va. Mem. Am. Def. Preparedness Assn., Soc. Am. Mil. Engrs., Engrs. Soc. West Pa. Researcher transparent armor, aircraft glazing, asbestos and glass tech.; patentee in field. Home: 200 Buchanan Pl Mount Lebanon PA 15228

SHORR, RONALD PHILIP, investment analyst; b. Chgo., Mar. 28, 1937; s. Ralph Louis and Babette Josephine (Zucker) S.; B.A., U. Mich., 1958; M.B.A., Harvard, 1961; postgrad. Columbia, 1965-66; m. Jean Cooper Fishack, July 1, 1960; children—David Baker, Scott Alden. Investment adviser, N.Y.C., 1961-63; with Hardy & Co., 1963-64, Roth, Gerard & Co., 1964-69; exec. v.p. Minbanco Corp., 1969-71; v.p. Dean Witter & Co., 1971-74; v.p. E.F. Hutton & Co., N.Y.C., 1974—. Served with U.S. Army, 1959-60. Chartered financial analyst. Mem. Am. Inst. Mining Engrs., N.Y. Soc. Security Analysts, N.Y. Metals and Mining Analyst Assn. (pres.). Contbr. chpt. to Economics of the Mineral Industries, 1976. Home: 75 East End Ave New York City NY 10028 Office: One Battery Park Plaza New York City NY 10004

SHORT, WILLIAM HOSLEY, architect; b. Warren, Mass., May 29, 1924; s. Walter Edwin and Mary Allen (Hosley) S.; A.B., Princeton U., 1949, M.F.A., 1952. Draftsman firm Holden, Egan & Assos., N.Y.C., 1952-54; planner Nat. Planning and Research Inc., Phila., 1954-55; architect firm Kenneth Kassler, Assos., Princeton, N.J., 1955-56; constrn. supr. Frank Lloyd Wright, Architect and Solomon R. Guggenheim Found., N.Y.C., 1956-60; partner firm Venturi & Short, Phila., 1960-63; prin. firm William H. Short, Architect, Princeton, 1963-73; partner firm Short and Ford, Architects, Princeton, 1974—. Mem. Princeton Joint Hist. Sites Commn., 1973—. Served with USAAF, 1943-46. Recipient AIA Homes for Better Living award, 1978; Sensible Growth merit award Nat. Assn. Home Builders, 1977. Mem. AIA. Club: Nassau (Princeton). Prin. works include: Lloyd Terrace Housing, Princeton, 1968; Guernsey Hall Condominium, Princeton, 1972; Princeton Community Housing, 1973-75. Home: 130 Stockton St Princeton NJ 08540 Office: RD 4 Box 864 Mapleton Rd Princeton NJ 08540

SHORTWAY, RICHARD ANTHONY, publishing co. exec.; b. Fairlawn, N.J., Feb. 17, 1924; s. Anthony and Blanche (Wiley) S.; student Western Res. U., 1942-43; m. Dorothy McDonald, Oct. 6, 1945 (div. Apr. 1963); children—Catherine Carina, Mary Lida; m. 2d, Sue Ann Taylor, Aug. 6, 1963 (div. Dec. 1969); m. 3d, Gretchen Swartzwelder, Nov. 27, 1971. Advt. rep. Womens Wear Daily, N.Y.C., 1946-50; advt. rep. Glamour mag., 1950-54, Eastern mgr., 1954-59, advt. mgr., 1959-63; advt. mgr. Vogue mag., 1963-64, advt. dir., 1964—, pub., 1970—. Served to 1st lt. USAAF, 1944-45. Decorated D.F.C., Air medal with oak leaf clusters. Mem. Advt. Sales Club, Mag. Pubs. Assn. Clubs: Westchester Country, Coveleigh (Rye, N.Y.). Home: 307 E 44th St New York City NY 10017 Office: 350 Madison Ave New York City NY 10017

SHOSHKES, LILA, interior designer; b. Bklyn., July 21, 1926; d. Samuel B. and Rhea (Gallay) Topal; B.A., Bklyn. Coll., 1947; student Pratt Inst., 1966-68; m. Milton Shoshkes, Sept. 25, 1948; children—Carol, Ellen, Ann, Deena. Interior designer Frank Grad & Sons, Newark, 1968-70, ISD, Inc., N.Y.C., 1970-71; individual practice interior design, South Orange, N.J., 1972—; cons. in field. Mem. Inst. Bus. Designers, Suburban Research Soc. Club: Braidburn Country. Contbr. articles to profl. jours. Office:

SHOTLAND, EDWIN, physicist; b. Palatinate, Germany, Dec. 18, 1908; s. Henry M. and Eugenia Eva (Loeb) S.; came to U.S. 1937, naturalized 1943; B.S., U. Munich, 1931, M.S., 1932; Dr. Phil., U. Heidelberg, 1934; m. Marianne Hess Blumenthal, May 19, 1946; children—Lawrence Martin, Michael David. Tchr. math. and physics German high schs., 1934-37; analytical engr. Kurman Electronics, N.Y.C., 1940-42; project engr. Chance Vought Aircraft, United Aircraft Corp., 1946-50; physicist and research project supr., prin. staff mem. Applied Physics Lab., Johns Hopkins, 1950—. Served in U.S. Army, 1942-45. Mem. Am. Phys. Soc., Philos. Soc. Washington, Washington Acad. Scis., Sigma Xi. Contbg. author to book series Modern Methods of Experimental Physics. Contbr. articles to profl. jours., also classified papers on missile control and guidance. Home: 418 E Indian Spring Dr Silver Spring MD 20901 Office: Johns Hopkins Rd Laurel MD 20810

SHOW, WHITLAW MISSIMER, osteo. physician, surgeon; b. Phila., Feb. 24, 1919; s. O. Whitlaw and Elizabeth S. (Missimer) S.; A.B., Kent State U., 1941; D.O., Phila. Coll. Osteopathy, 1946; m. Ruth Allen, Aug. 20, 1945; 1 son, John Allen. Chief stock clk. J. C. Penney Co., Massillon, 1937-38; with Republic Steel Mills, Massillon, Ohio, 1938-40; intern Lancaster (Pa.) Osteo. Hosp., 1945-46, Surg. resident 1947-50; pvt. practice osteo. medicine, Bird-In-Hand, Pa., 1950—; exec. staff, v.p. Lancaster Osteo. Hosp., pres.-elect med. staff; county dep. coroner, Lancaster, Pa., 1965-74, county coroner, 1976—. Former mem. Susquehanna Valley Regional Med. Program. Ambulance instr. ARC; ret. med. dir. Lane County Ambulance Assn.; past asst. fire chief. Past unit captain for Community Chest drives; founder, also committeeman Boy Scout Troop 8. Served to 2d lt. USMCR, 1941-43. Recipient Highest and 1st award most outstanding alumnus Kent State U., 1958; named Nat. Gen. Practitioner of Year, Kansas City, 1960, named Pa. Doctor of Year, 1960. Fellow Am. Coll. Osteo. Medicine and Surgery; mem. Lancaster County Med. Osteo. Soc. (pres. 1970-71), Am. Coll. Gen. Practitioners (past pres. Pa. div., sec. past chmn. state liaison with drug mfrs., past chmn. state vocational guidance, past chmn. med. exhibits, conv. chmn. state com., past dist. 5 chmn. ethic com.), Hosp. Alumni Staff (pres. 1965-66), Pa. County Coroners Assn. Mason (Shriner, 32 deg.), Rotarian (past pres.). Clubs: Lancaster County Shrine (pres.); Sertoma Internat. (life, dir. Eastern Lancaster County chpt.). Address: Rural Route 1 Bird-in-Hand PA 17505

SHOWERS, HERMAN BYRON, educator; b. Reading, Pa., Nov. 14, 1930; s. Herman S. and Melva E. (Youse) S.; A.B., Houghton Coll., 1952; M.Div., Temple U., 1955; Ed.M., Rutgers U., 1964, Ed.D., 1964; m. Jane M. Knabb, Aug. 30, 1952; children—David S., Thomas L., Shelley Ann. Sch. counselor pub. schs., Reading, Pa., 1959-61; asst. prof. psychology Monmouth Coll., W. Long Branch, N.J., 1961-65; lectr. in edn. Rutgers U., New Brunswick, N.J., 1964-65; prof., chmn. dept. counselor edn. Millersville (Pa.) State Coll., 1965—. Vice chmn. Lancaster County Republican Com., 1976. NDEA fellow, 1960. Mem. Am. Psychol. Assn., Phi Delta Kappa, Psi Chi, Kappa Delta Pi. Republican. Methodist. Club: Lancaster NE Rotary (pres. 1978-79). Home: 1432 Mission Rd Lancaster PA 17601 Office: Byerly Hall Millersville State Coll Millersville PA 17551

SHRAGER, MORTON WILLIAM, cardiologist; b. Phila., Dec. 5, 1930; s. Harry Eli and Lillian (Shotkin) S.; A.B., U. Pa., 1952, M.D., 1956; m. Simone Grunberg, Dec. 29, 1957; children—Jeffrey, Joseph, Monique. Rotating intern Albert Einstein Med. Center, No. div., Phila., 1956-57, med. resident, 1957-58; resident neurology Jefferson Med. Coll., 1958-59; resident cardiology Phila. Gen. Hosp., 1959-60; clin. asst. prof. medicine U. Pa. Sch. Medicine, Phila., 1971—; cons. medicine U. Pa. Service, VA Hosp., Phila., 1969—; asso. cardiology Presbyn.-U. Pa. Med. Center, Phila., 1973—; acting chief dept. medicine Women's Hosp., Phila., 1963-64; ward attending in medicine VA Hosp., Phila., 1966-69, Presbyn. Hosp. U. Pa., 1964—, Bryn Mawr (Pa.) Hosp., 1978—. Diplomate Am. Bd. Internal Medicine. Mem. Phila. Coll. Physicians, Philadelphia County Med. Soc. Home: 845 Hunt Rd Newtown Square PA 19073 Office: 3910 Powelton Ave Suite 207 Philadelphia PA 19104

SHRALOW, RHODA ROBIN, guidance counselor; b. Phila., July 23, 1938; d. Morris and Celya Robin; student U. Pa., 1956-58; B.A., Boston U., 1959; M.A., Villanova U., 1974; m. M. Melvin Shralow, June 22, 1958; children—Donna, William, Jeffrey. Tchr., Beth Hillel Nursery Sch., Phila., 1971-74; guidance counselor Delaware County Intermediate unit Nonpub. Sch. Services, Phila., 1974-75, guidance counselor, center leader, 1975—, practicum asst. Villanova U., summer 1975. Rec. sec. Haverford Jr. High Sch. PTA, 1974-75. Certified early childhood edn., edn. specialist I and II. Mem. Am. Personnel and Guidance Assn., Pa. Sch. Counselor Assn., LWV Haverford Twp. (rec. sec. 1973-75). Home: 824 Dover Rd Philadelphia PA 19151 Office: 2340 Westchester Pike Broomall PA 19008

SHREINER, CHARLES WESLEY, JR., ednl. adminstr.; b. Phila., Aug. 3, 1922; s. Charles W. and Mary C. S.; B.S. in Bus. Adminstrn., Temple U., Phila., 1949, LL.D., 1970; L.H.D. (hon.), Widener Coll., Chester, Pa., 1969; m. Shirley M. Shreiner; children—Charles W. III, Stacey B., Alix M. Asst. to headmaster Church Farm Sch., Paoli, Pa., 1949-55, asst. headmaster, 1955-64, headmaster, 1964—. Trustee Episcopal Acad., 1968—; bd. mgrs. Chester County Hosp., 1969—. Licensed headmaster, Pa. Mem. Headmasters Assn., Boarding Sch. Headmasters Assn. Middle States, Heads of Phila. Area Ind. Schs.; Pa. Assn. Ind. Schs. (pres. 1978-79), Nat. Assn. Episcopal Schs. (pres. 1979—). Home and Office: Box S Paoli PA 19301

SHRIER, ADAM LOUIS, oil co. exec.; b. Warsaw, Poland, Mar. 26, 1938; s. Henry Leon and Mathilda June (Czamanska) S.; came to U.S., 1943, naturalized, 1949; B.S., Columbia, 1959; M.S. (Whitney fellow), Mass. Inst. Tech., 1960; D.Eng. and Applied Sci. (NSF fellow), Yale, 1965; postdoctoral visitor U. Cambridge (England), 1965-66; J.D., Fordham U., 1976; m. Diane Kesler, June 10, 1961; children—Jonathan, Lydia, Catherine, David. With Esso Research & Engring. Co., Florham Park and Linden, N.J., 1963-65, 66-72, head environmental scis. research area, 1969-72; coordinator pollution abatement activities, tanker dept. Exxon Internat. Co., N.Y.C., 1972-74; project mgr., energy systems Exxon Enterprises Inc., N.Y.C., 1974-75, mgr. solar energy projects, 1975-77, gen. mgr. solar heating div., 1977-78, pres. solar thermal systems div., 1979—; dir. Solar Power Corp., North Billerica, Mass., Daystar Corp., Burlington, Mass.; adj. lectr. chem. engring. Columbia, N.Y.C., 1967-68, 68-69. Mem. Am. Inst. Chem. Engrs., Am. Chem. Soc., AAAS, N.Y. Acad. Scis., Am. Bar Assn. Contbr. to profl. jours. Patentee in field. Home: 60 Melrose Pl Montclair NJ 07042 Office: Exxon Corp 1251 Ave of Americas New York City NY 10020

SHRIER, DIANE KESLER, psychiatrist; b. N.Y.C., Mar. 23, 1941; d. Benjamin Arthur and Mollie (Wortman) Kesler; B.S. in Chemistry and Biology magna cum laude (Regents scholar 1957-61), Queen's Coll., City U. N.Y., 1961; student Washington U. Sch. Medicine, St. Louis, 1960-61; M.D., Yale, 1964; m. Adam Louis Shrier, June 10, 1961; children—Jonathan Laurence, Lydia Anne, Catherine Jane, David Leopold. Pediatric intern Bellevue Hosp., N.Y.C., 1964-65; psychiat. resident Albert Einstein Coll. Medicine-Bronx (N.Y.) Municipal Hosp. Center, 1966-68, child psychiatry fellow, 1968-70; staff cons. Family Service and Child Guidance Center of the Oranges, Maplewood, Milburn-Orange, N.J., 1970-73, cons., 1973—; pvt. practice, Montclair, N.J., 1970—; cons. Community Day Nursery, E. Orange, 1970—, Montclair State Coll., 1976-78; psychiat. cons. Bloomfield (N.J.) pub. schs., 1974-75; clin. instr. Albert Einstein Coll. Medicine, 1970-73; clin. asst. prof. psychiatry Coll. Medicine and Dentistry N.J., 1978—. Trustee Montessori Learning Center, Montclair, 1973-75. Diplomate Am. Bd. Psychiatry and Neurology. Fellow Am. Psychiat. Assn.; mem. Acad. Child Psychiatry, Am. Orthopsychiat. Assn., Tri-County Psychiat. Assn. (exec. com., rec. sec. 1977-78, 2d v.p. 1978-79), Am. Med. Women's Assn., Nat. Assn. Residents and Interns, Essex County Med. Soc., Phi Beta Kappa. Contbr. articles to med. jours. Address: 60 Melrose Dr Montclair NJ 07042

SHRIVER, RICHARD HANSON, banker; b. Balt., Aug. 17, 1933; s. Samuel Henry and Eleanor (Ringgold) S.; B.S. in Mech. Engring., Cornell U., 1956; M.S. in Indsl. Engring., Ohio State U., 1960; m. Barbara Ann Brown, June 24, 1960; children—Richard, Andrew. Head ops. research for mktg. Esso Research and Engring., 1965-66; pres. R. Shriver Asso., systems cons., Parsippany, N.J., 1966-74, chmn., 1974—; dir. telecommunications and command and control systems Dept. Def., 1976-77; sr. v.p. Chase Manhattan Bank, N.Y.C., 1977—; dir. J.L. Prescott Co., Passaic, N.J. Mem. bd. edn., Mt. Lakes, N.J., 1971-74; dir. telephone campaign Com. to Reelect Pres., 1972. Served with USAF, 1957-59. Recipient Medal for Distinguished Pub. Service, Dept. Def., 1977. Mem. Armed Forces Communications and Electronics Assn. Republican. Episcopalian. Clubs: Md., Cornell. Home: RD 3 Box 18 Waynesboro PA 17268 Office: 1 Chase Manhattan Plaza New York City NY 10005

SHULL, KENNETH EDGAR, water co. exec.; b. Ardmore Park, Pa., July 30, 1916; s. Alvin Edgar and Alma Barbara (Haupt) S.; B.S. with distinction, Phila. Coll. Pharmacy and Sci., 1938; m. Marie-Louise Cone, July 22, 1977; children—Richard L., Nancy Branca, David L. Chemist, bacteriologist Phila. Suburban Water Co., Bryn Mawr, Pa., 1938-41, chief chemist, 1941-44, supt. water treatment, 1944-52, dir. pub. relations and water quality control, 1956-58, v.p. pub. relations and quality control, 1958-59, v.p. treatment quality control and research, 1959—. Bd. dirs. Main Line br. A.R.C. Mem. Am. Water Works Assn. (Fuller award 1968, Research award 1975, nat. dir. 1962-65), Am. Chem. Soc. (dir. Phila. sect. 1949-57, editor Catalyst

1949-51), Mainline C. of C. (pres. 1968), AAAS, Am. Pub. Health Assn., Inst. Water Engrs. and Scientists (Eng.). Episcopalian. Club: Rotary (pres. Ardmore club 1953-54). Contbr. articles to profl. publs. Home: 1220 Morgan Ave Drexel Hill PA 19026 Office: 762 Lancaster Ave Bryn Mawr PA 19010

SHULMAN, FRANK JOSEPH, librarian; b. Boston, Sept. 20, 1943; B.A. in History magna cum laude, Harvard U., 1964; postgrad. Hebrew U. Jerusalem, 1964-65, U. Minn., summer 1966, Inter-Univ. Center for Japanese Lang. Studies, Tokyo, 1967-68; M.A. in E. Asian Studies, U. Mich., 1968, M.L.S., 1969, doctoral candidate, 1974. Bibliographer/librarian Center for Japanese Studies, U. Mich., Ann Arbor, 1970-75; head E. Asia Collection, U. Md. Libraries, College Park, 1976—; asst. devel. library resources for study of Asia, Hebrew U. Jerusalem, 1970-74; library cons. Groupe d'Etudes et de Documentation sur le Japon Contemporain, Ecole Pratique des Hautes Etudes, Sciences Economiques et Sociales, Paris, 1974. Carnegie fellow, 1969; Nat. Def. Fgn. Lang. fellow, 1965-69. Mem. Assn. Asian Studies (asst. editor Bibliography of Asian Studies 1970-72), Am. Hist. Assn. (com. E. Asian libraries), D.C. Library Assn., European Assn. Japanese Studies, Internat. Assn. Orientalist Librarians, Japan-Am. Soc., Middle East Librarians Assn., Interchange for Pacific Scholarship (council), Phi Kappa Phi, Beta Phi Mu. Author: Japan and Korea: An Annotated Bibliography of Doctoral Dissertations in Western Languages, 1877-1969, 1970; American and British Doctoral Dissertations on Israel and Palestine in Modern Times, 1973; (with others) The Allied Occupation of Japan, 1945-1952: An Annotated Bibliography of Western-Language Materials, 1974; others; contbr. numerous articles and revs. to scholarly jours. Home: 4313 Knox Rd #405 College Park MD 20740 Office: McKeldin Library U Md College Park MD 20742

SHULMAN, GERALD DENNIS, psychologist, clin. dir.; b. Phila., May 28, 1937; s. Herman and Dorothy (Malamed) S.; B.A., Temple U., 1958, M.A., 1960; m. Susie Branum, Dec. 5, 1974; children—Scott J., Hillary B. Clin. psychologist State Correctional Inst., Phila., 1961-62; clin. psychologist Chit Chat Farms, Wernersville, Pa., 1962-71, dir. therapy, 1971-72, exec. dir., 1972—; exec. dir. Caron Hosp., Wernersville, 1975—; mem. alcohol task panel Pres.'s Commn. Mental Health; founder, mem. bd., former chmn. pvt. rehab. sect. Alcohol Drug Problems Assn. N.Am. Licensed psychologist, Pa. Home: Box 277 Wernersville PA 19565

SHULTZ, HERBERT LLOYD, coll. adminstr., bus. exec.; b. N.Y.C., Apr. 4, 1918; s. Edwin DeNyse and Mary Ella (Smith) S.; A.B. with honors, Princeton, 1940; m. Barbara Hinkley Rodie, Dec. 6, 1941; children—Barbara Redfield, Herbert Lloyd, Anne Rodie. Polit. and legislative corr. A.P. Bur., Albany, N.Y., 1941-42; sales rep. various coal cos., 1945-51; v.p. v.p. Rodie Coal Co., Inc., Kingston, N.Y., 1951-61, pres., 1961—; v.p. devel. Vassar Coll., Poughkeepsie, N.Y., 1973—; pres. North River Coal Co., Inc., Kingston, 1961-73, Kingston Coal & Oil Co., Inc., 1961-73; pres., dir. R & S Pubs., Inc., Kingston, 1963-65; pub. Hudson River Pilot, 1963-65; pres. Spin-Line Co., Kingston, 1970-77; trustee, chmn. finance com. Rondout Savs. Bank, Kingston, 1960—; exec. com. Honamalino Agrl. Co., Inc., Kealakekua, Hawaii; dir., sec. Mid-Hudson Pattern for Progress, Inc.; dir. Winnisook, Inc., Kingston, 1956—, pres., 1957-62; dir. Central Hudson Gas and Electric Corp., Poughkeepsie. Ulster County chmn. capital funds drive Princeton; mem. Kingston Human Relations Commn., 1969—; chmn. Princeton Schs. Com., for Mid-Hudson Region, 1967-73. Bd. dirs., past pres. Kingston Boys Club Inc.; trustee, treas. Kingston Hosp., 1962-68 trustee Kingston Acad. Served as combat corr. 2d Div., USMC, 1943-45. Mem. NAACP (mem. chpt. exec. com. 1968—). Episcopalian (past vestryman). Clubs: Nassau (Princeton, N.J.); Angler's, Princeton (N.Y.C.); Winnisook (Olivera, N.Y.); Flyfishers (London). Contbr. articles on jazz history to Saturday Rev., others. Home: 62 Lounsbery Pl Kingston NY 12401 Office: Vassar Coll Poughkeepsie NY 12601

SHUMAN, STANLEY SAXE, investment banker; b. Cambridge, Mass., June 22, 1935; s. Saul Aaron and Sarah Lillian (Saxe) S.; B.A., Harvard, 1956, J.D., 1959, M.B.A., 1961; m. Ruth Helen Lande, Nov. 19, 1967; children—David Lande, Michael Adam. Admitted to Mass. bar, 1959; with Allen & Co. Inc., N.Y.C., 1961—, exec. v.p., 1970—, also dir., mem. exec. com.; v.p., dir. Internat. Foodservice Corp., Horizon Corp.; dir. N.Y. Post Corp., N.Y. Mag., Applied Devices Corp., News Am. Pub. Inc. Pres. Wiltwyck Sch., 1971-78; v.p., bd. dirs., mem. exec. com. Jewish Guild for the Blind; bd. dirs. Nat. Econ. Devel. Law Project, also chmn.; mem. Gov. Hugh Carey's Task Force on Unemployment; trustee The Dalton Sch.; mem. Emergency Fin. Control Bd. N.Y.C. Mem. Am. Bar Assn. (comml. arbitration com.). Home: 17 E 73d St New York City NY 10021 Office: 711 Fifth Ave New York City NY 10022

SHUSTER, CARL NATHANIEL, educator; b. Frenchtown, N.J., Feb. 16, 1890; s. Nathaniel Rittenhouse and Catharine (Draucker) S.; diploma Normal Sch., 1913; B.S., Tchrs. Coll. Columbia U., 1915; A.M., 1918; Ph.D., Columbia U., 1940; m. Edith Gilman, June 5, 1918; children—Carl, Nathaniel, John, Gilman, Jean Wessner. Tchr. elementary schs., 1907-10, high schs., 1913-17, adminstr., 1917-21; instr. Bowling Green U., summer 1920, 21, Pa. State U., summer 1925; instr. Columbia U., 1926-52, prof., head dept. math. N.J. State Coll., Trenton, 1929-56; head dept. math. Pennington Sch., 1956-57; tchr. Sch. Indsl. Arts, Trenton, 1956-57; vis. prof. Yeshiva U., 1953-57; head math. dept. U. Tampa (Fla.), 1957-60; prof. emeritus Trenton State Coll.; head math. dept., dir. Adirondack So. Sch., St. Petersburg, Fla.; vis. prof. Coll. Advanced Sci., N.H., summer 1962, U. Fla., summer 1963; also sr. sci. editor. Served with USNRF, 1917-18. Recipient alumni citation Trenton State Coll., 1961; Columbia Press Assn. Gold Key. Fellow AAAS, Fla. Council Sci.; mem. Fla. Acad. Sci., Assn. Math. Tchrs. N.J. (council 1926, permanent mem. 1955—, pres. 1952, charter mem.), Nat. Council Tchrs. Math. (dir. 1946-48, pres. 1948-49), Am. Math. Soc., Math. Assn. Am., Phi Delta Kappa. Clubs: Lions, Torch. Author: How to Use the Sextant, 1934; How to Use the Hypsometer and Clinometer, 1934; Field Work in Mathematics, 1936; Real Life Mathematics, Grades 3-8, 1938; Problems in Teaching the Slide Rule, 1940; Plane Geometry, 1955; The Scribner Arithmetics, Grade 7-8, 1955; Functional Mathematics, Grades 7-12, 1956; editorial bd. Math. Mag., 1946-60; contbr. numerous articles to jours. and mags.; originator computation with approximate numbers, 1918. Home: 2393 Pennington Rd Trenton NJ 08638 also 2035 26th Ave N Saint Petersburg FL 33713

SHUSTER, CARL NATHANIEL, JR., govt. ofcl., ecologist; b. Randolph, Vt., Nov. 16, 1919; B.Sc., Rutgers U., 1942, M.Sc., 1948, postgrad. summers 1953, 54, Ph.D. in Biology (fellow), N.Y. U., 1955; m. Helen Irwin, May 4, 1944; children—George Whitcomb, Kenneth Ashton, Chris Irwin, Carl Nathaniel III, Forrest, Winthrop Hilton. Asst. prof. biol. sci., dir. marine labs. U. Del., 1955-63; dir. Northeast Research Center USPHS, 1963-69, div. ecologist Bur. Water Supply, 1970-71; acting chief environ. evaluation br. EPA, 1971-72; asst. adviser for ecol. systems analysis Office Environ. Quality, FPC, Washington, 1972-75, acting adviser for environ. quality, 1974-75, ecol. systems analyst Office Energy Systems, 1975-77, coordinator marine coastal zone affairs, 1976—; acting dir. div. energy tech. and environ. Fed. Energy Regulatory Commn., Washington, 1977—; adj. prof. oceanography and zoology U. R.I., 1963-70, research asso. Grad. Sch. Oceanography, 1963-70. Mem. U.S. Nat. Mus. Smithsonian-Bredin Caribbean exptdn., 1958. Served with AUS, 1942-43; to 1st lt. USAAF, 1943-45. Recipient Silver Beaver award Boy Scouts Am., 1969; decorated Air medal with 3 oak leaf clusters, D.F.C. Fellow AAAS, N.Y. Acad. Scis.; mem. Am. Soc. Limnology and Oceanography, Am. Soc. Zoologists, Ecol. Soc. Am., Nat. Shellfisheries Assn., Del. Conservation Edn. Assn. (pres. 1959-63), Sigma Xi. Research in aquatic biology, estuarine and tidal marsh ecology; authority on ecology of Limulus. Home: 3733 N 25th St Arlington VA 22207 Office: Fed Energy Regulatory Commn 825 N Capitol St NE Washington DC 20426

SHUSTER, E.G. (BUD), congressman; b. Glassport, Pa., Jan. 23, 1932; s. Prather and Grace (Greinert) S.; B.S., U. Pitts., 1954; M.B.A., Duquesne U., 1960; Ph.D. in Econs. and Mgmt., Am. U., 1967; m. Patricia Rommel, Aug. 27, 1955; children—Peg, Bill, Debbie, Bobby, Gia. System analyst Univac div. Remington Rand (now Sperry Rand), 1956, then nat. account mgr., to 1960; dist. mgr. western Pa. RCA, 1960-62, mgr. operations, Washington, 1962-65, v.p. electronic data processing div., 1965-68; mgmt. cons., 1968-72; mem. 92-96th congresses from 9th Pa. dist. Owner, operator beef cattle farm, Everett, Pa., 1964—. Former trustee U. Pitts. Served with AUS, 1954-56. Named Republican Freshman Congressman of Month, 1973. Mem. Phi Beta Kappa, Omicron Delta Kappa, Sigma Chi. Clubs: Capitol Hill, 93d (Washington). Home: Star Route #5 Everett PA 15537 Office: 1110 Longworth House Office Bldg Washington DC 20515

SHUTACK, JOHN PATRICK, printing co. exec.; b. Manville, N.J., Oct. 7, 1925; s. John and Mary (Singel) S.; student pub. schs., Manville; m. Mary J. Sluck, May 23, 1953; children—John Gerard, Kevin Patrick. Reporter, printer Manville News, 1936-50; with I.N. Blue Printing Co., New Brunswick, N.J., 1950—, foreman, 1971—. Mem. Manville Bd. Edn., 1949-57; active mem. Camplain Vol. Fire Co., 1950—; pres. Manville Library Bd. Trustees, 1964—; pres. St. Mary's Catholic Ch. Choir, Manville, 1947, adult advisor to youth, 1974—; pres. dist. 7 Greek Catholic Union of the U.S.A., 1974—. Served with USMC, 1943-46. Mem. N.J. Library Trustees Assn., Internat. Typog. Union Local 103, VFW (life), Veterans of Manville. Democrat. Home: 15 S 5th Ave Manville NJ 08835

SHUTTLEWORTH, ANNE MARGARET, psychiatrist; b. Detroit, Jan. 17, 1931; d. Cornelius Joseph and Alice Catherine (Rice) S.; A.B., Cornell U., 1953, M.D., 1956; m. Joel R. Siegel, Apr. 19, 1959; children—Erika, Peter. Intern Lenox Hill Hosp., N.Y.C., 1956-57; resident Payne Whitney Clinic-N.Y. Hosp., 1957-60; pvt. practice medicine, specializing in psychiatry, Maplewood, N.J., 1960—; cons. Maplewood Sch. System, 1960-62; instr. psychiatry Cornell U. Med. Sch., 1960; mem. Com. to Organize New Sch. Psychology, 1970. Mem. AMA (Physicians Recognition award 1975, 78), Am. Psychiat. Assn., Am. Med. Women's Assn., N.Y. Acad. Scis., Acad. Medicine N.J. Home: 46 Farbrook Dr Short Hills NJ 07078 Office: 2066 Millburn Ave Maplewood NJ 07040

SHVETZ, ALEXANDER EPHRAIM, bus. exec.; b. Nikolaev, Russia, Sept. 4, 1913; s. Ephraim Gregoravitch and Esphir S.; came to U.S., 1945, naturalized, 1953; B.S., Harbin (China) Bus. Sch. Commerce, 1932; economist Advanced Sch., Sorbonne U., Paris, 1957, Ph.D. (hon.), Dr. Econ. Sci. (hon.), 1959; m. Eda D., Apr. 4, 1940; children—Jeannette Alexandra, Frederick Ronald. Chmn. bd., pres. Amerex Trading Corp., N.Y.C., 1946—, Amerex Group Cos., Asia, 1946—, Trans World Electronics, Asia, 1971—. Decorated Legion of Honor, Croix de Guerre (France); recipient Gold and Silver Cross, Red Cross Japan, 1951; Gen. Pershing medal Assn. Nationale des Croix de Guerre, 1939-45. Fellow Royal Soc. Arts (Eng.) (life); mem. Sovereign Greek Order St. Dennis of Zante (chancellor of exchequer 1958—), N.Y. Acad. Scis. (life), Renaissance Francaise (French Gold medal), French Nat. Assn. Profl. Engrs. (hon.), Nat. Legion Greek-Am. War Vets. in U.S. (Greek Cross Merit 1952). Jewish. Club: Am. (Asia). Home: 980 Fifth Ave New York City NY 10021 Office: Amerex Trading Corp 1372 Broadway New York City NY 10018

SIAR, ROBERT THOMAS, athletic adminstr., educator; b. Brookville, Pa., Sept. 26, 1932; s. Raul T. and Nellie L. (Kinder) S.; B.S. in Health and Phys. Edn., Slippery Rock State Coll., 1955; m. Susan F. Freeman, Jan. 26, 1957; children—Robert Matthew, Richard Thomas, Kimberly Susan. Tchr. and coach Kane Area (Pa.) High Sch., 1955-57, Johnsonburg (Pa.) High Sch., 1957-60; tchr. phys. edn., head football, wrestling and track coach Brookville (Pa.) High Sch., 1960-65; tchr. science, head wrestling coach Shaler High Sch., Glenshaw, Pa., 1965—; tchr. Buhl Planetarium of Arts and Scis., 1967-72; mem. teaching staff Sheridan Wrestling Clinic, Bethlehem, Pa., 1970, Annapolis (Md.) Wrestling Clinic, 1972; mem. adv. bd. Three Rivers All-Star Wrestling Clinic, 1971—. Recipient Wrestling Coach of Year award Western Pa. Interscholastic Athletic League, 1974; elected to Western Pa. Sports Hall of Fame, 1974. Mem. U.S. Wrestling Fedn. (adv. bd. 1974—), NEA, Pa. State Edn. Assn., Shaler Area Tchrs. Assn., Pa. Wrestling Coaches Assn. (rep. dist. 7 1969-76), Allegheny Mountain AAU Wrestling Assn. (chmn. 1968-74, 77-78), Western Pa. Interscholastic Athletic Wrestling Coaches Assn. (pres. 1968-76). Presbyterian. Editor Shaler Area Titan Grappler, 1973—. Home: 2616 Hamilton Ave Glenshaw PA 15116 Office: 1800 Mount Royal Blvd Glenshaw PA 15116

SIBALIS, DAN, mfg. co. exec.; b. Ploesti, Rumania, Sept. 6, 1940; s. Mony S. and Etta (Trachtenbrod) S.; came to U.S., 1964, naturalized, 1975; B.S. in Elec. Engring., Joseph Rangetz Inst., Bucharest, 1959; M.S. in Elec. Engring., State U. Bucharest, 1963. Chief engr. Cyclo-Sci., Inc., Palisades, Park, N.J., 1969-71; v.p. engring. Dynaguard Systems, Inc., div. P.S.I., N.Y.C., 1971-73; chief engr. Jim Walther Co., Mt. Vernon, N.Y., 1973-75; dir. engring. V.E. Power Door Co., Inc., Lindenhurst, N.Y., 1975-79; pres. Link Controls Inc., Bohemia, N.Y., 1979—; dir. Cyclo Scis., Inc.; cons. to power door industry, audio industry. Mem. IEEE. Inventor in field. Home: 90 Gold St New York City NY 10038 Office: 55 Knickerbocker Ave Bohemia NY 11716

SIBINOVIC, KYLE HARDING (MRS. STEVAN SIBINOVIC), microbiologist; b. Oceanside, N.Y., June 12, 1936; d. William Harry and Martha Ann Louise (Burtt) Harding; B.S., Cornell U., 1961; M.S., U. Ky., 1965; Ph.D., U. Ill., 1966; m. Stevan Sibinovic, July 26, 1963; children—Shirley, Alexander, Dragan. Research asso., instr. U. Ill., Urbana, 1962-67; asso. dir. Med. Lab., Litton Bionetics Inc., Kensington, Md., 1967-74, dir. microbiology dept., 1971-74, tech. dir. biomed. lab., 1974—; cons. med. indsl. microbiology. Mem. AAAS, Research Congress on Animal Diseases, Am. Soc. Tropical Medicine and Hygiene, Am. Soc. Microbiology, Soc. Indsl. Microbiology, Clin. Lab. Mgmt. Assn., Am. Pub. Health Assn., Conf. Pub. Health Lab. Dirs., Nat. Wildlife Fedn., Am. Forestry Assn., Oceanic Soc., Am. Soc. Parasitologists, Sigma Xi. Contbr. articles to profl. jours. Home: 7613 Carteret Rd Bethesda MD 20034 Office: 5516 Nicholsen Ln Kensington MD 20795

SIBLEY, JOHN JOSEPH, internist, cardiologist; b. S.I., Mar. 23, 1922; s. Robert Emmett and Mary Loretta (Schafer) S.; student Manhattan Coll., 1940-43; M.D., Columbia U., 1946; m. Marie Ann Cox, July 4, 1944; children—John J., Suzanne, Robert Emmett, Catherine M. Sibley Comeau. Intern, Bellevue Hosp., N.Y.C., 1946-47, resident in medicine, 1949-50; resident in medicine Bronx (N.Y.) VA Hosp., 1950-52; practice medicine specializing in internal medicine and cardiology, S.I., 1952—; mem. staff St. Vincent's Hosp.; mem. staff Doctor's Hosp. S.I., 1960—, dir. medicine, cardiology, 1975—; med. dir., trustee Carmel Richmond Nursing Home, S.I. Trustee Sacred Heart Ch., S.I.; mem. steering com. to form Parish Council Sacred Heart Ch.; mem. S.I. Vicariate Council. Served to capt. M.C., U.S. Army, 1947-49. Diplomate Am. Bd. Internal Medicine. Fellow A.C.P., Am. Coll. Cardiology; mem. Alumni Assn. Coll. Physicians, Surgeons (dir.), AMA, N.Y. State, Richmond County (N.Y.) med. socs. Home: 387 Oakland Ave Staten Island NY 10310 Office: 491 Bard Ave Staten Island NY 10310

SICK, WILLIAM NORMAN, JR., electronics co. exec.; b. Houston, Apr. 20, 1935; s. William Norman and Gladys Phylena (Armstrong) S.; B.A., Rice U., 1957; B.S. in Elec. Engring., 1958; m. Stephanie Anne Williams, Sept. 14, 1963; children—Jill Melanie, David Louis. With Tex. Instruments, Inc., 1958—, applications and sales engr., Dallas, Washington, Phila., 1958-61, mktg. mgr. silicon transistors, Dallas, 1961-64, gen. mgr. power products, 1964-68, mgr. strategic planning, 1968-70, mgr. microwave and custom programs, 1970-71; pres. Tex. Instruments, Asia Ltd., Tokyo, Japan, 1971-74, asst. v.p. strategic devel., gen. mgr. metals and controls Europe, 1974-76, v.p., mgr. materials and elec. product group Tex. Instruments, Attleboro, Mass., 1977—; pres. Tex. Instruments Internat. Trade Corp., Dallas, 1977; guest lectr. Sophia U., Tokyo, 1973. Dir. Tex. Instruments, Holland, Australia, Spain. Bd. dirs. Fairhill Sch., Dallas, 1977—. Recipient Francis award Rice U., 1956. Mem. IEEE, Japan-Am. Soc., Sigma Xi, Tau Beta Pi, Sigma Tau (award 1955). Episcopalian. Club: Bent Tree (Dallas). Contbr. articles to profl. jours. Home: 46 Algonquin Rd Canton MA 02021 Office: Tex Instruments Inc 34 Forest St Attleboro MA 02703

SIDAMON-ERISTOFF, CONSTANTINE, lawyer; b. N.Y.C., June 28, 1930; s. Simon and Anne Huntington (Tracy) S.-E.; B.S., Princeton U., 1952; LL.B., Columbia U., 1957; m. Anne Phipps, June 29, 1957; children—Simon, Elizabeth, Andrew. Admitted to N.Y. bar, 1958; exec. asst. to Congressman John V. Lindsay, 1965; asst. to Mayor Lindsay, 1966; commr. hwys. City of N.Y., 1967-69, transp. adminstr., 1969-73; mem. Met. Transp. Authority, State of N.Y., also pvt. practice law, transp. cons., N.Y.C., 1974-77; partner Sidamon-Eristoff, Morrison, Warren, Ecker & Schwartz, 1978—. Dir. Mid-Hudson Pattern for Progress; v.p., dir. Tolstoy Found., N.Y., 1975—, chmn., 1978—; city coordinator Lindsay mayoral campaign, 1965; campaign dir. Lindsay for Congress, 1964; bd. dirs. Yorkville Republican Club, 1962—; del. Rep. Nat. Conv., 1976; trustee Carnegie Hall, 1966—, Phipps Houses, N.Y.C., 1974—, Millbrook (N.Y.) Sch., 1971—, Am. Farm Sch., Thessaloniki, Greece, 1963—, Caramoor Center for Music and Arts, Katonah, N.Y., 1961—, Allaverdy Found., N.Y.C., 1962—. Served to 1st lt., arty. AUS, 1952-54; Korea. Decorated Bronze Star; recipient Honor award N.Y. State Soc. Profl. Engrs., 1969. Mem. Assn. Bar City N.Y., N.Y.C. Lawyers Assn., Am., N.Y. State bar assns., Am. Inst. Mining, Metall. and Petroleum Engrs., Phi Delta Phi, Delta Psi. Clubs: Century Assn., Knickerbocker, St. Anthony's, Racquet and Tennis. Home: 120 East End Ave New York City NY 10028 Office: 551 Fifth Ave New York City NY 10017

SIDECO, EDGAR CRUZ, physician; b. Manila, July 26, 1934; s. Anastacio Jimenez and Felisa (Cruz) S.; came to Can., 1961; naturalized, 1970; B.A., St. Thomas U., Manila, 1956; M.D., Far Eastern U., Manila, 1960; m. Carmelita Ongpauco, Dec. 28, 1960; children—John Eric, Robert Ian, Neil, Arne. Intern, Good Samaritan Hosp., Cin., 1961; resident in rehab., Rehab. Inst. Montreal, Que., Can., 1963-65; clin. research fellow Royal Victoria Hosp., Montreal, 1967-69; practice medicine specializing in rehab. medicine; physiatrist-in-chief Lethbridge Rehab. Center, Montreal, 1971-76; dir. phys. medicine and rehab. Queen Elizabeth Hosp., Montreal, 1976; cons. Montreal Protestant Hosp., Douglas Hosp., Montreal Chinese Hosp. Recipient most outstanding Filipino in Can. award, 1974; Can. Arthritis and Rheumatism grantee, 1968-70; certified specialist in rehab. medicine. Fellow Royal Coll. Medicine and Surgery Can.; mem. Que., Can. med. assns., Am. Geriatric Soc., Royal Soc. Medicine Eng., Can. Assn. Phys. Medicine and Rehab., Quebec Physiatry Assn. Roman Catholic. Home: 234 Strathcona Dr Mount Royal PQ H3R 1E7 Canada Office: 7005 Maisonneuve Blvd Montreal PQ Canada

SIDELL, WILLIAM, union ofcl.; b. Chgo., May 20, 1915; s. Samuel and Fannie (Freeman) S.; grad. high sch.; m. Frankie Scruggs, Aug. 14, 1936; children—Barton, Gary and Suzann (Mrs. Jerome Cook) (twins). With United Brotherhood of Carpenters and Joiners Am., 1939—, bus. mgr. local 721, Los Angeles, 1948-57, exec. sec., Los Angeles, 1957-63, mem. gen. exec. bd., 1963—, 2d gen. v.p., 1964-69, 1st gen. v.p., 1969-72, gen. pres., 1972—; mem. exec. council AFL-CIO, 1972—, mem. bldg. and constrn. trades dept. exec. council, 1972—; v.p. Calif. Labor Fedn., AFL-CIO, 1958-64; mem. exec. bd. Calif. State and Los Angeles County Bldg. and Constrn. Trades Council, 1957-63; sec. So. Calif. Conf. Carpenters, 1957-63. Mem. Calif. Gov.'s Adv. Commn. on Housing Problems, 1957-63, Mayor's Labor-Mgmt. Com., Los Angeles, 1957-63; mem. Pres.'s Labor-Mgmt. Constrn. Com., 1975—, constrn. adv. com. Fed. Energy Adminstrn., 1975—, labor policy adv. com. trade negotiations, 1975—. Trustee Carpenters Health and Welfare Trust So. Calif., Carpenters Pension Trust So. Calif., Carpenters Joint Apprenticeship Com. Fund So. Calif., Carpenters Vacation Savs. Plan So. Calif. Home: 2301 Glenallan Rd Silver Spring MD 20906 Office: 101 Constitution Ave NW Washington DC 20001

SIDER, RONALD RAY, musician, educator; b. Harrisburg, Pa., May 10, 1933; s. Christian Harold and Cora Mabel (Saylor) S.; Mus.B., Eastman Sch. Music, Rochester, N.Y., 1957, Mus.M., 1959, Ph.D., 1967; m. Beth Frances Kanode, July 31, 1971; 1 dau., Rhonda Beth. Prof. music Messiah Coll., Grantham, Pa., 1958—, chmn. dept., 1964-73; condr., mus. dir. Grantham Oratorio Soc., 1968—; organist-choirmaster Grace Methodist Ch., Harrisburg, 1973—; organ recitalist, guest condr. choir festivals. Asso. Am. Guild Organists (lectr., condr. workshops); mem. Am. Choral Dirs. Assn., Music Educators Nat. Conf. Composer anthems, author articles. Home: RD 3 Dillsburg PA 17019 Office: Messiah Coll Grantham PA 17027

SIDOTI, RAYMOND BENJAMIN, violinist, educator; b. Cleve., Aug. 21, 1929; s. Joseph and Carmella (Alletto) S.; Mus. B., Cleve. Inst. Music, 1951, Mus. M., 1954; postgrad. (Fulbright fellow) Santa Cecilia, Rome, 1957-58; D. Musical Arts, Ohio State U., 1972; m. Mary Sue Lawrence, June 14, 1971. Concert soloist and chamber musician, U.S., Europe, 1958—; chmn. string dept. Baylor U., 1972-73; coordinator strings, first violin Shiras String Quartet, No. Mich. U., 1973-75; prof. violin, coordinator chamber music Stephens Coll., 1975—; mem. faculty, soloist, concertmaster orch. Rome Festival Inst., summers 1973, 76, 77; State Dept. grantee Western Europe tours, 1959-68; concertmaster of chamber and festival orchs.

Mo. Symphony Soc., 1977-78. Served with U.S. Army, 1951-53. Mem. Coll. Music Soc., Cleve. Fedn. Musicians, Am. String Tchrs. Assn., Pi Kappa Lambda. Author: The Violin Sonatas of Bela Bartok: An Epitome of the Composer's Development, 1972. Home: 218 Newburg Ave Baltimore MD 21228 Office: Stephens Coll Columbia MO 65201

SIECZKOS, JOHN HENRY, mech. engr.; b. Zaklikow, Poland, Sept. 10, 1946; s. Stanley and Bernice (Stachyra) S.; came to U.S., 1960, naturalized, 1978; Asso. Applied Sci., Broome Community Coll., 1967; B.S., Rochester Inst. Tech., 1970; M.S., Worcester Poly. Inst., 1972; m. Mary Jane Frazier, Oct. 12, 1974. Quality assurance engr. Gen. Electric Co., Binghamton, N.Y., 1973-76, acting mgr. quality assurance, 1976-77, supr. farmout quality assurance, 1977-78, mgr. quality assurance, 1978—. NSF fellow, 1970-72. Mem. ASME (asso.). Home: 917 Oak Hill Ave Endicott NY 13760 Office: PO Box 5000 Binghamton NY 13902

SIEFKEN, HAROLD EDWARD, pub. adminstr.; b. Millville, N.J., Apr. 9, 1948; s. Oscar William and Emily Lavinia (Broadwater) S.; B.A., Eastern Nazarene Coll., 1970; M.S.W., Syracuse U., 1975; M.P.A., U. Maine, 1978; m. Brenda Shirley Swift, June 14, 1969; 1 dau., Lorica Elaina. coordinator community service Bur. Mental Retardation, Augusta, Maine, 1975-78; exec. dir. Group Home Found., Inc., Belfast, Maine, 1978—. Sec. bd. Gardiner Ch. of Nazarene, 1975-78. Mem. Pi Sigma Alpha. Home: Valley Rd Palermo ME 04354 Office: 37 High St Belfast ME 04915

SIEGEL, ALAN ALFRED, lawyer; b. Irvington, N.J., Dec. 7, 1939; s. Arthur A. and Mabel G. (Chandler) S.; A.B., Rutgers, 1961; M.A., Columbia, 1962; J.D., Rutgers, 1965; m. Betty Jane Oleksik, Aug. 1, 1976. Admitted to N.J. bar, 1965; asso. firm Toner, Vanderbilt, Michels & Light, Newark, 1968-69; partner firm Toner, Vanderbilt & Toner, Livingston, 1970-75, Vanderbilt and Siegel, Livingston, 1975—. Chancellor, Huguenot Soc. of N.J.; counsel Irvington Planning Bd., 1973-78; pres. Clinton Cemetery Assn., 1972—; chmn. Irvington Centennial Com., 1973-74; chmn. Irvington Bicentennial Commn., 1975-76; pres. Irvington Hist. Soc., 1978—; councilman-at-large Town of Irvington, 1978—. Served with U.S. Army, 1965-67. Recipient Citizenship award, Town of Irvington, 1974, Citizen of Yr. award, B'nai B'rith, 1975, Civic award Irvington C. of C., 1977. Mem. Am., N.J., Essex County bar assns. Republican. Methodist. Author: Out of Our Past, a history of Irvington, New Jersey, 1974. Home: 35 Clinton Terr Irvington NJ 07111 Office: 155 S Livingston Ave Livingston NJ 07039

SIEGEL, ARTHUR HERBERT, accountant; b. N.Y.C., Jan. 5, 1938; s. Joseph Kenneth and Gertrude (Hecker) S.; A.B., Columbia, 1958, M.B.A., 1960; m. Eleanor Novick, June 5, 1960; children—Joan Aileen, Linda Beth, Mark Eric. With Price Waterhouse & Co., 1960—, audit mgr. L.I. office, Huntington Station, N.Y., 1965-72, partner, Boston, 1972—. Past trustee, treas. Dix Hills Jewish Center; trustee, former treas. Temple Beth Avodah, 1974—. Mem. Am. Inst. C.P.A.'s, N.Y. State Soc. C.P.A.'s (past chpt. chmn. accounting and auditing procedures com. 1970-71), Nat. Assn. Accountants (chpt. pres. 1967-68), Mass. Soc. C.P.A.'s (chmn. accounting and auditing procedure com. 1975-77, chmn. health care com. and auditing procedure com. 1977-79, dir., 1976—, v.p., 1979—), Hosp. Fin. Mgmt. Assn., Beta Gamma Sigma, Phi Sigma Delta. Home: 50 Farina Rd Newton Centre MA 02159 Office: One Federal St Boston MA 02110

SIEGEL, ARTHUR IRVING, psychol. adminstr.; b. N.Y.C., Dec. 1, 1921; s. Nathan and Rose (Chustek) S.; A.B., N.Y. U., 1948, M.A., 1950, Ph.D., 1951; m. Estelle Fryburg, Sept. 18, 1949; children—Janet, Mark. Instr. psychology N.Y. U., N.Y.C., 1950-51; project dir. Inst. Research in Human Relations, Phila., 1951-55; dir. Applied Psychol. Services, Wayne, Pa., 1955—; cons. in field. Served with USCGR, 1942-46. Diplomate Am. Bd. Profl. Psychology. Fellow Am. Psychol. Assn.; mem. Human Factors Soc., Eastern, Pa. psychol. assns., Aerospace Med. Assn. Author: Professional Police Human Relations, 1964; Man-Machine Simulation Models, 1969. Contbr. articles to profl. publs. Home: 130 Pine Tree Rd Radnor PA 19087 Office: 404 E Lancaster Ave Wayne PA 19087

SIEGEL, EDWARD PAUL, surgeon; b. N.Y.C., Oct. 27, 1938; s. Ralph H. and Sara S.; B.A., U. Buffalo, 1959; M.D., N.Y. Med. Coll., 1964; m. Evelyn, June 1964; children—Amy, Wendy, Meredith, A. Scooter. Intern USPHS, 1964-65; resident in ophthalmology and ophthalmic surgery Mt. Sinai Hosp., N.Y.C., 1967-70; mng. dir. Eye Physicians & Surgeons P.A., Freehold, N.J., 1970—; mem. staff Freehold area hosps., Princeton Hosp.; asso. clin. prof. Rutgers U., 1971—. Served with USPHS, 1964-67. Fellow A.C.S., Am. Acad. Otolaryngology and Ophthalmology; mem. Pan Am. Soc. Ophthalmologists, Assn. Contact Lens Ophthalmologists, AMA, N.J. Assn. Otolaryngology and Opthalmology. Club: Lions. Office: 303 W Main St Freehold NJ 07728

SIEGEL, ELLIOT ROBERT, psychologist; b. N.Y.C., May 31, 1942; s. Samuel and Anne (Eisman) S.; B.A., Bklyn., 1964; M.A., Mich. State U., 1966, Ph.D., 1969; m. Nancy B. Linn, July 23, 1967; 1 dau. Erica Beth. Research and teaching asst. Mich. State U., 1964-69; research psychologist Mich. Dept. Mental Health, Lansing, 1966; research scientist Human Sciences Research, Inc., McLean, Va., 1969-70; research asso. Am. Psychol. Assn., Washington, 1970-72, mgr. and exec. editor for publs. devel., 1972-74, adminstrv. officer for sci. affairs, 1975-76; research scientist Lister Hill Nat. Center Biomed. Communications, Nat. Library Medicine, NIH, Bethesda, Md., 1976—; cons. AID, Pub. Broadcasting Environment Center, Biotechnology, Inc.; mem. Adv. Panels in Info. Sci. and Tech. Mem. AAAS, Am., D.C. psychol. assns., Internat. Communication Assn., Am. Soc. Info. Sci. (chmn. behavioral and social sci. 1974-75), Psi Chi. Asso. editor Jour. Am. Psychologist, 1975-76; exec. editor Jour. Supplement Abstract Service, 1971-75. Home: 10141 Cape Ann Dr Columbia MD 21046 Office: Nat Library Medicine NIH Bethesda MD 20014

SIEGEL, HENRY, med. examiner; b. N.Y.C., Oct. 16, 1910; s. William and Pauline (Berkowitz) S.; B.S., Coll. City N.Y., 1933; M.D. (Christian A. Herter fellow), N.Y. U., 1937; D.Sc. (hon.), 1976; m. Lillian Niefield, Aug. 1968; children—Edward Mark, Marian Irma. With Office Chief Med. Examiner City N.Y., 1928-70, exec. dep. chief med. examiner, 1961-70; intern Kings County Hosp., Bklyn., N.Y., 1937-39; resident 1939-41; chief med. examiner County Westchester, Valhalla, N.Y., 1970—; mem. faculty Downstate Med. Center State U., N.Y.C., 1950-55, Albert Einstein Coll. Medicine, 1955-58, Rutgers State U., New Brunswick, N.J., 1955—, N.Y. U. Coll. Medicine, 1960-70; prof. pathology N.Y. Med. Coll., N.Y.C., 1970—; cons. Bellevue Hosp., Beekman Downtown Hosp. (N.Y.C.), Merck Inst. for Therapeutic Research, AEC, 1961—, Grasslands Hosp., Westchester, 1970—, Blythedale Childrens Hosp., Westchester, 1970—. Served with M.C., AUS, 1944-46; ETO, CBI. Diplomate Am. Bd. Pathology. Fellow AMA; mem. Coll. Am. Pathologists, Am. Assn. Pathologists and Bacteriologists, Am. Soc. Clin. Pathology, Am. Acad. Forensic Scis. Contbr. articles to profl. jours. Home: Scarborough Manor Scarborough NY 10510 Office: Office Medical Examiner Grasslands Valhalla NY 10595

SIEGEL, HERBERT JAY, mfg. co. exec.; b. Phila., May 7, 1928; s. Jacob and Fritzi (Stern) S.; B.A., Lehigh U., 1950; m. Ann F. Levy, June 29, 1950; children—John C., William D. Sec., dir. Ofcl. Films, Inc., N.Y.C., 1950-55; v.p., dir. Bev-Rich Products, Inc., Phila., 1955-56; v.p., dir. Westley Industries, Inc., Cleve., 1955-58, Phila. Ice Hockey Club, Inc., 1955-60, chmn. bd. Ft. Pitt Industries, Inc., Pitts., 1956-58, The Seeburg Corp., Chgo., 1958-60, Centlivre Brewing Corp., 1959-61, Baldwin-Montrose Chem. Co.; chmn. bd. Gen. Artists Corp., 1960-63, pres., 1963-65; chmn. bd., pres., dir. Chris-Craft Industries, 1967—; dir. Baldwin Rubber Co., Mono-Sol Corp., Piper Aircraft Corp., 1976-77. Bd. dirs. Phoenix House, 1978—. Club: Friars. Home: 190 E 72d St New York City NY 10021 Office: 600 Madison Ave New York City NY 10022

SIEGEL, PAUL MICHAEL, psychometrist; b. Bklyn., Nov. 19, 1947; s. Herman Ralph and Sylvia (Marcus) S.; B.A., Richmond Coll., City U. N.Y., 1969, M.S., 1976; m. Candida R. Albino; 1 son, Robert Laurence. Psychometrist, S.I. Community Coll., N.Y., 1969-76; dir. adult counseling services Research Found. of City U. N.Y., 1976-77; dir. testing services Coll. of S.I., 1977—; pvt. practice therapy and vocat. counseling, 1974—. Recipient Vocat. Edn. Act grant, 1976-77; certified sch. counselor, N.Y. Mem. Am., N.Y. State personnel and guidance assns., Am. Coll. Personnel Assn., Nat., N.Y. State vocat. guidance assns., Assn. Measurement and Evaluation in Guidance, N.Y. State Coll. Personnel Assn., N.Y. State Assn. Measurement and Evaluation in Guidance. Jewish. Office: 715 Ocean Terr Staten Island NY 10301

SIEGFRIED, FRANKLIN, musician; b. Atlantic City, Aug. 22, 1917; s. Sylvester Franklin and Sephyrina (Daugert) S.; grad. Curtis Inst. Music, 1933; m. Marjorie Helen Ginsberg, June 4, 1942; 1 son, Barry Glenn. Violinist, Radio City Music Hall, N.Y.C., 1937-42, 47-50; Broadway musical shows include: Carousel, 1945-46, New Faces of 1952, Girl in Pink Tights, 1953-54, My Fair Lady, 1956-61, 76—, Little Me, 1963, High Spirits, 1965, On A Clear Day, 1966-67, Yllia Darling, 1969, CoCo, 1970-72, Jesus Christ Superstar, 1971-72, sec., treas. Avant Garde Records Inc., N.Y.C., 1966-68, pres., 1968—; sec., treas Vanguard Music Corp., N.Y.C., 1966-68, pres., 1968—. Served with USAF, 1942-43. Mem. Am. Fedn. Musicians. Home: 357 W 55th St Apt 3H New York City NY 10019 Office: 250 W 57th St New York City NY 10019

SIEGLER, WILLIAM A., JR., photographer; b. Spartanburg, S.C., May 1, 1947; s. William A. and Ann Theodosa (Shuler) S.; A.A.S., Rochester Inst. Tech., 1968; postgrad. Mt. St. Mary Coll., 1970-72; m. Lisa Ann Wagner, June 28, 1975. Free-lance profl. photographer, 1965-67; supr. photog. service lab. div. diagnostic radiology U. Rochester Med. Center, 1967-70; pres., owner Siegler Photograph Studios, Walden, N.Y., 1970—. Mem. 5th Dist. N.Y. State Vol. Ambulance and First Aid Assn., 1972—, chmn. publicity, 1972-75, del. at large, 1975. Recipient Nat. Merit award Profl. Photographers Am., 1976; 2 Exhbn. Blue Ribbons, Profl. Photographers Soc. N.Y., 1976. Mem. Profl. Photographers Am., Profl. Photographers Soc. N.Y. (treas. and editor newsletter Hudson Valley sect. 1975—, state del. 1976-79, pres. Hudson Valley sect. 1978-79), Greater Rochester Indsl. Photographers (charter 1967), Eastern Orange C. of C. Republican. Quaker. Club: Rotary (dir. 1976—) (Washingtonville). Home: PO Box 232 Washingtonville NY 10992 Office: 38 Orange Ave PO Box 422 Walden NY 12586

SIEGMAN, HENRY, clergyman; b. Germany, Dec. 12, 1930; s. Mendel and Sara (Scharf) S.; came to U.S., 1942, naturalized, 1948; rabbi, Torah Vodaath Sem., N.Y.C., 1951; B.A., New Sch. Social Research, 1961; postgrad. New Sch. Social Research, 1961-64; m. Selma Goldberger, Nov. 8, 1953; children—Bonnie, Debra, Alan. Nat. dir. community activities div. Union Orthodox Jewish Congregations Am., 1953-59; exec. sec. Am. Assn. Middle East Studies, 1959-64; dir. internat. affairs Nat. Community Relations Adv. Council, N.Y.C., 1964-65; exec. v.p. Synagogue Council Am., N.Y.C., 1965—; guest lectr. U. Ill., Columbia U., Williams Coll. An organizer White House Conf. Civil Rights, 1967; nat. vice chmn. Religion in Am. Life, 1966—; exec. com. Interreligious Com. on Peace, 1966—; chmn. Interreligious Com. Gen. Secs. (Nat. Council Chs.-U.S. Cath. Conf.-Synagogue Council Am.), 1973. Bd. dirs. Nat. Com. Against Discrimination in Housing, 1966—; steering com., exec. com. Nat. Urban Coalition. Served to 1st lt., chaplain, U.S. Army, 1952-54. Decorated Bronze Star; designated Distinguished Am. by Pres. U.S., 1970. Mem. AAUP, Rabbinical Council Am., Nat. Conf. Jewish Communal Service, Assn. Jewish Community Relations Workers. Contbr. articles to profl. jours. Editor Middle East Studies, 1959-64. Home: 287 Redmont Rd West Hempstead NY 11552 Office: 432 Park Ave S New York City NY 10016

SIEH, THEODORE, opera co. dir.; b. Hainan Island, China, Apr. 14, 1925; s. Sing Yu and Shing (Hwa) S.; student Hainan U., 1947-50; B.A., Chu Hai U. (Hong Kong), 1952; postgrad. Luth. Sem. (Hong Kong), 1952-54, U. Mich., 1955-56, Princeton Theol. Sem., 1955-57, Westminster Choir Coll., Princeton, 1956-57, Union Theol. Sem., 1958-60, Julliard Sch. Music, 1968-69; m. Eleanor Anne Becker, June 6, 1957; children—Peter, Catherine. Came to U.S., 1955, naturalized, 1961. Dir. coll. student work projects Ch. World Service, Hong Kong, 1954-55; choral dir. Reed Meml. Ch., Lyndhurst, N.J., 1959-61, St. John's Luth. Ch., Mamaroneck, N.Y., 1961-62, asst. minister in various Chinese chs., until 1969; producer, artistic dir. Bel Canto Opera Co., N.Y.C., 1969—. Served to capt. Nat. Chinese Spl. Airport Ground Force, 1945-47. Baptist (deacon). Home: 1281 Raleigh Rd Mamaroneck NY 10543 Office: 30 E 31st St New York City NY 10016

SIELLER, WILLIAM VINCENT, educator; b. Norfolk, Conn., Jan. 5, 1917; s. Pierre J. and Mary J. (Murphy) S.; student Syracuse U., 1938-41; A.B., U. Buffalo, 1948; M.A., Canisius Coll., 1952; certificate in advanced grad. studies U. Hartford, 1959. Supr. Navy shipping office United Aircraft Corp., E. Hartford, Conn., 1941-45; asst. prof. English, Canisius Coll., 1949-55; tchr. English, Pearson Sch., Winsted, Conn., 1956-66; lectr. English, N.W. Conn. Community Coll., Winsted, 1965-66, asst. prof., 1966-67, asso. prof., 1967-77, prof., 1977—, dir. arts and scis., 1967—, chmn. dept. English, 1970—. Mem. Poetry Soc. Am., Cath. Poetry Soc. Am., Acad. Am. Poets, Sigma Upsilon. Roman Catholic. Author: (poetry) This Transient Hour, 1939; Let Him Return, 1941; Green Water for a Granite Valley, 1970; Beyond All Seasons, 1971; Gather Back the Dream, 1973. Contbr. poems to lit. jours. Home: Ashpohtag Rd Norfolk CT 06058 Office: N W Conn Community Coll Winsted CT 06098

SIENKIEWICZ, JOHN CASIMIR, ins. co. exec.; b. Doylestown, Pa., Oct. 8, 1933; s. Casimir A. and Jane (Patton) S.; B.A., Princeton U., 1955; m. Patricia Davis, May 12, 1956; children—Mark Patton, Peter Casimir. Partner, Hutchinson, Rivinus & Co., ins. brokers, Phila., 1957-69; with Alexander & Alexander Services Inc., ins. brokers, Phila., 1969—, sr. v.p., dir. internat. ops., also dir.; dir. Am. Dredging Co., Phila. Served to lt. USNR, 1955-57. Clubs: Gulph Mills Golf, Racquet, Princeton (Phila.); Bedens Brook (Princeton); Pine Valley Golf (Clementon, N.J.). Home: 55 Winfield Rd Princeton NJ 08540 Office: 1211 Ave of Americas New York City NY 10036

SIERACKI, LOUIS ANTHONY, ret. physician; b. Chgo., Aug. 1, 1904; s. Frank and Lottie (Rutkowski) S.; B.S., Ind. U., 1927, M.D., 1929; m. Helen Altham, Oct. 26, 1932; children—Mary Louise, Robert Francis. Intern, St. Margaret's Hosp., Hammond, Ind., 1929-30; resident House of Good Samaritan Hosp., Boston, 1930-31; practice of medicine, Norwood, Mass., and Boston, 1937-72; med. dir. State Prison Colony Hosp., Norfolk, 1934-37, cons. 1937-70; dir. coronary care unit Norwood Hosp., 1969-72; research fellow in medicine Tufts Med. Sch., 1932-34. Diplomate Am. Bd. Internal Med. Fellow A.C.P., American Coll. Chest Physicians; mem. Am., Mass. thoracic socs., Am., N.E. heart assns., AMA, Mass. Med. Soc. Home: 699 Prestwick Ln New Seabury MA 02649

SIES, LUTHER FRANK, educator; b. Westminster, Md., July 29, 1927; s. Frank Noah and Hilda (Friese) S.; A.B., Western Md. Coll., 1948; B.S., Towson State Coll., 1950; M.Ed., Western Md. Coll., 1954; Ed.D., George Washington U., 1962; m. Leora Motta, Apr. 21, 1967. Speech and hearing cons. Loudoun (Va.) Pub. Schs., 1955-57; supr. speech pathology sect. Walter Reed Army Hosp., Washington, 1957-61; coordinator clin. speech pathology and audiology services State U. Iowa, Iowa City, 1961-63; chmn. speech dept. Towson State Coll., Balt., 1964-66; prof. Nassau Community Coll., Hempstead, N.Y., 1966-67; prof. Hunter Coll., N.Y.C., 1967-68; prof., dir. Speech and Hearing Clinic Lehman Coll., N.Y.C., 1968-73, 77—, head speech and hearing scis., 1977—; cons. Loudon County (Va.) Bd. Edn., Nassau County (N.Y.) Police Acad., Md. State Penitentiary, Balt., Iowa City VA Hosp., Children's Hosp., Washington, Cancer Clinic George Washington U. Hosp., Dept. Army, Prospect Hosp., Model Cities South Bronx-Propsect Hosp. Med. Found. Served with AUS, 1950-52. Mem. Am. Speech and Hearing Assn., Am. Congress Phys. Medicine and Rehab., Speech Assn. Am., Internat. Soc. Gen. Semantics, Gen. Semantics Inst., Sigma Alpha Eta, Phi Delta Kappa. Methodist. Author: Fundamentals of Speech, 1966; Aphasia Theory and Therapy; co-author: The Communication Contract; contbr. articles to profl. jours. Home: 101 W 23d St New York City NY 10011

SIESSER, PAUL, accountant, fin. cons.; b. N.Y.C., Sept. 7, 1935; s. Sol and Sarah (Gromb) S.; B.B.A., Coll. City N.Y., 1957; m. Carole Zeeman, June 10, 1957; children—Glenn, Barbra, Steven. Practice accounting, East Brunswick, N.J., 1968—; controller Hygrade Packaging Corp., Farmingdale, N.Y., 1964-66, Computer Applications Inc., N.Y.C., 1966-68; builder owner mgr. garden apt. projects and office bldgs.; organizer real estate projects. Enrolled agt. IRS. Mem. N.J. Assn. Pub. Accountants (pres. Middlesex chpt. 1975-77), East Brunswick C. of C., Nat. Soc. Pub. Accountants, Am. Taxation Assn., Assn. Enrolled Agts. Jewish. Home: 4 Coachman Ct East Brunswick NJ 08816 Office: 4 Cornwall Dr East Brunswick NJ 08816

SIFF, MARLENE IDA, artist, designer; b. N.Y.C., Sept. 20, 1936; d. Irving Louis and Dorothy Gertrude (Lahn) Marmer; B.A., Hunter Coll., 1957; m. Elliott Justin Siff, July 11, 1959; children—Bradford Evan, Brian Douglas. Tchr., Stewart Manor (N.Y.) Sch. System, 1957-59, Teaneck (N.J.) Sch. System, 1959-60; free lance interior designer Marlene Siff Interior Design Cons., Westport, Conn., 1966-70; interior designer indsl. plant Varo Inertial Products, Trumbull, Conn., 1970; corporate sec., treas., dir. Belmar Corp., Westport, 1972—; chmn. bd. Marlene Designs, Inc., Bridgeport, Conn., 1973-78, Marlene Siff-Design Studio, Westport, 1978—; design cons. Conn. Digestive Disease Soc. Active fund raising coms. Levitt Pavillion of Performing Arts, Westport PTA. Recipient Lower Conn. Mfrs. Assn. award for creating most beautiful working environment in lower Conn., 1970. Mem. Westport-Weston Arts Council, Nat. Council Jewish Women, Kappa Pi. Designer exterior, interior and grounds of her home and studio, 1965, decorative arts designs for wall hangings; designer signature collections under name Marlene for nat. mass market distbn. J.P. Stevens Co., Inc.; her pattern Tailored Elegance chosen by Easter Seal Home Service to decorate Grand Ballroom of Plaza Hotel, N.Y.C. for ann. charity ball, also designer invitation for ball, 1976; designer kitchen and dining area coordinate program for J.C. Penney Co., 1978. Home and studio: 15 Broadview Rd Westport CT 06880

SIFTON, CHARLES P., judge; b. N.Y.C., Mar. 18, 1935; s. Paul Field and Clare Sifton; student Harvard U., 19S3-56, Columbia U. Law Sch., 1958-61; m. Elisabeth Niebuhr, July 7, 1922; children—Sam, Toby, John. asso. firm Cadwalader, Wickersham & Taft, N.Y.C., 1961-62, 64-66; staff counsel U.S. Senate Fgn. Relations Com., 1962-63; asst. U.S. atty. Dept. Justice, N.Y.C., 1966-69; partner firm LeBoeuf, Lamb, Leiby & MacRae, N.Y.C., 1969-77; judge U.S. Dist. Ct. for Eastern Dist. N.Y., Bklyn., 1977—. Office: US Courthouse 225 Cadman Plaza Brooklyn NY 11201

SIFTON, PAUL GINSBURG, historian; b. N.Y.C., Apr. 17, 1927; s. Paul Field and Claire Eunice (Ginsburg) S.; A.B., George Washington U., 1951; M.A. (Univ. scholar 1952-53), U. Pa., 1953, Ph.D., 1960. Instr. English, Wayne State U., Detroit, 1953-55; lektor Amerikakunde, U. Kiel (W. Ger.), 1956-57; interpretive historian Independence Nat. Hist. Park., Phila., 1958-65; specialist early Am. history, manuscript div. Library of Congress, Washington, 1965—. Served with U.S. Army, 1945-46. Recipient A.D. Goddard award George Washington U., 1951; Fulbright grantee U. Grenoble (France), Sorbonne (Paris), 1951-52. Mem. Manuscript Soc. (dir. 1974-78), Delta Tau Delta. Democrat. Baptist. Contbr. articles to scholarly publs. Home: 2939 Van Ness St NW Washington DC 20008 Office: 10 E 1st St SE Washington DC 20540

SIGALL, MICHAEL WILLIAM, polit. scientist, lawyer, educator; b. N.Y.C., July 10, 1944; s. Leon and Hertha (Dubiner) S.; B.A., Coll. City N.Y., 1966; Ph.D., City U. N.Y., 1970; J.D., Fordham U., 1977; m. Roberta Diane Kramer, Mar. 9, 1975. Asst. prof. polit. sci. Finch Coll., N.Y.C., 1970-73; asst. prof. polit. sci. Wagner Coll., S.I., N.Y., 1973-77, adj. asst. prof., 1977—; admitted to N.Y. bar, 1978; asso. firm Shea Gould Climenko & Casey, 1977—. Mem. nat. commn. Jewish affairs Am. Jewish Congress, 1972—. Mem. Am. Polit. Sci. Assn., N.Y. Bar Assn., Am. Soc. Internat. Law, AAUP. Jewish. Author: (with Thomas A. Reilly) Political Bargaining, 1976; editor: (with Milton D. Ottensoser) The American Political Reality, 1972; (with T.A. Reilly) New Patterns in American Politics, 1975; contbr. articles to profl. jours. Home: 155 W 68th St New York City NY 10023 Office: 330 Madison Ave New York City NY 10017

SIGETY, CHARLES EDWARD, lawyer, health care exec.; b. N.Y.C., Oct. 10, 1922; s. Charles and Anna (Toth) S.; B.S., Columbia, 1944; M.B.A. (Baker scholar), Harvard, 1947; LL.B., Yale, 1951; m. Katharine K. Snell, July 17, 1948; children—Charles B., Katharine K., Robert G., Cornelius Edward, Elizabeth Snell. With Bankers Trust Co., 1939-42; instr. adminstrv. engring. Pratt Inst., 1948; instr. econs. Yale, 1948-50; vis. lectr. accounting Sch. Gen. Studies, Columbia, 1948-50, 52; admitted to N.Y. bar, 1952, D.C. bar, 1958; rapporteur com. fed. taxation U.S. council, Internat. C. of C., 1952-53; asst. to com. fed. taxation Am. Inst. Accountants, 1950-53; vis. lectr. law Yale, 1952; pres., dir. Video Vittles, Inc., N.Y.C., 1953-67; dep. commr. FHA, 1955-57; pvt. practice law, N.Y.C., 1952—; 1st asst. atty. gen. N.Y. State, 1958-59; bd. dirs., mem. exec. com. The Gotham Bank, N.Y.C., 1961-63; dir. N.Y. State Housing Finance Agy., 1962-63; pres. Florence Nightingale Nursing Homes, N.Y.C., 1965—,

Guild of N.Y. Nursing Homes, Inc., 1969-72; professorial lectr. Pratt Inst. Sch. Architecture, Bklyn., 1962-66; chmn. Council to Improve Long Term Health Care, Inc., N.Y.C.; inter housing cons., insp. housing in over 40 countries. Bd. dirs., sec., v.p. Nat. Council Health Care Services, Washington, 1969—; bd. dirs. Am. Hungarian Found. Served to lt. (j.g.) USNR, 1943-47. Mem. D.C. Bar, N.Y. County Lawyers Assn., Am. Bar Assn., Newcomen Soc. N.Am., Harvard Bus. Sch. Assn. (council 1966-69), Am. Coll. Nursing Adminstrs., Gerontol. Soc., Alpha Kappa Psi, Phi Delta Phi. Presbyn. Clubs: Yale, Harvard (N.Y.C.); Metropolitan (Washington); Harvard Bus. Sch. of N.Y.C. (pres. 1964-65, chmn. bd. dirs. 1965-66). Office: 175 E 96th St New York City NY 10028

SIGMAN, GORDON HILL, JR., engring. mgr.; b. Bklyn., Feb. 25, 1937; s. Gordon Hill and Marjorie B. S.; B.M.E., Worcester Poly. Inst., 1959; M.E.E., Drexel U., 1967; m. Eileen C. Slater, Mar. 29, 1963; children—Patricia M., Gordon H. III, Jeffrey S., Meghan E. Sr. project engr. Frankford Arsenal, Phila., 1962-68, chief aircraft fire control br., 1968-73, chief arty. inf. and tank fire control div., 1973-76; dir. fire control systems lab. Arradcom, U.S. Army, Dover, N.J., 1976-78; dir. Tactical Tech. Office Def. Advanced Research Projects Agy., 1978. Served with U.S. Army, 1959-62. Mem. ASME, IEEE, Research Soc. Am. Contbr. articles on fire control to tech. jours. Home: 11213 Split Rail Ln Fairfax Station VA 22039

SIGMON, JACKSON MARCUS, lawyer; b. Bethlehem, Pa., Apr. 15, 1918; s. William Louis and Jeanette (Marcus) S.; A.B., U. Pitts., 1938; M.A., Fletcher Sch. Internat. Law and Diplomacy, 1939; LL.B., Duke, 1942; student Balliol Coll., Oxford U., Eng., 1945; m. Ruth Friedman, Aug. 22, 1948; children—Mark Stephen, Hilary Diane, Jill Ann, Jan Alison, Willian Randolph, Erica Joan. Admitted to Pa. bar, 1943; pres. firm Sigmon and Ross, P.C., and predecessor firms, Bethlehem, 1946—; spl. dep. atty. gen. Pa., 1951-55, 63-72. Bethlehem rep., adv. bd. Northampton County com., Republican party, 1956—; counsel Northampton County Rep. Com., 1957—; Rep. state committeeman, 1958-72, asst. city solicitor, Bethlehem, 1962-66. Served from pvt. to 1st lt. AUS, 1942-46. Decorated Bronze Star medal, Croix de Guerre. Mem. Pa. Soc., Am., Pa. (ho. of dels. 1966-70, bd. govs. 1971-74), Northampton County (bd. govs., pres. 1963) bar assns., Am. Legion, D.A.V., Brith Sholom Community Center (dir.), Zionist Orgn. Am., Am. Judicature Soc., Am. Trial Lawyers and Def. Research Inst., Pi Lambda Phi, Pi Sigma Alpha, Sigma Kappa Phi. Mason (32 degree). Clubs: Optimist (pres. 1955); Moselem Springs Golf. Home: 3464 Mountainview Circle Bethlehem PA 18017 Office: 146 E Broad St Bethlehem PA 18018

SIGNORELLI, ALFRED ROMEO, social worker; b. Wakefield, R.I., Dec. 7, 1941; s. Victor and Catherine Victoria (Frustere) S.; B.A., U. R.I., 1963; M.S.W., U. Conn., 1968; m. Heather Smith, July 14, 1962; children—Lisa, Jon, Peter, Jane. Co-founder, cons. Little Brothers-Little Sister Inc., Kingston, R.I., 1967—; psychiat. social worker Bradley Hosp., East Providence, R.I., 1968-71; exec. dir. Sophia Little Home, Cranston, R.I., 1973—; pvt. practice marriage counseling, Wakefield, R.I., 1975-76; mem. R.I. Gov.'s Commn. Child Welfare and Childrens Services. Active United Way. Mem. Nat. Assn. Social Workers (pres. R.I. chpt.), Child Welfare League of Am. (exec. advisory bd. 1975-76), Acad. Certified Social Workers, Assn. Community Execs., Speakers Platform. Roman Catholic. Home: 11 Fairgrounds Rd West Kingston RI 02892 Office: 135 Norwood Ave Cranston RI 02905

SIGNORELLI, SALVATORE, orch. condr., educator; b. Rochester, N.Y., May 15, 1925; s. Frank and Carmela (Condello) S.; B.S., State U. N.Y., 1950, M.S., 1954, postgrad., 1954; postgrad. Hofstra U., 1967; m. Isabelle Marie Williford, Aug. 29, 1951; children—Marie, Anthony, Joseph. Tchr., Schroon Lake (N.Y.) Central Sch., 1950-51, Cortland (N.Y.) Pub. Schs., 1951-58; tchr. music East Williston (N.Y.) Sch., 1958—; performer, asso. condr. Gt. Neck (N.Y.) Symphony Orch., 1962-76; founder, dir. Young Artists Chamber Symphony, L.I., 1967-76, Virtuoso Ensemble, strings, 1975—; violin maker and restorer. Served with USNR, 1943-46; PTO. Mem. N.Y. State Sch. Music Assn. (string adjudicator 1953—), Nassau Music Educators Assn. (sec. 1957), L.I. String Festival Assn. (orch. chmn. 1966-67, v.p. 1968-70), Am. String Tchrs. Assn. (v.p. 1968-69). Roman Catholic. Home: 50 Robbins Dr East Williston NY 11596

SIGRIST, CHARLES A., diversified bldg. products mfg. co. exec.; b. Buffalo, Apr. 2, 1924; s. Charles A. and Agnes R. (Rothleder) S.; B.A., Millard Fillmore Coll., U. Buffalo, 1950; postgrad. Dartmouth, 1953; m. Elizabeth J. Smith, Apr. 25, 1957 (dec. July 1975); children—Roger, David, Darcy, Mark, Tracy, John, Polly; m. 2d, Lynnette D. Nelson, Aug. 13, 1977. Accountant, Am. Shipbuilding Co., Buffalo, 1949-50; office and credit mgr. Harry Lee & Sons, Chgo., 1950-53; controller Samuel Greenfield Co., Buffalo, 1954-57, Roblin Steel Co., North Tonawanda, 1957-67; corporate controller, asst. treas., sec. Roblin Industries, Inc., diversified hard goods mfr., Buffalo, 1967-72; controller, v.p. adminstrn. Flangeklamp Industries Inc., Buffalo, 1972—. Lectr. cost accounting, direct costing, planning. Served to 1st lt. USAAF, 1943-46; PTO. Mem. Financial Execs. Inst., Nat. Accountants Assn., Planning Execs. Inst., Am. Mgmt. Assn., U.S. Figure Skating Assn. (regional chmn. sanctions com. 1967). Home: 194 Glen Oak Dr East Amherst NY 14051 Office: 1971 Abbott Rd Buffalo NY 14218

SIKRI, ATAM PRAKASH, chem. engr.; b. Sheikhupura, Pakistan, Mar. 12, 1939; s. Narain Das and Sushila Devi (Rajpal) S.; B.A., Panjab U., 1957; B.S. in Chem. Engring., B.S. in Metall. Engring., U. Mich., 1963, M.S.E., 1965; Ph.D. (teaching fellow), U. Pa., 1971; m. Kiran Budhraja, Jan. 17, 1968; children—Anmol P., Ritika; came to U.S., 1960. Research engr. DuPont Co., Phila., 1965-66, 68-70; engring. mathematician Cities Service Co., Cranbury, N.J., 1970-72; sr. process devel. engr., project mgr. Johnson & Johnson, Somerville, N.J., 1972-74; sr. engr. Hoffmann LaRoche Co., Nutley, N.J., 1974-76; program mgr., chem. engr. Dept. of Energy, Washington, 1976—; mem. faculty Rutgers State U. N.J., Camden, 1970-71. Mem. Am. Inst. Chem. Engrs., Am. Chem. Soc. Home: 7117 Galgate Dr Springfield VA 22152 Office: Dept of Energy Fossil Fuel Extraction Washington DC 20545

SILBER, JOHN ROBERT, univ. pres.; b. San Antonio, Aug. 15, 1926; s. Paul G. and Jewell (Joslin) S.; B.A. summa cum laude, Trinity U., 1947; postgrad. Northwestern U., summer 1944, Yale Div. Sch., 1947-48, U. Tex. Sch. Law, 1948; M.A., Yale, 1952, Ph.D., 1956; L.H.D., Kalamazoo Coll., 1970, U. Evansville, 1975; LL.D., Maryville Coll., 1975, Coll. St. Scholastica, 1975; m. Kathryn Underwood, July 12, 1947; children—David Joslin, Mary Rachel, Judith Karen, Kathryn Alexandra, Martha Claire, Laura Ruth, Caroline Jocasta. Instr. philosophy Yale, 1952-55; asst. prof. U. Tex., Austin, 1955-59, asso. prof., 1959-62, prof. philosophy, 1962-70, chmn. dept. philosophy, 1962-67, Univ. prof. arts and letters, 1967-70, dean Coll. Arts and Scis., 1967-70; pres., Univ. prof., prof. philosophy and law Boston U., 1971—; vis. prof. U. Bonn, 1960; fellow Kings Coll. U. London, 1963-64. Chmn. Tex. Soc. to Abolish Capital Punishment, 1960-67; nat. adv. com. Big Thicket Assn.; edn. adv. com. New Eng. Aquarium; mem. Nat. Commn. United Methodist Higher Edn., 1974—. Bd. dirs. Nat. Humanities Faculty, 1968-72; exec. bd. Nat. Humanities Inst.; trustee Coll. St. Scholastica, WGBH Ednl. Found.; bd. visitors Air U. Recipient E. Harris Harbison award for distinguished teaching Danforth Found., 1966, Wilbur Lucius Cross medal Yale Grad. Sch., 1971. Fulbright Research fellow Germany, 1959-60, Guggenheim fellow, Eng., 1963-64. Mem. Am. Philos. Assn., Southwestern Philos. Soc. (pres. 1966-67), Nat. Assn. Ind. Colls. and Univs. (dir. 1976—), Am. Soc. Polit. and Legal Philosophy, Aristotelian Soc., Royal Inst. Philosophy, Phi Beta Kappa. Author: The Ethical Significance of Kant's Religion, 1960; Democracy: Its Counterfeits and Its Promise, 1976; editor: Religion Within the Limits of Reason Alone, 1960; Works in Continental Philosophy, 1967. Asso. editor Kant-Studien, 1968—. Contbr. articles to profl. jours. Home: 132 Carlton St Brookline MA 02146 Office: 147 Bay State Rd Boston MA 02215

SILBERFARB, PETER MICHAEL, psychiatrist; b. Jersey City, Oct. 28, 1938; s. Jacob I. and Leah (Wahl) S.; B.S., Bucknell U., 1960; postgrad. Grad. Sch. Arts and Sci., N.Y. U., 1960-61; M.D., Hahnemann Med. Coll., 1965; m. Anne Wagner, June 10, 1962; children—Benjamin Jacob, Leah Sarah. Intern, Hahnemann Med. Coll. Hosp., 1965-66; resident medicine Dartmouth Affiliated Hosps., 1966-68, resident in psychiatry, 1968-69, 71-73; dir. psychiat. inpatient service Dartmouth-Hitchcock Med. Center, Hanover, N.H., 1973-75, dir. psychiat. consultation service, 1977-78; chief psychiat. service Norris Cotton Cancer Center, Hanover, 1975—; practice medicine specializing in psychiatry, Hanover, 1973—; asso. prof. psychiatry and medicine Dartmouth Med. Sch., Hanover, 1977— dir. grad. edn. and residency tng., dept. psychiatry, 1978—; mem. staff Mary Hitchcock Meml. Hosp., Hanover; cons. VA hosps. Served to lt. comdr. USPHS, 1969-71. Diplomate Am. Bd. Psychiatry and Neurology, Nat. Bd. Med. Examiners. Mem. Am. Psychiat. Assn., Am. Psychosomatic Soc., Internat. Coll. Psychosomatic Medicine, Assn. for Research in Nervous and Mental Disease. Jewish. Contbr. articles to med. and psychiat. jours. Office: Dartmouth Med Sch Hanover NH 03755

SILBERMAN, H. LEE, pub. relations exec.; b. Newark, Apr. 26, 1919; s. Louis and Anna (Horel) S.; B.A., U. Wis., 1940; m. Ruth Irene Rapp, June 3, 1948; children—Richard Lyle, Gregory Alan, Todd Walter. Radio continuity writer Sta. WTAQ, Green Bay, Wis., 1940-41; reporter Bayonne (N.J.) Times, 1941-42; sales exec. War Assets Adminstrn., Chgo., 1946-47; copy editor Acme Newspictures, Chgo., 1947; reporter, editorial writer Wichita (Kans.) Eagle, 1948-55; reporter Wall St. Jour., N.Y.C., 1955-57, banking editor, 1957-68; 1st v.p., dir. corporate relations Shearson-Hammill & Co., N.Y.C., 1968-74; N.Y. corr. economist of London, 1966-72; editor-in-chief Finance Mag., N.Y.C., 1974-76; dir. fin. services group Carl Byoir & Assos., Inc., N.Y.C., 1976—, sr. v.p., 1978—. Served to capt. C.E., AUS, 1942-46. Recipient Loeb Mag. award U. Conn., 1965, Loeb Achievement award for distinguished writing on finance Gerald M. Loeb Found., 1968. Mem. N.Y. Fin. Writers Assn., Am. Soc. Bus. Writers, Am. Soc. Bus. Press Editors, Sigma Delta Chi, Phi Kappa Phi, Zeta Beta Tau, Phi Sigma Delta. Republican. Clubs: Overseas Press, Deadline (exec. council). Contbg. editor Securities Mag., 1966-70, Finance mag., 1970-74; contbr. articles to profl. jours. Home: 80 Miller Rd Morristown NJ 07960 Office: 380 Madison Ave New York City NY 10017

SILBERMANN, PETER THOMAS, cons. sanitary engr.; b. Wellington, Eng., Aug. 11, 1941; s. Richard and Gisela (Barratz) S.; came to U.S., 1950, naturalized, 1956; B.S. in Engring., U. Calif. at Los Angeles, 1964; M.S. in Indsl. Engring., Northeastern U., 1969; m. Carol Ann Lehrberger, Dec. 25, 1967; children—David Joel, Kerrie Beth. Project engr. Green Engring. Co., Boston, 1966-67, project mgr., 1968-71; project mgr. Anderson-Nichols Co., Boston, 1971-75, v.p., 1975-77, sr. v.p., 1978—; lectr. in field. Bd. dirs. Lake Cochituate Watershed Assn., Framingham, Mass., 1977-78; coach Natick Soccer Club. Registered profl. engr., Mass., N.Y., Calif., N.H., Maine, R.I., Conn. Mem. Am., Boston socs. civil engrs., Nat., Mass. (dir. Western Middlesex chpt.) socs. profl. engrs., Fed. Water Pollution Control Fedn., Am. Water Works Assn., Alpha Pi Mu. Jewish. Club: B'nai B'rith (dir. Boston 1977-78). Contbr. tech. papers in field. Home: 29 Liberty St Natick MA 01760 Office: 150 Causeway St Boston MA 02114

SILBERSTEIN, RICHARD M., psychiatrist; b. Pitts., Nov. 15, 1922; s. Joseph R. and Cecile Ruth (Balter) S.; A.B., Dartmouth Coll., 1944; M.D., U. Pitts., 1946; grad. Inst. Phila. Assn. for Psychoanalysis, 1957; m. Muriel Janice Rosoff, June 18, 1944; children—Wendy Alexandra, Jeffrey Soctt, Charles Henry. Intern, St. Francis Hosp., Pitts., 1946-47; resident in psychiatry Phila. Psychiat. Hosp., 1947-48, Mt. Sinai Hosp., Phila., 1949-50; instr. Hahnemann Med. Coll., 1949-52; clin. adminstr. Albert Einstein Center, Phila., 1950-52; practice medicine specializing in psychiatry, Phila., 1950-52; lectr. Inst. Phila. Assn. for Psychoanalysis, 1954-60; clin. asst. prof. psychiatry State U. N.Y. Med. Center, 1958-64; dir. child psychiatry St. Vincents Med. Center of Richmond, S.I., N.Y., 1967-74; dir. N. Richmond Community Mental Health Center, S.I., 1970—; vis. prof. Cornell U., 1968-69; clin. prof. psychiatry Cornell Med. Center, 1969-75; sr. lectr. State U. N.Y. Downstate Med. Center, 1970—; cons. in field. Served with USPHS, 1952-54, U.S. Army, 1973-76. NIMH grantee; recipient B'nai B'rith Human Relations award, 1964. Diplomate Am. Bd. Psychiatry and Neurology. Fellow Am. Acad. Child Psychiatry, Am. Orthopsychiat. Assn., Am. Psychoanalytic Assn., Am. Psychiat. Assn., N.Y. Acad. Medicine; mem. AMA (Physicians recognition award 1972, 75, 78), Am. Pub. Health Assn., Internat. Psychoanalytic Assn., N.Y. Council Child Psychiatry, N.Y. State Med. Soc. (life), Pan Am. Med. Assn. Republican. Jewish. Club: Richmond County Country. Asst. editor: Ency. of Psychoanalysis. Contbr. articles to profl. jours. Home and office: 144 Clinton Ave Staten Island NY 10301

SILBERT, NATHAN ERNEST, physician; b. Boston, Oct. 6, 1908; s. Harry and Rebecca (Kettleman) S.; grad. Tufts Coll. Pre-Med. Sch., 1928; A.B., Boston Coll., 1958; M.D., Kansas City U., 1933; student Harvard Sch. Pub. Health, 1935-36, spl. student Harvard Coll., 1939-40; clin. fellow, postgrad. dept. dermatology Mass. Gen. Hosp., 1951; m. Grace Claire Farrell, Nov. 10, 1942; children—Peter Kevin, Judith Ann, Gerald David. Intern, Cambridge (Mass.) Relief Hosp., 1933-34; gen. practice medicine, Somerville, Mass., 1934-42, specializing in allergic diseases, Lynn, Mass., 1946—; in allergy service, out-patient dept. Mass. Gen. Hosp., 1945-46; in dept. dermatology Allgemeines Krankenhaus, Vienna, Austria, 1956—; cons. allergist Danvers (Mass.) State Hosp., Benjamin Stickney Cable Meml. Hosp., Ipswich, Mass., St. John's Hosp., Lowell, Mass., Saugus (Mass.) Gen. Hosp., Lynn (Mass.) Hosp.; emeritus chief, sr. cons. allergic diseases Lawrence Quigley Meml. Hosp. and Soldiers Home, Chelsea, Mass., St. Joseph's Hosp., Lowell. Past dir. Myles Standish State Sch. Mentally Defective Children; pres. Nat. Allergy Seminar; ambassador Jewish Theolody Am.; bd. dirs. Allergy Found. Am.; past mem. Mass. Bd. Registration Nursing. Served from lt. to maj. AUS, 1942-46. Recipient Zeugnis in allergic diseases U. Vienna, 1958, Nat. Community Service award Jewish Theol. Sem. Am., 1972. Diplomate Am. Bd. Allergy and Immunology. Fellow Am. Coll. Allergists (pres. 1976-77, dir. pub. relations), Internat. Assn. Allergology, Am. Coll. Chest Physicians (chmn. internat. com. on allergy Fifth Internat. Congress Diseases Chest, Tokyo 1958; internat. sec. com. on allergology 6th Internat. Congress, Vienna, 1960), Am. Thoracic Soc., Am. Assn. Clin. Immunology and Allergy, Mass. Med. Soc., Am. Acad. Allergy; mem. Assn. Convalescent Homes and Hosps. for Asthmatic Children (past pres.), Am. Med. Writers Assn., N.E. Pediatric Soc., Assn. Certified Allergists (bd. govs.). Club: Harvard (Boston). Jewish (dir., past pres. temple, pres. temple). Contbr. articles to profl. jours.; pub., asso. editor News & Trends in Allergy. Home: 242 Puritan Rd Swampscott MA 01907 Office: 214 Ocean St Lynn MA 01902

SILLS, ARTHUR JACK, lawyer; b. Bklyn., Oct. 19, 1917; s. Herman Silverman and Ida (Rosenzweig) S.; B.A., Rutgers U., 1938; LL.B. (Kirkpatrick scholar 1938), Harvard, 1941; LL.D., Rutgers U., 1966; Litt.D., Newark State Coll., 1967; m. Mina Minzer, May 7, 1947; 1 dau., Hedy Erna. Admitted to N.J. bar, 1941; partner firm Wilentz, Goldman, Spitzer & Sills, 1950-62; pub. rate counsel N.J., 1958-61; atty. gen. N.J., 1962-70; now sr. partner firm Sills, Beck, Cummis, Radin & Tischman; dir. City Title Ins. Co., N.Y.C., Channel Cos., Inc., Packaging Products & Design Corp., Devel. Corp. Am. Counselor-lectr. counselors course Rutgers U., 1953-55; mem. character and fitness com. Middlesex County, 1959-62. Rutgers Douglas Hillel Found. Bldg. Corp.; chmn. State Law Enforcement Planning Agy., Police Tng. Commn., 1962-70, Gov.'s Interdepartmental Com. on Equal Opportunity, 1962-70; Adv. Com. to Atty. Gen. on Governmental Immunity; mem. Gov.'s Commn. on Pub. Broadcasting, N.J. Housing Finance Agy., N.J. Commn. on Interstate Cooperation, State Supreme Ct. Com. on Press Relations, State Atomic Energy Council; chmn. N.J. March of Dimes, 1963; former chmn. Gov.'s Com. on Poverty and Law; mem. Gov.'s Council Against Crime, Adv. Com. to Atty. Gen. on Govtl. Immunity, State Coordinating Council on Traffic Safety; commr. state Narcotics Adv. Council; trustee Garden State Ballet, New York Soc. Crippled Children and Adults, Rabbinical Coll. Am.; bd. dirs. WHYY-TV, Nat. Council for Responsible Firearms Policy, N.J. Anti-Defamation League; trustee WNDT-TV, J.F. Kennedy Community Hosp., Edison, N.J.; nat. comms. B'nai B'naith Hillel Found. Recipient Louis Brownlow Meml. prize, 1968, Pope Paul VI Humanitarian award, 1968. Mem. Am., Fed. (trustee), N.J., Middlesex County, Perth Amboy bar assns., Am. Judicature Soc., Nat. Conf. Bail and Criminal Justice (exec. bd.), Nat. Assn. Atty. Gens., Nat. Dist. Attys. Assn., Internat. Platform Assn., Phi Beta Kappa. Democrat. Jewish religion. Mem. B'nai B'rith (past pres.). Home: 204 Dellwood Rd Metuchen NJ 08840 Office: 33 Washington St Newark NJ 07102

SILLS, BEVERLY (BELLE SILVERMAN) (MRS. PETER B. GREENOUGH), coloratura soprano; b. Bklyn., May 25, 1929; d. Morris and Sonia (Bahn) Silverman; grad. pub. schs.; student voice Estelle Leibling, piano Paolo Gallico, stagecraft Desire Defrere; hon. doctorates Harvard U., N.Y. U., New Eng. Conservatory, Temple U.; m. Peter B. Greenough, 1956; stepchildren—Lindley, Nancy, Diana; children—Meredith, Peter B. Radio debut as Bubbles Silverman on Uncle Bob's Rainbow House, 1931; appeared on Major Bowes Capitol Family Hour, 1934-41, on Our Gal Sunday; toured with Shubert Tours, Charles Wagner Opera Co., 1950, 51; debut with N.Y.C. Opera Co., 1955, as Rosalinda in Die Fledermaus; debut San Francisco Opera, 1953, Vienna State Opera, 1967, Teatro Colon, Buenos Aires, 1968 La Scala, Milan, 1969, Royal Opera, Covent Garden, London, 1970, Teatro San Carlo, Naples, 1970, Deutsche Opera, 1971, Met. Opera, N.Y.C., 1975; recital debut, Paris, 1971; appeared throughout U.S., Europe, S. Am., including Teatro Fenice, Venice, N.Y. State Theatre, 1966, Boston Symphony, Tanglewood Festival, 1968, 69, Robin Hood Dell, Phila., 1969; star roles in Handel's Julius Caesar, Manon, La Traviata, Tales of Hoffman, Lucia di Lammermoor, Roberto Devereux, Anna Bolena, Maria Stuarda, Siege of Corinth, Barber of Seville, I Puritani, Rigoletto, Capuleti ed Montecchi, Don Pasquale, Thäis. Recipient Edison award for best classical opera rec., 1971; Handel medalion, N.Y.C. Mus. award, 1973; Emmy award for Profile in Music-Beverly Sills, 1976, Lifestyles with Beverly Sills, 1978; Woman of Year award Hasting Pudding Club, Harvard U., 1978. Author: Bubbles-A Self Portrait, 1976. Address: care Edgar Vincent Assos 145 E 52d St Suite 804 New York NY 10022

SILLS, H. DONALD, lawyer; b. Torrington, Conn., Dec. 15, 1908; s. Samuel L. and Elizabeth (Bondell) S.; LL.B., St. Johns U., 1930; m. Ruth Curtis Frank; 1 son, Charles Frank. Admitted to N.Y. bar, 1935, since practiced law in N.Y.C. Vice pres. Youth Haven Inc., N.Y.C., United Presbyn. Men's Council, N.Y. Presbytery. Served with USMC, World War II. Past judge adv. Marine Corps League. Mem. New Eng. Soc. N.Y. Presbyn. (deacon, elder). Club: Met. Home: 3 E 69th St New York City NY 10021 Office: 551 Fifth Ave New York City NY 10017

SILLS, RUTH CURTIS FRANK (MRS. H. DONALD SILLS), civic worker; b. N.Y.C.; d. Charles Stuart and Catherine (Curtis) Frank; m. H. Donald Sills; 1 son, Charles Frank. Chmn. bd., mem. exec. com. Internat. Debutante Ball; mem. N.Y. adv. com. World Council Christian Edn., 1965-67; vice chmn. N.Y. com. Easter Seal Soc. for Crippled Children, 1965-68; chmn. Arthur Rubinstein Concert, Carnegie Hall for Collegiate Sch., 1965; chmn. Pan Am. Fiesta, 1964, Spring Festival of Fragrance, 1965-68; pres. bd. Kidney Found. of N.Y., 1964-65; v.p. Muscular Dystrophy Assn.; chmn. spl. events N.Y. Heart Fund, Golden Jubilee 50th Anniversary, Marymount Sch. N.Y.; mem. devel. council Mother Cabrini Health Center; lectr. Hunter Coll. Center for Lifelong Learning; chmn. bd. dirs. devel. council Cabrini Med. Center; bd. dirs. Parkinson's Disease Found.; Trustee Met. chpt. Nat. Hemophelia Found.; bd. dirs. Walderman Med. Research Found., Pearl S. Buck Found., People for the UN. Mem. Womens Service League (past pres.). Presbyterian. Club: York. Author: Sweet Bitter Charity. Home: 3 E 69th St New York City NY 10021

SILSBY, HERBERT TRAFTON, II, lawyer; b. Brewer, Maine, Feb. 8, 1925; s. William S. and Myrle (Coombs) S.; A.B., Bowdoin Coll., 1947; student Boston U., 1947-49; m. Ruth Blaisdell, July 1, 1950; children—Paula D., Kathryn M. Admitted to Maine bar, 1949, practiced in Ellsworth; judge Municipal Ct., Ellsworth, 1951-55; partner firm Silsby and Silsby, Ellsworth, 1954-77; Justice Superior Ct., 1977—; pres. Union River Telephone Co., Aurora, Maine; dir. Union Trust Co. Ellsworth, 1966-77. Vice chmn. Coast Regional Health Facilities, 1973-76, chmn., 1976-77. Chmn., Maine Young Republican Clubs, 1954-57, chmn. Ellsworth City Council, 1967. Trustee, Hancock County (Maine) Pub. Reservation. Served with AUS, 1943. Named Jaycee of Year, Ellsworth Jr. C. of C., 1958-59. Mem. Am., Maine (gov., pres.) bar assns., N.E. Folklore Soc. (dir.), Ellsworth Jr. C. of C., Maine Hist. Soc. (standing com., exec. com., pres. 1973-76), Maine League Hist. Socs. and Museums (trustee), Hancock County Hist. Soc. (past pres.; mem. standing com.), Maine Trial Lawyers Assn. (gov.). Conglist. (dir. Maine conf., deacon, supt. Sunday Sch.). Mason (Shriner), Rotarian (sec. 1962). Author: History of Aurora, 1958; A Church Has Been Gathered, 1962; Brief History of Ellsworth. Home: 10 Pleasant St Ellsworth ME 04605 Office: Hancock County Court House Ellsworth ME 04605

SILTANEN, JOHN CARL, indsl. engr.; b. Kings County, N.Y., May 21, 1913; s. Karl and Fanny (Jusenius) S.; B.S. in Engring., N.Y.U., 1938; M.S., Calif. Inst. Tech., 1946; LL.B. LaSalle U., 1952, M. Indsl. Engring., 1958; diploma Air War Coll., 1963; m. Elinor Van Kan, May 30, 1942. Exptl. engr. Curtiss-Wright, 1938-39; group engr. Brewster

Aircraft Co., N.Y.C., 1939-41; asst. chief design engr. Vertol Aircraft Co., Morton, Pa., 1950-53; asst. quality mgr. Curtiss Wright Corp., Woodridge N.J., 1953-54; engring. project field mgr. Bendix Aviation Corp., Teterboro, N.J., 1954-56, Hollywood, Calif., 1956-60; product mgr. advanced systems Internat. Tel. & Tel. Co., Nutley, N.J., 1960-67; v.p. Yucair Transport, Inc.; gen. mgr. John Siltanen Assos., 1968—. Served to sgt. Finnish Air Force, 1933-34; pvt. N.Y. N.G., 1937-38; served from 2d lt. to col. USAAF, 1941-50. Mem. I.E.E.E., Am. Inst. Aeronautics and Astronautics, Archeol. Inst. Am., Soc. for Am. Archeology, Am. Helicopter Soc., Tau Beta Pi, Psi Upsilon. Republican. Lutheran. Home: 101 Prospect Ave Hackensack NJ 07601

SILVA, PHYLLIS JEANNE, newspaper editor, columnist; b. Norwood, Mass., Dec. 3, 1945; d. Anthony Francis and Gloria Mae (Williams) S.; grad. John Robert Powers Finishing and Modeling Sch., 1964; student Boston U., 1966-68. Cosmetics rep. Max Factor, Boston, 1964-65; with Brockton (Mass.) Daily Enterprise & Times, 1966—, writer radio-TV-entertainment column, 1968—, writer feature stories and travel articles, 1966—. Mem. Ladies of Press Brockton (pres. 1972-73), Am. Newspaper Guild, New Eng. Women's Press Assn. (dir., parliamentarian 1978-79), Nat. Acad. TV Arts and Scis. (charter mem. Boston/New Eng. chpt.), Am. Film Inst., NOW. Episcopalian. Home: 1218 Bay Rd Stoughton MA 02072 Office: Brockton Daily Enterprise & Times 60 Main St Brockton MA 02403

SILVA, RENE NARCISO, engr., water and waste treatment cons.; b. Havana, Cuba, Oct. 29, 1923; s. Benigno and Petra (Triana) S.; B.S. in Chemistry, U. Havana, 1947, M.S. in Agrl. Engring., 1949, postgrad., 1949-51; m. Isabel Maria Lopez-Silvero, Feb. 21, 1954; children—Rene José, Eduardo, Raul, Isabel María. Came to U.S. 1960, naturalized, 1966. Asst. to supt. Cuban Rayon Co., 1951-55; water treatment supr. Cuban Electric Co., 1955-60; tech. staff engr. Welsbach Corp., Phila., 1961-66; process engr., cons. clarification Permutit Co., Paramus, N.J., 1966-70; dir. research and devel. Ultra-Dynamics Corp., Paterson, N.J., 1970-71; water and waste treatment specialist Stone & Webster Engring. Corp., N.Y.C., 1971-75; sr. water and waste treatment engr. Sanderson and Porter, Inc., N.Y.C., 1975-77; cons. water and waste treatment, 1977—; pres. Compania Inmobiliaria Siltriana, S.A., Cuba, 1948-60, Compañia Arrendadora Trape, S.A., Cuba, 1950-60. Registered profl. engr., N.J. Mem. Am. Inst. Chem. Engrs. Club: Big Five (Miami, Fla.). Patentee in field. Home and Office: 555 Cliff St Ridgewood NJ 07450

SILVAIN, PETER BRULE, law enforcement ofcl.; b. White Plains, N.Y., Aug. 15, 1940; s. Ernest A. and Regina B. (Brule) S.; B.A., U. Md.; M.A., George Washington U.; M.P.A., U. No. Colo.; m. Patricia Carbotti, Aug. 24, 1963; 1 son, Peter Brule. Sgt., N.Y. State Police, 1962-69; cons. Internat. Assn. Chiefs of Police, 1969-73; chief law enforcement Bur. Land Mgmt., U.S. Dept. Interior, Washington, 1973—; lectr. criminal justice Washington area colls. and univs. Mem. bd. Boy Scouts Am.; mem. Pres.'s Reorgn. Project, 1977-78. Served with USMC, 1958-61. Recipient award for advancement of police sci. Am. Express Corp., 1970; commendation U.S. Dept. Interior, 1974. Mem. Internat. Assn. Chiefs of Police. Office: Bureau of Land Management Washington DC 20240

SILVER, CARL ELIHU, surgeon; b. Bronx, N.Y., May 10, 1935; B.A., U. Rochester, 1956; M.D., Upstate Med. Center, State U. N.Y., 1959. Intern, Mt. Sinai Hosp., N.Y.C., 1959; resident gen. surgery Montefiore Hosp., N.Y.C., 1960-65, staff, 1966—, chief head and neck surgery, 1974—; staff Yonkers (N.Y.) Gen. and Profl. Hosp., 1971—; asst. prof. surgery Albert Einstein Coll. Medicine, N.Y.C., 1972-77, asso. prof., 1977—; individual practice medicine, specializing in head, neck, tumor surgery Bronx, N.Y., 1965—. Fellow A.C.S.; mem. Soc. Head and Neck Surgeons, Am. Soc. Head and Neck Surgery, N.Y. Surg. Soc., Old Chatham Hunt Club. Contbr. articles to med. publs. head, neck surgery, as transplantation larynx, reconstrn. cervical esophagus, parathyroid surgery. Office: 111 E 210th St Bronx NY 10467

SILVER, LOUIS, nursing home adminstr.; b. Bialystok, Poland, Jan. 20, 1908; s. Jacob and Mollie S.; grad. Jewish Tchrs. Sem.; student Columbia, 1970; m. Fanny Silver; 1 dau., Judith Silver Butlein. Exec. dir. Workmen's Circle Schs., N.Y.C., 1944-51, Workmen's Circle Home and Infirmary for Aged, N.Y.C., 1951—. Bd. dirs. Jewish Daily Forward, Sta. WEVD. Pres. adminstrs' council Dirs. Vol. Homes for Aged, 1974—; mem. N.Y. Gov.'s. Task Force on Aged, 1974—. Fellow Am. Coll. Nursing Home Adminstrs., Am. Acad. Med. Adminstrs.; mem. Internat. Council on Social Welfare, Am. Pub. Health Assn., Weizmann Inst. Sci. Author: Jews in America, 1951; contbg. author books. Home: 3850 Sedgwick Ave New York City NY 10463 Office: Workmen's Circle Home and Infirmary for Aged 3155 Grace Ave New York City NY 10469

SILVER, ROBERT ALAN, fin. exec., art gallery exec.; b. Bklyn., May 5, 1936; s. Morris and Estelle (Raskin) S.; B.S. in Accounting, L.I. U., 1958; m. Sandra Topple, June 7, 1958; children—Carrie, Jill. Sr. accountant, David Kulok & Co., C.P.A.'s, N.Y.C., 1960-65; controller Great Eastern Lines Inc., Totowa, N.J., 1965-69; treas. Top Tile Bldg. Supply Corp., N.Y.C. 1969-72; treas. M.Knoedler & Co. Inc., Knoedler-Modarco S.A., Geneva, N.Y.C., 1972—, also Hammer Galleries, London, Knoedler Pub., N.Y.C. C.P.A., N.Y. Mem. N.Y. Soc. C.P.A., Am. Inst. C.P.A. Jewish. Home: 32 Sandburg Dr Morganville NJ 07751 Office: 19 E 70th St New York City NY 10021

SILVER, SIDNEY LEONARD, telecommunications engr.; b. N.Y.C., Mar. 17, 1921; s. Hyman and Mildred (Stern) S.; student Bklyn. Coll., 1938-39; B.E.E., Tex. A. and M. U., 1946; m. Lillian F. Platner, Aug. 21, 1948; children—Joy Selena. Broadcast engr. Radio Sta. WKIP, Poughkeepsie, N.Y., 1942-44; radio instr. New Paltz (N.Y.) State Tchrs. Coll., 1942-44; sound engr. CBS Labs., N.Y.C., 1946-47; supervisory engr. telecommunications sect. UN, N.Y.C., 1947—; guest lectr. City U. N.Y., 1974—. Served with USN, 1944-46. Mem. IEEE, Audio Engring. Soc., UN Parapsychology Soc. Club: UN Amateur Radio. Inventor in field; contbr. articles to profl. jours. Home: 73 22 181 St Flushing NY 11366 Office: PO Box 120 New York City NY 10017

SILVER, STANLEY, ednl. adminstr.; b. N.Y.C., Sept. 2, 1934; s. Morton Leon and Libby (Lifschitz) S.; B.A. in English, Hunter Coll., 1956; diploma in econs. and social planning U. P.R., 1967; certificate in statis. analysis U. Md., 1969; M.A. in Ednl. Adminstrn., Columbia, 1970, postgrad., 1970—; D.D. (hon.), Universal Life Ch., 1968; m. Heidi Jung, Dec. 2, 1967; children—Michael, Susan, Rebecca. Pub. relations asst. Inst. Internat. Edn., N.Y.C., 1956-57; jr. high sch. tchr., N.Y.C., 1957-59; asst. editor Challenge Mag., N.Y.C., 1959-60; ednl. planner Govt. P.R., San Juan, 1960-62; pres. P.R. Pub. Relations, Inc., San Juan, 1962-64; asst. to chmn. P.R. Planning Bd., San Juan, 1964-68; chief data processing Inst. Adminstrv. Research, Tchrs. Coll., Columbia, 1968-70; coordinator communications Great Neck (N.Y.) Pub. Schs., 1970-74; asst. supt. Dover (Pa.) Pub. Schs., 1974-77; exec. dir. Ednl. Services Inc., Dover, 1977—. Community relations cons. N.Y.C. Youth Bd., Popular Democratic party, San Juan, N.Y. State Sch. Bds. Assn., others; vis. lectr. U. P.R., Hofstra U., Pa. State U., York Coll.; group leadership trainer Nat. Tng. Labs., Charles Slack Assos. Mem. N.Y.C. Mayor's Youth Adv. Council, 1959; vice chmn. San Juan Planning Commn., 1962; mem. San Juan Ednl. Task Force, 1968; mem. Great Neck Citizens Adv. Bd., 1972; mem. planning com. United Community Fund, Great Neck, 1972-73. Trustee, Great Neck Community Sch., 1972, Hickory Dickory Day Care, 1976—. Recipient N.Y.C. Mayor's Citizenship award, 1959; San Juan Mayor's citation for outstanding community service, 1962; certificate of achievement Nat. Acad. Sch. Execs., 1972. N.Y. State Regents scholar, 1948-52; U.S. Office Edn. research fellow, 1968-70. Mem. Am. Ednl. Research Assn. (research utilization com. 1971-72), Am. Assn. Sch. Adminstrs. (nat. seminar chmn. 1974), NEA, Nat. Sch. Pub. Relations Assn., Ednl. Press Assn. Am., Acad. Polit. and Social Sci., L.I. Sch.-Community Relations Assn. (v.p. 1973), Phi Delta Kappa, Kappa Delta Pi. Club: Lions. Author: San Juan: Choices for Change, 1967; Public Education in Puerto Rico, 1968; Sex Stereotyping in the Public Schools: A Pilot Study, 1972; On Discipline, 1974. Office: 5770 Mountain Rd Dover PA 17315

SILVERA, AMERICO, mktg. and tech. cons. co. exec.; b. David, Republic of Panama, Oct. 12, 1912; s. Didacio and Asuncion (Mojica) S.; B.Sc., Instituto Nacional (Panama), 1932; B.Sc. in Architecture, Rensselaer Poly. Inst., 1937; m. Hildegard Else Seglig, June 18, 1937 (div. 1974); children—Robert K., Ronald E., Ricardo R.; m. 2d, Emma M. Morales, 1975; 1 son, Roger A. Came to U.S., 1933, naturalized, 1950. With Carrier Corp. from 1937, v.p., regional mgr. Africa/Middle East, Carrier Internat. Corp. subsidiary, N.Y.C., 1964-69, v.p. export sales, from 1969; now pres. Amersil Overseas, Inc., internat. mktg. and tech. cons. firm, Stony Point, N.Y. Mem. fed. adv. com. multilateral trade negotiations Dept. Commerce. Fellow Am. Soc. Heating, Refrigeration and Air Conditioning Engrs. (chmn. internat. relations com. 1961-64, Distinguished Service award 1964); mem. Air Conditioning and Refrigeration Inst. (internat. trade com. 1972—), Internat. Execs. Assn., Pan-Am. Soc. U.S.A., Soc. Internat. Devel., UN Assn. U.S.A. Contbr. tech. articles to trade jours. Patentee airblast freezing tunnel. Office: 1 Rosewood Dr Stony Point NY 10980

SILVERBERG, BERNARD, ins. agt.; b. Brooklyn, N.J., Aug. 29, 1933; s. Jack J. and Anna (Kuklin) S.; C.L.U., Am. Coll. Life Underwriters, Bryn Mawr, Pa., 1967; m. Frances L. Gotfrid, Jan. 7, 1956; children—Karen Rochelle, Donald Samuel. Agt., New Eng. Mut. Life Ins. Co., Hackensack, N.J., 1969-63, brokerage mgr., 1963-64; unit mgr. Mass. Mut. Life Ins. Co., 1964-66, gen. agt., Paramus, N.J., 1966—. Mem. fin. com. Bergen County Boy Scouts Am. Served with USAF, 1952-56; Korea. Named Underwriter of Year, N.J. Life Underwriters Assn., 1971; life and qualifying mem. Million Dollar Round Table. Mem. Ins. Industries Inner Circle, Emerson Planning Bd., Emerson Zoning Bd. Adjustment, Mass. Mut. Gen. Agts. Assn. (exec. com.), No. N.J. Gen. Agts. Assn. (past pres.), Bergen Passaic Assn. Life Underwriters (past pres.). Club: Masons. Home: 132 Longview Dr Emerson NJ 07630 Office: 3 Winslow Pl Paramus NJ 07630

SILVERMAN, BUDDY ROBERT STEPHEN, program analyst, govt. ofcl.; b. Washington, Apr. 15, 1949; s. Abraham George and Clara Mildred (Lavenstein) S.; M.A., Kent State U., 1972; Ph.D., Am. U., 1977. Writer, editor Office Sec. Def., Washington, 1972-75; mgmt. analyst Nat. Archives and Records Service, 1975-76; chief procedures sect. Office Export Adminstrn., U.S. Dept. Commerce, 1976-77; program analyst Office Sec. Treasury, 1977—. Patron, Aspin Hill Pet Cemetery, Silver Spring, Md., 1974—. Served with USCGR, 1967. Recipient Comptroller Gen. U.S. commendation, 1978. Mem. Am. Assn. Budget and Program Analysis. Contbr. numerous articles to profl. jours. Home: 6132 Farver Rd McLean VA 22101 Office: Office of Sec Treasury Room 2450 Washington DC 20220

SILVERMAN, CATHERINE SCLATER PARKER, state adminstr.; b. Portland, Maine, Apr. 9, 1921; d. Elliott MacDonald and Laura Virginia (Montague) P.; B.A., Sweet Briar Coll., 1943; M.A., Coll. City N.Y., 1964; Ph.D., City U. N.Y., 1972; m. Joseph Silverman, June 26, 1953; children—Jane Hoskins, Fay Elizabeth. Lectr., Coll. City N.Y., 1964-68, 70-72, Baruch Coll., 1969-70; asst. to editor Hamilton Papers, Columbia U., N.Y.C., 1971-72; asst. prof. history Hunter Coll., N.Y.C., 1972, State U. at Stony Brook, N.Y., 1972-73; sr. field rep. N.Y. Div. Human Rights, N.Y.C., 1972-77, asst. dir. regional affairs, 1977—. Pres. Community Finders, Laurelton, N.Y., 1977-78. NDEA fellow, 1965-67. Mem. Am., So. hist. assns., Orgn. Am. Historians, Inst. for Research History. Home: 129-11 232d St Laurelton NY 11413 Office: 2 World Trade Center New York City NY 10047

SILVERMAN, FRED, broadcasting corp. exec.; b. N.Y.C., Sept. 1937; grad. Syracuse U.; M. TV and Theatre Arts, Ohio State U.; m. Cathy Kihn; children—Melissa Anne, William Lawrence. With WGN-TV, Chgo.; exec. position WPIX-TV, N.Y.C.; dir. daytime programs CBS-TV, N.Y.C., v.p. programs, 1970-75; pres. ABC Entertainment, N.Y.C., 1975-78; pres., chief exec. officer NBC-TV, N.Y.C., 1978—. Office: NBC-TV 30 Rockefeller Plaza New York NY 10020*

SILVERMAN, FRED, hosp. exec.; b. N.Y.C., May 31, 1935; s. Joseph and Bella (Brenman) S.; B.B.A., City Coll. N.Y., 1958; postgrad. N.Y. U., 1962-68; m. Lois Silverman, Dec. 3, 1972; children—Mark, Gail, Karyn, Jeffrey. Mgr., central supply dept. Monteiore Hosp., Bronx, N.Y., 1958-62, asst. to adminstr. methods and procedures, 1962-63, asst. adminstr., 1963-69, dep. dir., 1973-77; adminstr. Hosp. Albert Einstein Coll. Medicine, N.Y.C., 1969-73; pres. Bronx-Lebanon Hosp. Center, 1977—; asso. clin. prof. pub. adminstrn., N.Y. U., N.Y.C., 1974—; asst. prof. City U. N.Y., N.Y.C., 1974—; lectr. in field; dir. FOJP Service Corp., Malpractice ins. corp. Bd. dirs. Birth Milah Sch. N.Y., 1969-73; health com. Task Force N.Y.C. Crisis, 1978—. Served with M.C., U.S. Army, 1958. Mem. Am. Coll. Hosp. Adminstrs., Am., Greater N.Y. (bd. dirs. 1978—) hosp. assns., Am. Pub. Health Assn., Hosp. Mgmt. Systems Soc., Hosp. Mgmt. Systems Soc. Greater N.Y., Pub. Health Assn. N.Y.C. Home: 28 Clubway Hartsdale NY 10530 Office: 1276 Fulton Ave Bronx NY 10456

SILVERMAN, HAROLD IRVING, pharmacist, educator; b. Lawrence, Mass., Apr. 27, 1928; s. Jack David and Norma (Illman) S.; B.S. cum laude, Phila. Coll. Pharmacy and Sci., 1951, M.S., 1952, D.Sc., 1956; postgrad. N.Y. U., 1965, Columbia, 1966, Rutgers, 1969; m. Arlene Jacobowitz, Nov. 25, 1951; children—Robert Lewis, Richard Larry. Asst. prof. Bklyn. Coll. Pharmacy and L.I. U., 1956-59, asso. prof., 1960-64; sr. scientist Warner Lambert Pharm. Co., 1959-60; vis. scientist Ciba Pharm. Co., 1961; with Knoll Pharm. Co., Orange, N.J., 1964-68, sci. dir., 1966-68, v.p., 1967-68; prof., chmn. dept. pharmacy Mass. Coll. Pharmacy, Boston, 1968-73, prof., dir. div. applied sci., 1973—, also asso. dean; lectr. New Eng. Coll. Optometry, 1971—, Sch. Medicine Boston U., 1971—; lectr. continuing edn. Am. Optometric Assn., 1971—; dir. health related indsl. firms; cons. pharm. and cosmetic industries, fed., municipal and state agencies, Boston Mus. Sci. Recipient E.A. Newcomb Meml. award, 1956, Lederle Research award, 1962, 63, Am. Optometric Assn. award, 1974. Grantee Pfeiffer Fund., Cooper Labs., Warner Lambert Research Inst., Smith, Kline and French Inst. Fellow Soc. Cosmetic Chemists; mem. Mass. Soc. Hosp. Pharmacists, Parenteral Drug Assn., Drug Info. Assn., Am., Mass. pharm. assns., AAAS, Am. Chem. Soc., Am. Soc. Pharmacists in Industry, N.Y. Acad. Scis., Am. Soc. Hosp. Pharmacists, Internat. Narcotics Officers Enforcement Assn., Rho Chi. Author: Pharmacology Manual for Optometrists, 1971, 74. Sci. editor: Pharmacy Letter; contbg. editor: Apothecary. Contbr. articles to profl. jours. Research in drug stability, pharmacokinetics; patentee drug dosage forms. Home: 45 Crest Rd Framingham MA 01701 Office: Div Applied Scis Mass Coll Pharmacy Boston MA 02115

SILVERMAN, HIRSCH LAZAAR, psychologist, educator; b. N.Y.C., June 19, 1915; s. Herman Bear and Ida (Mackta) S.; B.Sc., Coll. City N.Y., 1936; M.Sc. in Edn., City U. N.Y., 1938; M.A., N.Y.U., 1948, Seton Hall U., 1957; Ph.D., Yeshiva U., 1951; Sc.D., Lane Coll., 1962; LL.D., Fla. Meml. Coll., 1965; L.H.D., Ohio Coll. Podiatric Medicine, 1972; m. Mildred Friedlander, Mar. 1, 1942; children—Hyla Susan, Morton Maier, Stuart Edward. Tchr. high sch., Newark, 1936-39; psychiat. social worker Newark Dept. Pub. Affairs, 1939-42; chmn., asst. prof. philosophy Mohawk Coll., 1946-48; ednl. and vocational counselor Stevens Inst. Tech., 1948-49; asst. prof. psychology Rutgers U., 1949-53; dir. psychol. services, asst. supt. Nutley (N.J.) Bd. Edn., 1953-59; prof., chmn. grad. div. dept. ednl. and sch. psychology Yeshiva U., 1959-65, asst. dean grad. div., 1951-52; prof., chmn. grad. div. dept. ednl. adminstrn. and supervision Sch. Edn., Seton Hall U., South Orange, N.J., 1965—. Research clin. psychologist Columbus Hosp., Newark, 1963-73; clin. psychologist, mem. staff St. Vincent's Hosp., Montclair, N.J., 1971—; cons. clin. psychologist N.J. Hosp. for Rehab. Medicine, 1974—; vis. prof. psychology Lane Coll., Jackson, Tenn., 1961—; pvt. practice clin. psychology, Newark, West Orange, N.J., 1950—; psychol. cons. N.J. Rehab. Commn., 1953—; clin. psychologist Jewish Edn. Assn. Torah Workshop for Handicapped Children, Newark, 1954-76; lectr. psychology Paterson State Coll., 1957-59; asst. examiner N.Y.C. Bd. Examiners, 1958-67; chmn. N.J. Bd. Marriage Counselor Examiners, 1969-74; mem. N.J. Bd. Psychol. Examiners, 1975—; research cons. psychologist N.Y. Med. Coll., 1961-65; vis. prof., adminstrv. cons. Fla. Meml. Coll., 1962—. Chmn. N.J. region speakers bur. NCCJ, 1957-59. Trustee, Lane Coll., 1963-68. Served with AUS, 1942-46; PTO. Decorated Supreme Ordo Domus Hospitalis Sancthi Johannis Hierosolymitani Danias (Denmark); Order St. John of Jerusalem, Knight of Malta. Benjamin Franklin fellow Royal Soc. Arts; recipient Townsend Harris medal City U. N.Y., 1976. Diplomate in clin. psychology Am. Bd. Profl. Psychology. Fellow Coll. Preceptors (Eng.), Am. Assn. for Social Psychiatry, Am. Med. Writer's Assn., Assn. for Advancement Psychotherapy (hon.), Am. Pub. Health Assn., Philos. Soc. Eng. (hon. v.p. 1965—), Am. Assn. Marriage and Family Counselors, Royal Soc. Health, Royal Soc. Medicine (Eng.), World Acad. Arts. and Scis., Am. Psychol. Assn., Am. Orthopsychiat. Assn., Gerontological Soc., AAAS, mem. Acad. Psychologists in Marital Therapy (chmn. research com. 1964-67), Am. Bd. Forensic Psychology (vice chmn. 1978-80), Internat. Council Psychologists (treas. 1970-72), Am. Assn. Clin. Counselors (diplomate, v.p. Mid-Atlantic region chpt. 1961-64, 69—, dir. 1963-67), AAUP (past chpt. v.p.), Acad. Psychologists in Marital Counseling (pres. 1964-67), Am. Soc. Psychologists in Pvt. Practice (sec. 1974-76). Author numerous books, including: Psychology and Education: Selected Essays, 1961; Psychiatry and Psychology: Relationships, Intra-Relationships and Inter-Relationships, 1963; Marital Counseling: Psychology, Ideology, Science, 1967; Humanism, Psychology and Education, 1969; Out of Yesterday and Into Tomorrow: Selected Poems 1935-1970, 1970; Marital Therapy: Moral, Sociological and Psychological Factors, 1972; Dimensions of Education and Psychology: Essays in Behavioral Sciences, 1975; Vignettes of the Intellect, 1977. Asso. editor Social Sci. Jour., 1969. Contbr. numerous articles to profl. jours. Home: 123 Gregory Ave West Orange NJ 07052 Office: Grad Div Sch of Edn Seton Hall University South Orange NJ 07079

SILVERMAN, HYMAN JACOB, accountant, bus. cons.; b. Boston, Feb. 2, 1918; s. Samuel Morris and Sarah Edith (Silverman) S.; B.B.A., Coll. City N.Y., 1940; m. Selma Schlesinger, Dec. 20, 1941; children—Ellen Silverman Popper, Charles Jay. Sr. accountant Hendel & Hendel, N.Y.C., 1945-52; partner Sapir & Silverman, N.Y.C., 1952-56; pvt. practice, accounting, N.Y.C., 1956-71; sr. partner Silverman & Silverman, N.Y.C., 1971—. Served with AUS, 1941-45. Mem. Nat., Empire State assns. pub. accountants. Jewish religion. Club: Oddfellows. Home: 143-16 84th Dr Jamaica NY 11435 Office: 521 Fifth Ave New York City NY 10017

SILVERMAN, IRA, data processing co. exec; b. Petach Tikvah, Israel, Nov. 9, 1936; s. Sol and Miriam (Altman) S.; came to U.S., 1946, naturalized, 1952; B.S. in Elec. Engring., Bklyn. Poly. Inst., 1958; M.S. (Howard Hughes fellow), U. So. Cal., 1960; m. Natalie Lurie, June 15, 1958; children—Miryam, Daniel, Joseph. Engr., Howard Hughes Aircraft Co., Culver City, Calif., 1958-60; sr. systems analyst IBM, N.Y.C., 1960-63; pres. Analytic Computing Services, Inc., N.Y.C., 1963-70, Ira Silverman & Assos., 1970-72; pres. Natek Corp., Hackensack, N.J., 1972—. Instr. elec. engring. Los Angeles City Coll. Evening Sch., 1958-60. Mem. I.E.E.E., Data Processing Mgmt. Assn., Assn. for Computing Machinery, Eta Kappa Nu. Home: 161 S Woodland St Englewood NJ 07631 Office: 190 Moore St Hackensack NJ 07601

SILVERMAN, MARTIN, social worker, camp dir.; b. Springfield, Mass., Aug. 27, 1927; s. Joseph and Esther (Furman) S.; B.S., Springfield Coll., 1950; M.S., Sch. Applied Scis., Western Res. U., 1952; m. Sylvia Leigh Trees, Feb. 22, 1953; children—Linda, Paul, Jonathan. Exec. dir. Cambridge (Mass.) Jewish Community Center, 1952-66; field work instr. Boston U. Sch. Social Work, 1953—; owner, dir. Camp Kippewa for Girls, Winthrop, Maine, 1957—; mem. hdqrs. guidance staff Quincy (Mass.) pub. schs., 1966—; bd. dirs. New England Camping Assn., 1972-73. Served with AUS, 1945-47. Certified camp dir. Am. Camping Assn.; certified social worker Acad. Certified Social Workers. Mem. Am. Camping Assn., Maine Camp Dirs. Assn., Nat. Assn. Social Workers, Acad. Certified Social Workers, Mass. Tchrs. Assn., NEA, Quincy Edn. Assn. Contbr. articles to Camping Mag. Home: 60 Mill St Westwood MA 02090

SILVERMAN, MICHAEL ROBERT, coll. adminstr.; b. N.Y.C., Dec. 2, 1945; s. Sidney and Esther Ann (Krieger) S.; A.B. (N.Y. State Regents Scholar), Middlebury Coll., 1967; M.A., Columbia, 1968; Ph.D., N.Y. U., 1976. Tchr. pub. schs. N.Y.C., 1970-71; exec. asst. to dean adminstrn. Bronx Community Coll., 1973-76; asst. dir. office of community coll. programs N.J. Dept. Higher Edn., 1977—. Intern, AID, 1966; vol. VISTA, 1967; intern N.Y. State Senate, 1972-73. Mem. Am. Polit. Sci. Assn., Acad. Polit. Sci., Am. Acad. Polit. and Social Scis. Home: 4216 Fox Fun Plainsboro NJ 08536 Office: New Jersey Dept Higher Education 225 W State St Trenton NJ 08625

SILVERMAN, PAUL LEONARD, clin. psychologist; b. Newark, Apr. 29, 1937; s. Samuel and Ann (Shwam) S.; B.A., Rutgers U., 1959; M.A., U. Md., 1962, Ph.D., 1964; m. Judith Shapiro, June 18, 1961; children—Michael, Noah. Dir. psychol. tng. Area A Mental Health Program, Washington, 1965-68; pvt. practice clin. psychology, Montgomery County, Md., 1965—; chief psychologist D.C. Bur. Youth Services, 1968—; instr. Washington Sch. Psychiatry; cons. Potomac Found., Rockville, Md. Chmn., Montgomery County ACLU, 1972-73; bd. dirs. Nat. Capital Area ACLU, 1971-74. Recipient Charles Webster St. John Meml. award Rutgers U., 1959.

Licensed psychologist, Washington; certified psychologist, Md. Fellow Md. Psychol. Assn.; mem. Washington, Am. psychol. assns., Montgomery County Mental Health Assn. Home: 14315 Bauer Dr Rockville Md 20853 Office: 122 C St NW Washington DC 20001

SILVERMAN, RICHARD, direct mktg. cons.; b. Manchester, N.H., Feb. 21, 1925; s. Abraham B. and Bess (Finman) S.; B.J., U. Mo., 1948; m. Rosemary Arico, July 18, 1964; 1 dau., Eileen. Account exec. Mailograph Co., Inc., N.Y.C., 1949-51; direct mail copywriter Remington Rand Co., N.Y.C., 1952-53; direct mail mgr. Advance Pattern Co., N.Y.C., 1954; advt.-pub. relations dir. Universal Transistor Products Corp., Westbury, L.I., N.Y., 1954-58; copywriter Harrison Home Products, N.Y.C., 1958-60; sr. copywriter Schwab, Beatty & Porter, Inc., N.Y.C., 1960-65; self-employed advt. cons., Kew Gardens, N.Y., 1965—, free-lance financial writer, 1967—; editor Sophisticated Investing, financial adv. service, Palisades Park, N.J., 1967-73. Served with AUS, 1943-46. Mem. 100 Million Club, Direct Mktg. Writers Guild, Newsletter Assn. Am., Alpha Delta Sigma, Alpha Epsilon Pi. Mason. Author: $100 Gets you Started: Market Secrets For the Small Investor, 1965; The Shale Oil Industry, 1968; The Life Insurance Industry, 1968. Home: 83-33 Austin St Kew Gardens NY 11415

SILVERMAN, SAM MENDEL, physicist; b. N.Y.C., Nov. 16, 1925; s. Moshe Aaron and Gitel (Korenbaum) S.; B.Ch.E., Coll. City N.Y., 1945; Ph.D., Ohio State U., 1952; m. Jacqueline Greenberg, Sept. 12, 1948 (div. Apr. 1965); children—Ann, William, Nancy; m. 2d, Phyllis Rolfe, June 26, 1966; children—Gila, Aaron. Research asso. Ohio State U., Columbus, 1952-55; asst. prof. chem. physics U. Toledo, 1955-57; research physicist Air Force Cambridge Research Labs., Bedford, Mass., 1957—, chief polar atmospheric processes br. and dir. geopole obs., 1963-74; vis. research asso. Queens U., Belfast, 1963-64; vis. prof. Osmania U., Hyderabad, India, 1965-66; mem. adv. bd. Inst. Space and Atmospheric Studies U. Sask. (Can.), 1965-69. Mem. Town Meeting Lexington, Mass., 1973—. Served with USAAF, 1945-46. Fellow Am. Phys. Soc.; mem. Am. Geophys. Union. Contbr. articles to profl. jours.; abstractor psychology of politics Jour. Psychotherapy. Home: 18 Ingleside Rd Lexington MA 02173 Office: Air Force Geophysics Lab Bedford MA 01731

SILVERMAN, SIDNEY, coll. pres.; b. N.Y.C., June 23, 1912; s. Michael and Gussie (Zalesky) S.; B.S., Coll. City N.Y., 1933, M.S., 1940; Ed.D., N.Y. U., 1958; m. Esther Krieger, May 23, 1936; children—Richard Arthur, Michael Robert. Tchr. biology N.Y.C. Bd. Edn., 1936-48; prin. Taft Youth & Adult Center, N.Y.C., 1948-57; asst. dir. community edn. N.Y.C. Bd. Edn., 1957-59; dean adminstrn., dir. evening session Bronx Community Coll., 1959-67; pres. Bergen Community Coll., Paramus, N.J., 1967-77, pres. emeritus, 1977—; faculty N.Y. U., Coll. City N.Y. Bd. dirs. N.Y. Adult Edn. Council, 1952-57; sec. Council County Colls. N.J.; mem. adv. council Bergen County Community Fund. Chmn. Morrisania Hosp. Sch. Nursing, 1954-57. Bd. dirs. Pro Arte Choral, N.J. League for Nursing; pres. North Jersey Cultural Council; chmn. bd., former v.p. Israel Cancer Research Fund; mem. Bergen County Cultural Art Commn. mem. allied health edn. com. Hackensack Hosp. Mem. Nat. N.Y. (past. pres.) assns. pub. sch. adult educators, Adult Edn. Assn. U.S., N.Y. Acad. Pub. Edn., Doctorate Assn. N.Y., Am. Assn. Jr. Colls., UN Assn., ACLU, Assn. County Community Coll. Pres. Author: A Plan to Help Break the Nursing Shortage, 1960; Operation Second Change—a Pre-College Enrichment Studies Program, 1962. Home: Horizon Towers S Fort Lee NJ 07024

SILVERMAN, STUART RONALD, counselor; b. Bklyn., Dec. 3, 1939; s. Murray and Sophie (Radejefsky) S.; B.S. in Biology, Fairleigh Dickinson U. 1961; M.S. in Guidance and Sch. Counseling, Queens Coll. 1966; m. Frances Reiser, Dec. 24, 1961; children—Craig, Cindy, Glen. Tchr. biology MacArthur High Sch., Levittown, N.Y., 1961-66; guidance counselor Island Park (N.Y.) schs., 1966-68; high sch. counselor, coordinator and developer alternative sch. Deer Park (N.Y.) High Sch. 1968—; exec. dir. Human Effectiveness Tng. Assos., 1977—; group facilitator; Neighborhood Youth Corps career counselor Island Park Schs. and co-dir. L.I. Family Edn. Center, 1978—; cons. in field; workshop presenter. Recipient various research grants in field; participant in various govt. projects. Certified Am. Mental Health Counselors Assn. Mem. NEA, N.Y. Ed. Assn., Deer Park Tchrs. Assn., Am. (registry com.), N.Y. State (senator 1973—, chairperson statewide com. for profl. certification) personnel and guidance assns., N.Y. Sch. Counselor Assn. (exec. v.p. 1975-77, bd. govs. 1977-78), West Suffolk Counselors Assn. (chairperson profl. practices com. 1974—), Nat. Alliance for Family Life. Author: The Counselors' Guide to Colleges, 1975, 1978; editor N.Y. Sch. Counselor Newsletter 1973-75; contbr. articles to profl. jours. Home: 3419 Byron Pl Seaford NY 11783 Office: 30 Rockaway Ave Deer Park NY 11729

SILVERSTEIN, LEONARD, psychologist; b. Jersey City, May 15, 1934; s. David and Mae (Grubman) S.; B.S., N.Y. U., 1955, M.S., 1964; Ph.D. in Psychology, Adelphi U., 1973; m. Janet Marlene Price, Jan. 30, 1960; children—Randee, Laura. Tchr. N.Y. Pub. Schs., 1963-66; research asso. dept. neurology Albert Einstein Coll. Medicine Yeshiva U., 1966-67; human factors engr. Gumman Aerospace Corp., Bethpage, N.J., 1967-73; coordinator vocat. rehab. psychology Sound View Throgs Neck Community Mental Health Center, 1973-74; chief psychologist, coordinator psycho-social unit United Cerebral Palsy Treatment and Rehab. Center, Roosevelt, N.Y., 1974—; cons. in field. Served with USAF, 1956-59. Licensed psychologist, N.Y. State; certified rehab. counselor. Mem. Am. Psychol. Assn., Nat. Register Health Service Providers in Psychology, Am. Assn. Biofeedback Clinicians, Biofeedback Soc. Am., Sigma Xi, Phi Delta Kappa. Home: 10 Caravan Dr East Northport NY 11731 Office: 380 Washington Ave Roosevelt NY 11735

SILVESTRI, JAMES JOSEPH, psychotherapist; b. N.Y.C., Oct. 27, 1938; s. Philip James and Helen (Bartoli) S.; B.A., Lafayette Coll., 1960; M.S.W., N.Y. U., 1963; m. Bonnie, Feb. 25, 1961; children—Peter, Timothy. Sr. psychotherapist Family Service of Orange and Maplewood (N.J.), 1966-69; dir. social services Janet Meml. Home, Elizabeth, N.J., 1969-74; dir. group homes Ednl. Alliance, N.Y.C., 1974-76; clin. dir. Somerset Hills Sch., Warren, N.J., 1976-77; pvt. practice psychotherapy, Nutley, N.J., 1976—; cons. Mayors Council on Sr. Citizens, East Orange, N.J. Bd. dirs. Citizens League Elizabeth, 1968, pres., 1969. Served with USA, 1963-69. Mem. Nat. Assn. Social Workers, Nat. Inst. Psychotherapists, Acad. Cert. Social Workers, Nat. Psychiat. Inst., Register Clin. Social Workers. Roman Catholic. Office: 512 Franklin Ave Nutley NJ 07110

SIMELS, RICHARD NEIL, mech. engr.; b. N.Y.C., Sept. 5, 1949; s. Irving Seymour and Dora (Falker) S.; B.M.E., Duke U., 1971; M.A. (Research fellow), N.Y. U., 1974; M.B.A. in Mktg., Fordham U., 1978; m. Christie Ann Zodda, Aug. 12, 1972. Area engr. Pfizer, Inc., Bklyn., 1974-75; dept. head pharm. engring. Lederle Labs. Am. Cyanamid Co., Pearl River, N.Y., 1975—. Mem. Am. Mgmt. Assn. Research in workplace design, repetitive movements of wrist and indsl. injuries, muscular response to lifting, 1972-74. Home: 334 Central Ave Apt H7 Scarsdale NY 10583

SIMIC, IVAN S., automotive co. exec.; b. Belgrade, Yugoslavia, June 2, 1927; s. Slavko L. and Erna Simic; came to U.S., 1942, naturalized, 1945; B.A., Harvard Coll., 1948; m. Kathryn Ann Steiner, Aug. 24, 1969; children—Yvonne, Charles, Tamara. Vice pres. S & G Parts Mfg., Bklyn., 1954-59, Shenco Sales, Columbus, Ohio, 1960-65; v.p. Morris Bros. Auto Trucks and Parts Corp., Farmingdale, N.Y., 1966—, Power Automotive Industries Inc., Farmingdale, 1966—. Served with CIC, U.S. Army, 1948-54. Mem. Am. Ordnance Soc. Clubs: Centerport Yacht, Ambassador, Pan Am. Home: 32 Morahopa Rd Centerport NY 11721 Office: Morris Brothers 150 Finn Ct Farmingdale NY 11735

SIMKIN, DON HOWARD, dentist; b. N.Y.C., June 8, 1948; s. Theodor and Beatrice (Cooper) S.; A.B. in English, Syracuse U., 1969; D.D.S., N.Y. U., 1973. Pvt. practice gen. dentistry, Monticello, N.Y., 1973—, also Livingston Manor, N.Y. Chmn. Sullivan County Health Adv. Council of Hudson Valley Health Systems Agy.; past v.p. Sullivan County chpt. ARC.; mem. adv. council Adventures for Spl. Children. Home: Debruce Livingston Manor NY 12758 Office: 10 Prince St Monticello NY 12701 also Main St Livingston Manor NY 12758

SIMMERS, HARRY LEE, music educator; b. Rockingham County, Va., May 9, 1931; s. Paul H. and Margaret M. (Mundy) S.; B.S., Bridgewater Coll., 1954; Mus.M., Am. Conservatory Music, 1957; m. Betty Jean Kline, Aug. 15, 1953; children—Stephen, Bobbi Jean. Choral dir. Montevideo High Sch., Penn Laird, Va., 1953-54; minister of music First Church of the Brethren, Chgo., 1954-57; choral dir. Andrew Lewis High Sch., Salem, Va., Central Ch. Brethren, Roanoke, Va., 1957-64; grad. asst. W.Va. U., minister of music First Presbyterian Ch., Morgantown, W. Va., 1964-66; dir. choral activities Elizabethtown (Pa.) Coll., 1966—; minister of music St. Paul's United Methodsit Ch., Lancaster, Pa., 1968-75, Redeemer United Ch. of Christ, Hershey, Pa., 1975—; guest condr. various choral festivals; judge various high sch. choral festivals. Served alt. mil. duty, 1965-67. Mem. Nat., Pa. music educators assns., Am. Choral Dirs. Assn. (pres. Pa. chpt.), Pa. Collegiate Choral Assn. (past pres.). Mem. Brethren Ch. Home: 1015 College Ave Elizabethtown PA 17022 Office: Rider Meml Hall Elizabethtown Coll Elizabethtown PA 17022

SIMMONS, ADELE SMITH, coll. adminstr.; b. Amherst, Mass., June 21, 1941; d. Hermon Dunlap and Ellen (Thorne) Smith; B.A. with honors, Radcliffe Coll., 1963; D.Phil., Oxford U., 1969; m. John Leroy Simmons, Sept. 18, 1966; children—Ian, Erica. Dir. African Youth Leadership program Operation Crossroads, N.Y., Africa, 1963-64; asst. prof. history Jackson Coll., Medford, Mass., 1969-72, asst. dean, 1969-70, dean, 1970-72; dean student affairs Princeton U., 1972-77; pres. Hampshire Coll., Amherst, 1977—; dir. Marsh and McLennan Cos., 1978—. Trustee Carnegie Found. for Advancement of Teaching, 1978—, Southeastern Mass. U., 1971-72; bd. overseers Harvard U., 1972-78; mem. Pres.'s. Commn. on World Hunger, 1978—. Home: 15 Middle St Amherst MA 01002 Office: Cole Science Center Hampshire College Amherst MA 01002

SIMMONS, ALVIN JOSEPH, psychologist; b. New Bedford, Mass., Oct. 31, 1930; s. Joseph Ferreira and Elvira (Page) S.; B.S., Boston Coll., 1952; M.S., U. Mass., 1954, Ph.D., 1960; M.S. in Hygiene, Harvard, 1962; m. Eleanor Joan Brindel, Aug. 10, 1957; children—Christopher, Michael, Polly, John, Lacy. Community mental health fellow, psychologist, adminstrv. asst., coordinator research Mass. Gen. Hosp., Boston, also Human Relations Service, Wellesley Hills, Mass., 1957-65; asso. dir. John F. Kennedy Family Service Center, Inc., Boston, 1965-68; asst. psychologist Mass. Gen. Hosp., 1965-70, asso. psychologist, 1971—; chief community mental health Bunker Hill Health Center of Mass. Gen. Hosp., 1968-73; dir. pub. health, New Bedford, Mass., 1973-76; area dir. Mass. Dept. Mental Health, 1977—. Cons. Boston U., 1960-63; asst. prof. Boston Coll., 1965-69; asst. clin. prof. psychology, dept. psychiatry Harvard Med. Sch., 1970-78, asst. prof. psychology, lectr. Sch. Pub. Health, 1978—; cons. R.I. Gov.'s Council on Mental Health, 1964-65; instr. U. Mass., 1955-56, Regis Coll., Weston, Mass., 1958-60; Chmn. Indsl. Devel. Commn., Dartmouth. Fellow Mass. Psychol. Assn.; mem. Am. Psychol. Assn., AAAS, Am. Acad. Polit. and Social Sci., Am. Pub. Health Assn., Assn. Behavioral Sci. and Medicine Edn., Sigma Xi, Phi Kappa Phi. Lion. Author: Community Mental Health and Social Psychiatry: A Reference Guide, 1962; Health Fair for the Elderly, 1974; also articles and book revs. Home: 175 Rockland St South Dartmouth MA 02748 Office: New Bedford Health Dept New Bedford MA 02740

SIMMONS, FREDERICK CHARLES, wood industries cons.; b. Waverly, N.Y., Oct. 27, 1905; s. Frederick Charles and LaVantia (Russell) S.; B.S., Cornell U., 1928; M.F., Yale, 1932; m. Marina Azocar Doussoulin, July 15, 1964; children (by previous marriage)—Donna Sue (Mrs. Theodore F. Schwaab), Beverly Jane (Mrs. Stanley Lelinski). Asst. timber mgr. U.S. Forest Service, Phila., 1935-44, specialist logging and primary processing N.E. Forest Expt. Sta., Upper Darby, Pa., 1944-63; adviser mech. conversion of wood FAO, UN, Santiago, Chile, 1963-64; exec. sec., editor Northeastern Loggers Assn., Old Forge, N.Y., 1965-77; cons. wood industries, U.S., Can., Brit. Honduras, P.R., Chile. Mem. Soc. Am. Foresters, Forest Products Research Soc. Contbr. U.S. Dept. Agr. publs., also trade and tech. jours. Home and office: Main St Old Forge NY 13420

SIMMONS, GEORGE ALLEN, glass co. exec.; b. Birmingham, Ala., May 2, 1926; s. George Allen and Stella Lee (Reid) S.; B.S. cum laude, Birmingham-So. Coll., 1947; M.S., Ohio State U., 1949, Ph.D. (DuPont research fellow), 1952; m. Marilyn Naomi Boyer, June 9, 1951; children—Roger Allen, Gaile Lynette, Elaine Denise. Asst. prof. Birmingham-So. Coll., 1949-50, asso. prof., 1953-55; asst. prof. Purdue U., Lafayette, Ind., 1952-53; mgr. research services Pitts. Plate Glass, 1955-61, coordinator melting, 1961-62; spl. projects chief Owens-Illinois, Toledo, 1962-66, tech. dir. new product devel., 1966-69, sr. marketing mgr., 1969-71; tech. dir. Dominion Glass Co., Mississauga, Ont., Can., 1971-76; sr. v.p. research and devel. Thatcher Glass Co., Elmira, N.Y., 1976—. Fellow Am. Inst. Chemists, Am. Chem. Soc., Am. Ceramic Soc.; mem. ASTM (councilor 1959-62), Sci. Research Soc. Am. (chpt. sec. 1963-64), Can. Ceramic Soc. (div. dir. 1971-76), Phi Beta Kappa, Omicron Delta Kappa, Delta Sigma Phi. Unitarian. Contbr. articles to various publs. Patentee in field. Office: Box 265 Elmira NY 14902

SIMMONS, HARRY DADY, JR., physician; b. Chgo., June 10, 1938; s. Harry Dady and Ruth Carol (Finkelberg) S.; B.S., U. Ill., Urbana, 1960; Ph.D., Mass. Inst. Tech., 1966; M.D., State U. N.Y., 1977. NIH postdoctoral research fellow Inorganic Chem. Inst., Tech. Hochschule, Munich, Germany, 1966-67, Brandeis U., 1967-69; research chemist Allied Chem. Corp., Morristown, N.J., 1969-71; evening shift lab. supr. Kingsbrook Jewish Med. Center, Bklyn., 1971-74. Served with USNR, 1960-61. Mem. Am. Chem. Soc., Chem. Soc. London, AMA, Am. Meteorol. Soc. (asso.), N.Y. Acad. Scis., Sigma Xi, Phi Kappa Phi, Phi Lambda Upsilon. Home: 99 Bull Hill Rd Rt 44 Pittsfield MA 01201 Office: Berkshire Medical Center 725 North St Pittsfield MA 01201

SIMMONS, JOHN DEREK, economist, investment researcher; b. Essex, Eng., July 17, 1931; s. Simon Leonard and Eve (Smart) S.; B.S., Columbia, 1956; M.B.A., Rutgers U., 1959; postgrad. N.Y.U., 1959-62 ; m. Rosalind Wellish, Mar. 5, 1961; children—Peter Lawrence, Sharon Leslie. Came to U.S., 1952. Chief cost accountant Airborne Accessories, Hillside, N.J., 1952-57; sr. cost analyst Curtiss-Wright Corp., Wood Ridge, N.J., 1957; sr. financial analyst internat. group Ford Motor Co., Jersey City, 1958-60; research asso. Nat. Assn. Accountants, N.Y.C., 1960-64; asst. to v.p. finance Air Reduction Co., Inc., 1965-67; mgr. corporate planning Anaconda Wire and Cable Co., N.Y.C., 1968-69; financial cons. Rogers, Slade & Hill, Inc., N.Y.C., 1969-71; economist, investment research Fourteen Research Corp., N.Y.C., 1971—. Lectr. econs., mgmt., polit. sci. Rutgers U., 1957-65. Served to 1st lt. British Army, 1950-52. Mem. Am. Econ. Assn., Royal Econ. Soc. Contbr. articles on econs. of underdeveloped nations, polit. sci., mgmt., finance to U.S. and fgn. profl. and sci. jours. Home: 360 E 72d St New York City NY 10021 Office: 201 E 42d St New York City NY 10017

SIMMONS, KENNETH JON, health care adminstr.; b. Buffalo, July 12, 1945; s. Henry Casimir and Alicia Mary (Trzcinski) Spychaj; B.A., Canisius Coll., 1967, M.S., 1974; M.H.A., Med. Coll. Va., 1976; m. Barbara Ann Chmielewski, Aug. 24, 1968; 1 son, Mark Christopher. Asst. hosp. adminstr. Wyoming County Community Hosp., Warsaw, N.Y., 1976-78; asst. hosp. adminstr., dir. spl. services Monroe Community Hosp., Rochester, N.Y., 1978—. Mem. Wyoming County Alcoholism Prevention Com., 1977. Served with USAF, 1969-73. Mem. Am. Coll. Hosp. Adminstrs., Hosp. Fin. Mgmt. Assn., Am., Western N.Y. hosp. assns. Roman Catholic. Club: Soc. Preservation and Encouragement Barbershop Quartet Singing Am. (treas. Warsaw chpt. 1976-77). Office: 435 E Henrietta Rd Rochester NY 14603

SIMMONS, THOMAS MURRAY, lawyer; b. Chgo., Feb. 25, 1932; s. Roscoe C. and Althea (Merchant) S.; B.S. in Humanities, Loyola U., Chgo., 1953; J.D., Boston Coll., 1956; postgrad. in bus. adminstrn., Suffolk U., Boston; m. Gertrude Lustig, Nov. 30, 1963; children—Karen, Paul. Admitted to Mass. bar, 1956, also U.S. Supreme Ct. bar; practiced in Boston, 1956—; approved examiner titles Mass. Land Ct. Incorporator, past pres. Adult Edn. Inst. New Eng.; mem. nat. panel arbitrators New Eng. council Am. Arbitration Assn.; mem. adv. gen. bd. spl. classes Boston Pub. Schs., 1968; mem. Bd. Examiners City of Boston, 1969; area spl. gifts chmn. Am. Cancer Soc., 1967-68; mem. bd. Greater Boston Council Alcoholism, 1970, treas., 1973; bd. dirs. Boston chpt. NAACP, 1971-72, chmn. legal com., counsel to chpt., 1972-73; chmn. commn. promotion parish councils Roman Catholic Archdiocese Boston, 1969—, chmn. lay caucus, 1970, pres. Council Cath. Men, 1968; sec. Cath. Alumni Sodality Boston, 1969-76, pres., 1976; mem. bd. Cath. Interracial Council, 1969-71; nat. cons. Nat. Council Cath. Men; mem. bd. Nat. Council Cath. Laity, 1971—, 1st v.p., 1973, pres., 1978; exec. com. Nat. Cath. Community Service, 1971—. Bd. govs. USO. Recipient St. Thomas More award Nat. Council Cath. Men, 1970. Hon. mem. Greater Boston C. of C. Past legal editor New Eng. Real Estate Jour. Mem. Mass., Boston bar assns., Mass. Trial Lawyers Assn., Blue Key. Democrat. Office: 27 State St Boston MA 02109

SIMON, ARTHUR JAMES, plastic mfg. co. exec.; b. Bklyn., Feb. 12, 1927; s. Harry and Helen (Cline) S.; B.A., U. Ala., 1947; postgrad. Oxford (Eng.) U., 1948; M.B.A., U. Pa., 1949; m. Barbara Colby, July 11, 1955; children—Kevin Charles, Meri. Vice pres. Closure Research Assos., 1950-62; pres. Tho-Ro Products, Inc., Carlstadt, N.J., 1965—; F-A-C-T, Inc., Wilmington, Del., 1965—; dir. Vistas in Plastics, St. Thomas, V.I., 1966; dir. Eagle Closure Corp., N.Y.C., Stazon Fastener, Inc., Calba Corp., Towcin, Pa. Pres. Riverdale Community Council, 1968-69; dir. Philanthropic Fifty Assn. Served with AUS, 1945-48. Decorated Bronze Star medal; recipient Appreciation certificate City of New York, 1962. Mem. Soc. Plastics Industry, Forum Advancement Closure Tech. (past sec.), League of Presidents, Adminstrv. Mgmt. Soc., Am. Inst. Mgmt. (exec. council), Phi Beta Kappa. Home: 89 Andrea Ln Westwood NJ 07675 Office: 415 14th St Carlstadt NJ 07072

SIMON, BENJAMIN, psychiatrist, neurologist; b. Ponievej, Russia, May 31, 1903; s. Max and Eva (Yudelevit) S.; A.B., Stanford 1925, A.M., 1927, M.D., Washington U., St. Louis, 1931; m. Sarah Henderson Scrimshaw, June 5, 1935; children—Robert Currie, John Scrimshaw, Richard Henderson. Intern, St. Louis Isolation Hosp., 1931-32, Bernard Skin and Cancer Hosp., 1931-32, Barnes Hosp., St. Louis, 1932-33; residency, neurology, Boston City Hosp., 1933-34; clin. asst., asst. physician, sr. psychiatrist Worcester State Hosp., 1934-36, 1938-41; Rockefeller fellow, neurology Nat. Hosp., Queen Square, Eng., France, Belgium, Scandinavia, etc., 1937-38; med. registrar Nat. Hosp., Queen Sq., 1938; practice psychiatry and neurology 1932—; clin. dir. Conn. State Hosp., 1941-42, 46-49; med. dir. Ring Sanatorium and Hosp., 1949-50, dir., 1950-59; pres. Bay State Med. Assos., Boston, 1960-69, dir., 1969—; dir. psychiatry and edn. Westborough (Mass.) State Hosp., 1960-73, cons., 1973—; asst. clin. prof. psychiatry Tufts U. Sch. Medicine, 1964—; cons. psychiatry, VA Hosp., Bedford Mass., 1950—; cons. in neurology and psychiatry Symmes Hospital, Arlington, Mass., 1949—; asst. in physiology Stanford 1926-27; asst. clin. prof. psychiatry and mental hygiene, Yale, 1947-50; lectr. psychology and social relations Harvard, 1956—; attending psychiatrist Vets. Hosp., Newington, Conn., 1947-50; lectr. in psychiatry Conn. Post Grad. Seminars Neuropsy, 1947—; lectr., depts. of psychology, Yale, Wesleyan U., Trinity Coll., 1947-50; lectr. depts. of nursing and social work, Boston U., 1950—; lectr. dept. of nursing U. Conn., 1950—; lectr. Mass. Post Grad. Seminars in Psychiatry and Neurology 1951—; mem. faculty Comd. and Gen. Staff Coll., U.S. Army, Ft. Leavenworth, Kan., 1948; cons. Dept. Health. Edn. and Welfare, USPHS Policy and Standards br., div. Med. Care Adminstrn., chmn. Conn. Coop. Lobotomy Com., 1946-49, regional cons. Bur. Disability Ins., Social Security, 1974—; many hosp. affiliations. Served as capt. to lt. col. U.S. Army, 1942-46; neuropsychiatrist Gen. Dispensary, U.S. Army, N.Y. City, 1942-43; chief neuropsychiatry Mason Gen. Hosp., 1943-46, exec. officer, 1945-46. Awarded Legion of Merit, Army Commendation medal, Meritorious Service Unit award. Diplomate Am. Bd. Psychiatry and Neurology, Nat. Bd. Med. Examiners; diplomate Bd. of Mental Hosp. Adminstrs. Fellow Am. Psychiat. Assn. (life; com. on rehab. 1946-61, chmn. 1951-61, alternate area rep. 1966-70, area rep., chmn. council 1971-75), Am. Group Psychotherapy Assn. (chmn. pub. relations 1953-55, mem. exec. com. 1953-55, dir. 1954-57, 62—), A.A.A.S., Am. Acad. Neurology (chmn. sci. program com. 1951-52), Am. Assn. on Mental Deficiency, Mass. Med. Soc. (sr.; sec. sect. neurology, psychiatry, 1956, chmn. 1957), Am. Coll. Psychiatrists, (emeritus), Am. Acad. Psychoanalysis, Am. Coll. Psychoanalysts (founding), Internat. League Against Epilepsy (v.p. Am. br. 1951); mem. A.M.A. (chmn. adv. com. on occupational therapy edn. to council on med. edn. and hosps.; Physician's Recognition award 1969-72, 72-75, 76-79), Assn. for Research in Nervous and Mental Disease (sr.), Assn. Mil. Surgeons of U.S., Nat. Assn. for Mental Health, Mass. Assn. for Mental Health (profl. adv. com.), Mass. Psychiat. Soc. (v.p.), Mass. Soc. for Research in Psychiatry (mem. exec. com.). Nat. Assn. Pvt. Psychiat. Hosp. (hon.; pres. 1958), Group for Advancement of Psychiatry (life; chmn. com. on psychiat. nursing; chmn. com. on therapeutic care), Am. Occupational Therapy Assn. (med. adv.

council), Am. Registry Phys. Therapists (adv. bd., adv. com. to cons. in psychiatric rehab.), N.E. Soc. Psychiatry (life, councillor, 1951), Mass. Soc. for Research in Psychiatry (life; sec.-treas., 1950, v.p., 1951, pres., 1952), Mass. Psychiat. Soc. (pres., 1956, mem. exec. council, del. dist. br. assembly), Conn. State Med. Soc., Conn. and Boston Socs. for Neurology and Psychiatry, Conn. Soc. for Mental Hygiene, Assn. Gen. Hosp. Psychiatrists (dir.), Alpha Omega Alpha, Sigma Xi. Author: Rehabilitation of the Mentally Ill: Social and Economic Aspects: Toward Therapeutic Care; (with John G. Fuller) The Interrupted Journey; Crisis in Psychiatric Hospitalization, 1969; also numerous profl. publs. Home: 141 Hillside Ave Arlington Heights MA 02174 Office: Bay State Med Assos 10 Hawthorne Pl Charles River Park Boston MA 02114

SIMON, BERNARD, assn. exec.; b. West New York, N.J., May 7, 1920; s. Max and Mary (Kell) S.; B.S. in Journalism, N.Y. U., 1941; m. Dorothy Ligeti, May 24, 1942; children—Gary Leonard, Linda Fran, David Judah. Reporter, Religious News Service, N.Y.C., 1946-47; asso. dir. pub. relations Anti-Defamation League, B'nai B'rith, N.Y.C., 1947-55, dir. pub. relations B'nai B'rith, 1955-78, spl. asst. to pres., 1978—; editor The Nat. Jewish Monthly mag., Washington, 1970-71. Served with U.S. Army, 1942-46. Mem. Pub. Relations Soc. Am., Am. Jewish Pub. Relations Soc. Jewish. Mem. B'nai B'rith. Club: National Press (Washington). Home: 2405 Colston Dr Silver Springs MD 20910 Office: 1640 Rhode Island Ave NW Washington DC 20036

SIMON, ELLEN SHATTUCK, editor; b. Ashland, Kans., Dec. 19, 1921; d. Willis Henry and Ethel Grace (Luther) S.; diploma Cottey Coll. for Women, 1941; student Sch. Journalism, U. Mo., 1941-42; m. Alfred Philip Simon, Apr. 5, 1948; children—James Michael, Nancy Ellen. County reporter Evening Bull. Phila., 1961-74; mng. editor Springfield (Pa.) Press, 1975—. Ruling elder 1st Presbyterian Ch., Springfield; bd. dirs. Community Nursing Service Delaware County; chmn. Delaware County Christmas Seal campaign; mem. Youth Aid Panel Springfield Twp. Recipient Keystone Press awards, 1976, 78. Mem. Women in Communications, Pa. Soc. Newspaper Editors, PEO, Nat. Soc. Colonial Dames Am. Democrat. Clubs: Poor Richard of Phila. Home: 331 Spring Valley Rd Springfield PA 19064 Office: 204 Ballymore Rd Springfield Rd Springfield PA 19064

SIMON, GERALD AUSTIN, mgmt. cons.; b. N.Y.C., Aug. 19, 1927; s. William and Ray (Goldberg) S.; B.B.A., Coll. City N.Y., 1950; M.B.A., Harvard, 1956, postgrad. research fellow, 1956-58; 1 son, Dana Alexander. With various advt. firms, Phila., N.Y.C., Providence, 1950-54; research asst., doctoral research fellow Harvard Bus. Sch., 1956-58; vis. lectr. Northwestern U., Evanston, Ill., 1958-59; mng. dir. Cambridge Research Inst., 1959—. Served with USNR, 1945-46. Certified mgmt. cons. Mem. Inst. Mgmt. Cons. (founding mem., dir.), Assn. Cons. Mgmt. Engrs. (dir.), Harvard Bus. Sch. Assn. (exec. council), N.Am. Soc. Corp. Planning, Am. Arbitration Assn. Clubs: Harvard (N.Y.C., Boston), Belmont Hill, Harvard U. Faculty. Editor: Chief Executives Handbook, 1976. Home: 205 Walden St Cambridge MA 02140 Office: Cambridge Research Institute 15 Mount Auburn St Cambridge MA 02138

SIMON, HAROLD, radiologist; b. Trenton, N.J., May 13, 1930; s. John and Rae B. (Gilinsky) S.; M.D., Duke U., 1955; m. Jane L. Ludwig, Feb. 25, 1956; children—Steven Gregg, John Gregory. Intern, U.S. Naval Hosp., Chelsea, Mass., 1955-56; resident in radiology Mass. Gen. Hosp., Boston, 1958-61, Oak Ridge Inst. Nuclear Medicine, 1959; instr. radiology Med. Sch., Tufts U., Boston, 1961-63, clin. asst. prof. radiology, 1965, asso. clin. prof., 1971-77, clin. prof. radiology, 1977—; practice medicine specializing in radiology and nuclear medicine, Newton Lower Falls, Mass., 1963—; mem. staff Newton Wellesley Hosp., Newton, Mass., asso. chief radiology, 1977—; dir. Sch. Nuclear Med. Tech. Served with USNR, 1955-58. Diplomate Am. Bd. Radiology, Am. Bd. Nuclear Medicine. Fellow Am. Coll. Radiology; mem. AMA, Radiol. Soc. N.Am., New Eng. Roentgen Ray Soc., Mass. Med. Soc., Mass. Radiology Soc., Phi Beta Kappa, Phi Eta Sigma. Club: Pine Brook Country. Contbr. articles to med. jours.

SIMON, HERBERT ALEXANDER, social scientist; b. Milw., June 15, 1916; s. Arthur and Edna (Merkel) S.; A.B., U. Chgo., 1936, Ph.D., 1943, LL.D., 1964; D.Sc., Case Inst. Tech., 1963, Yale U., 1963; Fil. Dr., Lund U. (Sweden), 1968; LL.D., McGill U., 1970; Dr. Econ. Sci., Erasmus U. Rotterdam (Netherlands), 1973; m. Dorothea Pye, Dec. 25, 1937; children—Katherine Simon Frank, Peter Arthur, Barbara S. Candioto. Research asst. U. Chgo., 1936-38; staff mem. Internat. City Mgrs. Assn., also asst. editor Pub. Mgmt. and Municipal Year Book, 1938-39; dir. adminstrv. measurement studies Bur. Pub. Adminstrn., U. Calif., 1939-42; asst. prof. polit. sci. Ill. Inst. Tech., 1942-45, asso. prof., 1945-47, prof., 1947-49; also chmn. dept. polit. and social sci., 1946-49; prof. adminstrn. and psychology Carnegie-Mellon U., Pitts., 1949-65, Richard King Mellon univ. prof. computer scis. and psychology, 1965—, head dept. indsl. mgmt. 1949-60, asso. dean Grad. Sch. Indsl. Adminstrn., 1957-73, trustee, 1972—; Ford Distinguished lectr. N.Y. U., 1959. Cons. to Internat. City Mgrs. Assn., 1942-49, U.S. Bur. Budget, 1946-49, U.S. Census Bur., 1947, Cowles Found. for Research in Econs., 1947-60; cons. and acting dir. Mgmt. Engring. br. Econ. Cooperation Adminstrn., 1948; Vanuxem lectr. Princeton U., 1961; William James lectr. Harvard U., 1963, Sigma Xi lectr., 1964; Harris lectr. Northwestern U., 1967; Karl Taylor Compton lectr. M.I.T., 1968; Wolfgang Koehler lectr. Dartmouth, 1975; Katz-Newcomb lectr. U. Mich., 1976; Carl Hovland lectr. Yale U., 1976; Veno lectr., Tokyo, 1977; chmn. bd. dirs. Social Sci. Research Council, 1961-65; chmn. div. behavioral scis. NRC, 1968-70; mem. President's Sci. Adv. Com., 1968-71; cons. bus. and govtl. orgns. Chmn. Pa. Gov.'s Milk Inquiry Com., 1964-65. Recipient adminstrs. award Am. Coll. Hosp. Adminstrs., 1957; Distinguished Sci. Contbn. award Am. Psychol. Assn., 1969; Frederick Mosher award Am. Soc. Pub. Adminstrn., 1974. Distinguished fellow Am. Econ. Assn. (Ely lectr. 1977); fellow Econometric Soc., AAAS, Am. Acad. Arts and Scis., Am. Psychol. Assn., Am. Sociol. Soc.; mem. Inst. Mgmt. Scis. (v.p. 1954), Am. Polit. Sci. Assn., Assn. for Computing Machinery (A.M. Turing award 1975), Nat. Acad. Scis. (mem. com. sci. and pub. policy 1967-69, chmn. com. air quality control 1974; chmn. com. behavioral scis. NSF 1975-76), Soc. Exptl. Psychologists, Am. Philos. Soc., Phi Beta Kappa, Sigma Xi. Democrat. Unitarian. Clubs: Cosmos (Washington); Univ. (Pitts.). Author or co-author books relating to field, including: Adminstrative Behavior, 1947, 3d edit., 1976; Public Administration, 1950; Models of Man, 1956; Organizations, 1958; New Science of Management Decision, 1960, rev. edit., 1977; The Shape of Automation, 1965; The Sciences of the Artifical, 1968; Human Problem Solving, 1972; Skew Distributions and Business Firm Sizes, 1976; Models of Discovery, 1977. Home: 5818 Northumberland St Pittsburgh PA 15217

SIMON, JOSEPH HENRY, advt. art cons.; b. Rochester, N.Y., Oct. 11, 1913; s. Harry and Rose (Kurland) S.; student Syracuse U., 1937-38; m. Harriet Feldman, July 14, 1946; children—Jon, James, Melissa, Gail, Lori. Sports and edit. cartoonist Rochester Jour. Am., 1933-35, Syracuse (N.Y.) Herald, 1936-37; art editor Syracuse Jour. Am., 1937-39; editor Goodman Publs., N.Y.C., 1939-41; editor Harvey Features Syndicate, N.Y.C., 1946-50; editor, pub. Crestwood Publs., N.Y.C., 1950-70; cons. art dir. Burstein, Philips & Newman, advt., Great Neck, N.Y., 1965—; dir. research and devel. Warner Communications, N.Y.C., 1973—. Mem. L.I. div. U.S. Olympic Com., 1972, CARE Com., 1970-73, Happy Landing Fund, L.I., 1968-72, Hope for Youth, 1969—. Active citizens com. for Rockefeller, Javits, Keating, Lefkowtiz. Served with USCGR, 1942-45. Creator, Capt. America, 1939, Boy Commandso, 1941. Founder, Sick mag., 1960. Author: Sick Anthology, 1963, Ensicklopedia, 1970, A Funny Thing Happened on the Way to Tel-Aviv, 1967, Look Who's Talking, 1963. Art editor Olympic Publs., 1973. Home: 11 Arbutus Ln Stony Brook NY 11790 also 330 W 56th St New York City NY 10019 Office: Harvey Publs Inc Gulf & Western Bldg New York City NY 10023

SIMON, SIDNEY, osteo. physician; b. N.Y.C., Aug. 6, 1924; s. Edward A. and Anna (Postal) S.; student N.Y. U., 1942-46; D.O., Phila. Coll. Osteo. Medicine, 1950; m. Janet Norma Lonker, Aug. 22, 1948; children—Nancy Ann, Judy Ellen, Gail Beth. Intern, Met. Hosp., Phila., 1950-51; gen. practice osteo. medicine, N.Y.C., 1951-55, group practice, 1956—; mem. staff Leroy Hosp.-Osteo Clinic, N.Y.C., St. Barnabas Hosp., N.Y.C.; cons. Leroy Hosp., N.Y.C.; asso. clin. prof. medicine N.Y. Coll. Osteo. Medicine; chmn. dept. allergy and immunology N.Y. Coll. Osteo. Medicine at N.Y. Inst. Tech. Served with Med. Dept., U.S. Army. Decorated Purple Heart. Diplomate Am. Bd. Allergy and Immunology. Fellow Am. Acad. Allergists, Am. Coll. Allergists, Am. Assn. Clin. Allergy and Immunology, Am. Coll. Chest Physicians, Am. Assn. Certified Allergists, Osteo. Coll. Allergy and Immunology; mem. Westchester County (N.Y.), N.Y. allergy assns., Internat. Assn. Allergology, Am. (editorial cons.), N.Y. State N.Y.C. osteo. socs. Contbr. articles on allergy and immunology to profl. jours.; sculptor. Office: 1846 Victor St Bronx NY 10462

SIMON, STANLEY ROBERT, physician; b. Bklyn., Jan. 21, 1933; s. Morris Henry and Anne Mary S.; B.A., U. Buffalo, 1954; M.D., Chgo. Med. Sch., 1958; m. Ellen Meryl Burakof, Dec. 26, 1971; children—John, Paul, Marc. Intern and resident Newark Beth Israel Med. Center, 1958-62; practice medicine specializing in obstetrics and gynecology, S. Orange, N.J., 1964—; clin. faculty N.J. Coll. Medicine and Dentistry, Newark, 1968—; asso. attending St. Barnabas and Beth Israel med. centers; advisory bd. Broad Nat. Bank, Millborn, N.J. Served in M.C., U.S. Army, 1962-64. Diplomate Am. Bd. Obstetrics and Gynecology, Nat. Bd. Med. Examiners. Fellow Am. Coll. Obstetrics and Gynecology, A.C.S., Internat. Coll. Surgeons; mem. AMA, Pan Am., Essex County med. socs., N.J. Soc. Obstetricians and Gynecologists, Fertility Soc., Mental Health Assn., Am. Assn. Gynecol. Laparoscopists, Planned Parenthood Assn. Jewish. Clubs: B'nai B'rith, YMHA. Contbr. articles to med. jours. Office: 468 Irvington Ave South Orange NJ 07079

SIMON, WILLIAM, accountant; b. Bayonne, N.J., Aug. 12, 1938; s. Harold and Betty (Belitz) S.; B.S., Fairleigh Dickinson U., 1962; m. Harriet Lee Caposello; children—Garry, Jeffrey. Staff Peat, Marwick, Mitchell & Co., N.Y.C., 1962-68, mgmt. group, 1968-72, audit partner, 1972-77, SEC reviewing partner, 1977—; lectr., condr. seminars. Gen. chmn. accountants com. Anti-Defamation League N.Y.C., 1974—. Served with U.S. Army, 1956-58. C.P.A. Mem. Am. Inst. C.P.A.'s, N.Y. State Soc. C.P.A.'s (past chmn. fin. and leasing com., mem. fin. accounting standards com.), Nat. Assn. Accountants. Contbr. articles to profl. publs. Office: Peat Marwick Mitchell & Co 345 Park Ave New York City NY 10022

SIMON, WILLIAM DIEN, govt. ofcl.; b. Washington, Sept. 11, 1954; s. Jerome Martin and Harriett (Dienstein) S.; B.S. in Polit. Sci., U. Calif., Berkeley, 1976. Staff asst. to Rep. Thomas M. Rees of Calif., Los Angeles, 1974, Washington, 1975; paralegal San Francisco Neighborhood Legal Assisantce Found., 1975; adminstrv. asst. to dep. campaign dir. Jimmy Carter Presdl. campaign, Atlanta, 1976; adminstrv. asst. to Hamilton Jordan, 1976-77; dep. staff sec. to pres., Washington, 1977—. Coro Found. fellow, San Francisco, 1976. Jewish. Club: Commonwealth (San Francisco). Home: 241 8th St NE Washington DC 20002 Office: West Wing White House Washington DC 20500

SIMON, WILLIAM EDWARD, cons. psychologist; b. N.Y.C., Aug. 5, 1943; B.A., C.W. Post Coll., 1965; M.A., Bklyn. Coll., 1969; Ph.D., City U. N.Y., 1971. Research asst. City U. N.Y. Environ. Psychology program, 1967-69; adj. instr. psychology Nassau Community Coll., Garden City, N.Y., 1968-72; cons. ednl. psychologist Syosset (N.Y.) Pub. Schs., 1971-75; instr. to asso. prof. psychology Southampton (N.Y.) Coll., 1969-75; cons. psychologist Baldwin and Commack, N.Y., 1971—; staff psychologist Pilgrim Psychiat. Center, West Brentwood, N.Y., 1974—; adminstrv. dir. Island Consultation Center Inc., Commack, N.Y., 1975—; adj. asso. prof. counselor edn. C.W. Post Coll., 1974—; pres. William E. Simon Assos., 1976—. Mem. Am., Nassau County, Suffolk County, Eastern psychol. assns., Am. Sociol. Assn., Nat. Council Measurement Edn., Am. Assn. Marriage and Family Counselors (clin.), Am. Assn. Sex Educators, Counselors and Therapists (certified), AAAS, Am. Ednl. Research Assn., Council Exceptional Children, N.Y. Soc. Clin. Psychologists, Assn. Children with Learning Disabilities, Sigma Xi. Editorial adv. bd. Med. Malpractice Cost Containment Jour. Contbr. articles to profl. publs. Home: 678 Allwyn St Baldwin NY 11510 Office: 67 Harned Rd Commack NY 11725

SIMON, WILLIAM HENRY, information specialist; b. New Haven, Dec. 26, 1928; s. Henry Charles and Florence (Shaw) S.; A.A., Jr. Coll. Commerce, New Haven, 1948; B.A., U. Bridgeport, 1950; M.S. in L.S., Columbia, 1955; M.B.A., Western New Eng. Coll., 1964; m. Dorothy Elaine Beckett, Oct. 1, 1955; children—Stephen Eric, William Edward. Circulation desk asst. Sterling Meml. Library, Yale, New Haven, 1951-52; profl. asst. bus. and technology dept. Bridgeport Pub. Library, Bridgeport, Conn., 1955-56; chief librarian New Haven Research Library Olin-Mathieson Chem. Corp., New Haven, 1956-61; tech. info. supr. Nuclear Power Systems, Combustion Engring., Inc., Windsor, Conn., 1961, mgr. information and adminstrv. services, 1961—; research mgr. Miller, Starrett, West and Assos., Inc., mgmt. cons. and research firm, Hartford, 1961-62. Mem. Conn. adv. com. Inter-Library Coop., 1967-68; sub. chmn. adv. com. Conn. Pub. Library Standards, 1967-68. Chief merit badge counselor, dist. tng. chmn. Metacomet dist. Long Rivers Council Boy Scouts Am., asst. dist. commr., vigil honor mem. Order of Arrow, Nat. Eagle Scout Assn. Publicity chmn. Windsor Republican Com., mem. Windsor Town Com.; justice of peace, 1965-73. Chmn. bd. dirs. Windsor Pub. Library, USN, 1952-54. Recipient Gen. Scholar, Sch. Library Sci., Columbia, 1955. Vice-chmn. Windsor Red Cross Drive, 1962. Mem. Am. Soc. for Information Sci., Spl. Libraries Assn., Am. Soc. Metals, Am. Mgmt. Soc., Assn. Records Mgrs. Administs., Assn. Conn. Library Bds. (chmn. pub. relations and publicity com., del.), Nat. Rifle Assn. (instr.), Nuclear Records Mgmt. Assn. (publs. chmn.), NOW, Alpha Phi Omega, Beta Phi Mu. Episcopalian. Mason (32 degrees), Elk (chmn. youth activities com.). Club: Green Mountain. Home: 17 Priscilla Rd Windsor CT 06095 Office: Prospect Hill Rd Windsor CT 06095

SIMONE, JOSEPH, clergyman, educator; b. Bridgeport, Conn., Jan. 13, 1924; s. Dominic and Anna (Mastrianni) S.; B.A., Elon Coll., 1958; M.A., Andover Newton Theol. Sch., 1968; m. Viola Ruskay, June 27, 1953; children—J. Scott, Zachary D., Claudia A. Ordained to ministry Congl. Ch., 1960; pastor Congl. Ch., Chicopee Falls, Mass., 1958-61, 1st Congl. Ch., Farmington, N.H., 1961-63, Hope Congl. Ch., East Providence, R.I., 1963-65, All Souls Ch., Lowell, Mass., 1965-69; tchr. English, also guidance counselor, 1969—. Chmn. ecumenical commn. Greater Lowell Council Chs., 1967-68; founder Ecumenical Dialogue with Clergymen and Laymen, Lowell, 1966, Radio Ministry on Ecumenism, Lowell, 1966-69; chaplain Roger Hall Sch. for Girls, Lowell, 1965-69. Bd. dirs. Jewish-Arab Ednl. Fund, Lowell. Served with AUS, 1942-45. Mem. Andover Assn. Ministers United Ch. of Christ (adv. com. 1966—), Assn. Clin. Pastoral Edn., Am., Mass. sch. counselors assns., N.E.A., Nat. Vocational Guidance Assn., Am. Personnel and Guidance Assn., Sigma Mu Sigma (v.p. 1957). Mason. Home: 117 Jenkins Rd Andover MA 01810

SIMONS, RICHARD DUNCAN, justice N.Y. supreme ct.; b. Niagara Falls, N.Y., Mar. 23, 1927; s. William T. and Sybil I. (Swick) S.; A.B., Colgate U., 1949; LL.B., U. Mich., 1952; m. Muriel E. Genung, June 1951; children—Ross, Scott, Kathryn, Linda. Admitted to N.Y. bar, 1952; asst. corp. counsel, City of Rome, N.Y., 1955-58, corp. counsel, 1960-63; justice 5th Jud. Dist. N.Y. Supreme Ct., 1964—, asso. justice appellate div., 3d Dept., 1971-73, 4th Dept., 1973—. Served with USNR, 1945-47. Home: 1410 N George St Rome NY 13440 Office: Oneida County Court House Rome NY 13440

SIMONS, WILLIAM MARK, historian; b. Lynn, Mass., July 8, 1949; s. Shepherd and Elaine Sylvia S.; B.A. with honors in History (Dana scholar), Colby Coll., 1971; M.A. with honros, in History U. Mass., 1972; D.A. with honors in History (Dana scholar), Carnegie-Mellon U., 1977. Tchr. history Kingswood-Oxfrod Sch., West Hartford, Conn., 1972-74; instr. in history Carnegie-Mellon U., 1975-77; mem. faculty in residence, lectr. in Am. ethnic and family studies State U. N.Y., Oneonto, 1977—; cons. Allegheny Intermediate Unit, 1977, Pitts. Council Higher Edn., 1977; interviewer Pa. Hist. Museum and Commn., 1977; sessions chmn. Eastern Social Sci. Community Coll. Assn. Conv., 1977. Mem. Swampscott (Mass.) Town Meeting, 1973—. Recipient Book award Columbia Tchrs. Coll., 1970, honorarium Ethnic Studies Planning Commn. of Pitts. Council Higher Edn., 1977. Mem. Am. Hist. Assn., Smithsonian Assos., Phi Beta Kappa. Developer pilot program in ethnic studies for Western Pa. Sch. Dists., 1977-78; contbr. articles to profl., popular publs. Home: London PH-S 400 Paradise Rd Swampscott MA 01907 Office: Dept History Univ Coll Oneonta NY 13820

SIMONSON, ANDREW CRAIG, clergyman; b. Phila., Mar. 29, 1941; s. Andrew Simon and Marie Elizabeth (Montgomery) S.; A.B., Temple U., 1962; postgrad. (Merit scholar), U. Pa., 1964-66; B.D. cum laude, Eastern Bapt. Sem., 1966, M.Div., 1974, D.Min., 1979; Th.M. cum laude, Lexington Sem., 1973; m. Doreen Craig, June 16, 1962; children—Paul Craig, Geoffrey Andrew Craig, Alexandra Ianthe. Ordained to ministry Methodist Ch., 1963; asst. pastor Somerton Meth. Ch., Phila., 1959-61; pastor Washington Crossing (Pa.) Meth. Ch., 1961-63, St. Stephen's Meth. Ch., Phila., 1963-66, Providence Meth. Ch., Phila., 1966-68; chaplain U.S. Air Force, 1968-76; pastor Messiah United Meth. Ch., Lafayette Hill, Pa., 1976—; asst. prof. Greek, Eastern Bapt. Coll., 1966-67. Served with USAF, 1968-76. Decorated Air Force Commendation medal with oak leaf cluster. Mem. Am. Assn. Clin. Pastoral Edn., NIMH. Office: 527 Ridge Pike Lafayette Hill PA 19444

SIMOWITZ, SYLVIA, community service agy. exec.; b. N.Y.C., Sept. 10, 1919; d. Max and Rose (Unger) Popiol; student pub. schs., N.Y.C.; m. Arthur Simowitz, Jan. 4, 1941. Sec., Ronald Press, N.Y.C., 1936-39, Daniel Jones, N.Y.C., 1939-43; adminstrv. asst. War Dept., Army Service Forces, 2d Service Command, Ft. Jay, Governors Island, N.Y., 1943-46; bus. mgr. Simowitz Trucking Co., Bklyn., 1950-60; exec. asst. Samaritan Halfway Soc., Richmond Hill, N.Y., 1967-74, dep. dir., 1974—, sec. bd. dirs., 1972—. Borough pres. Queens Narcotics Steering Com., 1970—; treas. Greater New York Coalition on Drug Abuse, 1976—; mem. ARC Blood Program, 1941—, Assn. Vol. Agys. on Narcotic Treatment, 1967—, Therapeutic Communities Am., 1975—, Dist. 26 Drug Prevention Program Adv. Program, 1975—, Queensboro Council for Social Welfare, 1975—, Transitional Services for N.Y., Inc., Creedmoor Psychiat. Center, 1975—, City N.Y. Human Resources Adminstrn. Adv. Council, 1975—, Queens Preventive Medicine, Dentistry and Health Edn. Center, 1976—, Queens Treatment Coalition, 1976—, Mayor's Office Service Coordination, 1976—, Queens Borough Pres.'s Community Council on Substance and Alcohol Abuse, 1977—; sec. bd. dirs. Assn. Vol. Agys. on Narcotic Treatment, 1968—. Recipient Merit award Rotary Club, Queens, 1971, Service award Samaritan Parents Assn., 1971, Outstanding Service award Queens Community, 1972, Recognition award Samaritan Halfway Soc., 1973, 75, 10 Years Service award Bd. Dirs., 1976, Merit award Dist. 27 Drug Prevention and Edn. Program, 1974, Appreciation award Samaritan Family Assn., 1974, Community Service award Mesivta of Forest Hills, 1977, certificate of appreciation Kiwanis Club Mineola, 1977, citation merit Seward Park High Sch. Alumni Assn., 1978. Mem. Am. Mgmt. Assn. Home: 1725 York Ave New York City NY 10028 Office: 118-21 Queens Blvd Forest Hills NY 11375

SIMPICH, GEORGE CARY, investment banker; b. Washington, June 25, 1923; s. Frederick and Margaret (Edwards) S.; 1 dau., Juliet Elizabeth. Mem. advt. staff Washington Post, 1945-47, Nat. Geog. Mag., 1947-49; with Young & Rubicam Advt. Agy., 1949-51; with Davidson & Co., 1951-56; div. mgr. Fin. Programs, Inc., Washington, 1956-61; investment cons. V. Clarke & Co., Washington, 1961-66; mem. Butcher & Singer Investment Co., and predecessors, Washington, 1966-75, v.p. and resident mgr., Reston, Va., 1977—; bus. devel. White, Weld & Co., Inc., Washington, 1975-76; v.p. sales Johnston, Lemon & Co., Inc., Bethesda, Md., 1976-77. Served as pilot USAAC, 1943-45. Mem. Nat. Economists Club, Municipal Fin. Forum, Bond Club, Nat. Press Club. Republican. Episcopalian. Clubs: Reston Golf and Country; Del Ray. Home: 3309 Macomb St NW Washington DC 20008 Office: 11484 Washington Plaza W Suite 406 Reston VA 22090

SIMPSON, JEAN WHEELER, ednl. adminstr.; b. Hackettswown, N.Y., Sept. 10, 1931; d. Clarence and Anna (Weston) Wheeler; B.S. in Elementary Edn., SUNY, Potsdam, 1953, M.S. in Elementary Edn., 1955; m. Roy Simpson; children—Robert, Rea Jean, Roy. Elementary tchr. Adams (N.Y.) Union Free Sch., 1953-56; asso. prof. Congdon Campus Sch., Potsdam, N.Y., 1956-58; elementary and fed. aid adminstr. S. Jefferson Central Schs., Adams, N.Y., 1965—, also K-12 curriculum coordinator. Regional planner Jefferson-Lewis Bds. Coop. Ednl. Services, Watertown, N.Y., 1972-73. Coach A Spartan Bantam League Am. Jr. Bowling Congress, 1974-75. Certified in adminstrn., Supervision. Recipient media program award N.Y. Library Assn. Mem. Nat. Assn. Elementary Sch. Prins., Sch. Adminstrs. Assn. N.Y. State. Contbr. articles to various ednl.

magazines. Home: 12 Hungerford Ave Adams NY 13605 Office: Box 40 Adams NY 13605

SIMPSON, MARY MICHAEL, priest; b. Evansville, Ind., Dec. 1, 1925; d. Link Wilson and Mary Garrett (Price) S.; B.A., B.S., Tex. Women's U., 1946; grad. N.Y. Tng. Sch. for Deaconesses, 1949; grad. Westchester Inst. Tng. and Counseling and Psychotherapy, 1976. Missionary, Holy Cross Mission, Bolghun, Liberia, 1950-52; mem. order St. Helena, 1952—, academic head Margaret Hall Sch., Versailles, Ky., 1958-61, sister-in-charge convent, Bolahun, 1962-67, dir. of novices Order, 1968-74; pastoral counselor on staff Cathedral St. John the Divine, N.Y.C., 1974—, canon residentiary, canon counselor, 1977—; ordained priest Episcopal Ch., 1977. Mem. Assn. Women in Psychology, Am. Assn. Pastoral Counselors, Am. Assn. Marriage and Family Counselors, Feminist Therapy Collective. Home and Office: 1047 Amsterdam Ave New York City NY 10025

SIMPSON, ROBERT LLOYD, ednl. guidance cons.; b. Concord, N.H., Nov. 19, 1932; s. Lloyd Atherton and Mabel B. (Suitor) S.; B.Ed. with high honors, Keene State Coll., 1955; M.Edn., U. N.H., 1960, postgrad. 1960-74; m. Virginia Ruth Brooks, Aug. 18, 1956; children—Stephen Robert, Richard Lloyd. High sch. tchr. Portsmouth (N.H.) Sch. Dept., 1955-58, counselor, 1958-60, jr. high sch. prin., 1960-62, dir. guidance, 1962-76, ednl. guidance cons., 1976—; bd. dirs. Seacoast Counseling Service, 1971-78. Mem. Newfields (N.H.) Sch. Bd., 1968-71, chmn., 1969-71. Mem. NEA, N.H. Edn. Assns., Am., New Eng. (Outstanding New Eng. Ednl. Research award 1964), N.H. (named Outstanding Male Counselor 1970) personnel and guidance assns., Am., N.H. sch. counselors assns., Nat. Assn. Coll. Admissions Counselors, Assn. Portsmouth Tchrs., N.H. Seacoast Counselors Assn., Keene State Coll., U. N.H. alumni assns., Seacoast Social Service (chmn. 1970-74), Alpha Pi Tau Alumni Assn., Kappa Delta Pi. Congregationalist. Author: The Average Student and Coll. Admissions, 1964; contbr. articles to profl. jours. and mags. Home: RFD 2 Newmarket NH 03857 Office: Portsmouth High School Alumni Dr Portsmouth NH 03801

SIMPSON, RUSSELL GORDON, lawyer; b. Springfield, Mass., May 22, 1927; s. Archer R. and Ethel (Gordon) S.; B.A., Yale U., 1951; J.D., Boston U., 1956; postgrad. Law Sch., Harvard U., 1961, Parker Sch. Internat. Law, Columbia U., 1962; m. Bickley S. Flower, Sept. 11, 1954; children—Barbara G., Elisabeth B., Helen Blair. Advt. mgr. Burden Bryant Co., Springfield, 1951-53; admitted to Mass. bar, 1956, since practiced in Boston; asso. firm Goodwin, Procter & Hoar, 1956-64, partner, 1965—; sec. Lehrer and Madden, Inc.; dir. Bolsa Corp., Haskell Investment Corp., Bolsa Pub. Corp.; dir., mem. exec., compensation and audit coms. Stride Rite Corp.; mem. spl. com. to revise Mass. Corrupt Practices Act, 1961-62. Mem. adv. com., ambulatory care service Beth Israel Hosp., 1969-71; mem. Met. Boston Area Planning Council Coms. on Housing and Regional Orgn., 1969-75; mem. Milton Town Warrant Com., 1976—, chmn., 1978—; mem. Mass. Republican Com., 1959-67, mem. exec. com., 1959-67, chmn. exec. com., 1962-67; del. state Rep. convs., 1960, 62, 64, 66, 67, 70; alt. del. at large Rep. nat. conv., 1964; exec. dir. Mass. del. Rep. Nat. Conv., 1968; vice chmn. Milton Rep. Town Com., 1970-71; bd. visitors Boston U. Coll. Bus. Adminstrn., 1969-74; bd. dirs. Green Shoe-Stride Rite Charitable Found., Inc.; adv. com. civic service ednl. program Milton Acad. Served with USNR, 1945-46. Named Outstanding Young Man of Greater Boston, Greater Boston Jr. C. of C., 1963. Mem. Am. Soc. Internat. Law, Am. (Year 2000 com.; sect. on corp., banking and bus. law; panel on corp. law ednl. programs com. on corp. law), Mass. (chmn. subcom. legis. liaison and of liaison with auditors), Boston bar assns. Home: 76 Brook Hill Rd Milton MA 02187 Office: 28 State St Boston MA 02109

SIMS, ALBERT M., mktg. exec.; b. Bklyn., Jan. 22, 1930; s. Samuel Lee and Jennie (Rosenberg) S.; student Bklyn. Coll. 1954-55; B.S. in Physics, Adelphi Coll., 1960; m. Estelle Irene Deiner, Nov. 28, 1963; children—Suzanne, Lynda, Wendy. Field engr. Metro Greenhouse, Bklyn., 1953-54; analytic engr. Stratos div. Fairchild Co., Bayshore, N.Y., 1954-60; project engr. Lycoming div. AVCO, Stratford, Conn., 1960-61; program mgr. EDO Corp., N.Y.C., 1961-77; fed. mktg. mgr. Sperry Marine Systems, N.Y.C., 1977—; pres. Performance Engr., Smithtown, N.Y., 1958—; v.p., editor Patron Mag., Bayshore, 1956-58. Served with USNR, 1947-58. Mem. Am. Def. Preparedness Assn., Am. Inst. Aeros. and Astronautics, Nat. Security Indsl. Assn. Republican. Clubs: Smithtown Landing Country, Lake Hopatcong Yacht. Mgr. USN airborne mine clearing system which was major influence in peace negotiations with Vietnam, successfully cleared Suez Canal; contbr. numerous research papers in field. Address: 7 Cambridge Dr Smithtown NY 11787

SIMS, JAMES ERNEST, chemist; b. Pitts., June 23, 1927; s. James Edward and Wilhelmina Lydia (Rommel) S.; B.S., Westminster Coll., 1952; postgrad. U. Pitts., 1952-53; m. Barbara Ann West, Oct. 18, 1952; children—Debra Ann, Kimberly Ann, Bronwyn Louise. Chemist, Federal Labs. Inc., Saltsburg, Pa., 1952—, chemist in basic and applied research of fuels and propellants, 1965—; research and devel. projects Edgewood Arsenal Chem. and Research and Devel. Labs., 1965-67, Cornell Aeor. Labs., 1965-67. Scoutmaster, leader Boy Scouts Am., 1950-52; leader Boys Clubs Am., 1950-55. Served with USN, 1945-50. Mem. Am. Chem. Soc., Am. Def. Preparedness Assn., Smithsonian Assos. Republican. Patentee in field. Home: Rural Route 3 Hills Church Rd Export PA 15632 Office: Federal Labs Inc Saltsburg PA 15681

SIMUNEK, FRANK ALAN, archtl. interior designer, builder; b. N.Y.C., Oct. 22, 1948; s. Frank and Emily Simunek; B.A., Bradley U., 1970. Designer window displays, also interior design retail stores, 1970-77; pres., chmn. bd. Ravaan Designs, N.Y.C., 1977-78; designer, builder, cons. Allen & Co., N.Y.C., 1977—; mem. adv. panel Interior Design Mag. Active 76th St. Central Park Rehab. Club. Mem. World, Am. crafts councils, Men's Display Guild. Home: 42 E 76th St New York City NY 10021 Office: 315 W 36th St New York City NY 10021

SINAI, ALLEN L., economist; b. Detroit, Apr. 4, 1939; s. Joseph and Betty Paula (Feinberg) S.; A.B. in Econs., U. Mich., 1961, M.A. in Econs., 1966; Ph.D. in Econs., Northwestern U., 1969; m. Lee D. Etsten, June 23, 1963; children—Lauren B., Todd M. Instr., Northwestern U., Evanston, Ill., 1963-64, Lake Forest (Ill.) Coll., 1964-65; instr. U. Ill., Chgo., 1965-66 asst. prof. econs., 1966-71, asso. prof., 1971-75; vis. asso. prof. Sloan Sch., Mass. Inst. Tech., 1975-77; vis. asso. prof. Boston U., 1977-78; cons. Fed. Home Loan Bank of Chgo., 1966-67, Ill. Bell Telephone Co., 1969-70, Continental Ill. Bank of Chgo., 1970, Bur. Labor Statistics, 1971-72, Joint Econ. Com., U.S. Congress, 1972-73; sr. economist Data Resources, Inc., 1971-75, dir. fin. econs., 1975-77, v.p., 1977—. Mem. Am. Econ. Assn., Am. Statis. Assn., Econometric Soc. Contbr. articles in field to profl. jours. Home: 16 Holmes Rd Lexington MA 02173 Office: 24 Hartwell Ave Lexington MA 02173

SINAY, RALPH HEATWOLE, forest engr.; b. Norwich, Conn., Dec. 1, 1916; s. Albert James and Bessie Tillinghast (Crary) S.; B.S., Pa. State Coll., 1940; m. Mary Bernadette Crotty, Nov. 21, 1942; children—James Alexander, Margaret Ann. Engr.-in-tng. Conn. Hwy. Dept., Norwich, 1941; forest engr. Conn. Park and Forest Commn., Hartford, 1946-72; engr. Close, Jensen & Miller, cons., Wethersfield, Conn., 1972—. Served to lt. col. C.E., U.S. Army, 1941-46; PTO, ETO. Mem. Soc. Am. Foresters, Soc. Mil. Engrs., Conn. Assn. Land Surveyors, V.F.W. (comdr. post 1956-57, 69-70). Congregationalist. Club: Masons. Home: 35 Britt Rd East Hartford CT 06118 Office: 449 Silas Deane Hwy Wethersfield CT 06109

SINBACK, DONALD LEE, reliability and quality engr.; b. Princeton, Minn., May 31, 1945; s. Warner R. and Lyla Irene (Berrgren) S.; B.S., St. Lawrence U., 1967; postgrad U. Va., 1967-69; m. Marguerite Alma Harvey, Apr. 12, 1969; children—Katherine Clark, Matthew John. Mathematician, Adaptronics Inc., McLean, Va., 1969; sr. reliability and maintainability engr. Gen. Environments Corp., Springfield, Va., 1969-73; staff reliability and maintainability engr. Tensor Industries, Falls Church, Va., 1973-75; gen. engr. guidance reliability and maintainability Naval Air Systems Command, Washington, 1975-77, electronics engr./avionics system project engr., 1977—. Home: 8208 Oak Glen Rd Manassas VA 22110 Office: Naval Air Systems Command Washington DC 20361

SINCERBEAUX, ROBERT ABBOTT, found. officer, trustee; b. N.Y.C., July 22, 1913; s. Frank Huestis and Jessie (Batterson) S.; B.A. cum laude, Princeton, 1936; LL.B., Yale, 1939; m. Elizabeth Morley, Apr. 19, 1940; children—Richard M., Suzanne (Mrs. James M. Brian), Charles M. Admitted to N.Y. bar, 1940; asso. firm White & Case, N.Y.C., 1939-42, Simpson, Thacher & Bartlett, N.Y.C., 1942-43; asso. firm Sincerbeaux & Shrewsbury, N.Y.C., 1946-52, partner, 1952-72, of counsel, 1972—; trustee, pres. Eva Gebhard-Gourgaud Found. (historic preservation); mng. trustee Cecil Howard Charitable Trust; trustee, v.p. Woodstock Assos.; trustee Woodstock Found., Woodstock Hist. Soc., Ottauguechee Regional Land Trust; bd. overseers Old Sturbridge Village. Served with USNR, 1943-46; lt. comdr. Res. ret. Fellow Met. Mus. Art (life); mem. Soc. Colonial Wars, Soc. for Preservation New Eng. Antiquities (Vt. council). Episcopalian. Clubs: Short Hills; Down Town Assn. (N.Y.C.); Woodstock Country; The Round Table, Lakota, Nassau. Home: Uphill Farm Woodstock VT 05091 Office: One The Green Woodstock VT 05091

SINCLAIR, IAN DAVID, railroad co. ofcl.; b. Winnipeg, Man., Can., Dec. 27, 1913; s. John David and Lillian (Matheson) S.; B.A. in Econs., Wesley Coll., U. Man., 1937, LL.D., 1967; LL.B., U. Man. Law Faculty, 1941; m. Ruth Beatrice Drennan, July 17, 1942; children—Ian R., Susan L., Christine R., Donald L. Barrister, Guy, Chappell & Co., Winnipeg, 1937-41; called to Man. bar, 1941, apptd. Queen's counsel, 1961; lectr. torts U. Man., 1942-43; with Canadian Pacific Ltd., 1942—, asst. solicitor, 1942, solicitor, Montreal, Que., Can., 1946, asst. to gen. counsel, 1951;, gen. solicitor, 1953, v.p., gen. counsel, 1960, v.p. law, 1960-61, v.p., 1961-66, mem. exec. com., dir., 1961—, pres., 1966-72, chief exec. officer, 1969—, chmn. bd., 1972—; dir., exec. officer Canadian Pacific Air Lines, Ltd., subs. Midland Simcoe Elevator Co., Ltd., Canadian Pacific Investments, Ltd.; v.p., dir. Pan Canadian Petroleum Ltd., Cominco Ltd., Royal Bank of Can.; dir. subsidiaries Canadian Pacific Securities Ltd., Canadian Pacific Steamships Ltd., Canadian Pacific (Bermuda) Ltd., Pacific Logging Co. Ltd., Marathon Realty Co. Ltd., Soo Line RR Co., Great Lakes Paper Co Ltd.; dir. MacMillan Bloedel Ltd., Canadian Investment Fund, Union Carbide Corp., Union Carbide Can. Ltd., Canadian Fund Inc., Simpsons Ltd., Can. Marconi Co., Sun Life Assurance of Can. Ltd., Seagram Co. Ltd. Mem. Canadian adv. bd. Sun Alliance and London Ins. Group; mem. internat.adv. com. Chase Manhattan Corp. Mem. The Conf. Bd. N.Y., Canadian C. of C., La. Chambre de Commerce (Montreal), Montreal Bd. Trade. Clubs: Canadian Railway, Canadian, Mount Royal (Montreal); Rideau (Ottawa, Ont.). Office: Canadian Pacific Limited Windsor Sta Montreal H3C 3E4 PQ Canada

SINDEN, HARRY, profl. hockey team exec.; m. Eleanor Sinden; children—Nancy, Carol, Dawn, Julie. Player Hull-Ottawa Eastern Pro League hockey team; player-coach Kingston team, from 1961; coach numerous teams Central League until 1967; coach Boston Bruins Nat. Hockey League team, 1967-70, mng. dir., 1972-77, gen. mgr., alt. gov., 1977—; v.p. Storer Broadcasting Co.; TV hockey commentator, 1970-72. Coach Team Can., 1973. Coach Stanley Cup team, 1970. Address: care Boston Bruins Boston Gardens 150 Causeway St Boston MA 02114*

SINGER, BARRY MANA, physicist; b. N.Y.C., Feb. 15, 1940; s. Melvin A. and Janice G. (Slater) S.; B.S., U. Colo., 1961; M.S., N.Y. U., 1963; Ph.D., Polytech. Inst. N.Y., 1968; m. Helene Kalisch, Apr. 12, 1964; children—Claudine W., Eugene R. Engr., Machlett Labs., Stamford, Conn., 1961-63; sr. engr. Raytheon Co., 1963-65, sect. head, 1965-68; program mgr. Philips Labs., Briarcliff Manor, N.Y., 1969-71, sr. program mgr., 1971-77, dir. components and devices, 1978—; cons. Vita Corp., 1975-77, Amprex Electronics Co., 1975-76. Poly. Inst. N.Y. fellow, 1964-65; Raytheon Co. fellow, 1964-68. Mem. IEEE, Sigma Xi. Republican. Jewish. Contbr. articles in field to profl. jours.; patentee in field. Home: 401 E 86 St New York City NY 10028 Office: 345 Scarborough Rd Briarcliff NY 10510

SINGER, BERNARD ELIAS, lawyer; b. N.Y.C., Sept. 6, 1913; s. Henry A. and Rose (Mednick) S.; B.S. in Commerce, U. N.C., 1934; postgrad. N.Y. U., 1934-35; LL.B., Bklyn. Law Sch., 1938; m. Rose Scharf, Sept. 16, 1934; children—Henry A., Elizabeth Singer Mosely, Margery Singer Honig. Accountant, David Berdon & Co., N.Y.C., 1934-39; admitted to N.Y. bar, 1938; practiced law, 1941—; sr. partner firm Singer Hutner Levine & Seeman, and predecessors, N.Y.C., 1950—; dir. Chem. Patents Corp., Century Industries Inc. Mem. Am., N.Y. bar assns., Phi Beta Kappa, Beta Gamma Sigma. Clubs: B'nai B'rith (Harrison pres. 1952-53); Fenway Golf (Scarsdale, N.Y.). Home: Delevan Ln Harrison NY 10528 Office: 110 E 59th St New York City NY 10022

SINGER, ESTHER FORMAN (MRS. SIDNEY SINGER), artist; b. N.Y.C.; d. Maurice and Sarah (Shaller) Forman; R.N., Albert Einstein Hosp., Phila., 1944; B.A., N.Y.U., 1957; postgrad. Fairleigh Dickinson U., Madison, N.J., 1960-63, New Sch. Social Research, 1965-71; m. Sidney Singer, Oct. 29, 1950; children—Keith Arlen, Maurene Forman. Exhibited in one man shows Papermill Playhouse Galleries, 1965, Bambergers Dept. Store, 1965, Gallery 9-Chatham, 1967, Seton Hall U., 1969, Centenary Coll., Hackettstown, N.J., 1970, Bloomfield Coll., 1970, County Coll. of Morris, 1971, Mus. Modern Art, Paris, France, 1973 (1st prize), Gallery 52, 1973, N.J. State Mus., 1973, 76, Brandeis U., 1978, Morris Mus., Morristown, N.J., 1978; one-man show tour, 1973-75; exhibited numerous group shows throughout U.S.; represented in permanent collections at Finch Mus. Contemporary Art, N.Y.C., Newark Mus., Hudson River Mus., Yonkers, N.Y., N.J. State Mus., Trenton, Seton Hall U. Mus. Collection, N.Y. Hosp. Collection, Whitney Mus., others; art critic Am. Artist mag., Worrall Publs.; tchr. elementary sch. art class Recreation Center South Orange; guest lectr. B'nai B'rith, Deborah; guest panelist Channel 7 TV, 1967-68, radio, 1968-69. Judge local and regional art shows. Served as 1st lt. Army Nurse Corps, 1944-46. Recipient prize for painting Paris Mus. Modern Art. Mem. Artists Equity N.J., Artists Equity N.Y., Art Exhbns., Council, Old Bergen Art Guild, Painters and Sculptors Soc. N.J., Am. Vets. Soc. Artists, Miniature Art Soc. N.J. Address: 70 Glenview Rd South Orange NJ 07079

SINGER, FRED, educator; b. Bklyn., July 28, 1915; s. Harry and Tillie (Miller) S.; B.B.A., St. John's U., 1942; J.D., St. Louis U., 1952; m. Antoinette Scherer, Jan. 26, 1947; children—Ira, Harold. Instr., U.S. Army, Scott Field, Ill., 1942-45; revenue agt. IRS, St. Louis, 1945-53; admitted to Mo. bar, 1952, U.S. Supreme Ct. bar, 1966; appellate conferee appellate div. U.S. Dept. Treasury, N.Y.C., 1953-70; asst. prof. bus. law N.Y.C. Community Coll., 1970—; lectr. to bus. groups. Chmn. sch. bd. Israel Community Center, Levittown, N.Y., 1951-52. Mem. Fed. Bar Assn., Nat. Assn. Pub. Accountants, Tchrs. of Accounting at Two-Year Colleges, Phi Alpha Delta. Jewish. Contbr. articles on tax law to profl. jours. Home: 67-26 Groton St Forest Hills NY 11375 Office: 300 Jay St Brooklyn NY 11201

SINGER, GARY, advt. agy. exec.; b. Norwalk, Conn., Nov. 27, 1929; s. Benn and Sylvia (Shilepsky) S.; B.A., U. Bridgeport, 1959; m. Bunni Greenbaum, Aug. 28, 1953; children—Barry Scott, Timothy Paul. Vice pres. Ted Gravenson Inc., advt., N.Y.C., 1959-62; account mgt. Danial & Charles advt., N.Y.C., 1962-63; dir. pub. relations, state coordinator J.F.K. Library, Conn., 1963-65; dir. pub. relations group advt. Singer Co., N.Y.C., 1965-70; pres. Singer & Millar Inc., advt., Greenwich, Conn., 1970-77; partner Hall Decker McKibbin & Singer, Inc., Advt., N.Y.C., 1977—; dir. Thermetrics Corp., Orange, Conn., Peppermill Assos., Westport, Conn., Parsley, Inc., Norwalk, Aerospace Edn. Council, N.Y.C. Commr., Weston (Conn.) Little League, 1973-75; mem. Planning and Zoning Commn., 1973-75; v.p. Weston Charter Revision Commn., 1975-78; moderator Weston Town Meeting; chmn. Weston Democratic Town Com., 1975-77; founder, bd. dirs. Westport Community Theatre. Served with AUS, 1948-51; PTO. Mem. Assn. Indsl. Advertisers, Advt. Club Fairfield County, Pi Delta Epsilon, Pi Omega Chi. Club: Weston Racquet (pres.). Contbr. articles to profl. jours. Home: Pink Cloud Ln Weston CT 06883 Office: 1200 Summer St Stamford CT 06905

SINGER, ISAAC BASHEVIS, writer; b. Radzymin, Poland, July 14, 1904 (came to U.S. 1935, naturalized 1943); s. Pinchos Menachem and Bathsheba (Zylberman) S.; student Rabbinical Sem., Warsaw, Poland, 1920-27; m. Alma Haimann, Feb. 14, 1940; 1 son, Israel. With Hebrew and Yiddish publs. in Poland, 1926-35, Jewish Daily Forward, N.Y.C., 1935—. Recipient Nat. Book awards, 1970, 74. Fellow Jewish Acad. Arts and Scis., Nat. Inst. Arts and Letters, Polish Inst. Arts and Scis. in Am.; mem. Am. Acad. Arts and Scis. Club: Pen (N.Y.C.). Author: Satan in Goray, 1935, The Family Moskat, 1950, Gimpel The Fool, 1957, The Magician of Lublin, 1960, The Spinoza of Market Street, 1961, The Slave, 1962, Short Friday, 1964, In My Father's Court, 1966, The Manor, 1967, The Seance, 1968, The Estate, 1969; Enemies, A Love Story, 1972; A Crown of Feathers, 1973; Passions, 1976; also books for children including A Day of Pleasure, 1970. Address: 209 W 86th St New York NY 10024

SINGER, JOSEPH HOWARD, chem. co. exec.; b. San Francisco, Dec. 5, 1922; s. Jack and Julia (Sullivan) S.; B.A. cum laude, Stanford, 1950, M.A., 1951; m. Jacqueline Yvonne Auliac, Jan. 14, 1947; 1 dau., Patricia Jacqueline. Staff corr. Internat. News Service, Paris, France, 1951-53, Berlin bur. chief, 1953-56, chief diplomatic corr., Washington, 1956-57; Washington mgr. pub. relations Reynolds Metals, Washington, 1958-60, eastern pub. relations mgr., N.Y.C., 1960-63; dir. pub. relations Geigy Chem. Corp., Ardsley, N.Y., 1963-66; asst. pub. relations dir. Gen. Foods, 1966-72, dir. pub. relations, White Plains, N.Y., 1972-75; corp. dir. pub. relations Am. Hoechst Corp., Somerville, N.J., 1975—. Bd. govs. U.S.O., 1967—, nat. v.p., 1969—; chmn. journalism adv. bd. Coll. White Plains, 1970-74. Bd. dirs., v.p. Travelers Aid Internat. Social Services Am. Served to 1st lt. Mil. Police Corps, AUS, 1943-48; ETO. Mem. Calorie Control Council (chmn. pub. relations com. 1969-74), Packaging Inst. U.S.A. (chmn. pub. affairs adv. com. 1970-74), Pub. Relations Soc. Am. (pres. Westchester County chpt. 1971-72), Nat., Overseas press clubs, Delta Phi Epsilon. Home: 275 Hobart Ave Short Hills NJ 07078 Office: Am Hoechst Corp Route 202-206 N Somerville NJ 08876

SINGER, MARCIA B., educator; b. N.Y.C., Apr. 11; d. Meyer and Sadie (Brosterman) Bosniak; B.A., N.Y. U., 1943, M.A. in Edn., 1959; profl. diploma in guidance and counseling, Columbia Tchrs. Coll., 1971; m. Jules Singer, June 12, 1943; children—Barbara (Mrs. Allen Thomas), Nancy, Michael. Tchr. salesmanship for women, Port Washington and New Hyde Park, N.Y., 1959-60; tchr. course for women returning to labor market, Rockville Center (N.Y.) and Sewanhaka Sch. Dist., 1963-65, White Plains (N.Y.) Center and Nassau County, auspices, N.Y. U., 1963-65; counselor Manpower Devel. and Tng., 1965-67; guidance counselor Port Washington Sr. High Sch., 1967-68; asst. dean students N.Y. Inst. Tech., Old Westbury, N.Y., 1968—, also coordinator coll.-wide cultural com.; vocat. counselor for mature women, also pvt. practice and lectr. in field. Mem. adv. bd. Vol. Services Bur. Westchester County, New Sch. Social Research; bd. dirs. Nassau County Council Girl Scouts U.S.A.; mem. Roslyn Bicentennial Commn., 1975-76; mem. adv. bd. Oyster Bay Council Arts. Named Greek Faculty Woman of Year, Greek Soc., N.Y. Inst. Tech. Mem. Nat. Assn. Women Deans, Adminstrs. and Counselors, Am., L.I. personnel and guidance assns., Nat. County Bus. and Profl. Women's Assn., Eta Mu Phi, Alpha Phi Epsilon. Author courses in field. Home: 65 Green Leaf Hill Great Neck NY 11023 Office: NY Inst Tech Old Westbury NY 11568

SINGER, MARILYN PHYLLIS, mirror mfg. co. exec.; b. Lawrence, Mass., Jan. 5, 1931; d. David Nathan and Sarah Theresa (Silverman) Albert; A.B., Columbia U., 1971, M.A., 1973; m. Bernard Harris Singer, Apr. 24, 1949; 1 son, David William. Supr., Lawrence City Hosp. Lab., 1949; tchr. African history South Bronx High Sch., N.Y.C., tchr. spl. edn. students, 1973-75; sec. to pres. Friedman Bros., N.Y.C., 1954-63, v.p., 1976—. Mem. exec. bd. Reform Democratic Club, 1977-78; mem. Judicial Com., 1977-79; Dem. committeewoman 84th Assembly Dist., N.Y.C., 1978—; vol. tchr. spl. edn. Mem. Am. Hist. Soc., Mirror Mfrs. Assn. Club: Benjamin Franklin Dem. (Riverdale, N.Y.). Compiler research on old furniture; contbr. articles on social history of furniture to publs. Home: 4465 Douglas Ave Riverdale NY 10471 Office: 305 E 47th St New York City NY 10017

SINGER, NIKI (MRS. MICHAEL J. SHEETS), pub. relations co. exec.; b. Rochester, N.Y., Sept. 10, 1937; d. Goodman A. and Evelyn (Simon) Sarachan; B.A. cum laude, U. Mich., 1959; m. Warren Singer, Aug. 16, 1959 (div. Jan. 1973); m. 2d, Michael J. Sheets, Feb. 24, 1973; 1 dau., Romaine Kitty Sheets. Asst. promotion mgr. Fairchild Publs., N.Y.C., 1962-65; dir. women's interest div. Vernon Pope Co., N.Y.C., 1965-69, v.p., 1969-71; pres. Niki Singer, Inc., N.Y.C., 1972—. Home: 1035 Fifth Ave New York City NY 10028 Office: 400 Madison Ave New York City NY 10017

SINGER, ROBERT CLIFFORD, assn. exec.; b. Mt. Vernon, N.Y., Jan. 27, 1929; s. Henry A. and Gertrude (Berns) S.; B.S., N.Y. U., 1949, M.A., 1954; m. Elna M. Campbell, June 25, 1954. Account exec. Swanson & Dalzell, Inc., pub. relations, N.Y.C., 1954-55; asst. dir. advt. and promotion Inst. Life Ins., N.Y.C., 1955-63; sr. account exec. John Moynahan & Co., Inc., pub. relations, N.Y.C., 1964-65; pub. relations dir., adminstrv. mgr., v.p., asst. sec., dir. pub. affairs Soap and Detergent Assn., N.Y.C., 1965—. Instr. polit. sci. N.Y. U., 1955-56. Mem. Floral Park Bd. Zoning Appeals, 1968-73, village trustee, recreation commr., library commr., police commr., pub. works commr., dep. mayor, 1973—. Served with AUS, 1950-52. Mem. Pub.

Relations Soc. Am., Am. Soc. Assn. Execs., Chem. Communications Assn., Soc. Consumer Affairs Profls. in Bus. (charter), Am. Oil Chemists Soc., AAAS. Christian Scientist. Clubs: Masons (32 deg.), Shriners (dist. dep. grand master 1965-66); Garden City Country; Univ. (Washington); Union League. Home: 501 Tulip Ave Floral Park NY 11001 Office: 475 Park Ave S New York City NY 10016

SINGER, VERA, mail order co. exec.; b. Jersey City, July 11, 1932; d. Bohdan D. and Eva (Churik) Murdza; student pub. schs.; m. Lawrence Singer, Nov. 3, 1951; children—Richard Alan, Brian David. With Yogg & Co., Newark, 1948-67, owner firm (name now Menu Promotions/Yogg, 1977—; engaged in menu promotions and ideas, 1967—. Mem. Nat. Restaurant Assn., N.J. Restaurant Assn. Address: 208 River Rd Clifton NJ 07014

SINGH, AMARENDRA NARAYAN, physician; b. Gulni, Bihar, India; s. Gaya Prasad and Bimala; came to Canada, 1970; m. Gertraud Singh, Apr. 23, 1968; children—Sheila Kumari, Rejendra Narayan. Intern, Darbhanga Med. Coll. Hosp., 1961-62; royal post grad. Hammersmith Hosp., London, 1963-64, Inst. Neurology Queen Sq., 1964-65, dept. psychiatry Bristol (Eng.), U., 1965-68; sr. registrar dept. psychiatry Birmingham U., 1968-69; sr. psychiatrist Prince Albert Psychiatric Center, Sask., Can., 1970-71; med. dir. Northeastern Mental Health Center, South Porcupine, Ont., Can., 1971-72; dir. psychopharmacology unit Hamilton Psychiatric Hosp., McMaster U., Hamilton, Ont., 1972—. Recipient Queens scholarship, 1967, Morris Hallet award, 1962; also many grant and fellowships awarded by nat. and internat. med. socs. Fellow Royal Coll. Physicians (C.), Internat. Coll. Psychosomatic Medicine; mem. World, British, Canadian med. assns., World Psychiatric Assn., Internat. Platform Assn., Internat. Assn. Prevention of Suicide. Contbr. articles in field to profl. jours. Home: 7 Rhodes Ct Dundas ON L9H 5R5 Canada Office: Box 585 Hamilton ON L8N 3K7 Canada

SINGH, DARSHAN, chemist; b. Phagwara, India, Dec. 25, 1939; s. Amar and Maya (Devi) S.; B.S., Panjab U. (India), 1961, diploma and certificate in French, 1964, M.S., 1962, Ph.D., 1968; m. Rajinder Kaur, Jan. 30, 1972; 1 son, Raman Preet. Sr. research fellow Panjab U., 1967-69; prodn. mgr. Gibco, Santa Clara, Calif., 1971-73, supr. research and devel., Grand Island, N.Y., 1973-74, dir. biochem./clin. quality control, 1974—; tchr. State Univ. Coll., Buffalo, 1978—. Mem. Am. Chem. Soc., Automobile Assn. Western N.Y., Sikh Soc. Buffalo. Contbr. articles to sci. jours. Home: 105 Birkshire Grand Island NY 14072 Office: 3175 Staley Rd Grand Island NY 14072

SINGH, HAR SWARUP, economist; b. Nowshera, India, Dec. 28, 1928; s. Bharat and Dhoop (Kaur) S.; came to U.S., 1965; B.S., Agra U. (India), 1948, M.S., 1950; Ph.D., N.C. State U., 1958; m. Bijendri Devi, May 4, 1944; children—Satya Vir, Mahendra Paul, Sudha Rani. Inspector, Cooperative Socs., India, 1951-53; research Delhi Sch. Econs., Delhi U., India, 1954-55; dep. project dir. Long Term Projections of Agrl. Commodities, Nat. Council Applied Econ. Research, New Delhi, 1959-61; bus. economist, head econ. research units Delhi Cloth and Gen. Mills, Delhi, 1961-65; sr. economist in charge econ. research Internat. Cotton Adv. Com., Washington, 1965—. Mem. Smithsonian Instn., Am. Assn. Textile Tech., Textile Analysts Group, Am. Chem. Assn. Hindu. Club: Toastmasters (area gov. 1968-69). Research and publs. on econs., fiber and textile topics. Home: 4926 Andrea Ave Annandale VA 22003 Office: Internat Cotton Adv Com South Agr Bldg Washington DC 20250

SINGH, INDER JIT, anatomist, dentist; b. Gujranwala, India, Apr. 28, 1939; s. Sanpuran and Piar (Kaur) S.; came to U.S., 1960, naturalized, 1973; D.D.S., Punjab U., 1959; Ph.D., U. Oreg., 1969; Jr. and sr. house surgeon Govt. Dental Coll. and Hosp., Amritsar, India, 1959-60; Murry and Leonie Guggenheim Dental Clinic fellow in pedodontics, N.Y.C., 1960-61; from grad. asst. to instr. Dental Sch., U. Oreg., Portland, 1962-65, research asso. med. psychology Med. Sch., 1968-69; asst. prof. anatomy N.Y. U. Dental Center and Grad. Sch. Arts and Scis., 1972-74, asso. prof., 1974—; adj. asst. prof. Fordham U., 1970-71; adj. asst. prof. City Coll., City U. N.Y., 1973, vis. biomed. anatomist, 1973—. NIH spl. fellow, 1971-72. Fellow Gerontol. Soc.; mem. Sikh Cultural Soc. (treas. N.Y. 1972), Am. Assn. Anatomists, N.Y. Acad. Scis., Internat. Assn. Dental Research, AAAS, Anat. Soc. India, Sigma Xi. Democrat. Mem. editorial adv. bd. Sikh Sansar, San Francisco, 1973—. Home: 10 Waterside Plaza New York City NY 10010 Office: 345 E 24th St New York City NY 10010

SINGH, ISHWAR, educator; b. Gujarawala, West Pakistan, June 6, 1941; s. Jagat and Prakash (Kaur) S.; Ph.D., U. Hawaii, 1966; m. Ravinder Kaur, Mar. 3, 1969; children—Sunila, Pavan. Postdoctoral fellow U. Wash., Seattle, 1966-67; pool officer All India Inst. Med. Scis., New Delhi, 1968; postdoctoral fellow McMaster U., Hamilton, Ont., Can., 1969; teaching master Mohawk Coll., Hamilton, 1969—; summer research asso. McMaster U. Vol. UNICEF, 1975—. Recipient Gold medal Panjab U., 1962, Cultural Activity award East-West Centre, 1966; Teaching Excellence award Mohawk Coll., 1976; Govt. India scholar, 1963; East-West Centre Honolulu fellow, 1963-66. Fellow Chem. Inst. Can. (chmn. Hamilton sect. 1975-76); mem. Indian Students Assn. (pres. 1966), Am. Chem. Soc., Coll. Chemistry Can., India-Can. Soc., Sigma Xi. Office: 135 Fennell Ave W Hamilton ON L8N 3T2 Canada

SINGH, MAHENDRA PAL, physicist; b. Moradabad, India, May 1, 1930; came to U.S., 1957; s. Umrao and Kalavati S.; B.S., Allahabad U., 1948; M.S., Muslim U., Aligarh, 1953; Ph.D., Purdue U., 1964; m. Krishna Tanwer, June 12, 1948; children—Sunil, Arti, Anita. Lectr. Muslim U., Aligarh, India, 1953-57; research asst. Purdue U., Lafayette, Ind., 1958-64; sr. physicist GTE Automatic Electric Co., Northlake, Ill., 1964-72; mem. tech. staff GTE Labs., Inc., Waltham, Mass., 1972—; instr. Ill. Inst. Tech., Chgo., Elmhurst (Ill.) Coll. Mem. Am. Phys. Soc., Soc. Photo-optical Instrumentation Engrs., Sigma Xi. Hindu. Contbr. articles to profl. jours. Home: 78 Larchmont Ave Newton MA 02168 Office: 40 Sylvan Rd Waltham MA 02154

SINGH, PRABJIT, engr.; b. India, Apr. 16, 1948; s. Parkash and Rajbans (Kaur) S.; B.Tech. with honors, Indian Inst. Tech., 1969; M.S., Stevens Inst. Tech., 1973, Ph.D., 1977. Research asst. Stevens Inst., 1970-77; sr. engr. Airco, Inc., Murray Hill, N.J., 1977—. NSF grantee, 1972-77. Mem. Am. Soc. Metals, Electrochem. Soc., Am. Vacuum Soc. Home: 100 Hospital Plaza Apt 1108 Paterson NJ 07503

SINHA, ASHOK KUMAR, materials scientist; b. Patna, India, Feb. 23, 1944; s. Kedar Nath and Shanti (Prasad) S.; came to U.S., 1966; B.S. summa cum laude, Patna U., 1962; B. Engring. summa cum laude, Indian Inst. Sci., Bangalore, 1964; Ph.D., Oxford (Eng.) U., 1966; m. Rekha Verma, Feb. 19, 1969; children—Gita Anjali, Anoop Kumar. Research asso. metallurgy U. Ill., Urbana, 1966-68; research fellow in materials sci. Calif. Inst. Tech., Pasadena, 1968-70; mem. tech. staff Bell Telephone Labs., Murray Hill, N.J., 1970-76, supr. technology and diagnostics group, 1976—; cons., lectr. in field. Recipient Alumni Gold medal Indian Inst. Sci., 1965; Brit. Iron and Steel Research Assn. scholar, 1964-66; Calif. Inst. Tech. research fellow, 1968-70. Mem. Electrochem. Soc. (exec. com. electronics div., divisional editor jour.). Club: Bell Labs. Garden. Contbr. articles to profl. jours. Developed electronic materials, processes and devices, metals, alloys. Patentee fabrication of integrated circuits, compound semiconds. Home: 36 Fox Run Murray Hill NJ 07974 Office: Bell Labs 600 Mountain Ave Murray Hill NJ 07974

SINN, ROBERT SAMUEL, electronic co. exec., securities co. exec.; b. Phila. Mar. 9, 1930; s. Charles M. and Dorothea (Koenig) S.; A.B., U. Pa., 1952, M.S., 1957; 1 dau., Nina A. Engr. RCA, Camden, N.J., 1952-60; chmn. bd. Microwave Semiconductor Corp., 1968—, El Kins-Sinn Corp., 1967-75; pres. Ultronic Systems Corp., 1960-70, dir., 1967-72; pres. Robert S. Sinn Securities Inc., 1975—. Mem. IEEE, Young Pres.'s Orgn., Engrs. Club Phila., N.Y. Acad. Sci., Ops. Research Soc. Am. Club: Wall Street. Patentee in field. Home: Rosebud Farms Jobstown NJ 08041

SIPP, ELMER FRANKS, JR., mfg. co. exec.; b. Woodhaven, N.Y., Apr. 5, 1914; s. Elmer Franks and Maeola Magdaleine (Courrier) S.; E.E., Rensselaer Poly. Inst., 1935; Aero. Engr., Mass. Inst. Tech., 1941; m. Mildred Grace McCormack, June 17, 1942; children—Susan Sipp Potter, Peter E., Steven O. Mem. indsl. sales staff Nat. Carbon Co., N.Y.C., 1937-40, indsl. rep., 1946-49, asst. dist. mgr., Pitts., 1949-54; asst. mgr. govt. contracting Union Carbide Corp., N.Y.C., 1954-64, exec., 1964—. Served to comdr. USNR, 1941-46; PTO. Mem. Am. Def. Preparedness Assn., Metall Soc., Assn. U.S. Army, Ret. Offices Assn., Mass. Inst. Tech. Alumni Assn., Roman Catholic. Clubs: Skytop, Wings, Ponte Vedra, Key Biscayne Yacht, Mt. Anthony Country. Home: 47 Beechroft Rd Greenwich CT 06830 Office: 270 Park Ave New York City NY 10017

SIRIANNI, AURELIO FREDERICK, chemist; b. Soveria Mannelli, Italy, Mar. 14, 1915; came to Can., 1925, naturalized, 1926; s. Antonio and Maria Raffaela (Colosimo) S.; B.S. with honors in chemistry, Mt. Allison U., 1943; Ph.D., McGill U., 1946; m. Elsie Mary Haime, Feb. 23, 1949; children—Maria Rosa (Mrs. J.P. Gravelle), Margaret Anne, Michael Frederick, David Anthony. Chemist, NRC Can., Ottawa, Ont., 1946—, head colloid and clathrate chem. sect. Fellow Chem. Inst. Can.; mem. N.Y. Acad. Scis. Contbr. numerous tech. and sci. papers to profl. jours. Patentee. Home: 1187 Tawney Rd Ottawa ON K1G 1B5 Canada Office: Nat Research Council of Can Div of Chemistry Montreal Rd Labs Ottawa ON K1A 0R9 Canada

SIRKIN, DOUGLAS MICHAEL, physician; b. Buffalo, May 22, 1942; s. Allen and Rheda Ann (Greenstone) S.; student U. Buffalo, 1960-63; M.D., State U. N.Y., 1967; m. Sara Rachael Gerstman, June 4, 1967; children—Jonathan William, Michelle Francine. Intern, Millard Fillmore Hosp., Buffalo, 1967-68, resident in diagnostic radiology, 1968-71, attending physician in radiology and nuclear medicine, 1973—; asst. prof. Sch. Medicine, State U. N.Y., Buffalo, 1973—. Served with USAF, 1971-73. Decorated Air Force Commendation medal. Diplomate Am. Bd. Radiology, Am. Bd. Nuclear Medicine. Mem. AMA, Med. Soc. State N.Y., Erie County Med. Soc., Maimonides Med. Soc., Alpha Omega Alpha. Home: 259 Troy-Del Way Buffalo NY 14221 Office: 3 Gates Circle Buffalo NY 14209

SIRKIN, JACOB, psychiatrist; b. Syracuse, N.Y., Dec. 4, 1910; s. William and Mollie Sirkin; A.B., Syracuse U., 1931, M.D., 1934; m. Winifred E. Harris, June 18, 1952; 1 son, Stephen R. Intern, Newark (N.Y.) State Sch., 1934-35, resident, 1935-44; practice medicine specializing in psychiatry, 1934—; staff physician Newark State Sch., 1934-44; sch. psychiatrist Wayne County (N.Y.) pub. schs., 1949-56; dir. Wayne County Mental Health Clinic, 1956-67; chief psychiatry Clifton Springs (N.Y.) Hosp., 1968-71, asso. psychiatrist, 1971—; chief psychiatry Newark Hosp., 1968-73, cons., 1973—. Served to capt. U.S. Army, 1944-47. Fellow Am. Psychiat. Assn. (life); mem. N.Y. State, Wayne County med. socs. Republican. Jewish. Clubs: Elks., Masons. Contbr. articles to med. jours. Home: 127 Pineridge Dr Newark NY 14513 Office: 330 East Ave Newark NY 14513

SISK, ALBERT FLETCHER, JR., ins. agt.; b. Easton, Md., Nov. 25, 1928; s. Albert Fletcher and Helen (Marvel) S.; student Mercersburg Acad., 1945-46, Washington and Lee U., 1946-49; m. Mary Douglass Tweedy, Jan. 8, 1955; children—Douglass Fletcher, Geoffrey Price. With Albert W. Sisk & Son. Preston, Md., 1950-66; ins. agt. Conn. Gen. Life Ins. Co., 1968—; dir. Preston Trucking Co., Inc., Provident State Bank, Preston, Md. Trustee Meml. Hosp., Easton, Md., 1965-71, mem. Sch. of Nursing Com., 1969—. Served with USNR, 1952-54. C.L.U. Mem. Nat. Rifle Assn. Club: Chesapeake Bay Yacht. Home: Gilpin's Point Preston MD 21655 Office: 3 N Harrison St POB 118 Easton MD 21601

SISLER, HAMPSON ALBERT, ophthalmologist; b. Yonkers, N.Y., Aug. 13, 1932; s. Frank Albert and Mildred Anabelle (Hampson) S.; B.S., N.Y. U., 1954, M.D., 1957; m. Mary Dianne Newsum, Aug. 28, 1966. Intern Lenox Hill Hosp., N.Y.C., 1957-58; resident in ophthalmology N.Y. Eye and Ear Infirmary, 1958-61; practice medicine specializing in ophthalmology, N.Y.C., 1961—; attending surgeon N.Y. Eye and Ear Infirmary; instr. Postgrad. Inst. Ophthalmology, Am. Acad. Ophthalmology and Otolaryngology; cons. ophthalmologist Lederle Labs., Inc., Am. Optical Corp. Served with USAR, 1958-67. Diplomate Am. Bd. Ophthalmology and Otolaryngology. Fellow A.C.S., Am. Acad. Ophthalmology and Otolaryngology, Am. Soc. Ophthalmic Plastic and Reconstructive Surgery, Am. Guild Organists; mem. AMA, ASCAP. Composer, pub. sacred choral, organ and instrumental music; patentee opthalmic devices; originator several ophthalmic surg. ops. and techniques; producer films introducing original surg. methods and instruments; contbr. articles to profl. jours. Home: 34 W 12th St New York City NY 10011 Office: 13 W 13th St New York City NY 10011

SISLEY, EMILY LUCRETIA, psychologist, writer; b. North Charleroi, Pa., May 7, 1930; d. Frederick William and Harriet Watkins (Litman) S.; Ph.D. in Clin. Psychology, L.I. U., 1972. With editorial dept. Chem. Week, McGraw-Hill Pubs., N.Y.C., 1957-60; mng. editor med. jours. dept. Hoeber div. Harper & Row, N.Y.C., 1960-67; freelance editor and writer, N.Y.C., 1967—; supervising psychologist, dir. psychiat. day center Roosevelt Hosp., N.Y.C., 1971-77; pvt. practice psychotherapy, N.Y.C., 1977—; faculty dept. psychiatry Columbia U., 1976-78; lectr. in field. Mem. N.Y. Acad. Scis., Am. Psychol. Assn. Democrat. Cons. editor: Internat. Jour. Group Tensions, 1971-73; co-author: The Joy of Lesbian Sex, 1977; contbr. to profl. jours., lit. and popular mags. Office: 61 Gramercy Park N New York City NY 10010

SISMONDO, SERGIO FRANCESCO, social scientist; b. Livorno, Tuscany, Italy, Jan. 13, 1943; s. Enrico Maria and Verna (Foran) S.; B.A. in Econs., Cornell U., 1965; m. Liane Gray Cooper, Apr. 22, 1962; children—Sergio, Christine. Dir. research New Brunswick Newstart, Inc., Can., 1969-74; sr. policy analyst Dept. Regional Econ. Expansion, Govt. of Can., Ottawa, Ont., 1974-77, sr. policy analyst Dept. Nat. Health and Welfare, 1977—. Mem. Am. Acad. Polit. and Social Sci., Rural Sociol. Soc. Contbr. articles in field to profl. jours. Home: 555 Churchill Ave Ottawa ON Canada Office: Brooke-Claxton Bldg Tunney's Pasture Ottawa ON Canada

SISTEK, WALTER JOSEPH, cons. firm exec.; b. Balt., Jan. 4, 1940; s. Joseph and Margaret Agnes (Hughes) S.; B.S., U. Balt., 1968; m. C. Beverly Hartman, Nov. 4, 1961; children—Craig Joseph, Kiersten Anne. With Md. Nat. Bank, Balt., 1966-76, cons., v.p., dir. 1973-76; pres. Systech & Asso., Towson, Md., 1976—; pres. Aadels, Inc., Towson, Md., 1976—; sec., dir. Alexander & Michaels, 1976—. Mem. advisory com. Morgan State U., 1976—. Served with AUS, 1959-65. Mem. Assn. Internat. Consultants (founder, pres. 1971-73), Assn. Systems Mgmt. (past pres.). Roman Catholic. Home: 2825 Cubhill Rd Baltimore MD 21234 Office: 28 Alleghany Ave Suite 1307 Towson MD 21204

SITO, PETER STANLEY, mfg. co. exec.; b. Bklyn., Jan. 29, 1919; s. Thomas and Agnes (Novak) S.; student Acad. Advanced Traffic, 1945-47, econs. N.Y. U., 1947-49, Internat. Corr. Schs., 1950-52; m. Catherine J. Williams, Dec. 3, 1960. Supr. Chasers, Inc., cosmetics, Bklyn., 1945-50; asst. traffic mgr. Fairchild Engine & Airplane Corp., Farmingdale, N.Y., 1950-59; corporate traffic mgr. Staver Co., Inc., electronic components, Bay Shore, N.Y., 1959—; traffic adviser to Staver Thermal Products (U.K.) Ltd., Wickford, Essex, Eng. Instr. safe boating, conservation dept. N.Y. State Conservation Dept., 1968—. Served with USAAF, 1942-45. Decorated Purple Heart. Mem. Am. Soc. Traffic and Transp., Am. Soc. Internat. Execs., Internat. Platform Assn., U.S., Captree (treas. 1974—, bridge officer 1974—, mem. exec. com. 1974—, lt. comdr. 1974—) power squadrons. Contbr. articles on safe boating to mags. Home: 139 Bergen Ave West Babylon NY 11704 Office: 41-51 N Saxon Ave Bay Shore NY 11706

SITTEL, KARL, physicist; b. Frankfurt am Main, Germany, Oct. 10, 1916; s. Karl Wilhelm and Helene (Schmitt) S.; Master, Goethe U., Frankfurt Main, Germany, 1939, Ph.D., 1940; postgrad. Max Planck Inst. Biophysics, Frankfurt Main, 1946-47; m. Edith Emilia Ecker, May 16, 1953; 1 son, Frederick Karl. Came to U.S., 1947, naturalized, 1953. Research asso. Max Planck Inst. Biophysics, Frankfurt am Main, 1939-47; dir. Aerological Instrumentation Lab., German Marine Obs., Greifswald, Germany, 1941-45; physicist, group leader Naval Air Exptl. Sta., Phila., 1947-50; sr. staff physicist Franklin Inst., Phila., 1950-59; staff scientist, leader RCA, Moorestown, N.J., 1959-67; cons. scientist Gen. Electric Co., Phila., 1967—. Staff cons. Jefferson Med. Coll., 1953-56; partner Walsco Corp., Trenton, N.J., 1960-66; mem. radar workshop Def. Atomic Support Agy., 1962-67; asso. mem. Albert Einstein Med. Center Research Lab., 1969-71. Mem. council on basic scis. Am. Heart Assn., 1968—. Woehler Found. scholar, 1939-41. Mem. Elfun Soc., Am. Phys. Soc., Am. Inst. Physics, Sci. Research Soc. N.Am., Smithsonian Inst., Nat. Geog. Soc., N.Y. Acad. Scis., Franklin Inst. State Pa. Lutheran (mem. ch. council 1959-65). Club: Germantown Cricket (Phila.). Contbr. articles to profl. jours. Patentee in field. Home: 916 Denston Dr Ambler PA 19002 Office: POB 7560 Philadelphia PA 19101

SITTENFELD, ITAMAR, ins. co. exec.; b. Israel, Jan. 13, 1937; s. Erwin and Yocheved (Gruenberg) S.; came to U.S., 1965, naturalized, 1975; Asso. Applied Sci., N.Y.C. Community Coll., 1961; B.B.A., City U. N.Y., 1969; M.B.A., Fordham U., 1979; m. Anne-Marie A. Hausaux, June 24, 1963; 1 child, Eyal Thierry. Mgmt. analyst Dept. of Def., U.S. Army, Europe, 1962-65; accountant/cost-methods analyst Chem. Bank N.Y. Trust Co., N.Y.C., 1965-67; sr. systems analyst/project leader Programming Methods, Inc., N.Y.C., 1967-72, Computer Applications, Inc., N.Y.C., 1967-72; owner, gen. mgr. Silves, Ltd., N.Y.C., 1972-75; with Blue Cross and Blue Shield of Greater N.Y., N.Y.C., 1975—. Certified jr. engring. technician Inst. for Certification of Engring. Technicians; recipient declaration commendation City N.Y. Mem. Mu Gamma Tau. Home: 7 W 14th St New York City NY 10011

SIVOWITCH, ELLIOT NORMAN, museum specialist; b. Bklyn., Aug. 10, 1932; s. Jacob and Olga (Mirsky) S.; B.A., Syracuse U., 1954, A.M., 1957. Mus. specialist in telecommunications and electroacoustics Smithsonian Instn., Washington, 1961—. Mem. IEEE, Soc. Motion Picture and TV Engrs. (mgr. Washington sec. 1975-76), Audio Engring. Soc., Broadcast Edn. Assn., Am. Inst. Aeros. and Astronatuics, Catgut Acoustical Soc., Am. Radio Relay League. Editorial bd. Jour. Broadcasting, 1974—, Arno Press Hist. Studies in Telecommunications, 1974—. Home: 2122 Massachusetts Ave NW Washington DC 20008 Office: Div Electricity Smithsonian Inst Washington DC 20560

SJÖBERG, LEIF TORE, Scandinavian studies specialist; b. Boden, Sweden, Dec. 15, 1925; s. Ernst Albert and Maria Elisabeth (Falk) S.; came to U.S., 1958; Fil. kand., Uppsala (Sweden) U., 1952, Fil. mag., 1954, Fil. lic., 1968; m. Inger M. Wallervik, Jan. 31, 1959. Mem. faculty Vindelns (Sweden) Realskolan, 1954-56; lector King's Coll., Newcastle-upon-Tyne, Eng., 1956-58; lectr. Columbia U., 1958-65, asst. prof., 1965-68; asso. prof. Scandinavian studies and comparative lit. State U. N.Y., Stony Brook, 1968-72, prof., 1972—; mem. exec. com. N.Y. U. Colloquia on Comparative Lit., 1976—. Served with Swedish Army, 1947-48, 51. Decorated knight Royal Swedish Order Vasa; co-recipient Transl. award Swedish Acad., 1967, recipient Ida Bäckmann Stipendium, 1976. Mem. AAUP, Am. Scandinavian Found., Assn. Advancement Scandinavian Studies (v.p. 1965-67), Comparative Lit. Assn., Isländska sällskapet (Uppsala), Ibsen Soc. (Oslo). Translator: (with W.H. Auden) Markings (Dag Hammarskjöld), 1964, Selected Poems (Gunnar Ekelöf), 1971; A Reader's Guide to Gunnar Ekelöf's A Mölna Elegy, 1973; Pär Lagerkvist, 1976; editor Scandinavian sect. Twayne's World Authors Series, 30 books, 1965—. Home: 15 Claremont Ave New York City NY 10027 Office: German and Slavic Dept State U NY Stony Brook NY 11794

SKATOFF, MARY MARGARET, realtor; b. Boston, Apr. 16, 1921; d. Walter Joseph and Teresa (Morgan) Smith; student Mass. Real Estate Inst., 1967-70; m. Leonard Leo Skatoff, Sept. 29, 1940; children—Mary Jane Skatoff MacKay, Lenore Skatoff Stone, Leonard Leo. Founder, pres. Hatherly Realty, Rockland, Mass., 1962—; builder, designer Colonial Homes, 1973. Dir. Greater Brockton Multiple Listing Service, Inc., Rockland Credit Union; sec. Rockland Indsl. Devel. Commn., 1970-71, chmn., 1971-72. Recipient spl. commendation Nat. Conf. Christians and Jews, 1965. Mem. Greater Brockton Bd. Realtors (dir. 1970-72), Rockland C. of C., Mass. Assn. Real Estate Bds. (edn. com. 1972-73), Nat. Assn. Real Estate Bds., Nat. Fedn. Ind. Bus. Roman Catholic. Home: 275 Beach St Rockland MA 02370 Office: 437 Webster St Rockland MA 02371

SKEELS, DORR COVELL, ret. geologist, geophysicist; b. Wallace, Idaho, Aug. 6, 1908; s. Dorr and Blanche (Covell) S.; B.A., U. Mont., 1930; B.A., (Rhodes Scholar) Oxford (Eng.) U., 1933; Ph.D., Princeton U., 1936; m. Lydia Lowndes Maury, Sept. 19, 1934; children—David, Anne Skeels Kupersmith. Seismologist, Carter Oil Co., Tulsa, 1936-38; research geophysicist Standard Oil Co. (N.J.), N.Y.C., 1938-52; mgnt. asst. Imperial Oil Ltd., Edmonton, Ata., Can., 1952-55, sr. research asso., asst. mgr. exptl. research, Calgary, Can., 1955-56; research asso., Esso Prod. Research, Houston, 1966-71. Mem. Am. Assn. Petroleum Geologists, Am. Geophys. Union, Geol. Soc. Am. Democrat. Episcopalian. Contbr. to various sci. jours. Home and Office: 32 Chaffeeville Rd Storrs CT 06268

SKEEN, DAVID RAY, computer systems adminstr.; b. Bucklin, Kans., July 12, 1942; s. Claude E. and Velma A. (Birney) S.; B.A. in Mathematics, Emporia State U., 1964; M.S., Am. U., 1972, certificate in Computer Systems, 1973; m. Carol J. Stimpert, Aug. 23, 1964; children—Jeffrey Kent, Timothy Sean, Kimberly Dawn. Computer systems analyst to comdr.-in-chief U.S. Naval Forces, Europe, London, Eng., 1967-70; computer systems analyst Naval Command Systems Support Activity, Washington, 1970-73; dir. of data processing Office Naval Research, U.S. Navy Dept., Arlington, Va., 1973-78, dir. mgmt. info. systems Naval Civilian Personnel Command, Washington, 1978—; lectr. Inst. for Sci. and Pub. Affairs, 1973-76; cons. Electronic Data Processing Career Devel. Programs, 1975—; detailed to Pres.'s Reorgn. Project for Automated Data Processing, 1978. Pres. Fed. Automated Data Processing Users Group, Washington, 1978—. Served with USN, 1964-67. Recipient Outstanding Performance award, Interagy. Com. on Data Processing, 1976. Mem. Am. Mgmt. Assn., Assn. for Computing Machinery, Data Processing Mgmt. Assn. Contbr. articles to profl. jours. Home: 707 Forest Park Rd Great Falls VA 22066 Office: US Navy Dept Washington DC 20390

SKEGGS, HELEN R., microbiologist; b. Schuylkill Haven, Pa., Mar. 9, 1918; d. Hugh Todd and Mary (Standiford) Ryan; B.A., U. Wis., 1939; m. Paul L. Skeggs, Oct. 23, 1943. Med. technician Ohio Valley Gen. Hosp., Wheeling, W.Va., 1940-41, Meml. Hosp., Milford, Del., 1941, Women's Homeopathic Hosp., Phila., 1941-42; chemist Houdry Process Labs., Marcus Hook, Pa., 1942-43; research asst. pharmacology Sharp & Dohme, Glenolden, Pa., 1943-45, research asso. microbiol. chemistry, 1945-53; research asso. microbiol. chemistry Merck Sharp & Dohme, West Point, Pa., 1953-56; research asso. pharmacological chemistry, 1956-65, sr. research biologist clin. pathology, 1965-73, research fellow safety assessment, 1973-76, sr. research fellow, 1976—. Fellow AAAS, mem. Am. Soc. Microbiology, Med. Tech. Registry, Am. Soc. Clin. Pathologists, Am. Soc. Indsl. Microbiology, Am. Inst. Biol. Scis., N.Y. Acad. Sci., Am. Inst. Nutrition, Sigma Xi, Sigma Delta Epsilon (nat. pres. 1968-69, dir. 1971—). Contbr. numerous articles on microbial nutrition, microbiol. assay to sci. jours. Home: 505 Cricket Ave Ardsley PA 19038 Office: Merck Sharp & Dohme Research Labs West Point PA 19486

SKIADAS, GEORGE DEMETRIOS, physician; b. Messolongi, Greece, Apr. 23, 1924; s. Demetrios George and Argyre Demetri (Papanicolaou) S.; came to Can., 1958, naturalized, 1963; M.D., U. Athens, 1952; postgrad. U. Pitts., 1960; m. Angeline Pothitos, Feb. 2, 1958; children—Sophia, Diana-Argyre. Intern, Alexian Bros. Hosp., Chgo., 1953; resident radiology Montefiore Hosp., Pitts., 1954-56, Allegheny Gen. Hosp., Pitts., 1956-57; radiotherapy fellow U. Va. Hosp., Charlottesville, 1957-58; fellow Royal Victoria Hosp., Montreal, Que., Can., 1958-63; practice medicine specializing in radiology 1963—; mem. staff St. Justine Hosp., Montreal. Served with inf. Greek Army, 1947-50. Mem. Soc. Nuclear Medicine, Med. Assn. Athens, Coll. Gen. Practice Can., Can. Assn. Radiologists, Canadian Med. Assn., Coll. Physicians and Surgeons Can. Patentee in field. Address: 5253 Park Av 4th Floor Montreal PQ H2V 4P2 Canada

SKILLINGER, RICHARD THURMAN, transp. co. exec.; b. New Brighton, Pa., Oct. 7, 1936; s. Thurman Douglas and Florence Edna (Nicely) S.; student Geneva Coll., 1957-58; m. Marie George, Apr. 27, 1957; children—LuAnne, Nancy Lee. Terminal mgr. Helms Express Inc., Harrisburg, Pa., 1958-64; with Eazon Express Inc., various locations, 1964-70, dir. line haul, Pitts., 1969, regional mgr., 1970, ops. mgr. Preston Trucking Co. (Md.), 1970-76; v.p. ops. Hemingway Transport Inc., New Bedford, Mass., 1976—; mem. exec. policy com. T.E.I. Inc., 1978—. Elder, bd. dirs. Lutheran Ch. Served with USN, 1954-57. Mem. Am. Transp. Assn. (terminal ops. council), Am. Mgmt. Assn., Smithsonian Assos. Republican. Club: R.I. Country. Home: 1 Old Forge Rd Barrington RI 02806 Office: 438 Dartmouth St New Bedford MA 02740

SKINNER, DAVID COOPER, bookseller; b. Jersey City, Nov. 4, 1947; s. Samuel James and Elaine (Cooper) S.; A.B., Grinnell Coll., 1969; M.A., Northeastern U., 1973; m. Maureen Orman, Apr. 4, 1977. Mgr. optical lab., L. C. Optical Service, Cambridge, Mass., 1973-77; sole propr. Movie Madness Cinema Bookstore, Cambridge, 1977—. Mem. Am. Booksellers Assn. Home: 2 Arlington St Apt 2 Cambridge MA 02140 Office: 1642 Massachusetts Ave Cambridge MA 02138

SKINNER, JOHN HAYES, gerontologist; b. Elizabeth, N.J., Mar. 4, 1941; s. Rutherford Hayes and Florence (Biggs) S.; B.S., Va. State Coll., 1964; M.S., Columbia U., 1967, Ed.D., 1974; m. Beverly Jean Lanier, Oct. 26, 1973; children—Chad Malik, Jason Todd. Dir. recreation Mary Manning Walsh Home for Aged, N.Y.C., 1964-66; dir. recreation therapy Mt. Sinai Hosp. Services, Elmhurst, N.Y., 1967-69; sr. research scientist Biometrics-Gerontology Unit, N.Y. Dept. Mental Hygiene, N.Y.C., 1969-71; dir. research Nat. Council on Aging, Washington, 1971-74; regional program evaluation officer HEW, Region III, Phila., 1974-77; exec. dir. Phila. Health Mgmt. Corp., 1977—; cons., lectr. in field. Social Rehab. Services trainee, 1964-66; Adminstrn. Aging trainee, 1969-71. Mem. Gerontol. Soc., Nat. Caucus on Black Aged, Fed. Bus. Assn. Phila., Kappa Alpha Psi, Phi Delta Kappa, Kappa Delta Pi. Contbr. articles to profl. publs. Home: 10 Woodhurst Dr West Berlin NJ 08091

SKINNER, PATRICK JAMES, archbishop; b. St. John's, Nfld., Can., Mar. 9, 1904. Ordained priest Roman Cath. Ch., 1929; aux. to archbishop of St. John's, Nfld., Can., 1950; titular bishop of Zenobia, 1950-51; archbishop of St. John's, 1951—. Address: Basilica Residence POB 37 Bonaventure Ave St John's NF A1C 5H5 Canada

SKLADANOWSKI, DIANE MARIE, educator; b. Erie, Pa., Mar. 15, 1949; d. Chester Charles and Sophia Frances (Rogowski) S.; B.A. cum laude in Biology, Mercyhurst Coll., 1970; M.S. in Radiation Sci. and Protection, Rutgers U., 1971. Tchr. chemistry and physics Villa Maria Acad., Erie, Pa., 1973—. AEC fellow, 1970. Mem. Nat. Assn. Physics Tchrs., Health Physics Soc., Delta Epsilon Sigma. Roman Catholic. Home: 4350 Miller Ave Erie PA 16509 Office: 2403 West Lake Rd Erie PA 16505

SKLAR, S. HARVEY, pediatrician; b. N.Y.C., July 12, 1911; s. Jack and Tillie S.; B.S., City Coll. N.Y., 1933; M.S.P.H., Columbia U., 1934; M.D., Am. U., Beirut, Lebanon, 1939; m. Evelyn C. Boyle, Sept., 1942; children—Cheryl Lynne, Robyn Lynn, Hollis Lyne. Intern, North Hudson Hosp., 1939-40, Mt. Sinai Hosp., N.Y.C., 1941; resident in pediatrics Henrietta Egelston Hosp., Atlanta, 1941-42, Willard Parker Hosp. Contagious Diseases, N.Y.C., 1945, N.Y. Med. Coll., 1946; practice medicine specializing in pediatrics and clin. virology, Cliffside Park, N.J., 1946—; mem. staff Englewood (N.J.) Hosp., 1947—, Holy Name Hosp. Served to maj. U.S. Army, 1942-46. Diplomate Am. Bd. Pediatrics. Fellow Am. Acad. Pediatrics, Am. Pub. Health Assn., Royal Soc. Health (London); mem. AMA, N.J. State, Bergen County med. socs., N.J. State Pediatric Soc. Office: 647 Anderson Ave Cliffside Park NJ 07010

SKOLE, RICHARD DAVID, microbiologist; b. Pittsfield, Mass., Oct. 5, 1927; s. Jacob and Estelle Jean (Plotzky) S.; student Purdue U., 1945-48; B.S., U. Ariz., 1949; M.S., La. State U., 1951; m. Marcia Helen Lightstone, Sept. 23, 1956; 1 son, Michael James. Pres., Skole Ice Cream Co., Pittsfield, 1951-56; with quality control dept. Dairymen's League Coop. Assn., N.Y.C., 1956-57; indsl. microbiologist, lab. supr. Lewis Research Labs., Englewood, N.J., 1957-60; mgr. biol. research Amstar Corp., Bklyn., 1960—; asso. referee microbiol. tests Internat. Commn. for Uniform Methods of Sugar Analysis, 1970—. Judge Am. Inst. of City of N.Y., 1960—; active West Side Republican Club, 1960-68. Mem. Am. Soc. Microbiology, Soc. Indsl. Microbiology, Internat. Assn. Milk, Food and Environ. Sanitarians, Inst. Food Technologists. Republican. Jewish. Contbr. articles to sci. publs. Home: 94-01 58th Ave Elmhurst NY 11373 Office: 266 Kent Ave Brooklyn NY 11211

SKULSKI, ANDRONIK EMIL, pharmacist; b. Uniw, Ukraine, Oct. 25, 1928; s. Joseph and Melania (Redczuk) S.; came to U.S., 1960, naturalized, 1967; B.S., Sao Joaquim Coll. Philosophy, Lorena, Brazil, 1952; B.S., Fluminense Coll. Pharmacy, Rio de Janeiro, Brazil, 1959; m. Oksana Magockyj, Sept. 16, 1961; children—Myron, Goerge, Mark. Packaging supr. Merck-Sharp-Dohme, Brazil, 1958-61; with Fleuroma Fragrances, N.Y.C., 1961-64; tableting supr. Davis-Edwards Pharm. Co., Bronx, N.Y.C., 1964-67; research asst., research and devel. div. Pfizer Co., Bklyn., 1967-71; pharm. scientist, research and devel. div. Vick Co., Mt. Vernon, N.Y., 1971—. Mem. Am. Pharm. Assn., Ukrainian Med. Assn. Republican. Ukrainian Catholic. Office: 54 Vista Rd Wilton CT 06897

SKUPINSKI, BOGDAN KAZIMIERZ, artist; b. Poland, July 16, 1942; s. Kazimierz Stanislaw and Jrena Lucja (Kanar) S.; came to U.S., 1971, naturalized, 1976; B.A., Acad. Fine Arts, Krakow, Poland, 1969, M.A., 1971; certificate Ecole Nationale Superieure de Beaux Arts, Paris, 1971. Graphic artist; paintings include Proclamation, 1968, Escape, 1968, Return, 1969, Good Journey (permanent collection N.J. State Mus. 1971), The Stable, (permanent collection Library of Congress), 1971, Nouvel ordre, (annual prize Ministry of Cultural Affairs of France), 1970, Gare du Nord (award Commn. Fine Arts, Paris), 1970; pres. The MacMurchy Co. (N.Y.C.). Recipient Grand Prix, Nat. Salon Young Artists, 1968, People's Choice award 2nd Nat. Graphic Review, Krakow, 1969, annual Bartoczek and Bobrowski award Polish Ministry of Art and Culture, Warsaw, 1970, Cannon prize for graphics NAD, N.Y.C., 1971, 1st prize for prints and drawings Nat. Conn. Acad. Exhbn., Hartford, 1971; sci. fellow Acad. Fine Arts, Ecole Nationale Superieure de Beaux Arts, Kosciuszko Found.; fellow Pratt Inst. Mem. NAD, Conn. Acad. Fine Arts, Pratt Inst., Kosciuszko Found. Democrat. Roman Catholic. Graphic art includes anti-war themes, life and work of John F. Kennedy and Albert Michelson, 1969-76. Home: PO Box 849 215 W 104th St Cathedral Sta New York City NY 10025

SKURDENIS, JULIANN V., educator; b. Bklyn., July 13, 1942; d. Julius J. and Anna M. (Zilys) Skurdenis; A.B. with honors, Coll. New Rochelle, 1964; M.S., Columbia U., 1966; M.A., Hunter Coll., 1974; m. Lawrence J. Smircich, Aug. 21, 1965 (div. July 1978); m. 2d, Paul J. Lalli, Oct. 1, 1978. Young adult librarian Bklyn. Pub. Library, 1964-66; periodicals librarian, instr. Kingsborough Community Coll., Bklyn., 1966-67; acquisitions librarian Pratt Inst., Bklyn., 1967-68; acquisitions librarian, asst. prof. Bronx (N.Y.) Community Coll., 1968-75, head tech. services, asso. prof., 1975—. N.Y. State fellow, 1960-66, Columbia U. fellow, 1964-66, Pratt Inst. fellow, 1965. Mem. AAUP, NOW, N.Y. Library Assn., Library Assn. City U. N.Y., City U. N.Y. Women's Coalition. Author: Walk Straight thru the Square, 1976; More Walk Straight thru the Square, 1977. Office: Bronx Community Coll University Ave and 181st St Bronx NY 10453

SLABY, LOUIS RICHARD, cons. engr.; b. Cleve., Dec. 13, 1941; s. Louis and Helen Anne (Kovachs) S.; B.S.M.E., U. Pitts., 1965; M.B.A., Baruch Sch. Bus., 1970; postgrad. Rutgers U. Sch. Engring., 1972; m. Virginia Antoinette Remick, Jan. 22, 1966; children—Richard, Laura. Cons. engr. Richard A. Alaimo Assos., Passaic, N.J., 1974—; profl. football player Detroit Lions, 1966, N.Y. Giants, 1963-65; plant engr. Thomas J. Lipton, Inc., Flemington, N.J., 1968-74; cons. to various municipal agys. Registered profl. engr., N.J., Ohio, Pa. Mem. Am. Water Works Assn., ASME (asso.), Nat. Soc. Profl. Engrs., Hunterdon C. of C. (1st v.p. 1972-73). Lutheran. Club: Rotary. Home: 6 Elder Pl Denville NJ 07834 Office: 1 Howe Ave Passaic NJ 07055

SLACHTA, GREGORY ANDREW, urologist; b. Paterson, N.J., Mar. 17, 1946; s. Andrew Gregory and Mary Catherine (Shimko) S.; B.S., Pa. State U., 1966; M.D., Jefferson Med. Coll., 1968; m. Elaine Harrison, Sept. 3, 1967; children—Gregory Andrew, Lara Ann. Intern, Lankenau Hosp., Phila., 1968-69, resident gen. surgery, 1969-70; resident urology Temple U. Hosp., Phila., 1970-71, 73-75; practice medicine specializing in urology, Springfield, Mass., 1975—; mem. staffs Baystate Med. Center, Mercy Hosp.; cons. Shriners Hosp. for Crippled Children; clin. instr. surgery (urology) Tufts Med. Sch. Bd. dirs. Greater Springfield unit Am. Cancer Soc., chmn. profl. edn. com., 1978-79. Served to maj. M.C., U.S. Army, 1971-73. Decorated Army Commendation medal. Diplomate Am. Bd. Urology. Mem. AMA, Am. Fertility Soc., Am. Urol. Assn., Mass., Hampden Dist. med. socs., Springfield Acad. Medicine, A.C.S. Roman Catholic. Home: 9 Metacomet Rd Longmeadow MA 01106 Office: 120 Maple St Springfield MA 01103

SLACK, FLORENCE KANTOR (MRS. MELVIN F. SLACK), educator; b. N.Y.C.; d. Philip and May (Kreiness) Kantor; B.A., Hunter Coll., 1960, M.S., 1962; M.A. in Psychology, New Sch. for Social Research, 1972; m. Melvin F. Slack, Sept. 5, 1942; 1 dau., Brenda. With FHA, San Diego, 1943-45; tchr. Drake Bus. Sch., N.Y.C., 1961-62; tchr. N.Y.C. Bd. Edn., 1963—, coop. edn. coordinator Walton High Sch., Bronx, 1974-75, tchr. bus. lab.-bus. edn., 1976—; mem. Am. Research Centre in Egypt. Fellow Internat. Biog. Assn.; mem. Internat. Platform Assn., Kappa Delta Pi, Delta Pi Epsilon (chpt. newsletter editor Highlights 1963-67). Home: 9 Farrant Dr Parsippany NJ 07054 Office: Fort Hamilton High Sch 8301 Shore Rd Brooklyn NY 11209

SLACK, GEORGE HENRY, ins. co. exec.; b. Boston, July 9, 1926; s. George Henry and Geraldine Mary (Judge) S.; A.A., Suffolk U., 1950, J.D., 1959; grad. Exec. Program, Ind. U. Grad. Sch. Bus., 1964; m. Virginia Ann Lane, Oct. 30, 1954; children—Elizabeth Ann, Katherine Mary, Christopher Lee, Kevin Michael. Home office claims examiner Employers of Wausau, 1950-61; group mgr. br. ops. Am. States Ins. Co., 1961-64; claims mgr. Forum Ins. Co., 1964-66; asst. sec. Reins. Corp. N.Y., 1966-69; 2d v.p. Covenant Group, Hartford, Conn., 1969-70, v.p. ops., 1970-76; v.p. Security Group, 1976—. Co. chmn. United Fund, 1971-72; mem. fund raising com. YMCA, 1972-74; mem. fin. com. West Hartford Youth Hockey Assn., 1971—. Served with USNAF, 1943-46; PTO; with USAF, 1951-53; Korea. Recipient United Fund award, 1971-72. Mem. Ins. Assn. Conn., Am. Ins. Assn. Claim Exec. Council, Fedn. Ins. Counsel, New Eng. Claim Exec. Assn., Loss Exec. Assn., Am. Mgmt. Assn., Surplus Lines Assn., AIM. Republican. Roman Catholic. Clubs: Univ. of Hartford, Shennecossett Yacht, Pocasset Country, Lions. Home: 53 Wardwell Rd West Hartford CT 06107 Office: 1000 Asylum Ave Hartford CT 06101

SLADE, WALTER RALEIGH, JR., neurologist; b. Knightsdale, N.C., Nov. 11, 1918; s. Walter Raleigh and Blonnie (Pair) S.; B.S., St. Augustine's Coll., 1939; M.D., Meharry Med. Coll., 1947; m. Ruth Dealya Sims, Feb. 2, 1947. Tchr. math. Risley High Sch., Brunswick, Ga., 1939-40, Edenton (N.C.) Pub. Schs., 1940-44; intern Harlem Hosp., N.Y.C., 1947-48; resident in internal medicine Jewish Chronic Disease Hosp., 1948-50, chief resident, resident neurology, 1950-52; resident psychiatry VA Hosp., Bklyn., 1952-54, staff neurologist and psychiatrist, 1954-69, chief neurology, 1970—; clin. asso. prof. neurology State U. N.Y., Bklyn., 1973—; attending neurologist Kings County, Kingsbrook Jewish, Samaritan hosps. (all Bklyn.), Gracie Square Hosp., N.Y.C., Mat. Bapt. Camps, Boy Scouts. Diplomate Am. Bd. Psychiatry and Neurology. Fellow Am. Acad. Neurology, Am. Coll. Angiology (v.p. 1976); mem. AMA, Bklyn. Neurol. Soc. (pres. 1972) Bklyn. Psychiatry Soc., Kings County Med. Soc., Am. Geriatric Soc., Nat. Med. Assn., Am. Psychiat. Assn. Editor Jour. Angiology, 1971—. Home: 1344 E 22d St Brooklyn NY 11210 Office: 800 Poly Pl Brooklyn NY 11209

SLANETZ, CHARLES ARTHUR, JR., surgeon; b. Sayville, N.Y., Jan. 30, 1933; s. Charles Arthur and Madilyn Katherine (Geiger) S.; B.S. magna cum laude, Yale, 1953, M.D., 1957; m. Nancy Ann Edwards, July 16, 1960; children—Alfred Edwards, Priscilla Jennings, Carolyn Abigail, Phoebe Gillette. Intern, then resident in surgery Presbyn. Hosp., N.Y.C., 1957-63, clin. asst. surgeon, 1965—; attending surgeon Glen Cove (N.Y.) Community Hosp., 1970—; clin. asst. surgeon Columbia Presbyn. Med. Center, 1965—; instr. Columbia Coll. Physicians and Surgeons. Served to lt. comdr. USN, 1963-65. Diplomate Am. Bd. Surgery. Fellow A.C.S., N.Y. Colon and Rectal Soc. (exec. council 1975), N.Y. State, Nassau County med. socs., Phi Beta Kappa, Sigma Xi. Republican. Episcopalian. Club: Beaver Dam Winter Sports. Author articles, revs. in field. Home: 107 Ayer Rd Locust Valley NY 11560 Office: 10 Medical Plaza Glen Cove NY 11542

SLATCHER, WILLIAM AUGUSTUS, city ofcl.; b. Laurel, Del., Jan. 10, 1926; s. Augustus and Emma L. (Thomas) S.; student Salisbury State Tchrs. Coll., 1948; m. Virginia Ruth Starnes, Jan. 17, 1945; children—Jennifer, Craig Stephen, Maribeth. Electrician, E.I. duPont de Nemours & Co., Seaford, Del., 1945-54; elec. contractor Bill's Elec. Service, Seaford, 1954—; mem. council ministries State Del., 1970-73; pres. Del. League Govt., 1976—; mayor City of Seaford, 1969—. Served with USNR, 1942-45. Decorated Air medal with oak leaf cluster, Purple Heart. Methodist (dist. lay leader 1970—, mem. bd. properties 1970-73). Clubs: Lions (pres. 1969-70), Elks. Home: 522 Phillips St Box 86 Seaford DE 19973 Office: 1605 Middleford Rd Seaford DE 19973

SLATER, FORD CHAPMAN, bus. exec.; b. Detroit, July 30, 1932; s. Francis Marion and Ruby Julia (Chapman) S.; B.A. with honors, Mich. State U., 1954; m. Beverly Jane Martin, June 21, 1952; children—Jeffrey Todd, Michael Francis, Karen Lee, Kevin Gregory. With Gen. Electric Co., 1956—; with jet engine dept., Cin., 1956-58, mem. advt. and sales promotion dept., Schenectady, 1959-65, with light bulb dept., 1965-66, pub. relations exec., N.Y.C., Fairfield, Conn., 1967-76, mgr. communications resources, Fairfield, 1976—. Dir. Westport-Weston, Conn. United Fund; chmn. citizens advisory com. to Mayor, Glenville, N.Y. Served with USAF, 1954-56. Mem. Nat. Elec. Mfrs. Assn., Direct Mail Advt. Assn., Delta Sigma Phi, Alpha Delta Sigma. Republican. Congregationalist. Home: 11 Mary Jane Ln Westport CT 06880 Office: 3135 Easton Turnpike Fairfield CT 06431

SLATER, HELENE FORD SOUTHERN, pub. relations exec.; b. Phila.; d. William Bette and Henrietta Harriet (Ford) Southern; B.A., New Sch. for Social Research, 1955, M.A., 1959; postgrad. Yeshiva U., Coll. City N.Y., Fordham U., Temple U., Howard U.; m. Chester E. Slater, June 22, 1955 (div. Dec. 1968). Reporter, columnist, feature writer various newspapers, 1940—; pres. Southern-Slater Enterprises, pub. relations, N.Y.C., 1955—; supr. Bur. Attendance, Bd. Edn. City N.Y., 1970-73. Pub. relations officer Shirley Chisholm Community Action Corp., 1972. Recipient Outstanding Community Person award Radio Sta. WWRL, 1965; Achievement award Lambda Kappa Mu, 1971, Citation of Merit, 1973, Outstanding Soror of Yr., 1967, Distinguished Service Key, 1977. Mem. Nat. Assn. Media Women (nat. pub. relations dir. 1973—, Pres.'s award 1971, Founder's cup 1974), Nat. Assn. Coll. Women, N.Y.C. Howard U. Alumni (pres. 1975—), Nat. Assn. Negro Bus. and Profl. Women's Clubs. Editor: The Acorn, Lambda Kappa Mu Sorority Ann. House Organ, 1960-65, 78—; The Media Woman, Nat. Assn. Media Women Ann. House Organ, 1966-67. Home: 360 W 22d St New York City NY 10011

SLATER, MIRIAM, historian; b. Bklyn., Aug. 22, 1931; A.B., Douglass Coll., 1963; Ph.D., Princeton U., 1971; m. Paul Slater, May 1, 1948; children—Margaret, Leo. Sec., N.J., 1953-57; farmer, N.J., 1957-59; instr. Princeton U., 1969; asst. prof. history, master Dakin House, Hampshire Coll., Amherst, Mass., 1970-73, asso. prof. history, 1973—; charter mem. Com. for Concerns of Women in N.E. Colls. Woodrow Wilson fellow, 1964, 67; Davis Center fellow, 1973; Mellon Found. Wellesley fellow, 1979. Mem. AAUW, Am. Hist. Assn., Phi Beta Kappa. Office: Hampshire College Amherst MA 01002

SLATER, SIDNEY DONALD, investment banker; b. N.Y.C., Apr. 8, 1927; s. Moses and Rose (Warshaw) S.; B.A. cum laude, Syracuse U., 1949; M.A., Columbia, 1951, postgrad., 1955; m. Eve Munzer, Mar. 7, 1953; children—Donald, Julia. Investment cons. Standard & Poor's Corp., N.Y.C., 1951-53; lectr. econs. U. Conn., lectr. accounting and finance Upsala Coll., 1954-55; investment banking and dir. research Shields & Co., N.Y.C., 1955-58; investment banking and research Blyth, Eastman, Dillon & Co., N.Y.C., 1958-61, E.F. Hutton & Co., N.Y.C., 1962-64; pres. Good Rds. Machinery Corp., pres. MainTek, Inc., Canton, Ohio, 1965-67; pres. Amadon Corp., Boston, 1964—; lectr. econs. Babson Coll., Wellesley, Mass. Served with USNR, 1945-46. Mem. N.Y. Soc. Security Analysts, Boston Investment Club, Boston C. of C. (Exec. Club), Smaller Bus. Assn. New Eng., New Eng. Council, Tabard, Pi Sigma Rho, Pi Gamma Mu, Theta Beta Phi. Unitarian (chmn. finance com.). Author: The Strategy of Cash: A liquidity approach to maximizing the company's profits, 1974. Home: 21 Alden Rd Wellesley Hills MA 02181 Office: 31 Milk St Boston MA 02109

SLATER, THOMAS CORTLAND, chemist; b. Johnstown, Pa., Apr. 12, 1942; s. John C. and Hazel (Jones) S.; B.S., U. Pitts., 1965; postgrad. Indiana U. of Pa., 1966-68; m. Joanne Grembi, Sept. 1, 1962; 1 dau., Michele. Technologist, Conemaugh Valley Meml. Hosp., Johnstown, 1961-67, chief technologist, 1967-70; dir. labs. Slater Labs. Inc., Johnstown, 1970—; cons. Pa. State Rehab. Center Lab. Mem. Am. Assn. Bioanalysts, Pa. Assn. Clin. Labs. Republican. Clubs: Sunnehanna Country, Bachlors. Home: 1051 Goucher St Johnstown PA 15905 Office: 1111 Franklin St Johnstown PA 15905

SLATTERY, BRADLEY, writer; b. Vicksburg, Miss., Dec. 19, 1917; s. John Rodolph and Elizabeth Virginia (Bradley) S.; B.S. in Econs., N.Y. U., 1941; M.A. in Sociology, The New Sch., 1953; m. Barbara Redka, Oct. 2, 1966; 1 child—Carolee Slattery Webb. Owner, pub. Brad Lee Publs., Forest Hills, N.Y., 1951—; spl. assignment investigator Weisman Celler et al, N.Y.C., 1976-77; adminstr. IBI Security Services Inc., Jamaica, N.Y., 1971-74; critic for Nat. Writers' Club, Denver, 1968—; instr., coach Stevens Inst. Tech., Hoboken, N.J., 1946-49. Served with USAF, 1942-46. Recipient trophy for winning Timberpoint Doubles Championship in tennis, 1941; hon. mention Nat. Writers Club contest, 1959. Mem. Nat. Writers' Club (pres. N.Y.C. chpt. 1963-64, program chmn. 1961-70), Sigma Phi Epsilon (v.p. alumni bd. 1967-68), Internat. Platform Assn. Congregationalist. Author: So This Is Life, 1948; co-author: Your Store, 1949; author numerous pamphlets on social topics. Address: Box 8 Forest Hills NY 11375

SLATTERY, PAUL DAVID, psychologist; b. Lakewood, Ohio, May 5, 1942; s. Matthew Thomas and Mary Elizabeth (Pollack) S.; B.A., Am. U., 1971; M.A., U. Md., 1975; m. Janina Maria Bonczek, Aug. 8, 1970; 1 dau., Carolyn. Vol., Peace Corps, Chile, 1965-67, program officer, Washington, 1969-71; selection asso. Am. Psychol. Assn., Washington, 1971-72; personnel analyst Arlington County (Va.), 1975-76; research asso. Inst. for Behavior Research, Silver Spring, Md., 1974—; sr. analyst Gen. Research Corp., McLean, Va., 1976—; job devel. cons. Independent Found., Washington, 1975—. Mem. Am. Psychol. Assn. (asso.), Biofeedback Soc. Am., Md. Beekeepers Soc., D.C. Md. Biofeedback Soc. Office: Inst Behavior Research/BBC 2429 Linden Ln Silver Spring MD 20910

SLAVIK, JULIE CONSTANCE BRES (MRS. JURAJ LUDEVIT JAN SLAVIK), orgn. exec.; b. Wallace, Idaho, July 8, 1936; d. Allen Vincent and Frances (Jordan) Bres; B.A., Vassar Coll., 1958; m. Juraj Ludevit Jan Slavik, May 13, 1961; children—Juraj Michal Daniel II, William Nicolas Allen. Adminstrv. asst. Govt. Affairs Inst., 1959-61; sec. to gen. counsel Textile Mfrs. Inst., 1962-65; office mgr. Jr. League Washington, 1965-77; exec. dir. St. Francis Burial and Counseling Soc., Inc., Washington, 1977-78; adminstrv. sec. ednl. programs Sister Cities Internat., 1979—. Mem. jr. guild Davis Meml. Goodwill Industries, Washington, 1965-70; corr. sec. Washington Antiques Show, 1972; sec. Parents Assn. St. Patrick's Episcopal Day Sch., 1971-72; chmn. ball Washington chpt. Czechoslovak Nat. Council, 1965, mem. ball exec. com., 1971. Bd. dirs. St. Stephen's Community Center, 1964-69, pres., 1966-67, sec., 1967-69; bd. dirs. Modern Dance Soc., 1976—; mem. adv. bd. Rose Sch./Family Center, 1976-77; trustee St. Patrick's Episcopal Day Sch., 1976-77, exec. com. capital fund dr., 1973—; bd. dirs. St. Andrews Episcopal Sch., 1977-78, Jr. League, Washington. Episcopalian (aux. vestry 1971-73, mem. calling com. for new rector, mem. music, finance fund raising, organ, worship coms., choir, vestrywoman 1973-75, worship and nominating coms., parish register and vestrywoman 1977—, also mem. exec., worship and search coms., lic. lay leader/chaliast Diocese of Washington). Home: 5264 Loughboro Rd NW Washington DC 20016 Office: 1625 I St NW Suite 424 Washington DC 20006

SLAVIN, RICHARD EDWARD, III, historic site ofcl.; b. Washington, May 14, 1938; s. Richard Edward and Frances Temple (Haislip) S.; B.A., George Washington U., 1960, postgrad. 1965-66; M.A., State U. N.Y. at Oneonta, 1967. Illustrator, USN, Indian Head, Md., 1962, U.S. Army C.E., Gravelly Point, Va., 1963-65; asst. curator Carriage and Harness Mus., Cooperstown, N.Y., summer 1967; curator collections Valentine Mus., Richmond, Va., 1967-68; curator Olana Historic Site, N.Y. State Hist. Trust, Hudson, N.Y., 1968-73, dir. site, 1973-75; asso. curator, adj. prof. N.Y. State Hist. Assn., Cooperstown, 1975—; attended Am. Friends of Attingham Summer Sch., Eng., 1975; cons. in field. Trustee Friends of Hyde Hall. Scriven Found. scholar, 1967. Recipient Service award Hendrick Hudson chpt. D.A.R., 1973. Mem. Cooperstown Alumni Assn., Am. Victorian Soc., N.Y. State Hist. Assn., Nat. Trust Historic Preservation, Friends of Olana, Royal Oak Found., Tau Kappa Epsilon. Address: RD 2 Box 447 Cooperstown NY 13326

SLAVIN, WILLIAM MICHAEL, clergyman; b. Waterford, N.Y., Nov. 17, 1907; s. Augustin F. and Elizabeth A. (Fitzpatrick) S.; A.B., Georgetown U., 1929; M.A., St. Bonaventure U., 1930; postgrad. Christ the King Sem., 1930-34. Ordained priest Roman Catholic Ch., 1934; pastor Our Lady of Victory Ch., Troy, N.Y., 1959—; tchr. Cath. schs., Troy, 1934-41; resident Cath. chaplain Rensselaer Poly. Inst., 1936-41, 1946-59; named to rank Papal Chamberlain, 1959. Mem. Urban Renewal com. City of Troy, City of Troy Human Rights Commn.; bd. dirs. Rensselaer County chpt. ARC, Rensselaer County Mental Health Bd., Family and Childrens Service of Troy, LaSalle Inst., Cath. Central High Sch. of Troy, Community Mental Health Bds. Assn. of N.Y. State; pres. bd. trustees Troy Pub. Library; bd. govs. Georgetown U. Alumni Assn.; bd. consultors Diocese of Albany. Served in Chaplain Corps, USNR, 1942-46. Mem. Phi Kappa Theta. Clubs: Troy Country; Army and Navy of N.Y.; Lake Placid. Home: 55 N Lake Ave Troy NY 12180

SLAVIT, MICHAEL ROY, counseling therapist; b. Providence, Aug. 3, 1948; s. Leonard Albert and Irma Constance Slavit; student Bates Coll., 1966-68; A.B. in Psychology, Brown U., 1970; M.A. in Counselor Edn., U. R.I., 1975. Social caseworker South County Regional Center, North Kingstown, R.I., 1971-73; counseling intern Counseling Center, U. R.I., Kingston, 1974-75, lectr. extension div., 1976—; social caseworker Dr. Joseph H. Ladd Sch., Exeter, R.I., 1975—; instr. R.I. Municipal Police Tng. Acad., 1976; pvt. practice counseling therapy, 1978—; lectr., discussion leader Providence Alternative Learning Center, 1977. Instr. water safety ARC, 1967—. Mem. Am. Personnel and Guidance Assn., R.I. Assn. for Retarded Citizens. Club: Appalachian Mountain. Home: 292 Morris Ave Providence RI 02906 Office: 1052 Main St Warren RI 02885

SLAVOV, EUGENIA MARGARET, educator; b. Reims, France, Feb. 18, 1925; d. Michael Alexander and Elisabeth Vladimir (Maximovitch) Hintze; came to U.S., 1956, naturalized, 1962; LL.D., U. Rome, 1954; certificate U. Paris, 1964, U. Del., 1965, 69; m. Assen Ivanov Slavov, Sept. 9, 1951. Accountant, corr. Sperrwaffenarsenal, Linz-Ebelsberg, Austria, 1944-45; interpreter, Hdqrs. Allied Command, Linz, Austria, 1945; tchr. Latin, Russian, Spanish, French, Tower Hill Sch., Wilmington, Del., 1957-64; mem. faculty U. Del., Newark, 1964—, asst. prof. Russian, German, French and Italian, 1965—. Mem. Am.-Swiss Soc., Am. Contract Bridge League, Am. Assn. U. Profs. Italian (rep. for Del.), Wilmington Friends Italian Culture, Am. Assn. Tchrs. German, Am. Assn. Tchrs. Slavic and East European Langs., Alliance Francaise, Internat. Studies Assn., Pi Delta Phi, Delta Phi Alpha. Home: Fiske Ln Newark DE 19711

SLAWINSKI, STANLEY ALOYSIUS, state ofcl.; b. Jersey City, Oct. 8, 1938; s. Stanley Aloysius and Mae (Kiczek) S.; B.A., Seton Hall U., 1960; M.A., Cath. U. Am., 1964, E. Carolina U., 1968; Ph.D., U. Sarasota, 1973; m. Suzanne A. Sobieski, Jan. 27, 1968; children—Jennifer Lyn, Stacia Marie, Mark Steven. Chief service Willowbrook Devel. Center, N.Y. State Dept. Mental Hygiene, S.I., 1972-75, dep. dir., 1975-76, acting dir., 1976-79; dir. bur. community assistance Gov.'s Council Drug and Alcohol Abuse, Pa., 1976—; dep. dir. (clin.) N.Y. State Dept. Mental Retardation, 1979—; preceptor Rutgers U., New Brunswick, N.J., 1974-76; cons. in field; prof. psychology Sullivan County Coll., 1968-70. Amerpol scholar, 1956-60; research grantee U. Sarasota, 1972-73. Certified rehab. counselor. Mem. Am. Assn. Marriage and Family Counselors (clin.), Am. Assn. Personnel and Guidance Counselors, Nat. Rehab. Vocat. Counseling Assn., Am. Vocat. Guidance Assn., Am. Assn. Mental Deficiency, Kappa Delta Pi. Club: K.C. (4 deg.). Contbr. articles to profl. publs. on mental health, mental retardation. Home: 107 Holly Dr Mechanicsburg PA 17055

SLAYMAKER, SAMUEL REDSECKER, II, writer; b. Lancaster, Pa., Jan. 1, 1923; s. Samuel Cochran and Martha (Fletcher) S.; B.A., Cambridge U. (England); m. Sarah Elizabeth (Hazzard) Oct. 25, 1959; children—Elizabeth Duncan, Caroline Morgan Hale, Susan Frances, Samuel Cochran. Sales rep. Slaymaker Lock Co., Lancaster, Pa., 1947-64, advt. mgr., 1950-73, exec. v.p., 1964-73, sec. bd. dirs., 1955-73; free lance author, 1976—; books include: Tie a Fly, Catch a Trout, 1976; Simplified Fly Fishing; Captives Mansion; lectr. in field. Mem. Lancaster County Mfrs. Assn., Sales Exec. Club Lancaster, Am. for Competetive Enterprise, Soc. of Cincinnati (Md.), Pa. Soc. Sons of Colonial Wars, Pa. Soc. Sons Revolution, Pa. Soc. War 1812, Lancaster County Hist. Soc., Donegal Soc., Hist. Found. Pa., Trout Unltd., Theodore Gordon Fly Fishers, Fly Fishing Fedn., Am. League Anglers, Brotherhood of the Jungle Cock. Clubs: Lancaster Country, Hamilton of Lancaster, UnionoLeague, Anglers of N.Y. Contbr. articles in field to outdoors mags. Home: Rural Route 2 White Chimneys Gap PA 17527

SLEDD, HASSELL BRANTLEY, educator; b. Spring Hope, N.C., May 9, 1926; s. Arthur Purefoy and Elsie Josephine (Brantley) S.; student Furman U., 1943-44; A.B., U. N.C., 1948, M.A., 1949; Ph.D., Boston U., 1965; m. Pauline Benedict Rogers, Dec. 27, 1959; children—Margaret Westray, Meredith Ann, Andrew Douglas, James Arthur. Instr. in English, N. Tex. State Coll., Denton, 1949-51; reservations clk. United Air Lines, N.Y.C., 1951-54; mail order copywriter Prentice-Hall, N.Y.C., 1954-57; mgr. subscription promotion Atlantic Monthly mag., Boston, 1957-59; lectr. English, Boston U., 1959-61, intern in communications, 1961-63; lectr. Northeastern U., Boston, 1959-61, instr., 1963-65, asst. prof. English, 1965-69; asso. prof. English, Slippery Rock (Pa.) State Coll., 1969-72, prof., 1972—. Served with AUS, 1944-46. Recipient Eben Alexander Greek prize, 1948. Mem. Shakespeare Assn. Am., Renaissance Soc. Am., Boston Browning Soc. (v.p. 1966-69), Browning Inst., Tennyson Soc., Modern Lang. Assn., Coll. English Assn., Bibl. Soc. Univ. Va., Phi Beta Kappa. Democrat. Episcopalian. Club: Slippery Rock Rotary (pres. 1972-73, youth exchange officer, 1970-72, 74-76). Editor: Poets at Northeastern, a Series, 1968-69; Poems, Essays and a Letter Presented to Everett C. Marston, June, 1968; Self Study at Slippery Rock for the Middle States Assn., 1970; Self Study for the Nat. Council for the Accreditation of Teacher Education, 1971. Home: 276 Normal Ave Slippery Rock PA 16057 Office: Slippery Rock State Coll Slippery Rock PA 16057

SLEIGHT, JESSIE ADELE, ret. editor; b. Stony Brook, L.I., N.Y.; d. Charles Mills and Adella Abigail (Bayles) S.; student pub. schs.; pvt. study piano, organ. Staff mem. Mus. Am., asst. to A. Walter Kramer, 1920-21; asst. to editor George Matthew Adams Service, N.Y.C., newspaper syndicate, 1922-34, editor, 1935-64; exec. editor Washington Star Syndicate, 1965-67; organist St. James Episcopal Ch., St. James, L.I., 1942-55. Mem. Authors League Am., English-Speaking Union. Episcopalian. Club: Woman Pays. Home: PO Box 73 Stony Brook NY 11790

SLENN, JOHN RAYMOND, elec. equipment co. exec.; b. Phila., Apr. 29, 1933; s. Samuel and Nancy (Sharpe) S.; B.S., Temple U., 1954, postgrad. in Bus. Adminstrn., 1957; m. Elizabeth J. Berry, June 8, 1957; children—Kurt J., Lisa A. Exec. trainee State Farm Ins. Co., 1956-57; employment supr. I-T-E Circuit Breaker Co., Phila., 1957-64, sales application engr., 1964-65; advt. mgr. I-T-E Imperial Corp., Phila., 1965-69, personnel mgr., 1969-76; mgr. employee relations Gould Inc., Phila., 1976—. Served with U.S. Army, 1954-56. Accredited personnel exec. Mem. Am. Soc. Personnel Adminstrn., Mfrs. Assn. of Del. Valley, Indsl. Relations Assn. of Phila., Phila. Survey Group, Am. Mgmt. Assn., Mensa Internat. Home: 719 Stockton Circle Ridley Park PA 19078 Office: 601 E Erie Ave Philadelphia PA 19134

SLEVIN, JOANNA HELEN, interior designer; b. Newark, Sept. 21, 1950; d. Murry Applebaum and Beatrice Ceceila (Botvenick) Applebaum Seinfeld; stepdau. Benjamin Seinfeld; B.A., N.Y. U., 1971; certificate N.Y. Sch. Interior Design, 1972; postgrad. Parsons Sch. Design, 1976—; m. Ronald Slevin, Nov. 22, 1972. Apprentice in interior design Clarence House, N.Y.C., 1972; propr. Joanna Slevin Interiors, Little Falls, N.J., 1973—. Active Montclair (N.J.) chpt. Multiple Sclerosis Soc.; interior design chmn. Tennis Super Ball, 1977, 78; v.p. gen. program Livingston (N.J.) chpt. Cancer Care, 1974-76, corr. sec., 1976-77. Jewish. Office: 181 Long Hill Rd Suite 9-9 Little Falls NJ 07424

SLITOR, RICHARD EATON, economist; b. St. Paul, July 1, 1911; s. Ray Francis and Nelle (Eaton) S.; student U. Wis., 1928-30; S.B. magna cum laude, Harvard U., 1932; Ph.D., 1940; M.A. (Carnegie Teaching fellow), Colgate U., 1934; m. Louise Bean, Dec. 24, 1937; children—Prudence Van Zandt Slitor Crozier, Deborah Beckwith, Nicholas Wentworth, Christopher Wells Eaton. Instr., tutor econs. Harvard U., 1934-41, Radcliffe Coll., 1940-41; asso. prof., chmn. dept. econs. and bus. adminstrn. Mt. Union Coll., 1941-42; economist U.S. Dept. Treasury, 1942-72, chief bus. taxation staff, office tax analysis, 1961-63, asst. dir., 1963-72; prof. econs. U. Mass. at Amherst, 1967-68; econ. cons. Rand Corp., NSF, HUD, Fed. Res. Advisory Commn. on Intergovtl. Relations, 1972-78; cons. Nat. Commn. on Urban Problems, Colombian Fiscal Commn., Bogota, 1968. Fed. exec. fellow The Brookings Instn., 1963-64. Mem. Am. Statis. Assn., Am. Econ. Assn., Internat. Inst. Pub. Fin., Royal Econ. Soc., Nat. Tax Assn., Phi Beta Kappa. Episcopalian. Club: Harvard (Washington). Author: Federal Income Tax in Relation to Housing; contbr. articles and studies on taxation to profl. jours. Home: 9000 Burning Tree Rd Bethesda MD 20034

SLIVKA, ROBERT MICHAEL, mgmt. cons.; b. Cleve., July 27, 1941; s. Michael Edward and Agness Bernice (Strouhal) S.; B.S., Denison U., 1963; M.A., Bryn Mawr Coll., 1963, postgrad., 1963-68. Research psychologist Franklin Inst. Research Labs., Phila., 1966-68; dir. evaluation N.J. Urban Schs. Devel. Council, Trenton, 1968-71; v.p. Multi-Media Assos., Inc., Tucson, 1971-76, cons. Communication Tech. Corp., Marlton, N.J., 1976—; adj. prof. psychology Drexel U., 1968, Pa. State U., 1969-71, Trenton State Coll., 1971. Mem. Am. Psychol. Assn., Am. Ednl. Research Assn., Sigma Xi, Psi Chi, Phi Delta Kappa. Contbr. articles in field to profl. jours. Home: 6 A Dennison Dr East Windsor NJ 08520 Office: 64 E Main St Marlton NJ 08053

SLIWINSKI, EDWARD ROBERT, civil engr.; b. N.Y.C., Aug. 27, 1920; s. Frank and Anna (Hruby) S.; B.C.E., Cooper Union Coll. 1947; M.C.E., Polytechnic Inst. Bklyn., 1950, postgrad. chem. engring., 1950-53. Surveyor, cost estimator Roth-Schenker Construction Corp., N.Y.C., 1946-47; holder various engring. position Mobil Oil Corp., N.Y.C., 1947-70; prin. engr. stress analysis EBASCO Services, Inc., N.Y.C., 1970-72, supr. engr. stress analysis, 1972—. Capt. Cooper Union Development Fund Dr., N.Y.C., 1957; instr. Jr. navigation course Bayside (N.Y.) Power Squadron, 1961-68, chmn. Jr. navigation, 1969-72, chmn. navigation 1973-75; 3rd dist. chmn. U.S. Power Squadron, L.I. area, 1971; fin. sec. Bayside Power Squadron, 1972-76. Served with U.S. Army 1942-46. Recipient contribution award ASME, Boiler and Pressure Vessel Com. 1970; profl. engr. N.Y., Mich. Mem. ASME (design analysis sub-group, chmn. working group spl. topics, 1976—, ad-hoc com. examination and inspection standards, 1976—, high pressure tech. sub-com. 1977—, code activities com. 1953—). Republican. Roman Catholic. Patentee in field.

SLOAN, ALBERT RAYMOND, mfg. co. exec.; b. Los Angeles, Oct. 2, 1926; s. Albert C. and Grace (Brown) S.; B.S. in Mech. Engring., U. Calif. at Los Angeles, 1949; postgrad. Harvard; m. Janet M. Kelley, June 25, 1949; children—Nancy L., Carol A., Laurie E., Andrew C. With Continental Can Co., 1949—, v.p., asst. gen. mgr. metal div., N.Y.C., 1969-72, v.p., gen. mgr. mfg. operations, Chgo., 1972—; pres. Continental Can Internat. Corp., 1977—. Served with USNR, 1944-46. Mem. Delta Sigma Phi. Roman Catholic. Office: 72 Cummings Pt Rd Stamford CT 06902

SLOAN, BURTON, physician; b. Bronx, N.Y., Mar. 10, 1927; s. David and Eva S.; B.A., N.Y. U., 1950; M.D., U. Bern (Switzerland), 1957; m. Nanda Agnetti, Jan. 26, 1957. Intern, L.I. Coll. Hosp., Bklyn., 1957-58; resident Bklyn. Vets. Hosp., 1958-61; asso. dir. medicine Lutheran Med. Center, Bklyn., 1977—; clin. asst. prof. medicine State U. N.Y., 1975—. Served with U.S. Army, 1945-46. Mem. AMA, A.C.P., N.Y. State, Am., Bklyn. socs. internal medicine, Kings County, Ray Ridge (pres. 1973) med. socs. Home: 8205 Narrows Ave Brooklyn NY 11209 Office: 8846 7th Ave Brooklyn NY 11228

SLOAN, STEPHEN, real estate exec.; b. N.Y.C., June 21, 1932; B.A., Washington and Lee U., 1954; m. Nannette Barkin, Feb. 24, 1957; children—Suzanne, Robert. Engaged in real estate, 1957—; partner Milton Barkin Mgmt., 1959-71; pres. Lehman Realty Corp., Lehman Bros. Kuhn Loeb, Inc., N.Y.C., 1971-74; chmn. bd. World Record Fishing Club, Inc., N.Y.C., 1975—; pres. World-Wide Realty Corp. subs. World-Wide Volkswagen, N.Y.C., 1974—; dir. Pacific Design Center, Los Angeles, Realty Found., Aquirre. Chmn. Masters Angling Tournament, 1976—; trustee Horace Mann Sch., 1971—; bd. dirs. Am. League Anglers Edn. and Research Found. Mem. Internat. Game Fish Assn., Internat. Oceanographic Assn., Am. League Anglers (dir.), Nat. Coalition for Marine Conservation. Jewish. Clubs: Explorers, Deep Sea, Chubb Cay, City Athletic. Home: 510 Park Ave New York City NY 10022 Office: 1 Dag Hammarskjold Plaza New York City NY 10017

SLOBODIEN, HOWARD DAVID, surgeon; b. Perth Amboy, N.J., July 25, 1923; s. Albert Leo and Anna Frances (Sontag) S.; B.S., Rutgers Coll., 1943; M.D., N.Y. U., 1947; m. Sally Doris Yerkes, May 9, 1950; children—David, Donald, Daniel, Douglas. Intern, Morrisania City Hosp., N.Y.C., 1947-48, resident, 1948-52; practice medicine specializing in surgery, Perth Amboy, 1955—; pres. John F. Kennedy Med. Center, Edison, N.J., 1967-70, dir. surgery, 1975—; attending surgeon Gen. Hosp., Perth Amboy, dir. surgery, 1970-74; chief gen. surgery, past pres. med. staff Roosevelt Hosp., Edison; cons. surgery Meml. Hosp., South Amboy; clin. asst. prof. surgery Rutgers Med. Sch., 1971—, mem. advisory council Office Consumer Health Edn., 1973—; mem. advisory council Middlesex County Coll., 1968-78; v.p. Regional Health Facilities Planning Council, 1970-73. Pack committeeman Cub Scouts, 1960-64; active steering com. Metuchen YMCA, 1962. Served with USNR, 1943-45, USAF, 1952-54. Diplomate Am. Bd. Surgery. Fellow A.C.S.; mem. World, Am., Pan-Am. med. assns., N.J. (trustee 1972—, chmn. pub. relations council 1973-76), Middlesex County (pres. 1970-71) med. socs., Pan-Pacific Surg. Assn., Am. Geriatric Soc., Royal Soc. Health, Am. Acad. Med. Adminstrs., Royal Soc. Medicine, N.J. Acad. Med. Adminstrs., Royal Soc. Medicine, N.J. Acad. Medicine (trustee 1974-78), Middlesex County Med. Assts. Assn. (county med. adviser 1973—), N.J. Soc. Surgeons, Phi Beta Kappa. Clubs: Metuchen Country, Innisbrook, N.Y. U. Home: 34 Linden Ave Metuchen NJ 08840 Office: 500 Lawrie St Perth Amboy NJ 08861

SLOSBERG, MIKE, advt. exec., author; b. Phila., Aug. 29, 1934; s. Sam M. and Florence Slosberg; B.S. in Bus. Adminstrn., Denver U., 1960; m. Joan Shidler, Aug. 29, 1957; children—Sydney Ellen, Robert. With Young & Rubicam, 1960-78, sr. v.p., asso. creative dir., N.Y.C., 1970-78; exec. v.p., gen. mgr. subs. Wunderman, Ricotta and Kline, Inc., 1978—; author: (novel) The August Strangers, 1977; (cartoons) Klan-Destined, 1965. Served with USAF, 1953-57. Clubs: Players, Overseas Press, Friars (N.Y.C.). Home: 31 Sturges Hwy Westport CT 06880 Office: Young & Rubicam 285 Madison Ave New York City NY 10017

SLOTKOFF, BEATRIZ FLORES, dancer, choreographer; b. Mexico City, Jan. 2, 1932; d. Mariano Saleme and Maria Antonieta (Castro) Flores; came to U.S., 1962; student Nat. Inst. Fine Arts, Mex., 1945-48, Internat. Inst. Interior Design, Washington, 1970-73; m. Lawrence Martin Slotkoff, May 17, 1962; children—Xavier, Douglas, Andrea. Prof. dance, choreographer Nat. Inst. Fine Arts, Mexico City, 1947-62; dancer with José Limon, Mex., 1950-54; dance dir., choreographer U. Xalapa, Veracruz, Mex., 1955-59; world tour, 1957; performer in Dreams, by Anna Sokolow, 1961, in Opus 60, 1961; dance rep. of Mexican Embassy, Washington, 1966-70; prin. of TV show, Mexico, 1954-55; leading role in Mexican film, Roots, 1954; dance instr., Washington, 1968-73; free-lance performer and interior designer, D.C. and Md., 1975—. Home: 4514 Drummond Ave Chevy Chase MD 20015

SLURZBERG, ELIHU (LEE), market research cons.; b. Newark, Mar. 22, 1929; s. Herman Harry and Mildred (Nemhauser) S.; B.S., N.Y. U., 1952; M.B.A., 1956; m. Nancy Hope Miller, Dec. 30, 1956; children—Michael, Wendy. Dir. mktg. services J.B. Williams Co., N.Y.C., 1962-65; v.p., dir. survey div. Audits & Surveys, Inc., N.Y.C., 1965-68; exec. v.p., chief exec. officer Alfred Politz Research div. Computer Scis. Corp., N.Y.C., 1968-70; pres. Lee Slurzberg Research Inc., N.Y.C., 1970—; adj. instr. mktg. Baruch Coll., City U. N.Y.; dir. Compusamp, Inc. Mem. N.J. Tercentenary Com., 1964. Served with U.S. Army, 1946-48. Named Outstanding Young Man of Yr., Englewood, N.J., 1963. Mem. Am. Mktg. Assn., Pharm. Advt. Club. Jewish. Contbr. articles in field to profl. jours. Home: 379 Windsor Rd Englewood NJ 07631 Office: 120 E 56th St New York City NY 10022

SLUSSER, EUGENE ALVIN, electronics mfg. co. exec.; b. Denver, Mar. 13, 1922; s. Jesse Alvin and Grace (Carter) S.; B.S. in Physics, U. Denver, 1947; m. Anne L. Longley, Oct. 2, 1943; children—Robert, Jon, Carolyn. Staff mem. Mass. Inst. Tech. Radiation Lab., Cambridge, 1942-45; project engr. Heiland Research Co., Denver, 1945-47; cons. Gen. Telephone System, N.Y.C., 1947-51; project engr. Airborne Inst. Lab., Mineola, N.Y., 1951-53; v.p. N.E. Electronics Corp., Concord, N.H., 1953-58; chmn. bd., pres. Aerotronic Assos., Inc., Contoocook, N.H., 1958—; pres. N.H. Automatic Equipment Corp., Concord, 1962—; dir. Indianhead Nat. Bank, Concord. Chmn., Hopkinton (N.H.) Water Bd., 1962-69, Hopkinton Planning Bd., 1971-73, Hopkinton Pct. Bd. Adjustment, 1977-78. Comml. pilot. Mem. Nat. Pilots Assn., Aircraft Owners and Pilots Assn. Club: Masons. Patentee electronics field. Home: RFD 1 Concord NH 03301 Office: Riverside Dr Contoocook NH 03229

SMALL, HAROLD MELVIN, venture capital co. exec.; b. Springfield, Mass., Nov. 6, 1915; s. Samuel and Rose (Webb) S.; B.S. in Chem. Engring., Northeastern U., 1939; m. Josephine W. Hempenius, Dec. 29, 1954; children—Doris L., David A. Sales engr.

Filtration Engrs., Inc., Newark, 1940-44, asst. sales mgr., 1944-46, v.p., sales mgr., 1946-56, v.p., gen. mgr., 1956-58; v.p. Stockdale Engring. Co., Haddonfield, N.J., 1958-60; gen. sales mgr. Buflovak div. Blaw-Knox Co., Buffalo, 1960-61, gen. mgr. Buflovak div., 1961-64, v.p., gen. mgr. food and chem. equipment div., 1964-66; exec. v.p. Conax Corp., Buffalo, 1966-68, pres., 1968-70, gen. mgr., 1966-70, also dir.; pres. M & T Capital Corp., 1971—; dir. Brantford Devel. Co., Comptek Research Inc., Gaymar Industries Inc., Gen. Data Comm. Inc., Gor-Den Industries Inc., Atlas Mineral & Chem. Co., Transcontinent Records Inc., Smith Pipe & Steel Co., Andeo Industries Inc. Mem. Am. Inst. Chem. Engrs., Instrument Soc. Am., Chemists Club. Home: 78 Brandywine Dr Williamsville NY 14221 Office: 1 M & T Plaza Buffalo NY 14240

SMALL, ROBERT VAN DYKE, psychologist; b. Abbeville, Ala., Nov. 29, 1924; s. John and Della S.; B.A. Morehouse Coll., 1949; M.A., Atlanta U., 1950; Ms.D., Am. Bible Inst., 1969; postgrad. in psychotherapy Rutgers U., Masterson Group, Inc., N.Y.C.; hon. degree in human service Inst. Community Service, Eng. Prof. psychology Mercer Coll., Trenton, N.J., 1969—; cons. clin. psychologist N.J. State Prison. Commr. human rights, Newark, 1974—. Served with AUS, 1942-45. Decorated Bronze Star. Mem. AAUP. Democrat. Presbyterian. Author: The Legal Slaughter of Peace, 1956; The Victim, 1968; Undercurrents, 1971; Confrontations with Hang-Ups, 1973; Darkness Where Light Fails to Shine, 1976. Home: 680 Summer Ave Newark NJ 07104

SMALL, STANLEY ALAN, dentist; b. N.Y.C., Mar. 2, 1934; s. Louis A. and Gertrude (Greenblatt) S.; student Alfred U., 1951-55; D.D.S., N.Y. U., 1963, postgrad. in oral surgery, 1965-66; m. Amy Kathman, Mar. 30, 1962; children—Samantha Beth, Gabrielle Anne. Resident in oral surgery Bklyn.-Cumberland Med. Center, 1963-64, chief resident in oral surgery, 1965-66; asst. to dir., asso. attending oral surgeon Cath. Med. Center Bklyn. and Queens, Inc., 1974—; clin. asso. prof. hosp. dentistry, clin. asst. prof. oral and maxillofacial surgery Fairleigh Dickinson Coll. Dentistry, 1974-78; asso. attending oral surgery White Plains (N.Y.) Hosp. Diplomate Am. Bd. Oral Surgery. Fellow Am. Dental Soc. Anesthesiology; mem. Am. Soc. Oral Surgeons, Alpha Omega. Home: 39 Horsechestnut Rd Briarcliff Manor NY 10510 Office: 170 Maple Ave White Plains NY 10601

SMALL, WILFRED THOMAS, surgeon, educator; b. Boston, June 13, 1920; s. Fred Wentworth and Isabelle (Scott) S.; B.S., Bowdoin Coll., 1943; M.D., Tufts U., 1946; m. Muriel Yoe Gratton, Sept. 25, 1948; children—Wilfred Thomas, Richard Gratton, James Stewart, John Wentworth. Intern surg. service The Boston Children's Hosp., 1946-47, then research fellow; asso. in surgery Peter Bent Brigham Hosp., Harvard U., 1949-50; resident, chief resident in surgery New Eng. Med. Center, Tufts U., 1950-53; practice medicine specializing in surgery, Worcester, Mass., 1953—; asso. prof. surgery U. Mass., 1973—; mem. staff Meml. Hosp., 1953—, chief div. surgery, 1973—; instr. Harvard U., 1949-50, Tufts U., 1952-60. Bd. dirs. Worcester Boys Club; mem. Worcester Art Museum, Worcester County Music Assn. Served to lt. (j.g.) USN, 1947-49. Diplomate Am. Bd. Surgery. Fellow A.C.S. (pres. elect Mass. chpt.); mem. New Eng. Surg. Soc., New Eng. Cancer Soc., Soc. Surgery Alimentary Tract, Mass., Pan Am. med. socs., AMA, Am. Trauma Soc., Worcester Econs. Club (past pres.), Worcester Council on Fgn. Relations. Episcopalian. Clubs: Tatnuck Country, Sakonnet Golf. Contbr. articles to profl. jours. Home: 13 Butternut Hill Dr Worcester MA 01609 Office: 25 Oak Ave Worcester MA 01605

SMALLETZ, THEODORE WILLIAM, publishing co. exec.; b. Paterson, N.J., Sept. 9, 1946; s. Samuel and Amelia Elizabeth (Derr) S.; B.A., Rutgers U., 1968. Fin. trainee, corporate auditor RCA Corp., N.Y.C., 1968-70; mgr. cost accounting Random House, Inc., N.Y.C., 1970-73; staff auditor Prentice-Hall, Inc., Englewood Cliffs, N.J., 1974-75, mgr. accounting ops., 1975-77, group controller book pub. divs., 1977—. Mem. Am. Mgmt. Assn., Assn. Am. Pubs. Office: Prentice-Hall Inc Route 9W Englewood Cliffs NJ 07632

SMALLEY, PHILIP ADAM, JR., steel co. exec.; b. Latrobe, Pa., Nov. 9, 1941; s. Philip Adam and Stella Diane (Checco) S.; B.S. in Edn., Clarion State Coll., 1964, postgrad., 1966, State U. Fredonia, 1969; m. Saly M. Goedicke, Aug. 28, 1965; children—P. Adam, David Keith. Personnel asst. Allegheny Ludlum Steel, Natrona Heights, Pa., 1966-69, gen. supr. personnel, Dunkirk, N.Y., 1969-72; mgr. orgn. devel. Sharon (Pa.) Steel Corp., 1972-73, dir. personnel and human resoruces, 1973-78, v.p./personnel and orgn., 1978—; instr. in personnel adminstrn. State U., Fredonia, N.Y. Classification com. United Way of Shenango Valley. Served with M.P., U.S. Army, 1964-66. Mem. Am. Compensation Assn. (v.p. central region), Am. Soc. Personnel Adminstrn. (certified), Western Pa. Personnel Assn. Republican. Presbyterian. Club: Elks (exolted ruler 1969). Pub. speaker in field. Home: 4715 Scott Dr Sharon PA 16146 Office: Box 291 Sharon Steel Corp Sharon PA 16146

SMALLEY, RALPH RAY, educator; b. Starkey, N.Y., Aug. 26, 1919; s. James Ray and Edith Dell (Hammond) S.; B.S., Cornell U., 1950, M.S., 1951; Ph.D., U. Fla., 1961; m. Dorothy Gomera Smith, Mar. 16, 1946; children—Patricia Smalley Eldredge, David, Timothy. Asst. prof. agronomy Farmingdale Agrl. & Tech. Coll. N.Y., 1951-58; asst. turfgrass technologist U. Fla., Ft. Lauderdale, 1961-62; prof. plant sci. Cobleskill (N.Y.) Agrl. and Tech. Coll., 1962—, chmn. dept., 1965-71; vis. prof. Cornell U., 1973-74. Mem. Bd. Edn., Bd. Coop. Ednl. Services, 1971-75; trustee Cobleskill United Methodist Ch. Served with USMCR, 1942-46. Certified profl. agronomist. Mem. N.Y. State Agrl. Soc. (life), Am. Soc. Agronomy, N.Y. State Turfgrass Assn., N.Y. Acad. Scis., Soil Conservation Soc. Am., Nat. Agrl. Coll. Tchrs. Assn., Sigma Xi, Gamma Sigma Delta, Pi Alpha Xi. Home: PO Box 451 Cobleskill NY 12043 Office: Cobleskill Agricultural and Technical College Cobleskill NY 12043

SMARDZEWSKI, RICHARD ROMAN, chemist; b. Nanticoke, Pa., July 4, 1942; s. Anthony Charles and Helen (Kustis) S.; B.S., King's Coll., 1964; Ph.D., Iowa State U., 1969; m. Marguerita M. Fino, Oct. 1, 1977. Sci. Research Council fellow U. Leicester (Eng.), 1969-70; NSF research fellow U. Va., Charlottesville, 1971-72; NRC fellow Naval Research Lab., Washington, 1972-74, research chemist, 1974—; adviser NRC Associateship Program. Mem. Am. Chem. Soc., Chem. Soc. Washington, Sigma Xi. Fellow Am. Inst. Chemists. Contbr. articles to profl. jours. Home: 3711 Towanda Rd Alexandria VA 22303 Office: Code 6130 Naval Research Lab Washington DC 20375

SMART, JAMES GORDON, coll. adminstr.; b. Williamsport, Pa., Jan. 24, 1954; s. Gordon James and Marietta (Williamson) S.; B.A., Indiana U. of Pa. 1975; M.S., Ed. S., State U. N.Y. at Albany, 1977. Residence dir. State U. Coll. at Geneseo, N.Y. 1976-77; asst. dir. residence life Mansfield (Pa.) State Coll., 1977—. Mem. Am. Coll. Personnel Assn., Am. Personnel and Guidance Assn., Nat. Assn. Student Personnel Adminstrs. Club: Mansfield Ski. Home: Maple A Apt Mansfield State Coll Mansfield PA 16933 Office: Box 20 South Hall Mansfield State Coll Mansfield PA 16933

SMART, LOUIS EDWIN, JR., airline exec.; b. Columbus, Ohio, Nov. 17, 1923; s. Louis Edwin and Esther (Guthery) S.; A.B. magna cum laude, Harvard, 1947, J.D. magna cum laude, 1949; m. Virginia Alice Knouff, Mar. 1, 1944 (div. 1958); children—Cynthia Stephanie, Douglas Edwin; m. 2d, Jeanie Alberta Milone, Aug. 29, 1964; 1 son, Dana Gregory Milone. Admitted to N.Y. bar, 1950; asso. firm Hughes, Hubbard & Ewing, N.Y.C., 1949-56; partner firm Hughes, Hubbard & Reed, N.Y.C., 1957-64; pres. Bendix Internat., dir. Bendix Corp. and fgn. subsidiaries, 1964-67; sr. v.p. corporate affairs, dir., exec. and fin. coms. Trans World Airlines, Inc., 1967-77, chmn., chief exec. officer, 1977—; chief exec. officer Hilton Internat. Co., 1967-73, dir., 1967—; dir. So. Natural Gas Co., So. Natural Resources, Inc., Canteen Corp. Served to lt. (j.g.) USNR, 1943-46. Mem. Am. Bar Assn., N.Y. County Lawyers Assn., Phi Beta Kappa, Sigma Alpha Epsilon. Clubs: Downtown Athletic, Sky (N.Y.C.). Home: 535 E 86th St New York City NY 10028 also Coakley Bay St Croix VI 00820 Office: 605 3d Ave New York City NY 10016

SMART, MARY-LEIGH CALL (MRS. J. SCOTT SMART), farm operator, civic worker; b. Springfield, Ill. Feb. 27, 1917; d. S(amuel) Leigh and Mary (Bradish) Call; jr. coll. diploma Monticello Coll., 1934; student Oxford U., 1935; B.A., Wellesley Coll., 1937; M.A., Columbia U., 1939, postgrad., 1940-41; postgrad. N.Y. U., 1940-41; painting student with Bernard Karfiol, 1937-38; m. J. Scott Smart, Sept. 11, 1951 (dec. 1960). Dir. mgmt. Central Ill. Grain Farms, Logan County, 1939—; art collector, patron, publicist, 1954—; program dir., sec. bd. Barn Gallery Assos., Inc., 1958-69, pres., 1969-70, hon. dir., 1970-78; curator Hamilton Easter Field Art Found. Collection, 1978—; owner Lowtrek Kennel, 1957-73, Cove Studio Art Gallery, 1961-68 (all Ogunquit, Maine). Mem. acquisition com. DeCordova Mus., Lincoln, Mass., 1966-78; mem. chancellor's council U. Tex., 1972—; bd. dirs. Ogunquit C. of C., 1966, treas. 1966-67, hon. life mem., 1968—; bd. overseers Strawbery Banke, Inc., Portsmouth, N.H., 1972-75, 3d vice chmn., 1973, 2d vice chmn., 1974; bd. advisers Univ. Art Galleries, U. N.H., 1973—, v.p., bd. overseers, 1974—; chmn. outdoor display bd. Perkins Cove Assn., Ogunquit, 1973; mem. advisory com. Bowdoin Coll. Mus. Art Invitational Exhibit, 1975, '76 Maine Artists Invitational Exhbn. of Maine Am. Revolution Bicentennial Commn., 1976, Maine Coast Artists, Rockport, 1975—. Served to lt. jg. WAVES, 1942-45. Mem. Am. Fedn. Arts, Am. Assn. Museums, Mus. Modern Art, Springfield Art Assn., Boston Mus. Fine Arts, Solomon R. Guggenheim Mus., Portland Mus. Art., Jr. League of Springfield, Inst. Contemporary Art Boston (corporator). Republican. Episcopalian. Club: Western Maine Wellesley. Editor: Hamilton Easter Field Art Found. Collection Catalog, 1966; originator, dir. show, compiler of catalog Art: Ogunquit, 1967. Address: Surf Point York ME 03909

SMART, WALTER LEWIS, assn. exec.; b. Birmingham, Ala., Dec. 3, 1927; s. Arthur Frank and Cynthia Lavinia (Fisher) S.; A.B., Miles Coll, 1954; M.A., Atlanta U., 1956; m. Gaynell Clarita Guice, Aug. 25, 1955; children—David, Walter, Jeffrey, Steven, Philip. Dir. community devel. Germantown Settlement, Phila., 1956-61; asst. project dir. Boston Redevel. Authority, 1961-64, dir. family relocation, 1964-66, dir. social services, 1968-70; asst. dir. President's Commn. on Urban Problems, Washington, 1968-70; asso. dir. Nat. Fedn. Settlements and Neighborhood Centers, N.Y.C., 1970-72, exec. dir., 1972—; hon. sec. Internat. Fedn. Settlements and Neighborhood Centers, 1976—. Bd. dirs. Nat. Assembly Voluntary Social Welfare Agencies, Guiding Eyes for the Blind. Served with AUS, 1950-52. Ford Found. grantee, 1972. Mem. Nat. Council Social Welfare, Nat. Assn. Housing and Redevel. Ofcls. Democrat. Unitarian. Author: The Large Poor Family-A Housing Gap, 1968. Address: care Nat Fedn Settlements and Neighborhood Centers 232 Madison Ave New York City NY 10016

SMEAL, THEODORE SAMUEL, elec. engr.; b. Sykesville, Pa., Feb. 20, 1911; s. Samuel and Mary (Pavlick) S.; student Pa. State U., 1934-44; m. Gertrude Eckert, June 8, 1937; children—Janice Smeal King, Judith Smeal Olson. Elec. engr. Stackpole Carbon Co., St. Mary's, Pa., 1934-76. Active Boy Scouts Am., St. Mary's, Pa., 1924-76, recipient Silver Beaver award, 1955; trustee St. Mary's Pub. Library, 1953-59, librarian, 1959-76. Recipient Resolution for Community Service, Borough of St. Mary's Pa., 1966; Certificate of Appreciation for community service, Lions, 1976; certified librarian. Mem. IEEE, ALA, Pa. Library Assn., Soc. Mfg. Engrs., Am. Legion (distinguished service award, 1967). Republican. Roman Catholic. Home: 484 Spruce St Saint Marys PA 15857 Office: 127 Center St Saint Marys PA 15857

SMEDLEY, WILLIAM MICHAEL, chemist, educator; b. Cook County, Ill., Aug. 2, 1916; s. William M. and Margaret Elizabeth (McQueen) S.; B.S., Northwestern U., 1938, M.S., 1940; postgrad. U. Md., 1950-60; m. Margaret Thurston, Sept. 12, 1943; 1 dau., Jane Elizabeth. Instr., asst. prof., asso. prof., prof. organic chemistry U.S. Naval Acad., Annapolis, Md., 1948—; asst. prof. quantitative analysis U. Md., 1956-58; dir. research, v.p. Applied Sci. & Chem. Corp., Am. Chem. Co., Inc.; gen. partner Korab, Smedley & Co.; v.p., dir. Everett Factories (Mass.). Served to comdr. USNR, 1940-47. NSF Faculty Fellow U. Md., 1964-65. Mem. Am. Chem. Soc. Presbyn. (elder). Patentee in field. Home: 5017 Riverdale Rd Riverdale MD 20840

SMEDLEY, WILLIAM PAUL, surgeon; b. Kingston, Pa., June 7, 1934; s. William Paul and Regis M. (Farrell) S.; B.S., Kings Coll., 1956; M.D., Loyola U., Chgo., 1960; m. Catherine Ann Moran, June 20, 1959; children—William Paul, Paul Charles, Katie, Jane. Intern, Wilkes-Barre (Pa.) Gen. Hosp., 1960-61; resident Geisinger Med. Center, Danville, Pa., 1961-64; practice medicine specializing in surgery, Wilkes-Barre, Pa., 1966—; mem. staff Wilkes-Barre Gen. Hosp.; surg. cons. Wilkes-Barre VA Hosp., 1977—, Little Flower Manor, Wilkes-Barre, Armed Forces Examining Sta., Wilkes-Barre; cons. staff Nesbitt Meml. Hosp., Kingston. Served to capt. M.C., U.S. Army, 1965-69. Diplomate Am. Bd. Surgery. Mem. AMA, A.C.S., Pa., Luzerne County med. asocs., Am. Automobile Assn. (dir. local club 1974—). Roman Catholic. Clubs: K.C. (4th deg.), Westmoreland. Office: 480 Pierce St Kingston PA 18704

SMELTER, KATHERINE VAFAKAS, educator; b. Detroit, Dec. 30, 1941; d. Nicholas Andrew and Fannie (Pappas) Vafakas; B.S., Eastern Mich. U., 1965; M.Ed., Wayne State U., 1967, Ed.D., 1972; m. Bernard Joseph Smelter, July 21, 1975; 1 dau., Christine Katherine. Adminstrv. asst., instr. Wayne State U., Detroit, 1966-67; counselor, dept. chmn. Oakland Community Coll., Bloomfield Hills, Mich., 1967-72; asst. prof. dept. behavioral scis. Northwestern State U., Natchitoches, La., 1972-73; asst. prof. U. Windsor (Ont., Can.), 1973; asst. prof. U. Bridgeport, Conn., 1973-75; adj. asso. prof. L.I. U., Dobbs Ferry, N.Y., 1975—. Mem. Am. Personnel and Guidance Assn., Am. Assn. Counselor Edn. and Supervision, AAUP, Psi Chi. Contbr. articles in field to profl jours. and books. Home: Route 9 Garrison NY 10524

SMIRNOW, ROBERT, dentist; b. Bklyn., Feb. 3, 1924; s. Louis and Anna (Silbert) S.; student U.Pa., 1940-42, N.Y. U., 1941-42; D.D.S., U. Pitts., 1945, postgrad. New Sch., 1948-49, Albert Einstein Coll., 1965-72; m. Dorothy Wiggins, July 11, 1954; children—William, David. Practice gen. dentistry, Queens, N.Y., 1947-51, Manhattan, 1950-51, East Northport, N.Y., 1951—; clin. asst. Beth Israel Hosp., N.Y.C., 1947-51, preceptorship in orthodontics 1947-49, supr. preceptor, 1949-51; vis. research fellow Guggenheim Inst. Dental Research, N.Y.C., 1962, asso. research scientist, 1965-67; adj. asst. prof. Sch. Dentistry, Columbia U. Served with AUS, 1942-44, USNR, 1945-47. N.Y. U. Coll. Dentistry grantee, 1962, Nat. Inst. Dental Research grantee, 1964-67. Mem. 2d Dist., 10th Dist., Suffolk County dental socs., ADA, Internat. Assn. Dental Research, Internat. Assn. Orthodontics, Am. Prosthodontic Soc., AAAS, Am. Radio Relay League. Home: Route 3 Huntington NY 11743 Office: 7 Pulaski Rd East Northport NY 11731

SMITH, ALLEN ARTHUR, accountant; b. N.Y.C., Aug. 14, 1946; s. David and Sylvia Rachael (Glass) S.; B.B.A. in Accounting, Pace U., 1968; m. Suzanne Esther Schauer, Dec. 20, 1970. Mem. firm Harris, Kerr, Forster & Co., N.Y.C., 1968-72, mem. firm Robbins Green & Co., N.Y.C., 1972—. Trustee Am. Com. Shaare Zedek Hosp., Jerusalem, 1977—; treas. Young Israel of the West Side, 1972—. C.P.A., N.Y. State. Mem. N.Y. State Soc. C.P.A.'s (com. health care insts. 1975-78). Home: 186 Riverside Dr New York City NY 10024 Office: 522 Fifth Ave New York City NY 10036

SMITH, ALLEN DAVID, acct.; b. Torrington, Conn., Apr. 26, 1951; s. James Milford and Florence Helen (Strandberg) S.; B.S. in Bus. Adminstrn., Bryant Coll., 1973; postgrad., U. Hartford, 1973—; m. Barbara Sekulski, Sept. 1, 1973. Staff accountant Torrington Co. (Conn.), 1973-75, supr. gen. accounting, 1973-79, cost analyst, 1979—, also mem. supervisory com. Employees Credit Union. Active Boy Scouts Am. Mem. Nat. Assn. Accountants (asso. dir. Waterbury chpt.), Woodridge Lake Assn., Bryant Coll. Alumni Assn., Phi Epsilon Pi. Republican. Episcopalian. Clubs: Foreman's, Elks. Home: Marshapaug Rd Goshen CT 06756 Office: 59 Field St Torrington CT 06790

SMITH, ALLEN HENDERSON, III, mech. engr.; b. Phila., Dec. 17, 1948; s. Allen Henderson and Katherine Vosler (Clark) S.; B.S., Pa. State U., 1970; M.B.A., Drexel U., 1970; M. Engring., Widener Coll., 1979. Regional mgr. Schramm Inc., West Chester, Pa., 1970-71; project engr. Keebler Co., Phila., 1971-73, sr. project engr., 1973-75, plant engr., 1976-77, mgr. process tech., 1977-78; project mgr. SmithKline Corp., Phila., 1978—; cons. in field. Active Boy Scouts Am. Served with USNR, 1970. Registerd profl. engr., Pa., N.J., Ill. Mem. Penjerdel C. of C., Am. Inst. Indsl. Engrs., IEEE, Nat., Pa. socs. profl. engrs., Am. Inst. Plant Engrs. (certified), Instrument Soc. Am., Soc. Mfg. Engrs., ASME, Am. Quarter Horse Assn., Nat. Assn. Underwater Instrs. Republican. Episcopalian. Clubs: Engrs. Phila., Com. of '70, Main Line Scuba. Home: 2625 Church Rd Glenside PA 19038 Office: SmithKline Corp 1500 Spring Garden St PO Box 7929 Philadelphia PA 19101

SMITH, ALLEN NORMAN, research psychologist; b. N.Y.C., Mar. 7, 1937; s. Herman and Minerva (Goldberg) S.; B.A., Bklyn. Coll., 1958; M.S., Iowa State U., 1960; postgrad. George Washington U., 1961-63; m. Elaine Sierpinski, July 31, 1960; children—Jennifer Mila, Elissa Kim. Research psychologist personnel research field activity U.S. Navy, Washington, 1960-61, Bur. Ships, 1961-63, Internal Revenue Service, 1963-70, OEO, 1970-73; sr. social psychologist Office Human Devel. Services HEW, Washington, 1973—. Vice pres. Jewish Community Council Bowie (Md.), 1975-77; chmn. social action and youth com. Temple Solel, Bowie, 1972-76; chmn. United Jewish Appeal, Bowie, 1974-78. Recipient Certificate of Appreciation, Prince Georges County (Md.), 1968; Award for initiation of relevant research Alliance Child Devel. Assn., 1976; Scroll of Honor State of Israel Bonds, 1977; award merit United Jewish Appeal, 1974-78. Mem. Am., Eastern, Md. psychol. assns., Policy Studies Orgn., Council Applied Social Research, Evaluation Research Soc. Club: B'nai B'rith. Home: 2703 Federal Ln Bowie MD 20715

SMITH, ANDREW JOHN, physicist; b. Simpson, Pa., Nov. 29, 1936; s. Adam John and Martha Veronica (Kiehart) S.; B.S. in Physics, Pa. State U., 1961, M.S., 1964; M. Kathleen Elaine Yuninger, June 16, 1962; children—Tara Kate, Kristen Elizabeth, Erin Kathleen. Engr.-in-charge Nuclide Corp., State College, Pa., 1959-64, mgr. instrument testing, 1965-73; scientist Armstrong Cork Co., Lancaster, Pa., 1964-65; sr. scientist Westinghouse Electric Corp.-Bettis Atomic Power Lab., West Mifflin, Pa., 1973—. Chmn., Republican Party, Bethel Park, Pa., 1977—, mem. exec. com., 1976—. Served with U.S. Army, 1954-57. Mem. Am. Soc. for Mass Spectroscopy, Spectroscopy Soc. Pitts. Club: Toastmasters Internat. Contbr. tech. articles to profl. jours. Home: 2580 N Lightwood Ave Bethel Park PA 15102 Office: Westinghouse-BAPL PO Box 79 West Mifflin PA 15122

SMITH, ANN LACAMERA, health care co. exec.; b. N.Y.C., Apr. 7, 1917; d. Michael and Angelina (Sarpi) Lacamera; M.E., Rutgers U., 1946; student Kean Coll., 1970-74; m. Herman P. Smith, May 15, 1960. Sec. Ransome Machinery Co., Dunellen, N.J., 1936-40; asst. to gen. mgr. Worthington Corp., Harrison, N.J., 1940-50, office mgr., asst. to v.p. mktg., 1950-60; exec. sec. to pres. Ortho Pharm. Corp., Raritan, N.J., 1960-63, mem. staff, 1964-68; mgr. corp. personnel search Johnson & Johnson, New Brunswick, N.J., 1968—; lectr. Douglass Coll., Middlesex Coll., Princeton U., Kean Coll. Trustee YWCA, New Brunswick, 1973-74. Mem. Am. Soc. Personnel Adminstrn. Republican. Home: 451 Grove St North Plainfield NJ 07060 Office: 501 George St New Brunswick NJ 08903

SMITH, BARRY HAMILTON, neurosurgeon, neurobiologist; b. Orange, N.J., Oct. 6, 1943; s. Kenneth Wright and Harriet (Barr) S.; B.A., Harvard U., 1965; Ph.D., Mass. Inst. Tech., 1968; M.D., Cornell U., 1972; m. Carley Eldredge, Dec. 16, 1969; 1 son, Christopher Ridley. Resident surgeon N.Y. Hosp., 1972-75, Mass. Gen. Hosp., Boston, 1975-78; staff scientist, neuroscis. research program Mass. Inst. Tech., Cambridge, 1975, program dir., 1976-78; sr. staff surg. neurology br. NINCDS, NIH, 1978—. Trustee FOCUS, 1968—. NIH fellow, 1965-68; Med. Scientist fellow, 1969-72; A.C.S. Schering scholar, 1975-76. Mem. AMA, Soc. for Neurosci., Internat. Assn. for Study of Pain, Phi Beta Kappa, Sigma Xi. Club: Eastern Yacht. Asso. editor Brain and Behavioral Scis., 1976—. Home: 159 Prince George St Annapolis MD 21401 Office: Surg Neurology Br NINCDS Bldg 10A Room 3E68 NIH Bethesda MD 21401

SMITH, BARRY MARSHALL, publisher; b. Providence, May 19, 1931; s. Elmer Reid and Muriel Violet (Kettelle) S.; A.B., Colby Coll., 1953; postgrad. U. R.I., 1954-56, Boston U., 1956-60; m. Eleanor Frances Hackett, Aug. 17, 1957; children—Deborah Ellen, Karen Jeanne, Lynda Ann, Michael Barry. Instr., Vets. Meml. High Sch., Warwick, R.I., 1957-60; dir. Johnson & Wales Reading Inst., Providence, 1961-64; dir. admissions Johnson & Wales Coll., Providence, 1965-68; v.p. Programs For Achievement in Reading, Inc., Providence, 1969-75, pres., 1975—; corporator Citizens Savings Bank, Providence, 1976—. R.I. del. trustee Nat. Kidney Found., 1964-71; dir. Fitzgerald-Toole Advt. Agy., Providence, 1976—; bd. dirs. Norfolk Coll., 1974—, Milw. Stratton Coll., 1975—, Davis Coll., 1974—. Served with USAF, 1950-52. Mem. Am. Assn. Jr. Colls., Coll. Reading Assn., Internat. Reading Assn., Nat. Small Bus. Assn., Am. Assn. Collegiate Registrars and Admissions Officers, Nat. Assn. Concerned Vets (Life). Republican. Roman Catholic. Club: South County Rod and Gun. Author: SRA Reading Laboratory, 1957; Powereading, 1960; Democracy, 1966. Home: 73 Sedgefield Rd

North Kingstown RI 02852 Office: Abbott Park Pl Providence RI 02903

SMITH, BRUCE EVERETT, army officer; b. W. Stewartstown, N.H., May 3, 1941; s. Laurence Elliott and Eola Jewell Smith; B.S., U. N.H., 1963; M.B.A., Syracuse (N.Y.) U., 1972; grad. various mil. schs.; m. Jo-Ann Theriault, June 22, 1963; children—Stephanie Ann, Stephen Andrew. Commd. 2d lt. U.S. Army, advanced through grades to maj., 1971; service in Vietnam, 1966-67; dep. comptroller Edgewood Arsenal, Aberdeen (Md.) Proving Ground, 1972-74; asst. sec. gen. staff U.S. Army Material Devel. and Readiness Command, Alexandria, Va., 1974-77; assigned Naval War Coll., Newport, R.I., 1977—; dir., sec. MATCOM Fed. Credit Union, Edgewood Arsenal, 1972-74. Decorated Army Commendation medal, Joint Service Commendation medal, Bronze Star. Mem. Am. Soc. Mil. Comptrollers, Am. Def. Preparedness Assn., Alpha Zeta. Republican. Roman Catholic. Address: North Haverhill NH 03774

SMITH, CARL EDGAR, JR., bank exec.; b. Balt., Apr. 8, 1916; s. Carl Edgar and A. Louise S.; ed. Gilman Sch.; m. Dorothy L. Williams, June 12, 1947; children—Claire DeMaille, Anne Clark, Charles Edgar. With real estate investment co., 1938-39; prodn. clk. to sr. personnel officer Glen L. Martin Co., 1942; with Navy Dept., Washington, 1946-47; mortgage dept. Piper & Hill, 1947-53; v.p., then pres. Mchts. Mortgage Co., 1953-56; founder, pres. Constrn. Credit Corp., 1956-67; v.p. Merc. Safe Deposit & Trust Co., 1967-69; bus. and fin. cons., 1969-73; pres. Central Savs. Bank, Balt., 1973—; mem. Md. Banking Bd. and Regulation Bd. Bd. govs. Greater Balt. Com., chmn. edn. subcom.; various coms. St. David's Episcopal Ch., Balt. Served to lt. (s.g.) USN, 1942-46; PTO. Mem. Assn. Execs. of Nat. Assn. Mut. Savs. Banks (corporate sec. council), English Speaking Union (dir.), Asso. Mut. Savs. Banks Md. (sec.). Clubs: Md., Elkridge, Center (Balt.). Home: 4203 St Paul St Baltimore MD 21218 Office: PO Box 1316 Baltimore MD 21203*

SMITH, CATHERINE MARY DALMASO, nurse; b. Gt. Barrington, Mass., Apr. 24, 1920; d. Emilio and Fortuna F. Dalmaso; diploma Henry W. Bishop 3d Meml. Sch. Nursing, 1941; m. Frank D. Smith, Jr., Dec. 2, 1943 (div.); children—Judith Ann, Sandra Jeanne. Head nurse, inservice coordinator Berkshire Med. Center, Pittsfield, Mass., 1955-70; dir. nursing Valley View Nursing Home, Lenox, Mass., 1970-72; dir. nursing services Hillcrest Hosp., Pittsfield, 1972—. Served as lt. Nurse Corps, USAAF, 1941-43. Registered nurse, Mass. Mem. Am., Mass. nurses assn., Am. Soc. for Hosp. Nursing Service Adminstrs., Henry W. Bishop 3d Meml. Alumnae Assn. Roman Catholic. Club: Quota. Home: Route 49 Summit Rd Pittsfield MA 01201 Office: Tor Ct Pittsfield MA 01201

SMITH, CHARLES DANIEL, educator; b. Akron, Ind., Oct. 16, 1914; s. Cleotus Grindle and Faye (Leininger) S.; A.B., Ind. U., 1936; M.A., Washington U., St. Louis, 1949, Ph.D., 1954; m. Elliott Chambers, June 22, 1938 (dec. 1974); children—David Hughes, Alan, Julia. Instr., Washington U., St. Louis, 1946-53; asst. prof. Syracuse (N.Y.) U., 1954-64, asso. prof., 1964-74, prof. rhetoric, 1974—, chmn. dept. pub. address, 1965-69; cons. Hdqrs. Air Tng. Command, 1954, Am. Mgmt. Assn., 1957, Gen. Electric Co., Syracuse, 1957-69, IBM Corp., Princeton, N.J., 1963-65. Served to maj., inf., AUS, 1940-45. Mem. Speech Assn. Am., Royal Hist. Soc., Ret. Officers Assn., English Speaking Union, Dartmouth House (London). Asso. editor Quar. Jour. Speech, 1967-68; author: The Early Career of Lord North The Prime Minister, 1978. Home: 301 Salt Springs Rd Syracuse NY 13224 Office: 110 Sims Syracuse U Syracuse NY 13210

SMITH, CHARLES EDWARD, endocrinologist; b. Cin., Sept. 8, 1943; s. Clarence Vernon and Mary Rogers (Myers) S.; B.A. in Chemistry, Coll. Wooster, 1965; M.D., U. Cin., 1969; m. Hannelore Eipeltauer, Dec. 1968. Intern U. Cin., 1969-70; resident U. Utah, Salt Lake City, 1970-71; practice medicine specializing in internal medicine, East Sparta, Ohio, 1971; resident internal medicine Walter Reed Med. Center, Washington, 1974-76, fellow endocrinology, 1977—; chief medicine Kirk Army Hosp., Aberdeen, Md., 1976-77. Served with U.S. Army, 1971—. Mem. AMA. Republican. Presbyterian. Home: 11303 Palisades Ct Kensington MD 20795 Office: Walter Reed Med Center Dept Endocrinology Washington DC 20012

SMITH, CHARLES ELMER, club adminstr.; b. Columbus, Ohio, Oct. 5, 1915; s. Frank Rite and Nellie Beatrice (Matheny) S.; B.A., Ohio State U., 1936, B.Sc., 1937, M.Sc., 1940; postgrad. Denison U., Princeton U., U. Calif. at Berkeley, 1945-46; m. Cindy Grace Nestor, Oct. 5, 1944; children—Craig, Candace; m. 2d, Paula Adrienne Roye, Nov. 24, 1974; children—Paul, Jamie. Conf. leader Ohio Dept. Edn., Columbus, 1940-44; trainer War Manpower Commn., Fed. Prison Industry Bds., Columbus, 1941-44; coordinator Foreman Clubs, Columbus, 1944-48; lectr. various univs., 1948-59; gen. mgr. Athletic Club, Columbus, 1944-55; gen. mgr. Chevy Chase (Md.) Club, Inc., 1955—; speaker for pvt. club industry. Served from ensign to lt. comdr. USNR, 1942-46. Named to Hospitality Hall of Fame, 1966; named Mr. Club Mgr., Cornell U., 1961; recipient Order of Skillet award Food Service Execs., 1976, 77; certified club mgr., certified food exec. Mem. Nat., Washington restaurant assns., Nat. Food Service Execs. Assn., Central Ohio Mgmt. Assn., Nat. Capitol Club Mgrs. Assn. (pres.), Club Mgrs. Assn. Am., Internat. Club Execs. Assn., Club Mgmt. Inst. Republican. Methodist.

SMITH, CHARLES FRANK, circus exec.; b. Daisy, Ky., July 19, 1939; s. Frank and Alberta (Andersen) S.; B.C.S. in Accounting, Strayer Coll., 1963; m. Etta Jane Kearns, Sept. 23, 1957; children—Terri, Charles Frank, Deidre. Supr. cost accounting Page Communications, Inc., Washington, 1960-63; supr. accounting systems Leasco Systems & Research Co., Bethesda, Md., 1964-67; v.p. finance and adminstrn. Ringling Bros.-Barnum & Bailey Combined Shows, Inc., Washington, 1968—; dir. Barnett Bank of Winter Haven, N.A. Mem. Nat. Assn. Accountants. Republican. Baptist. Home: 16516 Jilrick St Rockville MD 20853 Office: 1015 18th St NW Washington DC 20036

SMITH, CHARLES FRANK, JR., educator; b. Cleve., Jan. 5, 1933; married, 2 children. M.Ed. in Adminstrn. and Supervision, Kent (Ohio) State U., 1963; Certificate of Advanced Studies in Sch. Adminstrn. and Supervision, Curriculum in Elementary Edn., Harvard, 1965; Ed.D. in Adminstrn. and Higher Edn., Mich. State U., East Lansing, 1969. Tchr. 5th grade Lorain (Ohio) Pub. Sch. System, 1960-62; asst. to dir. elementary edn. Flint (Mich.) Pub. Sch. System, 1965-66; instr. Mich. State U., 1966-68; asso. prof. dept. edn. Boston Coll., Chestnut Hill, Mass., 1968—. Mem. adv. task force State of Mass. Com. on Criminal Justice, 1974—; mem. adv. council State of Mass. Council on Bilingual Edn., 1972—. Mem. Am. Assn. Colls. for Tchr. Edn., Am. Assn. Sch. Adminstrs., Assn. for Supervision and Curriculum Devel., New Eng. Assn. for Supervision and Curriculum Devel., Dept. Elementary Sch. Prins., Nat. Council for Social Studies. Danforth assn., 1974. Specialist in curriculum and instrn., urban ed., tchr. tng. Home: 194 Parker St Newton Centre MA 02159 Office: Bost Coll Sch Edn Campion Hall 140 Commonwealth Ave Chestnut Hill MA 02167

SMITH, CHARLES WILLIAM, coll. adminstr.; b. Grimsby, Eng., Oct. 19, 1931; s. Harry and Lillian Annie (Anderson) S.; came to U.S., 1965; student Met. Coll., St. Albans, Eng., 1948-54; m. Hazel Rebecca Cooper Gray, Aug. 6, 1955; children—Patricia, Charles, Andrew, Anne, Mark. Sr. audit. asst. Alexander, Machennan, Trundell & Co., Kenya, 1955-58; sec., accountant Uganda Transport Co., Ltd., Kampala & Dist. Services Ltd., also sec. United Touring Co. Ltd., Uganda United Transport Ltd., 1959-63; chief fin. officer, lectr. Makerere U. Coll., Kampala, Uganda, 1963-65; v.p. bus. affairs Haverford (Pa.) Coll., 1965-72, cons., 1973-74; v.p. fin. Boston U., 1972-76, v.p. fin. and bus. affairs, 1976—; cons. Nairobi (Kenya) U., 1965, Coll. St. Scholastica, Duluth, Minn., 1975, Mgmt. Planning, Inc.; dir. Advent Capital Corp., Devonshire Capital Corp.; mem. Mass. Gov.'s Mgmt. Task Force, 1975-76; chmn. steering com. Econ. Impact Study of Colls. and Univs. on Boston Area, 1972-73. Mem. exec. com. Friends Coll., Kenya, 1971; bd. dirs. Partnership for Productivity, Annondale, Va., 1972—, Better Bus. Bur. Eastern Mass. Fellow Inst. Chartered Accountants; mem. Chartered Inst. Secs. (asso.), Northeast Regional Studies Assn., Mass. Soc. C.P.A.'s, Nat. Assn. Coll. and Univ. Bus. Officers (publs. com. 1976—). Author: Introduction to Bookkeeping, 1966; A Proposal for the Establishment of Friends College in Western Kenya, 1971. Home: 285 Goddard Ave Brookline MA 02146 Office: 881 Commonwealth Ave Boston MA 02215

SMITH, CHRISTOPHER LEE, advt. co. exec.; b. N.Y.C., Nov. 18, 1947; s. Carruth Lee and Ann Bruce (Gallagher) S.; B.A. with honors in Econs., Lake Forest Coll., 1969; M.B.A., U. Chgo., 1971. Asso. cons. Management Analysis Center, Chgo., 1971-73; v.p. Marsteller Inc., N.Y.C., 1973—, sr. research dir., 1976—; instr. advt. Northwestern U., Chicago, 1975-76, Manhattan Coll., Riverdale, N.Y., 1977. Served with USA Res., 1970-76. Mem. Am. Mktg. Assn., Bus./Profl. Advt. Assn., U. Chgo. Alumni Assn. Home: 160 E 48th St New York City NY 10021 Office: 866 3d Ave New York City NY 10022

SMITH, CLAY DEMPSTER, mech. engr.; b. Buffalo, Aug. 10, 1936; s. Wilmot Merle and Florence (Graves) S.; B.S. in Mech. Engring., U. Buffalo, 1960; m. Anne Kathleen Saxton, Sept. 5, 1959; children—Bradley Harrison, Amy Kathleen. Mech. engr. Trane Co., Syracuse, N.Y., 1960-67, Bristol Labs., Syracuse, 1967-72; pres. Clay D. Smith and Assos., cons. mech. engrs., LaFayette, N.Y., 1967—; pres. Otisca Industries, Ltd., LaFayette, 1972—. Mem. Am. Soc. Heating, Refrigerating and Air-Conditioning Engrs., Am. Inst. Mining Engrs., Nat. Soc. Profl. Engrs., Licensing Execs. Soc., AAAS, Optimists. Episcopalian. Contbr. articles to profl. jours. Home: PO Box 35 LaFayette NY 13084 Office: PO Box 186 LaFayette NY 13084

SMITH, CLOTILDE DURHAM, med. technologist; b. Raymond, Miss., Jan. 16, 1915; d. Curtis George and Chanie (Tillman) Durham; certificate med. technology Providence Hosp., Chgo., 1942; student Howard U., 1945-49; B.S., Roosevelt U., 1950; m. Henry M. Smith, Jr., Mar. 28, 1955. Med. technologist Sta. Hosp., Ft. Huachuaca, Ariz., 1942-44; supr. clin. microbiology Freedmen's Hosp. (now Howard U. Hosp.), Washington, 1945-67, chief med. technologist, 1968—; lectr., cons. clin. microbiology, coordinator edn. Mem. Registry Med. Technologists, Am. socs. Microbiologists, Med. Technologists, Clin. Pathologists, AAAS. Author: Manual of Microbiology for Clinical Labs, 1973; contbr. articles in field to profl. jours. Home: 1311 Delaware Ave SW Washington DC 20024 Office: 2041 Georgia Ave NW Washington DC 20060

SMITH, CUTHBERT HENRY, social worker; b. Ocala, Fla., Mar. 30, 1912; s. John Harold and Ella (Williams) S.; B.A., Howard U., 1947, M.S.W., 1949. Case supr. St. Christopher Sch., Dobbs Ferry, N.Y., 1956-58, dir. social service, 1959-60; supr. Wiltwyck Sch., N.Y.C., 1960-61; chief project social worker, child health care program Jewish Hosp. & Med. Center, Bklyn., 1967—. Mem. Nat. Assn. Social Workers (registered clin. social worker), Nat. Conf. Social Workers, Social Work Vocat. Bur., Am. Negro Commemorative Soc., Howard U. Sch. Social Work Alumni Assn. Contbr. articles to profl. jours. Home: 175 Willoughby St Brooklyn NY 11201 Office: 555 Prospect Pl Brooklyn NY 11201

SMITH, DAVID, chemist; b. Fall River, Mass., Nov. 7, 1939; s. Jacob Max and Bertha (Horvitz) S.; B.S., Providence Coll., 1961; Ph.D., Mass. Inst. Tech., 1965; m. Renee Lea Gutfreund, Nov. 23, 1967; children—Aliza, Miriam Zesel, Shimon Zimel, Noah Shmuel, Mordechai Yaakov. Instr. in chemistry Bklyn. Coll., 1965-68; asso. prof. chemistry Pa. State U., 1968—. Bd. dirs. Ohav Zedek Synagogue, Wilkes-Barre, Pa., 1971—; sec. Vaad Hakashres of Wyoming Valley (Pa.), 1972—; sec. sch. bd. United Hebrew Inst., Kingston, 1974-76, chmn. sch. bd., 1977—. Mem. Am. Chem. Soc., Am. Phys. Soc., Sigma Xi, Delta Epsilon Phi. Contbr. articles on molecular dynamics to profl. jours., 1967—. Home: 68 Second Ave Kingston PA 18704 Office: Pa State U High Acres Campus Hazleton PA 18201

SMITH, DAVID ENGLISH, pathologist; b. San Francisco, June 9, 1920; s. David English and Myrtle (Goodin) S.; A.B., Central Coll. Mo., 1941; M.D., Washington U., St. Louis, 1944; m. Margaret Elizabeth Bronson, June 9, 1948; children—Ann English Smith Aberle, David Bronson, Mary Margaret. Intern, Barnes Hosp., St. Louis, 1944-45, resident pathology, 1945-46; instr. pathology Washington U., St. Louis, 1948-51, asst. prof., 1951-54, asso. prof., 1954-55; prof. U. Va., Charlottesville, 1955-73, chmn. dept., 1958-73; asso. dir. Am. Bd. Med. Specialties, Evanston, Ill., 1974-75; prof. pathology Northwestern U., Chgo., 1974-75; v.p., sec., dir. undergrad. med. evaluation Nat. Bd. Med. Examiners, Phila., 1975—; adj. prof. U. Pa., Phila., 1975—. Bd. dirs. Phila. div. Am. Cancer Soc., 1977—. Served to capt. M.C., AUS, 1946-48. Mem. Internat. Acad. Pathology (pres. 1964-65), Am. Soc. Clin. Pathologists, Am. Assn. Pathologists, Phila. Pathology Soc., AMA, Am. Acad. Neurology, AAAS, Coll. Physicians of Phila., Sigma Xi, Alpha Omega Alpha, Phi Beta Pi, Alpha Epsilon Delta. Presbyterian. Contbr. articles to profl. jours. Home: 1320 Grenox Rd WynneWood PA 19096 Office: 3930 Chestnut St Philadelphia PA 19104

SMITH, DEAN, govt. ofcl.; b. N.Y.C., Aug. 10, 1925; s. Franklin Grant and Anna Lucille (Kranebell) S.; student N.Y. U., 1945-46, Columbia U., 1946-47, N.Y. Sch. Printing, 1946-47; m. Andree Marie Praileur, Aug. 9, 1947; children—David F., Christopher P. Editor, ShowBill Mag., N.Y.C., 1945-47; news editor Boulder City (Nev.) Daily News, 1947-49; owner, pub., editor Tucson Sun-News, 1949-51; dir. radio and TV news WBEN/WBEN-TV, Buffalo, 1951-53; dir. pub. sers. and promotion Indpls. Times, 1953-56; v.p., gen. mgr. Kendall Assos., Inc., N.Y.C., 1956-60; dir. Office Publs. and Info. Commerce Dept., Washington, 1961-70, dir. publs. div., 1970, asst. dir. Nat. Tech. Info. Ser., Springfield, Va., 1971—. Chmn. for fed. mail list policy Vice Pres.'s Com. on Right of Privacy. Bd. dirs. Commerce Fed. Credit Union. Served with AUS, 1943-45. Decorated Silver Star with oak leaf cluster, Bronze Star, Purple Heart with oak leaf cluster. Recipient award Ariz. Newspaper Assn., 1950; Ind. Photo Journalism award, 1954. Democrat. Clubs: Nat. Dem.; Federal City, International (Washington). Home: 2325 49th St NW Washington DC 20007 Office: 5285 Port Royal Rd Springfield VA 22161

SMITH, DEFOREST WEBB, real estate exec.; b. Bridgeport, Conn., Dec. 12, 1939; s. Winthrop Arthur and Louise (Moulton) S.; B.A. in Internat. Econs., Yale U., 1961; grad. Realtors' Inst.; m. Nancy Newlin Willett, Dec. 29, 1962; children—Marjorie Currier, Sarah DeForest, Alexis Hill. Pres. Century 21-George J. Smith & Son, realtors, Milford, Conn., 1974—; dir., owner Century 21 New Eng., Inc., Milford, 1973—; dir. Milford Savs. Bank. Chmn. Yale U. Alumni Schs. Com., 1964—. Certified comml. investment mem.; certified residential broker. Mem. Soc. Indsl. Realtors, Conn., Nat. assns. realtors. Club: Yale (dir.) (New Haven). Address: Smith Bldg Broad St at Green's End Milford CT 06460

SMITH, DENNIS, novelist; b. N.Y.C., Sept. 9, 1940; s. John and Mary Elizabeth (Hogan) S.; B.A., N.Y. U., 1970, M.A., 1972; m. Patricia Anne Kearney, Aug. 24, 1963; children—Brendan, Dennis, Sean, Deirdre and Aislinn (twins). Author: Report from Engine Co. 82, 1972; The Final Fire, 1975; Firehouse, 1977; Dennis Smith's History of American Firefighting, 1978; Glitter and Ash, 1979; The Aran Islands: A Memoir, 1979; founder, editor-in-chief FireHouse Mag., N.Y.C., 1976—; adj. asst. prof. Coll. New Rochelle, 1973-74; fireman, N.Y.C., 1963—. Bd. dirs. Boys Clubs Am., N.Y.C.; bd. dirs., v.p. Kips Bay Boys Club. Served with USAF, 1957-60. Recipient Christopher award for Non-Fiction, 1973. Mem. Author's Guild, Internat. Assn. Fire Fighters. Democrat. Roman Catholic. Home: 114 E 84th St New York City NY 10028 also Phillipsbrook Rd Garrison NY 10524

SMITH, DONALD ALVIN, advt. exec.; b. Boston, Aug. 3, 1920; s. Adelbert W. and Ella Roberta (Baker) S.; A.B. magna cum laude, Brown U., 1941; m. Elizabeth Fielden, Sept. 8, 1945; children—Judith Smith Hess, Jeffrey. Editor, Boy Scouts Am., N.Y.C., 1942-44; copywriter Benton & Bowles, Inc., N.Y.C., 1944-55; creative dir. Lynn Orgn., Inc., Wilkes-Barre, Pa., 1955-58, v.p., 1958-77; advt. mgr. Met. Wire Corp., Wilkes-Barre, 1977—; tchr. mass communications Pa. State U., Wilkes-Barre, 1971. Mem. Advt. Fedn. Am. (treas. 2d dist. 1961-63), Advt. Club Wilkes-Barre (pres. 1961-62), N.E. Pa. Advt. Club (pres. 1978-79), Phi Beta Kappa, Phi Delta Theta. Clubs: Back Mountain Kennel (pres. 1968-70), Westmoreland (Wilkes-Barre); Afghan Hound of Am. (pres. 1955-59, 61-66). Home: 559 Charles Ave Kingston PA 18704 Office: N Washington St and George Ave Wilkes-Barre PA 18705

SMITH, DONALD WILLIAM, paint co. exec.; b. Lockport, N.Y., Dec. 31, 1938; s. Elmer Francis (stepfather) and Anna Elizabeth (Keller) Hufnagel; student Canisius Coll., 1956-58; A.A.S. in Chemistry, Erie Community Coll., 1961; m. Kathryn Alice Duffy, May 27, 1967; children—Donald William III, Allison Marie, Erica Ann. Staff asst. Sandia Corp., Albuquerque, 1961-65; technologist Union Carbide Corp., Tonawanda, N.Y., 1966-67; safety engr. Bell Aerospace, Niagara Falls, N.Y., 1968-69; corporate indsl. hygienist Carborundum Co., Niagara Falls, 1970-71; mgr. safety and environ. affairs Pratt & Lambert, Inc., Buffalo, 1972—. Mem. occupational health com. Am. Lung Assn. Western N.Y., Buffalo Area C. of C.; v.p. North Tonawanda Am. Little League; bd. dirs. Western N.Y. Safety Conf. Registered profl. engr., Calif.; certified safety profl. Mem. Am. Soc. Safety Engrs. (treas. Niagara Frontier chpt.), Nat. Fire Protection Assn., Adhesives and Sealants Council (govt. relations com.), Am. Soc. Indsl. Security, Am. Indsl. Hygiene Assn. (pres. sect. 1970-71), Nat. Safety Mgmt. Soc., Nat. Paint and Coatings Assn. (chmn. occupational health research subcom.), Canadian Paint Mfrs. Assn. (occupational health and safety com.). Democrat. Roman Catholic. Home: 509 Meadowbrook Dr North Tonawanda NY 14120 Office: 75 Tonawanda St Buffalo NY 14207

SMITH, DONN J., real estate co. exec.; b. New Bethlehem, Pa., Feb. 26, 1927; s. Alfred H. and Hazel M. (Whiteman) S.; B.S. in Chem. Engring., Bucknell U., 1950; LL.B., George Washington U., 1956, J.D., 1968; m. Shirley S. Womeldorf, July 15, 1951; children—Gregory A.E., Glenn A.E. Plant chemist Sylvania Electric Products, Inc., Brookville, Pa., 1950-52, patent atty. trainee, 1952-56; admitted to Va. bar, 1956, U.S. Patent Office, 1953, Canadian Patent Office, 1973, patent atty. Westinghouse, Pitts., 1956-58, patent atty. sect. mgr., 1958-64; building contractor, Marrysville, Pa., 1964-65; asso. patent atty. firm Blenko, Leonard & Buell, Pitts., 1965-70; individual practice law specializing in patents, trademarks and copyrights, Pitts., 1970-76; mem. firm Smith & Carothers, Pitts., 1976-77; pres., chief exec. officer Donnwood, Inc., Donleybrook, Ltd., Sylvanettes, Ltd., Shirllane, Inc., Greensburg, Pa., 1976—, Glennfield, Inc., Shirldonne, Ltd., Greensburg, 1977—, Smithfield, Ltd., Smithvale, Inc., Greensburg, Pa., 1978—. Active Boy Scouts Am., 1967-74, YMCA Indian Guides, 1962-67. Served with U.S. Army, 1945-46. Club: Eagles. Home: 166 Round Top Rd Export RD3 PA 15632 Office: 402 Coulter Bldg Greensburg PA 15601

SMITH, E(DMUND) CARLYLE, real estate broker; b. Syracuse, N.Y., July 4, 1928; s. Edward J. and Grace (Michels) S.; B.S., Brockport State Tchrs. Coll., 1952; m. Clare Loeber, June 14, 1952; children—Julie, Larry, Cheryl, Vicki, David, Timothy. Reservation agt. Am. Airlines, Syracuse, 1952-53; traffic supt. N.Y. Telephone Co., Syracuse, 1953-58; traffic supt. Longley & Jones Real Estate, Syracuse, 1958—; pres. Multiple Listing Service Greater Syracuse Bd. Realtors, 1968, chmn. legis. com., 1968—. Mem. Dist. Atty. Advisory Council Syracuse, 1969—. Named Realtor of Yr., Syracuse, 1970. Mem. Syracuse Bd. Realtors (pres. 1968, 73), N.Y. State (chmn. conv. 1970), Syracuse (dir.) real estate bds., N.Y. State Assn. Real Estate Bds. (state legis. chmn.), Syracuse C. of C. (dir.), N.Y. State Golf Assn. (dir.). Clubs: Skyline Golf and Country (pres., dir.), Skaneareles Golf and Country, Bellevue Golf and Country. Home: 4229 Wolf Hollow Rd Syracuse NY 13219 Office: 935 James St Syracuse NY 13201

SMITH, EDWARD JAMES, coll. dean; b. Hays, Kans., Apr. 7, 1929; s. Edward Jacob and Margaret Louise (Boyer) S.; B.S., U. Notre Dame, 1952; M.S., U. Colo., 1955, Ed.D., 1958; m. Frances Carol Johnson, Aug. 25, 1954; children—Tangi, Holly, Kully, Karla, Shawn. Instr., coach U. Colo., Boulder, 1954-56, dean, 1959-63; dean U. N.Mex., Albuquerque, 1963-69; dean student affairs Plymouth (N.H.) State Coll., 1969—. Chmn. United Fund Drive, Albuquerque, 1968; vice chmn. ARC, Plymouth, 1969; mem. Plymouth Town Planning Bd., 1970; trustee Sceva Speare Hosp., Plymouth, 1970. Served to capt. USMCR, 1952-54. Mem. Nat. Assn. Student Personnel Adminstrs. (state dir. 1977—), Assn. Coll. and Univ. Housing Officers (regional pres. 1969), Nat. Assn. Fin. Aid Officers, Assn. Coll. and Univ. Staffing, Am. Personnel and Guidance Assn., Kappa Delta Pi. Club: Varsity (Plymouth). Home: 100 Tobey Rd Plymouth NH 03264 Office: Plymouth State College Plymouth NH 03264

SMITH, EDWARD SAMUEL, judge; b. Birmingham, Ala., Mar. 27, 1919; s. Joseph Daniel and Sarah Jane (Tatum) S.; student Ala. Poly. Inst., 1936-38; B.A., U. Va., 1941, J.D., 1947; m. Innes Adams Comer, May 5, 1942; children—Edward Samuel, Innes Comer Smith Richards. Admitted to Va. bar, 1947, D.C. bar, 1948, Md. bar, 1953; practiced in Washington, 1947-63, Balt., 1963—; asso., partner Blair, Korner, Doyle & Appel, 1947-54; partner Blair, Korner, Doyle & Worth, 1954-61; chief trial sect. Tax Div., U.S. Dept. Justice, 1961, asst. for civil trials, 1961-63; partner Piper & Marbury, Balt., 1963-78; apptd. asso. judge U.S. Ct. Claims, 1978—. Past pres., trustee St.

Andrew's Soc. Washington. Served to lt. USNR, 1941-46. Mem. Am., Fed., Md., Balt. City, D.C., Va. bar assns., Nat. Lawyers Club Washington, Lambda Chi Alpha. Democrat. Episcopalian. Clubs: Chevy Chase (Md.), Mountain Brook (Birmingham); Mchts. (Balt.). Home: 3708 Taylor St Chevy Chase MD 20015 Office: 717 Madison Pl NW Washington DC 20005

SMITH, ELSIE MAE, counselor, educator; b. Vicksburgh, Miss., July 8, 1943; s. Richard and Geneva Mae (Totten) Jones; B.S., State U. Coll., Buffalo, 1966; Ed.M., State U. N.Y., Buffalo, 1970, Ph.D., 1973. Tchr. English, Kenmore (N.Y.) East Sr. High Sch., 1966-69; counselor Buffalo Pub. Schs., 1969-70; counselor State U. Coll., Buffalo, 1970-72; asst. prof. counselor edn. Boston U., 1973-74; asst. prof. counselor psychology State U. N.Y., Buffalo, 1974-76, asso. prof., 1977—. Vol. Buffalo Cancer Crusade. Mem. Am. Psychol. Assn., Assn. Counselor Edn. and Supervision, Am. Ednl. Research Assn., Nat. Assn. Women Deans, Adminstrs. and Counselors, Urban League, NAACP, Jack and Jill Soc. Am. Author: Counseling the Culturally Different Black Youth, 1973; Group Counseling: Theory and Process, 1976. Contbr. articles to profl. jours. Editorial bd. Jour. Counseling Psychology, 1976-81, Personnel and Guidance Jour., 1976-78, Counselor Edn. and Supervision Jour., 1976-79. Office: 416 Christopher Blady Hall State U NY at Buffalo Amherst NY 14260

SMITH, ERIC, chemist; b. Woolwich, Eng., June 2, 1928; s. Terence George and Jessie Mary S.; came to U.S., 1956; B.Sc. with honors, Imperial Coll., London, 1947, Ph.D., 1949; postdoctoral fellow U. Conn., 1972-74; m. Patricia Kelley, Nov. 13, 1958 (div.); children—Karen Jessie Marie, Moira Ruth Ann. Sr. chemist Monsanto, Springfield, Mass., 1949-60; research asso. Olin, New Haven, 1960-72; mgr. applied chemistry Amicon, Lexington, Mass., 1975-77; sr. scientist Purdue Frederick Research Center, Yonkers, N.Y., 1977—; cons. Mem. Royal Inst. Chemistry. Unitarian. Contbr. articles on organic and polymer chemistry to profl. jours. Holder 30 U.S. patents. Home: 1116 Warburton Ave Apt 3N Yonkers NY 10701 Office: 99 101 Sawmill River Rd Yonkers NY 10701

SMITH, ERIC PARKMAN, r.r. exec.; b. Cambridge, Mass., Mar. 23, 1910; s. Benjamin Farnham and Helen Train (Blanchard) S.; A.B., Harvard U., 1932, M.B.A., 1934. Statistician, Fed. Coordinator Transp., Washington, 1934; with New Haven R.R., Boston, New Haven, 1934-53; with Maine Central R.R., Portland, 1953—, asst. treas., dir. cost analysis, 1970—; dir. J.P. Nourse Corp., Shepard & Morse Lumber Co. Trustee parish donations First Parish, Concord, Mass., 1960—; sec. adv. bd. Maine Central R.R. Co. Retirement Trust Plan. Mem. New Eng. R.R. Club (pres. 1973-74). Republican. Unitarian. Author: Verses on an Icelandic Vacation, 1965. Home: Academy Ln Concord MA 01742 Office: 242 St John St Portland ME 04102

SMITH, FRANCIS ALOYSIUS, JR., lawyer; b. Greenfield, Mass., Feb. 19, 1923; s. Francis Aloysius and Marie (Harrington) S.; B.S., U. Notre Dame, 1947; LL.B., Fordham U., 1950; m. Catherine C. O'Neill, Apr. 28, 1951; children—Brigid Marie, Mary-Ellen, Margaret Mary. Admitted to Conn. bar, 1951, Fed. bar, 1952; mem. firm Pullman Comley Bradley & Reeves, Bridgeport, Conn., 1951-58, partner, 1958—. Pres. lay advisory bd. Notre Dame, Easton, Conn. Served with U.S. Army, 1942-45. Decorated Bronze Star. Fellow Am. Coll. Trial Lawyers; mem. Am., Bridgeport, Conn. bar assns. Republican. Roman Catholic. Club: Algonquin. Home: 32 Southfield Rd Easton CT 06612 Office: 855 Main St Bridgeport CT 06604

SMITH, FRANCIS WAVERLY, def. contract exec.; b. Milo, Maine, July 11, 1921; s. Frank William and Gladys Jenny (Beal) S.; B.B.A., Northeastern U., 1956; postgrad. Dept. Def. Schs.; m. Anne Veronica Zick, Oct. 2, 1948; children—William Francis, Daniel Eric. Chief insp. U.S. Naval Ammunition Depot, Hingham, Mass., 1952-58, foreman ordnance, 1958-61; quality control dir. Insp. of Naval Material, Reading, Pa., 1961-64; chief quality assurance Def. Logistics Agency, Contract Mgmt. Area, Reading, 1964—. Bd. dirs. Berks County Easter Seal Soc. Served with USAAF, 1943-46. Certified profl. contracts mgr.; recipient Ann. award for Profl. Excellence, Def. Logistics Agency, 1975. Sr. mem. Am. Soc. for Quality Control (past chmn. Reading sect.); mem. Nat. Contract Mgmt. Assn. (bd. dirs.; past pres. E. Central Pa. chpt.), Am. Bus. Clubs (past pres. Spring Twp. chpt.). Methodist. Clubs: Green Valley Country, Masons, Shriners. Home: 213 Shakespeare Dr Cornwall Terr Reading PA 19608 Office: 45 S Front St Reading PA 19602

SMITH, FRANK JUNIUS, ins. co. exec.; b. Richmond, Va., Oct. 21, 1937; s. Albert Brown and Odeal (Seal) S.; B.S., Hampton Inst., 1960; M.B.A., Am. U., 1967; postgrad. Rensselaer Poly. Inst., 1972; m. Shirley Elizabeth Carter, June 4, 1960; children—Monica T., Frank Junius, Leah F. Methods engr. Melpar, Inc., Falls Church, Va., 1961-62; staff specialist Vitro Corp. Am., Silver Spring, Md., 1962-67; staff indsl. engr. Pratt & Whitney, East Hartford, Conn., 1967-69; supr. Conn. Gen. Ins. Co., Bloomfield, 1969-74; asst. dir. Travelers Ins. Co., Hartford, Conn., 1974—. Incorporator, Manchester Meml. Hosp., 1978. Recipient Award of Excellence, Am. Inst. Indsl. Engrs., 1978; Ujima award for service to the orgn. and Greater Hartford Community, 1976; Recruitment award Nat. Hampton Alumni Assn., 1978. Mem. Am. Inst. Indsl. Engrs. (pres. 1977-78), Assn. for Systems Mgmt., Assn. Internal Mgmt. Consultants. Roman Catholic. Club: Ellington Ridge Country. Home: 93 Ferguson Rd Manchester CT 06040 Office: 1 Tower Sq Hartford CT 06115

SMITH, FREDERICK ORVILLE, II, woodturning co. exec.; b. Cambridge, Mass., July 17, 1934; s. Harry Francis and Dorothy (Zeller) S.; A.B., Bowdoin Coll., 1956; m. Mabel-Roxie Moore, June 5, 1965; children—Sarah Zeller, Jennifer Joy, Erica Hildred. Exec. trainee Fred O. Smith Mfg. Co., New Vineyard, Maine, 1956, sec., 1960-65, v.p., clk., 1965-71, acting pres., treas., 1969-71, pres., treas., 1971—. Dir. CD, New Vineyard, 1961-70; vol. fireman, New Vineyard, 1960—; mem. Sch. Bd., 1968; notary pub.; justice peace; mem. nat. com. Young Republicans, 1960-62, Maine pres., 1962-64, New Eng. pres., 1963-65, dir. nat. fedn., 1963-65; Rep. fin. chmn. Franklin County, Maine, 1966-71, exec. com., 1972—; New Vineyard Rep. town chmn., 1972—; chmn. Franklin County Rep. Com., 1976—; chmn. Maine Rep. County Chmns.' Assn., 1976—; alt. del. Rep. Nat. Conv., 1968. Served with USNR, 1957-60; lt. comdr. Res. Mem. Woodturners and Shapers Assn., Maine Fish and Game Assn. (legis. rep. 1969), Porter Lake Fish and Game Assn. (pres. 1969), Maine Hardwood Assn. Congregationalist. Clubs: Sugarloaf (Maine) Ski, Masons, Shriners. Home: High St New Vineyard ME 14956 Office: Main St New Vineyard ME 04956

SMITH, GAIL PRESTON, physicist; b. Rochester, Pa., Jan. 25, 1915; s. Daniel and Sarah Amanda (Ketterer) S.; B.S., Geneva Coll., Pa., 1934; M.A., Syracuse (N.Y.) U., 1935; Ph.D., U. Mich., 1941; m. Martha Marian Cameron, June 8, 1937; children—Daniel Preston, Martha Marian. Instr. Battle Creek (Mich.) Coll., 1936, Geneva Coll., 1936-37; asst. U. Mich., 1937-41; mem. research staff Corning Glass Works (N.Y.), 1941—, dir. math. phys. and chem. analytical services and tech. liaison, 1970—. Chmn. adv. council Corning Sch. Dist., 1955-56, Citizens for Adequate Schs., 1957-58; physics vis. com. Clarkson Coll., Potsdam, N.Y., 1961-64, chmn., 1963-64. Recipient Distinguished Service Alumnus award Geneva Coll., 1959. Mem. Am. Phys. Soc. (chmn. N.Y. State sect. 1951-53), Am. Optical Soc., AAAS, Am. Ceramic Soc. (chmn. corp. assos. com. 1978—), N.Y. Acad. Scis., Soc. Glass Tech., Inst. Physics and Phys. Soc., Union Sci. Continentale du Verre, Sigma Xi, Sigma Pi Sigma. Home: 75 Caton Rd Corning NY 14830 Office: Corning Glass Works Sullivan Park Corning NY 14830

SMITH, GARY LEE, agrl. engr.; b. Confluence, Pa., Dec. 12, 1950; s. Charles Kenneth and Martha Mildred (Nickelson) S.; B.S., Pa. State U., 1973, M.S., 1975; postgrad. U. Md., 1976—. Test engr. Applied Research Lab., Pa. State U., University Park, 1973-75; extension agrl. engr., faculty in machine design and power systems, Dept. Agrl. Engring., U. Md., College Park, 1975—; cons. and lectr. in field. Energy project judge Prince Georges County Sci. Fair, 1976-77; region workshop leader Citizens Workshop program U.S. Dept. Energy. Recipient Am. Soc. Agrl. Engrs. Blue Ribbon Award for Excellence in Extension Methods, 1977. Mem. Am. Soc. Agrl. Engring., Nat. Inst. for Farm Safety, Coop. Extension Specialists Assn., Triangle. Club: Lions. Contbr. numerous articles to profl. jours.; patentee in field. Office: Dept Agrl Engring U Md College Park MD 20742

SMITH, GEORGE THOMAS, city ofcl. Randolph (N.J.); b. N.Y.C., Apr. 21, 1947; s. George Thomas and Margaret Teresa (MacDonald) S.; B.B.A., Nichols Coll., Dudley, Mass., 1968; M.A., Central Mich. U., 1974; LL.B., Blackstone Coll. Law, 1971; Ed.D., Calif. Western U., 1978; m. Caroline Alden Vose, July 28, 1973; 1 son, Sean Alden. With Up With People, Inc., Tucson, 1968-70, Coast Fed. Savs. & Loan Assn., Los Angeles, 1970-72, A & W Restaurants, Grand Ledge, Mich., 1972-73; dir. parks and recreation City of Randolph, 1974-78, dir. CD, 1975-78; asst. prof. Morris County Coll., 1974—; adj. prof. Kean Coll., 1974-77. Served to 1st lt. USAF, 1971-77. Decorated Red Service medal C.A.P., 1974; knights cross Order Constantine; comdrs. cross Sursum Corda; recipient Nat. award merit Sports Found., 1974-76; Paul Harris fellow Rotary Internat., 1977; named Jaycee of Year, Randolph Jaycees, 1976; recipient Nat. Jamboree award Boy Scouts Am., 1969, Eagle Scout award, 1964. Mem. Am. Park and Recreation Soc., Soc. Park and Recreation Educators, Nat., N.J. recreation and parks assns., N.J. Turf Grass Assn., Nat. Eagle Scout Assn., Nat. Pub. Parks Tennis Assn. (dir. 1977—), Am. Assn. Leisure and Recreation, Am. Radio Relay League, Randolph Jaycees, Split Rock Radio Assn. Roman Catholic. Clubs: Randolph Athletic, Randolph Rotary. Home: PO Box 444 Mount Freedom NJ 07970 Office: Morris County Coll Rt 10 Randolph NJ 07801

SMITH, GEORGE WILLIAM, psychiatrist; b. Mechanicsburg, Pa., Nov. 5, 1939; s. George Alvin and Laura Irene (Fishel) S.; B.S., Lebanon Valley Coll., 1961; M.D., Jefferson Med. Coll., Phila., 1965. Intern, Harrisburg Hosp., 1965-66; resident in psychiatry Eastern Pa. Psychiat. Inst., Phila., 1966-69; fellow in adolescent psychiatry U. Mich. Hosp., Ann Arbor, 1971-72; with Harrisburg Hosp. Mental Health/Mental Retardation Center, 1972—, cons. adolescent psychiatry and group psychotherapy, 1976—; clin. asst. prof. Pa. State U. Med. Coll., Hershey Med. Center, 1975—; mem. Dauphin County Sanity Commn., 1974-76; staff psychiatrist Inst. Human Identity, N.Y.C., 1973-76; Pa. Gov. appointee Pa. Council for Sexual Minorities, 1976-77. Served as maj. USAF, 1969-71; Vietnam. Fellow Am. Orthopsychiat. Assn.; mem. Am. Psychiat. Assn., Pa., Central Pa. psychiat. socs., Am. Soc. Adolescent Psychiatry, Phila. Soc. Adolescent Psychiatry, Soc. USAF Psychiatrists, ACLU, Am. Soc. Group Psychotherapy and Psychodrama, Am. Group Psychotherapy Assn., Am. Assn. Sex Educators, Counselors and Therapists, Am. Coll. Health Assn. Democrat. Home: 101 S 2d St #1218 Harrisburg PA 17101 Office: Harrisburg Hospital Mental Health Mental Retardation Center Harrisburg PA 17101

SMITH, GERRIT JOSEPH, educator; b. Syracuse, N.Y., Dec. 18, 1938; s. Gerrit Joseph and Margaret Mae (Guilfoyle) S.; B.S., Le Moyne Coll., 1960; M.S., Boston Coll., 1962; licentiate in philosophy Loyola Seminary, Shrub Oak, N.Y., 1966; Ph.D., Syracuse U., 1971; m. Aileen Mary McLoughlin, July 28, 1972. Teaching asst. Boston Coll., 1960, research asst. nuclear physics, 1961-62; teaching asst. Syracuse U., 1966, research asst. relativity physics, 1967-70, postdoctoral research asso. relativity, 1971; instr. phys. sci. study com. physics Regis High Sch., N.Y.C., 1970; asst. prof. philosophy Fordham U., 1972—. Mem. Am. Phys. Soc., Am. Philos. Assn. Democrat. Roman Catholic. Contbr. articles in field to profl. jours. Home: 630 E 187th St Bronx NY 10458 Office: Philosophy Dept Fordham Univ Bronx NY 10458

SMITH, GORDON ROSS, English scholar, educator; b. Monmouth County, N.J., May 23, 1917; s. Mortimer Dickerson and Elizabeth Clara (Ross) S.; B.S., Columbia U., 1948, M.A., 1949; Ph.D., Pa. State U., 1956; m. Jane Pakenham, Aug. 29, 1948; children—Gordon Ross, Corinna Pakenham. Instr. English, Waynesburg (Pa.) Coll., 1949-50; instr. English, Pa. State U., 1950-56, asst. prof., 1956-59, asso. prof., 1959-63, prof., 1963-66; Folger Shakespeare Library fellow, 1958; Fulbright lectr. Royal U. Malta, 1962-63; prof. English, Temple U., Phila., 1966—. Democratic Party committeeman, State Coll., Pa., 1952-56. Served with AUS, 1943-46. Mem. Modern Lang. Assn., Shakespeare Assn. Am., Internat. Shakespeare Assn. Author: A Classified Shakespeare Bibliography, 1936-58, 1963; Essays on Shakespeare, 1965; contbr. articles to scholarly jours. Home: 35 Red Oak Rd Oreland PA 19075 Office: English Dept Temple Univ Philadelphia PA 19122

SMITH, HALE, composer, arranger; b. Cleve., June 29, 1925; s. Hale and Jimmie A. (Clay) S.; Mus.B., Cleve. Inst. Music, 1950, Mus.M., 1952; m. Juanita Ruth Hancock, Feb. 15, 1948; children—Hale Michael, Marcel Hancock, Robin Alison, Eric Dale. Compositions performed by Louisville Orch., 1961, Cleve. Orch., 1966, Cin. Orch., 1967, New Haven Orch., 1968, Dallas Symphony Orch., 1970, N.Y. Philharmonic, Springfield Symphony, Amsterdam Philharmonic, 1971, Atlanta Symphony; Richmond Symphony, 1972; Houston Symphony, 1974, Detroit, Nat., Am. symphonies, 1976; arranger for pubs., jazz performers; editor E.B. Marks Music Corp., Sam Fox Music Pubs.; editor, gen. music adviser Frank Music Corp.; mus. cons. C.F. Peters Corp. Chmn. Freeport Arts Council, 1974; panelist Nat. Endowment for Arts, 1978; lectr., prof. music U. Conn. Mem. bd. ethics Village of Freeport, N.Y.; pres. Freeport Block and Civic Assn., 1965—. Served with AUS, 1943-45. Recipient B.M.I. Student Composer award, 1952, Cleve. arts prize, 1973. Mem. Am. Composers Alliance (bd. govs.), Bohemians. Composer: Duo for Violin and Piano, 1952; In Memoriam, 1953; Epicedial Variations, 1955; Two Love Songs of John Donne, 1958; Three Brevities for Solo Flute, 1960; Contours for Orch., 1960; Evocation, 1965; Somersault, 1964; Music for Harp and Orch., 1966; Orchestral Set (1952-68), Faces of Jazz, 1968, Expansions, 1967; Beyond The Rim of Day, 1970; By Yearning and By Beautiful, 1970; The Valley Wind; Anticipations, Introspections and Reflections, 1971; Comes Tomorrow, 1972; Concert Music for Piano and Orchestra, 1972; Ritual and Incantations for Orchestra, 1974; Introduction, Cadenzas and Interludes, 1974; Variations for Six Players, 1975; Innerflexions for Orchestra, 1977. Home: 222 Independence Ave Freeport NY 11520

SMITH, HAMILTON OTHANEL, microbiologist; b. N.Y.C., Aug. 23, 1931; s. Tommie Harkey and Bunnie (Othanel) S.; student U. Ill., 1948-50; A.B. in Math., U. Calif., Berkeley, 1952; M.D., Johns Hopkins U., 1956; m. Elizabeth Anne Bolton, 1957; children—Joel, Barry, Dirk, Bryan, Kirsten. Intern, Barnes Hosp., St. Louis, 1956-57; resident Henry Ford Hosp., Detroit, 1959-62; NIH postdoctoral fellow, dept. human genetics U. Mich., Ann Arbor, 1962-64, research asso., 1964-67; asst. prof. microbiology Johns Hopkins U. Sch. Medicine, 1967-70, asso. prof., 1970-73, prof., 1973—. Served to lt. M.C., USN, 1957-59. Recipient Nobel prize in medicine, 1978; Guggenheim fellow, 1975-76. Mem. Am. Soc. Microbiology, AAAS, Am. Soc. Biol. Chemists. Research and pubs. in field. Home: 8222 Carrbridge Circle Baltimore MD 21204 Office: 725 N Wolfe St Baltimore MD 21205

SMITH, HAROLD CHARLES, financial exec.; b. N.Y.C., Jan. 11, 1934; s. Harold E. and Hedwig Agnes (Gronke) S.; B.A. cum laude, Ursinus Coll. 1955; M.B.A., N.Y. U., 1958; B.D., Union Theol. Sem., 1958. Research dir. YMCA Retirement Fund, N.Y.C., 1958-65, asst. sec. investments 1965-75, asso. sec., 1975-77, v.p., 1977—; asso. prof. bus. fin. L.I. U., 1967-70. Mem. Congress Plaza Redevel. Commn., Bridgeport, Conn., 1972-76. Mem. Am. Econs. Assn., Acad. Profl. Certified Dirs., Assn. Profl. Dirs. YMCA's, Acad. Chartered Profl. Dirs. YMCA's, Fin. Analysts Fedn., N.Y. Soc. Security Analysts. Mem. United Ch. Christ. Clubs: Masons, Mchts. (N.Y.C.); Oronoque Village Country (Stratford, Conn.). Home: 215 W 259 St New York City NY 10471 Office: 291 Broadway New York City NY

SMITH, HAROLD WEBSTER, savs. and loan assn. exec.; b. Waterbury, Conn., July 23, 1911; s. James Emile and Margaret Loretta (Dunn) S.; B.A. cum laude, Dartmouth Coll. 1933; m. Elizabeth Grant Copenhaver, Nov. 10, 1945; children—Harold Webster, Robert, James, Margaret Smith, Ann. Asst. to dir. of U.S. Mint, 1933-35; with First Fed. Savs. and Loan Assn., Waterbury, 1935—, pres., dir., 1946—; dir. Canadian Internat. Power, Heminway Corp., Internat. Power Co., So. New Eng. Telephone Co., Baldwin-United Corp., Buell Industries. Corporator, bd. dirs. Naugatuck Valley Devel. Corp.; corporator, past bd. dirs. United Council and Fund, Greater Waterbury Indsl. Devel. Corp.; past treas. Waterbury Tercentennial Com.; trustee Post Coll., Waterbury Found.; corporator, past pres., trustee Waterbury Hosp. Served to lt. comdr. USNR, 1942-46. Mem. U.S. League Savs. Assn. (past dir.), Savs. and Loan League Conn. (past pres., dir.), Alpha Delta Phi. Democrat. Roman Catholic. Clubs: Waterbury, Waterbury Country; Conn. Srs. Golf Assn. Home: 22-B Heritage Circle Southbury CT 06488 Office: 50 Leavenworth St Box 191 Waterbury CT 06720

SMITH, HARRIS FREDERIC, chem. co. exec.; b. Newark, Sept. 4, 1919; s. Frederic William and Grace (Harris) S.; A.B., Princeton U., 1941; student Columbia U. Law Sch., 1941-42; m. Betty Jane List, Apr. 8, 1949; children—Timothy Laurence, Todd Atkin. Mem. sales dept. Weston Elec. Instrument Corp., Newark, 1948-49; lab. dir. Indsl. Radiant Heat Corp., Gladstone, N.J., 1949-54; sec. Acro Chem. Products Corp., Long Valley, N.J., 1955-60, pres., 1960—; dir. Fidelity Union Trust Co., Newark. Pres. Camp Speers-Eljabar YMCA, 1970-76; pres. Tewksbury Twp. Bd. Edn., 1952-56. Served with USNR, 1942-47. Republican. Presbyterian. Clubs: Skytop, Essex, Princeton (N.Y.C.), Tewksbury Balloon. Home: Rural Route 1 Box 41 Califon NJ 07830 Office: 20 Parker Rd Long Valley NJ 07853

SMITH, HARRISON HARVEY, newspaper pub. exec.; b. Wilkes-Barre, Pa., Oct. 24, 1915; s. Ernest Gray and Marjorie (Harvey) S.; literary-sci. diploma Wyoming (Pa.) Sem., 1936; postgrad. Medill Sch. Journalism Northwestern U., 1937-38; m. Joanne Christopher, June 7, 1940; children—Barbara Dewitt, Marjorie Harvey, Susan C.; m. 2d, Margaret Simons, July 18, 1947; children—Roseanne Jameson, Elizabeth Simons. Asst. pub. Wilkes-Barre Times-Leader, 1938-39, v.p., asst. sec., 1939-46, pres., 1946—; editor Wilkes-Barre Record, 1962-72; dir. 1st Eastern Bank of Wilkes-Barres. Chmn., Wyoming Valley chpt. ARC, 1954-55, chmn. NE Pa. Blood Center, 1955-56; v.p. Wilkes-Barre Gen. Hosp., 1954-76. Served with U.S. Mil. Govt., Korea, 1945-46. Recipient Distinguished Service Award U.S. Jr. C. of C., 1949. Mem. Am. Soc. Newspaper Editors, Nat. Conf. Editorial Writers, Am., Pa. (exec. com.) newspaper publishers' assns., Associated Press of Pa. (pres. 1953), Wyoming Hist. Soc. (pres. 1971-74), Sigma Delta Chi. Republican. Presbyterian. Clubs: Newcomen, Poor Richard (Phila.); Westmoreland (Wilkes-Barre); Masons. Home: RFD 5 Shrine View Dallas PA 18612 Office: 15 N Main St Wilkes-Barre PA 18711

SMITH, HERBERT DEWITT, ret. rubber co. exec.; b. Piedmont, Calif., Mar. 31, 1914; s. Herbert E. and Alice (Crocheron) S.; B.A., Yale U., 1937; m. Dorothy Parr, May 17, 1941;children—Meryl Crocheron Smith Renwick III, Herbert Cortelyou. Tire salesman U.S. Rubber Co., Detroit, 1946-49, dist. mgr., Newark, 1949-52, mgr. oil marketer sales, tire div., N.Y.C., 1953-56, dir. mfrs. sales, tire div., Detroit, 1956-58, gen. sales mgr. U.S. Royal Tires, N.Y.C., 1959-62, v.p. market U.S. Rubber Tire Co., N.Y.C., 1962-65, dir. market devel. U.S. Rubber Co., N.Y.C, 1965-68, v.p. Uniroyal Inc., (formerly U.S. Rubber), 1968-75; mem. nat. motor vehicle safety advisory council U.S. Dept. Transp., 1972-77. Past trustee Rumson (N.J.) Country Day Sch.; trustee Monmouth Med. Center, Long Branch, N.J. Served. to lt. comdr. USNR, 1940-46. Mem. Soc. Automotive Engrs., Army Ordnance Assn., Am. Petroleum Inst. Club: Seabrigh (N.J.) Beach (past trustee); Racquet and Tennis, Links, Yale (all N.Y.); Rumson Country (dir., pres.). Home: 140 Bingham Ave Rumson NJ 07760

SMITH, HILARY CRANWELL BOWEN, security analyst; b. Balt., Nov. 1, 1937; s. Henry Bowen and Alice Clayton Cranwell (Seward) S.; B.A., Colgate U., 1960; M.B.A., U. Va., 1967; m. Janet E. Simmons, June 9, 1962; children—Kent, Kendall, Hillary. Researcher, jr. analyst 1st. Nat. City Bank, N.Y.C., 1964-65; asst. v.p. Mercantile Safe Deposit & Trust Co., Balt., 1967-69; v.p. research Goldman Sachs Co., N.Y.C., 1969-74; v.p. E.F. Hutton & Co., N.Y.C., 1974-77; 1st v.p. Blyth Eastman Dillon Co., N.Y.C., 1977—. Mem. Wilton Town (Conn.) Retirement Bd., 1972-73; pres. Voice, 1972-73, George Cobb Fellowship, 1957-60. Served to lt. USNR, 1960-63. Mem. Paper and Forest Products Industry Analysts Group (pres. 1975-76), N.Y. Soc. Security Analysts. Presbyterian. Home: 334 Lake Ave Greenwich CT 06830 Office: 1221 Ave of the Americas New York City NY 10020

SMITH, HOWARD A., analytical chemist; b. St. Cloud, Minn., Nov. 8, 1930; s. Albert J. and Mathilda E. (Zinken) S.; B.S., St. Johns U., 1952; M.S., U. Colo., 1954; m. Nancy L. Schenk, June 20, 1953; children—Curtis, Lee, Judy, David. With E.I. Du Pont De Nemours & Co. Inc., N.J., Tex., Ky., Del., 1954—, head quality control dept., Louisville, 1966—, supt. environ. and energy mgmt., Deepwater, N.J., 1974-78, mgr. mfg. environ. and health, Elastomer chems. dept., Wilmington, Del., 1978—. Leader Beaumont (Tex.) council Boy Scouts Am., 1962-66, Old Ky. Home Council, 1966-74, Del-Mar-Va council, 1974—. Mem. AAAS, Am. Chem. Soc. (local chpt. treas., chmn. arrangement com.). Republican. Roman Catholic. Contbr. articles to sci. jours. Home: 15 Crestfield Rd Wilmington DE 19810 Office: Du Pont Elastomers Wilmington DE 19898

SMITH, HUGH ROBERTS HOVAL, lawyer; b. Chgo., Nov. 24, 1916; s. Hoval Arnold and Nina Cornelia (Roberts) S.; A.B., Yale U., 1939, LL.B., 1942; m. Marianne Morgan Moses, Nov. 7, 1942; children—Leslie, Lindsay, Morgan, Scott, Tilman. Admitted to D.C. bar, 1946, Md. bar, 1960; asso. firm Wilmer & Brown, Washington, 1946-50, mem. firm, 1950-62; mem. firm Wilmar, Cutler & Pickering, Washington, 1962—. Trustee Holton Arms Sch., Bethesda, Md., 1961—. Served to lt. USNR, 1942-46. Mem. Assn. Yale U. Alumni (gov. 1978—). Clubs: Chevy Chase (Md.) (past pres.); Yale (pres. 1976), Lawyers (sec. 1972—), Barristers (past pres.); Met. (Washington). Home: 6803 Meadow Ln Chevy Chase MD 20015 Office: 1666 K St NW Washington DC 20006

SMITH, J(OHN) GRAHAM, educator, bus. cons.; b. Staffordshire, Eng., Dec. 31, 1936; s. Henry and Mary Fraser (Aitken) S.; came to Can., 1965, naturalized, 1972; B.A. with honors, U. Nottingham (Eng.), 1958; M.A. in Econs., Ohio State U., 1961, Ph.D., 1964; m. Ricarda Brauer, Dec. 18, 1966; children—Andrew Fraser, Alexandra Mary Fraser. Instr. econs. Wellesley Coll., 1964-65; asst. prof. econ. and polit. sci. McGill U., Montreal, Que., Can.. 1965-67, asso. prof., 1967, prof. mgmt. and applied econs., 1974—, chmn. dept. econs., 1970-72; vis. sr. research fellow U. East Africa, Nairobi, Kenya, 1967-68, vis. sr. lectr. econs., 1968-69; vis. prof. U. Montreal, 1972-73; v.p., dir. IN.CEP., Ltd./Ltée, Montreal; dir. Modico Internat., Inc., Montreal, Regent Industries Ltd., Montreal; cons. to UN agys., Canadian fed. govt. depts., industry, trade, commerce. Recipient Can. Council awards. 1966, 67. Rockefeller award through McGill Program for Univs. Overseas, 1967-69, East African Teaching Found. award Ford Found., 1968. Mem. Canadian Council Internat. Cooperation, Institut Canadien des Affaires Internationales. Episcopalian. Co-author: The Conserver Soc., 1978; co-editor: Nationalism and the Multinational Enterprise, 1973. Contbr. articles to profl. jours. Home: 565 Grosvenor Ave Westmount PQ Canada Office: Faculty of Mgmt McGill U Montreal PQ H3C 3G1 Canada

SMITH, J(OHN) JOSEPH, fed. judge; b. Waterbury, Conn., Jan. 25, 1904; s. James Emile and Margaret Loretta (Dunn) S.; B.A., Yale U., 1925, J.D., 1927; m. Eleanor M. Murnane, Aug. 16, 1939; children—John Joseph, Richard P., Mary Eleanor Smith McCarthy, Mary Martha Smith Murphy. Admitted to Conn. bar, 1927; research fellow Yale Sch. Law, 1927-28; asso. firm Peasley & Klein, Waterbury, 1928; individual practice law, Waterbury, 1928-41; U.S. dist. judge Dist. of Conn., 1941-60; U.S. circuit judge 2d Circuit, 1960—, sr. circuit judge, 1971—. Mem. 74th through 77th Congresses from 5th Dist. Conn., Com. on Mil. Affairs, Steering Com.; active Democratic Nat. Congl. Campaign Com., 76th and 77th Congresses. Mem. Am., Conn., Waterbury bar assns., Am. Judicature Soc. Roman Catholic. Clubs: Wampanoag Country (West Hartford); Yale (N.Y.C.). Home: 27 Brenway Dr West Hartford CT 06117 Office: 450 Main St Hartford CT 06103

SMITH, JAMES ALMER, JR., psychiatrist; b. Montclair, N.J., May 30, 1923; s. James Almer and Carrie Elizabeth (Moten) S.; B.S., Howard U., 1946, M.D., 1948; m. Elsie Mae Brooks, Oct. 15, 1949; children—James Almer III, Rorger M., Margo A., Melanie K. Intern, Homer G. Phillips Hosp., St. Louis, 1948-49, resident in psychiatry, 1949-52; staff psychiatrist Hartley Salman Child Guidance Clinic, Hartford, Conn., 1955-60; asso. psychiatrist Springfield (Mass) Child Guidance Clinic, 1960—; cons. med. dir. Kolbourne Sch., Inc., New Marlborough, Mass., 1969—; cons. psychiatrist Valley View Farms, North Brookfield, Mass., 1970—. Mem. Springfield Human Relations Commn., 1961-62. Served with M.C., AUS, 1953-55. Recipient Human Service award Am. Acad. Human Services, 1974-75. Fellow Am. Orthopsychiat. Assn., Am. Assn. Psychoanalytic Physicians, Inc.; mem. Am. Psychiat. Assn. Baptist. Home: 96 Dartmouth St Springfield MA 01109

SMITH, JAMES FRANCIS, utilities exec.; b. Saugus, Mass., May 15, 1936; s. James Gregory and Marion Irene (Huckins) S.; A.B., Bentley Coll., 1956; m. Margaret Ellen Frame, Nov. 30, 1963; children—Ellen Hawley, James Gregory. Security analyst Boston Safe Deposit & Trust Co., 1956-58; pub. accountant Robert C. O'Connell, C.P.A., Boston, 1958-60; controller Precision Microwave Co., Saugus, 1960-65; with Orange and Rockland Utilities, Inc., 1965—, v.p., 1969-75, exec. v.p. fin. 1975-78, vice chmn., chmn. exec. com., 1978—, also dir. Trustee Tuxedo (N.Y.) Meml. Hosp.; affiliated Bay State Gas Co., Concord Electric Co., Exeter & Hampton Electric Co., Fitchburg Gas and Electric Light Co., Boston, 1965-75. Served with AUS, 1958-61. Mem. Am. Gas Assn., Edison Electric Inst., Fin. Execs. Inst. Clubs: Tuxedo (Tuxedo Park, N.Y.); Met. (N.Y.C.); Rockland Country (Sparkill, N.Y.). Home: Club House Rd Tuxedo Park NY 10987 Office 1 Blue Hill Plaza New York City NY 10965

SMITH, JEAN CHANDLER, ofcl. Smithsonian Instn.; b. Phila., Apr. 13, 1918; d. Chandler White and Philena Pennell (Cheetham) S.; A.B., Bryn Mawr Coll., 1939; M.S., Yale, 1953; M.L.S., Cath. U. Am., 1973. Reference librarian D.C. Pub. Library, 1939-43; translator C.Z., 1943-44; librarian Nat. Air Sta., Kaneohe Bay, Oahu, Hawaii, 1944-46; reference librarian, also research asso. Yale, 1947-58; acting chief acquisitions NIH Library, Bethesda, Md., 1959-63; chief reader services U.S. Dept. Interior, Washington, 1964-65; with Smithsonian Instn. Libraries, Washington, 1965—, asst. dir. instn. services, 1972-77, acting dir., 1977—. Mem. Friends of Library com. Bryn Mawr Coll., 1975—; sec., bd. dirs. Universal Serials and Book Exchange. Mem. Spl. Libraries Assn., ALA, AAAS. Clubs: Bryn Mawr Washington, Yale of Washington, Zonta. Home: 3601 Connecticut Ave Washington DC 20008 Office: Smithsonian Instn 1000 Jefferson Dr SW Washington DC 20560

SMITH, JEROME ROBERT, architect, educator; b. Oak Hill, W.Va., Apr. 17, 1938; s. Robert Hall and Lecy Mae (Havens) S.; B.Arch., Va. Poly. Inst., 1962; M.Arch. in Urban Design (Mellon fellow), Carnegie Inst. Tech., 1967; m. Margaret Smiley, Apr. 27, 1963; children—Melissa, Elaine. Designer, draftsman Hayes, Seay, Mattern and Mattern, Roanoke, Va., 1962-65; research architect Transp. Research Inst., Carnegie Inst. Tech., Pitts., 1966; architect Kohler, Misner, Daniels, Vienna, Va., 1967-68; asso. prof. archtl. tech. Anne Arundel Community Coll., Arnold, Md., 1968—, dir. program for archtl. technicians, 1968—; prin. Jerome R. Smith, Architect, Annapolis, Md., 1970—; major works include: Md. Capital Yacht Club, Annapolis, Barrel Shopping Mall, Blacksburg, Va., Hammock Island Marina-Pavilion, Pasadena, Md., Gray Residence, Annapolis, Allen Profl. Bldg., Annapolis, Warnock Residence, Battle Creek, Md., Astronomy Lab., Anne Arundel Community Coll., Haislip Residence, Davidsonville, Md. Registered profl. architect, Md., Pa., Va. Mem. AIA. Home: 210 Severn Grove Rd Annapolis MD 21401

SMITH, JOHN THOMAS, JR., psychologist; b. Columbia, Mo., Feb. 21, 1944; s. John Thomas and Jeannette Lucille (Cottrill) S.; B.S., U. Pitts., 1966, M.Ed., 1967, Ph.D. (NDEA fellow), 1971; m. Donna Sue Kwall, Aug. 22, 1968; 1 dau., Lauren Shana. Asst. to chancellor, asst. sec. bd. U. Pitts., 1968-71, instr. ednl. psychology, 1970-72, asso. registrar, 1971-72; asso. prof. ednl. psychology and psychology Indiana U. of Pa., 1972-73, summers 1974, 76, 77; psychologist, coordinator programs for gifted and talented ARIN Intermediate Unit, edn. agency, Indiana, Pa., 1973-75, psychologist, coordinator spl. edn., 1976-78, dir. spl. edn., 1978—; pvt. practice psychology, Indiana, Pa., 1973—. Bd. dirs. Indiana Area After-Sch. Center, 1974-77. Mem. Am., Eastern psychol. assns., Council Exceptional Children, Indiana Arts Council, Assn. for the Gifted, Pa. Assn. for Gifted Edn., Nat. Assn. Gifted Children, Indiana County (Pa.) Mental Health Assn., Phi Delta Kappa, Kappa Kappa Psi (hon.). Home: 120 Cambridge St Indiana PA 15701 Office: ARIN Intermediate Unit PO Box 175 Shelocta PA 15774

SMITH, JOSEPH MARSHALL, chem. co. exec.; b. Bayonne, N.J., July 26, 1921; s. Clarence Jenkins and Agnes McVicar (Marshall) S.; B.S. in Mech. Engring. with distinction, Akron U., 1947; m. Rosemarie Pilsitz, Feb. 1, 1947; children—Cynthia Ann, Joseph David, Michael John, Daniel Jamie, Mary Kay. Design engr. Babcock & Wilcox Co., Barberton, Ohio, 1938-40; with B.F. Goodrich Co., 1947—, plant engr., Pedricktown, N.J., 1970—. Mem. budget com. United Fund, Salem, N.J., 1971—. Served with C.E., AUS, 1942-46. Registered profl. engr., N.J., Ohio; cert. plant engr. Mem. VFW, Am. Legion, Tau Beta Pi, Sigma Tau. Roman Catholic. Home: 325 Westwood Dr Woodbury NJ 08096 Office: B F Goodrich Co PO Box 400 Pedricktown NJ 08067

SMITH, KATHLEEN TENER, banker; b. Pitts., Oct. 19, 1943; d. Edward Harrison, Jr. and Barbara Elizabeth (McCormick) Tener; B.A. summa cum laude, Vasser Coll., 1965; M.A., Harvard U., 1968; m.Roger Davis Smith, May 30, 1970; children—Silas Wheelock, Jocelyn Tener. Research asst. Harvard Grad. Sch. Bus. Adminstrn., 1967-69; with Chase Manhattan Bank, N.Y.C., 1969—, 2d v.p., 1972-73, v.p., 1973—. Class fund chmn. Vassar Coll., 1969-74. Mem. Am. Econ. Assn., Am. Fin. Assn., Phi Beta Kappa. Episcopalian. Club: Vassar (N.Y.C.). Home: 454 Route 32 N New Paltz NY 12561 Office: Financial Planning and Budgeting Dept Chase Manhattan Bank 1 Chase Manhattan Plaza New York NY 10015

SMITH, KENDRICK, fund raising cons.; b. N.Y.C., Jan. 6, 1922; s. Walter Murray and Doramont (Kendrick) S.; B.A., Amherst Coll., 1943; m. Margaret Ross Gray Sturtevant, Nov. 26, 1966; children—Deborah R. Sturtevant, Thomas C. Sturtevant, Kristin F. Sturtevant, Susan G. Sturtevant, K. Tasker. With Kersting Brown & Co., N.Y.C., 1946-63, v.p., sec., dir., 1963; fund raising cons., Wayland, Mass., 1963—; owner Info. Research Service; mem. Execs. in Edn.; judge Lilly Endowment Competition, 1976, 78. Trustee Beaver Country Day Sch., 1974. Served with USAAF, 1943-46; ETO. Home and Office: 12 Cole Rd Wayland MA 01778

SMITH, KENNETH JUDSON, JR., chemist, educator; b. Raleigh, N.C., Sept. 4, 1930; s. Kenneth Judson and Irene (Strickland) S.; A.B., E. Carolina U., 1957; M.A., Duke, 1959, Ph.D., 1961; m. Dorothy Margaret Ratcliffe, Mar. 6, 1953; children—Patricia Lynne (Mrs. Jackie Pittman), Pamela Jean. Research chemist Chemstrand Research Center, Durham, N.C., 1961-65, sr. research chemist, 1965-68; asst. prof. polymer research State U. N.Y. Coll. Environ. Sci. and Forestry, Syracuse, 1968-70, asso. prof., 1970-73, prof., 1973—, asst. dir. Polymer Research Center, 1971—, dir. Organic Materials Sci. Program, 1971-75, chmn. dept. chemistry, 1972—, mem. research found. joint com. on procedures, 1976—. Served with USMC, 1951-54. Mem. Am. Chem. Soc. (dir. Syracuse sect. 1977-79, chmn. 1978), AAAS, Soc. Plastics Engrs., Am. Chem. Soc., Sigma Xi, Phi Lambda Upsilon, Kappa Delta Pi. Contbr. articles to profl. jours. Home: 108 Scottholm Blvd Syracuse NY 13224

SMITH, LILLIAN LOUISE QUICK, counselor; b. Wilmington, N.C., Oct. 5, 1931; d. Earl Benjamin and Eloise Ernestine (Middleton) Quick; B.A. in Social Sci., Allen U., 1953; M.S. in Edn., Ind. U., 1966; postgrad. D.C. Tchr. Coll., 1973-74, Antioch Coll., 1974, U. Md., 1977-78; m. Olander James Smith, July 21, 1971. Tchr. English, Gt. Branch Sch., Orangeberg, S.C., 1953-54; tchr. social studies Sims High Sch., Union, S.C., 1954-55; instr. social studies, librarian Kettrell Coll., 1955-61; counselor Adkin High Sch., Kinston, N.C., 1961-63, Logan High Sch., Concord, N.C., 1963-64, Williston Sr. High Sch., Wilmington, N.C., 1964-68, Anacostia High Sch., Washington, 1968-69, Western High Sch., Washington, 1969-74, Sch. Without Walls, Washington, 1974—; participant numerous workshops. Named Tchr. of Yr., Sch. without Walls, 1977. Mem. Am. Personnel and Guidance Assn., D.C. Sch. Counselors Assn., Delta Sigma Theta. Methodist. Home: 1221 Massachusetts Ave NW Suite 824 Washington DC 20005 Office: Sch Without Walls 1619 M St NW Washington DC 20036

SMITH, MARILYNN KNOWLTON, librarian; b. Indpls., May 1, 1915; d. Lynn Orlando and Hazel Mary (Vliet) Knowlton; B.A., Butler U., 1936; M.A., U. Colo., 1951; M.S., Columbia U., 1964; m. David Lane Smith, Dec. 3, 1955 (dec. Nov. 1960). Council exec. Girl Scouts Am., Richmond, Ind., 1937-39, Ft. Wayne, Ind., 1939-41, Salt Lake City, 1942-43; various stenographic and clerical positions, 1943-49, 52-59, 61-62; librarian trainee Gen. Theol. Sem., N.Y.C., 1962-64; cataloger Library, State U. N.Y., Stony Brook, 1964-66; reference librarian U.S. Mil. Acad., West Point, N.Y., 1966-72, asst. librarian pub. services div., 1972—. Served with WAC, 1944-46. Mem. Am., N.Y. library assns., Spl. Libraries Assn., N.Y. Tech. Services Librarians, Women's Overseas Service League, Phi Kappa Phi, Kappa Delta Pi, Pi Gamma Mu, Phi Alpha Theta. Episcopalian. Home: 90 Main St Highland Falls NY 10928 Office: US Mil Acad Library West Point NY 10996

SMITH, MARK ALAN, personnel adminstr.; b. Lafayette, Ind., May 15, 1934; s. Mark Andrew and Sarah Fredissa (Palin) S.; B.A. in Mus. Edn., Ind. State U., 1957, B.S. in French, 1957; M.S. in Adminstrn., George Washington U., 1976; children by previous marriage—Michelle Renee, Janene Marie. Tech. writer Douglas Aircraft Co., Santa Monica, Calif., 1961-62; editor Copyright Law Office, Library of Congress, Washington, 1963-64; asst. dir. personnel Holy Cross Hosp., Silver Spring, Md., 1964-65, dir. personnel adminstrn., 1965—; instr. in personnel mgmt. and labor relations Strayer Coll., Washington, 1970-73; instr. Grad. Sch. Bus. Adminstrn., Washington extension Central Mich. U., 1975—; vis. lectr. Grad. Sch. Bus. Adminstrn., George Washington U., Washington, 1969, 70, 76; cons. to various hosps. in Md., Va. and Washington, 1967—. Served with CIC, U.S. Army, 1957-60. Mem. Am. Hosp. Assn., Am. Soc. for Hosp. Personnel Dirs. (mem. labor relations com. 1970), Am. Soc. for Personnel Adminstrn. (accredited exec. in personnel; mem. pub. affairs com. 1975), Am. Mgmt. Assn., Washington Personnel Assn., Hosp. Council of the Nat. Capital Area (pres. personnel dirs. div. 1969, 71), Md. Hosp. Personnel Adminstrn. Assn., Phi Delta Kappa, Phi Mu Alpha Sinfonia, Blue Key. Democrat. Contbr. articles on orgn. devel. to profl. jours. Home: 872 New Mark Esplanade Rockville MD 20850 Office: 1500 Forest Glen Rd Silver Springs MD 20910

SMITH, MARTIN, educator, guidance counselor, adminstr.; b. Bronx, N.Y., May 16, 1932; s. Edward and Anna (Kass) S.; B.S. in Edn., City Coll. of N.Y., 1956; M.A. in Social Sci., Bklyn. Coll., 1959, M.S. in Guidance and Counseling, 1962, profl. certificate in Adminstrn. and Supervision, 1966; doctoral candidate, Columbia U., 1969-72; m. Sydel Fine, Mar. 24, 1956; children—Wayne Howard, Sharon Michelle, Edward Charles. Tchr. social studies Bklyn. Jr. High Sch. No. 64, 1956-61; guidance counselor Manhattan (N.Y.) Jr. High Sch. #71, 1961-64; Bklyn. Jr. High Sch. #275, 1964-66; supr. guidance Community Sch. Dist. 24, Queens, N.Y., 1966-71; coordinator toward upward mobility program Bureau of Ednl. and Vocat. Guidance, NYC Bd. Edn., 1971-72, coordinator occupational guidance programs, 1972-78, coordinator support services in occupational guidance program, 1978—; adj. instr. guidance and counseling Hunter Coll., N.Y.C., 1967-69, Tchrs. Coll., Columbia U., N.Y.C., 1968, N.Y.C. Dept. Personnel, 1973-74; mem. N.Y. State Adv. Council on Career Edn., 1976—, mem. steering com., 1977—. Served with U.S. Army Mil. Police, 1952-54. Decorated European theatre ribbon. Certified sch. dist. admnstr., supr. secondary edn., principal secondary level, guidance counselor, social studies tchr., supr. guidance, all N.Y. State; recipient N.Y. State Regents' scholarship City Coll. N.Y., 1950-52, 54-56; outstanding state div. award, Nat. Vocat. Guidance Assn., 1977, 78. Mem. N.Y.C. Personnel and Guidance Assn. (pres. 1973-74, trustee 1968-69, conference chmn. 1972, co-chmn. legislative com. 1968-70), N.Y. State Vocat. Guidance Assn. (pres. 1976-78, editor Focus on Career Guidance Newsletter), N.Y.C. Assn. Suprs. of Guidance (treas. 1968-70, sec. 1976-78), Joint Assn. Suprs. of Bureau of Child Guidance and of Ednl. and Vocat. Guidance (treas. 1968-70), Am. Personnel and Guidance Assn., N.Y. State Personnel and Guidance Assn., Nat. Vocat. Guidance Assn., Am. Sch. Counselors Assn., N.Y. State Sch. Counselors Assn., Am. Assn. for Counselor Edn. and Supervision, N.Y. State Assn. for Counselor Edn. and Supervision, N.Y.C. Council of Suprs. and Admnstrs., Joint Assn. Bur. Child Guidance and Ednl. and Vocat. Guidance, N.Y.C. Assn. Suprs. Guidance, N.Y. Regional Council for Industry Edn. Cooperation, Bklyn. Mgmt. Club. Democrat. Jewish. Co-editor Career Guidance Newsletter, N.Y.C. Bur. Edn. and Vocat. Guidance, 1974-78; contbr. articles to profl. jours. Home: 1021 E 81st St Brooklyn NY 11236 Office: 110 Livingston St Room 418 NYC Bureau of Edn and Vocat Guidance Brooklyn NY 11201

SMITH, MARY ALICE, educator; b. Conestoga, Pa., Feb. 29, 1920; d. Martin W. and Agnes M. (Groff) Smith; B.S., Millersville State Coll., Pa., 1942; M.A., Columbia U., 1947; Ed.D., Pa. State U., 1958. Tchr. elementary schs., Lancaster County, 1942-48, tchr. spl. edn. for mentally retarded, 1948-53; coll. tchr., supr. kindergarten Lock Haven State Coll., 1953-63, dir. spl. edn., 1963-73, chairperson dept. specialized studies, 1974—, bd. dirs. Child Welfare Assn., 1965-77; bd. dirs. Community Service Assn., 1966-77, pres., 1978; bd. dirs. Crafts, Inc., 1967—, Enterprises for Handicapped, Inc. Mem. Nat., Pa. edn. assns., Am. Assn. for Mental Deficiency, Pa., Nat. assns. for retarded children, Council for Exceptional Children, Assn. for Childhood Edn. Internat., Pi Lambda Theta. Contbr. articles to profl. jours. Home: Conestoga PA 17516 Office: Lock Haven PA 17745

SMITH, MILTON JOSEPH, mfg. co. exec.; b. Youngstown, Ohio, Jan. 26, 1917; s. Mendle and Fanny Celia (Hansburg) S.; A.B., Western Res. U., 1937; postgrad. law Youngstown Coll., 1939-41; m. Fay Goldberg, Apr. 14, 1945; children—Nancy B. Smith Lombardi, Richard D., Steven R., Gary W. With Youngstown Window Shade Co., 1938; founder Skol Products Co., Struthers, Ohio, 1939-45; pres., treas. Trim Alloys, Inc., Randolph, Mass., 1945—. Pres. Aluminum Extruders Council, Chgo., 1960, 63. Served to lt. comdr. USNR, 1942-45. Registered profl. engr., Mass. Mem. Young Presidents Orgn., Mass. (pres. 1949), U.S. (v.p. 1950) jaycees. Clubs: Masons, Shriners, Randolph Rotary (treas. 1970-76). Home: Six Fawn Circle Randolph MA 02368 Office: care Trim Alloys Inc Box 355 Randolph MA 02368

SMITH, NICHOLAS NEVILLE, librarian; b. Malden, Mass., Dec. 25, 1926; s. H. Robert and Anne Benigna (Silvester) S.; B.A., U. Maine, 1950; M.L.S., Cdlumbia, 1959; m. Edyth Louise Kummerle, Sept. 29, 1956; 1 dau., Wanda Louise. Dir., Peekskill (N.Y.) Pub. Library, 1959-61; audio visual librarian North Country Library System, Watertown, N.Y., 1961-69; dir. Ogdensburg (N.Y.) Pub. Library, 1969—. Cons. anthrop. bibliography Nat. Mus. Can., 1967, Champlain Valley Hosp., Plattsburg, N.Y., 1968-69. Served with USAAF, 1944-46; ETO. Grantee Nat. Mus. Can., 1971-74, Am. Philos. Soc., 1955. Mem. ALA, Ind. Central Library Assn. (pres. 1977-78), N.Y. State Library Assn., Soc. Ethnomusicology. Episcopalian. Contbr. to Groves Dictionary of Music, 6th edit. Home: 1009 Hamilton St Ogdensburg NY 13669 Office: 312 Washington St Ogdensburg NY 13669

SMITH, OLIVER, theatrical producer-designer; b. Waupun, Wis., Feb. 13, 1918; s. Larue F. and Nina (Kincaid) S.; B.A., Pa. State U., 1939. Co-producer, designer plays; On the Town, 1945; Billion Dollar Baby, 1945; No Exit, 1946; Me and Molly, 1947; Gentlemen Prefer Blondes, 1949; Bless You All, 1950; In The Summer House, 1952; Clearing in the Woods, 1957; Time Remembered; Romulus, 1961; The Night of the Iguana; Lord Pengo, 1962; Barefoot in the Park, 1963; 110 in the Shade, 1963; The Girl Who Came to Supper, 1963; Dylan, 1963; The Chinese Prime Minister, 1964; Ben Franklin in Paris, 1964; Luv, 1964; Poor Richard, 1964; Odd Couple, 1965; designer of musicals: Brigadoon, 1946; High Button Shoes, 1946; Miss Liberty, 1949; Paint Your Wagon, 1952; Pal Joey, 1952; On Your Toes, 1955; My Fair Lady, 1956; Candide, 1955; Auntie Mame, 1956; West Side Story (Antoinette Perry award 1958); Jamaica; Destry; Flower Drum Song; Camelot; Beckett; Met. Opera; Traviata, 1958; Martha, 1961; Hello Dolly, 1963 (1963 Tony award); I Was Dancing, 1964; Candide, 1971; The Little Black Book, 1972; The Time of Your Life, 1972; Lost in The Stars, 1972; designer movies: Band Wagon, 1952; Oklahoma, 1955; Guys and Dolls, 1955; Porgy and Bess; Sound of Music; designer Unsinkable Molly Brown, 1960; co-dir. Am. Ballet Theatre, 1945—; designer ballets: Rodeo, 1942; Fancy Free, 1943; Fall River Legend, 1946; Swan Lake; Les Noces; exhbns.: Pa. State Coll., Mus. Modern Art, Bklyn. Mus., Chgo. Art Inst., Cocoran Gallery, Yale; produced Natural Affection; Tiger, Tiger; On the Town, London (all 1962-63). Recipient Donaldson award, 1946, 47, 49, 53, Antoinette Perry award, 1957, 58, 60, 61, 64, 65, Shubert Award, 1960; Pa. State U. Distinguished Alumni award, 1962. Mem. Triangle Soc., Acacia, Nat. Council Arts. Address: 70 Willow St Brooklyn NY 11201

SMITH, OWEN TELFAIR, lawyer; b. Bklyn., June 29, 1937; s. O. Telfair and Lauraine G. (Murphy) S.; B.A. in Econs. and Govt., Trinity Coll., 1959; postgrad. Georgetown U., 1961, St. John's Sch. Law, 1963. Admitted to N.Y. State bar, 1964; individual practice law, Oyster Bay, N.Y., 1964—; counsel N.Y. Senate Coms. on Crime and Correction, 1970—; asso. prof. C.W. Post Coll. of L.I. U. Chmn. Nassau County Planning Commn. Mem. Am., N.Y. State bar assns., Nat. Microfilm Assn., Info. Industry Assn., Am. Assn. Info. Roman Catholic. Clubs: The Creek, Wheatley Hills Golf, Nat. Lawyers (Washington); Univ. (Albany). Author: Professional Corporations, 1973; Wage and Price Freeze, 1973, Fletchers Corporation Forms, 1974; Fletchers Cyclopedia of Corporation, 1975; Real Estate Forms of Organization, 1975. Home and Office: Mill River Rd Oyster Bay NY 11771

SMITH, PATRICIA MARY, newspaper pub.; b. Toronto, Ont., Canada; d. James Patrick and Blanche (Smith) Kieley; student Loretto Abbey Coll., 1936-40; m. Samuel John Smith, Apr. 29, 1942; children—Sallie, Sheila, Wendy. Pub., editor Gates-Chili News, Inc., Rochester, N.Y., 1974—. Judge, Jr. Miss Pageant, 1976, 77, 78. Mem. Gates-Chili C. of C. (dir. 1975-77); hon. mem. Gates Vol. Ambulance Service. Roman Catholic. Office: 1269 Chili Av Rochester NY 14624

SMITH, PETER WALKER, instrument mfg. co. exec.; b. Syracuse, N.Y., May 19, 1923; s. Stanley S. and Elizabeth W. (Young) S.; B.Chem. Engring., Rensselaer Poly. Inst., 1947; M.B.A. cum laude, Harvard U., 1948; J.D. cum laude, Cleve. Marshall Law Sch., 1955; m. Lucile E. Edson, June 22, 1946; children—Andrew, Laurie Smith Falzone, Pamela Smith Schweppe Jr., Stanley. Admitted to Ohio bar, 1955; div. controller Raytheon Co., Lexington, Mass., 1958-66; v.p. finance indsl. systems group Litton Industries, Stamford, Conn., 1966-70; v.p. fin., treas. Copeland Corp., Sidney, Ohio, 1970-74; v.p. fin., treas., dir. Instrumentation Lab., Inc., Lexington, 1974-78; treas., chief fin. officer Ionics, Inc., 1978—. Served with AUS, 1943-46, 50-52. Registered profl. engr., Ohio. Mem. Fin. Execs. Inst., Sigma Xi, Tau Beta Pi. Home: 155 Monument St Concord MA 01742 Office: 65 Grove St Watertown MA 02172

SMITH, PHILIP ALAN, bishop; b. Belmont, Mass., Apr. 2, 1920; s. Herbert Leonard and Elizabeth (MacDonald) S.; B.A., Harvard U., 1942; B.D., Va. Theol. Sem., 1949, D.D., 1970; m. Barbara Ann Taylor, June 12, 1949; children—Sarah, Ann, Jeremy. Ordained priest Episcopal Ch., 1949; asst. rector All Saints Ch., Atlanta, 1949-51; rector Christ Ch., Exeter, N.H., 1952-59; asst. prof. pastoral theology Va. Theol. Sem., 1959-62, chaplain, 1962-70, asso. dean student affairs, 1967-70; suffragan bishop Diocese of Va., 1970-73; bishop of N.H., 1973—; mem. nat. exec. council Protestant Episcopal Ch. in U.S. Founder, 1st pres. Exeter Community Service Assn. Served with AUS, 1942-46. Home: 122 School St Concord NH 03301 Office: 63 Green St Concord NH 03301

SMITH, PHILLIP HARTLEY, steel co. exec.; b. Sydney, Australia, Jan. 26, 1927; s. Norman Edward and Elizabeth (Williams) S.; B.Engring. with 1st class honors in Mining and Metallurgy, U. Sydney, 1950; Metall. Engr., Mass. Inst. Tech., 1952; LL.D., Grove City Coll., 1975; m. Martha Frances Dittrich, June 4, 1955; children—Elizabeth Thomas, Johanna, Alice, Margaret, Sarah. Came to U.S., 1950, naturalized, 1960. Successively trainee, metallurgist, foreman Inland Steel Co., Indiana Harbor, Ind., 1952-55; successively trainee, metallurgist, dir. purchasing and planning La Salle Steel Co., Hammond, Ind., 1956-64; with Copperweld Corp., Pitts., 1964-77, pres., 1968-77, chmn., 1973, also dir. Trustee Gordon-Conwell Theol. Sem., Grove City Coll., Berea Coll. Served as cadet officer Australian Mcht. Marine, 1942-43, Royal Australian Fleet Aux., 1943. Recipient Nat. Open Hearth Steelmaking award, 1955. Presbyterian (ruling elder). Clubs: Univ. (Chgo.); Duquesne (Pitts.); Rolling Rock (Ligonier, Pa.). Editor: Am. Inst. M.E. Handbook, Mechanical Working of Steel, 1961. Patentee in field. Home: 102 Haverford Rd Pittsburgh PA 15238

SMITH, RAY THADDEUS, JR., anesthesiologist; b. Huntington, L.I., N.Y., Sept. 15, 1922; s. Ray Thaddeus and Viola Elizabeth (Swezey) S.; B.S., Franklin and Marshall Coll., 1943; M.D., Temple U., 1947; m. Nancy Lee Leadbetter, Sept. 16, 1945; children—Bonnie Lou Smith Tyler, Ray Scott, Betsy Ann Smith Anderson. Intern, U.S. Naval Hosp., Phila., 1947-48, resident in anesthesiology, 1949-51; resident in anesthesiology Children's Hosp., Phila., 1951; anesthesiologist Wesson Meml. Hosp., Springfield, Mass., VA Hosp., Florence, Mass., 1954-63, Hartford (Conn.) Hosp., Newington (Conn.) Children's Hosp., 1963-64, Baystate Med. Center, Springfield, 1964—, also dir. pain clinic. Coach U.S. Women's Internat. Rifle Teams, 1962, 63, 64, 69. Served with USNR, 1943-45, as lt. M.C., USN, 1947-54. Diplomate Am. Bd. Anesthesiology. Fellow Am. Coll. Anesthesiology; mem. Am. Soc. Regional Anesthesia, Am. Soc. Anesthesiologists, Gen. Soc. Colonial Wars, Mil. Order World Wars, Sons Revolution, SAR, Mil. Order Fgn. Wars U.S., Soc. Descs. Colonial Clergy, Hereditary Order Descs. Loyalists and Patriots Am. Revolution, Nat. Soc. Sons and Daus. Pilgrims, Sons of Union Vets. Civil War, Order Desc. Colonial Physicians and Chir urgiens. Inventor periscopic laryngoscope, R.T. Smith laryngoscope blade, pediatric unidirectional anesthesia valve. Home: 209 Merriweather Dr Longmeadow MA 01106 Office: 77 Boylston St Springfield MA 01100

SMITH, RAYMOND D(ANIEL), pub. co. exec.; b. St. Johnsville, N.Y., Aug. 4, 1912; s. Emery Augustus and Ada (Groff) S.; ed. pub. schs.; m. Blanche Virginia Wolfram, Feb. 11, 1960; 1 stepson, Charles H. Copeland. Newspaper advt. Union Star, Schenectady, 1929-31; chemist, dispatcher, gen. office Standard Oil N.J., Albany and N.Y.C., 1934-51; free lance photographer, 1944-50; pub. Cats mag., Washington, Pa., 1951—; instr. Henry George Sch. Social Sci., N.Y.C., 1948-50. Mem. AAAS, Henry George Found. Am., Am. Cat Fanciers Assn., Crown Cat Fanciers Fedn., Am. Contract Bridge League. Democrat. Presbyterian (elder). Editor: (with Blanche V. Smith) Complete Cat Encyclopedia; contbr. articles to profl. jours., also World Book, other encys.; poetry to In Praise of Cats, other anthologies. Home: Rural Delivery 3 Box 353-B Washington PA 15301 also 1928 Vernon Pl Daytona FL 32014 Office: PO Box 557 Skylark Dr Washington PA 15301

SMITH, RAYMOND EDWARD, health care adminstr.; b. Freeport, N.Y., June 17, 1932; s. Jerry Edward and Madelyn Holman (Jones) S.; B.S. in Edn., Temple U., 1953; M.H.A., Baylor U., 1966; children—Douglas, Ronald, Kevin, Raymond. Commd. 2d lt. U.S. Army, 1953, advanced through grades to lt. col., 1973; helicopter ambulance pilot, 1953-63; various hosp. adminstrv. assignments, 1963-73; personnel dir. Valley Forge (Pa.) Gen. Hosp., 1966; adminstr. evacuation hosp., Vietnam, 1967; dep. insp. Walter Reed Gen. Hosp., Washington, 1970; dir. personnel div. Office of Army Surgeon Gen., Washington, 1971-73, ret., 1973; adminstr. Health Care Centers, Phila. Coll. Osteo. Medicine, 1974-76; dir. bur. hosps. Pa. Dept. Health, Harrisburg, 1976—. Decorated Bronze Star, Legion of Merit. Mem. Am. Hosp. Assn., Am. Legion, Ret. Officers Assn., Kappa Alpha Psi. Episcopalian. Club: Masons. Home: 4525 Sequoia Dr Apt 239 Harrisburg PA 17109 Office: PO Box 90 7th and Forster St Harrisburg PA 17120

SMITH, RAYMOND JOSEPH, paper industry cons.; b. Bklyn., Oct. 15, 1938; s. Thomas Edward and Sophie (Naguszewska) S.; B.A., Georgetown U., 1960; postgrad., St. John's Law Sch., 1961-62; m. Bernice L. Curol, June 17, 1961; children—Raymond, Ellen, Paul, Michele. Trainee exec. sales Internat. Paper Co., N.Y.C., 1962-63, sales rep., 1963-65, nat. accounts mgr., 1965-66; sales mgr. Med. div. Disposables, Inc., Huntington Sta., N.Y., 1966-68, sales mgr. Med. and Indsl. div., 1968-70, v.p. marketing and sales, 1970-74; partner Frank & Smith Internat., cons. paper industry, Manhasset, N.Y., 1974—. Mem. Disposables Assn. (1st chmn. indsl. market research com.). Club: West Oak Recreation (dir., pres. 1978-79) (Oakdale, N.Y.). Home: 98 Hanson Pl Ronkonkoma NY 11779 Office: 14 Locust St Manhasset NY 11030

SMITH, RHOTEN ALEXANDER, polit. scientist, ednl. adminstr.; b. Dallas, Jan. 17, 1921; s. Rhoten Alexander and Ruth Elizabeth (Cooke) S.; student Tex. Wesleyan Coll., 1940, U. Tex., 1940-42; A.B., U. Kans., 1946, M.A., 1948; Ph.D., U. Calif., Berkeley, 1955; m. Barbara Maria Okerberg, Dec. 24, 1942; children—Susan Jane Smith Warren, Tyler Rhoten. Instr. polit. sci. U. Kans., 1947-49, 51-54, asst. prof., 1954-57, asso. prof., 1957-58; asso. dir. Citizenship Clearing House, N.Y.C., 1955-56, dir., 1958-61; prof. politics N.Y. U., 1958-61; dean Coll. Liberal Arts, Temple U., 1961-67; pres. No. Ill. U., DeKalb, 1967-71; provost U. Pitts., 1971—; research asso. Govt. Research Center, U. Kans., 1946-48, 51-58; research cons. Kans. Legis. Council, summer 1954, cons. survey higher edn., summer 1957; cons. Kans. Constl. Revision Commn., 1957-58; chief cons. polit. edn. program Maurice and Laura Falk Found., Pitts., 1958; cons. exec. devel. program Ford Found., 1960; adv. commn. gen. edn. N.Y. Community Coll., 1960-61; mem. Pub. Com. for Humanities in Pa., 1974-77. Advisor to chmn. Kans. Democratic Party, 1956-58. Served to 1st lt., USAAF, 1942-45. Fellow AAAS; mem. Am., Midwest polit. assns., Carnegie Mus. Natural History. Democrat. Author: The Life of a Bill, rev. edit., 1961; Republican Primary Fight: A Study in Factionalism (with C.J. Hein), 1958. Home: 717 Amberson Ave Pittsburgh PA 15213

SMITH, RICHARD EMERSON (DICK SMITH), makeup artist, sculptor; b. Larchmont, N.Y., June 26, 1922; s. Richard Roy and Coral (Brown) S.; B.A., Yale, 1944; m. Jocelyn De Rosa, Jan. 10, 1949; children—Douglas Todd, David Emerson. Founder, dir. makeup dept. NBC-TV, N.Y.C., 1945-59, developed monochrome and color TV make-up colors and techniques used for all systems; live TV, video tape, TV film; pioneered use of rubber and plastics in TV makeup; inventor spl. quick-change make-up techniques; creator foam latex character masks and features permitting facial expression; profl. sculptor; freelance makeup artist and cons., 1959—; make-up dir. Talent Assos., Ltd., N.Y.C., 1959-61; make-up dir. Requiem for a Heavyweight, 1961; make-up specialist for It's a Mad Mad Mad Mad World, 1962; make-up dir. Paramount's All The Way Home, 1962; The Cardinal, 1963; The World of Henry Orient, 1963; Marco the Magnificent, 1965, Me Natalie, 1968, Little Big Man, 1969-70, Who is Harry Kellerman, 1970, The Godfather, 1971, The Exorcist, 1972-73; The Godfather, Part II, 1973-74; The Sunshine Boys, 1975; The Heretic, 1976; The Sentinel, 1976; created makeup for Hal Holbrook TV prodn. Mark Twain Tonight, 1967; make-up cons. Midnight Cowboy, 1968, Taxi Driver, Murder by Death, Meeting at Potsdam, Marathon Man, 1975, The Deer Hunter, 1977, The Fury, 1977. Served as 2d lt. F.A., AUS. World War II. Recipient Emmy award for Mark Twain, 1967. Author: Make-Up Handbook, 1965. Contributor, consultant Vogue, Seventeen and other mags. Inventor patented lipstick applicator. Address: 209 Murray Ave Larchmont NY 10538

SMITH, RICHARD EUGENE, internist, oncologist; b. LongBranch, N.J., Dec. 4, 1934; s. Eugene T. and Anna May (Lane) S.; B.S., Mass. Inst. Tech., 1957; M.D. (Dennison scholar), Johns Hopkins U., 1961; m. Janice D. McDowell, Jan. 1, 1978; children—Stacy F., Sheridan J., Evan R. H. Intern, Johns Hopkins Hosp., 1961-62, fellow, 1962-66, resident, 1962-64; practice medicine specializing in oncology and internal medicine, Hagerstown, Md., 1968—; mem. staff Washington County Hosp., chief dept. medicine, 1973-76; bd. dirs. Washington County (Md.) chpt. Am. Cancer Soc., 1968-78, Western Md. Heart Assn., 1968-73. Served with M.C., U.S. Army, 1966-68. Recipient Borden award Johns Hopkins U., 1960. Mem. Washington County Med. Soc., Med., Chirurg. Soc. State Md. Republican. Office: 1708 Oak Hill Ave Hagerstown MD 21740

SMITH, RICHARD FRANCIS, JR., electronics co. exec.; b. Revere, Mass., Nov. 21, 1928; s. Richard Francis and Gertrude May (Cameron) S.; Asso. Elec. Engring., Northeastern U., 1954, B.B.A., 1956; m. Marion Costello, Sept. 11, 1949; children—Jean Marie, Richard Francis. Electronic engr. BLH Electronics Inc., Waltham, Mass., 1956-61, application engr., 1961-68, product mgr. process control sytems, 1968—. Served with USMCR, 1946-48. Mem. Instrument Soc. Am., Soc. Exptl. Stress Analysis. Republican. Roman Catholic. Contbr. articles to profl. mag. Home: Route 111 Applewood Condominium Boxborough MA 01720

SMITH, RICHARD LOUIS, JR., ins. co. exec.; b. St. Inigoes, Md., July 20, 1930; s. Richard Louis and Mary Edna (Taylor) S.; student Mt. St. Mary's Coll., 1948-49; m. Mary Regina Mueller, Dec. 2, 1950; children—Elaine, Janet, Richard, Dennis, Regina. Agt., Peoples Life Ins. Co., Washington, 1951—, v.p. mktg., 1970-74, sr. v.p. mktg., 1974-76, exec. v.p. mktg., 1976—, dir., 1972—; exec. v.p. mktg., dir. Home Life Ins. Co. Am. subs., 1977—. Past pres. PTA; chmn. Essex County (Va.) unit Am. Cancer Soc., 1964. Mem. Life Ins. Mktg. and Research Assn. (dir. 1976—), Am. Soc. Chartered Underwriters, Nat. Assn. Life Underwriters, Life Insurers Conf., D.C. C. of C., Hon. Order Ky. Cols. Roman Catholic. Clubs: Ruritan Nat., K.C. Home: 146 Mary's Mount Rd Harwood MD 20776 Office: 601 New Hampshire Ave NW Washington DC 20048

SMITH, ROBERT CHARLES, steel co. exec.; b. Pitts., Sept. 24, 1929; s. Kenneth Stewart and Annabelle Mary (Anderson) S.; B.S. in Elec. Engring., U. Pitts., 1955; m. Peggy Joan Hanson, Apr. 19, 1975. With U.S. Steel Corp., 1955-66, 75—, maintenance engr., lubrication and hydraulics engring., Pitts., 1975—; indsl. engr. Mobil Oil Co., 1966-74. Active local Boy Scouts Am. Republican. Presbyterian. Club: Shriners. Home: 2509 Holly Dr Pittsburgh PA 15235 Office: US Steel Corp 1 Library Pl Duquesne PA 15110

SMITH, ROBERT DOUGLAS, environ. engr.; b. Flint, Mich., Sept. 7, 1918; s. Robert Frances and Luella (Richter) S.; B.S.Engring. in Chem. Engring., U. Mich., 1950; postgrad. Wayne State U., 1951-52, Gen. Motors Inst., 1955-57; m. Shirley Avis Mindrop, Jan. 7, 1945; 1 dau., Christina Mindrop Smith Claxton. Paint chemist Ditzler Color div. Pitts. Plate Glass Co., Detroit, 1950-52; analytical engr., chemist Ternstedt div. Gen. Motors Co., Flint, Mich., 1952-53, lab. supr., 1953-55, waste treatment process engr., 1955-57; waste control engr., plastic div. Allied Chem. Corp., Toledo, 1957-64; pollution control engr. Kaiser Engrs., Chgo., 1964-70; environmental engr. Pullman-Swindell, Pitts., 1970-75; sr. process engr., water and waste treatment Dravo Corp., Pitts., 1975—. Served with ordnance U.S. Army, 1941-45. Registered profl. engr., Pa. Mem. Water Pollution Control Fedn. Pa., Am. Iron and Steel Engrs., TAPPI. Contbr. articles to tech. jours. Home: 520 Bower Hill Rd Pittsburgh PA 15228 Office: One Oliver Plaza Pittsburgh PA 15222

SMITH, ROBERT HENRY, internist; b. New Paris, Ohio, Apr. 11, 1923; s. Leo J. and Rhea (Davison) S.; M.D., Cornell U., 1948; m. Jean Ann Losacco, June 23, 1945; children—Richard, Douglas, John. Intern, Bellevue Hosp., N.Y.C., 1948-49; practice medicine, specializing in internal medicine Astoria Med. Group, Long Island City, N.Y., 1949-62; dir. profl. services Health Ins. Plan Greater N.Y., N.Y.C., 1962-65; internist Queensboro Med. Group, Floral Park, N.Y., 1965-72; pvt. practice internal medicine, Bellerose, N.Y., 1972—; staff physician L.I. Jewish, Deepdale, Mary Immaculate, Parkway hosps; cons. internal medicine Hillside Hosp. Served with U.S. Army, 1942-45, USAF, 1954-56. Mem. AMA, N.Y. State, Queens County med. scos., N.Y. Cardiology Soc., N.Y. Soc. Internal Medicine, Am., N.Y.C. pub. health assns., N.Y. Assn. Professions, Bayside Gables Civic Assn. Home: 27-15 215 St Bayside NY 11360 Office: 247-11 Union Turnpike Bellerose NY 11426

SMITH, ROGER DAVIS, lawyer; b. Yonkers, N.Y., May 21, 1923; s. Leon H. and Elizabeth (Elting) S.; S.B., Mass. Inst. Tech., 1948; LL.B., Yale U., 1953; m. Kathleen Wallis Tener, May 30, 1970; children—Silas Wheelock, Jocelyn Tener, Luke Ewing Taft. Product devel. engr. Gates Rubber Co., Denver, 1948-49; admitted to N.Y. bar 1953; asso. firm Carter, Ledyard & Milburn, N.Y.C., 1953-66; partner firm Jackson & Nash, and predecessor, N.Y.C., 1966—. Trustee Profl. Children's Sch., Inc., N.Y.C., 1968-74, pres., 1973-74; trustee, pres. Royal Coll. Surgeons Found., Inc., 1975—. Served to 1st lt. AUS, 1943-46, 51-52. Mem. Am., N.Y. bar assns., Assn. Bar City N.Y., Phi Alpha Delta, Sigma Alpha Epsilon. Club: Yale (N.Y.C.). Republican. Unitarian. Home: 454 Route 32 N New Paltz NY 12561 Office: 330 Madison Ave New York City NY 10017

SMITH, ROLAND WHITE, physician, artist; b. Westfield, Mass., Sept. 28, 1931; s. Howard S. and Alice W. (Woodruff) S.; B.A., U. Mass., 1957; M.D., U. Pa., 1961; children—April, Heather, Howard. Resident in anesthesiology U. Pa., Phila., 1962-64; anesthesiologist Sharon (Conn.) Hosp., 1964-69; asst. prof. anesthesiology Columbia, 1970-72; anesthesiologist Putnam Meml. Hosp., Bennington, Vt., 1972—. Recipient Borden Co. Found. award, 1961, Myers award for innovative earth-water sculpture, 1978. Diplomate Am. Bd. Anesthesiology. Inventor operating room replay monitor. Home and office: Pippin Knoll Bennington VT 05201

SMITH, RUSSELL FRANCIS, fin. planning and policies cons.; b. Washington, Mar. 26, 1944; s. Raymond Francis and Elma Gloria (Daugherty) S.; student East Carolina U., 1964, N.C. State U., 1964-65; B.S. with honors, U. Md., 1970, M.B.A., 1976. Exec. asst. mgr. Hotel Corp. Am. Internat. Inn and Mayflower Hotel, Washington, 1966-68; sr. venture capital cons. Initiative Investing Corp., Washington, 1968-69; pres., gen. mgr. Associated Trades Corp., Washington, 1970-74; cons. in fin., Greenbelt, Md., 1974-76; mng. cons. Bradford Nat. Corp., Washington, 1976-79; exec. asst. dir. OAO Corp., Washington, 1979—. Chmn. com. on wildlife Prince George's Humane Soc., Hyattsville, Md., 1968-71, Soc. for Prevention Cruelty to Animals, Hyattsville, 1971-75. Served with U.S. Army, 1963-66. Decorated Silver Star medal, Bronze Star medal with V device, Purple Heart. Mem. Am. Fin. Assn., Ops. Research Soc. Am., Am. Acctg. Assn., N.Am. Soc. Corp. Planners, Internat. Assn. Math. Modeling, Assn. M.B.A. Execs., Beta Gamma Sigma, Beta Alpha Psi. Republican. Home: 5921 Cherrywood Terr Greenbelt MD 20770 Office: AOA Corp 2101 L St NW Washington DC 20036

SMITH, SARAH SIMS, guidance counselor; b. Winston-Salem, N.C., Jan. 31, 1935; d. George Sanders and Myrtle (Reed) Sims; B.S., Winston-Salem U., 1957; M.A., George Washington U., 1970; postgrad. N.Y. U., 1959-60, U. Omaha (Overseas br.), 1973-74, U. D.C., 1974—, U. Va., 1976; children—Donald Anthony, Mark Andre. Tchr., Albert Harris Sch., Martinsville, Va., 1957-60, D.C. Pub. Schs., 1960-67; guidance counselor Lovejoy Sch., Washington, 1967-69, Bad Kreuznach (Germany) Elementary Sch., 1972-74, Friendship Ednl. Center, Washington, 1974—; former counselor Family Counseling Center, Bad Krueznach; conducted Human Relations Seminars, Germany, 1972-74, also Drug Abuse Workshops. Mem. Am. Personnel and Guidance Assn., Am., D.C. sch. counselors assns., Am. Fedn. Tchrs., Urban League, D.C. Elementary Counselors Assn., Smithsonian Assos. Democrat. Roman Catholic. Home: 3336 Carpenter St SE Washington DC 20020 Office: 4600 Livington Rd SE Washington DC 20032

SMITH, SEYMOUR ALAN, lawyer; b. N.Y.C., Nov. 15, 1913; s. Sol and Esther (Och) S.; LL.B. cum laude, John Marshall Coll., 1935; m. Marjorie Heft, June 1, 1939; children—Lawrence Douglas, Robert Thornton, Peter Jay. Admitted to N.J. bar, 1936, U.S. Supreme Ct. bar, 1957; counsellor at law, master in chancery N.J., 1940; partner firm Hein, Smith and Berezin and predecessor, Hackensack, N.J., 1944—; mem. adv. com. on profl. ethics N.J. Supreme Ct., 1973—. Mem. Am., N.J., Bergen County (chmn. unauthorized practice of law com. 1958—) bar assns. Club: Preakness Hills Country (Wayne, N.J., pres., 1975-77). Home: 50 Walnut Ct Englewood NJ 07631 Office: 25 E Salem St Hackensack NJ 07601

SMITH, STANLEY A., psychologist, educator; b. Bklyn., Sept. 3, 1937; s. Lou C. and Florence (Mann) S.; B.A., Adelphi U., 1959; M.A. in Psychology, Mich. State U., 1961; postgrad. Yeshiva U., 1964-65, New Sch. for Social Research, 1965-66; m. Carole M. Lesser, June 14, 1959; children—Jodi Lynn, Francine E. Research asst. Mich. State U., 1959-61; sr. clin. psychologist St. Lawrence State Hosp., Ogdensburg, N.Y., 1961; asst. prof. psychology State U. Coll., Potsdam, N.Y., 1961-64; sch. psychologist Carmel (N.Y.) Central Sch. Dist. #2, 1964—, dir. spl. edn., 1967-68; instr. gen. psychology Orange County (N.Y.) Community Coll., 1964-66; tchr. gen. and developmental psychology United Hosp., Port Chester, N.Y., 1964-66; mem. faculty New Rochelle (N.Y.) Hosp., 1965; mem. faculty U. Bridgeport (Conn.), summer 1965; lectr. child devel. and behavior Lakeland Central Sch. Dist., Mohegan Lake, N.Y., 1966-67; staff psychologist Yorktown Counseling Service, Yorktown Heights, N.Y., 1966—; propr., ednl. cons. Ednl. Diagnostic Service, Mohegan Lake, 1970—; partner Westchester-Putnam Counseling Service, Yorktown Heights, 1973-77; adj. asso. prof. Grad. Sch. Edn., C.W. Post Center/L.I. U., 1975—; mem. faculty Mercy Coll., Yorktown, 1975—. Mem. N.Y. State Educators of Emotionally Disturbed (sec. 1968-69, pres. 1971-72, plaque award 1972, 73, life mem.), Am., N.Y. State, Westchester County, St. Lawrence (pres. 1963-64) psychol. assns., Putnam County Sch. Psychologist's Assn. (v.p. 1967-69, pres. 1970-72), Psi Chi. Contbr. articles to profl. jours.; editor N.Y. State Psychologist Newsletter, 1964-65. Home: 1435 Ivy Rd Mohegan Lake NY 10547 Office: George Fischer Middle Sch 275 Fair St Carmel NY 10512

SMITH, STANLEY BABCOCK, JR., sci. instrument mfg. co. exec.; b. Dearborn, Mich., Feb. 27, 1930; s. Stanley B. and Charlotte E. (Schmaler) S.; B.S. in Chemistry, Mich. State U., 1951; M.S. in Physics, Wayne State U., 1956; postgrad. in mgmt. Am. Mgmt. Assn., 1965-70, Babson Inst., 1969, Northeastern U., 1973-75, U. N.H., 1975—; m. Barbara; 2 children. Chemist, spectroscopist Detroit Testing Lab., 1952-55; research engr. nuclear optical sect. Fort Motor Co., Dearborn, 1955-58; sales and service engr. Mich., Ind. and Ohio area Jarrell Ash Co., 1958-60, tech. dir. sales, Waltham, Mass., 1960-66; with Instrumentation Lab., Inc., Wilmington, Mass., 1966—, product mgr. mktg., 1969-71, mgr. research and devel. Analytical Instruments div., 1973—. Chmn. parish life 1st Parish Ch., United, Westford, Mass. Mem. Fedn. Analytical Chemistry and Spectroscopy Socs. (chmn. exhbn. Boston 1978 meeting), Soc. Applied Spectroscopy (chmn. New Eng. sect. 1974-75, chmn. nat. com. publicity 1971-72, sect. del. 1977—), Sci. Apparatus Mfr. Assn. (chmn. atomic absorption group, analytical instruments sect.), IEEE, ASTM (chmn. task group atomic absorption guidelines 1974—), New Eng. Computer Soc., Nat. Watch and Clock Collectors, Sigma Pi Sigma. Contbr. numerous articles on automobile exhaust gas analysis, emission spectroscopy, computers, atomic absorption, lab. and research and devel. mgmt., spectroscopic instrumentation to profl. jours. Home: 99 Lowell Rd Westford MA 01886 Office: Analytical Instrument Div Instrumentation Lab Inc Jonspin Rd Wilmington MA 01887

SMITH, STEVEN DENNIS, computer scientist; b. Charleston, W.Va., Nov. 15, 1945; s. Dennis Ray and Katherine Mondaine (Sands) S.; B.A., U. Richmond, 1968; postgrad. Va. Poly. Inst. and State U., 1969, 71-72. Programmer/analyst Hercules Inc., Radford (Va.) Army Ammunition Plant, also Wilmington, Del., 1968-72; supr.

computer systems and ops. Black, Crow and Eidness, Inc., Gainesville, Fla., 1972-74; sr. mem. tech. staff Computer Scis. Corp., Silver Spring, Md., 1974—. Active youth work Soccer Assn. Columbia (Md.), 1975—, Howard County Children's Phys. Devel. Clinic, 1976—. Mem. Am. Inst. Aeros. and Astronautics, Ops. Research Soc. Am., Soc. Indsl. and Applied Math., Math. Assn. Am. Home: 5868 Thunder Hill Rd Columbia MD 21045 Office: 8728 Colesville Rd Silver Spring MD 20910

SMITH, THOMAS LIONEL, mfg. co. exec.; b. Bradenville, Pa., July 27, 1924; s. Plummer Martin and Margaretta (Latchford) S.; teaching certificate U. Pitts., 1964; student Space Coll., Huntsville, Ala., 1954-55, Pa. State U., 1969-70; m. Eleanor Mary Hines, July 12, 1946; children—Beverly, Thomas, Timothy. Dir. maintenance U.S. Govt. Guided Missile Div., Pitts., 1952-72; maintenance supr. Seasonal Industries, Indiana, Pa., 1973-75; instr. electronics Greensburg (Pa.) Inst. Tech., 1975-76; supt. maintenance Gibson Electric Co., Delmont, Pa., 1976—. Dir. Civil Def., Latrobe, Pa., 1972-76; scoutmaster Boy Scouts Am., 1964-67. Served with USNR, 1943-46, U.S. Army, 1948-52: Korea. Recipient Sustained Superior Performance award U.S. Govt., 1957, 65. Mem. Am. Mgmt. Assn. Democrat. Presbyterian. Club: Elks. Contbr. articles to profl. jours. Home: 1084 Hillview Ave Latrobe PA 15650 Office: Gibson Electric Co Delmont PA 15626

SMITH, THOMAS MARSHALL, psychotherapist; b. Washington, Sept. 26, 1942; s. Asa Albert and Amelia Cary (Marshall) S.; B.A., N.Y. U., 1967; M.S., Columbia U., 1973; m. Susan Schwartz, Oct. 2, 1977. Staff psychotherapist New Hope Guild, N.Y.C., 1973-78; social worker Jewish Family Service, N.Y.C., 1973-74; pvt. practice psychotherapy, N.Y.C., 1973—; social worker U.S. VA, N.Y.C., 1974-78, coordinator methadone treatment program, 1978—; guest lectr. Columbia U. Sch. Social Work, 1975. Served with U.S. Army, 1963-65. Certified social worker, N.Y. State. Mem. Nat. Assn. Social Workers, Acad. Certified Social Workers, Nat. Psychol. Assn. for Psychoanalysis. Club: Fifth Ave. Racquet (N.Y.C.). Home: 425 W 23d St New York NY 10011 Office: 69 W 9th St New York NY 10011

SMITH, VALERIA LITCHFIELD MCKEE, former ednl. adminstr.; b. Bklyn., May 13, 1908; d. William Litchfield and Annie Valeria (Northup) McKee; student pvt. schs., U.S. Sch. Secs., 1927-38; m. Monroe Edwards Smith, Oct. 28, 1933; children—Cynthia Smith Austin, Valeria Smith Ritchie. Sec. to dir. devel. Northfield (Mass.) Schs., 1957-60; sec. Bement Sch., Deerfield, Mass., 1960-73, exec. sec., dir. admissions, 1971-73. Pres., N. Parish PTA, 1951, Jr.-Sr. PTA, 1953-55, Greenfield PTA Council, 1958-60; pres. Franklin County Womens Republican Club, 1956; former bd. dirs. Order of Rainbow for Girls. Mem. Mass. PTA (life), Mass. Geneal. Soc., Pocamtuch Valley Meml. Assn., Friends of Historic Deerfield, Greenfield Hist. Soc., Nat. Trust for Historic Preservation, Old Sturbridge Village Assn., Soc. Preservation New Eng. Antiquities. DAR. Episcopalian. Club: Greenfield Women's (asst. treas. 1975—). Home: Calico Farm 283 Barton Rd PO Box 384 Greenfield MA 01301

SMITH, VERN HENRY, scene designer, artist, educator; b. Kingston, Pa., Aug. 6, 1927; s. Lavern and Elizabeth Ryle (Reese) S.; M.F.A. (Leopold Schepp Found. Scholar, 1946-50, Van Swinderen Scholar, 1950-52), Am. U., 1952; M.A. in Theatre, Columbia U., 1963. Art chmn. elementary schs., Phillipsburg, N.J., 1954-58; chmn. high sch. art, Carteret Sch., West Orange, N.J., 1958-60; stage designer, instr. theatre dept., Rutgers U., Newark, 1960-63, asso. prof., stage designer, 1966—; asst. prof. stage design, tech-dir. Glassboro (N.J.) State Coll., 1963-66; stage designer, Parkway Playhouse, Burnsville, N.C., summers 1959-62, summer theatre Glassboro State Coll., 1963-66; artist murals for Mego Toys, N.Y.C., 1975-76; interior designer, Easton Display Co., N.Y.C., 1972-75; dir. Rutgers Newark Open Stage Players, 1978; one man shows: Paris, 1969, 78, Japan, 1970, Milan, 1972, N.Y., 1974, 77; designer over 150 coll. and off Broadway theatre prodns; represented in numerous pub. and pvt. collections in Europe and U.S. Recipient numerous awards for paintings including Prix de Paris, 1978. Mem. AAUP, Ward Nasse Gallery (N.Y.C.), Ligoa Duncan Gallery (N.Y.C.), Alpha Psi Omega. Democrat. Presbyterian. Dir.: Chinese Menu, Rutgers U., 1975, Emporer Jones, Rutgers U., 1973, Murder in the Cathedral, Haddonfield, N.J., 1968. Home: 215 Elm Ct Scotch Plains NJ 07076 Office: 392 High St Newark NJ 09023

SMITH, WALTER POWELL, educator; b. Hudson Falls, N.Y., Sept. 24, 1923; s. Frank Ray and Mary Etta (Trumble) S.; B.S., U. Idaho, 1948, M.S., 1952; D.Mus.Arts, U. Oreg., 1972; m. Marylon Haines, Mar. 15, 1953; children—Deborah, Michael, Randall, Jennifer. Music supr. pub. schs., Emmett, Idaho, 1948-51, Auburn, Wash., 1951-52, Klamath Falls, Oreg., 1952-54, West Hartford, Conn., 1956-58; prof. music Central Wash. Coll., 1955-56; chmn. dept. music Plymouth (N.H.) State Coll., 1958—; guest prof. U. Idaho, U. Oreg. music cons. Cardigan Mountain Sch. (Canaan, N.H.); condr. N.H. Honor Choir. Mem. New Eng. State Coll. Music Assn. (pres.), Music Educators Nat. Conf., N.H. Music Educators Assn., Phi Mu Alpha, Kappa Delta Pi, Phi Delta Kappa. Club: Masons. Editor Quarter Notes, 1972-76. Composer: U. Idaho Alma Mater, 1948, N.H. State Anthem, 1963. Home: Oak Ridge Rd Plymouth NH 03264 Office: Plymouth State Coll Plymouth NH 03264

SMITH, WARREN ALLEN, rec. studio corp. exec.; b. Minburn, Iowa, Oct. 27, 1921; s. Harry Clark and Ruth Marion (Miles) S.; B.A., U. No. Iowa, 1948; M.A., Columbia, 1949. Chmn. dept. English, Bentley Sch., N.Y.C., 1949-54, New Canaan (Conn.) High Sch., 1954—; pres., also chmn. bd. Variety Sound Corp., N.Y.C., 1961—; instr. Columbia, 1961-62. Pres. Taursa Fund, Piscataway, N.J., 1971. Served with AUS, 1940-44. Mem. Mensa, Am. Unitarian Assn., Brit. Humanist Assn., Humanist Book Club (pres. 1957-62), Bertrand Russell Soc. (v.p. 1977—), Mensa Investment Club (chmn. 1967-70), Internat. Press Assn. Book rev. editor The Humanist, 1953-58; syndicated columnist Scene from Manhattan in West Indian newspapers. Home: 1435 Bedford Apt 10-A Stamford CT 06905 Office: 130 W 42d St Room 551 New York City NY 10036

SMITH, WEAKS GARDNER, architect, civil engr.; b. Paducah, Ky., Aug. 7, 1922; s. Ephraim Weaks and Mary Virginia (Mollie) (Gardner) Smith; B.C.E., U. Fla., 1946; B.Arch., Washington U., St. Louis, 1951. Individual practice architecture, Paducah, 1951-55; staff Hartstern, Louis & Henry, architects, Louisville, 1955, LaPierre, Litchfield & Partners, architects, N.Y.C., 1955-57; plant engr. Western Electric Co., N.Y.C., 1958-63; sr. plant engr. Bell Telephone Labs., Murray Hill, N.J., 1963—; lectr. in field. Mem. Planning and Adjustment Bd. Paducah, 1952-55. Served with U.S. Army, 1943-46; PTO. Certified architect, Ky., N.Y., N.J.; registerd profl. engr., N.Y. Mem. A.I.A., Archaeol. Inst. Am., Soc. Am. Mil. Engrs., S.A.R., Sons Confederate Vets., Bourland Soc., Audubon Soc., Gold Prospectors Assn. Am., Pi Kappa Alpha. Republican. Episcopalian. Club: Filson (Louisville). Home: 48 Southgate Rd New Providence NJ 07974

SMITH, WENDELL MURRAY, mfg. co. exec.; b. N.Y.C., May 15, 1935; s. James Henry and Roberta (Foard) S.; A.B., Dartmouth Coll., 1957, M.S., 1958; m. Margaret MacGregor, Aug. 24, 1957; children—Karen Murray, Wendy Margaret, Kimberley Foard, Kathryn MacGregor, Jennifer Keith. Engr., Sikorsky Aircraft, Stratford, Conn., 1958-60; gen. sales mgr. Barnes Engring., Stamford, Conn., 1960-65; pres. Baldwin-Gegenheimer Corp., Stamford, 1965—, dir., 1969—; pres. Baldwin Tech. Corp., 1976—. Bd. dirs. Stamford Area Commerce and Industry Assn., 1972—, Stamford Symphony, 1973—, Stamford Devel. Corp., 1970—, Stamford Forum for World Affairs, 1974—, Jr. Achievement of Stamford, 1973—; trustee Stamford Hosp., 1977—. Mem. Graphic Arts Tech. Found., Printing Industries of Am., Nat. Printing Equipment Assn., Nat. Assn. Printers and Lithographers, Graphic Communications Computer Assn. (dir.), Research and Engring. Council, Young Pres.'s Orgn. Republican. Methodist. Club: Stamford Yacht (commodore). Home: 298 Ocean Dr E Stamford CT 06902 Office: 401 Shippan Ave Stamford CT 06902

SMITH, WILBERT HAYES, JR., nuclear engr.; b. Jackson, Miss., Sept. 12, 1923; s. Wilbert Hayes and Doretha Louise (Robinson) S.; student S.C. State Coll., 1939-41; B.S., Kent State U., 1950, postgrad., 1953-54; postgrad. Case Inst. Tech., 1959-66; M.B.A., Xavier U., 1973; D.Phys. Chemistry (hon.), Ill. Inst. Tech., 1974; m. Calvesta Carolyn Mitchell, Apr. 7, 1944; children—Alvin Wilbert, Richard Vernon, Stephen Sylvester. Tchr. math. and sci. Central High Sch., Cleve., 1954; pres. Southeast Builders, Inc., Cleve., 1954-56; phys. chemist, carbon products div. Union Carbide Corp., Parma, Ohio, 1956-66; research engr., structural fiberglass/polymer material prodn., comml. airplane div. Boeing Co., Renton, Wash., 1966-67, leader composite materials research sect., comml. airplane div., Seattle, 1967-68; engr./scientist, material and process tech. labs., group engring. div. Gen. Electric Co., Evendale, Ohio, 1968-73, nuclear reactor fuel element test and evaluation engr. Knolls Atomic Power Labs., Schenectady, 1974—; project mgr. ITT Research Inst., Chgo., 1973-74. Bd. dirs. Region O, Zone B., Lions Hearing Conservation Soc.; bd. dirs. Country Knolls South, Clifton Park, N.Y. Served to 1st lt. U.S. Army, 1950-52. Mem. Am. Phys. Soc., Internat. Conf. on Carbon, ASTM, Am. Soc. for Metallurgy, Soc. for Aerospace Profl. Engrs., Alpha Phi Alpha. Republican. Roman Catholic. Club: Lions. Home: 7 Timber Terr Clifton Park NY 12065 Office: Gen Electric Materials and Process Lab 1 River Rd Schenectady NY 12345

SMITH, WILLIAM CHARLES, lawyer; b. Batavia, N.Y., June 9, 1930; s. William and Verna (Busmire) S.; B.A., U. Buffalo, 1952; LL.B., Harvard, 1955; m. Lucia P. Pierce, July 10, 1954; children—William Charles, Leonard P., Victoria J. Admitted to Maine bar, 1955, D.C. bar, 1961; practiced in Portland, 1955-59, 61—; asso. Hutchinson, Pierce, Atwood & Allen, 1955-57, partner, 1958-59; atty. Office Tax Legis. Counsel U.S. Treasury Dept., 1959-61; partner firm Pierce, Atwood, Scribner, Allen, Smith & Lancaster, 1961—. Dir. Sanborn's Motor Express, Inc. Vice chmn. budget com. United Way, 1966-68, chmn., 1968-70, bd. dirs., 1968-74, 75—; mem. Nat. Budget and Consultation Commn., 1969-71; mem. Area V Mental Health Adv. Bd., 1972-75. Bd. dirs. Portland Goodwill Industries, Inc., 1967-69; trustee Portland Regional Opportunity Program, 1967-68, Portland Widow's Wood Soc., 1961—, pres., 1974-77; trustee Fryeburgh Acad. Mem. Am., Maine, Cumberland County bar assns., Am. Law Inst. Unitarian. Clubs: Portland Country, Cumberland (Portland). Home: 28 Orchard St Portland ME 04102 Office: 1 Monument Sq Portland ME 04111

SMITH, WILLIAM PETER, mktg. research co. exec.; b. N.Y.C., Jan. 17, 1937; s. William P. and Elsie M. (Stein) S.; B.A., City Coll. N.Y., 1967; m. Helen Doheny, Sept. 30, 1961; children—Kara, Nora, Tricia. Mem. staff beneficiary clause settlements and sales, Equitable Life Assurance Soc., N.Y.C., 1955-64, mem. staff mktg. info. service Equifax div., 1964-72, nat. accounts exec. Eastern div., 1973-75, mem. staff mktg. research and controlled mktg. service, 1975-76, area mgr. and trainer, sales and mktg., 1976-77. Named Best Mktg. Research Salesman, Mktg. Info. Service, 1973-75. Developer and salesman, hosting and theatre reporting service to motion picture industry, 1973. Home: 2 Eldor Ave New City NY 10956

SMITHGALL, ELIZABETH, educator; b. Lancaster, Pa., d. James B. and Edith (Mowrer) S.; B.S., Columbia U., 1929, M.A., 1934; postgrad. summers U. Calif. at Berkeley, 1939, N.Y. U., 1940, Temple U., 1954, U. Hawaii, 1962, Pa. State U., 1965, U. Pitts., 1967, U. London, 1970. Tchr., Lancaster Pub. Schs., 1923-50; supr. student teaching Dakota State Coll., 1950-52, Wis. State Coll., 1952-53, Plymouth State Coll., 1955-56; tchr. Thomas Jefferson Sch., Levittown, Pa., 1957-69, St. Michael Sch., Levittown, 1969—. Recipient Freedoms Found. Tchrs. medal, 1962; Nathan C. Schaeffer Meml. scholar, 1947; Hilda Maehling fellow, 1970; AAUW project grantee, 1978. Mem. Daus. Am. Colonists, D.A.R., Nat. League Am. Pen Women, AAUW, NEA, Kappa Delta Pi. Author: Lancaster and Children's Literature, 1950; compiler Developing World Understanding in Elementary Schools, 1954; Children's Books for Christmas Gifts, 1957; Human Relations in Education, 1962; Bibliography of Library Books for Beginning Readers, 1972. Contbr. articles to profl. jours.; contbr. poems to mags., anthologies. Home: 66 Huckleberry Ln Levittown PA 19055

SMITHWICK, ROBERT BRUCE, oil co. exec.; b. Phila., Apr. 25, 1928; s. Bruce and Thelma Lee (Head) S.; A.B., Elon Coll., 1950; postgrad. U. Va., 1950; m. Faye Branch, Mar. 6, 1950; children—Dorene, David, Robert, Amy. With Texaco Inc., 1953—, supt. sales tng., 1957-58, dist. sales supr., 1958-60, dist. sales mgr., 1960-61, asst. div. mgr., 1961-62, mgr. distbn. devel., N.Y.C., 1962-63, asst. div. mgr., 1963-64, Houston, 1964-66, div. mgr., 1966-68, gen. sales mgr., Denver, 1968-70, gen. mgr. personnel, 1970-71, gen. mgr. mktg. dept.-U.S., 1971, now gen. mgr. internat. aviation sales dept., White Plains, N.Y.; officer, dir. various off-shore subs. cos. Pres., Jr. Football Assn., 1974-75; adminstrv. bd. United Methodist Ch., 1964—; mem. presdl. adv. bd. Elon Coll. Served with U.S. Army, World War II. Mem. Am. Mgmt. Assn. Home: 21 Mill Stream Rd Upper Saddle River NJ 07458 Office: 2000 Westchester Ave White Plains NY 10650

SMOCK, RAYMOND WILLIAM, editor; b. Jeffersonville, Ind., Feb. 8, 1941; s. Richard and Lottie (Paciorek) S.; B.A., Roosevelt U., 1966; Ph.D., U. Md., 1974; m. Phyllis Lee Chadwick, Feb. 12, 1961. Research asst. Md. Constnl. Conv., 1967-68; asst. editor Booker T. Washington Papers Project, U. Md., 1967-74, co-editor, 1974—; pres. Instnl. Resources Corp., Laurel, Md., 1976—, also dir. Ford Found. fellow, 1970. Mem. Am., So. hist. assns., Orgn. Am. Historians, Assn. for Ednl. Communications and Tech. Author: (with Pete Daniel) A Talent for Detail: The Photographs of Miss Frances Benjamin Johnston, 1889-1910, 1974. Home: 12121 Dove Circle Laurel MD 20811 Office: History Dept U Md College Park MD 20742

SMODLAKA, VOJIN NIKOLA, physician; b. Belgrade, Yugoslavia, Nov. 14, 1912; s. Nikola J. and Leposava J. (Marinkovic) S.; came to US, 1961, naturalized, 1967; M.D., U. Belgrade, 1936; m. Melanie D. Jankovic, June 26, 1962; children—Snezana, Ivan, Bojana, Vesna. Intern, Meml. Hosp., Phila., 1962-63; resident N.Y. U., Bellevue Hosp., Goldwater Meml. Hosp., N.Y.C., 1963-65, 65-66; practice medicine specializing in physical medicine and rehab., 1966—; chmn. chair of sports medicine, dir. Inst. Sports Medicine of the State Inst. Physical Culture, Belgrade, 1946-60; physician Olympic Team, Yugoslavia, 1948-60; attending physician Methodist Hosp., Bklyn., 1967—, dir. dept. rehab. medicine, 1967—; clin. asso. prof. rehab. medicine State U. N.Y., Bklyn., 1973—; attending physician City Hosp., Elmhurst, N.Y., 1975—, Kingsbrook Jewish Hosp., Med. Center, Bklyn., 1976—; courtesy staff Doctors Hosp. S.I. (N.Y.), 1977; physician U.S. Olympic Soccer Team, 1977. Recipient Citation award, Am. Coll. Sports Medicine, 1975, Physicians Recognition award, AMA, 1977; Medal of Honor, Orbis Rheumatismi Annus, 1977; Gold medals, Minister Edn., France, 1952, Luxembourg, 1952. Fellow Am. Coll. Sports Medicine; mem. Am. Acad. Phys. Medicine and Rehab., Am. Congress Rehab. Medicine, N.Y. Acad. Medicine, AMA, N.Y. State, Kings County med. socs., Am.-Yugoslavian Med. Soc. (past pres.), Fedn. Am.-European Med. Socs. Home: 16 Signal Hill Rd Staten Island NY 10301 Office: Methodist Hosp 506 6th St Brooklyn NY 11215

SMOLANOFF, MICHAEL LOUIS, composer, educator; b. N.Y.C., May 11, 1942; s. Irving and Beatrice (Groopman) S.; B.S., Juilliard Sch. Music, 1964, M.S., 1965; Mus.D., Combs Coll., 1975. Research asst. Columbia, 1965-66; tchr. Juilliard Sch. Music, 1966; editor E.B. Marks Music Corp., N.Y.C., 1966-68; instr. Phila. Mus. Acad., 1968-71; prof. music Rutgers U., Camden, N.J., 1971—; cons. Amherst Electronic Studios. Served with USAF, 1966-70. Rutgers Research Council grantee, 1973; recipient ASCAP award, 1975-76. Mem. Nat. Assn. Am. Composers and Condrs., ASCAP, Juilliard Alumni Assn., Phi Mu Alpha Sinfonia. Composer: String Quartet, 1972; Concerto for Trombone, 1968; Celebration, 1975; Pages from a Summer Journal, 1974; others. Home: 20 A Brown Pl Bronx NY 10454 Office: Rutgers University Fine Arts Bldg Camden NJ 08102

SMOLINSKY, GISELA (GIZ) UNGURIAN, clin. child psychologist; b. Northampton County, Pa., Mar. 31, 1929; d. Emil M. and Helen (Buda) Ungurian; B.S., Ursinus Coll., 1949; M.A., Lehigh U., 1953; Ph.D., U. Pitts., 1968; m. Mervin P. Smolinsky, May 15, 1960. Psychologist, Woods Schs. Exceptional Children, Langhorne, Pa., 1954-55, Dept. Pub. Welfare, Commonwealth of Pa., Children's Div., Allen-Town State Hosp. and Western Pa. Diagnostic and Evaluation Center, Pitts., 1955-69; instr. U. Pitts., 1965-68; cons. psychologist Vitalistic Therapeutic Center, Allentown, 1972-74, Bethany Children's Home, Womelsdorf, Pa., 1969—, Lehigh Valley Child Care, Allentown, 1973—; instr. Marywood Coll., Scranton, Pa., 1977—; family therapy trainee Phila. Child Guidance Clinic. Certified sch. psychologist, Pa.; lic. psychologist, Pa. Mem. Am., Pa., Lehigh Valley psychol. assns., Internat. Transactional Analysis Assn., Pi Lambda Theta. Home: 3320 Green Meadow Dr Bethlehem PA 18017

SMOLLER, SAUL, pediatrician; b. Chelsea, Mass., Dec. 14, 1924; s. John and Goldie Smoller; B.S., U. Mass., 1945; M.D., Syracuse U., 1948; m. Sylvia Hafftka, May 15, 1971; children—Scott, Jordan. Intern, Harlem Hosp., N.Y.C., 1948-49, asst. resident pediatrics, 1949-50, chief resident pediatrics, 1950-51; sr. partner Smoller, Bernstein and Glatt, pediatrics group practice, Oceanside, N.Y., 1963—; attending staff dept. pediatrics Nassau County Med. Center, 1954—; pediatrics cons. N.Y.C. Dept. Health, 1954-59; asst. prof. clin. pediatrics State U. N.Y., Stony Brook, 1971—; vis. asst. prof. community health Albert Einstein Coll. Medicine, Bronx, N.Y., 1974—; asst. dir. dept. pediatrics South Nassau Communities Hosp., 1974—; sch. physician Oceanside Sch. Dist., 1969. Vice chmn. Oceanside Narcotics Council, 1972-74. Served with USN, 1944-46; with M.C., U.S. Army, 1952-54. Fellow Am. Acad. Pediatrics, Am. Pub. Health Assn., Nassau Acad. Medicine; mem. AMA, Am. Sch. Health Assn., N.Y. State, Nassau County med. socs., Nassau Pediatric Soc. (pres. 1977-78). Clubs: K.P.; Oceanside Lions (pres. 1970-71). Office: 3051 Long Beach Rd Oceanside NY 11572

SMOOT, LUCILLE D. HEIN (MRS. CHARLES EFFINGER SMOOT), govt. ofcl.; b. West Pittston, Pa., July 25, 1920; d. John Jonas and Elizabeth Boam (Coffee) Hein; student Am. U., 1940-45, Cornell U., 1969; m. Gerald Arthur Butler, Oct. 7, 1942 (div. July 1946); 1 son, Gerald Allan; m. 2d, Charles Effinger Smoot, Sept. 9, 1961. With Personnel Div., IRS, Washington, 1942—, successively asst. clerk, sr. clerk, personnel technician, personnel officer, 1942-59, employee relations specialist, 1959-66, labor mgmt. and employee relations spcialist, 1967-70, program leader for employee relations, 1970-72, chief conduct and appeals sect. 1972-74, spl. adviser labor relations, 1974-76, tech. adviser to dir. personnel, 1976-77, chief labor relations, 1977-78, tech. adviser to dir. personnel, 1978—; cons. ethical standards codes, 1977—. Past chmn. info. bur. Community Chest; past v.p. Young Peoples League, Nat. Symphony Orch., U.S. Savs. Bonds. Mem. Nat. Trust Historic Preservation, Am. Heritage Soc., Smithsonian Assos., Nat. Hist. Soc. Republican. Presbyterian. Clubs: Ski, St. Albans. Home: 2006 Columbia Rd Washington DC 20009 Office: Treasury Dept Washington DC 20224

SMYERS, DANIEL JEFFERSON, civil engr.; b. Pitts., May 21, 1920; s. Charles Wilson and Anna Minerva (Westwood) S.; B.S. in Civil Engring., Carnegie Mellon U., 1959; m. Gertrude Hargrave Reno, Mar. 3, 1945; 1 son, Daniel J. With Gulf Research & Devel. Co., 1957-64, Swindell-Dressler Co., 1964-67; project civil design engr. Dravo Corp., 1968-75; chief civil engr. Envisco Engring. Services, Carnegie, Pa., 1976-77, v.p., 1977—. Forum pres. Carnegie Mellon U., 1964; pres. North Hills Clan, 1966; treas. Pitts. Men's Clan, 1972—; pres. Wittmer Park Water Assn., 1969-74; mem. Allegheny Sanitary Authority Odor Control Task Force, 1970. Served with USN, 1941-45; PTO. Recipient Alumni Service award Carnegie Mellon U., 1969; registered profl. engr., Pa., Calif. Fellow ASCE (pres. Pitts. sect. 1974), Soc. Am. Mil. Engrs., Engrs. Soc. Western Pa., U.S. Power Squadron. Republican. Club: Oakmont Yacht. Home: 8657 Wittmer Rd Pittsburgh PA 15237 Office: 338 E Main St Carnegie PA 15106

SMYTH, DAVID, editor, author; b. Buenos Aires, Argentina, Feb. 7, 1929; s. Currell Hutchinson and Jessie Rodger (Dodds) S.; came to U.S., 1962, naturalized, 1970; M.A., Cambridge (Eng.) U., 1951; m. Elli Helene Dusterhoft, Nov. 9, 1968; 1 son, Clifford Dieter. Tech. writer, then copywriter, 1953-55; movie promotion writer, 1956; owner Ace Translation Agency, Buenos Aires, 1957-58; sec. Found. Econ. Edn., 1959; cables editor Buenos Aires Herald, 1960; lexicographer Simon & Schuster English-Spanish Dictionary, 1961; Latin Am. desk editor UPI, N.Y.C., 1962-63; Latin Am. desk editor AP, N.Y.C., 1963-73, world services fin. editor, 1973—; author: You Can Survive Any Financial Disaster, 1977; co-author: The Speculator's Handbook, 1974. Served with Argentine Army, 1952. Mem. N.Y. Fin. Writers Assn., Newspaper Guild. Inventor kitchen range lighter. Home: 23 Lake Ave Metuchen NJ 08840 Office: 50 Rockefeller Plaza New York City NY 10020

SMYTH, KENNETH HOWARD, agrl. engr.; b. Sherbrook, Que., Can., Oct. 20, 1948; s. Howard Ray and Ethel Mayota (Dougherty) S.; B.Sc. in Agrl. Engring., McGill U., 1972; m. Alison Margaret Mosher, Feb. 7, 1970; children—Jonathan Walter, Jeremy Howard. Pres., Maritime Drainage & Supplies Co., Brookfield, N.S., Can., 1972—; basketball coach N.S. Agrl. Coll., 1972—, mem. faculty, 1974—. Mem. Am. Soc. Agrl. Engrs., Canadian Soc. Agrl. Engrs., Assn. Profl. Engrs. N.S., Nat. Assn. Basketball Coaches. Home and office: PO Box 100 Brookfield NS B0N 1C0 Canada

SMYTH, ROGER LOUIS, psychologist; b. N.Y.C., Apr. 9, 1937; s. Ira and Esther (Sault) S.; B.A., Coll. City N.Y., 1968; M.A., Fordham U., 1971, Ph.D., 1973. Trainee VA Hosps., Manhattan, Bronx, Montrose and Bklyn., 1969-73; asst. prof. psychology Manhattan Coll., 1973-76; vis. prof. U. Redlands, Calif., 1974; cons. Project Headstart, Los Angeles, 1974; pvt. practice psychology, N.Y.C., 1974—; adj. instr. John Jay Coll., 1974-75; asso. clin. dir. 5th Ave. Center Counseling, N.Y.C., 1975-77; supervisory staff L.I. Community Coll., 1976—; adj. instr. LaGuardia Community Coll., 1977—; cons. Psychol. Selection Service, N.Y.C., 1977—; asst. prof. psychology N.Y. Inst. Tech., 1977—; guest lectr. Am. Internat. Sch., Vienna, 1978. Certified psychologist, N.Y. Mem. Am., N.Y., Eastern psychol. assns., N.Y. Soc. Clin. Psychology, Am. Group Psychotherapy Assn., Eastern Group Psychotherapy Soc., Nat., N.Y. State assns. humanistic psychology, Nat. Inst. Psychotherapies, Am. Orthopsychiat. Assn., Am. Assn. Sex Educators and Counselors, NOW, Sigma Xi. Democrat. Editorial bd. Psychotherapy, 1976—. Home and Office: 215 W 92d St New York City NY 10025

SNADER, DANIEL WEBSTER, educator, author; b. Akron, Pa., Jan. 25, 1907; s. John P. and Lizzie (Hummer) S.; B.S., Albright Coll., 1929; M.A., Columbia, 1935, Ed.D., 1942; m. Mae M. Snader (dec. 1955); 1 son, Jack R.; m. 2d, Ella C. Marth, July 28, 1956; m. 3d, Carolina Sicurella, Aug. 30, 1972; 1 son, Daniel Webster Jr. Tchr. pub. high schs., Pa., N.Y., 1929-36; critic-supr. math. tchrs. Ohio U., Athens, 1936-38; asst. prof. math., math supr. N.Y. State U. Albany, 1938-46; prof. math., edn. U. Ill., Urbana, 1946-61; specialist for math. U.S. Office Edn., Washington, 1959-62; prof. math., chmn. dept. State U. N.Y. Coll., Fredonia, 1962-72, now emeritus. U.S. ednl. cons. Gakko Tosho, Japanese Pub. Co.; cons. Ill. Secondary Sch. Curriculum Program; dir. NSF Insts. Mem. Math. Assn. Am., Nat. Council Tchrs. Math., Central Assn. Sci. and Math., Math.-Edn. Research Assn. Japan, NEA, N.Y. State Edn. Assn., Phi Eta Sigma, Phi Delta Kappa, Kappa Delta Pi, Pi Mu Epsilon, Alpha Pi Omega. Author: Individualization of Instruction in Math, 1942; numerous text books in math. Home and office: 164 Fizell Ave Dunkirk NY 14048

SNEDDEN, MARY JANE HEFFNER (MRS. HOMER GRANGER SNEDDEN), govt. ofcl.; b. McKeesport, Pa., Mar. 14, 1917; d. Samuel Harrison and Meda (Calhoun) Heffner; secretarial student Douglas Bus. Coll., McKeesport, Pa., 1936-37; student Duquesne U., 1942; m. Homer Granger Snedden, Nov. 6, 1943. Sec., legal dept. Westinghouse Air Brake Co., Wilmerding, Pa., 1940-44. Leader Brownie Scouts, Fayetteville, N.C., 1947-48. Pres. East McKeesport Recreation Bd., 1968-76; majority inspector, dist. 1, East McKeesport Election Bd., 1966-69; councilwoman Borough of East McKeesport, 1972—, chmn. fin., 1972-78, mem. fin. com., 1978—, chmn. st. com., 1978—, v.p. council, 1976—; mem. Rep. Com., Dist. 1, East McKeesport, 1971-76. Bd. dirs. Pre-Sch. for Exceptional Children Greater McKeesport Area, 1966—; trustee Allegheny Acad., 1969-74; mem. citizens adv. com. Gov.'s Traffic Safety Council, 1978—. Recipient Gov.'s award for outstanding contbn. to traffic safety Commonwealth of Pa., 1968-77. Mem. Pa. Huguenot Soc., D.A.R. (chpt. regent 1966-68, state vice chmn. U.S.A. Bicentennial com. 1971-74, state chmn. Am. history month 1974-75, state vice chmn. student loan and scholarship com. 1977-80), Internat. Platform Assn. Presbyn. Mem. Order Eastern Star (past matron, pres. McKeesport Past Matrons Club 1975-76). Club: Ligonier (Pa.) Country. Home: 722 Broadway East McKeesport PA 15035

SNELL, DAVID, writer; b. Minden, La., Mar. 28, 1921; s. John Barnard and Ada Jack (Carver) S.; student La. State U., 1939-43; children by previous marriage—Barry, Jan Whitfield; m. 2d, Dixie Baye Oliver, Sept. 1, 1956; children—Steven Mark, Sandra Robin. Reporter, Minden Herald & Webster Rev., 1936-37, Atlanta Constn., 1943-44; rewrite man U.P.I., N.Y.C. bur., 1946-47; reporter N.Y. Sun, 1947-50; radio, TV commentator WOR-Mut., 1950-52; reporter feature writer N.Y. World Telegram & Sun, 1950-55; mem. staff Life mag., 1955-69, corr. in Paris, France, 1957-61, London, Eng., 1961-62, asso. editor, 1962-63, sr. editor, 1963-69, author column Dateline America; pres. Internat. Writers Ltd.; dir. Internat. Spl. Projects Consultants, Inc. Served with AUS, 1945-46. Recipient George Polk Meml. award, 1952, Sportsmanship Brotherhood award, 1954, Citizenship award Am. Legion, 1938, Sci. award Bausch & Lomb, Inc., 1938; cited by Inst. Edn. by Radio-TV, Ohio State U., 1951. Mem. Sigma Nu. Unitarian. Contbr. to Life, Smithsonian, Signature, Today's Health, Saturday Rev., other mags. Artist in oil, also cartoonist pub. nat. mags. Office: 440 Pinehaven Houston TX 77024 also care Harold Matson Co Inc 22 E 40th St New York City NY 10016

SNELLING, CHARLES DARWIN, orchardist; b. Allentown, Pa., Jan. 26, 1931; s. Walter O. and Marjorie G. (Gahring) S.; B.S., Lehigh U., 1954; m. Adrienne C. Angeletti, Mar. 21, 1951; children—Adrienne C., Jonathan C., Marjorie P., Elizabeth H., Lesley C. Asst. to pres. N.Y. Transformer Co., Alpha, N.J., 1954-55; founder, pres., dir. Cryo-Therm, Inc., Fogelsville, Pa., 1955-72; pres. Trexler Orchards, Inc., Lehigh C-County, Pa., 1967-74; v.p. Mohr Orchards Inc., Allentown, 1967-74, pres., 1975—; dir. Boyertown Burial Casket Co Co., 1975—; chmn. bd. Applewood, Inc., 1971—. Mem. commerce tech. adv. bd. Commerce Dept., 1976-77; mem. Pres.'s Commn. on Personnel Interchange, 1976-77; trustee YMCA, Allentown, 1974—; trustee Cedar Crest Coll., Allentown, 1974—; trustee Allentown Art Mus., 1970—; dir. United Way, Lehigh County, 1965-67, 1976—; dir. Planned Parenthood Assn., Lehigh County, 1976-77; chmn. Lehigh Valley Energy Task Force, Allentown, Bethlehem, Easton, 1974—; pres. Allentown City Council, 1970-73; chmn. Republican Fin. Com. of Pa., 1977—; fin. cchmn. Lehigh County Rep. Com., 1975-77; del. Nat. Conv., 1976. Mem. AAAS, Am. Phys. Soc., Young Pres.'s Orgn., Franklin Inst. Mem. United Ch. of Christ. Clubs: Merion Cricket (Haverford, Pa.); Grenidier Island (Ont., Can.); Lehigh Country; Pa. Soc. (N.Y.C.). Patentee in field of cryogenics and thermodynamics. Home: 2949 Greeleaf St Allentown PA 18104 Office: 711 Hamilton Mall Allentown PA 18101

SNELLING, RICHARD ARKWRIGHT, gov. of Vt.; b. Allentown, Pa., Feb. 18, 1927; s. Walter Otheman and Marjorie (Gahring) S.; student Lehigh U., 1943; A.B., Harvard, 1948; m. Barbara T. Weil, June 14, 1947; children—Jacqueline (Mrs. Robert Pettit), Mark, Diane, Andrew. Chmn. bd. Shelburne Industries, Inc., Barreca Products Co., Inc., Wessel Hardware Co.; mem. Vt. Ho. of Reps., 1959-60, 72-74, 75-77; gov. of Vt., 1977—. Mem. Vt. Devel. Commn., 1960-62; chmn. Vt. Aeros. Commn., 1968-72, Vt. del. Republican Nat. Conv., 1960-68; Rep. nominee lt. gov. Vt., 1964, gov. Vt., 1966; chmn. Vt. Rep. Fin. Com., 1974—. Chmn. bd. dirs. Greater Burlington Indsl. Corp., 1960-62; trustee Med. Center Hosp. of Vt. Served with U.S. Army, 1944-46; ETO. Mem. Lake Champlain C. of C. (dir. 1962-64). Home: Harbor Rd Shelburne VT 05482

SNELLING, WILLIAM RODMAN, ednl. cons.; b. Pittsfield, Mass., Feb. 10, 1931; s. Samuel William and Beatrice (Bamforth) S.; grad. Deerfield Acad., 1949; A.B. magna cum laude (James Bowdoin scholar), Bowdoin Coll., 1953; postgrad. Harvard, 1953; M.Ed., Coll. William and Mary, 1956; D.Ed., U. Va., 1957; m. Anne Louise Kurtz, Jan. 27, 1953; children—Roxanne, Glenn Rodman. Tchr. math., coach Cradock Sch., Portsmouth, Va., 1953-54; tchr. Niskayuna Sr. High Sch., Schenectady, 1957-59, Phillips Andover Acad., 1958-59, Morgan Park Acad., Chgo., 1959-61; headmaster Detroit Country Day Sch., Birmingham, Mich., 1961-67, Tatnall Sch., Wilmington, Del., 1968-77. Research cons. Bur. Research N.Y. State Dept. Edn., 1957; cons. math. N.Y. State Dept. Edn., 1958; ednl. cons. Research Corp., 1967-68; pres. Ind. Sch. Mgmt., sch. cons. Served to 1st lt. Transp. Corps, AUS, 1954-56. Ford Found. grantee, 1953. Recipient Distinguished Service citation Detroit Country Day Sch., 1965. Mem. World Affairs Council Del., Cum Laude Soc., Nat. Assn. Ind. Schs. (dir.). Clubs: University, Whist. Author: Science in Liberal Arts Colleges, 1972. Editor, pub. Ideas & Perspectives, tri-weekly adv. letter ind. sch. mgmt. Home: 1100 Pennsylvania Ave Wilmington DE 19806

SNIDER, EDWARD MALCOLM, profl. hockey club exec.; b. Washington, Jan. 6, 1933; s. Sol C. and Lillian (Bonas) S.; B.S., U. Md., 1955; m. Myrna Gordon, July 11, 1954; children—Craig Alan, Jay Thomas, Lindy Lou, Tina Suzanne. Maj. stockholder, exec. v.p. Edge Ltd., Washington, 1957-63; v.p. Phila. Eagles Football Club, 1964-67; chmn. bd. Phila. Flyers Hockey Club, 1967—; co-chmn. bd. Spectrum Arena, Phila., 1971—. Chmn. bd. Nat. Hockey League Services, 1968—; bd. govs., Nat. Hockey League, 1967—, mem. fin. com., 1969—. Trustee St. Luke's Childrens Hosp., bd. dirs. Phila. Assn. Retarded Children, 1971—, Western br. JYC, 1973—, Police Athletic League, 1974—. C.P.A., Md. Office: The Spectrum Broad and Pattison Philadelphia PA 19148

SNIDER, HAROLD WAYNE, educator; b. Puyallup, Wash., Apr. 16, 1923; s. P. Marion and Grace Stevenson (Short) S.; B.A., U. Wash., 1946, M.A., 1950; Ph.D., U. Pa., 1955; m. Isobel Milne Dice, Jan. 20, 1961; stepchildren—Isobel Milne Given, John Kenneth Desmond. Instr. bus. U. Wash., 1952-54; asso. prof. Ill. Wesleyan U., 1954-57; asst. prof. U. Pa., Phila., 1957-64; prof., chmn. dept. ins. and risk Temple U., Phila., 1964—. Served with AUS, 1943-46. S.S. Huebner Found. fellow, 1950-52. Mem. Risk and Ins. Mgmt. Soc., Am. Mgmt. Assn., Am. Risk and Ins. Soc., Phi Beta Kappa, Beta Gamma Sigma. Club: Philadelphia Aviation Country. Author: Life Insurance Investment in Commercial Real Estate, 1956; (with Denenberg and others) Risk and Insurance, 1964; (with John Adams) The Automobile Accident Problem: Saskatchewan Approach, 1973; contbg. author The Job of Risk Management, 1962. Home: Box 256 Gwynedd PA 19436 Office: School Business Adminstrn Temple U Philadelphia PA 19122

SNIDERMAN, KENNETH WILFRED, cardiovascular radiologist; b. Toronto, Ont., Can., Jan. 29, 1945; s. Harold Roy and Anne Beatrice Sniderman; came to U.S., 1975; B.Sc. in Medicine, U. Toronto, 1970, M.D., 1970. Intern, Mt. Sinai Hosp., Toronto, 1970-71; clin. fellow in cardiovascular radiology Mass. Gen. Hosp., Boston, 1975-76; clin. fellow in cardiovascular radiology N.Y. Hosp.-Cornell U. Med. Coll., N.Y.C., 1976-77, asst. prof. radiology, 1977—. Diplomate Am. Bd. Radiology. Fellow Royal Coll. Physicians (Can.); mem. Canadian, Ont. med. assns., AMA, Canadian Assn. Radiologists. Home: 520 E 72d St New York City NY 10021 Office: 525 E 68th St New York City NY 10021

SNIDERMAN, MARVIN, dentist; b. Pitts., Oct. 23, 1923; s. Abraham and Rebecca (Hecht) S.; B.S. in Pharmacy, U. Pitts., 1943, D.M.D., 1947; m. Eleanore Jessie Cohen, Dec. 25, 1947; 1 dau., Abby. Pvt. dental practice Pitts., 1947-50, 53—; chief dental service Home for Crippled Children, 1947—; chief oral surgery dept. Pitts. Skin and Cancer Found., 1947-67. Mem. dental adv. com. Allegheny County Dept. of Health, div. dental health, 1958-70; mem. undergrad. and postgrad. faculty U. Pitts. Sch. Dental Medicine, 1962—, asso. prof. oral medicine, 1972—. Mem. health adv. com. Pitts. Bd. Pub. Edn., 1965-70; mem. dental health com. Mayor's Com. on Human Resources, Operation Head Start, 1965; mem. adv. com. on health Mayor's Com. on Human Resources, 1965-70; dental cons. USPHS, 1965—; dir. Delta Dental of Pa., 1971-78; health edn. com. Allegheny County Adv. Council, 1972-74, 78—; mem. dental adv. com. Office Med. Programs Pa. Dept. Pub. Welfare, 1976—; vis. lectr. Emory U., U. Pa., Polyclinic and French Med. Sch., N.J. Coll. Medicine Dentistry, Temple Dental Sch. Albert Einstein Coll. Medicine, N.Y.C. Served pvt. AUS, 1943-44, 1st lt. to capt., Dental Corp., 1950-53. Fellow Am. Coll. Dentists (pres. Pitts. sect. 1972), Acad. Dentistry for Handicapped (charter), Acad. Gen. Dentistry (charter), Soc. Oral Physiology and Occlusion (charter), Internat. Coll. Dentists (dep. regent 1970-76), Acad. Oral Medicine (academic, charter), Acad. Dentistry Internat. (charter), Acad. Stress and Chronic Disease (Charter); mem. Am., Pa. (vis. lectr.) dental assns., Am. Acad. Oral Medicine (charter), Am. Endodontic Soc. (charter), Am. Assn. Dental Editors, Am. Acad. Craniomandibular Orthopedics (charter), Internat. Assn. Study Pain, Am. Pain Soc. (Charter), Odontological Soc. Western Pa. (pres. 1965), Am. Soc. Dentistry for Children, Am. Prosthodontic Soc., Internat. Assn. Dental Research, AAAS, Am. Assn. Hosp. Dentists, Am. Assn. Dental Sch., Am. Acad. Implant Dentistry, Fedn. Prosthodontic Assns., Am. Endodontic Soc., Am. Dental Soc. Anesthesiology, Am. Analgesia Soc., Am. Acad. Dental Practice Adminstrn., AAUP, U. Pitts. Dental Alumni Assn. (pres. 1973-74), Am. Med. Writers Assn. Jewish religion. Editor: Odontological Bulletin of Western Pa., 1960-70, Pa. Dental Assn., 1970—; also articles in field; abstractor Jour. Oral Research Abstracts; cons., contbr. book revs. Jour. Am. Dental Assn. Home: 5633 Callowhill St Pittsburgh PA 15206 Office: 519 Jenkins Arcade Pittsburgh PA 15222

SNIFFEN, ALLAN MEAD, III, ednl. psychologist; b. Hackensack, N.J., May 7, 1926; s. Allan Burr and Margaret (Smith) S.; B.S. in Psychology Haverford Coll., 1950; M.A. in Spl. Edn., N.Y. U., 1951, Ph.D. in Ednl. Psychology, 1963; m. Eleanor Adele Sauer, Nov. 20, 1954; children—Allan Mead IV, Daniel Burr. Sr. teaching asst. psychology group N.Y. U. Sch. Commerce, N.Y.C., 1952-54; sch. psychologist City Sch. Dist. of New Rochelle (N.Y.), 1954-56; psychologist-counselor Bd. Coop. Ednl. Services, Bedford Hills, N.Y., 1956-67; head psychologist-counselor Guidance and Child Study Center, Yorktown Heights, N.Y., 1967-68, coordinator, 1972—; coordinator Guidance and Child Study Center, Carmel, N.Y., 1968-72. Pvt. practice psychology, Katonah, N.Y., 1958—, Pleasantville, N.Y., 1958-66, Bedford Hills, 1966—; coordinator Evening Counseling Service; asso. dir. research project Diagnosis Learning Disabilities. Mem. N.Y. State Com. on Learning Disabilities. Served with USNR, 1944-46. Diplomate Am. Bd. Profl. Psychology. Mem. Westchester, Putnam, Rockland personnel and guidance assns., Am., N.Y. State psychol. assns., NEA, N.Y. State Tchrs. Assn., Westchester Assn. Sch. Psychologists, No. Westchester Mental Health Assn. (vice chmn.), Am. Psychol. Assn., Am. Personnel and Guidance Assn., Nat. Register Health Service Providers in Psychology, SAR, Phi Delta Kappa, Kappa Delta Pi. Contbr. articles to profl. jours. Home: Wood Rd Bedford Hills NY 10507 Office: Northmore Dr Yorktown Heights NY 10598

SNOOK, ELWOOD BANKES, textile mfg. exec.; b. West Lawn, Pa., May 4, 1928; s. Elwood Dennis and Myrtle Ruth (Bankes) S.; student Albright Coll., 1945-47; m. Jean C. Tobias, Oct. 21, 1954; children—David, Pamela. Accountant, tax mgr. Gilbert, Assos., Inc., Reading, Pa., 1951-57; with Vanity Fair Mills, Inc., Reading, 1957—, asst. controller, 1973—; guest lectr. Albright Coll., Pa. State Coll. Auditor, Wilson (Pa.) Joint Sch. Dist., 1958-64; mem. audit com. United Way, 1964-67; active Boy Scouts Am.; borough councilman West Lawn, also chmn. finance com., 1968—. Served with USAF, 1947-48. Mem. Nat. Assn. Accountants (past chpt. pres.). Methodist. Club: Lions. Home: 2241 Fairview St West Lawn PA 19609 Office: 1045 Park Rd Wyomissing PA 19610

SNOW, ALBERT JOSEPH, educator; b. N. Tonawanda, N.Y., Jan. 9, 1935; s. Joseph T. and Alice B. (French) S.; B.S. in Chemsitry, St. John's U., 1957; M.S. in Sci. Edn., C.W. Post Coll., 1964; M.A. in Chemistry, Bowling Green State U., 1969; Ed.D. in Sci. Edn., U. Md., 1974; m. Anne M.V. Gloster, Apr. 25, 1959; children—Matthew B., Anne Gloster. Sci. tchr. Highland Prep. Sch., Jamaica, N.Y., 1957-59, Valley Stream (N.Y.) North High Sch., 1959-61; exhibits mgr. Oak Ridge Inst. Nuclear Studies, 1961-62; sci. tchr., dist. sci. coordinator, chmn. dept. Eastchester (N.Y.) Pub. Schs., 1962—; adj. prof. sci. edn. Coll. New Rochelle; cons. AAAS, Bur. Indian Affairs, Navajo Nation; panel mem. Native AMs. in Sci. of AAAS. Served with USAR, 1955-62. NSF grantee and fellow, 1960-71. Mem. AAAS, Nat. Indian Edn. Assn., Nat. Sci. Tchrs. Assn., Sci. Tchrs. Assn. N.Y., Westchester-Rockland Sci. Suprs. Assn., N.Y. State United Tchrs. Contbr. articles on the Am. Indian to profl. jours. Home: 216 Dante Ave Tuckahoe NY 10707

SNOW, EDWINA FEIGENSPAN (MRS. MACVICKER SNOW), editor, pub.; b. N.Y.C., July 14, 1927; d. Edwin Christian and Flora Marie (Russ) Feigenspan; student Barnard Coll., 1945-46, Columbia U., 1946, Julliard Sch. Music, 1943; m. David Dodge Osborn, June 1946 (div. 1951); children—Dana (Baroness Francois Andrea de Nerciat), Christopher Fairfield Osborn; m. 2d, MacVicker Snow, Dec. 19, 1964; children—Marina, Michael Snow. Model, John Robert Powers, N.Y.C., 1947-48, pub. relations dir. Powers cosmetics, 1948-50; model Ford Agy., N.Y.C., 1950-53, Jacques Heim, Paris, France, 1957; bilingual sec. Cofinindus, Brufina, Electrobel Belgian holding cos., 1960; co-editor, pub. Locust Valley (N.Y.) Leader, 1961-67; editor, pub. Oyster Bay (N.Y.) Guardian, 1967—; partner Locust Valley Pub. Co., Inc., 1965—; pres. Oyster Bay Pub. Co., Inc. Bd. dirs. Nassau chpt. ARC; benefit dir. Boys Town Italy, 1952-54. Mem. ASCAP, Am. Horse Protection Assn. Kiwanian (hon.). Home: Centre Island Oyster Bay NY 11771 Office: 188 W Main St Oyster Bay NY 11771

SNOW, JERRY ALLISON, physician; b. Guntersville, Ala., Jan. 9, 1940; s. Leon and Ora Mae (Hunkapiller) S.; B.A. cum laude, U. of South, 1961; M.D., Washington U., St. Louis, 1965. Intern, Boston City Hosp., 1965-66, resident in internal medicine, 1966-67, fellow in cardiology, 1967-69; research internist in cardiovasular disease Walter Reed Army Inst. Research, Washington, 1969-72; asst. chief cardiology VA Hosp., Washington, 1972-75, chief hemodynamics, 1975-76; asst. prof. medicine George Washington U., Washington, 1972-77; asst. clin. prof. medicine Georgetown U., Washington, 1974—; practice medicine specializing in cardiovascular disease medicine, Washington, 1977—; cons. in cardiovascular disease Nat. Naval Med. Center, Bethesda, Md., 1975—. Bd. dirs. nation's capital affiliate Am. Heart Assn., 1976—, also mem. nat. faculty for basic and advanced life support. Served from capt. to maj. M.C., U.S. Army, 1969-72. Diplomate Am. Bd. Internal Medicine. Fellow A.C.P., Am. Coll. Cardiology; mem. Am. Heart Assn. (fellow council on clin. cardiology), Am. Fedn. Clin. Research, Am. Physiol. Soc., Internat. Soc. Cardiology, AAAS, AMA, Med. Soc. D.C., Phi Beta Kappa. Republican. Episcopalian. Club: Annapolis Yacht. Contbr. articles to med. jours. Home: 2120 Yorktown Rd NW Washington DC 20012 Office: 4900 Massachusetts Ave NW Washington DC 20016

SNOW, MARGARET THROCKMORTON, physician; b. Sioux Falls, S.D., Oct. 8, 1926; d. Charlie Gross and Grace Luzela (Griffith) Throckmorton; A.B., Iowa Wesleyan Coll., 1942; M.D., George Washington U., 1946; children—Ann Snow Hobbs, Carmel Jeanne, Carol Joan, Nancy Lee Snow Nelson, Robert Lee, Dorothy Ann, John Charles. Intern, Garfield Meml. Hosp., Washington, 1946-47; resident Children's Hosp., Washington, 1947; practice medicine specializing in family practice, Washington, 1947—; preceptor, physicians asst. program George Washington Sch. Medicine, 1978; mem. staff George Washington U. Hosp., Washington, Washington Adventist Hosp., Takoma Park, Md., Holy Cross Hosp., Silver Spring, Md. Chmn. univ. bldg. fund Montgomery County U., 1967—. Precinct chmn. Republican party, Silver Springs, Md., 1969-71; mem. Montgomery County Symphony Orch., 1960-68; chmn. bd. govs. Nat. Colls. Sci. and Arts, 1965-66. Diplomate Nat. Bd. Med. Examiners, Am. Bd. Family Practice. Mem. AMA, Eastern Psychoanalytic Assn., Med. and Chirurg. Faculty Md., Montgomery County Med. Soc., Montgomery County C. of C. (sec. 1962-66), Smith Reed Russell Med. Honor Soc., Iota Phi Honor Soc. Club: Ski (Washington). Address: 9013 Flower Ave Silver Spring MD 20901 also Welcome Home Again Farms PO Box 84 Damascus MD 20750

SNOW, RONALD LOUIS, lawyer; b. Franklin, N.H., Aug. 3, 1935; s. Louis Joseph and Evangeline Mary (Pinard) S.; B.A., Dartmouth Coll., 1958; LL.D., Yale, 1961; m. Mary Ellen Holopainen, July 8, 1961; children—Mark R., Lisa K., Ronald. Admitted to N.H. bar, 1960; partner firm Orr and Reno, Concord, N.H., 1961—. Chmn. N.H. Ballot Law Commn., 1972—; chmn. Concord Area Drug Action, 1969-75; pres. Concord YMCA. Recipient Man of Year Award, Concord YMCA, 1972. Mem. Am., N.H. (past chmn. drug abuse program), Merrimack County bar assns., Def. Research Inst., Soc. Hosp. Attys. Republican. Roman Catholic. Club: Concord Country. Home: 87 Mountain Rd Concord NH 03301 Office: 95 N Main Concord NH 03301

SNOW, VERNON FRED, historian, philanthropist; b. Milw., Nov. 25, 1924; s. Howard Melvin and Violet Charlotte (Stalker) S.; B.A., Wheaton Coll., 1948; M.A., U. Chgo., 1949; Ph.D. (Adams fellow), U. Wis., 1953; m. Emily Jean Wry, June 17, 1949; 1 son, Jonathan. Asst. prof. history U. Oreg., Eugene, 1953-60; asso. prof. English history U. Mont., Missoula, 1960-66; prof. English history U. Nebr., Lincoln, 1966-74, Syracuse (N.Y.) U., 1974—; vis. prof. U. Wis., 1957; pres. John Ben Snow Found., Fayetteville, N.Y., 1967—; cons. World Book Ency., 1966—; cons., research fellow Yale U., 1974—. Am. Philos. Soc. travel research grantee, 1958, 65, 69; Economic Found. fellow, 1962; Royal Hist. Soc. fellow, 1969—. Author: The Noble Rebel: The Life and Times of Robert Devereux, Third Earl of Essex, 1970; JBS: the Biography of John Ben Snow, 1974; Parliament in Elizabethan England, 1977. Home: 5161 Winterton Dr Fayetteville NY 13066

SNOWE, OLYMPIA JEAN, Congresswoman; b. Augusta, Maine, Feb. 21, 1947; d. George John and Georgia (Goranites) Bouchles; B.A. in Polit. Sci., U. Maine, 1969. Mem. Maine Ho. of Reps., 1973-77; mem. Maine Senate, 1977-79; mem. 96th Congress from 2d Maine dist.; dir. Superior Concrete Co., Inc., 1973. Mem. Gov.'s Adv. Com. on U. Maine, Gov.'s Positive Action Com., Gov's Adv. Com. Drug Abuse and Alcoholism Prevention; formerly vice-chmn. Auburn (Maine) Republican City Com.; alt. del. Rep. Nat. Conv., 1976. Mem. Maine Women's Polit. Caucus, League Women Voters, Women's Hosp. Assn., Women's Lit. Union. Greek Orthodox. Office: 1729 Longworth House Office Bldg Washington DC 20515*

SNYDER, BARRY SHERWOOD, ins. co. investments exec.; b. Hartford Conn., Dec. 12, 1942; s. Israel and Shirley (Goldstein) S.; student bus. Manchester Community Coll., 1962-65; m. Linda Iris Forman, May 19, 1968; children—Jay Gregory, Lisa Beth. Computer operator Travelers Ins. Co., Hartford, 1962-64, supr. securities dept., 1964-68, sr. trader, investments, 1968-71, head trader investments securities dept.; mem. adv. bd. Autex Corp., N.Y.C. Served with USNG, 1961-62. Mem. Nat. Assn. Securities Dealers, Conn. Security Traders Assn., Hartford Soc. Fin. Analysts. Jewish. Home: 81 Kent Dr Manchester CT 06040 Office: Travelers Insurance Corp 1 Tower Sq Hartford CT 06115

SNYDER, C. DUANE, realtor; b. North Wales, Pa., Jan. 1, 1926; s. Charles B. and Anna R. (McDowell) S.; student U. Va.; m. Louise Camburn, Aug. 7, 1948; children—Jeffrey Keith, Debora L. Snyder Cramer, Harry E., Gerald William. Real estate salesman Kenneth Kratz Co., Lansdale, Pa., 1955-58, asso. broker, 1959-62, dir. sales, 1963-73, dir. appraisals, 1974—. Dir. Gen. Nash council Boy Scouts Am., 1960-61; capt. YMCA Fund Dr., 1972-75. Served with U.S. Army, 1944-46. Decorated Croix de Guerre. Mem. N. Pa. (dir. 1968—, pres. 1974, Realtor of Year 1975), Pa. (dir.) bds. realtors, Nat. Assn. Realtors, Del. Valley Council of Realtors, Pa. Soc. Republican. Presbyterian. Club: Rotary (dir. Lansdale 1973-74). Home: 739 Rosemont Ave Lansdale PA 19446 Office: 410 W Main St Lansdale PA 19446

SNYDER, GARY SHERMAN, poet; b. San Francisco, May 8, 1930; s. Harold Alton and Lois (Wilkie) S.; B.A., Reed Coll., 1951; postgrad. Ind. U., 1951-52, U. Calif. at Berkeley, 1953-56; m. Masa Uehara, Aug. 6, 1967; children—Kai, Gen. Lookout, Mount Baker Forest, 1952-53; research in Japan, 1956-57, 59-64; lectr. U. Calif. at Berkeley, 1964-65. Bollingen fellow, 1966-67; Poetry award Nat. Inst. Arts and Letters; Guggenheim fellow, 1968-69; recipient Pulitzer prize in poetry, 1975. Author: (poems) Riprap, 1959; Myths and Texts, 1960; Six Sections from Mountains and Rivers without End., 1965; A Range of Poems, 1966; The Back Country, 1968; Earth House Hold, 1969; Regarding Wave, 1970; Turtle Island, 1974; (essays) The Old Ways, 1977. Office: care New Directions 333 6th Ave New York City NY 10003

SNYDER, GERALD A., profl. assn. exec.; b. East Stroudsburg, Pa., Dec. 17, 1925; s. Oscar and Leah (Fisher) S.; B.S., Stroudsburg State Coll., 1949; M.A. Lehigh U., 1960; m. Kathleen Schlough, Oct. 11, 1946; children—Susan Snyder Good, Linda Snyder Schober. Tchr. schs., N.Y., N.J., Pa., 1950-64; field rep. N.J. Edn. Assn., 1964-68; asst. dir. legislation Pa. State Edn. Assn., 1964-70, dir. retirement and welfare, 1970—; acting exec. dir. Pa. State Ret. Tchrs. Assn., 1974—. Served with USAF, 1943-46. Life mem. NEA, Pa., N.J. edn. assns. Club: Masons (32 deg.). Home: 3406 Canby St Harrisburg PA 17109 Office: 400 N 3d St Harrisburg PA 17101

SNYDER, IVAN JAY, accountant, mail order and retail exec.; b. N.Y.C., Mar. 5, 1942; s. Solomon and Ida (Sherman) S.; B.B.A., Coll. City N.Y., 1966; m. Irene B. Saretsky, Nov. 14, 1944; children—Stephen Craig, Keith Ira. Supr. sr. accountant S.D. Leidesdorf & Co., N.Y.C., 1966-67; asst. corp. controller, asst. treas., v.p. ops. publs. div. Cadence Industries Corp., N.Y.C., 1969-75; pres. Superhero Enterprises, Inc., N.Y.C., 1975—, Heroes World Centers, Inc., 1977—; cons. various bus. Mem. Am. Inst. of C.P.A.'s, N.Y. Soc. C.P.A.'s. Home: 22 Deer Run Dr Randolph Township NJ 07801 Office: Randolph Plaza Center Grove Rd RTE 10 Randolph Township NJ 07801

SNYDER, JANE PETERS (MRS. ARTHUR LELAND SNYDER), pub. relations exec.; b. Manassas, Va., July 23, 1925; d. James Walker and Alma Dorothy (Cross) Peters; student George Washington U., 1943-45, Columbia U. Sch. Pub. Health, 1962; m. Arthur Leland Snyder, June 7, 1944; children—Susan Leland, James Peters. Reporter, Montgomery County (Md.) Sentinel, 1952-54, Chatham (N.J.) Courier, 1956-59, Morris County (N.J.) Daily Record, 1959-61; pub. relations asst. East Orange (N.J.) Gen. Hosp., 1962-64, United Hosp., Newark, 1964-65; dir. community relations Georgetown U. Hosp., Washington, 1966-68; dir. pub. relations Hosp. Council and Met. Regional Med. Program, Washington, 1968-70, Washington Hosp. Center, Washington, 1970—; lectr. George Washington U. Sch. Health Care Adminstrn., 1973, 78. Mem. Am. Soc. Hosp. Pub. Relations (dir. 1973-75), Acad. Hosp. Pub. Relations (treas. 1973, dir. 1974—, MacEachern awards 1963, 72-77). Home: 5235 Elliott Rd Washington DC 20016 Office: 110 Irving St NW Washington DC 20010

SNYDER, JOHN MENDENHALL, thoracic surgeon; b. Slatington, Pa., Aug. 1, 1909; s. James Wilson and Gertrude (Mendenhall) S.; B.S., Bucknell U., 1930; M.D., U. Pa., 1934; M.S. in Surgery, U. Minn., 1941; m. Betty June Wiltrout, Feb. 14, 1942; children—Sue Anne (Mrs. R. James Alexy, Jr.), John Sanford. Intern, Bryn Mawr (Pa.) Hosp., 1934-35; resident in medicine Western Res. U. Hosp., Cleve., 1935-36; fellow in surgery Mayo Clinic, 1936-41; practice medicine specializing in thoracic surgery, Bethlehem, Pa., 1945-77; mem. staff St. Lukes Hosp.; past cons. Mt. Trexler Sanitarium, Sacret Heart Hosp., Allentown State Hosp., Graden-Huetton Hosp., Easton Hosp., Muhlenberg Med. Center; vis. lectr. U. Pa., 1960. Mem. Air Pollution Commn., Bethlehem, 1967. Dir. med. sect., Civil Def., Bethlehem; chmn. pres. Lehigh Valley Regional Lung and Health Assn., 1978—. Served with AUS, 1941-45; served from capt. to col. M.C., surg. cons. 2d Army, AUS, 1953-58. Decorated Silver Star medal, Legion of Merit, Bronze Star medal. Fellow A.C.S., Am. Coll. Chest Physicians (past pres Pa. chpt.); mem. Am. Assn. Thoracic Surgery, Internat. Soc. de Chirurgie, Am. Thoracic Soc., AMA, Pan Am. Med. Assn., Pa. Assn. for Thoracic Surgery (past pres.), Pan Pacific Surg. Soc., N.Y. Acad. Sci., AAAS, Royal Soc. Medicine (Eng.), Am. Cancer Soc. (past. pres. chpt.), Delta Upsilon, Phi Chi. Republican. Episcopalian. Mason, Rotarian (past pres. Bethlehem club) Clubs: Lehigh; Valley of Allentown. Contbr. articles to profl. jours. Home: 139 E Market St Bethlehem PA 18018

SNYDER, JOHN ROBERT, med. technologist; b. Scranton, Pa., Jan. 30, 1950; s. Richard Allen and Ruth Ann (Asmus) S.; student Keystone Jr. Coll., 1967-68; B.S., Wilkes Coll., 1971; M.S., Elmira Coll., 1975; M.A. Mgmt. and Supervision, Central Mich. U., 1978; m. Millie L. Harvey, June 5, 1971; children—David, Jennifer. Med. technologist Robert Packer Hosp., Sayre, Pa., 1971-72, hematology surp., 1973-76; technologist Fairbanks (Alaska) Meml. Hosp., 1972-73; program dir. MetPath Sch. Lab. Medicine, Hackensack, N.J., 1976—. Certified med. technologist, specialist in hematology Am. Soc. Clin. Pathologists. Mem. Internat. Mgmt. Council, Am. Soc. Allied Health Professions, Am., N.J. socs. med. technology, Immunohematologists of N.J. Home: 112 3d Ave Westwood NJ 07675 Office: 60 Commerce Way Hackensack NJ 07606

SNYDER, JOSEPH, ophthalmologist; b. Phila., Dec. 13, 1937; s. Gilbert and Sophie (Paul) S.; B.A., U. Pa., 1958; M.D., Jefferson Med. Coll., 1962; m. Madrian Friedman, Aug. 9, 1964; children—Lori, Lee. Intern in internal medicine Jefferson Med. Coll. Hosp., Phila., 1962-63, resident, 1963-64; resident in ophthalmology George Washington U. Med. Center, Washington, 1967-70; practice medicine, specializing in ophthalmology, Silver Spring, Md., 1970—; clin. instr. ophthalmology George Washington U., 1970—; attending physician Washington Hosp. Center, 1970—. Vice-pres. Winding-Orchard Civic Assn., 1973-75. Served to sr. asst. surgeon USPHS, 1964-67. Diplomate Am. Bd. Ophthalmology. Fellow Am. Acad. Ophthalmology and Otolaryngology. Fellow A.C.S.; mem. AMA, Montgomery County Med. Soc., Med. and Chir. Faculty Md., Md. Acad. Ophthalmology (pres. 1975-76), Contact Lens Soc. Ophthalmologists, Phi Beta Kappa, Alpha Omega Alpha. Home: 1344 Winding Ln Silver Spring MD 20902 Office: 1109 Spring St Silver Spring MD 20910

SNYDER, JOSEPH JULIEN, corp. exec.; b. Findlay, Ohio, Oct. 29, 1907; s. Paul Julien and Mabel Sarah (Bair) S.; B.S., Carnegie Inst. Tech., 1931; M.B.A., Harvard, 1934; postgrad. Mass. Inst. Tech., 1943-44; m. Helen Torrance Colburn, Apr. 3, 1937; children—Clinton Lytle, Joseph MacGeorge, Susanne Colburn. Dir., Colonial Fund, Inc., 1954-75; v.p., dir. Colonial Mgmt. Assos., Boston, 1945-74; chmn. bd. Quanex Corp., Houston, 1942-53, dir., 1940—; dir. Transcontinental Gas Pipe Line Corp., 1951-78, Transco Cos., Inc., Houston, 1973-78; trustee Boston Five Cents Savs. Bank, 1950—; dir. Arthur D. Little, 1958-77, Liberty Mut. Ins. Cos., Montagu Boston Investment Trust Ltd., London; mem. staff Radiation Lab., Mass. Inst. Tech., 1944-45, asst. treas., 1946-50, treas., mem. exec. com., mem. corp., 1950-75, mem. investment com., 1950—, v.p., 1951-73, life mem. corp., treas. emeritus, financial cons., 1975—. Recipient Army-Navy Certificate Appreciation, 1946. Mem. Am. Inst. Chem. Engrs., Harvard Bus. Sch. Alumni Assn. (pres. 1943-44), Am. Acad. Arts and Scis., Beta Theta Pi, Clubs: Detroit; Downtown, St. Botolph (Boston); University (N.Y.C.). Home: 100 Memorial Dr Cambridge MA 02142 Office: 77 Massachusetts Ave Cambridge MA 02139

SNYDER, LARRY DONALD, engring. co. exec.; b. Erie, Pa., Sept. 10, 1940; s. Elmer William and Bernice Frances Snyder; B.S. in Indsl. Mgmt., Gannon Coll., 1968; m. Mary Louise Trevor, Dec. 10, 1959; children—Linda Ann, Mary Kay. Mgr. indsl. engring. Am. Meter Co., Erie, 1968-71, mgr. production control, 1971-73; dir. quality assurance, mgr. controlled products operation Autoclave Engrs., Inc., Erie, 1973—; cons. devel. quality assurance systems. Mem. Indsl. Mgmt. Club Erie County, Am. Soc. Quality Control, Am. Soc. Non-Destructive Testing. Republican. Roman Catholic. Home: 3910 Eliot Rd Erie PA 16508 Office: 2930 W 22d St Erie PA 16512

SNYDER, M. WILSON, former physician, surgeon; b. Polk, Pa., Oct. 5, 1912; s. Charles Peter and Mabel S. (Piper) S.; B.S. Bucknell U., 1933; M.D., Jefferson Med. Coll., 1937; M.S., Temple U., 1941; m. Gertrude Byers, Jan. 24, 1941; children—Wilson, Susan, Ann. Intern, Allegheny Gen. Hosp., Pitts., 1937-38, chief resident, 1938; fellow in ophthalmology Temple U., Phila., 1938-41; chief ophthalmology Sharon Gen. Hosp. (Pa.), 1946—; practice medicine specializing in ophthalmology, Sharon, 1946-78, ret., 1978; dir. Mchts. and Mfrs. Nat. Bank, Sharon. Served with M.C., U.S. Army, 1941-46. Diplomate Am. Bd. Ophthalmology. Mem. AMA, Pa. Med. Soc., Pa., Am. acads. ophthalmology and otolaryngology, Internat. Coll. Surgeons, other orgns. Republican. Episcopalian. Clubs: Sharon Country, Sharon Univ., Masons, Elks. Home: 620 Koehler Dr Sharpsville PA 16150

SNYDER, NATHAN, communications co. exec.; b. Hartford, Conn., Oct. 7, 1934; s. Saul and Betsy (Wand) S.; A.B., Harvard U., 1956; LL.B., Columbia U., 1963; postgrad. N.Y. U. Sch. Bus., 1967-68; m. Geraldine Wolff, Dec. 27, 1964; children—Hannah Abigail, Alexander Lowell Wolff. Admitted to N.Y. bar, 1963; with firm Paul, Weiss, Rifkind, Wharton & Garrison, N.Y.C., 1963-66; v.p., sec. Randolph Computer Corp., Greenwich, Conn., 1966-69, exec. v.p., gen. counsel, dir., 1969-73; exec. v.p., chief operating officer BanCal Tri-State Corp. (holding co. Bank of Calif.), 1974-76; v.p. acquisitions CBS Inc., N.Y.C., 1976—. Lectr., Grad. Sch. Mgmt., Golden Gate U., San Francisco. Vol. legal services Office Econ. Opportunity, 1963. Bd. dirs. New Canaan Community Nursery Sch., 1970. Served to lt. USNR, 1956-60. Harlan Fiske Stone scholar, 1964-65. Mem. Am. Bar Assn., Assn. Bar City N.Y. Clubs: Harvard (N.Y.C.); Hasty Pudding, Institute of 1770 (Harvard). Editor: Columbia Law Rev., 1962-63. Home: 163 Parish Rd New Canaan CT 06840 Office: 51 W 52d St New York City NY 10019

SNYDER, RICHARD A., state senator; b. Lititz, Pa., Mar. 26, 1910; s. Paris F. and Barbara (Ziegler) S.; student Moravian Coll., 1927-29; B.A., Franklin and Marshall Coll., 1931; LL.B., Temple U., 1942; m. Toylee McClinton, July 24, 1943. Admitted to Pa. bar, 1943; partner firm Barley, Snyder, Cooper, Barber, Lancaster, Pa., 1945-78, of counsel, 1978—; mem. Pa. Senate, 1962—; dir. Lancaster (Pa.) Indsl. Devel. Co. Chmn. Republican Com. Lancaster County, 1958-64; trustee Moravian Coll., Bethlehem, Pa. Served with CIC, AUS, 1942-45; ETO. Mem. Am. Legion (comdr., post 1948). Mason, Elk. Club: Hamilton. Home: 27 Orchard Rd Lancaster PA 17601 Office: 115 E King St Lancaster PA 17602

SNYDER, RICHARD DONALD, physician; b. Reading, Pa., Feb. 28, 1931; s. Ephraim Kinsey and Florence Rothermel (Rohrbach) S.; B.A., N.Y. U., 1953; M.D., N.Y. Med. Coll., 1957; M.S. in Health Adminstrn., U. Colo., 1973; m. Elaine Marie Paul, Aug. 28, 1969. Intern USPHS Hosp., S.I., N.Y., 1957-58; resident gen. surgery VA Hosp., East Orange, N.J., 1962; resident ear, nose and throat surgery Manhattan Eye, Ear and Throat Hosp., 1963-66; practice medicine specializing in otolaryngology, Cresskill, N.J., 1966-70, Las Cruces, N.Mex., 1970-72; USPHS fellow in health adminstrn. U. Colo. Med. Center, Denver, 1972-73; clin. asso. in surgery N.Y. Med. Coll., 1968-70, U. N.Mex. Med. Sch., 1970-73; adj. prof. audiology N.Mex. State U., 1970-72; dir. med. edn. com. Meml. Gen. Hosp., Roxborough, Phila., 1974-76; asst. clin. prof. medicine Allied Health, Hahnemann Med. Sch., Phila., 1976—. Tympanist, El Paso Symphony Orch., 1970-72. Served as lt. col., chief med. edn. USAF, 1973-74. Recipient award for outstanding articles in Med. Econs. Mag., 1969, 70. Diplomate Am. Bd. Otolaryngology. Mem. AMA, Del. Med. Soc., Am. Occupational Medicine Assn., Am. Acad. Family Physicians, World Future Soc. (coordinator chpt. 1975—), Phi Chi, Phi Mu Alpha Sinfonia. Rotarian. Contbr. articles to profl. jours. Home: 403 Lark Dr Newark DE 19713 Office: El duPont Co Glasgow Site Med Dept Wilmington DE 19898

SNYDER, ROBERT EDWARD, pharmacist; b. Balt., July 25, 1931; s. Fred Frederick and Emma Elizabeth (Hobson) S.; student Balt. City Coll., 1947-50; B.S., U. Md., 1955. Pharmacist, Read Drug & Chem. Co., Balt., 1957-58; pharmacist Morgan and Millard Pharmacy, Balt., 1958; staff pharmacist Md. Gen. Hosp., Balt., 1958-66, dir. pharmacy services, 1966—; clin. asst. prof. pharmacy U. Md., Balt., 1971-75. Mem. Md. Bd. Pharmacy, 1975—, sec.-treas., 1976-77. Served with Hosp. Corps, USN, 1955-57. Geigy Leadership awardee, 1970-71; Squibb Pres.'s awardee, 1970-71. Mem. Md. (W. Arthur Purdum award 1977), Am. socs. hosp. pharmacists, Am., Md. pharm. assns., Nat. Assn. Bds. Pharmacy, Alumni Assn. U. Md. Sch. Pharmacy. Democrat. Methodist. Home: 1101 St Paul St Apt 1903 Baltimore MD 21202 Office: Md Gen Hosp 827 Linden Ave Baltimore MD 21201

SNYDER, WILLIAM LLOYD, III, fin. cons.; b. Lancaster, Pa., Mar. 24, 1944; s. William Lloyd and Elizabeth (Colby) S.; B.A., Amherst Coll., 1966; M.B.A., Harvard U., 1968; m. Deirdre Rhoads, Aug. 20, 1966; children—Alexandra Dugan, Megan Colby, Andrew Rhoads. Partner, Butcher & Sherrerd, Phila., 1968-73; chmn. Intermodal Transp. Co., East Windsor, N.J., 1973-76; owner, chmn. Huff Paper Co., Phila., 1977—; owner, fin. cons. Snyder & Co., Phila., 1973—. Democrat. Mem. United Ch. of Christ. Clubs: Racquet (Phila.); Little Egg Harbor (N.J.) Yacht; Rehobeth Bay Sailing, Society Hill. Home: 3 Blackwell Pl Philadelphia PA 19147 Office: 1529 Walnut St Philadelphia PA 19102

SOBCZAK, THOMAS VICTOR, mfg. co. exec.; b. N.Y.C., Aug. 6, 1937; s. Edward Eugene and Josephine (Janas) J.; B.A., St. John's U., N.Y., 1959; postgrad. Hofstra U., 1965; Ph.D., Sussex Coll., Eng., 1972; m. Mary Ann Florio, Jan. 23, 1960; children—Thomas, Michael, Katherine, Elisabeth, Deanna, Jessica. Cost analyst Sperry Gyroscope Co., 1959-60; mgmt. systems specialist Kollsman Instrument Corp., 1960-62; cons. Airborne Instruments Lab., 1963-67, 1st. Nat. City Bank, N.Y.C., 1967-68; mgr. systems and EDP, PIC Design Corp., East Rockaway, N.Y., 1968-70; dir. info. processing Waldes Kohinoor Inc., Long Island City, N.Y., 1970—; cons. in field, lectr.; dir. Internat. Industrial Exchange (Australia), Mgmt. Info. Systems Pty, Ltd., N.Y.C., Mem. Baldwin Bicentennial Com., 1975—; cubmaster Boy Scouts Am., 1971-75, dist. roundtable chmn., 1974-76, chmn., 1976, coach counselor, 1973-78; mem. St. Christ Parish Council, Roman Catholic Ch., 1975-77, mem. Bishops Appeal Fund, 1975—. Served with U.S. Army Res., 1958-66. Named Exec. Reservist Sec. of Commerce, 1963—. Certified mfg. engr., N.Y.; registered profl. engr., Calif. Mem. Am. Mgmt. Assn., Soc. Mfg. Engrs. (sec. 1977-78, 1st v.p., chmn. elect 1978—), Computer and Systems Assn. (charter), Data Processing Mgrs. Assn., Nat. Def. Exec. Res. Assn. (dir. 1971-74, vice chmn. 1973-74). Numerical Control Soc. Republican. Clubs: LaGuardia Kiwanis (2d v.p.), Hofstra U., Ft. Hamilton Officers Open Mess. Author, contbg. author books, contbr. articles to profl. and other publs.; developer theory of significant milestone integration, APE theory of computer terminal security, also concept of simplified computer integrated mfg. Home: 2580 Grand Ave Baldwin NY 11510 Office: 47-16 Austel Pl Long Island City NY 11101

SOBOL, BRUCE J., physician; b. N.Y.C., June 10, 1923; s. Ira J. and Ida S. (Gelula) S.; B.A., Swarthmore Coll., 1947; M.D., N.Y. U., 1950; m. Barbara Sue Gordon, Apr. 30, 1951; children—Peter Gordon, Scott David. Intern, Bellevue Hosp., N.Y.C., 1950-51, resident, 1951-52, N.Y. Heart Assn. fellow, 1953-55; resident VA Hosp., Boston, 1952-53; practice medicine specializing in internal medicine, White Plains, N.Y., 1955-59; dir. pulmonary lab. Westchester County (N.Y.) Med. Center, Valhalla, 1959-78; dir. clin. research Boehringer Ingelheim, Ltd., Ridgefield, Conn., 1978—; research prof. medicine N.Y. Med. Coll. Bd. dirs. Westchester Community Services Council, 1977—; pres. Westchester Heart Assn., 1976-78. Served with inf. AUS, World War II; ETO. Diplomate Am. Bd. Internal Medicine. Fellow A.C.P., Am. Coll. Chest Physicians, N.Y. Acad. Scis.; mem. Am. Physiol. Soc., Am. Heart Assn., N.Y. Trudea Soc., Am. Thoracic Soc., Am. Fedn. Clin. Research. Contbr. numerous articles to profl. publs. Home: 275 Ridgebury Rd Ridgefield CT 06877 Office: Boehringer Ingelheim Ltd East Ridge PO Box 368 Ridgefield CT 06877

SOCEY, FRANCIS JOSEPH, meteorologist; b. Altoona, Pa., Sept. 16, 1913; s. Francis Joseph and Kathryn Helen (Hartman) S.; student Juniata Coll., 1936-40; m. Mary M. O'Rourke, Apr. 18, 1944 (div.); 1 dau., Margaret Ellen. Writer, Altoona Mirror and Tribune, 1931-42; meterologist Am. Machine & Fdy., Greenwich, Conn., 1951-61; meteorol. cons. Fleetweather, Hopewell Junction, N.Y., 1976—. Served with USAF, 1942-46. Mem. Am. Meteorol. Soc., Am. Geophys. Union. Roman Catholic. Contbr. articles to astrol. jours. Address: 10 Bryant Crescent White Plains NY 10605

SOCHA, WLADYSLAW WOJCIECH, med. researcher; b. Paris, July 3, 1926; s. Tadeusz and Anna (Klara) S.; M.A., Jagellonian U., 1952; M.D., Med. Acad. Cracow (Poland), 1959, teaching certificate, 1963; m. Adela Katherine Zacharko, Jan. 3, 1956. Asst. dept. pathology Cancer Inst., Warsaw, Poland, 1952-60; asso. prof. dept. forensic medicine Med. Acad., Cracow, 1955-63; dir. Inst. Pediatrics, Cracow, 1963-69; research prof. dept. forensic medicine Sch. Medicine, chief pathologist Lab. Exptl. Medicine and Surgery in Primates N.Y.U., N.Y.C., 1969—; asso. dir. Primate Blood Group Reference Lab. and WHO Collaborating Centre for Hematology of Primate Animals, 1977—. Served with Polish Home Army, 1941-45. Decorated Mil. Cross of Merit, Cross of Valor; recipient Polish Med. Soc. Ann. award, 1959; Polish Surg. Soc. award, 1960; Polish Acad. Sci. Ann. award, 1966. Mem. Am. Soc. Human Genetics, N.Y. Acad. Scis., AAAS, Polish Inst. Arts and Sci. in Am., Polish-Am. Med. Soc., Institut Pyreneen d'Etudes Anthropologiques Toulouse. Author, co-author various med. texts, 1963—; editor Jour. Med. Primatology; contbr. numerous articles on immunology, imunogenetics, pathology, anthropology to profl. jours. Home: 10 Townsend Ave Upper Grandview NY 10960 Office: 550 1st Ave New York City NY 10016

SOCHUREK, HOWARD (JAMES), photographer, corr.; b. Milw., Nov. 27, 1924; s. Edward Alloys and Gertrude (Herbst) S.; student Princeton U., 1942-44, Harvard (Nieman fellow), 1959-60; m. Tatiana Akhonin, May 9, 1965; 1 dau., Tatiana. Photographer Milw. Jour., 1946-49, Life mag., Time, Inc., 1950-70, corr. based in Singapore, 1950-52, Saigon, 1952-54, Paris, 1954-57, Moscow, 1958-59, N.Y. based covering world, 1960-70; pres. Howard Sochurek, Inc., 1970—. Photog. contbr. to Nat. Geog. mag. Served with AUS, 1944-46. Recipient Mag. Photographer of Yr. award U. Mo., 1957; Capa award Overseas Press Club, 1956. Mem. Am. Soc. Mag. Photographers. Clubs: Overseas Press (N.Y.C.); Bronxville Field. Home: 25 Oakledge Rd Bronxville NY 10708 Office: 680 Fifth Ave New York City NY 10019

SOCOLOW, ARTHUR ABRAHAM, geologist; b. Bronx, N.Y., Mar. 23, 1921; s. Samuel and Yetta (Solomon) S.; B.S., Rutgers U., 1942; M.A., Columbia, 1947, Ph.D., 1955; m. Edith S. Blumenthal, Apr. 10, 1949; children—Carl, Roy, Jeff. Photogrammetrist, U.S. Geol. Survey, 1942, 46; with Eagle Picher de Mexica, 1947; instr. geology So. Meth. U., 1948-50, dir. geology field camp in Colo., 1948-50; asst. prof. Boston U., 1950-55; asso. prof. U. Mass., 1955-57; econ. geologist Pa. Geol. Survey, 1957-61, dir., chief geologist, 1961—; geologist Def. Minerals Exploration Authority, Alaska, 1952; cons., 1949-57. Geol. adviser Boston Mus. Sci., 1955-57; lectr. mineral conservation Pa. State U., 1956—; mem. conf. earth sci. source materials NSF, 1959; mem., past chmn. Am. Commn. on Stratigraphic Nomenclature; chmn. research com. Interstate Oil Compact Commn.; permanent dir. Field Conf. of Pa. Geologists; mem. Pa. Gov.'s Adv. Com. Council Environmental Quality; chmn. Pa. Water Resources Coordinating Com. Served with USAAF, 1942-46. Fellow Geol. Soc. Am. (sec.-treas. N.E. sect.), Minerol. Soc. Am.; mem. AAAS, Soc. Econ. Geologists, AAUP, Phila. Geol. Soc. (past pres.), Am. Meteoritical Soc., Am. Geophys. Union, Nat. Assn. Geology Tchrs. (past regional pres.), Pa. Acad. Sci., Am. Assn. State Geologists (past pres.), Fgn. Policy Assn. (past chpt. pres.), Torch Clubs Internat. (past chpt. pres.), PTA (chpt. pres.), Sigma Xi. Editor: Bull. of Pa. Geology. Contbr.

articles to profl. jours. Home: 420 Larry Dr Harrisburg PA 17109 Office: Pa Geol Survey Harrisburg PA 17120

SODEN, EDWARD ROGER, systems cons.; b. Montclair, N.J., Sept. 28, 1929; s. Esley Floyd and Mabel (Hallas) S.; B.S. in Mgmt., Rutgers U., 1960; m. Nancy Virginia Gill, July 29, 1977; children—Gary William, Scott Edward. With Becton, Dickinson & Co., Rutherford, N.J., 1953—, corporate cons. systems mgr., 1968-70, mgr. inventory plan, 1970-71, corporate mgr. info. systems, 1971—. Active Boy Scouts Am., 1968-72. Served with USMC, 1950-52; Korea. Republican. Club: Pines Lake Men's (treas. 1972-74, pres. 1975, sec. 1979). Office: Becton Dickinson & Co Mack Centre Dr Paramus NJ 07652

SODEN, JAMES ARTHUR, lawyer, real estate investment co. exec.; b. Montreal, Que., Can., Oct. 20, 1922; s. Robert Bowden and Violet (McNamara) S.; B. Civil Law with honours, McGill U., 1950; m. Edna Amy McConkey, June 30, 1945; children—Ann, Robert, Margaret, Lesley. Called to Que. bar, 1950, created Queen's Counsel, 1968; mem. firm Wainwright, Elder, Laidley, Leslie, Chipman & Bourgeois, Montreal, 1950-57, Phillips, Bloomfield, Vineberg & Goodman, Montreal, 1957-76; pres. DWS Holdings Ltd., Montreal, 1977—; chmn., dir. Trizec Corp. Ltd., Montreal, 1960-76; chmn. bd., dir. Trizec Equities Ltd., Trizec So. Inc., Place Bonaventure Que., Inc., Mobile Home Communities, Inc., Tristar Western Ltd.; pres., dir. Central Park Lodges Can. Ltd., Scotia Winnipeg Devel. Ltd., Scarborough Shopping Centre Ltd.; pres. Trizec Devels. Inc. (U.S.A.); lectr. law McGill U., 1954-61, also Sir George Williams U. Mem. Que., Canadian nat. councils Boy Scouts Can. Bd. dirs. York-Finch Gen. Hosp., Toronto, St. Mary's Hosp., Montreal; bd. dirs. Canadian Inst. Pub. Real Estate Cos. Served with RCAF, 1942-45. Mem. Canadian, Montreal bar assns. Roman Catholic. Clubs: Mount Royal, St. James's. Home: 3559 Northcliffe Ave Montreal PQ Canada also Montgomery Centre VT Office: Suite 609 1801 McGill College Ave Montreal PQ H3A 2N4 Canada

SOFARELLI, ROBERT JOSEPH, veterinarian; b. N.Y.C., Dec. 6, 1945; s. Joseph Michael and Frances (Francioso) S.; B.A. (George Nasson scholar 1967), Nasson Coll., 1967; D.V.M., Cornell U., 1971; m. Holly Wadhams Walter, Aug. 3, 1968; 1 dau., Jillian Meinz. Student vet. asst. Cornell U. Small Animal Clinic, 1968-71; veterinarian Glens Falls (N.Y.) Animal Hosp., 1971-73; veterinarian, owner Saratoga County Veterinary Hosp., Saratoga Springs, N.Y., 1973—. Recipient Charles Gross Bondy award Cornell U., 1971, Upjohn award, 1971. Mem. Saratoga County Animal Welfare League (v.p. 1974-76), Am., Hudson Valley (heartworm com. 1974-75) vet. med. assns., Capital Dist. (hosp. improvement com. 1978—), N.Y. State vet. med. socs., Am. Animal Hosp. Assn., Am. Assn. Zoo Veterinarians, Defenders Wildlife, Wilderness Soc., Animal Protection Inst., Nat. Humane Soc., Saratoga Springs C. of C. (dir. 1978—), Omega Tau Sigma, Phi Zeta. Roman Catholic. Clubs: Rotary (asst. sec. 1974—). Office: PO Box 373 Saratoga Springs NY 12866

SOFFER, MARTIN HARVEY, planner, community cons.; b. Phila., Feb. 26, 1945; s. Bernard and Selma (Barrot) S.; student Tyler Sch. Fine Arts, 1963-64; A.A. in Applied Sci., Community Coll. Phila., 1969; B.S. in Social Sci., Pa. State U., 1971, M.R.P. in Urban and Regional Planning (Koontz Municipal scholar), 1972; M.P.A. candidate, Temple U., 1976—; m. Kathleen O'Neill, Aug. 24, 1969; 1 dau., Nicole. Editorial research asst., file and library supr. Washington Post, CBS, Phila., 1965-66; trust adminstr. Provident Nat. Bank, Phila., 1970; research asst. Pa. State U., Middletown, 1971-72; asso. planner State of Ga., Atlanta, 1972-73; comprehensive planner, community cons. Mullin & Lonergan Assos., Inc., Phila., 1973-75; pvt. cons. practice in planning, land use, 1975-76; environ. assessment analyst, land use specialist City of Phila., 1976-77, community service/facility planning analyst, 1977—. Served with U.S. Army, 1966-68. Decorated Silver Star, Air medal with bronze oak leaf cluster, Gallantry Cross with silver star (Vietnam); recipient Fine Arts award, Pa. Acad. Fine Arts. Mem. Am. Inst. Planners, Am. Soc. Planning Ofcls., Am. Soc. Pub. Adminstrn., Smithsonian Inst., also VA orgns. Club: Masons (32 deg.). Asst. editor: Central Pa. Planning News and Revs., 1971-72; contbr. articles on planning to profl. jours. Home: 1903 Lanark Bldg 9200 New Bustleton Ave Philadelphia PA 19115

SOFILLAS, GRACE SOPHIE JOANOU, journalist; b. Wheeling, W.Va., Oct. 29, 1932; d. John Frank and Gazel (Klochan) Joanou; B.S., W.Va. U., 1955; m. William C. Sofillas, Sept. 2, 1962 (div.); children—Constandino William, John Frank. Women's editor Intelligencer, Wheeling, 1957-62; comml. writer Sta. WLAN, Lancaster, Pa., 1963; women's editor Intelligencer Jour., Lancaster, 1963-73, reporter-columnist, religion editor, 1973—; co-owner Dino's Market, Lancaster, 1966-72. Correspondent, Orthodox Observor; editor newsletter Hellenic Orthodox Church of N. and S. Am. Recipient State Journalism award W.Va. Press Assn., 1960, Handicapped Profl. Women of Year award, 1973. Mem. Am. Legion Aux., Alpha Delta Pi. Home: 1300 Maple Ave Lancaster PA 17603 Office: 8 W King St Lancaster PA 17604

SOFINOWSKI, JOHN ROBERT, mech. engr.; b. Balt., May 21, 1950; s. John Joseph and Rita Maria (Fones) S.; B.S., U. Md., 1973; postgrad. in engring. adminstrn. George Washington U., 1977—; m. Sandra K. Shoap, June 29, 1974. Patent researcher Mfrs. Aircraft Assn., Arlington, Va., 1973-74; mech. project engr. Ward Machinery Co., Cockeysville, Md., 1974—. Mem. Smithsonian Inst. (asso.), Cousteau Soc., ASME (asso.), Am. Inst. Aeros. and Astronautics (asso.). Democrat. Roman Catholic. Home: 2218 Nodleigh Terr Jarrettsville MD 21084 Office: Ward Machinery Co Beaver Dam Rd Cockeysville MD 21030

SOHN, DONALD RICHARD, travel agy. exec.; b. N.Y.C., May 15, 1926; s. Maxwell Monroe and Florence (Bergoff) S.; A.B., St. Lawrence U., 1948; M.B.A., Harvard U., 1951, D.B.A., 1959; m. Gabriella Kozma, June 26, 1971; stepchildren—Francis Feith, Peter Feith. Instr., Mass. Inst. Tech., Cambridge, 1951-54; research asso. Harvard U., Cambridge, 1954-57; pres. United Pharmacal Corp., Cambridge, 1959-62; pres. Heritage Travel, Inc., Cambridge, 1965—; dir. Woodside Mgmt. Systems, Inc., 1975-77; bd. advisors Lexington Mgmt. Corp., 1974—. Dir., mem. exec. com. World Affairs Council of Boston, 1973—, v.p., 1975—; dir. Internat. Center of New Eng., 1975-78. Ford Found. grantee, 1955-56. Mem. Am. Soc. Travel Agts. (chmn. automation com. 1974-76), Am. Mktg. Assn., Greater Boston C. of C. Clubs: Execs., Harvard, Cambridge Boat, Appalachian Mountain, Harvard Bus. Sch. Home: 55 Black Oak Rd Weston MA 02193 Office: 238 Main St Cambridge MA 02142

SOICHET, SAMUEL, gynecologist; b. Rio de Janeiro, Brazil, Sept. 27, 1921; s. Julio and Sabina S.; came to U.S., 1947, 51, naturalized, 1958; M.D., State Rio de Janeiro Med. Sch., 1944; m. Jean Fineman, June 16, 1954; children—Roberto Joseph, Stefanie Brenda. Fellow, Chgo. Lying-In-Hosp., U. Chgo., 1947; intern, resident Harlem Hosp., 1951-55, attending physician, 1956-63; attending physician Beth Israel Hosp., N.Y.C., 1956-66, French Hosp., N.Y.C., 1959-66, St. Clare Hosp., N.Y.C., 1966-70; attending physician obstetrics/gynecology, cons. N.Y. Infirmary, N.Y.C., 1965—; clin. asst. prof. Cornell U. Med. Coll., 1970—; asst. attending physician N.Y. Hosp., N.Y.C., 1970—. Served with U.S. Army, 1943-45; ETO; Israeli Army, 1948-49. Leonard Found. Cancer Research grantee, 1971-74. Fellow Am. Bd. Obstetrics and Gynecology, Am. Coll. Obstetrics and Gynecology; mem. A.C.S., Brazilian Soc. Human Reprodn., N.Y. Gynecol. Soc. Jewish. Clubs: Young Men and Women Hebrew Assn., B'nai B'rith. Inventor Ypsilon intrauterine contraceptive and modulator for infertility, 1972—, ovarian and fallopian tube envelopes for reversible fertility, 1970-78. Home: 4 E 95th St Apt 6A New York City NY 10028 Office: 1088 Park Ave New York City NY 10028

SOK, JAMES EDWARD, pharmacist; b. Torrington, Conn., Dec. 19, 1946; s. William John and Blanche Barbara (Pavlik) S.; B.S. in Pharmacy (Conn. Pharm. Assn. scholar), U. Conn., 1969; m. Debra Lee Hamzy, Dec. 1, 1973. Staff pharmacist Sharon (Conn.) Hosp., 1970-71, dir. pharmacy services, lectr. pharmacology, 1971—; cons. pharmacist Geer Meml. Nursing Facility, Canaan, Conn., Whitridge Nursing Wing, Salisbury, Conn.; founder, pres. Pharmacy Cons. of Conn. Mem. profl. adv. com. W. Bradford Walker Community Health Assn., West Cornwall, Conn.; mem. Conn. Pub. Health Council, 1972—; alt. mem. Goshen (Conn.) Planning Commn., 1977—. Mem. Am., Conn. socs. hosp. pharmacists, Am., Conn., Litchfield County pharmacy assns., Mortar and Pestle, Kappa Psi. Republican. Roman Catholic. Club: Torrington-Winsted AeroModelers. Home: Shean Rd Goshen CT 06756 Office: Sharon Hosp W Main St Sharon CT 06069

SOKERKA, RICHARD ANDREW, editor; b. Passaic, N.J., Oct. 4, 1949; s. Andrew Richard and Emily Barbara (Adamkovic) S.; B.A. in Communication Arts, U. Notre Dame, 1971; m. Linda Lee Pickard, Sept. 21, 1975; 1 son, Scott Andrew. Sports editor Today Newspapers, Wayne, N.J., 1972-74, mng. editor, 1974-75, exec. editor, 1975—; sports info. dir. William Paterson Coll., Wayne; editor Wayne C. of C. Newspaper. Exec. bd. mem. Diocese of Paterson Cath. Youth Orgn. Mem. N.J. Press Assn. (first prize 1976, 77), Pica Club (N.J. chpt. 2d prize 1977), Community Newspapers of N.J., Notre Dame U. Alumni Assn. Club: N.J. Notre Dame. Roman Catholic. Home: 8 Elizabeth St Bloomingdale NJ 07403 Office: 1661 Route 23 Wayne NJ 07470

SOKOLOW, NICKOLAS N., plastics machinery co. exec.; b. Leningrad, Russia, June 20, 1916; s. Nikolai Mikhailovich and Ljubov Andrianovna S.; came to U.S., 1956, naturalized, 1962; student U. Leningrad, 1933-34; M.S.M.E. summa cum laude, Zhukovski Acad., 1936-41; m. Julia T. Sokolow, Nov. 12, 1949; children—Victor, Dimitri, Alexander. Chief engr. Portland (Maine) Machine Tool Co., 1956-60; project engr. Olin Chem. Corp., New Haven, 1960-65; mgr. new product devel. Koehring Corp., Fords, N.J., 1965-71; asst. v.p. engring. Beloit Corp., Dalton, Mass., 1971—. Registered profl. engr., Maine, Conn., Fla. Mem. Soc. Plastic Engrs. Russian Orthodox. Patentee in field. Home: Rt 2 Box 153-M1 Floral City FL 32636 Office: 401 South St Dalton MA 01226

SOKOLOWSKI, ANN RUTH, ednl. adminstr.; b. N.Y.C.. Sept. 30, 1941; d. Stanley and Stella (Sosna) S.; B.A., St. Joseph's Coll. for Women, 1963; postgrad. St. John's U., Jamaica, N.Y. Tchr., N.Y.C. Bd. Edn., 1963-67, 69—, asst. dean girls, 1971-75, dean, 1975—. Program dir. Missilier Service Club, Dept. Def., 1968, club dir. Hourglass Service Club 7th Inf. Div., Korea, 1968; mem. human relations team daily radio show Sta.-AFKN, 1967-68. Master tchr., N.Y.C. Bd. Edn. Mem. Internat. Platform Assn., Met. Museum Art, Self-Realization Fellowship. Office: John Adams High Sch Ozone Park NY 11417*

SOKOLSKY, GEORGE EPHRAIM, JR., data processing cons.; b. N.Y.C., Nov. 11, 1936; s. George Ephraim and Dorothy Elizabeth (Fiske) S.; B.A., Columbia, 1958; M.S., U. Mich., 1960; m. Helen Leslie Higinbotham, Oct. 13, 1961; children—Anne Elizabeth, Margaret Leslie. Systems engr. IBM, N.Y.C., 1968-73; mgr. corporate systems St. Joe Minerals Corp., N.Y.C., 1973-75, dir. data processing, 1974-77; sr. systems specialist Eastern States Bankcard Assn., New Hyde Park, N.Y., 1977-78; v.p. Exception Mgmt. Corp., N.Y.C., 1978—. Chmn. parks com., neighborhood action program, Washington Heights, 1971-73. Served to capt. USAF, 1960-66. Mem. Assn. Computing Machinery, Soc. Mining Engrs. Roman Catholic. Club: Mining. Home: 900 W 190th St New York NY 10040 Office: 21 W 76th St New York NY 10017

SOKOLYSZYN, ALEKSANDER S., librarian; b. Czernowitz, West Ukraine, Sept. 8, 1914; s. Stepan and Eufrozyna (Zaretzka) S.; Licencé en Droit, U. Czernowitz, 1938; Absolvent, Ivan Franko U. of Lwiw-W, 1941; D. Rerum Politicarum, Innsbruck U., 1947; M.L.S., Columbia, 1958; m. Sophia Antoniw, 1944; 1 dau., Aleksandra Nychka. Lawyer, Ukraine, 1938-44; reference librarian to UN, N.Y. Pub. Library, 1958; cataloger Yale Law Library, 1959-60; sr. librarian, fgn. book cataloger Bklyn. Pub. Library, 1961—; lectr. Ukrainian Harvard Inst. Bd. dirs. Ukrainian Congress Com. of Am., Inc.; exec. dir., sec.-gen. Astoria Captive Nations Com.; press chmn. Captive Nations Com. N.Y. Served with Ukrainian Bukovina Brigade, 1941-44. Mem. Shevchehnko Sci. Soc. in Am. (sci. sec.), Ukrainian Library Assn. Am. (sec. gen.), Ukrainian Lawyers Assn., Ukrainian Philatelic and Numis. Soc., Orgn. Def. Four Freedoms Ukraine (dir.; pres. 35th br.), Ukrainain Bukovinian Assn., Am. Assn. Advancement Slavic Studies, Tech. Services Librarians Greater N.Y. Democrat. Mem. Ukrainian Greek Oriental Ch. Author: Shevchenkology in English, 1967; Ucrainica in English, 1972; contbr. articles in field to profl. jours. Home: 46-02 30th Rd Long Island City NY 11103 Office: Grand Army Plaza Bklyn Pub Library Brooklyn NY 11238

SOLARZ, STEPHEN JOSHUA, congressman; b. N.Y.C., Sept. 12, 1940; s. Sanford and Ruth (Fertig) S.; B.A., Brandeis U., 1962; M.A., Columbia U., 1967; m. Nina Koldin, Feb. 5, 1967; children—Randy, Lisa. Mem. N.Y. Ho. of Reps. from 45th Dist., 1968-74; mem. 94th-96th Congresses from 13th Dist. N.Y., mem. Fgn. Affairs Com., Post Office and Civil Ser. Com. Mem. 61st Precinct Community Council, 1968—. Governing council Am. Jewish Congress; bd. dirs. Citizens Housing and Planning Council. Mem. N.Y. Americans for Democratic Action (state bd. 1971—). Democrat. Home: 241 Dover St Brooklyn NY 11235 Office: 1628 Kings Hwy Brooklyn NY 11229 also US Ho of Reps Washington DC 20515

SOLBERG, MYRON, food scientist, educator; b. Boston, June 11, 1931; s. Alexander and Ruth (Graff) S.; B.S. in Food Tech., U. Mass., 1952; Ph.D., Mass. Inst. Tech., 1960; m. Rona Mae Bernstein, Aug. 26, 1956; children—Sara Lynn, Julie Sue, Laurence Michael. Cons. to food industry, 1956-60, 64—; mem. research staff food tech. Mass. Inst. Tech., 1954-60; quality control mgr. Colonial Provision Co., Inc., Boston, 1960-64; sci. editor Meat Processing mag., Chgo., 1968-69; mem. faculty Rutgers U., 1964—, prof. food sci., 1970—; UN expert on food product qualtiy control, 1973-74; vis. prof. Technion, Israel Inst. Tech., Haifa, 1973-74. Pres., Highland Park (N.J.) Bd. Health, 1971-72. Served in USAF, 1952-54. Recipient numerous research grants. Fellow Am. Chem. Soc., AAAS; mem. Inst. Food Technologists (pres. N.Y. sect. 1971-72), Am. Soc. Microbiology, Am. Soc. Quality Control, Am. Meat Sci. Assn., N.Y., N.J. acads. sci. Contbr. articles to profl. jours. Home: 415 Grant Ave Highland Park NJ 08904 Office: Dept Food Sci Rutgers Univ New Brunswick NJ 08903

SOLETSKY, ALBERT Z., educator; b. N.Y.C., Apr. 25, 1937; s. David and Della (Cherey) S.; A.B., Columbia U., 1958, M.A., 1961, Ph.D., 1968. Lectr. Spanish, Queens Coll., 1965-66; asst. prof. Spanish, Fairleigh Dickinson U., 1968-74, asso. prof., 1974—, acting chmn. dept. modern langs., 1972. Dyckman Inst. scholar, 1966-67. Mem. AAUP, Modern Lang. Assn., Hispanic Inst. U.S. Author: A Study of the Vocabulary of the Germanía According to the Romances de Germanía and Bocabvlario of Juan Hidalgo, 1969; contbr. articles in field to profl. jours. Home: 124 W 79th St New York City NY 10024 Office: Fairleigh Dickinson U 1000 River Rd Teaneck NJ 07666

SOLEY, ROBERT LAWRENCE, surgeon; b. N.Y.C., Feb. 26, 1935; s. Max and Saide (Leader) S.; B.S., Yale U., 1956; M.D., N.Y. U., 1959; m. Judy Wasserman, June 16, 1963; children—John, Jill. Intern, Bellevue Hosp., N.Y.C., 1959-60; resident in gen. surgery Mt. Sinai Hosp., N.Y.C., 1960-65; resident in plastic surgery Hosp. of U. Pa., Phila., 1967-69; practice medicine specializing in plastic surgery, White Plains, N.Y., 1969—; attending surgeon Westchester County Med. Center, 1969—; attending surgeon White Plains Hosp., 1969—; clin. asst. prof. surgery N.Y. Med. Coll., Valhalla, 1972—. Served to capt. M.C., USAF, 1965-67. USPHS grantee, 1968-69. Diplomate Am. Bd. Plastic Surgery, Am. Bd. Surgery. Fellow A.C.S.; mem. Am. Soc. Plastic and Reconstructive Surgery, Am. Soc. Aesthetic Surgery, N.Y. State, Westchester County med. socs., Cleft Palate Assn., Am. Burn Assn. Home: 30 Griffen Ave Scarsdale NY 10583 Office: 170 Maple Ave White Plains NY 10601

SOLEYMANIKASHI, YUSSEF, physician; b. Iran, Nov. 15, 1938; came to U.S., 1965; s. Aghajan and Rouhi (Ohebsion) S.; M.D., Tehran Med. Sch., 1964; m. Louise Sedgh, June 7, 1965; children—Stephen, Edmund, Nancy. Intern, Monmouth Med. Center, Long Branch, N.J., 1965-66; resident in pediatrics Brookdale Hosp. Center, Bklyn., 1966-68, Meadowbrook Hosp., East Meadow, N.Y., 1968-69; fellow in pediatric allergy Nassau County Med. Center, 1969-71; practice medicine specializing in allergies, East Meadow, N.Y., 1972—, New Hyde Park, 1975—; asst. prof. clin. pediatrics SUNY at Stony Brook, 1976—; head pediatric allergy Beth Israel Med. Center, N.Y.C. 1972—; asst. attending pediatrician Nassau County Med. Center. Diplomate Am. Bd. Allergy and Immunology, Am. Bd. Pediatrics. Fellow Am. Coll. Allergists, Am. Acad. Allergy, Am. Assn. Certified Allergists; mem. AMA (recipient recognition award 1969, 76). Jewish. Contbr. articles to profl. jours. Office: 1250 Union Tpk New Hyde Park NY 11040

SOLIT, ROBERT WOLF, surgeon; b. Phila., Feb. 23, 1935; s. Jacob and Edith (Gross) S.; A.B., U. Pa., 1956; M.D., Jefferson Med. Coll., Phila., 1961; m. Linda Joan Tomkin, May 18, 1963; children—Richard Lawrence, David Brian, Lisa Alexandra, Douglas Andrew. Intern, Albert Einstein Med. Center, Phila., 1961-62; resident in surgery Jefferson Med. Coll. Hosp., Phila., 1962-66, trainee in cardiovascular surgery, 1968-69; practice medicine, specializing in surgery, Phila., 1969—; attending Albert Einstein Med. Center No. Div., Phila. Gen. Hosp., Thomas Jefferson Univ. Hosp.; instr. surgery Thomas Jefferson U., Phila., 1969-73, asst. prof., 1973, clin. asso. prof., 1978—. Served to capt. M.C., U.S. Army, 1966-68. S.E. Pa. Heart Assn. fellow, 1963-64; Am. Cancer Soc. fellow, 1964-66. Diplomate Am. Bd. Surgery, Am. Bd. Thoracic Surgery. Mem. AMA, Pa., Phila. County med. socs., Soc. Thoracic Surgeons, Pa. Thoracic Surg. Soc., Phila. Coll. Physicians, A.C.S., Phil. Acad. Surgery, Phila. Acad. Cardiology, Greater Del. Soc. Transplant Surgeons. Contbr. articles to profl. jours. Office: 111 S 11th St Suite 8229 Philadelphia PA 19107

SOLL, DAVID BENJAMIN, ophthalmologist; b. N.Y.C., Aug. 9, 1930; s. Hyman and Sara (Karansky) S.; B.A., N.Y. U., 1951, postgrad. Med. Sch., 1956-57, M.S. in Ophthalmology, 1963; M.D., Chgo. Med. Sch., 1955; m. Jean Shtasel, Dec. 23, 1956; children—Abby, Stephen, Warren, Adam. Intern, Phila. Gen. Hosp., 1955-56; resident Manhattan Eye, Ear & Throat Hosp., N.Y.C., 1957-59; instr. dept. ophthalmology U. Pa., Phila., 1961, asso., 1962-68, asst. prof., 1968-72, asso. prof., 1972-75, lectr., 1975—; chief Service B., Frankford Hosp., Phila., 1961-65, dir., 1965—; asso. asst. attending ophthalmologist Phila. Gen. Hosp., 1961-75, cons. in ophthalmology, 1975-77; attending in ophthalmology VA Hosp., Phila., 1961—; clin. affiliate dept. surgery Children's Hosp., Phila., 1961—; dir. dept. ophthalmology Phila. Geriatric Center, Phila., 1965—, Rolling Hill. Hosp. and Diagnostic Center, Elkins Park, Pa., 1969—; cons. plastic surgery Pa. Hosp., Phila., 1973-75, cons. ophthalmology, 1975-78; prof., chmn. dept. ophthalmology Hahnemann Med. Coll. and Hosp. of Phila., 1974—. Served with USPHS, 1959-61. Diplomate Am. Bd. Opthalmology. Fellow A.C.S., Am. Acad. Ophthalmology and Otolaryngology, Am. Soc. Ophthalmic Plastic and Reconstructive Surgery (pres. 1978), Phila. Coll. Physicians; mem. AMA, Pa. Acad. Ophthalmology and Otolaryngology, Am. Assn. Cosmetic Surgeons (pres.), Am. Acad. Facial Plastic and Reconstructive Surgery, Am. Assn. Ophthalmology, AAUP, Assn. Univ. Profs. in Ophthalmology, Robert H. Ivy Soc., Assn. Research in Ophthalmology, Pan. Am. Med. Assn., Pan Am. Ophthalmol. Found., Pa., Philadelphia County med. socs., U. Pa. Eye Alumni Soc., Alpha Omega Alpha, Pi Delta Epsilon, others. Contbr. articles to med. jours. Home: 1127 Devon Rd Rydal PA 19046 Office: 5001 Frankford Ave Philadelphia PA 19124

SOLL, RAPHAEL ISRAEL, ophthalmologist; b. N.Y.C., Apr. 10, 1934; s. William and Rose (Krant) S.; B.A., N.Y. U., 1955; M.D., State U. N.Y. Downstate Med. Sch., 1959; m. Davida Louise Kenvin, Sept. 1, 1957; children—Vicki Patrice, Alysse Lynn, Meri Lee. Intern, Beth El Hosp., Bklyn., 1959-60; resident ophthalmology Bklyn. Eye and Ear Hosp., 1960-62; pvt. practice medicine, specializing in ophthalmology and ophthalmic surgery, Westwood, N.J., 1962—; pres. Raphael I. Soll, M.D., P.A., 1963—; attending physician, chief dept. ophthalmology Pascack Valley Hosp. Diplomate Am. Bd. Ophthalmolgy. Fellow Am. Acad. Ophthalmology and Otolaryngology, A.C.S.; mem. Bergen County Med. Soc., Med. Soc. N.J., N.J. Acad. Ophthalmology, AMA, Am. Assn. Ophthalmology, Internat. Eye Found. Office: 400 Old Hook Rd Westwood NJ 07675

SOLOMON, ANTHONY JOSEPH, state ofcl.; b. Providence, Apr. 1, 1932; s. Joseph and Naza S.; student Providence Coll., 1951-53; B.S. in Pharmacy, R.I. Coll. Pharmacy, 1956; m. Sarah Symia; children—Michael A., Donna M., Sharon A., Anthony E. Owner, operator Anthony's Drug, Inc., Providence, 1957—; gen. treas. State of R.I., Providence, 1977—; mem. R.I. Ho. of Reps., 1966-76; mem. R.I. Gov's. Permanent Council on Drug Abuse; dir. Bank, Inc.; chmn. R.I. Investment Commn., R.I. Retirement Bd., R.I. Unclassified Pay Bd. Mem. R.I. Democratic Charter Commn., Nat. Dem. Charter Commn., R.I. Dem. Com. on Party Policy, Orgn. Mem. R.I. Pharm. Assn. Mem. Maronite Catholic Ch. Clubs: Lebanese-Am. Community Center, K.C., Lions, Knights of Lebanon. Home: 65 Modena Ave Providence RI 02908 Office: State Capitol Room 102 Providence RI 02903

SOLOMON, ANTHONY NICHOLAS, hair stylist; b. Troy, N.Y., July 31, 1942; s. Edward and Margaret (Carnevale) S.; m. Debra Wagner, June 19, 1976. East coast rep. Kovado, 1967-69; rep. Masterpiece for Men, Buffalo, 1970-71; rep. Clairol Co., 1971-73; owner, stylist Anthony's Phase I, Troy, N.Y., 1972—, Albany, N.Y.,

1979—. Served with USNR, 1965-67. Mem. Internat. Coiffure Am. Methodist. Home: 8 Dobert Ct Wynanskill NY 12198 Office: 118 4th St Troy NY 12180

SOLOMON, BERNARD SIMON, educator; b. N.Y.C., June 10, 1924; s. Israel and Rose (Stuchinski) S.; B.S. in Social Sci., Coll. City N.Y., 1946; M.A., Harvard U., 1949, Ph.D., 1952. Research asst. Harvard U., 1952-58; asst. prof. State U. N.Y., New Paltz, 1959-62; mem. faculty Queens Coll., Flushing, N.Y., 1962—, prof. dept. classical and Oriental langs., 1970—. Served with U.S. Army, 1943-45. Harvard-Yenching Inst. fellow, 1949-52; Fulbright fellow, 1955-56, summer 1966; N.Y. State fellow, summer 1964; Nat. Found. for Humanities sr. fellow, 1967-68; Am. Council Learned Socs. fellow, 1977-78. Democrat. Jewish. Author: The Veritable Record of the Tang Emperor Shun-Tsung, 1955. Home: 35 E 9th St New York City NY 10003 Office: Dept Classical and Oriental Langs Queens Coll Flushing NY 11367

SOLOMON, CHARLES MORRIS, lawyer; b. Phila., May 2, 1914; s. David B. and Hylda A. ; B.S. in Econs., U. Pa., 1935, J.D., 1938, LL.M. (Gowen fellow 1938-39), 1939; m. Vita J. Petrosky, Apr. 8, 1941; children—Robert Charles, Henry Andrew, Jon David. Spl. agt. FBI, 1940-45; admitted to Pa. bar, 1939; pvt. practice, Phila., 1939-40, 45—. Mem. Am., Pa., Phila., Fed., Inter-Am., Internat. bar assns., Soc. Former Spl. Agts. of FBI, Lawyers Club of Phila., Order of Coif, Beta Gamma Sigma, Pi Gamma Mu. Club: Locust-(Phila.). Home: 112 Glenview Ave Wyncote PA 19095 Office: 1401 Walnut St Philadelphia PA 19102

SOLOMON, GERALD BROOKS HUNT, congressman; b. Okeechobee, Fla., Aug. 14, 1930; s. Seymour and Rlee Eugenia (Hunt) S.; student Sienna Coll., Albany, N.Y., 1948-49, St. Lawrence U., Canton, N.Y., 1953-54; m. Freda Frances Parker, Feb. 5, 1955; children—Susan, Daniel, Robert, Linda, Jefrey. Town supr., chief exec., Queensbury, N.Y., 1967-72; legislator Warren County, N.Y., 1968-73; mem. N.Y. State Assembly, 1972-78, mem. agr., transp., local govts. and social services coms., 1972-78; mem. 96th Congress from 29th Dist. N.Y., Washington, 1979—; partner Asso. of Glens Falls (N.Y.), Inc., Ins. Agy., 1964-78; Solomon, Veysey, Dixon, Gohn Assos., Glens Falls, 1968-78; mem. adv. bd. State Bank of Albany (N.Y.), 1971—. Chmn., Warren County Social Service Com., 1968-72; active Eastern Adirondack Heart Assn., Adirondack Muscular Dystrophy Assn.; mem. Queensbury Central Vol. Fire Co., 1967—; bd. dirs. Adirondack Park Assn., Glens Falls Area Youth Center, Boy Scouts Am. Mem. Queensbury C. of C. (pres. 1972), Queensbury Jaycees (pres. 1964-65). Republican. Presbyterian. Clubs: Masons, K.T., Kiwanis (dir. Queensbury chpt. 1965-69), Grange. Home: 23 North Rd Queensbury Glens Falls NY 12801 Office: US Ho of Reps The Capitol Washington DC 20515*

SOLOMON, GERALD HARRY, real estate appraiser; b. New Castle, Pa., Sept. 18, 1923; s. Benjamin and Jenny (Neiman) S.; B.A., Transylvania Coll., 1950; student real estate various univs.; m. Sylvia Rossen, Apr. 21, 1966. Staff appraiser Pa. Dept. Hwys., Franklin, 1959-64, U.S. Army C.E., Pitts., 1964-65, supervisory appraiser, Balt., 1965-69; asso. regional appraiser GSA, Washington, 1969-73; chief appraiser U.S. Army C.E., Balt., 1973—. Served with USAAF, 1943-46; PTO, CBI. Mem. Am. Soc. Real Estate Appraisers (sr. real property appraiser), Am. Soc. Appraisers, Am. Right of Way Assn., Assn. Fed. Appraisers (past pres.). Home: 8 Charles Plaza Apt 801 NT Baltimore MD 21201

SOLOMON, MARTIN, ins. broker; b. Bklyn., May 25, 1935; s. Alex and Anna S.; B.S., Bklyn. Coll., 1957, student Law Sch., 1959; M.S., C.W. Post Coll., 1977; m. Lillian Cohen, Feb. 16, 1958; children—Cheryl, Richard. Pres., M. Solomon & Co., Inc., ins. brokers, Hicksville, N.Y., 1963—; v.p. C & R Budget Services Inc., Hicksville, N.Y.; partner Redwood Realty Co., Hicksville; pvt. practice vocat. and family counseling; tchr. mid life career assessment program Nassau Community Coll., Hicksville Adult Edn. Pres., Hicksville Jewish Center, 1969-71; Webelos leader Boy Scouts Am.; mgr. Little League teams. Served with AUS, 1957. Mem. Ind. Agts. Assn., Greater N.Y. Brokers Assn., Assn. Guidance Counselors. Jewish. Club: K.P. Home: 27 April Ln Hicksville NY 11801 Office: 90 Jerusalem Ave Hicksville NY 11801

SOLOMON, MORTON BERNARD, accountant; b. Freeport, N.Y., Dec. 28, 1929; s. David and Tillie (Rathsprecher) S.; B.S. in Commerce, Washington and Lee U., 1951; M.B.A., U. Pa., 1956; m. Marilyn Lee Zahm, Sept. 4, 1955; children—Laurie, Karen, Joyce. Staff accountant Peat, Marwick, Mitchell & Co., N.Y.C., 1956-61; controller, dir. H.L. Klion, Inc., Westbury, N.Y., 1961-65; exec. asst. dept. stock list N.Y. Stock Exchange, N.Y.C., 1965-68; partner Main Lafrentz & Co., N.Y.C., 1968—, nat. dir. accounting and auditing. Served to lt. USNR, 1952-55. C.P.A., N.Y. Mem. Am. Inst. C.P.A.'s, Nat. Assn. Accountants. Contbr. articles to profl. jours. Office: 280 Park Ave New York City NY 10017

SOLOMON, NATHAN AARON, physician; b. Bklyn., Oct. 31, 1922; s. Barney W. and Gertrude S.; B.S., City Coll. N.Y., 1942; M.S., N.Y. U., 1947, Ph.D., 1955; M.D., State U. N.Y., 1959; m. Florence Schneider, Mar. 25, 1944; children—William, Robert, Judith. Chief chemist, chief surg. resgarch Maimonides Med. Center, Bklyn., 1945-55, intern, 1959-60, resident, 1960-63, dir. nuclear medicine, 1964-70; practice medicine specializing in metabolism and nuclear medicine, N.Y.C., 1964—; dir. nuclear medicine State U. N.Y., Bklyn., 1970—, asso. prof., 1977—, prof. Downstate Med. Center, 1977—; cons. Bklyn.-Queens Hosp., VA Hosps., Bklyn. and Northport, Maimonides Hosp., Coney Island Hosp., Kings Hwy. Hosp. Recipient A. Cressy Morrison award N.Y. Acad. Scis., 1954; NIH spl. fellow, 1962-63. Mem. AMA, N.Y. Acad. Scis., Am. Assn. Clin. Chemists, Soc. Nuclear Medicine. Contbr. articles, chpts. to med. jours. and texts. Office: 1308 E 21st St Brooklyn NY 11210

SOLOVIJ, JURIJ, artist; b. Lviv, Ukraine, USSR, Jan. 6, 1921; s. Ivan and Katherine S.; came to U.S., 1952, naturalized, 1960; grad. Acad. Fine Arts, Lviv, 1944; m. Liselotte Metzger; 1 son, Jurij. Exhibited in numerous one man shows including Art Center Gallery, N.Y., 1959, Gunther Franke Gallery, Munich, 1971, St. Lawrence Arts Center, Toronto, 1972, N.J. State Mus., 1973, Phila. Art Alliance, 1975; group shows including Nat. Gallery, Munich, 1947, Mus. of Nurenberg, 1950, U. Chgo., 1960, N.Y. U., 1972, Minn. Mus. Art, 1976; represented in permanent collections: N.J. State Mus., N.Y. Pub. Library, Ukrainian Mus., N.Y., others. Author: About Things Greater Than Stars (Ukrainian), 1976. Home: 149 Wood St Rutherford NJ 07070

SOLYMOSSY, ALFRED AUSTIN, physician; b. Lorinczi, Hungary, Dec. 29, 1913; s. Aladar Aurel and Julianna (Berke) S.; came to U.S., 1959, naturalized, 1965; M.D., U. Budapest, 1942; M. Chirurg., 1945, M.P.H., 1954; m. Piroska Ilona Karacsonyi, Aug. 23, 1941; children—Robert Andras, Julia Rose. Intern, Lebanon Hosp., N.Y.C., 1960; dist. med. officer, Budapest, 1951-54; dir. Ministry of Health, Hungary, 1954-56; gen. practice medicine Raleigh-Boone Clinic, W.Va., 1966-68; sr. med. officer HEW, 1969—. Served to 2d lt. Hungarian Army, World War II. Fellow Royal Soc. Health; mem. AAAS, AMA, Nat. Aero. Assn., Nat. Geog. Soc. Mem. Hungarian Ref. Ch. Home: 12916 Twinbrook Pkwy Rockville MD 20851 Office: 5600 Fishers Ln Rockville MD 20857

SOM, ERNEST LASZLO, pilot, ednl. adminstr.; b. Debrecen, Hungary, July 29, 1935; s. Ernest and Vilma Maria (Erche) S.; came to U.S., 1959, naturalized, 1965; student Cistercitak Szent Bervat Coll., 1949-53; B.A., Art U., 1956; m. Elaine Joy, Aug. 5, 1967; children—Judith, Joane, Ernest, Tina. Artist, Austen Display Inc., N.Y.C., 1959-61; art dir./product mgr. Resident Display Inc., N.Y.C., 1961-71; workshop dir. Woman's Day mag. Fawcett Publ., N.Y.C., 1971-75; chief pilot, flight instr., pres. Empire Flight Center Inc., N.Y.C., 1975—; dir. flight operation Suburban Aviation. Mem. N.J. Hall of Fame, 1975. Mem. Airplane Owners and Pilots Assn., Nat. Assn. Flight Instrs., Nat. Pilots Assn. Nat. Soc. Lit. and Arts. Club: Wings. Office: 855 6th Ave New York NY 10001

SOMERSET, IRA JON, environ. engr.; b. Cambridge, Mass., Jan. 6, 1944; s. Joseph Elliot and Sadie T. (Geisinger) S.; B.S.C.E., U. Mass., 1966; M.S. (U.S. Fed. Water Quality Adminstrn. fellow 1966-68), Tufts U., 1968; m. Judith Kaplan, Nov. 9, 1968; children—Sara Toby, Joseph Elliot. Staff engr. USPHS, Davisville, R.I., 1968-74; regional shellfish specialist U.S. FDA, Balt., 1974-77, Boston, 1977—. Served with USPHS, 1968—. Recipient Merit award FDA, 1972, plaque USPHS, 1974. Mem. ASCE (mem. task com. on environ. effects), Water Pollution Control Fedn., Soc. Am. Mil. Engrs., Internat. Water Pollution Control Fedn., Commd. Officers Assn. USPHS, New Eng. Water Pollution Control Fedn., Sigma Xi. Publs. reviewer to Environ. Engring. jour. Office: 150 Causeway St Boston MA 02114

SOMERVILLE, WALTER RALEIGH, JR., govt. ofcl.; b. Macon, N.C., Feb. 17, 1930; s. Walter Raleigh and Bettie Lou (Hunt) S.; student Morgan State Coll., 1957-60; B.A. in Bus. Adminstrn., U. Md., 1970; m. Jean Renwick (Nava), Sept. 12, 1975; 1 dau., Pamela Nava. Personnel staffing specialist FAA, Washington, 1962-65; personnel mgmt. specialist OEO, 1965-67; personnel mgmt. specialist Office Sec. Transp., 1967-70; chief civilian equal opportunity div. USCG, Transp. Dept., 1970—, trainee Fed. Exec. Devel. Program, 1975-76. Mem. adminstrv. bd. Christ United Meth. Ch., Washington, also chmn. fin. com. Served with USAF, 1951-60. Mem. Am. Mgmt. Assn., Fed. Exec. Inst. Alumni Assn., NAACP, Internat. Personnel Mgmt. Assn., Nat. Assn. Human Rights Workers, Washington Urban League. Home: 1228 4th St SW Washington DC 20024 Office: 400 7th St SW Washington DC 20591

SOMJEN, GABOR, physician; b. Budapest, Hungary, Mar. 7, 1931; s. Paul and Elizabeth S.; came to U.S., 1956, naturalized, 1963; M.D., Med. U. Budapest, 1955; m. Agnes Komaromi, July 21, 1951; children—George Paul, Gregory John. Intern, Barnert Meml. Hosp., Paterson, N.J., 1962; resident in family practice Valley Hosp., Ridgewood, N.Y., 1957-58, Dover Gen. Hosp., 1958-63; staff Dover Gen. Hosp., 1963—; individual practice medicine specializing in family practice, Dover; chmn. dept. family practice, Wharton, N.J., 1976-78. Diplomate Am. Bd. Family Practice. Fellow Am. Acad. Family Practice; mem. AMA, N.J., Morris County (pres. 1974-75) med. socs. Home and Office: 100 Baker Ave Dover NJ 07801

SOMMER, ERNEST LORGE, accountant; b. Kassel, Germany, Dec. 13, 1926; s. Benjamin and Hedwig (Lorge) S.; came to U.S., naturalized, 1946; B.B.A., Pace Coll., 1949; M.S., Columbia U., 1954; m. Donna Anne Lapin, Aug. 25, 1951; children—Robert George, Jeffrey Andrew, Benjamin David. Lectr. Pace Coll., 1954-56; dir. elec. bus. equipment applications Monroe Calculator Machines div. Litton Industries, 1956-58; lectr. accounting, faculty supr. Coll. City N.Y., 1957-66; partner Sommer, Abraham & Gross (and predecessor firm), C.P.A.'s, 1966—; prin. Ernest L. Sommer & Co., C.P.A.'s, 1961-66; dir. Herbert Products, Inc., Westbury, N.Y., Rodney White Found., N.Y.C., Lynne and Charles Klatskin Found., Teterboro, N.J.; mem. adj. faculty Bergen Community Coll., 1970—. Bd. dirs., treas. Foster Parents Plan, Warwick, R.I. C.P.A., N.Y., N.J. Mem. Am. Inst. C.P.A.'s, Bergen County Estate Planners, N.Y. State, N.J. socs. C.P.A.'s. Jewish (treas. temple). Home: 28 Deer Trail Hillsdale NJ 07642 Office: 424 Madison Ave New York City NY 10017

SOMMER, FRANK HENRY, III, librarian, educator; b. Newark, July 30, 1922; s. George R. and Abigail Woodruff (Van Horn) S.; B.A., Yale U., 1943, Ph.D., 1950; diploma gen. archeology Cambridge U., 1948. Keeper folk art Winterthur Mus., 1958-63, head libraries, 1963—; instr. to full prof. U. Del., 1948—; cons. Nat. Gallery, 1971, Nat. Endowment Humanities, 1978; dir. Furniture Library. Henry fellow, 1947-48. Mem. Am. Assn. Archtl. Bibliographers, Soc. Archtl. Historians. Republican. Roman Catholic. Clubs: Grolier (N.Y.C.); Odd Volumes (Boston); Franklin Inn (Phila.); Elizabethan (New Haven). Contbr. articles to profl. jours. Address: Winterthur Mus Winterthur DE 19735

SOMMERS, ALLEN ABRAHAM, public relations agency exec.; b. N.Y.C., Oct. 26, 1918; s. Robert and Clara (Ressler) S.; student Temple U., 1936-38; m. Ruth Lehrer, Mar. 16, 1941; children—Erica Sommers Gero, Carl. Copyboy, reporter, editor Phila. Ledger, 1936-42; asst. city editor Easton (Pa.) Free Press, 1942; founder Sommers/Rosen Inc., Phila., 1946, chmn. bd., 1970—; mem. faculty Charles Morris Price Sch. Journalism and Advt., 1968-74. Leadership chmn. Allied Jewish Appeal-Israel Emergency Fund Phila., 1975—; bd. dirs. YMHA-YWHA Phila; pub. relations chmn. Jackson for Pres. Com. Pa., 1975-76. Mem. Phila. Pub. Relations Assn. (pres. 1969-70), Pub. Relations Soc. Am. (certified), Nat. Investment Relations Inst. (charter), Republican. Jewish. Clubs: Poor Richard, Gulph Mills Racket, B'nai B'rith. Author: (with Chet Smith) Iwo—Hell's Half Acre, 1945. Home: 115 David Rd Bala-Cynwyd PA 19004 Office: 1405 Locust St Philadelphia PA 19102

SOMMERS, BEN, shoe mfg. co. exec.; b. N.Y.C., Dec. 1, 1906; s. Abraham and Dora (Milgrim) Schusterman; student pub. schs. Bklyn.; m. Jean Gerstner, Dec. 25, 1928 (div. Nov. 1961); 1 dau., Carolyn; m. 2d, Estelle Goldstein Loshin, Dec. 2, 1962. With Capezio, Inc., N.Y.C., 1920-64, pres., 1940-64; pres. Capezio Found., 1952—; chmn. Capezio Ballet Makers, 1964-76. Organizer, treas. Navy Relief Dance Profession Victory Ball, N.Y.C., 1942; organizer, chmn. Dance Bus. Group, N.Y.C., 1954-70; organizer, treas. Alliance Three Arts (dance-theatre-fashion), 1971; dir. Ednl. Found. for Apparel Industry, Fashion Inst. Tech., N.Y.C., 1966—; organizer, bd. dirs. Nat. Assn. for Regional Ballet, N.Y.C., 1963—. Organizer, bd. dirs. Am. Assn. Dance Cos. Recipient Winnie-Coty award, Am. Fashion Critics award, 1952, Neiman Marcus award, 1953, Nat. Shoe Retailers award, 1961, Am. Shoe Designers award Leather Industries Am., 1963, Assn. Am. Dance Co. award, 1974, citation City N.Y., 1974. Address: 15 W 81st St New York City NY 10024

SOMMERS, WALDO, educator; b. Balt., May 27, 1908; A.B., Heidelberg Coll., 1927; postgrad. Northwestern U., 1927, Columbia U., 1931-32; M.A., Yale U., 1934; Ph.D., 1948; m. Cordelia Lucille Schmidt, July 20, 1937; children—Claire Sommers Rundle, Joan Sommers Steinkuller, David Henry, Paul Daniel. Mgr. br. regional office, asso. regional dir. U.S. Civil Service, 1939-59; asst. prof. sociology Maxwell Grad. Sch. Citizenship and Pub. Affairs, Syracuse (N.Y.) U., 1946-48; vis. prof., acting chmn. sociology Ohio Wesleyan U., 1949-50; prof. pub. adminstrn. George Washington U., 1959-73, prof. emeritus in residence, 1973—, coordinator intern scholarships, 1959—; cons. Brookings Instn., 1963-64; lectr. Nat. Def. U., summers 1966-67, 70-74, 77-78. Com. Econ. Devel. grantee, 1962-63. Mem. Am. Sociol. Assn., Am. Soc. Pub. Adminstrn., Internat. Personnel Mgmt. Assn., AAUP. Presbyterian. Club: Cosmos (Washington). Author: Reorganizing Federal Personnel Management, 1945-1960, 1963; books editor Personnel Adminstrn., 1961-65; contbr. to ency. Home: 7217 Oakridge Ave Chevy Chase MD 20015 Office: George Washington U Washington DC 20052

SONG, JAMES CHINHO, anesthesiologist; b. Seoul, Korea, July 30, 1942; s. Ki Hak and Shin Chung (Kang) S.; came to U.S., 1971, naturalized, 1977; M.D., Catholic Med. Coll., 1967; m. Susie Y. Choi, Mar. 28, 1970; children—Judy H., Edward W., Deborah K. Intern, Sister's Charity Hosp., Buffalo, 1971; resident St. Vincent's Med. Center, 1972-75; pediatric anesthesia fellow Boston Children's Med. Center, 1975; practice medicine specializing in anesthesiology, 1976—; asso. staff anesthesiologist Wilson's Meml. Hosp., Johnson City, N.Y., 1976—. Diplomate Am. Bd. Anesthesiology. Fellow Am. Coll. Anesthesiologists; mem. Am. Soc. Anesthesiologists, N.Y. State Soc. Anesthesiologists, Am. Soc. Regional Anesthesia. Home: 2637 Purdue Dr Vestal NY 13850 Office: 300 Main St Vestal NY 13850

SONGER, THOMAS FRASHER, II, engring. co. exec.; b. Brookville, Pa., Apr. 4, 1947; s. Thomas Frasher and Stella (Kane) S.; student Lycoming Coll., 1965-67; B.S., Pa. State U., 1970; m. Sara Hine, Nov. 28, 1968; children—Thomas Frasher III, Aaron. Sanitary engr. Allegheny County Health Dept., Pitts., 1970-72; civil and sanitary engr. Pa. State Engring., State College, 1972-76; co-owner, pres. Universal Technical Inc., State College, 1976—. Registered profl. engr., Pa. Mem. Nat., Pa. socs. profl. engrs., Am. Concreter Inst. Democrat. Roman Catholic. Home: 110 S Science Park Rd State College PA 16801 Office: 1234 E College Ave State College PA 16801

SONKIN, LAWRENCE SIDNEY, endocrinologist; b. N.Y.C., Apr. 7, 1920; s. Leo and Amy (Dickler) S.; B.S., City Coll. N.Y., 1941; M.S., U. Wis., 1942; Ph.D. in Pharamacology, U. Chgo., 1949, M.D. with honors, 1950; m. Patricia Jean Lafferty, May 26, 1977. Research asst. U. Chgo., 1942-50; intern N.Y. Hosp., N.Y.C., 1951, asst. resident, to 1953; practice medicine specializing in internal medicine; dir. home care program N.Y. Hosp., 1953-55; instr. medicine Cornell U. Sch. Medicine, N.Y.C., 1953-62, clin. asst. prof., 1962-71, clin. asso. prof., 1971—. Served to capt. U.S. Army, 1957-59. Diplomate Am. Bd. Internal Medicine. Fellow A.C.P.; mem. N.Y. Acad. Medicne, Endocrine Soc., Am. Diabetes Assn., N.Y. State, N.Y. County med. socs., Alpha Omega Alpha. Contbr. articles to med. jours. Office: 220 E 69th St New York City NY 10021

SONN, GEORGE FRANK, JR., chem. engr.; b. Point Pleasant, N.J., Jan. 19, 1936; s. George Frank and Mary (Lehner) S.; B.S. in Chem. Engring., N.C. State Coll., 1957; M.S., Rutgers U., 1960; m. Claire Savin, Jan. 25, 1960; children—Jeffrey, Randy. Tech. mgr. Colloids Inc., Newark, Newark, 1957-58, Inmont Corp., Clifton, N.J., 1958-72; mktg. dir., tech. coordinator Indol Chem. Co. Inc., Cliffwood, N.J., 1972—; cons. in color chemistry, 1974—. Mem. Am. Inst. Chem. Engrs. (award 1968), Am. Chem. Soc., N.Y. Printing Ink Soc., N.Y. Pigment Club, Am. Assn. Textile Chemists and Colorists, Inter Soc. Color Council. Contbr. articles to tech. publs. Patentee coloration of fibers. Home: 141 Mundy Ave Edison NJ 08817 Office: 433 County Rd Cliffwood NJ 07721

SONNEBORN, MEYER ROBERT, osteo. physician, educator; b. Bellaire, Ohio, Feb. 11, 1921; s. Malvin Lewis and Charlotte Irene (Herzeberg) S.; student Belmont (N.C.) Abbey Coll., 1939-41; B.S., Wofford Coll., 1946, M.A., 1948; D.O., Phila. Coll. Osteopathy, 1954; m. Lana Loreen Fisher, Dec. 4, 1943; children—Richard Allyn, Judith Ann Sonneborn Nardis, Meyer Robert, Arthur Aaron, Stephanie Allyson. Pvt. practice osteo. medicine, Wheeling, W.Va., 1955-61, Wind Ridge, Pa., 1961—; physician W. Greene (Pa.) High Sch., 1972—; mem. bd. dirs. Greene County Dept. Welfare, 1972—; faculty Hershey Med. Center, Pa. State U., 1975—; staff Greene County Meml. Hosp.; chief Greene County Coroner's Dept., 1969—; chmn. disaster unit Greene County chpt. ARC, 1972-76. Served with AUS, 1942-46; ETO. Mem. Am. Heart Assn., Am. Trauma Soc. (founding), Am. Osteo. Assn., Pa. Osteo. Med. Soc., VFW, Pa., Greene County med. socs., Pa. Soc. Gen. Practice, Am. Acad. Family Practice, Greene County Hist. Soc. Republican. Methodist. Clubs: Elks, Masons, Shriners. Address: PO Box 68 Wind Ridge PA 15380

SONNENBLICK, EDMUND HIRAM, cardiologist; b. New Haven, Dec. 7, 1932; s. Ira J. and Rosalind H. S.; B.A. summa cum laude, Wesleyan U., 1954; M.D. cum laude, Harvard U., 1958; m. Linda Bland, Dec. 21, 1954; children—Emily, Annie, Charlotte. Intern, resident in medicine Presbyn. Hosp., N.Y.C., 1958-60, 62-63; sr. investigator cardiology br. Nat. Heart Inst., Bethesda, Md., 1960-62; asso. prof. cardiology Harvard Med. Sch., Boston, also dir. cardiovascular research Peter Bent Brigham Hosp., 1967-75; prof. medicine, chief div. cardiology Albert Einstein Coll. Medicine, Bronx, N.Y., 1975—. Served as sr. surgeon USPHS, 1960-62. Mem. Phi Beta Kappa, Sigma Xi, Alpha Omega Alpha. Clubs: Woods Hole and Noroton Yacht, Harvard Boston. Editor Progress in Cardiovascular Diseases, 1973—; contbr. articles to profl. pubs.; author books on cardiovascular topics. Home: 138 Goodwives River Rd Darien CT 06820 Office: Albert Einstein Coll Medicine 1300 Morris Park Ave Bronx NY 10461

SONNENBLICK, JACK EARL, mortgage banker; b. N.Y.C., Oct. 1, 1923; s. Nathan J. and Lillian L. (Langman) S.; student Mass. Inst. Tech., 1941-43; m. Augusta Arline Dann, May 12, 1946; children—Jon D., Mary Ellen Sonnenblick Hirsch, Robert E. With Sonnenblick-Goldman Corp., mortgage banking, N.Y.C., 1946—, pres., 1974—, chmn., 1978—; founder, mng. trustee N. Am. Mortgage Investors, mem. N.Y. Stock Exchange, 1968-70; founder Mortgage Growth Investors, mem. Am. Stock Exchange, 1971; founder S-G Securities Inc., mem. Am. Stock Exchange, N.Y.C., 1973—. Mem. council govs. Albert Einstein Coll. Medicine; trustee N.Y. Bank for Savs., Horace Mann Barnard Sch. Served to 1st. lt. C.E., U.S. Army, 1943-46; ETO. Mem. Nat. Assn. Real Estate Investment Trusts (pres. 1971-72), Mortgage Bankers Assn. Am., N.Y. Real Estate Bd. (chmn. mortgage com. 1967-68). Clubs: Harmonie, Old Oaks Country, Turf and Field. Home: Sterling Rd Harrison NY 10528 Office: 1251 Ave of Americas New York City NY 10020

SONNENSCHEIN, HARRY, pediatrician, pediatric nephrologist; b. N.Y.C., Sept. 17, 1905; s. Louis and Anna (Cohen) S.; student Columbia U.; D.M.C., State U. N.Y., L.I. Coll. Hosp., 1928; m. Beatrice Lasner, Sept. 17, 1933. Intern, Maimonides Med. Center, N.Y.C., 1928-29; practice medicine specializing in pediatric nephrology, Bklyn., 1930-67; cons. pediatrician Maimonides Med. Center, Coney Island Hosp.; attending pediatrician State U. Hosp., Kings County Med. Center; asso. clin. prof. State U. N.Y.; exhibitor med. convs. U.S.; guest reviewer Am. Jour. Diseases of Children, 1967. Recipient certificate of merit AMA, 1962; Silver award Am. Soc. Clin. Pathologists and Am. Coll. Pathologists, 1968; diplomate Am. Bd. Pediatrics. Fellow Am. Acad. Pediatrics; mem. Am. Soc. Pediatric Nephrology, Internat. Pediatric Nephrology Assn. Contbr. articles in field to profl. jours. including 1st description of 2 cases of congenital cutaneous candidiasis, 1st clin. classification of childhood nephrosis without renal biopsy. Home and Office: 17 Maidstone Way Lakehurst NJ 08733

SONNICHSEN, HAROLD MARVIN, cons. chemist; b. Hancock, Minn., Apr. 4, 1912; s. Henry Matthew and Mary (Hults) S.; B.S., Tex. Western U., 1934; M.S., Harvard U., 1935, Ph.D., 1939; m. Thelma Lowenberg, Mar. 11, 1939; children—Susan Elizabeth, Harold Eric. Chemist, plant supr. E.I. Dupont de Nemours, Niagara Falls, N.Y., 1939-44; tech. service mgr. Permacel div. Johnson & Johnson, Inc., New Brunswick, N.J., 1944-48, asst. tech. dir., 1948-52, tech. dir., 1952-55, v.p., dir. research, 1955-60; dir. fiber and saturant research Dewey and Almy div. W.R. Grace & Co., Cambridge, Mass., 1960-64; v.p. Precision Tech. Products, Matwan, N.J., 1965-75; pres. H.M. Sonnichsen & Assos., Arlington, Mass., 1965—. Fellow Am. Inst. Chemists; mem. Am. Chem. Soc., AAAS, ASTM, TAPPI, Assn. Research Dirs., Chemists Club, Sigma Xi. Republican. Home: 37 Robin Hood Rd Arlington MA 02174 Office: 256 Salem St Woburn MA 01801

SONTHEIMER, MORTON, pub. relations co. exec.; b. N.Y.C.; s. Emanuel W. and Sadie (Alderman) S.; student Temple U.; m. Alice Sontheimer, July 3, 1948; children—Marcia Preciado, Donna Jo Sontheimer Acquavella. Reporter, feature writer, editor, various newspapers; later asst. to pres. Am. Heritage Found.; pres. Sontheimer and Co., Inc., N.Y.C., 1957—; cons. U.S. State Dept. on indsl. and tourism devel.; cons. to various fgn. govts. Vice chmn. Sex Info. and Edn. Council U.S. Served with AUS, 1943-45; PTO. Decorated Bronz Star with oak leaf cluster. Mem. Am. Soc. Journalists and Authors (past pres.). Author: Newspaperman, 1942; Attention Comrades, 1955. Contbr. articles and fiction to popular mags. Home: 200 E 57th St New York City NY 10022 Office: Sontheimer and Co Inc 445 Park Ave New York City NY 10022

SOOBITSKY, JOEL ROBERT, govt. youth program ofcl.; b. Middletown, Conn., Dec. 23, 1940; s. Azreal and Myrtle (Brenner) S.; B.S. (4-H Scholar), U. Conn., 1962; M.S. (Nat. 4-H Scholar), Kans. State U., 1963; student Merrill-Palmer Inst., 1967; Ph.D., Ohio State U., 1971; m. Cassandra McClain, Sept. 2, 1962; 1 son, Jayson Aaron. 4-H summer asst. U. Conn., 1961-62; coop. extension agt. Schenectady County, N.Y., 1963-70; program devel. specialist Dept. Agr., Washington, 1970-73, nat. 4-h program leader, 1973—, mem. nat. 4-H leadership devel. com., 1973-76, nat. 4-H urban devel. com., 1976—, nat. 4-H resource devel. com.; vis. prof. U. Ariz., 1973-74, U. R.I., 1975, U. Calif., 1976; cons. land-grant univs., U.S.; dir. B.S.W. Inc., 1975; sci. dept. adminstr., equal employment opportunity counselor Dept. Agr., 1978—. Coach baseball, basketball Wheaton Boys Club, 1975-77; judge WWDC Safety Patrol Program; active Kennedy High Sch. Parents, Tchrs. and Students Assn., 1975; exec. com. Chaddsford Civic Assn., Silver Springs, Md., 1972—; mem. White House Youth Council, 1974; mem. Fed. Interagency Council on Juvenile Delinquency, 1974-75; rep. 4-H on Nat. Collaboration for Youth; mem. Juvenile Delinquency Prevention Task Force, Youth Edn. and Employment Task Force, 1976, 77, 78; cons. Am. Assn. Ret. Persons Generation Alliance. Recipient Outstanding Young Man award Jaycees, 1968, Centennial medal Ohio State Expt. Sta., 1976, Distinguished Alumni award Ohio State U., 1976. Mem. Orgn. Profl. Employees Dept. Agr., Conn. 4-H Key Club, Nat. 4-H Congress, Nat. 4-H Conf. (rep. Conn. 1956, 59), Nat. Future Farmers Am. Conv., Nat. Collaboration of Youth, Nat. 4-H Agts. Assn., Alpha Gamma Rho, Gamma Sigma Delta, Epsilon Sigma Phi. Clubs: E.S. Activities (pres. 1974-76). Contbr. articles to profl. jours.; author 4-H publs. Home: 13848 Turnmore Rd Silver Spring MD 20906 Office: Room 6001 Dept Agr Washington DC 20250

SOOY, LESLIE THOMAS, neuropsychiatrist, educator; b. Atlantic City, Nov. 21, 1906; s. Walter Collins and Lida H. (Thomas) S.; B.S., Hahnemann Coll., 1928, M.D., 1929; m. Carrie Shaw Compton, June 7, 1928. Intern, West Jersey Hosp., Camden, N.J., 1929-30; practice medicine specializing in neurology and psychiatry, Pitman, N.J., 1931—; mem. staff Hahnemann Hosp., 1931-67; instr. histology and embryology Hahnemann Med. Coll., 1930-33, asst. dept. neurology and psychiatry, 1930-34, instr., 1934-37, lectr., 1937-50, asso. in neurology, 1950-56, asst. prof., 1956-67; civilian psychiatrist Army Induction Center, Camden, 1943-45; cons. neuropsychiatrist to VA, N.J. Rehab. Commn. Social Security div. HEW. Recipient Wisdom award of honor, 1970, Physician's Recognition award, 1976. Fellow Acad. Psychosomatic Med., Sci. Council of Internat. Coll. Angiology, Am. Geriatrics Soc., Am. Coll. Angiology; mem. Assn. Am. Med. Colleges, AMA, N.J. State, Gloucester County med. socs., Am. Psychiat. Assn., Am. Soc. Med. Psychiatry, Am. Acad. Neurology, World Med. Assn. (U.S. Com.), N.J. Neuropsychiat. Assn., Soc. Biol. Psychiatry, Pi Upsilon Rho. Clubs: Phila. Med., Phila. Union League, Masons. Home and Office: 202 W Holly Ave Pitman NJ 08071

SOPCHAK, ANDREW LEO, psychologist; b. Auburn, N.Y., Jan. 2, 1919; s. Andrew and Anna (Friga) S.; B.A., Syracuse U., 1946, M.A., 1948; Ph.D., Adelphi U., 1957; m. Mary Fechisin, Sept. 3, 1950; 1 son, Andrew M. Instr. psychology U. Maine, Orono, 1947-52; clin. psychologist, research fellow Meml. Hosp. Sloan Kettering Inst. for Cancer Research, N.Y.C., 1956-58; clin. instr. psychiatry Upstate Med. Center, State U. N.Y., Syracuse, 1961—; chief psychologist Onondage County (N.Y.) Child Guidance Center, Syracuse, 1961—; cons. DePaul Clinic, Rochester, N.Y., 1962-64, N.Y. State Office Vocat. Rehab., Syracuse, 1965—. Served with U.S. Army, 1942-43. Mem. Am., Eastern, N.Y. State psychol. assns., N.Y. Soc. Clin. Psychologists, AAUP, Am. Group Psychotherapy Assn., Nat. Rehab. Assn., Phi Delta Kappa. Contbr. articles to profl. jours. Home: 17 Heritage Circle Solvay NY 13209

SOPER, KENNETH JOSEPH, hosp. adminstr.; b. Balt., Nov. 1, 1940; s. William Joseph and Grace (Davis) S.; A.A. in Bus. Adminstrn., U. Balt., 1967, A.A. in Sales Mgmt., 1969, B.S. in Bus. Mgmt., 1973, M.B.A., 1979. Asst. div. mgr. Eastern Products Corp., Balt., 1965-70; admitting mgr., utilization control mgr. Church Hosp. Corp., Balt., 1970-71, dir. admitting and med. records, 1971-74, adminstrv. asst., 1974-77, asst. v.p., 1977—. Bd. dirs. Church Home and Hosp. Fed. Credit Union, 1972-75; scout leader Boy Scouts Am., 1967-71. Mem. Am. Coll. Hosp. Adminstrs., Am. Soc. Hosp. Engring., Am. Hosp. Assn., Md. Asst. Adminstrs., Club: Optimist (dir., sec. 1975—) (Balt.). Home: 340 Stevenson Ln Towson MD 21204 Office: 100 N Broadway Baltimore MD 21231

SORBIE, CHARLES, surgeon; b. Hamilton, Scotland, June 20, 1931; s. Charles and Hannah Hendry (Clark) S.; M.B., Glasgow U., 1953, Ch.B., 1953; m. Janet Wynne-Edwards, Apr. 27, 1957; children—Pamela Jane, Alison Wynne, Valerie Clark. Intern, Western Infirmary, Glasgow, Scotland, 1953-54, sr. registrar, 1963-65; resident in surgery Univ. Coll. W.I., Jamaica, 1954-56; resident in gen., pediatric and orthopaedic surgery Glasgow U. Teaching Hosps., 1956-61; clin. fellow Harvard U., Mass. Gen. Hosp., 1961-63; prof. surgery Queen's U., Kingston, Ont., Can., 1965—, chief div. orthopaedic surgery, 1967—; mem. attending staff Kingston Gen. Hosp. Fellow Brit. Orthopaedic Assn., Royal Coll. Surgeons Can., Edinburgh; mem. Can. Orthopaedic Research Soc. (past pres.), Can. Orthopaedic Assn. (sec.), Brit., Can. med. assns. Presbyterian. Clubs: Kingston Yacht, Kingston Tennis. Contbr. articles to med. jours. Home: 208 Alwington Pl Kingston ON K7L 4P8 Canada Office: Richardson House Queen's U Kingston ON K7L 3N6 Canada

SORBO, PAUL JOSEPH, JR., supt. schs.; b. New Britain, Conn., Oct. 31, 1927; B.S. in Bus. Edn., Central Conn. State Coll., New Britain, 1951; M.S. in Bus. Edn., U. Conn., Storrs, 1963, also postgrad.; m. Marian Kloje; 4 children. Tchr., Litchfield (Conn.) Pub. Schs., 1954-58; adminstrv. asst. Windsor (Conn.) Pub. Schs., 1963-65, asst. supt., 1965-69, supt., 1969—; faculty Central Conn. State Coll. Vice-pres. Hartford Easter Seal Rehab. Center, 1973-75, pres., 1977-79. Recipient Distinguished Service award Greater Hartford Council Economic Edn., 1976. Mem. Greater Hartford Council Econ. Edn. (chmn. 1969-71), Conn. Assn. Advancement Sch. Adminstrs., Am. Assn. Sch. Adminstrs., Conn. Assn. Sch. Adminstrs. (v.p. 1978-79); Conn. Joint Council Econ. Edn. (exec. com. 1977-79), Phi Delta Kappa. Home: 15 Timber Ln Windsor CT 06095 Office: 150 Bloomfield Ave Windsor CT 06095

SORCE, ANTHONY JOHN, artist; b. Chgo., Apr. 30, 1937; diploma Am. Acad. Art, Chgo., 1957; B.F.A., U. Notre Dame, 1961, M.F.A., 1962; married; 3 children. Tchr. art Nazareth Coll., Kalamazoo, 1962-67, Nazareth Coll., Rochester, N.Y., 1967-68, Pace U., 1969-72, Queens Coll., 1971-72; asst. prof. art Manhattan Community Coll., 1971—; one man exhbns., 1960—, latest being Wichita (Kans.) Art Mus., 1970, Jewish Mus., N.Y.C., 1970, O.K. Harris, N.Y.C., 1977, 79; group exhbns., 1957—, latest being Pace Graphics, N.Y.C., 1972, Aldreich Mus. Contemporary Art, Ridgefield, Conn., 1976; represented in permanent collections: Chase Manhattan Bank, Wichita Art Mus., Kalamazoo Inst. Art, Kalamazoo Coll., Upjohn Co. Pres. bd. dirs. Greenwich Village Montessori Sch., 1975-76. Ivan Mestrovic studio asst. U. Notre Dame, 1959-62; recipient Jacques Fine Arts Silver medal U. N.D., 1961; Guggenheim fellow, 1968-69; grantee Research Found. City U. N.Y., 1973-74, Research Found. State U. N.Y., 1974-75. Address: 463 West St Apt 1021 H New York City NY 10014

SOREFF, STEPHEN MICHAEL, psychiatrist; b. Manchester, Conn., Dec. 7, 1942; s. Louis and Rebecca (Zoken) S.; B.A., Tufts U., 1964; M.D., Northwestern U., 1969; m. Joan Eve Sud, Apr. 19, 1969; children—Alexandra Eytana, Benjamin Elhanan. Intern, Harborview Med. Center, Seattle, 1969-70; resident Maine Med. Center, Portland, 1970-73, dir. emergency psychiatry and psychiat. consultation, 1973—; assoc. clin. prof. psychiatry Tufts U., 1972—; vis. lectr. psychiatry Bowdoin Coll., Brunswick, Maine, 1973. Bd. dirs. Abilities and Goodwill Inc., Portland, 1975—; chmn. bd. visitors Augusta State Hosp., 1972-73. Diplomate Am. Bd. Psychiatry and Neurology. Mem. AMA (Physician's Recognition award 1972, 75), Maine Med. Assn., Am., Maine (pres. 1978-79) psychiat. assns., Sierra Club. Democrat. Jewish. Clubs: Appalachian Mountain, Mystic Seaport. Home: Cumberland ME 04110 Office: Maine Med Center Portland ME 04102

SORENSON, JAMES ROGER, med. sociologist, educator; b. Yakima, Wash., Feb. 9, 1943; s. Paul O. and Helen (Anderson) S.; B.A. magna cum laude, U. Wash., Seattle, 1965, M.A., 1966; Ph.D., Cornell U., 1970; m. Nancy E. O'Neal, May 24, 1968; 1 son, Peter M. Research asst. sociology U. Wash., 1965-66; asst. prof. sociology Princeton U., 1969-74; asso. prof. socio-med. scis. Boston U. Sch. Medicine, 1974—; sci. asso. Boston City Hosp., 1975—; mem. clin. research com. Nat. Found., 1974-75. NIMH fellow, U. Wash., 1965-66, Cornell U., 1966-70; recipient grants Russell Sage Found., 1970-75, Nat. Found., 1975-79, Nat. Fund for Med. Edn., 1976-77. Mem. Am., Eastern sociol. assns., AAAS, Inst. Soc., Ethics and the Life Scis., Phi Beta Kappa. Author: Social Aspects of Applied Human Genetics, 1971; contbr. articles to profl. jours. Home: 86 Forest St Wellesley Hills MA 02181 Office: 80 E Concord St Boston MA 02118

SORGIE, FRANK BERNARD, chem. co. exec.; b. Washington, Pa., Dec. 22, 1930; s. Frank David and Betty E. (Ross) S.; B.S. in Math., Waynesburg Coll., 1953; postgrad. Washington and Jefferson Coll., 1952; m. Dawn T. Chambers, Feb. 12, 1954; 1 dau., Valorie Dawn. Mem. ops. research staff Am. Standard Corp., N.Y.C., 1954-63; asst. to pres. Geigy Chem. Co., Ardsley, N.Y., 1963-66, dir. corporate comml. services, 1966-70; dir. corporate comml. service Ciba-Geigy Corp., Ardsley, 1970-72, dir. corporate personnel, 1972—; dir. Airwick Industries, Inc. Served with U.S. Army, 1953-54. Registered profl. engr., Calif. Mem. Am. Inst. Indsl. Engring. (sr.), Am. Mgmt. Assn., Am. Soc. Personnel Adminstrn. Republican. Presbyterian. Home: 89 Forest Rd Allendale NJ 07401 Office: 444 Saw Mill River Rd Ardsley NY 10502

SORHAINDO, ALPHONSO LORENZO, psychologist; b. Dominica, W. Indies, Apr. 10, 1942; s. Clive Anselm and Rosa (Frederick) S.; came to U.S., 1960, naturalized, 1969; B.A., Iona Coll., 1964; M.A., Conn. Coll., 1967; Ph.D., Ohio State U., 1970; m. Marie-Louise Blanchet; children—Alphonso Lorenzo, Kathryn Rosa, Jeanne Marie. Clin. instr. Ohio State U. Coll. Medicine, Dept. Psychiatry, Columbus, 1970-71; staff psychologist Cath. Social Services, Columbus, 1968-70; postdoctoral fellow in community psychology Center for Study of Social Intervention, Albert Einstein Coll. Medicine, Bronx, 1971-72; instr., group leader St. Vincent's Orphanage, Columbus, 1970-71; mental health cons., Iona Coll., part-time, 1971-72; instr., cons. psychologist Coop. Coll. Center of Westchester, Ednl. Opportunity Center of Westchester, Yonkers, N.Y., 1971-76; sr. clin. psychologist Div. Consultation and Edn., Brookdale Hosp., Bklyn., 1972-73; chief psychologist Manhattan Devel. Center, 1973-74, chief developmental center treatment services, 1974-76, dep. dir. treatment services, 1976—. Roman Catholic. Address: 164 Centre Ave Apt 3N New Rochelle NY 10805

SOSKIN, DAVID HOWELL, advt. agy. exec.; b. N.Y.C., Feb. 14, 1942; s. William and Virginia Mapes (Howell) S.; B.A. in English Lit., Knox Coll., 1964; m. Janet Meyer, Sept. 12, 1964; children—Christopher David, Rebecca Tier. Editor, asso. pub. bus. publs. div. Cowles Communications, Inc., N.Y.C., 1964-71; advt. mgr. Book-of-the-Month Club, Inc., N.Y.C., 1971-73, mktg. dir., 1973-75, corporate v.p. mktg. and advt., N.Y.C., 1975-78; pres. David Soskin Assos. div. of Lord, Geller, Federico, Inc., N.Y.C., 1978—; lectr. N.Y. U., Harvard U. Mem. Assn. Am. Pubs., Am., Can. direct mail mktg. assns. Mem. United Ch. of Christ. Clubs: N.Y. Univ.; Tokeneke (Darien, Conn.); John's Island (Fla.). Home: 10 Dellwood St Darien CT 06820 Office: 1414 6th Ave New York City NY 10019

SOTTERLY, JOSEPH FRANCIS, real estate and ins. broker; b. Orange, N.J., Sept. 14, 1921; s. John Francis and Anna Matilda (Confessore) S.; B.S., Seton Hall Coll., 1948; postgrad. Yale U. Sch. of Bus., 1949; m. Carol R. Sotterly. Pres., J.F. Sotterly & Assos., East Orange, N.J. Served as lt. USCG, 1942-45. Roman Catholic. Clubs: Newark Athletic, Knoll Country, Essex County Country. Home: 35 Cornell Dr Livingston NJ 07039 Office: 586 Central Ave East Orange NJ 07018

SOUCY, JEAN-CHARLES RENE, psychologist; b. Woonsocket, R.I., May 2, 1948; s. Jean-Paul and Jeanne (Pierel) S.; A.B. cum laude, Providence Coll., 1969; M.A., Boston Coll., 1972; certificate advanced grad. study R.I. Coll., 1975; m. Lorraine Jeanne Pichette, June 21, 1969; children—Michael, Daniel. Instr. in English, Chariho Regional High Sch., Richmond, R.I., 1969-70, St. Clare High Sch., Woonsocket, 1971-72; elementary sch. psychol. counselor Woonsocket Dept. Edn., 1972-74, counselor CETA program, summers 1975, 76, 77; sch. psychologist Woonsocket Jr. and Sr. High Schs., 1974—; cons. No. R.I. Assn. Retarded Citizens, Woonsocket Council Community Services, others. Mem. Am. Psychol. Assn., R.I. Sch. Psychologists Assn. (exec. bd.), Woonsocket Jaycees, Delta Epsilon Sigma. Certified sch. psychologist, R.I., Mass. Democrat. Roman Catholic. Home: 70 Woodland Rd Woonsocket RI 02895 Office: Cass Park Ednl Center Newland Ave Woonsocket RI 02895

SOUCY, W. ROLAND, environ. devel. engr.; b. Troy, N.Y., May 6, 1925; s. Wilfred and Marion (Voege) S.; B.Engring., Rensselaer Poly. Inst., 1945, M.Engring., 1948, postgrad., 1949; m. Elizabeth M. Bogle, Aug. 30, 1952. Structural engr. Bell Aircraft Corp., Buffalo, 1945; instr. Rensselaer Poly. Inst., 1945-49; project engr. Office of Gen. Services, Exec. Dept., State of N.Y., Albany, 1949—. Registered profl. engr., Maine, N.Y.; certified Nat. Council Engring. Examiners. Mem. Nat., N.Y. State (past v.p. Rensselaer County chpt.) socs. profl. engrs., Smithsonian Assos., Internat Platform Assn. Clubs: Albany Country, Aurania, Monarch (past pres.) (Albany). Patentee in field. Home: 8 Maple Ln N Loudonville NY 12211

SOULE, PHILIP PATRICK, SR., social worker, state ofcl.; b. Quincy, Mass., June 28, 1942; s. Melvin Dodge and Phyllis S. (Emerson) S.; B.A., St. John's Sem. Coll., 1964, M.A., 1966; M.Ed. in Counseling, U. N.H., 1978; m. Jane Justine Longley, Jan. 20, 1968; children—Philip Patrick, Celeste, Veronica, Estelle, Stephen. Asst. mgr. W.T. Grant Co., Laconia, N.H., 1969-71; ins. agt. Prudential Ins. Co., Laconia, N.H., 1971-72; social worker Child and Family Services, N.H. Div. Welfare, Concord, 1972-75, casework supr., 1975-77, dir. Concord Office, 1977—; cons. in field. Served with U.S. Army, 1966-69, USAR, 1969—; Vietnam. Decorated Bronze Star. Mem. Franklin (N.H.) Jaycees (pres. 1977), Am. Personnel and Guidance Assn., Res. Officers Assn., Am. Pub. Welfare Assn., N.H. State Employees Assn. Roman Catholic. Club: K.C. Home: 10 View St Franklin NH 03235 Office: 10 Pleasant St Extension Concord NH 03301

SOUTER, DAVID HACKETT, former atty. gen. N.H.; b. Melrose, Mass., Sept. 17, 1939; s. Joseph Alexander and Helen Adams (Hackett) S.; B.A., Harvard U., 1961, LL.B., 1966; Rhodes scholar, Oxford U., 1961-63. Admitted to N.H. bar; asso. firm Orr & Reno, Concord, 1966-68; asst. atty. gen. N.H., 1968-71, dep. atty. gen., 1971-76, atty. gen., 1976-79. Trustee, Concord Hosp., N.H. Hist. Soc. Mem. N.H. Bar Assn., Phi Beta Kappa. Republican. Episcopalian. Home: Weare NH 03281

SOUTH, FRANK EDWIN, physiologist, univ. adminstr.; b. Norfolk, Nebr., Sept. 20, 1024; s. Frank Edwin and Gladys (Brinkman) S.; A.B., U. Calif., Berkeley, 1949, Ph.D., 1952; m. Berna Deane Phyllis Casebolt, June 23, 1946; children—Frank Edwin, III, Robert Christopher. Asst. prof. physiology U. P.R. Sch. Medicine, 1953-54, U. Ill. Coll. Medicine, 1954-61; asso. prof. Colo. State U., 1961-62, prof., 1962-65; prof. U. Mo., 1965-76; prof., dir. Sch. Life and Health Scis. U. Del., 1976—; mem. governing bd., dir. Hibernation Info. Exchange, 1959—. Bd. dirs. Del. Lung Assn., 1976—, Del. Cancer Network, 1977—; mem. research com. Del. Heart Assn., 1977—; mem. med. advisory bd. A. I. DuPont Inst., Wilmington, Del., 1978—. Served with AUS, 1943-45. Decorated Purple Heart with oak leaf cluster, Silver Star. NIH Career Devel. awardee, 1961-65. Fellow AAAS, Sigma Xi; mem. Am. Physiol. Soc., Soc. Gen. Physiologists, Soc. Exptl. Biology, Medicine, Internat. Hibernation Soc. (governing bd., dir.), Am. Soc. Zoologists, Cryobiology Soc., U.S. Power Squadron, Oceanic Soc., Soc. Hist. Preservation. Episcopalian. Club: North East River Yacht. Contbr. numerous articles on physiology of hibernation, temperature regulation, renal function, marine mammals, artificial atmospheres, sleep to profl. jours. Office: Dir Sch Life and Health Scis U Del Newark DE 19711

SOUTHER, RICHARD STANLEY, journalist; b. Salisbury Beach, Mass., July 21, 1925; s. William Bartlett and Lillian Frances (Farnum) S.; grad. MacIntosh Bus. Coll., 1947; student No. Essex Coll., 1970-73; m. Deanna Jean Bradbury, Jan. 15, 1961; 1 son, Richard Stanley. Reporter Haverhill (Mass.) Jour., 1965-66; waterfront reporter New Bedford (Mass.) Standard Times, 1966-67; N.H. bur. chief Daily News, Newburyport, Mass., 1967-70; editor-in-chief Beach Comber, Hampton Union, Exeter Gazette, Derry Gazette, Smart Shopper, Seabrook, N.H., 1970-73; N.H. editor-journalist Daily News (Essex County Newspapers), Newburyport, 1974—. Cons. No. Essex Coll., 1970-73. Hon. mem. Meeting House Green Meml. and Hist. Assn., Hampton, N.H., 1972-73. Served with USAAF, 1943-46. Mem. Internat. Soc. Weekly Newspaper Editors, N.H. Archeol. Soc., New Eng. Antiquities Research Assn., New Eng. Outdoor Writers Assn., Am. Police and Fire News Reporters Assn., Nat. Soc. Lit. and Arts. Conglist. Home: 16 Bromfield St Newburyport MA 01950 Office: 23 Liberty St Newburyport MA 01950

SOUTHERLAND, EDNA EUGENIA SPEARMAN, counselor; b. Rose Hill, N.C., Apr. 16, 1931; d. Samuel Dolphus and Sudie (Boykin) Spearman; M.Ed., Am. U., 1971; m. Elonzia B. Southerland, Dec. 28, 1955. Tchr., Duplin County Pub. Schs., Rose Hill, 1955-62, D.C. Pub. Schs., 1962-73; counselor Watkin and Lenox elementary schs., 1973—; cons. in field. Chairperson career planning New Bethel Ch. God in Christ, Washington, 1968—. Mem. Am., Nat. Captial personnel and guidance assns., Am., D.C. sch. counselors assns., NEA (life). Democrat. Home: 427 Madison St NE Washington DC 20011

SOUTHERN, EILEEN (MRS. JOSEPH SOUTHERN), educator; b. Mpls., Feb. 19, 1920; d. Walter Wade and Lilla (Gibson) Jackson; B.A., U. Chgo., 1940, M.A., 1941; Ph.D., N.Y. U., 1961; m. Joseph Southern, Aug. 22, 1942; children—April, Edward. Concert pianist, 1940-55; instr. Prairie View U., Hempstead, Tex., 1941-42; asst. prof. So. U., Baton Rouge, 1943-45, 49-51; tchr. N.Y.C. Bd. Edn., 1954-60; instr. Bklyn. Coll., City U. N.Y., 1960-64, asst. prof., 1964—; asso. prof. York Coll., City U. N.Y., 1969-71, prof., 1972-75; prof. music and Afro-Am. studies, chmn. dept. Harvard U., 1976—. Active Girl Scouts U.S.A., 1954-63; chmn. mgmt. com. Queens Area YWCA, 1970-73. Mem. Internat., Am. (dir. 1974-76). musicol. socs., Renaissance Soc., NAACP, Alpha Kappa Alpha. Author: The Buxheim Organ Book, 1963; The Music of Black Americans: A History, 1971; Readings in Black American Music, 1972; founder, editor The Black Perspective in Music, 1973—; contbr. articles profl. jours. Home: 115-05 179th St Saint Albans NY 11434 Office: Harvard Univ Cambridge MA 02138

SOUTHERN, HUGH, theater exec.; b. Newcastle-on-Tyne, Eng., Mar. 20, 1932; s. Norman and Phyllis Margaret (Hiller) S.; B.A., King's Coll., Cambridge (Eng.) U., 1956; m. Jane Rosemary Llewellyn, Dec. 18, 1954; children—Hilary, William Norman. Asso. account exec. Fuller & Smith & Ross, N.Y.C., 1956-58; treas. Westport Country Playhouse (Conn.), 1958; adminstrv. mgr. Theatre Guild-Am. Theatre Soc., N.Y.C., 1959-62; asst. dir. Repertory Theater Lincoln Center, N.Y.C., 1962-65; gen. mgr. Nat. Repertory Theater, N.Y.C., 1965-67; mgmt. asso. San Francisco Opera, 1967-68; exec. dir. Theatre Devel. Fund, N.Y.C., 1968—; acting dir.

performing arts program N.Y. State Council Arts, N.Y.C., 1974-75, acting exec. dir., 1976; cons. in field. Pres. Opportunity Resources for Performing Arts, 1972-74; mem. N.Y.C. Mayor's Com. Cultural Policy, 1974-75; trustee Manhattan Country Sch., 1970—, chmn., 1971-74; bd. dirs. Vol. Urban Cons. Group, 1976—. Mem. New Drama Forum Assn. (v.p. 1974—), Century Assn. Home: 1270 Fifth Ave New York City NY 10029 Office: Theatre Devel Fund 1501 Broadway New York City NY 10036

SOUTHGATE, DONALD FREDERIC, former bus. cons.; b. Railroad Mills, N.Y., Aug. 20, 1893; s. William F. and Harriet F. (Edwards) S.; student U. Rochester, 1912-15; m. Edna R. Scutt, June 24, 1919; 1 dau., Betty H. Copywriter, Lyddon & Hanford Advt. Agency, Rochester, 1915-16; asst. advt. mgr. Standard Optical Co., 1917, advt. mgr., 1919-25, Shur-on Standard Optical Co., Inc., 1925-31, Shuron Optical Co., Inc., 1931-34, v.p. in charge advt., 1935-37, asst. to pres., 1938-40, comptroller, 1941-42, mgr. ophthalmic lens production, 1943-47, v.p. in charge sales promotion, 1947-49, sec., 1950, exec. v.p., 1953-54, pres., dir., 1954-60; then bus. cons., Geneva, N.Y.; now ret.; mem. advisory com. Lincoln Rochester Trust Co. Served to 2d lt. U.S. Army, 1918-19; AEF. Mem. VFW, Am. Legion. Home: RD 2 Phelps NY 14532

SOUTHWARD, BERNARD MORRISON, JR., correction counselor; b. Augusta, Ga., Nov. 24, 1944; s. Bernard Morrison and Lucille (Thompkins) S.; student Howard U., 1962-65; A.B. in Sociology and Psychology, Augusta Coll., 1971; A.M. in Sociology of Edn. (Coll. fellow), Columbia U., 1972. Substitute tchr. elementary and secondary schs. Richmond County (Ga.) Bd. Edn., 1966-71; correction counselor Clinton Correctional Facility, Dannemora, N.Y., 1973-74; correction counselor Green Haven Correctional Facility, Stormville, N.Y., 1974-76, sr. correction counselor, 1976—; corrections cons. Internat. Key Women Am.; cons. Marist Coll. Higher Edn. Opportunity Program Prison Program; cons. Think Tank, Inc., Green Haven Artists Collective, Project Build. Pres. Partners Ten, Dutchess County; participant Voter Registration Dr., Duchess County. Mem. Pub. Offender Counselor Assn., Am. Personnel and Guidance Assn., Nat. Assn. Black Social Workers, Smithsonian Assos., Am. Museum Natural History (asso.). Co-developer honor housing model (maximum security) Green Haven Correctional Facility, 1976; research on pre-release concept, 1976. Office: Drawer B Stormville NY 12582

SOUW, RAYMOND STEVEN, psychiatrist; b. Indonesia, Sept. 23, 1935; s. James and Netty (Yo) S.; M.B.B.S., U. Sydney (Australia), 1961; D.P.M., U. Melbourne (Australia), 1968; m. Fe E. Pizana, Dec. 1, 1962; 1 son, Peter Anthony. Psychiatrist, Royal Park Psychiat. Hosp., Melbourne, Australia, 1965-68, Munroe Wing, Regina, Sask., Can., 1970; child psychiatrist Queen's U., 1970-71; practice medicine, specializing in child and adolescent psychiatry and psychotherapy, Brantford, Ont., Can., 1972—; tchr. humanistic and existential philosophy and psychology. Fellow Royal Coll. Physicians Can.; mem. Australian and N.Z. Coll. Psychiatrists, Am. Humanist Assn., Royal Coll. of Psychiatrists (U.K.), Am., World psychiat. assns., Am. Orthopsychiat. Assn., Am. Acad. Child Psychiatry, AAAS, Can. Wildlife Fedn., Ont. Fedn. of Naturalists. Mem. Ch. of England. Office: Terrace Hill Med Center 217 Terrace Hill St Brantford ON N3T 1J8 Canada

SOXMAN, DON GERMAIN, physician; b. Monarch, Pa., Oct. 25, 1921; s. James Omer and Margaret (Victor) S.; B.S., Washington and Jefferson Coll., 1943; M.D., U. Pitts., 1946; postgrad. Harvard U., 1960; m. Dolores Ann Sandusky, July 2, 1954; children—Margaret Ellen, Jane Ann, James Thomas, Mary Susan, Pamela Dawn, Kirk Ephram. Resident internal medicine VA Hosp., Oakland, Pitts., 1959-60; pvt. practice gen. medicine, Connellsville, Pa., 1948-51, practice ltd. internal medicine, 1951—; sr. staff Connellsville State Gen. Hosp., chief of medicine and cardiology; dir., v.p. Connellsville Devel. Corp., 1960; dir. Sta WCVI, 1950-58. Mem. Bd. Health, Connellsville, 1962—; dir. Fayette County chpt. Am. Heart Assn., 1952-62, Am. Cancer Soc., 1949-57, pres., 1953, Easter Seal Soc., 1953-56. Served to lt. (j.g.) M.C., USNR, 1946-49. Recipient Outstanding Service award Fayette County chpt. Am. Cancer Soc., 1952. Fellow Internat. Coll. Angiology, Am. Coll. Angiology, Am. Coll. Chest Physicians (asso.); mem. Am. Coll. Physicians, Internat. Assn. Internal Medicine, Am. Diabetes Assn., Am. Geriatrics Soc., Aero. Space Med. Assn., AMA, Civil Aviation Med. Assn., Am., Pa. socs. internal medicine, Am. Coll. Cardiology (affiliate), Pa., Fayette County (pres. 1961) med. socs., SAR, Delta Tau Delta, Nu Sigma Nu, Phi Sigma, Alpha Kappa Alpha. Republican. Lutheran. Clubs: Masons, Shriners; Univ. (Pitts.); Pittsburgh Playhouse, Century; Pleasant Valley Country (Connellsville). Home: Wyndwood Off Dogwood Dr Connellsville PA 15425 Office: Profl Bldg Connellsville PA 15425

SPACE, THEODORE MAXWELL, lawyer; b. Binghamton, N.Y., Apr. 3, 1938; s. Maxwell Evans and Dorothy Marie (Boone) S.; A.B., Harvard U., 1960; LL.B., Yale U., 1966; m. Susan Shultz, Aug. 18, 1962; children—William Schuyler, Susanna. Admitted to Conn. bar, 1966; asso. firm Shipman & Goodwin, Hartford, Conn., 1966-71, partner, 1971—. Mem. Bloomfield (Conn.) Bd. Edn., 1973—, chmn., 1975—; treas. Citizens Scholarship Found., Bloomfield, 1971-73, bd. dirs., 1973—; mem. Bloomfield Human Relations Commn., 1973-75; mem. Bloomfield Town Democratic Com., 1976—; corporator Hartford Pub. Library, 1976—. Served to lt. (j.g.), USNR, 1960-63. Mem. Am., Conn., Hartford County bar assns. Club: Hartford. Home: 59 Prospect St Bloomfield CT 06002 Office: Shipman and Goodwin 799 Main St Hartford CT 06103

SPACHNER, SHELDON ARTHUR, metal forming process and systems devel. exec.; b. Chgo., Mar. 28, 1924; s. Arthur and Sadie S.; student U. Pa., 1943-44; B.S. in Physics, Northwestern U., 1948, M.S. in Physics, 1949; postgrad. in Physics and Metallurgy, U. Md., 1949-53; Ph.D. in Metall. Engring., Ill. Inst. Tech., 1957; m. Ruth J. Kraus, Oct. 24, 1959; 1 dau., Carol Jo. Sr. scientist Ill. Inst. Tech. Research Inst., Chgo., 1953-65; project engr. LTV Aerospace Corp., Dallas, 1965; head applications research group Curtiss-Wright Corp., Woodridge, N.J., 1965-66; sr. scientist RCA, Harrison, N.J., 1966-67; prin. scientist, asst. chief engr. Gulf & Western Advance Devel. & Engring. Center, Swarthmore, Pa., 1967—. Served with U.S. Army, 1942-45; ETO. Mem. Am. Soc. Metals (adv. tech. awareness council), ASTM, Soc. Mfg. Engrs. Contbr. articles on research and devel. mgmt., metalforming machinery, metalforming processes to profl. jours. Home: 400 Glendale Rd Apt G-168 Havertown PA 19083 Office: 101 Chester Rd Swarthmore PA 19081

SPADA, RICHARD, real estate broker, developer; b. S.I., N.Y., Nov. 10, 1946; s. Joseph and Mary (Ruberto) S.; student Wagner Coll., 1965-66, N.Y. U., 1967-68; grad. Realtor Inst. Pres. Spada Realty Corp., S.I., 1968—, Spada Constrn. Corp., 1974—; real estate broker S.I., 1971—; lectr. in field. Exec. com. S.I. Bd. Realtors, 1972-77, chmn. edn. com., 1975-76. Mem. Nat., Pa. State assns. realtors, Nat. Inst. Real Estate Brokers, Pocono Mountain Bd. Realtors, Pocono Mountain C. of C., Aircraft Owners and Pilots Assn. Club: Kiwanis (pres. S. Shore 1976-77). Home: PO Box 1452 East Stroudsburg PA 18301 Office: 43 N 7th St East Stroudsburg PA 18360

SPADAFORA, ANTHONY JOSEPH, elec. engr.; b. Phila., Aug. 26, 1942; s. Frank Matthew and Olga Rita S.; B.S. in E.E., Drexel U., 1965; m. Patricia A. Montone, July 24, 1965; 1 dau., Gina Marie. Asst. project engr. Bendix Corp., Towson, Md., 1965-68; sr. tech. staff mem. Bunker Ramo Corp., Silver Spring, Md., 1968-70; tech. asst. to v.p. engring. Frederick (Md.) Electronics, 1970-74; mgr. software engring. Siemens Corp., Cherry Hill, N.J., 1974—. Mem. Assn. Computing Machinery, Am. Mgmt. Assn. Republican. Roman Catholic. Club: K.C. Office: 18 Olney Ave Cherry Hill NJ 08034

SPAGNOLA, THOMAS ANTHONY, pharmacist; b. Camden, N.J., Aug. 24, 1938; s. Thomas Joseph and Josephine (Nocito) S.; B.S. in Pharmacy, Fordham U., 1961; m. Joanne Marini, June 29, 1963; children—Amy Alison, Adam Thomas. Mem. pharm. staff Cooper Med. Center, Camden, 1961—, asst. dir. pharmacy, 1968-73, dir. pharm. services, 1973—; adj. clin. instr. Temple U. Coll. Pharmacy, Phila.; cons. in field; mem. Mt. Laurel (N.J.) Bd. Health, 1968-72; mem. task force inflation N.J. Dept. Health, 1973-74. Mem. S. Jersey Instl. Pharmacists Assn. (pres. 1973-74), N.J. Soc. Hosp. Pharmacists (chpt. pres. 1977-78, state pres. elect 1978-79, membership chmn. 1976-77), Am. Soc. Hosp. Pharmacists, Am. Pharm. Assn. Roman Catholic. Home: 536 Perry Dr Mount Laurel NJ 08054 Office: Cooper Med Center 6th and Stevens Sts Camden NJ 08103

SPAGNUOLO, MARIO, physician; b. Naples, Italy, Apr. 14, 1930; s. Vincent and Giulia (Ronca) S.; came to U.S., 1948, naturalized, 1962; diploma Liceo Colletta, 1949; student Boston U., 1949-50; M.D., U. Naples, 1956; m. Kathryn Birchall, July 10, 1962; children—Mario, Sandra, Peter, Eugene. Intern, St. Clare's Hosp., N.Y.C., 1957-58; resident Irvington House, N.Y.C., 1958-60, fellow, 1960-61, clin. dir., 1963-71; asst. attending in medicine Bellevue Hosp., N.Y.C., Univ. Hosp., N.Y.C.; instr. medicine N.Y. U. Med. Sch., 1961-65; dir. Juvenile Rheumatoid Arthritis Clinic, Bellevue Hosp.; asst. prof. medicine, 1965—. Diplomate Am. Bd. Internal Medicine. Fellow A.C.P.; mem. Asso. Cardiac Leagues N.Y. (mem. med. adv. bd. 1966—), N.Y. Acad. Sci., Am. Fedn. Clin. Research. Contbr. papers on rheumatic fever, rheumatic heart disease, rheumatic diseases, and hosp. care to profl. lit. Home: 60 Amherst Dr Hastings-on-Hudson NY 10706 Office: 45 Ludlow St Yonkers NY 10705

SPAHN, MARY ATTEA, educator; b. Buffalo, July 16, 1929; d. George H. and Madeline Barbara (Bitar) Attea; student Nazareth Coll. at Kalamazoo, 1947; A.B., Nazareth Coll. at Rochester, N.Y., 1950; Ed.M., State U. N.Y. at Buffalo, 1952, Ed.D., 1966. Tchr., Clarence Central Schs., Clarence, N.Y., 1951-65; reading tchr. Sweet Home Central Schs., Amherst, N.Y., 1965-68; asso. prof. elementary edn. D'Youville Coll., Buffalo, 1968-70; prof. State U. Coll. N.Y., Buffalo, 1970—; coordinator Sweet Home secondary sch. summer reading program, 1968-70; cons. to Niagara Wheatfield, Clarence Central, Sweet Home schs. Mem. NEA, Internat. (pres. 1968 Niagara Frontier council), N.Y. State (sec. 1970) reading assns., Am. Ednl. Research Assn., United Univ. Profs., Nat. Council Tchrs. English. Author: Turning Children on Through Creative Writing, 1973; (poetry) Weep Willow Weep, 1974; Busy Bodies, 1975; contbr. articles to profl. jours. Home: 58 Buffalo Rd East Aurora NY 14052 Office: 1300 Elmwood Ave Buffalo NY 14222

SPALDING, HARLAN JOSEPH, dental technician; b. Somerville, Mass., Oct. 6, 1924; s. William Frederick and Henrietta Frances (Dow) S.; grad. U.S. Coast Guard Radar Operators Sch., 1943, U.S. Army Med. Field Service Sch., 1949; m. Carol Greenlaw, Dec. 11, 1948; children—Alan, Gail, Beverlie, Donna. Enlisted in U.S. Army, 1948, ret., 1965; chief dental lab. technician Haverhill (Mass.) Lab., 1965-68; owner Spalding Dental Lab., Nashua, N.H., 1968—. Served with USCG, 1942-46. Decorated Navy Commendation medal, Combat med. badge. Certified Dental Technician, N.H. Mem. Nat. Assn. Dental Labs., Dental Lab. Assn. N.H., Am. Automobile Assn., Officers Benefit Assn., VFW, Non-Commd. Officers Assn. Democrat. Home: 13 Greenlay St Nashua NH 03060 Office: 92 Main St Nashua NH 03060

SPALLINO, ANTHONY, funeral dir.; b. N.Y.C., Mar. 13, 1910; s. Guiseppe L. and Lucia (Failla) S.; grad. high sch. Owner, operator Paradise Flower Shop, Niagara Falls, N.Y., 1930-66; partner Spallino Funeral Home, Niagara Falls, 1935—, Spallino Devel. Co., 1950—, Waldorf Niagara Motor Lodge, 1959—. Mem. Niagara Falls Housing Authority, 1955—, chmn., 1959-60. Mem. Am. Funeral Dirs. Assn., N.Y. State, Erie-Niagara funeral dirs., Nat. Assn. Housing and Renewal Assn., Christopher Columbus Soc., Niagara Falls Hist. Soc. Republican. Roman Catholic. Home: 562 15th St Niagara Falls NY 14301 Office: 1300 Pine Ave Niagara Falls NY 14301

SPANGENBERGER, JOSEPH GEORGE, real estate broker; b. Newark, June 30, 1933; s. George Joseph and Gertrude A. (Farrell) S.; B.A., Rutgers U., 1955; M.B.A., N.Y. U., 1961; m. Mary Jacqmein, Sept. 14, 1957; children—Susan, Joseph, Kathryn, Elizabeth. Systems analyst Babcock & Wilcox, N.Y.C., 1957-59; retail rep., merchandising rep., real estate rep., regional real estate rep. Shell Oil Co., Newark, 1960-67; real estate rep., Tenafly, N.J., 1967-69; pvt. practice as real estate broker, Cresskill, N.J., 1970—. Mem. Cresskill Bd. Edn., 1967-73; chmn. Cresskill Heart Fund, 1971; mem. N.J. Cultural Council, 1976—; bd. dirs. Cresskill-Alpine Little League, 1970—, N.J. Symphony, 1965-70. Served with Signal Corps, AUS, 1955-57. Mem. Eastern Bergen County (sec. 1972-73), N.E. Bergen (sec. 1974-75, top selling awards 1975, 76, 77) multiple listing assns., Eastern Bergen County Bd. Realtors, Chi Psi. Roman Catholic. Clubs: Elks, Rotary (v.p. Cresskill-Demarest 1970-78). Home: Lambs Ln Cresskill NJ 07626 Office: 31 Union Ave Cresskill NJ 07626

SPANGLER, ELWYN FISHER, music educator, organist; b. Fredericksburg, Pa., Jan. 6, 1933; s. Lester and Edna Elizabeth (Fisher) S.; B.S., Lebanon Valley Coll., 1954; M.A., Columbia U., 1958, profl. diploma, 1968, Ed.D., 1977. Vocal music dir. Lebanon (Pa.) High Sch., 1964-71; sabbatical instr. Queens Coll., City U. N.Y., 1971-72; dir. vocal music Tenafly (N.J.) High Sch., 1978—; organist-dir. 2d Ref. Ch., Hackensack, N.J.; dir. Lebanon County Choral Soc., 1964-71. Former pres. Lebanon County Community Concert Assn. Served with AUS, 1954-56. Mem. Am. Guild Organists, Am. Choral Dirs. Assn., Assn. Choral Conductors, NEA, Music Educators Nat. Conf., Phi Mu Alpha Sinfonia, Kappa Delta Pi, Phi Delta Kappa. Home: 1 Sherman Sq 29A New York City NY 10023

SPANGLER, RONALD LEROY, television producer, aviation co. exec.; b. York, Pa., Mar. 5, 1937; s. Ivan L. and Sevilla (Senft) S.; student U. Miami (Fla.), 1955-59; children—Kathleen, Ronald, Beth Anne. Radio announcer Sta. WSBA, York, 1955-57; television producer-dir. Sta. WBAL-TV, Balt., 1959-65; pres., chmn. bd. LewRon TV, N.Y.C., 1965-74, Spanair Inc., Forest Hill, Md., 1974—; pres. Performance Machines Inc., Forest Hill. Winner 1st place sales awards Rockwell Bus. Aircraft, 1976, 77, 78. Mem. Video Tape Producers Assn. N.Y., Ferrari Club Am. Home: 2305 Warfield Dr Forest Hill MD 21050 Office: Forest Hill Indsl Airpark Forest Hill MD 21050

SPANOVICH, MILAN, civil engr.; b. Steubenville, Ohio, Feb. 19, 1929; s. Stanley and Katherine (Komazec) S.; B.S. in Civil Engring., Carnegie-Mellon U., 1956, M.S., 1957; m. Sylvia J. Tomko, Apr. 16, 1971. Instr., Carnegie-Mellon U., 1957-60; charter asso. E. D'Appolonia Assos., cons. engrs., Pitts., 1957-61; staff U. N.Mex., 1961-63; founder Engring. Mechanics, Inc., 1963, prin. engr., 1963—; Mem. founds. adv. com. Pitts. Bd. Standards and Appeals, 1968—. Recipient Pitts. Young Civil Engr. of Yr. award, 1969; registered profl. engr., Pa., N.Y., Ohio, Va., Fla., W.Va., Mich., N.Mex., Ky., Md., Colo., Del., N.J. Fellow ASCE (chmn. Pitts. bldg. code com. 1968—), Am. Cons. Engrs. Council; mem. Cons. Engrs. Council Greater Pitts. (pres. 1972-74), Engrs. Soc. Western Pa. (dir. 1971-73, 1978—), Nat., Pa. (chmn. ethics and practice com. 1963-67, chmn. legis. com. 1973-74, pres. Pitts. chpt. 1975-76) socs. profl. engrs., ASTM (chmn. task com. on relative density of granular soils 1959-63), Constrn. Specifications Inst., Am. Concrete Inst., Hwy. Research Bd., Internat. Soc. Soil Mechanics and Found. Engring., Pitts. Geol. Soc., Am. Arbitration Assn., Profl. Engrs. in Pvt. Practice (chmn. 1970-71), Soc. Explosives Engrs. Contbr. articles on soil mechanics to tech. jours.; patentee found. systems. Home: 216 Eton Rd Pittsburgh PA 15205 Office: 4636 Campbells Run Rd Pittsburgh PA 15205

SPAR, JEROME, meteorologist; b. N.Y.C., Oct. 7, 1918; s. Nathan and Celia (Meltzer) S.; B.S., Coll. City N.Y., 1940; M.S., N.Y. U., 1943, Ph.D., 1950; m. Frances Fernbach, Apr. 5, 1945; children—Susan, Richard. Instr. N.Y. U., 1946-50, asst. prof. meteorology, 1950-57, asso. prof., 1957-63, prof., 1963-73; dir. research U.S. Weather Bur., Washington, 1964-65; prof. meteorology dept. earth and planetary scis. Coll. City N.Y., 1973—. Served with weather service U.S. Army, 1942-46. Fellow Am. Meterol. Soc.; mem. Am. Geophys. Union, Royal Meteorol. Soc., AAAS. Author: The Way of the Weather, 1957; Earth, Sea, and Air, 1962. Home: 18 Fieldmere Ave Glen Rock NJ 07452 Office: City U NY Dept Earth and Planetary Scis Convent Ave at 138th St New York City NY 10031

SPARACINO, ROBERT RUDOLPH, bus. machines mfg. co. exec.; b. N.Y.C., Nov. 6, 1927; s. Philip and Mary (Valenza) S.; B.E.E., Coll. City N.Y., 1950; M.E.E., Bklyn. Poly. Inst., 1955; Sc.D., Mass. Inst. Tech., 1961; m. Marguerite Riff, Oct. 1, 1949; children—Jack, Michael, Paul. Project engr. Atlantic Electronics Corp., Port Washington, N.Y., 1950-54; chief engr., asst. sec. Penn-East Engring. Corp., Kutztown, Pa., 1954-58; research asst. Mass. Inst. Tech., Cambridge, 1958-59, 60-61; sect. head AC Electronics div. Gen. Motors Corp., Wakefield, Mass., 1961-62, lab. dir., 1962-63, dir. research and devel., Los Angeles, 1963-64, dir. research and devel., Milw., 1964-68, dir. engring., 1968-70; v.p., mgr. quality assurance dept. Bus. Products group Xerox Corp., Rochester, N.Y., 1970-71, v.p., mgr. product design and engring., 1971-73, v.p. tech. and engring., 1973—, sr. v.p. copier and duplicates devel. div., 1973-75, pres. Info. Tech. Group, 1975—. Served with AUS, 1946-47. Registered profl. engr., Pa. Mem. Am. Soc. for Quality Control, IEEE, Sigma Xi. Unitarian. Home: 7 Hickory Ln Rochester NY 14625 Office: Xerox Corp 800 Phillips Rd Webster NY 14603

SPARANO, VINCENT THOMAS, editor, writer; b. Newark, Apr. 7, 1934; s. Gaetano and Agnes (Martucci) S.; student Newark Coll. Engring., 1952-54; B.S., N.Y. U., 1959, postgrad., 1960; m. Elizabeth Frances Rooney, Nov. 21, 1959; children—Donna Marie, Michael Thomas, Matthew John, Ellen Elizabeth. Reporter, advt. dir. West Orange (N.J.) Tribune, 1958-59; asso. editor Sports Afield Mag., N.Y.C., 1959-60; sr. editor Outdoor Life mag., N.Y.C., 1960—; author columns Where-To-Go and Outdoor Life Field Guide; author: Outdoors Ency. (outstanding reference book 1973), 1972; The American Fisherman's Fresh and Salt Water Guide, 1976; free-lance mag. writer; editor and cons. to book pubs.; cons. to industry on devel. of outdoor sports equipment. Outdoor committeeman Fairfield Dist. council Boy Scouts Am., 1970—; mem. Mayor's Adv. Bd., Fairfield, 1972-73; trustee Camp Wyanokie Commn., Fairfield, 1976—. Served with AUS, 1954-56; ETO. Mem. Outdoor Writers Assn. Am. (sec.), Rod and Gun Editors Assn. Met. N.Y. (pres.), Nat. Rifle Assn. Sigma Delta Chi, Theta Chi. Roman Catholic. Clubs: Fairfield Sportsmen & Conservation Assn., Elks, K.C. Home: 17 Henning Dr Fairfield NJ 07006 Office: 380 Madison Ave New York City NY 10017

SPARKES, THOMAS, med. microbiologist, educator; b. Cambridge, Mass., June 2, 1918; s. Henry and Lillian M. (Mahoney) S.; B.S., Tufts U., 1941; M.S., U. Mass., 1943; m. Laurel E. Wheelock, June 5, 1942; children—Janet Sparkes Egbert, Judith Sparkes Cucinotta. Teaching fellow U. Mass., 1941-43; bacteriologist, Joseph E. Seagram & Sons, Lawrenceburg, Ind., 1943-45; bacteriologist/analytical chemist Swift & Co., Cambridge, Mass., 1945-50; commd. 1st lt. U.S. Army, 1950, advanced through grades to col., 1969; microbiologist Clin. Lab., cons. Surgeon Gen. European Command, W. Ger., 1965-68, Eastern U.S., Fort Meade, Md., 1968-70, ret. 1970; tchr. Severna Park (Md.) Bd. Edn., 1970-78; asst. prof. U. Maine, Augusta, 1978—; cons. in field. Decorated Legion of Merit; recipient A prefix Surgeon Gen.'s Office. Registered specialist microbiologist Am. Acad. Microbiology. Republican. Clubs: Ft. Meade Officer's, Masons (32 deg.). Home: Pleasant Point Cushing ME 04563 Office: Dept Sci Univ Maine Augusta ME 04330

SPATARO, FRANCIS CAJETAN, guild adminstr.; b. N.Y.C., Feb. 5, 1936; s. Francis Anthony and Gilda Teresa (de Simone) S.; B.A., L.I. U., 1959; M.A., N.Y. U., 1971; Licentiate in Religion, People's U. Americas, 1976; m. Bokeeta T. Craft, Aug. 1, 1968; children—Francesca, Peter. Tchr. ind. acads., pub. schs., N.Y. State, 1962-76; pres. Vilatte Guild, Bellerose, N.Y., 1976—; mem. staff Star of West, also Bahai Reporter mags., 1976—. Mem. pub. relations com. Nat. House of Justice U.S. and Can., 1976—. Served with AUS, 1959-62. Mem. N.J. Poetry Soc. Democrat. Home: 86-11 Commonwealth Blvd Bellerose NY 11426 Office: PO Box 431 South Orange NJ 07079

SPATARO, OLIMPIA, chemist, educator; b. N.Y.C., Dec. 3, 1933; d. John and Rebeca Varela; B.A., Hunter Coll., 1958; M.S. in Biology, Adelphi U., 1972, M.S. in Chemistry, 1973; postgrad. biology N.Y. U., 1975—; m. Joseph J. Spataro, Apr. 5, 1953; children—Joseph David, Linda, Diana, Cristina. Tchr. chemistry, phys. and biol. scis. N.Y.C. Bd. Edn., 1958—; clin. asso. Tchrs. Coll., Columbia U., N.Y.C., 1976—. Mem. NEA. Home: 2412 Kingsland Ave New York City NY 10469 Office: Evander Childs High School 800 E Gun Hill Rd New York City NY 10467

SPAULDING, DOROTHY C. (MRS. JAMES E. SPAULDING), state ofcl.; b. Hermansville, Miss., Aug. 10, 1910; d. William L. and Dora (Anderson) Coleman; A.B., Hunter Coll., 1931; M.A., Columbia U., 1934; LL.B., Bklyn. Law Sch., 1936; m. James E. Spaulding, Nov. 29, 1935. Employment sec. Bklyn. YWCA, 1931-35; with div. employment N.Y. State Dept. Labor, 1935—, sr. unemployment ins. mgr., 1951—, temporary unemployment ins. supt., 1955-59, unemployment ins. supt., 1962—; treas., dir. Azurest, Inc., 1954-68; supt. in charge Youth Services, N.Y.C., 1965-71; dir. manpower and community services, N.Y.C., 1967-70; mgmt. cons., 1970—. Pres., bd. dirs. Bklyn. Lung Assn.; trustee, v.p. bd. Bklyn. YWCA, 1922—; sec. adminstrv. com. Fedn. Protestant Welfare Agys. City N.Y., 1958-59, chmn. youth services com., del.; v.p. Interreligious Found. for

Community Orgn.; former chmn. nat. personnel and employee relations com., former nat. bd. dirs. YWCA; trustee Retirement Fund YWCA U.S.A.; mem. bd., counsel Coalition 100 Black Women; mem. personnel com. Vis. Nurses Assn. N.Y.C., U.S.O. Recipient Brotherhood award N.Y. State Civil Service Employees Joint Com., 1959; Achievement award Alpha Kappa Alpha, 1955; Merit award N.Y. chpt. Internat. Assn. Personnel in Employment Security, 1967; mem. Hunter Coll. Hall of Fame. Mem. Bklyn. Bar Assn., Bus. and Profl. Women's Club, Assn. Women Lawyers, Bklyn. L.I. Lawyers Assn., Met. Rose Soc. (sec. 1956-58), NAACP, Urban League, Am. Mgmt. Assn., YWCA (life), Alpha Kappa Alpha (life), Alpha Chi Alpha. Congregationalist (trustee). Home: 21 Saint James Pl Brooklyn NY 11205

SPAULDING, WILLIAM ROWE, banker; b. Cambridge, Mass., Nov. 26, 1915; s. William Rowe and Jennie Jane (Gillam) S.; B.S., U. N.H., 1938; M.B.A., Harvard U., 1940; m. Gertrude Ellen Mowry, June 7, 1947; children—Edward Albert, William Mathews. Trader, Kidder Peabody & Co., N.Y.C., 1940-41; asst. exec. v.p. Mut. Savs. Central Fund, Inc., Boston, 1946-58; v.p. Vance Sanders & Co., Boston, 1959-63; trustee Century Shares Trust, Boston, 1963-71, chmn., 1969-71; pres., chmn. Wakefield Savs. Bank (Mass.), 1971—; dir. Fidelity Group of Mut. Funds, Boston, Savs. Banks Investment Fund; trustee Savs. Banks Employees Retirement Assn., Gen. Ins. Guaranty Fund; v.p., dir. Mut. Savs. Central Fund, Inc. Chmn. bd. trustees Wakefield YMCA, 1976; trustee Melrose Wakefield Hosp., 1973; fin. v.p. Citizens Scholarship Found. Wakefield, 1963. Served with AUS, 1942-45, to lt. col. Mass. N.G., 1946-62. Decorated Bronze Star; Croix de Guerre (Belgium). Mem. pres.'s council U. N.H. Mem. Fin. Analysts Fedn. Congregationalist. Club: Union of Boston. Home: 35 Outlook Rd Wakefield MA 01880 Office: 357 Main St Wakefield MA 01880

SPEAR, ROBERT JOSEPH, info. systems mgr. and cons.; b. Chgo., Oct. 8, 1945; s. Edward William and Idamae (Obermeier) S.; B.A. cum laude, U. Notre Dame, 1967; M.S. in Fgn. Service, Georgetown U., 1970; m. Mary Helen Carol Gloss, Sept. 8, 1967; children—Eric Anthony, Timothy Michael. Tchr., Washington Pub. Schs., 1968; mgmt. intern Dept. of Navy, 1968; mgmt. info. systems specialist Naval Ordnance Systems Command, 1969-73, computer systems analyst, 1973-74; digital data systems adminstr. Naval Sea Systems Command, 1974-75; tech. dir., primary legal rep. McLaughlin Enterprises, Ltd., Tehran, 1975-76; v.p., tech. dir. McLaughlin Research Corp., Alexandria, Va., 1976—. Mem. long range planning com. Greenbelt Homes, Inc., 1974-77, mem. nominations and elections com., 1977—. Recipient certificate of accomplishment Naval Ordnance Systems Command, 1969, certificate of commednation, 1970, certificate of appreciation, 1974. Mem. Soc. Logistics Engrs. Democrat. Roman Catholic. Home: 1A Ridge Rd Greenbelt MD 20770 Office: 5200 Eisenhower Ave Alexandria VA 22304

SPEARS, LEON NAVARRO, JR., ins. agt.; b. New Orleans, Sept. 28, 1947; s. Leon Navarro and Estelle (Adams) S.; student Kingsborough Coll., 1965-68, Pace Coll., 1968-72, now Coll. Fin. Planning; m. Myschelle Grant, Oct. 25, 1970; children—Leon Navarro III, Seth. Instr. photography, basketball coach Miccio Police Athletic League Center, Bklyn., 1965-68; econ. devel. specialist, neighborhood youth corps dir. S. Bklyn. Community Corp., 1967-74; sales rep. Met. Life Ins. Co., Flushing, N.Y., 1974—. Local elder Manor Road Seventh-Day Adventist Ch. Recipient Service award Bklyn. Bd. Sports United Boro-wide Ofcls. Assn., 1977; Nat. Sales Achievement award Nat. Assn. Life Underwriters, 1976. Mem. Am. Mgmt. Assn., Am. Accounting Assn., Nat. Assn. Life Underwriters, Collegiate Basketball Ofcls. Assn., Internat. Assn. Approved Basketball Ofcls., Sports United Boro-Wide Ofcls. Assn. (pres.). Home: 88 Snug Harbor Rd Apt 2 Richmond NY 10310 Office: 136-56 39th Ave Flushing NY 11354

SPEARS, ROBERT RAE, JR., bishop; b. Rochester, N.Y., June 18, 1918; s. Robert Rae and Phebe (Wing) S.; A.B., Hobart Coll., 1940, D.D. (hon.), 1969; S.T.B., Gen. Theol. Sem., N.Y.C., 1943, S.T.D. (hon.), 1967; m. Charlotte Lee Luttrell, June 16, 1947; children—Robt. Rae III, Deborah Wing, Gregory Luttrell. Ordained priest Episcopal Ch., 1944; curate in Olean, N.Y., 1943-44; rector in Mayville, N.Y., 1944-48; canon St. Paul's Cathdral, Buffalo, 1948-50; rector in Auburn, N.Y., 1950-54; vicar Chapel of the Intercession, N.Y.C., 1954-60; rector Trinity Ch., Princeton, N.J., 1960-67; suffragan bishop Diocese West Mo., 1967-70; bishop of Rochester (N.Y.), 1970—. Pres. Met. Interch. Agy., Kansas City, Mo., 1968. Trustee Gen. Theol. Sem., 1955-75, Hobart Coll., 1970—, Bexley Hall Sem., 1975—. Home: 40 Douglas Rd Rochester NY 14610 Office: Episcopal Diocese of Rochester 935 East Ave Rochester NY 14607

SPEAS, ROBERT DIXON, aviation cons.; b. Davie Co., N.C. Apr. 14, 1916; s. William Paul and Nora Estelle (Dixon) S.; B.S., Mass. Inst. Tech., 1940; grad. Boeing Sch. Aero., 1938; m. Manette Lansing Hollingsworth, Mar. 4, 1944; children—Robert Dixon, Jay Hollingsworth. Aviation reporter Winston Salem Jour., 1934; sales rep. Trans World Airlines, 1937-38; engr. Am. Airlines, 1940-44, asst. to v.p., 1944-47, dir. maintenance and engring., cargo div., 1947-48, spl. asst. to pres., 1948-50; U.S. rep. A.V. Roe Can., Ltd., 1950-51; chmn. bd., pres. R. Dixon Speas Assos., Inc., aviation cons., 1951-76; chmn. bd., chief exec. officer Speas-Harris Airport Devel., Inc., 1974-76; chmn. bd., pres. Aviation Cons. Inc., 1976—. Mem. governing bd. Flight Safety Found., 1958-66, 78—; mem. council C.W. Post Coll., L.I. U., 1970-71; trustee Acad. Aeros., 1970—; bd. dirs. L.I. Assn. Commerce and Industry, 1969—. Awarded 1st award Ann. Nat. Boeing Thesis Competition, 1937; research award, Am. Air Transport Assn., 1942. Fellow Am. Inst. Aeros. and Astronautics (treas. 1963-64, council 1963-64, finance com. 1963-69); asso. fellow Royal Aero. Soc.; mem. Soc. Automotive Engrs. (v.p. 1955, mem. council 1964-66), Inst. Aero. Scis. (past treas.; council 1959-62, exec. com. 1962), Nat. Acad. Engring. (mem. alternate aircraft fuels com.), Manhasset C. of C. (pres. 1962), ASME. Club: Wings (v.p. 1959-60, 63-64, 67-68, council 1966, pres. 1968-69, dir. 1973-76, 77—). Author: Airplane Performance and Operations, 1945; Pilots' Technical Manual, 1946; Airline Operation, 1949; Technical Aspects of Air Transport Management, 1955. Home: 591 Park Ave Manhasset NY 11030 Office: 58 Hillside Ave Manhasset NY 11030

SPECHT, CARL, JR., wallcover mfg. co. exec.; b. Newark, July 8, 1949; s. Carl and Ann (Graham) S.; B.A. in Accounting, Bloomfield Coll., 1971; m. Teresa M. Piszczatowski, Aug. 19, 1972. Staff acct. Price Waterhouse & Co., Newark, 1971-74, sr. acct., 1974-75; sr. internal auditor Foster Wheeler Energy Corp., Livingston, N.J., 1975-76; mgr. gen. acctg. The Pantasote Co. of N.Y., 1977-78; controller Panta Astor, S. Kearny, N.J., 1978—. Served with U.S. A.R., 1970-76. C.P.A., N.Y., N.J. Mem. Am. Inst. C.P.A.'s, N.J. Soc. C.P.A.'s.; Nat. Assn. Accountants, Am. Inst. Corporate Controllers. Home: 2 Archibald Terr Kearny NJ 07032 Office: 85 Lincoln Hwy South Kearny NJ 07032

SPECK, ROBERT HURSEY, ret. naval officer, cons.; b. Oskaloosa, Iowa, Nov. 22, 1906; s. Harris Bert and Mildred (Redfern) S.; B.S., U.S. Naval Acad., 1927; student ordnance engring. U.S. Naval Postgrad. Sch., 1934-37; grad. Naval War Coll., 1949; m. Martha Blanchard Brackett, June 4, 1936; 1 son, Robert Hursey. Commd. ensign U.S. Navy, 1927, advanced through grades to rear adm., 1956; various assignments sea duty, 1927-59; chmn. ship characteristics bd. Navy Dept., 1959-61; comdr. Cruiser-Destroyer Force, Atlantic Fleet, 1961-63; chief Mil. Assistance Advisory Group, Netherlands, 1963-65, comdt. 4th Naval Dist., 1965-68, ret., 1968; cons.; gov. U.S. Naval Home, 1970-74. Pres. Independence Hall Assn.; nat. trustee Freedom Found. at Valley Forge. Decorated Bronze Star with combat V (2), Legion of Merit; comdr. Order of Merit (Italy). Clubs: N.Y. Yacht; Union League (chmn. com. boys work 1973-76), Merion Cricket (Phila.); Army-Navy (Washington); Army-Navy Country (Alexandria, Va.). Home: 132 Adrienne Ln Penn Valley Wynnewood PA 19096

SPECTOR, ARTHUR ROBERT, banker; b. Phila., Oct. 8, 1940; s. Irvin Edward and Beatrice Ruth (Actman) S.; B.S. with honors, Wharton Sch., U. Pa., 1962; J.D., magna cum laude, U. Pa., 1965; m. Miriam Anne Siegel, June 9, 1965; children—Adam Benjamin, Jeremy David. Admitted to Calif. bar, 1966, Pa. bar, 1968; partner firm Spector, Cohen, Hunt & Rosen, Phila., 1974—; chmn. bd. State Nat. Bank, Rockville, Md., 1975—. Chmn. Phila. Friends of Boys Town, Jerusalem; trustee Phila. Friends Hebrew U. Office: 11616 Rockville Pike Rockville MD 20852

SPECTOR, HENRY THEODORE, physician; b. N.Y.C., Aug. 25, 1933; s. Nathan Bernard and Betty Gertrude (Trieff) S.; B.S., Coll. City N.Y., 1955; M.D., Albert Einstein Coll. Medicine, 1959; m. Ann Deborah Masarof, Dec. 25, 1955; children—Elizabeth, Peter Salem. Intern, Boston City Hosp., 1959; resident in internal medicine Bronx VA Hosp., 1960-62, Montefiore Hosp., Bronx, 1964; surgeon USPHS, 1962-64; clin. instr. Tufts U. Sch. Medicine, Medford, Mass., 1962-64, Albert Einstein Coll., 1965-72; asst. clin. prof. medicine N.Y. Med. Coll., Valhalla, 1972—; practice medicine specializing in internal medicine and nephrology, White Plains, N.Y., 1965—; mem. staff White Plains Hosp.; mem. N.Y. Peer Rev. long term care com., 1977—; mem. health adv. bd. Richard Ottinger, White Plains, 1977—. Mem. Am., Internat. socs. nephrology, Westchester Acad. Medicine, Westchester County Med. Soc. Democrat. Jewish. Office: 56 Doyer Ave White Plains NY 10605

SPECTOR, JOHANNA LICHTENBERG (MRS. ROBERT SPECTOR), educator; b. Libau, Latvia; d. Jacob C. and Anna (Meyer) Lichtenberg; came to US., 1947, naturalized, 1954; D.H.L. Hebrew Union Coll., 1950; M.A., Columbia, 1960; m. Robert Spector, Nov. 20, 1939 (dec. 1941). Research fellow Hebrew U., Jerusalem, Israel, 1951-53; faculty Jewish Theol. Sem. Am., 1954—, dir., founder dept. ethnomusicology, 1962—, asso. prof. musicology, 1966-70, sem. prof., 1970—. Mem. Am. Anthrop. Assn., Soc. for Applied Anthropology, Am. Musicological Soc., Internat. Folk Music Council, World Union Jewish Studies, Asian (v.p. 1964—, acting pres. 1973, pres. 1974), African mus. socs., Soc. for Ethnomusicology (sec.-treas. N.Y. chpt. 1960-64), Soc. Preservation of Samaritan Culture (founder). Research in field. Author: Ghetto-und KZLieder, 1947; Samaritan Chant, 1965; Musical Tradition and Innovation in Central Asia, 1966; Bridal Songs from Sana Yemen, 1960; (documentary films) The Samaritans, 1971; Middle Eastern Music, 1973; About the Jews of India, 1976. Editorial bd. Asian Music. Contbr. articles to encys., various jours. Home: 400 W 119th St New York City NY 10027

SPEER, DAVID STOCKTON, surgeon; b. N.Y.C., Apr. 5, 1916; s. Arthur Robins and Mary Wilda (Powe) S.; A.B., Princeton U., 1938; M.D., Harvard U., 1943; m. Dorothy Ann Tippett, Feb. 26, 1955; children—David Tippett, Richard Stockton. Intern, N.Y. Hosp., N.Y.C., 1943-44, asst. resident, 1947-50, resident in surgery, 1950-51; practice medicine specializing in surgery, N.Y.C., 1951—; asst. attending surgeon, asst. prof. surgery Cornell U. Med. Sch., N.Y.C., 1970—; attending surgeon Doctors Hosp., N.Y.C. Served to capt. M.C., U.S. Army, 1944-46. Diplomate Am. Bd. Surgery. Mem. A.C.S., N.Y. State, New York County med. socs., AMA, Pan Am. Med. Assn., Am. Geriatric Soc., N.Y. Acad. Medicine. Republican. Presbyterian. Clubs: Racquet and Tennis, Englewood Field; Knickerbocker Country (Tenafly, N.J.). Home: 1530 Palisade Ave Fort Lee NJ 07024 Office: 430 E 63d St New York City NY 10021

SPEER, EDGAR B., steel co. exec.; b. Pitts., July 28, 1916; s. Edgar B. and Gladys (Kelly) S.; student U. Pa., also Harvard U. Bus. Sch.; m. Arlene R. Kline, Apr. 8, 1946; children—Edgar B. III, John Michael, Stephen Fox, Tony Scott. With U.S. Steel Corp., 1938—, gen. supt. Fairless works, 1955-58, became gen. mgr. steel ops., Pitts., 1958, adminstrv. v.p. central ops., 1959, adminstrv. v.p. steel ops., exec. v.p., pres., 1968-73, chmn. bd., chief exec. officer, 1973—, also dir.; dir. AT&T, Procter & Gamble. Bd. overseers U. Pa.; trustee Widener Coll., Waynesburg Coll. Mem. Am., Internat. iron and steel insts., Am. Iron and Steel Engrs., Bus. Council, Bus. Roundtable, Harvard Bus. Assn., Phi Gamma Delta. Home: Edgewood Rd Pittsburgh PA 15215 Office: 600 Grant St Pittsburgh PA 15230

SPEER, RAYMOND DANIEL, mktg. cons.; b. Edmonton, Alta., Can., Feb. 11, 1941; s. Murray Clifford and Helen Marie (Leroy) S.; B.Sc. in Elec. Engring. with distinction, U. Alta., 1967; m. Marilyn Anne Matthiessen, Dec. 27, 1962. Transmission engr. Alta. Govt. Telephones, Edmonton, 1967; applications engr. C.P. Clare Co., Chgo., 1967-68; mng. editor Electronic Design Mag., N.Y.C., 1968-72; pres. Speer Research Corp., N.Y.C., 1972—; lectr. in field. Mem. IEEE, Am. Mktg. Assn., Assn. Profl. Engrs. Alta. Roman Catholic. Club: N.Y. Athletic. Home: 230 E 79th St #19A New York City NY 10021 Office: 488 Madison Ave New York City NY 10022

SPEERS, JERROLD BOND, lawyer, state ofcl.; b. Cambridge, Mass., June 5, 1941; s. Ronald Thomas and Shirley Helen (Bond) S.; B.A., Colby Coll., 1963; LL.B., Georgetown U., 1966. Admitted to Maine bar, 1966; asso. firm Ralph M. Clark, Gardiner, Maine, 1966-67, Locke, Campbell & Chapman, Augusta, Maine, 1967-69, Lipman & Gingras, Augusta, 1972-74; spl. asst. to asst. sec. ednl. and cultural affairs Dept. State, Washington, 1969-70; partner firm Gingras, Speers & Gasink, Augusta, 1974-79; treas. State of Maine, Augusta, 1979—. Sec., Maine Senate, Augusta, 1966-69, senator, 1973-79, majority leader, 1975-79; bd. dirs. Maine Law Enforcement Planning and Assistance Agy., 1973-75, mem. grants com. 1974-75; mem. Maine Health Study Commn., 1974, Maine Commn. Interstate Coop., 1975-79, Atlantic States Marine Fisheries Commn., 1975-79, adv. com. Jud. Records, 1975—; chmn. Legis. Council, 1975-77; del. to People's Republic of China, Nat. Conf. State Legislatures, 1976, exec. com., 1977-78; U.S. del. Atlantic Alliance Young Polit. Leaders, NATO, Brussels, 1977; Maine coll. chmn. Young Republicans Nat. Fedn., 1961-62, nat. committeeman, 1962-64, nat. officer, 1963-65, nat. auditor, 1965; alt. del. Rep. Nat. Conv., 1964, del., 1968, 72; mem. Rep. Nat. Platform Com.; mem. Maine Rep. State Com., 1978—; trustee U. New Eng., 1978—. Mem. Am. Bar Assn., Kennebec (Maine), Bar Assn., Am. Judicature Soc. Congregationalist. Club: Lions. Office: State House Augusta ME 04330

SPEIRS, DORIS HUESTIS (MRS. J. MURRAY SPEIRS), artist, author; b. Toronto, Ont., Can.; d. Archibald Morrison and Florence Gooderham (Hamilton) Huestis; student Toronto Model Sch., 1900-02, Havergal Ladies Coll., 1902-15, U. Toronto, 1914-16, U. Ill., 1940-41; m. Wilfrid Gordon Mills, May 2, 1916 (div. June 1939); children—Adèle Barbara Mills Hearn, Iris Florence Mills Weir; m. 2d, John Murray Speirs, Aug. 1, 1941. One-man show studio J. E. H. MacDonald, Toronto, 1925, Prouts Neck, Maine, 1929, Jerrold Morris Gallery, Toronto, 1970, Toronto Heliconian Club, 1970, Robert McLaughlin Gallery, Oshowa, Ont., 1971, Lyceum Club and Women's Art Assn., 1974; exhibited in group shows Art Gallery of Toronto, Albright Art Gallery, The Station, Whitby Arts, 1972, others; represented in permanent collections at Nat. Gallery of Can., Art Gallery of Ont., McMichael Canadian Collection, Kleinburg, Ont., Robert McLaughlin Gallery, many pvt. collections in U.S., Can., Finland. Recipient with husband Ont. Conservation trophy, 1974; honored by Fedn. Ont. Naturalists, 1977, Nat. Mus. Natural Scis., Ottawa, 1975. Mem. Royal Ont. Mus., World Federalists Can., Art Gallery Ont., Fedn. Ont. Naturalists, Am., Brit. ornithologists' unions, Wilson Ornithol. Soc., Theta Beta Sigma. Clubs: Hamilton Nature, Heliconian of Toronto, Margaret Nice Ornithol. Translator: The Forehead's Lyre, poems from the Swedish of Lars von Haartman, 1962; Black Sails, 1976; author: Eastern, Western and Mexican Evening Grosbeak; (with J. Murray Speirs) Lincoln's Sparrow, 1968; Exercise for Psyche, poems (1922-1972), 1973; contbr. poems, essays to profl. jours. Home: Cobble Hill 1815 Altona Rd Pickering ON L1V 1M6 Canada

SPEISER, STUART MARSHALL, lawyer; b. N.Y.C., June 4, 1923; s. Joseph and Anne (Jonath) S.; student U. Pa., 1939-42; LL.B., Columbia U., 1948; m. Mary J. McCormick, Feb. 12, 1950; 1 son, James Joseph. Admitted to N.Y. bar, 1948, since practiced in N.Y.C. and Washington; mem. firm Speiser & Krause, 1957—; chmn. bd. Hydrophilics Internat., Inc., 1971-77. Served as pilot USAAF, 1943-46. Hon. atty.-gen., La., 1958—. Mem. Am. Bar Assn., N.Y. County Lawyers Assn. (chmn. subcom. law outer space 1958—), Am. Trial Lawyers Assn. (chmn. aviation law 1955-64), Am. Inst. Aeros. and Astronautics (asso.). Author: Preparation Manual for Aviation Negligence Cases, 1958; Death in the Air, 1957; Liability Problems in Airline Crash Cases, 1957; Private Airplane Accidents, 1958; Speiser's Negligence Jury Charges, 1960; Speiser's Aviation Law Guide, 1962; Lawyers Aviation Handbook, 1964; Recovery for Wrongful Death, 1966, 2d edit., 1975; Lawyers Economic Handbook, 1970; Attorneys' Fees, 1972; The Negligence Case - Res Ipse Loquitur, 1973; A Piece of the Action, 1977; Aviation Tort Law, 1978; bd. editors Jour. Post Keynesian Econs., 1977—. Home: Westover Ln Stamford CT 06902 Office: Pan Am Bldg 200 Park Ave New York City 10017

SPEKEN, RALPH HOWARD, psychiatrist; b. Pueblo, Colo., Oct. 16, 1941; s. Samuel Paul and Clara Esther (Berman) S.; B.A., Columbia U., 1964; M.D., U. Colo., 1968; m. Stephanie Mirsky; children—Seth, Shana. Intern, Montefiore Hosp., N.Y.C., 1968-69; fellow in pediatrics Tel Aviv U., 1968; resident in psychiatry Kings County Hosp., Bklyn., 1969-72; acting dir. emergency unit Rockland Community Mental Health Center, Pomona, N.Y., 1972-73; chief family service unit Bronx (N.Y.) Psychiat. Center, 1975-76; clin. dir. psychiatry Misericordia Hosp., Bronx, 1978—; grad. Nathan Ackerman Inst. for Family Therapy, 1977; chmn. Williamsbridge Subfedn. for Mental Health, 1978—; founder Fordham-Tremont Community Mental Health Center, 1978. Mem. synagogue relations com. Fedn. Jewish Philanthropies. Diplomate Am. Bd. Psychiatry and Neurology. Mem. Am. Psychiat. Assn. Co-author: Jewish Ethno-Psychiatry, 1977. Office: Misericordia Hospital 667 E 234th St Bronx NY 10466

SPELLER, LESLIE CLIFTON, physicist, educator; b. Windsor, N.C., June 10, 1942; s. Benjamin Franklin and Mamie B. Speller; B.S. in Math. and Physics, N.C. Coll., 1963; M.S. in Physics, Howard U., 1967, Ph.D., 1971; m. Lula Outlaw Bond, Mar. 28, 1964; children—Leslie Clifton, LaSonia Claudette. Teaching asst., teaching fellow, NSF research asst. Howard U., Washington, 1963-65, 65-66, 66-68; physicist Nat. Bur. Standards, Gaithersburg, Md., 1971-72; asso. prof. physics D.C. Tchrs. Coll., Washington, 1973-77, prof., 1977—; adj. research prof. Howard U.; coordinator coop. physics program Title III. Mem. Nat. Inst. Sci., Am. Phys. Soc., Aircraft Owners and Pilots Assn., AAUP, NEA, Sigma Xi, Sigma Pi Sigma. Democrat. Baptist. Research in electron energy losses and optical properties of solids. Home: 2309 Westview Dr Silver Spring MD 20910 Office: T-19 Room 211 U DC Washington DC 20001*

SPELLER, ROBERT ERNEST BLAKEFIELD, book pub. co. exec.; b. Chgo., Jan. 19, 1908; s. John Ernest and Florence (Larson) S.; student Columbia U., 1929; m. Maxine Elliott Watkins; children—Robert Ernest Blakefield, Jon Patterson. Mng. editor Fgn. Press Service, 1930-31; pres. The Mohawk Press, 1931-32, Robert Speller Pub. Corp., 1934-52, Record Concerts Corp., 1940-53, Robert Speller & Sons, Publishers, Inc., 1955—; pub. Hough's Ency. of American Woods, 1957—; pres. Transglobal News Service, 1960—, Norellyn Press, Inc., 1960—; chmn. bd., pres. Nat. Resources Publs., Inc., 1968—; sec., dir. Encoder Research & Devel. Corp., 1971—; pub. East Europe mag., 1970—; v.p., dir. Pecos Western Corp. Del., 1973—; dir. Gen. Research Corp. Mem. founding bd. USO; trustee Philippa Schuyler Meml. Found. Served with Signal Corps Publs. Agency, AUS, 1944-45. Mem. Gourmet Soc. (founder), Am. Legion. Club: Columbia Univ. (N.Y.C.). Home: 115 E 9th St New York City NY 10003 Office: 10 E 23d St New York City NY 10010

SPELLMAN, GLADYS NOON, congresswoman; m. Reuben Spellman; 3 children. Tchr., Prince George County (Md.) Pub. Schs.; mem. 94th and 95th Congresses from 5th Md. dist.; mem. Com. Banking, Fin. and Urban Affairs, Democratic Steering and Policy Com., Com. P.O. and Civil Service, chmn. Subcom. on Compensation and Employee Benefits. Mem. Prince George's County (Md.) Bd. Commrs., 1962-71, councilor at large, 1971. Mem. Adv. Commn. Intergovtl. Relations, 1967; mem. Nat. Labor-Mgmt. Relations Service; mem. Md. Gov.'s Commn. Law Enforcement and Adminstrn. Justice, Md. Gov.'s Commn. Function Govt.; chmn. Md. State Comprehensive Health Planning Adv. Council; past chmn. Washington Suburban. Transit Commn.; bd. dirs. Washington Met. Area Transit Authority. Democrat. Office: Room 308 Cannon House Office Bldg Washington DC 20515

SPELMAN, MALCOLM STEWART, cons. transp. engr.; b. Bklyn., Dec. 11, 1900; s. John Rodgers and Elsie Rankin (Warnock) S.; ed. Syracuse U. Coll. Forestry, 1919-20, Coll. Applied Sci., 1921-22; m. Elsie Wilson Biddleman, July 8, 1925; children—Alma Spelman Treen, Stewart Rodgers. Designer, project engr. J.R. Spelman, cons. bridge engrs., Nassau County, N.Y., 1922-23, 27-28; hwy. engring. insp. Lincoln hwy. Pa. State Hwy. Dept., Pitts., 1924; structural designer subway N.Y.C. Bd. Transp., 1925-26; bridge, bldg. designer J.G. White Engring. Corp., 1929; engr. maintenance, specifications engr. bridges including George Washington, tunnels including Lincoln, airports J.F.K., LaGuardia and Newark, Port of N.Y. Authority, 1930-52; specifications engr. turnpikes, bridges Howard, Needles, Tammen, Bergendoff, N.Y.C., 1952-56; prin. engr. M.S. Spelman Assos., cons. engrs. airports, mass transit to states, counties, towns, Rockville Center, N.Y., 1957—. Troop committeeman Boy Scouts Am., 1942-48, chmn. troop com., 1948-52; mem. Rockville Center Recreation Advisory Council, 1958-72; pres. Rockville Centre Youth Assn., 1956-68, v.p., 1968-72; warden fire and pub. works Nat.

CD, Rockville Center, 1942—; mem. Nassau County Republican Com., 1952-72, vice-chmn. Nassau County Rep. Fin. Com., 1935-40. Recipient 1st prize for Brookhaven Airport Ops. Bldg., L.I. Assn. Commerce and Industry, 1966. Registered profl. engr., N.Y., N.J., Conn. Fellow ASCE (life mem.); mem. Nat., N.Y. State (Community Service and Distinguished Service award Nassau chpt.) socs. profl. engrs., Syracuse Alumni Assn. (past pres. Nassau County), Phi Kappa Psi. Methodist (mem., com. chmn. ofcl. bd. 1932—). Club: Masons. Address: 5 Kenwood Ct Rockville Centre NY 11570

SPENCE, FRANCIS J., bishop; b. Perth, Ont., Can., June 3, 1926. Ordained priest Roman Catholic Ch., 1950; ordained titular bishop of N.S., aux. bishop Mil. Vicariate, 1967; bishop of Charlottetown (P.E.I., Can.), 1970—. Office: PO Box 907 Charlottetown PE C1A 7L9 Canada*

SPENCE, JANET BLAKE CONLEY (MRS. ALEXANDER PYOTT SPENCE), civic worker; b. Upper Montclair, N.J., Aug. 17, 1915; d. Walter Abbott and Ethel Maud (Blake) Conley; student Vassar Coll., 1933-35; certificate Katharine Gibbs Sch., 1936; m. Alexander Pyott Spence, June 10, 1939; children—Janet Blake Spence Kerr, Robert Moray, Richard Taylor. Formerly active Jr. League, Neighborhood House, ARC, Girl Scouts U.S.A.; active various community drives; chmn. Darien (Conn.) Assembly, 1955-56; sec., chmn. Wilton Jr. Assembly, 1961-63; subscription chmn. Candlelight Concerts Wilton, Conn., 1963-65; rec. sec. Pub. Health Nursing Assn. Wilton Bd., 1964-67; corr., rec. sec. Royle Sch. Bd., Darien, 1952-55; active program com. Washington Valley Community Assn. Mem. N.J. Symphony Orch. League (treas. Morris County br. 1978—), Vassar, Dobbs alumnae assns. Congregationalist. Clubs: Wilton, Garden, Valley Econs. (corr. sec. 1977-80), Spring Brook Country. Home: Hilltop Washington Valley Rd Morristown NJ 07960

SPENCER, ALBERT LAWRENCE, aerospace co. exec.; b. Bklyn., July 20, 1929; s. Gillian George and Pearl Rose S.; B.S. in Bus. Adminstrn., Community Coll. N.Y., 1959. Purchasing agt. Belock Instrument Corp., College Point, N.Y., 1952-62; purchasing dir. ELWICO, Westbury, N.Y., 1962-63; sr. subcontract adminstr. Grumman Aerospace Corp., Bethpage, N.Y., 1963—. Mem. Luth. Sch. for Deaf, Middleneck, N.Y., 1973—. Served with USAF, 1951. Certified purchasing mgr. Mem. Nat. Assn. Purchasing Mgmt., Purchasing Mgmt. of N.Y., Internat. Fedn. Purchasing Materials and Mgmt., Am. Def. Preparedness Assn. Democrat. Lutheran. Club: Police Boys of Nassau County. Author: Training The Man-Purchasing, 1968. Home: 22 John Ln Levittown NY 11756 Office: Grumman Aerospace Corp Bethpage NY 11714

SPENCER, DONALD FORD, electronics engr.; b. Dayton, Ky., Apr. 16, 1924; s. Merle Wilson and Mildred (Ford) S.; B.S., U. Cin., 1951; m. Phyllis Esther Parry, Dec. 30, 1950 (div. Sept. 1973); children—Barton Parry, Sherra Ford, Wendra Whitman. Electronic engr. USN Bur. Ships and Naval Research Lab., Washington, 1951-56; head air-to-surface missile guidance unit USN Bur. Aeros., 1956-59; chief avionics and guidance div. Office Communications and Electronics, Office Dir. Def. Research and Engring., 1959-70; electronics indsl. specialist Office Asst. Sec. Def., 1970—; pres. Va. Execs. Investments. Served with USNR, 1943-46. Registered profl. engr., D.C. Asso. fellow Am. Inst. Aeros. and Astronautics; mem. IEEE (sr.), Inst. Nav., Old Crows, Soc. Va., Pi Kappa Alpha. Presbyterian. Clubs: Masons; Annapolis Yacht; Washington Golf and Country. Home: 6621 Wakefield Dr Alexandria VA 22307 Office: The Pentagon Washington DC 20301

SPENCER, EDWARD HATHAWAY, lawyer; b. Zurich, Switzerland, July 1, 1909; s. Edward B.T. and Helen Imogen (Hathaway) S. (parents Am. citizens); B.A., Grinnell Coll., 1931; J.D., Harvard U., 1934; m. Harriet Critcherson, Dec. 31, 1934 (dec.); children—Anne C., Harriet C., Edward Hathaway; m. 2d, Olga Brom, Oct. 15, 1978. Admitted to N.Y. bar, 1936; asso. firm Sage, Gray, Todd & Sims, N.Y.C., 1934-42, partner firm, 1943—; dir. Howden Swann Ltd., Drake Ins. Co. N.Y. Chmn. N.Y.C. USO, 1954-56; pres. Bronxville Bd. Edn., 1968-70; bd. dirs. Greater N.Y. YMCA, 1958—; bd. dirs., treas. Nat. League Nursing, 1953-57. Mem. Am., N.Y. State bar assns., Assn. Bar City N.Y. Republican. Mem. Dutch Reformed Ch. Clubs: Down Town Assn.; Bronxville (N.Y.) Field (dir., sec.) Home: 1 Red Oak Rd Bronxville NY 10708 Office: 140 Broadway New York City NY 10005

SPENCER, FLORA CHARLOTTE, nurse; b. Heath, Mass., Nov. 18, 1935; d. John Oliver and Florence Elizabeth (Newton) Hillman; R.N., Franklin County Pub. Hosp., Greenfield, Mass., 1957; m. Roger Dewey Spencer, Sept. 28, 1957; 1 dau., Sheila Ann. Mem. staff Franklin County Pub. Hosp., 1957—, operating room supr., 1974—; mem. bldg. com. for new surgery unit, 1971—; examiner operating room technicians, 1974—. Mem. Am., Mass. nurses assns., Assn. Operating Room Nurses. Address: 46 Summer St Greenfield MA 01301

SPENCER, MICHAEL JON, social service and arts assn. exec.; b. N.Y.C., Feb. 14, 1938; s. Joseph and Ethel Spencer; B.A. cum laude, U. Calif., Los Angeles, 1960; m. Ruth Albert, Mar. 21, 1964; 1 dau., Joanna Albert. Founder, exec. dir. Hospital Audiences, Inc.; mem. Gov. Carey's Task Force on Cultural Affairs. Active Citizen's Com. for N.Y.C., Inc. named Arts Adminstr. of Yr., Arts Mgmt. mag., 1976-77. Mem. Friends of the Theatre and Music Collection, Mus. of City of N.Y., Phi Beta Kappa. Club: City (N.Y.C.). Home: 334 W 86th St New York City NY 10024 Office: 1540 Broadway New York City NY 10036

SPENCER, SALLY LOUISE, educator; b. Williamsburg, Pa., Apr. 1, 1931; d. Herbert Lincoln and Mildred (Pollard) Spencer; A.B., cum laude in English and History, Bucknell U., 1953; certificate Katharine Gibbs Sch., 1954; postgrad. Glassboro State Tchrs. Coll., 1955-56, Stroudsburg State Tchrs. Coll., 1956, Wilkes Coll., 1956, Tchrs. Coll., Columbia, 1957-58; M.A. in Student Personnel Administration, 1958; postgraduate N.Y. U., 1960—; m. David L. Hurwitz. Secretary, asst. to pub. relations dir. Conv. and Visitors Bur., Phila. C. of C., 1954-55; tch. English and history Pennsauken (N.J.) Jr. High Sch., 1955-57; sec. Tchrs. Coll., Columbia, 1957-58; counselor Cornell U., Ithaca, N.Y., 1958-59; dean women, asst. dean students So. Conn. State Coll., New Haven, 1959-63, asst. prof. history asst. to pres., 1965—. Mem. Am. Hist. Assn., Orgn. Am. Historians, Am. Assn. U. Profs., Am. Acad. Polit. and Social Scis., Modern Lang. Assn., Nat. Assn. Women Deans and Counselors, Am., Conn. (exec. bd. 1962-63), New Haven (pres. 1962-63) personnel and guidance assns., Am. Assn. U. Women, Mortar Bd., Phi Beta Kappa, Pi Delta Epsilon, Sigma Tau Delta, Phi Alpha Theta, Delta Delta Delta. Republican. Presbyn.

SPENCER, THOMAS, III, statistician; b. S.I., N.Y., June 25, 1939; s. Thomas and Anne (Riddell) S.; student Rutgers U., 1957-61; B.S., Newark Coll. Engring., 1964, M.S., 1969; M.S., Stevens Inst. Tech., 1967, Ph.D., 1976; m. Janet Folland, Dec. 26, 1965; children—Thomas IV, John. Asst. to elec. engr. Triangle Conduit & Cable Co., New Brunswick, N.J., 1961-62; tech. trainee Rigal Paper Co., Milford N.J., 1963; elec. engr. Electronic Assos., Inc., West Long Branch, 1964; instr. dept. math. Newark Coll. Engring., 1964-68; asst. prof. dept. math. Trenton (N.J.) State Coll., 1968-76; staff asso. in statistics AT&T, Basking Ridge, N.J., 1976-78; bus. research supr. econometric and stats. studies Bell Telephone Co. Pa., Phila., 1978—; cons. Nametre, Inc., Edison N.J., Tile Council Am., Princeton, N.J., Western Electric Corp., Princeton, N.J., Meta Sci., Inc., Westfield, N.J. Mem. Math. Assn. Am., Inst. Math. Statis. Inst. Math. and Its Applications, Math. Assn. (Eng.), Am. Statis. Assn., Sigma Xi, Tau Beta Pi, Eta Kappa Nu, Theta Chi. Lutheran. Home: Box 425 A Bergen Ave RD 1 Princeton NJ 08540 Office: Bell Telephone Co Pa One Parkway Philadelphia PA 19102

SPENCER, WILLIAM I., banker; b. Grand Junction, Colo., July 24, 1917; s. Eugene W. and Nellie (Haviland) S.; student Colo. Coll.; m. Kathryn Cope, June 5, 1943. With Chem. Bank, 1939-51; with Citibank, N.Y.C., 1951—, exec. v.p., 1965-68, exec. v.p. operating group, 1968-70, pres., chief adminstrv. officer, 1970—; dir. United Techs. Corp., FNCB Waltons Corp., First Nat. City Found., Sears, Roebuck & Co., Bedford-Stuyvesant Devel. & Services Corp. Chmn., Community Blood Council Greater New York; active Met. Opera Assn., U.S.-Korea Econ. Council; trustee Colo. Coll., N.Y. U. Med. Center. Mem. Transp. Assn. Am. (dir.), Bond Club, Econ. Club N.Y. Clubs: Boone and Crockett; Campe Fire of Am.; Sleepy Hollow Country. Home: 12 Beekman Pl New York City NY 10022 Office: 399 Park Ave New York City NY 10022

SPERBER, DANIEL, physicist; b. Vienna, Austria, May 8, 1930; s. Emmanuel and Nelly (Liberman) S.; came to U.S., 1955, naturalized, 1967; M.Sc., Hebrew U., 1954; Ph.D., Princeton U., 1960; m. Ora Yuvall, Nov. 29, 1963; 1 son, Ron Emanuel. Tng. and research asst. Israel Inst. Tech., Haifa, 1954-55, Princeton U., 1955-60; sr. scientist, research adviser Ill. Inst. Tech. Research Inst., Chgo., 1960-67, asso. prof. physics, 1964-67; asso. prof. physics Rensselaer Poly Inst., Troy, N.Y., 1967-72, prof., 1972—; Nordita prof. Niels Bohr Inst., Copenhagen, 1973-74. Served to capt. Israeli Army, 1950-52. Fellow Am. Phys. Soc.; mem. Israel Phys. Soc., N.Y. Acad. Scis., Sigma Xi. Jewish. Contbr. articles to profl. jours. Home: 1 Taylor Ln Troy NY 12180 Office: Dept Physics Renssalaer Poly Inst Troy NY 12181

SPERGEL, PHILIP, psychologist, rehab. dir.; b. Phila., Jan. 23, 1935; s. William V. and Sara (Cohen) S.; B.A., Temple U., 1956, M.A., 1959, Ed.D. in Counseling Psychology, 1968; m. Ruth Ellen Horowitz, Dec. 22, 1957; children—Patricia Dale, Steven Hersh, Jonathan Howard. Tchr. spl. edn. Phila. Sch. Dist., 1957-59; vocat. counselor to dir. profl. services Phila. Jewish Employment and Vocat. Service, 1959-69; dir. psychol. services Moss Rehab. Hosp., Phila., 1969—; cons. HEW; asst. clin. prof. rehab. medicine Temple U.; vis. prof. U. Glasgow (Scotland), LaSalle Coll. Mem. Am. Psychol. Assn., Eastern Psychol. Assn., Pa. Psychol. Assn., Phi Delta Kappa (Research Excellence award 1968). Home: 7620 Dorcas St Philadelphia PA 19111 Office: 12th and Tabor Rd Philadelphia PA 19141 also 1335 W Tabor Rd Philadelphia PA 19141

SPERL, VIRGINIA R., librarian; b. Orange, N.J., Jan. 3, 1 920; d. Adolph A. and Olga J. (Linn) S.; B.A., Randolph-Macon Woman's Coll., 1942; B.L.S., U. Minn., 1945. Library asst. New Britain (Conn.) Inst., 1942-43; asst. order dept. Harvard Law Library, 1945-46; library asst. Pa. Sch. Social Work, Phila., 1947; serials cataloger, then asst. catalog librarian med. Columbia U., 1947-58; chief cataloger Albert Einstein Coll. Medicine, N.Y.C., 1958-60; catalog librarian, then asst. librarian, asso. prof. Dowling Coll., Oakdale, N.Y., 1961—, acting dir., 1975-76. Mem. Am., N.Y. State, Suffolk County library assns., Spl. Libraries Assn., AAUP, AAUW, L.I. Archives Conf. Home: Sayville NY 11782 Office: Dowling Coll Oakdale NY 11769

SPERLING, ARTHUR LAWRENCE, oral-maxillofacial surgeon; b. Boston, June 23, 1939; s. William Bernard and Ethyl J. (Berry) S.; D.M.D., Tufts U., 1964; m. Harriet Louise Feldman, Aug. 11, 1961; children—Bradley Todd, Audrey Lynn. Resident in oral and maxillofacial surgery Mass. Gen. Hosp., Boston, 1964-67; teaching fellow Harvard U., 1966-67; practice dentistry specializing in oral-maxillofacial surgery, Hartford, Conn., 1969—; mem. faculty U. Conn. Sch. Dentistry and Medicine. Bd. dirs. Am. Heart Assn., Hartford. Served with USAF, 1967-69. Diplomate Am. Bd. Oral Surgery. Fellow Am. Dental Soc. Anesthesiology; mem. ADA, Am. Assn. Oral and Maxillofacial Surgeons, Conn. Soc. Oral and Maxillofacial Surgeons, Hartford, Middlesex dental socs., Internat. Soc. Oral Surgery. Home: 115 Black Birch St Wethersfield CT 06109 Office: 100 Constitution Plaza Hartford CT 06103 also 80 S Main St Middletown CT 06457

SPETTER, MATTHEW IES, educator; b. The Hague, Netherlands, Sept. 15, 1921; s. Adolph and Rieka (Dessauer) S.; came to U.S., 1951, naturalized, 1956; student Inst. Social Psychology, The Hague, 1939-41, Amsterdam City U., 1947-50, Leicester U. (Eng.), 1948; M.A., New Sch. for Social Research, 1955, Ph.D., 1957; postgrad. Inst. Practicing Psychotherapists, 1965-67; m. Ina Staercke, May 19, 1948 (dec. 1960); children—Sanne, Ruth Marguerita, Job Mattijs Uri; m. 2d, Sylvia Berke, Jan. 29, 1961. Fgn. editor Nat. Broadcasting Service, Hilversum, Netherlands, 46-48; polit. advisor to high commr. Republic Indonesia, The Hague, 1947-51; chief fgn. editor Vrij Netherland, 1948-51; lectr. fgn. affairs Antioch Coll., Yellow Springs, Ohio, 1951; columnist Yellow Spring News, 1951-54; chmn. dept. social ethics Fieldston Sch., Riverdale, N.Y., 1954-76; religious leader Riverdale-Yonkers Soc. for Ethical Culture, 1954—; tchr., chmn. dept. ethics Ethical Culture Schs., N.Y.C., Bronx, 1951-76; co-dir. Tng. Inst. for Humanist Philosophy, Columbia U., N.Y.C., 1959-62; chmn. permanent Internat. Workgroup on Family Counseling and Mental Health of Internat. Humanist and Ethical Union, 1970—; asso. prof. Peace Studies Inst., Manhattan Coll., 1976—; vis. prof. Bard Coll., 1958—, John Lovejoy Elliott Inst. for Human Relations, N.Y.C., 1954-66; broadcaster Voice of Am., to Netherlands, 1956-67; mem. fgn. affairs adv. com. Netherlands Ho. of Reps., 1948-51; alt. del. UN for Internat. Humanist and Ethical Union, 1971—; asso. editor Internat. Humanism, 1971—. Served with Dutch Resistance as liaison officer with Allied Intelligence, 1941-45, Dutch Security with U.S. Army, 1945-46. Sutro Found. fellow, 1952-55. Fellow Am. Sociol. Assn., Am. Assn. Marriage and Family Counselors (clin. mem.), Acad. for Religion and Psychiatry, Nat. Council Leaders of Am. Ethical Union, Nat. Council on Family Relations, Am. Psychol. Assn., Riverdale Mental Health Assn. Author: The Courage to Stand Alone, 1960; Man the Reluctant Brother, 1967; To Deny the Night, 1969; also articles in profl. jours. Home: 47 Jefferson Ave Hastings on Hudson NY 10706 Office: 4450 Fieldston Rd Bronx NY 10471

SPEVAK, IRVING BERTRAM, realtor; b. Albany, N.Y., Dec. 10, 1917; s. Bernard and Bella (Belkin) S.; student Coll. City N.Y., 1936-37, U. Nebr., 1937-39, vet. edn. program Vassar Coll., 1948-49; m. Miriam Lillian Pols, Dec. 10, 1940; children—Elaine Sherry, Albert Bennet. Mgr. G. R. Kinney Co., Inc., Riverhead, N.Y., 1940-43; ins. agt. Poughkeepsie, 1946—; realtor, Poughkeepsie, 1955—. V.P., dir. Jewish Community Center, Poughkeepsie, 1953-56. Served with USN, 1943-46; PTO. Mem. Dutchess County Bd. Realtors (pres. 1968-70), Nat. Assn. Real Estate Bds. (exec. officers council 1959-65), Jewish War Vets. (comdr. 1952), Am. Legion. Jewish religion (sec., v.p. Temple Men's Club 1951-55). Mason (past master). Patentee collar stay, food container. Address: 287 New Hackensack Rd Poughkeepsie NY 12602

SPICER, CHARLES FREDERICK, mech. engr.; b. Weltonville, N.Y., Nov. 29, 1933; s. Leon Eugene and Helen Ruth (Holden) S.; Asso. Applied Sci., Broome Community Coll., 1954; m. Anna Marie Robinson, Oct. 24, 1959; 1 son, David Charles. Draftsman Frederick Nicholson Co., Candor, N.Y., 1954-58, Mut. Designers, Owego, N.Y., 1958-59; designer Frederick Nicholson Co., 1959-60, Leigh St. John & Assos., Binghamton, N.Y., 1960-65; designer, cost estimator S.P. Ainslie Inc., Binghamton, 1965-68; asst. mgr. Power Engring. Corp., Binghamton, 1968-71; field engr. Louis N. Picciano Sr. Corp., Endicott, N.Y., 1971-73; tech. asst. N.Y. State Electric & Gas Corp., Binghamton, N.Y., 1973-74; facilities engr. Binghamton Container Corp., Conklin, N.Y., 1974; design mech. engr. McFarland-Johnson Engrs. Inc., Binghamton, 1974—. Sr. adviser Girl Scouts U.S.A., 1971-76; bd. dirs. Conklin Community Corp., 1973—. Mem. Am. Soc. Heating Refrigeration Air Conditioning Engrs. Republican. Club: Masons. Active ruling elder Ross Meml. Presbyn. Ch., Binghamton, 1967—. Home: RD 1 Box 430 Wilcox Rd Conklin NY 13748 Office: 171 Front St Binghamton NY 13905

SPIEGEL, HERBERT, psychiatrist, educator; b. McKeesport, Pa., June 29, 1914; s. Samuel and Lena (Mendlowitz) S.; B.S., U. Md., 1936, M.D., 1939; m. Natalie Shainess, Apr. 24, 1944 (div. Apr. 1965); children—David, Ann. Intern, St. Francis Hosp., Pitts., 1939-40; resident St. Elizabeth's Hosp., Washington, 1940-42; practice medicine specializing in psychiatry, N.Y.C., 1946—; attending psychiatrist Columbia-Presbyn. Hosp., N.Y.C., 1960—; clin. prof. dept. psychiatry Columbia Coll. Physicians and Surgeons, 1960—; mem. faculty Sch. Mil. Neuropsychiatry, Mason Gen. Hosp., Brentwood, N.Y., 1943-46; contbr. profl. advisory com. Am. Health Found.; mem. pub. edn. com., mem. smoking and health com. N.Y.C. div. Am. Cancer Soc.; mem. med. advisory com. Nat. Aid to Visually Handicapped. Served with M.C., AUS, 1942-46. Decorated Purple Heart; diplomate Am. Bd. Psychiatry. Fellow Am. Psychiat. Assn., Am. Coll. Psychiatrists; mem. Am. Orthopsychiat. Assn., Am. Psychosomatic Soc., Am. Soc. Clin. Hypnosis, Am. Acad. Psychoanalysis, AAAS, AMA, N.Y. County Med. Soc., Internat. Soc. for Clin. and Exptl. Hypnosis, William A. White Psychoanalytic Soc., N.Y. Acad. Medicine, N.Y. Acad. Scis. Author: (with A. Kardiner) War Stress and Neurotic Illness, 1947; (with D. Spiegel) Trance and Treatment: Clinical Uses of Hypnosis, 1978; mem. editorial bd. Preventive Medicine, 1972; contbr. articles to profl. publs. Home: 1065 Park Ave New York City NY 10028 Office: 19 E 88th St New York City NY 10028

SPIEGEL, LEONARD BERNARD, photography lab. exec., cons.; b. N.Y.C., Mar. 27, 1931; s. Ralph and Lillian (Spring) S.; B.S., N.Y. U., 1952; m. Kay Klein, Nov. 1, 1958. Vice pres. Modernage Photo Service, N.Y.C., 1956-59; pres. ASAP Photolab, Inc., N.Y.C., 1970—; cons. photog. exhbns. N.Y. State Council on Arts, N.Y.C., Internat. Center Photography, N.Y.C., Jewish Mus., N.Y.C., Minn. Mus. Fine Arts, Mpls., Mus. Modern Art, N.Y.C., Met. Mus. Art, N.Y.C., New Eng. Aquarium, Boston. Served with U.S. Air N.G., 1951-55. Mem. Profl. Photographers Am. (Merit award 1968), Soc. Photog. Scientists and Engrs., Assn. Profl. Color Labs. Office: 40 E 49th St New York City NY 10017

SPIEGEL, LEONARD E(MILE), biologist, educator; b. N.Y.C., Sept. 12, 1924; s. Leon A. and Rosina B. (Roth) S.; A.B., Drew U., 1948; M.S., Northwestern U., 1950; Ph.D., Cornell U., 1954; m. Alice Joan Hahn, Dec. 27, 1950; children—Frederick William, Michael Leonard, Martha Lynn, Melanie Anne, Lisa Marie. Wildlife mgmt. supr. Ohio Div. of Wildlife, Columbus, 1953-55; instr. biology Alpena (Mich.) Community Coll., 1955-57; asst. prof. Central Mich. U., Mt. Pleasant, 1957-61, asso. prof., 1961-62; extension wildlife conservationist Cornell U., Ithaca, N.Y., 1962-63; prof. biology Monmouth Coll., West Long Branch, N.J., 1963—, chmn. dept. biology, 1973—; environ. cons., West Long Branch, N.J., 1967—; tech. adviser West Long Branch Environ. Commn., 1972—; mem. N.J. State Mosquito Control Commn., 1976—. Mem. pastoral relations com. Old First United Methodist Ch., West Long Branch, 1976; bd. dirs. Community Center, West Long Branch, 1965-67. Served with USNR, 1943, USAAF, 1943-46. NSF grantee, 1960, 61, 69, ERDA grantee, 1975. Mem. Wildlife Soc. (pres. N.J. chpt. 1974-76), Am. Inst. Biol. Sci., AAAS, N.J. Acad. Sci., Mich. Assn. of Conservation Ecologists (founding mem.), Sigma Xi, Phi Kappa Phi, Beta Beta Beta. Democrat. Clubs: Explorers; S and M Hunt, N.J. Fedn. Sportsmen's. Author: (with J.D. Adams, C.A. Scheel, G.R. Gleason) Biology Laboratory Guide, 1963; (with C.A. Scheel, D.W. Benjamin) Experiences in Laboratory Biology, 1974; contbr. articles on ecology to sci. publs. Home: 56 Golf St West Long Branch NJ 07764 Office: Biology Dept Monmouth College West Long Branch NJ 07764

SPIEGEL, SIEGMUND, architect, profl. planner; b. Gera, Germany, Nov. 13, 1919; s. Jakob and Sara (Precker) S.; ed. Coll. City N.Y., 1939-40, Columbia U., 1945-50; m. Ruth Josias, Apr. 13, 1945; children—Sandra Renee, Deborah Joan. Came to U.S., 1938, naturalized, 1941. Draftsman, Mayer & Whittlesey, architects, N.Y.C., 1941-47, office mgr., 1947-55; pvt. practice architecture, East Meadow, N.Y., 1956—. Served with AUS, 1941-45; ETO. Decorated Purple Heart, Bronze Star, Croix de Guerre with palme (Belgium). Registered architect, N.Y., N.J., Mass., Md., Va., Pa., Conn., Ga., Tenn., N.H., Vt., Fla. Fellow Acad. Mktg. Sci.; mem. AIA, N.Y. State Assn. Architects, East Meadow C. of C. (pres. 1966). Club: Kiwanis. Contbr. articles to Progressive Architecture; prin. works include: Syosset (N.Y.) Hosp., 1962; Villa Victor Motel, Syosset, 1958; Cameo House apts., Hempstead, N.Y., 1960; Smith-town (N.Y.) Gardens, apt. devel., 1960; Capitol House, East Rockaway, N.Y., 1961; Reliance Fed. Savs. and Loan Assn. Bank, Queens, N.Y., 1961; Louden Hall Psychiat. Hosp., 1963; Human Resources Sch., Albertson, N.Y., 1964; Nassau Center for Emotionally Disturbed children, 1968; Harbor Club Apts., Babylon, N.Y., 1968, Reliance Fed. Bank, Albertson, 1967, Birchwood Glen Apt. Community, Holtsville, N.Y., 1972, North Isle Club and Apt. Community, Coram, N.Y., 1972; Birchwood Blue Ridge & Bretton Woods condominiums, 1974, Luther E. Woodward Sch. for Emotionally Disturbed Children, Freeport, N.Y., 1974, County Fed. Savs. and Loan Offices, Commack, N.Y., 1973; author Spiegel plan for conversion surplus sch. bldgs. to housing for elderly, 1975. Recipient grand prize for instnl. bldgs. (for Syosset Hosp.), L.I. Assn., 1963; grand prize Human Resources Sch., 1966; grand prize Stony Brook Profl. Bldg., 1966; Beautification award, Town Hempstead, N.Y., 1969; Archi award L.I. Assn., 1970, 74. Home: 1508 Hayes Ct East Meadow NY 11554 Office: 2035 Hempstead Turnpike East Meadow NY 11554

SPIEGEL, TED, photojournalist; b. Newark, June 15, 1934; s. Simon and Paula (Kleinman) S.; A.B., Columbia U., 1954; m. Signy Alice Espeland, July 29, 1966; children—David, Erik. Photographer, Wash. State Dept. Commerce, 1959-60; free-lance photojournalist, 1961—; pres. Involvement Media, Inc., books ednl. materials and films, South Salem, N.Y.; exhibited at Expo '67, 1st Triennale of Photography, Jerusalem, 1973; one man photographic show Wavehill Mus., N.Y. State Capitol, Nikon Gallery, 1978, Am. Mus. Natural History. Served with AUS, 1957-59. Mem. Assn. Conservation Trusts (trustee 1977—). Contbg. photographer Isles of the Caribees, 1966; Introduction to Sociology, 1968; Australia, 1968; The Renaissance, 1970; Great Religions, 1971; The Vikings, 1972; Golden Islands of the

Caribbean, 1972; author: Western Shores, 1975; writer, producer, dir. film A Walk in the Park, 1970. Contbr. to Nat. Geog., various mags.; spl. reports, cons. for Rockefeller Found., 1965—. Home: Laurie Ln South Salem NY 10590

SPIEGLER, ENRIQUE, vascular surgeon; b. Buenos Aires, Argentina, Aug. 19, 1928; s. Joseph and Laura (Teicher) S.; came to U.S., 1953, naturalized, 1965; B.S., Nat. Coll. Mariano Moreno, Buenos Aires, 1942-47; M.D., U. Buenos Aires, 1953; m. Gayle Green, Aug. 14, 1963; children—Philip Jason, Elena Victoria. Rotating intern Hosp. for Joint Diseases, N.Y.C., 1953-54, resident in surgery, 1954-55, chief div. vascular surgery, 1973—; jr. resident in surgery Montefiore Hosp., N.Y.C., 1955-56, sr. resident in surgery, 1956-57, chief resident in surgery, 1957-58, NIH research grantee in vascular surgery, 1959-60; chief resident in surgery Beth David Hosp., N.Y.C., 1958-59; practice medicine specializing in vascular surgery, N.Y.C., 1961—; mem. staff Doctor's Hosp., N.Y.C., Yonkers (N.Y.) Profl. Hosp.; prof. vascular surgery N.Y. Coll. Podiatry, 1969—. Diplomate Am. Bd. Surgery. Mem. N.Y. County Med. Soc., A.C.S., N.Y. Diabetes Assn., N.Y. Acad. Scis., Internat. Oceanographic Found., Am. Coll. Angiology. Home: Sterling Rd Harrison NY 10528 Office: 20 Fifth Ave New York City NY 10011

SPIER, NATHANIEL, surgeon; b. Bklyn., Jan. 13, 1934; s. Isidor and Anna (Kirschenbaum) S.; A.B., Bklyn. Coll., 1954; M.D., Downstate Med. Center, State U. N.Y., 1958; m. Toby Griff, June 8, 1957; children—Michael, Laurence, Neal, Randi. Intern, L.I. Jewish Hosp., New Hyde Park, N.Y., 1958-59, resident in gen. surgery, 1959-63; fellow in gen. surgery Lahey Clinic, Boston, 1965-66; practice medicine specializing in surgery, Great Neck, N.Y., 1966—; attending surgeon dept. surgery North Shore Univ. Hosp., Manhasset, N.Y.; asso. clin. prof. surgery Cornell Med. Coll., N.Y.C. Served to capt. M.C., AUS, 1963-65. Recipient Lindner Surg. award, 1958; diplomate Am. Bd. Surgery. Fellow A.C.S., mem. AMA, Nassau County Med. Soc., Nassau Surg. Soc., L.I. Gastroent. Soc., Alpha Omega Alpha. Contbr. articles to med. jours. Office: 275 Middle Neck Rd Great Neck NY 11023

SPIERS, TOMAS HOSKINS, JR., architect; b. Paris, Jan. 26, 1929; s. Tomas Hoskins and Blanca Genevive (DePonthier) S. (parents Am. citizens); student Mohawk Coll., 1946-48; B.A., Hobart Coll., 1951; M.Arch., Yale U., 1960; m. Nancy M. Fenold, Aug. 10, 1952; children—Merrick David, Jordan Henry, Corey Albert. Archtl. designer Pederson & Tilney, New Haven, 1955-60; mng. dir. Pederson & Tilney Italia SpA, Milan, Italy, 1960-66; v.p. European ops. Pederson/Tilney/Spiers, Milan, 1963-66; v.p. S.E. Asia, Louis Berger, Inc., Bangkok, Thailand, 1966-68; v.p. architecture Berger Assos., Harrisburg, Pa., 1968-75, v.p. design, 1975—, also dir.; lectr. archtl. restoration Pa. State U., 1975-76; cons. Pa. Hist. & Mus. Commn., Bur. Historic Sites; mem. advisory council Cheney -Lincoln-Temple Coll.-Industry Cluster, 1975-77. Bd. dirs. Urban League of Harrisburg, Inc., 1977-78. Served with USNR, 1951-55. Registered architect, Pa., N.J., N.Y., Mass., Md., Ohio, Conn., S.C., R.I., Ind., Va., W.Va., D.C., Fla., Ga. Mem. Am. Arbitration Assn. (arbitrator 1974—), AIA (com. on hist. resources 1977-78), ASCE, Soc. Am. Mil. Engrs. Works include: Liberal Arts Bldg., Pa. State U.; Regional Correctional Facility, Mercer, Pa. Home: 357 N 27th St Camp Hill PA 17011 Office: 101 Erford Rd Camp Hill PA 17011

SPIEWAK, KENNETH RALPH, investment broker; b. N.Y.C., Dec. 15, 1935; s. Peter B. and Bessie (Kaufman) S.; A.B., Brown U., 1958; postgrad. N.Y. U., 1958-59; m. Helene Luckman, June 17, 1961; children—Jill Ellen, David Jay. Investment broker Cohen, Simonson & Co., N.Y.C., 1958-59, H. Hentz & Co., N.Y.C., 1959-62, Brand, Grumet & Siegel, N.Y.C., 1962-64; v.p., dir. tech. research Scheinman, Hochstin & Trotta, Inc., N.Y.C., 1964-71; v.p. tech. research Reich & Co. Inc., N.Y.C., 1971-74; investment broker Bear Stearns & Co., N.Y.C., 1975-77, Loeb Rhoades, Hornblower & Co., N.Y.C., 1977—; cons. in field. Served with USAFR, 1959. Mem. Wall St. Technicians and Analysts Soc., N.Y. Mercantile Exchange. Author market letter and commentary, 1964-72. Home: 16 Old Farm Rd Great Neck NY 11020 Office: 1595 Northern Blvd Manhasset NY 11030

SPILLER, MORTIMER, sales promotion item mfg. co. exec.; b. LeRoy, N.Y., Dec. 28, 1922; s. Harry and Jennie; B.A., Miami U., Oxford, Ohio, 1946; M.B.A., City Coll. of N.Y., 1947; m. Harriet E. Eisenberg, Apr. 8, 1949; children—Lora, Jill, Harley. Pres., Mortimer Spiller Co., Inc., Buffalo, N.Y., 1959—, Jayel, Inc., Batavia, N.Y., 1960—; adj. prof. mktg. Buffalo State Coll., 1947-48; mktg. instr. City Coll. of N.Y., 1948-49. Served to sgt. U.S. Army, 1943-45. Recipient Bishop medal, Miami Univ., 1978. Mem. Zeta Beta Tau, Alpha Delta Sigma. Home: 163 High Park Blvd Buffalo NY 14226

SPILMAN, J. STANLEY, material handling crane co. exec.; b. Rushville, Ind., Oct. 10, 1927; s. Claude M. and June L. Spilman; B.S. in Mech. Engring., Purdue U., 1950; m. Patricia Coleman, Nov. 5, 1950; children—Ann, Susan. With Gen. Motros Corp., 1950-68, Eastern regional mgr. and nat. accounts mgr., 1967-68; sales mgr. Euclid Truck Inc., 1968-69; gen. sales mgr. contrn. equipment (payline) div. Internat. Harvester Co., 1969-74; pres. Carrington Co., Seattle and Alaska, 1974-75, HIAB Cranes & Loaders, Inc. of U.S.A., Newark, Del., 1976—. Pres. Homeowners Assn., Hudson, Ohio, 1965-67. Served with paratroops U.S. Army, 1946-47. Mem. Phi Delta Theta. Republican. Episcopalian. Club: Masons. Address: 904 DuPont Rd Westover Hills Wilmington DE 19807

SPINDLER, CLARENCE FRANCIS, cons. mech. and civil engr.; b. Olean, N.Y., Aug. 23, 1905; s. John Joseph and Josephine (Martiny) S.; C.E. (Regents scholar), Cornell U., 1927; m. Marjorie Jane McCune, Aug. 18, 1934; 1 dau., Patricia (Mrs. Richard H. Gustafson). Chief engr., maintenance of way and structure Schenectady Ry. Co., 1928-41; partner Teeling & Spindler cons. engrs., Albany, N.Y., 1946-67; pres., dir. Teeling, Spindler & Fink Engrs., Inc., Albany, 1967-72; owner, cons. engr. C.F. Spindler Assos., Latham, N.Y., 1972—. Cons., City Albany, 1958—. Mem. Gov. Rockefeller's N.Y. State Com. on Energy Conservation, 1972-73; mem. citizens com. on facilities Niskayuna Sch. System, 1959-61. Served with AUS, 1941-46; ETO. Mem. Nat., N.Y. State, Schenectady (treas., 1947-48) socs. profls. engr., Nat. Fire Protection Assn., Cons. Engrs. Council (chmn. nat. codes com., 1971-72, Eastern chpt. pres. 1966-67, dir. 1967-70), Am. Soc. Heating, Refrigerating and Air Conditioning Engrs. Roman Catholic. Club: Optimist (founding mem. Albany). Developed treatment system for recycle and reuse of nearly all water requirements for high rise apt. bldgs. Home: 1603 Baker Ave Schenectady NY 12309 Office: 8 Northway Ln Latham NY 12110

SPINDLER, FRANK MACDONALD, historian, clergyman; b. Columbus, Ohio, Dec. 17, 1917; s. Alva Reed and Mary Pearl (MacDonald) S.; B.A., U. Tex. at Austin, 1939; M.Div., Gen. Theol. Sem., 1948; M.A., U. Houston, 1955; Ph.D., Am. U., 1966; m. Evelyn Lyman Blanchard, July 17, 1956. Ordained priest Protestant Episcopal Ch., 1948; vicar, Crockett, Tex., Huntsville, Tex., 1948-50; rector, Hempstead, Tex., 1950-56; asst. minister, Balt., 1956-57; asso. rector St. Michael and All Angels Ch., Balt., 1957-62; curate St. Paul's Ch., Washington, 1962; asst. minister St. John's Ch., Washington, 1962-63; asst. minister Ch. Ascension and St. Agnes, Washington, 1963—; lectr. history U. Md., College Park, 1964-67; asst. prof. George Mason U., Fairfax, Va., 1967-73, asso. prof., 1973—. Trustee Quin Found., 1954-56. Served to capt. AUS, 1941-46. Named Prof. of Year, George Mason U., 1972-73, recipient grant, 1974-75. Mem. Am. Hist. Assn., Conf. Latin Am. History, Ch. Hist. Soc., Am. Inst. Archeology. Democrat. Home: 1233 4th St SW Washington DC 20024 Office: 4400 University Blvd Fairfax VA 22030

SPINDOLA-FRANCO, HUGO, cardiovascular radiologist; b. Mexico City, Sept. 1, 1938; s. Juan Spindola and Gloria Franco; came to U.S., 1964; B.A., Nat. U. Mex., 1957, M.D., 1963; m. Edith Balderas, June 29, 1961; children—Gloria, Jackeline, Claudia, Hugo. Intern Gen. Hosp. Mex., Mexico City, 1963, resident in radiology, 1965-66; intern Danbury (Conn.) Hosp., 1964, resident in pathology, 1967; resident in radiology Montefiore Hosp. and Med. Center, Bronx, N.Y., 1967-70, adj. attending radiologist 1974, head radiologic cardiology, 1974—; fellow in cardiovascular radiology Harvard U., 1970-71, instr. radiology, 1971-74; fellow in cardiovascular radiology Peter Bent Brigham Hosp., Boston, 1970-71, radiologist, 1971-74; cons. West Roxbury (Mass.) VA Hosp., 1972-74; asst. prof. radiology Albert Einstein Coll. Medicine, Yeshiva U., Bronx, 1974-77, asso. prof., 1977—; cons. Coll. Medicine and Dentistry N.J., Martland Hosp., 1977—. Diplomate Am. Bd. Radiology. Fellow Council on Cardiovascular Radiology, Am. Heart Assn.; mem. Sociedad Mexicana de Radiologia, Am. Coll. Radiology, Radiol. Soc. N. Am., Mass. Radiol. Soc., Am., N.Y. roentgen ray socs. Contbr. articles to med. jours. Home: 11 Union Ave Harrison NY 10528 Office: Dept Radiology Montefiore Hospital and Medical Center 111 E 210th St Bronx NY 10467

SPINETTA, FRANK, mortgage banker; b. Manhattan, N.Y., May 31, 1913; s. Arthur and Alice (Fucella) S.; B.Arch., Cooper Union Inst. Tech., 1933; m. Marie E. Graf, Sept. 5, 1937; children—Arthur, Frank Anthony, Elissa. Pres., Colonial Mortgage Corp. of D.C., 1962—; pres. N.Am. Investment and Devel. Corp., 1966—; pres. Spinetta and Co. of N.Y., N.Y.C., 1956—; dir. Dist. Realty Title Ins. Corp. Mem. Mortgage Bankers Assn. Am., Mortgage Banker Assn. N.Y., Nat. Home Bldrs. Assn. Republican. Roman Catholic. Clubs: Georgetown (gov.), Capitol Hill, N.Y. Athletic, N.Y. A.C. Yacht, Jockey (Miami); Ocean Reef (Fla.); Cat Cay (Bahamas). Home: 3900 Watson Pl NW Washington DC 20016 Office: 1101 17th St NW Washington DC 20036

SPINGARN, CLIFFORD LEROY, physician; b. Bklyn., May 8, 1912; s. Alexander and Eleanor (Trinz) S.; A.B., Columbia, 1933, M.D., 1937; m. Eleanor Harrison, June 9, 1937; children—John Harrison, Alexandra. Intern, Mt. Sinai Hosp., N.Y.C., 1937-40, asst. attending physician, 1946-63, asso. attending physician, 1963—, chief parasitology clinic, 1956—; attending physician Doctors Hosp., N.Y.C., 1968—, chmn. com. on continuing med. edn., 1976—; instr. pharmacology Columbia, 1940-42; pvt. practice internal medicine, N.Y.C., 1946—; asst. clin. prof. preventive medicine N.Y.U., 1956-68; asso. clin. prof. medicine Mt. Sinai Sch. Med. Served from lt. (j.g.) to lt. comdr. M.C., USNR, 1942-46; now lt. comdr. ret. res. Diplomate Am. Bd. Internal Medicine. Fellow N.Y. Acad. Medicine, A.C.P.; mem. N.Y. Soc. Tropical Medicine, Am. Soc. Tropical Medicine and Hygiene, Am. Soc. Parasitologists, AAAS, Am. Soc. Internal Medicine, Med. Soc. County N.Y. (chmn. grievance com. 1969-72, chmn. bd. censors 1978—), Scc. Internal Medicine County New York (pres. 1965-67), N.Y. State Soc. Internal Medicine, N.Y. Cardiological Soc. (dir. 1971-73), Phi Beta Kappa, Sigma Xi, Alpha Omega Alpha. Author numerous papers. Home: 201 E 79th St New York City NY 10021 Office: 66 E 80th St New York City NY 10021

SPIRER, EDWIN SHEV, social worker, hosp. adminstr.; b. N.Y.C., Feb. 15, 1947; s. Aaron Maurice and Naomi (Werblowsky) S.; B.A., C.W. Post Coll., 1968; cert. environ. planning, Victoria U., Manchester, Eng., 1971; M.S.W., Fordham U., 1972; m. Arlene Weber, June 27, 1974; 1 dau., Judith Ann. Groupworker, N.Y.C. Dept. Social Services, 1968-70, caseworker, 1972-73; social groupworker Bronx (N.Y.) House, 1970-71; community organizer Flushing Ave. Sr. Center, Bklyn., 1971-72; commd. lt. USPHS, 1973, advanced through grades to lt. comdr., 1979; staff social worker USPHS Hosp., S.I., N.Y., 1973-76; asst. asso. dir. for ambulatory care USPHS Hosp., Boston, 1976—; pvt. practice social work; cons. social work. Served with USAF, 1967-72. Cert. social worker, N.Y. State. Mem. Nat. Assn. Public Adminstrs., Nat. Assn. Social Workers, Aircraft Owners and Pilots Assn., Commd. Officers Assn. USPHS, Nat. Acad. Cert. Social Workers. Clubs: Naval Air Sta. South Weymouth (Mass.) Flying; Mystic Valley Gun (Malden, Mass.). Home: 77 Warren St Boston MA 02135 Office: USPHS Hosp 77 Warren St Boston MA 02135

SPIRIDIGLIOZZI, FRANCIS DONALD, mech. engr.; b. Utica, N.Y., Feb. 2, 1919; s. John and Filippa (Purchine) S.; student Delehanty Inst. N.Y., 1939; B.S. in Aero. Engring., Glenn L. Martin Coll. Aero. Engring., 1944; certificate in stationary and power plant engring. N.Y. State Civil Service Engring. Sch., 1952; m. Josephine LoPiccolo, May 8, 1943; 1 son, Robert Francis. Aero. tool engr. Glenn L. Martin Aircraft Co., Middle River, Md., 1943-48; chief project engr. Rockwell Industries, Utica, N.Y., and Pitts., 1948-58; chief project engr. Univac div. Sperry Rand Corp., Utica, 1959-66; supr. mfg. and design engring. Spl. Metals Corp. div. Allegheny Ludlum Industries, New Hartford, N.Y., 1966—; tchr. mech. and structural engring. Mohawk Valley Community Coll., Utica. Licensed tchr., N.Y.; registered profl. engr., Calif., Can.; certified mfg. engr. Soc. Mfg. Engrs.; profl. mgr. award Soc. for Advancement Mgmt.; certified mgr. U. Trinity and Internat. Indsl. Mgmt. Assn. Mem. Internat. Indsl. Mgmt. Assn., Assn. for Research and Enlightenment, Nat. Assn. Watch and Clock Collectors. Roman Catholic. Club: K.C. (Utica). Home: 1157 Leeds St Utica NY 13501

SPITZ, EMIL WILLIAM, optometrist; b. Bklyn., Nov. 29, 1921; s. Louis and Bertha (Weiss) S.; D.O., Pa. Coll. Optometry, 1940-43; postgrad. Ohio State Coll., 1956; m. Fay N. Zeidman, Dec. 3, 1944; children—Robert, Janet. Practice optometry, Reading, Pa., 1949—; visual cons. industries. Mem. Mayor's Adv. Com., Reading, 1965—; chmn. bd. Berks County Bd. Assistance, 1971-76. Served with M.C., U.S. Army, 1943-46. Mem. Berks County Optometric Soc. (pres. 1961, 70), Pa., Am. optometric assns., Am. Acad. Optometry, Am. Optometric Found. Clubs: B'nai B'rith, Sertoma. Home: 1619 Lorraine Rd Reading PA 19604 Office: 613 Franklin St Reading PA 19602

SPITZER, JEROME, ednl. adminstr.; b. N.Y.C., Oct. 30, 1936; m. Harry and Ray (Cohen) S.; B.S. cum laude, N.Y. U., 1958, M.A., 1959; m. Linda Kirsten, June 20, 1959; children—Jeffrey Alan, Richard Scott. Exec. dir. Camps Mikan-Recro, Arden, N.Y., 1964-73; dir. W.O.M.A.C.S. Acad., N.Y.C., 1970-73; supr. drug, health edn. and health services, N.Y.C. Bd. Edn., 1973—; mem. adj. faculty N.Y. U. Bd. dirs. Recreation Rooms and Settlement, Inc.; trustee Fedn. Jewish Philanthropies; mem. edn. com. Town Club of Scarsdale. Recipient Founders Day award N.Y. U., 1958. Mem. Am. Orthopsychiat. Assn., AAHPER, Am. Personnel and Guidance Assn., Am. Jewish War Vets. Club: B'nai B'rith. Producer TV documentary on sch. health services, 1974. Home: 5 Coralyn Rd Scarsdale NY 10583

SPITZER, ROBERT CLARK, lawyer; b. Chgo., Sept. 25, 1941; s. Sherman Tefft and Harriet Amy (Bradshaw) S.; B.A., Trinity Coll., Hartford, Conn., 1963; J.D., U. Chgo., 1966; m. Beverly Bacot Dickson, June 11, 1963; children—Catherine W., Ian C., David M., Todd B. With firm McNees, Wallace & Nurick, Harrisburg, Pa., 1966-67; admitted to Pa. bar, 1967; atty.-draftsman Pa. Constl. Conv., 1967-68; atty. Legis. Reference Bur., Harrisburg, 1967-69; asst. Office Dist. Atty. Dauphin County, Harrisburg, 1970-72; partner firm Nauman, Smith, Shissler & Hall, Harrisburg, 1973—. Chmn. exec. com. Yoke Crest Inc., 1971; bd. dirs. Big Brother Assn. Dauphin County, 1971, Tri County Easter Seal Soc., 1978; mem. Draft Bd. #55. Mem. Am., Pa., Dauphin County bar assns., Pa. Trial Lawyers Assn. Republican. Episcopalian. Clubs: Harrisburg Country, Pinehurst, Rotary. Photo exhbns., 1977-78. Home: 5509 River Rd Harrisburg PA 17110 Office: 6 N 3d St Harrisburg PA 17101

SPITZER, ROXANE BLUMBERG, nursing adminstr.; b. N.Y.C., July 5, 1939; d. Irving and Lillian (Gardos) Blumberg; B.S., Adelphi Coll., 1960; postgrad. Tchrs. Coll., Columbia U., 1972; m. Jay Spitzer, May 24, 1970; children—Michael, David, Deborah. Clin. supr. North Shore Univ. Hosp., Manhasset, N.Y., 1960-65; pub. health nurse Nassau County Dept. Health, Mineola, N.Y., 1965-68; asst. prof., mgmt. cons. C.W. Post Coll., Brookville, N.Y., 1972-75; asst. adminstr., dir. nursing St. John's Episcopal Hosp., Smithtown, N.Y., 1968-71, 75—; asso. prof. State U. N.Y. at Stony Brook, State U. N.Y. at Farmingdale; asst. prof. Adelphi U. Bd. dirs. Nassau-Suffolk Coordinating Council, 1977—, Middle County Adv. Dist. on Occupational Edn., 1977—; active Suffolk Heart Assn., Suffolk Com. on Mental Health. Mem. Am., N.Y. State nurses assns., Am. Hosp. Assn., Soc. for Nursing Service Adminstrs., Nassau-Suffolk Soc. Nursing Service Dirs. (chmn. 1976—), Nat. League for Nursing, Forum for Nursing Adminstrs., Sigma Theta Tau. Jewish. Contbr. articles to profl. jours. Home: 5 Howard Ct Smithtown NY 11787 Office: St John's Episcopal Hosp Route 25A Smithtown NY 11787

SPITZNAGEL, JOHN TETJE, pharm. co. exec.; b. Auborn, N.Y., Sept. 3, 1941; s. John Frederick and Mary B. (Armstrong) S.; B.A., Rider Coll., 1963; M.B.A. magna cum laude, Fairleigh Dickinson U., 1973; m. Yvonne A. Alexander, June 27, 1964; children—Yvonne T., John T. Pharm. sales rep. Warren Teed Co., Columbus, Ohio, 1964-66; sales rep. Warner-Chilcott Labs, Rochester, N.Y., 1966-68, product supr., Morris Plains, N.J., 1968-71; product advt. mgr. Roche Labs, Nutley, N.J., 1971-74, product mktg. dir., 1974—. Dir. Cromwell Hills (N.J.) Civic Assn., 1974-76. Recipient Hoke award Direct Mail Mktg. Assn., 1973; Ednl. TV Excellence award Ohio State U., 1975. Mem. Am. Mktg. Assn., Pharm. Advt. Club (dir.). Office: Roche Labs Kingsland Rd Nutley NJ 07110

SPIVACK, HENRY ARCHER, life ins. co. exec.; b. Bklyn., Apr. 15, 1919; s. Jacob and Pauline (Schwartz) S.; student Coll. City N.Y., 1936-42, Am. Coll., Bryn Mawr, Pa., 1962-65; m. Sadie Babe Meiseles, Jan. 1, 1941; children—Ian Jeffrey, Paula Janis. Comptroller, Daniel Jones, Inc., N.Y.C., 1947-59; field underwriter Union Central Life Ins. Co., N.Y.C., 1959—, mgr. programming dept., 1966-69, asso. mgr., 1977—; pension dir. Bleichroeder, Bing & Co., N.Y.C., 1975-77; employee benefit plan cons., instr. N.Y. State Ins. Dept., C.W. Post Coll. of Long Island U. Served with USN, 1943-46. Chartered life underwriter. Mem. Life Underwriters Assn. of N.Y., Am. Soc. Chartered Life Underwriters (chmn. N.Y. chpt. pension sect., vice-chmn. profl. liaison com.), Am. Soc. Pension Actuaries, Pensioneers at C.W. Post Coll. of Long Island U., Tax Inst. and Fin. Planning Inst. of C.W. Post Coll., Practicing Law Inst., Greater N.Y. Brokers Assn. Clubs: Knights of Pythias (life mem.; past dep. grand chancellor N.Y. State). Contbr. articles to ins. pubs.; lectr. and panelist confs. and seminars. Home: 1522 45th St Brooklyn NY 11219 Office: 555 5th Ave New York City NY 10017

SPLAVER, SARAH, psychologist; b. N.Y.C.; d. Morris and Rose (Farber) Splaver; Ph.D., N.Y. U., 1953. Pvt. practice counseling, psychologist-guidance cons., 1950—; dir. guidance Rhodes Sch., N.Y.C., 1946-50; editor, pub. Occu-Press, 1953-70; cons. on computerized guidance programs. Fellow Internat. Council Psychologists (co-chmn. on problems of children); mem. Am. Psychol. Assn., Am. Personnel and Guidance Assn. (life), Nat. Vocat. Guidance Assn., Assn. Religious and Value Issues in Counseling, Authors Guild, Am. Sch. Counselors Assn., AAAS, Breast Diseases Assn. Am. (pres.), Am. Rehab. Counseling Assn. Club: B'nai B'rith (v.p. educators chpt.). Author: Your Career-If You're Not Going to College, 2d edit., 1971; Your College Education-How to Pay for it, 1964, rev. edit., 1968; Your Personality and You, 1965; Your Handicap-Don't Let It Handicap You, 1967, rev. edit., 1974; Some Day I'll Be an Aerospace Engineer, 1967; Some Day I'll Be a Librarian. 1967; Some Day I'll Be a Doctor, 1967; The High School Student's Guide to Summer Jobs, 1967; You and Todays Troubled World, 1970; Paraprofessions: Careers of the Future and the Present, 1972; Nontraditional Careers for Women, 1973; Nontraditional College Routes to Careers, 1975; Career Choices in Psychology, 1976; Your Personality and Your Career, 1977; Your Mind and Breast Diseases, 1978; also articles in field; dir., Guidance Exchange; originator, editorial cons. Socioguidrama Series. Address: 3310 Rochambeau Ave Bronx NY 10467

SPLETE, ALLEN PETERJOHN, univ. exec.; b. West Carthage, N.Y., June 24, 1938; B.A. in Govt., St. Lawrence U., Canton, N.Y., 1960; M.A. in Polit. Sci. and Guidance, Colgate U., Hamilton, N.Y., 1962; Ph.D., Syracuse (N.Y.) U., 1968; m. Marilyn Detweiler; children—Heidi, Michael. Grad. preceptor Colgate U. Preceptorial Program, 1960-62; instr. Am. govt. U. Md., Heidelberg br., Karlsruhe, Germany, 1963-64; counselor on admissions U. Rochester, 1964-65; adminstrv. asst. to v.p. acad. affairs Syracuse U., 1965-68, asso. dean acad. affairs, exec. asst. to provost, asst. prof. higher edn., 1968-70, mem. council deans, 1965-70; mem. Middle States Evaluation Teams for Commn. on Higher Edn., 1969—, team chmn., 1975—; v.p. acad. planning and spl. program, asso. prof. higher edn. St. Lawrence U., Canton, 1970—, mem. adminstrv. adv. council, dept. heads council, 1970—, founder, dir. Ann. Confs. on Adirondack Park, 1971—, founder, chmn. Can. Week Program, 1972-76, chmn. univ. priorities com., 1972-77; mem. Presdl. Commn. on Co-edn., 1973-74, trustee com. on acad. affairs, 1973—, chief liaison officer Ford venture com., 1974-78, trustee com. on univ. planning, 1973—, chmn. spl. ad hoc library com., 1976-78; dir. Canton Savs. & Loan Assn.; cons. York (Pa.) Coll., 1974, Alliance Coll. (Pa.), 1977. Chmn. Village of Canton Planning Bd., 1974—; pres. St. Lawrence County Hist. Assn., 1977—; bd. overseers Gov. Silas Wright Hist. Center, 1974-77, chmn., 1975-76. Mem. Am. Assn. Higher Edn., Assn. Profs. Higher Edn., Am. Ednl. Research Assn., Soc. Coll. and Univ. Planning, Citizens to Save Adirondack Park, Nature Conservancy, St. Lawrence County Hist. Assn., Assn. Am. Colls. (pres.'s adv. council 1977—), Soc. Educators and Scholars (bd. editors and cons. Scholar and Educator 1977—), Omicron Delta Kappa, Beta Theta Pi. Editor Adirondack and Canadian Procs.; contbr. articles to profl. jours. Home: 14 Goodrich St Canton NY 13617

SPODEK, RICHARD GEORGE, lumber co. exec.; b. Bklyn., Jan. 3, 1939; s. Julius and Mildred S.; B.S., U. Vt., 1960; postgrad. Wharton Sch. U. Pa., 1977. With ABC TV, N.Y.C., 1960; with Gem Lumber Co., Inc., Rego Park, N.Y., 1960—, sec. treas., 1978—; dir. Monarch

Millwork Co., Inc. Home: 400 E 56th St New York City NY 10022 Office: 97-77 Queens Blvd Rego Park NY 11374

SPOKELY, DAVID GUY, mech. engr.; b. Huron, S.D., July 3, 1928; s. Guy G. and Marjorie U. (Urquhart) S.; B.S., Stanford U., 1950, M.S., 1951; children—David, Margaret Jean. Reliability and quality program mgmt. staff mem. Polaris missile program, U.S. Navy, 1957-60; system engr. satellite and nuclear space program Lockheed Aircraft, 1960-62; mgr. reliability and quality program Apollo program, NASA, 1962-70; system engr. aerosat and communication programs FAA, Washington, 1970-77, system engr. communications, 1977—; founder, dir., coordinator Alliance for Rail Commuter Progress, Inc., 1971—. Mem. Am. Soc. Quality Control, ASME. Presbyterian. Home: 3832 Tremayne Terr Wheaton MD 20906 Office: 2100 2d St SW Washington DC 20590

SPONZILLI, EDWARD GEORGE, lawyer; b. Newark, Mar. 30, 1948; s. Edward James and Dorothy Maria (Murillo) S.; B.A. magna cum laude (Henry Rutgers scholar, Nancy H. Dorr award), Rutgers Coll., 1971; M.A., Columbia U., 1972; J.D., Rutgers U., 1975; summer course Institut Catholique de Paris, 1971. Legal intern Essex County Prosecutor's Office, Newark, 1974-75; admitted to N.J. bar, 1975; law clk. to judge U.S. Dist. Ct. N.J., 1975-77; asso. firm Pitney, Hardin and Kipp, Morristown, 1977—; guest lectr. Rutgers Coll., Essex County Coll.; tutor Rutgers Coll., 1969-71. Mem. YMCA, Madison, N.J. Mem. Am., Fed., N.J., Essex County bar assns., Assn. Study of Negro Life and History, Orgn. Am. Historians, So., Am. hist. assns., Acad. Polit. Sci., Phi Beta Kappa, Phi Alpha Delta. Democrat. Roman Catholic. Clubs: Cranford Judo and Karate Center, Scarlet R Alumni Assn., Rutgers-Newark Law Sch. Alumni Assn. (exec. bd.), Rutgers Coll. Judo Club (treas. 1970-71), Columbia Grad. Faculties Alumni Assn., Kappa Sigma (trustee, sec. 1977-78, alumni advisor). Office: 163 Madison Ave Morristown NJ 07960

SPOONER, JOHN DAVIS, brokerage co. exec.; b. Boston, July 25, 1937; s. Herbert Monroe and Helen (Fine) S.; A.B., Harvard U., 1959; m. Susan L. Farnsworth, June 25, 1966; children—Scott, Nicholas Monroe, Amanda Davis. Asst. v.p. H. Hentz & Co. Inc., N.Y.C., 1961-63, in charge Boston office, 1963-73; v.p. Shearson, Hayden-Stone Inc., N.Y.C., 1973—; dir. Islandia Corp., Del.; instr. securities course Brookline (Mass.) Adult Edn. Center, 1962-70; lectr. finance. Active Boston Big Bros. Assn.; bd. dirs. Ford Hall Forum of Boston, Morgan Meml. Goodwill, Boston, Latimer Found.; trustee Inst. Contemporary Art, Boston; mem. Mayor's Com. Pro Boston, 1978—. Served with M.C., AUS, 1959-60. Mem. Authors Guild. Clubs: St. Botolph (Boston), Harvard of Boston; Owl (Cambridge, Mass.); The Country (Brookline); Belmont (Mass.) Country; Tennis and Racquet. Author: The Pheasant Lined Vest of Charlie Freeman, 1967; Three Cheers for War in General, 1968; Confessions of a Stockbroker (pseudonym Brutus), 1972; Class, 1973; The King of Terrors, 1974; contbg. editor Boston mag.; contbr. articles to mags. Home: 22 Newton St Weston MA 02193 Office: 28 State St Boston MA 02107

SPORN, LAWRENCE MARC, educator; b. N.Y.C., June 18, 1947; s. Michael and Frances (Greenfield) S.; B.A., Curry Coll., 1969; M.S.Ed., Monmouth Coll., 1977. Tchr. mathematics 7th and 8th grades Manalapan-Englishtown (N.J.) Regional Schs., 1970—; adviser Pine Brook Sch. Student Council; mem. Freehold Borough (N.J.) Juvenile Conf. Com.; trustee Rutgers Preparatory Sch. Alumni Assn. Bd. dirs. Freehold (N.J.) Area YMCA. Mem. Math. Assn. Am., Nat. Council Tchrs. Mathematics, Assn. Mathematics Tchrs. N.J., Am. Personnel and Guidance Assn., Nat., N.J. edn. assns. Jewish. Home: 46 Brinckerhoff Ave Freehold NJ 07728 Office: Pine Brook Sch Pease Rd Englishtown NJ 07726

SPOTNITZ, HENRY MICHAEL, thoracic surgeon; b. N.Y.C., July 7, 1940; s. Hyman and Miriam (Berkman) S.; A.B., Harvard U., 1962; M.D., Columbia U., 1966; m. Sharon Meryl Hertz, Jan. 2, 1977. Intern, Bellevue Hosp., N.Y.C., 1967; staff asso. Nat. Heart Inst., Bethesda, Md., 1967-69; resident in gen. and thoracic surgery Presbyn. Hosp., N.Y.C., 1969-75, asst. attending surgeon Columbia-Presbyn. Hosp., 1975—; asst. prof. surgery Coll. Physicians and Surgeons, Columbia U., N.Y.C., 1975—, dir. cardiovascular surgery research lab., 1976—; established investigator Am. Heart Assn., 1977—; asst. attending surgeon Harlem Hosp. Center, 1977—. Served with USPHS, 1967-69. Diplomate Am. Bd. Surgery, Am. Bd. Thoracic Surgery. Fellow A.C.S., Am. Coll. Cardiology; mem. Am. Heart Assn., N.Y. State Med. Assn., Am. Assn. Artificial Internal Organs, AAAS, Am. Fedn. Clin. Research, Soc. Univ. Surgeons. Contbr. articles in cardiovascular surgery to med. jours. Home: 444 E 86th St New York City NY 10028 Office: 161 Fort Washington Ave New York City NY 10032

SPRADLIN, THOMAS RICHARD, lawyer; b. Pauls Valley, Okla., June 9, 1937; s. Julius Everett and Mary Jane (Thompson) S.; A.A. with distinction, George Washington U., 1958, A.B. with distinction, 1959, J.D. with honors, 1963; m. Della Marie Martinez, Mar. 18, 1968; 1 son, Trevor Richard. Admitted to Va. bar, 1963, D.C. bar, 1967, U.S. Supreme Ct. bar, 1968; clk. FBI, Washington, 1955-56; asst. to Sen. Mike Monroney, 1956-63; asso. firm Clifford, Warnke, Glass, McIlwain & Finney, Washington, 1967-72, partner, 1973—; dir. Univ. Assos., Inc., Washington; dir. Applied Practical Tng. Inc., Arlington, Va., Am. Trade and Fin. Co., Arlington. Served to capt. U.S. Army, 1963-67. Mem. Am., Fed., D.C., Va. bar assns., Lamar Soc., Order of Coif, Phi Beta Kappa, Phi Delta Phi, Pi Gamma Mu, Delta Sigma Rho. Asso. editor George Washington Law Rev., 1961-62. Home: 6118 Tilden Ln Rockville MD 20852 Office: 815 Connecticut Ave NW Washington DC 20006

SPRAGGINS, STEWART, mfg. co. exec.; b. Pheba, Miss., May 17, 1936; s. Sherman Johnson and Lithia (Spencer) S.; A.A., Mary Holmes Coll., 1959; B.A., Knoxville Coll., 1962; M.Ed., Fairfield U., 1971; m. Georgene Caldwell, Apr. 30, 1966; 1 dau., Renee Ericka. Asst. phys. dir. Greater Bridgeport (Conn.) YMCA, 1962-63, phys. dir., 1963-66, exec. of phys. edn. and membership depts., 1966-70; Met. Outreach exec. Greater Oklahoma City YMCA, 1970-72; exec. dir. YMCAs of the Oranges, Central Br., Orange, N.J., 1972-74; exec. dir. Harlem br. Greater N.Y. YMCA's, Rio de Janeiro , Argentina, 1967; mem. Nat. Black YMCA Task Force, 1975, Fedn. Concerned YMCA Assns., 1967-71; chmn. YMCA Tri-State Spl. Program Planning Com., 1970; YMCA commr. for Basketball, N.E. Region, 1970-71; chmn. drug abuse com. Greater Bridgeport Council Chs., 1970-71; adviser Greater Bridgeport Inter-Faith Council, 1974-76; corp. mgr. urban/community affairs J.P. Stevens & Co., Inc., N.Y.C., 1976—. Bd. dirs. James Varick Center, Deux Found. Served with AUS, 1974. Mem. Assn. Profl. Dirs., Conn. (pres. 1968-69, N.E. (v.p. 1969-70) phys. dirs. socs., Nat. YMCA Phys. Edn. Soc., Nat. YMCA Adminstrn. Soc., Bridgeport Umpires Assn., Phi Beta Sigma. Presbyterian. Club: 1800 (Bridgeport). Address: JP Stevens & Co Inc 1185 Ave of Americas New York City NY 10036

SPRAGUE, CONSTANCE CAMPBELL, therapist; b. Springfield, Mass., May 12, 1923; d. Charles Burton and Beatrice Millicent (Houston) Campbell; B.A., Wellesley Coll., 1945; M.S., U. Bridgeport, 1976; m. Richard E. Sprague, Feb. 3, 1945 (div. May 1969); children—Peter Campbell, Anne Dodd, Robert Houston. Staff mem. Danbury (Conn.) Mental Health Clinic, 1977—; prin. R.S.L. Counseling Services, Ridgefield, Conn., 1977—; cons. Sr. Retirees Adv. Bd. Mem. planning and adv. bd. YWCA of Greater Bridgeport Center for Women. Mem. Am., Conn. personnel and guidance assns. Congregationalist. Clubs: Jr. League of Bridgeport; Fairfield Villages Wellesley. Home and office: 5 Quince Ct Ridgefield CT 06877

SPRAGUE, GEORGE FREMONT, ret. pub. co. exec.; b. Drew, Maine, Dec. 4, 1908; s. Marion E. and Maude (Scott) S.; B.S., Colby Coll., 1931; m. Lillias Jeannette Reed, Dec. 26, 1933; 1 son, Christopher Reed. Tchr. and coach Lee (Maine) Acad., 1931-33; salesman, vocat. counsellor, exec. Curtis Pub. Co., Phila., 1933-45; asst. circulation mgr. Reader's Digest, 1945-66; mgr. Reader's Digest Services, Inc., 1958-66, v.p., dir. ednl. publs. and projects, 1966-71; sec. Select Mags., 1962-66; exec. v.p. Quality Sch. Plan, 1964-71; v.p., dir. Reader's Digest Assn., 1969-71; ret., 1971. Mem. Mt. Kisco Citizens Com. on Sch. Centralization, 1952-55, Mt. Kisco Recreation Commn., 1953-58, Mt. Kisco Planning Bd., 1956-61, Westchester Coll. Scholarship Com., 1955-61, Westchester County Assn. Edn. Com., 1956-58; bd. dirs. Mt. Kisco Boys' Club, 1948-72, pres., 1956-58; bd. dirs. United Fund of No. Westchester, 1960-62, v.p., 1962-63; sec. bd. trustees N. Westchester Hosp. 1962-72; trustee Knox County Hosp., 1971—; trustee Lee Acad., 1971—, pres., 1976—; trustee Pen Bay Med. Center, 1973—. Home: Owl's Head ME 04854

SPRAGUE, L(LOYD) DEAN, govt. exec., lectr., author; b. Corning, N.Y., Mar. 21, 1922; s. Lloyd Drummond and Iva (Gorton) S.; student Am. U. (Cairo, Egypt), 1939-40; B.A. magna cum laude, Amherst Coll., 1943; postgrad. Am. U., Biarritz, France, 1945-46; M.A., Syracuse U., 1950, Ph.D., 1959; postgrad. U. Pa., 1954, U. Pitts., 1958, George Washington U., 1955-57; m. Edna Smith, Dec. 17, 1949; children—Linda Ann, John Lloyd. Instr. polit. sci. Syracuse (N.Y.) U., 1949-52; budget analyst Dept. Navy, Washington, 1952-58; budget officer Office Sec. Def., Washington, 1958-62; planning officer Dept. Def., Washington, 1963-77, exec. editor budget and program newsletter, 1977—; asso. professorial lectr. George Washington U., Washington, 1966-69, professorial lectr., 1969—; vis. lectr. Syracuse U., 1966-70. Served with AUS, 1943-46. Mem. Am. Polit. Sci. Assn., Am. Soc. Pub. Adminstrn., Assn. for Pub. Program Analysis, Phi Delta Theta, Phi Beta Kappa. Methodist. Author: The Suppression of Dissent During the Civil War and World War I, 1960; Freedom Under Lincoln, 1965. Home: 11113 Ardwick Dr Rockville MD 20852

SPRIGGS, DAVID CARLTON, sch. adminstr.; b. Dayton, Ohio, Feb. 22, 1935; s. Earl Eugene and Viola Evelin (Sigafoos) S.; B.S. in Bus. Adminstrn., Miami U., Oxford, Ohio, 1957. Asst. to pres. Miami Jacobs Jr. Coll., Dayton, 1961-64; dean, v.p. Davis Jr. Coll., Toledo, 1964-68; regional mgr., sch. dir. Lear Siegler Edn. Div., Detroit and Washington, 1968-72; dir. curriculum and new sch. devel. CBS Inc., N.Y.C. and Chgo., 1972-74; gen. mgr. UEI, Inc., Louisville, 1974-75; pres., partner Georgetown Sch. Sci. and Arts, Ltd., Washington, 1975—; v.p., dir. Ednl. Opportunities Exchange, Inc., Washington, 1977—. Leader, Boy Scouts Am.; bd. dirs. Temple Sch. Md., 1978. Served with USAR, 1958-64. Mem. Nat. Assn. Allied Health Schs. (pres. elect), Am. Vocat. Assn., Am. Personnel and Guidance Assn., Nat. Bus. Edn. Assn., Eastern Bus. Tchrs. Assn., Nat. Assn. Trade and Tech. Schs., Phi Theta Pi (past nat. pres.), Phi Gamma Delta, Alpha Kappa Psi. Republican. Methodist. Club: Masons, Shriners. Home: 2720 Wisconsin Ave NW Apt 2 Washington DC 20007 Office: 2233 Wisconsin Ave NW Washington DC 20007

SPRING, JOHN KENNETH, trustee; b. Des Moines, Apr. 7, 1919; s. Alvin Julius and Pearl Susan (Krueger) S.; B.A., Yale U., 1941; M.B.A., Harvard U., 1943; m. Helen Claflin, Oct. 12, 1945; children—Helen, John, Susan, William. Investment broker Shearson Hammill & Co., N.Y.C., 1946-48; trust officer State St. Bank, Boston, 1948-60; partner Welch & Forbes, Boston, 1960—; dir. New Eng. Mut. Life Ins. Co., State St. Boston Fin. Corp., State St. Bank & Trust Co., Millipore Corp., Compugraphic Corp., Maximum, Inc.; gen. partner Ampersand Assos. Trustee Children's Hosp., Boston, Children's Mus., Boston; treas., trustee Wellesley Coll., 1960-78. Served with USNR, 1943-46. Mem. Boston Security Analysts Soc., Inst. Chartered Fin. Analysts. Congregationalist. Clubs: Boston Econ., Somerset. Home: 285 Elm St Concord MA 01742 Office: 73 Tremont St Boston MA 02108

SPRINGER, HANS GUENTHER, coll. adminstr.; b. Hamburg, Germany, July 8, 1943; s. Gerhard Wilhelm and Hertha H.A. (Ross) S.; came to U.S., 1952, naturalized, 1969; A.A., Niagara County Community Coll., 1969; B.A., Concordia Coll., 1977; m. Marie E. Eisemann, Aug. 15, 1965; children—Kathryn Marie, John William. With Hens & Kelly Inc., Buffalo, 1961-62; mgr. biochemistry lab. facilities Buffalo Gen. Hosp., 1964-75, lectr. Sch. Med. Tech., 1970-75; asst. devel. dir. Concordia Coll., Bronxville, N.Y., 1976—. Treas. Fish, 1972-75; driver Tri-Community Vol. Ambulance Service. Mem. Assn. Advancement of Med. Instrumentation, Am. Assn. Clin. Chemists, Concordia Hist. Inst., Assn. Luth. Devel. Execs. (charter mem.), Deferred Giving Group N.Y.C. Republican. Lutheran. Club: Lions. Mem. research adv. panel Med. Lab. Observer jour., 1970-76. Home: 220 Midland Ave Tuckahoe NY 10707 Office: Concordia Coll Bronxville NY 10708

SPRINGER, JOHN KELLEY, hosp. exec.; b. Salem, Ohio, May 11, 1931; s. Wilbur Johnson and Nellie Marie (Kelley) S.; A.B., Dartmouth Coll., 1953; M.H.A., U. Mich., 1960; m. Jane Lee Parsons, Oct. 13, 1956; children—Kelley Lynn, Dana Lee, Susan Elizabeth, Nellie Jane, Adminstrv. resident Mary Hitchcock Meml. Hosp., Hanover, N.H., 1959-60, asst. adminstr., 1960-64, asso. adminstr., 1964-69, adminstr. for ops., 1969-71; asso. exec. dir. Hartford (Conn.) Hosp., 1971-73, exec. dir., 1974—, pres., 1977—; pres. Combined Hosps. Alcoholism Program, Inc., 1972-75; lectr. Sch. Pub. Health, Yale U., 1975. Deacon, First Ch. of Christ Congl., West Hartford, 1975—; bd. dirs. Urban League Greater Hartford, 1973-76, Greater Hartford chpt. ARC, Hartford Sem. Found. Served to capt. USMC, 1953-58; col. Res., 1958-75. Mem. Am. Coll. Hosp. Adminstrs., New Eng. Hosp. Assembly (pres. 1972), Conn. Hosp. Assn. (chmn. council on govt. 1973—), Am. Hosp. Assn. Clubs: Hartford; Hartford Tennis. Home: 47 Brenway Dr West Hartford CT 06117 Office: 80 Seymour St Hartford CT 06115

SPRINGFIELD, FRANKLYN BRUCE, psychoanalyst; b. N.Y.C., June 6, 1933; s. Harry and Renee (Stempa) S.; B.A., New Sch. Social Research, 1955; M.S., City Coll. N.Y., 1956; Ph.D., N.Y. U., 1960. Psychol. intern N.J. Neuro-Psychiat. Inst., Princeton, 1956-57; pvt. practice psychoanalysis, N.Y.C., 1957—; clin. psychologist N.J. State Prison, Trenton, 1957-58, Arthur Brisbane Child Treatment Center, 1958-59; prin. clin. psychologist Essex County Guidance Center East Orange, N.J., 1959-62; dir. psychology dept. N.Y. Psychiat. Center, 1960-70, dir. dept. child guidance Livingston (N.J.) pub. schs., 1962-63; instr. N.Y. U., 1959-60; asso. prof. L.I. U., 1966-67; supr. Met. Center Mental Health, 1972—; cons. Am. Mgmt. Psychologists, 1966-68. Mem. Am. Psychol. Assn., N.Y. Soc. Clin. Psychologists, Am. Acad. Psychotherapists. Office: 15 W 72d St New York City NY 10023

SPRINKLE, MELVIN CLINE, electronic and acoustical engr.; b. Martinsburg, W.Va., Mar. 22, 1916; s. Melvin Jacob and Susan (Hensel) S.; A.B. with honors, Shepherd Coll., 1938; postgrad. George Washington U., 1958-62, U. Mo. at Rolla, 1970, Purdue U., 1971, Mass. Inst. Tech., 1972; m. Gladys Virginia Miller, June 28, 1941; children—William Melvin, Janet Elaine Sprinkle Gilbert, Kenneth Alan. Engr., Radiomarine Corp., N.Y.C., 1940-41; radio engr. Signal Corps, War Dept., Washington, 1941, Bur. of Ships, Navy Dept., 1941-46; sales engr. Altec Lansing Corp., N.Y.C., 1946-51, Shrader Sound, Washington, 1952-53, Ampex Corp., Redwood City, Calif., 1953-56, Prodn. Research Corp., Thornwood, N.Y., 1956-57; project engr. Page Communication Engrs., Inc., Washington, 1958-70; cons. audio-acoustical engr., 1970-75; project engr. N.J. Communication Corp., Kenilworth, 1975-76; chief audio engr. Dynacom div. Dynaelectron Corp., Alexandria, Va., 1976-78; cons. audio-acoustical engr., 1978—; instr. audio system and design Eastman Sch. Music, Rochester; rec. seminars, 1972—. Troop com. Boy Scouts Am., Kensington, Md., 1957-59, 64-68. Registered profl. engr. D.C., N.J., Md. Mem. Audio Engring. Soc. (charter), Acoustical Soc. Am. Republican. Methodist. Club: Masons (32 deg.) (grand high priest D.C. 1974, post master). Contbr. articles on audio and acoustic subjects to profl. jours. and mags. Engr. sound system N.Y. Giants Football Stadium. Home and office: 3403 Saul Rd Kensington MD 20795 Office: PO Box 10 Kensington MD 20795

SPRINKLE, ROBERT MARSHALL, internat. ednl. exchange exec.; b. Granite City, Ill., Dec. 12, 1936; s. Marshall Roseboro and Jean Pomeroy (Miller) S.; B.A., U. Colo., 1959; student N.Mex. State U., 1963-64, U. Mich., 1964-65; m. G(ladys) Sandra Fisher, Mar. 31, 1967; 1 dau., Lisa Jean Harrison. Dir. pub. relations, editor, dir. Internat. Student Visitor Service, USNSA/Ednl. Travel, Inc., N.Y.C., 1960-63; grad. asst., counselor N.Mex. State U. Guidance Center, 1963-64; program adviser, adminstrv. coordinator U. Mich. Internat. Center, 1964-67; exec. dir., sec.-treas., dir. Internat. Assn. for Exchange of Students for Tech. Experience U.S., Inc., Columbia, Md., 1967—, mem. internat. advisory com.; mem. exec. com. U.S. Nat. Commn. for UNESCO, Washington, 1970-74, mem. membership com. 1974-75, nominating com., 1974-75. Served to capt. AUS, 1959-60. Mem. Am. Assn. Higher Edn., Am. Fgn. Service Assn., Am. Soc. Engring. Edn., Am. Soc. Pub. Adminstrn., Am. Soc. Tng. and Devel., Assn. World Edn., Nat. Assn. Fgn. Student Affairs, Soc. Citizen Edn. in World Affairs, Soc. Internat. Devel., Empire State Ry. Mus. Inc., Railroadians of Am. Inc., South Street Seaport Mus. Inc. Republican. Baptist. Office: 217 American City Bldg Columbia MD 21044

SPROULL, ROBERT LAMB, physicist, univ. pres.; b. Lacon, Ill., Aug. 16, 1918; s. John Steele and Chloe Velma (Lamb) S.; A.B., Cornell U., 1940, Ph.D., 1943; m. Mary Louise Knickerbocker, June 27, 1942; children—Robert F., Nancy M. Research physicist RCA Labs., 1943-46; faculty Cornell U., 1946-63, prof. physics, 1956-63, dir. lab. atomic and solid state physics, 1959-60, dir. materials sci. center, 1960-63, v.p. acad. affairs, 1965-68; v.p., Provost U. Rochester, 1968-70, pres., 1970—; dir. Advanced Research Projects Agy., Dept. Def., Washington, 1963-65; prin. physicist Oak Ridge Nat. Lab., 1952; physicist European Research Assos., Brussels, Belgium, 1958-59; lectr. NATO, 1958-59; chmn. Def. Sci. Bd., 1968-70; sci. adv. com. Gen. Motors Corp., 1971—, chmn., 1973—; fellow Center for Advanced Study in Behavioral Scis., 1973; dir. Security Trust, John Wiley & Sons, Sybron Corp., United Technologies Corp., Xerox Corp. Trustee Cornell U., 1972-77, Deep Springs Coll., 1967-75. Mem. Telluride Assn. (pres. 1945-47). Author: Modern Physics, 1956. Editor Jour. Applied Physics, 1954-57. Home: 692 Mt Hope Ave Rochester NY 14620

SPUHLER, HAROLD AYLESWORTH, fed. agy. ofcl.; b. Tucumcari, N.Mex., Sept. 16, 1915; s. Frank Jacob and Hettie (Aylesworth) Spuhler; B.S., Tex. Tech. Coll., 1948; S.M., Mass. Inst. Tech., 1950; Ph.D., U. Ill., 1960; m. Fay Long, Oct. 7, 1936; 1 son, Karl Francis. With Internat. Harvester Co., 1937-42; asst. prof. Tex. Tech. Coll., 1950-53, asso. prof., 1954-56, prof., head dept. elec. engring., 1960-65; staff asso. grad. sch. facilities sect. NSF, Washington, 1966-70, head Inst. Planning and Evaluation Group, 1970-71, dept. head Office Oceanographic Facilities and Support, 1971-73, cons., 1973-74, program mgr. advanced energy research and tech., 1974-76, dir. resource systems program, 1976-78, program mgr. engring. applications 1978—; research asso. Elec. Engring. Research Lab., U. Ill., 1956-60; cons. in field. Served with USNR, 1942-45. Mem. AAAS, IEEE (chmn. awards com. S. Plains sect. 1963), Am. Soc. Engring. Edn. (editorial com. 1961-71), Am. Inst. Physics, Soc. Coll. and Univ. Planners, Western Interstate Commn. on Higher Edn. (adv. panel space analysis manuals project), Sigma Xi, Phi Kappa Phi, Tau Beta Pi, Eta Kappa Nu, Sigma Pi Sigma. Home: 2000 S Eads St Arlington VA 22202 Office: 1800 G St NW Washington DC 20550

SPUNT, SHEPARD ARMIN, mgmt. and financial cons.; b. Cambridge, Mass., Feb. 3, 1931; s. Harry and Naomi (Drooker) S.; B.S., U. Pa., 1952, M.B.A., 1956; m. Joan Murray Fooshee, Aug. 6, 1961 (dec. June 1969); children—Erica Frieda and Andrew Murray (twins). Owner, Colonial Realty Co., Brookline, 1953—; sr. asso. Gen. Solids Assos., 1956—; chmn. bd., clk. Gen. Solids System Corp., 1971-74; trustee Union Capital Trust; incorporator Liberty Bank & Trust Co. Chmn., Com. for Fair Urban Renewal Laws, 1965—. Pres. N.E. Council of Young Republicans, 1964-67, 69-71, vice chmn. Young Republican Nat. Fedn., 1967-69, dir. region 1, 1964-67, 69-71; mem. Brookline (Mass.) Republican Town Com., 1960—; del. Atlantic Conf. Young Polit. Leaders, 1973; treas. Ten. Men of Mass., 1973—. Bd. dirs. Brookline Taxpayers Assn., 1964—, v.p., 1971-72, pres., 1972—. Registered profl. engr., Mass. Mem. Nat. Soc. Profl. Engrs., Am. Mgmt. Assn., Rental Housing Assn., Greater Boston Real Estate Bd., Navy League. Mason. Author: (with others) A Business Data Processing Service for Small Business Practitioners, 1956, latest rev. edit., 1959; A Business Data Processing Service for Medical Practitioners, 1956. Patentee in field; author, sponsor consumer protection legislation Mass. Gen. Ct., 1969—. Home: 177 Reservoir Rd Chestnut Hill MA 02167 Office: 21 Elmer St Cambridge MA 02138

SPYROU, PANAGIOTIS GEORGE, thoracic surgeon; b. Florina, Greece, Mar. 22, 1936; s. George Lazaros and Sofia Eugenia (Mirtsou) S.; came to U.S., 1969, naturalized, 1973; M.D., U. Thessaloniki Med. Sch., 1962; Doctorate, U. Athens Med. Sch., 1971; m. Alice May Roberts, Nov. 11, 1977. Intern, Presbyn.-U. Pa. Med. Center, 1969-70; resident in gen. surgery Hahnemann Med. Coll. Hosp., Phila., 1970-73, resident in thoracic-cardiovascular surgery, 1973-75, instr. cardio-thoracic surgery, 1975; practice medicine specializing in thoracic and cardiovascular surgery, Penn Sauken, N.J., 1975—; mem. staff Our Lady of Lourddes Hosp., Camden, N.J., 1976—, dir. thoracic cardiovascular surgery, 1977—; mem. staffs Hahnemann Med. Coll. Hosp.; asst. prof. surgery Coll. Medicine and Dentistry N.J., 1977—. Served with M.C., Greek Army, 1962-64. Diplomate Am. Bd. Surgery, Am. Bd. Thoracic Surgery; cert. Ednl. Council Fgn. Med. Grads., fed. licensure exam. Fellow Am. Coll. Cardiology (asso.), Am. Coll. Angiology (asso.), Internat. Coll. Angiology, Internat. Coll. Surgeons, Royal Coll. Health; mem. AMA, Pa., N.J. med. socs. Home: 3707 Country Club Rd Philadelphia PA 19131 Office: Browning Road Medical Center Penn Sauken NJ 08109

SQUADRA, JOHN HARLEY, artist, designer; b. N.Y.C., June 25, 1932; s. Enrico L. and Mary (Ludington) S.; B.F.A., R.I. Sch. Design, 1953; m. Daisy Stieber, Oct. 10, 1953; children—Christopher, Carol. Designer, Leo Jiranek, N.Y.C., 1952-58; color coordinator Hamilton Cosco, Inc., Columbus, Ind., 1965-67; designer Poloron Products, Inc., New Rochelle, N.Y., 1967-69; pvt. practice indsl. and graphic design, Rowayton, Conn., 1969—; exhibited surrealist paintings Bridgeport Mus. Art, Sci. and Industry, 1978. Served with U.S. Army, 1954-56. Mem. Rowayton Arts Center. Home and Office: 151 Highland Ave Rowayton CT 06853

SQUEGLIA, NICHOLAS LOUIS, JR., quality control engr.; b. New Haven, Mar. 7, 1933; s. Nicholas Louis and Phyllis S.; A.S. in Indsl. Engring., U. New Haven, 1960, A.S. in Indsl. Mgmt., 1963; m. Joan Arlene Coates, June 29, 1957; children—Vanessa, Nicholas, Jaqueline. Gen supr. product quality AVCO Lycoming, Stratford, Conn., 1964-71; pres., mgmt. cons. Acutime Systems Inc., Milford, Conn., 1971-72; dir. quality control and inspection N.Y.C. Transp. Adminstrn., 1972-76; quality engr. modernization Olin Corp.-Winchester Western div., New Haven, 1976—; part-time instr. quality control. Advisor, Jr. Achievement, 1977-78. Served with U.S. Army, 1953-55. Certified quality engr. Mem. Am. Soc. Quality Control (past chmn. New Haven sect.). Author: Sampling Plans, 1969; Sampling Plans for Zero Defects, 1978. Home: 218 Hawthorne Ln Orange CT 06477 Office: 275 Winchester Ave New Haven CT 06504

SQUIRE, ALBERT TEGG, state ofcl.; b. Rochester, N.Y., July 14, 1925; s. Andrew Bradford and Lillian Mae (Tegg) S.; B.S., Rensselaer Poly. Inst., 1948; postgrad., 1963-64; postgrad. U. Rochester, 1952-53; m. Lois Nancy Rothfuss, Sept. 3, 1950; children—Andrew Bradford, Margaret Anne. Project engr. Lozier Engrs., Inc., Rochester 1952-60; sr. staff engr. Kordite Corp., Macedon, N.Y., 1960-62; plant engr. Standard Packaging Corp., Buter, Pa., 1962-63; chief engr. Tek Hughes Corp., Watervliet, N.Y., 1963-66; asso. engr. Myrick & Chevalier, Albany, N.Y., 1966-68; dir. bur. rodent and control N.Y. State Dept. Health, Albany, 1968-72, dir. bur. milk and food sanitation, 1972—. Pres., dir. Bradford-Park Corp., Elnora, N.Y., 1963—. Cons. engr. Village of Macedon, 1960-62. Served with USNR, 1943-46, 50-51. Registered profl. engr., N.Y., Ohio, Pa., Ind., Ill. Mem. Rotarian (past pres. Watervliet). Patentee chem. metal cleaners. Home: 311 River Rd Schaghticoke NY 12154 Office: Empire State Plaza Albany NY 12237

SQUIRE, HERBERT EARL, JR., elec. engr.; b. Bayshore, N.Y., Oct. 12, 1944; s. Herbert Earl and Marian Sophie (Reiser) S.; B.S. in TV and Radio, Ithaca (N.Y.) Coll., 1967; m. Laurie Melinda Rubin, Aug. 6, 1975. Program dr. Sta. WICB-AM & FM, Ithaca, 1966-67, chief engr., 1964-66; engr. Empire State Sports Network, summers 1964-67; disc jockey, engr., newsman Sta. WPAC-AM & FM, Patchogue, N.Y.; designer highly specialized telecommunications systems for WOR Radio, Metromedia, others; instr. radio N.Y. Inst. Tech., 1970-71; engring. supr. Sta. WOR-AM, N.Y.C., 1967—, asst. chief operator, 1973-74. Mem. Soc. Broadcast Engrs., Nat. Acad. TV Arts and Scis. Luthern. Home: 46 Schenck Ave Great Neck NY 11021 Office: WOR Radio 1440 Broadway New York NY 10018

SQUIRES, BONNIE STEIN, poet; b. Phila., May 12, 1940; d. Joseph and Lillian (Ponnock) Stein; B.S. in Edn., U. Pa., 1962, M.A. in English, 1965; m. Melvin Squires, June 11, 1961; children—Deborah Rose, David Abram. Tchr. English, Yeadon (Pa.) High Sch., 1962-64; summer sch. tchr., substitute tchr., homebound tutor Lower Merion (Pa.) Sch. Dist., 1962-66; columnist Jewish Exponent, 1970-74; instr. poetry Main Line Night Sch., Phila., 1977-78; master tchr. Brit. European Center, French exchange program, summers 1977, 78; entertainment editor Main Line Jewish Expression, 1978. Vice pres. Lower Merion-Narbeth Democratic Com., 1970-74, Lower Merion Dem. Women, 1970—; women's div. v.p. Am. Jewish Congress, 1975—, Am. Friends Hebrew U., 1972—. Recipient 1st prize N. Am. Mentor Mag., 1974, 77. Mem. Pa., Ky. poetry socs., St. David's Writers Conf. (conf. editor 1975—), Nat. Council Tchrs. English, Phila. Writers Conf., Dickens Fellowship, U. Pa. Alumni Assn., Phi Beta Kappa, Kappa Delta Epsilon, Pi Lambda Theta. Jewish. Author: New Eden, 1977. Editor: A New Nation, 1976. Home: 11 Arthur's Round Table Wynnewood PA 19096 Office: PO Box 664 Ardmore PA 19003

SQUIRES, LINDLEY STURGES, electronics design and mfg. co. exec.; b. Rutland, Vt., Oct. 10, 1932; s. Lindley Sturges and Harriet Sophia (Ward) S.; A.B. in Physics, Middlebury Coll., 1956; B.S. in Elec. Engring., Mass. Inst. Tech., 1956; m. Edwina Christine Rachels, June 16, 1973; children—Lorene Herriette, Livia Jo. Engr., ITT Fed. Labs., 1956-59; sr. engr. ITT Labs., 1959-61, project engr., 1961-64, sect. head ITT Avionics div., 1964-67, mgr. electronic design, 1967-71, program mgr., 1971-73, program dir., 1973-76, v.p., dir. program mgmt., 1976—. Mem. Am. Def. Preparedness Assn., Soc. Logistics Engrs., Tau Beta Pi, Eta Kappa Nu. Home: 418 Valley Rd Upper Montclair NJ 07043 Office: 390 Washington Ave Nutley NJ 07110

SRIVASTAVA, SURESH CHANDRA, research chemist; b. Aligarh, India, Jan. 1, 1939; s. Jang B. and Shakuntala Devi S.; came to U.S., 1969, naturalized, 1977; B.S., Agra U., 1955, M.S., 1957; Ph.D., U. Allahabad, 1960; m. Maria Castillo, Sept. 16, 1968; children—Stephen, Neil. Research asso. Ga. Inst. Tech., Atlanta, 1969-71; chemist Research Triangle Inst., Research Triangle Park, N.C., 1971-74; clin. asst. prof. radiology Downstate Med. Center, State U. N.Y., Bklyn., 1974-75; scientist, med. dept. Brookhaven Nat. Lab., Upton, N.Y., 1975—. AEC fellow, 1962-65. Mem. Am. Chem. Soc., Soc. Nuclear Medicine. Contbr. articles to profl. jours. Home: 8 Penelope Dr Setauket NY 11733 Office: Brookhaven Nat Lab Upton NY 11973

STAAB, JOSEPH RAYMOND, govt. ofcl.; b. Hays, Kans., Jan. 2, 1932; s. Joseph Leo and Esther Isea (Eaton) S.; B.S., Ft. Hays State U., 1958; postgrad., Kans. State U., 1958-59; m. Joan Annette Schumacher, Nov. 25, 1961; children—Gregory Joseph, William Eric. Regional audit mgr. GAO, FAA, USAF, OEO, Washington, Los Angeles, Chgo., 1959-67; account exec. Dean Witter & Co., Inc., Pasadena, Calif., 1967-69; financial planner Powell, Johnson & Assos., Inc., Pasadena, 1969-70; sr. fin. analyst Standard & Poor's Corp., Los Angeles, 1970-71; mgmt. cons., Los Angeles, 1971-74; supervising mgmt. analyst FAA, Seattle, 1974-76, Washington, 1977—; dir. Center for Small Bus., Urbana (Ohio) Coll., 1976-77. Served with USN, 1952-56. Mem. Assn. Govt. Accts., Ellis County Hist. Soc., Ft. Hays State U. Alumni Assn., Sigma Tau Gamma. Home: 7112 Carnation Ct Springfield VA 22152 Office: FAA AMS-530 800 Independence Ave SW Washington DC 20591

STABELL, DONALD EDWARD, physicist, programmer,; b. North Tonawanda, N.Y., Feb. 2, 1942; s. Harold Joseph and Annie (Barnes) S.; B.S. cum laude, Canisius Coll., 1963; Ph.D., U. Pitts., 1968; m. Karen Hawkes, Jan. 16, 1960; children—Howard, Phillip, Angela, Patrick. Sr. asso. physicist IBM Corp., East Fishkill, N.Y., 1968-73, staff engr./physicist, 1973-74, staff engr./physicist, Poughkeepsie, 1974-78, reliability engr., 1978—. Tchr. engring. physics Dutchess Community Coll., 1969-75; cons. U.S. Bur. Mines, Bruceton, Pa., 1967-68, Nuclear Materials and Engring. Corp., 1967. NASA trainee, 1965-68. Contbr. articles to profl. jours. Home: Pancake Hollow Rd Route 2 Box 538 Highland NY 12528 Office: IBM D/F88 B/052 PO Box 390 Poughkeepsie NY 12602

STABILE, CHARLES JOSEPH, printing co. exec.; b. Bklyn., June 7, 1932; s. Joseph Robert and Eleanor S.; certificate vocat. edn. Central Conn. State Coll., 1968; m. Lorraine Salvo, Nov. 22, 1956. Supr. human relation area files Yale U., New Haven, 1953-57; supr. Casco Products, Bridgeport, Conn., 1957-60, Am. Machine Foundry Co., Stamford, Conn., 1960-70; mgr. adminstrv. services Am. Jewish Com., N.Y.C., 1970-76; gen. mgr. Congress Printers Inc., New Haven, 1976-77; owner, gen. mgr. Fairfax Press, West Haven, Conn., 1977—. Mem. In-Plant Printing Mgmt. Assn. Home: 785 Dennis Dr Orange CT 06477

STABILE, ROSE TOWNE, bldg. mgmt. cons.; b. Sunderland, Eng.; d. Stephen and Amelia Bergman; ed. English schs., Tchr's. Coll. Columbia U.; m. Wilfred Kermode, (dec. Feb. 1934); m. 2d, Arthur Whittlesey Towne, May 29, 1936 (dec. July 1954); m. 3d, G. Norbert LeVeillie, June 10, 1961 (div.); m. 4th, Fred Stabile, May 30, 1970. Formerly auditor Whitehall, London; activities and membership dir. N.Y. League of Girls Clubs, N.Y.C.; real estate exec., also bldg. mgr. State Tower Bldg., Syracuse, N.Y.; also designer and decorator; cons. State Tower, pub. relations, 1975—; lectr. real estate dept. Syracuse U. Sponsor, Assn. Crippled Children and Adults N.Y. State; active Syracuse Symphony, Everson Mus., alumni and meml. funds Amherst Coll. and Harvard U. Mem. English Speaking Union (membership com.), Bus. and Profl. Women's Clubs, Syracuse Real Estate Bd., Nat., N.Y. assns, real estate bds., Nat. Assn. Bldg. Owners and Mgrs., N.Y. Soc. Real Estate Appraisers, Syracuse C. of C., Friends of Reading, LWV, Assn. of UN. Clubs: Women of Rotary, Internat. Center Syracuse, Corinthian. Unitarian (chmn. service com. 1956-57). Home: 304 Malverne Dr Syracuse NY 13208 Office: State Tower Bldg Syracuse NY 13202

STABLER, DONALD BILLMAN, business exec.; b. Williamsport, Pa., Dec. 23, 1908; s. George W. and Etta Mae (Billman) S.; B.S. in Civil Engring., Lehigh U., 1930, M.S., 1932, LL.D., 1974; m. Dorothy L. Witwer, Aug. 10, 1952; 1 dau., Beverly Anne. Engr., Pa. Supply Co. and Walter M. Mumma, contractor, Harrisburg, Pa., 1932-40; owner Donald B. Stabler, contractor, Harrisburg, 1940—; chmn. bd. Stabler Constrn. Co., Harrisburg, 1955—; pres., chmn. bd. Protection Services Inc., 1955—, State Aggregates, Inc., Harrisburg, 1964—, DBS Transit Co., Harrisburg, 1965—, Stabler Cos., Inc., Harrisburg, 1976—; chmn. bd. Eastern Industries, Inc., Wescosville, Pa., 1976—; pres., dir. Surf House, Inc., Surfside, Fla.; dir. Dauphin Deposit Bank & Trust Co., Millers Mut. Ins. Co., Harrisburg. Mem. Com. of 100, Miami Beach, Fla. Chmn. bd. The Road Info. Program (TRIP), Washington; bd. dirs. Polyclin. Med. Center, Harrisburg, Miami Heart Inst., Miami Beach, Miami Opera; corporate mem. bd. trustees Lehigh U., Bethlehem, Pa. Recipient L-in-Life award N.Y. Lehigh Club, 1972; Silver Hard hat award Constrn. Writers Assn., 1973, award Nat. Auto Dealers, 1978. Mem. Am. Rd. and Transp. Builders Assn. (dir.; award 1974), Asso. Pa. Constructors (dir., adv. bd., pres. 1949-50), U.S., Pa., Harrisburg Area (past adm.) chambers commerce, Am. Soc. Hwy. Engrs. (award 1975), Harrisburg Builders Exchange, Nat., Pa. socs. profl. engrs., Lehigh U. Alumni Assn. (pres. 1965-66), Navy League, Pa. Soc. N.Y., Pi Delta Epsilon, Chi Epsilon. Presbyterian. Clubs: Masons, Shriners, Jesters, Tall Cedars, Elks, Rotary, Saints and Sinners, Harrisburg Country, Tuesday (Harrisburg); Union League Phila.; Bal Harbor (Fla.); Beach Colony (Coral Gables, Fla.); Saucon Valley Country (Bethlehem, Pa.); Coral Reef Yacht (Miami, Fla.); Indian Creek Country, Surf (bd. govs., pres. 1974-76), (Miami Beach, Fla.); Le Mirador Country (Switzerland). Home: Stray Winds Farm 4001 McIntosh Rd Harrisburg PA 17112 also 236 Bal Bay Dr Bal Harbour FL 33154 Office: 635 Lucknow Rd Harrisburg PA 17110

STACHNIEWICZ, STEPHANIE ANNE, nurse, health facility adminstr.; b. Clifton Heights, Pa., Nov. 20, 1921; d. John and Mary (Pyrczak) S.; grad. Phila. Gen. Hosp. Sch. Nursing, 1947; B.S. Nursing Edn., U. Pa., 1956, certificate in pub. health, 1956, M.S. in Nursing, 1967. With Phila. Gen. Hosp., 1947-77, supr. outpatient dept., 1963-67, asso. dir. nursing service, 1967-72, dir. nursing service and Sch. Nursing, 1972-77, clin. instr. Sch. Nursing, 1953-63; dir. Nursing City of Phila. Nursing Home, 1977-78, nursing home adminstr. N.E. unit, 1978—; participant History of Nursing, TV program; coordinator self breast exam. program Am. Cancer Soc.; speaker on careers in nursing, alcoholic, drug abuse program; participant profl. seminars. R.N., lic. nursing home adminstr., Pa. Mem. Alumnae Assn. Phila. Gen. Hosp. Sch. Nursing (pres. 1969-71), Alumnae Assn. U. Pa., Am., Pa. nurses assns., Pa., Southeastern Pa. (chmn. Deans and Dirs. Conf. Group 1969-71), Nat. (council diploma programs) leagues nursing, Am. Hosp. Assn., Am. Soc. Hosp. Nursing Service Adminstrs., Profl. and Bus. Woman's Assn., AAUW, Grad. Nurse Assn. Phila. Gen. Hosp., Politically Responsible Nurses, Sigma Theta Tau. Democrat. Ukrainian Catholic. Author: (with J. Axelrod) The Double Frill—A History of the Philadelphia General Hospital School of Nursing, 1978. Office: 700 Civic Center Blvd Philadelphia PA 19104

STACKHOUSE, CHARLES MOULTON, JR., social worker; b. Orange, N.J., Apr. 26, 1947; s. Charles M. and Pauline (Colabelli) S.; B.A., Ottawa U., 1969; M.A., Montclair State Coll., 1971; certificate in alcoholic studies, Rutgers U., 1972, certificate in tng., 1973, certificate in mgmt., 1978; M.P.A. candidate, Rutgers U.; m. Evelyn June Binder, May 29, 1971. Social worker Bur. Local Ops., Wayne, N.J., 1969-74; asst. social work supr. Greystone Park (N.J.) Psychiat. Hosp., 1974—. Recipient hon. award Dept. Mental Health of State Kans., 1968. Mem. Am., N.J. psychol. assns., Nat. Assn. Social Workers, Am. Mgmt. Assn., Psi Chi. Research in attitudes. Home: Jenny Jump Estates PO Box 197 Hope NJ 07844 Office: Greystone Park Psychiatric Hosp Greystone Park NJ 07950

STADDEN, WARREN CARL, architect, civil engr., planner; b. Watertown, N.Y., June 30, 1922; s. David Irland and Annabel Grace (Clark) S.; B.S., Bucknell U., 1947; student Princeton U., 1943-44, Inst. Design and Constrn., 1953-54; m. Jean Marie Russo, Aug. 31, 1946; children—Arlene, Robert, Barbara. Archtl., structural bldg. designer, 1948—; pvt. practice, Roselle, N.J., 1955—; mayor of Roselle, 1964-65; tchr. Rutgers U., 1954-59; mem. planning bd. Borough of Roselle; fallout shelter analyst U.S. Dept. Def., 1962—; mem. N.J. Interprofl. Com. on Urban Affairs. Served as sgt. AUS, 1943-46. Profl. engr., N.J., N.Y., Pa., Mass., Hawaii; registered architect, N.J., Pa., Hawaii. Mem. Nat. (chmn.), N.J. (chmn., sec.-treas.), Union County (pres.) socs. profl. engrs., N.J. Soc. Architects, AIA, Bldg. Ofcls. Assn. N.J., N.J. Soc. Profl. Planners, N.J. Cons. Engrs. Council, Soc. Am. Value Engrs., Internat. Platform Assn., Pi Mu Epsilon, Phi Eta Sigma, Tau Beta Pi. Presbyterian (elder). Club: Lions (pres. Roselle). Address: 315 E 5th Ave Roselle NJ 07203

STADNICKI, STANLEY WALTER, JR., toxicologist; b. Norwich, Conn., Sept. 30, 1943; s. Stanley Walter and Beatrice Catherine (Dumais) S.; B.A., Assumption Coll., Worcester, Mass., 1965; M.A., Clark U., Worcester, 1970; Ph.D., Worcester Poly. Inst., 1976; m. Jeanne Marie Couture, Sept. 6, 1965; children—Sandra, Scott, Steven, Robert. Grad. fellow dept. biology Clark U., Worcester, Mass., 1965-67; neurophysiologist dept. toxicology pharmacology Mason Research Inst., Worcester, 1967-70, sect. head, 1970-75, research scientist, 1975-76; toxicologist dept. drug safety evaluation Pfizer, Inc., Med. Research Labs., Groton, Conn., 1976-78, sr. toxicologist, 1979—. NIH tng. fellow, 1966-67. Mem. AAAS, IEEE, Soc. Toxicology, N.Y. Acad. Scis., Am. Soc. Pharmacology and Exptl. Therapeutics. Contbr. articles in field to profl. jours. Home: 66 Quailcrest Rd East Lyme CT 06333 Office: Pfizer Inc Groton CT 06340

STAFFIER, PAMELA MOORMAN, psychologist; b. Passaic, N.J., Dec. 7, 1942; d. Wynant Clair and Jeannette Frances (Rentzsch) Moorman; B.A., Bucknell U., 1964; M.A. in Psychology, Assumption Coll., Worcester, Mass., 1970, C.A.G.S., 1977; Ph.D., Union Grad. Sch., 1978; m. John Staffier, Jr., Apr. 5, 1975. Psychologist, Westboro (Mass.) State Hosp., 1965, prin. psychologist, also asst. to supt., 1973-75; psychologist Moriarty Mental Health Clinic; psychiat. cons. local gen. hosp.; research psychologist Wrentham (Mass.) State Sch., 1966, Cushing Hosp., Framingham, Mass., 1967; prin. psychologist, also asst. to supt. Grafton (Mass.) State Hosp., 1967-72; individual practice psychology pvt. community mental health clinic, 1974—. Mem. Am. (asso.), New Eng., Mass. psychol. assns., Assn. Advancement Psychology, Nat. Register Health Service Providers in Psychology. Research, publs. on state hosp. closings, biochem. basis of Schizophrenia. Home: 5 Mohawk Circle Westboro MA 01581 Office: 314 Grafton St Shrewsbury MA 01545

STAFFORD, ROBERT THEODORE, U.S. senator; b. Rutland, Vt., Aug. 8, 1913; s. Bert L. and Mabel R. (Stratton) S.; B.S., Middlebury Coll., 1935; postgrad. U. Mich., 1936; LL.B., Boston U., 1938, LL.D., 1959; LL.D., Norwich U., 1960, Middlebury Coll., 1960, St. Michaels Coll., 1967; U. Vt., 1970; m. Helen C. Kelley, October 15, 1938; children—Madelyn, Susan, Barbara, Dianne. Admitted to Vt. bar, 1938; city prosecutor, Rutland, 1939-42; state's atty. Rutland County, 1947-51; dep. atty. gen. of Vt., 1953-54, atty. gen., 1954-56, became lt. gov., 1957; gov. Vt., 1959-61; partner Stafford, Abatiell & Stafford, 1938-46; sr. partner Stafford & LaBrake, 1946-51; mem. 87th-89th, 90th-92d Congresses, Vt.-at-large; appointed U.S. Senator, 1971, elected, 1972, re-elected, 1976. Served as lt. comdr. USN, 1942-46, 51-52, now capt. Res. Mem. V.F.W., Am. Legion. Clubs: Elks, Lions. Home: 64 Litchfield Ave Rutland VT 05701 also 3541 Devon Dr Falls Church VA 22042 Office: Dirksen Senate Office Bldg Washington DC 20510

STAGE, GINGER ROOKS, psychologist; b. Allentown, Pa., Sept. 23, 1946; d. John Myers and Catherine Estella (Graser) Rooks; B.A. magna cum laude, Moravian Coll., 1968; M.A., Temple U., 1969; m. Robert Roy Stage, Aug. 23, 1969; 1 son, Stephen Robert. Instr. psychology Pa. State U., 1969-74; psychologist St. Francis Community Mental Health Center, Pitts., 1974—; pvt. practice psychol. counseling, Coraopolis, Pa., 1978—. Mem. Am., Greater Pitts. psychol. assns., Western Pa. Group Psychotherapy Assn. Episcopalian. Home: 112 Wessex Hills Dr Coraopolis PA 15108 Office: 950 5th Ave Coraopolis PA 15108

STAGG, PAUL ALBERT, surgeon; b. Pineville, La., Oct. 5, 1926; s. Albert Manly and Pauline Amelia (Barron) S.; B.S., La. Coll., 1948; M.D., La. State U., 1953; M. Pub. Adminstrn., George Washington U., 1963; m. Patricia Ann Whitaker, Mar. 28, 1953; children—Peggy Stagg McComas, Carol, Janet, Linda. Intern Porter Hosp., Denver, 1953-54; resident in surgery USAF, VA Hosp., Nashville, 1954-56, Univ. Hosp., Louisville, 1956-58; commd. 1st lt. M.C., USAF, 1954, advanced through grades to col., 1968, chief surgeon Dover AFB, Del., 1958-62; comdr. USAF Hosp., Sembach AB, W.Ger., 1963-66, Reese AFB, Tex., 1966-69, USAF Hosp., Udorn Royal Thai AFB, Thailand, 1969-70, dep. surgeon AF Systems Command, Andrews AFB, Md., 1970-74, ret., 1974; pvt. practice gen. surgery, Cambridge, Md., 1974—; mem. staff Dorchester Gen. Hosp. and Eastern Shore Hosp. Center, Cambridge. Bd. dirs. county chpt. Am. Cancer Soc. Decorated Legion of Merit, Air medal, Bronze Star. Diplomate Am. Bd. Surgery. Fellow A.C.S., Am. Coll. Preventive Medicine; mem. AMA, Am. Legion, Aerospace Med. Assn., Flying Physicians Assn. Clubs: Cambridge Yacht, Rotary Internat. Home: PO Box 804 Cambridge MD 21613 Office: 4 Aurora St Cambridge MD 21613

STAHL, FRANK LUDWIG, civil engr.; b. Fuerth, Germany, Jan. 29, 1920; s. Leo E. and Anna (Regensburger) S.; B.S. in Civil Engring., Tech. Inst. Zurich, Switzerland, 1945; m. Edith Cosmann, Aug. 31, 1947; children—David, Robert. Came to U.S., 1946, naturalized, 1949. With Ammann & Whitney, Cons. Engrs., N.Y.C., 1946—, project engr., 1955-67, asso., 1968-76, sr. asso., 1977—. Fellow Am. Soc. C.E. (Thomas Fitch Rowland prize 1967); mem. Am. Inst. Steel Constrn., Am. Soc. for Testing and Materials (vice chm. com. A-1 on steel, stainless steel and related alloys, chmn. steel reinforce-subcom.), Engring. Found. (research council on riveted and bolted structural joints), Internat. Asso. Bridge and Structural Engring. Contbr. articles to profl. jours. Works include: Verrazano-Narrows Bridge, Throgs Neck Bridge, improvements to Golden Gate Bridge. Home: 209-11 28th Rd Bayside NY 11360 Office: 2 World Trade Center New York City NY 10048

STAHL, LADDIE L., elec. co. exec.; b. Terre Haute, Ind., Dec. 23, 1921; s. Edgar Allen and Martha (Llewellyn) S.; B.S.C.E., Purdue U. 1942; grad. U.S. Army Command and Gen. Staff Coll., Ft. Leavenworth, Kans., 1948; M.S.E. Johns Hopkins U. 1950; m. Thelma Mae Beasley, Dec. 11, 1942; children—Stephanie, Laddie, Jr., Craig. Commd. 2d lt. U.S. Army, 1942, advanced through ranks to maj. gen. 1966; comdr. arty. battery, ops. officer armoured div., Europe 1942-45; instr. ops. guided missiles, Ft. Bliss, Tex., 1950-53; war planner Dept. Army Gen. Staff Pentagon, 1953-54; comdr. 98th Div. (tng.), Rochester, N.Y., 1964-75; mgr. product planning and mkt. research Missile and Space Vehicle Dept. Gen. Elec. Co., Phila., 1954-59, mgr. tech. planning, gen. engring. labs. 1959-60, mgr. advanced tech. applications 1960-64, mgr. info. engring. lab. 1964-65, mgr. research and development applications, 1965-74, mgr. planning and resources, electronics sci. and engring., corporate research and development 1974-76, mgr. electronics systems programs operation, elec. sci. and engring. 1976—; cons. U.S. Army Aviation Systems, 1973-75; mem. advisory group U.S. Army Electronics Cmd. 1970-71, chmn. 1971-74; bd. dirs. Instructional Industries, Inc., Communities Corp. of Am., Inc., 1974—. Served with U.S. Army 1942-54, to maj. gen. with USAR 1954-77. Decorated distinguished service medal, Legion of Merit. Mem. Am. Defense Preparedness Assn., Am. Inst. Aeronautics and Astronautics, IEEE, Tau Beta Pi, Chi Epsilon. Clubs: Mohawk of Schenectady; Edison; Army and Navy. Contbr. text for grad. course in guided missiles. Home: 29 Fairway Ln Rexford NY 12148 Office: Gen Elec Co Research & Development Ctr PO Box 8 Schenectady NY 12301

STAHL, MARILYN BROWN, interior designer; b. Boston, Dec. 11, 1929; d. Benjamin and Nettie (Glazer) Brown; B.S., Mass. Coll. Art, 1951; m. Alvan Stahl, July 1, 1951; children—Robert, Barry, Kimberly. Instr. painting, Newton, Mass., 1957-63; free-lance fabric designer, 1960-63; owner gallery, Newton, 1963-66, M.B. Stahl Interiors, Chestnut Hill, Mass., 1966—. Address: 15 Manet Circle Chestnut Hill MA 02167

STAHR, ELVIS J(ACOB), JR., conservationist, educator, lawyer; b. Hickman, Ky., Mar. 9, 1916; s. Elvis and Mary Anne (McDaniel) S.; A.B., U. Ky., 1936; B.A. (Rhodes scholar, 1936-39), U. Oxford, 1938, B.C.L., 1939, M.A., 1943; Diploma in Chinese lang., Yale, 1943; LL.D., Brown U., Concord Coll., U. Fla., Hanover Coll., Ind. U., Ind. State U., U. Ky., La. State U., U. Md., Northwestern U., U. Notre Dame, U. Pitts., U. Tampa, Tex. Christian U., Waynesburg Coll., W.Va. Wesleyan Coll.; Litt.D., U. Cin., U. Maine; D.Sc., Norwich U.; D.H.L., De Pauw U., Rose Poly Inst., Transylvania U.; D.Environ. Sc., Rollins Coll.; D. Pub. Adminstrn., Bethany Coll.; D. Mil. Sci., Northeastern U.; Ph.D., Culver-Stockton Coll.; m. Dorothy Howland Berkfield, June 28, 1946; children—Stephanie Ann Stahr Metzger, Stuart Edward Winston, Bradford Lanier. Admitted to N.Y. State bar, 1940, Ky. bar, 1948, U.S. Supreme Ct. bar, 1950; asso. firm Mudge, Stern, Williams & Tucker, N.Y.C., 1939-41, sr. asso., 1946-47; asso. prof. law U. Ky., 1947-48, prof., 1948-56, dean Coll. Law, 1948-56, provost, 1954-56; vice chancellor-the professions U. Pitts., 1957-58; pres. W.Va. U., Morgantown, 1958-61; spl. asst. to sec. of Army, Washington, 1951-52, 1961-62; pres. Ind. U., 1962-68, Nat. Audubon Soc., N.Y.C., 1968—; dir., mem. exec. com. Acacia Mut. Life Ins. Co.; dir. Univ. Assos., Inc., Chase Manhattan Corp., Chase Manhattan Bank, Saxon Industries, Alliance to Save Energy; dep. chmn. bd. Fed. Res. Bank Chgo., 1966-68. Mem. Constn. Rev. Commn., Ky., 1949-56, Ind., 1967-68; incorporator Argonne Univs. Assn., 1965, trustee, 1965-67; chmn. higher edn. advisory com. Edn. Commn. States, 1966-68; mem. nat. conservation com. Boy Scouts Am., 1969—; mem. Pres.'s Aviation Advisory Commn., Washington, 1970-73; mem. U.S. del. UN Conf. on Human Environment, Stockholm, 1972; mem. advisory council Gas Research Inst., Center for Internat. Environment Info.; mem. Joint U.S.-USSR Com. on Cooperation for Protection of Environment, 1974; mem. Nat. Commn. World Population Year, 1974; mem. U.S. del. Internat. Whaling Commn., London, 1975, 78; mem. Nat. Petroleum Council, 1974—; vice-chmn. Citizen's Com. Natural Resources, 1978—; chmn. com. on equality of opportunity Am. Council on Edn., 1964-67, commn. fed. relations, 1965-68; mem. exec. bd. Am. Com. for Internat. Conservation, 1978—. Trustee Com. Econ. Devel., 1964—; nat. chmn. USO, 1973-76; dir.-at-large Am. Cancer Soc., 1970-76. Served to lt. col. U.S. Army, 1940-45. Decorated Spl. Breast Order of Yun Hui (2), Army Navy and Air Force medal 1st class (Chinese); Bronze star medal with oak leaf cluster (U.S.); Order of Grand Cruz (Peru); recipient Centennial medal U. Ky., 1965; Sesquicentennial medal U. Mich., 1967, Kentuckian of Year award Ky. Press Assn., 1961; Meritorious Civilian Service medal Dept. of Army, 1953, Distinguished Civilian Service medal, 1971. Mem. Assn. U.S. Army (past pres., chmn.), SAR, S.R., Nat. Audubon Soc., Disciples of Christ Hist. Soc., The Kentuckians N.Y.C. (pres. 1976-78, life trustee), Phi Beta Kappa, Order of Coif, Sigma Chi (Balfour award 1936; named Significant Sig 1961), Omicron Delta Kappa, Phi Delta Phi, Tau Kappa Alpha Merton Soc. (Oxford, Eng.), Blue Key, Beta Gamma Sigma (hon.). Presbyterian. Clubs: Century, Explorers, Pilgrims (N.Y.C.); Army-Navy, Cosmos (Washington); Field (Greenwich, Conn.); Nantucket Yacht; Boone and Crockett. Co-author: Economics of Pollution, 1971; contbr. articles to profl. jours. Home: Martin Dale Greenwich CT 06830 Office: Audubon Hdqrs 950 3d Ave New York NY 10022

STAINBACK, THOMAS NATHANIEL, coll. pres.; b. Saranac Lake, N.Y., Oct. 19, 1923; s. Ashley Forest and Sarah Virginia (Peacock) S.; B.S., Ithaca Coll., 1951; m. Aida Di Filippo, Oct. 11, 1958. Pres., Jersey City C. of C., 1957-64; exec. v.p. Greater Cin. C. of C., 1965-69, N.Y. C. of C., N.Y.C., 1969-73; pres. N.Y. C. of C. and Industry, N.Y.C., 1973-76; pres. Paul Smiths (N.Y.) Coll., 1976—; dir. Lake Placid Co.; mem. adv. bd. Farmers Nat. Bank, Saranac Lake. Served to sgt. AUS, 1942-46. Recipient 1st Distinguished Alumni award Paul Smiths Coll. Mem. Am. C. of C. Execs. (past pres.), N.J. Assn. C. of C. Execs. (past pres.), N.Y. State Assn. Jr. Colls. Clubs: Masons (32 deg.), Rotary. Home and office: Box 92 Paul Smiths NY 12970*

STALEY, RICHARD ALLEN, assn. exec.; b. Pitts., Dec. 8, 1926; s. Benjamin Maxwell and Dorothy (Gottfried) S.; B.S. cum laude, Lehigh U., 1948; m. Jean Burns, July 3, 1948 (dec. May 1975); children—Richard M., Barry N.; m. 2d, Sabra Miller, Mar. 3, 1979. Chief money and capitol market sec. Internat. Monetary Fund UN, Washington, 1948-50; chief research Nat. Assn. Securities Dealers, Washington, 1950-52; research exec. div. research and econs. Am. Trucking Assn., Washington, 1952—. Pres., Staley & Co. investment adviser, 1952-65, Richard A. Staley transp. cons., Arlington, Va., 1968—. Pres., Civic Assn., 1969-71; founder S. Arlington Coalition, 1971. Mem. adv. faculties Lehigh U., 1964-67, No. Va. Community Coll., 1973—. Chmn. Fiscal Affairs Adv. Commn., Arlington, Va., 1970-72; mem. Arlington Transp. Commn., 1976—; mem. Arlington Republican Com., 1969—, vice chmn., 1978—. Served with USNR, World War II. Ky. Col.; recipient trucking industry awards. Mem. Atlantic Econ. Assn., Inst. Transp. Engrs., Transp. Research Bd. Rep. Episcopalian. Mason; mem. Order Old Bastards, Com. of 100 of Arlington. Clubs: Questionnaire, SAAB. Author: Trucks and Our Changing Cities, 1974; Visual Impact of Trucks in Traffic, 1977. Editor: Research Rev., 1961—. Contbr. articles to profl. jours. Home: 1221 S Buchanan St Arlington VA 22204 Office: 1616 P St NW Washington DC 20036

STALLINGS, JAMES HENRY, govt. ofcl.; b. Bryan, Tex., Sept. 20, 1892; s. William Daniel and Emma Elizabeth (Josey) S.; B.S., Tex. A. and M. U., 1914; M.S. (Research fellow), Iowa State U., 1917, Ph.D., 1926; m. Pearl Louise Drummond, Aug. 1, 1923; children—George Drummond, James Henry. Asst. prof. Iowa State U., 1919-20; head soils dept. Tex. A. and M. U., 1920-26; agronomist Penny-Gynn Inst., 1926-28, Nat. Fertilizer Assn., 1929-33; regional dir. Soil Conservation Service, U.S. Dept. Agr., 1934-37, organizer, dir. flood control program, Washington, 1937-42; dir. fertilizer program War Food Adminstrn., Washington, 1942-44; prin. research specialist Soil Conservation Service, 1945-59; soil sci. editor Biol. Abstracts, 1952—, Webster's Internat. Dictionary. Mem. N.Y. Acad. Scis., Soil Sci. Soc. Am., Agronomy Assn., Internat. Platform Assn., Sigma Xi. Author: Soil Conservation, 1957; Soil Use and Improvement, 1957. Contbr. articles to profl. jours. Originator no-tillage method of farming; pub. abstracts of all pub. research findings related to soil conservation in U.S. and Can. Address: 5146 Nebraska Ave NW Washington DC 20008

STALLWORTH, JOHN WILLIAM, city ofcl.; b. Jersey City, Apr. 30, 1931; student pub. schs.; m. Sandra; children—Carla, April. Mayor's aide, Jersey City, 1977-78, exec. sec. to mayor, dir. Mayor's Office, 1978—; v.p. Jersey City Battleship Commn. Bd. dirs. Jersey City chpt. ARC, Polit. Unity Assn.; trustee Concerned Black Citizens. Served with USMCR, 1951-54. Recipient Meritorious Service award Neighborhood Youth Corps, 1969; also various certificates appreciation. Mem. NAACP (certificate Merit 1972), PTA, Union St. Block Assn., Concerned Community Women (hon., Community Service award 1977), N.J. Black Caucus (voting del.). Address: 240 Union St Jersey City NJ 07304

STALVEY, HAROLD DIXON, physician, educator; b. Hartsville, S.C., June 19, 1921; s. Dixon I. and Helen V. (McDonald) S.; B.S. magna cum laude, Furman U., 1942; M.D., Vanderbilt U., 1947; grad. Boston Psychoanalytic Inst., 1960; m. Frances Woodward, Apr. 24, 1948; children—John Robert Dixon, Richard Laurence. Intern, resident Vanderbilt U. Hosp., 1947-49, Taunton (Mass.) State Hosp., 1949-50, Boston VA Hosp., 1953; Staff psychiatrist, cons. Mass. Mental Health Center, 1954-76; clin. asst. and asst. attending psychiatrist McLean Hosp., Belmont, Mass., 1958-66; chief cons. psychiatrist Wellesley Coll., 1961-77; mem. psychiat. staff Newton Wellesley Hosp., 1973—; mem. faculty Harvard Med. Sch., 1954—, mem. faculty Boston Psychoanalytic Inst., 1965—; regional interviewer Vanderbilt U. Med. Sch., 1960—; evaluating psychiatrist Peace Corps, 1964-65; clin. asso. in psychiatry Mass. Gen. Hosp., 1976—. Served with AUS, 1943-46, USPHS, 1950-52. Diplomate Am. Bd. Psychiatry and Neurology. Fellow Am. Psychiat. Assn., Mass. Med. Soc.; mem. Am. Psychoanalytic Assn., Phi Chi, Alpha Omega Alpha. Office: 108 Windsor Rd Waban MA 02168

STAMPS, GEORGE MORELAND, communications cons.; b. Kuling, Ki., China, June 15, 1924 (parents Am. citizens); s. Drew Fletcher and Elizabeth Camilla (Belk) S.; B.S. magna cum laude, Wake Forest U., 1947; M.A. (Elizabeth Lowndes Scholar), Columbia U., 1949; postgrad. Polytech. Inst. Bklyn., 1950-52; m. Helen Leone Paty, Nov. 29, 1946; children—Margaret Evalyn, Robert Fletcher, Thomas Paty, John Belk. Instr. physics, math. State U. N.Y. Maritime Coll., Bronx, 1949-51; physicist Hogan Labs Inc., N.Y.C., 1951-54, asst. chief engr., 1954-58, dir. tech. sales, 1958-59; dir. tech. sales Hogan Faximile Corp., N.Y.C., 1959-60; mgr. market research Telautograph Corp., Los Angeles, 1960, chief engr., asst. to pres. mktg., 1960-62; staff engr. Magnavox Research Labs., Torrance, Calif., 1963-65, Magnafax program mgr., 1963-65; mgr. indsl. mktg., Magnavox Corp., Urbana, Ill., 1965-67, mgr. mktg. ops. 1967-70, mgr. bus. devel., Ft. Wayne, Ind., 1971-73; mgr. bus. devel., corp. staff Xerox Corp., Stamford, Conn., 1973-76; facsimile communications cons. Westport, Conn., 1976—; electronic mail cons. several maj. communications cos. Bd. dirs. Champaign-Urbana Civic Symphony Orch., 1970-71; elder, trustee New Hyde Park Presbyterian Ch., 1955-60, St. Peters by the Sea Presbyn. Ch., Portuguese Bend, Calif., 1962-65, McKinley Meml. Presbyn. Ch., Champaign, Ill., 1967-71. Served to lt. USAF, 1942-45; lt. col. Res. (ret.). Decorated Air Medal with two oak leaf clusters. Mem. Am. Microfilm Assn., Am. Phys. Soc., IEEE, Electronic Industries Assn. (chmn. facsimile sect. 1963-66, chmn. communications terminals and interfaces sect. 1966-73, founder TR-29 facsimile tech. com. 1962), Communications Soc. (officer Ft. Wayne chpt. 1972-73), Phi Beta Kappa, Omicron Delta Kappa. Democrat. Patentee (10 U.S., fgn.) facsimile and photogrammetry processes; contbr. reports, articles in field to publs. Home and Office: 268 Hillspoint Rd Westport CT 06880

STANDEN, DONNA SONDRA KOMAR (MRS. JOHN L. STANDEN), editor; b. Red Bank, N.J., Dec. 1, 1936; d. Herman Harvey and Margaret Casper (Goldfarb) Komar; student Wellesley Coll., 1955-56; m. Maurice Gordon Stempler, Nov. 24, 1956 (div. July 1963); children—Charles Jacob, Margaret Blair; m. 2d, John Lucas Standen, July 15, 1965. Reporter Red Bank Register daily, 1955-56, 64-65; reporter, women's reporter Asbury Park (N.J.) Press, 1965-66; feature writer Trenton Times, 1966-68; copy editor Phila. Bulletin, 1968-73, asst. editor spl. sect. Focus, 1973-74, news editor, 1974—. Mem. Women in Communications, Wellesley Coll. Alumnae Assn., Sigma Delta Chi. Home: 303A Kingston Terr RD 4 Princeton NJ 08540 Office: Philadelphia Bulletin 30th at Market St Philadelphia PA 19101

STANGLER, BERNARD BENEDICT, nurseryman; b. LeCenter, Minn., Dec. 19, 1917; s. Henry and Anna (Beran) S.; B.S., U. Minn., 1941; Ph.D., Cornell U., 1949; m. Inez E. Todnem, Sept. 10, 1942; children—Mary, Paul, Carol, Jean, Susan, Nancy. Pres., chmn. bd. Land O'Trees Nursery, Williamsville, N.Y., 1949—; pres., chmn. bd., Menne Corp., North Tonawanda, N.Y., 1963—; v.p., treas., chmn. bd. Arbordale Nursery, Getzville, N.Y., 1968—; mem. advisory bd. N.E. local Marine Midland Banks, 1966—. Bd. dirs. Ken Post Found., Ithaca, N.Y. Mem. N.Y. State (past pres., Hall of Fame award 1971), Western N.Y. State (past pres.) nurserymen's assns. Club: Lions (past local pres.). Home: 600 Park Club Ln Williamsville NY 14221 Office: 600 Park Club Ln Williamsville NY 14221

STANKO, CHESTER MICHAEL, ednl. counselor; b. Buffalo, Mar. 22, 1924; s. Walter and Victoria (Wojniak) S.; B.Ed., U. Buffalo, 1948, M.Ed., 1951; m. Angeline Caruana, June 19, 1948; children—Joan, Thomas. Formerly asst. supt. Greenhaven (N.Y.) Public Schs.; formerly tchr., coach public schs. Buffalo, East Aurora, Bishop Timon High Sch., Bishop Ryan High Sch.; asst. prof. Erie Community Coll.; counselor Burgard Vocat. High Sch., Buffalo, 1978—; panelist Focus on Youth series Channel 29, WUTV. Served with U.S. Army, 1943-45; ETO. Mem. Am. Personnel and Guidance Assn., Buffalo Sch. Counselors Assn., Buffalo Schoolmasters Assn., Am. Sch. Councelor Assn., Assn. Measurement and Evaluation in Guidance, Nat. Vocat. Guidance Assn., N.Y. Educators Assn., Western N.Y. Guidance Assn., Polish Union Am. (dir.), NEA, Phi Delta Kappa, Phi Epsilon Kappa. Democrat. Roman Catholic. Club: Am. Legion. Home: Tomcyn Dr Amherst NY 14221 Office: 400 Kensington Ave Buffalo NY 14212

STANKO, DAVID MICHAEL, mktg. exec.; b. Johnson City, N.Y., Aug. 25, 1943; s. Michael Andrew and Lillian (Stanley) S.; B.M.E., U.S. Merchant Marine Acad., 1965; student SUNY, Binghamton, 1968; m. Ann Hulbert, July 18, 1970; children—Eileen, Andrew. Quality control systems engr. Gen. Electric Co., Binghamton, N.Y., 1966-68, weapon control sales engr., 1968-71, nuclear systems sales mgr., Valley Forge, Pa., 1971-75, mgr. mktg. aero. satellite program, Valley Forge, 1975-77, mgr. mktg. subsect. Space div., Valley Forge, 1977—. Served with USNR, 1968. Office: PO Box 8555 Philadelphia PA 19101

STANLEY, CAROLINE HART, librarian; b. Washington, July 28, 1911; d. Lester Abbot and Angie May (Nuckols) S.; B.A., U. Ariz., 1933; B.S. in L.S., Columbia, 1934. Librarian, D.C. Pub. Library, 1934-39, 40-42; children's librarian Tucson Pub. Library, 1939-40; reference librarian War Dept. Library, 1942-46; librarian U.S. Info. Library, Sydney, Australia, 1947, Navy Spl. Services, 1948-53; library adviser Dept. Army, 1953-64; personnel officer D.C. Pub. Library, 1964-66; library research analyst George Washington U., 1962-72; librarian U.S.-Japan Trade Council, Washington, 1972-76; chmn. com. to revise qualifications standards for U.S. Govt. libraries, 1956; mem. panel U.S. Civil Service Examiners, 1958; mem. task force recruitment librarians Fed. Library Com., 1966-67. Recipient certificate of achievement Dept. Army, 1964. Mem. Nat. Writers Club, Nat. League Am. Pen Women, Smithsonian Assos., Internat. Platform Assn., D.C. Soc. Crippled Children, Washington Animal Rescue League, Humane Soc., Nat. Symphony Assos., Nat. Trust Historic Preservation, Corcoran Gallery Art, U. Ariz. Alumnae Assn., Phi Kappa Phi, Chi Delta Phi, Kappa Alpha Theta. Democrat. Presbyterian. Clubs: 20th Century, George Washington U. (Washington). Author guides, articles, pamphlets, bibliographies. Home: 2853 Ontario Rd NW Washington DC 20009

STANLEY, EARL R, lawyer; b. Windham, Ohio, Mar. 9, 1921; s. Harry Grimm and Grace Arda (Waller) S.; B.S. in Edn., Kent State U., 1943; J.D. with honors, George Washington U., 1949, LL.M., 1950; m. Alberta R. Royal, Jan. 29, 1945; children—Ann Royal, Margaret Alison. Admitted to D.C. bar, 1949, U.S. Supreme Ct. bar, 1955; atty.-advisor FCC, Washington, 1949-53; asso. firm Dow, Lohnes & Albertson, Washington, 1953-54, partner, 1954—; dir. Fetzer Broadcasting Co., Kalamazoo; guest lectr. Kent State U. Sch. Telecommunications, 1968-73. Served with USNR, 1943-46. Recipient Distinguished Achievement award Kent State U. Sch. Speech, 1970. Mem. Am., Fed. Communications bar assns., Bar Assn. D.C., George Washington U. Law Assn. (dir.), SAR, Delta Theta Phi (Diamond Crowned badge 1973). Methodist. Clubs: Masons, Shriners, Congl. Congressional Country (Bethesda, Md.); Oceana Country (Shelby, Mich.). Home: 11005 Stanmore Dr Potomac MD 20854 Office: 1225 Connecticut Ave NW Washington DC 20036

STANLEY, (MARION) EDWARD ENZELEAUX, author, broadcasting exec.; b. Aurora, Nebr., Jan. 31, 1903; s. Marion Francis and Ethzelda (Rush) S.; A.B., U. Nebr., 1926; LL.D., 1966; m. Pauline Gund, Oct. 18, 1927; children—Michael, David. Journalist, U.S. and abroad, 1920-39; mem. exec. editorial staff AP, 1928-38; dep. dir. overseas br. OWI, 1940-43; pub. relations Earl Newsom Assos., 1944-45; exec. editor Coronet and Esquire, 1946; dir. pub. affairs NBC, 1950-68, pres., 1968—, Tchrs. Guides to Television, Inc., 1978; pres. Lab. for Research in Relevant Edn., 1978. Clubs: Century Assn., Univ., (N.Y.C.); Cosmos (Washington). Author: Thomas Forty and The Rock Cried Out, 1947. Home: 116 E 66th New York City NY 10021 Office: Box 564 Lenox Hill Sta New York City NY 10021

STANLEY, JOAN GLORIA, mktg. and sales exec.; b. Hoboken, N.J., June 14, 1939; d. Alexander John and Elfrieda Katherina (Matula) S.; student New Sch. Social Research, 1959-60, N.Y. U., 1960-63. Vice pres. N.Y. Apt. Exchange, N.Y.C., 1965-70; dir. sales promotions Zsa Zsa Internat., N.Y.C., 1970-72; dir. spl. projects Nat. Audubon Soc., N.Y.C., 1972—; cons. Mem. Nat. Soc. Fund Raising Execs., Direct Mail Fundraisers Assn. Home: 35 E 35th St New York City NY 10016 Office: National Audubon Soc 950 3d Ave New York City NY 10022

STANLEY-BROWN, EDWARD GARFIELD, pediatric surgeon; b. Cleve., Nov. 11, 1923; s. Rudolph and Katharine (Oliver) Stanley-B.; student U. Va., 1942-44; M.D., U. Pa., 1948; postgrad. surg. anatomy Cornell U. Sch. Medicine, 1953; m. Jeanne Claire Olson, Nov. 1, 1952; children—Jeanne Drake, David Garfield, Elizabeth Powell. Intern, Columbia div. Bellevue Hosp., N.Y.C., 1948-49, asst. resident, 1949, chief surg. resident, 1953-55; asst. resident Presbyterian Hosp., N.Y.C., 1950-51; attending surgeon Bellevue Hosp., 1959-65, St. Luke's Hosp., N.Y.C., 1959—; practice medicine specializing in pediatric surgery, N.Y.C., 1955—; cons. House St. Giles the Cripple, Bklyn., 1969—; instr. in surgery Columbia U., 1955-59, asso. in surgery, 1959-65, asst. clin. prof. surgery, 1965-74, asso. clin. prof., 1974—. Served as capt. M.C., U.S. Army, 1951-52; Korea. Diplomate Am. Bd. Surgery. Fellow A.C.S., Am. Acad. Pediatrics (surg.); mem. Am. Pediatric Surg. Assn., N.Y. Pediatric Surgeons, New York County, N.Y. State med. socs., N.Y. Clin. Soc., St. Nicholas Soc. Republican. Episcopalian. Clubs: Charaka, Ridgewood (N.J.) Country, Siaconset (Nantucket Island, Mass.) Casino. Author: Pediatric Surgery for Nurses, 1961; contbr. numerous articles to med. jours. Home: 860 Roslyn Rd Ridgewood NJ 07450 Office: 962 Park Ave New York City NY 10028

STANNARD, CARL ROY, JR., physicist, educator; b. Syracuse, N.Y., July 24, 1935; s. Carl Roy and Ruth (McCloy) S.; B.S., Syracuse U., 1956, Ph.D., 1964; M.S., Cornell U., 1960; m. Lonnelle Gay Hickox, Sept. 17, 1967; children—Kent Geoffrey, Ross McCloy. Lectr. physics Syracuse U., summer 1961, research asso., 1963-64, vis. prof., summer 1965; asst. prof. State U. N.Y., Binghamton, 1964-70, asso. prof., 1970—, dir. undergrad. program in physics, 1970-78, dir. Harpur Coll.-Broome Community Coll. joint degree program, 1973-77, chmn. dept. physics, 1978—; mem. proposal rev. panel NSF, 1975, reviewer fund for improvement post-secondary edn., 1978. NSF grantee, 1971-75; Fund for Improvement Post-Secondary Edn. grantee, 1974-77. Mem. Am. Phys. Soc., Am. Assn. Physics Tchrs., Phi Beta Kappa, Sigma Xi, Phi Kappa Phi, Sigma Pi Sigma. Author: Physics of Technology Modules series: The Stroboscope, 1975; The Solenoid, 1975; project dir. Physics of Technology Modules series, 1975; contbr. articles on computer assisted instrn., photoconductivity to profl. jours. Office: Physics Dept State U NY Binghamton NY 13901

STANOCH, THOMAS PAUL, capital goods mfg. co. exec.; b. Jersey City, Jan. 18, 1951; s. Paul Stanley and Josephine Jane (Warakomski) S.; B.E. in Chem. Engring., Stevens Inst. Tech., 1972; M.B.A., Kent State U., 1975; m. Lenore Catherine Zubrycki, Oct. 27, 1973. Sr. research engr. Babcock & Wilcox, Alliance, Ohio, 1972-75, bus. devel. coordinator, N.Y.C., 1975-77, planning cons., 1977—. Mem. Am. Mktg. Assn., Am. Inst. Chem. Engrs., N. Am. Soc. Corp. Planners, Tau Beta Pi, Chi Psi. Home: 972 Richard Ct Teaneck NJ 07666 Office: 161 E 42d St New York City NY 10017

STANSBURY, CLAYTON CRESVELL, psychologist, educator; b. Havre de Grace, Md., Mar. 20, 1932; s. Clayton Cresvell and Mary Louise (Vessels) S.; B.S., Morgan State U., 1955; M.S., Howard U., 1962; Ph.D., U. Md. 1972; m. Catherine Laverne Posey, Dec. 22, 1957. Instr. psychology Howard U., 1962-63, 65-67; teaching asst. U. Md., 1963-65; counselor Morgan State U., 1967-70, asst. dean freshman program, 1970-73, dept. chmn. psychology, 1973-75, dir. lower div., 1975-77, acting dean student affairs, 1977-78, v.p. for student affairs, 1978—. Bd. dirs. YMCA, Balt.; active Boy Scouts Am. Served with U.S. Army, 1955-57. Mem. Am., Md. psychol. assns., NAACP, Psi Chi. Democrat. Methodist. Author: Portrait of a Colored Man: Clayton C. Stansbury, Sr., 1977; Fifty Years of Humanitarian Thoughts by Clayton C. Stansbury, Sr., 1978. Home: 3215 Elba Dr Baltimore MD 21207 Office: Cold Spring Ln and Hillen Rd Baltimore MD 21239

STANTON, IVENS V., fin. co. exec.; b. N.Y.C., Feb. 27, 1929; s. Harry and Yetta (Kalmowitz) S.; B.A., Syracuse U., 1954; m. Joyce Needleman, Jan. 28, 1970; children—Marshall Scott, Alison Eve, Lynn Erica. Editor Simon & Schuster Co., N.Y.C., 1954-55; editor, bus.-fin. news dept. N.Y. Times, N.Y.C., 1955-62; fin. news dir. PR Newswire, N.Y.C., 1962-66; pres. Ivens Stanton Assos. Inc., N.Y.C., 1966—; dir. Meridian Advt. Inc., Wildwood Group Inc., Ivey Group Inc.; cons. oil and gas firms. Served with Signal Corps, U.S. Army, 1951-53. Mem. Communications Alumni Soc. Syracuse U. (pres. 1967—), Police Conf. N.Y. (hon.). Contbr. articles in field to profl. jours. Office: 101 Park Ave New York City NY 10017

STANTON, SEYMOUR, forest products co. exec.; b. N.Y.C., Feb. 13, 1923; s. Jack and Bess S.; B.S., N.Y. U., 1948; m. Marlynn Slocum, Apr. 10, 1949; children—Richard Jay, Barry Jon, Lori Jo. Supervising sr. accountant C.P.A. firms, N.Y.C., Los Angeles, 1948-57; v.p. fin. Mark Hild & Assos., Los Angeles, 1957-60, Sacher Properties Inc., N.Y.C., 1960-63, No. Instrument Corp., Bayshore, N.Y., 1963-66; gen. mgr. Eastern U.S., Boise Cascade Corp. realty group, N.Y.C., 1966—; fin. cons. Transp. Mgmt. Services, Tarrytown, N.Y., 1973—. Mgr., Little League, Hillcrest Lakers Boys Club, Yonkers, 1963-68, dir., 1964-65; trustee Temple Emanu El, Yonkers, 1972-77. Served with AUS, 1941-45. Decorated Air medal, Purple Heart, Bronze Star;

C.P.A., N.Y., Calif. Mem. N.Y. State Soc. C.P.A.'s. Hebrew. Club: Masons. Home: 8 Whitman Rd Yonkers NY 10710 Office: 437 Madison Ave New York City NY 10022

STANTON, VIVIAN BRENNAN (MRS. ERNEST STANTON), educator; b. Waterbury, Conn.; d. Francis P. and Josephine (Ryan) Brennan; B.A., Albertus Magnus Coll., 1939; M.S., So. Conn. State Coll., 1962, 6th yr. degree, 1965; postgrad. Columbia U.; m. Ernest Stanton, May 31, 1947; children—Pamela L., Bonita F., Kim Ernest. Tchr. English, history, govt. Milford (Conn.) High Sch., 1940-48; tchr. English, history, fgn. Born Night Sch., New Haven, 1948-54, Simon Lake Sch., Milford, 1960-62; guidance counselor, psychol. examiner Jonathan Law High Sch., Milford, 1962-73, Nat. Honor Soc. adviser, 1966-73, mem. Curriculum Councils, Graduation Requirement Council, Gifted Child Com., others, 1940-48, 60-73; guidance dir. Foran High Sch., Milford, 1973—, career center coordinator, 1976—. Active various community drives; mem. exec. bd. Ridge Rd PTA, 1956-59; mem. Parent-Tchr. council Hopkins Grammer Sch., New Haven; mem. Human Relations Council, North Haven, 1967-69. Mem. Nat. Assn. Secondary Schs. and Colls. (evaluation com.; chmn. testing com.), AAUW, Conn. Personnel and Guidance Assn., Conn. Sch. Counselors Assn., Conn. Assn. Sch. Psychol. Personnel, Conn., Milford (pres. 1945-47) edn. assns. Home: 44 Marlborough Rd North Haven CT 06473 Office: Foran High School Foran Dr Milford CT 06460

STANTON, WALTER O., electronics co. exec.; b. Canton, Ohio, Sept. 29, 1914; s. Bela Hayden and Edna (Keckley) S.; Elec. Engring., Wayne State U.; m. Mary Ann Wilcox; children—Sharon (Mrs. Robert Russell), Diana (Mrs. Grant Thornbrough), Pamela Stanton. Pres. Pickering & Co., Inc., 1948—, Stanton Magnetics, Inc., 1966—; dir. Servo Corp. Am. Chmn. Inst. of High Fidelity, 1961-63, pres., 1964-67. Fellow Audio Engring. Soc. (pres. 1957); mem. Chief Exec.'s Forum. Home: Rural Delivery 1 Syosset NY 11791 Office: Sunnyside Blvd Plainview NY 11803

STANTON-HICKS, MICHAEL D'ARCY, physician, educator; b. Adelaide, South Australia, June 3, 1931; s. Cedric and Florence (Haggitt) S-H.; came to U.S., 1972; M.B., B.S., U. Adelaide, 1961; m. Kristina Litsmark, Sept. 2, 1967; children—Erik, Leif. Intern, Queen Elizabeth Hosp., Adelaide, 1961-62; resident Central Lasarett, Falun, Sweden; registrar anesthesiology Lasarett Koping, Sweden, 1966-67; registrar anesthesiology Postgrad. Med. Sch., Hammersmith, London, 1967-68; practice medicine specializing in anesthesiology, London, 1967, Stockholm, 1968, Seattle, 1969, Adelaide, 1970, Worcester, Mass., 1975—; asst. dir. anesthesiology Sodersjukhuset, Stockholm, 1968-69; staff anesthesiologist Queen Elizabeth Hosp., Adelaide, 1970-72; instr. anesthesiology U. Wash., Seattle, 1969-70, asst. prof., 1972-75; prof., chmn. anaesthesia U. Mass., Worcester, 1975—; mem. staff VA Hosp., Seattle, Harborview Med. Center, 1969-70, 72-75. Served as flight lt. Royal Australian Air Force, 1962-65. Fellow Royal Soc. Medicine, Faculty of Anaesthetists; mem. Assn. Anaesthetists of Gt. Britain and Ireland, Australian Soc. Anaesthetists, Societas Anaesthesiologica Sueciae, Australian Med. Assn., Internat. Assn. for Study of Pain, Am. Soc. Anesthesiologists, Mass. Soc. Anesthesiology, Soc. Acad. Anesthesia Chmn. Club: Army, Navy Airforce. Research in regional anaesthesia and local anesthetics. Home: 10 Otsego Rd Worcester MA 01609 Office: U Mass Med Center Worcester MA 01605

STANWICH, EUGENE EDWARD, librarian; b. Niagara Falls, N.Y., May 6, 1948; s. Edward T. and Lillian L. S.; A.A., Niagara County Community Coll., 1968; B.A., State U. N.Y., Buffalo, 1970, M.L.S., 1975; m. Nancy Jean Forbach, Oct. 6, 1973; children—Brett, Jill, Jack. Library media specialist Emerson Vocat. High Sch., Buffalo, 1970-71, Amherst Jr. High Sch., Snyder, N.Y., 1973—, chmn. sch. library media specialists, 1975—. Served with U.S. Army, 1971-73. Mem. ALA, Sch. Library Assn. Western N.Y., Toy Train Operating Soc. Office: Library Media Center Amherst Jr High Sch Snyder NY 14226

STAPINSKI, STEPHEN EDWARD, civil engr.; b. Lawrence, Mass., Jan. 20, 1953; s. Edward M. and Irene F. (Tuminowski) S.; B.S. in Civil Engring., Merrimack Coll., 1974; M. in Civil Engring., Northeastern U., 1978. Civil engr. Commonwealth of Mass. Dept. Pub. Works, 1976-77; surveyor A.H. Leman Constrn. Co., Kingston and Woodstock, N.Y., 1971-72, Stevens Assos., Salem, N.H., 1974; engr. Rust Constrn. Co., Beverly, Mass., 1974-75; treas. Merrimack Engring. Services, Inc., 1975—, v.p., 1977—; instr. civil engring. Merrimack Coll., North Andover, Mass., 1976—. Chmn. Haverhill (Mass.) Conservation Commn., 1975—. Mem. ASCE, Soc. Profl. Engrs. in Pvt. Practice, Nat. Soc. Profl. Engrs., Boston Soc. C.E., Haverhill C. of C., Delta Phi Kappa. Democrat. Roman Catholic. Club: Elks. Home: 49 5th Ave Haverhill MA 01830 Office: 66 Main St Andover MA 01810

STAPLER, ALBERT BROADUS, JR., hosp. adminstr.; b. Metter, Ga., Apr. 15, 1921; s. Albert Broadus and Lillie Mae (Carter) S.; student Washington schs.; m. Helen Hinson, Apr. 17, 1948; children—Susan Lynn, Alan Barry. With USPHS, 1942—; lab aide NIH, 1942-46; with supply mgmt. div. hosps. and clinics in Detroit, Seattle and Balt., 1946-61; supply mgmt. and adminstrn. officer Staten Island and Norfolk, Va., 1961-75; asso. dir. adminstrn. USPHS Hosp., Staten Island, 1976—. Served with U.S. Army, 1942-45. Mem. Am. Hosp. Assn. Democrat. Methodist. Club: Staten Island Lions. Home: Quarters 6 USPHS Hosp Staten Island NY 10304 Office: USPHS Hosp Bay and Vanderbilt Sts Staten Island NY 10304

STAPLES, BASIL GEORGE, chemist; b. Eliot, Maine, Aug. 13, 1914; s. Victor R. and Gladys (Langley) S.; B.S., U. Maine, 1935, M.S. in Biochemistry, 1936; m. Jeannette Maria Morgan, June 10, 1935; children—John Eliot, George David. Foreman depts. Gen. Chem. Co., Balt., and Claymont, Del., 1936-42; shift supt. U.S. Rubber Co., South Charleston, W.Va., 1942-45; research fellow The Pfaudler Co., Rochester, N.Y., 1945-64, tech. service engr., 1964-66, engring. specialist, 1966-67, sr. engr., 1967—. Fellow Am. Inst. Chemists, Am. Ceramic Soc. (v.p. 1974-75, Pask-Coffeen-Rigterink award 1972); mem. Nat. Inst. Ceramic Engrs., ASTM (exec. vice chmn. 1974—, chmn. com. on gaskets 1976—), Am. Chem. Soc., Nat. Assn. Corrosion Engrs. (chmn. Niagara Frontier sect. 1969, trustee Niagara Frontier sect. 1976—), Alpha Zeta, Alpha Gamma Rho. Republican. Methodist. Contbr. articles on ceramic engring. to profl. jours.; patentee in field. Home: 275 Colwick St Rochester NY 14624 Office: 1000 W Ave Rochester NY 14603

STAPLES, NORMAN APPLETON, banker; b. St. Croix, V.I., Dec. 12, 1919; s. Appleton H. and Johanne (Svitzer) S.; B.S., U. N.C., 1946; student Am. Inst. Fgn. Trade, Phoenix, 1947; m. Dec. 18, 1944 (div. 1975); 2 sons, 2 daus. With Merrill Lynch, Pierce, Fenner & Smith, Stamford, Conn., 1948-50; with Chem. Bank N.Y. Trust Co. (name changed to Chem. Bank), N.Y.C., 1951—, v.p., 1965—. Served as pilot USNR, 1942-45. Mem. St. Anthony Hall, Naval Aviation Commandery. Clubs: Univ. (N.Y.C.); Turf and Field, Pilgrims (N.Y.); Bath, Royal Automobile (London). Office: Chem Bank Secretariat Bldg UN New York City NY 10017

STAPLES, TERRENCE EDWIN, trust investments exec.; b. Peterborough, Ont., Can., Nov. 13, 1935; s. Gerald Edwin and Marion Irene (McKinnon) S.; B.A., U. Toronto, 1958, diploma in bus., 1972; m. Patricia Anne Bent, Aug. 26, 1961; children—Catherine Anne, Sarah Christine, Colin Edwin. Investment clk. Royal Trust Co., London, Ont., 1958-62; officer Montreal Trust Co., Montreal and Toronto, 1962-65; investment mgr. Met. Trust Co., Toronto, 1965-66; supr. estate, trust, agency div., Nat. Trust Co., Toronto, 1966-69; mgr. pension fund Ont. Hydro, Toronto, 1969-75, asst. treas., 1975—; dir. Pension Fund Properties Ltd., Pension fund Realty Ltd.; pres. Pension Investment Assn. Can., 1977—; investment cons. Progressive Conservative Party (Can.), 1975-76; vis. lectr. York U., Toronto. Mem. Toronto Soc. Fin. Analysts, Toronto Soc. Bus. Economists. Mem. United Ch. Can. Home: 104 Bessborough Dr Toronto ON Canada Office: 700 University Ave Toronto ON M5G 1X6 Canada

STAPLETON, THOMAS DAVID, physician; b. Auburn, N.Y., Dec. 10, 1912; s. John Edward and Anna (McDermott) S.; A.B., Georgetown U., 1934, M.D., 1938; m. Wilhelmina Eileen Meagher, Apr. 6, 1942; children—David Sheila, Miriam, William. Intern Georgetown U. Hosp., Washington, 1938-40; practice gen. medicine, Auburn, N.Y., 1940-42; resident Bklyn. Eye and Ear Hosp., Bklyn., 1946-48; practice medicine specializing in ophthalmology Auburn, 1948—; staff mem. Auburn Meml. Hosp.; staff mem. Mercy Hosp., Auburn, pres. staff, 1958. Bd. dirs. United Fund; vice chmn. bd. trustees Auburn Community Coll. Served from lt. (j.g.) to lt. comdr., USNR, 1942-46. Decorated Bronze Star medal, Purple Heart (U.S.). Diplomate Nat. Bd. Med. Examiners. Mem. Pan-Am. Assn. Ophthalmology, A.M.A., N.Y. State, Cayugo County med. socs., Bklyn. Eye and Ear Hosp. Alumni Assn., Internat. Platform Assn., Central N.Y. Eye and Ear Assn., N.Y. Pa. League (pres. Auburn community baseball orgn. 1959-62, chmn. bd. 1962—, v.p. 1962—), Georgetown U. Alumni Assn. (bd. govs.), Auburn C. of C., Am. Legion. Roman Catholic. K.C., Elk (dir.). Home: 130 Walnut St Auburn NY 13021 Office: Auburn Savs Bank Bldg Auburn NY 13021

STARASOLER, STANLEY, dentist; b. Bklyn.; s. Samuel and Fannie (Landesberg) S.; A.B., N.Y. U., 1944; D.D.S., U. Pitts., 1948, D.M.D., 1969; m. Alice Suzanne Goldstein, Jan. 8, 1956; children—Tracy, Lewis. Intern oral surgery and gen. anesthesia Greenpoint Hosp. and Dept. of Hosps., N.Y.C., 1948-49; clin. asst. oral surgery Greenpoint Hosp., 1950, asst. oral surgery, 1960; asst. in oral surgery Greenpoint Hosp. unit Mt. Sinai Hosp.; practice dentistry, Woodhaven, 1953—; sect. chief oral surgery dept. Greenpoint Hosp. unit Bklyn. Jewish Hosp., 1965-75; attending gen. dentistry staff Bklyn. Jewish Hosp. and Med. Center, Greenpoint Hosp. Unit, 1975—; mem. staff L.I. Jewish-Hillside Med. Center, Jewish Inst. for Geriatric Care; dir. Internat. House Nutrition, 1976; past pres. combined dental staffs Greenpoint Hosp. and Bklyn. Jewish Hosp. and Med. Center. Served to 1st lt., Dental Corps, AUS, 1951-53. Fellow Am. Soc. Advancement of Gen. Anesthesia in Dentistry, Royal Soc. Health (Eng.); mem. Internat. Platform Assn., Pan-Am. Med. Assn., Pan-Am. Odontological Soc., N.Y. Acad. Scis., ADA, 11th Dist., Queens County (chmn. pub. health edn.) dental socs., AAAS, Fedn. Dentaire Internationale, Am. Soc. Geriatric Care Internat. Acad. Anesthesiology, Alpha Omega. Clubs: N.Y. U. Varsity; Century (U. Pitts.). Author articles in field. Home: 29 Country Village Ln Manhassett Hills NY 11040 Office: 8656 Woodhaven Blvd Woodhaven NY 11421 also Fresh Meadows Exec Plaza 61-18 190th St Fresh Meadows NY 11365

STARBUCK, SHIRLEY, artist; b. Bklyn.; d. Sidney Hilton and Maria Ponce de Leon (French) S.; student Art Students League, 1945-46; m. Baxter Ragsdale Still, Jr., May 27, 1949 (div. Apr. 1954); 1 dau., Susan. Art dir. Ted. Bates & Co., N.Y.C., 1944-49, Doherty, Clifford, Steers & Shenfield, N.Y.C., 1954-59, Norman, Craig & Kummel, N.Y.C., 1959-62; free lance designer, illustrator, calligrapher. Red Cross vol., sketching patients in mil. hosps. Mem. Washington Calligraphers Guild, DAR, Soc. Mayflower Descs. in State N.Y., Nat. League Am. Pen Women. Republican. Club: Tavern Cay Sailing (Abaco, Bahamas). Address: 2022 Columbia Rd NW Washington DC 20009

STARESINA, DENISE MARIE, mfg. co. exec.; b. Cleve., May 18, 1951; d. Nicholas Edward and Lucille Cecelia (Horley) S.; B.A., Mich. State U., 1974. Adminstrv. mgmt. trainee Pitney Bowes, Stamford, Conn., 1974-75, Richmond, Va., 1975, adminstrv. mgr., Lansing, Mich., 1975-76, product analyst, Norwalk, Conn., 1976-78, product planner, 1978—. Recipient award of Excellence, Pitney Bowes, 1976. Mem. Nat. Assn. Female Execs., Mich. State U. Alumni Assn., Phi Gamma Nu. Home: 3 Blackberry Ln Ridgefield CT 06877 Office: 380 Main St Norwalk CT 06852

STARGARDTER, HANS, mech. engr.; b. Breslau, Germany, Apr. 16, 1927; s. Alfred and Katherine (Bucka) S.; B.S., Fla. So. Coll., 1951; m. Henrietta Stepner, June 7, 1951; children—Herman, Ben, Paul, Susan, Anne. Sales engr. Fairbanks Morse, N.Y.C., 1951-53; engr. Gen. Electric Co., Cin., 1953-62, Sundstrand Corp., Denver, 1962-63; sr. asst. project engr., project mgr. Pratt & Whitney Aircraft, East Hartford, Conn., 1963—; lectr. Pa. State U., 1967, U. Tenn., 1968. Scoutmaster, Boy Scouts Am., 1955-65. Registered profl. engr., Ohio. Mem. ASME (exec. com. Hartford sect.). Democrat. Jewish. Contbr. articles to profl. jours. Patentee in field. Home: 9 Prospect St Bloomfield CT 06002 Office: 400 Main St East Hartford CT 06108

STARK, ELI HERMAN, osteo. physician; b. Monticello, N.Y., Feb. 21, 1926; s. Morris and Celia (Shapiro) S.; D.O., Phila. Coll. Osteo. Medicine, 1951; m. Anita Rothenberg, June 18, 1949; children—Richard, Ira, Jay, Lauri. Exec. dir. Massapequa Gen. Hosp., 1967-73; asst. dean student affairs N.Y. Coll. Osteo. Medicine, also chmn. dept. family medicine, prof. medicine, 1976—, editorial dir. Osteo. Annals, 1973—. Served with U.S. Army, 1944-46. Decorated Bronze Star; diplomate Nat. Osteo. Bd., Am. Coll. Gen. Practioners (chmn. council edn. and evaluation). Fellow Am. Coll. Gen. Practioners (pres. 1975), Am. Sch. Health Assn.; mem. Am. Med. Writers Assn., Am. Osteo. Assn. (v.p., trustee; Gen. Practioner of Year award 1977), N.Y. State Osteo. Soc. (pres. 1971-73), Am. Acad. Med. Adminstrs., Royal Soc. Health. Editor: Clin. Rev. Series Osteo. Medicine, 1975. Home: 1072 Old Britton Rd North Bellmore NY 11710 Office: 1046 Bellmore Rd North Bellmore NY 11710

STARK, JEFFREY MICHAEL, chem. co. exec.; b. N.Y.C., Jan. 3, 1943; s. Nathan and Ruth (Derman) S.; A.B. in Econs., Lafayette Coll., 1963; M. in Indsl. and Labor Relations, Cornell U., 1965; m. Patricia Joan Birnbaum, June 21, 1964; children—David Alan, Robert Jay, Rachel Lynne. Profl. placement specialist Am.-Standard, Inc., N.Y.C., 1965-67, personnel supr. church products dept., Monson, Mass., 1967-68; tng. supr. Continental Can. Co. Inc., Pitts., 1968-70, indsl. relations staff rep. Eastern Metal div., N.Y.C., 1970-71; Eastern region employee relations mgr. Metal div. N.L. Industries, Inc., Perth Amboy, N.J., 1971-73, mgr. mgmt. devel. MBJ group, N.Y.C., 1973-74, dir. employee relations indsl. chems. div. NL Industries, Inc., Highstown, N.J., 1974—; ind. cons. on orgn., employee relations. Served as sgt. USAR, 1967-73. Named Jaycee of the Quarter, 1972. Mem. Am. Soc. Personnel Adminstrn., Lafayette Coll., Cornell Indsl. Labor Relations alumni assns., Franklin Twp. Jaycees (dir. 1973), Smithsonian Assos., Friends of E. Brunswick Library, Alpha Chi Rho. Jewish. Author: (with R. Duino) Annotated Bibliography, Selected Readings on Shift Systems, 1964. Home: 6 Plymouth Ln East Brunswick NJ 08816 Office: PO Box 700 Hightstown NJ 08520

STARK, JESSE DONALD, physician; b. N.Y.C., Dec. 3, 1899; s. Eugene J. and Helen (Goldberger) S.; A.B., Cornell U., 1921; M.D., Jefferson Med. Coll., 1925; studied Berlin, Vienna, Munich, 1925, 1930; m. Florence C. Seligmann, 1933 (dec.); m. 2d, Sara Miller Suchoff, Dec. 20, 1968. On staff Polyclinic Hosp., N.Y.C., 1934-35, Met. Hosp., N.Y.C., 1935-39; cons. roentgenologist, Ft. Jay, Governor's Island, N.Y., 1935-41; vis. roentgenologist, Gouverneur Hosp., N.Y.C., 1939-41, chief roentgenologist, 1946-61; attending cons. roentgenologist, VA Hosp., Bronx, N.Y., 1946-47; instr. radiology, N.Y. U. Coll. Medicine, 1935-49, asst. clin. prof. radiology, 1953-64, attending radiologist Clinic, 1935-41; asso. attending radiologist Univ. Hosp., 1954-58; instr. radiology N.Y. U.-Bellevue Post Grad. Med. Sch., 1949, asst. clin. prof. radiology, 1950-53; exec. dir. x-ray dept. Bird S. Coler Hosp., 1961-64, roentgenologist, 1964-71; dir. x-ray dept. Prospect Hosp., Bronx, 1968—; cons. to the Surgeon Gen. U.S. Army, 1947-48, West Point Sta. Hosp., 1947, First Army, 1947—, Army of Occupation, Germany and Austria, 1948. Served as 2d lt., inf., U.S. Army, World War I; lt. col. M.C., AUS, 1941-50; col. M.C. U.S. Army Res., 1950; chief of X-Ray service and instr. U.S. Mil. Acad., West Point, N.Y., 1941-46. Decorated chevalier Mil. Order of St. Stephen, comdr. Mil. Order of St. Salvadore, Gold Medal, Order of Macedonia; medal for merite scientifique Inst. of Humanities of Republic of France; Order of Lafayette; chevalier Legion of Honor, Croix de Guerre (hon.) (France); surgeon gen. Order of Lafayette; Gold Medal of Merit (Free Poland); diplomate Am. Bd. Radiology. Fellow Am. Coll. Radiology, Royal Coll. Health (Eng.); mem. N.Y. Acad. Scis., 7th Regiment Assn., N.Y. Soc. Med. Jurisprudence, Inst. Humanities Republic France, Radiology Soc. N. Am., AAAS, Soc. Am. Wars. AAUP, N.Y. Roentgen Soc., AMA, Assn. Mil. Surgeons U.S., Mil. Order World Wars, Res. Officers Assn., N.Y. Physicians Art Assn., West Point Soc. N.Y. Clubs: Army Navy (Washington); Cornell, Old Guard (N.Y.C.). Home: 965 Fifth Ave New York City NY 10021 Office: 51 E 90th St New York City NY 10028

STARK, RICHARD BOIES, surgeon; b. Conrad, Iowa, Mar. 31, 1915; s. Eugene and Hazel (Carson) S.; A.B., Stanford U., 1936; U. Heidelberg, 1936-37; M.D., Cornell U., 1941; m. Judy Thornton, Oct. 31, 1967. Intern, Peter Bent Brigham Hosp., Boston, 1941-42; asst. resident surgery Childrens Hosp., Boston, 1942; plastic surgeon Northington Gen. Hosp., Ala., 1945-46, Percy Jones Gen. Hosp., Mich., 1946; postwar fellow anatomy and embryology Stanford U., 1946-47; asst. resident and resident surgery, plastic and gen. surgery VA Hosp., Bronx, N.Y., N.Y. Hosp., 1947-50; instr. surgery Cornell U., 1950-52, asst. prof., 1952-55, asso. prof., 1955; asst. attending surgeon N.Y. Hosp., 1950-55; asst. prof. surgery Columbia U., 1955-58, asso. prof., 1958-73, prof. clin. surgery, 1973—; asso. attending surgeon St. Luke's Hosp., N.Y.C., 1955-58, attending surgeon, 1958—; cons. Walter Reed Med. Center, 1970-77. Chmn. Medico Advisory Bd., 1976-77; mem., v.p. CARE Bd.; v.p. Wellborn Found., N.Y.C. Served with AUS, plastic surgeon, 1943-46. Decorated Bronze Star (U.S.); Medal of Honor (2) (Vietnam); cavallero Order of San Carlos (Colombia); diplomate Am. Bd. Plastic Surgery (pres. 1967-68). Fellow A.C.S.; mem. Am. Assn. Plastic Surgeons, Am. Soc. Plastic and Reconstructive Surgery (pres. 1966), Found. Am. Soc. Plastic and Reconstructive Surgery (pres. 1961-65), Am. Surg. Assn., Soc. Univ. Surgeons, French, Brasilian, Colombian, Argentina socs. plastic surgeons, Brit. Assn. Plastic Surgery, Peruvian Acad. Surgeons, N.Y. Surg. Soc., N.Y. Acad. Medicine (pres. Friends Rare Book Room), N.Y. State Med. Soc. (pres., sec. med. history), Halsted Soc. (pres. 1973-74), James IV Assn. Surgeons, Am. Soc. Aesthetic Plastic Surgery (pres. 1974-75), Author: Plastic Surgery, 1962; Cleft Palate, 1968; Plastic Surgery at the New York Hospital 100 Years Ago; contbr. 30 chpts. to books, 170 articles to profl. jours.; asso. editor Plastic Reconstructive Surgery, 1969-74; editor Annals Plastic Surgery, 1977—. Home: 35 E 75th St New York City NY 10021 Office: 115 E 67th St New York City NY 10021

STARK, ROBERT MARTIN, mathematician, civil engr.; b. N.Y.C., Feb. 6, 1930; s. Alexander and Julia (Gross) S.; A.B., Johns Hopkins U., 1951; M.A., U. Mich., 1952; Ph.D., U. Del., 1965; m. Carol LaSage, Jan. 13, 1955; children—Bradley R., Timothy D., Steven M., Candice B. Research scientist Bausch and Lomb, Rochester, N.Y., 1955; instr. Rochester Inst. Tech., 1956-57; asst. dean engring., asst. prof. mathematics Cleve. State U., 1957-62; instr. U. Del., 1962-64, asst. prof. civil engring., ops. research, 1964-68, asso. prof., 1968-76, prof., 1976—; vis. asso. prof., Mass. Inst. Tech., 1972-73; cons. in field. Office Naval Research grantee, 1974—; NSF grantee, 1966-70; U.S. Army Research Office grantee, 1967-68. Mem. AAAS, Phila. Ops. Research Soc. (pres. 1970), Ops. Research Soc. Am., ASCE, Inst. Mgmt. Sci. Author: (with R.L. Nicholls) Mathematical Foundations for Design: Civil Engineering Systems, 1972; research, publs. ops., applied probability. Home: One Fox Ln Newark DE 19711 Office: U Del Dept Math Sci Newark DE 19711

STARK, THOMAS MICHAEL, justice N.Y. Supreme Ct.; b. Riverhead, N.Y., Feb. 13, 1925; s. John Charles and Mary Ellen (Gaynor) S.; B.S. cum laude, Holy Cross Coll., 1945; LL.B., Harvard U., 1949; m. Jane Claire Crabtree, Dec. 30, 1954; children—Elizabeth Mary, Ellen Gaynor. Admitted to N.Y. bar, 1950; asso. firm Zaleski & Jablonka, Riverhead, 1949-51; individual practice, Riverhead, 1951-63; town atty., Riverhead, 1953; justice of peace, mem. town bd., Riverhead, 1956-57; mem. Riverhead Bd. Edn., 1960-63; judge county ct., County of Suffolk, 1963-68; justice 10th Jud. Dist. Supreme Ct. N.Y., Riverhead, 1969—; panel discussion leader Ann. Conf. N.Y. State Trial Judges, 1970-78; chmn. criminal law subcom. N.Y. State Trial Judges Benchbook, 1970-75; vice chmn. com. on criminal jury instrns. N.Y. State Office Ct. Adminstrn., 1975—. Mem. exec. bd., v.p. Suffolk County council Boy Scouts Am., 1955-58. Mem. exec. com., co-leader Riverhead, Suffolk County Republican Com., 1961-62. Served as ensign USNR, World War II. Recipient Silver Beaver award Boy Scouts Am., 1957. Mem. Suffolk County Bar Assn. (sec. 1959-62, 3d v.p. 1962-63). Home: Bay Woods Aquebogue NY 11931 Office: Suffolk County Courthouse Riverhead NY 11901

STARKEY, NORMAN BERNE, aerospace engr.; b. Gary, Ind., Oct. 20, 1949; s. James Edward and Beulah Lucille (Roberts) S.; B.S., U. Md., 1972, M.S., 1978; m. Veronica O'Dea, Sept. 2, 1972; 1 son, Robert Sean. Engring. co-op student NASA Goddard Space Flight Center, Greenbelt, Md., 1970-72, flight structures engr., 1972—; participated in joint NASA/European Space Agency mission planning confs. Vice pres. bd. dirs. Homeowners, 1978. Mem. Am. Inst. of Aeros and Astronautics, Phi Kappa Phi, Sigma Gamma Tau, Tau Beta Pi. Club: NASA/Goddard Chess. Home: 2213 Notely Ln Crofton MD 21114 Office: NASA Goddard Space Flight Center Greenbelt MD 20771

STARR, MICHAEL BARRY, dentist; b. Bklyn., Jan. 26, 1948; s. Herbert J. and Ida (Polakoff) S.; B.A., Bklyn. Coll., 1973; D.D.S., N.Y.U., 1976. Gen. practice dentistry, Fresh Meadows, N.Y.; instr. operative dentistry Coll. Dentistry, N.Y. U., N.Y.C., 1977—. Mem. ADA, Acad. Gen. Dentistry, N.Y. State, 1st Dist. dental socs., Am.

Analgesia Soc. Home: 4150 Ocean Ave Brooklyn NY 11235 Office: 61-17 190th St Queens NY 11365

STARRETT, LOYD MILFORD, lawyer; b. St. Louis, Aug. 13, 1933; s. Loyd George and Edna (Switzer) S.; A.B. magna cum laude, Harvard U., 1953, LL.B. magna cum laude, 1958; m. Elaine Virginia MacGray, Apr. 8, 1967; children—Lucinda, Sarah Jean, Loyd Benjamin, Patricia Mary, Charles Daniel. Admitted to Mass. bar, 1959; law clk. Covington & Burling, Washington, 1957, Cahill, Gordon, Reindel & Ohl, N.Y.C., 1958, Chief Judge Calvert Magruder, U.S. Ct. Appeals First Circuit, Boston, 1958-59; Milton research fellow Harvard Law Sch., 1958-60; asso. Foley, Hoag & Eliot, Boston, 1959-63, partner, 1963—. Dir. Park Mobile, Inc. and affiliated cos., A.W. Hastings & Co., Inc. and subs. First v.p. Cape Ann Interfaith Commn., Gloucester, Mass., 1970-72, treas., 1972—; moderator Town of Rockport (Mass.), 1975-78, 78—, chmn. Rockport Growth Policy Com., 1976-78; vice chmn. Rockport Zoning Bd. Appeal, 1976—. Bd. dirs. Rockport Joint Youth Fellowship, 1969-73, coordinator, 1967-69, exec. dir., 1969-71, treas. 1971—; bd. dirs. Am. Bapt. Chs. of Mass., 1977—; bd. dirs. Adoniram Judson Bapt. Assn., 1974—, vice moderator, 1977-79. Served to 1st lt. USAF, 1953-55; maj. Res., ret. Mem. teaching teams Trial Advocacy Workshops Harvard Law Sch., 1975-78. Mem. Am. Soc. Hosp. Attys., Am., Mass., Boston bar assns., Am., Mass. trial lawyers assns., Am. Judicature Soc., Assn. ICC Practitioners, Mass. Moderators Assn., Air Force Assn., CAP, Res. Officers Assn. Baptist (chmn. bd. deacons 1968-73, 77—, supt. ch. sch. 1974-77). Home: 23 Granite St Rockport MA 01966 Office: 10 Post Office Sq Boston MA 02109

STASHEFF, CHRISTOPHER BORIS, educator; b. Mt. Vernon, N.Y., Jan. 15, 1944; s. Edward and Evelyn (Maher) S.; B.A., U. Mich., 1965, M.A., 1966; Ph.D., U. Nebr., 1972; m. Mary Margaret Miller, June 7, 1973; children—Isobel, Edward, Genevieve. Floor crew U. Mich. TV Center, 1961-67; adminstrv. asst. U. Nebr. and Nebr. Ednl. TV Council for Higher Edn., 1967-68; asst. prof. dept. speech and theatre Montclair State Coll., Upper Montclair, N.J., 1972—. Roman Catholic. Author: The Warlock in Spite of Himself, 1969; King Kobold, 1970. Office: Montclair State Coll Valley Rd and Normal Ave Upper Montclair NJ 07043

STASIOWSKI, PATRICIA MONICA, nurse; b. Everett, Mass., Jan. 28, 1938; d. Pasquale and Mary (DiFilippo) Duragano; grad. Melrose-Wakefield Hosp. Sch. Nursing, 1959; student Boston U., 1963-68, Merrimack Coll.; m. William A. Stasiowski, Apr. 21, 1961. Surg. nursing instr. Melrose-Wakefield Hosp., Melrose, Mass., 1960-69; surg. dept. head Whidden Meml. Hosp., Everett, Mass., 1970-74; surg. coordinator Lynn (Mass.) Hosp., 1974-78. Mem. Assn. Operating Room Nurses (pres. Mass. chpt. I). Home: 119 Johnson Rd Winchester MA 01890

STATHIS, NICHOLAS JOHN, lawyer; b. Calchi, Dodecanese Islands, Greece, Feb. 27, 1924 (father Am. citizen); s. John and Sylvia (Koutsonouris) S.; student Columbia U., 1942-43, 44-48, A.B., 1946, J.D., 1948. Admitted to N.Y. bar, 1949; asso. James Maxwell Fassett, N.Y.C., 1948-50; asst. counsel to spl. com. to investigate organized crime in interstate commerce U.S. Senate, Washington, 1951; trial atty. Fidelity & Casualty Co. N.Y., N.Y.C., 1952; law sec. to Harold R. Medina, judge U.S. Ct. Appeals for 2d Circuit, N.Y.C., 1952-54; spl. dep. atty. gen. N.Y. State Election Frauds Bur., Dept. Law, 1956; asso. firm Watson Leavenworth Kelton & Taggart, N.Y.C., 1954-60, partner, N.Y.C., 1961—; lectr. Practising Law Inst., 1968-69. Pres., exec. dir., bd. dirs. Found. for Classic Theatre and Acad., 1973—; bd. dirs. Concert Artists Guild, 1974—, Pirandello Soc., 1976—. Served with AUS, 1943-44. Mem. Assn. Bar City N.Y., Am., N.Y. State bar assns., Am., N.Y. patent law assns. Democrat. Greek Orthodox. Contbr. articles to profl. jours. Home: 53 Duncan Ave Jersey City NJ 07304 Office: 100 Park Ave New York City NY 10017

STAUB, HENRY PAUL, pediatrician; b. Berlin, Germany, Sept. 13, 1919; s. Ludwig O. and Erna L. (Zitzke) S.; B.A., Augsburg Coll., 1943; B.S., U. N.D., 1945; M.D., U. Ill., 1947; M.S., U. Minn., 1950; m. Marie T. Wasthues, July 14, 1951; children—Doris M. Petrie, Joan L., Barbara E., Julie A., Nancy L., Mary H. Intern, Mpls. Gen. Hosp., 1947-48, resident, 1948-50; practice medicine specializing in pediatrics, Mpls., 1950-66; asst. prof. pediatrics U. Minn., Mpls., 1967; dir. dept. pediatrics E.J. Meyer Meml. Hosp., Buffalo, 1970-77; asso. prof. pediatrics State U. N.Y., Buffalo, 1970—, A. Conger Goodyear prof. pediatrics, 1977-79; mem. physician adv. com. Vis. Nurse Assn., Buffalo, 1973—; mem. bd. Pastoral Counseling Center, Buffalo, 1973—; mem. health adv. com. Community Action Orgn. Erie County, Buffalo, 1977—. Served to capt. M.C., U.S. Army, 1943-46, 51-52. Recipient Distinguished Alumnus citation Augsburg Coll., 1970. Mem. Am. Acad. Pediatrics (mem. com. on Indian health, chpt. chmn.), AMA, Am. Pub. Health Assn., Minn. Acad. Medicine. Author: Ambulatory Care in Children, 1977. Home: 203 Woodbridge Ave Buffalo NY 14214 Office: 219 Bryant St Buffalo NY 14222

STAUB, ROBERT ANDRE, mgmt. cons.; b. Paris, Apr. 2, 1934; s. Francis R. and Margot (Hechinger) S.; came to U.S., 1938, naturalized, 1945; B.B.A., U. Miami, 1956; m. Sandra Lee Hess, Feb. 14, 1967; children—Robert Andre, Margot Gabriele. Mgmt. trainee Ford div. Ford Motor Co., Dearborn, Mich., 1956, personnel mgr., 1957-60; dir. personnel Allstate Ins. Co., Hartford, Conn., 1960-61; chmn. bd., pres. Staub, Warmbold & Assos. Internat. Inc., N.Y.C., 1962—; adviser to sec. treasury, 1978—, U.S. commr. customs, 1978—. Trustee French and Polyclinic Med. Center, also vice chmn. med. affairs, chmn. planning and devel. com., mem. exec. com.; bd. dirs. Girls Clubs of N.Y.; mem. men's com. Madison Sq. Boys Club; bd. govs. USO. Mem. Assn. Exec. Recruiting Cons. (dir.), Am. Mgmt. Assn., IEEE, Young Pres. Orgn., Lambda Chi Alpha. Presbyterian. Clubs: Pisces (Washington); La Gorce Country, Palm Bay (Miami, Fla.); Royal Cercle Gaulois (Brussels); N.Y. Athletic, Doubles, El Morroco. Home: 200 E 62d St New York City NY 10021 also 720 NE 69th St Miami FL 33138 Office: 919 3d Ave New York City NY 10022

STAUFFER, TOM GOODMAN, physician; b. St. Louis, Jan. 14, 1920; s. Dickson Shaw and Cyrene (VanderLippe) S.; A.B., Washington U., St. Louis, 1940, M.D., 1943; certified grad. N.Y. Psychoanalytic Inst., 1958; m. Anne Dance Kennard, June 15, 1948; children—Margery A. Stauffer Meeks, Kennard S., Jean F. Intern, internal medicine Vanderbilt U. Hosp., Nashville, 1944; asst. resident, resident psychiatry N.Y. Hosp., Westchester div., White Plains, 1944-48, asst. attending psychiatrist Westchester div., 1965-76, asso. attending, 1976—; clin. asst. prof. psychiatry Med. Coll. Cornell U., N.Y.C., 1965-76, clin. asso. prof., 1976—, chmn. faculty Westchester div., 1978—; staff psychiatrist Four Winds Sanitarium, Katonah, N.Y., 1948-50; individual practice psychiatry, psychoanalysis, White Plains and Briarcliff Manor, N.Y., 1948—; attending psychiatrist White Plains Hosp., 1950-55, Lawrence Hosp., Bronxville, N.Y., 1967—, United Hosp., Port Chester, N.Y., 1967—; chief psychiatrist Sarah Lawrence Coll., 1959—, dir. health services, 1973—; psychiat. cons. White Plains pub. schs., 1948-75, Briarcliff Coll., 1963-64, Youth Consultation Service, White Plains, 1948-51, Westchester Community Mental Health Bd., 1960-62. Pres. elect. Jr.-Sr. High Sch. PTA, Briarcliff Manor, 1968-69, pres., 1969-70; v.p. Friends of Music, Briarcliff Manor, 1960-63, pres., 1963-65, bd. dirs., 1965-70; chmn. outdoor com. Troop 95, Taconic council Boy Scouts Am., Briarcliff Manor, 1963-65, vice chmn., 1965-66, chmn. troop, 1966-67; mem. advisory bd. Fair Housing Commn., Briarcliff Manor, 1965-70; mem. Westchester Community Mental Health Bd., 1970-76, chmn., 1972-76; bd. dirs. Met. (N.Y.C.) Coll. Mental Health Assn., 1969-75, pres., 1973-74. Served to capt. M.C., AUS, 1951-53; C.Z.; diplomate Am. Bd. Psychiatry and Neurology. Fellow Am. Psychiat. Assn., Am. Coll. Health Assn.; mem. Westchester Psychiat. Soc. (pres. 1966-67, chmn. nominating com. 1967-68, distinguished service award 1977), Group for Advancement Psychiatry, Am., N.Y. (co-chmn. Extension Sch. Dialogue with Educators 1967-74), Westchester (pres. 1974-75) psychoanalytic socs., Med. Soc. of Westchester County (dir. 1972-75), AMA, Phi Beta Kappa, Sigma Xi, Phi Delta Theta (pres. 1940), Phi Beta Pi. Congregationalist. Author: (with Dr. Eddy, Stauffer and others on Com. on Coll. Student, Group for Advancement of Psychiatry) Sex and the College Student, 1966; (film) A Nice Kid Like You, 1970; The Educated Woman, 1975. Home: 238 Chappaqua Rd Briarcliff Manor NY 10510 Office: 499 N Broadway White Plains NY 10603 also 238 Chappaqua Rd Briarcliff Manor NY 10510

STAVE, CARL EDWARD, physician; b. Paterson, N.J., Jan. 30, 1942; s. Thomas Lewis and Sadye Marrion (Goldberg) S.; B.A., Rutgers U., 1963; M.D., Tufts U., 1967; m. Norma Ann Weinberg, Aug. 22, 1964; children—Todd M., Nancy T. Intern, Maimonides Hosp., Bklyn., 1967-68; resident in obstetrics and gynecology Pa. Hosp., Phila., 1968-71; practice medicine specializing in obstetrics and gynecology, Hyattsville, Md., 1973—. Served with USAF, 1971-73. Fellow Am. Coll. Obstetrics and Gynecology; mem. Am. Assn. Sex Educators, Councilors and Therapists, Am. Assn. Gynecol. Laparoscopists, Am. Fertility Soc., Prince Georges County Med. Soc., Phi Delta Epsilon. Republican. Jewish. Club: Potomac Tennis. Home: 10109 Logan Dr Potomac MD 20854 Office: 6525 Belcrest Rd Hyattsville MD 20782

STAVISKY, ELI, oral surgeon; b. Scranton, Pa., Jan. 22, 1940; s. Andrew and Helen (Macheska) S.; B.A., Lycoming Coll., 1961; D.D.S., Temple U., 1965; postgrad. N.Y. U., 1967-68; m. Paula Ovens, Aug. 4, 1962; children—Tanya, Elena, Natasha. Intern oral surgery Bklyn. Cumberland Med. Center, 1968-69, resident, 1969-70; individual practice oral surgery, Scranton, 1970—. Served to capt. USAF, 1965-67. Diplomate Am. Bd. Oral Surgery. Mem. Am. Soc. Oral Surgery, Pa. Soc. Oral Surgery, Am., Pa., Scranton Dist. (pres. 1976-77) dental assns. Russian Orthodox. Clubs: Scranton Country, Lycoming Coll. Alumni (exec. bd. 1973- 76). Home: 700 Glenburn Rd Clarks Summit PA 18411 Office: 1 Adams Plaza Scranton PA 18503

STAVOLA, JOHN JOSEPH, obstetrician, gynecologist; b. Hartford, Conn., Feb. 4, 1929; s. Felix Joseph and Lucy Marie (Martino) S.; B.S., Holy Cross Coll., 1951; M.D., N.Y. Med. Coll., 1956; m. Sylvia Caroline Gaworski, Dec. 20, 1951; children—Beth Ann, John Joseph, Joseph. Intern, St. Francis Hosp., Hartford, 1956-57; resident obstetrics and gynecology Hartford Hosp., 1957-60; practice medicine specializing in obstetrics and gynecology, Hartford, 1962—; mem. staff Hartford Hosp.; clin. asst. prof. dept. obstetrics and gynecology U. Conn., Farmington, 1975—. Served with M.C., USNR, 1960-62. Diplomate Am. Bd. Obstetrics and Gynecology. Fellow Am. Coll. Obstetricians and Gynecologists; mem. AMA, Conn. Med. Soc., Hartford County Med. Assn. Democrat. Roman Catholic. Home: 91 Forster St Hartford CT 06106 Office: 78 Retreat Ave Hartford CT 06106

STAYMAN, SAMUEL M., investment co. exec.; b. Worcester, Mass., May 28, 1909; s. Morris and Francis R. (Mittel) S.; A.B., Dartmouth Coll., 1930, M.B.A., 1931; m. Marjorie Schmukler, May 1, 1941 (dec. Feb. 1961); 1 dau., Susan Stayman Madorsky; m. 2d, Josephine L. Wacht, Sept. 21, 1962. Pres. Vt. Woolen Mills, 1939-51, Stamina Mills, 1952-65, S.M.S.A. Corp., N.Y.C., 1955—; mng. partner Stramd & Co., N.Y.C., 1966—. Trustee Am. Contract Bridge League Charity Found., 1970—. Mem. Am. Contract Bridge League. Clubs: Beach Point, Cavendish, Harmonie. Author: Expert Bidding at Contract Bridge, 1951; The Complete Stayman System of Contract Bidding, 1957; Do You Play Stayman?, 1965. Originator Stayman conv. method of bidding; U.S. contract bridge champion, 1942, 44, 46, 47, 50, 51, 53, 55, 59, 65; world bridge champion, 1950, 51, 53. Address: 850 Third Ave New York City NY 10022

STAYTON, WILLIAM RALPH, educator; b. Kelso, Wash., Dec. 25, 1933; s. Ralph Willard and Marguerite (Hunter) S.; B.A., U. Redlands, 1956; M.Div., Andover Newton Theol. Sem., 1960; Th.D., Boston U., 1967; m. Kathleen Boucher, Sept. 4, 1954; children—Mark William, John Hunter, Cheryl Kathleen, Robert Paul. Ordained to ministry Baptist Ch., 1959; asso. minister First Bapt. Ch., Newton Centre, Mass., 1956-61; minister First Bapt. Ch., Gloucester, Mass., 1961-68; minister-in-residence New Eng. Bapt. Hosp., Boston, 1968-71; chief, family life and sex edn., div. family study, dept. psychiatry U. Pa. Sch. Medicine, Phila., 1972—, asst. prof. family study in psychiatry 1975-77; asst. prof. psychiatry and human behavior Thomas Jefferson U. Med. Coll., Phila., 1977—; lectr. Swarthmore Coll., Widener Coll., Am. U. Named B'nai B'rith Man of Year, 1968. Licensed psychologist, Pa. Mem. Am., Pa. psychol. assns., Am. Assn. Sex Educators, Counselors and Therapists (certified sex educator and therapist), Am., New Eng. socs. clin. hypnosis, Nat. Council Family Relations, Am., Pa. assns. marriage and family counselors, Assn. for Creative Change, Eastern Assn. Sex Therapists, Soc. for Psychol. Study Social Issues, Sex Info. and Edn. Council U.S., Soc. for Sci. Study of Religion, Acad. Religion and Mental Health, Assn. for Clin. Pastoral Edn. Democrat. Club: Masons. Home: 188 Blackberry Ln Malvern PA 19355 Office: 14 Elliott Ave Bryn Mawr PA 19010

STEARN, DANIEL RICHARD, assn. exec.; b. Pitts., Apr. 9, 1923; s. Joseph Anthony and Mary Katherine (Lipinska) S.; B.A. in Journalism, Duquesne U., 1950; m. Margaret Theresa Wagner, Aug. 5, 1950; children—Mary Margaret, Susan Marie. Staff corr. UP, Pitts., 1950-56; mem. pub. relations staff Crucible Steel Co., Pitts., 1957-58; account exec. Lando, Inc., Pitts., 1958-61; mgr. pub. relations Instrument Soc. Am., Pitts., 1961-67; mgr. mktg. services Air Pollution Control Assn., Pitts., 1972—; pub. relations cons.; sr. scientist Div. Sponsored Research of Carnegie-Mellon Inst., 1972—. Served with USAAF, 1942-45. Mem. Nat. Assn. Expn. Mgrs., Am. Soc. Assn. Execs., Council Engring. and Sci. Soc. Execs. Democrat. Roman Catholic. Home: 219 Haugh Dr Pittsburgh PA 15237 Office: PO Box 2861 Pittsburgh PA 15230

STEARNS, FRANK BARNEY, educator, musician; b. Brattleboro, Vt., June 7, 1941; s. Barney Avery and Anne (Yurkus) Stearns; Mus.B., Westminster Choir Coll., 1963; M.A., U. Pitts., 1970; M.Ed., Slippery Rock (Pa.) State Coll., 1975; m. Patricia Ann Beckman, Aug. 9, 1969; children—Jin Soo, David. Minister music Connellsville (Pa.) U.P. Ch., 1963-67; dir. music Zion's Reformed Ch., Greenville, Pa., 1967—; tchr. music Buckeye Local Schs., Ashtabula, Ohio, 1968-70, Greenville Area Sch. Dist., Greenville, Pa., 1971—. Pvt. music tchr., Greenville, 1967—; community music dir. Orpheus Choral Soc., 1969—; organist, recitalist; violist Greenville Symphony Orch., 1972—. Bd. dirs. Greenville Symphony Orch., 1970-73, 75-78, Greenville Community Concerts Assn., 1970—. Mem. Am. Guild Organists, Am. Fedn. Musicians, Organ Hist. Soc., Choristers Guild, Mercer County Hist. Soc. Club: Greenville Orpheus (program chmn. 1969-70, choral dir. 1969—). Home: 6 Columbia Ave Greenville PA 16125 Office: 260 Main St Greenville PA 16125

STEARNS, LLOYD WORTHINGTON, investment adviser, oriental artifact cons.; b. Somerville, Mass., Feb. 16, 1910; s. Charles Victor and Flora D. (Liscom) S.; B.S. in Indsl. Engring., N.Y. U., 1934; m. Adelaide Church, May 23, 1935; 1 dau., Adelaide Liscom (Mrs. Peter Duncan McRae). Indsl. security analyst Adminstrv. and Research Corp., 1934-38; asst. to treas., v.p. Northam Warren Corp., 1938-41; with Met. Life Ins. Co., 1941-75, sr. procedure analyst, mgmt. cons., exec. asst. to sr. v.p., exec. v.p., 1941-60, sec., emergency com., 1950-75; coll. relations cons.; dir. Soundscriber, Inc.; pres., dir. Dispoz Sani Products, Ltd. Dir. Mil. Pub. Inst., Inc. sec. N.Y. State Life Ins. Civil Def. Adv. Com., 1954-64. Corporate mem. N.Y. World's Fair 1964-65 Corp.; mem. nat. def. com. U.S. C. of C. and N.A.M.; mem. joint com. emergency operation Am. Life Conv.-Life Ins. Assn. Am.; mem. corps com. Lincoln Center for Performing Arts, 1959-62; v.p., treas., dir., vice chmn. N.Y. com. Nat. Strategy Seminars, Inc.; dir. Nat. Inst. Disaster Moblzn., Inc., Battery Park Colonnade Assos., Inc.; sec. French-Polyclinic Fund, Inc. Trustee French Hosp., N.Y.C., N.Y. Polyclinic Med. Sch. and Hosp. Served with AUS, 1941-46; col. res. Decorated Legion of Merit; recipient Outstanding Civilian Service medal U.S. Army; decorated comdr. Crown of Italy, comdr. Sts. Maurice and Lazarus (Italy); War Cross Commemorative Royal Yugoslav Army. Mem. Am. Ordnance Assn. (dir., chmn. programs), Am. Legion, Soc. Colonial Wars (council), S.A.R. (bd. mgrs.), N.Y. Soc. Mil. and Naval Officers World Wars (sec.), Assn. U.S. Army (pres. N.Y. chpt. 1961-62, regional pres. 1963-64), Def. Orientation Conf. Assn., N.Y. Chamber Commerce, Newcomen Soc., U.S. Naval Inst., Phi Gamma Delta. Episcopalian. Mason. Clubs: University (N.Y.C.); Army and Navy (Washington). Home and office: 410 Main St Keene NH 03431

STEARNS, ROBERT LOUIS, pub. relations exec.; b. Logan, Iowa, Sept. 22, 1924; s. Robert Louis and Blanche Gwendolyn (Murfield) S.; B.A., Mich. State U., 1949; m. Irene Marron Stearns, Nov. 24, 1952; children—Catherine, Robert M., Michael Q., Barbara I., Jonathon P. Police reporter, real estate editor Pontiac (Mich.) Press, 1949-51; staff writer Phila. Bull., 1951-55, N.Y. Daily News, 1955-57; account exec. S. Rider & Assos., N.Y.C., 1957-61, Carl Blair & Assos., N.Y.C., 1961-65; mgr. pub. relations Xerox Corp., Rochester, N.Y., 1965—; pub. relations cons. AMA, 1974-75, Strong Meml. Hosp., Rochester, 1974-75. Served with U.S. Army, 1942-46, USAFR, 1946-60. Recipient Pall Mall Big Story award, 1955. Mem. Pub. Relations Soc. Am. (dir. Rochester chpt. 1975-76); Distinguished Service award 1974). Home: 7 Ross Brook Dr Rochester NY 14625 Office: 006 Xerox Sq Rochester NY 14644

STECK, EDGAR ALFRED, chemist; b. Phila., Dec. 24, 1918; s. Elwyn Alfred and Martha Marguerite (Feicke) S.; A.B., Temple U., 1939; M.S., U. Pa., 1941, Ph.D., 1942; postgrad. N.Y. U., U. Chgo.; m. Mildred D. Anselment, Apr. 24, 1947; children—Marlene D., Alfred E. Group leader Sterling-Winthrop Research Inst., Rensselaer, N.Y., 1942-58; dir. medicinal chem. research Johnson & Johnson, New Brunswick, N.J., 1958-60; dir. research and devel. Wilson Lab., Chgo., 1960-61, McKesson Labs., Bridgeport, Conn., 1965-66; sr. scientist Nalco Chem. Co., Chgo., 1961-65; project dir. parasitic diseases Walter Reed Army Inst. Research, Washington, 1967—; adj. prof. medicinal chemistry Rensselaer Poly. Inst., Troy, N.Y., 1951-57; mem. sci. working group parasitic diseases WHO, 1977—. Recipient certificate of achievement Office Sci. Research and Devel., Washington, 1946, certificate of outstanding achievement U.S. Army, 1978. Mem. Tropical Medicine Assn. Washington (pres. 1977-78), Am., Royal socs. tropical medicine and hygiene, Helminthological Soc. Washington, Am. Chem. Soc., Chem. Soc. London, Chem. Soc. Washington. Author: The Chemotherapy of Protozoan Diseases, 1972. Contbr. articles to profl. jours. Patentee. Home: 1913 Edgewater Pkwy Silver Spring MD 20903 Office: Div Exptl Therapeutics Walter Reed Army Inst Research Washington DC 20012

STECKIW, EUGENE, anesthesiologist; b. Ukraine, June 8, 1921; s. John and Euphrosina (Chychula) S.; student State Med. Inst. Lviv, 1939-44, Ludwig Maximillian U., Glessen, 1944-45, Munich, 1946-47; M.D., U. Munich, 1947; postgrad. N.Y. U., 1951-52; m. Nila Bezkorowainy, Feb. 25, 1949; children—Andrew, Roma. Intern, Mercy Hosp., Buffalo, 1949-51; resident Meyer J. Meml. Hosp., Buffalo, 1952, Buffalo Gen. Hosp., 1953-54; anesthesiologist USPHS Hosp., Balt., 1956-58; pvt. practice medicine specializing in anesthesiology Kenmore (N.Y.) Mercy Hosp., 1958-70, Sisters Hosp., Buffalo, 1970—. Attending anesthesiologist State U. N.Y., Buffalo, 1972—. Mem. AMA, Am., N.Y. socs. anesthesiologists, N.Y. State Med. Soc., Ukrainian Med. Soc. N.Am. Home: 61 Snughaven Ct Tonawanda NY 14150 Office: 5353 Main St Williamsville NY 14221

STEEDLE, ROGER CRAIG, lawyer; b. Phila., Sept. 17, 1942; s. Robert Herbert and Mary Marjorie (Keil) S.; A.B., Dickinson Coll., 1964; J.D., Dickinson Sch. Law, 1967. Admitted to N.J. bar, 1967; asso. firm Lloyd, Megargee and Steedle, and predecessor, Atlantic City, 1967-69, jr. partner, 1969-75; sr. partner firm Lloyd Megargee Steedle & Connor, Pleasantville, N.J., 1975—. Mem. Linwood (N.J.) City Council, 1973-74; Rep. County committeeman, 1975, 76, 77, 78; pres. Linwood Rep. Club, 1975; bd. dirs. Atlantic County YMCA, to 1975. Served with USAF, 1967-74. Mem. Am., N.J., Atlantic County (trustee 1971, 75, treas. 1972-74) bar assns., N.J. Def. Assn. (trustee 1977, 78), Am. Judicature Soc., Am. Arbitration Assn., Trial Attys. N.J., Assn. Ins. Attys., Def. Research Inst., N.J. Fedn. Planning Ofcls., N.J. Inst. Municipal Attys., N.J. State C. of C., Dickinson Law Sch. Alumni Assn. (exec. bd. 1973—), Am. Legion (judge adv. 1976—), Alpha Chi Rho. Republican. Methodist. Clubs: Atlantic City Jaycees (v.p. 1972), N.J. Jaycees, Kiwanis, Masons. Home: 1050 Bartlett Dr Linwood NJ 08221 Office: 600 Fire Rd Pleasantville NJ 08232 also 1421 Atlantic Ave Atlantic City NJ 08401

STEEGE, BETTY K. (MRS. PETER O. STEEGE), ednl. adminstr.; b. Rochester, Pa., Sept. 9, 1932; d. Charles and Ethyln Ruth (Lambert) Tarazano; B.S., Edinboro State Coll., 1954; M.Ed., U. Pitts., 1970, Ph.D., 1977; m. Henry Albert Gardner, Jr., Dec. 27, 1953 (div. Jan. 1968); children—Elizabeth Ann, Trilby Lee; m. 2d, David J. Williams, Aug. 26, 1968 (dec. June 23, 1973); m. 3d, Peter O. Steege, Jan. 9, 1975. Art tchr. Rochester Area Sch. Dist., 1954; tchr. art, mech. drawing Monaca (Pa.) Sch. Dist., 1955-70; dir. Urban Center, dean acad. services Community Coll. Beaver County, Monaca, Pa., 1970-74; adminstrv. asst. to pres. Community Coll. Allegheny County, Pitts., 1974-76, dean pub. affairs and devel., 1976—. Sec., Rochester Planning and Zoning Commn., 1960-72; mem. legislation adv. com. Pa. Bd. Edn., 1967-68; mem. adv. bd. on quality edn. assessment Pa. Dept. Pub. Instrn., 1968; mem. edn. adv. com. Rochester Area Sch. Dist., 1966-67; charter mem., dir. Chippewa Playhouse, Beaver, Pa., 1960-61, sec., 1961; charter mem., dir. Regent Theatre, Beaver Falls, 1961-62, v.p., 1961; mem. Beaver County Emergency Med. Council, 1973-75; mem. com. on instnl. master planning Pa. Dept. Edn., 1974-76. Bd. dirs. Beaver County Children Aid and Family Service, Beaver-Butler-Lawrence Counties Comprehensive Health Planning Assn., 1972-76. Named One of Outstanding Young Women in Am. leaders of women's orgns., 1965. Mem. Pa. Art Edn. Assn. (sec. 1970-72), Pa. Fedn. Women's Clubs (state bd. 1964-74, bicentennial chmn. 1973-76). Presbyterian. Home: 1150 Bank St Beaver PA 15009 Office: Community Coll of Allegheny County Pittsburgh PA 15222

STEELE, BERT L., telephone co. exec.; b. Erie, Pa., Apr. 27, 1918; s. John L. and Hannah R. S.; B.A., U. Pa., 1949; m. Emma A. Klemm, June 25, 1949; children—Diane, David, Cynthia. Personnel asst. Gen. Telephone Co. Pa., Erie, 1949-52, adminstrv. asst., 1952-53, dir. indsl. relations, 1953-57, dir. personnel, 1957; personnel adminstr. GTE Service Corp., N.Y.C., 1957-60, dir. personnel, 1960-66, v.p. personnel telephone ops., 1966—. Mem. Ind. Telephone Pioneers (nat. pres. 1978). Republican. Lutheran. Home: 195 W Haviland Ln Stamford CT 06903

STEELE, CHARLES WILLIAM, physician; b. Chillicothe, Mo., Dec. 1, 1905; s. William D. and Kathryn L. (Seiberling) S.; A.B., U. Mo., 1927, M.A., 1929; M.D., Harvard, 1931; m. Ruby Mabelle Cram, Apr. 21, 1931; children—Charles William, Mary Louise, Richard Earl, Linda Maybell. Intern in pathology and on 4th med. service, Boston City Hosp., 1931-34; resident in medicine Central Maine Gen. Hosp., Lewiston, 1934-35; practice medicine specializing in internal medicine and cardiology, Lewiston and Auburn, Maine, 1936—; cardiologist, sr. attending physician Central Maine Med. Center, 1937-71, chief cardiac clinics, 1955-71; chief cardiac clinics Central Maine Med. Center, Lewiston, Rumford Community Hosp., Bath (Maine) Meml. Hosp., 1955-71; cons. in internal medicine Med. and Surg. Hosp., VA, Togus, Maine, 1947—, Social Security Adminstrn., Bur. Hearing and Appeals, HEW; cons. div. health, moblzn. USPHS, 1960-72; cons. in cardiology Rumford Community Hosp., Bath Meml. Hosp.; cons. internal medicine and cardiology Augusta Gen. Hosp.; asso. staff Maine Gen. Hosp., Portland. Mem. Pub. Safety Council, 1950-54; state dep. civil def. dir. Med. and Spl. Weapons Def., State of Maine, 1949-56; spl. advt. to state dir. Maine Civil Def. and Pub. Agy. on Health and Spl. Weapons Def., 1957-70; mem. Fed. Civil Def. Adminstrn., regional med. adv. com.; mem. health and spl. weapons com. U.S. Civil Def. Council, 1956—, chmn. med. and spl. weapons com., 1958—. Served from maj. to lt. col., M.C., AUS, 1942-46; col. M.C. Res., 1946-65, ret. 1966; comdg. officer 333d Gen. Hosp., 1954-62. Recipient Freedoms Found. award, 1952; Robins award for outstanding community service by a physician, 1964; Phizer award of merit U.S. Civil Def. Council, 1960; award Am. Soc. Internal Medicine. Diplomate Am. Bd. Internal Medicine, Pan Am. Med. Assn. Fellow A.C.P., AMA (mem. com. on civil def. 1955-62); mem. Am., N.E., Maine (dir., pres. 1953) heart assns., Internat. Soc. Internal Medicine, Am. Soc. Clin. Pharmacology and Therapeutics, Mil. Order World War (Maine charter mem.), Arthritis and Rheumatism Found., N.E. chpt. (med. and sci. com.), Maine (pres. 1963-65), Am. (med. service com. 1964-65) socs. internal medicine, Am. (com. emergency med. care 1961-62), N.E. diabetic assns., Maine Med. Assn., Am. Chem. Soc., Assn. Mil. Surgeons U.S., Res. Officers Assn. of U.S., Phi Beta Kappa, Sigma Xi, Alpha Omega Alpha. Baptist. Clubs: Rotary, Exec. (Lewiston-Auburn). Author of articles on cardiology and internal medicine in Jour. Med. Med. Assn. and other med. jours.; also author numerous brochures and pamphlets on civil def. Home: 1 Wakefield St Lewiston ME 04240 Office: 472 Main St Lewiston ME 04240

STEELE, HOWARD LOUCKS, govt. ofcl.; b. Pitts., Jan. 27, 1929; s. Howard Bennington and Ruby Alberta (Loucks) S.; B.S., Washington and Lee U., 1950; M.S., Pa. State U., 1952; Ph.D., U. Ky., 1962; m. Sally E. Funk, June 6, 1952 (div. 1977); children—John F., David A., Patricia A.; m. 2d, Jane R. Cornelius, July 30, 1977. Sales mgr. Greenville (Pa.) Dairy Co., 1952-56; owner H.L. Steele Bulk Milk Hauling, Greenville, Pa., 1955-60; asst. prof. Clemson (S.C.) U., 1956-57, asso. prof., 1957-64; asso. prof. Ohio State U., Columbus, 1964-71; with Office Internat. Cooperation and Devel. U.S. Dept. Agr., Washington, 1971—, project mgr. AID, Bolivia, 1977—; instr. U. Md., College Park, 1974—; vis. prof. U. Sao Paulo, Piracicaba, Brazil, 1964-66; partner Kingwood Acres Farm, Rockwood, Pa., 1966—. Mem. Am. Agrl. Econs. Assn., Internat. Assn. Agrl. Economists. Mason (Shriner). Contbr. articles to profl. jours. Home: care USATD/Bolivia APO Miami FL 34032 Office: Room 100 Pomponia Plaza OICD Dept Agr 14th St and Independence Ave Washington DC 20250

STEELE, JAMES BRUCE, JR., newspaper reporter; b. Hutchinson, Kans., Jan. 3, 1943; s. James Bruce and Mary (Peoples) S.; B.A., U. Mo., 1967; m. Nancy Saunders, June 25, 1966. Labor writer Kansas City (Mo.) Star, 1962-67; dir. info. Laborers' Internat. Union of N.Am., AFL-CIO, Washington, 1967-70; urban affairs and investigative reporter Phila. Inquirer, 1970—. Recipient Am. Polit. Sci. Assn. award distinguished reporting pub. affairs, 1971; George Polk Meml. award of L.I.U. for met. reporting, 1971; Sigma Delta Chi award gen. reporting, 1971, Heywood Brown award, 1973, George Polk. Meml. award for spl. reporting, 1973, Gavel award Am. Bar Assn., 1973, Sidney Hillman award, 1973, John Hancock award for bus. reporting, 1973, Bus. Journalism award U. Mo., 1973, Pulitzer prize, 1975. Office: 400 N Broad St Philadelphia PA 19101

STEELE, MARK WILLIAM, physician; b. N.Y.C., Mar. 5, 1932; s. Harold Henry and Zoe (Steinberg) Rosenstiel; A.B. magna cum laude, Kenyon Coll., 1953; M.D., State U. N.Y., Bklyn., 1957; m. Shirley May Straitiff, Oct. 1, 1959; children—Ann Belle, Victoria Grace, Emily Helen. Intern, Yale Med. Center, 1957-58, resident, 1958-60, asst. prof. pediatrics, U. Pitts. Sch. Medicine, 1968-74, asso. prof., 1974—; practice medicine, specializing in pediatrics and genetics, Pitts., 1968—; attending staff, dir. div. med. genetics Children's Hosp., Pitts., 1968—; cons. staff U. Pitts. Health Center Hosps., 1968—, Home Crippled Children Pitts., 1976—; chmn. genetics sci. adv. com. Health-Research Service Found., Pitts., 1968-74. Served as capt. M.C., USAF, 1960-63. NIH research fellow Johns Hopkins Sch. Medicine, 1966-68; NIH Cancer Inst. research grantee 1971-77; Health-Research Service Found. Pitts. grantee, 1969-76; Nat. Found. March Dimes grantee, 1971—; Am. Cancer Soc. grantee, 1969. Diplomate Am. Bd. Pediatrics. Fellow Am. Acad. Pediatrics; mem. Allegheny County Med. Soc., Soc. Pediatric Research, Am. Soc. Human Genetics, Genetics Soc. Am., Kenyon Coll. Alumni Assn. (pres. Pitts. chpt. 1975-79), Phi Beta Kappa, Alpha Omega Alpha. Jewish religion. Club: Edgewood (Pitts.). Research in field. Contbr. articles to profl. jours. Home: 6947 Reynolds St Pittsburgh PA 15208 Office: U Pitts Sch Medicine Pittsburgh PA 15213

STEELE, ROBERT DONALD, civil engr.; b. Denver, Mar. 2, 1922; s. William Donald and Lydia Wilhelmina (Nyquist) S.; B.S.C.E. (N.Y. State Regents scholar), Cornell U., 1943; m. Constance Marie Gustavson, Apr. 23, 1944; children—Pamela Marie, Robert Donald. With Ebasco Services Inc., N.Y.C., 1946—, supervising engr., 1960-69, corp. chief engr. dept., 1969-76, cons. civil engr., 1977—, condr. co. seminars on nuclear power plants design, 1967-75; participant research projects AEC, NASA, 1960-67. Served to 1st lt. field arty., U.S. Army, 1943-46; ETO. Decorated Air medal with 2 oak leaf clusters; registered profl. engr. in 27 states, including N.Y. Fellow ASCE; mem. Am. Welding Soc., Nat. Council Engring. Examiners (certified), Rod and Bob, Chi Epsilon, Phi Delta Theta. Republican. Lutheran. Home: 130 Cherry St Katonah NY 10536 Office: 2 Rector St New York City NY 10006

STEELE, WILLIAM RICHARD, photographer; b. Chester, Pa., June 7, 1935; s. William Richard and Eliz Alberta (Smith) S.; ed. high sch.; 1 dau., Barbara L. Owner Richard Steele Studio Photography, Toms River, N.J., 1958—; head photography duCret Sch. Arts, Toms River, 1975—; pres. Keystone Agency, real estate, Toms River, 1969—, v.p. Tyler-Steele Assos., N.Y.C., Toms River, 1973—. Mem. adv. com. Ocean County Coll., Toms River, N.J., 1970—. Recipient numerous photog. awards. Mem. Prof. Photographers Assn. Am., Profl. Photographers Assn. N.J., Nat. Press Photographers Assn., Nat. Soc. Lit. and Arts. Club: USCG Aux. (founder and 1st. comdr. Flotilla 71 1973-75). Home: Money Island Summit Ave Toms River NJ 08753 Office: 1201 Hwy 37E Toms River NJ 08753

STEEN, CHARLES EDWIN, III, collectors' arms dealer; b. Newark, May 27, 1935; s. Charles Edwin and Rose Francis (Willkehr) S.; student Newark Coll. Engring., 1959-60; m. Marie Adele Bryan, Aug. 22, 1959; children—Valerie Gail, Charles Edwin IV. Founder, pres. Sarco, Inc., Stirling, N.J., 1971—. Served with USMCR, 1954-57. Mem. Nat. Rifle Assn. (life), Am. Def. Preparedness Assn., various gun collectors assns. Republican. Presbyterian. Office: 323 Union St Stirling NJ 07980

STEERS, EDWARD, microbiologist; b. Bethlehem, Pa., July 15, 1910; s. John Edward and Elizabeth Louise (Hess) S.; B.S. in Chemistry, Moravian Coll., 1932; M.S. in Biology, Lehigh U., 1937; Ph.D., U. Pa., 1949; m. Mary Mae Hochella, Sept. 26, 1930; children—John Edward, Edward, Mary Elizabeth. Prof., Moravian Coll., Bethlehem, 1932-45; research asso. U. Pa. Sch. Medicine, 1945-49, asso. prof. microbiology in medicine, dir. clin. microbiology William Pepper Lab., Hosp. U. Pa., 1956-63; asso. prof. bacteriology U. Md. Sch. Medicine, 1949-56; prof. bacteriology N.Y. Med. Coll., 1964-66; dir. microbiology Bklyn.-Cumberland Med. Center, 1966-70, dir. labs., 1967-70. Clin. prof. pathology State U. N.Y. Downstate Med. Center, 1966-70, prof. pathology, 1970-74, also dir. clin. labs., chmn. Sch. Med. Tech., 1972-74; prof. dept. biology L.I. U., 1967-70; attending cons. in microbiology and infectious diseases Mercy Hosp., Scranton, Pa., 1974—, Moses-Taylor Hosp., 1974—, Community Med. Center, 1974—. Fellow Am. Acad. Microbiology; mem. Soc. Am. Microbiology, Wayne County (Pa.), Lackawanna (Pa.) hist. socs., Wyo. Hist. and Geol. Soc. Republican. Episcopalian. Contbr. numerous articles to sci. jours. Home: Box 199-C Paupack PA 18451 Office: 403 Med Arts Bldg Washington Ave Scranton PA 18501

STEERS, NEWTON IVAN, JR., former congressman; b. Glen Ridge, N.J., Jan. 13, 1917; s. Newton Ivan and Claire L. (Herder) S.; grad. Hotchkiss Sch., 1935; A.B. in Econs., Yale, 1939, J.D., 1948; certificate advanced meteorology Mass. Inst. Tech., 1943; m. Nina G. Auchincloss, June 8, 1957; children—Newton Ivan III, Hugh A., Burr G. Asst. in plant mgmt. E.I. duPont de Nemours Co., Inc., Parlin, N.J., 1939-40, asst. tech. supt. tests, Seaford, Del., 1940-41; asst. works mgr. Gen. Aniline & Film Corp., 1948-51; asst. to br. chief AEC, 1951, div. dir., 1952, asst. gen. mgr., 1953, commr., 1953; pres., dir. Atomics, Physics & Sci. Fund, Inc., Washington, 1953-65; ins. commr. State of Md., 1967-70; mem. Md. Senate, 1971-76; mem. 95th Congress from 8th Dist. Md. Trustee, chmn. fin. com. Columbia Lighthouse for Blind. Chmn., Md. Republican Com., 1964. Capt. USAF Res.

STEFANSKI, RAYMOND ARTHUR, biologist; b. Goodman, Wis., July 2, 1940; s. Rudolph Frank and Frances (Dziedzic) S.; B.S., U. Wis., 1963; M.S., Utah State U., 1965; Ph.D., U. Toronto, 1969. Postdoctoral researcher Cambridge (Eng.) U., 1969-72; research scientist Mass. Inst. Tech., Cambridge, 1972-75; sr. biologist Govt. of Ont., Toronto, 1975—. Ont. Grad. Studies fellow, 1967-69; Research Lab. of Electronics fellow, 1973; NIH fellow, 1974-75. Mem. Brit. Ornithologists Union, Sigma Xi. Clubs: Manomet, Long Point bird observatories. Contbr. articles in field to profl. jours. Home: 25 Lascelles Blvd Apt 1015 Toronto ON M4V 2C1 Canada Office: Wildlife Branch M N R Queens Park Toronto ON M7A 1W3 Canada

STEFFA, LOUIS JOHN, cons. chemist; b. Phila., Oct. 13, 1936; B.A. in Biochem. Scis., Harvard U., 1959; Ph.D. (NIH predoctoral fellow 1963-64; hon. Taggert scholar 1963-64), U. Pa., 1965; NIH postdoctoral fellow, 1965-66. Research asst. organic chemistry U. Pa., 1960-61; research chemist plastics investigation Eastern utilization research and devel. div. Dept. Agr., Wyndmoor, Pa., 1966-68; cons. chemist, Meadbwbrook, Pa., 1968—. Mem. Phi Lambda Upsilon. Contbr. to profl. jours. Address: 1004 Spring Valley Rd Meadowbrook PA 19046

STEFFEN, ALAN LESLIE, med. entomologist; b. Ansonia, Ohio, Feb. 27, 1927; s. Henry William and Maude (DuBois) S.; A.B., Miami U., Oxford, Ohio, 1948; M.Sc. in Entomology, Ohio State U., 1949; m. Genevieve Carlyle, Dec. 27, 1950. Tech. dir. Commonwealth Sanitation Co., Pitts., 1955-59; malaria adviser AID, Indonesia, 1959-65; area malaria adviser AID and USPHS, Songkhla, Thailand, 1965-66; sr. malaria adviser USPHS, Kathmandu, Nepal, 1966-71; sr. adviser AID, Addis Ababa, Ethiopia, 1971-76, Nepal, 1976-78, Pakistan, 1978—; cons. on urban pest control to Dominican Republic, 1956; cons. to Ethiopia on agrl. pest control, 1972-76. Served on Poison Info. Bd., Pitts., 1955-59. Served with AUS, 1945-46. Recipient Meritorious Honor award Dept. State, 1972. Mem. Entomol. Soc. Am., Royal Sco. Tropical Medicine and Hygiene, Am. Registry of Profl. Entomologists, Am., German philatelic socs., Am. Topical Assn. Lutheran. Club: Masons. Home and Office: Islamabad ID Dept of State Washington DC 20520

STEG, LEO, research dir.; b. Vienna, Austria, Mar. 30, 1922; s. Jacob and Clara (Gellert) S.; B.S., Coll. City N.Y., 1947; M.S., U. Mo., 1948; Ph.D., Cornell U., 1951; m. Doreen Ethel Ray, June 12, 1947; children—Paula Jamie, Ellen Leslie, Audrey Leigh. Came to U.S., 1941, naturalized 1946. Chief engr. Fed. Design Co., N.Y.C., 1946-47; instr. mech. engring. U. Mo., 1947-48; instr. mech. and math. Cornell U., Ithaca, N.Y., 1948-51, asst. prof., 1951-55; systems engr., missile and space div. Gen. Electric Co., Phila., 1955-56, mgr. space sci. lab., 1956—. Cons. to space scis. bd. Nat. Acad. Scis., other govt. agys. Past chmn. bd. Long Beach Island Found. Arts and Scis. Named Engr. of Year, Phila., 1965. Registered profl. engr., Pa. Fellow Am. Inst. Aero. and Astronautics (editor-in-chief jour. 1962-67), AAAS; mem. Phila. Acad. Scis. (founding), Franklin Inst. Phila. (bd. mgrs.), Sigma Xi, Phi Kappa Phi. Clubs: Cosmos, Cornell of N.Y. Contbr. articles to profl. jours.; also editor books. Home: 1616 Hepburn Dr Villanova PA 19085 Office: POB 8555 Philadelphia PA 19101

STEIGER, FREDERIC, artist; b. Solwutz, Austria, Oct. 21, 1905; s. Michael and Ida (Schaeffer) S.; m. Ruby Eleanor Fevens; children—Trudy, Linda. Exhibited one-man shows including Carroll Galleries and Roberts Gallery, Toronto, 1947, Odeon Theatre-Galleries, Toronto and Ottawa, 1951, Ho. of Assembly, St. John's, Nfld., Arts Club Montreal, 1960, L'Art Francaise Gallery, Montreal, 1961, T. Eaton Galleries, 1972, Cummerford Gallery, N.Y.C.; group exhbns. include: Vancouver Art Gallery, Royal Can. Acad., Montreal and Toronto, 1941-45, Ont. Soc. Artists, 1938-50; represented in permanent collections IBM, Hallmark Collection Can. Art, Imperial Oil Ltd., Toronto Pub. Library; executed 40 portraits now in Nfld. Parliament Bldg., also portrait William G. Davis, premier Ont., 1976. Unitarian. Home: 316 The Kingsway Apt 201 Islington ON M9A 3V2 Canada Studio: 406 Bloor St E Toronto ON M4W 1H4 Canada

STEIMLE, EDMUND AUGUSTUS, JR., hosp. exec.; b. Boston, Mar. 5, 1947; s. Edmund Augustus and Rosalind Weinert (Ball) S.; A.B., Hamilton Coll., 1969; M.B.A., Suffolk U., 1976; m. Helen Michaela O'Callahan, Apr. 17, 1971; children—Kimberly, Erin. Group underwriter Liberty Mut. Ins. Co., Boston, 1969-71; unit mgr. Mass. Gen. Hosp., Boston, 1971-76; asst. dir. gen. profl. services South Shore Hosp., South Weymouth, Mass., 1976—. Mem. Am., Mass. hosp. assns., Health Care Mgmt. Assn., Am. Acad. Med. Adminstrs., Mass. Unit Mgmt. Assn. Lutheran. Club: Cohasset Tennis and Squash. Home: 25 Woodway St Cohasset MA 02025 Office: South Shore Hospital 55 Fogg Rd South Weymouth MA 02190

STEIN, BETTY CANOWITZ, pub. exec.; b. Columbus, Ohio, Apr. 19, 1917; d. Abe J. and Fannie (Bonowitz) C.; B.Sc., Ohio State U., 1937; postgrad. Columbus Gallery Fine Arts Sch., 1938, Art Inst. Pitts., 1956; m. Milton Stein, June 8, 1941; children—Frannie (Mrs. Ronald B. Ein), Bernard David. Sec.-treas. Long & Stouder Co., Columbus, Ohio, 1938; asst. training dir. F & R Lazarus Co., Columbus, 1939; milinery buyer F & R Lazarus & Co., 1940-41; substitute art tchr. Pitts. pub. schs., 1958-59; asst. to bus. mgr. U. Pitts. Press, 1959, bus. mgr., 1964—. Mem. Women in Communications, Women's Nat. Book Assn., Ohio State U. Alumni Assn., Ladies Hosp. Aid Soc., Hadassah. Home: 700 Forbes Ave Apt 1002 Pittsburgh PA 15219 Office: 127 N Bellefield Ave Pittsburgh PA 15260

STEIN, CHARLES FRANCIS, JR., lawyer, corp. exec.; b. Balt., June 19, 1900; s. Charles F. and Ella Willson (Griffith) S.; A.B., Johns Hopkins, 1920, postgrad., 1920-22; J.D., U. Md., 1923; m. Jean Renneburg, May 14, 1932; children—Charles Francis III, Jean Alexandra (Mrs. William Kouwenhoven). Admitted to Md. bar, 1923, since practiced in Balt.; mem. Hennighausen & Stein, 1923-49; pvt. practice, 1949—; pres. Balt. Permanent Bldg. Assn.; dir. Edward Renneburg & Sons Co., 1943—, gen. counsel, 1945—; counsel Wyman Park Fed. Savs. & Loan Assn., 1940—, dir., 1955—; dir. Md. Title Guarantee Co., Dir., gen. counsel German Aged Peoples Home Balt., 1939—. Served from pvt. lt., U.S. Army, 1918. Mem. Am. Bar Assn., AAAS, Soc. War 1812 (pres. Md. 1956-58), Soc. Cincinnati Md. (sec. 1968-76, pres. 1976—), Soc. Colonial Wars, German Soc. Md. (pres.), So. Md. Soc. (pres. 1970), S.A.R. (gold medal for good citizenship 1973), Soc. for History of Germans in Md. (pres. 1971-76), Huguenot Soc. (chancellor gen.), Mil. Order Loyal Legion U.S. Democrat. Club: Masons (32 deg.). Author: History of Calvert County, Maryland; Our National Anthem—The Star-Spangled Banner, 1964; History of the Southern Maryland Society. 1965; The Origin and History of Howard County Maryland, 1973; History of the Grand Lodge Ancient Free and Accepted Masons of Maryland, 1951-76. Home: 17 Midvale Rd Baltimore MD 21210 Office: 231 St Paul Pl Baltimore MD 21202

STEIN, ELLEN GAIL, urban planner; b. N.Y.C., May 19, 1951; d. Manuel W. and Bella (Skutel) S.; B.A., State U. N.Y., Stony Brook, 1972; M.Urban Planning, Hunter Coll., 1976. Mgmt. intern Office of Mayor, N.Y.C., 1975; sr. research asso. Nassau-Suffolk Regional Med. Program, Melville, N.Y., 1976-77; asso. staff analyst planning and mgmt. analysis unit. N.Y.C. Dept. Correction, 1977—. Recipient Regents Scholar Incentive award, 1968-72. Mem. Am. Soc. Planning Ofcls. Home: 67 Park Terr E New York City NY 10034 Office: 100 Centre St New York City NY 10013

STEIN, FRITZ HENRY, art gallery dir.; b. N.Y.C., July 25, 1932; s. Harve Carl and Hope Louise (Jonas) S.; B.A., U. R.I., 1955; postgrad. N.Y. Sch. Interior Design, 1965; m. Diane Louise Mayer, May 28, 1968; children—Andrea, Pamela, Kimberly. Art dir. G. Fox Co., Hartford, Conn., 1955-60; co-owner Constitution Galleries, West Hartford, Conn., Gloucester, Mass., 1960-63; interior designer Silberman's of Norwich (Conn.), 1963-71; owner, mgr. Stone Ledge Studio Art Galleries, Noank, Conn. Mem. Town Meeting, Groton, Conn., 1977—. Mem. Noank Hist. Soc. (v.p.). Republican. Congregationalist. Club: Rotary. Home: 88 Pearl St Box 193 Noank CT 60340 Office: 59 High St Box 237 Noank CT 06340

STEIN, GEORGE HENRY, photog. engr.; b. Chelsea, Mass., Aug. 1, 1942; s. Henry I. and Evelyn M. (Robenolt) S.; B.S., Colo. State U., 1964; postgrad. Northeastern U., 1967-68, 70-71, U. Glasgow (Scotland), 1969, Southeastern Mass. U., 1975-76; m. Mary L. Shanley, Feb. 26, 1965; children—Tanya, Russell. Process engr. Douglas Aircraft Co., Santa Monica, Calif., 1964-66; process engr. Polaroid Corp. Film Div., Waltham, Mass., 1966-68, vendor devel. engr. Polaroid (U.K.) Ltd., Vale-of-Loven, Scotland, 1968-70, sr. engr.-photog. evaluation, negative mfg. div. Polaroid Corp., New Bedford, Mass., 1970-76, prin. engr.-photog. evaluation Sesame div., Norwood, Mass., 1976—. Mem. elementary sch. bldg. com. Mattapoisett, Mass., 1973-75, chmn. indsl. devel. com., 1974-76. Mem. Soc. Photog. Scientists and Engrs., Omicron Delta Kappa. Home: 16 Cushing Ave Hingham MA 02043 Office: One Upland Rd Norwood MA 02062

STEIN, GLADYS MARIE, pianist, educator; b. nr. Meadville, Pa., Oct. 19, 1900; d. Henry and Albertha (Hood) S.; grad. Pa. Coll. Music, 1922, New Eng. Conservatroy Music, 1924; grad. Aeolian Hall Sch. Music Research, 1927; pvt. student of pipe-organ and violin; pvt. tchr. piano, Meadville, 1921-22, Boston, 1923-24, Erie, Pa., 1925-29; organizer, dir. Stein Sch. Music, Erie, 1930-50; pvt. tchr., Erie, 1950—; lectr. on rhythm band for Ludwig & Ludwig Co., 1936-45, also author rhythm band book Tuned Time Bell Rhythm Band Instr., 1936; author articles, stories for Kindergarten-Primary mag., Erie Daily Times, Christian Sci. Monitor, Music Tchrs. Rev., Etude mag., others, 1927—; condr. piano tchr. workshops. Mem. Music Tchrs. Nat. Assn., Pa. (Distinguished Service award 1973), Erie (organizer 1970, pres. 1970-72, certification officer 1968—), music tchrs. assns., Nat., Walnut Creek rifle assns., Internat. Platform Assn. Author: Keyboard Tunes, 1949; composer numerous piano pieces, also for rhythm bands. Address: 427 W 31st St Erie PA 16508

STEIN, HAROLD AARON, ophthalmologist; b. Niagara Falls, Ont., Can., May 24, 1929; s. Louis and Sadie (Levine) S.; M.D., U. Toronto, (Ont.), 1953; M.Sc., U. Minn., 1958; diploma in ophthalmic medicine and surgery, London, 1958; m. Anne Bochner, Dec. 17, 1952; children—Raymond Stein, Laurie Stein, Gary Stein. Intern, Mt. Sinai Hosp., Toronto, 1953-54; resident Mayo Clinic, Rochester, Minn., 1954-57; practice medicine, specializing in ophthalmology, Toronto, 1958—, Scarborough, Ont. 1958—; chief dept. ophthalmology Scarborough Gen. Hosp., 1960—; attending physician Mt. Sinai Hosp., Toronto, 1958—; dir. Joint Commn. Allied Health Personnel. Fellow Royal Coll. Physicians Surgeons Can. Mem. Can., Ont. med. assns., Am. Assn. Ophthalmology, Can. Ophthalmol. Assn. Jewish religion. Club: York Racquet. Author: The Ophthalmic Assistant, 3d ed., 1976; Introductory Manual for the Ophthalmic Assistant, 1974; Fitting Guide for Hard and Soft Contact Lenses, 1977; asso. editor Contact and Intraocular Med. Jour., Internat. Contact Lens Jour.; contbr. articles to profl. jours. Home: 97 Douglas Dr Toronto ON

M4W 2B2 Canada Office: 170 Bloor St W Toronto ON M5S 1T9 Canada

STEIN, JESS, publisher, editor; b. N.Y.C., June 23, 1914; s. Elias and Regina (Goldenberg) S.; A.B., Wayne State U., 1933; M.A., U. Chgo., 1934, postgrad., 1934-36; m. Dorothy Gerner, Mar. 7, 1943; children—Regina (Mrs. Bruce H. Wilson, Eric. Editor, Scott Foresman & Co., Chgo., 1934-42; with Office of Censorship, Washington, 1942-45; with Random House, Inc., N.Y.C., 1945—, head coll. and reference depts., 1950-59, v.p., 1959—, dir., 1967-74. Dir. L.W. Singer Co., N.Y.C., Random House Can. Ltd., Toronto; v.p. Alfred A. Knopf, Inc., N.Y.C., 1967-74; dir. RH Sch. and Library Services, Inc.; pres. Jess Stein Assos., 1974—; cons. U. Mass. Press, 1975-78, Internat. Reading Assn., 1976—; advisor Hall of Fame, Jerusalem, 1976—. Mem. Westchester County Democratic Com., 1956-58; mem. White Plains (N.Y.) City Dem. Com., 1954-58. Mem. Am. Textbook Publs. Inst. (dir. 1961-64, treas. 1964), Coll. Pub. Group (chmn. 1960-61), Linguistic Soc. Am., Nat. Council Tchrs. English, Modern Lang. Assn., Dictionary Soc. Am., Am. Hist. Assn., Coll. English Assn., Dialect Soc., AAAS, Am. Geog. Soc., N.A.A.C.P., Am. Civil Liberties Union, Urban League. Club: Dutch Treat (N.Y.C.). Co-author: Why You Do What You Do, 1956. Editor translator (pseudonym Isai Kamen) Tolstoy's Kreutzer Sonata, 1957, Great Russian Stories, 1959. Mng. editor Am. Coll. Dictionary, 1947—, editor, 1957—; editor Am. Everyday Dictionary, 1949—, American Vest Pocket Dictionary, 1951—, Basic Everyday Encyclopedia, 1954—, Vest Pocket Rhyming Dictionary, 1960—, Modern American Dictionary, 1957—; editor-in-chief Random House Dictionary English Language, 1966—, Ballantine Paperback; editorial dir. Random House dictionaries, 1966—; editor: Irving's Life of George Washington, 1975; editor-in-chief Random House Coll. Dictionary (rev. edit.), 1975—; editorial dir. Random House Ency., 1977—. Home: 11 Sherman Ave White Plains NY 10605 Office: 201 E 50th St New York City NY 10022

STEIN, MARK, ophthalmologist; b. Munich, W. Germany, July 14, 1946; s. Henry and Hannah (Kesten) S.; came to U.S., 1951, naturalized, 1957; B.A. cum laude, Brooklyn Coll., 1967; M.D., Albert Einstein Coll. of Medicine, 1971; m. Toby Wietschner, June 22, 1968; children—Erika Beth, Scott Howard. Intern, Beth Israel Hosp., N.Y.C., 1971-72, resident in ophthalmology 1972-75; practice medicine specializing in ophthalmology, N.Y.C., 1975—; mem. staff Mt. Sinai Hosp., Brunswick Hosp., Mid-Island Hosp., Nassau County Med. Center; clin. instr. dept. ophthalmology Mt. Sinai Sch. of Medicine, N.Y.C., 1976—. Diplomate Am. Bd. Ophthalmology. Fellow Am. Acad. of Ophthalmology and Otolaryngology; mem. Am. Assn. of Ophthalmology, Am. Contemporary Soc. of Ophthalmology, N.Y. State, Nassau County med. socs., Nassau Acad. Medicine, AMA, Long Island Ophthalmological Soc., Internat. Glaucoma Congress. Office: 2084 Bedford Ave Bellmore NY 11710

STEIN, MELVIN ARNOLD, accountant; b. N.Y.C., Sept. 7, 1932; s. William H. and Lillian (Goldberg) S.; B.S. in Accounting, N.Y. U., 1953; m. Barbara Blumencranz, Dec. 17, 1955; children—Susan, Karen. Accountant various firms, 1955-61; pvt. practice accounting, Jericho, N.Y., 1961-75; partner Stein and Stein, C.P.A., Hicksville, N.Y., 1975—. Served in U.S. Army, 1953-55. Mem. Am., N.Y. Inst. C.P.A.s, C.W. Post Tax Inst. Club: N.Y. Univ. Home: 519 Links Dr E Oceanside NY 11572 Office: One Frederick Pl Hicksville NY 11801

STEIN, MONA LOLA, rehab. counselor; b. Elizabeth, N.J., Jan. 15, 1939; d. Irving and Anne Rose (Allen) Lampert; B.A. Kean Coll. 1967; M.S., U. Scranton, 1974; children—Mitchell Keith, Jeffrey. Editorial asst. Inst. Radio Engrs., N.Y.C., 1958-60; substitute tchr. Woodbridge and Edison, N.J., 1967-68; rehab. intern Lourdesmont Sch., Clarks Summit, Pa., 1973, Luzerne-Wyoming County Mental Health-Mental Retardation Center, Wilkes-Barre, Pa., 1974; cons., interviewer research dept. U. Scranton, 1974-75; vocat. rehab. counselor, coordinator Mt. Carmel Guild, Newark, 1975-77, supr. CETA clerical program and job placement, 1977—. Recipient certificate of appreciation Nat. Assn. Retarded Citizens, 1978. Mem. Am. Personnel and Guidance Assn., Nat. Vocat. Guidance Assn., N.J. Assn. Rehab. Facilities. Author research paper in field. Home: 7 Van Wyk Rd Lake Hiawatha NJ 07034 Office: 450 Market St Newark NJ 07102

STEIN, STUART WILLIAM, urban planner; b. N.Y.C., Nov. 29, 1929; s. Herman J. and Tillie (Berger) S.; B.Arch., Mass. Inst. Tech., 1952, M.C.P., 1954; m. Sandra Ginsburg, May 22, 1955; children—Thomas, Peter, Catherine, Jennifer. Prin. planner R.I. Devel. Council, 1954-57; partner Blair Assos., Urban Planning Consultants, Providence, 1957-59; pres. Blair & Stein Assos., Providence and Washington, 1959-62; asso. prof. urban planning Cornell U., 1962-68, prof., 1968—, asso. dean Coll. Architecture, Art & Planning, 1969-71, chmn. dept. urban planning and devel., 1971-75, prof. urban planning, 1975—. Mem. N.Y. State Bd. Historic Preservation, 1977—; mem. City of Ithaca City Council, 1972-73; chmn. Ithaca City Planning Bd., 1978—. Mem. Am. Inst. Planners, Am. Soc. Planning Ofcls., Interam. Planning Soc., Nat. Trust for Historic Preservation. Democrat. Jewish. Home: 1018 E State St Ithaca NY 14850 Office: 106 W Sibley St Cornell U Ithaca NY 14853

STEIN, THEODORE ANTHONY, physiol. chemist; b. St. Louis, Aug. 30, 1938; s. Leonard A. and Mathilda (Ellwangen) S.; B.S., St. Louis U., 1960; M.S., So. Ill. U., 1970; m. Jeanette Heidemann, Aug. 30, 1975. Research instr. Washington U. Sch. Medicine, 1972-75; research supr. surgery L.I. Jewish Hosp., 1975-76, research coordinator in surgery, 1977—; asst. prof. surgery State U. N.Y. at Stony Brook, 1978—. NIH grantee, 1962. Mem. N.Y. Acad. Sci., Am. Fedn. Clin. Research, AAAS. Republican. Roman Catholic. Contbr. numerous articles to med. jours. Home: 10 Glamford Ave Port Washington NY 11050 Office: Long Island Jewish Hosp New Hyde Park NY 11040

STEIN, VIRGINIA KRAMER, clin. psychologist; b. N.Y.C., July 22, 1924; d. Sidney David and Nora (Atkins) Kramer; A.B., Hunter Coll., 1944; postgrad. in occupational therapy Tufts U., 1945; M.A., San Fra. cisco State Coll., 1954; certificate sch. psychology, Newark State Coll., 1967; m. Jerome David Stein, Jr., Sept. 7, 1947; children—Christopher David, Jonathan Atkins. Cons. psychologist Bur. Vocat. Rehab., Oakland, Calif., 1948-57, Bonnie Brae Farm Boys, Millington, N.J., 1958-69, Princeton (N.J.) Day Sch., 1964—; fellow in clin. psychology Langley Porter Neuropsychiat. Clin., U. Calif. Sch. Medicine, San Francisco, 1954-55; pvt. practice clin., sch. and vocat. psychology, 1954—. Vis. lectr. in psychology Vis. Homemakers Assn. Rutgers U., 1960-62. Mem. profl. adv. com. Somerset County Mental Health Assn., 1968—, 1st v.p., trustee; chmn. Bridgewater Twp. Citizens for Kennedy, 1959-60; trustee N. Country Sch., Lake Placid, N.Y. Licensed psychologist, N.J., Pa. Mem. Am., N.J. psychol. assns., Nat., N.J. assns. sch. psychologists, Orton Soc., Council Advancement Psychol. Professions and Scis., Assn. Women in Psychology, Psychologists in Pvt. Practice, Nat. Rehab. Assn., Nat. Rehab. Counseling Assn., Assn. Advancement Psychology. Democrat. Mem. Reformed Ch. Home: 357 William St Somerville NJ 08876 Office: Princeton Day Sch PO Box 75 The Great Rd Princeton NJ 08540

STEIN, WILLIAM H., packaging co. exec.; b. Bklyn., Mar. 29, 1935; s. Sam and Madeline (Lucas) S.; B.S., Lehigh U., 1957; postgrad. U. Miami, 1958; m. Dolores Suenderhauf, Aug. 24, 1957; children—Linda Joan, William Martin. Plant engr. Oneida Packaging Products, Inc., subs. Reed-Deeron Corp., Clifton, N.J., 1958-67, asst. v.p., 1967-69, v.p. mfg., 1969-74, exec. v.p., asst. sec., 1974, dir., pres., chief exec. officer, 1970—, v.p. parent co., Wellesley, Mass., 1975—; dir. Plastic Piping System, Inc., Plainfield, N.J. Employer trustee Health and Welfare Trust Fund United Paperworkers Internat. Union. Comml. Pilot. Mem. Am. Mgmt. Assn., TAPPI. Patentee in field. Home: 38 Maria Dr Hillsdale NJ 07642 Office: 10 Clifton Blvd Clifton NJ 07015

STEIN, WILLIAM HOWARD, biochemist; b. N.Y.C., June 25, 1911; s. Fred M. and Beatrice (Borg) S.; grad. Phillips Exeter Acad., 1929; B.S., Harvard, 1933; Ph.D., Columbia, 1938, D.Sc. (hon.), 1973; D.Sc. (hon.), Yeshiva U., 1973; m. Phoebe Hockstader, June 22, 1936; children—William Howard, David F., Robert J. Asst., Rockefeller Inst. Med. Research, N.Y.C., 1939-43, asso., 1943-49, asso. mem., 1949-52, mem., 1952; prof. Rockefeller U., 1955—. Vis. prof. U. Chgo. 1960, Harvard, 1964. Fellow Am. Swiss Found., 1956; Harvey lectr., 1957; mem. med. adv. bd. Hebrew U. Hadassah Med. Sch., Israel, 1947-61; Phillips lectr. Haverford Coll., 1962; Philip Schaffer lectr. Washington U., St. Louis, 1965; sci. counselor Nat. Inst. Neurol. Diseases and Blindness, 1961-66. Trustee Montefiore Hosp., N.Y.C., 1947-74. Recipient (with Stanford Moore) Kaj Linderstrom-Lang award, 1972; (with Stanford Moore and Christian B. Anfinsen) Nobel prize in chemistry, 1972; Columbia Grad. Faculty and Alumni Assn. award excellence, 1973. Fellow AAAS; mem. Am. Acad. Arts and Scis., Nat. Acad. Scis., Am. Soc. Biol. Chemists (chmn. editorial com. 1958-61) Am. Chem. Soc. (Electrophoresis award 1964, Richards medal 1972 both with Stanford Moore), U.S. Nat. Com. Biochemistry (chmn. 1965-68), Biochem. Soc., (London), N.Y. Acad. Sci., Harvey Soc., Sigma Xi. Editorial bd. Jour. Biol. Chemistry, 1962-64, asso. editor, 1964-68, editor, 1968-71. Contbr. to sci. jours. Home: 530 E 72d St New York City NY 10021 Office: Rockefeller Univ 66th St and York Ave New York City NY 10021

STEINBERG, ARTHUR IRWIN, periodontist, educator; b. Pitts., Sept. 16, 1935; s. Ben and Sylvia (Jacobs) S.; B.S. in Microbiology, U. Pitts., 1957, D.M.D. cum laude, 1963, postgrad. in radiobiology, 1957-59; diploma in periodontology-microbiology (USPHS fellow), Harvard, 1966; m. Barbara Fay Ehrenkranz, May 23, 1959; children—Sharon Jill, Mindy Ruth, Michael Eli. Asst. prof. periodontology State U. N.Y. at Buffalo, 1966-67; asso. prof. periodontology Temple U., Phila., 1967-68, asso. prof. grad. periodontology, 1968-70; attending periodontist Phoenixville (Pa.) Hosp., 1971—, now mem. infections control com., by-laws com., religious affairs com., 1977—; mem. staff Suburban Gen. Hosp., Norristown, Pa., 1972—, Phoenixville Hosp., 1976—; asst. prof. periodontics U. Pa., 1973—; mem. continuing edn. faculty U. Pitts., 1973—; Fulbright-Hays lectr. Nat. U. Ireland, Cork, 1970-71; vis. prof. Cork Dental Sch. and Hosp., 1971—; dentist in pediatrics Charlestown (Mass.) Boys Club, 1965-66; speaker Periodontists Conv., Chgo., 1966, N.J. Coll. Medicine and Dentistry, Conn. Dental Assn., 1967, U. Ind. Schs. Dentistry and Medicine, Phila. Ann. Dental Sci. Session, 1969, N.J. Dental Assn., 1970, Wilmington chpt. Sigma Epsilon Delta, 1974, Lehigh Valley Dental Soc., 1974, Inst. Medicine, Bucharest, Rumania, 1976; participant Project Head Start, Childrens Hosp., Boston, 1966. Fellow Am. Coll. Dentists, Coll. Physicians Phila.; mem. AMA, Am. Dental Assn., AAUP, Harvard Dental, Fulbright (dir. 1977—) alumni assns., Pa. Soc. Periodontists (chmn. ins. com. 1967-69), Harvard Odontological Soc., Fulbright Alumni Assn., Nat. Fulbright-Alumni Assn. (a founder 1976, v.p. fin. affairs 1976—), Am. Acad. Periodontology (ins. com. 1969, hosp. care com. 1973—, continuing edn. speaker 1976 conv.; nominating com. chmn. Pa. region to exec. council 1975), Sigma Xi, Omicron Kappa Upsilon, Psi Omega (dep. councillor Zeta chpt. 1977—). Clubs: Masons (32 deg., Shriner), Rotary (dir. 1973—, chmn. found. com., chmn. internat. service 1974—), B'nai B'rith, Harvard of Phila., Pottstown (Pa.) Area Study (pres. 1976—). Contbg. author: Dentistry and the Allergic Patient, 1973. Contbr. numerous articles to profl. jours. Home: 1681 Pheasant Ln Norristown PA 19401 Office: 135 Nutt Rd Phoenixville PA 19460

STEINBERG, SAMUEL HARRY, hosp. adminstr.; b. Phila., May 20, 1948; s. Sidney and Molly (Feldman) S.; B.S., Pa. State U., 1972; M.B.A., Temple U., Phila., 1977; m. Karen Ann Base, Sept. 11, 1971; 1 dau., Jennifer Dana. Food service dir. Saga Food Service, Menlo Park, Calif., 1973-74; food service dir., then asst. v.p. Episcopal Hosp., Phila., 1974-77; asst. dir. Thomas Jefferson U. Hosp., Phila., 1977—, also mem. hosp.-med. staff relations com. Served with U.S. Army, 1967-70; Vietnam. Decorated Army Commendation medal; recipient Ellsworth Milton Statler award Pa. State U., 1972. Mem. Am. Hosp. Assn., Am. Coll. Hosp. Adminstrs., Hosp. Assn. Pa., Del. Valley Hosp. Council. Home: 413 Rock Glen Dr Wynnewood PA 19096 Office: Thomas Jefferson Univ Hosp Philadelphia PA 19107

STEINBERG, SAUL PHILLIP, data processing co. exec.; b. Bklyn., Aug. 13, 1939; s. Julius and Anne (Cohen) S.; B.S. in Econs., Wharton Sch., U. Pa., 1959; m. Barbara Herzog, May 28, 1961 (div. 1977); children—Laura, Jonothan, Nicholas. Founder, Leasco Corp., N.Y.C., 1961; chmn. bd., pres., chief exec. officer Reliance Group, Inc., N.Y.C., 1962—; chmn. exec. com., chmn. fin. com., dir. Reliance Ins. Co., 1968—. Overseer Wharton Grad. Sch. Fine Arts. Trustee L.I. Jewish-Hillside Med. Center, Saul Steinberg Found.; dir. Juvenile Diabetes Found.; bd. dirs. Circle in Sq., United Cerebral Palsy Found.; asso. trustee U. Pa.; mem. vis. com. Mass. Inst. Tech. Recipient Humanitarian award Am. Jewish Com., 1973. Mem. Am. Mgmt. Assn., Young Pres.'s Orgn. Office: 919 Third Ave New York City NY 10022

STEINBRENNER, GEORGE MICHAEL, III, shipbuilding co. exec., baseball exec.; b. Rocky River, Ohio, July 4, 1930; s. Henry G. and Rita (Haley) S.; B.A., Williams Coll., 1952; postgrad. Ohio State U., 1954-55; m. Elizabeth Joan Zieg, May 12, 1956; children—Henry G. III, Jennifer Lynn, Jessica Joan, Harold Zeig. Asst. football coach Northwestern U., 1955, Purdue U., 1956-67; treas. Kinsman Transit Co., Cleve., 1957-63; pres. Kinsman Marine Transit Co., 1963-67, dir., 1965—; pres., chmn. bd. Am. Ship Bldg. Co., Cleve., 1967—; owner N.Y. Yankees, Bronx, N.Y.; dir. Gt. Lakes Internat. Corp., Gt. Lakes Assos., Cin. Sheet Metal & Roofing Co., Nashville Bridge Co., Nederlander-Steinbrenner Productions. Mem. Cleve. Little Hoover Com., group chmn., 1966; chmn. Cleve. Urban Coalition; vice chmn. Greater Cleve. Growth Corp., Greater Cleve. Jr. Olympic Found. Served to 1st lt. USAF, 1952-54. Named Outstanding Young Man of Yr., Ohio Jr. C. of C., 1960, Cleve. Jr. C. of C. 1960; Chief Town Crier, Cleve., 1968; Man of Yr., Cleve. Press Club, 1968. Mem. Greater Cleve. Growth Assn. (dir.). Office: care New York Yankees Yankee Stadium Bronx NY 10451*

STEINBRUCKNER, BRUNO FRIEDRICH, educator; b. Linz/Donau, Austria, Aug. 22, 1941; s. Bruno and Michaela Maria (Wimberger) S.; came to U.S., 1965, naturalized, 1973; Ph.D., U. Innsbruck, 1965; m. Claudia Jane Frey, Mar. 9, 1973. Asst., U. Innsbruck, spring 1965; mem. faculty Am. U., 1965—, prof. German Studies 1973—, chmn. dept. lang. and fgn. studies, 1975—. Mem. Am. Goethe Soc. (pres. 1971-73), Am. Assn. Tchrs. German (chpt. corr. sec. 1965-66), Nat. Humanities Faculty. Author: Dialektographie des oberen Mühlviertels, 1976; Ludwig Thoma, 1978; also articles. Contbg. author: Encyclopedic Dictionary of Religion, 1979. Home: PO Box 747 McLean VA 22101 Office: Dept Lang and Foreign Studies American Univ Washington DC 20016

STEINER, JEROME, psychiatrist; b. Newark, July 16, 1929; s. Sidney and Frieda P. (Zorn) S.; A.B., U. Chgo., 1949; M.A., 1952; M.D., State U. N.Y., 1962. Intern dept. pediatrics Kings County Hosp., Bklyn., 1962-63; resident N.Y. State Psychiat. Inst. and Vanderbilt Clinic, Columbia Presbyn. Hosp., N.Y.C., 1963-66; practice medicine, specializing in psychiatry N.Y.C., 1966—, Miami, Fla., 1971—; instr. psychiatry Albert Einstein Coll. Medicine, Bronx, N.Y., 1966-67; asst. attending psychiatrist Vanderbilt Clinic, Columbia-Presbyn. Med. Center, N.Y.C., 1966-75, asso. attending psychiatrist, 1975—; attending psychiatrist Gracie Square Hosp., N.Y.C., 1966—; instr. Coll. Phys. and Surg., Columbia, 1967-72, asso. in clin. psychiatry, 1972-76, asst. prof. clin. psychiatry, 1976—; psychiatrist-in-charge group therapy program Vanderbilt Clinic, Presbyn. Hosp., 1970-72, supr. group therapy, 1972-73; attending psychiatrist N.Y. State Psychiat. Inst., N.Y.C., 1971—, Roosevelt Hosp., N.Y.C., 1971-75; dir. group therapy program Washington Heights Community Mental Health Service, N.Y.C., 1972-77; exec. dir. Miami Center Group Treatment and Tng., 1972-73; lectr. in clin. psychiatry U. Miami Sch. Medicine, Coral Gables, Fla., 1973-76; vis. lectr. Marist Bros. Coll., Poughkeepsie, N.Y., 1975; dir. edn. and tng. Harlem Valley Psychiat. Center, Wingdale, N.Y., 1975-76, asst. dir. and dir. profl. affairs, 1976-78; dir. mental health services St. Francis Hosp., Poughkeepsie, N.Y., 1978—; dir. Bio-Psych Center, White Plains, N.Y.; cons. and lectr. in field. Adv. bd. Am. Thanatology Found. Diplomate Am. Bd. Psychiatry and Neurology. Mem. N.Y. Soc. Clin. Psychiatry, Am. Psychiat. Assn. (chmn. com. on allied professions 1970-72; mem. or chmn. other coms.), Am. Soc. Adolescent Psychiatry, Am., Eastern group psychotherapy assns. Democrat. Jewish religion. Mng. Editor: Jour. Psychoanalysis in Groups, 1971-72. Editor: Groups, A Jour. Group Process and Treatment, 1972-77. Contbr. articles to profl. jours. Address: PO Box 488 Dover Plains NY 12522 also 300 E 54th St Apt 8H New York City NY 10022

STEINER, RALPH LEE, environ. engr.; b. Reading, Pa., Feb. 7, 1944; s. Roland Leighton and Vivian S.; B.C.E., Drexel U., 1966, M.S. in Environ. Engring., 1967, Ph.D. in Environ. Engring., 1973; m. Kaaren Lee Stauffer, June 19, 1966; children—Christopher Lee, Margot Louise. Research asso. Drexel U., 1974; project engr. Gilbert Assos., Reading, 1975, Enviro/Earth, Ltd., Phila., 1975—, AGES Corp., Phila., 1975-77; v.p. AGES Corp., 1977—; dir. Applied Tech. Assos. Mem. ASCE, Am. Chem. Soc., Water Pollution Control Assn., Owen J. Roberts Friends of the Arts. Mem. United Ch. of Christ. Club: Laurelwood Swim. Research on hydraulic and chem. characteristics of milled refuse, subsurface pollution from san. landfills. Home: 829 Worth Blvd Pottstown PA 19464 Office: 215 S Broad St Philadelphia PA 19107

STEINER, ROBERT FRANK, phys. biochemist; b. Manila, Philippines, Sept. 29, 1926; s. Frank and Clara Nell (Weems) S.; A.B., Princeton U., 1947; Ph.D., Harvard U., 1950; m. Ethel Mae Fisher, Nov. 3, 1956; children—Victoria, Laura. Chemist, Naval Med. Research Inst., Bethesda, Md., 1950-70, chief Lab. Phys. Biochemistry, 1965-70; prof. chemistry U. Md., Balt., 1970—, chmn. dept. chemistry, 1974—. Served with AUS, 1945-47. Recipient Superior Civilian Achievement award Def. Dept., 1966; NSF research grantee, 1971; NIH research grantee, 1973. Fellow Washington Acad. Sci.; mem. Am. Soc. Biol. Chemists. Club: Princeton (Washington). Author: Life Chemistry, 1968; Excited States of Proteins and Nucleic Acids, 1971; editor: Jour. Biophys. Chemistry, 1972—. Home: 2609 Turf Valley Rd Ellicott City MD 21043 Office: 5401 Wilkens Ave Baltimore MD 21228

STEINER, ROGER JACOB, educator; b. South Byron, Wis., Mar. 27, 1924; s. Jacob Robert and Alice Mildred (Cowles) S.; A.B., Franklin and Marshall Coll., 1945; M.Div., Union Theol. Sem., 1947; M.A., U. Pa., 1958, Ph.D., 1963; m. Ida Kathryn Posey, Aug. 7, 1954; children—David Posey, Andrew Posey. Ordained to ministry Methodist Ch., 1947; pastor chs., N.Y., 1945-54, New Lisbon, Wis., 1954-56, Parkside, Pa., 1956-61; U. Pa./U. Bordeaux (France) inter-univ. teaching exchange fellow, lectr. U. Bordeaux, 1961-63; instr. U. Del., 1963-64, asst. prof. modern langs., 1964-71, asso. prof., 1971—. Pres., bd. dirs. Newark (Del.) Twin Towns Assn., Inc.; founding mem., bd. dirs. Del. Council on Internat. Visitors; chmn. Herbert H. Lank Exchange fellowship U. Montreal (Que., Can.)/U. Del. Served with USNR, 1942-46. Recipient Williamson medal Franklin and Marshall Coll., 1945; Am. Philos. Soc. grantee, 1971. Mem. Modern Lang. Assn. Am., Am. Assn. Tchrs. French, Am. Assn. Tchrs. Spanish and Portuguese, Mediaeval Acad. Am., Société Rencesvals, Internat. Arthurian Soc., Internat. Courtly Lit. Soc., Am. Council on Teaching Fgn. Langs., AAUP, Phi Beta Kappa (pres. Alpha chpt. of Del. 1975-76). Republican. Author: Two Centuries of Spanish and English Bilingual Lexicography, 1590-1800, 1970; The New College French and English Dictionary, 1972. Contbr. articles to profl. jours. Home: 10 Korda Dr Newark DE 19713 Office: Dept Langs and Lit U of Del Newark DE 19711

STEINER, STUART, coll. pres.; b. Balt., July 24, 1937; s. Louis and Lillian (Block) S.; B.S., U. Md., 1959; grad. certificate Fla. State U., 1962; M.S.W., U. Pa., 1963; J.D., U. Balt., 1967; M.A., Tchrs. Coll. Columbia U., 1972; m. Rosalie Weiner, Sept. 12, 1962; children—Lisa, Susan, David, Robyn. Caseworker, then supr. and dir. juvenile ct. services Balt. Dept. Social Services, 1960-64; dir. referral center Health and Wealfare Council Met. Balt., 1964; dir. admissions and placement Hartford Jr. Coll., Bel Air, Md., 1965-67; dean students Genesee Community Coll., Batavia, N.Y., 1967-68, dean coll., 1968-75, pres., 1975—; pres. State U. N.Y. West; mem. council pres.'s State U. N.Y. Bd. dirs. Genesee County Community Chest, Health Sci. Agy. Western N.Y. Heisler scholar, 1960-61; Kellogg fellow, 1971-72; Sigma Delta scholar, 1958-59. Mem. Am. Assn. Higher Edn., Jr. Coll. Council Middle Atlantic States (v.p.), Am. Coll. Personnel Assn., Batavia C. of C., Jr. Coll. Council Middle Atlantic States (exec. com.). Club: Rotary. Contbr. articles to profl. jours. Home: 33 Woodcrest Dr Batavia NY 14020 Office: Genesee Community Coll Batavia NY 14020

STEINERT, RICHARD JACOB, mfg. co. exec.; b. Hasbrouck Heights, N.J., Oct. 28, 1935; s. Henry Herman and Helen Florence (Werner) S.; B.S. in Mech. Engring., Newark Coll. Engring., 1958, M.S., 1962; children—Robert, Katherine, Richard Jacob, Ronald; m. 2d, Wendy Laura Wendt, Aug. 8, 1975. Project engr. Worthington Corp., East Orange, N.J., 1959-63; prodn. engr. Owens-Ill. Glass Co., North Bergen, N.J., 1963-64, prodn. mgr., Barranquilla, Colombia, S.Am., 1965-66, mold and machine repair supr., North Bergen, 1966-67, plant engr., North Bergen, 1967-73, mgr. engring., Mansfield, Mass., 1973-75; mgr. staff projects Thatcher Glass Mfg. Co., Elmira, N.Y., 1975-76, gen. mgr. engring. services, 1976—. Mem. N.J. League for Hearing Handicapped, 1966-75, Internat. Parents Orgn. Alexander Graham Bell Assn., 1966-75; treas. Millburn (N.J.) Ave. Sch. for Deaf. Registered profl. engr., N.J., Mass.; certified plant engr. Mem. Am. Inst. Plant Engrs. (sec. met. N.J. chpt. 1967-73, sec. Twin Tiers chpt. N.Y. 1973—), N.J. Soc. Profl. Engrs. (pres. Hudson County chpt. 1966-73, profl. conduct com. 1972-73, Young Engr. of Year 1969), N.Y. State Soc. Profl. Engrs. Mason. Clubs: North Jersey Gun (Fairfield, N.J.); Roseland (N.J.) Rifle Team; Chemung County Rod and Gun. Home: 409 Highland Ave Horseheads NY 14845 Office: PO Box 265 Elmira NY 14902

STEINFINK, MURRAY, chem. engr., bus. exec.; b. N.Y.C., July 17, 1940; s. Jack and Stella; B.S. in Chem. Engring., Coll. City of N.Y., 1963; M.S. in Polymeric Materials, Bklyn. Poly. Inst., 1969; m. Susan Rose Wachs, June 15, 1963; children—Jaime, Jeremy. Product devel. chemist DuPont Co., Wilmington, Del., 1963-66; group leader adhesives products div. PPG Industries, Bloomfield, N.J., 1966-69; tech. dir. New Eng. Laminates Inc., Stamford, Conn., 1969-70; v.p. Skeist Labs. Inc., Livingston, N.J., 1970-73; dir. mktg. Ciba-Geigy Corp., Ardsley, N.Y., 1973-76; v.p. M. Lowenstein and Sons, Inc., N.Y.C., 1976—, also pres. Splty. Products div.; adj. prof. chem. engring. dept. Poly. Inst. Bklyn. Mgr. Monsey Little League. Mem. Comml. Devel. Assn., Soc. Plastics Engrs., Am. Chem. Soc., Am. Inst. Chem. Engrs. Jewish. Patentee in field. Home: 329 Strawtown Rd New City NY 10956 Office: 1430 Broadway New York City NY 10018

STEINHART, DEAN RAYMOND, ednl. adminstr.; b. Allentown, Pa., May 6, 1930; s. Raymond Curtis and Zelia (Johns) S.; B.S., Kutztown State Coll., 1957; M.A., Franklin and Marshall Coll., 1963; M. Ed., Pa. State U., 1962; m. Norma Myers, Apr. 20, 1952; children—Eric Charles, Carl David. Tchr. sci. Elizabethtown (Pa.) Area High Sch., 1957-59, tchr. biology, sci. coordinator sch. dist., 1959-68, prin. high sch., 1968-73, dir. secondary edn., high sch. and jr. high sch., 1973-77, asst. dist. supt. instruction and profl. supervision, 1977—; cons. in field; evaluator Middle States Assn. Colls. and Secondary Schs. Bd. dirs. No. Lancaster County Med. Center; active Boy Scouts Am.; trustee Evangelical Congregational Ch., Lawn, Pa. Served with USMCR, 1948-52. NSF fellow, 1960-63; recipient Outstanding Citizen award Bus. and Profl. Women, Elizabethtown, 1970; Law and Order award Elizabethtown Optimists, 1974. Mem. Elizabethtown C. of C. (dir. 1972-76), Assn. Supervision and Curriculum Devel. (asso.), Nat., Pa. assns. secondary sch. prins., Nat. Sci. Tchrs. Assn., Nat. Sheriffs Assn., Phi Delta Kappa. Republican. Clubs: Rotary, Milton Grove Sportsmans. Contbr. articles to profl. jours. Home: RD 2 PO Box 239 Mount Joy PA 17552 Office: 600 E High St Elizabethtown PA 17022

STEINHAUS, PHILLIP LEE, organist, educator; b. Kalamazoo, Jan. 1, 1934; s. Ties Philip and Elizabeth (Yonker) S.; B. Music, U. Mich., 1955, M. Music, 1957; D. Music, Parsons Coll., 1961. Organist, choirmaster, All Saints Ch., Pontiac, Mich., 1953-60; organist, choirmaster, carillonneur, The Kirk in the Hills, Bloomfield Hills, Mich., 1960-64, St. John's Ch., Washington, 1964-66; dir. music, Ch. Advent, Boston, 1968-77; instr., Am. U., Washington, 1964-66, Peabody Conservatory, Balt., 1965-66, Boston Conservatory, 1972—; exec. v.p., dir., Aeolian-Skinner Organ Co., Boston, 1966-69; dir. music Ossabaw Island Project Found. Films on Art and Architecture Renaissance, Bloomfield Hills, Mich., 1963-64. Mem. Am. Guild Organists, Assn. Anglican Musicians. Recitals, radio broadcasts, recordings U.S. and Europe. Home: 298 Bradford St Provincetown MA 02657 Office: 8 The Fenway Boston MA 02118

STEINHAUS, RICHARD ZEKE, lawyer; b. N.Y.; B.S., N.Y. U., 1951; J.D., Bklyn. Law Sch., 1955; L.H.D., N.Y. Coll. Podiatric Medicine, 1975; m. Joan Goodman, June 24, 1951; children—Peter Michael, Richard Zeke. Accountant, Marks & Marks, C.P.A.'s, N.Y.C., 1951-55; admitted to N.Y. bar 1956, D.C. bar, 1961; pvt. practice N.Y.C., 1956-76; mem. firm Blinder, Steinhaus & Hochhauser, N.Y.C., 1965-76, Washington, 1961-70; vis. lectr. Ithaca Coll. President Camp Vacamas Assn., 1965-68; acting police judge, Dobbs Ferry, 1965-66. Served with USN, 1945-47. Mem. Am. (mem. tax sect.), Internat., N.Y. State, Westchester bar assns., Warren County (N.Y.) Bar Assn., N.Y., Westchester magistrates assns., Assn. Bar City of N.Y. Democrat. Jewish. Clubs: Fort Orange (Albany, N.Y.); Alpine Suisse (Zermatt). Home: 33 Saranac St Dobbs Ferry NY 10522 Office: 80 S Broadway Tarrytown NY 10591

STEINHORN, PAUL, physician; b. N.Y.C., July 31, 1919; s. Morris and Rose (Lechner) S.; B.A., N.Y. U., 1941; M.D., Temple U., 1944; m. Adele Lyons, Apr. 16, 1950; children—Charles Ira, Leonard Kurt. Intern, Jewish Hosp. Bklyn., 1944-45; resident in radiology Queens Hosp. Center, 1950-52, Mt. Sinai Hosp., N.Y.C., 1954-55; individual practice medicine, specializing in radiology, Elmhurst, N.Y., 1970—; radiologist LaGuardia Med. Group, Elmhurst, 1970—, dir. radiology, 1977—, also bd. dirs.; mem. staff L.I. Jewish Hillside Med. Center, New Hyde Park, LaGuardia Hosp., Forest Hills. Served with USNR, 1945-46, 52-54. Mem. Am. Coll. Radiology, Radiol. Soc. N.Am., L.I. Radiol. Soc. (past pres.), Nassau County, N.Y.State med. socs. Democrat. Jewish. Home: 121 Bacon Rd Old Westbury NY 11568 Office: 86-15 Queens Blvd Elmhurst NY 11373

STEINIGER, WILLIAM HOWARD, career counselor; b. Florence, S.C., July 1, 1944; s. Gustav William and Dorothy (Salisbury) S.; B.S., State U. N.Y., 1967; M.S., State U. N.Y., 1972. Tchr. pub. schs., Newburgh, N.Y., Walden, N.Y., and Schenectady, 1966-71; acad. advisor State U. N.Y., Albany, 1971-72; career edn. specialist Career Acad., Milw., 1972-73; career edn. coordinator Bethlehem Central Schs., Delmar, N.Y., 1973-74; group home dir. Vandenheyden Hall, Troy, N.Y., 1974-76; pres. Nat. Center for Career Devel., Albany, N.Y., 1976—; instr. Hudson Valley Community Coll., Troy, N.Y., 1976-78; lectr. in field. Pres. PTA, Newburgh Schs., 1966-67. Mem. Am., N.Y. personnel and guidance assns., Nat. Vocat. Guidance Assn. Internat. Transactional Analysis Assn., N.Y. State Vocational Guidance Assn. Author: Sibling Order and Career Decisionmaking, 1972; Guide for State U. of N.Y. for Admissions Policies for Transfer Students, 1971. Home: 68 Point of Woods Dr Albany NY 12203 Office: 12 Colvin Ave Albany NY 12206

STEINLE, JOHN GERARD, health orgn. exec.; b. Havre, Mont., Nov. 8, 1916; s. Francis X. and Ada L. (de Lorimier) S.; B.S., St. Mary's Coll., 1936; M.A., U. So. Calif., 1937; LL.B., St. Louis City Coll. Law, 1941; M.S., Syracuse U., 1947; m. Joan E. Sinnott, Aug. 14, 1945, (div. June 1972); children—Susan (Mrs. Raymond Bebko), Elizabeth (Mrs. Jesse McFarland), Gretchen (Mrs. Sanford Prater), Jacquelynn (Mrs. Nickolas Leisos), Abbe Anne (Mrs. Michael Finn), Robyn; m. 2d, Bianca Santisteban, July 15, 1972. Adminstr. St. Louis City Infirmary, 1939-42; chief hosp. adminstrn. sect. USPHS, Washington, 1947-51, hosp. program dir., N.Y.C., 1951-54; pres. John G. Steinle & Assos., Garden City, N.Y., 1954-70; pres. Health Orgns., Systems and Planning Corp., Garden City, 1970-75; pres. John G. Steinle and Assos., Inc., 1975—. Lectr. hosp. adminstrn. Columbia, 1952-59. Trustees Adelphi U., Garden City, 1953-62; chmn. bd. Madison Park Hosp., Bklyn., 1955-61. Served with AUS, 1942-46. Decorated Silver Star, Purple Heart. Mem. Assn. Med. Colls., AIA, Acad. Hosp. Cons. (pres. 1964-66), Internat. Hosp. Assn. Club: Princeton (N.Y.C.). Author: (with Ivan Belknap) The Community and Its Hospitals, 1963. Editor: Health and Hosp. Encys., 1974. Contbr. articles to profl. jours. Home: 151 Piermont Rd Norwood NJ 07648 Office: 50 E Palisade Ave Englewood NJ 07631

STEINMAN, CHARLES ROBERT, physician; b. Bklyn., Aug. 3, 1938; s. Alan M. and Estelle (Hartman) S.; A.B., Princeton U., 1959; M.D., Columbia U., 1963; m. Heidi Sims Fiske, Jan. 8, 1978. Intern, Presbyn. Hosp., N.Y.C., 1963-64, resident, 1964-65, 68-69, fellow in rheumatology, 1967-68, 69-70; asst. prof. medicine Mt. Sinai Sch. Medicine, 1970-77, asso. prof., 1977—; practice medicine specializing in internal medicine and rheumatology, N.Y.C., 1970—; mem. staff Beth Israel Hosp., VA Hosp., Bronx, Mt. Sinai Hosp. Mem. med. and sci. com. Lupus Found. Am., N.Y. Rheumatism Assn. Served with USPHS, 1965-67. NIH grantee, 1971—. Diplomate Am. Bd. Internal Medicine. Mem. AAAS, Am. Fedn. for Clin. Investigation, Am., N.Y. rheumatism assns., Harvey Soc., N.Y. Acad. Sci. Club: Princeton (N.Y.C.). Office: 1 E 100th St New York City NY 10029

STEINMAYER, ALWIN GUSTAV, JR., aerospace engring. exec.; b. Milw., Feb. 4, 1925; s. Alwin Gustav and Mary (Currie) S.; B.S., Mass. Inst. Tech., 1947, postgrad., 1947-50; postgrad. U. Calif., Los Angeles, 1969; m. Agnes P. Rizzo, May 6, 1948; children—Karen Marie, Janet Lee. Mem. staff Mass. Inst. Tech., 1947-50; asst. to plant mgr. McGraw Edison, Kyle plant, 1950-53; systems engr. missiles div. Bendix Co., South Bend, Ind., 1953-56; pre-design project engr. Bell Aircraft, Buffalo, 1956-60; mgr. advanced systems programs Gen. Electric Co., Phila., 1960—. Recipient Cordiner award, 1963. Mem. Am. Inst. Aeros. and Astronautics. Episcopalian. Clubs: Mac, Masons. Home: 558 Leopard Rd Berwyn PA 19312 Office: 3198 Chestnut St Philadelphia PA 19101

STEITZ, EDWARD STEPHEN, athletics adminstr., educator; b. Bklyn., Nov. 7, 1920; s. Charles and Magdeline (Esch) S.; B.S., Cornell U., 1943; Ed.M., Springfield Coll., 1948, D.Phys. Edn., 1963; m. June M. Harrison, Jan. 18, 1946; children—Steve, Nancy, Robert. Instr. phys. edn. Springfield (Mass.) Coll., 1948-52, asst. to dir. Sch. Phys. Edn., 1950-54, asst. dir. athletics, 1954-56, dir. athletics, 1956—, prof. phys. edn., 1963—, head coach varsity basketball, 1956-66; cons., lectr. on athletics and phys. edn. to various countries in Europe, 1958-77, Can., 1959-76, S.Am., 1968-76, Japan, 1964, Panama, 1971, 73, India, 1965, 72; U.S. rep. to World Congress of Basketball at Olympic Games, Rome, 1960, Tokyo, 1964, Mexico City, 1968, Munich, 1972, Montreal, 1976; mem. U.S. State Dept.'s Panel of Experts on Internat. Sports, 1968-76; pres. Basketball Fedn. U.S., 1968-75; vice chmn. U.S. Olympic Com., 1968-72; mem. exec. com. Nat. Basketball Rules Com. of U.S. and Can., 1967-78; nat. chmn. YMCA Basketball Championship com., 1957-65; dir. Western Mass. High Sch. Basketball Championships, 1956-71; coach of New Eng. All-Star Team, ann. Hall of Fame All-Star Game, 1966; mem. exec. com. New Eng. Conf. on Athletics, 1970-76; cons. on basketball rules interpretation of movies, 1956-76; nat. interpreter of basketball rules of U.S. and Can., 1967-78. Mem. nat. rules com. Little League Baseball, 1952-63; trustee Naismith Meml. Basketball Hall of Fame, 1961—. Served with U.S. Army, 1942-46; ETO. Elected to Dutchess County (N.Y.) Basketball Hall of Fame, 1976; recipient Walter Brown award, 1973, Disting. Alumnus award Springfield Coll., 1974; named Outstanding Servant of the Public, Channel 22. Mem. State and Nat. Assns. of Health, Phys. Edn. and Recreation, Nat. Assn. Coll. Athletic Dirs. Am., Nat. Assn. Basketball Coaches, Nat. Basketball Coaches Assn. (award 1974), New Eng. Basketball Coaches Assn. (pres. 1965-66), New Eng. Football Ofcls. Assn., New Eng. Wrestling Assn. (exec. com. 1967-69), Nat. Coll. Athletic Assn. (internat. relations com. 1973-79), Internat. Assn. Approved Basketball Ofcls. (rules interpreter 1956—), Coll. Basketball Ofcls. Assn. (hon.). Author: Illustrated Basketball Rules, 1976; contbr. to profl. publs.; editor: Basketball Case Book, 1965-78; trophy for nat. tournament in India named in his honor. Home: 141 Elm St E Longmeadow MA 10128 Office: Springfield College Springfield MA 01109

STELE, RICHARD BARRY, chiropractor; b. N.Y.C., Feb. 27, 1940; s. Aaron and Anne (Brook) S.; student Ohio State U., 1957-60; D. Chiropractic, Columbia Inst. Chiropractic, 1963; m. Ellyne Feldman, May 29, 1969; children—Erika Beth, Nicole Alissa. Individual practice chiropractic medicine, Howard Beach, N.Y., 1964-70, Montville, N.J., 1970—; cons. in field. Mem. Am., N.J. chiropractic assns. Jewish. Clubs: K.P., Rotary (pres. Montville Twp. 1975-76, dist. gov.'s aide 1977-78). Office: 339 Main Rd Route 202 Montville NJ 07045

STELZER, IRWIN MARK, economist; b. N.Y.C., May 22, 1932; s. Abraham and Fanny (Dolgins) S.; B.A. cum laude, N.Y. U., 1951, M.A., 1952; Ph.D., Cornell U., 1954; m. Elaine Waldman, June 18, 1950 (div. 1964); 1 son, Adam David; m. 2d, Agnes Sasaki, Aug. 30, 1966 (div. 1976). Financial analyst Econometric Inst., 1952; teaching fellow Cornell U., 1953-54; instr. U. Conn., 1954-55; researcher Twentieth Century Fund, 1953-55, economist W.J. Levy, Inc., 1955-56; sr. cons., v.p. Boni, Watkins, Jason and Co., Inc., 1956-61. Lectr. N.Y. U., 1955-56, Coll. City N.Y., 1957-58; researcher Brookings Instn., 1956-57; pres. Nat. Econ. Research Assos., Inc., 1961—; chmn. com. on adequate power sup ply FPC. Mem. Cornell U. Council. Pres. bd. dirs. Emerson Sch., 1970-72; bd. dirs. U.S. Nat. Com., World Energy Conf. Mem. Am. Econ. Assn., Am. Statis. Assn., Nat. Assn. Bus. Economists, So. Econ. Assn., Japan Soc., Phi Beta Kappa Assos., Phi Beta Kappa. Author: Selected Antitrust Cases: Landmark Decisions. Contbr. articles in econ. field. Asso. editor Antitrust Bull. Home: 31 E 79th St New York City NY 10021 Office: 80 Broad St New York City NY 10004

STEMMY, THOMAS JOSEPH, accountant, educator; b. Shenandoah, Pa., July 29, 1938; s. Thomas W. and Jean C. (Shemansky) S.; B.S. in Econs., Villanova U., 1960; M.Mgmt. Sci., Nat. Grad. U., 1977; m. Linda B. Cook, June 9, 1962; 1 dau., Lynn M. Fed. tax auditor IRS, Washington, 1960-63, rep. in pub. relations programs, 1961-63; tax auditor D.C. Govt., Washington, 1963; accountant, tax adviser T.J. Stemmy & Co., College Park, Md., 1963-73, Stemmy, Tidler & Co., College Park, 1973—; instr. U. Md., College Park, 1967-76; instr. fed. taxation Prince George's Community Coll., 1974-76; dir. Lakewood Harbor Estates, Inc., Fredericksburg, Va. Campaign mgr. for Mayor of College Park, 1968; mem. Md. Crime Investigating Commn., 1976—; treas. Prince Georges County Cleanup Com., 1967-72; pres. College Park Bd. of Trade, 1971; mem. Am. Security Council, 1971—; mem. Estate Planning Council Prince George's County; mem. Md. Ednl. Found., 1975-76; tchr. Confraternity Christian Doctrine, St. Matthias Ch. Served with AUS, 1960-66. Recipient Key to the City award College Park, 1971; C.P.A., Md., Washington. Mem. Md. Soc. C.P.A.'s, Md. State Sheriffs Assn., Md. State Toboggan Team Assn. (chmn. 1975), Am. Legion, Gamma Phi. Republican. Roman Catholic. Clubs: Kiwanis, Elks. Home: 9532 Elvis Ln Seabrook MD 20801 Office: 7338 Baltimore Ave College Park MD 20740

STEPAHIN, JOHN MATTHEW, coll. adminstr.; b. Butlter, Pa. Nov. 26, 1948; s. Alexander M. and Mary (Soley) S.; B.A. in Psychology, Pa. State U., 1970, M.Ed. in Student Personnel and Counseling, 1972; postgrad. in Adminstrn. and Research U. Pitts.; m. Marion Evette Allegre, Sept. 5, 1970. Asst. coordinator residence hall program Pa. State U.,1970-72; counselor/coordinator career resource center Community Coll. Allegheny County, Boyce campus, 1972-76, asst. prof. counseling, 1972-76, dir. job. placement, South campus, 1976—; cons. career devel., job. placement services; author, project dir. various fed. grants. Certified counselor, Pa. Mem. Am. Personnel and Guidance Assn., Nat. Employment Counselors Assn., Am. Coll. Personnel Assn., Pa. Sch. Counselors Assn., Mon-Yough C. of C. (edn. com.). Author: Placement Manual, 1976. Home: 323 Karen Dr Elizabeth PA 15037 Office: 1750 Clairton Rd Route 885 West Mifflin PA 15122

STEPANISHEN, PETER RICHARD, engr., educator; b. Boston, Jan. 20, 1942; s. Peter and Helen (Furmenek) S.; B.S. (Douglas Aircraft scholar 1962), Mich. State U., 1963; M.S., U. Conn., 1966; Ph.D. (Gen. Dynamics sponsorship program), Pa. State U., 1969; m. Lenore Thomas, June 27, 1970. Engr., Gen. Dynamics/Elec. Boat, Groton, Conn., 1963-66, sr. systems engr., 1966-70, research specialist, 1970-74; asst. prof. ocean engring. U. R.I., Kingston, 1974-77, asso. prof., 1977—; cons. in acoustics to pvt. industry and naval labs. Recipient A.B. Wood medal and prize Inst. Acoustics, Eng., 1977; NIH grantee in med. ultrasonics, 1976-78. Fellow Acoustical Soc. Am.; mem. IEEE, Am. Inst. Ultrasound in Medicine, Am. Soc. Nondestructive Testing, Sigma Xi. Contbr. reports on underwater acoustics, articles to tech. jours. Home: 1 Treetop Dr Westerly RI 02891

STEPHENS, EVERETT WATSON, ednl. adminstr.; b. Springfield, Mass., June 7, 1913; s. James Strickney and Jennie Lena (Watson) S.; B.A., Am. Internat. Coll., 1936; M.A., Hartford Seminary Found., 1937; postgrad. Boston U., 1940-42; Ed.D. (hon.), Calvin Coolidge Coll., 1962; m. Mary Louise Thompson, Aug. 13, 1938; children—Alan T., James L., Louisa Mae. Instr. psychology, English Anatolia Coll., Thessaloniki, Greece, 1937-40; asst. prof. psychology, vocat. Guidance Boston U., 1942-46; dir. counseling, placement Babson Coll., Babson Park, Mass., 1946-52, dean students 1952-62, v.p. devel., 1962-66, v.p. pub. affairs, 1966—, dean Sch. Continued Mgmt. Edn., 1970—. Chmn. bd. trustees Anatolia Coll., 1970—; bd. dirs. Jr. Achievement; moderator Town of Southboro (Mass.), 1956-61, mem. sch. com., 1961-66. Mem. Am. Coll. Personnel and Guidance Assn., Nat. Vocat. Guidance Assn., Eastern Coll. Personnel Officers Assn., Council for Advancement and Support Edn., Coll. Placement Council, Blue Key Nat. Honor Soc., Delta Sigma Pi. Mem. Churches of Christ. Author: Career Counseling and Placement in High Education, 1970; contbr. articles on tests and measurements, attitude measurement, personnel relations, counseling, job placement, master planning in higher edn. to profl. jours. Home: 1 Sears Rd Southboro MA 01772 Office: Babson Coll Babson Park MA 02157

STEPHENS, HUGH MART, marine safety exec.; b. Mpls., Apr. 3, 1924; s. George A. and Jane (Mart) S.; m. Nancy J. Johnson, May 12, 1945; 1 son, Craig H.; m. 2d, Barbara N. Karlin, June 22, 1950 (dec. June 1965); children—Mary D., Dean J., Kirk R.; m. 3d, Elizabeth Piltz Moring, Mar. 5, 1966. Seaman, deck officer Am. flag vessels, 1943-50; dredging supt. Henry DuBois Sons Co., N.Y.C., 1951-52; asst. to mgr., marine div. Isthmian S.S. Co., N.Y.C., 1953-55; supr. vessel performance Navios Corp., Nassau, Bahamas, 1955-59; marine supt., marine mgr. Naess Shipping Co., N.Y., 1960-66; V.P. Mgmt. and Shipping Transport, Inc., N.Y.C., 1966-67; exec. dir. Marine Safety Inst., 1967; founder, pres. Ships' Operational Safety, Inc., 1967—; pres. Nautical Holdings Corp.; dir. Lizgraphics. Sec. exec. com. marine sect. Nat. Safety Council; mem. Nat. Cargo Bur. Recipient Cameron award, marine sect. Nat. Safety Council, 1971, 72, 74; registered profl. engr., Calif.; certified safety profl.; licensed master and 1st class pilot USCG. Mem. Am. Petroleum Inst. (fire and safety com.), Nat. Cargo Bur., Am. Soc. Safety Engrs., Nat. Safety Mgmt. Soc., Council Am. Master Mariners, Inst. of Nav. (U.S. and U.K.), Nat. Fire Protection Assn. Unitarian. Contbr. articles to profl. publs. Producer Safety on Slides Series audio-visuals for seamen. Editor, pub. Lifeline, Sealution and 20 other multilingual safety, pollution prevention. monthlies co-producer video film Morale and Physical Fitness. Home: 103 Huntington Rd Port Washington NY 11050 Office: 284 Main St Port Washington Harbor NY 11050 also 312 John Anderson Dr Ormond Beach FL 32074

STEPHENS, JOHN WELLINGTON, econ. cons.; b. Brownwood, Tex., June 24, 1934; s. L.M. and J.E. (McFarlin) S.; A.B., Harvard U., 1955; M.A., Am. U., 1960; m. Toni Hanlon, Jan. 26, 1963; children—Alexander Whitehall, Christopher John. Fgn. service officer U.S. Govt., Aden, Rotterdam and Washington, 1958-64; sr. asso. Cresap, McCormick & Paget, N.Y.C., 1965-68; cons., N.Y.C., 1968-71; v.p. Chase Manhattan Bank, N.Y.C., 1971-74; cons. internat. economist to fin. instns., N.Y.C., 1974—; guest lectr. Grad. Sch. Bus. Adminstrn., U. Mich., Ann Arbor, 1974-77. Served to 1st lt. USAF, 1955-58. Mem. Am. Fgn. Service Assn., N.Y. Assn. Bus. Economists. Club: Harvard. Author: Investment in Egypt, 1974.

STEPHENS, LA VERNE IDA, ins. exec.; b. Chgo., July 25, 1935; d. Langley A. and Cleo M. (Powell) Waller; B.B.A., Coll. Ins., N.Y.C., 1970; M.B.A., Fordham U., 1975; divorced. With Met. Life Ins. Co., N.Y.C., 1954—, group sales rep., 1978—. Home: 233-12 139th Ave Laurelton NY 11422 Office: 1 Madison Ave New York City NY 10010

STEPHENS, MARGARET JOY BRANDENBURG, librarian; b. Elizabeth, N.J., Feb. 3, 1927; d. Arthur Henry and Margaret (Leonard) Brandenburg; B.A., Woman's Coll. U. N.C., 1948; M.L.S., Rutgers U., 1969; m. William Gustave Stephens, Dec. 18, 1948; 1 dau., Lee Elizabeth (Mrs. Robert William Wollenberg). Jr. high sch. librarian Elizabeth Bd. Edn., 1958-61; high sch. librarian Roselle Park (N.J.) Bd. Edn., 1961—. French horn player Elizabeth Civic Orch., 1958—, v.p., 1970-78, pres., 1978—; French horn player Union County Symphony, 1972—. Co-chmn. library com. N.Y. Soc. for Ethical Culture, 1969-72, library dir., 1973—, del. Am. Ethical Union Assembly, 1971, 72, 76. Mem. ALA, NEA, N.J. Edn. Assn., Roselle Park Edn. Assn. (v.p. 1977—), League Women Voters Roselle (treas. 1969-71), Garden State Theatre Organ Soc. Home: 416 Birch St Roselle Park NJ 07204 Office: 185 W Webster Ave Roselle Park NJ 07204

STEPHENS, WARREN CLAYTON, JR., mfg. co. exec.; b. Mobile, Ala., Apr. 6, 1942; s. Warren Clayton and Ellen Story (Fretz) S.; B.A., Notre Dame U., 1964; M.B.A., Stanford U., 1966; m. Millicent A. Wynne, Dec. 28, 1963; children—Warren Clayton III, Brent Christopher, Craig Gordon, Keith Wynne. Second v.p. Chase Manhattan Bank, N.Y.C., 1966-69; corp. v.p., div. pres. Genway Corp., Chgo., 1969-72; v.p., treas. Wheelabrator Frye, Inc., Hampton, N.H., 1972—, also pres. various subsidiaries. Nat. alumni sec. U. Notre Dame, 1964-74. Mem. Bus. and Industry Assn. N.H. (chmn. taxation com. 1976-78, dir. 1977—), Notre Dame Alumni Assn., Stanford Bus. Sch. Assn. Roman Catholic. Contbr. articles to profl. jours. Home: 36 Pine St Exeter NH 03833 Office: Liberty Ln Hampton NH 03842

STEPHENS, WILLIAM THEODORE, lawyer; b. Balt., Mar. 31, 1922; s. William A. and Mildred (Griffin) S.; student Balt. City Coll., 1939-41, U. Md., 1946-47; A.B., J.D., George Washington U., 1950, postgrad., 1951; m. Arlene Alice Lesti, June 2, 1958; children—William Theodore, Renée Adena. Admitted to Md. bar, 1950; also D.C., Va. bars; mem. firm J.L. Green, Washington, 1950-51, J.M. Cooper, Washington, 1952-54; practiced in Washington, 1955—; prin. owner, dir. BARBCO, Inc. (Nev.); dir. Exotech, Inc. and subs., Gaithersburg, Md., KHI Corp., Fairfax, Va.,

Hamilton Bank & Trust Co., Bailey's Cross Roads, Va.; dir. Frat. Housing Corp., Washington. Exec. com. Nat. Com. on Uniform Traffic Laws and Ordinances. Trustee Ophthalmic Research Found., Washington, Fairfax-Brewster Sch., Falls Church, Va., Am. Bikeways Found., Washington. Served to 1st lt. U.S. Army, 1941-46. Mem. Am. Bar Assn. (sec. taxation 1959—, sec. corps., banking and bus. law 1960—). XVI Corps Assn. (pres. 1967), Kappa Alpha order (Ct. of Honor), Delta Theta Phi. Clubs: Commonwealth (Cal.), University, Captiol Hill, Army-Navy Country (Washington); Fairfax Racquet (dir.); Racquet International, Jockey (Miami, Fla.). Home: 6636 Tansey Dr Falls Church VA 22042 also 881 Ocean Dr Key Biscayne Fl 33149 Office: Regency Club McLean 1800 Old Meadow Rd McLean VA 22101 also 1050 17th St NW Suite 900 Washington DC 20036

STEPHENSON, JAMES HAWLEY, physician; b. St. Louis, Mar. 29, 1919; s. Carl and Olive Elizabeth (Diall) S.; student Raja Yoga Arcane Sch., 1945-65; student in Postural Dynamics with Ida Rolf, 1948-50; B.A., Cornell U., 1948, M.D., 1951; student homeopathy E.W. Hubbard, 1952-55; postgrad. N.Y. Soc. Analytical Psychology, 1955-57; m. Maria Vittoria Monti, May 26, 1974; children—Skye, Heather, Natalia. Exec. trainee Harper Bros. Pub. Co., N.Y.C., 1939-41; intern Santa Clara County Hosp., San Jose, Calif., 1951-52; practice medicine specializing in internal medicine, N.Y.C. and Greenwich, Conn., 1953—; cranial osteo. trainee Howard Lippincott, 1959-63; trustee, dir. research Am. Inst. Homeopathy, Council for Homeopathic Research and Edn. Pres. Medicauto, Inc., Internat. Hahnemannian Assn., Am. by Choice, Inc., Metallum Antiquum; trustee Found. for Integrative Edn.; co-chmn. Am. Assn. for UN. Served with AUS, 1941-42; to 1st lt. USAAF, 1941-46; Eng. Decorated Air medal, Purple Heart; diplomate Am. Bd. Homeotherapeutics. Mem. Conn., Fairfield County, N.Y. State med. socs., Am. Inst. Homeopathy, La Societe Medicale de Biotherapie, N.Y. State, New York County, Conn. homeopathic med. socs., AAAS. Republican. Episcopalian. Author: Hahnemannian Provings, 1924-59, 1960; Index Medicus Homoeopathicus Cumulativus, 1963-65; (with others) The Homeopathic Pharmacopoeia of the United States, 7th edit., 1968; A Doctor's Guide to Helping Yourself with Homeopathic Remedies, 1976; A Doctor's Auto Checkup List, 1978; editor Jour. Am. Inst. Homeopathy, 1958-68; U.S. editor Acta Homoeopathica, 1968—. Home: 1078 Sasco Hill Rd Southport CT 06490 Office: 66 E 83d St New York City NY 10028

STEPHENSON, JUNIUS WINFIELD, environ. engr.; b. N.Y.C., Feb. 4, 1922; s. Junius W. and Ruth S. (Walther) S.; B.C.E., Union Coll., 1944; m. Josephine Romano, May 14, 1977; children by previous marriage—Carol Anne, Linda Story, Patricia Lynn, Robert Scott. Instr. in engring. Union Coll., Schenectady, 1943-44; design engr. Havens & Emerson, Inc., N.Y.C., 1944-53, field engr., 1953-54, project engr., 1954-62, asso., 1962-70, prin., Saddle Brook, N.J., 1970—; cons. solid waste mgmt. and air pollution control. Vestryman, Christ Ch., Pelham, N.Y., 1948-58, St. Peter's Ch., Port Chester, N.Y., 1961-75, St. Peter's Ch., Rochelle Park, N.J., 1977—. Recipient Silver Beaver award Boy Scouts Am., 1956; registered profl. engr., N.Y., N.J., Conn., Pa., Va., Wis., N.C., Maine, Mich., Tenn. Diplomate Am. Acad. Environ. Engring. Fellow ASCE; mem. ASME (Distinguished Service award 1976, chmn. solid waste processing div. 1965-66, 79-80), Water Pollution Control Fedn., Nat. Soc. Profl. Engrs., Air Pollution Control Assn., Am. Cons. Engrs. Council, Inst. Solid Wastes, Am. Pub. Works Assn., Internat. Solid Wastes and Pub. Cleansing Assn. Episcopalian. Contbr. numerous articles on solid waste mgmt. to profl. jours.; editor: Incinerator and Solid Waste Technology, 1975. Home: 38 Sunset Rd Demarest NJ 07627 Office: Havens & Emerson Inc 299 Market St Saddle Brook NJ 07662

STEPHENSON, WILLIAM EUGENE, pub. relations co. exec.; b. Leesburg, Fla., July 7, 1925; s. James Harold and Ethel (Spires) S.; B.B.A. cum laude, Cleve. State U., 1950; m. Antoinette Bertone, Aug. 2, 1947; children—David J., James Harold, Mark John. With Am. Cyanamid Co., 1951-73, pub. relations mgr. agrl. div., Princeton, N.J., 1970-73; sr. partner Ellis Assos., N.Y.C., 1973-77; pres. W.E.S. Pub. Relations, Inc., East Windsor, N.J., 1977-78; v.p. Paluszek & Leslie Assos., 1978—. Mem. East Windsor Twp. Planning Bd., 1977-78, chmn., 1978—; mem. Econ. Devel. Com., East Windsor Twp., 1972-77, chmn., 1974-77. Served to 1st lt. AUS, 1944-46. Recipient Silver Beaver award Gulf Ridge council Boy Scouts Am., 1968. Mem. Pub. Relations Soc. Am. (accredited). Roman Catholic. Home: 6314 Cottonwood Ln Apollo Beach FL 33570 Office: Warren Plaza W East Windsor NJ 08520 also PO Box 22102 Tampa FL 33622

STEPHENSON, WILLIAM HERMAS, life sav. mfg. equipment co. exec.; b. Raleigh, N.C., May 12, 1897; s. Charles Henry and Annie Evelena (Jones) S.; A.B., U. N.C., 1918; LL.B., S.J.D., U. Tex., 1922; m. Esther C. Myers Nov. 26, 1942 (dec. Aug. 1959); children—Dorothy Esther, William Hermas; m. 2d, Irene W. Stephan, Mar. 16, 1968. Admitted to Tex. bar, 1922, N.Y. bar, 1923, Calif. bar, 1924; practiced in Dallas, 1922-28; founder, operator Am. Mines & Metals Corp., Mina, Nev., 1929-34; developer research 1st automatic resuscitator AMA, 1935-40, launched 2d resuscіator, 1940-45; founder Stephenson Corp., Red Bank, N.J., 1946—, chmn. bd., 1962—; v.p. Life Support Systems, Inc., Stamford, Conn.; v.p. Alcar Metals Corp., Highlands, N.J., Iconex Systems, Inc., Stamford; mktg. dir. Bow Waves Inc., Atlantic Highlands, N.J. Founder Inst. World Affairs, Mondsee, Austria, 1934; co-founder Internat. Rescue and First Aid Assn., 1948. Served to lt. USNRF, World War I. Mem. N.J. Council on Historic Sites, Sierra Club, Phi Beta Kappa, Sigma Chi, Tau Kappa Alpha, Sigma Upsilon. Presbyterian (trustee, ruling elder). Clubs: Masons, Navesink Country (Middletown, N.J.); Circumnavigators (N.Y.C.). Home and Office: Monmouth Hills Highlands NJ 07732

STEPITA-KLAUCO, MATEJ, behavioral scientist; b. Martin, Czechoslovakia, Sept. 8, 1939; s. Matej and Marie (Jurcickova) S.-K.; came to U.S., 1972; M.D., Charles U., Prague, Czechoslovakia, 1962. Asst. prof. exptl. pathology Charles U., 1962-66; research asso. in physiology Czechoslovak Acad. Scis., Prague, 1966-68; research asso. in pharmacology Royal Carolina Inst., Stockholm, 1968-70; staff scientist in neuropharmacology Draco Research Labs., Lund, Sweden, 1970-72; asst. prof. biobehavioral scis. U. Conn., Storrs, 1972-78. USPHS grantee, 1974—; NSF grantee, 1978—. Mem. Soc. for Neuroscis., Am. Soc. for Mass Spectrometry. Contbr. articles to sci. jours. Home: Box 85A Willington Hill Rd Storrs CT 06268 Office: U-154 Biobehavioral Sci U Conn Storrs CT 06268

STERLING, JAMES LEWIS, fin. exec.; b. Port Huron, Mich., Mar. 2, 1929; s. James Richard and Agnes Mathilda (Leonard) S.; A.A., Port Huron Jr. Coll., 1949; B.A., Mich. State U., 1956; m. Frances Louise Kraft, Sept. 29, 1951; children—Gregory, Robert Renee. Auditor, Herkner & Frazier, C.P.A.'s, Benton Harbor, Mich., 1956-59; controller Adams Electronics, Inc., Bangor, Mich., 1959-63; pres., gen. mgr. Shelby Corp. (Ohio), 1963-67; v.p. fin. Dare, Inc., Troy, Ohio, 1967-68; gen. mgr. Simmond Precision Products, Dayton, Ohio, 1968-70; dir. Sawyer Sch. Bus., Buffalo, 1970-72; pvt. practice accounting, 1972-73; treas. Powers Mfg., Inc., Elmira, N.Y., 1973—. Bd. dirs. Capabilities, Inc.; treas. Chemung County Indsl. Devel. Agency. Served with USAF, 1950-52. Mem. Am. Mgmt. Assn., Am. Inst. C.P.A.'s, Nat. Assn. Accountants. Roman Catholic. Club: Elmira Country. Home: 244 Orchard Dr Big Flats NY 14814 Office: Powers Mfg Inc 1140 Sullivan St Elmira NY 14901

STERLING, KEIR BROOKS, historian, educator; b. N.Y.C., Jan. 30, 1934; s. Henry Somers and Louise Noel (de Wetter) S.; B.S., Columbia U., 1961, M.A., 1963, Profl. Diploma, 1965, Ph.D., 1973; m. Anne Cox Diller, Apr. 3, 1961; children—Duncan Diller, Warner Strong, Theodore Craig. Asst. to dean Sch. Gen. Studies, Columbia U., N.Y.C., 1959-65, research grantee, Eng., 1965-66; instr. in history Pace U., N.Y.C. and Pleasantville, N.Y., 1966-71, asst. prof., 1971-74, asso. prof., 1974-77, prof., 1977—; lectr. in gen. counselling, Bklyn. Coll., City U. N.Y., 1967-68; asst. academic dean, adj. asst. prof. history, coordinator Am. studies program, dir. summer session Marymount Coll., Tarrytown, N.Y., 1968-71; asst. dean Rockland Community Coll., State U. N.Y., Suffern, N.Y., 1971-73; vis. prof. Mercy Coll., Westchester Community Coll., King's Coll., 1971, 75, 78—; co-project dir. Am. Ornithologists Union Centennial Hist. Project, 1976—; cons. Arno Press, Inc., 1973-78, Council State Colls. of N.J., 1974-75. Mem. Bicentennial Com. Tarrytown, 1975-76. Served with U.S. Army, 1954-56. Grantee Theodore Roosevelt Meml. Fund, Am. Mus. Natural History, 1967, Nat. Geog. Soc., 1977, NSF/Am. Soc. Mammalogists, 1978. Mem. Am. Soc. Mammalogists, Am. Ornithologists Union (co-chmn. Centennial Hist. Com., mem. Archives Com., grantee, 1976, 77), Am. Hist. Assn., Orgn. Am. Historians, Am. Soc. Environ. History (sec., mem. governing bd.; editor newsletter), History of Sci. Soc., AAUP, Am. Mil. Inst., Am. Studies Assn., Soc. Bibliography in Natural History, Rhinebeck (N.Y.) Hist. Soc. (trustee, chmn. Oral Hist. Com.), Phi Alpha Theta. Democrat. Episcopalian. Author: Last of the Naturalists: The Career of C. Hart Merriam, 1974, 77; editor: Notes on the Animals of North America (B.S.Barton), 1974; gen. editor, contbr.: The International History of Mammalogy, 1979—; editor, contbr. to numerous works in history Am. and European natural scis. Home: 31 Chestnut St Rhinebeck NY 12572 Office: Choate House Pace University Pleasantville NY 10570 also Dept Ornithology American Museum Natural History Central Park W at 79 St New York City NY 10024

STERN, DONALD ELLSWORTH, JR., scientist; b. New Haven, Oct. 17, 1950; s. Donald Ellsworth and Marianne Jane (Boswell) S.; student State U. N.Y., 1975; B.A. in Chemistry, So. Conn. State Coll., 1976; postgrad. Mass. Inst. Tech., 1977, U. New Haven, 1977—; m. Sharon Donna Cooper, Mar. 29, 1969; 1 son, Timothy. Toiletries lab. technician Schick Safety Razor Co. (now Warner Lambert Co.), Milford, Conn., 1969, later devel. lab. technician, asst. engr. and jr. engr., now project scientist, 1976—; owner, mgr. DES Assos., photog. services, 1974—. Mem. Optical Soc. Am., Soc. Photog. Scientists and Engrs., Am. Soc. for Metals, Electron Microscopy Soc. Am. Research on optical and electron microscopy, x-ray spectrochem. analysis, photoelastic stress analysis, videography, high speed cinematography, pattern recognition and info. processing using digital computers. Home: Riverhill Rd Southbury CT 06488 Office: 10 Webster Rd Milford CT 06460

STERN, E(RWIN) MARK, clin. psychologist; b. N.Y.C., Dec. 5, 1929; s. David Samuel and Esther (Swimmer) S.; B.S., Boston U., 1952; M.S., Pa. State U., 1953; Ed.D., Columbia U. (Grant Found. fellow), 1955; m. Virginia Fraser Underwood, Oct. 11, 1967; children—Sarah Rebecca, Cailean Fraser. From supr. to chief psychologist N.Y. Clinic for Mental Health, N.Y.C., 1961-63; from asst. to prof. grad. div. pastoral counseling Iona Coll., New Rochelle, N.Y., 1965—; adj. prof. Seton Hall U., 1967-77; faculty Am. Inst. Psychotherapy and Psychoanalysis, 1975—; individual practice clin. psychology, N.Y.C., 1956—. Diplomate Am. Bd. Profl. Psychology. Mem. Am., N.Y. State psychol. assns., Am. Acad. Psychotherapists, N.Y. Soc. Clin. Psychologists. Democrat. Roman Catholic. Author: Psychotheology, 1970; editor Voices: The Art and Sci. of Psychotherapy, 1977—, Jour. Pastoral Counseling, 1968-77; contbr. articles to profl. publs. Home: Hampton Ln Amagansett NY 11930 Office: 215 E 11th St New York City NY 10003

STERN, EDWARD LEE, publishing co. exec.; b. N.Y.C., Sept. 11, 1935; s. Abraham and Bertha (Lurie) S.; B.S., N.Y. U., 1957, M.B.A., 1960; m. Rhoda Swann, June 17, 1962; children—Susan, David. Asst. creative dir. Doubleday Inc., N.Y.C., 1963-66; mktg. dir. Newsweek Books, N.Y.C., 1966-69; v.p. Downe Communications, Inc., N.Y.C., 1969-70; v.p. Grosset & Dunlap, Inc., N.Y.C., 1970—, pres. advt. agency subs. 51 Madison Assos., 1971—; instr. advt. and promotion N.Y. U. Mem. Direct Mktg. Writers Assn., Am. Assn. Pubs., Direct Mktg. Assn., Pubs. Advt. Club. Author: Prescription Drugs and Their Side Effects, 1975, rev. edit., 1978. Home: 1033 Channel Dr Hewlett Harbor NY 11557 Office: Grosset & Dunlap 51 Madison Ave New York City NY 10010

STERN, EMANUEL RICH, pharm. co. exec.; b. N.Y.C., Nov. 26, 1918; s. Hyman and Clara (Rich) S.; B.S., Coll. City N.Y., 1938; m. Anita Brooks, Oct. 13, 1945; children—Howard J., Marsha F. Med. examiner's office St. John's Hosp., N.Y.C., 1939-40; with USPHS, War Dept., Ala., 1940-43; with Block Drug Co., Inc., Jersey City, 1943—, v.p. quality assurance, 1976—. Pres., East Brunswick (N.J.) Bd. Health, 1962-65. Fellow Am. Inst. Chemists; mem. Am. Chem. Soc., AAAS, Am. Soc. Quality Control (sr.) (chmn. drug and cosmetic sect. 1967-68), Proprietary Mfg. Assn. (mfg. controls com. 1976—). Jewish. Home: 64 Farms Rd East Brunswick NJ 08816 Office: Block Drug Co Inc 257 Cornelison Ave Jersey City NJ 07302

STERN, FRANCES MERITT, psychologist, educator; b. Springfield, N.J., Apr. 24, 1938; d. Morris and Gertrude (Diamond) Milberger; B.A., Newark State Coll., 1960, M.A., 1962; Ph.D., N.Y. U., 1972; postgrad. Temple U., 1976; m. Floyd Stern, June 14, 1959. Asso. prof. psychology Kean Coll. N.J., Union, 1967—; dir. Inst. Behavioral Awareness, Springfield, 1973—; condr. seminars for health delivery profls., workshops profl. orgns.; cons. Nat. Dairy and Nutrition Council, N.Y. and N.J.; lectr in field. Recipient Founders Day award N.Y. U., 1973. Mem. Am., Eastern, N.J. psychol. assns., Am. Soc. Tng. and Devel., Assn. Advancement Behavior Therapy. Author: Mind Trips to Help You Lose Weight, 1976. Contbr. articles McCalls, Glamour, and profl. jours.; author handbook. Home: 810 S Springfield Ave Springfield NJ 07081 Office: PO Box 532 Springfield NJ 07081

STERN, HERBERT JAY, fed. judge; b. N.Y.C., Nov. 8, 1936; s. Samuel and Sophie (Berkowitz) S.; B.A., Hobart Coll., 1958, LL.D. (hon.), 1974; J.D., U. Chgo., 1961; LL.D. (hon.), Seton Hall U., 1973; L.H.D. (hon.), Newark State Coll., 1973; Litt.D. (hon.), Montclair State Coll., 1973; D.C.L. (hon.), Bloomfield Coll., 1973; children—Jason Andrew and Jordan Ezekial (twins). Admitted to N.Y., N.J. bars; asst. dist. atty. New York County, 1962-65; trial atty., organized crime and racketeering sect. Dept. Justice, Washington, 1965-69; chief asst. U.S. atty. Dist. N.J., Newark, 1969-70, U.S. atty., 1971-74; judge U.S. Dist. Ct., Dist. N.J., Newark, 1974—; adj. prof. Seton Hall U. Law Sch. Mem. Am., Fed. (N.J. chpt.), Essex County bar assns., Am. Judicature Soc. Office: US Courthouse Newark NJ 07101

STERN, PAUL HERTZLER, museum curator; b. Elizabethtown, Pa., Feb. 17, 1902; s. Jacob Hoffman and Sarah (Hertzler) S.; B.A., Lehigh U., 1924; M.S., Lebanon Valley Coll., 1930; m. Grace Lloyd, Nov. 29, 1934; children—Joyce Stern Hesketh, Joan Stern Longenecker, Peggy Stern Hassey, Paul Hertzler. Tchr. chemistry and physics, coach wrestling and tennis Manheim (Pa.) High Sch., 1924-42; automobile dealer Paul H. Stern, Inc., Manheim, 1941-60; pres. Manheim Auto Auction, Manheim, 1946-69; curator Auto Mus., Manheim, 1969—; dir. Manheim Savs. & Loan Co. Served to lt. AUS, 1924-34. Mem. Ch. of Christ. Clubs: Hershey Antique Auto (pres. 1966); Chrysler Restorers (pres. Manheim 1961-63), Masons, Shriners, Lions (pres. 1936-37). Home: 426 Orchard Ln Manheim PA 17545 Office: 121 S Main St Manheim PA 17545

STERN, RONALD IVAN, psychotherapist; b. Bklyn., July 1, 1946; s. Lawrence and Dorothy (Goodman) S.; B.A. in Psychology Monmouth Coll., 1968; M.S. in Counseling Psychology, Springfield Coll., 1970; Ph.D. in Counseling, U. Pitts., 1972; m. Randee; children—Jason, Barri, Casey. Worked in drug abuse programs, Pitts., 1970-72, throughout N.J., 1972-74; pvt. practice psychotherapy, Syosset, N.Y., 1975-77, Woodbury, N.Y., 1978—; youth worker, human relations counselor Plainview-Old Bethpage Central Sch. Dist., Plainview, N.Y., 1974—; established with Dr. Jeff Lubin Center for Learning and Behavioral Disorders, Woodbury, 1978; lectr., cons. in field. Active Nassau County Drug and Alcohol Dept. Served with USAR, 1968-74. Mem. Am. Personnel and Guidance Assn. Jewish. Author: The Experience of Being-Anxious, 1972. Contbr. articles on youth in crisis, family relationships. Office: 136 Woodbury Rd Woodbury NY 11797

STERN, RUDI, artist; b. New Haven, Nov. 30, 1936; s. Kurt Guenter and Else Emily (Jacobi) S.; B.A., Bard Coll., 1958; M.A., U. Iowa, 1960. Kinetic light artist, 1964—; co-founder, 1969, since co-dir. Global Village Video Resource Center, Inc., video documentaries, cons., programs, N.Y.C.; neon artist in sculpture, environments, gallery and workshops, 1972—; tchr. neon art Let There to Be Neon Workshop, N.Y.C., 1972—; tchr. exptl. video New Sch., 1971-73; mus. exhbns. include Lights in Orbit, Milw. and Mpls., 1967, Vibrations, Archtl. League N.Y., 1967-68, Options, Inst. Contemporary Art, Chgo., 1968, Expts. in Art and Tech., Bklyn. Mus., 1968, Theater of Light, Austin Art Center, Hartford, Conn., 1968, Vision and TV, Brandeis U., 1970, Contemplation Environments, Mus. Contemporary Crafts, N.Y.C., 1970, Light/Motion/Sound, Hudson River Mus., 1970, Light Sculpture, U. N.C., 1975; gallery exhbns. include Lights in Orbit, Howard Wise Gallery, 1966, also Festival of Light, 1967; The Visionaries, Easthampton Gallery, N.Y.C., 1967; Art Today, N.Y. State Fair Syracuse, summer, 1967; Fun on 57th St., Howard Wise Gallery, N.Y.C., 1967; Let There Be Neon, 1972—; Neon, Hallmark Gallery, 1973; also lectr., demonstrations and environments in kinetic light and neon; commd. sculpture for Malcolm Forbes collection, 1968. Grantee Rockefeller Found., 1971, 72, 76, John D. Rockefeller III Fund, 1971, N.Y. State Council Arts, 1970, 71, 72, 75, 76, Nat. Endowment Arts, 1971, 74, 76. Home: 155 Chambers St New York City NY 10007 Office: Let There Be Neon 451 W Broadway New York City NY 10012

STERN, SILVIU ALEXANDER, educator; b. Bucharest, Rumania, June 18, 1921; s. Henry H. and Bianca B. (Joseph) S.; came to U.S., 1946, naturalized, 1954; B.S. in Chem. Engring., Israel Inst. Tech., Haifa, 1945; M.S., Ohio State U., 1948, Ph.D. in Phys. Chemistry, 1952; m. Reneé E. Oziel, Mar. 21, 1973; children by previous marriage—Michael L., Laurence D. Research fellow dept. chemistry Cryogenic Lab., Ohio State U., 1948-52, postdoctoral research asso. dept. chem. engring., 1952-55; research supr., group leader, research engr. Linde div. Union Carbide Corp., Tonawanda, N.Y., 1955-67; academic visitor chemistry dept. Imperial Coll. Sci. and Tech., London, 1975; prof. chem. engring. dept. chem. engring. and materials sci. Syracuse (N.Y.) U., 1967—. NSF grantee, 1968-71, AEC grantee, 1969-75, NIH grantee, 1969-70, 73-78, ERDA Energy Dept. grantee, 1975-77. Mem. Am. Inst. Chem. Engrs., Am. Chem. Soc., AAAS, AAUP, Internat. Inst. Refrigeration (U.S. nat. com. 1962-69), Sigma Xi, Phi Lambda Upsilon. Mem. editorial bd. Jour. of Membrane Sci., 1975—. Office: Syracuse U Dept Chem Engring and Materials Sci Syracuse NY 13210

STERN, STEPHEN HARVEY, med. and pharm. products co. exec.; b. N.Y.C., Jan. 3, 1943; s. Joseph and Mollie (Pfeffer) S.; B.A., City Coll. N.Y., 1965; Ph.D. (Faculty Research grantee 1972), City U. N.Y., 1973; m. Dorothy Modell, Nov. 25, 1964; children—Shari, Lori. Med. research asso. Pfizer Corp./Roerig Div., N.Y.C., 1973-75; research scientist, dept. cardiovascular research, Inst. Rehabilatative Medicine, N.Y. U. Med. Center, N.Y.C., 1975-76; mgr. biologic graft research, dir. clin. research Meadox Medicals, Inc., Oakland, N.J., 1976—. Mem. Am. Chem. Soc., Am. Assn. Tissue Banks, Parenteral Drug Assn. Developer human umbilical vein graft. Home: 140-10 DeKruif Pl New York City NY 10475 Office: 103 Bauer Dr PO Box 530 Oakland NJ 07436

STERN, WALTER PHILLIPS, investment exec.; b. N.Y.C., Sept. 26, 1928; s. Leo and Marjorie (Phillips) S.; A.B., Williams Coll., 1950; M.B.A., Harvard U., 1952; m. Elizabeth May, Feb. 12, 1957; children—Sarah May, William May, David May. With Lazard Freres & Co., N.Y.C., 1953-54; asso. Drexel, Burnham Lambert Group, Inc., N.Y.C., 1954-60, partner, 1960-71, sr. exec. v.p., dir. 1972-73; sr. vice chmn., dir. Capital Research Co., Los Angeles, 1973—, also mng. dir. Eastern ops.; chmn. bd. New Perspective Fund, Inc., 1973—, Fundamental Investors, Anchor Growth Fund; dir. Income Fund Am., Growth Fund Am., Capital Group Inc.; pres., chief exec. officer Capital Strategic Services, Inc., 1973—; pres. Capitol Guardian Mgmt. Co.; instr. N.Y.U., 1956-62, 70-73. Mem. fin. com. Hadassah; bd. dirs. Westchester chpt. Am. Jewish Com., Inst. for Jewish Policy Planning and Research; trustee Fin. Accounting Found., treas., 1975—; vice chmn., trustee Hudson Inst., 1973—; trustee Tel Aviv U., 1976—; pres., bd. dirs. Research Project on Energy and Econ. Policy, 1974—; treas., trustee Fin. Analysts Research Found., 1976—. Served as 1st lt. USAF, 1952-53. Mem. N.Y. Soc. Security Analysts (dir.), Inst. Chartered Fin. Analysts (pres. 1976-77, trustee), Fin. Analysts Fedn. (pres. 1971-72), Phi Beta Kappa. Jewish. Clubs: Williams, Econ. Harvard, Board Room (N.Y.C.); Sunningdale Country (Scarsdale, N.Y.). Contbr. articles to profl. publs. Home: 450 Ft Hill Rd Scarsdale NY 10583 Office: 299 Park Ave New York City NY 10017

STERNLICHT, BENO, research and devel. co. exec.; b. Nowy Sacz, Poland; s. Hugo Charles and Helena (Anisfeld) S.; B.S., Union Coll., 1950; M.S., Columbia, 1951, Ph.D., 1954, D.Sc. (hon.), 1970; children—Mark David, Eric Alan. Staff engr. Thermal Power Systems Gen. Engr. Lab., Gen. Electric, 1951-54, specialist-applied mechanics Gen. Engring. Lab., 1954-58, cons. engr. Gen. Electric, Schenectady, 1958-61; tech. dir., chmn. bd., co-founder Mech. Tech., Inc., Latham, N.Y., 1961—; pres. 97 Fort Washington Corp., N.Y.C., 1961—, Huben Assos., Corp., N.Y.C., 1959—, Ameast Distbrs. Corp., N.Y.C., 1959—, Starlight Holding Corp., N.Y.C., 1959—, 172 E. 4th St. Corp., N.Y.C., 1956—; dir. Small Diesels Ltd., India, New Eastern India Ltd. Pres., VITA (Vols. for Internat. Tech. Assistance), 1965-71, chmn. bd., 1971-73; chmn. NASA Com. on Energy Tech. and Space Propulsion; mem. NASA Research and Tech. Adv. Council, 1970—. Mem. ASME (Machine Design award 1966), Am. Inst. Aeros. and Astronautics, Nat. Acad. Sci., Am. Soc. Lubrication Engrs., Sigma Xi, Tau Beta Pi., Navy League U.S. Author, editor books. Patentee in field. Home: 2520 Whamer Ln Schenectady NY 12309 Office: 968 Albany-Shaker Rd Latham NY 12110

STERNLICHT, MANNY, psychologist; b. N.Y.C., July 21, 1932; s. Oscar and Blanche (Sternlicht) S.; B.A., Coll. City N.Y., 1953, M.A., 1954; Ph.D., Yeshiva U., 1960; m. Madeline Goldstein, Apr. 10, 1954; children—Elliot F., Harold C., Jeffrey M., Riva R. Clin. psychologist intern Kings County Hosp., N.Y.C., 1957-58; asst. prof. psychologist Rockford Coll., 1958-60; clin. psychologist Inst. Juvenile Reserach, N.Y.C., 1959-60; prin. psychologist Willowbrook State Sch., 1960-69, asst. dir., 1969-72, dep. dir., 1973—; individual practice psychology, S.I., N.Y., 1962—; prof. psychology Yeshiva U., 1965—; cons. S.I. Aid for Retarded Children, 1961—. Mem. ednl. adv. bd. S.I. Brain-Injured Assn., 1966—; bd. dirs. S.I. Family Service. Fellow Am. Psychol. Assn., Am. Assn. Mental Deficiency, Am. Group Psychotherapy Assn. Author: Personality Development and Social Behavior in the Mentally Retarded, 1972; The Psychology of Mental Retardation, 1977. Contbr. articles, chpts. to profl. lit. Home: 263 Martin Ave Staten Island NY 10314 Office: Victory Blvd Staten Island NY 10314

STERNS, INDRIKIS, educator; b. Liepaja, Latvia, Oct. 13, 1918; s. Otto and Katherin (Upmalis) S.; came to U.S., 1962, naturalized, 1967; B.A., U. Pa., 1964, M.A., 1965, Ph.D., 1969; m. Marta Meters, Mar. 28, 1943; children—Aija, Silvija. Librarian, U. Pa., Phila., 1962-66; instr. Lehigh U., Bethlehem, Pa., 1967-68; instr. history Muhlenberg Coll., Allentown, Pa., 1968-69, asst. prof., 1969-75, asso. prof., 1975—. Mem. Am. Hist. Assn., Medieval Acad. Am. Lutheran. Home: 1134 Webster Ave Allentown PA 18103 Office: Muhlenberg College Allentown PA 18104

STERTZ, STEPHEN ALLEN, historian; b. N.Y.C., Aug. 2, 1944; s. Philip Bernard and Anne (Herman) S.; B.S., Columbia U., 1968; postgrad. City U. N.Y., 1968, 69-70, U. Pa., 1968-69, (Gilman fellow) Johns Hopkins U., 1970-72; Ph.D. in History, U. Mich., 1974. Research asst. Dillon, Agnew & Marton, N.Y.C., 1975-76; asso. in continuing edn. Bloomfield (N.J.) Coll., 1976; free-lance editor DMS, Inc., Greenwich, Conn., 1977—; adj. instr. history St. Francis Coll., Bklyn., 1977—; researcher Bronx County Hist. Soc., 1978—. Candidate for N.Y. Legislature, 1970. Am. Philos. Soc. grantee, 1978. Mem. Archaeol. Inst. Am., Am. Philol. Assn., Am. Hist. Assn., Am. Assn. Ancient Historians, Am. Numis. Soc., N.Y. Classical Club, Classical Assn. Atlantic States, Am. Classical League. Clubs: Constantian Soc., Halsbury. Contbr. articles to hist. jours. Office: Bronx County Hist Soc 3266 Bainbridge Ave Bronx NY 10476

STETSON, JOHN BOYDSTON, engring. co. exec.; b. Utica, N.Y., Nov. 27, 1928; s. Everett and Vinna (Boydston) S.; B.S., U.S. Naval Acad., 1950; B.C.E., Rensselaer Poly. Inst., 1953; M.S. in Engring., Princeton, 1960; m. Margaret C. Tyler, Mar. 17, 1951; children—John B., Andrew T., James B., Martha A. Commd. ensign U.S. Navy, 1950, advanced through grades to lt. comdr. CEC, 1963; assigned, Latin Am.; ret., 1963; pres. Dale Engring. Co., Utica, 1963—; mng. partner Stetson Parternship, architects and engrs., Utica, 1970—; trustee Savs. Bank Utica; dir. Comml. Travellers Ins. Co., Duofold, Inc. Trustee Munson Williams Proctor Inst., Utica; mem. bd. edn. Holland Patent Central Schs., 1966-76. Mem. ASCE, Soc. Am. Mil. Engrs. Presbyterian. Clubs: Fort Schuyler, Rotary (Utica); Army-Navy (Washington). Home: Trenton Falls Rd Barneveld NY 13304 Office: 185 Genesee St Utica NY 13501

STETTZ, STANLEY EDWARD, lawyer; b. Scranton, Pa., Mar. 2, 1934; s. Stanley M. and Irene A. (Sheffick) S.; B.S. magna cum laude, Scranton U., 1961; student Dickinson Law Sch., 1961-64; m. Elaine Victor, Aug. 31, 1957; children—Susan, Melanie. Admitted to Pa. bar, 1964; pres. firm Teel, Stettz, Shimer and DiGiacomo, Ltd., Easton, Pa., 1966—. Chmn. bd. trustees Easton YWCA, 1975—; solicitor Forks Twp., 1969—; active ARC, United Way, community concerts. Served with USAF, 1953-57. Mem. Am., Pa., Northampton County bar assns. Club: Rotary. Home: 616 Paxinosa Ave Easton PA 18042 Office: 616 Alpha Bldg Easton PA 18042

STEUER, NEIL BURT, geologist, airline transport pilot, flight instr.; b. Cleveland Heights, Ohio, Jan. 2, 1924; s. Harry and Jeannette (Kanner) S.; B.A. in Geology, U. Calif., Los Angeles, 1950; m. Marjorie Macy, Jan. 17, 1962. Geologist, Shell Oil, 1950-54, Sunray Oil, 1954-55; gen. mgr. Tungsten Mine, Fresno, Calif., 1955-56; sr. geologist Sonoma Quicksilver Mine, Guerneville, Calif., 1956-58, Kaiser Aluminum Co., Hilo, Hawaii, 1956-58, Petrobras, Belém, Brazil, 1958-60; engring. geologist AEC, Washington, 1961-75, program mgr. NRC/State Coop. Regional Geology Seismology Programs, U.S. Nuclear Regulatory Commn., 1974—; cons. in field. Served with AUS, 1942-45. Recipient certificate for contbns. to Brazil expdn. NSF, 1966. Mem. Am. Assn. Petroleum Geologists, Geol. Soc. Am., Am. Inst. Profl. Geol. Scientists, Am. Nuclear Soc., Aircraft Owners and Pilots Assn. Clubs: Quiet Birdmen, Explorers (fellow, sec. Washington group), (N.Y.C.); Westerners, Masons, FAA Flying Club (v.p., safety officer 1975-77) (Washington). Author: Journal of the First Official Reconnaissance for an Interoceanic Sea Level Canal, Panama, 1965; Journal of the Expedition Solar Eclipse, Brazil, 1966; contbr. articles to profl. jours. Home: 10022 Stedwick Rd Gaithersburg MD 20760 Office: US Nuclear Regulatory Commn Washington DC 20555

STEVENS, DANIEL JAMES, elec. engr.; b. Meriden, Conn., Apr. 25, 1951; s. Franklyn Ralph and Dorothy Ann (Knapp) S.; B.S. in Elec. Engring. magna cum laude, U. Bridgeport, 1973; M.S., Syracuse U., 1977; m. Charlotte Aron, Dec. 31, 1973. Engr., designer Sikorsky Aircraft Co., Stratford, Conn., 1972-74; process engr. IBM, East Fishkill, N.Y., 1974-78; sr. engr. GCA, Burlington, Mass., 1978—; v.p. Hudson River Chair Co., Inc., Croton on Hudson, N.Y., 1978—. Dana scholar, 1970-73; Carpenter scholar, 1969; Rebecca scholar, 1969; Elks Scholar, 1969; Conn. scholar, 1969. Mem. U. Bridgeport Presidents Scholar Assn., IEEE, ARISTEA, Sigma Pi Sigma. Clubs: Fishkill Soccer (pres.). Patentee in test pattern for photo lithography tools. Home: 42 Marshall St Billerica MA 01865 Office: GCA Middlesex Turnpike Burlington MA

STEVENS, ELISABETH GOSS (MRS. ROBERT SCHLEUSSNER, JR.), author, journalist; b. Rome, N.Y., Aug. 11, 1929; d. George May and Elisabeth (Stryker) Stevens; B.A., Wellesley Coll., 1951; M.A. with high honors, Columbia U., 1956; m. Robert Schleussner, Jr., Mar. 12, 1966 (dec. 1977); 1 dau., Laura Stevens. Editorial asso. Art News Mag., 1964-65; art critic and reporter Washington Post, Washington, 1965-66; freelance art critic and reporter, 1966—; contbr. art critic The Wall Street Jour., N.Y.C., 1969-72; art critic Trenton (N.J.) Times, 1974-77; art critic Balt. Sun, 1978—. Recipient art critics' fellowship Nat. Endowment for the Arts, 1973-74. Mem. Coll. Art Assn. Am., Am. Soc. Journalists and Authors, Authors Guild, Am. Studies Assn., Soc. Archtl. Historians. Contbr. articles, poetry and short stories to jours., nat. newspapers and popular mags. Home: 6604 Walnutwood Circle Baltimore MD 21212

STEVENS, JOHN PAUL, asso. justice U.S. Supreme Ct.; b. Chgo., Apr. 20, 1920; s. Ernest James and Elizabeth (Street) S.; A.B., U. Chgo., 1941; J.D., Northwestern U., 1947; m. Elizabeth Jane Sheeren, June 7, 1942; children—John Joseph, Kathryn, Elizabeth Jane, Susan Roberta. Admitted to Ill. bar, 1949, practiced in Chgo.; law clk. to U.S. Supreme Ct. Justice Wiley Rutledge, 1947-48; asso. firm Poppenhusen, Johnston, Thompson & Raymond, 1948-50; asso. counsel sub-com. on study monopoly power, com. on judiciary U.S. Ho. of Reps., 1951; partner firm Rothschild, Hart, Stevens & Barry, 1952-70; U.S. circuit judge, 1970-75; asso. justice U.S. Supreme Ct., 1975—. Lectr. anti-trust law Northwestern U. Sch. Law, 1953, U. Chgo. Law Sch., 1954-55. Mem. Atty. Gen.'s Nat. Com. to Study Anti-Trust Laws, 1953-55. Served with USN, 1942-45. Decorated Bronze Star. Mem. Chgo. Bar Assn. (2d v.p. 1970), Order of Coif, Phi Beta Kappa, Psi Upsilon, Phi Delta Phi. Office: US Supreme Ct 1 First St NE Washington DC 20543

STEVENS, JOSEPH ROBERT, coll. adminstr.; b. Bronx, Feb. 12, 1933; s. Leo and Luba (Malmed) S.; B.A., N.Y. U., 1954; M.S., Yeshiva U., 1963; M.A., St. John's U., 1967; postgrad. George Peabody Coll., 1976—; m. Susan Gardos, Dec. 31, 1962; children—Douglas Franklin, Veronica Judy S. Prin., Roosevelt Sch., Stamford, Conn., 1958-60; tchr. Glen Cove (N.Y.) High Sch., 1960-61, audio-visual coordinator, 1961-63, dept. chmn. social studies, 1963-67, dean, 1967-70; prin. John F. Kennedy Sch., Berlin, Germany, 1970-73; edn. services officer USAF, Berlin, 1973-75; European coordinator, asso. dir. Office Ednl. Services, George Peabody Coll. for Tchrs., Nashville, 1975—. Served with U.S. Army, 1955-57. PTA Fellowship award, 1962. Mem. Am. Profl. Guidance Assn., Phi Delta Kappa. Address: PSC Box 1148 7274 Air Base Group APO NY 09193

STEVENS, NANCY DUNCAN, educator; b. Passaic, N.J.; d. Herbert Chester and Anna (Dunn) Stevens; A.B., Barnard Coll., 1947; M.A., N.Y. U., 1950, Ph.D., 1960. Asst. vocat. bur. Vassar Coll., 1947-48; sec., asst. placement office Coll. City N.Y., 1949-50; asst. registrar N.J. State Tchrs. Coll., Newark, 1950-53; research asso. div. advanced studies N.Y. U., 1953-54, asst. dir. placement services, 1954-60; asso. dir. career counseling placement Hunter Coll., N.Y.C., 1960-68, 70-76, dir., 1976—, asst. prof. counseling and student devel., 1960-71, asso. prof. 1971—, coordinator Ellen Morse Tishman Meml. Seminars, 1974—, coordinator gen. counseling and academic advisement, 1968-70, dir. H.E.O. project for educationally disadvantaged students, 1969-70; vis. asst. prof. dept. guidance and student personnal N.Y.U., summers 1957-68, vis. asso. prof. counselor edn., 1972-73. Recipient Gordon A. Hardwick award Middle Atlantic Placement Assn., 1968. Mem. Am. Coll. Personnel Assn. (vice chmn. placement commn. 1967-68), Nat. Vocat. Guidance Assn. (editorial bd. Vocat. Guidance Quar. 1972-74), City U. N.Y. Career Counseling and Placement Assn. (chmn. 1975-77), Eastern Coll. Personnel Officers, Met. N.Y. Assn. Applied Psychology, Am., N.Y. State (mem. exec. council 1967-68), N.Y. (pres. 1967-68) personnel and guidance assns., N.Y. U. Edn. Alumni Assn. (v.p. 1964-67), N.Y. Personnel Mgmt. Assn., Met. N.Y. Coll. Placement Officers Assn. (chmn. profl. standards com. 1962-65, historian, chmn. employment com. 1975—), Internat. Assn. Personnel Women, Personnel Assn. of N.Y. (2d v.p. 1966-67). Author articles in field. Home: 50 E 8th St New York City NY 10003 Office: 695 Park Ave New York City NY 10021

STEVENS, NICHOLAS GEORGE, former educator; b. Pitts., Sept. 30, 1911; s. Samuel and Mary (Mervosh) Stepanovich; A.B., U. Pitts., 1933, A.M., 1940; A.M. in L.S., U. Mich., 1949; postgrad. Columbia Sch. L.S., Rutgers U.; m. Elizabeth F. Renwick, Sept. 18, 1948. Tchr., Pitts. Pub. Schs., 1936-42; student asst. history U. Pitts., 1932-33, 36-40; tchr. Vets. high sch. program, Pitts., 1946-48; asso. prof. history, library sci. Kutztown (Pa.) State Coll., 1949-55, prof., dir. div. library sci., 1955-77. Vis. prof. Tex. Women's U., 1954, Marshall U., Huntington, W.Va., 1958, 59, Villanova U., 1960, 61, 64; cons. in field. Mem. Gov. Pa. Adv. Council on Library Devel., 1973-77. Served with USAAF, 1942-46. Recipient Outstanding Educator's award Pa. Dept. Edn., 1964; citation for service Kutztown State Coll., 1975, also citation from alumni assn., 1975; Distinguished Service award U.S. Jaycees, 1976-77. Mem. Am. (chmn. tchrs. sect. library edn. div. 1971-72), Pa. (pres. 1963-64; award of merit 1976, Distinguished Service award 1977) library assns., Pa. Sch. Librarians Assn. 75 Club, Phi Alpha Theta, Alpha Beta Alpha, Phi Delta Kappa. Mason (Shriner), Lion (pres. Kutztown 1958-59). Contbr. articles to profl. jours. Editor library bulls. Home: 616 Highland Ave Kutztown PA 19530

STEVENS, ROY WHITE, microbiologist; b. Troy, N.Y., Sept. 4, 1934; s. Edward M. and Bernice B. (White) S.; B.S., State U. N.Y., Albany, 1956, M.S., 1958; Ph.D., Albany (N.Y.) Med. Coll., 1965; m. Shirley A. Brehm, Aug. 4, 1956; children—Scott D., Mark G. Sr. research scientist serology and immunology labs., div. labs. and research N.Y. State Dept. Health, Albany, 1967-70, asso. research scientist, 1970-73, prin. research scientist, 1973—. Served with USAF, 1961-62. Diplomate Am. Bd. Med. Microbiology. Mem. AAAS, N.Y. State Assn. Pub. Health Labs., Am. Soc. Microbiology. Home: 507 Acre Dr Schenectady NY 12303 Office: NY State Dept Health Empire State Plaza Albany NY 12201

STEVENS, WILLIAM JOHN, trade assn. exec.; b. Dusseldorf, Germany, Aug. 23, 1915; s. Peter and Margaret (Kaumanns) S.; brought to U.S., 1923, naturalized, 1931.; student McCall Sch. Printing, 1933; student assn. mgmt. Northwestern U., 1947; m. Dorothy V. Santangini, Feb. 14, 1937. With Ruttle, Shaw & Wetherill, Phila., 1931-34; partner New Era Printing Co., Phila., 1934-37; plant mgr. Marcus & Co., Phila., 1937-41; supt. Edward Stern & Co., Phila., 1941-46; exec. sec. Nat. Assn. Photo-Lithographers, N.Y.C., 1946-50, exec. v.p. 1961-64, pres., 1964-71; pres., chief operating officer NPEA Exhibits, Inc., N.Y.C., 1971—; owner Dorval Co.; exec. sec. Met. Lithographers Assn., N.Y.C., 1946-50; asst. to v.p. Miehle Co., N.Y.C., 1950-56, mgr. Phila. dist., 1956-61. Cons., Sales Devel. Inst., Phila., 1960—; mem. Am. Bd. Arbitration, 1962—; chmn. adv. commn. on graphic arts N.Y.C. Community Coll., 1962—; mgr. PRINT 80 Graphic Arts Exposition. Named Industry Man of Year, Nat. Assn. Photo-Lithographers, 1954, Man of Year, N.Y. Litho Guild, 1962; Distinguished Service medal Printing Impressions Publ. Mem. Am., N.Y. socs. assn. execs., Graphic Arts Assn. Execs. (past pres.), Am. Soc. Appraisers (asso.), Tech. Assn. Graphic Arts, Nat. Assn. Litho Clubs (founder, pres. 1947, Industry award 1947, sec. 1964-71), N.Y. Club Printing House Craftsmen. Clubs: Philadelphia Litho (pres. 1945); N.Y. Litho (N.Y.C.). Author: How To Prepare Copy for Offset Lithography, 1948. Contbr. articles to trade publs. Inventor Hicky-piker for lithographic pressmen, quick match color file. Home: 431 Lakeview Dr Oradell NJ 07649 Office: 230 W 41st St New York City NY 10036

STEVENSON, BENJAMIN HAYNES, JR., educator; b. Newark, Nov. 23, 1940; s. Benjamin Haynes and Dorothy (Andrwews) S.; B.S.M.E., Newark Coll. Engring., 1962; M.S., Cornell U., 1966; Ph.D., N.Y. U., 1971; m. Justine Edwina Baumgarten, Aug. 22, 1970; children—Victoria Anne, Benjamin Haynes III. Cons. engr. Berger Assos., Orange, N.J., 1962; research collaborator Brookhaven Nat. Lab., Upton, N.Y., 1970-72; asso. prof. physics, chmn. Engring. Sci. div. and head Nuclear Lab., N.J. Inst. Tech., 1965—. Recipient Founders Day award N.Y. U., 1971. Mem. Am. Nuclear Soc. (dir. N.Y. Met. sect.), Am. Phys. Soc., Sigma Xi. Contbr. articles in field to profl. jours. Home: 110 W Hill Rd Colonia NJ 07067 Office: 323 High St Newark NJ 07102

STEVENSON, CHARLES SUMMERS, obstetrician, gynecologist; b. Balt., Nov. 12, 1907; s. David Hays and Grace Thomas (Summers) S.; B.S., Princeton U., 1930; M.D., Johns Hopkins U., 1934; m. Alice deGueldry Stevens, Sept. 21, 1935; children—Charles S., Frances Kellogg, Edith Twining, Ann Valiant. Intern in gynecology and female urology Johns Hopkins Hosp., Balt., 1934-35, resident, 1934-39; house officer Boston Lying-In Hosp., 1939-40, resident, 1947-48; asso. pathology Johns Hopkins U. Sch. Medicine, Balt., 1934-36, asst. inst. gynecology and female urology, 1936-39; asso. obstetrics Harvard Med. Sch., Cambridge, Mass., 1947-48; prof., chmn. dept. gynecology and obstetrics Sch. Medicine, Wayne State U., Detroit, 1948-72; practice medicine specializing in obstetrics and gynecology, Detroit, 1948-72, Wolfeboro, N.H., 1973—; chief gynecologist-obstetrician Huggins Hosp., Wolfeboro, 1975—; co-founder Maternal Mortality Study Com., Mich. State Med. Soc., 1949, mem. com., 1949-64, chmn., 1964-72; mem. med. advisory com. Iran Found., 1952-72; examiner Am. Bd. Obstetrics and Gynecology, 1961-64. Served with USNR, 1943-46. Recipient Spl. award, Detroit Med. Soc., 1962; diplomate Am. Bd. Obstetrics and Gynecology. Fellow A.C.S., Am. Coll. Obstetricians and Gynecologists; mem. Central Assn. Gynecologists and Obstetricians, Am. Soc. for the Study of Sterility, W.Va. Obstetrical Gynecological Soc., Pacific Coast Fertility Soc., Alpha Omega Alpha, Sigma Xi. Republican. Presbyterian. Clubs: Princeton Quadrangle, Pithotomy, Grosse Ile Yacht, Masons. Contbr. articles monographs, chpts. to med. jours., texts. Home: Mt Israel Rd Center Sandwich NH 03227

STEVENSON, DEAN T., bishop; b. Pottsville, Pa., Aug. 16, 1915; s. Paul Arthur and Martha (Taylor) S.; B.A., Lehigh U., 1937, M.A., 1949, D.D.(hon.), 1969; S.T.B., Gen. Theol. Sem., N.Y.C., 1940, S.T.D., 1962; m. Doris Quier, July 5, 1942; children—James Stevenson, Frederic G., Ruth M. Ordained priest Episcopal Ch.; curate Cathedral Ch. of Nativity, Bethlehem, Pa., 1940-42; dean Leonard Hall, Bethlehem, 1946-57; archdeacon of Bethlehem, 1957-66; bishop of Harrisburg, Pa., 1966—. Trustee Lehigh U., Gen. Theol. Sem. Served as chaplain AUS, 1942-46. Decorated Bronze Star. Recipient Sports Illustrated award, 1962. Mem. Lehigh U. Alumni Assn. (pres. 1968-69), V.F.W. Home: 944 Indiana Ave Lemoyne PA 17043 Office: 221 N Front St Harrisburg PA 17101

STEVENSON, JAMES BRADDOCK, newspaper publisher; b. Franklin, Pa., Mar. 23, 1911; s. Edgar Taft and Ferne (Braddock) S.; A.B., Bucknell U., 1932; m. Katharine Haskell, Sept. 14, 1933; 1 son, James Haskell; m. 2d, Marjorie Manelick, July 26, 1974. Advt. mgr. Titusville (Pa.) Herald, 1932-56, treas., 1936-56, pres., publisher, 1956—; dir. Pa. Bank & Trust Co. Mem. adv. bd. Drake Well Park. Chmn. Pa. Hist. and Museum Commn., 1961-72; pres. Hist. Found. Pa., 1974—; bd. dirs. Western Pa. Conservancy, 1962—. Mem. Pa. Newspaper Pubs. Assn. (pres. 1965). Republican. Presbyn. Home: RD 1 Box 229C Youngsville PA 16371 Office: 209 W Spring St Titusville PA 16354

STEVENSON, LOIS WELLMAN HADDOCK (MRS. FREDERICK LEON STEVENSON), journalist; b. Mpls., Jan. 1927; d. Royal Wellman and Jean (Emmerick) Haddock; B.A., U. Calif. at Berkeley, 1949, B.S. with honors, 1960; m. Frederick Leon Stevenson, Apr. 8, 1944; 1 dau., Elizabeth Ann. Sec. to mayor and city council City of San Diego, 1952-53; analytical chemist Bendix Aviation Corp., Burbank, Calif., 1954-55; math. computer Poroloy Equipment Co., Van Nuys, Calif., 1956-57; pet columnist Courier-News, Somerville, N.J., 1968-75, Star-Ledger, Newark, 1971—; tchr. non-fiction writing, adult sch., Watchung, N.J., 1973—; free-lance writer for various mags., newspapers. Bd. dirs. N.J. br. Humane Soc. U.S., 1968-71, dir. edn., 1968-73. Recipient certificate award Humane Soc. U.S., 1974. Mem. Nat. Fedn. Press Women, N.J. Press Women, Women in Communications, Outdoor Writers Assn. Am., Dog Writers Assn. Am. (awards for best feature articles 1971, 72, 73, 74, 75), Quill and Scroll. Clubs: Words and Music (pres. 1971-73), Plainfield Music. Address: 49 Rock Road W Green Brook NJ 08812

STEVENSON, ROBERT EDWIN, former petroleum co. exec., cons.; b. Iowa City, Jan. 5, 1917; s. Russell A. and Edna Lorraine (Kampenga) S.; B.B.A., U. Minn., 1939; M.B.A., N.Y. U., 1954; grad. Exec. Devel. Program, Stanford U., 1958; m. Pauline Louise McCracken, Sept. 1, 1939; children—Jean Stevenson Simpson, Robert Harold. With Mut. Implement and Hardware Co., Owatonna, Minn., 1939-43, Aero. div. Mpls.-Honeywell Regulator Co., Mpls., 1943-44; with Exxon Corp. and affiliated cos., 1944—; sr. tax accountant Esso Standard Oil Co., Baton Rouge, 1944-48; head, div. deptl. adminstrn. Standard Oil Co. (N.J.), N.Y.C., 1948-59; asst. controller Carter div. Humble Oil & Refining Co., Tulsa, 1960-64, accounting research coordinator, Houston, 1964-72; coordinator accounting research Exxon Corp., N.Y.C., 1972-77; cons., 1977—; advisor Accounting Prins. Bd., 1964-71. Recipient certificate of appreciation Am. Petroleum Inst., 1967. Mem. Am. Accounting Assn. (nat. v.p. 1970-71), Fin. Execs. Inst., Am. Petroleum Inst., Nat. Assn. Accountants, Beta Alpha Psi (nat. adv. bd. 1975—). Republican. Presbyterian. Club: Masons. Contbr. articles to profl. jours. Home and office: 38 Heritage Hill Rd New Canaan CT 06840

STEVENSON, ROBERT STANLEY, bus. forms mfg. co. exec.; b. Rochester, N.Y., Mar. 5, 1926; s. John Douglass and Margaret Alice (Gales) S.; B.S., Rochester Inst. Tech., 1965; m. Florence Amy Hill, June 29, 1946; children—Robert Stanley, Richard Tyrone, Roxanna (Mrs. Terry Latimore), René (Mrs. Jessee Myricks), Craig. Mgr., State Theatre, Caledonia, N.Y., 1946-53; quality control lead man Sylvania Electric Co., Batavia, N.Y., 1953-54; pre-press supr. Specialized Printed Forms Co., Caledonia, 1954-71; pres., chief operating officer Stanlee Bus. Forms, Inc., Rochester, 1971—. Mem. Livingston County (N.Y.) County Sheriff's Dept., Geneseo, 1967—, dir., 1968-71; adv. bd. Spencerport Bd. Coop. Edn. Services High Sch., 1972—. Served with USNR, 1944-46; PTO. Mason (master). Home: 1541 McVean Rd Caledonia NY 14423 Office: 185 Murray St Rochester NY 14606

STEWART, ALBERT CLIFTON, chem. co. exec.; b. Detroit, Nov. 25, 1919; s. Albert Queely and Jeanne Belle (Kaiser) S.; B.S., U. Chgo., 1942, M.S., 1948; Ph.D., St. Louis U., 1951; m. Colleen Moore Hyland, June 25, 1949. Sr. chemist nuclear div. Union Carbide Corp., Oak Ridge, 1951-56, group leader carbon products div., Parma, Ohio, 1956-60, asst. dir. research and devel., consumer products, 1963-67, mktg. mgr. chems. and plastics div., N.Y.C., 1967-73, internat. bus. mgr., 1973-77, dir. sales NE region, 1977; lectr., cons. in field. Mem. Oak Ridge Town Council, 1953-56; treas. Dormitory Authority State N.Y., 1972-76; panel arbiters Am. Arbitration Assn.; bd. dirs. N.Y. Philharmonic Soc., Am. Mus. Natural History. Served with USNR, 1944-46. Fellow Am. Inst. Chemists, AAAS; mem. Am. Chem. Soc., Radiation Research Soc., Am. Nuclear Soc., N.Y. Acad. Scis., Sigma Xi. Contbr. articles to profl. jours. Patentee in field. Home: 50 E 89th St New York City NY 10028 Office: Union Carbide Corp One University Plaza Hackensack NJ 07601

STEWART, ALEXANDER DOIG, bishop; b. Boston, Jan. 27, 1926; s. Alexander Doig and Catherine Muir (Smith) S.; A.B. cum laude, Harvard, 1948, M.B.A., 1961; M.Div. cum laude, Union Theol. Sem., N.Y.C., 1951; m. Laurel Gale, June 5, 1953. Ordained priest Episcopal Ch., 1951; asst. Christ Ch., Greenwich, Conn., 1950-52; priest-in-charge St. Margaret's Parish, Bronx, N.Y., 1952-53; rector St. Mark's Episcopal Ch., Riverside, R.I., 1953-70; bishop Episcopal Diocese Western Mass., Springfield, 1970—; mem. faculty Barrington Coll., 1955-70. Mem. budget and program com. Episcopal Ch. U.S.A.; mem. com. theology House of Bishops; trustee denomination pension fund. Chmn. Urban Renewal, E. Providence, R.I., 1967-70; vice chmn. United Fund Springfield, 1972; mem. schs. and scholarship com. R.I. chpt. Harvard Coll., 1960-70. A founder, 1959, since mem. bd. dirs., sec. corp. Health Havens, Inc., E. Providence; trustee Barrington Coll., 1971—, Providence County Day Sch., 1964-70; me. mem. corp. St. Elizabeth's Hosp., Providence, 1954-70, Springfield Hosp., 1970—. Mem. Religious Research Assn. Clubs: Hartford (Conn.); Harvard (R.I. and Springfield, Mass.). Author: Science and Human Nature (Wainwright House award), 1960; The Shock of Revelation, 1967; also articles. Home: 75 Severn St Longmeadow MA 01106 Office: 37 Chestnut St Springfield MA 01103

STEWART, CARLOS GUILLERMO, govt. ofcl.; b. Dayton, Ohio, Feb. 11, 1942; s. Leo E. and Gladys E. Stewart; B.A, Howard U., 1965, M.Ed., 1974; m. Rosalind Thomas, Oct. 12, 1975; children—Dora, Melanie, Carla. Community service worker Nat. Capital Housing Authority, Washington, 1966-68; research asst. Office of Edn., HEW, Washington, 1968-72, edn. program specialist, 1973—. Recipient Man of Yr. award from Israel Met. CME Ch., 1972. Mem. Am. Personnel and Guidance Assn., Am. Assn. Higher Edn. Roman Catholic. Club: Foxtrappe. Home: 7710 Maple Ave Takoma Park MD 20012 Office: US Office Edn 7th & D Sts Room 3711 Washington DC 20202

STEWART, CHARLES LYMAN, lawyer; b. Norwich, Conn., Sept. 6, 1924; s. Charles Lyman and Mary (Lewis) S.; B.A. magna cum laude, Amherst Coll., 1950; LL.B., Yale U., 1954; m. Sharon P. Campbell, Feb. 20, 1971; children—Charles Lyman III, Marjorie Lewis, Campbell Lamont. Admitted to N.Y. bar, 1954, since practiced in N.Y.C.; mem. firm Donovan, Leisure, Newton & Irvine, 1954-56, Dunnington, Bartholow & Miller, 1959—; asst. U.S. atty. Eastern dist. N.Y., 1956-59; dir. Tiffany & Co. Bd. dirs. Kane Found., Beekman Estate, Sheltering Arms Children's Service. Served to 1st lt. with AUS, 1943-45, U.S. Army, 1951-52. Mem. Phi Beta Kappa, Delta Upsilon, Phi Delta Phi. Clubs: Racquet and Tennis, Yale, Metropolitan Opera (dir.) (N.Y.C.); Rockaway Hunting, Lawrence Beach. Home: 80 East End Ave New York City NY 10028 Office: 161 E 42d St New York City NY 10017

STEWART, CHARLES WILLIAM, theatre dir.; b. Columbia, Mo., May 22, 1936; s. Francis Frost and Edith Lee (Payne) S.; student Knox Coll., 1954-57; A.B., U. Miami, Coral Gables, Fla., 1958, postgrad. 1961-62; m. Jane Ellen Ratcliffe, July 27, 1957; children—Elizabeth Laura, Melissa Anne, Jeremy Maxwell. Asst. producer Am. Shakespeare Theatre, Stratford, Conn., 1963-65, adminstr. dir., 1965-67, mng. dir., 1973-76; mng. dir. Playhouse in the Park, Cin., 1967-69, Hartford (Conn.) Stage Co., 1969-73, 76—; mem. bd. Hartford Stage Co., 1973-76; cons. Found. for Expansion and Devel. Am. Profl. Theatre, Nat. Endowment Arts, Nat. Endowment Humanities, 1977; mem. R.I. Council Arts Instl. Support Com., 1975-78; lectr. U. Bridgeport, 1965-66, U. Hartford, 1971, Yale U., 1976—; v. chmn. Stratford Cultural Commn. 1965-67; asst. dir. Shakespeare Inst., U. Bridgeport 1965-67; theatre chmn. Greater Hartford Arts Festival 1971-73, 78. Served to 1st lt. U.S. Army 1959-61. Recipient Ford Foundation Adminstrv. Intern grantee, 1962-63. Mem. League Resident Theatres (exec. com. 1977—), Nat. Theatre Conf. Democrat. Home: 134 Great Swamp Rd Glastonbury CT 06033 Office: 50 Church St Hartford CT 06103

STEWART, GEORGE DANIEL, univ. adminstr.; b. Montclair, N.J., Nov. 8, 1925; s. Robert G. and Mary (Sanftleben) S.; A.B. in Econs., Syracuse U., 1951; postgrad. N.Y. U., 1953-55; m. Carroll Fletcher, Feb. 19, 1955; children—Glen, Gail. Investment analyst C.J. Lawrence & Sons, N.Y.C., 1951-59; sr. investment analyst Dominick & Dominick, N.Y.C., 1960-63; dir. instl. research James H. Oliphant & Co., N.Y.C., 1963-65; asst. treas. Johns Hopkins, 1965-69, treas., 1969—. Vice pres. Md. Children's Aid and Family Service Soc.; chmn. adv. investment com. Md. State Retirement System; trustee, sec.-treas. Fgn. Service Edn. Found.; trustee Common Fund for Nonprofit Orgns., 1974—. Served with USAAF, 1943-46. Mem. Balt. Soc. Security Analysts. Club: Gibson Island. Home: Brooklandville MD 21022 Office: 34th and Charles Sts Baltimore MD 21218

STEWART, JAMES BUCHANNON, mech. engr.; b. Rahway, N.J., Aug. 27, 1933; s. Walter Everett and Nellie Kight (Burgess) S.; B.Mech. Engring., Cornell U., 1956; postgrad. Pratt Inst., 1959-60; certificate bus. mgt., St. Procopius Coll., 1972; m. Judith Esther Zucker, June 12, 1956; children—Katherine, Margaret, Martha Irene. Indsl. designer Westinghouse Electric Corp., Metuchen, N.J., 1959-64; sr. indsl. designer Sunbeam Corp., Chgo., 1964-66, design supr., 1966-68, devel. engr., 1968-70; mgr. engring. Empire Metal Products, Chgo., 1970-72; mgr. indsl. design Magnavox Co., Fort Wayne, Ind., 1972-75, product mgr. small screen television, 1975-76; v.p. research and devel. Metaframe Corp. div. Mattel, Elmwood Park, N.J., 1976—; cons. in field. Served with USNR, 1956-58. Mem. Indsl. Designers Soc. Am., Soc. Plastics Engrs., Internat. Inst. Oceanography. Unitarian. Contbr. articles to profl. jours. Office: 41 Slater Dr Elmwood Park NJ 07407

STEWART, JAMES JOSEPH, pharmacist; b. Bklyn., Mar. 19, 1925; s. James B. and Katherine (Bulmer) S.; B.S. in Pharmacy, St. John's U., 1950; m. Eileen Rose Nelson, Aug. 30, 1947; children—James, Eileen, Margaret, John, Thomas, Donald, Kathleen, Theresa, Keith. Asst. to med. dir. Am. Export Lines, 1947-48; pharmacy intern Clayton & Edwards Pharmacy, 1948-50; surg. supply salesman Fulton Surg. Co., 1950-52; pharmacist, purchasing agt. Rockefeller U., N.Y.C., 1952—, supt. purchases, 1970—, chief pharmacist, 1965—. Coach Little League, 1975-77; cub master Cub Scouts, 1960-63; scout master Boy Scouts Am., 1964-66. Served with USNR, 1943-46; PTO. Mem. Am. Hosp. Pharmacy Assn., Nat. Assn. Ednl. Buyers, Am. Soc. Hosp. Pharmacists. Democrat. Roman Catholic. Home: 829 Doughty Ave Long Island NY 11010

STEWART, JOHN CAMERON, chem. co. exec.; b. Warren, Pa., June 16, 1942; s. John Harvey and Dorothy (Hand) S.; B.S. in Chemistry, Pa. State U., 1964; M.S. in Chemistry, Stevens Inst. Tech., 1967; M.B.A. in Fin., Drexel U., 1972; 1 dau., Melinda MacDonald. Sr. research chemist, reaction motors div. Thiokol Chem. Co., Denville, N.J., 1964-67; project mgr. new venture devel., mem. economic fin. planning staff Sun Oil Co., Phila., 1967-72; mgr. fin. planning Far East div. Fuji Xerox, Xerox Corp., Stamford, Conn., 1972-76; mgr. planning, mergers and acquisitions Tenneco Chems., Inc., Saddle Brook, N.J., 1976—. Mem. Assn. M.B.A. Execs., Am. Chem. Soc. Republican. Episcopalian. Office: Tenneco Chemicals Park 80 Plaza West 1 Saddle Brook NJ 07662

STEWART, JOSEPH TURNER, JR., diversified co. exec.; b. N.Y.C., Apr. 30, 1929; s. Joseph Turner and Edna (Pride) S.; S.B. with honors, U.S. Mcht. Marine Acad., 1951; M.B.A., Harvard U., 1954; m. Carol Graham, Aug. 7, 1954; children—Lisa D., Alison D. Systems analyst Warner Lambert Co., Morris Plains, N.J., 1954-56, budget supr. internat., 1956-60, asst. div. controller consumer products group, 1960-62, div. controller group, 1962-66, dir. adminstrn. and finance, proprietary drug div., 1966, dir. Lactona products div., 1967; controller Beech-Nut subs. Squibb Corp., N.Y.C., 1968, v.p. finance, 1968-71, v.p. planning, corporate staff parent corp., 1971—; dir., mem. investment com. Minority Equity Capital Co., Inc. Mem. N.Y. adv. council Banco Popular de P.R., 1969-72. Vice pres., finance chmn. Urban League Essex County, N.J., 1963-66; pres. exec. council Harvard Bus. Sch. Assn., 1971-75; mem. vis. com. bd. overseers Harvard Bus. Sch., 1976—; bd. dirs. CARE. John Hay Whitney Opportunity fellow, 1952-54. Recipient Alumni Outstanding Profl. Achievement award U.S. Mcht. Marine Acad., 1971. Mem. Am. Mgmt. Assn., Inst. Mgmt. Sci., Am. Mus. Natural History, Mus. Modern Art. Episcopalian (vestryman 1962-68). Club: Harvard (N.Y.C.). Home: 7 Alden Rd Glen Ridge NJ 07028 Office: 40 W 57th St New York City NY 10019

STEWART, KENNETH EDWARD, hosp. adminstr.; b. Clinton, Mass., Mar. 10, 1930; s. Kenneth E. and Alice (Tracy) S.; student Clark U., 1962-65, Quinsigamond Community Coll., 1964-66; m. Beverly Ann Axton, July 12, 1952; children—Kenneth, Kevin, Kim, Kerry, Kathy. Sales rep. Brulin & Co., 1961-64; dir. dept. prodn. control and preventive maintenance Colonial Press Inc., Clinton, Mass., 1964-67; mgr. bldg. service dept. St. Vincent Hosp., Worcester, Mass., 1967-72, adminstrv. asst., gen. services div., 1972—; pres., cons. engr. White Wings Industries, Worcester, 1977—. Mem. Local Health Bd., 1952, Recreation Commn., 1957; chmn. Sch. Com., 1965. Served with USNR, 1948-49. Mem. Environ. Mgmt. Assn., Nat. Assn. Accountants. Republican. Roman Catholic. Club: K.C. Home: 474 Coburn Ave Worcester MA 01604 Office: 25 Winthrop St Worcester MA 01604

STEWART, POTTER, asso. justice U.S. Supreme Ct.; b. Jackson, Mich., Jan. 23, 1915; s. James Garfield and Harriet Loomis (Potter) S.; student Hotchkiss Sch.; B.A. cum laude, Yale U., 1937, LL.B. cum laude, 1941, LL.D., 1959; fellow Cambridge U., Eng., 1937-38; m. Mary Ann Berties, Apr. 25, 1943; children—Harriet Potter Stewart Virkstis, Potter, David Berties. Admitted to Ohio bar, 1941, N.Y. bar, 1942; asso. firm Debevoise, Stevenson, Plimpton & Page, N.Y.C., 1941-42, 45-47; asso. Dinsmore, Shohi, Sawyer & Dinsmore, Cin., 1947-50, mem. firm, 1951-54; U.S. judge Ct. Appeals, 6th Circuit, 1954-58; asso. justice U.S. Supreme Ct., 1958—. Mem. com. White House Conf. on Edn., 1954-55. Mem. Cin. City Council, 1950-53, vice mayor, 1952-53. Served as lt. USNR, 1943-45. Mem. Am., Ohio, Cin. bar assns., Am. Law Inst., Yale Law Sch. Assn. (exec. com.), Order of Coif, Phi Beta Kappa, Delta Kappa Epsilon, Phi Delta Phi. Episcopalian. Clubs: Camargo, Commonwealth, Commerical, University (Cin.); Chevy Chase (Washington); Century (N.Y.C.); Bohemian (San Francisco). Home: 5136 Palisade Ln Washington DC 20016 Office: Supreme Ct Bldg Washington DC 20543

STEWART, ROBERT BRADLEY, assn. exec.; b. N.Y.C., July 21, 1944; s. Richard More and Noel (Russell) S.; B.A., U. Vt., 1968; postgrad. Wharton Sch. Finance and Govt., U. Pa., 1969; m. Irene Aja, Jan 7, 1967; children—Robert Bradley, Christine Ann. Staff trainee Vt. Dept. Mental Health, Waterbury, 1968; exec. dir. Vt. League Cities and Towns, Montpelier, 1969—; chmn. bd. New Eng. Municipal Center, Durham, N.H., 1975—, Vt. Municipal Employees Retirement Bd., 1975—; bd. dirs. Nat. League Cities, Washington, 1975-77; mem. nat. com. Nat. Conf. Pub. Employee Retirement Systems, 1976—; mem. nat. bd. Am. Inst. Mgmt. Research and Tng., 1975—. Chmn. Montpelier City Cancer Crusade, 1970. Mem. Am., Vt. (pres. 1973-74) socs. assn. execs., Montpelier Amateur Hockey Assn. (pres. 1975-76), Can-Am Hockey League (treas. 1975-76). Democrat. Episcopalian. Club: Elks. Home: 4 Crestview Dr Montpelier VT 05602 Office: 118 Main St Montpelier VT 05602

STEWART, WILLIAM GARRETT, cons. co. exec.; b. Independence, Mo., Oct. 29, 1922; s. Milton William and Esther (Long) S.; B.S., U.S. Mil. Acad., 1945; M.S., in Civil Engring., Harvard, 1953; M.A. in Internat. Affairs, George Washington U., 1965; m. Zigride Margarete Graudins, Sept. 14, 1946; children—Aino Stewart Leedom, William Garrett, II. Commd. 2d lt. C.E., U.S. Army, 1945, advanced through grades to col., 1966; assigned Ger., Greenland, Japan and Vietnam; engr. group comdr., Vietnam, 1968; dist. engr., Chgo., 1969-71; chief Engr. Strategic Studies Group, 1971-73; ret., 1973; v.p. environmental and resources mgmt. Linton & Co. Inc., Washington, 1973-76, pres., 1976—. Decorated Legion of Merit (2), Bronze Star (2), Air medal (3), Joint Service Commendation medal, Army Commendation medal (2); Vietnamese Cross of Gallantry with palm. Registered profl. engr., Mass., Maine, Vt. Mem. Soc. Am. Mil. Engrs. (past post pres.). Episcopalian. Author articles and defense studies. Home: 6190 Hardy Dr McLean VA 22101 Office: 1015 18th St NW Washington DC 20036

STEYER, ROY HENRY, lawyer; b. Bklyn., July 1, 1918; s. Herman and Augusta (Simon) S.; A.B., Cornell U., 1938; LL.B. cum laude, Yale, 1941; m. Margaret Fahr, Feb. 21, 1953; children—Hume R., James P., Thomas F. Admitted to N.Y. bar, 1941; pvt. practice N.Y.C., 1941—, partner Sullivan & Cromwell, 1953—. Chmn. Yale Law Sch. Fund, 1957-59; trustee N.Y.C. Sch. Vol. Program, 1974-78. Served from ensign to lt. USNR, 1943-46. Mem. Am., N.Y. State, N.Y. County (dir. 1972-78) bar assns., Assn. Bar City N.Y., Am. Judicature Soc., Am. Coll. Trial Lawyers, Yale Law Sch. Assn. (v.p. 1961-67), N.Y. Law Inst., Order of Coif, Phi Beta Kappa, Phi Kappa Phi. Clubs: Broad Street, Yale of New York. Home: 112 E 74th St New York City NY 10021 Office: 125 Broad St New York City NY 10004

STICHT, ROBERT LARSON, real estate exec.; b. Flushing, N.Y., June 18, 1945; s. Otto William and Helen (Larson) S.; student Athens Coll., 1965-67; B.S., U. Tenn., 1970. Vice pres. C.A. Bilinkas & Co., Newark, 1970-73; with U.S. Trust Co., N.Y.C., 1973-75; mgr. office leasing Eric Bram & Co., East Brunswick, N.J., 1975—. Campaign mgr. for Michael Shalit, Middlesex County Freeholder, 1977-78. Mem. Indsl. Real Estate Brokers Assn. N.Y. Met. Area, Am. Indsl. Real Estate Salesmen Assn., German Am. C. of C. Clubs: Princeton Meadows Ski, Bamm Hollow Country. Contbg. editor In-Site, 1977—. Home: 2908 Hunters Glen Dr Plainsboro NJ 08536 Office: 77 Milltown Rd East Brunswick NJ 08816

STICK, MARVIN EARL, data processing research scientist; b. Boston, Dec. 21, 1942; s. Benjamin and Anna (Koshky) S.; B.S., Boston Coll., 1964; M.A., Boston U., 1966, postgrad., 1966-71; postgrad. Northeastern U., 1966-72; certificate cobol programming Control Data Inst., 1973; m. Marilyn Joan Meyers, Aug. 14, 1966; children—Paula, Michael. Research scientist Space Data Analysis Lab., Boston Coll., 1966—; asst. prof. computer sci. and math. Boston State Coll., 1966—; cons. computer programming Boston, Fitchburg and Salem State Colls.; lectr. Mass. Bay Community Coll. Treas., Temple Aliyah, Needham, Mass., 1976. Mem. Am. Inst. Aeros. and Astronautics, Nat. Council Tchrs. Math., Math. Assn. 2-Year Colls. Contbr. articles to profl. jours. Home: 272 Greendale Ave Needham MA 02194 Office: Boston State Coll 625 Huntington Ave Boston MA 02115 also Space Data Analysis Lab 885 Centre St Newton MA 02159

STICKLER, DANIEL LEE, hosp. adminstr.; b. Fairmont, W.Va., Jan. 4, 1938; s. Elmer Daniel and Ruby Lee (Ball) S.; B.C.E., W.Va. U., 1960; M.P.H., U. Pitts., 1970; m. Donna Lou Johnson, Apr. 16, 1960; children—Dwight Lorne, Dwayne Lee, Douglas Lynn. Chief engr. VA Hosp., Amarillo, Tex., 1963-66; exec. engr. Presbyterian-Univ. Hosp., Pitts., 1966-67, dir. support services, 1967-68, adminstrv. resident, 1969-70, asst. dir., 1970-71, asso. dir., 1971-72, adminstr., 1972-76, exec. dir., 1976—; adj. asso. prof. U. Pitts. Grad. Sch. Pub. Health, 1974—. Registered profl. engr., Tex. Mem. Am. Coll. Hosp. Adminstrs., Am. Hosp. Assn., Internat. Hosp. Fedn., Am. Pub. Health Assn. Methodist. Club: Univ. (Pitts.). Home: 140 Penham Ln Pittsburgh PA 15208 Office: 230 Lothrop St Pittsburgh PA 15213

STICKLER, MITCHELL GENE, computer systems engr.; b. Fairmont, W.Va., Sept. 19, 1934; s. Elmer Daniel and Ruby Lee (Ball) S.; B.S. in Elec. Engring., W.Va. U., 1960; M.S. in Elec. Engring., U. Pitts., 1962; postgrad. Lehigh U., 1962-64; m. Janet Elaine Mankins, Aug. 6, 1960; children—Mitchell, Matthew, Mark, Patrick, Jason. Engr., Westinghouse Electric Corp., Youngwood, Pa., 1960-62; mem. tech. staff Bell Telephone Labs., Allentown, Pa., 1962-64, supr., 1964-68; v.p., dir. Virtual Computer Services, Union, N.J., 1968-70; systems cons. Pentamation Enterprises, Inc., Bethlehem, Pa., 1970—. Served with USAF, 1954-57. Registered profl. engr., Pa. Mem. IEEE (computer group 1960—), Nat. Soc. Profl. Engrs. Home: Route 2 Schnecksville PA 18078 Office: One Bethlehem Plaza Bethlehem PA 18018

STICKLEY, DENNIS W., writer, investment cons., real estate broker; b. Pitts., Feb. 23, 1938; M.B.A., Madison Coll., 1972; m. Dorothy Janet Cush, Oct. 22, 1965; children—Dennis, Andrew, Annina, Sean, Kathryn. Broker real estate, 1978—; investment cons., 1978—; free-lance writer; author articles and booklets on home buying and financing residential investment.

STIEGLITZ, WILLIAM IRVING, aviation and automotive cons.; b. Chgo., June 7, 1911; s. Irving Edward and Helene C. (Wolf) S.; student Swarthmore Coll., 1928-31; B.S., Mass. Inst. Tech., 1932; m. Florence C. Burt, Nov. 19, 1977; 1 son, David T. From asst. chief to chief tech. engr. Central Aircraft Corp., Keyport, N.Y., 1938-41; chief aerodynamics and flight testing Fleetwings div. Kaiser Corp., Bristol, Pa., 1941-44; spl. lectr. aerodynamics Princeton (N.J.) U., 1942-43; design engr. to mgr. design safety and reliability div. Republic Aviation Corp., Farmingdale, N.Y., 1944-64; owner, prin. William I. Stieglitz Assos., Huntington, N.Y., 1964—; adj. asst. prof. physics C.W. Post Coll., 1956-59. Fellow Am. Inst. Aeros. and Astronautics (asso.); mem. Royal Aero. Soc., Soc. Automotive Engrs., Soc. Air Safety Investigators (chpt. v.p. 1971-73), System Safety Soc. (chpt. chmn. 1971-72, 77-78), Human Factors Soc. Club: Wings. Contbr. articles in field to profl. jours. Home: 9 Howard Dr Huntington NY 11743 Office: 9 Howard Dr Huntington NY 11743

STIFF, DAVID PARKER, pathologist; b. Evanston, Ill., Mar. 30, 1931; s. Gary Packard and Helen Winona (Chalmers) S.; A.B. magna cum laude, Dartmouth Coll., 1953, postgrad. Med. Sch., 1952-54; M.D., U. Mich., 1956. Intern, Pa. Hosp., Phila., 1956-57; resident, fellow in pathology N.Y. U.-Bellevue Med. Center, N.Y.C., 1957-59; resident Bellevue Hosp., 1959-60, asst. pathologist, 1960-61; instr. pathology N.Y. U. Med. Center, 1960-63, asst. clin. prof., 1963-66; mem. attending staff St. Vincents Med. Center, Bridgeport, Conn., 1963—, attending pathologist, 1970—, dir. blood bank, 1967—; asso. dir. St. Vincent Med. Center-Park City Hosp. Sch. Med. Tech., 1964; lectr. biology Fairfield U., 1964-75; asso. clin. faculty in med. tech. Quinnipiac Coll., Hamden, Conn., 1969—; v.p., med. dir. Columbia Biologicals, Inc., Fairfield, Conn.; mem. med. adv. com. Conn. Hemophilia Soc., Conn. Red Cross Blood Program; mem. adv. com. on plasmapheresis and blood banking Conn. Dept. Health. Served with USAR, 1961-63. Fellow Coll. Am. Pathologists (life), Am. Soc. Clin. Pathologists; mem. Conn. State, Fairfield County med. socs., Am. Assn. Blood Banks, Pan Am., Bridgeport med. assns., Conn. Soc. Pathologists, Fairfield County Pathology Soc., Phi Beta Kappa, Alpha Epsilon Delta, Alpha Omega Alpha. Republican. Contbg. author: Dolan's Comprehensive Review for Medical Technologists, 1968. Home: Arnolda E Charlestown RI 02813 Office: 2820 Main St Bridgeport CT 06606

STIGLIANO, ANTHONY GERARD, physician; b. Bklyn., Oct. 3, 1914; s. Ferdinand Michael Anthony and Geraldine Johanna (Capece) S.; M.D., L.I. Coll. Medicine, 1939; m. Josephine Helen Spina, June 14, 1947; children—Joan Marie, Phyllis Ann, Diane Marie, Anthony Gerard. Intern, St. Mary's Hosp., Bklyn., 1939-41; chief resident, resident in charge of croup, meningitis and poliomyelitis Kingston Ave. Hosp. for Contagious Diseases, Bklyn., 1941-43; with Kenny Inst. for Polio, Mpls., 1944; asst. resident in pediatrics N.Y. Hosp. and Babies Hosp., Columbia Presbyn. Med. Center, N.Y.C., 1943-44; practice medicine, specializing in pediatrics, Bklyn., and Williston Park, N.Y., 1944—; cons. pediatrician Meth. Hosp., Bklyn., 1978—, Cath. Med. Center, Bklyn., 1968—, Queens and Nassau Hosp., Mineola, N.Y., 1970—; attending pediatrician St. Vincent's Hosp. and Med. Center, Manhattan, 1962—. Mem. univ. council St. John's U., Jamaica, N.Y.; trustee Cardinal Spelman Philatelic Mus., Weston, Mass. Mem. Bklyn. Acad. Pediatrics, AMA, Nassau County Pediatric Soc., N.Y. Acad. Medicine, Knights of Malta, Equestrian Order Holy Sepulchre of Jerusalem (knight comdr.). Roman Catholic. Home: 128 Wetherill Rd Garden City NY 11530 Office: 62 8th Ave Brooklyn NY 11217 also 22 Hillside Ave Williston Park NY 11596

STIGLITZ, MARTIN RICHARD, elec. engr.; b. Vienna, Austria, Mar. 24, 1920; s. Georg Adolph and Maria (Brun) S.; came to U.S., 1939, naturalized, 1942; B.S., Northeastern U., 1957, M.S. in Electronics Engring., 1959; M.B.A. in Mgmt., Western New Eng. Coll., 1977; m. Lenna Schoenberg, Dec. 10, 1950. Mech. engr. S.A. Woods Machine Co., Boston, 1939-51; electronics engr., research scientist Air Force Cambridge Research Labs., Hanscom AFB, Bedford, Mass., 1945-75; research electronics scientist Rome Air Devel. Command electromagnetic scis. div. U.S. Air Force, Bedford, Mass., 1975—; dir. Solar Energy Tech. Inc., Bedford. Served with 11th Airborne div. U.S. Army, 1942-45. Decorated Air medal. Mem. IEEE, Sigma Xi. Patentee solid state devices, med. instruments. Home: 30 Woodpark Circle Lexington MA 02173

STILLER, EUNICE BARBARA HERMAN, guidance counselor; b. Bklyn., Aug. 21, 1924; d. Irving Philip and Helen (Meisel) Rabinowitz; M.A., Columbia U., 1948; certificate Gestalt Inst. Cleve., 1976; m. Alfred Stiller, Sept. 12, 1971; 1 dau. by previous marriage, Shelley Herman Schiller. Personnel dir. Air Materiel Command, Newark, 1946-47; rehab. counselor N.Y. State Employment Service, N.Y.C., 1948-51; guidance counselor N.Y.C. Bd. Edn., 1958—; lectr. Bklyn. Coll. Mem. Am., N.Y. State, N.Y.C. personnel and guidance assns., Gestalt Inst. Cleve., Phi Delta Kappa. Home and Office: 1675 E 18th St Brooklyn NY 11229

STILLINGS, IRENE CORDINER (MRS. GORDON A. STILLINGS), club woman; b. Boston, Aug. 17, 1918; d. Matthew Wilson and Susan F. (Mason) Cordiner; student Radcliffe Coll., 1936-39; diploma Burdett Coll., 1941; m. Gordon A. Stillings, May 13, 1945; children—David Gordon, Susan Irene. Sec., bookkeeper Boston Refrigerator Co., 1941-42; sec., tchr. Burdett Coll., 1942-44; sec., bookkeeper Gertrude Rittenburg, Boston, 1944-46. Town chmn. Heart Fund, Woodland, Maine, 1953-61; Brownie leader Girl Scouts U.S.A., 1954-58; v.p. Woodland Woman's Club 1961-63; sec. P.T.A., 1961-62; chmn. Baileyville Superintending Sch. Com., 1962-64; chmn. women's activities Nat. Found., E. Washington County, 1959-61; pres. Hosp. Aid, 1961-63; chmn. Newcomers Coll. group YWCA, 1965-66, chmn. theatre group, 1968-70, pres. Suburbanites, 1970-71; Stamford chmn. Experiment in Internat. Living, 1965-68. Bd. dirs. YWCA of Stamford, chmn. ann. Antique Show benefit. Mem. Mass. Hort. Soc., St. Luke's Guild (treas. 1954-63), Theta Alpha Chi. Episcopalian. Clubs: Radcliffe; Stamford Woman's (treas., program com., co-chmn. Am. home dept. 1974, 75). Home: 277 West Hill Rd Stamford CT 06902

STILLMAN, ALFRED WILLIAM, JR., elec. engr.; b. Biloxi, Miss., Sept. 11, 1942; s. Alfred William and Marie Ann (Hengen) S.; A.A., Am. River Coll., 1966; B.S. in Elec. Engring., Calif. Poly. State U., 1970, B.S. in Applied Math., 1970, M.S. in Applied Math., 1973; M.E. in Indsl. Engring., Tex. A. and M. U., 1976; postgrad. elec. engring. N.J. Inst. Tech., 1977—; m. Cheryl Ann Power, June 19, 1971; children—Shannon Lynn, Laura Marie. Engring. intern U.S. Army Materiel Command, Texarkana, Tex., 1973-75, electronic systems staff maintenance engr., Ft. Monmouth, N.J., 1975-77, mil. tactical data system integrated logistics support mgr. Office of Project Mgr., ARTADS, Ft. Monmouth, 1977-78, tactical ADP ILS mgr., ILS dir. CORADOM, Ft. Monmouth, 1978—. Served with USAF, 1962-66. Mem. IEEE, Am. Inst. Indsl. Engrs., Nat. Soc. Profl. Engrs., Soc. Logistics Engrs., Solar Energy Soc. Am., Am. Def. Preparedness Assn., AAAS, Tau Beta Pi. Presbyterian. Club: Acacia. Home: 325 Barcelona Dr Toms River NJ 08753 Office: US Army CORADCOM Attn DRDCO-ILS-B Fort Monmouth NJ 07703

STILLMAN, MARY ELIZABETH, librarian; b. Phila., Oct. 31, 1929; d. Ernest E. and Rosalie (Burhans) S.; B.A., Wilson Coll., Chambersburg, Pa., 1950; M.S., Drexel U., Phila., 1952; Ph.D. (fellow 1963-65), U. Ill., 1966. Librarian, USAF, 1953-63, Export-Import Bank U.S., 1965-68; asst. prof. Drexel U., 1968-72; mem. faculty Albright Coll., Reading, Pa., 1972—, prof., librarian, 1975—; editor Drexel Library Quar., 1969-72; cons. research info. system Social and Rehab. Service, 1972-74. Mem. ALA (reviewer Subscription Books Bull. 1972—), Pa. Library Assn. (dir. pub. relations task force 1974—, editor bull. 1973—), Spl. Libraries Assn., Am. Soc. Info. Sci., AAUP. Contbr. articles to profl. jours. Home: 1516 Greenview Ave Reading PA 19601 Office: Albright Coll Reading PA 19604

STILLWAGGON, CAROL ANNE, nurse; b. Newark, Mar. 7, 1933; d. John James and Estelle Marie (Baldus) Stillwaggon; R.N., St. Mary Hosp., Passaic, N.J., 1953; B.S. in Nursing, Seton Hall U., 1959; M.S. in Nursing Edn., St. Louis U., 1961. Staff nurse, head nurse, supr., instr. St. Mary's Hosp., Passaic, 1953-59; asst. supr. intensive care St. Mary's Hosp., St. Louis, 1961-63; asso. dir. Sch. Nursing, St. Elizabeth Hosp., Elizabeth, N.J., 1965-68, asso. dir. hosp. nursing service, 1968-74; asst. adminstr. nursing service and edn. St. Barnabas Med. Center, Livingston, N.J., 1974—. Active North Caldwell Civic Assn., 1969-71. Mem. Am. Nurses Assn., Am. Soc. for Nursing Service Adminstrs., Sigma Theta Tau. Office: St Barnabas Med Center Old Short Hills Rd Livingston NJ 07039

STIMMEL, BARRY DAVID, physician; b. N.Y.C., Oct. 9, 1939; s. Abraham and Mabel D. (Bovit) S.; B.S., Bklyn. Coll., 1960; M.D., State U. N.Y., Bklyn., 1964; m. Barbara Ellen Barovick, June 6, 1970; 1 son, Alexander. Intern, Mt. Sinai Hosp., N.Y.C., 1964-65, resident, 1967-70; asso. dean acad. affairs, admissions and student affairs Mt. Sinai Sch. Medicine, City U. N.Y., 1971—, asso. prof. medicine, also mem. doctoral faculty Grad. Sch. Biol. Scis., 1975—; asso. attending cardiology Mt. Sinai Hosp., 1975—, exec. dir. methadone maintenance and aftercare treatment program, 1972—; mem. med. adv. bds., cons. med. programs. Served with USNR, 1965-67. Diplomate Nat. Bd. Med. Examiners, Am. Bd. Internal Medicine. Mem. Am. Assn. Higher Edn., Soc. Study Addiction to Alcohol and Other Drugs, Inst. Study Drug Addiction, Am., N.Y. Heart assns., Am., N.Y. State socs. internal medicine, Soc. Internal Medicine County N.Y. (exec. bd.), AAUP, Am. Coll. Cardiology. Author: Heroin Dependency: Medical, Social and Economic Aspects, 1975; Cardiovascular Effects of Mood Altering Drugs, 1979; also articles. Home: 1185 Park Ave New York City NY 10028 Office: Mt Sinai Sch Medicine 100th St and Fifth Ave New York City NY 10029

STINEBRING, RUSSELL CHARLES, elec. products co. exec.; b. Niagara Falls, N.Y., Aug. 23, 1927; s. Clifford Thomas and Signa Theresa (Arvidson) S.; B.S. in Phys. Sci., U. Buffalo, 1952; certificate Northeastern U., 1969; m. Ruth Jeannette Ambler, Jan. 22, 1949; children—David Robert, Cheryl Ann. Quality supr. nuclear fuels div. Sylvania Electric Co., Hicksville, N.Y., 1953-56; devel. engr. Westinghouse Corp., Pitts., 1956-62; sr. staff cons. Avco Corp., Lowell, Mass., 1962-69; mgr. materials evaluation research and devel. Gen. Electric Co., Phila., 1969-78; mgr. reliability Wilson Greatbatch Co., Clarence, N.Y., 1978—; cons. high temperature materials for Air Force Materials Lab., 1966-69. Served with USAAF, 1945-47. N.Y. State Bd. of Regents scholar, 1946-50. Mem. Nat. Materials Adv. Bd. Mem. Soc. for Nondestructive Testing, Am. Soc. Metals, ASTM. Mem. Christian Missionary Alliance Ch. (dir.). Contbr. articles to profl. jours. Home: 665 Mountain View Dr Lewiston NY 14092 Office: 10000 Wehrle Dr Clarence NY 14031

STINEHELFER, HAROLD EUGENE, assn. exec.; b. Bucyrus, Ohio, Apr. 22, 1924; s. Roy Ellsworth and Florence Elizabeth (Readyhough) S.; B.S. in Elec. Engring., Bklyn. Poly. Inst., 1948, M.S., 1951; m. Dorothy Edith Whiteman, June 3, 1944; children—Harold E., Carol E., Sharon Ruth Stinehelfer Brown. Research engr. Western Union Telegraph Co., N.Y.C., 1948-53; chief engr. frequency Standards Inc., Red Bank N.J., 1953-55; mem. tech. staff Bell Telephone Labs, Whippany, N.J., 1955-66; mem. tech. staff Microwave Assos., Inc., Burlington, Mass., 1966-67, mgr. computer sci., 1967—. Served with USAF, 1942-45. Mem. IEEE, Profl. Soc. Engrs. Club: Translation Assistance Soc. (pres. 1975-76). Home: 21 Daniel Dr Burlington MA 01803 Office: 63 South Ave Burlington MA 01803

STIRRAT, WILLIAM ALBERT, electronic engr.; b. Syracuse, N.Y., Nov. 5, 1919; s. Robert William and Doris (White) S.; B.S. in Physics, Rensselaer Poly. Inst., 1942, postgrad., 1949-50; postgrad. Rutgers U., 1951-58, Fairleigh Dickinson U., 1971; m. Bernice Amelia Wilson, July 13, 1958; children—Valerie Lynne, Dorothy Grace, William Ellsworth. With Gen. Electric Co., Schenectady, 1941-44; instr. physics Clarkson Coll. Tech., 1947-49; electronic engr. U.S. Army Electronics Research and Devel. Command. Ft. Monmouth, N.J., 1950—. Chmn. pub. relations Battleground dist. Monmouth council Boy Scouts Am., 1970-77. Mem. Old Crows, IEEE (sr., editor N.J. Coast sect. Scanner 1974-75), Internat. Platform Assn. Episcopalian. Club: Central Jersey Natural Food (pres. 1970). Author: (with Alex North) Unchained Melody, 1936. Asso. editor IEEE Transactions on Electromagnetic Compatability, 1970-76. Patentee in field. Contbr. articles to tech. jours. Home: 218 Overbrook Dr Freehold Township NJ 07728 Office: US Army EW Lab DELEW-V Fort Monmouth NJ 07703

STITELY, DORIS MAE, nurse; b. Irwin, Pa., Sept. 30, 1928; d. Arthur Edward and Hannah (Bullock) Stitely; R.N., Allegheny Gen. Hosp., 1949; B.S., U. Pitts., 1968, M.N., 1971. Nurse, Allegheny Gen. Hosp., Pitts., 1949-56, 64-75; head nurse U. Oreg. Med. Sch. Hosp., Portland, 1956-64; dir. nurses Lee Hosp., Johnstown, Pa., 1975—. Mem. Am., Pa. nurses assns., Am. Soc. Nursing Service Adminstrs., Am. Heart Assn., Hosp. Council Western Pa., Nat. League Nurses, Hosp. Assn. Pa., U. Pitts. Alumni Assn., Sigma Theta Tau. Methodist. Home: 1205 Norwood St Johnstown PA 15904 Office: Lee Hospital 320 Main St Johnstown PA 15901

STIVER, MYRTLE PEARL, nurse, bus. exec.; b. Osprey Twp., Ont., Can., Nov. 9, 1908; d. Henry and Abbie Olga (Smith) Stiver; R.N., Toronto Western Hosp., 1932; certificate Pub. Health Nursing, U. Toronto, 1940; B.S. in Nursing, Columbia, 1947. Individual practice nursing, Toronto, Ont., 1932-39; staff nurse Victorian Order Nursing, Toronto, 1940-41; staff nurse Toronto Dept. Health, 1941-43; nurse cons. Ont. Dept. Health, 1943-48; dir. pub. health nursing Ottawa Dept. Health, 1948-52; gen. sec.-treas. Canadian Nurses Assn., Montreal, 1952-60, hon. life mem., 1966—, exec. dir., Ottawa, 1960-63; exec. sec.-treas. Canadian Nurses' Found., 1963-64; co-owner Croft, Canadian handcraft shop, Baysville, Muskoka, Ont., 1963-75. Mem. nat. nursing adv com. Victorian Order Nurses Can., 1952-63, Can. Civil Def., 1952-62; mem. dental med. services adv. bd. Canadian govt., 1955-62; mem. vocat. adv. com. Dist. Muskoka Bd. Edn., 1969—. Bd. dirs. Canadian Citizenship Council. Recipient Centennial medal Govt. Can., 1968. Fellow Am. Pub. Health Assn.; mem. Bus. and Profl. Women's Club (v.p. Bracebridge 1969-71, pres. 1971-73), Zonta Internat. (pres. Ottawa 1961-63), Venerable Order St. John Jerusalem (comdr. sister), Ont. Pub. Health Assn. (hon. life mem.). Baptist (deacon). Club: University Women's (Toronto, Montreal). Author: (with Christine Livingston) Patient Care in the Home, 1965. Address: 360 Wellington St N Box 2112 Bracebridge ON Canada

STIVER, WILLIAM EARL, govt. ofcl.; b. Madison, Ind., Mar. 30, 1921; s. John Virgil and Anna Lynne (Ryker) S.; student Hanover Coll., 1947-49; B.S., U. Calif. at Berkeley, 1951, M.B.A., 1952; m. Norma A. Cull, June 11, 1944; children—Vicki, Raymond, Gena, John. With Fed. Ser., Bur. Census, Commerce Dept., Suitland, Md., 1952—, chief budget and finance div., 1963-73, dep. asso. adminstrn. Social and Econ. Stats. Adminstrn., 1973-75, spl. asst., asso. dir. for adminstrn. and field ops. Bur. of Census, 1975—. Served with AUS, 1942-43, 45-46. Recipient Silver medal Commerce Dept., 1969. Mem. Phi Beta Kappa, Beta Gamma Sigma. Home: 8104 Kerby Pkwy Ct Oxon Hill MD 20022 Office: Federal Office Bldg No 3 Suitland MD 20233

STOCKER, GERARD CRAIG, mgmt. engr.; b. Paterson, N.J., Dec. 13, 1944; s. Gerard Herman and Anna Marie (Abel) Stocker; B.Engring., Stevens Inst. Tech., 1965; M.S. in Mgmt. Engring., Newark Coll. Engring., 1968; m. Helen Mary Smith, Sept. 18, 1965; children—Gerard Craig II, Krisanne Laraine. Design engr. Chevron Oil Co., Perth Amboy, N.J., 1965-67; process engr. Witco Chem. Co., Oakland, N.J., 1967-69; sales mgr. Mesco Tectonics, Inc., Clifton, N.J., 1969-72; v.p. engring. and mktg. Thomas Assos., Inc., Westfield, N.J., 1972—; cons. liquified petroleum gas field. Registered profl. engr., N.J., N.Y., Ohio, Pa., Md., Del., W.Va., Ind., La., Mich., N.C. Mem. Nat. Soc. Profl. Engrs., Am. Inst. Chem. Engrs., Alpha Sigma Phi. Home: 1312 Dartmouth Terr Union NJ 07083 Office: 200 North Ave E Westfield NJ 07091

STOCKTON, WILLIAM JAMES, psychiatrist, psychoanalyst; b. Paris, Tex., July 30, 1929; s. William James and Charlotte (Landers) S.; M.D., U. Okla., 1952; m. Irma Louise Ford, Aug. 21, 1953; children—Rebecca Louise, Charlotte Kathryn, Deborah Lynn. Intern Walter Reed Gen. Hosp., Washington, 1956-57, resident, 1957-60; pvt. practice medicine specializing in psychiatry, psychoanalysis, Washington, 1964—; asso. clin. prof. George Washington U.; mem. teaching staff Georgetown U. Sch. Medicine, Walter Reed Gen. Hosp., St. Elizabeth's Hosp.; tng. and supervising analyst Balt.-D.C. Inst. for Psychoanalysis. Mem. citizens' com. D.C. Bar Assn. Served as maj. M.C., U.S. Army, 1955-64. Fellow Am. Psychiat. Assn.; mem. Washington Psychiat. Soc. (pres. 1977—), AMA, Am. Psychoanalytic Assn., Med. Soc. D.C., Balt.-D.C. Soc. and Inst. for Psychoanalysis. Democrat. Presbyterian. Home: 2715 Daniel Rd Chevy Chase MD 20015 Office: 1800 R St NW Washington DC 20009

STODDARD, WILLIAM BERT, JR., investment economist; b. Carbondale, Pa., Oct. 6, 1926; s. William Bert and Emily (Trautwein) S.; student Lafayette Coll., 1944-45; B.S., N.Y. U., 1950, A.M., 1952; m. Carol Marie Swartz, Feb. 28, 1970; 1 dau., Emily Coleman. Asst. chief accountant, budget dir. Hendrick Mfg. Co., Carbondale, Pa., 1952-54, asst. dir. prodn., 1956-68, also dir.; credit corr. U.S. Gypsum Co., N.Y.C., 1954-56; investment counselor, Carbondale, 1968-73, Ridgefield, Conn., 1973—; dir. First Nat. Bank Carbondale, 1968-73; bd. dirs. Lackawanna County Mfrs. Assn., Scranton, Pa., 1960-73. Treas., trustee Aldrich Museum Contemporary Art, Ridgefield, 1976—; bd. dirs. Ridgefield Library and Hist. Assn., 1977—, 1977—. Served with U.S. Army, 1946-47. Mem. Nat. Assn. Accountants, Am. Def. Preparedness Assn., Phi Alpha Kappa, Phi Delta Theta. Republican. Methodist. Clubs: N.Y. U. (N.Y.C.); Waccabuc (N.Y.) Country. Home: 59 Bridle Tr Ridgefield CT 06877 Office: 23 Catoonah St Ridgefield CT 06877

STOESSEL, HENRY KURT, artist; b. Chemnitz, Germany, Apr. 17, 1909; s. Henry and Anna (Scmiedicke) S.; came to U.S., 1910, naturalized, 1917; student Chgo. Art Inst., 1925-28, Ray Schs. (Chgo.), 1925-27, Grand Central Sch. Art (N.Y.C.), 1928-30, of Eric Pape, 1930-31, New Sch. Social Research, 1938-39; 1 dau. by previous marriage, Roxana Ellen. Free-lance illustrator, N.Y.C., 1930-31; art dir. Arnold Hoffman Studios, N.Y.C., 1931-38; head (founder) Stoessel Studios, Inc., N.Y.C., 1938-75; pres. Stoessel Graphics, Inc., 1960—; chmn. bd. Flight Arrivals Internat., Inc., N.Y.C.; v.p., dir. Pan Am. Lithographing Corp.; 21 paintings in collection at U.S. Air Force Mus., pvt. collections. contbr. illustrations to nat. mags. Recipient 61 awards for graphic design and fine art. Advanced pilot U.S. Power Squadrons, N.Y.C. Mem. Soc. of Illustrators, Long Beach Art Assn., Am. Artists Profl. League (Acrylic award 1976). Club: Salmagundi. Home: 116 Pinehurst Ave New York City NY 10033

STOETZNER, ERIC WOLDEMAR, newspaper exec.; b. Leipzig, Germany, Mar. 11, 1901; s. Woldemar and Emma (Wolf) S.; student U. Leipzig, 1922; Dr. Econ. Sci., Frankfurt am Main, 1925; m. Fridel Henning-Gronau, Dec. 20, 1927 (dec. Sept. 1967); 1 dau., Renée. Came to U.S., 1938, naturalized, 1944. Advt. dir., bus. mgr., mem. bd. Frankfurter Zeitung, Germany, 1930-38; bus. mgr. mag. of Schurz Found., Phila., 1939-43; research analyst of pub. N.Y. Times, 1944-45, dir. fgn. bus. promotion, 1945-50, dir. fgn. advt., 1950-70, internat. cons., 1970—. Bd. dirs. Stamford Forum World Affairs. Decorated chevalier de l'ordre du Merite Commercial de la France; officer's cross, German Order of Merit, 1953. Mem. Internat. Advt. Assn. (internat. v.p. 1956-59, hon. life). Quaker. Club: Rotary (chmn. internat. service div. N.Y.). Home: 376 Westover Rd Stamford CT 06902

STOFKO, KARL PETER, dentist; b. Bristol, Conn., Dec. 8, 1938; s. Charles Joseph and Isolde Louise (Jestinsky) S.; B.A., Gettysburg Coll., 1960; D.D.S., U. Mich., 1964. Gen. practice dentistry, Moodus, Conn., 1965—. Adviser, East Haddam (Conn.) Youth Recreation Council, 1972; mem., chmn. East Haddam Bicentennial Commn., 1974-77; mem. East Haddam Historic Dist. Commn., 1976—. Bd. dirs., sec. East Haddam Pub. Health Nursing and Community Health Service, 1974—. Mem. Middlesex County Dental Soc. (pres. 1971-72), Cappella Cantorum, East Haddam Hist. Soc. (v.p. 1974-77). Congregationalist (deacon 1967-74, pres. cemetery assn. 1972—, supt. 1972—, treas. ch. 1975—). Home: Orchard Rd East Haddam CT 06423 Office: WF Palmer Rd Moodus CT 06469

STOKELY, HUGH LAWSON, JR., economist; b. Newport, Tenn., Jan. 6, 1933; s. Hugh Lawson and Nellie Roberta (Runnion) S.; A.B., U. Tenn., 1952; postgrad. N.Y. U. Grad. Sch. Bus., 1966-67; 1 son, David Kerr. Asso. economist, cons. Far and Middle East, Chase Manhattan Bank, N.Y.C., 1962-67; chief economist Keystone Custodian Funds, Boston, 1967-70; sr. v.p., dir. investment research and econs. Girard Bank, Phila., 1970-75; v.p., dir. econs. Bradley Woods & Co., Inc., Washington, 1975-78; pres. Hugh Stokely Assos., 1978—; mem. econ. adv. bd. U.S. Dept. Commerce, 1973-74; pub. Washington Economist Monthly, 1975—; mem. bd. Fed. Statistics Users Council. Served to comdr. USNR, 1953-62. Fellow Fin. Analysts Fedn.; mem. N.Y. Soc. Security Analysts, Am. Econ. Assn., Am. Statis. Assn., Nat. Assn. Bus. Economists, Middle East Inst., Asia Soc., Greater Phila. C. of C. (past chmn. econ. adv. group, council regional econ. policy), Greater Boston C. of C. (past chmn. research com.), Phi Kappa Phi, Beta Gamma Sigma, Lambda Chi Alpha. Club: Fed. City (Washington). Office: 144 Duddington Pl SE Washington DC 20003

STOKES, WILLIAM E.D., JR., geologist, lawyer, economist; b. N.Y.C., Jan. 5, 1896; s. William E. D. and Rita de Alba (de Acosta) S.; student Yale (Sheffield Sci. Sch.), 1915-17; Chgo. Law Sch., 1920-23; m. Lucia H. Hobson, Aug. 16, 1938; children—Houston Hobson, Sylvia. Asso. with Fisher, Boyden, Kales, and Bell, 1923-24; pres. Chesapeake Western Ry. Co., 1926-37; pres. Kessto Corp., 1926-37, Onward Constrn. Co., 1926-47, Stokes Properties Inc., 1938—. Trustee, sec. Berkshire Country Day Sch.; trustee Berkshire Garden Center. Chmn. Lenox Park Commn. Served as lt. USNR, World War I, lt. comdr., World War II; central insp. officer Torpedo Program, U.S.S. Albemarle planning officer Navy Catalog Office. Mem. Econometric Soc., Am. Econ. Assn., Berzelius, S.R., Colonial Lords of Manors, Order 3 Crusades, Am. Inst. Mining and Metall. Engrs., Am. Mining Congress, Alpha Delta Phi, Phi Delta Phi. Clubs: University (Wash.); Union (N.Y.C.); Lenox (sec.), Radio Am. (fellow); Country of Pittsfield; Royal Bermuda Yacht. Author articles and pamphlets Aviation Survey, 1937, Origin of the Gold Pennyweight, 1938, Planetary Configurations and Stock Market Sentiment and others. Editorial writer Am. Friends Rhodesia News Letter; former feature editor La Liberte, New Eng. Jour., Green Mountain Rev., Up-State New Yorker. Address: Thistlewood Farm Box 864 Lenox MA 01240

STOLBA, LEONARD BIDWELL, architect; b. Middletown, Conn., June 13, 1932; s. Joseph Ladeslav and Emma Leona (Bidwell) S.; A.B., Wesleyan U., 1954; B.Arch., M.S. in Building Engring. and Constrn., Mass. Inst. Tech., 1963; m. Ann Dorothy McClure, May 4, 1955. Designer, Carl Koch & Assos., Boston, 1963; project architect S.S. Eisenberg Assos., Boston, 1963-66; office mgr. Lord & Den Hartog, Boston, 1966-67; tech. dir. architecture, planning Parsons, Brinckerhoff, Quade & Douglas, N.Y.C., 1967-70, resident architect, Toledo, 1974-76, asst. v.p., prodn. mgr., Boston, 1976—; v.p. design Spacemakers subs. Internat. Paper then div. AC&S, Canton, Mass., 1970-74; instr. Boston Archtl. Center. Served with USMCR, 1954-76, col., 1976. Registered architect, Mass., N.Y. State, Conn., R.I., Ohio. Mem. AIA (corporate), Soc. Mil. Engrs., Marine Corps Reserve Officers Assn. (past pres., Boston chpt.). Republican. Home: 5 Littles Ln Marshfield MA 02050 Office: Parson Brinckerhoff Quade & Douglas 177 Milk St Boston MA 02109

STOLLEY, RICHARD BROCKWAY, journalist; b. Peoria, Ill., Oct. 3, 1928; s. George Brockway and Stella (Sherman) S.; B.S. in Journalism, Northwestern U., 1952, M.S., 1953; LL.D. (hon.), Villa Maria Coll., Erie, Pa., 1976; m. Anne Elizabeth Shawber, Oct. 2, 1954; children—Lisa Anne, Susan Hope, Melinda Ruth, Martha Brockway. Sports editor Pekin (Ill.) Daily Times, 1944-46; reporter Chgo. Sun-Times, 1953; mem. staff Life mag., 1953-72, bur. chief Los Angeles, 1961-64, Washington, 1964-68, sr. editor, Europe, 1968-70, asst. mng. editor, N.Y.C., 1971-73; mng. editor People mag., N.Y.C., 1974—. Served with USN, 1946-48. Recipient Alumni Merit award Northwestern U., 1977. Mem. Am. Acad. Polit. and Social Sci., Nat. Press Club, Overseas Press Club, Kappa Tau Alpha, Sigma Delta Chi. Home: 6 Minerva Pl Old Greenwich CT 06870 Office: Time-Life Bldg New York City NY 10020

STOLNACKE, RICHARD ARTHUR, hosp. adminstr.; b. Worcester, Mass., July 8, 1929; s. Arthur John and Alma E. (Gustafson) S.; A.B., Clark U., 1952; M.S., Columbia U., 1957; m. Margaret E. Jones, Nov. 5, 1955; children—Elizabeth E., Jonathan Luce. Asst. adminstr. Lutheran Hosp. of Md., Balt., 1957-61, adminstr., 1961-63; adminstr. South Nassau Communities Hosp., Oceanside, N.Y., 1963-70; exec. dir., dir. United Hosp., Port Chester, N.Y., 1970-74, pres., 1974—; lectr. Columbia Sch., Pub. Health and Adminstrv. Medicine; preceptor Cornell U. Grad. Sch. Bus and Pub. Adminstrn.; guest faculty Hosp. Med. Staff Conf., U. Colo. Sch. Medicine. Chmn. L.I. Task Force Health Manpower, 1968; rep. Nassau/Suffolk Comprehensive Health Planning Council, 1968-70; mem. Nassau/Suffolk Hosp. Council; com. on exploring exec. bd. Nassau County council Boy Scouts Am., 1970. Bd. dirs. Nassau County Heart Assn. Served with AUS, 1953-55. Fellow Am. Pub. Health Assn., Am. Coll. Hosp. Adminstrs.; mem. Am. Hosp. Assn., Hosp. Assn. N.Y. (adv. com. on hosp. mgmt. engring. program, chmn. edn. com. 1972). Contbr. articles to profl. jours. Home and Office: Haywain Way Wellfleet MA 02667

STOLP, LAUREN ELBERT, speech pathologist; b. Sprague, Wash., July 10, 1921; s. Charles Albert and Sarah Christine (Campbell) S.; A.B., Eastern Wash. State U., Cheney, 1946; M.S., Ind. State U., 1951; m. Nadine McWhorter, Jan. 29, 1946 (dec. 1976); children—Lauren Elyce Stolp Nasseri, Marla Eve Stolp Sullivan; m. 2d., Barbara Duncombe Lang, Mar. 3, 1978. Pvt. practice speech pathology Houston, 1947-49; instr. spl. edn. Ind. State U., Terre Haute, 1949-53; dir. Lower and Middle Schs., Pa. Sch. for Deaf, Phila., 1953-61, prin. Middle Sch., 1961-68; head speech dept. All Saints' Hosp., Phila., 1971—; dir. Lauren E. Stolp Assos., speech pathologists, Roslyn, Pa., 1976—; cons. in field. Pres. Upper Moreland High Sch. Home and Sch. Assn., 1964-66. Served with USCGR, 1942-45. Fellow Am. Assn. Mental Deficiency; mem. Am., Pa. speech and hearing assns., Am. Acad. Pvt. Practice Speech Pathology and Audiology, Am. Forestry Assn., Acoustical Soc. Am. Republican. Methodist. Club: Lions (pres. Upper Moreland, Pa., 1964-65). Home: 14 Laughlin Ln Philadelphia PA 19118 Office: 2347 Kenderton Ave Roslyn PA 19001

STOLTING, RICHARD RONALD, market and media research adminstr.; b. Bklyn., May 27, 1947; s. William Henry and Theresa Emma (Pierro) S.; B.S. in Psychology, Fordham U., 1968; M.S. in Indsl. and Consumer Psychology, Purdue U., 1970; m. Jean Marie Sutherland, Sept. 8, 1973; children—Jennifer, Laura, Deborah. Aptitude tester Johnson O'Connor Research Found., N.Y.C., 1966-68; instr. psychology, in charge testing for introductory psychology program Purdue U., West Lafayette, Ind., 1969-70; mktg. research analyst Lever Bros. Co., N.Y.C., 1969-70; survey research project dir. Appel, Haley Fouriezos Research Co., N.Y.C., 1971-72; research cons. Haley, Overholser & Assos., New Canaan, Conn., 1973-74; project dir. AHF Mktg. Research Co., N.Y.C., 1974-76; v.p. Simmons Market Research Bur., Inc., N.Y.C., 1976—. Mem. Am. Psychol. Assn. (asso.). Author: A Teacher's Guide to Psychology: A Social Approach, 1970. Home: 40 Maple St Garden City NY 11530 Office: 219 E 42d St New York City NY 10017

STOLZ, ALAN JAMES, youth camp exec.; b. N.Y.C., May 7, 1931; s. Irving H. and Pearl M. (Maltz) S.; A.B., Wabash Coll., Ind., 1953; postgrad. Columbia, 1954-55, N.Y.U., 1953-54; D.Hum. (hon.); m. Sandra Grace Miller, Apr. 8, 1956; children—Gary, Maryann. Partner, officer several real estate cos., N.Y.C., 1952—; pres. Camp Cody Inc., West Ossipee, N.H., 1960—; cons. youth camping legislation U.S. Congress, White House, HEW; guest lectr., panelist on youth camping. Nat. sec. Nat. Camping Edn. Com., 1971-75; active Boy Scouts Am., 35 yrs. Served to sgt. Ordnance Corps, AUS, 1955-57. Mem. N.H. Camp Dirs. Assn. (pres. 1970-75), New Eng. (bd. dirs. 1970—), N.Y. (bd. dirs. 1972—) camping assns., New Eng. (bd. dirs. 1971—), N.Y. (bd. dirs. 1970—) assns. pvt. camps, Am. Camping Assn. (nat. pub. relations cons. 1971—, nat. dir. 1973—, dir. pub. relations N.Y. 1973—, nat. legis. chmn. 1973—). Author documents and proclamations pertaining to youth camping. Contbr. articles to profl. jours. Home: 5 Lockwood Circle Westport CT 06880 Office: 529 Fifth Ave New York City NY 10017 and Ossipee Lake Rd West Ossipee NH 03890

STOLZ, JONATHAN LAVERY, radiologist; b. Phila., Nov. 21, 1942; s. John Conwell and Vivian (Lavery) S.; B.S., Trinity Coll., 1965; M.D., Temple U., 1969; postgrad. U. Pa., 1970-73; m. Sandra Vincent, Apr. 20, 1974; 1 dau., Amanda Keatley. Intern Charity Hosp., New Orleans, 1969-70; resident and fellow in radiology U. Pa. Hosp., Phila., 1970-73, chief resident, 1973, jr. staff radiologist, 1973-74; practice medicine specializing in radiology, Phila., 1973—; asst. instr. radiology U. Pa., 1970-73, instr., 1973-74; staff radiologist Community Gen. Hosp., Reading, Pa., 1974—, chief dept. radiology, 1974—, dir. outpatient service, 1975—; attending radiologist Reading Rehab. Hosp., 1975—. Diplomate Am. Bd. Radiology. Mem. Am. Coll. Radiology, Pa., Berks County med. socs., Radiol. Soc. N. Am., AMA, Pa. Radiol. Soc., Pa. Soc. Nuclear Medicine, Daniel Boone Nat. Found. (dir.), Psi Upsilon. Republican. Episcopalian. Contbr. articles to med. jours. Home: 18 Junco Dr Wyomissing PA 19610 Office: Dept Radiology Community Gen Hosp Reading PA 19601

STONE, AL, hotel exec.; b. Fort Anne, N.Y., Dec. 30, 1927; s. Ercelle Carrol and Geraldine (Bradway) S.; grad. Profl. Sch. Bus., 1973; m. Joan Frances Hotaling, May 28, 1949; 1 son, Bradley H. Asst. mgr. Hotel McAlpin, N.Y.C., 1948-52; mgr. Woodstock Hotel, N.Y.C., 1952-55; mgr. motor hotels Marriott Industries, Washington, 1955-61; gen. mgr. Summit (N.J.) Suburban Hotel, 1961-72, pres., gen. mgr., 1972—, also dir.; dir. ops. Sheraton Northlake Inn, Atlanta. Served with USMCR, 1944-46. Recipient community service award Summit Kiwanis Club, 1974. Mem. N.J. Hotel and Motel Assn. (dir. 1973—, v.p. 1976—, pres.'s club award 1974-76, presdl. meritorious achievement award 1978). Club: Masons. Home: 54 Robbins Ave Berkeley Heights NJ 07922 Office: 570 Springfield Ave Summit NJ 07901

STONE, ALAN JOHN, mfg. co. exec.; b. Dansville, N.Y., Sept. 9, 1940; s. Guthrie Boyd and Doris Irene (Wolfanger) S.; B.S. in Mech. Engring., Rochester Inst. Tech., 1963; M.B.A., U. Pitts., 1964; m. Sandra Barber, Aug. 22, 1964; children—Teri, Timothy, Michael. Engring. aide Xerox Corp., Webster, N.Y., 1960-63; gen. mgr. plastic component div. Stone Conveyor Co., Inc., Honeoye, N.Y., 1964-67, v.p. sales, 1968; co-founder, pres. dir. Stone Constrn. Equipment Inc., Honeoye, 1969—; founder, pres., dir. Canandaigua Apts. Inc. (N.Y.), 1968—; v.p., dir. Baker Rental Service, Inc., 1973-76; dir. Bunnington Corp., 1972-77. Mem. Town of Richmond (N.Y.) Planning Bd., 1970-75, chmn., 1970-71; mem. Honeoye (N.Y.) Central Sch. Bd. Edn., 1971-76, pres. 1973-74; chmn. Cub Scout com. 1975-77; mem. Ontario County Overall Economic Devel. Com., 1976—. Mem. Honeoye C. of C. (chmn. indsl. com. 1974—), Rochester C. of C., Assn. M.B.A. Execs. Mem. Ch. of Christ. Patentee in field. Home: Egypt Valley Rd Honeoye NY 14471 Office: 32 E Main St Honeoye NY 14471

STONE, ALBERT HENRY, sales and operations exec.; b. Englewood, N.J., Jan. 27, 1928; s. Benjamin and Sara Gertrude (Dorf) S.; student Denison U., 1945-46, Union Coll., Schenectady, 1946-47, Rutgers U., 1947-50; m. Elinore Francine Fishman, Aug. 26, 1951; 1 son, Steven Austin. Buyer, Bamberger's Dept. Store, 1954-59; mdse. mgr. Grand Union Co., 1959-67; with Hoffritz Cutler Co., 1967-75; exec. v.p. Dalia, Inc. div. Joyeria y Plateria de Guernica, Carlstadt, N.J., 1975-78; internat. sales mgr. New Hermes, Inc., 1978—; dir. Samson Mfg. Co. Mem. Bergen County Democratic Com., 1962-73. Served with USNR, 1945-57. Mem. Housewares Club N.Y., China and Glass Assn., N.J. Meadowlands C. of C., Orgn. for Rehab. and Tng. Clubs: Masons, Lions. Home: 105 Hudson Ave Tenafly NJ 07670 Office: 20 Cooper Sq New York NY 10003

STONE, ALLAN, licensing and TV producers co. exec.; b. N.Y.C., Jan. 5, 1926; ed. Hamilton Coll., Clinton, N.Y., 1941-43, N.Y. State Maritime Acad., Fort Schuyler, 1943-44; m. Barbara Stone, May 9, 1947; 3 children. Asst. to pres. Gallery Artists Co., N.Y.C., 1946-47; sr. v.p. Howdy Doody merchandising, promotion, and exploitation Kagran Corp., N.Y.C., 1947-55; founder, pres. Stone Merchandising Assos., N.Y.C., 1955-60; founder, pres. Licensing Corp. Am., N.Y.C., 1960-70; partner, pres. Media Assos. Inc., N.Y.C., 1970-72; founder, pres., chmn. Hamilton Projects Inc., N.Y.C., 1972—. Served with U.S. Mcht. Marine, USNR, 1943-46. Home: 13 Grenfell Dr Great Neck NY 11020 Office: Hamilton Projects Inc Olympic Tower 645 Fifth Ave New York NY 10022

STONE, CARL HENRY, computer co. exec.; b. Yankton, S.D., July 2, 1924; s. Carl B. and Ruth L. (Fernald) S.; B.A., Miami U., Oxford, Ohio, 1949; B.Arch., U. Tex., 1950, M.S., 1960; m. Viviane Bomanji, 1945; children—Claudia Anne, Douglas Fernald. Engr., mgr. Union Carbide Nuclear Co., Oak Ridge, 1952-62; mgr. bus. sci., fin. div. Gen. Electric Co., Lynn, Mass., 1965-67; dir. info. processing Bull-Gen. Electric Co., Paris, 1967-70; fin. advisor Honeywell-Bull Corp., Paris, 1970-75, bus. planning N. Am. ops. Honeywell Corp., Waltham, Mass., 1976-77; bus. strategist Digital Equipment Corp., Maynard, Mass., 1977—; dir. Firepro, Inc., Wellesley, Mass., 1975—; cons. in field. Mem. Am. Mgmt. Assn., Assn. Computing Machinery, Soc. Mfg. Engrs., Am. Inst. Indsl. Engrs., SAR. Clubs: Cercle Interallie (Paris); Wellesley, Wellesley Country. Home: 81 Albion Rd Wellesley Hills MA 02181 Office: Digital Equipment Corp Parker St Maynard MA 01754

STONE, CARLETON GOSHEN, artist; b. Biddeford, Maine, Sept. 30, 1911; s. Ernest Cole and Mary Andrews (Goshen) S.; student Pittsfield Artists Sch., Internat. Sch., Scranton, Pa.; pupil T. Bailey, H. Cowgill, Walker; m. Florence I. Weir, May 1, 1965; children—Carletina I. Stone Brann, Gail W. Truitt. Employed in various govt. positions, intermittently, 1939-63; employed with law enforcement agys., intermittently, 1957-64; pvt. art tchr., 1967—; exhibited in one man shows including: Fenway Art Center, Albany, N.Y., 1929, Chabot Acres Recreation Bldg., Vallejo, Calif., 1947; exhibited in group shows including: Pittsfield (Mass.) Art Mus., 1928, Rams Gallery, Oakland, Calif., 1957, Brick Store Mus., Kennebunk, Maine, 1967, Elsinor Gallery, Denmark, Maine, 1965, Tool Shed Gallery, Norway, Maine, 1965, Carriage House Gallery, Portsmouth, N.H., 1974, Stonecrest Fine Arts Gallery, Cornish, Maine, 1973, Portland (Maine) Mus. Fine Arts; represented in permanent collections including: Maine State Museum, Augusta, also numerous pvt. collections. Served with U.S. Army, 1932-33. Mem. Internat. Soc. Artists (charter), Soc. N. Am. Artists, York Art Assn. Home: PO Box 81 Route 113 East Baldwin ME 04024

STONE, DIANE LIPSON, psychiatrist; b. N.Y.C., Aug. 1, 1945; d. George and Evelyn Gloria (Goldman) Lipson; A.B., U. Pa., 1966; M.D., Columbia U., 1970; m. Jeffrey B. Stone, May 12, 1974. Intern, Roosevelt Hosp., N.Y.C., 1970-71; resident Columbia-Presbyn. Med. Center, N.Y.C., 1971-74; dir. psychiat. emergency services Roosevelt Hosp., N.Y.C., 1974-77; asso. psychiatrist Columbia Presbyn. Hosp., N.Y.C., 1977—. Mem. Am. Psychiat. Assn., N.Y. County Med. Soc. Jewish.

STONE, ERNEST LYNN, educator; b. New Haven, Nov. 25, 1907; s. Wilbur Clayton and Emma (Benedict) S.; B.F.A., Yale U., 1936; postgrad. Tchrs. Coll. Columbia U., 1940; m. Semmeh Hall Sanjiyan, Jan. 11, 1928;children—Mary Victoria (Mrs. Russell Edward Leary), Ernest Lynn, Judith Cushing (Mrs. Leon Vincent Grabar). Art tchr. Bassett Jr. High Sch., New Haven, 1931-38, Hillhouse High Sch., New Haven, 1938-40; supr. art edn. New Haven Pub. Schs., 1940-70; asst. prof. art So. Conn. State Coll., 1943-61. Conn. coordinator for art in opera N.Y. Met. Opera Guild, 1950-60. Recipient 1st medal award, mural painting Soc. Beaux Arts-Architects (N.Y.), 1927, 29. Mem. Nat. Ret. Tchrs. Assn., Conn. Arts Assn., Assn. Ret. Tchrs. Conn., Conn. Watercolor Soc., Conn. Soc. Founders and Patriots (gov. 1965-66). Clubs: New Haven Paint and Clay (pres. 1949-52), Civitan (pres. 1961-62, dir. 1962-68, 72-78), Yale, New Haven Congregational (pres. 1945-46). Home: 139 Beecher Rd Woodbridge CT 06525

STONE, JAMES LESTER, social worker; b. Syracuse, N.Y., May 31, 1940; s. Lester Herbert and Mary (Cowley) S.; B.A., Syracuse U., 1962, M.S.W., 1964; m. Joan McDermott Borzelle, Aug. 5, 1967; children—Jeffrey Borzelle, Michael McDermott, Andrew Cowley. Onondaga County dep. dir. detention care, Syracuse, 1962-63; tchr. Fayetteville-Manlius (N.Y.) Schs., 1964-65; asst. dir. Edmond Fitzgerald Start Center, N.Y. State Div. Youth, Middletown, 1965-67; dir. Rochester (N.Y.) Urban Youth Home, 1967-73; asst. supt. N.Y. State Div. for Youth Tng. Sch., Industry, 1973-74, supt., 1974-78; dir. Livingston County Dept. Mental Health, Mt. Morris, N.Y., 1978—; lectr., Rochester Inst. Tech., 1968-71; cons. Community Service Bur. Upstate N.Y., 1968-71; field faculty Syracuse U., 1969—; mem. adv. com. Youth Residence Center Greater Rochester; mem. youth services system adv. com. Rochester-Monroe County Youth Bd. Chmn. tng. subcom. Monroe County Children's Detention Com.; exec. bd., chmn law com. Assn. for Community Transitional Services. Mem. N.Y. Air N.G., 1962. Mem. Am. Group Psychotherapy Assn., Nat. Assn. Social Workers, Am. Orthopsychiat. Assn., Acad. Certified Social Workers, Council Social Agys. (del. assembly 1967—). Home: 66 Yorktown Dr Webster NY 14580 Office: Murray Hill Mount Morris NY 14510

STONE, JUSTIN HOWARD, dentist; b. Kings County, N.Y., Apr. 5, 1931; s. Louis and Sarah (Goldberg) S.; B.A. cum laude, U. Buffalo, 1952; D.D.S., U. Pa., 1955; m. Diana Joy Lesgold, Dec. 23, 1956; children—Douglas, Alison, Amanda. Intern, Kingsbrook Med. Center, Bklyn., 1957-58, resident anesthesiology, 1958-59; pvt. dental practice, Newark, 1960-66, East Orange, N.J., 1966—; chief pain control, sr. attending, v.p. Dental Health Center, Newark Beth Israel Hosp., 1963—. Chmn. dentist's div. United Fund of Newark and West Hudson, 1962; mem. exec. bd. Nat. Found. Dentistry for Handicapped, 1976—, chmn. Newark-Essex coordinating com. Campaign of Concern Dentistry for Handicapped; dental service for the handicapped St. Barnabas Med. Center, Livingston, N.J. Served with Dental Corps, USNR, 1955-57. Fellow N.J. Acad. Medicine, Am. Dental Soc. Anesthesiology, Am. Soc. for Advancement Gen. Anesthesia in Dentistry; mem. N.J. Dental Soc. Anesthesiology (pres. 1970-71), Acad. Dentistry for Handicapped (treas. 1976-77, v.p. 1978—), Am., N.J. (exec. bd.) socs. dentistry for children Am. Dental Assn., N.J. Dental Soc., Internat. Anesthesia Research Soc., U. Buffalo (life), U. Pa. alumni socs., Sigma Alpha Mu, Sigma Epsilon Delta, Alpha Omega. Home: 35 Arden Rd Mountain Lakes NJ 07046 Office: 123 S Munn Ave East Orange NJ 07018

STONE, RICHARD THOMAS, bank ofcl.; b. Bridgeport, Conn., Mar. 7, 1948; s. James J. and Violet Elsie (Damer) S.; B.S. in Materials Engring., U. New Haven, 1972; m. Cynthia Jane Elwell, Nov. 24, 1972; 1 son, Geoffrey Lawrence. Asst. dept. head bank bldgs. Conn. Nat. Bank, Bridgeport, 1972-75, supt. of bldgs., 1975-78, bank bldgs. officer, 1978—. Lector and usher St. Augustine's Cathedral, Bridgeport, 1966—, mem. parish council, 1971-73; v.p. Diocese of Bridgeport Pastoral Council, 1974—. Mem. Assn. Energy Engrs., Nat. Rifle Assn. Roman Catholic. Home: 97 Anson St Bridgeport CT 06606 Office: 888 Main St Bridgeport CT 06602

STONE, ROBERT ELDRED, archeol. assn. adminstr., mech. engr.; b. Chester, N.H., July 26, 1929; s. Harold I. and Anna L. (Ahlberg) S.; student Merrimack Coll., 1955-57; m. Dorothy Harriette Fullonton, Feb. 3, 1951 (div. 1977); children—Dennis Wayne, Kathy Ann. Asso. engr. Western Electric Co., N. Andover, Mass., 1957—; pres., founder Mystery Hill Caves, Inc., N. Salem, N.H., 1957—; research dir., 1957; founder New Eng. Antiquities Research Assn., 1964, pres., 1964-75, chmn. bd., 1964-75, editor Newsletter, 1957; lectr. Am. pre-historic culture NBC-TV program, 1970; cons. Mystery Hill documentary In Search of, ABC-TV, 1977. Served with USCG, 1949-52. Mem. N.H., Conn., Eastern States archaeol. socs., Western Electric Pioneers. Episcopalian. Contbr. articles on Am. ancient history to profl. jours. Address: NEARA 29 Highland Ave Derry NH 03038

STONER, FERN GOODE, sch. ofcl.; b. Forest City, N.C., Feb. 22, 1924; d. Roland Erastus and Julia Elice (Harton) Goode; student Gardner-Webb Coll., 1941-43; B.A., Berea Coll., 1945; M.A., George Washington U., 1968 m. Bruce Maynard Stoner, Dec. 18, 1976; children by previous marriage—Victor W., Aaron A. Tchr. English, Waynesville, N.C. schs., 1945-47; with Bell Telephone Co., Charlotte, N.C., 1947-48; tchr. Fayetteville, N.C., 1948-52, Forestville, Md., 1952-53, Suitland, Md., 1953-55; tchr. French, Montgomery Blair High Sch., Silver Spring, Md., 1955-57; counselor Bowie (Md.) Jr. High Sch., 1967-68, Beltsville (Md.) Jr. High Sch., 1968-72, Bladensburg (Md.) Sr. High Sch., 1972-74, Kent Jr. High Sch., Landover, Md., 1975—. Mem. Am. Personnel and Guidance Assn., Am. Sch. Counselors Assn., Assn. Counselors and Ednl. Suprs. Democrat. Episcopalian. Home: 8400 Potomac Valley Court Oxon Hill MD 20021 Office: Kent Junior High School Landover MD 20786

STONIER, CHARLES EDWARD, economist, planner; b. Hamburg, Germany, Nov. 8, 1920; s. John and Elaine (Cooper-Meese) S.; B.S. cum laude, Syracuse U., 1947; M.B.A., U. Pa., 1948, Ph.D., 1955; m. Margaret Adams, Sept. 1, 1946; children—Jennifer Sue Mercer, Mark Adams (dec.), Richard Todd, David John, Peter Scott. Lectr., Rutgers U., 1948-50; asst. prof. transp. Pa. State U., 1950-54; asst. prof., asso. prof. econs. Hofstra U., 1954-63, dir. Center Bus. and Urban Studies, 1966-67; exec. dir. Nassau County Planning Commn., Mineola, N.Y., 1963-66; cons. Ford Found., Calcutta, India, 1967-68; sr. economist, overseas cons. assignments Louis Berger, Inc., East Orange, N.J., 1968-74; economist S.E. Asia Agy. for Transport and Communications Devel., 1974—. Vis. prof. econs. Queens Coll., N.Y., 1964-65. Mem. Nassau-Suffolk Regional Planning Bd., 1965-66; research dir. Joint Legislative Com. Edn. Law State N.Y., 1965-66. Served with AUS, 1943-45. Mem. Am. Econ. Assn., Soc. Internat. Devel., Internat. Fedn. Housing and Planning, Am. Soc. Planning Ofcls. Contbr. numerous articles to profl. jours. Home: care Cooper 260 Marlborough Rd Brooklyn NY 11226 Office: SEATAC Box 1078 Kuala Lumpur Malaysia

STOOLMAN, HERBERT LEONARD, pub. relations co. exec.; b. Newark, Apr. 6, 1917; s. Abe C. and Ida H. (Sinar) S.; A.B., Catawba Coll., 1937; B.S., Temple U., 1939; postgrad. Harvard, 1938; m. Sarah Janice Cutler, Apr. 6, 1944; children—Cathy Lynn (Mrs. Richard Schwartz), Robert Henry. Pub., East Camden Newspapers, 1941-57; pres. Stoolman Assos., Camden, N.J., 1946—; dir. pub. relations Camden County, N.J., 1953—. Mem. Camden County Econ. Devel. Commn., 1963—, Camden County Cultural and Heritage Commn., 1973—. Served with USAF, 1942-46. Recipient Nat. award Nat. Assn. of Counties, 1969, 72, 78; Nat. award Am. Indsl. Devel. Council, 1963. Mem. Am., N.J. hosps. pub. relations assns., S. Jersey, Phila. pub. relations assns., N.J. Press Assn., N.J. Indsl. Devel. Assn., Camden County Ethics Commn., Am., N.J. assns. county pub. relations officers. Lion (dir. pub. relations). Home: 811 Redman Ave Haddonfield NJ 08033 Office: 315 Cooper St Camden NJ 08102

STOOP, NORMA MCLAIN, author, photographer; b. Panama, C.Z.; d. Harry Edward and Gladys (Brandon) McLain; student Penn Hall Jr. Coll., Carnegie Inst. Tech., New Sch., N.Y. U.; m. William J. Stoop, Jr., Sept. 20. Contbg. editor Dance Mag. and After Dark, N.Y.C., 1969-71, asso. editor, 1971—, sr. editor After Dark, 1978—; also photographer, film critic. Recipient Dance awards Dance Tchrs. Club of Boston, Dancing Ambassador of Friendship, 1977. Mem. Dance Critics Assn., Nat. Acad. TV Arts and Scis. (N.Y. chpt.), Poetry Soc. Am., Overseas Press Club, Nat. Press Women, Dance Masters Am. Contbr. poems to Tex. Quar., Chgo. Rev., N.Y. Times, Arts in Society, Quest, Atlantic Monthly, Christian Sci. Monitor, others, 1958—, essays to Book Week in N.Y. Herald Tribune; represented in Best Poems of 1973; dance photog. exhibit Harvard U., 1975. Home: 1 Lincoln Plaza 23D New York City NY 10023 Office: 10 Columbus Circle New York City NY 10019

STOOPS, JOHN, educator; b. Tarentum, Pa., Mar. 10, 1925; s. Charles Crawford and Ellen (Street) S.; B.S. in Edn., State Coll., California, Pa., 1948; M.S., U. Pa., 1949, Ed.D., 1960; m. Muriel Brugger, Aug. 2, 1947; children—Cathy Ellen, John Albert, Judy Lynn, Charles Billingsly. Tchr. Claymont (Del.) pub. schs., 1948-54; sr. high sch. prin., dir. adult edn. Neshaminy Sch. Dist., Langhorne, 1954—, asst. supt., 1961-62; instr. grad. courses Lehigh U., Bethlehem, 1959-61, prof. edn., head dept., 1962—, dean Sch. Edn., 1966-76, Distinguished prof. philosophy, 1975—, dir. Inst. for Ednl. Studies and Evaluation, 1975—; pres. Schoolmaster's Inc., 1975—; dir. elementary sch. assembly Middle States Assn., 1978—; coordinator Center for Ednl. Diagnosis, 1977—; ednl. cons. instns. higher edn., govt. agys., accrediting bodies; project dir. study elementary sch. evaluation Middle States Assn. Colls. and Schs. Mem. Pa. Comm. for Humanities in Schs., 1962—, Pa. Adv. Com. on Tchr. Edn., 1963—; chmn. programming Lehigh Valley Ednl. TV. Served with USNR, 1943-46. Mem. Philosophy of Edn. Soc., Nat. Assn. Secondary Sch. Prins., Assn. Supervision and Curriculum Devel., Phi Delta Kappa. Author: Religious Values in Education, 1967; Education of Inner Man; Philosophy and Education in Western Civilization; Histories of Education from Summeria to Modern Times; Guide to Preparation of a Philosophy of Education; contbr. articles to profl. jours. Home: 454 Linden Ave Coopersburg PA 18036 Office: Lehigh U Bethlehem PA 18015

STORM, JOHN HERSHEY, journalist; b. Cleve., Nov. 24, 1935; s. John Manley and Evelyn Claire (Hershey) S.; student (Scholar) Northwestern U., 1954-55; B.A. in Journalism (Scholar), U. Tulsa, 1957; postgrad. George Washington U., 1961-62; m. Janet Elizabeth Greeley, Nov. 25, 1967. Reporter, editor Tulsa Daily World, 1957-59, Washington Evening Star, 1959-62; copy editor, spl. project editor, N.Y. Times, N.Y.C., 1962-65, nat. news, 1962-75, editor Sunday real estate sect., 1975—. Solo violist Tulsa Philharmonic, 1955-58. Served with U.S. Army, 1959. Club: Marshall Chess. Home: 55 Park Ave New York City NY 10016

STORM, MARY ELIZABETH, lawyer; b. Frederick, Md., Jan. 11, 1940; d. Edward Daniels and Mildred Elizabeth (Raum) S.; student St. John's Coll., Annapolis, 1958-60; B.A., Hood Coll., 1962; J.D., George Washington U., 1966. Admitted to Md. bar, 1967; mem. firm Storm & Storm, Frederick and Emmitsburg, Md., 1967—; instr. estate planning Frederick Community Coll., 1969-70, mem. adv. com. asso. degree nursing program, 1970-77, recorder, 1970-72. Mem. LWV, 1967—, Hosp. Aux., 1967—; mem. Md. Comprehensive Health Planning Council, 1971-77, vice chmn., 1975-77; mem. Md. Statewide Health Coordinating Council, 1977—, vice chmn., 1977—; 2d v.p. Md. Young Democrats, 1961; bd. dirs., sec. Girl Scout council Central Md., 1972-73; bd. dirs. Frederick Orgn. for Rehab., 1970-71. Mem. Nat. Assn. Women Lawyers (del. Md. 1969-73), Frederick County (rec. sec. 1971—), Am., Md. (council, com. family and juvenile law

777 WHO'S WHO IN THE EAST

1968-70) bar assns., AAUW, Am. Health Planning Assn. (dir. 1976—), Md. Fedn. Women's Clubs (dir. jr. clubs 1970-72), Phi Delta Delta. Democrat. Presbyterian. Clubs: Hood, Frederick Women's Civic, Zonta (pres. 1971-72, gov. dist. 3 1976-78). Home: 321 S Market St Frederick MD 21701 Office: 114-A W Church St Frederick MD 21701

STORROW, JAMES J., JR., mag. publisher; b. Boston, May 7, 1917; s. James J. and Margaret (Rotch) S.; B.S., Harvard, 1940, postgrad., 1940-41; m. Patricia Blake, June 26, 1940 (dec. May 1962); children—Gerald B., Peter, James J., Margaret R.; m. 2d, Linda Eder Jamieson, Dec. 15, 1962. Dir., North Shore Players, Inc., Marblehead, Mass., 1939-41; office mgr., asst. treas. Baush Machine Tool Co., Springfield, Mass., 1941-43; treas. Brooks Green Co., Boston, 1946, Gen. Microfilm Co., Cambridge, Mass., 1947—, The Stamp Show, Inc., N.Y.C., 1953-55, Trident Films, Inc., N.Y.C., 1961—; pres. Henry Thayer Co., Cambridge, 1947-53; pub. The Nation mag., N.Y.C., 1965—; dir. Farrar, Straus & Giroux, Inc., Mid Atlantic Fund Inc. Chmn. Joint Council on Fgn. Affairs, Boston, 1947; mem. Brookline (Mass.) Democratic Town Com., 1958-61; bd. dirs. Housing Assn. Met. Boston, 1948-53, Cath. Guild for All the Blind, Newton, Mass., The Med. Found.; trustee New Eng. Coll. Pharmacy, 1956-62. Served with USNR, 1943-45. Clubs: Coffee House, The Players, Century (N.Y.C.); Harvard (Boston and N.Y.C.). Home: 25 East End Ave New York City NY 10028 Office: 333 6th Ave New York City NY 10014

STORZER, GERALD HOWARD, educator; b. Green Bay, Wis., Feb. 20, 1938; s. Charles Alfred and Mary Agnes (Stich) S.; B.A. magna cum laude, Lawrence U., 1960; postgrad. U. De Laval (Que.), 1959; postgrad. (Fulbright fellow) U. de Montpellier (France), 1960-61; M.A. (Woodrow Wilson fellow), U. Wis., 1963, Ph.D., 1967. Instr. French, U. Wis., Madison, 1964-65; instr. French studies Brown U., Providence, 1965-67; vis. prof. Tougaloo (Miss.) Coll., 1966-67; asst. prof. French, Brown U., Providence, 1967-73; asst. prof. French, Bklyn. Coll., City U. N.Y., 1973-76; asso. prof. Bklyn. Coll. City U. N.Y., 1977—; instr. English, Montpellier, France, 1960-61, Montreal, Can., 1969-70; leader to France expt. in internat. living, 1961, 62; cons. Tougaloo Coll., 1966, Talladega Coll., 1968. Howard Found. grantee, 1969-70; Am. Philos. Soc. grantee, 1969-70. Mem. Modern Lang. Assn., African Studies Assn., African Lit. Assn., City U. N.Y. Profl. Staff Congress, Pi Delta Phi. Author: Dictionary of Modern French Idioms, 1976; contbr. articles in field to profl. jours. Home: 416 W 23d St New York City NY 10011 Office: Dept Modern Langs Brooklyn Coll City U NY Brooklyn NY 11210

STOSSER, ROBERT JAMES, data processing co. exec.; b. N.Y.C., Feb. 28, 1940; s. James Raymond and Elizabeth Anna (Miles) S.; B.S. in Edn. and English, Fordham U., 1966; postgrad. Fairfield U., 1975; m. Ann Harkins, Dec. 28, 1963; children—Kathleen, Mary Beth, Geralyn. Br. mgr. Prentice-Hall, Inc., Englewood Cliffs, N.J., 1965-70, Itel Corp., White Plains, N.Y., 1970-72; nat. sales mgr. Numerax, Inc., Englewood Cliffs, 1972-73; regional v.p. sales ADP, Inc., N.Y.C., 1973—. Served with AUS, 1959-62. Named to Sales Hall of Fame, ADP, Inc., 1978. Roman Catholic. Home: 4 Winthrop Rd Bethel CT 06801 Office: ADP Inc 425 Park Ave New York City NY 10022

STOTT, THOMAS EDWARD, mech. engr.; b. Beverly, Mass., May 14, 1923; s. Thomas Edward and Mildred (Ayers) S.; B.S., Tufts U., 1947; m. Mary Elizabeth Authelet, Feb. 26, 1944; children—Pamela, Randi, Wendy, Thomas Edward III, Diana. Design engr. shipbldg. div. Bethlehem Steel Corp., Quincy, Mass., 1956-59, project engr., 1959-60, sr. engr., 1960-63, project coordinator, 1963-64; pres. Stal-Laval, Inc., Elmsford, N.Y., 1964—, also dir.; dir. Thomas Stott & Co., MacKenzie Boat Yard; trustee Stal-Laval Employees Pension Trust. Trustee Egremont Congregational Ch., 1975-78. Served with USN, 1944-46; PTO. Registered profl. engr., Mass. Fellow ASME (exec. sec. gas turbine div.); mem. Am. Nat. Standards Inst. (chmn. nat. com.), Conseil Internat. Machines á Combustion (U.S. nat. com.), Soc. Naval Architects and Marine Engrs. (ships machinery com.), Marine Tech. Soc. Republican. Home: PO Box 134 Cummaquid MA 02637 Office: 400 Executive Blvd Elmsford NY 10523

STOUDENHEIMER, RICHARD GEORGE, adminstrv. physicist; b. Cleve., Dec. 10, 1918; s. Charles Roger and Laura Edith (Cassidy) S.; B.A., Coll. Wooster, 1940; M.S., Syracuse U., 1942; m. Ruth Lancaster Saylor, July 8, 1950; children—Susan, Samuel Richard. Design engr. phototube and image tube RCA Electronic Components Devices, Harrison, N.J., 1942, Lancaster, Pa., 1943-53, leader advanced devel. image tube, 1953-69, leader application engring. image tube, 1969-72; tchr. physics high sch., Birdsboro, Pa., 1973-74; sr. project engr. Fidelity Electric Co., Lancaster, 1975—; U.S. Rep., image tube standards com., NATO, 1959. Area chmn. Coll. Wooster Fund Raising, 1959-63. Recipient Arthur H. Compton prize Highest Honors Physics, Coll. Wooster, 1940. Mem. IEEE (chmn. subcom. phototube image tube standards 1954-58), Am. Phys. Soc., Central Pa. Coll. Wooster Alumni Club (pres. 1952), Sigma Pi Sigma. Republican. Presbyterian. Contbr. articles on phototubes and image tubes to tech. jours.; patentee in field. Home: 425 Ruth Ridge Dr Lancaster PA 17601 Office: 332 N Arch St Lancaster PA 17604

STOVALL, ROBERT HENRY, economist; b. Louisville, Feb. 16, 1926; s. Harold Samuel and Agnes Clara (Hinkle) S.; B.S., Wharton Sch. U. Pa., 1948; postgrad. U. Copenhagen, 1948-49; M.B.A., N.Y. U., 1957; m. Inger Gerda Bagger, Sept. 29, 1951; children—Sten Torben, Harold Samuel II, Inger Benedikte, Robert Henry, Jr. analyst E.F. Hutton Co., N.Y.C., 1953-57, market letter writer, 1960-67, sr. security analyst, 1957-60, mgr. investment research dept., 1960-61, gen. partner research, 1961-66, chmn. investment policy com., 1966-67; v.p., dir. research Nuveen Co., N.Y.C., 1968-69; gen. partner research Reynolds Securities Inc., N.Y.C., 1969—, v.p. research, 1970-71, 1st v.p. investment policy com. chmn., 1971—; dir. investment policy Dean Witter Reynolds, Inc., 1978—; panelist Wall St. Week PBS-TV, 1977—; columnist Forbes' mag., 1966-76. Bd. adjustment Mountain Lakes, Morris County, N.J., 1973—; bd. advisors St. Clair's Hosp., Denville, N.J.; trustee N.Y. U., 1977—. Served to capt. U.S. Army, 1943-46. Mem. N.Y. Soc. Security Analysts (dir. 1974-76, 78—), Grad. Sch. Bus. Adminstrn. Alumni Assn. N.Y. U. (pres. 1977-78), Mensa, Nat. Assn. Bus. Economists Inst. Chartered Fin. Analysts, Wall St. Forum, Financial Forum. Republican. Roman Catholic. Clubs: N.Y. U. Finance (pres. 1974-75), Union League, DownTown Assn., Kentuckians. Home: 26 Condit Rd Mountain Lakes NJ 07046 Office: Dean Witter Reynolds Inc 120 Broadway New York City NY 10005

STOVER, CARL FREDERICK, found. exec.; b. Pasadena, Calif., Sept. 29, 1930; s. Carl Joseph and Margareta (Müller) S.; B.A. magna cum laude, Stanford U., 1951, M.A., 1954; m. Catherine Swanson, Sept. 3, 1954; children—Matthew Joseph, Mary Margaret, Claire Ellen; m. 2d, Jacqueline Kast, Sept. 7, 1973. Instr. polit. sci. Stanford, 1953-55; fiscal mgmt. officer Office Sec. Dept. Agr., 1955-57; asso. dir. conf. program pub. affairs Brookings Instn., 1957-59, sr. staff mem. govtl. studies, 1960; fellow Center for Study Democratic Instns., Santa Barbara, Cal., also asst. to chmn. bd. editors Ency. Brit., 1960-62; sr. polit. scientist Stanford Research Inst., 1962-64, dir. pub. affairs fellowship program Stanford, 1962-64; pres. Nat. Inst. Pub. Affairs, Washington, 1964-70; pres. Nat. Com. U.S.-China Relations, 1971-72; pres., dir. Federalism Seventy-Six, Inc., 1972-74; dir. cultural resources devel. Nat. Endowment for Arts, Washington, 1974-78; pres. Cultural Resources, Inc., Washington, 1978—; cons. to govt., 1953—; pvt. profl. cons., 1970—. Treas., Nat. Com. U.S.-China Relations, 1966-71, bd. dirs., 1966-74; bd. dirs. Coordinating Council Lit. Mags., 1966-68, H.E.A.R. Found., 1976—; trustee Inst. of Nations, 1962-76, Nat. Inst. Pub. Affairs, 1967-71, Kinesis, Ltd., 1972—. Fellow A.A.A.S.; mem. Am. Soc. Pub. Adminstrn., Am. Soc. for Cybernetics, Fedn. Am. Scientists, Soc. Internat. Devel., Nat. Acad. Pub. Adminstrn. (hon.), Phi Beta Kappa Assos. (hon.), Phi Beta Kappa. Democrat. Presbyn. Club: City Tavern (Washington). Author: The Government of Science, 1962; The Technological Order, 1963. Founding editor Jour. Law and Edn., 1971-73. Home: 1280 21st St NW Washington DC 20036 Office: 1019 19th St NW Washington DC 20036

STOVER, HERMAN DINSMORE, distillers assn. exec.; b. Portland, Maine, Nov. 14, 1918; s. Herman Dinsmore and Leona Frye (Johnson) S.; student Northeastern Bus. Coll., Portland, 1938; certificate pub. adminstr. U. Maine, 1967; m. Faith Janice Clark, Sept. 15, 1940; children—Carole (Mrs. Stanley Roger Tupper, Jr.), Susan Elaine. Purchasing agt. New Eng. Shipbldg. Corp., 1941-43, 45-46, Bakar Refrigeration Corp., 1947-53; adminstr. Maine State Liquor Commn., 1953-68; dir. pub. and trade relations Distilled Spirits Inst., Washington, 1968-72; v.p. adminstrn. Distilled Spirits Council U.S., Inc., Washington, 1972—. Mem. Me. Gov's. Standardization Com., 1962-68; past pres. Maine State Employees Assn.; mem. Sch. Bldg. Com., Augusta, Maine, 1967-68. Trustee Ft. Western, Augusta, 1967-68. Served with USAAF, 1943-45. Mem. Am. Soc. Assn. Execs., C. of C. U.S., Maine State Soc. Washington (past pres.). Mason (Shriner). Club: Nat. Press (Washington). Home: 8425 Willow Forge Rd Springfield VA 22152 Office: 1300 Pennsylvania Bldg Washington DC 20004

STOVER, RICHARD ROBERT, pharm. co. exec.; b. Mpls., Feb. 6, 1944; s. Robert Donald and Leona M. (Heinbockel) S.; B.A. in Econs., U. Pa., 1967; postgrad. N.Y. U., 1967-70; m. Sara Frances Hatton, Nov. 24, 1973; children—Forrest Shaw, Sara Avant. Security analyst Mfrs. Hanover Trust Co., N.Y.C., 1967-69, asst. trust officer, 1969-70, asst. v.p., 1970-71; security analyst Mitchell Hutchins, Inc., N.Y.C., 1971—, asst. v.p., 1972-73, v.p., 1973-77; v.p. Kuhn Loeb & Co., Inc., N.Y.C., 1977; ass. to v.p. fin. Pfizer, Inc., N.Y.C., 1978, dir. pharm. and diagnostic planning, 1978—. Mem. N.Y. Soc. Security Analysts, Health Industry Analysts Group (former pres.). Clubs: Apawamis. Home: 36 Grove St New York City NY 10014 Office: 235 E 42 St New York City NY 10017

STRACHAN, RONALD RICHARD, tube mfg. co. exec.; b. Waterbury, Conn., Aug. 7, 1935; s. John Donald F. and Metty R. (Pawloski) S.; grad. Cheshire Acad.; B.S., Georgetown U., 1956; postgrad. U. Conn. Law Sch., 1957-58; m. Anne Louise Williams, Apr. 27, 1963; children—Susan Anne, John Williams, Richard, Thomas Mitchell. Sales, Anaconda Am. Brass Co., Waterbury, 1956-59; v.p. Consol. Tube Fabricating Corp., Waterbury, 1959-72, pres., 1972-74, treas., 1960-74, also dir.; v.p., treas. Wire-Form, Inc., 1972, pres., 1972-74; pres., treas. E.S.P. Lock Corp., Leominster, Mass., 1974—, Three Point Products Inc.; pres. Mass. Colony Corp.; incorporator Banking Center regional bd. City Nat. Bank. Chmn. Central Bus. Dist. Renewal; mem. Central Naugatuck Valley Planning Commn., Waterbury Urban Renewal Agy.; chmn. Waterbury Urban Renewal Agy. Bd. dirs. Mental Health Assn., 1962-71, pres., 1963-70; bd. dirs. Easter Seal Rehab. Center. Mem. Mfrs. Assn. Conn., Greater Waterbury C. of C. (v.p., dir.), Smaller Mfg. Assn. Waterbury (dir., pres.), Waterbury Sales Exec. Club, Georgetown U. Alumni Assn. Clubs: Waterbury, Country; Weston Golf. Home: 60 Buckskin Dr Weston MA 02193 also Birchs Broomby Village Peru VT 05152 Office: 375 Harvard St Leominster MA 01453

STRACHMAN, PHILIP, lawyer, accountant; b. N.Y.C., Nov. 29, 1917; s. Rubin and Rose (Weintraub) S.; B.B.A., Coll. City N.Y., 1941; J.D., Georgetown U., 1949; LL.M., George Washington U., 1951; m. Flora V. Kemp, Dec. 27, 1942; children—Doreen, Lewis, Joel, Hedy. Auditor, GAO, Washington, 1942-47; internal revenue agt. U.S. Treasury, Washington, 1948-53; chief Navy indsl. funds U.S. Def. Dept., Washington, 1953-60; chief accounting programs div. FAA, Washington, 1960-73; comptroller L'Enfant Plaza Properties, Inc., Washington, 1973-75; instr. accounting U. Md., 1976—; prin. Philip Strachman, law and accounting taxes and fin. cons., Washington and Md., 1953—; admitted to D.C. bar, U.S. Supreme Ct. bar; instr. comptrollership, fin. mgmt. U.S. Navy, Wharton Sch. Finance, 1954, FAA, 1960-73; mem. Washington Inst. Select Comm. to Assist Congress in System and Audit. Treas. Civic Assn., 1950; auditor supr. Credit Union, 1960; commr. Boy Scouts Am., 1950. Served with U.S. Army, 1943-46. C.P.A., Md. Mem. Am., D.C. bar assns., Am., D.C. insts. c.p.a.'s. Jewish religion. Clubs: Alumni Georgetown Law Sch. George Washington Law Sch. Contbr. various articles to profl. Jours. Home and Office: 12204 Connecticut Ave Silver Spring MD 20902

STRACHOCKI, ALPHONSE, health care adminstr.; b. New Bedford, Mass., May 29, 1923; s. Paul and Frances K. S.; student Princeton U., 1943-44; B.S., U. Mass., 1950; M.S., Columbia U., 1955; m. Ruth Blackburn, Apr. 28, 1962. Hosp. adminstr. Indian Health Hosp., USPHS, 1955-58; cons. hosp. program USPHS Hill-Burton program, 1958-60; hosp. cons. Indian Health Service, 1960-63, asst. chief office program planning and evaluation, 1963-65; specialist hosp. mgmt. NIH, Bethesda, Md., 1965-66, hosp. adminstrv. specialist Medicare program, 1966-67, hosp. cons. regional med. program, 1967-70, chief health care adminstrn. Indian Health Service, 1970—; chmn. Inter-agency for Fed. Health Care Execs, 1973-76. Served with U.S. Army, 1942-45. Decorated Purple Heart. Fellow Am. Pub. Health Assn.; mem. Fed. Health Care Execs. Assn. (pres. 1978), Am. Hosp. Assn. Am. Mgmt. Assn., Columbia U. Alumni Assn. Republican. Home: 13 Eton Overlook Rockville MD 20850 Office: 5600 Fishers Ln Rockville MD 20857

STRACK, JOSEPH GEORGE, author, editor; b. Long Island City, N.Y., July 3, 1904; s. George Pius and Margaret (Ackerman) S.; student pub. schs.; m. Marie Elizabeth Rankin, June 1, 1935 (dec. Aug. 1977). Editor, Herrschaft-Willenbrock Publs., L.I. Weeklies, N.Y., 1927-30; pub. relations, N.Y.C., 1930-34; asst. to commr. N.Y.C. Dept. Welfare, 1934-41; pub. relations officer N.Y. State Dept. Social Services, Albany, 1941-70, cons., 1974; cons. N.Y. State Welfare Conf., 1943-73, N.Y. State Dept. Civil Service, 1947, N.Y. State Joint Legis. Com. Mental Retardation and Handicap, 1959-64, Welfare Research, Inc., Albany, 1977. Founder, dir. Nat. Inst. Publicity Writing, Albany, 1964—. Social services cons. N.Y. State, 1973. Gen. mgr. Queens Symphony Orch., N.Y.C., 1926-34. Served as capt. U.S. Army, 1943-44. Recipient award for outstanding service to dentistry Am. Assn. Dental Editors, 1973; award for article Dentistry and Presidents, Internat. Coll. Dentists, 1976. Mem. Am. Acad. History of Dentistry, Am. Assn. Dental Editors, Union Concerned Scientists, Center for Sci. in Public Interest, Sierra Club, Am. Orchid Soc., Whale Protection Fund, Indoor Lighting Soc. Am., Nat. Com. for Effective Congress, Common Cause, Public Citizen, Nat. Taxpayers Union, Gray Panthers, NOW, Nat. Council To Control Handguns, IPI in Public Interest. Club: University (Albany). Author: No Sign of Murder, 1940; Time to Kill, 1940; Marked for Murder, 1941; Democracy Cares, 1941; Motive for Murder, 1957; The Added Years, 1960; Index of Inadequacy and Indigency in the United States, 1963; How to Do Publicity Successfully, 1964; contbr. numerous articles in field to profl. jours. Founder, editor Social Service Outlook, Albany, 1966-70. Editor TIC mag., Albany, 1948—; Contacts mag., Albany, 1976—. Home: Willowbrook North Chatham NY 12132

STRADER, WILLIAM CLYDE, hosp. adminstr.; b. Weston, W.Va., July 8, 1934; s. William Foster and Luna Mae (Jefferies) S.; B.B.A., Fla. State U., 1969; m. Ruth Elizabeth Emmons, June 28, 1972; children—Carl C., William Clyde, James J., Brian D., Robert W., Jennifer L., Sal N. Joined Med. Service Corps, U.S. Navy, 1953, advanced through grades to lt. (j.g.), 1973; engaged in adminstrn. and aviation physiology, ret., 1973; dir. materials mgmt. Doctors Meml. Hosp., Baton Rouge, 1973-74, Andrew Kaul Meml. Hosp., St. Marys, Pa., 1974-75, Warren Gen. Hosp., Warren, Pa., 1975—; cons. materials mgmt. Decorated Purple Heart, Air medal. Mem. Am. Hosp. Assn., Hosp. Assn. Pa., Hosp. Council Western Pa., Dirs. Hosp. Purchasing, Soc. Materials Mgmt., Am. Mgmt. Assn., Fleet Res. Assn., VFW. Home: 209 Onondaga Ave Warren PA 16365 Office: 2-12 Cresent Park W Warren PA 16365

STRAHAN, CHARLES, JR., psychoanalyst; b. Balt., Feb. 6, 1921; s. Charles and Ethel Virginia (Fisher) S.; B.S., Dickinson Coll., 1942; M.D., U. Md., 1945; grad. Balt.-D.C. Psychoanalytic Inst.; m. Jean Phyllis Stevens, June 23, 1945; children—Donna Kirk, Christine Anne, Holly Leigh. Intern, Mercy Hosp., Balt., 1945-46; resident in psychiatry VA Hosp., Perry Pt., Md., 1946-49, staff psychiatrist, 1949-51; pvt. practice medicine, specializing in psychiatry, Wilmington, Del., 1952—; instr. U. Pa. Sch. Medicine, 1953-54; asst. prof. clin. psychiatry Thomas Jefferson U.; cons. Emily Bissel Hosp., Children's Home, Friends Sch., Wilmington. Served with M.C., U.S. Army, 1946-48. Fellow Am. Psychiat. Assn.; mem. Am. Psychoanalytic Assn., Balt.-D.C. Soc. Psychoanalysis, New Castle County Med. Soc., Med. Soc. Del., AAAS. Home and Office: 2105 Kentmere Pkwy Wilmington DE 19806

STRAIN, PAULA MARY, librarian; b. Brooke County, W.Va.; d. Paul Russell and Margaret (Evans) S.; A.B., Bethany Coll., 1937; B.S., Carnegie Inst. Tech., 1938; student U. Pitts., 1940-41. Asst. librarian Westminster Coll., 1939-40; asst. librarian Carnegie-Ill. Steel Corp., Pitts., 1940-42, librarian, 1942-44; librarian U.S. Naval Photog. Interpretation Center, Washington, 1946-48, liaison and selection officer Library of Congress, 1948-57; sr. research analyst Library of Congress, 1957-60; tech. librarian Electronics Systems Center, IBM, Owego, N.Y., 1960-68; head librarian Booz Allen Applied Research, Inc., Bethesda, Md., 1968-70; mgr. info. services MITRE Corp., McLean, Va., 1970—. Served with USNR, 1944-46. Mem. bd. mgrs. Finger Lakes Trail Conf., 1962-68. Mem. AAUW, Women's Nat. Book Assn., Appalachian Trail Conf., Spl. Libraries Assn. Clubs: Potomac Appalachian Trail (pres. 1970-72, Washington); Adirondack Mountain. Author articles various periodicals and jours. Home: 8315 N Brook Ln Bethesda MD 20016 Office: 1820 Dolley Madison Blvd McLean VA 22102

STRAIT, ALMUTH VANDIVEER, JR., dentist; b. Yonkers, N.Y., June 29, 1938; s. Almuth Vandiveer and Hilda Louise (Brandt) S.; B.A., U. Conn., 1961; D.D.S., Temple U., 1965; postgrad. Ind. U., 1965-66; m. Kathleen Joan Milligan, Dec. 21, 1963; children—Tara Elizabeth, Jonathan Vandiveer. Gen. practice dentistry, Indpls., 1965-66, Old Greenwich, Conn., 1968—; chief periodontics Boston Naval Shipyard, 1966-68; mem. dental staff Greenwich Hosp.; pres. Jay Vandiveer Ltd. Served to lt. USNR, 1966-68. Recipient Harris award for scholarship Temple U., 1963-65. Mem. Acad. Gen. Dentistry, Am. Soc. Preventive Dentistry Am., Conn., Western Fairfield County, Greenwich dental assns., Am. Analgesia Soc., Fedn. Dentaire Internationale, Nat. Audubon Soc., Am. Soc. Dentistry Children, Conn. Conservation Assn., Nat. Wildlife Fedn., U.S. Jr. C. of C. (past dir. Greenwich chpt.), John Cameron Hon. Med. Soc., U.S. Power Squadron, Old Greenwich Art Soc., Beta Sigma Gamma (past v.p.), Xi Psi Phi (nat. hon. award). Republican. Congregationalist (deacon). Lit. editor Temple Dental Rev., 1963-65. Home: 15 Pierce Rd Riverside CT 06878 Office: 182 Sound Beach Ave Old Greenwich CT 06870

STRANAHAN, ROBERT PAUL, JR., lawyer; b. Louisville, Oct. 29, 1929; s. Robert Paul and Anna May (Payne) S.; A.B., Princeton U., 1951; J.D., Harvard U., 1954; m. Louise Perry, May 12, 1956; children—Susan Dial, Robert Paul, Carol Payne. Admitted to D.C. bar, 1954, Md. bar, 1964; practiced in Washington, 1957—; asso. firm Wilmer & Broun, 1957-62; partner Wilmer, Cutler & Pickering, 1963—; professorial lectr. in law Nat. Law Center George Washington U., 1969-72. Served to 1st lt., USMCR, 1954-57. Mem. Am., Fed., D.C. bar assns. Clubs: Princeton, Met., Gridiron (Washington); Chevy Chase (Md.). Home: 5316 Cardinal Ct Bethesda MD 20016 Office: 1666 K St NW Washington DC 20006

STRANC, SISTER MARY CELAINE, librarian; b. Buffalo, July 28, 1913; d. Frank and Katherine (Antoniak) Strano; B.S. in Edn., Mt. St. Joseph Coll., Buffalo, 1950; M.L.S., State U. N.Y., Geneseo, 1966. Joined Congregation of Sisters of St. Felix; tchr., librarian, Buffalo, 1956-70; acad. librarian Villa Maria Coll., Buffalo, 1970—, head librarian, 1972—, coordinator library asst. program, 1970—, asso. prof., 1973-78, prof., 1978—; supr. Felician Sch. Libraries, 1970-71; dir. Model Cities Library Tech. Program, from 1973; chmn. Western N.Y. Cath. Librarian Conf., 1971-73. Certified supr. in pub. service, media mgmt. specialist; recipient HEW grant, 1970. Mem. AAUP, ALA, Assn. Ednl. Communications and Tech., Cath., N.Y. library assns., Council Library Tech., Western N.Y. Ednl. Communications Assn., Nat. Council Tchrs. of English. Roman Catholic. Contbr. to Cath. Library World, 1963, Media Handbook, 1976. Office: 240 Pine Ridge Rd Buffalo NY 14225

STRANGE, JOHN PHILLIP, safety equipment co. exec.; b. Canonsburg, Pa., Dec. 26, 1915; s. William and Laura (Phillips) S.; B.S., Waynesburg Coll., 1937; postgrad. Harvard Bus. Sch., 1967; m. Esther Alice Bluett, Aug. 12, 1939 (dec.); children—John Phillip, Alan W.; m. 2d, Almeda Morrow West, July 22, 1978. With Mine Safety Appliances Co., Pitts., 1937-48, 50—, research advisor to v.p. research and engring., 1977—; sr. research engr. Stanolind Oil & Gas

Co., Tulsa, 1948-50. Trustee Waynesburg Coll. Fellow Instrument Soc. Am.; mem. Am. Phys. Soc., ASTM, Air Pollution Control Assn., Am. Def. Preparedness Assn. Contbr. articles to profl. jours. Home: 4109 Calla Dr Murrysville PA 15668 Office: 201 N Braddock Ave Pittsburgh PA 15208

STRASBERG, LEE, theatrical dir.; b. Budzanow, Austria, Nov. 17, 1901; s. Baruch Meyer and Ida (Diner) S.; student Boleslavsky-Ouspenskaya, Am. Lab. Theatre; D.F.A., Fla. State U., 1977; m. Nora Z. Orecaun (dec.); m. 2d, Paula Miller, Mar. 16, 1934 (dec.); children—Susan, John; m. 3d, Anna Mizrahi, Jan. 7, 1968; children—Adam Lee Baruch, David Lee Isaac. Came to U.S., 1909, naturalized, 1936. Made first appearance as dir., actor Chrystie Street Settlement House, N.Y.C., 1925; began profl. career, 1925, actor Processional, Theatre Guild, also Garrick Gaieties 1, 1925; stage mgr. Garrick Gaieties II, 1926; asst. stage mgr. to Alfred Lunt-Lynne Fontanne, The Guardsman; actor in Red Rust, Green Grow the Lilacs; founder Group Theatre, N.Y.C., 1930, dir., 1930-37, including House of Connelly, Night Over Taos, Success Story, Men in White (Pulitzer prize winner), Gold Eagle Guy, Johnny Johnson; dir. All The Living, also Clash by Night, Fifth Column; co-producer Country Girl, 1950; dir. The Big Knife, 1949, Skipper Next to God, 1948, Godfather, Part II, 1974, Cassandra Crossing, 1977; artistic dir. Actors' Studio, N.Y.C., 1948—, Actors' Studio Theater, Inc., 1962-66; artistic dir. The Silent Partner, Felix; dir. The Three Sisters, 1964; film debut in The Godfather, Part II, 1974; lectr. Harvard, Brown U., Yale, Brandeis U., Northwestern U. Established Lee Strasberg Inst. of Theatre, N.Y.C. and Los Angeles, 1969. Recipient Kelcey Allen award, N.Y.C., 1961; Centennial Gold medal award for execellence in dramatic arts Boston Coll., 1963, Handel medallion, 1976. Author articles on the theatre. Contbr. to Ency. Brit., Ency. Spettacolo, Funk and Wagnall Ency., Ency. Americana. Address: 135 Central Park W New York NY 10023

STRASSER, ARNOLD, labor economist; b. N.Y.C., Oct. 8, 1932; s. N.I. and Edith (Deringer) S.; B.S., N.Y. U., 1957, postgrad., 1957-61; m. Alice Epstein, July 7, 1963; children—Kurt A., Eric A. N.Y. State Pub. Adminstrn. intern, 1957-58; sr. economist Office Research and Statistics, N.Y. State Div. Employment, 1958-63; dir. compensation structure studies U.S. Bur. Labor Statistics, 1963-67, dir. wage trend and constrn. compensation projects, 1967-69, dir. ann. earnings and employee benefit projects, 1969-72; dep. chief economist, dir. div. case econ. and policy Exec. Office Pres. Pay Bd., Washington, 1972-73; dir. econ. analysis Office Wage Stblzn., Cost of Living Council, 1973-74; analytical statistician Statis. Policy div. Office Mgmt. and Budget, Exec. Office Pres., 1974-77, Regulatory Policy and Reports Mgmt. div., 1977—. Mem. met. Washington council Govt.'s Transp. Citizen Advisory Com., 1978—; mem. exec. bd. Mishkan Torah Congragation, Greenbelt, Md., 1974—, fin. sec., 1975-78, exec. v.p., chmn. fin. com., 1978—. Mem. Am. Econ. Assn., Indsl. Relations Research Assn. Contbr. numerous articles to profl. jours. Home: 106 Julian Ct Greenbelt MD 20770 Office: New Exec Office Bldg Washington DC 20503

STRASSER, JOHN ALBERT, research scientist; b. Sydney, N.S., Can., Jan. 28, 1945; s. Albert Gus and Lillian (Tetanish) S.; diploma in Engring. (univ. scholar), St. Francis Xavier U., 1965; B.Metall. Engring., N.S. Tech. Coll., 1967, Ph.D., 1972; M.S., Pa. State U., 1968; m. Gayle Pearl Valerie Moore, Aug. 15, 1970; 1 son, Andrew Albert. Research scientist Dept. Energy, Mines and Resources, Ottawa, Ont., Can., 1971-73; chief research engr. Sydney Steel Corp., 1973—. Spl. lectr. Dalhousie U., 1969-70; lectr. metallurgy Sydney Steel employees, 1974. Pres., Dept. Energy, Mines and Resources Recreational Assn., 1973. Recipient Bart Griffin Meml. award St Francis Xavier U., 1965. NRC grantee, 1969-71. Mem. A.A.A.S., Canadian Inst. Mining and Metallurgy, Engring. Inst. Can., Atlantic Group for Research in Indsl. Metallurgy (chmn. bd. dirs.), N.S. Tech. Coll. Alumni Assn. (exec. mem. Ottawa br. 1972-73). Clubs: Lingan Golf and Country (Sydney); Sydney Curling. Contbr. articles to profl. lit. Home: 16 Woodill St Sydney NS Canada Office: PO Box 1450 Sydney NS Canada

STRATFORD, CAROL ANN (MRS. FRANCIS A. STRATFORD, JR.), occupational therapist; b. Columbus, Ohio, Dec. 17, 1946; d. Earl Brent and Gladys May (Wade) Deering; A.A., Brevard Jr. Coll., 1966; B.S., U. Fla., 1968; m. Francis A. Stratford, Jr., Aug. 4, 1973. Staff occupational therapist Hosp. Albert Einstein Coll. Medicine, Bronx, N.Y., 1968-74; sr. research therapist Inst. Rehab. Medicine N.Y. U. Med. Center, N.Y.C., 1975—. Registered occupational therapist. Mem. Am., N.Y. State, Met. N.Y. Dist. occupational therapy assns. Methodist. Contbr. articles to profl. jours. Home: 20 Waterside Plaza New York City NY 10010 Office: 400 E 34th St New York City NY 10016

STRATON, ANDREW CHARLES, fin. planner; b. Boston, July 26, 1923; s. Charles Andrew and Olympia Jacoblevna (Bonetzky) S.; A.B., U. Calif., Berkeley, 1954; M.S., George Washington U., 1965; postgrad. Naval War Coll., 1965; m. Olympia Richardovna Wisnevsky, Jan. 28, 1945; children—Daniel A., Walter A. (dec.), Alexandra, Lawrence. Methods engr. Yale & Towne Mfg. Co., Stamford, Conn., 1940-42; aviation cadet U.S. Navy 1943-45, commd. ensign, 1945, advanced through grades to comdr., 1966; served in various squadrons and aircraft carriers, alternating with staff duty shore assignments, 1945-73, ret., 1973; mem. sales staff Conn. Gen. Ins. Co., Providence, 1974-76; owner, operator Eastern Fin. Services, Warren, R.I., 1976—. Troop leader Boy Scouts Am., dir. Little League, 1959-61. Mem. Internat. Assn. Fin. Planners, Nat. Assn. Life Underwriters, Ret. Officers' Assn., Corvair Soc. Am. Clubs: Barrington Lions, Brown U. Navy. Home: 164 Touisset Point Rd Warren RI 02885 Office: Eastern Fin Services PO Box 195 Warren RI 02885

STRATTON, JOHN CARYL, Realtor; b. Chgo., July 11, 1920; s. John Frederick Otto and Dorothy Marjorie (Young) S.; B.S. cum laude, Princeton U., 1949; grad. Conn. Realtors Inst.; m. Lucille Waterhouse Hall, Mar. 13, 1974; children by previous marriages—Caryl Stratton Killing, John Caryl II, Susan Hall Levy, Evelyn Hall Brenton, Kenneth B. Hall. Chief liaison engr., Avco Mfg. Co., Stratford, Conn., 1950-55; pres. Yankee Engring. Service, Newtown, Conn., 1955-65; pres. Stratton Realty, Newtown, 1965—; dir. Autoswage Products Inc.; lectr. U. Conn., 1968-74, Western Conn. State Coll., 1975—. Chmn. Zoning Commn. Newtown, 1971-77. Served with USAF, 1942-46. Decorated D.F.C., Air medal with oak leaf cluster. Mem. Am. Inst. Aeros. and Astronautics, Newtown Bd. Realtors (pres. 1974, dir. 1975—), Conn. Assn. Realtors (comml. investment div.), Nat. Assn. Realtors, Nat. Inst. Real Estate Brokers, Nat. Assn. Real Estate Appraisers, Soc. Real Estate Appraisers, Am. Right of Way Assn., Realtors Nat. Mktg. Inst., Nat. Inst. Farm and Land Brokers, Nat. Assn. Real Estate Counselors, Nat. Assn. Rev. Appraisers, Sigm Xi. Republican. Congregationalist. Clubs: N.Y. Athletic, Princeton.

STRATTON, SAMUEL STUDDIFORD, congressman; b. Yonkers, N.Y., Sept. 27, 1916; s. Paul and Irene (Russell) S.; A.B., U. Rochester, 1937; M.A., Haverford Coll., 1938; M.A., Harvard, 1940; LL.D., Hartwick Coll., 1967, Coll. of St. Rose, 1974, Union Coll., 1978; m. Joan Harris Wolfe, Dec. 17, 1947; children—Lisa (Mrs. Martin Gonzalez), Debra, Kevin, Kim, Brian. Sec. to Congressman Thomas H. Eliot (Mass.), Washington, 1940-42; dept. sec. gen. Far Eastern Commn., Dept. State, Washington, 1946-48; lectr. Union Coll., Schenectady, 1948-50, lectr. Rensselaer Poly. Inst., 1953-54; TV newscaster; investment counselor First Albany Corp., Albany, N.Y., 1957; mem. 86th-87th Congresses from 32d N.Y. Dist., mem. 88th-91st Congresses from 35th N.Y. Dist., 92d Congress from 29th N.Y. Dist., 93d-95th Congresses from 28th N.Y. Dist., mem. armed services com., chmn. investigations subcom. City councilman, City of Schenectady, 1949-55; elected mayor, 1955; mem. Schenectady Municipal Housing Authority, 1950-51, chmn. 1951; hon. trustee U. Rochester. Served with USNR, World War II; staff Gen. Mac Arthur, PTO, 1942-46; in Korea, 1951-53; capt. USNR ret. Decorated Bronze Star medal (2). Mem. VFW, Amvets, Am. Legion, Res. Officers Assn., Navy League, Phi Beta Kappa, Psi Upsilon. Democrat. Presbyterian. Clubs: Masons (32 deg.), Kiwanis. Home: 244 Guy Park Ave Amsterdam NY 12010 Office: Rayburn House Office Bldg Washington DC 20515

STRATTON, WALTER LOVE, lawyer; b. Greenwich, Conn., Sept. 21, 1926; s. John McKee and June (Love) S.; student Williams Coll., 1943; A.B., Yale, 1948; LL.B., Harvard, 1951; m. Helen Marie Elting, Sept. 11, 1954; children—John, Michael, Peter, Lucinda. Admitted to N.Y. bar, 1952; asso. Casey, Lane & Mittendorf, N.Y.C., 1951-53, Donovan, Leisure, Newton & Irvine, N.Y.C., 1956-63, partner, 1963—; asst. U.S. atty. So. dist. N.Y., N.Y.C., 1953-56. Served with USNR, 1945-46. Fellow Am. Coll. Trial Lawyers; mem. Am., N.Y. State bar assns. Clubs: Round Hill (Greenwich); Fairfield County Hunt (Westport); Minneapolis. Home: Round Hill Rd Greenwich CT 06830 Office: 30 Rockefeller Plaza New York City NY 10020

STRAUB, CHESTER JOHN, lawyer; b. Bklyn., May 12, 1937; s. Chester and Ann (Majewski) S.; A.B., St. Peter's Coll., 1958; LL.D., U. Va., 1961; m. Patricia Morrissey, Aug. 22, 1959; children—Chester, Michael, Christopher, Robert. Admitted to N.Y. State bar, 1962, U.S. Supreme Ct., 1978; asso. firm. Willkie, Farr & Gallagher, N.Y.C., 1963-71, partner, 1971—; mem. N.Y. State Assembly, 1967-72, N.Y. State Senate, 1973-75. Mem. Democratic Nat. Com., 1976—; vice chmn. N.Y. City Dem. Com., 1974—; co-chmn. platform com. N.Y. State Dem. Com., 1975-76; personal aide Senator Robert F. Kennedy, 1968; mem. Cardinal's Com. of Laity for Catholic Charities N.Y., 1974—; vice chmn. Bklyn. Community Dist. Planning Bd.; chmn. fin. com. Eastern dist. com. Boy Scouts Am.; bd. dirs. Bklyn. Legal Services Corp.; trustee N.Y. League for Histadrut, Greenpoint YMCA. Served with U.S. Army, 1961-63. Mem. Am., N.Y. State, Bklyn. bar assns., Assn. Bar City N.Y., Greenpoint-Williamsburg Health Council, Pulaski Bus. and Profl. Men's Assn., Kosciuszko Found., Assn. Sons of Poland. Office: Willkie Farr & Gallagher 1 Citicorp Center 153 E 53 St New York City NY 10022

STRAUB, FRANK, investment cons.; b. Queens County, N.Y., May 20, 1912; s. Frank and Margaret Rosalia (Gerkin) S.; B.C.S., N.Y. U., 1937; m. Laura Mangano, June 30, 1973. Securities analyst White, Weld & Co., N.Y.C., 1946-60, United Funds, N.Y.C., 1960-62; investment mgr. Equitable Life Assurance Soc., N.Y.C., 1962-64; v.p. Paine, Webber, Jackson & Curtis, N.Y.C., 1964-69; pvt. practice investment consulting, Chester, Conn., 1969—. Served with U.S. Army, 1942-46. Mem. N.Y. Soc. Security Analysts, Chartered Fin. Analysts (Charlottesville, Va.), Transp. Analysts. Lutheran. Clubs: Moodus Country, Lyman Golf, Rotary. Author: Airlines Into the Future, 1968; Transportation Trends, 1964. Home: Parkers Point Chester CT 06412 Office: Box 6 Chester CT 06412

STRAUCH, BERISH, plastic and reconstructive surgeon; b. N.Y.C., Sept. 19, 1933; s. Herman and Anna S.; B.A., Columbia Coll., 1955; M.D., Columbia U., 1959; m. Rena Feuerstein, June 12, 1955; children—Robert J., Laurie E. Intern, Columbia div. Bellevue Hosp., 1959-60; surg. resident Montefiore Hosp. Med. Center, N.Y.C., 1960-64; hand surgery resident Roosevelt Hosp., N.Y.C., 1961; plastic surgery resident Stanford (Calif.) U., 1966-68; chief plastic surgery service Albert Einstein Coll. Medicine and Montefiore Hosp. and Med. Center, Bronx, N.Y., 1978—. Served to capt. M.C., U.S. Army, 1964-66. Mem. Am. Soc. Plastic and Reconstructive Surgeons, Am. Assn. Plastic Surgeons, Am. Soc. Surgery of Hand, Internat. Soc. Reconstructive Microsurgery. Author: Symposium on Microsurgery, 1976; contbr. articles to profl. jours. Office: 3331 Bainbridge Ave Bronx NY 10467

STRAUCH, GEORGE JOSEPH, lawyer; b. N.Y.C., Apr. 24, 1933; s. Charles and Anna (Karten) S.; B.A., N.Y. U., 1955, M.A., 1957; LL.B., Bklyn. Law Sch., 1959, J.D., 1967. Admitted to N.Y. State bar, 1960; asso. firm Jason Meth, N.Y.C., 1959-63; individual practice law, Jackson Heights, N.Y., 1963—. Bklyn. Law Sch. scholar, 1956-57. Mem. Am., Queens County bar assns., N.Y. County Lawyers Assn., N.Y. State Land Title Assn., Am. Judicature Soc., Phi Delta Kappa. Democrat. Jewish. Club: Lions. Office: 37-60 82d St Jackson Heights Queens NY 11372

STRAUCH, GERALD OTTO, surgeon; b. Three Rivers, Mich., July 26, 1932; s. Gerald Otto and Helen Jeanette (Zierle) S.; grad. U. Mich., M.D., 1957; m. Margaret Mary Spindler, Aug. 20, 1955; children—David Mark, Susan Mary, Jean Ellen. Intern, R.I. Hosp., Providence, 1957-58; resident in surgery, 1958-62; practice medicine specializing in surgery, Stamford, Conn., 1964—; clin. asso. prof. surgery N.Y. Med. Coll. Served to capt. AUS, 1962-64. Diplomate Am. Bd. Surgery. Fellow A.C.S.; mem. New Eng., Frederick A. Coller surg. socs., Soc. for Surgery of Alimentary Tract, Collegium Internationale Chirurgiae Digestivae, Surg. Soc. N.Y. Med. Coll., Conn. Soc. Am. Bd. Surgeons, Am. Trauma Soc., AMA, Assn. Mil. Surgeons U.S., Conn. State, Fairfield County med. socs., Stamford Med. Assn., Am. Assn. Surgery of Trauma. Republican. Roman Catholic. Clubs: Wee Burn Country, Landmark. Contbr. numerous articles to profl. jours. Office: 70 Mill River St Stamford CT 06902

STRAUSS, ALBERT JAMES, paper mfg. cons.; b. Washington, Dec. 23, 1910; s. Albert A. and Lydia (Thompson) S.; A.B., George Washington U., 1935; m. Violet R. Haney, Nov. 27, 1935. Central purchasing agt. Hecht. Co., Washington, 1947-49; purchasing agt. E.F. Drew, Boonton, N.J., 1949-52; v.p. purchasing and transp. Riegel Paper Corp., N.Y.C., 1952-72; v.p. purchasing and distbn., dir. Riegel Products Corp., 1972-77; cons., 1977—. Mem. Am. Paper Inst. (chmn. materials com. 1960-62), Pulp Consumers Assn. (dir.), Lehigh Valley Purchasing Assn. (dir. 1958-59), Nat. Assn. Purchasing Agts., Am. Mgmt. Assn. Contbr. articles to profl jours. Home: RD 8 Box 247 Flemington NJ 08822 Office: Riegel Products Corp Milford NJ 08848

STRAUSS, AMELIE LEE, dance therapist; b. Fulda, Germany, Dec. 15, 1933; d. Abraham and Stephanie (Hahn) Wertheim; came to U.S., 1939, naturalized, 1944; certificate State Tchrs. Sem., Israel, 1954; B.A. magna cum laude, Bklyn. Coll., 1974; m. Eliezer Strauss, Nov. 10, 1954; children—Samuel, Ailon. Tchr. intermediate schs. Israel Ministry Edn., Raanana, 1953-57; instr. modern dance N.Y.C. Bd. Adult Edn., also pvt. tchr., 1964-69; staff dance therapist Bellevue Hosp. and psychiat. div. N.Y. U. Med. Center, N.Y.C., 1967-69; coordinator creative arts therapy program, activity therapy dept. psychiat. div., Bellevue Hosp., 1969—; instr. dance therapy N.Y. U., N.Y.C., 1973-78; pvt. practice dance therapy; lectr.; cons. in field. Bd. dirs. Center Expressive Analysis, 1977—. Mem. Am. Dance Therapy Assn. (registered), Am. Personnel and Guidance Assn., Assn. Humanistic Psychology. Democrat. Jewish. Home: 120 Bennett Ave New York City NY 10033 Office: Activity Therapy Dept Bellevue Psychiat Hosp 400 E 30th St New York City NY 10016

STRAUSS, DOROTHY BRANDFON, marriage, family and sex therapist, psychologist; b. Bklyn.; d. Marcus and Beatrice (Wilson) Brandfon; B.A., Bklyn. Coll.; M.A., N.Y. U., Ph.D., 1963; m. Hyman Strauss, Oct. 19, 1947; 1 dau., Josette S. Gershen. Asso. dir. Center for Treatment Sexual Dysfunction, clin. asso. prof. psychiatry Downstate Med. Center, State U. N.Y., Bklyn.; mem. NIMH research team, dept. psychiatry U. Pa. Sch. Medicine; prof. Kean Coll. N.J., also coordinator grad. study in psychology; pvt. practice sex and marital therapy, Bklyn.; spl. instr. group dyanmics AUS Signal Corps, 1967-70. Certified sex therapist. Mem. Eastern Assn. Sex. Therapy, Am., N.J. psychol. assns., Am. Psychosomatic Soc., Soc. Clin. and Exptl. Hypnosis, N.J. Geriatric Soc., Am. Assn. Marriage and Family Therapists, Kappa Delta Pi, Pi Lambda Theta. Home: 1700 Ditmas Ave Brooklyn NY 11226

STRAUSS, GEORGE HERSCHEL, polit. scientist; b. Cleve., Jan. 2, 1937; s. Harry and Carrie (Axelrod) S.; A.B., Oberlin Coll., 1959; M.Pub. Affairs (U.S. Steel Found. fellow), Woodrow Wilson Sch. Pub. Affairs, 1961; Ph.D., N.Y. U., 1973. Cons., Inst. Pub. Adminstrn., N.Y.C., 1964; research asso. Comm. City Finances, N.Y.C., 1964-65; lectr. polit. sci. Coll. City N.Y., 1968-70, William Paterson Coll., Wayne, N.J., 1972-73; sr. project mgr. Cambridge Opinion Studies, N.Y.C., 1973-74; project dir. Bur. Audit and Control, Office City Comptroller, City of N.Y., 1974-78; dir. community relations Jewish Bd. Family and Children's Services. County comitteeman Manhattan County Democratic Com., 1971—; pres. W. 89th St. Park Block Assn., 1970. Fulbright fellow, 1961-62; Richard Harrison Bull fellow, 1966. Mem. Am. Soc. Pub. Adminstrn., Child Welfare League Am., Am. Polit. Sci. Assn., Am. Acad. Polit. and Social Sci., Phi Beta Kappa. Contbr. articles to profl. jours. Home: 39 W 89 St New York City NY 10024 Office: Jewish Bd Family and Children's Services 120 W 57th St New York City NY 10019

STRAUSS, MARTIN HEINZ, mfg. co. exec.; b. Hoechheim, Germany, May 21, 1927; s. Ben and Rose (Sommer) S.; grad. high sch.; m. Ellen Lindauer, Oct. 27, 1951; children—Gary, Joanne. Came to U.S., 1939, naturalized, 1944. With Kahn & Feldman, Inc., N.Y.C., 1945-57, export mgr., 1950-57; with Plicose Mfg. Corp. div. Diamond Shamrock, N.Y.C., 1957-68; traffic mgr., exec. v.p. Dura Commodities Corp., Harrison, N.Y., 1968—. Served with USNR, 1944-45. Vice pres. Jewish Community Center, Harrison, N.Y., 1963—. Honored by Jewish Theol. Sem., 1970. Mem. B'nai B'rith (pres.). Home: 515 Harrison Ave Harrison NY 10528 Office: 111 Calvert St Harrison NY 10528

STRAUSS, RAYMOND BERNARD, physician; b. N.Y.C., Mar. 25, 1930; s. Victor M. and Fannie (Price) S.; A.B., Washington U., St. Louis, 1950; Ph.D., U. Fla., 1956; M.D., Case-Western Res. U., 1958; m. Lois Kelly, June 12, 1958; children—Steven Douglas, Keith Andrew. Intern dept. medicine U. Hosps., Cleve., 1958-59, asst. resident surgery, 1959-60; resident otolaryngology Columbia-Presbyn. Med. Center, N.Y.C., 1960-63; practice medicine, specializing in otolaryngology and facial plastic surgery, Englewood, N.J., 1963—; attending otolaryngologist Englewood Hosp., asso. attending otolaryngologist St. Lukes Hosp.; asst. otolaryngologist Vanderbilt Clinic and Presbyn. Hosp., N.Y.C.; instr. otolaryngology Coll. Phys. and Surg. Columbia U.; dir. No. Valley-Englewood Savs. and Loan Assn. Bd. dirs. Dwight-Englewood Sch. Served to capt. M.C., AUS, 1964-66. Recipient Coakley Meml. prize in otolaryngology, Columbia, 1958. Marie and Henry Heiner fellow in otolaryngology, 1961-62. Diplomate Am. Bd. Otolarynogology. Fellow A.C.S., Internat. Coll. Surgeons, Am. Acad. Facial Plastic and Reconstructive Surgery, Am. Assn. Cosmetic Surgeons, Am. Acad. Ophthalmology and Otolaryngology; mem. Am. Speech and Hearing Assn., AMA, N.J., Bergen County, N.Y. County med. socs., Bergen County Soc. Otolaryngologists (past pres.), N.Y. Laryngol. Soc. (sec.-treas.), N.Y. Bronchoscopic Soc. (pres.), N.Y. Otological Soc., Royal Soc. Medicine, Phi Beta Kappa, Alpha Omega Alpha, Nu Sigma Nu. Presbyn. (elder, pres. bd. trustees). Rotarian (past pres.). Clubs: Englewood (pres.), Knickerbocker Country. Home: 436 Lewelen Circle Englewood NJ 07631 Office: 216 Engle St Englewood NJ 07631

STRAUSSNER, SHULAMITH LALA ASHENBERG, social worker, educator; b. Lodz, Poland, Mar. 2, 1947; d. Samuel and Ruth (Apelcwig) Ashenberg; B.A., CCNY, 1969; M.S.W., Fordham U., 1972; certificate in psychoanalytic psychotherapy, tng. inst. for Mental Health Practitioners, N.Y.C., 1978; m. Joel H. Straussner, Dec. 28, 1969. Psychiat. social worker N.Y. Hosp. Westchester Div., 1972-74; pvt. practice psychoanalytic psychotherapy, N.Y.C., 1973—; psychiat. social worker Smithers Alcoholism Treatment and Tng. Center, Roosevelt Hosp., N.Y.C., 1974-78; mem. faculty Tng. Inst. for Mental Health Practitioners, 1977—, Touro Coll., 1978—; cons. on alcoholism; Recipient award for outstanding community project Assos. of Tng. Inst. for Mental Health, 1978; certified social worker, N.Y. State. Mem. Acad. Certified Social Workers, N.Y. Soc. Clin. Psychologists (asso.), Nat. Assn. Social Workers. Contbr. chpts. to books, articles to profl. jours.

STRAYER, VERNON JOHN, ry. exec.; b. Johnstown, Pa., Feb. 7, 1917; s. Forest R. and Elma E. (Fyock) S.; B.S., Juniata Coll., 1946; m. Betty M. Fisher, Mar. 24, 1946; children—Timothy J., Stephen J., Douglas J. Bradley J., Kim J. Looper, Bethlehem Steel Co., Johnstown, Pa., 1941-42; spl. agy. FBI, Richmond, Va. and Louisville, Ky., 1946-52; labor relations E.I. DuPont de Nemours & Co. Inc., Louisville, 1952-55; supr. personnel Youngstown & No. Ry. (Ohio), 1955-62; claim agt. safety and tng. Union R.R. Co., East Pittsburgh, Pa., 1962—. Twp. supr., also supt. police Franklin Twp. (Pa.), 1965-68; mem. Republican com. Franklin Twp., 1962-66. Served with M.I., USAAF, 1942-46; PTO. Mem. Am. Soc. Safety Engrs., Soc. Former Agts. F.B.I., Fedn. Fly Fishermen, Titusville Rod and Gun Club. Home: RD 1 Export PA 15632 Office: 666 Linden Ave East Pittsburgh PA 15112

STREAN, BERNARD MAX, JR., cartographer; b. Pensacola, Fla., Mar. 6, 1936; s. Bernard Max and Janet (Lockey) S.; A.B., Earlham Coll., 1959; M.S., So. Ill. U., 1965; m. Florence Jones, May 7, 1973. Cartographic survey aide U.S. Geol. Survey, Arlington, Va., 1959, oceanographer sediment lab. Washington, 1963-64, hydrographic surveys, 1964-67, oceanographer marine geology, 1967-77, cartographer Def. Mapping Agency-Hydrographic Center, 1977—. 1967—. Mem. Am. Assn. Petroleum Geologists, Am. Geophys. Union, Geol. Soc. Am., Nat. Geog. Soc., Seismol. Soc. Am., Internat. Assn. Volcanology and Chemistry of Earth's Interior. Episcopalian. Home: 6111 Colonial Terr Camp Springs MD 20031 Office: Def Mapping Agency-Hydrographic Center Washington DC 20390

STRECKO, MICHEL, physicist; b. Montreal, Que., Can., Dec. 17, 1953; s. Anton and Jeannine (Cocciardi) S.; M.Physics, U. Que., Montreal, 1976; m. Danielle Jodoin, Dec. 24, 1975;

children—Jean-Sebastien, Julie. Faculty Universite du Que. a Montreal, Montreal, 1973—, asst. in research, 1975-76, physicist, 1976—. Mem. Am. Phys. Soc., IEEE, Am. Soc. Microbiology, Canadian Assn. Physics, Am. Philatel. Soc., Royal Philatel. Soc., Federation Quebecoise de Philatelie (dir.) Eastor Laurentien (pres.), Can. Mem. Parti Quebecois. Roman Catholic. Club: Nexialisme. Author: Physics and Virology, 1976; Theory of Group in Virology, 1977; contbr. articles to profl. jours. Home: 1145 24e Ave Saint-Antoine des Laurentides PQ J7Z 3J1 Canada Office: Université du Quebec a Montreal Dept Physique CP 8888 Succursale A Montreal PQ H3C 3P8 Canada

STREET, JAMES HARRY, educator; b. New Braunfels, Tex., Nov. 17, 1915; s. James William and Kate (Goldenbagen) S.; B.A. magna cum laude, U. Tex., 1940, M.A., 1947; Ph.D., U. Pa., 1953; D.Econ. Sci. (hon.), Nat. U. Asuncion (Paraguay), 1955; M.A. (hon.), U. Cambridge (Eng.), 1972; m. Mabel Carroll, Jan. 16, 1944; children—John William, Janet Pauline. Reporter, editor New Braunfels Herald, 1933-36; social sci. analyst U.S. Bur. Agr. Econs., Washington, 1941-43; civilian pub. service U.S. Forest Service, Cooperstown, N.Y. and Phila., 1943-46; instr. econs. U. Pa., Phila., 1946-48; asst. prof. econs. Haverford (Pa.) Coll., 1948-52; asst. prof. Rutgers U., New Brunswick, N.J., 1952-55, asso. prof., 1955-59, prof. econs. 1959-76, distinguished prof. econs., 1976—, chmn. econs. dept., 1977—; vis. prof. Nat. U. Asuncion, Paraguay, 1955; vis. lectr. various univs. S.Am., 1957-58; Fulbright lectr. U. San Marcos, Peru, 1963; econ. specialist Central Am. social studies seminars, summers 1965-72; Fulbright lectr. Nat. U. Mex., 1970; vis. scholar U. Cambridge, 1972-73. Bd. dirs. Metuchen Free Pub. Library, 1963-68. Mem. Am. Econ. Assn., Assn. Evolutionary Econs., Conf. Latin Am. History, Latin Am. Studies Assn., Royal Econ. Soc., Council Internat. Exchange Scholars, Phi Beta Kappa (chpt. pres. 1967-68). Editor: Ideas and Issues in the Social Sciences, 1950; author: The New Revolution in the Cotton Economy, 1957. Contbr. articles to profl. jours. Home: 11 Lexington Dr Metuchen NJ 08840 Office: 192 College Ave New Brunswick NJ 08903

STREET, ORMAN ELERY, educator; b. Revillo, S.D., Jan. 5, 1903; s. Thomas and Gertrude (Barlow) S.; B.S., S.D. State Coll., 1924; postgrad. Mass. Agrl. Coll., 1924-26; M.S., Mich. State Coll., 1927, Ph.D., 1933; m. Mary Fayette Kent, June 20, 1929; children—Harold K., Priscilla M. (Mrs. William K. Tucker), Martha F. (Mrs. Jesse A. Eller), Margaret E. (Mrs. William R. Lear). Plant physiologist Conn. Agr. Expt. Sta., Tobacco Substa., Windsor, Conn., 1929-39; agronomist tobacco investigations Bur. Plant Industry, U.S. Dept. Agr., Lancaster, Pa., 1939-49; prof. agronomy Pa. State Coll., 1945-49; asso. prof. agronomy U. Md., 1949-54, prof., 1954-69, emeritus prof., 1969—; acting climatologist U. Md., 1973—. cons. Chun Cheng Found., Republic China, 1969-70; cons. Standard Brands, Inc.; cons. U.S. tobacco culture Spanish Ministry Agr., 1976. Recreation dr., YMCA, Windsor, Conn., 1935-39, park commrs., 1936-38. Bd. dirs. Md. Tobacco Improvement Found., 1950—. Recipient Cigar Mfrs. Research award, 1963, award for outstanding research Md. Crop Improvement Assn., 1973; Tobacco Sci. Yearbook dedicated to him, 1975. Mem. Am. Soc. Plant Physiology, Am. Inst. Biol. Scis., Seminar Botanicus, Sigma Xi, Alpha Zeta, Phi Sigma. Contbr. articles in field to expt. sta. bulls., sch. jours. Home: 4003 Hillwood Ct Beltsville MD 20705 Office: U Md College Park MD 20742

STREETER, TAL, sculptor; b. Oklahoma City, Aug. 1, 1934; s. Paul Waller and Pauline Viola (Roberts) S.; B.F.A., U. Kans., 1956, M.F.A., 1961; m. Dorothy Ann Sheets, June 26, 1957; 1 dau., Lissa. Exhibited in one-man shows, N.Y.C., yearly 1965—; exhibited in group shows at N.Y. World's Fair, 1965; Whitney Mus., N.Y.C., 1965, Larry Aldrich Mus., Ridgefield, Conn., 1968, 70, Sheldon Art Mus., Lincoln, Nebr., 1970; represented in permanent collections including Mus. Modern Art, N.Y.C., San Francisco Mus. Art, Nat. Fine Arts Collection at Smithsonian, Washington, Wadsworth Atheneum, Newark Mus., Smith Coll. Mus. Art, High Mus., Atlanta, Ark. Art Center, Little Rock, Storm King Art Center, Corcoran Gallery, Contemporary Arts Mus., Houston, Neuberger Mus. vis. artist-in-residence Dartmouth, 1963, U. N.C., 1970, 72, 73, Penland Sch. of Crafts, 1974, 75, 76, 77; prof. State U. N.Y. at Purchase, 1973—. Fulbright lectr., Korea, 1971. Collaborations in Art, Sci. and Tech./N.Y. State Council on Arts grantee, 1976. Author: The Art of the Japanese Kite, 1974; contbr. Ency. of Japan, 1978. Home: Old Verbank Sch Millbrook NY 12545

STREETER, THOMAS WINTHROP, stockbroker; b. N.Y.C., Feb. 23, 1922; s. Thomas W. and Ruth (Cheney) S.; grad. St. Paul's Sch., 1940; A.B., Dartmouth, 1947, M.S., 1948; m. Barbara Brown, Sept. 7, 1946; children—Mary, Thomas Winthrop III, Deborah. Trainee, Am. Optical Co., Southbridge, Mass., 1948-50; sales engr. Diehl Mfg. Co., Somerville, N.J., 1950-57; v.p. Meyer & Depew Co., Inc., Union, N.J., 1957-59; asso. Neville Rodie & Co., N.Y.C., 1959-63; partner G.C. Haas & Co., N.Y.C., 1963-66; chmn. Haas Securities Corp., N.Y.C., 1966-77, Spaulding Securities Corp., N.Y.C., 1977—. Served with AUS, 1942-45: CBI. Club: Downtown Assn. (N.Y.C.). Home: 253 W 101st St New York City NY 10025 Office: 120 Broadway New York City NY 10005

STREITFELD, NINA (FELBER), pub. relations exec.; b. N.Y.C., Dec. 10, 1931; d. Alexander and Vivien (Kressh) Weinstein; B.A. with honors, Swarthmore Coll., 1953; M.A., Columbia U., 1956; m. Franklin H. Streitfeld, Dec. 20, 1959 (div. 1969); children—Laura, David John; m. Lloyd Hauser, Feb. 8, 1971 (div. 1976). Editor, ABC, 1953-54; asst. info. dir., asst. editor The Near East, Near East Coll. Assn., 1955; dir. publicity Travelers Aid Soc. N.Y., 1956-58; acting and asst. dir. pub. relations and devel. Vis. Nurse Assn. Bklyn., 1958-59; pub. relations coordinator Child Study Assn. Am., 1959-60; cons., Westport, Conn., 1961-68; v.p. promotion Adams Oil Corp., Bklyn., 1968-76; dir. pub. relations Leisure Tech. Corp., Lakewood, N.J., 1977; cons. U.S. Rep. James H. Scheuer, N.Y.C., 1976-77, 78. Trustee, Mid-Fairfield Child Guidance Center, Norwalk, Conn., 1960-68, bd. sec., mem. exec. com., 1964-66; com. chmn., pack 121, Boy Scouts Am., Rockaway, 1975-77. Hannah H. Leedom fellow Swarthmore Coll., Columbia U., 1953-56. Mem. Public Relations Soc. Am., Fairfield County Public Relations Assn., Publicity Club N.Y. (bd. mem. 1960-62). Democrat. Jewish. Home: 20 Pin Oak Ct Westport CT 06880

STRENG, RUDOLPH JOSEPH, computer systems designer; b. N.Y.C., Nov. 17, 1936; s. Rudolf and Margaret F. (Frercks) S.; A.A., Wesley Jr. Coll., 1958; postgrad. Union Coll. (Barbourville, Ky.), 1960; m. Joan Wolf, Apr. 6, 1963; children—Kimberly Lynn, R. Craig. Owner Nutmeg of Norwalk, Inc., (Conn.), 1974—; computer systems project leader Homequity, Wilton, Conn., 1977—. Mem. Common Council, Norwalk, 1962-64; mem. Redding Rep. Town com., 1976—; pres. Redding Young Reps., 1977, v.p., 1976, dir., 1978. Served with USNR, 1958-62. Mem. Ch. of Christ. Club: YMCA Indian Guides (regional adv. bd. 1976, nat. exec. com. 1977, chief N.E. U.S. 1978—, Outstanding Vol. YMCA Parent Child Programs 1976, 77). Home: 76 Gallows Hill West Redding CT 06896 Office: 249 Danbury Rd Wilton CT 06897

STRENGER, LAWRENCE, neurosurgeon; b. N.Y.C., Oct. 19, 1930; s. Max and Rose S.; A.B., Syracuse U., 1950; M.S., N.Y. U., 1951; M.D., Chgo. Med. Sch., 1955; m. Mildred B. LeVine, Dec. 20, 1953; children—Scott William, Jonathan, Keith David. Intern, resident gen. surgery St. Raphael Hosp., New Haven; resident neurosurgery St. Vincent Hosp., N.Y.C.; practice medicine specializing in neurosurgery, Atlantic City; mem. staff Shore Meml. Hosp.; asso. clin. prof. neurosurgery Hahnemann Med. Coll., Phila. Trustee Fedn. Jewish Agencies; bd. mgrs. Friends Sch., Atlantic City, 1977—. Served to capt. USAF, 1957-59. Fellow A.C.S., Am. Coll. Angiology; mem. AMA, N.J., Atlantic County (pres. 1976-77) med. socs., Phila., Mid Atlantic, N.J. (pres. 1978-79) neurosurg. socs., Am. Assn. Neurosurg. Surgeons, Congress Neurosurg. Surgeons, N.Y. Acad. Sci., N.J. Acad. Medicine, U.S. Power Squadron, Atlantic City C. of C. Clubs: Margate City Yacht, Masons. Contbr. articles to profl. jours. Home: 9004 Ventnor Ave Margate NJ 08402 Office: 3625 Boardwalk Atlantic City NJ 08401

STRETCH, GEORGE EDWARD, editor; b. White Plains, N.Y., Nov. 17, 1926; s. Edwin Nelson and Helen (Rawls) S.; student U. Bridgeport, 1946; m. Shirley L. Kling, Apr. 4, 1953; children—Leslie Ann (Mrs. Stephen Barker), Joel Harry. Reporter, New Haven Journal-Courier, 1949-52; editor Branford (Conn.) Rev., 1952-53; editor East Haven (Conn.) News, 1953, 56; reporter Cape Cod Standard-Times, Hyannis, Mass., 1953-55; asso. editor Newtown (Conn.) Bee, 1956-62; editor, gen. mgr. Sakonnet Times, Portsmouth, R.I., 1967-71; editor The Darien (Conn.) Rev., 1962-67, 1971—. Served with USNR, 1944-45. Mem. New Eng. Press Assn. (dir. 1966-67, 70-71), Overseas Press Club Am. Republican. Congregationalist. Home: Shaw Rd Little Compton RI 02837 Office: 20 West Ave Darien CT 06820

STRIANO, VINCENT ROCCO, fireproof products co. exec.; b. Bronx, N.Y., June 18, 1924; s. Gennaro and Fedora (Robusto) S.; B.M.E., Coll. City N.Y., 1948; m. Luisa A. Cangello, Mar. 5, 1945; children—Geraldine Striano Robustelli, Allan, James, Richard, Christine. Engr., Southworth Mgmt., N.Y.C., 1948-49; engr., Fireproof Products Co., Bronx, N.Y., 1949-57, chief engr., 1957-64, v.p., 1964-71, exec. v.p., 1971-74, pres., 1974—, also dir. Served with AUS, 1943-46; PTO. Registered profl. engr., N.Y. Mem. Concrete Reinforced Steel Inst. (dir., chmn. Atlantic states region), N.Y. Soc. Profl. Engrs., Concrete Industry Bd. N.Y. Republican. Roman Catholic. Club: Athletic. Home: 2632 Windmill Dr Yorktown Heights NY 10598 Office: 500 E 132d St Bronx NY 10454

STRIANSE, SABBAT JOHN, cosmetic cons.; b. Bklyn., Nov. 16, 1913; s. Angelo E. and Maria (Spinelli) S.; student Bklyn. Coll., evenings 1931-37; B.S., L.I. U., 1941; m. Dorothy Ryan, Sept. 7, 1942; children—Patricia (Mrs. Michael Toglia), Kathleen (Mrs. Sidney Lawrence), Carol (Mrs. Edmund Silvia). Pharmacist, Walgreen Drug Co., N.Y.C., 1941-42; chemist Chem. Warfare Service, U.S. Army, 1942-45; research chemist George W. Luft Co., Inc., L.I. City, N.Y., 1945-48; sr. research chemist Warner-Hudnut, Inc., N.Y.C., 1948-50; tech. dir. Sofskin div. Vick Chem. Co., Bloomfield, N.J., 1950-56; dir. research Shulton, Inc., Clifton, N.J., 1956-59; dir. research Yardley Research Labs., Little Falls, N.J., exec. dir. Yardley & Co. Ltd., London, Eng., 1959-68, v.p. research Yardley of London, Inc., Totowa, N.J., 1968-75, also dir.; controller research Brit.-Am. Cosmetics, Ltd., 1971-75; pres. Stri-Tech Inc., Caldwell, N.J., 1975—. Fellow Am. Inst. Chemists, Soc. Cosmetic Chemists (past pres., com. chmn., Service award 1966, medal award 1973); mem. Internat. Fedn. Socs. Cosmetic Chemists (past pres., Outstanding Service award 1965), Cosmetic, Toiletry and Fragrance Assn. (editorial bd.), Am. Chem. Soc., Acad. Pharm. Scis., Am. Pharm. Assn., AAAS, Textile Research Inst., N.Y. Acad. Scis., (hon.) Belgium, Italian socs. cosmetic chemists. Co-editor Case of the Diversification Dilema, 1965. Editorial bd. Cosmetics: Sci. and Tech., 1972. Contbr. articles to profl. jours. Patentee in field. Home and office: 40 Westville Ave Caldwell NJ 07006

STRICKLIN, CARL SPENCER, religious assn. exec.; b. Baconton, Ga., Nov. 23, 1917; s. Daniel Spencer and Alberta (Clarkson) S.; B.S. in Bus. Adminstrn., certificate in fin., Boston U., 1950; m. Constance Allen, Aug. 26, 1949; 1 dau., Sandra Lee. Clk. stock control Eastern Air Lines, Miami, Fla., 1947; auditor Ernst & Ernst, Boston, 1950-54; asst. bus. mgr. Mass. Bible Soc., Boston, 1954-64, bus. mgr., 1964-74, dir., 1974-77, editor Comment, semi-monthly publ., 1974-77. Treas., trustee Daystar Found., Inc., non-profit retirement home, Needham, Mass. Served with Q.M.C., U.S. Army, 1942-46. Mem. Mass. Soc. C.P.A.'s., Mass. assns. pub. accountants, Nat. Soc. C.P.A.'s, Aircraft Owners and Pilots Assn., Norwood Aviation Club, Young Man's Christian Union Camera Club (treas.). Republican. Clubs: Masons (Shriners). Home and Office: 1019 Webster St Needham MA 02192

STRICKMAN, ROBERT LOUIS, chemist; b. N.Y.C., Aug. 13, 1911; s. Louis and Mollie (Sarver) S.; student Coll. City N.Y., 1928, N.Y. U., 1929-31; m. Rose Potoker, Mar. 21, 1935; children—Barbara Ann (Mrs. Emanuel Reiter), Melvyn Bruce. Co. dir. Flatbush Labs., Bklyn., 1955-63; co-owner, asso. dir. Elm Path Lab., Jackson Heights, N.Y., 1948-50; dir. research Haematype, Inc., Jamaica, L.I., 1952-54; lab. cons., 1954-56; dir. research Calorabic Materials, Inc., Pearl River, N.Y., 1961-64; pres. Allied Testing & Research, Hillsdale, N.J., 1966-72. Adviser on environ. matters to sec. of health State of Md.; mem. Pres.'s Study Group on Control of Hazardous Polluting Substances, 1970. Trustee Robert L. Strickman Found. Recipient award Nat. Inventors Council, 1967. Mem. Am. Chem. Soc., AAAS, Am. Soc. Metals, Am. Inst. Chem. Engrs., N.Y. Acad. Scis., N.Y. State Soc. Bioanalysts, Chemists Club, N.Y., Am. Inst. Biol. Scis. Patentee in field. Home and Office: Lawrence Rd RD 1 Bridgeton NJ 08302

STRIDSBERG, ALBERT BORDEN, editor bus. writer, educator; b. Wyoming, Ohio, July 22, 1929; s. Carl Alexander Herbert and Edith Vivian (Farley) S.; B.A., Yale, 1950; postgrad. U. Poitiers (France), 1950-51, Am. U. Beirut (Lebanon), 1953-54. Copywriter, Swink, Inc., Marion, Ohio, 1955-58; account supr. McCann-Erickson, Brussels, 1958-60; account supr. J. Walter Thompson Co., Amsterdam, Netherlands, 1960-63, asst. to exec. v.p. internat., N.Y.C., 1963-67, cons., N.Y.C. and London, 1967-69, internal cons. on spl. projects, acquisitions and diversification, N.Y.C., 1969-73; ind. cons., writer on advt. and mktg., N.Y.C., 1973—; editor Advt. World mag., N.Y.C., 1975-77; editor Corporate Advt. Newsletter, 1978—; cons. Internat. Advt. Assn., 1974—; adj. asso. prof. N.Y.U., 1966—. Served with U.S. Army, 1951-53. Fulbright fellow, 1950-51; Ford fellow, 1953-54. Mem. Internat. Advt. Assn., Am. Mktg. Assn., Inst. Mgmt. Scis. Episcopalian. Clubs: Yale (N.Y.C.); Elizabethan (New Haven). Author: Effective Advertising Self-Regulation, 1974; Controversy Advertising, 1977. Home: 300 E 46th St New York City NY 10017 Office: World Wide Info Service 660 1st Ave New York City NY 10016

STRIGNANO, JOSEPH ROBERT, indsl., furniture, environmental designer; b. N.Y.C., June 25, 1932; s. Salvatore S. and Mary (Santogade) S.; student N.Y. Sch. Interior Design, Pratt Inst., Sch. Art, Columbia; m. Ann Wald, June 13, 1954; children—Barbara, Marc. Designer, Ernest Furniture Corp., N.Y.C., Nemirow Furniture Corp., N.Y.C., Standbuilt Furniture Corp., N.Y.C., Valley Furniture Corp., N.Y.C.; designer, v.p. Longacre Furniture Corp., N.Y.C., State of Newburgh Furniture Corp., N.Y.C.; pres. J.R. Strignano Assos., Inc., Product, Interior, Archtl. and Environmental Design, 1969—; cons. Directional Furniture Corp., John Stuart Furniture Corp., Design Inst. Am., Laurel Lighting, Armico Furniture Corp., Green Metal Furniture Corp., Penn. Valley Furniture Corp.; conceptual or cons. designer Colonie Hill, Hauppage, N.Y., Southampton (N.Y.) Inn, additions to Gurney's Inn, Montauk, N.Y., 1st Nat. Bank of Bayshore, Fed. Ct. House, Hauppage, Suffolk Meadows Race Track, Yaphank, N.Y., Canyon Club, Armonk, N.Y. Served with AUS, 1952-55. Chair, desk designs selected for permanent collection Museum of Modern Art, N.Y.C. Home: 300 E 56th St New York City NY 10022

STRIKE, DONALD PETER, chemist; b. Mt. Carmel, Pa., Oct. 24, 1936; s. Peter and Verna (Dugan) S.; B.S., Phila. Coll. Pharmacy and Sci., 1958; Ph.D., Iowa State U., 1963; m. Sally Cavanaugh, July 28, 1972; children—Brian, Samantha. NIH research fellow U. Southampton (Eng.), 1963-64; research chemist Wyeth Labs., Radnor, Pa., 1965-69, group leader, 1969-77, research mgr., 1977—. Mem. Am. Chem. Soc., Phila. Organic Chemists Club, Phi Delta Chi, Phi Lambda Upsilon. Democrat. Roman Catholic. Home: 445 Ivan Ave Saint Davids PA 19087 Office: Wyeth Labs Radnor PA 19087

STRINE, HARRY CORNELIUS, III, educator; b. Danville, Pa., Jan. 18, 1943; s. Harry Cornelius and Helen Elizabeth (Barron) S.; B.A., Susquehanna U., 1964; M.A., Ohio U., 1969; m. Mary Ann Bolig, June 14, 1969; children—Harry Cornelius, Sean Bolig. Teaching asst. speech U. Md., Coll. Park, 1964-66; tchr. English, speech Shamokin (Pa.) Area High Sch., 1966-70; instr. speech communication and theatre arts Bloomsburg (Pa.) State Coll., 1970-73, asst. prof., 1973—, also dir. forensics. Chmn. manpower com. Cub scouts Bloomsburg council Boy Scouts Am., 1976. Mem. Am., Nat., Pa. (sec.-treas. 1978-79) forensic assns., Speech Communication Assn., Speech Communication Assn. Pa., Pi Kappa Delta (gov. province of colonies 1978-80), Alpha Psi Omega. Republican. Lutheran. Clubs: Elks, K.T. Home: 250 Sunnyside Ave Bloomsburg PA 17815 Office: Bloomsburg State Coll Bloomsburg PA 17815

STRINGFIELD, VICTOR TIMOTHY, hydrogeologist; b. Franklinton, La., Sept. 10, 1902; s. William Smith and Laura Amelia (Harvey) S.; B.S., La. State U., 1925; M.S., Washington U., St. Louis, 1927; m. Jessica Fairfax Hill, Oct. 19, 1929; children—Barbara Louise, Beverly Anne. Geologist, Tex. Co., Amarillo, 1927; instr. geology Okla. A. and M. Coll., Stillwater, 1927-28; asst. prof. geology and mineralogy N.Mex. Sch. Mines, Socorro, 1928-30; geologist N.Mex. Bur. Mines, Socorro, 1928-30; geologist, research hydrologist U.S. Geol. Survey, Washington, 1930—; cons. FAO UN, 1965-72. Recipient O.E. Meinzer award Geol. Soc. Am., 1970. Fellow Geol. Soc. Am.; mem. Soc. Econ. Geologists, Am. Assn. Petroleum Geologists, Geol. Soc. Washington, Internat. Assn. Hydrogeologists, Am. Geophys. Union. Contbr. articles to profl. publs. Home: 4208 50th St NW Washington DC 20016 Office: US Geol Survey Reston VA 22092

STRINIC, LILA FRANCES, counselor; b. Clairton, Pa., June 6, 1934; d. Andrew F. and Stella Marie (Sammartin) Chasko; B.A., Duquesne U., 1955; M.Ed., U. Pitts., 1958; postgrad. U. London, 1959, U. Colo., 1957, Hunter Coll., 1963; M.A. equivalent, U. Wis., 1964; postgrad. Columbia U., 1964-65, U. Pitts., 1967-68, 75-78, Loyola U., 1973, Harvard U., 1974; m. Matthew V. Strinic, Jan. 28, 1967; children—Luke, Mary Monica. Editorial asst. U. Pitts. Press, 1955-56; tchr. English, journalism Clairton (Pa.) pub. schs., 1956-61; tchr., counselor White Plains (N.Y.) High Sch., 1961-63; counselor Sleepy Hollow High Sch., Tarrytown, N.Y., 1964-66, Thomas Jefferson High Sch., W. Jefferson Hills, Pa., 1966-67; counselor Pitts. pub. schs., 1967-78. Co-chmn. human relations com., mem. bd. govs., Duquesne U., Pitts., 1974-75. Frick fellow, U. London, 1959; NDEA fellow, U. Wis., 1963-64; NDEA summer fellow, Columbia U., 1965; certified tchr., counselor, N.Y., Pa.; licensed real estate sales woman. Mem. Pitts. Counselors Assn., Am. Psychol. Assn., Am., Pa. personnel and guidance assns., Am. Fedn. Tchrs., Assn. for Counselor Edn. and Supervision, Assn. Humanistic Edn. and Devel., Assn. for Specialists in Group Work, Make Today Count, Duquesne Alumni Assn., Pitts. Psychoanalytic Center. Democrat. Roman Catholic. Editor: World Lits., 1956, Pitt Mag., 1956. Home: 220 Temona Dr Pittsburgh PA 15236

STRNISA, FRED V., physicist; b. Cleve., Nov. 20, 1941; s. Fred V. and Josephine J. (Pajk) S.; B.S. in Physics, Case Western Res. U., 1963; M.S. in Physics, John Carroll U., 1967; Ph.D. in Physics, State U. N.Y., 1972; m. Diana I. Anderson; children—Jeanette, Jennifer, Jeannine. Engr., lamp div. Gen. Electric Co., Cleve., 1963-67, physicist Knolls Atomic Power Lab., Schenectady, 1967-69; research asso. State U. N.Y., Albany, 1969-73; sr. scientist N.Y. State Atomic Energy Council, Albany, 1973-76, N.Y. State Energy Office, Albany, 1976-77; program mgr. N.Y. State Energy Research and Devel. Authority, Albany, 1977—. Fellow Sunya Inst. for Study of Defects in Solids; mem. Am. Phys. Soc., Am. Nuclear Soc., Health Physics Soc., Sigma Xi, Sigma Pi Sigma. Contbr. articles to profl. jours. Home: Box 389-A RD 1 Pattersonville NY 12137 Office: Empire State Plaza Albany NY 12223

STROBRIDGE, TRUMAN RUSSELL, historian; b. Sault Ste. Marie, Mich., Oct. 15, 1927; s. Roy Jamie and Ethel Augusta (Goodeman) S.; B.A., Mich. State U., 1951, M.A., 1957; grad. student Am. U., 1959-62; m. Mary Margaret Witeck, Aug. 25, 1959; 1 son, Lance Jamie. Archivist, Nat. Archives, 1959-61; historian USMC, 1961-63; command historian Alaskan Command Joint Chiefs of Staff, Anchorage, 1964-67; sr. historian Office Comdr.-in-Chief Pacific Joint Chiefs Staff, Honolulu, 1967-70; service historian USCG, Washington, 1970—; high sch. tchr., Onconto, Wis., 1958-59; instr. history U. Alaska, 1964-67. Served with USAAF, 1946-47. Nat. Archives scholar, 1959. Mem. Am. Hist. Assn., Orgn. Am. Historians, Co. Mil. Historians, Am. Mil. Inst. Republican. Baptist. Author: Chronology of Aids to Navigation 1716-1939, 1974; U.S. Coast Guard Annotated Bibliography, 1972; co-author: Western Pacific Operations: History of U.S. Marine Corps in World War II, 1971. Contbr. profl. jours. Home: 4721 Koester Dr Woodbridge VA 22193 Office: G-APA/83 US Coast Guard 400 7th St SW Washington DC 20590

STROH, EDWARD WALDEMAR, ednl./vocat. counselor; b. Weehawken, N.J., Aug. 1, 1928; s. Waldemar and Veronica S.; B.S., Columbia U., 1957; M.A., Montclair State Coll., 1965; Ph.D., Fla. State U., 1976; m. Constance Mae Bogert, June 20, 1953; children—Katherine, Valerie, Edward. Tchr., Leonia (N.J.) Pub. Schs., 1953-57; tchr. River Dell Regional Schs., Oradell, N.J., 1957-64, counselor edn., vocation, 1964—. Mem. Randolph (N.J.) Drug Action Council, 1976-77, v.p., 1977-78. Mem. Am. (licensure rep. N.J. 1977—), N.J. (v.p. 1977—) personnel and guidance asssns., NEA, Am. Psychol. Assn. Democrat. Methodist. Home: 19 Dogwood Trail Randolph NJ 07801

STROH, OSCAR HENRY, agrl. engr.; b. Harrisburg, Pa., Jan. 11, 1908; s. Simon Henry and Alice (Feaser) S.; B.S., U. Fla., 1948; student Command and Gen. Staff Coll., 1944, Armed Forces Indsl. Coll., 1954; m. Geraldine Bradshaw, Dec. 18, 1936; children—Jon Robert, Dana Evelyn. Ofcl. photographer U. Fla., 1938-40; civil engr. U.S. Govt., 1952-67, Commonwealth of Pa., 1967-73; cons. engr., Harrisburg, 1973—. Pa. forest fire warden, 1931-71. Bd. dirs. Central Dauphin Sch. System, 1953-65, Daniel Boone Nat. Found., Birdsboro, Pa., 1969—, Fishing Creek Valley Community Assn., 1949—; bd. govs. Am. Coll. Heraldry. Served to lt. col. AUS, 1940-47, 50-52; Korea. Registered profl. engr., Pa., Vt. Mem. Nat. Soc. Profl. Engrs., Constrn. Specifications Inst., Co. Mil. Historians, Assn. Ret. Intelligence Officers, S.A.R. (sec.), Mil. Order World Wars. Mason (32 deg.). Club: Sojourners. Author: Thompson's Battalion, 1975. Contbr. biweekly hist. column Paxton Herald, 1973—. Home and office: RD 4 Box 925 Harrisburg PA 17112

STROH, OSCAR SIMON, steel import co. exec.; b. Vienna, Austria, Jan. 20, 1914; s. Leopold M. and Bertha S. (Blatt) S.; LL.D., U. Vienna, 1938; m. Eve G. Sondheimer, Jan. 6, 1946; 1 son, Peter. Came to U.S., 1940, naturalized, 1945. Traffic mgr. Sopic Corp., N.Y.C., 1940-48; with Standard Internat. Co., Mt. Vernon, N.Y., 1948-72, pres., 1967-72; with B.S. Livingston, N.Y.C., 1972—, v.p., 1973—; cons. Trefil Arbed Co., N.Y.C. Mem. hospitality com. UN, N.Y.C., 1965—; cons. Mem. Am. Inst. Imported Steel (past dir.), Am. Arbitration Assn. (arbitrator). Home: 3050 Fairfield Ave Riverdale NY 10463 Office: Trefil Arbed Co 825 3d Ave New York City NY 10022

STROHL, JAMES EMERSON, counselor; b. Allentown, Pa., Dec. 7, 1950; s. Darle Albert and Lorraine Anna (Schlegel) S.; B.S., Stroudsburg East State Coll., 1972; M.Ed., Kutztown State Coll., 1977; m. Linda Lissette Mertz, Mar. 22, 1975. Tchr., Nitschmann Jr. High Sch., Bethlehem, Pa., 1974-77; counseling intern Allentown Coll., Center Valley, Pa., 1977, residence dir., 1978; counselor Liberty High Sch., Bethlehem, 1978—. Served with USNR, 1972-78. Mem. Am., Pa. personnel and guidance assns., Am. Coll. Personnel Assn., Pa. Sch. Counselors Assn., Assn. Humanistic Psychology, NEA, Pa. Edn. Assn., Polit. Action Com. for Edn. Mem. United Ch. Christ. Home and office: Tocik Hall Allentown Coll Center Valley PA 18034

STRONG-TIDMAN, VIRGINIA ADELE, bus. services co. exec.; b. Englewood, N.J., July 26, 1947; d. Alan Ballentine and Virginia Leona (Harris) S.; B.S., Albright Coll., 1969; postgrad. U. Pitts., 1970-73; m. John Fletcher Tidman, Sept. 23, 1978. Exec. trainee, Allied Store Corp., Pomeroy's Reading, Pa., 1969-70; home economist/product testing coordinator/market research analyst Heinz U.S.A., Pitts., 1970-74; mktg. mgr. new products Ky. Fried Chicken Corp., Louisville, 1974-76; account exec. Mktg. and Research Counselors Inc., Dallas, 1976-77, dir., Pitts., 1977—. Mem. Pitts. C. of C., Am. Mktg. Assn. Episcopalian. Home: 2113 St James Pl Wexford PA 15090 Office: Marketing and Research Counselors Inc 4 Allegheny Center Suite 810 Pittsburgh PA 15212

STROTHER, JOHN ALAN, mfg. co. exec.; b. Hartford, Conn., Dec. 27, 1927; s. Alfred Carter and Mary Stoughton (Parsons) S.; student Norwich U., 1945; B.S., Trinity Coll., Hartford, 1950; M.S.E., Princeton, 1954; m. Helene Therese McCurdie, June 16, 1951; children—Kathleen, Jean, Nancy. Jr. physicist USN Underwater Sound Lab., New London, Conn., 1950-52; mem. tech. staff RCA Labs., Princeton, N.J., 1954-58; engring. mgr. RCA Astro Electronics, Princeton, 1958-61, engring. mgr., 1966—; project engr. Electro Mech. Research, Inc., Sarasota, Fla., 1961-62; engring. mgr., Princeton, 1962-66. Served with Signal Corps, AUS, 1946-47. NSF fellow, 1952-53, 53-54. Registered profl. engr., N.J. Mem. Phi Beta Kappa, Sigma Xi, Sigma Pi Sigma. Contbr. chpt. to text, articles to profl. jours. Home: 201 Grover Ave Princeton NJ 08540 Office: RCA Astro Electronics POB 800 Princeton NJ 08540

STROUD, JAMES STANLEY, lawyer; b. Wimbledon, N.D., Jan. 26, 1915; s. Herbert Montgomery and Amanda Getchel (Longfellow) S.; A.B., Jamestown Coll., 1936; J.D., U. Chgo., 1939; m. Marjorie Marsh Hovey, Sept. 11, 1940; children—Jay Stanley, Steven Hovey. Admitted to Ill. bar, 1939, D.C. bar, 1972; draftsman Ill. Municipal Code Commn., Chgo., 1939-40; bill drafter Ill. Legis. Reference Bur., Springfield, 1941; asso. firm Mayer, Brown & Platt, Chgo., 1941-57, partner, 1957—, Washington office, 1972—. Bd. dirs. Chgo. Community Renewal Found., 1962-70, Community Renewal Soc., 1964-70. Served with C.I.C., U.S. Army, 1942-44, J.A.G., 1944-46. Mem. Am., D.C., Fed. Energy bar assns. Republican. Methodist. Club: Nat. Lawyers, Washington. Home: 3620 Lido Pl Fairfax VA 22030 Office: Suite 400 888 17th St NW Washington DC 20006

STROWGER, RICHARD JOHN, accountant; b. Buffalo, Feb. 23, 1939; s. Earl B. and Dorothy (Hoffman) S.; B.S., Syracuse U., 1960; m. Barbara J. Reslink, May 20, 1967; children—Ryan J., Bradley R. With Price Waterhouse & Co., Buffalo, 1960-62, 64-67, Syracuse, N.Y., 1967—, sr. accountant, 1965-69, mgr., 1969-75, audit partner, 1975—. Bd. dirs. UN Assn. Central N.Y., 1972-73, 76—, pres., 1973-76; bd. dirs. Internat. Center of Syracuse, 1977—. Served with U.S. Army, 1962-64. C.P.A. Mem. Am. Inst. C.P.A.'s, N.Y. State Soc. C.P.A.'s, Am. Hosp. Assn., Hosp. Fin. Mgmt. Assn. (principles and practices bd. 1978—). Clubs: World Trade Central N.Y., University, Cavalry, Limestone Tennis, Lions (dir. 1977-78, v.p. 1978—). Author articles in field. Home: 101 Stanwood Ln Manlius NY 13104 Office: One Mony Plaza Syracuse NY 13202

STRUBLE, ROBERT STANLEY, steel co. exec.; b. Morristown, N.J., Aug. 4, 1923; s. Ernest A. and Adele (Hall) S.; B.S. in Commerce, Rider Coll., 1948; m. Lamond Doig, Apr. 21, 1946; children—L. Lynn, Janet D., Meg M., Kim M. Staff accountant Haskins & Sells, 1948-49; control accountant cyclone fence div. U.S. Steel Corp., Newark, 1949-54, supr. cost analysis Am. Steel & Wire div. Waukegan, Ill., 1955-60, sr. systems designer Chgo., 1961-65, supr., sr. cost analyst supply div., Chgo., 1965, mgr. cost and statistics, 1966-71, dist. mgr. U.S. Steel Supply div., Conshohocken, Pa., 1971-74; mgr. ops., comptroller Charles F. Guyon, Inc., Harrison, N.J., 1974-76, v.p. ops., comptroller, 1976—. Chmn., Waukegan Republican Com., 1962-66; vice chmn. Lake County (Ill.) Republican party, 1964-66. Served with USAAF, 1942-45. Decorated D.F.C., Air medal with silver oak leaf cluster. Mem. Am. Legion, V.F.W., Nat. Assn. Accountants. Clubs: Masons (32 deg.), Newton Country, Rotary, Lake Lenape (Andover, N.J.). Home: Route 1 Box 703 Newton NJ 07860 Office: 900 S 4th St Harrison NJ 07029

STRUCKUS, EDWARD JOSEPH, city ofcl.; b. Worcester, July 21, 1925; s. Joseph Adam and Mary Elizabeth (Sinaskas) S.; B.S. in Group Work and Community Orgn., Springfield (Mass.) Coll., 1949; M.Ed., Worcester State Coll., 1957; m. Theresa K. Khoury, Apr. 1948; children—Michael Joseph, Joseph Edward. Program dir. Settlement House, Dorchester, Mass., 1949-52; sport therapist Brockton (Mass.) VA Hosp., 1952-54; recreation therapist Westborough (Mass.) State Hosp., 1955-56; tchr. phys. edn. Worcester Pub. Schs., 1956-57; gen. recreation supr. Worcester Parks and Recreation Commn., 1957-68, supt. parks, forestry and recreation, 1968—. Bd. dirs. United Fund, 1959-63, Great Brook Valley Community Center, 1960-65; sponsor Worcester Area Assn. Retarded Children summer camp; mem. Worcester City Democratic Ward Com., 1962-72; mem. Pres.'s Council Phys. Fitness and Sports. Served with USAAF, 1943-45. Recipient award Worcester Park and Recreation Commn., 1957, Mass. House Reps., 1960, 67, John F. Kennedy Assn., 1962, Mass. Recreation and Park Soc., 1966; Outstanding Letter of Recognition, Vice Pres. Lyndon B. Johnson, 1962; Eugene A. Parsons Meml. award for hort. achievement, 1968; Recognition award Boy Scouts Am., 1968; Recognition plaque for continuous support live music programs in Worcester, Worcester Musicians Union Local 143, 1974; Achievement award Worcester Area Assn. Retarded Children, 1976; letter of appreciation for fish and game programs Worcester County Fish and Game Assn., 1977; Nat. Vol. Service award Nat. Recreation and Park Assn., 1977; Merit of Achievement and Gold Medal award Sports Found. USA, Inc., 1978. Mem. Mass. Recreation and Park Soc., Mass. Adult Edn. Assn., Mass. Lifelong Learning Assn., C. of C. (chmn. sr. citizen hobby and craft assn.), Am. Assn. Zool. Parks, Am. Park and Recreation Soc. (spl. achievement award with Nat. Recreation and Park Assn. 1978), Am. Forestry Assn., Mass. Assn. Health, Phys. Edn. and Recreation, Worcester City Adminstrs. Assn., Worcester Hort Soc., New Eng. Park Assn., DAV (comdr., life mem.), Lithuanian Naturalization and Social Club (dir.), Lithuanian Charitable Soc., Worcester Auto Club. Home: 5 Pratt St Worcester MA 01609 Office: 455 Maine St Worcester MA 01608

STRUPCZEWSKI, JAMES ANTHONY, city ofcl.; b. New Bedford, Sept. 20, 1936; s. Anthony and Annette (Rostocki) S.; B.S. in Bus. Adminstrn., Bryant Coll., 1966; m. Apr. 18, 1970. Internat auditor Uniroyal, Detroit, 1966; with N.Y. State Dept. Audit and Control, Albany, 1967-71; asst. city auditor City of New Bedford, 1971-74, city auditor/budget analysis, 1974—; lectr. in field. Chmn. City of New Bedford Retirement System, 1974—; treas. Southeastern Regional Transit Authority, 1975—; mem. New Bedford Airport Commn., 1974—. Served with U.S. Army Res., 1955-57. Mem. EDP Auditors Assn., Mass. Municipal Accountants and Auditors Assn., Municipal Fin. Officers Assn. Democrat. Roman Catholic. Home: 1075 Braley Rd New Bedford MA 02745 Office: 133 William St New Bedford MA 02740

STRUZYNA, GEORGE ARTHUR FELIX, mech. engr.; b. Breslau, Germany, July 13, 1920; came to U.S., 1958; naturalized, 1964; s. Joseph and Elise (Leppmann) S.; Diplom-Ingenieur, Hanover Inst. Tech. (Germany), 1950; postgrad. U. Bristol (Eng.), 1949, Veasey Coll. Engring. (South Africa), 1954-56; m. Erika Hertha Schomburgk, May 27, 1950; children—Reinhart W., Dieter G., Dorothee E. Asst. to plant mgr. German Highgrade Steel Co., Remscheid, 1950; design engr., plant engr. Bayer AG, Leverkusen, Germany, 1951-53; chief engr. No. 1 ammonia plant African Explosives and Chem. Industries, Johannesburg, South Africa, 1954-57; chief engr., v.p. engring. Verona Chem. Corp., Union, N.J.,1958-76; dir. engring. services Mobay Chem. Corp., Pitts., 1976—. Chmn. bd. dirs. German Lang. Sch., Union, 1964-68. Served with Germany Army, 1940-45. Decorated Iron Cross 1st and 2d class; registered profl. engr., N.J., S.C. Mem. Nat. Soc. Profl. Engrs. (chpt. pres. 1974-75), ASME, Inst. Mech. Engrs. (London), Center for Internat. Security Studies (founder mem.). Republican. Presbyterian. Contbr. articles to profl. jours. Home: 203 Roscommon Pl McMurray PA 15317 Office: Penn Lincoln Pkwy W Pittsburgh PA 15205

STRYKER, JAY WILLIAM, JR., radiation biophysicist; b. Trenton, Aug. 22, 1941; s. Jay William and Eleanor Whitney (Reed) S.; B.A., Trenton State Coll., 1963; M.S. (USPHS fellow), Rutgers U., 1970; m. Janet Elaine Cole, Jan. 17, 1978; children—Jeff, Brett, Barry, David, Anne, Catherine, Sander, George. Tchr. sci. Peace Corps, Zomba, Malawi, Africa, 1964-66; lectr. in radiation Rutgers U., 1968-69; radiation safety officer, lectr. U. Mass., Amherst, 1969-78, now research asso. dept. physics and astronomy; lectr. Orchard Hill Residential Coll., 1972—; dir. Conn. Valley Cottage Industries; mem. nuclear incidents advisory team Mass. State Police and Pub. Health; speaker in field. Mem. AAAS, Health Physics Soc., Internat. Radiation Protection Assn., Nat. Safety Council, New Eng. Indsl. Hygiene Assn., Solar Energy Soc., Space Colony Soc., World Future Soc., Amherst Ry. Soc., Sigma Xi. Unitarian. Designer cart for handicapped; composer: Nocturnes and Hymns, 1978; composer musical play: Dance in The Sunshine, 1978. Home: 47 Garage Rd Sunderland MA 01375 Office: Dept Physics and Astronomy U Mass Amherst MA 01003

STRYKER-RODDA, KENN, editor, genealogist; b. Arlington, N.J., July 7, 1903; s. Samuel Hockings and Cora Augusta (Stryker) Rodda; B.A., Princeton U., 1923; M.A., N.Y. U., 1925; D.Litt., Webster U., 1927; m. Harriet Mott, Dec. 29, 1924; children—Paul Mott, Ellsworth Natton, Andrea. Tchr., Pennington (N.J.) Sem., 1923-25; head English dept. Massanutten Acad., Woodstock, Va., 1925-27; dean Colby Acad., Bklyn., 1927-68; editor N.Y. Geneal. and Biog. Soc., N.Y.C., 1965—; certified genealogist, 1965—. Charter commr. Union County Cultural and Heritage Commn., 1970; mem. heritage com. N.J. Bicentennial Commn., 1975—. Recipient Outstanding Service award N.J. Hist. Commn., 1977; named Genealogist of Year, Utah Geneal. Soc., 1977. Fellow Am. Soc. Genealogists (past pres.), Nat. Geneal. Soc. (past pres.), Geneal. Soc. N.J. (past pres.); trustee League Hist. Soc. N.J. (past. gen. chmn.), Bd. Certification Genealogists (vice chmn. 1966—); mem. L.I. Hist. Soc. (dir., mem. exec. com. 1952-77). Author: Long Island Genealogical Source Materials, 1962; Digging for Ancestors in the Garden State, 1970; Boy Scout Merit Badge Manual: Genealogy, 1973; co-editor New York Historical Manuscripts: Dutch series, 1974—; contbr. articles to profl. jours. Home: 421 Summit Ave South Orange NJ 07079 Office: 122 E 58th St New York City NY 10022

STUART, ALDEN TAYLOR, ret. coll. ofcl.; b. Lockport, N.Y., July 13, 1908; s. Ira Alonzo and Mary Pettis (Baker) S.; B.S., St. Lawrence U., 1929; M.S., Cornell U., 1937; Ed.D., Syracuse U., 1956; m. Marion Ernestine Edwards, Aug. 19, 1936; children—Ursula E. (Mrs. Joseph T. Hedges), David Alan, Jacqueline Gertrude. Chemist, DuPont Cellophane Co., Buffalo, 1929-30; tchr. sci., math. Angelica Central Sch. (N.Y.), 1931-33; supervising prin. Canaseraga (N.Y.) Central Sch., 1933-40; supt. schs. Perry (N.Y.) Pub. Schs., 1940-46, Wellsville (N.Y.) Pub. Schs., 1946-56, Patchogue (N.Y.) Pub. Schs., 1956-64; adj. prof. Alfred (N.Y.) U., 1954-56, C.W. Post Coll., 1956; dir. div. edn. Southampton (N.Y.) Coll. of L.I. U., 1964-73. Mem. Allegany County (N.Y.) council Boy Scouts Am., 1948-54, Allegany County Tb and Health Bd., 1946-56, Suffolk County (N.Y.) Mental Health Bd., 1957-62; mem. parks adv. com. Town of Southampton. Trustee Suffolk County Dept. Parks, Recreation and Conservation. Mem. NEA (life), Nat. Soc. Study of Edn., AAUP, Phi Delta Kappa, Beta Theta Pi. Republican. Presbyterian (mem. bd. trustees). Mason, Rotarian. Contbr. articles to profl. jours. Home: 39 St Andrews Rd Southampton NY 11968

STUART, CHARLES HARPELL, historian; b. Worcester, Mass., Apr. 1, 1930; s. Raymond Robinson and Viola Gertrude (Harpell) S.; A.B., Houghton Coll., 1952; M.A., Bradley U., 1954; postgrad. Pa. State U., 1953-54, Andover-Newton Theol. Sch., 1954-55, Ecole Coloniale, Brussels, 1955-56; Ph.D., Boston U., 1969; m. Jeannette Brownell Spinny, Aug. 1, 1952; children—Charles Edward, Jeanne Elizabeth, Glen Raymond, Patricia Grace. Grad. asst. Bradley U., Peoria, Ill., 1952-53; grad. asst., instr. Pa. State U., University Park, 1953-54; ednl. missionary Bd. Internat. Ministries of Am. Baptist Chs. in U.S.A., Zaire, 1954-68; prof. history, acting dept. chmn. West Chester (Pa.) State Coll., 1968—; bd. dirs. Am. Bapt. Hist. Soc., 1971, pres., 1978—; moderator Bapt. Ch. W. Chester, 1973—. Mem. Am. Hist. Assn., African Studies Assn., AAUP. Contbr. book revs. to Internat. Jour. African Hist. Studies. Home: 812 S Church Ave West Chester PA 19380 Office: Main 502 West Chester State Coll West Chester PA 19380

STUART, JOHN M., lawyer; b. N.Y.C., Apr. 3, 1927; s. Winchester and Maude (Marberger) S.; B.A., Columbia, 1948, LL.B., 1951; m. Marjorie Louise Browne, Dec. 11, 1954; children—Jane, Alice, Richard. Admitted to N.Y. State bar, 1951, since practiced in N.Y.C.; asso. firm Reid & Priest, 1951-64, partner, 1965—. Asst. sec. Minn. Power &Light Co., 1951-64. Recipient Internat. Brotherhood Magicians award, 1958, 60, First prize sci. fiction Phila. Writers Conf., 1958. Mem. Am., N.Y. County bar assns., Sons of Revolution (life). Republican. Methodist. Contbr. articles to mags. Magician, W. German TV magic spl., 1965; appeared in Spy at the Magic Show benefit for Project Hope, Manhasset, N.Y., 1967; producer, co-author off-Broadway show Make Me Disappear, 1969; co-author: (novel) You Don't Have to Slay a Dragon, 1976. Home: 31 Westgate Blvd Plandome NY 11030 Office: 40 Wall St New York City NY 10006

STUART, WILLIAM CLARKSON, III, real estate exec.; b. Newport News, Va., May 25, 1926; s. William Clarkson and Susan Reid (Williams) S.; student Augusta Mil. Acad., Ft. Defiance, Va., 1940-44; m. Patricia Polk Morgan, June 12, 1950; children—William Clarkson, Alice Rhett, Patricia Morgan, Henry Morgan. Loan officer Mut. Home and Savs. Assn., Newport News, 1946-48; real estate salesman, asst. sales mgr. Boss & Phelps, Inc., Washington, 1948-51; real estate sales mgr. J. Rupert Mohler, Inc., Washington, 1951-56; pres. Stuart and Maury, Inc., Washington, 1956—. Mem. exec. com. Downtown Progress, D.C., 1974. Realtor, D.C., Md., Va., Del.; named D.C. Realtor of Year, 1974. Mem. Washington (past pres.), Montgomery County bds. Realtors, Md., Nat. (past dir.) assns. Realtors, Met. Washington Bd. Trade (past dir.), Omega Tau Rho. Republican. Episcopalian. Clubs: Chevy Chase, Rehoboth Beach Country, Henlopen Acres Beach. Home: 4960 Sentinel Dr Bethesda MD 20016 Office: 5010 Wisconsin Ave NW Washington DC 20016

STUART, WILLIAM DAVID, elec. engr.; b. Boyleston, Ind., June 25, 1932; s. John Edward and Mabel Ann (Weaver) S.; B.S. in E.E., Purdue U., 1955, M.S., 1957; postgrad. Ohio State U., 1959-75; m. Barbara Josephine Vandervort, Nov. 10, 1956; children—David Joseph, Karen Lynne. Engr., Farnsworth Electronics Co., Fort Wayne, Ind., 1955-57; research asso. Ohio State U., 1959-61; project leader Battelle Columbus Labs. (Ohio), 1961-75; group leader IIT Research Inst., Annapolis, Md., 1975—. Commr. Girls Softball, 1973-75; mem. com. Boy Scouts Am., 1968-72; chmn. student adv. services sci. Columbus Tech. Council, 1972-75. Served to 1st lt. AUS, 1957-58. Purdue Alumni scholar, 1951-55; Merit scholar, 1950-55. Registered profl. engr., Ohio, Md. Mem. IEEE (sr. mem.; chmn. Columbus, treas. Balt.), Am. Geophys. Union, Assn. Old Crows, Sigma Xi, Eta Kappa Nu. Democrat. Mem. Ch. of Christ. Author: Radar Cross Section Handbook, 1970. Home: 109 Claiborne Rd Edgewater MD 21037 Office: N Severn Annapolis MD 21402

STUART, WILLIAM EDWARD CAMPBELL, assn. exec.; b. Surry, N.C., Apr. 21, 1930; s. Raleigh Anderson Donathan and Ellen Luella (Jones) S.; B.S., Clemson U., 1950; M.A., U. Chgo., 1953; Ph.D., U. N.C., 1956; m. Hectorina Manuella y Sanchez, Sept., 1973; 1 dau., Angelika. Asst. attache Am. embassy, Djarkarta, Indonesia, 1956-57; asst. prof. Appalachian State Coll., Boone, N.C., 1958; dir. indsl. relations Ala. Turbine Corp., Mobile, 1965-69; pres. Sanchez Internat., San Juan, P.R., 1969-73, now dir.; pres. Stuart-Donathan Assos., Washington, 1973—; dir. Personnel Inst., Washington, 1973—; exec. v.p. Conn. Ave Assn.; dir. Hardy Products, Inc., Lacaze Acad., Rolphco, Inc.; lectr. George Washington U., Fed. City Coll. Mem. Pres's Hire the Handicapped Task Force; advisor J.O.B.S. Program; dir. Project Assist, 1975; sponsor D.C. Status of Women Program, 1976; sustaining mem. D.C. Republican Party. Served to maj. USMCR, 1950. Designated hon. capt. The Black Watch, Royal Highland Regt., 1959. Mem. Am. Mgmt. Assn., Am. Ordnance Assn., C. of C. U.S., Met. Washington Bd. Trade, NEA, Alpha Epsilon Rho. Unitarian. Clubs: Army-Navy, Aviation, Pilot Mountain Country, Marine Corps League. Author: Indonesia - Land of Promise, 1960; Personnel Development as an MBO Tool, 1970; The Executive Selector, 1975. Home: 610 Bashford Ln Alexandria VA 22314 Office: 1000 Connecticut Ave NW Washington DC 20036

STUBBS, DONALD CLARK, educator; b. Providence, R.I., Mar. 6, 1935; s. Edward Joseph and Margaret Eleanor (Clark) S.; A.B., Cath. U. Am., 1959, M.S., 1966; m. Lorraine A. Stubbs, Apr. 3, 1969; 1 son, Derek Clark. Tchr., Bishop Loughlin Meml. High Sch., Bklyn., 1959-61; tchr. Bishop Bradley High Sch., Manchester, N.H., 1961-66; tchr., chmn. sci. dept. LaSalle Mil. Acad., Oakdale, N.Y., 1966-69; tchr., chmn. sci. dept. Ponaganset Regional High Sch., Glocester, R.I., 1969—. NSF grantee, 1967-68. Mem. NEA, Ponaganset Tchrs. Assn. Democrat. Roman Cath. Home: 51 Woodland Ave Esmond RI 02917

STUBBS, JOHN JAMES, physician; b. Scott Haven, Pa., Aug. 27, 1911; s. Alfred and Lily Catherine (Cannon) S.; B.S., U. Pitts., 1932, M.D., 1936; m. Louisa Brinton, Aug. 3, 1939; children—John James, Margaret Louisa Stubbs Astley. Intern Western Pa. Hosp., 1936-37, resident in internal medicine, 1937-39, now mem. staff; practice medicine specializing in gerontology, Pitts., 1939—; med. dir. Collins Nursing Home, Pitts., 1969—. Served to maj. AUS, World War II. Mem. AMA, Pa., Allegheny County med. socs., Soc. Gerontology, Am. Soc. Geriatrics, Alpha Omega Alpha, Sigma Pi. Republican. Presbyterian. Clubs: Masons, Longue Vue, University. Home: 5025 5th Ave Apt B1 Pittsburgh PA 15232 Office: 506 Highland Bldg Pittsburgh PA 15206

STUDDIFORD, WALTER BEEKMAN, univ. ofcl.; b. Bridgewater, N.J., Jan. 18, 1928; s. Walter C. and Anna V. (Saums) S.; B.A. cum laude, Hope Coll., 1950; M.A., U. Minn., 1951, Ph.D., 1960. Research asso. Counseling Service, Princeton (N.J.) U., 1961-63, lectr. dept. of psychology, 1961-69, research asso. Office of Coll. Ops., 1963-65, asst. dir., 1965-69, asst. registrar Office of the Registrar, 1969—; dir. State Bank of Raritan Valley. Clk. of Consistory Third Ref. Dutch Ch. of Raritan, N.J., 1966-76; mem. Theol. Commn., Ref. Ch. in Am., 1968-74. Mem. Am. Psychol. Assn., Ednl. Research Assn., AAAS, N.J. Acad. Sci., Am. Statis. Assn., Assn. for Computing Machinery. Republican. Contbr. articles on psychology to profl. publs. Home: 170 Old York Rd Bridgewater NJ 08807 Office: Princeton University 3 W College Princeton NJ 08540

STUDDS, GERRY EASTMAN, congressman; b. Mineola, N.Y., May 12, 1937; s. Eastman and Beatrice (Murphy) S.; B.A., Yale, 1959, M.A. in Teaching, 1961. Fgn. service officer Dept. State, Washington, 1961-63; exec. asst. to presdl. cons. for a nat. service corps White House, 1963; legis. asst. to Sen. Harrison Williams, 1964; tchr. St. Paul's Sch., Concord, N.H., 1965-69; mem. 93d-95th congresses from 12th Dist. Mass.; candidate U.S. Congress, 1970. Del. Democratic Nat. Conv., 1968. Home: 16 Black Horse Ln Cohasset MA 02025 Office: Ho of Reps Washington DC 20515

STUEBER, GUSTAV, cons. engr.; b. Elberfeld, West Germany, Dec. 25, 1909; s. Joseph and Maria (Ross) S.; fundamental engring. certificate Tech. Sch., Cologne, West Germany, 1926; certificate U. Madison, 1940; m. Gertrude Martha Niere, Dec. 7, 1935; children—Loretta M., Gertrude (Mrs. Kenneth Eysel), Eric. Came to U.S., 1926, naturalized, 1931. With Sverdrup & Parcel Cons. Engring., 1935-39, Pitts. Des Moines Steel Co., 1939-42, Rust Engring. Co., 1942-43, United Engrs. & Constructors, Phila., 1943-45, Norfolk & Western Ry. Co., 1945-49, Dravo Corp., Pitts., 1949-50, pvt. practice as cons. engr., Pitts., 1950—. Charter mem. sci. seminar Peters Twp. (Pa.) High Sch. Former med. bd. view Washington County (Pa.) Ct. Named to Constrn. Industry Hall of Fame, Pitts., 1974. Mem. Am. Soc. Mil. Engrs., ASCE (life), Soc. Cons. Engrs. (charter), Nat., Pa. (past pres. Washington County chpt.) socs. profl. engrs., Cons. Engrs. Council, Pitts. Cons. Engrs. Council (charter). Author: Modern Welded Structures, 1963, 70. Contbr. articles to profl. jours. Home: 720 E McMurray Rd McMurray PA 15317 Office: 1039 Brookline Blvd Pittsburgh PA 15226

STUEBING, EDWARD WILLIS, research phys. scientist, educator; b. Cin., Sept. 9, 1942; s. Edward Norman and Ruth Marcella (Glass) S.; B.S., U. Cin., 1965; M.A. in Chemistry, Johns Hopkins, 1969, Ph.D. in Chem. Physics, 1970; m. Mary Ann Brown, Dec. 22, 1961; children—Barbara Jean, Jennifer Jane. Research physicist U.S. Army Frankford Arsenal, Phila., 1970-77; adj. asst. prof. chemistry Drexel U., 1974-77; research phys. scientist Chem. Systems Lab., U.S. Army, Aberdeen (Md.) Proving Ground, 1977—; cons. computer applications, math. Served with AUS, 1970-71. NSF trainee, 1965-70. Mem. Am. Phys. Soc., Am. Chem. Soc., Assn. for Computing Machinery, Internat. Soc. for Quantum Biology, Phi Beta Kappa, Sigma Xi, Phi Lambda Upsilon (chpt. pres. 1968-69), Lambda Chi Alpha. Democrat. Contbr. articles to profl. jours. Home: 1411 Purdue Ct Bel Air MD 21014

STUENKEL, ARTHUR EMIL, food co. exec.; b. Hinsdale, Ill., Apr. 21, 1926; s. Emil H. and Atense N. (Mandel) S.; B.S. in Naval Sci. and Tactics, also B.M.E., Purdue U., 1948; postgrad. U. Chgo., 1949-51; m. Lois Jean Otto, May 3, 1952; children—Gail Virginia, Donna Jean. With CPC Internat. Inc., 1947—, asst. to gen. mgr. mfg., Chgo., 1962-64, dir. investment planning, N.Y.C., 1965-68, exec. asst. to exec. v.p., corp. mfg. and engring., Englewood Cliffs, N.J., 1968-70, v.p. finance indsl. div., Englewood Cliffs, 1971-78, v.p. and exec. asst. indsl. diversified unit, 1978—; dir. Acme Resin Corp., Amerchol Corp., Penick Corp., Peterson/Puritan, Inc. Served to lt. (j.g.) USNR, 1944-46, 53-54. Mem. Theta Chi. Republican. Lutheran. Home: 106 Mill Brook Circle Norwood NJ 07648 Office: CPC Internat Inc International Plaza Englewood Cliffs NJ 07632

STUENKEL, HERBERT EDWARD, health care adminstr.; b. Concordia, Mo., Feb. 18, 1923; s. Edward and Martha (Holsten) S.; B.S. in Edn., Concordia Coll., River Forest, Ill., 1945; M.A., San Francisco State U., 1954; postgrad. U. Calif., Berkeley, 1954-56; m. Betty Jane Kuddes, Jan. 7, 1945; children—Elizabeth Ann Stuenkel Friedrich, Mark Herbert. Dir. religious edn. Redeemer Lutheran Ch., Kansas City, Mo., 1944-46; prin. St. Paulus Luth. Sch., San Francisco, 1946-63; exec. dir. Balt. Luth. High Sch., 1963-69, Luth. High Sch. Orange County (Calif.), 1969-75, Luth Care for Aging, San Francisco, 1975-79, Gen. German Aged People's Home, Balt., 1979—. Founder Luth. high sch., Balt., 1965, Orange, Calif., 1973. Mem. Luth. Acad. Scholarship, Phi Delta Kappa. Republican. Club: Greenspring (Towson, Md.). Home: The Ridgely 2409 205 E Joppa Rd Towson MD 21204 Office: 22 S Athol Ave Baltimore MD 21229

STULA, MICHAEL JAMES, govt. ofcl.; b. N.Y.C., July 9, 1914; s. Fred and Irene (Melnik) S.; B.S., Ia. State U., 1938; m. Pauline A. Wickson, July 5, 1941; children—Linnea W., Jocelyn D. Insp. United Aircraft Co., East Hartford, Conn., 1940-42, foreman, 1942-45; owner Stula Agy., Colchester, Conn., 1945—; commr. Conn. Bd. Fisheries and Game, Hartford, 1957—, also chmn. Mayor, Colchester, Conn., 1953-61. Trustee Cragin Meml. Library, Bacon Acad. Mem. New Eng. Outdoor Writers Assn., Nat. Assn. Real Estate Bds. Roman Catholic. Elk, Lion. Address: 53 S Main St Colchester CT 06415

STULL, DONALD LEROY, architect; b. Springfield, Ohio, May 16, 1937; s. Robert and Ruth (Callahan) S.; B.Arch. (Dwight Smith scholar), Ohio State U., 1961; M.Arch., Harvard U., 1962; m. Patricia Ann Ryder, Dec. 29, 1959; children—Cydney Lynn, Robert Branson, Gia Virginia. Designer, George Mason Clark, Architect, Columbus, 1958-61; designer Boston Fed. Office Bldg Architects, Cambridge, Mass., 1961-62; project dir. Samuel Glaser & Partners, Boston, 1962-66; pres. Stull Assos., Inc., Boston, 1966—. Mem. faculty Yale U., Harvard U. Mem. policy com. Harvard Grad. Sch. Design, 1970-71, mem. alumni council, 1969-71, Loeb Fellowship com., 1970—; mem. Myer com. Yale, 1970-71, mem. pres.'s vis. com. Sch. Architecture, 1973—; mem. Boston-Hist. Preservation Commn., 1970; mem. adv. com. Mass. Housing and Finance Agy., Mass. Dept. Community Affairs, 1970-71; chmn. Mass. Bldg. Code Commn., 1973-75; cons. Roxbury Action Program, Boston, 1970—; v.p. Black Grove, Miami, Fla., 1970-75. Bd. dirs. Mus. Afro-Am. History, New Urban League Boston; former bd. dirs. Interfaith Housing Corp.; trustee Shaw U., 1973-75, Mus. Contemporary Art. Recipient Alpha Rho Chi medal Ohio State U., 1961, Texnikoi Honorary, 1960, named Centennial Year Distinguished Alumni, 1970; Regional Design award A.I.A., 1970; named one of Ten Outstanding Young Men of Am., Boston Jaycees, 1970. Mem. AIA, Boston Soc. Architects (dir. 1969), Bldg Ofcls. Code Adminstrs., Boston Archtl. Center, Mass. Soc. Architects, NAACP. Office: 431 Marlborough St Boston MA 02115

STUMPF, T(HOMAS) ROBERT, graphic cons.; b. Queens Village, N.Y., Oct. 23, 1909; s. Conrad O. and Eleanor (Barwood) S.; B.S., Trinity Coll., 1932; postgrad. N.Y. U., New Sch. Social Research, 1932-37; m. Clara Rumpe, June 10, 1958. With Marchbanks Press, N.Y.C., 1932-34, Mergenthaler Linotype Co., Bklyn., 1934-42; graphic designer, Standard Oil Co. (N.J.), N.Y.C., 1946-63, on loan to Iranian Oil Operating Cos. to establish graphic audio visual sect., Tehran, 1958-60; graphic cons., N.Y.C., 1963—. Faculty graphic arts dept. N.Y. U., 1933-35; graphic asst. New Sch. Social Research, 1934-37. Served to lt. comdr. USNR, 1942-46. Mem. Pub. Relations Soc. Am., Typophiles, Delta Phi. Club: Grolier. Address: 36 Corrigan St Southampton NY 11968

STUNKARD, HORACE WESLEY, zoologist; b. Monmouth, Iowa, Aug. 23, 1889; s. Hiram Wesley and Lula May (Hopkins) S.; B.S. magna cum laude, Coe Coll., Cedar Rapids, Iowa, 1912, Sc.D., 1937; A.M., U. Ill., 1914, Ph.D., 1916; Sc.D., N.Y. U., 1954; m. Frances Grace Klank, June 12, 1920 (dec.); children—Albert James, Eunice Stunkard Latham. Mem. faculty N.Y. U., 1916-54, emeritus prof. biology, 1954—; research asso. dept. fossil and living invertebrates Am. Mus. Natural History, N.Y.C., 1921—. Served with A.C., U.S. Army, 1917-1919; AEF in France. Guggenheim fellow, 1931-32; Oberländer Trust fellow, 1938-39; recipient Gold medal Am. Mus. Natural History, 1971; Leuckart medal German Parasitological Soc., 1974. Mem. Am. Micros. Soc. (past pres.), Am. Soc. Parasitologists (past pres.), Soc. Systematic Zoologists (past pres.), N.Y. Acad. Scis. (past pres.; A. Cresy Morrison prize 1929, Pregel prize 1973), N.Y. Soc. Tropical Medicine (past pres.), AAAS (past v.p.), Am. Soc. Zoologists (past v.p.), Am. Assn. Anatomists, Am. Soc. Naturalists, Am. Soc. Tropical Medicine and Hygiene, Royal Soc. Tropical Medicine, Soc. Zoologique France. Contbr. articles to profl. jours. Home: 5000 Waldo Ave Bronx NY 10471 Office: Am Museum Central Park West New York City NY 10024

STUNKARD, JIM A., veterinarian; b. Sterling, Colo., Jan. 25, 1935; s. James Leith and Gladys Leone (Winey) S.; B.S., Colo. State U., 1957, D.V.M., 1959; M.S., Tex. A. and M. U., 1966; m. Patricia Gayle Dotson, Sept. 2, 1967; children—Todd Matthew, Cory Leith. Clinician, Glasgow (Ky.) Animal Hosp., 1959-61; commd. 1st lt. USAF, 1961, advanced through grades to lt. col. reserves, 1975; chmn. veterinary med. scis. dept. Naval Med. Research Inst., Bethesda, Md., 1966-71; resigned regular commn., 1971, med. augmentee Armed Forces Inst. Pathology, Washington; owner, clinician Bowie (Md.) Animal Hosp., 1971—, Crofton Animal Hosp., Gambrills, Md., 1975—; pres. SMA, Inc.; referral veterinarian for exotic animal medicine; veterinary cons. NIH. Mem. D.C. Acad. Vet. Medicine (pres. elect), D.C. Vet. Med. Assn. (pres.). Home: 959 Mayo Rd Edgewater MD 21037 Office: 1044 Hwy 3N Gambrills MD 21054

STURGES, FLORENCE MARGARET (MRS. DWIGHT RICHARD STURGES), librarian; b. Boston, July 2, 1908; d. Edgar Saxon and Charlotte Jane (Case) Stanley; student New Eng. Conservatory, 1928-30; student Boston Pub. Library Tng. Sch., 1931-33; diploma Curry Coll., 1940; m. Dwight Richard Sturges, Oct. 12, 1935. Children's librarian Boston Pub. Library, 1932-41; children's librarian Wellesley (Mass.) Free Library, 1943-70, reference librarian, 1943-70; children's librarian, asst. librarian Skidompha Library, Damariscotta, Maine, 1970—. Cons. in establishment of library at Children's Hosp., Boston, 1956-60; pres. New Eng. Round Table of Children's Librarians, 1960-62; mem. Sci. Mus. Book Com., Boston, 1962-68; Caroline M. Hewins lectr., Boston, 1959. Mem. Bronte Soc. of Eng., Nat. Book League, Am. Pen Women (book rev. editor 1968-70). Clubs: Women's Club. Author hist. studies; contbr. articles to lit. publs. Home: Old County Rd Damariscotta ME 04543 Office: Skidompha Library Damariscotta ME 04543

STURGES, JOHN SIEBRAND, ins. co. exec.; b. Greenwich, Conn., Feb. 12, 1939; s. Harry Wilton and Elizabeth Helen (Niewenhouse) S.; A.B., Harvard U., 1960; M.B.A., U. So. Calif., 1965; certificate EDP, N.Y. U., 1972, certificate life ins. Life Office Mgmt. Assn., 1967; m. Anastasia Daphne Bakalis, May 6, 1967; 2 daus., Christina Aurora, Elizabeth Athena. With Equitable Life Assurance Soc. U.S., N.Y.C., 1965—, supr. systems devel., 1965-67, project mgr., 1967-70, mgr. adminstrv. services, 1970-71, dir. compensation, 1971-75, asst. v.p., personnel, 1975-77, v.p. adminstrv. and devel. resources, 1977—. Vestryman, St. Peter's Episcopal Ch., Freehold N.J., 1974—, corp. sec., 1976—, lay reader, 1972—. Served to lt. USNR, 1960-65. Mem. Commerce Assos., Life Office Mgmt. Assn. (salary adminstrn. com., 1972-75), Am. Soc. Personnel Adminstrn., Health Ins. Assn. Am. (personnel com., 1972—), N.Y. Personnel Mgmt. Assn. (chmn. tng. and devel. com. 1972-77), Am. Compensation Assn., Beta Gamma Sigma (dir. N.Y. 1978—), Phi Kappa Phi. Republican. Home: 8 Winnipeg Ct Morganville NJ 07751 Office: 1285 Ave of the Americas New York City NY 10019

STURM, RUTH FOSTER, lawyer; b. Bklyn., Jan. 3, 1911; d. Ernest and L. Elsie (Foster) Sturm; B.A., Vassar Coll., 1932; LL.B., Columbia U., 1935; postgrad. U. Lausanne (Switzerland), summer 1929, U. Berlin (Germany), summer 1931. Admitted to N.Y. bar, 1936, asso. with Walter F. O'Malley, Esq., N.Y.C., 1936-42; law asst. Ct. Appeals, State of N.Y., 1942-44, U.S. Customs Ct., 1944-76. Mem. Com. Edn. and Employment of Women, 1964-65; mem. adv. com. Hudson River Valley Commn., 1965-66. Mem. Nat. Council Women, N.Y. Mem. County Lawyers' Assn., Fed. Bar Assn., Bus. and Profl. Women's Club (Tarrytowns pres., 1948-50, N.Y. State safety chmn., 1950-52, by-laws chmn. 1953-58, 2d v.p., 1958-60, 1st v.p. 1960-62, pres. 1962-64, parliamentarian 1971-76), Phi Beta Kappa, Kappa Beta Pi. Republican. Presbyterian. Author: A Manual of Customs Law, 1974, supplement, 1976. Home: Hudson House Ardsley-on-Hudson NY 10503

STURMAN, ROBERT HARRIES, neurol. surgeon; b. Austin, Minn., Jan. 8, 1923; s. Everett Nelson and Hannah (Harries) S.; A.B. in Chemistry, Colgate U., 1943; M.D., Yale U., 1950; m. Gloria Laverne Weyand, June 24, 1944; children—Peter, Everett, Bruce, Jeffrey. Rotating intern, Waterbury (Conn.) Hosp., 1950-51, asst. resident in gen. surgery, 1951-53, attending neurosurgeon, 1959, chief sect. of neurosurgery, 1974—, cons. in neurology, 1959—; asst. resident, fellow in neurosurgery, Hartford (Conn.) Hosp., 1953-54; fellow in neuropathology, Sch. Medicine, Yale U., New Haven, 1954, clin. asso. in neurosurgery, 1972-75, clin. instr. neurosurgery, 1976—; fellow in neurology, Columbia Presbyn. Med. Center, N.Y. Neurol. Inst., N.Y.C., 1955; chief resident in neurosurgery, sr. clin. instr. in neurosurgery, U. Hosp., Med. Sch. U. Mich., Ann Arbor, 1955-56; attending neurosurgeon, St. Mary's Hosp., Waterbury, 1959-68, courtesy staff, 1968-73, chief sect. neurosurgery, 1973—; clin. asso. in neurosurgery, Health Center, U. Conn., Hartford, 1972—; asso. attending neurology and neurosurgery, Newington (Conn.) Children's Hosp., 1960—; cons. in neurosurgery and neurology, Meriden (Conn.) Meml. Hosp., 1958-66, New Milford (Conn.) Hosp., 1956—, Sharon (Conn.) Hosp., 1956—, Southbury (Conn.) Tng. Sch., 1956—. Bd. trustees McTernan Sch., Waterbury, 1963-68, Cerebral Palsy Assn., Waterbury, 1958-67, Reading Research, Inc., Waterbury, 1960-65, Waterbury Area Easter Seal Rehab. Center, 1968—; med. advisory bd. Waterbury Chpt. Nat. Found., 1960—. Served to lt. USNR, 1943-46. Diplomate Am. Bd. Neurol. Surgery. Fellow A.C.S.; mem. Waterbury, New Haven County, Conn. State (sec. treas. sec. neurosurgery, 1965-69, chmn. sec., 1970-71, alt. mem. socio-econ. com. sect., 1976—) Med. Socs., AMA, N.Eng. Neurosurg. Soc. (bd. trustees, 1965-67, alt. mem. socio-econ. com., 1976—), Congress Neurol. Surgeons, Am. Assn. Neurol. Surgeons (socio-econ. com.), Pan Am., Pan Pacific Surg. Socs., Soc. for Cryosurgery, Conn. Chpt. A.C.S., Council State Neurosurg. Socs. Republican. Episcopalian. Contbr. articles to profl. publs., papers to confs. Home: Sage Rd Woodbury CT 06798 Office: 1211 W Main St Waterbury CT 06708

STURMAN, ROBERT MORRIS, physician; b. N.Y.C., June 28, 1926; s. Joseph and Dinah (Harris) S.; A.B. with honors, Columbia U., 1946; M.D., N.Y.U., 1949, M.Sc. in Ophthalmology, 1956. Rotating intern Mt. Sinai Hosp., N.Y.C., 1949-50; basic scis. ophthalmology Post-Grad. Med. Sch., N.Y.U.-Bellevue Med. Center, 1950-51; research fellow in ophthalmology Columbia-Presbyn. Med. Center, 1951-52; resident in ophthalmology Mt. Sinai Hosp., 1954-56, staff ophthalmology, 1956—, asst. attending ophthalmic surgeon, 1958; practice medicine, specializing in ophthalmology, N.Y.C., 1957—; staff Trafalgar, Park East hosps., N.Y.C.; instr. ophthalmology Mt. Sinai Sch. Medicine, 1964—. Served from lt. (j.g.) to lt., M.C., USNR, 1952-54. Recipient Pulitzer scholarship, Columbia U., 1943-46. Diplomate Am. Bd. Ophthalmology. Mem. Am. Acad. Ophthalmology and Otolaryngology, Assn. Research Ophthalmology, N.Y. Soc. Clin. Ophthalmology, AMA, N.Y. State, N.Y. County med. socs., Pan-Am. Med. Assn., Pan-Am. Assn. Ophthalmology, AAAS, Nat. Parks Assn., Phi Beta Kappa. Contbr. articles to profl. jours. Home: 401 E 88th St New York City NY 10028 Office: 8 E 84th St New York City NY 10028

STURTEVANT, PETER MANN, JR., journalist; b. Northampton, Mass., Feb. 27, 1943; s. Peter Mann and Katherine (Hobson) S.; B.A., Wilmington Coll. (Ohio), 1965; M.A., U. Iowa, 1967; m. Anne Elizabeth Fitzpatrick, July 12, 1969; 1 dau., Amanda. Assignment editor, asso. producer Washington Bur., CBS News, 1967-71, asst. bur. chief, Vietnam bur., 1971, bur. chief, 1972-73, chief NE bur., N.Y.C., 1973, nat. editor, 1973—; teaching asst. journalism U. Iowa, Iowa City, 1966-67. Recipient distinguished alumni award Wilmington Coll., 1975. Mem. Sigma Delta Chi, Alpha Phi Gamma. Episcopalian. Home: 90 Riverside Dr New York City NY 10024 Office: 524 W 57th St CBS News New York City NY 10019

STUTMAN, LEONARD JAY, research scientist, cardiologist; b. Boston, Apr. 8, 1928; s. Herbert Hyman and Nellie (Wiener) S.; B.S., Mass. Inst. Tech., 1948; M.A., Boston U., 1949; M.D., U. Rochester, 1953; m. Jeanne Ann Soblen, Dec. 23, 1951; children—Peter, David, Marc, Robin. Intern, resident medicine Bellevue Hosp., 1953-57; chief, med. services br. WPAFB, Dayton, Ohio, 1957-59; spl. advanced research fellow NIH, Nat. Heart Inst. 1959-61; instr. in clin. medicine N.Y. U. Coll. Medicine, 1956-61, asst. prof. pathology, 1961-65; head coagulation research lab. St. Vincent's Hosp. and Med. Center, N.Y., 1965—; attending physician St. Vincent's Hosp.; sr. attending physician medicine, sr. cardiologist Nyack (N.Y.) Hosp.; med. dir. Presdl. Life Ins. Co., Nyack. Dir. cardiac epidemiology study Ford Found. Vera Inst., 1971—; mem. com. on fibrinolytic agts. and myocardial infection NIH; mem. Internat. Com. on Thrombosis and Hemostasis; vis. mem. arteriosclerosis group Rockefeller U., 1976—. Served as capt. USAF, 1957-59. Fellow Am. Coll. Cardiology, AAAS, A.C.P., N.Y. Acad. Medicine; mem. Am. Soc. Hematology, AMA, N.Y. Med. Soc., N.Y. Acad. Sci., Sigma Xi. Contbr. articles to profl. jours. Home: 250 Town Line Rd West Nyack NY 10994 Office: 153 W 11th St New York City NY 10011

STUTZ, KENNETH JOHN, accounting exec.; b. Reading, Pa., Mar. 11, 1945; s. Frederick Francis and Kathleen Veronica (Grace) S.; B.S. in Accounting, U. Scranton, 1967; m. Sylvia Ann Menegat, Aug. 28, 1965; children—Theresa, Kenneth John. Sr. accountant Arthur Andersen & Co., Phila., 1967-71; controller Host Enterprises, Inc., Lancaster, Pa., 1971-73; partner Stockton Bates & Co., Harrisburg, Pa., 1973—. Fund raiser, United Fund, St. Joseph's Hosp., Lancaster; v.p. Hempfield PTO. Mem. Am., Pa. (chmn. com. on pub. services, also mem. other coms.) insts. C.P.A.'s, W. Shore Chpt. C.P.A.'s. Democrat. Roman Catholic. Clubs: Budweiser Town (charter), Grues Fours and Assos. (charter). Home: 61 W Elizabeth Dr Landisville PA 17538 Office: 1110 Fernwood Ave Camp Hill PA 17011

STYSKAL, HENRY, JR., electronics exec.; b. N.Y.C., Dec. 25, 1926; s. Henry and Annette (Sokol) S.; B.S., Worcester Poly. Inst., 1950; student Pa. State U., 1957, 58, Worcester Poly. Inst., 1962-64; m. Shirley Louise Johnson, June 2, 1951; children—Roger Henry, Gary William, Karen Shirley. Design engr. Rice Barton Corp., Worcester, Mass., 1950-51; design engr. Persons Majestic Co. Inc., Worcester, 1951-52; engring. instr. Alden Hydraulic Labs. of Worcester Poly. Inst., 1952; project engr. Philco Corp., Phila., 1952-59; engr. sect. mgr. Sylvania Electric Products, Inc., Woburn, Mass., 1959-62, prodn. mgr., 1962-68, chief engr., mktg. mgr., 1968-70; ops. mgr. Viatron Computer Systems Corp., Bedford, Mass., 1970; v.p. mktg. Helana Corp., Laredo, Tex., 1970-72; gen. mgr. Infoton, Inc., Burlington, Mass., 1972-74; pres. Teledyne TAC, Woburn, Mass., 1974—; dir. Additive Tech. Corp., North Chelmsford, Mass. Pres., Chelmsford Community Civic Assn., 1961-63, bd. dirs., 1960-64. Served with USNR, 1944-46. Mem. Semicondr. Equipment Mfrs. Inst., Am. Mgmt. Assn., Smithsonian Assos., Am. Bowling Congress, Lambda Chi Alpha. Home: 10 Donna Rd Chelmsford MA 01824 Office: 10 Forbes Rd Woburn MA 01801

SUÁREZ, RAFAEL, elec. engr.; b. Aibonito, P.R., Jan. 24, 1921; s. Miguel Angel and Antonia (González) S.; B.S.E.E., N.Mex. State U., 1950; postgrad. Newark Coll. Engring., 1953-56; m. Juana Concepción Aviles, July 15, 1950; children—Hector Xavier, William Oscar, Margarita. With Gen. Gable Corp., Union, N.J., 1951—, sr. research engr., 1960-68, sr. quality assurance engr., 1968-72, sr. elec. engr., research staff specialist, 1972—. Served with U.S. Army, 1943-46. Mem. IEEE. Patentee test equipment for measurements of high voltage cables. Home: 445 Remsen Ave Avenel NJ 07001 Office: 800 Rahway Ave Union NJ 07083

SUAREZ, RAMON URGEL, urologist; b. Hilongos, Leyte, Philippines, Dec. 22, 1936; s. Heracleo Z. and Elena Z. (Urgel) S.; came to U.S., 1965; M.D., Southwestern U., 1962; m. Nenita U. Lanaria, June 21, 1964; children—Ramon L., Ronald, Robert. Intern, Franklin Sq. Hosp., Balt., 1965-66; resident surgery St. Agnes Hosp., Balt., 1966-68; resident urology Albert Einstein Med. Center, Phila., 1968-71; practice medicine specializing in urology; mem. staffs Good Samaritan Hosp., Lebanon Valley Gen. Hosp. Diplomate Am. Bd. Urology. Fellow A.C.S.; mem. AMA, Pa. Med. Soc., Phila. Urologic Soc. Roman Catholic. Club: Rotary (dir. 1977-78). Home: 246 Crooked Ln Lebanon PA 17042 Office: 437 Chestnut St Lebanon PA 17042

SUCHOFF, BENJAMIN, educator; b. N.Y.C., Jan. 19, 1918; s. Aaron and Sadie (Leishin) S.; B.S., Cornell U., 1940; postgrad. Juilliard Sch. Music, 1940-41, 46-47; M.A., N.Y. U., 1949, Ed.D., 1956; m. Eleanor Rosen, Nov. 16, 1949; children—Michael Alan, Susan Carol, Deborah Ann. Dir. music Hewlett-Woodmere Union Free Sch. Dist., Hewlett, N.Y., 1950-78; dir. Spl. Collections and Commpute Program Center for Contemporary Arts and Letters, State U. N.Y. at Stony Brook, 1973—, now prof. arts and letters; lectr. Columbia Tchrs. Coll., 1973. Cons. computer applications for music research, 1971—. Dir. N.Y. Bartók Archive, Lynbrook, N.Y., 1953—; trustee Estate of Béla Bartók, Cedarhurst. Served to capt. AUS, 1941-45. Recipient Founders Day award N.Y. U., 1954. Am. Council Learned Socs. grantee in aid computerized music research, 1966. Mem. ASCAP, Am. Musicol. Soc., Soc. for Ethnomusicology, NEA, Coll. Music Soc., Assn. for Computing Machinery, Internat. Folk Music Council, Internat. Music Soc., N.Y. State Sch. Music Assn. Author: Guide to the Mikrokosmos of Béla Bartók, 1970; Curriculum Guide to Electronic Music, 1973; Electronic Music Techniques, 1975. Editor: Rumanian Folk Music (Bartók), vols. 1-3, 1967, vols. 4, 5, 1975; Turkish Folk Music from Asia Minor (Bartók), 1975; Belá Bartók Essays, 1976; Yugoslav Folk Music (Bartók), vols. 1-4, 1978. Composer, arranger works for choruses, symphonic band, orch., instrumental ensemble. Home: 2 Tulip St Cedarhurst NY 11516 Office: Center for Contemporary Arts and Letters State U Stony Brook NY 11794

SUDDUTH, SOLON SCOTT, obstetrician-gynecologist; b. Georgetown, Ky., Sept. 23, 1936; s. Solon B. and Dorothea Penn (Allphin) S.; A.B. magna cum laude, Princeton U., 1958; M.D., Johns Hopkins U., 1962; m. Charlotte Pratt, Aug. 20, 1960; children—Andrew, Robert, Jennifer, Matthew. Intern, Boston City Hosp., 1962-63, jr. resident in surgery, 1963-64; resident in obstetrics and gynecology Boston Hosp. for Women, Harvard Med. Sch., 1966-69; practice medicine, specializing in obstetrics and gynecology, Exeter, N.H., 1969—; staff obstetrician-gynecologist Exeter Hosp., 1969—; courtesy staff Boston Hosp. for Women; chief obstetrics Exeter Hosp., 1971—. Bd. dirs. Exeter Youth Hockey, 1971-74.

Served to lt., USNR, 1964-66. Recipient Physician's Recognition award AMA, 1977. Diplomate Am. Bd. Obstetrics and Gynecology. Fellow Am. Coll. Obstetricians and Gynecologists, Obstetrical Soc. Boston; mem. Mass., N.H., Rockingham County med. socs. Republican. Episcopalian. Clubs: Harvard (Boston); Kittansett, Beverly Yacht, Pithotomy. Office: Exeter-Hampton Ob-Gyn Profl Assos Hampton Rd Exeter NH 03833

SUE-A-QUAN, ERROL ALBERT, orthopedic surgeon; b. Georgetown, Guyana, June 27, 1938; s. Albert Henry and Rubina Evelyn (Lou-Hing) Sue-A-Quan; came to Can., 1967, naturalized, 1975; M.B. Ch.B., U. Edinburgh, 1963; M.S., U. Toronto, 1970; m. Pene lope Ann Mook-Sang, July 27, 1964; children—Andrew, Gregory, Carolyn, Andrea, Simone, Anthony. Intern Western Gen. Hosp., Edinburgh, 1963-64, Royal Infirmary Edinburgh, 1964; resident Princess Margaret Rose Orthopedic Hosp., Edinburgh, 1965-66, Western Gen. Hosp., 1966-67, Royal Infirmary, 1967, St. Michael's Hosp., Toronto, Ont., Can., 1967-68, Hosp. for Sick Children, Toronto, 1968-69; practice medicine specializing in orthopaedic surgery Don Mills and Scarborough, Ont., 1970—; demonstrator in anatomy Edinburgh Med. Sch., 1964-65; hon. lectr. U. Toronto, 1971—. Fellow Royal Coll. Surgeons Edinburgh, Royal Coll. Surgeons Can.; mem. Can. Med. Assn., Acad. Medicine Toronto, Am. Acad. Orthopedic Surgeons, Can. Orthopedic Assn. Anglican. Home: 8 Silversand Pl West Hill ON M1E 4J1 Canada Office: 2877 Ellesmere Rd West Hill ON M1E 4C1 Canada

SUFLAS, WILLIAM VASEL, restaurateur; b. Bridgeport, Pa., Aug. 15, 1923; s. James and Paraskeve S.; B.A., Ursinus Coll., 1945; m. Dorothy S. Stafre, June 12, 1949; children—Steven William, Barbara June. Partner, The Town Restaurant, Phila., 1946-65; pres., owner, mgr. Heritage Foods Inc./Grand Coach Restaurant, Maple Shade, N.J., 1965—. Chmn., North Br. YMCA, Phila., 1960; trustee St. Thomas Greek Orthodox Ch., Cherry Hill, N.J., 1967. Served to lt. (j.g.) USNR, 1943-46: CBI. Named to Hospitality Mag. Hall of Fame, 1965. Mem. Nat., Pa. (past pres.), N.J. (dir.), Phila. (past pres.) restaurant assns. Home: 272 Buckner Ave Haddonfield NJ 08033 Office: State Hwy 73 Maple Shade NJ 08052

SUGAR, DONALD ANDREW, surgeon; b. Passaic, N.J., Aug. 20, 1935; s. Andrew E. and Alva L. (Thulin) S.; A.B., Columbia, 1957; M.D., N.Y. Med. Coll., 1961; m. Janet Ann Oros, Oct. 16, 1965; children—Dianea, Donald Andrew, Julia Ann, Andrew John. Organic chemist Hoffman-LaRoche, Nutley, N.J., 1956-57; intern New Britain (Conn.) Gen. Hosp., 1961-62; resident in surgery Orange (N.J.) Meml. Hosp., 1962; resident E. Orange (N.J.) VA Hosp., 1963-66; pvt. practice medicine, East Orange, 1962-66; instr. N.J. Coll. Medicine, 1964-65; chief of surgery Ft. Steward Army Base, Ga., 1966-68; chief emergency service Franklin (N.J.) Hosp., 1968—, trustee, 1974—. Served with U.S. Army, 1968-69. Diplomate Am. Bd. Surgery. Recipient AMA Physicians Recognition award, 1970, 76. Lutheran. Home and Office: 1 Deerfield Dr Franklin NJ 07416

SUGERMAN, ABRAHAM ARTHUR, psychiatrist; b. Dublin, Ireland, Jan. 20, 1929; s. Hyman and Anne (Goldstone) S.; B.A., Trinity Coll., 1950, M.B., B. Chir., B.A.O., 1952; Sc.D., State U. N.Y., 1962; m. Ruth Nerissa Alexander, June 5, 1960; children—Jeremy, Michael, Adam, Rebecca. Came to U.S., 1958, naturalized, 1963. House officer Meath Hosp., Dublin, 1952-53, St. Nicholas Hosp., London, Eng., 1953-54; sr. house physician Brook Gen. Hosp., London, 1954; registrar in psychiatry Kingsway Hosp. Derby and Kings Coll. Med. Sch., Newcastle, Eng., 1955-58; clin. psychiatrist Trenton (N.J.) Psychiat. Hosp., 1958-59, cons. psychiatry, 1964—; research fellow Downstate Med. Center, Bklyn., 1959-61; chief investigative psychiatry sect. N.J. Bur. Research, Princeton, 1961-73; cons. research, asso. psychiatrist Carrier Clinic, Belle Mead, N.J., 1968-72, dir. outpatient services, 1972-74, 77-78, med. dir., 1974-77; dir. research Carrier Clinic Found., Belle Mead, 1972—; cons. psychiatry Med. Center, Princeton, N.J., 1972—; clin. asso. prof. psychiatry Rutgers Med. Sch., New Brunswick, N.J., 1972-78, clin. prof., 1978—; contbg. faculty Grad. Sch. Applied and Profl. Psychology, Rutgers U., 1974-78. Bd. dirs. N.J. Mental Health Research and Devel. Fund, Princeton, 1968-74; v.p. Jewish Family Service, Trenton, 1972-78; 1st v.p. Trenton Hebrew Acad., 1972-75; mem. bd. sci. advisers Found. Thanatology. Diplomate in psychiatry Am. Bd. Psychiatry and Neurology. Fellow Am. Psychiat. Assn. (mem. Hofheimer research bd. 1970-73), Am. Coll. Neuropsychopharmacology, Am. Coll. Clin. Pharmacology, AAAS; mem. Am., Royal colls. psychiatrists, AMA, Brit. Med. Assn., Soc. Biol. Psychiatry, Assn. Research Nervous and Mental Diseases, Eastern Psychol. Assn., Soc. Gen. Systems Research. Editor: (with Ralph E. Tarter) Alcoholism: Interdisciplinary Approaches to an Enduring Problem, 1976, Expanding Dimensions of Consciousness, 1978; contbr. articles to profl. jours. Home: 125 Roxboro Rd Lawrenceville NJ 08648 Office: Carrier Found PO Box 147 Belle Mead NJ 08502

SUH, DONG S., internat. trade co. exec.; b. South Korea, June 12, 1939; s. Jung H. and Myung S. Suh; came to U.S., 1961, naturalized, 1973; B.S. in Accounting and Fin., N.Y. U., 1966; m. Eunice K. Hong, Nov. 22, 1961; children—Eugene, Sharon. Accountant, Arthur Young & Co., N.Y.C., 1966-72, audit mgr., 1972; v.p., corp. controller Kay Corp., N.Y.C., 1972-73, v.p., chief fin. officer, 1974—. Served with Republic Korea Army, 1959-60. C.P.A., N.Y. Mem. Am. Mgmt. Assn., Am. Inst. C.P.A.'s, N.Y. State Soc. C.P.A.'s. Presbyterian. Club: N.Y. Downtown Athletic. Home: 11 Pine Hollow Ct Greenlawn NY 11740 Office: Kay Corp 88 Pine St New York City NY 10005

SUH, KENNETH KYONG SUK, physician; b. Jinchon, Korea, Jan. 15, 1939; came to U.S., 1964, naturalized, 1974; M.D., Seoul Nat. U., 1963; m. Alice Suh, Sept. 10, 1971; children—Soonie, Tewon Edwards, Benjamin Won. Intern, St. Mary Hosp., Hoboken, N.J., 1964-65; resident in internal medicine Albert Einstein Med. Center, Phila., 1966-67, VA Hosp., Long Beach, Calif., 1966-67, hematology VA Hosp., San Francisco, 1967-68, oncology Lemuel Shattuck Hosp., Boston, 1971-72; practice medicine, specializing in internal medicine, hematology, Jamestown, N.Y., 1977—; staff YWCA Hosp. and Jamestown Gen. Hosp.; cons. in field. Diplomate Am. Bd. Internal Medicine and Hematology. Mem. Am. Soc. Clin. Oncology. Home: 70 Pleasantview Dr Jamestown NY 14701

SUKMAN, CHARLES ARTHUR, psychologist; b. Chgo., Jan. 15, 1916; s. Max and Adela (Drucker) S.; B.S., Ind. U., 1940, M.S., 1942; Ed.D., U. Sarasota, 1973; m. Naomi Joy Tyson, Jan. 25, 1941; children—Carol Ann, Marsha Lynn. Counselor, Ind. U. Guidance Center, Bloomington, Ind., 1946-49; dir. employee relations Army Air Force PX Services, N.Y.C., 1949-56; asst. supt. pupil services Levittown (N.Y.) Pub. Schs., 1956-70; adj. prof. L.I. U., 1960-70; dir. guidance Locust Valley (N.Y.) Central Sch. Dist., 1970—; pvt. practice psychology, Locust Valley, 1960—; cons. staff Nassau Hosp., Mineola, N.Y., 1967-68; mem. adv. bd. Central Islip State Hosp. Sch. Nursing. Mem. Bd. Edn., Coll. DuLeman, Versoix Switzerland. Served with AUS, 1943-46. Mem. N.Y. State Assn. Pupil Personnel Adminstrs. (past pres.), Am. Personnel and Guidance Assn. (del. nat. conv.). Contbr. articles to profl. jours. Home: 17 Purdue Rd Glen Cove NY 11542 Office: 27 Plaza Locust Valley NY 11560

SULEIMAN, ANVER SILVINO, edn. exec.; b. N.Y.C., Oct. 25, 1931; s. Adhem and Thomasina (Foglia) S.; B.S., N.Y. U., 1956; m. Penelope Giannaris, Aug. 1, 1953; children—Tina Marie, John Anver, Tamara Lee, James Anver. Account rep. Remington Rand, N.Y.C., 1954-55; indsl. applications specialist Monsanto Chem. Co., Springfield, Mass., 1955-58; v.p., gen. mgr. Valco Inc., St. Petersburg, Fla., 1958-61; pres. Internat. Plastics Industry Cons., Inc., N.Y.C., 1962-67; pres. Reading Devel. Center, N.Y.C., 1968-69; pres. N.Y. Mgmt. Center, Inc., N.Y.C., 1969-75; exec. dir. Bur. Bus. and Tech. Inc., 1975—; lectr. N.Y. U., 1963-72. Chmn. Bicentennial Program, Gt. Neck, N.Y. Served with Signal Corps, AUS, 1951-53. Mem. Am. Soc. Tng. and Devel., Soc. Plastics Industry, Soc. Plastics Engrs., Adult Edn. Assn., Assn. Continuing Higher Edn. Club: New York University (N.Y.C.). Editor: Plastics Ednl. Guide, 1967; Plastracts, 1963-72; Dean and Director, 1975—. Home: 60 Radnor Rd Great Neck NY 11023 Office: Bur Bus and Tech 101 Park Ave New York City NY 10017

SULHAM, GLENN ALTON, assn. exec.; b. West Haven, Conn., Feb. 5, 1923; s. Glenn Harrison and Rhey Ione (Prevost) S.; student Montpelier Sem., 1938-39; B.Personnel, Champlain Coll., 1957; m. Emma Albertine Bjorn, Oct. 2, 1947; 1 son, Grant Carroll. With E.M. Loew's Theatres, Boston, 1941-46, Drown Motor Car Co., 1946-48; owner Glenn A. Sulham's Auto Sales, Barre, Vt., 1948-68; mgr. mem. services Barre Granite Assn., 1968—. Trustee Granite Group Ins., Barre Belt Pension. Alderman Barre City, 1956-58, 60-64; chmn. Citizen's Adv. Com. Barre, 1964-67; bd. dirs. Vt. Assn. Mental Health; mem. Vt. Apprenticeship Council; Vt. rep. to New Eng. Shippers Adv., 1972—. Mem. Asso. Industries Vt., Vt. State Exec. Assn., Central Vt. C. of C. Unitarian-Universalist. Clubs: Universalist Men's, Can., Barre Country, Lake Mansfield Trout, Mason, Elk, Order of Eastern Star. Home: 20 Delmont Ave Barre VT 05641 Office: 51 Church St Barre VT 05641

SULLIVAN, A(NNA) MANNEVILLETTE, metallurgist, editor; b. Washington, Aug. 18, 1913; d. Francis Paul and Villette (Anderson) Sullivan; student Wellesley Coll., 1931-33; A.B., George Washington U., 1935; postgrad. Cath. U., 1935-36, M.S., U. Md., 1955. Asst. metallurgist, geophys. lab. Carnegie Inst. Washington, 1942-45; metallurgist Nat. Bur. Standards, Washington, 1945-46, U.S. Naval Research Lab., Washington, 1947-78; dep. tech. editor ASME Trans., Jour. Engring. Materials and Tech., 1978—. Mem. Am. Soc. Metals, ASTM, ASME, Sigma Xi, Alpha Delta Pi. Iota Sigma Pi. Clubs: Altrusa Internat. Research in fracture of metals with spl. reference to fracture mechanics. Home: 4000 Massachusetts Ave NW Washington DC 20016 Office: Naval Research Lab Code 8430 Washington DC 20375

SULLIVAN, ARTHUR EUGENE, engring. cons.; b. Medford, Mass., Aug. 13, 1931; s. Robert William and Clare Helen (Rodgers) S.; B.S., Boston Coll., 1953; M.S., Harvard U., 1957; m. Rosemary Anne Keiran, June 21, 1958; children—Maura Anne, Mark Jerome, Paul David. Designer firm McCarron & Sullivan, Inc., Boston, 1955-56; clk. firm Robert W. Sullivan, Inc., Boston, 1956-62, v.p., 1962-67, pres., 1967—; prof. san. engring. tech. Franklin Inst. Boston, 1975—; dir. Hillside Cambridge Bank. Mem. Medford City Council, 1962-68, dep. mayor, 1966-68; chmn. Medford Housing Authority, 1973-75; v.p. Lawrence Meml. Hosp., 1972—. Served with AUS, 1953-55. Named Outstanding Citizen of Year, Grace Episcopal Ch., 1969. Registered profl. engr., Mass., Maine, N.H., Vt., R.I., D.C. Mem. Nat. Soc. Profl. Engrs., ASCE, Am. Soc. Plumbing Engrs., Nat. Environ. Health Assn., Nat. Fire Protection Assn., Cons. Engrs. Council New Eng. (pres. 1975-76), Medford Plan and Civic Assn., Boston Coll., Harvard U. alumni assns. Democrat. Roman Catholic. Contbr. articles to profl. jours. Patentee in field. Home: 138 Fells Ave Medford MA 02155 Office: 38 Newbury St Boston MA 02116

SULLIVAN, DANIEL JOSEPH, educator; b. N.Y.C., Apr. 22, 1928; s. Daniel Joseph and Margaret Mary (O'Brien) S.; B.S., Fordham U., 1950, M.S., 1958; Ph.D. in Entomology, U. Calif. at Berkeley, 1969; postgrad. U. Innsbruck (Austria), 1958-62, U. Vienna (Austria), summer 1958, U. Strasbourg, summer 1962. Asst. prof. entomology dept. biol. scis. Fordham U., Bronx, N.Y., 1969-74, asso. prof., 1974—; tchr. McQuaid High Sch., Rochester, N.Y., 1955-57; research asso., dept. entomol. scis. U. Calif., Berkeley, 1977-78; NSF research grantee, 1970-71. Mem. N.Y. Entomol. Soc. (pres. 1973-75), Entomol. Soc. Am., Soc. Ecology, Sigma Xi (pres. Fordham chpt. 1971-72). Roman Catholic. Contbr. articles to profl. jours. Address: Dept Biol Scis Fordham U Bronx NY 10458

SULLIVAN, DONALD JEROME, justice N.Y. Supreme Ct.; b. N.Y.C., July 18, 1929; s. Joseph and Johanna (Sweeney) S.; B.A., Iona Coll., New Rochelle, N.Y., 1951; J.D., Bklyn. Law Sch., 1954; m. Theresa Carway, Jan. 28, 1956; children—Theresa Ann, Daniel, Douglas. Mem. N.Y. Ho. of Reps. from 1st Assembly Dist., 1959-65; judge N.Y.C. Civil Ct., 1966-69; justice 1st Jud. Dist. N.Y. Supreme Ct., Bronx, 1970—. Democrat. Home: 22 Throggs Neck Blvd Bronx NY 10465 Office: 850 Grand Concourse Bronx NY 10451

SULLIVAN, DOROTHY RONA, state ofcl.; b. Boston, Jan. 7, 1941; d. Lewis Robert and Dorothy (Hopkins) Sullivan; B.A., Boston U., 1963; M.Ed., State Coll. Boston, 1966; C.A.G.S., Boston U., 1972; postgrad. Northeastern U., 1970-71, Boston Coll., 1974-78. Research asst., lay med. editor Boston Lying-in Hosp., 1963-64; employment counselor Mass. Div. Employment Security, Boston, 1964-66, sr. employment counselor, 1966-67, prin. employment counselor, 1967-70, employment office mgr., 1970-75, supr., 1975-78, chief, research dept., 1978—. Supr. community counselor interns and rehab. adminstrn. interns Northeastern U. Grad. Sch. Edn., 1968-74; supr. pub. adminstrn. interns Suffolk U., 1976; mem. regional adv. subcom. on mental retardation Mass. Dept. Mental Health, 1969. Mem. Jamaica Plain Community Council Health, Edn. and Welfare Subcom., 1967-69; recorder Gov.'s Conf. on Rehab., 1970, mem. Gov.'s Commn. Employment of Handicapped, 1972—, Pres.'s Com. Employment of Handicapped, 1975—, Gov.'s Com. Status of Women, White House Conf. on Small Bus., 1978. Exec. bd. Greater Boston council Camp Fire Girls; R.S.V.P. advisory bd. Boston Commn. Affairs of the Elderly, 1977-78. Mem. Nat. Vocat. Guidance Assn., Nat. Rehab. Assn. (Mass. sec. 1971-72, exec. bd. 1972-74, v.p. 1974-75, pres. 1976-77), Am. Fedn. State, County and Mcpl. Employees (exec. bd. local 164 1972-73, 74-76), Am. Personnel and Guidance Assn. (nat. recorder conf. 1968), Am. Acad. Polit. and Social Sci., Rockport, Cape Cod art assns., Smaller Bus. Assn. New Eng. Author: Boston Employment Service Guide, 1969. Contbr. articles to profl. jours. Home: 33 Morey Rd Roslindale MA 02131 Office: Employment Security Bldg Govt Center Boston MA 02114

SULLIVAN, EDWARD JOSEPH, electrotype co. exec.; b. Concord, N.H., May 17, 1915; s. Edward J. and Ida (Packard) S.; student St. Anslem's Coll., 1935-36; m. Dorothea M. Ash, Sept. 30, 1944; children—James Ash, Maureen Packard. Treas., Merrimack Electrotyping Corp., 1950-55, pres., 1955—; treas. Sheraton Properties Corp., 1961—; exec. v.p. Blanchard Press Corp., 1968-69; pres. Tridel Housing Devels., 1970—, Ho-Tei Corp., St. Thomas, V.I.; dir. Concord Fed. Savs. Bank; pres. Allied Photo Engraving Corp., 1964. Mem. Concord Hosp. Corp.; chmn. bldg. fund Carmelite Monastery, Concord, 1950, St. Peters Ch. for Bishop Brady High Sch. Bldg. Fund, 1961; citizens com. Concord Housing Authority; commr. Concord Urban Renewal Assn.; v.p., bd. dirs. Diocesan Bur. Housing, Inc., Manchester, N.H., 1975—; bd. dirs. Carpenter Center, Manchester, N.H.; mem. U.S. Commn. on Civil Rights; bd. dirs. Concord chpt. ARC, Concord Hosp. Served with USNR, 1942-46. Mem. Internat. Assn. Electrotypers and Stereotypers Union, Internat. Assn. Electrotypers and Stereotypers, Inc., Am. Legion, Aircraft Owners and Pilots Assn., Printing Inst. Am., One Hundred Club N.H. Elk. Republican. Roman Catholic. Club: Serra (v.p.). Kiwanian, K.C. Home: 99 Manor Rd Concord NH 03301 Office: 99 Manor Rd Concord NH 03301

SULLIVAN, EUGENE JOSEPH, counseling psychologist; b. Providence, Apr. 28, 1919; s. Arthur Aloysius and Mabel Hannah (Heck) S.; A.B., Providence Coll., 1940; C.A.G.S., Boston U., 1960; Ed.D. (hon.), Our Lady of Providence Coll., 1971; m. Josephine R. Cahill, June 7, 1941; children—Gene, Arthur, Diane. Tchr., guidance worker pub. schs., Providence, 1940-43; counseling psychologist Providence Regional Office U.S. VA, 1946-62; chief counseling psychologist U. R.I. Extension, Providence, 1962—; cons. psychologist Our Lady of Fatima Hosp. Served with U.S. Army, 1943-46, 50-52. Recipient outstanding service award VA, 1958; grantee psychol. testing police R.I. Gov's. Justice Commn., 1972-77; certified psychologist, R.I. Mem. Am., R.I. Psychol. Assns., Am., R.I. personnel and guidance assns., Nat., R.I. Rehab. Assns., Roman Catholic. Author research monograph, 1977. Home: 6 12th St Providence RI 02906 Office: University Rhode Island Div University Extension Providence RI 02908

SULLIVAN, GEORGE JOSEPH, exec. recruiting firm exec.; b. New Haven, Feb. 22, 1917; s. Thomas Andrew and Delia Agnes (Burke) S.; Ph.B., Providence Coll., 1940; m. Janet Marie Dalton, Sept. 16, 1950; children—Patricia Marie, Robert Burke, Casey Thomas. Spl. agt. FBI, 1942-50; asso. Thorndike Deland Assos., N.Y.C., 1950-53; dir. corporate recruiting ACF Industries, N.Y.C., 1953-55, asst. to corp. v.p. mfg. and engring., 1955-56, pres. nuclear energy products div., 1955-56, dir. indsl. relations, advanced products div. and asst. to pres. Carter Carburetor div., 1956-59; v.p., dir. Wright-Porter, Inc., N.Y.C., 1959-62; pres., chmn. bd. dirs. George Sullivan Assos., Inc., Rumson, N.J. and N.Y.C., 1962—. Mem. Assn. Exec. Recruiting Consultants, Am. Mgmt. Assn., Soc. Former FBI Spl. Agts. Roman Catholic. Clubs: Union League (N.Y.C.); Sea Bright Lawn Tennis and Cricket (Rumson, N.J.); Sea Bright (N.J.) Beach. Address: 62 Rumson Rd Rumson NJ 07760

SULLIVAN, BROTHER JEREMIAH STEPHEN, coll. pres.; b. Boston, June 25, 1920; s. John Joseph and Bridget Claire (Quirke) S.; B.A., Catholic U. Am., 1943; M.A. in Classics, Manhattan Coll., 1950; M.A. in Philosophy, Boston Coll., 1955; S.T.L., Catholic U. Am., 1957, S.T.D., 1959. Joined Bros. Christian Schs., 1938; tchr. St. Peter's High Sch. S.I., N.Y., 1943-48, St. Mary's High Sch., Waltham, Mass., 1948-53; instr. theology De La Salle Coll., Washington, 1953-59; asst. prof. theology Manhattan Coll., Bronx, N.Y., 1959-63, asso. prof., 1963, acad. v.p., 1963-70, exec. v.p., provost, 1970-75, pres., 1975—. Mem. Coll. Theology Soc. (dir. 1959-70), Catholic Theol. Soc. Am., Catholic Bibl. Assn., Nat. Cath. Ednl. Assn., Am. Assn. Higher Edn., AAUP, Phi Beta Kappa, Delta Mu Delta. Contbr. articles to profl. jours. Address: Manhattan Coll Bronx NY 10471

SULLIVAN, JOHN CORNELIUS, JR., lawyer; b. Erie, Pa., Oct. 23, 1927; s. John Cornelius and Catherine J. (Carney) S.; B.A. in Econs., Allegheny Coll., 1953; LL.B., Dickinson Sch. Law, 1959; m. Helen E. Kennedy, Feb. 3, 1951; children—John Cornelius, Timi Ann, Michael, Elisabeth. Sales rep. IBM Corp., 1953-56; admitted to Pa. bar, 1960; mem. firms Nissley, Clecker & Fearen, Harrisburg, Pa., 1959-63, Nauman, Smith, Shissler & Hall, Harrisburg, 1964—; asst. city solicitor City of Harrisburg, 1964-68, city solicitor, 1968-70; gen. counsel Harrisburg Redevel. Authority, 1964-68, Harrisburg Municipal Authority, 1964—; solicitor Silver-Spring Twp., 1970—; dir. accounts and fin. City of Harrisburg, 1963; mem. Pa. House of Reps., 1963-64. Chmn. bd. dirs. Harrisburg Pub. Library, 1965-73; mem. Harrisburg Hosp. Adv. Bd., 1965—; bd. dirs. WITF TV/FM. Mem. Am., Pa., Dauphin County (Pa.) (dir.) bar assns., Nat. Inst. Municipal Law Officers, The Pa. Soc. (N.Y.C.), Phi Gamma Delta. Asso. editor Dickinson Law Rev., 1958-59; editor Dauphin County Reporter, 1961-63. Home: Sample Bridge Rd RD 4 Mechanicsburg PA 17055 Office: 6 N 3rd St Harrisburg PA 17108

SULLIVAN, JOHN JOSEPH, JR., psychiatrist; b. Boston, June 9, 1929; s. John Joseph and Mary (Mahoney) S.; A.B. cum laude, Coll. of Holy Cross, 1951; M.D., Tufts U., 1955; m. Jean Marie Waller, July 31, 1954; children—Stephen J., Michael W., Edward J., Gregory F., Kevin R. Intern, Cambridge (Mass.) City Hosp., 1955-56; resident State Hosp., Worcester, Mass., 1956-57, Connecticut Valley Hosp., Middletown, Conn., 1959-61, VA Hosp., West Haven, Conn., 1960, Yale U. and Grace New Haven Hosp., 1961; attending psychiatrist St. Joseph Hosp., Stamford, Conn., 1961-68, chief, 1968—; attending psychiatrist Stamford Hosp., 1961—; practice medicine specializing in psychiatry, Stamford, 1961—; instr. psychiatry N.Y. Med. Coll., 1974—. Served to capt. M.C., USAF, 1957-59. Diplomate Am. Bd. Psychiatry and Neurology. Fellow Am. Psychiat. Assn.; mem. AMA, Stamford (sec. 1966, v.p. 1975, pres. 1976), Fairfield County, Conn. State (del. state conv. 1970—), med. socs., Conn. Psychiat. Soc. (councilor 1975, pres. 1976). Club: Burning Tree Country. Office: 144 Morgan St Stamford CT 06905

SULLIVAN, JOHN PATRICK, health adminstr.; b. Brockton, Mass., Aug. 19, 1936; s. William Edward and Catherine (Brides) S.; A.B., Boston Coll., 1962, M.S.W., 1964; m. Rosemary Woods, Dec. 28, 1963; children—Debra Ann, Kimberly Ann, Shaun Patrick. Social worker Judge Harry K. Stone Clinic, Brockton, 1964—, head psychiat. social worker, 1968—; adminstrv. asst. to dir., acting asso. area dir. VA Hosp., Brockton, 1967—, community placement supr., part-time 1967—; psychotherapist Dr. Busfield Clinic and Staff, Quincy, Mass., part-time 1968—; research interviewer Sandoz Pharm. Co., Hanover, N.J., 1969—; pvt. practice as psychotherapist, Scituate, Mass., 1969—; mental health adminstr., 1972; pres. Brockton Area Human Resources Group, Inc. Mem. mental health adv. com. Region VII Mass., 1967-69. Bd. dirs. Sun House Trust, Inc. Served with USNR, 1955-57. Mem. Nat. Assn. Social Workers (participant nat. leadership tng. program Chgo. 1969-71), Am. Assn. Marriage and Family Counselors, Am. Assn. Sex Educators and Counselors, Nat. Council on Family Relations, Am. Orthopsychiat. Assn., Mass. Mental Health Social Workers Assn. (pres. 1968-69), Boston Coll. Alumni Assn. (exec. bd.). Home: 40 Arborway Dr Scituate MA 02066 Office: 165 Quincy St Brockton MA 02401

SULLIVAN, JOSEPH MICHAEL, life ins. co. exec.; b. Phila., Jan. 12, 1925; s. Denis T. and Catherine G. (Cavanaugh) S.; B.S., St. Joseph's Coll., 1951; postgrad. Temple U. Sch. Law, 1951-52, Am. Coll. Life Underwriters, 1969; m. Maureen A. Crowe, Aug. 8, 1953; children—Sharon Anne, Mary Eileen, Joseph Michael, Brian Alexander, Robert Denis, Matthew Judge, Mary Kristine. Spl. Investigator Retail Credit Co., 1949-52; spl. agt. Lincoln Nat. Life Ins. Co., 1952-55; asst. mgr. Bankers Life Co. Des Moines, 1955-60; regional mgr. Pacific Mut. Life Ins. Co., Phila., 1960-69; pres. Sullivan & Co., Phila., 1969—; adv. Council Pacific Mut. Life Ins. Co.,

Newport Beach, Calif.; dir. McGettigans Travel Bur., Inc., Phila., Walsh & Walsh, N.Y.C., Nat. Assos., Inc., Cape May, N.J. Pres., Council Civic Assns. Springfield (Pa.), 1957-59; asso. capt. Malvern Weekend Retreat League, Phila. 1964-65; mem. ins. com. Cath. Charities Dr., Phila., 1959-65; bd. govs. St. Joseph's Coll., Phila. Committeeman, Republican party Springfield Twp., 1955-58. Mem. coll. council St. Joseph's Coll. Served with AUS, 1943-46. Recipient Order of Arrow award Boy Scouts Am., 1943. C.L.U. Mem. Phila. Assn. Life Underwriters, Nat. Def. Exec. Res., Order of Arrow (asso. mem.), Cath. Guild for Blind, St. Joseph's Coll. Alumni (treas., v.p. evening div. 1953-54), Am. Legion, V.F.W., Greater Phila. C. of C. (mem. tax, manpower resources coms. 1966-67, mem. com. on higher edn. 1969-70), U.S. Naval Inst., Nat. Assn. Security Dealers, Phila. Estate Planning Council, Million Dollar Round Table. Home: 37 W Golf View Rd Merion Golf Manor Havertown PA 19083 Office: Suite 1130 1617 JF Kennedy Blvd Philadelphia PA 19103 also 116 Strafford Bldg Wayne PA 19087 also 127 John St New York City NY

SULLIVAN, JOSEPH TIMOTHY PATRICK, lawyer; b. N.Y.C., Nov. 17, 1895; s. Timothy Patrick and Hannah (McCarthy) S.; Ph.B., Yale, 1916; LL.B., Fordham U., 1924; m. Grace Darby, Jan. 25, 1933 (dec. 1940); children—Sally (Mrs. David Fox), Maureen (Mrs. Joseph Rollins, Jr.), Timothy Patrick. Admitted to N.Y. bar, 1925, since practiced in N.Y.C.; pres. Sullivan Enterprises, Inc., N.Y.C., 1950—. Foreman Second Panel Sheriff's Jury, N.Y. County; co-founder Just One Break, Inc. Del., Democratic Nat. Conv., 1952, 56, 60. Trustee N.Y. Eye and Ear Infirmary, Coll. Mt. St. Vincent. Mem. Am., Washington, N.Y. State bar assns., Bar Assn. City N.Y., Am. Irish Hist. Soc. (pres. gen. emeritus). Clubs: Yale, Brook (N.Y.C.); California (Los Angeles). Home: 50 Vanderbilt Ave New York City NY 10017

SULLIVAN, MARGARET RITA, librarian; b. Fall River, Mass., Oct. 12; d. Algernon Desmond and Abbie Angela Sullivan; B.S., M.Ed., Boston U.; postgrad. Bristol Community Coll., 1970-71. Tchr. English, Joseph Case High Sch., Swansea, Mass., librarian, 1968—. Librarian Women's Program radio sta. WALE, Fall River; recreation supr. Fall River; chmn. Recreation of Model Cities. Sec. Fall River Park Bd., 1956—. Mem. women's bd. Union Hosp. Mem. Am., Mass., New Eng. library assns. Swansea Tchrs. Assn. (sec.), AAUW, Mass. Tchrs. Assn., South Shore Librarians Assn., Boston U. Alumni Assn., Nat. Soc. Lit. and the Arts, Friends of the Library, Friends of Animals, Holy Name Women's Guild, Pi Lambda Theta. Clubs: College, Catholic Woman's (Fall River). Home: 860 President Ave Fall River MA 02720 Office: Joseph Case High Sch Swansea MA 02777

SULLIVAN, RICHARD PARKER, ins. co. exec.; b. Bklyn., July 15, 1938; s. Hugh J. and Margaret M. (Kelleher) S.; B.A., Hofstra U., 1960; m. Dee Dee Stellato, Sept. 28, 1963; children—Pamela Jane, Kathleen, Margaret, Brian Parker. Group sales rep. Conn. Gen. Life Ins. Co., Garden City, N.Y., 1960-64, account mgr., 1964-71, mgr., Newark, 1971-76, regional v.p., Hartford, Conn., 1976—. Chmn. fund drive United Fund, Fanwood, N.J.; trustee United Fund, Plainfield. Republican. Roman Catholic. Clubs: Warren (N.J.) Country; Golf (Avon, Conn.); Hartford. Home: 65 Daventry Hill Avon CT 06001 Office: Conn Gen Life Ins Co Hartford CT 06152

SULLIVAN, ROBERT FRANCIS, rehab. counselor; b. Elmira, N.Y., Jan. 7, 1927; s. Eugene Henry and Rose Mary (Hayes) S.; B.A., St. Bernard's Sem., Rochester, N.Y., 1947, Syracuse (N.Y.) U., 1951; m. Rose Mary Caccia, Aug. 21, 1970; children—Kathleen, Robert, Therese, Maureen, Marianne, Michael, Timothy. Personnel mgr., asst. to treas. LeValley McLeod, Inc., Elmira, 1948-65; dir. fed. on-job tng. program Chemung and Schuyler counties, Econ. Opportunity Program, Inc., Elmira, 1966-71; mgr. purchasing and credit Goff Supply Corp., Horseheads, N.Y., 1971-72; housing adviser HUD, Corning, N.Y., 1972-73; coordinator on-job tng. programs C. of C. Chemung County, Elmira, 1973-74; program coordinator social and vocat. rehab. mentally retarded, Community Services unit Rome (N.Y.) Developmental Center, N.Y. State Dept. Mental Hygiene, 1974—. Mem. Chemung County Bd. Suprs., 1958. Served with USAF, 1950-53. N.Y. State Regents scholar, 1944; certified rehab. counselor, N.Y. Mem. Am. Personnel and Guidance Assn., Am. Rehab. Counseling Assn. Republican. Roman Catholic. Club: Elks. Home: 956 Pauline Ave Pine City NY 14871 Office: 435 N Main St Herkimer NY 13350

SULLIVAN, ROGER BRECK, univ. adminstr.; b. Ogdensburg, N.Y., Dec. 28, 1950; s. Roger Preston and Velma Irene (O'Shaughnessy) S.; B.A., State U. N.Y., Potsdam, 1973; M.A., Bowling Green State U., 1974; m. Jane Elizabeth Henry, Aug. 18, 1973; 1 son, Shaun Daniel. Grad. asst. in coll. student personnel adminstrn. Bowling Green State U., 1973-74; asst. dir. student activities Adrian Coll., 1973-74; residence hall dir. State U. N.Y., Oswego, 1974-76, asst. to asso. dean students, 1976-77; admissions officer State U. N.Y., at Utica/Rome, Utica, 1977—. Vol. driver Oswego Meals-on-Wheels, 1976-77; co-chmn. Oswego Muscular Dystrophy Dance Marathon, 1977. Mem. Am. Personnel, Guidance Assn., Assn. Coll. Personnel Adminstrs., State U. N.Y. Coll. Admission Personnel, Assn. New Student Personnel Adminstrs., Theta Omega Phi. Congregationalist. Club: Lions (dir., chmn. youth com. Oswego club 1977). Developer, author ofcl. recognition procedure for nat. fraternities, sororities at State U. N.Y., Oswego, 1977. Home: 27 Utica St Clinton NY 13323

SULLIVAN, ROY FRANCIS, hearing and noise cons.; b. Bklyn., Apr. 7, 1938; s. Francis T. and Sally R. (Wilsek) S.; B.A., Bklyn. Coll., 1960, M.A., 1962; Ph.D., City U. N.Y., 1972; children—Glenn Peter, Evan Christopher. Asso. prof. audiology Adelphi U., Garden City, N.Y., 1973—; chief research cons. N.Y. League for Hard of Hearing, 1974—; coordinator Carlyle Labs., Inc., N.Y.C., 1963—; cons. noise and hearing U.S. Environmental Protection Agy., Region II Noise Br., N.Y.C., 1973-74; chief div. audiology L.I. Coll. Hosp., Bklyn., 1963-73; mem. grad. faculty Adelphi U., Garden City, part-time 1964-73, N.Y. U., 1966, 1971-72, Columbia U. Tchrs. Coll., 1964, State U. N.Y. Downstate Med. Center, 1963; profl. staff mem. U.S. Senate Com. on Aging, 1973; cons. Meth. Hosp., Bklyn., 1962-66, Bklyn. Eye and Ear Hosp., 1969-71; bd. examiners N.Y.C. Bd. Edn., 1965-73; cons. Nat. Center Deaf-Blind, 1971-76, Indsl. Home for Blind, 1975—; cons. hearing conservation programs Newsday, Oxford Pendaflex; bd. sci. advisers Muzak Corp., 1975—, Am. Electromedics Corp., 1976—, Sears Corp., 1977—. Recipient 1st award for sci. merit for exhibit Am. Speech and Hearing Assn., 1970. Mem. Acoustical Soc. Am., Am. Speech and Hearing Assn. (legis. Councillor 1976—), Audiology Study Group N.Y. (pres. 1970-71), Pre-Sch. Hearing Council L.I. (vice-chmn. 1970-74, chmn. 1974—), Internat. Audiology Soc., Am. Psychol. Assn., Am. Assn. U. Profs., L.I. (1st v.p. 1978-79), N.Y. State (del. 1978-79) speech and hearing assns. Home: 50 Willow St Garden City NY 11530 Office: Dept Speech Adelphi U Garden City NY 11530

SULLIVAN, THOMAS MICHAEL, med. center adminstr.; b. Indiana, Pa., Sept. 5, 1942; s. Michael Joseph and Berthe Marguerite (Zabeau) S.; B.S., Indiana U., of Pa., 1964; M.S., Johns Hopkins U., 1974; m. Jean Ann Boxler, June 26, 1965; children—Dennis John, Maureen Lynn. Bacteriology technician Conemaugh Valley Meml. Hosp., Johnstown, Pa., 1964-65; serologist, 1967-68; supr. immunology, coagulation cytogenetics, hematology, urinalysis Greater Balt. Med. Center, Balt., 1968—; cons. pvt. labs.; lectr. Essex Community Coll., also USPHS. Served with AUS, 1965-67, to maj. U.S. Army Res. Mem. Am. Soc. Microbiology, Am. Mgmt. Assn. Republic. Roman Catholic. Home: 107 Thorden Rd Reisterstown MD 21136 Office: 6701 N Charles St Towson MD 21204

SULLIVAN, THOMAS MICHAEL, engring. co. exec.; b. Waltham, Mass., May 27, 1938; s. D. Bradley and Anne V. (Weiner) S.; B.S. in Accounting, Boston Coll., 1959, M.B.A., 1964; m. Jane M. Marks, Nov. 28, 1959; children—Thomas M., Elizabeth A., Andrew Douglas. With Gillette Co., Boston, 1961-63, United Shoe Machinery Co., Boston, 1963-65, Warren Bros. Co., Cambridge, Mass., 1965-73; v.p., treas. Dufresne-Henry Engring. Corp., North Springfield, Vt., 1973—; cons. in field; acquisition specialist, mgmt. cons. Active Boy Scouts Am., Little League Baseball; bd. dirs. Fall Mountain YMCA; mem. Weathersfield Planning Commn. Served to lt. AUS, 1959-61. Mem. Fin. Analysts Assn., C. of C., Boston Coll. Alumni Assn. Home: Cady Hill Rd Perkinsville VT 05151 Office: Dufresne-Henry Engring Corp Precision Park North Springfield VT 05150

SULLIVAN, WILLIAM HALLISEY, JR., football league exec.; b. Lowell, Mass., Sept. 13, 1915; s. William H. and Vera F. Sullivan; A.B., Boston Coll., 1937, postgrad., 1938-39; postgrad. Harvard U., summer 1938; m. Mary K. Malone, Dec. 29, 1941; children—Charles W., Kathleen Marie, Mary Jeannie, Nancie Vera, William Hallissey III, Patrick Jerome. Publicity dir. Boston Coll., 1938-40; spl. asst. to dir. athletics U. Notre Dame, 1941-42; dir. pub. relations U.S. Naval Acad., 1942-46, Boston Braves, 1946-52; owner All Star Sports, Inc., 1952-55; asst. to pres. Met. Coal & Oil Co., Dorchester, Mass., 1955-56, v.p., 1956-58, pres., 1958-78; pres. Am. Football League, 1963-69, chmn. TV com., merger com. of Nat. and Am. football leagues; v.p. Pittston Co., 1978—; pres. New Eng. Patriots Football Club; dir. Commonwealth Nat. Bank Boston, Allied Concrete Co., Vol. Coop. Bank, Better Home Heat Council. Kiddie Kamp Corp., Better Bus. Bur. Met. Boston, Nat. Football League Properties, Inc., Nat. Football League Film, Inc.; incorporator Union Savs. Bank. Chmn. Greater Boston Stadium Authority, 1962—; chmn. Christmas Seal campaign Mass. Tb Assn., 1963-64. Bd. dirs. Catholic Counseling Service, Mass. Eye Research Corp., Stonehill Coll.; mem. Pres.'s Council Boston Coll. Served with USNR, 1942-46. Mem. New Eng. Fuel Dealers Assn. Knight of Malta. Clubs: Indian Creek Country; Hundred of Mass. (dir.); Algonquin (Boston); Woodland Golf; Vesper Country; Fort Hill; Oyster Harbors. Home: 5 Bay State Rd Wellesley Hills MA 02181 Office: One Federal St 29th Floor Boston MA 02110

SULZBERGER, ARTHUR OCHS, newspaper exec.; b. N.Y.C., Feb. 5, 1926; s. Arthur Hays and Iphigene (Ochs) S.; B.A., Columbia, 1951; LL.D., Dartmouth, 1964, Bard Coll., 1967; L.H.D., Montclair Coll., 1972; m. Barbara Grant, July 2, 1948 (div. 1956); children—Arthur Ochs, Karen Alden; m. 2d, Carol Fox, Dec. 19, 1956; children—Cathy Jean, Cynthia Fox. With N.Y. Times Co., N.Y.C., 1951—, asst. treas., 1958—, pres., pub. 1963—, also dir. and chmn.; dir. Times Printing Co., Chattanooga, Gaspesia Pulp and Paper Co., Ltd. Can. Mem. exec. com. Bur. Advt., ANPA. Trustee Met. Mus. Art, Columbia U.; bd. dirs. Center Inter-Am. Affairs, N.Y. Conv. and Visitors Bur., Hundred Year Assn. Served to capt. USMCR, World War II, Korea. Mem. S.A.R. Clubs: Overseas Press, Explorers (N.Y.C.); Metropolitan (Washington); Century Country (Purchase, N.Y.); Rockrimmon (Stamford, Conn.). Office: 229 W 43d St New York City NY 10036

SUMBERG, ALFRED DONALD, profl. assn. exec.; b. Utica, N.Y., Nov. 22, 1928; s. Samuel M. and Rachel Frances (Silverstein) S.; student Utica Coll., 1946-48, Hebrew Union Coll., 1948-50; A.B., U. Cin., 1950, M.A., 1951; Ph.D., U. Wis., 1960; m. Dolly Primakow, June 26, 1955; children—Susan Diane, Laurie Darlene. Instr. in history U. Wis., Racine and Kenosha, 1955-56; prof. history and econs. E. Stroudsburg (Pa.) State Coll., 1956-67; asso. sec., dir. govt. relations AAUP, Washington, 1967—; dir. Pa. Cultures Research Program, E. Stroudsburg State Coll., 1961-67. Founder, pres., Monroe County Sch. Employees Fed. Credit Union, 1960-67; vice chmn. adv. bd. dirs. First Fed. Savs. and Loan Assn. of Wilkes-Barre; coordinator SBA Mgmt. Inst., 1965-67; pres. Monroe County Hist. Soc., 1965-67. Mem. Am. Hist. Assn., Orgn. Am. Historians, Am. Econ. Assn., Nat. Economists Club, U.S. Capitol Hist. Soc., Nat. Trust Historic Preservation, Phi Alpha Theta, Kappa Delta Pi. Jewish. Clubs: U. Wis. Alumni (pres. 1978), U. Cin. Alumni (pres. 1972-74, Distinguished Alumni Service award 1976) (Washington). Contbr. essays, sects. to books in field of twentieth century history, faculty bargaining and govt. regulation of higher edn. Home: 1309 Fallsmead Way Rockville MD 20854

SUMBRY, LOUIS CLYDE, JR., chemist; b. Avon Park, Fla., Apr. 2, 1947; s. L. C. and Maggie Bell (Jackson) S.; B.S. in Chemistry, Fla. A. and M. U. 1969; m. Ernestine Coleman, June 24, 1967; 1 dau., Angela Denise. Jr. chemist/chem. engr. Owens-Ill., Valdosta, Ga., summer, 1968; dir. high sch. program Fla. State U., Tallahassee, 1969; chemist, prodn. supr., lab. supr. ICI Am., Chattanooga, 1969-74; corrosion chemist Gulf Sci. and Tech. Co., Pitts., 1974—; instr. math/sci. enrichment program Schenley High Sch., Pitts., 1977-78. Initiator project SEED programs Fla. State U., 1969, U. Tenn., 1971. Mem. Am. Chem. Soc., Nat. Assn. Corrosion Engrs., Nat. Tech. Assn. Democrat. Baptist. Clubs: Men of Sixth, Big Bros. of Chattanooga. Home: 20 Foster Sq Pittsburgh PA 15212 Office: PO Box 2038 Pittsburgh PA 15230

SUMMA, DON JOSEPH, accountant; b. Flushing, N.Y., Sept. 29, 1926; s. Joseph and Louise (Rosa) S.; B.A., Columbia, 1946, M.S., 1948; m. Helen Staples, June 12, 1949; children—Jeffrey Donaldson, James Douglas. Accountant, Arthur Young & Co., N.Y.C., 1948—, partner, 1958—, dir. taxes, 1959-66, nat. dir. tax practice, 1966-75, mng. partner, Newark, 1975—, also former mem. mgmt. com. U.S. and Europe; mem. accounting faculty Columbia, 1949-65, adj. prof., 1965-70. Vice chmn. com. on legacies and bequests A.R.C., N.Y.C., 1969—; past pres., v.p. Rumson United Community Appeal; mem. White House Task Force on Bus. Taxation, 1969-70, Adv. Group to Commr. Internal Revenue, 1966-67, Adv. Group on Tax Adminstrn., N.Y.C., 1966-69; trustee, treas. Tax Inst. Am., 1971-73; mem. steering com. to study adminstrv. procedures of Internal Revenue Service, Adminstrv. Conf. U.S., 1974-76. Mem. com. on trust and estate gift plans Rockefeller U., 1973—; bd. dirs. Tax Mgmt. Adv. Bd. Bur. Nat. Affairs, Inc., 1970—; trustee, v.p. Nat. Center for Automated Information Retrieval, 1972-76. Served with AUS, 1945-46. C.P.A., N.Y., N.J. Mem. Am. Inst. C.P.A.'s (governing council 1965-67, 70-76, v.p. 1975-76), N.Y. State Soc. C.P.A.'s (pres. 1973-74, dir.), Phi Beta Kappa, Beta Gamma Sigma, Beta Alpha Psi (hon.). Clubs: Rumson (N.J.) Country: Seabright (N.J.) Beach; Metropolitan, Columbia U. (bd. govs. 1963-69), Accountants (bd. govs. 1965—, pres. 1976-78) (N.Y.C.); Metropolitan (Washington); Essex (Newark). Author: Assignment of Income, 1958. Editor: Working With the Revenue Code, 1970-71; mem. editorial bd. Fed. Income Taxation of Banks and Financial Institutions, 1963, 65, 67, Tax Adviser, 1972—, Jour. Corporate Taxation, 1974—. Home: 12 Sailer's Way Rumson NJ 07760 Office: 520 Broad St Newark NJ 07102

SUMMERS, ROBERT SAMUEL, lawyer, author, educator; b. Halfway, Oreg., Sept. 19, 1933; s. Orson William and Estella Belle (Robertson) S.; B.S. in Polit. Sci., U. Oreg., 1955; postgrad. (Fulbright scholar) U. Southampton (Eng.), 1955-56; LL.B., Harvard U., 1959; postgrad. Oxford U. (Eng.), 1964-65, 74-75; m. Dorothy Millicent Kopp, June 14, 1955; children—Brent, William, Thomas, Elizabeth, Robert. Admitted to Oreg. bar, 1959, N.Y. bar, 1974; asso. firm King, Miller, Anderson, Nash and Yerke, Portland, Oreg., 1959-60; asst. prof. law U. Oreg., 1960-63, asso. prof., 1964-68; vis. asso. prof. law Stanford U., Calif., 1963-64; prof. law U. Oreg., 1968-69; prof. law Cornell U., Ithaca, N.Y., 1969-76, McRoberts prof. law, 1976—; vis. prof. law Ind. U., 1969, U. Mich., 1974, U. Warwick (Eng.), 1975, U. Miami (Fla.), 1976-78, U. Sydney (Australia), 1977; cons. Cornell Law Project in pub. schs., N.Y., 1969-74, Law in Am. Soc. project Chgo. Bd. Edn., 1968-69; instr. Nat. Acad. Jud. Edn., 1976—. Social Sci. Research Council fellow in legal philosophy, 1964-65. Mem. Am. Law Inst., Assn. Am. Law Schs. (chmn. jurisprudence sect. 1972-73), Am. Soc. for Polit. and Legal Philosophy (v.p. 1977-78), Internat. Assn. Philosophers of Law, Phi Beta Kappa. Republican. Congregationalist. Author: (with Howard) Law, Its Nature, Functions and Limits, 1965; (with Speidel and White) Teaching Materials on Commercial Transactions, 1969; (with White) The Uniform Commercial Code, 1972; (with Hubbard and Campbell) Justice and Order Through Law, 1973; (with Bozzone and Campbell) The American Legal System, 1973; contbr. numerous articles on jurisprudence and legal philosophy to scholarly jours.; contbr. book reviews in field; editor: Essays in Legal Philosophy, 1968, More Essays in Legal Philosophy, 1971. Home: 116 McIntyre Pl Ithaca NY 14850 Office: Cornell Law School Ithaca NY 14853

SUMMERSCALES, WILLIAM, educator; b. Silsden, Yorkshire, Eng., Aug. 5, 1921; s. Edmund and Margaret (Newns) S.; B.A., B.Th., Eastern Nazarene Coll., 1944-45; M.Div., San Francisco Theol. Sem., 1956; M.A., U. Toronto (Ont., Can.), 1966; Ph.D., Columbia, 1969; m. Ruth B. Sickler, 1945 (div. 1969); children—Marjorie Summerscales Wright, Stephen T. (dec.); m. 2d, Elpida Tsonides, 1970. Came to U.S., 1953, naturalized, 1957. Minister chs., Toronto, Vancouver, B.C., Calif., 1945-60; sec. adult edn. and coll. planning hdqrs. staff Presbyn. Bd. Edn., Phila., 1960-66; adminstrv. asso. Horace Mann-Lincoln Inst., adminstrv. asso. div. ednl. instns. and programs Tchrs. Coll., Columbia, 1967-69, asso. prof. edn., 1969—, dir. placement, 1969-72, dir. instl. devel., 1972—. Served as 1st lt. USAFA, 1958-60. Mem. Phi Delta Lambda. Author: Affirmation and Dissent—Historical Study of Columbia University and World War I, 1970; co-author: Jesus—The Four Gospels Combined in Modern English, 1974. Home: 400 W 119th St New York City NY 10027

SUMNER, KENNETH, health care co. exec.; b. N.Y.C., Sept. 29, 1942; s. Samuel and Nettie (Levin) S.; B.S., Union Coll., 1964; Ph.D., State U. N.Y. Upstate Med. Center, 1969; m. Mary Arline Sroka, Nov. 30, 1969; 1 son, Joel Sumner. Postdoctoral fellow U. Chgo., 1969-71; faculty Bridgewater (Mass.) State Coll., 1971-76, asst. prof. chemistry, 1971-74, asso. prof., 1974-76; clin. research scientist Warner-Lambert Research Inst., Morris Plains, N.J., 1976-78, mgr. clin. investigation, 1978—. Manuscript reviewer Biochimica Biophysica Acta, Amsterdam, The Netherlands, 1971, Prentice-Hall Pubs., Englewood Cliffs, N.J., 1972-76. Predoctoral trainee Pub. Health Service, Syracuse, N.Y., 1964-69, post-doctoral trainee, 1969-71. Mem. Am. Assn. Clin. Chemistry, Regulatory Affairs Profl. Soc. Home: 153 S Hillside Ave Succasunna NJ 07876

SUN, BENEDICT CHING-SAN, educator; b. Nanking, China, Nov. 5, 1934; s. Kuang Yu and Ta Chen (Chiang) S.; Ph.D., U. Ill., 1967; m. Alice Kau-Hwa Mao, Sept. 18, 1965; children—Christina, David, Eileen. Came to U.S., 1956, naturalized, 1969. Asso. tool engr. Boeing Airplane Co., Renton, Wash., 1959-60; jr. engr. IBM Corp., San Jose, Calif., 1960-63; faculty N.J. Inst. Tech., 1967—, asso. prof. stress analysis, design, 1970—. Cons. Stone & Webster Engring. Corp., N.Y.C., Boston, 1970-74. Mem. ASME, Am. Soc. Engring. Edn., Chinese Soc. Mech. Engrs. (jr.), Soc. Plastic Engrs., Pi Mu Epsilon, Pi Tau Sigma. Home: 17 Sunset Dr Whippany NJ 07981 Office: 323 High St Newark NJ 07102

SUN, ELEANOR, chemist; b. Tiensin, China, May 12, 1948; d. Shih Ming and Sarah (Lee) Sun; came to U.S., 1959, naturalized, 1965; B.S., Wright State U., 1971, M.S., 1974. Nurse asst. Kettering (Ohio) Meml. Hosp., 1968; scientist Mead Digital Systems, Dayton, Ohio, 1973-76; research scientist Chicopee Inc., Milltown, N.J., 1976—. Mem. Am. Chem. Soc. Republican. Author: The Relationship Between the Chemistry of the Toxic Heavy Metal Mercury, Chelation, and Algal Growth, 1974. Home: 65B Taylor Ave East Brunswick NJ 08816 Office: 2 Ford Ave Milltown NJ 08850

SUNDARESAN, PERUVEMBA RAMNATHAN, biochemist; b. Madras, India, Aug. 11, 1930; s. Peruvemba A. and Saraswathi (Subramanian) R.; B.S., U. Banaras, 1950, M.S., 1953; Ph.D., Indian Inst. Sci., Bangalore, India, 1958; m. Gloria B. Marquez, Dec. 23, 1970; children—Sita, Ramesh. Came to U.S., 1961, naturalized, 1973. Research asso. Radiocarbon Lab., U. Ill., Urbana, 1961-62; research asso. dept. nutrition food sci. Mass. Inst. Tech., Cambridge, 1962-64; vis. sci. research asso. U.S. Army Research Inst. Environ. Medicine, Natick, Mass., 1964-66, research biochemist, 1966-68; chief Lipids Lab., Research Inst. St. Joseph Hosp., Lancaster, Pa., 1968-77; chemist div. toxicology FDA, Washington, 1978—; cons. Millersville (Pa.) State Coll., 1972-77, VA Hosp., Washington, 1973-77. Sr. Research fellow Council Sci. Indsl. Research, New Delhi, India, 1959-61; NIH grantee, 1970-77. Mem. Am. Inst. Nutrition, Am. Soc. Biol. Chemistry, Bio-chem. Soc. (U.K.), AAAS, Am. Oil Chemists Soc., Sigma Xi. Contbr. articles to various publs. Office: Div Toxicology Bur Foods FDA 200C St Washington DC 20204

SUNDERLAND, RAY, JR., ins. co. exec.; b. N.Y.C., Nov. 12, 1913; s. Ray and Rose (Goehl) S.; grad. Pace Coll., 1948, Exec. Program in Bus. Adminstrn., Columbia, 1968; m. Melva Joyce Mace, June 13, 1943; 1 son, Joel Wayne. With comptroller's dept. Brown Bros. Harriman & Co., N.Y.C., 1934-40; sr. auditor on staff Price Waterhouse & Co., N.Y.C., 1940-50; with N.Y. Life Ins. Co., N.Y.C., 1950—, gen. auditor, 1969-71, v.p., comptroller, 1971-75, sr. v.p., 1975—. Pres. community scholarship fund, local sch. dist., Locust Valley, N.Y., 1958-62, pres. parents club, 1958-62. Served to capt. USAAF, 1942-45. C.P.A., N.Y. Mem. Am. Inst. C.P.A.'s, Columbia U. Grad. Sch. Bus. Exec. Alumni Assn. Home: 3 Wood Ln Locust Valley NY 11560 Office: 51 Madison Ave New York City NY 10010

SUNDLUN, BRUCE GEORGE, lawyer, bus. exec.; b. Providence, Jan. 19, 1920; s. Walter I. and Jane Z. (Colitz) S.; B.A., Williams Coll., 1942; LL.B., Harvard U., 1949; student Air Command and Staff Sch., 1948; m. Joyanne T. Carter, Aug. 5, 1974; children by previous marriage—Tracy, Stuart, Peter, Michael R.E. Carter, Cintra Ellis Carter. Admitted to R.I. and D.C. bars, 1949; asst. U.S. atty., Washington, 1949-51; spl. asst. to U.S. atty. gen., Washington, 1951-54; partner firm Amram, Hahn & Sundlun and predecessor, Washington, 1954-72, Sundlun, Tirana & Scher, 1972-76, counsel, 1976—; v.p., gen. counsel, dir. Outlet Co., Providence, 1960-76, pres., chief exec. officer, 1976—; pres. Exec. Jet Aviation, Inc., Columbus, Ohio, 1970-76, chmn. bd., 1976—; incorporator, dir. Communications Satellite Corp., Worthington Industries, Guest Research, McLean,

Va. Chmn. Inaugural Medal Com., Washington, 1961, 65; vice chmn. Inaugural Parade Com., Washington, 1961; mem. Adv. Group on Nat. Aviation Goals, 1961; pres. Washington Internat. Horse Show, 1970-75, trustee, 1975—; pres. Ocean State Performing Arts Center, 1978—; bd. visitors U.S. Air Force Acad., 1978—; del. Democratic Nat. Conv., 1964, 68. Served to capt. USAAF, 1942-45; col. Res., ret. Decorated D.F.C., Air medal with oak leaf cluster, Purple Heart; chevalier Legion d'Honneur (France). Mem. Greater Providence C. of C. (dir. 1976—), Delta Upsilon. Clubs: Hope, Squantum Assn., Dunes, University, Turks Head, Spouting Rock Beach Assn., Bristol Yacht (R.I.); Federal City, 1925 F St. (Washington); Fauquier; Middleburg (Va.) Tennis Assn., Orange County (Va.) Hunt; Saratoga Reading Room. Home: 33 Power St Providence RI 02903 also Salamander Farm The Plains VA 22171 Office: Outlet Company 176 Weybosset St Providence RI 02902

SUNDQUIST, RALPH ROGER, JR., educator; b. Yakima, Wash., Dec. 9, 1922; s. Ralph Roger and Elaine Suzanne (Fager) S.; student Yakima Valley Jr. Coll., 1940-42; M.A., U. Chgo., 1948; M.Div. (Cuyler Preaching fellow), Union Theol. Sem., 1951; Ph.D., Columbia U., 1970; m. Bernita May Woodruff, Sept. 16, 1945; children—Eric Thorsten, Karin Olds, Nils Fredrik. Ordained to ministry Presbyterian Ch., 1951; pastor First Presbyn. Ch., Franklinville, N.Y., 1952-58; editor, adminstr. bd. Christian edn. United Presbyn. Ch., Phila., 1958-62; mem. faculty 1965-73, prof. religion and edn. Hartford Sem. Found., 1965-73, adj. faculty, 1976—; pvt. cons. in edn. and religion, 1973—. Co-dir. Ecumenical Inst. Religious Studies, Assumption Coll., Worcester, Mass., 1972, lectr., 1975, 77, 79. Chmn. div. Christian edn. Conn. Council Chs., Hartford, 1966-76; bd. dirs., past treas., chmn. Greater Hartford Campus Ministry, 1966—; vice chmn. Conn. Commn. on United Ministries in Higher Edn.; chmn., bd. dirs. Ch. Edn. Center, Hartford, 1975—. Served with AUS, 1942-45. Mem. Am. Acad. Religion, Am. Schs. Oriental Research, Assn. Profs. and Researchers in Religious Edn., Nat. Soc. for Study Edn., Religious Edn. Assn., Soc. Bib. Lit. Author: Consider Your Ministry, 1963; Whom God Chooses: The Child in The Church, 1964; mem. editorial bd. Jour. Religious Edn., 1976—; contbr. articles to religious and ednl. jours. Home: 9 Livingston Rd Bloomfield CT 06002 Office: 481 Farmington Ave Hartford CT 06105

SUNDY, GEORGE JOSEPH, refractories research engr.; b. Nanticoke, Pa., Apr. 22, 1936; s. George Joseph and Stella Mary (Bodurka) S.; B.S., Pa. State U., 1958; m. Stella Pauline Miechur, May 21, 1966; children—Sharon Ann, George Joseph III. Research engr. Bethlehem Steel Corp. (Pa.), 1959—. Mem. Am. Ceramics Soc., Keramos, Sigma Tau. Democrat. Roman Catholic. Patentee in field. Home: 3815 Dartmouth Dr Bethlehem PA 18017 Office: Homer Research Labs Bethlehem PA 18016

SUNG, PEI, physicist; b. China, Mar. 12, 1936; s. Tze Kai and S. F. (Yao) S.; came to U.S., 1961; B.S., Cheng-Kung U., Tainan, Taiwan, 1958; M.S., U. Wash., 1963, Ph.D., 1967; m. Cheng-Yu Meng, June 18, 1966; 1 dau., Jane. Sr. research chemist Allied Chem. Corp., Morristown, N.J., 1967-70; dir. research Ceramco Inc. subs. Johnson & Johnson Co., N.Y.C., 1970-74, research asso. Johnson & Johnson Dental Co., East Windsor, N.J., 1974—. Mem. Am. Soc. Metals, Am. Ceramic Soc., Internat. Assn. Dental Research. Patentee dental materials, crystal growth, metalceramic composite, nuclear materials. Home: 5 Woodhollow Rd Lawrenceville NJ 08648 Office: Johnson & Johnson Dental Co 20 Lake Dr East Windsor NJ 08520

SUNKIN, IRVING BURTON, cosmetics and pharm. mfg. co. exec., lawyer; b. N.Y.C., July 9, 1932; s. Nathan and Fay (Ackerman) S.; student Washington U., St. Louis, 1949-50; B.A., N.Y. U., 1953; J.D. (Harlan Fiske Stone scholar), Columbia, 1958; m. Mirel Jacobs, Dec. 5, 1953; children—Neil Michael, Andrew Alan, Ellen. Admitted to N.Y. State bar, 1958; asso. firm Paul, Weiss, Rifkind, Wharton & Garrison, N.Y.C., 1958-65; gen. atty. Revlon, Inc., N.Y.C., 1965-68, asst. sec., 1968-71, corp. sec., 1971-74, v.p., sec., 1974—; div. counsel USV Pharm. Corp., Tuskahoe, N.Y., 1968-71, corporate sec., 1971—; corporate sec. Nat. Health Labs. Inc., La Jolla, Calif., 1971—, Coburn Optical Industries, Inc., Muskogee, Okla., 1975—, Barnes-Hind Pharm. Inc., Sunnyvale, Calif., 1976—, Armour Pharm. Co., Phoenix, 1977—, Lewis-Howe Co., St. Louis, 1978—. Served with AUS, 1953-55. Mem. Assn. Bar City N.Y. Jewish (trustee temple 1963-65). Editor Columbia Law Rev., 1956-58. Home: 60 East End Ave New York City NY 10028 Office: Revlon Inc 767 Fifth Ave New York City NY 10022

SUNSERI, ANTHONY, dentist; b. Pitts., Nov. 24, 1927; s. Emanuele and Mary Josephine (Incardona) S.; B.S., U. Pitts., 1950, postgrad. in zoology, 1950-51, Pharmacy Sch., 1951-52, D.D.S., 1956; m. Palma Marie Palermo, Sept. 12, 1959; children—Anthony Joseph, Palma Jo. Practice gen. dentistry, Pitts., 1956—. Instr. crown and bridge U. Pitts. Sch. Dentistry, 1963—; lectr. hydrocolloid in crown and bridge to various dental groups Pitts. area. Served with Service Corps, AUS, 1946-47. Mem. Am., Pa. dental assns., Odontological Soc., Italian Sons and Daus. Am., Phi Kappa, Psi Omega. Roman Catholic. Rotarian, Lion. Home: 1345 Craigview Dr Pittsburgh PA 15243 Office: 1535 Broadway Ave Pittsburgh PA 15216

SUNSHINE, NANCY JEAN, psychologist; b. N.J., May 2, 1935; d. Kenneth Hastings and Amy May (Colbeth) Van Valkenburg; B.S., Cornell U., 1956; M.A., Queens Coll., 1967; Ph.D., City U. N.Y., 1971; m. Robert Milton Sunshine, Aug. 10, 1957 (dec. Dec. 1965); children—Winifred Joyce, Christopher James; m. 2d, Richard H. Seroff, Jan. 2, 1978. Psychol. clk. Manhattan State Hosp., N.Y.C., 1968-70; intern psychologist Kings County Hosp., Bklyn., 1970-71; psychotherapist L.I. Consultation Center, N.Y.C., 1971—, supr., 1977—; individual practice psychotherapy, 1971—; psychol. asso. Psychol. Service Center, 1972—; asst. editor Found. for Interdisciplinary Biocharacterization, 1972. Mem. Am., Eastern, N.Y. psychol. assns., N.Y. Soc. Clin. Psychologists. Contbr. articles to profl. jours. Home: 61-41 Saunders St Rego Park NY 11374

SUNTAG, CHARLES, mfg. co. exec.; b. N.Y.C., Feb. 17, 1914; s. Benjamin and Mollie (Hahn) S.; B. Chem. Engring., Cooper Union, 1942; M.S., Stevens Inst., Tech., 1958; m. Henrietta Bell, Dec. 25, 1942; children—Michael C., David T. Supervising insp. ordnance U.S. Army, N.Y.C., also supervising naval insp. U.S. Navy Dept., Clifton, N.J., 1941-46; sr. quality engr. Curtiss Wright Co., Wright Aero. div., Woodridge, N.J., 1955-56; dir. quality assurance Gen. Precision Labs., Bloomfield, N.J., 1956-58; mgr. qualiity control ITT, Nutley, N.J., 1958-67; dir. quality assurance Consol. Diesel Electric Co., Old Greenwich, Conn., 1967—; lectr., cons. in field. Mem. Am. Soc. Quality Control (cert. quality and reliability engr.; past nat. com. chmn. reliability reporting; sr. mem.), Am. Ordnance Assn. (past nat sec. quality tech.), Am. Def. Preparedness Assn., Nat. Security Indsl. Assn. (chmn. Army liaison com.). Home: 90 Cedar Heights Rd Stamford CT 06905 Office: 1500 Post Rd Old Greenwich CT 06870

SUOZZI, JOSEPH ANTHONY, justice state supreme ct.; b. Italy, Aug. 22, 1921; s. Michael and Rosa (Ciampa) S.; came to U.S., 1923; B.S., Fordham U., 1943; LL.B., Harvard U., 1948; m. Marguerite Holmes, Feb. 14, 1953; children—Joseph Michael, Rosemary, William, Christopher, Thomas. Admitted to N.Y. bar, 1948; pvt. practice, Glen Cove, 1948-60; judge Glen Cove City Ct., 1949-55; mayor-supr. City Glen Cove, 1956-60, justice 10th jud. dist. N.Y. State Supreme Ct., Mineola, 1961—, asso. justice 2d dept. appellate div., 1976—. Del. Nat. Conf. State Trial Judges, 1971-72; faculty adviser Nat. Coll. State Trial Judges, 1970, 77; chmn. judiciary relations com. 10th and 11th Jud. Dist., 1973—. Served to 1st lt. USAAF, 1943-45. Decorated D.F.C., Air medal with 3 oak leaf clusters. Home: 9 September Ln Glen Cove NY 11542 Office: Supreme Ct Bldg Mineola NY 11501

SUPINSKI, CATHERINE JOSEPHINE CURRAN (MRS. EDMUND SUPINSKI), librarian; b. N.Y.C., Aug. 27, 1915; d. Francis Joseph and Mary (Jordan) Curran; B.A., Hunter Coll., 1936; M.A., Columbia, 1937, B.S. in Library Sci., 1943; m. Edmund Supinski, June 2, 1951. Asst. librarian Nat. Indsl. Conf. Bd., N.Y.C., 1943-48; librarian N.Y. C. of C., N.Y.C., 1948-64, Dumont (N.J.) High Sch., 1964—. Mem. Spl. Libraries Assn. (N.Y. pres. 1950-51, internat. 2d v.p. 1953-54), ALA, NEA, N.J., Bergen County, Dumont edn. assns., N.J., Bergen County (rec. sec. 1967-68) sch. librarians assns., N.J. Secondary Tchrs. Assn. Home: 30 Kinderkamack Rd Woodcliff Lake NJ 07675 Office: Dumont High Sch New Milford Av Dumont NJ 07628

SUPIRO, LESTER DANIEL, tech. and mgmt. cons.; b. Little Falls, N.Y., Dec. 17, 1921; s. Julius and Helen (Miller) S.; student Coll. City N.Y., 1939-42; B.S., N.Y. U., 1943. Cons., chem. engr., 1945-48; mgr. Sty-Jar Products, Inc., 1948-51; asst. to pres. Internat. Testing Labs., Inc., 1951-53; treas., mgr. M & R Refractory Metals, Inc., 1953-60, pres., 1960-69; treas. Spot-Testers, Inc., 1952-69, dir., 1952-70; ind. tech. and mgmt. cons., 1969—. Served to capt. USAAF, 1942-45. Decorated Legion of Merit, Army commendation ribbon. Mem. Aircraft Owners and Pilots Assn., N.Y.U. Alumni Assn. Contbr. articles in field to various publs. Inventor hexamine process for mfg. tungsten, molybdenum; patentee metal processes. Office: 1530 Palisade Ave Fort Lee NJ 07024

SUPRANOVICZ, JOHN MICHAEL, cons. elec. engr.; b. Manchester, N.H., Feb. 22, 1922; s. Nicholas and Julia (Dudziak) S.; B.S. in Elec. Engring. with honors, U. Mass., 1950; m. Mary Rose, Dec. 28, 1947; children—Julia E. (Mrs. Richard Dolgin), Mary Deborah, Michael J. Elec. engr. Cleverdon, Varney & Pike, Boston, 1950-62; elec. engr., office mgr. R.G. Vanderweil, Boston, 1962-64; owner, prin. John M. Supranovicz, Engrs., Wilmington, Mass., 1964—; elec. cons. Avco, Wilmington, Mass. Served with Signal Corps, AUS, 1943-45. Registered profl. engr., Mass., R.I., Maine, N.H., Nat. Council Engring. Examiners. Mem. Cons. Engrs. Council, Illuminating Engring. Soc. Elk. Home: 14 S Amos St Tewksbury MA 01876 Office: 388 Main St Wilmington MA 01887

SURACI, CHARLES XAVIER, JR., govt. ofcl.; b. Washington, Feb. 10, 1934; s. Charles Xavier and June (Hunter) S.; student Pa. Mil. Coll., 1952-53; grad. Nat. Acad. Broadcasting, 1959; student Columbia Union Coll., 1962-63, 72, Catholic U., 1969; grad. Civil Air Patrol Staff Coll., 1974; B.S., Calif. Christian Coll., 1977, H.H.D. (hon.), 1977; m. Florence Patricia De Mino, May 23, 1970. Served with U.S. Air Force, 1953-57; enlisted CAP, 1957, commnd. 1st lt., 1961, advanced through ranks to col., 1974, founder Wheaton-Silver Spring Cadet Squadron, comdr. Nat. Capital Wing, 1973-76, now dep. chief staff cadet activities Middle East region; with Harry Diamond Lab., U.S. Army, Washington, 1963—, material publs. asst. 1963-68, now asst. to motor transp. officer. Mem. youth com. YMCA, Silver Spring, Md., 1962-69, mem. bd. mgmt., 1967—; bd. dirs. Am. Youth Com.; mem. Montgomery County (Md.) Juvenile Ct. Com., 1977—; Recipient Leader and Service award Silver Spring YMCA, 1968, 69; Meritorious Service award CAP, 1969; certificate of commendation from Pres. Nixon, 1970; Exceptional Service award Congressman Lester Wolff of N.Y., 1972; award Montgomery County C. of C., 1973; commendation Gov. of Tenn., 1975; certificate of appreciation Harry Diamond Lab., U.S. Army, 1977; letter of commendation Mayor Walter Washington, 1977; Outstanding Patriotic Civilian Service award, 1977; named Air Man of Month USAF, 1956. Mem. Air Force Assn. (dir.), Am. Security Council (dir.). Roman Catholic (mem. choir). Club: Andrews AFB Officers (Washington). Home: 3906 Halsey St Kensington MD 20795

SURDOVAL, DONALD JAMES, financial exec.; b. N.Y.C., Aug. 26, 1932; s. Donald J. and Catherine A. (Slevin) S.; B.B.A., Manhattan Coll., 1954; m. Patricia Fitzpatrick, May 28, 1955; children—Donald, Lisa, John, Catherine, Brian. Mgr., Touche Ross & Co., 1956-63; treas. Mohican Corp., 1963-65; asst. controller, then v.p., controller Litton Industries, 1965-68; v.p., controller Norton Simon Inc., 1968—; dir. Fuller O'Brien Paint Co. Bd. dirs. Calvary Hosp., N.Y.C. Served to 1st lt. USMCR, 1954-56. C.P.A., N.Y. Mem. Fin. Execs. Inst. Club: Hackensack Golf. Home: 87 Winding Way Woodcliff Lake NJ 07675 Office: 277 Park Ave New York City NY 10017

SURMELI, SUPHI, psychiatrist; b. Antakya, Turkey, Jan. 18, 1931; s. Saban and Munire (Beyaz) S.; Degree Sci., U. Istanbul, 1949, M.D., 1954; m. Guner Erdal, Mar. 24, 1965; children—Sahir, Sedat, Mine. Intern, St. Francis Hosp., Poughkeepsie, N.Y., 1958-59; resident Harlem Valley State Hosp., Wingdale, N.Y., 1959-60, Hudson River State Hosp., Poughkeepsie; practice medicine specializing in psychiatry; mem. staff Harlem Valley State Hosp., 1959, 67, Hudson River State Hosp., 1960-61, Kingston Gen. Hosp., 1966; acting dir. SENG Center, Seaford, N.Y., 1968-71; asst. clin. dir. South Oaks Hosp., Amityville, N.Y., 1972—; asst. prof. clin. psychiatry U. Stony Brook, 1975—. Served to lt. Turkish Army, 1954-56. Recipient Good Citizenship award Dept. Edn., Ministry Edn. Turkey. Mem. Am. Psychiat. Assn., Am. Coll. Clin. Pharmacology, AMA, N.Y., Nassau med. assns., Neuropsychiat. Soc., Turkish Am. Physicians Soc., Turkish Am. Soc. Moslem. Clubs: Anadolu, Am. Turkish Islamic Cultural Center, Turkish Sport (pres. 1974-75). Home: 225 Harbour Ln Massapequa Park NY 11762 Office: 400 Sunrise Hwy Amityville NY 11701

SUSA, PHILIP MICHAEL, elec. products co. exec.; b. Sharon, Pa., Apr. 30, 1939; s. Paul Andrew and Julia Dorothy (Chernitsky) S.; B.A., Gannon Coll., 1961; M.B.A. in Personnel Adminstrn., Fairleigh Dickinson U., 1973; m. Suzanne Margaret Sonken, July 18, 1964; children—Anthony, David, Jeanne. Personnel supr. trainee Internat. Paper Co., N.Y.C., 1965, personnel supr. container plant, Cin., 1966, Whippany, N.J., 1966-69; personnel mgr. Pyrotronics, Inc., Cedar Knolls, N.J., 1969; personnel mgr. Boonton Electronics Corp., mfg. electronic test and measurement equipment com., Parsippany, N.J., 1970-72, personnel dir., 1972—. Chmn. legislators liaison staff Morris County Employers Legis. Com., 1972-73; capt. United Fund of Morris County, 1968. Bd. dirs. Morris County Indsl. Recreation Assn., 1971—; adv. bd. Boonton High Sch. Coop. Indsl. Edn. Program, 1971-75; mem. indsl. adv. bd. Coll. St. Elizabeth, 1972—; mem. adv. com. Morris County Jr. Achievement, 1973-74. Served to 1st lt. USAF, 1962-65. Accredited personnel exec. Mem. Am. Soc. Personnel Adminstrn., Am. Mgmt. Assn., North Jersey Personnel Assn. (v.p. 1973-74, pres. 1974-75), Morris County C. of C. (mem. wage and salary survey com. 1972-76, vice chmn. personnel mgrs. com. 1974, chmn. 1975). Roman Catholic. K.C. (3 deg.). Home: 133 Hillside Ave Succasunna NJ 07876 Office: Route 287 at Smith Rd Parsippany NJ 07054

SUSAN, FRANK AUSTIN, physician; b. McKeesport, Pa., Oct. 1, 1908; s. Matt and Jasperine (Doimovic) S.; B.S., U. Pitts., 1930; M.D., George Washington U., 1932; m. Clarece Bland, July 15, 1933; 1 dau., Evelyn Bland (Mrs. Vincent C. Hungerford). Intern, Providence Hosp., Washington, 1932-33; physician Civilian Conservation Corps, while M.C., U.S. Army Res., 1933-35, highest rank being capt.; pvt. practice medicine, Indian Head, Md., 1935-78; dir. Bank of So. Md., La Plata. Mem. AMA, Md. State, Charles County med. assns., Am. Acad. Family Practice, Indian Head Bus. Assn., Charles County C. of C. Democrat. Episcopalian. Home: Route 1 Box 164 H Indian Head MD 20640

SUSMAN, ABRAHAM BERNARD, physician; b. Kingston, Ont., Can., Aug. 14, 1903; s. Max and Annie (Chananie) S.; came to U.S., 1928, naturalized, 1933; B.A., Queen's U., 1925, M.D., 1928; m. Rose Elson, Feb. 19, 1933; 1 son, David Gerson. Intern, Binghamton (N.Y.) City Hosp., 1928-29; resident pediatrics Children's Hosp., Buffalo, 1929-30; former dir. pediatrics Beth David Hosp., N.Y.C.; dir. pediatrics N.Y. Polyclinic Med. Sch. and Hosp., N.Y.C., 1958-65, prof. pediatrics, 1958-65; individual practice medicine, specializing in pediatrics, N.Y.C., 1932—. Vice-pres. Friends of Queens U., Kingston, 1972—, mem. univ. council, 1973—. Diplomate Am. Bd. Pediatrics. Mem. AMA, N.Y. State, N.Y. County med. socs., N.Y. Soc. Queens U. (past pres.). Home: 114 W 70th St New York City NY 10023

SUSSKIND, SIEGFRIED, elec. mfg. co. exec.; b. Nuremberg, Germany, Nov. 27, 1919; s. Maurice and Frieda (Schmal) S.; B.S., Lycée Janson de Sailly, Paris, 1936; E.E., Ecole superieur d'électricité, Paris, 1938; m. Gisela Baer, July 6, 1941; children—M. Roy, Joyce Renee Susskind Hancock. Vice pres. Waldorf Instrument Corp., Huntington, N.Y., 1952-59; pres. Instruments Systems Corp., Westbury, N.Y., 1959-63, Omnivend Corp. (merged with Matrix), Hicksville, N.Y., 1964-65, Matrix Research & Devel. Corp. (merged with Eastern Air Devices), Nashua, N.H., 1965-69; pres., chief exec. officer Eastern Air Devices, Inc. (now Electro Audio Dynamics, Inc.), Dover, N.H. and Great Neck, N.Y., 1966—; also dir.; dir. Peerless Fabrikkerne, Copenhagen, Denmark, Etablissements Bretton, Cluses, France. Home: Feeks Ln Locust Valley NY 11560 Office: 98 Cutter Mill Rd Great Neck NY 11021

SUSSMAN, BERNARD JULES, neurol. surgeon; b. N.Y.C., Jan. 4, 1926; s. Irving and Sally (Schanzer) S.; M.D., N.Y. U., 1950; m. Clare Ann Stein, Aug. 17, 1956. Intern, Bellevue Hosp., N.Y.C., 1950-51; resident in neurology N.Y. Neurol. Inst., N.Y.C., 1951-53; resident in neurosurgery Beth Israel Hosp., N.Y.C., 1953-54, Mt. Sinai Hosp., N.Y.C., 1954-56, Montefiore Hosp., N.Y.C., 1956-57; practice medicine specializing in neurol. surgery, Plainfield, Perth Amboy, N.J., 1957-67; lectr. neurosurgery Howard U. Coll. Medicine, Washington, D.C., 1967-69, asso. prof., 1969-72, prof., 1972—; neurosurgery cons. U.S. govt., Virgin Islands, 1978. Served with AC, U.S. Army, 1944-46. Recipient Honors Achievement award Angiology Research Found., 1965; citation Howard U. Research Com., 1971; NIH, Am. Heart Assn. grantee; diplomate Am. Bd. Neurol. Surgery. Fellow Am. Heart Assn. Council on Stroke; mem. Am. Assn. Neurol. Surgeons, Internat. Soc. Psychiat. Surgery (founding mem.), Internat. Med. Soc. Paraplegia, Internat. Coll. Angiology, AMA, Am. EEG Soc., Washington Acad. Neurosurgery. Successfully set civil rights precedent in Superior Ct. N.J. case, 1966. Developed methods of stroke treatment using enzymes; developer, patentee method for removing herniated intervertebral discs with enzyme collagenase, 1967-75. Contbr. articles to med. jours. Home: 2400 Tilden St NW Washington DC 20008 Office: 2041 Georgia Ave Howard U Hosp Washington DC 20060

SUSSMAN, HAROLD IRWIN, periodontist; b. N.Y.C., Nov. 4, 1938; s. Bernard and Evelyn (Rabinowitz) S.; B.S., Coll. City N.Y., 1959; D.D.S., Columbia, 1964; M.S.D., N.Y. U., 1968; m. Jacqueline Altman, Feb. 25, 1971; children—Bradford Jay, Clifford Jon, Samara Beth, Tamatha Britt. Gen. practice dentistry N.Y.C., 1966-68, specializing in periodontics, N.Y.C., 1968—; attending staff Mt. Sinai Hosp., N.Y.C., 1971-73, Bklyn. Jewish Hosp., N.Y.C., 1974-75, Meth. Hosp., 1976-77; instr. Community Coll., N.Y.C., 1966-67; asst. clin. prof. N.Y. U., 1968-76; staff lectr. dept. continuing edn. Brookdale Dental Center, N.Y.C., 1974-78; mem. Peer Rev. Com. N.Y. State, 1976—, chmn. periodontic sect. Manhattan div., 1976-78. Served with USNR, 1964-66; lt. comdr. Res. Certified Am. Acad. Oral Medicine. Mem. Research Scientists Am., Am. Acad. Periodontology, ADA, 1st Dist. Dental Soc., Caduceous Soc., Alpha Omega. Jewish. Contbr. articles to profl. jours. Home: 64 Popham Rd Scarsdale NY 10583 Office: 67 Park Ave New York City NY 10016 also 64 Popham Rd Scarsdale NY 10583

SUSSMAN, RALPH MAURICE, physician; b. N.Y.C., Apr. 15, 1908; s. Jacob and Taube Etta (Gertler) S.; student Columbia U., 1924, 26-28; M.D., L.I. Coll. Medicine, 1932; m. Frances Irene Goldberg, Sept. 12, 1929; children—Elizabeth Anne Sussman Socolow, Victoria Amy; m. 2d, Gertrude Hoddes Sneider, July 14, 1974. Intern, Beth Israel Hosp., N.Y.C., 1932-33, resident, 1933-35; practice medicine specializing in cardiology, N.Y.C., 1941—; adj. physician Beth Israel Hosp., N.Y.C., 1941-47, asso. physician, 1947-60, attending, 1960-77; asso. clin. prof. dept. medicine (cardiology) Mt. Sinai Sch. Medicine City U. N.Y., N.Y.C., 1972-77; mem. staff Drs. Hosp., also chmn. com. coronary care. Bd. govs. Downstate Med. Center, 1970—; mem. Arthur Ross Found., 1975—; physician Draft Bd., 1942-45. Dazian Found. recipient, 1949-50. Diplomate Am. Bd. Internal Medicine. Fellow R.C.P. (asso.), N.Y. Acad. Medicine, A.C.P. (life), Am. Coll. Cardiology, Clin. Council Cardiology of Am. Heart Assn.; mem. N.Y. Cardiologic Soc. (trustee 1975-78), Soc. Internal Medicine N.Y. County (sec. 1977-78), Am. Geriatric Soc., N.Y. Acad. Scis., AMA, Alumni Assn. Downstate Med. Center (pres. 1974). Jewish. Editor Lichonian, 1932; contbr. articles to med. jours. Home: 15 E 91 St New York City NY 10028 Office: 1148 Fifth Ave New York City NY 10028

SUSSMAN, ROBERT B., physician, psychiatrist; b. N.Y.C., May 22, 1932; s. Samuel and Eva (Kapinsky) S.; B.A., N.Y. U., 1953; M.D., U. Buffalo, 1957; M.S. in Adminstrv. Medicine, Columbia U., 1967; m. Marianne Lowenkopf, Aug. 16, 1964; children—Caroline, Jonathan. Intern, Maimonides Hosp., Bklyn., 1957-58; resident in psychiatry Stanford Med. Center, Palo Alto, Calif., 1958-60, Hillside Hosp., Queens, N.Y., 1962-63; clin. asst. in psychiatry Hillside Hosp., Glen Oaks, N.Y., 1963-64; mem. staff Roosevelt Hosp., N.Y.C., 1964-65; spl. asst. in geriatric psychiatry N.Y.C. Community Mental Health Bd., 1967-70; clin. dir. Four Winds Hosp., Katonah, N.Y., 1970-72; attending physician United Hosp., Port Chester, N.Y., 1971—, dir. div. alcoholism services, 1978—; pvt. practice medicine, specializing in psychiatry, Scarsdale, N.Y., 1963—; clin. asst. prof. psychiatry N.Y. Med. Coll., N.Y.C., 1974—. Served with USPHS, 1960-62. Fellow A.C.P., Am. Psychiat. Assn.; mem. Am. Pub. Health Assn., Westchester County Psychiat. Soc., Westchester County Med. Soc. Jewish. Home: 19 Hayhurst Rd New Rochelle NY 10804 Office: 192 Garth Rd Scarsdale NY 10583

SUTER, GEORGE AUGUST, internat. mgmt. cons. co. exec.; b. Zurich, Switzerland, July 22, 1934; s. Jakob George and Ann (Hagi) S.; M.Comml.Sci., Coll. St. Michael, 1954; m. Annelise Growe, July

2, 1962; children—Jeanine, Marcel. Vice-pres. mktg. Pantaplass, Zurich, 1954-62; mktg. mgr. Semperit A.G., Zurich, 1962-69; pres. Altexina A.G., Zurich, Switzerland, 1969-73; pres. George A. Suter Assos., Inc., Pitts., 1973—; dir. KaGa Security Locks, Inc., Pitts., Bracker Corp., Pitts. Mem. Door and Hardware Inst. Clubs: Pitts. Press, Alcoma Country. Office: One Oliver Plaza Pittsburgh PA 15222

SUTHERLAND, DONALD JAMES, investment co. exec.; b. Teaneck, N.J., Jan. 2, 1931; s. Conrad James and Lavinia Marie (Peters) S.; A.B., Princeton U., 1953; M.B.A., Harvard U., 1958; children—Paige, Donald, Shelley, Julie. Regional sales mgr. Dahlstrom Corp., Jamestown, N.Y., 1958-60; asso. McKinsey & Co., Inc., N.Y.C., 1961-64; v.p. Laird, Inc., N.Y.C., 1965-67, New Ct. Securities Corp., N.Y.C., 1968-70; pres., Quincy Assos., Inc., N.Y.C., 1970-75; pres., corp. gen. partner Quincy Partners, N.Y.C., 1975—; chmn. bd. Crane Hoist Engring. Corp., 1975—, Am. Spring & Wire Splty. Co., Inc., 1977—, Muehlhausen Bros. Spring & Mfg. Co., Inc., 1977—; dir. Mark Controls Corp., Century Glove, Inc., Hager, Inc., PBA, Inc. Mem. Nassau County (N.Y.) Planning Commn., 1965-68; mem. nat. adv. council Hampshire Coll., 1972—; trustee Sheltering Arms Children's Service, N.Y.C., 1973-75, St. Michael's Coll., 1973—. Served to lt., j.g., USN, 1953-56. Democrat. Roman Catholic. Clubs: Creek, Twenty-Nine. Contbr. articles to profl. jours. Home: High Farms Rd Glen Head NY 11545 Office: PO Box 154 Glen Head NY 11545

SUTHERLAND, GEORGE LESLIE, chem. co. exec.; b. Dallas, Aug. 13, 1922; s. Leslie and Madge Alice (Henderson) S.; B.A., U. Tex. at Austin, 1943, M.A., 1947, Ph.D., 1950; m. Mary Gail Hamilton, Sept. 9, 1961; children—Janet Leslie, Gail Irene, Elizabeth Hamilton. With Am. Cyanamid Co., various locations, 1951—, asst. dir. research and devel., Princeton, N.J., 1969-70, dir. research and devel., agr. div., Princeton, 1970-73, v.p. med. research and devel., Pearl River, N.Y., 1973—, dir. Med. Research div., 1978—. Served with USN, 1944-46. Mem. Assn. Research Dirs. (pres. 1975-76), AAAS, Am. Chem. Soc., Chem. Soc. London. Home: 42 Sky Meadow Rd Suffern NY 10901 Office: Middletown Rd Pearl River NY 10965

SUTHERLAND, JOHN CAMPBELL, pathologist; b. Tamingfu, Hopei, China, Oct. 28, 1921; s. Francis Campbell and Ann Findlay (Bowman) S.; A.B., N.W. Nazarene Coll., 1941; M.D., Marquette U., 1946; m. Eunice Lucille Kindschi, June 16, 1950; 1 son, John Mark. Med. missionary Raleigh Fitkin Meml. Hosp., Swaziland, 1956, Ethel Lucas Meml. Hosp., Republic South Africa, 1956-61, 62-67; intern Milw. Luth. Hosp., 1946-47; resident St. Francis Hosp., Wichita, 1950-52, Washington U., St. Louis, 1952-54; acting head dept. biology N.W. Nazarene Coll., Ida., 1961-62; chief resident, acting instr. pathology Stanford (Calif.) U., 1967-68; pathologist Balt. Cancer Research Center, Nat. Cancer Inst., 1968—; mem. faculty U. Md. Med. Sch., Balt., 1974—, asso. prof. pathology, 1976—. Trustee, Eastern Nazarene Coll., Quincy, Mass., 1972-73. Served with USAF, 1947-49. Mem. Internat. Acad. Pathology, Am. Assn. Cancer Research, Am. Assn. Pathologists. Republican. Mem. Ch. of Nazarene. Home: 23 Chiara Ct Towson MD 21204 Office: 655 W Baltimore St Baltimore MD 21201

SUTHERLAND, JOHN PATRICK, journalist; b. Kansas City, Mo., June 12, 1920; s. Joseph Frederick and Hazel Marie (Hogan) S.; A.B., U. Mo., 1947, B.Jour., 1948; m. Virginia Claire Shockley, Oct. 19, 1942. Reporter, Spirit Lake (Ia.) Beacon, 1937; asst. editor Barrick Pub. Co., 1948-50; mem. Washington staff Wall Street Jour., 1951-52; White House corr. U.S. News and World Report, Washington, 1953-74, sr. editor, 1974-76, congl. corr., 1976—. Chmn. bd. trustees Merriman Smith Meml. Fund, Washington, until 1972. Served to lt. F.A. U.S. Army, World War II; PTO. Recipient Journalism Excellence award Nat. Press Found., 1977. Mem. White House Corrs. Assn. (pres. 1971-72), Mil. Order Carabao. Roman Catholic. Clubs: Cosmos, Nat. Press. (Washington); Old Dominion Boat (Alexandria, Va.). Author: Man of Waterloo, 1966. Office: US News and World Report 2300 N St NW Washington DC 20037

SUTHERLUND, DAVID ARVID, lawyer; b. Stevens Point, Wis., July 20, 1929; s. Arvid E. and Georgia M. (Stickney) S.; B.A., U. Portland, 1952; J.D., U. N.M., 1957. Admitted to D.C. bar, 1957; atty. I.C.C., Washington, 1957-58; counsel Am. Trucking Assn., Washington, 1958-62; asso. and partner Morgan, Lewis & Bockius, Washington, 1962-72; counsel firm Turney & Turney, Washington, 1972-75; partner Fulbright & Jaworski, Washington, 1975—. Exec. dir. Film, Air & Package Carriers Conf., Washington, 1962-72; dir. and gen. counsel Nat. Film Service, 1962-75. Vice chmn. Nat. Capitol Area council Boy Scouts Am., 1975—. Served with U.S. Army, C.I.C., 1952-54. Mem. Am., Fed., D.C. Bar assns., Assn. Bar D.C., Motor Carrier Lawyers Assn., ICC Practitioners Assn., Am. Arbitration Assn., Am. Judicature Soc. Clubs: Nat. Lawyers Club, Lawyers Club N.Y.; Lakewood Country; International (Washington). Founder, chmn. bd. govs. Transp. Law Jour., 1969-74. Home: 2130 Bancroft Pl NW Washington DC 20008 Office: 1150 Connecticut Ave NW Washington DC 20036

SUTKOWSKI, ERNEST HAROLD, ednl. adminstr.; b. Middletown, Conn., Oct. 7, 1931; s. Joseph Francis and Julia Ethel (Waylock) S.; B.S., Central Conn. State Coll., 1955; postgrad. (Edn. scholar) Syracuse U., 1957; m. Jeanne Marie Blovat, Nov. 23, 1957; children—Mary Elizabeth, Joseph Francis II, Nancy Ann, Karen Julia, Jennifer Bernice. High sch. tchr. Bd. Edn., Little Falls, N.Y., 1956-58; sales rep. McGraw-Hill Book Co., N.Y.C., 1958-64, sales mgr., 1964-66; exec. v.p. Berkeley Schs., East Orange, Ridgewood, N.J., Hicksville, White Plains, N.Y., N.Y.C., 1966-73; chmn. bd., pres. Westchester Bus. Inst., White Plains, N.Y., 1973—. Exec. v.p. Atlantic Med. TV Network, 1970—. Mem. Nat., Eastern bus. edn. assns., New Eng.-N.Y. State Ind. Bus. Sch. Adminstrs. Group, N.Y. State Assn. Registered Pvt. Bus. Schs. (sec.), N.Y. Bus. Tchrs. Assn. (dir.), N.Y. Personnel and Guidance Assn. Home: 68 Armour Rd Mahwah NJ 07430

SUTNICK, ALTON IVAN, physician; b. Trenton, N.J., July 6, 1928; s. Michael and Rose (Horwitz) S.; B.A., U. Pa., 1950, M.D., 1954; postgrad. Drexel Inst. Tech., 1961-62, Temple U., 1969-70; m. Mona Reidenberg, Aug. 17, 1958; children—Amy Ilene, Gary Benjamin. Rotating intern, then resident in anesthesiology Hosp. U. Pa., 1954-56, resident in medicine, 1956, USPHS postdoctoral research fellow, 1956-57; asst. instr. aesthesiology, then asst. instr. medicine U. Pa. Med. Sch., 1955-57; from asso. in medicine to asso. prof., 1965-75; resident in medicine, then chief resident Wishard Meml. Hosp., Ind. U. Med. Center, Indpls., 1957-57, 60-61, resident instr., 1960-61; USPHS postdoctoral research fellow Temple U. Hosp., Phila., 1961-63, instr., then asso. in medicine, 1962-65; research physician Inst. Cancer Research, Phila., 1965-75, asso. dir., 1972-75; clin. asst. physician Pa. Hosp., 1966-71; dir. clin. devel. Am. Oncologic Hosp., Phila., 1973-75; vis. prof. medicine Med. Coll. Pa., 1971-75, prof., 1975—; exec. v.p. health affairs, 1976—, dean, 1975—; attending physician Hosp. Med. Coll. Pa., VA Hosp., Phila.; bd. dirs. Phila. Health Mgmt. Corp., 1977—; mem. numerous other med. coms., med. adv. coms. Pres. bd. dirs. Phila. Concerto Players, 1964-66; bd. dirs. Phila. Council Internat. Visitors, 1972-77, Phila. Chamber Ensemble, 1977-78. Served to capt. M.C., AUS, 1958-60. Diplomate Am. Bd. Internal Medicine. Fellow A.C.P., Coll. Physicians Phila.; mem. Assn. Am. Med. Coll. Council Deans, Am. Fedn. Clin. Research (chpt. pres. 1964-65), Am. Assn. Cancer Research, Am. Soc. Clin. Oncology, Assn. Am. Cancer Insts., Am. Cancer Soc. (dir. Phila. chpt. 1974—, chmn. awards com. 1976), Am. Lung Assn., AMA (Arnold and Marie Schwartz award 1976), AAAS, Am. Heart Assn., Pan Am. Med. Assn., Phila. Cancer Coordinting Assn., N.Y. Acad. Scis., Pa. Heart Assn., Heart Assn. Southeastern Pa., Pa., Phila. County (chmn. com. internat. affairs 1964-72) med. socs., Pa. Lung Assn., Soc. des Medecins Militaires Francais, Sydenham Coterie, Phi Beta Kappa, Sigma Xi, Alpha Omega Alpha. Contbr. numerous articles to med. jours., mem. editorial bds. profl. jours. Address: Medical Coll Pa 3300 Henry Ave Philadelphia PA 19129

SUTRO, FREDERICK CHARLES, JR., chem. co. exec.; b. Basking Ridge, N.J., June 21, 1920; s. Frederick Charles and Elizabeth Tallman (Winne) S.; student U. Ariz., 1939-40; B.S. in Indsl. Engring., Yale U., 1943; m. Sheila Kelley, Nov. 6, 1943; children—Tracy (Mrs. Charles Horter), Tina Tallman. Tech. rep. N.Y. area Bakelite Co. div. Union Carbide Corp., 1944-51; mgr. comml. research and devel. PM Industries, Inc., Stamford, Conn., 1951-54; sales supr. plastics Spencer Chem. Co., Kansas City, Mo., 1954-57, mgr. tech. service, 1957-58, product mgr., 1959-60; mktg. mgr. Cabot Corp., Boston, 1960-64, asst. to v.p. devel., 1964-66; gen. mgr. plastics dept. USS Chems. div. U.S. Steel Corp., Pitts., 1966-78, asst. to v.p. planning and devel., 1978—; dir. Koro Corp., Hudson, Mass. Served as 2d lt. USAAF, 1943-44. Mem. Soc. Plastics Engrs. (nat. council 1955-61, v.p. 1958, pres. 1959), Plastics Pioneers Assn., Soc. Plastics Industry (dir. 1973—, exec. com. 1974—, chmn. pub. affairs com. 1974-76, treas. 1976—), Yale Engring. Assn. (sec. 1946-49), Phi Gamma Delta. Clubs: Chatham Beach and Tennis; Yale (N.Y.C.); Harvard-Yale-Princeton (Pitts.); Allegheny Country (Sewickley, Pa.). Home: 647 Grove St Sewickley PA 15143 Office: US Steel Corp 600 Grant St Pittsburgh PA 15230

SUTTON, CLYDE CLARENCE, food service dir.; b. Millville, N.J., Jan. 10, 1954; s. Alonzo J. and Doris R. (Pfleghar) S.; certificate in food service supervision Cumberland County Vocat. Tech. Sch., 1975. Cook, Millville (N.J.) Hosp., 1972-73, mgmt. trainee, 1973-74, asst. food service mgr., 1974-75, food service dir., 1975—; N.J. rep. for Mid Atlantic Health Congress-Dietary Profl. Devel. Programs, 1977-79. Mem. Hosp. Food Dirs. Assn. Phila. (mem. symposium com. 1977-78), Internat. Food Service Execs. Assn., Am. Soc. Hosp. Food Service Adminstrs., Hosp. Food Service Dirs. of Phila. and So. Jersey (dir.). Methodist. Home: RD 3 PO Box 122 Millville NJ 08332 Office: High and Harrison Ave Millville NJ 08332

SUTTON, GEORGE HILLS, III, mgmt. cons. co. exec.; b. New Rochelle, N.Y., July 29, 1929; s. George Hills and Lillian Annette (Watkins) S.; B.S., U. Bridgeport, 1951; m. Nancy Tufts, May 3, 1968; children—Catherine, Carol Sue, George Hills, Sherry Lynne. Account mgr. AT&T, Los Angeles, 1953-59; corporate mgr. communications and utilities N.Am. Aviation Inc., Los Angeles, 1959-63; mgr. adminstrv. services Litton Industries, Los Angeles, 1963-66; group mgr. Coopers & Lybrand, N.Y.C., 1966-73; pres. Ruxton Assos., Sherman, Conn., 1973—; faculty N.Y. Inst. Fin. Nat. chmn. Communicators for Nixon, 1972; campaign treas. Boughton for Mayor City Danbury, 1976. Served with USAF, 1951-52. Certified mgmt. cons. Mem. Tele-Communications Assn. (pres. 1961-62), Inst. Mgmt. Cons.'s. Am. Arbitration Assn. Club: Masons. Contbg. author: Stock Market Handbook, 1971. Home: Orchard Rest Rd Sherman CT 06784 Office: PO Box L Sherman CT 06784

SUTTON, JOHN JOSEPH, III, rehab. counselor: b. Clearfield, pa., Aug. 6, 1945; s. John Joseph and Violet May (Knepp) S.; B.A., Columbia U., 1972; M.A., N.Y. U., 1976; grad. Am. Mus. Dramatic Acad., 1969; m. Phyllis Jean Roach, Oct. 31, 1970. Specialist, cons. theatre arts program N.Y. State Bd. Edn., Bronx, 1969-71: tchr. Immaculate Conception Elementary Sch., Secaucus, N.J., 1972-73: employment interviewer N.Y. State Employment Service, N.Y.C., 1973-75: rehab. counselor Fedn. Employment and Guidance Service, N.Y.C., 1976-77, supr. profl. services, 1977—; lectr. in field. Served with USAF, 1963-67. Certified rehab. counselor NY State. Mem. Nat., Am. rehab. counseling assns., Nat. Rehab. Assn., Am. Personnel and Guidance Assn. Home: 200 E 21st St New York City NY 10010 Office: 2432 Grand Concourse Bronx NY 10432

SUTTON, JONATHAN STONE, architect, landscape architect, planner; b. Columbus, Ohio, July 31, 1944; s. Charles Reuel and Theodora (Stone) S.; B.A., Amherst Coll., 1966; M.Arch., M. Landscape Architecture, U. Pa., 1970; m. Karen Marie Johnson, May 21, 1970; children—Eva Marie, Theodora Stone, Karen Amelia. Draftsman, Pierre Zoelly, Architect, Zurich, Switzerland, 1966; designer Weissman/Spohn, Phila., 1967, Magruder House, LaJolla, Calif., 1968; research asst. regional planning br. Delaware River Port Authority, Phila., 1969, computer applications group center for ecol. research in planning and design U. Pa., 1970; partner Adaptive Design, computer-assisted ecol. planning, Phila., 1970; architect, landscape architect Wallace, McHarg, Roberts & Todd, Phila., 1971—, asso. partner, 1973—; instr. U. Pa. Grad. Sch. Fine Arts, 1972-75; Laredo Taft lectr. U. Ill., 1974. Mem. Citizen's Council of Delaware County (Pa.), tech. subcom. Suburban Zoning Task Force, Fellowship Commn. Recipient Anna Baker Heap prize in art Amherst Coll., 1966, Arthur Spayd Brooke Meml. prize in design U. Pa., 1970; numerous office project awards; registered architect, Pa.; registered landscape architect, Ky. Mem. AIA, Am. Soc. Landscape Architects (award of Merit 1971, Brad Williams medal 1974, 76), Am. Inst. Planners, Am. Soc. Planning Ofcls., Nature Conservancy, Soc. Archtl. Historians, Sierra Club, Housing Assn. Delaware Valley, Wallingford Community Arts Center. Democrat. Presbyterian. Clubs: Racquet; Wallingford Swim; Pier 30 Tennis. Home: 335 Plush Mill Rd Wallingford PA 19086 Office: 1737 Chestnut St Philadelphia PA 19103

SUTTON, LEON MURAD, physicist; b. Los Angeles, Nov. 8, 1942; s. Murad Abraham and Adele (Ancona) S.; B.S., Mass. Inst. Tech., 1962; postgrad. (Fulbright fellow) U. Paris, 1962-63; Ph.D., Princeton U., 1970. Research asso. Stanford U., 1969-70; instr., adj. asst. prof. physics City Coll., City U. N.Y., 1970-73; owner, operator L.M. Sutton Mgmt. Co., N.Y.C., 1973—; partner MCAT Rev. Course Inc., East Orange, N.J., 1974-76; owner, operator Sutton Nursing Rev., N.Y.C., 1975—. Mem. nat. governing bd., vice chmn. N.Y. state governing bd. Common Cause. Mem. Am. Phys. Soc., AAAS, Sigma Xi. Home: 900 W End Ave New York City NY 10025 Office: 225 W 34th St Suite 918 New York City NY 10001

SUTTON, PERCY E., lawyer; ed. Prairie View Coll., Hemstead, Tex., Tuskegee Inst., Hampton Inst., Columbia, Bklyn. Law Sch.; m. Leatrice Sutton; children—Pierre Monte, Cheryl Lynn. Admitted to N.Y. State bar; mem. N.Y. Assembly, 1964-67; former pres. Borough of Manhattan. Counsel, Harlem United Block Assn., Harlem Council on Jobs and Freedom; co-chmn. United Council Harlem Orgns.; mem. lay adv. bd. Harlem Hosp.; cons. Student Non-Violent Coordinating Com.; pres. N.Y. br. NAACP; legal counsel N.Y. Congress on Racial Equality, Baptist Ministers Conf. of Greater N.Y.C. Bd. dirs. Am. Com. on Africa, Harlem Neighborhood Assn., African Am. Inst. Served to capt. USAAF, World War II. Office: 801 2d Ave New York City NY 10007

SUTTON, PETER A., bishop; b. Chandler, Que., Can., Oct. 18, 1934. Ordained priest, Roman Catholic Ch., 1960; ordained bishop of Labrador-Schefferville (Que.), 1974. Office: 303 AP Low CP 700 Schefferville PQ G0G 2T0 Canada

SUTTON, RICHARD LAUDER, lawyer; b. Dover, Del., July 4, 1935; s. Richard and Anna Kimber (Massey) S.; A.B. with distinction, U. Del., 1957; LL.B., Yale, 1960; m. Violette Witwer, June 25, 1960; children—Jane Valentine, Richard Mohler. Admitted to Del. bar, 1961; law clk. to Judge Edwin D. Steel, U.S. Dist. Ct., Wilmington, Del., 1960-61; asso. firm Morris Nichols Arsht & Tunnell, Wilmington, 1961-65, partner, 1966—; mem. antitrust and trade regulation com. U.S. C. of C., 1976—. Chmn., Del. Gov.'s Higher Edn. Commn., 1976; dir., mem. exec. com. Greater Wilmington Devel. Council; trustee Wilmington Pub. Library; bd. dirs. Grand Opera House, Inc. Mem. Am., Del. bar assns., Phi Beta Kappa, Phi Kappa Phi, Omicron Delta Kappa, Phi Delta Phi. Clubs: Wilmington, Wilmington Country, Pine Valley Golf, Bidermann Golf. Home: 10 Barley Mill Dr Wilmington DE 19807 Office: PO Box 1347 Wilmington DE 19899

SUTTON, ROBERT FRANKLIN, coll. librarian; b. Washington, Mar. 25, 1921; s. Don Franklin and Harriet (Roberts) S.; B.S., D.C. Tchrs. Coll., 1945; M.A., U. Pa., 1951; M.L.S., Rutgers U., 1960, postgrad., 1961-62; m. Clarice Nettie Collier, June 29, 1946 (div. Sept. 1960); children—Robert Franklin, Haldon Collier. Clk., Hecht Co., Washington, 1941-42; assignee Civilian Pub. Service, 1942-46; curator E.F. Smith Meml. Collection, U. Pa., Phila., 1949-54; librarian Ursinus Coll., Collegeville, Pa., 1954-58; asso. librarian Monmouth Coll., West Long Branch, N.J., 1958—. Sec. bd. dirs. William Jeanes Meml. Library, Lafayette Hill, Pa. Mem. Phila. Area Tech. Service Librarians Assn. (pres. 1958-59), Am., N.J., Pa. library assns., Am. Assn. U. Profs., Am. Civil Liberties Union, SANE. Mem. Soc. Friends (nat. coll. program com. Am. Friends Service Com. 1964-68). Home: 4026 School House Ln Plymouth Meeting PA 19462 Office: Monmouth Coll West Long Branch NJ 07764

SUTTON, SUZY, lectr., entertainer; b. Phila., Aug. 16, 1924; d. Nathaniel and Esther (Saks) Snyderman; student Phila. Dance Acad., 1963-65; m. Maurice Kaufmann, Aug. 14, 1944 (dec. Nov. 1977); children—Ellen Ann, Martha Dell. Nightclub entertainer, 1940-64; lectr., entertainer, 1965—; cons., trainer communication skills, 1970—; producer TV pub. affairs programs, 1974-75; writer, producer, hostess, radio commentator, 1974—; character dancer Pa. Ballet Co., 1968-75. Served with WAF, 1943-46. Mem. AGVA, Am. Guild Mus. Artists, Screen Artists Guild, Artists Equity, AFTRA, Women in Communication, WAC Vets., Internat. Platform Assn. (gov.), Nat. Speakers Assn. Jewish. Home and Office: 253 Shawmont Ave Philadelphia PA 19128

SUTTON, WILLIAM JAMES, III, assn. exec.; b. Tex., Feb. 5, 1930; s. William James and Helen (Holmes) S.; B.S., U.S. Mil. Acad., 1953; audited U. Paris, Heidelberg (Germany) U.; grad. Arty. Sch., 1953, Arty. and Missile Sch., 1960, Nuclear Weapons Sch., 1964, Spl. Warfare Sch., 1965, Mil. Assistance Inst., 1965, Command and Staff Coll., 1971, in Arabic, Def. Lang. Inst., 1972, Def. Computer Inst., 1974, Criminal Investigation Sch., 1974; postgrad. George Washington U.; m. Sanelma Tarkka, Dec. 28, 1963; children—Sharon, William James IV. Commd. 2d lt. U.S. Army, advanced through grades to lt. col. F.A.; ops. officer Joint Chiefs of Staff, Washington; ops. adv. to Prince and minister def. Saudi Arabia; dir. ops. U.S. Army Criminal Investigation Command, Washington; ret., 1975; chief ops. Nat. Rifle Assn., Washington, 1975—, dir. nat. championships; speaker, tchr. in field. Mem. council Messiah Lutheran Ch., Alexandria, Va. Decorated Army Commendation medal, Meritorious Service medal, Joint Service Commendation medal. Mem. Internat. Assn. Chiefs Police, Co. Mil. Historians, Internat. Platform Assn., Nat. Trust Hist. Preservation, West Point Soc. D.C., Ret. Officers Assn. Contbr. articles to profl. publs., texts. Home: 6917 Stoneybrooke Ln Alexandria VA 22306 Office: 1600 Rhode Island Ave Washington DC 20036*

SUYDAM, THOMAS WILLIAM, mgmt. services exec.; b. Gloversville, N.Y., Apr. 24, 1945; s. William Andrew and Ella Christine (Van Denburgh) S.; B.S. in Bus. Adminstrn., Babson Coll., Wellesley, Mass., 1966, M.B.A., 1968. Vice pres. L & L Growth Fund, Inc., Wellesley, 1967; instr. Bryant and Stratton Jr. Coll., Boston, 1968, Nichols Coll. Bus. Adminstrn., Dudley, Mass., 1970; accountant George J. Dorfman & Co., C.P.A., Gloversville, 1971; chmn., pres. Van-Dam Mgmt. Corp., Gloversville, 1972-78; partner George J. Dorfman & Co., C.P.A., Johnstown, N.Y., 1978—. Mem. Am. Inst. C.P.A.'s, N.Y. State Soc. C.P.A.'s. Office: 338 N Comrie Ave Johnstown NY 12095

SUZUKI, KOTARO, obstetrician, gynecologist; b. Tokyo, Sept. 13, 1934; s. Yasuzo and Nobuko (Miyazawa) S.; came to U.S., 1962; M.D., Keio U. Sch. Medicine, 1960, Ph.D., 1969; m. Bridget Kennedy, Jan. 16, 1965; 1 son, Kenneth Kotaro. Intern, Albert Einstein Coll. Medicine, Bronx Municipal Hosp. Center, 1962-63; asst. resident in obstetrics and gynecology Lincoln Hosp., Bronx, 1963-64; sr., chief resident St. Mary's Hosp., Bklyn., 1964-66; NIH postdoctoral fellow Columbia Coll. Physicians and Surgeons, N.Y.C., 1966-69, asst. prof. obstetrics and gynecology, 1969-70; asst. prof. Harvard Med. Sch., Boston, 1970-76, also dir. semi-ann. postgrad. course in fetal monitoring; asst. obstetrician-gynecologist Beth Israel Hosp., Boston, 1970-73, asso. obstetrician-gynecologist, 1974—, head obstetrical physiology sect., 1970-76, fetology, 1974-76, dir. High Risk Obstet. Clinic, 1974-76; asso. prof. obstetrics and gynecology and pediatrics Boston U. Sch. Medicine, 1976—; asso. dir. dept. obstetrics and gynecology, chief obstetrics, dir. high risk obstet. clinic Boston City Hosp., 1976—. Recipient Physicians Recognition award AMA, 1969-72; 2d award 6th World Congress Gynecology and Obstetrics, 1970; USPHS grantee, 1966-69, Mass. Heart Assn. grantee, 1971-72, Milton Fund grantee Harvard U., 1971-72, Charles H. Hood Found. grantee, 1974, Beth Israel Hosp. grantee, 1971-72, 75-76. Diplomate Am. Bd. Obstetrics and Gynecology. Fellow Am. Coll. Obstetricians and Gynecologists; mem. Japanese Obstetrical and Gynecol. Soc., Am. Fedn. Clin. Research, Soc. Exptl. Biology and Medicine, Internat. Corr. Soc. Obstetricians and Gynecologists (cons. panel), Boston Obstetrical Soc., Royal Soc. Medicine (Eng.) (affiliate). Contbr. chpts., articles to med. publs. Home: 24 Apple Crest Rd Weston MA 02193 Office: Boston City Hosp Boston MA also 720 Harrison Ave Boston MA 02118

SVARC, EMILE DRAGAN, ophthalmologist; b. Zagreb, Yugoslavia, Nov. 26, 1936; s. Dr. Djuro and Olga (Vasiljevic) S.; came to Can., 1969, naturalized, 1974; M.D., U. Zagreb, 1962; m. Milica Magovac, Dec. 21, 1963. Gen. practice medicine, Yugoslavia, 1962-65; resident in medicine Ichilov Municipal Hosp., Tel Aviv, 1965-66; intern Booth Meml. Hosp., Flushing, N.Y., 1966-67; resident in ophthalmology North Shore Hosp., Manhasset, N.Y., 1967-68, Jewish Gen. Hosp., Montreal, 1969-72; pvt. practice specializing in ophthalmology, Montreal, 1972—; staff physician Jewish Gen., Queen Mary Vets. hosps.; dir. low vision clinic Jewish Gen. Hosp.; lectr. ophthalmology

McGill U. Fellow Royal Coll. Physicians and Surgeons (Can.); mem. Can. Med. Assn., Can., Montreal ophthalmol. socs., Internat. Intraocular Implant Club, Am. Intraocular Implant Soc., Montreal Clin. Soc. Research on intravenous application of fluorescent protein conjugates in ophthalmology. Home: 5775 Cote des Neiges Montreal PQ H3S 2S9 Canada Office: 3755 Cote Saint Catherine Rd Montreal PQ H3T 1E2 Canada

SVETLICH, WILLIAM GEORGE, govt. ofcl.; b. Detroit, Sept. 8, 1929; s. George I. and Mary S.; B.Sc. cum laude, Wayne State U., Detroit, 1951, M.Sc., 1952; postgrad. (research doctoral fellow) Northwestern U., 1952-53; M.B.A. (Univ. scholar), U. Mich., 1960; diploma Indsl. Coll. Armed Forces, 1975. Commd. 2d lt. USAF, 1951, advanced through grades in Res. to col., 1973—; tech. program mgmt. Lockheed Missiles & Space Co., Sunnyvale, Calif., 1961-63; tech. program mgr. NASA, Cleve., 1963-64; sr. staff planner Hdqrs. U.S. Air Force, Pentagon, Washington, 1964-72, sci. and tech. advisor Joint Chiefs of Staff, 1972-75, sr. staff asst., planning, systems acquisition and program devel. Office of Sec. Def., 1975—, adviser to asst. sec. comptroller, 1976; adviser to dir. on reorgn., 1978. Decorated Legion of Merit; recipient Outstanding award Dept. Def., 1973. Mem. Mil. Ops. Research Soc., Air Force Assn., Am. Inst. Aeros. and Astronatuics. Author govt. publs. on nat. def. policy, strategic and gen. purpose forces, NATO interoperability, econ. analysis and systems acquisition. Home: 4107 Rocky Mount Dr Washington DC 20031 Office: Office of Secretary Defense The Pentagon Washington DC 20301

SVILOKOS, NIKOLA ANDREW, systems analyst; b. Zagreb, Yugoslavia, Oct. 25, 1931; s. Pavo Joseph and Katinka Dare (Kobila) S.; B.Sc. magna cum laude with honors in Math., Loyola Coll., Montreal, Que., Can., 1953; A.M. magna cum laude, Harvard, 1959; Mathematician, engr. Canadair Ltd., Montreal, 1956-58; research mathematician Dow Chem. Co., Williamsburg, Va., 1959-60; ops. research analyst Bankers Trust Co., N.Y.C., 1961-63; applied mathematician Allied Chem. Co., N.Y.C., 1963-65; system analyst N.Y. Stock Exchange, N.Y.C., 1965—; pres. Evening Math., Inc., N.Y.C., 1965—. Mem. Am. Math. Soc., Math. Assn. Am., N.Y. Acad. Scis., Harvard Soc. Advanced Study and Research. Roman Catholic. Club: Tinccum Swim and Golf. Research on flutter in aerodynamics, de-icing in thermodynamics, fiber formation, color analysis, security analysis and indexes, abstract tensor analysis, number theory. Home: 1060 Park Ave New York City NY 10028 Office: 55 Water St New York City NY 10028

SVOKOS, STEVE GEORGE, pharm. co. exec.; b. Wierton, W.Va., June 22, 1934; s. George and Irene (Makrinos) S.; B.S. in Chemistry, Bklyn. Coll., 1956; M.S. in Biol. Chemistry, State U. N.Y., 1962, Ph.D. in Biol. Chemistry, 1964; m. Chrysanthe Lampadarios, Sept. 11, 1960; children—George, Rena, Anthony. Chemist quality control and research Lederle Labs. div. Am. Cyanamid Corp., Pearl River, N.Y., 1956-60, research chemist medicinal chemistry dept., 1965-69; regulatory liaison Ayerst Labs. div. Am. Home Products Corp., N.Y.C., 1969-72; dir. regulatory and tech. affairs Knoll Pharm. Co., Whippany, N.J., 1972—. Served with AUS, 1958. Fellow Chem. Soc.; mem. Am. Chem. Soc., N.Y. Acad. Scis., Sigma Xi, Alpha Chi Sigma, Phi Lambda Upsilon. Patentee in field. Home: 59 1st Ave Westwood NJ 07675 Office: 30 N Jefferson Rd Whippany NJ 07981

SWAIN, ETHEL M., steel co. exec.; b. Lambertvill, N.J., Sept. 27, 1917; d. Harold Ross and Edith (Gregg) S.; student Temple U. 1952-54. Legal sec., Lambertville, N.J., 1935-41; asst., personal sec. to pres. Magnetic Pigment Co., Monmouth Junction, N.J., 1941-43; accounting clk., asst. to office mgr. Frederick H. Levey Co. div. Columbian Carbon Co., 1943-51; asst. to wage and salary adminstr. U.S. Pipe and Foundry, Burlington, N.J., 1951-52, cost accountant, Burlington and Birmingham, Ala., 1953; credit clk., cost accountant, gen. ledger accountant SPS Techs. Inc., Jenkintown, Pa., 1953-62, supr. div. accounting, corporate accounting, 1962-67, corporate consolidations accountant, 1967-71, supr. corporate and consolidation accounting, 1971-73, adminstrv. asst. to chmn. bd., 1973—. Mem. Nat. Assn. Accountants, Bus. and Profl. Womens Club. Methodist. Club: Order Eastern Star. Home: 901 The Benson East Jenkintown PA 19046 Office: 916 The Benson East Jenkintown pA 19046

SWAIN, ROBERT VICTOR, san. engr.; b. Dillwyn, Va., Feb. 2, 1940; s. Frank Robert and Virginia Odell (Doss) S.; B.S. in Physics, Carson-Newman Coll., 1961; B.C.E., Va. Poly. Inst., 1964, M.S. in San. Engring., 1967; m. Norma Foley, Aug. 28, 1965; 1 son, John Victor. Design engr. Gannett Fleming Dorddry and Carpenter, Inc., Harrisburg, Pa., 1965-72; chief engr. Glace and Glace, Inc., Harrisburg, 1972—. Bd. dirs. First Baptist Ch. Registered profl. engr., Pa., Va., W.Va., Ark., Del. Mem. ASCE, Water Pollution Control Fedn., Water Pollution Control Assn. Pa. (chmn. govtl. affairs com.), Am. Water Works Assn., Water Pollution Control Operators Assn., Lake Meade Property Owners Assn., Va. Tech. Alumni Assn. Republican. Contbr. article to profl. publ. Home: 110 Ridgewood Dr Camp Hill PA 17011 Office: 2771 Paxton St Harrisburg PA 17111

SWAIN, WILLIAM GRANT, landscape architect; b. Covington, Ky., Sept. 5, 1923; s. George Wellington and Emma (Holmes) S.; B.Arch., Carnegie-Mellon U., 1952; m. Marjorie Page Reno, Dec. 21, 1957; children—Margaret Page, Jill Holmes. Asso. firm Ralph E. Griswold Assos., Pitts., 1948-57; partner firm Griswold, Winters, Swain & Mullin, Pitts., 1957-75; pres. GWSM, Inc., 1975—. Vis. lectr. colls., univs.; chmn. Interprofl. Council Environ. Design, 1975—; vis. Mem. Mayor's Community Improvement Com., Monroeville, Pa., 1963-66, 77; mem. Pa. Art Commn.; bd. dirs. Western Pa. Conservancy, Landscape Architecture Found. Served as 1st lt. inf. AUS, 1943-46; ETO. Decorated Purple Heart. Recipient service award Carnegie-Mellon U., 1963. Fellow Am. Soc. Landscape Architects (pres. 1973-74). Club: University (Pitts., dir.). Home: 413 Harper Dr Monroeville PA 15146 Office: 1101 Greenfield Ave Pittsburgh PA 15217

SWAINE, ROBERT LESLIE, chemist; b. Boston, Mar. 20, 1923; s. Aldeverd Harold and Annette (Harris) S.; B.S., Northeastern U., 1948; m. Barbara Elizabeth Allen, Mar. 26, 1949; children—Robert Leslie, David Allen, Donald Richard. Sr. research chemist Arthur D. Little, Inc., Cambridge, Mass., 1948-70; v.p. tech. operations Can. Dry Corp., Greenwich, Conn., 1970—. Served with AUS, 1942-46, ETO. Decorated Purple Heart with oak leaf cluster. Mem. Inst. Food Technologists, Am. Chem. Soc., N.Y. Acad. Sci., Soc. Cosmetic Chemists (treas. 1966-67), Royal Soc. Health, Soc. Flavor Chemists. Clubs: Masons, Chemists' (N.Y.C.). Home: 155 Riverside Ave Riverside CT 06878 Office: Old Track Rd Greenwich CT 06830

SWALES, GEORGE ALOYSIUS, mil. health care exec.; b. Leonardtown, Md., July 22, 1937; s. George Robert and Mattie Mae (Mason) S.; B.S., George Washington U., 1975; m. Clara Mae Wicks, Apr. 4, 1964; children—Timothy Bai, Gerald Anthony. Enlisted U.S. Navy, 1955, commd. ensign, 1970, advanced through grades to lt. comdr., 1979; hosp. corpsman, 1956-69, head med. records br., Adminstrv. Command, Naval Tng. Center, San Diego, 1970-72; head acctg. and stats. br. Bur. Medicine and Surgery, Dept. of Navy, 1973-74; adminstrv. asst. Nat. Naval Med. Center, Bethesda, Md., 1974-75, regional health care coordinator, 1975-76, head enlisted personnel br., 1977-78, chief manpower mgmt. service, 1978—. Vice pres. Seabrook Recreation Council, 1975-76; del. Prince George's County Schs. Parents Adv. Council, 1976-77. Democrat. Roman Catholic. Club: K.C. Home: 10306 Chautauqua Ave Lanham MD 20801 Office: Manpower Mgmt Service Nat Naval Med Center Bethesda MD 20014

SWAMY, SRIKANTA M.N., elec. engr., dean; b. Bangalore, India, Apr. 7, 1935; s. M.K. Nanjundiah and M.N. Mahalakshamma (Kashipathaiah) S.; B.Sc. (Hons.), Mysore U., 1954; diploma Indian Inst. Sci., Banglore, 1957; M.Sc., U. Sask., 1960, Ph.D., 1963; m. Leela Sitaramiah, June 5, 1964; children—Saritha, Nikhilesh, Jagadish. Research asst., dept. elec. engring. U. Sask. (Can.), 1959-63, lectr. math., 1961-63; scientist Indian Inst. Tech., Madras, 1963-64; asst. prof. math U. Sask., Regina, 1964-65; asst. prof. elec. engring. N.S. Tech. Coll., Halifax, 1965-66, asso. prof., 1966-67, prof., 1967-68; prof. U. Calgary (Alta.), 1969-70; prof. Concordia U., Montreal, Que., 1968-69, prof., chmn. dept. elec. engring. 1970-77, dean engring., 1977—. Mem. Am. Soc. Engring. Edn., IEEE (sr.), Math. Assn. Am., Am. Math. Soc. Asso. editor Fibonacci Quar., Circuits and Systems, 1974. Contbr. articles to profl. jours. Home: 660 Verdure St Brossard PQ Canada Office: Dean of Engring Concordia U Montreal PQ Canada

SWAN, CHARLES, lawyer; b. Elmira, N.Y., Feb. 11, 1914; s. Charles and May (Maxon) S.; student Cornell U., 1932-33, LL.B., J.D., 1943; B.S. in Commerce, U. N.C., 1941; m. Florence Myers, Sept. 5, 1939; children—Mary Jane Swan Belinky, Eleanor Myers, John C. Teller, bookkeeper Chemung Canal Trust Co., Elmira, 1931-38; admitted to N.Y. bar, 1943; atty. firm Mudge, Stern, Williams & Tucker, N.Y.C., 1943-45, Mandeville, Buck, Teeter & Harpending, Elmira, 1945-47; mem. firm Swan & Frawley, Elmira, 1947-54; individual practice law, Elmira, 1954—. Pres., treas., dir. Chemung Valley Realty Corp., Southport Shopping Center Corp., Swan-Elmira Realty Corp.; v.p., dir. Elmira Drug of Southport, Inc.; sec., dir. Standard Operating Service of Chemung, Inc., Van Auken Mill Supplies & Equipment, Inc.; sec., treas. dir. Gilbert's Service Center, Inc.; v.p., sec., dir. John H. Cook, Jr., Painting Contractors, Inc. Chmn., Woodlawn Cemetery Commn. Mem. Am., N.Y. State, Chemung County bar assns., N.Y. County Lawyers Assn., Chemung County C. of C., Am. Judicature Soc., Phi Delta Phi. Democrat. Episcopalian (vestryman). Clubs: Elmira City, Elmira Country, N.Y.C. Lawyers, Cold Brook, Cornell (N.Y.C.), Fur, Fin and Feathers, Elks, Watkin Yacht. Home: 655 Fassett Rd Elmira NY 14901 Office: 463 W Church St Elmira NY 14901

SWANBORN, EDWIN DONALD, harpsichordist, organist; b. Boston, May 25, 1948; s. Edwin Ferdinand and Jean MacLeod (Burgess) S.; studied with Dr. Anthony Newman, Music Sch. at Juilliard, 1967-72; studied with Gustav Leonhardt, 1973, Anton Heiller, 1974; m. Nancy Lucile McMahon, July 23, 1970. Performing harpsichordist, organist, specializing in Early Music performance practices; solo recitalist, 1967—; concerto soloist orchs. or as guest artist with various chamber ensembles throughout East Coast; recorder numerous radio, TV concerts Boston, Atlanta; European debut, France, 1975; asst. condr. Northeastern U. Choral Soc., 1970—; solo harpsichordist Atlanta Virtuosi, 1978—; dir. Boston Baroque Chamber Players, 1969—; pvt. studio tchr. music, Boston, 1967—; guest lectr. Northeastern U., Boston, 1967—. Found. Camargo Cassis grantee, 1975. Mem. Am. Guild Organists, Atlanta Virtuosi Found., New Eng. Pianoforte Tchrs. Assn., Boston Musician's Assn., Am. Mus. Instrument Soc., Atlanta Fedn. Musicians. Address: 24 Mapleton St Brighton MA 02135

SWANK, RICHARD BRUCE, publisher; b. Ames, Iowa, Apr. 20, 1931; s. Frederick Charles and Florence Ovanda (Batman) S.; student Johns Hopkins U., 1949-50; B.A., Iowa U., 1953; m. Jean Florence Goodspeed, Dec. 30, 1955; children—Scott, Mark, Andrew, Steven. Various exec. positions Reuben H. Donnelley Corp., N.Y.C., 1963-70, v.p. staff, 1970-72, v.p., Phila., 1975-78, sr. v.p., N.Y.C., 1978—; v.p., chmn. R.H. Donnelley Internat., Ltd., London, 1972-75; dir. Reuben Donnelley Ltd., London, Thomson Yellow Pages, Ltd., Farnborough, Eng. Served as lt. AUS, 1953-55. Mem. Am. Mgmt. Assn., Dirs. Inst. (London), Delta Upsilon. Episcopalian. Clubs: Urban (gov.); Univ. (N.Y.C.); Phila. Country; Apawamis Country; Manursing Island. Office: 825 Third Ave New York City NY 10022

SWANKOSKI, MICHALINE ANN, nurse; b. Allentown, Pa., Mar. 19, 1941; d. Charles Thomas and Antoinette Henrietta (Yancoski) S.; grad. Sacred Heart Hosp. Sch. Nursing, Allentown, 1961; B.S. in Nursing, Villanova U., 1967; M.S. in Nursing, U. Pa., 1975. Staff nurse Sacred Heart Hosp., Allentown, 1961-62, Phila. VA Hosp., 1962-64; instr. Bryn Mawr (Pa.) Hosp. Sch. Nursing, 1967-69; head nurse Delaware County Meml. Hosp., Drexel Hill, Pa., 1970-71, inservice edn. coordinator, 1971-75; asst. dir. nursing Lock Haven (Pa.) Hosp., 1975-76, dir. nursing, 1976—. Mem. Am., Pa. nurses assns., Am., Pa. hosp. assns., Alumnae Assn. Sacred Heart Hosp., Sch. Nursing Alumnae Assn. Villanova U., Sigma Theta Tau. Office: Lock Haven Hosp 4th and Nelson Sts Lock Haven PA 17745

SWANNER, GRACE MAGUIRE (MRS. ROY O. SWANNER), physician; b. Albany, N.Y., Dec. 5, 1901; d. Joseph A. and Mary D. (Stevens) Maguire; B.S., State U. of N.Y., 1923; M.A., Columbia U., 1927; postgrad. U. Chgo., 1929; M.D., Albany Med. Coll., 1933; m. Roy O. Swanner, Apr. 25, 1936; children—Roy Stevens, Katherine Vaughan. Intern, Albany Med. Center, 1933-34; resident Jersey City Med. Center, 1934-35, Margaret Hague Hosp., Jersey City, 1934-35, Overlook Hosp., Summit, N.J., 1935-36; gen. practice medicine, Saratoga Springs, N.Y., 1936-75; mem. staff Saratoga Hosp., also bd. mgrs.; health officer town of Wilton (N.Y.), 1937-39; town of Greenfield (N.Y.), 1948-72. Lectr. pub. health Skidmore Coll., Saratoga Springs, 1944-46; acting med. dir. Saratoga Spa, 1953, 55-58, med. cons., 1969-72. Bd. dirs. Am. Cancer Soc. Mem. AMA, N.Y., Saratoga County med. socs., N.Y. Health Officers Assn., AAUW (chpt. pres. 1959-61). Home and Office: 107 Lake Ave Saratoga Springs NY 12866

SWANSON, ALBERT ARTHUR, historian, historic planner; b. Everett, Wash., Feb. 21, 1920; s. Carl Albert and Clarissa Anne (Corey) S.; spl. courses Northeastern U.; m. Shirley Elaine Haskell, Sept. 6, 1946; children—Kristine Elaine, Victoria (Mrs. Daniel Donovan). Ship officer U.S. Army Engrs. from Seattle to Skagway, Alaska, 1941-42; owner, operator Commn. Sales Co., 1950-62; ship restoration historian South St. Seaport Mus., N.Y.C., 1968-70; historian, historic planner Met. Dist. Commn., Boston, 1970—. Lectr. on Boston Harbor and islands; historian, historic planner Bunker Hill Monument and Battlefield; lectr. on Boston and met. parks; in charge hist. restoration Ft. Independence and Ft. Warren, Dorothy Quincy Homestead; organizer Tall Ships Visit, sec. Operation Sail '76, Boston. Founder, Hist. Mus. New Eng.; dir. Save Our Shore. Episcopalian (warden, vestryman). Club: Masons. Home: 5 Bagley St Danvers MA 01923 Office: 20 Somerset St Boston MA 02108

SWANSON, CARL EVERT, engring. exec.; b. Lysekil, Sweden, Feb. 3, 1918; s. Enock Adrian and Signe Vilhelmina (Johansson) S.; came to U.S., 1925, naturalized, 1929; B.S. in Chem. Engring., N.J., Inst. Tech., 1943; postgrad. in Phys. Chemistry, Stevens Ins. Tech., 1943-47; m. Gertrude Ruhs, June 26, 1943; children—Philip, Neil. Radio crystal technician Western Electric Co., Kearny, N.J., 1937-38; engring. technician Gen. Electric Co., Hoboken, N.J., 1938-41; cathode ray tube and fluorescent powder engr. RCA, Harrison, N.J., 1941-43; sr. devel. engr. Nat. Union Radio Corp., Newark, 1943-46; fluorescent lamp engr., chief chemist Duro Test Corp., N. Bergen, N.J., 1946-68, asst. dir. engring., dir. quality control, 1968—. Mem. Electrochem. Soc., Illuminating Engring. Soc., Am. Chem. Soc., Am. Soc. Quality Control, U.S. affiliate Internat. Electrotech. Commn. Author and co-author patents on cathode ray tube processing, electropolishing of metals and incandescent and fluorescent lamp constrn. Home: 26 Morton Pl North Arlington NJ 07032 Office: 2321 Kennedy Blvd North Bergen NJ 07047

SWANSON, CARL SYLVESTER, typographer; b. Douglas, Ariz., Oct. 6, 1924; s. Carl S. and Addie (Blum) S.; student U. Ariz., 1941-43; m. Margaret Catherine Todd, Aug. 19, 1944; children—Ronald, Richard, Rodger. Printer Kogan Printing Co., Balt., 1945-48, 49-53, 54-57, Mills-Frizzell-Evans, Balt., 1948-49, A. S. Abell Co., Balt. Sun, Balt., 1953-54; owner Swanson Typesetting Service, Balt., 1957—. Served with AUS, 1943-45. Decorated Bronze Star with 2 oak leaf clusters, Purple Heart, Combat Infantry badge. Republican. Episcopalian. Patentee of game. Home: 15 Dublin Drive Lutherville MD 21093 also Burning Tree Ct Bethany Beach DE 19930 Office: 5205 York Rd Baltimore MD 21212 also 232 Cockeysville Rd Cockeysville MD 21030

SWANSON, ERNEST ALLEN, JR., educator; b. Miami, Fla., Apr. 9, 1936; s. Ernest Allen and Thelma Eileen (Hilton) S.; B.A., Emory U., 1958, Ph.D., 1964; m. Barbara Ann Thomas, June 20, 1967. Grad. asst. anatomy Emory U., Atlanta, 1962-64, instr., 1964-65; instr. anatomy U. Va., Charlottesville, 1965-67; asst. prof. anatomy Temple U., Phila., 1967-72, asso. prof., 1972—. Mem. Ga. Acad. Sci., So., Soc. Anatomists, Am. Assn. Anatomists, Am. Assn. Dental Schs., AAUP, Sigma Xi, Pi Delta Epsilon, Omicron Delta Kappa, Alpha Omega (hon.), Xi Psi Phi (hon.). Home: 38 Hastings Ave Havertown PA 19083 Office: 3223 N Broad St Philadelphia PA 19140

SWANSON, ROGER FULTON, indsl. engr.; b. Sioux City, Iowa, Oct. 12, 1930; s. Elmer Fulton and Beulah Mae (Fisher) S.; student Wayne State U. (Nebr.), 1949-50; E.E., U. Nebr., 1957; B.S.I.E., Iowa State U., 1961; postgrad. U. Va., 1972-73; m. Orchid Swanson, Aug. 15, 1959; children—Corinne, Annette, Craig. Staff, Collins Radio Corp., Cedar Rapids, Iowa, 1957-61; staff McClellan AFB, Sacramento, 1961-64, hdqrs. U.S. Weapons Command, Rock Island, Ill., 1964-65, Maintenance Engring. Agy., U.S. Continental Army, Aberdeen, Md., 1965-67; mgmt. systems service, dept. medicine and surgery VA, 1967-69, engring. service, Washington, 1969-78, dept. medicine and surgery bldg. mgmt. service. 1978—, now engaged in program devel. and coordination for VA Hosps.; cons. in field. Vice-pres. Francis Scott Key PTA, 1968-69. Served with USAF, 1950-54; Korea. Mem. Assn. Advancement Med. Instrumentation. Lutheran. Home: 3208 Wood Ave Burtonsville MD 20730 Office: Veterans Adminstrn 810 Vermont Ave NW Washington DC 20420

SWART, ROBERT J., dentist; b. Elmira, N.Y., July 11, 1925; s. Donald Aubrey and Mazie (putnam) S.; student Ark. State Coll., 1944-45; A.B., U. Buffalo, 1949, D.D.S., 1953; m. Virginia Sutter, Aug. 20, 1949; children—Susan Sutter, Robert Carlton. Intern, Rockland Hosp., N.Y.C., 1953-54; gen. practice dentistry, Rochester, N.Y., 1954—; lectr. Am. U., Lebanon, 1965; lectr. Rochester Dental Assistant Sch., 1960—; lectr. U. Rennes (France), 1963, Rochester Bus. Inst., 1956-57, U. Buffalo, 1968, N.Y. Acad. Dental Practice Adminstrn., Buffalo, Al Sigl Center, 1970. Pres., Crippled Children's Soc. Monroe County (N.Y.), 1974-77; pres. Easter Seal Soc. N.Y. State, 1977-79; bd. dirs. Handicapped Children's Camp, Monroe County; mem. Medicaid Rev. Bd. of Monroe County, 1965—. Served to lt. USAAF, 1944-45. Mem. Monroe County Dental Soc. (pres. 1963-64, dir. 1964-69), 7th. Dist. Dental Soc. (pres. 1973-74, chmn. pub. and profl. relations 1965-69), Internat. Coll. Dentists, Flying Dentists Soc., Rochester Dental Study Club, Am. Acad. of Anesthesiology, Am. Dental Assn. (lectr. 1967-68), Acad. of Medicine of Rochester (award of merit 1976), Dental Soc. State of N.Y. (chmn. council on membership 1972-75), N.Y. State Acad. of Dental Practice (pres. 1971-73), Rochester pilots Assn., Civic Music Assn., Omicron Kappa Upsilon, Xi Psi Phi, Tau Kappa Epsilon. Presbyterian. Clubs: Rotary (pres. 1975-76): Oak Hill Country, Masons. Home: 164 Schofield Rd Honeoye Falls NY 14472 Office: 1580 Elmwood Professional Center Rochester NY 14620

SWARTWOUT, JOHN BAXTER, optometrist; b. Cohoes, N.Y., June 2, 1922; s. Walton Leslie and Margaret Mary (Baxter) S.; student Rensselaer Poly. Inst., 1946-48; B.S. in Optometry, Columbia U., 1950; O.D., Mass. Coll. Optometry, 1963; m. Dorothy Frieda Porter, June 4, 1949; children—John, Frank, Glen. Gen. practice optometry, Troy, N.Y., 1950-76, Latham, N.Y., 1952—; mem. profl. adv. bd. Albany (N.Y.) chpt. Assn. for Children with Learning Disabilities, 1969—, Tri-City Tutorial Center, Cohoes, 1969-74; advisor outreach program State Coll. Optometry State U. N.Y., 1975—; lectr. in field. Served with USAAF, 1942-46. Fellow Am. Acad. Optometry, Coll. Optometrists in Vision Devel.; mem. Eastern N.Y. Optometric Soc., N.Y. State (Distinguished Service award 1973, asso. editor jour. 1975—), Am. optometric assns., Aniseiconic Forum, Optometric Extension Program (dir. 1976—), Optometric Center N.Y., Omega Epsilon Phi. Episcopalian. Contbr. articles to profl. jours. Office: Park Ave and Route 7 Latham NY 12110

SWARTZ, DONALD PERCY, physician; b. Preston, Ont., Can., Sept. 12, 1921; s. Simon Wingham and Lydia (Ethell) S.; B.A., U. Western Ont., 1951, M.D. cum laude, 1951, M.Sc. cum laude, 1953; m. Norma Mae Woolner, June 24, 1944; children—Ian Donald, Rhonda Swartz Peterson. Intern, Victoria Hosp., London, Ont., 1951-52; resident Johns Hopkins U., Balt., 1954-58; asst. prof. obstetrics and gynecology U. Western Ont., London, 1958-62; prof. Columbia U., N.Y.C., 1962-72, also dir. obstetrics and gynecology Harlem Hosp.; prof., chmn. dept. Albany (N.Y.) Med. Coll., 1972—. Vice pres., pres. Assn. Planned Parenthood Physicians, 1972-74. Served with RCAF, 1942-45. NRC Can. fellow; Am. Cancer Soc. fellow, Markle scholar. Fellow Royal Coll. Surgeons Canada, Am. Coll. Obstetricians and Gynecologists, Am. Gynecologic Soc., Am. Fertility Soc., Royal Soc. Health. Asso. editor Advances in Planned Parenthood. Home: 24 Devon Rd Delmar NY 12054 Office: 47 New Scotland Ave Albany NY 12208

SWARTZ, JAMES RICHARD, investment co. exec.; b. Pitts., Oct. 4, 1942; s. Frank Thomas and Mary Elizabeth (Roth) S.; A.B., Harvard, U., 1964; M.S. in Indsl. Adminstrn., Carnegie-Mellon U., 1966; m. Susan Lee Shallcross, June 18, 1966; children—James Scott, Karin Lynn, Kristin Lee. Asst. to v.p mfg. Campbell Soup Co., Camden, N.J., 1966-68; sr. asso. Cresap, McCormick & paget, N.Y.C., 1968-72; asst. v.p. G.H. Walker, Laird Inc., N.Y.C., 1972-74; v.p. Citicorp Venture Capital Ltd., N.Y.C., 1974-78; gen. partner VENAD Assos., N.Y.C., 1978—; pres. N.Y. Venture Forum, 1977-78; dir. WellTech, Inc., Loehmann's, Inc., Phys. Acoustics Corp., Cambridge Telecommunications, Inc., Transatlantic Venture Capital, Ltd. Mem. West Windsor Twp. Conservation Com., 1973-74. Mem. Nat.

Venture Capital Assn., Assn. Corporate Growth. Republican. Episcopalian. Clubs: Harvard, Board Room, Racquet and Tennis (N.Y.C.); Harvard (N.J.); Bedens Brook. Home: 15 Hibben Rd Princeton Junction NJ 08540 Office: 280 park Ave New York City NY 10017

SWARTZ, LILLIAN BURTON, editor; b. Ansonia, Conn., Mar. 16, 1897; d. James and Caroline (Prisk) Williams; student George Washington U.; m. Bert O. Swartz, July 7, 1921 (dec. Sept. 1959); 1 dau., Jean E. (Mrs. Ivan B. Colburn). Chief sect. Civilian Personnel div. Office Sec. Army, Washington, then chief Policy, Regulations and Procedures br.; editor weekly Community Reporter, Mt. Airy, Md., 1966—. Recipient achievement award Sec. Army. Mem. Md., Del., D.C. Press Assn. Mem. Order Eastern Star (grand matron Md. 1964-65, chmn. cancer research gen. grand chpt. 1973-76). Home: Route 6 Mount Airy MD 21771 Office: Main St Mount Airy MD 21771

SWARTZ, WARREN LESTER, newspaper exec.; b. Lancaster, Pa., Aug. 18, 1919; s. Oliver Julius and Dorothea Anna (Bechtold) S.; student Franklin and Marshall Coll., 1937-39; B.S. in Edn., State Tchrs. Coll. at Millersville, Pa., 1941; m. Emma Kathryn Moore, Nov. 3, 1943; children—Sharon Louise (Mrs. Howard G. Butler), and George Philip. Master Peekskill (N.Y.) Mil. Acad., 1946, head jr. sch., 1946-47; adminstrv. asst. Lancaster (Pa.) Newspapers, Inc., 1947-55, asst. sec. 1955-56, asst. treas. 1956-61, treas. 1961—; asst. treas. Intelligence Printing Co., 1956-77, treas., 1977—; asst. treas. Gen. Engraving, Inc. 1956-77, treas., 1977—. Chmn. Lancaster Airport Authority. Served from apprentice seaman to lt., USNR, 1941-46; capt. Res. Mem. Nat. Assn. Accountants, Res. Officers Assn., Newspaper Purchasing Mgmt. Assn. (pres. 1963-64), Stuart Cameron McLeod Soc., Lancaster Assn. Commerce and Industry, Phi Sigma Pi. Republican. Presbyn. Club: Hamilton. Home: Troy Dr Route 2 Lititz PA 17543 Office: 8-10 W King St Lancaster PA 17604

SWEARER, HOWARD ROBERT, coll. pres.; b. Hutchinson, Kans., Mar. 13, 1932; s. Edward Mays and Elloise (Keeney) S.; A.B., Princeton U., 1954: M.A., Harvard U., 1956, Ph.D. 1960; m. Janet Lois Baker, June 19, 1954; children—Nicholas Baker, Howard Randolph, Richard William. Prof. polit. sci. U. Calif. at Los Angeles, 1960-67; program officer-in-charge office European and internat. affairs Ford Found., N.Y.C., 1967-70; pres. Carleton Coll., Northfield. Minn., 1970-77, Brown U., Providence, 1977—. Dir. Ninth Dist. Fed. Res. Bank, Mpls. Mem. Commn. Govtl. Relations Am. Council Edn. Mem. Minn. Humanities Commn. Bd. dirs. German Marshall Fund U.S., Spring Hill Conf. Center, Orono, Minn. Served to 1st lt. U.S. Army, 1958-59. Mem. Council Fgn. Relations, Phi Beta Kappa (senator). Office: Office of Pres Brown Univ Providence RI 02912

SWEENEY, EUGENE THOMAS, educator; b. Greenwich, Conn., May 12, 1920; s. Eugene Augustine and Agnes Clothilde (Joyce) S.; M.A., U. Chgo., 1950, Ph.D., 1961; m. Emily E. Ariewitz, Mar. 21, 1947; children—Lee, Bayard, Ian. Research asst. U. Chgo., 1952-53, dir. World Politics Program, 1953-56, lectr. history, 1953-56; asso. historian Nat. Found. for Infantile Paralysis, N.Y.C., 1956-57; mem. faculty U. Hartford (Conn.), 1957-58, asst. prof., 1958-61, asso. prof., 1961-70, dean of students, 1968-70, prof. history, 1970—. Chmn. Hartford Bicentennial Com., 1974-76; mem. policy bd. Our Roots, 1975-76; chmn. Bloomfield (Conn.) Bd. Tax Rev., 1969-71; mem. Bloomfield Bd. Edn., 1971-75, chmn., 1974-75. Served to sgt. USAAF, 1942-45; ETO. Mem. Am., New Eng. hist. assns., Soc. Historians for Am. Fgn. Relations, Orgn. Am. Historians. Democrat. Author: The Medical Services Div. of the NFIP, 1957; contbr. articles to profl. jours. Home: 27 Hoskins Rd Bloomfield CT 06002 Office: Hartford West Hartford CT 06117

SWEENEY, FRANCIS JOSEPH, JR., mech. engr.; b. N.Y.C., Dec. 1, 1926; s. Francis Joseph and Margaret (Cronin) S.; Sr.; B.S. in Mech. Engring., Rensselaer Poly. Inst. 1947, B.M.E. 1947; postgrad. in mech. engring. Columbia U. 1948; M.M.E., Poly. Inst. of Bklyn. 1953; m. Carol Marie Cavanagh, Apr. 23, 1949; children—Kathleen, Francis, III, James, John, Mary, Patricia, Erin, Robert, Michael, Philip, David. Sr. draftsman EBASCO Services, Inc., N.Y.C., 1947-48, mech. engr. 1948-54, field contruction engr. Wilmington, N.C., 1954-55; sr. prin. and supervising mech. engr. N.Y.C., 1956-68, cons. mech. engr. 1970-74, chief engr. mech. nuclear design engring. 1975-77, v.p. engring. 1978—; sr. mech. engr. Westinghouse Elec. Corp., Pitts., 1955-56; mgr. staff engring. Commonwealth Assos., Inc., Jackson, Mich. 1968-69; mgr. conceptual engring. Stone & Webster Engring. Boston 1969-70. Mem. indsl. adv. council N.Y.C. Community Coll.; squadron edn. officer N. River Power Squadron, N.Y.C. 1978—. Served with USNR, 1944-46. Profl. engr. registered various states. Mem. ASME, Am. Nuclear Soc., Nat. Soc. Profl. Engrs. Clubs: Roosevelt Rod and Gun, Statuit Boat, Knights of Columbus. Contbr. research reports, papers in field. Home: 90 Old Forge Rd Scituate MA 02066 Office: 2 Rector St New York City NY 10006

SWEENEY, HUGH JOHN, cons. mech. engr.; b. Bklyn., Apr. 21, 1942; s. John Joseph and Evelyn Veronica (Joyce) S.; student Cath. U. Am., 1959-62; B.M.E., Pratt Inst., Bklyn., 1966; postgrad. U. Bridgeport, 1966-67; m. Ann Joan Honeycutt, June 11, 1966; children—Michael, Scott, Heather. Design engr. Syska & Hennessy Inc., N.Y.C., 1962-65, Sikorsky Aircraft Co., Stratford, Conn., 1966-67; service engr. Pan Am. World Airways, N.Y.C., 1967-70; pvt. practice cons. engring. Norwalk, 1970—. Mem. Norwalk Fair Rent Commn., 1975-77; alt. mem. Norwalk Zoning Bd. Appeals, 1976—; pres. Norwalk Young Republican Club, 1976-77; Norwalk coordinator, reelection U.S. Senator Lowell Weicker, 1976. Mem. Norwalk C. of C., Nat. Soc. Profl. Engrs., Am. Soc. Heating, Refrigeration and Air Conditioning Engrs., Conn. Engrs. Pvt. Practice, Am. Soc. Plumbing Engrs. Roman Catholic. Registered profl. engr. Conn. Designer solar-heated bldgs. Home: 10 Marlin Dr Norwalk CT 06854 Office: 69 East Ave Norwalk CT 06851

SWEENEY, JAMES FRANCIS, steel co. exec.; b. Pitts., Dec. 27, 1928; s. James Augustine and Emelie Irene (Hollerman) S.; B.S., U. Pitts., 1950, M.Litt., 1954, postgrad., 1954-56; m. Mary Audrey West, Nov. 2, 1951; children—Kathi Elizabeth, Michael James. Geologist, J&L Steel Co., Pitts., 1948-51; with U.S. Steel Corp., Pitts., 1953—, mgr. facility planning-raw materials, 1968-75; tech. dir. raw materials and lake shipping, 1975—. Served to lt. USNR, 1951-53. Fellow Geologic Soc. Am.; Mem. Am. Inst. M.E., Coal Mining Inst. Clubs: Oakmont Yacht (Pitts.), Masons, Shriners. Home: 6837 Saltsburg Rd Pittsburgh PA 15235 Office: 600 Grant St Pittsburgh PA 15235

SWEENEY, JOHN J., lawyer; b. N.Y.C., Dec. 28, 1924; s. John J. and Rose H. (Galligan) S.; B.A., St. Johns U., 1952, LL.B., 1951, J.D., 1968; m. Rita V. Colleran, Aug. 27, 1955; children—Jean Maria, John J., Peter F., Thomas P., Michael J., Rose Anne. Admitted to N.Y. bar, 1951; mem. firm Sweeney, Cunningham & Krieg, P.C. (formerly Sweeney, O'Donognue & Cunningham), N.Y.C.; pres. Arthur Manor Assn., Scarsdale, N.Y., 1969-71; pretrial master Civil Ct., N.Y.C., 1964-68; spl. master Supreme Ct. N.Y. County, 1977—. Mem., arbitrator N.Y. State Mediation Bd. Pres. Guild Catholic Lawyers Archdiocese N.Y., 1969-71; pres. Catholic Big Bros., 1971-73. Served with inf. AUS, World War II. Decorated Silver Star, Bronze Star, Purple Heart with oak leaf cluster; Combat Inf. badge. Mem. N.Y. State Trial, N.Y.C. Trial, (gov. 1969—), N.Y. County lawyer assns., Am. Arbitration Assn. (arbitrator). K.C. (grand knight 1956-57). Editor Nat. Democratic Club bull., N.Y.C., 1965-70. Home: 223 Boulevard Scarsdale NY 10583 Office: Sweeney Cunningham & Krieg PC 800 3d Ave New York City NY 10022

SWEENEY, MARY ELIZABETH, educator; b. North Versailles, Pa., June 1, 1930; d. Albert Alexander and Agnes Marie (Gawlak) Rutka; B.S., U. Pitts., 1952, M.Ed., 1962, Ph.D., 1976; m. Steve J. Sweeney, Aug. 8, 1953; children—Steven, Louise, Ramon. Jr. engr. Westinghouse Electric Co., East Pittsburgh, Pa., 1952-54; med. researcher Falk Clinic, U. Pitts., 1956-58; tchr. chemistry, physics South Huntingdon High Sch., Ruffsdale, pa., 1961—. Mem. Sewickley Twp. Planning Bd., 1976; chmn. community affairs commn. Greensburg Diocesan Council of Catholic Women. Mem. Nat. Assn. Research in Sci. Teaching, Nat. Sci. Tchrs. Assn., Assn. for Edn. Tchrs. Sci., Pa. Sci. Tchrs. Assn. (dir., pres.-elect 1979-80), NEA, Pa. Acad. Scis., Jean Piaget Soc., U. Pitts. Alumni Assn., polish Women's Alliance, Polish Nat. Alliance, Christian Mothers (past pres.). Roman Catholic. Home: RD 1 Box 233 West Newton PA 15089 Office: 99 Lowber Rd Herminie PA 15637

SWEENEY, ROBERT JOHN, lawyer; b. Glendale, L.I., N.Y., Mar. 5, 1918; s. John Patrick and Claire M. (Evers) S.; B.B.A., Pace Coll., 1950; LL.B., St. John's U., 1956; m. Martha Loddigs, Oct. 31, 1942; children—Robert J., Martha A. Admitted to N.Y. bar, 1957, since practiced in Freeport; mayor Freeport, 1961-73; dep. county atty. Nassau County, 1973-76, sr. dep. county atty., 1976, chief dep. county exec., 1977; spl. counsel Villages Freeport and Lynbrook, 1973—. Mem. Gov.'s Spl. Electric Power Com., 1967. Pres. Village Party of Freeport, 1972-75. Served to capt. with F.A., AUS, 1952. Mem. Am., N.Y. State, Nassau County bar assns. N.Y. Trial Lawyers Assn., Nassau Lawyers Assn., Municipal Electric Utilities Assn. N.Y. (past pres.), Nassau County Village Ofcls. Assn. (past pres.), N.Y. State Conf. Mayors, Assn. Bar City N.Y., Freeport C. of C. (dir. 1973-75), Am. Legion, Nat. Council Christians and Jews, Phi Delta Phi. Republican. Roman Catholic, Kiwanian. Elk. Home and office: 99 Lester Ave Freeport NY 11520

SWEENY, CHARLES DAVID, chemist; b. Freeport, Pa., May 22, 1936; s. Charles A. and Ruth (Beale) S.; B.S., Pa. State U., 1960; m. Barbara K. Scheid, Feb. 12, 1977. Technician, Alcoa Research Labs., New Kensington, Pa., 1954-58; spectroscopist Am. Color & Chem. Corp., Lock Haven, Pa., 1963-66, supr. analyt. labs., 1966—. Scoutmaster, W. Branch council Boy Scouts Am., 1966-76, counselor, 1976—, chmn. adminstrv. bd., 1975—. Served with AUS, 1960-63. Mem. Am. Chem. Soc., Inter Soc. Color Council (chmn. strength of colorants-dyes com. 1975—), Am. Assn. Textile Chemists and Colorists (chmn. weathering com. 1978—). United Methodist. Contbr. articles to profl. jours. Patentee effluent treatment. Office: Mt Vernon St Lock Haven A 17745

SWEET, DONALD HERBERT, mfg. co. exec.; b. Washington, Mar. 8, 1925; s. George Henderson and May (DeLawder) S.; B.A. in Econs., Gettysburg Coll., 1949; m. Mary Nelle Hart, Feb. 12, 1955; children—Kara Lee, Kimberly Adair, Allison Bryan. With Dept. Navy, Washington, 1949-56, RCA, Cape Canaveral, Fla. 1956-57, Am. Bosch ARMA Corp., Garden City, L.I., 1957, Raytheon Co., Waltham, Mass., 1957-60, Arthur D. Little Inc., Cambridge, Mass., 1960-63; dir. employment Celanese Corp., N.Y.C., 1963—; chmn. N.Y. Employment Council. Mem. Nat. personnel com. Boy Scouts Am. Served with USN, 1943-46; PTO. Recipient Pericles award Employment Mgmt. Assn./Deutsch, Shea & Evans, 1976. Mem. Employment Mgmt. Assn. (pres. 1970-72, sr. adviser to bd. 1974—), Am. Soc. Personnel Adminstrn., N.Y. Personnel Mgrs. Assn. Presbyterian. Author: The Modern Employment Function, 1973; The Job Hunters Manual, 1975; Decruitment, A Guide for Managers, 1975; co-author: Job Hunting for the College Graduate, 1978; contbr. numerous articles to profl. publs. Office: 1211 6th Ave New York City NY 10036

SWEET, JOHN HOWARD, publisher; b. Emerson, Man., Can., Mar. 21, 1907; s. Henry Charles and Hannah (Mooney) S.; student U. Manitoba, 1923-26; m. Lillian Flora Martin, Sept. 11, 1926; 1 son, John Allan; m. 2d, Anne Ethel Wallace, Oct. 4, 1940; children—Anthony Howard, Elizabeth Anne. Asst. circulation mgr. AMA, 1926-29; circulation mgr. Traffic World, 1929-37; v.p. Poor's Pub. Co., 1937-40, Dickie Raymond, Inc., 1940-42; circulation mgr. World Report, 1946-48; with U.S. News and World Report, 1948—, circulation dir., 1948-51, exec. v.p., pub., 1951-59, pub., 1959-78, pres., 1959—, chmn. bd., chief exec. officer, 1973—. Served as lt. comdr. USNR, 1943-45. Mem. Conf. Bd., Mag. Pubs. Assn. (dir.). Presbyterian (trustee). Clubs: Princess Anne Country (Virginia Beach); Nat. Press. Internat., Army and Navy, Congressional Country, Met. (Washington). Home: 2124 Bancroft Pl NW Washington DC 20008 Office: 2300 N St NW Washington DC 20037

SWEET, MARC STEVEN, food co. exec.; b. Bklyn., Aug. 15, 1945; s. Edward I. and Bess G. (Freiman) S.; B.B.A. (trustees scholar), Pace Coll., 1967; postgrad. Columbia Sch. Bus., 1967-68; m. Naomi Charna Fishbein, Aug. 22, 1971; children—Erica Rebekah, Miriam Shoshana. Sr. staff auditor Arthur Young & Co., 1969-71; asst. corp. controller Liberty Fabrics of N.Y., Inc., 1971-72; corp. accounting mgr. Tetley Inc., 1972-75, corp. budget mgr., 1975—. Asst. scoutmaster Boy Scouts Am., 1963-66, mem. Flatbush dist. com., 1965-67, Eagle Scout, recipient Gold palm. C.P.A., N.Y. Texaco Co. scholar. Mem. Am. Inst. C.P.A.'s, N.Y. State Soc. C.P.A.'s, Planning Execs. Inst. Home: 1282 E 29th St Brooklyn NY 11210 Office: 522 Fifth Ave New York City NY 10036

SWEET, ROBERT THOMAS, banker; b. Hartford, Conn., June 18, 1938; s. Howard Francis and Catherine Elizabeth (Chesanek) S.; B.A., Trinity Coll., 1960; LL.B., U. Balt., 1966; M.A., Cath. U., 1973; m. Bonita Neumeister, June 29, 1963. Asst. dir. research, asst. v.p. Dean Witter, Investment Bankers, N.Y.C., 1969-71; v.p., trust investment officer Riggs Nat. Bank of Washington, 1971—. Lectr. on investments George Washington U., Am. U.; adviser Singapore Stock Exchange, 1974, Korean govt., 1976, Venezuelan Govt., 1978. Active Washington chpt. ARC; mem. Community Planning Bd., N.Y.C., 1970; bd. dirs. Vol. Clearing House D.C. Served with U.S. Army, 1962. Mem. Fin. Analysts Fedn. (internat. analysts com.), Washington (dir. 1972-73, pres., chmn. bd. 1974-75), N.Y. socs. security analysts, Am. Fin. Assn., Nat. Economists Club, Pi Gamma Mu. Clubs: Hyannis (Mass.) Yacht; Internat. of Washington. Contbr. articles to profl. jours. Home: 4934 Western Ave Chevy Chase MD 20016 Office: 800 17th St NW Washington DC 20006

SWEET, ROSS BENNETT, ins. co. exec.; b. Solvay, N.Y., May 31, 1917; s. Wallace and Vella E. (Bennett) S.; student Cornell U., 1947-48, Beloit Coll., 1961-63; m. Alice E. Lisdell, Dec. 26, 1942; children—R. Brickley, Erick W., Mary Beth. Asst. cashier First Nat. Bank, Dryden, N.Y., 1945-56; exec. v.p., cashier Unadilla Nat. Bank (N.Y.), 1956-59; sec., treas. Farmers & Traders Life Ins. Co., Syracuse, N.Y., 1959-69, fin. v.p., treas., 1969—, also dir. Chmn. corp. SODAC. Served to capt. AUS, 1939-45. Republican. Methodist. Clubs: Masons (32 deg.), Rotary. Home: 2 W Lake St Skaneateles NY 13152 Office: 960 James St Syracuse NY 13201

SWEET, STANLEY ADAMS, JR., ret. clothing mfg. co. exec.; b. N.Y.C., Aug. 14, 1916; s. Stanley Adams and Grace Avery (Ingersoll) S.; B.A., Yale U., 1941; postgrad. N.Y. U., 1943; m. Barbara Whittlesey McGraw, May 6, 1944; 1 dau., Nancy Adams Sweet Master. Asst. sales mgr. Reinhold Pub. Corp., N.Y.C., 1941-49; with sales dept. Sweet-Orr & Co., N.Y.C., 1949-57, exec. v.p., treas., 1952-58, pres., 1958-66, chmn. bd., 1966; adviser, mem. sales dept. B. Oppenheim Co., Inc., N.Y.C., 1967-73. Trustee Edwin Gould Found. for Children, N.Y.C., 1949—, Lake Placid Edn. Found.; vestryman St. Eustace Ch. Mem. Union Made Apparel Assn. (dir.). Presbyterian (deacon). Clubs: Yale (N.Y.C.); Lake Placid (N.Y.). Home: Mirror Lake Dr Lake Placid NY 12946

SWENSON, HAROLD FRANCIS, consumer goods mfg. co. exec.; b. N.Y.C., Apr. 28, 1915; s. Charles Henry and Ethel Marie (Igoe) S.; A.B., Manhattan Coll., 1938; student Fordham U. Law Sch., 1938-41; m. Mildred Chandler, Dec. 31, 1943; 1 dau., Sally (Mrs. Richard Reisner). Spl. agt. FBI, 1941-47; indsl. relations exec. Gulf Oil, San Tome, Venezuela, 1947-52; employee relations and security exec. Sears, Roebuck & Co., Chgo., 1953-54; with State Dept., Washington, 1955-65, Def. Dept., Washington, 1965-68; pres., chief exec. officer, dir. Bishop's Service Inc., N.Y.C., 1969-73; surveys, mktg. and fgn. ops. exec. Intertel Inc., Washington, 1974-78; law dept. and security exec. Chesebrough Pond's Inc., Greenwich, Conn., 1978—. Polit. attache U.S. Embassy, Buenos Aires, Argentina, 1956-62. Served with USMCR, 1944-46. Mem. Soc. Former FBI Agts., Internat. Assn. Chiefs of Police, Beta Sigma. Clubs: Chantilly Golf and Country (Centerville, Va.); Bad Ems Golf Alumni (Washington); Silvermine Golf and Country (Norwalk, Conn.). Home: Georgetown N Greenwich CT 06830 Office: 33 Benedict Pl Greenwich CT 06830

SWENSON, JON MALCOLM, granite co. exec.; b. Concord, N.H., Feb. 29, 1936; s. Guy Andrew and Mildred Hopewell (Bolan) S.; B.A., Dartmouth Coll., 1959; postgrad. U. Innsbruck, Austria, 1961; M.B.A., Harvard U., 1963; m. Suzanne Murth, Jan. 29, 1966 (div. 1976); m. Jolanta Vojtek, Dec. 18, 1976. With John Swenson Granite Co., Inc., Concord, 1963-74, pres., 1968-74, chmn. bd. dirs., 1972-74; dir. F.A.S.T. Ltd., natural stone industry, Saudi Arabia, 1974-76; dir. Tech. Mktg. Corp., Dallas, Arab-Am. Stone Erectors, Inc., Dubai, U.A.E., Tech. & Mktg. Services Corp.; adviser to Fayez Family interests in Saudi Arabia, 1976. Chmn., Gov.'s Com. on UN, N.H., 1972-75; vice chmn. Nat. UN Day Com., 1972-74; pres. Arts Council Concord, 1972-74; mem. N.H. Republican State Com., 1966-68. Served with C.E., AUS, 1959-60. Recipient Distinguished Service award UN Assn. U.S.A., 1972. Mem. New Eng. Granite Assn. (pres. 1973-76), Concord C. of C., Newcomen Soc. Episcopalian. Clubs: Rye Beach (Rye, N.H.); Ski of Arlberg (Austria). Home: 71 Washington St Concord NH 03301 Office: 8577 Manderville Dallas TX 75231

SWENSON, LARRY GRANT, educator; b. Queens Village, N.Y., Aug. 4, 1931; s. Samuel Jonathan and Hedvig Louise (Andersen) Svenssen; B.A. in History, Hofstra U., 1964, certificate advanced study in ednl. adminstrn., 1978; M.S. in Guidance and Counseling, Queens Coll., 1968; m. June 15, 1957 (div.); children—Andrew, Timothy. Tchr. N.Y.C. Bd. Edn., 1958-63, Bay Shore (N.Y.) schs., 1963-66; vocat. counselor Bay Shore (N.Y.) schs., 1966-73; career edn. coordinator Suffolk County schs., 1973-75; dir. Career Guidance Center, Patchogue, N.Y., 1975-77; counselor Shoreham-Wading River High Sch., Shoreham, N.Y., 1977—; adj. asso. prof. edn. C.W. Post Center, L.I. U., 1972—; cons. decision-making program Coll. Entrance Exam. Bd.; lectr. edn. Dowling Coll., 1976; instr. N.Y. Inst. Tech., 1977. Vice pres. Life-Skills Center, Inc. Served with USAF, 1950-54. Mem. Am., N.Y. State, East End personnel and guidance assns., Western Suffolk Counselors Assn. (pres. 1970-71), N.Y. State Vocat. Guidance Assn. (pres. 1971-72), N.Y. State United Tchrs. Shoreham-Wading River Tchrs. Assn., Phi Delta Kappa. Presbyterian. Home: 24 Watergate Ln Patchogue NY 11772 Office: Shoreham-Wading River High Sch Route 25A Shoreham NY 11786

SWERN, LEONARD, mfg. co. exec.; b. N.Y.C., Feb. 12, 1925; s. Philip and Ida (Sternfield) S.; A.B. in Physics, Columbia U., 1945, M.A. in Physics, 1947; m. Nancy Ann Peter, Sept. 25, 1948. Sr. engr. Sperry Gyroscope Co., Great Neck, N.Y., 1949-54, sect. head, 1954-59, head dept. applied physics, 1959-60, asst. to v.p. research and devel., 1960-69; dir. tech. programs Sperry Rand Corp., N.Y.C., 1969—; mem. industry panel on sci. and tech. NSF, 1975—. Served with U.S. Army, 1945-46. Fellow IEEE; mem. Am. Phys. Soc. Contbr. articles on microwave physics to profl. jours. Office: 1290 Ave of Americas New York City NY 10019

SWETT, PHILIP EUGENE, constrn. co. exec.; b. Hinsdale, Ill., Feb. 6, 1931; s. Floyd A. and Wilhelmena E. (Joscelyn) S.; B.Engring., Yale, 1953; m. Ann Parkhurst, July 24, 1954; children—Barbara, Richard, Jay, Gail, Philip Eugene. Field engr. M.W. Kellogg Co., N.Y.C., 1953-54, methods and standards engr., 1955-59; resident engr. Consoer Townsend Assos., Chgo., 1954-55; pres., gen. mgr. Nalews, Inc., Laconia, N.H., 1959—; dir. Laconia Peoples Nat. Bank & Trust Co., Maj. Pool Equipment Corp., Clifton, N.J.; pres. Lakes Region Airport Properties, Inc. Mem. adv. bd. N.H. Vocat. Tech. Coll., 1974—; bldg. com. chmn. Gilford (N.H.) Middle/High Sch., 1973—; pres. N.H. Music Festival, 1972-74. Registered profl. engr., N.Y., N.H., Fla., S.C., Maine, R.I., Mass., Vt., Ga., N.C., Pa. Mem. Associated Builders and Contractors, Inc. (nat. dir., chpt. pres. 1972), Nat. Soc. Profl. Engrs., Am. Inst. Constructors, Water Pollution Control Fedn., Am. Mgmt. Assn. Clubs: Winnipesaukee Yacht, Guilford Outing. Home: RFD 3 Laconia NH 03246 Office: PO Box 656 Laconia NH 03246

SWETT, STEPHEN FREDERICK, JR., educator; b. Englewood, N.J., Sept. 14, 1935; s. Stephen Frederick and Frances (Gulotta) S.; B.A., Montclair State Coll., 1959, M.A., 1965; Ed.D. in Ednl. Adminstrn., Rutgers U., 1976; m. Annette Palazzolo, Nov. 18, 1961; children—Susan, Kimberly Ann, Stephen Laurence. Tchr., Long Branch (N.J.) High Sch., 1961-62, Roselle Park (N.J.) High Sch., 1962-73; research asst. Rutgers U., New Brunswick, N.J., 1973-74; instructional supr. Elmwood Park (N.J.) Schs., 1974-76, Morris Hills Regional Schs., Denville, N.J., 1976-77; asst. prin. Lawrence High Sch., Lawrenceville, N.J., 1977—; participant NSF Inst. in physics, chemistry and math. Seton Hall U., 1964, Newark Coll. Engring., 1965, Stevens Inst. Tech., summers 1966-68. Served with AUS, 1959-61. Mem. Roselle Park Edn. Assn. (pres. 1971-73). Nat. Soc. Study Edn., Am. Assn. Physics Tchrs., Am. Inst. Physics, Am., N.J. assns. sch. adminstrs., Nat. Assn. Secondary Sch. Prins., N.J. Assn. Secondary Sch. Prins. and Suprs., Phi Delta Kappa. Research on sch. finance. Home: 12 Louis St Old Bridge NJ 08857 Office: Lawrence High Sch North Princeton Pike Lawrenceville NJ 08648

SWICK, LUCILLE, performing artist; b. Athens, Ala., Aug. 31, 1930; d. James H. and Agnes E. (Neely) Sims; student Orlando (Fla.) Jr. Coll., 1949-50, Orlando Fla. Sch. of Modeling, 1951; m. Thomas Swick, Mar. 22, 1958 (dec. Jan. 17, 1976); children—Nanette M. Swick Harrison, Carol Anne. Singer, guitarist Radio Sta. WORZ, Orlando, 1956-58, WLOF, Orlando, 1955-56, WDBO, Orlando, 1950-54; mem. N.J. Council on the Arts, 1977—. Mem. Phillipsburg

Town Council, 1977—. Recipient numerous awards for country and western music performances. Mem. So. Quartets Assn. Home: 651 Elder Ave Phillipsburg NJ 08865

SWIECICKA-ZIEMIANEK, MARIA A. .L., educator; b. Wilno, Poland: d. George S. and Frances Swiecicki; came to U.S., naturalized; Ph.D., U. Pa., 1971; m. Janusz B. Ziemianek, May 15, 1976. Mem. faculty Temple U., Phila., 1968—, asst. prof. German and Russian, 1972-76, asso. prof., 1976—; lectr. in field. Co-chmn. Temple Ethnic Festival, 1975, 77. Kosciuszko Found. fellow, 1973. Mem. Polish Inst. Arts and Scis. in Am. (council, chmn. chpt., council), Polish Am. Hist. Assn. (adv. council), AAUP, Modern Lang. Asn., Am. Assn. Tchrs. Slavic and East European Langs., Delta Phi Alpha. Roman Catholic. Author: The Memoirs of Jan Chryzostom z Goslawic Pasek, 1978. Contbr. articles to profl. jours.; recorded series of radio programs Poles in Phila., Sta. KYW. Home: Rural Route 1 Glenwood Dr Washington Crossing PA 18977 Office: Dept Germanic and Slavic Langs Temple Univ Philadelphia PA 19122

SWIFT, LEROY RUSSELL, ofcl. HEW; b. N.Y.C., Dec. 11, 1912; s. Joseph John and Amanda (Henry) S.; B.S., Howard U., 1931, M.D., 1936; M.P.H., U. Mich., 1942; children—Killian Brumfield, Peter Van Hanagan. Intern, City Hosp., St. Louis; resident Lincoln-Duke Hosp., Durham, N.C., 1936-37, attending chief obstetrics and gynecology, 1942-62; dir. coll. health service N.C. Central U., Durham, 1942-52, adj. prof. health edn., 1952-70; spl. asst. to dir. Bur. Health Manpower Edn., NIH, HEW, Bethesda, Md.; med. cons. Region II, USPHS, HEW, 1973-74; med. analyst N.Y.C. Dept. Health and Hosp. Corp., 1974—; faculty cons. dept. obstetrics and gynecology Coll. Medicine, Howard U., 1973-74; cons. N.Y.C. HRA Family Planning Clinics, 1975-76. Mem. Bishops's Urban Crisis Com., N.C. Diocese P.E.Ch. Rosenwald fellow; Rockefeller fellow. Diplomate Am. Bd. Obsetetrics and Gynecology. Fellow Internat. Coll. Surgeons, Am. Soc. Abdominal Surgeons; mem. Nat. Med. Assn. (nat. chmn. obstetrics and gynecology 1959). Editorial bd. Jour. Nat. Med. Assn. Contbr. articles to med. jours. Home: 111-28 175th St Jamaica NY 11433

SWIFT, ROBERT ANTON, metall. engr.; b. Hempstead, N.Y., Jan. 21, 1940; s. William A. and Anna D. (Bartosh) S.; B.Met.E., Poly. Inst. Bklyn., 1961; M.Mat.E., Drexel Inst. Tech., 1969; Ph.D., Drexel U., 1974; m. Christiane Marchionda, Nov. 30, 1963; 1 son, Joseph William. Research engr. Veeco Instruments, Plainview, N.Y., 1961-64; devel. engr. Martin Marietta, Balt., 1964-65; research physicist IRC, Inc., Phila., 1965-67; research engr. Lukens Steel Co., Coatesville, Pa., 1967-76, supr. metall. devel., 1976—. Mem. Coatesville Area PTA Council, 1974-77. Served to 1st lt. U.S. Army, 1961-63. Mem. Am. Soc. Metals, ASME, Am. Welding Soc. (McKay-Helm award 1976), Metal Properties Council. Roman Catholic. Contbr. articles to profl. jours. Home: 1523 Fox Run Dr Coatesville PA 19320 Office: Lukens Steel Co Coatesville PA 19320

SWIGART, EDMUND KEARSLEY, hist. mus. adminstr., educator; b. Milw., Mar. 30, 1931; s. Harry M. and Lucie C. (Emerson) S.; B.A. in English, Yale, 1954, M.S. in Conservation, 1956; postgrad. Rutgers U., summer 1962; m. Deborah Waite Herold, Sept. 11, 1954; children—Lucie Thayer, Edmund Kearsley III, Paul Marshall. Field research scientist Housatonic Valley Planning Assn., New Haven, 1955-56; instr. summer tchr. workshops Nat. Audubon Soc., Damariscotta, Maine, 1956, Greenwich, Conn., 1957-58; lectr. and cons. on archaeology and conservation, 1956—; instr. biology, earth sci. Gunnery Sch., 1956-59, 60-73, instr. archaeology, 1973-76, instr. ecology, 1976—, chmn. sci. dept., 1965-72, chaplain, 1962-70, dir. Gunnery Precoll. Program in Archeology, 1977—; bus. mgr. cons. to Am. Indian Archeol. Inst., Washington, Conn., 1974-76, dir., 1976—, founder, pres. bd., 1972—; chmn. Biol. Scis. Curriculum Study, Conn., 1964-66; dir. Gunn Meml. Mus., Washington, Conn., 1969-76, mem. mus. com., 1969—; 1st. chmn. Washington (Conn.) Conservation Commn., 1970-72; bd. dirs. Housatonic Valley Assn., 1978—, Eliot Pratt Outdoor Garden Center, 1978—; mem. com. of sponsors Mus. of the Am. Indian. Sunday sch. tchr., vestryman St. John's Episcopal Ch., Washington, Conn., 1962-64; trustee Steep Rock Assn., 1957-59, 70—. Recipient award of merit Conn. League Historic Socs., 1975. Mem. Archeol. Soc. Conn. (dir. 1971—), Am. Nature Study Soc., Pa., N.J. archeol. Socs., Eastern States Archeol. Fedn. (treas. 1974—), Nat., Litchfield Hills (newsletter editor 1958-59, v.p., 1958-59, dir. 1958-59) audubon socs., Wildlife Soc., Conn. Sci. Tchrs. Assn. Republican. Congregationalist. Clubs: Lions, Masons, Rod and Gun, Adirondack League. Contbr. articles on history of Am. Indians to profl. publs. Home: Roxbury Rd Washington CT 06793 Office: PO Box 85 American Indian Archeological Institute Washington CT 06793

SWINBURNE, LAURENCE JOSEPH, writer; b. N.Y.C., July 2, 1924; s. Laurence Trimble and Marie Louise (Floris) S.; A.B., Princeton U., 1949 (cum laude) ; M.Ed., Rutgers U., 1958; m. Irene Joan Kallini, June 14, 1947; children—Virginia Louise, Susan Elizabeth. Salesman, D. Van Nostrand, Mid Atlantic states, 1949-51; salesman Rand McNally Co., N.J., 1952-56, sales promotion mgr., Chgo., 1957-59; mgr. sales promotion Wesleyan Univ. Press, Middletown, Conn., 1959-61, Doubleday & Co., Garden City, N.Y., 1961-63; v.p., Gt. Soc. Press, N.Y.C., 1963-65; editor McGraw-Hill Co., N.Y.C., 1965-68; v.p. Educreative Systems, N.Y.C., 1968-72, dir., 1968-72; pres. Swinburne Press/ pres. Swinburne Readability Lab., East Norwich, N.Y., 1972—. Pres. Oyster Bay (N.Y.) High Sch. PTA, 1963; trustee Oyster Bav Library, 1965-68, pres. friends library, 1975—; pres. Confraternity of Christian Doctrine, Oyster Bay, 1972-73. Served with USMCR, 1943-45. Recipient Notable Book award children ALA, 1977, Notable Book for Children award Children's Book Council, 1977. Mem. Author's Guild, Nat. Council Tchrs. English, Internat. Reading Assn., Delta Kappa Phi. Roman Catholic. Clubs: Princeton N.Y., K.C. Author numerous books for children, as Behind the Sealed Door, 1977. Contbr. stories, articles to children's publs.; producer ednl. filmstrips, audiovisual programs schs., libraries. Home and office: 49 Cord Pl East Norwich NY 11732

SWITAK, HEATHER JOAN, nurse; b. Sidney, Brit. Columbia, Can., Jan. 2, 1947; d. Ernest Francis and Helen Merrielee (Booth) White; grad. Kingsway Coll. and Branson Hosp. Sch. Nursing Ontario, 1968; B.S. in Behavioral Sci., Atlantic Union Coll., 1974; m. Robert Arthur Paul Switak, June 29, 1969. Staff nurse, relief charge nurse New Eng. Meml. Hosp., Stoneham, Mass., 1968-70, coordinator nursing orientation 1970-72, team leader 1972, inservice edn. instr. 1972-74, dir. staff development 1974—. Certified basic life support instr.-trainer Am. Heart Assn. Mem. Am., Mass. nurses assns., NE Council Hosp. Inservice Educators, Assn. Seventh-day Adventist Nurses (Greater Boston chpt.). Address: 5 Woodland Rd Stoneham MA 02180

SWITZER, STEVEN MLADEN, data processor; b. Zagreb, Yugoslavia, May 9, 1934; s. Arthur and Frieda (Roman) S.; came to U.S., 1949, naturalized, 1954; B.Chem.Engring., Coll. City N.Y., 1956, M.B.A., 1964; M.Chem.Engring., Rensselaer Poly. Inst., 1958; m. Ruth Schattner, Dec. 24, 1962; children—Susan, Jeffrey. Analyst, programmer Am. Cyanamid Co., Wayne, N.J., 1959-64; sr. analyst Shell Chem. Co., N.Y.C., 1964-67; project leader Texaco Inc., N.Y.C., 1967-70; asst. mgr. systems and programming Ins. Services Office Co., N.Y.C., 1970—. Served with U.S. Army, 1957-58. Mem. Am. Inst. Chem. Engrs. Home: 108 Luquer Rd Port Washington NY 11050 Office: 2 World Trade Center New York City NY 10048

SWOPE, CHARLES EVANS, banker, lawyer; b. West Chester, Pa., June 16, 1930; s. Charles S. and Edna (McAllister) S.; B.S., Bucknell U., 1953; J.D., Washington and Lee U., U. Va., 1959; student Judge Adv. Gen. Sch., 1957, Indsl. Coll. Armed Forces, 1966, Command and Staff Coll., 1969. Asso. firm Gawthrop & Greenwood, Attys., West Chester, Pa., 1959; pres., sr. trust officer 1st Nat. Bank, West Chester, 1965—, also dir.; pres. Eachus Dairy Co.; dir. Denney-Reyburn Co., Madison Co., Penjerdel, 1st Nat. Bank West Chester, Automobile Assn. Chester County; lectr. corporation law. Pres., West Chester Civic Assn., 1964; co-chmn. Chester County Heart Assn. Drive, West Chester Community Center Bldg. Drive, 175th Anniversary West Chester. Mem. Nat. Football Found. and Hall of Fame; dir. Chester County council Boy Scouts Am., 1961-72; bd. dirs. Chester County Service, Swope Found. Trust, West Chester Coll. Found.; chmn. Easter Seal Soc. Chester County. Trustee, West Chester State Coll., 1963, 72, pres. bd. trustees, 1966-72; trustee Chester County Devel. Fund, Charles S. Swope Scholarship Fund, Hatfield Home. Served to maj. USMCR, 1952-55; now col. res. Recipient Coll. Football Centennial award, 1970; Outstanding Citizen award C. of C. Greater West Chester, 1974; Marine Corps commendation; Meritorious Service award Gen. Anthony Wayne Soc. Chester County, 1976. Mem. Pa. Bankers Assn. (chmn. legislative com. 1965, 70), U.S. Naval Inst., Assn. Coll. Trustees Pa., Am. Soc. Internat. Law, Nat. Eagle Scout Assn., Pa. Soc. Greater West Chester C. of C. (pres. 1963), Marine Corps League Chester County (vice comdt. 1960-72), Freedoms Found., Am. Legion, Chester County Hist. Soc., Marine Corps Res. Officer Assn. (judge adv. gen.), Marine Corps Assn., Marine Corps League, Pa. C. of C., Navy League U.S., Washington and Lee Law Sch. Assn., Bucknell, West Chester State Coll. alumni assns., Pa. Economy League, Nat. Trust Preservation Historic Landmarks, Nat. Wildlife Assn., Maxwell Football Club, Phi Alpha Delta, Phi Kappa Psi. Republican. Methodist (ofcl. bd.). Clubs: West Chester (Pa.) Golf and Country; Union League (Phila.) Italian Social; Sky Top; Great Oaks Yacht and Country; Radley Run Golf and Country; Masons; Rotary (pres. West Chester, Pa., 1968-69); Elks. Home: Rosedale Ave and Church Ct West Chester PA 19380 Office: 9 N High St West Chester PA 19380

SWOPE, GEORGE WENDELL, clergyman, educator; b. Norfolk, Va., Feb. 2, 1916; s. Dr. George W. and Nellie (Guthrie) S.; student Drexel U., 1940-41, U. Pa., 1941-42; A.B., Eastern Coll., 1945; Th.B., Eastern Bapt. Theol. Sem., 1945, D.D., 1958, M. in Divinity, 1972; S.T.B., Temple U., 1946; m. Winifred A. Devlin, June 26, 1940; children—George Wendell, Gregory Willard, Winifred Ruth. Ordained to ministry Bapt. Ch., 1945; pastor, Essington, Pa., 1940-43, Camden, N.J., 1943-46; dir. evangelism, Christian edn. Am. Bapt. Conv., 1946-54; pastor East Orange, N.J., 1954-58, Kenova, W.Va., 1958-63, Port Chester, N.Y., 1963-70; registrar Westchester Community Coll., 1970-74, asst. dir. guidance services, 1975—. Pres. Nat. Alumni Assn., Eastern Bapt. Theol. Sem., 1956-58; pres. N.J. Bapt. Ministers Council, 1955-57, East Orange Protestant Council, 1955-56; mem. pastor's adv. com. Am. Bapt. Publs., 1957-62; vice chmn. press relation com. Am. Bapt. Conv., 1958-62, chmn. nominations com., 1962; chmn. commn. on Christian unity W.Va. Council Chs., 1958-60; pres. Port Chester Council Chs., 1969-70; mem. dept. evangelism Fed. Council of Chs., Nat. Council Chs. Chaplain East Orange His. Soc., 1957-58, mem. moderator council ordination Met. N.Y. Bapt. City Soc., also v.p.; chmn. ministers div. Planned Parenthood Assn. So. Westchester County; mem. Port Chester Anti-Poverty Commn.; chmn. mayor's commn. on community improvement Port Chester; chmn. Nat. Com. Engaged in Freeing Minds, 1976—. Mason (past master), Rotarian (pres.). Club: Westchester Country. Home: 61 Tower Hill Dr Port Chester NY 10573 also High St Bradford NH 03221

SYELES, ALBERT MAC, radiation scientist; b. Vari, Bereg Mege, Hungary, Nov. 15, 1911; s. John and Ester (Mester) Szeles; came to U.S., naturalized, 1928; student metallurgy Columbia U., 1941, Cath. U., Washington, 1943; Electronic Engr., U.S. Naval Ordnance Lab., 1970; m. Regina Mary Margaret O'Donnell, Apr. 29, 1939; children—Alice Jean Syeles O'Donnell, Albert Michael. Various positions Nassau Smelting & Refining Co. subs. Western Electric Co., Tottenville, S.I., N.Y., 1932-42; phys. sci. aide U.S. Naval Gun Factory, Washington, 1942-45; engring. aide U.S. Naval Ordnance Lab., White Oak, Md., 1945-48, phys. sci. aide, 1948-52, 57-61, technologist-gen., 1952-57, phys. sci. technician, 1961-75, with U.S. Naval Surface Weapons Center, 1975—. Mem. bd. U.S. Civil Service Examiners Sci. and Tech. Personnel Potomac River Naval Command, panel examiner, 1958-61; team mem. Md. Internat. Geophys. Yrs., 1961-63. Recipient Meritorious Civilian Service award U.S. Naval Ordnance Lab., 1951; citation Search for Submarine Thresher, 1964; Metall. Engring. awards, others. Mem. AAAS, Am. Soc. Metals, Am. Def. Preparedness Assn., Am. Hungarian Found., Soc. Old Bats, White Oak Lab. Astronomy Club. Contbr. articles to profl. publs. Patentee in field. Home: 591 University Blvd E Silver Spring MD 20901 Office: US Naval Surface Weapons Center White Oak Lab Silver Spring MD 20910

SYKES, DONALD JOSEPH, chem. co. exec.; b. Buffalo, Mar. 16, 1936; s. Joseph John and Josephine Mary; B.S., Rochester Inst. Tech., 1958; m. Suzanne Kay Marble, May 28, 1960; children—Kathryn, Jeffrey. Dir. research Cormac Chem. Corp., Long Island City, N.Y., 1959-63; research mgr., asst. dir. research then dir. research Philip A. Hunt Chem. Corp., Palisades Park, N.J., 1963—, asst. v.p. research, 1977-79, group v.p., 1979—. Served with U.S. Army, 1958-59. Mem. Am. Chem. Soc., Soc. of Photographic Scientists and Engrs. Holder patents in field. Home: 8 Sunset Ln Upper Saddle River NJ 07458 Office: Roosevelt Pl Palisades Park NJ 07650

SYKES, MARTHA MOORE, pub. relations co. exec.; b. Atlanta, Dec. 15, 1927; d. Schmidt A. and Martha Jo (Mays) Moore; student Randolph-Macon Woman's Coll., 1943-45; B.S., Juilliard Sch. Music, 1948. Founder, sec./treas. Nelson Sykes Assos., pub. relations, N.Y.C., 1960-67; partner McDavid, Richmond & Rudd, pub. relations, N.Y.C., 1967-70, v.p., 1970-75; partner, exec. v.p. McDavid/Sykes Assos., N.Y.C., 1975—. Founder, pres. N.Y.C. Opera Guiild, 1959; bd. dirs. N.Y.C. Opera, exec. com. Opera Guilds Internat., 1977—; alumna adviser bd. trustees Randolph-Macon Woman's Coll., 1977—. Day proclaimed in her honor by mayor City of Birmingham (Ala.) Apr. 16, 1977. Mem. Women Execs. in Pub. Relations, Pub. Relations Soc. Am., Am. Women in Radio and TV, Delta Delta Delta, Mu Phi Epsilon. Democrat. Club: Randolph-Macon. Address: McDavid/Sykes Assos 919 3d Ave New York City NY 10022

SYKU, ANTON ZEF, therapist; b. Lezhe, Albania, Aug. 25, 1931; came to U.S., 1971, naturalized, 1976; s. Zef Kel and Filomena Lush (Turkaj) S.; Respiratory therapist St. Vincent's Hosp., Melbourne, Australia, 1957; m. Filomena Curanaj, Feb. 11, 1961. Chief respiratory therapist, dir. services St. Vincent's Hosp., Melbourne, 1962-71; asst. dir. respiratory therapy White Plains (N.Y.) Hosp., 1973-74; chief respiratory therapist, dir. respiratory and pulmonary services Jewish Meml. Hosp., N.Y.C., 1974—. Sec., Pan Albanian Vatra orgn., 1975—. Mem. Am. Assn. Respiratory Therapy, Am. Coll. Respiratory Therapy, Albanian Am. Cath. League (sec.). Republican. Albanian Catholic. Home: 2869 Grand Concourse Bronx NY 10468

SYLVESTER, MELVIN ROBERT, librarian; b. New Orleans, Mar. 25, 1939; s. John Gilbert and Myrtle (Howard) S.; B.A. (scholar), Dillard U., 1961; M.S. in L.S., L.I. U., 1966, M.Ed., 1973; m. Frances Modica, June 20, 1964; children—Lori Alaine, Kyle Eugene. Reference circulation library asst. Dillard U., New Orleans, 1961-62; head circulation dept. C.W. Post Center Library, Brookville, N.Y., 1962-64, head periodicals dept., 1964—. Mem. Nat. Frat. Policy Com., Indpls., 1973—; mem. Martin Luther King Ednl. Adv. Com., Brookville, N.Y., 1974—; pub. info. chmn. N. Oyster Bay unit Am. Cancer Soc., Melville, N.Y., 1971—, mem. adv. bd. Friendship House, Glen Cove, N.Y., 1975—; mem. com. on handicapped Glen Cove Schs., 1978—; bd. dirs. Boys Club, Glen Cove, 1978—. Recipient Outstanding Service award, 1969, 70. Mem. N.Y., Nassau County (sec. coll. and univ. div. 1973—) library assns., L.I. U. Alumni Assn., Tau Kappa Epsilon (pres. 1971-72, Outstanding Service award Theta Kappa chpt. 1969, 70, Adviser's award 1974). Club: Melvil Dui Marching and Chowder Assn. Author: Periodical Literature for Black Studies, 1972; A Library Handbook to Basic Source Materials in Guidance and Counseling, 1973. Contbr. articles to profl. jours. Home: 50 Robinson Ave Glen Cove NY 11542 Office: CW Post Center Library Northern Blvd Brookville NY 11546

SYLVESTRE, JEAN GUY, nat. librarian of Can.; b. Sorel, Que., Can., May 17, 1918; s. Maxime Arthur and Yvonne Marie (Lapierre) S.; B.A., U. Ottawa, 1939, B.Ph., 1940, M.A., 1942, D.L.S. (hon.), 1969, D.Litt. (hon.), 1970, LL.D. (hon.), 1974, 75; m. Françoise Poitevin, Feb. 27, 1943; children—Marie, Jean, Paul. Translator, Dept. Canadian Sec. of State, 1942-44; editor Wartime Info. Bd., 1944-45; asst. pvt. sec. to minister of justice, 1945-47; pvt. sec. to sec. of state for external affairs, 1947-48; pvt. sec. to prime minister, 1948-50; adminstrv. officer Dept. Resources and Devel., 1950-53; asst. librarian Library of Parliament, Ottawa, Ont., 1953-56, asso. parliamentary librarian, 1956-68, nat. librarian of Can., 1968—; chmn. Gov. Gen.'s Lit. Awards, 1960-62; organizer, chmn. World Poetry Conf., Expo, 1967; chmn. Can. Council Com. on Aid-to-Publs., 1960-68; pres. Conf. Nat. Librarians, 1974-78; lectr. U. Ottawa Library Sch., 1954-71; chmn. Can. del. UNISIST Conf., 1970, NATIS Conf., 1974; chmn. nat. libraries sect. IFLA, 1978—; v.p. Canadian Library Week Council, 1965-67; bd. dirs. Canadian Writers Found., pres., 1960-61. Fellow Royal Soc. Can. (hon. sec. 1959-62, pres. sect. 1 1963-64, hon. librarian 1969—, pres. 1973); mem. Académie canadienne-française, Société des Ecrivains canadiens, Canadian Library Assn. (life), Library Assn. Ottawa. Clubs: Le Cercle Universitaire (Ottawa); Rivermead Golf (Lucerne, Que.). Author: Louis Francoeur, journaliste, 1941; Situation de la poésie canadienne, 1941; Anthologie de la poésie canadienne-française, 1943, 58, 64, 66, 68, 74; Poétes catholiques de la France contemporaine, 1944; Sondages, 1945; Impressions de théâtre, 1950; Amours, délices et orgues, 1953; Panorama des lettres canadiennes-françaises, 1964; Canadian Writers, 1964; Literature in French Canada, 1967; A Century of Canadian Literature, 1967; editor: A Canadian Errant (J.P. Manion), 1960; Canadian Universities Today, 1961; Structures sociales du Canada français, 1967; contbr. articles in field to profl. jours. Office: 395 Wellington St Ottawa ON K1A 0N4 Canada

SYLVIA, LAWRENCE CHARLES, pathologist; b. Shanghai, China, May 31, 1933; s. Lawrence Arthur and Zenaida M.; B.A., U. Conn., 1956; M.D., Tufts U., 1960; m. Ima Stacy, Sept. 10, 1955; children—Damian, Todd, Stacy. Intern, Mallory Inst. Pathology Boston City Hosp., 1960-61, resident in pathology, 1961-64; resident in pathology Yale U., New Haven, 1964-65; practice medicine specializing in pathology, Long Br., N.J., 1967—; mem. staff Monmouth Med. Center, Long Branch, N.J., 1967—, dir. labs., 1978—; asso. prof. Hahnemann U. Mem. Am., N.J. (past pres.) assns. blood banks, AMA, Am. Soc. Cytology, Internat. Acad. Cytology, Mass., N.J., Monmouth County (pres.) med. socs. Roman Catholic. Office: Monmouth Med Center Long Branch NJ 07740

SYMONDS, JOHNNIE PIRKLE, psychologist; b. Wynnewood, Okla., Apr. 5, 1900; d. John Thomas and Lillie Belle (Driver) Pirkle; B.A., U. Tex., 1920, M.A., 1921; postgrad. Columbia Tchrs. Coll., 1921-22, 26-27, 28-29, 30-31; m. Percival Mallon Symonds, Dec. 25, 1922. Research asst. dept. psychology U. Tex., Austin, 1919-21; research asso. Inst. Ednl. Research Tchrs. Coll. Columbia U., N.Y.C., 1921-22; psychologist Family Service Soc., Yonkers, N.Y., 1937-47; ret., 1960. Mem. Am., N.Y. State psychol. assns., Am. Assn. Applied Psychology. Editor, Jour. Cons. Psychology, 1937-47; contbr. articles to psychol. jours. Home: 106 Morningside Dr New York City NY 10027

SYMONS, HARRY CLAY, educator; b. Pottstown, Pa., Dec. 21, 1922; s. William Smith and Elizabeth (Faith) S.; B.A., Pa. State U., 1946, M.A., 1953; postgrad. Bryn Mawr Coll., 1963-66; m. Eva Elizabeth Finkbiner, June 25, 1944; children—Jane K. (Mrs. J. Barrie Frees), Harry Clay. Grad. asst. Pa. State U., 1946-47; instr. econs. Ursinus Coll., Collegeville, Pa., 1947-52, asst. prof., 1952-70, asso. prof., 1970—. Dir. Elverson Nat. Bank. Cons. Gov.'s Office Dept. Revenue, 1956-57, also small bus. Sch. dir. South Coventy Twp., Pa., 1947-65; pres. South Coventry Sch. Dist., 1949-65; v.p. Owen J. Roberts Sch. Dist., 1954-59, pres., 1959-60, chmn. tax bd., 1965-67, mem. of tax bd., 1968—, chmn. tax adv. bd., 1970; vice chmn. planning commn. South Coventry Twp. Trustee W. Chester State Coll., chmn. bd., 1961-63. Mem. Am. Econ. Assn., AAUP, Omicron Delta Epsilon. Democrat Baptist. Home: RD 2 Pottstown PA 19464 Office: Dept Econs Collegeville PA 19426

SYMONS, JOANNE LYMAN, polit. party ofcl.; b. Bklyn., Feb. 25, 1941; d. Hal and Irene (Fife) Lyman; B.A., Bklyn. Coll., 1962; m. Alan George Symons, June 15, 1963; children—Noel, Jeremy. Mem. N.H. Ho. of Reps., 1973-76, asst. minority leader, 1975-76. Pres. Democratic Women N.H., 1974-76; congl. dist. coordinator Udall for Pres., 1975-76; campaign mgr. Grandmaison for U.S. Congress, 1976; chmn. N.H. Dem. Com., 1977—; del. Am. Council Young Polit. Leaders, Soviet-Am. conf., 1976. Home: 32 Rayton Rd Hanover NH 03755 Office: 77 N Main St Concord NH 03301

SYREK, RICHARD WILLIAM, mfg. co. exec.; b. Teaneck, N.J., Oct. 12, 1947; s. Steven Stanley and Mary (Turco) S.; B.S., N.J. Inst. Tech., 1972; postgrad. bus. Pace U., 1979—; m. Maryann Sticco, Oct. 16, 1971. Engring. asso. Western Electric Co., Kearny, N.J., 1968-69; indsl. engr. Relay Instrument div. Westinghouse Electric Co., Newark, 1969-71; indsl. engr. Am. Tack & Hardware Co., Inc., Monsey, N.Y., 1971-76, indsl. engring. mgr., 1976-77, planning and systems mgr., 1977—. Asst. minister, trustee co chmn. bldg. fund com. Psychic Sci. Temple of Metaphysics. Home: 111 Kenilworth Rd Ridgewood NJ 07450 Office: 25 Robert Pitt Dr Monsey NY 10952

SYRJALA, EDITH A., dairy, food council dir.; b. Boston, Nov. 25, 1933; d. Savele and Rachel S.; B.S., Simmons Coll., 1955; M.Ed., Boston U., 1968; M.P.H., U. N.C., 1969. Dietetic intern Beth Israel Hosp., Boston, 1955-56, chief therapeutic dietician, 1956-64; asst. prof. nutrition Boston U. Sch. Nursing, 1964-68; ednl. coordinator dietary dept. Peter Bent Brigham Hosp., Boston, 1969-72; asst. dir. New Eng. Dairy and Food Council, Boston, 1972-73, exec. dir.,

1973—. Served to lt. col. USAR, 1963—. Mem. Am., Mass. dietetic assns., Am., Mass. pub. health assns., Nutrition Today Soc., Mass. Council Food Nutrition & Health, Mass. Health Council, N.E. Health Edn. Assn., Soc. for Nutrition Edn. Clubs: Zonta, Assos. Author: Meal Time, Happy Time—A Guide for Parents of 5-12 Year-Olds, 1972. Home: 35 Pierce Rd Watertown MA 02172 Office: 1034 Commonwealth Ave Boston MA 02215

SYROVATKA, EUGENE CHARLES, assn. exec.; b. Prague, Czechoslovakia, Sept. 15, 1916; s. Eugene and Vladana (Gregr) S.; student Law Sch., Charles U., Prague, 1935-39; Dr. Laws, 1946; m. Veronica M. Kozak, Sept. 23, 1945. Came to U.S., 1949. With Nat. Bank of Czechoslovakia, 1939-42. Soc. for Chem. and Metall. Prodn., Prague, 1942-45; with Czechoslovakian Ministry Fgn. Affairs, 1945-49, as attache (Washington), consul (Montreal, Can.), sec. (Mexico. D.F.); exec. dir. Del. Acad. Medicine. Wilmington, 1949—, New Castle County Med. Soc., Wilmington, 1950—; exec. sec. Del. Soc. Internal Medicine, Wilmington, 1963—; exec. v.p. Med. Dental Bur. Mem. Am. Assn. Med. Execs., Czechoslovakian Soc. Arts and Sci. in Am., AMA, Am. Pub. Health Assn. Clubs: University, Whist (Wilmington). Home: 1405 Veale Rd Wilmington DE 19810 Office: 1925 Lovering Ave Wilmington DE 19806

SYSOL, HENRY FRANK, JR., constrn. co., real estate devel. exec.; b. Dunkirk, N.Y., June 18, 1941; s. Henry Frank and Geneva Frances (Holman) S.; student Am. U., 1961-62, Ga. Inst. Tech., 1961-62; m. Annette Speziale, Sept. 1, 1962; children—Kimberly Ann, Lynn Marie, Brad Henry. Project engr. with heavy constrn. firms, 1962-64; project mgr. various comml. bldg. firms, 1964-71; founder H. Sysol Constrn. Co., Fredonia, N.Y., 1971, inc., 1973, pres., 1973—; founder, pres. H.F. Sysol & Assos.; gen. mng. partner One Temple Sq. Assos., 1977—; pres. H. Sysol Mgmt. Co., Inc.; v.p., dir. Old Main Housing Devel. Corp. Lic. real estate sales, N.Y. Mem. Nat. Builders Marketing Bd. (distinguished mem.). Roman Catholic. Clubs: Westfield Rod and Gun, Fishing of Am., Pennhills Country, Lakewood Rod and Gun. Home: 124 Lambert Ave Fredonia NY 14063 Office: One Temple Square PO Box 346 Fredonia NY 14063

SYWAK, ZOFIA, archivist; b. Mosciska, Poland, Mar. 26, 1941; d. Wasyl I. and Aniela (Lyszczek) Sywak; came to U.S., 1949; naturalized, 1955; B.A., Alburtus Magnus Coll., 1964; M.A., St. John's U., 1966, Ph.D., 1975. Research asso. Yale U., 1962-64; tchr. Bklyn. Diocese, 1964-66; mgr. N.Y. Telephone Co., N.Y.C., 1966-68; lectr. Poznan (Polan) U., 1969; free-lance translator and interpreter, Warsaw, Poland, 1968-70, New Haven, 1970-74; archivist New Haven Colony Hist. Soc., 1975-78; archivist, asst. dir. James A. Kelly Inst. Local Hist. Studies St. Francis Coll., 1978—. IREX fellow, 1977-78; Alfred Jurzykowski grantee, 1977; Kosciuszko Found. grantee, 1968-70, 72. Mem. Am. Assn. for the Advancement Slavic Studies, Am. Hist. Assn., Jozef Pilsudski Inst. Am., Polish Inst. Arts and Scis. in Am., Soc. Am. Archivists, New Eng. Archivists Assn., New Eng. Slavic Assn., Ukrainian Nat. Women's League Am. (regional sec. 1975-77). Co-author: Poles in America: Bicentennial Essays, 1978. Contbr. articles to profl. jours. Home: 258 W Elm St New Haven CT 06515 Office: 180 Remsen St Brooklyn NY 11201

SZAMEK, PIERRE ERVIN, research anthropologist; b. Budapest, Hungary, July 12, 1920; s. Eugene Jeno and Olga S.; grad. The Pingry Sch., Elizabeth, N.J.; B.A., Upsala Coll., 1942; M.A., Columbia U., 1944; A.M., Princeton U., 1946, Ph.D. (Henry M. Bergen Jr. fellow, Univ. fellow), 1947. Corr., Central European Press Service, 1939; etymol. asst. in linguistic anthropology to Dr. Harold H. Bender, etymol. editor The Webster Dictionary, 1947-48; vis. post-doctoral research fellow Princeton U., 1947-48; edni. broadcasting CBS, N.Y.C., 1948-65; vis. prof. anthropology Drew U., 1966-67, N.J. State Coll., 1968-71; research anthropologist, Newark, 1950—; mem. panel radio show Invitation to Learning, 1948-63; anthrop. cons. CBS-TV, 1950-65; lectr. in field. Served with USCGR, 1942-43. Decorated knight Order of Star (Italy); knight officer Gold Cross of Royal Order of Phoenix (Greece); knight Order of St. Agatha (San Marino); chevalier de l'Ordre des Palmes Académiques (France); officer Order St. John (Gt. Britain);. Fellow Royal Anthrop. Inst. Gt. Britain and Ireland; mem. AAUP, Am. Oriental Soc., Am. Acad. Polit. Sci., N.J. Acad. Sci. Author: Invitation to Learning, 1966; numerous publs. in fgn. press, Am. jours.

SZAWRANSKYJ, WILLIAM MICHAEL, city ofcl.; b. Gunsberg, Germany, Sept. 27, 1946; s. Michael and Elizabeth (Kukuruza) S.; came to U.S., 1953, naturalized, 1967; B.S., Tenn. Tech. U., 1969; m. Helen Medianik, July 22, 1967; children—Peter, Anna, Natalie, Pauli. Design engr. Woodward Assos., Webster, N.Y., 1969-70; project mgr. Sear-Brown Assos., Rochester, N.Y., 1970-73; sr. asso. Passero-Scardetta Assos., Rochester, 1973-78; commr. pub. works Town of Webster (N.Y.) 1978—; line officer fire dept., 1975—; mem. Webster Democratic Com., 1976—. Registered profl. engr. and land surveyor, N.Y. Mem. Nat. Soc. Profl. Engrs., ASCE (award 1975), Rochester Engring. Soc., Am. Congress on Surveying and Mapping, N.Y. State Profl. Engrs., Ukrainian Engrs. Mem. Am. Ukrainian Catholic Ch. Club: Ukrainian Home of Rochester. Home: 798 Lauren Ct Webster NY 14580 Office: 1000 Ridge Rd Webster NY 14580

SZAZ, ZOLTAN MICHAEL, polit. scientist; b. Budapest, Hungary, Jan. 3, 1930 (came to U.S. 1950, naturalized, 1955); s. Geza and Magda (Nagy) S.; student U. Munich (Germany), 1949-50; B.A. cum laude, St. John's U., Minn., 1951; M.A., Cath. U. Am., 1952, Ph.D., 1956; m. Jayne Anne Davis, Sept. 7, 1957; children—Claire Ann, Annamaria, Mary Carol, Christopher Michael. Washington corr. Radio Free Europe, 1953-55; editor Free World Forum, bi-monthly jour. fgn. affairs, 1958-61; instr., asst. prof. grad history dept. St. John's U., 1960-64; lectr. history and govt. Seton Hall U., 1965-66, asso. prof. govt., 1966-68; exec. dir. Am. Inst. on Problems of European Unity, Washington, 1968-75; v.p. Am. Fgn. Policy Inst., 1975—; asso. prof. polit. sci. Troy (Ala.) State U., 1971-72; internat. trade cons., 1977—; cons. Am. Security Council, 1978—. Chmn., Internat. Relation Commn., D.C. Young Republicans, 1955-58; Young Rep. leader 11th Jud. Dist. State of N.Y., 1962-64; v.p. Everett McKinley Dirksen Forum, Washington, 1969-71. Recipient Godl medal Arpad Acad. Arts and Scis., 1973. Mem. Am., Internat. polit. sci. assns., Am. Hungarian Fedn. (sec. and cons. internat. relations), Nat. Confedn. Am. Ethnic Groups (sec. 1978—), Pi Gamma Mu. Author: Germany's Eastern Frontiers, 1960; Die deutsche Ostgrenze, 1961; (with others) MBFR at the Crossroads, 1974. Home: 6811 Supreme Ct Springfield VA 22150 Office: 499 S Capitol St Washington DC 20003

SZELL, THOMAS RUDOLF MIKLOS, chemist; b. Hereny, Hungary, May 29, 1926; s. Elemer Odon and Martha Camilla (Nemeth-Bejcz) S.; came to U.S., 1970; diploma chem. engring. Tech. U. Budapest, 1950, Dr. Techn., 1961; M.Ed., U. Szeged, Hungary, 1957, Dr. Nat., 1958; C.Sc., Acad. Hungary, 1960, D.Sc., 1975; m. Klara Molnar, Aug. 12, 1952; children—Timea Klara, Agnes Martha. Asst. prof. chemistry U. Szeged, 1950-53, adj., 1955-63; postdoctoral fellow Nat. Research Council, Ottoawa, 1963-64; asso. prof. U. Szeged, 1964-70; head sci. dept. UN Internat. Sch., N.Y.C., 1970—; guest prof. India, 1967; vis. scientist, West Berlin, 1969; lectr. 11 countries; external referee doctoral theses, India; cons. Internat. Sch. of Manila. Served with Hungarian Army, 1944-45. Named Outstanding Educator, Hungarian Ministry of Edn., 1967, 69. Mem. Chem. Soc. London, Am. Chem. Soc. (certificate 1971, 76), Nat. Sci. Tchrs. Assn., Arpad Acad. Hungarian Scientists Abroad, Assn. Hungarian Chemists. Contbr. articles on chem. edn. and organic chemistry to profl. jours. Developed a new chromone synthesis via enolesters. Home: 157 Hudson Ave Tenafly NJ 07670 Office: UN International School 24 50 East River Dr New York NY 10010

SZEMRAJ, EDWARD RICHARD, librarian, educator; b. Buffalo, N.Y., Aug. 7, 1934; s. Edward Michael and Anna (Skowron) S.; B.A., U. Buffalo, 1956; postgrad. (Prefect fellowship) Niagara U., 1956-57; M.S., Canisius Coll., 1959; M.L.S. (grad. asst. scholarship 1970-71), State U. Coll. at Geneseo, 1971; m. Geraldine T., June 27, 1959; children—James, John. Tchr. English, Lyndonville (N.Y.) Central Sch., 1957-59; tchr. English and Russian, librarian Maryvale Sr. High Sch., Cheektowaga, N.Y., 1960—; trustee Pub. Library Bd., Cheektowaga. Vice-chmn. permanent chair of Polish culture Canisius Coll., Buffalo, 1974—. Served with U.S. Army, 1959-60. N.Y. State grantee Colgate U., 1966. Mem. Am., N.Y. State library assns., Sch. Librarians Assn. of Western N.Y., Maryvale Tchrs. Assn., N.Y. State United Tchrs., Am. Fedn. of Tchrs., Am. Assn. of Tchrs. of Slavic and E. European Langs., Nat., Maryvale edn. assns., N.Y. State Educators Assn. Democrat. Roman Catholic. Clubs: Polish Union of Am. Home: 15 Normandy Ave Buffalo NY 14225 Office: 1050 Maryvale Dr Cheektowaga NY 14225

SZENT-GYORGYI, ALBERT, biochemist; b. Budapest, Hungary, Sept. 16, 1893; s. Nicholas and Josephine (Lenhossek) S.-G.; M.D., U. Budapest, 1917; Ph.D., Cambridge, Eng., 1927; m. Marcia Houston, 1975. Came to U.S., 1947, naturalized, 1955. Prof. med. chemistry, Szeged, 1931-45; prof. biochemistry U. Budapest, 1945-47, dir. research Inst. Muscle Research, Marine Biol. Labs., 1947—; now sci. dir. Nat. Fund Cancer Research. Recipient Nobel prize in medicine, 1937, Lasker award Heart Assn., 1954. Mem. Acad. Scis. Budapest (pres.), Nat. Acad. Budapest (v.p.), Nat. Acad. Scis., Council of Edn. (chmn.). Author: Oxidation, Fermentation, Vitamins, Health and Disease, 1939; Muscular Contraction, 1947; The Nature of Life, 1947; Contraction in Body and Heart Muscle, 1953; Bioenergetics, 1957; Submolecular Biology, 1960; Bioelectronics, 1968; The Crazy Ape, 1970; What Next?, 1971; Electronic Biology and Cancer, 1976. Office: Marine Biological Labs Box 187 Woods Hole MA 02543

SZEP, PAUL MICHAEL, editorial cartoonist; b. Hamilton, Ont., Can., July 29, 1941; s. Paul Joseph and Helen (Langhorne) Szep; came to U.S., 1966, A.O.C.A., Ont. Coll. Art, 1964, hon. degree, 1975; hon. degree Framingham State Coll., 1975; m. Angela Diane arton, Feb. 27, 1965 (div. 1976); children—Amy, Jason. Sports cartoonist Hamilton Spectator, 1958-61: graphics designer Financial Post, Toronto, Ont., 1965-66; editorial cartoonist Boston Globe, 1966—. Lectr. various univs. Served with F.A., Royal Canadian Army, 1957-58. Recipient Pulitzer prize, 1974, 77; award Sigma Delta Chi, 1974, 77. Club: Hatherly Golf and Country. Author: In Search of Sacred Cows, 1967; Keep Your Left Hand High, 1969; At This Point in Time, 1973; The Harder They Fall, 1975; Them Damned Pictures, 1978. Home: 191 Buckminster Rd Brookline MA 02046 Office: Boston Globe Boston MA 02107

SZEPLAKI, JOSEPH, librarian, historian, bus. exec.; b. Hatvan, Hungary, Apr. 17, 1932; s. Joseph and Julianna (Gazsi) S.; came to U.S., 1956, naturalized, 1963; M.L.S., Apaczai Csere Janos Coll. of Pedagogy, Library Sch., Budapest, Hungary, 1954; m. Clara Irmai, Jan. 24, 1957; children—Victor Aniko. Chief librarian, Trade Union Library, Budapest, Hungary, 1955-66; asst. acquisitions librarian Brandeis U. Library, Waltham, Mass., 1963-65, acting head of acquisitions, 1965-66, head of acquisitions, 1966-67; supr. tech. services Info. Dynamics Co., Reading, Mass., 1967-68; head of serials Ohio U. Library, Athens, 1969-74; head of acquisitions U. Minn. Libraries, Mpls., 1974-77; v.p. Monitor Systems Inc., Washington, N.J., 1977—; cons. for Hungarian collection of the Immigration History Research Center, 1974—. Mem. ALA, Internat. Pen Club, Am. Assn. for Study Hungarian History, Hungarian Assn. of Cleve. (Silver medal award 1972, Gold medal award 1973), Internat. Social Sci. Honor Soc. Author: The Hungarians in America, 1975; Louis Kossuth, 1976; Hungarians in the U.S. and Canada, 1977; also bibliographies; contbr. aritcles on history and Hungarian culture to Am. and Hungarian periodicals and newspapers. Address: 36 Canterbury Rd Phillipsburg NJ 08865

SZILAGYI, GEORGE, microbiologist, educator; b. Carei, Rumania, Dec. 30, 1916; s. Adolph and Lotte (Kepecs) S.; M.D., Regele Ferdinand U. and Franz Joseph U., 1942; m. Magdalena Virag, Aug. 11, 1945; children—Edith (Mrs. Michael Lehrer), Andrew. Came to U.S., 1962, naturalized, 1969. Lab. physician, microbiologist Lab. Hygiene, Oradea, Rumania, 1942-49; chief dept. labs. Antiepidemic Center, Satu-Mare, Rumania, 1949-62; prof. microbiology Med. Edn. Center, Satu-Mare, 1950-62; research asso. Montefiore Hosp., N.Y.C., 1963-69; dir. microbiology Albert Einstein Coll. Hosp., N.Y.C., 1969—, asst. prof. depts. microbiology, immunology, lab. medicine Albert Einstein Coll. Medicine, 1971—; asst. prof. biology Fordham U., Bronx, N.Y., 1976—. Fellow Am. Acad. Microbiology; mem. Med. Mycology Soc. N.Y., Am. Soc. Microbiology, N.Y. Acad. Scis., Am. Pub. Health Assn., AAAS. Contbr. articles to profl. jours. Home: 67-71 Yellowstone Blvd New York City NY 11375 Office: 1825 Eastchester Rd Bronx NY 10461

SZILASI, WILLIAM JOSEPH, securities co. exec.; b. Passaic, N.J., Dec. 23, 1942; s. William James and Erma (Straub) S.; B.S., Rutgers U., 1971; postgrad. N.Y. Law Sch., 1977—; m. Rosemarie Ricciardi, July 26, 1964; 1 son, William James. Accountant, N.J. Bank, Paterson, 1963-65, Nabisco, Fair Lawn, N.J., 1965-67, Rayfield, Albano & Leaf, C.P.A.'s, Newark, 1967-69; v.p. Mitchell, Hutchins Inc., N.Y.C., 1969-77; v.p. compliance Paine Webber Jackson & Curtis, Inc., N.Y.C., 1977—; allied mem. N.Y. Stock Exchange. Served with USMCR, 1960-63. Mem. Nat. Assn. Securities Dealers, Securities Industry Assn., Futures Industry Assn. Republican. Roman Catholic. Club: Ocean Acres Country. Home: 6 9th St Barnegat NJ 08005 Office: 25 Broad St New York City NY 10005

SZLOCH, MICHAEL MIECZYSLAW, civil engr.; b. Boryslaw, Poland, Aug. 24, 1923; s. Walenty and Ann (Szumacher) S.; came to U.S., 1951, naturalized, 1956; student Huddersfield (Eng.) Tech. Coll., 1947-50, Northeastern U., 1951-57; m. Mary Ann Nestor, Feb. 19, 1955; 1 son, Michael Noel; 2 daus., Carmel Ann, Marlene Ann. Civil structural engr. C. A. Maguire Assos., Boston, 1957-60, Badger Mfg., Cambrdige, Mass., 1960-63; sr. strucutral design engr. Stone & Webster Engring. Corp., Boston, 1964-70; lead strucutral engr. C. T. Main Co., Boston, 1970-74; supervising civil engr. Burns & Roe, Inc., Stamford, Conn., 1976—; cons. in field. Served with 2nd Polish Corps, 8th British Army, 1944-47. Registered profl. engr., Mass., Conn., La., Fla. Mem. Polish Army Vets. Assn. (pres. cultural club 1960-62, post comdr. 1973-74), Am. Soc. C.E., Mass. Soc. Profl. Engrs. Home: 28 Windsor Rd Stoneham MA 02180

SZOGYEN, JOHN RODOLPHE MARIA CHARLES, cons.; b. Budapest, Hungary, Oct. 7, 1924; s. Tibor and Karola (Gussenbauer) S.; student Josef Nador U., Budapest, 1942-48, Swiss Fed. Inst. Tech., Zurich, 1949-50; B.Applied Sci., U. B.C., 1951; M.B.A., Fairleigh Dickinson U., 1977; m. Beatrice Delmar, Mar. 28, 1945; 1 dau., Carla. Came to U.S., 1962, naturalized, 1971. Various engring. positions, 1951-58; chief rotating machine engr. English Electric Co. of Can., St. Catharines, Ont., 1958-62; mgr. mfg. Electrodynamic div. Gen. Dynamics Corp., Avenel, N.J., 1963-67; v.p. mfg. Howe Richardson Scale Co., Clifton, N.J., 1967-69, v.p. ops., 1969-71; mng. dir. Reliance Electric Co. (Europe), Brussels, Belgium, 1971-73; gen. mgr. materials and mfg. Am. Dist. Telegraph Co., Clifton, 1973-76; v.p. ADT Internat., N.Y.C., 1976-78; tchr. night sch. hydraulics course, 1956-59. Registered profl. engr., Ont., N.J. Mem. IEEE, ASME, Am. Mgmt. Assn., Soc. Mfg. Engrs., Instrument Soc. Am., Assn. Profl. Engrs. Ont., N.J. Soc. Profl. Engrs., Clifton C. of C., Assn. Suisse des Electriciens, Newcomen Soc. N.Am. Club: Glen Ridge Country. Contbr. articles to profl. jours.; patentee in field. Home: 25 Douglas Rd Glen Ridge NJ 07028 Office: 20 Bridewell Pl Clifton NJ 07015

SZOGYI, ALEX, educator, author; b. N.Y.C., Jan. 27, 1929; s. Arpad and Vera Irene (Hoffmann) S.; B.A., Bklyn. Coll., 1950; M.A., Yale, 1954, Ph.D., 1958. Mem. faculty Yale, 1952-55, Wesleyan U., 1955-61; mem. faculty Hunter Coll., N.Y.C., 1961—, prof. Romance langs., 1971—, chmn. dept., 1970-77; mem. exec. bd. French doctoral program City U. N.Y.; translator plays, book reviewer. Decorated chevalier dans l'ordre des palmes académiques, 1974; recipient Distinguished Alumnis award Bklyn. Coll., 1974; French Govt. fellow, 1950-51; Danforth Found. fellow, summer 1959; Guggenheim Found. fellow, 1962-63. Mem. Modern Lang. Assn., Am. Assn. Tchrs. French (pres. Met. chpt. 1978—), P.E.N., Am. Comparative Lit. Assn., Soc. des Professeurs de Français en Amérique, Les Amis de George Sand, Dramatists Guild, Phi Beta Kappa, Pi Delta Phi, Sigma Delta Pi. Author: Anthologie d'Humour Français, 1970. Translator: (Temkine) Grotowski, 1972; also all of Chekhov's plays, and plays of Gorki, Giraudoux, Anouilh, Marquis de Sade, Verga, George Sand, Strindberg, Feydeau. Editor: Candide (Voltaire), 1962; George Sand Studies. Home: 61 Jane St New York City NY 10014 Office: 695 Park Ave New York City NY 10021

SZORADI, CHARLES, architect; b. Matyasfold, Hungary, Nov. 2, 1923; s. Nandor and Margit (Tittl) Stift; came to U.S., 1957, naturalized, 1962; Master's degree Architecture Sch., Budapest Inst. Tech., 1950; m. Barbara Hill, Sept. 18, 1964; children—Charles Attila, Stephen Hill. Architect, planner Hungarian Central Planning Office, 1950-56; architect Chatelain, Gauger & Nolan, Washington, 1957-60, Keyes, Lethbridge & Condon, Washington, 1962-68; architect, planner Doxiadis Assos., Washington, 1968-71; chief architect Daniel, Mann, Johnson & Mendenhall, 1972; prin. Charles Szoradi, AIA, architect and planner, Washington, 1973—. Served with Hungarian Army, 1944. Nat. Endowment for Arts grantee, 1974-75. Mem. AIA, Am. Planning Assn., Potomac River Sailing Assn. Home: 2822 28th St NW Washington DC 20008 Office: 1710 Connecticut Ave Washington DC 20009

SZOVERFFY, JOSEPH, educator, author; b. Clausenbourgh, Rumania, June 19, 1920; s. Louis and Anna (de Simkovith) S.; B.A., St. Emeric Coll., Budapest, 1939; M.A.T., State Coll. Budapest, 1944; Ph.D., Budapest U., 1943; Dr. Philologiae Habilitatus, Fribourg U., Switzerland, 1950. Came to U.S., 1962. Faculty mem. Budapest U., 1943-48, Fribourg U., Switzerland, 1949-50, Glenstal Coll., Ireland, 1950-52; research archivist Irish Folklore Commn., Univ. Coll., Dublin, Ireland, 1952-57; asst. prof. U. Ottawa (Can.), 1957-59; asso. prof. U. Alta., 1959-62; asso. prof. medieval German lit. Yale U., 1962-65; prof. Medieval studies and German lit. Boston Coll., 1965-70, also dir. grad. studies and acting chmn.; prof., chmn. dept. comparative lit. State U. N.Y. at Albany, 1970-77, lifetime faculty exchange scholar, 1974—; vis. prof. CESCM, U. Poitiers (France), 1961; vis. prof. Harvard U., 1968, Loeb Classical lectr., 1967, hon. research asso., 1975—, mem. Harvard Ukrainian Research Inst., 1975—; vis. scholar Dumbarton Oaks Center Byzantine Studies (Harvard U.), Washington, 1977-78; mem. Sch. Hist. Studies, Princeton (N.J.) Inst. for Advanced Study, 1978—, Nat. sec.-gen. Foederatio Emericana, Budapest, 1943-46; council alderman of Guild Medieval and Renaissance Studies, Alta., Can., 1960-62. Bd. dirs. Inst. for Early Christian Iberian Studies. Guggenheim fellow, 1961, 69; Publ. grantee, 1963, 65, 71, 75; Calhoun Coll. fellow Yale U., 1963-65; Am. Council Learned Socs. grantee, 1960, 64, 66; medieval seminar fellow State U. N.Y., 1973—; Nat. Endowment for Humanities fellow, 1978. Mem. Medieval Acad. Am., Am. Folklore Soc. (mem. council 1958-61), Am. Philol. Assn., Conn. Acad. Arts Scis., Am. Assn. Tchrs. German, Am. Cath. Hist. Assn., Internat. Verein. German. Author: St. Christoph und sein Kult (Budapest), 1943; Irisches Erzaehigut (Berlin), 1957, An Ungáir (Dublin). 1958; Lyrische Dichtung des Mittelalt. I-III (Berlin), 1964-66; Mirror of Medieval Culture, 1965; Iberian Hymnody, 1971; Peter Abelard's Hymnarius Paraclitensis, vols. I and II, 1975; Hymns of the Holy Cross, 1976; Germanic Studies on Medieval Literature, 1977. Editor: Medieval Classics, 1974—; Baroque, Romanticism and the Modern Mind, 1975—; co-editor Mittellat. Jahrb., Cologne, Germany, 1970—. Mem. editorial bd. Mediaevalia, 1975—. Home: 1514 Beacon St Brookline MA 02146 Office: Princeton Inst for Advanced Study Sch of Hist Studies Princeton NJ 08540

SZUHAY, JOSEPH ALEXANDER, educator; b. Cambridge, Ohio, Feb. 28, 1925; s. David and Barbara (Orosz) S.; B.S. in Phys. Edn., U. Iowa, 1953, Certificate in Phys. Therapy, 1954, M.S., 1956, Ph.D., 1961; m. Joy Naomi Youppi, Nov. 21, 1946; children—Paige Melanie (dec.), Brooke Jana. Recreation therapist Iowa Hosp. for Severely Handicapped Children, Iowa City, 1952-53; instr. U. Iowa Sch. Phys. Therapy, Iowa City, 1954-61; phys. therapist Steindler Orthopedic Clinic, Mercy Hosp., Iowa City, part-time 1959-61; dir. vocational guidance adult day care program Southeastern Mental Health Center, Sioux Falls (S.D.) Coll., 1961-64, lectr. psychology, 1962-64; dir. rehab. counseling program U. Scranton (Pa.), 1964-74, prof., chmn. dept. human resources, 1974—. Vocat. cons. Bur. Hearings and Appeals, Social Security Adminstrn., HEW, 1962—, mem. policy adv. com. Social and Rehab. Services, 1971-75, Rehab. Services Adminstrn. commr., 1975-76; ednl. cons. Pa. Bur. Visually Handicapped, 1968-69; cons. clin. and counseling psychology VA Hosps., 1971—; spl. projects cons. Teledyne Econ. Devel. Co., 1973—; vis. cons. Regional Research Inst., U. Wis., 1973—; cons. adv. council on rehab. counseling, 1974-76; mem. manpower task force Gov.'s Comprehensive Vocational Rehab. Commn., 1967-68; mem. Gov.'s Regional Commn. on Health Care Bill, 1974. Bd. dirs. Alcoholism and Drug Abuse Council Northeastern Pa., 1965-71, pres., 1967-69, chmn. edn. com., 1966, 69, 70; bd. dirs. United Neighborhood Services Lackawanna County, 1965-70, pres., 1968-69; bd. dirs., U. Scranton rep. Allied Services for Handicapped, 1967-78; bd. dirs. Lackawanna County chpt. Nat. Found., 1969-72; bd. dirs., pres. Treatment and Rehab. Center Northeastern Pa., 1970-75; bd. dirs. Scranton and Lackawanna County unit Vis. Nurses Assn., 1972-74, Scranton Mental Health and Mental Retardation, 1971-78. Certified rehab. counselor; licensed psychologist, Pa. Fellow Pa. Psychol. Assn.; mem. Am. (chmn. ethics com. 1965-70), Pa. personnel and guidance assns., Am., Northeastern Pa. psychol. assns., Nat., Pa. (dir.) rehab. assns., Nat. Council Rehab. Edn. (dir. region II 1969-71, region III 1971-72, 77—, chmn. nominating com. region III 1971, chmn. legislation com. region III, 1972—, pres. 1974-75), Phi Delta Kappa (treas. U. Iowa chpt. 1958-60, treas. U. Scranton chpt. 1970—). Contbr. articles to profl. jours. Book reviewer Psychiatry and

Social Sci. Rev., Bestsellers. Home: 66 Woodland Way Clarks Summit PA 18411 Office: U Scranton Monroe and Linden Sts Scranton PA 18510

SZURGOCINSKI, LEONARD MIECZYSLAW, indsl. co. ofcl.; b. Carentan, France, May 12, 1948; s. Leonard and Krystyna (Ostrowski) S.; came to U.S., 1957, naturalized, 1962; B.S. in Indsl. Mgmt., Lowell Tech. Inst., 1971; m. Teresa Anna Borysewicz, May 21, 1972; children—Krystyna, Dorothy. Machine operator, prodn. and inventory control ISM Corp., Boston, 1972-74; with Minn. Mining and Mfg. Co. (formerly ISM Corp.), Northboro, Mass., 1974-76; quality control mgr. Thomas Smith Co., Worcester, Mass., 1976—. Mem. Am. Soc. Quality Control Democrat. Roman Catholic. Home: 94 Sussane Dr Whitinsville MA 01588 Office: 288 Grove St Worcester MA 01605

SZUTOWICZ, PAUL MICHAEL, import-export co. exec.; b. Berwick, Pa., Apr. 2, 1944; s. Paul Michael and Louise Mary (Norce) S.; B.S., Mount St. Mary's Coll., 1966; M.S., St. John's U., 1968, M.B.A., 1974; m. Louise B. Ferraro, Apr. 11, 1970. Chemist Schwarz/Mann div. Becton-Dickenson Corp., Orangeburg, N.Y., 1968-69; asst. sales mgr. Aceto Chem. Co., Inc., Flushing, N.Y., 1969-74; asst. dir. sales Napp Chem. Inc., Lodi, N.J., 1974-77; mgr. import-export R.W. Greff & Co., Inc., Old Greenwich, Conn., 1977—. NSF Research assistantship, 1967-68. Mem. Sales Assocs. of the Chem. Industry, Chgo. Drug Exchange, Beta Gamma Sigma, Sigma Xi. Republican. Roman Catholic. Home: 169-56 25th Ave Whitestone NY 11357 Office: 1445 E Putnam Ave Old Greenwich CT 06870

SZWAJKOWSKI, HERMAN ROBERT, guidance counselor; b. Phila., July 20, 1945; s. Herman G. and M. Stephanie (Kucment) S.; B.A. cum laude, La Salle Coll., 1968; M.Ed., Trenton State Coll., 1974; m. Mary Coia Szwajkosski, June 27, 1970. Tchr., guidance counselor Bishop Conwell High Sch., Archdiocese Phila., Roman Cath. Ch., Levittown, Pa., 1968—, mem. archdiocese Human Relations Coordinators Com., human relations coordinator for sch., 1969-71; counselor Nat. Assn. Coll. Admission Counselors, 1977, 78. Cert. guidance counselor and tchr., Pa., N.J. Mem. Assn. Cath. Tchrs. (sr. del. from sch. 1968-71), Am. Personnel and Guidance Assn., Secondary, Pa., Bucks County sch. counselors assns., Nat. Empolyment Counselors Assn., Assn. Cath. Tchrs., Secondary, Pa., Bucks County sch. counselors assns., Am. Fedn. Tchrs., Action Children's TV, Holy Name Soc., St. John the Baptist Home and Sch. Assn. Home: RD 1 The Cedar Nok Pipersville PA 18947 Office: Bishop Conwell High Sch Levittown Pkwy Levittown PA 19054

TABIN, EMANUEL NATHEN, health care co. exec.; b. Bronx, N.Y., Apr. 6, 1927; s. Leon and Fanny (Pitler) T.; student CCNY, 1945-46, Columbia U., 1974-75, Colby Coll., 1963; m. Evid Solomon, July 30, 1960; children—Audrey Hope Sacca, Sanford Russell, Leslie Sara. Pres. Richmond County Hearing Aid Center, S.I., N.Y., 1961-78; pres. Emanuel N. Tabin Assos., Inc., S.I., 1973—; cons. Dept. Health, State of N.Y., 1978—. Served with USAAF, 1944-45. Certified occupational hearing conservationist. Mem. N.Y. Guild Hearing Aid Dispensers (past pres.), N.Y. State, Nat. hearing aid socs. Democrat. Jewish. Clubs: B'nai B'rith, K.P. Office: 1736-38 Victory Blvd Staten Island NY 10314

TABLER, D. JANE PIEKARSKI, musician, educator; b. Wilkes-Barre, Pa., Mar. 27; d. Joseph William and Jean Marian (Garron) Piekarski; Mus.B. (Oliver Ditson scholar), New Eng. Conservatory, Boston, 1954; Mus.M., Catholic U., Washington, 1959; postgrad. Am. Conservatory Music, Fontainebleau, France, 1961; m. Grayson Brust Tabler, June 23, 1965. Instr. music Coll. Misericordia, Dallas, Pa., 1955-57; tchr. music Kingston (Pa.) pub. Schs., 1959-65, Montgomery County (Md.) Pub. Schs., 1966-68, Prince George's County (Md.) Pub. Schs., 1968—; flutist Wilkes-Barre Symphony Orch., 1948-65, Scranton (Pa.) Symphony Orch., 1948-65, Wyoming Valley (Pa.) Symphony Orch., 1948-65, Montgomery County Symphony Orch., 1966-68, Prince George's County Symphony Orch., 1965-66, Georgetown Symphony Orch., Washington, 1968—. Mem. Am. Fedn. Musicians, NEA, AAUW, Mozart Club Wilkes-Barre, Audubon Soc. Home: 3700 Kenilworth Dr Chevy Chase MD 20015

TACHMINDJI, ALEXANDER JOHN, naval architect, marine engr.; b. Athens, Greece, Feb. 16, 1928 (came to U.S., U.S. 1950; naturalized 1958); s. John and Athena (Andreades) T.; B.Sc., Kings Coll. Durham (Eng.) U., 1949, B.Sc. (hons.); 1950; M.S., Mass. Inst. Tech., 1951; postgrad. U. Md., 1951-54; m. Diane Primeau, Dec. 4, 1965. Head research and propeller br. D.W. Taylor Model Basin, U.S. Navy Dept., Washington, 1951-59; with Inst. for Def. Analyses, Arlington, Va., 1959-72, asst. dir. sci. and tech. div., 1963-67, dep. dir., 1967-69, dir. systems evaluation div., 1969-72, dir. Tactical Tech. Office, Def. Advanced Research Projects Agy., 1972-73, dep. dir. DEF Advanced Research Projects Agy., 1973-75; chief scientist Mitre Corp., 1975-76, v.p., 1976—; U.S. mem. Internat. Cavitation Com., 1955-59, also U.S. chmn. Am. Cavitation Com. Recipient U.S. Navy Meritorious Civilian award, 1955; Sec. Def. Meritorious Civilian Service medal, 1975. Fellow Am. Inst. Aeros. and Astronatuics (asso.), Royal Instn. Naval Architects; mem. Soc. Naval Architects and Marine Engrs. (chmn. panel hydroelasticity 1967-73, mem. hydrodynamics com. 1967—), N.E. Inst. Engrs., A.A.A.A.S., N.Y. Acad. Sci., Sigma Xi. Club: Cosmos (Washington). Patentee ventilated propeller. Home: 4915 Sedgwick St Washington DC 20016 Office: Mitre Corp Westgate Research Park McLean VA

TADDEI, ROMANO, electronics co. exec.; b. Guastalla, Italy, June 6, 1934; s. Zeffiro and Dina (Franzoni) T.; came to U.S., 1973; B.S. in Engring., Witwatersrand U., 1956; M.S.E.E., Columbia U., 1979; m. Licia Peluffo, Apr. 5, 1959; children—Laura, Silvana, Marco. Research and devel. mgr. Fuchs Elec. Industries, Alberton, South Africa, 1959-62; nat. field service mgr. Olivetti Africa, Ltd., Johannesburg, South Africa, 1962-66; product design group leader engring. div. Olivetti & Co., Ivrea, Italy, 1966-73, spl. assignment from home office to U.S., 1973—, mgr. East Coast Tech. Center div., N.Y.C., 1977—. Mem. IEEE, Assn. Computing Machinery, Soc. Info. Display, Am. Mgmt. Assn. Roman Catholic. Patentee in field. Home: 62 Carlton Ln Harrington Park NJ 07640 Office: 500 Park Ave New York City NY 10022

TADINI, FRED ATHELIO, ret. mfg. co. exec.; b. N.Y.C., Feb. 8, 1918; s. John and Mary (Serra) T.; student U. Md., 1957-58; m. Marie P. Brown, Jan. 4, 1942; children—Letitia, Loraine. Enlisted U.S. Army, 1941, advanced through grades to lt. col., 1957; ret., 1961; adminstrv. asst. Ford Instrument Div., Sperry Rand Corp., Long Island City, N.Y., 1961-62, materials control gen. supr., 1963-68, v.p. facilities, from 1969, then v.p. div.; purchasing mgr. Kreisler Mfg. Corp., North Bergen, N.J.; cons. H. Jordan Cons., 1974—. Pres., Planning Ednl. and Research Found., 1965—, treas., 1966-72; customer service mgr. Singer Corp., Ozone Park, N.Y., 1972—. Bd. dirs. Soltanoff Chiropractic Found. Decorated Bronze Star medal, Silver Star; recipient N.Y. State Distinguished Service Cross. Mem. Am. Prodn. and Inventory Control Soc. (pres. 1965-66), Am. Ordnance Assn., Ret. Officers Assn., Ft. Jay Officers Mess, Am. Legion, Ft. Hamilton Officers Mess, Res. Officers Assn. U.S., Ford Inst. Div. Suprs. Club (v.p. 1960—). Mason, Toastmaster. Club: Pompeii Fathers. Home: 138 W Houston St New York City NY 10012

TAFFEL, SHERMAN DENNIS, mgmt. cons., ednl. adminstr.; b. Long Branch, N.J., Nov. 6, 1945; s. Benjamin R. and Pearl P. (Polansky) T.; student Syracuse U., 1963-65, U. Okla., 1965-69; B.A., Antioch Coll., 1972; M.Ed., Pa. State U., 1973; postgrad. U. Md., 1977—. Therapist, Central State Hosp., Norman, Okla., 1969-70; dir. edn. Grassroots, Inc., Columbia, Md., 1970-71; research asst. Pa. State U., 1973; adminstr., planning specialist, office advanced planning and devel. Balt. City Pub. Schs., 1974—; cons. U. Md. Sch. Pharmacy, 1978—; mem. adj. faculty Antioch Coll., 1971—; bd. dirs. Ednl. and Environ. Planners, Treasure Lake, Pa., 1976—. Bd. dirs. Student Action, U. Okla., 1969-70, Antioch Coll. Policy Bd., 1970-71, Center for Resolution Global Problems Resulting from Technotronic Evolution, Balt., 1978—. Served with USNR, 1968-69. Mem. World Future Soc., Am. Inst. Planners, Am. Edn. Research Assn., Ops. Research Soc. Am. Democrat. Club: B'nai Brith. Home: RD 4 PO Box 49 Treasure Lake PA 15801

TAFFET, SAUL S., film producer, dir.; b. Newark, Oct. 19, 1918; s. Louis and Bertha (Schimmel) T.; student U. Mich., 1936-38; B.S. in Edn., U. Ill., 1940; Pres., founder TelematedMotion Pictures, N.Y.C., 1947—; head, coordinator Sch. Continuing Edn. film program N.Y. U., 1962—, adj. asso. prof., 1971—; film cons. Nat. Endowment Humanities. Served to capt. USAAF, 1942-46. Recipient Silver medal Venice Film Festival, Golden Eagle award Council Internat. Nontheatrical Events, Christopher award (2). Nat. Endowment Humanities grantee, 1974. Mem. Nat. Acad. TV Arts and Scis., Info. Film Producers Am. Home: 110 Bleecker St New York City NY 10012 Office: 51 E 42d St New York City NY 10017

TAFT, ARNOLD JAY, chem. co. exec.; b. N.Y.C., Jan. 28, 1933; s. Herman J. and Miriam Leah (Rabstein) T.; B.S., City U. N.Y., 1955; M.A., Bklyn. Coll., 1960; Ph.D. (research fellow, Hatco Chem. Co. fellow), Rutgers U., 1970; m. Phyllis Arlene Goodman, Aug. 2, 1964; children—Lisa Raquel, Stacy Dawn. Med. technologist VA Hosp., Bklyn., 1957-59; biochemist E.R. Squibb & Sons, New Brunswick, N.J., 1960-66; sr. chemist Johnson & Johnson Co., New Brunswick, 1970-73; devel. mgr. Coated Products Inc., Monmouth Junction, N.J., 1973—; teaching fellow Sch. Chemistry, Rutgers U., 1966-67. Served with U.S. Army, 1957. Lic. bio-analytical lab. dir. Mem. Am. Chem. Soc., Am. Assn. Bioanalysts, Phi Lambda Upsilon. Patentee in synthesis and use of biodegradable polymers. Home: 2 Willis Ct East Brunswick NJ 08816 Office: Coated Products Inc PO Box 276 Black Horse Ln Monmouth Junction NJ 08852

TAFT, ROBERT STEPHEN, lawyer, educator; b. N.Y.C., Nov. 1, 1934; s. Harold A. and Mae Vivian (Gray) T.; B.A., Dartmouth U., 1956; LL.B., Columbia U., 1959; LL.M., N.Y. Law Sch., 1960; m. Marlene Rosalie Medwin, June 22, 1958; children—Leslie Ann, Peter Stephen. Admitted to N.Y. State bar, 1959; practiced in N.Y.C., 1960—; asso. firm Reid and Priest, 1960-67; partner firm Hatfield, Brady and Taft, 1967-77, Miller, Montgomery, Sogi, Brady & Taft, 1977—; lectr. Practicing Law Inst., N.Y.C., 1967-75, Ark. Law Sch., Little Rock, 1968, N.Y. U. Tax Inst., N.Y.C., 1973—; prof. law N.Y. Law Sch., 1972—; cons. to U.S. Dept. Treasury, 1970-71; dir. Robert F. Warner, Inc., Whitehouse Products Corp. Pres. Great Neck (N.Y.) Grace Ave. Sch. PTA, 1971-72; mem. adv. bd. Odyssey House, 1970—, bd. dirs., 1975—; trustee Practicing Law Inst. Found., 1970—. Mem. Am., N.Y. State, Nassau County bar assns., Soc. of Am. Magicians. Author: (with Arnold S. Anderson) New York Practice-Personal Taxes, 1975; contbr. articles to legal jours.; tax columnist N.Y. Law Jour., 1972—. Home: 85 Nassau Dr Great Neck NY 11021 Office: 200 Park Ave New York City NY 10017

TAGGART, JOSEPH HERMAN, economist; b. Wakefield, Mass., Dec. 29, 1902; s. David and Josephine (Jess) T.; Ph.B., Yale U., 1924; M.B.A., Harvard U., 1927; Ph.D., Columbia U., 1938; LL.D. (hon.), L.I. U., 1964, U. Lagos, Nigeria, 1968. Instr., Lehigh U., 1927-28; asst. prof. to prof. econs. U. Kans., 1928-46; prof. fin. Rutgers U., 1947-52, prof. econs., 1952-56; prof. fin. Grad. Sch. Bus. Adminstrn., N.Y. U., 1956-71, asso. dean, 1956-59, dean, 1959-70, exec. dean schs. of bus., 1962-70, dean emeritus, prof. fin. emeritus, 1971—; economist, bus. cons. Dept. Commerce, 1941-42, chief fin. and tax research unit, 1945; econ. adviser commr. in Europe, dir. planning Fgn. Liquidation Commn., Washington, 1945-46; econ. adviser, chmn. munitions bd. Dept. Def., 1946-52; U.S. rep. Western Union Mil. Supply Bd., London, 1949-50; cons. Def. Prodn. Adminstrn., 1951-52; mem. U.S. del. Internat. Conf. Am. States, Bogota, Colombia, 1948; pub. gov. Am. Stock Exchange, 1966-72; dir. Fed. Paper Bd. Co., Inc., Tishman Realty & Constrn. Co.; trustee Hubbard Real Estate Investments. Mem. adv. council W. Paul Stillman Sch. Bus., Seton Hall U., Sch. Arts, N.Y. U. Served to maj. AUS, 1942-45. Gallatin fellow N.Y. U., 1977—. Home: 37 Washington Sq W New York City NY 10011 Office: 100 Trinity Pl New York City NY 10006

TAGGART, LESLIE DAVIDSON, lawyer; b. Glasgow, Scotland, Aug. 28, 1910; s. Frederick James and Petrina W. (Paterson) T.; A.B., Columbia U., 1931, LL.B., 1934; m. Mary Mason Kerr, Sept. 27, 1940; children—Georgia M. Taggart Brackett, William K., Patricia A., Douglas G. Admitted to N.Y. bar, 1934; practice law, N.Y.C., 1934—; sr. partner Watson, Leavenworth, Kelton & Taggart; lecturer. Practicing Law Inst. Former sec. St. Andrews Soc. N.Y. State. Mem. N.Y. Patent Law Assn. (past dir.) U.S. Trademark Assn. (past dir.), Am. Bar Assn., Am. Coll. Trial Lawyers, Burns Soc. N.Y. (past pres.), Phi Beta Kappa, Phi Sigma Kappa, Conglist. Clubs: University, Columbia University (past treas., gov.) (N.Y.C.); Patterson (Fairfield, Conn.). Home: 2 Melwood Ln Westport CT 06880 Office: 100 Park Ave New York City NY 10017

TAGLIAFERRI, LEE GENE, investment banker; b. Mahanoy City, Pa., Aug. 14, 1931; s. Charles and Adele (Cirilli) T.; B.S., U. Pa., 1957; M.B.A., U. Chgo., 1958; m. Maryellen Stanton, Apr. 28, 1962; children—Mark, John, Mary Ann. Div. comptroller Campbell Soup Co., Camden, N.J., 1958-60; securities analyst Merrill, Lynch, Pierce, Fenner & Smith, Inc., N.Y.C., 1960-62; asst. v.p. U.S. Trust Co. of N.Y., 1962-71; v.p. corp. fin. div. Laidlaw & Co., Inc., N.Y.C., 1972-73; pres. Everest Corp., N.Y.C., 1973—; dir. Fairfield Communities Land Co., UEC, Inc., LRA, Inc., Industrialized Bldg. Systems, Inc. Past pres. West Windsor Community Assn.; trustee West Windsor Little League, West Windsor Football League, Schuyler Hall, Columbia; trustee, treas. Madison Sq. Boys Club. Served with U.S. Army, 1953-55. Clubs: K.C.; U. Pa., Princeton (N.Y.C.). Home: 77 Lillie St Princeton Junction NJ 08550 Office: 1 Penn Plaza New York City NY 10001

TAGUE, BARRY ELWERT, stock broker; b. Phila., June 17, 1938; s. Edward James, Jr. and Eleanor May (Elwert) T.; student Bucknell U., 1956-59; m. Dorothy Elizabeth Beausang, May 14, 1960; children—Kimberly, Nancy, Barry Elwert, Edward James III. Partner, E.J. Tague & Co., Phila., 1959-68; partner Barry E. Tague & Co., Phila., 1968; exec. v.p., vice chmn. Raymond, James & Assos., Inc., Phila., 1968-76; pres. Tague Securities Corp., Bryn Mawr, Pa., 1976—; chmn. bd. Bryn Mawr Group and Bryn Mawr Corp., 1976—; gov. Phila.-Balt.-Washington Stock Exchange, Inc., 1967-77, vice chmn. bd., 1973-74, chmn. bd., 1974-76, also trustee; dir. Stock Clearing Corp. of Phila., 1973-76. Active Litte League Baseball, 1961-65, 76—; pres. Sch. PTA, 1971-72. Served with USMCR, 1959-65. Named Man of Year, Raymond James & Assoc., Inc., 1970. Mem. Kappa Sigma. Republican. Episcopalian. Clubs: Le Mirador Country (Lake Geneva, Switzerland); Waynesborough Country (Paoli, Pa.). Office: 931 Haverford Rd Bryn Mawr PA 19010

TAHAN, THEODORE WAHBA, radiotherapist, educator; b. Alexandria, Egypt, Jan. 22, 1936; came to Can., 1972; s. Cesar W. and Wedad E. (Zarrifeh) T.; M.B. B.Ch., Alexandria U., 1961, D.M.R. and E., 1964, doctorate radiotherapy, 1969; C.S.P.Q., Quebec, 1972; m. Mary Ann James, Nov. 17, 1962; 1 son, Alain. Demonstrator radiotherapy Alexandria Med. Sch., 1964-69, lectr., 1969-71; asst. prof. radiotherapy Sherbrooke (Que., Can.) Med. Sch., 1972-75, asso. prof., 1975—. Mem. Egyptian, Canadian med. assns., Egyptian Radiology Soc., Canadian Assn. Radiologists, Canadian Oncology Soc., Assn. Medecins de Langue Francaise, Radiol. Soc. N.Am. Home: 1885 Grime St Sherbrooke PQ Canada Office: Sherbrooke Med Sch Sherbrooke PQ Canada

TAHLER, EMANUEL DAVID, microbiologist; b. N.Y.C., June 30, 1916; s. Nathan and Bertha (Ascher) T.; B.S. in Chemistry with honors, L.I.U., 1938; postgrad. Bklyn. Coll., 1938-40, Rensselaer Poly. Inst., 1940-48; m. Caroline Leitstein, Dec. 17, 1950; children—Norman, Robin. Bacteriologist, N.Y. State Dept. Health, Div. Labs. and Research, Albany and N.Y.C., 1940-54; sr. bacteriologist, Dept. Mental Hygiene, Pilgrim Psychiat. Center, West Brentwood, 1954—; bacteriologist, North Shore Med. Group Huntington, N.Y., 1959—, Brunswick Hosp. Center, Amityville, N.Y.; bacteriologist Suffolk County Med. Examiner. Registerd microbiologist and specialist microbiologist Nat. Registry of Microbiologists. Mem. Am. Soc. for Microbiology. Co-author: Journal of Investigative Dermatology, 1950. Home: 8 Horizon Dr Huntington NY 11743 Office: Pilgrim Psychiat Center Bldg 82 Lab West Brentwood NY 11717

TAI, GEORGE MARSHALL, obstetrician, gynecologist; b. Kowloon, Hong Kong, Dec. 23, 1941; s. En Shui and Lan Chan (Wong) T.; came to U.S., 1955, naturalized, 1973; A.B., Haverford Coll., 1962; M.D., Jefferson Med. Coll., 1966; m. Deborah Krown, Sept. 11, 1971; 1 dau., Samantha. Intern, Meth. Hosp., Phila., 1966-67, resident, 1967-70; practice medicine specializing in obstetrics and gynecology, Atlantic City, 1972—, Somers Point, N.J., 1975—; mem. staffs Atlantic Ob-Gyn Group, Shore Meml. Hosp., Somers Point, Atlantic City Med. Center. Fellow Am. Coll. Obstetrics and Gynecology, ACS; mem. Atlantic County, N.J. med. socs., N.J. Obstet.-Gynecol. Soc. Methodist. Office: Mainland Med Center 1750 Zion Rd and New Rd Northfield NJ 08225

TAIRA, FRANK MORIHIKO, artist, sculptor, silversmith; b. San Francisco, Aug. 21, 1913; s. Morinobu and Ritsuko T.; student Calif. Sch. Fine Arts, 1935-38, Columbia U., 1945, Art Students League, 1956. Exhibited in one-man show at Hudson Guild Gallery, N.Y.C., 1967; exhibited in group shows at San Francisco Mus. Art, 1940, Oakland Municipal Gallery, F.A.R. Gallery, 1967, A.C.A. Gallery, 1957, NAD, 1976, Allied Artists Am., 1976, Internat. Soc. Artists, 1978, others; represented in pvt. collections; pvt. art tchr. Topaz Art Sch., Utah, 1941-43; china and glass decorator, 1945-50. Recipient law prize Calif. Sch. Fine Arts, 1938; 1st prize Com. for Awards of the Sch., Cambridge, Mass., 1942; award Nat. Arts Club, 1968. Mem. Internat. Soc. Artists, Artists Equity N.Y. Home: 458 W 49th St New York City NY 10019

TAIT, JOSEPH LLOYD, veterinarian; b. Jamaica, W.I., May 5, 1935; s. Guillermo Gabriel and Nihlet (Loudon) T.; came to U.S., 1960; B.S., N.Y. U., 1964, V.M.D., U. Pa., 1968; m. Lizette Alma Hutchinson, Jan. 3, 1968; children—Patricia Elaine, Lisa Janice. Dir. vet. services Med. Sch. N.Y. U., N.Y.C., 1968-69; practice veterinary medicine, N.Y.C., 1969—; cons. veterinarian Am. Soc. Prevention Cruelty Animals, N.Y.C., 1976—. Mem. Community Bd. Delafield Hosp., 1973-75; chmn. Community Planning Bd. 9, Manhattan, 1975—; mem. Manhattan Borough Bd.; dir. Harlem Commonwealth Council, 1977—, Area 145 Inc., 1977—. Mem. AMVA, N.Y.C. (pres. 1974-75), N.Y. State (polit. edn. com. 1974-76) vet. med. assns., Met. Vet. Assn. (sec. 1970), Am. Assn. Lab. Animal Sci. Democrat. Contbr. articles to profl. jours. Home: 807 Riverside Dr Apt 6G New York City NY 10032 Office: 454 W 145th St New York City NY 10031

TALABISCO, JOHN JOSEPH, bus. services co. exec.; b. Pottsville, Pa., Nov. 14, 1940; s. John M. and Josephine E. T.; student U. Miami (Fla.), 1960-63; m. Barbara E. Briggs, Apr. 22, 1971; 1 dau., Jacqueline E. Gen. mgr. CRC, N.Y.C., 1966-69; pres., chmn. bd. Botal Assos. Inc., N.Y.C., 1969—. Served with U.S. Army, 1963-65. Mem. Nat. Computer Assos. (pres.), Employment Mgrs. Assn., Nat. Employment Assn., Asso. Personnel Agency N.Y. Office: Botal Assos Inc 405 Lexington Ave New York City NY 10017

TALARICO, ANTHONY RUDOLPH, investment exec.; b. North Adams, Mass., July 13, 1914; s. Felix Anthony and Clementina (Folino) T.; B.S. in Bus. Adminstrn., Bryant Coll., 1938; m. Helen Roberts, Feb. 14, 1946; children—Teresa and Jean (twins). Accountant, Frank's Motor Sales, North Adams, 1949-62; stock broker Wood Walker & Co., Pittsfield, Mass., 1962-69, First Albany Corp., Pittsfield, Mass., 1969-71; registered rep. Hornblower & Weeks, Pittsfield, 1971-77; investment exec. Shearson Hayden Stone, Pittsfield, 1977—. Trustee North Adams Pub. Library, 1959—; chmn. Hoosac Tunnel Centennial Com., 1973. Served with U.S. Army, 1942-45. Mem. Am. Philatelic Soc., Am. Legion, VFW, Sons of Italy. Republican. Roman Catholic. Club: Mt. Greylock Coin. Home: 54 Foucher Ave North Adams MA 01247 Office: 100 N St Pittsfield MA 01201

TALBERT, PRESTON TIDBALL, chemist, educator; b. Washington, Feb. 17, 1925; s. James Loraine and Grace Anna (Johnson) T.; B.S. cum laude, Howard U., 1950, M.S., 1952; Ph.D., Washington U., St. Louis, 1955; m. Rebecca L. Chandler, Aug. 8, 1956. Postdoctoral fellow U. Wash., Seattle, 1955-59; asst. prof. Howard U., Washington, 1959-63, asso. prof., 1963-70, prof., 1970—, asso. chmn. dept. bio-organic chemistry, 1966—. Served with USAF, 1943-46. Nat. Heart Inst. fellow, 1957-59. Mem. Am. Chem. Soc., A.A.U.P., A.A.A.S., N.Y. Acad. Scis., Beta Kappa Chi. Democrat. Methodist. Contbr. articles to profl. jours. Home: 400 Old Stone Rd Silver Spring MD 20904 Office: Dept Chemistry Howard University Washington DC 20059

TALBOT, IRWIN NORMAN, mgmt. cons., educator; b. N.Y.C., Dec. 29, 1923; s. Gustave Adolph and Ruth (Greenberg) Teitelbaum; B.A., Lafayette Coll., 1945; M.P.A., N.Y. U., 1969, Ph.D., 1971; m. Lita Marilynn Schmidt, Jan. 26, 1963; 1 son, Robert Glenn. Pres., Irwin N. Teitelbaum Co., N.Y.C. and Teaneck, N.J., 1946-55; v.p. Kendall Constrn. Co., S. River, N.J., 1955-58; with Kislak Mortgage Corp., Newark, 1958-63; v.p. Globe Mortgage Co., Hackensack, N.J., 1963-68; asso. prof. pub. adminstrn., chmn. dept. polit. sci., coordinator pub. adminstrn. program Newark State Coll., 1972-73; asso. prof. Fairleigh Dickinson U., 1973-76; lectr. N.Y. U., 1975—; cons. in mgmt. devel. to health care facilities, other orgns.; lectr. in field. Mem. Union County (N.J.) Optional County Charter Act Com.,

1971-72, Bergen County (N.J.) Overall Econ. Devel. Plan Com., 1975—. Served to lt. USN, 1942-46; PTO. Recipient Founders' Day award N.Y. U., 1971. Mem. Am. Soc. Pub. Adminstrn., Soc. Advancement Mgmt., Am. Polit. Sci. Assn., Acad. Polit. Sci., Regional Plan Assn. Author: Regional Administration: The Role of the County in Connecticut and New Jersey, 1971. Contbr. articles to profl. jours. Home: 23 Ellen Ct Hillsdale NJ 07642 Office: PO Box 22 Hillsdale NJ 07642

TALBOT, MILDRED FISHER, orgn. exec.; b. Champaign, Ill., Feb. 3, 1915; d. Pearl and Minnie Ethel (Darmer) Fisher; B.A., U. Ill., 1936; m. Phillips Talbot, Aug. 18, 1943; children—Susan, Nancy, Bruce Kenneth. Asst. to dean women U. Ill., Urbana, 1936-39; dir. Alumni Relations Office and Student-Faculty Union Bldg., U. Ill., Chgo., 1939-42; with ARC, CBI, 1942-43, OSS, CBI, 1943-44, U.S. Army Services of Supply, China, 1944-45; nat. sec. Nat. Council Women of U.S., Inc., N.Y.C., 1970-72, nat. pres., 1974-76. Mem. N.Y. State Citizens Com. for Pub. Edn., 1958-60; bd. dirs. Elder Craftsmen Showcase, N.Y.C., 1974—, pres. Elder Craftsmen, Inc., 1978—; bd. dirs. Overseas Edn. Fund LWV, 1970-74, mem. Asia Commn., 1970-76. Recipient Meritorious Service award U.S. Army, 1945. Mem. Pan Pacific and S.E. Asia Women's Assn. (co-founder Washington chpt. 1962). Democrat. Presbyterian. Club: Cosmopolitan (N.Y.C.). Home: 200 E 66th St New York City NY 10021

TALENFELD, HILDA FRIEDMAN (MRS. MEYER MAIER TALENFELD), real estate and ins. broker; b. Pitts., Dec. 28, 1903; d. Jacob and Esther (Sheffler) Friedman; B.S., U. Pitts., 1926, postgrad., 1945-48; pvt. study piano and violin; m. Meyer M. Talenfeld, May 1, 1927; 1 dau., Marquita Pettler. Real estate and ins. broker Talenfeld Real Estate Co., 1927—. Mem. 14 women Commn. U.S. Govt. to inspect missile installations in South and Southwest U.S., 1966. Recipient Margaret Enright prize U. Pitts., 1925. Mem. AAUW, Am. Numis. Assn., Greater Pitts. Real Estate Bd. (pres. women's council), Nat. Assn. Real Estate Boards (gov. Pa. women's council 1966-67; pres. Pitts. chpt. women's council, v.p. regional women's council 1969-70, recipient Service medal), Bus. and Profl. Women, Officers Open Mess-Pitts. Air Def., Internat. Platform Assn., Nat. Assn. Real Estate Brokers, Pa. Realtors Assn. Inst. Real Estate Mgmt., ORT, Hadassah, Delta Phi Epsilon, Omega Tau Rho. Clubs: Highland Park Community, Women's City (Pitts.). Home: 5640 Callowhill St Pittsburgh PA 15206 Office: 1436 5th Ave Pittsburgh PA 15219

TALER, JOSEPH, physician; b. Rozwadow, Poland, Jan. 10, 1923; s. Abraham and Zofia (Tobias) T.; M.D., Philipps U., Marburg-Lahn, Germany, 1950; m. Bronislawa Frenkiel, June 20, 1948; children—George Abraham, Gustava Elizabeth. Intern, resident in internal medicine Sinai Hosp., Balt., 1951-54; practice medicine, Glen Burnie, Md., 1954—; chief div. family practice North Arundel Hosp., Glen Burnie, 1965—; mem. staff Sinai Hosp., 1954—. Diplomate Am. Bd. Family Practice. Fellow Am. Acad. Family Physicians, Royal Acad. Health (Eng.), Am.-Israeli Med. Assn.,; mem. AMA, Pan Am. Med. Assn. (v.p. family practice sect.), Anne Arundel County Med. Soc. Jewish. Office: 95 Aquahart Rd Glen Burnie MD 21061

TALIAFERRO, JAMES HUBERT, JR., speech scientist, educator; b. Chattanooga, Feb. 21, 1924; s. James Hubert and Ida Estelle (Gilbert) T.; student Davidson Coll., 1942-43; B.S., U. Denver, 1948; M.S., Columbia, 1949; Ph.D., N.Y. U., 1976. Advt. exec. McCann-Erickson Inc., N.Y.C., 1951-53, Grey Advt. Agy., N.Y.C., 1953-55, Kenyon & Eckhardt Inc., N.Y.C., 1955-61, Sullivan Stauffer Colwell & Bayles, N.Y.C., 1961-68; instr. speech Bklyn. Coll., City U. N.Y., 1968-75, asst. prof., 1975—; pres. Communiskills Inc.; cons. in field; asso. producer New Am. Playwright Series, 1970; asso. dir. Reading for Blind, Bklyn. Coll., 1976—; drama critic Housatonic Valley Pub. Co. newspapers, 1973—. Chmn., Found. for Mus. of Am. Theatre, 1974—. Served with U.S. Army, 1943-45. Mem. Am. Soc. Theatre Research, Internat. Communication Assn., Speech Communication Assn., Eastern Communication Assn., Huguenot Soc. Am., SAR. Democrat. Episcopalian. Author plays: Inside Out, 1963; Tour de Force, 1963; also articles, papers. Home: 320 E 57th St New York City NY 10022 Office: Bklyn Coll Brooklyn NY 11210

TALLEY, HARRY DARLINGTON, JR., hwy. engr.; b. Ridley Park, Pa., Oct. 16, 1926; s. Harry Darlington and Marie Curtis (Bishop) T.; B.S., Drexel Inst. Tech., 1950; m. Mary Grace Wolfenden, Sept. 23, 1949; children—Lois A., M. Patricia, Michele J. Project engr., McCormick-Taylor Assos., Phila., 1960-61, Urban Engrs. Inc., Phila., 1961-63; sr. project engr. Urban Engrs. Inc., 1963-66, chief hwy. engr., 1966—; adj. instr. countinuing edn. Drexel U., 1967—. Served with USNR, 1944-45. Texas. Christ Ch. Valley Forge, Wayne, Pa., 1972—. Registered profl. engr., Pa. Mem. Am. Soc. Hwy. Engrs. (pres. Del. Valley sect. 1977-78). Republican. Home: 279 Heather Rd King Prussia PA 19406 Office: 306 S 19th St Philadelphia PA 19103

TALLEY, JOHN (JACK) VICTOR, state ofcl.; b. Hartford, Conn., Apr. 4, 1934; s. Victor John and Olive F. (Farquhar) T.; B.S., U. Conn., 1978; m. Mary Jane Lashay, Aug. 19, 1955; children—John, Guy, Cheri. Programmer analyst Hartford Ins. Group (Conn.), 1960-61; supr. systems and programming Hamilton Standard div. U.T.C., Windsor Locks, Conn., 1961-74; info. systems adminstr. State of Conn. Info. Systems Div., Hartford, 1974—. Mem. Soc. Mgmt. Info. Systems, Data Processing Mgmt. Assn., Nat. Assn. State Info. Systems. Democrat. Roman Catholic. Club: Elks. Home: 526 Vernon St Manchester CT 06040 Office: 340 Capitol Ave Hartford CT 06115

TALLIA, EUGENE JOHN, helicopter mfg. co. exec.; b. Bridgeport, Conn., Oct. 18, 1936; s. Mario Robert and Florence Virginia T.; A.S., U. New Haven, 1973; m. Nadine R. Heche, Apr. 23, 1960; children—Glenn Eugene, Cheryl Ann. With Sikorsky Aircraft Co., Stratford, Conn., 1955—, asst. program mgr. Utility Tactical Transport Aircraft System, 1972-74, mktg. mgr. Utility Tactical Trnasport Aircraft System, 1974-77, v.p. govt. relations, Washington, 1977—. Bd. dirs. Barnum Festival Soc., 1973-74. Served with U.S. Army, 1955-57. Mem. Am. Def. Preparedness Assn., Assn. U.S. Army, Am. Helicopter Soc., Army Aviation Assn. Am. (nat. v.p. 1976-79, regional v.p. 1975-78), Navy League U.S. (regional v.p. 1978), Nat. Security Indsl. Assn., Air Force Assn., Marine Corps Aviation Assn., U. New Haven Alumni Assn. Roman Catholic. Clubs: K.C., Bethesda Country, Army and Navy, Nat. Aviation, Georgetown. Home: 11204 Willowbrook Dr Potomac MD 20854 Office: Sikorsky Aircraft 1125 15th St NW Washington DC 20005

TALMADGE, JULIA, nurse; b. Pa.; diploma nursing, U. Pa., 1946, B.S. magna cum laude, 1954, M.S., 1962. Mem. staff U. Pa. Hosp., Phila., 1946—, asst. dir. nursing service charge med. div., 1954-59, asst. dir. nursing service, 1959-61, dir. nursing service, 1961—. Mem. Am., Pa., Phila. County Dist. nurses assns., Southwestern Pa. League Nursing, W.Phila. Mental Health Consortium (dir.), alumni assns. U. Pa. Hosp. Sch. Nursing, U. Pa. Grad. Sch. Edn., Sigma Theta Tau.

TAM, FRANCIS MANKEI, educator; b. Macao, Asia, Dec. 7, 1938; s. Anthony W. and Agatha Y. (Young) T.; came to U.S., 1960, naturalized, 1973; A.B., U. Calif., Berkeley, 1963; M.S., U. Minn., 1967. High sch. tchr. Institute Salesiano, Macao, Asia, 1959; teaching asst. U. Minn., Mpls., 1964-65, research asst., 1965-66; asst. prof. physics Frostburg (Md.) State Coll., 1967—. Mem. Am. Geophys. Union, Am. Meterol. Soc., Am. Assn. Physics Tchrs. (v.p. Appalachian sect. 1977-78, pres. 1978-79), Sigma Pi Sigma, Sigma Zeta. Democrat. Roman Catholic. Home: 33 Teaberry Ln Frostburg MD 21532 Office: Dept Physics Frostburg State College Frostburg MD 21532

TAMBOLI, AKBAR RASUL, cons. engr.; b. India, July 20, 1942; s. Rasul M. and Chandbi C. Tamboli; came to U.S., 1965, naturalized, 1968; B.Engring., U. Poona, 1964; M.S., Stanford U., 1967; m. Rounkbi G Tamboli, May 20, 1969; children—Tahira, Ajim. Sr. engr. Miller Assos., Pottsville, Pa., 1967-69; asso. Edwards & Hjorth, N.Y.C., 1970-76; sr. partner A.R. Tamboli & Assos., Verona, N.J., 1976—. Mem. ASCE, Am. Concerete Inst., Am. Inst. Steel Constrn.

TAMM, EDWARD ALLEN, U.S. circuit judge; b. St. Paul, Apr. 21, 1906; s. Edward Allen and Lucille Catherine (Buckley) T.; student Mt. St. Charles Coll., Helena, Mont., 1923-25, U. Mont., 1926-28; LL.B., Georgetown U., 1928-30, LL.D., 1965; J.S.D., Suffolk U., 1971; LL.D., Carroll Coll., 1974; m. Grace Monica Sullivan, Jan. 30, 1934; children—Edward Allen, Grace Escudero. Ofcl., FBI, 1930-48; judge U.S. Dist. Court for D.C., 1948-65, U.S. Ct. Appeals for D.C., Circuit, 1965—; chief judge, U.S. Temporary Emergency Court of Appeals, 1972—; admitted to bar Minn. and U.S. Supreme Ct. Spl. adviser to U.S. delegation UN Conf. on Internat. Orgn., 1945; mem. com. on jud. adminstrn. Jud. Conf. U.S., 1969—, chmn. rev. com., 1969—. Trustee St. Joseph Coll.; bd. dirs. Police Boys Club, Washington. Served to lt. comdr., USNR. Decorated comdr. Legion of Merit (Ecuador); Order of Balboa (Panama); recipient Judiciary award, 1970, Distinguished Alumnus award Georgetown U., 1964. Mem. Met. Bd. Trade, USCG Aux., Am. (mem. adv. com. on judges function 1969—, spl. com. on prevention and control crime 1969—, Fed., D.C. (hon.) bar assns., Am. Law Inst., Gourmet Soc., Am. Judicature Soc., Friendly Sons St. Patrick, U.S. Power Squadron, Sons Union Vets, John Carroll Soc., President's Cup Regatta Assn., La Confrerie des Chevaliers du Tastevin, Confrerie de la Chaine des Rotisseurs, Newcomen Soc., Sigma Nu. Roman Catholic. Clubs: Columbia Country; Ocean City Light Tackle; Nat. Lawyers; Seaview Country. Home: 3353 Runnymede Pl NW Washington DC 20015 Office: US Ct Appeals DC Circuit Washington DC 20001

TAMPONE, DOMINIC, retail store exec.; b. Italy, May 9, 1914; s. Gabriel and Constance (Pierro) T.; came to U.S., 1920, naturalized, 1937; student bus. adminstrn. Alexander Hamilton Inst., electronics and physics RCA Inst. With Hammacher Schlemmer, N.Y.C., 1929—, pres., 1958—; also pres. Invento Products Corp., N.Y.C., 1960—, Three New Yorkers Mfg. Co., 1962—, Plummer McCutcheon, N.Y.C. Served with U.S. Army, 1943-46; ETO. Decorated Knight Order of Merit of Italian Republic. Home: 36 Sutton Pl S New York City NY 10022 Office: 147 E 57th St New York City NY 10022

TAMPONE, MARGARET ANN, counselor, sch. psychologist; b. N.Y.C., Oct. 1, 1951; d. Gary Joseph and Margaret Marcella (Pearson) Tampone; B.A. with honors in Psychology, Russell Sage Coll., 1973; M.Ed. in Counseling Psychology, Boston Coll., 1976. Asst. tchr., special skills tchr. LaBoure Ctr., S.Boston 1974-75; counselor, sch. psychologist Mission Ch. High Sch., Roxbury, Mass. 1976—, dir. guidance 1976—. Mem. Bos-Line Council for Children, Boston 1976—; mem. Help for Children, Boston 1976—, sec., 1977—. Certified guidance counselor, sch. psychologist, tchr., Mass.; recipient ESAA grants, 1976, 77, 78. Mem. Am. Sch. Counselor Assn., Am. Personnel and Guidance Assn., Am. Psychological Assn. Contbr. article in field to profl. newsletter. Home: 43 Parker Hill Ave Boston MA 02120 Office: 69 Alleghany St Boston MA 02120

TAN, TJIAUW-LING, educator, psychiatrist; b. Pemalang, Java, Indonesia, June 2, 1935; s. Ping-Hoey and Liep-Nio (Liem) Tan; came to U.S., 1967; naturalized, 1972; B.S., U. Indonesia Faculty Medicine, 1957, M.D., 1961; postgrad. U. Indonesia, Jakarta, 1961-65, U. Calif. at Los Angeles, 1967-71, Pa. State U., 1971-72; m. Esther Joyce Kho, June 2, 1961; children—Paul Budiman, Robert Yuling, Alice Ayling. Lectr. psychiatry U. Indonesia, Jakarta, 1965-67; psychiat. cons. Central Gen. Hosp., Jakarta, 1965-67; postdoctoral fellow U. Calif. at Los Angeles Brain Research Inst., 1967-69; asst. research psychiatrist, dept. psychiatry Neuropsychiat. Inst. U. Calif. Los Angeles, 1969-70; asst. prof. psychiatry Pa. State U., 1972—; chief inpatient psychiatry Milton S. Hershey Med. Center, 1972—, dir. Behavior Therapy Clinic, co-dir. Biofeedback Lab., 1975—; cons. psychiatry Family and Children's Service Lebanon County, Lebanon, Pa., 1971—, Bd. dirs. Retarded Children's Assn. Dauphin County, Inc., 1971-73. Diplomate Am. Bd. Psychiatry and Neurology. Fellow Am. Psychiat. Assn.; mem. Pa., Central Pa. psychiat. socs., Pa. Med. Assn., Dauphin County Med. Soc., Assn. Advancement Behavior Therapy, Biofeedback Soc. Am., N.Y. Acad. Scis., AAAS, Assn. Psychophysiol. Study of Sleep, Am. Assn. Fgn. Med. Grads., Nat. Assn. Residents and Interns. Contbr. articles to profl. jours. Home: 182 Bradley Ave Carol Acres Hummelstown PA 17036 Office: Dept Psychiatry Pa State U Coll Medicine 500 University Dr Hershey PA 17033

TANENBAUM, HOWARD LEON, ophthalmologist, educator; b. Montreal, Que., Can., Sept. 8, 1935; s. Hyman Bernard and Bessie (Green) T.; B.Sc., McGill U., Montreal, 1957, M.D., C.M., 1961; m. Havie Chinks; children—Roberta, Henry Caplan, David. Intern, Jewish Gen. Hosp., Montreal, 1961-62; resident U. Colo. Med. Center, Denver, 1962-63, Kingston (Ont.) Gen. Hosp., 1963-66; instr. medicine U. Colo., Denver, 1962-63; practice medicine specializing in ophthalmology, Montreal, 1968—; asso. prof. ophthalmology McGill U., 1976—; mem. staff Montreal Gen. Hosp., 1968—, dir. retina and diabetic eye clinic, 1968-70; mem. staff Jewish Gen. Hosp. Montreal, 1968—, ophthalmologist in chief, 1970—; cons. to hosps.; project dir. Lady Davis Inst. Med. Research. Retina Found. Boston fellow, 1967-68. Fellow Royal Coll. Physicians and Surgeons Can., Am. Acad. Ophthalmology; mem. Med. Coll. Can. (licentiate), Que. Assn. Ophthalmology, Canadian Med. Assn., Montreal Clin. Soc., Montreal Ophthal. Soc., Assn. Research and Vision in Ophthalmology. Jewish. Club: Cote de Liesse Racquet. Contbr. articles to profl. jours. Home: 44 Somerville Westmount PQ Canada Office: 3755 Cote Ste Catherine Rd Montreal PQ Canada

TANENBAUM, WALTER IRA, adminstrv. exec.; b. N.Y.C., July 17, 1939; s. Leonard and Louise (Salidor) T.; B.S., N.Y. U., 1962; M.B.A., City U. N.Y., 1968; m. Barbara Lynn Pyenson, July 7, 1968; children—David Ian, Marc Evan. Systems engr. Consol. Laundries Corp., N.Y.C., 1962-66; supr. indsl. engring. Singer Co., N.Y.C., 1966-69; asso. dir. Montefiore Hosp. and Med. Center, N.Y.C., 1969-78; sr. mgr. Peat, Marwick, Mitchell & Co., 1978—; instr. mgmt. sci. Fairleigh Dickinson U., 1968—, adj. asst. prof. Rensselaer Poly. Inst., 1974—; cons. in field. Recipient Founders Day award N.Y. U., 1962; N.Y. U. acad. achievement scholar. Mem. Am. Inst. Indsl. Engrs. (sr.), Hosp. Mgmt. Systems Soc., ECHO. Home: 47 Waterford Dr Wheatley Heights NY 11798 Office: Peat Marwick Mitchell & Co 345 Park Ave New York NY 10022

TANENHOLTZ, STANLEY DONALD, engr., physicist, cons.; b. Boston, Mar. 10, 1931; s. Jack and Lena (Miller) T.; A.B., Boston U., 1958; M.S. in Physics, Northeastern U., 1967; m. Helene Burke, June 1, 1958; children—Laurel, Holly, Fern. Research physicist Natick Labs.(Mass.), 1958-70; founder, pres. Electric Transport Systems, Southboro, Mass., 1970-74; mgr. project engring. Reed & Prince Mfg. Co., Worcester Mass., 1974-75; product engr. USM Corp., Seabrook, Mass., 1976-77; cons. Technol. Devel. Cons., Southboro, 1972—; adj. prof. Bentley Coll., 1978—. Treas. Town of Southborough, Mass., 1975-77. Served with U.S. Army, 1953-55. Certified mfg. engr. Mem. Am. Phys. Soc., Soc. Mfg. Engrs., Soc. Automotive Engrs., Electric Vehicle Council, IEEE. Contbr. numerous articles to profl. publs. Designer electric vehicles and wind generators; patentee in field. Home: 153 Middle Rd Southborough MA 01772

TANG, MAN-CHUNG, constrn. exec.; b. Canton, China, Feb. 22, 1938; s. Fay-Pown and Jing-Tze (Ho) T.; B.S.C., Chu Hai Coll., 1959; Diploma Engring., Tech. U., Darmstadt, 1963, Dr.-Eng., 1965; m. Yee-Yun-Fung, Aug. 26, 1966; children—Chin-Chung, Chin-Ning. Bridge engr. Gutehoffnungshutte, West Germany, 1965-68; sr. structural engr. Severud-Perrone-Sturm-Conlin-Bandel, N.Y.C., 1968-70; v.p., chief engr. Dyckerhoff & Widmann, constrn., N.Y.C., 1970—; exec. v.p. DRC Consultants, Inc., N.Y.C., 1978—; structural cons. Mem. Am. Soc. C.E., Nat. Soc. Profl. Engrs., Prestressed Concrete Inst., Am. Concrete Inst., Internat. Assn. Bridge and Structural Engrs. Author publs. in stability theory of structures, long-span bridges, concrete design. Home: 83-23 Midland Pkwy Jamaica Estates NY 11432 Office: 529 Fifth Ave New York City NY 10017

TANG, ROBERT LEE-CHING, investment analyst; b. Hong Kong, Oct. 12, 1946; s. Wai Tong Tang and Sophie Lai-Kum Tai; B.A. (grantee) U. Chgo., 1968. Fin. investment analyst, v.p. McLeod, Young, Weir, & Co. Ltd., Toronto, 1972-78; v.p. McLeod Young Weir Inc., N.Y.C., 1978—; trust adminstr. Can. Permanent Trust Co., Toronto, 1969-71. Mem. Fin. Analysts Fedn., Toronto Soc. Fin. Analysts, Royal Geog. Soc. (Eng.), Royal Meteorol. Soc. (Eng.). Club: Canadian (Toronto). Contbr. research reports to profl. jours. Home: Apt 15F Connaught Tower 300 E 54th St New York City NY 10022 Office: McLeod Young Weir Inc 1 State St Plaza New York City NY 10004

TANIS, DAHLIA JOAN, constrn. co. exec.; b. Totowa, N.J., Nov. 7, 1936; d. Harry and Rosemary (Etrie) Longo; ed. Drake's Comml. Coll., 1954; m. James Tanis, June 20, 1955 (dec.); 1 dau., Deborah M. With 1st Nat. Bank, Clifton, N.J., 1976; owner, operator Hollywood Indsl. Co., drill sales, Wayne, N.J., 1970-73; v.p. A.B. Constrn. Co. Inc., boiler constrn., Paterson, N.J., 1973—. Republican. Roman Catholic. Home: 58 Hazen Ct Wayne NJ 07470 Office: 67 Danforth Ave Paterson NJ 07501

TANNENBAUM, BERNICE SALPETER, civic worker; b. N.Y.C.; d. Isidore and May Franklin; B.A., Bklyn. Coll., 1934; m. Nathan Tannenbaum; 1 son, Richard Salpeter. Pres. L.I. Region, Hadassah, 1954-57; nat. chmn. Jr. Hadassah, 1957-60; co-chmn. nat. conv. Nat. Hadassah, 1961-62, chmn. dept. press/radio/TV, 1961-64, nat. sec., 1964-68, nat. v.p., nat. youth aliyah chmn., 1968-71, nat. chmn. Zionist affairs, 1971-75, chmn. First Mid-Winter Conf., Israel, 1968, chmn. fund raising Hadassah Med. Orgn., 1975-76, nat. pres., 1976—, mem. exec. bds., Nat. Conf. Soviet Jewry, Am.-Israel Pub. Affairs Com., World Jewish Congress-Am. Sect., World Zionist Orgn.; mem. presidium Zionist Gen. Council, Gen. Assembly, Jewish Agency; bd. dirs. United Israel Appeal, Jewish Nat. Fund; mem. exec. com. Am. Zionist Fedn.; mem. governing bd. World Jewish Congress, 1976, Hebrew U., Jerusalem, 1976; mem. Conf. Pres's. Maj. Jewish Orgns., 1976—. Editor: The Hadassah Idea, Analysis and Action, 1972-75; editorial bd. Hadassah Mag., 1972—. Office: care Hadassah 50 W 58th St New York City NY 10019

TANNENBAUM, DONALD MARTIN, accountant; b. Hackensack, N.J., Oct. 14, 1932; s. Benjamin H. and Helen (Worms) T.; B.A., U. Pa., 1954, J.D., 1959; LL.M., N.Y. U., 1962; m. Doris Cohen, Apr. 11, 1954; children—Jay, Deborah. Partner, Oppenheim, Appel, Dixon & Co. N.Y.C. Admitted to N.Y. bar, 1961; past adj. asst. prof. grad. div. Bernard Baruch Coll. City U. N.Y. Served to 1st lt. AUS, 1954-56. C.P.A., N.Y. Mem. Am. Inst. C.P.A.'s, Am. Bar Assn., N.Y. State Soc. C.P.A.'s (past chmn. fed. tax com.). Club: Masons. Home: 19 Kenwood Ln Matawan NJ 07747 Office: 1 New York Plaza New York City NY 10004

TANNER, CHUCK, profl. baseball team mgr.; b. 1930. Player, mgr. numerous minor league teams, 1946-55, 60-61, 62-71; player Milw. Braves, 1955-57, Chgo. Cubs, 1957-58, Cleve. Indians, 1959-60, Los Angeles Angels (name changed to Calif. Angels), 1961-62; mgr. Chgo. White Sox, 1971-75; mgr. Oakland Athletics, 1976-77; mgr. Pitts. Pirates, 1977—. Recipient Rookie of Year award Milw. Braves, 1955; Major League Mgr. of Year award The Sporting News, 1972, Am. League Mgr. of Year award AP, 1972; Rookie of Year award Chgo. White Sox, 1971, Good Guy Ambassador award, 1972. Address: care Pitts Pirates Three Rivers Stadium 600 Stadium Circle Pittsburgh PA 15212*

TANNER, DANIEL, educator; b. N.Y.C., Sept. 22, 1926; s. John and Lillian (Jupiter) T.; B.S. with honors, Mich. State U., 1949, M.S., 1952; Ph.D. (University scholar), Ohio State U., 1955; m. Laurel Nan Jacobson, July 11, 1948. Asst. prof. edn. San Francisco State Coll., 1955-60; asso. prof. edn., coordinator Midwest program on airborne TV instrn. Purdue U., 1960-62; asso. prof. edn. Northwestern U., 1962-64; asso. prof. research div. tchr. edn. City U. N.Y., 1964-66; prof. edn. U. Wis.-Milw. Sch. Edn., 1966-67; prof. edn., dir. grad. programs in curriculum theory and devel. Grad. Sch. Edn. Rutgers U., 1967—, chmn. dept. curriculum and instrn., 1969-71, faculty research fellow, 1974-75; vis. lectr. Tchrs. Coll. Columbia, summer 1966; vis. prof. Emory U., summer 1968, State U. N.Y. at Binghamton, winter 1968; vis. scholar U. London Inst. Edn., 1974-75. Mem. rev. bd. coll. work-study program U.S. Office Edn., 1965; cons. Chgo. Sch. Survey, 1964-65, Center Urban Edn., N.Y.C., 1964-65, West Chicago (Ill.) Sch. Survey, 1963-64, Nat. Ednl. TV Center, N.Y.C., 1963, U. Tex. Med. Center, 1961-62, Exhbn. Radio and TV, Ohio State U., 1961-63, Campbell County (Va.) Sch. Survey, 1970, Memphis Schs., 1977-78. Fellow AAAS, John Dewey Soc.; mem. Am. Ednl. Research Assn., AAUP, Am. Polit. Sci. Assn., Am. Ednl. Studies Assn., Phi Kappa Phi, Phi Delta Kappa (Service award 1957). Author: Schools for Youth; Change and Challenge in Secondary Edn., 1965; Secondary Curriculum: Theory and Development, 1971; Secondary Education: Perspectives and Prospects, 1972, Using Behavioral Objectives in the Classroom, 1972; Curriculum Development: Theory into Practice, 1975; contbg. author: Readings in Educational Psychology, 1965; Yearbook of the Association for Student Teaching, 1962; The Great Debate, Our Schools in Crisis, 1959; Educational Issues in a Changing Society, 1964; Programs, Teachers and Machines, 1964; Views on American Schooling, 1964; The Training of America's Teachers, 1975; co-author: Teen Talk: Curriculum Materials in Communications, 1971. Contbg. editor Educational Leadership, 1969-74. Contbr. articles to nat. mag., ednl. jours. Home: Highwood Rd Somerset NJ 08873 Office: Grad Sch Edn Rutgers U New Brunswick NJ 08903

TANNER, JACK GENE, ins. co. exec.; b. Spencer, W.Va., Mar. 7, 1940; s. Ira John and Arlene (Harper) T.; LL.B., LaSalle U., 1965; B.S., St. John's U., 1977; m. June Rita Sheehan, Sept. 3, 1966; 1 son, Craig Andrew. Examiner, Hartford Ins. Co., N.Y.C., 1963-65; examiner bond claims Continental Ins. Co., N.Y.C., 1965-70; v.p. Intelligence Services Inc., Syosset, N.Y., 1970-71; mgr. bond claims Home Ins. Co., N.Y.C., 1971—. Served with USNR, 1958-62. Mem. Execss Bond Reins. Assn. (vice chmn.). Republican. Mormon. Club: Masons. Home: PO Box 243 25 John Tuttle Rd New Kingston NY 12459 Office: 59 Maiden Ln New York City NY 10038

TANNERS, HENRY, psychologist; b. Bklyn., Mar. 29, 1942; s. Nathan P. and Esther Lillian (Zuckerman) Tanners; B.A., Bklyn. Coll., 1964; M.S., Queens Coll., 1966; Ph.D., U. Iowa, 1972; m. Sandra Rhoda Epstein, Mar. 19, 1967; children—Lisa Sue, Adam Craig. Sch. psychologist North Babylon (N.Y.) Union Free Sch. Dist., 1966-69, 72—; adminstrv. asst. Spl. Tng. Inst. on Problems Sch. Desegregation, U. Iowa, 1970-72; psychotherapist Advanced Center for Psychotherapy, Garden City, N.Y., 1973-76, Therapeutic Consultation Center, Hauppauge, N.Y., 1974-76; adj. faculty, asst. prof. dept. psychology Nassau Community Coll., Garden City, 1973—; pvt. practice psychology Hauppauge, 1976—, Smithtown Psychiat. Group, 1976-77. Mem. Bipartisan Sch. Bd. Nominating Com., Iowa City, 1970. City U. N.Y. Bd. Higher Edn. fellow, 1964-65. Mem. Am., Suffolk County (pres. elect) psychol. assns., Am. Orthopsychiat. Assn., Am. Assn. for Advancement Tension Control, Adj. Faculty Assn. Nassau Community Coll., Suffolk County Acad. Psychology (pres.), Phi Delta Kappa. Author curriculum materials, articles. Democrat. Jewish. Club: K.P. Home: 20 Hill Ln Smithtown NY 11787 Office: 5 Jardine Pl North Babylon NY 11703 also 111 Smithtown By-pass Hauppage NY 11787

TANSELLE, GEORGE THOMAS, educator; b. Lebanon, Ind., Jan. 29, 1934; s. K. Edwin and Madge R. (Miller) T.; B.A. magna cum laude, Yale, 1955; M.A., Northwestern U., 1956, Ph.D., 1959. Instr., Chgo. City Jr. Coll., 1958-60; instr. U. Wis., Madison, 1960-61, asst. prof., 1961-63, asso. prof., 1963-68, prof. English, 1968-78. Mem. Planning Inst. Commn. on English, 1961; mem. exec. com. Center for Edits. Am. Authors, 1970-73; mem. advisory com. for drama for bicentennial Kennedy Center, 1974-75; mem. exec. com. Center for Scholarly Editions, 1976-77; v.p. Guggenheim Found., 1978—. Recipient Kiekhofer Teaching award U. Wis., 1963; Jenkins award for bibliography, 1973. Guggenheim fellow, 1969-70; Am. Council Learned Socs. fellow, 1973-74; Nat. Endowment Humanities fellow, 1977-78. Mem. Modern Lang. Assn. Am. (mem. exec. com. bibliog. evidence group 1974-75), Modern Humanities Research Assn., Bibliog. Soc. London, Bibliog. Soc. Australia, Bibilog. Soc. Am. (mem. council 1970—, vice chmn. publs. com. 1974-76), Bibliog. Soc. U. Va., Oxford, Cambridge, Edinburgh, Can. bibliog. socs., Printing Hist. Soc. (Am. corr. 1970—), Am. Printing Hist. Assn., Pvt. Libraries Assn., Manuscript Soc. (dir. 1974—), Am. Antiquarian Soc. (mem. publs. com. 1972—, mem. council 1974—), Nat. Council Tchrs. English, Book Club of Calif., Typophiles, Wis. Acad. Scis., Arts and Letters, Phi Beta Kappa. Clubs: Caxton, Grolier. Author: Royall Tyler, 1967; Guide to the Study of United States Imprints, 1971. Bibliog. editor: The Writings of Herman Melville, 1968—. Mem. editorial bd. Contemporary Literature, 1962—, Abstracts of English Studies, 1964—, Paper of Bibliog. Soc. Am., 1968—, Resources for American Literary Study, 1971—, Analytical and Enumerative Bibliography, 1977—. Contbr. articles to profl. jours. Home: 410 W Washington St Lebanon IN 46052 Office: care John Simon Guggenheim Meml Found 90 Park Ave New York City NY 10016

TANSER, PAUL HARRY, cardiologist, educator; b. Chatham, Ont., Can., Dec. 7, 1938; s. Harry Ambrose and Isabel Grace (Saporito) T.; M.D. magna cum laude, U. Ottawa, 1962; m. Catherine Lydia Weaver, Sept. 1, 1962; children—Christopher Paul, Carl Rodney. Intern. Royal Victoria Hosp., Montreal, Que., Can., 1962-63, resident, 1963-68; practice medicine specializing in cardiology; asso. prof. medicine McMaster U., Hamilton, Ont., 1975—; staff Royal Victoria Hosp., Montreal; cons. cardiology Queen Elizabeth Hosp.; head service, asst. physician-in-chief cardiology St. Josephs Hosp., 1975—. Fellow Royal Coll. Physicians Can., A.C.P., Am. Coll. Cardiology, Internat. Coll. Angiology; mem. Can., Montreal cardiovascular socs., Am. Heart Assn., Hamilton Acad. Medicine, Can. Med. Assn. Author numerous publs. in field. Office: St Josephs Hosp Charlton Ave E Hamilton L8N 1Y4 Canada

TANTON, THOMAS GEORGE, physician; b. Jersey City, June 7, 1942; s. George William and Ruth Gladys (Both) T.; B.A., Rutgers U., 1963; M.D., U. Bologna, 1969; m. Gloria Ruggiero, Dec. 13, 1969; children—Andrea, Michael. Intern, Walter Reed Gen. Hosp., 1970-71, resident in pediatrics, 1971-73; practice medicine specializing in pediatrics, 1975—; clin. instr. pediatrics Georgetown U. Med. Center, 1976—; mem. staff Montgomery Gen. Hosp., Olney, Md., Georgetown U. Med. Center, Washington. Served to maj. MC U.S. Army, 1969-75. Fellow Am. Acad. Pediatrics; mem. Med. Soc. Montgomery County, Georgetown U. Med. Center, Morgagni Med. Soc. Club: Potomac Men's Sr. Hockey. Office: 18111 Prince Philip Dr Olney MD 20832

TANZER, MARTIN SHELDON, environ. cons. firm exec.; b. N.Y.C., July 19, 1944; s. Lawrence and Estelle (Krasnow) T.; B.S., Bklyn. Coll., 1966; M.S., C.W. Post Coll., 1968; Ph.D., Heed U., 1977; 1 son, Jason. Research scientist Off Shore Sea Devel. Corp., N.Y.C., 1967-70; mgr. U.S. Testing Environ. Group, Hoboken, N.J., 1970-73; mgr. bus. devel.-environment services Sanderson & Porter, N.Y.C., 1973-77; mgr. bus. devel. E.G. & G. Environ. Consultants, Waltham, Mass., 1977-79; cons., Waltham, 1979—; lectr. in field. Certified in water Quality analysis N.J. Bd. Health. Mem. N.Y. Acad. Scis., Water Pollution Control Fedn., AAAS, Nat. Wildlife Fedn. Contbr. articles to profl. jours. Office: 5805 Stearns Hill Rd Waltham MA 02154

TARANTA, ANGELO, rheumatologist; b. Rome, Apr. 18, 1927; s. Giovanni and Luigina (Visca) T.; M.D. cum laude, U. Rome, 1949; m. Bruna Norsa, Sept. 7, 1957; children—Adriana, Paola. Intern, Univ. Hosp., Rome, 1949-50, resident, 1950-52; resident St. Mary's Hosp., Rochester, N.Y., 1952-53, Irvington (N.Y.) House, 1953-54; practice medicine, specializing in rheumatology, N.Y.C., 1965—; adj. asst. prof. microbiology N.Y. U. Sch. Medicine, N.Y.C., 1958-60, asst. prof. medicine, 1960-65, asso. prof., 1966-75; prof. medicine, chief rheumatology/immunology N.Y. Med. Coll., 1975—; asso. dir. Irvington House Inst., N.Y.C., 1965-71; dir. medicine Cabrini Health Care Center, N.Y.C., 1973—; cons. Task Force on Heart Disease in the Young, Nat. Heart and Lung Inst., 1977—; chmn. Council on Cardiovascular Disease in the Young, 1975-77. Bd. dirs. Am. Heart Assn., 1975-77. Am. Rheumatism Assn. fellow, 1957-58. Diplomate Am. Bd. Internal Medicine. Mem. Am. Soc. Clin. Investigation, Am. Assn. Immunologists, Am. Rheumatism Assn., N.Y. Acad. Medicine, Harvey Soc. Editor: (with E. Kaplan) Infective Endocarditis: An American Heart Assn. Symposium, 1977; mem. editorial bd. Bull. N.Y. Acad. Medicine. Home: 93 Hudson Terr Yonkers NY 10701 Office: 227 E 19th St New York City NY 10003

TARASI, LOUIS MICHAEL, JR., lawyer; b. Cheswick, Pa., Sept. 9, 1931; s. Louis M. and Ruth (Records) T.; B.A., Miami U., Oxford, Ohio, 1954; LL.B., U. Pa., 1959; m. Patricia R. Finley, June 19, 1954; children—Susan Louise, Louis Michael III, Beth Marie, Brian R., Patricia A., Matthew John. Admitted to Pa. bar, 1960, U.S. Supreme Ct. bar, 1969; asso. Burgwin, Ruffin, Perry, Pohl & Springer, Pitts., 1959-65. partner, 1965-68; sr. partner Conte, Courtney & Tarasi, Pitts. and Baden, Pa., 1968-70, Conte, Courtney, Tarasi & Price, 1970-78; partner firm Tarasi & Tighe, Pitts., 1978—. Cons.; lectr.; research asst. U. Pa. Law Sch., 1958-59. Mem. St. Vincent de Paul Penal Com., Pitts., 1964—. Bd. govs., sec. St. Thomas More Soc. Pitts., 1963—. Served with AUS, 1954-56. Mem. Am., Pa., Allegheny County bar assns., Pa. (asso. editor, pres.-elect), Western Pa. (editor, parliamentarian), Am. trial lawyers assns. Roman Catholic. Clubs: Allegheny, Pitts. Athletic Assn., Lewis Law. Home: 940 Beaver St Sewickley PA 15143 Office: Tarasi & Tighe 510 3d Ave Pittsburgh PA 15219

TARDIF-HÉBERT, J., artist; b. Bagotville, Que., Can., Jan. 19, 1934; d. Theodule and Marie (Boudreau) T.; B.A., U. Toronto, 1973; B.sp. histoire, U. Que., 1974. One-man shows: Salle la Coquille, Jonquière, Que., 1975, Festival des Artisans, Ste. Rose du Nord, Que., 1975, Arvida, Que., 1976, La Chasse Galerie, Toronto, Ont., 1976, Alma, Que., 1977; group shows: Vancouver (B.C.) Art Gallery, 1974, Chicoutimi (Que) Arts Soc., 1974, 75, 76, Galerie La Minerve, Quebec, 1975, 76, Print Drawing Council Can.; Calgary, Alta., 1977, Scarborough Town Centre, 1978; works represented in pvt. collections, Can., U.S. Mem. Canadian Conf. Arts, Société des Artistes Processionnels du Québec, Société des Arts de Chicoutimi, Société Historique du Saguenay.

TARLOV, EDWARD, neurosurgeon; b. N.Y.C., Nov. 18, 1938; s. Isadore M. and Fella T.; A.B. cum laude, Harvard U., 1960; A.M., U. Chgo., 1964, M.D., 1965; m. Suzanne Roffler, Jan. 18, 1969; children—Nicholas E., Katherine S. Intern, Johns Hopkins Hosp., Balt., 1965-66; clin. asso. in surg. neurology NIH, Bethesda, Md., 1966-68; house physician in neurology Nat. Hosp., London, 1968-69; vis. scientist Anat. Inst., Oslo, 1969; research asso. Mass. Inst. Tech., Cambridge, 1970; resident in neurosurgery Mass. Gen. Hosp., Boston, 1969-73, chief resident, 1973, neurosurg, staff, 1972—; neurosurgeon Lahey Clinic Found., Boston, 1977—, also New Eng. Deaconess, New Eng. Bapt. hosps. Served to lt. comdr. USPHS, 1966-68. Diplomate Am. Bd. Neurol. Surgery. Fellow A.C.S.; mem. Am. Assn. Neurol. Surgeons, Congress Neurol. Surgeons, New Eng. Neurosurg. Soc. Club: Harvard. Contbr. articles on neurosurgery to med. jours. Office: Lahey Clinic Found 605 Commonwealth Ave Boston MA 02115

TARNAY, ROBERT STEVENS, lawyer; b. N.Y.C., May 13, 1913; s. Victor William and Irma (Stevens) T.; A.B., U. Mich., 1934; J.D. with distinction, George Washington U., 1938; m. Anne Marie Larson, Sept. 5, 1936; 1 dau., Alice Anne. Admitted to D.C. bar, 1938, Conn. bar, 1938; spl. asst. to atty. gen. Dept. of Justice, Washington, Phila., Calif. and Hawaii, 1938-45; corp. adminstrv. law practice, Washington, 1945—; editor, pub. Washington Banktrends. Pres., chmn. bd. Tarsch Co., Washington; pres., dir. Gen. Pub. Co.; exec. v.p., chief exec. officer Cashier and Restaurant Tng. Sch., Inc.; exec. v.p., gen. counsel Mini Rhea, Designer, Inc.; pres. Mechtronics, Inc.; operating trustee Schiarone Popcorn Devices, Inc., Washington. Active local, state juvenile delinquency work, 1940—; financial chmn. local chpt. Girl Scouts of Am. 1954-56; chmn. area Community Chest Budget, 1957-66; mem. P.T.A. Council, Family and Welfare Council. Mem. Am. Bar Assn., Bar Assn. of D.C., State Bar Assn. of Conn., Order of Coif, Phi Alpha Delta, Kappa Sigma Phi, Phi Kappa Tau, Conglist. Author numerous articles, related econ. works. Home: Willow Oak Farm Route 1 Box 88F Newburg MD 20664 Office: 734 15th St Suite 503 Washington DC 20005

TARPLEY, THOMAS MARVIN, JR., oral pathologist, govt. scientist; b. Albany, Ga., Apr. 23, 1934; s. Thomas Marvin and Laura Barnett (Bierman) T.; D.D.S., Emory U., 1961; M.S., Georgetown U., 1973; M.A., George Washington U., 1978; m. Patricia Ann Newman, Sept. 23, 1964. Intern. USPHS Hosp., S.I., N.Y., 1961-62; resident in oral pathology Nat. Inst. Dental Research, NIH, Bethesda, Md., 1968-72, staff oral pathologist Lab. Oral Medicine, 1972-73, head oral pathology, 1973-74, exec. sec. oral biology and medicine study sect. div. research grants NIH, 1974—; vis. staff oral pathologist AFIP, Washington, 1970-73; clin. instr. pathology Sch. Georgetown U., 1970-75; clin. asso. prof. dept. pathology Uniformed Services U. Health Scis., Bethesda, Md., 1978—; cons. U.S. Naval Dental Center, Bethesda. Served with AUS, 1954-57, USPHS, 1961—. Diplomate Am. Bd. Oral Pathology. Fellow Am. Acad. Oral Pathology; mem. Am. Dental Assn., AAAS, Internat. Assn. Dental Research, Washington Soc. Pathologists, Internat. Assn. Pathology, Assn. Mil. Surgeons U.S., Commd. Officers Assn. USPHS, Phi Delta Kappa, Psi Omega. Mason. Author: (with John E. Horton and William F. Davis) Mechanisms of Localized Bone Loss; contbr. numerous articles to profl. publs. Home: 7115 Ridgewood Ave Chevy Chase MD 20015 Office: Westwood Bldg Nat Insts Health Bethesda MD 20014

TARR, CHARLES EDWIN, physicist, educator; b. Johnstown, Pa., Jan. 14, 1940; s. Charles Larned and Mary Catherine (Wright) T.; B.S. in Physics (Morehead scholar 1957-61), U. N.C., Chapel Hill, 1961, Ph.D., 1966; m. Bex Suzanne Harrell, Sept. 4, 1964 (div. Feb. 1977); m. 2d, Gudrun Kiefer, Nov. 18, 1977. Research asso. U. N.C., Chapel Hill, 1966, U. Pitts., 1966-68; mem. faculty U. Maine, Orono, 1968—, asso. prof. physics, 1973-78, prof., 1978—, chmn. dept., 1977—; gast docent U. Groningen (Netherlands), 1975-76; cons. in field. NASA grantee, 1970-72, NSF grantee, 1972—. Mem. AAAS, Am. Phys. Soc., AAUP, Am. Assn. Physics Tchrs., Sigma Xi. Quaker. Contbr. articles to profl. jours. Home: 519 College Ave Orono ME 04473 Office: Dept Physics Univ Maine Orono ME 04473

TARRANTS, WILLIAM EUGENE, govt. ofcl.; b. Liberty, Mo., Dec. 9, 1927; s. Joseph Eugene and Mildred Jane (Wright) T.; B.Indsl. Engring., Ohio State U., 1951, M.S., 1959; Ph.D., N.Y. U., 1963; m. Mary Jo Edman, Jan. 19, 1952; children—James Timothy, Jennifer Lynn. Instr. indsl. engring. Ohio State U., Columbus, 1958-59; asst. prof., research asso. N.Y. U., N.Y.C., 1959-64; chief accident research div. Bur. Labor Statistics, U.S. Dept. Labor, Washington, 1964-67; dir. manpower devel. div. Nat. Hwy. Traffic Safety Adminstrn., U.S. Dept. Transp., Washington, 1967—. Cons. safety program evaluation Indsl. Commn. Ohio, 1959; research asso. ops. research group Ohio State U., Columbus, 1958-59; guest lectr., instr. safety courses. Served with USAF, 1951-57. Registered profl. engr., Ohio, N.Mex., Calif. Fellow Am. Soc. Safety Engrs. (dir., v.p. research and tech. devel. 1968-72, 1st v.p. 1975-76, pres. 1977-78), mem. Am. Nat. Standards Inst. (standards com.), Am. Inst. Indsl. Engrs., System Safety Soc., Human Factors Soc., Vets. of Safety, Am. Soc. Safety Research (trustee 1972—), Indsl. Conf., Nat. Safety Council (chmn. research projects com. 1973—, exec. com. 1977—), AAAS. Mem. Evang. Covenant Ch. (chmn. 1976—). Author: A Selected Bibliography of Reference Materials in Safety Engineering and Related Fields, 1967; Dictionary of Terms Used in the Safety Profession, 1971; Selected Readings in Safety, 1973; The Evaluation of Safety Program Effectiveness, 1978; Measurement of Safety Performance, 1978. Mem. editorial adv. bd. Accident Analysis and Prevention 1969—; bd. cons. editors Behavioral Research in Traffic Safety, 1970—; editorial bd. Jour. Safety Research, 1974—. Contbr. articles to profl. jours. Home: 12134 Long Ridge Ln Bowie MD 20715 Office: 400 7th St SW Washington DC 20590

TARSOLY, BALAZS KOLOZSVARY, air motor and tool mfg. co. exec.; b. Komadi, Bihar, Hungary, Aug. 2, 1923; s. Balazs K. and Irma K. (Bujdoso) T.; came to U.S., 1956, naturalized, 1962; 1 son, Huba Peter. Owner, mgr. Balazs K. Tarsoly Exptl. Shop, Amityville, N.Y., 1962—; owner, mgr. K. Tarsoly Machine Shop for Prodn. & Exptl. Work, Amityville, N.Y., 1971—; cons. Mem. Am. Def. Preparedness Assn., Am. Soc. Metals, Soc. Broadcast Engrs. Republican. Home: 52 Maple Place Amityville NY 11701

TASHJIAN, AETNA MYRON, electronic co. exec.; b. Watertown, Mass., Sept. 28, 1932; s. Eknadeos and Sara (Lokantajian) T.; student Northeastern U., 1956-58; m. Araksie Kalajian, Oct. 31, 1954; children—Stephen, Gary, Roxanne. With Radio Corp. of Am., Burlington, Mass., 1956-67; project engr. Raytheon, Lexington, Mass., 1968—, project mgr. space radar, 1968-70, program mgr. air traffic control precision approach radars, 1970—. Served with USAF, 1952-56. Mem. U.S. Air Force Assn. Mem. Armenian Apostolic Ch. Club: Ch. Men's. Home: 11 Clemmons St Southboro MA 01772 Office: Boston Post Rd Wayland MA 01778

TASMAN, WILLIAM SAMUEL, ophthalmologist; b. Phila., Aug. 9, 1929; s. Isaac Samuel and Selma (Stern) T.; B.A., Haverford Coll., 1951; M.D., Temple U., 1955; postgrad. U. Pa., 1956-57; m. Alice Lea Mast, Mar. 31, 1962; children—Jamie, Alice and Graham (twins). Intern, Phila. Gen. Hosp., 1955-56; resident Wills Eye Hosp., Phila., 1959-61; asso. prof. Temple U. Health Scis. Center, Phila., 1966-71; asso. surgeon Retina Service, Wills Eye Hosp., Phila., 1962-74, attending surgeon, 1974—; prof. ophthalmology Thomas Jefferson U., Phila., 1974—; practice medicine specializing in ophthlamology, Phila., 1962—; attending surgeon Chestnut Hill Hosp., Phila., 1965—; asso. surgeon in ophthalmology Children's Hosp. of Phila., 1976—; co-dir. Retina Service, Wills Eye Hosp., 1976—. Fund raiser, Retina Research and Devel. Found., 1968-75. Served with USAF, 1957-59. Recipient Zentmayer award, ACP, 1970; Honor award, Am. Acad. Ophthalmologists and Otolaryngologists, 1974; Billings Gold Medal award, Am. Med. Assn., 1976; NIH grantee, 1972—. Mem. ACS, Am. Med. Assn., Phila. Retina Soc., Jules Gonin Retina Soc., Am. Acad. Ophthalmology and Otolaryngology, Pan Am. Assn. Ophthalmology, Pa. Acad. Ophthalmology and Otolaryngology, Am. Ophthalmological Soc., Phila. Mus. Art. Presbyterian. Clubs: Phila. Cricket, Haverford. Contbr. articles in field to profl. jours.; author: Retinal Diseases in Children, 1971; Diseases of the Peripheral Retina, 1979; editorial bd. Jour. Survery of Ophthalmology, 1971—, Am. Med. Assn. Archives of Ophthalmology, 1972-76. Home: 8500 Ardmore Ave Philadelphia PA 19118 Office: 187 E Evergreen Ave Philadelphia PA 19118

TASSIE, DOUGLAS PRAY, machine designer; b. Mt. Lake Park, Md., Dec. 31, 1925; s. Robert Clifford and Beatrice Leola (Bridge) T.; student Wentworth Inst., 1946-48; m. Allison Peabody, Aug. 24, 1956; children—Holt Clifford, Leola Ruby. Engring. draftsman Sutorbilt Corp., Los Angeles, 1950-51; engring. designer Gen. Electric Co., Burlington, Vt., 1951—, advance design specialist, 1971—. Mem. Bd. Selectman, St. George, Vt., 1962-70; mem. Sch. Bd. St. George, 1970-78. Recipient Managerial award Gen. Electirc Co., 1974. Mem. Am. Def. Preparedness Assn. Republican. Mem. Ch. Nazarene. Patentee in mechanism design and automatic gun armament systems. Home: St George RFD Williston VT 05495 Office: General Electric Co Lakeside Ave Burlington VT 05401

TASSINARI, SILVIO JOHN, nuclear chemist; b. N.Y.C., June 2, 1922; s. Ceasar and Adrean (Bacchiani) T.; B.S., St. Michael's Coll., 1943, M.S., 1947; Ph.D., Internat. U., 1949; m. Lorraine I. Murtha, Oct. 18, 1952; children—Patricia Jeanne, Barbara Lynne. Nuclear chemist Brookhaven Nat. Lab., Upton, N.Y., 1951-71, radiation safety officer and health physicist, 1952; nuclear chemist, tech. dir. nuclear medicine VA Hosp., Bklyn., 1971-72; nuclear chemist Sch. Nuclear Med. Tech., VA Hosp., Northport, N.Y., 1972—; cons. nuclear medicine Catholic Med. Center, Bklyn. and Queens, N.Y., C.W.Post Coll., Brookville, N.Y., John F. Kennedy Med. Center, Sch. Nuclear Med. Tech., Edison, N.J. Vice pres. Smithtown Central Sch. Dist. Bd. Edn., 1954-67. Served with USNR, 1942-45, USNR, 1966-70. Fellow Am. Soc. Radiologic Technologists; mem. Soc. Nuclear Medicine, Am. Inst. Chemists, U.S.Naval Inst. Republican. Roman Catholic. Home: 47 Moriches Rd Nissequogue St James NY 11780 Office: Nuclear Med Service VA Hosp Northport NY 11768

TATEL, ALLAN BRUCE, accountant; b. Boston, Jan. 21, 1947; s. William and Phyllis (Swartz) T.; B.S. in Bus. Adminstrn., Northeastern U., 1969; M.B.A., Suffolk U., 1977; m. Rita Stokes, Nov. 4, 1973; children—Jeffrey Scott, Heather Lynn. Asst. to comptroller Northeastern U., Boston, 1968-69; sr. accountant Haskins & Sells, Boston, 1969-71; accounting mgr. Standex Internat. Corp., Andover, Mass., 1971-74; accounting mgr. M. Hoffman & Co., clothing mfr., Boston, 1974—. Notary pub., Mass. Mem. Nat. Assn. Accountants, Assn. M.B.A. Execs., Am. Accounting Assn., Am. Mgmt. Assn., Inst. Internal Auditors, Am. Taxation Assn. Club: K.P. Home: 10 Acorn Dr Randolph MA 02368 Office: 160 N Washington St Boston MA 02114

TATES, DONALD EUGENE, pub. relations cons.; b. Boston, Feb. 19, 1943; s. Horace E. and Jean Lev (Newbold) T.; student Chamberlayne Jr. Coll., Boston, 1961, Lee Inst., 1962, Northeastern U., 1968, Harvard, 1969, Dale Carnegie course, 1970, N.Y. State U. Sch. Continuing Edn., 1972. Staff liaison officer printing, pub. div. Avco Corp., Boston, 1967-69, sr. pub. relations rep. Lycoming div. (aerospace), Stratford, Conn., 1969-71; pub. relations cons. my Friend the Policeman, Inc., Boston, 1972-73; membership coordinator Nat. Assn. Minority Consultants and Urbanologists, Washington, 1973-74; pub. relations cons. in pvt. practice, Washington, 1974—. Licensed real estate broker. Mem. Pub. Relations Soc. Am., Direct Mktg. Club Washington. Club: Nat. Press. Address: 1234 Massachusetts Ave NW Washington DC 20005

TATOSSIAN, ARMAND, painter; b. Alexandria, Egypt; Sept. 26, 1948; s. Charles Garo and Annie T.; came to Can., 1961, naturalized, 1968; student McGill U., 1967-69, J. Majzner, Montreal, Can., 1966-67, Adam Sherriff Scott, Montreal, 1967-72, Cararra Acad., Bergamo, Italy, 1970. One man shows: Double Take Art Gallery, N.Y.C., 1968, Galerie Gauvreau, Montreal, 1968, 70, 71, Molesworth Gallery, N.Y.C., 1969, Mt. Stephen Club, Montreal, 1972, Studio des artistes Canadiens, Inc., Quebec City, 1973, Galerie Bernard Desroches, Montreal, 1973, 75, Gallery St. Laurent, Ottawa, Ont., 1976, Nat. Gallery Armenia, Yerevan, U.S.S.R., 1976, A.GB.U. Gallery, N.Y.C., 1977, Dominion Corinth, Ottawa, 1978, Kaspar Gallery, Toronto, 1978; group shows include: Chakrian Gallery, N.Y.C., 1968, Galerie Gary Ustel, Toronto, 1970; represented in permanent collections: Canadian Foundry Supplier and Equipment Ltd., Montreal, Civitas Corp., Montreal, Concordia, U., Montreal, Crites and Riddell Ltd., Montreal, Lebanese Syrian Canadian Assn., Montreal, McGill U., Montreal Amateur Athletic, Mus. Fine Arts of Soviet Armenia, Musee de Quebec, Nat. Gallery Can., Royal Bank Can., Montreal, Univ. Club Montreal; prof. art Concordia U., from 1971; chmn. cultural com. Armenian Gen. Benevolent Union, Montreal, 1976-77. Mem. Royal Canadian Acad. Arts, Armenian Orthodox Clubs: Mt. Stephen (Montreal); Calgary Petroleum; Engrs. (Toronto), Los Angeles Athletic. Home: 4488 St Catherine W Penthouse 1 Montreal PQ Canada

TATSCH, JAMES HENDERSON, geologist, geophysicist; b. Eldorado, Tex., Dec. 7, 1916; s. Henry Charles and Ella Mae (Specht) T.; B.S., U.S. Naval Acad., 1940; postgrad U. Ariz., 1960-63; m. Helen Gailis, July 23, 1946; children—James Alexis Wolfgang, Karyn Jo. Sr. staff research scientist Collins Radio Co., Cedar Rapids, Ia., 1963-64; commd. 2d lt. U.S. Marine Corps, 1940, advanced through grades to lt. col., 1960; assignments include Quantico, 1941, Guadalcanal, 1942, Bougainville, 1943, Guam, 1944, Okinawa, 1945, Washington, 1948-52, Japan, 1955-56, Venezuela, 1959-60; ret., 1960; corp. engrng. scientist Ingersoll Milling Machine Co., Rockford, Ill., 1965-67; prin. engr. Raytheon Co., Sudbury, Mass., 1967-70; pres. Tatsch Assos., Sudbury, 1970—. Decorated Bronze Star. Mem. AAAS, British Assn. Advancement Sci., Am. Geophys. Union, Seismological Soc. Am., Geochemical Soc., Soc. Exploration Geophysicists, European Assn. Exploration Geophysicists, S.E. Asia Petroleum Exploration Soc., N.W. Mining Assn., Nuclear Research Council, Geotherm Research Council. Lutheran. Author: The Earth's Tectonosphere, 1972, 2d edit., 1977; Mineral Deposits, 1973; The Moon, 1974; Petroleum Deposits, 1974; Copper Deposits, 1975; Gold Deposits, 1975; Uranium Deposits, 1976; Geothermal Deposits, 1976; Earthquakes, 1977; Coal Deposits, 1979. Contbr. articles to profl. jours. Home and office: 120 Thunder Rd Sudbury MA 01776

TATTERSON, BENJAMIN FRANKLIN, engrng. cons.; b. Reedy, W.Va., Aug. 18, 1913; s. Ora Monroe and Mattie May (Riddle) T.; A.B. in Edn., Glenville State Coll., 1936; M.S. in Chemistry, W.Va. U., 1940; m. Clerissa Ann Hathaway, Aug. 17, 1941; children—David F., Gary B. Tchr. chemistry and physics Roane County Schs., Spencer, W.Va., 1936-38; open hearth chemist Weirton Steel Co. (W.Va.), 1940-41; prof. chemistry Glenville (W.Va.) State Coll., 1941-42; chief field ops. engr. Koppers Co. Inc., Pitts., 1942-45, sr. project engr., 1950-74, ret., 1974, engrng. cons., 1974-77, sr. staff engr., 1977—; research fellow Mellon Inst. Indsl. Research, 1945-50. Charter mem. Pitts. Baptist Ch., deacon, trustee, tchr. men's Bible class, 1962-70. Mem. Am. Chem. Soc., Eastern States Blast Furnace and Coke Plant Assn., Phi Lambda Upsilon. Republican. Co-author: History and Genealogy of the Poling Family, 1978; patentee coal chem. processing. Home: 975 McNeilly Rd Pittsburgh PA 15226 Office: Koppers Bldg Pittsburgh PA 15219

TATTLE, ALAN MICHAEL, counselor, educator; b. Lynn, Mass., Jan. 30, 1937; s. Samuel and Esther (Marcus) T.; B.S. in Bus. Adminstrn., Boston U., 1958, Ed.M., 1959, postgrad.; postgrad. UCLA, Harvard U., U. S.C. Tchr. bus. Breed Jr. High Sch., Lynn, 1959-63; English High Sch., Lynn, 1963-69, guidance counselor, 1969—; data processing instr. North Shore Community Coll., Beverly, Mass., 1966-69; tchr. data processing Essex County (Mass.) Prison, 1969; sr. lectr. in data processing Northeastern U., 1977—; mem. adv. bd. Mass. State Bd. Edn., 1977—. Mem. of corp. United Way of Mass. Bay, 1977—; dist. chmn. Heart Fund, Lynn, 1959-60; mem. Lynn Zoning Bd. Appeals, 1977—; trustee Danvers State Hosp., 1977—. Gen. Electric Found. fellow, 1977. Mem. Am. Personnel and Guidance Assn., Mass. Sch. Counselors Assn., Lynn Adminstrs. Assn., Lynn Tchrs. Union (pres. 1970-72), Nat. Vocat. Guidance Assn., Data Processing Mgmt. Assn. (v.p. edn. 1967-69), Phi Delta Kappa, Delta Pi Epsilon. Home: 31 Basset St Lynn MA 01902 Office: 50 Goodridge St Lynn MA 01902

TATUM, GEORGE BISHOP, educator; b. Cleve., Aug. 1, 1917; s. Alfred Marion and Myra (Williams) T.; grad. Western Res. Acad., Hudson, Ohio; A.B., Princeton, 1940, M.F.A., 1947, Ph.D., 1949; m. Alma Standish Merry, May 1, 1942; children—Susan, John Richard, Daniel. Instr., Princeton, 1947; asst. prof. history art, vice dean Sch. Fine Arts, U. Pa., 1948-53, asso. prof., chmn. dept. history of art, 1954-58, prof. history of art, 1962-67; H. Rodney Sharp prof. history of art U. Del., Newark, 1967-78. Research asso. Henry Francis du Pont Winterthur Mus., 1965-78; sr. fellow history of landscape architecture Dumbarton Oaks, 1967-68. Adv. bd. Historic Am. Bldgs. Survey, Nat. Park Service, 1966-72, chmn. 1969-71; mem. Old Lyme Hist. Dist. Commn., 1978—; mem. New Castle County (Del.) Beautification Bd., 1970-78; mem. Nat. Collection Fine Arts Commn., Smithsonian Instn., 1971—, chmn., 1976—; trustee Connecticut River Found., 1978—, Lyme Acad. Fine Arts, 1978—. Served to capt. USAAF, 1942-46. Fellow Royal Soc. Arts; mem. Coll. Art Assn., Soc. Archtl. Historians (pres. 1966-68), Am. Soc. Eighteenth Century Studies, Am. Studies Assn., AIA (hon.), Victorian Soc. Am. (dir. 1968-71, v.p. 1971-74), Old Lyme Hist. Soc. (trustee 1970-76, pres. 1978—), Phila. Soc. Preservation Landmarks (dir. 1963-76), Phi Beta Kappa, Tau Sigma Delta (hon.), Phi Kappa Phi (hon.). Author: (with others) Philadelphia Architecture in the Nineteenth Century, 1953; (with Alfred H. Bill) A House Called Morven, 1954; Penn's Great Town: Two Hundred Fifty Years of Philadelphia Architecture in Prints and Drawings, 1961; (with others) The Arts in America: The Colonial Period, 1966; Philadelphia Georgian, 1976; also articles in field. Home: Academy Ln Old Lyme CT 06371

TAUB, EDWARD, psychologist; b. Bklyn., Oct. 22, 1931; s. Samuel Hart and Ida (Kimmel) T.; B.A., Bklyn. Coll., 1953; M.A., Columbia U., 1959; Ph.D., N.Y. U., 1970; m. Mildred Ann Reynolds, Aug. 13, 1959. Research asst. psychology Columbia, N.Y.C., 1956; research asst. neuropsychology dept. exptl. neurology Jewish Chronic Disease Hosp., Bklyn., 1957-60, research asso., 1960-68; chief behavioral biology center Inst. for Behavioral Research, Silver Spring, Md., 1968—; asst. prof. Sch. Medicine, John Hopkins, Balt., 1970—. Dept. Def. grantee, 1966-75, NIH grantee, 1970—. Fellow Am. Psychol. Assn.; mem. Soc. Neurosci., Biofeedback Research Soc. (exec. bd.), Psychonomic Soc., Am. Physiol. Soc., Soc. for Psychophysiol. Research, AAAS, Eastern Psychol. Assn., Sigma Xi, Psi Chi. Editorial bd. Biofeedback and Self-Regulation, 1975—; contbr. numerous articles to profl. jours. Home: 1812 Metzerott Rd Adelphi MD 20783 Office: Inst for Behavioral Research 2429 Linden Ln Silver Spring MD 20910

TAUB, JESSE, oil co. exec.; b. Bronx, N.Y., July 25, 1927; s. Saul and Rae (Weinstock) T.; B.S., Bradley U., 1950; m. Shirley Jane Rippen, Aug. 3, 1952; children—Robert Michael, Cathy Ellen. Account supr. firm Harshe Rotman, N.Y.C., 1951-58; acct. supr. firm Fred Rosen Assos., N.Y.C., 1958-61; with firm John DeNigris Assos., N.Y.C., 1961—, account supr., 1970-71, v.p., dir. 1971-75; dir. advt. and pub. relations Shaheen Natural Resources Co., Inc., N.Y.C., 1975-76, v.p., 1976—; v.p., dir. MacMillan Ring-Free Oil Co., Inc., 1976—; dir. Precision Polymers Inc., Mountainside, N.J., Precision ThermoPlastics Inc., Charlotte, N.C., Derby Plastics Inc., Temple, Tex. Mem. pub. relations adv. com. N.Y. council Boy Scouts Am., 1966-68; press aide to pres. N.J. State Senate, 1966-68. Chmn. pub. relations Middlesex County Democratic Orgn., 1966-70. Served with USNR, 1942-45. Home: 10 Colonial Ct Edison NJ 08817 Office: 90 Park Ave New York City NY 10016

TAUB, STEVEN IRWIN, chem. engr.; b. N.Y.C., Oct. 7, 1942; s. Joseph and Reah (Gunspan) T.; B. Engrng., City Coll. City U. N.Y., 1965; M.S., Newark Coll. Engrng., 1967; Ph.D., Carnegie Mellon U., 1971; m. Hilary Anne Kurzweil, Nov. 1, 1970; 1 son, Lowell Matthew. Process engr. Airco Inc., Middlesex, N.J., 1965-67; NASA trainee, Bur. of Mines fellow, Carnegi Mellon U., Pitts., 1967-70; sr. engr. E. I. duPont De Nemours & Co., Inc., Wilmington, Del., 1970-74; dir. research and devel. I.U. Conversion Systems, Inc., Phila., 1974-78; v.p. process engrng. devel. Stablex Corp., Radnor, Pa., 1978—; lectr. Widener Coll., 1972—; Am. Inst. Chem. Engrs. rep. to modify Del. Profl. Engrng. law, 1973-74. Mem. New Castle County 208 Commn., 1974-77. Registered profl. engr., Del., Pa. Mem. Am. Inst. Chem. Engrs., Nat. Soc. Profl. Engrs. Jewish. Contbr. articles to profl. jours.; patentee in field. Home: 2409 Allendale Rd Wilmington DE 19803 Office: Two Radnor Corporate Center Radnor PA 19087

TAUBER, GILBERT, environ. cons.; b. N.Y.C., Apr. 20, 1935; s. Joseph Harry and Frances (Lifschitz) T.; B.A., Coll. City N.Y., 1956; M.U.P., Hunter Coll., 1978; m. Susanne Weil, Dec. 25, 1960 (div. 1974); children—Sarah E., Katherine J. Publicity dir. Dover Publs., Inc., N.Y.C., 1958-59; asst. promotion dir. N.Y. Conv. and Visitors Bur., N.Y.C., 1960-65; pub. info. officer State of N.Y. Hudson River Valley Commn., Tarrytown, 1965-71; cons. N.Y. U. Inst. Environ. Medicine, 1971-76, Hudson River Mus., Yonkers, N.Y., 1974-76, Rockefeller Found., 1975, N.Y. State Dept. Environ. Conservation, 1976-77, Ecol. Analysts, Inc., 1976—; lectr. archtl. and historic walking tour program Mus. City N.Y., 1959-61; mem. N.Y. Gov.'s Com. for Earth Day, 1970; chmn. Hudson River study adv. com. N.Y. State Dept. Environ. Conservation, 1978—. Served as pub. info. specialist U.S. Army, 1957-58. Mem. Am. Inst. Planners, Hudson River Environ. Soc. (dir. 1978—), Hudson River Research Council, Westchester Recycling Conf. (program chmn. 1971). Author: (with Samuel Kaplan) The New York City Handbook, 1966, rev. edit., 1968; The Hudson River Tourway, 1977. Address: Gate Hill Rd Stony Point NY 10980

TAUBKIN, IRVIN S., pub. relations cons.; b. N.Y.C., Nov. 14, 1906; s. William and Fannie (Stern) T.; student U. Wis., 1923-24, N.Y. U., 1924-26; m. Kiyoko Tsuboi, Aug. 11, 1964. Reporter, Dallas Morning News, 1928-34; correspondent Tex., N.Y. Times, 1928-34, copywriter, asst. promotion mgr., 1934-43; promotion dir. Bur. Advt., Am. Newspaper Pub. Assn., 1945-47; with N.Y. Times, 1947—, gen. mgr. Internat. Edition, Paris, 1960-61, promotion dir., 1961-69, pub. relations dir., 1969-71; partner Goldstein & Taubkin, Pub. Relations, N.Y.C., 1971—. Served with AUS, 1943-45. Mem. Internat. Newspaper Promotion Assn. (past pres.), Pub. Relations Soc. Am. Republican. Clubs: Nat. Press, Overseas Press, N.Y. Press. Home: 180 West End Ave New York City NY 10023 Office: 260 Madison Ave New York City NY 10016

TAUBMAN, HERBERT, orthodontist; b. N.Y.C., Mar. 31, 1925; s. Harry and Celia (Helfman) T.; D.D.S., U. Pa., 1947; certificate orthodontics N.Y. U., 1961; B.A., Hofstra U., 1968; m. Lenore Kopf, Oct. 29, 1949; children—Arthur, Leslie, Lowell. Practice dentistry ltd. to orthodontics, Valley Stream, N.Y., 1955—; chief orthodontics Maimonides Med. Center, Bklyn. mem. staff LaGuardia Hosp., Forest Hills, N.Y. Instr. orthodontics N.Y. U. Dental Sch., N.Y.C., 1961-63. Served with AUS, 1943-44, Dental Corps, USNR, 1952-54. Diplomate Am. Bd. Orthodontics. Mem. Am. Assn. Orthodontists, European, N.Y. U. orthodontic socs., N.Y. State., 10th Dist., Rockaway (treas.) dental socs., Sigma Epsilon Delta. Mason. Home: 1349 W Boxwood Dr Hewlett Harbor NY 11557 Office: 258 Munro Blvd Valley Stream NY 11581

TAUBMAN, JOSEPH, lawyer, author, editor; b. N.Y.C., Dec. 1, 1918; s. Max and Yetta (Shubert) T.; B.A., Cornell U., 1940, LL.B., 1942; LL.M. in Taxation, N.Y.U., 1952, J.S.D., 1955; m. Lillian Newman, June 12, 1943; children—Daniel, Fred, Susan. Admitted to N.Y. State bar, 1943; asso. firm Wolfson, Caton & Moguel, N.Y.C., 1946-51; practiced in N.Y.C., 1951-55, 70-75; house counsel Columbia Pictures, N.Y.C., 1956-65; asso. firm Rubin, Wachtel, Baum & Levin, N.Y.C., 1965-70; partner firm Feig & Taubman, N.Y.C., 1975—; v.p., sr. editor Law-Arts Publishers, N.Y.C., 1969—; lectr. State U.N.Y. Binghamton, 1975—, New Sch., N.Y.C., 1977—; chmn. bd. Am. Inst. Performing and Fine Arts Mgmt., Inc., N.Y.C., 1974—; v.p., trustee, counsel Com. to Combat Huntington's Disease, Inc., N.Y.C., 1970—. Served with U.S. Army, 1943-46. Mem. Am. Bar Assn., Assn. Bar City N.Y., N.Y. County Lawyers Assn., Fed. Bar Council, Copyright Soc. USA, Authors Guild, P.E.N. Am. Center, N.Y. State Bar Assn., Phi Beta Kappa. Author: Performing Arts Management and Law, 1972—; Joint Venture and Tax Classification, 1957; Copyright and Antitrust, 1960; Separate Stations, 1963, Editor: Financing a Theatrical Production, 1964; The Business and Law of Music, 1965; Subsidiary Rights and Residuals, 1968 Creative Intention, 1974; Professional Sports and the Law, 1977; Sleepwalking Nights by August Strindberg (trans. Arvid Paulson); founder, editor profl. quar. Performing Arts Review, 1969—; editor Antitrust Bulletin, 1961-66. Home: 159 W 53d St New York City NY 10019 Office: 159 W 53d St Suite 14F New York City NY 10019

TAVES, CAROLINE DILGARD, guidance counselor; b. Omaha, Aug. 14, 1915; d. Henry J. and Carrie Ellen (Davis) Dilgard; A.A., Bethel Jr. Coll., 1941; B.A., Hamline U., 1943; M.A., U. Minn., 1959; postgrad. Johns Hopkins U., 1969; m. Marvin J. Taves, Dec. 25, 1942 (div. Apr. 1976); children—John, Peter. Tchr. Minn. high schs., 1941-43; social worker State of Minn., 1943-45; mem. staff U. Minn., 1956-62; counselor, Roseville, Minn., 1959-62, Arlington, Va., 1962-63; social work adminstr., Alexandria, Va., 1966-67; counselor Southwestern High Sch., Balt., 1967—. Vol. polit. worker, fundraiser for charities. Recipient award for excellence in history DAR, 1932. Mem. Am. Personnel and Guidance Assn., Nat. Vocat. Guidance Assn., Kappa Delta Epsilon, Pi Gamma Mu, Alpha Kappa Delta. Democrat. Presbyterian. Home: 8779 Oxwell Ln Laurel MD 20811 Office: Southwestern High Sch 200 Font Hill Ave Baltimore MD 21223

TAVES, ERNEST HENRY, psychiatrist, psychoanalyst; b. Aberdeen, Idaho, Feb. 1, 1916; s. Henry C. and Louisa (Hardy) T.; A.B., Columbia, 1937, M.A., 1938, Ph.D., 1941; postgrad. (Hodgson fellow) Harvard, 1939-40; M.D., N.Y.U., 1945; m. Judith Brasher de Forest, July 29, 1949; 1 son, Henry. Intern, Bellevue Hosp., N.Y.C., 1945-46, resident, 1948-51; practice medicine specializing in psychiatry and psychoanalysis, N.Y.C., 1950-53, Cambridge, Mass., 1954—; co-founder, pres. Directions Inc., Cambridge, 1967—. Mem. vis. com. dept. astronomy Harvard, 1976—; sci. cons. Com. for Sci. Investigation of Claims of Paranormal, 1978—. Served with M.C., U.S. Army, 1947-48. Diplomate Am. Bd. Psychiatry and Mem. Sci. Fiction Writers Am., Sigma Psi, Sigma Delta Chi. Clubs: Dublin (N.H.) Lake, St. Botolph, Port Royal. Author: (with Donald H. Menzel) The UFO Enigma, 1977. Contbr. numerous short stories to popular mags., including Playboy, Galaxy, Worlds of If. Home and Office: 12 Hubbard Park Cambridge MA 02138

TAVITIAN, HENRY OHANES, psychiatrist; b. Sofia, Bulgaria, Mar. 13, 1934; M.D. with highest honors, Higher Inst. Medicine, 1960. Intern, Flushing (N.Y.) Hosp. and Dispensary, 1963-64; resident in psychiatry Manhattan Psychiat. Center, Ward's Island, N.Y., Columbia U.-N.Y. State Psychiat. Inst., 1964-65, Downey (Ill.) VA Hosp.-Northwestern U., 1965-67; clin. asst. psychiatry Northwestern U., Chgo., 1967; sect. chief psychiatry service, later dir. and chief in-patient unit, substance abuse program psychiatry outpatient clinic and consultation service Bronx (N.Y.) VA Hosp., 1968—; asst. prof. clin. psychiatry Mt. Sinai Sch. Medicine and sr. lectr. N.Y. Sch. Psychiatry, Ward's Island, N.Y., 1973—; practice medicine, specializing in psychiatry, Bronx, 1968—; lectr. in field. Diplomate Am. Bd. Psychiatry and Neurology. Fellow Am. Psychiat. Assn.; mem. AMA (Physician's Recognition award 1969, 75), Am. Ontoanalytic Assn., Bronx Soc. Neurology and Psychiatry (pres. 1975—). Contbg. author Progress in Neurology and Psychiatry, 1966-68. Home: 90-45 56th Ave Elmhurst NY 11373 Office: VA Hosp 130 W Kingsbridge Rd Bronx NY 10468

TAVOULAREAS, WILLIAM PETER, oil co. exec.; b. Bklyn., Nov. 9, 1919; s. Peter William and Mary (Palisi) T.; B.B.A., St. John's U., 1941, J.D., 1948; m. Adele Maciejewska, Aug. 13, 1941; children—Peter, Patrice, William. Admitted to N.Y. bar, 1948; with Mobil Oil Corp. 1947—, v.p. plans and programs Mobil Internat. Oil Co., 1961-63, v.p. charge supply and distbn. and internat. sales parent co., 1963-65, sr. v.p., dir., mem. exec. com., 1965-67, v.p. charge supply, transport and Middle East and Indonesian affairs, pres. N. Am. div., 1967-69, corp. pres., 1969—, vice chmn. exec. com., dir.; dir. Gen. Foods Corp., Bankers Trust Co., Bankers Trust N.Y. Corp. Trustee St. John's U., Athens Coll., St. Paul's Sch.; bd. govs. N.Y. Hosp.; bd. dirs. Near East Coll. Assn. Served with U.S. Army, World War II. Mem. Harbor Acres Assn., Beta Gamma Sigma. Knights of Malta. Clubs: Pinnacle, North Hempstead Country. Office: 150 E 42d St New York City NY 10017

TAWIL, JOSEPH, archbishop, Greek Cath. Ch.; b. Dec. 25, 1913. Ordained priest Greek Catholic Ch., 1936; consecrated archbishop of Myra in Lycia, 1960; exarch for Melkites in U.S., 1970-76; eparch of Melkite, Diocese of Newton, 1976—. Address: 19 Dartmouth St West Newton MA 02165

TAYLOR, ALAN JAMES, publisher, film producer; b. Milo, Maine, Sept. 24, 1949; s. James Stanley and Genieve (Olson) T.; grad. Broadcasting Radio and TV Acad., 1968. Pres. Classic Film Mus. Inc., Dover-Foxcroft, Maine, 1973—, Classic Internat. TV Co., 1973—; tchr. Career Acad., Boston, 1969; staff announcer Eternal Word radio program, 1976—; distbr. Ray Harryhausen Fantasy Collection; host TV series Classic Showcase, 1969, Science-Fiction Fantastic, 1974; mgr. Sta. WTOS/WSKW, 1978—. Mem. Writers Guild Am. East, Dover-Foxcroft Jaycees (award 1974). Democrat. Baptist. Club: Kiwanis. Author: How to Make a Monster, make-up and costume guide, 1976; A Film Portfolio of Sherlock Holmes, 1976; A Film Portfolio of Shirley Temple, 1976; (with Mrs. Sue Roy) Behind-The-Scenes in Motion Pictures: Make-Up and Effects, 1978; contbr. articles to Starlog/Future mag.; recorded Hot Child in the City (gold record). Developer format Earth. Address: Taylor Film Prodns Ltd 1/3 Union St Dover-Foxcroft ME 04426

TAYLOR, BARBARA JO ANNE HARRIS, civic and polit. worker; b. Providence, Sept. 9, 1936; d. Ross Cameron and Anita (Coia) Harris; student Tex. Christian U., 1952, Salve Regina Coll., 1952-53, Our Lady of the Lake Coll. and Convent, 1953-54, St. Mary's U., summer 1954, Incarnate Word Coll., 1954-55; B.S. cum laude, Georgetown U., 1963; m. Richard Powell Taylor, Dec. 19, 1959; 1 son, Douglas Howard. Adminstrv. asst. profl. devel. and welfare NEA, Washington, 1956-59; asst. to dir. Georgetown U., Washington, 1956-59; exec. asst. All Am. Conf. to Combat Communism, Washington, 1960; Spl. legis. asst. mil. affairs to chmn. mil. research and devel. subcom. U.S. Senate Armed Services Com., 1971-72. Mem. exec. bd. Salvation Army Aux., D.C., 1967—, chmn. membership com., 1969-70, co-chmn., 1970-72, chmn. fund-raising com., 1968-69, co-chmn., 1971-72, 73-74, mem. exec. com. of exec. bd., 1970—, treas., mem. fin. com., 1970-71, v.p., 1971-72, historian, 1972—, editor Our Watchword Newsletter, 1968-69, chmn. nominating com., 1974-75, spl. awards for exceptional vol. service, 1969, 72; mem. exec. bd. Welcome to Washington Internat., 1969—, bd. advisers, 1969—, dir. workshop, 1969—; exec. bd. Am. Opera Sch. Soc., Washington, 1970—, v.p., 1974—; Episcopal Ch. Home for Aged Women's Aux., 1970—, Episc. Center for Emotionally Disturbed Children Women's Aux., 1970—; exec. bd. St. David's Episc. Ch. Aux., 1970-72, 73-74, v.p., 1970-72, 73-74, chmn. program com., 1970-72, 73-74; bd. dirs., treas. Spanish-Portuguese Study Group, 1970-72; mem. exec. bd. League Republican Women D.C., 1964-67, 75—, treas., 1964-67; mem. nat. council Women's Nat. Rep. Club, N.Y.C., 1969—, chmn. Washington-Md.-Va. legis. com., 1970-75, co-chmn. ann. conf., 1971, 74; mem. Nat. Fedn. Rep. Women, 1964—; mem. governing bd. Capital Speakers Club, 1973—, chmn. by-laws com., 1973-74; mem. exec. bd. Nat. Vols. in Action, 1975—. Mem. Internat. Platform Assn., Spanish-Portuguese Study Group, Nat. Lawyers Wives, Lawyers Wives D.C., DAR (nat. vice chmn. nat. bd. 1977—, nat. vice chmn. meml. service com. 1977—, mem. nat. resolutions com. 1977—, (nat. vice chmn. nat. bd. 1977—, nat. vice chmn. meml. service com. 1977—, mem. nat. resolutions com. 1977—, nat. vice chmn. mus. docent com. 1974-77, del. congress 1973—; state historian 1978—, mem. state bd. mgmt. 1973—, mem. exec. com. 1978—; numerous other offices), Nat. Soc. Children Am. Revolution (sr. nat. asst. registrar 1978—, mem. sr. nat. bd. mgmt. 1978—, sr. nat. exec. com. 1978—). Clubs: Internat., Capitol Hill, Washington (internat. com. 1971-75); Congressional Country (Potomac, Md.). Home: 8801 Belmart Rd Potomac MD 20854

TAYLOR, BERNARD FRANKLIN, virologist, educator; b. Charles Town, W.Va., Mar. 21, 1930; s. Beverly Douglas and Harriet Elizabeth (Dotson) T.; B.S. in Biology cum laude, Storer Coll., Harpers Ferry, W.Va., 1952; M.S. in Microbiology and Pub. Health, Mich. State U., 1959; Ph.D. in Microbiology, Rutgers U., 1972; M.A. in Adminstrn., Rider Coll.; m. Sylvia A. Spriggs Jan. 28, 1957; children—Bernard F., Michael L. Bacteriologist, Bur. Virology, Mich. Dept. Health, Lansing, 1954-56, virologist, acting chief bur., 1956-59; sci. inst., asst. football coach Elizabeth City (N.C.) State Tchrs. Coll., 1959-60; virologist div. labs. and epidemiology N.J. Dept. Health, Trenton, 1960-61, sr. virologist, 1961-62; prin. virologist, 1962-67, chief virologist, 1967—; co-adj. prof. biology Trenton State Coll., 1972—. Campaign chmn. United Way, 1973; mem. Mercer County (N.J.) Juvenile Conf. Com. Served with airborne inf. U.S. Army, 1946-49. Mem. Am. Soc. Microbiologists, Am. Acad. Microbiology, Nat. Registry Microbiologists, Theodbald Smith Soc., Nat. Found. Infectious Diseases, Sigma Xi, Beta Kappa Chi, Alpha Phi Alpha. Democrat. Club: Mason. Author publs. in field. Home: 438 Walnut Ave Trenton NJ 08609 Office: PO Box 1540 Trenton NJ 08625

TAYLOR, BERNARD UNDERHILL, singer, voice tchr.; b. Olean, N.Y., Jan. 8, 1897; s. Benjamin Underhill and Harriet (McFarland) T.; student Columbia Tchrs. Coll., 1931-33; pvt. study music in Europe; m. Jeannette Hayes, Oct. 13, 1919; 1 dau., Jean Anne. Founder pres. Ft. Worth Conservatory Music, 1919-29; mem. vocal faculty Juillard Sch. Music, N.Y.C., 1932-53; pvt. tchr. singing, N.Y.C., 1953—; tchr. vocal master classes and clinics in schs. and univs.; editor, classic Italian songs, and German art songs, oratorio arias; editor vocal albums. Served with U.S. Army, 1917-19. Decorated Croix de Guerre (France). Mem. Am. Acad. Tchrs. Singing, Nat. Assn. Tchrs. Singing (founder, pres.), N.Y. Singing Assn. (Pres.). Republican. Home: 464 Riverside Dr New York City NY 10027

TAYLOR, DONALD SHERMAN, engrng. exec.; b. Berkeley, Calif., Mar. 7, 1932; s. David Guernsey and Dolores Antoinette (Sherman) T.; B.S. in Engrng., U. Calif., Berkeley, 1953; postgrad. George Washington U., 1961-63; m. Betty Jean Austin, Feb. 2, 1957; children—Diana Gail, Donald Sherman, Dewayne Austin. Indsl.

engr. Colgate-Palmolive Co., Berkeley, 1958-61; engring. mgr. Naval Ordnance Sta., Indian Head, Md., 1961—, head engring. dept., 1975—. Pres. PTA, Murray Hill Citizens Assn; active Boy Scouts Am., Cub Scouts; bd. dirs. Prince Georges County Assn. Retarded Citizens. Served to comdr. USNR, 1953-58, now Res. Nominee William A. Jump award U.S. Navy, 1967; hon. life mem. PTA, 1973. Mem. Armed Forces Mgmt. Assn., Am. Def. Preparedness Assn., Naval Res. Assn., Am. Inst. Indsl. Engrs. Republican. Home: 8135 Murray Hill Dr Oxon Hill MD 20022 Office: Naval Ordnance Station Indian Head MD 20640

TAYLOR, ERVIN FRANCIS, med. instrument mfg. co. exec.; b. Chillicothe, Ohio, Aug. 6, 1926; s. Francis Pittenger and Mary Eliza (Ingmire) T.; B.A., Ohio State U., 1950; m. Pamala May Grunkemeyer, Nov. 1, 1952; children—Mark Waring, Michele Diane. Sr. quality engr. Westinghouse Electric Corp., Cheswick, Pa., 1956-58; quality control cons. Martin Marietta Co., Balt., 1958-62; product mgr. Gen. Electric Co., Milw., 1962-76; corp. dir. quality control Am. Cystoscope Makers, Inc., Stamford, Conn., 1976—; adj. prof. quality control U. Balt., Johns Hopkins U., Drexel U., West Conn. State Coll. Registered profl. engr. Fellow Am. Soc. Quality Control; mem. Assn. Advancement Med. Instrumentation, Regulatory Affairs Profls. Soc. Contbr. articles to profl. publs., editorials to Newsletter Biomed. Safety and Standards. Home: 310 Echo Valley Ln Newtown Square PA 19073 Office: 300 Stillwater Ave Stamford CT 06902

TAYLOR, FRANCIS CHARLES, librarian; b. Hartford, May 23, 1923; s. Charles Henry and Charlotte (Fitzgerald) T.; B.A., Franklin and Marshall Coll., 1947; B.S. in L.S., U. Ill., 1948, M.S. in L.S., 1949; m. Jane Carolyn Stevens, June 16, 1948; children—Elizabeth Louise, Lauri Anna. Head bus. and tech. dept. Wichita (Kan.) City Library, 1949-51; chief librarian Wichita div. Boeing Airplane Co., 1951-55; asst. librarian Providence Pub. Library, 1955-59, asso. librarian, 1960-61, librarian, 1968-78; ret., 1978; asso. librarian St. Louis Pub. Library, 1961-66, librarian, 1966-68; lectr. library sci. Univ. Coll., Washington U., St. Louis, 1962-67, U. R.I., 1973-74. Bd. dirs. Adult Edn. Council Greater St. Louis, 1964-67; trustee R.I. Sch. of Design, Providence, 1968—. Served with USNR, 1943-46. Mem. ALA, New Eng. (pres. 1971-72), R.I. library assns., Beta Phi Mu. Episcopalian. Home: 6 Elton Rd Barrington RI 02806

TAYLOR, FRANK LEONARD, health care mgmt. engr.; b. Lemoyne, Pa., July 1, 1925; s. Hugh A. and Florence J. T.; B.S., U.S. Mil. Acad., 1947; M.S., Ga. Inst. Tech., 1956; m. Susan Etter, June 8, 1947; children—Diane S., Frank D. Commd. 2d lt. U.S. Army, 1947, advanced through grades to col., 1971; test engr., Ft. Knox, Ky., 1956-59; ops. officer 14th Armored Cavalty Regt., Fulda, Ger., 1959-62; exec. Army Research & Devel. Pentagon, Washington, 1963-66, 67-70; comdr. Armored Cavalry Squadron, 7th Inf. Div., Korea, 1966-67; chief Combat Weapons Div., Ft. Belvior, Va., 1970-73, ret., 1973; sr. mgmt. cons. Princeton (N.J.) Hosp. Assn., 1973-75; dir. mgmt. engring. Harrisburg (Pa.) Hosp., 1975—. Army staff rep. Pres.'s Blue Ribbon Def. Panel. Decorated Legion of Merit with oak leaf cluster, Bronze Star; registered profl. engr., Pa. Mem. Am. Inst. Indsl. Engrs. (v.p. chpt.), Hosp. Mgmt. Systems Soc., Am. Hosp. Assn. Republican. Presbyterian. Clubs: Racquet, Allenberry. Home: RD 2 Oakhill Dr Boiling Springs PA 17007 Office: S Front St Harrisburg PA 17101

TAYLOR, GORDON STEVENS, plant pathologist; b. Danbury, Conn., Nov. 12, 1921; s. Ernest Leach and Mabel Florence (Taylor) T.; B.S. in Horticulture with high distinction, U. Conn., 1947; M.S. and Ph.D. in Phytopathology, Iowa State U., 1952; m. Elizabeth F. Campbell, July 30, 1946; 1 dau., Nancy Beth. Asst. plant pathologist Conn. Agrl. Expt. Sta., Windsor, 1952-53, chief agrl. scientist, 1960, asst. to dir. in charge Valley Lab., 1953—. Served as pilot USAAF, 1944-46. Decorated D.F.C., Air medal with oak leaf cluster; recipient Cigar Mfrs. award and plaque, 1969. Mem. Am. Phytopath. Soc., AAAS, Am. Inst. Biol. Sci., Air Pollution Control Assn. Congregationalist. Club: Windsor Civitan. Research on diseases of potatoes and tobacco. Home: 812 Matianuck Ave Windsor CT 06095 Office: PO Box 248 Windsor CT 06095

TAYLOR, HAROLD ALLEN, JR., mineral commodity analyst; b. San Jose, Calif., June 27, 1936; s. Harold Allen and Marie Anna (Briody) T.; B.A., Brown U., 1958; M.A., U. Minn., 1968; m. Theresa Josephine Kustritz, Aug. 29, 1963; children—Harold A., III, Ruth F., Jonathan L.E. Project leader office Mineral Supply, U.S. Bur. of Mines, Mpls., 1968-70, commodity specialist div. ferrous metals, Washington, 1970-74; commodity analyst U.S. Internat. Trade Commn., Washington, 1974—. Coordinator Emergency Furniture Bank, 1973-78; chmn. North Arlington Parish Council, 1976; precinct capt. Arlingtonians for a Better County, 1975, area chmn., 1976. Mem. Am. Inst. M.E., Am. Geog. Soc., World Future Soc., Toastmasters (sec. 1971, ednl. v.p. 1977, pres. 1978), Nova Catholic Community (sec. 1975), Sigma Gamma Epsilon. Contbr. articles to profl. jours. Home: 6321 N Eleventh Rd Arlington VA 22205 Office: US Internatl Trade Commn 8th and E Sts NW Washington DC 20436

TAYLOR, HARRY WINFIELD, obstetrician/gynecologist; b. Zanesville, Ohio, Dec. 10, 1921; s. Harry Winfield and Clara Naomi (Wymer) T.; B.A., Washington and Jefferson Coll., 1942; M.D., Temple U., 1945; m. Mary EllenWarren, Sept. 14, 1944; children—Pamela Lee, Wendy Lee, Alicia Marie. Intern, Phila. Gen. Hosp., 1945-46, resident in obstetrics/gynecology, 1949-52, attending physician, 1952-59, asst. dir., 1953-54; practice medicine specializing in obstetrics/gynecology, Pennsville, N.J., 1954—; attending staff Salem County (N.J.) Meml. Hosp., 1956—, chmn. dept. obstetrics and gynecology, 1956-70; attending staff Wilmington (Del.) Med. Center, 1959—; clin. asst. prof. Jefferson Med. Coll., Phila., 1952—. Served to capt. U.S. Army, 1946-48. Diplomate Am. Bd. Obstetrics and Gynecology. Mem. AMA, Salem County (pres. 1972-73), New Castle med. socs., Del., N.J., Phila. obstetrical socs., Am. Coll. Obstetrics and Gynecology. Republican. Quaker. Contbr. articles in obstetrics and gynecology to med. jours. Home: RFD 3 Box 234 Kings Hwy Woodstown NJ 08098 Office: Milltown Med Center 3101 Limestone Rd Wilmington DE 19808 also Cordrey Profl Bldg Carroll Ave Pennsville NJ 08070

TAYLOR, JAMES GORDEN, county adminstr.; b. Anderson, Ind., Mar. 31, 1946; s. Jack Leland and Norma Jane (Gill) T.; B.A., Cleve. State U., 1968; M.S., George Peabody Coll. Tchrs., 1977; m. Mary Elizabeth Buvalic, June 15, 1968; children—Heather Ann, Jason Joseph. Mmgt. trainee Montgomery Wards, Cuyahoga Falls, Ohio, 1968-69; staff tng. dir. Monmouth County (N.J.) Comprehensive Employment, Tng. Agy., 1977—. Served with USAF, 1969-77. Mem. Am. Personnel and Guidance Assn., Nat. Employment Counselors Assn., Nat. Vocat. Guidance Assn., Assn. Counselor Edn. and Supervision. Republican. Home: 1710 Fifth Ave Spring Lake NJ 07762 Office: 1929 Corlies Ave Neptune NJ 07753

TAYLOR, JEREMY, railroad exec.; b. Bklyn., Aug. 6, 1926; s. Winthrop and Nina Whelan (Brown) T.; B.A., Cornell U., 1949, LL.B., 1952; m. Jean Kathleen Weber, May 14, 1955; children—William W., Neal F., Kent L., Andrew C., Mary B., Gordon P., Jeremy. Trainee N.Y. Central R.R., N.Y.C., 1952-53, asst. supr. power and train operation, Indpls., 1953-55, transp. asst., 1955-56, asst. motive power controller, N.Y.C., 1956-58, asst. supr. system ops. bur., N.Y., 1958-60, supr., 1960-61, transp. engr., N.Y.C., 1962, asst. trainmaster, Toledo, 1962, terminal supt. E. St. Louis, Mo., 1963, transp. supt. Chgo., 1963-64, Buffalo, 1964-65, div. supt., 1965-66, dist. transp. supt., N.Y.C., 1966, Cleve., 1967, gen. mgr., Indpls., 1967-68; gen. mgr. Penn Central Transp. Co., Indpls., 1968, New Haven, 1969; v.p. ops. L.I. R.R., Jamaica, N.Y., 1969-77, ret.; dir. Indpls. Union R.R., 1967-68, Cin. Union Terminal Co., 1967-68, Dayton Union R.R., 1967-68, Terminal R.R. Assn. St. Louis, 1968—, Peoria and Pekin Union Union R.R., 1968—. Served with USMCR, 1944-46. Mem. Kappa Alpha, New York R.R. Club. Author: A Sampling of Penn Central, 1973; The Fifty Best of New York Central System, Book Three, 1978. Home: 11 Longwood Dr Huntington Station NY 11746

TAYLOR, JOHN LEWIS, clergyman; b. Venice, N.Y., Feb. 28, 1931; s. Leslie Gordon and Rachel Eleanor (Briggs) T.; student Bible and Theology Moody Bible Inst., 1964-70; m. Jane Marie Saville, Sept. 12, 1950; children—Neil G., John M., Daniel L., Jeffrey L., Jennie L. Truck driver, 1950-54; owner, operator trucking bus., Auburn, N.Y., 1954-58; youth worker, counselor Syracuse (N.Y.) Rescue Mission, 1959-63, counselor, 1971—; counselor Chgo. Christian Indsl. League, 1963-69; ordained to ministry Baptist Ch., 1971; pastor Burbank (Ill.) Bapt. Temple, 1965-71; asso. pastor 2d Bapt. Ch., Auburn, 1971-75, sr. pastor, 1975—; speaker Sta. WMHR-FM, Syracuse. Served with USN, 1949-50. Mem. Internat. Union Gospel Missions, Conservative Bapt. Assn. Am., Evang. Ch. Alliance, Fingerlakes CBA Fellowship (sec.-treas.). Home: Route 4 Franklin St Rd Auburn NY 13021 Office: 1 N Herman Ave Auburn NY 13021

TAYLOR, JOSHUA CHARLES, educator, art historian; b. Hillsboro, Oreg., Aug. 22, 1917; s. James Edmond and Anna L.M. (Scott) T.; student Mus. Art Sch., Portland, Oreg., 1935-39; B.A., Reed Coll., 1939, M.A., 1946; M.F.A., Princeton U., 1949, Ph.D., 1956. Designer for theatre, 1936-41, San Francisco Opera Ballet, 1936-37; Reed Coll., 1939-41; tchr. history art Princeton, 1948-49; faculty U. Chgo., 1949-74, chmn. 1st year program humanities in coll., 1954-58, William Rainey Harper prof. humanities, prof. history art, 1963-74; dir. Nat. Collection Fine Arts, Smithsonian Instn., 1970—; lectr. in U.S., also on TV, 1953—; lectr. Inst. Interuniversitario, Argentina, 1962; spl. research 19th and 20th century painting and artistic theory Italy, U.S. Mem. adv. com. 20th Century art Art Inst. Chgo.; bd. dirs. Am. Fedn. Arts, Mus. Contemporary Art, Chgo.; faculty adv. com. Ency. Brit.; mem. adv. bd. Lillie P. Bliss Internat. Study Center, Mus. Modern Art; council Archives Am. Art. Served to maj. inf. AUS, 1941-46; ETO. Fellow Royal Soc. Arts; mem. bd. Coll. Art Assn. Am., Internat. Inst. Conservation Historic and Artistic Works, Assn. Art Mus. Dirs., Am. Assn. Museums, Phi Beta Kappa. Author: William Page, The American Titian, 1957; Learning to Look, 1957; Futurism, 1961; Graphic Works of Umberto Boccioni, 1961; Vedere prima di credere, 1970; To See is to Think: Looking at American Art, 1975; also articles. Home: 1250 31st St NW Washington DC 20007 Office: Nat Collection Fine Arts 8th and G Sts NW Washington DC 20560

TAYLOR, LAWRENCE WILLIAM, JR., aero. engr.; b. Kansas City, Kans., Feb. 3, 1933; s. Lawrence W. and Eula Xarifa (Hill) T.; B.S., U. Kans., 1955; M.S., U. So. Calif., 1959, Engr., 1963; m. Mary Lee Mattingly, Dec. 18, 1971; children—Lawrence William III, David Kent, Lisa Kay. Research engr. Dryden Flight Research Center, NASA, 1955-70, research engr., project mgr. Langley Research Center, 1970-75, dep. dir. aeronautics Guidance, Control and Info. Systems, NASA Hdqrs., Washington, 1975—; pres. Investment Analysis Co., Alexandria, Va. Served with USAF, 1955-57. Recipient Spl. Achievement award NASA. Mem. Am. Inst. Aeros. and Astronautics (Outstanding Contbn. award), Tau Beta Pi, Sigma Gamma Tau. Contbr. articles to profl. jours. Home: 6519 Tower Dr Alexandria VA 22306 Office: 600 Independence Ave SW Washington DC 20541

TAYLOR, LISA SUTER, museum dir.; b. N.Y.C., Jan. 8, 1933; d. Theo and Martina (Weincerl) von Bergen-Maier; student Corcoran Sch. Art, 1958-65, Georgetown U., 1958-62, Johns Hopkins U., 1956-58; D.F.A. (hon.), Parsons Sch. Design, 1977; m. Bertrand L. Taylor, III, Oct. 30, 1968; children—Lauren, Lindsay. Adminstrv. asst. Pres.'s Fine Arts Com., 1958-62; membership dir. Corcoran Gallery of Art, 1962-66; program dir. Smithsonian Instn., Washington, 1966-69; dir. Cooper-Hewitt Mus. Decorative Arts and Design, Smithsonian Instn., N.Y.C., 1969—; mem. adv. bd. N.Y. State Assn. Museums, Center for Residential Space Design, Fashion Inst. Tech. N.Y., Center for Holographic Art. Mem. vis. com. Bank St. Coll. Recipient Exceptional Service award Smithsonian Instn., 1969, Gold medal, 1972, Thomas Jefferson award, 1976; Bronze Apple award Am. Soc. Indsl. Designers, 1977. Mem. Am., N.Y. State, N.Y.C. museum assns., Am. Craftsmans Council, Archtl. League, Ceramics Circle, Needle and Bobbin Club, Am. Soc. Interior Designers (hon.). Co-dir. film: A Living Museum, 1968. Office: 2 E 91st St New York NY 10028*

TAYLOR, PAUL HOWARD, educator, engr.; b. Chelsea, Mass., Aug. 29, 1916; s. George F. C. and Georganna G. (Pike) T.; B.S., N.C. State U., 1941; M.S. in Regional Planning, U. Mass., 1973; postgrad. Columbia U., 19—; m. Mildred Mundy, Oct. 4, 194; children—Nancy D. Taylor Harrow, Paul H., William M., Mildred E. With N.Y.C. Govt., 1943-66; mgr. loss prevention, naval reactors div. Combustion Engring. Co., Windsor, Conn., 1966-68; dir. corporate security United Nuclear Corp., New Haven, 1968-69; exec. v.p. ARMSAC, Wethersfield, Conn., 1969-72; pres. Paul H. Taylor Assos., Longmeadow, Mass., 1972—; tchr. evening div. Springfield (Mass.) Tech. Community Coll., 1975—. Decorated Order of Merit (Italy). Mem. Am. Soc. Safety Engrs. (past pres. Connecticut Valley chpt.), Am. Soc. Indsl. Security (past chmn. Conn. chpt.), Sons of Norway. Home and Office: 93 Edgewood Ave Longmeadow MA 01106

TAYLOR, PHILIP LAWRENCE, psychologist; b. Boston, Sept. 18, 1944; s. Philip Sellew and Iris Elizabeth (Lowe) T.; A.B., Harvard U., 1966; M.A., N.Y. U., 1971, Ph.D., 1975; m. Francine Zuzzolo, Dec. 15, 1973. Dir. research N.Y. Community Tng. Inst., Inc., N.Y.C., 1970-72; dir. criminology City U. N.Y., 1972-73; research and cons. psychologist, Lancaster, Pa., 1974—; prof. psychology Capitol Campus of Pa. State U., Middletown, 1974—; research cons. Allegheny County Cts., Gov.'s Justice Commn. Pa. Bd. dirs. early intervention program Holy Spirit Hosp., Camp Hill, Pa., chmn., 1977; adv. bd. Women in Crisis, Inc. (Harrisburg, Pa.). NIMH fellow, 1966-70; USPHS fellow, 1978; licensed psychologist, Pa. Mem. Am., Pa. (exec. com., pres. community psychology div.) psychol. assns. Democrat. Unitarian. Club: Golden Meadow. Contbr. articles to profl. jours. and book. Home: 157 Hamilton Rd Lancaster PA 17603 Office: Captiol Campus Pa State U Middletown PA 17057

TAYLOR, RICHARD POWELL, lawyer; b. Phila., Sept. 18, 1925; s. Earl Howard and Helen (Martin) T.; student Cornell U., 1946-48; B.A., U. Va., 1950, J.D., 1952; m. Barbara Jo Anne Harris, Dec. 19, 1959; 1 son, Douglas Howard Martin. Admitted to Va. bar, 1952, D.C. bar, 1956; law clk. Judge Armistead M. Dobie, U.S. Ct. Appeals 4th Circuit, 1952-53, practiced in Washington, 1956—; asso. firm Steptoe and Johnson, 1956-61, partner, 1962—, chmn. transp. dept., 1978—; sec. corp. counsel Slick Corp., 1963-69, asst. sec., 1969-72, dir., 1965-68; sec., corp. counsel Slick Indsl. Co., 1963-72; sec., dir. Slick Indsl. Co. Can. Ltd., 1966-72; gen. counsel Intercontinental Forwarders, Inc., 1969—, sec., 1969-72, dir., 1972—; gen. counsel Am. Opera Scholarship Soc., 1974—. Served to lt. (j.g.) Air Intelligence, USNR, 1953-56. Mem. Am. (vice chmn. aviation com. pub. utility sect., 1974—, co-chmn. 1975—), Fed., Fed. Power, D.C., Va. bar assns., Am. Judicature Assn., Internat. Platform Assn., Order of Coif, Raven Soc., Chi Phi, Delta Theta Phi. Republican. Episcopalian (vestrymen). Clubs: International, Nat. Aviation, Potomac Polo, Capitol Hill, Congressional Country. Home: 8801 Belmart Rd Potomac MD 20854 Office: 1250 Connecticut Ave NW Washington DC 20036

TAYLOR, RICHARD WIRT, psychiatrist; b. Merchantville, N.J., Dec. 10, 1923; s. Ernest Lee and Beatrice (Barrington) T.; student Yale, 1942-43, U. Chgo., 1944; B.S., U. Ill., 1946, M.D., 1948; m. Joan Carolyn Koslosky, July 6, 1957; children—Laura Lee, Martha Caroline. Intern, Jefferson Hosp., Phila., 1948-50; resident in psychiatry U. Mich. Hosp., Ann Arbor, 1950-53; staff psychiatrist VA Hosp., Coatesville, Pa., 1953-54, East Orange, N.J., 1955-56; pvt. practice psychiatry, Summit, N.J., 1956-66, Chatham, N.J., 1966—; mem. attending staff Overlook Hosp., Summit, N.J., 1956-78, chief dept. psychiatry, 1972-74; courtesy staff St. Barnabas Hosp., Livingston, N.J., 1957—; cons. Psychiatry-Family Service Bur., Newark, 1957-76; lectr. mental health Newark Coll. Engring., 1958-59. Mem. profl. adv. com. Union County Assn. Mental Health, 1957-58; mem. Summit commn. on Drug Abuse, 1972-73. Served with U.S. Army, 1943-46. Diplomate Am. Bd. Psychiatry and Neurology. Mem. Am., N.J., Union County med. assns., Am., N.J., Tri-County psychiat. assns. Office: 12 Parrott Mill Rd Chatham NJ 07928

TAYLOR, ROBERT B., lawyer; b. Kew Gardens, N.Y., July 29, 1944; s. Robert D. and Lorraine V. (Barre) T.; B.A., Queens Coll. City U. N.Y., 1966; J.D., St. John Law Sch., 1970; m. Barbara A. Castellano, June 12, 1976. Admitted to N.Y. bar, 1971, U.S. Supreme Ct. bar, 1976; partner firm Trainello and Taylor, Esqs., Astoria, N.Y., 1970-72; asso. atty. firm Corner, Finn, Cuomo and Charles, Esqs., Bklyn., 1972-75; mng. atty. Corner, Finn, Dwyer and Charles, Esqs., Bklyn., 1975-77; asst. gen. counsel Americana Hotels, Inc., 1977—. Staff tchr. vol. Harlem Prep. Sch., 1970; trustee Nat. Urban League, 1972-75. Mem. Am., N.Y. bar assns., Assn. Bar City N.Y. Home: 101 Storer Ave Pelham NY 10803 Office: 605 Third Ave New York City NY 10016

TAYLOR, ROBERT LINDELL, mfg. co. exec.; b. Albany, N.Y., May 3, 1942; s. William Merritt and Marion (Nielson) T.; student Monmouth Coll., 1966-69; m. Mary Louise Schlechtweg, Dec. 18, 1965; 1 dau., Lorraine Marion. Engring. technician RCA Space Center, Hightstown, N.J., 1965-66; sr. digital technician Electronic Assos., Eatontown, N.J., 1966-68; v.p., prin. G T Research, Imlaystown, N.J., 1968-69; mgr. quality control consumer specialty products div. ITT, Clark, N.J., 1970—; elec. cons. automation and machine control systems. Mem. Millstone (N.J.) Twp. Bd. Edn., 1972-78. Served with U.S. Army, 1961-65. Democrat. Methodist. Club: Florence (N.J.) Yacht. Patentee in field. Home: Route 526 Imlaystown NJ 08526 Office: 133 Terminal Ave Clark NJ 07066

TAYLOR, RON VIVIAN, graphic designer; b. N.Y.C., Apr. 30, 1918; s. Ronald Vivian and Elfrieda (Martinez) T.; B.A., Pratt Inst., 1940; m. Lillian M. Clark, July 2, 1944; children—Pamela Lee, Cameron. Asso. art editor McCall's, Inc., 1946-52; art dir. McFadden Publs., N.Y.C., 1952-57; presentation editor Lebhar Friedman Publs., N.Y.C., 1968-71; asso. art dir. Time, Inc., N.Y.C., 1961-64; exec. art dir. Famous Schs., Internat., Westport, Conn., 1965-69; pres. Taylor Assos., Stratford, Conn., 1969—. Served with USAAF, 1941-44. Republican. Congregationalist. Clubs: Masons (Floral Park, N.Y.); Elks (Ft. Lauderdale, Fla.); Rotary (Stratford, Conn.). Home: 223A Shoshoni Ln Stratford CT 06497 Office: 3333 Main St Stratford CT 06497

TAYLOR, SUSAN JANE (SUZY), interior designer; b. Van Wert, Ohio, Mar. 27, 1946; d. Harold A. and Gwenelyn (Hughes) T.; B.S. in Interior Design, U. Cin., 1969. Room designer, advt. dept. Armstrong Cork Co., Lancaster, Pa., 1969-72; staff interior designer Apt. Life Mag., Des Moines, 1972-73; interior design cons. Better Homes & Gardens, Des Moines, 1973-75; free lance designer, editorial cons., N.Y.C., 1976—. Mem. Am. Soc. Interior Designers. Contbr. furniture designs to nat. mags.; room designs featured in advt. Home and Office: 127 W 79th St New York City NY 10024

TAYLOR, TOSSIE EDWARD, JR., biologist, educator; b. Rich Square, N.C., Feb. 13, 1935; s. Tossie Edward and India (Jordan) T.; B.S., N.C. Central U., 1961, M.S., 1962; Ph.D., U. R.I., 1974; m. Joyce Tretta Jenkins, Aug. 29, 1960; 1 son, Cedric Pierre. Instr. biology Morris Coll., Sumter, S.C., 1962-63; asso. prof. biology Del. State Coll., Dover, 1963-70, 72-76, Cheyney (Pa.) State Coll., 1976—; Nat. Urban League fellow in diagnostic research Hoffman La Roche, Nutley, N.J., 1967. Served with U.S. Army, 1955-58. NSF grantee U. P.R., 1966. Mem. Am. Soc. Cell Biology, Electron Microscopy Soc. Am., AAUP, AAAS, Omega Psi Phi. Democrat. Contbr. articles to profl. jours. Home: 824 Miller Dr Dover DE 19901 Office: Box 269 Cheyney State Coll Cheyney PA 19319

TAYLOR, WARREN JUSTIN, thoracic surgeon; b. Boston, Nov. 2, 1921; s. William John and Virginia Stewart (Thompson) T.; A.B., Dartmouth Coll., 1943; M.D., Columbia U., 1945; m. Marjorie Marian Hutchins, Sept. 15, 1945; children—Wayne Jonathan, Leigh Whitham, Jane Stewart, Virginia Martha. Intern, Mary Hitchcock Meml. Hosp., Hanover, N.H., 1945-46, resident in anesthesia, 1948-49; resident in surgery VA Hosp., White River Junction Vt., Mary Hitchcock Meml. Hosp., 1949-52, chief surg. resident VA Hosp., White River Junction, 1952-53; surgeon VA Hosp., Rutland Heights, Mass., 1953-55; fellow in thoracic surgery Malden (Mass.) Hosp., 1955-57, sr. surgeon, 1957—, chief thoracic surgery, 1966-73, surgeon in chief, 1973—; instr. surgery Harvard Med. Sch., 1961-68, clin. asso. in surgery, 1969-70, asst. clin. prof., 1970-74; clin. instr. Tufts Med. Sch., 1967—; asso. clin. prof. surgery Boston U. Sch. Medicine, 1974—; mem. cons. staff numerous hosps. Served to maj., M.C., AUS, 1945-59. Mem. Winchester Bd. Health, 1962-74. Diplomate Am. Bd. Surgery, Am. Bd. Thoracic Surgery. Fellow A.C.S., Am. Coll. Chest Physicians (treas. 1974—), Am. Coll. Cardiology; mem. Mass. Med. Soc., Am. Thoracic Soc., AMA, Soc. Thoracic Surgeons, Internat. Cardiovascular Soc., Boston Surg. Soc., Mass. Heart Assn., Am. Assn. Thoracic Surgery, New Eng. Cardiovascular Soc. Contbr. articles to med. jours. Home: 10 Edgehill Rd Winchester MA 01890 Office: 101 George P Hassett Dr Medford MA 02155

TAYLOR, WILLIAM ARTHUR, JR., physician; b. Wilmington, Del., Feb. 18, 1941; s. William Arthur and Margaret U. T.; A.B., U. Del., 1962; M.D., Hahnemann Med. Coll., 1966; m. Evelyn D. Hunt, Dec. 23, 1965; children—Billy, Jay. Intern in surgery, Hosp. U. Pa., Phila., 1966-67; resident in medicine Wilmington (Del.) Med. Center,

1969-71, chief resident in medicine, 1971-72, sr. attending physician, 1976—, asso. dir. Infectious Disease Research Lab., 1975—; NIH fellow in infectious disease Thorndike Lab. and Channing Lab., Med. Sch., Harvard U., Boston, 1972-73; instr. in medicine and infectious disease Harvard Med. Unit, Boston City Hosp., 1972-73; practice medicine specializing in internal medicine, Wilmington, 1974—; asst. prof. medicine Jefferson Med. Coll., Phila., 1974—; cons. in medicine and infectious diseases St. Francis Hosp., Wilmington, A. I. DuPont Inst., Wilmington; vice chmn. infections com. Wilmington Med. Center, mem. publs. com.; chmn. infections disease com. St. Francis Hosp., Wilmington. Served with M.C. U.S. Army, 1967-69, Diplomate Am. Bd. Internal Medicine, also subsplty. infectious diseases. Mem. Del. Lung Assn. (trustee), Del. Med. Soc. (venereal disease com.). Club: Wilmington Country. Asso. editor Del. Med. Jour.; wine and food editor Del. Today mag.; co-author textbook and book sects.; contbr. articles in field to profl. jours.; free lance writer. Home: 2402 Grant Ave Wilmington DE 19806 Office: 1306 N Broom St Wilmington DE 19806

TAYLOR, WILLIAM DAVIS, newspaperman; b. Boston, Apr. 2, 1908; s. William Osgood and Mary (Moseley) T.; student Harvard, 1927-31; m. Mary Hammond, 1931 (dec. 1947); children—William Osgood, Ann Rumrill; m. 2d, Ann Caroline Macy, Nov. 1947; children—Thomas Macy, Margaret Mosley, Wendy Elizabeth, James Morgan. With Globe Newspaper Co., 1931—, became treas., 1937, gen. mgr., 1940, chmn., pub. Boston Globe, 1955—; dir. Met.-Sunday Newspapers, Inc., Million Market Newspapers, Inc. Mem. exec. bd. Boston council Boy Scouts Am. Bd. overseers Harvard; trustee Noble and Greenough Sch., Dedham, Mass. Mem. Am. Newspaper Pubs. Assn. (dir.). Episcopalian. Club: Harvard (bd. govs.) (Boston). Home: 32 Old Farm Rd Dedham MA 02026 Office: 135 Morrissey Blvd Boston MA 02125

TAYLOR, WILLIAM HERBERT, cons. civil engr.; b. Camden, N.J., Oct. 30, 1928; s. Samuel Herbert and Mary Lavenia (Skeggs) T.; B.S., Princeton U., 1950; M.S., U. Pa., 1956; m. Helga M.E. Nepple, Mar. 6, 1951; children—Jeffrey P., James D., Anne L. Partner, Taylor Engring. Assos., cons. engrs. and urban planners, Mt. Laurel, N.J., 1952-60; prin., chmn. bd. Taylor, Wiseman & Taylor, Mt. Laurel, 1960—; surveyor gen. Western Div. N.J., 1963—; dir. Fidelity Mut. Savs. & Loan Assn., 1975—. Chmn. Boro of Haddonfield Planning Bd., 1976—; dir., chmn. facilities com. Cooper Med. Center, 1976—; trustee So. N.J. Devel. Council, 1974—. Served to lt. (j.g.), USNR, 1950-52. Registered profl. engr., N.J., N.Y. Mem. ASCE, Nat. Soc. Profl. Engrs., Am. Cons. Engrs. Council, Am. Littoral Soc., Water Pollution Control Fedn., Am. Arbitration Assn., Princeton Engring. Assn., Navy League U.S. Editor Coastal Zone Mgmt. Publs., 1977—. Office: 306 Fellowship Rd Mt Laurel NJ 08054

TEACH, GUSTA MORGAN, land development co. exec.; b. Chestnut Hill, Mass., Mar. 13, 1924; d. Clyde Brooke and Maud Ethel (Goodrich) Morgan; B.S., Md. Coll. Women, 1944; m. Fredric Hersom Giddings, June 10, 1944; children—Brooke, Fritz, Suzanne Scott, Morgan, Bruce; m. 2d, Robert Adams Teach, Sept. 24, 1977. Salesperson Hilltop Place of New London (N.H.), Inc., 1970-71, sales mgr., v.p., dir., 1971-74; sales mgr. Hilltop Trust, New London, N.H., 1974-79; pres. Crossroads of Sports, New London, 1967-70; dir. King Ridge Ski Area. Licensed real estate broker, N.H. Mem. New London Outing Club, Lake Sunapee Yacht, U.S. Combined Training Assn., U.S. Pony Clubs, Inc. (gov.). Home: Brentwood Farm New London NH 03257 Office: Hilltop Place New London NH 03257

TEACHOUT, ROGER SAGE, polit. scientist, educator; b. Syracuse, N.Y., Nov. 17, 1921; s. Almon Henry and May (Sage) T.; B.A., Syracuse U., 1948, M.A., 1953; Ph.D., U. Md., 1971; div. 1978; children—Roger Sage II, Jaime Janville. Asst. prof. polit. sci. U. Maine, Augusta, 1969-70, asso. prof., 1970-72, prof., 1972—; asso. dir. Nat. Strategy Seminar, Nat. War Coll., 1962; mil. manpower adviser Republic of China, 1965-67; dir. ops. New Eng. Polit. Research Inst., Inc., 1971—; mediator Maine Labor Relations Bd., 1976—. Served with USAAF, World War II; USAF, Korea and Vietnam. Recipient Better Life award Am. Nursing Home Assn., 1973. Mem. Am. Acad. Polit. and Social Sci., Soc. Profls. in Dispute Resolution, Pi Sigma Alpha. Democrat. Presbyterian. Author: (with Palmer et al) The Legislative Process in Maine, 1973. Editor: A Study of Policy Making (Nickerson, Shin and Teachout), 1971. Home: RFD 5 Augusta ME 04330 Office: Univ Maine Augusta ME 04330

TEAGUE, ABNER FRANKLIN, govt. ofcl.; b. Gainesville, Tex., May 25, 1919; s. John Abner and Martha Leo (Chandler) T.; B.S. in Chem. Engring., Tex. Tech. U., 1942; M.S. in System Mgmt. Scis., U. So. Calif., 1969; m. Doris Beatrice New, Dec. 30, 1946; children—Barbara Jan Teague Holloman, Julia Ann, James Abner; m. 2d, Nora Katharine Henderson, June 26, 1971; 1 stepson, Cecil Dow James. With Camp Evans Signal Lab., Belmar, N.J., 1942-44, Naval Ordnance Sta., Inyokern, Calif., 1946-51, Navy Dept. Bur. Ordnance, Washington, 1952-56; head A/C rocket propellants Phillips Petroleum/Astrodyne, Inc., McGregor, Tex., 1956-59; project engr. TRW Systems, Redondo Beach, Calif., 1959-64, project mgr. propulsion satellite subsystem, 1964-71, sr. engr., 1959-71; engr. Naval Weapons Engring. Support Activity, Washington, 1971-77, Joint Cruise Missile Project office, Tomahawk Booster/Pyrotechnic Project engr., Washington, 1977—. Pres. Patrick Henry PTA, 1956; bd. dirs. Rollings Hills Little League, 1964; chmn. parents com. Boy Scouts Am., 1966-67. Served with USNR, 1944-46. Registered profl. engr., Tex., Calif. Mem. Am. Inst. Chem. Engrs., N.Y. Acad. Scis. Episcopalian. Clubs: Masons, Tex. Tech. Letterman's Assn. Patentee multiple thrust propellant charge. Home: 8072 Fairfax Rd Alexandria VA 22308 Office: JCMPO (PM3) Nat Center No 1 Dept of Navy Washington DC 20360

TEAHAN, FREDERICK HATCH CHRISTOPHER, found. exec.; b. N.Y.C., Mar. 11, 1922; s. James Thomas and Teresa (Hatch) T.; M.A., Columbia, 1948; Ph.D., Trinity Coll., Dublin, Ireland, 1952. Instr. English, Wagner Coll., N.Y., 1951; ednl. advisor USAF, Middlesex, Eng., 1952-55; asst. dir. research, prof. English, Getulio Vargas Found., Rio de Janeiro, 1955-60; cons. Council Higher Edn. Am. Republics, Inst. Internat. Edn., N.Y.C., 1960-63; exec. dir. Found. Pub. Relations Research and Edn., N.Y.C., 1963—; edn. dir. Pub. Relations Soc. Am., N.Y.C., 1963—, Pub. Relations Student Soc. Am., 1968—. Served with USAF, 1942-45. Mem. Philos. Soc., Assn. Edn. Journalism, Internat. Pub. Relations Assn. Author: Jonathan Swift and the Age of Handel, 1948; Musical Criticism in Seventeenth and Eighteenth Century England, 1952. Home: 37 E 29th St New York City NY 10016

TEAMAN, CHARLES RICHARD, marketing research co. exec.; b. Bklyn., Feb. 17, 1937; s. Henry and Rebecca B. (Burg) T.; B.A., Queens Coll. City U. N.Y., 1959; M.A., L.I. U., 1962; m. Judith Ann Shipman, May 28, 1969; children—Gary Randall, Hollys Ann, Daniel Edwin. Analyst A.C. Nielsen, 1959-61; analyst Colgate-Palmolive Co., N.Y.C., 1961-63, group mgr., 1963-64; dir. research MacManus, John & Adams (now Darcy/MacManus/Masius), Chgo., 1964-66; asso. dir. research Tatham, Laird & Kudner, Chgo., 1966-68; sr. v.p., also dir., Burgoyne Inc., Cin., 1968-70; corporate prin., pres., treas. Wilson Group Inc. (now Teaman/Lehman Assos. Inc.), Stamford, Conn., 1970—; lectr. in field. Served with N.Y. Army N.G., 1959-65. Mem. Am. Mktg. Assn., Market Research Assn., Psi Chi. Home: 523 Ridgebury Rd Ridgefield CT 06877 Office: 300 Broad St Stamford CT 06901

TEATES, NOAH GROVE, JR., stretch bundling machinery mfg. co. exec.; b. Washington, Dec. 17, 1942; s. Noah Grove and Edna (Merrick) T.; student Emory and Henry Coll., 1961-65; M.Commerce, U. Richmond, 1971; m. Judith Anne Haddock, Nov. 24, 1967; children—Noah Grove, Seth Turner. Jr. indsl. engr. FMC Corp., Fredericksburg, Va., 1965-67; indsl. engr. Richmond Engring. Co. (Va.), 1967-69; founder, chief officer Leaf Co., Wheaton, Md., 1971-78; pres., chmn. bd. Systemation, Inc., Wheaton, 1978—; prin. N. Grove Teates & Assos.; municipal composting cons. Bd. dirs. Richmond Wesleyan Found., 1968-69. Mem. Am. Inst. Indsl. Engrs. (v.p. 1968-71). Patentee large scale composting shredders, stretch bundling machinery. Home: 2707 Weisman Rd Wheaton MD 20902

TEBET, DAVID WILLIAM, TV exec.; b. Phila., Dec. 27, 1920; s. Joshua and Edith (Dechowits) T.; student Temple U., 1941. Pub. relations staff legitimate theatre prodns. for John C. Wilson, Theatre Guild, others; plays include Blithe Spirit, Bloomer Girl, Quadrille, 1943-55; pub. relations Max Leibman Prodns., 1950—; v.p. Talent NBC-TV, N.Y.C., 1959; v.p. NBC, Inc. 1959-75, sr. v.p., 1975—. Advisory bd. Stephens Coll., Columbia, Mo. Named man of yr. Conference of Personal Mgrs. West, 1977. Club: Friars (bd. govs., chmn. spl. events com., exec. chmn. ann. testimonial dinner). Home: Beverly Hills Hotel Beverly Hills CA 90210 Office: NBC 300 Rockefeller Plaza New York City NY 10020 also West Alameda Burbank CA 91523

TECE, ALP SUNQUR, psychiatrist; b. Tarsus, Turkey, Mar. 13, 1934; s. Ruhi and Ayse T.; M.D., Med. Sch. Istanbul U., 1960; came to U.S., 1961; m. Renan Ozbilge, Nov. 9, 1967; children—Basak, Hande. Intern Youngstown (Ohio) Hosp. Assn., 1961-62; resident Pilgrim State Hosp., 1962-65; staff psychiatrist Pilgrim Psychiat. Center, Brentwood, N.Y., 1967—, Community Mental Health Center, part time, 1970—. Served to lt. Turkish Army, 1965-67. Mem. Am. Psychiat. Assn., L.I., Turkish Am. physicians assns. Home: Box 112 W Brentwood NY 11717 Office: 5 Wicks Rd Brentwood NY 11717

TEDESCHI, ROBERT JAMES, chem. co. exec.; b. Woodside, L.I., N.Y., July 25, 1921; s. Romolo Valentine and Maria Antonette (Prezzi) T.; A.B., Cornell U., 1944, M.S., 1945, Ph.D., 1947; m. Jean Lois Scruggs, June 21, 1953; children—Marc, Lisa, Thomas. Sr. chemist Am. Cyanamid Co., Bound Brook, N.J., 1947-53; sect. head Air Reduction Co., Murray Hill, N.J., 1953-60, supr., Piscataway, N.J., 1960-71; asso. dir. research and devel. Air Products and Chems. Co., Piscataway, 1971—. Active Boy Scouts Am.; mem. bd. edn. Readington Township, N.J., 1964-67. Accredited profl. chemist Am. Inst. Chemists. Fellow Am. Inst. Chemists; mem. Am. Chem. Soc., N.Y. Acad. Scis., Organic Catalysis-Reactions Soc., Sigma Xi, Alpha Chi Sigma. Republican. Roman Catholic. Contbr. articles to profl. jours. Patentee in field. Home: RD 3 Box 143 Whitehouse Station NJ 08889 Office: Air Products and Chemicals Co Piscataway NJ 08854

TEDESCO, FRANK MARIO, chemist; b. Bklyn., May 6, 1945; s. Anthony George and Nina Emily (Sorrentino) T.; A. Chem. Tech. (N.J. State scholar), U. Dayton, 1967, B. Tech. (N.J. State scholar), 1967; M.B.A., Fairleigh Dickenson U., 1977; m. Cheryl Ann Smith, July 5, 1969; children—Michael, Daniel. Research chemist I, ITT Rayonier Inc., Whippany, N.J., 1967-73, research chemist II, 1973-77, research group leader II, 1977—. Served with U.S. Army, 1969-71. Mem. Am. Chem. Soc., TAPPI, Am. Mgmt. Assn., Assn. M.B.A's. Roman Catholic. Research on cellulose acetate. Home: 124 Crease Rd Budd Lake NJ 07828 Office: ITT Rayonier S Jefferson Rd Whippany NJ 07981

TEDRICK, RICHARD NEWMAN, acoustic physicist; b. Chgo., May 10, 1931; s. Floyd Newman and Testy Isora (Schoby) T.; student Wright Jr. Coll., Chgo., 1948-50, student Ill. Inst. Tech., 1950-52; B.S. in Physics, U. Tex. at El Paso, 1956; m. Vonicille Haire, July 11, 1953; children—Samuel, Yvonne. Chief acoustical research group White Sands (N.Mex.) Missile Range, 1956-61; contract scientist NASA, Huntsville, Ala., 1961-63, acoustical engr., 1963-67; supr. acoustics group Garrett AiResearch Co., Phoenix, 1967-74; chief environ. regulatory br. Office Environ. and Energy, FAA, Washington, 1974—. Served with U.S. Army, 1952-54. Recipient Sustained Superior Performance awards NASA, 1963, FAA, 1975, 76, 78. Mem. Acoustical Soc. Am., Am. Inst. Physics, Audio Soc. Am., Mensa. Contbr. articles to profl. jours. Inventor remote-controlled acoustic monitoring system, 1959, others in field. Home: 8810 Parliament Dr Springfield VA 22151 Office: Office Environ and Energy FAA AEE-220 800 Independence Ave SW Washington DC 20591

TEETER, JAMES HERRING, surgeon; b. Taneytown, Md., Aug. 22, 1927; s. John Stuff and Margaret Ann (Roop) T.; A.B., Gettysburg Coll., 1950; M.D., U. Md., 1954; m. Annie Mae McDaniel, Sept. 10, 1949; children—Timothy, Paul, Jonathan. Intern, Mercy Hosp., Balt., 1954-55; resident in surgery Church Home Hosp., Balt., 1955-57, Franklin Sq. Hosp., Balt., 1957-59; practice medicine specializing in surgery, Waynesboro, Pa., 1959—; attending surgeon Waynesboro Hosp., 1959—, chief surgery, 1974—; pres. Surg. Assos. Waynesboro Ltd., 1977—. Past bd. dirs. Children's Aid Soc., New Life Treatment Center, Union Rescue Mission. Served with U.S. Army, 1946-47. Diplomate Am. Bd. Surgery. Fellow A.C.S.; mem. AMA, Pa., Franklin County, Christian med. socs. Republican. Mem. Brethren Ch. Club: Rotary. Home: RD 6 Box 406 Waynesboro PA 17268 Office: 45 Roadside Ave Waynesboro PA 17268

TEFT, LEON WILLIAM, educator; b. N.Y.C., Oct. 6, 1935; s. Leon William and May Carrie (Benedict) T.; B.A. summa cum laude, U. Bridgeport, 1961; A.M., Clark U., 1962, Ph.D., 1966; m. Janice Gordon, Sept. 6, 1958; 1 son, Gregory Lee. Faculty, U. Bridgeport (Conn.), 1965—, prof. psychology, 1974—, summer chmn. dept., 74—; lectr. So. Conn. State Coll., Coll. New Rochelle, Stamford (Conn.) Pub. Schs. Sec.-treas. Assn. New Eng. Field Trial Clubs, 1976—; bd. dirs. Shoreline Assn. Retarded and Handicapped, 1974—. Served with USMCR, 1953-56. NIMH grantee, 1964-66; NSF grantee, 1967. Mem. Am., Eastern psychol. assns., N.Y. Acad. Scis., New Eng. Open Bird Dog Championship (pres.), Associated Field Trial Clubs Conn. (sec.), Psi Chi, Phi Delta Kappa. Republican. Contbr. articles in field to profl. jours. Home: 68 Stepstone Hill Rd Guilford CT 06437 Office: South Hall U Bridgeport Bridgeport CT 06602

TEGLAS, CSABA, city planner; b. Hungary, Jan. 13, 1930; naturalized Can. citizen; degree in Architecture, Tech. U. Budapest, 1952; degree in Town and Regional Planning (Central Mortgage and Housing Corp. Can. fellow), U. Toronto, 1961; m. Rowena E. Walker, Apr. 10, 1965; children—Nicholas Miklos, Gordon Csaba. Sr. designer City of Toronto (Ont.) Planning Bd., 1962-65; head master plan sect. Expo 67, Montreal, Que., Can., 1965-67; sr. design asso. Raymond, Parish, Pine & Weiner, Inc., Tarrytown, N.Y., 1967—; lectr. in N.Y. area colls. Mem. Am. Inst. Planners (bd. examiners), Can. Inst. Planners. Contbr. articles on planning to profl. jours. Home: 136 Clinton St White Plains NY 10604 Office: 555 White Plains Rd Tarrytown NY 10591

TEICHMANN, HOWARD MILES, writer; b. Chgo., Jan. 22, 1916; s. Jack and Rose (Berliner) T.; B.A., U. Wis., 1938; m. Evelyn Jane Goldstein, Apr. 2, 1939; 1 dau., Judith Robin. Prof. English, Barnard Coll., Columbia U., N.Y.C., 1946—; v.p. Shubert Theatres, 1962-72; biographer, playwright, N.Y.C., 1953—, biographies include: George S. Kaufman, An Intimate Portrait, 1972, Smart Aleck, the Wit and World of Alexander Woollcott, 1976; plays include: The Solid Gold Cadillac, 1953, Miss Lonelyhearts, 1957, The Girls in 509, 1958, Julia, Jake & Uncle Joe, 1960, Rainy Day in Newark, 1963; dir. Dramatists Play Service; lit. critic for N.Y. Times, Washington Post, Chgo. Tribune, Phila. Inquirer; writer for radio, TV, and nat. mags. Adminstr., Sam S. Shubert Found., 1962-72; bd. dirs. Broadway Assn., 1964-71. Sr. editor Overseas br. Office War Info., 1942-43; served with U.S. Army, 1943-45. Recipient award Women's Overseas Press Club, 1942, Peabody award, 1953, Emmy award, 1954, Distinguished Service award, Sch. Journalism U. Wis., 1959. Mem. Dramatists Guild (treas.), AFTRA, Actors Fund, Writers Guild East. Home and Office: 863 Park Ave New York City NY 10021

TEITELBAUM, HERBERT ULYSSES, architect; b. Bklyn., Nov. 25, 1923; s. Irvin and Mildred (Berman) T.; B.Arch., Cooper Union U., 1948; M.B.A., Columbia U., 1959; m. Lucia M. Hellmich, May 19, 1949; children—Bradley David, Graham Kimble. Resident architect Vollmer Ostrower Asso., Saratoga Springs, N.Y., 1956-58; in charge constrn. George Diamond Assos., N.Y.C., 1958-60; partner Handren, Sharp Assos., N.Y.C., 1968-73; project mgr. Dormitory Authority of State N.Y., N.Y.C., 1973—; mem. faculty architecture Columbia U., 1953-59, Mondell Inst., 1958-64. Active Boy Scouts Am., 1935—, mem. exec. com. Rockland County council, 1976, exec. bd., 1976—. Served with USN, 1941-46, USMC, 1949-53. Decorated Sivler Star, Legion of Merit, Bronze Star, Purple Heart (U.S.); officer Order Brit. Empire (Eng.); recipient award Boy Scouts Am., 1966-77. Mem. Am. Ordnance Assn., Soc. Am. Mil. Engrs., Rockland Hist. Assn. Methodist. Free lance research for mil. writers. Home: 107 Parkway Dr S Orangeburg NY 10962 Office: 41 E 42d St New York City NY 10007

TEITELBAUM, HUBERT I., judge; b. Pitts., July 2, 1915; s. Jack and Anna (Wolk) T.; A.B., U. Pitts., 1937, J.D., 1940; m. Maja Wahrheit, Dec. 2, 1949; children—Hugh, Bruce. Admitted to Pa. bar, 1940; teaching fellow Sch. Law U. Pitts., 1940; adj. prof. law Duquesne U., 1948—; spl. agt. FBI, 1940-43; pvt. practice law; Pitts., 1949-55; first asst. U.S. atty., 1955-58; U.S. dist. atty. Western Dist. Pa., 1958-61; U.S. dist judge, 1971—. Dir. Three Rivers Bank & Trust Co., 1964-71. Trustee Montefiore Hosp., Pitts., Woodville State Hosp., Carnegie, Pa. Served to capt. AUS, 1944-49; lt. col. Res. Mem. Am., Fed., Pa., Allegheny County bar assns., Am. Law Inst., Am. Judicature Soc., Am. Legion, Order of Coif. Clubs: Pitts. Athletic Assn., Pitts. Press, Nat. Lawyers, Lawyers of Allegheny County, Wildwood Golf, Westmoreland Country, Variety, Amen Corner, Masons, Shriners. Home: 4913 Wallingford St Pittsburgh PA 15213 Office: US Post Office and Courts Pittsburgh PA 15219

TEITELBAUM, IRVING, psychotherapist; b. N.Y.C., May 5, 1923; s. Chiel and Sadie (Reinhard) T.; B.A., Bklyn. Coll., 1947; M.S., Yeshiva U., 1951; Ph.D. (Mack Dreyfus scholar), Dropsie U., 1964; m. Phyllis Lee Abrams, Mar. 6, 1958; children—Shifra, Ozer. Therapist, Temple Emanuel Family Counseling Center, 1965-68; asst. prof. Queensborough Community Coll., 1968-70; dir. Temple Emanuel Family Counseling Center, 1970-72; staff psychologist Bklyn. Community Counseling Center, 1968-72; psychotherapist Community Guidance Service, N.Y.C., 1967-70; practice psychotherapy, N.Y.C., 1964—; dir. Met. Counseling Center, 1976—; chief psychotherapist satellite clinic Interbon Counseling and Developmental Center, Bklyn., 1977—. Exec. dir. Jewish Aid Soc. for Ex-Offenders, 1977—. Certified sch. psychologist, N.Y.; certified vocat. rehab. counselor. Mem. AAUP, Am. Personnel and Guidance Assn., Assn. Applied Psychoanalysis, Am., N.Y. State, Bklyn. psychol. assns., Queens County Mental Hygiene Soc. (dir. 1969-71), Nat. Alliance Family Life (clin.), Doctorate Assn. for N.Y. Educators, Nat. Rehab. Assn., Mental Health Professions (dir.). Address: 1508 48th St Brooklyn NY 11219

TEITELBAUM, MARCEL, psychologist; b. Antwerp, Belgium, Apr. 3, 1934; s. Josef and Mirla (Wolf) T.; came to U.S., 1940, naturalized, 1947; B.A., Yeshiva U., 1955, M.S., 1957, Ph.D. (Ford Found. Fund for Advancement Edn. fellow), 1965; m. Liane Charlotte Slesinger, June 8, 1958; children—Howard Dennis, Marc Allan, Suzanne Rena. Sch. psychologist East Meadow (N.Y.) Pub. Schs., 1957-61, Levittown (N.Y.) Pub. Schs., 1961-64; chief psychologist, chmn. spl. services, sch. psychologist Uniondale (N.Y.) Pub. Schs., 1964—; pvt. practice psychology, Hempstead, N.Y., 1965—; instr. Queens Coll., City U. N.Y.; teaching asso. Hofstra U.; lectr. C.W. Post Coll. Licensed psychologist, certified sch. psychologist, N.Y. State. Mem. Am., Nassau County (N.Y.) psychol. assns., Uniondale Tchrs. Assn., NEA, N.Y. State Tchrs. Assn. Home: 8 Laurel Ct West Hempstead NY 11552 Office: 230 Hilton Ave Hempstead NY 11550

TEITELBAUM, SEYMOUR, dentist; b. N.Y.C., Feb. 3, 1927; s. Charles and Ray (Nurick) T.; B.S., L.I. U., 1950; D.D.S., N.Y.U., 1955; postgrad. Bklyn. Coll., 1950; m. Lilian Ostrovsky, Jan. 7, 1960; children—Lizanne, Michael, Lorne. Intern Bronx-Lebanon Hosp. Center, 1955, then adj. attending; practice dentistry, specializing in preventive, restorative dentistry, N.Y.C., 1957-62, Briarcliff Manor, N.Y., 1963—; dental staff Phelps Meml. Hosp. Served with USAAF, 1944-46. Past chmn. United Jewish Appeal, Briarcliff Manor. Fellow Soc. Oral Physiology and Occlusion, Am. Acad. Gen. Dentistry, Fedn. Prosthetic Orgns., Royal Soc. Health, Am. Prosthodontic Soc.; mem. AAAS, First, Ninth dist. (profl. edn. com.) dental socs., Am. Acad. Implant Dentistry, Am. Analgesia, So. New Eng. Acad. Practice Adminstrn., Westchester Acad. Gen. Dentistry (pres.), Am. Soc. Preventative Dentistry, Westchester Acad. Restorative Dentistry, Am. Dental Assn., Tappan Zee, Western Westchester dental study groups, Fedn. Internat. Dentaire, Park Chester Rifle and Revolver Assn., Alpha Omega. Odd Fellow; mem. B'nai B'rith. Home and office: 1312 Pleasantville Rd Briarcliff Manor NY 10510

TEITELL, CONRAD LAURENCE, lawyer; b. N.Y.C., Nov. 8, 1932; s. Benson and Belle (Altman) T.; A.B., U. Mich., 1954; LL.B., Columbia, 1957; LL.M., N.Y.U., 1968; m. Adele Mary Crummins, May 26, 1957; children—Beth Mary, Mark Lewis. Admitted to N.Y. State bar, 1958, D.C. bar, 1968; mem. firm Prerau & Teitell, N.Y.C., 1964—; dir. Philanthropy Tax Inst., Old Greenwich, Conn., 1964—. Trustee Am. Arthritis Found., N.Y. Lung Assn., Hendrix Coll. Served with U.S. Army, 1957. Recipient Distinguished Service to Higher Edn. award Am. Coll. Pub. Relations Assn., 1970. Mem. Nat. Assn. Coll. and Univ. Attys., Am. Soc. Hosp. Attys., Am. Bar Assn. (co-chmn. com. on charitable giving, trusts and founds.), N.Y. County Lawyers Assn., Assn. Bar City N.Y. Author: Deferred Giving-Explanation, Specimen Agreements, Reporting Forms, 2 vols., 1976; editor Taxwise Giving. 1964—; contbr. articles to field to profl. jours. Home: 44 Binney Ln Old Greenwich CT 06870 Office: 375 Park Ave New York City NY 10022 also 13 Arcadia Rd Old Greenwich CT 06870

TELAK, MARLENE MARY, coll. adminstr.; b. Balt., May 18, 1950; d. Casimir Stanley and Wilhelmina (Balling) T.; B.S., U. Md., 1972; M.Ed., Am. U., 1976. Interior designer Montgomery Ward & Co., Hecht Co., Washington, 1972-74; adminstrv. sec., internat. student and faculty exchange Am. U., Washington, 1974-76; fin. aid adminstr. No. Va. Community Coll., Alexandria, 1976—. Mem. Am. Personnel and Guidance Assn., Am. Coll. Personnel Assn., So. Assn. Student Fin. Aid Adminstrn. Democrat. Roman Catholic. Home: 413 Hamilton Ave Silver Spring MD 20901 Office: Northern Virginia Community College 3001 N Beauregard St Alexandria VA 22311

TELFER, JOHN DELBERT, univ. adminstr.; b. Mifflintown, Pa., Dec. 21, 1926; s. James Glasgow and Ruth Adelia (Hart) T.; student Widener Coll., 1944; B.Arch., U. Mich., 1951, M. City Planning, 1961; LL.D. (hon.), Eastern Mich. U., 1974; m. Virginia Norma Kilgore, July 31, 1948; children—Carleton K., Carlyle H. (twins). Jr. partner, design chief AOA Schmidt Asso. Architects, Detroit, 1955-57; prof., head div. engring. Abadan (Iran) Inst. Tech., 1957-59; univ. planner U. Mich., Ann Arbor, 1960-68; asst. v.p. for phys. planning Columbia U., N.Y.C., 1968-71; v.p. for facilities planning State U. N.Y., Buffalo, 1972—, adj. prof. architecture, 1975—. Trustee United Theol. Sem., Dayton, O., 1972—; chmn. City Planning Commn., Ypsilanti, Mich., 1962-67; bd. dirs. Morningside Heights, Inc., N.Y.C., 1968-71, Audubon New Community, Amherst, N.Y., 1974—, Nat. Center for Coll. and Univ. Planning, Balt., 1976—. Served with inf. U.S. Army, 1945-47. Fellow Royal Soc. Health; mem. Am. Inst. Planners (profl. planner), Soc. Coll. Univ. Planning (founder 1966, exec. dir. 1966-72, pres. 1974-78, Distinguished citation 1972), Amherst C. of C., Widener PMC Coll. Alumni Assn., Tau Sigma Delta. Presbyterian. Home: 4838 Smiley Terr Clarence NY 14031 Office: State U NY Buffalo 521 Capen Hall Buffalo NY 14260

TELLER, MYRTLE ROGERS BRILLIANTINE, heavy machinery mfg. co. exec.; b. Birmingham, Ala., Aug. 6, 1922; d. Oliver Conrad and Minnie Gladys (Nunnally) Rogers; student U. Ala., Tuscaloosa, Mercer County Coll., Trenton, N.J.; m. Bruno Brilliantine, Aug. 17, 1941 (dec. Jan. 1968); children—Bruce, Lance, Randall, Janet; m. 2d, Martin P. Teller, Nov. 22, 1975 (dec. Jan. 1977). Various secretarial positions, 1944-46; office mgr. Indsl. Machine Tool Co., Trenton, 1958-62; with DeLaval Turbine div. Transamerica Corp., 1962—, sr. buyer, supr. customer repair/service group, Trenton, 1978—; notary public, 1956-75. Active local PTA, Cub Scouts, Heart Assn. Mem. Purchasing Agts. Club Trenton, DeLaval Turbine Mgmt. Assn. Roman Catholic. Club: Order Eastern Star. Address: 72 Hardwick Dr Trenton NJ 08638

TELLIER, LEO JOSEPH, JR., tech. analyst; b. Cameron, Tex., Nov. 14, 1945; s. Leo Joseph and Dorothy Marcella (Ondreas) T.; B.A. in Geology and Earth Scis. magna cum laude, St. Mary's U., San Antonio, 1974; M.S. in Edn., U. So. Calif., 1977; m. Katherine R. Keil, June 14, 1974; 1 stepdau., Dianna N. Anderson. With USAF Security Service in Turkey, 1964-65, Italy, 1965-67, S. Korea, 1969-70, Japan, 1970-72, Berlin, 1975—. Decorated Commendation medal. Mem. Am. Inst. Aeros. and Astronautics, Nat. Space Club, Air Force Assn., Nat. Space Inst., Am. Soc. Aerospace Edn. Roman Catholic. Home: 7A AM Hegewinkel Apt # 7 1000 Berlin 37 Office: 6912 Scty Sq Attn DOA/T APO New York City NY 09611

TELLING, RAYMOND GORDON, accountant; b. Danville, Ill., Sept. 7, 1922; s. Gordon R. and Fern D. (Hodge) T.; B.S. in Accounting, U. Ill, 1947; m. Bonnie J. Buttrey, May 7, 1949; children—Martha Telling Witrak, Jennifer Hays, Thomas, James. Sr. accountant Price Waterhouse & Co., Chgo., 1947-52; asst. controller W.F. Hall Printing Co., Chgo., 1953-59; pres., dir. Demco Library Supplies, Inc. and Finer Products, Inc., Madison, Wis., 1960-68; pres., dir. Telling & Potter, C.P.A.'s, Plattsburgh, Ticonderoga and Malone, N.Y., 1969—. Bd. dirs., mem. exec. com., treas. Champlain Valley Physicians Hosp, Plattsburgh, N.Y. Served with USAAC, 1943-47. C.P.A., Ill., Wis., N.Y. Mem. Am. Inst. C.P.A.'s, N.Y., Vt. socs. C.P.A.'s. Episcopalian. Clubs: Masons, Shriners, Elks. Home: 14 Coastland Dr Plattsburgh NY 12901 Office: Lake Shore Rd Plattsburgh NY 12901

TEMMER, STEPHEN FRANCIS, electronics co. exec.; b. Vienna, Austria, May 28, 1928; s. Frederic M. and Margaret D. (Jeiteles) T.; came to U.S., 1939, naturalized, 1945; student Mass. Inst. Tech., 1946-47. Vice-pres., chief engr. Gotham Recording Corp., N.Y.C., 1950-57, pres. Gotham Audio Corp. div., 1957—, pres. Gotham Export Corp. div., 1968—; gen. mgr. Sta. WBAI-FM, N.Y.C., 1956-58; lectr. Banff (Alta., Can.) Center Performing Arts, 1976—. Fellow Audio Engring. Soc. (v.p. internat. 1973-75, 77-79); mem. IEEE (sr.), Soc. Motion Picture & TV Engrs., Acoustical Soc. Am., Disk Recording & Reproducing Com. Nat. Assn. Broadcasters. Home: 767 Greenwich St New York City NY 10014 Office: 741 Washington St New York City NY 10014

TEMPEST, JEANNE BRUNEAU, newspaper editor; b. West Haven, Conn., Aug. 20, 1930; d. Arthur Magloir and Marie Mathilde (Hupe) Bruneau; A.A., Jr. Coll. Commerce, 1950; m. Anthony John Alderette, Jan. 22, 1952 (dec. 1962); children—Richard, Marc, Paula, James, Ronald, Artyth; m. 2d, Norman Arthur Tempest, Dec. 28, 1963 (div.); children—Jeffrey, Scott. Society stringer New Haven Jour. Courier, 1950; reporter West Haven Town Crier, 1951-52; reporter Granite State News, Wolfeboro, N.H., 1968-70, asso. editor, 1970-71; asso. editor Rochester (N.H.) Courier, 1971-75, editor-in-chief, 1975—. Bd. dirs. N.H. Odyssey House; pres. adv. bd. Salvation Army, 1974-77. Mem. New Eng. (dir.), N.H. (past pres.) press assns., N.H. Press. Women (sec.), Edn. Writers Assn., Strafford County Homemakers Assn. (dir.). Roman Catholic. Club: Altrusa of Rochester (pres.). Home: 4 Giroux St Somersworth NH 03878 Office: Jarvis Ave Rochester NH 03867

TEMPLE, PAUL NATHANIEL, lawyer, investor; b. Cin., Mar. 19, 1923; s. Paul Nathaniel and Alice Marie (White) T.; A.B., Princeton U., 1944; J.D., Harvard U., 1948; m. Karen Borgstrom, Aug. 3, 1944; children—Pamela Temple Abell, Lise Temple Greenberg, Robin Elinor, Thomas D. Admitted to Calif. bar, 1948, D.C. bar, 1950; asso. firm Pillsbury, Madison and Sutro, San Francisco, Washington, 1948-51; atty., exec. Celanese Corp., N.Y.C., 1952-54; internat. concessions negotiator Standard Oil N.J., N.Y.C., 1954-60; pres. Esso Affiliates, Spain, 1961-65; exec. v.p. Gas Natural S.A., Barcelona, 1965-69; pres., co-founder Weeks Natural Resources, Ltd., Westport, Conn., Hamilton, Bermuda, 1970-76; chmn. Energy Capital, Inc., Rosslyn, Va., 1977—, also investor petroleum exploration. Served to ensign USNR, 1944-45. Recipient Civil Merit decoration, Spain, 1969. Mem. Am. C. of C. (pres. Spain 1969), State Bar Calif., Bar Assn. D.C., Inst. Noetic Scis. (co-founder, dir.), Fellowship Found. (v.p., dir.). Episcopalian. Clubs: Mid-Ocean (Bermuda); Puerta de Hierro Golf (Madrid, Spain); Royal Prat Golf (Barcelona, Spain). Asso. producer film Born Again, 1977-78. Home: 2700 Calvert St NW Washington DC 20008 Office: Suite 900 1800 N Kent St Rosslyn VA 22209

TEMPLE, RILEY KEENE, lawyer; b. Richmond, Va., July 9, 1949; s. David Lorenzo and Helen Burnette (Jones) T.; A.B., Lafayette Coll., 1971; J.D., Georgetown U., 1974. Admitted to Va. bar, 1975, D.C. bar, 1978; atty. Corp. for Pub. Broadcasting, Washington, 1974-75, asst. gen. counsel, 1975-77; counsel U.S. Senate Judiciary Com., Washington, 1977-78, U.S. Senate Com. on Govtl. Affairs, 1978-79; sr. counsel RCA Global Communications, Inc., N.Y.C., 1979—. Mem. Nat. Bar Assn., Communications Task Force, Pi Lambda Phi. Republican. Episcopalian. Office: 178 E 80th St New York NY 10021

TEN CATE, ADRIAN GOBEL, ophthalmologist, b. Netherlands, July 14, 1932; s. John and Joan (Ambrosius) T.; M.D., Queens U., 1962. Intern, Montreal (Que., Can.) Gen. Hosp., 1962-63, resident, 1963-64; resident Kingston (Ont., Can.) Gen. Hosp., 1964-66, 67; practice medicine specializing in opthalmology, Brockville, Ont., 1967—; dir. Ormond Leaseholds Ltd., Besancourt Publishers. Fellow Royal Coll. Surgeons (Can.); mem. Leeds and Greenville Med. Soc., Ont. Med. Assn., Can. Opthal. Soc., Brockville and District Hist. Soc. (past pres.). Mem. United Ch. of Canada. Editor: Brockville, A Pictorial History, 1972; Pictorial History of the Thousand Islands, 1977. Home: Rural Route 1 Brockville ON K6V 5T1 Canada Office: 135 Ormond St Brockville ON K6V 5Y2 Canada

TENER, HAMPDEN EVANS, III, chem. co. exec.; b. Pitts., Oct. 10, 1932; s. Hampden Frost and Virginia Louise (Letson) T.; B.A., Amherst Coll., 1954; m. Carol Williams, June 18, 1960; children—Tracy T., Kelly E., Hampden E. Archtl. product sales Alcoa Corp., Pitts., 1958-62; plastic resin sales Avisun Corp., Rochester, N.Y., 1962-66; product mgr. Milacron Chem., New Brunswick, N.J., 1966-69, mktg. mgr., 1969-72; v.p., gen. mgr. Interstab Chems., Inc., New Brunswick, 1973—, also dir. Served as pilot USNR, 1955-58. Mem. Nat. Paint and Coatings Assn., Soc. Plastics Engrs. Clubs: Echo Lake Country, Westfield Tennis. Home: 619 Tremont Ave Westfield NJ 07090 Office: 500 Jersey Ave New Brunswick NJ 08903

TENG, YU-LING, chemist; b. Kiang-Se, China, Aug. 9, 1944; s. Chun-Hau and Shu-Hua (Young) T.; B.S. in Chemistry, Chun-Yuan Coll., 1964; M.A. in Analytical Chemistry, L.I. U., 1967; Ph.D. in Electroanalytical Chemistry, U. Mich., 1973. Analytical chemist Union Indsl. Research Inst., Taiwan, China, 1964-65; mgr., chemist Chinese Pottery Center, N.Y.C., 1974; instr. Middlesex County Coll., Edison, N.J., 1974-76; chief analytical chemist, mgr. Photocircuits Corp., Glen Cove, N.Y., 1976—. Fenwick fellow, 1970-71. Mem. Am. Chem. Soc., Am. Electroplater's Soc., Inst. printed Circuits, Photocircuits Tech. Assn., Phi Lambda Upsilon. Researcher electroanalytical chemistry, wet and instrumental analysis, development and improvement of analytical methods, microanalysis, electro and electroless plating. Home: 141-40 Pershing Circle Briarwood NY 11435 Office: 31 Sea Cliff Ave Glen Cove NY 11542

TENNANT, HARRY LARENZE, editor; b. Seymour, Iowa, Aug. 17, 1909; s. Frank F. and Myrtle (Tennant) Rouse; B.A., State U. Iowa, 1933; postgrad. U. Calif. at Berkeley, 1936; m. Margaret Alice Free, Feb. 14, 1942. Reporter, S.W. Newspress, Los Angeles, 1934; pub. relations Shuberts Theatrical Co., Los Angeles, San Francisco, 1935-38; writer UPI, Omaha, Lincoln, Nebr. and Phila., 1940; city editor Ames (Iowa) Daily Tribune, 1941; corr. Chgo.-N.Y. Jours. of Commerce, Washington, 1945-50, Vision Mag., 1961-65; editor Watson Publs., Washington, 1952-66; U.S. editorial dir. Interavia Pubs., Geneva, 1955-69; editor Cahners Publs., Washington, 1965—, Biomed. News, Washington, 1971-74. Served with U.S. Army, 1942-45. Recipient Explorer I 10th Anniversary medal, 1969; 1st prize typog. excellence Nat. Composition Assn., 1972; Jesse H. Neal Editorial Achievement award, 1975, 76, 77. Mem. Nat. Space Club, White House, State Dept. corrs. assns., Aviation and Space Writers Assn., Nat. Space Writers Assn., Aero Club, Nat. Press Club, Sigma Phi Epsilon. Contbr. articles to profl. jours. Home: 3705 Mill Creek Rd Haymarket VA 22069 Office: Nat Press Bldg Washington DC 20045

TENNENBAUM, ROBERT, architect, planner; b. Vienna, Austria, June 12, 1936; s. Mark and Ernestine (Chayes) T.; B.Arch., Pratt Inst. Sch. Arch., 1959; M.City Planning, Yale U., 1961; m. Marcelle S. Aiss, June 18, 1961; children—Ann, Eve. Urban designer Nat. Capital Planning Commn., Washington, 1961-62, Doxiadis Assos., Planners, Washington, 1962-63; chief architect and planner Rouse Co., Columbia, Md., 1963-69; v.p. planning and urban design R.B.A., Engrs., Planners and Architects, Columbia, 1969-72; prin. Tennenbaum Assos., Columbia, 1972—; prof., dir. grad. community planning program Sch. Social Work and Community Planning, U. Md., Balt., 1976—; past tchr. urban devel. asst. program Balt. Community Colls., New Communities Seminars Program, U. No. Colo.; lectr. urban design and new towns. Democrat. Jewish. Home: 5422 Wild Turkey Ln Columbia MD 21044

TENNIES, ARTHUR CORNELIUS, clergyman; b. Boston, Apr. 15, 1931; s. Raymond Ara and Frances Eden (Fiske) T.; B.S., Grove City Coll., 1953; B.D., Louisville Presbyn. Sem., 1956; M.S., Butler U., 1968; m. S. Janet Trowbridge, Sept. 6, 1959; children—Diane Alicia, Linda Marie, Susan Dawn, Philip Arthur. Ordained to ministery Presbyterian Ch., 1956; pastor, Vernon, Ind., 1956-58, Lewisville, Ind., 1958-64, Burrows, Ind., 1965-66; asso. exec. for ch. planning and research N.Y. State Council Chs., Syracuse, 1967-75; asso. for non-met. ministry United Presbyn. Program Agy., N.Y.C., 1973-76; pastor Tuscarora Presbyn. Ch. and United Ch. Mt. Morris (N.Y.), 1976—. Mem. Research Assn., World Future Soc. Author: A Church for Sinners, Seekers and Sundry Non-Saints, 1974. Contbr. Small Churches Are Beautiful, 1977, also articles to profl. jours. Home and office: 32 Stanley St Mt Morris NY 14510

TENNYSON, MARJORIE LEIGH, coll. adminstr.; b. Youngstown, Ohio, May 7, 1953; d. Edson Leigh and Shirley Lou (Forward) T.; B.S., Pa. State U., 1974, M.Ed., 1977. Geol. field asst. U. Wash., Seattle, 1972, 73; student personnel asst. Coll. Edn., Pa. State U., 1974-77; asst. to dean student life services, resident dir. Clarion State Coll. (Pa.), 1977—, dir. assn. women students, 1977-78. Emergeyncy med. technician Pa. Dept. Health, 1971—; resource person Pa. Dept. Transp. on Bicycle Legis., 1975-76. Mem. Am. Personnel and Guidance Assn., Am. Coll. Personnel Assn., Nat. Ski Patrol, Phi Delta Kappa. Republican. Presbyterian. Club: Nittany Valley Track. Home: Apt 1 Ballentine Clarion PA 16214 Office: 228 Egbert Hall Clarion State Coll Clarion PA 16214

TENOPYR, MARY LOUISE WELSH (MRS. JOSEPH TENOPYR), psychologist; b. Youngstown, O., Oct. 18, 1929; d. Roy Henry and Olive (Donegan) Welsh; A.B., Ohio U., 1951, M.A., 1951; Ph.D., U. So. Calif., 1966; m. Joseph Tenopyr, Oct. 30, 1955. Psychometrist, Ohio U., Athens, 1951-52, also housemother, Sigma Kappa; personnel technician to research psychologist USAF, 1953-55, Dayton, Ohio, 1952-53, Hempstead, N.Y.; indsl. research analyst to mgr. employee evaluation Rockwell Internat., El Segundo, Calif., 1956-70; asso. prof. Calif. State Coll. at Los Angeles, 1966-70; asso. research educationist U. Calif. at Los Angeles, 1970-71; program dir. U.S. Civil Service Commn., 1971-72; mgr. human resources research Am. Tel. & Tel., N.Y.C., 1972—; lectr. U. So. Calif., Los Angeles, 1967-70. Vice chmn. research com. Tech. Adv. Com. on Testing, Fair Employment Practice Commn. Cal., 1966-70; adviser on testing Office Fed. Contract Compliance, U.S. Dept. Labor, Washington, 1967-70. Fellow Am. Psychol. Assn.; mem. Internat. Council Psychologists, Nat. Council on Measurement in Edn., Psychometric Soc., Eastern Psychol. Assn., Internat., Met. N.Y. assns. applied psychology, Am. Ednl. Research Assn., Sigma Xi, Sigma Kappa, Psi Chi, Alpha Lambda Delta, Kappa Phi. Mem. editorial bd. Jour. Applied Psychology. Contbr. articles to profl. jours. Home: 557 Lyme Rock Rd Bridgewater NJ 08807 Office: 295 N Maple Ave Basking Ridge NJ 07920

TEPPER, BLOSSOM WEISS, clin. psychologist; b. Bklyn., Oct. 15, 1921; d. Meyer and Anna (Lax) Weiss; B.A., Bklyn. Coll., 1942; M.Ed., Lehigh U., 1962, Ed.D. in Clin. and Counseling Psychology, 1967; m. Louis Tepper, Apr. 17, 1942 (dec. Aug. 1978); children—Irene Tepper Homa, Allan M. Tchr. sci., guidance counselor Blue Mountain Sch. Dist., Schuylkillhaven, Pa., 1958-64; grad. asst., instr., asst. prof. Lehigh U., Bethlehem, Pa., 1964-71; dir. home and sch. visitor project Luzerne County Schs., Wilkes-Barre, Pa., 1968-71; adj. profl. Wilkes Coll., Wilkes-Barre, 1969-71; clin. psychologist base service unit, dir. Mental Health Mental Retardation, Pottsville, Pa., 1971-72, Easton, Pa., 1972-75; clin. psychologist, mental retardation and developmental disabilities specialist Northampton County Mental Health/Mental Retardation, Bethlehem, Easton, 1975—; cons. community living program for mental retardation, 1975—. Fellow Pa. Psychol. Assn.; mem. Am. Personnel and Guidance Assn., Pa. Personnel and Guidance Assn., Am. Psychol. Assn., Eastern Psychol. Assn., Am. Assn. on Mental Deficiency, Am. Assn. Psychiat. Services for Children, Am. Assn. for Higher Edn. (charter, life mem.), Hadassah (life). Democrat. Jewish. Developer exptl. program for tng. sch. social workers. Home: Bridle Path Woods Apt C12 Bethlehem PA 18017 Office: 2009 Lehigh St Easton PA 18042

TERMAN, JOSEPH, mgmt. and mktg. cons.; b. Chgo., June 5, 1924; s. Abraham and Agnes (Glick) T.; B.A., Crane Coll., 1945; m. Pearl Scharfman, July 10, 1949; children—Diane and David (twins). Mdse. mgr. Petries, N.Y.C., 1946-57, Lady Lynn Stores, Chgo., 1957-65, Three T's, N.Y.C., 1965-69; owner, operator Joe Terman Cons., N.Y.C., 1969—. Mem. Am. Mgmt. Assn., Nat. Retail Mchts. Assn., Nat. Small Bus., Ind. Consultants Assn. Club: Mr. Sword Found. Creator Open-To-buy Program. Office: 310 Lexington Ave New York City NY 10016

TERRANOVA, CARMELO, psychologist; b. Buffalo, Nov. 11, 1932; s. Salvatore and Theresa Pauline (D'Auria) T.; B.A., U. Buffalo, 1955; M.S., Canisius Coll., 1962; Ph.D., State. U. N.Y., Buffalo, 1969; m. Marie Elizabeth Sinaguglia, June 1, 1957; children—Terese-Marie Christine, Roseanne Patricia, Salvatore Joseph, Carl John, John Theodore, Elizabeth Anne. Statistician, State U. N.Y., Buffalo, 1966-68; asst. prof. State U. N.Y. Coll., Oneonta, 1968-69, asso. prof., acting chmn. dept. psychology, 1969-70; sr. research asso. Ednl. Research Council Am., Cleve., 1970-74; dir. instl. research City U. N.Y., Lehman Coll., Bronx, 1974-75; asso. psychologist J. N. Adam Developmental Center, Perrysburg, N.Y., 1975-76; supervising psychologist Mental Health Clinic, Niagara Falls, N.Y., 1976—; practice psychology, 1976—; adj. prof. psychology State U. Coll., 1976—; research and evaluation design cons.; measurement cons. for fed. agys., sch. dists., others. Served with U.S. Army, 1955-57. Mem. Am., Western N.Y. psychol. assns., Assn. Advancement Behavior Therapy, Am. Soc. Clin. Hypnosis, Psychometric Soc., Am. Ednl. Research Assn., Mensa. Author computer programs; contbr. articles to profl. jours.; developed psychol. tests. Home: 18 Woodward Ave Buffalo NY 14214 Office: 6325 Sheridan Dr Amherst NY 14221

TERRELL, JAMES CLETYS, guidance counselor; b. Alton, Kans., Oct. 28, 1930; s. Floyd Christopher and Cecile Blanche (Thornburg) T.; B.A., Kans. Wesleyan U., 1952; M.S., Fort Hays (Kans.) State Coll., 1959, (NDEA fellow 1960, 63), Ed. Specialist, 1964; m. M. Carmelita Hood, Jan. 7, 1953; children—Michael, Catherine, Denise (dec.), Rosanne, Christine. Tchr., counselor Claflin (Kans.) High Sch., 1955-64; counselor Newark (Del.) Sch. Dist., 1964-67, Elkton (Md.) High Sch., 1967-70; dir. guidance Concord High Sch., Wilmington, Del., 1970—; instructional asso. U. Del., Newark, 1970—. Served with U.S. Army, 1952-54. Mem. NEA, Del. Edn. Assn., Am. (senator N.E. region 1977—, chmn. ethics com. 1978), Del (pres. 1977) personnel and guidance assns., Am., Del. (pres. 1976) sch. counselor assns., Am. Legion (post comdr. 1958). Home: 501 Brennen Dr Newark DE 19713 Office: 2501 Ebright Rd Wilmington DE 19810

TERRIS, LILLIAN DICK, psychologist; b. Bloomfield, N.J., May 5, 1914; d. Alexander Blaikie and Herminia Genevieve (Doscher) Dick; B.A., Barnard Coll., 1935; Ph.D., Columbia U., 1941; m. Louis Long, Apr. 22, 1935 (dec. 1968); 1 son, Alexander; m. 2d, Milton Terris, Feb. 6, 1971. Instr. psychology Sarah Lawrence Coll., Bronxville, N.Y., 1937-40; jr. personnel technician Social Security Bd., 1941; sr. personnel technician Office of War Info., 1941-43; dir. profl. examination service Am. Pub. Health Assn., N.Y.C., 1943-71, pres., 1971—. Recipient award, Nat. Environ. Health Assn., 1976. Fellow Am. Coll. Hosp. Adminstrs. (hon.); mem. Am. Psychol. Assn., Am. Pub. Health Assn., AAAS, Phi Beta Kappa, Sigma Xi. Contbr. articles on assessment of competence in health professions to profl. jours. Home: 1120 Fifth Ave New York City NY 10028 Office: 475 Riverside Dr New York City NY 10027

TERRY, EDWARD ALLISON, JR., civil engr., govt. ofcl.; b. Atlanta, Nov. 14, 1940; s. Edward A. and Annie Ayres (Lewis) T.; B.C.E., Auburn U., 1963; postgrad. Catholic U., 1967, Pa. State U., 1974, U.S. Dept. Agr. Grad. Sch., 1975, 78; m. Lady Marion Andridge, June 4, 1962; children—Louise Ayres, Edward Allison, Elizabeth Anne. Hwy. engr. Fed. Hwy. Adminstr., Dinosaur, Colo., 1965, 66, Harrisburg, Pa., 1965-66, San Francisco, 1966-67, Washington, 1967, Tallahassee, 1967-68, asst. area engr., 1968-69, area engr., 1969-74, regional materials engr., Arlington, Va., 1974-76, dist. engr., Balt., 1976—. Soccer coach Edmonson Recreation Council, 1977—. Served to 1st lt. U.S. Army, 1963-65. Recipient Outstanding Performance Rating award Fed. Hwy. Adminstrn., 1969, 72. Registered profl. engr., Ala. Mem. Assn. Asphalt Paving Technologists, Res. Officers Assn. U.S., Tau Kappa Epsilon. Presbyterian (ordained ruling elder 1975—, Sunday sch. tchr. 1971-73, 78, youth adviser 1973-74; ordained deacon 1972-73, supt. Sunday schs., 1975-76). Home: 10 Madison Mills Ct Baltimore MD 21228 Office: Suite 220 The Rotunda 711 W 40th St Baltimore MD 21211

TESLA, IWAN, geographer; b. Nastasiw, Ukraine, Aug. 19, 1902; s. Jacob and Thekla (Bilakh) T.; came to Can., 1948, naturalized, 1954; M.A., U. Lviv, 1932, Ph.D., 1939; Ph.D., Ukrainian Free U., Munich, Germany, 1946; m. Julia Maria Mycyk, Sept. 30, 1939; children—Bohdan-Daniel, George, Marichka. Asst. to Prof. H. Arctowski, Inst. Meteorology and Geophysics, U. Lviv, 1932-39; lectr. climatology Ukrainian Free U., Munich, Germany, 1946-48; sec. gen. Shevchenko Sci. Soc. Can., Toronto, Ont., 1949-54; faculty Dept. Mines and Tech. Surveys, Ottawa, Ont., 1956-69. Fellow Shevchenko Sci. Soc., Ukrainian Free Acad. Scis.; mem. Can. Assn. Geographers, Assn. Am. Geographers. Author: Geography of Ukraine, 1942; Historical Atlas of Ukraine, 1976. Editor Ukrainian tchrs. jour. Ukrainska Shkola, 1940-45. Research macroclimatical variations. Home: 8 Tormey St Ottawa ON K1N 5V8 Canada

TESLER, MAX A., gastroenterologist; b. N.Y.C., Jan. 29, 1931; s. James and Bertha (Snyder) T.; B.A., N.Y. U., 1951, M.D., 1955; m. Nancy Linda Blumenthal, Nov. 11, 1956; children—Kenneth, Robert, Douglas. Intern, Bellevue Hosp., N.Y.C., 1955-56, asst. resident, 1956-57, research fellow Cornell div., 1961-62; chief resident N.Y. U. Hosp., 1959-60; research Fellow Yale Med. Center, New Haven, 1960-61; practice medicine specializing in gastroenterology, N.Y.C., 1962—; chmn. bd. dirs. Biometric Testing Inc., 1970—, Broadway Capital Corp. Served to maj. USAF, 1957-59. Diplomate Am. Bd. Internal Medicine. Mem. Am. Gastroent. Assn., Am. Soc. Gastroent. Endoscopy, N.Y. Soc. Gastroenterology, Am. Assn. Hosp. Med. Edn. Clubs: Atrium. Home: 110 De Vriese Ct Tenafly NJ 07670 Office: 30 Central Park S New York City NY 10019

TESORO, GEORGE ALFRED, lawyer; b. Rome, Feb. 6, 1904; s. Alfred and Anna (Russi) T.; came to U.S., 1940, naturalized, 1946; D.J., U. Rome, 1925, D. Pol. Sci., 1929, Ph.D., 1930; m. Gilda De Mauro, Mar. 18, 1934; children—Alfred W., Alexandra L. Tesoro Miller. Corp. lawyer, tax expert, Rome, 1927-38; instr., lectr. econs. and taxation U. Rome, 1930-35; asso. prof. pub. fin. and taxation U. Bari (Italy), 1935-38; news editor, announcer sta. WOV, N.Y.C., 1941-42; lectr. econs. Lawrence Coll., Appleton, Wis., 1942; vis. prof., lectr., adj. prof. econs. Am. U., 1942-55; econ. analyst, chief sec. Fgn. Econ. Adminstr., 1944-46; with Div. Econ. Devel. and Office Western European Affairs, U.S. Dept. State, 1946-55, fgn. service officer, 1955-65, sr. econ. officer, counselor U.S. Mission, Geneva, 1956-65; admitted to D.C. bar, 1948; counsel firm Cox, Langford, & Brown, Washington, 1965-69, Coudert Bros., Washington, 1969—. Chmn. bd. trustees Am. U. Rome, 1975—. Decorated comdr. Merito Della Repubblica, 1971. Mem. Am., D.C., Fed. bar assns., Am. Soc. Internat. Law, Am. Fgn. Service Assn., Washington Fgn. Law Soc. Clubs: Cosmos, Nat. Lawyers (Washington); Met. (N.Y.C.). Author books in field. Home: 4000 Massachusetts Ave NW Washington DC 20016 Office: One Farragut Sq S Washington DC 20006

TESSLER, ALLAN ROGER, lawyer, bus. exec.; b. Phila., Sept. 29, 1936; s. Irving and Rhoda (Marinoff) T.; B.A. (Knickerbocker scholar), Cornell U., 1958, LL.B., 1963; m. Frances Goudsmit, June 17, 1958; children—Andrea Leslie, Christopher Lee, Karla Beth. Admitted to N.Y. bar, 1963; asso. firm Cleary, Gottlieb, Steen & Hamilton, N.Y.C., 1963-67; with arbitrage dept. Leob, Rhoades & Co., N.Y.C., 1967-68; U.S. rep. Butlers Bank Ltd., N.Y.C., 1968; mng. partner Devon Securities, N.Y.C., 1969-72; exec. v.p. Ladenburg, Thalmann & Co., Inc., N.Y.C., 1972; pres., chmn. bd. Fifth Ave. Coach Lines Inc., N.Y.C., 1972-73; pres. Slater, Walker of Am., 1972-73, Slater, Walker of Am. Ltd., 1973-75; counsel firm Spengler, Carlson, Gubar & Churchill, N.Y.C., 1975-76; partner firm Shea Gould Climenko & Casey, N.Y.C., 1976—; dir. Horizon Corp., Exec. Life Ins. Co. N.Y., Checker Motors Corp. Served with USN, 1958-61. Mem. N.Y. Bar Assn., Order of Coif, Phi Kappa Phi. Club: Harmonie (N.Y.C.). Home: 4 Blueberry Hill Rd Irvington NY 10533 Office: Shea Gould Climenko & Casey 330 Madison Ave New York City NY 10017

TESSLER, HERBERT ALAN, architect, constrn. cons.; b. Lido Beach, N.Y., Jan. 26, 1931; s. Benjamin and Yetta (Samuels) T.; B. Arch., Pratt Inst., 1954, M.Arch., 1956; m. Eva Wilkenfeld, Sept. 6, 1952; children—Warren Scott, Linda Norene, Jill Sandi. Urban renewal specialist Brown & Guenther, Architects, N.Y.C., 1956-57; airport architect Port N.Y. Authority, N.Y.C., 1957-62, mgr. planning World Trade Center, 1962-68; dir. design and constrn. N.Y. State Urban Devel. Corp., 1968-75; v.p., gen. mgr. McKee, Berger, Mansueto, Constrn. Consultants, 1975-76; pres. Herbert Tessler Architect, architects and constrn. cons., 1976-77; prin. Tessler & Panero, Architects and Constrn. Cons., 1977—. Past pres. Lido Homes Civic Assn. Recipient 1st prize Chgo. Planning Competition, 1954, Exec. Dir.'s award Achievement Port N.Y. Authority, 1964; named Outstanding Young Am., Chgo. Jaycees, 1954. Mem. AIA, Am. Acad. Architects and Related Scis. in Govt. (chmn. bd. dirs. 1967—), N.Y. Soc. Architects, Am. Soc. Planning Ofcls. Home and Office: 177 Lagoon Dr W Lido Beach NY 11561

THAKKER, ASHOK BHAGWANDAS, aluminum co. exec.; b. Bombay, India, Aug. 9, 1947; s. Bhagwandas P. and Champa B. (Lakhpatia) T.; came to U.S., 1970; B.C.E., Bombay U., 1970; M.S., S.D. Sch. Mines and Tech., 1971; Ph.D., Va. Poly. Inst. and State U., 1974; m. Sarla A. Bhate, Dec. 30, 1975. Research asst. Va. Poly. Inst. and State U., Blacksburg, 1972-73, instr., 1973-74; sr. engr. Alcoa Research Lab., Aluminum Co. Am., Alcoa Center, Pa., 1974—. Registered profl. engr., Va. Mem. ASTM, Am. Inst. Aeros. and Astronautics, Soc. Exptl. Stress Analysis, Sci. Research Soc. N.Am., Sigma Xi. Club: Toastmasters (adminstrv. v.p. Alcoa chpt.). Contbr. articles in field to profl. jours. Home: 230 Rockingham Rd Pittsburgh PA 15238 Office: Alcoa Tech Center Alcoa Center PA 15069

THALACKER, DONALD WILLIAM, architect/art adminstr.; b. Detroit, July 29, 1939; s. Arbie Otto and Jeanne (Emmett) T.; B.A., Washington and Lee U., 1961; B.Arch. with highest honors, U. Calif. at Berkeley, 1967; m. Helene Marie Heldenstein, Sept. 7, 1968; children—Christian, Francoise. Architect, Skidmore, Owings, & Merrill/Wuster, Bernardi & Emmons, San Francisco, 1967-70; architect GSA, San Francisco, 1970-71, Washington, 1971—, dir. art-in-architecture program, 1972—; lectr. in field. Served with U.S. Army and Res., 1961-67. Mem. Nat./Internat. Sculpture Conf., Delta Tau Delta. Club: Edgemoor (Bethesda, Md.). Author: The Place of Art in the World of Architecture, 1979. Home: 11 Magnolia Pkwy Chevy Chase MD 20015 Office: GSA Washington DC 20405

THALBERG, JOSEPH HYMAN, lawyer; b. New Haven, Apr. 5, 1904; s. Abraham J. and Minnie (Hyman) T.; LL.B., Bklyn. Sch. of St. Lawrence U., 1925; m. Florence Wittenberg, July 14, 1930; children—Stanton P., Sara E. Admitted to Conn., bar, 1927, Supreme Ct. Conn., 1927, U.S. Dist. Ct., 1931, U.S. Supreme Ct. bar, 1936, Tax Ct. U.S., 1946; practiced in New Haven, 1927-32, Southington, Conn., 1932—; counsel Town of Southington, 1960-62, 70-71. Dir. Southington Savs. Bank. Prosecutor of Town Court, Southington, 1943-45, 53-55. Bd. dirs., past pres. YMCA; pres. Southington Community Chest, 1949-51; chief air raid warden, Southington, World War II. Mem. Meriden-Wallingford-Southington (past pres.), Am., Conn., Hartford County, Meriden bar assns., Nat. Fedn. Jewish Men's Clubs (dir., past pres. Conn. Valley region), Southington C. of C. (pres. 1948-49). Jewish religion (pres. temple 1965-67; pres. temple mens' club 1955-57). Mason (32 deg., Shriner), Odd Fellow (past grand), Eagle. Club: Exchange (past pres.). Home: 45 Buckland St Plantsville CT 06479 Office: 24 N Main St Southington CT 06489

THALER, DAVID, newspaper editor; b. Newark, Oct. 19, 1940; s. Aaron and Ida (Bederman) T.; B. Journalism, U. Mo., 1962; m. Sara Elizabeth Bryant, June 3, 1962 (div.); children—Philip Nathan, Anne Courtney; m. 2d, Judith Anne Lewis, Dec. 22, 1977. Reporter, Belleville (N.J.) Times-News, 1956-58; reporter, Bayonne (N.J.) Times, 1960; mng. editor, Palos (Ill.) Regional, 1962-63; regional news editor Ry. Age Weekly, Chgo., 1963-64; asso. editor Am. Builder, N.Y.C., 1964-66, mng. editor, 1966-68; asst. to chmn. bd. U.S. Homes Corp., West Orange, N.J., 1969-70; contbg. editor House & Home, N.Y.C., 1969-70; editor and pub. The Bayshore Ind., Keyport, N.J., 1970—; pres. Monmouth Communications Corp., Keyport, 1970—. Mem. Mayor's Citizen adv. com., Keyport, 1973—, journalism adv. com. Brookdale Community Coll., 1972—; chmn. Keyport Improvement Com., 1974. Recipient Jesse H. Neal Editorial Achievement award Nat. Assn. Bus. Publs., 1967. Mem. Matawan (dir. 1973-74), Keyport (dir., 1974) chambers commerce, Kappa Tau Alpha. Jewish religion. Home: POB 81 Keyport NJ 07735 Office: POB 81 Keyport NJ 07735

THALER, WARREN ALAN, chemist; b. N.Y.C., Jan. 7, 1934; s. Jack and Lillian (Cwirn) T.; B.S. cum laude, Coll. City N.Y., 1956; M.A., Columbia, 1958, Ph.D., 1961; m. Harriet Sandra Raynes, June 17, 1956; children—Alaine Caryn, Lauren Sue. With Exxon Research and Engring. Co., Linden, N.J., 1960—, research asso. corp. research lab., 1972-78, sr. research asso. corp. research lab., 1978—. Mem. Am. Chem. Soc., N.Y. Acad. Scis., Phi Beta Kappa, Sigma Xi, Phi Lambda Upsilon. Jewish. Club: B'nai B'rith (local pres. 1970-71, dist. gov. 1971-74). Author: (with Richard M. Kellogg) Methods in Free Radical Chemistry, Vol. 2, 1969. Contbr. articles to profl. jours. Patentee in field. Home: 133 Deerfield Ln Matawan NJ 07747 Office: Exxon Research and Engring Co Linden NJ 07036

THAR, F. A., assn. exec.; b. Paw Paw, Mich., Oct. 26, 1940; s. James Ferdinand and Olga Louise (Schmidt) T.; B.A., Mich. State U., 1964; postgrad. Boston U., 1964-65, Am. U., 1969-73, U. Ga., 1978; m. Siri Ashelman, Jan. 28, 1967; children—Jonathan Justin, Christina Sheri. U.S. del. 1st World Agr. Fair, New Delhi, 1960; U.S. del. Internat. Farm Youth Exchange, Israel, 1962, Mich. pres. 1963-64; condr. citizenship seminars Nat. 4-H Found., 1964; research writer Mich. State U., 1964; staff store front UMCA, Roxbury, Mass., 1964-65; program officer Govtl. Affairs Inst., 1965-73; participant White House Conf. on Internat. cooperation, 1967, White House Conf. on Balanced Growth, 1978; spl. asst. natural resources and environ. mgmt. Nat. Govs. Assn., Washington, 1973-75, liaison with Fed. Energy Adminstrn., 1974, spl. asst. to staff dir. Transp., Commerce and Tech. Com., 1975-78; staff dir. Internat. Trade and Fgn. Relations Com., 1979—; guest lectr. urban planning Am. U. Active soccer team and Boy Scouts Am., Chevy Chase, Md., 1974-78; exec. com. Nat. Com. Uniform Traffic Laws and Ordinances; policy com. Transp. Research Bd., 1977—. Recipient grant Friends Com. on Nat. Legis., 1965. Mem. Am. Polit. Sci. Assn., Asia Soc., Nat. Council Community Services to Internat. Visitors, Am. Sociol. Assn., Chevy Chase Citizens Assn. Christian. Author: Rural Youth Michigan, 1964; Influence of International Travel on Vocational Choice, 1964; Early Education in Israel, 1962; Foreign Students at Boston U., 1965. Home: 5618 Nebraska Ave NW Washington DC 20015 Office: Hall of the States 444 N Capitol St Washington DC 20001

THARION, ROSELLE LAVINA, psychologist; b. Greenville Junction, Maine, Jan. 26, 1924; d. Charles Emanuel and Eva Mae (Smith) Johnson; B.A. cum laude, Colby Coll., 1946; M.A., Boston U., 1947; postgrad. Curry Coll., Bridgewater State Coll., Boston U., Southeastern Mass. U., Worcester State Coll., 1966-77; m. July 26, 1947; children—Karen, Deborah, Janet, Laurel. Social worker Dept. Pub. Welfare, Middleboro, Mass., 1946; staff mem. Office Ednl. Research, Dartmouth Coll., Hanover, N.H., 1946-47; social worker, psychometrist Middleboro Pub. Schs., 1967-69, psychologist, 1969-72, adjustment counselor, psychologist, 1972-75, spl. needs counselor, 1975—. Bd. dirs. Citizens Scholarship Found., 1966-68, Middleboro Lakeville Mental Health Center, 1964-74, Area Mental Health and Retardation Bd., 1969-75, Taunton Mental Health Center. Mem. Am. Personnel and Guidance Assn., Mass. Assn. Children with Learning Disabilities, Mass. Sch. Counselors Assn., Mass. Psychol. Assn., Mass. Sch. Psychologists Assn., Mass. Tchrs. Assn., Nat. Tchrs. Assn., Phi Beta Kappa, Delta Kappa Gamma, Pi Gamma Mu. Congregationalist. Club: Reservoir Heights Country. Home: 4 Oliver St Middleboro MA 02346 Office: Burkland Sch Mayflower Ave Middleboro MA 03246

THARP, TWYLA, choreographer; b. Portland, Ind., July 1, 1941; d. William A. and Lecile C. T.; B.A., Barnard Coll., 1964; D. Performing Arts (hon.), Calif. Inst. for Arts, 1978; 1 son, Jesse Huot. Choreographer numerous works, 1965—, including Duece Coupe, 1973, As Time Goes By, 1973, Happily Ever After, 1976 (for Joffrey Ballet); Push Comes to Shove, 1976 (for Mikhail Baryshnikov and Am. Ballet Theatre); After All, 1976 (for figure skater John Curry); artistic dir. Twyla Tharp Dance Found., N.Y.C., 1970—; choreographer for film: Hair (United Artist). Recipient Creative Arts citation Brandeis U., 1972; John Simon Guggenheim fellow, 1971, 74; Nat. Endowment for Arts grantee, 1973—; Creative Artists Pub. Service Program grantee, 1974-75. Co-producer TV prodns.: Eight Jelly Roll, 1974, Making Television Dance, 1978; appeared in Making Televions Dance. Office: 38 Walker St New York City NY 10013

THAU, HAROLD ADRIAN, rec. co. exec.; b. N.Y.C., Sept. 4, 1934; s. Morris and Shirley (Fisbein) T.; B.B.A., Coll. City N.Y., 1956; M.S., Columbia, 1958; m. Dorothy Golden, Aug. 4; children—Michael, Amy. Partner, Rosenblum, Rubin, Burn & Thau, C.P.A.'s, N.Y.C., 1962-72; pres. Royalty Controls Corp., N.Y.C., 1972—, also dir.; sec. John Denver Enterprises, Inc., N.Y.C., 1976—; partner Windstar Prodns., Aspen, Colo., 1976—; pres. Windsong Records, Inc., N.Y.C., 1976—; sec., dir. John Jer Prodns., Inc., Beverly Hills, Calif., 1975—. Dir. The Windstar Found., Aspen, Colo., 1976—. C.P.A., N.Y. Home: 19 Saugatuck River Rd Weston CT 06880 Office: 1345 Ave of Americas New York City NY 10019 also 1234 Summer St Stamford CT 06905

THEBERGE, LEONARD JOSEPH, lawyer; b. Oceanside, N.Y., May 17, 1935; s. Lionel J. and Antoinette Marie (Tomasulo) T.; B.A., Columbia U., 1957; certificate U. Paris, 1954; LL.B., N.Y. Law Sch., 1960; M.A., U. Oxford, 1968; m. Virginia Elizabeth Rice, Aug. 1, 1963; children—Michele Elizabeth, Christina Grace-Anne, Valerie Bennett. Admitted to N.Y. bar, 1961, D.C. bar, 1962, Mass. bar, 1969, Mich. bar, 1972; asst. U.S. atty. Eastern Dist. N.Y., 1963-66; atty. FTC, Washington, 1961-62; internat. counsel Upjohn Co., Kalamazoo, 1969-72; v.p. corp. services Rohr Industries, San Diego, 1972-74; pres. Nat. Legal Center for Pub. Interest, 1975—; cons. Pacific Legal Found., 1975—. Mem. Mich. Hist. Soc., 1972-73, Natural Hist. Soc. San Diego, 1973-75, San Diego Hist. Soc., 1973—; chmn. Kalamazoo Hist. Commn., 1971-72; bd. dirs. St. Peters Coll. Oxford Found., 1969-75, U.S. Com. for Study Conflict, 1974-75, Mountain States Legal Found., Mid-Am. Legal Found., Capital Legal Found. Recipient Meritorious Service award FTC, 1962. Fellow Royal Econ. Soc.; mem. Am., Fed., Internat. bar assns., Oxford Soc., Columbia Coll. Assn., Old Blue Rugy Football Club. Mng. editor The Internat. Lawyer, 1969; editor: Current Legal Aspects of Doing Business in Europe, 1971; Multinational Corporation Checklist for Foreign Subsidiaries, 1975. Home: 5801 Huntington Pkwy Bethesda MD 20014 Office: Suite 810 1101 17th St NW Washington DC 20036

THELEN, EDMUND, research exec.; b. Berkeley, Calif., May 8, 1913; s. Paul and Alice (Arnold) T.; B.S., U. Calif., Berkeley, 1934; m. Helen Naomi Betton, Oct. 30, 1965; children—Nancy Anne, Joan Arnold Thelen Hanson. Asst. chemist Certain-Teed Products Corp., Richmond, Calif., 1934-35; chemist O. C. Field Gasoline Corp., Santa Maria, Calif., 1936-41; asst. mgr. Eclipse Pioneer div. Bendix Corp., Teterboro, N.J., 1946-47; sr. research chemist Franklin Inst. Research Labs., Phila., 1947-51, mgr. colloids and polymers br., 1951-74, v.p., dir. phys. and life scis. dept., 1974-76, Inst. fellow, sec. com. on sci. and the arts, 1976—; mem. Council for Delivery of Dental Care, 1970—; bd. govs. Franklin-Hahnemann Inst. Occupational and Environ. Health, 1975—, Mayor's Sci. and Tech. Adv. Com. on Environment, 1973—; instr. dental medicine Hahnemann Med. Coll. and Hosp., 1964-74; v.p., dir. Pa. Environ. Council, 1974—. Served with USN, 1941-45; to comdr. USNR, 1941-66. Recipient spl. recognition award Am. Soc. Landscape Architects, 1974. Mem. AAAS, ASTM, Hwy. Research Bd., Franklin Inst., Sierra Club (Eastern Pa. group chmn. 1968, Atlantic chpt. vice chmn. 1971-73, founding chmn. Pa. chpt. 1974), Friends of the Earth, Nat. Audubon Soc. Sigma Xi. Club: Toastmasters Internat. (dist. gov. 1959-60). Patentee asphalts, dropwise condensation, safe fibres to replace asbestos; head devel. team, co-author book on Porous Pavement for Runoff Control, 1978; contbr. papers to tech. publs. Home: 658 Davis Ln Strafford PA 19087 Office: Franklin Inst 20th and Parkway Philadelphia PA 19103

THEODORE, FREDERICK HAROLD, ophthalmologist; b. N.Y.C., Apr. 4, 1908; s. Benno and Luba (Biscow) T.; A.B., Columbia Coll., 1927, M.D., 1931; m. Jeanne Sincoff, Feb. 6, 1940; children—Andrea, William. Intern, Mt. Sinai Hosp., N.Y.C., 1931-34, resident in ophthalmology, 1934-36; practice medicine specializing in ophthalmology, N.Y.C., 1936—; attending ophthalmic surgeon Manhattan Eye, Ear and Throat Hosp., 1958—; asso. clin. prof. N.Y. U., 1951-73; clin. prof. Mt. Sinai Sch. Medicine, 1970—; cons. in field. Served with U.S. Army, 1942-45. Schoenberg Meml. lectr., 1968; recipient Jacobi medallion Mt. Sinai Alumni, 1973. Sr. author: Ocular Allergy, 1958; editor, contbr. Complications After Cataract Surgery, 1965. Mem. editorial bd. Pediatric Ophthalmology, 1964—; asso. editor Eye, Ear, Nose and Throat Monthly, 1963—. Contbr. chpts. to books, numerous articles on infections and allergy of eye to profl. jours.; pioneer in sterility of ophthalmic drugs, eye infection diagnosis and treatment. Home: 1120 Park Ave New York City NY 10028 Office: 625 Park Ave New York City NY 10021

THEODORE, THOMAS RONALD, research cons.; b. Manchester, N.H., Jan. 3, 1946; s. Paul Raco and Flora (Chicos) T.; C.B.S., Boston U., 1966; S.B., Mass. Inst. Tech., 1968; postgrad. Joint Program in Health and Tech., Harvard-Mass. Inst. Tech., 1974—; m. Mary Lou Sallee, Sept. 7, 1975; 1 dau., Lauren Marie. With Bolt, Beranek & Newman-Prototech div., Cambridge, Mass., 1964-70, Chickering, Boston, 1970-71; ind. research cons. bio-physics, Arlington, Mass., 1971—; instr. anatomy Boston U., 1968-69; cons. physiol. man-machine instrumentation lab. criteria, 1973; cons. Theta Tech., Wethersfield, Conn., 1976; cons. clin. dir. Hairgenics, Inc., Cambridge, Mass., 1978. Active ARC blood drive, 1970-72. Mem. Am. Coll. Sports Medicine (certified), Am. Inst. Aeros. and Astonautics, Assn. Surg. Technologists, Internat. Assn. for Hydrogen Energy, Boston Athletic Assn. (med. unit), Am. Def. Preparedness Assn., Inst. for Am. Strategy, Am. Security Council, Pan-Am. Albanian Fedn. Vatra. Club: Order DeMolay. Inventor: Caloric Computer L71, 1973; inventor method of improving the conduction of sound in stethescope tubing, electrophysiol. measurements of the human heart using technique of concentration polarization. Address: 57 Jame St Arlington MA 02174

THERIAULT, ROMEO JOSEPH, assn. exec.; b. Paquetville, N.B., Can., Sept. 16, 1922; s. Joseph Honore and Marie Monique (Godin) T.; student pub. schs., Paquetville, N.B., student Holy Cross Father Coll. 1938-42. Sec. to Police Magistrat, Paquetville, N.B., 1943-44; with M.A. Green Co., Waterbury, Conn., 1953-61; exec. dir. Northeastern N.B. Vets. Assn., Bathurst, N.B., 1973—; exec. dir Mobile Info. Centre, Bathurst, N.S., 1972—; commr. oath, Province of N.B., 1974—. Served with Royal Canadian Air Forces, 1951-53. Sherbrooke U. grantee, 1972-73; Inst. Cultural and Social Jean XXIII grantee, 1974. Mem. Canadian Social Devel. Conf. (dir. 1976-77), Atlantic Devel. Conf., Nat. Anti-Poverty Orgn., Canadian Council on Development, Canadian Legion, Nova Scotia l'Assn., Nouvelle Vie Inc. Liberal Party. Roman Catholic. Club: Order of the Good Time. Author: Repetoire des Services Communautaire du Nord-Est du N.B., 1975, 2nd. edit., 1976. Home: 478 King Ave Bathurst NB Canada Office: 231 Main St Bathurst NB Canada

THERRIEN, ROBERT WILFRID, constrn. co. exec.; b. Manchester, N.H., Oct. 31, 1929; s. Alfred Wilfrid and Fedora Alma (Morin) T.; student U. N.H., 1948-49; B.A., St. Anselm's Coll., 1952; postgrad. Boston U., 1953-54; m. Beverly L. Ferron, Aug. 15, 1954; children—Robert Wilfrid, Clara Elena, David, Mary. Pres., Al Melanson Co., Inc., Keene, 1953—; treas. R & M Realty, Keene, 1961, Vt. Roofing Co., Inc., Rutland, 1962—, Tri State Acoustical, Inc., Keene, and Rutland, Vt., 1967—; dir. Keene Co-op. Bank. Pres., Daniel Webster council Boy Scouts Am., 1975-78; bd. dirs. YMCA, Monadnock United Fund; trustee N.H. Cath. Charities, Inc., 1968-75. Recipient Silver Beaver award Boy Scouts Am., 1962. Mem. Nat., New Eng. (dir.) roofing contractors assns., C. of C. (dir.). Clubs: Elks, Moose, K.C. (4 deg.), Rotary. Home: Sawyer Crossing Swanzey NH 03431 Office: 353 West St Keene NH 03431

THIBAULT, ARNOLD FRANCIS, constrn. co. exec.; b. Digby, N.S., Can., Jan. 8, 1948; s. James Edward and Elise Marie (Saulnier) T.; came to U.S., 1950, naturalized, 1969; B.S. in Civil Engring., Merrimack Coll., 1969; M.S., Northeastern U., 1972, postgrad., 1972-74; m. Donna Lee Butterfield, Aug. 23, 1969. Resident engr. bridge constrn. div. Washington Hwy. Dept., 1969-70; chief engr., estimator Hub Found. Co., Inc., Wellesley, Mass., 1974-75; contract mgr. George Hyman Constrn. Co., Bethesda, Md., 1975—; cons. engring., constrn., mgmt., 1973—. Mem. several condominium coms. Served to capt. Med. Service Corps, U.S. Army, 1970-74. Registered profl. engr., Maine, N.H., Vt., Mass., R.I., Conn., N.Y., D.C., Fla., Va., Md. R.I. scholar, 1965-69, Ednl. Opportunity grantee, 1965-69, Merrimack scholar, 1967-69. Mem. ASCE, Nat. Soc. Profl. Engrs., Boston Soc. Civil Engrs., Am. Soc. Engring. Educators, Internat. Soc. Soil Mechanics and Foundation Engrs., Sigma Xi, Mu Chi Epsilon, Theta Xi. Home: 18357 Lost Knife Circle Apt 304 Gaithersburg MD 20760 Office: 4930 Del Ray Ave Bethesda MD 20014

THIELSCH, HELMUT JOHN, pipe materials co. exec., metall. engr.; b. Berlin, Germany, Nov. 16, 1922; s. Kurt and Anna- Sibylle (Pape) T.; came to U.S., 1939, naturalized, 1954; B.S., Auburn U., 1943; postgrad. U. Mich., 1943-45, Lehigh U., 1948; m. Margaret E. McKenna, Aug. 1952; children—Barbara Anne, Donald Kurt, Deborah Lee, Helmut John. Research engr. Allis Chalmers Co., Milw., 1945-46; metall. engr. Black, Sivalls & Bryson, Inc., Kansas City, Mo., 1946-47; research engr. Lukens Steel Co., Coatsville, Pa., 1948-49; engr. Welding Research Council, N.Y.C., 1949-52; dir. research Eutectic Welding Alloys Co., 1952-53; v.p. dir. research and devel. ITT Grinnell Corp., Providence, R.I., 1954—; cons. on failure anlysis to industry, pub. utilities, equipment builders, 1954—. Registered profl. engr., R.I., Mass., N.J., Maine, Ga., Calif. Fellow ASME, Am. Welding Soc., Nat. Assn. Corrosive Engrs., Am. Soc. for Metals, Am. Soc. for Nondestructive Testing, Am. Chem. Soc., Am. Mgmt. Assn., Am. Nuclear Soc., Am. Soc. Quality Control, Sigma Xi. Author: Defects and Failures in Pressure Vessels and Piping, 1965; contbr. articles in field to profl. jours.; patentee in field. Home: 140 Shaw Ave Cranston RI 02905 Office: 260 W Exchange St Providence RI 02901

THIES, PHOEBE LORENE ANDERSON, educator; b. Jamestown, N.Y., Feb. 17, 1918; d. George and Doretta Cecelia (Lindbeck) Anderson; diploma Fredonia Normal Sch., 1939; B.S., State U. N.Y. Fredonia, 1955; M.S. magna cum laude, N.Y. State U. Coll. Buffalo, 1965; certificate advanced study (Fed. fellow), Syracuse U., 1966; postgrad. Calif. State Tchrs. Coll., 1970, U. Nebr., 1977—; m. Earl LeRoy Thies, Jr., Apr. 4, 1942 (dec. 1965); children—Dan Reese, Jackie Lynne (Mrs. Arthur L. Jackson, Jr.), Michael Earl, Patricia Cecelia. Kindergarten tchr., Portville, N.Y., 1939-41, Jamestown, N.Y., 1941-42, 52-61; helped to inaugurate trainable classes, tchr. trainable mentally retarded Charles St. Sch., Jamestown, N.Y., 1961-65; supr.-head spl. edn. dept. Jamestown Pub. Schs, 1966-72, tchr. pre-primary educable mentally retarded Love Sch., 1969-72, tchr. jr. high educable class Washington Jr. High, 1972-76, Lincoln Jr. High, 1976-78; resource-room tchr. R.R. Rogers Elementary Sch., 1978—; part-time instr. human services Jamestown Community Coll., 1972—. Helped establish Spl. Olympics in Chautauqua County, 1970—; v.p. Northside Community Center, 1968-71; mem. Human Rights Commn., 1968-76; cook Camp Onyahsa, 1969-77; Jamestown area coordinator Buffalo Variety Club Camperships for Mentally Handicapped Children, 1968—. Bd. dirs. Chautauqua County Assn. Mental Health, 1970-73, Chautauqua County chpt. A.R.C., 1963-65, 70-73. Ruth Frazier scholar Delta Kappa Gamma, 1977-78. Mem. Assn. for Childhood Edn. (pres. 1962-63), N.Y. State Tchrs. Mentally Handicapped, Council for Exceptional Children (pres. 1971-72), NEA, N.Y. State Edn. Assn., Jamestown Tchrs. Assn. (Spl. award for community service 1976), Assn. for Children with Learning Disabilities (adv. bd. 1972-74), Am. Assn. for Mental Deficiency, P.T.A. (life), Delta Kappa Gamma. Home: 47 Clyde Ave Jamestown NY 14701

THIGPEN, EDWARD LESTER, graphics co. exec.; b. Balt., June 16, 1938; s. Lester V. and Thelma B. (Bolland) T.; B.A., Western Md. Coll., 1959; S.T.B., M.S.T.(hon.), Wesley Theol. Sem., Washington, 1963; Ph.D., Am. U., 1972; postgrad. George Washington U., Vanderbilt U., So. Methodist U., 1973-75; m. Betsy A. Bowman, June 22, 1963; children—Deborah Leslie, Edward II. Ordained to ministry United Methodist Ch., 1963; minister chs., Balt., York, Pa., 1960-78; adminstr. York County (Pa.) Hosp. and Home, 1965-66; dir. personnel Thonet Industries div. Simmon Co., York, 1966-70; v.p., dir. personnel York Graphic Co. (Pa.), 1970—, v.p., dir. personnel York Graphic Service, Inc., 1970—; exec. dir. Printing Industries of Va., Charlottesville, 1978—; pastor Adamsville United Meth. Ch., 1976—; instr. behavioral sci. York Coll.; mgmt. cons. Recipient award St. Johns Soc., 1960, Outstanding Citizen award Am. Legion, 1962, citation Gov. Raymond Shaffer, 1967. Mem. Am. Mgmt. Assn., Am. Soc. Tng. and Devel., Am. Soc. Personnel Dirs., C. of C., Nat. Alliance Businessmen (dir.), Council Chs., Indsl. Relations Council, Mfrs. Assn. (sec.-treas.). Democrat. Clubs: Lions, Rotary, Masons. Contbr. personnel adminstrn. and religious articles to various jours. Home: 3175 Brookside Ave Dover PA 17315 Office: PO Box 865 Charlottesville VA 22902

THIMM, ALFRED LOUIS, economist, coll. adminstr.; b. Vienna, Austria, Dec. 10, 1923; s. Hartwig B. and Olga F. (Felsner) T.; came to U.S., 1939, naturalized, 1943; B.A. cum laude, N.Y. U., 1948, M.S., 1949, Ph.D. (Univ. fellow 1955, N.Y. State War Service scholar 1955), 1959; m. Patricia Mullen, Dec. 18, 1954; children—Alfred L., Peter H. Asst. prof. econs. St. Lawrence U., 1953-55; research fellow dept. econs. N.Y. U., 1955-56; asso. prof. econs. and indsl. engring., depts. bus. adminstrn. and indsl. engring. Clarkson Coll., 1956-59; asso. prof. econs. Union Coll., Schenectady, 1960-62, Ford Found. research grantee, summers 1960, 62, dir. grad. program indsl. adminstrn., 1962-68, prof. econs. and indsl. adminstrn., dir. Inst. Adminstrn. and Mgmt., 1968—; mgm. cons. govt. agencies, industry; asso. STOCHOS, Inc., 1973; Fulbright research scholar Technische Hochschule, Graz, Austria, 1967-68; vis. prof. U. Munich (W. Ger.), 1972, vis. research prof. Institut fuer Entscheidungs und Organisationsforschung, 1974-75. Treas. Galway (N.Y.) Republican Club. Mem. Am. Econ. Assn., Am. Statistics Assn., Econ. History Assn. Lutheran. Author: (with Josef Finkelstein) Economists and Society: From Aquinas to Keynes, 1973; (with Eberhard Witte) Neue Richtlinien in der Amerikanischen Management Theorie, 1976, Entscheidungstheorie: Texte und Analysen, 1977; Business Ideologies in the Reform-Progressive Era, 1880-1914, 1976; contbr. articles to profl. jours. Home: RD 1 Galway NY 12074 Office: Union Coll Schenectady NY 12308

THOBURN, CRAWFORD RANDALL, musician, educator; b. Cleve., Oct. 23, 1933; s. Crawford Bennett and Mary Randall (Hinds) T.; B.A., Allegheny Coll., 1954; Mus.M., Boston U., 1960; m. Ingrid Elizabeth Samzelius, Dec. 26, 1955; children—Matthew Bennett, Sarah Katherine, Laura Elisabeth, Martha Suzanne. Grad. asst. to dean students Allegheny Coll., 1954-55; grad. asst. in choral conducting Boston U., 1959-60; mem. faculty Wells Coll., Aurora, N.Y., 1960—, chmn. dept. music, 1965-69, prof. music, 1973—, chmn. div. creative and performing arts, 1975-77; dir. music Saegertown (Pa.) Methodist Ch., 1951-55, St. Paul Lutheran Ch., Arlington, Mass., 1957-60, United Ministry of Aurora, 1961—; tenor soloist and recitalist; adjudicator choral festivals. Elder Presbyterian Ch. Served with USAF, 1955-58. Mem. Am. Choral Dirs. Assn., Music Educators Nat. Conf. Democrat. Club: Masons. Author choral arrangements and edits., articles and revs.; head choral rev. sect. Choral Jour. Home: Orchard Ln Aurora NY 13026 Office: Wells Coll Aurora NY 13026

THOM, CHARLES RICHARD, justice N.Y. Supreme Ct.; b. Storrs, Conn., Apr. 17, 1913; s. Charles and Ethel Winifred (Slater) T.; B.A., George Washington U., 1934, LL.B., 1936; m. Dorothy Lee, June 29, 1941; children—Kathryn Thom Fitzgerald, Margaret Thom Ferraro. Admitted to N.Y. bar, 1937; practiced in Port Jefferson, 1937-52; asst. dist. atty., Suffolk County, 1952-56, chief asst. dist. atty., 1957-59, police commnr., 1959-62, judge Family Ct., 1962-68; justice 10th Jud. Dist. N.Y. Supreme Ct., Riverhead, 1969—. Pres. Suffolk County council Boy Scouts Am., 1962-64. Bd. dirs. Mather Meml. Hosp., Port Jefferson, 1946-71. Served with AUS, World War II. Decorated Bronze Star with 2 oak leaf clusters, Combat Inf. badge. Mem. Phi Alpha Delta. Republican. Home: 125 Bleeker St Port Jefferson NY 11777 Office: Court House Riverhead NY 11901

THOM, JAMES THEOPHILUS, educator; b. Georgetown, Guyana, Apr. 27, 1916; s. Emanuel and Susan T.; came to U.S.; 1971, B.A., U. London, 1951, M.A., 1961, Ph.D., 1969; m. Ruth Violet Lashley; children—James Tylden, Janice, Hazel, Helen, Raymond. Tchr. elementary sch. Guyana, until 1940, vice-prin., 1941-48; tchr. high sch. Montserrat Secondary Sch., B.W.I., 1948-53; prin. Valley Secondary Sch., Anguilla, B.W.I., 1953-57; dist. supt. schs. Guyana Ministry Edn., Georgetown, 1957-65, dep. chief supt., 1965-70, acting chief supt., 1965-66, 69; asso. prof. edn. Bowie (Md.) State Coll., 1971-74, prof., 1974—; lectr. counseling and guidance. Bd. dirs. Anguilla div. St. Kitts Red Cross, 1954-56; chmn. Guyana Civil Service Assn., sr. profl. and tech. sect., 1965-70; council Guyana Red Cross, 1968-70. Decorated Guyana Independence medal, 1969; recipient 5 year service certificate State of Md., 1971-76. Mem. AAUP, Md. Assn. Higher Edn., Assn. Tchr. Edn. Md., Caribbean-Am. Intercultural Orgn. (life), Am. Personnel and Guidance Assn., Assn. Counce Counselor Edn. and Supervision. Episcopalian. Home: 12504 Millstream Dr Bowie MD 20715

THOM, JOSEPH M., librarian; b. Bronx, N.Y., Oct. 22, 1919; s. Harry and Jennie Thom; B.A., N.Y. U., 1948, M.A., 1949; M.S. in L.S., Columbia, 1950; postgrad. Washington U., St. Louis, 1951-53, Ohio U., 1958-59; m. Lillian Rosenstein, Sept. 1, 1945; children—Janice Eleanor, Eric Frederick. Library asst. N.Y. U., 1940-42, 46-49; library fellow Bklyn. Coll., 1949-50; chief reference dept. Washington U., 1950-53, instr. librarianship, 1950-54; dir. Research Information Service of St. Louis, 1954-55; supr. records and library Goodyear Atomic Corp., 1955-60; became dir. libraries Yeshiva U., 1960; librarian Port Jefferson (N.Y.) Schs.; instructional TV and library cons. design and services. Served with AUS, 1942-45. Mem. ALA, Suffolk Sch. Library Media Assn. (pres. 1974—). Editor: Reference Sources in Education, 1953; Personnel Notes and News. Compiler: Reference Sources in Political Science, 1953. Contbr. articles. Home: Setauket NY 11733 Office: Port Jefferson Schs Port Jefferson NY 11777

THOMAE, EDMUND GEORGE, fin. co. exec.; b. Schenectady, Apr. 16, 1912; s. William Carl and Wilhelmina (Boehne) T.; student Bentley Coll., 1931; B.B.A., Northeastern U., 1937; m. Alice Larson, Aug. 10, 1935; 1 dau., Carol Thomae Barrett. Sr. accountant Price Waterhouse & Co., Boston, 1937-47; treas. Stone & Forsyth Co., Cambridge, Mass., 1947-60, Boston Harbor Marina Co., 1960-64; comptroller Hunneman & Co., Boston, 1964-75; fiscal officer Jamaica Plain APAC, Inc. (Mass.), 1975—; treas. Boston Harbor Marina Co., 1960-64. Mem. Mass. Soc. C.P.A.'s, Am. Mgmt. Assn. Home: 1 Woodside Dr Milton MA 02186 Office: 30 Bickford St Jamaica Plain MA 02130

THOMAE, HERBERT LOUIS, jewelry co. exec.; b. Attleboro, Mass., Sept. 14, 1904; s. Charles and Margaret (Carl) T.; grad. high sch.; m. Constance D. Witherell, July 23, 1938; children—Irving H., Christopher C. With Charles Thomae & Son, Inc., Attleboro, 1921—, pres. 1958—; dir. Jewelers Bd. of Trade, pres., 1969-71. Mem. 100 Club of Mass. Mem. Navy League, Amateur Telescope Makers of Boston. Mason (32 deg.); Cousteau Soc., Boston Mus. Sci. Clubs: Boston Jewelers (Hon. pres. 1957-58), Diamond Peacock, King Philip Shriners. Home: 123 Berwick Rd Attleboro MA 02703 Office: 15 Maynard St Attleboro MA 02703

THOMAS, ALAN, candy co. exec.; b. Evansburg, Pa., Jan. 1, 1923; s. William Roberts and Letta (Garrett) T.; student Rutgers U., 1941-42, 46-47; B.S., Pa. State U., 1949; M.S., U. Minn., 1950, Ph.D., 1954; m. Marguerite Atria, July 1, 1972; children—Garrett Lee, Michael Alan, Randall Stephen, Brett Eliot. Instr., Temple U., Phila., 1950-51, U. Minn., St. Paul, 1951-54; research asst. Bowman Dairy Co., Chgo., 1954-56; research project mgr. M&M Candies div. Mars, Inc., Hackettstown, N.J., 1956-60, product devel. mgr., 1961-64, chocolate research dir. 1964; v.p. research and devel. Mars Candies, Chgo., 1964-67, M&M/Mars div., Hackettstown, 1967-77, v.p. sci. affairs, 1977—. Chmn. industry council of industry liaison panel Food and Nutrition Bd., Nat. Acad. Scis./NRC, 1972-73. Served to 1st lt. inf. U.S. Army, 1942-46. Recipient research award Nat. Confectioners Assn. U.S., 1971. Mem. AAAS, Am. Dairy Sci. Assn., Am. Assn. Cereal Chemists, Inst. Food Technologists, Grocery Mfrs. Am. (chmn. tech. com. for food protection 1975-76), Am. Assn. Candy Technologists, Gamma Sigma Delta, Phi Kappa Phi. Home: 82 Bald Eagle Panther Valley Hackettstown NJ 07840 Office: M&M/Mars Div Mars Inc High St Hackettstown NJ 07840

THOMAS, ARTHUR LOUIS, editor; b. N.Y.C., 1928; s. Arthur Waldorf and Suzanne Henriette-Lucie (Hervieu) T.; A.B., Columbia U., 1951; Ph.D., Princeton, 1956; m. Charlotte Bernadette Harrieu, Nov. 19, 1977. Chem. engr., research supr. E.I. du Pont de Nemours & Co., Inc., Parlin, N.J., 1956-59; chem. engr. Standard Ultramarine & Color Co., Huntington, W.Va., 1960-65; sr. research scientist MHD Research, Inc., also Plasmachem, Inc., Newport Beach, Calif., 1965-68; instr., asst. profl. chemistry Calif. Poly. State U., San Luis Obispo, 1969-72; vis. asst. prof. Columbia, 1973; sci. editor Ronald Press Co., N.Y.C., 1974-77; free-lance editor, 1977—. Mem. Am. Chem. Soc., Am. Inst. Chem. Engrs., AAAS. Republican. Episcopalian. Author: (with Frank H. Moser) Phthalocyanine Compounds, 1963. Home: 20 Brookside Dr Greenwich CT 06830

THOMAS, BASIL ANARGYROS, judge; b. Greece, Oct. 17, 1914; s. Steven and Helen (Koulias) T.; student Coll. William and Mary, 1930-31; LL.D., U. Balt., 1935; m. Helen Pappas, May 18, 1944; 1 son, Steven A. Admitted to Md. bar, 1935; practiced in Balt.; adminstrv. asst. to mayor Balt., 1948-49, asst. city solicitor, 1949-54; judge Municipal Ct., Balt., 1961-68; judge Supreme Bench of Balt., 1968—. Trustee C & J Coventaros Found. Served to 1st lt. CIC, AUS, 1942-46; PTO. Clubs: Lions (past pres.), Hillendale Country (past pres.) (Balt.). Home: 5606 N Charles St Baltimore MD 21210 Office: Courthouse Baltimore MD 21202

THOMAS, CAROL LOUISE JOSEPH (MRS. CHARLES RAYMOND THOMAS), community planning co. exec.; b. Poughkeepsie, N.Y., Aug. 29, 1923; d. Harold Kritzman and Charlotte Carolyn (Freiberg) Joseph; student Vassar Coll., 1941-43, Boston U., 1943, 49; A.B. cum laude, Syracuse U., 1948; M.A., U. Conn., 1950; postgrad. Mass. Inst. Tech., 1950; m. Charles Raymond Thomas, Mar. 21, 1943; children—Charles Joseph, Katharine Louise. Freelance community planner, 1950-58; partner Sonthoff & Thomas, community planners, 1958-61; pres., treas. Thomas Assos., community planners, 1961-69; dir. Thomas Assos. div. Universal Engring. Corp., Boston, 1969-78; pres. Thomas Planning Services, Inc., Boston, 1978—. Dir. Summer Inst. in Community Planning for Minority Groups, Dept. Housing and Urban Devel., 1969; asst. prof. community planning and area devel. U. R.I. Grad. Curriculum in Community Planning and Area Devel., 1967—, vis. lectr., 1964-65, asst. prof., 1965-71, adj. prof., 1972—; lectr. Boston State Coll., 1970—, Harvard Grad. Sch. Design, 1974—. Active various community drives; mem. Gov.'s Adv. Com. on Planning, 1963-68, Gov.'s Adv. Com. on Civil Def., 1966-68, Wayland (Mass.) Town Govt. Com., 1958-72; chmn. scholarship awarding com. P.T.A., Wayland, 1965-72. Pres., Arlington (Mass.) Women's Republican Club, 1954-55; vice-chmn. town com. Rep. party, Arlington, 1953-55; sec. town com. Rep. party, Wayland, 1957-59, 68—, vice-chmn., 1959-61; del. state conv. Rep. party, 1954-58. Mem. Am. Soc. Planning Ofcls., AAUP, Am. Inst. Planners (pres. New Eng. chpt. 1965-67, chmn. jury of awards 1969-71, bd. examiners 1969-78), Mass. Fedn. Planning Bds. (dir.). Republican. Unitarian (mem. parish com. 1958-60, adult edn. com. 1973). Author articles in field. Home: 151 Tremont St Boston MA 02111 Office: 100 Boylston St Boston MA 02116

THOMAS, CHARLES EDMOND, anesthesiologist; b. Balt., Mar. 21, 1933; s. James Clayton and Emily Marie (Shimek) T.; grad. Columbia Union Coll., 1955; D.O., Kansas City Coll. Osteopathic Medicine and Surgery, 1959; m. Aug. 23, 1955; m. Lillian C. Thomas; children—James Phillip, Lane Lynn, Cheryl-lee, Karen, Kevin Charles. Intern Doctors Hosp., Columbus, Ohio, 1959-60; resident in anesthesiology Detroit Osteopathic Hosp., 1960-62; staff anesthesiologist Bi-County Community Hosp., 1962-70, Detroit Osteopathic Hosp., 1962-70; chief dept. anesthesiology Annie Warner Hosp., Gettysburg, Pa., 1970-72; staff anesthesiologist Crippled Childrens Hosp., Elizabethtown, Pa., 1970-75; chief dept. anesthesiology Hanover (Pa.) Gen. Hosp., 1975—; pres., chmn. bd. Anesthesia Assos. Detroit, 1962-69. Recipient grant Pfizer Co. Diplomate Am. Bd. Anesthesiology. Mem. Am. Soc. Anesthesiologists, Pa. Osteopathic Med. Assn., Pa. Soc. Anesthesiologists, Internat. Anesthesia Research Soc., Am. Osteopathic Assn., Am. Thoracic Soc., Am. Osteopathic Coll. Anesthesiology. Republican. Club: Lions. Home and office: 300 Baltimore Ave Hanover PA 17331

THOMAS, DALE JOHN, bus. equipment co. exec.; b. Lansing, Mich., June 26, 1940; s. William Gentry and Ruth Agnes (Mattson) T.; B.A. in Mgmt., Mich. State U., 1962, M.B.A. in Mktg., 1965; m. Barbara Lee Andrews, July 6, 1963; children—Jennifer Lee, Christopher John. Traffic supr. N.Y. Telephone Co., N.Y.C., 1962-64; product planner Pitney Bowes, Inc., Stamford, Conn., 1965-70, asst. to chmn. bd., 1970-71, project mgr. new ventures, 1971-75, product line mgr., 1975-78, dir. prodn. line mgmt., 1978—; mem. Conn. Gov.'s Commn. Services Expenditures. Pres., Luth. Housing Corp., Bridgeport, Conn., 1974—; councilman Our Saviours Luth. Ch., 1969-75, sec., 1970-72, pres., 1972-75. Served with U.S. Army, 1966-68. Mem. Am. Mktg. Assn. (nat. dir. 1973-75, Outstanding Service award 1975), Republican. Mem. editorial rev. bd. Indsl. Mktg. Mgmt. Jour., 1975—; writer editor column Mktg. Mgmt. Viewpoint, Mktg. News, 1971-75. Home: 176 Carroll Rd Fairfield CT 06430 Office: 380 Main Ave Norwalk CT 06852

THOMAS, DONALD WAYNE, govt. ofcl.; b. Bradenton, Fla., Aug. 19, 1935; s. Jesse and Lydia Emma (Merkens) T.; B.Indsl. Engring., U. Fla., 1958; M.S. in Govtl. Adminstrn., George Washington U., 1968. Staff indsl. engr. Robins AFB, Ga., 1959-60, 62-64, U.S. Naval Ordnance Plant, Macon, Ga., 1960-61, Brookley AFB, Ala., 1961-62, Hdqrs. USAF, Washington, 1964-67; staff. indsl. engr., staff Office Sec. Navy, Office Civilian Manpower Mgmt., Washington, 1967-69, adminstrv. officer, 1969-72, spl. asst. for manpower utilization, 1972-74, manpower mgmt. specialist Office Civilian Personnel, 1974-77, manpower mgmt. specialist office of Dep. Asst. Sec., 1977—. Recipient Superior Achievement award Dept. Navy, 1969. Registered profl. engr., Vt. Mem. Am. Inst. Indsl. Engrs. (sr.), Nat. Soc. Profl. Engrs., Am. Soc. Pub. Adminstrn. Club: Univ. (Washington). Home: 4101 Cathedral Ave NW Washington DC 20016 Office: Office of Dep Asst Sec Dept Navy Washington DC 20390

THOMAS, EAPEN, gastroenterologist; b. Quilon, Kerala, India, Aug. 27, 1939; s. Koithodathil Eapen and Mary (Kurvilla) T.; came to U.S., 1973; M.B.B.S., Christian Med. Coll. (India), 1963; M.D., Med. Coll. Trivandrum (India), 1966; m. Anne Mathew, July 4, 1966; 1 son, Rohan Eapen. Tutor in medicine Med. Coll., Trivandrum, India, 1966; asst. prof. medicine Stanley Med. Coll., Madras, India, 1966-70; lectr. in medicine U. Adelaide (Australia), 1970-73; asst. prof. medicine N.Y. Med. Coll., N.Y.C., 1973-77, asso. prof. medicine, 1977—. Diplomate Am. Bd. Internal Medicine. Fellow Royal Australasian Coll. Physicians, Royal Coll. Physicians of Can., ACP; mem. Am. Gastroenterological Assn., Am. Soc. Gastrointestinal Endoscopy. Contbr. articles in clin. gastroenterology to med. jours. Home: 19 Brookdell Dr Hartsdale NY 10530 Office: NY Med Coll New York City NY 10029

THOMAS, ETHEL COLVIN NICHOLS (MRS. LEWIS VICTOR THOMAS), educator; b. Cranston, R.I., Mar. 31, 1913; d. Charles Russell and Mabel Maria (Colvin) Nichols; Ph.B., Pembroke Coll. in Brown U., 1934; M.A., Brown U., 1938; postgrad. Boston U., Fisk U., Rutgers U.; m. Lewis Victor Thomas, July 26, 1945 (dec. Oct. 1965); 1 son, Glenn Nichols. Tchr. English, Cranston High Sch., 1934-39; social dir. and adviser to freshmen, Fox Hall, Boston U., 1939-40; instr. to asst. prof. English Am. Coll. for Girls, Istanbul, Turkey, 1940-44; dean freshman, dir. admission Women's Coll. of Middlebury, Vt., 1944-45; tchr. English, Robert Coll., Istanbul, 1945-46; instr. English, Rider Coll., Trenton, N.J., 1950-51; tchr. English, Princeton (N.J.) High Sch., 1951-61, counselor, 1960-62, 72—, college counselor, 1962-72. Gen. Electric Summer Guidance Inst. Fellow, 1966. Mem. NEA, AAUW, Nat. Assn. Women Deans, Adminstrs. and Counselors, Am. Personnel and Guidance Assn., Met. Mus. Art, Kappa Delta Pi. Presbyn. Clubs: Princeton Bus. and Profl. Women's (Woman of Year 1977); Brown University (N.Y.C.); Nassau. Home: 154 Prospect Ave Princeton NJ 08540 Office: Princeton Regional Schs Princeton NJ 08540

THOMAS, FELYCE, educator; b. N.Y.C., Oct. 21, 1932; d. Abram and Hattie (Geen) Landau; B.A. in Psychology, Hunter Coll., N.Y.C., 1954; M.A. in Elementary Edn., Paterson State Coll., Wayne, N.J., 1963; m. Marvin Thomas; 1 dau., Suzette. Tchr., Pub. Sch. 107, N.Y.C., 1955-58; reading workshop dir. St. Joseph's Village, Rockleigh, N.J., 1971; perceptual tng. specialist Perceptual Motor Center, Boonton, N.J., 1970-71; reading specialist Heights Elementary Sch., Oakland, N.J., 1959-77, reading dir., 1978—. Mem. Internat. Reading Assn., Nat., N.J. edn. assns. Certified in elementary teaching, N.Y. State; elementary teaching, elementary and secondary reading Supervision, N.J. Home: 42 Normandy Dr Parsippany NJ 07054 Office: 315 Ramapo Valley Rd Oakland NJ 07436

THOMAS, JOHN MELVIN, physician; b. Carmarthen, Gt. Britain, Apr. 26, 1933; s. Morgan and Margaret (Morgan) T.; M.B., Ch.B., Univ. Coll. Wales, U. Edinburgh, 1958; m. Betty Ann Mayo, Nov. 3, 1958; children—James, Hugh, Pamela. Intern, Robert Packer Hosp., Sayre, Pa., 1958-59, chief surg. resident, 1963; asso. surgeon Guthrie Clinic Ltd., Sayre, Pa., 1963-69; pres. med. staff Robert Packer Hosp., Sayre, Pa., 1968-69, chmn. dept. surgery, 1969—; prof. Hahnemann Med. Sch., 1972—; pres., bd. dirs. Guthrie Clinic Ltd., Sayre, Pa. Chmn. Licensure and Accountability, Gov.'s Conf., 1974. Bd. dirs. Donald Guthrie Found. for Research; mem. exec. bd. trustees Robert Packer Hosp. Mem. Am. Coll. Surgeons, A.M.A., Am. Group Practice Assn., Pa., Bradford County med. scos., Central N.Y. Surg. Soc., Soc. Surgery Alimentary Tract, Am. Soc. Parenteral and Enteral Nutrition. Presbyn. Clubs: Shepard Hills Country, Moselem Springs Golf. Home: Box 113 Walker Hill Waverly NY 14892 Office: Guthrie Clinic Ltd Sayre PA 18840

THOMAS, JOHN WESLEY, JR., surgeon; b. St. Matthews, S.C., May 30, 1919; s. John W. and Harriett J. (Whitmore) T.; B.A., Lincoln U., 1940; M.D., Howard U., 1944; m. Irma Vivian Verdun, Nov. 25, 1944; children—Vivian Alma Rankin, Vicki Daryl Richardson, Janis Page, Eric Whitmore. Intern, Freedmans Hosp., Howard U., Washington, 1944-45; resident in surgery Douglass Hosp., Phila., 1945-46; resident in surgery Hosp. of U. Pa., 1950-53, 55-56; practice medicine specializing in surgery, Phila., 1956—; dir. of outpatient dept. Mercy-Douglas Hosp., Phila., 1956-69, chief sect. gen. surgery Mercy-Douglas Hosp., 1956-67, asst. dir. dept. surgery, 1964-67, dir. dept. surgery, 1967-73, attending surgeon, 1956-67; attending surgeon Women's Hosp. of Phila., 1958-68, Sacred Heart Hosp., Chester, Pa., 1959-65, Hahnemann Hosp., Phila., 1970-74; asst. chief of surgery Hahnemann div. Phila. Gen. Hosp., 1973-74; attending surgeon Mercy Cath. Med. Center, Phila., 1973—; asso. dept. surgery Hosp. of U. Pa., 1956-74; prof. surgery Hahnemann Med. Coll., Phila., 1970-74; asso. clin. prof. surgery U. Pa., Phila., 1974—. Served to capt., M.C., U.S. Army, 1953-55. Diplomate Am. Bd. Surgery. Fellow A.C.S., Phila. Coll. Physicians; mem. Pa. State, Eastern Pa., Phila. County med. socs., Nat. Med. Assn., Chi Delt Mu, Sigma Pi Phi. Methodist. Contbr. articles on surgery to med. jours. Home: 5900 Spruce St Philadelphia PA 19139 Office: Hosp of the Univ of Pennsylvania 3400 Spruce St Philadelphia PA 19104

THOMAS, LLOYD ALLEN, pediatrician; b. N.Y.C., Nov. 3, 1922; s. Lionel Septimus and Ethel Maud (Allen) T.; B.S., City Coll. N.Y., 1943; M.D., Howard U., 1946; m. Mary Elaine, June 9, 1946; children—Fern, Guy, Tobi. Intern, Harlem Hosp., N.Y.C., 1943-44, resident in pediatrics, 1945-46; resident in pediatrics N.Y. Foundling Hosp., 1944, Willard Parker Hosp., 1945, Emma Pendleton Bradley Home, 1946; practice medicine specializing in pediatrics, Bklyn., 1953—; mem. staff State U. Hosp., Brookdale Hosp. Med. Center, Kings County Hosp. Center; clin. asso. prof. State U. N.Y., Downstate Med. Coll. Mem. aux. bd. Bklyn. Urban League, 1954-58; bd. dirs. Willa Hardgrow Mental Health Clinic, 1960—; mem. advisory com. Parenting program Medgar Evers Coll. Served to capt. M.C., U.S. Army, 1951-53. Fellow Am. Acad. Pediatrics; mem. Nat. Med. Assn., Kings County Med. Soc. (past pres. pediatric sect.). Presbyterian. Home and office: 825 Lincoln Pl Brooklyn NY 11216

THOMAS, LOUIS JAMES, union ofcl.; b. Hazleton, Pa., Aug. 29, 1942; s. Ralph Charles and Ruth Geneva (Damato) T.; student East Stroudsburg State Tchrs. Coll., 1962-64, Harrisburg Area Community Coll., 1969, Onondaga Community Coll., 1976-77; m. Sandra Jean Smiley, June 20, 1964; children—Ralph James, Brian Joseph, Anthony John, Joseph Jeffrey. Vice-pres. Coffee Time Indsl. Catering, Inc., 1965-66; field office mgr. Hempt Bros. Constrn. Co., Harrisburg, Pa., 1969-70; internat. rep. Dist. 50 United Mine Workers Am., 1970-72; staff rep. United Steelworkers Am., AFL-CIO, Syracuse, N.Y., 1972—. Served with U.S. Army, 1966-69. Decorated Bronze Star. Democrat. Roman Catholic. Office: 104 Magnolia St Syracuse NY 13204

THOMAS, ROBERT G., film and TV producer; b. Orange, N.J., July 21, 1943; s. Gerald G. Maurillo and Vera T.; student in TV and Radio Arts, U. Bridgeport, 1961-63; B.S. in Bus. Admnstrn., Fairleigh Dickinson U., 1967, postgrad., 1967; m. Bernadette Fietti, Nov. 1, 1968; children—Robert, Michael. Producer ednl. radio programs WPKN-FM, Bridgeport, Conn., 1962; asst. stage mgr. Meadowbrook Dinner Theatre, Cedar Grove, N.J., 1963; cameraman, dir. TV test commls. Van Guard Telefilms, 1964; producer, dir. TV shows WPIX-TV, WOR-TV, WNBC-TV, live Spanish programs, commls. MGM Telestudios, Video Tape Center, commls., network programs Tele-tape Corp., ednl. programs, WNET-TV, sports WKBG-TV, Madison Sq. Garden, sports remotes, Hughes Sports Network, all N.Y.C., 1964-67, WNJU-TV, Newark, N.J., 1967, pres., owner, producer Bob Thomas Prodns., N.Y.C. and Bloomfield, N.J., 1968—; film commr., appointee N.J. Gov., 1977-79; major works include pub. affairs TV series The Jersey Side (5 Emmy nominations 1977), and numerous advt. films including Road-Eo (gold medal Internat. Film and TV Festival N.Y.), 1974, Water is My Middle Name (silver medal Internat. Film and TV Festival N.Y.), 1975, A-P-A Sales (silver medal Internat. Film and TV Festival N.Y., excellence award U.S. Indsl. Film Festival, spl. jury award L.I. Internat. Film Festival, certificate of recognition Film Council of Greater Columbus), 1975, N.J.-200 Years (bronze medal Internat. Film and TV Festival N.Y., honor award Advt. Club North Jersey), 1976. Mem. Nat. Acad. TV Arts and Scis., Motion Picture and TV Devel. Commn. Inventor holographic images of 3-D photography and curbside cinema, a portable projection system for outdoor presentations. Home: 7 Jason Ct Wayne NJ 07470 Office: PO Box 1787 Wayne NJ 07470 and 55 W 42nd St New York NY 10036

THOMAS, RUTH ANN, counselor, educator; b. Scottdale, Pa., May 2, 1937; d. Kenneth W. and Eleanor (Rexroad) Hodge; diploma magna cum laude Zion Bible Inst., 1958; B.S. cum laude, Calif. (Pa.) State Coll., 1968; M.Ed., Indian (Pa.) U., 1971; m. David E. Thomas, July 26, 1975. Sec., clk. Bryce Brothers Crystal, Inc., Mt. Pleasant, Pa., 1960-65; tchr. Southmoreland Sch. Dist., Scottdale, Pa., 1968-71; tchr. Mt. Lebanon Sch. Dist., Pitts., 1971-72, counselor, learning cons., 1972—. Frick scholar, 1967-68. Mem. Am., Pa. personnel and Guidance assns., Am., Pa., Allegheny County sch. counselor assns., NEA, Pa. Edn. Assn., Kappa Delta Pi, Delta Kappa Gamma. Office: Markham Sch Pittsburgh PA 15228

THOMAS, SARAH ELIZABETH BARKER, nurse, ofcl. ofcl.; b. Keene, N.H., Mar. 4, 1936; d. Sheldon Livermore and Florence Elizabeth (McClintock) Barker; diploma Mt. Auburn Hosp. Sch. Nursing, 1957; certificate in operating room tech. Yale-New Haven Hosp., 1958; student Western Res. U., 1959-60, Keene State U., 1961, New Eng. Coll., 1976-79; m. Wesley Lloyd Thomas, Nov. 24, 1962; children—Jennifer, Mark, Susanna. Operating room supr. Elliot Community Hosp. (now Chesire Hosp.), Keene, 1958; charge nurse metabolic research unit Univ. Hosp., Cleve., 1959-61; head nurse, operating room clin. instr. Mt. Auburn Hosp., Cambridge, Mass., 1962-63; staff nurse Exeter (N.H.) Hosp., 1969-71, in charge intensive care unit, 1971-73, in charge in-service, 1972-73, dir. nursing service, 1973—. Mem. Exeter Bicentennial Commn., 1974-76, Exeter Vocation Edn. Commn., 1976—. Recipient Exec. Devel. award New Eng. Hosp. Assn., 1974, 75, recognition Exeter Sch. Bd., 1977. Mem. Vis. Nurses Assn. (dir.), Dirs. Assembly, N.H. Exeter Hist. Soc., Women's Fellowship. Republican. Congregationalist. Home: 35 Pine St Exeter NH 03833 Office: 10 Buzell Ave Exeter NH 03833

THOMAS, WILLIAM JOHN, microbiologist; b. Sharon, Pa., Oct. 11, 1924; s. William George and Blanche Corinne (Canon) T.; B.S., Westminster Coll., 1948; M.S., U. Md., 1951; Ph.D., U. Pa., 1959; m. Betty Elizabeth Gathers, Sept. 3, 1949; children—Paula Thomas McCracken, Jonathan William (dec.). Sect. leader Ft. Detrick, Frederick, Md., 1951-56; research asso. Wister Inst., Phila., 1956-58; group leader Nat. Drug Co., Phila., 1958-65; sr. research virologist Merrell Nat. Labs., Swiftwater, Pa., 1965-78; research asso. The Salk Inst., 1978—. Dir. The Burnley Workshop. Pres., Mt. Pocono (Pa.) Municipal Authority, 1972-74. Served with USNR, 1943-46. Recipient Distinguished Alumni award Westminter Coll., 1973. Fellow Am. Pub. Health Assn; mem. Soc. Cryobiology, Tissue Culture Assn., Am. Soc. Microbiology, Ret. Officers Assn. Republican. Methodist. Clubs: Shawnee Country, The Manor. Patentee stockmarket game Stocknight. Office: Route 611 Swiftwater PA 18370

THOMOPOULOS, ANTHONY DENNIS, broadcasting exec.; B.S. in Fgn. Service, Georgetown U., 1959; m. Pipina Linakis, June 25, 1961; children—Anne, Denis, Mark. With NBC, 1959-64; dir. fgn. sales, then v.p., exec. v.p. Four Star Entertainment Corp., 1964-70; dir. programming selectavision div. RCA, 1970-71; v.p. TV mktg. Tomorrow Entertainment, 1971-73; with ABC, 1973—, v.p. prime time programs entertainment div., N.Y.C., 1973-74, v.p. prime time TV creative ops., 1974-75, v.p. spl. programs, 1975-76, v.p. TV div., 1976-78, pres. entertainment div., 1978—. Address: care ABC 1330 Ave of Americas New York NY 10019

THOMPSON, ARDITHEARL, psychologist; b. Ky.; d. Anderson and Georgia Edith (Craft) Campbell; M.Ed., U. Pitts., 1968; psychology certification Duquesne U., 1971; Ph.D., Heed U., 1975; m. Paul Albert Thompson; 1 son, Paul Douglas. Vocat. counselor, psychol. intern Vocat. Rehab. Center, Pitts., 1969-70; psychol. intern North Allegheny Schs., 1970-71; psychologist Allegheny Intermediate Unit #3, Pitts., 1971-72, Deer Lake and Hampton sch. dists., 1972-76; pvt. practice psychology, Allison Park, Pa., 1976—. Pres., McKnight Woman's Club, Pitts., 1957-58; sec. Council Rehab. Agys., Pitts., 1970-71; bd. dirs. Howe (Ind.) Mothers Assn., 1968-70, life mem. NDEA scholar, 1967-68. Mem. Am., Pa. personnel and guidance assns., Am., Pa. psychol. assns., Nat. Assn. Sch. Psychologists. Clubs: ASME Aux., So.; Symphony North. Author: (with Rizzo and Walk) To Reverse the Failure Syndrome, 1972. Home: 8217 Bramble Ln Pittsburgh PA 15237 Office: 4482 Mount Royal Blvd Allison Park PA 15101

THOMPSON, BRADBURY (JAMES), designer; b. Topeka, Mar. 25, 1911; s. James Kay and Eunice (Bradbury) T.; A.B., Washburn U., 1934, D.F.A. (hon.), 1965; m. Della Deen Dodge, Aug. 28, 1939; children—Leslie Dodge (Mrs. George W. Woideck, Jr.), Mark Bradbury, David Dodge, Elizabeth (Mrs. John E. Riley). Art dir. Capper Publs., Inc., 1934-38, Rogers-Kellogg-Stillson, 1938-42; asso. chief art sect. OWI State Dept., 1942-45; art dir. Mademoiselle mag., 1945-59, Living for Young Homemakers, 1947-49; editor-designer Westvaco Inspirations, 1938-62; design dir. Art News mag., Art News Ann., 1945-72; design cons. Westvaco Corp., 1951—, Famous Artists Schs., 1959-71, Pitney-Bowes, 1959—, McGraw-Hill mags., 1960—, Time-Life Books (Library of Art, 1965, Library of America, 1966, Foods of the World, 1966, The Swing Era, 1970), Field Enterprises Ednl. Corp., 1965-78, Harvard Bus. Rev., 1965-67, Cornell U., 1965-73. Exhibited one man show AIGA Gallery, N.Y.C., 1959, 75, Washburn U., 1964, Cornell U., 1969; exhibited group shows Alliance Graphique Internationale, Europe 1955-67, Harvard, 1965, Yale, 1976, Mus. Modern Art, N.Y.C. Faculty, Yale Sch. Art and Architecture, 1956—. Mem. Citizens Stamp Adv. Com., 1969—, 1st Fed. Design Assembly, 1973. Bd. advisers Parsons Sch. Design, 1949-55; bd. govs. Phila. Mus. Coll. Art, 1956-59; bd. dirs. Perrot Meml. Library, 1966—; Am. Arbitration Assn., 1976-78; trustee Washburn U., 1972—. Recipient awards AIGA, 1948—; Gold T-Square Nat. Soc. Art Dirs., 1950; medals Art Dirs. Club, 1945, 47, 51 (2), 55, named to Hall of Fame, 1977; Gold medal Sao Paulo Bienal, 1965, Silver medal, 1963. Mem. Art Dirs. Club N.Y. (v.p., dir.), Am. Inst. Graphic Arts (dir., Gold medal 1975), Alliance Graphique Internationale, Soc. Illustrators, Alpha Delta, Delta Phi Delta. Clubs: Dutch Treat; Riverside Yacht. Conglist. Author: Modern Painting and Typography, 1947; The Monalphabet, 1945; Alphabet 26, 1950. Designer for books including Painting Toward Architecture, 1948; Photo-Graphic, 1949; Abstract Painting, 1951; Annual of Advt. Art, 1943, 54; Graphic Arts Prodn. Yearbook, 1948, 50; The Fiction Factory, 1955; Westvaco Am. Classics, 1958—; The First 300 Years, 1967; Homage to the Book, 1968; The Quality of Life, 1968; The American Revolution: Three Views. Designer U.S. stamps: Brussells Fair, 1958; Am. Music, 1964; Search for Peace, 1967; Finland Independence, 1967; Herman Melville, 1970; John Sloan, 1971; Missouri Centennial, 1971; Christmas, 1972, 73, 74, 75, 76, 78, Universal Postal Union, 1974; Lexington and Concord, 1975; Bunker Hill, 1976; Washington at Princeton, 1977; Lafayette, 1977; Surrender at Saratoga, 1977. Home: Jones Park Riverside CT 06878

THOMPSON, DAVID DUVALL, physician; b. N.Y.C., June 1, 1922; s. Homer C. and Clara (Smith) T.; B.A., Cornell U., 1943, M.D., 1946; m. Lynn Poucher, Dec. 22, 1945; children—David D., Richard M., Catherine R., Peter L. Intern, resident N.Y. Hosp., N.Y.C., 1946-50; head div. metabolism N.Y. Hosp., 1957-65, acting physician in chief, 1965-67; dir. Soc. of N.Y. Hosp., 1967—. Vis. prof. hosp. adminstrn. Cornell U. Trustee Mut. Life Ins. Co. N.Y. Mem. med. adv. bd. Kidney Found. N.Y., 1963-66; trustee Mary Imogene Bassett Hosp. Recipient Lederle Med. Faculty award, 1955-57. Fellow A.C.P.; mem. A.M.A., Am. Physiol. Soc., Harvey Soc., Am. Soc. Clin. Investigation, Am. Fedn. Clin. Research, Soc. Med. Adminstrs., AAAS, Assn. Am. Med. Colls., Am. Heart Assn., Am. Hosp. Assn., Hosp. Adminstrs. Club N.Y., Hosp. Assn. N.Y. State, Med. Soc. County N.Y., N.Y. Acad. Medicine, N.Y. Soc. Internal Medicine, Sigma Xi. Club: University. Home: 11 Creston Ave Tenafly NJ 07670 Office: 525 E 68th St New York City NY 10021

THOMPSON, DOUGLAS LLEWELLYN, pharmacist; b. Regina, Sask., Can., June 24, 1934; s. James A. and Wilhelmine (Hehn) T.; B.Sc., U. B.C., Vancouver, 1958; M.Sc. in Pharmacy, State U. Iowa, 1963; m. Anne Paula van de Poel, Oct. 11, 1963; children—Sandra, Sheri. Dir. pharmacy Nanaimo Regional Gen. Hosp. (B.C., Can.), 1963-65; product devel. pharmacist Ayerst Labs., Inc., Rouses Point, N.Y., 1965-68; mng. editor Internat. Pharm. Abstracts, Am. Soc. Hosp. Pharmacists, Washington, 1968—. Mem. Am. Soc. Hosp. Pharmacists, Am. Pharm. Assn., Internat. Pharm. Fedn., Am. Soc. Indexers, Sigma Xi. Club: Potomac Curling. Home: 12009 Glen Mill Rd Potomac MD 20854 Office: 4630 Montgomery Ave Bethesda MD 20014

THOMPSON, EDWARD KRAMER, editor, publisher; b. Mpls., Sept. 17, 1907; s. Edward T. and Bertha E. (Kramer) T.; A.B., U. N.D., 1927, H.H.D., 1958; m. Marguerite M. Maxam, May 14, 1927 (div.); children—Edward T. Colin R.; m. 2d, Lee Eitingon, Apr. 1, 1963. Editor, Foster County Independent, Carrington N.D., 1927; city editor Fargo (N.D.) Morning Forum, 1927; picture editor, asst. news editor Milw. Jour., 1927-37; asso. editor Life, 1937-42, asst. mng. editor, 1945-49, mng. editor, 1961, editor, 1961-68; spl. asst. to sec. state, 1968; editor, pub. Smithsonian mag., 1969—. Served to lt. col. USAAF, 1942-45. Decorated Legion of Merit; Order Brit. Empire; named to N.D. Hall of Fame, 1968; named Editor of Year, Nat. Press Photographers Assn., 1968; recipient Joseph Henry medal Smithsonian Instn., 1973. Mem. Phi Beta Kappa, Sigma Delta Chi. Home: 2934 Macomb St NW Washington DC 20008 Office: Smithsonian Instn Washington DC 20560

THOMPSON, ELLEN KUBACKI, microbiologist, med. writer; b. Bethesda, Md., July 21, 1950; d. Edward Leonard and Ellen Angelina (Battaglia) Kubacki; A.B., Miami U., Oxford, Ohio, 1972; m. Richard Kent Thompson, Jan. 25, 1975. Asst. microbiologist Hoffmann-La Roche Inc., Nutley, N.J., 1972-77, med. writer, 1977—; lectr. in field. Mem. Am. Soc. Microbiology, Am. Med. Writers Assn., Theobald Smith Soc., Miami U. Alumni Assn. No. N.J., Concerned Women of Roche, Hoffmann-La Roche Employee Assn., Sigma Xi, Sigma Kappa. Home: 35 Fairfield Rd Kingston NJ 08528 Office: Hoffmann-La Roche Inc Bldg 1 Nutley NJ 07110

THOMPSON, FRANK, congressman, lawyer; b. Trenton, N.J., July 26, 1918; s. Frank and Beatrice (Jamieson) T.; student Wake Forest Coll., 1941, LL.B., 1948; LL.D., Rider Coll., 1962; LL.D. (hon.), Princeton; m. Evelina Gleaves Van Metre, Jan. 10, 1942; children—Anne Gleaves Thompson Henderson, Evelina Porter Thompson Lyons. Admitted to N.J. bar, 1948, elected N.J. Gen. Assembly, 1949—; asst. minority leader, 1950, minority leader, 1954; mem. 84th-96th Congresses from 4th Dist. N.J., mem. com. edn. and labor, com. house adminstrn., chmn. labor-mgmt. relations subcom., chmn. Trustee John F. Kennedy Center for Performing Arts. Served as comdr. USNR. Decorated Bronze Star, Gold Star, Combat Commendation Medal. Mem. Naval Res. Assn. Club: Players (N.Y.). Home: 455 W State St Trenton NJ 08618 Office: 2109 Rayburn House Office Bldg Washington DC 20515

THOMPSON, FRANK JOSEPH, accountant; b. Milw., Oct. 1, 1913; s. Jan and Valerya (Adamczyk) Tomaszewski; student U. Wis., 1939-43, Marquette U., 1943-44; m. Gertrude Liker, Feb. 24, 1936; children—Joan Thompson O'Neill, James Patrick. Purchasing agt., Inst. Paper Chemistry, Appleton, Wis., 1944-47; steel buyer Harnischfeger Corp., Milw., 1947-50; dir. purchases Mueller Climatrol, Milw., 1950-57; pvt. practice accounting, South Egremont, Mass., 1957—; sec., dir. Dickinson's Express Inc., Canaan, Conn., 1969—. Served with USMC, 1929-32. Mem. Nat. Assn. Pub. Accountants, Nat. Assn. Enrolled Agts., Nat. Assn. Notary Publics. Republican. Roman Catholic. Home: Mt Washington Rd South Egremont MA 01258 Office: PO Box 304 South Egremont MA 01258

THOMPSON, GEORGE LEE, mfg. co. exec.; b. Denver, June 12, 1933; s. George H. and Frances M. (Murphy) T.; B.S. in Bus., U. Colo., 1957; postgrad. in Advanced Mgmt., N.Y. U., 1969; m. Jean G. Meier, Aug. 25, 1957; children—Shannon, Tracy, Bradley. With GTE Sylvania, Danvers, Mass., 1957-65, nat. sales mgr., 1965-67, mktg. mgr., 1967-68, v. p. sales Entertainment Products, Batavia, N.Y., 1968-73, dir. mktg., Stamford, Conn., 1973-74; v. p. mktg. Servomation Corp., N.Y.C., 1974-76, exec. v.p., 1976-78; exec. v.p. The Singer Co., Elizabeth, N.J., 1978—. Mem. Republican Town Com., Wilton, Conn., 1976. Served to lt. USN, 1951-54. Decorated Air medal, UN medal; recipient Most Valuable Promotion award Nat. Restaurant Assn., 1976. Mem. Am. Home Sewing Assn., Illuminating Engring. Soc., Am. Mgmt. Assn., Internat. Assn. Food Service Mgmt., Chi Psi. Episcopalian. Clubs: Wilton Riding (gov.), Navesink Country, Newcomen. Home: 6 Northover Pl Middletown NJ 07701 Office: 321 1st St Elizabeth NJ 07207

THOMPSON, GEORGE WALTER MURRY, JR., educator; b. Richmond, Va., Oct. 12, 1931; s. George Walter Murry and Inez (Arrington) T.; B.A., Va. Union U., 1954; M.Div., So. Bapt. Theol. Sem., 1957; M.A., U. Chgo., 1962, Ph.D., 1974; m. Sarah Elizabeth Walden, June 2, 1955; 1 dau., Sarita. Ordained to ministry Bapt. Ch., 1955; pastor 2d Bapt. Ch., Hinton, W.Va., 1962-63, Providence Bapt. Ch., Phila., 1975—; asso. prof. theology and ethics, Payne Theol. Sem., Wilberforce, Ohio, 1963-70; coordinator Consortium for Higher Edn. Religion Studies, Dayton, Ohio, 1970-72; prof. East Stroudsburg (Pa.) State Coll., 1972—; vis. asso. prof. applied theology Harvard, 1975-77. Mem. Soc. Study Black Religion, Central Pa., Am. philos. assns., Am. Assn. Study Afro-Am. Life and History, UN Assn., Assn. Pa. State Coll. and Univ. Faculties, Pa. Assn. Higher Edn., NAACP, Soc. Creative Philosophy, Nat. Collegiate Honors Council, Michael Polanyi Philos. Soc., Am. Acad. Religion, Council Study of Religion, NOW, Bapt. Ministers Conf. Phila., Phila. Bapt. Assn. Club: Harvard Faculty. Contbr. articles to profl. jours. Home: 8325 Temple Rd Philadelphia PA 19150 Office: East Stroudsburg State Coll Dept Philosophy East Stroudsburg PA

THOMPSON, GORDON ELLEF, mgmt. cons.; b. Wautoma, Wis., May 15, 1933; s. Ellef N. and Florence A. (Gutreuter) T.; B.S., Marquette U., 1954; M.B.A., Harvard U., 1961. Instr. fin., asst. dean Sch. Bus. Adminstrn., Georgetown U., Washington, 1961-63, Found. for Econ. Edn. fellow, 1963; cons. Checchi and Co., Washington, 1963-65; investment officer Internat. Fin. Corp., Washington, 1965-69; investment officer 1st Nat. City Overseas Investment Corp., N.Y.C., 1969-70; dir. ambulatory detoxification program N.Y.C. Dept. Health, 1971-73; pres. Lindland Assos., N.Y.C., 1974—. Served from ensign to lt. USN, 1955-59. Mem. Soc. Internat. Devel., Asia Soc. Club: Harvard (N.Y.C.). Home and office: 127 E 69th St New York City NY 10021

THOMPSON, HAROLD ROY, JR., physicist; b. West Chester, Pa., June 6, 1953; s. Harold Roy and Edith May (Morris) T.; B.S., Carnegie-Mellon U., 1975; M.A., Princeton, 1977. Research asst. Princeton Plasma Physics Lab., 1975—. Mem. East Brandywine (Pa.) Vol. Fire Dept., 1973—. Mem. Am. Phys. Soc., Soc. Physics Students, AAAS, Tau Beta Pi, Phi Kappa Phi. Democrat. Methodist. Home: Route 1 PO Box 223 Downingtown PA 19335 Office: Princeton U James Forrestal Campus Plasma Physics Lab Princeton NJ 08540

THOMPSON, HELEN LOUISE, nurse; b. Mercer, Pa., Oct. 21, 1926; d. George Wesley and Ethel Margaret (Anderson) Kelso; grad. Youngstown Hosp. Sch. Nursing, 1948; B.S.Ed., Edinboro State Coll., 1972; m. Delmont Reed Thompson, Aug. 28, 1948. Nurse, Youngstown (Ohio) Hosp., 1948-53, Pa. Dept. Health, Harrisburg, 1953-58; supr. obstetrics Greenville (Pa.) Hosp., 1958-69, dir. nursing, 1969—. Mem. Am. Nurses Assn., Mercer County Cancer Soc., Northwestern Pa. Nursing Service Adminstrs. Forum. Presbyterian. Home: Route 1 Greenville PA 16125

THOMPSON, HOWARD ELLIS, mfg. co. exec.; b. L.I., N.Y., Sept. 10, 1931; s. Ellis John and Clara (Duncan) T.; B.S. in Marine Engring., N.Y. Maritime Coll., 1953; M.S., Poly. Inst. Bklyn., 1967; m. Joan. A. Downer, Sept. 25, 1954; children—Christopher, Susan. With Lunn Industries, Wyandanch, N.Y., 1959—, pres., dir., 1974—. Served to lt. USNR, 1955-59. Mem. Soc. Plastics Industries, L.I. Assn. Commerce and Industry, Am. Security Council. Republican. Club: Centerport Yacht. Office: Lunn Industries Inc Straight Path Wyandanch NY 11798

THOMPSON, J. FOSTER, govt. ofcl.; b. Ashtabula, Ohio, Sept. 12, 1922; s. James Bell and Rosemary (Foster) T.; B.B.A. cum laude, Western Res. U., 1948, LL.B., 1950, J.D., 1968; certificate Indsl. Coll. Armed Forces, 1967; m. Elizabeth I. Welsh, Sept. 14, 1946; children—Gail Aragon, Paul Welsh. Admitted to Ohio bar, 1950, N.Y. bar, 1957; atty.-adviser Army Ordnance Dist., Cleve., 1950-57; gen. counsel Army Ordnance Dist., Rochester, N.Y., 1957-59; mem. firm Thompson & Hayes, Rochester, 1959-68; contracting officer Def. Contract Adminstrn. Service, Rochester, 1968-73; head Office of Naval Research, Rochester, 1973—; spl. legal adviser Pres.'s Commn. on Fed. Procurement. Served with USAAF, 1943-45; PTO. Certified profl. contracts mgr. Mem. Fed. Bar Assn. (charter), Fed. Govt. Accountants Assn., Am. Def. Preparedness Assn. (life, nat. dirs.'commendation), U.S.C.G. Aux. (flotilla staff officer 1969-72), Fed. Exec. Assn. Rochester (v.p. 1977, pres. 1978), Navy League (officer Rochester council), Home Acres Tract Assn. (past pres.), U.S. Naval Inst. (asso.), Genesee Conservation League, VFW, Delta Theta Phi, Phi Kappa Epsilon. Episcopalian. Office: Office Naval Research Room 323 Fed Bldg Rochester NY 14614

THOMPSON, JACOB, state ofcl., Indian affairs exec.; b. Syracuse, N.Y., June 11, 1931; s. Jacob Herne and Priscilla T.; student Univ. Coll., 1971-72; m. Geralda Cornelius, Apr. 25, 1959; children—Vernon, Brian. Ironworker, Syracuse, 1951-76; pres. Oneida Indian Nation, 1960-77; exec. dir., Mass. Commn. on Indian Affairs, Boston, 1976—; mem. bd. Gov.'s Indian Interstate Council to Represent Indians of N.E. Region, 1977; cons. Am. Indian Policy Rev. Commn., 1976; dir. Oneida Indian Soc., Inc.; adminstr., dir. Iroquois Arts and Crafts Exhbn., Everson Mus., Syracuse, 1972. Com. chmn. Boy Scouts Am. and Cub Scouts, 1959-64. Recipient award

N.Y. Iroquois Conf. Inc., 1974. Mem. Nat. Congress of Am. Indians, Oneida Indian Nation (chmn. exec. bd.) bds. edn., housing, health, recreation, cultural and econ. devel., N.Y. State Health Commn. (adv. council), Madison County Comprehensive Health Planning Council, N.Y. Iroquois Conf., Inc., N.Y. State Sub-Com. on Indian Affairs, St. Lawrence U. Native Am. Spl. Services Program, Nat. Indian Edn. Assn., Coalition Eastern Native Ams.; exec. mem. Oneida Nation Tri-Council; mem. ALPHA Health Planning Task Force. Conducted research on history of Oneida Indian Nation, speaker on subject, also litigation for Indian rights. Home: 2 West Rd Oneida Territory Oneida NY 13421 Office: Mass Commn on Indian Affairs One Ashburton Pl Room 1004 Boston MA 02108

THOMPSON, JAMES LANTZ, consumer finance co. exec.; b. Huntingdon, Pa., Dec. 16, 1937; s. James Goodhart and Natalie Virginia (Lantz) T.; B.A. in Bus. Adminstrn., Eastern Ill. U., 1960; m. Carole Ann Kopac, June 24, 1967; children—Gregg Lantz, Lisa Goodhart, Hamilton Lantz. Various positions Lock Haven Co., Hanover and Tyrone, Pa., 1960-64, co. auditor Budget Plan, Huntingdon, 1964; asst. to pres., 1967-70, exec. v.p., 1970-73, pres., 1973—; pres., chmn. bd. Gen. Finance Service Corp., Huntingdon, 1973—; pres. Pa. Consumer Finance Assn., Huntingdon, 1976-77. Pres. Huntingdon Bus. and Industry, 1976-77. Served with U.S. Army, 1961. Mem. Nat. Consumer Finance Assn. (dir. 1974—, mem. adminstrn. com.), Republican. Presbyterian. Clubs: Rotary, Elks, Huntingdon Country (dir. 1974—). Home: Taylor Highlands Huntingdon PA 16652 Office: 326 Penn St Huntingdon PA 16652

THOMPSON, LAURIE JANE, advt. exec.; b. Middletown, N.Y., Apr. 9, 1930; d. Rex A. and Genevieve E. (McCann) Thompson; B.A., Hunter Coll., 1978; m. D. Arkin, 1947 (div. 1951); 1 son, Stephen; m. 2d, J. Finegan, 1954 (div. 1956); children—Wayne, Jonathan. Supr. media services, coordinator on Procter & Gamble, Benton & Bowles, Inc., 1952-56; media buyer, coordinator Lever advt. Ogilvy & Mather, Inc., 1956-59; media dir., coordinator Warner-Chilcott Labs. advt. Lambert & Feasley, Inc., N.Y.C., 1959-67, media cons., 1967-70; media dir. Wesson & Warhaftig, Inc., 1970-73; media coordinator Chesebrough-Pond's Inc., Greenwich, Conn., 1973—. Vice pres. Pub. Sch. No. 9 P.T.A., 1964-65; advt. coordinator Pharm. Advt. Club Project Hope Com., 1961-67. Republican. Presbyterian. Home: 490 West End Ave New York City NY 10024 Office: 33 Benedict Pl Greenwich CT 06830

THOMPSON, RALPH NEWELL, chem. co. exec.; b. Boston, Mar. 4, 1918; s. Ralph and Lillian (Davenport) T.; B.S., Mass. Inst. Tech., 1940; m. Virginia Kenniston, Jan. 31, 1942; children—Pamela, Nicholas, Diana. Research engr. Middlesex Products Corp., Cambridge, Mass., 1940-42; tech. dir. Falulah Paper Co., Fitchburg, Mass., 1945-48; staff engr. Calgon div. Hagan Corp., Pitts., 1948-54, research mgr. Calgon div., 1954-58; mgr. chem. research and devel. Hagan Chems. & Controls, Inc., Pitts., (co. name changed to Calgon Corp.), 1958-63, dir. research and engring., 1963-67, v.p., 1967-70; mgr. corporate devel. Pa. Indsl. Corp., Clairton, Pa., 1970, v.p., 1971-74; gen. mgr. chem. div. Thiokol Corp., Trenton, N.J., 1974-76, group v.p. chem., Newtown, Pa., 1976—; dir. Mulford Co., Inc., Boston, Thiokol (Can.) Ltd., Thiokol Chems. Ltd. (Eng.), Toray-Thiokol Co. Ltd. (Japan), Ventron Corp., Beverly, Mass. Mem. Mt. Lebanon Civic League, 1950-74. Served from ensign to lt. USNR, 1942-45; now lt. comdr. Res. (ret.). Recipient Goodrequ medal in chemistry Goodreau Meml. Fund, 1936. Fellow Am. Inst. Chemists; mem. TAPPI, N.Y. Acad. Scis., Soc. Chem. Industry, Soc. Rheology, A.I.M., Mil. Order World Wars, Pa. Soc. Presbyterian. Home: 1006 Lehigh Dr Yardley PA 19067 Office: Thiokol Corp PO Box 1000 Yardley-Newtown Rd Newtown PA 18940

THOMPSON, RONALD EDWARD, research chemist; b. Greensburg, Pa., Dec. 24, 1948; s. Earl Edward and Edna Emma (Patton) T.; B.S., Point Park Coll., 1970; M.S., Pa. State U., 1975. Quality control engr., Mine Safety Appliances Co., Murrysville, Pa., 1973-74, research chemist, 1974—. Advisor Explorer Post, Westmoreland-Fayette council Boy Scouts Am., 1972-76; bd. dirs. Esquires Sr. Drum and Bugle Corps. Mem. Am. Chem. Soc., Smithsonian Assos. (nat.), Am. Radio Relay League. Republican. Lutheran. Club: Foothills Amateur Radio. Home: 1616 Harrison Ave Jeanette PA 15644 Office: 200 N Braddock Ave Pittsburgh PA 15208

THOMPSON, SIDNEY ORVILLE, ins. co. exec.; b. Leonard, N.D., Mar. 20, 1920; s. Sabien Oliver and Anna (Benson) T.; jr. coll. degree State Sch. Sci., Wahpeton, N.D., 1939; B.C.S., Benjamin Franklin U., Washington, 1949; m. Mercedes Huppeler, Apr. 14, 1941; children—Pamela Gene, Gretchen Marie, Craig Sidney. With Internal Revenue Service, 1940-42, 45-50; mgr. pension dept. New Eng. Life Ins. Co., N.Y.C., 1950-61, treas. Leaders Assn., Boston, 1959; v.p., treas. Langson Corp., N.Y.C., 1960—; pres. Thompson Pension Employee Plans, N.Y.C., 1964—; asso. gen. agt. New Eng. Life Ins. Co.; organizer, dir., chmn. bd. Hudson Valley Nat. Bank, Yonkers, N.Y. Lectr. pension and profit sharing systems Purdue U., 1953, 54, U. Conn., 1961, U. P.R., 1961, U. N. H., 1962, Active local Community Chest, A.R.C. Served to chief petty officer USNR, 1941-45; PTO. Mem. Leaders Assn. Boston (pres. 1963). Clubs: Union League (N.Y.C.); Winged Foot Country (Mamaroneck, N.Y.); Westchester Hills Golf (White Plains, N.Y.); Adirondack League (Old Forge, N.Y.); Camp Fire of Am. Contbr. to ins. publs. Office: Route 1 Box 83 S Bedford Rd Pound Ridge NY 10576 also 1051 Villa Nueva Dr Litchfield Park Phoenix AZ 85340

THOMPSON, THOMAS FREDERICK, fin. and managerial cons.; b. N.Y.C., Mar. 27, 1901; s. Thomas and Ingeborg (Nelson) T.; B.C.S., N.Y.U., 1926, M.C.S., 1931; m. Dorothy J. Johnson, June 18, 1933; children—Carol Ann (Mrs. Oswald A. Krebs, Jr.), Ellen Dorothy (Mrs. Norman O Lorensen). Office boy Mass. and Waldstein Co., Newark, 1915-16, machine bookkeeper, 1916-18; bookkeeper Hyatt Roller Bearing Co., Harrison, N.J., 1918-19, asst. dept. head, 1919-20; budget clk. Nat. Council Bd. and Internat. Com., YMCA, N.Y.C., 1922-24, chief accountant, 1924-27, dep. controller, 1927-29; jr. pub. accountant Touche, Ross, Bailey and Smart, N.Y.C., 1929-35, sr. pub. accountant, 1936-41; accountant Met. Life Ins. Co., N.Y.C., 1941-48, investment analyst, accountant, 1949-61, mgr. indsl. bond and stock investments, 1961-66; fin. and managerial cons., 1966-75; chmn. finance com., dir. West Farms Land Trust, Inc., Waterford, 1975—. Mem. Waterford Charter Commn., 1977—. C.P.A., N.Y. Member Am. Inst. C.P.A.'s, N.Y. Soc. C.P.A.'s, Nat. Retail Mchts. Assn., Met. Controllers Assn. N.Y.C., N.Y. Soc. Security Analysts, Westchester County Grand Jurors Assn., Westchester Power Squadron, Nat. Hist. Soc., Arthritis Found., Accounting Research Assn., Am. Econs. Found., Smithsonian Assos., Met. Opera Guild, Goodspeed Opera House Found., Beta Gamma Sigma. Address: 9 Division St Waterford CT 06385

THOMPSON, WARREN HENRY, counselor; b. Framingham, Mass., Mar. 28, 1918; s. Herbert William and Esther Eleanor (Enright) T.; B.S., Northeastern U., 1941, M.Ed., 1965. Engr., Foxboro Co. (Mass.), 1944-51; tchr. math. and sci., Gloucester (Mass.) Vocat. High Sch., 1951-53; instr. math. and electricity Wentworth Inst., Boston, 1953-64; guidance counselor Newton (Mass.) Tech. High Sch., 1964-67; chairperson pre-tech. dept. Vt. Tech. Coll., Randolph Center, 1967—; asso. participant Biol. Humanics Center, Cambridge, Mass., 1975—. Trustee Orange County (Vt.) Mental Health Services, 1972-75; pres. Goodwill Assos. of Morgan Meml. Goodwill Industries, Boston, 1959-62; Dem. com. Randolph, Vt., 1972—, county com., 1974-77. Mem. Am. Personnel and Guidance Assn., Am. Coll. Personnel Assn., AAAS, Am. Tech. Edn. Assn., Internat. Platform Assn. Religious Soc. Friends. Home: RD 2 Randolph Center VT 05061

THOMPSON, WILLIAM BOND, physicist; b. Portland, Maine, Apr. 4, 1943; s. Philip Pickering and Mary (Rines) T.; B.S., Dartmouth, 1965; Yale, 1972; m. Sylvia Wiles, June 19, 1965; children—William C., Melanie L. Sr. research physicist Varian/Extrion Corp., Gloucester, Mass., 1972-74, 75—, Mass. Gen. Hosp., Boston, 1975; dir. Maine Radio and TV Corp., Portland. Gibbs fellow, 1966. Mem. Am. Phys. Soc., AAAS, Sigma Xi. Home: 8 Lawrence Rd Swampscott MA 01907 Office: Varian/Extrion Corp PO Box 1226 Gloucester MA 01930

THOMPSON, WILLIAM PARKHURST, educator; b. Corning, N.Y., Feb. 6, 1930; s. William C. and Anne Charlotte (Parkhurst) T.; B.S., Syracuse U., 1953, M.S., 1956, Ed.D., 1968; m. Jane Ellen Cooper, Aug. 3, 1974; children—Pamela A., Katherine J., William Parkhurst. Broadcaster, Sta. KVOL, Lafayette, La., 1953-54; asst. prof. speech Keuka Coll., Keuka Park, N.Y., 1956-59; faculty Corning Community Coll., 1959—, prof., 1967—; communication cons. Corning Glass Works. Pres. Corning Philharmonic Soc., 1968-70, Corning Workshop Players, 1965-67, Corning Area Arts Council, 1968-73. Mem. AAUP (chpt. pres. 1974—), Eastern Communication Assn., Speech Communication Assn., N.Y. Speech Assn., Pi Delta Epsilon, Alpha Psi Omega. Presbyterian (elder). Contbr. articles to profl. jours. Home: 4016 Rockwell Ave 12B Horseheads NY 14845 Office: Corning Community College Corning NY 14830

THOMPSON, WILLIAM PHELPS, lawyer, ch. ofcl.; b. Beloit, Kans., Sept. 14, 1918; s. William Frederick and Vera (Phelps) T.; student Bethel Coll., North Newton, Kans., 1935-36; A.B., McPherson (Kans.) Coll., 1939. J.C.D., 1956; J.D., U. Chgo., 1942; LL.D., Coll. Emporia, 1965, U. Dubuque, 1966, Missouri Valley Coll., 1967, LaSalle Coll., Phila., 1974; L.H.D., Tusculum Coll., 1977; m. Mary Alice Wood, Jan. 23, 1949; children—Judith Thompson Koop, William Wood, Margaret. Admitted to Kans. bar, 1942; practiced in Wichita, 1946-66; partner firm Hershberger, Patterson, Jones & Thompson, 1951-66. Mem. gen. Council Synod Kans., United Presbyn. Ch. U.S.A., 1958-64, chmn. budget and fin. com., 1959-62; mem. gen. council Gen. Assembly, United Presbyn. Ch. U.S.A., 1958-64, vice chmn., 1960-64, mem. budget and fin. com., 1958-64, chmn., 1960-64, moderator 177th Gen. Assembly, 1965, stated clk., 1966—; dir. Wichita Council Chs., 1954-59, v.p., 1954, pres. 1955, chmn. trustees, 1957-59; dir. Westminster Found., Synod Kans., 1955-62; mem. central com. World Council Chs., 1966—, exec. com. commn. on internat. affairs, 1973-75; exec. com., mem. gov. bd. Nat. Council Chs. Christ in U.S.A., 1966—, chmn. gen. planning and program com., 1969-72, pres., 1976-78; exec. com. World Alliance Reformed Chs., 1966—, pres., 1970-77. Pres., Civic Progress, Wichita, 1961; mem. Mayor of Wichita's Adv. Com. on Water, 1955, Adv. Com. Civic Center, 1962. Bd. dirs. Wichita Community Planning Council, 1952-60, pres., 1959; bd. dirs. Wichita Community Chest, 1955-57, Wichita Civic Music Assn., 1953-63, Wichita Council Campfire Girls, 1960-65, Wichita Symphony Soc., 1960-64, 65-66; bd. dirs. United Fund Wichita and Sedgwick County, 1957-66, chmn. fund raising campaign, 1964, v.p., 1965; trustee Midwest Med. Research Found., 1965-66. Served to capt. USAAF, 1942-46. Mem. Am., Kans., Wichita bar assns., Order of Coif, Pi Kappa Delta, Phi Delta Phi. Home: 60 Ross Stevenson Circle Princeton NJ 08540 Office: Room 1201 475 Riverside Dr New York City NY 10027

THOMS, DONALD RAYMOND, psychotherapist; b. S.I., N.Y., Mar. 17, 1949; s. Raymond Richard and Mildred (Pearson) T.; Asso. Sci., Grayson County Jr. Coll., 1969; B.S., Sam Houston State U., 1971; postgrad. Coll. S.I., 1978; m. Linda Ann Nicholas, Mar. 3, 1973; 1 son, Brandon Scott. Psychiat. team leader, adminstrv. supr. North Richmond Community Mental Health Center, S.I., 1972—; counselor Community Counseling Center Coll. S.I., 1976—. Mem. Am. Personnel and Guidance Assn., Am. Rehab. Counseling Assn. Lutheran. Home: 640 Drumgoole Rd E Staten Island NY 10312

THOMSON, CHARLES ALEXANDER HOLMES, cons., polit. scientist; b. Titaghur, India, Feb. 20, 1913; s. James and Shirley Holmes (Smith) T.; came to U.S., 1916, naturalized, 1928; B.A., Pomona Coll., 1934; M.A. (fellow), Claremont Coll., 1935; M. A. (fellow), Harvard, 1944, Ph.D., 1949; m. Adele Stuart Meriam, Aug. 30, 1940; children—John Stuart, Janet Elizabeth. Mem. staff Brookings Instn., Washington, 1936, 40, dir. edn. div., 1949-55, sr. staff mem., 1951-59; staff dir. Presidents Communications Policy Bd., 1950-51; sr. staff mem. Rand Corp., Santa Monica, 1959-69; chmn. research council Research Analysis Corp., McLean, Va., 1969-72; sr. tech. staff mem. Gen. Research Corp., McLean, 1972-75, cons., 1975-77; cons. polit. communications, hort., 1975—. Mem. Council Chevy Chase View, Md., 1952-59, 69-72. Served to col. U.S. Army, 1941-46. Decorated officer Order British Empire; Bronze Star. Fellow A.A.A.S.; mem. Phi Beta Kappa. Author: The Overseas Information Service of the U.S. Government, 1948; Authoritarianism and the Individual, 1950; Television and Presidential Politics, 1956; The 1956 Presidential Campaign, 1960; editor, co-author Successful Gardening, 1975; The Research Analysis Corporation, 1975. Home: 4013 Franklin St Kensington MD 20795

THOMSON, CHRISTIAN ROSS, fire protection specialist; b. Montreal, Que., Can., Oct. 27, 1929; s. Christian Aldrom and Jane Mary (Dolphin) T.; B.Sc., Carleton U., 1954; m. Dorothy Noel, Oct. 31, 1953; children—Katharine Joanne, Christine Elizabeth, Karen Jane, Sarah Ann. Insp., Canadian Underwriters Assn., Montreal, 1953-56; fire protection engr. Canadian Pacific Ry. Co., Montreal, 1956-57, supr. ins. and fire protection, Winnipeg, Man., 1957-65; dir. fire research Canadian Wood Council, Ottawa, Ont., 1965—. Mem. Soc. Fire Protection Engrs. (dir.), ASTM, Nat. Fire Protection Assn. Mem. Anglican Ch. Club: Masons. Home: 68 Westpark Dr Ottawa ON K1B 3E5 Canada

THOMSON, FRANK, hotel exec.; b. Raton, N.Mex., June 29, 1934; s. David and Carrie (Mancini) T.; B.S. in Bus. Adminstr., U. Denver, 1956; m. Marvel L. Atchison, June 26, 1955; children—Mark, Lawrence Arthur, Beverly Lorraine. Gen. mgr. Yucca Hotel, Raton, N.Mex., 1958-60, Heart O'Denver Motor Hotel, Denver, 1960-68, Hampshire House Hotel, Denver, 1965-68, Radisson Denver Hotel, Denver, 1968-75; pres. Hotel & Restaurant Mgmt., Inc., Denver, 1965-70; v.p. Radisson Denver Corp., 1968-75; now dist. dir. region III Holiday Inns, Inc., Rochester, N.Y. Pres. Colo. Visitors Bur., 1975-76. Served with USAF, 1956-58. Named Hotel Man of Year Colo./Wyo. Hotel and Motel Assn., 1966. Mem. Greater Denver Hotel Assn. (pres. 1969-70), Colo./Wyo. Hotel and Motel Assn. (pres. 1970-71), Am. Hotel and Motel Assn. (vice chmn. com. 1961-75), U. Denver Hotel and Restaurant Mgmt. Sch. Alumni Assn. (pres. 1965). Methodist (chmn. bd. trustees 1970-75). Clubs: Optimist, Skal (Rochester, N.Y.). Home: 69 Nettlecreek Rd Fairport NY 14450 Office: 120 Main St East Rochester NY 14604

THOMSON, GERALD EDMUND, physician, educator; b. N.Y.C., 1932; s. Lloyd and Sybil (Gilbourne) T.; M.D., Howard U., 1959; m. Carolyn Webber, children—Gregory, Karen. Intern, State U. N.Y.-Kings County Hosp. Center, Bklyn., 1959-60, resident in medicine, 1960-62, chief resident, 1962-63, N.Y. Heart Assn. fellow nephrology, 1964-65, asst. vis. physician, 1963-70, clin. dir. dialysis unit, 1965-67; practice medicine specializing in internal medicine, N.Y.C., 1963—; attending physician State U. N.Y. Med. Bklyn. Hosp., 1966-70; instr. medicine State U.N.Y., Bklyn., 1963-68, clin. asst. prof. medicine, 1968-70; asso. chief med. services Coney Island Hosp., Bklyn., 1967-70; asso. attending physician Presbyn. Hosp., 1970—; dir. nephrology Harlem Hosp. Center, N.Y.C., 1970-71, dir. med. services, 1971—, pres. med. bd., 1976—; asso. prof. medicine Columbia Coll. Phys. and Surg., 1970-72, prof., 1972—. Mem. Health Research Council City of N.Y., 1972—; mem. hypertension adv. com. N.Y.C. Health Services Adminstrn., 1972-75; mem. adv. bd. N.Y. Kidney Found., 1971—; mem. Health Research Council, State of N.Y., 1975—; mem. hypertension info. and edn. adv. com. NIH, 1973-74, N.Y. State Adv. Com. on Hypertension, 1977—; mem. med. adv. bd. Nat. Assn. Patients on Hemodialysis and Transplantation, 1973—; mem. com. on mild hypertension Nat. Heart and Lung Inst., 1976; bd. dirs. N.Y. Heart Assn., 1973—, chmn. com. high blood pressure, 1976—; chmn. com. hypertension N.Y. Met. Regional Med. Program, 1974-76. Diplomate Am. Bd. Internal Medicine. Fellow A.C.P.; mem. AAAS, Am., N.Y. (pres. 1973-74) socs. nephrology, Am. Fedn. Clin. Research, Soc. Urban Physicians (pres. 1972-73), Am. Soc. for Artificial Internal Organs, N.Y. Acad. Medicine (mem. com. medicine in soc. 1974-76), Alpha Omega Alpha. Mem. adv. bd. Jour. Urban Health, 1974—. Home: 118 Whitman Dr Brooklyn NY 11234 Office: Harlem Hosp Center 506 Lenox Ave New York City NY 10037

THOMSON, JAMES CUTTING, educator; b. Chgo., June 12, 1909; s. James Clark and Helen (Shaw); A.B., Middlebury Coll., 1929; Tchrs.' certificate Hochschule fur Musik, Berlin, Germany, 1934; M.A., Baylor U., 1940; M.A., Yale, 1948; Ph.D., N.Y.U., 1959; m. Selma Margaret Wertime, July 24, 1948; children—Ralph Gordon, Jean Ellen, Margaret Celia, Vivian Elizabeth. Asst. prof. violin Coll. Ozarks, Clarksville, Ark., 1934-35; asst. prof. violin and chamber music Baylor U., 1935-42; with Nat. Security Agy., Washington, 1951-52; chmn. music dept. Wilson Coll., Chambersburg, Pa., 1952-63; asso. prof. music history and lit. U. Kans., Lawrence, 1963-68; prof., chmn. music history and lit. West Chester (Pa.) State Coll., 1968-75; with H & R Block, 1977, 78. Served with Signal Corps, AUS, 1942-45. Recipient Kellogg Fugue prize Yale, 1949; Fulbright lectr., Iran, 1962. Mem. Am. Musicol. Soc., Internat. Music Soc., Pa. Assn. Higher Edn., N.E.A., Pi Kappa Lambda. Republican. Episcopalian. Mason. Author: Aria, 1941; The Works of Caron, a Study in Fifteenth Century Style, 1959; An Introduction to Philippe Caron, 1964; Music Through the Renaissance, 1968; Les Oeuvres Complete de Philippe (?) Caron, Vol. I, 1971, Vol. II, 1974; (pseudonym Adam Chase) Smoke No More!, 1976. Contbr. articles to profl. jours. Recitals on harpsichord, voilin, viola da gamba, 1976-77. Home: 1638 Green Ln RD 3 West Chester PA 19380

THOMSON, MELDRIM, former gov. N.H.; b. 1912; m., 4 children. Founder, former pres. Equity Pub. Co., Oxford, N.H.; gov. State of N.H., 1973-78. Republican.

THOMSON, RODERICK ALBERT EDWARD, med. technologist; b. Boston, Feb. 18, 1926; s. Roderick E.S. and Daphne M. (Hamilton) T.; diploma Eastern Sch. for Physcian's Aides, 1947—; student U. Rochester (N.Y.), 1966-68, 75; m. Theresa A. Thomson, Sept. 16, 1950; children—Roderick Kevin, Brenda Michele Thomson Aklile, Cheryl Gail. Med. technologist Chenango Meml. Hosp., Norwich, N.Y., 1948-51; chief clin. lab. services unit, Norwich Pharmacal Co., tech. asso. dept. of radiation biology and biophysics U. Rochester, 1958-67, sr. tech. asso., 1967-69, sr. tech. asso. radiation oncology, 1970-75, sr. tech. asso., adminstrv. asst. for animal health program dept. of radiation biology and biophysics, 1975—; sr. scientist Biomed. Research, Zaret Found., Inc., Oahu, Hawaii, 1968-70. Mem. 19th Ward Community Assn., Rochester, 1970—. Served with USCG, 1944-46; PTO, ETO. Mem. Soc. for Exptl. Biology and Medicine, Radiation Research Soc., Am. Med. Technologists, Aerospace Med. Assn., Royal Soc. of Health (London), N.Y. State Registry of Med. Technologists, Sigma Xi. Contbr. numerous articles on radiation biology to profl. jours. Home: 46 Winbourne Rd Rochester NY 14611 Office: Dept of Radiation Biology and Biophysics Rochester NY 14642

THOMSON, SELMA WERTIME, musician, educator; b. Chambersburg, Pa., Oct. 3, 1917; d. Rudolf H. and Flora Edith (Montgomery) Wertime; B.A., Wilson Coll., Chambersburg, 1938; M.A., N.Y. U., 1940; m. James Cutting Thomson, July 24, 1948; children—Jean, Margaret, Vivian. Tchr. music pub. schs., Pa. and Md., 1940-46; mem. faculty So. Conn. State Coll., 1946-51, U. Kans., 1965; asso. prof. music Kutztown (Pa.) State Coll., 1970—. Mem. Music Educators Nat. Conf., NEA, Pa. Music Educators Conf., LWV (local bd. mem.), Nat. Wildlife Fedn., Nat. Audubon Soc. Presbyterian. Home: 1638 Green Ln Rural Delivery 3 West Chester PA 19380 Office: Kutztown State Coll Kutztown PA 19530

THORBURN, PETER ALAN, fragrance and flavor co. exec.; b. Pangbourne, Eng., Jan. 12, 1943; s. Thomas and Gladys Mary (Gordon) T.; came to U.S., 1973; student East London Sch. Commerce, 1962-64, Internat. Corr. Inst. Mktg. Schs., 1968-70; m. Patricia Lilian Parkes, July 24, 1970; children—Robert Anthony, Peter Thomas, Samantha Clare. Mgmt. trainee Mobil Oil Co., London, 1961-63, supply exec., 1963-66; sales exec. Antoine Chiris/U.O.P. Fragrances, Epsom, Eng., 1966-70; mng. dir. V. Mane Fils Ltd., Haywards Heath, Eng., 1970-73, pres. V. Mane Fils Inc., Fairfield, N.J., 1973—; dir. V. Mane Fils Ltd. Eng. Mem. Soc. Cosmetic Chemists, Inst. Food Technologists, Brit. Soc. Flavourists (Eng.). Republican. Episcopalian. Club: Montclair Dramatic Club (pres. 1977—). Home: 101 Yantacaw Brook Rd Upper Montclair NJ 07043 Office: 16 Spielman Rd Fairfield NJ 07006

THORN, DONALD BARRY, educator; b. N.Y.C., Apr. 30, 1945; s. Saul and Frances (Chilk) T.; B.A., Syracuse U., 1965; M.S., So. Conn. State Coll., 1970; M.A. (Jesse Smith Noyes Found. fellow, NSF fellow), Columbia, 1971, Ed.D., 1979; m. Verna Sue Lapin, Dec. 19, 1971. Sci. coordinator Bds. of Coop. Ednl. Services, Yorktown Heights, N.Y., 1967-73; instr. biology Westchester Community Coll., Valhalla, N.Y., 1974, Irvington (N.Y.) High Sch., 1974—. Bd. dirs. Quakerbridge Sch., Ossining, N.Y., 1965—; pres. Jewish Reconstructionist Congregation Anshe Dorshe Emes, Ossining, N.Y., 1977-79. Mem. Nat. Assn. Research in Sci. Teaching, Club: B'nai B'rith Tri-community (corr. sec. 1973-74, v.p. 1976-77), Nat. Sci. Tchrs. Assn., Sci. Tchrs. Assn. N.Y. State, Nat. Assn. Biology Tchrs., Electron Microscopy Soc. Am. Home: 63 Van Wyck St Croton-on-Hudson NY 10520 Office: Irvington High School N Broadway Irvington NY 10533

THORN, SUSAN HOWE, interior designer; b. Washington, Apr. 22, 1941; d. James Bennett Cowdin and Lois (Fiesenger) Howe; A.B. cum laude, Syracuse U., 1962; postgrad. N.Y. Sch. Interior Design, 1965, lighting design Parsons Sch. Design, 1975-77; m. William D. Thorn,

June 22, 1963; children—Melissa Ann, William David. Owner, designer, Susan Thorn, Interiors, Cross River, N.Y., 1965—; designer total building, Cooper Labs, Bedford Hills, N.Y., 1973, total redesign, Nycrest Corp., Cold Spring, N.Y., 1973-75, showrooms, model rooms stylist and coordinator, France Voiles Co. Inc., N.Y.C., 1976, total design new corp. hdqrs. in Gen. Dynamics Bld. (with Marjorie Borradaile Helsel), Robert E. Eastman Co., N.Y.C., 1967; designer offices, stores, employee areas comml., pub., residential clients, including Waccabuc (N.Y.) Country Club, 1969, S. Salem (N.Y.) Library; instr. adult edn. dept. John Jay High Sch., Jr. League No. Westchester, Caramoor Mus.; speaker civic orgns. Mem. Am. Soc. Interior Designers (profl.), Internat. Assn. Lighting Designers (asso.). Episcopalian. Club: Waccabuc Country. Writer weekly decorating column in The Patent Trader, 1965-66; contbr. articles to newspapers. Home: Route 121 Cross River NY 10518

THORNBER, HUBERT ELWYN, assn. exec.; b. Brookings, S.D., July 18, 1900; s. William T. and Martha A. (Cuckow) T.; B.S. in Civil Engring., S.D. State Coll., 1922; certificate hwy. engring. U. Mich., 1924; certificate battalion comdr. U.S. Army Inf. Sch., 1940; grad. U.S. Army Command and Staff Sch., 1941; m. Winnifred Ann Griffiths, Mar. 22, 1924 (dec.); children—Hubert Elwyn, Richard W., Winnifred Ann (Mrs. James Earl Clites, Jr.); m. 2d, Blanche C. Coursey, Apr. 6, 1974. Jr. testing engr. Ill. Hwy. Dept., 1922-23; asst. construction engr., also asst. personnel dir. Pa. Dept. Hwys., 1924-40, civil engr., 1954-56, dir. dept. fiscal mgmt., 1956-63; exec. sec. Pa. Assn. Cons. Engrs., 1967-68, Cons. Engrs. Council Pa., 1968-70; Pa. staff dir. Pa. Profl. Engrs. in Pvt. Practice, 1970-73; prof. mil. sci. and tactics Pa. State Coll., Indiana, 1950-53. Served to maj. U.S. Army, 1941-42, to lt. col., to 1954. Decorated Legion of Merit; officer Order Brit. Empire; officer French Order Maritime Merit; chevalier French Legion of honor; D'Argent, French Medal Recognition. Mem. Ret. Officers Assn., Am. Legion, V.F.W., Engrs. Soc. Pa. (dir. 1962-65, fin. sec. 1967-69, treas. 1972-73), Am. Soc. Hwy. Engrs. (dir. 1963-65, v.p. 1965-66), U. Mich. Alumni Assn. (chpt. pres. 1961-63), Brotherhood St. Andrew (nat. councilman 1957-60). Episcopalian (laymen's league treas. 1961-64, v.p. 1965-66). Home: 542 Benton St Harrisburg PA 17104

THORNBERG, FREDERICK KELLEY, architect; b. Fulton, N.Y., Apr. 27, 1924; s. Fred V. and Gladys (Kelley) T.; B.Arch., Syracuse U., 1951; m. Phyllis Sinclair Dean, June 25, 1949; children—Frederick Dean, Ann Stephens Thornberg Jorgenson. Draftsman, Austin Co., Roselle, N.J., 1951-52; draftsman J. C. Van Nuys & Assos., Architects, Somerville, N.J., 1952-57, job capt., 1957-58; partner Scrimenti Swackhamer & Perantoni, Architects, Somerville, 1958-59; partner Thun & Thornberg, Architects, Basking Ridge, N.J., 1959-61; asso. architect Bauer & Corbett, Architects, Newark, 1961-71; v.p. Corbett Thornberg Stechow and Jordan, Architects, Newark, 1972—, also dir.; sec. Summit (N.J.) Bldg. Code Bd. Appeals, 1968, chmn., 1969-77. Served with AUS, 1943-46. Mem. AIA, N.J. Soc. Architects, N.J. Exec. Assn., U.S. Power Squadron (co-chmn. auction com. 1975-76, chmn. pub. relations and publicity com. 1977—). Club: Beacon Hill (Summit). Home: 26 Garden Rd Summit NJ 07901 Office: 60 Park Pl Newark NJ 07102

THORNBROUGH, ALBERT A., mfg. co. exec.; b. Lakin, Kans., 1912; grad. Kans. State Coll., 1935; student Harvard, 1937. Dep. chmn. bd., pres., chief exec. officer Massey-Ferguson Ltd., Toronto, Ont., Can. Mem. Farm Equipment Inst. (pres. 1962-63). Office: 200 University Ave Toronto ON M5H 3E4 Canada

THORNBURG, DONALD RICHARD, metallurgist; b. Pitts., Oct. 16, 1933; s. John Wilson and Theresa Katherine (Reffert) T.; B.Met. E., Rensselaer Poly. Inst., 1955; M.S., Carnegie Mellon U., 1963, Ph.D., 1972; m. Kathryn Jean Figler, Aug. 7, 1971; children—Donald Wilson, Joseph James, Natalie Jean. Jr. to sr. engr. Westinghouse Electric Corp., Pitts., 1958-68; fellow engr., 1970—. Served with USAF, 1955-57. NSF fellow, 1968-69. Mem. Am. Soc. Metals, Am. Inst. Mining and Metall. Engrs., AAAS, Sigma Xi. Democrat. Roman Catholic. Contbr. articles to profl. jours. Patentee in field. Home: 387 Barclay Ave Pittsburgh PA 15221 Office: 1310 Beulah Rd Pittsburgh PA 15235

THORNBURGH, RICHARD LEWIS, state ofcl., lawyer; b. Pitts., July 16, 1932; s. Charles G. and Alice (Sanborn) T.; B.E., Yale, 1954; LL.B. with high honors, U. Pitts., 1957; LL.D., Washington and Jefferson Coll., 1976; m. Virginia Walton Judson, Oct. 12, 1963; children—John Kendall, David Bradford, Peter Lewis, William Field. Admitted to Pa. bar, 1957, U.S. Supreme Ct. bar, 1965; with legal dept. Aluminum Co. Am., Pitts., 1957-59; mem. firm Kirkpatrick, Lockhart, Johnson & Hutchison, Pitts., 1959-69, 77-79; U.S. atty. for Western Pa., Pitts., 1969-75; asst. atty. gen. criminal div. U.S. Dept. Justice, 1975-77; gov. of Pa., 1979—. Del., Pa. Constl. Conv., 1967-68, sec. judiciary com.; chmn. Allegheny Regional Planning Council for Pa. Gov.'s Justice Commn., 1969-73. Mem. men's adv. bd. Home for Crippled Children, 1966—. Republican candidate U.S. Congress, 14th Congl. Dist., 1966. Mem. Am., Pa. (ho. of dels.), Allegheny County bar assns., Am. Judicature Soc., Am. Bar Fedn. Home: 412 S Linden Ave Pittsburgh PA 15208 Office: Office of Gov State Capitol Harrisburg PA 17120

THORNBURY, THOMAS GLIDDEN, lawyer; b. Cleve., May 5, 1931; s. Purla Lee and Gertrude Elinor (Glidden) T.; B.S., Miami U., Oxford U., 1953; LL.B., U. Mich., 1958; m. Cynthia Jane Schrock, Sept. 11, 1954; children—Jane Ellen, Thomas Lee, David Bruce. Admitted to Mich. bar, 1958, Ind. bar, 1958; atty. Lincoln Nat. Life Ins. Co., Fort Wayne, Ind., 1958-60, asst. counsel, 1960-65, asst. gen. counsel, 1965-68, asso. gen. counsel, 1968-69, 2nd v.p., 1969-71, v.p., gen. counsel, 1971-74; v.p., tax councel Lincoln Nat. Corp., 1975-76; tax dir. Hartford Fire Ins. Co., 1976—. Pres. New Glenwood Civic Assn., Ft. Wayne, Ind., 1974-75. Served to lt. USNR, 1953-55. Mem. Ind., Allen County bar assns., Am. Life Ins. Assn., Assn. Life Ins. Counsel, Ft. Wayne Estate Planning Council, U. Hartford Tax Inst. (mem. advisory bd.), Tax Execs. Inst. Home: 16 Sanctuary Dr Simsbury CT 06070 Office: Hartford Plaza Hartford CT 06115

THORNE, RALPH WEYMOUTH, banking exec.; b. Williamsport, Pa., Nov. 23, 1935; s. Ralph Weymouth and Joan (Stearns) T.; B.A., Pa. State U., 1958; grad. N.Y. Inst. Fin., 1968, Bucknell Trust Sch., 1972; m. Holly Carl Lyon, July 1, 1967; children—Patrick Todd, Tara Lyon, Travis Stearns. Gen. traffic mgr. Darling Valve & Mfg. Co., Williamsport, 1958-68; registered rep. Blair & Co., Inc., Williamsport, 1968-70; investment officer trust dept. Fidelity Nat. Bank Pa., Williamsport, 1970-73; trust adminstrn. officer Central Counties Bank, State College, Pa., 1973-77; trust officer Union Nat. Bank, Lewisburg, Pa., 1977-78; bus. devel. Fidelity Nat. Bank Pa., Williamsport, 1978—. Treas., Family and Children's Service, 1973-74; mem. Lycoming County Republican Finance Com., 1962; treas. Lycoming County Rep. Com., 1972-74; bd. dirs. Lycoming Child Day Care Center. Mem. Pi Kappa Pi, Alpha Mu. Lutheran. Clubs: Dunwoody Big Bear Fish and Game, Ross. Home: RD 3 Montoursville PA 17754 Office: 101 W Third St Williamsport PA 17701

THORNER, HORACE EDWARD, psychologist, educator, author, librarian; b. Boston, Aug. 3, 1909; s. Maurice H. and Lydia S. (Dann) T.; grad. cum laude, Thayer Acad., 1927; A.B. cum laude, Harvard U., 1931, A.M., 1932. Studied and worked with Dr. I. H. Coriat, founder Boston Psychoanalytic Inst., 1932-43; teacher Williston Acad., 1943-70, dir. Plimpton Library and mem. com. for new schedule; now engaged in free lance writing. Chmn. Easthampton div. Harvard Grad. Sch. Found. Spl. investigator war industry personnel for Dunn and Bradstreet under Provost Marshal's office, 1943. Sec. nat. library com. meeting Secondary Edn. Bd. on relation of library to sci. and math., N.Y.C., 1958. Recipient spl. tribute Western New Eng. Chess Fedn., 1970. Fellow Internat. Inst. Arts and Letters, Royal Soc. Arts (London); hon. fellow Nat. Cum Laude Soc.; mem. Nat. Council Teachers of English, U.S. Chess Fedn. Unitarian. Clubs: Harvard, Easthampton Rod and Gun, Appalachian Mountain. Author: (3-act play) The Man Who Shot God, 1951, rev. edit., 1953; Hawthorne, Poe, and a Literary Ghost; The Sources of The Gold Bug; (novel) Murder for Everybody, 1958; also numerous articles on creative imagination; translator complete verse, The Rubaiyat of Omar Khayyam, 1942, rev., 1955, London; The Iliad of Homer, 1948, Index to the Novel, 1956, rev., 1961; For Better or for Verse, 1966; Conversations with John Keats, 1968; the Lost Colonies of Virginia, 1976; Newly Collected Shorter Poems, 1978. Home: Swift River Cummington MA 01026

THORNTON, FRANK REGIS, indsl. engr.; b. Pitts., Sept. 14, 1909; s. Patrick Henry and Margaret Ruth (Walsh) T.; B.S. in Indsl. Engring., U. Pitts., 1935; m. Marion Frances Kelly, Dec. 29, 1931; children—Lawrence Raymond, Marion Martha. With Sears, Roebuck & Co., Pitts., 1935-40; with Martin Marietta Co., Balt., 1941-64; microfilm technician and records mgmt. officer Balt. County Dept. Pub. Works, Towson, Md., 1964—. Active Boys Scouts Am., Towson, 1949-64; past football coach Balt. City League. Mem. Nat. Microfilm Assn. Roman Catholic. Clubs: Kiwanis (pres. 1963, lt. gov. 1972-73), K.C. Home: 1829 Loch Shiel Rd Towson MD 21234 Office: 111 W Chesapeake Ave Baltimore MD 21204

THORNTON, ROBERT WHEELER, structural engr.; b. Trumbull, Conn., Dec. 24, 1922; s. Edwin William and Laura (Wheeler) T.; B.S. in Engring., U. Conn., 1950; m. Clare Lucy Gerard, June 7, 1947; children—Gail Wheeler Thornton Shipman, Laura Jo Thornton James, Geoffrey Gerard. Draftsman, Ebasco Services, 1950-51; estimator H.J. High, Orlando, Fla., 1951-52; structural designer Westcott of Mapes, New Haven, 1952-53; estimator Gellatly Constrn. Co., Bridgeport, Conn., 1953-56; sec., gen. mgr. Thornton Co., Trumbull, 1956-62; pvt. practice as cons. engr., Strafford, Vt., 1963—; pres. Thornton, Inc., Sprucewold Lodge, Boothbay Harbor, Maine, 1968—; mgr. Thornton Constrn., Trumbull, Conn., 1976—. Trustee pub. funds, Strafford, 1966-69. Sec. town com. Republican party, 1966-69. Served with USMCR, 1942-46; PTO. Registered profl. engr., Vt., N.H. Mem. Strafford Athletic Assn. (chmn. 1965-67). Conglist. (treas. 1965-68). Clubs: Masons (32 deg., past master); Sprucewold Beach (founder). Home: Sharon VT 05065

THORPE, GEOFFREY LASCELLES, psychologist, clin. dir.; b. Guildford, Surrey, Eng., Mar. 29, 1946; s. Denis Lascelles and Barbara Joan (Mason) T.; arrived U.S., 1975; B.A. with honors, U. Wales, 1968; B.Phil., U. Liverpool, 1970; Ph.D. (Fulbright travel grantee 1971-73), Rutgers U., 1973; m. Carol Louise Stoutenberg, July 7, 1973; 1 child—Elizabeth Joan. Pschologist Lancaster Moor Hosp., Eng., 1970-71; sr. psychologist Birch Hill Hosp., Rochdale, Eng., 1973-74; clin. coordinator Bangor (Maine) Mental Health Inst., 1975-76; clinician Counseling Center, Bangor, 1976-77, clin. dir. out-patient services, 1977-78, dir. inpatient services, 1978—; cooperating asst. prof. U. Maine, Orono, 1976—; editorial cons. for jour., 1975—; pvt. practice psychology, Bangor, 1975—. Licensed psychologist, Maine, 1975; certified by Nat. Register of Health Service Providers in Psychology. Mem. Am., Maine psychol. assns., Brit. Psychol. Soc., Assn. Advancement Behavior Therapy, Brit. Assn. for Behavioral Psychotherapy. Mem. Ch. of Eng. Club: Campaign for Real Ale (Britain) Researcher in field; contbr. chpt. to textbook, numerous articles in field to profl. jours. Home: PO Box 32 East Holden ME 04429 Office: Counseling Center 43 Illinois Ave Bangor ME 04401

THORPE, GERALD L., educator; b. Pontiac, Mich., Mar. 1, 1938; s. Earl W. and Mildred A. T.; B.A., Wayne State U., 1962, Ph.D., 1974; M.A., Harvard, 1963; m. Connie M. Ferguson, Oct. 27, 1956; children—Kenneth E., Jeffry A., Susan V. Tchr. Soc. Studies and English, Meadowbrook Jr. High Sch., Newton, Mass., 1963-65; tchr. pub. schs., Grosse Pointe, Mich., 1965-67; instructor Wayne State U. Coll. Ed., Detroit, 1967-70; prof. U. Penn., Indiana, Penn., 1970—; research dir. Ecological consortium S.W. Penn., dir. Wilburn Center Com. Affairs; supr. White Twp., Indiana County, Pa., 1975—. Mem. Democratic County Exec. Com., Democratic State Platform Com. Mem. N.E. Political Sci. Assn., AAAS, Pa. Assn. Township Suprs., Phi Delta Kappa, Phi Beta Kappa. Democrat. Methodist. Clubs: Allied, Indiana Country. Author: Conflict: A Simulation of a Disarmed World, Confrontation: The Cuban Missile Crisis. Home: 2537 Evergreen Indiana PA 15701 Office: 101 Keith Hall Indiana U Of Penn Indiana PA 15701

THORPE, LEON FERBER, real estate mgmt. exec.; b. Pitts., May 29, 1940; s. Benjamin and Freda (Ferber) T.; B.A., Harvard, 1961, LL.B., 1964; children—Joshua, David. Admitted to Mass. bar, 1964, Pa. bar, 1967; asso. firm Hale and Dorr, Boston, 1964; partner B. Thorpe & Co., Pitts., 1965-69; owner, mgr. Leon Thorpe Realty Co., Pitts., 1969—. Vice-chmn. Western Pa. area Harvard Law Sch. Fund, 1970-74; class agt. Shadyside Acad., 1973-78; asso. chmn. Bldg. and Real Estate div. United Jewish Fedn., 1975-78. Mem. Allegheny Bar Assn. Jewish. Clubs: Concordia, Harvard-Yale-Princeton, Standard (Pitts.) Home: 1445 N Highland Ave Pittsburgh PA 15206 Office: 414 Frick Bldg 437 Grant St Pittsburgh PA 15219

THRESHMAN, GEORGE THOMAS, profl. sales rep.; b. Bronx, N.Y., Aug. 18, 1944; s. Morton George and Isabelle Katherine (Euell) T.; B.B.A. in Mgmt., Ft. Lauderdale (Fla.) U., 1970, M.B.A., 1971; m. Clara Inez Venegas, Feb. 4, 1974. Fgn. br. accountant Am. Fgn. Ins. Co., N.Y.C., 1972-73; pharm. sales rep. Parke Davis & Co., Saddle Brook, N.J., 1973—. Served with U.S. Army, 1964-66. Mem. S.E. Conn. Pharm. Assn., Assn. M.B.A. Execs., Ft. Lauderdale U. Alumni Assn. (founder, pres. 1970-71), Friends Greenwich Library. Democrat. Roman Catholic. Clubs: Ascension Beach, Elks. Home: 61 East Ave Milford CT 06460

THROCKMORTON, WILLIAM ROBERT, SR., socioloigst; b. Washington, Feb. 28, 1923; s. Robert William and Katharine Eleanor (Crook) T.; A.B., George Washington U., 1954, postgrad., 1954-58; m. Sharon Ann Jarrett, Aug. 18, 1961; children—Theresa Cecilia, Elizabeth Jean, Thomas Cleon. Br. mgr. Western Union Tel. Co., Washington, Alexandria, Va., 1941-44, 46-48; library asst. Washington Pub. Library, 1948-49; clk., stenographer So. Ry., Washington, 1949-50; spl. class tchr., pub. schs., Washington, 1954-56; probation officer Arlington County Juvenile Ct., 1957; research asst., population research project George Washington U., 1957; instr. Washington Sch. for Secs., 1958-60; asst. to counsel and office mgr. U.S. Senate, 1960-66; manpower analyst US Labor Dept., 1966—; asst. professorial lectr. sociology George Washington U., 1960-76. Keyman, United Givers Fund, 1969-72; mem. and treas. Fairfax County Commn. on Women, 1977—. Served with USAAF, 1944-46; Korea, Japan. Recipient Distinguished Achievement award Dept. Labor, 1974. Mem. Lester F. Ward (treas. 1954), So., D.C. sociol. socs., Am. Sociol. Assn., AAUP, Am. Soc. Criminology, Alpha Kappa Delta. Democrat. Roman Catholic. Club: George Washington Faculty. Home: 6021 Old Rolling Rd Alexandria VA 22310 Office: 601 D St NW Room 9006 Washington DC 20213

THUERING, GEORGE LEWIS, engr., adminstr.; b. Milw., Sept. 2, 1919; s. Louis Charles and Elsie (Luetzow) T.; B.S., U. Wis., 1941, M.E., 1954; M.S., Pa. State U., 1949; m. Lillian May Cline, Dec. 7, 1945 (dec.); 1 dau., Jean Carol (Mrs. Carl Ameringer); m. 2d, Betty L. McBride, Aug. 9, 1975. Mfg. engr. Lockheed Aircraft Corp., Burbank, Calif., 1941-47, supr. plant layout, Marietta, Ga., 1951-52; faculty Pa. State U., University Park, 1947—, asso. prof. indsl. engring., 1952-56, prof., 1956—, dir. mgmt. engring., 1961—. Cons. engr. Registered profl. engr., Pa. Fellow Soc. Advancement Mgmt.; mem. Am. Soc. M.E. (chmn. mgmt. div. 1976-77, mem. exec. com. mgmt. div. 1973-77, chmn. papers rev. com. 1969-73), Am. Inst. Indsl. Engrs. (dir. student affairs 1972-74), Mem. Am. Soc. Engring. Edn. (chmn. indsl. engring. div. 1956-57), Sigma Xi, Tau Beta Pi, Pi Tau Sigma, Alpha Pi Mu. Contbr. articles to profl. jours. Home: 436 Homan Ave State College PA 16801 Office: 207 Hammond Bldg University Park PA 16802

THUMM, FRED WILLIAM, lighting fixture co. exec.; b. Teaneck, N.J., Nov. 20, 1937; s. Fred Albert John and Dorothea (Niehaus) T.; student Fairleigh Dickinson U., 1956-64; m. Margaret Ann Dievler, July 15, 1961; children—Fred William, Donna Lynn. Chief draftsman Indsl. Gauges, West Englewood, N.J., 1956-59; project engr. Fed. Design & Service Co., Riveredge, N.J., 1959-64; chief engr. N.Y. Pressing Machine Co., Paterson, N.J., 1965-69; plant mgr. Kurt Versen Co., Westwood, N.J., 1969—; partner, cons. engr. Prend, Inc.; cons. Enair, Inc. Mem. Soc. for Advancement Mgmt., North Jersey Reformed Ch. Young Adults (past pres.). Patentee in field. Home: 407 Ridgewood Ave Wyckoff NJ 07481 Office: 10 Charles St Westwood NJ 07675

THUNE, MARY LEE, clothing mfg. co. exec.; b. Balt., July 12, 1931; d. Fredrich William and Hazel Isabel (Cook) T.; student Drexel U., 1948-50, Parsons Sch. Design, 1951; 1 dau., Caryl Lee. With Modern Merchandising Bur., N.Y.C., 1952-56, Daniel & Charles, N.Y.C., 1956-58; account exec. Arndt, Preston, Chapin, Lamb & Keen, N.Y.C., 1958-61; merchandising editor Glamour Mag., N.Y.C., 1961-63; advt./promotion dir. N. Erlanger, Blumgart, N.Y.C., 1963-64; fashion/promotion dir. Lady Manhattan div. Manhattan Industries, N.Y.C., 1964-67; product, styling coordinator Doyle, Dane, Bernabach, N.Y.C., 1967-71; fashion dir. Vanity Fair Mills, N.Y.C., 1972-76, v.p., 1976—; free-lance market cons., N.Y.C., 1979—. Mem. Fashion Group, Round Table of Fashion Execs. Republican. Episcopalian. Home: 220 Central Park S Apt 4-D New York City NY 10019 Office: Vanity Fair Mills 640 Fifth Ave New York City NY 10019

THURMOND, GERALD PITTMAN, lawyer; b. Madison, Ga., Aug. 20, 1936; s. Gilbert Duard and Viola Elnora (Pittman) T.; B.B.A., U. Ga., 1958, J.D. cum laude, 1964; m. Ann Sexton, May 21, 1960; children—Gerald Pittman, William R., Susan A. Admitted to Ga. bar, 1963, Pa. bar, 1970, D.C. bar, 1976; atty. Troutman, Sams, Schroder & Lockerman, Atlanta, 1964-68; staff atty. gen. counsel Gulf Oil Corp., Pitts., 1963-73, asst. to exec. (chmn. bd., pres. and exec. v.p.'s), 1973, adminstrv. v.p., 1974-75, Washington counsel, 1975—. Gulf Oil Co. employee chmn. United Fund of Houston, 1975; mem. adv. com. Sch. Pub. Affairs of Tex. So. U., 1973-75. Served to 1st lt. AUS, 1958-60. Mem. Am., D.C., Ga., Allegheny County bar assns., Tex.-Mid Continent Oil and Gas Assn. (dir.), Houston C. of C., Ga. State Soc. (dir.), Phi Kappa Phi. Presbyterian. Clubs: Kenwood Golf and Country, Nat. Lawyers, Internat., Capitol Hill. Home: 5207 Falmouth Rd Washington DC 20016 Office: 1025 Connecticut Ave NW Washington DC 20036

TICHAUER, ERWIN RUDOLPH, educator; b. Berlin, Germany, Apr. 27, 1918; s. Bruno and Jolan (Gruber) T.; diplom engr. Technische Hochschule, Danzig, 1938; D.Sc., Albertus U., Königsberg, 1940; m. Helen Spitzer, Feb. 27, 1946. Came to U.S., 1964, naturalized, 1971. Dep. dir. team 1065F, UNRRA, Europe, 1946-47; chief engr. Famic, Santiago, Chile, 1947-50; design engr., works mgr. Pope-Mayne & So., Brisbane, Australia, 1950-53; sr. lectr. indsl. engring. and ergonomics Royal S. Sydney Hosp., U. N.S.W., Sydney, 1960-63; productivity expert UN, Latin American, 1956-59; cons. indsl. engr., Brisbane, 1953-56; prof. indsl. engring. Tex. Technol. U., Lubbock, 1964-67; prof., dir. div. biomechanics Center for Safety and Inst. Rehab. Medicine N.Y. U., N.Y.C., 1967-77, prof., dir. programs in ergonomics and biomechanics, 1977—. Illustrious vis. prof. Nat. U., San Marcos, Lima, Peru, 1958; spl. lectr. U. Queensland, Brisbane, 1953-59; mem. adv. panel grad. safety program N.C. State U., Raleigh, 1968—; cons. biomechanics Waterbury (Conn.) Hosp., 1969—, Helen Hayes Hosp.; mem. com. on prosthetics research VA, NRC, Nat. Acad. Scis., div. med. scis. Nat. Acad. Engring. Mem. trustees com. N.J. Inst. Tech. Served as security officer U.S. Mil. Govt., ETO, 1945-46. Recipient Gilbreth medal Soc. for Advancement Mgmt., 1969; Met. Life award Nat. Safety Council, 1972; Golden Plate award Am. Acad. Achievement, 1970. Fellow Royal Soc. Health, N.Y. Acad. Scis.; mem. N.Y. Acad. Medicine (chmn. biomed. engring. sect. 1969-73), Am. Inst. Indsl. Engrs. (Baker Distinguished Research award 1972, research chmn. work measurement div. 1973—), Am. Nat. Standards Inst., ASME (chmn. safety div. 1974-75), Internat. Standards Orgn. (tech. adv. group on ergonomics). Author: The Biomechanical Basis of Ergonomics: Anatomy Applied to the Design of Work Situations, 1978. Editorial adv. bd. Jour. Biomechanics, 1967—. Coordinator abstracts in work physiology Jour. Occupational Medicine. Contbr. articles to profl. jours. Home: 330 E 33d St New York City NY 10016 also Ergonomics and Biomechanics Lab NY U Washington Sq New York City NY 10003

TICHY, CHARLES, JR., educator; b. Louisville, Feb. 25, 1940; s. Charles and Mildred T.; B.A. with distinction, Ariz. State U., 1963; M.A. in German, 1965; M.A. in Slavic Langs., Ohio State U., 1967; m. Christy Ann Williams, Mar. 23, 1968; children—Andrea, Laura. Instr. Russian and German, Slippery Rock (Pa.) State Coll., 1967-70, asst. prof., 1970-73, chmn. dept. modern langs. and cultures, 1973—, asso. prof., 1978—, also area program coordinator Expt. in Internat. Living; adviser Career Lab, Placement Center, Black Cultural Media Info Center; mem. Speakers Bur. Title IV Nat. Def. fellow Slavic langs., 1965-66, 71-72; dir. Fgn. Lang. Projects Pa. High Schs. Mem. Modern Langs. Assn. Pa. State Modern Lang. Assn. (exec. council), Tchrs. Assn. Slavic and Eastern European Langs., Am. Council Tchrs. of Fgn. Langs., NE Modern Lang. Assn., Dobro Slovo, Alpha Mu Gamma. Contbr. articles to profl. jours. Home: 217 Kelly Blvd Slippery Rock PA 16057 Office: Dept Modern Langs and Cultures Slippery Rock State Coll Slippery Rock PA 16057

TIEDEMAN, GRETCHEN THOMAS, artist; b. Washington, June 9, 1919; d. Dorsey Opie and Gretchen (Gorton) Thomas; student Mt. Vernon Jr. Coll., Washington, 1936-38, Corcoran Sch. Art, 1939-40; m. Robert Komfort Tiedeman, Aug. 23, 1941; children—Trudi (Mrs. John A. Puravs), Thomas Van Dohlen. Art tchr. Mt. Vernon Jr. Coll., 1939-40; designer, 1943-45; founder, tchr. Packahack Coop. Nursery Sch., Wayne, N.J., 1953-59; exhibited paintings in shows including Wayne Library; pvt. art tchr.; portraits in collections Navy Mus., Packanack Community Ch., St. Michael's Episcopal Ch., Wayne. Mem. Wayne Hist. Commn., 1969—, chmn., 1972; Wayne chmn. Am. Bicentennial Commn., 1973—. A founder Wayne chpt. Fedn. Republican Women; mem. county com. Rep. Party, 1960-68; chmn. Nixon Now, 1968; co-chmn. Nixon campaign, 1968; bd. govs. Rep. Club. Bd. dirs. United Givers Packanack Lake. Mem. D.A.R., Daus. Am. Colonists, Colonial Dames 17th Century. Episcopalian. Club: Packanack Lake Golf. Home: 23 Spruce Terrace Wayne NJ 07470

TIEN, CHI, educator; b. Peking, China, Oct. 8, 1930; s. Pei-lin and I-chih (Cheng) T.; came to U.S., 1953, naturalized, 1970; Ph.D., Northwestern U., 1958; m. Julia Cheng, June 12, 1960; children—Anita, Ellen. Asst. prof. U. Tulsa, 1957-59; asst. prof., asso. prof. U. Windsor (Ont.), 1959-63; asso. prof. Syracuse (N.Y.) U., 1963-66, prof., 1966—, chmn. dept. chem. engring. and material sci., 1970—; cons. to industry and govt. Mem. Am. Inst. Chem. Engrs., AAUP, AAAS, Chem. Inst. Can., Assn. Profl. Engrs. Can. Contbr. articles to profl. jours. Home: 318 Roe Ave Syracuse NY 13210 Office: Syracuse U Syracuse NY 13210

TIERKEL, ERNEST SHALOM, state ofcl., veterinarian; b. Phila., July 2, 1917; s. David Baer and Esther (Ginsberg) T.; A.B., Pa. U., 1938, D.V.M., 1942; M.P.H., Columbia U., 1946; m. Ruby Reams Steele, July 13, 1958; 1 son, David Baer; 1 stepson, Michael Steele. Pub. health veterinarian Bur. Animal Industry Dept. Agr., N.Y.C., 1942-45; officer-in-charge rabies research unit, virus lab. Communicable Disease Center, USPHS, Montgomery, Ala., 1946-49, engaged in epidemiology and internat. health work for Communicable Disease Center, Altanta, Richmond, Geneva, Washington and New Delhi, 1949-68, asst. surgeon gen. USPHS, 1969-73; chief bur. disease control Del. Div. Pub. Health, Dover, 1973—; mem. expert panel rabies WHO, 1950—. Diplomate Am. Bd. Veterinary Pub. Health Assn. Fellow Am. Pub. Health Assn.; mem. Nat. Conf. Pub. Health Veterinarians (pres. 1956-57), AVMA (chmn. com. disease rev. council pub. health 1955-62), U.S. Livestock San. Assn. (chmn. com. rabies 1958). Home: 189 S Fairfield Dr Dover DE 19901 Office: Bur Disease Control Del Div Pub Health Capital Sq Dover DE 19901

TIERNEY, WILLIAM THOMAS, mech. engr.; b. Bklyn., Apr. 11, 1918; s. William Thomas and Rose Cecelia (Monahan) T.; B.M.E., N.Y. U., 1940; m. Mary Vivienne Adams, Oct. 2, 1943; children—William J. (dec.), John James, Christine Marie. Mech. engr. Texaco Inc., Beacon, N.Y., 1940-41, project leader engring. research, 1946-50, asst. supr. spl. engine research dept., 1950-53, asst. dir. research, 1953-58, asst. supt. Beacon Labs., 1958-60, corp. automation coordinator, 1960-70, project mgr. automotive engine devels., 1970—. Mem. Wappingers Central Sch. Dist. Bd. Edn., 1959-69. Served with Corps Engrs., U.S. Army, 1941-46; ETO. Registered profl. engr., N.Y. State. Mem. Soc. Automotive Engrs. Club: Rotary (Fishkill, N.Y.). Contbr. articles to tech. publs. Patentee in automotive engine and component devels. Home: Lyndon Rd Fishkill NY 12524 Office: Texaco Inc PO Box 509 Beacon NY 12508

TIERNO, PHILIP MARIO, JR., microbiologist; b. Bklyn., June 5, 1943; s. Philip M. and Phyllis (Tringone) T.; B.S., R.L. Conolly Coll., L.I. U., 1965; M.S., N.Y. U., 1974, Ph.D., 1976; m. Josephine Martinez, Apr. 2, 1967; children—Alexandra Lorraine, Meredith Anne. Microbiologist Lutheran Med. Center, Bklyn., 1965-66; chief research microbiologist hemodialysis unit VA Hosp., Bronx, N.Y., 1966-70; chief microbiology div. N.Y. U. Med. Center Goldwater Meml. Hosp., F.D. Roosevelt Island, N.Y., 1970—; asso. and cons. microbiologist Maimonides Med. Center, Bklyn.; adj. asst. prof. Bloomfield (N.J.) Coll., 1975—, N.Y. U., 1976—. Pres., Flushing Taxpayers Assn., 1973-77; bd. dirs. Comprehensive Health Planning Agy. City N.Y., 1974-75. Mem. N.Y. Acad. Scis., Am. Acad. Microbiology, AAAS, Am. Pub. Health Assn., Am. Soc. Microbiology, Phi Sigma, Alpha Epsilon Delta. Club: Optimists (v.p. Norwood 1978—). Contbr. articles to profl. jours. Research on hemodialysis sanitizing technique, antibiotic assay method, serotyping Staphylococcus epidermidis, and aminopeptidase profiles of bacteria. Home: 30 Carter St Norwood NJ 07648

TIFFANY, MARQUERITE BRISTOL, educator; b. Syracuse, N.Y., Mar. 31; d. Dr. Ernst L. and Clara Frances (Bristol) Tiffany; B.S., Syracuse U., 1922; A.M., Columbia U., 1930, also postgrad. Tchr. grades and high sch. art, music, Sidney and Herkimer, N.Y., 1919-20; indsl. arts supr. West Orange (N.J.) grade schs., 1921-27; tchr. fine and indsl. arts Montclair (N.J.) Jr. High Sch., 1927-29; prof., head art dept. Wm. Paterson Coll., Paterson, N.J., 1929-56; faculty Fairleigh-Dickinson U., 1956-64; summer sch. tchr. N.J. State Tchrs. Coll., Newark, Montclair, Kutztown State Coll., Lock Haven State Tchrs. Coll. Pa., Rutgers U., Ariz. State Coll. Instr. art classes for Sr. Citizens YMCA and YWCA Exhbns. of paintings in N.Y., Me., N.J., Portland, Oreg.; represented in permanent collection Paterson Mus., also numerous pvt. collections; exhibited weaving Newark Mus., 1968-76; demonstrator painting and weaving. Mem. Internat. Miniature Art Assn., Internat. Platform Assn., Nat. League Am. Pen Women (past N.J. state pres.), Paterson Mus. Art League (past pres.), Coll. Art Assn., AAUP, Met. Opera Guild (N.J. chmn. Arts in Opera contest 1952-58), Assn. Hand Weavers (pres. 1968-70), AAUW (dir.), Eastern Arts Assn. (citation), Am. Artists Profl. League (corr. sec. 1962-77), Nat. N.J. art edn. assns., Gotham Painters, NEA, N.J. Edn. Assn., Mus. Modern Art (Art Commn.), Met. Mus. Art, Vocat. Guidance Assn., English Speaking Union, D.A.R., Ridgewood, FairLawn, Paterson art assns., ANTA, N.Y.C. Sch. Art League, Montclair Mus. Art Tchrs. Assn. (past pres.), Am. Acad. Dramatic Arts, Chi Omega (past pres.), Kappa Delta Pi, Pi Lambda Theta. Clubs: Womens Press of N.J.; Century Theatre (past pres.) (N.Y.C.); Paterson Womens (chmn. lit. group, pres. 1977-78); Chaucer Guild. Contbr. articles to profl. jours. Home: 330 E 33d St Paterson NJ 07504

TIFFANY, ROBERT JARED, ins. co. exec.; b. Redwood Falls, Minn., Sept. 8, 1919; s. Dougald Milne and Jennie (Peabody) T.; student U. Minn., 1938-41; m. Clarine Marsh, Jan. 1, 1943; children—Robert Jared Jr., William Springer, Julie Foy. With Equitable Life Assurance Soc. U.S., Abilene, Tex., 1946—, v.p. agy. dept., N.Y.C., 1965—; dir. Citizens Nat. Bank, Abilene. Chmn., Abilene Pub. Library Bd., 1960-65, Abilene United Fund Campaign, 1963. Mem. City Council, mayor pro-tem, Abilene, 1955-57. Served to capt. U.S. Army, 1941-46. Named Outstanding Young Man Abilene, 1947, Outstanding Citizen Abilene, 1964. Mem. Am. Soc. C.L.U.'s (past trustee), Acacia, Presbyn. (elder). Mason. Author: Glimpses of Greatness, 1966. Home: Deep Woods Ln Old Greenwich CT 06870 Office: 1285 Ave of Americas New York City NY 10019

TILDEN, WILLIAM TATEM, financial exec.; b. Phila., Sept. 19, 1913; s. Herbert Marmaduke and Hazel (Megargee) T.; grad. The Haverford Sch.; A.B., Princeton U., 1936; grad. student U. Pa., 1938; C.P.A., Cades Sch., 1947; m. Marjorie Marquissee, Sept. 20, 1940; children—William Tatem IV, Geoffrey G., Victor M. Security salesman Hamphil Noyes & Co., N.Y.C., Phila., 1936-38; asst. to gen. mgr. John Wanamaker, Phila., 1938-40; acctg. supr., C.P.A., Barrow, Wade, Guthrie & Co., Arthur F. Morton Co., Phila., 1946-52; treas., controller Benjamin Foster Co., Phila., 1952-55; sec.-treas. Chemway Corp., Wayne, N.J., 1955-62, dir., 1960-62; sec.-treas. Crookes-Barnes Labs., Inc., Wayne, 1956-62; v.p. finance N.Y. Trap Rock Corp., West Nyack, N.Y., 1962-65, dir., 1963-65; v.p. finance The Fyr-Fyter Co., N.Y.C., 1963-65, chmn. bd., 1965-66; pres. Rock Industries, Inc., 1965-67; v.p. Ciba Pharm. Co., 1967-72; adv. bd. Midlantic Nat. Bank. Bd. dirs., v.p. N.J. Mental Health Assn., 1969-74. Served with AUS, 1941-46. C.P.A., Pa. Mem. Am. Inst. C.P.A.'s, Financial Execs. Inst. (dir. mem. relations 1972). Clubs: Baltusrol Golf (Springfield, N.J.); Princeton (N.Y.C.), Princeton Charter (Princeton). Home: 6 Middleton Rd The Landings on Slidaway Island Savannah GA 31409 Office: 633 3d Ave New York City NY 10017

TILGNER, CHARLES, III, engring. co. exec.; b. Mineola, N.Y., Feb. 16, 1935; s. Charles and Edna H. (Doscher) T.; B.S.E., Princeton U., 1956; m. Linda R. Altman, June 9, 1957; children—Charles, David. Project engr. Dynamic Devels. Inc., Oyster Bay, N.Y., 1956-61; asst. to dir. Hydrofoil Programs, Grumman Aircraft Engring. Corp., Bethpage, N.Y., 1961-63; mgr. research and devel. Dodge Inds. Inc., Hoosick Falls, N.Y., 1963-65; pres. Nutrionics Machine Corp., Hoosick Falls, 1969—; v.p., gen. mgr. Dodge Machine Co., Inc., Hoosick Falls, 1965-78, dir., 1965—; mgr. engring. and devel. Chem. Fabrics Corp., North Bennington, Vt., 1978—. Bd. dirs. Bennington Free Library, 1967—, treas. 1969-72, 1974-76, 77—, chmn. 1976-77; mem. Bennington Town Planning Commn., 1965-72, chmn. 1970-72; mem. Bennington Regional Commn. 1972—, sec. 1974-76, chmn., 1976-78; mem. S.W. Vt. Econ. Devel. Council, 1976-78. Registered profl. engr., N.Y., Vt., N.H. Mem. Nat., Vt. socs. profl. engrs., ASME, Princeton Engring. Assn. Unitarian. Clubs: Mt. Anthony Country; Cloister Inn (Princeton). Home: PO Box 137 Bennington VT 05201 Office: Chem Fabrics Corp Water St North Bennington VT 05257

TILLES, HENRY HERMAN, mech. engr.; b. Krakow, Poland, Oct. 25, 1908; s. Salomon F. and Esther (Rosenzweig) T.; came to U.S., 1945, naturalized, 1952; Ingenieur, German Tech. U., 1932; postgrad. Bklyn. Poly. Inst., 1948-49; m. Esther Dym, Apr. 15, 1935; 1 dau. Surveyor, Palestine, 1935-38, Egypt, 1937; asst. power plant engr. Consol. Refineries, Ltd., Haifa, Israel, 1938-45; designer Combustion Engring. Co., N.Y.C., 1946-47; mech. engr. Sanderson & Porter, Inc., N.Y.C., 1947-51, 55-73; with Gibbs & Hill, Inc., N.Y.C., 1951-53; supervisory mech. engr. Burns & Roe, Inc., Woodbury, N.Y., 1973—; chief engr. and engring. mgr. Seltec, Rio de Janeiro, Brazil, 1968-71. Mem. ASME, Nat. Soc. Profl. Engrs. Home: 32 Range Dr Merrick NY 11566 Office: 185 Crossways Park Dr Woodbury NY 11797

TILLEY, DAVID BROWN, SR., lawyer; b. Evanston, Ill., Oct. 30, 1928; s. Milton Popple and Winifred Lulu (Holly) T.; B.S. magna cum laude, Lafayette Coll., 1957; J.D., Cornell U., 1966; m. Alice Crane Pearsall, Aug. 31, 1951; children—David B., Ferris Pearsall. Asst., personnel Atlas Powder Co., Wilmington, Del., 1957; dir. personnel and labor relations Chemtron Corp. (name changed to Pearsall Corp.), Phillipsburg, N.J., 1957-63; admitted to Conn. bar, 1966, U.S. Supreme Ct. bar, 1973, practiced in Litchfield, 1966—; mem. firm Guion & Stevens, 1966—. Trustee, Center Congregational Ch., Torrington, Conn. Served with USAF, 1950-54. Mem. Am., Conn., Litchfield Country bar assns., Am. Judicature Soc., My Country Soc. (dir.), Litchfield (Conn.) Hist. Soc. (dir.), Phi Beta Kappa. Republican. Home: RD 3 Richards Rd Litchfield CT 06759 Office: Box 338 Litchfield CT 06759

TILLEY, LARRY GORDON, physician; b. Bel Air, Md., Nov. 25, 1935; s. George and Lucy Evelyn T.; B.S., Roanoke Coll., 1957; M.D., U. Md., 1961; m. Edith Purnell Proctor, June 14, 1958; children—David Gordon, Brian Douglas, Mark Andrew. Intern, USPHS, Boston, 1961-62; asst. resident in medicine Md. Gen. Hosp., Balt., 1964-65; practice medicine specializing in family practice, Balt., 1965-72, partner Med. Health Group, Balt., 1977—, asso., 1972-77: staff Md. Gen. Hosp., Balt., 1965-72, Franklin Sq. Hosp., 1968—. Served with USPHS, 1961-64. Diplomate Am. Bd. Family Practice. Fellow Am. Acad. Family Physicians: mem. Am. Med. Assn. Republican. Methodist. Home: 2814 Falls Mont Dr Fallston MD 21047 Office: 1012 Old North Point Rd Baltimore MD 21224

TILLINGHAST, META IONE, civic worker; b. Newark, Nov. 14; d. Ralph Vincent and Florence Virginia (MacDonald) Muldoon: student Leland Powers Sch. of Spoken Word, Boston; m. Frederick William Tillinghast, Apr. 20; children—Anne (Mrs. Robert Riley), Patricia (Mrs. Charles McLaughlin). Bd. dirs. Balt. chpt. ARC, 1955-58, chmn. Queen Anne's chpt. 1964-66, nat. bd. govs., 1966-69, Md. state fund chmn., 1969-71, Delmarva div. chmn. mems., funds, 1971-73, vols., 1971-74, coordinator community relations Eastern area, 1975-77, chmn. vols. Eastern field office, 1977—; dir. ch. plays; chmn. United Fund Baltimore County (Md.) Women's div., 1950. Named vol. of year Md., ARC, 1965; recipient award Gen. Fedn. Women's Clubs, 1952. Mem. Md. No. Dist. Fedn. Women's Clubs (pres. 1953-55). Clubs: Women's Glyndon (pres. 1949-51), Talbot County Women's (pres. 1962-64), Women's Ten Hills (pres. 1940-42). Home: Queenstown MD 21658 Office: 605 N Saint Asaph St Alexandria VA 22314

TILLOCK, EUGENE EDWARD, educator, nursing home adminstr.; b. N.Y.C., Feb. 14, 1928; s. Steve and Catherine (Woloshin) T.; B.S. in Accounting, L.I. U., 1948; M.S. in Hosp. Adminstrn., Columbia U., 1953, M.A. in Health Edn., 1957, Ed.D. in Health Edn., 1960; m. Frances Teresa DiMarco, Sept. 17, 1955; children—Theresa, Carol Ann, Eugene Edward, Catherine, Stephen, Paul. Adminstrv. resident USPHS Hosp., S.I., N.Y., 1952-53; asst. adminstr. Cortland (N.Y.) Meml. Hosp., 1953-55; adminstrv. asst. to psychiatrist-in-chief N.Y. Hosp, 1956-67; asst. dir. Highland View Hosp., Cleve., 1957-65; adminstr. Western Res. Convalescent Home, Kirtland, Ohio, 1966-67; dir. instl. research Onondaga Community Coll., Syracuse, N.Y., 1967-69; asso. dir., acting dir. Am. Coll. Nursing Home Adminstrn., Washington, 1969-70; regional ednl. coordinator New Eng. Hosp. Assembly, U. N.H., Durham, 1970-74; adminstr. Union Mission Nursing Home, Haverhill, Mass., 1974—; pres. Systems Educators, Inc., Durham, 1967—, Modern Life Systems Inc., Milw.; prof. health adminstrn. St. Joseph's Coll., N. Windham, Maine, 1972-75; lectr. in health adminstrn., ednl. cons. to colls. and univs.; mem. nat. com. on aging Nat. Conf. Cath. Charities, Washington, 1972-79; bd. dirs. Nat. Geriatrics Soc., 1973-79, pres., 1977-79; mem. founding bd. Durham Housing Assn., 1973-75; pres. N.H. League for Nursing, 1972-75; bd. dirs. North Essex Mental Health Assn., 1976-78. Served to tech. 4th grade, U.S. Army, 1946-48; Korea; served with USPHS inactive res., 1960—. Recipient Curtis Wheeler award Boys' Club N.Y., 1946; Better Life award N.H. Assn. Licensed Nursing Homes, 1971. Mem. Am. Pub. Health Assn. (life), Nat. Soc. Autistic Children (edn. chmn. 1968), Am. Coll. Nursing Home Adminstrs. (pres. N.H. chpt. 1971-72, past treas.), New Eng. Gerontol. Assn. (pres. 1973-79), Nat. Geriatrics Soc. (pres. 1976-79), Mexican Am. Geriatrics Soc. (founding pres. 1978), Sociedad de Geriatria y Gerontologia de Mexico (hon.). Democrat. Roman Catholic. Club: Ky. Col. Contbg. editor Nursing Homes, 1969-76; cons. ednl. editor So. Hosps., 1963-67; editor: Aging and Leisure Living; contbr. articles to profl. jours. Home: 81 Cutts Rd Durham NH 03824 Office: Union Mission Nursing Home 150 Water St Haverhill MA 01830

TILTON, WEBSTER, JR., gen. contractor: b. St. Louis, Sept. 11, 1922; s. Webster and Eleanor (Dozier) T.; master brewers degree, U.S. Brewers Acad., 1949: m. Grace Drew Wilson, Feb. 14, 1948 (div. Oct. 1959); 1 son, Webster III; m. 2d, Nancy McBlair Payne, Jan. 5, 1963. Asst. brewing technologist F&M Schaffer Brewing Co., Bklyn., 1948-52: factory sales rep. Cole Steel Equipment Co., N.Y.C., 1957-68; dist. sales mgr. Scantlin Electronics, Inc., Washington, 1968-70; sales rep. Comml. Washer & Dryer Sales Co., Washington, 1970-72; propr. Webster Tilton, Jr., contractor, Washington, 1972—. Served from cadet to chief mate USNR, 1942-45. Episcopalian. Home: 3719 Fulton St NW Washington DC 20007 Office: 1120 Connecticut Ave NW Washington DC 20036

TILY, STEPHEN BROMLEY, III, banking exec.; b. Phila., July 7, 1937; s. Stephen Bromley and Edith Helen (Straub) T.; B.A., Washington & Jefferson Coll., 1960; postgrad. Temple Sch. of Law, 1962-63; m. Janet Anita Walz, July 10, 1965; children—Deborah Powell, Stephen Bromley, James Charles. Trust officer Indsl. Valley Bank & Trust Co., Phila., 1968-71; v.p. Farmers Bank of the State of Delaware, Wilmington, 1971-77; exec. v.p., chief operating officer Del. Charter Guarantee & Trust Co., 1977—; tchr. Am. Inst. of Banking, Valley Forge chpt. Served in USAR, QMC, 1960-61. Mem. Fin. Analysts of Wilmington, Inc., Internat. Found. of Employee Benefit Plans. Home: 410 Churchill Dr Berwyn PA 19312 Office: PO Box 8963 Wilmington DE 19899

TIMMERMAN, ROBERT WILSON, mech. engr.; b. Abington, Pa., July 27, 1944; s. Clarence Arthur and Mildred Wilson (Slack) T.: student Wesleyan U., 1961-62; B.S., Cornell U., 1965, M. Engring., 1966: postgrad. Northwestern U., 1971-72 , U. Pa., 1972-74; m. Nancy Jean Spinka, Sept. 28, 1974. Project engr. Monsanto Co., 1966-68: engr. Stone & Webster Engring. Corp., 1966-71; mech. engr. United Engrs. and Constructors, (city and Boston, 1974-75; sr. mech. engr. R.W. Beck & Assos., Wellesley, Mass., 1975-76; prin. Robert Wilson Timmerman, Cons. Engr., Boston, 1976—. Mem. ASME (mem. exec. com. Boston sect.), Am. Soc. Heating, Refrigerating Air Conditioning Engrs. Presbyterian. Patentee in field. Home and office: 25 Upton St Boston MA 02118

TIMOUR, JOHN ARNOLD, librarian; b. Hartford, Conn., Jan. 20, 1926; s. John Alfred and Karin Elizabeth (Levin) T.; B.A., Miami U., Oxford, Ohio, 1951; postgrad. Fla. State U., 1951-52; M.A., George Washington U., 1960; M.L.S., U. Md., 1969; m. Betty Jo Lord, Mar. 23, 1952; children—Jon, David, Alan. Dir. library services Conn. Regional Med. Program, Yale U., New Haven, 1969-73; tng. and MEDLARS liaison officer Nat. Library Medicine, Bethesda, Md., 1966-69; dir. Mid-Eastern Regional Coll. Physicians Med. Library, Phila., 1973-75; univ. librarian Thomas Jefferson U., Phila., 1975—; adj. prof. library sci. Drexel U., 1976-78; lectr. library sci. So. Conn. State Coll., 1970-71; instr. Command and Gen. Staff Coll., U.S. Army Res., 1970-73. Served with USN, 1943-46, USAF, 1951-53. Mem. Med. Library Assn. (Ida and George Eliot prize essay award 1974, dir. 1978—), Spl. Libraries Assn., Health Scis. Communications Assn., ALA, Conn. Assn. Health Scis. Libraries, Beta Phi Mu. Episcopalian. Contbr. articles to profl. jours. Home: 144 Marne Ave Haddonfield NJ 08033 Office: 1020 Walnut St Philadelphia PA 19107

TIMPSON, JAMES, cons. engr.; b. N.Y.C., July 1, 1926; s. Carl William and Marcelle (Vallon) T.; student Wesleyan U., 1944-45; B.S., Rensselaer Poly. Inst., 1947, B.M.E., 1948; m. Annadel Beckers, Apr. 27, 1957; children—James, Annadel. Test engr. Gen. Electric Co., Schenectady, 1948-50; asst. to chief engr. Yale & Towne Mfg. Co., Stamford, Conn., 1950-52; field engr. Hewitt Robins, Inc., N.Y.C., 1952-62; v.p. Soros Assoc., Cons. Engrs., N.Y.C., 1962—. Served to lt. (j.g.), USNR, 1944-46. Mem. ASME, Am. Inst. Mining Metall. Petroleum Engrs., Am. Ry. Engring. Assn., Soc. Naval Architects and Marine Engrs. Republican. Roman Catholic. Clubs: N.Y. Yacht, Country of Fairfield, Pequot Yacht, Mining. Contbr. articles to profl. jours. Home: 896 Burr St Fairfield CT 06430 Office: 575 Lexington Ave New York City NY 10022

TINDALL, JEFFRY HAIGH, educator; b. Phila., Aug. 16, 1942; s. William Hall and Ruth (Haigh) T.; B.S., Bethany Coll., 1965; M.Ed., Am. U., 1969, Ph.D., 1971; postdoctoral Tavistock Inst., U. Leicester (Eng.), 1973, 74. Tchr. biology Langley High Sch., Fairfax, Va., 1965-68; instr., asst. prof. Rutgers U., New Brunswick, N.J., 1971-76, asst. prof. Med. Sch., Inst. Mental Health Sci., Group Psychotherapy Program, Grad. Sch. Applied Profl. Psychology; asst. prof. Fordham U. at Lincoln Center Grad. Sch. Edn. and Counseling Services, 1977—; asso. A.K. Rice Inst., Washington-Balt. Center, Washington Sch. Psychiatry. Mem. Am. Psychol. Assn., Am. Assn. Marriage and Family Counselors, Am. Personnel Guidance Assn., Assn. Specialists in Group Work, Am. Orthopsychiat. Assn. Home: Stanton NJ 08875 Office: Fordham U at Lincoln Center New York City NY 10023

TING, ER YI, physician, educator; b. Shantung, China, June 3, 1919; s. Yu Chuang and Mary (Chang) T.; M.D., Nat. Def. Med. Coll., Shanghai, China, 1948; m. Theresa Wang, Nov. 8, 1958; children—Selene, Sandra, Selwyn. Came to U.S., 1954, naturalized, 1967. Intern, Shanghai Gen. Hosp., 1947-48, instr. medicine, 1948-54; resident Nat. Def. Med. Center, Taipei, Taiwan, 1948-52; resident Bronx (N.Y.) Municipal Hosp. Center, 1954-56, staff physician, 1957-63; dir. Pulmonary Function Research Lab., N.Y. Med. Coll. Met. Hosp. Center, N.Y.C., 1963—; asso. attending physician Flower and 5th Av. Hosp., Met. Hosp. Center, 1963—; practice medicine specializing in internal medicine, N.Y.C., 1964—; cons. physician St. Vincent's Hosp., S.I., N.Y.; postdoctoral fellow U. Buffalo, 1956-57; instr. medicine State U. N.Y., 1957-59, Albert Einstein Coll. Medicine, 1959-63; clin. asso. prof. medicine N.Y. Med. Coll., N.Y.C., 1963—. Served with Chinese Nationalist Army, 1940-44. Mem. AAAS, A.M.A., Am. Physiol. Soc., Am. Thoracic Soc., Am. Coll. Chest Physicians, Fedn. Clin. Research, Med. Soc. N.Y. Home: 224 Highwood Ave Tenafly NJ 07670 Office: 50 Bayard St New York City NY 10013

TING, SAMUEL CHAO CHUNG, physicist; b. Ann Arbor, Mich., Jan. 27, 1936; s. Kuan H. and Jeanne (Wong) T.; B.S. in Engring., U. Mich., 1959, M.S., 1960, Ph.D., 1962; m. Kay Louise Kuhne, Nov. 23, 1960; children—Jeanne Min, Amy Min. Ford Found. fellow CERN (European Orgn. Nuclear Research), Geneva, Switzerland, 1963; instr. physics Columbia, 1964, asst. prof., 1965-67; group leader Deutsches Elektronen-Synchrotron, Hamburg, West Germany, 1966; asso. prof. physics Mass. Inst. Tech., Cambridge, 1967-68, prof., 1969—, Thomas Dudley Cabot prof., 1977—. Program cons. Div. Particles and Fields, Am. Phys. Soc., 1970. Recipient Nobel prize in Physics, 1976; Ernest Orlando Lawrence award, 1976; Erigen medal Soc. Engring. Sci., 1977; Am. Acad. Sci. and Arts fellow, 1975. Fellow Academica Sinica; mem. Nat. Acad. Sci. Asso. editor Nuclear Physics B., 1970; editorial bd. Nuclear Instruments and Methods, 1977—; contbr. articles to profl. jours. Home: 15 Moon Hill Rd Lexington MA 02173 Office: Dept Physics Massachusetts Inst Technology 51 Vassar St Cambridge MA 02139

TINGLE, WILLIAM HERBERT, physicist: b. Pernassus, Pa., Aug. 31, 1917; s. William Cecil and Norma Margaret (McRoberts) T.; B.S. magna cum laude, U. Pitts., 1949; m. Annetta Marie Johnson, Dec. 8, 1945; children—William H.C. IV, Susan Tingle Krumpe. Instr., U. Pitts., 1949-50; research engr. Spectrochem. Analysis, Alcoa, Alcoa Center, Pa., 1950-60, sect. head electro-optical instrumentation, 1960-73, scientific asso. analytical instrumentation and process control, 1973—; tech. advisor Internat. Standards Com. on Light Metals and Administers for Am. Nat. Standards Inst., Secretariat of Internat. Standards Orgn. Working Group on Spectrochem. Analysis of Light Metals, 1970—. Served with inf., U.S. Army, 1942-45. Recipient Sigma Pi Sigma Physics Honorary award, 1949; ASTM Award for Distinguished service, 1974; H. V. Churchill award for meritorous service, ASTM, 1977. Mem. ASTM, Soc. for Applied Spectroscopy, Optical Soc. Am., Am. Chem. Soc., Spectroscopy Soc. Pitts., Scientific Research Soc. N.Am., Am. Inst. Physics, Sigma Pi Sigma. Club: U.S. Yacht Racing Union. Contbr. articles in field to profl. jours.; patentee in field. Home: 3104 Leechburg Rd New Kensington PA 15068 Office: Alcoa Tech Center Alcoa Center PA 15069

TINKHAM, WILLIAM KNIPE, historian, educator; b. Dartmouth, Mass., Feb. 22, 1916; s. William Nelson and Mabel Winsor (White) T.; student New Coll., Oxford U. (Eng.), 1945-47; A.B., Boston U., 1954; A.M., Harvard U., 1957; postgrad. Tufts U., 1958-59; m. Caroline Brown, Oct. 23, 1965. Br. mgr. New Bedford (Mass.) Instn. for Savs., 1936-42, 47-50; lectr. history Lasell Jr. Coll., Newton, Mass., 1959-60; instr. history Boston State Coll., 1962-66, asst. prof., 1966-68, asso. prof., 1968—. Served with U.S. Army, 1942-45. Mem. Mediaeval Acad. Am., Mass. Soc. Mayflower Descs., Am. Ch. Union (v.p. New Eng. br. 1960-70), AAUP, English-Speaking Union, Beacon Hill Civic Assn., Am. Hist. Assn., Plimouth Plantation, Old Dartmouth Hist. Soc., Harvard Grad. Soc. Advanced Study and Research, New Coll. Soc. Oxford, Guild of Friends Winchester Cathedral, Friends of Lambeth Palace Library London, Phi Alpha Theta. Republican. Episcopalian. Clubs: Harvard, Wamsutta. Home: 10 Otis Pl Boston MA 02108 Office: 625 Huntington Ave Boston MA 02115

TINSLEY, THOMAS VINCENT, JR., accounting co. exec.; b. Wilkes-Barre, Pa., Oct. 16, 1940; s. Thomas Vincent and Mary Clare (Green) T.; B.S. in Accounting, U. Scranton, 1963; grad. in programming Electronic Computer Programming Inst., 1966; m. Katherine Alice Swan, Oct. 15, 1966; children—Sara Elisabeth, Tracy Swan. Jr. accountant Peat, Marwick, Mitchell & Co., Balt., 1963-64; accounts receivable mgr., import accounting mgr. Aimcee Wholesale Corp., N.Y.C., 1964-65; sr. accountant Richards, Ganly, Fries & Preusch, N.Y.C., 1965-66, Morris J. Weinstein, Groothius & Co., N.Y.C., 1966-69; supr. Brach Lane Hariton & Hirshberg, N.Y.C., 1969-70; owner, mgr. Thomas V. Tinsley, Jr., C.P.A., Wilkes Barre, Pa. and N.Y.C., 1970—; notary pub., Luzerne County, Pa.; div. chmn. United Way 1975 Campaign of Wyoming Valley. Served with USMCR, 1960-66. C.P.A., N.Y., Pa., N.J. Mem. Am. Arbitration Assn., Am. Accounting Assn., Am., Pa. insts. C.P.A.'s, Accounting Research Assn., Nat. Assn. of Accountants, N.J., N.Y. State socs. C.P.A.'s, Am. Numis. Assn., Nat. Rifle Assn. Democrat. Roman Catholic. Clubs: N.Y. Athletic, World Trade Center, K.C. Home: Box 366 White Birch Ln Glen Summit Mountaintop PA 18707 OFfice: Suite 500 10 W Northampton St Wilkes Barre PA 18701

TINTER, MICKEY, jewelry co. exec.; b. Germany, June 21, 1947; s. Boris and Nina Tinter; came to U.S., 1949, naturalized; B.B.A., C.W. Post Coll., 1970; m. Janet A. Alexander, May 30, 1975; 1 son, Adam. Owner Gold By Weight, N.Y.C., 1975—. Mem. Internat. Brotherhood Magicians. Address: 20 W 47th St New York City NY 10036

TINTLE, CARMEL JOSEPH, pub. relations exec.; b. Paterson, N.J., Sept. 25, 1924; s. Herbert J. and Agnes (Merna) T.; student Seton Hall U.; B.S., Fordham U., 1951; postgrad. N.Y. U.; m. Alice M. Hayes, Sept. 1, 1948; children—Joseph, Alice Maureen. Editorial asst. Newsweek Mag., N.Y.C., 1946-50; news editor Beverage Retailer Weekly, N.Y.C., 1950-52; city editor Paterson Sunday Eagle, 1950-52; staff writer Carl Byoir & Assos., Inc., N.Y.C., 1952-59, asst. account exec., 1959-64, asso. account exec., 1964; account supr. Grey Pub. Relations, Inc., N.Y.C., 1964; v.p. Schenley Affiliated Brands Corp. subsidiary of Schenley Industries, N.Y.C., 1964-72, sr. v.p., 1972-74; v.p. corporate affairs Am. Distilling Co., 1975—. Served to ensign U.S. Maritime Service, 1943-46. Mem. Pub. Relations Soc. Am. (1st v.p.), Cath. Inst. Press, Cath. Artists Radio and TV Advt., North Jersey Highlands Hist. Soc., S.A.R., N.J. Hist. Soc., St. Patrick Guard of Honor N.J. Clubs: N.Y. Press, K.C. Home: Winding Way E Convent NJ 07961 Office: 245 Park Ave New York City NY 10017

TIONGSON, JOSE ARAMIL, physician; b. San Pablo City, Philippines, Jan. 17, 1928; s. Teofilo Maclang and Gregoria Paulino (Aramil) T.; A.A., U. Santo Tomas (Philippines), 1948, M.D., 1953; m. m. Carmen Alcala, Nov. 15, 1954; children—Marie, Charles, Christine, Bella. Intern, U. Santo Tomas; resident N.Y. U. Med. Center, 1961-63, Columbia Presbyn. Harlem Med. Center, 1964; practice medicine, specializing in orthopaedic and hand surgery, 1964—; cons. orthopaedic and hand surgery, Georgetown Hosp., Guyana, S.A., 1967-72; med. supt. Maltaica Hosp., Guyana, 1967-69; chief rehab. med. service Albany VA Hosp., 1972—; asst. clin. prof. clin. rehab. medicine Albany Med. Coll., Union U., 1972—. Fellow Philippine Coll. Surgeons; mem. Am., Philippine med. assns., Philippine Orthopaedic Assn., Am. Congress Rehab. Medicine, Assn. Med. Rehab. Dirs. Coordinators, Am. Arbitration Assn., Am. Geriatric Soc., Carribean Hand Soc., Assn. Mil. Surgeons U.S. Office: Albany VA Hosp Albany NY 12208

TISCHLER, HERBERT, geologist; b. Detroit, Apr. 28, 1924; s. Louis and Hermina (Leb) T.; B.S., Wayne U., 1950; M.A., U. Calif. at Berkeley, 1955; Ph.D., U. Mich., 1961; m. Annette Zeidman, Aug. 10, 1954; children—Michael A., Robert D. Instr., Wayne State U., Detroit, 1956-58; asso. prof. No. Ill. U., DeKalb, 1958-65; prof., chmn. dept. earth scis. U. N.H., Durham, 1965—. Served with USCG, 1943-46. Fellow Geol. Soc. Am.; mem. Am. Assn. Petroleum Geologists, Paleontological Soc., Soc. Economic Paleontologists and Mineralogists, Nat. Assn. Geology Tchrs. Home: 36 Oyster Rd Durham NH 03824 Office: Dept Earth Scis U NH James Hall Durham NH 03824

TISCHLER, ISRAEL LEON, optometrist; b. Atlantic City, Oct. 27, 1925; s. Morris and Ida R. (Banner) T.; D.Optometry, Pa. Coll. Optometry, 1950. Practice optometry, Atlantic City, 1951—. Mem. Citizens' Advisory Bd. Atlantic City Community Devel. Served with AUS, 1943-46. Mem. Am., N.J. optometric assns., Atlantic-Cape May Optometric Soc. (past pres., named optometrist of year 1972), N.J. Pub. Health Assn., N.J. Vision Service Assos. (past pres.), Am. Assn. Workers for the Blind. Jewish. Club: Masons. Home: 217 S Victoria Ave Atlantic City NJ 08401 Office: 1517 Pacific Ave Atlantic City NJ 08401

TISDALE, BARBARA, librarian; b. Boston, Dec. 24, 1913; d. Charles Henry and Nancy (Wood) Tisdale; A.B. cum laude, Radcliffe Coll., 1935, postgrad., 1942-43; B.S. in L.S., Syracuse U., 1940; postgrad. Queens Coll., 1958-65, U. Milan, Rome, Italy, summer 1970; M.A., N.Y.U., 1971. Asst. catalogue dept. Harvard U. Library, 1936-39; librarian various schs., Mass., 1940-42; asst. librarian, cataloger Northeastern U. Library, Boston, 1942-43; librarian high sch., Bristol, Conn., 1943-45; reference and circulation asst. bus. dept. Columbia U. Library, N.Y.C., 1945-46; extension librarian Great Neck (N.Y.) Library, 1946-50, Lakeville br. librarian, 1951—, sec. art com., 1970-77. Deaconess, vice chmn. bd. elders Community Ch. Mem. ALA, Nassau County, N.Y. library assns., League Women Voters Great Neck. Club: Radcliffe (L.I. book sale chmn. 1961, 62 (L.I.). Home: 24 Terrace Circle Great Neck NY 11021 Office: 475 Great Neck Rd Great Neck NY 11021

TISSERAND, PETER JOHN, auto service co. exec.; b. Middelburg, Netherland, Nov. 5, 1934; s. Marimus Laurus and Alida Wilhelmina (Albaela) T.; came to U.S., 1960; children—Alfondso, Raymonde, Frits, Peter John, Patricia. Auto mechanic Truck Transportation Co., Bandung, Indonesia, 1949-50, Wander Ltd., Assen, Holland, 1956-57, County Cars, Inc., Media, Pa., 1960-61; shopforeman Sumardi Import Co., Djakarta, Indonesia, 1950, J.H. Coek & Sons, Assen, 1953-54, Steele Motors, Inc., Clifton Heights, Pa., 1961-63; maintenance engr. Vredestein Goodrich, Enschede, Holland, 1957-60; owner, mgr. MB Service Center, Glenolden, Pa., 1963—. Served with Dutch Army, 1954-56. Home: 115 President Ave Rutledge PA 19070 Office: 129 N MacDade Blvd Glenolden PA 19036

TITE, ELIZABETH GRACE, chemist; b. Southbridge, Mass., Apr. 7, 1937; d. Gregory Louca and Androniq (Zhidro) T.; B.S., U. Mass., 1958; M.S., U. N.H., 1962. Tchr. chemistry Tantasqua High Sch., Sturbridge, Mass., 1958-65; asst. prof. chemistry Holyoke (Mass.) Community Coll., 1965-68, asso. prof., 1968-74, prof., 1974—; pilot tchr. for chem. edn. material study, participant in chem. study text and course analysis Harvard; instr. high sch. chemistry tchrs. in NSF program for chemistry U. Conn., Storrs; NSF grantee Mich. State U., summer, 1962. Chmn. bd. dirs. St. Nicholas Albanian Orthodox Ch., Southbridge, 1976. NSF grantee, summers, 1967, 72, 73; AEC grantee, summer, 1969. Mem. Am. Chem. Soc., New Eng. Assn. Chemistry Tchrs. (editor newsletter 1978—), Mass. Community Coll. Faculty Assn., NEA. Home: N Main St Charlton MA 01507 Office: Dept Chemistry Holyoke Community Coll 303 Homestead Ave Holyoke MA 01040

TITONE, CHARLES SALVATORE, ophthalmologist; b. N.Y.C., Dec. 9, 1928; s. Charles and Frances T.; B.A., N.Y. U., 1949; certificate of med. studies, M.D., U. Lausanne (Switzerland), 1954; m. Patricia Ann Taormina, June 20, 1959; children—Charles, Frank, Francesca, Joseph. Intern, L.I. Coll. Hosp., Bklyn., 1955; resident State U. N.Y.-Kings County Med. Center, Bklyn., 1956-59; practice medicine spcializing in opthalmology, Jackson Heights, N.Y., 1963—; mem. staff Manhattan Eye, Ear and Throat Hosp., Cath. Med. Center Bklyn. and Queens, Astoria Gen. Hosp., Physicians Hosp., Kings County Hosp. Center; clin. instr. State U. N.Y. Med. Center. Served as capt. M.C., U.S. Army, 1959-61. Fellow Am. Acad. Ophthalmology and Otolaryngology, A.C.S.; mem. AMA, Med. Soc. State N.Y., N.Y. State Soc. Surgeons, Queens County Med. Soc., Société Française d'Ophthalmologie, Contact Lens Soc. Ophthalmologists, Nat. Med. Vets. Soc., Soc. Cryosurgery, Soc. Cryo-Ophthalmology. Home: 1 Beacon Hill Rd Port Washington NY 11050 Office: 37-42 73d St Jackson Heights NY 11372

TITONE, VITO JOSEPH, state justice; b. Bklyn., July 5, 1929; s. Vito and Elena L. (Ruisi) T.; B.S., N.Y. U., 1952; J.D., St. John's U., 1956; m. Margaret A. Viola, Dec. 30, 1956; children—Stephen, Matthew, Elizabeth, Elena. Admitted to N.Y. bar, 1956; partner firm Maltese, Titone & Anastasi, N.Y.C., 1956-68; asst. counse, pres. pro tem N.Y. State Senate, 1965; counsel jud. com. N.Y. State Constl. Conv., 1966; asso. justice appellate div. 2d Jud. Dept., N.Y. State Supreme Ct., 1969—, supervising justice criminal div. Adj. prof. U. City N.Y., 1972—; adj. prof. St. John's U. Law Sch., 1971—, bd. dirs. criminal justice program. Trustee, bd. dirs. S.I. YMCA; bd. dirs. Bklyn. Eye and Ear Hosp.; trustee S.I. council Boy Scouts Am. Served with U.S. Army, 1951-54. Mem. Am., N.Y. State, Richmond County bar assns., Am. Judicature Soc., Assn. Supreme Ct. Justices, Am. Legion (mem. nat. com.), V.F.W. Home: 1 Duncan Rd Staten Island NY 10301 Office: Supreme Ct Chambers Staten Island NY 10301 also 45 Monroe Pl Brooklyn NY 11201

TITSWORTH, (CHARLES) DAYTON, advt. agy. exec.; b. Greenwich, Conn., Dec. 31, 1943; s. Henry Dayton and Mary (Brown) T.; A.B., Syracuse U., 1965; m. Weltha Roberts, Apr. 19, 1969; children—Gregory Dayton, Susan Taylor. Asst. mktg. dept. Young & Rubicam, N.Y.C., 1965-66, project dir. research dept., 1966-67, asst. mktg. exec., 1967-68; account exec. Ted Bates & Co., N.Y.C., 1968-71, J. Walter Thompson Co., N.Y.C., 1971-74, v.p., account supr., 1974-78, v.p., mgmt. supr., 1975—; speaker in field. Publicity chmn. Republican Town Com., Westport, Conn., 1976-77; chmn. Citizens for Proper Planning, Westport, 1975. Served with Army N.G., 1965-71. Congregationalist. Club: Cedar Point Yacht (Westport). Home: 5 Tower Ridge Westport CT 06880 Office: J Walter Thompson Co 420 Lexington Ave New York City NY 10017

TIZES, REUBEN, physician; b. Ploesti, Rumania, May 22, 1930; s. Abraham L. and Hannah (Moscovici) T.; came to U.S., 1959, naturalized, 1963; M.D., Hebrew U., Jerusalem, 1956; M.P.H., Columbia, U., 1969; m. Carol Wiener, Nov. 27, 1959; children—Bruce Randolph, Andrea Celeste, Simone Melissa. Intern, Samaritan Hosp., Troy, N.Y., 1959-60; resident in medicine Queens Gen. Hosp., Jamaica, N.Y., 1960-61, King County Hosp. Center, Bkly., 1961-62, Met. Hosp., N.Y.C., 1962-63; practice medicine specializing in family practice, internal medicine and preventive medicine, Hewlett, N.Y., 1963—; mem. staff internal medicine S. Nassau Community Hosp., Oceanside, N.Y., 1963—; TB clinician, physician-in-charge chest clinics Bur. Tb, N.Y.C. Dept. Health, and Tb coordinator Kings County Hosp. Center, 1964-69; dir. respiratory diseases and Tb control officer Nassau County (N.Y.) Dept. Health, 1969-71; commr. health Orange County (N.Y.) Dept. Health, 1972-73; dir. dept. ambulatory care Newark Beth Israel Med. Center, 1974; dir. dept. ambulatory care services and community health Kingsbrook Jewish Med. Center, Bkly., 1974-77; dir. dept. medicine rehab. div. Peninsula Hosp. Center, Far Rockaway, N.Y., 1977—; clin. asst. instr. dept. medicine State U. N.Y. Downstate Med. Center, Bklyn., 1965-67, clin.instr., 1967-70, asst. prof. environ. medicine and community health, 1970-75, clin. asso. prof., 1975—; cons. examiner Nassau County Cancer Detection Center, 1963-72. Served to maj. M.C., Israel Def. Army, 1957-59. Diplomate Am. Bd. Family Practice, Am. Bd. Preventive Medicine. Fellow A.C.P., Am. Coll. Chest Physicians, Am. Coll. Preventive Medicine, Am. Coll. Angiology, Am. Pub. Health Assn.; mem. AMA (physician Recognition award 1969-72, 72-75), Am. Thoracic Soc., N.Y. State, Nassau County med. scos., Nassau Acad. Medicine, Am., N.Y. State, Nassau County socs. internal medicine. Jewish. Contbr. numerous articles on pub. health, internal medicine, preventive medicine to med. jours. Home and Office: 49 Pierrmont Rd Hewlett Bay Park Hewlett NY 11557

TJADER-HARRIS, MARGUERITE, author, editor; b. N.Y.C., Nov. 24, 1901; d. Richard and Margaret (Thorne) Tjader; B.A., Columbia, 1925; m. Overton Harris, May 23, 1922 (div. 1933); 1 son, Hilary Harris. Lit. sec. Theodore Dreiser, 1933-34, 43-44; editor Direction mag., 1938-45; author: (novel) Borealis, 1929; Theodore Dreiser, A New Dimension, 1975; Mother Elisabeth, 1972; also numerous articles; editor: (Dreiser) Notes on Life, 1974. Mem. Women's Internat. League Peace and Freedom, Fellowship of Reconciliation, Am. European Friendship. Democrat. Roman Catholic. Address: Vikingsborg Tokeneke Trail Darien CT 06820

TJOFLAT, JAMES AMUND, candy co. exec.; b. Pitts., Aug. 12, 1937; s. Gerald Benjamin and Sarita Dorothy (Romero) T.; B.A., Ohio State U., 1960; m. Nancy Kay Morse, June 6, 1964; children—James Amund Jr., Susan, Thomas. With Charmin Paper div. Procter & Gamble Co., 1960-66; salesman Alkon Products Inc., Cin., 1966-67; salesman Heath Candy Co., Cin., 1967-70, Western regional mgr., 1970-71, nat. field sales mgr., Kansas City, 1971-73; dir. QSP div. Heath Candy fund raising Reader's Digest Assos., Inc., Pleasantville, N.Y., 1973—. Solicitor, United Fund, Cin., 1963-67; troop com. Boy Scouts Am., 1977—, asst. dist. pres., 1976; bd. dirs., mgr. Roxbury Little League. Served with AUS, 1961-66. Mem. Am. Mgmt. Assn., Nat. Candy Wholesalers Assn., Ohio State U. Alumni Assn., Pi Kappa Alpha. Republican. Presbyterian. Home: 85 Shelter Rock Rd Stamford CT 06903 Office: PO Box 301 Pleasantville NY 10570

TOBIN, GEORGE RAYMOND, JR., photog. engr.; b. Rochester, N.Y., Jan. 19, 1931; s. George R. and Alma L. (Merz) T.; student Rochester Inst. Tech., 1949-52, U. Rochester, 1955-63; m. Janet Hogan, Nov. 23, 1961; children—Marcy, Pamela, George Raymond III. With Eastman Kodak Co., Rochester, 1949—, engr. engring. div., 1973—. Vice chmn. N.W. Hosp. Com., 1964-74; mem. adv. com. Rochester Blue Cross; active Com. for Civic Improvement, Greece Transp. Task Force; councilman Town of Greece (N.Y.), 1970-73, 75-76. Served with Signal Corps, U.S. Army, 1953-55. Mem. Illuminating Engring. Soc., Soc. Photog. Scientists and Engrs., Rochester Soc. Photog. Scientists and Engrs., Rochester Illuminating Engrs. Soc. (bd. mgrs.), Rochester Area C. of C. Republican. Luterhan. Patentee. Office: Engring Div Kodak Park Rochester NY 14650

TOBIN, JOHN JOSEPH, physician; b. Bklyn., May 28, 1934; s. John Joseph and Mae (Ferchland) T.; B.S., Coll. Holy Cross, 1956; M.D., N.Y. Med. Coll., 1960; m. Mary Rose Dempsey, June 22, 1957; children—John Mark, Margaret Rita, Mary Cecilia, Elizabeth Anne. Rotating intern, Naval Hosp., Stalbans, 1960-61, Fleet Marine Force Camp. LeJeune, N.C. and Med. Battalion, Mediterranean, 1961-62; resident internal medicine Naval Hosp., Boston, 1962-65; asst. dir. Exec. Health Examiners, N.Y.C., 1968-70; sr. clin. teaching fellow Boston U. Sch. Medicine, 1967-69; clin. asso. Mary Immaculate and L.I. Jewish Hosp., N.Y.C., 1969-70; practice medicine specializing in internal medicine and family practice, Darien, Conn., 1970—; asst. attending internal medicine Stamford (Conn.) Hosp., 1970—, St. Joseph Hosp., Stamford, 1970—; med. dir. A.R.C., Darien, 1970—; chmn. adv. bd. health Darien, 1971-73. Mem. bicentennial com. Darien, 1975-77; trustee Andrew Shaw Meml. Scout Cabin, Darien, 1975—; parish council St. Thomas More Ch., 1971-73, 77—; troop dir., med. advisor Boy Scouts Am., Darien, 1970—. Served with USN, 1959-68, USMC, 1960-61. Diplomate Am. Acad. Family Practice. Mem. Am. Med. Assn., Fairfield County Med. Soc., Conn. Med. Soc., Stamford Med. Soc. (bd. dirs. 1976), Conn. Acad. Family Practice, N.Y. Acad. Medicine, Undersea Med. Soc., Am. Heart Assn. Republican. Roman Catholic. Clubs: Kiwanis (dir. 1972-75, pres. 1973-74), Fairfield County of Holy Cross (dir. 1977—), K.C., YMCA Scuba (pres. 1977—). Contbr. articles in field to med. jours. Home: 18 Birch Rd Darien CT 06820 Office: 17 Old Kings Hwy S Darien CT 06820

TOBIN-ASHE, ANNE, family systems therapist; b. Albany, N.Y.; d. John M. and Anna (Scheibly) Tobin; B.A., Coll. St. Rose; Ed.M., U. Mass., 1975, Ed.D., 1979; m. Matthew T. Ashe; children—Mary, Marice, Matthew, Brian. Montessori directress Whitby Sch., Greenwich, Conn., 1969-73; leader workshops in communication skills and family systems, 1973-79; teaching asst. U. Mass., Amherst, 1975-78, vis. lectr., 1979; postgrad. tng. in family systems theory Georgetown U., 1976-79; family systems therapist Catholic Family and Community Services, Stamford, Conn., 1977—. Mem. Am. Assn. Marriage and Family Therapists, Nat. Council on Family Relations, Am. Personnel and Guidance Assn., AAUW. Home: 87 Echo Hill Dr Stamford CT 06903 Office: 384 N State St Stamford CT

TODD, EDWARD PAYSON, govt. ofcl.; b. Newburyport, Mass., Jan. 26, 1920; s. Glendon Forrest and Stella May (Cashman) T.; B.S., in Physics, Mass. Inst. Tech., 1942; Ph.D., U. Colo., 1954; m. Barbara Adams Wright, June 17, 1950; children—Glendon Gardner, Nathaniel Adams, Charles Payson. Research physicist United Shoe Machinery Corp., Beverly, Mass., 1946-49; supr. applied research Pitney Bowes, Inc., Stamford, Conn., 1954-57; tech. dir. Lab. for Atmospheric and Space Physics, U. Colo., Boulder, 1957-63; asso. program dir. for atmospheric scis. NSF, Washington, 1960-61, program dir. for aeronomy, atmospheric scis. sect., also NSF-Nat. Center Atmospheric Research liaison, Washington, 1963-65, acting head atmospheric scis. sect. Math. and Phys. Scis. div., 1963-64, spl. asst. to asso. dir. for research, 1965-66, dep. asso. dir. for research, 1966-70, dep. asst. dir. for research, 1970-75, dept. asst. dir. astron., atmospheric, earth and ocean scis., 1975-77, dir. div. polar programs, 1977—, chmn. interdeptl. com. for atmospheric scis., 1972-78, chmn. interagy. arctic research coordinating com., 1977-78. Mem. Falls Church (Va.) Sch. Bd., 1968-75. Served to capt. Signal Corps, U.S. Army, 1942-46. Recipient Distinguished Service award NSF, 1971, Superior Accomplishment award, 1977. Mem. Am. Geophys. Union (council mem. 1970-72), Am. Meterol. Soc. Home: 312 Van Buren St Falls Church VA 22046 Office: NSF 1800 G St NW Washington DC 20550

TODD, JOHN DAVID, psychologist; b. St. Louis, Aug. 6, 1947; s. John and Catherine (Laning) T.; B.A., Widener Coll., 1969; M.A. in Edn., Seton Hall U., 1974; postgrad. Boston U.; m. Christine A. McCullough, Aug. 14, 1971. Employment counselor Newark Concentrated Employment Program, 1969-72; vocat. counselor Newark Constrn. Trades Tng. Corp., 1973-74; mental health coordinator, div. legal medicine, Mass. Dept. Mental Health, Concord, 1975; psychotherapist Melrose (Mass.)-Wakefield Hosp., 1976-78; cons. psychologist Human Resource Inst. Boston at Lawrence, Mass., 1978—; staff psychologist Benjamin S. Cable Meml. Hosp., Ipswich, Mass., 1978—; counselor, supr. Cambridgeport Problem Center, Cambridge, Mass. Treas. Plainfield (N.J.) Boy's Sports League, 1971-72; bd. dirs. N. Jersey Community Union, 1973; treas. Boys' Club of Newark - Big Brothers Club, 1973-74. Recipient award for outstanding achievement Big Bros. Basketball League, 1974; teaching fellow Boston U., 1975-76. Mem. Am. Personnel and Guidance Assn., Nat. Vocat. Guidance Assn., Assn. Counselor Edn. and Supervision, N. Atlantic Regional Assn. Counselor Edn. and Supervision, Theta Chi. Presbyterian. Clubs: Quannapowitt Yacht (vice commodore). Research in relationship of need satisfaction in leisure and age. Home: 29 Carr Rd Saugus MA 01906 Office: Cable Hosp County Rd Ipswich MA 01938

TODD, JOHN PHILLIP ARNOLD, architect; b. North Stonington, Conn., Aug. 26, 1926; s. James Arnold and Isabel Nisbet (Downs) T.; B.A., Haverford Coll., 1950; B.Arch. with honors (Graham Found. fellow), U. Pa., 1962; m. Ruth Elsa Schoenwetter, Oct. 5, 1964 (div. 1977); children—Regula Elsbeth, Phillip Arnold. Prin., John P.A. Todd, architect, Phila., 1969—; partner Todd & Cope, Architect/Developers, 1978—; vis. critic architecture U. Pa., Drexel U., Temple U.; mem. land use planning com., aesthetics com., Community Assn., Chestnut Hill, Pa.; archtl. works include park bldgs. Jacobsburg (Pa.) State Park, 1974; dormitories Haverford (Pa.) Coll., 1975; Youth Cultural Center, Rosemont, Pa., 1976; restoration Rockland Mansion, Phila., 1977. Served with U.S. Army, 1946-47. Mem. AIA, Pa. Soc. Architects, Phila. Art Alliance, Fairmount Park Art Assn. Quaker. Club: Univ. Barge (Phila.). Home: 131 W Springfield Ave Philadelphia PA 19118 Office: 140 N 17th St Philadelphia PA 19103

TODD, MIRIUM JACKSON, govt. ofcl.; b. Phila., July 27, 1944; d. Howard C. and Marian E. Jackson; B.S. Howard U., 1970, M.Ed., 1971; m. Oria H. Todd, Aug. 26, 1972. Sch. counselor Pickett Middle Sch., Phila., 1972; sch. counselor Lea U.-Related Sch., Phila., 1972; equal opportunity specialist HEW, Phila., 1972-78, Dept. Labor, Phila, 1978—; former HEW regional liaison for pub. higher edn. in Va. Active Phila. Mus. Art, Afro Am. Hist. and Cultural Mus., Zool. Soc. Phila. Recipient spl. achievement award HEW, 1975; certified guidance counselor, Pa. Mem. Am. Personnel and Guidance Assn., Nat. Vocat. Guidance Assn., Kappa Delta Pi. Methodist. Home: 3901 Conshohocken Ave Philadelphia PA 19131 Office: 325 Chestnut St Philadelphia PA 19106

TODD, NORMA JEAN ROSS, govt. ofcl.; b. Butler, Pa., Oct. 3, 1920; d. William Bryson and Doris Mae (Ferguson) Ross; student spl. courses Pa. State U., 1944-46, Yale U., 1954-57; m. Alden Frank Miller, Jr., Apr. 16, 1940 (dec. Feb. 1975); 1 son, Alden Frank III; m. 2d, Jack R. Todd, Dec. 1977. Exec. mgr. Donora (Pa.) C. of C., 1950-57, Donora Community Chest, 1950-57; office mgr. Donora Golden Jubilee, 1951; staff writer Herald-Am., Donora, 1957, city editor, 1957-70; asso. editor Daily Herald, Donora, 1970-73; service rep. Pitts. Teleservice Center, Social Security Adminstrn., HEW, 1977—. Mem. Mayor's Adv. Council, Donora, 1965-69, Citizens' Adv. Council, Donora, 1965-69; mem. Donora Bd. Edn., 1954-60, pres., 1960; mem. Donora Borough Council, 1970-72; bd. dirs. Mon Valley chpt. ARC, 1964—, sec. bd., 1966—; bd. dirs. Washington-Greene County Tourist Promotion Agy., 1970—, sec., 1972—; bd. dirs. Washington County History and Landmarks Found. 1971—, sec., 1975—; bd. dirs. Mon Valley council Camp Fire Girls, 1965—, Mon Valley Drug and Alcoholism Council, 1971—; bd. dirs. United Way Mon Valley, 1973—, chmn. pub. relations, 1973-74. Mem. Pa. Soc. Newspaper Editors, Pitts. Press Club, Donora C. of C. (pres. 1971-72), D.A.R. (regent Monongahela Valley chpt. 1974-77). Clubs: Order Eastern Star (worthy matron 1966-67), White Shrine of Jerusalem (high priestess 1973-74), Order of Amaranth (royal matron 1966, dist. dep.); Donora Forecast (pres. 1962-63), Donora Unidon (pres. 1965-66, 56-57). Home: Overlook Terrace Donora PA 15033

TODD, WEBSTER BRAY, JR., airline exec.; b. N.Y.C., Dec. 1, 1938; s. Webster Bray and Eleanor Prentice (Schley) T.; student Ecole de Française Moderne, U. Lausanne (Switzerland), 1956-57; A.B., Princeton U., 1961; D. Aero. Sci. (hon.), Embry-Riddle Aero. U., 1976; m. Sheila Mitchell O'Keefe, Oct. 24, 1964; children—William Walker, Whitney de Forest, James Bridger. Vice pres. Basking Ridge Aviation Co. (N.J.), 1962-63; pres. Princeton Aviation Corp. (N.J.), 1963-69, Princeton Air-Research Park Co., 1965-69; spl. asst. to chmn. CAB, Washington, 1969-71; exec. dir. White House Conf. on Aging, 1971-72; nat. dir. Older Ams. Com. for Re-election of Pres., 1972; spl. asst. to pres. The White House, 1973-74; insp. gen. fgn. assistance State Dept., Washington, 1974-76; chmn. Nat. Transp. Safety Bd., Washington, 1976-77; v.p. Frontier Airlines, Denver, 1978—; mem. N.J.Gen. Assembly, 1967-69; group dir. Inaugural Com., 1973. Trustee Millbrook (N.Y.) Sch. Mem. Quiet Birdmen, Nat. Pilots Assn., Nat. Aeros. Assn. Clubs: Met., Kenwood, Somerset Hills Country. Publisher jazz albums: Songs You Forgot to Request, 1968; Lazy River Jazz Band, 1977. Home: 5017 Fort Sumner Dr Washington DC 20016 Office: 8250 Smith Rd Denver CO 80207

TODMAN, WILLIAM SELDEN, TV producer and program packager; b. N.Y.C., July 31, 1916; s. Frederick Simpson and Helena Diana (Orlowitz) T.; B.S., Johns Hopkins, 1938; B.A., N.Y. U., 1941; m. Frances Holmes Burson, Dec. 17, 1950; children—Lisa Susan, William Selden. Free lance radio writer and producer, 1938-41; writer, producer WABC, 1941-43; producer, agy. supr. Blow Co., also writer, dir. Connie Boswell Show for Blue Network, 1943; writer, dir. Anita Ellis Sings, 1944; writer Treasury Salute dramas, 1945-46; partner Goodson-Todman Prodns., N.Y.C., 1946—; developer, producer TV programs It's News to Me, What's My Line, The Web, By Popular Demand, The Name's the Same, I've Got a Secret, Two for the Money, Beat the Clock, Judge for Yourself, To Tell the Truth, The Price is Right, Jefferson Drum, Play Your Hunch, Split Personality, The Rebel, Philip Marlowe, Say When, One Happy Family, Don Rickles Show, Snap Judgement, He Said She Said, Password, others; pres. Goodson-Todman Prodns., Mid-Atlantic Newspapers, Central States Pub. Co., Inc.; v.p. Capitol City Pub. Co., Inc., Seattle Broadcasting Co. (Washington), New Eng. Newspapers, Am. Tribune Pub., Inc.; v.p., dir. Acme Newspapers, Inc., New Eng. Newspapers, Inc., N.E. Pub., Inc., Pearless Publs., Inc., Shenandoah Valley Pub. Corp.; exec. v.p., pres., dir. Goodson-Todman Broadcasting Inc., Milford Pub., Inc., Riverdale Pub., Inc.; dir. Central States Pub., Inc., Mid-Hudson Publs., Inc. Lectr. Queen's Coll., 1947. Chmn. radio-TV, stage artists and musicians div. United Jewish Appeal, 1954, 56; chmn. broadcasting ind. campaign Fedn. of Jewish Philanthropies N.Y., 1961-63; chmn. N.Y. Heart Fund. Mem. Phi Epsilon Pi. Author: Winner Take All Home Quiz Book (with Mark Goodson), 1949. Contbr. to Television, Advertising and Production Handbook, 1954. Home: 17 Heathcote Rd Scarsdale NY 10583 also 1045 S Ocean Blvd Palm Beach FL 33480 Office: 375 Park Ave New York City NY 10022 also 6430 Sunset Blvd Hollywood CA 90028

TODOROVIC, PETAR, educator; b. Belgrade, Yugoslavia, Nov. 10, 1932; s. Nikola D. and Milica (Savic) T.; came to Can., 1973; B.S., Belgrade U., 1958, Ph.D., 1964; m. Zivadinka Babic, Dec. 31, 1964; children—Natasha, Michal, Stevan. Docent, Belgrade U., 1958-66; asso. prof. Colo. State U., Ft. Collins, 1966-73; research prof. probability and engring. U. Montreal (Que., Can.), 1973—; cons. AEC in Vienna, Inst. Devel. Water Resources (Belgrade), U.S. Dept. Agr., U.S. Geol. Survey. Grant Nat. Research Council Can., 1974—, NSF, 1971-73. Mem. Inst. Math. Statistics, Am. Geophys. Union, N.Y. Acad. Sci., Math. Assn. Am. Contbr. articles to sci. jours. Home: 5 Vincent D Indy Ave Outremont PQ N2V 2S7 Canada Office: 2500 Ave Marie Guyard Montreal PQ H3C 3A7 Canada

TODRANK, GUSTAVE HERMAN, clergyman, educator; b. Huntingburg, Ind., Apr. 9, 1924; s. Christian William and Lillian Cathrine (Ahrens) T.; B.A., DePauw U., 1948; S.T.B., Boston U., 1951, Ph.D. (Sch. Theology Alumni fellow), 1956; M.A., Colby Coll., 1971; m. Elizabeth Chalmers, June 25, 1949; children—Stephen Knight, Josephine. Ordained to ministry United Ch. of Christ, 1951; pastor North Congregational Ch., Newton, Mass., 1951-56; instr. philosophy and religion Colby Coll., 1956-58, asst. prof. philosophy and religion, 1958-62, asso. prof, 1962-70, prof. philosophy and religion specializing in cultural euthenics, 1970—. Served with USAAF, 1943-46. Mem. Am. Acad. Religion (nat. chmn. religion and ecology group), Am. Philos. Assn., Phi Beta Kappa. Author: The Secular Search for a New Christ, 1969. Home: 38 Pleasant St Waterville ME 04901 Office: Lovejoy 314 Colby Coll Waterville ME 04901

TOEWS, CORNELIUS JACOB, endocrinologist; b. Altona, Man., Can., Mar. 22, 1937; s. Jacob and Helen (Hiebert) T.; B.Sc. in Medicine, U. Man., 1963, M.D., 1963; Ph.D. in Biochemistry, Queen's U., 1967; m. Hilda Martens, 1961. Intern, Winnipeg (Man.) Gen. Hosp., 1963-64; resident internal medicine Royal Victoria Hosp., Montreal, 1966-68; fellow in medicine Peter Bent Brigham Hosp., Boston, 1968-70; lectr. dept. medicine Harvard, 1970-71; asst. prof. dept. medicine and biochemistry McMaster U., 1971-73, asso. prof., 1973—. Med. Research Council Can. scholar, 1971—; grantee Ont. Heart Found. Fellow Royal Coll. Physicians Can.; mem. Am. Diabetes Assn., Can. Soc. Clin. Investigation, Can. Soc. Endocrinology and Metabolism, Can. Diabetes Assn. Home: 2083 Highview Dr Burlington ON Canada Office: Dept Medicine McMaster U Med Center Hamilton ON Canada

TOFFOLON, EDWARD PETER, gastroenterologist; b. New Britain, Conn., May 11, 1943; s. Ettore and Elvira T.; B.A., Holy Cross Coll., 1965; M.D., Tufts U., 1969; m. Anne M. Kochanek, Aug. 17, 1968; children—Amy, Rebecca. Intern, Bronx Municipal Hosp.-Einstein Med. Complex, 1969-71; resident in medicine U. Calif. at San Francisco, 1971-72; gastrointestinal fellow Mass. Gen. Hosp., Boston, 1972-74; clin. asst. prof. medicine U. Conn. Med. Sch., Farmington, 1974—; practice medicine specializing in gastroenterology, Kensington, Conn., 1974—. Mem. A.C.P., Conn. Med. Soc., Alpha Omega Alpha. Home: Office: 9 High Rd Kensington CT 06037

TOFIAS, ALLAN, accountant; b. Boston, Apr. 13, 1930; s. George I. and Anna (Seidel) T.; B.A., Colgate U., 1951; M.B.A., Harvard U., 1956; children—Bradley N., Laura J. Staff accountant Peat, Marwick, Mitchell & Co., Boston, 1956-60; mng. partner Tofias, Fleishman, Shapiro & Co., Brookline, Mass., 1960—. Mem. town meeting, com. on fin. planning, Brookline, 1970—. Served to lt. USN, 1951-54. Mem. Mass. Soc. C.P.A.'s, Am. Inst. C.P.A.'s. Home: 110 Wallis Rd Brookline MA 02167 Office: 21 Longwood Ave Brookline MA 02146

TOKARZ, STANLEY RICHARD, civil engr.; b. Holden, Mass., Jan. 20, 1923; s. Peter and Gladys T.; B.S. in C.E., Worcester Tech. Inst., 1950; m. Helen Marie Micolites, Sept. 29, 1951; children—Deborah, Brian. Civil engr. Worcester County Hwy. Engring. Dept., 1953-57; gen. airport engr. FAA, Boston, 1957-59; asst. chief engring. div. VA Hosp., Rutland Heights, Mass., 1959-63; chief engring. div. VA Hosp., West Roxbury, Mass., 1963-64, Kansas City, Mo., 1964-65, Togus, Me., 1965-72; chief engring. service VA Hosp., Providence, 1972-74, Bedford, Mass., 1974—. Instr. CAP, Augusta, Maine, 1968-70. Served to 1st lt. USAAF, 1942-46, USAF, 1951-53; lt. col. Res., 1946-70 (Ret.). Decorated Air medal with 2 oak leaf clusters; named Sportsman of Year Am. Legion Dept. of Me., 1967; registered land surveyor, profl. engr., Mass. Mem. New Eng. Hosp. Engring. Soc., Am. Hosp. Assn., Am. Legion. Democrat. Roman Catholic. Home: 383 Worcester St West Boylston MA 01583 Office: Springs Rd Bedford MA 01730

TOKUHATA, GEORGE KAZUNARI, educator, health scientist; b. Matsue, Japan, Aug. 25, 1924; s. Yujiro and Hama (Watanabe) T.; B.A., Keio U. (Tokyo), 1950; M.A., Miami U., Oxford, Ohio, 1953; Ph.D., State U. Iowa, 1956; Dr. Pub. Health, Johns Hopkins, 1962; m. Sumiko Matsui, June 10, 1949. Came to U.S., 1950, naturalized, 1959. Research asst. Scripps Found. for Population Research, Miami U., 1951-53; instr. State U. Iowa, Iowa City, 1954-56; research scientist Mich. Dept. Mental Health, Lansing, 1956-59; postdoctoral fellow Johns Hopkins U. Med. Center, Balt., 1959-61; spl. asst. div. dir. div. chronic diseases USPHS, Washington, 1961-62, prin. epidemiologist, 1962-63; asso. prof. preventive medicine U. Tenn., Memphis, 1963-67; dir. div. research and biostatistics Pa. Dept. Health, Harrisburg, 1967—; asso. prof. community medicine Temple U., Phila., 1967—; prof. epidemiology and biostatistics U. Pitts., 1967—. Cons. pub. health research. Fellow Am. Pub. Health Assn., Am. Sociol. Assn.; mem. Soc. Epidemiologic Research, N.Y. Acad. Scis. Contbr. numerous articles to profl. jours. Home: 410 Rupley Rd Camp Hill PA 17011 Office: PO Box 90 Harrisburg PA 17120

TOLES, WILLIAM HENRY, baking co. exec.; b. Poughkeepsie, N.Y., Aug. 5, 1919; s. William Henry and Ann (Fuzzeymore) T.; student Johnson C. Smith U., 1939-42; B.A., Howard U., 1949, M.A., 1949, M.S.W., 1950; m. Gloria Marie Allen, June 20, 1953; children—William H. III, Allen Wesley. Exec. dir. Catherine St. Community Center, Poughkeepsie, 1950-59; asso. dir. N.Y. Urban League, N.Y.C., 1960-67, dir., 1967, now chmn. bd. dirs.; equal employment officer, dir. urban affairs ITT, Continental Baking Co., Inc., Rye, N.Y., 1967-72, dir. urban affairs, equal employment officer, 1973-77, v.p., 1977—. Cons., Nat. Alliance Bus. Men, 1968-70, Inst. Criminal Justice, Queens County, N.Y., N.Y. State dept. Frontiers Internat., 1968-70; mem. judicial rev. bd. Appellate Div. N.Y.C., 1973—; v.p. exec. bd. dirs. Boy Scouts of Am., 1970—; chmn. campaign ARC, 1970. Bd. dirs. Central Queens YMCA, Queensboro Library Council. Served with USAAF, 1942-46. Mem. Nat. Assn. Social Workers, Nat. Assn. Intergroup Relations Ofcls., Queens County Grand Jurors Assn., NAACP, Nat. Assn. Market Developers, Acad. Certified Social Workers, N.Y. Urban League (chmn. bd. dirs.), Greater Jamaica C. of C. (pres. 1975-76), Nat. Conf. Christians and Jews (dir. 1976—). Methodist (trustee). Mason, Kiwanian (dist. lt. gov. 1973-74), Elk. Home: 104-27 192d St Hollis NY 11412

TOLK, NORMAN HENRY, atomic physicist; b. Idaho Falls, Jan. 9, 1938; s. Henry and Merle (Ricks) T.; A.B. (Univ. Nat. scholar 1956-60, Gen. Motors scholar 1956-60), Harvard, 1960; Ph.D., Columbia, 1966; m. Marilyn Ann Neubauer, Dec. 19, 1961; children—Jeffrey, Bentley, David, Rebecca, Amy. Research asso. dept. physics Columbia, 1966-67, lectr., 1967-68, adj. asst. profl., 1968-69; mem. tech. staff Bell Telephone Labs., Murray Hill, N.J., 1968—; vis. univ. fellow Australian Nat. U., summer 1975; lectr. Free U. Berlin, Freiburg, Chgo., Columbia, Yale. Mem. Am. Phys. Soc. Mormon. Editor: Inelastic Ion-Surface Collisions, 1977. Contbr. articles on atomic and astrophysics to profl. jours. Inventor Scaniir surface analysis device, neutral implantation. Home: 19 Franklin Rd Mendham NJ 07945 Office: 600 Mountain Ave Murray Hill NJ 07974

TOLL, DAVID, pediatrician; b. Cleve., May 6, 1925; s. Herman I. and Mollie (Neuger) T.; B.A., Harvard U.; M.D., Western Res. U., 1948; m. Bridget Ann Fryer; children—Job, Abel, Seth. Intern, Children's Hosp., Boston, 1948-50; resident in pediatrics Mass. Gen. Hosp., 1951-52; practice medicine specializing in pediatrics, St. Johnsbury, Vt., 1952—; med. dir. Child Health Center, St. Johnsbury, 1952—; cons. Vt. Health Dept., N.H. Health Dept., 1952—; preceptor Stanford, Dartmouth, Case Western Res., U. Vt. med. schs. Mem. AMA, Vt. Med. Assn., Am. Acad. Pediatrics, New Eng. Pediatric Soc., Am. Acad. Med. Dirs. Home: RFD 2 North Danville VT 05819 Office: 95 Main St Saint Johnsbury VT 05819

TOLL, JOHN SAMPSON, univ. pres.; b. Denver, Oct. 25, 1923; s. Oliver Wolcott and Merle d'Aubigne (Sampson) T.; B.S. with highest honors, Yale, 1944; A.M., Princeton, 1948, Ph.D., 1952; D.S., U. Md., 1973; D.S., U. Wroclaw (Poland), 1975; LL.D., Adelphi U., 1978; m. Deborah Ann Taintor, Oct. 24, 1970; children—Dacia Merle Sampson, Caroline Taintor. Mng. editor, acting chmn. Yale Sci. mag., 1943-44; with Princeton, 1946-49, Proctor fellow, 1948-49; Friends of Elementary Particle Theory Research grant for study in France 1950; theoretical physicist Los Alamos Sci. Lab. 1950-51; staff mem., asso. dir. Project Matterhorn Forrestal Research Center, Princeton, 1951-53; prof. chmn. physics and astronomy U. Md., 1953-65; pres., prof. physics State U. N.Y. at Stony Brook, 1965-78, dir. State U. N.Y. chancellor's panel on univ. purposes, 1970; pres., prof. physics U. Md., College Park, 1978—; chmn. com. faculty research, 1956-59. Physics cons. to editorial staff Nat. Sci. Tchrs. Assn., 1957-61; U.S. del., head sci. secretariat Internat. Conf. High Energy Physics, 1960; mem.-at-large U.S. Nat. Com. Internat. Union Pure and Applied Physics, 1960-63; chmn. research adv. com. on electrophysics to NASA, 1961-65; mem. gov. Md. Sci. Resources Adv. bd. 1963-65; chmn. NSF Adv. Panel for Physics, 1964-67; mem. N.Y. Gov.'s Adv. Com. on Atomic Energy, 1966-68; mem. commn. plans and objectives for higher edn. Am. Council on Edn., 1966-69; mem. N.Y. adv. council for Advancement of Indsl. Research and Devel., 1970—. Recipient Benjamin Barge prize in math. Yale, 1943, George Beckwith medal for Proficiency in Astronomy, Yale 1944, Nat. Gold Plate award Am. Acad. Achievement, 1968, Outstanding Citizen award Denver Centennial, 1958; named outstanding tchr. Men's League U. Md., 1965. Fellow Am. Phys. Soc.; mem. Am. Assn. Physics Tchrs., AAUP, Washington Acad. Scis., Philos. Soc. Washington, Assn. Higher Edn. Nat. Sci. Tchrs. Assn., Fedn. Am. Scientists (chmn. 1954), Yale Engring. Assn., Phi Beta Kappa, Sigma Xi (award for sci. achievement U. Md. chpt. 1965), Phi Kappa Phi, Sigma Pi Sigma. Contbr. articles to sci. jours. Research on elementary particle theory and scattering. Address: Univ Md College Park MD 20742

TOLLER, GLADYS SCHWARTZ, educator, psychologist; b. Phila., Sept. 6, 1925; d. Samuel Simon and Dorothy (Elgart) Schwartz; B.S. in Bus. Adminstrn., Temple U., 1948, Ed.M., 1951, Ed.D., 1967; m. Benjamin Esiah Toller, Mar. 30, 1950; 1 dau., Gale Elgart. Supr. jr. unit Temple U. Lab. Sch. reading clinic, Phila., 1956-60; reading cons. in pvt. practice, 1960-66; corrective reading tchr. Rosetree Media Sch. Dist., Media, Pa., 1966-67; asso. prof. elementary and secondary edn. Cheyney (Pa.) State Coll., 1967-70, prof. reading, 1970—, also mem. com. for new dean, 1973-74. Reading cons. Media Friends' Sch., 1963-64; head reading tchr. Smedley Jr. High Sch., Chester City Sch. Dist., 1965-66. Recipient silver medallion Mental Health Assn. S. Eastern Pa. Fellow Pa. Psychol. Assn. (mem. com. on tng. and standards); mem. Am. Psychol. Assn., Phila. Soc. Clin. Psychologists, Internat., Delaware Valley reading assns., Am. Assn. Univ. Profs., AAUW, NEA, Pa. State Edn. Assn., Assn. Pa. Colls. and Univ. Faculties, Delaware County Assn. for Children with Learning Disabilities, Del. Assn. for Gifted Children, S.E. Pa. Mental Health Assn., Kappa Delta Pi. Jewish (trustee Temple Beth Emeth (Wilmington, Del.) 1965-68, pres. Couples Club 1966-68, mem. social action com. 1973-74, religious edn. com. 1975—). Club: Knowlton Swim. Home: 630 Marydell Dr West Chester PA 19380 Office: Cheyney State College Cheyney PA 19319

TOLLESON, JOHN LEWIS, hosp. adminstr.; b. Cambridge, Mass., Jan. 6, 1949; s. Lewis Jackson and Rose M. (Corazzini) T., Jr.; student Boston Coll. 1967-69. Social dir. Harvard U. Summer Sch., Cambridge, 1969, head proctor, 1969; dir. food, beverages, front office Cambridge Hotels, Inc., Hotel Continental, 1969-72; asst. dir. food services Seiler Corp., Mt. Auburn Hosp., Cambridge, 1972-74; dir. food services Seiler Corp., Framingham (Mass.) Union Hosp., 1974-78, Univ. Hosp., Boston U. Med. Center, 1978—, lectr. food service labor relations, instr. dietetics. Mem. Town Meeting Watertown (Mass.), 1975—; pres. Watertown Lions Club, 1977—. Recipient outstanding achievement award Watertown Lions Club, 1976. Mem. Am. Hosp. Assn. Home: 805 Mount Auburn St Watertown MA 02172 Office: 25 Evergreen St Framingham MA 01701

TOLLIVER, JONATHAN COOPER, mktg. research exec.; b. Flemingsburg, Ky., Oct. 21, 1925; s. John Cooper and Bessilene (Hysong) T.; grad. high sch. Producer, Children's Fine Arts Guild, N.Y.C., 1959-63; treas. region 14, Children's Theatre Conf., N.Y.C., 1963-66, regional gov., 1966-68; comptroller, mem. exec. com. nat. governing bd. Children's Theatre Assn., Washington, 1968-74; exec. v.p., sec. Miller & Taliaferro, Inc., N.Y.C., 1973—. Bd. dirs. Children's Performing Arts Center, N.Y.C. Mem. Am., Children's theatre assns., Assn. Internat. du Theatre pour l'Enfance et la Jeunesse, Geneal. Soc. of Original Wilkes County, Episcopal Actors Guild, English Speaking Union. Translator: (pseudonym John D. Cooper) Ruy Blas (Victor Hugo), 1956. Home and office: 1270 Fifth Ave New York City NY 10029

TOLMIE, KENNETH DONALD, artist, author; b. Halifax, N.S., Can., Sept. 18, 1941; s. Archibald and Evelyn (Murray) T.; B.F.A. with honors, Mt. Allison U., 1962; student Alex Colville; m. Ruth Heloise MacKenzie, Aug. 8, 1962; children—Sarah Katharine, Jane Marianna. Exhibited in one man shows including: Dorothy Cameron Gallery, Toronto, Ont., Can., 1964, Lofthouse Gallery, Ottawa, Ont., 1969, Wallack Galleries, Ottawa, 1972, Canadian Soc. Graphic Art, London, Ont., 1973; Wells Gallery, Ottawa, 1974, 75; exhibited in group shows including: Royal Acad., London, 1963, Banfer Gallery, N.Y.C., 1963, Nat. Gallery Can. Waterc represented in permanent collections including: Nat. Gallery of Can., Montreal Mus. Fine Arts, Burnaby Art Gallery. Chmn. Visual Arts Ottawa, 1974-75. Author, illustrator: Tale of an Egg, 1975 (selected as 1 of 10 best Canadian children's books 1975). Home: Rural Route 3 115 South St Bridgetown NS B0S 1C0 Canada

TOMASSON, HELGI, dancer; b. Reykjavik, Iceland, 1942; student Sigridur Arman, Erik Bidsted, Vera Volkova, Sch. Am. Ballet, Copenhagen's Tivoli Pantomime Theatre; m. Marlene Rizzo, 1965; children—Kristin, Eric. Debut with Tivoli Pantomime Theatre, 1958; with Joffrey Ballet, 1961-64; soloist Harkness Ballet, 1964-70; prin. dancer N.Y.C. Ballet, 1970—. Office: care N Y C Ballet Lincoln Center New York NY 10023*

TOMAZINIS, ANTHONY RUDOLF, educator; b. Larissa, Greece, June 24, 1929; s. Rudolf A. and Christofily (Papamargaritou) T.; B.C.E., Schs. Nat. Tech. U. Greece, 1952; M. City Planning, Ga. Inst. Tech., 1959; Ph.D. in Planning, U. Pa., 1963; m. JoAnn R. Frank, June 24, 1962; children—Christina, Marina, Alexis. Came to U.S., 1956, naturalized, 1966. Mem. faculty U. Pa., Phila., 1962—, asso. prof. city planning, 1966-77, prof. city and regional planning, 1977—, asso. prof. civil engring., 1968-77, chmn. transp. research group, inst. environ. studies, 1967—, dir. Transp. Studies Center, 1969-76, chmn. univ.-wide program in transp., 1977—. Pres. A.R. Tomazinis & Assos., Inc., cons. transp. and urban planning. Transp. planning cons. Del. Valley Regional Commn., 1965-72, Doxiadis & Asso., Athens,

Greece, 1961-64, Orgn. for Econ. Cooperation and Devel., Paris, France, 1970-74, Govt. Iran, 1976; mem. travel forecasting com., com. on interdisciplinary edn. in transp. Transp. Research Bd.; Fulbright prof. city planning U. Paris, 1973-74; cons. Institut de Recherche des Transports, Paris, 1973-74. Served with Greek Armed Forces, 1953-54. Decorated Medal of Meritorious Acts H.M. King of Greece, 1949. Mem. Am. Inst. Planners, Inst. Transp. Engrs. (asso. editor High Speed Ground Transp. Jour., Transp. Planning and Tech.), Am. Hellenic League (Phila. pres. 1967-71, dir. 1971—), AAAS, Regional Scis. Assn., Am. Soc. Planning Ofcls., Univ. City Arts League, Fedn. Am. Hellenic Socs. of Greater Phila. (pres. 1977—). Club: Hellenic University. Home: 15 University Mews 45th and Spruce Sts Philadelphia PA 19104

TOMLINSON, J. RICHARD, railroad exec.; b. Newton, Pa., Mar. 26, 1930; s. Robert K. and Margaret (Wright) T.; B.A., Swarthmore, 1952; postgrad. George Washington U., 1952-53, U. Mich., 1955-57, Drexel Inst. Tech., 1954-57, Am. U., 1965; m. Barbara Elizabeth Brazill, Apr. 30, 1955; children—Karin Kathleen, Kimberly Ann. Mgmt. analyst Dept. State, Washington, 1952-53; with Old Republic Life Ins. Co., Washington, 1953-54; supr. financial analysis Ford Motor Co., Detroit, 1954-61; cons. McKinsey & Co., Washington, 1961-65; v.p. finance, dir. passenger services, Reading Co., Phila., 1965-69, v.p. finance Rollins Internat., Inc., 1969-71; exec. v.p. Amtrak, Washington, 1972-74; partner Louis T. Klander & Assos., Phila., 1974—; exec. v.p. Penn Central Transp. Co., 1975—. Named Man of the Month, Phila. C. of C., 1967. Mem. Transp. Research Forum, Soc. Investment Analysts. Clubs: Union League (Phila.); Stone Harbor (N.J.) Yacht. Home: 1656 Susquehanna Rd Rydal PA 19046 Office: 1700 Market St IVB Bldg Philadelphia PA 19107

TOMLINSON, WILLIAM WEST, univ. adminstr.; b. Salem, Ohio, Nov. 28, 1893; s. Lindley and Miriam Belle (Lease) T.; A.B., Swarthmore Coll., 1917; L.H.D., Susquehanna U., 1954; LL.D., Gettysburg Coll., Phila. Coll. Osteopathy, 1954; LL.D., Phila. Coll. Textiles and Scis., 1959; m. Rebecca Kirkpatrick Scott, Mar. 6, 1923; children—Jane Tomlinson Myhre, William, Rebecca Tomlinson Lindblom. With Scott Paper Co., Chester, Pa., 1922-37, dir., 1934-37; William W. Tomlinson & Assos., Phila. 1937-42; sec. Temple U., 1942-44, v.p. 1944—; mem. bd. mgrs. Swarthmore Coll., 1944-48. Chmn. projects com., mem. exec. and edn. coms. Pres.' People-to-People program; spl. ednl. missions to Germany, 1955, 56, 58. Bd. mgrs. Armed Services YMCA. Phila., 1940—, chmn. bd. 1953-58; dir. YMCA of Met. Phila., pres., 1964-65; mem. nat. council YMCA, 1964-70, armed services com., 1960—, mem. internat. com., 1963-70; mem. bd. govs. USO, 1971-73; vice chmn. Phila. United Charities campaign, 1939; pres. Phila. Tb and Health Assn., 1959-63. Hon. trustee Phila. Coll. Textiles and Scis.; life trustee Temple U.; chmn. bd. trustees Penn Center Acad., Phila., 1968-72. Ensign USNRF, World War I. Recipient Freedoms Found. award, 1951, 64, 76; Distinguished Service award Boy Scouts Am., 1961; Russell H. Conwell award, 1966, Phila. Outstanding YMCA Layman award, 1968; Distinguished Service medal Huguenot Soc. Pa., 1974. Mem. English-Speaking Union, Am. Acad. Polit. and Social Sci., Acad. Polit. Sci., Franklin Inst., Am. Scandinavian Found., Pa. Hist. Soc., Mil. Order World Wars, Newcomen Soc. Eng., Swarthmore Coll. Alumni Assn. (pres. 1935-37), Phi Beta Kappa, Alpha Phi Omega, Pi Gamma Mu, Delta Sigma Rho, Delta Upsilon. Presbyterian. (elder). Clubs: Union League Rotary, Merion Cricket (Phila.). Author: Time Out to Live, 1939; The Flickering Torch, 1942; There is no End, 1953; also articles and pamphlets. CBS script, This I Believe, 1952 on Voice of America to 97 countries. Moderator radio series Anatomy of Freedom, 1960—. Home: Cheswold and Elbow Lns Haverford PA 19041 Office: Temple U Philadelphia PA 19122

TOMPKINS, JAMES BALLANTINE, assn. exec.; b. Gloversville, N.Y., Jan. 23, 1922; s. Leslie James and Beulah (Tayntor) T.; B.S., Springfield Coll., 1947, M.Ed., 1949; m. Anne Novotny, Aug. 30, 1947; children—Robert James, Charlene Anne, Richard James. Youth dir. Country Club Br. YMCA, Kansas City, Mo., 1947-49, exec. dir. Linwood Br., Kansas City, Mo., 1949-52; exec. dir. Community YMCA-YWCA, Eastern Delaware County, Lansdowne, Pa., 1952-56; asso. area exec. youth services North Central Area Council YMCA's, Milw., 1957-64; exec. youth services YMCA, N.Y.C., 1964-67, dir. program services, 1967-75, v.p. program services, 1975-76, group v.p., 1976—. Mem. Mayors Urban Task Force, N.Y.C., 1968-70; group work, recreation com. Community Council N.Y., 1967-75, vice chmn., 1969-75. Bd. dirs. YWCA and YWCA Day Care, Inc., 1970—, treas., 1972-74, v.p., 1975—. Served with USAAF, 1942-46. Mem. Assn. Profl. YMCA Dirs. Am. (1st v.p. 1966-69), Am. Camping Assn., Nat. Social Welfare Assembly, Nat. Assn. Social Workers. Methodist. Home: 25 Herbert Ave White Plains NY 10606 Office: 422 9th Ave New York City NY 10001

TONELLI, JOSEPH P., union ofcl.; b. Grove City, Pa., Feb. 26, 1908; Ph.D. (hon.), Fu Jen Catholic U.; D.C.S. (hon.), St. Johns U., Jamaica, N.Y.; m. Mary Lombardi, July 26, 1924; children—James, Maria Tonelli Sciorra. With Schorsch Co., Bronx, N.Y., 1928-39; pres. United Paperworkers Internat. Union, Flushing, N.Y., 1939—; mem. exec. council, indsl. union dept. AFL-CIO; mem. adv. council Social Security Adminstrn. Commr., Adirondack Park Agy., 1971-75; N.Y. State Racing commr., 1974—; mem. pres.'s air quality bd. U.S. EPA, 1974-75. Recipient Menorah award (Prime Ministers Silver medal) State of Israel, Humanitarian award Villanova (Pa.) U.; decorated knight Order St. Gregory the Gt., Sovereign Mil. Order of Malta. Home: 315 Crestwood Ave Yonkers NY 10707 Office: 820 2d Ave New York City NY 10017

TONER, MICHAEL JOSEPH, psychologist; b. N.Y.C., June 12, 1941; s. Hugh Aloysius and Jean Marie (Brown) T.; A.B., Holy Cross Coll., 1963; M.A., Fordham U., 1967; m. Mary Margaret Breen, Aug. 20, 1967; children—Micahel, Laura, Timothy, Daniel. Tchr., Baghdad (Iraq) Coll., 1963-65; social worker Lincoln Hall, N.Y.C., 1966-69; sch. psychologist Hempstead (N.Y.) Pub. Schs., 1969-70; psychologist NE Nassau Psychiat. Center, Kings Park, N.Y., 1970-77; treatment team leader Suffolk Developmental Center, Melville, N.Y., 1977—; dir. Community Consultation Center, Centereach, N.Y., 1974—; adj. lectr. N.Y.C. Community Coll.; lectr. Suffolk County Community Coll. Mem. Am. Psychol. Assn., Assn. for Advancement Behavior Therapy. Democrat. Roman Catholic. Author articles on child rearing. Home: 30 Brookfield Ln Centereach NY 11720 Office: Suffolk Developmental Center Melville NY 11746

TONG KAI MING, surgeon; b. Nan-King, China, Sept. 24, 1935; s. Hoi Shung and Sau Ying (Chan) T.; M.D., Nat. Def. Med. Center, Taipei, Taiwan, 1962; m. Huey Li Luo, Dec. 29, 1966; children—Lorraine, Eugene. Immigrated to Can., 1968. Intern Md. Gen. Hosp., Balt., 1963-64; surg. resident Huron Rd. Hosp., Cleve., 1964-68; resident pathology Ottawa (Can.) Gen. Hosp., 1968-69; practice gen. surgery, London, Ont., Can., from 1970; mem. staff Van Buren (Maine) Community Hosp. Fellow Royal Coll. Surgeons Can. Home: 55 Main St Van Buren ME 04785 Office: 161 Main St Van Buren ME 04785

TONNESEN, STANLEY TERRY, research scientist; b. Bklyn., Feb. 2, 1935; s. Magne and Alma (Hansen) T.; B.A., N.Y. U., 1956; m. Marion Olsen, Aug. 19, 1961; children—Janet, David, Kevin. Research scientist Ciba-Geigy Pharm. Corp., Summit, N.J., 1960—; bd. dirs. Christian Research Inst., Anaheim, Calif., 1968—; pres. Christ Union Chapel, Culver Lake, N.J., 1976—; chmn. bd. Calvary Evang. Free Ch., Essex Fells, N.J., 1968-70, elder, 1970-74; bd. dirs. Normanoch Assn., Inc., 1971—, chmn. pub. relations com., 1973—; bd. dirs. Dover (N.J.) Christian Nursing Home, 1968—. Served with USAF, 1956-60. Mem. Am. Sci. affiliation, Golf Leagues Essex County (dir.), Fundamental Ch. Bowling League (pres., treas. 1964—). Club: Culver Lake Men's (pres.). Research in behavioral pharmacology, endocrinology and cardiovascular fields. Home: 17 Green Dr East Hanover NJ 07936 Office: Ciba-Geigy Pharm Corp Morris Ave Summit NJ

TOOMEY, JEANNE ELIZABETH, writer, conservationist; b. N.Y.C., Aug. 22, 1921; d. Edward Aloysius and Anna Margaret (O'Grady) Toomey; student Hofstra U., 1938-40, Fordham Law Sch., 1940-41, Coll. St. Rose, Albany, N.Y., 1975; B.A., Southampton Coll., 1976; m. Peter E. Terranova, Sept. 29, 1951 (dec. Sept. 1968); children—Peter, Sheila; m. 4th, Jim R. Gray, Dec. 5, 1972. With N.Y. Jour.-Am., 1955-61, Reno (Nev.) Evening Gazette; with N.Y. local desk, stringer AP, 1963-76; editor weeklies Tahoe Chronicle, This Week at Tahoe, 1964-65; editor Bronx Home News, Manhattan East, L.I. Post, 1966-67; people's editor Knickerbocker News, Albany, N.Y., 1975-76; columnist Woodbridge (N.J.) News Tribune; news broadcaster radio stas. WLNG, Sag Harbor, L.I., WWRJ, Southampton; writer for mags. Family Weekly, Modern Maturity, Family Circle, Cats; contbr. chpt. to book Psychiatry and Human Experience. Chmn. com. to establish wildlife refuge in Hackensack Meadows, 1968-69. Recipient N.Y. Women's Press Club award for best series pub. by N.Y.C. newspaper, 1960; Patrolmen's Benevolent Assn. award, 1960; Nev. Press Assn. Best Feature award, 1961. Mem. Wilderness Soc., Defenders of Wildlife, Overseas, N.Y. press clubs, Newswomen's Club N.Y., Silurians. Address: Gondola Gardens North Sea Rd Southampton NY 11968

TOOMEY, LAURA CAROLYN, psychologist; b. Manchester, Conn., Mar. 29, 1929; d. David Clark and Olive (Hutchinson) Toomey; B.S. cum laude, Bates Coll., 1950; M.A., U. Conn., 1954, Ph.D., 1961; student Trinity Coll., 1952-53. Research asso. Inst. of Living, Hartford, Conn., 1958-61, research psychologist, 1961-64; psychologist Community Child Guidance Clinic, Manchester, 1959-63, chief psychologist, 1963-64; psychologist Psychiat. Unit, Springfield (Mass.) Hosp., 1964-66, chief psychologist 1966-73; psychologist Connecticut Valley Hosp., Middletown, 1973—, coordinator clin. psychology tng., 1974—; cons. Andover (Conn.) Schs., 1963-64; asst. prof. U. Conn., 1962-63; supr. Springfield Para-Psychiat. Tng. Project, 1968-73. Mem. Am. (div. 31 rep. 1973-75), Conn. (council 1977—), Mass. psychol. assns., Phi Beta Kappa, Sigma Xi. Author: (with Marvin Raznikoff) Evaluation of Changes Associated with Psychiatric Treatment, 1959. Contbr. articles to profl. jours. Home: 40 Steele Crossing Rd Bolton CT 06040 Office: Connecticut Valley Hosp Middletown CT 06457

TOONKEL, LAWRENCE ELLIOTT, phys. scientist; b. Bronx, N.Y., Dec. 14, 1949; s. Alfred and Theresa (Pritzker) T.; B.A. magna cum laude, Hofstra U., 1971; M.S. in Applied Math., State U. N.Y., Stony Brook, 1972; m. Wendy Joan Shotsky, July 3, 1972; children—Matthew, Nancy. Phys. scientist AEC, 1972-74, ERDA, 1974-77; phys. scientist environ. measurements lab. Dept. Energy, N.Y.C., 1977—. Mem. N.Y. Acad. Scis., Free Sons of Israel. Jewish. Home: 86 Trafalgar Sq Lynbrook NY 11563 Office: 376 Hudson St New York City NY 10014

TOOT, FREDERICK PETER, YMCA dir.; b. Amsterdam, N.Y., July 16, 1939; s. John Texter and Dorothy Jane (Wolfgang) T.; B.S., Springfield (Mass.) Coll., 1961; m. Janet Marilyn Wulff, June 24, 1961; children—Gregory Paul, Scott Wulff. Dir. youth and camp Gloversville (N.Y.) YMCA, 1961-65; dir. youth, family and camp depts. Pawtucket (R.I.) YMCA, 1965-71; exec. dir. Cheshire County YMCA, dir. Camp Takodah, Keene, N.H., 1971-77; exec. dir. Pittsfield (Mass.) YMCA and mem. bd. dirs. Central Berkshire United Way, 1977—; dir. Keene Day Care Center, Monadnock Area pastoral counseling services; moderator, Swanzey Congl. Ch., Swanzey Center, N.H. Recipient Danforth Found. award, 1957. Mem. Assn. Profl. Dirs. YMCA, Am. Camping Assn. Club: Masons, Shriners, Rotary. Home: 1428 North St Pittsfield MA 01201 Office: 292 North St Pittsfield MA 01201

TOOTHMAN, EDWIN HUGH, acoustical engr.; b. Mannington, W.Va., Oct. 1, 1932; s. Charles Adam and Syvilla May (Fluharty) T.; B.S., Fairmont State Coll., 1960; postgrad. U. Pitts., 1960-62; m. Anita Louise Antel, June 16, 1955; children—Connie Louise, Eric Edwin, Kim Lynette, Wendy Lynae. Proposal engr. Pa. Transformer Co., Canonsburg, 1957-58; research asst. U. Pitts., 1958-62; sr. noise control engr. Bethlehem Steel Corp. (Pa.), 1962—. Chmn. tech. task group Fastener Industry Noise Control Research Program, 1975—. Pres., East Hills Civic Assn., 1971-72; pres. Gov. Wolf Sch. PTA, 1968-69. Served with USAF, 1950-53. Mem. Am. Indsl. Hygiene Assn., Acoustical Soc. Am. (pres. Delaware Valley chpt. 1971-72), Engrs. Club Lehigh Valley, Am. Iron and Steel Inst. (chmn. subcom. noise 1973—). Home: 2932 Avon Rd Bethlehem PA 18017 Office: Bethlehem Steel Corp Room B-252 Martin Tower Bethlehem PA 18016

TOPJIAN, NISHAN, fin. mgmt. cons.; b. Beirut, May 16, 1952; s. Souren Nishan and Sirvart Nikabet (Saghatelian) T.; came to U.S., 1969, naturalized, 1977; B.S. in Econs., Drexel U., Phila., 1976; M.B.A., Baruch Coll., N.Y.C., 1978. Fin. analyst Am. Internat. Group, N.Y.C., 1977; cons., mgmt. services div. Majic Enterprises, N.Y.C., 1978—. Active local Big Bros. Am. Grantee Drexel U. Alumni Assn., 1975-76. Mem. Armenian Evang. Coll. Assn. (treas.), Alumni Assn. Drexel U. (dir. 1977—), Nat. Assn. Ski Instrs. Club: Stuyvesant Yacht. Home: 84 State St Brooklyn Heights NY 11201 Office: 70 Pine St New York City NY 10005

TOPPING, MARVIN WOODROW, govt. ofcl.; b. Poquoson, Va., July 17, 1911; s. Joseph and Amelia (Bunting) T.; B.A., Randolph-Macon Coll., 1932; S.T.B., Boston U., 1936, postgrad., 1937-39; m. Louise E. Marshall, Dec. 3, 1938; children—John Marvin, Jean Carol. Dir. admissions, pub. relations Union Coll., Barbourville, Ky., 1943-47; dir. pub. relations Med. Coll., Va., 1947-50; exec. dir. Am. Coll. Pub. Relations Assn., Washington, 1950-56; vice chancellor Nebr. U., 1956-57; asst. dir. devel. George Washington U., 1957-62; founder, Pres. Coll. & Univ. Personnel Cons., Washington 1962-74; minority counsel subcom. on spl. small bus. problems com. on samll bus. U.S. Ho. of Reps., 1974—. Contbr. articles to profl. publs. Pioneer 1st ann. Survey Philanthropy to Higher Edn. Home: 9909 E Bexhill Dr Kensington MD 20795 Office: 2435 Rayburn House Office Bldg Washington DC 20515

TORAN, CAVIT MEHMET, cons. engring. co. exec.; b. Bursa, Turkey, Nov. 22, 1927; s. Fevzi Huseyin and Huriye Serife (Diker) T.; came to U.S., 1947, naturalized, 1956; B.S., Brown U., 1951; M.S., Poly. Inst. N.Y., 1953; m. Zeynep; children by previous marriage—Errol, Alev. Elec. engr., Howard Needles Tammen & Bergendoff, cons. engrs. and planners, N.Y.C., Fairfield, N.J., 1953-54, asst. elec. engr., 1956-58, asst. elec. project engr., 1958-71, elec. project engr., 1971—, also elec. project mgr., Fairfield. Registered profl. engr. N.J. Mem. IEEE, Turkish-Am. Cultural Assn. Muslim. Home: 65 Tyson Place Bergenfield NJ 07621 Office: 330 Passaic Ave Fairfield NJ 07006

TORELLO, ROBERT JAMES, economist; b. New Haven, Jan. 6, 1934; s. James and Louise T.; B.A., U. Conn., 1959; M.A., So. Conn. State Coll., 1973; m. Priscilla Ann Lutz, Aug. 12, 1966; children—Stacie, Amy. Fin. officer New Haven Redevel. Agy., 1960-68; exec. dir. Derby (Conn.) Redevel. Agy., 1968-74; dir. devel. Town of Hamden (Conn.), 1974—. Adv. council Albertus Magnus Coll.; area devel. com. mem. New Haven C. of C.; econ. devel. com. mem. Hamden C. of C. Recipient Presdl. award New Haven Jr. C. of C., 1970; Honor award AIA, 1972. Mem. Am. Inst. Planners, Nat. Assn. Housing and Redevel. Ofcls. Author: Bolivia, 1972; Money, Wages and Economic Growth, 1972; Money, Prices and Economic Growth in Brazil, Bolivia and Mexico, 1961-70, 1977. Home: 54 Hampton Park West Branford CT 06405

TORG, JOSEPH STEVEN, surgeon; b. Phila., Oct. 25, 1934; s. Jay and Elva (May) T.; A.B., Haverford Coll., 1957; M.D., Temple U., 1961; m. Barbara Jane Groenendaal, May 23, 1959; children—Joseph Steven, Elisabeth, Jay M. Intern, San Francisco Gen. Hosp., 1961-62; resident in orthopaedic surgery Temple U. Health Scis. Center, Phila., 1964-68, Shriner's Hosp. for Crippled Children, Phila., 1966-67; practice medicine specializing in orthopedic surgery, Phila., 1968—; instr. orthopaedic surgery Temple U. Sch. of Medicine, Phila., 1968-70, asst. prof., 1970-75, asso. prof., 1976-78; prof. orthopaedics Sch. Medicine, U. Pa., Phila., 1978—, dir. Sports Medicine Center, 1978—, physician to dept. intercollegiate athletics, 1978—; mem. staff St. Joseph's Hosp., U. Pa. Hosp., Children's Hosp. Phila.; cons. Phila. Flyers of the NHL; sports medicine cons. to div. of health and phys. edn. Sch. Dist. of Phila.; mem. subcom. on sports medicine Pa. Dept. of Health. Bd. dirs. Robert Maxwell Meml. Football Club, 1976. Served to capt., M.C., U.S. Army, 1962-64. Recipient Bronze award Am. Acad. Pediatrics, 1967, Layman Honor award Pa. State Assn. for Health, Phys. Edn. and Recreation, 1970, Commendation award Phila. Pub. High Sch. Football Coaches, 1974; diplomate Am. Bd. Orthopaedic Surgery. Fellow Am. Acad. Orthopaedic Surgeons, A.C.S., Am. Coll. Sports Medicine (trustee 1975-78), Phila. Coll. Physicians; mem. Pa. State, Phila., Eastern, Va. (hon. mem.) orthopaedic socs., Pa. State, Phila. County med. socs., AMA, Nat. Athletic Trainers Assn. Contbr. numerous articles on sports medicine and surgery to profl. jours. Home: 401 Conestoga Rd St Davids PA 19087 Office: Hosp Univ Pa 34th and Spruce St Philadelphia PA 19104

TORINA, MARY HELEN, dietitian, food service adminstr.; b. Washington, Sept. 5, 1945; d. Michael W. and Ann (Sershen) Torina; B.S., Mich. State U., 1967; student U. Del., 1963-65. Therapeutic dietitian L.I. Jewish Hosp., New Hyde Park, N.Y., 1968-69; asst. dir. dietary services Holy Cross Hosp., Silver Spring, Md., 1970-72, dir. dietary services, 1972—. Mem. Am., Md. dietetic assns., Soc. for Advancement Food Service Research, Am. Soc. for Hosp. Food Service Adminstrn. (pres. Mid. Atlantic chpt. 1976). Roman Catholic. Office: 1500 Forest Glen Rd Silver Spring MD 20910

TORMES, YVONNE MARIA, ednl. adminstr.; b. Ponce, P.R., Sept. 25, 1935; d. Leopold Tormes Garcia and Eulalia Providencia Gotay; B.A., Hunter Coll., 1956; M.A., N.Y. U., 1969. Claims rep. for Bur. of Old Age and Survivors Ins., Social Security Adminstrn., N.Y.C., 1956-57; case aid in interim care dept. N.Y. Foundling Hosp., N.Y.C., 1957; research asso. psychopharmacology research and treatment unit Research Found. of N.Y. State U., N.Y.C., 1960-64; jr. project dir. Gen. Foods Corp., White Plains, N.Y., 1964-65; research asso. children's div. Am. Humane Assn., N.Y.C., 1965-67, asst. dir., 1967-68; cons. on study of migrant farm workers, Div. of Migration and Employment, Commonwealth of P.R., 1968-69; lectr. dept. human relations Baruch Coll. of U. City N.Y., 1969-71; research asso. U. City N.Y., N.Y.C., 1968-70, dir. research and evaluation Regional Opportunity Center Program, 1970-71, adminstr. Coll. Discovery Program, 1972—; dir. program evaluation Human Resources Adminstrn., Manpower and Career Devel. Agy., N.Y.C., 1972; mem. adv. bd. Nat. Scholarship and Service Fund for Negro Students, 1973—, Pre-trial Service Agy., 1973—, Eric Clearinghouse on Urban Edn., 1974—, Consortium for Bilingual Conselor Edn., 1972-74; mem. statewide com. on ednl. opportunity, N.Y. State, 1973—. Mem. Am. Assn. of Higher Edn., Assn. for Supervision and Curriculum Devel., Am. Sociol. Assn., Am. Acad. Arts and Scis., Council for Basic Edn., N.Y. State Personnel and Guidance Assn., Nat. Congress for Minorities' Edn. Contbr. articles on child abuse, ednl. evaluation and curriculum to profl. publs. Home: 53 Joralemoir St Brooklyn NY 11201 Office: 315 Park Ave S New York City NY 10010

TORNABENE, HUGH SALVATORE, astrophysicist, educator; b. Liverpool, Eng., Dec. 27, 1932; s. Onofrio John and Norah (Green) T.; Ph.D., U. Liverpool, 1957. Came to U.S., 1965. Sci. officer U.K. Atomic Energy Authority, Harwell, Eng., 1956-59; mem. S.J., 1959-72; ordained priest Roman Catholic Ch., 1968; fellow Research Inst. Natural Sci., Woodstock Coll., 1965-69; prof. physics Bowie (Md.) State Coll., 1969—. Mem. AAUP, Am. Phys. Soc. Home: 6020 Westchester Park Dr #t(1) College Park MD 20740 Office: Bowie State Coll Bowie MD 20715

TOROK, ANDRE ENDRE, textile designer; b. Veresegyhaz, Hungary, Mar. 19, 1929; s. Endre I. and Maria (Romsics) Török; came to U.S., 1959, naturalized, 1964; student Art Sch., Hungary, 1948-50. Stylist, mdsg. dir. Crown Prints, Spartanburg, S.C., 1976; print stylist, head art dept., Knit Away, Inc., N.Y.C., 1972-75; artist-designer textile companies, N.Y.C., 1977—; fashion cons. N.Y.C.; producer fashion shows, N.Y.C., Phila., Dallas; designs pub. fashion and profl. mags.; exhibitor Bicentennial Art Exhibition, Calif. State Mus. Sci. and Industry, Los Angeles, 1976. Sec. N.Y. br. Hungarian Freedom Fighters Fedn. Mem. World Fedn. Hungarian Artists. Republican. Roman Catholic. Clubs: Barry Goldwater Rep., James Monroe Conservative (N.Y.C.). Home: 34-57 82d St New York City NY 11372

TOROK, TIBOR, mfg. co. exec.; b. Budapest, Hungary, May 27, 1935; s. Joseph and Piroska (Szegedi) T.; came to U.S., 1957, naturalized, 1962; B.S. in M.E., Poly. Inst. (Budapest), 1954; M.S. in Indsl. Engring., Tech. U. Budapest, 1956; m. Helen Odum, July 4, 1967; children—Derek, Marika. Mgr. mfg. and engring. Greenwald Industries, Bklyn., 1967-72; v.p. mfg. Wing Industries, Inc., Linden, N.J., 1972-77; v.p. operations The Valtronic Corp., Bronx, 1977—. Pres., Workers Revolutionary Council, Budapest, 1956. Mem. Am. Def. Preparedness Assn., Am. Security Council, Am. Mgmt. Assn. Home: 102 Cresci Blvd Hazlet NJ 07730

TORONTO, NICHOLAS ANTHONY, JR., physician; b. Johnstown, Pa., June 1, 1935; s. Nicholas Anthony and Ruth Iona (Murphy) T.; B.S., U. Pitts., 1956, M.D., 1960; m. Bernice Ann Havranek, Aug. 28, 1958; children—Tami Lynn, Nicholas Joseph. Intern, Lancaster Gen. Hosp., 1961; resident in gen. practice U.S. Air Force Hosp., Andrews AFB, 1963-64; gen. practice medicine, Saegertown, Pa., 1967-72; asso. prof. family practice U. Nebr., 1972-77; dir. W St. Clinic, Family Health Center, Omaha, Nebr.,

1972-77; dir. family practice residency Forbes Health System, Pitts., 1977—; asst. clin. prof. community medicine U. Pitts. Sch. Medicine, 1977—; v.p. med. staff Meadville City Hosp., 1971, pres., 1972. Bd. dirs. Douglas/Sarpy County Heart Assn.; pres. Crawford County Mental Health Assn., 1972. Served with USAF, 1961-67. Diplomate Am. Bd. Family Practice. Fellow Am. Acad. Family Physicians; mem. Soc. Tchrs. Family Medicine, AMA. Methodist. Home: 301 N Pasadena Dr Pittsburgh PA 15215 Office: 500 Finley St Pittsburgh PA 15206

TOROP, PAUL, psychiatrist; b. N.Y.C., Oct. 18, 1940; s. Ralph and Betty (Goodkin) T.; B.A., Yale U., 1962; M.D., Harvard U., 1966; m. Karen Barbara Bass, Dec. 19, 1965; children—Jonathan, Daniel. Intern, Mt. Zion Hosp., San Francisco, 1966-67; resident in psychiatry McLean Hosp., Belmont, Mass., 1967-70; psychiatrist Andrews AFB, Washington, 1970-72; chief inpatient psychiatry Undercliff Health Center, Meriden, Conn., 1972-74; pvt. practice medicine specializing in psychiatry, Middletown, Conn., 1973—; mem. staff Middlesex Meml. Hosp., Middletown; asst. clin. prof. Yale, 1973—. Served with USAF, 1970-72. Diplomate Am. Bd. Psychiatry and Neurology. Mem. Am., Conn. psychiat. socs., AMA, Middlesex County Med. Assn. Office: 109 Broad St Middletown CT 06457

TOROSYAN, ABRAHAM, visual designer; b. Istanbul, Turkey, Jan. 18, 1942; s. Hirant and Marika (Gova) T.; came to U.S., 1968; M.F.A., Acad. Fine Arts, Istanbul, 1968; m. Koharik Gumusyan, June 24, 1967; children—Roben, Cloe. One-man shows of paintings include: Pangalti, 1961; Getronagan, 1962, 63, 64, 65, 66, Kinali, 1963, Avsa, 1963, Izmir, 1964, Barcelona, Spain, 1965; group shows: German Culture Center, Istanbul, 1966; asst. display mgr. Bond's Clothing Co., Boston, 1968-70, Jordan Marsh Co., Burlington, Mass., 1970-73; free lance visual designer, trade show designer, West Peabody, Mass., 1973—. Named to Best 30 Young Turkish Artists, 1966. Translator 4 books on Byzantique era; research in medieval Arminian miniatures. Home and Office: 15 Hamilton Rd West Peabody MA 01960

TORRE, ARTHUR JOHN, pediatrician; b. Paterson, N.J., Sept. 23, 1946; s. Arthur M. and Margaret Joan (Kornafer) T.; A.B., Rutgers U., 1966; M.D., Coll. Medicine Dentistry N.J., 1970; m. Ruth Carolyn Krieger, Aug. 9, 1969; children—Suzanne, Christine, Carolyn, Elizabeth. Intern in pediatrics Martland Hosp. unit N.J. Med. Sch., Newark, 1970-71, pediatric resident, 1971-72, pediatric teaching fellow, clin. instr. and chief resident in pediatrics, 1972-73; practice medicine specializing in pediatrics and pediatric allergy, Paterson and Little Falls, N.J., 1974—; attending pediatrician St. Joseph's Hosp., Paterson, 1973—; clin. asst. prof. N.J. Med. Sch., Newark, 1976—; cons. pediatrician Mt. St. Joseph's Childrens Center, N.J., 1977—, Paterson Boys Community, 1976—, St. Thomas More Sch., Fairfield, N.J., 1977—; adj. attending Children's Hosp., Newark, 1975—, Passaic Gen. Hosp., 1973-77. Served to maj. N.J. Army N.G., 1970-76. Recipient Physicians Recognition Award, Am. Med. Assn., 1973, 76; diplomate Am. Bd. Pediatrics, Nat. Bd. Med. Examiners. Fellow Am. Acad. Pediatrics, Am. Coll. Allergists; mem. N.J. Med. Soc., N.J. Allergy Soc., N.J. Thoracic Soc., Alpha Epsilon Pi. Roman Catholic. Home: 11 Summit Ave Fairfield NJ 07006 Office: 608 21st Ave Paterson NJ 07513 also 105 Rt 23 Little Falls NJ 07424

TORRE, FRANK JOSEPH, psychotherapist, counselor, educator; b. Bklyn., Apr. 21, 1946; s. Anthony and Jennie (Guiliano) T.; B.A., City Coll. N.Y., 1967; M.A., Columbia U., 1969; certificate of fellowship Am. Inst. Psychotherapy and Psychoanalysis, 1977; m. Sonia Maria Green, Aug. 9, 1975. Sr. psychiatric technician St. Vincent's Hosp., NYC, 1966-70; asst. admnstrv. rehab. counselor Boerum Hill Home for Adults, Bklyn., 1970-71; asst. prof., counselor Coll. of Staten Island, N.Y., 1971—; pvt. practice psychotherapy, N.Y.C., 1971—. Mem. AAUP, Am., N.Y. State personnel and guidance assns., N.Y. Soc. Clin. Psychologists. Democrat. Roman Catholic. N.Y. State Rehab. Counseling Assn. (exec. bd. 1974—). Home: 88 Cray Terrace Fanwood NJ 07023 Office: 715 Ocean Terrace Staten Island NY 10301

TORRE, JOSEPH PAUL (JOE), profl. baseball exec.; b. Bklyn., July 18, 1940. First baseman Milw. Braves (name changed to Atlanta Braves), 1961-68; first baseman St. Louis Cardinals. Nat. League baseball team, 1969-70, 73-77, third baseman, 1971-72, team capt., player rep.; mgr. N.Y. Mets, 1977—. Address: care NY Mets William A Shea Stadium Roosevelt Ave and 126th St Flushing NY 11368*

TORRES, ANIBAL, scientist; b. Lares, P.R., May 23, 1934; s. Jose Antonio and Eloisa (Rodriquez) T.; A.A.S., State U. N.Y., 1953; B.S. in Food Sci. and Tech., U. Ga., 1955; m. Maria Diaz Diaz, Sept. 1, 1963. Chemist, Ungerer and Co., N.Y.C., 1955-58; flavor chemist Seeley and Co., Nyack, N.Y., 1960-62; sr. flavor chemist Haarman and Reimer Corp., Union, N.J., 1962-65; sr. research scientist Pfizer Inc., Groton, Conn., 1965—. Served with U.S. Army, 1958-60. Mem. Inst. Food Technologists, Am. Chem. Soc. Democrat. Roman Catholic. Patentee in field. Home: 7 Trumbull Rd Waterford CT 06385 Office: Eastern Point Rd Groton CT 06340

TORRES, ERIKA VOGEL, coll. adminstr.; b. Fulda, W. Germany, Mar. 22, 1939; d. Hermann Joseph and Ella Mathilda (Schneider) Vogel; came to U.S., 1962, naturalized, 1966; A.A., Institut Beatae Mariae Virginis, Fulda, 1960; postgrad. Padagogische Hochschule, Ludwigsburg, W. Germany, 1970-72; B.S., U. Bridgeport, 1973, M.S., 1975, 6th year profl. diploma, 1977; postgrad. Germanic langs. lit. City U. N.Y.; m. Angelo Torres, Jr., Mar. 2, 1974; children—Karen Doris, Christopher Hans, Alexandra Eran. Tchr., counselor U.S. Army Edn. Centers, various locations in Europe, 1966-71; tchr. N. Branford (Conn.) High Sch., 1974-75; sec. to registrar U. Bridgeport, 1972-74, sec., adminstrv. asst. to asst. dean arts and scis., 1975-76, admissions counselor Div. Continuing Edn., 1976-77, instr. German, 1976-77, dir. grad. admissions, 1977-79; on-site coordinator, needs assessment specialist Post Coll., Waterbury, Conn., 1979—. Mem. Am. Assn. Collegiate Registrars and Admissions Officers, Am. Assn. Tchrs. German, Am. Personnel and Guidance Assn., AAUW. Home: 97 Wilson St Bridgeport CT 06605 Office: Post College 800 Country Club Rd Waterbury CT 06708

TORRES, IVAN LINCOLN, educator; b. Quito, Ecuador, May 18, 1948; s. Miguel A. and Blanca I. (Castro) T.; came to U.S., 1965; A.A., Northampton County Area Community Coll., 1970; B.S. cum laude, E. Stroudsburg State Coll., 1972; M.Ed., Kutztown State Coll., 1974; postgrad. Pa State U., Reading, 1974-76; doctoral candidate Nova U., 1978—; m. Elaine Ayers, May 10, 1969. Tchr., Pocono Mountain High Sch., Swiftwater, Pa., 1972-73; residence hall dir. Kutztown (Pa.) State Coll., 1973-74; asso. prof. Reading (Pa.) Area Community Coll., 1974—; gifted program coordinator Berks County Intermediate Unit #14, Reading, 1976—; counselor, cons., lectr. in field. Bd. dirs. Berks County Prison Soc., 1975—, Advances of Berks County, 1977; v.p. Reading-Berks Spanish Speaking Council, 1976-77; vol. trainer for Women in Crisis, 1976—, People Against Rape, 1975—; mem. edn. com. Am. Heart Assn., 1976, gen. adv. com. Reading Muhlenberg Vocat. Tech. Sch., 1976—; commr. Reading House Authority, 1978—. Mem. Pa. Sch. Counselors Assn. (conv. speaker 1978), Am. Personnel and Guidance Assn. (conv. speaker, 1978), Pa. Personnel and Guidance Assn. (conv. speaker 1978), Assn. Counselor Edn. and Supervision, Am. Coll. Personnel Assn., Assn. Humanistic Edn. and Devel., Pa. Assn. Two-Year Colls. (conv. speaker 1978), Pa. Assn. Study and Edn. of Mentally Gifted, Council Exceptional Children (conv. speaker 1977), Berks Area Counselors Assn. Office: Box 1706 Reading PA 19604

TORRES, LUIS ANTONIO, accountant; b. Ponce, P.R., Apr. 3, 1922; s. Juan and Dionisia (Zambrana) T.; came to U.S., 1960; student Catholic U. Puerto Rico, 1950-52, Pohs Inst., N.Y.C., 1967—, Baruch Coll., N.Y., 1973-74; B.B.A., Mercy Coll., 1978; m. Estela Caridad, July 15, 1970; children—Marlene, Hector Luis. Various positions in accounting, auditing, Puerto Rico, 1956-62; examiner Walter E. Heller Co. Inc., 1962-63; gen. auditor Rosenthal & Rosenthal Inc., N.Y.C., 1963-66; asst. to controller Puerto Rico Cement Corp., Ponce, 1966-67; auditor Internat. Ladies Garments Worker's Union, N.Y.C., 1967-68; with N.Y.C. Income Tax Bur., 1968-69; individual practice tax accounting, Jackson Heights, N.Y., 1969-71; sr. accountant, asst. comptroller Hunts Point (N.Y.) Multi-Service Center Inc., 1971—. Served with U.S. Army, 1943-46. Mem. Nat. Soc. Pub. Accountants, Am. Legion (past post comdr.). Clubs: Lions (pres. Pan Am. chpt. 1977-78, outstanding service award). Home: 37-37 Warren St Jackson Heights NY 11372

TORREY, WILLIAM ARTHUR, profl. hockey team exec.; b. Montreal, Que., Can., June 23, 1934, B.S., St. Lawrence U., 1957. Dir. pub. relations to bus. mgr. Pitts. Hornets Am. Hockey League team, 1960-68; exec. v.p. Calif. Golden Seals, 1968-72; gen. mgr. N.Y. Islanders (both Nat. Hockey League teams), 1972—. Address: care New York Islanders 1155 Conklin St Farmingdale NY 11735

TORRICELLI, THOMAS EDWARD, architect, civil engr.; b. N.Y.C., Apr. 27, 1923; s. Frank and Rose (Garafalo) T.; student Pratt Inst., 1942-44, 46-48, Columbia U., 1948-50; m. Helen Ciolfi, Nov. 8, 1947; children—Janet, Carol. With A.F. Gilbert architect, N.Y.C., 1946-47, Eggers & Higgins, architects, N.Y.C., 1947-51, Ira H. Davey, architect, Tenafly, N.J., 1951-53, asso., 1954-57; partner Davey & Torricelli, architects and engrs., Hackensack, N.J., 1957-65; individual practice architecture and engring., Hackensack, 1965—; prin. works include Long Meml. Sch., Saddle Brook Twp., N.J., 1961, Palm St. Elementary Sch., Washington Twp., N.J., 1962, Montvale Meml. Sch. Annex, N.J., 1962, Westwood High Sch., 1963, Montvale Fieldstone Sch., 1965, Little Ferry Middle Sch., 1968, Lodi High Sch., 1972, Hackensack City Hall Complex, 1974, Bergen County Animal Shelter, 1978. Boro engr. Lodi, N.J., 1962; mem. council, mem. planning bd. Borough of Woodcliff Lake, N.J. Served to 2d lt. C.E., U.S. Army, 1944-46. Registered profl. engr., N.J. Registered architect, N.J., N.Y., Conn., Pa., Fla. Mem. Am. Inst. Architects, N.J. Soc. Architects, Architects League No. N.J. (dir.), Nat. Council Archtl. Registration Bds., Soc. Mil. Engrs., Nat. Soc. Profl. Engrs. Home: 19 Winding Way Woodcliff Lake NJ 07680 Office: 215 Union St Hackensack NJ 07601

TORSNEY, PHILIP JOSEPH, allergist, immunologist; b. Orange, N.J., Apr. 6, 1932; s. Philip Joseph and Gretrude Madeline (O'Brien) T.; B.S., Georgetown U., 1953, M.D., 1957; m. Virginia Honora Kunkel, Nov. 20, 1954; children—Philip, Catherine, Colleen. Intern, U.S. Naval Hosp., Phila., 1957, resident, 1958-61; resident Temple U. Hosp., 1961-62; practice medicine specializing in allergy and immunology, Red Bank, N.J., 1967—; mem. staffs Med. Center, Long Branch, N.J., Riverview Hosp., Red Bank; clin. asst. prof. Hahnemann Med. Coll., Phila., 1971—. Served with USN, 1956-66. Diplomate Am. Bd. Internal Medicine, Am. Bd. Clin. Allergy Immunology. Fellow A.C.P., Am. Coll. Chest Physicians, Am. Acad. Allergy. Republican. Roman Catholic. Contbr. articles in field to med. jours. Home: 15 Holly Tree Ln Rumson NJ 07760 Office: 1 Branch Ave Red Bank NJ 07701

TOSE, LEONARD H., profl. football team exec.; b. Bridgeport, Pa.; s. Mike Tose; grad. U. Notre Dame, 1937. With Tose Trucking Co., Bridgeport, 1946—, now pres.; pres. K & S Canning Co., Bridgeport; pres., owner Phila. Eagles Nat. Football League team, 1969—. Donor Phila. Sch. System Varsity Football Program, 1971. Address: Philadelphia Eagles Veterans St Broad St and Patterson Ave Philadelphia PA 19148*

TOSELLO, MATTHEW, clergyman, missions dir., tchr., lectr.; b. Cuneo, Italy, Aug. 30, 1934; s. Stefano and Maddalena (Cerato) T.; came to U.S., 1962, naturalized, 1975; B.A. in Philosophy and Theology, Consolata, Torino, Italy, 1958; B.A. in English, Duquesne U., 1965, M.A. in English, 1966, Ph.D. in English, 1970; postgrad. Yale U., Princeton U., Columbia U. Ordained priest Roman Catholic Ch., 1962; tchr. English, Holy Apostles Coll., Cromwell, Conn., 1970-73; asso. prof. English, Hartford (Conn.) U., 1970-71, New Haven U., 1971-73; asso. faculty English, Quinnipiac Coll., North Haven, Conn., 1972, Paterson (N.J.) State Coll., 1973-74, U. Pitts., 1969; superior and mission promotion dir. Consolata Soc., Pitts., 1974—; dir. Makonde Art Mus., Pitts.; tour guide, Middle East, 1975, 76, 78. Mem. Modern Lang. Assn., Dante Soc. Am., Internat. Platform Assn., AAUP, NE Modern Lang. Assn., Sigma Tau Delta. Democrat. Roman Catholic. Contbr. articles in field to popular and scholarly publs. Home: 7110 Thomas Blvd Pittsburgh PA 15208

TOTH, ALFRED LUKACS, economist, educator; b. Shelton, Conn., Dec. 18, 1917; s. Andrew and Helen Ilona (Lukacs) T.; B.S., U.S. Mil. Acad., 1943; M.S., U. Pa., 1949, postgrad., 1964-68; postgrad. Columbia, 1950-51; grad. Command and Gen. Staff Coll., 1959; m. Marian Norma Davies, Apr. 21, 1947; children—Jerry Geza, Christopher Keats, Geoffrey Alfred, Richard Kingsley. Commd. 2d lt. U.S. Army, 1943, advanced through grades to lt. col., 1956; instr. math. U.S. Mil. Acad., 1949-52; gen. staff officer Central Army Group, Germany, 1952-54; comdr. spl. weapons unit Def. Atomic Support Agy., 1956-58; chief tng. Army Air Def. Center, 1959-60; comdr. 5th Missile Bn., 562d Arty. and NORAD air def. comdr., Shreveport, La., 1960-61; chief plans JUSMAG, Thailand, 1962-63; chief plans br. Research and Devel. Directorate, Army Materiel Command, 1964; ret., 1964; teaching fellow U. Pa. Wharton Sch., 1965-68; asst. prof. econs. Boston U., 1968-69; econ. cons. Mathematica, Princeton, 1968; asso. prof. PMC Colls., 1969-70. Bd. dirs., treas. Internat. Sch., Bangkok, Thailand, 1962-63. Decorated Silver Star medal, Bronze Star medal with V and oak leaf cluster, Purple Heart with oak leaf cluster. Recipient citations for pub. service Shreveport C. of C., Sec. Army, others, 1961; named Hon. citizen Minden, La., 1961. Mem. Am. Econ. Assn., Econometric Soc., Shreveport Jr. Astron. Soc. (hon. life). Episcopalian. Author: Economics of Vietnam, 1968. Home: 310 Chamounix Rd St Davids PA 19087

TOTH, MARIAN DAVIES, educator, author; b. Great Falls, Mont.; d. John Davies and Zetta (Allen) D.; B.A. magna cum laude, Eastern Coll., 1967; M.A., U. Pa., 1970, Ed.D., 1977; m. Alfred L. Toth, Apr. 21, 1947; children—Jerry Geza, Christopher Keats, Geoffrey Alfred, Richard Kingsley. Tchr., Internat. Sch., Bangkok, Thailand, 1961-64; tchr. English, Conestoga High Sch., Berwyn, Pa., 1968-72; prin. Juniata Valley High Sch., Alexandria, Pa., 1977-78; dir. lang. arts East Brunswick (N.J.) Schs., 1978—. Mem. gov.'s task force on career edn., State of Pa., 1973-74; bd. alumni trustees Eastern Coll., 1978—. Recipient Superior Teaching award Tredyffrin/Easttown Sch. Dist., 1970; Disting. Pub. award Theta Sigma Phi, 1973; named Honored Author, Kutztown State Coll.-Pa. Library Assn., 1975. Mem. Nat. Pen Women, Nat. Assn. Supervision and Curriculum Devel., Assn. Am. Secondary Sch. Adminstrs., Phi Delta Kappa, Phi Lambda Theta. Episcopalian. Author: Tales from Thailand, 1970; contbr. articles to profl. jours. Home: 310 Chamounix Rd Saint Davids PA 19087

TOTH, ROBERT CHARLES, journalist; b. Blakely, Pa., Dec. 24, 1928; s. John and Tillie (Szuch) T.; B.S. in Chem. Engring., Washington U., St. Louis, 1952; M.S. in Journalism, Columbia, 1955; postgrad. Harvard, 1960-61; m. Paula Goldberg, Apr. 12, 1954; children—Jessica, Jennifer, John. Started as engr. in Army Ordnance Dept., 1952-54; reporter Providence Jour., 1955-57; sci. reporter N.Y. Herald Tribune, 1957-62, N.Y. Times, 1962-63; mem. staff Los Angeles Times, 1963—, bur. chief, London, Eng., 1965-70, diplomatic corr., 1970-71. White House corr., 1972-74, bur. chief. Moscow, 1974-77. Served with USMC, 1946-48. Pulitzer Travelling scholar, 1955; Nieman fellow Harvard, 1960-61. Recipient George Polk award in Journalism, 1978. Home: 21 Primrose St Chevy Chase MD 20015 Office: Los Angeles Times 1700 Pennsylvania Ave NW Washington DC 20006

TOTTEN, FRANK NORMAN, JR., historian; b. Morrilton, Ark., Sept. 5, 1934; s. Frank Norman and Minnie Era (Bryant) T.; B.A., Hendrix Coll., 1957; M.Div., Boston U., 1959, M.A., 1969, Ph.D., 1977; m. Martha Ann Lach; children—Mark Alan, Julianne. Ordained minister Meth. Ch., 1958; pastor Newton (Mass.) Meth. Ch., 1962-66; overseas tour condr. Maupintour Assos., Lawrence, Kans., 1966; dir. admissions Boston U. Sch. Theology, 1966-69, lectr. history Boston U. Met. Coll., 1967-69; asst. prof. history Bentley Coll., Waltham, Mass., 1969-76, asso. prof., 1976—, chmn. history dept., 1974—; lectr. in field. Recipient Nat. Meth. Sem. award, 1958; Boston U. Sch. Theology Alumni fellow, 1959-60: Lilly grantee, 1960-61. Fellow Epigraphic Soc. Mem. Am. Hist. Assn., Am. Numis. Assn., Am. Numis. Soc., Archaeol. Inst. Am., Oriental Numis. Soc., New Eng. History Tchrs. Assn. (exec. com. 1972—, editorial bd. 1973—), Epigraphic Soc. (v.p. 1974—), Blue Key, Alpha Psi Omega, Alpha Chi. Editor: New Eng. Social Studies bull., 1978—. Contbr. articles profl. publs. anthropology, archaeology, history, linguistics, numismatics. Home: 16 Belmont St Newton MA 02158 Office: Bentley Coll Waltham MA 02154

TOUHILL, CHARLES JOSEPH, JR., environ. engr.; b. Newark, Aug. 27, 1938; s. Charles Joseph and Caroline Ann (Lesaius) T.; B.C.E., Rensselaer Poly. Inst., 1960, Ph.D., 1964; S.M., Mass. Inst. Tech., 1961; diploma U. Wash., 1970; m. Helen Elizabeth O'Malley, June 11, 1960; children—Gregory Joseph, Stephen Mark, Christopher Alan, Kathleen Elizabeth. Engr., Gen. Electric Co., Richland, Wash., 1964; research engr. Battelle Meml. Inst., Richland, 1965-66, mgr. water and wastewater research unit, 1966-68, mgr. water and land resources dept., 1968-71; v.p. Engring.-Sci. Inc., Washington, 1971-72; v.p. Envisors, Inc., Rockville, Md., 1972-73; sr. program mgr. EQSI, Rockville, 1973-74; chmn., chief exec. officer Morris Knowles Inc. environ. engring. cons., Pitts., 1974-75; v.p. Green Internat., Inc., Sewickley, Pa., 1975-77; pres. Touhill, Shuckrow & Assos., Inc., Pitts., 1977—. Adj. prof. U. Wash., 1965-71. Mem. Com. of 100 of Rensselaer Newman Found., 1970—. Recipient Caird prize Rensselaer Poly. Inst., 1960; USPHS fellow, 1961-64. Registered profl. engr., Pa., Washington, N.Y., Md., W.Va., Ohio. Diplomate Am. Environ. Engrs. Acad. (trustee 1971-77). Mem. Internat. Assn. on Water Pollution Research (alternate sr. mem. U.S. nat. com. 1970-72), ASCE, Am. Inst. Chem. Engrs., (chmn. environ. div. 1977), Am. Chem. Soc., Water Pollution Control Fedn., Am. Water Works Assn., Sigma Xi, Tau Beta Pi, Chi Epsilon. Roman Catholic. Author: (with F.A. Butrico, I.L. Whitman) Resource Management in Great Lakes Basin, 1971. Mem. editorial bd. Environ. Sci. and Tech., 1975-77. Contbr. articles to profl. jours. Patentee wastewater treatment. Home: 2206 Almanack Ct Pittsburgh PA 15237 Office: PO Box 11022 Pittsburgh PA 15237

TOUSSIE, MICHAEL ISAAC, constrn. co. exec.; b. Bklyn., Dec. 10, 1949; s. Isaac Samuel and Marie (Sasson) T.; B.B.A. cum laude (Bernard Baruch scholar), Coll. City N.Y., 1970. Staff accountant J.K. Lasser & Co. (C.P.A.'s), N.Y.C., 1970-71; sr. accountant Arthur Andersen & Co., N.Y.C., 1971-73, v.p. finance Toussie World Enterprises, Inc., N.Y.C., 1971—, v.p. accounting, dir. Toussie Enterprises, Inc., Medford, N.Y., 1975—; v.p. finance and accounting, dir. Levitt House, Inc., Medford, 1976-77; v.p. finance and accounting Droden-Drowitz, Inc., Medford, N.Y., 1976—; dir. Environ. Solutions, Inc., 1976-77. Mem. Council Concerned Youth, Bklyn., 1976—. Bernard M. Baruch scholar, 1976. Mem. Am. Inst. C.P.A.'s, N.Y. Soc. C.P.A.'s. Democrat. Jewish. Home and office: 2014 E 5th St Brooklyn NY 11223

TOUSSIE, SAMUEL ROOSEVELT, investment banker, builder; b. Bklyn., May 9, 1934; s. Isaac Samuel and Marie (Sasson) T.; grad. high sch.; m. Nancy Hanan, Dec. 26, 1966; children—Marie, Victoria, Isaac, Ralph, David. Sec., dir. Merry Mites, Hiline, Small Talk, N.Y.C., until 1966; pres. Toussie Devel. Co., Toussie Land Co., Toussie Enterprises, Inc., Toussie World Enterprises, Inc., Toussie Oil & Gas Co., Medford, N.Y., 1966—; pres., dir., chief exec. officer Environ. Solutions, Inc., Levitt House. Editor, Community Jour., 1950-60. Chmn. Heart Fund. Mem. Nat. Assn. Securities Dealers. Jewish. Clubs: Masons; Bklyn. Yacht; Jogging; Sports. Home: 2014 E 5th St Brooklyn NY 11223 Office: 500 Expressway Dr S PO Box 572 Medford NY 11763

TOVEY, JOSEPH, investment banker; b. Tel Aviv, Nov. 5, 1938; s. Samuel and Rachel (Weiman) T.; came to U.S., 1940, naturalized, 1947; B.S. summa cum laude, Bklyn. Coll., 1959; M.B.A., N.Y. U., 1961, Ph.D., 1969; m. Anita Beverly Losice, Feb. 20, 1961; children—David, Debra, Nissan Chaim, Seth Reuven, Shayna Nava. Staff accountant Machtiger, Green & Co., N.Y.C., 1959-60, Loeb & Troper, N.Y.C., 1960-61; tax researcher Lybrand, Ross Bros. & Montgomery, 1961-63; planning asso. Mobil Oil Corp., N.Y.C., 1963-67; asst. v.p. A.G. Becker & Co., N.Y.C., 1967-70; asso. Roth, Gerard & Co., N.Y.C., 1970-73; v.p. Faulkner, Dawkins & Sullivan, Inc., N.Y.C., 1973-76, Shields Model Roland Inc., N.Y.C., 1976-77; partner Tovey & Co., 1977—; pres. Joint Trading Ltd., 1977—. Mem. exec. bd. Agudath Israel Am., 1963-67. C.P.A., N.Y. Mem. Newcomen Soc. N.Am., Am. Finance Assn., Am. Inst. C.P.A.'s, N.Y. Soc. C.P.A.'s, N.Y. Soc. Security Analysts, Nat. Assn. Petroleum Investment Analysts, N.Y. U. Alumni Assn. Jewish. Club: N.Y. U. (N.Y.C.). Author: (with H.C. Smith) Federal Tax Treatment of Bad Debts and Worthless Securities, 1964; asso. editor Tax Letter, 1961-66; contbr. articles to profl. jours. Home: 1170 E 19th St Brooklyn NY 11230 Office: 20 Exchange Pl New York City NY 10005

TOWER, CATHERINE, hosp. adminstr.; b. Quincy, Mass., Oct. 16, 1924; d. Orlie Leonard and Hilda Irene (MacKinnon) Anderson; M.S. in Nursing Adminstr., Boston U., 1964; diploma Worcester City Hosp., 1947; B.S.N., Boston Coll., 1960; m. John Tower, Aug. 24, 1947; children—Katheryn Elizabeth, Mark Steven. Staff nurse Worcester (Mass.) City Hosp., 1948-49; supr., 1954-56; staff nurse Quincy (Mass.) City Hosp., 1949-50; staff nurse Worcester Hahnemann Hosp., 1957-58, asst. instr. Worcester Hahnemann Hosp. Sch. Nursing, 1958-60, instr., 1960-61, dir. nursing service, 1961—, project dir. family nurse practitioner program, 1975-78; mem., vice chmn. Bd. Registration in Nursing Mass., 1977—. Mem. Am., Mass. (pres. 1973-75) nurses assns., Nat., Mass. leagues nursing, Am. Soc. Nursing Service Adminstrs., Sigma Theta Tau. Congregationalist. Home: 7 Dartmoor Dr Shrewsbury MA 01545 Office: 281 Lincoln St Worcester MA 01605

TOWER, DONALD BAYLEY, physician, govt. ofcl.; b. Orange, N.J., Dec. 11, 1919; s. Walter Sheldon and Edith Florence (Jones) T.; A.B., Harvard U., 1941, M.D., 1944; M.Sc., McGill U., Montreal, 1948, Ph.D., 1951; m. Arline Belle Croft, Aug. 5, 1947; 1 dau., Deborah Alden Tower Fretwell. Intern in surgery U. Minn. Hosp., Mpls., 1944-45; research fellow neurochemistry Montreal Neurol. Inst., 1947-48, 49-51, asst. resident in neurosurgery, 1948-49, asso. neurochemist, 1951-53; instr., then asst. prof. exptl. neurology McGill U. Med. Sch., 1951-53; joined USPHS, 1953, asst. surgeon gen., 1975; chief sect. clin. neurochemistry Nat. Inst. Neurol. Diseases and Stroke, NIH, HEW, Bethesda, Md., 1953-61, chief lab. neurochemistry, 1961-74, dir. Nat. Inst. Neurol. and Communicative Disorders and Stroke, 1974—; clin. asso. prof. neurology Georgetown U. Med. Sch., 1953—; chmn. U.S. neurochemistry del. to USSR, 1969; temp. adviser neuroscis. WHO, 1976—. Recipient Distinguished Service medal USPHS, 1977; John and Mary R. Markle scholar acad. medicine, 1951-53. Mem. Am. Acad. Neurology, AAAS, Am. Neurol. Assn., Internat., Am. socs. neurochemistry, Am. Soc. Biol. Chemists, Canadian Neurol. Soc., Canadian Physiol. Soc., Internat. Brain Research Orgn., Soc. Neuroscis., Washington Acad. Medicine. Author: Neurochemistry of Epilepsy, 1960; also numerous research papers. Editor: The Nervous System, 3 vols., 1975; chief editor Jour. Neurochemistry, 1968-73. Office: NIH Bldg 31 Room 8A52 Nat Inst Neurol and Communicative Disorders and Stroke Bethesda MD 20205

TOWNE, WILLIAM CHESTER, educator; b. Boston, May 20, 1943; s. Edward Stickney and Veronica Kathleen (Dwyer) T.; B.S., State Coll. Bridgewater, Mass., 1965, M.Ed., 1973. Tchr. educable retarded Sippican Sch., Marion, Mass., 1965-66; tchr. trainable retarded Las Vegas (Nev.) Schs., 1966-70, Everett A. McDonald Elementary Sch., Warminster, Pa., 1970-74; ednl. adviser trainable mentally retarded programs Montgomery County Intermediate Unit 3, Norristown, Pa., 1974-75; supr. spl. edn. Intermediate Unit 23, 1974-77, supr. Western Montgomery County Sch., 1975-76; program supr. Shore Collaborative, Medford, Mass., 1977—. Cons. Head Start Program, Las Vegas, 1969; utilization cons. Instructional TV, Las Vegas, 1970; co-chmn. Joint Conf. on Mental Retardation, 1970; project dir. Plymouth Meeting Mall Demonstration Class, 1974. Instl. rep. Boulder Dam Area council Boy Scouts Am., 1967-70; leader Cub Scouts, 1968-69. Bd. dirs. Margaret Friedenthal Found. Recipient Outstanding Young Educator award, 1968; named Outstanding Young Man, 1970. Fellow Internat. Inst. Community Services; mem. Am. Assn. on Mental Deficiency, Council for Exceptional Children (pres. Nev. chpt. 406 1970, pres. Pa. chpt. 348 1972, gov. 1973), Internat. Inst. for Sci. Study Mental Deficiency, Internat. Platform Assn., Royal Health Soc., Kappa Delta Pi. Co-producer: Public School Activities for the Mentally Retarded, 1968. Home: 5 Putnam St Charlestown MA 02129 Office: Shore Collaborative 10 Hall Ave Medford MA 02155

TOWNSEND, PAUL ROBERT, mech. engr.; b. Brockton, Mass., Mar. 20, 1946; s. William Everett and Eleanor Dorothy (Borgeson) T., Jr.; B.S., Mech. Engring., Northeastern U., 1969; M.S. in Engring., Catholic U. Am., 1971; M.A.T., Mass. Inst. Tech., 1974; m. Francine Fazio, June 2, 1968; children—Frank William, John David. Project engr. Nat. Bur. Standards, Washington, 1969-71; project engr. Codman & Shurtleff, Randoloph, Mass., 1975-76, mgr. implant design and materials engring., 1976-77, dir. engring., 1977—. Recipient Spl. Commendation for Superior Performance, Nat. Bur. Standards, 1970. Mem. Ortho. Research Soc., Sigma Xi, Pi Tau Sigma. Roman Catholic. Contbr. articles to profl. jours. Home: 169 Beach Ave Hull MA 02045 Office: Randolph Indsl Pk Randolph MA 02368

TOWNSEND, PAULINE MAE, nursing adminstr.; b. Needham, Mass., June 14, 1925; d. Irving Raymond and Marion Louise (Rice) Wallis; R.N., Faulkner Hosp., 1946; postgrad. Somerset County Coll.; m. Donald Howland Townsend, Oct. 6, 1945; children—Glenn, Gary, Wendy, Paul. Critical care nurse No. Westchester Hosp., Mt. Kisco, N.Y., 1967; vol. nurse St. Mary's Hosp., Paddington, London, Eng., 1968-73; critical care nurse Somerset Hosp., Somerville, N.J., 1973-75, dir. central service, 1975—; adv. bd. nursing Somerset County Tech. Inst. Bd. dirs. Somerset County Heart Assn., 1976; pres. United Methodist Women Soc., Centerville, N.J., 1975. Mem. Am. Soc. Hosp. Central Service Personnel, Am. Nurses Assn. Republican. Organizer first registered central service technician course Votech Inst., 1975. Home: 4 Dreahook Rd Somerville NJ 08876 Office: Rehill Ave Somerville NJ 08876

TOWNSEND, RAYMOND LAWRENCE, ednl. adminstr.; b. St. Joseph, Mo., Oct. 3, 1924; s. Ray Lawrence and Elta May (Scott) T.; student Goldy-Beacon Jr. Coll., 1942-43, Coll. South Jersey, 1946-48; B.A., U. Del., 1951, M.A., 1957; postgrad. Temple U., 1962-67; m. Helen Emily West Jefferson, June 20, 1953; children—W. Jefferson, David L., Ruth M., John R. Personnel mgr. Ludlow Corp., Wilmington, Del., 1948-51; tchr., chmn. social studies, curriculum coordinator De La Warr Sch. Dist., 1951-66, dir. adminstrv. services, 1966—; cons. Del. Ednl. TV Network, 1961-62. Served with AUS, 1943-46. Mem. Internat. Assn. Sch. Bus. Ofcls., Am., Del. assns. sch. adminstrs., Res. Officers Assn., VFW. Republican. Methodist. Clubs: Masons. Home: 610 Duncan Rd Wilmington DE 19809 Office: De La Warr Sch Dist New Castle DE 19720

TOWNSLEY, LOUIS FRANK, educator; b. Cedarville, Ohio, Sept. 28, 1934; s. Cassius Marcellus and Lillian Margaret (Paullin) T.; B.A., U. Fla., 1959, M.A., 1961; postgrad. U. Vienna, 1959-60; Ph.D., U. Md., 1972. Prof. German and classical langs. Gallaudet Coll., Washington, 1962—, prof., 1975—, chmn. dept., 1966—. Served with U.S. Army, 1954-57. Fulbright scholar, 1959-60. Mem. Modern Lang. Assn., Am. Assn. Tchrs. German, AAUP (chpt. pres. 1974-75), Alliance Francaise. Democrat. Roman Catholic. Home: 2604 Finley St Wheaton MD 20902 Office: Gallaudet Coll Washington DC 20002

TOYE, CLIVE ROY, profl. soccer exec.; b. Plymouth, Eng., Nov. 23, 1932; s. Thomas Roy and Irene Phyllis (Turner) T.; came to U.S., 1967, naturalized, 1976; Joint Certificate, Oxford and Cambridge, 1949; m. Christine Venloe DeLaine Bussell, Nov. 3, 1956; children—Gaynor Lee, Robert Alexander Grant. Sports writer Express and Echo, Exeter, Eng., 1953-57, Birmingham (Eng.) Mail, 1957-60; chief soccer writer London Daily Express, 1960-67; corr. BBC, 1955-67; v.p., gen. mgr. Balt. Bays, N.Am. Soccer League, 1967-68; dir. adminstrn. and info. N.Am. Soccer League, N.Y.C., 1969-70, mem. exec. com., 1971—, competition com., 1977—; v.p., gen. mgr. N.Y. Cosmos, 1971-75, pres., 1975-77; pres., part owner Chgo. Sting, 1977—. Founder Exeter Festival of Sport, 1953; mem. council U.S. Soccer Fedn., 1969—. Served with Royal Corps of Signals, 1951-53; Korea. Named Exec. of Yr., N.Am. Soccer League, 1967. Mem. Sports Writers Assn., Association de Presse Sportive. Mem. Ch. of Eng. Clubs: Town (Scarsdale, N.Y.); Larchmont (N.Y.) Yacht. Author: Soccer, 1967; Playing Soccer the Professional Way 1973. Office: 333 N Michigan Ave Chicago IL 60601

TRAA, RICHARD LOUIS, restaurant co. exec.; b. Pitts., June 8, 1942; d. Louis Arthur and Ruth Christine (Kirschner) T.; B.A., Wilmington Coll., 1965; M.B.A., Miami U. (Ohio), 1966; m. Ruth Melinna Dildilian, Aug. 27, 1966; children—Andrew Richard, Matthew Ara. Instr. econ. and bus. Wilmington (Ohio) Coll., 1966-68; pres. Traa Corp., Pleasantville, N.J., 1976—; dir. Fiber Glass Industries, Inc., Amsterdam, N.Y., 1976—. Mgmt. adv. council Wilmington Coll., 1978—; bd. govs. Shore Meml. Hosp., Somers Point, N.J., 1975—, v.p., 1978-79; councilman City of Linwood (N.J.), 1976; mem. Linwood Planning Bd., 1977—, pres., 1977; bd. dirs. Linwood Nursery Sch., 1973—, pres., 1978—; bd. dirs. Children's Oncology Services, Inc. of Phila., 1975—, pres., 1977-78, mem. nat. adv. bd., 1977—. Recipient Nat. Found. March of Dimes Service award, 1970; Phila. Eagles Touchdown award against Leukemia, 1976; Am. Cancer Soc. Service award, 1977; Wond Sports award, 1977; Wall St. Jour. Student Achievement award, 1965. Mem. Am. Mgmt. Assn., Restaurant Bus. Adv. Panel. Club: Atlantic City Country. Home: 214 Morris Ave Linwood NJ 08221 Office: 776 Black Horse Pike Suite 3 Pleasantville NJ 08232

TRACEY, EDWARD JOHN, physician, surgeon; b. Norwalk, Conn., July 26, 1931; s. Edward John and Clara (Hammond) T.; B.A., Yale U., 1954; M.D., N.Y. Med. Coll., N.Y.C., 1958; m. Ann Marie Schenk, Sept. 7, 1957; children—Sharon, Scott. Intern, Bellevue Hosp., N.Y.C.; resident in surgery N.Y. U.-Bellevue Med. Center, N.Y.C., 1958-63; attending surgeon Norwalk Hosp., 1965—, asst. dir. dept. surgery, 1975—, trustee, 1972; surgeon courtesy staff St. Joseph's Hosp., Stamford, Conn., 1978—; dir. Mchts. Bank & Trust Co., Norwalk, 1975—. Served to lt. comdr. USNR, 1963-65. Diplomate Am. Bd. Surgery. Mem. ACS, AMA, Conn., Fairfield County, Norwalk (pres. 1976-77) med. socs. Clubs: Catholic (pres. 1974-75), Shore and Country (Norwalk). Home: Old Saugatuck Rd East Norwalk CT 06855 Office: 124 East Ave Norwalk CT 06851

TRACEY, JAMES ALLISON, JR., adminstrv. tool room programmer; b. Balt., Mar. 30, 1924; s. James Allison and Helen Eugina (Cox) T.; student pub. schs., Towson, Md.; m. Ethel Viola Almony, July 31, 1948; 1 dau., Joan Ethel. Tool designer Westinghouse Air Arm Div., 1953-54; with Black and Decker Mfg. Co., Hampstead, Md., 1969—, unit tool estimator, 1959-68, group leader tool design, 1968-69, programmer tool room, 1969—. Registered profl. engr., Calif. Mem. Soc. Mfg. Engrs. (sr., certified). Republican. Home: 32 Northwood Dr Timonium MD 21093 Office: 626 Hanover Pike Hampstead MD 21074

TRACHTENBERG, ALAN, educator; b. Phila., Mar. 22, 1932; s. Isadore and Norma Trachtenberg; A.B. in English, Temple U., Phila., 1954; M.A., U. Conn., 1956; Ph.D. in Am. Studies, U. Minn., 1962; m. Betty Glassman, Dec. 21, 1952; children—Zev, Elissa, Julia. Instr., U. Minn., 1956-61; mem. faculty Pa. State U., 1961-69, prof. English, 1969; vis. prof. English and Am. studies Yale U., 1969-70, mem. faculty, 1970—, prof., 1972—, dir. grad. studies Am. studies, 1970-72, 74-75, chmn. Am. studies, 1971-73. Fellow Am. Council Learned Socs., 1968-69, Center Advanced Study Behavioral Scis., 1968-69. Mem. Am. Studies Assn., Modern Lang. Assn. Author: Brooklyn Bridge: Fact and Symbol, 1965; Democratic Vistas, 1986-1880, 1970; The City: American Experience, 1972; Memoirs of Waldo Frank, 1973; Critics of Culture, 1976. Home: 972 Prospect St Hamden CT 06511 Office: American Studies Program Yale Univ New Haven CT 06520

TRACHTENBERG, MARVIN LAWRENCE, educator, art historian; b. Tulsa, June 6, 1939; s. William and Leona (Fox) T.; B.A., Yale U., 1961; M.A., N.Y. U., 1963, Ph.D., 1967; m. Heidi Feldmeier, Nov. 10, 1961; children—Malcolm Blake, Gordon Charles. Asst. prof. fine arts Inst. Fine Arts, N.Y. U., 1967-69, asso. prof., 1969-76, prof., 1976—, mem. humanities council, 1976—; mem. vis. com. dept. fine arts Harvard U., 1976. Nat. Endowment for Humanities fellow, Florence, Italy, 1974-75; I. Tatti fellow Harvard U. Center for Renaissance Studies in Florence, 1974-76; Kress Found. postdoctoral fellow, Italy, France and Germany, 1970; Fulbright fellow U. Florence, 1964-66; Bernard Berenson fellow N.Y. U., 1966-67. Mem. Coll. Art Assn., Soc. Archtl. Historians. Club: Bellport Yacht. Author: The Campanile of Florence Cathedral - Giotto's Tower, 1971 (Hitchcock prize Soc. Archtl. Historians 1973); The Statue of Liberty, 1976. Office: Inst of Fine Arts 1 E 78th St New York City NY 10021

TRACHTENBERG, STEPHEN JOEL, univ. pres.; b. Bklyn., Dec. 14, 1937; s. Oscar and Shoshana (Weinstock) T.; B.A., Columbia U., 1959; J.D., Yale, 1962; M.Pub. Adminstrn., Harvard U., 1966; m. Francine Zorn, June 24, 1971; children—Adam Maccabee, Ben-Lev. Admitted to N.Y. State bar, 1964, U.S. Supreme Ct. bar, 1967; atty. AEC, N.Y.C., 1962-65; aide to Congressman Brademas of Ind., Washington, 1965; spl. asst. U.S. edn. commr. U.S. Office Edn., HEW, Washington, also sec. White House Edn. Task Force, 1966-68; Winston Churchill fellow, Eng., 1968-69; asso. prof. polit. sci. Boston U., 1969-77, asso. dean, 1969-70, dean, 1970-74, asso. v.p., 1974-76, v.p. acad. services, 1976-77; faculty asso. Harvard Grad. Sch. Edn., 1973—; cons. Ford and Danforth founds., 1973—; dir. Mass. Ednl. Seminar, 1974-77, pres., prof. law U. Hartford (Conn.), 1977—. Elector Hartford Atheneum, 1977—; corporator Hartford Hosp., Mt. Sinai Hosp., 1977—; mem. econ. adv. bd. Conn. Bank & Trust Co.; commr. B'nai B'rith Hillel, 1975—; bd. dirs. Am. Jewish Com., 1974—, Hartford Process, 1978—. Recipient Martin Luther King, Jr. Center award for service to minority youth, 1972; N.Y.C. Rexford Urban Govt. award, 1955; New Haven Municipal Legal Aid citation, 1961; named One of 10 Outstanding Young People, Boston C. of C., 1970; Harvard Adminstrn. fellow, 1965-66; Wilton Park fellow, 1967-68, Morse Coll. fellow Yale U., 1977. Mem. Am. Bar Assn., Am. Conf. Acad. Deans, Soc. Med. Jurisprudence, English Speaking Union, AAUP, Am. Assn. Higher Edn., Am. Soc. Pub. Adminstrn., Phi Beta Kappa (One of 100 Young Leaders of Acad. 1978). Clubs: University, Tumblebrook, Harvard (N.Y.C.); Cosmos. Contbr. articles to newspapers, mags. and profl. jours. Home: 85 Bloomfield Ave Hartford CT 06105 Office: U Hartford West Hartford CT 06117

TRACY, ALLEN WAYNE, mfg. co. exec.; b. Windsor, Vt., July 25, 1943; s. J. Wayne and Helen (Bernard) T.; B.A., U. Vt., 1965; M.B.A. cum laude, Boston U., 1974; m. Karla Noelte, Dec. 14, 1968; 1 dau., Tania. Retail salesman Exxon Corp., Boston, 1965-72; mfg. mgr. Leonard Silver Mfg. Co., Inc., Boston, 1974-78; pres. OESM Corp., N.Y.C., 1978—. Mem. Bd. Selectmen, Town of Ashland, 1977—; chmn. Ashland Study Town Govt. Com., 1976-77. Served with U.S. Army, 1965-68. Mem. Mass. Slectmans Assn., Middlesex County Selectmans Assn., Beta Gamma Sigma. Office: 144 Addison St Boston MA 02128

TRACY, CHARLES HAYDEN, physician; b. Schenectady, Sept. 2, 1924; s. Charles Hayden and Harriet (MacKallor) T.; B.S., Union Coll., 1948; M.D., Albany Med. Coll., 1952; m. Sigrid Margaret Johanson, Apr. 12, 1958; children—Adrienne Margaret, Charles Hayden III, David Leander, Peter Andrew, Kimberly Harriet, Jennifer Lynn. Intern Norwalk (Conn.) Hosp., 1952-53; resident Cornell U. Infirmary and Clinic, Ithaca, N.Y., 1953-54; practice medicine, Dundee, N.Y., 1954-59; became asst. med. dir. Eaton Labs. Div., Norwich (N.Y.) Pharmacal Co., 1959, then was med. dir. Norwich Products div.; med. dir. Batten, Barton, Durstine & Osborn, Inc., N.Y.C., 1969-71; med. dir. Sauter Labs., Nutley, N.J., 1971-74, Vick Divs. Research & Devel., Mt. Vernon, N.Y., 1974; med. dir. Norcliff Thayer Inc., 1974—; pub. Cider Mill Press, Wilton, Conn. Served as sgt. M.C., AUS, 1943-46. Diplomate Nat. Bd. Med. Examiners. Mem. A.M.A., Am. Med. Writers Assn., Kappa Sigma. Republican. Presbyn. Author various articles pub. in profl. jours. Home: 77 Piper's Hill Rd Wilton CT 06897 Office: Norcliff Thayer Inc 1 Scarsdale Rd Tuckahoe NY 10707

TRAENKNER, FREDERICK OSWALD, aluminum co. exec.; b. Natrona, Pa., Oct. 18, 1917; s. Henry John and Helen Louise (Schlicker) T.; B.S., Pa. State U., 1941; m. Helena Cornelia Glink, Nov. 15, 1940; children—Linda Rae Traenkner Atkinson, Alan Ray, Patricia Ann Traenkner Paloncy. With Aluminum Co. Am., 1941-69, primary products metallurgist, 1965-69; tech. dir. Nat. Aluminum Co., Pitts., 1969—. Active Boy Scouts Am., 1955-64. Mem. Am. Soc. for Metals, Aluminum Assn., Am. Inst. Mining, Metall. and Petroleum Engrs., Am. Soc. for Testing Materials. Republican. Patentee liquid top method of casting, homogenizing aluminum alloy billets. Home: 109 Laurelwood Dr Pittsburgh PA 15237 Office: 2800 Grant Bldg Pittsburgh PA 15219

TRAFAS, CLAUDE JAN, hosp. ofcl.; b. Poznan, Poland, June 24, 1923; s. Jan and Agnes (Czaja) T.; came to U.S., 1950, naturalized, 1954; B.S., Kent State U., 1962; postgrad. Ohio State U., 1964-66; m. Marcella E. Sulenski, July 24, 1954; 1 dau., Cynthia V. Tech. engr. Hoover Co., N. Canton, Ohio, 1956-61; purchasing agt. Ohio State U., Columbus, 1962-66; mgr. purchases Hershey (Pa.) Med. Center, 1966-69; dir. purchases Wilmington (Del.) Med. Center, 1969—. Fellow Am. Acad. Med. Adminstr.; mem. Nat., Del. assns. purchasing mgmt. Home: 523 Faraday Rd Hockessin DE 19707 Office: Wilmington Medical Center PO Box 2653 Wilmington DE 19805

TRAFFORD, JOHN THOMAS, developing, real estate, building cos. exec.; b. Providence, Dec. 13, 1942; s. Joseph Henry and Marie G. (Brown) T.; student Bryant Coll., 1966-67, U. R.I., 1967-70; m. Carol A. Perri, Dec. 26, 1966. Ins. underwriter Home Ins. Co., Providence, 1966-70; underwriter Providence Washington Ins. Co., Providence, 1970-71; salesman Morgan Battey Realtors, North Kingston (R.I.), 1971-72; pres. Trafford, Inc., Realtors, Builders, Coventry, R.I. 1973—, John T. Trafford Ltd. Homebuilders, Inc. Del., Democratic Conv., R.I., 1974. Served USNR, 1960-62, with U.S. Army, 1962-65. Mem. Kent County (R.I.) Bd. Realtors, Nat. Assn. Realtors, R.I. Builders Assn. (legis. com.), R.I. Polit. Action Com., Coventry C. of C. Mem. Christian Ch. Clubs: Shriner's, Masons, Warwick (R.I.) Elks. Home: 18 Stonegate Dr Coventry RI 02816 Office: 884 Tiogue Ave Coventry RI 02816

TRAGER, BERNARD HAROLD, lawyer; b. New Haven, July 18, 1906; s. Harry and Ida (Ruttenberg) T.; LL.B., N.Y. U., 1928; m. Mina Rubenstein, Aug. 25, 1929; children—Roberta E. Trager Cohen, Philip S. Admitted to Conn. bar, 1929; sr. partner firm Trager & Trager, 1965—. Trustee People's Savs. Bank. Chmn., Conn. Bd. Pardons, 1959-73; chmn. Bridgeport Mayor's Commn. on Human Rights, 1958-62, Nat. Community Relations Adv. Council, 1953-57; pres. Conn. Conf. Social Work, 1948-49; v.p. Am. Jewish Congress, 1958-60; mem. Nat. Exec. Council United Synagogue Am. 1957-59; mem. Bridgeport Fin. Adv. Commn. 1966-75. Dir. Council Jewish Fdns. and Welfare Funds, 1954-61, United Hias Service, 1956-58; trustee Nat. Health & Welfare Retirement Assn., 1955-68, U. Bridgeport, 1973—, Bridgeport Area Found., Inc.; bd. dirs. Bridgeport Hosp. Mem. Am. (mem. Ho. of Dels. 1964-66), Conn. (pres. 1964-65), Bridgeport (pres. 1959-61) bar assns., N.Y. U. Law Alumni Assn. (bd. dirs. 1958-62). Clubs: Algonquin (pres. 1978-79), Birchwood Country, N.Y. U., Nat. Lawyers. Home: 25 Cartright St Bridgeport CT 06604 Office: 1305 Post Rd Fairfield CT 06430

TRAGER, LAWRENCE, accountant; b. N.Y.C., Aug. 11, 1929; s. Harry and Anna (Freundlich) T.; B.B.A., Coll. City N.Y., 1950; M.B.A., N.Y. U., 1960; m. Jacqueline Silverman, June 25, 1955; children—Paul, Peter. Pres. Trager Glass & Co., C.P.A.'s, N.Y.C. Served with AUS, 1951-53. C.P.A., N.Y. Mem. Am. Inst. C.P.A.'s, N.Y. State Soc. C.P.A.'s, N.Y.C. Wine and Food Soc. (treas., dir.), Confrerie de la Chaine des Rotisseurs, Les Amis Du Vin, Jewish War Vets. Mason. Office: 515 Madison Ave New York City NY 10022

TRAGER, NEIL JAY, food co. exec.; b. Bklyn., Jan. 8, 1939; s. David and Elizabeth (Lerner) T.; B.S. in Food Tech., Del. Valley Coll. Sci. and Agr., 1960; m. Patricia Palmer, Apr. 3, 1976; 1 son, Adam Scott. Food technologist King Cola Corp., Newark, 1960-61; with Modern Maid Food Products Inc., Garden City, N.Y., 1961—, corp. dir. research, devel. and quality control, 1968-76, dir. labs., 1976—. Mem. Am. Chem. Soc., Inst. Food Technologists, Am. Assn. Cereal Chemists, Del. Valley Alumni Assn., Am. Numis. Assn. Home: 1866 Jeffrey Ct Wantagh NY 11793 Office: 200 Garden City Plaza Garden City NY 11530

TRAIN, ARTHUR RICHARD, investment co. exec.; b. N.Y.C., May 4, 1936; s. Irwin Paul and Belle T.; student Bklyn. Coll., 1957, Adelphi Acad., 1953; m. Sandra Joy Klarfeld, Apr. 21, 1963; children—Valerie, Lynn. With Shearson Hammill, Inc., N.Y.C., 1964—, sr. portfolio mgr., 1966—; with Shields, Model, Roland Inc., N.Y.C., 1971—, v.p. investment mgmt.; pres., chief investment officer Constellation Mgmt. Inc., N.Y.C., 1978—. Active Nassau County Police Boys' Club. Mem. N.Y. Soc. Security Analysts (certified sr. security analyst), N.Y. State Sheriffs Assn. (hon.), Fin. Analysts Fedn., Nat. Free Lance Photographers Assn., U.S. Chess Fedn., N.Y. Vet. Police Assn. (hon.). Office: Constellation Mgmt Inc 61 Broadway New York City NY 10006

TRAIN, JOHN, investment counselor; b. N.Y.C., May 25, 1928; s. Arthur Cheney and Helen (Coster) T.; B.A., Harvard U., 1950, M.A., 1951; postgrad. Sorbonne (France), 1951-52; m. Maria Teresa Cini di Pianzano, 1961 (div. 1976); children—Helen, Nina, Lisa; m. 2d, Frances Cheston, July 23, 1977. Founder, mng. editor Paris Review, 1952-54; pres. Train, Smith Counsel, and predecessor firms, N.Y.C., 1959—; columnist Forbes mag., 1977—; pres. Chateau Malcasse, Lamarque-Margaux, Bordeaux, France, 1970—; dir. Adela Investing Co., Luxembourg. Bd. dirs. Pine St. Fund, N.Y.C.; chmn. Italian Emergency Relief Com., 1976-77; trustee Harvard Lampoon, Cambridge, Mass., 1974—. Served with U.S. Army, 1954-56. Recipient Commendatore, Ordine del Merito Della Repubblica (Italy), 1977; Commendatore, Ordine Della Solidarieta (Italy), 1968; Chevalier, Ordre Franco-Outremerien, France, 1963. Clubs: Century, Racquet and Tennis, Travellers, St. Nicholas Soc., Order of Colonial Lords of Manors, The Pilgrims. Author: Dance of the Money Bees, 1973; Remarkable Names, 1977; Remarkable Occurrences, 1978; contbr. articles to profl. jours. Office: 345 Park Ave New York City NY 10022

TRAINA, ALBERT SALVATORE, pub. co. exec.; b. Bklyn., Apr. 30, 1927; s. Salvatore and Guilia (LeBarbara) T.; B.S. (N.Y. State War Service scholar), Seton Hall U., 1950; postgrad. Columbia 1950-51; M.B.A., N.Y. U., 1954; m. Vail Devereux, June 22, 1957; children—Caroline Vail, Robert Brooks. Circulation promotion advt. space salesman Fairchild Publs., N.Y.C., 1951-53; eastern advt. mgr. Modern Bride mag., Ziff Davis, N.Y.C., 1953-58; adv. mgr. Bride and

Home mag. Hearst Mags., N.Y.C., 1958-60, pub., 1960-64; pub. Sports Afield mag., N.Y.C., 1964-65, Town and Country mag., N.Y.C., 1966-67, Harpers Bazaar mag., N.Y.C., 1967-70; pres., pub. Bartell Media Corp., N.Y.C., 1970-74; pres. Ziff-Davis Mag. Network, 1974—; corp. v.p. Ziff-Davis Pub. Co., 1975—. Active United Community Fund, Scarsdale, N.Y. Served with USNR, 1945-46. 1947. Mem. N.Y. U. Grad. Sch. Bus. Adminstrn. Alumni Assn. (dir.), N.Y. U. Alumni Fedn. (communications com. 1970—). Clubs: Fox Meadow Tennis (Scarsdale); Shenorock Shore (Rye, N.Y.); Union League (N.Y.C.). Home: 2 Taunton Rd Scarsdale NY 10583 Office: 205 E 42d St New York City NY 10017

TRAMAGLINI, SALVATORE LAWRENCE, JR., cable and wire mfg. co. exec.; b. Ossining, N.Y., Dec. 4, 1941; s. Salvatore Lawrence and Barbara Ann (Pekic) T.; B.B.A., Pace U., 1972, M.B.A., 1978; 1 dau., Kimberly Ann. Lead operator IBM Corp., Yorktown, N.Y., 1965-69; ops. mgr., programmer Technicon Corp., Tarrytown, N.Y., 1969-72; mgr. data processing ops. Empire Nat. Bank, Newburgh, N.Y., 1972-74; mgr. info. systems dept. Phelps Dodge Cable & Wire Co., Yonkers, N.Y., 1974—. Served with USNR, 1962-64. Mem. Data Processing Mgmt. Assn., Am. Prodn. and Inventory Control Soc. Home: 3004 Ferncrest Dr Yorktown NY 10598 Office: PO Box 391 Yonkers NY 10702

TRANKIEM, KHIET, chemist; b. Hue, Vietnam, Jan. 15, 1937; s. Hai and Dao (Tranthi) T.; came to U.S., 1963, naturalized, 1975; B.S. (Japanese Govt. grantee 1958-63), Tokyo Inst. Agr. and Tech., 1963; M.S. (Thanh Hoa Co. grantee 1963-65), Lowell Tech. Inst., 1965; m. Phu-Loc Ho-Thi, Aug. 20, 1966; children—Marguerite P.A., Christine T.A. Research chemist E.I. DuPont de Nemours & Co., Inc., Wilmington, Del., 1966-76, tech. coordinator, 1976-78, product mgr., 1978—. Pres., Vietnamese Students Group, New Eng., 1965, Vietnamese Cath. Students Assn. in Am., 1967. Republican. Roman Catholic. Home: 963 Sara Dr Springfield PA 19064 Office: Rm B1236 Wilmington DE 19898

TRANTHAM, WALTER EARL, JR., transp. equipment mfg. exec.; b. Cuero, Tex., July 4, 1920; s. Walter Earl and Mabel (Duffey) T.; student Rice Inst., 1937-39; B.A.E., Tex. A. and M. U., 1942; student Am. U., 1943-44; Sc.D., Hamilton U., 1974; m. Eleanor MacDougall, Oct. 30, 1943; children—Walter Earl, Duffey Douglass. Dir. ops. Microwave Tube div. Hughes Aircraft Co., Los Angeles, 1959-61; v.p., dir. mktg. Radcom group Litton Industries, Silver Spring, Md., 1961-63; dir. S.E. ops. U.S. Def. group ITT, Washington, 1963-66; pres., chief exec. officer Tasker Industries, Van Nuys, Calif., 1966-68; v.p., dir. advanced programs Canoga Electronics Corp., 1968-70; mgr. transp. control systems Comml. Electronics div. Sylvania Electric Products, Inc., subs. Gen. Telephone & Electronics, Inc., Waltham, Mass., 1970-71; mgr. transp. control systems GTE Info. Systems, Bedford, Mass., 1971-72; dir. govt. ops. Servo Corp. Am., Hicksville, N.Y., 1972-75; v.p., gen. mgr. Marine Electric Ry. Products div., Inc., Bklyn., 1975—. Bd. regents Casa Loma Coll., 1966-71. Served to lt. col. USMC, 1942-55; col. Res., ret., 1975. Fellow AIM; mem. IEEE, Am. Inst. Aero. and Astronautics, Am. Mgmt. Assn., Electronic Industries Assn. (dir. 1966-70, 73-75, chmn. Mass. transp. bd. 1968-72, exec. bd. 1974-75), Armed Forces Communications Electronics Assn. (v.p., nat. treas. 1959-62, v.p. 1967-70), Nat. Security Indsl. Assn. (mgmt. adv. bd. 1966-68), Assn. Am. R.R.'s (S.C. div.), Am. Ry. Engring. Assn., Locomotive Maintenance Officers Assn., Marine Corps Res. Officers Assn. (v.p. 1971—). Home: 2605 Faber Ct Falls Church VA 22046 Office: 600 4th Ave Brooklyn NY 11215 also 1629 K St NW Washington DC 20006

TRAPP, LOUIS ANDRE, JR., lawyer; b. N.Y.C., July 21, 1930; s. Louis A. and Katheren (Schuster) T.; A.B., Rutgers U., 1951; LL.B., Columbia, 1956; m. Margaret P. Martines, Apr. 13, 1956; children—Amy Sayre, Louis A. III. Admitted to N.Y. bar, 1957; asso. firm Reynolds, Richards, LaVenture, Hadley & Davis, N.Y.C., 1956-65, partner, 1966—; justice Village Plandome (N.Y.), 1967-76, trustee, 1976—. Chief Plandome Vol. Fire Dept., 1972-74; bd. dirs. N.Y. Young Republican Club, 1957-59; trustee Soc. of St. Johnland, 1971-76, v.p., 1975-76; bd. dirs., sec. Halcyon Found.; bd. dirs., v.p. St. Johnland Nursing Home, Inc., 1975-76. Served to 1st lt. USAF, 1951-53. Mem. Assn. Bar City N.Y., Am. N.Y. State bar assns., N.Y. Law Inst., N.Y. County Lawyers Assn., N.Y. State Magistrates Assn., Phi Delta Phi. Republican. Episcopalian (vestry). Clubs: Downtown Assn. (N.Y.C.); Plandome Field and Marine (pres. 1969-70). Home: 35 Central Dr Plandome NY 11030 Office: 67 Wall St New York City NY 10005

TRASK, FRANKLIN ALBERT, theatrical producer; b. Boston, Aug. 17, 1911; s. Albert Maynard and Bertha Mae (Horne) T.; B.S. in Edn., Boston U., 1930, Ed.M., 1965; A.M., Columbia, 1967; Ph.D., N.Y. U., 1968; Ph.D. (hon.), Staley Coll.; m. Alison Hawley, Feb. 14, 1936. Theatrical producer Cape Cod Summer Theatres, 1938—; prof. speech, head drama dept. Cedar Crest Coll., Allentown, Pa.; founder, adminstrv. dir. Trask Center for Performing Arts, Plymouth, 1974—; v.p. Plymouth Hist. Outdoor Drama. Developer, builder homes, Plymouth, Mass. Trustee Andover-Newton Theol. Sch. Mem. Nat. Assn. Dramatics (chmn. bd.). Author: The Actors' Shakespeare. Home: Center Hill Rd Plymouth MA 02381

TRAUB, ALAN CUTLER, physicist; b. Hartford, Conn., Jan. 20, 1923; s. Samuel and Sadie (Cohn) T.; B.S., Trinity Coll., Hartford, 1947; M.S., U. Cin., 1949, Ph.D., 1952; m. Lois Sylvia Speckter, Aug. 5, 1951; children—Lauren Jean, Karen Lynne, Linda Gail. Staff mem. Am. Optical Co., Southbridge, Mass., 1952-56; research physicist Fenwal, Inc., Ashland, Mass., 1956-60, research mgr., 1960-61, chief research engr., 1961-63; tech. staff mem. MITRE Corp., Bedford, Mass., 1963-70; chief scientist Foto-Mem Corp., Natick, Mass., 1970-71; pvt. practice as cons., 1971-72; sr. postdoctoral research fellow Tufts U., Medford, Mass., 1972-73; engring. physicist Identicon Corp., Waltham, Mass., 1973-74; advanced devel. mgr. Vanzetti Infrared & Computer Systems Inc., Canton, Mass., 1974—. Served with AUS, 1943-46. Mem. Optical Soc. Am. (sec. New Eng. sect. 1956-57). Patentee in field. Home: 56 Donna Rd Framingham MA 01701

TRAUB, ROBERTA HARRIET, med. record technician; b. Lawrence, Mass., Oct. 9, 1934; d. Max Robert and Sadye J. (Sobil) Weinstein; A.S., No. Essex Community Coll., 1975; m. Neil Robert Raub, June 25, 1952; children—Jeri Faith, Seth Matthew, Craig David, Stacy Hope. Dir. med. records Dr. J. Robert Shaughnessy Chronic Diesease/Rehab. Hosp., Salem, Mass. also audit asst. med. and nursing audit coms. Mem. Am., Mass. (scholarship and pub. relations com.) med. record assns. Clubs: Hadassah, Temple Emanuel Sisterhood; Dr. J. Robert Shaughnessy Chronic Disease/Rehab. Hosp. Aux. Home: 100 Argilla Rd Andover MA 01810 Office: Off Jefferson Ave Salem MA 01970

TRAUGER, JOHN FREDERICK, educator; b. Middletown, N.Y., Aug. 30, 1916; s. John Webster and Mabel Helen (Fenstermacher) T.; student Colgate U., 1934-35, Antioch Coll., 1935-37; A.B. in Econs., Bucknell U., 1940; M.L.S., State U. N.Y., Geneseo 1970; m. Peggie S. Sears, July 7, 1942; children—John Terry, Barbara Ann (Mrs. Theodore Francioso), Patricia Lynn (Mrs. John Allen), Evamae Robin. Sales trainee Vick Chem. Co., N.Y.C., 1940-41; photographer editorial services dept. Standard Oil Co. (Ohio), Cleve., 1946-63; supr. photography, photomedia dept. Corning Glass Works, 1964-66; instr. prof. photography Rochester (N.Y.) Inst. Tech., 1966-68, counselor evening coll., 1966-68, dir. biomed. photography and biomed. communications, 1968-73, instr. photography phosomarketers and basic color, 1974—; mem. adv. com. biomed. photography U. Calif. at Los Angeles. Active Boy Scouts Am. Served to cap. USAAF, 1942-46. Mem. Profl. Photographers Am., Biol. Photographers Assn. (gov.), Health Scis. Communications Assn. Home: 20 Wendover Rd Rochester NY 14610

TRAUGOTT, FRITZ ARTHUR, cons. engr.; b. Austria, Mar. 18, 1928; s. Johann and Maria Traugott; came to U.S., 1952, naturalized, 1959; M.E., Fed. Govt. Engring. Inst., Vienna, 1948; postgrad. Syracuse (N.Y.) U., 1952; m. Frances Fortier, June 15, 1957. Project engr. Stefan Amman & Sohn, Vienna, 1948-52, dist. engr., 1953-55; engr. internat. tng. Carrier Air Conditioning Corp., 1952-53; supr. project engr. Robson & Eoese, Inc., cons. engr., Syracuse, N.Y., 1955-65; v.p., mng. partner mech. div., dir., 1965—; lectr. Syracuse U., 1972—. Named Engr. of Year, City of Syracuse, 1969. Mem. N.Y. State Cons. Engrs. Assn., Am. Soc. Heating, Refrigeration and Air Conditioning Engrs. (past regional chmn.), Tech. Club Syracuse. Republican. Roman Catholic. Clubs: Rotary (dir.), Century (Syracuse); Cazenovia Ski. Contbr. articles to profl. jours. Home: 3996 Pompey Hollow Rd Cazenovia NY 13035 Office: 2401 Burnet Ave Syracuse NY 13206

TRAUM, JEROME S., lawyer; b. Newark, Sept. 26, 1935; s. Max and Evelyn (Fein) T.; A.B., U. Mich., 1956, J.D. with distinction, 1959; m. Lynda Sturner, Apr. 16, 1972; children—David, Norman, Daniel. Admitted to N.Y. bar, 1960, U.S. Supreme Ct. bar; asso. firm Chadbourne, Parke, Whiteside & Wolff, N.Y.C., 1959-62; asso., partner firm Spear and Hill, N.Y.C., 1962-67; partner firm Janklow and Traum, N.Y.C., 1967—; adj. prof. fed. securities regulation Syracuse U. Coll. Law, 1975. Bd. dirs. Open Channel, Inc., 1971-77; trustee Jose Limon Dance Found., 1968. Mem. Assn. Bar City N.Y., Am. (com. on fed. regulation securities), FCC bar assns., Order of Coif. Club: Marco Polo (N.Y.C.). Bd. editors U. Mich. Law Rev., 1958-59. Home: 935 Park Ave New York City NY 10028 Office: 375 Park Ave New York City NY 10022

TRAURIG, ALLEN ROBERT, urol. surgeon; b. Elizabeth, N.J., May 13, 1934; s. Milton and Freda (Gross) T.; A.B., Wayne State U., 1955, M.D., 1958; m. Sondra Gloria Kronick, Sept. 3, 1962; children—Michael, William. Intern, Grace Hosp., Detroit, resident in urology Yale U. Coll. Medicine, 1964-66; pvt. practice medicine specializing in urol. surgery, Waterbury, Conn., 1966—; urol. surgeon, treas. Urol. Assos. of Waterbury, P.C., 1972—; chief dept. urology Waterbury Hosp., 1976—; chief dept. urology St. Mary's Hosp., Waterbury, 1976—; asst. clin. prof. urology Yale U. Coll. Medicine. Vice-pres. Western Conn. Jewish Community Center, 1976—; v.p. Beth El Synagogue, 1976—. Served with USNR, 1960-63. Mem. New Haven County Med. Soc., Am. Urol. Assn., Conn. Med. Soc., AMA, Waterbury Med. Assn. (pres. 1977). Mem. B'nai B'rith. Home: 166 Avalon Circle Waterbury CT 06710 Office: 1211 W Main St Waterbury CT 06710

TRAUTLEIN, JOSEPH JAMES, physician; b. N.Y.C., Apr. 15, 1940; s. Eugene C. and Margaret Agnes (Dorney) T.; B.A., Fordham U., 1962; M.D., N.Y. Med. Coll., 1966; m. Joan Marie Starosta, Oct. 10, 1966; children—Ann, Tom, Rob. Intern, Jersey Shore Med. Center, Neptune, N.J., 1966-67; jr. asst. resident N.Y. Med. Coll., 1967-68; sr. resident Case Western Res. U., 1970-72, chief resident, 1972, teaching fellow, 1970-72; asst. prof. medicine div. internal medicine Milton S. Hershey Med. Center, Pa. State U., 1972-76, asso. prof., 1977—, med. dir. Center for Air Environ. Studies, 1975—, chief outpatient medicine, 1972—, dir. employee health program, 1974-77, dir. student health program, 1974—, med. supr. anti-coagulation clinic and chief otorhinolaryngology/allergy clinic, 1975; chmn. Hershey Conf. on Allied Health Careers, 1974-78; bd. dirs. Central Pa. Blood Bank, 1975-78, treas., 1978—; bd. dirs. Harrisburg (Pa.) Area ARC, 1975-78; chmn. South Central Pa. Health Edn. Consortium, 1978. Served as capt. USAFR, 1968-70. Diplomate Am. Bd. Internal Medicine. Fellow A.C.P., Am. Coll. Clin. Pharmacology, Am. Coll. Utilization Rev. Physicians; mem. Pa., Dauphin County med. scos., Am. Fedn. Clin. Research, Am. Acad. Allergy, Pa. Allergy Assn. (regent 1976-78, pres. elect 1978-79). Ryzantine Catholic. Clubs: Lions, St. Ann's Holy Name Soc. (pres.). Contbr. articles to med. jours.; editor: Aerosols Airways and Astham, 1978. Home: 6430 Colchester Ave Harrisburg PA 17111 Office: Milton S Hershey Med Center 500 University Dr Hershey PA 17033

TRAVAGLINI, BARBARA CARLSON (MRS. ALFONSO FREDERICK TRAVAGLINI), steel co. exec.; b. Easton, Pa., Nov. 4, 1925; d. Gurard Oscar and Margaret Bailey (Berry) Carlson; student Bryn Mawr Coll., 1943-44, Moore Coll. Art, 1944-48; m. Alfonso Frederick Travaglini, June 15, 1946; children—Gunard Carlson, Frederick Carlson, Mark Carlson. Dir., v.p., sec. G.O. Carlson, Inc., Thorndale, Pa., 1956—. Pres. Coatesville Hosp. Aux., 1967-72, 1st v.p., 1972—; treas. Chester County Airport Authority. Vice pres. bd. mgrs. Coatesville Hosp.; sec., treas. Gunard Berry Carlson Meml. Found.; trustee Saint Francis Coll., Lafayette Coll. Republican. Roman Catholic. Author: The Kelly Green Cow, 1949; Henry Hippo, 1972; columnist As I See It and A Woman's Pen. Home: 4000 Hazelwood Ave Thorndale PA 19372 Office: G O Carlson Inc Thorndale PA 19372

TRAVELL, CLARK, corp. exec.; b. N.Y.C., Aug. 29, 1923; s. J. Willard (M.D.) and Edith (Talcott) T.; A.B. cum laude, Princeton, 1945; m. Joan Agnes Balch, Oct. 9, 1945 (div. June 1966); children—Susan Talcott Travell Johnson, Blair Bates Travell McMorrow, Jill Gordon, Phyllis Balch. Export dept. Phelps Dodge Copper Products Corp., N.Y.C., 1948-50; asso. William A.M. Burden & Co., N.Y.C., 1951-62; exec. v.p., sec. Austral Oil Co., Inc., 1951-67; cons. oil, gas and mineral investments, 1967—. Asst. treas. United Republican Finance Com. for N.Y. State, 1955-59. Trustee Solebury Sch., New Hope, Pa., 1950-56, 61-65; trustee, treas. The Browning Sch., N.Y.C., 1953-74, trustee, v.p., 1974-75, chmn., pres., 1975—. Served as capt., pilot USAAF, 1942-45. ETO. Decorated Air Medal with 5 clusters (U.S.); Croix de Guerre avec palme (France). Clubs: University (N.Y.C.); Quandrangle (Princeton). Office: Watrous Point Rd Old Saybrook CT 06475

TRAVERS, WARREN, cons. engr.; b. Paterson, N.J., Sept. 23, 1925; s. Charles Henry and Helen (Thompson) T.; B.S. with honors in Civil Engring., Pa. State U., 1950; m. Laurie Cecilia Bender, June 1, 1960; children—Thomas Warren, Danelle Stephani, Susan Lee, James Ernest, Ellen Laurie. Asso., Edwards & Kelcey, cons. engr., Newark, 1950-62; pres. Travers Assos., Inc., Dallas, Tex. and Clifton, N.J., 1962—. Mem. planning bd. Wyckoff, N.J., 1966-69. Served with USN, 1943-45; PTO. Registered profl. engr., 15 states. Mem. Inst. Transp. Engrs. (dir. 1966-67, pres. N.Y. Met. sect. 1964), N.J. Fedn. Planning Ofcls. (mem. adv. council 1968), ASCE, Transp. Research Bd., Nat. Soc. Profl. Engrs., Chi Epsilon, Sigma Tau. Designer multi-level plan for Dallas central bus. dist., 1969. Home: 70 Hummingbird Ct Wyckoff NJ 07481 Office: 1128 Main Ave Clifton NJ 07011

TRAVERSE, ALFRED, educator; b. Port Hill, P.E.I., Can., Sept. 7, 1925; s. Alfred Freeman and Pearle (Akerley) T.; S.B., Harvard U., 1946, A.M., 1948, Ph.D., 1951; certificate botany Kings Coll., Cambridge, Eng., 1947; M.Div., Episcopal Theol. Sem. S.W., 1965; m. Elizabeth Jane Insley, June 30, 1951; children—Paul, Martha, John, Celia. Teaching fellow Harvard U., 1947-51; coal technologist U.S. Bur. Mines, Grand Forks, N.D., 1951-55; head Fuels Microscopy Lab., Denver, 1955; palynologist Shell Devel. Co., Houston, 1955-62; cons. palynologist, Austin, Tex., 1962-65; asst. prof. geology U. Tex., Austin, 1965-66; asso. prof. geology and biology Pa. State U., University Park, 1966-70, prof., 1970—; ordained to ministry Episcopal Ch., 1965; asst. priest St. Matthew's Ch., Austin, Tex., 1966, St. Paul's Ch., Philipsburg, Pa., 1966-75; vicar St. John's Ch., Huntingdon, Pa., 1975—; adj. prof. geobiology Juniata Coll., 1977—; mem. Internat. Commn. Palynology, 1973-77, pres., 1977—; on-board scientist Glomar Challenger, 1975. Recipient research grants NSF, 1966-78, Best Paper award Am. Assn. Stratigraphic Palynologists, 1973. Fellow Geol. Soc. Am., AAAS; mem. Bot. Soc. Am. (sect.-treas. paleobot. sect. 1957-60, chmn. sect. 1960-61), Paleontol. Soc., Internat. Assn. Plant Taxonomists (sec. com. on fossil plants 1969—), Am. Assn. Stratigraphic Palynologists (sec.-treas. 1967-70, pres. 1970-71). Club: Harvard of Central Pa. (mem. schs. com. 1966-77). Mem. editorial bd. Catalog of Fossil Spores and Pollen, 1957-66, editor-in-chief, 1966-76. Home: RD 2 Box 390 Huntingdon PA 16652 Office: 435 Deike Bldg University Park PA 16802

TRAVIN, MILTON SAMUEL, oral surgeon; b. N.Y.C., May 9, 1912; s. Samuel and Clara (Katz) T.; D.D.S., U. Buffalo, 1936; 1 dau. by previous marriage, Sandra Jean; m. 2d, Lois Beryl Christiansen, May 26, 1961. Intern Gouverneur Hosp., N.Y.C., 1936-37; pvt. practice oral surgery, Bklyn., 1939—; chief dental dept., dir. oral surgery Kings Hwy. Hosp., Bklyn., 1952—, Flatbush Gen. Hosp., Bklyn., 1951—, Caledonian Hosp., Bklyn., 1952—; chief dept. dentistry and sect. oral surgery, dir. advanced oral surgery tng. program Bklyn./Cumberland Med. Center, 1961—; attending oral surgeon Bklyn. Hosp., Kingsbrook Jewish Hosp., Bklyn., 1964—; cons. Bklyn. VA Hosp., 1961—, Goldwater Meml. Hosp., 1972—. Served with AUS, 1942-46; ETO. Diplomate Am. Bd. Oral Surgery, Bd. Oral Surgery N.Y. State. Fellow Internat. Coll. Anesthetists, N.Y. Acad. Dentists, Am. Coll. Dentists, Am. Soc. Oral Surgeons, Am. Soc. for Advancement Gen. Anesthesia in Dentistry (pres. 1963-65), Am. Dental Soc. Anesthesiology, L.I. Acad. Odontology, N.Y. Acad. Dentists; mem. 2d Dist. Dental Soc. (pres. 1970, editor bull.), Dental Soc. State N.Y. (book reviewer, abstractor ofcl. jour.), Am. Dental Assn., Am. Acad. Oral Pathology, Am. Soc. Anesthesiologists, N.Y. State Soc. Anesthesiologists, N.Y. State Dental Soc. Anesthesiology, N.Y. State Soc. Oral Surgeons, Internat. Anesthesia Research Soc., Barrettonian Soc. Pierre Fauchard Acad., Am. Assn. Hosp. Dentists. Home: 1396 E 51st St Brooklyn NY 11234 Office: 1 Hanson Pl Suite 1318 Brooklyn NY 11243

TRAVIS, MARY EILEEN (MRS. ARTHUR J. TRAVIS), librarian; b. New Glasgow, N.S, Can., Mar. 16, 1931; d. Louis Michael and Mary Cummane (Hallisey) Connolly; B.A., St. Francis Xavier U., 1952; B.L.S., McGill U., 1953; LL.D., St. Thomas U., 1976; m. Arthur J. Travis, Sept. 1, 1958; children—Mary Patricia, John Louis. Librarian bookmobile Pictou County Library, New Glasgow, 1953-55, head children's dept., 1955-58; head children's dept. St. John (N.B.) City Library, 1960-63, city librarian, 1963-67, regional librarian, 1969—. Condr. radio show Book Review, CFBC-FM, St. John, 1966—, TV show Mag. CHSJ-TV, St. John, 1966—. Mem. St. John Mayor's Com., 1972—; mem. St. John Bd. Trade, 1970—, mem. council, 1975—. Bd. dirs. Netherwood Sch. for Girls, 1969—, Sch. Dist 19, Kings County, N.B., 1968—, N.B. Opera Co., 1965-73, St. John Arts Council, 1968—. Named Woman of Year, St. John, 1973. Mem. Can., Nat. (mem. adv. bd. 1972-74), Ottawa, Atlantic Provinces (pres. 1969-70, co-chmn. bibliog. com. 1975—) library assns., Can. Assn. Children's Librarians (sec. 1967), Catholic Women's League (pres. Rothesay, N.B. chpt. 1966), N.S. Drama League (pres. 1957), Can. Pony Club, Electic Club. Roman Catholic. Home: PO Box 302 Rothesay NB Canada Office: Saint John Regional Library 20 Hazen Ave Saint John NB Canada

TREATMAN, PAUL, supt. schs.; b. N.Y.C., Nov. 19, 1924; s. Meyer and Sadie (Rosenblum) T.; B.A., Bklyn. Coll., 1948; M.A., N.Y. U., 1949, Ph.D., 1954; m. Elaine Cohen, Aug. 28, 1946; children—Abbe Jo Treatman Vaccaro, Scott. Tchr. pub. elementary schs., N.Y.C., 1948-51, 54-56, curriculum specialist, 1951-54, asst. prin., 1956-62, prin., 1962-67, 68-71, prin. jr. high sch., 1971-73, supt. schs., 1973—; ednl. cons. to gov. V.I., 1967-68. Mem. Community Planning Bd., Bklyn., 1972-73. Served with U.S. Army, 1943-45. Decorated Bronze Star medal. Mem. Am. Assn. Sch. Adminstrs., N.Y.C. Assn. Supts., N.Y.C. Elementary Sch. Prins. Assn., N.Y.C. Jr. High Sch. Prins. Assn., Canarsie Educators Assn. (co-pres. 1974—). Democrat. Jewish religion. Author: Assistant Principal and Principal, 1957; The Principal as a Teacher of Teachers, 1971. Home: 1469 E 103d St Brooklyn NY 11236 Office: School Dist 6 665 W 182 St New York City NY 10033

TREEN, JOSEPH MAYES, journalist; b. Chgo., Nov. 12, 1942; s. Alfred Elbert and Mary Esmeralda (Mayes) T.; B.A. in English, U. Wis., 1964; postgrad. Mo. Sch. Journalism, 1964-65; M.A. in Journalism, Syracuse U., 1967. Asso. editor County Beautiful Found., Waukesha, Wis., 1965-66; copy editor, reporter Syracuse (N.Y.) Herald-Jour., 1966-67; reporter, editor, overseas corr. Newsday, Garden City, N.Y., 1968—; instr. typography U. Mo., 1965. Served with U.S. Army, 1968-69. Mem. N.Y. Press Club, Internat. Printing and Graphic Communications Union. Author: (play) The Orderly Room, 1978; contbr. articles to Rolling Stone mag., 1974-76. Home: 138 E 16th St Apt 4A New York City NY 10003 Office: 1500 Broadway Room 2201 New York City NY 10036

TREGLOS, RAPHAEL, communications co. exec.; b. Tournan, France, July 6, 1945; s. Jean and Denise M. (Droit) T.; came to U.S., 1976; grad. Ecole Superieure D'Electricite, Malakoff, France, 1968; m. Michele G. Dias, Dec. 21, 1973; children—Jean-Baptiste, Nicolas. Engr., then mgr. ops. Cie. Francaise des Cables Telegraphiques, Paris, 1970-76; asst. mgr., then v.p. U.S. ops. French Telegraph Cable Co., N.Y.C., 1976-78; pres., chief exec. officer, dir. FTC Communications, Inc., N.Y.C., 1978—; dir. PQ Telesystems, Ltd., London. Mem. Soc. des Ingenieurs E.S.E., Am.-French C. of C. in U.S. (counsellor). Roman Catholic. Home: 2 Split Tumber Pl Riverside CT 06878 Office: 25 Broad St New York City NY 10004

TREI, ALICE ROSALIE, occupational therapist; b. Estonia, Oct. 17, 1909; d. Prüdu and Müna (Kraun) Roost; came to U.S., 1929, naturalized, 1938; certificate occupational therapy, Columbia U., 1948; B.S., N.Y. U., 1954; m. Peter Trei, Sept. 20, 1928 (dec. Jan. 1962); children—Astra (Mrs. Felix Bottenhorn), Alan. Occupational therapist N.Y. State Psychiat. Inst., N.Y.C., 1948-53, head occupational therapist, 1953—; instr. clin. occupational therpy Columbia, 1964—. Recipient Outstanding Employee award N.Y. Dept. Mental Hygiene, 1975. Mem. Am., N.Y. State (treas. 1959-62, 69-73), Met. N.Y. Dist. occupational therapy assns., World Fedn. Occupational Therapists. Home: 15 Sickles St New York City NY 10040 Office: 722 W 168th St New York City NY 10032

TREIBL, HANS GEORGE, chemist; b. Vienna, Austria, Aug. 7, 1914; s. Robert and Ida (Salzer) T.; came to U.S., 1950, naturalized, 1955; M.S., State Research Inst., Vienna, 1935; m. Gertrude Schacherl, Nov. 22, 1951. Petro-chemist Cathay-Oil Co., Shanghai, China, 1939-49; coal assayer Luscar Coal Ltd. (Alta., Can.), 1949-50; chief chemist Hydrocarbon Chems. Co., Newark, 1951-57; research chemist Diamond-Alkali Co., Newark, 1957-58; chief chemist Standard Chlorine Chem. Co., Kearny, N.J., 1958—; cons. in field. Fellow Am. Inst. Chemists; mem. Am. Chem. Soc. Contbr. articles on naphthalene and naphthalene derivatives to profl. publs. Home: 155 Riverside Dr New York City NY 10024 Office: 1025 Belleville Turnpike Kearny NJ 07032

TREICHLER, RAY, tech. services mgr.; b. Rock Island, Ill., Sept. 10, 1907; s. Wallace and Pearl (Cushman) T.; B.S., M.S., Pa. State U., 1929; Ph.D., U. Ill., 1939; m. Kathryn Amelia Blakeley, June 13, 1942. Asst. state chemist Tex. Agrl. Expt. Sta., Tex. A. and M. Coll., College Station, 1929-40; chief, chemistry and biochemistry research Fish & Wildlife Service Labs., U.S. Dept. Interior, Laurel, Md., 1941-44; chief, biol. activities Office of Quartermaster Gen., U.S. Army, Washington, 1945-53; chief, toxic agents br. Rand D. Command, Army Chem. Center, Md., 1953-56, asst. to dir. med. research Chem. Warfare Labs., 1956-58; research adminstr. USAF, Bolling Field, Washington, 1958-68; technical services mgr. H.D. Hudson Mfg. Co., Washington, 1968—. Fellow N.Y. Acad. Scis.; mem. Am. Chem. Soc., Entomol. Soc. Am., Am. Soc. Tropical Medicine and Hygiene, Am. Mosquito Assn., Am. Soc. Agrl. Engrs., ASTM, Sigma Xi, Gamma Sigma Delta. Mason. Research in pesticides application equipment, prevention deterioration, chemistry and formulations pesticides, pesticide dissemination systems. Contbr. articles on vitamins, basal energy and endogenous nitrogen metabolism, nutrition, composition fishery products, toxic compounds, prevention material deterioration. Home: 4740 Connecticut Ave NW Washington DC 20008 Office: H D Hudson Mfg Co 1625 I St NW Washington DC 20006

TREIMAN, SAM BARD, educator; b. Chgo., May 27, 1925; s. Abraham and Sarah (Bard) T.; student Northwestern U., 1942-44; S.B., U. Chgo., 1948, S.M., 1949, Ph.D., 1952; m. Joan Little, Dec. 27, 1952; children—Rebecca, Katherine, Thomas. Instr., Princeton U., 1952-54, asst. prof., 1954-58, asso. prof., 1958-63, prof. physics, 1963—. Served with USNR, 1944-46. Mem. Am. Phys. Soc., Nat. Acad. Sci., Am. Acad. Arts and Scis. Author: (with M. Grossjean) Formal Scattering Theory, 1960; (with R. Jackia and D. Gross) Current Algebra and Its Applications, 1972. Contbr. articles to profl. jours. Home: 60 McCosh Circle Princeton NJ 08540

TREIRAT, EDUARD, design engr.; b. Estonia, May 25, 1912; came to U.S., 1949, naturalized, 1955; marine engring. diploma Marine Coll. Tallinn (Estonia), 1942; student Baltic U., Hamburg, Germany, 1946-47; B.S. in Engring., Fairleigh Dickinson U., 1957; postgrad. Stevens Inst. Tech., 1957-59; m. Maimo Paabo, Oct. 17, 1941. Asst. mgr. planning dept. Revaler Werft Tallinn Estonia, 1942-44; lectr. Nav. and Marine Engrs. Sch., Flensburg, Ger., 1946-49; toolmaker Bergenfield Devel. Co., Dumont, N.J., 1950-52; design engr. Star Kimble Electric Co., Bloomfield, N.J., 1952-56; design engr. Walter Kidde & Co., Belleville, N.J., 1956-61, engring. supr., 1961-71, chief design engr., 1971-76; sr. staff engr. advanced products devel. Valcor Engring. Corp., Kenilworth, N.J., 1976—; dir. Gen. Valve Co., East Hanover, N.J.; also cons. Served with Estonian Army, 1931-32. Decorated Sharpshooters medal. Lutheran. Club: Eüs. Patentee in field; also articles. Office: 365 Carnegie Ave Kenilworth NJ 07033

TREITLER, BYRON MORTON, surgeon; b. N.Y.C., Apr. 21, 1931; s. Morris and Nettie (Kessler) T.; B.A., N.Y. U., 1951; M.D., State U. N.Y. at Bklyn., 1955; m. Rhoda Chaprack, May 15, 1960; children—Michael Eric, Betsy Dale. Intern L.I. Jewish Hosp., New Hyde Park, N.Y., 1955-56, resident, 1956-60, staff surgeon, 1962—; dep. comdr., chief surgery 3565th USAF Hosp., James Connally AFB, Tex., 1960-62; practice medicine specializing in surgery, East Meadow, N.Y., 1962—; mem. staff Hempstead Gen. Hosp., 1962—, dir. surgery, 1975—, chmn. med. bd., 1975-77; staff surgeon Nassau Hosp., Mineola, N.Y., 1968—; clin. instr. surgery State U. N.Y. at Bklyn., 1962-71; asst. prof. clin. surgery State U. N.Y. at Stony Brook, 1973—; surg. cons. N.Y. State Aid Program for Handicapped Children, N.Y. State Ins. Fund. Chmn. membership com. L.I. Cancer Council, 1978. Diplomate Am. Bd. Surgery. Fellow ACS; mem. Nassau Surg. Soc., N.Y. State, Nassau County med. socs., N.Y. State Soc. Surgeons. Home: 81 Finch Dr Roslyn NY 11576 Office: 591 Merrick Ave East Meadow NY 11554

TRENCHER, MARK L., ins. co. exec.; b. Bad Nauheim, Germany, July 12, 1948; s. Naftali and Toni (Landau) T.; came to U.S., 1951; naturalized, 1956; B.A. cum laude, Bklyn. Coll., 1969; M.S., N.Y. U., 1971; m. Sandra Kaminetsky, Sept. 15, 1970; children—Steven, Elana. Ordained rabbi, 1971; mgr. research and long range planning Prudential Property and Casualty Ins. Co., Woodbridge, N.J., 1972-76; mgr. corp. planning Aetna Life & Casualty Co., Hartford, Conn., 1976—; adj. prof. Kean Coll., N.J., 1974-75, Rutgers U., 1975-76, U. Hartford, 1977—; cons. in operations research and mgmt. sci. Treas. Young Israel of West Hartford, 1977—; dir., mem. religious and secular bds. edn. Hebrew Acad. of Greater Hartford, 1977—. Mem. Am. Statis. Assn., Soc. Ins. Research, N.Am. Soc. for Corp. Planning, Developer computer statistical and econ. analysis systems. Home: 50 Miamis Rd West Hartford CT 06117 Office: Aetna Life & Casualty Co 151 Farmington Ave Hartford CT 06156

TRENT, JAMES ALFRED, govt. ofcl.; b. Bklyn., May 25, 1946; s. Alfred and Helen (Vanasco) T.; Asso. Applied Sci., State U. N.Y. at Farmingdale, 1966; B.Landscape Architecture, U. Ga., 1969. Jr. landscape architect Dept. Pub. Works N.Y.C., 1969-70, asst. landscape architect, 1970—. Pres. Creedmoor Civic Assn. Inc., Bellerose, N.Y., 1970—; mem. ornamental hort. adv. commn. Occupational Edn. Adv. Council, N.Y.C. Bd. Edn., 1973—; founder, pres. Colonial Farmhouse Restoration Soc. of Bellerose, 1975—; 1st v.p. Eastern Queens Civic Council, 1975—. Mem. Queens County Com. Republican party, 1968—; 1st v.p. Midland Rep. Club, N.Y. 23d Assembly Dist., 1970-76. Named Grad. of Year, State U. N.Y. at Farmingdale Alumni Assn., 1966, Humanitarian of 1977, 105th Policy Precinct Community Council. Fellow Internat. Biog. Assn.; mem. N.Y.C. Municipal Engrs., Friends of Jamaica History. Roman Catholic. Art editor Civil Service Merit Council Inc., 1972—. Home: 242-29 90th Ave Bellerose NY 11426 Office: Room 1416 Municipal Bldg New York City NY 10007

TRENT, ROBERT LEE, realtor; b. Somerset, Pa., May 1, 1928; s. Mervin Mckinley and Grace Marie (Walker) T.; student pub. schs., Somerset; m. Mildred Elizabeth Tasker, Sept. 17, 1950; children—Pattie Ann, Matthew Allen. Operator heavy equipment, supr. A. H. Sweeney Co., Legonier, Pa., 1957-60; coil winder Uptegraft Transformer Co., Somerset, 1960-67; supr. property and equipment Red Bird Mission Field, Ky., 1967-69; plumber Plumbers and Pipe Fitters Local Union 354, Latrobe, 1969-72; salesman James F. Custer, Realtor, Somerset, 1972-74; owner, mgr. Christian Book Store, Somerset, 1973—; real estate broker Robert L. Trent Real Estate, 1974—. Served with USAF, 1952-56. Mem. Somerset C. of C., Christian Book Sellers Assn., Nat., Pa. assns. realtors, Am. Mgmt. Assn. Republican. Mem. Christian and Missionary Alliance Ch. Home: 833 W Main St Somerset PA 15501

TRESCOTT, ALFRED PHILLIP, SR., radiologist; b. Bloomsburg, Pa., Apr. 1, 1930; s. Paul Henry and Stella Henrietta (Potts) T.; A.B., Swarthmore Coll., 1951; M.D., Case Western Res. U., 1955; m. Bettie Sue Gallimore, June 12, 1954; children—Alfred Phillip, Carol. Intern, Bryn Mawr (Pa.) Hosp., 1955-56; resident in radiology Robert Packer Hosp., Sayre, Pa., 1958-61; radiologist Soldiers and Sailors Meml. Hosp., Wellsboro, Pa., 1962-75, N. Penn Health Centers, Blossburg, Pa., 1975—; pvt. medicine specializing in addictive disease, 1975—. Bd. dirs. Clear Brook Lodge, Shickshinny, Pa., N. Penn Comprehensive Health Services, Blossburg; mem. Wellsboro Boro Council, 1969. Served to capt. M.C., USAF, 1956-58. Diplomate Am. Bd. Radiology. Mem. AMA, Tioga County (past pres.), Pa. med. socs., Am. Coll. Radiology, Am. Inst. Ultrasound in Medicine, Alcohol and Drug Problems Assn. N. Am., Pa. Radiol. Soc., Am. Med. Soc. Alcoholism, Biofeedback Soc Am., Am. Heart Assn. Mem. Soc. of Friends. Home and Office: 18 West Ave Wellsboro PA 16901

TRESNOWSKE, JOHN, lawyer; b. Perth Amboy, N.J., May 26, 1921; s. Basil and Catherine (Luceico) T.; B.Sc. magna cum laude, L.I. U., 1947; LL.B., Bklyn. Law Sch., 1949; m. Valerie Hubrecht, Apr. 3, 1961; children—Charles R., Richard W. Admitted to N.Y. State bar, 1949, U.S. Supreme Ct. bar, 1959; pvt. practice law, N.Y.C., 1949—; corporate dir. and officer various companies, corporations and firms; arbitrator civil ct., N.Y.C., 1963—. Judge advocate N.Y. County. Served with communications, USAAF, 1942-45. Mem. Soc. Optimates, N.Y. County Lawyers' Assn., VFW, L.I. U. Council. Republican. Episcopalian. Mason. Home: 1199 Park Ave New York City NY 10028 Office: 233 Broadway New York City NY 10007

TREU, JESSE ISAIAH, physicist; b. N.Y.C., Apr. 10, 1947; s. Ahbe Jay and Charlotte (Ratner) T.; B.S. in Physics, Rensselaer Poly. Inst., 1968; M.A. in Physics, Princeton U., 1971, Ph.D., 1973; m. Marissa Adeline Fellner, Nov. 15, 1970; children—Abigail Virginia, Dara Jill. Physicist, Gen. Electric Co., Schenectady, 1973-75, Liaison scientist Components and Materials Group, 1975-77; program mgr. Technicon Inst. Corp., Tarrytown, N.Y., 1977—. Served with USAR, 1969-75. NSF trainee, 1971-72. Mem. Am. Phys. Soc., Biophysical Soc., AAAS, Am. Assn. Physicists in Medicine, Sigma Xi, Sigma Pi Sigma, Tau Epsilon Phi. Research on hemoglobin quantum mechanics and biomed. instrumentation. Contbr. articles in field to profl. jours. Home: 280 Hardscrabble Rd Briarcliff Manor NY 10510 Office: Technicon Inst Corp Tarrytown NY 10591

TREVASKIS, RICHARD WHITE, psychiatrist: b. Cumberland, Md., Mar. 12, 1915; s. Richard White and Grace (Curnow) T.; B.S., Harvard Coll., 1937, M.D., U. Md., 1941; postgrad. U. Pa., 1949; m. Marion Haney, Aug. 5, 1943; Intern, Chester County Hosp., W. Chester, Pa., 1941-42; resident psychiatry Western Psychiat. Inst. U. Pitts. Med. Center, 1949-50; teaching fellow psychiatry U. Pits., 1950; individual practice medicine specializing in psychiatry Cumberland, Md.; cons. psychiatry Newton D. Baker VA Hosp., Martinsburg, W.Va., 1962-67; chmn. dept. psychiatry Sacred Heart Hosp., Cumberland, 1967-73; dir.psychiat. services Allegany County (Md.) Mental Health Center, 1958—; dir. Prolixin Clinic Mental Health Center, Cumberland, 1973—. Served to lt. comdr. M.C., USNR, 1942-46. Mem. Med. and Chir. Faculty Md., Am. Psychiat. Assn. Democrat. Diplomate Am. Bd. Psychiatry and Neurology. Clubs: Deep Creek Yacht, Deer Haven Yacht, Cumberland Country; Kenwood Country (Bethesda, Md.). Home: 115 Luteman Rd Cumberland MD 21502 Office: 220 Baltimore Ave Cumberland MD 21502

TREVOR, BRONSON, economist, corp. exec.; b. N.Y.C., Nov. 12, 1910; s. John Bond and Caroline Murray (Wilmerding) T.; A.B., Columbia Coll., 1931; m. Eleanor Darlington Fisher, Nov. 8, 1946; children—Eleanor, Bronson, Caroline. Own bus., 1931—; dir., asst. sec. Northwestern Terminal R.R., 1952-58; chmn. board Texinia Corp. Former dir., chmn. finance committee Gen. Hosp. of Saranac Lake; mem. The Council for Agrl. and Chemurgic Research. Am. Forestry Assn. Mem. New York County Republican Com., 1937-39; leader in primary election campaigns N.Y. County, 1937, 38, 39 to free local Rep. party orgn. from left-wing affiliations. Served with U.S. Army, 1942, World War II. Mem. N.Y. State C. of C., S.A.R., Soc. Colonial Wars. Clubs: Union, Knickerbocker, Racquet and Tennis, Nat. Republican, Piping Rock. Author: (pamphlet) The United States Gold Purchase Program, 1941; also numerous articles on econ. subjects. Home: Paul Smiths NY 12970 Office: Box 182 Oyster Bay NY 11771

TREVOR, FREDERICK ARTHUR, ret. dentist; b. East Boston, Mass., Oct. 31, 1899; s. Charles Francis and Florence Winifred (Freeman) T.; D.M.D., Harvard U., 1922; m. Blanche Mosley, June 12, 1925; children—Frederick Arthur, Joyce Trevor Bostder, Robert Freeman. Clk., William H. Willis Pharmacy, Reading, Mass., 1917-18, 20-21; practice dentistry, Melrose Highlands, Mass., 1922-36, Melrose, Mass., 1936-75; instr. oral pathology Harvard Dental Sch., 1922-43. Chmn. Melrose Dental Com., 1955-65. Recipient Distinguished Alumnus plaque Harvard Sch. Dental Medicine, 1972. Mem. Internat. Coll. Dentists (past regent), Am. Dental Assn. (past chmn. health and sci. exhibits com., chmn. council on membership), Mass. Dental Soc. (past pres., chmn. Past Pres. Club), Am. Acad. Dental Sci. (past pres.), Harvard Odontological Soc. (past pres.), Harvard Dental Alumni Assn. (past pres.), East Middlesex Component Dist. Dental Soc. (past trustee), Omicron Kappa Upsilon. Conglist. (deacon). Lion, Rotarian. Club: Waukewan Golf. Home: 1 Wagon Wheel Trail Meredith NH 03253

TRIBBLE, DAGMAR HAGGSTROM, artist; b. N.Y.C.; d. Olaf Albin and Ida (Sabini) Haggstrom; student Parsons Sch. Design, N.Y. and Paris, 1928, Art Students League, 1930-32, Farnsworth Sch. of Painting, 1949-50; m. Elston J. Tribble, July 15, 1933; 1 dau., Martha Watkins (Mrs. James Malcolm McKinnon). Tchr. fashion illustration Parsons Sch. Design, 1929-32; designer sportswear and beachwear Travelo Corp., N.Y.C., 1933-45. One-man shows at The Beard Sch., Orange, N.J., Monmouth Coll., West Long Branch, The Present Day Club, 1968, 71, M.S. Kungsholm, 1971, M.S. Sagafjord, 1971, United Nat. Bank, Fanwood, N.J., 1972, Present Day Club, Princeton, 1974-75, 77, others; exhibited in group shows at Cape Cod Art Assn., 1963, Knickerbocker Artists Ann. Exhbn., 1963, Westfield Art Assn. State Show, 1963, 64, Hunterdon County Art Center Ann., 1963, 64, Catherine Lorillard Wolfe Art Show, 1964, Nat. Arts Club shows, also Met. Mus. Art, Nat. Academy, N.Y.C., Am. Water Color Soc. Ann., Nat. Assn. Women Artists Ann., 1967—, Nat. Assn. Women Artists Internat., Paris, France, 1969, Am. Watercolor Soc. anns., 1967—, Garden State Watercolor Soc. anns., 1970—, Am. Watercolor Soc. Ann. Traveling Exhbn., 1972, Federated Art Assns. N.J. mem. show, 1977; represented in pvt. collections; tchr. watercolor painting Princeton Adult Sch., 1976. Recipient Agnes B. Noyes award, 1962; Windsor Newton award, 1963; Captain's Barn award for Watercolor Westfield Art Assn. State Show, 1964; Steinback Co. award for watercolor Festival of Fine Art Exhbn., 1964; Am. Artist medal of merit Am. Watercolor Soc., 1965; Jane C. Stanley Meml. prize Nat. Assn. Women Artists, 1966, Squibb award, 1973, Lawrenceville Triangle award, 1973. Mem. Am. (finance chmn. 1965-68), Garden State (pres. 1970—) watercolor socs., Nat. Assn. Women Artists, Princeton Art Assn. (pres. 1968-69). Club: Nat. Arts (N.Y.C.). Home: 12 Battle Rd Princeton NJ 08540

TRICOMI, VINCENT JAMES, obstetrician, gynecologist; b. N.Y.C., Sept. 16, 1921; s. Frank and Amelia (Pafumi) T.; A.B., Syracuse U., 1942; M.D., State U. N.Y. Downstate Med. Center, Bklyn., 1950; m. J. Marie Abair, Dec. 29, 1949; children—Frank, Mary, Nancy, Ellen, Charles, Linda. Intern, Kings County Hosp., Bklyn., 1950-51, resident, 1951-55; practice medicine specializing in obstetrics and gynecology Bklyn., 1955—; instr. obstetrics, gynecology State U. N.Y. Downstate Med. Center, Bklyn., 1955-57, asst. prof., 1957-63, asso. prof., 1963-69, clin. prof., 1969-73, asst. dean, 1971-73, prof., 1973—, asso. dean, 1973—; obstetrician, gynecologist-in-chief Bklyn.-Cumberland Med. Center, Bklyn., 1965—, dir. med. affairs, 1970; cons. Luth. Med. Center, Kings County Med. Center. Mem. exec. bd. Bklyn. unit Am. Cancer Soc. Served with U.S. Army, 1942-45. Bowen Brooks scholar, 1954-55. Diplomate Am. Bd. Obstetrics and Gynecology. Fellow A.C.S., Am. Coll. Obstetricians and Gynecologists (chmn. sect. 2 dist. 2 1969, sec. dist. 2, 1973—, chmn. dist. 2, 1978), N.Y. Obstet. Soc. (treas. 1975-77, 2d v.p. 1977-78, 1st v.p. 1978—), Bklyn. Gynecol. Soc. (pres. 1974-75); mem. Soc. Gynecol. Investigation, Coordinating Com. for Control of Cancer of Uterine Cervix N.Y.C. (chmn. 1966-68), Royal Soc. Medicine (affiliate). Asso. editorial bd. N.Y. State Jour. Medicine. Home: 25-31 West Dr Douglaston NY 11363 Office: 121 DeKalb Ave Brooklyn NY 11201

TRIESCHMAN, ALBERT EWELL, tng. sch. dir.; b. Balt., Sept. 20, 1931; s. Albert Ewell and Charlotte Adelaide (Borcherding) T.; A.B. magna cum laude, Franklin and Marshall Coll., 1951; Ph.D., Harvard U., 1960; m. Nancy Ann Eaton, June 25, 1955; children—Thomas Eaton, Karl Hendricks, Matthew Odell. Supervising psychologist Children's Hosp. Med. Center, Boston, 1958—; founder, dir. Walker Home and Sch., Needham, Mass., 1961—; former staff psychologist Judge Baker Guidance Center; former lectr. Clark U., Worcester; mem. faculty Harvard Med. Sch.; mem. Task Force for children, Joint Mental Health Com. U.S., 1968. Former bd. dirs. Harvard Pre-Sch.; former pres. bd. dirs. Community Nursery Sch., Lexington; bd. dirs. Fenn Sch., Concord; former bd. govs. Group Care Cons. U. N.C. Rantoul fellow, 1951-52; Naumberg scholar, 1957-58. Mem. Am. Orthopsychiat. Assn., Am. Assn. Childrens Residential Centers (pres.), Phi Beta Kappa, Pi Gamma Mu, Phi Alpha Theta. Author: The Other 23 Hours, 1969; Children Away From Home, 1972. Contbr. articles to profl. jours. Home: 2 Grimes Rd Lexington MA 02192 Office: 1968 Central Ave Needham MA 02192

TRIHAS, LEFTERIS MINAS, ops. research analyst; b. Mansura, Egypt, Dec. 15, 1936; s. Minas John and Anastasia (Zotos) T.; came to U.S., 1957; B.A., N.Y. U., 1962, M.S. (scholar), 1968, grad. Advanced Certificate Program in Fin., Grad. Sch. Bus. Adminstrn., 1976; m. Maria Garyfalidakis, Oct. 20, 1963; 1 dau., Anastasia. Faculty, N.Y. U., 1962-63; systems engr. cons. data processing IBM, N.Y.C., 1963-68, mgmt. sci. cons., educator Ednl. Center, 1968-69; operations research analyst, office of pres. IBM World Trade Corp., N.Y.C., 1969-72; systems engr., information systems cons. IBM, N.Y.C., 1973—. Cons. Hellenes from Egypt, 1965-66, Students from Greece, N.Y. U., 1960-61. Mem. Am. Mgmt. Assn., Assn. for Computing Machinery, Am. Statis. Assn., Inst. Mgmt. Sci. Clubs: IBM 555, Hellenic Univ. (N.Y.C.). Office: IBM Utilities Br Office 205 E 42d St New York City NY 10017

TRILLI, HARVEY JAMES, engring. co. exec.; b. Pitts., Oct. 11, 1929; s. Everest C. and Alice G. (Hinch) T.; B.S., U. Pitts., 1950, M.S., 1958; m. Nancy Lee Clendening, June 5, 1954; children—Gary, Gail Glen, Sally, Lauren. Various positions Pullman Swindell Inc., Pitts., 1964-73, v.p. engring. and constrn., 1973-74, sr. v.p., 1974-76, exec. v.p., 1976-77, pres., 1977—; dir. Gordian Assos. Bd. dirs Jr. Achievement Pitts. Served with C.E., U.S. Army, 1954-56. Mem. Pitts. C. of C., Machinery and Allied Products Inst. (council 1976—), Am. Iron Steel Inst., ASCE, Iron and Steel Assn., Am. Mgmt. Assn., Pitts. Athletic Assn. Clubs: Duquesne, Longue Vue. Registered profl. engr., Pa. Office: 441 Smithfield St Pittsburgh PA 15222

TRIMBATH, ERNEST RAY GORMAN, architect; b. Johnstown, Pa., Apr. 14, 1913; s. John and Margaret Mae (Bryan) T.; grad. Bklyn. Arch. Engr. Inst., 1933; C.E., U. Pitts., 1936; diploma architecture, Am. Sch. Chgo., 1946; pvt. tutor U. Pa., 1946; Certificate Civil Engring., Wagner Inst., 1950; Certificate in Structural Engring., Internat. Corrs. Schs., 1951; m. Dorothy Poehler Ballinger, Apr. 13, 1946; 1 son, David Charles (dec.). With Henry M. Rogers, registered architect, Johnstown, Pa., 1933-40, successively apprentice, detailer, draftsman, supr., 1935-40; archtl. draftsman Beaver County Housing Architects, Ackley, Bradley, Marsof & Stonorov, Pitts., 1940, designer, 1940; with Frankford Arsenal, Dept. Army, Ordnance Corps, Phila., 1941-53, asst. to constrn. engr., 1950-53; architect, coordinator Fridy, Gauker, Truscott & Fridy, Inc., Phila., 1953-57; prin. architect Fort Washington Indsl. Architect, 1958-67; dir. Fridy, Gauker & Fridy, Architects & Engrs., 1968; mgr. architecture and planning Albright & Friel div. Betz Environ. Engrs. Inc. (now Bet-Converse-Murdock), Phila., 1969-73, 78—; dir. Plymouth Archtl. and Planning Assos., Inc., 1973—. Dir., sr. architect Northampton Twp. Indsl. Devel. Com., 1960; trustee Northampton Civic Assn., Bucks County, Pa., 1958; sch. dir., chmn. bldg. com. Council Rock Sch. dist., Bucks County, Pa., 1967-71. Served with AUS, 1944-46. Decorated Purple Heart. Mem. AIA, Pa. Assn. Architects, Am. Registered Architects. Mason. Club: T Square (Phila.). Home: 33 Mallard Rd Holland PA 18966 Office: 1 Plymouth Meeting Mall Plymouth Meeting PA 19462

TRIMBLE, WILLIAM CATTELL, JR., lawyer; b. Buenos Aires, Argentina, Feb. 7, 1935; s. William Cattell and Nancy Gordon (Carroll) T.; A.B., Princeton, 1958; LL.B., U. Md., 1964; m. Barbara Janney, June 19, 1960; children—William C., Margery M. Admitted to Md. bar, 1965; asso. firm Cross, Shriver, Bright & Washburne, Balt., 1965-69; asso. firm Ober Grimes & Shriver, Balt., 1969-70, partner, 1970—, mng. partner, 1973—; mem. Gov.'s Commn. to Revise Annotated Code of Md., 1975—. Trustee, The Valley Sch., 1963-75, pres. bd. trustees, 1968-73; trustee St. Paul's Sch. for Girls, 1974-78, Garrison Forest Sch., 1975—. Served to lt. USNR, 1958-61. Mem. Am., Md. State bar assns., Bar Assn. Balt. City. Episcopalian. Clubs: Colonial (Princeton), Md., Greenspring Valley Hunt., Soc. of the Cin. Home: Valley Rd D3 Owings Mills MD 21117 Office: 1600 Maryland Nat Bank Bldg Baltimore MD 21202

TRIMBLE, WINFRED EUGENE, psychol. cons.; b. Plainview, Tex., Feb. 26, 1934; s. Herbert W. and Lois Elaine (Bell) T.; B.A., Gordon Coll., 1960; M.A. in Ednl. Psychology, U. No. Colo., 1962; Ph.D. in Counseling, Walden U., Fla., 1973; m. Mildred Elizabeth Norwood, Oct. 14, 1960; children—Rebecca Lynn, Douglas Eugene. Asso. dir. Christian Youth Inc., Boston, 1960-62; instr. psychol. statistics U. No. Colo., Greeley, 1963-64; asst. prof. psychology Gordon Coll., Wenham, Mass., 1964-66; research psychologist Directorate of Civilian Personnel, Hdqrs. USAF, Washington, 1966-67; cons. psychologist Adminstrv. Office, Office of the Sec., Dept. of Navy, Washington, 1967-69, dir. personnel measurement staff Office of Civilian Manpower Mgmt., 1970-74; dir. Potomac Assn.

for Transactional Analysis, Silver Spring, Md., 1974—; cons. to NIH, U.S. Peace Corps, U.S. Supreme Ct., United Air Lines, Dept. Def., Montgomery County (Md.) Schs. Bd. dirs. Nat. Presbyn. Sch. Served with U.S. Army, 1954-56. HEW grantee, 1956. Mem. Am., Md. psychol. assns., Am. Personnel and Guidance Assn., Nat. Vocat. Guidance Assn., Internat. Transactional Analysis Assn., Nat. Employment Counselors Assn., Am. Sci. Affiliation. Presbyn. Author manuals on job analysis and performance evaluation. Home: 1201 Burton St Silver Spring MD 20910 Office: 8730 Georgia Ave Silver Spring MD 20910

TRIMPI, HOWARD DENNIS, physician, surgeon; b. Newark, Apr. 27, 1917; s. Richard Howard and Florence (Dennis) T.; A.B., Emory U., 1940. M.D., 1943; M.S. in Medicine, Temple U., 1950; m. Viviane Geib, Nov. 28, 1944 (div. Apr. 1958); children—Leslie, John, William, Jane; m. 2d, Charlene Deubler, May 16, 1959; children—Richard, Barbara. Intern Milwaukee County Gen. Hosp., 1944, jr. resident surgery, 1945, sr. resident surgery, 1946; resident surgery U.S. Naval Hosp., Great Lakes, Ill., 1947; resident colon and rectal surgery Temple U. Hosp., Phila., 1948-50; in pvt. practice colon and rectal surgery, Phila., 1950-56; instr. Marquette Med. Sch., Milw., 1945-46, Temple U. Med. Sch., 1948-50, asst. prof. proctology, 1953-54; asso. prof. surgery Hahnemann Med. Sch., Phila., 1955-57; mem. staffs Temple U. Hosp., 1950-54. Northeastern Hosp., 1953-55, Frankfort Hosp., 1954-56, U.S. VA Hosp., Phila., 1953-56, Pa. Hosp., 1954—, St. Mary's Hosp., 1951—, Hahnemann Hosp., 1955-57, Stetson Hosp., 1952-55, Sacred Heart Hosp.; chief div. colon and rectal surgery Allentown and Sacred Heart Hosp. Center, 1976—; asst. chief surgery Allentown Gen. Hosp., 1969-71; mem. staff Muhlenberg Med. Center; cons. colon and rectal surgery, Phila. Freemason Meml. Hosp.; med. adviser Lehigh Valley Community Coll., Pa. Blue Shield; lectr. 18th century medicine Lehigh U. Served from ensign to lt. M.C., USNR, 1942-49; chief med. officer U.S.S. Gen. Wm. Mitchell AP114, 1947-48. Recipient Hermance Award for paper on proctology Am. Proctologic Soc., Milw., 1953. Diplomate Am. Bd. Colon and Rectal Surgery, Internat. Soc. Univ. Colon and Rectal Surgeons. Fellow Royal Soc. Medicine, Pa. Soc. Colon and Rectal Surgeons (pres.), Am. Geriatric Soc., Am. Med. Authors, A.C.S., Phila. Coll. Physicians, Am. Soc. Colon and Rectal Surgery, Am. (hon.), Internat. (hon.) colls. angiology; mem. Am., Pa. socs. colon and rectal surgeons, AMA, Pa. State (interspecialty com.), Lehigh County (cancer com.), Pan American, Lehigh Valley med. socs., Lehigh Valley Proctologic Soc. (cancer com.), Am. Therapeutic Soc., Am. Fedn. Clin. Research, Internat. Acad. Law and Sci. (past pres.), Pa. Soc., Phi Delta Theta, Phi Chi. Mason (32 deg., Shriner). Clubs: Lehigh Valley, Kiwanis (Meritorious Service award 1962), Allentown Chess (pres.). Asso. editor: Lex et Scientia. Home: 2205 Lehigh Pkwy N Allentown PA 18103 Office: Liberty Sq Med Center 501 N 17th St Allentown PA 18104

TRINKAUS, JOHN PHILIP, biologist; b. Rockville Centre, N.Y., May 23, 1918; s. Charles Edward and Fransiska Magdalena (Krueger) T.; B.A., Wesleyan U., Middletown, Conn., 1940; M.A., Columbia U., 1941; Ph.D., Johns Hopkins U., 1948; m. Madeleine Francine Marguerite Bazin, Oct. 6, 1963; children—Gregor, Tanya, Erik. Mem. faculty Yale U., 1948—, prof. cell and developmental biology, 1964—, master Branford Coll., 1966-73; chmn. Gordon Research Conf. on Cell Contact and Movement, 1979; mem. staff Woods Hole (Mass.) Marine Biol. Lab., 1953-57, 78. Served to capt. USAAF, 1942-46. Guggenheim fellow, 1959-60; NSF grantee, 1952-76; NIH grantee, 1974—. Mem. Am. Soc. Zoologists, Am. Soc. Cell Biology, Am. Soc. Developmental Biology, Internat. Inst. Embryology, ACLU (program chmn. New Haven 1952-58). Clubs: Yale (N.Y.C.); Mory's. Author: Cells into Organs—The Forces That Shape the Embryo, 1969; also articles. Home: Moose Hill Rd Guilford CT 06437 Office: Dept Biology Yale Univ New Haven CT 196520

TRIOLO, DOMINICK JOSEPH, chem. co. adminstr.; b. N.Y.C., Mar. 20, 1915; s. Domenico and Jennie (Giamparolo) T.; Electrician in Elec. Wiring, Murry Hill (N.Y.) Vocat. High Sch., 1934; Technician in Electronics, YMCA Vocat. Sch., N.Y.C., 1936; technologist in Animal Biology, Am. Assn. Lab. Animal Sci., N.Y.C., 1967; m. Mildred Senior, Oct. 9, 1938 (div. 1960); children—Patricia, Jeannine, Eileen; m. 2d, Janet Tyler, Nov. 19, 1961; children—Sandra, Cynthia. Foreman animal sci. dept. Columbia U., N.Y.C., 1939-42; civil service supr., dept. hosp. animal sci. N.Y. State U., N.Y.C., 1943, Columbia U., N.Y.C., 1943-68, also part-time elec. technician, aerospace dept. Bklyn. Poly. Inst., 1956-68; mgr. animal sci. dept. Ciba Geigy Chem. Corp., Ardsley, N.Y., 1969—; tchr., lectr. in animal sci. for tng. programs Am. Assn. Lab. Animal Sci., 1970—. Certified animal technologist, N.Y. Mem. Am. Assn. Lab. Animal Sci. Roman Catholic. Club: York Country (Ardsley). Home: PO Box 43 Thompson Ridge NY 10985 Office: 444 Saw Mill River Rd Ardsley NY 10502

TRIPLETT, GARY JOE, lawyer, chem. co. exec.; b. Van, W. Va., May 17, 1926, s. General Francis and Vivian Ethel (Eastep) T.; student Ala. Poly. Inst., 1944-45; A.B., W.Va. U., 1949, LL.B., 1951; m. Loretta James Findley, Apr. 18, 1953; children—Martha Sloan, Grace Stout. Admitted to W.Va. bar, 1951; law clk. U.S. Dist. Ct., Charleston, W.Va., 1951-52; mem. firm Jackson, Kelly, Holt & O'Farrell, Charleston, 1952-58; atty. Union Carbide Corp., South Charleston, 1958-69, atty. in charge South Charleston regional office law dept., 1969-72, energy, environ. affairs counsel, N.Y.C., 1972-76, sr. group counsel, 1976-78, sr. regional counsel, 1978—. Instr. comml. law Am. Inst. Banking, 1956-57; pres. W.Va. State Bar, 1970-71, chmn. bd., 1971-72; bd. dirs. Kanawha-Clay chpt. A.R.C., vice chmn., 1971-72. Served with USNR, 1945-46. Mem. Am. Bar Assn. (mem. standing com. assn. communications 1972-75), Phi Delta Phi, Psi Chi, Delta Nu Tau, Beta Theta Pi. Presbyterian. Mem. editorial bd. W.Va. Law Rev., 1949-51. Home: 74 Eastview Ave Pleasantville NY 10570 Office: Union Carbide Corp Law Dept 270 Park Ave New York City NY 10017

TRIPP, BENJAMIN RILEY, research and devel. co. exec.; b. Ayden, N.C., Sept. 15, 1934; s. Levi Redden and Nancy Elizabeth (Dail) T.; student E. Carolina Coll., 1952-53; B.E.E., N.C. State U., 1956, M.S., 1958; postgrad. State U. of N.Y. at Buffalo, 1961-65, Cornell U. (Calspan grad. fellowship), 1965-66; m. Evelyn Videau Joyner, June 7, 1958; children—Benjamin Riley, Michael Keith. Research engr. Radiation, Inc., Orlando, Fla., 1958-61; head dept. avionics Calspan Advanced Tech. Center, Buffalo, N.Y., 1961—; lectr. N.C. State U., 1956-58, State U. of N.Y. at Buffalo, 1961-65. Mem. Am. Def. Preparedness Assn., Assn. of Old Crows, Inst. of Electrical and Electronics Engrs., Am. Inst. Aeros. and Astronautics, Sigma Xi, Eta Kappa Nu, Tau Beta Pi. Baptist. Contbr. tech. papers to profl. jours. Home: 315 Windsor Ln East Aurora NY 14052 Office: PO Box 400 Buffalo NY 14225

TRIPP, TERRANCE BLAINE, chemist; b. Hollis, Maine, Aug. 6, 1937; s. Lloyd Leslie and Iva (Usher) T.; B.S. in Chemistry, U. Maine, Orono, 1959, M.S., 1961, Ph.D., 1967; m. Eugenia L. Murray, June 14, 1959; children—Valarie Dell, T. Daniel. Jr. chemist Sprague Electric Co., N. Adams, Mass., 1961-63, sr. chemist, 1967-70; instr. in chemistry U. Maine, Orono, 1963-67; asso. prof. chemistry U. Maine, Presque Isle, 1970-76, prof., 1976—; research participation contract with Oak Ridge Associated Univs., 1972—; liaison officer to Am. Assn. State Colls. and Univs. Mem. Presque Isle Zoning Bd. Appeals, 1975—; chmn. Presque Isle Band Boosters Assn.; sr. deacon Congregational Ch., Presque Isle, 1975. NDEA summer fellow, 1964, 65, 66. Mem. Sigma Xi. Clubs: Masons (Saco, Garfield, Aroostook), Order Eastern Star. Contbr. articles to sci. jours. Home: 128 Canterbury St Presque Isle ME 04769 Office: U Maine Presque Isle ME 04769

TRITT, JOHN EUGENE, ednl. adminstr.; b. Shippensburg, Pa., Jan. 12, 1937; s. Paul Wesley and Mabel (Swartz) T.; B.S., Shippensburg State Coll., 1959; M.Ed., U. Md., 1969; m. Jane Kramer, Aug. 11, 1957; children—James Todd, Jennifer Anne. Tchr. bus. edn., Frederick, Md., 1959-61; asst. in adminstrn. Bd. Edn. of Frederick County, Frederick, 1961-63, supr. purchasing and budgeting, 1963-65, dir. adminstrv. services, 1965-77, asst. supt., 1977—. Mem. grad. faculty Western Md. Coll. Gen. campaign chmn. United Givers Fund, 1975; pres. United Way, 1976. Bd. dirs. Frederick County YMCA, v.p. finance, 1975. Mem. Assn. Sch. Bus. Ofcls. U.S. and Can. (mem. elections com. 1970, by-laws com. 1975, internat. liaison rep. 1978, dir. 1979—), Assn. Sch. Bus. Ofcls. Md. and D.C. (pres. 1969), Am. Assn. Sch. Adminstrs., Phi Delta Kappa. Methodist (mem. adminstrv. bd., tchr., treas. 1977, chmn. finance com. 1978). Kiwanian (local chmn. finance com. 1970, dir. 1978). Home: Route 8 Eastview Frederick MD 21701 Office: 115 E Church St Frederick MD 21701

TRIVEDI, DINO C., hosp. adminstr.; b. India, Feb. 6, 1946; s. C. J. and A. C. T.; m. Nina, Aug. 12, 1974. Chief accountant Sprigarden Center, Inc., Phila., 1971-74; sr. accountant Hahnemann Med. Coll. and Hosp., Phila., 1974-76, mgr. transp. dept., fiscal coordinator, 1976—. Home: 4408 School Ln Drexel Hill PA 19026 Office: Hahnemann Med Coll and Hosp 230 N Broad St Philadelphia PA 19102

TRIVEDI, NIKHIL CHANDRAKANT, engr.; b. Navasari, India, Nov. 4, 1948; s. Chandrakant N. and Sheela H. (Divecha) T.; came to U.S., 1967, naturalized, 1977; B.Sc., U. Bombay, 1967; M.S., U. Nev., 1970; Ph.D., U. Minn., 1974. Metall. engr. Milchem Inc., Battle Mountain, Nev., 1969; research engr. Pfizer Inc., Easton, Pa., 1974-76, sr. research engr., 1976-77, mgr. mfg. devel., 1977—. Mem. AAAS, Am. Chem. Soc., Am. Inst. Mining, Metall. and Petroleum Engrs., Can. Inst. Mining and Metallurgy. Office: 640 N 13th St Easton PA 18042

TROBERG, LARS OSKAR, carbon co. research metallurgist; b. Aland, Finland, Nov. 16, 1922; s. Karl Oskar and Augusta Johanna (Helin) T.; came to U.S., 1949; B.S. in Chem. Engring., Tech. Coll., Helsinki, Finland, 1945; M.S. in Metallurgy, Stevens Inst. Tech., Hoboken, N.J., 1951; m. Beverly Joann Hoffman, Jan. 14, 1953. Research in metallurgy Hoganas Co. (Sweden), 1945-49; instr. metallurgy Stevens Inst. Tech., Hoboken, N.J., 1950-51; research metallurgist Keystone Carbon Co., St. Marys, Pa., 1954—. Westinghouse Elec. Corp. fellow in metallurgy, 1951. Mem. Am. Soc. Metals, Metal. Soc. of Am. Inst. Mining Engrs., Am. Powder Metallurgy Inst. Contbr. articles in field to profl. jours. Home: 645 Sherry St St Marys PA 15857 Office: 1935 State St St Marys PA 15857

TROIANO, JAMES ANTHONY, jewelry mfg. co. exec.; b. Providence, Dec. 4, 1947; s. Nicholas and Ida Sara (Ursillo) T.; student Bryant Coll., 1965-66, Tarkio Coll., 1966, Roger Williams Coll., 1967-68, U. R.I., 1967; m. Patricia Williams, Nov. 20, 1971; children—Nicole, James. Pres., M. & C. Mfg. Co., Providence, 1969-75; quality control mgr. Catamore Co., East Providence, R.I., 1975-77; quality assurance Monet/Ciani, Providence, 1977—; broker, real estate Troiano Realty, 1974—. Mem. Am. Soc. Quality Control, ASTM. Home: 40 Echo Ln Cranston RI 02920 Office: Monet/Ciani Chestnut St Providence RI

TROLL, JOHN HANS, research corp. exec.; b. Vienna, Austria, Apr. 20, 1919; s. Stephan V. and Anne (Thune) T.; student U. Vienna, 1937-38; B.A., Harvard, 1941, M.A., 1944; postgrad. Columbia, 1948-50; m. Lillian Ellman, June 21, 1941; children—Kathren, Jeanne, James Gregory; m. 2d, Enid R. Williams, Sept. 4, 1963. Came to U.S., 1938, naturalized, 1942. Engr. Western Electric Co., Kearney, N.J., N.Y.C., 1944-47; project engr. Fried Electronics Co., N.Y.C., 1947-50; v.p. Avion Instrument Co., Paramus, N.J., 1950-54, Electronics Corp. Am., Cambridge, Mass., 1954-59; cons., N.Y.C., 1959-64; pres., dir. Pyrotel Corp., Marmaraoneck, N.Y., 1964-66; v.p. Ovitron Corp., Cheshire, Conn., 1966-69; pres., dir. Ecologic Resources Corp., N.Y.C., 1969-71, Environ. Research and Applications, 1971-73, Natural Energy Corp., N.Y.C., 1973—. Sr. mem. IEEE. Author: The BHF, 1948. Contbr. articles to profl. jours. Patentee in field. Home: Cedar Rd E Katonah NY 10536 Office: Natural Energy Corp 375 Park Ave New York City NY 10022

TROPF, WILLIAM JACOB, physicist; b. Chgo., Jan. 14, 1947; s. William Jacob and Ardith Shirley (Clausen) T.; B.S., Coll. William and Mary, 1968; Ph.D., U. Va., 1973; m. Cheryl Lynn Griffiths, Aug. 31, 1968. Teaching asst. U. Va., 1968-70, research asst., 1970-73; project dir. B-K Dynamics, Inc., Rockville, Md., 1973-77; sr. physicist Applied Physics Lab., Johns Hopkins U., Laurel, Md., 1977—. Served with U.S. Army, 1973. Mem. Am. Phys. Soc., Optical Soc. Am., Am. Def. Preparedness Assn., Sigma Xi, Sigma Pi Sigma. Democrat. Club: Sigma Chi Alumni Assn. (Washington). Home: 13060 Saint Patricks Ct Highland MD 20777 Office: Johns Hopkins Rd Laurel MD 20810

TROPP, RICHARD ABRAHAM, govt. ofcl.; b. N.Y.C., Apr. 27, 1948; s. Leon and Stephanie T.; B.A., Coll. City N.Y., 1968; J.D., Yale U., 1971. Teaching fellow, adj. instr. polit. sci. Yale U., 1969-71, mem. task force genetics and reprodn. Med. Sch., 1971-77; legis. asst. to U.S. Senator Charles E. Goodell, 1970-71; spl. counsel Com. Study Incarceration, Field Found., N.Y.C., 1971; cons. Office of Sec., HEW, 1972-74; cons. Office of Adminstr., Fed. Energy Office, 1974; spl. counsel Presdl. Clemency Bd., The White House, 1974-75; cons. HEW and Dept. Labor, 1976-77, Office of Sec., HEW, 1978—. Regional dir., bd. govs. legis. services Yale Law Sch., 1969-71; mem. adv. bd. Nat. Assn. Pretrial Services Agencies, N.Y.C. Trustee Washington Community Sch. Music, 1977-78. Schapiro scholar, 1968; recipient Goldman Meml. award Coll. City N.Y., 1968, Ward medal, 1968. Mem. Areopagus, Blue Key, Phi Beta Kappa, Pi Sigma Alpha, Omicron Delta Epsilon, Phi Alpha Theta. Club: Wittes '68. Address: Office of Sec Dept HEW Humphrey Bldg 415F Washington DC 20201

TROTT, ROSMARY CLIFFORD (MRS. JAMES E. TROTT), writer; b. Mt. Vernon, N.Y., Mar. 8; d. Edward Farnsworth and Beatrice (Wright) Clifford; student Bates Coll., 1942, Columbia U., 1947-48; L.H.D., Internat. U., Ceylon, Internat. U. Pakistan; m. James Edwin Trott, Feb. 8, 1930; children—Donald Victor, Rosemary Diane. Feature writer Portland (Maine) Evening News, 1930; reporter, feature writer Gannett Publs., 1942-46, Brunswick (Maine) Record, 1942-47; feature writer Lewiston (Maine) Jour., 1945—; radio copy writer, WPOR, 1948-49; news dir. WLOB, 1957—; Maine staff corr. Dealerscope Mag., N.E., Waltham, Mass., 1969—; tchr. Woodfords Sch., Portland. Dir. Maine Women's State Relief Corps, 1948-50; women's dir. Freeport area CD; founder Poetry Day in Maine; Maine state chairman for Nat. Art Week; state chmn. Poetry Day, mem. world com., nat. com.; state chmn. Maine Poetry Week, 1950—; founder Maine Poetry Sunday, 1968, Am. Poetry Sunday, 1969; Maine chmn. Maine World Poetry Day, 1968—; Maine winner World Poetry Day Exhibit, 1961; Maine chmn. Authors' Nat. Library Week, 1959; judge Maine State Writers' Conf., juvenile fiction contest, 1960; poetry chmn. exhibits; Maine dir. Am. Art Week, 1966; chmn., judge state competition Maine Poetry Week, 1969; pub. relations dir. Second World Congress Poets, Taiwan, 1973, floor leader Third World Congress, Balt., 1976; hon. life mem. Nat. Poetry Day Com., 1975; dir. Freeport Poetry Centre. Named Hon. Poet Laureate Nature, United Poets Laureate Internat.; Internat. Woman of Year in Poetry, 1975; recipient Gold medal Pres. Marcos; UN Day award; 1st prize World Poetry Competition, 1967, Poetry Soc. N.H., 1967, Nat. Poetry Day, State of N.J.; others. Fellow Internat. Biog. Soc.; mem. Nat. League Am. Pen Women (N.E. regional chmn. of poetry 1954, pres. Pine Tree br. 1960, nat. poetry chmn.; co-chmn. biennial poetry banquet Washington, 1962; nat. ballad chmn. 1961-62, 1st prize non-fiction 1976, 1st prize publicity), Maine Poetry Day Assn. (pres. 1959), Poetry Fellowship (sec. 1948), Maine Hist. Soc., Am. Poetry League (1st prize features 1959), Press Women, Studi e Scambi Internazionli, Freeport, Yarmouth hist. socs., Cosmosythesis League Australia (hon. life), Poetry Soc. Fla. (hon.), Maine Poets and Writers Guild. Clubs: Freeport Woman's (chmn. service com. 1970), Order Eastern Star (officer 1978—). Author: Sea Mist and Balsam, 1958; Path of Roses; By Wind and Water, 1970; also articles and poetry to numerous mags. Editor: From One Bright Spark, 1959; editorial bd. As Maine Writes, 1948; Maine Indians in Story and Legend, 1950; The Pen Woman's Year, 1950; contbr. columns to Freeport Post, 1972—, column Taste of Salt, 1976. Home: Blueberry Hill Freeport ME 04032 Office: 115 2d Ave Waltham MA

TROTTA, ANTHONY RALPH, mech. engr.; b. Old Forge, Pa., Mar. 9, 1921; s. Ralph and Angeline (Genell) T.; B.S. in Chem. Engring., Pa. State U., 1949; M.B.A., U. Scranton, 1975; m. Carmella Dante, July 29, 1950; children—Angela Thomas, Anthony A. Chem. engr. U.S. Naval Engring. Exptl. Sta., Annapolis, Md. and U.S. Naval Air Rocket Test Sta., Dover, N.J., 1950-53; sr. design engr. Air Products and Chems. Inc., Allentown, Pa., 1953-62; cryogenic engr. and cons. Rocket Systems div. NASA, Plum Beach Sta., Sandusky, Ohio, 1962-64; head electric propulsion lab. Goddard Space Flight Center, NASA, Greenbelt, Md., 1964-69; chief prodn. engring. div. U.S. Army Tobyhanna (Pa.) Depot, 1969—. Mem. St. Mary's Holy Name Soc. Served with USAF, 1939-45. Roman Catholic. Club: K.C. Home: 301 Smith St Old Forge PA 18518 Office: Tobyhanna Army Depot Tobyhanna PA 18466

TROTTA, GERI (GERALDINE), writer, editor; b. N.Y.C.; d. Pasquale and Katherine (Marconi) Trotta; B.A., Barnard Coll.; postgrad. Columbia U.; m. Mark Shaw, Dec. 1948 (div. Feb. 1960). With Harper's Bazaar, feature and travel editor, 1959-71; contbg. editor Mademoiselle, 1947-59, Gourmet, 1972—; travel and feature writer for nat. mags. Recipient George Hedman Travel Writers' award, 1970; awards for features Pacific Area Travel Assn., 1977, 78. Mem. N.Y. Travel Writers (pres. 1969-71), Soc. Am. Travel Writers (chmn. N.E. chpt. 1975-77), Am. Soc. Authors and Journalists, Les Dames D'Escoffier. Author: Veronica Died Monday, 1952; Dead as Diamonds, 1956; Dune House, 1960. Address: 142 E 30th St New York City NY 10016

TROUBETZKOY, ALEXIS SERGE, sch. adminstr.; b. Paris, France, Mar. 6, 1934; s. Serge Gregory and Luba A. (Obolensky) T.; came to Can., 1953, naturalized, 1958; B.A., Sir George Williams U., 1958; postgrad. Bishops U., 1960; m. Helene de Klebnikoff, July 8, 1967; children—Anne, Andre. Housemaster, Bishop's Coll. Sch., Lennoxville, Que., Can., 1958-66; asst. to headmaster St. Stephen's Sch., Rome, Italy, 1966-68, Appleby Coll., Oakville, Ont., Can., 1968-70; headmaster Selwyn House Sch., Montreal, Que., 1970—. Served with Royal Canadian Navy Res., 1954-65. Mem. Canadian Headmasters Assn. (sec.-treas. 1973), Comite d'Honneur-Napoleonic Soc., Que. Assn. Ind. Schs. (dir. 1968, v.p.), Zeta Psi. Mem. Orthodox Ch. Am. Home: 444 Argyle Ave Montreal PQ H3Y 2H8 Canada Office: 95 Cote St Antoine Rd Montreal PQ H3Y 2H8 Canada

TROUP, FRANK FLEISHER, lawyer; b. Pitts., Sept 20, 1905; s. Charles Baldwin and Myrtle May (Fleisher) T.; A.B., U. Pitts., 1926, LL.B., 1929; m. Margaret Gertrude Pickering, Dec. 25, 1939. Admitted to Pa. bar, 1929, U.S. Supreme Court bar, 1965; pres., dir. Homewood Masonic Hall Assn., 1954-67; Allegheny County agt. Berks Title Ins. Co., 1949-76, atty., 1976—. Mem. Am., Pa., Allegheny County bar assns., Internat. Acad. of Law and Sci., Pa. Soc., Pi Kappa Alpha. Republican. Lutheran. Clubs: Pittsburgh Athletic Assn.; Lawyers (Allegheny County); Elkview Country (Pa.). Home: 1014 Blackridge Rd Pittsburgh PA 15235 also (summer) Newton Lake Carbondale PA 18407 Office: 335 Fifth Ave Pittsburgh PA 15222

TROUT, MONROE EUGENE, pharm. co. adminstr., physician; b. Harrisburg, Pa., Apr. 5, 1931; s. David Michael and Florence Margaret (Kashner) T.; A.B., U. Pa., 1953, M.D., 1957; LL.B., Dickinson Sch. of Law, 1964, J.D., 1969; m. Sandra Louise Lemke, June 11, 1960; children--Monroe Eugene, Timothy William. Intern Great Lakes (Ill.) Naval Hosp., 1957-58; resident Portsmouth (Va.) Naval Hosp., 1959-61; practice medicine specializing in internal medicine, Harrisburg, 1961-64; chief med. dept. Harrisburg State Hosp., 1961-64; dir. drug regulatory affairs Pfizer, Inc., N.Y.C., 1964-68; med. dir. Winthrop Labs., N.Y.C., 1968-70; med. dir. Sterling Drug, Inc., N.Y.C., 1970-74, v.p., 1974-78, sr. v.p., 1978—, mem. research bd., 1973—; adj. asso. prof. Bklyn. Coll. of Pharmacy, 1967—; spl. lectr. legal medicine Dickinson Sch. of Law, Carlisle, Pa., 1962—; cons. to HEW, 1973-74, sec. Commn. on Med. Malpractice, 1971-72; mem. profl. adv. bd. Comml. Credit Corp., 1976-78, Control Data Corp., 1978—. Bd. dirs. New Canaan (Conn.) Interch. Service Commn., 1965-69, Lake Club Inc., 1973-76; mem. New Eng. Synod Bd. of Social Ministry, 1965-67; Republican dist. leader, New Canaan, 1966-68; trustee Dickinson Sch. of Law, 1973—, Athlete's Kidney Found., Albany Med. Coll.; trustee Cleveland Clinic, 1971—. Served to lt. comdr. USNR, 1956-61. Recipient Alumni award of merit U. Pa., 1953, Physicians Recognition award AMA, 1969, 72, 77. Fellow Am. Coll. of Legal Medicine (v.p. 1969-72, pres. 1972-74, editorial bd. 1972, bd. govs. 1967-76, Pres.'s award 1976, 78); mem. Med. Execs. (pres. 1974-76), AMA, Pharm. Mfg. Assn. (med. steering com. 1974). Bd. editors Forensic Sci., 1971—, Hosp. Formulary, 1969—. Contbr. numerous articles on legal medicine, forensic sci. to profl. jours.; contbr. chpts. on medicine and law to various books. Home: 81 Mariomi Rd New Canaan CT 06840 Office: 90 Park Ave New York City NY 10016

TROUTWINE, CHARLOTTE TEMPERLEY, psychologist, adminstr., educator; b. Newton, Mass., Nov. 27, 1906; d. Joseph and Libbie (Kempton) Temperley; B.S., Simmons Coll., 1927; student Boston U., 1947-49; M.A., Northeastern U., 1966; m. Arklay S. Richards, Nov. 28, 1928 (div. 1942); children—Whitman Albin, Lincoln Kempton, Sylvia Caroline; m. 2d, Harry Troutwine, May 3, 1945 (div. 1954); m. 3d, Charles E. McCrum, 1961 (div. 1965); m. 4th, Lester Lewis Walsh, Feb. 16, 1968 (div. Feb. 1972); m. 5th, George Braun, Feb. 6, 1975 (dec. Oct. 1975). Pvt. sec. pres. Hygrade Sylvania Electric Corp. Salem, Mass., 1927-28; pvt. and dept. exec. sec. Dr.

Stanley Cobb, Bullard prof. neuropathology Harvard Med. Sch., 1928-31; part-time work, various positions, 1931-51; exec. dir. Postgrad. Med. Inst., 1951-57; mgr. Postgrad. Information Services, Lederle Labs. div. Am. Cyanamid Co., Pearl River, N.Y., 1957-60; exec. sec. postgrad. med. edn., Hahnemann Med. Coll. and Hosp. also exec. dir. Mary Bailey Inst. Cardiovascular Research, 1961. Caseworker Friends of Framingham Reformatory; counselor Falmouth High Sch., Falmouth, Mass., 1966-74. Speaker for Am. Epilepsy League. Mem. Mass. Tchrs. Assn. (life), Spiritual Frontiers Assn. (life), N.E.A. (life), Nat. Ret. Tchrs. Assn. (life), Nat. Assn. Sch. Counselors (charter, life), Assn. Research Enlightenment, Soc. Mayflower Descs. (life), Simmons Coll. Alumnae Assn., AAUW, Med. Soc. Execs. Assn. (emeritus), Am. Soc. Psychical Research, States Med. Postgrad. Assn. (past sec.), Mass. Psychol. Assn., Am. Spiritual Healing Assn. (healing mem., mem. adv. bd.), Spiritual Frontiers Fellowship (life), World Fedn. Healers (healer mem.). Mem. Soc. of Friends. Author articles in field. Home: 10 Waterside Dr North Falmouth MA 02556

TROWBRIDGE, CALVIN DURAND, JR., consumer products co. exec., lawyer; b. Chgo., Apr. 6, 1934; s. Calvin Durand and Lillias (Webster) T.; B.A., Yale U., 1956; LL.B., Harvard U., 1959; m. Lee Claire Doran, Nov. 28, 1959; children—Calvin Durand III, Lee Crane, David Kent, Nina. Admitted to Ill. bar, 1959, Calif. bar, 1969, N.Y. State bar, 1974, partner firm Isham, Lincoln & Beale, Chgo., 1967-68; asst. sec. Norton Simon, Inc., N.Y.C., 1968-70, asso. gen. counsel, 1970-73, gen. counsel, 1973—, v.p., sec., 1975—. Mem. Am., Calif. bar assns., Assn. Bar City N.Y. Office: 277 Park Ave New York City NY 10017

TROWBRIDGE, PHILLIP EDMUND, surgeon; b. Hartford, Conn., Oct. 17, 1930; s. John Henry and Isabelle Storrey (Warner) T.; B.A., Trinity Coll., Hartford, 1952; postgrad. Harvard U., 1955; M.D., Tufts U., 1959; m. Fay Elaine Russell, June 23, 1956; children—Kimberly, Heather, Allison, John, David. Intern, Hartford Hosp., 1959-60, resident in surgery, 1960-65, mem. staff, 1965—; practice medicine specializing in surgery, Hartford, 1965—; cons. McLean Home, Simsbury, Conn., 1972—, VA Hosp., Newington, Conn., 1965-74, 75—; clin. asso. U. Conn. Sch. Medicine, 1974—. Bd. dirs. West Hartford St. Ministry, 1974—; corporator Hartford Sem. Found., 1975-77, trustee, 1977—. Served to 1st lt. USAF, 1952-54. Diplomate Am. Bd. Surgery. Fellow A.C.S.; mem. Hartford, Conn. State, Hartford County (dir.) med. socs., Am. Burn Assn., Internat. Soc. Burn Injuries, Am. Trauma Soc., Conn. Bd. Surgeons, AMA, Theta Xi. Republican. Baptist. Contbr. articles to profl. publs. Home: 14 Dodge Dr West Hartford CT 06107 Office: 85 Jefferson St Hartford CT 06106 also 1005 B Farmington Ave West Hartford CT 06107

TROWBRIDGE, RICHARD STUART, virologist, cell biologist; b. Cambridge, Mass., Apr. 3, 1942; s. Walter Henry and Lamia Andree (Sanderson) T.; B.S., U. Mass., 1964, M.S., 1966, Ph.D., 1970; m. Sue Hitchcock, June 12, 1965; 1 son, John Richard. Research scientist dept. virology N.Y. State Inst. Basic Research in Mental Retardation, S.I., 1970-72, sr. research scientist, 1972-77, research scientist V, 1977—, grant adminstr., 1977—, vice chmn. human rights com., 1974-76, chmn., 1976-77. Bd. dirs. Research Found. for Mental Hygiene, Inc., 1978—, also mem. instnl. rev. bd. and affirmative action com. Active Boy Scouts Am. Nat. Inst. Allergy and Infectious Diseases grantee, 1974-77. Mem. Am. Soc. Microbiology, Tissue Culture Assn. Contbr. articles to profl. jours. Home: 180 Woodward Ave Staten Island NY 10314 Office: NY State Inst Basic Research in Mental Retardation 1050 Forest Hill Rd Staten Island NY 10314

TROXELL, RAYMOND ROBERT, JR., supt. schs.; b. Easton, Pa., July 11, 1932; s. Raymond Robert and Mary (Cooney) T.; B.A., Lafayette Coll., 1955; M.A. in Internat. Relations, Lehigh U., 1962, M.A. in Ednl. Adminstrn., 1963; m. Barbara Foulk, Aug. 6, 1955; children—Gayle, Pamella, Lynn Rae. Successively tchr., social studies dept. chmn., pub. relations dir., curriculum coordinator, prin. Easton Area Sch. Dist., 1956-65; successively curriculum coordinator, asst. supt., ESEA Title III project dir., supt. schs. West York (Pa.) Area Sch. Dist., 1966—. Vis. prof. ednl. adminstrn. Western Md. Coll.; evaluator commonwealth schs. program Pa. Dept. Edn., Pa. Model Schs. Program; participant Internat. Seminar on Edn., Eastern Europe, 1971. Bd. dirs. Jr. Achievement of York, York chpt. ARC, United Way. Served with USCG. Recipient award Valley Forge Freedoms Found., 1963, Outstanding Tchr. award, 1963, Am. Educators medal, 1975. Mott Found. fellow, 1964; Ford Found. grantee; Kettering Found. grantee. Mem. Am., Pa. assns. sch. adminstrs., Nat., Pa. sch. bds. assns., Nat. Assn. Secondary Sch. Prins., Nat. Council Social Studies, Am. Acad. Polit. and Social Scis., Center for Study of Presidency, Council on Basic Edn., Nat., Pa. assns. supervision and curriculum devel., Am. Judicature Soc., York C. of C. (v.p.), Nat. Alliance Businessmen, Phi Delta Kappa, Kappa Phi Kappa. Club: York Exchange (past pres.). Contbr. articles to profl. jours. Home: 2613 Sunset Ln York PA 17404 Office: 2605 W Market St York PA 17404

TRPIS, MILAN, scientist, educator; b. Mojsova Lucka, Slovakia, Czechoslovakia, Dec. 20, 1930; s. Gaspar and Anna (Sevcikova) T.; came to U.S., 1971, naturalized, 1977; M.S., Comenius U., Bratislava, 1956; Ph.D., Charles U., Prague, 1960; m. Ludmila Tonkovic, Dec. 15, 1956; children—Martin, Peter, Katarina. Research asst. Slovak Acad. Sci., Bratislava, 1953-56, sci. asst., 1956-60, scientist, 1960-62, ind. scientist, 1962-69; ecologist-entomologist East Africa-Aedes research unit, WHO, Dar es Salaam, Tanzania, 1969-71; asst. faculty fellow dept. biology U. Notre Dame, 1971-73, asso. faculty fellow, 1974-78; asso. prof. med. entomology Johns Hopkins U. Sch. Hygiene and Pub. Health, 1974-78, prof., 1978—; research asso. U. Ill., Urbana, 1956-57, Can. Dept. Agr., Lethbridge, Alta., 1957-58; dir. Biol. Research Inst. Am., 1975—. Recipient Slovak Acad. Sci., 1st prize for research project. Mem. AAUP, Am. Inst. Biol. Sci., AAAS, Am. Mosquito Control Assn., Am. Soc. Parasitologists, Am. Soc. Tropical Medicine, Entomol. Soc. Am., Johns Hopkins U. Tropical Medicine Club, Sigma Xi. Editor Jour. Biologia, 1956-71, Jour. Entomol. Problems, 1960-72, zool. sect. Jour. Biol. Works, 1960-71. Contbr. articles to profl. jours. Home: 1504 Ivy Hill Rd Cockeysville MD 21030 Office: Johns Hopkins U 615 N Wolfe St Baltimore MD 21205

TRUDEAU, PIERRE ELLIOTT, Canadian prime minister; b. Montreal, Que., Can., Oct. 18, 1919; grad. Jean de Bre'beuf Coll., 1940; ed. Harvard, U. Paris, London Sch. Econs., U. Montreal; LL.D., U. Alta., 1968, Queen's U., 1968, Duke U., 1974 D.Litt., U. Moncton, 1969; others; m. Margaret Sinclair (separated 1977); children—Justin, Alexandre Emmanuel, Charles Emile Michel. Created Queen's Counsel, 1969; Formerly minister of justice; now prime minister. Mem. Que., Ont. bar assns., Royal Soc. Can., others. Author: Re'ponses, 1967; Federalism and the French Canadians, 1968; co-author: Deux Innocents in Chine, 1961; contbr. articles to jours., books. Office: Office of Prime Minister 24 Sussex Dr Ottawa ON K1M 1M4 Canada

TRUDEAU, THEODORE JOSEPH, state legislator; b. Hillsgrove, R.I., Jan. 22, 1916; s. Walter Albert and Agnes Mary (Bedard) T.; student Western New Eng. Coll., 1960-62; m. Claire C. LeTourneau, Sept. 5, 1938; children—Robert H., John R., Roger W., James E. Various positions Springfield (Mass.) Armory, 1939-67, program coordinator, 1961-67; prodn. adminstrn. specialist Armament div. Gen. Electric Co., Springfield Ops., 1967-70; mem. Mass. Ho. of Reps., 1973—. Faculty, Springfield Tech. Community Coll., 1971. Chief warden Springfield Civil Def., 1950-55; police commr. Springfield, 1965-72; pres. Indian Orchard Civic Assn., 1960-62. Pres., Ward 8, Springfield Republican Com., 1971-72; mem. Wilbraham Rep. Town Com., 1973—. Bd. dirs. Pioneer Valley chpt. Nat. Found.-March of Dimes. Served with U.S. Army, 1945-46. Mem. Am. Inst. Indsl. Engrs. (past chpt. pres.). K.C. Home: 19 Pearl Ln Wilbraham MA 01095 Office: Room 146 State House Boston MA 02133

TRUEBLOOD, DAVID MARTIN, retirement community dir.; b. Indianola, Iowa, July 26, 1925; s. D. Elton and Pauline C. (Goodenow) T.; B.N.S., U. Notre Dame, 1946; A.B. in Physics, Earlham Coll., 1947; m. Margaret Elizabeth, June 20, 1947; children—Rachel Lynn, David Craig, Peter Martin, Christopher Scott. Asst. supr. photo-engraving dept. Sandura, Inc., Fullerton, Pa., 1947-52; with Standard Pressed Steel Co., 1954-70; asso. dir. retirement community Foulkeways, Gwynedd, Pa., 1970-74; exec. dir. Pine Run Community, Doylestown, Pa., 1974-76, Broadmead, Cockeysville, Md., 1976—; mem. com. to draft legis. on life care contracts Md. Dept. Aging; cons. in field. Served with USN, 1944-46, 1952-54. Licensed nursing home adminstr., Pa. Mem. Am. Assn. Homes for the Aging, Balt. County C. of C. (mem. health care com.). Mem. Soc. Friends. Club: Rotary. Home and Office: 13801 York Rd Cockeysville MD 21030*

TRUITT, (MARY) ANN, sch. psychologist; b. Washington, Aug. 31, 1941; d. Stephen and Ruth May (Moreland) Truitt; B.S., D.C. Tchrs. Coll., 1962; M.A., Columbia, 1963; Ph.D., Heed U., 1974. Tchr. spl. edn. in jr. high schs. Prince Georges County (Md.) Pub. Schs., 1963-68, sch. psychologist, 1968—. Instr. Western Md. Coll. Grad. Sch., Westminster, 1971—. Mem. NEA, Nat. Assn. Sch. Psychologists, Md., Prince Georges County (pres. 1975-77) psychol. assns., Md., Prince Georges County tchrs. assns. Author: Read Better, 1969, rev. edit., 1975. Home: 5101 River Rd Apt 1610 Chevy Chase MD 20016 Office: 6366 Greenbelt Rd Greenbelt MD 20770

TRUMP, FREDERICK TAYLOR, ct. reporter; b. Bloomsburg, Pa., Oct. 21, 1936; s. Ralph and Agnes Belinda (Taylor) T.; B.A., Bloomsburg State Coll., 1968; m. Nancy Carol Rubenstein, Mar. 3, 1956; children—Jeffrey Scott, Michelle Rene. Registered profl. reporter 26th Judicial Dist. Commonwealth Pa., Bloomsburg, 1962—; free lance reporter, 1971—; sec. Bloomsburg Fair Assn., 1972—; lectr. in field. Chmn. Columbia County Democratic party, 1972-74; mem. Columbia County Prison Bd., 1975—; trustee Danville State Hosp., 1972—. Mem. Am., Pa. shorthand reporters assn., Columbia County Hist. Soc., Pa. Bd. Judicial Rev. Lutheran. Clubs: Kiwanis, Rotary, Mason (Shriner), Elk, Moose. Author: Night of Miracles, play, 1965; Moment of Decision, short story, 1974; A Meeting At the Well, play, 1976. Organized Bloomsburg Boys' Club, 1971. Home: 528 W 3d St Bloomsburg PA 17815 Office: Ct House W Main St Bloomsburg PA 17815

TRUXAL, JACOB RUGH, psychologist; b. Unity Twp., Pa., Oct. 30, 1919; s. Albert Nevin and Katherine Blanche (Shaw) T.; B.A., Westminster Coll., 1943; M.Ed., U. Pitts., 1947; D.Ed., Pa. State U., 1973; m. Frances Emogene Whitacre, Dec. 22, 1948. Sch. psychologist Greensburg, Vandergrift, and New Kensington pub. schs., 1947-53; supr. spl. edn. Pa. Dept. Edn., Harrisburg, 1953-62; psychologist Pa. Bur. Correction, Dept. Justice, Harrisburg, 1962—; psychol. cons. Pa. Bur. Vocat. Rehab., Harrisburg, 1967—; adj. prof. psychology York (Pa.) Coll., 1965—, Pa. State U., 1954—, Antioch Coll., Columbia, Md., 1973—. Registered psychologist, Pa. Fellow Am. Assn. Mental Deficiency, Am. Assn. Correctional Psychologists, Am., Pa. psychol. assns., State Edn. Assn. (pres. 1959-61), Lycoming County Assn. Blind (pres. 1956-57), VFW. Republican. Mem. United Ch. Christ. Club: Masons. Served with USN, 1943-46. Home: 215 E Hill Crest Dr Carlisle PA 17013 Office: Box 598 Camp Hill PA 17011

TRYON, EDWARD POLK, educator; b. Terre Haute, Ind., Sept. 4, 1940; s. Philip Freeland and Elizabeth Marsh (Banker) T.; A.B., Cornell, 1962; Ph.D., U. Calif. at Berkeley, 1967. Research asso. Columbia U., N.Y.C., 1967-68, asst. prof., 1968-71; asst. prof. physics Hunter Coll. City U., N.Y.C., 1971-73, asso. prof., 1974-79, prof., 1979— (on leave 1977-78); vis. mem. Inst. Advanced Study Princeton, 1977-78. Hon. Woodrow Wilson fellow, 1962-64; NSF fellow, 1962-64. Mem. Am. Phys. Soc., N.Y. Acad. Scis., Phi Beta Kappa, Sigma Xi, Phi Kappa Phi. Contbr. articles to profl. jours. Office: Dept Physics Hunter Coll New York City NY 10021

TRYON, PHILIP TREMAINE, bus. exec.; b. Manhattan, Mont., July 23, 1916; s. Victor Weld and Grace (Brown) T.; B.A., U. Man. (Can.), Winnipeg, 1936; M.B.A., Harvard U., 1938; m. F. June Bradfield, Sept. 14, 1940; children—June Lynne, Sally Victoria. Supt., Bemis Bag Co., Vancouver, B.C., Can., 1938-41; indsl. engr., 1946; prodn. mgr. Dominion Bridge Co., Vancouver, 1941-45; chief indsl. engr. H.J. Heinz Co., Leamington, Ont., Can., 1946-50, coordinator overseas mfg., Pitts., 1950-53; asst. to pres. Edwin M. Knowles China Co., Newall, W.Va., 1953-54; prodn. control mgr., works mgr., gen. mgr. Dresser Indsl. Valve & Instrument div. Dresser Industries, Inc. (formerly Manning, Maxwell & Moore, Inc.), Stratford, Conn., 1954-68, v.p., 1963-68; mem. adv. com. Conn. Nat. Bank, Stratford, 1959-68; v.p. Berwind Corp., Phila., 1968, v.p., 1969-74; chmn. bd. dirs. Mateer Co., Wayne, Pa., Strong-Scott Mfg. Co., Mpls., K-G Industries, Inc., Rosemont, Ill., Bindicator Co., Detroit, Hutt GmbH, Leingarten, Germany, Reitz Mfg. Co., Santa Rosa, Calif., Burt Machine Co., Balt., 1969-73, Frank M. Weaver & Co., Inc., Lansdale, Pa., 1973-75; DeKalb (Ill.) Forge Co., Neapco Inc., Pottstown, Pa., Perfect Equipment Corp., Murfreesboro, Tenn., 1974—, Berwind (Pa.) Ry. Service Co., 1975; v.p., dir. Sinto Berwind, Nagoya, Japan, 1972—; dir. P.R. Lighterage Co., San Juan, Berwind Lines, Inc., San Juan, Indsl. Molasses P.R., Borinquen Lines, Inc., San Juan, 1974-75. Chmn., Stratford campaign United Fund Eastern Fairfield County, 1958, co-chmn. labor-mgmt. com., 1959, 3d v.p., 1959-60, bd. dirs., 1961-68; chmn. awards com. Jr. Achievement Western Conn., 1959-60; marshal Parade of Champions, Barnum Festival Soc., 1959, exec. aide, 1960-61; bd. assos. U. Bridgeport. Mem. Bridgeport Engring. Inst. (adv. com. 1960-68), Mfrs. Assn. Bridgeport (Community relations com. 1959-68), Bridgeport (past v.p., past dir.), Conn. chambers commerce, Delta Kappa Epsilon. Clubs: Merion Golf (Ardmore, Pa.); Union League (Phila.). Home: 945 Mt Moro Rd Villanova PA 19085 Office: 3000 Centre Sq W 1500 Market St Philadelphia PA 19102

TSAI, CHEN FAI, chem. engr.; b. Taiwan, Feb. 7, 1946; s. Kuo Yuan and Ou Chai T.; came to U.S., 1969; M.S., U. N.H., 1971; Ph.D., Tex. A. and M. U., 1976; m. Aimee Hung Yien Lui, Aug. 26, 1972; 1 dau., Emily Joy. Process engr. Chang Chun Petrochem. & Plastic Co., Taiwan, 1967-69; research asst. U. N.H., Durham, 1969-71, Tex. A. and M. U., College Station, 1971-76; chem. process analyst U.S. Indsl. Chems. Co., N.Y.C., 1976—. Mem. Am. Inst. Chem. Engrs., Assn. for Computing Machinery, Omega Chi Epsilon, Phi Lambda Upsilon.

TS'AO, IGNATIUS JIH-HSIN, educator; b. Hsüchow, Kingsu Province, China, Jan. 27, 1933; came to U.S., 1962, naturalized, 1971; J.D., U. Madrid, 1961; m. Grace Wang, Sept. 5, 1963. Mem. faculty State U. N.Y. at Oneonta, 1966—; cons. studies in Soviet thought, 1968—. Mem. Assn. for Asian Studies, Am. Polit. Sci. Assn. State U. N.Y. Research Found. grantee. Founder, chief editor Asian Thought and Society: An Internat. Rev., 1976—. Contbr. articles on Chinese Communist ideological issues to jours. Home: 1 Bugbee Rd Oneonta NY 13820 Office: State U NY Oneonta NY 13820

TSAO, MIKE CHIA-CHENG, mech. engr.; b. Shantung, China, Aug. 10, 1939; s. Chen Jen and Shen Hwey (Liu) T.; B.S., Nat. Cheng Kung U., 1961; M.S., Tufts U., 1965; Ph.D., Carnegie-Mellon U., 1969; came to U.S., 1963, naturalized, 1975; m. Anna Chao-Ying Ting, Aug. 7, 1965; children—Jack W.L., Connie W.L. Research officer U. Oxford (Eng.), 1969-71; sr. engr. Westinghouse Research Labs., Pitts., 1971—. Registered profl. engr., Pa. Mem. ASME, Acoustical Soc. Am., Sigma Xi. Republican. Home: 54 Hauck Dr Pittsburgh PA 15235 Office: Westinghouse Research Labs Pittsburgh PA 15235

TSAO, TSEN CHA, engring. cons.; b. Shanghai, China, Oct. 16, 1901; s. Jin-Poo and Pearl (Shen) T.; B.S., Chaio Tung U. (China), 1924; M.S., Harvard U., 1929; Ph.D. (hon.), China Acad., 1973; m. Christina Ching, Dec. 20, 1969; children—Victor, Anthony, Frank, Alice, Julia, Priscilla. Came to U.S., 1949, naturalized, 1954. Prof. elec. engring. Nat. Chekiang U., China, 1929-32; dir., chief engr. Chekiang Telephone Adminstrn., China, 1932-38; commr. telecommunications 3rd War Zone, China, 1938-42; ministerial dir. for post and telecommunications, China, 1943-45; commr. pub. utilities Met. Shanghai, 1945-49; system engr. Consol. Edison Co., N.Y.C., N.Y., 1950-58; sr. research scientist Columbia U., Electronics Research Lab., N.Y.C., 1958-71; dir. Chris Assos., N.Y.C., 1971—; cons. telecommunication engring. Trustee Buddhist Assn. U.S., 1972—. Recipient Distinguished Service award Chinese Inst. Engrs., 1964, Phi Tau Phi, 1973. Fellow AAAS, IEEE; mem. Chinese Inst. Engrs. (chmn. central planning bd. 1977—), Inst. Elec. Engrs (British), ASME, Radio Club Am. Contbr. articles to profl. jours. Address: 351 E 84 St New York City NY 10028

TSAO, UTAH, chem. design mgr.; b. Shanghai, China, June 6, 1913; s. Hui Chung and Chiao Pi (Chiang) T.; B.S., Tatung U., 1933; M.S., Chiao Tung U., 1936; D.S., U. Mich., 1940; m. Hazel A.C. Lin, Aug. 17, 1940; children—Thomas, Preston. Process engr. The Lummus Co., N.Y.C., 1942-52; staff engr. C.E. Lummus Co., Bloomfield, N.Y., 1952-62, mgr. chem. plant design, 1963—; dir. China Petrochem. Devel. Corp., Taiwan. Recipient Personal Achievement award Chem. Engring. mag., 1978. Mem. Chinese Inst. Engrs. (achievement award 1971, pres. 1967-68), Internat. Inst. Jersey City (v.p. 1974, pres. 1975-76), Am. Inst. Chem. Engrs. Democrat. Patentee in field. Home: 1887 Kennedy Blvd Jersey City NJ 07305 Office: 1515 Broad St Bloomfield NJ 07003

TSE, OLIVER WAI-BUN, photography lab. co. exec.; b. Canton, China, Apr. 14, 1931; s. Kon Pak and Sun Wah (Chan) T.; came to Can., 1966, naturalized, 1971; diploma in journalism, Hong Kong, 1953; m. Florane Fuk-Wun Yee, Apr. 1, 1959; children—Quinbert, Queenie, Clara. Speaker, instr., print show judge in photography, Hong Kong, 1960-66, also photographer, exhibiter, various countries; photographer, dept. head Ave. Advt. Art, Inc., Montreal, Que., Can., 1966-68; dir. Jasco Color Corp., Montreal, 1969-72; pres. Champion Color Lab., Montreal, 1973—. Fellow Chinese Photog. Assn. Hong Kong, S.E. Asia Photog. Soc. Singapore (hon.); mem. Profl. Photographers Am., Royal Photog. Soc. Gt. Britain (asso.). Contbr. articles to profl. jours. Home: 8170 Saguenay Ave Brossard PQ J4X 1H7 Canada Office: 1434 St Catherine St W Suite 104 Montreal PQ H3G 1R4 Canada

TSENG, ANTHONY TAI, mgmt. cons.; b. Shanghai, China, Sept. 19, 1922; s. Herbert P. and F. T. (Wu) T.; B.S. in Indsl. Engring., Chiao-Tung U., Shanghai, 1947; M.S. in Indsl. Engring., Purdue U., 1950; m. Sophia Lane, Jan. 30, 1947; children—Robert Howe, Vivian Fifi. Came to U.S., 1948, naturalized, 1955. Sr. indsl. engr. Beldon Mfg. Co., Richmond, Ind., 1950-52; dir. indsl. engring. Diamond Nat. Corp., Middletown, Ohio, 1952-60; v.p. phys. distbn. and mgmt. engring. Hudson Pulp and Paper Corp. N.Y.C., 1960-71; pres. Phys. Distbn. Dynamics, Port Chester, N.Y., 1971—. Speaker to numerous nat. mgmt. assns. in U.S. Sr. mem. Inst. Indsl. Engrs. Clubs: Rotary. Contbr. articles to profl. jours. Address: 15 Sleepy Hollow Rd Port Chester NY 10573

TSIMORTOS, ANNE MARIE JACQUELINE, fgn. exchange, gold and numis. co. exec.; b. Bordeaux, France, June 2, 1928; d. Fernando Alejandro and Madeleine (Joffre) Lus y Lafita; came to U.S., 1954, naturalized, 1976; student Institut d'Études Classiques, Bordeaux, 1946, Faculte des Lettres, Bordeaux, 1950; m. Andrew S. Tsimortos, Oct. 10, 1953. Mgr. Rockefeller Center operation Manfra, Tordella & Brookes, Inc., N.Y.C., 1965-70, asst. v.p., 1970-74, v.p., 1974—, also dir. Contbr. articles to profl. jours. Home: 340 E 64th St New York City NY 10021 Office: care Manfra Tordella & Brookes Inc 30 Rockefeller Plaza New York City NY 10020

TSO, MARGARET YU-YI LU, occupational therapist; b. Shantung, China, Nov. 4, 1920; d. Tai-Sheng and Ling-Yi (Tsiang) Lu; came to U.S. 1948, naturalized, 1961; B.S., Yen-Ching U., China, 1946; A.B., Lindenwood Coll., 1949; O.T.R., Western Mich. U., 1951; M.Ed., U. Md., 1953; m. Tien-Chioh Tso, Aug. 28, 1949; children—Elizabeth Lu, Paul Lu. Social worker rehab. center, China, 1946-48; therapist Pa. State Hosp., Wernerville, 1951, Health Dept. Prince George's County, Md., 1957-67; dir. occupational therapy dept. Univ. Nursing homes; cons. occupational therapist Prince Georges and Montgomery Counties, Md., 1972-74; resource therapist pub. schs., Prince Georges County, 1974-75; sr. therapist U.S. Soldiers' and Airmen's Home, Washington, 1975—; cons. in field. Recipient Art Achievement awards 1965, 67, 68, 74, 75. HEW grantee, 1964. Mem. Am., D.C., Md. occupational therapy assns. Baptist. Club: Washington Chinese Artists. Author: Activities Program in Long Term Care Facilities, 1974, 2d edit., 1976; contbr. articles in field to profl. jours.; inventor (with C.T. Antonio) vest-sling. Home: 4306 Yates Rd Beltsville MD 20705 Office: 3700 N Capital St NW Washington DC 20315

TSONGAS, ALEXANDER GEORGE, aerospace engr.; b. Karditsa, Thessaly, Greece, Jan. 2, 1905; s. George K. and Basiliki (Balafas) T.; came to U.S., 1916, naturalized, 1927; B.S. in Aero. Engring., Mass. Inst. Tech., 1928; m. Bertha Roussos, July 5, 1936; children—George, Mary, Theodora, Katherine. Jr. aero. engr. U.S. Air Force, Wright Field, Dayton, Ohio, 1928-29; asst. chief engr. Moth Aircraft, Lowell, Mass., 1929-30; chief tech. sect. Curtiss Robertson Airplane Co., St. Louis, 1930-33; structures engr. Curtiss Airplane Co., Buffalo, 1933-35; chief engr. Howard Aircraft, Chgo., 1935-36; asst. chief engr., chief engr. Stinson Aircraft, Wayne, Mich., 1939-45; project coordinator, dynamics engr. Consol. Vultee, San Diego, 1945-50; structures project engr. Grumman Aircraft Co. (now Grumman Aerospace Corp.), Bethpage, L.I., N.Y., 1950-70, structural cons. 1974—. Mem. Am. Inst. Aeros. and Astronautics, Hellenic Univ. and Cultural Soc. L.I. Republican. Greek Orthodox. Patentee in field. Address: 20 Avalon Rd Garden City NY 11530

TSONGAS, PAUL EFTHEMIOS, U.S. Senator; b. Lowell, Mass., Feb. 14, 1941; s. Efthemios and Katina Tsongas; B.A., Dartmouth Coll., 1962; LL.B., Yale U., 1967; M.P.A., Harvard U., 1973; m. Nicola Sauvage, Dec. 21, 1969; children—Ashley, Katina. Peace Corps vol., Ethiopia, 1962-64, tng. coordinator, W.I., 1967-68; admitted to Mass. bar; dep. asst. atty. gen. Commonwealth of Mass., 1969-71; individual practice law, 1971-74; mem. 94th-95th congresses from 5th Mass. Dist.; mem. U.S. Senate from Mass., 1979—. Mem. Gov.'s Com. on Law Enforcement, 1968-69; city councillor City of Lowell, 1969-72; county commr. Middlesex County (Mass.), 1973-74. Democrat. Greek Orthodox. Office: Senate Office Bldg Washington DC 20510*

TSOUCALAS, NICHOLAS, Supreme Ct. justice State N.Y.; b. N.Y.C., Aug. 24, 1926; s. George Michael and Mary (Monogenis) T.; B.S. in Bus. Adminstrn., Kent State U., 1949; LL.B., N.Y. Law Sch., 1951; m. Catherine Avavantinos, Nov. 21, 1954; children—Stephanie, Georgia. Admitted to N.Y. bar, 1953; practiced in N.Y.C., 1953-55; asst. U.S. atty. So. Dist. N.Y., 1955-59; supr. census 17th and 18th Congl. dists. N.Y.C., 1959-60; chmn. Neversink River Watershed Commn., 1962-63; judge criminal ct. N.Y.C., 1968—; acting justice N.Y. State Supreme Ct., 2d Jud. dept. Mem. exec. com. N.Y. County Republican Com., 1960-68; committeeman N.Y. State Rep. Com., 1965-66. Served with USNR, 1944-46, 51-52. Recipient Nathaniel Goldstein award. Mem. Am., Fed., N.Y. State, Queens bar assns., N.Y. County Lawyers Assn., Immigration and Nationality Lawyers Assn. Mem. Greek Orthodox Ch. Home: 88-25 63d Ave Rego Park NY 11374 Office: 125-01 Queens Blvd Kew Gardens NY 11415

TSUNG, CLARENCE PAI-AN, elec. engr.; Shanghai, China, Aug. 3, 1932; s. Liang H. and Ching H. (Au) T.; came to U.S., 1954, naturalized, 1973; B.S., Nat. Tawian U., 1953, Coll. Ordnance, Taipei, 1954; M.E.E., Poly. Inst. Bklyn., 1956; m. Helena Shin-Yi Wang, Aug. 8, 1959; children—Michael, Philip. Research fellow Poly. Inst., Bklyn., 1954-55, teaching fellow, 1955-58; elec. engr. Singmaster & Breyer, N.Y.C., 1958-59, Guy B. Panero, N.Y.C., 1959-60; dir. research Syska & Hennessy, Inc., engrs., N.Y.C., 1960—; cons. engring. grad. program N.Y.U., 1970—; mem. ad hoc com. on energy policy State of N.Y., 1972-74; mem. Elec. Industry Evaluation Panel, 1972—, N.Y.C. Code Revision and Interpretation Com., 1965—, Nat. Elec. Code Com., 1974—. Co-chmn. Cardinal's Com. of Laity, Archdiocese of N.Y.; adviser Am. Council for Emigres in the Professions. Fulbright scholar, 1954. Mem. IEEE (sr.), Illuminating Engrs. Soc., (Archievement award 1970), Chinese Inst. Engrs., AAAS. Contbg. editor: IEEE Recommended Practice of Electric Systems for Commercial Bldgs., 1974. Home: 829 Blanche Ave Norwood NJ 07648

TU, CONRAD CHIN-YUI, computer systems analyst; b. Taiwan, Oct. 24, 1927; s. Hsin Hoi and Ping Moy (Lai) T.; B.S., Taiwan Normal U., 1952; M.S., U. R.I., 1965; m. Margaret Yun-Ting Peng, Apr. 20, 1953; children—Sampson Hinchiu, Donald Hinchin, Steve Hinchen. Research asst. U. R.I., 1962-65; research asso. N.J. Coll. Medicine, Newark, 1965-68; jr. systems analyst Bristol Myers Products, Hillside, N.J., 1968-71; sr. program analyst Sandoz, Inc., East Hanover, N.J., 1971—. Mem. Biometrics Soc., Assn. Computing Machinery, AAAS, Drug Info. Assn. Home: 512 Barkers Mill Rd Hackettstown NJ 07840 Office: 25 Hanover Rd East Hanover NJ 07932

TU, KAI-WEN, computer scientist, applied mathematician; b. Kwantung, China, May 14, 1946; s. Liang and To-Ying (Chan) Tu; came to U.S., 1963, naturalized, 1967; B.S. in Chem. Engring., U. Wis., 1966; Ph.D. in Computer Sci., U. Ill., 1972; m. Carolyn M. Ling, June 7, 1969; children—Carl, William. Research mathematician Babcock & Wilcox Co., Alliance, Ohio, 1972-73; asst. prof. computer sci. Rutgers U., New Brunswick, N.J., 1973-75; project mgr. Occidental Petroleum Corp., Grand Island, N.Y., 1975—. Mem. Assn. for Computing Machinery, Soc. Indsl. and Applied Math., Am. Inst. Chem. Engrs., Am. Math. Soc. Contbr. articles to profl. jours. Reviewer, Applied Math. Jour. Home: 39 Robin Hill Williamsville NY 14221 Office: Occidental Petroleum Corp Grand Island NY 14302

TUBBS, LEVESTER, univ. adminstr.; b. Elba, Ala., Dec. 18, 1938; s. Plaze and Lillie T.; B.S., Allen U., 1961; M.S.Ed., N.C. A&T State U., 1961; Ed.D., U. Mo., 1975; m. Mary Alice Patterson, July 8, 1961; children—Daryl Tyrone, Delia Terese, Tiffany Danielle. Tchr., Palm Beach County Schs., West Palm Beach, Fla., 1961-64; dean men Allen U., Columbia, S.C., 1965-67; asso. dir. 13-coll. curriculum program N.C. A&T State U., Greensboro, 1967-69; dean students, dir. devel. Lincoln U., 1969-73; vice chancellor student affairs U. Mass., Boston, 1973—. Mem. Nat. Assn. Student Personnel Adminstrs., Am. Assn. Univ. Adminstrs., Am. Assn. Higher Edn., Nat. Assn. State Univ. and Land Grant Colls., Am. Personnel and Guidance Assn., Coll. Personnel Assn., Alpha Phi Alpha. Home: 61 Eisenhower Circle Wellesley MA 02181 Office: U Mass Boston MA 02125

TUCCI, GERALD FRANK, mfg. exec.; b. N.Y.C., Sept. 9, 1926; s. Frank and Mary (Fattizzi) T.; student Dartmouth, 1943-44; Sc.B. in Naval Sci., Brown U., 1946, Sc.B. in Mech. Engring., 1948; M.B.A. with distinction Harvard, 1950; m. Eva Gunilla Gyllander, May 14, 1968; children—Francis Henrik, Michael Fredrik. Amy Christina. With Am. Can Co., Jersey City, 1950-51, Artcraft Hosiery Mills, 1951-52; with Leach & Garner Co. and Gen. Findings Co., Attleboro, Mass., 1953-63, v.p., 1960-63; with Micro Contacts Inc., Hicksville, L.I., 1963—, pres., 1963—; chmn., chief exec. officer Hallmark Findings, Inc., Hicksville, 1965—; v.p. Mold-A-Matic Corp., Oneonta, 1968—; pres. Micro Pneumatic Logics, North Miami Beach, Fla. Served to lt. (s.g.) USNR, 1944-47. Mem. Beta Theta Pi. Republican. Roman Catholic. Home: 18 Plum Beach Point Rd Sands Point NY 11050 Office: 62 Alpha Plaza Hicksville NY 11801

TUCCI, NICHOLAS, psychologist; b. Reading, Pa., Dec. 22, 1936; s. Alfonso and Angeline T.; B.S., Kutztown State Coll., 1959, M.S. in Edn., 1966; certificate advanced grad. study Temple U., 1973; m. Patricia Ann Miller, Oct. 24, 1964; children—Gregory Colin, Pamela Ann. Tchr. sci. Scotch Plains (N.J.) Fanwood High Sch., 1959-61; tchr. Spanish, head lang. dept. Fleetwood (Pa.) High Sch., 1962-73; sch. psychologist Berks County Intermediate Unit 14, Reading, Pa., 1973—; lectr. psychology Alvernia Coll., Reading, 1976-77; cons. non-pub. schs., Pottstown, Pa., 1976—. Mem. advisory bd. Cath. Social Agy.; mem. parent-child programs com. YMCA; mem. local com. Cub Scouts. Mem. Am., Pa. psychol. assns., Nat. Assn. Sch. Psychologists, NEA, Pa. Edn. Assn., Berks Area Psychol Soc. (treas.), Berks County Intermediate Unit Edn. Assn. (treas.), Phi Delta Kappa. Democrat. Roman Catholic. Home: 400 Friedensburg Rd Mt Penn Reading PA 19606 Office: 3010 St Lawrence Ave Reading PA 19606

TUCK, MURRAY, accountant, ins. exec.; b. Bklyn., Nov. 12, 1920; s. Samuel and Rose (Green) T.; grad. with honors Pace Inst. Sch. of Accounting, N.Y.C., 1945; student Pace Inst. of Ins., 1949-50; m. Leah Samuels, Aug. 6, 1972; 1 dau. by previous marriage, Susan (Mrs. S. Chomsky); stepchildren—Edward Schultz, Charlotte (Mrs. K. Hoek), Larry Schultz. Jr. Accountant, Morris Traum & Co., C.P.A.'s, Bklyn., 1938-39; jr. accountant Mathew Weiss & Co., C.P.A.'s, Bklyn., 1939-40, supervising sr. accountant 1940-45; asst. dept. head of internal audit dept. United Mchts. and Mfrs., Inc., N.Y.C., 1945-52; comptroller TransRadio Press Service, Inc., N.Y.C., 1952-57, Bus. Factors, Inc., N.Y.C., 1957-62; pvt. practice accounting, Farmingdale, N.Y., 1950—; prin. Murray Tuck, ins. broker, Farmingdale, 1950—; ins. cons. to Assn. for the Help of Retarded Children, Inc., Nassau, N.Y., 1965—, Suffolk, N.Y., 1967—. Pres., Farmingdale Sr. High Sch. PTA, 1963-65; chmn. Farmingdale Community Scholarship Fund, 1962-67; sec., v.p. Group for Childrens Welfare, Central Islip, N.Y., 1961-65; treas. Farmingdale Little League Assn., 1956-78; treas. Farmingdale Youth Council, Inc., 1956-78; founder and donor Farmingdale Community award, 1962-65, Farmingdale Fireman award, 1962-65; co-committeeman Farmingdale Salvation Army, 1960-61; mem. Farmingdale Adult Edn. Adv. Com., 1955-60; mem. Farmingdale Police Aux., 1960-70; air raid warden, Farmingdale, 1944-50; notary public, state of N.Y., 1960; Republican Committeeman, Farmingdale, 1966-76; bd. dirs. Advancement for Commerce and Industry, Inc., pres., 1971-73, bd. dirs., 1974-78. Recipient Farmingdale Classroom Tchrs. Honor award, 1963, Certificate of Appreciation Farmingdale CAP, 1964, Distinguished Service plaque Advancement for Commerce and Industry, 1972, 74, Certificate of Service, Farmingdale Youth Council, 1964, Certificate of Merit, N.Y. Gov. Rockefeller, 1961. Accredited in accountancy and taxation Nat. Accreditation Council; enrolled to practice with U.S. Treasury Dept. Mem. Nat. Soc. of Pub. Accountants, Mut. Ins. Agts. of N.Y., Nat. Assn. of Ins. Agts., C.W. Post Coll. Accounting Inst., C.W. Post Coll. Tax Practicioners Forum. Jewish religion. Contbr. numerous articles on ins. to various mags. and newspapers; editor ARC Lamplighter, 1965-69. Home: 388 Fulton St Farmingdale NY 11735 Office: 388 Fulton St Farmingdale NY 11735

TUCKER, BURTON FRANK, dentist; b. Bklyn., Dec. 9, 1926; s. Joseph Louis and Frances Muriel (Lipgar) T.; student Coll. City N.Y., 1947; D.D.S., U. Pitts., 1959; m. Nanette Verk, Nov. 22, 1956; children—Jay Howard, Lloyd Martin. Dist. mgr. J.F. Jelenko Co., Inc., N.Y.C., 1948-53; practice dentistry, Pitts., 1959—; instr. crown and bridge restorative dentistry U. Pitts. Sch. Dentistry, 1962-69. Co-chmn. cancer drive Penn Hills, 1960; active Zionist Orgn. Am. Served with USNR, 1944-46. Mem. Acad. Gen. Dentistry, Am. Analgesia Soc., Pitts. Dental Research Club, Pitts. Odontological Soc. (past pres. E. Suburban br.), Penn Hills C. of C. (past pres.). Jewish (dir. synogogue). Clubs: Rotary, B'nai B'rith. Home: 1489 Laurel Dr Pittsburgh PA 15235 Office: 10529 Lindberg Ave Pittsburgh PA 15235

TUCKER, CYNTHIA DELORES NOTTAGE, former state ofcl., civic leader; b. Phila., Oct. 4, 1927; d. Whitfield and Captilda (Gardiner) Nottage; student Temple U., Pa. State U., U. Pa.; L.L.D., Villa Maria Coll., Erie, Pa., 1972; m. William M. Tucker, July 21, 1951. Sec., Commonwealth of Pa., Harrisburg, 1971-77. Vice Pres. Pa. chpt. NAACP; nat. v.p. Fedn. Democratic Women; mem. nat. adv. bd. Womens Polit. Caucus; vice chmn. Pa. Black Democratic Com., 1966—; chmn. Women for Dem. Action, 1967—; sec., mem. Phila. Zoning Bd. Adjustment, 1968-70; former vice chmn. Pa. Dem. Com., 1970—; mem. exec. com. Dem. Nat. Com.; bd. dirs. Nat. Black United Fund, Dr. Martin Luther King Center for Social Change, New Sch. Music, Phila. Tribune Charities; mem. Commonwealth bd. Med. Coll. Pa.; bd. assos. Messiah Coll. Recipient Service and Achievement award NAACP, 1964; Phila. Tribune Charities Ann. award; Community Service award Opportunities Industrialization Center, Emma V. Kelley Achievement award Nat. Elks, 1971; named Best Dressed Woman of Year, Ebony Mag., Woman of Year Pa. Beauticians Assn., 1971; Community Service award Quaker City chpt. B'nai B'rith; named One of 100 Most Black Influential Ams., Ebony mag. Mem. Bus. and Profl. Women's Club, Nat. Alpha Kappa Alpha. Home: 6700 Lincoln Dr Philadelphia PA 19119

TUCKER, ELEANOR DOROTHY, educator; b. Orange, N.J., Apr. 27, 1918; d. Andrew Noble and Velma Irene (Gwaltney) Tucker; A.B., Va. Union U., 1942; M.A., Columbia Tchrs. Coll., 1947, profl. diploma, 1950; postgrad. Temple U., 1951, U. Del., 1955, 73. Prin., tchr. Prince Edward Elementary Sch., Rice, Va., 1942-43, Hadensville (Va.) Elementary Sch., 1943-46; tchr. Newport News (Va.) elementary schs., 1946-47; mem. faculty Rust Coll., Holly Springs, Miss., 1947-50, Miss. Vocat. Coll., Itta Bena, 1951-53, Morris Coll., Sumter, S.C., 1953-54 asst. prof. edn. William Henry High Sch., Dover, Del., 1954-66, Dover High Sch., 1966—; asst. supr. migrant edn. State of Del., 1967; asst. supr. migrant edn. program Capital Sch. Dist., Dover, 1969-78. Mem. AAUW, NEA, Nat., Capital edn. assns., Soc. Research Child Devel., LWV, Delta Kappa Gamma, Kappa Delta Pi. Mem. A.M.E. Ch. Club: Order Eastern Star. Home: PO Box 334 Dover DE 19901 Office: 625 Walker Rd Dover DE 19901

TUCKER, HOWARD MCKELDIN, investment banker; b. Washington, Apr. 1, 1930; s. Howard Newell and Bessie Draper (McKeldin) T.; B.A., U. Va., 1954; M.B.A., N.Y. U., 1956; m. Julia Spencer Merrell, Feb. 1, 1952; children—Deborah, Mark, Alexander, H. David. Investment research J.P. Morgan & Co., N.Y.C., 1954-59; pension investment dept. Morgan Guaranty Trust Co., N.Y.C., 1959-61; registered rep.-analyst Mackall & Coe, Washington, 1962-69; dir. internat. dept., analyst Legg Mason Wood Walker & Co., Washington, 1969—; dir. Monarch Enterprises, Inc., Uniflight, Inc.; mem. task force on balance-of-payments U.S. Dept. Treasury, 1967—. Trustee Nat. Cathedral Sch. for Girls, 1972-78; chmn. missionary devel. fund Episcopal Diocese of D.C., 1974; vestryman Christ Episcopal Ch., Georgetown, 1972-75; del. Va. Republican Conv., 1968; co-dir. Andover-Exeter Washington Intern Program, 1976—. Served in USN, 1950-56. Chartered fin. analyst. Mem. Washington Soc. Investment Analysts, Fin. Analysts Fedn., Nat. Press Club, Nat. Economists Club. Club: Met. (Washington). Contbr. articles to fin. jours.; book revs. to Washington Post. Home: 1207 28th St NW Washington DC 20007 Office: 1747 Pennsylvania Ave NW Washington DC 20006

TUCKMAN, MARVIN ALFRED, periodontist; b. Paterson, N.J., Apr. 14, 1925; s. Max and Sarah (Sunderland) T.; B.S., Ind. U., 1947, D.D.S., 1947; Certificate in Periodontia, N.Y. U., 1951; m. Claire Marcus, Jan. 25, 1948; children—Drew Evan, Jane Enid. Gen. practice dentistry, Paterson, N.J., 1947-51, practice limited to periodontics, Paterson, 1953-74, Fair Lawn, N.J., 1974—; chief periodontics sect., attending dentist Barnert Meml. Hosp. Center, Paterson; instr. periodontics, oral medicine Sch. Dentistry, Fairleigh Dickinson U., 1959-63, asst. prof., 1963-73, asso. prof., 1973—; cons. periodontia Passaic County Cerebral Palsy Clinic. Served with USNR, 1944-45; periodontist, 1st lt. Dental Corps, U.S. Army, 1951-53. Diplomate Am. Bd. Periodontology. Fellow Am. Coll. Dentists, Internat. Coll. Dentists, Am. Acad. Oral Medicine; mem. Am., Northeastern, N.J. (pres. 1965-66) socs. periodontists, N.J., Passaic County (pres. 1959-60) dental socs., Am. Acad. Periodontology, Internat. Assn. for Dental Research, Am. Dental Assn., Alpha Omega (pres. alumni chpt. 1960-61), Omicron Kappa Upsilon. Editor: The Dialog, Fairleigh Dickinson U., 1972—. Home: 18 Garwood Rd Fair Lawn NJ 07410 Office: Fair Lawn Med-Dental Bldg 25-15 Fair Lawn Ave Fair Lawn NJ 07410

TUFF, RONALD, city ofcl.; b. Newark, June 6, 1950; s. Solomon B. and Anna K. Tuff; B.S. in Polit. Sci., Wilberforce U., 1972; M. in Pub. Adminstrn., Fairleigh Dickinson U., 1976. Mgmt. analyst Port Authority of N.Y., 1970; asso. dir. admissions Wilberforce (Ohio) U., 1970; cons. to NAACP, Newark, 1971-72; sales rep. Greyhound Bus Co., Wilberforce, 1972; adminstrv. aide to mayor City of Newark, 1972-73, adminstrv. analyst to bus. adminstr., 1973-75, dir. taxicab div., 1975—. Chmn. membership com. Robert Treat council Boy Scouts Am., 1973-75; mem. exec. bd. Cultural Center, Newark, 1974—; treas. Clark County (Ohio) Young Democrats, 1970-71; del. Naval Acad. Fgn. Affairs Conf., 1971. Recipient Youth of Yr. award Frontiers Internat., 1973; John J. McCloy fellow, 1977. Mem. Am. Mgmt. Assn., Internat. Conf. City Mgrs., Am. Soc. for Pub. Adminstrn., Fraternal Order of Police, Omega Psi Phi. Home: 373 S 19th St Newark NJ 07102 Office: City of Newark 920 Broad St B21A Newark NJ 07102

TUFFIASH, WILLIAM ALAN, physician; b. Newark, N.J., Nov. 30, 1944; s. Joseph Selig and Edith (Teitelbaum) T.; A.B., Franklin and Marshall Coll., 1966; M.D., Temple U., 1970; m. Rae Lynne Berger, Apr. 14, 1973; children—Michael, Scott. Intern, resident in internal medicine Upstate Med. Center, Syracuse, N.Y., 1970-73; fellow in allergy and immunology U. Mich., Ann Arbor, 1973-75; mem. staff allergy br., dept. internal medicine Nat. Naval Hosp., Bethesda, Md., 1975-77; practice medicine specializing in allergy, Allentown, Pa., 1977—; mem. staff Allentown Hosp., Sacred Heart Hosp., Allentown-Sacred Heart Hosp. Center. Served with USNR, 1975-77. Diplomate Am. Bd. Internal Medicine, Am. Bd. Allergy and Immunology. Mem. A.C.P., Am. Acad. Allergy, Pa., Lehigh County med. socs., Pa., Phila. allergy socs. Office: 1125 S Cedar Crest Blvd Allentown PA 18103

TUFTS, WESLEY MELBOURNE, design engring. cons.; b. Milton, Mass., Aug. 8, 1927; s. Howard Lorimer and Ruth Elizabeth (lfcWilliams) T.; B.S. in Mech. Engring., Northeastern U., Boston, 1951; certificate plastics engring. U. Wis., 1968; m. Virginia Hughes, Feb. 21, 1951; children—Robert, Denise, Janice, Deborah. Sr. prodn. engr. Warner Electronics/Pace Controls Corp., Needham, Mass., 1960-68; prodn. mgr. Microsystems Tech. Corp, Burlington, Mass., 1968-71; v.p. engring. Nautron Corp., Braintree, Mass., 1971-76, dir., 1971—; pres. Omni Design Assos., Medway, Mass., 1976—. Served with AUS, 1946. Mem. IRE (vice chmn. Boston 1960-64), Soc. Plastics Engrs. (Design award 1968), Am. Boat and Yacht Council, U.S. Golf Assn. (asso.). Club: Glen Ellen Country. Patentee in field. Office: PO Box 20 Medway MA 02053

TUFTY, JAMES VAN WAGONER, advt. and pub. relations exec.; b. Evanston, Ill., Mar. 11, 1929; s. Harold and Esther (Van Wagoner) T.; B.A. in Journalism and Advt., Mich. State U., 1953; postgrad. Alliance Francaise, Paris, 1963; m. Mary Elizabeth White, June 6, 1967; children—Patti Alyn, James Van Wagoner, Valentina Ivern. Field rep. Young & Rubicam, Inc., N.Y.C., 1956-58, asst. all-media buyer, Chgo., 1958-60, sr. all-media buyer, Los Angeles, 1960-62; journalist Tufty News Service, Paris, 1962-64, sec.-treas., 1956—; media dir. Am. Baker's Coop., Teaneck, N.J., 1964-65; supr., account rep. J. Walter Thompson Co., Inc., Washington, 1965-72; pres., chmn. bd. The Ad Agy., Inc., Washington, 1972—, Communications Sales, Inc., Washington, 1975—. Served with U.S. Army, 1953-56. Mem. Nat. Press Club, Advt. Club Washington. Democrat. Presbyterian. Home: 3209 Military Rd NW Washington DC 20015 Office: 900 National Press Bldg Washington DC 20045

TUKEY, HAROLD BRADFORD, JR., educator; b. Geneva, N.Y., May 29, 1934; s. Harold Bradford and Ruth (Schweigert) T.; B.S., Mich. State U., 1955, M.S., 1956, Ph.D., 1958; m. Helen Dunbar Parker, June 25, 1955; children—Ruth Thurbon, Carol Cameron, Harold Bradford. Mem. faculty Cornell U., 1959—, prof. floriculture and ornamental horticulture, 1970—; cons. P.R. Nuclear Center, Rio Piedras, 1965-66; vis. prof. U. Calif., Davis, 1972; lectr. Internat. Atomic Energy Sch., Hanover, Ger., 1968, Amkara, Turkey, 1965, Santiago, Chile, 1968; Longwood Gardens lectr., 1972; Ward Meml. lectr. Norfolk (Va.) Bot. Garden, 1972; Williamsburg (Va.) Garden symposium lectr., 1975, 78; mem. coms. Nat. Acad. Scis.-NRC. Served to 2d lt. AUS, 1958. AEC fellow, 1955-58; NSF postdoctoral fellow, 1958-59. Mem. Internat. (U.S. del. to council, v.p. 1978—), Am. (dir., sect. chmn. 1971-72) socs. hort. sci., Am. Hort. Soc. (dir. 1972—, exec. com. 1976—, v.p. 1978-80), Internat. Plant Propagators Soc. (pres. 1976), Bot. Soc. Am., Sigma Xi (past chpt. pres.), Phi Kappa Phi, Alpha Zeta, Pi Alpha Xi, Presbyterian. Club: Ithaca Rotary (past pres.). Home: 20 Woodlane Rd RD 2 Ithaca NY 14850 Office: Dept Floriculture and Ornamental Horticulture Cornell U Ithaca NY 14853

TULCHINSKY, DAN, physician; b. Tel Aviv, Dec. 8, 1938; s. Dov and Lena (Falkowitz) T.; M.D., Hebrew U., Jerusalem, 1966; m. Becky Versano, Aug. 28, 1962; children—Amir, Doron, Guy. Intern, Tel-Hashomer Hosp., U. Tel Aviv, 1965; resident in obstetrics U. Ill. Hosps., 1966-69; practice medicine specializing in obstetrics and gynecology, Los Angeles, 1969-73, Boston, 1973—; head physician dept. obstetrics and gynecology Harbor Gen. Hosp., Torrance, Calif., 1970-73; asst. prof. UCLA, 1970-73, Harvard Med. Sch., 1973-76; asso. prof. Boston Hosp. for Women/Harvard, 1976—, dir. fertility and endocrine clinic, 1976—, dir. endocrine lab., 1973—. Served with Israeli Army, 1956-58. Diplomate Am. Bd. Obstetrics and Gynecology. Mem. Soc. Gynecol. Investigation, Endocrine Soc., Am. Fedn. Clin. Research, Am. Fertility Soc. Jewish. Contbr. articles to profl. jours. Office: 221 Longwood Ave Boston MA 02115

TULIPANO, EMILIO JOHN, business exec.; b. Italy, June 20, 1946; s. Saverio and Lucy T.; 1 dau., Lisa. Owner, treas. Needham Clipper, Inc. (Mass.), 1975—. Served with USMC, 1963-67. Mem. Nat. Businessmen's Assn. Roman Catholic. Office: 1095 Great Plain Ave Needham MA 02192

TULL, ROGER JAMES, chemist; b. Duluth, Minn., Jan. 9, 1922; s. Harry P. and Margaret (Boyd) T.; B.S. in Chemistry, Mich. State U., 1944; Ph.D. in Chemistry (Rohm and Haas fellow), U. Ill., 1949; m. Susan E. Moore, Mar. 25, 1945; children—Eric, Barbara, James, Karen, Nancy. Chemist, Eastman Kodak, Rochester, N.Y., 1944-46; sr. chemist Merck & Co., Rahway, N.J., 1949-57, mgr. process research, 1957-69, dir. process research, 1969-77, sr. dir. process research, 1977—; research cons. Monclair State Coll., Upper Montclair, N.J., 1969-72. Dir. planning State Fedn. Dist. Bds. Edn., Bd. Edn., Metuchen, N.J., 1966-72, dir. legislation, 1969-72. Mem. AAAS, Am. Chem. Soc., Phi Lambda Upsilon, Alpha Chi Sigma. Contbr. articles to various publs. Patentee in field. Home: 48 Spring St Metuchen NJ 08840 Office: Merck and Co Inc Rahway NJ 07065

TULL, WILLIS CLAYTON, JR., librarian; b. Crisfield, Md., Feb. 22, 1931; s. Willis Clayton and Agnes Virginia (Milbourne) T.; B.S., Towson (Md.) State Coll., 1957; M.L.S., Rutgers U., 1962; m. Taeko Itoi, Dec. 18, 1952. Tchr., Hereford Jr.-Sr. High Sch., Parkton, Md., 1957-59; aide Enoch Pratt Free Library, Balt., 1959-61, profl. asst., 1962-64; coordinator adult services Washington County Free Library, Hagerstown, Md., 1964-67; asst. area librarian Eastern Shore Area Library, Salisbury, Md., 1967; br. librarian Balt. County Pub. Library, Pikesville, Md., 1968-71, asst. area br. librarian, Essex, Md., 1971-72, sr. info. specialist, Catonsville, Md., 1972—. Second legislative dist. committeeman Republican Central Com. Balt. County, 1971-72. Served with U.S. Army, 1949-52. Mem. ALA, Center for Study

Democratic Instns., Freedom to Read Found., Friends Hist. Assn., Md., Unitarian, Universalist hist. socs., World Future Soc., Md. Library Assn. (publicity com. 1964-67, chmn. intellectual freedom com. 1969-70), Md. Assn. Adult Edn. (regional coordinator Western Md. 1965-67), Unitarian and Universalist (founder, dir. 1971—), Md. (award of merit 1975) geneal. socs., Kappa Delta Pi (v.p. Epilson Alpha chpt. 1956-57). Editor, pub.: Tull Tracing, 1971—; ch. and cemetery records editor Md. Geneal. Soc. Bull., 1972-73; editor, pub. By the Mill Born, 1976—. Contbr. to profl. and geneal. jours. Home: 10605 Lakespring Way Cockeysville MD 21030 Office: 1100 Frederick Rd Catonsville MD 21228

TULLER, BURL ARTHUR, cons. co. exec.; b. Ottumwa, Iowa, Apr. 20, 1926; s. Arthur LeRoy and Gertrude Evona (Jackson) T.; B.A., U. Calif. at Berkeley, 1951, M.A., 1952, Ph.D., 1955; m. Bernice Lillian McClure, Jan. 30, 1949; children—Burl Arthur, Douglas Edward. Various positions Amoco Prodn. Co., 1955-68; v.p., gen. mgr. profl. services div. CEIR, Washington, 1968-70; dir. ops. Am. Research Bur., Washington, 1970-71; pres. Tuller Assos., Washington, 1971—, Info. Analysis Corp., Washington, 1974—. Served with AUS, 1943-45. Mem. Am. Mgmt. Assn., Data Processing Mgmt. Assn., Soc. for Mgmt. Info. Systems, Soc. Exploration Geophysicists, Potomac Geophys. Soc.

TULLER, WENDY JUDGE, cons.; b. Cranston, R.I., Dec. 17, 1943; d. Alfred Carman and Anna Louise (Waterman) Judge; A.B., Brown U., 1965; M.L.S., U. R.I., 1969. Elementary sch. librarian Providence Pub. Sch. System, 1965-69; mgr. Xerox Corp., various locations, 1969-75, Carter Hawley Hale Stores, Inc., Los Angeles, 1975; cons. Sibson & Co., Inc., Princeton, N.J., 1975—. Mem. Am. Soc. Personnel Adminstrn., Am. Soc. Tng. and Devel., Internat. Assn. Personnel Women. Home: 21-06 Deer Creek Dr Plainsboro NJ 08536 Office: 1101 State Rd Princeton NJ 08540

TULLY, JAMES HENRY, JR., state ofcl.; b. Bklyn., May 19, 1931; s. James Henry and Mary Frances (Dobbins) T.; m. Eileen Conway, July 4, 1959; children—Ann, Lauren, Susan, James, Kathleen. Admitted to N.Y. bar, 1961; mem. firm Wood, Redmond & Tully, N.Y.C., 1964-72, Manning, Carey, Redmond & Tully, N.Y.C., 1972-74; mem. N.Y. State Assembly, 1966; del. N.Y. State Constnl. Conv., 1967; commr. taxation and fin. pres. N.Y. Tax Commn., Dept. Taxation and Fin., Albany, 1975—. Pres., N.Y.C. Council Vol. Child Care Agys., 1968-70; bd. dirs. Little Flower Children Services, 1964-72, Park Slope N. Child Devel. Center, 1970-74; pres. Park Slope Civic Council, 1960. Served to lt., inf., U.S. Army, 1953-55. Recipient Children's Hope award, 1975. Mem. Bklyn. Bar Assn. Democrat. Roman Catholic. Home: 220 S Main St Albany NY 12208 Office: State Campus Bldg 9 Albany NY 12227 also 2 World Trade Center New York City NY 10047

TULLY, MICHAEL JOHN, fin. cons.; b. Bronx, N.Y., July 3, 1940; s. Patrick J. and Margaret C. (Van de Walle) T.; B.A., Fordham U., 1962, postgrad. in Bus. Adminstrn., 1969; m. Mary C. Comiskey, Jan. 2, 1959; children—Michael J., Patrick J., Sean P., Thomas F. Underwriter, Equitable Life Ins. Co., White Plains, N.Y., 1962-64; credit analyst, credit dept. Chase Manhattan Bank, N.Y.C., 1964-66, trainee spl. devel. program, 1966-67, asst. treas. commodity fin. div., 1967-69; v.p. comml. lending, money market ops. Fidelity Internat. Bank, N.Y.C., 1969-71. sr. v.p., 1971-73; v.p. fin., treas. Mocatta Metals Corp., Fed. Coin & Currency, Inc., N.Y.C., 1973-77, sr. advisor for finance Monata Metals Corp., 1977—; dir. Jefferson Nat. Bank, LaFargeville, N.Y.; trustee Mocatta Group Pension Trust; cons. serving numerous hard and soft commodity merchants, brokers, mfrs. Treas., Citizens for Spano, 1971-72; bd. dirs. Friends of Yorktown Mus., 1976. Mem. Brit.-Am. C. of C. Democrat. Roman Catholic. Home: Crompond Corners 2594 Old Yorktown Rd Yorktown Heights NY 10598 Office: 25 Broad St New York City NY 10004

TUNG, HSI-LIN, surgeon; b. Hong Kong, Nov. 12, 1924; s. C.W. and W.T. (Lo) T.; came to U.S., 1948, naturalized, 1958; M.D., Yale-in-China Med. Coll., 1949; m. Pola Tung, Aug. 20, 1977; children by previous marriage—Arthur, Paul, Grace, James, David. Rotating intern Washington Med. Center, 1948-49; surg. intern Albany (N.Y.) Med. Coll. Med. Center, 1949-50; pathology intern Yale-New Haven Med. Center, 1950-51; resident in gen. surgery Yale U., 1951-54; chief resident in thoracic surgery Conn. State Hosp., Raybrook (N.Y.) Hosp., 1954-56; practice medicine, specializing in gen. surgery Manchester, N.H., 1956—; pres. med. staff Notre Dame Hosp., Manchester, 1970-71; co-chmn. dept. surgery Cath. Med. Center, Manchester, 1977-78, v.p., 1976-77. Bd. dirs. YMCA, Manchester, 1965; pres. N.H. Philharmonic Orch., 1968-70, 1st violinist, 1956—; deacon 1st Congl. Ch., Manchester, 1972-73; mem. parents council St. Paul's Sch., Concord, N.H. 1972-77. Diplomate Am. Bd. Surgery. Fellow A.C.S.; mem. N.H. Med. Soc. Address: 913 Elm St Manchester NH 03101

TUNNELL, NORMAN DAVID, banker; b. Dallas, Mar. 21, 1942; s. Joseph T.; B.A., Baylor U., 1963; M.B.A., U. Pa., 1965; J.D., Columbia U., 1972; m. Phyllis Yurik, Sept. 25, 1965; 1 son, Trevor. Cost analyst Tex. Instruments, Inc., Attleboro, Mass., 1965-66, prodn. control supr., 1966-67, departmental controller, 1967-69; admitted to N.Y. bar, 1973; asso. firm White & Case, N.Y.C., 1972-74; v.p. Bankers Trust Co., N.Y.C., 1974—. Mem. Young Mortgage Bankers Assn., N.Y. Bldg. Congress, Mortgage Bankers Assn. (asso.), Am., N.Y. bar assns. Home: 59 Edgecliff Terr Yonkers NY 10705 Office: 280 Park Ave New York City NY 10017

TUNNESSEN, WALTER WILLIAM, JR., pediatrician; b. Hazleton, Pa., July 25, 1939; s. Walter William and Grace Louise (Schaller) T.; B.A., Lafayette Coll., 1961; M.D., U. Pa., 1965; m. Nancy Louise Layton, Aug. 24, 1963; children—Walter William, Anne Layton. Pediatric intern Children's Hosp. Phila., 1965-66, asst. chief resident physician, 1966-67; chief resident in pediatrics Hosp. U. Pa., Phila., 1967-68, dir. nurseries, instr. pediatrics, 1970-72; asst. prof. pediatrics State U. N.Y. Upstate Med. Center, Syracuse, 1972-75, asso. prof., 1975—; asso. attending State U. Hosp. and Crouse Irving Meml. Hosp., Syracuse; Robert Wood Johnson clin. scholar Yale U., 1978-79. Served to capt. USAF, 1968-70. Recipient Knockers Soc. award for Outstanding Teaching, State U. N.Y., 1974. Diplomate Am. Bd. Pediatrics. Mem. Am. Acad. Pediatrics, Ambulatory Pediatric Assn., Soc. Pediatric Dermatology. Episcopalian. Co-editor: Clinical Diagnosis Quiz (Pediatrics), 1976; editor Clini-Pearls, 1978; asso. editor Meditel, 1970—. Home: 107 Paddock Dr Dewitt NY 13214 Office: 750 E Adams St Syracuse NY 13210

TUNNEY, ARLENE ROCHELLE, archtl. designer; b. N.Y.C., Apr. 6, 1946; d. Samuel and Lilian (Koenigsberg) Kohnop; B.F.A., Pratt Inst., 1966, postgrad., 1966-68; m. Hugh L. Tunney Jr., Mar. 15, 1968 (dec. 1977). Vice pres. in charge design Mosaic Tile Co., N.Y.C., 1966-68; designer Bache & Co., N.Y.C., 1968-69, Montgomery Winecoff Assos., N.Y.C., 1969-70; chief of design Expanded Space Design, N.Y.C., 1970-73; owner, archtl. designer Tunney Assos., Hastings on Hudson, N.Y., 1973—. Chmn. Hastings on Hudson (N.Y.) Conservation Commn., 1976-78; mem. Hastings Parks and Recreation Commn., 1977-78; trustee Hastings Creative Arts Council, Temple Beth Shalom. Mem. Westchester Assn. Women Bus. Owners (dir. 1978—). Club: Hastings Women's. Office: 135 Southside Ave Hastings on Hudson NY 10706

TUNNICLIFFE, WILLIAM WARREN, graphics co. exec.; b. Washington, Apr. 22, 1922; s. Homer Warren and Christine (Hobbs) T.; B.E.E., Worcester Poly. Inst., 1943; M.A. in Engring. Scis. and Applied Physics, Harvard, 1951; m. Ruth Loretto Loftus, June 23, 1951; children—Peter Warren, Virginia Warren, Elizabeth Loftus, William Loftus. Staff mem. Mass. Inst. Tech. Radiation Lab., 1943-44; head electronics sect. Boston U. Optical Research Lab., 1946-51; electronics engr. Barkley & Dexter Labs., Inc., Fitchburg, Mass., 1953-55; mgr. Eastern engring. office Offner Electronics, Inc., Somerville, Mass., 1955-56; systems engr., project mgr., program mgr. Raytheon Co., Wayland, Mass., 1956-63; v.p. Info. Dynamics Corp., Reading, Mass., 1963-65; program mgr. Courier-Citizen Co., Lowell, Mass., 1965-68, v.p., 1969-72; nat. sales mgr. Graphic Services, an Am. Standard co., 1972, pres., 1973-74; pres. Tunnicliffe Assos., Inc., 1974—; gen. mgr. Woodland Communications Co. div. W.E. Andrews Co., Bedford, Mass., 1975; program dir. pre-press systems Graphic Communications Computer Assn., 1976-77; v.p. Walter T. Armstrong, Phila., 1977-78; program mgr. Bobst Graphic Inc., Hauppauge, N.Y., 1979—; cons. Raytheon Co., 1964-66, Courier-Citizen Co., 1972, Chrysler Corp., 1974. Bd. dirs., v.p. Horace and Florence Mayer Found., Inc., Balt.; organizing chmn. bd. dirs. Printing Research Inst. for New Techs. Inc., Washington, 1968-69, chmn. bd., pres., 1970-74. Served as lt. (j.g.) USNR, 1944-46, lt., 1951-53; capt. Res., 1967. Recipient Walter Sherman Gifford Jr. Trophy. Mem. Am. Soc. Info. Scis., Armed Forces Communications and Electronics Assn., Internat. Word Processing Assn., Assn. Computing Machinery, IEEE, Nat. Micrographics Assn., Soc. Motion Picture and TV Engrs., Inst. Printing (London), Printing Industries Am., Graphic Communications Computer Assn. (chmn. character generation com. 1967-74, dir. 1970-74, v.p. 1973-74), Printing Industries New Eng. (co-chmn. computer conf. 1967), Nat. Composition Assn., Research and Engring. Council of Graphic Arts Industry, Naval Res. Assn., Res. Officers Assn., U.S. Naval Inst., Sci. Research Soc. Am., Sigma Xi. Clubs: Harvard (Boston); Appalachian Mountain. Home: 39 Central St Winchester MA 01890 also Beard Brook Rd Hillsborough NH 03244 Office: 100 Parkway Dr S Hauppauge NY 11787

TURCOTTE, FERNAND WILFRID, physician; b. Sherbrooke, Que., Can., June 28, 1941; s. Forest Leonidas and Gemma Aline (Thibault) T.; B.A., Coll. St. Croix, 1962; M.D., U. Montreal, 1966; M.P.H., Harvard, 1971; m. Georgine Saint-Laurent, Aug. 13, 1964; children—Colin, Sandrine. Intern, Maisonneuve and St-Luc hosps., Montreal, 1966-67; asst. prof. preventive medicine Laval U. Med. Sch., 1971-78, asso. prof., 1978—; chief dept. pub. health Centre Hospitalier de l'Université Laval, 1975—; trustee Centre de Readaptation Quebec, 1975; lectr. Ecole Nat. d'Adminstrn. Publique, 1973—; cons. in field. Served with Canadian Army, 1967-70, Nat. Health Council Can. grantee, 1972-74, 77-78. Mem. Canadian (chmn. health services div. 1972-74), Am. pub. health assns., Am. Coll. Preventive Medicine, Canadian Assn. Tchrs. Social and Preventive Medicine, Canadian Med. Assn., Assn. des Epidemiologistes de lang. française. Club: Montreal Harvard. Home: 883 Chanoine Scott Sainte-Foy PQ G1V 3N5 Canada Office: Dept Preventive Medicine U Laval Quebec PQ Canada

TURGEON, LOUIS PHILLIPPE, hosp. exec.; b. Sillehy, Que., Can., Sept. 15, 1944; s. Jean Louis and Jeanne (Daignault) T.; M.A. in Commerce, U. Sherbrooke (Que.); m. Johanne Raby, May 29, 1971. Asst. accounter Consol. Bathurst Co., Montreal, Que., 1970-71; fin. analyst Que. Govt., Quebec City, 1971-72, systems analyst, 1972-74; dir. fin. Hosp. St. Croix, Drummondville, Que., 1974—. Mem. Adminstr. A Conseil. Home: 75 Despeupliers Drummondville PQ J2B 3C8 Canada Office: 570 Heriot Drummondville PQ J2B 1C1 Canada

TURGEON, RALPH ASHER, restaurant exec.; b. New Haven, May 29, 1929; s. Ralph Archie and Frances Louise (Holben) T.; B.S., Cornell U., 1951; M.B.A., U. Buffalo, 1959; m. June Dolores Williamson, Aug. 7, 1954; 1 dau.; Marjorie Louise. Vice pres. Turgeon Assos., Inc., Buffalo, 1952-61; pres. Amherst Towers, Inc., Buffalo, 1961-70; chmn. bd., pres. Turgeon Bros., Inc., North Tonawanda, N.Y., 1970. Mem. adv. bd. food service adminstrn. Erie Community Coll., 1969—; trustee United Way of Erie County, 1972-75. Served to 1st lt. Q.M.C., U.S. Army, 1951-53. Mem. Nat., N.Y. (pres. 1972), Buffalo (pres. 1961-62), Western N.Y. restaurant assns., Cornell Soc. Hotelmen of Western N.Y. (pres. 1956-57), Confrerie De la Chaine Des Rotisseurs. Republican. Presbyterian. Clubs: Park Country (pres. 1975), Mason. Home: 35 Farmington Rd Williamsville NY 14221 Office: 84 Sweeney St North Tonawanda NY 14120

TURK, OSCAR, hosp. adminstr.: b. Rochester, N.Y., Apr. 10, 1915; s. Benjamin and Bessie (Adler) T.; B.A., U. Rochester, 1936; B.B.A., Niagara U., 1941; M.A., U. Chgo., 1950; m. Elizabeth Helen Harrison, Sept. 16, 1944; children—Jonathan, Laurie, David, Karen, Bennett, Suzanne. Chief social worker VA Hosp., Kecoughtan, Va., 1947-49; clin. psychiat. social worker VA Hosp., Canandaigua, N.Y., 1950-51; cons. Nat. Tb Assn., N.Y.C., 1951-55; asso. dir. health sect. Community Council of Phila., 1955-58; dir. health sect. United Community Services of Greater Milw., 1958-63; exec. dir. Community Services for the Blind, Atlanta, 1963-66; mem. faculty dept. sociology Ga. State U., 1964-66; prof. social work Atlanta U., 1966-67; coordinator admission discharge planning, dir. patient community relations Bird S. Coler Meml. Hosp., N.Y.C., 1967—. Mem. various community health agy. bds., several state health dept. task forces. Served with Med. Service Corps, U.S. Army, 1941-45. Mem. Nat. Assn. Social Workers, Soc. Patient Reps., Delta Mu Delta. Home: 133-24 Sanford Ave Flushing NY 11355 Office: Bird S Coler Meml Hosp Roosevelt Island New York City NY 10044

TURKALY, LOUIS GENE, word processing and text editors mfg. co. exec.; b. Wheeling, W.Va., Dec. 7, 1945; s. Louis Joseph and Catherine Theresa (Yugovich) T.; B.S., Wheeling Coll., 1967; m. Darry Maureen Decker, Dec. 14, 1968; 1 son, David Louis. Coordinator advanced communications systems Singer Corp., N.Y.C., 1972-75; coordinator telecommunications engring. Exxon Corp., N.Y.C., 1975-76; mgr. product planning Vydec Co., affiliate Exxon Enterprises, Florham Park, N.J., 1976—. Served to capt. USAF, 1967-72. Mem. Assn. Data Communication U sers. Home: 29 Joyce Dr Succasunna NJ 07876 Office: 9 Vreeland Rd Florham Park NJ 07932

TURKSEN, ISMAIL BURHAN, indsl. engr.; b. Turgutlu, Turkey, Dec. 20, 1937; s. Huseyin and Asiye (Harcanoglu) T.; came to Can., 1970, naturalized, 1976; B.S., U. Pitts., 1960, M.S., 1962, Ph.D., 1969. Asst. prof. indsl. engring. U. Toronto (Ont., Can.), 1970-74, asso. prof., 1974—. Served to 1st lt. Turkish Ground Forces, 1965-66. Mem. Am. Inst. Indsl. Engrs. (dir. Canadian affairs 1974-75, mem. internat. task force 1975-76, v.p. 1978—, trustee, 1978—), Canadian Operational Research Soc., Turkish Ops. Research Soc., Assn. Profl. Engrs. Ont. Bd. advisors Ency. Computer Sci. and Tech., 1970—. Contbr. articles to profl. jours. and encys. Home: 720 Spadina Ave Toronto ON M5S 2T9 Canada Office: Dept Indsl Engring U Toronto Toronto ON M5S 1A4 Canada

TURNDORF, HERMAN, physician; b. Paterson, N.J., Dec. 22, 1930; s. Charles R. and Ruth (Blumberg) T.; A.B., Oberlin Coll., 1952; M.D., U. Pa., 1956; m. Sietske Huisman, Nov. 24, 1957; children—David, Michael Pieter. Instr. surgery Hosp. U. Pa., 1957-59; asst. anesthetist med. sch. Harvard, Mass. Gen. Hosp., 1961-63; asso. attending anesthesiologist Mt. Sinai Hosp., N.Y.C., 1963-70, asst. dir. dept. anesthesiology, 1963-70, clin. prof. anesthesiology, med. sch., 1966-70; prof., chmn. dept. anesthesiology W.Va. U. Sch. Medicine and Med. Center, Morgantown, 1970-74, N.Y. U. Sch. Medicine, 1974—; dir. anesthesiology N.Y. U. Hosp., 1974—, Bellevue Hosp. Med. Center, 1974—; cons. anesthesiology U.S. Naval Hosp., Portsmouth, Va., Manhattan VA Hosp., 1974—. Served to lt. M.C., USNR, 1959-61. Diplomate Am. Bd. Anesthesiology. Fellow Am. Coll. Chest Physicians, Am. Coll. Clin. Pharmacology and Chemotherapy, Am. Coll. Anesthesiologists (gov. 1977—); mem. N.Y. Acad. Scis., N.Y. Acad. Medicine, Soc. Critical Care Medicine. Home: 37 Hyatt Rd Briarcliff Manor NY 10510

TURNER, CLARICE PATRICIA (MRS. CHARLES HYGHE DEBNAM), physician; b. Wilmington, Del.; d. Patrick William and Helen (Henderson) T.; B.S., Temple U., 1944; M.D., Meharry Med. Coll., 1949; m. Charles Hyghe Debnam, Oct. 15, 1950; children—Charlene Patricia, Christopher Charles Patrick. Intern, Hubbard Hosp., Nashville, 1949-50, resident St. Agnes Hosp., 1950-51; psychiat. resident Del. State Hosp., New Castle, 1952-55; psychiat. cons. Dept. Research, New Castle, Del., 1955-57, Del. Dept. Mental Health, Wilmington, 1960-61; cons. Del. League for Planned Parenthood, 1965-75; dir. in-patient hosp. So. New Castle County Community Mental Health Center, 1975—. Bd. dirs. Childrens Bur. Del., 1965-66. Mem. New Castle County Med. Soc., Am. Acad. Family Physicians, Del. Acad. Gen. Practice, AMA. Episcopalian. Home: 1809 Newport Rd Wilmington DE 19808 Office: So New Castle County Mental Health Center Newark DE 19711

TURNER, DOLORES WALKER, educator; b. Manning, S.C., Nov. 21, 1935; d. Wilfred J. and Edris (Jackson) Walker; B.A. in Music, Fisk U., 1957; M.A. in Music, U. Ala., 1966; M.S. in Counseling, Johns Hopkins U., 1977; m. Richard Martin Turner, III, June 15, 1957; children—Michael Shawn, Edris LaVerne. Acting chmn. dept. music Stillman Coll., 1957-58, 63-64, 66-67, instr. music, music librarian, 1960-68; curator Negro Collection, Fisk U., 1968-69; music tchr. Nashville/Davidson County Pub. Schs., 1969-71, Balt. City Pub. Schs., 1971-72, Baltimore County Pub. Schs., 1972—. Area capt. Am. Cancer Soc., Balt., 1971—; team mem. Am. Heart Assn., Balt., 1972-73; mem. exec. com. Liberty Crest-Shirley Hill Improvement Assn., Balt., 1971-75; mem. network telephone com. Common Cause, Balt., 1976—. Danforth asso., 1959—. Mem. AAUW, Md. Music Educators Assn., Music Educators Nat. Conf., NEA, Phi Delta Kappa, Delta Sigma Theta, Pi Kappa Lambda. Democrat. Baptist. Home: 3412 Croydon Rd Baltimore MD 21207 Office: 106 Bloomsbury Ave Baltimore MD 21228

TURNER, DONALD HUNTER, advt. agy. exec.; b. Toronto, Ont., Can., Jan. 13, 1933; s. James Shortt and Gladys Marian Jean (Hunter) T.; came to U.S., 1941, naturalized, 1954; student Hunter Coll., 1951-53, Sch. Visual Arts, 1955-57; m. Janice Canterella, May 21, 1955; children—Darren Bradford, Denise Starr. With J. Walter Thompson Co. Inc., N.Y.C., 1957; artist Adpix, N.Y.C., 1958; art dir., writer, TV producer Morse Internat. Co., N.Y.C., 1959-66; creative supr. Marschalk Co., N.Y.C., 1966-68; pres., creative dir. Don Turner & Partners Inc., N.Y.C., 1968-71; v.p., asso. creative dir. Brandywynne Assos. div. Benton & Bowles, N.Y.C., 1971-73; head creative group Kenyon & Eckhardt, N.Y.C., 1973-74; creative dir. Doubleday Advt. Co., N.Y.C., 1974-77; exec. v.p., dir. creative services, also prin. Michel/Cather Inc., N.Y.C., 1977—, also dir.; also fine arts painter. Served with C.E., U.S. Army, 1953-55; ETO. Recipient award Bus. Press Am., 1977, Andy award Advt. Club N.Y., 1978, Am. Marketing Assn. award, 1977, Creativity award Art Direction mag., 1976. Mem. Nat. Acad. TV Arts and Scis., Phi Alpha Sigma, Alpha Delta Tau. Illustrator children's books Western Pub. Co., 1973-74. Home: 854 Van Buren St Baldwin Harbor NY 11510 Office: Michel/Cather Inc 488 Madison Ave New York NY 10022

TURNER, GEORGE ANDREW, educator; b. Montclair, N.J., Feb. 23, 1930; s. Isaac and Mary Turner; B.S. in Edn. and History, Wiley Coll., 1955; M.S. in Sci., Carnegie Mellon U., 1956; M.A. in Learning Disabilities, Columbia U., 1960; Ed.D. in Counselor Edn. and Psychology, Pa. State U., 1972; married; 1 dau., Clarice E. Counselor, Farmingdale (N.Y.) Union Free Sch. Dist., 1956-73; dir. guidance Wyandanch (N.Y.) Union Free Sch. Dist., 1973-78; dir. pupil personnel services, Hempstead, N.Y., 1978—. Pres. Minority Tchrs., Scholarship Fund, 1972-74. Mem. Am., Western Suffolk (County, N.Y.), L.I. personnel, guidance assns., N.Y. State United Tchrs., N.Y. Guidance Assn., Am. Assn. Sch. Adminstrs., L.I. Minority Edn. Assn., NEA, Assn. Black Psychologists, Assn. Non White Concerns, Phi Delta Kappa. Club: Kiwanis. Specialist in career edn. and environ. assessment for minority students. Home: 65 Rhodes Ave Hempstead NY 11550 Office: 265 Peninsula Blvd Hempstead NY 11550

TURNER, JAMES CASTLE, labor union ofcl.; b. Beaumont, Tex., Nov. 4, 1916; s. James Castle and Lydia (Carley) T.; A.B., Catholic U. Am., 1940; m. Mary Pauline Curtis, Apr. 14, 1934; children—Vivian, Daniel, Brian, Lisa, Lauran. Bus. mgr., bus. rep. local 77, Internat. Union Operating Engrs., Washington, 1940-71, nat. v.p., 1956-72, gen. sec.-treas., 1972-75, gen. pres., 1975—. Del., Democratic Nat. Conv., 1952, 56, 60, 64; vice chmn. D.C. Dem. Central Com., 1950-60, 63-67; Dem. nat. committeeman for D.C., 1960; mem. D.C. City Council, 1967-68. Mem. Nat. Planning Assn., Nat. Dem. Club, Nat. Press Club, Blue Key. Episcopalian. Clubs: Touchdown, Internat. editor Internat. Engr., 1972-75. Office: Internat-Union Operating Engrs 1125 17th St NW Washington DC 20036

TURNER, LEWIS, former mfg. exec.; b. Atlanta, Dec. 4, 1904; s. Lewis and Joan (Elsas) T.; M.E., Cornell U., 1925; m. Marjorie Salmon, Nov. 7, 1947; 1 son, Lewis. Dir., mfg. exec. Fulton Bag & Cotton Mills, 1926-36; v.p. Dollin Corp., mfrs. die castings, Irvington, N.J., 1939-61, exec. v.p., 1946-61; spl. partner Coleman & Co., N.Y.C., 1946-61; v.p. Precision Castings Co., Irvington, 1961; ltd. partner Bache & Co., 1964-69. Pres. Bronx River Neighborhood Centers, 1965-67, 69; bd. dirs. Citizens Union, 1965-75, vice chmn., 1971-75; bd. dirs. Play Sch. Assn., 1962-69, v.p., 1967-69, treas., 1975—; bd. dirs. Citizens Union Research Found., 1972-76, v.p., 1974-76; bd. dirs. Nat. Bd. Rev. Motion Pictures, 1974—. Served to capt. USAAF, 1942-45. Decorated Combat Star Alaskan Theatre. Mem. ASME (life). Clubs: Navesink County (Middletown, N.J.); Mayacoo Lakes Country (West Palm Beach, Fla.); Beach (Palm Beach, Fla.). Home: 163 Seminole Ave Palm Beach FL 33480 also 812 Fifth Ave New York City NY 10021 also 490 Navesink River Rd Red Bank NJ 07701

TURNER, PAUL ALFRED, govt. ofcl.; b. Chgo., Jan. 20, 1926; s. George Spencer and Mary Ann (Hugo) P.; B.S., Am. U., 1958, postgrad., 1959-60; m. Janet Audrey Staub, July 16, 1955; children—John Spencer, Catherine Ellen, Nancy Ann. Supervisory budget analyst Harry Diamond Labs., Washington, 1963-67; budget analyst Research, Devel., Test and Evaluation Program, also sr.

budget analyst, research and devel. Budget div. U.S. Army, Washington, 1967-77, chief Research, Devel., Test and Evaluation Budget Team, Office Dep. Chief of Staff for Research, Devel. and Acquisition, 1977—; dir. Harry Diamond Lab./Nat. Bur. Standards Fed. Credit Union, 1962-67. Active Boy Scouts Am. Recipient commendation for outstanding fed. service U.S. Dept. Army, 1974-77. Mem. Armed Forces Mgmt. Assn. Roman Catholic. Home: 11521 Patapsco Dr Rockville MD 20852

TURNER, PAUL CHARLES, computer co. ednl. specialist; b. Bklyn., Oct. 14, 1945; s.John Ashby and Anna May (Bunn) T.; certificate ednl. devel., N.Y. U., 1978; student St. John's U.; m. Marilyn Yvonne Bastian, Dec. 23, 1974; children—Shane John, Paul Charles II. Interviewer/counselor Tng. Resources for Youth Inc., Bklyn., 1967-68; program asst. supr. N.Y.C. Bd. Edn., Bklyn., 1968; personnel interviewer IBM, Bklyn., 1968-78, ednl. specialist, 1978—; lectr. in field; exhibited photography Bernard Baruch Coll., N.Y.C., 1972, throughout Met. N.Y. area, 1973. Served with USAF, 1964-66. Recipient Honor prize for photography, Sindelfinger, Germany, 1971; named man of year Nat. Assn. Negro Bus. and Profl. Women's Club, 1978. Mem. Am. Soc. Tng. and Devel., Nat. Rifle Assn., Profl. Photographers Guild. Bd. dirs. Crown Heights Ednl. Com., Bklyn. Home: 501 New York Ave Brooklyn NY 11225 Office: IBM 585 DeKalb Ave Brooklyn NY 11205

TURNER, RALPH EMERSON, former indsl. trade relations exec.; b. Chgo., July 11, 1912; s. Ralph Emerson and Hulda Victoria (Malm) T.; B.S. in Engring. Physics, U. Ill., Urbana, 1936; m. Laura V. Wegner, Dec. 25, 1936; children—William R., Barbara Turner Schloemer, Linda B., Thomas C. Mgmt. trainee Wis. Steel Co., Chgo., 1936-40; heating engr. steam engring. dept. Youngstown Sheet & Tube Co., East Chicago, Ind., 1940-41; x-ray sales engr. Gen. Elec. X-ray Corp., Rochester, N.Y., 1941-48, regional service mgr., N.Y.C., 1948-56; indsl. radiographic specialist Eastman Kodak Co., Rochester, 1956-65, dir. indsl. trade relations Radiographic Markets div., 1965-77. Recipient Merit award Am. Soc. Testing and Materials, 1976. Fellow Am. Soc. Non-Destructive Testing (chmn. bd. dirs. 1972-73, pres. 1971-72), Am. Soc. Testing and Materials (chmn. com. on non-destructive testing 1970-72), Am. Foundry Soc. (chmn. Rochester sect. 1971-72), ASME, Am. Nuclear Soc. Presbyterian. Home: 28 Chelmsford Rd Rochester NY 14618

TURNER, ROBERT EDWARD, psychiatrist, educator; b. Hamilton, Ont., Can., June 8, 1926; s. Robert William and Alice May (Johnson) T.; B.A. with honors in Zoology and Chemistry, McMaster U., 1948; M.D., U. Toronto, 1952; m. Gene Anne Stewart, Sept. 27, 1952; children—Margaret, John, Robert, Richard. Intern Hamilton Gen. Hosp., 1952-53; resident Bristol (Eng.) Mental Hosps. Group, 1953-55; practice medicine specializing in forensic psychiatry, Toronto, Ont.; dir. Forensic Clinic, Toronto Psychiat. Hosp., 1958-66; sr. psychiatrist forensic service Clarke Inst. of Psychiatry, Toronto, 1966, chief forensic service, 1967-69, med. dir., 1969-77; asst. prof. dept. psychiatry U. Toronto, 1964-68, prof., 1973-77, prof. forensic psychiatry, 1977—; psychiatrist in charge, dir. Met. Toronto Forensic Service, 1977—; cons. in psychiatry Law Reform Commn. of Can., 1972—; mem. legal task force com. on mental health services Ont. Council Health, 1978—. Pres. Kenneth G. Gray Found., 1971—; bd. dirs. Clin. Inst. Addiction Research Found. Ont., 1973—; dep. warden Cathedral Ch. of St. James, Toronto. Fellow Royal Coll. of Physicians and Surgeons of Can., Am. Psychiat. Assn.; mem. Canadian (dir. 1974-76), Ont. (pres. 1975-76) psychiat. assns., Canadian, Ont. med. assns., Med.-Legal Soc. of Toronto, Royal Coll. Psychiatrists. Author: Pedophilia and Exhibitionism, 1964; contbr. articles on psychiatry and law to profl. jours. Home: 64 Russell Hill Rd Toronto ON M4V 2T2 Canada Office: 999 Queen St W Toronto ON M6J 1H4 Canada

TURNER, ROGER RAVON, broadcasting co. exec.; b. Matewan, W. Va., July 15, 1939; s. John and Cora Lee (Vance) T.; ed. Alderson Broaddus Coll., 1957-61; m. Shirley Gail Lemley, Oct. 24, 1958; children—Craig, Kimberli, Kevin. With Sta. WHJC, 1954-57, WBUC, 1957-61, KSLN-TV, 1961-62, KAFM, 1962-66, KMNS, 1966-69; gen. mgr. WEBC, Duluth, Minn., 1969-70; v.p., gen. mgr. WNAX, Yankton, S.D., 1970-73; exec. v.p. Park Broadcasting Midwest, Inc., 1971-73; v.p. all radio with responsibility for 14 stas. in 8 states Park Broadcasting Inc., Ithaca, N.Y., 1973—. Served with SAC, USAF, 1961-65. Mem. Sertoma (pres. local chpt. 1968, lt. gov. Nebr. 1969), Nat. Assn. Broadcasters. Home: 104 Midway Rd Ithaca NY 14850 Office: Park Broadcasting Terrace Hill Ithaca NY 14850

TURNER, SHIRLEY, coll. ofcl.; b. Dover, N.J., July 3, 1941; d. Robert N. and Catherine E. Kersey; B.S., Trenton State Coll., 1964; M.A., Ridge Coll., 1971; postgrad. Rutgers U., 1976—; m. Donald Turner, June 19, 1963; children—Jacqueline, Donald. Tchr., Trenton Bd. Edn., 1966-70; asst. dir., counselor equal opportunity program Rider Coll., Lawrenceville, N.J., 1970-73, dir. Office Career Devel., 1973—; pres. Tri-Kersey, Inc., Dover, N.J., 1977—; notary pub., N.J., 1975—. Rep. to edn. and cultural panel Trenton Model Cities Policy Com., 1970-72; bd. dirs. Trenton chpt. Nat. Urban League, 1975—; mem. grants and personnel coms. N.J. Council on Arts, 1974—. Mem. Middle Atlantic Placement Assn. (profl. com., chmn. affirmative action com. 1977-78), Am. Personnel and Guidance Assn., Nat. Vocat. Guidance Assn., Nat. Assn. Student Personnel Adminstrs., Nat. Assn. Bd. Realtors, NAACP (exec. bd. Trenton chpt. 1970). Democrat. Baptist. Home: 22 Allwood Dr Lawrenceville NJ 08648 Office: 2083 Lawrenceville Rd Lawrenceville NJ 08648

TURNER, STANSFIELD, govt. ofcl.; b. Chgo., Dec. 1, 1923; s. Oliver Stansfield and Wilhelmina Josephine (Wagner) T.; student Amherst Coll., 1941-43, D.C.L., 1976 LL.D., 1976; B.S., U.S. Naval Acad., 1946; M.A. (Rhodes scholar), Oxford U., 1950; L.H.D., Roger Williams Coll., 1976; D.Ed., Bryant Coll., 1977; LL.D., Salve Regina Coll., 1977; m. Patricia Busby Whitney, Dec. 23, 1953; children—Laurel, Geoffrey W. Commd. ensign U.S. Navy, 1946, advanced through grades to adm., 1975; comdr. Carrier Task Group 6th Fleet, 1970-71; dir. systems analysis div. Office Chief Naval Ops., 1971-72; pres. Naval War Coll., Newport, R.I., 1972-74; comdr. U.S. 2d Fleet, 1974-75; comdr. in chief Allied Forces So. Europe, 1975-77; dir. CIA, Washington, 1977—. Decorated D.S.M., Legion of Merit with oak leaf cluster, Bronze Star. Christian Scientist. Contbr. articles to profl. publs. Office: CIA Washington DC 20505

TURNER, THOMAS, bus. exec.; b. Phila., June 21, 1915; s. Thomas Caldwell and Ethel (Hartson) T.; B.S., U.S. Naval Acad., 1937; m. Constance Babbitt, Sept. 28, 1940; children—Thomas Caldwell, John Edward, Constance Cope. Founder, Thomas Turner Co., Inc., Bellows Falls, Vt., pres., 1946-74; founder, treas. Riparius, Inc., Ponte Vedra, Fla., 1970—; chmn. bd. Hanover Bank & Trust (N.H.), 1973—; chmn. bd. Northeastern Culvert Corp., 1969—, pres., treas., 1976—; pres. United Bank Corp., Hanover, 1977—. Mem. Internat. Exec. Service Corps, Ghana, 1969, Colombia, 1971; incorporator Walpole Savs. Bank (N.H.), 1956—. Trustee Rockingham Meml. Hosp., Bellows Falls; bd. dirs. Vt. Council on World Affairs. Served to lt. col. USMCR, 1942-46. Clubs: Chevy Chase (Washington); Ponte Vedra, Sawgrass (Ponte Vedra, Fla.). Home: Walpole NH 03608 Office: Northeastern Culvert Corp Westminster Station VT 05159 also Box 742 Ponte Vedra FL 32082

TUROV, DANIEL, investment exec.; b. Bklyn., Jan. 15, 1947; s. Bernard and Mildred (Stevelman) T.; B.A. in Econs., Coll. City N.Y., 1969; m. Rosalyn B. Kalishock, Aug. 25, 1968; children—Joshua Nathaniel. Account exec. Walston & Co., N.Y.C., 1969-72, Thomson McKinnon Securities, N.Y.C., 1972-75; sr. v.p. Faulkner Dawkins & Sullivan, Inc., N.Y.C., 1975-77; sr. v.p. Cowen & Co., N.Y.C., 1977—; mem. faculty N.Y. Inst. Finance, New Sch. Social Research. Mem. N.Y. Instl. Options Soc. Author: Investment Hedging: The Conservative Approach to Aggressive Investing, 1979; contbr. articles to profl. publs. Home: Box 58 Ramsey NJ 07446 Office: Cowen & Co 1 Battery Park Plaza New York City NY 10004

TURSI, PETER BUDD, metals co. exec.; b. Phila., Mar. 4, 1919; s. Fred and Mary (Nociti) T.; student Drexel Inst. Tech., Temple U., 1941-48; m. Marjorie Shinn, Dec. 26, 1941; children—Gail (Mrs. Robert W. Smith), Marjorie (Mrs. James F. Costello). With Riverside Metals Corp. (N.J.), 1947—, works mgr., 1967-70; v.p., gen. mgr., 1971—, also dir. Guest lectr. metallurgy dept. Temple U. Mem. Riverside Zoning Bd., 1960-63; pres. Riverside Bd. Edn., 1964-66. Mem. Am. Soc. Metals (soc.-Temple U. ednl. com. for metallurgy 1955-60), Am. Inst. Mining, Metall. and Petroleum Engrs. Episcopalian. Rotarian. Home: 512 Weeks St Riverside NJ 08075 Office: 1 Pavilion St Riverside NJ 08075

TUTTLE, DOUGLAS EDELL, graphics co. exec.; b. Franklin, Pa., Jan. 10, 1915; s. Sterling Leroy and Bickford (Ledoux) T; student Pratt Inst., 1936; m. Evelyn E.C. Schilling, May 21, 1938; children—Lois Joy Tuttle Little, Wendelin Holly Tuttle Pokorny, Linda Jane Tuttle Jestice. Chemist, Continental Paper & Bag Corp., 1933-35; research dir. Crescent Ink & Color Co., 1935-38; product mgr. Interchem. Corp., 1938-66; v.p. mktg. Pamarco, Inc., Roselle, N.J., 1966—, also dir.; dir. Kirkridge, Inc., 1966-73; lectr. in field. Mem. graphic arts adv. com. Rochester Inst. Tech., 1973—; bd. dirs. Found. Flexographic Tech. Assn., 1976—. Recipient Elmer G. Voigt award Graphic Arts Industry, 1962. Mem. Packaging Inst., TAPPI, Am. Mktg. Assn., Flexographic Tech. Assn. (founder, charter mem.; sec. 1959-64, dir. 1959-64), Nat. Pilots Assn., Airplane Owners and Pilots Assn. Presbyterian (elder). Club: Wings (N.Y.C.). Author: Fellow Flexographer, monthly bull. Mem. editorial adv. com., publ. com. Flexographic Tech. Jour. Contbr. articles various publs. Home: 1000 Mary Allen Ln Mountainside NJ 07092 Office: 235 E 11th Ave Roselle NJ 07203

TUTTLE, FREDERICK BURTON, educator, govt. ofcl.; b. New Haven, July 12, 1908; s. Burton L. and Alta M. (Carter) T.; B.A., Yale U., 1930, Ph.D., 1942; postgrad. U. So. Calif., George Peabody Coll., U. Mich.; m. Mary Emily Armstrong, Sept. 3, 1936 (dec. July 1972); children—Frederick Burton, James, Allen, Margaret Emily; m. 2d, Eleanor B.P. Stiefel, June 14, 1975. Tchr. and prin. New Haven Pub. Schs., 1936-46; adviser edn. CAA, Washington, 1946-49; supt. schs., Westerly, R.I., 1949-52; dir. summer session, dir. placement, prof. edn. State U. Coll., Plattsburgh, N.Y., 1952-58, asso. dean, dir. grad. studies, 1958-63; dept. dir. ednl. programs NASA, 1963-70, dir. ednl. programs, 1970—; vis. prof. U. R.I., George Washington U., R.I. Coll. Mem. adv. com. CAP; exec. bd. Am. Soc. Aerospace Edn.; chmn. Brewer Com. for Aerospace Edn. Served as 1st lt. USMC, World War II. Recipient certificate of service Nat. Celebration, Fiftieth Anniversary of Powered Flight; citations N.Y. State Assn. Elementary School Prins. for service to edn. in N.Y., Plattsburgh Rotary Club for service to community, Plattsburgh Alumni Assn. for service to Coll.; Frank G. Brewer trophy for service to aerospace edn. Nat. Aeros. Assn. Mem. Nat. Council Social Studies, NEA, Am. Assn. Sch. Adminstrs., Nat. Sci. Tchrs. Assn., S.A.R., Order Founders and Patriots, S.R., Soc. Colonial Wars, Soc. Colonial Clergy, Soc. Colonial Govs., Baronial Order Magna Charta, Order of Crown of Charlemagne. Episcopalian. Clubs: Cosmos (Washington); Mory's (New Haven), Masons. Editor: Aviation Education Reports, 1949, 50; aviation edn. number. Nat. Elementary Prin., New Haven Tchrs. Jour., Sci. Edn. in Space Age; contbr. articles to periodicals. Home: 3133 Connecticut Ave NW Washington DC 20008

TVERT, RONALD MICHAEL, accountant; b. Bronx, N.Y., Dec. 15, 1937; s. Irving Eugene and Bernice (Levin) T.; B.B.A., Western Res. U., 1959; m. Mary Ellen Gilden, June 28, 1959; 1 dau., Lori Joy. Accountant Maurice Singer & Co., C.P.A.'s, Port Chester, N.Y., 1960-61; pvt. practice accounting, Yonkers, N.Y., 1961-68; partner Krawchick and Tvert, C.P.A.'s, Larchmont, N.Y., 1968-72; sr. partner Ronald M. Tvert & Co., C.P.A.'s, Yonkers, 1972—; guest lectr. colls. and profl. groups. Founder Woodlands Community Temple, Greenburgh, N.Y.; mem. Westchester Estate Planning Council. C.P.A., N.Y. State. Rotary Paul Harris fellow. Mem. Am. Inst. C.P.A.'s, N.Y. State Soc. C.P.A.'s, Nat. Found. Pension, Welfare and Edn. Funds, Iona Tax Inst. Jewish. Club: Rotary (pres. 1973-74, 75-76). Home: 31 Southern Rd Hartsdale NY 10530 Office: 984 N Broadway Yonkers NY 10701

TWITCHELL, H(ERBERT) KENASTON, JR., state ofcl.; b. London, Eng., July 2, 1928 (parents Am. citizens); s. Herbert Kenaston and Marian (Smith) T.; student Princeton, 1946-48; m. Lydia Margaret Bentley, July 21, 1962; children—Alexander Kenaston, Margaret Agnes, Andrew Frederic Bentley. With Moral Re-Armament Inc., N.Y.C., 1953-74, travelled in Africa, Europe, Asia, dir. various youth confs., corp. sec., 1965-69, chmn., exec. dir., 1969-73; dist. dir. Vt. Dept. Social Welfare, Bennington, 1974—. Pres., Friends of Retarded Citizens; trustee United Counseling Service. Served to 2d lt. AUS, 1950-51. Decorated Bronze Star. Editor: Corporation News Service, 1959-64. Home: 13 Monument Circle Bennington VT 05201 Office: 203 North St Bennington VT 05201

TWYON, JANE, advt. exec.; b. N.Y.C., June 29, 1946; d. Joseph Arthur and Ruth (Gilbert) Hanff; Asso.Sci., Lasell Jr. Coll., 1964; student Boston U., 1966; m. Patrick Michael Twyon, Oct. 5, 1968; 1 dau. Ashley Branwen. With Compton Advt. Agy., Inc., N.Y.C., 1970—, asso. spot TV Supr., 1974-76, v.p. asso. media dir., 1976—. Bd. dirs. Drama Ensemble Repertoire Theatre Co., 1974-76. Mem. Am. Assn. Advt. Agys. (mem. TV/radio policy com. 1977—). Home: 401 E 81st St New York NY 10028 Office: 625 Madison Ave New York NY 10022

TYBER, MURRAY AARON, rheumatologist; b. Toronto, Ont., Can., Jan. 22, 1934; s. Charles Jeffrey and Anna Guta (Kamucewicz) T.; M.D., U. Toronto, 1958; m. Anita Greenwood, Dec. 21, 1957; children—Kevin, Sheldon, Leora. Intern, Toronto E. Gen. Hosp., 1958-59, asso. staff arthritis, 1965—; clin. investigator Charles Frosst Co. Ltd., Toronto, 1968-69; practice medicine specializing in rheumatology, Toronto. Trustee Banting Research Found. Toronto. Surgeon-lt. Royal Canadian Navy Res., 1952-59. Mem. Ont. Coll. Physicians Surgeons, Toronto E. Med. Soc., Canadian Arthritis and Rheumatism Soc., Inter-Urban Arthritis Soc., U. Toronto Med. Alumni Assn. (pres. 1977—). Jewish. Contbr. articles in field to med. jours. Home: 47 Apollo Dr Don Mills ON Canada Office: 1483 Danforth Ave Toronto ON M4J 1N5 Canada

TYLER, MARGO HILLS, pub. relations exec.; b. Salt Lake City, Sept. 4, 1921; d. Harold Haven and Mary Edith (Roberts) Hills; B.A., U. Utah, 1942; m. Converse Tyler, Sept. 30, 1950. Asst. city editor Salt Lake Telegram, Salt Lake City, 1942-45; adminstrv. asst. Safety Services, Am. Nat. Red Cross, Washington, 1945-55; dir. pub. relations Am. Cancer Soc., Washington, 1957-65; dir. pub. relations Am. Assn. Motor Vehicle Adminstrs., Washington, 1966-68; dir. pub. info. Coll. of V.I., St. Thomas, 1968-70; mgr. info. services Nat. 4-H Council, Washington, 1970—. Mem. adv. council nat. orgns. Corp. for Pub. Broadcasting, 1971-77, exec. com., 1973-75, 77; co-founder Pub. Info. Assn. St. Thomas, 1969. Mem. Pub. Relations Soc. Am. (dir. 1962-64, 67, 72-73), Montgomery County Press Assn., Mortar Bd., Phi Beta Kappa, Phi Kappa Phi, Delta Gamma. Editor: (with Walter John) Adventures in Vision, 4-H Leader's Guide for Eye Care Education, 1976. Office: 7100 Connecticut Ave Washington DC 20015

TYLER, RICHARD DALE, entrepreneur; b. Binghamton, N.Y., Nov. 13, 1922; s. Floyd R. and Ruth (Smith) T.; B.S., Wharton Sch., U. Pa. 1943; m. Irene E. Brown, Dec. 8, 1943; children—Richard Dale, Jeffrey, Craig, Michael, Timothy, Thomas. Salesman to mktg. mgr. Gen. Electric Co., Schenectady, 1946-55; gen. sales mgr., asst. gen. mgr Overhead Door Co., Hartford City, Ind., 1955-61; pres. Lindsay Co., St. Paul, 1961-65; v.p., gen. mgr. Kawneer Co., Inc., Niles, Mich., 1965-67; v.p., gen. mgr. archtl. and indsl. products div. aluminum group Olin Corp., Phila., 1971-1974; chmn. bd. Ku Bar Bearings, Inc., Cambridge, Mass., treas., dir. Altech Industries, Allentown, Pa.; former mem. advisory bd. 1st Pa. Bank. Past pres. Water Conditioning Found.; past bd. dirs. Water Conditioning Research Council. Bd. dirs. Niles United Fund. Served to 1st lt., inf. U.S. Army, 1943-45; ETO. Decorated Purple Heart. Presbyterian. Club: Huntingdon Valley (Pa.) Country. Home: 1460 Gunpowder Rd Rydal PA 19046 Office: KuBar Bearings Inc 21 Erie St Cambridge MA 02139

TYLER, RICHARD FREDERIC, hosp. adminstr.: b. Cin., Apr. 18, 1940; s. Richard Smith and Torre (Atkinson) T.; B.A., U. Cin., 1963; postgrad. Cornell U., 1964-65; M.B.A., Am. U., 1970, Ph.D., 1975; m. Jacqueline Anne Steinke, Aug. 10, 1974; 1 dau., Torri Anne. Hosp. adminstrv. resident Good Samaritan Hosp., Cin., 1965-66; adminstrv. asst. Balt. City Hosp., 1966-68; asst. hosp. adminstr. Georgetown U. Hosp., Washington, 1970-73; med. sch. faculty Georgetown U., Washington, 1972—, adj. clin. prof., 1975—; pres. R.F.T. Assocs., P.A., Hosp. Mgmt. Cons., Annapolis, Md., 1975—; asso. prof. bus. and hosp. adminstrn. Anne Arundel Community Coll., 1978—. Mem. Anne Arundel County (Md.) Health Care Careers Council, 1975—; mem. Anne Arundel Gen. Hosp. Emergency Fund, 1976—, Chesapeake Bay Found., 1970—; patron, Annapolis Symphony Orch., 1975—. Fellow Am. Coll. Hosp. Adminstrs.; mem. Assn. Tchrs. Preventive Medicine, Am. Hosp. Assn., Md. Assn. Higher Edn., Am. Mgmt. Assn., Assn. for Computing Machinery, U.S. Yacht Racing Union. Republican. Episcopalian. Clubs: Annapolis Yacht, Leland Yacht. Home: 114 Duke of Gloucester St Annapolis MD 21401

TYNAN, EDWARD LYLE, tech. mktg. engr.; b. Poughkeepsie, N.Y., May 18, 1935; s. Joseph Edward and Doris Marie (Williams) T.; B.S. E.T., Midwestern U., 1957; grad. program Wesley Coll., 1978; m. Winona Phillips, Apr. 8, 1960; children—Joseph E., Theresa W., Christina M. Sr. tng. instr. Fed. Civil Services, Tex., Ga., N.Y., 1956-61; supr., sr. service engr. Bendix Corp., Teterboro, N.J., 1961-70, tech. mktg. exec., 1970—; acad. instr. Avionics; inst. light aircraft, CAP. Served with USAF, 1952-56. Mem. Am. Inst. Aeros. and Astronautics, Am. Mgmt. Assn., Smithsonian Assos., IEEE, Nat. Assn. Remotely Piloted Vehicles, Phi Theta Kappa. Roman Catholic. Club: Masons. Home: 906 Wilson Dr Dover DE 19901 Office: Bendix Corp Teterboro NJ 07608

TYNES, WILLIAM JOSEPH, III, clin. instrumentation co. exec.; b. Stamford, Conn., Apr. 29, 1946; s. William Joseph and Ellen Waterbury (Copeland) T.; B.S. in Engring., U. Conn., 1969. Project mgr. CBS Labs., Stamford, 1969-75; mgr. instrument devel. J.T. Baker Diagnostics Div., Bethlehem, Pa., 1975—. Mem. IEEE, Eta Kappa Nu. Home: 1066 New Haven Ave Milford CT 06460 Office: 540 New Haven Ave Milfrod CT 06460

TYSON, CHARLES ROEBLING, JR., advt. agy. exec.; b. Phila., Nov. 5, 1936; s. Charles Roebling and Barbara (Kurtz) T.; student Princeton, 1954-57; A.B., U. Pitts., 1960; m. Anna Newbold Starr, Apr. 28, 1962; children—Charles Roebling III, Mary Starr, Anna Bell. Mgmt. trainee N.W. Ayer & Son, Inc., Phila., 1960-61, plans/mktg. dept., 1961-63, account mgr., 1963-66, mem. creative dept., 1966-74, creative dir., 1971-74, v.p., 1972-74; pres. Tyson & Partners, Phila., 1974—. Co. chmn. United Fund Drive, Phila., 1962, advanced gifts chmn., 1967-72; advt. vol. Council Fin. Aid to Edn., Phila. Mayor's Youth Opportunity Council, 1966, 67, 68; trustee Pa. Sch. Deaf, 1968-70, So. Home for Children, Phila., 1971-74, Rider Coll., Lawrenceville, N.J., 1976—. Bd. dirs. Internat. House, Phila., 1977—. Served with USMC, 1957-59. Recipient numerous awards art dirs.' shows, Phila., Chgo., N.Y.C., Internat. Broadcast award TV commls., 1970-73, N.Y.C.'s The One Show, 1973. Mem. Parkside Angling Assn. Republican. Episcopalian. Clubs: Philadelphia, Cricket (Phila.); Ivy (Princeton). Home: 1725 E Willow Grove Ave Philadelphia PA 19118 Office: 399 Market St Philadelphia PA 19106

TYSON, LUTHER EWING, ch. ofcl. b. Temple, Tex., Oct. 19, 1922; s. Jos Mickel and Venevian Brack (Murphy) T.; A.B., Bethany Coll., 1944; S.T.B., Boston U. Sch. Theology, 1947, Ph.D., Grad. Sch., 1968; m. Mary Louise Griffis, Oct. 10, 1942; children—Joanna Griffis, Jonathan Pope. Ordained to ministry Congregational Christian Ch., 1950; asso. pastor Evan. Congregational Ch., Needham, Mass., 1949-50; pastor, St. Stephen's United Methodist Ch., Marblehead, Mass., 1950-54, Grace United Meth. Ch., Haverhill, Mass., 1954-58; exec. sec., Boston Area Com. on Indsl. Relations, 1958-66; dir. Dept. Econ. Life, Bd. of Ch. and Society, United Meth. Ch., Washington, 1966—; adj. prof. Boston U. Sch. Theology, 1959, 61, 74; dir., pres. Pax World Fund, 1971-78; chmn. com. for Polit. Renewal, Haverhill, 1956. Valentine fellow, Boston U., 1947-48, Swift fellow in instl. econs. 1962. Mem. Am. Sociol. Assn., Am. Soc. for Sci. Study Religion, Am. Soc. Christian Ethics. Democrat. Contbr. articles to religious jours. Home: 8739 Oxwell Ln Laurel MD 20811 Office: 100 Maryland Ave NE Washington DC 20002

TYTELL, PEARL LILY (MRS. MARTIN KENNETH TYTELL), examiner disputed documents; b. N.Y.C., Aug. 29, 1918; d. Harry and Yetta (Feigenbaum) Kessler; student St. John's U., 1941-43; B.S., N.Y. U., 1962, M.A., 1968; m. Martin Kenneth Tytell, May 23, 1943; children—Peter, Pamela. Examiner disputed documents, N.Y.C., 1950—; lectr. N.Y. U., 1955-57; mem. faculty N.Y. Inst. Criminology, N.Y.C., 1958; cons. govtl. agys., law firms, expert witness in city, state, fed. cts. U.S. and Commonwealth P.R., also Bahamas, France. Sec. Along The Hudson Home Owners Assn., 1960—. Mem. AAAS, Internat. Assn. Chiefs of Police (asso.), Eastern Bus. Tchrs. Assn. Club: New York University. Co-author: The Confrontation of Anonymous Letter Writers. Home: 3031 Scenic Pl Riverdale NY 10463 Office: 116 Fulton St New York City NY 10038

TZIMAS, NICHOLAS ACHILLES, physician; b. Greece, Apr. 18, 1928; s. Achilles Nicholas and Evanthia B. (Exarchou) T.; M.D., U. Athens (Greece), 1952; m. Helen J. Papastylopoulos, Apr. 22, 1958; children—Yvonne, Christina. Intern St. Mary's Hosp., Hoboken, N.J.,

1955-56; resident in gen. surgery Misericordia Hosp., N.Y.C.; resident in orthopedic surgery Bellevue Hosp., N.Y.C., 1957-60; instr. orthopedic surgery N.Y. U. Sch. Medicine, 1961-63, asst. clin. prof., 1963-65, asso. clin. prof., 1965-71; clin. prof., 1971—; mem. staff Univ. and Bellevue hosp., chief children's orthopedics, 1966—; orthopedic cons. Inst. Rehab. Medicine, N.Y. U., 1966—, St. Agnes Hosp., White Plains, N.Y., 1972—; advisory com. Bur. Handicapped Children, N.Y.C., 1975—. Served with M.C., Greek Army, 1952-55. Fellow Am., Internat. colls. surgeons; mem. N.Y. Acad. Medicine, N.Y. State, N.Y. County med. scos., Am. Acad. Orthopedic Surgeons, Am. Congress Rehab. Medicine, Am. Acad. Cerebral Palsy. Mem. Greek Orthodox Ch. Author articles on Spina Bifida child mgmt. Home: 33 Edgewood St Tenafly NJ 07670 Office: 566 1st Ave New York City NY 10016

UBANS, JURIS KONRADS, educator; b. Riga, Latvia, July 12, 1938; s. Konrads and Elina (Gailitis) U.; came to U.S., 1950, naturalized, 1957; student Yale, 1965; B.F.A. (Hiram Gee fellow, Helen B. Stoeckel fellow), Syracuse U., 1966; M.F.A., Pa. State U., 1968; postgrad. Cosanti Found., 1972; m. Mara Isaks, June 6, 1965. Dir. art gallery U. So. Maine, Gorham, 1968—, asst. prof. art, 1968-73, asso. prof., 1973—, chmn. dept. art, 1974—. Bd. dirs. Concept Sch. Art, Portland, Maine, 1970-73; bd. dirs., pres. Film Study Center, Portland, 1972—. Served with AUS, 1957-59. Mem. Am. Film Inst., Am. Fedn. Arts, Coll. Art Assn. Am., Mus. Modern Art, Internat. Mus. Photography, Bowdoin Coll. Mus., Portland Mus. Art, Maine Hist. Soc. Office: University Maine Gorham ME 04038

UDINE, EDGAR, pharm. co. exec.; b. Newark, Jan. 14, 1930; s. Joseph and Etta (Abramson) U.; B.S. in Biol. Scis., Rutgers U., 1950; m. Helene Cohen, June 20, 1951; children—Richard Douglas, Glen Robert, Lori Michelle. With Charles Pfizer & Co., Inc., 1954-65, mktg. dir. Roerig div., N.Y.C., 1964-65; dir. mktg. USV Pharm. Co. div. Revlon, N.Y.C., 1966, v.p. mktg., 1967-69, exec. v.p., 1969-70; pres. Ethos Mgmt. Corp., Orange, N.J., 1970-71, also Hudson Pharm. Corp.; v.p. Cadence Industries Corp., N.Y.C., 1971-74; pres. Bio-Med. Scis., Inc., 1974-77; exec. v.p. Erika, Inc. and v.p. Nat. Med. Care, Rockleigh, N.J., 1977—. Served to 1st lt. USAF, 1950-53. Mem Tau Delta Phi. Republican. Home: 4 Ellis Pl West Caldwell NJ 07006 Office: 1 Erika Plaza Rockleigh NJ 07647

UDIS, SANFORD WILLIAM, radiologist; b. Fall River, Mass., Aug. 3, 1919; s. Teavy and Mollie (Goldstein) U.; A.B., Brown U., 1941; M.D., Boston U., 1944: m. Beverly Tarle, Sept. 12, 1948; children—Andrew H., Jonathan. Intern, Boston City Hosp., 1944-45; resident in radiology Beth Israel Hosp., Boston, 1947-50; dir. dept. radiology Truesdale Hosp., Fall River, Mass., 1952-75; chmn. radiology dept. Union-Truesdale Hosp., Fall River, 1975—; dir. Fall River Trust Co. Trustee Brown U., Union Truesdale Hosp.; bd. visitors Boston U. Sch. Medicine. Served with U.S. Army, 1945-47. Diplomate Am. Bd. Radiology. Fellow Am. Coll. Radiology; mem. Radiol. Soc. N. Am. Home: 9 Courtney St Fall River MA 02720 Office: 1030 President Ave Fall River MA 02720

UDOFF, HOWARD STEPHAN, pharm. co. exec.; b. Queens, N.Y., May 20, 1940; s. Louis and Josephine (Barnett) U.; B.S. in Pharmacy, Bklyn. Coll. Pharmacy, 1963; M.S., Purdue U., 1966; m. Susan Carole Bergen, June 29, 1963; children—Douglas, Allison, Shari. Chemist, CIBA Pharm. Corp., 1965-67; asst. mgr. quality assurance Endo Labs., Garden City, N.Y., 1968-73; mgr. quality assurance Ortho Pharm. Co., Raritan, N.J., 1974-75, group mgr., 1975-78, mgr. quality assurance systems and automation, Mem. Am. Chem. Soc., AAAS, Rho Chi. Home: 7 Galaxy Ct Belle Mead NJ 08502 Office: US Route 202 Raritan NJ 08869

UEBEL, J. JOHN, chemist, educator; b. Chgo., Dec. 25, 1937; s. Jacob and Elsie (Loibl) U.; B.A., Carthage Coll., 1959; M.S., U. Ill., 1962, Ph.D., 1964; m. Kathleen Ann Garman, Aug. 23, 1958; children—Virginia, John, Mark. Chemist, Ill. Water Survey, Urbana, 1958; research asso. U. Mich., Ann Arbor, 1964; asst. prof. U. N.H., Durham, 1964-68, prof. chemistry, 1972—; vis. prof. U. Calif. at Riverside, 1971; vis. scientist Eastman Kodak Co., 1978-79. Cons. to publishers and chem. industry. Treas. Ch. Sch., Durham United Ch. of Christ, 1968-69, chmn. nomaniation com., 1976. Sun Oil fellow, 1961; NSF grantee, 1965-70; NSF faculty fellow, 1978-79. Mem. Am. Chem. Soc., Sigma Xi, Gamma Kappa Alpha. Contbr. articles to profl. jours. Office: Parsons Hall Chemistry Dept Durham NH 03824

UELAND, MARK, architect; b. Mpls., May 12, 1935; s. Rolf and Margaret Anna (Lavery) U.; A.B. (scholar 1953), Harvard U., 1959; B.Arch., U. Pa., 1961, M.Arch., 1964; m. Elizabeth J. Pritchard, Aug. 26, 1960; children—Mara Elizabeth, Anne Clara, Michael Andreas. Asst. architect Vincent Kling and Partner, Phila., 1962-64; project architect Geddes, Brecher, Qualls & Cunningham, Phila., 1964-67; partner Ueland & Junker, Phila., 1967—; adj. asst. prof. architecture Temple U., 1972-73, Drexel U., Phila., 1974—; lectr. U. Pa., 1967-69, 73-74. Chmn. housing div. Mayor's Sci. and Tech. Adv. Council, 1975—; v.p. Chestnut Hill Community Assn., 1975-76; bd. dirs. Chestnut Hill Hist. Soc., 1973-74; trustee Chestnut Hill Hosp., 1977—. Served with AUS, 1956-58. Henry Adams fellow, 1961. Mem. AIA, Pa. Soc. Architects, Am. Arbitration Assn., Phila. C. of C., Com. of Seventy. Republican. Roman Catholic. Clubs: Phila. Cricket, Harvard; Fox (Cambridge, Mass.). Home: 8316 Shawnee St Philadelphia PA 19118 Office: 1616 Walnut St Philadelphia PA 19103

UFBERG, SAUL HOWARD, chiropractic physician; b. Detroit, Mar. 26, 1921; s. Barney and Faye (Saperstein) U.; student Pa. State U., 1939; D.C., Can. Meml. Chiropractic Coll., 1952; m. Arline Wolman, Dec. 30, 1945; children—Ross, Sharon. Gen. practice chiropractic medicine, Wilmington, Del., 1952—; mem. postgrad. faculty Nat. Coll. Chiropractic, Lombard, Ill., 1968-76. Served with USAAF, 1940-45. Decorated Bronze Star (3). Diplomate Am. Bd. Chiropractic Orthopedics, Am. Coll. Chiropractic Roentgenology. Fellow Internat. Coll. Chiropractors; mem. Am. Chiropractic Assn. (del.), Del. Assn. Chiropractic Physicians (past pres.), Am. Council Chiropractic Orthopedics (past pres.), Am. Council on Chiropractic Roentgenology, Am. Coll. Roentgenology, Jewish War Vets. of Wilmington. Democrat. Jewish. Club: Masons. Editor Orthopedic Quiz, Jour. Am. Chiropractic Assn., 1968-76. Home and Office: 2205 Baynard Blvd Wilmington DE 19802

UGUCCIONI, ROBERT, personal services exec.; b. Scranton, Pa., Aug. 30, 1936; s. Otto and Christine U.; student U. Md., 1955-56; m. Marilyn Nolan, Aug. 26, 1973; children—Robert, Cindy, Michael. Dir. pub. relations Lake Wallenpauapck Assn., Paupack, Pa., 1965-67; exec. dir. Pocono Mountains Vacation Bur., Inc., Stroudsburg, Pa., 1967—; mem. tourist advisory council Fed. Energy Adminstrn. Bd. dirs. YMCA. Sec., Jacob Stroud Corp., 1978—. Served with USAF, 1955-58. Mem. Travel Industry Adv. Council (exec. com.), Travel Pa. Assn. (pres.), Hotel Sales Mgmt. Assn. (dir.), Pa. Hotel Motel Inn Assn., Pa. C. of C., Discover Am. Travel Orgn. Clubs: Elks. Home: RD 2 Box 565 East Stroudsburg PA 18301 Office: 1004 Main St Pocono Mountains Vacation Bureau Stroudsburg PA 18360

UH, DAVID KEUN, civil engr.; b. Korea, Jan. 28, 1935; s. Kwang Sun and Hyo Sook (Lee) Uh; came to U.S., 1956, naturalized, 1968; student Friends Bible Coll., 1956, Bethany Nazarene Coll., 1956-57; B.S. in Engring., U. Mich., 1961; M.S., Columbia U., 1968; m. Meong Jae Kim, June 4, 1966; children—Benjamin, Steven. Design engr. Allied Chem. Corp., 1963-66; sr. design engr. Frederick Snare Corp., 1966-68; project engr. Edwards & Hjorth, 1968-70; sr. engr. Soros Assos., Inc., 1970-73; prin. engr., cons. civil engr. dept. Ebasco Services Inc., 1973— (all N.Y.C.); cons. on offshore nuclear power plant and offshore coal handling, 1973—. Mem. governing bd. dirs., sec. Korean Cultural Center, Inc., 1969-72, 74—, editor News Bull., 1970-72. Mem. ASCE, Kyunggi Alumni Assn. Am. (exec. dir. 1971—), Kyunggi Alumni Assn. N.Y. (pres. 1969-72), Korean Student Assn. N.Y. (pres. 1962-63), U. Mich. Alumni Assn. (life). Republican. Home: 24 Woodbine St Coram NY 11727 Office: 21 West St New York City NY 10006

UHLER, IRVIN VALENTINE, oral surgeon; b. Easton, Pa., May 25, 1913; s. Norman Clifford & Lelia (Messinger) U.; student, Muhlenberg Coll., 1931-32; D.D.S., Temple U., 1937; postgrad. in oral surgery. U. Mich,, 1947-48; m. Gloria Rodgers Thompson. Intern Allentown (Pa.) Gen. Hosp., 1937-38; gen. practice dentistry, Allentown 1938-43; ltd. practice oral surgery, Lancaster, Pa., 1948—; chief oral surgery Lancaster Gen. Hosp., 1960-78; oral surgeon Lancaster Cleft Palate Clinic, 1948—; instr. oral surgery Grad. Sch. Medicine U. Pa., 1959-69; cons. oral surgery VA Hosp., Lebanon, Pa., 1949-71, Good Samaratin Hosp., 1949-71, Ephrata (Pa.) Community Hosp., 1949-72, Hershey (Pa.) Community Hosp., 1956-68, Milton Hershey Sch., 1950-69, St. Josephs Hosp., Lancaster, Pa., 1949—; lectr. Bd. dirs. Pa. div. Am. Cancer Soc., 1963-69, 70-76, 77—, pres. Lancaster County unit, 1972-74. Served from lt. (j.g.) to comdr., USN, 1943-45. Diplomate Am. Bd. Oral Surgery. Fellow Internat. Coll. Dentists, Internat. Assn. of Oral Surgeons (founder), Am. Coll. Dentists; mem. Am. Soc. Oral Surgeons (founding pres.), Am. Dental Assn., Am. Coll. Oral and Maxillofacial Surgeons (pres. 1975-76), Middle Atlantic Soc. Oral Surgeons (past pres.), Pa., Phila. (past. pres.) socs. oral surgeons, Lancaster County Hist. Soc. (life), Pa. Soc. Clubs: Pittsburgh Press, Pittsburgh Athletic Assn.; Hamilton, Lancaster Country, Rotary (Lancaster, Pa.); Variety. Contbr. articles to profl. jours. Home: 2610 Old Orchard Rd Mondamin Farm Lancaster PA 17601 Office: 548 N Duke St Lancaster PA 17602

UHRMAN, CELIA, artist, poet; b. New London, Conn., May 14, 1927; d. David Aaron and Pauline (Schwartz) U.; B.A., Bklyn. Coll., 1948, M.A., 1953; Ph.D., U. Danzig, 1977; postgrad. Tchrs. Coll., Columbia U., 1961, City U. N.Y., 1966, Bklyn. Mus. Art Sch., 1956-57, Ph.D. (hon.), Litt.D., 1973. One-woman shows: Leffert Jr. High Sch., Bklyn., 1958, Flatbush C. of C., N.Y.C., 1963, Conn. C. of C., New London, 1962; exhibited in group shows: Smithsonian Instn., Washington, 1958, Springfield (Mass.) Mus. Fine Arts, 1959, Bklyn. Mus., 1959, Old Mystic (Conn.) Art Center, 1959, Carnegie Endowment Internat. Center, N.Y.C., 1959, Lyman Allyn Mus., New London, 1960, Palacio de La Virreina, Barcelona, Spain, 1961, YWCA, Bklyn., 1962, UFT Art Exhibit, N.Y.C., 1963, Soc. of 4 Arts, Palm Beach, Fla., 1964, Perspective 68, Monte-Carlo, Monaco, 1968, George W. Wingate High Sch., Bklyn., 1967, Premier Salon Internat., Charleroi, Belgium, 1968, Palme d'or Beaux Arts, Monte-Carlo, 1970, 72, Dibuix-Joan Miro Premi Internacional, Barcelona, 1970; N.Y. Art Festival, 1970, Internat. Platform Assn. Art Show, Washington, 1971, 73, Ovar Mus., Portugal, 1974, others; represented in permanent collections: Bklyn. Coll., Ch. of Evangel, Bklyn.; tchr. N.Y.C. Sch. System, 1948—; partner Uhrman Studio, 1973—; hon. rep. U.S., Centro Studi E Scambi Internazionali, Rome, mem. internat. com., 1969—. Hon. life mem. World Poetry Day Com., Inc. and Nat. Poetry Day Com., 1977. Recipient award Freedoms Found., George Washington medal of honor, 1964; Diplome d'Honneur Palme d'Or des Beaux Arts Exhbn., Monaco, 1969, 72, Diploma and Gold medal, 1972; decorated Order of Gandhi Award of Honour, Knight Grand Cross, 1972; personal poetry certificate WEFG Stereo, 1970; Gold Laurel award Esposizione Internazionale D'Art Contemporain, Paris, 1974; named Poetry Translator Laureate World Acad. Lang. and Lit., 1972; Poet of Mankind Acad. Philosophy, 1972. Mem. Internat. Arts Guild (Monte-Carlo), World Poetry Soc. Intercontinental (rep. at large 1970—), Internat. Acad. Poets (founding fellow). Author: Poetic Ponderances, 1969; A Pause for Poetry, 1970; Poetic Love Fancies, 1970; A Pause for Poetry for Children, 1973; The Chimps Are Coming, 1975; also poems. Home: 1655 Flatbush Ave Apt and Studio C602 Brooklyn NY 11210

UJHELY, VALENTINE ANTHONY, physician; b. Budapest, Hungary, July 9, 1896; s. Balint and Emilia (Blav) U.; Med. diploma, Royal Hungarian U., 1920; m. Olga-Marit Hildeborg Ness, May 16, 1943 (dec.); m. 2d, Ruth L. Vartaw, July 9, 1977. Came to U.S., 1923; naturalized, 1930. Resident Met. Sanatorium, Budapest, 1920-23; physician in charge psychotherapy city and state hosps., Phila., Milw. and Providence, 1923-30; physician in charge psychotherapy VA Hosp., N.Y.C., Bath, N.Y., Brecksville, Ohio and Cleve., 1941-46; neuropsychiatrist Municipal Hosp., Washington, 1946-47; chief neuropsychiatrist Walter Reed Army Hosp., Washington, 1947-48; med. rating specialist, sec. bd. neuropsychiat. cons. Vet.'s Benefit Office, VA, Washington, 1948-65; practice medicine specializing in psychiatry, psychoanalysis and neurology, Washington, 1964—; neuropsychiat. dir. Hildeborg House Research Project, Washington, 1950-63; med. dir. Bionomic Research League and Library, 1964—. Served as 1st asst. med. officer Hungarian Army, 1918-19. Recipient pin 30 years service U.S. Govt., 1959, award sustained superior performance VA, 1960. Diplomate Am. Bd. Psychiatry and Neurology. Mem. Acad. Mental Health and Religion (charter), Am. Acad. Neurology, Am. Psychiat. Assn., AMA, So. Med. Assn., Cleveland Park Citizens Assn. Contbr. articles to profl. jours. Research visuo-acoustical instrumentation hypnoanalysis. Address: 3307 Macomb St NW Washington DC 20008

ULIN, RICHARD IRWIN, physician; b. N.Y.C., May 26, 1936; s. Albert Jay and Ruth Charlotte (Newman) U.; B.S. in Zoology, Franklin and Marshall Coll., 1958; M.D., Columbia U., 1962; m. Susan Borkow, Mar. 30, 1958; children—David, John. Intern Hosp. Joint Diseases, N.Y.C., 1962-63, resident, 1963-67; fellowship in children's orthopedics Rancho Los Angeles Hosp., Los Angeles, 1967-68; practice medicine specializing in orthopedic surgery, N.Y.C., 1968—; asst. clin. prof. orthopedic surgery Mt. Sinai Sch. Medicine, N.Y.C., 1973—. Served with NG, 1963-69. Recipient Smith award Hosp. Joint Diseases, 1962, also Kleinberg award, 1967. Diplomate Am. Bd. Orthopedic Surgery. Mem. N.Y. County, N.Y. State med. socs., Am. Acad. Orthopedic Surgeons, N.Y. State Soc. Orthopedic Surgeons. Clubs: South Yaremouth Tennis, Stone House Yacht. Home: 21 E 87th St New York City NY 10028 Office: 1095 Park Ave New York City NY 10028

ULLMAN, ROBERT, corp. exec.; b. Bklyn., May 11, 1908; s. Harry and Beatrice (Baslow) U.; student pub. schs.; m. Marie Michaelson, Aug. 15, 1935. Pres. Mercury Equipment Mfg. Corp., N.Y.C., 1934; partner Century Dryer Co., N.Y.C., 1935-36; pres. Ullman Products Corp., 1937—, Ullman Devices Corp., Ridgefield, Conn., 1937—; asso. dir. State Nat. Bank of Conn. Col. staff Gov. La. Recipient State of Conn. Employers award. Club: Cedar Point Yacht (Westpoint, Conn.). Patentee drying and hand tools. Office: 664 Danbury Rd Ridgefield CT 06877

ULLRICH, JAMES ARTHUR, educator; b. Passaic, N.J., Apr. 22, 1933; s. Arthur Jacob and Mary Josephine (Wood) U.; B.S. in Edn., N.J. State Tchrs. Coll., 1955; postgrad. Columbia U., 1959, Abilene Christian Coll., 1958, Lois Albright Sch. Music, 1959-61; M.A., Paterson State Coll., 1960. Tchr., Samuel R. Donald Sch., Bloomingdale, N.J., 1955-71, asst. prin., 1968-70; tchr., asst. prin. Walter T. Bergen Sch., Bloomingdale, 1971-78; prin. Samuel R. Donald Sch., Bloomingdale, 1978—. Treas., Bloomingdale PTA, 1959-61, sec., 1961-62. Served with Adj. Gen. Corps, AUS, 1956-58. Mem. Intercontinental Biog. Assn., NEA (life), Speech Communication Assn. Am., N.J. Congress Parents and Tchrs. (life), N.J. Edn. Assn., Passaic Council Educators, Bloomingdale Tchrs. Assn. (pres. 1964-65, 67-68), Am. Assn. UN. Home: 222 Lakeview Ave Paterson NJ 07503 Office: Samuel R Donald School Captolene Ave Bloomingdale NJ 07403

ULLUCCI, PAUL ANTHONY, chemist, toxicologist; b. Providence, May 17, 1946; s. Paul and Dorothy Janet (Ricci) U.; B.S. in Chemistry, Providence Coll., 1968; m. Dianne Elizabeth Strobel, Jan. 13, 1968; children—Paul Anthony, Beth Ann. Chemist, R.I. Hosp., Providence, 1968-70, supr. toxicology lab., 1973—; chemist Instrumentation Lab., Lexington, Mass., 1970-73; instr. instrumental methods of analysis, Med. Tech. Sch., R.I. Hosp. Prin. edn. St. Robert Bellarmine Ch., Johnston, R.I. Mem. Am. Chem. Soc. (divs. Analytical and Medicinal Chemistry), Soc. Applied Spectroscopy. Roman Catholic. Contbr. articles to tech. publs., papers to sci. confs. Home: 25 Spring St Johnston RI 02919 Office: 593 Eddy St Providence RI 02902

ULMAN, LUCY THIMANN, assn. exec.; b. Vienna, Austria, Jan. 21, 1933; d. Joseph and Maria (Tauber) Thimann; came to U.S., 1939, naturalized, 1945; B.S., Boston U., 1958, M.Ed., 1965; Ed.D., 1974; Ph.D., Heed U., 1973; m. Theodore B. Ulman, Feb. 20, 1954 (div. June 1971); children—Karen Sue, Janet Lee, Geoffrey Samuel, Linda Ann. Sch. adjustment counselor Needham (Mass.) Pub. Schs., 1964-67; staff psychologist Leslie B. Cutler Child Guidance Clinic, Norwood, Mass., 1965-69; asst. prof. Lesley Coll., Cambridge, Mass., 1967-72; v.p., cons. Universal Freedom, Inc., Newton, Mass., 1970—; clin. dir. Chestnut Hill Psychotherapy Assos.; asso. prof. Newton Coll. Sacred Heart, 1972-75; clin. dir. Universal Freedom, Inc., 1970—; individual practice psychol. counseling, Newton, 1962-70; prof. Heed U., 1972-75, Mass. Coll. Optometry, Framingham State Coll., 1973-75. Mem. exec. bd. PTA, Mason Rice Sch., Newton, 1966-69; bd. dirs. Washingtonian Hosp., Jamaica Plain, Mass. Mem. Heed U. Alumnae Assn. (dir.), Am., Mass., N.E. psychol. assns., Am. Group Psychotherapy Assn., Am. Personnel and Guidance Assn., Am. Assn. Sex Educators and Counselors, Am. Assn. Marriage and Family Counselors, AAUP. Address: 11 Riverview Terr Dover MA 02030

ULRICH, LORRAINE ANNE, editor; b. Chgo., Aug. 24, 1928; d. Ranieri and Anita Carolyn (Benedetti) Bonaguidi; student Northwestern U., 1946; B.S. in Journalism, U. Ill., 1950; postgrad. Moser Bus. Coll., U. Chgo.; m. Gene W. Ulrich, Aug. 30, 1952; 1 son, Christopher. Asst. editor Florists' Rev., Chgo., 1950-53, Nat. Underwriter, Chgo., 1955-56; asso. editor Jour. Housing, Chgo., 1956-61; mng. editor Drug and Cosmetic Industry mag., N.Y.C., 1961-62; sr. editor Hearst Mags., N.Y.C., 1962-63; asso. editor Tchr. mag., Darien, Conn., 1963-70; co-founder, mng. editor Early Years, also Early Year's Parent, Darien, 1970-78; mng. editor How To, N.Y.C., 1978—. Recipient awards for stories Edn. Press Assn. Mem. Ednl. Press, Nat. Fedn. Press Women. Club: Greenwich Boat and Yacht. Home: 49 Breezemont Ave Riverside CT 06878 Office: 380 Madison Ave New York City NY 10017

ULTAN, LLOYD, historian; b. Bronx, N.Y., Feb. 16, 1938; s. Louis and Sophie U.; B.A. cum laude, Hunter Coll., 1959; M.A., Columbia U., 1960. Asso. Edward Williams Coll., Fairleigh Dickinson U., Hackensack, N.J., 1964-74, asst. prof. history, 1974-75, asso. prof., 1975—; cons. in field. Gen. sec. Bronx Civic League, 1964-67; v.p. bd. trustees Bronx County Hist. Soc., 1965-67, 77—, curator, 1968-71, pres., 1971-76; founding mem., dir. Bronx Council on Arts, 1968-71; chmn. Bronx County Bicentennial Commn., 1973-76. Bronx Borough Pres.'s Bicentennial Adv. Com., 1974-76; program guidelines com. N.Y.C. Dept. Cultural Affairs, 1976-77. N.Y. State Regents Coll. Teaching fellow, 1959; elected to Hunter Coll. Alumni Hall of Fame, 1974; Fairleigh Dickinson U. Ten Yr. awardee, 1975. Mem. Am. Hist. Assn., AAUP, N.Y. Hist. Soc., Phi Alpha Theta, Alpha Chi Alpha, Sigma Lambda. Editor, Bronx County Hist. Soc. Jour., 1964—. Home and office: 91 Van Cortlandt Ave W Bronx NY 10463

ULYAT, HARRY LEE, JR., clin. lab. adminstr.; b. Dallas, July 17, 1935; s. Harry Lee and Mary Marthelene (Heathcock) U.; A.B., Asbury Coll., 1958; postgrad. Salvation Army Sch. Officers, 1959-60; M.S. in Med. Biology (HEW Allied Health grantee), C.W. Post Coll., 1972, M.P.S. in Health Care Adminstrn., 1976; m. Virginia Carole Cochran, Mar. 20, 1957; m. 2d Mary McAuley Stewart, June 27, 1970; children—Melody, Harry, Timothy, Melynda, Annamarie. Adminstrv. officer Salvation Army, Washington, 1960-62, Valdosta, Ga., 1963-64; adminstrv. asst. dept. nursing U. Ky., Lexington, 1965-66; med. technologist and clin. chemist trainee Booth Meml. Hosp., Flushing, N.Y., 1966-69; med. technologist Nassau Hosp., Mineola, N.Y., 1970-71; clin. services adminstr. Brookhaven Nat. Lab. Med. Research Center, Upton, N.Y., 1972—. Mem. Am. Hosp. Assn., Am. Pub. Health Assn., Am. Soc. Clin. Pathologists, Am. Soc. Med. Technologists, Am. Assn. Clin. Lab. Suprs. Adminstrs. Republican. Episcopalian; mem. Salvation Army. Home: 11 Deepdale Dr Rocky Point NY 11778 Office: Medical Research Center Upton NY 11973

UMLAND, HERBERT CHRISTIAN, JR., banker; b. Paterson, N.J., Oct. 12, 1946; s. Herbert Christian and Margaret Emily (O'Grady) U.; B.S. in Bus. Adminstrn., Villanova U., 1968; postgrad. Stonier Grad. Sch. Banking, 1973-76; M.B.A. in Mgmt., Fairleigh Dickinson Coll., 1978; m. Mary Lynn Kittel, Oct. 5, 1968; children—Amy, Rebecca. With Midlantic Nat. Bank/Citizens, Englewood, N.J., 1968—, v.p., 1973—, area devel. supr., 1977—. Pres. Indsl. Assn. Northvale, Norwood and Rockleigh (N.J.), 1973; regional chmn. Bergen County Heart Fund, Hackensack, N.J., 1974-77, mem. exec. and dir. com., 1975-76, chmn. county wide campaign, 1975-76; mem. City Englewood Econ. and Indsl. Devel. Com., 1975-76. Mem. Am. Inst. Banking, Englewood C. of C. (treas., dir. 1974-76), C. of C. and Industry No. N.J. (membership com. 1974-75, 78 co-chmn. 1975). Roman Catholic. Club: Englewood Rotary (treas., dir. 1975-79). Home: 537 Spencer Dr Wyckoff NJ 07481 Office: 16 Highwood Ave Tenafly NJ 07670

UNANGST, ROBERT WALKER, surgeon; b. Newark, Aug. 31, 1917; s. Ernest Walker and Anne (Robertson) U.; B.A., Dartmouth Coll., 1940; M.D., N.Y. U. Coll. Medicine, 1943; m. Phyllis Johnston, Mar. 1, 1976; children—Robert, Anne, Margaret, Mary; stepchildren—Donald, James, Amy, David. Intern, U.S. Naval Hosp., Bklyn., 1944; resident in surgery Mary Hitchcock Meml. Hosp., Hanover, N.H., 1947-53; practice medicine specializing in surgery, Huntington, N.Y., 1954—; chief surgery Huntington Hosp., 1970—; asst. prof. surgery U. State U. N.Y., Stony Brook, 1975—. Served with USNR, 1943-47. Diplomate Am. Bd. Surgery. Fellow A.C.S.; mem.

AMA. Home: 8 Talmadge Rd Northport NY 11768 Office: 180 E Pulaski Rd Huntington Station NY 11746

UNDERSTEIN, ROBERT STANLEY, accountant; b. Washington, D.C., Jan. 16, 1942; s. Jack and Mildred (Holtz) U.; B.S. in Commerce, U. Va., 1963; J.D., Am. U., 1967; m. Susan Heyman, Aug. 25, 1963; children—Adam, Allison, Amy. Mng. and sr. partner firm Jack Understein Co., Washington; cons. Diplomat Nat. Bank, 1975; dir. Free State Bank, Potomac, Md.; treas., bd. dirs. Washington dist. adv. council SBA; mem. U.S. del. to Japan, Am. Council Young Polit. Leaders, 1973. Mem. Am., D.C., Md. insts., C.P.A.'s. Home: 7710 Brookville Rd Chevy Chase MD 20015 Office: 5272 River Rd #740 Washington DC 20016

UNDERWEISER, IRWIN PHILIP, lawyer; b. N.Y.C., Jan. 3, 1929; s. Harry and Edith (Gladstein) U.; B.A., City Coll. N.Y., 1950; LL.D., Fordham U., 1954; LL.M., N.Y. U., 1961; m. Beatrice J. Kortchmar, Aug. 17, 1959; children—Rosanne, Marian, Jeffrey. Admitted to N.Y. State bar, 1954; asso. Scribner & Miller, N.Y.C., 1951-54, 56-62; partner Feuerstein & Underweiser, N.Y.C., 1964-73, Underweiser & Fuchs, N.Y.C., 1973-77, Underweiser & Underweiser, 1977—; v.p., sec., dir. Sunshine Mining Co., Kellogg, Ida., 1965-70, chmn. bd., 1970-78, pres., 1971-74, v.p., 1978—; vice chmn., dir. Underwriters Bank and Trust Co., N.Y.C., 1969-73; sec., dir. Berel Industries, Inc., N.Y.C., 1964—; dir. Anchor Post Products, Inc., chmn. bd., 1976-78. Gen. counsel, mem. bus. council The Friends City Center Music and Drama, 1966-67; pres. W. Quaker Ridge Assn., 1969-70; treas. Scarsdale Neighborhood Assn. of Presidents, 1970-71. Bd. dirs. Silver Inst., Inc. Served with AUS, 1954-56. Mem. Am., N.Y. State bar assns., Assn. Bar City N.Y., Phi Beta Kappa, Phi Alpha Theta. Home: 7 Rural Dr Scarsdale NY 10583 Office: 250 Park Ave New York City NY 10017

UNGER, CHRISTOPHER PELHAM, physician; b. Lancaster, Pa., Oct. 15, 1944; B.S., Ursinus Coll., 1965; M.D., U. Pa., 1969. Intern, New Eng. Deaconess Hosp., Boston, 1969-70, resident internal medicine, 1970-71; resident pediatrics Children's Hosp. Med. Center, Boston, 1972; resident, also fellow family practice Harvard Family Health Care program, Boston, 1971-73; clin. fellow medicine Harvard Med. Sch., Boston, also resident Peter Bent Brigham Home Care program, 1972-73; emergency physician Sibley Meml. Hosp., Washington, 1975-76; emergency physician Emerge Inc., Concord (Mass.) Med. Center, 1972-73; individual practice medicine specializing in family practice Washington, also Bethesda, Md., 1978—. Served to lt. comdr., M.C., USNR, 1965-75. Diplomate Am. Bd. Family Practice; licensed physician Mass., Md., D.C. Fellow Am. Acad. Family Physicians (charter); mem. Physicians Forum, AMA, Soc. Tchrs. Family Medicine, Harvard Med. Alumni Assn., Royal Soc. Medicine Md. Acad. Family Practice, D.C., Montgomery County (Md.) med. socs., Cub and Key. Home: 7801 Moorland Ln Bethesda MD 20014 Office: 8218 Wisconsin Ave Bethesda MD 20014

UNGER, WALTER PETER, dermatologist, educator; b. Toronto, Ont., Can., Apr. 8, 1939; s. Harry and Mary (Vladovitz) U.; M.D., U. Toronto, 1963; m. Marcia Ruby Raxlen, May 23, 1963; children—Jeffrey, Nicole, Robin, Rory-Ellen, Alexander, Amanda, Russell, Caroline, Andrew. Intern, New Mt. Sinai Hosp., Toronto, 1963-64; resident St. John's Hosp. for Diseases of the Skin, London, Eng., 1964-65; chief resdient in dermatology Skin and Cancer Hosp., Phila., 1966-67; resident in medicine Sunnybrook Hosp., Toronto, 1967-68; practice medicine specializing in dermatology, Toronto, 1968—; chief dept. dermatology Wellesley Hosp., Toronto, 1973—; mem. staff Doctors Hosp., Toronto, 1968—; asst. prof. dept. medicine (dermatology) U. Toronto, 1973—, dep. coordinator dermatology div., 1972—; pres. Dermatologists Adminstrv. Services, Ltd., Toronto, 1970—. Recipient Bickle award U. Toronto, 1960; diplomate Am. Bd. Dermatology. Fellow A.C.P., Royal Coll. Physicians; mem. Am. Acad. Dermatology, Ont. Med. Assn., St. John's Dermatologic Soc. of London, Am. Soc. for Dermatol. Surgery. Jewish. Author: Hair Transplantation (med. text), 1978. Contbr. articles to profl. pubs. Home: 26 Alexandra Wood Toronto ON M5N 2S1 Canada Office: 2156 Yonge St Toronto ON M4S 2A5 Canada

UNICK, RUSSELL ROY, pharmacist; b. Philipsburg, Pa., Feb. 13, 1949; s. Russell V. and Catherine Elizabeth (Heeman) U.; B.S. in Pharmacy with highest honors, U. Pitts., 1972; m. Sandra Jo McWilliams, Oct. 7, 1972; children—Catherine Danielle, Alison Jene. Intern, pharmacist Ibberson Drug Store, Philipsburg, 1972-74; staff pharmacist Clearfield (Pa.) Hosp., 1974-75, dir. pharmacy services, 1977—; pharmacist Cowdrick's Drug Store, Dubois, Pa., 1975-76; staff pharmacist Philipsburg State Gen. Hosp., 1976-77. Mem. Clearfield County unit Am. Cancer Soc.; advisor explorer post Bucktail council Boy Scouts Am.; mem. pastor-parish com. Grace United Methodist Ch., Philipsburg. Eagle Scout; mem. Nat. Honor Soc., 1967; recipient Merck award, 1972. Mem. Rho Chi (v.p. 1972). Home: Route 2 Mount Joy Rd Clearfield PA 16830 Office: 809 Turnpike Ave Clearfield PA 16830

UNIS, MAX JAY, mech. engr.; b. Phila., Mar. 5, 1914; s. Sam and Ida Unis; B.S. in Mech. Engring., Drexel U., 1936; m. Esther Odesser, June 8, 1940; 1 son, Richard. Purchasing engr. Molded Insulation Co., Phila., 1940-43; tool and gage design engr. Radio Condenser Co., Camden, N.J., 1943-50; research asso. U. Pa., 1950-65; pres. Gage Lab. Corp., Phila., 1965—; bd. dirs. Nat. Conf. Standards Labs.; cons. seminars, symposiums. Fellow Am. Soc. Quality Control; mem. U.S. Metric Assn. Clubs: B'nai B'rith. Patentee corner constrn.; co-inventor photo-electric colorimeter. Office: Gage Lab Corp Buck Rd North of County Line Huntingdon Valley PA 19006

UNKOVIC, NICHOLAS, lawyer; b. Chgo., Aug. 24, 1906; s. Kosto and Josephine (Polic) U.; A.B., Harvard U., 1928; LL.B., Dickinson Law Sch., 1932; m. Mary D. Clark, Oct. 26, 1935; children—Mary Madelon Unkovic Sheedy, Constance Clark Unkovic Kerr, Christine Anita Unkovic Valentine, John Clark, Nicholas Clark. Admitted to Pa. bar, 1932, since practiced in Pitts.; sr. partner Reed, Smith, Shaw & McClay, 1948—; dir. Mine Safety Appliances Co., Kennametal, Inc. Dir. Allegheny Roundtable; mem. Pa. Labor Law Com., Mercy Hosp., WQED Pitts. Ednl. TV Sta. Mem. Am., Pa., 3d Jud. Circuit, Allegheny County bar assns., Indsl. Relations Research Assn., Am. Arbitration Assn. (dir.). Clubs: Duquesne, Harvard-Yale-Princeton, Pitts. Athletic Assn., Harvard (Western Pa.); Rolling Rock. Home: 5023 Frew Ave Pittsburgh PA 15213 Office: Union Trust Bldg Pittsburgh PA 15219

UOTINEN, KYOSTI GUS, research dentist; b. Finland, Apr. 7, 1936; s. William E. and Vappu (Kortelainen) U.; D.D.S., U. Buffalo, 1960; M.S. in Pharmacology, Georgetown U., 1963-65; S.M., Mass. Inst. Tech., 1976; m. Fannie S. Maki, July 4, 1964. Dental officer U.S. Army, Mass., Korea, 1960-63, dental research officer, 1964-68; lectr. Georgetown U., 1965-68; asso. dir. advanced theory and sci. dental practice course Walter Reed Army Med. Center, Washington, 1967-68; clin. practice dentistry, Townsend, Mass., 1970-78. Fellow Royal Soc. Health; mem. Am. Dental Assn., Officers' Christian Fellowship, Aircraft Owners' and Pilots' Assn. Home: 70 Elm St West Townsend MA 01474 Office: 25 Harvard St Worcester MA 01608

UPCRAFT, M. LEE, univ. adminstr.; b. Syracuse, N.Y., Oct. 15, 1938; s. Milton John and Mabel (Hendricks) U.; B.A., State U. N.Y. at Albany, 1960, M.A., 1961; Ph.D., Mich. State U., 1967; m. Edith Lillian Skadberg, June 23, 1962; children—Kirsten Marie, John Gunnar. Tchr. social studies Hudson Falls (N.Y.) Central Sch., 1961-63; head resident adviser Mich. State U., East Lansing, 1963-66, asst. to dean, dir. student relations Justin Morrill Coll., 1966-69; dir. student activities, acting dean of students Pa. State U., University Park, 1969-72, dir. residential life programs and student assistance center, asst. prof. dept. counselor edn., asso. mem. Grad. Sch., 1972—; cons. Lewisburg (Pa.) Fed. Penitentiary, 1971-74. Mem. Am. Personnel and Guidance Assn., Am. Coll. Personnel Assn. (spl. task force on group procedures), Nat. Assn. Student Personnel Adminstrs., Pa. Assn. Student Personnel Adminstrs., Phi Delta Kappa, Kappa Phi Kappa, Kappa Delta Rho. Contbr. articles to profl. jours. Home: 188 Lenor Dr State College PA 16801 Office: 335 Boucke Bldg PA State U University Park PA 16802

UPGREN, ARTHUR REINHOLD, JR., astronomer; b. Mpls., Feb. 21, 1933; s. Arthur Reinhold and Marion Elizabeth (Andrews) U.; B.A., U. Minn., 1955; M.S., U. Mich., 1958; Ph.D., Case-Western Res. U., 1961; m. Josephine Joan Koswoski, Jan. 7, 1967; 1 dau., Amy Joan. Research asso. Swarthmore Coll. 1961-63; astronomer U.S. Naval Obs., Washington, 1963-66; asst. prof. astronomy Wesleyan U., Middletown, conn., 1966-73, asso. prof., chmn. dept. astronomy, dir. Van Vleck Obs., 1973—; vis. lectr. Yale U., 1967; v.p., exec. officer Found. Astrophys. Research, N.Y.C. Am. Philos. Soc. grantee, 1962; NSF grantee, 1967—. Mem. Internat. Astron. Union, Royal Astron. Soc., Am. Astron. Soc., Sigma Xi. Democrat. Contbr. numerous articles, revs. to profl. jours. Office: Van Vleck Obs Wesleyan U Middletown CT 06457

UPSON, STUART BARNARD, advt. agy. exec.; b. Cin., Apr. 14, 1925; s. Mark and Alice (Barnard) U.; B.S., Yale, 1945; m. Barbara Jussen, Nov. 2, 1946; children—Marguerite Nichols, Anne English, Stuart Barnard. With Dancer, Fitzgerald, Sample, Inc., N.Y.C., 1946—, sr. v.p., 1963-66, exec. v.p., 1966-67, pres., 1967-74, chmn., 1974—, also chief exec. officer; dir. Manhattan Life Ins. Co. Bd. dirs. Fresh Air Fund, N.Y. Served with USNR, 1943-46. Mem. St. Elmo Soc. Clubs: Wee Burn Country (Darien); Mpls.; Yale, Sky (N.Y.C.). Home: 68 Stephen Mather Rd Darien CT 06820 Office: 347 Madison Ave New York City NY 10017

UPSTON, JOHN EDWIN, fgn. affairs officer; b. Maxwell AFB, Ala., Apr. 17, 1935; s. John E. and Claudia (Smith) U.; student Va. Mil. Inst., 1954-55; A.B., Stanford, 1958; m. Barbara Craven, Aug. 23, 1969; children—John Edwin, III, Michael Gignoux, Bennett Coit, Leland Craven. Founding adminstr. Mental Research Inst., Palo Alto, Calif., 1959-61, dir., 1961—; bus. developer, N.Y.C., San Francisco, 1961—; v.p., dir. Broadcast Devel. Corp.; mem. mgmt. planning staff Dept. State, Washington, 1964-65, adviser Internat. Orgn. Affairs, 21st, 22d UN Gen. Assembly, mem. permanent U.S. Mission to UN, N.Y.C., 1966-69; exec. dir. Sec. of State's Com. Facilitate Travel, 1970—; spl. asst. dep. Under Sec. of State for Mgmt., 1970—; exec. dir. secretariat, exec. sec. U.S. Nat. Commn. for UNESCO, Bur. of Internat. Orgn. Affairs, Dept. of State, 1972—; U.S. adviser 17th Gen. Conf. UNESCO, Paris, 1972, 19th Gen. Conf., Nairobi, Kenya, 1976, U.S. del. to regional UNESCO confs., Bucharest, Rumania, Varna, Bulgaria; asso. Burnham & Co., investment bankers, N.Y.C., 1969—; founder, pres. Caribbeana Council, Washington and Barbados, W.I., 1977; cons. Warner Bros. Records, Burbank, Calif.; creator, producer Career, Westinghouse Broadcasting Network TV series, 1961. Bd. dirs. Tolstoy Found. Hon. mem. Population Crises Com., Washington. Recipient Superior Honor award State Dept., 1973. Club: Knickerbocker (New York). Home: 4602 Tournay Rd Westmoreland Hills MD 20016 also 2 E 62d St New York City NY 10021 Office: Dept State Washington DC 20520 also 1625 I St NW Washington DC 20006 also Caribbeana Council Regina Ct Maxwell Garden Christ Church Barbados West Indies

UPTHEGROVE, FRANKLIN JOHN, clergyman; b. Lima, Ohio, Dec. 18, 1921; s. George F. and Mary E. (Thomas) U.; B.S. in Edn., Ohio U., 1958; B.D., Crozer Theol. Sem., 1961, M. Div., 1972; postgrad. Conwell Sch. Theology, 1963-65, Hartford Sem., 1964; D.D.(hon.), Eastern Neb. Christian Coll., 1970; m. Margaret children—Sylvia M. Gable, Barbara J. Richardson, Rita J.; stepchildren—Robert H. Reid, Milton Reid, Joseph Reid. Ordained to ministry United Ch. of Christ, 1961; pastor Mt. Zion Baptist Ch., Athens, Ohio, 1954-58, 1st Bapt. Ch., Rutland, Ohio, 1954-58, St. Paul's Bapt. Ch., Utica, N.Y., 1966—; organizer Antioch United Ch. of Christ, Phila., 1961, pastor, 1961-66. Substitute tchr. secondary edn., Phila., 1960-66, Utica, 1966—. Mem. youth com. North br. Phila. YMCA, 1964-66; spl. examiner personnel dept. Civil Service, Phila., 1965-66; chmn. housing com. Utica Community Action Commn., 1966—; chmn. bd. Utica Community Action, Inc.; exec. dir. Commn. Human Relations City of Utica; gen. counsel Mohawk Valley Community Coll. Bd. dirs. Cosmopolitan Center, Utica, Utica Found. Served with USNR, 1943-46. Recipient citation Chapel of Four Chaplains, 1965. Mem. N. Central Ministerium (Phila. pres. 1966), Inter-Ch. Child Care Soc. Phila. (bd. dirs.). Home: 2231 Douglass Crescent Utica NY 13501 Office: 1 Kennedy Plaza City Hall 219 Leah St Utica NY 13502

UPTON, ARTHUR CANFIELD, pathologist, educator; b. Ann Arbor, Mich., Feb. 27, 1923; s. Herbert Hawkes and Ellen (Canfield) U.; grad. Phillips Acad., Andover, Mass., 1941; B.A., U. Mich., 1944, M.D., 1946; m. Elizabeth Bache Perry, Mar. 1, 1946; children—Rebecca A., Melissa P., Bradley C. Intern Univ. Hosp., Ann Arbor, 1947, resident, 1948-49; instr. pathology U. Mich. Med. Sch., 1950-51; pathologist Oak Ridge Nat. Lab., 1951-54, chief pathology-physiology sect., 1954-69; prof. pathology, State U. N.Y. Med. Sch. at Stony Brook, 1969—, chmn. dept. pathology, 1969-70, dean Sch. Basic Health Scis., 1970-75; now dir. Nat. Cancer Inst., NIH, Washington. Mem. various coms. nat. and internat. orgns. Served with U.S. Army, 1943-46. Recipient Ernest Orlando Lawrence award for atomic field, 1965. Mem. Am. Assn. Pathologists and Bacteriologists, Internat. Acad. Pathology, Radiation Research Soc. (councilor 1963-64, pres. 1965-66), Am. Assn. Cancer Research (pres. 1963-64), Am. Soc. Exptl. Pathology (pres. 1967-68), AAAS, Gerontol. Soc., Sci. Research Soc. Am., Soc. Exptl. Biology and Medicine, Phi Beta Kappa, Phi Gamma Delta, Alpha Omega Alpha, Nu Sigma Nu. Asso. editor Cancer Research; mem. editorial bd. Lab. Investigation, Nuclear Medicine, Excerpta Medica, Internat. Jour. Cancer, Internat. Union Against Cancer. Home: 7 Colgate Ct Shoreham NY 11786 Office: Nat Cancer Inst 330 Independence Ave SW Washington DC 20201

URBAN, GEORGE PENNOCK, III, electronics co. exec.; b. Buffalo, Oct. 13, 1942; s. George Pennock and Jane (Wells) U.; B.S. in Elec. Engring., U. Miami, 1966; M.E.E., U. Pa., 1969; M.B.A., Canisius Coll., 1971; m. Jean Taylor Enos, Feb. 7, 1974; 1 child, Christy Taylor. Design engr. Sylvania Electronics, Buffalo, 1966-67, sr. design engr., 1969-71; project coordinator Moore Bus. Forms, Niagara Falls, N.Y., 1971-73; with product mktg. dept. Sprague Electric Co., Worcester, Mass., 1973-74; pres. BUG Electronics, Inc., Dover, Mass., 1974—. Republican. Episcopalian. Club: Dedham (Mass.) Country and Polo. Office: BUG Electronics Inc PO Box 456 Dover MA 02030

URBAN, HENRY ZELLER, newspaperman; b. Buffalo, July 11, 1920; s. George Pennock and Florence Lenhard (Zeller) U.; B.S., Yale U., 1943; m. Ruth deMoss Wickwire, Apr. 28, 1948; children—Ruth Robinson, Florence de Moss, Henry Zeller, Ward Wickwire. Treas., George Urban Milling Co., 1946-53, now dir.; with Buffalo Evening News., 1953—, asst. bus. mgr., 1957-62, bus. mgr., 1962-71, treas., dir., 1971-74, pres., pub., 1974—; dir. G. F. Zellers Sons, Inc. Bd. dirs. Travelers Aid Soc., 1953-59, Buffalo Fine Arts Acad., 1960-63, 72—, YMCA; trustee Elmwood-Franklin. Sch.; bd. regents Canisius Coll., 1972—; adv. bd. Medaille Coll., 1968. Served to lt. USNR, 1942-46. Mem. N.Y. State Pubs. Assn. (dir. 1976—), Buffalo C. of C. Clubs: Mid-day, Rotary, Tennis and Squash, Buffalo, Buffalo Athletic, Buffalo Country, Saturn Pack (Buffalo); Sankaty Head (Nantucket), Nantucket Yacht; Cragburn. Home: 57 Tudor Pl Buffalo NY 14222 Office: 218 Main St Buffalo NY 14205

URBAN, THOMAS ELLIS, children's home adminstr.; b. Mt. Pleasant, Pa., Aug. 31, 1940; s. Albert Thomas and Mable Elizabeth (Bittner) U.; A.B., W.Va. Wesleyan Coll., 1963; M.A., Boston U., 1967, M.S.T., 1967; m. Edith Carrie Brown, Aug. 8, 1964; children—Phillip Scott, Beth Ellen. Minister of edn. West Pa. Conf., United Methodist Ch., Irwin and Bradford, 1967-71; dir. alcohol and drug abuse program Cameron, Elk, McKean and Potter Counties Mental Health-Mental Retardation, Bradford, 1971-73; exec. dir. Children's Home of Bradford, 1973—; cons. Pa. Dept. Edn. Bd. dirs. ARC. Mem. Pa. Assn. Children's Instns., Nat. Registry Emergency Med. Technicians and Paramedics. Presbyterian. Club: Kiwanis. Home: 52 Cornen St Bradford PA 16701 Office: 800 E Main St Bradford PA 16701

URBANIAK, EUGENE T., lawyer; m. Elsie Haumann, June 18, 1938; 1 dau., Betsy. Dep. atty. gen. N.J.; dir. div. Legal Affairs, N.J. Dept. Instns. and Agys.; counsel N.J. Parole Bd., 1936-71; now gen. counsel Asso. Gen. Contractors N.J., various pension funds. Former mem. Trenton Bd. Edn. Trustee Trenton council Girl Scouts U.S.A. Mem. Am., N.J., Mercer County bar assns., Am. Judicature Soc., Am. Polish Congress. Elk. Clubs: Trenton Country; Seaside Park Yacht (trustee). Contbr. articles to profl. pubs. Home: 24 River Dr Trenton NJ 08618 Office: 28 W State St Trenton NJ 08607

URCIUOLI, J. ARTHUR, investment banker; b. Syracuse, N.Y., Nov. 13, 1937; s. Joseph R. and Nicolette Anne (Phillips) U.; B.S., St. Lawrence U., 1959; J.D., Georgetown U., 1966; m. Margaret Jane Forelli, Aug. 13, 1966; children—Karen Sloan, Christian Arthur. Admitted to N.Y. bar, 1966; atty. firm Brown, Wood, Fuller, Caldwell & Ivey, N.Y.C., 1966-69; asso., investment banking div. Merrill Lynch, Pierce, Fenner & Smith, N.Y.C., 1969-70, v.p., mgr. internat. fin. dept., 1970-72; pres. Merrill Lynch, Pierce, Fenner & Smith Securities Underwriter Ltd., Paris, 1972-74; dir. internat. fin. Merrill Lynch, Pierce, Fenner & Smith Inc., N.Y.C., 1974-77, mng. dir. Merrill Lynch Capital Markets Group, 1977—; dir. Merrill Lynch Internat. Bank Ltd., London. Trustee St. Lawrence U., 1976—. Served to capt. USMC, 1959-63. Republican. Congregationalist. Clubs: City Midday (N.Y.C.); Riverside (Conn.) Yacht; Rocky Point (Old Greenwich, Conn.). Contbr. articles to profl. jours. Home: 14 Fairgreen Ln Old Greenwich CT 06870 Office: 1 Liberty Plaza 165 Broadway New York City NY 10006

URCUYO, LEONEL, adult and child psychiatrist; b. Rivas, Nicarague, Apr. 25, 1943; s. Alfredo and Elena (Vidaurre) U.; B.Sc., Instituto Rosendo Lopez, 1961; M.D., U. Madrid, 1967. Rotating intern St. Mary's Meml. Hosp., McGill U., Montreal, Que., Can., 1968-69; resident psychiatry N.Y.U., Bellevue Med. Center, N.Y.C., 1969-72, fellow in child and adolescent psychiatry, 1973-75; candidate-in-tng. Am. Inst. Psychoanalysis, N.Y.C., 1970-75; practice medicine specializing in adult and child psychiatry and psychoanalysis; asst. attending psychiatrist Univ. Hosp., Bellevue Hosp., N.Y. U.; chief psychiatrist, dir. med. edn., residency tng. Kingsboro Psychiat. Center, Bklyn.; dir. child and adolescent psychiatry Gouverneur Hosp.; asst. prof. psychiatry State U.N.Y. Downstate Med. Center, Bklyn; asst. prof. Am. Inst. Psychoanalysis Karen Horney Psychoanalytic Clinic, 1977—. Diplomate Am. Bd. Psychiatry and Neurology. Fellow Am. Acad. Psychoanalysis; mem. AMA, Am. Psychiat. Assn., Am. Acad. Child Psychiatry, N.Y. Council Child Psychiatry, Menninger Found., Assn. Advancement Psychoanalyis, AAAS, N.Y. Soc. Research Child Devel., N.Y. State, N.Y. County med. socs. Contbr. articles in field to profl. jours. Office: 201 E 66th St Suite 18-K New York City NY 10021

URFER, RICHARD PETERSON, investment banker, cattle breeder; b. Spring Green, Wis., June 28, 1936; s. Walter Chester and Alice Mae (Peterson) U.; B.S., U. Wis., 1958; M.B.A., Harvard U., 1964; m. Cynthia Leigh Vaughan, June 22, 1968; children—Jocelyn Leigh, Gilbert Fielding, Courtney Vaughan. Asst. to treas. Allis-Chalmers Mfg. Co., Milw., 1960-62; asso. Morgan Stanley & Co., N.Y.C., 1964-67; pres., chief exec. officer, dir. DCL, Inc., Jersey City, 1967-69; dir. Office of Fgn. Direct Investments, Commerce Dept., Washington, 1969-70; spl. cons. to Sec. of Commerce for Internat. Fin. Affairs, Washington, 1971; sr. v.p., dir. Blyth Eastman Dillon & Co., N.Y.C., 1971-73, Atlantic Capital Corp., N.Y.C., 1973—; propr. Urfer Farms, 1973—; dir. United Silk Mills Ltd., Plains Resources Inc., WJS Inc. Mem. nat. council Salk Inst. Served to 2d lt. AUS, 1959. Mem. N.Y. Soc. Security Analysts, Council Fgn. Relations. Republican. Clubs: Union, India House, Harbor. Contbr. articles in field to profl. jours. Home: Willowbrook Farm Blue Mill Rd Morristown NJ 07960 Office: 40 Wall St New York City NY 10005

URSTADT, CHARLES JORDAN, state ofcl.; b. N.Y.C., Oct. 27, 1928; s. Charles G. and Claire (Jordan) U.; A.B., Dartmouth Coll., 1949, M.B.A., 1951; LL.B., Cornell U., 1953; m. Elinor McClure Funk, Mar. 23, 1957; children—Charles D., Catherine C. Admitted to N.Y. State bar, 1953, since practiced in N.Y.C.; asso. atty. Nevius, Brett & Kellogg, 1953-58; asst. sec., atty. Webb-Knapp, Inc., 1958-63; v.p., sec., counsel Alcoa Residences, Inc., 1963-67; dep. commr. N.Y. State Div. Housing, 1967-69, commr., 1969-73; chmn. Battery Park City Authority, 1968—; chmn. Constrn. Users Council; trustee N.Y. Bank for Savs., Hubbard Real Estate Investment Trust; dir. Cooper Labs.; mem. adv. bd. Chase Manhattan Bank. Bd. dirs. Nat. Corp. for Housing Partnerships; trustee Pace U., Beekman Hosp. Served to lt. USNR, 1954-56. Mem. Theta Delta Chi, Phi Delta Phi. Republican. Mem. Dutch Reformed Ch. Club: Masons. Office: 40 Rector St New York City NY 10006

URSTADT, SUSAN POWERS (MRS. J. JEFFREY URSTADT), lit. agt.; b. N.Y.C., Nov. 29, 1942; d. Joshua Bryant and Susan (Moore) Powers; B.A., Wheaton (Mass.) Coll., 1964; m. Jeffrey Urstadt, Oct. 8, 1966; children—Bryant Earle, Jeffrey Jordan. Publicity asso. J.P. Lippincott Co., N.Y.C., 1966-69; fgn. pubs. rep., 1969-75; pres. Susan P. Urstadt Inc., fgn. pubs. rep. and lit. agt., N.Y.C., 1975—. Mem. Ind. Lit. Agts. Assn. Presbyterian. Address: 125 E 84th St New York City NY 10028

URSUL, GEORGE RICHARD, historian, educator; b. Hamilton, Ont., Can., Oct. 11, 1937; s. George and Doris U.; A.B., McMaster U., 1960; M.A., Harvard U., 1961, Ph.D. (William Lyon MacKenzie King Fellow, 1966), 1966; m. Ruth Baker, Oct. 11, 1969; 1 dau., Christina Elizabeth. Tutor in history, Harvard U., Cambridge, Mass., 1961-63; asst. prof. history and social scis., Fisher Jr. Coll., Boston, 1969-73; instr. to prof. history, Emerson Coll., Boston, 1963—, chmn. history dept., 1973—, Presdl. Emissary, 1975, dir. summer sch. abroad, 1967-78. Decorated Patriarchal Cross (Romania). Fellow Royal Soc. Arts (London), Royal Acad. Arts and Scis.; mem. Am., South End Hist. Assns., AAUP, Soc. for Propogation of the Gospel among Indians, Handel and Haydn Soc. (dir.), Gibson House (Boston, dir.), Am. Romanian Cultural Assn (v.p.). Eastern Orthodox. Clubs: Harvard (Boston), St. Botolph (Boston), Harvard Musical Assn., Harvard Travellers Assn. (Boston). Contbr. articles to publs. Home: 45 Concord Sq Boston MA 02118

URSZENYI, LASZLO GABOR, service orgn. exec.; b. Budapest, Hungary, July 15, 1933; s. Bertalan and Klara (Vas) U.; came to Can., 1960, naturalized, 1967; M.Da., Hungarian Acad. Theater and Film Arts, 1956; B.A., U. Toronto, 1970; m. Katalin Dezse, Apr. 1, 1957; children—Susan, Christine, Stephen. Mgr., Lenakrom Industries, Ghana, 1957-59; office mgr. Elite Plywood Co. Ltd., Toronto, Ont., Can., 1961-62; ins. salesman Indsl. Ins. Co. Ltd., Toronto, 1962-63; purchasing agt. Toronto Camera Indsl. Sales Ltd., 1963-68; exec. dir. Cath. Youth Orgn., Toronto, 1968—. Hon. chmn. Cath. Com. for Scouting, 1968-75; mem. Social Planning Council Metro Toronto, 1968—; mem. Nat. Cath. Council Social Services, 1968-74. Recipient Eagle of the Cross, 1968, Pro Deo et Juventute, 1971. Mem. Canadian Purchasing Agts. Assn., Ont. Recreation Soc., Ont. Handgun Assn. Pioneered Cath. Youth Orgn. community service programs in Toronto. Home: 40 Sunny Glenway Suite 202 Don Mills ON M3C 2Z2 Canada Office: care CYO 570-A Jarvis St Toronto ON M4Y 2H9 Canada

USCHAK, ELLEN ANN, devel. engr.; b. Latrobe, Pa., June 28, 1947; d. Pete and Ella Margaret U.; B.A. in Chemistry, Seton Hill Coll., 1972; student Approved Sch. Med. Tech., 1965-67; M.S. in Chemistry, Indiana U. of Pa., 1974. Spl. chemist Latrobe Area Hosp., 1967-71; biochemist, med. technician Monsour Hosp., Jeannette, Pa., 1971-72; teaching asst. chem. dept. Indian U. of Pa., 1972-74; devel. engr. catalyst carrier dept. Carborundum Co., Latrobe, 1974—. Mem. Am. Chem. Soc., Northeastern Catalysis Soc., Carborundum Mgmt. Club (sec.). Byzantine Catholic. Office: Carborundum Co Box 311 Latrobe PA 15650

USCHALD, WILLI ANDREAS, educator; b. Holzhammer, Germany, Mar. 18, 1926; s. Johann and Kunigunde (Brunner) U.; came to U.S., 1951, naturalized, 1961; M.A., Mich. State U., 1952, Ph.D., 1957. Instr. English and French, P.O.W. U., Beaconsfield, Eng., 1945-46; dir. lang. tng. Kaw-Siemens and Verein Merkur of Germany, 1947-51; asst. prof. French and German, Harpur Coll., Binghamton, N.Y., 1958-63; prof., chmn. dept. fgn. langs. State U. N.Y. at Cortland, 1963-67, prof., dir. internat. programs, 1967—. Recipient Amicitia prize Nurnberg, 1947. Mem. Renaissance Soc. Am., Modern Humanities Research Assn., Modern Lang. Assn., Am. Assn. Tchrs. of French, Am. Assn. Tchrs. of German, Soc. for Intercultural Edn., Tng. and Research. Lutheran. Home: 52 Lamont Circle Cortland NY 13045 Office: Internat Programs State U NY Cortland NY 13045

USHER, ELIZABETH REUTER (MRS. HARRY T. USHER), librarian; b. Seward, Nebr.; d. Paul and Elizabeth (Meyer) Reuter; diploma Concordia Tchrs. Coll., Seward; B.S. in Edn., U. Nebr., 1942; B.S. in L.S., U. Ill., 1944; m. Harry Thomas Usher, Feb. 25, 1950. Tchr., Zion Luth. Sch., Platte Center, Nebr., St. Paul's Luth. Sch., Paterson, N.J.; library asst. charge res. book reading room U. Nebr., 1942-43; asst. circulation librarian Mich. State U., 1944-45; librarian Cranbrook Acad. Art, Bloomfield Hills, Mich., 1945-48; catalog and reference librarian Met. Mus. Art, N.Y., 1948-53, head cataloger and reference librarian, 1953-54, asst. librarian, 1954-61, chief of art reference library, 1961-68, chief librarian, 1968—, acting librarian, 1954-57. Trustee N.Y. Met. Reference and Research Library Agy., 1968—, sec. bd., 1971-77, v.p., 1977—. Mem. Spl. Libraries Assn. (pres. 1967-68, past dir. 1950-63, 66-69), Coll. Art Assn. (chmn. libraries session 1972-73), N.Y. Library Club, Arlis N.A. Lutheran. Contbr. articles to profl. jours. and library publs. Home: 5 Peter Cooper Rd New York City NY 10010 Office: Met Museum Art Fifth Ave and 82d St New York City NY 10028

USHER, ESTHER, librarian; b. Lynn, Mass., Oct. 10, 1917; d. Arthur L. and Ada J. (Nichols) U.; B.S., Simmons Coll., 1938. Cataloger, Essex Inst., Salem, Mass., 1938-42, asst. librarian, 1943-45, asso. librarian, 1956; asst. editor Essex Inst. Hist. Collections, Salem, 1943-55; cataloger Jackson E. Moreland Library, Boston, 1956-57, librarian, 1957-72; librarian United Engrs. & Constructors Inc., Boston, 1972—. Recipient Simmons Coll. Alumnae Service award, 1977. Mem. Am., Mass. library assns., Spl. Libraries Assn., Photog. Soc. Am. Club: North Shore Simmons. Office: 100 Summer St Boston MA 02110

USINOWICZ, WALTER VICTOR, JR., mfg. co. exec.; b. Paterson, N.J., June 20, 1947; s. Walter Victor and Wilma Elizabeth (Riker) U.; B.S., Lehigh U., 1969; M.B.A., N.Y. U., 1973; m. Sheri Lynn Bentel, June 8, 1968; children—Tara Christine, Jeffrey Garrett. Internal auditor, cost accountant, asst. cost supr., product mgr. Maxwell House div. Gen. Foods Corp., Hoboken, N.J., 1969-73; cost analyst, fin. analyst W.R. Grace & Co., N.Y.C., 1973-74; sr. fin. analyst, div. controller, dir. advance planning Becton, Dickinson & Co., Orangeburg, N.Y., 1974—. Mem. Montclair Jr. C. of C. (dir. 1974), Nat. Assn. Accountants, Am. Assn. M.B.A.'s. Roman Catholic. Home: 44 Beverley Rd Upper Montclair NJ 07043 Office: Mountain View Ave Orangeburg NY 10962

USSERY, HARRY MACRAE, engring. and constrn. co. exec.; b. Rockingham, N.C., Jan. 27, 1920; s. Robert Roy and Maggie Estelle (MacRae) U.; A.A., Wake Forest U., 1947; J.D., George Washington U., 1950; m. Olive Dual Simmons, Mar. 19, 1949. Admitted to D.C. bar, 1950; asso. firm Geiger & Harmel, Washington, 1950-52; partner firm McNeill & Ussery, Washington, 1952-53; gen. counsel, dir. Harry R. Byers, Inc., Washington and Denver, 1953-59; procurement counsel Martin Marietta Corp., Denver, 1959-62; authorized agt. RCA, Camden, N.J., 1962-69; staff counsel, mgr. internat. subcontract ops. Burns and Roe Constrn. Corp., Paramus, N.J., 1969-74; legal counsel, mgr. internat. subcontract ops. Burns and Roe Indsl. Services Corp., Paramus, 1975—; cons. in field. Served with USAF, 1941-45. Recipient Community Chest Campaign awards, 1951, 52; mem. Aviation Hall of Fame. Mem. Am. Bar Assn., Am. Judicature Soc., Nat. Contract Mgmt. Assn., George Washington Law Assn., Wake Forest Alumni Assn., Delta Theta Phi. Republican. Presbyterian. Clubs: St. Andrew's Soc., Clan MacRae Soc., Delaware Valley Jaguar, Colony (Medford Lakes, N.J.). Chief moderator and dir. District Roundtable, Sta. WWDC, Washington, 1950-53. Home: 306 Village Pl Wyckoff NJ 07481 Office: PO Box 663 Paramus NJ 07652

USSIA, SAMUEL, cons. engr.; b. Sawerton, Mo., Sept. 24, 1923; s. John and Anastasia (Astorino) U.; Dott. Ing. in Elec. Engring., U. Naples (Italy), 1949, Dott. Ing. in Mech. Engring., 1955; m. Tonia De Santis, Aug. 29, 1949. Chief elec. and mech. engr. Officine Elettromeccaniche Meriodionan, Naples, 1950-53; head elec. and mech. div. U.S. Navy Pub. Works, Naples, 1953-58; chief engr. Cons. Engrs., Inc., Boston, 1958-60, pres., 1960-65; pres. Samuel Ussia & Assos., Inc., Brighton, Mass., 1965—; vis. lectr. dept. architecture Mass. Inst. Tech. Served as officer arty. Italian Army, 1949. Decorated knight Republic of Italy commendatore Republic of Italy; recipient Heritage Exemplification award, 1977. Mem. Am. Soc. Plumbing Engrs. (pres. Boston chpt. 1973-74), Profl. Engrs. in Pvt. Practice, Nat. Soc. Profl. Engrs., Dante Alighieri Soc. (pres. 1976—). Roman Catholic. Club: Rotary. Author tech. articles. Home: 164 Newton St Brookline MA 02146 Office: 167 Corey Rd Brookline MA 02146

VACANTI, CHARLES JOSEPH, JR., anesthesiologist; b. Rochester, N.Y., Dec. 7, 1936; s. Charles and Rose (Lagonegro) V.; B.A., U. Toronto, 1958; M.D., State U. N.Y. at Syracuse, 1962; grad. certificate mgmt. Am. U., 1968; m. Susan Carol Napolitano, June 18, 1960; children—Suzanne Mary, Karen Marie, Valerie Anne, Charles Joseph, Julie Anne. Intern, St. Mary's Hosp., Rochester, 1962-63, attending anesthesiologist, 1970—, med. dir. intensive care unit, 1972—, sec. med. and dental staff, 1973-75, chmn. dept. anesthesiology, 1976—; chmn. anesthesiology service Lakeside Meml. Hosp., Brockport, N.Y., 1976—; mem. N.Y. State Dept. Health Bd. Profl. Med. Conduct, 1978—. resident anesthesiology Nat. Naval Med. Center, Bethesda, Md., 1964-67, staff anesthesiologist, 1967-68; chmn. dept. anesthesiology Naval Hosp., Portsmouth, Va., 1968-70; mem. No. hosp. council N.Y. Finger Lakes Health Services Agy., 1976-77. Served to lt. comdr. M.C., USN, 1963-70. Diplomate Am. Bd. Anesthesiology, Nat. Bd. Med. Examiners. Fellow Am. Coll. Anesthesiologists, N.Y. Acad. Scis., Rochester Acad. Medicine, Soc. Advanced Med. Systems; mem. AMA (Physician Recognition award 1969, 72, 75, 79), N.Y., Monroe County (treas. 1977-78, pres. 1979-80) med. socs., Am. (del.), N.Y. (asst. sec. 76, dir. 1976—) socs. anesthesiologists. Home: 19 Fletcher Rd Pittsford NY 14534 Office: 909 W Main St Rochester NY 14611

VACANTI, KENNETH ANDREW, engr.; b. Rochester, N.Y., Nov. 23, 1947; s. Frank Anthony and Phyllis Jessie (La Monaco) V.; Asso. Applied Sci., Rochester Inst. Tech., 1973; B.S., 1977; m. Patricia M. O'Hara, Feb. 5, 1972; 1 son, Kyle. Inventory control auditor Xerox Corp., Webster, N.Y., 1970-72, quality control technician, 1972-73, quality control engr., 1973-76, mfg. foreman, 1976-77, sr. tech. foreman 9400 duplicating system, 1977—. Served with U.S. Army, 1967-70. Mem. Rochester Soc. Quality Control Engrs., Am. Legion. Mem. Am. Independent Party. Roman Catholic. Home: 756 Sugar Creek Trail Webster NY 14580 Office: 800 Phillips Rd Webster NY 14580

VACCARELLA, GERARD, JR., psychologist; b. Jersey City, June 26, 1948; s. Gerard Peter and Mary Roberta (Mueller) V.; B.A., Fairleigh Dickinson U., 1971, M.A. cum laude, 1972; postgrad. New Sch. for Social Research, 1973—; m. Gloria Anne Minnick, Aug. 10, 1974. Psychologist, Mt. Carmel Guild, Newark, 1972-73, Passaic Community Coll., Paterson, N.J., 1973-75, Mental Health Clinic, Passaic, N.J., 1976—; affiliate Inst. Mental Health Edn., Englewood, N.J., 1978—. Mem. Am. (asso.), N.J. (asso.) psychol. assns., Mensa, Psi Chi. Home: 119 Oak Grove Ave Hasbrouck Heights NJ 07604

VACCARO, JOSEPH PASCAL, educator; b. Cambridge, Mass., Feb. 7, 1935; s. Orazio E. and Margaret G. (Grosso) V.; B.B.A., Boston Coll., 1957; M.B.A., Suffolk U., 1969, J.D., 1976; m. Patricia A. Murphy, June 29, 1963; children—Paul J., Anne M., Theresa M., Rose P. Mem. mgmt. exec. tng. program J.M. Field's, Natick, Mass., 1957; mgr. Leaning Tower Pizza, West Yarmouth, Somerville, Mass., 1959-60; owner, mgr. Vaccaro's Iron Rail Restaurant, Waltham, Mass., 1961-66; instr. mktg. Burdett Coll., Boston, 1966-71; asst. prof. mktg. Suffolk U., Boston, 1971—; mktg. advisor Remme Assn.; small bus. cons. Chmn. Democratic ward com. Served with AUS, 1957-59. Mem. Am. Mktg. Assn. (certificate of recognition), Am. Advt. Fedn., Am. Acad. Advt., Suffolk U., Boston Coll. alumni assns., Delta Sigma Pi, Holy Name Soc. (past pres.), Newton Jr. C. of C. (past pres.). Roman Catholic. Author: Decision Making with Cases in Marketing; Consumer Behavior Cases: A Marketing Management Approach; contbr. articles in field to profl. publs. Home: 36 Oakwood Rd Auburndale MA 02166 Office: 41 Temple St Boston MA 02114

VACHON, BRIAN, journalist; b. Washington, Oct. 3, 1941; s. John and Emily Millicent (Leeper) V.; student Villanova U., U. Tenn.; m. Nancy Virginia Cargill, Nov. 14, 1972. Sci. editor Saturday Review mag., N.Y.C., 1971—; editor Vermont Life, Montpelier; freelance writer, 1968—; instr. Vt. history U. Vt., Montpelier, 1975-76; instr. writing Norwich U., 1976—. Served with USAR, 1964-69. Mem. Vt. League Writers, Vt. Hist. Soc. Club: Vt. 251. Author: A Time to be Born, 1971. Office: 61 Elm St Montpelier VT 05602

VAIL, VAN HORN, educator; b. Buffalo, Dec. 23, 1934; s. Curtis Churchill and Faith Newbrook (Ely) V.; B.A., U. Wash., 1956; M.A., Princeton U., 1961, Ph.D., 1964; m. Michele Juliette Edelstein, May 5, 1969; 1 son, Mark Curtis. Instr., Princeton U., 1962-65, asst. prof., 1965-66; asst. prof. Middlebury (Vt.) Coll., 1966-69, asso. prof., 1969-75, prof. German, 1975—, chmn. dept. German, 1970-73. Served with U.S. Army, 1956-58. Fulbright scholar, 1958-59. Mem. Modern Lang. Assn. Author: German in Review, 1967; Der Weg zum Lesen, 1967, 2d edit., 1974; Modern German, 1971, 2d edit., 1978; Tonio Kröger als Weg zur Literatur, 1974. Home: Cider Mill Rd Middlebury VT 05753 Office: Sunderland Hall Middlebury Coll Middlebury VT 05753

VAILLANCOURT, DONALD CHARLES, supermarket exec.; b. Newark, Dec. 30, 1943; s. Vincent Joseph and Margaret Kathleen (Pasch) V.; B.A., Thomas Edison Coll., Princeton, N.J.; LL.B., LaSalle U., 1969; m. Kathleen F. MacKewen, Aug. 8, 1964. Suburban reporter Newark Star Ledger, 1962-64; night editor Newark bur. UPI, 1964-65; reporter, editor Newark Evening News, 1965-71; dir. pub. relations Grand Union Co., Elmwood Park, N.J., 1971-76, dir. corporate communications and consumer affairs, 1976—. Recipient Honor award for food industry achievement Cornell U., 1976. Mem. Pub. Relations Soc. Am., Publicity Club N.Y.C., North Jersey Press Club, Nutley Jaycees, Sigma Delta Chi. Episcopalian. Home: 467 Chestnut St Nutley NJ 07110 Office: 100 Broadway Elmwood Park NJ 07407

VAJDA, JOHN JAY, lab. instrument mfg. co. exec.; b. Szeged, Hungary, Jan. 24, 1940; s. Nicholas M. and Lenke (Fried) V.; came to U.S., 1957, naturalized, 1962; B.A. in Biochemistry, N.Y. U., 1965; grad. certificate in instrumental analysis Rutgers U., 1966; m. Barbara Feuer, June 27, 1965; children—Lynn Ann, Michelle Lee. Lab. technician Union Carbide Co., Bound Brook, N.J., 1960-63; sr. lab. technician Am. Standard, Piscataway Twp., N.J., 1963-65; chemist Photovolt Corp., N.Y.C., 1965-69, project mgr., 1969-77, product mgr., 1977—. Mem. exec. bd. Order of Arrow, Thomas A. Edison council Boy Scouts Am., 1977; No. N.J. chmn. B'nai B'rith Young Adults, 1964-65. Served with U.S. Army, 1958-59. Mem. Regulatory Affairs Profls. Soc., N.Y. Acad. Scis., Smithsonian Instn., Mus. Natural History. Patentee in field of lab. instruments devel. Home: 124 Grove Ave Ave Woodbridge NJ 07095 Office: 1115 Broadway New York NY 10010

VALANIA, JOSEPH JOHN, power and petrochem. fabricating co. exec.; b. Alden Station, Nanticoke, Pa., May 18, 1943; S. John Anthony and Mary Ann (Makara) V.; student U. Md., 1962-64, U. LaSalle Extension, 1968-70; m. Patricia Ann Haun, May 22, 1965; children—Brian Joseph, Andrea Marie. Source insp. Air Products & Chems., Inc., Allentown, Pa., 1965-70; non destructive exam. supr., quality control engr., shift supt. Foster Wheeler Energy Corp., Mountaintop, Pa., 1970-77; mgr. quality assurance Bombardier Inc., Montreal, Que., Can., 1978—. Served with U.S. Army, 1962-65. Mem. Am. Legion. Democrat. Roman Catholic. Home: 93 Martin St Hudson PA 18705 Office: 1505 Dickson St Montreal PQ H1N 2H7 Canada

VALBUENA-BRIONES, A(NGEL) JULIAN, educator; b. Madrid, Jan. 11, 1928; s. Angel Valbuena-Prat and Francisco Briones; came to U.S., 1956, naturalized, 1963; Licenciado summa cum laude U. Murcia, Spain, 1949; Ph.D. cum laude, U. Madrid, 1952; m. Barbara Northrup Hobart, Nov. 9, 1957; children—Teresa, Vivian. Lectr., Oxford U., Eng., 1953-55; asst. prof. Spanish lit. U. Madrid, 1955-56; vis. lectr. U. Wis., 1956-58; asst. prof. Spanish lit. Yale U., 1958-60; Elias Ahuja prof. Spanish, U. Del., 1960—. U. Wis. grantee, 1957; Consejo Superior de Investigaciones Cientificas of Madrid grantee, 1970-71. Mem. Modern Lang. Assn. Am., Asociacion Internacional de Hispanistas, Instituto de Literatura Iberoamericana, Hispanic Soc. Am., Am. Assn. Tchrs. Spanish, Portuguese, Sigma Delta Pi. Clubs: Greenville Country (Wilmington, Del.); Blue and Gold (Newark, Del.). Author books, most recent being: Primera Parte de las comedias de Calderon, 1974; Calderon y la Comedia Nueva, 1977. Home: 203 Nottingham Rd Newark DE 19711 Office: U Del Dept Langs and Lit Newark DE 19711

VALENT, HENRY, lawyer; b. Watkins Glen, N.Y., July 21, 1915; s. Joseph and Nellie (Vickio) V.; A.B., Cornell U., 1936, LL.B., 1938; m. Joan Ella Blanchard, May 10, 1952; children—Nellie Mae, Joseph Arthur, Oscar Blanchard, Albert Warren, Henry William. Admitted to N.Y. bar, 1938; gen. practice law, Watkins Glen, N.Y., 1938-41, 46—; atty. Glen Nat. Bank, Watkins Glen, 1946—. Partner, Glenfield & Baxter Dairies of Watkins Glen; owner Finger Lakes Broadcasting Co. (WFLR, Dundee, N.Y.); dir. Glen Nat. Bank and Trust Co.; dir., sec. Hi-Speed Checkweigher Co., Inc. Sec. Watkins Glen Youth Center, Inc.; pres. Watkins Glen Grand Prix Corp. Bd. dirs. Schuyler Hosp., Sullivan Trail council Boy Scouts Am. Served from 2d lt. to lt. col., Inf., AUS, 1941-46, Am., Asiatic, PTO. Mem. Am., N.Y. State (grievance com.), Schuyler County bar assns., Watkins Glen C. of C., Am. Legion, Cornell Law Sch. Assn., Holy Name Soc. Roman Catholic. Mem. Red Men (Gt. Incohonee), Rotarian (Watkins-Montour). Author: Road Racing at Watkins Glen. Home: RD 2 Watkins Glen NY 14891 Office: 400 Franklin St Watkins Glen NY 14891

VALENTI, LEO FRANK, electronics co. exec.; b. Cleve., Dec. 23, 1925; s. Jospeh and Concetta (Giallanza) V.; B.E.E., Case Inst. Tech., 1946; m. Rosalie Regina Caputo, Oct. 29, 1949; children—Robert, Thomas, Paul, Mark, Cynthia. Chief engr. Brush-Devel. (Clevite), Cleve., 1947-58; engring. mgr. RCA, Moorestown, N.J., 1958-61; v.p. engring. Techni-Rite, Inc., East Greenwich, R.I., 1961-69, Gulton Industries, Inc., East Greenwich, 1969—; co-owner, dir. Techni-Rite Electronics, Inc.; faculty adviser Hall Inst., Providence. Served with USAAF, 1946-47. Mem. Instrument Soc. Am. Republican. Roman Catholic. Patentee in field. Home: 1185 Carrs Pond Rd East Greenwich RI 02818 Office: Route 2 and Middle Rd East Greenwich RI 02818

VALENTI, ROBERT JOSEPH, aquaculturist; b. Bklyn., Aug. 14, 1942; s. William and Eleanor V.; B.A. in Biology, L.I. U., 1963, M.S. in Marine Scis., 1966; Ph.D. in Biol. Scis., N.Y. U., 1973. Dir. vertebrate studies Aquatic Scis., Inc., Boca Raton, Fla., 1971-73; sr. research scientist, dir. ichthyology lab. N.Y. Ocean Sci. Lab., Montauk, 1973-77; dir. Multi Aquaculture Sytems, Inc., Amagansett, N.Y., 1976—; adj. asso. prof. marine scis. L.I. U., Greenvale, N.Y., 1973—. Mem. Am. Fisheries Soc. (certified fisheries scientist, dir. fish culture sect. 1976-77), Am. Inst. Fisheries Research Biologists, Am. Soc. Ichthyologists and Herpetologists, World Mariculture Soc., Japanese Soc. Sci. Fisheries. Roman Catholic. Office: Cranberry Hold Rd Amagansett NY 11930

VALENTINE, CHARLES FRANCIS, ednl. adminstr.; b. Vineland, N.J., May 17, 1934; m. Quinton D. and Mary (Parenti) V.; B.S. summa cum laude, Glassboro (N.J.) State Coll., 1956, M.A., 1965; postgrad. Temple U., 1972, Seton Hall U., 1972, Montclair (N.J.) State Coll., 1973-74, William Paterson Coll., N.J., 1974-75, Trenton (N.J.) State Coll., 1974, Nova U., 1977—. Tchr. Vineland (N.J.) Bd. Edn., 1956-65, prin., supr., 1965-77; adj. staff instr. Glassboro State Coll., 1974; co-chmn. Vineland Pub. Schs. Environ. Edn. Com., 1973—, Vineland Pub. Elementary Sch. Curriculum Writing Project, 1974-75, chmn., 1976—; co-chmn. job availability and outlook com. Cumberland County Work Edn. Council, 1977—; dir. thorough and efficient edn. and supplemental programs Vineland Pub. Schs., 1978—; participant 8th ann. Nat. Vocat. Edn. Personnel Devel. Seminar, Madison, Wis., 1974; co-chief investigator to develop learning packages for P.R., 1975-77. Pres. Greater Vineland United Fund, 1972-73, bd. dirs., 1972—, pub. schs. chmn., 1966-68; scoutmaster South Jersey council Boy Scouts Am., 1956-62, asst. scoutmaster, 1952-56, committeeman, 1962—; dir. Camp Kimble, South Jersey council Boy Scouts Am., Bridgeton, 1961-64, mem. extension com., 1973-74, activity chmn. Cumberland dist., 1976; v.p. Vineland PTA Dist., 1977—; mem. pastoral planning com. St. Isidore Ch., Vineland, 1973—; bd. dirs. Vineland YMCA, 1975—. Recipient Scouters Tng. award Boy Scouts Am., 1959, Silver Beaver award, 1976; Pres.'s award Vineland United Fund, 1968, 69, 72; St. George award Camden Catholic Diocese, 1969; Outstanding Young Educator award Vineland Jaycees, 1968-69; Liberty Bell award Cumberland County Bar Assn., 1969. Mem. NEA (life), Nat. Assn. Elementary Sch. Prins. (life), N.J., Vineland (v.p.) edn. assn., N.J. Assn. Environ. Edn., Vineland Prins. Assn. (pres. 1976-77), N.J. Hist. Soc. (adv. council 1977—, edn. com. 1978), Cumberland County Hist. Soc. (life), Vineland Hist. and Antiquarian Soc. (life), Glassboro State Coll. Alumni Assn. (life), Phi Delta Kappa (life), Kappa Delta Pi (life). Clubs. South Jersey Schoolmen's (pres. 1974—), K.C., Order of Arrow (life). Home: 1762 Washington Ave Vineland NJ 08360 Office: Vineland Pub Schs 106 W Landis Ave Vineland NJ 08360

VALENTINE, RALPH JAMES, chem. engr.; b. Mahwah, N.J., May 11, 1922; s. Richard Van and Matilda (Fisher) V.; B. Chem. Engring., Pratt Inst., 1943; postgrad. Stevens Inst. Tech., 1948-51, Case Inst. Tech., 1952, Fairleigh Dickinson U., 1965, 67; m. Irene M. Sandberg, Feb. 13, 1944; children—Ralph James, Dorothy June, Leonard Bradley, Christine Marie. Devel. engr. Western Electric div. Am. Tel. & Tel. Co., 1946-49; chem. process engr. Lederle Labs. div. Am. Cyanamid Co., Pearl River, N.Y., 1949-51, asst. supt. chem. prodn., 1951-52, corrosion and materials engr., 1952-56, sr. chem. engr. design and constrn. chem. and pharm. prodn. facilities, cons.

corrosion and materials engring. problems, 1956-73, sr. chem. project engring. mgr. Engring. and Constrn. div., Wayne, N.J., 1973—. Cons. chemist, corrosion specialist. Served to 1st lt. USAAF, 1943-46. Fellow Am. Inst. Chemists; mem. N.J. Inst. Chemists, Nat. Assn. Corrosion Engrs., Sea Horse Inst., Vasa Order of Am. (N.J. dist. 6 exec. bd.). Mem. Reformed Ch. of Am. (elder, v.p. consistory). Home: 244 Lincoln Blvd Emerson NJ 07630 Office: Am Cyanamid Co Wayne NJ 07470

VALENTINO, JOHN, bank exec.; b. Bklyn., Nov. 21, 1940; s. Francis S. and Phyllis J. (Manganello) V.; B.A., Columbia U., 1962, M.B.A., 1969; m. Marguerite Carol Sigelakis, Apr. 8, 1967; children—Jennifer Anne, John Francis, Christopher William. Exec. trainee Continental Ins. Co., N.Y.C., 1962-63; with Irving Trust Co., N.Y.C., 1969—, v.p., mgr. securities industry dept., 1975—; mem. com. on cooperation with securities industry Robert Morris Assos., 1975—. Served to capt. USAF, 1963-67. Generoso Pope scholar, 1958-62; N.Y. Regents scholar, 1958-62. Mem. Nat. Assn. Securities Dealers (panel arbitrators 1975—), Securities Industry Assn., Beta Sigma Rho. Democrat. Roman Catholic. Club: Marine Park Tennis. Home: 578 Ridgewood Ave Glen Ridge NJ 07028 Office: One Wall St New York City NY 10015

VALERINO, DONALD MATTHEW, pharmacologist; b. Syracuse, N.Y., June 23, 1941; s. Michael A. and Catherine (Mahar) V.; B.S., Rensselaer Poly. Inst., 1963; Ph.D., U. Vt., 1970; m. Linda Esther Fasoldt, Sept. 14, 1963; children—Brad Eric, Brooke Lee. Chemist, Hazelton Lab., Vienna, Va., 1963-65; fellow Nat. Cancer Inst., Bethesda, Md., 1970-72; instr. Milton S. Hershey Med. Sch., Pa. State U., 1972-74, asst. prof., 1974-75; criteria mgr., pharmacologist Nat. Inst. Occupational Safety and Health, Rockville, Md., 1975—; cons. Paul de Haen Co., 1971. Mem. Montgomery County Bd. Social Services, Rockville. Mem. Sigma Xi. Contbr. articles to profl. jours. Home: 128 Tulip Dr Gaithersburg MD 20760 Office: Nat Inst Occupational Safety and Health 5600 Fishers Ln Rockville MD 20857

VALERIO, HELEN JOSEPHINE, restaurant co. exec.; b. Chelsea, Mass., Nov. 23, 1938; d. William P. and Helen (Hoffman) Kazukonis; m. Michael A. Valerio, Oct. 6, 1957; children—Michael A., Laura L., Linda M. Accountant Piece O Pizza, of Am. Inc., Arlington, Mass., 1958-63; treas. Papa Gino's of Am., Inc., Needham Heights, Mass., 1963—. Mem. Fin. Execs. Inst., Nat., Mass. restaurant assns. Roman Catholic. Clubs: Weston Community League, St. Julia's Women's (pres. 1977-78). Home: 150 Concord Rd Weston MA 02193 Office: 111 Cabot St Needham Heights MA 02192

VALERIO, MICHAEL AMANDO, restaurant chain exec.; b. Villa Latina, Italy, Aug. 1, 1931; s. Peter Alfrado and Mary (Panetta) F.; came to U.S., 1936, naturalized, 1946; student E. Boston High Sch.; m. Helen J. Kazukonis, Oct. 6, 1957; children—Michael Amando, Laura L., Linda M. Founder, pres. restaurant chain Papa Gino's of Am., Inc., Needham Heights, Mass., 1954—. Bd. dirs. Conservative Caucus, Mass., v.p. found. Morality in Media. Served with AUS, 1950-53. Recipient Faith in Mass. Award, 1973. Mem. Mass., Nat. restaurant assns. Republican. Roman Catholic. Home: 150 Concord Rd Weston MA 02193 Office: 111 Cabot St Needham MA 02194

VALES, JOSEPH JOHN, mgmt. cons.; b. Portchester, N.Y., Sept. 21, 1945; s. Ramon Jaurrieta and Carmelina (Albuquerque) V.; B.B.A., U. Notre Dame, 1967; M.B.A., Columbia, 1969; m. Louise Loughman, Aug. 28, 1971; 1 dau., Christie. Advt. account exec. J.W. Thompson, N.Y.C., 1969-72; sr. advt. account exec. Wells, Rich, Greene, N.Y.C., 1973-75; venture mgr. Booz, Allen & Hamilton, N.Y.C., 1975—; lectr. and cons. in field. Served with Air N.G., 1967-73. Samuel Bronfman fellow dem. bus., 1968-69. Mem. Active Core Execs., Am. Mktg. Assn., Assn. Internat. des Etudiants en Sciences Economiques et Commerciales, Beta Gamma Sigma. Clubs: K.C., Manursing Island. Home: 19 Redfield St Rye NY 10580 Office: Booz Allen & Hamilton 245 Park Ave New York City NY 10017

VALINSKI, DENNIS JOHN, sculptor; b. Carbondale, Pa., Nov. 30, 1946; s. John Stanley and Aneil Christine Valinski; B.F.A., U. Dayton, 1968; B.F.A., Sch. of Dayton Art Inst., 1968; M.F.A., Sch. of Chgo. Art Inst., 1975. Exhibited in one-man shows at Gallery at 210 Fifth Ave, N.Y.C., 1973, 74, 76; exhibited in group shows at Storm King Art Center, Cornwall, N.Y., 1973, 74, 79, Chgo. Art Inst., 1974, 75, Mus. of Contemporary Crafts, N.Y.C., 1976, Johnson Mus. of Cornell U., Ithaca, N.Y., 1977, Tehran (Iran) Mus. Art, 1977, others; lectr. Sarah Lawrence Coll., Bronxville, N.Y., 1975. Nat. Endowment of Arts grantee, 1975, 77; Tiffany Found. grantee, 1974-75; N.Y. State Council on Arts grantee, 1974. Mem. Participation Project Found., Johnson Mus. Art. Home and Office: 266 River Rd Edgewater NJ 07020

VALIQUETTE, JEAN GUY, psychiatrist; b. Quebec, Que., Can., Oct. 5, 1938; s. Maurice and Claire (Brunet) V.; came to U.S., 1966; B.A., U. Montreal, 1959, M.D., 1964; m., Aug. 25, 1962; children—Diane, Jean-Luc. Intern, U. Montreal (Can.), N.Y. Sch. Psychiatry, 1964-69; psychiatrist, v.p. Smithtown (N.Y.) Psychiat. Group, 1972—; chief of service Kings Park (N.Y.) Psychiat. Center, 1966-72. Served with Royal Can. Navy, 1958-63. Diplomate Am. Bd. Psychiatry and Neurology. Fellow Royal Coll. Physicians and Surgeons (Can.); mem. Can. Med. Assn., Am., Can. psychiat. assns., Suffolk County Med. Soc. Roman Catholic. Home: Office: 98 Maple Ave Smithtown NY 11787

VALLAS, ALEX JAMES, hosp. exec.; b. Norfolk, Va., July 14, 1932; s. James George and Elpiniki (Kalesaki) V.; student Coll. William and Mary, 1952-54, Northeastern U., 1965-66; m. Jeanne Myers, Feb. 16, 1958; children—Catherine Marie, Niki Helene. Procurement and property officer in Fgn. Service, assigned to Am. embassies at Vienna, Moscow, Rome, Reykjavik, Baghdad, Karachi, 1955-63; dir. materials mgmt. Magee Women's Hosp., Pitts., 1963—; lectr. Am. Hosp. Assn. Certified purchasing mgr. Mem. Am. Soc. Hosp. Purchasing and Materials Mgmt. (pres. 1978), Nat. Assn. Purchasing Mgmt. (v.p. 1978—), Purchasing Mgmt. Assn. Pitts. (pres. 1975-76), Hosp. Purchasing and Materials Mgmt. Assn. Western Pa. (pres. 1972-73), Internat. Fedn. Purchasing (U.S. hosp. coordinator 1968-70). Republican. Greek Orthodox. Asso. editor: Aljian's Purchasing Handbook, 1978; mem. editorial bd. Hosp. Purchasing Mgmt., 1978; contbr. articles to profl. jours. Home: 576 Catskill Dr Pittsburgh PA 15239 Office: Forbes and Halket Sts pittsburgh PA 15213

VALLE, RAYMOND, mktg. exec.; b. N.Y.C., Nov. 11, 1947; s. Stephen Joseph and Helen (Delsignore) V.; B.A., Hofstra U., 1968; M.A., New Sch. for Social Research, 1970, postgrad.. 1970—; m. Angela Marie Arena, Aug. 1, 1970. Lectr. govt. Dowling Coll., Oakdale, N.Y., 1972-73, instr., 1974; teaching asst. New Sch. for Social Research, N.Y.C., 1970-76; instr. Nassau Coll., Garden City, N.Y., 1973-76, Hofstra U., Hempstead, N.Y., 1974-76, N.Y. Inst. Tech., Old Westbury, N.Y., 1975-76; govt. accounts mgr. Burroughs Corp., 1976-77; govt. accounts mgr. Raytheon Corp., 1977-78, major accounts mgr., 1978—. Mem. county com. Queens County Republican Club, 1973—. Mem. Am., Northeastern, Ga. polit. sci. assns. Roman Catholic. Contbr. articles to profl. jours., also papers to profl. panels. Home: 300 Beverly Rd Douglas Manor NY 11363

VALLE, STEPHEN KURT, rehab. psychologist, health services exec.; b. Yonkers, N.Y., Aug. 2, 1949; s. Dante Ugo and Helen Clara (Englemann) V.; B.A. in Psychology, Barrington Coll., 1971; M.Ed., Pa. State U., 1972; Sc.D., Boston U., 1976; m. Mary Elizabeth Johnson, Sept. 4, 1971. Dir., Alcoholism Counseling Center, Taunton, Mass., 1973-74; exec. dir. Taunton Council on Alcoholism, 1974-75, Taunton Substance Abuse Commn., 1975-76, alcoholism services Cape Counseling Center, Hyannis, Mass., 1976—; chief psychol. services Mt. Pleasant Hosp., Lynn, Mass.; dir. psychol. services Am. Internat. Health Services, Inc.; chief psychology Doctors Hosp., Worcester, Mass.; cons. Morton Hosp., Taunton; instr. Stonehill Coll., Mass. Maritime Acad., Barrington Coll.; mem. Nat. Commn. for Credentialing Alcoholism Counselors. Bd. dirs. Mass. Council on Alcoholism, 1974-75, Eastern Area Alcohol Edn. and Tng. Program. Recipient Fellowship award Buttonwood Found., 1967-74, Outstanding Citizenship award PTA, 1967, Barrington Coll. Alumni Assn. award, 1971; Shepp Found. grantee, 1972. Mem. Am. Assn. Marriage and Family Counselors (clin.), Am. Psychol. Assn., Alcohol and Drug Problems Assn. Am., Am. Personnel and Guidance Assn., Nat. Rehab. Assn., Am. Rehab. Counseling Assn. Home: 22 Green Dr North Dartmouth MA 02747 Office: 101 N Common St Lynn MA 01902

VALLIN, MARTA EMELIA, coll. counselor; b. Panama, Jan. 19, 1936; d. David Eligio and Isabel (Aguilar) Dumbar; B.A., U. Panama, 1964; student Yale U., 1965; M.S., U. Bridgeprot, 1974; D.Ed., Nova U., 1977; m. Karl-Gunnar Vallin, Dec. 16, 1967; 1 son, Lars-Eric. Elementary sch. tchr. Ministry of Edn., Panama, 1956-59, Instituto Pan-Americano, Panama, 1959-65; adult edn. teacher New Haven Bd. Edn., 1965-68; counselor Neighborhood Youth Corps, New Haven, 1969-73; adminstr. Spanish gen. edn. devel. test New Haven Bd. Edn., 1973-74; counselor South Central Community Coll., New Haven, 1973—; cons. Albertus Magnus Coll., 1978, U.S. Forest Service, 1978; participant representing Latin-Am. women on TV program Conn. Women, 1977. Mem. Concerned Citizens for Deaf Com. of New Haven, 1977—. Mem. Latin-Am. Women of New Haven (pub. relations officer 1977—, edn. com. chairperson 1977—), League United of Latin-Am. Citizens U.S. (sec. 1976-77), Junta for Progressive Action Inc. (mem. edn. com. 1970—), Spanish Cultural Assn. (dir. 1976-77), Am. Ednl. Research Assn., Am. Psychol. Assn., Am. Assn. Higher Edn., Am. Assn. Higher Edn. Women Caucus, Congress Com. Community Colls., Conn. State Employees Assn., Conn. Assn. Bilingual-Bicultural Edn., Am. Personnel and Guidance Assn., Nat. Epilepsy Found. Am., Nat. Assn. Physically Handicapped, Conn. Lung Assn., Nat. Paraplegia Found., Conn. Community Coll. Counselor Assn., Internat. Center New Haven. Office: 60 Sargent Dr New Haven CT 06511

VALOON, JACK ANDREW, enamal products and plating co. exec.; b. McKeesport, Pa., Mar. 2, 1918; s. Andrew John and Josephine Pearl (Edwards) V.; student Carnegie Inst. Tech., 1937-39; m. Catherine N. Carr, Sept. 22, 1944; children—Nancy Lee, Janis Lynn. With U.S. Steel Co., McKeesport, 1937-40, Scaife Co., Oakmont, Pa., 1941-60; with Enamel Products Plating Co., McKeesport, 1960—, plant mgr., 1961-64, v.p., 1964-67, exec. v.p., 1967-68, pres., 1968—. Adv. bd. White Oak Boys Club, 1965, Mon-Yough Jr. Achievement, 1968, McKeesport Recreational League, 1972; active Boy Scouts Am., 1971—; elder Riverside Presbyn. Ch., 1968-76; adv. bd. Union Nat. Bank, 1973—. Recipient award of Merit Jr. C. of C., 1974, United Way, 1975; profl. mgr. citation Soc. for Advancement Mgmt., 1975. Mem. Mon Yough C. of C. (pres. 1973), Soc. for Advancement Mgmt., NAM, Nat. Coil Coaters Assn., Smaller Mfrs. Assn., Smithsonian Assos., Tristate Indsl. Assn. (dir. 1970). Clubs: Oakmont Country, Youghiogheny Country, Lions (pres. 1961), Masons, Shriners, Jesters. Home: 826 15th St Oakmont PA 15139 Office: 3500 Walnut St McKeesport PA 15132

VALOVIC, STEFAN JOHN, engring. co. exec.; b. Cicero, Ill., Dec. 20, 1929; s. Stefan and Elizabeth (Kostelny) V.; B.S. in Fire Protection and Safety Engring., Ill. Inst. Tech., 1952; LL.B., John Marshall Law Sch., 1960; m. Barbara Bowers Camporeale, Dec. 10, 1966; children—Elizabeth, Stefanie. Fire protection engr. Cook County Inspection Bur., Chgo., 1956-58, W.A. Alexander & Co., Chgo., 1958-60; admitted to Ill. bar, 1960, Calif. bar, 1964; fire protection engr. Standard Oil of Calif., San Francisco, 1961-63, ins. analyst, 1963-66; sr. ins. rep. Kaiser Aluminum & Chem. Corp., Oakland, Calif., 1966-69, dir. ins., 1969-76; asst. ins. mgr. Stone & Webster Engring. Corp., Boston, 1976—. Served with USNR, 1952-56. Mem. Am. Bar Assn., Calif. State Bar, Risk and Ins. Mgmt. Soc., Soc. Fire Protection Engrs. Contbr. articles to profl. jours. Office: 245 Summer St Boston MA 02107

VAN ALSTYNE, JAMES REED, county ofcl.; b. Hudson, N.Y., June 5, 1932; s. Harry and Martha Elizabeth (Day) VanA.; B.S. in Edn., State U. N.Y., Oneonta, 1953, M.S. in Edn., 1961, postgrad. in adminstrn., Albany, 1961-68: m. Joan Ruth Taylor, May 25, 1957; children—Amy Renee, Meg Louesa. Tchr., Germantown (N.Y.) Central Sch., 1955-58; supervising prin. Stottville (N.Y.) Union Free Sch., 1958-66; prin. elementary sch. Hudson (N.Y.) Sch. Dist., 1966-75; commr. social services Columbia County Hudson, 1975—; asso., field staff State U. N.Y., Albany; councilman Town of Stockport (N.Y.), 1968-75. Republican. Methodist. Home: Box 26 Columbiaville NY 12050

VAN BASSELAERE, LEONARD JULES, elec. engr.; b. Racine, Wis., July 20, 1924; s. Leonard and Verona (Vereb) Van B.; B.S.E.E., U. Wis. 1950; m. Necija Dankers, Oct. 23, 1950. Tech. rep., field engr. Philco Corp., Phila. 1950-53, elec. engr. 1953-65; elec. engr. Am. Elec. Labs., Lansdale, Pa. 1965-67, maintainability engr. 1967—, human factors engr. 1969—, system safety engr. 1973—. Mem. Pa. Outdoor Edn. Conservation Assn., Allentown 1972—, v.p, 1972-73, pres. 1973-74, exec. bd. 1974—. Served with USN 1943-46; PTO. Decorated Phillipine Liberation medal, Bronze Star. Mem. IEEE, AAAS, Am. Def. Preparedness Assn., Am. Security Council (bd. dirs. 1978—), Nat. Rifle Assn., Bucks County Fish and Game Assn. Roman Catholic. Home: 1120 Brennan Dr Warminster PA 18974 Office: PO Box 552 Richardson Rd Lansdale PA 19446

VAN BELLINGHAM, LEON GEORGE, communications cons.; b. Lawrence, Mass., Jan. 18, 1926; s. Leon and Maud (Rust) Van B.; B.A., Columbia U., 1950; divorced; children—Wendy, Heidi, Katrina, Vanessa. With First Nat. City Bank, N.Y.C., 1950-53; exec. network programming NBC, 1953-64; chmn. bd., pres. Internat. Sci. Ltd., 1964-69; v.p. Larue Media Brokers, N.Y.C., 1969-71; v.p. corp. devel. Cablecom Gen. Inc., Denver, 1971-74; communications cons., N.Y.C., 1974—; owner, mng. dir. Manhattan Squash Club, N.Y.C., 1975—. Served with USNR, 1944-46. Mem. U.S., Met. squash racquet assns., Nat. Cable Communications Assn., Nat. Assn. Broadcasters. Clubs: N.Y. Athletic, Columbia Varsity C, Touchdown of N.Y. Home: 180 Central Park S New York City NY 10019 Office: 1114 Ave of Americas New York City NY 10036

VAN BEUREN, JOHN ARCHBOLD, investment co. exec.; b. N.Y.C., Sept. 20, 1932; s. Archbold and Margaret (Ziegler) van B.; B.A., Yale U., 1954; M.B.A., Columbia U., 1960; M. Arch., U. Pa., 1977; m. Hope Hill, June 26, 1954; children—Barbara, Archbold D., Andrea. Staff, Bankers Trust Co., N.Y.C., 1957; asso. Brundage, Story & Rose, N.Y.C., 1960-63; treas. Continental Communications Corp., N.Y.C., 1964-65; pres. Robbins Co., Attleboro, Mass., 1965-66; pres. Continental Communications Corp., N.Y.C., 1966-73; prin. van Beuren Estates, Newport, R.I., 1973—; dir. Indsl. Nat. Bank, Providence. Treas., also trustee St. George's Sch., 1977—; trustee Preservation Soc. Newport County (R.I.), 1977—; investment com. Newport Hosp., 1978—. Served with U.S. Army, 1955-56. Episcopalian. Clubs: Spouting Rock Beach Assn.; Union (N.Y.C.); Newport Country, Ida Lewis Yacht (Newport). Home: 15 Indian Ave Middletown RI 02840 Office: PO Box 399 51 Touro St Newport RI 02840

VAN BEYNUM, WILLIAM JOHN, librarian; b. Chgo., May 31, 1912; s. Clarence W. and Lulu Belle (O'Brien) Van B.; student Bard Coll., 1931-33; B.S., U. Conn., 1936; M.S., So. Conn. State Coll., 1961. Casualty field underwriter Travelers Ins. Co., 1937-41, 1946-52; office mgr. Hedenberg-MacBean Agy., Cranford, N.J., 1952-55; corr. Middleton (Conn.) Press, 1955-76; administrv. asst. Russell Pub. Library, Middletown, Conn., 1957-59, head librarian, 1963-78; ret., 1978. Exec. dir. Conn. Nat. Library Week, 1962; asst. treas., treas. Middlesex County chpt. A.R.C., 1964-69, 70-78, acting chmn., 1969-72; sec. Portland Conn. Conservation Commn., 1965-73; v.p. Conn. Assn. Conservation Commn., 1967-68. Bd. dirs. Com. for a New Eng. Bibliography, 1969—, Rockfall Corp., conservation trust, 1972—, Greater Middletown Preservation Trust, 1973—; trustee Godfrey Meml. Library, Middletown, 1962—, chmn. bd., 1967—; mem. Midstate (Conn.) Regional Planning Agy., 1968—, treas., 1975-78, chmn., 1978—; treas. Conn. Areawide Waste Treatment Planning Bd., 1978—. Served to capt. with AUS, 1941-46. Mem. Am. (council mem. 1965-69), New Eng., Conn. (pres. 1962-63, editor publ. 1959-62) library assns., Middlesex County Hist. Soc. (pres., 1959—), Conn., N.Y. State hist. socs., Am. Assn. State and Local History, Middletown Old Burying Ground Assn. Episcopalian. Clubs: Faculty (Wesleyan U.); Middletown University (pres. 1968-69); Meriden Motorcycle (asst. treas. 1970, sec. 1971-75); Welsh Corgi (Pembroke). Home: Middle Haddam Rd Portland CT 06480

VAN BLARCUM, BARBARA HAPPE, food service/lodging exec.; b. Toronto, Ont., Can., Mar. 27, 1945; d. William Henry and Jane Hammond (Barnes) Happe; B.A., Purdue U., 1968, M.S., 1969; m. James Corbett Van Blarcum, June 19, 1965. Secondary sch. French tchr., Ind. and Ga., 1969-71; with Marriott Corp., Washington, 1972—, now dir. corp. info.; Vol. tchr. English to foreigners, 1973-76. NDEA fellow, 1968; Rotary scholar, 1963. Mem. Pub. Relations Soc. Am. (accredited; nat. exec. com. investor relations sect. 1977), Nat. Investor Relations Inst. Republican. Episcopalian. Home: 11324 Rambling Rd Gaithersburg MD 20760 Office: Washington DC 20058

VAN BRUNT, H(OWELL) L(LOYD), poet, lectr.; b. Tulsa, July 18, 1936; s. Howell Harold and Elva Gladys (Johnson) Van B.; A.A., Alan Hancock Jr. Coll., 1956. Poet in residence Pa. Council on the Arts, 1975-76, 76-77, 77-78; poet; lectr. colls. and univs.; poetry editor of The Pushcart Prize, 1976—; contbg. editor to The Smith, 1965—; poetry books include: Uncertainties, 1968; Indian Territory, 1974; Feral, 1976; For Luck: Poems 1962-77; contbr. poetry to Am. Poetry Rev., Sat. Rev., The Nation, Natural History, Christian Sci. Monitor, anthologies; poetry editor The Oconee Rev. Mem. Poetry Soc. Am., Nat. Union Journalists (U.K.). Home: 53 Leroy St Apt 2A New York City NY 10014

VAN CAMPENHOUT, JACQUES LOUIS, obstetrician and gynecologist; b. Can., Apr. 2, 1933; s. Ernest and Marie Louise (Dewit) Van C.; M.D., U. Louvain, Belgium, 1958; m. Francoise Moreaux, June 18, 1960; children—Catherine, Isabelle, Eric. Practice medicine specializing in obstetrics and gynecology, Montreal, Que.; chief dept. obstetrics and gynecology Notre Dame Hosp., Montreal, 1972—; asst. prof. U. Montreal, 1964-70, asso. prof., 1969-74, prof., 1974—, chmn. dept., 1972—. Research fellow USPHS, 1962-63. Fellow Royal Coll. Surgeons (Can.), Am. Coll. Obstetricians and Gynecologists; mem. Assn. des Medecins de langue francaise du Can., Am., Canadian fertility socs., Soc. Obstetricians and Gynecologists Can., Soc. for Study Fertility (pres. elect), Assn. Profs. Obstetrics and Gynecology Am. (council), Assn. Profs. Obstetrics and Gynecology Can., Canadian Investigators in Reproduction, Internat. Fedn. Gynecologists and Obstetricians, Assn. Obstetricians and Gynecologists of Que., Fedn. internationale des Obstetriciens-gynecologues de langue francaise. Contbr. articles to med. jours. Home: 91 Beaumont St W Saint Bruno PQ Canada Office: 2065 Alexandre Deseve Montreal PQ H2L 2W5 Canada

VANCE, CYRUS ROBERTS, lawyer, sec. state; b. Clarksburg, W.Va., Mar. 27, 1917; s. John Carl and Amy (Roberts) V.; B.A., Yale, 1939, LL.B., 1942; LL.D., Marshall U., 1963, Trinity Coll., Hartford, Conn., 1966, Yale, 1968, W.Va. U., 1969, Brandeis U., 1971; m. Grace Elsie Sloane, Feb. 15, 1947; children—Elsie Nicoli, Amy Sloane, Grace Roberts, Camilla (Mrs. James H. Higgins, III), Cyrus Roberts. Admitted to N.Y. bar, 1947, U.S. Supreme Ct. bar, 1960; asst. to pres. Mead Corp., 1946-47; with Simpson, Thacher & Bartlett, N.Y.C., 1947-56, partner, 1956-61, 67-77; gen. counsel Dept. Def., 1961-62; sec. of army, 1962-63; dep. sec. def., 1964-67; spl. rep. of the Pres., Cyprus, 1967, Korea, 1968; U.S. negotiator Paris Peace Conf. on Vietnam, 1968-69; sec. state, 1977—; spl. counsel, preparedness investigating subcom. Senate Armed Services Com., 1957-60; cons. counsel spl. Com. on Space and Astronautics, U.S. Senate, 1958; chmn. com. on adjudication of claims Adminstrv. Conf. of U.S., mem. Com. to Investigate Alleged Police Corruption in N.Y.C., 1970-72; chmn. bd. Union Settlement Assn., Inc., 1953-61; trustee Yale, 1968-78; chmn. bd. trustees Rockefeller Found., 1975-76. Served to lt. USNR, 1942-46. Recipient Medal of Freedom, 1969. Fellow Am. Coll. Trial Lawyers; mem. Am. Bar Assn., Assn. Bar City N.Y. (pres. 1974-76). Office: Dept State Washington DC 20520

VANCE, GEORGE PAUL, naval engr.; b. Bklyn., Apr. 1, 1936; s. George Edward and Anna Marie (Chainese) V.; B.S., U.S. Coast Guard Acad., 1957; M.S., U. Mich., 1963; Ph.D., U.R.I., 1974; m. Rita Mary Mullen, Feb. 8, 1958; children—George Paul, Jr., Karen Francis, Dennis Edmound. Commd. ensign U.S. Coast Guard, 1957, advanced through grades to comdr., shipboard engr., 1957-60; comdg. officer U.S. Coast Guard Loran Sta., 1960-61; engring. officer icebreaker 1963-65; chief engr. ship design office U.S. Coast Guard Hdqrs., Washington, 1965-68; prof. engring. U.S. Coast Guard Acad., New London, Conn., 1968-77; ret., 1977; research engr. Army Cold Regions Research and Engring. Lab., Hanover, N.H., 1977—; cons. Exxon, Sun Shipbldg. and Dry Dock; Arctic researcher Gen. Dynamics; adj. prof. U. Conn. NSF grantee, 1973. Mem. Waterford Water and Sewer Commn., 1973-75; pres. Cohanzie PTA, 1973-74. Licensed profl. engr., Mich. Mem. Am. Soc. Naval Engrs., Marine Tech. Soc., Sigma Chi. Roman Catholic. Contbr. articles to profl. jours. Home: 29 Greentree Dr Waterford CT 06385 Office: Army Cold Regions Research and Engring Lab Hanover NH 03755

VAN DE BOVENKAMP, SUE ERPF, charitable orgn. exec.; b. N.Y.C., Oct. 16, 1938; d. George Norton and Bettina Lions (Hearst) Mortimore; student Gardner Sch., Art Students League, Cooper Union; m. Armand Grover Erpf, 1965; children—Cornelia Aurelia, Armand Bartholomew; m. 2d, Gerrit Pieter Van de Bovenkamp, Aug. 11, 1973. Pres., Arkville Erpf Fund, Arkville, N.Y., 1971-76, founder, chmn. Erpf Catskill Cultural Center, 1972-77. Trustee, founder N.Y. Zool. Soc., 1975-77; fellow in perpetuity Met. Mus. Art, 1977; life fellow Pierpont Morgan Library; mem. bd. council of friends Whitney Whitney Mus. Am. Art, 1971—; trustee, mem. adv. council, dept. art history and archaeology Columbia U., 1972—, asso. univ. seminar on uses of the oceans, 1977; mem. Agribus. Council; active Phila. Atheneum, 1971—, Municipal Art Soc., 1972—, Victorian Soc., 1971—, World Wildlife Fund, 1973—; adv. council Catskill Center for Conservation and Devel., 1971—; mem. pres.'s council Columbia U., 1973—, Mus. City N.Y., 1972—, also Guggenheim Mus., Mus. Modern Art, Asia Soc., Smithsonian Mus. Office: The Arkville Erpf Fund 640 Park Ave New York City NY 10021

VANDENBERG, JOHN DAVID, aircraft co. exec.; b. Paterson, N.J., Aug. 28, 1926; s. Harold A. and Mathilda (Veneman) V.; A.B., Columbia, 1950, M.A., 1953; postgrad. Purdue U., 1957-58; m. Doloros M. Shaffer, May 24, 1975; children by previous marriage—Donna Claire, Carol Ellen; step-children—Joseph Dale, Margaret Mary, Cynthia Ann. Research Asso. Dunlap & Assos., Stamford, Conn., 1950-53; chief, human engring. unit Picatinny Arsenal, Dover, N.J., 1953-56; human factors specialist Grumman Aircraft Engring. Corp., Bethpage, N.Y., 1959-61; human factors supr. Lockheed Electronics Co., Plainfield, N.J., 1962-77, asst. dept. mgr., 1967-69, engring. br. adminstr., 1970, mgr. mktg. adminstrn., 1971, asst. to chief engr. MK86 gunfire control system, 1971-73, spl. asst. to gen. mgr. products and systems div., 1973-75; mgr. engring. services Aircraft Radio and Control div. Cessna Aircraft Co., Boonton, N.J., 1977—. Served with USNR, 1944-46. Mem. IEEE, Human Factors Soc., Ergonomics Research Soc., Soc. for Information Display, AAAS, Internat. Assn. Torch Clubs, Sigma Xi. Contbr. articles to publs. Home: 21 Moss Ave Westfield NJ 07090 Office: Aircraft Radio and Control Div Cessna Aircraft Co Boonton NJ 07005

VAN DEN DAELE, LELAND DOUGLAS, psychologist, psychoanalyst, educator; b. Long Beach, Calif., Sept 28, 1939; s. Leopold Francis and Dorthy (Krolick) Van Den D.; A.B., U. San Francisco, 1962; M.S., Purdue U., 1964, Ph.D. (David Ross fellow), 1967; m. Ann Soderstrom, Nov. 2, 1967 (div.): 1 son, Brendan Brice. Asst. prof. child devel. Child Devel. Lab., U. Ill., Urbana, 1966-70, mem. Center Human Ecology, 1966-70, asso. prof., 1970-72; NIH sr. postdoctoral fellow Ednl. Testing Service, Princeton, N.J., 1970-72, vis. research psychologist, 1972-73; vis. asso. prof. psychology and edn. Tchrs. Coll. Columbia, U., N.Y.C., 1973-75; adj. asso. prof. psychology Queens (N.Y.) Coll., CU NY, 1976; asso. prof. Univ. Coll. and Grad. Sch. Applied and Profl. Psychology, Rutgers U., New Brunswick, N.J. 1976—; cons. Internat. Biol. Program, Milton Olive Found., Holmes County, Miss., 1968-72, Langley Porter Neuropsychiat. Inst., U. Calif. San Francisco, 1969, Bur. Children's Services, N.Y.C., 1976—; v.p. Candidates Assn. Am. Inst. Psychoanalysis; clin. asst. Karen Horney Psychoanalytic Inst. and Clinic, N.Y.C., 1975-77, adj. psychoanalyst, 1977—. Mem. Am. Psychol. Assn., Internat. Soc. Behavior Devel., Jean Piaget Soc. (contbg. editor newsletter 1975—), Soc. Research Social Biology, Soc. Research Child Devel. Asst. editor: Am. Jour. Psychoanalysis, 1978—; author chpts. in books; contbr. articles to profl. jours. Research in field. Home: 400 West End Ave Apt 6B New York City NY 10024 Office: Karen Horney Psychoanalytic Clinic 329 E 62d St New York City NY 10021

VANDEN DORPEL, RONALD DALE, coll. adminstr.; b. Hackensack, N.J., Apr. 21, 1947; s. Cornelius and Ona Jane (May) Vanden D.; B.A., Ohio State U., 1969; A.M., Brown U., 1971; m. Diane Marilyn Strock, Aug. 16, 1969. Exec. asst. to pres. Bryant Coll., Smithfield, R.I., 1977, dir. coll. resources, 1978—; asso. R.I. Ecumenical Center for Ch. and Univ. Consultation. Served to capt. USAF, 1971-76, USAFR, 1977—. Mem. Council Advancement and Support of Edn., Am. Assn. Univ. Adminstrs., Am. Hist. Assn., Res. Officers Assn., Charitable Baptist Soc., Assos. John Carter Brown Library, Phi Alpha Theta, Phi Eta Sigma, Scabbard and Blade. Baptist (deacon). Club: Brown of R.I. Contbr. revs. and articles on history of intelligence to Naval War Coll. Rev., 1977—. Home: 11 Secluded Ct Cumberland RI 02864 Office: Bryant Coll Smithfield RI 02917

VAN DER BURGH, CHARLES EDWIN, III, mgmt. cons.; b. N.Y.C., May 20, 1941; s. Charles E. and Alison (Philips) van der B.; B.A., Williams Coll., 1963; M.B.A., Harvard U., 1966. Account exec. U.S. Trust Co., N.Y.C., 1963-64; sr. cons. Booz, Allen & Hamilton, Internat., 1966-70; sr. asso. Internat. Cons. Assos. (C.I.) Ltd., Europe, 1970—; pres. Internat. Cons. Assos. (U.S.A.) Ltd., Washington, 1974—; dir. Covert, Crispin & Murray, Inc., Internat. Network Systems, Inc.; cons. trade devel. U.S. Dept. Commerce, Bur. East West Trade, 1971-74. Mem. Inst. Mgmt. Cons., Am. Mgmt. Assn., Mgmt. Center Europe, Am. Mktg. Assn. Clubs: Travellers (Paris); Williams (N.Y.C.); Capitol Hill, City Tavern (Washington). Home: 1 Place de l'Alma Paris France 75016 Office: 522 21st St NW Washington DC 20006

VAN DER CLUTE, DEAN SANDISON, architect; b. Hillsdale, N.J., Dec. 28, 1928; s. William Walton and Grace (Sandison) Van der C.; B.Arch., Carnegie Mellon U., 1952; children—Dean Sandison, Diana Grace, Martha Ann, Douglas Cobbe, Sandra Lee. Designer, W.W. Van der Clute, Architect, Cranford, N.J., 1947-58, David Ludlow, Architect, Summit, N.J., 1959; chief designer Tectonic Assos., Architects and Engrs., Sommerville, N.J., 1959, Minoru Yamasaki & Assos., Southfield, Mich., 1959-60; partner Van der Clute & Spies Architects, Cranford, 1960—; owner Sub Sea Divers; instr. scuba diving Fordham U., Union Coll. Mem. admission council Carnegie Mellon U., 1966—. Served with AUS, 1952-54. Recipient Gold medal Nomahegan Swim and Racket Club, 1963, awards for underwater photography. Mem. N.J. Soc. Architects, AIA, N.J. Council Diving Clubs, YMCA Inst. Scuba Instrs., Littoral Soc., Sigma Nu. Republican. Mem. Ref. Ch. Am. Clubs: Manta Ray Diving (pres. 1973-76), Cranford Kiwanis (pres. 1974-75). Editor Sub Sea Jour., 1975-78. Home and Office: 500 Centennial Ave Cranford NJ 07016

VANDERLYN, CHARLES PIERRE, economist, govt. ofcl.; b. The Hague, Holland, May 30, 1929; s. Martin and Dina (Abas) Mendels; came to U.S., 1939, naturalized, 1944; B.S., U. Md., 1953; M.B.A., U. City N.Y., 1962; m. Barbara Ellen Tilghman, May 26, 1962; children—Peter Mark, Nancy Tilghman, Derek Whitnall. Market research analyst Knoll Assos., N.Y.C., 1962-64, Kendall Co., N.Y.C., 1964-65; mgr. mktg. services Earle M. Jorgensen Co., Phila., 1965-67; economist Office Emergency Preparedness, Washington, 1967-68; program mgr. individual on-site wastewater treatment systems EPA, Washington, 1968—. Served to 1st lt. USAF, 1953-55. Mem. Am. Mktg. Assn., Soc. Govt. Econs., Am. Econ. Assn., Assn. Pub. Program Analysis, Res. Officers Assn., Lambda Chi Alpha. Home: 3817 S 16th St Arlington VA 22204 Office: EPA Office of Water Planning and Standards Washington DC 20460

VANDERPOOL, WYNANT DAVIS, JR., architect; b. Morristown, N.J., Apr. 12, 1914; s. Wynant Davis and Cornelia Grinnel (Willis) V.; A.B., Princeton U., 1936, M.F.A., 1940; m. Ann West Wheeler, Jan. 22, 1965; children—Wynant Davis, Helena, Madeleine. Designer, J.H. and W.C. Ely, architects, Newark, 1940-42, Skidmore, Owings and Merrill, architects, 1945-46, partner Faulkner, Stenhouse, Fryer & Faulkner, architects, Washington, 1965-68, Faulkner, Fryer & Vanderpool, architects, Washington, 1968—. Mem. Bd. Archtl. Cons.'s for Georgetown, Commn. Fine Arts; pres. Historic Georgetown Inc., Washington, 1971-77; trustee Holland Soc., N.Y., 1974—. Trustee Found. Preservation Historic Georgetown, 1970—; mem. citizens adv. com. to D.C. bar, 1974-77. Served to lt. USNR, 1942-45. Mem. AIA, Century Assn. N.Y., Historic House Assn. Am. (dir. 1978—). Episcopalian (sr. warden 1973). Club: Mid-Ocean (Tuckerstown, Bermuda); Chevy Chase, Met. (Washington); Coffee House (N.Y.). Home: 1330 30th St NW Washington DC 20007 Office: 2000 L St NW Washington DC 20036

VANDER VOORT, GEORGE FREDERIC, metall. engr.; b. Phila., Sept. 1, 1944; s. Frederic Clarendon and Frances Catherine (Hosenfeld) V.; B.S., Drexel U., 1967; M.S., Lehigh U., 1974; m. Brenda L. Schlaner, June 20, 1970; children—Robert Thomas, Juliana. With Bethlehem Steel Corp. (Pa.), 1967—, engr. metall. services and investigations research dept., 1972—; instr. phsy. metallurgy Pa. State U., Allentown, 1969-78. Mem. Am. Soc. for Metals, Acad. Metals and Materials, ASTM (com. metallography), Internat. Metallographic Soc. (v.p.). Roman Catholic. Home: 3740 Brandeis Ave Bethlehem PA 18017 Office: Bethlehem Steel Corp Homer Research Labs Bethlehem PA 18016

VAN DEUSEN, COURTLAND, III, radiologist; b. Tsingtau, Shantung, China, Sept. 1, 1917; s. Courtland and Mary (Lorenz) Van D.; B.S., Wooster Coll., 1939; M.D., U. Pa., 1943; m. Dorothy Grace Smith, June 27, 1942; children—Christina, Courtland, Edward, Laurence. Intern, Pa. Hosp., Phila., 1943-44, resident, 1944-47; practice medicine, specializing in radiology, Niagara Falls, N.Y., 1948—; radiologist Meml. Hosp., Niagara Falls, 1948-70; courtesy radiologist Mt. St. Mary's Hosp., Niagara Falls, 1950, DeGraff Meml. Hosp., Tonawanda, N.Y., 1948-50. Dist. v.p. Boy Scouts Am., Niagara Falls, 1950; pres. United Way of Niagara, 1968-70; pres. Council Social Agencies, 1965; bd. dirs. Salvation Army, Niagara Falls, 1970; elder First Presbyn. Ch., Lewiston, N.Y., 1953-56, mem. council, 1970-77, deacon, 1951-53, trustee, 1957-60; bd. dirs. Western N.Y. Health Systems Agy., 1976. Served with AUS, 1944-46; ETO. Recipient Physicians Recognition award AMA, 1977—. Fellow Am. Coll. Radiology; mem. NCCJ, AMA, N.Y. State, Niagara County med. socs., Niagara Falls Acad. Medicine, Radiol. Soc. N. Am., Am. Bd. Radiology, Buffalo, N.Y. State, Eastern radiol. socs. Republican. Presbyn. Clubs: Youngstown Yacht, Royal Canadian Yacht; Rotary (past pres.) (Niagara Falls). Home: 1 Main St Youngstown NY 14174 Office: 817 Main St Niagara Falls NY 14301

VANDEWALL, LAVERNE ROBERT, JR., pharmacist; b. Rochester, N.Y., Jan. 27, 1952; s. LaVerne Robert and Joan M. (Bartholomew) V.; B.S., Albany Coll. Pharmacy, 1975; Pharm.D., Duquesne U., 1977; m. Rosina Damulis, July 26, 1975. Intern in pharmacy Highland Hosp., Rochester, summers 1973, 74, St. Mary's Hosp., Rochester, summer 1975; hosp. residency Mercy Hosp., Pitts., 1976-77; dir. pharmacy Windber (Pa.) Hosp. and Wheeling Clinic, 1977—; instr. biopharmaceutics and dosage form lab. Duquesne U., Pitts., 1975-76, clin. pharmacy and therapeutics, 1976-77. Mem. Am. Soc. Hosp. Pharmacists, Cambria-Somerset-Bedford County Pharm. Assn. Office: Windber Hosp and Wheeling Clinic 600 Somerset Ave Windber PA 15963

VAN DIEN, JOHN EDWARD, research lab. co. exec.; b. Ridgewood, N.J., Jan. 30, 1909; s. John D. and Ella (Joralemon) Van D.; B.S., Tri State U., 1937; postgrad. N.Y. U., 1942; m. Elizabeth Irene Wynn, Feb. 14, 1930. Clk., DeCoppet & Doremus, N.Y.C., 1930-34; chemist Sohio Oil Refinery, Lima, O., 1937-38; draftsman Ohio Steel Foundries, Lima, 1938; spectrochemist Curtis Wright Corp., Paterson, N.J., 1938-42, Aluminum Co. Am., New Kensington, Pa., 1942-45; cons. spectrochemist Applied Spectrochem. Labs., Glen Rock, N.J., 1945-60; dist. mgr. Applied Research Labs., Inc., Glendale, Calif., 1951-60; pres. SpectroChem. Labs., Inc., Franklin Lakes, N.J., 1960—. Mem. Optical Soc. Am., Am. Chem. Soc., ASTM, Soc. Applied Spectroscopy (designer soc. medal), Ridgewood (N.J.) Art Assn., Sigma Mu Sigma. Club: Masons. Contbr. to Handbook of Analytical Chemistry. Home: 36 Cumberland Rd Glen Rock NJ 07452 Office: 545 Commerce St Franklin Lakes NJ 07417

VAN DUZER, ALBERT WIENCKE, clergyman; b. Newburgh, N.Y., July 15, 1917; s. Albert Barton and Clara Helen (Wiencke) Van D.; A.B., Trinity Coll., Hartford, Conn., 1940; Th.B., Gen. Theol. Sem., 1945, S.T.D., 1966; B.D., Phila. Div. Sch., 1954, D.D., 1967; m. Marion R. Lippincott, Apr. 31, 1939; children—Daryl Van Duzer Gorczycki, Margaret Lynn Van Duzer Ryan, Marianne Gayle Van Duzer Carson. Ordained to ministry Episcopal Ch., 1946; curate Grace Ch., Merchantville, N.J., 1946-47, rector, 1949-66; rector Ch. of Advent, Cape May, N.J., 1947-49; suffragan bishop N.J. Diocese, 1966-72; bishop coadjutor of N.J., 1972-73, bishop of N.J., 1973—. Past youth dir., past pres. Youth Cons. Service N.J. Diocese; Camden (N.J.) County rep. White House Conf. Aging, 1957; mem. Bd. Examining Chaplains N.J., 1957-66; past chaplain Merchantville Fire Co. Trustee Evergreen's Home Aged, Camden County Children's Shelter, Camden County council Girl Scouts Am. Named Man of Year Merchantville Fire Co. Trustee Evergreen's Home Aged. Recipient Medal of Honor, Diocese N.J., 1962, Boyle award citizenship and community service Camden County Bar Assn., 1965; named hon. canon Trinity Cathedral, Trenton, N.J., 1957. Mem. Camden County Health and Welfare Assn. (mem. bd.), Nat. Assn. Social Service. Clubs: Masons (33 deg.; past grand chaplain N.J.), Kiwanis, Lions. Home: 31 Delaware Ave Trenton NJ 08628 Office: 808 W State St Trenton NJ 08618

VAN DYKE, WILLIAM ADOLPHUS, JR., aerospace engr.; b. Greenville, Tex., Jan. 6, 1935; s. William Adolphus and Estella (Davis) Van D.; B.S. in Math., E. Tex. State U., 1958; student in Mech. Engring., So. Meth. U., 1959-60; postgrad. Trinity Coll., 1966-68; m. Patricia Ann Edwards, Sept. 28, 1952; children—William Kelsey, Vicki Lynn, Jay Patrick. With TEMCO, Greenville, 1953-65; sr. engr. Corp. Systems Center div. United Aircraft Corp., Farmington, Conn., 1965-69; sect. mgr. Saunders Assos. Inc., Bedford, Mass., 1969-71; project leader Harris Corp., Palm Bay, Fla., 1971-76; sect. leader 2D Radar Engring. Automation Industries/Vitro Lab., Silver Spring, Md., 1976—; cons. Dept. Navy. Layman Bible tchr. Presbyn. Ch., bd. deacons and elders, 1960—; mem. exec. bd. Circle Ten council Boy Scouts Am., 1962-65. Served with USN, 1958. Mem. Soc. Allied Weight Engrs. Democrat. Contbr. articles to profl. jours. Patentee in field. Home: Route 1 Box 89-57 Summit Dr Ijamsville MD 21754 Office: 14000 Georgia Ave Silver Spring MD 20910

VAN GORDER, JOHN FREDERIC, found. ofcl.; b. Jacksonville, Fla., Mar. 22, 1943; s. Harold Burton and Charlotte Louise (Anderson) Van G.; grad. Dover (Eng.) Coll.; A.B., Dartmouth Coll., 1965; postgrad. Air Force Inst. Tech., 1967-68; M.S. in Adminstrn., George Washington U., 1973; postgrad. U. Va., Coll. William and Mary, Northeastern U., Cath. U. Am., Babson Coll., Fordham U. Law Sch., 1977—; m. Sandra Joan Hagen, June 4, 1977; 1 dau., Alyssa Jane. Weapons controller Aerospace Def. Command, Ft. Lee, Va., 1965-67; buyer electronics systems div. Air Force Systems Command, Bedford, Mass., 1968-69; project mgr. research and devel. Hdqrs. U.S. Air Force, Washington, 1969-73, br. chief personnel, 1973-74, presdl. social aide White House, 1970-73; asso. Louis C. Kramp & Assos., Washington, 1975; program officer J.M. Found., N.Y.C., 1975—. Mem. exec. com. Mayor's Vol. Action Council, 1977-78; chmn. N.Y.C. steering com. Nat. Congress on Volunteerism and Citizenship; mem. bd. govs. N.Y. Jaycees Found., Inc., 1978-79. Served to capt. USAF, now Res. Named Outstanding Young Man of Va., 1974. Mem. U.S. (nat. v.p. 1973-74), Internat. (senator, v.p. 1975, rep. to UN 1976), D.C. (pres. 1972-73) Jaycees, S.A.R., Soc. Mayflower Descs., Student Bar Assn. (class pres. 1978-79), Alpha Delta Phi. Republican. Episcopalian. Mason. Club: Toastmasters (local pres. 1969-70, area gov. 1970-71) (Bedford, Mass.); First Assembly Dist. Republican (bd. govs. 1977—), Young Republican (N.Y.C.). Home: 30 Woods Ave Bergenfield NJ 07621 Office: 60 E 42d St New York City NY 10017

VAN HAMEL, ATTY THOMAS ANTHONY SWART, audiovisual technician; b. Kingsport, Tenn., June 7, 1940; s. Thomas A. and A.B. Camille Van H.; B.A. in Psychology, U.S. Air Force Inst., 1969; 1 son, Michael. Enlistedas pvt. U.S. Army, 1960, advanced through grades to staff sgt., 1967; chief classification interviewer, 1966-69, transition counselor, 1969-70, ret., 1970; audio-visual technician Ednl. Testing Service, Princeton, N.J., 1970—; profl. photographer. Bd. dirs. YMCA; mem. soccer bd. Decorated Bronze Star medal, Air medal, Purple Heart. Mem. Nat. Audio Visual Technicians, Profl. Photographers Assn., VFW, Am. Legion. Republican. Roman Catholic. Home: 326 Hale St Pennington NJ 08534 Office: Rosedale Rd Princeton NJ 08540

VAN HARE, GEORGE FREDERICK, JR., mfg. co. exec.; b. Jersey City, N.J., Oct. 8, 1923; s. George Frederick and Anna Price (Kuckler) Van H.; B.Ch.E., Pratt Inst., 1948; m. Marjorie Hall Ross, Nov. 8, 1952; children—George Frederick, David Ross, John Andrew, Mary Elizabeth. Project engr. Chem. Constrn. Co., N.Y.C., 1948-56; sr. project engr. Am. Cyanamid Co., Wayne, N.J., 1956-67, mgr. materials handling, 1967-73, chief materials handling engr., 1973—. Pack com. chmn. Fairfield County council Boy Scouts Am., 1967-69, troop com. chmn., 1971-73, com. mem. at large, 1974-77. Served with USAAF, 1942-45. Registered Profl. Engr., N.Y., N.J. Mem. Internat. Material Mgmt. Soc. (internat. v.p. 1977-79), Am. Inst. Chem. Engrs. Republican. Congregationalist. Patentee field hydrometallurgy. Home: 38 Red Bird Rd Stamford CT 06905 Office: 859 Berdan Av Wayne NJ 07470

VAN HORN, ROBERT EMERY, real estate exec.; b. Kenmore, N.Y., May 9, 1945; s. Emery Lamartine and Pauline Agnes (Shepson) Van-H.; student Am. U.; m. Barbara Clair Broseker, Jan. 12, 1973; adopted dau., Donna Creel. Sales mgr. Lenora Gordon, Inc., Annapolis, Md., 1972-74; sales mgr. Chris Coile & Assos., Inc., Annapolis, 1974-75, 76-77, v.p., 1977—, mktg. mgr. Realtronics Computer Systems, McLean, Va., 1975-76; dir. Annapolis br. Second Nat. Bldg. & Loan Assn., 1977—, chmn. bd., 1978, 79. Mem. Soc. Prevention Cruelty to Animals Anne Arundel County (pres. 1974-76, dir. 1973—), Nat., Md. assns. realtors, Am. Soc. Profl. Salesmen (v.p. Washington met. sales club chpt. 1977-78). Home: 1330 Waterbury Rd Crownsville MD 21032 Office: 101 N Center St Westminster MD 21157

VAN HYUCK, ALFRED PHILLIPS, city planner; b. N.Y.C., Jan. 22, 1933; s. Phillips Maybee and Helen Louise (Ashfield) Van H.; B.A., Dartmouth Coll., 1955; M.Regional Planning, U. N.C., 1959; m. Mary Elizabeth Jones, July 2, 1935; children—John, Nancy. Dir. city planning Herbert H. Smith Assos., W. Trenton, N.J., 1959-63; dir. urban renewal as Ford Found. advisor Calcutta Met. Planning Orgn., India, 1963-67; pres. Padco Inc., Washington, 1967—. Chmn., Lower Makefield Town Planning Bd., Makefield, Pa., 1961-63. Served to 1st lt. U.S. Army, 1955-57. Nat. Sears Roebuck fellow in city planning, 1957-59. Mem. Am. Inst. Planners, Soc. Internat. Devel. Mem. Soc. of Friends. Club: Cosmos. Contbr. articles in field to profl. jours.; editor: (with John D. Herbert) Urban Planning the Developing Countries, 1968; (with Jack Hornung) Citizens Guide to Urban Renewal, 1962. Home: 2773 N Wakefield St Arlington VA 22207 Office: 1834 Jefferson Pl NW Washington DC 20036

VANÍCEK, PETR, geodesist; b. Susice Czechoslovakia, July 18, 1935; s. Ivan and Irena (Blahovcová) V.; Ing. (Geodesy), Czech. Tech. U. Prague, 1959; Ph.D. in Math. Physics, Czech Acad. Scis., Prague, 1968; m. Jana Vancurová, Apr. 9, 1960; children—Filip, Stépán, Anna. Came to Can., 1969, naturalized, 1975. Geodesist, Inst. Surveying, Prague, 1959-63; computer cons. Czech Tech. U., Prague, 1963-67; Natural Environment Research Council sr. research fellow Tidal Institut, U. Liverpool (Eng.), 1967-68; sr. sci. officer Natural Environment Research Council, U.K., 1968-69; NRC Can. postdoctoral fellow Fed. Govt., Ottawa, 1969-71; prof. geodesy U. N.B., Fredericton, 1971—; vis. prof. U. Paraná (Brazil), summers 1975, 76; vis. scientist U.S. Geol. Survey, Menlo Park, Calif., 1977; sr. vis. scientist U.S. Nat. Acad. Scis., 1977; sec. NRC Subcom. on Geodesy, 1972-73; mem. Canadian Nat. Com. on Geodynamics, 1975—; nat. corr. on geodesy Canadian Geophys. Union, 1975-77, mem. exec. com., 1977—; mem. study groups on recent crustal movements, inertial positioning, large networks and determination geoid Internat. Union Geodesy and Geophysics, 1971, 73; Can. rep. Commn. on Recent Crustal movements. Fellow Geol. Assn. Can., Explorers Club; mem. Am. Geophys. Union, N.Y. Acad. Scis., Canadian Inst. Surveying, Canadian Lawn Tennis Assn. Club: Cross-Country Skiing (U. N.B.). Author: (with V. Pleskot, others) Základy Programování Pro Ural, vol. I, 1964, II, 1965; (with J. Culík, T. Hrusková); contbr. sect. Satellite Geodesy and Geodynamics to Ency. Soil Sci. and Applied Geology; contbr. articles to profl. lit.; editor: Procs. Internat. Symposium of N.Am. Geodetic Networks, 1974; Procs. Canadian Geophs. Union Symposium on Satellite Geodesy and Geodynamics, 1975. Home: 180 Charing Crescent Fredericton NB E3B 4R7 Canada

VAN KLEECK, PETER, hotel co. exec.; b. Hartford, Conn., Feb. 1, 1938; s. LeRoy Winfield and Myrtis (Parker) V.; B.A. with honors, Mich. State U., 1960; m. Gail Heustis, Sept. 19, 1959; children—Kimberli, Peter Kenneth. Mgmt. trainee Sheraton Corp., Boston, Louisville, 1960-62, field insp., Chgo., 1962-63, adminstrv. asst. to gen. mgr. Sheraton-Blackstone Hotel, Chgo., 1963-64, resident mgr. Sheraton Dallas, Sheraton Boston Hotels, 1964-70, mgr. Sheraton Waikiki, Hawaii, 1970-71, asst. dir. support, devel. N.Am. ops. Sheraton Corp., Boston, 1971—; v.p., dir. ops. support Sheraton Corp., Boston. Active United Way, Chgo., Dallas, Boston. Mem. Hotel Sales Mgmt. Assn., Dallas C. of C. Eipscopalian. Clubs: Cosmopolitan, Lasso (Dallas). Home: 3 Hartford St Dover MA 02030 Office: 60 State St Boston MA 02209

VAN KLOBERG, EDWARD JOSEPH, III, univ. dean; b. N.Y.C., Jan. 9, 1942; s. Edward J. and Eustelle Mary (Molyneux) Van K.; B.A. in History and Lit., Rider Coll., 1965; M.A., American U., 1968, postgrad., 1965-68. Lectr. in history Am. U., Washington, summer, 1968, teaching fellow, 1969-70, asst. to chmn. dept. history, 1969-70, dir. Office of Transfer, Grad. Admissions, and Fin. Aid, 1972-74, asso. dean, 1974-75, dean Office of Admissions, 1975—, asst. to v.p. for acad. affairs, 1975-76, rep. to D.C. Grad. Consortium of Univs., 1968-69. Mem. advisory com. Ednl. Opportunity Center, Washington, 1976—; mem. advisory bd. Enrollment Analysis Inc.,

Phila., 1975—; mem. bd. advisors Close Up Found., Washington, 1976—; trustee Opportunity Project for Edn. Now, Washington, 1973-76. Mem. Am. Hist. Assn., Am. Personnel and Guidance Assn., Nat. Assn. of Coll. Admissions Counselors, Nat. Assn. Student Personnel Adminstrs., AAUP, Am. Assn. of Collegiate Registrars and Admissions Officers, Alpha Phi Omega, Pi Delta Kappa (editor newsletter 1976-77), Phi Alpha Theta (sec. 1971-), Pi Alpha Alpha. Contbr. articles on ednl. adminstrn. to profl. publs. Home: 4008 47th St Washington DC 20016 Office: American Univ Washington DC 20016

VANKOUGHNETT, GEORGE LIMBERT, food co. exec.; b. Napanee, Ont., Can., Dec. 1, 1915; s. John Ferguson and Minnie Etta (Van Alstyne) vanK.; certificate mktg. mgmt. U. Western Ont., 1956; m. Dorothy Cowling, Aug. 1, 1942; children—Gregory, Kathleen. Nat. sales promotion mgr. Seagram's Distillers Ltd., Montreal, Que., 1952-54; devel. mgr. Seagram Overseas Corp., Montreal, 1954-58, dir. mktg., 1958-64; dir. mktg. Nat. House Coffee, Ltd., Montreal, 1964-67; pres. Exec. Coffee Service, Ltd., Montreal, 1967—; lectr. mktg. U. Montreal, 1957-60, Concordia U., 1962-64, U. Waterloo, 1965-66. Served with Canadian Army, 1939-45. Decorated Canadian Vol. Service medal and Clasp, Efficiency medal and 2 clasps, Queen's Jubilee medal; recipient Presdl. Commendation Advt. and Sales Execs. Club Montreal, 1966; Kiwanis Lt. Gov.'s Bronze Plaque, 1962. Mem. United Empire Loyalist Assn. Can. (charter pres. heritage br. 1972-74), Advt. and Sales Exec. Club Montreal (pres. 1964-65), Nat. Coffee Service Assn. (dir. 1975-76), Internat. Coffee Service Inst. (chmn. 1972—), Order of Meritorious Heritage (chancellor). Progressive Conservative. Anglican Ch. Clubs: Kiwanis (lt. gov. 1961-62), Masons. Office: 2291 46th Ave Lachine Quebec H8T 3C9 Canada

VAN LANDINGHAM, LEANDER SHELTON, JR., patent lawyer; b. Memphis, July 15, 1925; s. Leander Shelton and Bertha (Shumaker) Van L.; B.S. in Chemistry, U. N.C., 1948, M.A. in Organic Chemistry, 1949; J.D., Georgetown U., 1955; m. Henrietta Adena Stapf, July 5, 1959; children—Ann Henrietta, Leander Shelton III. Patent adviser Dept. Navy, Washington, 1953-55; admitted to D.C. bar, 1955, since practiced in Washington met. area; cons. patent, trademark and copyright law, chem. patent matters, 1955—. Served to lt. USNR, 1943-46, 1951-53. Mem. Am. Chem. Soc., Sci. Assn., Fed., Am., D.C. bar assns., Am. Patent Law Assn., Am. Judicature Soc., Sigma Xi, Phi Alpha Delta. Methodist. Home: 10726 Stanmore Dr Potomac Falls Potomac MD 20854 Office: Suite 507 2001 Jefferson Davis Hwy Arlington VA 22202

VAN LEIGHT, PETER ROBERT, communications exec.; b. Bklyn., Apr. 18, 1935; s. Eugene and Irma (Fink von Finkenstein zu Hohenstein) Van L.; B.A., Brown U., 1957; M.Archaeology, Mexico City U., 1956; m. Joan Aimee van Schreik, 1958, div., 1970; children—Nicole, Erik; m. 2d, Nancy Elizabeth Arnold, May 20, 1972; 1 dau., Courtney. Advt. staff exec. Time Inc., N.Y.C., 1961-63; advt. sales exec. Conde Nast Publs., N.Y.C., 1963-67; v.p. advt. sales N.Y. Mag., 1967-74; advt. sales dir., v.p. Saturday Rev., N.Y.C., 1974-76; sr. v.p., dir. mktg. Am. Banker, N.Y.C., 1976—; chmn. Internat. Subaquatic Indistries Inc.; mem. Post Master's Gen. Adv. Com., 1970-71. Served to USN, 1958-61. Recipient Meyer Sniffen award Union League Club, 1969. Mem. Mag. Pubs. Assn., Nat. Acad. TV Arts and Scis., U.S. Darting Assn., Subscription Fullfillment Mgrs. Assn., New Eng. Soc., Vets. Corps. Arty. N.Y. Clubs: Union League, Bombay Bicycle. Home: 16 Old Orchard Dr Weston CT 06883 Office: 325 West End Ave New York City NY 10023

VAN METER, RALPH MARMON, gynecologist; b. Bridgeton, N.J., Sept. 29, 1911; s. Harmon L. and Lillie V. (Harvey) Van M.; A.B., Temple U., 1941, M.D., 1944; m. Margaret Minch, Aug. 19, 1939; children—Janice, Lawrence, Gretchen. Intern, Pa. Hosp., Phila., 1944-45, resident obstetrician, gynecologist, 1945-46, 47-48, asst. gynecologist, 1951-74, gynecologist, 1974—; chief of obstetrics and gynecology, Burlington County Meml. Hosp., 1950-72; asso. gynecologist, 1972—. Served to capt. M.C. U.S. Army, 1945-47, 53. Fellow Am. Coll. Obstetricians and Gynecologists (chmn. N.J. sect., 1966-69); mem. N.J., Burlington County (pres., 1960-61) med. socs., N.J. Obstetrical and Gynecol. Soc., AAAS, N.J. Obstetrical and Gynecol. Travel Club (exec. com.). Address: 244 W Main St Moorestown NJ 08057

VANN, JOHN DANIEL, III, librarian, educator; b. Raleigh, N.C., June 14, 1935; s. John Daniel and Sybil Dean (Wilson) V.; student summers Northwestern U., 1952, Furman U., 1953-54; B.A., U. N.C., 1957; M.A., Yale U., 1959, Ph.D., 1965; postgrad. Columbia U. Tchrs. Coll., 1962-63; M.Librarianship, Emory U., 1971; postdoctoral scholar Stanford U., 1977-78; m. Ellen Jane Rogers, June 21, 1969; children—John Daniel IV, Justin Fitz Patrick. Asso. prof. history Campbell Coll., 1961-63; bibliographer European history, lit., asst. reference librarian Newberry Library, Chgo., 1963-65; prof. history Calif. Baptist Coll., 1965-66; dir. library, prof. history Bapt. Coll., Charleston, S.C., 1966-69; librarian Keuka Coll., Keuka Park, N.Y., 1969-71; chief librarian, prof. library, chmn. dept. S.I. Community Coll., City U. N.Y., 1971-76; dep. chief librarian, prof. library Coll. Staten Island, City U. N.Y., 1976—. Trustee Maplewood (N.J.) Pub. Library. Council on Library Resources acad. library mgmt. intern, 1977-78. Mem. Am. Hist. Assn., ALA (chmn. sect., coms.), Bibliog. Soc. Am., Library Assn. City U. N.Y., Mediaeval Acad. Am., Archons of Colophon, Beta Phi Mu, Phi Alpha Theta. Baptist. Club: Rotary. Contbr. articles to profl. jours. Home: 26 Hickory Dr Maplewood NJ 07040 Office: 715 Ocean Terr New York City NY 10301

VAN NOSTRAND, JOAN FEDELL (MRS. LYMAN G. VAN NOSTRAND), statistician, govt. ofcl.; b. Pitts., Oct. 1, 1944; d. John Charles and Rose M. (Madia) Fedell; B.S. cum laude, Am. U., 1966; m. Lyman G. Van Nostrand, Aug. 25, 1972. Statistician, Office Dir. Nat. Center Health Statistics, HEW, Washington, 1966-67, survey statistician health facilities statistics br., 1968-70, asst. chief br., Rockville, Md., 1971-74, chief long term care statistics br., 1974—; liaison to cons. panel on long term care U.S. Vital and Health Statistics Com., 1976—; del. Internat. Conf. on Women in Health, 1975; mem. Young Profls. Adv. Council to Adminstr. Health Services and Mental Health Adminstrn., 1971-72. Mary Graydon scholar, 1962-66. Mem. Am. Statis. Assn., Gerontol. Soc., Internat. Assn. Survey Statisticians, Am. Pub. Health Assn., Phi Kappa Phi, Psi Chi. Contbr. articles and statis. surveys on nursing facilities and costs to profl. pubs. Home: 10765 Deborah Dr Potomac MD 20854 Office: 3700 East West Hwy Hyattsville MD 20782

VAN PATTEN, MICHAEL ROBERT, accountant; b. Niskayuna, N.Y., July 17, 1948; s. Earl Rowland and Margaret (Smith) Van P.; B.B.A. cum laude, Siena Coll., 1971; M.S., State U. N.Y., Albany, 1972; m. Judith A. Synfelt, Oct. 16, 1971; children—Brittany Michelle, Kelly Michele. Sr. accountant Peat Marwick Mitchell & Co., Albany, 1972-74; accounting systems analyst Norton Co., Troy, N.Y., 1974; mgr. gen. accounting, div. dir. taxes, 1974-75; controller CR Wood Enterprises, Lake George, N.Y., 1975-76; pvt. practice accounting, Latham, N.Y., 1977—; asst. prof. accounting Siena Coll., Loudonville, N.Y., 1975—; cons. SBA. Campaign chmn. Schenectady Republican Com., 1977; asst. commr. Schenectady Babe Ruth League, 1977; exec. dir. Econ. Revitalization Com., VISTA, 1977-78. Served to capt. N.Y. Army N.G., 1965—. C.P.A., N.Y. Mem. Am. Inst. C.P.A.'s, N.Y. State Soc. C.P.A.'s, Am. Assn. Accountants, Nat. Assn. Accountants, AAUP. Methodist. Club: Edison. Home: 1092 Brierwood Blvd Schenectady NY 12308 Office: 1202 Troy Schenectady Rd Latham NY 12110

VAN RAAY, JANICE ELIZABETH, artist, photographer; b. Bklyn., May 27, 1942; d. Gradus Hermanus Jacobus and Mildred Amanda (Buckneberg) Van R.; student Abracheff Sch. Art, 1960-67; student N.Y. U., 1960-63, New Sch. for Social Research, 1963-65; m. David Paul Curtis, Mar. 24, 1968; 1 son, Cassidy Jonathan. One-woman shows include: Hansen Galleries, N.Y.C., 1974, 77, N.Y. Pub. Library, 1977, U. Tenn., 1978; group shows include: Galeries Raymond Duncan, Paris, 1966, Allied Artists Am., 1966, Audubon Artists Ann. Exhbn., 1967, Ogunquit (Maine) Art Center, 1963-68; represented in permanent art collections including: Mus. Modern Art, N.Y. Pub. Library, U. Tenn., Chattanooga, U. Exeter (Eng.), Archiv Conz, Asolo, Italy; exhibited photographs in one-woman shows: Focus II Photo Gallery, N.Y.C., Discovery Gallery, N.Y.C., N.Y. Pub. Library; exhibited photographs in group shows: Documenta V, Kassel, W. Ger., U. Toronto, 1972, Finch Coll., N.Y., 1971, U. Wash., 1971; represented in permanent photograph collections including: Mus. Modern Art, Archiv Sohm, W. Ger., N.Y. Pub. Library, U. Tenn.; lectr. art and photography Bklyn. Pub. Library. Mem. Sons of Norway. Author: Second Coming, 1977; Verhaltens Forscher, 1978; G.A.A.G. Guerrilla Art Action Group, 1978. Home: 135 Eastern Pkwy Brooklyn NY 11238

VAN RENSSELAER, SERENA MILES, breeder dogs; b. N.Y.C., Jan. 29, 1912; d. Robert Mickle and Serena Chestnut (Williams) Miles; student Barnard Coll., 1929-30, N.Y. Sch. Applied Design, 1930-31; m. Hendrik B. Van Rensselaer, Oct. 25, 1932; children—Hendrik B., Stephanie Van Rensselaer (Koven), Robert M. Breeder purebred Old English Sheepdogs, Fezziwig Kennels, Basking Ridge, N.Y., 1935—. Mem. Sussex Hills Kennel Club (dir. 1971-72), Old English Sheepdog Club Am. (del. to Am. Kennel Club 1975—, dog portraitist, ofcl. illustrator 1959—), Colonial Dames Am. Democrat. Episcopalian. Author: The Breed Manual of the Old English Sheepdog Club of America, 1974. Contbr. articles Old English sheepdogs to dog mags., lectr. in field. Home: RFD Youngs Rd Box 120 Basking Ridge NJ 07920

VAN ROOSBROECK, WILLY WERNER, research physicist; b. Antwerp, Belgium, Aug. 10, 1913; s. Gustave Leopold and Marie Joanna (De Graef) van R.; came to U.S., 1916, naturalized, 1921; A.B., Columbia, 1934, M.A., 1937; m. Marjorie Anna Covert, Oct. 7, 1945. Mem. tech. staff Bell Labs., Murray Hill, N.J., 1937-78; cons., 1978—. Recipient Van Buren prize in math., Columbia, 1934. Fellow Am. Phys. Soc.; mem. AAAS, Phi Beta Kappa. Contbr. articles to profl. jours. Home: 19 Whittredge Rd Summit NJ 07901

VAN ROOSEN, DONALD COLLETT, pollution control co. exec.; b. Boston, Aug. 11, 1923; s. Hugo and Ellen (Halck) Van R.; A.B. in English, Harvard, 1948; m. Nancy Johnston Crough, June 10, 1950; children—Christine, Laurie, Hugh. Dist. mgr. Hercules Gasket & Rubber Co., Buffalo, 1953-56; asst. sales mgr. Manton-Gaulin Mfg. Co., Everett, Mass., 1956-63, div. mgr., dir. market research Gaulin Corp., 1965-70; dist. mgr. McGraw-Hill Co., Boston, 1963-65; div. mgr., corporate marketing mgr. Columbia Precision Corp., Wilmington, Mass., 1970-73; dir. internat. marketing Applicon Inc., Burlington, Mass., 1973—; asst. to pres. Airtek Corp., Newton, Mass., 1977—. Organizer, Worcester County (Mass.) Republican Com., 1956; mem. Winchester Rep. Com., 1954-56. Pres., Friends of Harvard Fencing, 1969—; pres. Minuteman council Boy Scouts Am., 1976—; pres. New Eng. div. Amateur Fencing League Am., 1970-71. Served with inf. AUS, 1943-45; ETO. Decorated Silver Star, Bronze Star with oak leaf cluster, Purple Heart with 2 oak leaf clusters; Croix de Guerre (France). Recipient Dist. Merit award Boy Scouts Am., 1973, Silver Beaver award, 1977. Mem. Am. Inst. Chem. Engrs., Am. Mgmt. Assn., Am Marketing Assn. (dir. indsl. marketing group). Clubs: Harvard, Appalachian Mountain (Boston). Home: 12 Woodside Rd Winchester MA 01890 Office: One Wells Ave Newton MA 02154

VAN SICKLE, JOHN BABCOCK, classicist, educator; b. Freeport, Ill., Sept. 30, 1936; s. John Rowley and Mary Kathryn (Babcock) Van S.; A.B. cum laude, Harvard U., 1958, Ph.D., 1966; A.M., U. Ill., 1959; m. Giulia Battaglia, Dec. 28, 1965. Instr., then asst. prof. classical studies U. Pa., 1965-71; vis. asso. prof. classics Brown U., 1971-72; prof.-in-charge, vis. prof. Intercollegiate Center for Classical Studies (Stanford U.), Rome, 1972-74; asso. prof. Bklyn. Coll. and Grad. Sch., City U. N.Y., 1976-78, prof. classics, 1978—; Fulbright fellow, Rome, 1963-65; fellow Humanities Center Johns Hopkins U., 1969-70; jr. fellow Trustees for Harvard U. Center for Hellenic Studies, Washington, 1974-75. Recipient Summer stipend Nat. Endowment for Humanities, 1978; Guggenheim fellow, 1978-79. Mem. Am. Philol. Assn. Soc. Promotion Roman Studies, Soc. Promotion Hellenic Studies, Classical Assn. (Gt. Brit.). Vergilian Soc. Am. Author: The Design of Virgil's Bucolics, 1978; contbr. articles, revs. to profl. jours.; Atlantic states editor Classical Jour., 1978; corr. editor Quaderni Urbinati di Cultura Classica, 1977; guest editor Arethusa, 1976. Home: 380 Riverside Dr 6 T New York City NY 10025 Office: Classical Studies City U NY Grad Center 33 W 42d St New York City NY 10036

VAN SICLEN, CORNELIA, interior designer; b. Jamaica, N.Y.; d. George Tyler and Estelle (VanDime) Watts; student Packer Collegiate Inst.; m. Ira Emerich, Oct. 17, 1958. With Elisabeth Draper Inc., N.Y.C., 1945-46, Neiman Marcus, Dallas, 1946-47, Smythe, Wrquart & Marckwald Inc., N.Y.C., 1947-48, Elsie McNeil Inc., N.Y.C., 1949, John Gerold Asso., N.Y.C., 1955-57; pvt. practice interior design, N.Y.C., 1949-55; interior designer asso. Jones & Erwin Inc., N.Y.C., 1957-76; owner, mgr. Cornelia Van Siclen, N.Y.C. 1976—. Trustee, Old Merchants House Inc., 1968—; trustee Chapin Home for Aging, 1971-78. Mem. Am. Soc. Interior Designers. Republican. Club: Decorators (pres. 1977—). Home and office: 45 Sutton Place S New York City NY 10022

VAN SPLINTER, GERALD ARTHUR, travel advt. mgr., mag. exec.; b. Passaic, N.J., June 28, 1930; s. John Kerns and Ruth Mae (Horton) Van S.; B.B.A., Upsala Coll., 1953; m. Anne Iverson, Sept. 12, 1953; children—Kyle Anne, Gerald Arthur. Sales rep. U.S. Steel Co., N.Y.C., 1957-63; v.p. Haff Supply Co., Amityville, N.Y., 1963-65; asst. Eastern advt. mgr. Los Angeles Times, N.Y.C., 1965-67; travel advt. mgr. Nat. Geog. Mag., N.Y.C., 1968—; chmn. media mktg. com. U.S. Travel Data Center. Co-chmn. Multiple Sclerosis Tennis Tournament, Suffolk County, N.Y., 1975—. Served to lt. USNR, 1953-56. Mem. Caribbean Hotel Assn., Caribbean Tourism Assn., Pacific Area Travel Assn., Am. Soc. Travel Agts., Discover Am. Travel Orgns., Am. Hotel and Motel Assn. Republican. Presbyterian. Home: 17 Intervale Rd Setauket NY 11733 Office: 1251 Ave of Americas New York City NY 10020

VAN SWOL, NOEL WARREN, educator; b. N.Y.C., Dec. 30, 1941; s. Erwin Anton and Hildegard van S.; B.A., Am. U., 1964; M.A., Columbia U., 1967; M.S., Syracuse U., 1972. Asst. underwriter Comml. Union Ins. Group Ltd., N.Y.C., 1964-66; tchr. social studies jr. high sch., Bklyn., 1966-67, Liberty (N.Y.) Central High Sch., 1967-69; instr. student personnel Sullivan County (N.Y.) Community Coll., 1969-70; tchr. social studies E. Syracuse-Minoa (N.Y.) High Sch., 1970—, coordinator social studies, 1976—; cons. to trainer of tchr. trainers project Syracuse U., 1971-74. Vice pres. Fremont (N.Y.) Taxpayers and Civic Assn., 1971; mem. Task Force Against Nuclear Pollution, Inc. Tchr. Leadership Devel. fellow, 1971. Mem. Am. Hist. Assn., N.Y. State Hist. Assn., Am. Polit. Sci. Assn., Assn. Supervision and Curriculum Devel., Nat., N.Y. State, Central N.Y. councils social studies, Orgn. Am. Historians, Soc. for History Edn., Upper Delaware Scenic River Assn. Republican. Home: Rt 97 Long Eddy NY 12760

VANTINE, A. WILLIAM, ednl. adminstr.; b. Buffalo, Mar. 19, 1935; B.S. in Elementary Edn., SUNY, Buffalo, 1958, M.S. in Secondary Edn., 1961, Ed.D. in Ednl. Adminstrn., 1970; married; 4 children. Adminstrv. asst. Cheektowaga (N.Y.) Central Sch. Dist., 1967-69; mgmt. cons. Thealan Assos., Albany, N.Y., 1969-70; dir. personnel Mt. Lebanon Sch. Dist., Pitts., 1970-73; supt. Abington Heights Sch. Dist., Clarks Summit, Pa., 1973—. Bd. dirs. Visiting Nurse Assn., 1974—; mem. exec. com. State Adv. Council on Vocat. Edn. Mem. Am., Pa. Assn. Sch. Adminstrs. (pres.-elect N.E. Pa. chpt.), Assn. Ednl. Negotiators, Phi Delta Kappa. Office: 218 E Grove St Clarks Summit PA 18411

VAN TONGEREN, HERK, sculptor, arts adminstr.; b. Holland, Mich., Aug. 19, 1943; s. Harold Vernon and Sally Ann Van T.; B.A., U. Colo., 1968, M.F.A., 1970; 1 son, Trygve Erling. Instr., U. N.C., Greensboro, 1971-74; asst. mgr. Art Castings Colo., Loveland, 1974-75; asst. prof. art San Diego State U., 1975-77; exec. dir. Johnson Atelier Tech. Inst. Sculpture, Princeton, 1978—; dir. corp. offices Internat. Sculpture Center, Princeton, 1978—; mem. faculty U. B.C. (Can.), summers 1976-77; lectr. U. Mass., Amherst, summer 1978; one-man shows: U. Colo., 1969, U. N.C., Greensboro, 1973, San Diego State U., 1975, Burnaby Art Gallery, Vancouver, B.C., Can., 1977; group shows include: Denver Art Mus., 1969, Dean Gallery Mpls., 1970, U. N.C. Weatherspoon Art Gallery, 1970, 72, Salem Coll. Fine Arts, 1971, Mint Mus., Charlotte, N.C., 1972, 73 (2), Gallery Contemporary Art, Winston-Salem, N.C., 1973, Calif. State U., Los Angeles, 1976 (honorable mention), Riverside (Calif.) Art Mus., 1976, Livingston Coll., Rutgers U. 1978, Mill Valley Art Gallery, San Francisco, 1978; represented in permanent collections: Burnaby Art Gallery, U. Colo., Weatherspoon Art Gallery U. N.C., also numerous pvt. collections; condr. workshops in field. Recipient honorarium Duke U., 1974, Coll. Marin, 1976, SUNY, Purchase, 1978, Art Students League, N.Y.C., 1978; U. Colo. scholar, 1968-69, 69-70, research grantee, 1967-68, 68-69, 69-70, material grantee, 1967, 69; U. N.C. at Greensboro grantee, 1973; Soc. B.C. Sculptors grantee, 1976. Mem. Sculptors Soc. B.C. (hon.). Editor Sculptor's News Exchange, 1978—. Home: ETTL Farm Rosedale Rd Princeton NJ 08540 Office: 743 Alexander Rd Princeton NJ 08540

VAN VECHTEN, FREDERICK RUST, lawyer; b. Little Falls, N.Y., May 4, 1916; s. Frederick Rust and Alma (Newell) Van V.; grad. Hotchkiss Sch., 1934; B.A., Yale, 1938, LL.B., 1941. Admitted to N.Y. bar, 1942; asso. Webster Sheffield Fleischmann Hitchcock & Chrystie, N.Y.C., and predecessor firms, 1941-42, 45-64, mem. firm Webster & Sheffield, 1965—. Trustee Rye (N.Y.) Hist. Soc., pres., 1973-76; trustee Rye YMCA, pres. 1966-69. Served to lt. USNR, 1942-46. Fellow Am. Coll. Probate Counsel; mem. Assn. Bar City of N.Y. (chmn. com. on trusts, estates, surrogate's cts. 1969-72), St. Nicholas Soc. N.Y.C. Presbyn. (former trustee). Clubs: Apawamis (Rye); Yale (N.Y.C.). Home: 28 Walnut St Rye NY 10580 Office: 1 Rockefeller Plaza New York City NY 10020

VAN VLECK, JOHN HASBROUCK, physicist; b. Middletown, Conn., Mar. 13, 1899; s. Edward Burr and Hester Laurence (Raymond) Van V.; A.B., U. Wis., 1920, Sc.D., 1947; A.M., Harvard U., 1921; Ph.D., 1922, Sc.D., 1966; Sc.D., Wesleyan U., 1936, U. Md., 1955, Rockford Coll., 1961, U. Chgo., 1968, U. Nancy (France), 1961, U. Minn., 1971; Dr. honoris causa, U. Grenoble, 1950, U. Paris, 1960; Sc.D. honoris causa, Oxford (Eng.) U., 1958; m. Abigail June Pearson, June 10, 1927. Instr. physics Harvard U., 1922-23, asso. prof. math. physics, 1934-35, prof., 1935—, chmn. physics dept., 1945-49, Hollis prof. math. and nat. philosophy, 1951-69, emeritus, 1969—, dean engring. and applied physics, 1951-57; asst. prof. physics U. Minn., 1923-26, asso. prof., 1926-27, prof., 1927-28; prof. theoretical physics U. Wis., 1928-34. Vis. lectr. Stanford, 1927, 34, 41, U. Mich., 1933, Columbia U., 1934, Princeton U., 1937; Lorentz prof., Leiden, 1960; Eastman prof. Oxford (Eng.) U., 1961-62; head theory group Radio Research Lab., Harvard U., 1943-45; cons. Radiation Lab., Mass. Inst. Tech., 1942-45; asso. editor various phys. jour. Guggenheim Meml. Found. fellow, 1930. Decorated chevalier Legion of Honor (France); recipient Albert A. Michelson award Case Inst. Tech., 1963; Irving Langmuir award in chem. physics Gen. Elec. Found., 1965; Nat. Medal of Sci., 1966; Distinguished Service award U. Wis. Alumni Assn., 1967, Cresson medal Franklin Inst., 1971; Lorentz medal Netherlands Acad., 1974; co-recipient Nobel prize in physics, 1977. Fellow Am. Phys. Soc. (councillor 1932-35, pres. 1952-53), AAAS (v.p. 1960), Am. Acad. Arts and Scis. (v.p. 1956-57); mem. Nat. Acad. Sci., Am. Philos. Soc., Internat. Acad. Quantum Molecular Sci., Am. Math. Soc., Holland Soc. N.Y. (medal 1969), Netherlands Phys. Soc., Phi Beta Kappa, Sigma Xi; hon. mem. Societe Francaise de Physique; fgn. mem. Royal Netherlands Acad. Scis., Royal Soc. Sci. Uppsala, Royal Swedish Acad. Sci., Royal Soc. London, Acad. des Sciences (France). Presbyterian. Author: Quantum Principles and Line Spectra, 1926; The Theory of Electric and Magnetic Susceptibilities, 1932. Address: Lyman Lab Harvard U Cambridge MA 02138

VAN VORIS, FIL E., bus. exec.; b. Bklyn., July 16, 1917; s. Millard Filmore and Pearl (Everett) Van V.; Metall. Engr., Colo. Sch. Mines, 1939; postgrad. Mass. Inst. Tech., 1956; M.B.A. with honors, State U. N.Y., Buffalo, 1972; m. Jean Wigton, Sept. 4, 1941; children—Lee, Peter, Matthew. With Bethlehem Steel Co., 1939-56, asst. mgr. Steel div., 1950-56; mgr. tech. service, gen. mgr. tech. service product devel. Union Carbide Co., Niagara Falls, N.Y. and N.Y.C., 1956-72; v.p. sales St. Joe Minerals Corp., N.Y.C., 1972-75, v.p. planning, 1975-76; v.p., gen. mgr. recycling div., natural resource group Gulf & Western Industries, Inc., Bethlehem, Pa., 1976-77; pres. Van Voris Assos., Scarborough, N.Y., 1978—; asso. prof. and dir. Center Mgmt. Devel., Sch. Mgmt., State U. N.Y. at Buffalo, 1978—. Chmn., United Gifts Fund, Niagara Falls, 1966-67. Mem. Am., Brit. iron and steel insts., Am. Inst. Mining, Metall. and Petroleum Engrs. (past chmn.), Am. Soc. Metals, Zinc Inst. (v.p., mem. exec. com. 1975), Lead Industries Assn. (v.p., mem. exec. com.), Cleve. Engring. Soc., Met. Econ. Soc. N.Y.C., Colo. Sch. Mines Alumni Assn. (pres. N.Y.C. 1974-75), Mining Club N.Y.C. Republican. Episcopalian. Clubs: Pine Valley Golf; Sleepy Hollow Country (Scarborough). Contbr. articles to profl.

jours. Home: 7 Scarborough Circle Scarborough NY 10510 Office: Scarborough PO Scarborough NY 10510

VAN WINKLE, ARTHUR D., real estate and ins. exec.; b. Rutherford, N.J., Mar. 11, 1911; s. Charles A. and Helen (Decker) Van W.; grad. Babson Inst., 1932; m. Gretchen Horn, Feb. 23, 1934 (div. Oct. 1973); children—Joan (Mrs. David F. Cunningham), Daniel Horn, Linda (Mrs. Thomas W. Watkins III); m. 2d, Adelaide Shaffer Campbell, Nov. 1, 1973. Past pres. A.W. Van Winkle & Co., 1932-49; chmn. bd. Van Winkle & Liggett, gen. real estate, ins. brokers, 1949-76, chmn. bd., 1976—; pres. Central Guaranty Mortgage & Title Co., 1958-68, Rutherford Equities, 1972—; pres., treas. Rutherford Investment Co., 1972—, Mystic Island Co., 1960—; v.p., dir. Chelsea Title & Guaranty Co., Atlantic City, 1968—; dir. United Jersey Bank, United Jersey Banks Holding Co. Past pres., mem. N.J. Assn. Real Estate Bds., N.J. chpt. Am. Inst. Real Estate Appraisers, South Bergen County Bd. Realtors. Past pres. Rutherford YMCA. Trustee Centenary Coll. for Women, Hackettstown, N.J.; gov. Hackensack (N.J.) Hosp.; mem. adv. bd. Ladies Residence, Hackensack, N.J. Mem. Holland Soc. N.Y., Inst. Real Estate Mgmt., Nat. Assn. Real Estate Brokers, Rutherford C. of C. (dir. 1943). Republican. Presbyn. (past trustee). Mason, Elk, Rotarian (past. pres.). Clubs: Masons Island Yacht (past commodore) (Mystic, Conn.); Hackensack Golf. Home: 125 Prospect Ave Hackensack NJ 07601 also Mason's Island Mystic CT also 1000 Lowry St Delray Beach FL Office: 85 Orient Way Rutherford NJ 07070

VANZANDT, DOROTHY PERKINS, nutritionist; b. Wilmington, Del., Sept. 4, 1913; d. Charles Furry and Florence Ella (Porter) Perkins; B.S., Pa. State U., 1935; teaching certificate, U. Md., 1956; M.S., Tex. Woman's U., 1967, Ph.D., 1969; m. Mordecai Moore VanZandt, July 3, 1937; children—Suellen, Stephen Charles, John Michael. Home econ. rep. Pa. Coop. Extension Service, New Bloomfield, Pa., 1935-37; Farm Security Adminstrn., Lewisburg, Pa., 1938-40; tchr. Pimmit Hills Elementary Sch., Fairfax County, Va., 1956-57; tchr. home econs. Gurrie Central Jr. High Sch., LaGrange, Ill., 1959-66; food and nutrition specialist, acting asst. dir. extension home econs. Md. Coop. Extension Service, College Park, Md., 1969—. Mem. Md., Am. home econ. assns., Md., Am. dietetic assns., AAUW, Kappa Kappa Gamma, Omicron Nu, Iota Sigma Pi, Epsilon Sigma Phi. Club: Altrusa. Home: 11809 Stonington Pl Silver Spring MD 20902 Office: 1202 Symons Hall Univ Md College Park MD 20742

VARANO, DOMINICK, dentist; b. Reggio Calabria, Italy, Feb. 23, 1931 (parents Am. citizens); s. Salvatore and Rose (Cianflone) V.; A.A.S. (Stenberg Meml. medal N.Y.C. Community Coll., 1952; student (Founders Day award) N.Y. U., 1958, D.D.S. (Thaler award), 1962; m. Kathleen Blodgett, Aug. 17, 1963; children—Sal Raymond, Kenneth, Mark. Pvt. practice dentistry, Bklyn., 1962—; asst. clin. prof. N.Y. U. Coll. Dentistry, 1962—. Mem. Bay Ridge Community Council, 1968—, Bay Ridge Civic Assn., 1970—. Served with USAF, 1952-56. Recipient certificate honor Soc. Dental Research, 1962. Mem. ADA, Bay Ridge (pres. 1970-72), 2d Dist., Italian dental socs., Omicron Kappa Upsilon. Home: 1024 79th St Brooklyn NY 11228 Office: 365 77th St Brooklyn NY 11209

VARGA, NICHOLAS, educator; b. Elizabeth, N.J., Sept. 13, 1925; s. Joseph and Anna (Bucko) V.; student Syracuse U., 1943; B.S., Boston Coll., 1951, M.A., 1952; postgrad. Columbia U., 1948-51; Ph.D., Fordham U., 1960; postgrad. Morgan State U., 1968, Case Western Reserve U., 1977; m. Margaret Joan Skinner, Sept. 8, 1951; children—Deidre Kayne, Damian Guy, Colin Peire. Instr., Loyola Coll., Balt., 1955-59, asst. prof., 1959-62, acting chmn. Dept. History, 1962-64, chmn. Dept. History, 1964-67, asso. prof., 1962-66, prof. history, 1967—, archivist, 1977—; cons. Am. Hist. Assn. Study of NDEA summer insts., 1966. Adv. bd. United Nations Assn. Md., 1966-69, pres., 1968-69; cons. Mayor's Urban Service Corps, 1964; pres. Woodbourne Jr. High Sch. PTA, 1967-68; mem. Balt. City Bicentennial Commn., 1972-76; mem. Howard County bicentennial commn., 1975-76; mem. archdiocesan commn. on ecumenism and interreligious affairs, 1970—. Served with U.S. Army, 1943-47. Decorated Bronze Star Medal, Purple Heart. Mem. Am. Cath. Hist. Assn., Am. Hist. Assn., Orgn. Am. Historians, N.Y. Hist. Assn., Md. Hist. Soc., AAUP, Phi Alpha Theta. Byzantine Catholic. Contbr. articles in field to profl. jours.; book reviewer Sunday Sun, 1961-70. Home: 5183 Orchard Green Columbia MD 21045 Office: 4501 N Charles St Baltimore MD 21210

VARGAS, FERNANDO RODOLFO, studio exec.; b. San Jose, Costa Rica, Sept. 22, 1928; s. Elias and Elena (Zamora) V.; student RCA Inst., 1954. Engr., Audiosonic Rec. N.Y.C., 1953-61; v.p., dir. Variety Sound Corp., N.Y.C., 1962—. Address: Room 551 130 W 42d St New York City NY 10036

VARGAS, ROBERT, psychologist; b. Key West, Fla., Jan. 28, 1938; s. Victor and Caridad (Gonzalez) V.; B.E., U. Miami, 1962, B.A., 1963, M.Ed., 1964; M.S., Barry Coll., 1964; Ph.D., U. Fla., 1968; D.Sc. (hon.), Ohio Christian Coll., 1968; D.Sc., Thomas A. Edison Coll., 1974, D.D., Sch. Theology, 1976; M.D., United Am. Med. Coll., 1975. Cons. problems of desegregation and human growth Kirby-Smith Elementary Sch., Gainesville, Fla., 1965-66; instr. psychology Sante Fe Jr. Coll., Gainesville, 1966-67; counselor to residents, head counselor div. housing U. Fla., Gainesville, 1966-67, sr. research asso., 1968; dean student personnel services Southeastern Community Coll., Whiteville, N.C., 1968-69; asso. prof. counseling services Catonsville Community Coll., Balt., 1969-72, prof., 1972-77; psychologist dept. pediatrics and psychiatry Johns Hopkins Hosp., Balt., 1971-75, asst. prof. pediatrics and med. psychology Johns Hopkins U., 1971-75, instr. psychiatry, 1971-75; dir. counseling and psychol. services Youth Crisis and Counseling Center of Lighthouse, Inc., Catonsville, Md., 1971-73; vice chmn., then chmn. Md. State Bd. Examiners Psychologists, 1975-77; pvt. practice psychology, Catonsville, 1977—. Certified psychologist, Md., Pa., D.C., N.C., Fla. Diplomate Am. Bd. Profl. Psychology. Fellow Am. Orthopsychiat. Assn., AAAS, Md. Psychol. Assn. (chmn. pub. info. com. 1970-74), Royal Soc. Health; mem. Nat. Council Grad. Edn. Psychology, Am., N.C., Southeastern psychol. assns., Am. Ednl. Research Assn., AAUP, Soc. Psychophysiol. Research, Bio-feedback Soc., Assn. Humanistic Psychology, Psychologists Interested in Study Psychoanalysis, Am., Md. personnel and guidance assns., Md. Acad. Scis., Soc. Adolescent Medicine, Md. Assn. Jr. Colls., Phi Delta Kappa. Contbr. articles in field to profl. jours. Home: PO Box 3290 Catonsville MD 21228 Office: 101 Newburg Ave Catonsville MD 21228

VARNDELL, CHARLES ROBERT, cons. engring. exec.; b. Uniontown, Pa., July 5, 1924; s. Jacob Richard and Ruth O. (Brown) V.; B.S., U. Md., 1946; m. Elinor Power, July 10, 1954; children—Carolyn R., John P. Asst. bridge engr. Md. State Rds. Commn., Balt., 1946-50; civil engr. CAA, Anchorage, 1950-51; structural engr. Alaska R.R., Anchorage, 1951-52; structural engr. Rummel, Klepper & Kahl, Balt., 1952-55, head bridge dept., 1955-64, asso., 1964-68, partner, 1968—. Fellow ASCE; mem. Soc. Am. Mil. Engrs., Engring. Soc. Balt., Inst. Rapid Transit (asso.), Md. Acad. Scis., Am. Ry. Engring. Assn., Am. Rd. and Transp. Builders Assn., Prestressed, Am. concrete insts., Tau Beta Pi. Methodist. Club: Monument River Sportsmen's Assn. (Houlton, Maine). Home: 2117 Fernglen Way Baltimore MD 21228 Office: 1035 N Calvert St Baltimore MD 21202

VARNEY, CHARLES WESLEY, JR., ins. exec.; b. Rochester, N.H., Nov. 17, 1912; s. Charles Wesley and Matilda (Shepherd) V.; student New Hampton Sch., 1931; A.B., Dartmouth Coll., 1935; m. Marjorie Wainwright, Mar. 4, 1938; children—Cynthia Bisbee, Susan Helfenstein. Partner Charles W. Varney & Co., Rochester, 1935, sr. partner, 1948-63, sole owner, 1963-66, pres., also treas., 1966—; asst. treas. Grange Mut. Fire Ins. Co., 1941, treas., 1942, pres., dir., 1948—; pres. Rockingham Farmers Mut. Fire Ins. Co., Grange Ins. Bldg., Inc.; pres., treas. Varney Realty, Inc.; dir. Rochester Savs. Bank & Trust Co., Profile Bankshares, Mut. Data Inc.; adv. bd. Peerless Ins. Co. Trustee Nute High Sch. and Library, Frisbee Meml. Hosp., Eastern States Expn., Gafney Home for the Aged; bd. overseers Old Sturbridge Village. Mem. N.H. Legislature, 1937-38. Mem. N.H., Rochester hist. socs. Republican. Methodist. Mason (Shriner), Elk, Odd Fellow, Rotarian. Home: 2 Dartmouth Ln Rochester NH 03867 Office: 17 Wakefield St Rochester NH 03867

VARONA, ALBERTO JORGE, educator; b. Havana, Cuba, Apr. 19, 1921; s. Alberto A. Varona and Guillermina Valdes de la Paz; Doctor en Leyes, U. Havana, 1942; M.A. in Spanish and Spanish Am. Lit., U. Miami, 1966, Ph.D. in Spanish and Spanish Am. Lit., 1970; m. Gladys Martin, Aug. 3, 1946; children—Gladys M. Varona Lacey, Elena. Pub. defendant, Oriente, Cuba, 1943-45; prof. criminology and penal law U. Oriente, 1948-52; chief of labor dept., Oriente Province, Cuba, 1952-53; dir. labor ministry, Havana, Cuba, 1953-54; mem. Cuban Ho. of Reps., 1955-58; instr. Spanish, Hamilton Coll., Clinton, N.Y., 1965-66; asst. prof. Spanish, Wells Coll., Aurora, N.Y., 1966-71, asso. prof., 1971—. Recipient Premio Nacional Ricardo Dolz, U. Havana, 1942; John Barret prize, U. Miami, 1966. Mem. Modern Lang. Assn., Am. Assn. Tchrs. Spanish and Portuguese. Roman Catholic. Author: Cuba ante el mundo, 1960; Francisco Bilbao, revolucionario de America, 1973. Home: Main St Aurora NY 13026

VARSHNI, YATENDRA PAL, physicist; b. Allahabad, India. May 21, 1932; s. Hari Pal and Bhagyawati V.; B.Sc., U. Allahabad, 1950, M.Sc., 1952, Ph.D., 1956; came to Can., 1960. Asst. prof. U. Allahabad, 1955-60; postdoctoral fellow NRC, Ottawa, Ont., Can., 1960-62; asst. prof. U. Ottawa, 1962-65, asso. prof., 1965-69, prof., 1969—. Fellow Am., Indian phys. socs., AAAS, Inst. Physics U.K., Chem. Soc. U.K.; asso. fellow Brit. Interplanetary Soc.; mem. Am., Can. astron. socs., Can. Assn. Physicists, Royal Astron. Soc. Can., Am. Assn. Physics Tchrs., European Phys. Soc. Contbr. numerous articles to profl. jours. Home: Apt 17 350 Chapel St Ottawa ON K1N 7Z6 Canada Office: Dept Physics U Ottawa Ottawa ON K1N 6N5 Canada

VASI, CARMELO, chem. engr.; b. N.Y.C., Nov. 17, 1936; s. Frank Paul and Mary (Amoroso) V.; B.S. in Chem. Engring., Newark Coll. Engring., 1964; m. Lorraine M. Curcio, Apr. 15, 1974; children—Frank Paul, Lisa Ann, Lynn Marie, Sal Joseph. Mfg. mgr. Matheson Gas Products Co., East Rutherford, N.J., 1964-70; mgr. prodn. and customer service J.T. Baker Chm. Co., Phillipsburg, N.J., 1970-72; plant engr. Linde Spl. Gas div. Union Carbide Corp., Keasbey, N.J., 1972-73; plant engr. Sci. Gas Prodn. Co., South Plainfield, N.J., 1973-76; plant and developmental mgr. Synthatron Corp., Edgewater, N.J., 1976—. Mem. Am. Chem. Soc. Conservative Democrat. Roman Catholic. Patentee in field of prodn. of electronic and semicondr. gases. Home: 4 Hampton Pl Nutley NJ 07110

VASQUEZ, ANTHONY FOTI, clergyman; b. Cassaro, Italy, Oct. 11, 1908; s. Joseph and Carmelina (Foti) V.; A.B., Bucknell U., 1937; B.D., Crozer Theol. Sem., 1938, M.Div., 1976; D.D., Colonial Acad., 1958; m. Concetta Di Caprio, Oct. 9, 1937; children—Judith Vasquez Fonash, Vivian Claire Vasquez Stork. Ordained to ministry Bapt. Ch., 1937; dir. boys' work Phila. Bapt. Assn., 1937-41, dir. Christian edn. and youth activities, 1945-53; pastor Dietz Meml. Ch., Bklyn., 1941-45, St. John's Ch., Phila., 1953—; tchr. drama Bapt. Inst. Christian Workers, Bryn Mawr, Pa., 1954; tchr. Eastern Pa. State Penitentiary, 1946-54. Chmn. com. info. and understanding S. Phila. Citizens Com. Human Relations, 1962; mem. Phila. Fellowship. Commn., 1958-66; leader, founder Internat. Fellowship and Goodwill dels. to meet with heads of govt; apptd. Ambassador of Goodwill, City of Phila., 1969; pres. Christian Testimony to the Jew, 1971—; pres. S. Phila. Clergy Conf., 1976; trustee Phila. Assn., Crozer Theol. Sem., S. Phila. chpt. Am. Cancer Soc. Recipient Harvey Bartle honor award Phila. Bapt. Assn., 1953; Gen. Alumni Assn. citation and medallion Bucknell U., 1957; citation Italian Bapt. Conv. Am., 1961; recipient Human Relations award Phila. Commn. Human Relations, 1969; named in honor resolution Phila. City Council, 1968; Italo-Am. Press and Radio Bicentennial medallion of merit; hon. Pa. ambassador, 1973; hon. tribute Mayor and City of Phila., 1977. Mem. Italian Bapt. Assn. Am. (editor New Aurora 1955, pres. 1959-61),Italian Interdenominational Ministers Conf. Phila. and Vicinity, Am. Fedn. Italian Evangelicals (exec. sec. 1960). Author one-act plays, pageants. Home: 314 Richfield Rd Upper Darby PA 19082 Office: Saint John's Bapt Ch 13th and Tasker Sts Philadelphia PA 19148

VÁSQUEZ, FRED, chemist; b. Barranquilla, Colombia, Feb. 1, 1940; s. Manuel M. and Elizabeth A. (Gambier) V.; came to U.S., 1968, naturalized, 1976; B.S. in Chemistry and Pharmacy, Atlántico U., 1964; postgrad. Newark Coll. Egring., 1969-70; m. Marina Arcila, June 20, 1964; children—Lizbeth Marina, Fred. Dir. quality control Aluminum Anodizing Co., Barranquilla, 1963-64; tech. dir. Shulton (A. Balaguer Cd. S.A.), 1964-68; research chemist Bishop Industries, Union, N.J., 1968-70; sect. head analytical services Beecham Products Co., Clifton, N.J., 1970—. U.S. State Dept. fellow, 1963. Mem. Soc. Cosmetics Chemists, Am. Chem. Soc. Democrat. Roman Catholic. Home: 38 Fremont Terr Oak Ridge NJ 07438

VASSAR, BARBARA ELLEN, counselor; b. Springfield, Mass., July 25, 1930; d. Albert Leo and Grace Kathryn (Duffy) Benhard; student Am. Internat. Coll., 1947-49; B.A. in Psychology cum laude, Central Conn. State Coll., 1975, M.S. Edn. in Guidance and Counseling, 1976; m. William Gerald Vassar, June 21, 1952; children—William Gerald, James Paul, Richard Gregory, Carol Ann. Sec., Mass. Mut. Life Ins. Co., Springfield, 1949-53; grad. asst. in psychology Central Conn. State Coll., 1975-76; ednl. counselor, follow-through counseling program Dept. Correction Prison Sch., Conn. Correctional Instn., Cheshire, 1976-78; guidance counselor Roosevelt Middle Sch., New Britain, Conn., 1978—. Mem. parent adv. com. Martin Kellogg Middle Sch., Newington, Conn., 1972-73, 76-77. Recipient Outstanding Contbn. to Psychology Dept. citation Central Conn. State Coll., 1976; certified guidance counselor, Conn. Mem. Am. Personnel and Guidance Assn., Nat. Vocat. Guidance Assn., Pub. Offender Counselor Assn., Psi Chi (v.p., sec.-treas. local chpt. 1975-76). Democrat. Roman Catholic. Home: 47 Dowd St Newington CT 06111 Office: 40 Goodwin St New Britain CT 06051

VASSELL, MILTON OLIVER, physicist; b. Jamaica, W.I., May 8, 1931; s. Septimus Joseph and Ruby Venetia (Watson) V.; B.A. cum laude (Univ. Fgn. Students Tuition grantee), N.Y. U., 1958, Ph.D. in Physics (Univ. fellow), 1964; m. Dorine Mazrine Black, Sept. 6, 1958; children—Karyn Hope, Sheldon Oliver. Tech. asst. Courant Inst. Math. Scis., N.Y. U., 1956-58, lectr. physics Coll. Engring., 1959-64, grad. asst., 1960-64; mem. tech. staff G. C. Dewey Corp., N.Y.C., 1958-63; research scientist GTE Labs., N.Y.C., 1964-72, Waltham, Mass., 1972—. Recipient Founders Day award N.Y. U., 1958, 64; Black Achievers in Industry award N.Y. Harlem YMCA, 1972. Mem. Am. Phys. Soc., Phi Beta Kappa, Sigma Xi, Pi Mu Epsilon, Sigma Pi Sigma. Methodist. Club: Rotary (Acton, Mass.). Contbr. articles to profl. jours. Home: 33 Flint Rd Acton MA 01720 Office: 40 Sylvan Rd Waltham MA 02154

VASSILIOU, ANDREAS HAJI, mineralogist; b. Ora, Larnaca, Cyprus, Nov. 30, 1936; s. Vassilis Nicolaou and Paraskevi (Maou) V.; came to U.S., 59, naturalized, 1975; B.S., Columbia U., 1963, M.A., 1965, Ph.D., 1969; m. Marika Hensel, Sept. 7, 1965; 1 child, Alexia. Asst. prof. Rutgers U., Newark, 1969-75, asso. prof., 1975—, chmn. dept. geology, 1977—; cons. mineral.-geochem. problems to pvt. cos. Mem. Geol. Soc. Am., Mineral. Soc. Am., AAUP, Sigma Xi. Greek Orthodox. Contbr. articles in field to profl. jours. Home: 15 Neptune Ct Somerset NJ 08873 Office: Geology Dept Rutgers U Newark NJ 07102

VASSILIOU, EUSTATHIOS, chemist; b. Athens, Greece, Aug. 22, 1934; s. Theodore and Evlalia (Porfiriou) V.; B.Sc. in Chem. Engring., Nat. Tech. U. of Athens, Greece, 1958; Ph.D. in Chemistry (State Scholarships Found. of Greece scholar 1961-63, NATO grant 1963-64), Victoria U., Manchester, Eng., 1964; m. Kleoniki I. Vassiliou; children—Theodore, Helen, Evelyn. Analyst, Materials Test Center of Creek Armed Forces, Athens, 1959-60; research scientist Nuclear Research Center, Athens, 1964-66, D.S. Bersis, Athens, 1964-66; post-doctoral researcher, fellow Harvard U., 1966-67; research chemist E.I. DuPont de Nemours & Co., Inc., Wilmington, Del., 1967-73, staff chemist, Phila., 1973-78, research asso. Marshall Research and Devel. Lab., Phila., 1978—. Served with Greek Army, 1959-60. Mem. Am. Chem. Soc., Assn. of Harvard Chemists. Greek Orthodox. Clubs: Hellenic Univ. of Wilmington. Contbr. articles in field to profl. jours.; holder numerous patents in field. Home: 12 S Townview Ln Newark DE 19711 Office: 3500 Grays Ferry Ave Philadelphia PA 19146

VAUGHAN, HERBERT WILEY, lawyer; b. Brookline, Mass., June 1, 1920; s. David D. and Elzie (Wiley) V.; student U. Chgo., 1937-38; A.B. cum laude, Harvard, 1941, LL.B. 1948; m. Ann Graustein, June 28, 1941. Admitted to Mass. bar, 1948; asso. firm Hale and Dorr, Boston, 1948-54, jr. partner 1954-56, sr. partner, 1956-77, co-mng. partner, 1977—. Corporator, Boston Five Cents Savs. Bank. Mem. Am., Mass., Boston bar assns. Clubs: Union (Boston); Bay; Badminton and Tennis; Longwood Cricket. Home: 119 Jericho Rd Weston MA 02193 Office: 60 State St Boston MA 02109

VAUGHAN, RALPH CARNELL, fin. services co. exec.; b. Williamsburg, Va., May 12, 1949; s. Alfonso and Sarah Frnces (Brown) V.; student Clarion State Coll., 1967-68; B.S., Central State U., Wilberforce, Ohio, 1971; postgrad. bus. U. Pitts., 1973-74; m. Marilyn Orvette Porter, June 26, 1971. Indsl. credit analyst Westinghouse Credit Corp., Pitts., 1971-72; dist. mgr. Jemini Internat., Cleve., 1972-73; contract adminstr. Westinghouse Nuclear Energy Systems Co., Monroeville, Pa., 1973-74; fin. mktg. rep. Service Bur. Co./Control Data Corp., Pitts., 1975-77; pres. Internat. Payment Services, Pitts., 1974—; partner Neil/Lee Assos., 1976—. Chmn. Overall Econ. Devel. Planning Commn. Allegheny County; mem. labor and industry com. NAACP, housing com. Urban League. Bd. dirs. NEED Ednl. Found. Mem. Bus. and Profl. Assn. Pitts. (pres.), Pitts. Jaycees, Assn. M.B.A. Execs., Wilkensburg C. of C., Urban Council on Econ. Strategies, Nat. Bus. League, Manchester Fed. Credit Union (pres.), Central State U. Alumni Club, Alpha Phi Alpha, Alpha Kappa Mu. Republican. Baptist. Clubs: Kiwanis. Office: 5518 Baum Blvd Pittsburgh PA 15232

VAUGHN, ROBERT DONALD, ret. army officer, govt. ofcl.; b. Iola, Kans., Mar. 27, 1925; s. Ralph Herbert and Alice (Dille) V.; B.A., U. Md., 1954; M.B.A., U. Ala., 1960; postgrad. Command and Gen. Staff Coll., 1964, Nat. War Coll., 1970; m. Ruthe Irene De Bow, Aug. 23, 1946; children—Marta Kristine, Robert Donald, John Patrick. Commd. 2d lt. U.S. Army, 1950, advanced through grades to col., 1970; commissary officer SHAPE, 1951-54; co. comdr., 1955-56; adviser MAAG, Iran, 1957-58; staff officer Inventory Control Point, Germany, 1960-63: chief Civil Schs. Program, 1964-67; bn. comdr. support command comdr. G-4, 1st Cav. Div., Vietnam, 1967-68; monitor M-16 Rifle, 1968; dep. comdr. Atlanta Gen. Depot, 1970-71; comdr. Burtonwood Army Depot, U.K., 1971-73; dir. mgmt. Office Dep. Chief Staff, Logistics Dept. Army, 1973-74, ret., 1974—; with Combined Mgmt., Washington, 1975-77; asst. dep. adminstr. VA, Washington, 1977—. Decorated Legion of Merit with 2 oak leaf clusters, Bronze Star with oak leaf cluster, Air medal. Mem. Nat. Honor Soc., Beta Gamma Sigma. Democrat. Presbyn. (deacon 1969-76, elder 1978—). Clubs: Lions (pres. club 1978—); Army Navy Country. Home: 203 Yoakum Pkwy Apt 1726 Alexandria VA 22304 Office: 1025 Vermont Av Washington DC 20005

VEATCH, ROBERT MARLIN, med. ethics researcher; b. Utica, N.Y., Jan. 22, 1939; s. Cecil Ross and Regina (Braddock) V.; B.S., Purdue U., 1961; M.S., U. Calif. at San Francisco, 1962; B.D., Harvard U., 1964, M.A., 1970, Ph.D., 1971; m. Laurelyn Kay Lovett, June 17, 1961; children—Paul Martin, Carlton Elliot. Teaching fellow Harvard U., 1968-70; research asso. in medicine Coll. Physicians and Surgeons, Columbia U., 1971-72; asso. for med. ethics Inst. of Society, Ethics and Life Scis., Hastings-on-Hudson, N.Y., 1970-75, sr. asso., 1975—; mem. vis. faculty various colls. and univs. Mem. Soc. for Health and Human Values, Am. Soc. Christian Ethics. Author: Value-Freedom in Science and Technology, 1976; Death, Dying, and the Biological Revolution, 1976; Case Studies in Medical Ethics, 1977. Editor or co-editor: Bibliography of Society, Ethics and the Life Sciences, 1973, rev. edit., 1978; The Teaching of Medical Ethics, 1973; Death Inside Out, 1975; Ethics and Health Policy, 1976; Teaching of Bioethics, 1976; Population Policy and Ethics, 1977. Asso. editor Ency of Bioethics; mem. editorial bd. Jour. AMA, 1976—; mem. editorial Adv. bd. Forum on Medicine, 1977—; contbg. editor Hosp. Physician, 1975—. Contbr. articles to profl. jours. Home: 50 Old Farm Rd Chappaqua NY 10514 Office: 360 Broadway Hastings-on-Hudson NY 10706

VECCHIA, EUGENE FRANK, electronics exec.; b. Revere, Mass., June 16, 1925; s. Frank and Genevieve (Franzese) V.; engring. certificate, Wentworth Inst., 1948; m. Marie Del Vecchio, Apr. 15, 1951; 1 son, Eugene Frank. Electronics technician Mass. Inst. Tech., Cambridge, 1951-55; engr. RCA, Waltham, Mass., 1955-57; pres. Electronic Cable Corp., Cambridge, 1957-61; exec. v.p. Flow Corp., 1961-65, Conel Corp., Chester, Pa., 1966-69; pres. Cable Systems & Assembly, Inc., Everett, Mass., 1969—; dir. Precision Connector Designs, Inc. Served with USNR, 1943-46, 50-51. Mem. IEEE, Am. Ordnance Assn. Democrat. Roman Catholic. Home: 23 Bixby St Revere MA 02151

VEGA, MARIANO, JR., ednl. adminstr.; b. Naguabo, P.R., Oct. 8, 1949; s. Mariano and Eugenia (Flores) V.; student St. Peter's Coll., 1971; A.B., Montclair State Coll., 1972, M.A., 1977; postgrad., Rutgers U., 1972; m. Gail A. Smith, July 14, 1973. Youth counselor

Neighborhood Youth Corp., Jersey City, 1970-72; bilingual ednl. cons. Puertorriquenos Asociado for Community Orgn., Jersey City, 1973-75; bilingual team tchr., Newark, 1972; sensitivity trainer, Boston, 1974; asst. dir. admissions Montclair State Coll., Upper Montclair, N.J., 1972-77; spl. asst. to exec. commr. for ednl. programs HEW, Washington, 1977—; bilingual/bicultural counselor. Vice chmn. bd. dirs. Puerto Rican Congress N.J., 1973; del. Puerto Rican Conv. N.J., 1971-77; advisor Ski Club Montclair State Coll., 1974-77. Nat. Fellow in Edn., Aspira-Rockefeller Fellows Programs, 1977-78. Mem. Am. Fedn. Tchrs., Am. Personnel and Guidance Assn., Coll. Student Personnel Assn., Assn. Non White Concerns, Am. Sch. Counselors Assn. Democrat. Clubs: Ski (Montclair State Coll.); La Familia (Washington). Winner ski awards: first place ballet ski, Alan Schonberger Sch., 1977, silver medal, Slalom Ski Sch., Killington, Vt., 1978, bronze medal NASTAR Giant Slalom, Killington, 1978, bronze medal Giant Sloalom, Sugarbush, Vt., 1976. Home: 201 Eye St SW Apt 341 Washington DC 20024 Office: 400 Maryland Ave Washington DC 20202

VEGA, PAZ MINA, chemist; b. Manila, June 4, 1933; d. Simplicio R. and Augustina T. Mina; B.S., U. Philippines, 1959; M.S., Marquette U., 1964; m. Jaime G. Vega, Jan. 18, 1964; children—Veronica Marie, Virginia Rosario. Research asst. U. Philippines, 1959-61; teaching asst. Marquette U., 1961-63; plant chemist Philippine-Am. Film Industries, Inc., 1964-70; chemist Photo Service div. GAF Corp. (Guardian Industries 1978—), Phila., 1970—. NSF fellow, 1963. Mem. Soc. Photog. Scientists and Engrs. (asso.), Sigma Xi. Roman Catholic. Home: 5340 N Broad St Philadelphia PA 19141 Office: GAF 20th and Logan Sts Philadelphia PA 19141

VEGA, RICHARD LAWRENCE, communications systems co. exec.; b. Hollister, Calif., Oct. 9, 1935; s. Joseph Leon and Alvera Carrie (Grassini) V.; student City Coll. San Francisco, 1953-54, U. Ind., 1954-55; B.E.E., Heald Coll., 1957; children—Maureen, Richard, Vincent. Design engr. Denver Aerospace div. Martin-Marietta Corp., 1957-62; head test ops. dept. Aerospace Corp., Los Angeles, 1962-72; v.p. Microband Corp. Am., N.Y.C., 1972-74, also dir.; pres. Telecommunications Systems, Inc., Balt., 1974—, also dir.; dir. Microwave; tech. cons. broadcasting and aerospace industries; early researcher microwave portion of radio spectrum. Mem. Am. Inst. Aeros. and Astronautics, Engring. Soc. Balt. Democrat. Roman Catholic. Contbr. tech. articles to trade jours. Home: PO Box 28 Pasadena MD 21122 Office: 28 Alleghany St Towson MD 21204

VEILLETTE, REJEAN MARCEL, physician, city health ofcl.; b. Ste-Genevieve de Batiscan, Que., Can., May 16, 1936; s. Paul Georges and Juliette Berthe (Massicotte) V.; B.A., St. Joseph's Sem., Trois-Rivières, Que., 1957; M.D., Laval U., Quebec, Que., 1962; m. Claire Hudon, July 8, 1961; children—Marie-Jose, Pierre Hudon. Resident in surgery Notre-Dame Hosp., Montreal, Que., 1962-66; physician sch. health Montreal Health Dept., 1967-72, well baby clinics, 1967-72, family planning program, 1968-72; med. dir. Montreal Cath. Sch. Commn., 1972—, Montreal Instn. for Elderly. Mem. Que. Profl. Corp. Physicians, Canadian Med. Assn., Fondation les Anciens de l'Université Laval, Association des Medecins de langue française du Canada. Roman Catholic. Home: 359 de Mortagne Boucherville PQ J4B 1B7 Canada Office: 3737 E Sherbrooke Montreal PQ H1X 3B3 Canada

VEIRS, ALVIN BASTABLE, JR., constrn. co. exec.; b. Bethesda, Md., Apr. 12, 1945; s. Alvin and Barbara A. (Smith) V.; B.S. in Bus. Adminstrn., Am. U., 1969; m. Edith Stanley Allnutt, Aug. 27, 1966; children—Christopher, Meredith, Courtney. Vice-pres. A.B. Veirs, Inc., Rockville, Md., 1969-71; dir. land devel. Carl M. Freeman Assos., Inc., Silver Spring, Md., 1971-75, v.p., sec., 1976—. Bd. dirs. Inverness Homeowners Assn., 1972, Inverness Recreation Assn., 1973, Bristow Village Homeowners Assn., 1973, Tanterra Home and Recreation Assn., 1974. Mem. Community Assn. Inst. (Washington), Am. Diabetes Assn., Smithsonian Assos. Democrat. Roman Catholic. Home: 2402 Chilham Pl Potomac MD 20854 Office: 1400 Spring St Silver Spring MD 20910

VELARDE, REYNALDO AMOS, mathematician; b. Embudo, N.Mex., May 22, 1942; s. Jose Efren and Ciprenia V.; B.A., Gallaudet Coll., 1968. Mathematician, Community Service Adminstrn., Exec. office U.S. Pres., Silver Spring, Md., 1968—. Mem. Deaf Opportunities Enterprises, Nation's Capitol Deaf Bowling Assn. (pres. 1977-78, treas. 1978-79). Home: 2001 Fordham St Hyattsville MD 20783

VELKOFF, HYMAN, mfg. co. exec.; b. N.Y.C., Apr. 16, 1914; s. Louis and Dora (Aronoff) V.; B.B.A., Coll. City N.Y., 1937; m. Sylvia Black, June 12, 1938; children—Kenneth, Janet Velkoff Simone. Profl. football Bklyn. Dodgers, 1935-37; with Central States Diversified, N.Y.C., 1940—, v.p., 1954-62, exec. v.p., 1962—; dir. Indsl. Forest Products, Balt. Served to 1st lt. Q.M.C., AUS, 1943-45. Mem. Def. Supply Assn., Nat. Flexible Packaging Assn., Paper Bag Inst., Am. Logistics Assn. Home: 243 Taylor Rd West Hempstead NY 11552 Office: 122 E 42d St New York City NY 10017

VELTRI, BRENDA JOYCE, personnel exec.; b. Newark, Mar. 30, 1947; d. Salvatore Gerard and Dorothy Madeline (Covello) V.; B.A. in Polit. Sci., Rutgers U., 1969; M.A. in Rehab. Counseling, Seton Hall U., 1974. Budget examiner City of Newark, 1969-73, sr. personnel technician, 1973, prin. personnel technician, 1973-75, mgr. manpower planning, 1975, personnel dir., 1975—; instr. in pub. personnel adminstrn. Rutgers U. extension div., 1976; vol. counselor Irvington Youth Resources Center, 1974-76. Pres., Rutgers Young Democratic Club, 1969; pres. Greater Newark chpt. Friends of N.J. State Opera, 1978—, exec. bd., 1978—; chairperson Tng. Planning Com. Hudson, Essex and Union Counties, 1977—; personnel com. Crossroads Health Plan; v.p. Urban Mgmt. Assts. Newark, 1975—, Municipal Careerwomen Newark, 1977—. Recipient Profl. Achievement award UNICO, 1974; Rehab. Services Adminstrn. grantee, 1972-74. Mem. Am. Personnel and Guidance Assn., Internat. Personnel Mgmt. Assn., N.J. County and Municipal Personnel Dirs. and Officers Assn. (sec. 1977-78), Am. Rehab. Counseling Assn. N.J. (chmn. 1975). Home: 62 Peck Ave Newark NJ 07107 Office: 920 Broad St Newark NJ 07102

VELZY, CHARLES R., sanitary engr.; b. Lamont, Mich., Oct. 9, 1891; s. Frank and Luella (Angell) V.; B.M.E., Ill. U., 1914; m. Ethel L. Brunkow, Aug. 18, 1923; children—Donald Harwell, Charles Oral, Robert Allen, Howard Edward. Time-study engr. John Deere and Co., Moline, Ill., 1915-16; asst. prodn. engr. P. B. Yates Machine Co., Beloit, Wis., 1918-20; project engr. Greeley and Hansen, Chgo., 1920-32, head N.Y.C. office, 1942-46; plant supt. Buffalo Sewer Authority, 1938-42; project engr. Buck, Seifert and Jost, N.Y.C., 1946-48; partner Nussbaumer Clarke and Velzy, cons. san. engrs., N.Y.C., 1948-66; pres. Charles R. Velzy Assos., Inc., Armonk, N.Y., 1966—; cons. engr. War Dept., 1941-42. Served to lt. USNR, 1917-18. Recipient Distinguished Grad. award U. Ill., 1972. Mem. ASTM (chmn. coms., award of Merit 1970), N.Y. State Water Pollution Control Assn. (pres. 1942-43, Bedell award 1964), Am. Waterworks Assn., Am. Pub. Works Assn., Air Pollution Control Assn., Profl. Engring. Soc., ASCE, ASME, Water Pollution Control Fedn., Delta Phi, Tau Beta Pi. Methodist. Clubs: White Plains Coll., Masons. Contbr. articles to profl. jours. Home: 22 Earlwoode Dr White Plains NY 10606 Office: 355 Main St Armonk NY 10504

VENDOME, GENNARO, computer systems exec.; b. Naples, Italy, June 20, 1946; s. Rocco and Giuseppa (Petito) V.; came to U.S., 1954, naturalized, 1959; student N.Y.C. Community Coll., 1964-66. Jr. exec. positions N.Y. Telephone Co., N.Y.C., 1968-75; v.p. sales Computron Co., N.Y.C., 1972—; partner Vendome Properties, N.Y.C., 1973—, mng. dir. Vendome Holding Co., N.Y.C., 1976—; co-founder Nino's Fast Food Stores, N.Y.C., 1975—. Mem. Congl. Adv. Com. Community Affairs. Served with U.S. Army, 1966-68. Mem. Am. Mgmt. Assn., N.Y. State Chiefs Police Assn. Home: 3671 Hudson Manor Terr Riverdale NY 10463 Office: Computron Systems Corp 888 7th Ave New York City NY 10019

VENETSANOPOULOS, ANASTASIOS NICOLAOS, elec. engr., educator; b. Athens, Greece, June 19, 1941; s. Nicolaos Anastasios and Elli (Papacondilis) V.; diploma Athens Coll., 1960; diploma in elec. and mech. engring. Nat. Tech. U., Athens, 1965; M.S., Yale, 1966, M.Phil., 1968, Ph.D., 1969. Came to Can., 1968. Asst. in instrn. engring. and applied sci. Yale, 1966-68, research asst., 1968-69; lectr. U. Toronto (Ont., Can.), 1968-69, asst. prof. elec. engring., 1970-73, asso. prof., 1973—, chmn. communications group dept. elec. engring., 1974-78, asso. chmn. elec. engring., 1978—, mem. elec. engring. exec. com., 1974—, mem. elec. engring. grad. student staff com., 1971-75, elec. engring. curriculum com., 1972—. Cons. elec. engring. Consociates Ltd. Mem. allocations and agy. relations com. United Community Fund, Toronto, 1971-75; pres. Hellenic-Canadian Cultural Soc., 1972-75; sec. gen. Greek Community Met. Toronto, 1973-75. Recipient John Vakis award Athens Coll., 1960. Univ. scholar Greek Inst. Nat. Scholarships, 1961-63; Fulbright travel grantee in U.S.A., 1965; NRC Council grantee, 1969—; Def. Research Bd. Can. grantee, 1972-75. Registered profl. engr., Greece, Ont. Mem. IEEE (finance chmn. internat. symposium on circuit theory 1973, tech. program chmn. internat. conf. on communications 1978, vice chmn. Toronto sect. 1976-77, chmn. 1977—), Engring. Inst. Can., Assn. Profl. Engrs. Ont., Assn. Profl. Elec. Engrs. Greece, Assn. Profl. Mech. Engrs. Greece, Can. Soc. Elec. Engring. (chmn. Toronto sect. 1975-77, nat. dir. 1976—), AAAS, Yale Sci. and Engring. Assn., N.Y. Acad. Scis., Tech. Chamber of Greece, Am.-Hellenic Ednl. Progressive Assn. (v.p. Toronto sect. 1973-75, pres. Toronto sect. 1975-77), Intercultural Council (chmn. ednl. com. 1971—, sr. v.p. 1977—), Sigma Xi. Contbr. articles to profl. jours. Home: 260 Wellesley St E Toronto ON M4X 1G6 Canada Office: Dept Elec Engring U Toronto Toronto ON M5S 1A4 Canada

VENGLARCHIK, ANDREW STEFAN, JR., ins. co. exec.; b. Monaca, Pa., Nov. 23, 1922; s. Andrew Stefan and Mary Martha (Stas) V.; student Western Res. U., 1945-50. Clk.-typist Comml. Motor Freight Co., Cleve., 1941; jr. buyer S. K. Wellman div. Abex Corp., Bedford, Ohio, 1941-66; pres. Slovak Gymnastic Union Sokol of U.S.A., East Orange, N.J., 1967—; pres. Sokol Apts., Inc., Astoria, N.Y., 1975—. Mem. N.J. Ethnic Communities Congress, N.J. Bicentennial Ethnic Council, Nat. Ethnic Racial Alliance of Am. Revolution Bicentennial Commn. Mem. AAU, Nat., N.J. (pres. 1976-77), N.Y. fraternal congresses. Roman Catholic. Clubs: Slovak Gymnastic Union Sokol of U.S.A., Nat. Slovak Soc. of U.S.A. Home and office: 276 Prospect St East Orange NJ 07017

VENTIMIGLIA, JOSEPH JOHN, surgeon; b. N.Y.C., May 20, 1923; s. John B. and Santina Q. V.; B.S., Manhattan Coll., 1948; M.D., N.Y. Med. Coll., 1952; m. Eleanor G. Vitagliano, Dec. 12, 1976; children—Salvatore, Michael. Intern, Meadowbrook Hosp., Hempstead, N.Y., 1952-53; gen. practice medicine, Portland, Maine, 1953-55; resident in gen. surgery VA Hosp., West Haven, Conn., 1955-57, 58-60, chief resident, 1959-60, staff gen. surgeon, 1960—; Am. Cancer Soc. fellow Yale-New Haven Hosp., 1957-58; asst. clin. prof. Yale U., New Haven, 1974—, physician univ. health services, 1962—. Served with USNR, 1943-46. Diplomate A.C.S. Mem. AMA, Conn., New Haven County med. socs., Conn. Soc. Am. Bd. Surgeons, Guilford Art League. Home: 105 Laurie Ln Orange CT 06477

VENTRY, PAUL GUERIN, physician, ofcl. Dept. Def.; b. Ossining, N.Y., Sept. 1, 1934; s. Victor and Catherine (Dillon) V.; B.S., Manhattan Coll., 1957; M.D., Syracuse U., 1962; m. Betty Anne Baildon, Aug. 20, 1960. Commd. 1st lt. M.C., U.S. Army, 1962, advanced through grades to lt. col., 1971; intern Walter Reed Gen. Hosp., 1962-63, resident in internal medicine, 1963-66, fellow in immunology, 1966, fellow in allergy, 1967, chief med. outpatient clinic, 1971, allergy cons. to Surgeon Gen., Europe, 1967-70, ret., 1971; chief adult services Montgomery County (Md.) Health Dept., 1972; med. dir. Goddard Space Flight Center, NASA, 1973; partner Med. Assos., D.C., Washington, 1974; med. dir. Civilian Employees Health Service Dept. Def., Washington, 1975—; asst. clin. prof. medicine George Washington U., 1973—. Mem. Am. Occupational Med. Assn. (asso.), A.C.P., Am. Pub. Health Assn., Am. Acad. Allergy, Royal Soc. Medicine, British Allergy Soc., Potomac C. of C., Washington Performing Arts Soc., D.C., Montgomery County med. soc., Alpha Kappa Kappa. Contbr. articles to med. jours. Home: 7813 Masters Dr Potomac MD 20854 Office: Room 1 E 356 The Pentagon Washington DC 20310

VENTURELLA, VINCENT STEVEN, chemist, educator; b. Pitts., Aug. 24, 1930; s. Stephano and Rosalie (Noto) V.; B.S., U. Pitts., 1954, M.S., 1956, Ph.D. (George A. Kelly Sr. fellow), 1960; m. Mary Lou Sontheimer, July 10, 1954; children—Collette, Keith, Jeffrey. Instr. chemistry U. Pitts., 1957-60; asst. prof. chemistry Fordham U., N.Y.C., 1960-63; analytical research chemist Abbott Labs., North Chicago, Ill., 1963-64; asst. prof. Temple U., Phila., 1964-67; mgr. analytical research Hoffmann La Roche, Inc., Nutley, N.J., 1967-71, analytical sect. chief, 1972-75, asst. mgr. analytical devel., 1976-78, mgr. analytical devel., 1978—; research sect. chief Bur. Customs, N.Y.C., 1971-72. Tchr., Rutgers U., New Brunswick, N.J., 1969-70, Fairleigh Dickinson U., Rutherford, N.J., 1973—. Vol., Ambulance Unit, Cedar Grove, N.J., 1974—; mgr. Cedar Grove Jr. Baseball League; coach Cedar Grove Jr. Football League; mem. Cedar Grove Drug Abuse Subcom., 1971-72, Cedar Grove Bd. Edn., 1978—. NIH Research grantee, 1961-62. Mem. Am. Chem. Soc., Am. Pharm. Assn., Am. Inst. Chemists, N.Y. Acad. Scis., Soc. Applied Spectros, N.Am. Thermal Analysis Soc., Internat. Soc. Magnetic Resonance, AAAS, Sigma Xi, Phi Lambda Upsilon, Rho Chi, Contbr. articles to sci. jours. Home: 9 Ring Pl Cedar Grove NJ 07009 Office: 340 Kingsland St Nutley NJ 07110

VERANO, ANTHONY F., banker; b. West Harrison, N.Y., Jan. 4, 1931; s. Frank and Rose (Viscome) V.; student Am. Inst. Banking, 1956-60, Bank Adminstrn. Inst., U. Wis., 1962-64, N.J. Bankers Data Processing Sch., 1966-68; m. Clara Cosentino, July 8, 1951; children—Rosemarie, Diana Lynn. Clk., The County Trust Co., White Plains, N.Y., 1949, teller, 1949-52, jr. teller, 1952-53, sr. teller, 1953-57, asso. auditor, 1957-60, sr. auditor, 1960-61; asst. auditor State Nat. Bank Conn., Bridgeport, 1961, auditor, 1962—; instr. Am. Inst. Banking. Served with USN, 1951-52. Chartered bank auditor. Mem. Bank Adminstrn. Inst., Inst. Internal Auditors, Am. Accounting Assn. Home: 59 Bugg Hill Rd Monroe CT 06468 Office: 2834 Fairfield Ave Bridgeport CT 06605

VERBIAR, CLIFFORD PAUL, aerospace co. exec.; b. Bklyn., July 30, 1948; s. Paul and Mary (Oreste) V.; B.S. in Research Physics (N.Y. Regents scholar), State U. N.Y., Stony Brook, 1971; m. Linda Susan Liquori, July 24, 1976. Mech. engr. Instrument Systems Corp., Huntington, N.Y., 1970-71; test engr. Fairchild Space and Def. Systems, Syosset, N.Y., 1971-76, sr. staff engr., 1976-77, program mgr., 1977-78, prodn. control mgr., 1978—; cons. design of digital or linear circuitry. Recipient Superior award Engring. Tech. Soc., 1964, 65, 66. Mem. Inst. Environ. Sci. Republican. Roman Catholic. Home: 6 Harrison Ave Centereach NY 11720 Office: 300 Robbins Ln Syosset NY 11791

VERDUN, HAROLD CHARLES, food co. exec.; b. Washington, July 21, 1943; s. Harold Charles and Matiel Cora Verdun; B.S. in Bus. Adminstrn., Georgetown U., 1964; m. Angelita Hipolito, Sept. 7, 1968. Auditor, M.B. Hariton & Co., Washington, 1966-67; sr. auditor Coopers & Lybrand, C.P.A.'s, N.Y.C., 1967-74; sr. auditor Gen. Foods Corp., White Plains, N.Y., 1974-75, dist. sales service mgr., Liverpool, N.Y., 1975—. Served to capt. AUS, 1964-66. Mem. Nat. Assn. Accountants, Syracuse C. of C., Mfrs. Assn. Syracuse, Delta Nu Alpha. Home: 345 Scott Ave Syracuse NY 13224 Office: 7475 Henry Clay Blvd Liverpool NY 13088

VERGARA, WILLIAM CHARLES, electronic engr.; b. Far Rockaway, N.Y., July 6, 1923; s. R.C. and Lena (Corio) V.; student Coll. City N.Y., 1943-44, U.S. Naval Acad., 1945; B.E.E., Rensselaer Poly. Inst., 1945; m. Patricia Yvonne White, Apr. 27, 1946. Electronics engr. Allen D. Cardwell Corp., Plainville, Conn., 1947-48; chief engr. Bendix Corp., Balt., 1948—; instr. Hillyer Jr. Coll., 1947; mem. Md. Gov.'s Sci. Advisory Council, 1970—. Served with USN, 1943-46. Mem. IEEE, Nat. Assn. Sci. Writers, Md. Acad. Scis. (vice chmn. sci. council). Author: Science in Everyday Things, 1957; Mathematics in Everyday Things, 1959; Electronics in Everyday Things, 1961; Science—The Never-Ending Quest, 1965; Science in the World Around Us, 1973; usage panel cons. Harper Dictionary of Contemporary Usage, 1974-75; contbr. articles in field to profl. jours. Patentee in field. Home: 910 Dunellen Dr Towson MD 21204 Office: Communications Div Bendix Corp E Joppa Rd Baltimore MD 21204

VERNER, ELLIOTT KIRK, ednl. adminstr.; b. Phila., Mar. 20, 1930; s. Harry Jacques and Helen Lucretia (Kirk) V.; A.B., Johns Hopkins U., 1952; m. Joan Stover Howard, Dec. 27, 1951; children—Margaret, Edward, Elizabeth, David. Tchr., St. Paul's Sch., Brooklandville, Md., 1952; with trust dept. Md. Nat. Bank, 1956-60; tchr. Gilman Sch., 1960-67; founder Adirondack Mountain Sch., 1967, headmaster, 1967—; founder Adirondack Wilderness Camp, Long Lake, N.Y., 1964—. Served to lt. USNR, 1953-56. Presbyterian (trustee). Clubs: Elkridge (Balt.); Johns Hopkins. Address: Jennings Park Rd Long Lake NY 12847

VERNET, PETER STANLEY, ins. co. exec.; b. Providence, Feb. 15, 1947; s. Harold Stanley and Rosalind H (Harrison) V.; Asso. Sci., Roger Williams Jr. Coll., 1967; B.S., Bryant Coll., 1972; m. Linda Elizabeth Fondetti, Sept. 7, 1974; 1 son, Christopher. Dept. mgr. Outlet Co., Warwick, R.I., 1971-74, F.W. Woolworth Co., Warwick, 1974-75; sales mgr. Sheraton Hotel, Warwick, 1975-76; sales rep. Heirloom Collection, New Eng. ter., 1976; sales rep. Met. Ins. Co., West Warwick, 1977—. Class chmn. Bryant Coll. Reunion, 1977, chmn. reunion festival, 1978. Served with U.S. Army, 1969-71. Decorated Bronze Star medal, Purple Heart, Air medal, Combat Infantrymen's badge. Mem. Nat. Assn. Life Underwriters. Episcopalian. Home: 200 Vaughn Ave Warwick RI 02886 Office: 100 Quaker Ln West Warwick RI 02893

VERNI, JAMES MICHAEL, indsl. gases co. exec.; b. Utica, N.Y., Apr. 13, 1944; s. Ernest A. and Mary Ann V.; B.A. in Biology, Utica Coll., 1967; m. Mary Lourdes Manfredo, June 10, 1967; children—James, Christopher. Tchr. biology Utica (N.Y.) Free Acad., 1967-68; tchr. sci. Foley Jr. High Sch., Herkimer, N.Y., 1968-69; med. rep. A.H. Robins Co., Utica, State of N.H., 1969-73; med. rep. Ayerst Labs., S. Shore, Mass., 1973-74; med. rep. Liquid Carbonic Corp., Eastern Mass. and R.I., 1974-78, mgr. northeast specialty gas sales, 1978—. Chmn. exec. com. Moby Dick Council Boy Scouts Am., Wareham, Mass., 1977—. Mem. Wareham Hist. Soc. Roman Catholic. Club: Couples of Marion, Mass. Home: 2 Kings Cross Rd West Wareham MA 02576 Office: 1635 Shawsheen St Tewksbury MA 01876

VERNICK, MILANI LEE, educator; b. N.Y.C.; d. Joseph Leon and Beatrice (Carlin) V.; B.A., Queens Coll., City U. N.Y., 1972; m. Lawrence Maurice Kushner, June 23, 1946 (div. Jan. 1970); children—Robb Adam, Leslie Meryl. Instr. synchronized swimming Silver Spring (Md.) Community Pools, 1961-65; dir. aqua shows Oakview Recreation Corp., 1961-65; owner Milani's Studio of Polynesian Ballet, Silver Spring, 1962—; mem. Aqua Gems, synchronized swimming troupe, 1964-75, dir., 1966-67; dir. Moanas, Polynesian dance troupe, 1969—; instr. dance Free U. Md., 1974-75; mktg. cons. TSG & Assos., 1974; mem. staff Open U., Washington, 1975—; mgr. Weight Control Inst., 1975; pres. Weigh To Go, Inc., 1975—; ethical hypnotist, 1975—. Luau coordinator local country clubs, hotels, 1966—; troop leader Girl Scouts U.S.A., Silver Spring, 1963-65; mem. Suburban Md. Fair Housing, 1963. Mem. Internat. Platform Assn., LWV, Modern Dance Council Washington, Am. Dance Guild, Nat. Soc. Lit. and Arts, Assn. Advancement Ethical Hypnosis, Internat. Transactional Analysis Assn., Greater Washington Inst. Transactional Analysis. Address: 9628 Cottrell Terr Silver Spring MD 20903

VERRAL, CHARLES SPAIN, author; b. Highfield, Ont., Can., Nov. 7, 1904; s. George William and Kate Elizabeth (Peacocke) V.; grad. Upper Can. Coll., 1923; student Ont. Coll. Art, Toronto, 1923-26; m. Jean Willis Mithoefer, Mar. 19, 1932; 1 son, Charles Spain. Comml. artist, N.Y.C., 1927-30; editor, art dir. Clayton Publs., N.Y.C., 1930-35; free-lance writer, 1935-60; writer, asso. editor Golden Press Dictionary, N.Y.C., 1960-61; writer, staff editor Harper Ency. Sci., N.Y.C., 1961-62; writer, editor Reader's Digest Assn., N.Y.C., 1962-74; free-lance writer, 1974—. Author Street and Smith Publs. mag. series, Bill Barnes (under name George L. Eaton), 1934-43; continuity writer United Features Syndicate newspaper strip Hap Hopper, 1941-47; radio script writer Mandrake the Magician, 1940-41. Mem. Authors Guild, Mystery Writers Am. Episcopalian. Author: Captain of the Ice, 1953; Champion of the Court, 1954; Mighty Men of Baseball, 1955; Wonderful World Series, 1956; Winning Quarterback, 1960; Jets, 1962; Robert Goddard, Father Space Age, 1963; Babe Ruth, Sultan of Swat, 1976; Casey Stengel, Baseball's Great Manager, 1978; others. Contbr. articles and short stories to numerous mags. and anthologies. Home and office: 79 Jane St New York City NY 10014

VERSCHINGEL, ROGER HILAIRE CHARLES, chemist; b. Montreal, Que., Can., Jan. 19, 1928; s. Achille Joseph and Paula Esther (Bernaert) V.; B.S., Sir George Williams U., 1949; Ph.D., McGill U., 1955; m. Selena Anna Mary Lang, June 27, 1959. Lectr. chemistry Sir George Williams U., 1954-56, asst. prof., 1956-61, asso. prof., 1961-67, prof., 1967—, chmn. dept., 1968-73, dean Faculty of Sci., Sir George Williams campus Concordia U., 1973-77. Recipient Can. Centennial medal, 1967, NRC grant, 1950-53, Mappin medal,

1950. Mem. Canadian Assn. Univ. Tchrs. (exec. and fin. com. 1968-70), Chem. Inst. Can., Am. Chem. Soc., Royal Inst. Chemistry, Order of Chemists of Que. Home: 200 Gaspe St Nuns Island Montreal PQ H3E 1E6 Canada Office: 1455 De Maisonneuve Blvd W Montreal PQ H3G 1M8 Canada

VERTUCCI, NICHOLAS RALPH, mfg. co. exec.; b. Bronx, N.Y., Dec. 10, 1943; s. Salvatore Michael and Maria (Cocca) V.; B.B.A., St. Francis Coll., 1968; postgrad. Pace U., 1974-75; m. Annamarie Thurston; children—Maria Ann, Nicholas, Denise Lynn. Accountant, Peat, Marwick, Mitchell & Co., White Plains, N.Y., 1966-71; dir. accounting Western Union Telegraph Co., Upper Saddle River, N.J., 1971-73; controller Rapifax Corp., Fairfield, N.J., 1973-74, Simmonds Precision Products, Inc., Tarrytown, N.Y., 1974—; adviser Advanced Mgmt. Research Council. Treas., Rosary Acad. Parents Guild, 1976-77, pres., 1977-79. C.P.A., N.Y. Mem. Am. Inst. C.P.A.'s, N.Y. State Soc. C.P.A.'s, Nat. Assn. Accountants, Inst. Mgmt. Accounting. Club: Rockland Valley Golf. Home: 7 Baldwin Pl New City NY 10956 Office: 150 White Plains Rd Tarrytown NY 10591

VERY, DONALD LEROY, lawyer; b. Pitts., Aug. 19, 1933; s. Rocco and Elizabeth (Garfold) V.; B.A., Duquesne U., 1955; J.D., U. Notre Dame, 1958; m. Norma Claire Wandrisco, June 30, 1956; children—Donald Leroy, Dianne, David, Daniel, Douglas, Dennis. Admitted to Pa. bar, 1959, U.S. Dist. Ct. Western Dist. Pa., 1959, U.S. Ct. Appeals, 3d Circuit, 1961; asso. partner Camphell, Thomas & Burke, Pitts., 1959-63, partner, 1964-70; partner Tucker Arensberg Very & Ferguson, and predecessor, 1971—; asst. dir. In-Dev-Or, The Ins. Devel. Orgn. Bus. Sch.; mem. admiralty rules com. U.S. Dist. Ct. Western Dist. Pa., 1967—; examiner Pa. State Bd. Law Examiners, 1968-71. Lectr. U. Pitts. Sch. Gen. Studies, 1971-75, adj. prof. admiralty law, 1976—. Sec. Parks Commn., Bethel Park Borough, Pitts., 1966-68. Mem. Allegheny County (pres. 1978), Pa., Am. bar assns., Am. Judicature Soc., Am. Trial Lawyers Assn., Maritime Law Assn. U.S. Author: The Law-Make It Work for You, 1974. Opinion editor Pitts. Legal Jour., 1964-68, editor-in-chief, 1968—; editor Pa. Bar Quar., 1969—. Home: 90 Red Path Trail Upper St Clair Twp Pittsburgh PA 15241 Office: Pittsburgh National Bldg Pittsburgh PA 15222

VERZYL, JUNE CAROL, art gallery ofcl.; b. Huntington, N.Y., Feb. 5, 1928; d. Leo Daniel and Louisa C. (Scherer) Convery; student Parsons Sch. Design, 1947-48; m. Kenneth H. Verzyl, Mar. 6, 1953; 1 dau., Kim Greer. Gallery dir. Verzyl Art Gallery, Northport, N.Y., 1966—. Co-founder Independent Asharoken Citizens Party, 1966; mem. Village of Asharoken Bd. Elections, 1966-76. Mem. Northport Hist. Soc. Pub. numerous catalogs, brochures on exhibitions, 1966—. Home: 25 Bevin Rd Northport/Asharoken NY 11768 Office: 377 Route 25A Northport NY 11768

VERZYL, KENNETH HENRY, art gallery dir.; b. Sunnyside, N.Y., Sept. 18, 1922; s. Henry Kenneth and Florence Noreen (Greer) V.; grad. N.Y. State Agrl. and Tech. Inst., 1942; m. June Carol Convery; 1 dau., Kim Greer. Mayor, Village of Asharoken (N.Y.), 1970-76, police commr., 1974-76, trustee, 1969-70; dir. Verzyl Art Gallery, Northport, N.Y., 1966; one-man shows: Mus. of the Confederacy, Richmond, Va., 1972, Nicholas Roerich Mus., N.Y.C., 1973, E.Northport (N.Y.) Pub. Library, 1974, Berkshire Mus., Pittsfield, Mass., 1974, many others; group shows include: Parrish Mus., Southampton, N.Y., 19—, Guild Hall, Easthampton, N.Y., 19—; represented in permanent collections: Nicholas Roerich Mus., E. Northport Pub. Library. Served with USMCR, 1942-45. Mem. Guild Hall Easthampton, Northport Hist. Soc., Am. Fedn. Arts N.Y.C. Democrat. Clubs: Masons, Salmagundi (N.Y.C.). Home: 25 Bevin Rd Northport/Asharoken NY 11768 Office: 377 Route 25A Northport NY 11768

VESCI, JOSEPH VINCENT, accountant; b. Phila., Dec. 26, 1940; s. Joseph Francis and Susie Ann (Visco) V.; B.S., LaSalle Coll., 1965, M.B.A. candidate, 1977—; m. Lorraine D'onofrio, Nov. 21, 1970; children—Susan C., Joseph C., Rosemarie. Supr. trainee I-T-E Imperial Corp. (subs. Gould, Inc. 1976), Phila., 1967-68, financial analyst, 1968-71, supr. budgets and reporting, 1971-74, mgr. gen. accounting, 1974-78; corporate budget and accounting systems dir. Extracorporeal Med. Spltys., Inc. subs. Johnson & Johnson, King of Prussia, Pa., 1978—. Republican. com. rep., Phila., 1967-71, 60-64. Served with USN, 1964-67. Mem. Pa. Assn. Notaries. Roman Catholic. Club: The Drexelbrook. Home: 2517 Marshall Rd Drexel Hill PA 19026 Office: Extracorporeal Med Spltys Royal and Ross Rds King of Prussia PA 19406

VESEY, FRANK ARCHIBALD, opthalmologist; b. Kaposvar, Hungary, June 22, 1902; s. Isidor Wesel and Theresa (Kuttner) V.; came to U.S., 1937, naturalized, 1943; M.D., Royal Hungarian Elisabeth U., 1928; m. Olga Reti, June 2, 1928; 1 stepson, Peter E. Rotating intern County Hosp. Somogy, St. Rokers Hosp., Budapest, Count Apponyi Albert Polyclinic, Budapest, Jewish Hosp., Budapest, Kunucca Skin Hosp., Budapest, 1927-28; externist in ophthalmology County Hosp. Somogy, 1928-31; resident in opthalmology Manhattan Eye Ear and Throat Hosp., 1941-47; successively instr., lectr., asst. prof., asso. prof. N.Y. Polyclinic Med. Sch., 1947-51, 59-67; mem. faculty N.Y. Med. Coll., 1960-67; organizer, dir. N.J. Mobile Eye Clinic, 1946-49; chief dept. ophthalmology N.W. Clinic, Minot, N.D., 1952; research in glaucoma Toledo Inst. Med. Research, 1954-59; sr. physician VA Clinic, Toledo, 1954-59; chief div. opthalmology VA Center, Mountain Home, Tenn., 1967-69; chief div. opthalmology Bklyn. Med. Group, 1969-72; opthalmologist Yorkville Med. Group, N.Y.C., 1972—. Served to 1st lt. M.C., AUS, 1943-46; ETO. Diplomate Am. Bd. Opthalmology. Fellow Soc. Eye Surgeons, Royal Soc. Health (London); mem. AMA, Am. Acad. Opthalmology and Otolaryngology, N.Y. Soc. Clin. Ophthalmology, Assn. Research in Ophthalmology. Republican. Club: B'nai B'rith. Contbr. articles to sci. jours. Home and office: 644 W 204th St New York City NY 10034

VESTERGAARD, PER BJORN, physician; b. Florence, Italy, Aug. 30, 1920; s. Kristian and Augusta (Larsen) V.; M.D., U. Copenhagen, 1947; m. Inger Dehli, June 4, 1949; children—Birthe, Tom Christian, Ellen Marie. Intern, Herning County Hosp., Denmark, 1947-48; resident Univ. Clinic, Aarhus, Denmark, 1948-49; research asso., dir. labs. Hans Hosp., Roskilde, Denmark, 1949-53; sr. research med. biochemist Rockland State Hosp. Research Facility, Orangeburg, N.Y., 1953-58, asso. research scientist, 1958-66, prin. research scientist, 1966-76, chief psychiat. research, 1976—. Recipient Gold medal in theoretical medicine U. Copenhagen. 1949. Mem. AAAS, Am. Chem. Soc., N.Y. Acad. Sci., Danish Med. Soc., Sigma Xi. Home: 140 Old Tappan Rd Old Tappan NJ 07675 Office: Rockland Research Inst Orangeburg NY 10962

VETERE, ROBERT LOUIS, project engr., plastics co. exec.; b. Elizabeth, N.J., July 24, 1949; s. Robert and Pearl Elizabeth (Burlone) V.; B.S., Rensselaer Poly. Inst., 1972, M.B.A., 1974; postgrad. Seton Hall U., 1976—; m. Brenda Lee Viehweger, May 26, 1979. Teaching asst. mktg. and advt. Rensselaer Poly. Inst., Troy, N.Y., 1972-74; prodn. supr. Union Carbide Corp., Wayne, N.J., 1974, indsl. engr., 1974-75, bus. analyst-distbn., 1975-78, product mgr., N.Y.C., 1978—. Mem. Nat. Council Phys. Distbn. Mgmt. Roman Catholic. Office: Union Carbide Corp 55 Haul Rd Wayne NJ 07470

VICK, EDWARD HOGE, JR., advt. exec.; b. N.Y.C., Feb. 27, 1944; s. Edward Hoge and Margaret Jane (Sprankle) V.; A.B., U. N.C., 1966; M.S. (Journalism grantee), Northwestern U., 1971; 1 son, Joshua D. Account exec. Benton & Bowles, Inc., N.Y.C., 1971-75; mgmt. supr. Ogilvy & Mather, Inc., N.Y.C., 1975—, v.p., 1976—. Served to lt. USNR, 1966-69. Decorated Bronze Star medal (2). Mem. St. Andrew's Soc. Republican. Presbyterian. Author: An Examination of the Creative Process, 1971. Home: 106 E 81 St New York City NY 10028 Office: 2 E 48th St New York City NY 10017

VICKERS, JAMES HUDSON, veterinary pathologist, govt. ofcl.; b. Columbus, Ohio, Apr. 21, 1930; s. Carl J. and Betty O. (Schaer) V.; B.Sc., Ohio State U., Columbus, 1952, D.V.M., 1958; M.S., U. Conn., Storrs, 1966; m. Valerie Janet May, Apr. 5, 1964; 1 son, Dana Carlton. Zoo veterinarian Columbus Zoo, 1958-60; staff veterinarian Lederle Labs., Pearl River, N.Y., 1960-64, pathologist, 1964-68, head dept. pathology, 1968-70; v.p., dir. research Primelabs, Inc., Farmingdale, N.J., 1970-73; dir. pathobiology and primatology br. Bur. Biologics, FDA, Bethesda, Md., 1973—; lectr. in primatology N.Y. State U. Coll. Medicine, N.Y.C., 1970-73; FDA rep. to primate steering com. HEW, 1974—. Served to 1st lt. Signal Corps, AUS, 1952-54. Diplomate Am. Coll. Veterinary Pathologists. Mem. AMVA, Am. Assn. Zoo Veterinarians, Soc. Toxicology, Am. Assn. Neuropathologists, Am. Assn. Lab. Animal Practitioners, Am. Coll. Veterinary Med., Avian Pathologists, Phi Sigma Kappa. Narrator, prin. subject film Safari for Science, 1965. Contbr. numerous articles in field to profl. jours. Home: Box 142M24 RFD 1 Ijamsville MD 21754 Office: Bureau of Biologics 8800 Rockville Pike Bethesda MD 20014

VICKERS, STANLEY M., allergist; b. Bklyn., Oct. 19, 1927; s. Hyman and Henrietta V.; B.A., Columbia Coll., 1948, M.D., 1953; m. Esther Molinoff, Dec. 30, 1962; children—Sara B., Julia F. Intern, Bellevue Hosp., N.Y.C., 1953-54; resident in pediatrics Babies Hosp., N.Y.C., 1954-56, in allergy R.A. Cooke Inst. Allergy, Roosevelt Hosp., N.Y.C., 1958-59; individual practice medicine, specializing in pediatrics, Sayville, N.Y., 1956-58, in allergy, Huntington, N.Y., 1959—; chief allergy clinic Northport (N.Y.) VA Hosp., 1973—; asst. prof. clin. medicine State U. N.Y. at Stony Brook, 1973—. Served with U.S. Army, 1946-47. Diplomate Am. Bd. Pediatrics, Am. Bd. Allergy and Immunology. Fellow Am. Coll. Allergists, Am. Acad. Allergy, Am. Acad. Pediatrics; mem. Suffolk County (sec. 1956—), N.Y. State med. socs., Nassau-Suffolk Allergy Soc. Jewish. Club: Racquet Huntington. Office: 68 Nassau Rd Huntington NY 11743

VICKERSON, CHARLES EDWARD, clergyman; b. Sault Ste Marie, Ont., Can., July 29, 1941; s. Harry James and Nellie May (Longhurst) V.; B.A., Concordia U., Montreal, Que., Can., 1970; B.Th., McGill U., Montreal, 1973. Jr. exec. trainee McConnel-Eastman Advt. Agy., Toronto, Ont., 1960-63; jr. account exec. Spitzer, Mills and Bates Advt. Agy., Toronto, 1963-65; media dir. Stanfield, Johnson and Hill Advt. Agy., Montreal, 1965-67; ordained to ministry United Ch. Can., 1973; minister Milk River (Alta., Can.) United Ch., 1973-74, Rawdon (Que.) United Ch., 1974—; organizer Jesus People Revival Movement, Sta. CFCF-TV, Montreal, 1967-71, Talk-In, My Bag, Nat. Canadian TV Network; participant World Congress Evangelization, Lausanne, Switzerland, 1974. Exec. officer Ont. Progressive Conservative Party, 1960-65, Nat. Young Progressive Conservative Party, 1965-67. Active in war resistance movement, Can., 1967-69. Home: 431 4th Ave Rawdon PQ J0K 1S0 Canada

VICKS, ALBERT PAUL, trade assn. exec.; b. Erie, Pa., Mar. 2, 1915; s. Charles A. and Victoria A. (Caiola) V.; B.B.A., Duquesne U., 1939; m. Dorothy A. Zipperle, Jan. 5, 1952; 1 dau., Kathryn Ann. Engineman, Pa. R.R., Erie, 1941-45; owner Vicks' Food Market, Erie, 1945-49; exec. dir. Home Owned Food Stores Assn., Erie, 1949-52; founder, adminstr. Pa. Food Mchts. Assn., 1952—; pres. H.O. Gold Stamp Co., Erie, 1956-74; mem. Pa. Gov.'s Food Industry Com., 1970—; dir. Union Bank & Trust Co. Trustee St. Vincent's Hosp., Erie. Served with USAAF, 1940-41. Mem. Nat. Assn. Retail Grocers (Distinguished Service award 1973), Food Industry Assn. Execs. (pres. 1965-66), Pa. Soc. Clubs: Aviation, Univ., K.C., Asparagus. Contbr. columns to trade papers. Home: 3322 Forest Dr Erie PA 16505 Office: 2426-30 Parade St Erie PA 16512

VICTOR, BARRY ALAN, sculptor, painter; b. Rochester, N.Y., May 11, 1949; s. Louis and Evelyn (Brown) V.; A.A., Albany Jr. Coll., 1969; B.S. in Art Edn., State U. N.Y., New Paltz, 1972; m. Diana diGrandi, June 25, 1974. Sculptures, paintings in one-man shows Albany Art Gallery, 1969, Ann Leonard Art Gallery, 1975, B.A. Victor Gallery, Hyde Park, N.Y., 1977—; work pub. in Artist U.S.A., 1976-79; instr. summer art classes for adults and children; work represented pvt. collections U.S. and Europe. Mem. C. of C., 1977—. Recipient gold medals. Mem. Albany Art Gallery, Ann Leonard Art Gallery (Woodstick; N.Y.), asso. mem. Dutchess County Artists Assn. Jewish. Home: 3 Mansion Dr Hyde Park NY 12538

VICTOR, ELYSE GAIL, bilingual counselor; b. Boston, Nov. 20, 1952; d. Sumner Edward and Cynthia Beverly (Finn) Victor; B.A. in Psychology and Spanish, Hamilton Coll., 1974; M.Ed. in Counseling, Tufts U., 1977. Counseling intern Dorchester Mental Health Center, 1975-76, Batchelder Sch., 1975-76, Northshore Guidance Center, 1976-77, Salem State Coll., 1976-77; vis. instr. Tufts U., 1976, resident dir., Sept. 1975-1977; bilingual counselor Chelsea (Mass.) Sch. System, 1977—. Mem. Am. Personnel and Guidance Assn., Am. Sch. Counselor Assn., Nat. Assn. Bilingual Edn. Home: 115 Devonshire Rd Waban MA 02168 Office: Shurtleff Sch Bilingual Office Chelsea MA 02168

VICTOR, MARIO THOMAS, devel. co. exec.; b. Ridgway, Pa., Aug. 15, 1914; s. Frank and Lucrezia Borgia (DePamphli) V.; B.S., St. Bonaventure Coll., 1936; M.E., Pa. State U., 1939; m. Margaret E. Shaver, June 12, 1955; children—Carol, Margaret, Marcia, Michael, Frank. Sales engr. Keystone Carbon Co., St. Marys, Pa., 1939-48, sales mgr., 1946-48; gen. mgr., chmn. pres. Internat. Powder Metal Corp., Ridgway, Pa., Kent, Ohio and Colorado Springs, Colo., 1948-68; pres. powder metallurgy div. Alleghany Ludlum Steel Corp., Ridgeway, 1963-68, cons., 1968-78; pres. Laurel Acres Devel. Corp., Ridgway, 1978—. Pres. boro council, City of Ridgeway, 1958-63; mem. Bd. Labor and Industry, State of Pa., Harrisburg, 1958-68. Served with OSRD, 1941-45. Mem. Powder Metal Parts Assn., Soc. Automotive Engrs., Metal Parts Industries Fedn. Clubs: Kiwanis, Elks. Contbr. articles to profl. jours. Home: 522 Hyde Ave Ridgway PA 15853 Office: 220 Race St Ridgeway PA 15853

VIDA, JULIUS ADALBERT, pharm. co. exec. b. Losonc, Czechoslovakia, May 30, 1928; s. Julius George and Elizabeth Losonczy V.; came to U.S., 1957, naturalized, 1962; diploma in chemistry Pazmany Peter U., Budapest, Hungary, 1950; M.S., Carnegie Inst. Tech., 1959, Ph.D., 1960; m. Martha Botelle, Sept. 1, 1973; 1 dau. by previous marriage, Julie E.; children—Andre B., Nicholas D. Chemist, dept. head Egyt, Budapest, 1950-56; chemist Merck Co., Inc., Rahway, N.J., 1957-58; research fellow Harvard U., 1961-62; staff scientist Worcester (Mass.) Found. for Exptl. Biology, 1962-67; sect. head Kendall Co., Lexington, Mass., 1967-75; dir. chemistry, internat. div. Bristol-Myers Co., N.Y.C., 1975—; vis. lectr. Columbia U., 1977—; adj. prof. medicinal chemistry Northeastern U., Boston, 1972-75. Mem. Am. Chem. Soc., Assn. Harvard Chemists, Sigma Xi. Author: Androgens and Anabolic Agents, 1969. Editor, contbr. chpts. Anticonvulsants, 1977. Contbr. chpts. to books, articles on medicinal chemistry to profl. jours. Patentee in field. Office: Bristol-Myers Co 345 Park Ave New York City NY 10022

VIDLER, VIRGINIA ELLEN, writer; b. Buffalo, Aug. 24, 1928; d. Clifford Milton and Florence Mae (Hescock) Dawson; student Rochester Inst. Tech., 1947-49, Bryant and Stratton Bus. Inst., 1950; m. Edward White Vidler, June 30, 1951; children—Beverly, Ellen, Donald Edward. Clk.-typist N.Y. Telephone Co., Buffalo, 1950; exec. sec. Moog Valve Co., East Aurora, N.Y., 1951-52; freelance writer, 1952—; bookkeeper, corp. officer Vidler's Inc., East Aurora, 1967—; town and village historian East Aurora. Hon. adoptee Wolf Clan of Seneca Indians. Mem. Nat. League Am. Pen Women (pres. west N.Y. br. 1978—), N.Y. State Municipal Historians Assn., East Aurora C. of C., Aurora (hon. life), Seneca Indian Nation hist. socs. Author: American Indian Antiques, Arts and Artifacts of the Northeast, 1975; Sugarbush Antiques, 1979. Home: 309 Pardale Ave East Aurora NY 14052

VIEMEISTER, PETER EMMONS, bus. exec.; b. Mineola, N.Y., 1929; s. August Louis and Janet (Emmons) V.; B.M.E. (Grumman scholar), Rensselaer Poly. Inst., 1950; S.M. (Sloan Fellow), Mass. Inst. Tech., 1969; m. Suzanne Neelands, 1951 (div. 1965); children—Clay N., Read L., Susan B., Katherine A.; m. 2d, Revelle Hamilton, 1975. With Lippincott & Margulies, N.Y.C., 1945; with Grumman Aircraft, Bethpage, N.Y., 1946-57, mgr. bus. planning, 1960-65; pres. Grumman Data Systems Corp., Bethpage, 1969-73; chmn. bd. Computility, Inc., Boston, 1971-73; v.p. Grumman Corp., 1973—; dir. Grumman Allied Industries; adj. asso. prof. Dowling Coll., 1972-73. Mem. Citizens Parks Com., 1963; chmn. bd. Empire State Coll. Found., 1976-77; bd. dirs. S.C. Energy Research Inst., 1977—. Mem. Am. Assn. Automotive Medicine, Sigma Xi, Tau Beta Pi. Author: The Lightning Book, 1961; Psychosystems, 1973. Inventor behavior simulator. Office: Grumman Corp Bethpage NY 11714

VIERAS, FRANK, physician; b. San Juan, P.R., Oct. 7, 1947; s. Ricardo and Angela Ursula (Alejandro) V.; B.S. magna cum laude, U. P.R., 1968, M.D., 1972; m. Vilma Reyes, Dec. 22, 1971; children—Frances Sulmarie, Vilma Monique. Commd. 2d lt. M.C., U.S. Air Force, 1971, advanced through grades to lt. col., 1979; med. intern U.S. Air Force Med. Center, Keesler AFB, Biloxi, Miss., 1972-73; resident in nuclear medicine U. Ark. Med. Scis., Little Rock, 1973-76; chief nuclear biology div. Armed Forces Radiobiology Research Inst., Bethesda, Md., 1976—; sr. cons. nuclear med. clinic Nat. Naval Med. Center, 1977—; lectr. radiation biology Uniformed Services U. Health Scis., Bethesda, 1977—. Diplomate Am. Bd. Nuclear Medicine. Mem. Am. Coll. Nuclear Physicians, AMA, Soc. Nuclear Medicine, Nat. Assn. Residents and Interns, Md. Med. Soc. Contbr. articles to med. jours. Office: Armed Forces Radiobiology Research Inst Nuclear Biology div Nat Naval Med Center Bethesda MD 20014

VIETH, WILLIAM HENRY, civil engr.; b. Washington, Oct. 21, 1927; s. Kenneth and Mary Frances (Stamper) V.; B.S., U. Md., 1954; m. Anna Aloisia Spindler, Dec. 1, 1946; children—Sonja Anne, Sylvia Frances, Kenneth James. Instrument man, survey party chief, J. R. McCrone, Jr. and Assos., Annapolis, Md., 1948-49; design engr., cons. civil engr., Greenhorne and O'Mara, Hyattsville, Md., 1953-57; cons. civil engr., corp. sec. John E. Harms, Jr. and Assos., Inc., Pasadena, Md., 1957—. Served with U.S. Army, 1945-48. Mem. Nat., Md. Socs. Profl. Engrs., Am. Water Works Assn., Profl. Engrs. in Pvt. Practice. Democrat. Episcopalian. Club: Internat. of Annapolis. Home: 268 King George St Annapolis MD 21401 Office: PO Box 5 Pasadena MD 21122

VIGNOLA, ANDREW MICHAEL, banker; b. N.Y.C., Sept. 6, 1938; s. Michael John and Mary Elizabeth (Romano) V.; student in Bus. Adminstrn., Coll. City N.Y., 1956-59; m. Barbara Francis Hummel, Aug. 22, 1959; children—Ellen Ann, Andrew Michael, Robert Eugene. Programmer trainee 1st City Nat. Bank N.Y., N.Y.C., 1959-60; programmer analyst Soc. for Savs., Hartford, Conn., 1960-63; mgr. on-line data center NCR Corp., Boston, 1963-67; cons., sr. partner Computer Assistance, Inc., Hartford, 1967-72; v.p., info. systems service div. Soc. for Savs., Hartford, 1972—; pres. Solar Services, Inc. subs. Soc. for Savs., 1977—; mem. faculty Conn. Savs. Bank Sch.; lectr. in field. Mem. Data Processing Mgmt. Assn. (pres., chmn. bd. Hartford chpt. 1976-77), Assn. System Mgmt. (profl.). Contbr. articles to profl. jours. Home: 161 N Timber Ln Cheshire CT 06410 Office: 1290 Silas Deane Hwy Wethersfield CT 06109

VIGNONI, JOHN CHARLES, JR., hosp. adminstr.; b. Quincy, Mass., Sept. 22, 1947; s. John Charles and Elsie Norma (Melchionno) V.; student Bryant and Stratton Jr. Coll., 1966-68; B.B.A., U. Palm Beach, 1970, M.B.A., 1971; m. Paula Eileen Daley, May 19, 1973; 1 dau., Tara Ann. Unit mgr. Quincy (Mass.) City Hosp., 1971-73, central service mgr., 1973-76, asst. dir. gen. services, 1976—, safety com. chmn., 1973-76. Home: 48 Hayden St Quincy MA 02169 Office: 114 Whitwell St Quincy MA 02169

VIGUE, JAMES FRANCIS, investment advisor; b. Waterville, Maine, May 16, 1949; s. Harold Lionel and Evangeline (Julia) V.; B.A., Colby Coll., Waterville, 1972; m. Susan I. Bassi, June 28, 1975. Vice pres. Donald O. Smith Co., Waterville, 1973-77; regional mgr. 1st Affiliated Securities, Waterville, 1977—; pres. Capital Planning Assos., Waterville, 1972—, Realvest, Waterville, 1974—; tchr. real estate courses Thomas Coll. Registered investment advisor; certified fin. planner; registered ins. cons., real estate advisor. Mem. Nat. Assn. Securities Dealers (certified fin. prin.), Internat. Assn. Fin. Planners, Assn. Certified Fin. Planners. Home: 28 Cherry Hill Dr Waterville ME 04901 Office: 100 Silver St Waterville ME 04901

VIKLUND, WILLIAM EDWIN, banker; b. Bklyn., June 12, 1940; s. Edwin O. and Anna I. (Kvarnstrom); B.A., L.I. U., 1960; m. Joyce Eleanor Larson, Apr. 14, 1962; children—Mark, David, Andrea. Vice-pres., mortgage officer Anchor Savs. Bank, N.Y.C., 1967-71; v.p. C.I. Planning Corp., N.Y.C., 1972; sr. v.p. Bankers Trust Co., N.Y.C., 1972—; mem. adv. bd. Real Estate Inst. N.Y. U. Trustee Augustana Home for Aged, 1976—; bd. govs. N.Y. Bldg. Congress, 1977. Mem. N.Y. Real Estate Bd., Mortgage Bankers Assn. Club: Plandome (N.Y.) Country. Home: 110 Grist Mill Ln Plandome Manor NY 11030 Office: 280 Park Ave New York City NY 10017

VILKITIS, JAMES RICHARD, ecologist; b. Rush, Pa., Oct. 31; s. Joseph Edgar and Kathryn Ann (Fetchkowsky) V.; B.S., Mich. State U., 1965; M.S., U. Idaho, 1968; Ph.D., U. Mass., 1970, postgrad., 1971-72. Ecol. resource cons., biostatistician Regional Planning and Design Assos., Amherst, Mass., 1969-71; leader spl. big game project Maine Dept. Inland Fisheries and Game, Augusta, 1970-71; natural resource ecologist, planner Carlozzi, Sinton and Vilkitis Inc., Amherst, 1971—; lectr. div. continuing edn. U. Mass., Amherst, 1971—, research asso. Inst. Man and Environment, 1973-74; asst. prof. biol. scis. Mt. Holyoke Coll., S. Hadley, Mass.; partner Rams Head Leather Works Ltd., Ann Arbor, Mich., 1976-77; owner, operator TCL Leather, Amherst, 1977—. Bd. dirs. Amherst Resource

Center, 1978—. Mem. Wildlife Soc., Project Mgmt. Inst., NE Deer Study Group, Trout Unltd., Phi Sigma, Xi Sigma Pi. Home: RFD 2 W Pelham Rd Amherst MA 01002 Office: PO Box 831 Amherst MA 01002

VILLAFANE, EDWARD, JR., clergyman, rehab. home exec.; b. Ponce, P.R., Nov. 27, 1936; s. Eduardo and Carmen (Rivera) V.; D.D. (hon.), Universal Life Ch., 1974; m. Anna Padro, Mar. 18, 1969; children—Veronica Villafane Silva, Eric. Ordained to ministry Universal Life Ch., 1967; adminstr. Damascus Youth Center for Drug Abuse, Mountaindale, N.Y., 1965-67, also minister Universal Life Ch., Phoenix, 1974—; dir. Anchor House Religious Drug Center, Bklyn., 1967-68; founder, exec. dir. Way-Out Home for Addicts, Inc., Bronx, N.Y., 1970—; mem. Nat. Puerto Rican Drug Abuse Corp., 1975—, bd. dirs., 1975—; cons. in field to numerous local civic, religious groups. Served with USAF, 1954-55. Recipient 12 certificates from various religious orgns. Home: 1044 Morris Ave Bronx NY 10456 Office: 520 E 148 St Bronx NY 10455

VILLANUEVA, E. GARY CUENCA, JR., physician; b. Lipa City, Philippines, Dec. 27, 1934; s. Engracio Kalaw and Rosario (Cuenca) V.; came to U.S., 1970, naturalized, 1976; A.A., U. Santo Tomas, 1953, M.D., 1958; m. Imelda Garcia, May 4, 1963; children—Donna-Mae, Elaine, Gerald, Paul, Joseph. Intern, St. Johns Riverside Hosp., Yonkers, N.Y., 1960; med. resident Martland Med. Center, Newark, 1960-61, Maimonides, Coney Island Hosp., Bklyn., 1962-65; fellow in nutrition and metabolism Tulane U. Sch. Medicine, 1965; cons. metabolic diseases Family Clinic Hosp., Manila, Philippines, 1970; vis. internist Chinese Gen. Med. Center, Manila, 1970; primary care physician Brookdale Med. Center Hosp., Bklyn., 1970-73, med. dir., attending physician Lutheran Hosp. of Bklyn., 1972-79, sec., mem. exec. bd., 1974—; lectr. nutrition-biochemistry and physiology U. Santo Tomas, Faculty Medicine, Faculty Pharmacy and Biochemistry. Trustee, Luth. Hosp. Assn. N.Y., 1975-76, 79. Recipient Outstanding Mentor award U. Santo Tomas Pharm. Supreme Council, 1970, award of merit Luth. Hosp., 1974; named Outstanding Med. Educator, Luth. Hosp., 1976, Citizen of Month E. New Yorker, 1977; Jour. award Philippine Med. Assn., 1978, Meritorious Service award, 1978. Mem. Am. Acad. Med. Dirs., A.C.P., Am., N.Y. State, S.I. socs. internal medicine, Am., Philippine med. assns., Assn. Philippine Practicing Physicians in Am., N.Y. State, Kings County med. socs., Internat. Coll. Angiology. Roman Catholic. Author: Laboratory Manual in Intermediary Metabolism, 1969-70; Exodus-New Voices in American Poetry, 1973; The Gospel, 1978. Home: 738 Hylan Blvd Staten Island NY 10305

VILLARREAL, JAMES ALPHONSE, psychol. counselor; b. Manila, Sept. 11, 1937; s. Carlos Villarreal and Rosario Carrion; came to U.S., 1968, naturalized, 1974: A.B. in English, San Beda Coll., Philippines, 1961: M.A. in Psychology, Ateneo U., Philippines, 1967: M.Ed. in Counseling Psychology, Temple U., 1978. Dir. counseling services San Beda High Sch., Philippines, 1966-68; prof. psychology and philosophy San Beda Coll., 1964-68; asst. prof. psychology and philosophy, counselor Alvernia Coll., Reading, Pa., 1969-74; counseling supr. CORA Services, Phila., 1974—; ofcl. Spanish interpreter Berks County (Pa.) Cts., 1970: lectr.; counselor parent groups; cons. Religious Life Renewal, Sisters of the Cross, Washington Province. Mem. Am. Personnel and Guidance Assn., Berks County Mental Health/Mental Retardation Assn., Am. Sch. Counselors Assn., Pa. Assn. Counselor Edn. and Supervision. Roman Catholic. Office: 733 Susquehanna Rd Philadelphia PA 19111

VINCENT, DONALD EDWARD PERRY, librarian; b. Martin's Ferry, Ohio, Dec. 26, 1922; s. George Nicholas and Anne (Martochko) P.; B.A., U. Buffalo, 1949; A.M. in L.S., U. Mich., 1952, M.A. in Polit. Sci., 1957, Ph.D. in L.S., 1974; m. Nancy Elizabeth Suliburk; children—Daniel Perry, Jerett Edward. Cataloger, Wayne State U., Detroit, 1952-58, bibliographer, 1958-59, lectr. in library sci., 1957-59; dir. library services U. Mich., Dearborn, 1959-62; univ. librarian U. N.H., Durham, 1962—. Vice chmn. N.H. Library Council, 1970-71, chmn., 1971-72; mem. Region I Archives Council, 1971-73; mem. N.H. Gov.'s Com. for Better Libraries, 1962-63, N.H. Advisory Council on Libraries, 1972-78. Served to lt. (j.g.) USN, 1943-47. Mem. ALA, New Eng. (pres. 1975-76, 76-77), N.H. (v.p. 1963-65) library assns., New Eng. Library Info. Network (chmn. exec. com. 1967-72), Phi Kappa Phi, Beta Phi Mu. Home: Riverview Rd Durham NH 03824

VINCENT, MARC-AURÈLE, ednl. adminstr.; b. Hull, Qué., Can., Apr. 6, 1934; s. Aurèle and Germaine (Lacourcière) V.; B.A., B.Ph., U. Ottawa, Can., 1956, B.A. (hon.), 1957, B.S. in Math. and Physics (hon.), 1961, Th.B., 1963, M.A. in Philosophy, 1965, Th.M., 1965, M.S. in Physics, 1966; D.Sc. in Physics, U. Paris, 1971; m. Françoise Desjardins, Mar. 20, 1976; children—Jean-Luc, Brigitte, Benoît. Instr., research asst. Faculty of Sci., U. Ottawa, Ont., 1965-66, post-doctoral fellow, dept. math., 1971-72, head supr. of 1st year physics labs., dept. physics, 1971-72; tng. supr. Centre de Recherches en Sciences Apliquées à l'Alimentation (Cresala) U. Québec, Montréal, 1972-73, lectr. (part-time) in physics, 1972-73, research coordinator, 1973-74, asst. dir. planification and mgmt., 1974-76, dean of studies Hull campus, 1977—, research dir., 1978—, cons. in physics, 1973—, mem. bd. dirs. Cresala, 1972—; exec. sec. 2d Internat. Symposium on Ozone Tech., Montréal, 1975. Mem. Am. Phys. Soc., Société d'Astronomie du Québec, Am. Math. Soc., Société Française de Physique, Internat. Ozone Inst. (chmn. N.Am. exec. com. 1977—), Assn. Canadienne Française pour l'Avancement des Scis. Roman Catholic. Contbr. articles on nuclear physics to sci. jours. Home: 226 Ave Greensway Vanier ON K1L 7V4 Canada Office: Centre d'études universitaires dans l'Ouest Québéçois U Québec CP 1250 Succursale B Hull PQ J8X 3X7 Canada

VINCENT, NORMAN ROBERT, physician; b. Sydney, Australia, Mar. 13, 1932; came to U.S., 1961, naturalized, 1976; s. Sidney Norman and Gladys May (Eichler) V.; M.D., U. B.C., 1961; m. Beverley Eilleen Watts, Aug. 20, 1955; children—Lisa Marianne, Christopher Robert. Intern, St. Vincents Hosp., Bridgeport, Conn., 1961-62, resident in radiology, 1962-65; resident in radiology Bellevue Hosp. Med. Center, N.Y.C., 1963; attending radiologist St. Vincents Hosp., Bridgeport, 1965—, dir. div. nuclear medicine, 1970—. asst. clin. prof. Yale New Haven Hosp., 1975—. Diplomate Am. Bd. Radiology, Am. Bd. Nuclear Medicine. Mem. Am. Coll. Radiology, Soc. Nuclear Medicine, Radiol. Soc. Conn., Conn. Med. Soc., Fairfield County Med. assn., Coll. physicians and Surgeons B.C., Alpha Omega Alpha. Asso. editor Clinical Nuclear Medicine, 1975—. Office: 10 Washington Ave Bridgeport CT 06604

VINCENT, ROBERT CLARENCE, JR., lawyer; b. N.Y.C., May 21, 1938; s. Robert Clarence and Elizabeth Mandeville (Bracher) V.; B.A., Dartmouth Coll., 1961; LL.B., Columbia U., 1965; m. Barbara McMahon Bolich, Aug. 26, 1961; children—Page Pendleton, Caroline Talman, Robert Clarence. Admitted to N.Y. bar, 1965; practiced in N.Y.C., 1965—; asso. firm Skadden, Arps, Slate, Meagher & Flom, 1965-71, partner, 1971—; dir. Barclays Bank N.Y., Nat. Securities Corp., Windward Corp., Bankmanagers Corp., Knirps Internat. Ltd., Mespo Umbrellas Ltd. Office: 919 3d Ave New York City NY 10022

VINCENT, THEODORE HAROLD, journalist, photographer; b. Pittsfield, Mass., July 18, 1910; s. Harry Harold and Maude Adelle (Gardiner) V.; grad. Progressive Sch. Photography, 1948, Newspaper Inst. Am., 1954; m. Ruth Alvina Sampson, Nov. 22, 1937; children—Theodore Harold, Mary-Elizabeth Vincent Sampson. Div. mgr. Sears, Roebuck and Co., New Bedford, Mass., 1940-42, 45-47; freelance photojournalist, Wesport, Mass., 1950-65; columnist World Outdoors, The New Bedford Standard-Times, 1961-74, staff writer-photographer, 1965-76, outdoor editor, 1966-74, environ. conservation natural resources spl. writer, 1973-76, ret., 1976; lectr., tchr. in field; spl. writer Cape Cod Times, 1977—. Dir. Environ.-Solar Energy Research Project, Edgartown, Mass., 1974; tech. sub-com. mem. Pilgrim Area Resource Conservation and Devel. Project, 1971; resource adviser info. and edn. Resource Conservation and Devel. Council, 1975, mem. council representing Dukes County Commns., Dukes Conservation Dists., 1977. Served with U.S. Army, 1942-45. Recipient Jim Hurley Meml. sportsmanship award, 1964; award outstanding contributions to youth and conservation, Mahar Regional Sch., Orange, Mass., 1968; award of merit State Maine, 1969; named to Fishing Hall Fame, 1968. Mem. New Eng. Outdoor Writers Assn. (pres. 1967), Environ. Writers Assn. Am. Research in developing environ. land use to utilize insulation properties of earth and other alt. sources of energy, 1973—. Home: 18 Glenwood Ave Westport MA 02790 Office: Off W Tisbury Rd RFD Box 35A Edgartown MA 02539

VINE, HANNAH MOLLIE, food services dir.; b. Bklyn., Dec. 12, 1925; d. Nathan and Lillian (Chamikles) Siegel; grad. Kings County Hosp. Sch. Nursing, N.Y.C., 1943-46; A.A., Bklyn. Coll., 1947; student art Adelphi Coll., 1960-62, interior design Willsey Inst. Art Interior Design, 1962, food service mgmt., dietetic assistance Seldon Community Coll., 1975-76; m. Tovia Aaron Vine, Feb. 22, 1949; children—Mark Emmanuel, Libby Nadine Vine Rosenfeld, Morrey Morton. Pvt. duty nurse Star Registry, 1948-49, 50, 51; interior designer Libby Decorators, Island park, N.Y., 1952-75: instr. interior design Willsey Inst. Art Interior Design, 1963: tchr. interior design Uniondale (N.Y.) High Sch., 1964; instr. spl. subjects Hebrew Inst. L.I., Hebrew Acad. Long Beach, 1964-75; dir. food services Nassau Nursing Home, Oceanside, N.Y., 1975—. pres. Ladies of Bachurei Chemed Synagogue, Long Beach, N.Y., 1971-76; pres. L.I. Dist. Women's Br. Union Orthodox Gonregations Am., Nat. Com. for Furtherance Jewish Edn.; chmn. bd. ladies Bachurei Chemed Youth Synagogue. Recipient Founders and Pres's. award L.I. chpt. Nat. Com. for Furtherance Jewish Edn., 1977, plaque for service Nat. Conf. Synagogue Youth, 1975. Mem. Hosp. Insnl. Ednl. Food Service Soc. (pres. L.I. dist.), N.Y. State Hosp. Instl. Ednl. Food Service Soc., Am. Soc. Hosp. Food Adminstrs., Nassau Suffolk Hosp. Food Adminstrs. Assn. Democrat. Author diet man., syllabus for home econs. and policies and procedures man. for Nassau Nursing Home. Home: 118 W Olive St Long Beach NY 11561 Office: Nassau Nursing Home 2914 Lincoln Ave Oceanside NY 11572

VINER, EDWARD DAVID, physician; b. Middletown, N.J., Oct. 24, 1935; s. Edward A. and Amelia I. (Amerise) V.; B.A. cum laude, Harvard U., 1956; M.D., U. Pa., 1960; m. Judith Benson, Apr. 5, 1969; children—Carol, Beth, James, Jennifer, Julia. Intern, Hosp. U. Pa., Phila., 1960-61, resident in internal medicine, 1961-63, fellow in hematology, 1964-65; practice medicine specializing in hematology, oncology, Phila., 1965—; acting dir. dept. medicine Pa. Hosp., Phila., 1967-69, head hematology oncology sect., 1967—; asso. prof. clin. medicine U. Pa. Sch. Medicine, 1974—. Diplomate Am. Bd. Internal Medicine. Mem. AMA, Am. Soc. Hematology, Am. Soc. Clin. Oncology, Phila. County Med. Soc., Phila. Coll. Physicians, Phila. Hematology Soc., Am. Cancer Soc. (bd. dirs. Phila. chpt.), Lupus Assn. Delaware Valley (bd. dirs.), Alpha Omega Alpha. Home: 1633 Montgomery Ave Villanova PA 19085 Office: Pa Hosp 8th and Spruce Sts Philadelphia PA 19107

VINICK, RICHARD LAURENCE, pub. relations exec.; b. Schenectady, May 4; s. Samuel and Del (Rosenzweig) V.; grad. Am. Acad. Dramatic Arts, 1948. Actor, east coast stock prodns., radio, TV, 1946-50; publicity dir. Simon & Schuster, Inc., N.Y.C., 1950-58; pub. relations rep. Air France, N.Y.C., 1958-66; pub. relations exec. Daniel J. Edelman, Inc., N.Y.C., 1966-71, Harshe-Rotman & Druck, Inc., N.Y.C., 1971-73, Edward Gottlieb & Assos., Ltd., 1973-77, Gross & Assos./Pub. Relations, Inc., 1978—. Mem. Pub. Relations Soc. Am., Actors Equity Assn., Actors Fund Am. Home: 437 E 74th St New York City NY 10021 Office: 592 Fifth Ave New York City NY 10036

VIOLA, LEONARD JOHN, chemist; b. Yonkers, N.Y., May 21, 1924; s. Constantine Frank and Hilma Marie (Ronkainen) V.; B.S., U. Louisville, 1949, M.S. (USN fellow), 1951; postgrad., Poly. Inst. N.Y., 1952-55; m. Jane Katerine Taylor, June 12, 1949; children—Leonard John, Katherine Marie, Judy Ann, Susan, Lynn. Scientist, chemist Warner-Lambert Co., Morris Plains, N.J., 1952-55; dir. research Caryl Richards Inc., N.Y.C., 1955-57; pres. Visom Inc., Yonkers, 1957-63; group leader Richardson Merril, Inc., Mt. Vernon, N.Y., 1963—. Served with USAAF, 1942-45. Decorated Air Medal with 2 oak leaf clusters, Purple Heart. Mem. Am. Chem. Soc., Am. Pharm. Soc. Patentee foam cleansers; contbg. author Cosmetics Sci. and Tech., vol. 2., 1972. Home: 94 Colonial Pkwy Yonkers NY 10710

VIOLANTE, THOMAS ROBERT, advt. cons.; b. New Haven, June 7, 1946; s. Samuel Robert and Elizabeth Jean (Paparella) Forte V.; A.B., New Haven Coll., U. New Haven, 1969; postgrad. So. Conn. State Coll., 1970-71. Advt. and mktg. mgr. Fair Haven Camera Shops, Inc., New Haven, 1971-72; pvt. practice advt. design cons.; graphics dir. Universal Electronic Seal Corp., Norwalk, Conn., 1973; past dir. advt., media, and communications Corometrics Med. Systems, Inc., Wallingford, Conn.; lectr. U. New Haven; pres. TRV Property Adminstrs.; pres. Innervisions Advt., Meriden, Conn.; mgr., past pres. Blackstone Village Condominium Assn. #1, Meriden. Recipient design award Hopper/Georgia Pacific Paper Co., 1977, advt. recognition awards McGraw-Hill Pub. Co., 1973-77. Mem. Modern Lang. Assn., Conn. Condominium Council (charter), Community Assns. Inst. (asso.). Editor: A Primer of Neonatal Heart Rate Monitoring (Luis Cabal), 1977; writer music (several recordings): co-inventor patient record/storage system. Office: 12 Curtis St Meriden CT 06450

VIRGULAK, FRANCIS EDWARD, security service adminstr., ret. city ofcl.; b. Norwalk, Conn., Apr. 2, 1916; s. Francis Joseph and Velma Veronica (Vadas) V.; grad. Bridgeport Engring. Inst., 1939, U.S. Armed Forces Inst., 1946, FBI-Nat. Acad., 1951, Command Tng. Inst. Babson Coll., 1969; m. Anne Veronica Baltovich, July 22, 1939; children—Barbara Virgulak Keeny, Francis Edward, James F. With Yankee Metal Products Corp., Norwalk, Conn., 1934-44, personnel mgr., 1942-44, asst. factory supt., 1944-46; with Norwalk Police Dept., 1946-76, lt., 1959-60, capt., 1960-61, insp., 1961-67, chief police, 1967-76; regional adminstr. IBI Security Service, Inc., Bridgeport, Conn., 1976—; security officer So. Norwalk Savs. Bank; founder, pres. Fairfield County Fraudulent Check Assn.; faculty Internat. Police Services Acad., Washington and Vienna, Va., 1952-57; nationwide lecture tour Fed. Bur. Narcotics and Dangerous Drugs, 1970; organizer, implementer 1st drug edn. program to be presented in pub. schs., 1960; organizer co-op. enforcement squads aimed at apprehending dealers and pushers narcotics and illicit drugs; chmn. S.W. Region Criminal Justice Supervisory Bd., 1969—. Bd. dirs. Howland Found., Hooper Found., Spear Drug Program, Greater Norwalk Community Council; mem. Bishop's Commn. Human Rights and Opportunities, Diocese of Bridgeport. Served with USNR, 1944-46. Named Norwalk High Sch. Alumnus of Year, 1965; Outstanding Hungarian of Year, 1967; recipient Norwalk Jewish Center Sportsman's award, 1966; Cath. War Vets. Outstanding Service to God, Country and Home award, 1968; citation for meritorious service Bur. Narcotics and Dangerous Drugs, 1971; Distinguished Service award Police Commrs. Assn. Conn., 1974; numerous service club certificates for services. Mem. Internat. Acad. Criminology, Internat., New Eng., Conn., Fairfield County chiefs of police assns., FBI Nat. Acad. Assos. (pres. 1971), Norwalk Athletic Assn. (charter). Roman Catholic (pres. Holy Name Soc. 1963-64). Clubs: K.C. (4 deg.); South Norwalk Boat; Norwalk Quartette. Home: 66 Quintard Ave South Norwalk CT 06854

VIRUS, JOHN ROBERT, cologne co. exec.; b. Johnstown, Pa.; s. John and Christina Anna (Urias) V.; student pub. and pvt. schs., Johnstown. Founder, owner, operator Brandy Harvest Colognes, N.Y.C., 1962—. Office: 53-06 39th Ave Woodside Queens New York City NY 11377

VITA, DOMINICK CHARLES, sch. and community counselor; b. Norwalk, Conn., Nov. 29, 1950; d. Rocco A. and Mary V.; B.A., Assumption Coll., 1972; M.A., Fairfield U., 1974; 6th year profl. diploma U. Bridgeport, 1975; Ph.D., Heed U., 1976; m. Maureen Margaret McGovern, Jan. 15, 1972; children—Melissa Marie, Dominick Christopher, Carrie Anne. Tchr., Cathedral High Sch., Bridgeport, Conn., 1972-76; counselor Roton Middle Sch., Norwalk, Conn., 1976—; counseling psychologist Norwalk Cath. Family and Community Service, 1977—; asst. prof. Coll. Health Scis. U. Bridgeport, 1978—. Mem. Greater Norwalk C. of C. (dir. vocat. exploration program), Conn., Am. personnel and guidance assns., Nat. Psychol. Assn., Am. Assn. Applied Psychology, Nat. Vocat. Guidance Assn. Roman Catholic. Home: 15 Old Witch Ct Rowayton CT 06853

VITANZA, ANGELO ANTHONY, psychologist; b. N.Y.C., Sept. 26, 1918; s. Thomas and Mary (Carlano) V.; emigrated from Sicily, 1903; B.A., N.Y. U., 1949, M.A., 1953, Ph.D., 1957. Intern in psychology Creedmoor State Hosp., Queens, N.Y., 1955, staff psychologist, 1958; psychotherapist L.I. Consultation Center, Rego Park, Queens, 1959-61; adminstrv. dir. Fifth Ave. Center Counseling and Psychotherapy, N.Y.C., 1961—; pvt. practice psychol. counseling, N.Y.C., 1959—; treas. Greenwich Inst. Psychoanalytic Studies, N.Y.C., 1961—. Served with U.S. Army, 1941-45. Decorated Bronze Star (2). Mem. Am. Psychol. Assn., N.Y. Soc. Clin. Psychologists. Club: Marshall Chess. Contbr. tech. papers to field. Office: 10 W 10th St New York City NY 10011

VITEK, CLEMENT GERARD, newspaper librarian; b. Balt., Mar. 6, 1920; s. John Rudolf and Elizabeth Remegia (Cvach) V.; student Balt. Bus. Coll., 1939-40, Loyola Coll., Balt., 1966-68; m. Grace Carolyn Easter, Oct. 17, 1941; 1 son, Brent Gerard. With Balt. Sun, 1938—, chief librarian, 1950—. Served with USNR, 1944-46. Mem. Spl. Libraries Assn., Md. Hist. Soc., Md. Library Assn., Nat. Press Club, Nat. Micrographics Assn. Democrat. Roman Catholic. Home: 8705 Wendell Ave Baltimore MD 21234 Office: 501 N Calvert St Baltimore MD 21202

VITELLI, ELINOR MARIE, hosp. adminstr.; b. Sebago, Maine, Dec. 22, 1920: d. Chester Arthur and Avis Pearl (Richardson) Wormhood; diploma Maine Eye and Ear Infirmary, 1941; m. Bartholomew S. Vitelli, Apr. 26, 1943; children—Bartholomew S., Chester Patrick, Marie Elizabeth, Christine Marie. Staff nurse Maine Eye and Ear Infirmary, Portland, 1941; sch. nurse Maine State Sch. for Boys, Portland, 1942; staff nurse Ellis Hosp., Schenectady, 1943-44, Sunnyview Hosp. and Rehab. Center, Schenectady, 1945—, v.p. nursing services, 1976—; dir. Health Systems Agency Northeastern NY, 1975—; mem. adv. com. BOCES Vocat. Program, Albany and Schenectady, 1971—. Mem. Am., N.Y. State nurses assns., Nat. League Nursing, Hosp. Assn. Northeastern N Y. Republican. Baptist. Home: 1414 Belmont Ave Schenectady NY 12308 Office: 1470 Belmont Ave Schenectady NY 12308

VITETTA, FRANCIS GUY, architect; b. Mamaroneck, N.Y., Apr. 8, 1932; s. Guy and Theresa M. (Rapolla) V.; B.S. in Archtl. Engring., U. Pa., 1955; m. Dorothea Henry, Mar. 17, 1957; children—Guy, Stacy, Robin. Archtl. draftsman Wm. Cramp Scheetz Architect, Phila., 1957-60; project architect Harkins & Alvare, Architects & Planners, Norristown, Pa., 1960-63; chief architect Day & Zimmermann Assos., Phila., 1963-66, mng. partner, 1966—; prin. Francis G. Vitetta, Westville, N.J., 1966—. Served to 1st lt. USAF, 1955-57. Mem. Beta Theta Pi (dir.). Republican. Roman Catholic. Archtl. works include: N.J. Vineland City Hall, 1971; Morton Sch., Phila. (AASA jury citation for design 1971), 1970; Mt. Laurel (N.J.) Middle Sch.; Phila. Acad. Fine Arts restoration, 1974; 1st Bank U.S. restoration, Phila., 1974, 76; Garden State Hosp., Evesham Twp., N.J., 1973; Echelon Mall, Voohres Twp., N.J. (Distinguished Bldg. award A.I.A.); Cumberland County (N.J.) Vocational-Tech. Sch. (Sch. of Yr. award N.J. Dept. Edn.); Pa. Acad. Fine Arts Restoration, 1976; restoration and Renovations Bellview Stratford Hosp., Phila.; 1979; Camden (N.J.) VA Hosp., 1979. Home: Box 352 Springhouse PA 19477 Office: 1818 Market St Philadelphia PA 19103 also 919 Broadway Westville NJ 08093

VITT, SAM B., advt. co. exec.; b. Greensboro, N.C., Oct. 23, 1926; s. Bruno Caesar and Gray (Bradshaw) V.; A.B., Dartmouth Coll., 1950; m. Marie Foster, Oct. 30, 1955; children—Joanne Louise, Michael Bradshaw, Mark Thomas. Exec. asst. TV film CBS, N.Y.C., 1950-52; broadcast media buyer Benton & Bowles, Inc., N.Y.C., 1952-54; broadcast media buyer Biow Co., N.Y.C., 1954-55, asso. account exec., 1955-56; broadcast media buyer Doherty, Clifford, Steers & Shenfield, Inc., N.Y.C., 1956-57, media supr., 1958-59, v.p., media supr., 1960, v.p., asso. media dir., 1960, v.p., media dir., 1960-63, v.p. in charge media and broadcast programming, 1963-64; v.p., exec. dir. media-program Ted Bates & Co., Inc., N.Y.C., 1964-66, sr. v.p. exec. dir. media-program dept., 1966-69; founder, pres. Vitt Media Internat., Inc., N.Y.C., 1969—; advt. dir. Banking Law Jour., 1955-69; lectr. advt. N.Y. U., 1973, 74, Am. Mgmt. Assn., 1974, 75, Assn. Nat. Advertisers, 1967, 69, 70, Advt. Age Media Workshop, 1975, 77. Dir. N.Y.C. Comml. Devel. Corp., 1966-69; chmn. radio-TV reps. div. Greater N.Y. Fund, 1962, chmn. pub. div., 1963; dir. advt. Info. Services, Inc., 1964-65; mem. Nat. UN Day, 1973, vice chmn., 1974, asso. chmn., 1975, co-chmn., 1976, 77; bd. govs. N.Y. Young Republican Club, 1957-58, editor Directory, 1956-57. Recipient Media award Sta. WRAP, Norfolk, Va., 1962; award of Merit Greater N.Y. Fund, 1963; Gold Key Advt. Leadership award Sta. Reps. Assn., 1967; certificate merit Media/Scope, 1967, 69; Ann. honors Ad Daily, 1967. Mem. Am. Assn. Advt. Agys. (broadcast media com. corr. 1958-63, media operating com. on consumer mags. 1964-65), Internat. Radio and TV Soc. (timebuying and selling seminar com. 1961-62), UN Assn. Am. (dir. 1977), Sigma Alpha Epsilon. Clubs: Manor Park Beach (Larchmont, N.Y.); N.Y. Athletic (N.Y.C.); Roxbury Run Country (Denver, N.Y.). Presbyterian. Contbg. editor, columnist Madison Ave., 1963-68; editorial cons. Media/Scope, 1968-69; cover story guest editor Media Decisions,

1967; contbg. editor: Handbook of Advertising Management, 1970; contbr., cons. Advertising Procedure, 5th edit., 1966, 6th edit., 1973, 7th edit., 1977; contbr. Exploring Advertising, 1970; producer record album The Body in the Seine. Home: 3 Roosevelt Ave Larchmont NY 10538 also Roxbury Run Roxbury NY Office: 1114 Ave of Americas New York City NY 10036

VITTORINI, CARLO, publisher; b. Phila., Feb. 28, 1929; s. Domenico and Helen (Whitney) V.; B.A., U. Pa., 1950; m. Alice Hellerman, Oct. 10, 1953; children—Carolyn, Stephen W. With Chilton Publ., Phila., 1950-51; copy writer Farm Jour., Phila., 1951-53; with Saturday Evening Post, N.Y.C., 1953-60, asst. promotion engr., sales rep., 1953-60; asso. advt. sales mgr. Look mag., N.Y.C., 1960-65; with Redbook Publ. Co., N.Y.C., 1965—, advt. dir., 1966-69, pres., 1973—; pres. Charter Pub. Co., 1974—, Harlequin Mags., Inc., 1978—. Mem. Mag. Pub. Assn. (dir. 1973), Psi Upsilon. Episcopalian. Clubs: Sky (N.Y.C.); Bedford Golf and Tennis (Bedford, N.Y.). Home: Upper Hook Rd Katonah NY 10536 Office: 230 Park Ave New York City NY 10017

VIVERA, ARSENIO BONDOC, physician; b. Cebu City, Philippines, Oct. 29, 1931; s. Arsenio R. and Ramona del Mar (Bondoc) V.; A.A., Cebu Coll., U. Philippines, 1950, M.D., 1954. Intern, Philippines Gen. Hosp., 1954-55; resident in medicine Beekman-Downtown Hosp., N.Y.C., 1955-57, Detroit Meml. Hosp., 1957-58; resident in allergy Robert A. Cooke Inst. Allergy, Roosevelt Hosp., N.Y.C., 1958-59, fellow in allergy, 1959-61; sr. cons. scientist Philippines Nat. Inst. Sci. and Tech., Manila, 1961-62; practice medicine specializing in allergy, N.Y.C.; chief allergy dept. attending physician N.Y. Polyclinic Med. Sch. and Health Center, 1972-77, adj. prof., 1972-77; clin. asst. attending physician Robert A. Cooke Inst. Allergy, 1969—; asst. attending physician N.Y. Infirmary, N.Y.C., 1969—, St. Vincent's Hosp. and Med. Center, N.Y.C., 1977—. Diplomate Am. Bd. Allergy and Immunology. Fellow Am. Acad. Allergy, Am. Coll. Allergists, Am. Assn. Clin. Immunology and Allergy; mem. N.Y. Allergy Soc., AMA, N.Y. Acad. Scis., Am. Geriatric Soc., N.Y. State, N.Y. County med. socs. Office: 155 E 55th St New York City NY 10022

VIZY, KALMAN NICHOLAS, research physicist; b. Gyor, Hungary, July 7, 1940; s. Joseph and Helen Julianna (Meleg) V.; came to U.S., 1954, naturalized, 1962; B.Engring. Sci., Cleve. State U., 1964; M.S., John Carroll U., 1967; m. Mary Anne Smith, Aug. 31, 1968; children—Anne Katharine, Edward Kalman. Apprentice design engr. Warner & Swasey, Cleve., 1959-64; tchr. and dept. head scis. Byzantine Ednl. Center, Parma, Ohio, 1964-67; research physicist Eastman Kodak Research Labs., Rochester, N.Y., 1967—; adj. faculty Rochester Inst. Tech., 1968—. Mem. Rochester-Rennes Sister Cities Com., 1977—; mem. Ogden (N.Y.) Republican Com., 1974—. Registered profl. engr., N.Y. State. Mem. Am. Soc. Photogrammetry (certified photogrammetrist; autometric award 1975), Nat., N.Y. State socs. profl. engrs., ASME, Am. Assn. Physics Tchrs., Am. Assn. Physicists in Medicine, Optical Soc. Am. (house chmn. 1975), Soc. Photog. Scientists and Engrs. (inter-soc. rep. 1975—). Inventor in field. Home: 16 Clearview Dr Spencerport NY 14559 Office: Eastman Kodak Research Labs Rochester NY 14650

VLADECK, BOBB CHARNEY, surgeon; b. N.Y.C., Mar. 27, 1943; s. William Charney and Irene (Lichterman) V.; A.B., Columbia U., 1963; M.D., Albert Einstein Coll. Medicine, 1967; m. Cheryl Deborah Wiener, May 25, 1968; children—Andrew, Naomi, Michael. Intern, Mt. Sinai Hosp., N.Y.C., 1967-68, resident, 1968-73, NIH trainee, 1971-73, instr. in surgery, 1973: practice medicine specializing in gen. surgery, Monsey, N.Y., 1974—; mem. staff Community Hosp. Rockland (county, N.Y.), 1974—, dir. surgery, 1976—, asso. bd. govs., 1977—; mem. staff Good Samaritan Hosp., Suffern, N.Y., Nyack (N.Y.) Hosp. Served to lt. comdr. USN, 1973-74. Diplomate Am. Bd. Surgery. Fellow A.C.S.; mem. med. socs. Rockland County, State N.Y., AMA. Research, publs. on shock. Office: 3 College Rd Monsey NY 10952

VLADUTIU, ADRIAN OCTAVIAN, physician; b. Bucharest, Rumania, Aug. 5, 1940; s. Octavian A. and Veturia N. (Chirescu) V.; came to U.S., 1969, naturalized, 1974; M.D. with honors, Bucharest Sch. Medicine, 1962; m. Georgirene D. Therrien, Sept. 4, 1971; 1 dau., Christina Lynn. Instr. pathology Bucharest Sch. Medicine, 1965-68, asst. prof., 1968-71; research fellow Clin. Research Inst. Montreal (Que., Can.), 1968-69; intern medicine Millard Filmore Hosp., Buffalo, 1971-72; resident in clin. pathology Meyer Meml. Hosp., Buffalo, Buffalo Gen. Hosp., 1972-74; research asst. prof. microbiology State U. N.Y. at Buffalo, 1969-71, clin. asst. prof. pathology, 1974-77, asso. prof. pathology, 1977-79, research asso. prof. medicine, 1979—; dir. immunopathology lab. Buffalo Gen. Hosp., 1974—; individual practice clin. pathology, specializing in immunopathology, Buffalo, 1974—; cons. in field. Med. Research Council Can. fellow, 1968-69, Buswell fellow, 1969-71. Recipient physician recognition awards AMA, 1972, 76, 78. Fellow A.C.P., Assn. Clin. Scientists, Coll. Am. Pathologists; mem. Assn. Immunologists, N.Y. Acad. Scis., Am. Fedn. Clin. Research, Am. Soc. Clin. Pathologists, Soc. Exptl. Biol. Medicine. Contbr. articles to profl. publs. genetics of autoimmunity, immunopathology. Home: 80 Oakview Dr Amherst NY 14221 Office: 100 High St Buffalo NY 14203

VLAHAKIS, JOHN GEORGE, chem. engr.; b. Lynn, Mass., Aug. 12, 1944; s. George John and Evelyn (Penokas) V.; B.S., Tufts U., 1966, M.S., 1968; Ph.D., Syracuse U., 1972; m. Gail Linda Goldmeier, Jan. 30, 1970. Research asst. Syracuse (N.Y.) U., 1968-72; chem. engr. U.S. Army Mobility Equipment Research and Devel. Center, Ft. Belvoir, Va., 1972-74; chem. engr.-tech. staff Mitre Corp., McLean, Va., 1974-76; sr. process design specialist U.S. Dept. Energy, Washington, 1976—. NSF trainee, 1970-71; Presdl. intern in sci. and engring., 1972. Mem. Am. Inst. Chem. Engrs., Internat. Ozone Inst. Contbg. author Electrotechnology for Wastewater Treatment and Separation Methods, 1977. Home: 417 Pitt Mews Alexandria VA 22314 Office: Dept Energy Washington DC 20545

VLCEK, JOSEPH FRANK, mech., elec. engr.; b. Zleby, Czechoslovakia, May 31, 1914; s. Louise John and Francisca V.; B.S., U. Prague, 1933, M.S., 1935, Ph.D., 1937, 48; came to U.S., 1956, naturalized, 1961; m. Jarmila Betty Tluchor, Apr. 5, 1942; children—Joseph Vincent, Vera Mary Kelsey. Various positions Czechoslovakia, 1929-35, 37-48; prin. Refugee Camp High Sch., Nuremberg, W.Ger., 1949-50; design engr. U.S. Army, Heidelberg, W.Ger., 1950-56, Wilberding Co., Washington, 1956-57; sr. engr. Chesapeake Instrument Corp., Shadyside, Md., 1957-62; pres., chief scientist Applied Poly. Research Corp., Annapolis, Md., 1962-69; gen. mgr. Applied Research and Tech. Inc., Glen Burnie, Md., 1968-74; agt. for U.S. and Western hemisphere of Atlantic Trust Co., Fairview, N.J., 1974—; asso. prof. engring. tech. Prince George's Community Coll., Largo, Md., 1975-76; sr. engr. Cons. Engr. Services, Sewell, N.J., 1976—. Served with Czeckoslovakian Army, 1935-37. Decorated Medal of Merit. Mem. ASME, Instrument Soc. Am., Soc. Plastics Engrs., AIM (pres.'s council 1969), Soc. Tech. Writers and Pubs., Internat. Platform Assn. Lutheran. Clubs: Sokol, Civitan. Researcher infrared, radar, sonar, oceanography instrumentation. Home: 140 Corte de Cantanio La Cascata Clementon NJ 08021 Office: Cons Engr Services County House Rd off Delsea Dr Fairview NJ 08080

VLCEK, JOSEPH ROBERT, utility co. exec.; b. Cleve., Aug. 15, 1933; s. Joseph J. and Mildred A. (Koubeck) V.; Asso. Degree in Bus. Mgmt., Fisher Jr. Coll., 1978; m. Joan M. Walsh, June 16, 1956; children—Pamela J., Joseph J. Plant clk. Columbia Gas of Ohio, Parma, 1956-61, plant and service supr., Bowling Green, Ohio, 1961-69, plant supr., 1969-73; gen. foreman, gas div. Middleborough (Mass.) Gas and Electric Dept., 1973-74, gas. supt., 1974—. Mem. Bowling Green Bd. Zoning Appeals, 1969-72, chmn., 1972-73. Served with USCG, 1952-56. Mem. Nat. Assn. Corrosion Engrs. (dir. Boston chpt. 1976—, nat. dir. 1976—), Am. Soc. Gas Engrs., Am. Inst. Indsl. Engrs., New Eng. Gas Assn. Roman Catholic. Home: PO Box 11 488 Long Point Rd Lakeville MA 02346 Office: Town Hall Nickerson Ave Middleborough MA 02346

VOGEL, ABRAHAM P., men's knit goods mfg. co. exec.; b. Bklyn., June 20, 1941; s. Max S. and Eva (Zerden) V.; B.A., Dakota Wesleyan U., 1963; married; 2 children. Personnel safety supr. Greyhound, N.Y. Worlds Fair, 1963-65; personnel asst. Hewitt Robins div. Litton Industries, Florence, Ky., 1965-69; mgr. employee relations Questor Corp., Toledo, 1969-73; asst. dir. human resources Lionel Leisure, Inc., Phila., 1973-74; dir. personnel Warminster (Pa.) Gen. Hosp., 1975-77; dir. personnel Robert Bruce div. Consol. Foods Corp., Phila., 1977—. Mem. employer adv. council Pa. Bur. Employment Security. Mem. Am. Soc. Personnel Adminstrn. (accredited exec. in personnel), Nat. Fire Protection Assn. Club: Elks. Office: C and Westmoreland Sts Philadelphia PA 19134

VOGEL, ALEXANDER S., ophthalmologist; b. N.Y.C., Mar. 20, 1937; s. Charles M. and Sarah K. (Steir) V.; B.A., N.Y. U., 1954-58; M.D., State U. N.Y., 1962; m. Claire Abramowitz, Aug. 21, 1960; children—Larraine, Richard, Alison, Jon. Intern, Kings County Hosp., N.Y.C., 1962-63; resident in ophthalmology Mt. Sinai Hosp., N.Y.C., 1966-69; pvt. practice medicine specializing in ophthalmology, White Plains, N.Y., 1969—; mem. staffs Mt. Sinai Hosp., N.Y.C., White Plains, St. Agnes hosps., White Plains. Served to capt. AUS, 1963-65. Diplomate Am. Bd. Ophthalmology. Fellow A.C.S.; mem. N.Y. State, Westchester County med. socs., Am. Acad. Ophthalmology and Otolaryngology, Alpha Omega Alpha. Office: 33 Davis Ave White Plains NY 10605

VOGEL, FERDINAND PETER, photographer; b. Vienna, Austria, Sept. 9, 1900; s. Daniel and Gisella (Fuchs) V.; Master Photography, Bavarian State Coll. Photography, Munich, 1929; m. Lili Heid, July 23, 1943; 1 dau., Linda F. Came to U.S., 1937. Movie cameraman Universal Picture Co., Berlin, Germany, 1930-34; owner Vogel Studio, N.Y.C., 1939—. Tchr. photography Bklyn. Mus. Art Sch., 1948. Mem. Profl. Photographers Am. Author: With the Camera in Grönland, 1932. Address: PO Box 781 Ansonia Sta New York City NY 10023

VOGEL, FRANCIS EDWIN, rehab. counselor; b. Holyoke, Mass., Nov. 24, 1939; s. William George and Elda Mae V.; A.A., Holyoke Community Coll., 1960; B.A., U. Mass., 1966; M.A., U. Conn.; m. Patricia Pecevich, June 18, 1966; 1 son, Eric Matthew. Supr., Conn. Div. Vocat. Rehab., Manchester, 1968-73, dist. supr., div. workmens rehab., Manchester, 1973—. Founder, People Interested in Narcotic and Drug Abuse; pvt. practice addictive personalities, 1975—. Served with U.S. Army, 1960-64. Mem. Am. Personnel and Gudince Assn., Am. Group Work Assn. Democrat. Roman Catholic. Home: 46 Heather Ln Manchester CT 06040 Office: 633 Washington St Middletown CT 06457

VOGEL, GEORGE SIGMUND, physician; b. Bklyn., May 22, 1912; s. Sigmund and Bessie (Cohen) V.; B.S., N.Y.U., 1932; M.D., U. Hamburg, 1936; m. Franzi Leopold, June 22, 1938; children—Susan Marcia, Michael Lee. Intern Lutheran Hosp., Manhattan, N.Y.C., 1937-39; practice medicine, Croton-on-Hudson, N.Y., 1943—; attending physician Phelps Meml. Hosp., North Tarrytown, N.Y., pres. med. staff, 1966-67, chmn. gen. practice dept., 1969-72; hon. attending staff Peekskill Hosp., N.Y.; surg. N.Y.C. R.R., 1944—; sch. physician Croton-Harmon Sch. System, 1953—; police surgeon, Croton-on-Hudson; med. dir. Cedar Manor Nursing Home, Ossining, N.Y., 1976—; asso. med. dir. Brandywine Nursing Home, Briarcliff, N.Y., 1976—. Served to 1st lt. M.C., AUS. Named Man of Year, Croton-on-Hudson C. of C., 1976. Diplomate Am. Bd. Family Practice. Mem. Am., N.Y. State, Westchester County med. assns., Am. Acad. Family Practice (chpt. sec., chpt. v.p., pres. Westchester chpt. 1973—). Jewish religion (dir.). Mason, Lion. Home: 19 Meadowbrook Dr Ossining NY 10562 Office: 87 Grand St Croton-on-Hudson NY 10520

VOGEL, JOHN MICHAEL, lawyer; b. Redlands, Calif., Nov. 1, 1945; s. Frank Edward and Beatrice (Jonas) V.; B.A., Occidental Coll., 1966; J.D., N.Y. U., 1969. Admitted to N.Y. bar, 1970; asso. firm Windels Merritt & Ingraham, N.Y.C., 1969-70; trial lawyer Office of Chief Trial Atty., U.S. Air Force, Ohio, 1970-74, Office of Gen. Counsel, Navy Dept., Washington, 1974—. Mem. Spl. White House Study Group on Calif. Problems, 1972. Bd. dirs. Dayton Repertory Theatre, Town Hall Players. Served to capt. USAF, 1970-74. Recipient George Washington medal Freedoms Found., 1972. Mem. Am. Bar Assn. Home: 1101 S Arlington Ridge Rd Arlington VA 22202 Office: Dept Navy Washington DC 20360

VOGEL, JULIUS A., JR., pediatrician; b. Pitts., Sept. 2, 1933; s. Julius A. and Eunice V. (John) V.; B.S., U. Pitts., 1955, M.D., 1959; m. Sandra Elaine Johnston, Aug. 2, 1957; children—Suzanne, Edward, Philip, Matthew. Intern, Mercy Hosp., Pitts., 1959-60; resident Children's Hosp. Pitts., 1960-63; practice medicine specializing in pediatrics, Beaver, Pa., 1964—; mem. sr. staff Med. Center Beaver County, 1972—; courtesy staff Children's Hosp., Pitts., 1963—. Bd. dirs. Center Area Sch. Dist., Monaca, Pa., 1970—, Beaver County YMCA, 1975-76. Served to capt. USAF, 1963-65. Diplomate Am. Bd. Pediatrics. Mem. Am. Acad. Pediatrics, AMA, Pa., Beaver County med. socs., Pitts. Pediatric Soc. Republican. Home: 126 Windy Ghoul Beaver PA 15009 Office: 336 College Ave Beaver PA 15009

VOGEL, STANLEY MORTON, educator; b. Norwalk, Conn., Jan. 21, 1921; s. Morris and Betty (Jacobson) V.; A.B., N.Y. U., 1942; M.A., Yale U., 1945, Ph.D., 1949. Instr., Princeton U., 1947-48; faculty Suffolk U., Boston, 1948—, prof. English, 1958—, chmn. dept., 1961—; propr. Boston Athenaeum, 1971—. Served with USAAF, 1943-45. Mem. Modern Lang. Assn., Coll. English Assn., Phi Beta Kappa, Phi Alpha Theta, Phi Alpha Tau. Author: German Literary Influences on the American Transcendentalists, 1955, 2d edit., 1970; (with Ella Murphy) Hymarx Outline Series: American Literature, 2 vols., 1961, The English Novel in the Nineteenth Century, 1967. Home: 69 Hancock St Boston MA 02114 Office: Suffolk U Beacon Hill Boston MA 02114

VOGELBACH, THEODORE OSCAR, cons. engring. co. exec.; b. North Arlington, N.J., May 18, 1935; s. Oscar and Eleanor Woods (Lindsay) V.; student Rensselaer Poly. Inst., 1953-54, Newark Coll. Engring., 1956-59; m. Elaine Monica Mara, May 5, 1956; children—Denise Ann, Gretchen Marie, Kerstin Elizabeth. Draftsman, designer, project leader Vogelbach & Baumann, Scotch Plains, N.J., 1954-66; sr. designer, engr. Wigton-Abbott Corp., Plainfield, N.J., 1966-69; design engr. IBM Corp., Fishkill, N.Y., 1969-70, mech. cons., 1972-73; design engr. Foster-Wheeler Corp., Livingston, N.J., 1970-71; sr. project and design engr. J.T. Baker Chem. Corp., Philipsburg, N.J., 1971; sr. project engr. VOL Industries Inc., Hawthorne, N.J., 1971; mech. engr. Airco/Boc Cryoplants Corp., Murray Hill, N.J., 1971-72; mech. cons. Allied Chem. Corp., Morristown, N.J., 1973-75; mech. cons. T.O. Vogelbach, Raritan, N.J., 1975-76, pres., dir. T.O. Vogelbach Inc., 1976—. Registered profl. engr., N.Y., N.J. Mem. Soc. Am. Mil. Engrs. (sustaining mem.; dir. N.J. post), Am. Def. Preparedness Assn., Nat. Rifle Assn. (life). Home and Office: 110 Avonridge Rd Raritan NJ 08869

VOGELPOEL, ANTHONY PETER, mfg. co. exec.; b. Amsterdam, Netherlands, Apr. 7; s. Johannes Anthonius and Anna Catharina (Van D.) V.; came to U.S., 1960, naturalized, 1966; certificate, Ryerson Inst. Tech. (Can.), 1956; certificate, U. Toronto (Can.,), 1959; B.S. cum laude, Boston U., 1964; postgrad. Northeastern U., 1964-65; m. Ilse Lina Kuhn, Jan. 7, 1969; children—Amelie, Louise. Quality control technician Raytheon Can., Kitchener, Ont., 1959-60; sr. quality control engr. Raytheon Co., Newton, Mass., 1960-66; corporate quality cons. The Singer Co., Elizabeth, N.J., 1966-69; corporate mgr. quality assurance and reliability N. Am. Philips Corp., N.Y.C., 1969—. Registered profl. engr., Calif. Mem. Nederlandse Genealogische Vereniging (co-founder, 1st pres. 1946), Arleitskreis Siegen (W. Germany), Deutsche Gesellschaft Fuer Qualitaet, Am. Soc. for Quality Control, Internat. Word Processing Assn., Boston U. Alumni Assn. Republican. Lutheran. Contbr. articles to profl. jours. Home: 7896 Red Fox Dr Manlius NY 13104 Office: 100 E 42nd St New York City NY 10017

VOGT, ROY SCHOPPAUL, mgmt. cons.; b. Wilmington, N.C., Apr. 9, 1919; s. Henry and Florence Johanna (Schoppaul) V.; B.A., Haverford Coll., 1941; postgrad. Grad. Sch. Bus. Harvard U., 1965, 69; m. Winifred Dorothy Sorg, June 23, 1951; children—Henry, Virginia. Asst. to pres. Haverford (Pa.) Coll., 1944-45; mgr. adminstrn. dept. Smith, Kline & French Labs., 1945-51; purchasing mgr. Crawford Mfg. Co., Richmond, Va., 1951-55; sr. adminstrv. officer Princeton, U., 1955-71; treas., chief bus. officer Windham Coll., Putney, Vt., 1971-76; treas., sec. Fitz, Vogt & Assos. Ltd., Brattleboro, Vt., 1977—; tree farmer, Vt.; officer Brattleboro Score chpt. SBA, 1978—. Chmn. ARC, Princeton, 1958, Community Chest, 1957, bldg. com. Calvary Bapt. Ch., 1957-58; bd. mgrs. N.J. Bapt. Conv., 1957-60, mem. finance com., 1957-60; mem. alumni council Haverford Coll., 1965, also exec. com. alumni mem Corp. Haverford Coll., 1966. Mem. Woodlot Owners Assn., Phi Beta Kappa, Alpha Tau Omega. Clubs: Founders Haverford Coll., Varsity Haverford. Address: Kipling Rd Brattleboro VT 05301

VOGT, WILLIAM HENRY, III, lawyer; b. Pearl River, N.Y., Dec. 22, 1930; s. William Henry, Jr. and Ida May (Thornton) V.; B.S., Mass. Inst. Tech., 1952; LL.B., Harvard, 1955; m. Dorothy M.S. Wilson, April 10, 1964; children—Mary, Alice, Amy, Jennifer. Admitted to N.Y. bar, 1955, U.S. Supreme Ct. bar, 1960; mem. firm Watson, Leavenworth, Kelton & Taggart, N.Y.C., 1958—, partner, 1964—. Served with USAF, 1956-58. Office: 100 Park Ave New York City NY 10017

VOLKHARDT, JOHN MALCOM, food co. exec.; b. Englewood Cliffs, N.J., Apr. 13, 1917; s. George Thomas and Evelyn (Mitchell) V.; A.B. cum laude, Brown U., 1939; children—Jacqueline, Janet, Dana. With Vick Chem. Co., N.Y.C., 1939-48; gen. mgr. No. Warren Co., Stamford, Conn., 1948-56; gen. mgr. Rit div. Best Foods Co., N.Y.C., 1956-58; with Best Foods div. CPC Internat., Englewood Cliffs, 1959—, exec. v.p., 1968-72, pres., 1972—; pres. CPC N.Am., 1978—; dir. S.B. Thomas, Learn, Inc. Mem. adminstrv. bd. Alpine (N.J.) Methodist Ch., 1970—; mem. nat. devel. bd. Youth Hostels, 1972; bd. dirs. Bergen County council Girl Scouts U.S.A., 1973-76; trustee Nutrition Found. Mem. Am. Mgmt. Assn., Grocery Mfrs. Assn., Conf. Bd. Clubs: Knickerbocker Country; Met.; Canadian. Home: 1530 Palisade Ave Fort Lee NJ 07024 Office: Internat Plaza Englewood Cliffs NJ 07632

VOLL, JOHN OBERT, historian; b. Hudson, Wis., Apr. 20, 1936; s. Obert Frank and Ruth Olivia (Seaberg) V.; A.B. summa cum laude, Dartmouth Coll., 1958; A.M. (Danforth fellow), Harvard U., 1960, Ph.D. (Ford. Found. fellow, Harvard teaching fellow), 1969; m. Sarah Lynne Potts, June 12, 1965; children—Sarah Layla, Michael Obert. Instr. history U. N.H., Durham, 1965-69, asst. prof., 1969-74, asso. prof. 1974—. Mem. bd. Ecumenical Ministry U. N.H., 1974-78, pres., 1975-77; chmn. social action Durham Community Ch., 1974-75, mem. ch. council, 1977-78. Sheldon travelling fellow, 1960-61; U. N.H. summer fellow, 1969; Nat. Endowment Humanities fellow, 1971-72. Mem. New Eng. Hist. Assn. (sec. 1975-78), N.H. Council on World Affairs (dir. 1978—), Am. Hist. Assn., Middle East Studies Assn., African Studies Assn., Am. Oriental Soc., Middle East Inst., N.H. Council World Affairs. Mem. United Ch. of Christ. Author: Historical Dictionary of the Sudan, 1978. Contbr. articles to profl. jours. Home: PO Box 51 Durham NH 03824 Office: Dept History Univ NH Durham NH 03824

VOLPE, ROBERT, physician; b. Toronto, Ont., Can., Mar. 6, 1926; s. Aaron G. and Esther (Shulman) V.; M.D., U. Toronto, 1950; m. Ruth Vera Pullan, Sept. 5, 1949; children—Catherine, Elizabeth, Peter, Edward, Rose Ellen. Intern, U. Toronto, 1950-51, resident in medicine, 1951-52, 53-55, fellow in endocrinology, 1952-53, 55-57, sr. research fellow dept. medicine, 1957-62, McPhedran fellow, 1957-65, asst. prof., 1962-68, asso. prof., 1968-72, prof., 1972—; attending staff St. Joseph's Hosp., Toronto, 1957-66; active staff Wellesley Hosp., Toronto, 1966—, dir. endocrinology research lab., 1968—, physician-in-chief, 1974—. Served with Royal Canadian Navy Vol. Res., 1943-45. Recipient Goldie medal for med. research U. Toronto, 1971; Med. Research Council Can. grantee, 1955—. Fellow Royal Coll. Physicians (Can.), Royal Soc. Medicine, ACP; mem. Canadian Soc. Endocrinology and Metabolism (past pres.), Canadian Soc. Clin. Investigation, Am. Thyroid Assn. (1st v.p. 1975-76), Endocrine Soc., Am. Fedn. Clin. Research, Soc. Nuclear Medicine, AAAS. Clubs: Donalda, Alpine Ski, U. Toronto Faculty. Author: Systematic Endocrinology, 1973; also numerous research articles, especially on immunology of thyroid disease; editorial bd. Annals Internal Medicine, Clin. Endocrinology. Home: 3 Daleberry Pl Don Mills ON M3B 2A5 Canada Office: Wellesley Hosp Toronto ON M4Y 1J3 Canada

VOLPE, S. PETER, constrn. co. exec.; b. Malden, Mass., Apr. 14, 1917; s. Vito and Filomena (Benedetto) V.; grad. Wentworth Inst., 1939; D.Engring. Sci. (hon.), Merrimack Coll., 1971; m. Armita A. Palmerino, June 14, 1942; children—Janet (Mrs. Ronald V. Livesey), Peter J. With Volpe Constrn. Co., Inc., Malden, 1935—, treas., 1953—, pres., 1969—; treas. Fifty-Four Realty Corp., Malden, 1958—; hon. dir. Malden Trust Co.; v.p., dir. Fellsway Coop. Bank, Malden; mem. adv. bd. Lumbermens Mut. Casualty Co. Mem. adv. bd. Suffolk U., 1968—. Bd. overseers Old Sturbrige Village; bd. dirs. Constrn. Scis. Research Found., Horizons for Youth; mem. com. on probation State of Mass.; chmn. bd. trustees Merrimack Coll. Served with Seabees, USNR, 1943-45. Mem. Cons. Constructors Council Am., Soc. Am. Mil. Engrs. (nat. dir., past pres. Boston), Holy Name Soc., Asso. Gen. Contractors Mass. (pres. 1961-62), Mass. Bldg. Congress (pres. 1957), Nat. Inst. Bldg. Scis. (dir.), Asso. Gen. Contractors Am. (past pres.), Am. Inst. Constructors, Am. Arbitration Assn., Sons Italy in Am., Malden C. of C., VFW (past post comdr.), Holy Name Soc. Roman Catholic. Kiwanian. Clubs: Salem Country (Peabody, Mass.); 100 of Mass. (dir.); Engineers (Boston). Author: Construction Management Practice, 1972. Office: 54 Eastern Ave Malden MA 02148

VONDERAHE, ALAN GEORGE, printing services co. exec.; b. Bridgeport, Conn., July 18, 1942; s. George Roland and Virginia Grace (Simons) V.; student Middlebury Coll., 1961-65; m. Marilynn May Owens, Nov. 12, 1966; children—Katherine Owens, Matthew Alan, Kurt Markham. Sales rep. Coll. Life Ins. Co. Am., Los Angeles, 1967-68; v.p. sales, marketing and promotion Vonderahe Printing Services, Inc., Livingston, N.J., 1968—. Cons. to industry; active Children's Asthma Research Inst. and Hosp. Past mem. bd. govs., pres., trustee Newark Acad. Mem. Brookside Semi-Wild Assn. (co-chmn.), Chi Psi (pres. Alpha Mu chpt. 1966). Republican. Presbyn. Author: (poem) Speedthink, 1972. Profl. musician, writer, arranger. Home: 48 Berkeley Circle Basking Ridge NJ 07920 Office: 81 Dorsa Ave Livingston NJ 07039

VON HOLDEN, MARTIN HARVEY, psychologist; b. Bronx, N.Y., May 29, 1942; s. Leon and Gertrude (Fishbein) Von H.; B.A., N.Y. U., 1964; M.A., U. Toledo, 1965; postgrad. N.Y. U.; m. Virginia T. Brown, Dec. 17, 1971; 1 son, Mark Walter; children by previous marriage—Sandi Gwen, David Lawrence, step-dau., Theresa Ann Brilli. Sr. psychologist N.Y. State Dept. Mental Hygiene, Rockland State Hosp., Orangeberg, 1966-67, team leader, 1970-71, dir. interdisciplinary tng. team, 1971-73; chief of service Metro Unit, Harlem Valley Psychiat. Center, Wingdale, N.Y., 1973-74, dep. dir. programs, 1974-75; dep. dir. treatment services Pilgrim Psychiat. Center, West Brentwood, N.Y., 1975-76; dir. Matteawan State Hosp., Beacon, N.Y., 1977; dir. Central N.Y. Psychiat. Center, Marcy, N.Y., 1977—; asso. dir. Inst. for Motivation Research, Croton-on-Hudson, N.Y., 1965-73; dir. Martin H. Von Holden Assos., motivation research, Fairlawn, N.J., 1970-74; cons. psychologist, group therapist Green Haven Correctional Facility, Stormville, N.Y., 1970-77; cons. psychologist, group therapist Auburn Correctional Facility, Auburn, N.Y., 1977—. Served to capt. Med. Service Corps, U.S. Army, 1967-70. Decorated Army Commendation medal; recipient James Gordan Bennett prize N.Y. U., 1964. Mem. Am. Psychol. Assn., Am. Correctional Assn., Am. Assn. Correctional Psychologists, Am. Assn. Mental Health Adminstrs., N.Y. State Dept. Mental Hygiene Assn. of Mental Hosp. Dirs., Marcy C. of C., Order of Arrow, Psi Chi. Democrat. Jewish. Contbr. articles to profl. jours. Home: PO Box 185 Marcy NY 13403 Office: Central NY Psychiatric Center PO Box 300 Marcy NY 13403

VON KEMENCZKY, MIKLOS, inventor, elec. engr., composer and arranger; b. Budapest, Hungary, Dec. 14, 1919; s. Arpad and Maria (Reisz) Kemenczei Kemencky; came to U.S., 1962, naturalized, 1972; E.E., Jozsef Nador Muegyetem, Budapest, 1944; m. Ingeborg Link, Dec. 11, 1947; 1 dau., Judith; m. 2d, Romana Gulich, June 18, 1957; children—Sylvia, Oliver. Technician, Hungarian Def. Inst., 1938-42; design engr. Gamma Optical Mfg. Co., 1942-47; researcher Hungarian Automatization Institut, 1947-55; ind. inventor, 1956-59; tech. dir. Kemenczky Establishment, Liechstenstein, 1959-64; dir. research, tech. dir. G.D. Co., Elizabeth, N.J., 1965—; cons.; composer and arranger. Mem. United Inventors and Scientists, Am. Def. Preparedness Assn., Smithsonian Assos. Contbr. articles to profl. jours. Holder 25 U.S. and 30 fgn. patents. Home: 112 Warrenville Rd Green Brook NJ 08812

VONKEVICZKY, COLMAN STEPHEN, former army officer, research scientist; b. Ruttka, Hungary, Aug. 21, 1909; s. Kalman deKevice and Karoline (Musza) Keviczky; M. Mil. Sci. and Engring, Royal Hungarian Ludovica Mil. U., 1932; m. Yolanda Von Makkay, June 23, 1963; 1 son by previous marriage—Attila B. Served with Royal Hungarian Army Gen. Staff, 1932-45; mil. and sci. study of Unidentified Flying Objects, 1952-66; mem. UN Secretariat staff Office Pub. Info., 1964-66; founder, project dir. Intercontinetal Galactic Spacecraft UFO Research and Analytic Network, N.Y.C., 1966—. Recipient Signum Laudis, Pope Paul VI; UN Mem. medal. 1965. Mem. Am. Inst. Aeros. and Astronautics, Hermann Oberth Rocket Soc. (W.Ger.). Contbr. articles to profl. jours. Home: 35-40 75th St Jackson Heights NY 11372

VON MEHREN, ROBERT BRANDT, lawyer; b. Albert Lea, Minn., Aug. 10, 1922; s. Sigurd Anders and Eulalia (Anderson) von M.; A.B. summa cum laude, Yale U., 1942; LL.B. magna cum laude, Harvard U., 1946; m. Mary Katharine Kelly, June 26, 1948; children—Carl Sigurd, John Milsted, Katharine, Jane, Margaret. Admitted to N.Y. bar, 1946, U.S. Supreme Ct., 1954; asso. mem. firm Debevoise, Plimpton, Lyons & Gates, 1946, 48-57, partner, 1957—; law clk. Judge Learned Hand, U.S. Circuit Ct. Appeals 2d circuit, 1946-47, Justice Stanley Reed, U.S. Supreme Ct., 1947-48; legal counsel prep. commn. IAEA, 1956-57; mem. exec. com., bd. dirs. Practising Law Inst., 1972—. Bd. dirs. Legal Aid Soc., N.Y.C., 1961-66, Axe-Houghton Found., N.Y.C.; trustee La Fondation des Etats-Unis, Paris, 1966-70, Nightingale-Bamford Sch., N.Y.C. Fellow Am. Bar Found.; mem. Assn. Bar City N.Y. (past officer several coms., mem. exec. com. 1978—), Internat. Law Assn. (exec. com. Am. br.), Am. Bar Assn., Am. Soc. Internat. Law, Union Internat. des Avocats (rapporteur U.S. on enforcement fgn. country judgments), Council Fgn. Relations. Contbr. numerous articles legal jours.; editor Harvard Law Rev., 1943-46, pres. Vol. 59, 1945-46. Clubs: Century Assn., University (N.Y.C.). Home: 925 Park Ave New York City NY 10028 Office: 299 Park Ave New York City NY 10017

VON RINGELHEIM, PAUL HELMUT, sculptor; b. Vienna, Austria; s. Henry and Rosita (Altschuler) von R.; B.S., Bklyn. Coll., 1956; M.A., Fairleigh Dickinson U., 1958; postgrad. Art Students League, N.Y.C., 1958-59; Fulbright scholar in sculpture, Acad. Fine Arts, Munich, 1960-61. Tchr. printmaking Bklyn. Mus. Sch., 1957-58; prof. sculpture Sch. Visual Arts, N.Y.C., 1967-71; one-man shows at Niveau Art Gallery, N.Y.C., 1958, Am. House, Berlin, Munich and Hamburg, 1960-61, Rose Fried Gallery, N.Y.C., 1964, 67, Fairleigh Dickinson U., 1964, New Vision Galleries, London, 1964, O.K. Harris Gallery, N.Y.C., 1971-73, Mitzi Landau Gallery, Los Angeles, 1974, N.Y. Cultural Center, 1975, OK Harris Gallery, N.Y.C., 1976, 78; exhibited in group shows at Bklyn. Mus. Ann., 1958, Gunther Franke, Munich, 1961, New Eng. Exhbn., Silver Mine Guild Council (Silver prize), 1962, Whitney Ann., 1963, 65, Mus. Modern Art, N.Y.C., 1964, Whitney Mus., 1964, O.K. Harris Gallery, Providence, 1964, Ben Uri Gallery, London, 1965, S.I. Mus., N.Y.C., 1965, Byron Gallery, N.Y.C., 1965, Jewish Mus., N.Y.C., 1966, 68, Cleve. Mus., 1966, Obelisk Gallery, Boston, 1967, Albright-Knox Gallery, Buffalo, 1967, Rose Art Mus., Brandeis U., 1967, Am. embassy, Brussels, 1967, Mus. Modern Art, N.Y.C., 1967, 69, Hessischeslanders Mus., Daensstadt, Germany, 1967, Mus. Paymons-Von Bellninger, Rotterdam, Netherlands, 1967, New Sch. Social Research, N.Y.C., 1968, Meml. Hall, Boston, 1968, Finch Coll., N.Y.C., 1968, Bridgehampton (L.I.) Galleries, 1968, Hardin Simmons U., Abilene, Tex., 1968, Cedar Rapids (Iowa) Art Assn., 1968, Decatur (Ill.) Art Center, 1968, Greenville County (S.C.) Mus., 1968, St. Cloud (Minn.) Coll., 1968, U. Tex., Austin, 1968, Roanoke (Va.) Art Center, 1968, Westmoreland County Mus., Greensburg, Pa., 1969, Frick Mus., Pitts., 1969, Temple U. Music Festival, 1969, Dance Set for Chimera by Murray Louis, N.Y.C., 1969, Cultural Affairs Commn., N.Y.C., 1969-70, Internat. Sculpture Show, Govt. Center, Boston, 1971, Monumenta, Newport, R.I., 1974, Nebr. Bi-Centennial Interstate 80 Project, 1976, Flair, Columbia Mall, Columbia, S.C., Tex. Eastern, Houston, 1977, Moment, Taubman Center, Sterling Heights, Mich.; Endless Force, Pres. Gerald R. Ford, Palm Springs, Calif.; commd. Going My Way, Meml. to Bing Crosby, Los Angeles, 1978; designer cover Time mag. and Partisan Rev.; represented in permanent collections at Welton Becket Assos., Broadway Maintenance Corp., Carter Wallace Corp., N.Y.C., CBS, N.Y.C., Fairleigh Dickinson U., Haus Der Kunst, Munich, Martin Found., Mus. Modern Art, N.Y.C., Mus. Modern Art, Tel Aviv, Israel, Mus. Modern Art, Tokyo, Japan, Twentieth Century Fund, N.Y.C., Wheaton Coll., Whitney Mus. Am. Art, Hrsicher Landes Mus., Damstatd, Germany, Time and Life Collection, N.Y.C.; archtl. commns. include World Peace Monument, U.S. Pavilion, New York Worlds Fair, 1963-64, lands, 1967, New Sch. Social Research, N.Y.C., 1968, Meml. Hall, Boston, 1968, Finch Coll., N.Y.C., 1968, Bridgehampton (L.I.) Galleries, 1968, Hardin Simmons U., Abilene, Tex., 1968, Cedar Rapids (Iowa) Art Assn., 1968, Decatur (Ill.) Art Center, 1968, Greenville County (S.C.) Mus., 1968, St. Cloud (Minn.) Coll., 1968, U. Tex., Austin, 1968, Roanoke (Va.) Art Center, 1968, Westmoreland County Mus., Greensburg, Pa., 1969, Frick Mus., Pitts., 1969, Temple U. Music Festival, 1969, Dance Set for Chimera by Murray Louis, N.Y.C., 1969, Cultural Affairs Commn., N.Y.C., 1969-70, Internat. Sculpture Show, Govt. Center, Boston, 1971, Monumenta, Newport, R.I., 1974, Nebr. Bi-Centennial Interstate 80 Project, 1976, Flair, Columbia Mall, Columbia, S.C., Tex. Eastern, Houston, 1977, Moment, Taubman Center, Sterling Heights, Mich.; Endless Force, Pres. Gerald R. Ford, Palm Springs, Calif.; commd. Going My Way, Meml. to Bing Crosby, Los Angeles, 1978; designer cover Time mag. and Partisan Rev.; represented in permanent collections at Welton Becket Assos., Broadway Maintenance Corp., Carter Wallace Corp., N.Y.C., CBS, N.Y.C., Fairleigh Dickinson U., Haus Der Kunst, Munich, Martin Found., Mus. Modern Art, N.Y.C., Mus. Modern Art, Tel Aviv, Israel, Mus. Modern Art, Tokyo, Japan, Twentieth Century Fund, N.Y.C., Wheaton Coll., Whitney Mus. Am. Art, Hrsicher Landes Mus., Damstatd, Germany, Time and Life Collection, N.Y.C.; archtl. commns. include World Peace Monument, U.S. Pavilion, New York Worlds Fair, 1963-64, Bronx Park 11, Steel Directional #17, N.Y.C., 1968, Gateway, New York, Unimark Internat. Tangential 32, N.Y.C., 1969, Continum III, Worcester (Mass.) Center, Westinghouse Nuclear Center, Fulcrum, Pitts., 1971, Vortex in Red, Houston, 1975, numerous others. Dir. fine arts bd. Fairleigh Dickinson U., Fine Arts Commn., 1974-75. Recipient Outstanding Young Man of Year award for world peace sculpture Fed. Pavilion, New York Worlds Fair, 1964. Mem. Archtl. League City of N.Y. Clubs: Lambs (hon.), Explorers. Home: 9 Great Jones St New York City NY 10012

VON SZITANYI WALEWSKA, MARGIT, artist; b. Hungary, Dec. 19, 1920; d. Rudolph and Alexandra (Chlebowski) von Szitanyi; grad. Fine Art Acad. Warsaw, 1939; m. Joseph von Szitanyi, Dec. 11, 1948. One woman shows: Gallery Bernheim, 83 Faubourg St. Honore, La Palette Blue, Paris; Galeria Tritone, Rome; Gilhaus, Naples, Italy, Munich, Germany, Vienna, Austria; N.Y.C. Center Gallery, 1946-73, Internat. Gallery, N.Y.C., 1946-73; represented in permanent collection: Museo Vaticano, Rome. Instr., Yoga Soc. N.Y. Home: 631 W 185th St W New York City NY 10033

VON TAUBER, ROBERT F., diplomat, chemist; b. Vienna, Austria, Jan. 11, 1902; s. Bernard and Antonia (Klaphote) von T.; M.S., State U. Vienna, 1926, Ph.D., 1930; J.D., Blackstone Coll. Law, 1955; LL.D. (hon.), Philathea U. (Can.), 1970; m. Olga Maria Beck. Gen. mgr. Nevsiedler Paper Co., A.G., Vienna, 1926-36; tech dir., chief chemist Brightwater Paper Co., Adams, Mass., 1946-50; cons. chemist in paper and pulp, Phila., 1950—; consul gen. of Haiti in Phila., 1956-67, N.Y.C., 1967—. Decorated comdr. Order Honneur et Merite (Haiti); Knight 1st class Order of Merit (Austria); Grand Cross of Black Star (French Colonial); grand-officer Order Toussaint Louverture. Mem. Soc. Fgn. Consuls in N.Y., Am. Chem. Soc., AAAS, Am. Acad. Polit. and Social Sci., Pam Am. Union. Clubs: Stony Brook Yacht; Racquet (Jamaica). Home: 198 West Neck Rd Huntington NY 11743 Office: 60 E 42d St New York City NY 10017

VONTRESS, CLEMMONT EYVIND, educator; b. Bowling Green, Ky., Apr. 22, 1929; s. Benjamin Franklin and Elizabeth (Brown) V.; B.A., Ky. State U., 1952; M.S., Ind. U., 1956, Ph.D., 1965; m. Mary Delma Hockersmith, Apr. 12, 1951; 1 son, Amasa Delano. Instr. English, So. U., Baton Rouge, 1956-57; English tchr. George Washington High Sch., Indpls., 1957-58; dir. counseling Crispus Attucks High Sch., Indpls., 1958-65; asso. prof. edn. Howard U., Washington, 1965-69; prof. edn. George Washington U., Washington, 1969—, pres. Urban Learning, Tng. and Research Assos., Inc., 1975—. Served with U.S. Army, 1953-55. Mem. Nat. Capital, Am. personnel and guidance assns., Nat. Vocat. Guidance Assn., AAUP, Assn. Counselor Educators and Supervisors, D.C. Psychol. Assn., Phi Delta Kappa. Author: Counseling Negroes, 1971. Office: Dept Edn George Washington U Washington DC 20052

VON WECHMAR, RUEDIGER EBERHARD (BARON), German diplomat; b. Berlin, Nov. 15, 1923; s. Irnfried and Ilse von Wechmar; grad. Hans Richert Coll., Berlin, 1940; corr. student U. Minn., 1943-46; m. Rosemarie Warlimont, Mar. 15, 1947; children—Stephanie, Alexander; m. 2d, Susanne Woldenga, Nov. 16, 1961; 1 dau., Yvonne. Reporter, fgn. corr. German News Agy., also UP, 1946-58; press officer German consulate gen., N.Y.C., 1958-63; fgn. corr. German TV in Vienna, 1963-68; dept. govt. spokesman, Bonn, 1969-72; state sec. for info. and govt. spokesman, 1972-74; ambassador, permanent rep. Fed. Republic of Germany to UN, 1974—, mem. Security Council, 1977—. Served to st lt. German Army, 1941-45; prisoner-of-war Am. Army, 1943-46. Recipient various decorations from fgn. countries. Mem. Free Democratic Party. Office: 600 3d Ave New York City NY 10016

VOORHEES, DONALD EDWARD, artist; b. Neptune, N.J., May 6, 1926; s. James Henry and Blanche Elizabeth (Hankinson) V.; student Acad. Arts, Newark, 1946-50, Art Students League N.Y., 1970-73; m. Janice A. Watson, Apr. 26, 1953 (div. Dec. 1974); children—Nancy, Patricia, Kathleen; m. Theresa S. Martin, Mar. 21, 1976. Advt. artist N.Y. Artists, Inc., N.Y.C., 1950-52; photoengraver Asbury Park (N.J.) Press daily and Sunday newspaper, 1952-60; supt. graphic arts Newark Star Ledger daily and Sunday, 1960-77; instr. watercolors Guild Creative Art, Shrewsbury, N.J., 1964—, also privately; one-man shows: Guild Creative Art, 1968, 74, Old Mill Art Assn., Tinton Falls, N.J., 1969, Raylyn Art Center, Lakewood, N.J., 1973-76; exhibited in group shows: N.J. Watercolor Soc. State Ann., Morris Mus., 1954-75, Knickerbocker Artists Ann., Nat. Arts Club, 1971-75, Am. Watercolor Soc. 105th Ann., 1972, 75; represented in permanent collection Asbury Park Soc. Fine Arts, also numerous pvt. collections; mem. art adv. commn. Monmouth County (N.J.) Bd. Freeholders, 1969—. Served with USNR, 1944-46: PTO. Recipient Mary T. Lawrence Meml. award N.J. Watercolor Soc. State Ann., 1971, Mary Alvord award Hudson Valley Artist, 1975. Mem. Am. (asso.), N.J. (v.p. 1973-74, pres. 1975-76) watercolor socs., Salamagundi Club (award 1975). Address: 35 Center Ave Atlantic Highlands NJ 07716

VOORTHUYZEN, PETER, clergyman; b. Netherlands, Jan. 5, 1927; s. Jacob and Jannetje (Van Dam) V.; came to U.S., 1958, naturalized, 1969; student sacred music Northeastern Bible Coll., Essex Fells, N.J.; M.Div., Gordon Div. Sch., 1968. Ordained to ministry Am. Bapt. Ch., 1970; pastor, Amherst, N.H., 1964-68, Litchfield and Sabattus, Maine, 1968-76; pastor 1st Bapt. Ch. of Canastota (N.Y.), 1977—; research chemist Merck Sharp, Dohm, Rahway, N.J., 1960; with Research Assos., Inc., Bernardsville, N.J., 1958-60, Philips Duphar, Netherlands, 1952-58; numerous violin concerts and recitals; lectr. in field. Mem. Am. Chem. Soc. Patentee in field. Address: 113 Ball Ave Canastota NY 13032

VOROSMARTI, JAMES, JR., physician, naval officer; b. Palmerton, Pa., Oct. 18, 1935; s. James and Ruth Smith (Mohler) V.; A.B., Lafayette Coll., 1957; M.D., Jefferson Med. Coll., 1961; postgrad. (fellow) State U. N.Y., Buffalo, 1970-72; m. Carol Ann Schoch, June 21, 1959; children—James III, Richard Stefan, Erika Lynn. Commd. lt. U.S. Navy, 1961, advanced through grades to capt., 1975; intern U.S. Naval Hosp., Portsmouth, Va., 1961-62; sr. med. officer, submarine base dispensary and submarine escape tng. tank, Pearl Harbor, 1965-66; postdoctoral fellow dept. physiology SU NY, Buffalo, 1970-72; med. officer deep submergence systems project, San Diego, 1966-70; exchange med. officer R.N. Inst. of Naval Medicine and R.N. Physiol. Lab., Alverstoke, Eng., 1972-75; dep. dir. Naval Med. Research Inst., Bethesda Md., 1975-78; program mgr. diving and submarine med. research Naval Med. R&D Command, Bethesda, 1978—. Diplomate Nat. Bd. Med. Examiners, Am. Bd. Preventive Medicine. Fellow Am. Coll. Preventive Medicine, Am. Acad. Family Practice, A.C.P., mem. Am. Physiol. Soc., Undersea Med. Soc. (pres. 1977-78), Am. Occupational Med. Assn., Assn. Mil. Surgeons U.S., Oceanic Soc., Nat. Maritime Hist. Soc., Friends of Earth, Nat. Trust for Historic Preservation. Editor: Undersea Biomed. Research, 1979—. Contbr. articles on diving research to sci. publs. Home: 16 Orchard Way S Rockville MD 20854 Office: Naval Med Research and Devel Command Bethesda MD 20014

VOS, HUBERT DANIEL, consumer products co. exec.; b. Paris, Aug. 2, 1933 (parents Am. citizens); s. Marius and Aline (Porge) V.; B.A., U. Paris, 1954; M.P.A., Princeton U., 1956; m. Susan Hill, Apr. 18, 1958; children—Wendy, James. Dir. fin. internat. Packers Ltd., Chgo., 1957-64; controller internat. div. Monsanto Co., St. Louis, 1964-69; v.p. corporate planning and fin. Smith Kline & French Labs., Phila., 1969-72; sr. v.p. fin., mem. exec. office Comml. Credit Co., Balt., 1972-74; sr. v.p. fin. Norton Simon, Inc., N.Y.C., 1974—, also dir.; dir. Leesona Corp. Mem. Am. Mgmt. Assn. (fin. planning council), Fin. Execs. Inst., Nat. Assn. Accountants. Home: 340 Lake Ave Greenwich CT 06830 Office: 277 Park Ave New York City NY 10017

VOSS, DONALD HENRY, clergyman, psychologist, lawyer; b. Grand Rapids Mich., June 2, 1927; s. Henry D. and Grace (Smit) V.; A.B., Calvin Coll., 1949; M.Div., Evang. Sem., 1955; M.S., No. Ill. U., 1957; Ph.D., Mich. State U., 1966; J.D., Akron U., 1975; m. Elizabeth Ann Hart, July 3, 1953; children—Erica, Douglas, Kerry. Ordained to ministry United Ch. Christ, 1955; pastor, 1955-60; asst. dir. admissions Mich. State U., 1960-61, adminstrv. asst., v.p., 1961-62; prof. psychology, chmn. social sci. dept. Lansing (Mich.) Community Coll., 1963-67; prof. psychology Slippery Rock (Pa.) State Coll., 1967—, dir. counseling services, 1967-72. Served with USNR, 1945-46. Mem. Am. Psychol. Assn., AAAS, Am. Bar Assn., Am. Psychology-Law Soc., Internat. Platform Assn., Assn. Pa. State Coll. and Univ. Faculties (exec. com. 1969-71), Phi Delta Kappa. Author: Emerging Ethics, 1969. Home: 248 Maple St Slippery Rock PA 16057

VOSS, HOWARD EVAN, physician; b. N.Y.C., July 23, 1935; s. James and Rose V.; B.A., Union Coll., 1957; M.D., N.Y. U., 1961; m. Lorraine Glasser, June 29, 1958; 1 son, Daren. Intern, resident in medicine Bellevue Hosp., N.Y.C., 1961-64; postdoctoral fellow in allergy and immunology NIH, 1964-65; practice medicine specializing in allergy and clin. immunology, Stamford, Conn., 1968—; asst. prof. clin. medicine N.Y. U. Sch. Medicine, 1968-77; clin. asso. prof. N.Y. Med. Coll., 1977—. Served to capt., M.C., U.S. Army, 1966-68. Diplomate Am. Bd. Internal Medicine, Am. Bd. Allergy and Immunology. Fellow A.C.P., Am. Acad. Allergy; mem. N.Y. Allergy Soc. (pres.), New Eng. Soc. Allegy (pres. 1978-79), Phi Beta Kappa. Contbr. articles to med. jours. Office: 144 Morgan St Stamfrod CT 06905

VOZELLA, JOHN JOSEPH, photog. co. exec.; b. Portsmouth, N.H., Feb. 16, 1925; s. Joseph Anthony and Carmela (Memmolo) V.; B.S., Mass. Inst. Tech., 1945; M.S., Columbia U., 1947; m. Caroline Laura Wescott, Nov. 29, 1952; children—John, Joseph, Stephen. Asst. to gen. supt. Riley Stoker Corp., Worcester, Mass., 1948-52; asst. steam and power supt. Oxford Paper Co., Rumford, Maine, 1952-56; plant engr. St. Croix Paper Co., Woodland, Maine, 1956-59; sr. mgr. Polaroid Corp., Cambridge, Mass., 1959—. Exec. chmn. Polaroid Labs. for United Way Fund, 1972—. Served with USNR, 1945. Recipient Reading Athletic Dir.'s award, 1972. Registered profl. engr., Maine. Mem. Mass. Inst. Tech. Alumni Assn. (chmn. Reading, Mass. 1968, 69). Home: 420 South St Reading MA 01867 Office: 730 Main St Cambridge MA 02139

VUCKOVICH, CAROL YETSO (MRS. MICHAEL VUCKOVICH), librarian; b. East Liverpool, Ohio, Sept. 23, 1940; d. Stephen A. and Louise (Sever) Yetso; B.S., Geneva Coll., 1966; M.L.S., U. Pitts., 1968; m. Michael Vuckovich, Sept. 24, 1970. Computation analyst Crucible Steel div. Colt Industries, Midland, Pa., 1958-62; library dir. Community Coll. Beaver County, Monaca, Pa., 1968—, instr. human anatomy and physiology, 1970—. Mem. Am., Pa. library assns., Spl. Libraries Assn., Am. Inst. Biol. Scis., Am. Anti-Vivisection Soc., Nat. Wildlife Fedn., Coll. and Research Libraries. Home: 21 Elm St Midland PA 15059 Office: Center Grange Rd Monaca PA 15061

VUOSO, FRANK, systems engr.; b. N.Y.C., Mar. 12, 1948; s. George and Anne (Mesopotanese) V.; B.S. in Computer Sci., Loyola Coll., Md., 1975; m. Josephine Calabro, Oct. 12, 1968; children—Frank, Paul Bryan. Systems programmer Woodward & Lothrop, Washington, 1971, First Nat. Bank, Balt., 1971-72, Balt. Gas & Electric Co., Balt., 1972-75; sr. system programmer, asst. tech. systems mgr., Equitable Trust Co., 1975-77; systems engr. Paradyne Corp., Ft. Lee, N.J., 1977—; cons. in computer systems. Leader Watchung council Boy Scouts Am., 1978—. Served with USAF, 1967-71. Mem. Data Processing Mgmt. Assn. Roman Catholic. Club: Dive and Rescue. Home: 1 Riviera Dr Somerville NJ 08876 Office: 2175 Lemoine Ave Ft Lee NJ 07024

VYASANAKERE, SATYANARAYANA RAO, surgeon; b. Vyasanakere, India, June 9, 1936; s. Rama Rao and Laksmi Bai (Chikkerahally) V.; came to U.S., 1964; M.B., B.S., Govt. Med. Coll., Mysore, India, 1962; 1 son, Madhusudhana. Intern, resident in gen. surgery Watts Hosp., Durham, N.C., 1966-71, New Hanover Meml.

Hosp., Wilmington, N.C., 1969-70; practice medicine, specializing in gen. surgery, Salisbury, Md., 1971—; mem. staff Peninsula Gen. Hosp., Salisbury. Diplomate Am. Bd. Surgery. Fellow A.C.S., Royal Coll. Surgeons Can.; mem. Wicomico County Med. Soc., Md. Med. Chirurg. Soc., AMA. Hindu. Home: 1224 Orchard Circle Salisbury MD 21801 Office: 231 Florida Ave Salisbury MD 21801

VYNER, MARY BAINBRIDGE, pianist, composer, educator; b. Uniontown, Pa., Oct. 4, 1933; d. John Andrew and Mary (Anderson) Bainbridge; student Carnegie Tech. U., 1946-50; Mus.B., Phila. Musical Acad., 1952, Mus.M., 1953, Mus.D., 1954; m. Louis Vyner, Feb. 20, 1960. Concert pianist, numerous locations, 1950—; composer 19 concertos for piano and orch., 4 symphonic tone poems for orch., 4 sonatas for piano, 4 preludes for piano, Bicentennial symphony with narrator; mem. faculty Phila. Musical Acad., 1961—, Franklin and Marshall Coll., Lancaster, Pa., 1968-71; founder, dir. Lancaster (Pa.) Conservatory of Music, 1953—. Mem. AAUP, Lancaster Musical Art Soc. (pres. 1962-64), Nat. Fedn. Music Clubs, Musicians Union Local 294. Presbyterian. Author: Creative Harmony, 1953, Creative Counterpoint, 1954. Home: 681 Valley Rd Lancaster PA 17601 Office: PO Box 1152 Lancaster PA 17604

WACHENHEIM, EDGAR, III, investment co. exec.; b. N.Y.C., Oct. 14, 1937; s. Edgar and Elizabeth (Lewis) W.; B.A., Williams Coll., 1959; M.B.A. (George F. Baker scholar), Harvard, 1966; m. Sue Ann Wallach, June 4, 1962; children—Lance Robert, Kim, Chris Andrew. Sr. analyst Goldman, Sachs & Co., N.Y.C., 1966-69; exec. v.p. Central Nat. Corp., N.Y.C., 1969—; dir. RSR Corp., Sejak Corp., Gerbaz Corp. Bd. dirs. Wallach Found., Orient Point Assn., Mamaroneck, N.Y.; mem. citizens budget adv. com. Bd. Edn., Union Free Sch. Dist. Mem. N.Y. Soc. Security Analysts. Clubs: Beach Point (gov., sec.), Harvard Bus. Sch. of N.Y.; Williams; Adirondock Mountain. Home: 850 Orienta Ave Mamaroneck NY 10543 Office: care Central Nat Corp 100 Park Ave New York City NY 10017

WACHMAN, MARVIN, univ. pres.; b. Milw., Mar. 24, 1917; s. Alex and Ida (Epstein) W.; B.S., Northwestern U., 1939, M.A., 1940; Ph.D., U. Ill., 1942; LL.D., U. Pa., 1964, Lincoln U., 1970, Del. Valley Coll. Sci. and Agr., 1973; D.H.L., Gratz Coll., 1973; Litt.D., Jewish Theol. Soc. Am., 1973; L.H.D., Colgate U., 1975, Widener Coll., 1976; m. Adeline Lillian Schpok, Apr. 12, 1942; children—Kathleen M., Lynn A. Asst. in history U. Ill., 1940-42; instr. Biarritz Am. U., Biarritz, France, 1945-46; vis. asst. prof. San Diego State Coll., summer 1948, U. Minn., 1950; asso. prof. history U. Md. in Europe, 1952-53; instr. Colgate U., 1946-47, asst. prof., 1947-52, asso. prof., 1952-56, prof., 1956-61, dir. upper class core program, 1956-61; pres. Lincoln U., 1961-70; v.p. acad. affairs Temple U., Phila., 1970-73, pres., 1973—; dir. Salzburg (Austria) Seminar in Am. Studies, 1958-60; Am. specialist U.S. Dept. State, Africa, 1965, 68; dir. Bell Telephone Co. Pa., Phila. Savs. Fund Soc. Mem. Pa. Higher Edn. Assistance Agy., Colgate Nat. Council, Crime Commn. Corp. Phila., Phila. Com. Fgn. Relations; mem. adv. council Expt. In Internat. Living; bd. dirs. Crime Prevention Assn. Phila., Greater Phila. Partnership, Jour. History Ideas, Phila. Contributionship, African Acad. Arts and Research, Phila. Orch. Assn., Phila. Acad. Music; trustee Phila. Award, Temple U., Jewish Publ. Soc. Am., Abington Meml. Hosp., Acad. Music Phila., African Student Aid Fund; bd. overseers Coll. V.I.; bd. visitors Eckerd Coll. Served pvt. to sgt., AUS, 1942-46. Mem. NAACP, Am. Studies Assn. (past mem. exec. com.), AAUP (past pres. Colgate U. chpt.), Am. Hist. Assn., ACLU, Pa. Assn. Colls. and Univs. (past pres.), Nat. Assn. State Univs. and Land-Grant Colls. (vets. affairs com., com. vol. support), Assn. Am. Colls. (commn. coll. adminstrn. 1967-69, task force on presdl. selection and career devel. 1973—), Phi Beta Kappa. Author: History of Social-Democratic Party of Milwaukee, 1897-1910; also articles in field. Home: 321 E Evergreen Ave Philadelphia PA 19118 Office: Temple U Broad and Montgomery Sts Philadelphia PA 19122

WACHTEL, HOWARD RICHARD, lawyer; b. N.Y.C., Mar. 28, 1927; s. Stanley and Miriam (Ducoffe) W.; student U. Ill., 1944-47; LL.B., Columbia, 1951; m. Audrey Berk, Sept. 17, 1954; children—Julia, Emily. Admitted to N.Y. bar, 1951; practiced in N.Y.C., 1953—; asso. LeBoeuf, Lamb, Leiby & MacRae, 1953-62, partner, 1962—. Lectr. Antitrust Inst. Am. Bar Assn. Chmn. N.Y.C. Com., N.Y. Young Republican Club, 1953-55. Served with U.S. Mcht. Marine, 1944-46; to lt. comdr. USCGR, 1951-53. Mem. Am. Bar Assn. (chmn. trade assn. com., antitrust sect.), Bar Assn. City N.Y. Home: 28 Justamere Dr Ossining NY 10562 Office: 140 Broadway New York City NY 10005

WACHTEL, NATHAN, dentist, educator; b. N.Y.C., Mar. 21, 1921; s. Herman Louis and Helen (Rosenbaum) W.; A.B., N.Y.U., 1942, D.D.S., 1945; m. Edith Kohler, June 29, 1950 (dec. July 1978); children—Eric Hillary, Jeffrey Holden. Gen. practice dentistry, N.Y.C., 1947-50; practice specializing in periodontics, oral medicine, oral diagnosis, N.Y.C., Stamford, Conn., 1950—; instr. periodontics N.Y.U., 1947-55, asst. clin. prof., 1955-58, asso. prof., 1965-71, asso. prof. preventive dentistry and community health, 1971-73, sr. clin. asst. in periodontics Polyclinic Hosp., also Post Grad. Med. Sch., 1948-53; attending in periodontics, in charge U. Hosp., N.Y.U.-Bellevue Med. Center, 1953-58. Scoutmaster, cubmaster Boy Scouts Am., N.Y.C., 1947-56. Served as lt. (j.g.) USNR, 1943-47. Diplomate Am. Bd. Periodontia. Fellow Am. Acad. Oral Medicine, Internat., Am. colls. dentists; mem. Am. Dental Assn., Am. Acad. Periodontology, Am. Acad. Dental Medicine, Omicron Kappa Upsilon. Contbr. articles to profl. jours. also sects. to textbooks in field. Asst. editor: Jour. Dental Medicine, 1953-69. Home: 203 E 72d St New York City NY 10021 Office: 800-A Fifth Ave New York City NY 10021 also 480 Bedford St Stamford CT 06902

WACHTER, WILLIAM W., JR., elec. constrn. co. exec.; b. Pitts., June 17, 1930; s. William H. and Mildred H. (Jacob) W.; B.S. in Bus. Adminstrn., U. Pitts., 1957; postgrad. in electronics Gateway Tech. Sch., 1960; postgrad. in mgmt. Pa. State U., 1961; m. Irene T. Batelli, Feb. 4, 1956; children—William H., Denise Lynn. Projects mgr. and asst. br. mgr. Lord Electric Co., Inc., Pitts., 1957-69, br. mgr., Cleve., 1969-73, v.p., regional mgr., Boston, 1973—; cons. Contract Admnstrn. Assos., Boston, 1978—. Dir. Bethel Park. Vol. Fire Dept., 1964-66; bd. fire engrs. Stow (Mass.) Fire Dept., 1975-77; mem. Indsl. Devel. Commn., Stow, 1975—. Served with U.S. Army, 1952-54. Mem. Assn. Iron and Steel Engrs., Nat. Elec. Contractors Assn., Dirs. Electric Inst., Elec. Contractors Assn. of Greater Boston (dir. 1976—), VFW, Am. Legion. Republican. Lutheran. Clubs: Elks, Masons. Home: 101 Kerkland Dr Stow MA 01775 Office: 86 Coolidge Ave Watertown MA 02172

WADDELL, SUE MARY, psychotherapist; b. Winston-Salem, N.C., Jan. 9, 1932; d. William Bayne and Marigold (Evans) W.; R.N., City Meml. Hosp., Winston-Salem, 1951; B.S., Marywood Coll., 1956; certificate in adminstrn. East Carolina U., 1969, M.A. in Counseling Services (Hugo E. Meml. scholar), 1969; Ph.D., U. Sarasata (Fla.), 1973; postgrad. Phila. Sch. Modern Psychoanalysis, 1978—. Profl. student nurse City Meml. Hosp., Winston-Salem, 1948-51; clin. nurse Dr. Hugh Thompson & Firm, Raleigh, N.C., 1951-53; joined Sisters of the Immaculate Heart of Mary, Scranton, Pa., 1953; clin. nurse Rex Hosp., Raleigh, 1951-53, St. Joseph Hosp., Carbondale, Pa., 1956-59; pastoral psychotherapist; dir. of counseling services Pope John XXIII Sch., Balt., 1969-70, Immaculate High Sch., N.Y.C., 1970-71; coordinator of project help East Carolina U., Greenville, N.C., 1971-72; dir. Marywood Coll. Counseling Center, Scranton, Pa., 1973-74; asso. dir. psychiat. nursing services, dir. clin. edn. services Northwestern Inst. of Psychiatry, Fort Washington, Pa., 1974-77; pvt. practice, psychotherapy, Phila., 1978—; guest lectr. depts. counselor edn. and psychology East Carolina U., 1969-70; clin. cons. in area workshops for counselors and psychologists Dept. of Pub. Instruction, N.C., 1971-72; psychol. cons. So. Assn. of Schs. and Colls., 1970-72. Certified counselor, N.C., N.Y. Mem. Nat. Assn. for Humanistic Psychology, Am., Pa. personnel and guidance assns., Kappa Delta Pi. Author: Human Perspectives in Educational Research, 1973; contbr. article to profl. jour. Home: 4000 Gypsy Ln Philadelphia PA 19144 Office: 4000 Gypsy Ln Philadelphia PA 19144

WADE, CAROLE KAY, interior designer; b. Fairmont, W.Va., Apr. 5, 1947; d. Lewis H. and Hazel M. (West) Manko; A.A., Fairmont (W.Va.) State Coll., 1970; postgrad. N.Y. Sch. Interior Design, 1974-75; m. Michael R.A. Wade, Aug. 25, 1974. Pub. affairs asst. Export-Import Bank of U.S., Washington, 1970-72; owner Carole Wade Concepts, Interior Design Instruction, Washington, 1975-76; proprietor Carole Wade Interior Design, N.Y.C., 1976—; instr. refresher projects N.Y. U.; charcoal drawings exhbn. Corcoran Mus. Art, Washington, 1973. Mem. campaign staff Senator Edmund Muskie for pres., 1972. Recipient Home Fashion Forum spl. award Montgomery Ward & Co., 1976. Contbr. articles to jour. Changing Type, 1975. Office: 250 E 63rd St New York City NY 10021

WADE, DONALD ZAHN, bank exec.; b. Quarryville, Pa., July 26, 1910; s. Harry Keene and Ida (Zahn) W.; certificate Columbia Inst. Commerce, 1932; Am. Inst. Banking, 1936; m. Mabel Rosemond Goss, Dec. 26, 1940. Teller, Farmers Nat. Bank, Quarryville, 1929-39; bank examiner Pa. State Dept. Banking, 1939-44; exec. v.p. Bank of Matamoras (Pa.), 1946-47, pres., dir., 1947-70, pres., chief exec. officer, 1970—; exec. v.p. Security Bank & Trust Co., Stroudsburg, Pa. Mem. Pa. State Banking Bd. Bd. dirs. Pike County chpt. ARC, 1953—, Hudson-Delaware council Boy Scouts Am., 1956—, Tri-State area United Fund; dir., officer Pike County Assn.; chmn. Pike, Monroe counties N.E. Pa. chpt. Blue Cross Blue Shield, Wilkes Barre; mem. com. for evaluating land sites Delaware Valley Sch. Dist., Milford, Pa., mem. Sch. Authority; agrl. rep. Pike County, 1957—; county chmn. Pike County Savs. Bond Com.; dir. Water Resources Assn. of Delaware River Basin, Port Jervis Devel. Corp., Pike County Indsl. Devel. Corp.; mem. com. N.E. Pa. Indsl. Devel. Commn.; bd. dirs., mem. comprehensive planning com. Tocks Island Regional Adv. Council. Dir. St. Francis Hosp., Port Jervis, N.Y., pres., 1965-66. Served USNR, 1944-46. Mem. Am. (country bankers com. 1961-69, exec. council 1962-65), Pa. (chmn. group 3 council of administration 1957-59, state pres. 1961-62, exec. council 1962-65, trustee ednl. found. 1962-66) bankers assns., Ind. Bankers Assn. Am. (dir.), Pa. Soc., Am. Legion, Port Jervis (dir.), Pike County (dir.) chambers commerce. Methodist. Mason (Shriner). Clubs: Lions, Rod and Gun (Matamoras); Lords Valley Country (gov., 1st pres.) (Hawley, Pa.); Irem Temple Country (Dallas, Pa.); Lehigh Valley (Allentown, Pa.); Union League (Phila.). Home: 710 Delaware Dr Metamoras PA 18336 Office: Security Bank & Trust Co Stroudsburg PA 18360

WADE, FURMAN, garage exec.; b. Mt. Morris, Pa., Aug. 13, 1927; s. Furman and Margaret (Renner) W.; student pub. schs.; m. Audra F. Stewart, June 29, 1956; children—Michael A., Mark Edward, Rebecca Ann. With Wades Body and Frame Shop, Waynesburg, Pa., 1952—, pres., 1960—; pres. Wades Mobile Home, Waynesburg, 1969—, Southwestern Pa. Coal Hauling, Inc.; owner Wades Radiator Repair, Waynesburg, 1972—. Mem. Waynesburg Sch. Bd.; committeeman Waynesburg Democratic Com. Served with USAR, 1943-45. Mem. Pa. Motor Truck Assn. (v.p.), Am. Automobile Assn. (dir.), VFW, DAV. Clubs: Moose, Lions. Home: Rural Route 2 Waynesburg PA 15370 Office: 71 N Maiden Waynesburg PA 15370

WADE, PETER CAWTHORN, chemist; b. Washington, Feb. 15, 1944; s. Howard W. and Cora M. (Farrier) W.; A.B. with honors, Middlebury Coll., 1966; Ph.D., U. Washington, 1971; m. Tamara Chaikowski, June 18, 1966; 1 son, Douglas. Research investigator Squibb Inst. Med. Research, Princeton, N.J., 1971—. Mem. Pennington (N.J.) Borough Planning Bd., 1976—. Shell Oil fellow, 1969-70; DuPont fellow, 1971. Mem. Am. Chem. Soc., AAAS. Contbr. articles to profl. jours. Patentee in field. Home: 415 Hale St Pennington NJ 08534 Office: PO Box 4000 Princeton NJ 08540

WADSWORTH, CHARLES YOUNG, lawyer; b. Winchester, Mass., Jan. 16, 1911; s. Lewis L. and Vera (Young) W.; grad. Phillips Exeter Acad., 1928; A.B., Harvard, 1932, LL.B., 1935; m. Virginia Dorr, June 18, 1938; children—Christopher D., George D., Anne D. Admitted to Mass. bar, 1935; mem. firm Hill & Barlow, Boston, 1935—, partner, 1938—. Dir. Barnstable Water Co., Boston, treas., 1962—; dir. Dorr Woolen Co., Newport, N.H., treas., 1947—; dir. Edgartown Water Co., Boston, Gen. Engring. & Constrn. Corp., Boston, Pinnacle Mfg. Corp. Moderator, Town of Lincoln, Mass., 1961-67. trustee Longfellow House Trust; com. mem. Permanent Charity Fund Inc. Mem. Am. (Ho. of Dels.), Mass. (ho. of dels. 1967—, treas. 1969-74, pres. 1975-76) bar assns., Am. Law Inst., Am. Coll. Probate Counsel (mem., treas. clients security bd.). Author: (with Benjamin A. Trustman, Richard B. Johnson) Town Meeting Time, 1962. Asst. editor: Rule Against Perpetuities (Gray), 1942; editor: Settlement of Estates (Newhall), 4th edit., 1958—; Massachusetts Trust and Will Manual, 1967. Home: Sandy Pond Rd Lincoln MA 01773 Office: 225 Franklin St Boston MA 02110

WADSWORTH, HOWARD MARVIN, marketing exec.; b. Syracuse, N.Y., Apr. 20, 1907; s. Marvin Orin and Elizabeth (Aylward) W.; student Syracuse U. extension, 1927; m. Helen Kathrine Matthews, May 28, 1936 (div. Dec. 1965); children—H. Duane, Fay Lydia (Mrs. Ralph R. Whitney, Jr.); m. 2d, June Miller Baker, Sept. 21, 1966. Founder, sr. partner Wadsworth & Lees, Syracuse, 1930-42; partner, gen. mgr. Uni-Tel., Liverpool, N.Y., 1940—; owner, gen. mgr. Wadsworth Mfg. Assos., Liverpool, 1942-60, pres., 1960-72, chmn., 1968—; mgr. marketing Warren Components Corp. (Pa.), 1949-68, chmn., 1969, pres., chief exec., 1972—; founder, v.p. marketing Greenfield Components (Mass.), 1959-61; exec. v.p., dir. Allegheny Glasseal, Warren, 1959-61; v.p. marketing, dir. Saegertown Glasseals, Saegertown, Pa. and San Rafael, Calif., 1961-62; pres. Wadsworth Pacific Mfg. Assos., Palo Alto, Calif., 1961-71; chmn. Carler Products, Inc., Syracuse, 1963-71, Coastal Communications Corp., Carson City, Nev., 1966-68; v.p., sec., dir. Petrex, Inc., Warren, 1972—; marketing cons. Aerospace Electronics, Miami Springs, Fla. Mem. Liverpool Vol. Fire Dept., 1935-38; dir. Oneida Lake Assn., Syracuse. Served with USCGR, 1940-45. Mem. N.Y. State Soc. Plastic Engrs., Electronic Reps. Assn., Atlantic Salmon Assn. (Montreal, Can.). Presbyn. Clubs: Governors, Lotos (N.Y.C.); Capital Hill (Washington); University, Penn Athletic (Phila.); Liederkranz, Tigris AAO NMS (Syracuse); Nautique, Jacques Cartier de Gaspe (Gaspe, Que., Can.); Conewango (Warren); Internat. Atlantic Salmon Found. (St. Andrews, N.B., Can.). Mason Patentee in field. Home: Box 16 Johnson Rd S Bernhards Bay NY 13028 also 3450 Osler St Vancouver BC Canada Office: 181 Blackberry Rd Liverpool NY 13088

WADSWORTH, MARION FRANCES EDDY (MRS. LESLIE R. WADSWORTH), ednl. adminstr.; b. Swansca, Mass., Oct. 30, 1916; d. Robert Palmer and Hazel Frances (Baker) Eddy; student Columbia U., 1939, Simmons Coll., 1940-44; B.S., Boston U., 1950; M.Ed., U. Mass., 1976; m. Leslie R. Wadsworth, Oct. 5, 1951; 1 dau., Cynthia Louise. Instr. nursing Union Hosp. Sch. Nursing, Fall River, Mass., 1940-44, dir. edn., 1945-49; instr. social studies New Eng. Bapt. Hosp. Sch. Nursing, Boston, 1950-52; inservice program dir. Belchertown (Mass.) State Sch., 1965—; vis. lectr. social studies Children's Hosp., Boston, 1950-51, Peter Bent Brigham Hosp., Boston, 1950-51. Mem. task force on civil rights for older women NOW. Mem. Am. Assn. Mental Deficiency, Internat. Platform Assn., Pi Gamma Mu, Alpha Sigma Nu. Congregationalist. Home: 79 Taylor St Granby MA 01033 Office: PO Box 486 Belchertown MA 01007

WAESCHE, R(ICHARD) H(ENLEY) WOODWARD, research co. exec.; b. Balt., Dec. 20, 1930; s. J(oseph) Edward and Margaret Steuart (Woodward) W.; B.A., Williams Coll., 1952; postgrad. U. Ala., 1956-58; M.A., Princeton U., 1962, Ph.D., 1965; m. Lucy Spotswood White, June 29, 1957; children—Charles Russell, Ann Spotswood. Research asst. Princeton U., 1961-64; research scientist Rohm & Haas Redstone div., Huntsville, Ala., 1954-59, sr. research scientist, 1964-66; sr. research engr. United Technologies Research Center, East Hartford, Conn., 1966—; cons. Goodyear Corp., 1959-60, Princeton U., 1965. Chmn. Fine Arts Com., Glastonbury, Conn., 1975—. Served with AUS, 1952-54. Guggenheim fellow, 1959-61. Mem. Am. Phys. Soc., Combustion Inst., Am. Inst. Aeros. and Astronautics (chmn. propellants and combustion tech. com. 1975—), Sigma Xi. Contbr. articles to profl. jours.; asso. editor Jour. Spacecraft and Rockets. Home: 281 Strickland St Glastonbury CT 06033 Office: Silver Ln East Hartford CT 06108

WAGMAN, GERALD HOWARD, biochemist; b. Newark, Mar. 4, 1926; s. David and Sophie (Milinsky) W.; B.S., Lehigh U., 1946; M.S., Va. Poly. Inst., 1947; m. Rhoda Kirschner, Dec. 9, 1948; children—Jan Donald, Neil Mark. Tech. research asst. Squibb Inst. for Med. Research, New Brunswick, N.J., 1947-49, research asst., 1954-57; mgr. Yankee Radio Corp., N.Y.C., 1950-54; asso. biochemist Schering Corp., Bloomfield, N.J., 1957-58, biochemist, 1958-65, sr. biochemist, 1966-68, sect. leader, 1969-70, mgr. antibiotics dept., 1970-74, asso. dir. microbiol. scis.-antibiotics, 1974-76, asso. dir. microbiol. scis. and head screening lab., 1977-78, dir. microbiol. strain lab., 1979—. Council mem. Troop 23 Boy Scouts Am., 1964-66; communications officer East Brunswick Civil Def. and Disaster Control, 1966-71; mem. sci. adv. com. East Brunswick Bd. Edn., 1960-68. Recipient Pub. Service award Am. Radio Relay League, 1965. Fellow Am. Inst. Chemists; mem. AAAS, Am. Chem. Soc., Am. Soc. Microbiology, Am. Inst. Biol. Scis., Soc. Indsl. Microbiology, N.Y., N.J. acads. scis., Soc. Applied Bacteriology (Gt. Britain), Sigma Xi, Tau Delta Phi. Author: Chromatography of Antibiotics, 1973. Editorial bd. Antimicrobial Agents and Chemotherapy, 1971-74. Co-editor: Isolation, Separation and Purification of Antibiotics, 1978. Contbr. articles to profl. jours. Patentee in field. Home: 62 Farms Rd Circle East Brunswick NJ 08816 Office: Galloping Hill Rd Kenilworth NJ 07033

WAGNER, CHARLES WILLIAM, twp. ofcl.; b. Mapeth, N.Y., May 29, 1934; s. Charles Anthony and Pauline (Wagner) Palagonia; Mktg. Degree, Holiday Inn U., 1972; m. Betty Rose Sconyers, July 27, 1975; children—Jay Charles, Belinda Breedlove, Joe Mark Breedlove. Sales mgr. Sunshine Co., Ltd., Hamilton, Bermuda, 1962-74; dist. dir. sales and mktg. parent owned cos. of Holiday Inn, Bermuda, N.Y., Ala., Ga. and Fla., 1972-75; gen. mgr. George Washington Motor Lodge, Whitehall, Pa., 1975-79; treas. Whitehall Twp., 1979—. Acting chmn. Whitehall Twp. Planning Commn., 1978-79; pres. Whitehall-Coplay Library, 1977—; mem. Mayor's Com. for Summer Youth Employment, Allentown, Pa., 1977-79; mem. adv. bd. Vocat.-Tech. Sch., Lehigh County, Pa., 1976—; bd. dirs. Allentown/Lehigh County Conv. and Tourism Bd., 1975-79. Served with USN, 1952-56; Korea. Mem. Travel Protective Assn., Whitehall (pres. 1978-79), Allentown (pub. relations dir. 1975-79) chambers commerce, Lehigh Valley Restaurant Assn. (dir. 1978-79). Democrat. Clubs: Rotary (pres. 1975-79), Exchange (dir. 1975-79). Home: 1024 N Poplar St Whitehall PA 18052 Office: Whitehall Twp Municipal Bldg Whitehall Township PA 18052

WAGNER, CLIFFORD CONFER, optometrist; b. West Reading, Pa., May 13, 1927; s. Benjamin Sonday and Ruth Gladys (Confer) W.; O.D., Pa. Coll. Optometry, 1951; m. Doris Mildred Allwein, Sept. 9, 1951; 1 son, Jeffrey Lee. Pvt. practice optometry specializing in contact lenses, Hamburg, Pa. Chmn. Hamburg Citizens for Gus Yatron U.S. Ho. of Reps., 1968, 70, 72, 74, 76; active Boy Scouts Am. Mem. Pa. (dir. 1956-77), Am. (keyman 1968—, polit. action com.), optometric assns., Am. Optometric Found., Berks County Optometric Soc. (pres. 1965-67, named Optometrist of Year 1976, Achievement award 1978), Vision Welfare League Pa., Am. Legion, Beta Sigma Kappa (pres. 1976-77). Republican. Lutheran. Clubs: Hamburg Exchange (pres. 1966-67), Heidelburg Country, Schuylkill Valley Racquet, Masons; Flying Dutchmen Ski (Berks County, Pa.). Home and office: 72 N 4th St Hamburg PA 19526

WAGNER, FLORENCE, metals recycling exec.; b. McKeesport, Pa., Sept. 23, 1926; d. George and Sophia (Petros) Zeleznik; B.A. magna cum laude, U. Pitts., 1977; m. Francis Xavier Wagner, June 18, 1946; children—Deborah Elaine Wagner Franke, Rebecca Susan, Melissa Catherine Wagner Good, Francis Xavier, Robert Francis. Sec. to pres. Tube City Iron & Metal Co., Glassport, Pa., 1944-50; cons. Raw Materials, Inc., Pitts., 1955; gen. mgr. Carson Compressed Steel Products, Pitts., 1967-69; partner Universal Steel Products, Pitts., 1970-71; gen. mgr. Josh Steel Co., Braddock, Pa., 1971—; trustee Profit-Sharing trust, Pension trust. Mem. Pitts. Symphony Soc., Pitts. Ballet Theater Guild. Mem. Soc. Pub. Adminstrn. (founder U. Pitts. br.), Acad. Polit. Sci., U.S. Strategic Inst. Alpha Sigma Lambda (past treas., sec., pres.) Republican. Roman Catholic. Club: Clairton (Pa.) Anglers. Home: 672 Ridgefield Ave Pittsburgh PA 15216 Office: 46 6th St Braddock PA 15104

WAGNER, FREDERICK BALTHAS, III, fluid flow engr.; b. Phila., July 21, 1946; s. Frederick Balthas and Jean Eleanor (Lockwood) W.; A.A.S. in Design Tech., Acad. Aeros., 1968; B.S. in Aerospace Tech., N.Y. Inst. Tech., 1970; m. Jeanne Elizabeth German, Oct. 27, 1973. Engr., aeronautical tech. Boeing Vertol Co., Ridley Park, Pa., 1971-74; engr. Sanders and Thomas, Inc., Pottstown, Pa., 1974-75; fluid flow engr. Kontes Mfg. Co., Vineland, N.J., 1976—; cons. Princeton (N.J.) Combustion Labs., 1977—. Served with Air N.G., 1970-76. Recipient Alumni Assn. award Acad. Aeros., 1971. Mem. Am. Def. Preparedness Assn. Republican. Methodist. Club: Lions. Contbr. articles to profl. jours. Home: 105 Walker Dr Boyertown PA 19512 Office: 1000 Spruce St Vineland NJ 08360

WAGNER, KARL THOMAS, machine tool mfg. co. exec.; b. Sidney, Ohio, Mar. 18, 1919; s. Karl John and Katherine (Dillon) W.; student U. Cin., 1937-39; B.S.M.E., Tri-State U., 1942; m. Virginia Russell, May 31, 1944; children—Karen Wagner Nickels, Karl Thomas. With Monarch Machine Tool Co., Sidney, Ohio, 1937-40; salesman Harrington, Wilson, Brown, N.Y.C., 1946-48; with Machinery Assos. Inc., Narberth, Pa., 1949—; pres. 1969—. Served to lt. (j.g.) USNR,

1944-46. Mem. Am. Machine Tool Distbrs. Assn. (dir. 1973-76), Soc. Mfg. Engrs. Republican. Clubs: Phila. Country, Sky Top, Union League, Seaview Country, Bachelors Barge. Home: 726 Harriton Rd Bryn Mawr PA 19010 Office: 134 Narberth Ave Narberth PA 19072

WAGNER, LOUIS EDWARD, chem. waste treatment processing co. exec.; b. Buffalo, N.Y., Mar. 12, 1937; s. Louis F. and Lucille S. (Olson) W.; A.A. in Chemistry, U. Buffalo, 1961, B.S. in Mgmt., 1963, M.B.A., 1964; m. Mary M. Fitzgerald, Sept. 13, 1958; children—Maribeth, Thomas F. Research chemist in polymer and chem. recycling research Amercoat Corp., Buffalo, 1954-63, asst. lab. mgr., 1961-63, plant mgr., Buffalo and Ft. Erie, Ont., Can., 1963-69; founder, pres. Chem-Trol Pollution Services, Inc., Blasdell, N.Y., 1969-76; founder, pres. Newco Chem. Waste Systems, Inc., Niagara Falls, N.Y., 1976—; lectr. chem. waste treatment, 1969—. Mem. Am. Chem. Soc., N.Y. State Conservation Assn., Fed. Water Pollution Assn., Am. Forestry Assn., Am. Nat. Standards Inst., Associated Industries N.Y. State, Western N.Y. Air and Water Pollution Control Socs., Young Pres.'s Assn., Jacques Cousteau Soc., Buffalo C. of C. Club: Park Country. Home: 8 Eltham Dr Eggertsville NY 14226 Office: 4626 Royal Ave Niagara Falls NY 14303

WAHEED, KHALID, internat. trade and investment exec.; b. Lahore, Pakistan, Jan. 1, 1936; s. Abdul and Saida (Mir) W.; came to U.S., 1973, naturalized, 1974; B.S., Purdue U., 1955; m. Akhter Firdaus, Apr. 7, 1956; children—Laila, Munize, Nadia, Scheherazade, Ayesha, Osman, Omar. Pres., chmn., chief exec. officer Ferozsons Labs., Ltd., Rawalpinda, Pakistan, 1955-74; mng. dir. Pakistan Tourism Devel. Corp., 1972; adminstrv. v.p. Ketchum & Co., Inc., N.Y.C., 1974-76, pres., chief exec. officer, 1976-78; chmn, chief exec. Ferozsons Inc., Stamford, Conn., 1978—, Scandia Cosmetics Internat. Inc., 1978—, Dahlia Parfums Inc., N.Y.C., 1978—. Mem. Sigma Nu, Kappa Psi. Author: Man and State, 1968; Winds of Change, 1970. Home: 109 Webbs Hill Rd Stamford CT 06903

WAHL, RAY FRANKLIN, educator; b. Northampton, Pa., Apr. 27, 1913; s. Morris Deysher and Carrie (Benninger) W.; Ph.B., Muhlenberg Coll., 1934; M.A., N.Y.U., 1953, Ph.D., 1967; m. Marie Minnie Kibler, Dec. 26, 1936; 1 dau., Rae Marie. Tchr. English, social studies, researcher, historian, Northampton (Pa.) High Sch,, 1934-66; instr., researcher N.Y.U., summers, 1951-57; reporter, photographer advt. Call-Chronicle Newspaper, Allentown, Pa., 1941-59; adviser in safety edn. Pa. Dept. Pub. Instrn., 1966-67; asso. safety edn. NEA, 1967-69; asst. dir. occupational safety and safety tng. Bur. Occupational and Indsl. Safety, Pa. Dept. Labor and Industry, 1969-70; dean Luzerne Community Coll. (Pa.), 1970-71; chief div. course devel. Office of Tng. and Edn., U.S. Labor Dept., 1971-74; vis. prof. Pa. State U., 1974—. Chmn. Northhampton Borough Civil Service Commn., 1948-54; mayor, Northampton, 1958-62; dir. Northampton County Chpt. Am. Cancer Soc. Pres. bd. dirs. Northampton Borough Sch. Employees Credit Union, 1950-66. Served from pvt. to 1st lt., U.S. Army, 1943-46. Mem. NEA, Pa. Edn. Assn., Northampton Tchrs. Assn. (past pres.), Nat. Driver Edn. Assn., Pa. Assn. Safety Educators, Pa. Mayors Assn., V.F.W., Am. Legion, Res. Officers Assn. (pres. Lehigh Valley chpt., 1963, mem. nat. air force affairs com.; pres. dept. Pa. 1965-66), Am. Soc. Safety Engrs., Nat. Safety Mgmt. Soc., Phi Delta Kappa, Kappa Phi Kappa, Lambda Chi Alpha. Democrat. Mem. Evang. & Reformed Ch. Mason. Author various hist. works. Mem. original programed learning research and writing team, USAF Res., 1962. Address: 1723 Hokendauqua Ave Northampton PA 18067

WAHLBERG, ERIC CLIFTON, engring. devel. co. exec.; b. Plainfield, N.J., May 25, 1910; s. Carl Victor and Anna Elizabeth (Anderson) W.; B.S. in Elec. Engring., Newark Coll. Engring., 1933; m. Grace Alberta Merkel, June 2, 1935; children—Carolyn Mae, Nancy Edith. Devel. engr., Condenser Corp. Am., South Plainfield, N.J., 1935-37; engr. petroleum storage facilities H. S. Bell Co., Bayonne, N.J., 1937-39; field engr. Asiatic Petroleum Co., Bayonne, 1939-41; head devel. govt. projects Electrolux Corp., Old Greenwich, Conn., 1941-56; various positions Am. Machine & Foundry Co., Greenwich, 1956-63, mgr., 1963-66; pres. Wahlred Co., Stamford, Conn., 1966—; cons. in field. Mem. IEEE (sr.). Patentee in field. Home, office: 32 8th St Stamford CT 06905

WAINER, MELVIN HENRY, real estate appraiser; b. Wilmington, Del., Mar. 19, 1921; s. Louis Juda and Dora (Korngold) W.; B.S., Pa. State U., 1946; m. Mary Louise Hoover, Oct. 9, 1949; children—Constance Ann, Pamela Louise Wainer Weisman, Debra Lynn, Wendy Lu. Pres. Pony Boy Vending Service, Inc., Lancaster, Pa., 1939-61; salesman real estate Charles Adler & Son, Inc., Lancaster, 1961-65; pres. Melvin H. Wainer Real Estate, Inc., Lancaster, 1965—. Bd. dirs. Lancaster Boys' Club, 1971-72, 75-76. Served with AUS, 1942-45. Decorated Purple Heart. Mem. Am. Soc. Appraisers (pres. chpt. 80 1974-75, sr. mem.), Greater Lancaster Bd. Realtors, Nat., Pa. assns. realtors. Club: Wheatland Sertoma (charter, pres. 1971-72, chmn. bd. dirs. 1972-73). Home: 10 Pilgrim Dr Lancaster PA 17603 Office: 102 Village Green Ln Lancaster PA 17603

WAINWRIGHT, CARROLL LIVINGSTON, JR., lawyer; b. N.Y.C., Dec. 28, 1925; s. Carroll Livingston and Edith Katherine (Gould) W.; B.A., Yale U., 1949; LL.B., Harvard U., 1952; m. Nina Walker, July 2, 1948; children—Delos Walker, Mark Livingston. Admitted to N.Y. bar, 1953; asso. firm Milbank, Tweed, Hope & Hadley, N.Y.C., 1952-58, 60-62; partner firm Milbank, Tweed, Hadley & McCloy, 1963—. Mem. State Commn. on Jud. Conduct, 1974—. Asst. counsel Gov. N.Y., 1959-60. Trustee Am. Mus. Natural History, Cooper Union for Advancement Sci. and Art, Boys' Club N.Y.; trustee Ch. Pension Fund and Affiliates; mem. univ. council Yale. Served with USMCR, 1943-46. Mem. Am., N.Y. State bar assns., Assn. Bar City N.Y. (treas. 1970-73, v.p. 1975-76), Am. Coll. Probate Counsel. Clubs: Century Assn., Union, River (N.Y.C.); Maidstone (pres. 1970-73) (East Hampton, N.Y.). Home: 1120 Fifth Ave New York City NY 10028 Office: 1 Chase Manhattan Plaza New York City NY 10005

WAINWRIGHT, RICHARD ADOLPH, owner elec. co.; b. Creston, Iowa, Apr. 15, 1931; s. Theodore Lee and Annetta (Schlepp) W.; Engring. diploma, Capitol Inst. Tech., 1954, D.Sc., 1976; m. Hilda Ohenian Alexander, Feb. 18, 1977; children—Richard L., Deborah A. (Mrs. John Wenth), Jonathan M., Stephen A., David B. Instr., lectr. elec. engring. Capitol Inst. Tech., Kensington, Md., 1954-57, trustee, 1968—, vice chmn. bd., 1976-77, chmn., 1977—; design engr. Page Communications Engr., Washington, 1957-59; cons. Rixon Electronics, Silver Spring, Md., 1959-60; chief research, chief engr. Telonic Engring. Co., Laguna Beach, Calif., 1960-62; pres. I-Tel, Inc., Kensington, 1962-68, chmn. bd., dir. engring., 1968-71; sr. partner, dir. engring. Cirqtel, Kensington, 1971-72, mng. partner, 1973-74; owner, cons. Cirqtel Inc., 1974—; founder, pres. Wainwright & Cromwell, 1976—. Served with USN, 1948-52. Recipient Achievement award E.H. Reitzke, 1961, United Inventors and Scientists Am., 1973. Mem. I.E.E.E., Am. Phys. Soc., Am. Austrian Soc. Club: Arts (Washington). Author poems; contbr. articles to profl. jours. Patentee in field. Address: care Clark & Cromwell 8414 Ramsey Ave Silver Spring MD 20910

WAITZKIN, STELLA, artist; b. Bklyn., Nov. 17, 1920; d. Isidor and Saide Rosenblatt; student N.Y. U., Alfred U., Columbia U.; children—Fred, Bill. One-woman exhibitions include: Yale U., 1974, Fordham U., N.Y.C., 1975, James Yu, N.Y.C., 1974, 75, 77; group exhibitions include: Art Inst., Dayton, Ohio, 1979, Renwick Gallery, Washington, 1977, Dalhousie Art Gallery, Halifax, N.S., 1978; represented in permanent collections: Nat. Collection Art, Washington, Va. Mus., N.Y. U., Newark (N.J.) Mus., Butler Mus., N.Y. State Coll., Potsdam. Home: 222 W 23d St New York City NY 10011

WAKAMORI, TAKASHI, physician; M.D., Hokkaido U., 1953. Intern, Sagamihara Nat. Hosp., Kanagawa, Japan, 1954; resident otolaryngology N.Y. Polyclinic Med. Sch. and Hosp., 1962-65; chief resident otolaryngology Albert Einstein Med. Coll., N.Y.C., 1965; fellow Queen's Gen. Hosp.-L.I. Jewish Hosp., 1966-69; fellow Lenox Hill Hosp., N.Y.C., 1974-75; practice medicine, Teaneck, N.J., 1975—. Diplomate Am. Bd. Otolaryngology. Mem. Am. Acad. Ophthalmology and Otolaryngology, N.J., Bergen County med. socs. Office: 960 Teaneck Rd Teaneck NJ 07666

WAKEFIELD, FREDERICK IRVING, rubber mfg. co. exec.; b. Stewartstown, N.H., Nov. 21, 1923; s. Julian Edward and Anne Mae (Abbott) W.; B.S., U. N.H., 1944; m. Helen Winifred Smith, Nov. 29, 1944; children—Joane Ruth, Richard Alan, Karen Ann, Lynn Elizabeth, Susan Mary. Design engr. to mgr. engring. Simplex Wire & Cable Co., Newington, N.H., 1953-70; engring. mgr. Cable div. ITT, San Diego, 1970-71; mgr. mfg. engring. Simplex Wire & Cable Co., North Berwick, Maine, 1971-72; pres. Wakefield Engring. Co., Durham, N.H., 1972-73; mgr. mfg. devel. Davidson Rubber Co., Dover, N.H., 1973—; cons. in field. Mem. Town of Durham Planning Bd., 1968-70; mem. Town of Durham Long Range Planning Com. Schs., 1966-70. Served with USN, 1944-46. Registered profl. engr., N.H. Mem. ASME, Wire Assn. Republican. Roman Catholic. Home: 48 Mill Pond Rd Durham NH 03824 Office: Davidson Rubber Co Indsl Park Dover NH 03820

WAKELEE, ROBERT LOUIS, JR., indsl. engr.; b. Derby, Conn., Sept. 1, 1936; s. Robert Louis and Edith Louise (Hawks) W.; B.A., Chapman Coll., Orange, Calif., 1969; M.S. in Systems Mgmt., U. So. Calif., 1974; m. Adah Mae Terrill, May 25, 1963; children—Kieth Robert, Kent Walter. Engr. time standards Chgo. Pneumatic Tool Co., Utica, N.Y., 1977—. Served to sr. master sgt., USAF, 1956-77. Decorated Meritorious Service medal, Commendation medal. Mem. Am. Inst. Indsl. Engrs. (sr.), Am. Mgmt. Assn. Mem. United Ch. Christ. Clubs: Masons, Shriners. Home: 123 Glen Rd S Rome NY 13440 Office: 2200 Bleeker St Utica NY 13440

WAKSLAK, HARRY ARON, clergyman, psychologist; b. Stockholm, Oct. 29, 1948; s. Israel and Dora Wakslak; came to U.S., 1953, naturalized, 1953; B.S., Bklyn. Coll., 1969; D.D., Mesivta Talmudical Sem., 1972; PH.D., Hofstra U., 1974; m. Rivka Morgenstern, Nov. 17, 1973; children—Avigail, Menachem. Rabbi, 1974; clin. intern Maimonides Med. Center, Bklyn., 1973; instr. Hofstra U., 1971; sch. psychology cons. N.Y. Bd. Edn., N.Y.C., 1973—, Hebrew Acad. for Spl. Children, 1975—; psychology cons. Lawrence Nursing Home, Queens, N.Y., 1974—; clin. psychologist Brunswick Hosp. Center for Phys. Med. and Rehab., Amityville, L.I., 1973—; rabbi Young Israel of Belle Harbor, 1974—; lectr. to religious and psychol. orgns., 1974—; chaplain Sr. Citizens Center-Gustave Hartman YMHA, 1976—; mem. Yeshiva of Belle Harbor Bd. Edn., 1975—. Certified sch. psychologist, licensed clin. psychologist, N.Y. State; recipient Outstanding Alumnus award Yeshiva Torah Vodaath, 1976. Mem. Am. Psychol. Assn., Nat. Rehab. Assn., Assn. for Advancement Behavior Therapy, Rabbinical Alliance Am., Young Israel Rabbis (dir.). Home and Office: 193 Beach 122d St Belle Harbor NY 11694

WALCH, DAVID BEAN, univ. dean; b. LaGrande, Oreg., May 19, 1936; s. Charles Lloyd and Lila (Bean) W.; B.S., Eastern Oreg. Coll., 1960; M.S. in L.S., U. Ill.; 1962, certificate advanced studies, 1969; Ph.D., U. Utah, 1973; m. Phyllis Collins, June 23, 1959; children—Shane, Shawna, Sherece, Curt, Shalene. Tchr., LaGrande, 1960-61; asso. librarian Ch. Coll. of Hawaii, Laie, 1962-64, dir. library services, 1965-67; asst. prof. library sci. U. Utah, Salt Lake City, 1967-74; dean acad. services SUNY, Buffalo, 1974—. Cons. library orgn. C&W Library Cons., 1969—. Katerine Sharp fellow, 1960-61. Mem. Am., Utah library assns. Mormon (bishop 1965—). Author: Cataloging and Classification of Non-Print Materials, 1970. Home: 246 Sprucewood Williamsville NY 14221 Office: SUNY Buffalo 1300 Elmwood Ave Buffalo NY 14221

WALCOTT, DAVID NATHANIEL, pharmacist; b. Cambridge, Mass., Dec. 22, 1922; s. James Adaniel and Keziah Ann (Cummings) W.; B.S., Ferris State Coll., 1953; postgrad. Boston State Coll., 1968, U. So. Calif., 1977; m. Phyllis Eleanor Barrow, June 24, 1951. Research chemist New Eng. Center Hosp., Boston, 1956; asst. chief dept. pharmacy Newton Wellesley Hosp., Newton, Mass., 1957-59, Malden (Mass.) Hosp., 1960-64; asst. chief, dept. mental health Cushing State Hosp., Framingham, Mass., 1965; dir. pharmacy Solomon Mental Health Center, Lowell, Mass., 1966—. Served with USAAF, 1944-46. Registered pharmacist, Mich., Mass. Mem. Am. Soc. Hosp. Pharmacists, Omega Psi Phi. Republican. Episcopalian. Office: Solomon Mental Health Center 391 Varnum Ave Lowell MA 01854

WALD, ALVIN STANLEY, biomed. engring. research scientist; b. N.Y.C., May 17, 1934; s. Hyman and Ida W.; B.E.E., Cooper Union, 1955; M.E.E., Poly. Inst. Bklyn., 1961; Ph.D., N.Y. U., 1974; m. Mary Jack Light, Aug. 28, 1977; children—Danis Cory Lloyd, Lemuel Gardner Lloyd. Sr. engr. Bulova Research and Devel. Labs., Woodside, N.Y., 1961-64; biomed. engring. research scientist Med. Center, Dept. Neurosurgery, N.Y. U., N.Y.C., 1964—, asst. prof. exptl. neurosurgery; mem. neurol. device panel Bur. Med. Devices, FDA. Served with U.S. Army, 1956-58. N.Y. State Regents scholar, 1951-55; N.Y. State Health Research Council grantee, 1976-77; certified clin. engr. Mem. AAAS, Am. Physiol. Soc., IEEE, N.Y. Acad. Scis. Contbr. research articles to profl. sci. jours. Adapted mass spectrometer for in vivo blood gas analysis; developed instrumentation for intracranial pressure monitoring. Home: 3 Bridges PO Box 36 West Redding CT 06896 Office: 550 First Ave New York City NY 10016

WALD, BERNARD JOSEPH, lawyer; b. Bklyn., Sept. 14, 1932; s. Max and Ruth (Mencher) W.; B.B.A. magna cum laude, Coll. City N.Y., 1953; J.D. cum laude, N.Y. U., 1955; m. Francine Joy Weintraub, Feb. 2, 1964; children—David Evan, Kevin Mitchell. Admitted to N.Y. bar, 1955; since practiced law in N.Y.C.; partner, mem. firm Herzfeld & Rubin, N.Y.C., 1964—. Mem. Am., N.Y. State bar assns., Assn. Bar City N.Y., N.Y. County Lawyers Assn., Beta Gamma Sigma, Beta Alpha Psi. Home: 520 LaGuardia Pl New York City NY 10012 Office: 40 Wall St New York City NY 10005

WALD, FRANCINE JOY WEINTRAUB (MRS. BERNARD J. WALD), physicist; b. Bklyn., Jan. 13, 1938; d. Irving and Minnie (Reisig) Weintraub; student Bklyn. Coll., 1955-57; B.E.E., Coll. City N.Y., 1960; M.S., Poly. Inst. Bklyn., 1962, Ph.D., 1969; m. Bernard J. Wald, Feb. 2, 1964; children—David Evan, Kevin Mitchell. Engr., Remington Rand Univac div. Sperry Rand Corp., Phila., 1960; instr. Poly. Inst. Bklyn., 1962-64, adj. research asso., 1969-70; lectr. N.Y. Community Coll., Bklyn., 1969, 70; instr. sci. Friend Sem., N.Y.C., 1975—, chmn. dept. sci., 1976—. NDEA fellow, 1962-64. Mem. Am. Phys. Soc., Am. Assn. Physics Tchrs., Sigma Xi, Tau Beta Pi, Eta Kappa Nu. Home: 520 LaGuardia Pl New York City NY 10012

WALD, GEORGE, educator; b. N.Y.C., Nov. 18, 1906; s. Isaac and Ernestine (Rosenmann) W.; B.S., N.Y. U., 1927; M.A., Columbia, 1928, Ph.D., 1932; M.D. (hon.), U. Berne, 1957; D.Sc., Yale, 1958, Wesleyan U., 1962, N.Y.U., 1965, McGill, 1966, Amherst Coll., 1968, Rennes, 1970, U. Utah, 1971, Gustavus Adolphus, 1972; m. Frances Kingsley, May 15, 1931 (div.); children—Michael, David; m. 2d, Ruth Hubbard, 1958; children—Elijah, Deborah. NRC fellow at Kaiser Wilhelm Inst., Berlin and Heidelberg, U. Zurich, U. Chgo., 1932-34; tutor biochem. scis. Harvard, 1934-35, instr. biology, 1935-39, faculty instr., 1939-44, asso. prof. biology, 1944-48, prof., 1948—, Higgins prof. biology, 1968-77, prof. emeritus, 1977—; vis. prof. biochemistry U. Calif., Berkeley, summer 1956; Nat. Sigma Xi lectr., 1952; chmn. divisional com. biology and med. scis. NSF, 1954-56; Guggenheim fellow, 1963-64; Overseas fellow Churchill Coll., Cambridge U., 1963-64; participant U.S.-Japan Eminent Scholar Exchange, 1973; guest China Assn. Friendship with Fgn. Peoples, 1972. Recipient Eli Lilly prize from Am. Chem. Soc., 1939; Lasker award Am. Pub. Health Assn., 1953; Proctor medal Assn. Research in Ophthalmology, 1955; Rumford medal Am. Acad. Arts and Scis., 1959; Ives medal Optical Soc. Am., 1966; Paul Karrer medal in chemistry U. Zurich, 1967; co-recipient Nobel prize for physiology, 1967; T. Duckett Jones award Helen Hay Whitney Found., 1967, Bradford Washburn medal Boston Mus. Sci., 1968; Max Berg award, 1969; Priestley medal Dickinson Coll., 1970. Fellow Nat. Acad. Sci., Am. Acad. Arts and Scis., Am. Philos. Soc. Co-author: General Education in a Free Society, 1945; Twenty Six Afternoons of Biology, 1962; also science papers on vision and biochem. evolution. Home: 21 Lakeview Ave Cambridge MA 02138

WALD, LAWRENCE, accountant; b. Bklyn., Mar. 12, 1933; s. Meyer and Rose (Kloner) W.; B.S., N.Y. U., 1954; m. Alice Donowitz, Oct. 3, 1954; children—Susan Michelle, Alan Scot. Auditor, Kestenbaum & Kass, C.P.A.'s, N.Y.C., 1954-55, Lowett & Schall, C.P.A.'s, N.Y.C., 1958-60; accountant Jack I. Rosen, C.P.A., N.Y.C., 1960-62; v.p. finance Gotham Industries Inc., N.Y.C., 1962-77, Milor Corp., Leominster, Mass., 1977—, Bee Plastics Corp., 1977—, Gotham Chgo. Corp., 1977—. Treas. Ross Hall Heights Civic Assn., 1968. Served with AUS, 1955-57. Mem. Am. Inst. C.P.A.'s, N.Y. Soc. C.P.A.'s. Home: 55 Ross Hall Blvd N Piscataway NJ 08854 Office: 511 Lancaster St Leominster MA 01453 also 2660 N Clybourn Ave Chicago IL

WALD, PHILIP MARTIN, physician; b. N.Y.C., Feb. 28, 1929; s. Heiman Z. and Pauline Wald; B.S., Bklyn. Coll. Pharmacy, 1955; M.D., U. Rome, 1968; m. Eva Heublum, Sept. 8, 1957; 1 dau., Marla Frances. Intern, Beth Israel Med. Center, N.Y.C., 1968-69, resident, 1969-74; practice medicine specializing in obstetrics and gynecology, N.Y.C., 1974—; asso. attending obstetrician and gynecologist Beth Israel Med. Center, N.Y.C.; asso. attending obstetrician and gynecologist, dir. ultrasonography lab. Cabrini Med. Center, N.Y.C., 1977—. Served with USMC, 1948-51. Diplomate Am. Bd. Obstetrics and Gynecology. Fellow A.C.S., Am. Coll. Obstetricians and Gynecologists; mem. AMA, Am. Inst. ultrasound in Medicine, Flying Physicians Assn. Home: 360 E 72d St New York NY 10021 Office: 145 E 16th St New York NY 10003

WALDAU, HELEN FRANCES, educator; b. Torrington, Conn., Mar. 21, 1925; d. Teofil and Michaelena (Plaga) Budney; B.A., U. Conn., 1953, 6th yr. certificate, 1968; M.A., U. Hartford; divorced; children—Geoffrey, Christopher, Peter, Sandra. Mem. faculty Hopewell Sch., Glastonbury, Conn., 1966—, supr. U. Conn. open edn. interns, 1971-75. Fellow U. Conn., 1967-68. Mem. NEA, Conn., Glastonbury edn. assns., Greater Conn. Council for Open Edn. (charter), Glastonbury Task Force for Gifted Edn., Psi Upsilon Omicron. Home: 154 Wood Pond Rd Glastonbury CT 06033

WALDEN, RICHARD HENRY, physician; b. N.Y.C., Aug. 5, 1913; s. Henry W. and Eva (Birke) W.; D.D.S., N.Y. U., 1938; M.D., L.I. Coll. Medicine, 1943; children—Richard Henry, Kenneth, Peter, Terri Ann. Intern, Kings County Hosp., 1938-39, resident, 1939-40, 43-45; practice medicine specializing in plastic surgery and maxillo facial surgery; attending, chief plastics surgery Nassau Hosp., Mineola, Mercy hosps.; asso. prof. plastic and maxillo facial surgery SU NY, Stoney Brook, 1975—; dir. N. Shore Univ. Hosp. Cleft Palate Center. Served to capt. M.C., U.S. Army, 1945-47. Mem. Am. Soc. Maxillo Facial Surgeons (pres. 1977-78), Am. Assn. Plastic Surgeons, Am. Soc. Plastic and Reconstructive Surgery, Am. Cleft Palate Assn., Nassau County Med. Soc., L.I. Plastic Surg. Group (pres. 1968-78). Republican. Contbr. articles to profl. jours. Home: 19 Victorian Ln Brookville Long Island NY 11545 Office: 110 Willis Ave Mineola NY 11501

WALDEN, WILLIAM DAVID, physician; b. Vienna, Austria, Nov. 23, 1929 (parents Am. citizens); s. Hugo and Ann (Marion) Wallenfels; B.S., U. Calif. at Los Angeles, 1951; M.D., N.Y. U., 1959; m. Elinor Klotz, July 27, 1952; children—Jonathan Jay, Ann Elizabeth. Intern, Beth Israel Hosp., N.Y.C., 1959-60; resident obstetrics and gynecology Cornell Med. Center, N.Y. Hosp., N.Y.C., 1960-63; practice medicine specializing in obstetrics and gynecology, N.Y.C., 1963—; clin. asst. prof. obstetrics and gynecology Cornell U. Med. Coll.; chief gynecol. service Center Reproductive and Sexual Health, N.Y.C. Served to lt. (j.g.), USNR, 1952-55. Decorated UN medal, Korean Service medal with two stars; hon. police surgeon Police Dept. N.Y.C. Diplomate Am. Bd. Obstetrics and Gynecology. Fellow Am. Coll. Obstetricians and Gynecologists, N.Y. Gynecol. Soc.; mem. Am. Fertility Soc. Home: 142 West End Ave New York City NY 10023 Office: 936 Fifth Ave New York City NY 10021

WALDHAUSEN, JOHN ANTON, cardiothoracic surgeon; b. N.Y.C., May 22, 1929; s. Max H. and Agnes H. (Stettner) W.; B.S. magna cum laude, Coll. Great Falls, 1950; M.D., St. Louis U., 1954; m. Marian Trescher, June 4, 1957; children—John H., Robert Rodney, Anthony Gordon Scarlett. Intern, Johns Hopkins Hosp., 1954-55, resident, 1955-57; clin. asso. Nat. Heart and Lung Inst., NIH, 1957-59; resident Hosp. U. Pa., 1959, Ind. U. Med. Center, 1960-62; practice medicine, specializing in cardiothoracic surgery, Indpls., 1962-66, Phila., 1966-70, Hershey, Pa., 1970—; mem. staff Milton S. Hershey Med. Center, 1970—; from instr. to asst. prof. Ind. U. Med. Center, 1962-66; asso. prof. surgery U. Pa. Sch. Medicine, Phila., 1966-70; prof., chmn. Dept. Surgery, Pa. State U. Coll. Medicine, The Milton S. Hershey Med. Center, 1970—, sr. mem. grad. faculty, 1970—, vice chmn. med. policy bd., 1971-72, interim provost, dean, 1972-73, asso. dean health care, 1973-75. Served with USPHS, 1957-59. Recipient USPHS Career Devel. award, 1964; USPHS grantee, 1964-69; diplomate Am. Bd. Surgery, Am. Bd. Thoracic Surgery. Mem. Allen O. Whipple Surg. Soc., Am. Acad. Pediatrics, AAAS, Am. Assn. for Surgery of Trauma, Am. Coll. Cardiology, A.C.S. (chpt. pres. 1974-75), Am. Fedn. Clin. Research, Am. Heart Assn., AMA, Am. Physiol. Soc., Am. Soc. Artificial

Internal Organs, Am. Assn. Thoracic Surgery, Am. (mem. com. issues), Central surg. assns., Internat. Cardiovascular Soc. (chpt. recorder 1969-74), Pa. Assn. Thoracic Surgery (pres. 1977-78), Societe Internat. de Chirurgie, Soc. Clin. Surgery (treas. 1972—), Soc. Surg. Chmn., Soc. Thoracic Surgeons, Soc. Univ. Surgeons, Thoracic Surgery Dirs. Assn. (pres. 1977—), Soc. Vascular Surgery, Sigma Xi, Alpha Omega Alpha. Contbr. chpts. to books, articles to med. jours. Home: RD 1 PO Box 158G Annville PA 17003 Office: M S Hershey Med Center Pa State U Hershey PA 17033

WALDMAN, JEFFREY, metallurgist, educator; b. Phila., Jan. 10, 1941; s. Albert Berger and Rita Joanne (Weitzenkorn) W.; B.S. in Metall. Engring., Drexel Inst. Tech., 1963; Sc.D. in Metallurgy (Whitney fellow), Mass. Inst. Tech., 1967; m. Judith Shulman, Dec. 23, 1962; children—Stacey, Jonathan, Karen. Drexel Inst. Tech. coop. student RCA, Somerville, N.J., 1959-61; metallurgist Frankford Arsenal, Phila., summers 1963, 64, 1968-77, U.S. Army Armament Research and Devel. Command, Dover, N.J., 1977—; sr. research engr. Western Electric Co., Princeton, N.J., 1967-68; instr. evening coll. Drexel U., 1968-71, prof., 1975—, adj. prof. dept. metallurgy, 1973. Recipient Spl. Act awards Frankford Arsenal, 1969, 71, also Suggestion award, 1969. Mem. Research Soc. N.Am. (treas. Frankford Arsenal chpt.), Frankford Arsenal Mgmt. Assn., Am. Soc. Metals, Am. Inst. Metall., Mining and Petroleum Engrs., Am. Def. Preparedness Assn. (liaison), Sigma Xi, Tau Beta Pi, Phi Kappa Phi, Alpha Sigma Mu. Contbr. articles to profl. jours.; patentee in field. Home: 3894 Donna Dr Huntingdon Valley PA 19006 Office: US Army Armament Research and Devel Command Dover NJ

WALDMAN, LESTER JESSE, assn. exec.; b. N.Y.C., Mar. 5, 1907; s. Henry and Ruth (Rindskopf) W.; student U. Cin., 1927-29; B.S., L.I.U., 1931, LL.D. (hon.), 1975; LL.B., St. Lawrence U., 1931; J.D., Bklyn. Law Sch., 1969; m. Blanche Weinstein, July 29, 1947; 1 son, Michael. Admitted to N.Y. bar, 1932; practiced in N.Y.C., 1933-48, mem. Henry and Lester J. Waldman, 1933-48; with Anti-Defamation League of B'nai B'rith, 1949-73, regional dir., 1949-52, program dir., 1952-54, exec. asst. nat. dir., 1954-73; counsel, dir. planning N.Y. Soc. for Deaf, 1973-77, exec. dir., 1977—; spl. dep. atty. gen. N.Y., 1937; lectr. L.I. U., 1950-54. Del. White House Conf. on Edn., 1955, Arden House Round Table on Edn., 1954-76. Dir. League for Jewish Deaf; dir. N.Y. Soc. for Deaf, pres., 1964-68. Trustee Fedn. Jewish Philanthropies, Temple Emanu-El, 1969-71, pres. Men's Club, 1969-71. Served from pvt. to 1st lt. U.S. Army, 1942-46. Mem. Long Island U. Alumni Assn. (pres. 1933-42), Am. Psychol. Assn. Phi Epsilon Pl. Republican. Mason; mem. B'nai B'rith. Home: 340 E 64th St New York City NY 10021 Office: 344 E 14th St New York City NY 10003

WALDO, HENRY CHANNING, forest industries cons.; b. East Randolph, Vt., July 6, 1904; s. Willis Henry and Lena May (Ferris) W.; B.S. in Forestry, U. Maine, 1927; m. Mary Mildred Maguire, Sept. 4, 1928; 1 son, William Channing. Forest engr. Parker Young Co., Lincoln, N.H., 1927-33; asst. ranger U.S. Forest Service, Laconia, N.H., 1933-34, dist. ranger, 1934-41, asso. forester, 1941-43; chief pulpwood unit Office Price Adminstrn., Washington, 1943-45; mgr. wood dept. Franconia Paper Corp., 1945-71; proprietor Waldo Land Mgmt. Service, Lincoln, N.H., 1971—; trustee Plymouth Guaranty Savs. Bank, Plymouth, N.H., 1962—; dir., acting pres. No. R.R., pres., 1976—; mem. N.H. Bd. Registration of Land Surveyors, 1970-71; cons. in field. Chmn. Lincoln Sch. Bd., 1953-55; chmn. budget com. Lincoln, 1965-75; chmn. N.H. Gov.'s Taxation Com., 1952-55, 74-75; chmn. Granite State Forest Industries Com., 1953-66; mem. Conv. to Revise N.H. Constn., 1957-71; active Daniel Webster council Boy Scouts Am., ARC; trustee N.H. State Prison, 1972-76. Recipient New Eng. Council award good forest mgmt., 1960; N. Eastern Loggers Assn. award practicing forestry, 1961. Registered land surveyor, N.H., Maine, Vt. Mem. Soc. Am. Foresters, N. Eastern Loggers Assn. (pres. 1955-57), New Eng. Lumbers Assn. (dir., pres. 1953-54), Can. Pulp and Paper Assn., Nat. Def. Exec. Res. (emeritus), SAR, Xi Sigma Pi, Phi Sigma. Address: Box 38 Pollard Rd Lincoln NH 03251

WALDRON, JAMES BELLORD, ophthalmologist; b. Christchurch, N.Z., Sept. 17, 1938; s. Randolph Vivian Eustace and Virginia Dorothy (Bacon) W.; B.A., U. N.Z., 1960; M.B. Ch.B., U. Otageo, 1964; m. Esther Ann Boler, July 1, 1970; 1 son, Jay. Intern, Christchurch Hosp., N.Z., 1965-66, intern Christ Hosp., Cin., 1966-67; resident in ophthalmology Montreal Gen. Hosp., 1968-71; practice medicine specializing in ophthalmology, Montreal, PQ, Can., 1972—; chief ophthalmology Reddy Meml. Hosp., asst. ophthalmologist Montreal Gen. Hosp., lectr. ophthalmology McGill U. Mem. Corp. Professionnelle des Medecins du Quebec, Coll. Physicians and Surgeons Ont., Can. Med. Assn. Home: 11 Gladstone Ave Westmount PQ H 3Z1Z3 Canada Office: suite 614 1538 Sherbrooke St W Montreal PQ H3G 1L5 Canada

WALEN, HARRY LEONARD, ednl. adminstr.; b. Winchester, Mass., June 26, 1915; s. Harry Leonard and Alice (Garland) W.; A.B. cum laude, Harvard, 1937, A.M., 1942; m. Elizabeth Rowe Benson, June 26, 1939; children—Harry Benson, Kimball Frederick, Robert Leonard. Tchr., Los Alamos Ranch Sch., 1937-42, head English dept., 1939-42; tchr. English, Groton (Mass.) Sch., 1942-46; instr. English, faculty marshal Newton Jr. Coll., 1946-51; English and journalism tchr. Newton High Sch., Newtonville, Mass., 1946-51, adminstr., 1951-55; directing editor secondary sch. English textbooks Ginn & Co., Boston, 1955-61; prin. Needham (Mass.) High Sch., 1961-72, career, post-secondary counselor, 1972—. Mem. Interviewing Com. for Overseas Grants and Fellowships, 1961—; mem. planning com. Task Force on High Sch. Graduation Requirements, Mass. Dept. Edn., 1976-79. Adviser, Jewish War Vets. Brotherhood program, 1971-72, 73—; corporate mem. U.S.S. Mass. Meml. Com., Inc., 1972—; chmn. edn. com. N.E. conf. Nat. Council Christians and Jews, 1972—, mem. study mission to Israel, 1974; vice-chmn. New Eng. Conf. on Quality of Life, Boston, 1973; mem. Newton Regional Adv. Manpower Planning Bd., 1973-77. Pres. YMCA Counseling Services Greater Boston, 1976—. Recipient citation Nat. Council Tchrs. English, 1969; citation U.S. Commr. Edn., 1971; Certificate of Appreciation, City of Newton, 1971; Half Million Miler plaque United Airlines, 1974. John Hay fellow in humanities, 1965, Commonwealth fellow Mass. State Dept. Edn., 1972. Mem. Nat. Council Tchrs. English (asso. chmn. nat. conv. 1965, mem. steering com. 1966-69, asso. chmn. com. on English learning environments 1969-72, chmn. Hall of Fame 1976—, parliamentarian nat. conv. Chgo. 1976), Nat. Assn. Secondary Sch. Prins. (chmn. curriculum com. 1970-71), Headmasters Assn., New Eng. Assn. Tchrs. English (life mem., pres. 1962-64, 65-66, chmn. ann. C.S. Thomas award com. 1975—), Mass. Secondary Sch. Prins. Assn. (chmn. curriculum com. 1967-74, mem. exec. bd. 1968-74, diploma standards com. 1973—, Bronze plaque 1974), New Eng. Assn. Schs. and Colls. (mem. exec. bd. 1969-70), Mass. Council Tchrs. English (mem. founding com. 1970—), Friends Jackson Homestead (pres. 1973-75), Newton's Hist. Soc. (life, chmn. 1976—, trustee Trust Fund 1974—), Los Alamos (N.Mex.) Hist. Soc. (life), Greater Boston Guidance Club, Mass. Sch. Counselors Assn., New Eng. Historic and Geneal. Soc., Order Founders and Patriots (life), Plimoth Plantation, Mass. Schoolmasters Club (pres. 1973-74, hon. life), S.A.R. (pres. Minuteman chpt. 1975-77, v.p. Mass. State soc. 1977—), Mass. Soc. Mayflower Desc. (life), Old Plymouth Colony Desc., Huguenot Soc., Flagont Trencher, Desc. Colonial Clergy, Order of Crown of Charlemagne, Piscataqua Pioneers, Sons and Daus. of First Settlers of Newbury, Pilgrim John Howland Soc. (life). Conglist. (chmn. N.H. Bd. Christian Edn. 1974-75, pres., trustee weekday ch. sch. 1975-76). Mason (32 deg.). Clubs: Harvard, Harvard Faculty, Authors, English Lunch (pres. 1975—), Friday Evening (Boston); The Neighbors (Newton). Author: The Family Travel-Camper, 1955; (with E. Gordon and others) Types of Literature: American Literature: English Literature, 1964. Editor: The English Leaflet, 1947-54. Contbr. articles, poems to profl. jours. and periodicals. Home: Penzance Rd Rockport MA 01966

WALES, FLORENCE ALBERTA, ret. librarian, writer; b. Niagara Falls, N.Y.; d. Charles C. and Christeana (Retallack) Wales; M.L.S., Syracuse U., 1954. Dir., Niagara Falls Pub. Library, 1954-73. Bd. dirs. Friends of Library, YWCA; bd. dirs. Porta-Niagara Girls Club, 1955—, treas., 1967—. Mem. Assn. Profl. Women Writers (treas. 1974-76), AAUW, Niagara Falls C. of C., Niagara Falls Hist. Soc., Beta Phi Mu. Presbyterian. Club: Zonta (past sec., dir. Niagara Falls). Home: 711 8th St Niagara Falls NY 14301

WALGREN, DOUG, congressman; b. Rochester, N.Y., Dec. 28, 1940; B.A., Dartmouth Coll., 1963; LL.B., Stanford U., 1966; m. Carmala Vincent. Admitted to Pa. bar, 1967, Calif. bar, 1966; staff atty. Neighborhood Legal Services, 1967-68; individual practice law, 1969-72; corporate counsel Behavioral Research Labs., Inc., Palo Alto, Calif., 1973-75; mem. 95th-96th Congresses from 18th Pa. Dist. Democrat. Office: 117 Cannon House Office Bldg Washington DC 20515

WALK, PAUL KENNETH, psychologist, educator; b. Lehighton, Pa., Nov. 1, 1914; s. Francis E. and Margaret (Hildebrand) W.; A.B., U. Pitts., 1956, M.Ed., 1957, postgrad., 1963; m. Dorothy E. Wistran, Oct. 8, 1949; 1 son, Gerald Kenneth. Social scientist U.S. Bur. Census, Washington, 1940-41, supr. social econ. research, 1941-44; orgn. and bus. developer Easter Coops., Inc., also Council for Coop Devel., N.Y.C., 1945-51; social worker Pressley House, Pitts., 1954-56; clin. and cons. psychologist Gumbert Sch., Pitts., 1958-61; tchr. pub. schs., Montour, 1956-58, psychologist, guidance coordinator Bethel Park, Pa., 1958-67; psychologist N. Allegheny Schs., Pitts., 1967-74; instr. psychology Pa. State U., 1966-71; pvt. practice. Mem. NEA, Pa. Edn. Assn., Community Services of Pa., Am., Pa. psychol. assns., Phi Eta Sigma, Kappa Phi Kappa. Mason (Shriner). Home: 1540 W Ingomar Rd Franklin Park Borough Pittsburgh PA 15237 Died May 1, 1974.

WALKER, BURT, mktg. cons.; b. Bklyn. Mar. 9, 1936; s. Arnold N. and Goldie (Buch) W.; B.E.E., Poly. Inst. Bklyn., 1957, M.S., 1967; postgrad. N. Y. U., 1967-68; m. Mindy M. Kantor, June 13, 1957; children—Scott E., Andrew R. Project engr. research and devel. dept. Western Union Telegraph Co., N.Y.C., 1957-61; project mgr. electro-optical systems Kollsman Instrument Corp., Syosset, N.Y., 1961-67; mgr. new product planning Dynamics Corp. Am., Long Island City, N.Y., 1967-69; founder, corporate dir. Nardcom Corp., Melville, N.Y., 1967-71, dir. mktg., 1969-71; mgr. new bus. devel., maj. shareholder Comtech Labs., Inc., Smithown, N.Y., 1971-75; pres. Walker Telecommunications Corp., Old Bethpage, N.Y., 1975—. Served to 1st lt. C.E., AUS, 1958-59. Mem. IEEE, Air Force Communications and Electronics Assn. (sec. N.Y. chpt. 1968). Patentee in field. Home: 4 Millford Ct Plainview NY 11803 Office: PO Box 70 Old Bethpage NY 11804

WALKER, EUNICE MIRIAM ARNAUD, govt. ofcl., writer; b. Monett, Mo.; d. Emile and Pauline (Barriquand) Arnaud; student S.W. Mo. State U.; B.A., U. Ark.; postgrad. George Washington U., 1956; m. Joseph Edward Walker (div.); children—Diane Walker Smith, Carole Cecile Walker Baker; m. 2d, William Roy Little. Reporter, feature writer The Monett (Mo.) Times, The Kansas City (Mo.) Star; publs. writer Woodrow Wilson Centennial Celebration Commn., Washington, 1957; pub. relations writer Senator Joseph S. Clark, Washington, 1958-59; asst. pub. relations Ho. of Reps. Com. on Sci. and Astronautics, 1959-61; info. specialist ACDA, Washington, 1961-65, policy reports officer, 1965-70; pub. info. officer U.S. Dept. Agr., Washington, 1970—; free lance writer, 1956—. Mem. LWV, Nat. League Am. Penwomen, Nat. Press Club, Nat. Fedn. Press Women, Assn. Agr. Coll. Editors, Nat. Hist. Soc., Am. Hist. Soc., Nat. Archives, Smithsonian Assos., Nat. Women's Polit. Caucus, Nat. Trust Historic Preservation, Huguenot Soc. Club: City Tavern (Washington). Author: Woodrow Wilson, 1958; contbr. articles to various publs. Home: 205 James Thurber Ct Falls Church VA 22046 Office: US Dept Agr South Bldg Washington DC 20250

WALKER, GENE ALDEN (MRS. CLARE J. CRARY), artist; b. New Albany, Ind.; d. Herbert Graham and Clara (Perry) W.; grad. Pratt Inst., 1920; spl. courses NAD, 1940; m. Clare J. Crary, June 30, 1943. One-woman shows: Grand Central Galleries, N.Y.C., 1946; group shows: NAD, Nat. Arts Club, Grand Central Galleries, Allied Artists, Pen and Brush, Am. Water Color Soc., Carnegie Inst., Butler Mus., Phila. Water Color Soc., John Herron Art Inst., Toledo Mus., Speed Mus., Louisville, Wildenstein Galleries; represented in permanent collections: NAD, N.Y.C., Montgomery Mus. Art, Ala., pvt. collections, Bd. dirs. Watson Meml. Home, The Warren Found., No. Allegheny Conservation Assn. Recipient numerous art awards including Maynard prize for portrait NAD, 1943, Cooper prize Nat. Assn. Women Artists, 1943, First prize award John Herron Art Mus., 1950, Portrait prize Nat. Assn. Women Painters, 1946. Mem. Nat. Arts Club, Nat. Assn. Women Artists, Warren Art League, Grand Central Galleries, Allied Artists, Audubon Artists, Pen and Brush. Clubs: Woman's, Warren, Philomel (Warren, Pa.). Illustrator: Western Range Plant, 1939. Home: 508 Liberty St Warren PA 16365

WALKER, JOHN ROBERT, naval officer; b. Fayette, Mo., May 5, 1927; s. Reginald Hampton and Mary Evelyn (Holman) W.; B.S., U.S. Naval Acad., 1949; M.S. in Mgmt., U.S. Naval Postgrad. Sch., 1969; m. Emma Colleen Parker, Oct. 21, 1950; children—John Reginald, Patricia Anne, Mary Kathryn. Commd. ensign U.S. Navy, 1949, advanced through grades to capt., 1969; served on destroyers, minesweepers, atomic submarines, 1949-62; establisher, nuclear power sch., Mare Island, Calif., 1958; various assignments, submarine bldg. and repair, naval shipyards, Portsmouth, N.H., Mare Island, 1962-64, 67-69; repair officer Submarine Tender Proteus, 1964-66; dep. head, engring. dept. Naval Ship Engring. Center, Hyattsville, Md., 1971-74; officer in charge, Carderock site, David Taylor Naval Ship Research and Devel. Center, Bethesda, Md., 1974—. Named Distinguished Alumnus Central Meth. Coll., 1958. Mem. Am. Soc. Naval Engrs., USN Inst., Nat. Eagle Scout Assn. Democrat. Methodist. Home: 14817 Bauer Dr Rockville MD 20853

WALKER, KENNETH FRANCIS, physician, author; b. Croydon, Eng., Feb. 28, 1924; s. Walter Francis and Annie Mabel (Harrison) W.; B.A., U. Toronto, 1946; M.D., Harvard, 1950; came to Can., 1927, naturalized, 1941; m. Susan D. Turner, Feb. 8, 1956; children—Robert, John, Brett, Diana. Intern, Strong Meml. Hosp., U. Rochester, 1950-51, Montreal Gen. Hosp., 1951-52; resident in gynecology Harvard, 1953-56; practice medicine specializing in gynecology, Niagara Falls, Ont., Can., 1956—; cons. in gynecology Niagara Falls Gen. Hosp., Douglas Meml. Hosp., Ft. Erie, Can., Niagara-on-the-Lake Hosp.; dir. Lincoln Trust & Savs. Co., St. Catharines, Ont. Mem. Buffalo Gynecol. Soc., Ont. Med. Assn. Club: Niagara Falls. Author: (under pseudonym W. Gifford-Jones) Hysterectomy, 1961; On Being a Woman, 1971; The Doctor Game, 1975; What Every Woman Should Know About Hysterectomy, 1976; also syndicated column The Doctor Game. Home: 9237 Niagara River Pkwy Rural Route 3 Niagara Falls ON Canada Office: 6150 Valley Way Niagara Falls ON L2E 1Y3 Canada

WALKER, P. DAVID, printing co. exec.; b. N.Y.C., Feb. 3, 1941; s. J. Philip and Edith T. (Cluett) W.; B.A., Parsons Coll., 1963; M.B.A., Harvard, 1971; m. Susan Randall; children—Lisa, Dana, Sally, Hope. Vice-pres. Corporate Aviation, Suffield, Conn., 1963-65; asst. to pres. Beckett Aviation Corp. div. Chesapeake & Ohio R.R., Youngstown, Ohio, 1965-70; pres. Fitzpatrick Printers, Inc., Manchester, N.H., 1970—. Dir. devel. Pine Haven Boys Center, Allenstown, N.H. Served as officer U.S. Army and Res., 1958-65. Mem. Printing Industries Am., Profl. Photographers Am., Am. Helicopter Soc., Automobile Competition Com. U.S., Fedn. Internat. de l'Automobile, Internat. Motor Sports Assn., Nat. Skeet Shooting Assn. (life). Home: Foundry St Amherst NH 03031 Office: 338 Lincoln St Manchester NH 03103

WALKER, PRESTON JASON, clin. psychologist; b. Elkins, W.Va., Apr. 7, 1946; s. Roscoe Preston and Bessie Estella (Hartman) Judy; A.B. (Bd. Govs. scholar), W.Va. State U., Morgantown, 1968, M.A. (NIMH grantee), 1971, Ph.D. in Clin. Psychology, 1975. Cons. psychologist Albert Gallatin Sch. Dist., Fayette County, Pa., 1970-71; staff psychologist Weston (W.Va.) State Hosp., 1973-74; unit chief psychologist Fairfield Hills Hosp., Newtown, Conn., 1974—. Mem. Am. Psychol. Assn., Assn. Advancement of Psychology, Common Cause. Home: Watertown Hall Mile Hill South Rd Apt 218-219 Box W Newtown CT 06470 Office: care Psychological Services Fairfield Hills Hosp Newtown CT 06470

WALKER, ROBERT ARNOLD, pension cons.; b. Springfield, Mass., Oct. 28, 1930; s. Douglass J. and Louise A. (Eginton) W.; B.A., Columbia U., 1952; m. Jean E. Griswold, July 19, 1952; children—Lori Ann, Sandra E., James A. With Mass. Mut. Life Ins. Co., Springfield, 1954-61; v.p., treas. Pension Assos., Inc., Springfield, 1961—. Bd. dirs. Met. Springfield YMCA, 1968—, v.p., 1975—; trustee Old First Ch. (United Ch. Christ), Springfield, 1973—, moderator, 1971-73, sr. deacon, 1969-71; dir. Longmeadow chpt. Am. Field Service, 1977. Served with U.S. Army, 1952-54. Recipient Layman of Yr. award Met. Springfield YMCA, 1974. Mem. Springfield C. of C. (chmn. breakfast com. 1977—), Internat. Found. Employee Benefits, Nat. Assn. Accountants, Am. Soc. Pension Actuaries (asso.). Republican. Congregationalist. Club: Kiwanis (pres.) (Springfield). Home: 98 Coventry Ln Longmeadow MA 01106 Office: 1243 Main St Springfield MA 01103

WALKER, ROBERT HARRIS, educator; b. Cin., Mar. 15, 1924; B.S. Northwestern U., 1945; M.A., Columbia U., 1950; Ph.D., U. Pa., 1955; m. Grace V. Burtt; children—Amy, Rachel, Matthew. Edn. specialist U.S. Mil. Govt., Japan., 1946-47; instr. Carnegie Tech., 1950-51, U. Pa., 1953-54; asst. prof., dir. Am. studies U. Wyo., 1955-59; asso. prof. George Washington U., 1959-63, dir. Am. studies program, 1959-66, 68-70, prof. Am. civilization, 1963—; dir. Edn. and Pub. program Nat. Endowment for Humanities, 1966-68. Served with USNR, 1943-46, 50. Harrison fellow, 1952-53, 54-55; Washington Star research grantee, 1966-67; Fulbright and other specialist grants to Japan, Germany, Sweden, Thailand, Iran and Greece, 1964-75; fellow Woodrow Wilson Internat. Center, 1972-73. Mem. Am. Studies Assn. (nat. pres. 1970-71), Phi Beta Kappa. Club: Cosmos. Author: American Studies in the U.S., 1958; Poet and the Guilded Age, 1963; Life in the Age of Enterprise, 1967; American Studies Abroad, 1975; Reform Spirit in America, 1976; American Studies: Topics and Sources, 1976; editor Am. Quarterly, 1953-54, Am. Studies Internat. (sr.), 1970—; Am. Studies Series for Greenwood Press, 1972—. Home: 3915 Huntington St NW Washington DC 20015 Office: George Washington Univ Washington DC 20052

WALKER, ROBERT SMITH, congressman; b. Bradford, Pa., Dec. 23, 1942; s. Joseph E. and Rachel Viola (Smith) W.; student William and Mary Coll., 1960-61; B.S., Millersville State Coll., 1964; M.A., U. Del., 1968; m. Sue E. Albertson, Apr. 13, 1968. Tchr., Penn Manor High Sch., Lancaster, Pa., 1964-67; legis. asst. to Congressman Edwin D. Eshleman, U.S. Ho. of Reps., Washington, 1967-74, adminstrv. asst., 1974-76; mem. 95th Congress from 16th Dist., Pa.; press room dir. Republican Nat. Conv., 1972; dir. Inaugural Ball, 1973. Pres., trustee Bethany Presbyn. Ch., 1975. Served with Pa. N.G., 1967-73. Recipient Freedom Found. award, 1973; named Outstanding Young Man of Am., 1970. Mem. Internat. Platform Assn., Am. Legion, Lancaster County Hist. Soc. Clubs: Capitol Hill; Old l(ickory Racquet. Author: (with others) Congress-The Pennsylvania Dutch Representatives; co-author: Can You Afford This House. Contbr. articles to nat. mags. Home: 6065 Parkridge Dr East Petersburg PA 17520 Office: US Ho of Reps Washington DC 20515

WALKER, ROBERTA HAM (MRS. DAVID HONORE WALKER), psychologist; b. Sumter, S.C., Aug. 20, 1940; d. John Henry and Eliza (Pringle) Ham; B.A., Hampton Inst., 1962; Ed.M., Temple U., 1978; m. David Honore Walker, Apr. 30, 1966. Speech clinician Easter Seal Soc. Phila., 1962-64, adminstr., 1966-77; speech clinician Magee Meml. Rehab. Center, Phila., 1964-66; pvt. practice speech, Phila., 1965-70; cons. speech Inglis House, Phila., 1967—, Parents Network Delaware Valley, 1970-74. Recipient Legion of Honor award Chapel of Four Chaplins, 1973; Service award Optimist Club, 1972. Certified psychologist, Pa., N.J. Mem. Council for Exceptional Children, Phila. Speech and Hearing Assn. (v.p. 1965-66), Delaware Valley Assn. for Edn. Young Children, Del. Valley Assn. for Children with Learning Disabilities, Walnut Street Theatre Soc., Piaget Soc., Delta Sigma Theta. Home: 141 Woodshade Dr Newark DE 19702

WALKER, SHIRLEY C. (MRS. MELVIN LEE WALKER), educator; b. N.Y.C.; d. Harold Edward and Dagmar (McCabe) Cheatum; B.A. cum laude, Howard U., 1947; M.A. in Guidance and Counseling, Hunter Coll., 1956; M.S. in Edn., advanced certificate in sch. psychology, Bklyn. Coll., 1970; m. Melvin L. Walker, Apr. 4, 1953; 1 dau., Julie Patrice. Mem. staff N.Y.C. Bd. Edn., 1948-71, sch. psychologist Bur. Child Guidance, 1970-71; sch. psychologist intern, ednl. clinic and teaching asst. Bklyn. Coll., 1968-69, sr. counselor HEOP grant, 1969-70; lectr. ednl. psychology York Coll., City U. N.Y., Jamaica, 1972—, also coordinator field experiences and student teaching in elementary sch.; cons., chmn. Protestant Bd. Guardians Remedial Reading Program for Delinquent Youth, 1963-64; participant Piagetian Edn. Inst., Geneva, 1978. Chmn. art exhibit United Negro Relief, 1963; mem. Flatbush Community Council, 1965-66; mem. guild Bklyn. Home Aged Colored People, 1968-69; chmn. art exhibit Willia Hardgrow Mental Health Clinic, 1966, 67, bd. dirs., 1963—; com. mem. Grace Roos Community Music Sch., 1978—. Mem. Nat. Assn. Sch. Psychologists, N.Y. State Psychol. Assn., NAACP, Urban League, Jack and Jill Am., Bklyn. and L.I. Lawyers Wives (pres. 1967-69). Fellow Menninger Found. (charter), Alpha Kappa Alpha; mem. Kappa Delta Pi. Democrat. Author children's stories, hist. scripts, also newspaper articles. Home: 183 Maple St Brooklyn NY 11225 Office: 150-14 Jamaica Ave Jamaica NY 11432

WALKER, VINCENT HENRY, govt. ofcl.; b. Lowell, Mass., Oct. 14, 1915; s. Daniel Henry and Annie Jane (Gookin) W.; J.D., Boston Coll. Law, 1939; B.C.S., Benjamin Franklin U., 1951; m. Irene Iris Johnson, Nov. 16, 1946; children—Patricia Anne (Mrs. John Armstrong III), J. Melinda (Mrs. Gaetano Monterosso). Admitted to Mass. bar, 1940, Fed. Tax Ct. bar, 1952, U.S. Supreme Ct. bar, 1965, D.C. bar, 1979; partner firm, 1940-42; gen. mgr., counsel, joint venture land and subdiv. devels. and sales, South and Southwestern U.S., 1946-60; FHA regional atty., Southeastern U.S. and Virgin Islands, later FHA Washington Hdqrs. and Mid Atlantic region, 1960, zone ops. exec. asst., Southwestern U.S., 1960-61; AID State Dept. contract specialist, chief comml. contracts br., adviser to Govt. of Sudan for contract negotiations, developed conversion of AID contracts to Automatic Data Processing System in Vietnam, AID Office of Contract Services, Washington, 1961-69; internat. trade policy specialist, chief trade policy br., acting dir. indsl. resources div., AID Office of Procurement, 1969-72; internat. trade specialist, agrl. commodities mgr., procurement support div., AID Office of Commodity Mgmt., 1972-75; contracts specialist, policy, AID Office Contracts Mgmt., 1975—. Hon. mem. bd. dirs. Am. Opera Scholarship Soc.; contbr. incorporating atty. Lowell Light Opera Guild, 1942. Served to lt. comdr. USNR, 1942-46. Named hon. citizen City of Lexington (Ky.), 1970. Mem. Lowell, Middlesex County, Mass. bar. assns., Nat. Trust for Historic Preservation, Smithsonian Assos., Wolf Trap Assos., D.A.V. Author and interagy. collaborator AID govt. and world-wide legal and regulatory publs., export program directives, notices to U.S. industry, internat. posts and orgns., 1970—. Author, pub. weekly Agrl. Commodity Supply, Price, Trends, Report, 1972-75. Founding editor Keith Acad. Alumni mag., 1940-42. Photog. works published various media in U.S. and fgn. countries, 1970—. Home: 9908 Julliard Dr Bethesda MD 20034 Office: AID State Dept SER/CM Washington DC 20523

WALKER, WENDELL KIRSHMAN, librarian; b. Battle Creek, Mich., Jan. 9, 1908; s. John Franklin and Clara (Kirshman) W.; B.A. Western Mich. U., 1930; certificate U. Exeter, Eng., 1931; B.S. in L.S., Columbia, 1947; m. Marjorie Knapp Balch, June 27, 1953. Library asst. Grand Lodge, Mason, N.Y., 1932-34, librarian, 1934-42, dir. library and mus., 1946—, grand sec., 1963—. Served to capt. AUS, 1942-45, maj., 1951-53; lt. col. Res. Mem. Spl. Libraries Assn. (past chpt. pres.), ALA, Am. Geog. Soc., Assn. of U.S. Army, Res. Officers Assn. Mason (33 deg., Shriner, K.T.). Home: 101 W 12th St New York City NY 10011 Office: 71 W 23d St New York City NY 10010

WALKER, WILLIAM JEFFERSON, JR., physicist, mil. officer; b. Norfolk, Va., Dec. 13, 1936; s. William Jefferson and Frances Juanita (Nummy) W.; B.S., Va. Mil. Inst., 1958; M.S., U. Kans., 1964; Ph.D., U. Fla., 1971; m. Anne Thomas Fyfe, Dec. 26, 1957; children—Donna Lee, Catherine Anne, William Jefferson III. Commd. 2d lt. USAF, 1958, advanced through grades to lt. col., 1976; ret., 1978; base bioenviron. engr. Castle AFB, Calif., 1958-60; staff bioenvironmental engr. Air Force 7th Air Div., High Wycombe, Bucks, U.K., 1960-62; research health physicist Air Force Weapons Lab., Kirtland AFB, N.M., 1964-68; chief med. physics Malcolm Grow USAF Med. Center, Andrews AFB, Washington, 1971-78; health physicist div. fuel cycle and material safety U.S. Nuclear Regulatory Commn., Washington, 1978—; cons., owner Med. Physics Services, 1972-78; pres. Physics Control, Inc., 1975-78; mem. cons. staff Clinton (Md.) Community Hosp., 1973-77; chmn. adv. com. radiol. tech. program Prince George's Community Coll., Md., 1972—; cons. in med. physics Children's Hosp. Nat. Med. Center, 1975-78. Registered profl. engr., Vt. Diplomate Am. Bd. Health Physics. Mem. Am. Assn. Physicists in Medicine (sec.-treas. Mid-Atlantic chpt. 1973-76, pres.-elect 1976), Health Physics Soc., Nuclear Medicine, Mensa, Sigma Xi. Baptist. Home: 4501 Herend Pl Fairfax VA 22032 Office: US Nuclear Regulatory Commn Washington DC 20555

WALKUP, HARRY ERNST, physician, ret. govt. ofcl.; b. Mount Hope, W.Va., Feb. 15, 1919; s. Homer Allen and Lillie Belle (Harris) W.; A.B., W.Va. U., 1940; M.D., U. Md., 1943; postgrad. U. Pa. Sch. Surgery, 1948-49; m. Mary Roe Groves, Mar. 13, 1945; children—Mary, Harry, Margaret, Robert. Intern, St. Joseph's Hosp., Balt., 1944, resident, 1944-46; resident VA Hosp., Oteen, N.C., 1946-48, chief surg. services, 1955-61; practice medicine specializing in gen. and thoracic surgery, Asheville, N.C., 1949-50; dep. dir. surg. services VA Central Office, Washington, 1961-62; dir. research and statistics Nat. Tb Assn., N.Y.C., 1962-65; dir. VA Center, Wilmington, Del., 1965-76, ret., 1976. Cons. program on mgmt. and orgn. sci. Cornell U., Ithaca, N.Y., 1966-70; chmn. Gov.'s ad hoc com. to develop Del.'s Health Care Delivery and Use Program, 1969-72. Bd. dirs. mycology program U. Ky., Lexington, Del. Tb, and Health Assn., Del. Heart Assn. Mem. Assn. Del. Hosps. (pres. 1972), Am. Assn. for Thoracic Surgery (sr.), So. Thoracic Surg. Assn. (founders group). Home: RFD 1 Worton MD 21678

WALL, ALBERT, editor; b. Birmingham, Ala., Apr. 23, 1919; s. Louis and Frances (Morse) W.; B.A., Vanderbilt U., 1940; m. Mary Sprague, Feb. 16, 1947; children—Katharine, Anthony. Asst. editor Newsweek Mag., N.Y.C., 1947-62, asso. editor, 1962-64; sr. editor Roche Med. Image, N.Y.C., 1966-69, asst. mng. editor, 1969-71; asst. mng. editor Med. Tribune, N.Y.C., 1971, mng. editor, 1972; editorial coordinator Med. World News, N.Y.C., 1972-74; editor-in-chief McGraw Hill World News, N.Y.C., 1974-76, World Environment Report, N.Y.C., 1976—. Chmn. Dobbs Ferry (N.Y.) Democratic Com., 1952-60. Served with inf. AUS, 1941-45. Decorated Combat Infantryman's badge. Mem. Am. Med. Writers Assn. (pres. N.Y. Met. chpt. 1973-74), Nat. Assn. Sci. Writers, Overseas Press Club (gov.), Am. Soc. Mag. Editors, Phi Beta Kappa, Sigma Delta Chi. Clubs: Tarrytown Yacht, Overseas Yacht. Editor: First Lady of the Lighthouse (Winifred Holt Mather), 1952. Home: 133 Bellair Dr Dobbs Ferry NY 10522 Office: 345 E 46th St New York City NY 10017

WALL, IRVING M., lawyer; b. Montreal, Can., May 13, 1924; s. Abraham Max and Eva Pearl (Gorfein) W.; came to U.S., 1940, naturalized, 1941; A.B., N.Y. U., 1947, LL.B., 1950; m. Marcia Maier, Dec. 14, 1947; children—Allison Heidi, Donald Roger, Barbara Harris, Beth Russell. Admitted to N.Y. bar, 1951, since practiced in N.Y.C.; co-producer TV interview show The Hot Seat, 1947-49; sch. dist. atty. Freeport (N.Y.) Pub. Schs., 1965—; officer, dir. Select Theatres, Inc., Shubert Orgn., Inc., Shubert Found. Campaign cons., mgr. Rudolf Halley, pres. N.Y.C. Council, 1950. Served with AUS, 1941-44; ETO. Decorated Purple Heart. Mem. N.Y. State Bar Assn., Bar Assn. City N.Y., N.Y. State Assn. Sch. Bd. Attys. Jewish. Clubs: Harbor Point Racquet and Yacht; Rockville Racquet; Lambs (past dir., chmn. house com.) (N.Y.). Home: 174 N Brookside Ave Freeport NY 11520 Office: 415 Madison Ave New York City NY 11017

WALL, SHANNON JEROME, union ofcl.; b. Portland, Oreg., Mar. 4, 1919; s. Edward C. and Hope C. (Scartum) W.; student U. Wash., 1939-41; m. Lucy Mildred Davis, May 10, 1952; children—Sean Michael, Maureen Hope, Kevin Edward. Bus. agt. Nat. Maritime Union, N.Y.C., 1951-58, v.p., 1958-69, sec.-treas., 1969-73, pres., 1973—. Vice pres. indsl. union dept. AFL-CIO; mem. exec. bd. AFL-CIO, co-chmn. labor/mgmt. com., Washington; vice chmn. Seafarers sect. Internat. Transport Workers Fedn., London, Eng. Bd. dirs. City Center of Music and Drama, Inc. Served with U.S. Mcht. Marines, 1942—. Office: 346 W 17th St New York City NY 10011

WALLACE, ARNOLD DELANEY, SR., broadcasting exec.; b. Salisbury, Md., Feb. 1, 1932; s. George Linwood and Margaret Elizabeth (Townsend) W.; B.A., Howard U., 1952; B.S. magna cum laude, Rutgers U., 1977, postgrad., 1977—; m. Theresa Fredericks Brooks, Sept. 27, 1950; children—Deborah, Terry, Arnold, Michael, Stephen, Stephanie. Communications engr. WCAU-TV, Phila., 1963-72, dir. community affairs, 1972—. Mem. Pennsauken (N.J.) Bd. Edn., 1971—, v.p., 1973-75, pres., 1975-77. Bd. dirs. Juvenile Diabetes Found. N.J. Urban League, Phila.; mem. nat. adv. com. Merabash Mus. Black History, New Egypt, N.J.; bd. dirs. Phila. Mayor's Commn. Drug and Alcohol Abuse, Phila., Urban League, Phila., N.J. Commn. for Humanities mem. media com. Crippled Childrens Soc. Pa. Recipient awards Phila. Commn. Human Rights, Assn. Study Afro-Am. Life and History, Council Spanish Speaking Orgns. Mem. N.J. Sch. Bds. Assn. (ednl. finance com.), Negro Airmen Internat. (internat. publicity chmn. 1969—), Aircraft Owners and Pilots Assn., Corp. Social Responsibility Assn., World Affairs Council, Alpha Sigma Lambda. Omega Psi Phi. Mem. A.M.E. Ch. (vice chmn. bd. trustees). Mason, (Shriner), Kiwanian. Clubs: TV and Radio Advt., Willingboro Country. Producer, dir. documentary film Journey to Paradise-Barbados; exec. producer film 2000 and Beyond. Home: 3405 Gladwyn Ave Pennsauken NJ 08109 Office: CBS-TV City Line Ave and Monument Rd Philadelphia PA 19131

WALLACE, DONALD FOOTE, dentist, state ofcl.; b. Port Henry, N.Y., Sept. 7, 1910; s. Rollin Lee and Annie Laura (Murdock) W.; student Union Coll., 1928-31; D.D.S., U. Buffalo, 1934; m. Jane Elizabeth Powell, Apr. 14, 1936; children—James Donald, Richard Powell. Practice dentistry, Troy, N.Y., 1935-42, 46-60; sec. N.Y. State Bd. Dental Examiners, Albany, 1960-71; exec. sec. N.Y. State Bd. for Dentistry, 1971—; hon. mem. med.-dental staff Samaritan Hosp., Troy, 1960—. Cons. USPHS, 1965-69, council on dental edn. Am. Dental Assn., 1965—; chmn. N.E. Regional Bd. Dental Examiners, 1967—. Exec. bd. Uncle Sam council Boy Scouts Am., 1951-64, pres., 1957-58, mem. adv. council to exec. bd., 1964—, recipient Silver Beaver, 1964. Served to maj. Dental Corps, AUS, 1942-46. Fellow Am. Coll. Dentists; mem. Am. Assn. Dental Examiners (pres. 1971-72), Am. Dental Assn., Dental Soc. State N.Y. (Jarvie Burkhart award 1969, bd. govs. 1955-58), 3d Dist. Dental Soc. N.Y. (pres. 1954), Troy Dental Study Club (pres. 1947), Omicron Kappa Upsilon (hon.), Phi Delta Theta. Home: 36 Belle Ave Troy NY 12180 Office: 99 Washington Ave Albany NY 12230

WALLACE, GEORGE WILSON, pub. co. exec.; b. Springville, N.Y., Dec. 23, 1914; s. George Francis and Estelle Rea (Wilson) W.; B.S., U. Pa., 1939; m. Mary Jane Stokes, May 2, 1942; 1 dau., Susan Wallace. Accountant, Niagara Hudson Power Co., Buffalo, 1932-37; asst. promotion dir. spot sales NBC, N.Y.C., 1940-42, copywriter, 1945-46, promotion dir. owned and operated stas., 1946-47, promotion mgr. radio network, 1947-48, TV network, 1948-49, mgr. sales planning and research, 1949-50, dir. advt. and promotion, 1950-51; promotion dir. internat. editions Reader's Digest, N.Y.C., 1951-56, dir. merchandising, 1956-62, dir. trade relations, 1962-75, dir. trade relations and merchandising, 1975—. Bd. dirs. USO Greater N.Y., 1970—, United Way Mamaroneck, 1971-72, ARC Mamaroneck, 1962-72. Served with inf. U.S. Army, 1942-45. Decorated Silver Star, Bronze Star, Purple Heart with cluster. Mem. Am. Mktg. Assn., Am. Soc. Travel Agts., Wharton Sch. Alumni Soc. Republican. Episcopalian. Clubs: Union League N.Y.; Larchmont Yacht, University (Larchmont); Palm Bay Jockey; Racquet (Miami, Fla.). Home: 711 Forest St Mamaroneck NY 10543 Office: Reader's Digest 200 Park Ave New York City NY 10017

WALLACE, JAMES PETER, advt. agy. exec.; b. Montreal, Que., Can., Apr. 21, 1946; s. Joseph J. and Lillian Emma (Adams) W.; ed. McGill U., Can., 1964-67; m. Sandra MacDonald, Apr. 2, 1971; children—Derek, Amy. Exec. v.p. Nat. Standard Photoengraving Inc., Montreal, 1971-72; exec. v.p. Wallace, Moore & Co. Ltd. Montreal, 1972-73, chmn. bd., pres., 1973—; pres., chmn. bd. Wednesday Communications Ltd., Comvestor Ltd.; chmn. bd. Agence de Publicité Contact Inc.; pres., chmn. bd. Wallace, Moore & Co. Ltd.; dir. WalBros. Investments Ltd., Naples, Fla. Mem. Montreal Bd. Trade, Bus. and Prof. Advt. Assn. (pres.). Club: Montreal Press. Home: 5999 Monkland Ave Montreal PQ Canada Office: Place Bonaventure Montreal PQ Canada

WALLACE, JANE HOUSE, geologist; b. Ft. Worth, Aug. 12, 1926; d. Fred Leroy and Helen Gould (Kixmiller) W.; A.B., Smith Coll., 1947, M.A., 1949; postgrad. Bryn Mawr Coll., 1949-52. Geologist, U.S. Geol. Survey, 1952—, chief Pub. Inquiries Offices, Washington, 1964-72, spl. asst. to dir., 1974—. Recipient Meritorious Service award Dept. Interior, 1971, Distinguished Service award, 1976. Mem. geol. socs. Am., Washington (treas. 1963-67), Sigma Xi (asso.). Home: 2450 Huidekoper Pl NW Washington DC 20007 Office: US Geol Survey 110 Nat Center Reston VA 22092

WALLACE, RAYMOND P(AUL), patent agt., cons.; b. Dunn, Wash.; s. John L. and Olive E. M. (Lindley) W.; A.B., U. Calif., 1941, M.A., 1947; D.Litt., Western U., 1950. Teaching asst. U. Calif., 1942, nuclear engr. Radiation Lab., 1942-50, chief patent engr., 1950-53; chief patent engr., head patent dept. Mycalex Corp. Am., 1953-55; head patent dept., research div. Curtiss-Wright Corp., 1957-61, patent dept., 1961-75; cons., 1975—. Registered profl. engr., Calif. Recipient Atomic Energy Citation from War Dept., 1945. Fellow Inst. Am. Genealogy, Am. Heraldic Soc.; mem. Heraldry Soc. Eng. (life), IEEE (sr.), Am. Soc. Metals, Am. Soc. Bookplate Collectors and Designers, N.J. Patent Law Assn., Sigma Xi, Phi Sigma, Psi Chi. Author: The Three Small Republics, 1947; The Chiefs of Wallace, 1947; Contribution to the History of Neutral Moresnet, 1948; The Royal House of Liechtenstein, 1951; Ethnogeny of Easter Island and Its Kings, 1951. Contbr. articles to profl. publs. Responsible for inventions in atomic energy devel. Home: 77 Orange Rd Montclair NJ 07042

WALLACE, RICHARD POWELL, lawyer; b. Troy, N.Y., Apr. 28, 1941; s. Donald Foote and Jane Elizabeth (Powell) W.; A.B., Brown U., 1963; LL.B., Union U., 1967, J.D. cum laude, 1967; m. Elizabeth Lee Allen, June 20, 1964; children—Stephen Allen, Lee Elizabeth, Scott Powell. Investment analyst R.I. Hosp. Trust Co., Providence, 1964-65; confidential law asst. appellate div. N.Y. Supreme Ct., 3d dept., Albany, N.Y., 1967-68; admitted to N.Y. State bar, 1967; asst. dist. atty. Rensselaer County, N.Y., 1970-71; partner, firm Martin, Noonan, Hislop, Troue & Shudt, Troy, Albany, N.Y., 1968—; dir., sec. Blanchard Indsl. Supplies, Inc.; dir. Marine Midland Bank-Capital Region Bd.; trustee Herold Charitable Trust; faculty mem. Emma Willard Sch. Mem. exec. bd., sec., gen. com. Gov. Clinton council Boy Scouts Am., 1974—; trustee, sec. Troy Cemetery Assn., 1974—; mem. exec. com., sec. Vis. Nurse Assn. Troy, Inc., 1975—; mem. allocations div. United Way Mohawk-Hudson Area, Inc., 1976, bd. dirs., 1974—; trustee Troy Pub. Library, 1974—, sec., 1977; trustee Albany Acad., 1977—. Recipient Silver Beaver award Boy Scouts Am., 1973, Cardozo Prize, Albany Law Review, 1967. Mem. Justinian Soc., Commercial Law League Am., Am., N.Y. State (mem. standing com. on estate planning), Rensselaer County, Albany County bar assns., N.Y. State Trial Lawyers Assn., Estate Planning Council Northeastern N.Y., Greater Troy C. of C., Albany Acad. Alumni Assn. (mem. bd. 1972—, 1st v.p. 1976, pres. 1977—), Sigma Chi. Clubs: Brown (treas. 1975—); Rotary (pres. 1974-75), Country (Troy, N.Y.). Office: 21 2d St Troy NY 12180 also 99 Washington Albany NY 12210

WALLACE, THOMAS FRANCIS, jewelry mfg. co. exec.; b. Boston, Nov. 23, 1943; s. Thomas Edward and Pauline Louise (Ross) W.; B.S. in Bus. Adminstrn., Bryant Coll., 1964; postgrad Boston Coll., 1964-65; m. Kathleen Veronica Gonet, May 28, 1966; children—Denise Veronica, Thomas Gregory. Mfrs. rep. Wallace Assos., Boston, 1964-75; sales rep. O.C. Tanner Co., Salt Lake City, 1975—. Named Jaycee of the Year, 1970. Mem. U.S. Jaycees (nat. v.p. 1974-75), Mass. Jaycees (pres. 1973-74). Republican. Roman Catholic. Club: Elks. Office: PO Box 1228 Plymouth MA 02360

WALLACE, WILLIAM KEITH, beverage exec.; b. Montreal, Que., Can., Feb. 11, 1932; s. W.H. and Elcy (Harrison) W.; B.A., St. Lawrence U., Canton, N.Y., 1955; advanced mgt. course Exec. Devel. Inst., Montreal; 1959; m. Marjorie Conkling, Apr. 7, 1956; children—William, Kimberly, Kathleen. Vending machine salesman Seven-Up Montreal Ltd., 1955-59, mgr. vendor dept., 1959-61, asst. gen. mgr., 1961-64, pres., 1964—. Mem. Montreal Bd. Trade; dir. Conv. and Visitors Bur. Greater Montreal; bd. dirs. Zeller Osteo. Clinic. Mem. Canadian C. of C., Advt. and Sales Execs. Club Montreal, Can. Automatic Merchandising Assn., Young Pres.'s Orgn., Montreal Execs. Assn. Mem. United Church Can. (past pres. men's club, bd. mem. Mount Royal United Ch.). Kiwanian (pres. Montreal 1973-74). Clubs: Mount Royal Curling, Royal Montreal Golf, Mt. Stephen. Home: 2125 Sunset Rd Mount Royal PQ H3R 2Y5 Canada Office: Seven-Up Montreal Ltee 3700 Thimens Blvd St Laurent PQ H4R 1T8 Canada

WALLACE, WILLIAM RAY, architect; b. Calvin, Okla., June 6, 1927; s. Raymond Fern and Flossie Myrtle (Milner) W.; B.S., U. Okla., 1953; m. Charlene Mae Joyner, June 4, 1950; children—David Allen, Nancy Carol, Thomas Ray (dec.). Apprentice architect, structural engr. Coston-Frankfurt-Short, Architects, Engrs., Oklahoma City, 1952-55; chief structural engr., asso., 1956-60, v.p., mgr. br. office, Bethlehem, Pa., 1960-64, partner, 1964-67; partner Coston-Wallace, Architects, Engrs., Planners (now called Wallace & Watson), 1967—; adj. prof. civil engring. Lehigh U., 1968-69; dir. Pocono Recreation, Inc., Bethlehem Risk; partner Bethlehem Plaza Mall; dir. Lehigh Valley Indsl. Park. Mem. exec. com. Com. Greater Bethlehem; bd. dirs., mem. exec. com. Bethlehem chpt ARC, dir. South side Non-Profit Housing Corp.; mem. exec. com. Minsi Trails council Boy Scouts Am. Mem. AIA, Nat. Soc. Profl. Engrs., Soc. Coll. and Univ. Planners, Hist. Bethlehem (dir.), Nat. Fire Protection Assn., Nat. Trust Hist. Preservation, Bethlehem Area C. of C. (past pres.), Pa. Soc. Architects (dir.). Republican. Baptist. Clubs: Saucon Valley Country, Rotary, Bethlehem. Home: 527 Pine Top Trail Bethlehem PA 18017 Office: Suite 900 1 Bethlehem Plaza Bethlehem PA 18018

WALLACH, AMEI MARIONE, journalist; b. N.Y.C., Sept. 21, 1941; d. Gert M.K. and Gerda (Lewenz) W.; student U. Chgo., 1959-61; B.S. in Comparative Lit., Columbia U., 1965; m. Charles Tebo, June 17, 1972. Editorial trainee McGraw Hill, Inc., N.Y.C., 1965, asso. editor cover stories and features Merchandising Week, 1966-68; reporter, reviewer UPI, 1968-69; editor Modern Living sect. Newsday, Garden City, N.Y., 1969-72, cultural affairs writer, columnist, 1972—; lectr., seminar leader in field. Recipient Front Page award in columnist category Newswomen's Club of N.Y., 1970, Clarion award for article Andrew Wyeth, a Painter's World, Am. Women in Communication, 1977. Among initiators Newsday Part II, expanded modern living sect.; contbr. to Art News, Antiques World, Horizon, Conn. mag. Home: 210 E 68th St New York NY 10021 Office: Newsday 1500 Broadway New York NY 10036*

WALLACH, ESTELLE, mag. publishing exec.; b. Bklyn., Oct. 1, 1938; d. Isidore and Ida (Schecht) W.; student N.Y. U., 1957-58. Account exec. McFadden, Strauss & Irwin (now ICPR), N.Y.C., 1969-73; dir. pub. relations Essence mag., N.Y.C., 1975—. Mem. Mag. Pubs. Assn. (pub. relations com.), Pub. Relations Soc. Am., Women in Communications, Nat. Acad. TV Arts and Scis., Actors Equity, Publicity Club N.Y. Home: 150 E 18th St New York City NY 10003 Office: Essence 1500 Broadway New York City NY 10036

WALLACH, FRANCES, recreation co. exec.; b. N.Y.C.; d. Adolf and Adele (Wind) Gross; M.A., Columbia U., 1972, postgrad., 1972—; m. Gilbert Wallach, June 5, 1949; children—Mark Foster, Merryl Eve, Jonathan Floyd. Supt. recreation program devel. Nassau County (N.Y.) Dept. Recreation and Parks, 1965-72; cons. Game Time Inc., Litchfield, Mich., 1972—; instr. leisure edn. Columbia U., N.Y.C., 1972—; pres. Total Recreation Mgmt. Services Inc., N.Y.C., 1972—. Mem. Nat., N.Y. recreation and parks assns., AAHPER. Office: 239 Central Park W New York NY 10024

WALLACH, FREDERICK, lawyer; b. Duisburg, Germany, Dec. 21, 1907; s. Herrmann and Elsie (Weil) W.; student U. Heidelberg, 1926, U. Munich, 1927; LL.B., 1929, J.D., U. Bonn, 1935; J.D., Columbia, 1949; M.B.A., N.Y.U., 1952; grad. Command and Gen. Staff Coll., Ft. Leavenworth, Kan., 1962; m. Elizabeth Hoelzl nee Dannheiser, June 3, 1940 (dec. July 1976); 1 son, Donald F. Asst. judge Duisburg, Germany, 1934 (dismissed by Hitler); lawyer, corp. counsel, Stuttgart, 1934-38; interned Dachau, 1938, exiled, 1939; came to U.S., 1940, naturalized, 1942; asso. Omgus Pub. Safety Br., 1946-47; admitted to N.Y. bar, 1950, since practiced in N.Y.C. Mem. Center for Study Democratic Instns. Served from pvt. to 1st lt., AUS, 1941-45; maj. Res. Mem. Wisdom Hall of Fame, Am. Bar Assn., Am. Judicature Soc., Am. Security Council, World Peace Through Law, Ret. Officers Assn., Epigraphic Soc. Club: Village Bath (Manhasset, N.Y.). Author: The Post-War Western German Banking System, 1952; Introduction to European Commercial Law, 1953. Contbr. articles newspapers, mags. Address: 64-48 Bell Blvd Bayside NY 11364

WALLACH, ROBERT CHARLES, physician; b. Bklyn., Jan. 2, 1935; s. Irving T. and Saralta W.; B.A. with honors (N.Y. State Regents scholar), Swarthmore Coll., 1956; M.D., Yale U., 1960; m. Judith Leffert, Apr. 1, 1968. Intern, Beth Israel Hosp., N.Y.C., 1960-61, resident in obstetrics and gynecology, 1961-65; fellow in gynecol. oncology State U. N.Y., Bklyn., 1965-66; practice medicine specializing in obstetrics and gynecology, N.Y.C., 1966—; chief obstetrics and gynecology Gouverneur Hosp., N.Y.C., 1966-76; dir. obstetrics and gynecology Beth Israel Med. Center, N.Y.C., 1977—; prof. clin. obstetrics and gynecology Mt. Sinai Sch. Medicine, N.Y.C., 1977—; lectr. State U. N.Y., Bklyn. Fellow Am. Coll. Obstetricians and Gynecologists; mem. A.C.S., Soc. Gynecol. Oncologists, Am. Fertility Soc., N.Y. Acad. Medicine, N.Y. Acad. Sci., N.Y. Cancer Soc., Am. Pub. Health Assn., N.Y. Obstetrical Soc., Internat. Soc. for Study Vulvar Disease. Office: 10 Perlman Pl New York City NY 10003

WALLENDER, HARVEY W., assn. exec.; b. Port Arthur, Tex., Jan. 7, 1943; s. Harvey W. and Annie Laurie (Kirkpatrick) W.; B.A., U. Tex., 1965; M.B.A., Columbia, 1969, postgrad., 1974-76; m. Irene Z.

St. John, June 21, 1972; children—Lauren Marie, Austin Kirkpatrick. Financial officer Internat. Basic Economy Corp., N.Y.C., 1969-72; pres. TransOceanic Fishing Corp., N.Y.C., 1972—; v.p. Council of Americas, exec. v.p., dir. Fund Multinat. Mgmt. Edn., N.Y.C., 1972—; cons. Sears, Roebuck & Co., Charter Med. Corp., Kuhn, Loeb & Co.; mem. U.S. del. to InterAm. Working Group Fgn. Ministers Brasilia, Caracas, 1973, to sci. and tech. group UNCTAD, Geneva, 1975; mem. adv. com. on transnat. enterprises Dept. State, 1977-78. Served to 1st lt. Spl. Forces, Airborne, U.S. Army, 1966-68. Recipient Diploma of Honor, Bolivian Govt., 1968; Bronfman scholar Columbia, 1974. Mem. Phi Delta Theta. Presbyterian. Author: (with Jack Behrman) Technology Transfer within Wholly Owned Subsidiaries, 1976; editor: Technology Transfer and Development: An Historical and Geographic Perspective, 1974; contbr. monographs and articles in field. Home: 1148 Fifth Ave New York City NY 10028 Office: 684 Park Ave New York City NY 10021

WALLER, WILLIAM EDWARD, bio-electronics engr.; b. Hartford, Conn., Feb. 5, 1947; s. John and Lucille W.; B.S., N.Y. Inst. Tech.; m. Carol Ann Bateman, Oct. 28, 1967; children—William C., Scott E. Test equipment and product devel. engr. Lambda Electronics Co., Melville, N.Y., 1968-69, design engr., 1969-70; chief test equipment engr. Fairchild Camera and Instruments Co., Copaigue, N.Y., 1970-71; chief engr. Waller Cons. Co., Cooperstown, N.Y., 1971-72; electronics engr. Mary Imogene Bassett Hosp., Cooperstown, N.Y., 1972—; cons. in design, devel. pub. service radio; chmn. Cable TV Advisory Com. Chmn. Cooperstown Winter Carnival, 1973-74; marshall Cooperstown Parade, 1974-75; mem. Cooperstown Fire Dept. Mem. Assn. Advancement Med. Electronics, N.Y.-Pa. Med. Instrumentation Assn., Central N.Y. Soc. Hosp. Engrs., Clubs: Lions (Cooperstown); Otsego County (N.Y.) Radio (pres.). Home: 77 Beaver St Cooperstown NY 13326 Office: Mary Imogene Bassett Hosp Atwell Rd Cooperstown NY 13326

WALLERSTEIN, LEIBERT BENET, economist; b. Bklyn., July 5, 1922; s. William Mark and Rachel Leah (Goldberg) W.; B.A., U.Mex., 1950; M.A., U. Minn., 1953; m. Alice Stehle, Mar. 26, 1968. Research asst. U. N.Mex., 1951; research asst., research fellow U. Minn., 1952-53; asst. employee relations U.S. Dept. Navy, Washington, 1954-55; economist, manpower specialist, editor U.S. Dept. Labor, Washington, 1955-67; economist U.S. HUD, Washington, 1967-69, U.S. Dept. Transp., Washington, 1969—; mem. faculty U. Md., 1966-67, Georgetown U., 1967-69; cons. Comm. on Correctional Manpower, 1967, System Devel. Corp., 1966. Served with U.S. Army, 1946-47. Mem. Am. Econ. Assn., Am. Soc. Govt. Economists, Nat. Economists Club. Home: 3505 Thornapple St Chevy Chase MD 20015 Office: care Dept Transp 400 7th St SW Washington DC 20590

WALLES, PETER PAUL, ophthalmologist; b. Bklyn., Sept. 26, 1942; s. Peter John and Tillie W.; B.S., St. Johns U., 1964; M.D., N.J. Coll. Medicine, 1969; m. Carolyn Louise Booth, June 14, 1969; 1 son, Jeffrey Pierce. Intern, Meadowbrook Hosp., East Meadow, N.Y., 1969-70; resident in ophthalmology Nassau County Med. Center, East Meadow, 1970-73; retinal fellow, med. and surg. diseases of retina U. Mich., Ann Arbor, 1973-74; practice medicine specializing in ophthalmology, Cherry Hill, N.J., 1974—; chief sect. retinal disease Cooper Med. Center, Camden, N.J., 1976—; chief vitreo retinal service West Jersey hosps., Camden, Voorhees, Berlin, N.J., 1976—; asso. in opthalmology U. Pa. Med. Sch. Scheie Eye Inst., 1974—. Bd. dirs. N.J. chpt., Am. Diabetic Assn., 1976. Served to maj. USAR. Diplomate Am. Bd. Opthalmology. Fellow A.C.S.; mem. Am. Acad. Ophthalmology, Am. Assn. Ophthalmology, Research to Prevent Blindness. Home: 8 Winter Pl Cherry Hill NJ 08003 Office: The Lynlee Bldg 69 Haddonfield Berlin Rd Cherry Hill NJ 08034

WALLIN, GARY PHILLIP, communications equipment co. exec.; b. Newark, Nov. 8, 1940; s. Irving and Rose (Greenberg) W.; B.S., Upsala Coll., 1958-62; m. Diana Nushie Pavlak, Nov. 21, 1965; children—Ian Robert, Amy Gwen, Michael Adam. Engr., Welch Communications Corp., Dover, N.J., 1962-64; asst. to v.p. Edison Electronics, Boonton, N.J., 1965; service mgr. Motorola, Inc., Franklin Park, Ill., 1965-69; owner, pres. Comex Systems, Inc., Comex, Inc., Manchester, N.H., 1969—; dir. Exec. Exchange, Inc., Communications Engrs. Co., Inc.; cons. in field. Justice of the peace, Manchester, 1971—; bd. dirs. Jewish Community Center; asso. chmn. nat. Young leadership cabinet United Jewish Appeal; dir. local temple; bd. dirs., treas. Federated Arts of Manchester, Jewish Community Council. Mem. IEEE, Radio Club Am., Electronic Industries Assn., AAAS, Soc. Am. Magicians, Internat. Brotherhood Magicians (sec. 1964), Hundred Club N.H. Club: Manchester Country. Patentee in field. Home: 1092 Union St Manchester NH 03104 Office: Comex Inc 720 Union St Manchester NH 03104

WALLIN, JUDITH KERSTIN, physician; b. Paris, Apr. 23, 1938 (parents Am. citizens); d. Theodore Bror and Ella Charlotte (Butler) W.; B.S., Elizabeth Coll., Elizabethtown, Pa., 1960; M.D., Temple U., 1964. Intern in pediatrics Bellevue Hosp., N.Y.C., 1964-65, resident, 1965-67, attending pediatrician, 1967—; instr. pediatrics N.Y. U. Sch. Medicine, N.Y.C., 1967-71, asst. prof. clin. pediatrics, 1971-74, asst. prof., 1974—. Diplomate Am. Bd. Pediatrics, Nat. Bd. Med. Examiners. Recipient Educate for Service through Profl. Achievement award and O. F. Stambaugh Chemistry Alumni award Elizabethtown Coll., 1978. Home: 300 E 33d St New York City NY 10016 Office: Dept Pediatrics Bellevue Hosp 27th St and 1st Ave New York City NY 10016

WALLING, W(ILBER) DONALD, educator; b. Hudson Falls, N.Y., Sept. 14, 1915; s. William D. and Julia (Griffin) W.; A.B., Union U., 1937; M.A., Columbia, 1940, Ed.D., 1951; m. Jean Marion Sears, Dec. 30, 1950; children—Michael, William, Peter, Jon, Richard. Tchr., West Orange (N.J.) High Sch., 1940-42; research asso. N.Y. State Edn. Dept., Albany, 1947-53; dir. research N.Y. State Commn. on Sch. Bldgs., Albany, 1954; asst. supt. for bus. affairs Hicksville (N.Y.) Pub. Schs., 1955; prof., dir. field studies and research Rutgers U., 1956—. Ednl. cons., 1950—; cons. N.J. Sch. Bldg. Guide Adv. Com. Served to capt. USAAF, 1942-46. Mem. Council Ednl. Facility Planners, N.E. Council Schoolhouse Constrn., AAUP, Phi Delta Kappa. Home: 2 Louise Dr Milltown NJ 08850 Office: Rutgers U New Brunswick NJ 08903

WALLIS, CHARLES L(ANGWORTHY), educator, clergyman; b. Hamilton, N.Y., May 1, 1921; s. Robert Scott and Caroline (Langworthy) W.; B.A., U. Redlands, 1943; M.A., U. Rochester, 1945; M.Div., Colgate Rochester Div. Sch., 1945; m. Betty Barbe Watson, Aug. 16, 1947. Ordained to ministry Bapt. Ch., 1944; minister, Canandaigua, N.Y., 1943-47; chaplain U.S. Vet's Hosp., 1944-46; instr. English, Keuka Coll., 1945-47, asst. prof., 1947-52, asso. prof., 1952-59, prof., 1959—, chmn. dept. English, 1959-70, lectr. philosophy, 1952-61; minister Keuka Coll. Ch., 1947-65, Keuka Park Ch., 1965—. Research fellow Minister Research Found., Los Angeles, 1955-58; mem. exam. com. Japan Internat. Christian Univ. Found., 1972—; bd. dirs. Am. Bapt. Hist. Soc., 1961-67; mem. acads. selection com. 33d Congl. Dist., 1970—, chmn., 1975—. Chmn. Yates County Republican Com., 1965—; del. N.Y. State Rep. Conv., 1962-66, Rep. Nat. Conv., 1968, 72. Recipient medallion Civil War Centennial Commn. Mem. Am. Assn. U. Profs., Coll. English Assn., N.Y. Hist. Assn., Am. Acad. Religion, Nat. Council Tchrs. English, Soc. of Biblical Lit., Poetry Soc. Am. Am., N.Y. folklore socs., Tau Kappa Alpha, Pi Delta Epsilon, Pi Kappa Delta, Delta Alpha. Mason (master 1965); mem. Order Eastern Star (patron 1961, 63). Rotarian (pres. 1962-63, Rotarian of Yr. 1976). Author: Selected Poems of John Oxenham, 1948; Poems of Edwin Markham, 1950; Treasury of Sermon Illustrations, 1950; The Funeral Encyclopedia, 1953; Stories on Stone: A Book of American Epitaphs, 1954; Worship Resources for the Christian Year, 1954; Speakers' Illustrations for Special Days, 1956; Treasury of Story-Sermons for Children, 1957; Table of the Lord, 1958; Notable Sermons from Protestant Pulpits, 1958; (with others) Twentieth Century Bible Commentary, 1955; (with Dr. Charles L. Allen) Christmas in Our Hearts, 1957; Riverside Sermons of Harry Emerson Fosdick, 1958; Candle, Star and Christmas, 1959; A Treasury of Poems for Worship and Devotion, 1959; The Greatest Sermons of George H. Morrison, 1959; When Christmas Came to Bethlehem, 1963; (with J. Ferguson) Prayers for Public Worship, 1958; Lenten-Easter Sourcebook, 1961; 1010 Sermon Illustrations from the Bible, 1962; Eighty-eight Evangelistic Sermons, 1964; The Treasure Chest, 1965; Speakers Resources from Contemporary Literature, 1965; Flapdoodle, Trust and Obey, 1966; Words of Life, 1966; The Eternal Light, 1966. General editor: Harper's Ch. Life Series, Harper's New Anvil Library. Editor: Pulpit Preaching, 1951-72; Pulpit Digest, 1972—; N.Y. Folklore Quar., 1955-63; The Ministers Manual, 1967—; 365 Table Graces for the Christian Home, 1967; Close Your Eyes When Praying, 1968; Holy, Holy Land, 1968; The Charles L. Allen Treasury, 1970; Our American Heritage, 1970; American Epitaphs: Grave and Humorous, 1973; Christmas, 1977; The Complete Sourcebook for the Lord's Supper, 1978. Contbg. editor Harper & Row, 1952—. Daily radio program For Heaven's Sake, 1967—; writer newspaper column Lakeside Pulpit, 1968—, Religion Beat, 1976—. Home: E Bluff Dr Keuka Park NY 14478 Office: Box 1 Keuka Coll Keuka Park NY 14478

WALLIS, GORDON TODD, banker; b. Salt Lake City, Aug. 15, 1919; s. James Benjamin and Jessie (McAlister) W.; B.A., Columbia, 1940; LL.B., N.Y.U., 1948; m. Dorothy Jean Merrill, June 15, 1946; children—Judith (Mrs. Clifton Fenton), Deborah (Mrs. Joseph Rei). With Irving Trust Co., N.Y.C., 1940—, asst. sec., 1948-53, asst. v.p., 1953-55, v.p., 1955-64, sr. v.p., 1964-65, exec. v.p., 1965-69, vice-chmn., 1969-70, chmn., 1970—, dir., 1969—; pres., Charter N.Y. Corp., 1970-72, chief exec. officer, 1970—, chmn., 1972—, also dir.; dir. Gen. Telephone & Electronics Corp., J. Walter Thompson Co., Wing Hang Bank, Ltd., Sterling Drug, Inc., F.W. Woolworth Co., Internat. Comml. Bank, Ltd. Trustee N.Y. U.; bd. dirs. United Fund Greater N.Y., Downtown-Lower Manhattan Assn., Inc., Econ. Devel. Council N.Y.C. Served to capt. USAAF, 1942-46. Mem. Council Fgn. Relations, UN Assn. (dir.), Conf. Bd., Internat C. of C. (trustee U.S. council), N.Y. Chamber Commerce and Industry. Clubs: Links, University (N.Y.C.). Home: Washington CT 06793 Office: 1 Wall St New York City NY 10015

WALLIS, JOSEPH ANTHONY, advt. exec.; b. Cattaro, Austria, Aug. 30, 1917; s. Josef Anton and Beatrix (Tropper) W.; Phil. C., U. Zurich (Switzerland), 1956; M.B.A., N.Y. U., 1962; m. Johanna Hurni, Mar. 30, 1963. Came to U.S., 1956, naturalized, 1962. Asst. sales mgr. Velan Engring. Cos., Zurich, 1946-49; sales mgr. Globus Trading Corp., Zurich, 1949-53; internat. credit analyst Swiss Credit Bank, N.Y. agy., N.Y.C., 1956-63, head advt. office, head office Zurich, 1963-64; mgr. marketing data analysis, Bur. of Advt. Am. Newspaper Pubs. Assn., N.Y.C., 1965-73; mgr. marketing services Newspaper Advt. Bur., Inc., N.Y.C., 1973—. Mem. Am. Marketing Assn., Advt. Data Processing Assn., Sales and Marketing Execs. Internat., Swiss-Am. C. of C. (Zurich). Clubs: New York University (N.Y.C.); American (Zurich). Home: 340 E 51st St New York City NY 10022 Office: 485 Lexington Ave New York City NY 10017

WALLIS, WILLIAM C., investment banker; b. Pitts., Feb. 28, 1939; s. Wayne G. and Louise Ada (Russell) W.; B.A., Lycoming Coll., 1962; m. Davea McCahill Horning, Apr. 12, 1963; children—William, Wayne G., Michele Marie. With Merrill Lynch Pearce Fenner & Smith, N.Y., 1963-64; commodity exec. Eastman Dillon Union Sel & Co., 1964-69; investment exec. Woodcock Cummings Taylor and French, 1969-71; instl. sales exec. F.S. Moseley, N.Y.C., 1971-73; commodity exec. Shearson Hayden Stone, 1973-74; investment banker, Boonton, N.J., 1975—; chmn. Interlox Punch & Die Corp., Boonton, 1975—; chmn. Wallmont, Inc., Montclair, N.J.; mem. N.Y. Cotton Exchange. Chmn. bd. mgrs. Silver Lake YMCA, Stockholm, N.J., 1974-78. Mem. Soc. Mfg. Engrs. Republican. Presbyn. Clubs: Downton Athletic; Mountain Lakes. Home: 428 Upper Mountain Ave Upper Montclair NJ 07043 Office: N Main St Box 267 Boonton NJ 07005

WALLMAN, GEORGE, hosp. adminstr., food services specialist; b. U.S., Apr. 10, 1917; s. Joseph and Celia (Kascawal) W.; student pub. schs., N.Y.C.; m. Benita B. Kaufman, June 11, 1941. Dir. food and banquet services Normandy Hotel, Hollywood, Calif., 1945-47; dir. food services Med. Center N.Y.C., 1947-64; menucologist and cons. to hosps., 1964-67; dir. food services Montefiore Hosp., Pitts., 1967—; mem. Cancer Rehab. Project, U. Pitts.; lectr. on food to orgns., cos.; cons. in field to pub. schs., homes, hosps. for aged, on new products to cos.; lectr. Exercise is Not Enough show NBC-TV. Mem. Am. Hosp. Assn., Nat. Restaurant Assn., Am. Fedn. Musicians. Contbg. editor Today's Chef, 1978—. Home: 1420 Centre Ave Pittsburgh PA 15219 Office: Montefiore Hosp Fifth Ave at Darragh Pittsburgh PA 15213

WALLNER, LUDWIG JOHN, ednl. adminstr.; b. N.Y.C., Sept. 14, 1941; s. Ludwig and Antonette (Maier) W.; A.A., Orange County Community Coll., 1961; B.S., State U. Coll., Oswego, N.Y., 1964, M.S., 1967; certificate of advanced studies State U. Coll., Cortland, 1977; m. Carolyn E. Holzer, Dec. 19, 1964; children—Heidi Elizabeth, Kurt Andrew. Tchr. indsl. arts Gillette Rd. Middle Sch., Clay, N.Y., 1964-66, guidance counselor, 1966-69, head guidance counselor, 1969-73, asst. prin., 1973—. Mem. Sch. Adminstrn. Assn. N.Y., North Syracuse Adminstrs. Assn., Phi Delta Kappa, Epsilon Pi Tau, Kappa Delta Pi. Republican. Episcopalian. Home: 4005 Pawnee Dr Liverpool NY 13088 Office: RD 4 Clay NY 13041

WALMAN, JEROME, author, producer; b. Charleston, W.Va., June 19, 1937; s. Joe and Madeline Minnie (Levy) W.; student W.Va. U., Boston U., Berkley Sch. Music, Boston; m. Mary Joan Granara, Sept. 5, 1960. Producer mus. compositions at Carnegie Hall, Broadway theatre, 1962, 63; practicing psychotherapist in spl. hypnosis and music therapy, 1964—; designer Jerome Walman Systems Applied Hypnosis, 1969; dir., producer TV show Enterprises Unlimited, 1978—; producer I Murdered Mary, N.Y.C., 1976, Last Call, N.Y.C., 1977, TV Mag., 1978; lectr. East-West Center, N.Y.C., 1978. Mem. Music Therapy Internat., Meditation and Mental Devel. Center N.Y., Memory Improvement and Concentration Center Am. Author papers on hypnosis, psychic phenomena and memory, music therapy. Address: 400 E 59th St Apt 9F New York City NY 10022

WALROD, TRUMAN HARRINGTON, assn. exec.; b. Des Moines, July 6, 1924; s. Truman Spencer and Flora Maude (Trowbridge) W.; A.B., Drake U., Des Moines, 1949, M.A., 1953; Ph.D. in Pub. Adminstrn., Guglielmo Marconi. Internat. U., Rome, Italy, 1960; m. Anne Deinek, Apr. 26, 1949; children—James Deinek, Catherine Alexandra. Mem. staff sta. KRNT, Des Moines, 1945-47, WXYZ-TV, Detroit, 1956-58; mgr. Daniels Broadcasting Co., Rapid City, S.D., 1960-63; dir. community, pub. affairs Fetzer TV, Inc., Cadillac, Mich., 1963-66; dir. pub. affairs Nat. Sheriff's Assn., Washington, 1966—; instr. seminars, workshops Nat. Sheriffs Assn. Ann. Informative Confs., 1966-75, Nat. Jail Chaplains Seminar, Arlington, Va., 1973-76. Served with U.S. Army, World War II. Named Knight Comdr., Order of St. Dennis of Zanta (Greece), 1971; Hon. Atty. Gen., State of La., 1968, Col., 1969. Mem. Nat. Sheriffs Assn., Internat. Assn. Chiefs of Policy, World Intellectual Soc. (Athens, Greece), S.A.R. (dir. pub. relations nat. soc. 1973-74), Sigma Delta Chi, (past editor publs. Washington). Mason (32 deg.). Author: The Role of Sheriff: Past-Present-Future, 1968; Manual on Jail Adminstration, 1969. Editor: Manual of Training for Sheriffs, 1970. Home: 6004 Kerrwood St Burke VA 22015 Office: Nat Sheriffs Assn 1250 Connecticut Ave Washington DC 20036

WALSH, LAWRENCE E(DWARD), lawyer; b. Port Maitland, N.S., Can., Jan. 8, 1912; s. Cornelius Edward and Lila May (Sanders) W., brought to U.S., 1914, naturalized, 1922; A.B., Columbia U., 1932, LL.B., 1935; LL.D., Union, 1959, St. John's U., 1975, Suffolk U., 1975, Waynesburg Coll., 1976, Vt. Law Sch., 1976; m. Mary Alma Porter; children—Barbara Marie, Janet Maxine (Mrs. Wiggins), Sara Porter, Dale Edward, Elizabeth Porter. Admitted to N.Y. bar, 1936, spl. asst. atty. gen. Drukman Investigation, 1936-38; dep. asst. dist. atty. N.Y. County, 1938-41; asst. counsel to gov. N.Y., 1943-49, counsel to gov., 1950-51; counsel Pub. Service Commn., 1951-53; gen. counsel exec. dir. Waterfront Commn. N.Y. Harbor, 1953-54; U.S. judge So. Dist. N.Y. 1954-57; U.S. Dep. Atty. Gen., 1957-60; dep. head with rank of ambassador U.S. Delegation to Paris Meetings on Vietnam, 1969; partner Davis Polk & Wardwell, 1961—. Dir. Richardson-Merrell, Inc.; trustee Mut. Life Ins. Co. N.Y. Chmn. N.Y. State Moreland Commn. on Alcoholic Beverage Control Law, 1963-64, Mayor Lindsay's Task Force on Law Enforcement, 1965-66; counsel to N.Y. state ct. on the judiciary, 1971-72; mem. N.Y. State Commn. on Legislative and Judicial Salaries; 2d circuit mem. U.S. Circuit Judge Nominating Commn., 1978. Trustee William Nelson Cromwell Found., Columbia U. Fellow Am. Coll. Trial Lawyers, Am. Bar Found.; mem. Am. (pres. 1975-76), N.Y. State (pres. 1966-67), Internat. Bar Assn., N.Y. County Lawyers Assn., Assn. Bar City N.Y., Am. Judicature Soc., Am. Law Inst. (council), Inst. Jud. Adminstrn., Law Soc. Eng. and Wales (hon.), Canadian, Mexican bars (hon.), Columbia U. Alumni Fedn. (pres, 1968-69), Beta Theta Pi. Clubs: India House, The Century. Home: 320 E 72d St New York City NY 10021 Office: 1 Chase Manhattan Plaza New York City NY 10005

WALSH, ROBERT REDDINGTON, engr.; b. Wilmington, Del., Nov. 4, 1927; s. Michael J. and Nancy (Ahrens) W.; E.E., U. Del., 1950; A.B., St. Mary's Coll., Balt., 1954. Engr., E.I. duPont Co., 1954-59; research engr., 1959-60; chief engr. Reynolds Broadcasting Co., 1957-60; asst. dir. applied physics All Am. Engring Co., 1960-61, dir. mktg. and product devel., comml. products div., 1961-63, dir. research, 1963-66; v.p., gen. mgr. Technidyne, Inc., Wilmington, 1967-70; asst. advt. and pub. relations Wilmington Trust Co., 1971-73; product design cons. Advanced Tech. Products, Inc., Newark, Del., 1973-76; asst. treas. Wilmington Trust Co., 1976—. Tchr. adult edn. program Wilmington Pub. Schs., 1956-60. Served with USAAF, 1946-47. Mem. IEEE, AAAS. Patentee in field. Home: 1301 N Harrison St Apt 402 Wilmington DE 19806

WALSH, THOMAS JOSEPH, neuro-ophthalmologist; b. N.Y.C., Sept. 18, 1931; s. Thomas Joseph and Virginia (Hughes) W.; B.A., Coll. Fordham, 1954; M.D., Bowman Gray Med. Sch., 1958; m. Sally Ann Maust, June 21, 1958; children—Thomas Raymond, Sara Ann, Mary Kelly, Kathleen Meghan. Intern, St. Vincent's Hosp., N.Y.C., 1958-59; resident ophthalmology Bowman Gray Med. Sch., Winston-Salem, N.C., 1961-64; fellow neuro-ophthalmology Bascom Palmer Eye Inst., Miami Fla., 1964-65; practice medicine specializing in neuro-ophthalmology, Stamford, Conn., 1965—; dir. neuro-ophthalmology service, asst. prof. ophthalmology and neurology Yale Sch. Medicine, New Haven, Conn., 1965-74, asso. prof., 1974—; dir. Ophthalmology Stamford Hosp., 1978—; mem. staffs Stamford Hosp., St. Joseph Hosp., Yale New Haven Hosp. Cons., Surgeon Gen. Army in neuro-ophthalmology Walter Reed Hosp., Washington, 1966—, Vets. Hosp., West Haven, 1965—, Silver Hill Found., New Canaan, Conn., 1974—; frequent lectr. various univs. Mem. adv. bd. Stamford Salvation Army, 1972—; mem. med. bd. Darien (Conn.) Nurses Assn., 1972—; surgeon Darien Fire Dept., 1969—. Served with AUS, 1959-61. Centennial fellow Johns Hopkins, 1976. Mem. AMA, Conn., Fairfield County med. socs., Acad. Ophthalmology, Acad. Neurology, Am. Assn. Neurol. Surgeons, Soc. Med. Cons. to Armed Forces. Lion. Contbr. articles to various publs. Home: 11 Salt Box Ln Darien CT 06820 Office: 1100 Bedford St Stamford CT 06905

WALTER, CHARLES RUSSELL, JR., air force officer; b. Evanston, Ill., June 19, 1936; s. Charles Russell and Alvira (Bleil) W.; B.A., Mich. State U., 1959; postgrad. Springfield Coll., Air and Command Staff Coll., 1975, Air War Coll., 1977; m. Margo Ellen Walter, Nov. 24, 1968; children—Laura Catherine, Charles Russell. Commd. 2d lt. U.S. Air Force, 1959, advanced through grades to lt. col., 1974; assigned to officers clubs, Wiesbaden, Germany, 1959, London, Eng., 1960-62, Mobile, Ala., 1963-64, Sacramento, Calif., 1965-66, Clark AFB, Philippines, 1966-67, Honolulu, 1969-70; mgr. Andrews Officers Club Complex, Washington, 1971, Kessler Officers Club, Biloxi, Miss., 1972; club officer Bolling Officers Club, Washington, 1973—; mem. faculty No. Va. Community Coll.; cons. NATO, 1978. Mem. Club Mgrs. Assn. Am., Nat. Restaurant Assn. (Gold award 1978), Food Service Exec. Assn. (dir. Hawaii chpt. 1969-70), Mich. State U. Alumni Assn., Bolling Officers' Open Mess, Beta Theta Pi Alumni. Home: 628J Westover Ave Bolling AFB Washington DC 20332

WALTER, KENNETH GEORGE, auto. accessory co. exec.; b. Bklyn., Nov. 8, 1942; s. Nicholas Conrad and Mildred Christine (Weiser) W.; A.A.S., Delhi Tech. Coll., 1963; m. Norma Mischler, Nov. 23, 1963; children—Christian, Kevin. Purchasing agt. Chemicolloid Labs., Inc., Garden City Park, N.Y., 1963-71; purchasing agt. Del-Met Corp., Walton, N.Y., 1971-72, dir. purchasing, 1972—; lead time panel mem. Purchasing mag., 1975-78; aluminum com. chmn. Purchasing Mgmt. Assn. Commodity Report, 1977-78. Commr. Franklin-Treadwell Fire Dist., 1974-77; chief Treadwell Volunteer Fire Dept., 1978; hunter tng. instr. N.Y. State Dept. Environ. Conservation, 1964-78; bd. dirs. Treadwell TV Cable, 1978. Recipient Purchasing Mag. Value Improvement award, 1977. Mem. Nat. Assn. Purchasing Mgmt., Purchasing Mgmt. Assn. of Syracuse and Central N.Y., Am. Soc. Metals. Club: Masons. Home: PO Box 268 Main St Treadwell NY 13846 Office: Del-Met Corp 44 West St Walton NY 13856

WALTER, ROBERT LOUIS, nurse; b. Wilkes-Barre, Pa., Sept. 10, 1946; s. Frederick C. and Sophia (Tanski) W.; grad. Kings Park (N.Y.) State Hosp. Sch. Nursing, 1967; student Trenton State Coll., 1971-73; m. Lynne Podeswa, Apr. 21, 1968; children—Tara Michelle, Cynthia Carol. Nurse, Commonwealth of Pa., 1968—, mem. infection control com., 1977—, clin. supr., 1975—, nurse coordinator Boarding Home/Nursing Home Relocation, Phila., 1976—; tax cons. and preparer, 1970—; notary pub., Pa., 1970—. Mem. various coms. St. Mark Ch., Bristol, Pa., 1970—. Mem. Am., Pa., Bucks County nurses assns., Pa. Assn. Notaries. Home: 7010 N Radcliffe St Bristol PA 19007 Office: Phila State Hosp Roosevelt Blvd Philadelphia PA 19114

WALTERS, BETTE J., lawyer; b. Norristown, Pa., Sept. 5, 1946; d. Albert Bradford and Elizabeth Moore (Daymon) W.; B.A., U. Pitts., 1967; J.D., Temple U., 1970, LL.M. in Taxation, 1974. Admitted to Pa. bar, 1970; law clk., asso. counsel William R. Cooper, Lansdale, 1969-72; student staff asst. legal aid br. Temple U., 1967-70; practice in North Wales, Pa., 1972—; house counsel Alco Standard Corp., Valley Forge, Pa., from 1973, now asst. counsel; spl. asst. to pub. defender Montgomery County, 1973-75; staff atty. Montgomery County Legal Aid Service, 1973, bd. dirs., 1973-75. Sponsor North Penn High Sch. Sr. Career Study Program, 1972-73, 73-74; mem. Community Orgn. for Personal Enrichment, 1971-74. Recipient Legal Aid award Temple U. Law Sch., 1970. Mem. Am., Pa., Montgomery County bar assns., Nat. Assn. Women Lawyers, Wissahickon Valley Watershed Assn. Home: #18 Etienne Arbordeau Berwyn Baptist Rd Devon PA 19333 Office: PO Box 834 Valley Forge PA 19482

WALTERS, RONALD GORDON, educator; b. Sacramento, Apr. 23, 1942; s. Russell Goodrum and Arvilla (Scholfield) W.; A.B., Stanford U., 1963; M.A., U. Calif., Berkeley, 1965, Ph.D. (Max Farrand fellow 1969-70), 1971; m. Charlotte Higgins, July 25, 1965; 1 son, Nathaniel Bradford. Acting instr. U. Calif., Berkeley, 1968-70; instr. history Johns Hopkins U., Balt., 1970-72, asst. prof., 1972-75, asso. prof., 1975—. Nat. Endowment for Humanities fellow, 1974-75; Rockfeller Found. fellow, 1977-78. Mem. Am., So. hist. assns., Orgn. Am. Historians, Phi Beta Kappa. Democrat. Home: 3300 Beech Ave Baltimore MD 21211 Office: History Dept Johns Hopkins University Baltimore MD 21218

WALTERS, WALTER HENRY, univ. dean; b. Troy, Ala., Dec. 19, 1917; s. Walter Henry and Julia (Coleman) W.; B.S., Troy State U., 1939; Ph.M., U. Wis., 1947; M.F.A., Western Res. U., 1949, Ph. D., 1950; m. Geraldine Ross, Sept. 18, 1947; children—Ross Atwell, Ann Coleman, Kirk Madison. Tchr. pub. schs., Ala., 1939-42; mem. faculty U. Wis., 1946-48; mem. faculty Pa. State U., 1950—, chmn. dept. theatre arts, 1954-66, producer Mateer Playhouse, 1958-62, producer Pa. State Festival Theatre, 1963-66, dean Coll. Arts and Architecture, 1968—, dir. Univ. Arts Services, 1973—; cons. in field, 1955—; mem. adv. council Am. Acad., Rome, 1968—. Mem. Commonwealth Pa. Council Arts, 1969-71, chmn. theatre adv. panel, 1972; chmn. fine arts commn. Nat. Assn. State Univs. and Land-Grant Colls., 1975—; bd. dirs., sec.-treas. Am. Research Inst. for Arts, 1975—. Served with USNR, World War II. Decorated Meritorious Service citation. Fellow Am. Theatre Assn., U.S. Inst. Theatre Tech. (bd. dirs. 1976-78, editor newsletter 1966-68, 1st v.p. 1970-71, pres. 1971-72); mem. Internat. Council Fine Arts Deans (chmn. 1973-74), Theatre Assn. Pa., Am. Theatre Assn., Univ. and Coll. Theatre Assn. (dir. 1970-71). Mem. editorial adv. bd. Arts in Soc., 1969—. Home: 1358 Greenwood Circle State College PA 16801 Office: Arts Bldg Pa State U University Park PA 16802

WALTON, RALPH GERALD, psychiatrist; b. Darlington, Eng., Aug. 18, 1942; came to U.S., 1951, naturalized, 1957; s. Kenneth and Paula Walton; B.A., U. Rochester, 1963; M.D., State U. N.Y., Syracuse, 1967; m. Ellen Liebling, Feb. 15, 1970; children—Deborah Joy, Rachel Beth. Intern, U. Rochester Med. Center, 1967-68, resident, 1968-71; mem. faculty, dir. drug and alcohol treatment program, clin. dir. inpatient unit U. Rochester Sch. Medicine, 1973-76; practice psychiatry, Jamestown, N.Y., 1976—; chief of psychiatry Jamestown Gen. Hosp., 1976—; attending physician WCA Hosp., Jamestown Gen. Hosp., Strong Meml. Hosp.-U. Rochester Med. Center; cons. Jamestown Bd. Edn. Mem. Chautauqua County Bd. Mental Health, 1976—; actor Jamestown Little Theatre Prodns., 1976, 77. Served as maj. M.C., U.S. Army, 1971-73. Diplomate Am. Bd. Psychiatry and Neurology, Nat. Bd. Med. Examiners. Mem. Am. Psychiat. Assn., Med. Assn. Isthmian C.Z., Chautauqua County Med. Soc., Med. Soc. N.Y. State. Contbr. articles to profl. jours. Home: 321 Arlington Ave Jamestown NY 14701 Office: 102 Forest Ave Jamestown NY 14701

WALTZER, STEWART PAUL, gallery dir.; b. N.Y.C., Mar. 17, 1948; s. Samuel and Mildred (Lefkowitz) W.; B.A., N.Y. U., 1970, M.A., 1971. Personal asst. to painter Kenneth Noland, 1971-73; dir. Andre Emmerich Gallery Downtown, N.Y.C., 1973-74, Tibor de Nagy Gallery, N.Y.C., 1974-77, Meredith Long Contemporary, N.Y.C., 1977—. Democrat. Jewish. Office: 7 W 57th St New York City NY 10019

WANG, CHIH CHUN, chemist; b. Peking, China, Oct. 9, 1932; s. Hsi Hwan and Hilda (Young) W.; came to U.S., 1958, naturalized, 1971; B.Sc., Nat. Taiwan U., 1955; M.Sc., Kans. State U., 1959; Ph.D., Colo. State U., 1962; postdoctoral U. Kans., 1963; m. Betty Rei-Chi Tung, Mar. 29, 1969; children—Joyce S., Francis P., Bessie. Mem. tech. staff RCA Labs., David Sarnoff Research Center, Princeton, N.J., 1963-73, fellow, 1973—. Recipient Outstanding Achievement awards RCA Labs., 1965, 67, 69, Inventor Recognition award, 1974. Mem. Am. Chem. Soc., Electrochem. Soc., Am. Phys. Soc., Am. Vacuum Soc., Sigma Xi, Phi Lambda Upsilon, Sigma Pi Sigma. Contbr. articles to profl. jours.; patentee in field. Home: 41 Maple Stream Rd East Windsor NJ 08520 Office: RCA Labs Princeton NJ 08540

WANG, JEN CHIN, physician; b. Taiwan, June 20, 1943; s. Chi-Twen and Huan-Roon W.; M.D., Nat. Taiwan U., 1969; m. Jan Wha Wang, Oct. 28, 1972; children—Anne, Sunny. Intern, Elmhurst Gen. Hosp., Queens, N.Y., 1971-72; resident in medicine Brookdale Hosp. Med. Center, Bklyn., 1972-74, research asst., asst. attending physician sect. hematology-oncology, 1976—. Mem. A.C.P., Tissue Culture Assn. Contbr. articles to med. jours. Home: 1132 E 98th St Brooklyn NY 11236 Office: Brookdale Hosp Med Center Linden Blvd Brooklyn NY 11212

WANG, KUNG-LEE, economist, ops. analyst, govt. ofcl.; b. Pei-Tai-Ho, Hopei, China, Aug. 12, 1925; s. Cheng-Fu Wang and Funghin Liu; came to U.S., 1947, naturalized, 1954; B.A., Yenching U., 1947; M.A., Brown U., 1950; M.B.A., Columbia U., 1958; M.P.A., Harvard U., 1965; m. Christine Wen, Aug. 15, 1959 (div.); 1 son, Christopher Ching-Yu. Accountant in charge fiscal mgmt. Bushwick Hosp., Bklyn., 1952-55; economist, civilian and mil. ops. analyst, internat. affairs C-E-I-R., Inc., Washington, 1955-60, cons. 1960-61; chief qualitative econs. analysis Bur. Mines, U.S. Dept. Interior, Washington, 1960—; cons. Asian econ. affairs Research Analysis Corp., McLean, Va., 1961-68; dir. Internat. Data Applications Inc., 1969-71; econ. ops. adviser to ministry econs. affairs Republic of China, 1969-71; cons. ops. research office John Hopkins, Bethesda, Md., 1960-61; ethnic advisor U.S. OEO, 1972-75. Pres., chmn. bd. dirs. Civic League of Brookmont, 1963-64; coordinator Chinese-Am. Leadership Council, 1971-73, pres. Rho Psi Found., Inc., 1966—; charter nat. pres. Orgn. Chinese-Ams. Inc., 1973-77. Nat. Inst. Pub. Affairs fellow, 1965. Mem. Am. Inst. Mining, Metall. and Petroleum Engrs. (charter pres. mineral econs. Washington sect. 1975—), Am. Soc. Pub. Adminstrn., Western Regional Sci. Assn., Am. Econs. Assn., Rho Psi. Chinese Christian Ch. Contbr. articles to profl. jours. Home: 1940 Dundee Rd Rockville MD 20850 Office: Div Economic Analysis US Bur Mines Washington DC 20241

WANG, LAWRENCE KONGPU, engr., educator; b. Chiangshan, Chekiang, China, Nov. 20, 1940; s. Pu Chen and Hsiu Yu Wang; B.S. in Civil Engring., Nat. Cheng Kung U., Tainan, Taiwan, China, 1962; M.S. in Civil and Structural Engring., U. Mo., 1965; M.S. in Sanitary Engring. U. R.I., 1967; Ph.D. in Environ. Engring. (fellow), Rutgers U., 1972; m. Mu-Hao Sung, June 8, 1968; children—John Chungkuei, Norman Chungshing, Betty Chungmei. Asst. engr. Yun Lee Cons. Co., Taiwan, 1963-64; research asst. U. of Mo., 1965-66, U. Rhode Island, 1966-67; research fellow Rutgers U., 1967-70; san. engr. Hackensack Water Co. (N.J.), 1970-71; environ. engr. Calspan Corp. (formerly Cornell Aeronautical Lab., Cornell U.), 1971-74; adj. asso. prof. Rensselaer Poly. Inst., 1974—; adj. prof. Nat. Cheng Kung U., 1974—; asso. prof. Stevens Inst. Tech., 1977—; cons. in field. Recipient Kenneth Allen Meml. award, 1978. Licensed profl. engr., N.Y.; registered profl. engr., Pa., Del. Mem. Am. Inst. Chem. Engrs., Am. Chem. Soc., Inst. of Environ. Scis., Am. Water Works Assn., Del. Assn. Profl. Engrs., Assn. Environ. Engring. Profs., Sigma Xi. Contbr. numerous articles in field to profl. jours. Patentee in field. Home: 44 Continental Dr West Nyack NY 10994 Office: Dept Mech Engring Stevens Inst Tech Hoboken NJ 07030

WANG, N(IAN) T(ZU), UN ofcl.; b. Shanghai, China, July 25, 1917; s. Pah-Yuan and Su-Teh (Tu) W.; A.B., Columbia, 1941; A.M. (Austin, Saltontall scholars, Univ. fellow), Harvard, 1943, Ph.D., 1945; m. Mabel U, Sept.21, 1942; children—June, Kay (Mrs. Leighton Chen), Cynthia, Geraldine, Newton. Instr., Columbia, 1949-51; with UN, N.Y.C., 1951—, chief, econ. survey sect., 1964-73, leader mission to Jamaica, 1967, leader Eastern African Team, 1968-69, asst. dir. charge planning and projections br., 1972-73, asst. dir. charge financial resources devel. br., 1973-75, asst. dir. in charge info. analysis div., 1975-76, dir., 1977—; vis. prof. U. Pitts., 1962, City U. N.Y., 1968; adj. prof. Columbia U., 1978. Mem. Econometric Soc., Am. Econ. Assn., Royal Econ. Soc., Phi Beta Kappa. Author: New Proposals for the International Finance of Development, 1967; Cooperation for Economic Development of Eastern Africa, 1971; Taxation and Development, 1976. Contbr. articles to profl. jours. Home: 25 Lincoln St Larchmont NY 10538 Office: UN New York City NY 10538

WANG, TEH PO, mfg. co. exec.; b. Macao, China, Feb. 22, 1926; s. Ying Fong and Wing Ping (Ho) W.; came to U.S., 1948, naturalized, 1964; B.S., Chiao-Tung U., 1947; M.S., U. Pa., 1950, Ph.D. (Univ. scholar), 1955; m. Marina Yi-Shen, Oct. 9, 1954; children—Kenneth Wei-Han, Nora Wei-Ming, Michael Wei-Kang. Asst. instr., then research asst. U. Pa., 1950-54; with Wilbur B. Driver Co. subsidiary GTE Sylvania, mfrs. alloy wire and strip, Newark, 1954—, supervising engr., 1968-74, dir. research, 1974—. Recipient Alumni citation U. Pa., 1975. Mem. Am. Inst. Mining and Metall. Engrs., Am. Soc. Metals, ASTM (chmn. subcom. 1977—), Metal Sci. Club N.Y.C. (pres. 1976-77), West Essex Chinese Assn. (pres. 1975-76). Baptist. Author, patentee in field. Home: 9 Timber Dr North Caldwell NJ 07006 Office: 1875 McCarter Hwy Newark NJ 07104

WANG, YINPAO, artist, author, educator; b. Soochow, China, Mar. 11, 1915; s. Chuan Chun and Chin Fong (Chiang) W.; M.B.A., U. Pa., 1938; m. Yung Lan Cheng, Jan. 20, 1970. Regional mgr. Farmers Bank of China, 1941-47; prof. Kwansi U., Kweilin, China, 1945-47; prof. S.W. Coll. Finance and Commerce, Kweilin, 1945-47; exec. v.p. Havana Trading Corp., N.Y., 1948-52; product devel. mgr. Garden State Tanning, Inc., Fleetwood, Pa., 1959-62; U.S. rep. Mitsuyu & Co., Osaka, Japan; pres. Parfait Products Corp., 1959—; cons. automotive, vinyl, ceramic, leather industries; dir. Exchange Control Commn., China, 1941-43; mem. Examination Yuan, Govt. of China, 1942-47. One-man shows at Columbia U., N.Y. World's Fair 1964-65, Detroit Inst. of Art Mus., Ward Eggleston Galleries, Crocker Galleries, Werbe Galleries, Crespie Gallery, Lynn Kottler Galleries, Woodmere Gallery, N.Y. Pub. Library, Nat. Gallery China, many others; represented in permanent collections at Henry Ford Mus., Gracie Mansion, Mus. Fla. Coll., Nat. Mus. China, J.C. Penney Collections. Served to maj. gen. Chinese Army, 1942-45. Recipient Key to City of Harrisburg, Pa., 1964; Internat. awards AID, 1961, 63; Grumbacher Merit award, 1954; ann. award Resources Council, 1973. Fellow Royal Soc. Arts (London); mem. Nat. Press Club, Nat. Soc. Arts and Letters, Phila. Art Alliance, Internat. Platform Assn. (spl. award 1967). Author: The Mysterious Fifth Dimension, 1953; Fundamental Techniques of Chinese Painting, 1968; An Assessment of the New Chinese Landscape, 1971; First Generation, 1975. Home: 87 Kent Dr East Greenwich RI 02818 Office: Harry Wang & Co 306 Emmons Dr Princeton NJ 08540

WANK, GERALD SIDNEY, dentist; b. Bklyn., Jan. 20, 1925; s. Joseph and Sadie (Ikowitz) W.; B.A., N.Y.U., 1945, D.D.S., 1949; certificate in orthodontia, Columbia, 1951; certificate in periodontia, Colombia, 1956; m. Gloria Baum, June 4, 1949; children—David, Stephen, Daniel. Intern oral surgery Bellevue Hosp., 1949-50; practice dentistry, specializing in oral rehab. and periodontal prosthetics, N.Y.C., Great Neck, N.Y., 1949—; instr. dept. periodontia, oral medicine N.Y.U. Dental Sch., 1956-63, asst. clin. prof. dept. periodontia, 1963-67, asst. prof. periodontia, oral medicine, postgrad. tchr. dept. fixed partial prosthesis until 1970, clin. asso. prof. dept. periodontia, oral medicine Coll. Dentistry, 1970-77, clin. prof., 1977—, postgrad. dir. periodontia, 1968-71; staff lectr. periodontology Harvard U. Sch. Dental Medicine, 1973-74; vis. lectr. Albert Einstein Coll. Medicine, N.Y.C. Community Coll. Sch. Dental Hygiene; sr. asst. attending N. Shore Univ. Hosp., 1977—; cons. orthodontic panel N.Y. State. N.Y.C. depts. health; former postgrad. instr. 1st Dist. Dental Soc. Postgrad. Sch.; lectr. various socs., N.Y. U. Mem. com. admissions N.Y. U. Coll. Dentistry, 1975—, chmn. fund raising, 1976—. Served to capt. USAF, 1953-55. Fellow Acad. Gen. Dentistry, N.Y. Acad. Dentistry, Internat. Coll. Dentists, Am. Coll. Dentists, Am. Acad. Oral Medicine (pres. N.Y. sect. 1971-72), Am. Pub. Health Assn.; mem. N.Y. Coll. Dentists (dir.), Dental Soc. N.Y.C. (dir. 1st dist.), Fedn. Dentaire Internat., Am. Assn. Dental Sch., N.Y. State Pub. Health Assn., AAUP, Pan Am. Med. Assn. (life), AAAS, ADA, Am. Acad. Periodontology, Sci. Research Soc. Am., Northeastern Soc. Periodontia, Am. Acad. Dental Medicine, Acad. Gen. Dentistry, Internat. Acad. Orthodontia, N.Y. U. Coll. Dentistry Alumni Assn. (dir., sec. 1973-74, v.p. 1974-75, pres. 1976-77), Am. Soc. Anesthesiology, Am. Assn. Endodontists, N.Y. U. Coll. Dentistry Dental Assos. (charter mem.), N.Y. U. Gallatin Assos., Alumni Fedn. N.Y. U., Omicron Kappa Upsilon, Alpha Omega. Jewish. Mason. Clubs: Fresh Meadow Country (Great Neck, N.Y.); N.Y. University; Century (charter) (N.Y. U. Coll. Dentistry). Contbr. to Practice of Periodontia, 1960; Dental Clinics of North America, 1972; Manual of Clinical Periodontics, 1973; also articles to profl. jours. Home: 40 Bayview Ave Great Neck NY 11021 Office: 40 Bayview Ave Great Neck NY 11021 also 14 E 60th St New York City NY 10022

WANKO, GEORGE J., univ. adminstr.; b. Drums, Pa., Feb. 27, 1937; s. John P. and Mary M. (Merker) W.; B.S., Pa. State U., 1964; M.S., Syracuse U., 1966; Ph.D., Catholic U. Am., 1975. Dir. men's residences Cath. U. Am., Washington, 1966-67, asst. dean of men, 1967-69, asso. dean resident life, 1969-73, dean student life, 1973—, bd. dirs. Fed. Credit Union, 1977—, organizer workshops in student personnel services; guest lectr. George Washington U. Sch. Edn., Md. Sch. Nursing, Cath. U. Sch. Social Service and Edn. Advisor, Cath. U. chpt. Blue Key Nat. Hon. Soc., 1970—. Served with U.S. Army, 1957-60. Recipient resident advisor scholarship Pa. State U., 1963-64, Syracuse U., 1964-66; S. Dean service award Cath. U. Athletic Dept., 1977. Mem. Am. Assn. Higher Edn., Am. Personnel and Guidance Assn., Nat. Assn. Student Personnel Admnstrs., Nat. Cath. Ednl. Assn., Alpha Delta Gamma, Phi Kappa Theta. Contbr. research paper in field. Home: 11300 NE 2d Ave Miami FL 33161 Office: St Bonaventure Hall Catholic U Am Washington DC 20064

WANLESS, RONALD WALTER, advt. agency exec.; b. New Haven, Aug. 22, 1946; s. W. Roland and Clara Olive (Boyden) W.; B.A. in English, Quinnipiac Coll., 1968. Sr. account exec. Diener/Hauser/Bates div. Ted Bates Advt., N.Y.C., 1972—. Republican. Congregationalist. Home: New Haven CT Office: Diener Hauser Bates 25 W 43d St New York City NY 10036

WARACH, BERNARD, social agy. exec.; b. N.Y.C., Feb. 10, 1921; s. Joseph and Frances (Farber) (dec.) W.; B.S., Coll. City N.Y., 1940; M.S.W., U. Pitts., 1942; m. Shirley Wagner, May 5, 1950 (dec.); children—Joshua, Jonathan, Beth; m. Marie Sieff Norkin, May 30, 1976. Field rep. Agrl. Marketing Adminstrn., U.S. Dept. Agr., W.Va., also Vt., 1942-44; welfare officer Displaced Persons Program, UNRRA and U.S. Zone, Germany, 1944-48; asso. dir. Irene Kaufmann Settlement, dir. Emma Kaufmann Camp, 1948-52; exec. dir. Mosholu-Montefiore Neighborhood Center, N.Y.C., 1952-54; asso. gen. dir. Asso. YM and YWHA, N.Y.C., N.Y., 1954-62, gen. dir., 1962-68; exec. dir. Jewish Assn. Services for Aged, N.Y.C., 1968—. Lectr., Sch. Social Work Adelphi U., Hunter Coll., N.Y. U., Hebrew Union-Jewish Inst. Religion, New Sch. Social Research, 1956-77. Mem. Nat. Assn. Social Workers, Nat. Assn. Jewish Center Workers, Gerontol. Soc., Phi Beta Kappa. Jewish. Contbr. articles to profl. jours. Home: 10 Hampshire Rd Great Neck NY 11023 Office: 222 Park Ave S New York City NY 10003

WARBER, ESTHER MAXINE, psychologist; b. Grand Haven, Mich., Mar. 21, 1923; s. Alex and Helena (Schippers) W.; B.S., U. Mich., 1951; M.S. in Psychology (Vocat. Rehab. grantee 1956-58), Wayne State U., 1958; postgrad. in pub. adminstrn. Nova U. Lab. technician U. Mich., 1949; asst. Doctor Gurskis, Detroit, 1950-53; supr. Blue Cross, Detroit, 1953-56; vocat. rehab. specialist State of Mich. Vocat. Rehab., Detroit, 1956-58; pub. health vocat. rehab. specialist City of Detroit, 1958-62; tchr. pub. health Peace Corps, Ecuador, 1962-64, community action worker, 1964-67; vocat. rehab. specialist City of Washington, 1964-67; counseling psychologist VA, Boston, 1967—; counseling psychologist Vets. Resource Bd., U. Mass., 1972-74, mem. adv. bd. Employee Services, 1974-78; mem. Humphrey's Human Resources Commn., Washington, 1967; vol. Domestic Community Action, 1965-67. Served with WAVES, 1943-46. Mem. Am. Soc. Pub. Adminstrn., Am. Personnel and Guidance Assn. (chmn. membership 1967-70), Am. Psychol. Assn., Nat. Vocat. Rehab. Assn., Women Overseas Service League, Wayne U. Alumni Assn., Women of Wayne. Methodist. Club: Am. Legion. Contbr. articles to Mich. Hist. Collections, Peace Corps Bulls. Office: JFK Bldg Govt Center VARO Boston MA 02203

WARBURG, STEPHANIE WENNER, artist; b. Kalamazoo, Dec. 29, 1941; d. William Franklin and Charlotte Sophia (Rossi) Wenner; B.S., Coll. Architecture and Design, U. Mich., 1963; M.F.A., Tchrs. Coll., Columbia U., 1965. Chmn. dept. art Latin Sch. Chgo., 1969-72; instr. drawing, watercolor and visual elements of design Chamberlayne Jr. Coll., Boston, 1975—; dir. art related activities Boston Parks Dept., summer 1978; exhibited in group shows Mystic (Conn.) Art Mus., 1968, Slater Mus., Norwich, Conn., 1969, Gilman Gallery, Chgo., 1970-72, Lord and Taylor Gallery, N.Y.C., 1969-77. Funchal, Madeira, Portugal, 1973, Famous-Barr, St. Louis, 1974, Paine Furniture Co. Gallery, Boston, 1975—; artistic cons. New Eng. Conservatory Music, 1975. Bd. dirs. Jr. League Boston, 1975-77, chmn. house, 1975-77; mem. women's bd. dirs. Mus. Sci., Boston, 1974—, chmn. internat. focus programs, 1977—; mem. Beacon Hill Circle for Charity, Boston, 1974—; justice of peace, New London, Conn., 1967. Recipient art awards Conn. chpt. Am. Cancer Soc., 1967, 68, award for painting East Lyme (Conn.) Art Assn., 1968. Mem. DAR, Kappa Alpha Theta. Home: 50 Commonwealth Ave Boston MA 02116 Office: 128 Commonwealth Ave Boston MA 02116

WARD, HAROLD WALTON, former union welfare fund exec.; b. Nanticoke, Pa., Nov. 26, 1905; s. Edwin Alexander Kerry and Myrtle Elizabeth (Garrison) W.; student Girard Coll., 1913-23, Temple U. H.S., 1925-26, Bucknell U. Jr. Coll., 1933-36; m. Betty Bertha Mandeville, Aug. 17, 1929; children—Constance (Mrs. Maurice Woolard), Edwin Mandeville. With Wilkes-Barre (Pa.) Record, 1930-37; legislative corr. A.P., Harrisburg, Pa., 1937-42, regional, capitol and labor editor, Washington, 1942-51; pub. relations officer United Mine Workers Am. Welfare and Retirement Fund, Washington, 1951-74. Bd. govs. Union Mills (Md.) Homestead Found. Mem. Nat. Press Club, Pub. Relations Soc. Am., Am., Pa., Hanover hist. socs. Home: Pine Grove Rd RD 1 Hanover PA 17331

WARD, JOAN GAYE, psychologist; b. Englewood, N.J., May 22, 1934; d. James A. and Eda D. W.; M.A., New Sch. Social Research, 1965; Ph.D., N.Y. U., 1973, postdoctoral, 1975—. Research asso. Mktg. Survey and Research Corp., N.Y.C., 1962-67; counselor N.Y. U., 1967-68; psychologist in tng. Bur. Child Guidance, Bronx, N.Y., 1968-69, psychologist, 1969—; individual practice psychotherapy, N.Y.C., 1969—; instr. N.Y. U., 1970-71. Mem. Am., Eastern psychol. assns., N.Y.C. Assn. Sch. Psychologists. Home: 395 Riverside Dr New York City NY 10025

WARD, JOHN BERNARD, cosmetic co. exec.; b. Asbury Park, N.J., Dec. 27, 1926; s. Raymond J. and Julia (Mraz) W.; B.S., Rutgers U., 1950; M.Sc., Purdue U., 1951, Ph.D., 1964; m. Jeanne Van Moerkerken, Feb. 24, 1951; children—Patricia, Susan, Kenneth. Head pharm. pilot plant White Labs., 1951-55; sr. chemist, group leader Wallace & Tiernan, 1955-58; group leader Strasenburgh Labs., 1959-62, head product devel., 1964-65; asst. dir. pharm. devel. Johnson & Johnson, New Brunswick, N.J., 1965-70; mgr. product devel. Avon Products, Suffern, N.Y., 1970-75; dir. sci. and regulatory affairs Vick Chem. Co., 1975-76; mgr. cosmetics and skin care sect. Consumer Research Center, Am. Cyanamid, Clifton, N.J., 1976-78; asso. prof. indsl. pharmacy Arnold and Maria Schwartz Coll. Pharmacy and Health Scis., L.I. U., 1978—. Adviser Jr. Achievement, Kenilworth, N.J., 1952-53; active Cub Scouts, ARC Blood Bank, New Brunswick, 1968-70. Served with AUS, 1945-46. Fellow Am. Found. Pharm. Edn., Soc. Cosmetic Chemists; mem. Am. Pharm. Assn., N.Y. Acad. Scis., Sigma Xi, Rho Chi. Patentee in field. Home: 135 Norman Dr Ramsey NJ 07446

WARD, JOSEPH FRANCIS, publishing co. exec.; b. Jersey City, Mar. 25, 1929; s. Francis William and Josephine (Haynes) W.; B.S. in Mgmt., St. Peter's Coll., 1957; postgrad. in Data Processing, N.Y. U., 1962-63, m. Joan B. Wysocki, Apr. 24, 1954; children—Joseph S., Bernadette J. Office mgr. Prentice Hall Inc., Englewood Cliffs, N.J., 1954-57, mgr. office services, 1957-65; asst. v.p. Inst. Bus. Planning,

Englewood Cliffs, 1965-78, v.p., 1978—. Chmn., Secaucus (N.J.) Planning Bd., 1960-66; Dem. candidate for mayor of Secaucus, 1971; pres., charter mem. Secaucus Babe Ruth Baseball League, 1959. Served with U.S. Army, 1951-53. Recipient Distinguished Citizen award Hudson County Police Chiefs Assn., 1964. Mem. Am. Legion (state comdr. 1969-70), Assn. U.S. Army, Air Force Assn., St. Peter's Coll. Alumni Assn. Roman Catholic. Home: 950 Schopmann Dr Secaucus NJ 07094 Office: IBP Plaza Englewood Cliffs NJ 07632

WARD, MADELEINE REBECCA SUPLEE, interior decorator; b. Phila., Dec. 4, 1908; d. William Zerns and Emma Theresa (Ward) Suplee; student Temple U., 1927, Pa. State Coll., 1933-34, Pa. Mus. Sch. Indsl. Art, 1934-35, N.Y. Sch. Interior Decoration, 1935-36; m. Douglas Henry Ward, Mar. 2, 1940; 1 son, James Burton III, Interior decorator, Hampton Bays, L.I., N.Y., Mem. Am. Assn. Ret. Persons, Hampton Bays Civic Assn. Democrat. Mem. Order Eastern Star. Address: Box 211 Private Rd Hampton Bays NY 11946

WARD, NICHOLAS DONNELL, lawyer; b. N.Y.C., July 30, 1941; s. Francis Xavier and Sarah DeLamater (Donnell) W.; B.A., Columbia, 1963; LL.B., Georgetown U., 1966; m. Elizabeth Reed Lowman, Sept. 6, 1968. Admitted to D.C. bar, 1967; asso. firm Hamilton and Hamilton, Washington, 1967-72, partner, 1973—; panelist Am. Law Inst.-Am. Bar Assn. Program, 1975—; instr. U. Md. Ct. Mgmt. Inst., 1975-77; instr. legal asst. program Sch. Summer and Continuing Edn. Georgetown U., 1977; mem. adv. com. on fiduciary rules D.C. Superior Ct., 1975—. Ann. corp. mem. Washington Children's Hosp., 1971—; trustee Confederate Meml. Assn., 1975-77, pres., 1976-77; trustee Benjamin Franklin U., 1976—. Served with USAR, 1966-72. Decorated officer Mil. and Hospitaller Order St. Lazarus of Jerusalem, knight Ordo Constantini Magni. Fellow Am. Coll. Probate Counsel; mem. Washington Estate Planning Council, Bar Assn. D.C. (editor Will and Testamentary Trust Forms 1974, Supplement, 1979, certificate of Appreciation 1976, 78, sec. com. probate, chmn. com. estates and guardianship sect. young lawyers), Downtown Jaycees (dir. 1971-73, Man of Year award 1972), Nat. Gavel Soc., Order Loyal Legion U.S. (chancellor in chief 1977—), Huguenot Soc. Washington (pres. 1975-77), SAR (pres. 1976-77), Soc. War 1812 (pres. 1976-78), SR (sec. D.C. chpt. 1973—, nat. gen. sec. 1976—), Soc. Mayflower Descs. in D.C. (gov. 1978—), Aztec Club of 1847 (pres. 1977—), Soc. Colonial Wars (sec. 1973—), Barrister Inn (pres. 1977-78), Alpha Delta Phi, Phi Delta Phi. Episcopalian. Clubs: Univ. of Washington, Barristers; Union (N.Y.C.); Metropolitan, Cosmos (Washington). Editor Am. Revolution Roundtable of D.C. newsletter, 1975-77, pres., 1978-79. Home: 6654 Barnaby St NW Washington DC 20015 Office: 600 Union Trust Bldg Washington DC 20005

WARD, PHILIP HENRY, III, lawyer; b. Phila., Aug. 7, 1920; s. Philip Henry Jr. and Ruth Coke (MacNamara) W.; A.B. cum laude, Princeton U., 1942; J.D., Harvard, 1948; m. Margaretta Dodge, Aug. 25, 1967; children—Philip Henry IV, Susan Ward Stitzer. Admitted to Pa. bar, 1949, since practiced in Phila.; partner firm Montgomery, McCracken, Walker & Rhoads, 1960—. Permanent del. Jud. Conf. 3d Circuit. Vice pres. Phila. Crime Commn. Trustee Phila. Coll. Art, Chestnut Hill Acad., 1963-70, Springside Sch., 1963-69. Served to capt. AUS, World War II; PTO. Decorated Silver Star, Bronze Star, Purple Heart. Mem. Phila. Bar Assn. (chmn. sect. corp. banking and bus. law 1969-70), Am. Arbitration Assn. (panel arbitrators), Wilderness Club (past pres.), Com. of 70 (past chmn.), Wissahickon Valley Watershed Assn. (past chmn.), Pohoqualine Fish Assn., Juristic Soc., Pa. Soc., Newcomen Soc. N.Am. Clubs: Philadelphia Cricket, Racquet (sec.), Lawyers, Union League, Anglers (Phila.). Home: 8605 Seminole Ave Philadelphia PA 19118 Office: 3 Parkway Philadelphia PA 19102

WARD, ROBERT JOSEPH, judge; b. N.Y.C., Jan. 31, 1926; s. Joseph G. and Honor V. (Hess) W.; S.B., Harvard U., 1945, LL.B., 1949; m. Florence C. Maisel, Apr. 15, 1951; children—Laura Alice, Carolyn. Admitted to N.Y. bar, 1949; practiced in N.Y.C., 1949-51, 61-72; asst. dist. atty. New York County, 1951-55; asst. U.S. atty. So. Dist. N.Y., 1956-61; judge U.S. So. Dist. N.Y., 1972—. Served with USNR, 1944-46. Mem. Am., N.Y. State bar assns., Assn. Bar City N.Y. Office: US Dist Ct US Courthouse Foley Sq New York City NY 10007

WARD, RODMAN, JR., lawyer; b. Wilmington, Del., Apr. 8, 1934; s. Rodman and Dorcas (Andrews) W.; B.A., Williams Coll., 1956; LL.B., Harvard U., 1959; m. Susan S. Hill, Oct. 10, 1959; children—Margery, Emily Tatnall, Rodman, III, Jenifer Janvier. Admitted to Del. bar, D.C. bar, 1959; asso. firm Prickett & Prickett, Wilmington, 1959-64, partner, 1965-67; partner firm Prickett, Ward, Burt & Sanders, Wilmington, 1967—. Dir. Corp. Service Co., Wilmington, 1964—. Sec. rules com. Ct. Chancery; trustee, mem. finance, investment coms. Wilmington Med. Center, 1971—; chmn. New Castle County Housing Authority, 1972-73; trustee, v.p. Lalor Found.; bd. dirs. U. Del. Library Assos. Served to capt. USAF, 1960-63, Mem. Am., Del. (vice chmn. com. on corp. law) bar assns., Assn. Bar City of N.Y. (com. on corp. law 1977-79), Am. Judicature Soc., Wilmington World Affairs Council (co-founder, dir.), Del. Hist. Soc. (dir.). Clubs: Wilmington, Wilmington Country; Vicmead Hunt. Mem. editorial bd. Am. Law Jour. Home: 52 Selborne Dr Wilmington DE 19807 Office: 1310 King St Wilmington DE 19899

WARD, SAMUEL M., accountant; b. N.Y.C., Mar. 12, 1932; s. Harry and Lena W.; B.B.A., Baruch Sch., U. City N.Y., 1954; m. Audrey Propp, June 27, 1963; children—Elise, Rachel, Jennifer. Staff, Margold, Erskin & Wang, N.Y.C., 1954-59, N.Y. State Investigation Commn., N.Y.C., 1959-62; accountant, prin. S.M. Ward Co., N.Y.C., 1962—. Vice-pres. Young Israel Synagogue, 1975—. Mem. Nat. Soc. Pub. Accountants. Address: 386 Park Ave S New York City NY 10016

WARD, THOMAS VINCENT, cons. engr.; b. Brookline, Mass., Dec. 10, 1938; s. Thomas Francis and Josephine Hanna (Hughes) W.; B.S., Northeastern U., 1962; postgrad. Portia Law Sch., 1962-63. Lab. technician G. L. Cabot Corp., Cambridge, Mass., 1957-58; mech. designer Computer Control Corp., Framingham, Mass., 1958-60; sr. mech. designer St. Regis Paper Co., E. Providence, R.I., 1960-62; lead mech. engr. Stone & Webster Engring. Corp., Boston, 1962-69; asst. engring. group supr. Bechtel Corp., Vernon, Calif., 1969-73; project mgr. C. T. Main, Inc., Boston, 1973—; cons. mech. engr. nuclear and fossil electric generating stas. Registered profl. engr., Mass. Mem. Am. Mgmt. Assn., Internat. Mensa Soc., ASME, Am. Water Works Assn., Nat., Mass. socs. profl. engrs. Clubs: Palmers Cove Yacht, Pelagic Sailing (vice commodore 1968-69), Undersea Explorers. Contbr. articles in field to profl. jours. Home: 100 Grand View Ave Apt 12D Quincy MA 02170 Office: CT Main Inc SE Tower Prudential Center Boston MA 02199

WARD, VERNON UNDERHILL, bus. mgr.; b. N.Y.C., June 22, 1936; s. Thomas Paul and Winifred (Underhill) W.; A.B., Dartmouth Coll., 1957; postgrad. Woods Hole Marine Biol. Lab., 1956, Hofstra Coll., 1959, Rutgers U., 1962, U. N.H., 1966; m. Sallie H. Tomasi, Aug. 14, 1971. Sales and engring. rep., dir, market research Special Electric Co., Milw., 1958; tchr. gen. sci. Locust Valley (N.Y.) High Sch., 1959; dept. head, lower sch., McBurney Sch., N.Y.C., 1959-60; instr. biology Hill Sch., Pottstown, Pa., 1960-62; sales rep. Macalaster Bicknell Co., Cambridge, Mass., 1963-65; sales mgr. Caley-Whitmore Corp., Somerville, Mass., 1965-66; agt. and tech. specialist Sun Life of Can., Manchester, N.H., 1966-69; cons. Internat. Personnel Cons., Hanover, N.H., 1969-70; pres., treas. Iron Horse Antiques, Inc., Hubbardton, Vt., 1970—. Undergrad. instr. botany Dartmouth, 1956—. Recipient Nathan Jenks Biology prize, 1956. Mem. Early Am. Industries Assn. (dir., chmn. whatsit com., mem. publs. com.), Early Trades and Crafts Soc., Antique Tools and Trades in Conn., Antique Crafts and Trades in Vt., Soc. History Tech., Tools and Trades of Mass., Internat. Platform Assn., Soc. for Preservation Old Mills, Mid-West Tool Collectors Assn., Brit.-Am. Rykhenological Soc., Ohio Tool Collectors Assn. Address: RD 2 Poultney VT 05764

WARD, VICTORIA FRANCINE, ednl. counselor; b. Phila., May 12, 1951; d. John and Margaret Covington; grad. Community Coll. Phila., 1971; B.Elementary Edn., Pa. State U., 1972; M.Edn., Antioch Grad. Sch., 1977. Asst. coordinator Students and Neighbors Action Program, Phila., 1970-72; tchr. Phila. Pub. Sch. System, 1972-76, elementary sch. counselor, 1976—. Mem. Women in Edn., Am. Personnel and Guidance Assn., Am. Sch. Counselors Assn., Bus. and Profl. Women Phila. and Vicinity, Antioch Grad. Sch. Alumni Assn., Delta Sigma Theta. Democrat. Presbyterian. Home: 4823 N Warnock St Philadelphia PA 19141 Office: 22d and Moore Sts Philadelphia PA 19145

WARD, W. RALPH, clergyman; b. Boston, Oct. 16, 1908; s. William Ralph and Janie (Johnston) W.; A.B., Baker U., 1929, D.D., 1950; S.T.B., Boston U., 1932, S.T.M., 1933, D.D., 1963; LL.D., Mt. Union Coll., 1960; S.T.D., Syracuse U., 1961; L.H.D., Keuka Coll., 1963; m. Arleen Burdick, June 3, 1933; children—Ralph A., David B., Gerald W.R. Ordained to ministry Meth. Ch., 1933; pastor, Mass., R.I., Conn., 1930-48, Mt. Lebanon Ch., Pitts., 1948-60; bishop Northeastern Jurisdicitional Conf., Syracuse, 1960-72, N.Y. area, 1972—. Pres. United Meth. Devel. Fund, N.Y. State Council Chs., 1970-73; mem. Bd. Christian Concerns Meth. Ch.; pres. Council Bishops United Meth. Ch., 1975-76. Trustee Hartford Sem. Found., Syracuse U., Bethune-Cookman Coll., Folts Home, Drew U., St. Paul's Sch. Theology, Washington, Bethel Meth. Home, Ossining, N.Y., Mt. Union Coll., Troy Conf. Geriatric Found., Saratoga Springs, N.Y., Meth. Hosp. Bklyn. Recipient Freedoms Found. award, 1950, Man of Year award B'nai B'rith, Pitts., 1954. Mem. Theta Chi Beta, Zeta Chi. Address: United Meth Center 210 Boston Post Rd Rye NY 10580

WARDLY, GEORGE ALFRED, JR., physicist, engr.; b. Teaneck, N.J., Jan. 29, 1940; s. George A. and Valma C. (Riggs) W.; B. Engring. Physics (McMullen scholar, Alcoa scholar), Cornell U., 1963; M.A. (NDEA fellow), Princeton U., 1965, Ph.D. in Physics and Engring., 1968; children—Deborah E., Jason B. Research asst. Princeton (N.J.) U., 1965-67; research engr. in microlithography IBM T.J. Watson Research Center, Yorktown, N.Y., 1967-78; program mgr. test engring. IBM World Trade Americas/Far East Corp., Mt. Pleasant, N.Y., 1978—. Mem. IEEE, Sigma Xi. Contbr. articles in field to profl. jours.; patentee in field. Home: 2279 Mark Rd Yorktown NY 10598 Office: IBM World Trade Americas/Far East Corp Route 9 Mount Pleasant NY 10591

WARE, CHARLES HARVEY, JR., chem. engr.; b. N.Y.C., July 8, 1927; s. Charles Harvey and Lillian Josephine (Miller) W.; B.S.E., Princeton, 1949; M.S. (Allied Chem. fellow), U. Pa., 1957, (duPont fellow), Ph.D., 1959; m. Elizabeth Joan Brayton, Sept. 27, 1952; children—Ellen Elizabeth, Laura Margaret. Salesman, SISCO, New Brunswick, N.J., 1949-52; jr. process engr. Atlantic Refining, Phila., 1952-56; with Texaco, Beacon, N.Y., 1959-74, sr. research chem. engr., 1965-70, group leader, 1970-74; cons. Commercialization Insights, Poughkeepsie, N.Y., 1974—. Adj. asso. prof. Columbia, 1968-69; cons. Sch. Chem. Engring. U. Pa., 1969-71; co-developer Texaco Yale Student Cons. Team Project, 1973; adj. prof. U. Pa., 1975, Manhattan Coll., 1978—; feature editor Computers and Chem. Engring., 1976—. Bd. dirs. George Washington Carver Fund scholarship, Poughkeepsie, N.Y., 1968-71, 74-75, pres., 1974-75. Served with AUS, 1952-54. Mem. Am. Chem. Soc., Am. Inst. Chem. Engrs. (chmn. machine computation com. 1973-76, nat. speakers bur. 1975—, lectr. Today series 1975—, exec. com. computers and systems tech. div. 1978—), Am. Mgmt. Assn., Am. Statis. Assn., Catalysis Soc., Sigma Xi. Unitarian. Clubs: Poughkeepsie Squash; Princeton (N.Y.C.). Patentee in field. Address: 33 Sandi Dr Poughkeepsie NY 12603

WARE, FRANCES LEE, govt. govt. ofcl.; b. Louisville, Dec. 13, 1919; d. Willie Lionel and Florence (Brown) Ware; A.B., U. Louisville, 1940; postgrad. George Washington U., Syracuse U. Aide U.S. Govt. Printing Office, Washington, 1943-50, planner, 1950-60; printing specialist, publishing services br. Internal Revenue Service, Washington, 1960-62, mgmt. services officer, 1962-72, asst. operations mgr., 1972-73, operations mgr., 1973—. Recipient Career Ednl. award, 1969. Mem. Am. Soc. Pub. Adminstrn., Am. Assn. U. Women, Internat. Personnel Mgmt. Assn., Franklin Tech. Soc., Columbia Women George Washington U. (publicity chmn. 1967-72, treas. 1972-74, v.p. 1974-76, pres. 1977—), Bus. Profl. Women's Club D.C. (treas. 1975-76, 2d v.p. 1977—), Phi Delta Gamma (chpt. historian 1967-68, nat. editor 1963—, chpt. pres. 1969-70). Club: University Women's (v.p. D.C. 1960-62, pres. 1968-70). Home: 4201 Massachusetts Ave NW Washington DC 20016 Office: 1111 Constitution Ave NW Washington DC 20224

WARE, GRACE ELIZABETH, social worker; b. Pitts., Nov. 13, 1933; d. Alphonse Marion and Loretta Henderson (McConnell) Moore; B.A., Fisk U., 1955; M.S.W., U. Pitts., 1960, M.P.H., 1973; m. Leonard Ware, Apr. 1, 1961; children—Thomas Aaron, Janine Elizabeth, Laura Anne Lucinda. Dir. Orange Ave. YWCA, Roanoke, Va., 1955-58; social worker Mich. Dept. Mental Health, Pontiac, 1960-61; Allegheny Gen. Hosp., Pitts., 1961-63, Allegheny County Child Welfare Services, Pitts., 1963-66; asst. dir. family service unit LEAP, Pitts., 1966-69; social work cons. Pa. Dept. Health, Pitts., 1969—. Preceptor, U. Pitts. Grad. Sch. Public Health, 1971—; co-chmn. Allegheny County Center for Victims of Violent Crimes, 1973—. Mem. Nat. Council Negro Women, Nat. Assn. Social Workers, Acad. Certified Social Workers, Western Pa. Public Health Council. Republican. Baptist. Club: Order of Eastern Star. Home: 7409 Mt Vernon St Pittsburgh PA 15208 Office: 300 Liberty Ave Pittsburgh PA 15222

WARFIELD, ROBERT WELMORE, research chemist; b. Long Branch, N.J., Oct. 11, 1926; s. Everett W. and Mildred (Marriner) W.; B.S. in Chemistry, U. Va., 1950; m. Mildred T. Stewart, Nov. 12, 1955; children—Richard S., Garrett W. With U.S. Bur. Mines, College Park, Md., 1950-55; research chemist U.S. Naval Surface Weapons Center, Silver Spring, Md., 1955—. Recipient Meritorious Service award Bur. of Mines, 1954, Dept. of Interior, 1955, Naval Ordnance Lab., 1961. Sr. mem. Am. Chem. Soc. Author: Analytical Applications of Electrical Resistivity Measurements on Polymers, 1977; Static High Pressure Measurements on Polymers, 1978. Contbr. chpts. to books, articles to profl. jours. Patentee in field. Home: 22712 Ward Ave Hereford Hills Germantown MD 20767 Office: Naval Surface Weapons Center Silver Spring MD 20910

WARING, JOHN ALFRED, research writer, editor, cons.; b. San Francisco, Dec. 30, 1913; s. John A. and Mary (Wheeler) W.; student pub. schs. Yachting, marine editor Chgo. Tribune, 1934-47; editor Kellogg Messenger, Kellogg Switchboard & Supply Co., Chgo., 1945-49; research cons. Baxter Internat. Econ. Research Bur., Inc., investment counselling, N.Y.C., 1951-52; research asst. marketing research dept. Fuller, Smith & Ross, Inc., advt., N.Y.C., 1953; research writer, cons. Twentieth Century Fund, N.Y.C., 1953-54; research cons. Ford Motor Co., Dearborn, Mich., 1955; chief researcher Internat. Fact Finding Inst., Lawrence Orgn., pub. relations cons., N.Y.C., Washington, 1957-58; lectr. on energy, tech. and history World Power Conf., Montreal, 1958, First Energy Inst., Am. U., Washington, 1960, Nat. Archives, Washington, 1962, Smithsonian Mus. History and Tech., Washington, 1968; guest lectr. social responsibility in sci. U. Md., 1972, guest lectr. sci. and environment, 1974; lectr. Internat. Conf. on Energy and Humanity, Queen Mary Coll., U. London, 1972, World Energy Conf., Detroit, 1974, History of Sci. Soc., 1974; research cons. PARM Project, Nat. Planning Assn., Washington, 1961-62; cons. Sci., Tech. and Fgn. Affairs Seminar, Fgn. Service Inst., U.S. Dept. State, 1965; cons. U.S. energy statistics Smithsonian Instn., U.S. Bur. Census, 1960—; research cons. Program of Policy Studies in Sci. and Tech., George Washington U., 1967-68; del. U.S. commn. UNESCO Conf., San Francisco, 1969; inaugural lectr. Future of Sci. and Soc. in Am. Seminar U.S. Civil Service Commn., Washington, 1970; editorial cons. Nat. Acad. Engring., Washington, 1971; research cons., analyst Seminar Sch., Indsl. Coll. Armed Forces, Ft. Lesley J. McNair, Washington, 1958-74; researcher Office Plans and Programs, U.S. Army Med. Dept., Washington, 1975-76; asst. editor Def. Systems Mgmt. Rev. mag. Def. Systems Mgmt. Coll., Ft. Belvoir, Va., 1977-78; ret., 1979. Mem. Soc. History of Tech. (charter), History Sci. Soc., Technocracy Inc., AAAS, Washington Acad. Scis., Washington Soc. Engrs. (sec.), Phi Beta Kappa Assn. in D.C., Internat. Soc. Gen. Semantics, Am. Humanist Assn., Washington Ethical Soc. Contbg. editor: Progressive World Mag., 1962—; technol. trends editor The Futurist Mag., 1968—. Contbr. chpts. to books; compiler statis. tabulations. Home: 8502 Flower Ave Takoma Park MD 20012

WARMAN, JOHN BOYLE, clergyman; b. Uniontown, Pa., Apr. 9, 1915; s. Robert Densmore and Minnie Lillian (Conaway) W.; A.B., Western Md. Coll., 1937; B.D., Andover Newton Theol. Sch., 1941; Ed.M., U. Pitts., 1951; D.D., Allegheny Coll., 1958, Western Md. Coll., 1962, Lebanon Valley Coll., 1974; m. Annie Owings Sansbury, June 15, 1939; children—John Sansbury, Irene (Mrs. Vernard Taulbee, Jr.), Oden Robert. Ordained to ministry Methodist Ch., 1941; pastor 1st Meth. Ch., Butler, Pa., 1950-58, 1st Meth. Ch., Pitts., 1958-62, Baldwin Community Ch., Pitts., 1965-72; bishop Harrisburg (Pa.) area United Meth. Ch., 1972—; supt. Pitts. dist. Meth. Ch., 1962-65. Mem. Pitts. Human Relations Commn., 1962-67. Trustee Mt. Union Coll., 1962-65, Lebanon Valley Coll., 1974—, Dickinson Coll., 1974—. Served with USNR, 1945-46. Mem. Tau Kappa Alpha. Democrat. Mason (33 deg.). Home: 1 Frances Dr Harrisburg PA 17109 Office: 900 S Arlington Ave Harrisburg PA 17109

WARMAN, KENNETH EDWARD, JR., personnel exec.; b. Easton, Pa., Aug. 13, 1937; s. Kenneth Edward and Ruth Kiefer (Helm) W.; B.A., Yale U., 1959; M.S., Rutgers U., 1969; m. Sarah Jane Fox, Dec. 19, 1959; children—Linda Jane, Shelly Lynn, Kenneth Edward III. Tech. recruiter Lukens Steel Co., Coatesville, Pa., 1962-64; dir. placement Johnson & Johnson, New Brunswick, N.J., 1964-71; mgr. coll. relations Allied Chem. Co., Morristown, N.J., 1971-72; dir. recruiting Peat, Marwick, Mitchell, N.Y.C., 1972-73; corporate personnel mgr. Foster Wheeler Corp., Livingston, N.J., 1973-77; dir. human resources Rapidata, Inc., Fairfield, N.J., 1977—. Chmn. major firms United Fund of Central Jersey, 1969. Served to capt. USMC, 1959-62. Mem. Middle Atlantic Placement Assn., Coll. Placement Council, Am. Mgmt. Assn., Am. Soc. Personnel Adminstrs. Republican. Lutheran. Home: 76 Seymour Terr Piscataway NJ 08854 Office: 20 New Dutch Ln Fairfield NJ 07006

WARNER, BARBARA JEAN, hosp. exec.; b. Bklyn., Sept. 22, 1942; d. Wilmer Dehn and Myra Isabelle (Pittman) W.; diploma Monmouth Med. Center Sch. Nursing, 1964; B.S., Adelphi U., 1971, M.S., 1973. Staff nurse, Vis. Nurses Assn., Atlantic City, 1968-69; staff nurse, psychiat. unit Mercy Hosp., Rockville Centre, N.Y., 1969-72; clin. nursing instr. State U. N.Y., Farmingdale, 1972-73; instr. nursing Villanova U. (Pa.), 1973-74; dir. edn Haverford (Pa.) State Hosp. Mem. Monmouth Med. Center Nurses Alumni Assn., Am. Nurses Assn., Sigma Theta Tau. Baptist. Office: 3500 Darby Rd Haverford PA 19041

WARNER, FRANCIS JAMES, physician, neuropathologist; b. Warsaw, Poland, Oct. 3, 1897; came to U.S., 1903, naturalized, 1925; s. Samuel and Molly (Smith) W.; B.A., U. Iowa, 1922; M.A. in Anatomy, U. Mich., 1925; M.D., Loyola U. Med. Sch., 1919. Postgrad. student in anatomy (in lieu of internship) U. Mich., 1924-25, instr. clin. neurology, 1931-32; instr. clin. neurology U. Md., 1938-39; research asso. in neuro-anatomy U. Calif., 1943-44; lectr. neuro-anatomy U. Utah, 1946-48; resident in neurology Henry Ford Hosp., Detroit, 1951-52; guest investigator in neuro-pathology Nat. (Queen's Sq.) Hosp., London, 1954-56; instr. neurology Temple U., 1957-75, asst. prof., 1975—. Diplomate in neuropathology Am. Bd. Pathology. Fellow Zool. Soc. of London, Royal Soc. Medicine (London), AAAS; mem. Am. Micros. Soc., Am. Assn. Anatomists, Am. Soc. Ichthyologists & Herpetologists, Am. Soc. Zoologists, Anatomical Soc. Gt. Britain and Ireland, Assn. Research in Nervous & Mental Disease, Am. Psychiat. Assn., Ill. Acad. Sci., AMA, Am. Assn. Neuropathologists, N.J. Soc. Clin. Pathologists, Sigma Xi. Home: PO Box 523 Philadelphia PA 19105 Office: Sch Medicine Temple U Philadelphia PA 19122

WARNER, FRANK WILLIAM, photographic specialist; b. Berne, N.Y., May 22, 1920; s. Aaron H. and Dorah (Deitz) W.; grad. pub. schs.; m. Grace M. Gerard, June 13, 1942; children—Deborah Jean, Brian Gerard. Asst. state photographer Nat. Youth Adminstrn., Albany, N.Y., 1941-42; chief photographer Gen. Electric Co., Schenectady, 1942, 1945-61; supervising photographer Niagara Mohawk Power Corp., Albany, 1961-76, photographic specialist, 1976—; conf. dir. Empire State Photocon, 1978; judge I Love New York Exhbn., 1978. Served with USAAF, 1942-45. Mem. Capital Dist. Assn. Photography in Industry (First Service award 1965, Profl. Protographers Am. Nat. award 1969, Spl. award 1973, life), Profl. Photographers Soc. N.Y. (life, Speakers award 1965, Bronze Service award and medal 1965, Silver Service award and medal 1967, Gold Service award and medal 1968, Exec. Council award 1968, Indsl. Photique award 1969, 72, 74, State award 1971, 72, 74, 75, 76, Pres.'s award 1971, hon. Gold Service award and medal 1973), Am. Soc. Photography, Profl. Photographers Am. (M. Photography degree 1965, Photographic Craftsman degree 1968, Indsl. Div. award 1969, nat. award 1978, sr. dir.). Mason (Shriner). Contbr. articles to The Professional Photographer mag. Home: State Farm Rd Voorheesville NY 12186 Office: Niagara Mohawk Power Corp 126 State St Albany NY 12207

WARNER, GLORIA MARMAR (MRS. RICHARD R. PICHEL WARNER), psychiatrist; b. N.Y.C., July 24, 1933; d. William W. and Celia (Dantzig) Marmar; B.A., Barnard Coll., 1952; M.D., N.Y. U.,

1959; postgrad. Columbia Psychoanalytic Clinic for Tng. and Research, 1972-76; m. Richard R. Pichel Warner, July 4, 1953; children—Jon J.P., Keith R.P., Douglas C.P., Lynn S.P. Intern Montefiore Hosp., N.Y.C., 1959-60; research fellow medicine and gastroenterology Mt. Sinai Hosp., N.Y.C., 1961-63, resident psychiatry, 1963-66, staff psychiatrist, 1966-69, asst. attending psychiatrist, 1969-76; asst. attending psychiatrist N.Y. Hosp. Med. Center, 1976—; instr. Mt. Sinai Sch. Medicine, City U. N.Y., 1965-69, clin. asso. psychiatrist, 1967-73, asst. clin. prof. psychiatry, 1973-76; asst. clin. prof. psychiatry Cornell U. Med. Sch., 1976-78, adj. asst. clin. prof., 1978—; asst. clin. prof. psychiatry Columbia U. Coll. Phys. and Surg., 1978—; mem. faculty Center for Psychoanalytic Tng. and Research, Columbia U., 1978—; sch. psychiatrist Mt. Sinai Hosp. Sch. Nursing, 1966-69. Diplomate Am. Bd. Psychiatry and Neurology. Mem. AMA, N.Y. State, N.Y. County med. socs., Am. Psychoanalytic Assn. (asso.), Am. Psychiat. Assn., Am. Fedn. Clin. Research, Am. Assn. Group Psychotherapy, Am. Med. Womens Assn., Assn. Psychoanalytic Medicine, N.Y. Acad. Scis., Alpha Omega Alpha. Contbr. articles to profl. jours. Office: 1160 5th Ave New York City NY 10029

WARNER, PATRICIA ANNE, educator; b. Northampton, Mass., Apr. 14, 1954; d. Edward Clark and Mary Elizabeth (Martin) W.; B.A., Eisenhower Coll., 1975. Saga Food Service mgr. trainee Nazareth Coll., Rochester, N.Y., 1975-76, mgr. Union Coll., Schenectady, 1976-77, U. Vt., Burlington, 1977-78; instr. hospitality food service mgmt. Holyoke (Mass.) Community Coll., 1978—. Active Girl Scouts U.S.A., 1977—. Mem. Western Mass. Food Services Execs. Assn., Mass. Community Coll. Council. Roman Catholic. Home: Montague Rd Sunderland MA 01375 Office: Holyoke Community Coll Homestead Ave Holyoke MA 01040

WARNER, RAWLEIGH, JR., oil co. exec.; b. Chgo., Feb. 13, 1921; s. Rawleigh and Dorothy (Haskins) W.; grad. Lawrenceville (N.J.) Sch., 1940; A.B. cum laude, Princeton, 1943; m. Mary Ann deClairmont, Nov. 2, 1946; children—Alison H. Pyne, Suzanne Parsons. Sec., treas. Warner Bard Co., Chgo., 1946-48; with Continental Oil Co., 1948-53, asst. treas., Houston, 1952-53; treas. Socony-Vacuum Overseas Supply Co., 1953-55; asst. treas. Mobil Overseas Oil Co., 1955-56; mgr. econs. dept., then mgr. Middle East dept. Socony Mobil Oil Co. Inc., 1956-59; regional v.p. Mobil Internat. Oil Co., 1959-60, exec. v.p., 1960-63, pres., 1963-64; exec. v.p., dir. Mobil Oil Corp. (formerly Socony Mobil Oil Co., Inc.), 1964, pres., 1965-69, chmn. bd., chief exec. officer, 1969—; dir. Caterpillar Tractor Co., Chem. Bank-Chem. N.Y. Corp., Am. Tel. & Tel. Co., Am. Express Co., Am. Express Internat. Banking Co. Chmn. council on univ. resources Princeton. Trustee Woodrow Wilson Internat. Center for Scholars. Served to capt. F.A., AUS, 1943-46. Decorated Purple Heart, Bronze Star, Silver Star. Mem. Am. Petroleum Inst. (dir.). Republican. Presbyterian. Clubs: Augusta (Ga.) Nat. Golf; Links, Pinnacle (N.Y.C.); New Canaan Country; Blind Brook (Port Chester, N.Y.); Island, Jupiter Island, Seminole (Hope Sound, Fla.); Chicago. Office: 150 E 42d St New York City NY 10017

WARNER, WILLIAM WHITESIDES, author, Smithsonian Instn. Exec.; b. N.Y.C., Apr. 2, 1920; s. Charles Jolly and Leonora (Haberle) W.; A.B., Princeton U., 1943; m. Kathleen Berryman McMahon, June 14, 1951; children—John B., Alletta B., Georgiana B., Alexandra DeP., Elizabeth S., Andrew. With USIA, Dept. State, 1951-62; exec. sec., program coordinator for Latin Am., Peace Corps, 1962-63; dir. office internat. activities Smithsonian Instn., Washington, 1964-67, asst. sec. for public service, 1967-73, research asso., 1973—. Served with USNR, 1944-46. Mem. Rachel Carson Trust for Living Environ. (v.p. 1966-73), Audubon Naturalist Soc. for Central Atlantic States (v.p. 1961-64), Sigma Xi. Episcopalian. Club: Federal City. Author: Beautiful Swimmers-Waterman, Crabs and the Chesapeake Bay (recipient Phi Beta Kappa Book award, Christopher award, Pulitzer prize for gen. non-fiction 1977), 1976. Contbr. articles in field to various mags. Office: Office Asst Sec Sci Smithsonian Instn Washington DC 20460 also care Little Brown & Co 34 Beacon St Boston MA 02106*

WARREN, ALAN, chemist; b. Phila., Dec. 20, 1936; s. S. Reid, Jr. and Marian E. (Stradling) W.; B.A. in Chemistry, U. Pa., Phila., 1958; m. Lorraine Benedetto, Oct. 17, 1973. Research chemist of detergents in research and devel. dept. PQ Corp., Primos, Pa., 1958-63, tech. service rep., Phila., 1963-66, mgr. research and devel. services, 1966-71; market devel. specialist P. Q. Internat. div., Valley Forge, Pa., 1972-75, mktg. dept. Specialty Chems. div., Valley Forge, 1976-77, research and devel. bus. ops. mgr. research and devel. div., Lafayette Hill, Pa., 1977—, also editor co. tech. house organ, 1964-72. Bd. dirs. Queen Village Neighbors Assn., Phila., 1969-75, sec., 1971-73, v.p., 1973-75. Fellow Am. Inst. Chemists (accredited); mem. Am. Chem. Soc., AAAS. Democrat. Home: Box 17124 Philadelphia PA 19105 Office: Research and Devel Center Box 258 Lafayette Hill PA 19444

WARREN, BERTRAM, psychiatrist; b. Roselle Park, N.J., July 9, 1932; s. Samuel and Anna Sylvia (Kozak) W.; B.S., Rutgers U., 1953; M.D., State U. N.Y. at Syracuse, 1957; m. Ann C. Wunderlich, June 15, 1957; children—Susan, Miriam. Intern, Meadowbrook Hosp., East Meadow, N.Y., 1958; resident in psychiatry Lyons (N.J.) VA Hosp., 1961-64; staff psychiatrist Union County Psychiat. Clinic, Elizabeth, N.J., 1964-66, sr. staff psychiatrist, 1966-73, clin. dir., 1973—; pvt. practice psychiatry, Fanwood, N.J., 1965—; faculty N.J. Med. Sch., 1976; psychiatrist-at-large, past v.p. N.J. Assn. Mental Health Agys. Served to capt. M.C., AUS, 1958-61. Dipolmate Nat. Bd. Med. Examiners. Mem. Union County, N.J. med. socs., AMA, Am., N.J. psychiat. assns., Social Welfare and Research Council, Am. Assn. Psychiat. Services for Children. Home: 86 N Martine Ave Fanwood NJ 07023 Office: 1358 South Ave Plainfield NJ 07062

WARREN, BETTY DEANE, artist; b. N.Y.C.; d. Alonzo Vincent and Dorothy Deane (Devor) Warren; student N.A.D., N.Y.C., 1937-42; student Cape Sch. Art, 1937-42, 1949; m. Stuart Lancaster, May 12, 1950; children—John Warren, Michael Dean; m. 2d, Jacob H. Herzog, 1960. Tchr. drawing, painting Albany (N.Y.) Inst. History and Art, 1959-75; owner, dir. Malden Bridge (N.Y.) Sch. Art, 1964—; one-person shows Albany Inst. History and Art, U. N.C., Berkshire Mus., Hartwick Coll., Pen and Brush Club, Shaker Mus., U. N.C., Mexico; exhibited art in group shows Allied Arts Am., Tampa Mus., Am. Watercolor Soc., Knickerbocker Artist, Nat. Arts Club, Am. Artists profl. League, Cooperstown (N.Y.) Ann., numerous others; represented in permanent collections at numerous colls., pub. instns., and pvt. collections. Recipient Purchase prize Albany Inst. History and Art, 1964; Gold medal Catherine Lorrilard Wolfe Nat. Annual, 1964, grand prize Cooperstown Nat. Ann., 1966, Kathleen Grumbacher medal C. L. Wolfe Club, 1970. Mem. Grand Central Art Galleries, Portraits, Inc., Nat. Arts Club. Am. Artists Profl. League, Nat. League Am. Pen. Women. Address: 76 Western Ave Albany NY 12203 also Malden Bridge NY 12115 also Ajijic Jalisco Mexico

WARREN, CAROL HORTENSEN, librarian; b. Motley, Minn., Sept. 5, 1919; d. Horton Alonzo and Madge Kathryn (Webster) Mosher; B.A., Eastern Nazarene Coll., 1963; M.A., Boston U., 1965; M.S. in L.S., Simmons Coll., 1967; postgrad. U. N.H., 1968-69; m. Robert Harold Warren, Nov. 20, 1940; children—Robert Joseph, Patricia Carol (dec.), John Horton, Judith Lynn. With Mass. Assn. for Blind, Boston, 1962, 64; tchr. Woodward Sch., Quincy, Mass., 1963-64; with Boston Pub. Library, 1965-66; asst. reference librarian Bentley Coll., Waltham, Mass. 1966-67; asst. librarian Colby Sawyer Coll., New London, N.H., 1967-70, N.H. Tech. Inst., Concord, 1970-71; reference librarian, asst. prof. Stonehill Coll., North Easton, Mass., 1971-74, asst. dir., 1974—; faculty Bridgewater (Mass.) State Coll., 1973. Chmn. bd. trustees Landsdowne Condominiums, 1976-78. NSF grantee Dartmouth Coll., 1969. Mem. AAUP, Am. Com. for Irish Studies, Am. Hist. Assn., ALA, New Eng. Library Assn., New Eng. Library Info. Network (task force govt. documents), Phi Alpha Theta, Phi Delta Lambda. Baptist. Home: PO Box 548 New London NH 03257 Office: Stonehill Coll Library North Easton MA 02356

WARREN, LOUIS BANCEL, lawyer; b. Monmouth Beach, N.J., Aug. 30, 1905; s. Schuyler Neilson and Alice Edith (Binsse) W.; B.A. with honors in Jurisprudence, Trinity Coll., Oxford U., 1927; M.A., D.J., Columbia U., 1930; m. Rosalie Watson, June 9, 1934; children—Hope Wilberforce (Mrs. Charles E. Shaw), Rosalie Starr (Mrs. Paul S. Byard), Louis Bancel. Admitted to N.Y. bar, 1930; asso. Larkin, Rathbone & Perry, now Kelley Drye Warren, N.Y.C., 1930-40, mem. firm, 1940—. Mem. compensation com., dir. Chrysler Corp., 1957-76; dir. Chrysler France; dir. Chrysler U.K. Ltd., Chrysler Espana, Hammerson Holdings (U.S.A.), Inc., Am. European Assos., Inc. Sec. bd. dirs., pres. Am. Ditchley Found., 1962-73; bd. dirs. France-Am. Soc.; bd. visitors Columbia Law Sch., 1953-77; trustee Homeland Found.; exec. com. Correctional Assn. N.Y. Served with 101st Cav., N.Y. N.G., 1927-30; with USCG, 1943-45; participant strategy discussions U.S. Naval War Coll., 1966. Decorated comdr. Order Brit. Empire; chevalier French Legion of Honor; knight comdr. Order of St. Gregory the Gt. (Vatican); Officer's Cross of Merit, Sovereign Order of Malta; officier Ordre des Arts et des Lettres (France). Fellow Pierpont Morgan Library, 1962—; hon. fellow Columbia U., 1978. Mem. Assn. Bar City N.Y., Internat., Am., N.Y. State bar assns., Am. Judicature Assn., Am. Soc. Internat. Law, St. Nicholas Soc., Pilgrims Soc., St. George's Soc., French Inst., Alliance Francaise, English-Speaking Union. Clubs: Century Assn., Knickerbocker, Racquet and Tennis (N.Y.C.); Somerset Hills Country, Somerset Lake and Game (Bernardsville, N.J.); Detroit. Contbr. articles to legal jours. Home: Ballantine Rd Bernardsville NJ 07924 Office: 350 Park Ave New York City NY 10022

WARREN, ROBERT AULENBACH, engr.; b. Phila., Feb. 11, 1942; s. Myron Maskell and Grace Gaynor (Aulenbach) W.; B.S., Webb Inst., 1965; M.S., Drexel U., 1970; postgrad. U. So. Calif., 1975—; m. Christine Franklin Vail, Sept. 18, 1965; children—Robert Douglas, Cynthia Grace. Marine engr. Phila. Naval Shipyard, 1965-68; pres. Robert A. Warren Marine Consultants, 1969—; gen. engr. Naval Air Engrng. Center, Phila., 1968-73, cyrogenic sect. head, 1968-71, long-range planning engr., 1971-73; gen. engr., asst. for program appraisal Research and Tech. Group, also VSTOL aircraft/ship interface mgr. Naval Air Systems Command, Washington, 1973—, chmn. middle mgmt. council, 1977-78. Pres., Timber Hill Homeowner's Assn., Turnersville, N.J., 1970-71; vestryman St. Christopher's Episcopal Ch., 1978—. Mem. Am. Boat and Yacht Council, Soc. Naval Architects and Marine Engrs., Am. Soc. Naval Engrs., Navy League, Am. Soc. Pub. Adminstrn. Republican. Home: 7916 Springfield Village Dr Springfield VA 22152 Office: Naval Air Systems Command Research and Technology Group Washington DC 20361

WARREN, SKIP OWEN, constrn. co. exec.; b. Tulsa, Nov. 25, 1931; s. Clarence Albert and Betty (Palmer) W.; B.A., Okla. State U., 1953; J.D., U. Tulsa, 1960; m. Carol Ann Smith, Dec. 8, 1961; children—Scott Alan, Storme Lawrence, Skip Richard, Gary Dennis. Admitted to Okla. bar, 1960; atty. advisor U.S. Army C.E., Tulsa, 1960-64, chief counsel, engr. dist., Sacramento, 1964-66, asst. gen. counsel, Washington, 1966-67, chief counsel, engr. div., Ohio River, Cin., 1967-73; v.p., counsel Perini Corp., Framingham, Mass., 1973—. Served with USAF, 1955-58. Named Fed. Profl. Employee of Year, Fed. Exec. Bd., Cin., 1971. Mem. Am. (pub. contracts sect., forum com. on constrn.), Fed., Okla., Mass. (pub. contracts sect.) bar assns., Am. Arbitration Assn., Soc. Am. Mil. Engrs., Phi Alpha Delta, Beta Theta Pi. Democrat. Presbyterian. Contbr. article to profl. jour. Home: 19 Woodland St Sherborn MA 01770 Office: 73 Mt Wayte Ave Framingham MA 01701

WARSHAVSKY, BELLE BENNETT (MRS. HENRY WARSHAVSKY), educator; b. N.Y.C., Apr. 14, 1917; d. Maurice and Sarah (Brown) Bennett; B.B.A., St. Johns U., 1940; M.S., Hofstra Univ., 1957; postgrad. Bernard Baruch Sch. Bus. Adminstrn., 1949; N.Y. U., 1962; profl. diploma reading, 1965; Ph.D., Walden U., 1975; m. Henry Warshavsky, Feb. 22, 1941; children—Barry Alyn, Beth, Benes. Pvt. sec. real estate div. Home Owners Loan Corp., N.Y.C., 1935-39; personnel interviewer N.Y. State Arsenal, Bklyn., 1940-41; brokerage agt. Mut. Trust Life Ins. Co., N.Y.C., 1950-55; instr. Central Sch. Dist. No. 4, Plainview, N.Y., 1955-60, cons. reading, 1961—, dir. Summer Reading Sch., 1965-66; instr. reading Dist. in Service Course, 1962—, Kindergarten Workshops, 1961-63, Reading Clinic, Hofstra U., 1965-66; adj. instr. Queensborough Community Coll., 1970—. Leader, Girl Scouts U.S.A. 1940-42; instr. 1st aid Adults Civil Def., 1941; welfare commr. Saddle Rock Civic Assn., 1962—. Mem. Nat. Soc. Study Edn., NEA, N.Y. State, Nassau County tchrs. assns., Classroom Tchrs. Assn. (v.p., sec. 1958-60), Great Neck Edn. Assn., Nassau County, Internat. reading assns., Internat. Platform Assn., Sigma Tau Delta. Contbg. author: The Non-Graded Primary—A Case History, 1966. Home: 35 Cooper Dr Great Neck NY 11023 Office: Central Sch Dist No 4 Plainview NY 11803

WARSHAWSKY, ALBERT, accountant; b. Asbury Park, N.J., Oct. 2, 1935; s. Harry and Eva (Holland) W.; B.B.A., U. Mich., 1957, M.B.A., 1958; m. Felicia Dawn Jacob, Aug. 14, 1966; children—David Sereno, Leah Vanessa. Sr. accountant Apfel & Englander, C.P.A.'s, N.Y.C., 1959-65; mgr. Price Waterhouse & Co., N.Y.C., 1965—. Served with USMCR, 1958. Mem. Am. Inst. C.P.A.'s, N.Y. State Soc. C.P.A.'s, Beta Alpha Psi, Alpha Epsilon Pi. Home: 200 E 78th St New York City NY 10021 Office: 153 E 53d St New York City NY 10022

WARSLEY, PAUL DANIEL, publishing co. exec.; b. Pa., June 18, 1916; s. Paul and Catherine W.; certificate accounting Fairleigh Dickinson Coll., 1956; m. Elizabeth Fitzgerald, Oct. 3, 1942; children—Janice Elizabeth, Daniel Paul. Bus. mgr. Auxilium Latinum Mag., Elizabeth, N.J., 1945-60; dir. Nat. Latin Honor Soc., Wheaton, Md., 1960—. Served with U.S. Army, 1942-45. Mem. Nat. Property Adminstrn. Assn., Retired Tchrs. Assn., Toastmasters Internat. Roman Catholic. Home: PO Box 6008 Wheaton MD 20906 Office: 17900 Georgia Ave Olney MD 20832

WARWICK, DONALD PHILLIP, educator; b. Rogers City, Mich., June 10, 1934; s. Howard John and Winifred Marie (Smillie) W.; B.S., Sacred Heart Coll., 1954-56; M.A., U. Detroit, 1956-58; Ph.D., U. Mich., 1958-63; m. Ellen Rita Donohue, Aug. 29, 1959; children—Christopher John, Elizabeth Winifred, Margaret Mary. Study dir. Survey Research Center, U. Mich., Ann Arbor, 1964-66; dir., lectr. comparative program Harvard, 1967-71; prof. sociology York U., Toronto, Ont., Can., 1971-75, prof. sociology, adminstr. studies, 1975-76; fellow Harvard Inst. Internat. Devel., 1976—; project mgr. Inst. Soc. Ethics, Life Scis., 1973—. Trustee Latin Am. scholarship program Am. Univs., 1972-75, chmn. bd. trustees, 1973-74. NSF fellow. Mem. Am. Sociol. Assn., Soc. Psychol. Study Social Issues. Democrat. Roman Catholic. Author: A Theory of Public Bureaucracy, 1975. Office: 1737 Cambridge St Harvard Inst Internat Devel Cambridge MA 02138

WASDYKE, JACK CONRAD, ednl. adminstr.; b. Passaic, N.J., Jan. 7, 1942; B.S. in Social Scis., Fairleigh Dickinson U., 1964; M.A. in Remedial Reading, William Paterson Coll., Wayne, N.J., 1968; married; 2 children. Tchr. English, Union City (N.J.) Pub. Schs., 1964-67; reading coordinator Pascack Valley Regional Sch. Dist., Hillsdale, N.J., 1967—; instr. Bergen Community Coll., Paramus, N.J., 1971-72 1971-72; dist. assessment coordinator Pascack Valley Regional Sch. Dist., Hillsdale, N.J., 1973-77; prin. Franklin Sch., Saddle Brook (N.J.) pub. schs., 1977—. Certified tchr. Mem. Pascack Valley Regional, Bergen County, N.J., Nat. edn. assns., Bergen County Elem. Sch. Prins. Assn., Kappa Delta Pi. Home: 59 Spindler Terrace Saddle Brook NJ 07662 Office: Franklin Sch Caldwell Ave Saddle Brook NJ 07662

WASE, ARTHUR WILLIAM, physicist; b. Jersey City, Nov. 16, 1919; s. Charles Louis and Martha Maud (Francois) W.; B.A., Columbia U., 1947; Ph.D., Rutgers U., 1951; Ph.D. (hon.), U. Del Caucua (Colombia), 1962; m. J.P. Francey, Sept. 1, 1941; children—Peter Ives, Cheryl Louise. Asso. prof. Hahnemann Med. Coll., 1952-61, prof. biochemistry, 1962—; Fulbright prof. U. Bruxelles and Inst. Jules Bordet, 1956-57; mgr. biosci. Colgate Company, 1961-63; sr. research fellow, health physicist research labs. Merck Sharpe & Dohme, Rahway, N.J., 1963—; cons. radiation RCA. Served with U.S. Army, 1941-45, 47. Recipient medal of Honor, U. Bruxelles, 1957; citation Inst. Jules Bordet, 1957. Mem. AAAS, Am. Cancer Soc., Am. Heart Assn., Am. Nuclear Soc., Health Physics Soc., N.J. Acad. Sci. Contbr. articles in field to profl. jours. Home: 213 Valentine St Highland Park NJ 08904 Office: Merck Inst PO Box 2000 Rahway NJ 07065

WASHINGTON, CRAIG STEPHEN, educator; b. Chgo., Jan. 22, 1949; s. Charles and Anna Lee (Lott) W.; B.S. in Environ. Health and San. Sci., Ind. State U., 1971; M.S. in Agy. Counseling, Ind. State U., 1973; Ed.D. in Counseling Psychology, U. Mass., 1976; m. Gloria Faye Wise, Aug. 21, 1971. Group leader H. Ralph Johnston Regional Youth Community, Terre Haute, Ind., 1972-73; community mental health worker Katherine Hamilton Mental Health Center, Terre Haute, 1973-75; counselor educator U. Mass., Amherst, 1975-76; chmn. health and pub. services No. Va. Community Coll., Alexandria, 1976—; instr. Johns Hopkins U., Balt.; cons. Acad. for Ednl. Devel., Washington. Mem. Am., Va. personnel and guidance assns., Assn. Specialists in Group Work, Va. Assn. Specialists in Group Work, Assn. of Non-White Concerns. Contbr. articles to profl. jours. Office: 3001 N Beauregard St Alexandria VA 22311

WASHINGTON, WALTER E., former mayor Washington; b. Dawson, Ga., Apr. 15, 1915; s. William L. and Willie Mae (Thornton) W.; A.B., Howard U., 1938, LL.B., 1948; postgrad. Am. U., 1939-43; LL.D., Fisk U., Georgetown U., 1968, Catholic U., Boston U., 1969, George Washington U., Princeton U., 1970; L.H.D., Bishop Coll., 1970; J.D., Washington Coll. (Md.), 1972, Ind. Central Coll., 1972, Boston Coll., 1972, Carnegie-Mellon U., 1973, Howard U., 1974, Trinity Coll., 1974; m. Bennetta Bullock; 1 dau., Bennetta Hayward. Admitted to D.C. bar, 1948, U.S. Supreme Ct. bar, 1952; with Nat. Capital Housing Authority, Washington, 1941-66, exec. dir., 1961-66; chmn. N.Y.C. Housing Authority, 1966-67; apptd. mayor commr. Washington, 1967-75, mayor, 1975-78; mem. adv. bd. U.S. Conf. of Mayors; vice chmn. Nat. League of Cities. Mem. ins. panel Nat. Adv. Commn. on Civil Disorders; v.p. United Community Funds and Councils Am.; trustee John F. Kennedy Center for Performing Arts; bd. dirs. Washington Council Chs., Washington area Boy Scouts Am., United Planning Orgn., Big Bros. Am. Recipient Alumni award Howard U., 1963; Career Service award Nat. Civil Service League, 1965; Archdiocesan award, 1968; award NCCJ; Nat. Bar Assn. award; Health and Welfare Council award; Distinguished Service awards Howard U. Law Alumni Assn., 1974, Capitol Press Club, 1974; Silver Beaver award Boy Scouts Am., 1973; Nat. Jewish Hosp. award for outstanding service, 1973. Mem. Am. Bar Assn., Washington Urban League (dir.), Order of Coif. Democrat. Clubs: Masons (32 deg.); Cosmos, Federal City (Washington), Nat. Lawyers; City N.Y. Home: 408 T St NW Washington DC 20001

WASHIO, HIROSHI, physician; b. Nagaoka, Niigata-ken, Japan, Jan. 1, 1932; s. Kakuho and Hiro W.; came to U.S., 1958, naturalized, 1975; student U. Chiba (Japan), 1951-53; M.D., Tokyo Med. and Dental U., 1957; m. Yachio Inagaki, May 17, 1958. Teaching fellow in plastic surgery Health Center Hosps. of U. Pitts., 1964-66; asso. plastic surgeon Tokyo Met. Police Hosp., 1966-69; asst. attending surgeon St. Luke's Hosp. Center, N.Y.C., 1969—; instr. clin. surgery Columbia U., 1970—. Recipient 1st prize Scholarship Contest, Ednl. Found. of Am. Soc. Plastic Surgeons, 1968. Mem. A.C.S., Am. Soc. Plastic and Reconstructive Surgeons, N.Y. County Med. Soc. Clubs: Nippon, Met. (N.Y.C.). Contbr. articles to profl. jours. Home: 45 E 89th St New York City NY 10028 Office: 580 Park Ave New York City NY 10021

WASKO, MATTHEW FRANCIS, educator; b. Martin, Pa., Jan. 11, 1914; s. Michael and Mary (Rusnak) W.; B.A., Waynesburg Coll.; M.Ed., U. Pitts., 1952; m. Merline Bakewell, June 29, 1940; children—Byron Matthew, Mark Stephen. High Sch. tchr., Brownsville (Pa.) High Sch., 1941-79, chmn. biology dept., 1941-79. Chmn., Citizens Adv. Com., 1973-74. Served with USMC, 1942-45, lt. col. Res. ret. Named Tchr. of Year, Radio Sta. KQV, Pitts., 1950; named to Waynesburg Coll. Football Hall of Fame, 1976. Mem. NEA, Res. Officers Assn., Pa. Sch. Edn. Assn., Coaches Assn. (past pres.), Am. Legion (past post comdr.), VFW. Author: Poems-Mine May Become Yours, 1976. Home: 709 Howard St Brownsville PA 15417

WASSERMAN, JACK, lawyer; b. N.Y.C., Feb. 20, 1913; s. Samuel and Sabine (Hoffman) W.; A.B., Coll. City N.Y. 1932; J.D. cum laude, Harvard U., 1935; m. Marie Krempa, June 7, 1941; children—Lorraine DeVera, Michael Owen. With Harvard Legal Aid Soc., 1934-35; admitted to N.Y. bar, 1936, D.C. bar, Pa. bar, U.S. Supreme Ct. bar, Bd. Immigration Appeals, ICC, FCC; practiced in N.Y., 1936-41; atty. Bd. Immigration Appeals, 1941-42; sr. atty. Alien Enemy Control Unit, 1942-43; mem. Bd. Immigration Appeals, 1943-46; atty. Alien Enemy Litigation Sect., 1946-47; asst. gen. counsel Citizens Com. on Displaced Persons, 1947-48; partner firm Wasserman, Orlow, Ginsberg & Rubin, Washington. Mem. Assn. Immigration and Nationality Lawyers (former nat. pres., legis. rep.), N.Y. State, D.C., Pa., Fed., Am. bar assns., Nat. Lawyers Club, Phi Beta Kappa. Author: Immigration Law and Practice. Contbr. articles on immigration to mags. Home: 4405 Sedgwick St Washington DC 20016 Office: 1707 H St NW Washington DC 20006

WASSERMAN, MARVIN DAVID, pharm. co. exec.; b. Bklyn., Aug. 29, 1933; s. Abraham and Bella (Tessler) W.; B.S., L.I. U., 1955; M.S., Columbia U., 1957. Dir. quality assurance Sterling Drug, N.Y.C., 1959-67; corporate dir. quality assurance Endo Labs. div. E. I. duPont De Nemours & Co., Inc., Garden City, N.Y., 1967-70; v.p., dir. scientific and regulatory affairs, quality assurance ops. Am. Home Products, Whitehall Labs., div. N.Y.C., 1970—; teaching fellow Columbia U., N.Y.C., 1955-57. Vice chmn. fund raising com. Columbia U., 1965-67, mem. trustee nominating com., 1969-70; cons. for drug quality control UN, 1967-68. Served with USAR, 1958-64. Licensed pharmacist, N.Y., N.J., Fla. Mem. Am. Pharm. Assn., Acad. Pharm. Sci., Mfg. Control Sect. of Proprietary Assn., Soc. Cosmetic Chemists, Rho Chi, Phi Beta Kappa, Sigma Xi. Contbr. articles in field to profl. jours. Home: 36-25 Parsons Blvd Flushing NY 11354 Office: 685 Third Ave New York City NY 10017

WASSERMAN, RUTH, nurse; b. N.Y.C., Aug. 28, 1930; d. Harry and Dora W.; R.N., Bellevue Hosp., N.Y.C., 1948; B.S., Hunter Coll., N.Y.C., 1955; M.A., N.Y. U., 1958. Staff nurse Morrisania Hosp., N.Y.C., 1948-49, dir. nursing, 1969-76; charge nurse, supr.-tchr. Hosp. Joint Diseases, N.Y.C., 1951-55; supr., asst. dir. nursing Met. Hosp., N.Y.C., 1956-69; asso. exec. dir. nursing service and edn. Met. Hosp. Center, 1977—; sec. Morrisania Hosp. Community Bd., 1972-76. Served with Army Nurse Corps, 1949-50. WHO fellow, 1970. Mem. Am. (council nursing facilitators), N.Y. State (sec. dirs. nursing practice and service) nurses assns., Pub. Health Assn., Am. Hosp. Assn., Am. Soc. Nursing Services Adminstrs., Deans and Dirs. Greater N.Y., Bellevue Hosp., Hunter Coll., N.Y. U. alumni assns. Office: 1901 1st Ave New York City NY 10029

WASSERSTROM, STEVEN, investment analyst; b. Wilkes-Barre, Pa., Nov. 26, 1947; s. Samuel and Ruth (Bell) W.; B.S. in Accounting, Wilkes Coll., Wilkes-Barre, 1969; m. Wanda Paula Scheuer, Oct. 4, 1970; children—Rachel May, Heather Ann. Dir. research Sartorius & Co., N.Y.C., 1969-72; with Grenel & Co., N.Y.C., 1972-73; with Gruntal & Co., N.Y.C., 1973-78, asst. mgr. option dept., 1975-77; with L. F. Rothschild, Unterberg, Towbin, Hackensack, N.J., 1978—; tchr. N.Y. U. Certified fin. planner; chartered fin. analyst. Mem. N.Y. Soc. Security Analysts (sr.), Fin. Analyst Fedn. Contbr. articles to profl. jours. Home: 25 Willow Ln Tenafly NJ 07670 Office: LF Rothschild Unterberg Towbin Continental Plaza 411 Hackensack Ave Hackensack NJ 07601 Hackensack Ave Hackensack NJ 07601

WASSON, WILLIAM GEORGE, oil co. exec.; b. Bradford, Pa., Sept. 10, 1918; s. Albert Dorr and Fleury Clara (Morris) W.; student pub. schs., Bradford; m. Betty Jean Irons, July 10, 1940; children—William Barry, Thomas Lee. With Felmont Oil Corp., Olean, N.Y., 1968—, v.p., 1978—; automobile dealer, 1937-68; air taxi operator, 1964-70; pres. Wasson Motors Inc., Olean, 1967—, Jadeland Devel. Inc., Olean, 1967—; v.p. Chrysler Dealer Advt. Assn., 1960-68. Pres. Olean United Fund, 1958-72, Seneca council Boy Scouts Am., 1960-61; mem. Olean Bd. Edn., 1955-60, Olean Planning Commn., 1968. Served with USAAF, 1942-45. Recipient Silver Beaver award Boy Scouts Am., 1960. Mem. Am. Petroleum Inst., Pa. Oil and Gas Assn., N.Y. State Oil Producers Assn., Olean C. of C. (v.p., dir. 1952—; Community Service award 1972), N.Y. State Auto Dealers Assn. (v.p. 1952-68). Republican. Methodist. Clubs: Bartlett, Rotary (past pres. Olean), Shriners. Home: 1605 Stardust Ln Olean NY 14760 Office: 1446 Buffalo St Olean NY 14760

WASTIE, ARTHUR EDWARD, gas engr.; b. Bklyn., Aug. 7, 1909; s. Harry W. and Margaret (Bennett) W.; B.S., Villanova U., 1932; gas engr. Columbia, 1935; m. Clotilde M. Monaghan, Sept. 21, 1935; children—Peter A., Catherine (Mrs. John J. Gleason), Margaret A. (Mrs. Robert Comba), Christopher E. Distbn. and sales engr. Bklyn. Union Gas Co., 1932-44; indsl. sales engr., mgr. Phillips Petroleum Co., 1944-51; v.p., chief engr. Thomas Assos., 1951-57; v.p., chief engr. Drake & Townsend, Inc., 1957-66; chief engr. N.Am. Utility Constrn. Corp., N.Y.C., 1966-73; pres. A.E. Wastie & Assos., Inc., cons. engr., 1973—. Pres. Community Players, Inc., 1974-76; mem. adv. bd. Manhattan Coll. Registered profl. engr. Mass., N.Y., N.J., Ill., N.C., S.C., Ga., Va., Ill. Mem. Nat. Soc. Profl. Engrs., ASME, Am. Gas Assn. Contbr. articles to profl. jours. Patentee in gas systems. Home and office: 643 Dorian Rd Westfield NJ 07090

WAT, JAMES KAM-CHOI, jeans mfg. co. exec.; b. Hong Kong, Sept. 9, 1949; s. Biu and Yuk-ping (Tang) W.; gen. certificate of edn., New Method Coll., U. London, 1969; m. Miranda K. Leong, Oct. 6, 1974; 1 son, Bryan K. Sales exec. Tonan Mdse. (H.K.) Ltd., Hong Kong, 1969-70; asst. bus. exec. Texwood Ltd., Hong Kong, 1970-72, asst. mgr., 1972-74, sales mgr., 1974-77; bus. mgr., gen. mgr. Texwood Inc. (U.S.A.), N.Y.C., 1977—; v.p. Jive Sportswear, Inc., N.Y.C., 1978—. Home: 17 Capi Ln Port Washington NY 11050 Office: 1441 Broadway Suite 1440 New York City NY 10018

WATANABE, KYOICHI ALOISIUS, chemist; b. Amagasaki City, Japan, Feb. 28, 1935; s. Yujiro Paul and Yoshiko Francisca (Hashimoto) W.; B.A., Hokkaido U., 1958, M.A., 1960, Ph.D., 1963; m. Kiyoko Agatha Suzuki, Nov. 22, 1962; children—Kanna, Kay, Kenneth, Kim, Kelly, Katharine. Came to U.S., 1963. Lectr., Sophia U., Tokyo, 1963; research asso. Sloan Kettering Inst. for Cancer Research, N.Y.C., 1963-66, Rye, N.Y., 1968-72, asso. mem., 1972—. Research fellow U. Alta., Edmonton, 1966-68; asso. prof. Sloan-Kettering div. Cornell U. Med. Coll., N.Y.C., 1972—. Mem. Pharm. Soc. Japan, Am. Chem. Soc. Contbr. to profl. jours. Home: 28 Wilton Rd Port Chester NY 10573 Office: Sloan Kettering Inst 145 Boston Post Rd Rye NY 10580

WATANABE, RUTH, librarian; b. Los Angeles, May 12, 1916; d. Kohei and Iwa (Watanabe) Watanabe; B.Mus., U. So. Calif., 1937; A.B., 1939, A.M., 1941, M.Mus., 1942; student Eastman Sch. of Music, Rochester, N.Y., 1942-46, Columbia, 1947; Ph.D., U. Rochester, 1952. Instr. piano, music theory, Los Angeles, 1934-41; counsellor and personnel work Eastman Sch. Music, U. Rochester, 1943-46, instr. music history, 1946-62, asso. prof. musicology, 1962-78, prof., 1978—; program annotator Am. Music Festival, 1956-71, dir. music library workshop, 1957—; program annotator Rochester Philharmonic Orch., 1959—; staff mem. in charge of circulation Sibley Music Library, Rochester, 1943-47, acting librarian, 1947-58, librarian 1948—; instr. English, U. Rochester, 1946-47; cons. music libraries, 1968—; adj. prof. Sch. Library Sci., State U. Coll. at Geneseo, 1975—. Contbr. adult edn. program Rochester Civic Music Assn., 1963-75. Lectr. on music; book reviewer, 1966—. Mem. Am. Assn. U. Women (Pa.-Del. fellowship 1949-50, 1st v.p. Rochester 1964-65, mem. N.Y. State bd. 1965-66, mem. nat. com. on soc.'s reflection in arts 1967-69, nat. com. Am. fellowships awards 1969-74, br. pres. 1969-71), Internat. Assn. Music Libraries (2d v.p., commn. on conservatory libraries), Am. Musicol. Soc., Music Library Assn. (v.p. 1968-70, mem. editorial bd. 1967—, pres.-elect 1978—), ALA, Civic Music Assn. Rochester, Dorcas chpt. YWCA, Phi Beta Kappa (pres. Iota of N.Y. chpt. 1977-78), Phi Kappa Phi, Mu Phi Epsilon (gen. chmn. nat. conv. 1956, nat. librarian 1958-60), Pi Kappa Lambda (sec.-treas. chpt. 1975—), Delta Phi Alpha, Epsilon Phi, Delta Kappa Gamma (v.p. Eta chpt. Pi State 1972-76). Club: Soroptimist (chmn. N. Atlantic Conf. 1961, pres. 1964-66). Author: Introduction to Music Research, 1967; Madrigali-Il Verso, 1978. Editor Scribners New Music Library, vols. 2, 5, 8, 1973. Contbr. articles to jours. Home: 111 East Ave #610 Rochester NY 14604 Office: Eastman Sch Music Rochester NY 14604

WATERHOUSE, GARY GEORGE, retail food chain exec.; b. McKeesport, Pa., Jan. 23, 1942; s. George Henry and Hazel Rhoda (Stevens) W.; B.A., Grove City Coll., 1963; m. Alice Adele Wilcox, Oct. 15, 1966; children—Camille Alice, Chrstie Adele. Mgmt. trainee Three Rivers Bank & Trust Co., 1965-66; with Great A & P Tea Co., Inc., various locations, 1966—, internal auditor, 1970-72, asst. treas. Altoona div., 1972-73, treas. Pitts. div., 1974-75, controller, 1976-77, regional mgr. fin. reporting and analysis, Keystone office, Valley Forge, Pa., 1977—, also sec. exec. bd. Chmn. finance and stewardship com. Wilson United Presbyn. Ch., 1972, elder, 1972—. Served with USN, 1963-65. Home: 110 W Glamorgan Ct Exton PA 19341 Office: PO Box 841 Valley Forge Plaza Valley Forge PA 19481

WATERHOUSE, KEITH, surgeon, educator; b. Derby, Eng., May 10, 1929; s. Arthur R. and Marion (Tock) W.; came to U.S., 1953, naturalized, 1964; B.A., Cambridge (Eng.) U., 1950; M.B., Oxford U. Med. Sch. 1953; M.A., 1957; m. Anne Therese Milotzky, Jan. 14, 1955; children—Katherine Anne, Vincent, Maria Ursula, Isabelle, Christopher. Intern, Bklyn. Hosp., 1953-54; resident Kings County Hosp., Bklyn., 1957-59; practice medicine specializing in urol. surgery, Bklyn., 1959—; instr. surgery State U. N.Y., Bklyn. 1959-61, asst. prof., 1961-62, asso. prof., 1962-65, prof. surgery, 1965-69, head div. urology, 1962-69, prof., chmn. dept. urology, 1969—; dir. urology Kings County Hosp., Bklyn., 1962—; cons. urology St. Mary's Hosp., Passaic, N.J., Samaritan Hosp., Bklyn., St. Charles Hosp., Port Jefferson, N.Y., Bklyn. VA Hosp., St. Francis Hosp., Poughkeepsie, N.Y., Arden Hill Hosp., Goshen, N.Y., Brookhaven Meml. Hosp., Patchogue, N.Y., Jewish Hosp. Bklyn., Luth. Med. Center, Columbus Hosp., N.Y.C., Wyckoff Hosp. Bklyn. Served to capt. M.C., Royal Army, 1955-57. Recipient William H. Burpeau award N.J. Acad. Medicine, 1973; diplomate Am. Bd. Urology. Mem. Am. Acad. Pediatrics (pres. sect. on urology 1976), Bklyn. Urol. Soc. (pres. 1966-67), N.Y. State Med. Soc., Internat. Soc. Urology, Am. Urol. Assn. (pres. N.Y. sect. 1971-72, mem. coordinating council 1975-76), Genitourinary Surgeons. Contbr. articles to med. jours. Office: 450 Clarkson Ave Brooklyn NY 11203

WATERMAN, DONALD CALVIN, designer, educator; b. Erie, Pa., Aug. 17, 1928; s. Mark Calvin and Gladys L. (Aikens) W.; diploma Cleve. Inst. Art, 1952; B.F.A., Syracuse U., 1957, M.F.A., 1959; m. Virginia Ann Wressell, Sept. 6, 1952; children—Catherine Ann, Mark Del, Robert Calvin. Instr. art Mexico City Coll., 1953; chief designer Industrias Ruiz Galindo S.A., Mexico D.F., 1953-55; instr. indsl. design Syracuse (N.Y.) U., 1955-60, prof. fabric design, 1960—, resident adviser Semester in Mex., Cholula, 1973, London Art Program, 1976-77, Textile Arts Summer Session, London, 1978, chmn. dept. textile arts, 1970—; resident designer U.S. Pavillion, Internat. Trade Fair, Zagreb, Yugoslavia, summer 1956, Bari, Italy, summer 1957, Lima, Peru, summer 1959; partner Waterman Design, Manlius, N.Y., since 1969—; work commd. by F. Schumacher & Co., Riverdale Fabrics, Cohama Fabrics (all N.Y.C.), S.M. Hexter Co., Cleve., Maharam Fabric Corp., Haphauge, N.Y., Imperial Wallcoverings, Cleve., Sunworthy Wallcoverings Ltd., Toronto, Ont., Can., Liberty of London, Warner & Co., London. Served with U.S. Army, 1946-48. Mem. Surface Design Assn., AAUP. Unitarian. Home: 7398 Silverwood Dr Manlius NY 13104 Office: 407 Lyman Hall Syracuse U Syracuse NY 13210

WATERMULDER, DAVID BRAINERD, clergyman; b. Sioux City, Iowa, Nov. 16, 1920; s. Gustav A. and Henrietta (Hospers) W.; A.B., U. Kans., 1942; postgrad. Union Theol. Sem., 1942; B.D., Princeton Theol. Sem., 1945, Th.M., 1947; postgrad. Mansfield Coll., Oxford, Eng., 1953; D.D., Parsons Coll., 1955; LL.D., Davis and Elkins Coll., 1973; m. Ruth Jane Gullyes, July 20, 1946; children—Paul Gustav, Peter Joseph, Martha Ruth. Ordained to ministry Presbyn. Chs., 1945; pastor, Hightstown, N.J., 1945-50, Watertown, N.Y., 1950-55, Oak Park, Ill., 1955-62, Bryn Mawr, Pa., 1962—; vis. lectr. McCormick Theol. Sem., 1956-62; pres. United Presbyn. Bd. Nat. Missions, 1963-73; mem. gen. council, 1962, mem. judicial commn., 1957-62. Trustee Presbyn.-U. Pa. Med. Center, Princeton Theol. Sem., Wilson Coll., Pathway Sch., A.D. Mag. Named Exchange Preacher Gt. Britain Nat. Council Chs., 1953, Nat. Ch. Preacher United Presbyn. Delegation, World Council Chs., 1968. Author: Proclamation for Advent, 1974. Home: 121 Fishers Rd Bryn Mawr PA 19010 Office: 625 Montgomery St Bryn Mawr PA 19010

WATERS, CHARLES EDWARD, mktg. co. exec.; b. Phila., Aug. 22, 1950; s. Charles Edward and Marion Louise (Williamson) W.; B.S. in E.E., Villanova U., 1972. Lead programmer Valley Forge Labs., Devon, Pa., 1970-72; applications programmer UNI-COLL Corp., Phila., 1973; systems programmer, 1973-76, mgr. interactive systems, 1976-78; mgr. systems and data processing DSG, Inc., Phila., 1978—. Office: 1737 Chestnut St Philadelphia PA 19103

WATERS, FRANCIS P., investment adviser; b. N.Y.C., Apr. 21, 1931; s. Francis J. and Nora (Hegarty) W.; B.A. cum laude, St. John's Coll., 1953; LL.B., St. John's U., 1955; LL.M., Columbia, 1956; m. Nuala M. Kilbride, Oct. 2, 1965. Admitted to N.Y. bar, 1956, U.S. Supreme Ct. bar, 1960; asso. firm Barr, Robbins & Palmer, N.Y.C., 1960-61, Hawkins, Delafield & Wood, N.Y.C., 1961-64; individual law practice, N.Y.C., 1964-67. Chmn. bd. Internat. Investment Counsellors, 1967—. Served as 1st lt. Judge Adv. Gen.'s Corp., AUS, 1957-60. Mem. Am. Bar Assn., N.Y. State Bar Assn. Home: 45-49 41st St Long Island City NY 11104 Office: 1 Hainault Park Foxrock Dublin 18 Ireland

WATERS, LEWIS THOMAS, urban and regional planner; b. Dallas, July 6, 1939; s. Lewis Boyd and Grace Louise (Sprau) W.; B.A., B.S., Rice U., 1962; M.Arch., Harvard U., 1964; M.Community Planning and Area Devel., U. R.I., 1966; Ph.D. in Urban and Regional Planning, U. Edinburgh (Scotland), 1970; m. Patricia Kingsbury Lane, Aug. 25, 1973. Archtl. designer with archtl. and engring. firms in Dallas, Houston and Boston, 1960-65; urban designer The Planning Services Group, Boston, 1965; planning cons., Kingston, R.I., 1965-66; planning designer Freeman-Fox/Wilber Smith Assos., Edinburgh, 1968-69; planning cons. Dere St. Design Group, Edinburgh, 1970; dir. urban studies Nat. Capital Planning Commn., Washington, 1971-72; urban and regional planner Fed. Dept. Town and Country Planning, Kuala Lampur, Malaysia, 1972-73; chief systems planning D.C. Govt. Office Municipal Planning, 1973-78; dir. planning, resources and energy tech. Advanced Tech., Inc., McLean, Va., 1978—; lectr. univs. U.S. and abroad; mem. Potomac River Basin Conf., 1975—; alt. mem. D.C. Water Resources Planning Bd., 1975-78. Black-Brollier scholar, 1960. Mem. Internat. City Mgrs. Assn. Contbr. articles to profl. jours. Office: 1329 E St NW Suite 600 Washington DC 20004

WATERS, THOMAS LYLE, univ. adminstr.; b. Susquehanna, Pa., Mar. 11, 1929; s. Theodore E. and Lucile (Taylor) W.; B.E.E., Youngstown State U., 1953; M.S. in Systems Mgmt., Fla. Inst. Tech., 1973; M.S. in Edn., U. So. Calif., 1975; Ph.D., Am. U., 1979; m. Evelyn Yvonne Miller, June 11, 1956; children—Wendy May, Timothy Alan. Commd. 2d lt. U.S. Army, 1953, advanced through grades to lt. col., 1968; chief staff 13th Splty. Brigade, 1972-73; ret., 1976; asst. dir. continuing engring. edn. George Washington U., D.C., 1977-79; coordinator Center Student Career Services Rensselaer Poly. Inst., 1979—. Commr. Boy Scouts Am., scouting program chmn., camp dir., substaining membership enrollment chmn., neighborhood commr., active Sea Explorer com. Recipient Medal Appreciation Boy Scouts Korea, 1975; registered profl. engr. Mem. Am. Guidance And Personnel Assn., Am. Coll. Personnel Assn., Nat., Tex. socs. profl. engrs., Soc. Logistics Engrs., Am. Def. Preparedness Assn., Soc. Am. Mil. Engrs., Assn. U.S. Army. Lutheran. Clubs: Mt. Vernon Tennis World. Developer first math. model evaluation ABM system. Home: PO Box 459 West Sand Lake NY 12196 Office: Center Student Career Services Rensselaer Poly Inst Troy NY 12181

WATERS, WILLIAM ERNEST, microelectronics exec.; b. Toronto, Ont., Can., Aug. 18, 1928; s. Charles Lacy and Margaret (Boulden) W.; B. Applied Sci., U. Toronto, 1950; m. Evelyn Elizabeth Phillips, Jan. 18, 1952; children—Kenneth Geoffrey, Brian Gregory, Kimberly William. Gen. mgr. Hoskins Alloys of Can. Ltd., Toronto, 1953-59; pres. Waters Metal Products Ltd., Niagara Falls, Ont., 1960—, Waters Metal Products, Inc., Buffalo, 1960-69, Watmet Inc., Buffalo, 1968—; pres. Microtectonics Inc., 1969-71. Served with RCAF, 1946-52. Mem. Engring. Inst. Can., Ont. Assn. Profl. Engrs., Can. Soc. Elec. Engring., Mfrs. Agts. Nat. Assn. (dir. 1973-77), Internat. Soc. Hybrid Microelectronics, Beta Theta Pi. Club: Niagara Falls Golf and Country. Home: 5060 Woodland Dr Lewiston NY 14092

WATKINS, ANNE LOUISE, nursing adminstr.; b. Staten Island, N.Y., June 12, 1936; d. Dennis Franklon and Cora Julia (McCulley) Grady; degree in practical nursing, Central Sch. Practical Nursing, 1951; A.Applied Sci., Staten Island Community Coll., 1969; B.A. in psychology with honors, Richmond Coll., 1976, postgrad. 1977; m. Thomas Watkins, Nov. 3, 1956; children—Thomas Michael, Stephen, Phyllis Anne. Licensed practical nurse Greenpoint Gen. Hosp., Bklyn., 1956, S.I. Devel. Center, 1959-67, staff registered nurse, 1969-70, head nurse, 1970-71, supr. nurse adminstr., 1971-77; dir. nursing United Cerebral Palsy Assn., Inc., Unit 6 at Karl D. Warner Devel. Center, S.I., 1977—; condr. nursing seminars for nurses at Willowbrook Devel. Center. Recipient Award of service S.I. Devel. Center; Certificate of Merit, N.Y. State Suggestion No. 35,073. Mem. S.I. Community Coll. Alumni Assns., Richmond Coll. Alumni Assn. Mem. Mt. Calvary Holy Ch. of Am. Address: 146 Pheasant Ln Willingboro NJ 08046

WATKINS, DONALD THOMAS, univ. adminstr.; b. Wilkes Barre, Pa., Apr. 3, 1943; s. Charles William and Elizabeth (Connors) W.; B.S., Bloomsburg State Coll., 1964; postgrad. Newark Coll., 1965-66; M.S., N.C. A. and T. State U., 1972; postgrad. Trenton State Coll., 1970-71; Ed.D., Pa. State U., 1976. Tchr. biology Jamesburg (N.J.) High Sch., 1964-67, Carteret (N.J.) High Sch., 1967-72; coordinator student teaching Pa. State U., University Park, 1974-75, adminstrv. asst. for academic affairs, McKeesport, Pa., 1975-76, coordinator, regional Latin Am. student teaching program C.Z., 1976—. NSF fellow, 1969-71. Mem. Nat. Assn. for Research in Sci. Teaching, Nat. Assn. Biology Tchrs., Assn. Tchr. Educators, Phi Delta Kappa, Phi Kappa Phi. Home: 245 Boland Ave Wilkes Barre PA 18702 Office: Pennsylvania State U University Park PA 16802 also Box 536 Balboa CZ

WATKINS, EUGENE LEONARD, surgeon; b. Worcester, Mass., Jan. 4, 1918; s. George Joseph and Marcella Katherine (Akels) W.; A.B. with honors in biology, Clark U., 1940; M.D. (Hood scholar), Harvard U., 1943; m. Victoria Peake, Sept. 23, 1944; children—Roswell Peake, Priscilla Avery. Intern Roosevelt Hosp., N.Y.C., 1944; resident in surgery, 1944-46, sr. asst. resident in surgery, 1948-49, resident surgery, 1949-50; fellow in surgery, clin. research fellow, Mass. Gen. Hosp., Boston, 1947-48; practice medicine specializing in surgery, N.Y.C., 1950-56, Morristown, N.J., 1950—, Denville, N.J., 1956—, Boonton, N.J., 1961—; mem. staff Morristown Meml. Hosp., 1950, vice chmn. dept. surgery, 1974-76, chmn., 1959-61; cons. surgeon St. Clare's Hosp., Denville, N.J., Riverside Hosp., Boonton, N.J., Community Med. Center, Morristown; courtesy surg. staff Roosevelt Hosp., N.Y.C.; asst. clin. prof. surgery Rutgers U. Coll. Medicine and Dentistry, New Brunswick, N.J., 1972—; v.p. chmn. finance com. Morristown Bd. Health, 1954-56. Served to 1st lt., AUS, 1946. Diplomate Am. Bd. Surgery. Fellow A.C.S. (chmn. N.J. Adv. Com. 1965-77, chmn. N.J. State com. Trauma, 1960); mem. N.J., Morris County med. socs., AMA, Am. Thoracic Soc., AAAS, Harvard Med. Soc. N.Y. (pres. 1960-61), West Side Med. Soc., Roosevelt Hosp. Alumni Assn. Republican. Presbyn. Clubs: Harvard (N.Y.C.), Morristown, Morristown Field. Development spring-loop surg. suture holder. Home: Spring Valley Rd Morristown NJ 07960 Office: 2 Franklin Pl Morristown NJ 07960

WATKINS, GLENN AMOSS, JR., architect; b. Baltimore County, Md., May 3, 1921; s. Glenn Amoss W.; student U. Fla., 1943, Johns Hopkins U., 1953-56; grad. Md. Inst., Balt., 1947; m. Daisy Adele Lehman, June 27, 1944; children—Barbara Joyce Watkins Aiken, Karen Lea Watkins Webner, Kimberly Glenn Watkins Ford. With archtl. firms in Balt., 1947-59; founder, 1959, propr. firm, Balt.; prin. works include Washington County Office Bldg., Howard County Office Bldg., also libraries in Howard County, Randallstown, Parkville, Perryhall, Cambridge, Woodlawn. Pres., dir. Kingsville Vol. Fire Dept.; bd. dirs. Kingsville Coordinating Council. Served to 1st lt., fighter pilot USAAF, 1942-46; PTO. Mem. AIA, Balt. Engring. Soc., Northeastern Library Assn. (v.p., dir.), Engring. Soc. Howard County, Bldg. Congress and Exchange Balt. Democrat. Methodist. Clubs: Kingsville Rotary (pres., dir.); Balt. Aero. Home: 11944 Jerusalem Rd Kingsville MD 21087 Office: 11944 Jerusalem Rd Kingsville MD 21087

WATKINS, PHILLIP LEWIS, electronic engr.; b. Gaithersburg, Md., July 30, 1924; s. Grover Cleveland and Florence Mae (Foster) W.; B.E.E., George Washington U., 1950. Electronic engr. Naval Research Lab., Washington, 1951—, spl. projects Office Dir. of Research, 1973-76, space systems div., 1976—; mem. Electronics Internat. Adv. Panel, 1974, 75. Mem. nat. adv. bd. Am. Security Council, 1970, 73; patron Radio Free Asia, 1970, 71; sponsor Nat. Right to Work Found., 1973. Served with USNR, 1943-46, 50-51; PTO, Korea. Mem. IEEE, Naval Res., Navy League, Am. Def. Preparedness Assn., AAAS, V.F.W. Patentee electronics. Home: 1101 Brooke Dr Rockville MD 20851 Office: Naval Research Lab Code 7560 Washington DC 20375

WATKINS, ROBERT GOODMAN, motor transp. co. exec.; b. St. Helena, Md., June 26, 1921; s. George Robert and Hilda Jane (Smerbeck) W.; B.S. in Bus. Adminstrn., Pa. Mil. Coll. (name changed to Widener Coll. 1972), 1942; m. Hilda Govers West, Oct. 10, 1942; children—Robert G., George Elgin. Vice pres. Blue Line Transfer Co., Inc., Chester, Pa., 1946-53, chmn., 1970—; pres. Watkins System, Inc., Chester, 1953-78, chmn., 1978—; partner Apollo Devel. Co., Chester, 1969—; mem. pres.'s council Gen. Motors Corp., 1962, 77. Served to maj., Transp. Corps., AUS, 1942-46. Mem. Teamsters Union (life, hon.), Quiet Birdmen. Clubs: Ocean Reef (Key Largo, Fla.); Radley Run Country (West Chester, Pa.). Home: Winhill RD 5 West Chester PA 19380 Office: Watkins System 2d and Palmer Sts Chester PA 19016

WATLINGTON, JOSEPH, JR., ins. broker; b. Phila., Aug. 22, 1924; s. Joseph and Susie (Banks) W.; B.A., Temple U., 1947; m. Marion Spencer, July 9, 1949; children—Joseph Richard, Leigh Ellen. Visitor, social worker Pa. Dept. Pub. Assistance, Phila., 1947-48; ins. salesman N.C. Mut. Life Ins. Co., Phila., 1948; with Watlington & Cooper, Phila., 1948—, pres., 1967—; pres. Personnel Resources, Inc., 1974—; chmn. Nat. Urban Ins. Co., 1971-74; broker 1st Pa. Bank Ins. cons. Sch. Dist. Phila., others; instr. Community Coll. Phila., 1972. Vice pres. Afro-Am. Hist. and Cultural '76 Bicentennial Corp. Phila. Bd. dirs., pres. Lighthouse, 1971-72; bd. dirs. Urban Studies Center, LaSalle Coll., 1969-72, Nat. Bonding Service Found., 1969-75, Upward Exec. Tng. Inst., Afro-Am. Hist. and Cultural Museums. trustee W. Kuhn Day Camp, Coll. Settlement Phila.; pres. Black Unitarian-Universalist Caucus Delaware Valley, 1970-71; chmn. The Citizens, Phila. Allied Action Commn.; treas. Edn. to Work Council. Served with AUS, 1943-45. Mem. Nat. Assn. Ins. Agts. and Brokers, Pa. Assn. Ins. Agts., Mutual Assn. Ins. Agts., Tri-State Assn. Ins. Agts., Ins. Soc. Phila. (dir.), Greater Phila. C. of C. (dir.), Alpha Phi Alpha. Unitarian (past trustee, ann. fund chmn.). Clubs: Downtown, Urban (Phila.). Home: 6447 Magnolia St Philadelphia PA 19119 Office: 3734 Germantown Ave Philadelphia PA 19140

WATMAN, JEROME, profl. engr.; b. N.Y.C., May 30, 1934; s. Sol and Rebecca B. (Charmatz) W.; B.S.C.E., U. Ala., 1959; M.S.C.E., N.Y.U., 1966; m. Gloria Weiss, Mar. 29, 1958; children—Aaron H., Richard M., Marcie E. Engr., N.Y. Water Services, Long Island, 1959-62, Metcalf & Eddy, N.Y.C., 1962-63; sr. engr. Buck, Seiffert & Jost, Englewood Cliffs, N.J., 1963-64; chief engr. Elam & Popoff Cons. Engrs., Glen Rock, N.J., 1964-69; asso. and chief engr. Lee T. Purcell Assos., Paterson, N.J., 1969—. Served with U.S. Army, 1954-56. Registered profl. engr., N.Y., N.J., Fla. Mem. ASCE, Am. Water Works Assn. Chi Epsilon. Jewish. Home: 2 N Eckerson Ln Spring Valley NY 10977 Office: 60 Hamilton St Paterson NJ 07505

WATSON, ALFRED MICHAEL, bishop; b. Erie, Pa., July 11, 1907; s. Thomas and Catherine (Fahey) W.; student Gannon Coll., Erie, 1925-27; A.B., St. Mary U., Balt., 1928, A.M., 1930, S.T.B., 1934. Ordained priest Roman Cath. Ch., 1933; prof. Mercyhurst Coll., Gannon Coll., 1934-44; rector St. Peter Cathedral, 1944-69; aux. bishop, Erie, 1965-69, bishop, 1969—. Address: 205 W 9th St Erie PA 16501

WATSON, ARTHUR RICHARD, zoo dir.; b. Cleve., June 25, 1915; s. George Henry and Martha Helen (Ratensperger) W.; student Cleve. Coll., Western Reserve U.; m. Marybeth Wiemer Anderson, Nov. 2, 1967; 1 dau. by previous marriage—Lois Ruth Watson Ferber. Asst. to dir. Cleve. Zoo, 1942-48; dir. Balt. Zoo, 1948—; master of ceremonies, producer TV program, This Is Your Zoo, 1949-59, 71-72, Radio Zoo program, Sta. WCAO, 1966-76; incorporator, bd. trustees Wild Animal Propagation Trust. Mem. at large bd. dirs. Boy Scouts Am., 1976. Recipient McCormick award, 1949; certificate of merit, TV Guide, 1952-53; Notable Service award, Advt. Club of Balt., 1954; Hats Off award, DeMolay, 1956; commendation Am. Legion, 1958, 68; citation U.S. Hall of Fame Soc., 1968. Mem. Am. Assn. of Zool. Parks and Aquariums, Balt. Zool. Soc., Audubon Soc., Variety Club (treas. 1962), Sierra Club, Md. Press Club, Balt. Pub. Relations Council. Unitarian. Clubs: Kiwanis (bd. dirs. 1953) (Hampden-Mt. Wash.); St. Georges Soc. of Balt., The Timber Ridge Bassets (Hanpstead, Md.); Six Napoleona (Sherlockian Literary Soc.); Order of DeMolay (past-master-counsellor, Coeur de Lion chpt.), Md. Sportsmen's Luncheon (pres. 1977-78). Zool. editor: Parks and Recreation mag., 1952-53. Home: 4700 Forest Park Ave Baltimore MD 21207 Office: Druid Hill Park Baltimore MD 21217

WATSON, EDWIN BEN, mech. engr.; b. Titusville, Pa., Mar. 23, 1918; s. Harold Benson and Bessie (Leary) W.; B.M.E., U. Rochester, 1939; M.S. in Engring., Cornell U., 1943; m. Betty E. Bemont, Feb. 14, 1941; children—Judith, Elizabeth, Sarah, Mary, Robert. Asso. prof. mech. engring. Cornell U., Ithaca, N.Y., 1946-59; chief engr.-diesel Bendix Corp., Sidney, N.Y., 1959-65, mgr. diesel products, 1965—; cons. mech. engr., 1946-59. Pres. bd. mgrs. Sidney Hosp., 1970—; bd. dirs. Sidney United Way, 1975-78, Health Systems Agy. N.E. N.Y., 1976—. Registered profl. engr., N.Y. Mem. Sidney C. of C. (dir. 1972-77), ASME, Soc. Automotive Engrs., Phi Beta Kappa, Tau Beta Pi. Methodist. Club: Rotary (past pres. Sidney). Patentee diesel fuel injection. Home: 35 W Main St Sidney NY 13838 Office: Bendix Corp Sidney NY 13838

WATSON, JACK HEARN, JR., lawyer, govt. ofcl.; b. El Paso, Tex., Oct. 24, 1938; s. Jack Hearn and Winifred (Milliron) W.; B.A., Vanderbilt U., 1960; LL.B., Harvard U., 1966; m. Teena Stern Mohr; children—Melissa, Lincoln. Admitted to Ga. bar, 1965; asso. firm King & Spalding, Atlanta, 1966-71, partner, 1972-77; asst. to Pres. for intergovtl. affairs, sec. to Cabinet, Washington, 1977—; counsel Met. Atlanta Commn. on Crime and Juvenile Deliquency, 1966-67. Mem. Fulton County Mental Health Adv. Com., 1968-70; mem. Citizens Adv. Council on Urban Devel., 1970-72; pres. Met. Atlanta Mental Health Assn., 1971-72; chmn. Ga. Gov.'s Study Commn. on Alcohol, 1971-72, Ga. Alcoholism Adv. Council, 1972; chmn. bd. Ga. Dept. Human Resources, 1972-77; nat. fin. dir., chmn. Ga. fin. campaign Jimmy Carter's Presdl. Campaign; head policy planning office Carter-Mondale Campaign, head Carter/Mondale Transition, 1976-77. Served as officer USMC, 1960-63. Mem. Am., Ga., D.C. bar assns., Phi Beta Kappa, Phi Eta Sigma, Omicron Delta Kappa. Office: The White House Washington DC 20500

WATSON, MARY STONE, educator; b. Marcellus, N.Y., May 24, 1909; d. James Horace and Ethel (Cowles) Stone; B.Oral English, Syracuse U., 1931; M.A., U. Md., 1965; m. Harry P. Watson, June 27, 1936; children—Ruth Watson Lancaster, Robert S., Rollin J., Harry P., Douglas J., Donald M., Sara L. High sch. tchr. English, speech, drama, N.Y., Pa., Md., 1931-37, 62-64; asso. prof. speech Essex Community Coll., Baltimore County, Md., 1965-78, prof., 1978—, also head speech and drama dept.; lectr., condr. workshops in communications, 1965—; faculty in parent and child communication YMCA. Home: 108 W 39th St Apt 8 Baltimore MD 21210

WATSON, THOMAS JONES, III, communications co. exec.; b. Pitts., Mar. 28, 1932; s. Thomas J. and Anna (Stack) W.; B.S., U. Pitts., 1954; m. Patricia L. Zoll, Apr. 4, 1953; children—Thomas Jones IV, LuAnn. With AT&T Co., Pitts. and N.Y.C., 1956-69, account mgr., 1962-64, supr. mktg., 1964-69; asst. v.p. mktg. Western Union Tel. Co., Upper Saddle River, N.J., 1969-78; v.p. major accounts mktg. Northern Telecom Inc., Nashville, 1978—. Served with U.S. Army, 1954-57. Mem. Am. Mgmt. Assn. Republican. Episcopalian. Clubs: Ramsey Golf and Country, Fiddlers Elbow Country, Masons. Home: 263 Canterbury Dr Ramsey NJ 07446 Office: 163 Morristown Rd Bernardsville NJ 07924

WATSON, WILBUR HENRY, gerontologist, educator; b. Cleve., Apr. 14, 1938; s. Lovest Lee and Marjorie Christine (Williford) W.; B.A., Kent State U., 1964, M.A., 1966; Ph.D. (NIMH fellow), U. Pa., 1972; m. Shirley Lucy Washington, June 17, 1960; children—Stephen, Sheryl Lynn. Coordinator survey research and group work services for adolescents League Pk. Center, Hough Area, Cleve., 1965-66; instr. sociology Kent State U., 1966-67; lectr. sociology Lincoln U. (Pa.), 1968; designer, supr. field research Center for Research on Acts of Man, U. Pa., 1968-69; asso. prof. sociology Cheyney (Pa.) State Coll., 1969-70; asst. prof. sociology Rutgers Coll., 1970-74, Temple U., Phila., 1973-77; research dir. Nat. Center on Black Aged, 1977—; prof., chmn. sociology and anthropology Morgan State U., 1978—; cons. Transcentury Corp., Washington, 1967, State U. N.Y., 1974, Phila. Bd. Edn., 1975; research sociologist, cons. Stephen Smith Geriatric Center, Phila., 1970—; research adviser Phila. Geriatric Center, 1970-73. Chmn. steering com. Project Learn, Exptl. Elementary Sch., Phila., 1970-71. Nat. Endowment for Humanities fellow Princeton, 1972-73. Mem. Gerontol. Soc., Nat. Caucus on Black Aged (a founder), Am. Sociol. Assn., Soc. Sci. Study Social Problems, Am. Acad. Arts and Scis., Assn. Stud African Am. Life and History, Assn. Social and Behavior Scientists, Assn. Black Sociologists. Democrat. Baptist. Clubs: Nucleus (Cleve.); Poor Richards (Phila.). Author: (with R.J. Maxwell) Human Aging and Dying, 1977; Stress and Old Age, 1979. Editor Black Sociologist quar., also Caucus Black Sociologists' Newsletter, 1975—; contbr. articles to profl. lit.

WATT, JAMES D., fin. cons.; b. N.Y.C., Dec. 20, 1946; s. Douglas Benjamin and Ray (Mantel) W.; B.A. in English, Iona Coll., 1969. Former asso. editor Scholastic Mags., N.Y.C.; pres. Re-Inovations Ltd., N.Y.C., 1974-76; account exec. Merrill, Lynch, Pierce, Fenner & Smith, N.Y.C., 1977-78, Oppenheimer & Co., N.Y.C., 1978—. Tchr., vol. with Pres. Johnson's War on Poverty Program, Elmsford, N.Y., 1965-66; contbr. J.O.B. program, N.Y.C. Democrat. Roman Catholic. Home: 132 W 88th St New York City NY 10024 Office: One New York Plaza New York City NY 10004

WATT, RICHARD MARTIN, author, corp. exec.; b. La Grange, Ill., Nov. 10, 1930; s. Richard R. and Gertrude (Martin) W.; A.B., Dartmouth Coll., 1952; m. Sandra Elizabeth Fitch, July 11, 1953 (div. Aug. 1970); children—Kimberly Anne, Linda Kathryn, David Rockwell; m. 2d, Nancy Johnstone Clure, Sept. 16, 1972. Advt. mgr. Crossfield Products Corp., Roselle Park, N.J., 1955-64, sales mgr., 1964-67, corp. sec., 1967-72, v.p., 1972—, also dir. Served to lt. (j.g.) USNR, 1952-55. Mem. Am., British hist. assns., French Inst., Fgn. Policy Assn., Co. Mil. Historians, Conf. Group Central European History. Clubs: Glen Ridge Country; Dartmouth College. Episcopalian. Author: Dare Call It Treason, 1963; The Kings Depart, 1969; Future Indefinite. Home: 211 Forest Ave Glen Ridge NJ 07028 Office: Mountainside Rd RD #2 Mendham NJ 07945

WATT, THOMAS LORNE, dermatologist; b. Denver, July 14, 1935; s. Sherman A. and Lois M. (Hitt) W.; A.B., Dartmouth Coll., 1957; M.D., Harvard U., 1960; m. Mette Arup, Aug. 22, 1959; children—Charles Thomas, Sherman A., Kathryn A. Intern, Mary Hitchcock Meml. Hosp., Hanover, N.H., 1960-61; resident, Dartmouth Med. Sch. affiliated hosps., Hanover, 1961-65; staff dermatologist Monroe (Wis.) Clinic and clin. instr. dermatology U. Wis., Madison, 1965-68, 70-71; practice medicine, specializing in dermatology, Bangor, Maine, 1971—; head, sect. dermatology Eastern Maine Med. Center, Bangor, 1975—; adv. bd. rep. Nat. Program for Dermatology, 1973—. Mem. Orono (Maine) Traffic Safety Com., 1977; bd. dirs. Penobscot Valley Regional Health Planning Bd., 1974-75. Served with U.S. Army, 1968-70. Decorated Bronze Star. Diplomate Am. Bd. Dermatology. Fellow Am. Acad. Dermatology; mem. Penobscot County Med. Soc., Maine Med. Soc., AMA, New Eng., Atlantic dermatologic socs. Republican. Episcopalian. Club: Penobscot Valley. Author: (with Andrew Ognibine) History of U.S. Army Medical Corps, 1969. Home: 18 Lexington Rd Orono ME 04473 Office: 263 State St Bangor ME 04401

WATTS, GLENN ELLIS, union ofcl.; b. Stony Point, N.C., June 4, 1920; s. George Dewey and Nellie Viola (Ellis) W.; student Wilson Tchrs. Coll., 1938-41; m. Bernice Elizabeth Willett, Nov. 8, 1941; children—Glenn Ellis II, Sharon Elizabeth Ann Watts Cardany, Marianne Elizabeth Watts Cardany. With Chesapeake & Potomac Telephone Co., Washington, 1941-48; with Communication Workers Am. (formerly Nat. Fedn. Telephone Workers), 1942—, pres. div. 36, Washington, 1948-51, dir. dist. 2, 1951-56, asst. to pres., 1956-65, v.p., 1965-69, v.p. indsl. union dept. AFL-CIO, 1968—, sec.-treas. union, 1969-74, pres., 1974—; v.p., exec. council AFL-CIO, 1974—. Past treas. Washington Housing Assn.; Past chmn. James E. West dist. Nat. council Boy Scouts Am., 1969-71, Silver Beaver award, 1965; past mem. Home Rule for D.C. Com.; pres. Health and Welfare Council of Nat. Capitol Area, 1967-69; mem. Postal Tel. and Tel. Internat., v.p., 1978—; gen. chmn. United Giver's Fund, 1968-70, pres., 1971-75; chmn. exec. com. United Way of Am., 1971-78; mem.-at-large Democratic Nat. Com., 1974—; trustee, sec.-treas. Am. Inst. Free Labor Devel., 1974—; governing bd., treas. Nat. Urban Coalition, 1970—; hon. vice chmn. Am. Trade Union Council for Histadrut, 1974—; trustee Nat. Planning Assn., 1974—, Ford Found., 1975—, Aspen Inst., 1978—; mem. President's Commn. on Mental Health, 1978, President's Commn. on the Holocost, Trilateral Commn., 1976—, Helsinki Watch Com., 1978—; bd. dirs. New Directions, 1978—, Alliance To Save Energy, 1977—, Am. Productivity Center, 1978—. Democrat. Methodist. Home: 3929 Oliver Chevy Chase MD 20015 Office: 1925 K NW St Washington DC 20006

WATTS, HERBERT ERROL, mfg. co. exec.; b. Bklyn., June 18, 1928; s. Errol Fredrick and Iris Watts (Marshall) W.; midshipman U.S. Mcht. Marine Acad., 1947-50; student Columbia U., 1960-61, C.W. Post Coll., 1962-64; m. Blanche Rita Popiolek, May 29, 1954; children—Iris Mary, Dana, Lisa Marie. With GTE Met. Lab. & Lighting Co., various locations, 1952—, mgr. nuclear engring., 1968-75, v.p. engring. mfg. and materials internat., 1975—; dir. Kondo Electric Co., Nippon Electric Co. Sylvania, Metaldyne Co. Bd. dirs. Northport Methodist Ch. Served to lt. USNR, 1954-57; Korea. Mem. Am. Soc. Metals, ASME, Am. Mgmt. Assn. Home: 23 Crooked Pond Dr Boxford MA 01921 Office: 100 Endicott St Danvers MA 01923

WATTS, RAYMOND DAY, lawyer; b. Cin., Oct. 24, 1924; s. Thomas Raymond and Dorothy Mildred (Day) W.; B.A., Antioch Coll., 1949; J.D., Georgetown U., 1953; m. Anne Pennybacker, June 18, 1948; 1 dau., Kathryn. Reporter, Niles (Ohio) Daily Times, 1949-50; asst. to U.S. Rep. James G. Polk, 1950, 54; profl. staff mem. House Spl. Com. to Investigate Campaign Expenditures, 1952, counsel, 1956; admitted to D.C., Md. bars, 1954; pvt. law practice, Washington, 1954-58, 78—; counsel Senate Small Bus. Com., 1958-74, gen. counsel, 1975-77; of counsel firm Blum, Parker & Nash, Washington, 1978—. Chmn., Rockville (Md.) Bd. Appeals, 1963-71; sec. bd. dirs. Pennybacker Found., 1965-73; trustee Antioch Coll., 1974-75; mem. Am. Vets. Com. Served with AUS, 1943-46. Decorated Combat Inf. badge. Mem. Am., Inter-Am., Fed. bar assns., Solar Energy Industries Assn., Solar Energy Inst. Am., Am. Solar Energy Assn., Friends of Earth. Home: 2264 Glenmore Terr Rockville MD 20850 Office: Suite 408 1015 18th St NW Washington DC 20036

WATTS, WARREN WAYNE, minister, pastoral counselor; b. Severn, Md., Apr. 27, 1940; s. James Henry and Lula Idella (Sherman) W.; A.B., Western Md. Coll., 1962; M.Div., Wesley Theol. Sem., Washington, 1966; m. Patricia Ann Cross, Apr. 6, 1963; children—Warren Keith, Deborah Ann. Ordained to ministry, 1963; ordained elder, full conf. mem., Balt. Conf. United Methodist Ch., 1966; chaplain intern Springfield (Md.) State Hosp., 1961, Md. Reformatory for Women, Patuxent (Md.) Inst. for Men, 1962, Sibley Meml. Hosp., Washington, 1965; pastoral counselor Washington Pastoral Counseling Service, 1970—; dir. Tri County Pastoral Counseling Service, Martinsburg, W.Va., 1973—. Mem. Am. Assn. Marriage and Family Counselors (supr.), Am. Assn. Clin. Pastoral Educators, Am. Assn. Pastoral Counselors. Clubs: Lions, Ruritan. Co-author: Getting It Said and Done, 1973; First Letter of John, 1973; Deeper Furrows, 1976; contbr. prayers to Minister's Manual 1973. Home: 8 Decker Ave Hagerstown MD 21740 Office: 222 W Burke St Martinsburg WV 25401

WAUGH, BASCOM SLEMP, physician; b. Glade Springs, Va., Dec. 9, 1908; s. Wiley Benjamin and Gillyard (Johnson) W.; B.S., Morgan State Coll., 1930; M.D., Meharry Med. Coll., 1935; postgrad. U. Pa., 1952-53; m. Alberta Inez Foye, Dec. 20, 1943; 1 dau., Dianne Anita. Intern, Freedmens Hosp., Washington, 1935-36; practice medicine specializing in internal medicine, Camden, N.J.; staff Cooper Hosp.; dir. medicine Camden County Hosp. Complex; asst. in medicine Jefferson Med. Coll., 1957, instr. medicine, 1962—, asso. in clin. medicine, 1966-70, asst. prof. clin. medicine, 1970—. Served as capt. USAAF, 1942-46. Diplomate Am. Bd. Internal Medicine. Fellow A.C.P.; mem. AMA, Am. Heart Assn., Nat. Med. Assn., Aerospace Med. Assn. Home: 352 Bellevue Ave Haddonfield NJ 08033 Office: 1882 S 10th St Camden NJ 08104

WAWAK, PHYLLIS JANE, chemist; b. Yonkers, N.Y., Apr. 10, 1938; d. Stephen and Anna (Kostesky) W.; B.S., Coll. Mount St. Vincent, 1960; postgrad. Hunter Coll., 1963-65, 76; M.A., U. Iowa, 1962. Chemist, Sloan Kettering Inst., N.Y.C., 1960-62; with N.Y. U. Med. Sch., N.Y.C., 1963, Union Carbide Research Inst., 1965-68, SunChem., Carlstadt, N.J., 1968-72, Columbia Coll. Physicians and Surgeons-N.Y. State Psychiatric Inst., N.Y.C., 1973-76, Aspen Systems, N.Y.C., 1977—. Mem. Am. Inst. Chemists. Catholic.

WAXMAN, HERBERT JACOB, accountant; b. N.Y.C., Jan. 19, 1913; s. Isidore and Alice (Jacobowitz) W.; student N.Y. U., 1929, Coll. City N.Y., 1930, 38; m. Vivian Sarah Krischer, May 28, 1939; children—Jill, Jonathan. Jr. accountant Gray, Scheiber Co., C.P.A.'s, N.Y.C., 1931; office mgr. Breslauer & Fliegler, produce dealers, N.Y.C., 1932-40; C.P.A. in individual pvt. practice, N.Y.C., 1940-60, 72-75; partner Waxman, Pepper & Gotbetter, C.P.A.'s, and successors, N.Y.C., 1960-72, Waxman & Goldman, C.P.A.'s, Great Neck, N.Y., 1975—. Mem. budget adv. com. Great Neck Bd. Edn., 1970-71; trustee, dir. Great Neck Library Assn.; founder, trustee, past pres. Temple Emanuel, Great Neck; pres. Margaret Court Civic Assn., Great Neck; bd. dirs. officer N.Y. Quar. Poetry Found. Recipient Distinguished Leadership award Reform Jewish Appeal, 1969; C.P.A., N.Y. Mem. N.Y. State Soc. C.P.A.'s. Contbr. articles on taxes and bus. to trade publs., 1940-74; author: Where Worm Grows Fat, 1975; contbr. poems to lit. jours. Home and Office: 29 Margaret Ct Great Neck NY 11024

WAYMAN, JOHN GEIB, lawyer; b. Pitts., Feb. 2, 1912; s. William Arthur and Wilhemina (Geib) W.; B.A., Washington and Jefferson Coll., 1934; J.D., Duquesne U., 1941; m. Marion McCormick, March 30, 1932; 1 son, John William. Admitted to Pa. bar, 1942, U.S. Supreme Ct. bar, 1963; factory mgr. U.S. Glass Corp., Pitts., 1934-37; traffic and export mgr. Imperial Oil & Gas Products Co., 1938-42; asso. firm Reed, Smith, Shaw & McClay, Pitts., 1942-57, partner, 1957—. Mem. Allegheny County, Pa., Am. bar assns., Am. Judicature Soc., Soc. for Advancement and Mgmt., Am. Def. Preparedness Assn. Republican. Presbyterian. Clubs: Duquesne, St. Clair Country. Home: 2611 Fairgreen Dr Pittsburgh PA 15241 Office: 747 Union Trust Bldg Pittsburgh PA 15219

WAYSON, CHARLES HENRY, communication co. exec.; b. Balt., Jan. 5, 1942; s. Charles Francis and Marian (Berger) W.; B.S., Towson State U., 1974; postgrad. Morgan State U., 1975—; m. Carol Lee Thompson, May 2, 1963; children—Michelle Lynn, Charles Jeffrey, Susan Lynn. With Kane Transfer Co., Balt., 1966-67; with Western Electric Co., Cockeysville, Md., 1967—, program analyst, 1972—, mktg. staff Am. Tel. & Tel., 1977—. Bd. dirs. Rodgers Forge Community Assn., 1968—; precinct exec. Republican party, 1971-74. Served with AUS, 1962-65. Named Towson Jaycee of Yr., 1973-74. Mem. Am. Mktg. Assn., Am. Wine Soc. Roman Catholic. Home: Fawn Dr Clinton Twp Hunterdon County NJ 07921 Office: Am Tel & Tel Bedminster NJ 07921

WEARY, THOMAS SQUIRES, lawyer; b. Junction City, Kans., Feb. 15, 1925; s. Ulysses S. and Ina (Kirkpatrick) W.; A.B. cum laude, Harvard, 1946, LL.B., 1950; m. Helen G. Stephenson, Nov. 25, 1967. Admitted to Pa. bar, 1950; practice law, Phila., 1950—; mem. firm Saul, Ewing, Remick & Saul, Phila., 1961—; dir. Westco, Inc., Thunderbird Petroleums, Inc., Alces Holding, Ltd., Radnor Assos., Ltd., Consol. Producing Co., Consol. Crude Oil Co., Thunderbird Oil & Gas, Inc., Westco Farmlands, Inc., Diamond Asphalt Co., Pay-N-Save Petroleums, Inc., Westland Oil Co., Omni-Exploration, Inc. Lectr. Am. Law Inst., 1964—. Bd. dirs. Acad. Vocal Arts, Phila. Served to lt. (j.g.) USNR, 1945-49. Mem. Scotch-Irish Soc. of U.S. (sec. 1957-72, pres. 1972-74), Hon. Order Ky. Cols., Internat. Platform Assn., Am. Arbitration Assn. (arbitrator). Clubs: Harvard (sec. 1952-56. exec. com. 1962-66), Racquet, Orpheus (Phila.); Merion Cricket (Haverford, Pa.); Edgemere (dir., sec. 1970-74) (Pike County, Pa.). Home: 210 Curwen Rd Rosemont PA 19010 Office: 3800 Centre Sq W Philadelphia PA 19102

WEATHERLY (THOMAS ELIAS WEATHERLY, JR.), poet; b. Scottsboro, Ala., Nov. 3, 1942; s. Thomas Elias and Lucy Belle (Golson) W.; student Morehouse Coll., 1958-60, Ala. & M. Coll., 1960-61, Columbia, 1974; m. Susan Ellene Christoffersen, Dec. 1, 1973; children—Regina Nicholson, Thomas Elias III. Tchr. poetry workshops, N.Y.C., 1967-69; instr. art dept., poetry workshop, Rutgers U., Newark, N.J., 1970; poet-in-residence, Bishop Coll., Dallas, 1970-71, Morgan State Coll., Balt., 1971-72; tchr., poetry in the schs. projects, N.Y.C., Montclair, N.J., 1972-74; dir. Bklyn. Poetry Project, 1973-74; tchr. pub. schs., Somerset, N.J. and Richmond, Va., 1974; poetry tchr. for Free Space, Women's House of Detention, N.Y.C., 1975-76; tchr. Poets in Schs. Program, State of N.Y., 1975—; tchr. Leesburg (N.J.) State Prison, 1978, Poets in Schs. program State of N.J., 1978—; vis. lectr. State U. N.Y., Buffalo, 1977. Chmn. George Schuyler chpt. Young Ams. for Freedom, 1973-75. Mem. Omega Psi. Republican. Mem. First Spinozan Ch. of N.Y. (Eastern grand master 1977—). Author: Maumau American Cantos, 1970; Natural Process, 1970; Thumbprint, 1971. Home: 194 1st Ave New York City NY 10009

WEAVER, DANIEL CONWAY, anesthesiologist; b. Rawson, Ohio, Jan. 6, 1924; s. Paul Herman and Violette Anderson (Conway) W.; B.S., U. Chgo., 1945, M.D., 1947; 1 dau., Alix Lynn. Intern, Butterworth Hosp., Grand Rapids, Mich., 1947-48; Bingham fellow in anesthesiology New Eng. Center Hosp., 1950, resident in anesthesiology, 1950-53; practice medicine specializing in anesthesiology, Boston; asst. chief Anesthesia Sect., VA Hosp., Boston, 1977—; asso. prof. anesthesiology Tufts U. Sch. Medicine, Boston, 1977—. Diplomate Am. Bd. Anesthesiology. Mem. Am. Soc.

Anesthesiologists, New. Eng. Soc. Anesthesiologists, Mass. Soc. Anesthesiologists, Internat. Anesthesia Research Soc. Contributing author: Bulletin Am. Rock Garden Soc., 1969. Home: Apt C907 77 Pond Ave Brookline MA 02146 Office: Boston VA Hosp 50 Huntington Ave Boston MA 02130

WEAVER, DONALD ROBERT, pathologist; b. Mercer, Pa., Mar. 7, 1930; s. Mark Donald and Margaret Evelyn (McClees) W.; student Princeton U., 1948-49; B.S., Allegheny Coll., 1952; M.D., Temple U., 1956; m. Jane Anne Sayre, June 15, 1955; children—Cynthia, Valerie, Amy, Mark, Matthew. Intern, Hamot Hosp., Erie, Pa., 1956-57; gen. practice medicine, Titusville, Pa., 1957-62; fellow in pathology Cleve. Clinic, 1962-66; asso. in pathology Guthrie Clinic, Sayre, Pa., 1966-67, co-chmn. dept. pathology, 1967—, med. dir., 1974—; asso. prof. pathology Hahnemann Med. Coll., Phila., 1972—; instr. pathology Ithaca (N.Y.) Coll., 1973—. Bd. dirs. Donald Guthrie Found. Diplomate Am. Bd. Pathology. Fellow Coll. Am. Pathologists, Am. Soc. Clin. Pathologists; mem. Am. Soc. Hematology, Internat. Acad. Pathology. Presbyterian. Contbr. articles to sci. jours. Home: 710 W Lockhart St Sayre PA 18840 Office: Guthrie Clinic Sayre PA 18840

WEAVER, EDGAR SHELDON, real estate and constrn. exec.; b. Schenectady, June 22, 1925; s. Caius Edgar and Grace Marion (Patterson) W.; B.S. in Civil Engring., U. Okla., 1951; grad. Advanced Mgmt. Program, Harvard U., 1967; m. Jeanne Ann Bisgrove, Sept. 13, 1950; children—Christine A. JoAnn M., Weaver Whitehouse, Nancy L. With Gen. Electric Co., Schenectady, 1951—, resident constrn. mgr., 1965-68, regional constrn. mgr. internat. and spl. projects, 1968—; pres., dir. Gen. Electric Realty Corp. Past pres. PTA. Served with AUS, 1943-46. Registered profl. engr.; licensed realtor. Mem. Nat. Assn. Realtors. Clubs: Elfun Soc., Woodlin Swim and Racquet, Northway Heights Country, Admirals. Author articles in field. Office: Gen Electric Co Bldg 36 1 River Rd Schenectady NY 12345

WEAVER, ELLEN GAIL, educator; b. Providence, Dec. 24, 1954; d. Paul and Barbara Eunice (Wales) Weaver; B.A., R.I. Coll., 1976, M.A., 1978. Staff asst. R.I. Coll., Providence, 1973-76, grad. asst./cons., 1976-77; career coordinator Norton (Mass.) High Sch., 1977—. Mem. Am. Personnel and Guidance Assn., Am. Coll. Personnel Assn., Nat. Vocat. Guidance Assn., R.I. Career Edn. Assn., Phi Alpha Theta. Editor bi-monthly newsletter Mobile Career Edn. Project, 1977. Home: 29 Westfield Rd Warwick RI 02888 Office: Norton High School Norton MA 02766

WEAVER, ERIC JAMES, ednl. adminstr.; b. Purley, Surrey, Eng., May 14, 1938; s. Edward Arthur and Amelia Cecily (Ealden) W.; came to U.S., 1947, naturalized, 1963; A.B. (Univ. scholar), Princeton, 1958; S.T.B., Gen. Theol. Sem., 1961, M.Div., 1972; M.S., City Coll. City N.Y., 1968; profl. diploma Hofstra U., 1973, postgrad., 1973—; m. Joyce Lynn McKean, Aug. 19, 1973; children—Stephanie Lynn, Heather Elizabeth, Jonathan Eric. Research asso. Meadow Brook Nat. Bank, West Hempstead, N.Y., 1957-61; dir. Christian edn. and youth work Ch. of the Holy Cross, Bklyn., 1958-61; vicar, Ch. of the Messiah, Central Islip, N.Y., and St. Michael and All Angel's Ch., Gordon Heights, N.Y., 1961-63; tchr. spl. edn. The Nassau County Vocational Edn. and Extension Bd., N.Y., 1963-67; supr. central adminstrn, Nassau Bd. Coop. Ednl. Services, 1967-70, asst. prin. Rosemary Kennedy Sch. for Trainable Mentally Retarded, Wantagh, N.Y., 1970-73; dir. spl. edn. Middle County Schs., Suffolk County, N.Y., 1973—. Capt., Aux. Police, County of Suffolk, N.Y., 1962-69. Bd. dirs. Traffic Safety Bd., County of Nassau, N.Y., 1969-71, Robin Park Civic Assn., Huntington, N.Y., 1963-66; trustee Police Hall of Fame. Fellow Am. Assn. Mental Deficiency; mem. The Interagency Council on Recreation for the Handicapped (dir. 1970-73), Council for Exceptional Children (pres. 1973-74), Council Adminstrs. Spl. Edn., Internat. Assn. Sci. Study Mental Deficiency, L.I. Assn. Spl. Edn. Adminstrn. (sec. 1975-76, v.p. 1976-77, pres. 1977-78), Assn. Help Retarded Children, Am. Ednl. Research Assn., Am. Assn. Sch. Adminstrs., Sch. Adminstrs. Assn. N.Y. State, Phi Delta Kappa. Republican. Episcopalian. Author monographs: The Sources of the First Gospel, 1958; Rudolf Bultman and Entmythologisierung, 1961; Ocular, Manual, and Podiatric Dominance in a Severely Retarded Older Adolescent Population, 1968. Home: 8 Oceanside Ct Northport NY 11768 Office: 43d St Centereach NY 11720

WEAVER, JOHN ARTHUR, chemist, physician; b. Hemingway, S.C., Nov. 23, 1940; s. Arthur C. and Winnie Mae (Williams) W.; B.S., Va. Union U., 1964; M.S., Howard U., 1968, Ph.D., 1970, M.D., 1978; m. Yvonne Jackson, Dec. 18, 1970. Clin. lab. technician Med. Coll. Va., Richmond, 1964, 65, 66; chemist Dept. Pub. Health, Washington, 1967, FDA, Washington, 1968; asso. prof. chemistry N.C. Agrl. and Tech. State U., Greensboro, 1970-74, 75-78; resident in radiology Howard U. Hosp., Washington, 1979—. Recipient Garnett Ryland award Va. Union U., 1964; NDEA fellow, 1966-68, Am. Chem. Soc. petroleum research fellow, 1969-70, Agrl. and Tech. Ednl. grantee, 1970-71, Piedmont grantee, 1971-72, NSF grantee, 1972-74, NIH grantee, 1972-74, N.C. Bd. Sci. and Tech. grantee, 1972-73. Mem. AAAS, AMA, Student Nat. Med. Assn., Am. Med. Student Assn., N.Y. Acad. Sci., N.C. Acad. Sci., Am. Chem. Soc., Phi Beta Sigma, Beta Kappa Chi. Contbr. articles to profl. jours. Home: 1111 Burketon Rd Hyattsville MD 20783

WEBB, CLIFFORD WELLINGTON, educator; b. Prescott, Ont., Can., May 21, 1925; s. Walter George and Ruby Marguerite (Lake) W.; B.A., U. Western Ont., London, 1951, M.A., 1952; Ph.D. (Sir Joseph Flavelle scholar, Open fellow, Royal Soc. predoctoral fellow), U. Toronto (Ont., Can.), 1956; m. Nellie Myers Thompson, May 21, 1949; children—Marianne Webb Pierrot, Jayne, Thomas. Adminstrv. officer Pub. Service of Can., Ottawa, Ont., 1952-53; instr. philosophy U. Toronto, 1955-56, asst. prof., 1956-60, asso. prof., 1960-76; cons. in field Intendes Research Found., Toronto, 1970—. Served with Royal Can. Air Force, 1943-46. Mem. Can. Philos. Assn., U. Toronto Faculty Assn. Conservative. Mem. Anglican Ch. Club: United Empire Loyalist (Toronto). Contbr. articles in field to Jour. of Philosophy, Maclean's jour., Globe and Mail. Home: 9 Liszt Gate St Apt #513 Willowdale ON M2H 1G6 Canada Office: Dept of Philosophy Univ of Toronto 215 Huron St Toronto ON Canada

WEBB, ELMON DODD, theatrical designer; b. Shreveport, La., Apr. 22, 1936; s. Clarence H. and Dorothy (Dodd) W.; M.F.A., Tulane U., 1961; postgrad. Yale U., 1961-62; m. Virginia Dancy Webb, Aug. 15, 1969; children—John, Larkin. Production designer Long Wharf Theatre, New Haven, 1968-77, Syracuse Stage, 1976-78, Pitt. Pub. Theatre, 1977-78, Nat. Health, N.Y.C., 1976; art dir. CBS TV, 1969-77, NBC TV, 1978—. Mem. Nat. Acad. TV Arts Scis. (bd. govs. 1971-73), United Scenic Artists of Am. (sec.). Photographs of productions appeared in photographic and theatrical mags.; work represented in Contemporary Stage Design, U.S.A., Smithsonian. Home and Office: 105 W 72nd St New York City NY 10023

WEBB, J. RICHARD, appliance co. exec.; b. Orlando, Fla., Feb. 28, 1940; s. L.C. and C.M. (Campbell) W.; B.S. in Indsl. Mgmt., Fla. State U., 1962; postgrad. in Mgmt. Devel., Harvard, 1971; m. Judith A. Paulsen, Dec. 21, 1963: children—Scott R., Craig A. With corporate purchasing program Westinghouse Electric Corp., Pitts., 1963-71, mgr. purchasing home comfort div., Edison, N.J., 1971-73, exec. asst., v.p. mktg. maj. appliance group, 1973-75, dir. bus. planning heating and cooling divs., 1976-77, pres. Luxdire Inc. subs., Elyria, Ohio, 1978—; mgr. nat. distbn. White-Westinghouse Appliance Co., Pitts., 1975-76; pvt. cons. distbn. and purchasing. Mem. Harvard PMD Assn., Nat. Assn. Purchasing Mgmt., Nat. Council Phys. Distbn. Mgmt. Home: 131 Old Orchard Dr Hudson OH 44236 Office: Westinghouse Bldg Room 2181 Pittsburgh PA 15222

WEBB, WILLIAM READING, dentist; b. Phila., June 6, 1896; s. William Reading and Annie (Matchett) W.; D.D.S., U. Pa., 1916; postgrad., 1917; B.S., Temple U., 1918; m. Helene Block, Aug. 25, 1927 (dec. Jan. 1961); m. 2d, Mary V. Carr, Mar. 9, 1962 (dec. June 1969); m. 3d, Theodosia Immekus, Oct. 2, 1969. Practice dentistry, Phila., 1916-23, N.Y.C., 1923-70; vis. oral surgeon Queens Gen. Hosp., N.Y.C., 1935-55, cons. 1955—. Mem. Queens dist. atty.'s adv. bd., 1957; mem. med. adv. bd. SSS, 1940-47. Recipient Selective Service medal U.S. Congress, 1947. Fellow Am. Coll. Dentists, Internat. Coll. Dentists, N.Y. Acad. Dentistry, L.I. Acad. Odontology; mem. Am. (past del.), N.Y. State, 2d Dist., North Queens (charter), Queens Dist. (past pres.), Chgo. dental socs., Am. Denture Soc., Soc. Dentistry for Children, Federation Dentaire Internationale, Pierre Fauchard Acad., N.Y. State Assn. of Professions (charter), Chapala Soc., Associacion des Colonos de Chula Vista, Am. Banjo Frat., Alpha Tau Omega, Psi Omega. Elk. Club: Admirals (N.Y.C.). Address: 34-41 79th St Jackson Heights NY 11372

WEBBER, JOHN BENTLEY, orthopaedic surgeon; b. Morristown, N.J., Jan. 27, 1941; s. George Bentley and Gladys (Moody) W.; B.A., Lehigh U., 1962; M.D., Temple U., 1966; m. Mary Christina Thometz, Feb. 25, 1978. Intern Rochester (N.Y.) Gen. Hosp., 1966-67; resident Temple U. Med. Center, Phila., 1967-70; Sterling Bunnell fellow in hand surgery Pacific Med. Center, San Francisco, 1971; practice medicine specializing in orthopaedic surgery, surgery of hand, Phila., 1973—; chief dept. orthopedic surgery Phila. Gen. Hosp., 1973-76; asso. prof. dept. orthopedic surgery and rehab. Hahnemann Med. Coll. and Hosp., Phila., 1973—, chief sect. on hand surgery, 1973—; cons. in hand surgery Municipal Med. Services, Phila., 1973—; USPHS, Phila, 1973-76; burn center St. Agnes Med. Center, Phila., 1973—. Served to maj. USAF, 1971-73. Fellow Am. Acad. Orthopedic Surgeons, A.C.S.; mem. Am. Soc. for Surgery of the Hand, Eastern, Phila. orthopedic socs., Bunnell Hand Club, Phila. Hand Group, AMA, Pa., Phila. County med. socs., Assn. for Academic Surgery. Republican. Congregationalist. Clubs: Union League (Phila.), Phila. Country, Phila. Athletic. Home: 2200 Delancey Pl Philadelphia PA 19103 Office: 216 N Broad St Philadelphia PA 19102

WEBBER, MICHAEL DAVID, mgmt. cons.; b. Enid, Okla., May 27, 1940; s. Mike and Lorine (Loomis) W.; B.B.A., U. Okla., 1962; M.B.A., U. Pa., 1964; m. Janet Joyce Dodson, June 30, 1962; children—Michael David II, Meredith. Research asst. E.I. DuPont de Nemours & Co., Inc., Phila., 1962-63; research fellow Mgmt. Sci. Center. U. Pa.. 1963-64; mgmt. analyst N.Am. Air Def. Command Hdqrs., Colorado Springs, Colo.. 1964-67; mgmt. cons. A.T. Kearney, Inc., Chgo., 1967-72, prin., 1972-76, v.p., 1976-77, dir., pres. Kearney Mgmt. Consultants Ltd., Toronto, Ont., Can., 1975-77; v.p. Booz, Allen & Hamilton, Inc., N.Y.C., 1977—. Mem. Ravinia Benefit Com., 1969-75. Served to 1st lt. USAF, 1964-67. Mem. Inst. Mgmt. Scis., Operations Research Soc. Am., Am. Mgmt. Assn., Am. Mktg. Assn., Delta Sigma Pi. Club: Milbrook. Home: 18 Woodside Dr Greenwich CT 06830 Office: 245 Park Ave New York City NY 10017

WEBBINK, PATRICIA GLIXON, psychologist; b. N.Y.C., Feb. 13, 1943; d. S. Arthur and Jane (Amberg) Glixon; B.A., Conn. Coll., 1965; M.A., Duke U., 1970, Ph.D., 1974. Asst. dir. Dept. of Recreation Day Camp, Washington, 1963; research asst., infant evaluator Edn. Improvement Project, Durham, N.C., 1965-66, 68; clin. psychologist Prince George's County Health Dept., Cheverly, Md., 1970-71; pvt. practice psychotherapy, Washington area, 1971—; mem. faculty U. Md., 1973, 78, Am. U., 1976, George Washington U., 1977. Certified psychologist, Md.; licensed psychologist, D.C., N.C. Mem. Am., Md., D.C. psychol. assns., Assn. Women in Psychology, Assn. Feminist Therapists. Home: 6033 Broad St Brookmont MD 20016

WEBER, ALFRED LEO, radiologist; b. Fulda, Germany, Sept. 23, 1926; s. Aloys and Anna (Ruhl) W.; came to U.S., 1953, naturalized, 1957; M.D., U. Munich (W. Ger.), 1953; married; children—Rachael, Gloria Jean, Debbie, Chester. Resident in pathology U. Munich Med. Sch., 1952, resident in internal medicine U. Munich Med. Sch. Hosps., 1952-53; rotating intern Toledo Hosp., 1953-54; resident in internal medicine Herman Kieter Hosp., Detroit, 1954-55; resident in radiology Mass. Gen. Hosp., Boston, 1956-59, asst. in radiology, 1959-62, asst. radiologist, 1962-67, asso. radiologist, 1967-71, radiologist, 1971—; asst. in radiology Harvard U. Med. Sch., 1959-62, instr., 1962-68, clin. asso. in radiology, 1968-69, asst. prof. radiology, 1969-73, asso. prof., 1973—; asso. radiologist Mass. Eye and Ear Infirmary, Boston, 1969-73, chief radiology, 1973—. Diplomate Am. Bd. Radiology. Mem. New Eng., Am. Roentgen Ray Soc. (Bronze medal for exhibit 1963, certificate of merit for exhibit 1962, 70, 72, 75), Radiol. Soc. N.Am., Mass. (council), Virchow-Pirquet med. scos., West African, German, Mass. radiol. scos., Am. Coll. Radiology, AMA, Brit. Inst. Radiology. Contbr. numerous articles to med. jours. Home: 79 Whittier Rd Milton MA 02186 Office: 243 Charles St Mass Ear and Eye Infirmary Boston MA 02114

WEBER, CLARENCE ADAM, author; b. Winfield, Kans., May 2, 1903; s. William J. and Pearl L. (Hunter) W.; A.B., Ill. Coll., 1924; M.A., U. Ill., 1929; Ph.D., Northwestern U., 1943; m. Mary E. Beaty, Aug. 7, 1925; children—Jane Weber Ruck, Betty L. (Mrs. Charles A. Dewey). Head dept. math, coach Oakland Twp. High Sch., Oakland, Ill., 1924-27; supt. schs. Hume, Galva, Cicero, Ill., 1927-44; asso. prof. edn. U. Conn., Storrs, 1945-46, dir. Fort Trumbull br., 1946-50, prof. edn., 1950-66, prof. emeritus, 1967—, chmn. dept. sch. adminstrn., 1950-66, dean Sch. Edn., 1960-61. Corporator Windham Meml. Hosp., Willimantic, Conn., 1966—. Mem. Am. Assn. Sch. Adminstrs., Phi Delta Kappa. Mason, Rotarian (dist. gov. 1965-66). Author: Organization and Administration in Public Education in Connecticut, 1951; Personal Problems of School Administrators, 1954; Fundamentals of Education Leadership, 1955; Industrial Leadership, 1956; Leadership in Personnell Management, 1970; Roots of Rebellion, 1970; What the People Ought to Know about School Administration, 1971; Welcome to the Rotary Club, 1971; Mary E. Weber, a biography, 1977; Autobiography, 1978; Diamonds in the Driveway, 1978; (with Jean Poull) Songs of Cajean, 1979. Home: 491 North Eagleville Rd Storrs CT 06268

WEBER, DAVID ALEXANDER, physicist; b. Lockport, N.Y., Mar. 6, 1939; s. Fred Leonard and Gladys (Woodcock) W.; B.S., St. Lawrence U., 1960; Ph.D. (AEC Grad. Lab. fellow), U. Rochester, 1970; m. Sandra Jean Watson, Aug. 26, 1961; children—Sarah Deirdre, David Alexander. Asst. attending physicist, lab. chief radioactive isotopes sect. Div. Med. Physics, Meml. Sloan-Kettering Cancer Center, N.Y.C., 1961-68; asst. prof. radiology U. Rochester (N.Y.), 1970-75, asst. prof. radiation biology and biophysics, 1970—, acting chief Div. Nuclear Medicine, 1974-75, asso. prof. radiology, 1975—; mem. med. adv. com. N.Y. State Dept. Health, 1973—. Roswell Park Meml. Inst. summer fellow, 1961. Mem. Soc. Nuclear Medicine (med. internal radiation dose com. 1976—; pres. computer council 1978), Am. Assn. Physicists in Medicine and Biology, Health Physics Soc. (chpt. pres. 1974-75). Home: 93 Fonthill Park Rochester NY 14618 Office: 601 Elmwood Ave Rochester NY 14642

WEBER, GERALD JOSEPH, U.S. judge; b. Erie, Pa., Feb. 1, 1914; s. Joseph J. and Ruth M. (Sullivan) W.; A.B., Harvard, 1936; LL.B., U. Pa., 1939; m. Berta M. Drechsel, Aug. 21, 1947; children—Thomas, William, Mary. Admitted to Pa. bar, 1940; civilian with U.S. Forces in Austria, 1946-47; practice law, Erie, 1947-64; city solicitor Erie, 1951-61; U.S. dist. judge Western Dist. Pa., 1964—, now chief judge. Served with U.S. Army, 1942-45. Decorated Bronze Star. Home: 4207 Beech Ave Erie PA 16509 Office: US Court House Erie PA 16501 also US Court House Pittsburgh PA 15219

WEBER, HENRY THOMAS PAUL, pub. relations exec. and counselor; b. Watertown, N.Y., Feb. 22, 1911; s. Henry Edward and Ellen Elizabeth (Purtell) W.; B.A., U. Windsor (Ont., Can.), 19—; postgrad. Harvard U. Bus. Sch., 1963; m. Alice Ruth Marlatt, Oct. 14, 1939; children—Mary Weber McGovern, Gael Weber Jaeger, Jr., Henry Ross. Can. corr. Detroit News, 1930-34; asst. publicity dir. Detroit Community Fund, 1935-39; dir. pub. relations Mpls. Community Fund, 1940-42; exec. dir. Elizabeth (N.J.) Community Chest, 1946-47; asso. exec. dir. Community Chests and Councils Am., N.Y.C., 1960-70; dir. Washington office United Way Am., 1969-73; nat. dir. United Community Campaigns Am., N.Y.C., 1960-72; exec. cons. United Way Am., Alexandria, Va., 1970-73; counselor community relations, Maplewood, N.J., 1973—; dir. United Def. Fund, 1950-54; mem. bd. Nat. Social Welfare Assembly, 1963-67; vice chmn. Nat. Communications Council, 1955-63; mem. bd. Nat. Council Aging, 1972-73; mem. editorial adv. bd. Pub. Relations News; mem. bd. Goodwill Industries; lectr. community relations U. Minn., Columbia, Rutgers U., Farleigh Dickenson U., N.Y. U. Served to lt., USNR, 1942-46. Mem. Pub. Relations Soc. Am. (Silver Anvil award 1960), Overseas Press Club, Advt. Club. N.Y. Editor: People & Events, A History of the United Way, 1976; author (with others) Management for Health & Welfare, 1966; exec. editor Community, Mag., 1950-60. Home: PO Box 3072 Chapel Hill NC 27514 Office: 99 Park Ave New York City NY 10016

WEBER, JOHN BENEDICT, banker, educator; b. Buffalo, Apr. 11, 1926; s. John August and Loretta (Kolkmeyer) W.; B.B.A., Canisius Coll., 1952, M.B.A., 1976; m. Frances J. Steck, June 4, 1949; children—John Benedict, William T., Paul J., Christopher R., Richard A., Mary Frances, Edward C. Title officer Abstract & Title Ins. Corp., 1946-56; asst. sec., asst. controller Transcontinent Television Corp., 1956-65; treas., controller, asst. sec. Crescent Niagara Corp., 1960-68, treas., asst. sec. Northeastern Pa. Broadcasting, Inc., 1958-68, treas., asst. sec., dir. Bridgeport Hardware Mfg. Corp., 1964-68; pres., treas., dir. Frontier Savs. & Loan Assn., 1969-74; sec., dir. Taylor Travel Service Inc., 1969—; dir. McCoy Med. Enterprises, Inc., 1970—; treas., dir. Claddagh Commn. Inc., 1978—; chmn. adv. bd. Erie Savs. Bank, 1974—; mem. N.Y. Bd. for Pub. Accountancy, 1974—; bus. cons., 1968—. Mem. faculty Canisius Coll., 1970—, State U. N.Y. Coll. at Fredonia, 1971—. Treas., Citizens Com. for Observance of Lord's Day, 1961—. Served with USAAF, 1944-45. Mem. Christian Family Movement (nat. treas. 1961-68), Financial Exec. Inst. (nat. dir. 1969-70, nat. adv. council 1970-73), Nat. Assn. Accountants, Am. Accounting Assn., Nat. Assn. Pub. Accountants, Air Force Assn., Financial Mgmt. Assn., Amherst C. of C. Roman Catholic. Club: Lancaster Country (treas. 1973-78). Home: 149 Wickham Dr Williamsville NY 14221 Office: 30 S Cayuga Rd Williamsville NY 14221

WEBER, RICHARD GLEN, metallurgist; b. Stamford, Conn., Sept. 4, 1943; s. Rene Paul and Helen Josephine (Koproski) W.; B.S. in Mech. Engring., U. Conn., 1967, M.S. in Metallurgy, 1969; D.Sc., Inst. Nat. Polytechnique de Lorraine, 1975; m. Ruta Ripa, Jan. 27, 1968; children—Laila Renee, Natalie Nicole. With Pitney-Bowes, Inc., Stamford, 1963-67, Sikorsky Aircraft Co., Stratford, Conn., 1969; faculty U. Conn., Storrs, 1970, Nancy Sch. Mines, France, 1970; research metallurgist Paris Sch. Mines, 1971-73; sr. metallurgist Machlett Labs., Inc., Stamford, 1973—; vice-chmn. dept. mech. engring. Bridgeport Engring. Inst. Mem. Stamford Bd. Edn., 1976—, Loaned Exec. Program, United Way, 1977. Recipient 1st Place award in color metallography Internat. Metallographic Soc., 1974. Mem. Am. Soc. Metals, Nat. Sch. Bds. Assn., Pi Tau Sigma, Phi Kappa Phi. Roman Catholic. Clubs: Polish Am. Businessmen and Profls.; Holy Name Athletic. Home: 166 Dannell Dr Stamford CT 06905 Office: 1063 Hope St Stamford CT 06907

WEBER, THOMAS WILLIAM, educator; b. Orange, N.J., July 15, 1930; s. William A. and Dorothy (Negus) W.; B.Chem. Engring., Cornell U., 1953, Ph.D., 1963; M.S. in Chem. Engring., Newark Coll. Engring., 1958; m. Marianne S. Hartmann, June 4, 1966; children—Anne Louise, William Alois. Chem. engring. in econs. and planning Esso Research & Engring., Linden, N.J., 1955-58; instr. Cornell U., 1961-62; asst. prof. State U. N.Y., Buffalo, 1963-66, asso. prof. chem. engring., 1966—. Cons., Nuclear Materials. Named Prof. of Year, Tau Kappa Chi, 1965; licensed profl. engr., N.Y. Mem. Am. Inst. Chem. Engrs. (chmn. Western N.Y. sect. 1969-70, Profl. Achievement award Western N.Y. sect. 1978), Am. Soc. for Engring. Edn. (chmn. instrumentation div. 1975-77), Tech. Socs. Council Niagara Frontier (sec. 1973-75, pres. 1975-76), Sigma Xi, Phi Kappa Phi, Tau Beta Pi, Theta Xi. Presbyn. Club: Swedish of Buffalo (pres. 1974-76). Author: An Introduction to Process Dynamics and Control, 1973. Home: 52 Autumnview Dr Williamsville NY 14221

WEBSTER, CARMEN JACQUELINE (MRS. HARRY M. KELLY), r.r. co. exec.; b. Houston, Apr. 25; d. Jefferson Charles and Nettie Alice (Fitchett) Duncan; B.S., Coll. Bus. and Pub. Adminstrn., N.Y. U., 1941; m. Harold Franklyn Webster, May 20, 1940; m. 2d, Harry M. Kelly, June 21, 1973. Asst. sales mgr. Scholl Mfg. Co., N.Y.C., 1938-39; supr. N.Y.C. Dept. Welfare, 1939-40; pres. Model R.R. Equipment Corp., N.Y.C., 1942—, also co-pub. The News, 1950-60, drama editor, 1954—, pub., 1960-62; pres. Rail Chief Products Co., N.Y.C., 1944-52; dir. Dunjen Pub. Corp., Hartsdale, N.Y., 1950-62. Permanent patron Bellevue Med. Center, N.Y. U., 1950-52; pub. relations co-chmn. Greenburgh Republican Com., 1954-60; mem. N.Y. State Legis. Adv. Com., 1971—; bd. dirs. Myopia Internat. Research Found., Futura Home Found. Recipient Madden Meml. award, N.Y. U., 1953, N.Y. U. Alumni Meritorious Service award, 1969. Mem. Hobby Industry Assn. Am. (packaging award 1950, spl. contbn. award 1976, best promotional idea award 1952, dir. retail div. 1968-71, 74—, life mem.), N.Y. U. Commerce Alumni Assn. (v.p. 1950-52), N.Y. U. Club (founder 1957), N.Y. U. Alumnae Club (pres. 1940-41), Outer Circle of Drama Critics of N.Y. Theatre Working Press, Soroptomist Internat. (pres. Central Westchester Club 1959-60, dir. 1960-63, life mem.), Nat. Assn. Model R.R. Mfgrs. (dir., sec. 1943-47), Nat. Model R.R. Assn., N.Y. U. Alumni Fedn. (dir. 1952-55, dir. emeritus 1966), Beta Gamma Sigma (dir. 1969—), Am. Contract Bridge League. Clubs: No. Westchester (N.Y.) Country; N.Y. Univ. (dir.). Editor: Manual and Catalog for all Gauges, 1950; Handbook and Catalog for HO Model Railroaders, 1953. Patentee in field.

WEBSTER, CLINTON WALLACE, educator; b. Webster, N.D., Mar. 8, 1919; s. David E. and Gelena Petra (Lenes) W.; B.A., U. N.D., 1941; B.S., Mich. Tech. U., 1950; M.A., Hofstra U., 1968; m. Dorothy Ann Thorne, July 2, 1948; children—Michael D., Richard A., Gary C. Tchr. lang. Mil. Inst., Millersburg, Ky., 1941; instr. Spanish, Mich. Tech. U., Houghton, 1948-50; metallurgist Cerro Corp., Peru, S.Am., 1950-55, Braden Copper Co., Chile, S.Am., 1956-59; asst. smelter supt. Phelps Dodge Corp., N.Y.C., 1959-61; tchr. fgn. langs. Massapequa (N.Y.) Pub. Schs., 1962—. Served with AUS, 1941-46. Decorated Purple Heart. Mem. Am. Soc. Metals, Am. Inst. Metall. Engrs., Am. Assn. Tchrs. Spanish and Portuguese. Republican. Home: 17 Jefferson Ave Hicksville NY 11801 Office: Carman Mill Rd Massapequa NY 11758

WEBSTER, DAVID ARTHUR, life ins. co. exec.; b. Downs, Ill., July 20, 1937; s. Harold Sanford and Carmen Mildred (Moore) W.; B.S., U. Ill., 1960; m. Anna Elizabeth Prosch, June 10, 1956; children—Theodore David, Elizabeth Anna, Arthur Lee, William Harold. Actuarial asst. Mass. Mut. Life. Ins. Co., Springfield, 1960-64; cons. actuary George Stennes & Assos., Mpls., 1964-68; v.p., actuary Piedmont Life Ins. Co., Atlanta, 1968-72, Pacific Fidelity Life Ins. Co., Los Angeles, 1972-74; v.p., chief actuary U.S. Life Corp., N.Y.C., 1974-76, exec. v.p., 1976—, dir., 1976—. Fellow Soc. Actuaries; mem. Am. Acad. Actuaries, N.Y. Actuaries Club. Club: Fairmont Country. Home: 101 Hobart Ave Summit NJ 07901 Office: 125 Maiden Ln New York City NY 10038

WEBSTER, JAMES KELSEY, III, acad. librarian; b. Buffalo, May 13, 1933; s. J. Kelsey and Dorothy (Wetmore) W.; B.A., U. Buffalo, 1956; M.L.S., State U. N.Y., Geneseo, 1966; m. Carol J. Mast, Apr. 25, 1959;children—James Kelsey IV, Alexander Daniel. With Calspan Corp., Buffalo, 1956-76, sr. librarian, tech. library, 1965-70, head librarian, 1970-76; dir. Sci. and Engring. Library, State U. N.Y. at Buffalo, 1976—; mem. planning com. N.Y. State Regents Intersystem Coop. Library Services. Town chmn. United Fund of Erie County, 1962-63, mem. allocation rev. com., 1964, county sect. chmn., 1966; chmn. Akron-Newstead Recreation Com., 1968-70; mem. Transp. Safety Information Com., 1969—. Mem. Newstead Republican Com., 1964-71, sec., 1966-71; mem. Erie County Republican Com., 1964-71; mem. Newstead Republican Club, Newstead Young Republican Club (treas. 1967). Trustee, Village of Akron, N.Y., 1967-70, Western N.Y. Library Resources Council, 1970—, pres. bd. trustees, 1976; coordinating com. SLA/Transp. Research Info. Services, 1973—. Mem. Spl. Libraries Assn. (chmn. transp. div. 1977-78, pres. Upstate N.Y. chpt. 1978-79), Am. Soc. Engring. Edn., State U. N.Y. Librarians Assn., ACLU, Assn. Coll. and Research Libraries, Akron C. of C. (pres. 1966), Nat. Jogging Assn. (life), Sierra Club, Gordon Highlanders Pipe Band, Sigma Phi Epsilon. Methodist. Home: 8 Cedar St Akron NY 14001 Office: Sci and Engring Library State U NY at Buffalo Buffalo NY 14260

WEBSTER, JOHN ARCHIBALD, JR., distbn. co. exec.; b. Boston, Dec. 21, 1935; s. John A. and Mildred B. (Bridgeman) W.; B.S. in Bus. Admnstrn., Boston U., 1957; m. Ann S. Hersey, Nov. 29, 1958; children—John A. III, Jeffrey H., Scott A. Salesman, J.A. Webster, Inc., North Billerica, Mass., 1958-69, v.p., sales mgr., 1969-76, pres., 1976—; pres. E. Med. Inc., Midland Park, N.J., 1972—; dir. Bio-Ceutic Labs., 1974-76, Med-Tech. Inc., 1976—. Mem. Am. Veterinary Distbrs. Assn. (bd. dirs. 1976-78, pres. 1978-79), Nat. Assn. Wholesalers (bd. trustees, 1979). Clubs: Nashawtuc Country, Country of New Seabury. Home: 39 Maynard Farm Rd Sudbury MA 01776 Office: Chelmstord Rd North Billerica MA 01862

WEBSTER, RAEY WILLIAM SNODGRASS, computer mfg. co. adminstr.; b. Philippines, Jan. 15, 1941; s. James D. and Ethel (Kegan) W.; A.B., B.S. in Chemistry and Econs., Mercer U., 1963; M.S. in Mgmt. Sci. and Accounting, State U. N.Y., Binghamton, 1974; m. Gail Thompson, Jan. 4, 1964. Staff systems analyst IBM, Endicott, N.Y., 1967-74, dept. mgr. warehouse systems and ops., 1974-75, project programmer, mgr. mfg. requirements systems, 1975-76, project programmer, mgr. program devel. support, Sterling Forest, N.Y., 1976—. Treas., Warwick (N.Y.) Shade Tree Commn. Served to lt. USN, 1964-67. Scholarship citation, Kappa Alpha, 1959. Mem. Am. Inst. C.P.A.'s, N.Y. Penn Divers, Nat. Assn. Underwater Instrs. Home: 22 Crescent Ave Warwick NY 10990

WEBSTER, ROSA CORNICE, personnel adminstr.; b. Virginia Beach, Va., May 20, 1947; d. Curtis Brown and Lillian Butler (Clark) Cornick; B.S. in Physics, Norfolk (Va.) State Coll., 1969; M.S., Old Dominion U., 1977; m. Joe Louis Webster, Jan 1, 1966; children—Crystal Lynnette, Barbara DoJoi. Physicist, then personnel mgmt. specialist NASA Langley Research Center, Hampton, Va., 1969-76, position classification specialist, 1976—. Pres., Crossroads Elementary Sch. PTA, 1973-74; v.p. jr. usher bd. Mt. Zion Ch. of God Holiness. Mem. Nat. Tech. Assn. (past chpt. pres.), Classification and Compensation Soc., Norfolk State Coll. Alumni Assn. Author papers in field. Office: NASA Langley Research Center Hampton VA 23665*

WEBSTER, THOMAS GLENN, psychiatrist; b. Topeka, Jan. 23, 1924; s. Guy Welland and Iva Amanda (Keefover) W.; A.B., Ft. Hays (Kans.) State Coll., 1946; M.D., Wayne State U., Detroit, 1949; m. Mary Tupper Dooly, June 27, 1948; children—Warnie Louise, Guy Weyman, David Michael. Intern Los Angeles County Gen. Hosp., 1949-50; resident in psychiatry Mass. Mental Health Center, Boston, 1953-55, in child psychiatry Mass. Mental Health Center, 1955-56, James Jackson Putnam Children's Center, Boston, part-time, 1956-58; dir. presch. program for retarded children Greater Boston, 1958-62; coordinator 3d year med. student psychiatry clerkship Harvard U. Med. Sch.-Mass. Mental Health Center, 1960-63; practice medicine specializing in psychiatry, Boston, 1953-62, Bethesda, Md., 1963-72, Washington, 1972—; tng. specialist psychiatry, then chief continuing edn. br. NIMH, Bethesda, 1963-72; prof. psychiatry George Washington U. Med. Sch., 1972—, chmn. dept. psychiatry and behavioral scis., 1972-75. Pres. Woodhaven Citizens Assn., 1971-72. Served with AUS, 1943-46; as sr. asst. surgeon USPHS, 1951-53. Fellow Am. Psychiat. Assn., Am. Coll. Psychiatrists, Am. Coll. Psychoanalysts; mem. Assn. Acad. Psychiatry (pres. 1976-78), Group Advancement Psychiatry. Home: 8506 Woodhaven Blvd Bethesda MD 20034 Office: 2150 Pennsylvania Ave NW Washington DC 20037

WECHMAN, ROBERT JOSEPH, educator, textile co. exec., social scientist; b. N.Y.C., Sept. 23, 1939; s. David Samuel and Blanche (Udell) W.; B.A., City U. N.Y., 1961, M.A., 1964; M.A., Columbia, 1966; Ph.D., Syracuse U., 1970; post-doctoral U. Pa., 1974; m. Stephanie Helene Kellman, June 18, 1967; children—Craig Samuel, Evan Mitchell, Darren Max. Tchr. history, N.Y.C., 1961-63, Dobbs Ferry (N.Y.) High Sch., 1963-66; instr. history Elmira (N.Y.) Coll., 1966-70; vis. lectr. history and polit. sci. State U. N.Y., Corning, summers 1967, 70—; asst. prof. history, coordinator urban studies Hartwick Coll., Oneonta, N.Y., 1970-74; asst. v.p. Candy Textile Co., 1977—; adj. prof. social sci. New Sch. for Social Research, also State U. N.Y., Rockland Community Coll., 1974—, Empire State Coll., 1974-77, Bergen Community Coll., 1976—. Cons. urban affairs State U. N.Y., Corning, 1969-70; cons. Choice Jour., 1972—. Mem. Oneonta Bd. Ethics, 1971-74, Oneonta Anti-Pollution Commn., 1972-74; mem. Otsego County Bicentennial Commn., 1972-74; committeeman Rockland County Republican Com., 1978—. Served with AUS, 1959. Mem. Orgn. Am. Historians, AAUP, Am. Hist. Assn., Council for Basic Edn., Univ. Centers for Rational Alternatives, Phi Alpha Theta, Delta Tau Kappa. Republican. Author: Urban America: A Guide to the Literature, 1971; The Eager Immigrants, 1972. Editor: Critical Issues in Modern American Life, 1968; The Crisis in Population, 1969. Reviewer for hist. jours. Home: 9 Verdin Dr New York City NY 10956

WECHSLER, ALAN LEWIS, lawyer, assn. exec.; b. N.Y.C., Apr. 19, 1940; s. Max and Mollie (Finkelstein) W.; B.A., N.Y.U., 1961; J.D., Bklyn. Law Sch., 1964; m. Nancy Gleicher, June 16, 1963; children—Sandra, Amy. Admitted to N.Y. bar, 1964; partner firm Wallman and Wechsler, N.Y.C., exec. dir. N.Y. Paper Merchants Assn., 1964—; dir. Simco Stores, Inc. Mem. exec. com. Paper div. United Jewish Appeal-Fedn. Jewish Philanthropies. Served to capt., inf. U.S. Army, 1963-66. Mem. N.Y. State Bar Assn., N.Y. State Trial Lawyers Assn., Am., N.Y. State socs. of assn. execs. Jewish. Clubs: Canyon (Armonk, N.Y.), Fiat Lux 1079. Home: 47 Old Lyme Rd Chappaqua NY 10514 Office: 292 Madison Ave New York City NY 10017

WECHSLER, HERBERT, lawyer, educator; b. N.Y.C., Dec. 4, 1909; s. Samuel and Anna (Weisberger) W.; A.B., Coll. City N.Y., 1928; LL.B., Columbia U., 1931; LL.D., U. Chgo., 1962, Harvard U., 1967; m. Elzie S. Stix, May 29, 1933 (div. 1957); m. 2d, Doris L. Klauber, Apr. 13, 1957. Admitted to N.Y. bar, 1933; editor Columbia U. Law Rev., 1929-31, instr. law, 1931-32, asst. prof., 1933-38. asso. prof., 1938-45. prof., 1945—, on leave 1940-46; law sec. to Mr. Justice Harlan F. Stone, 1932-33; counsel to minority leader N.Y. State Constl. Conv., 1938; asst. atty. gen. N.Y. (assigned Bklyn. investigation), 1938-40; exec. sec. U.S. Bd. Legal Examiners, 1941-42; mem. adv. com. on rules criminal procedure U.S. Supreme Ct., 1941-45; spl. asst. to atty. gen. of U.S., 1940-44; asst. atty. gen. of U.S., in charge war div., U.S. Dept. of Justice, 1944-46; tech. advisor to U.S. mems. Internat. Mil. Tribunal, 1945-46; vis. prof. Harvard Law Sch., 1956-57, Oliver Wendell Holmes lecturer, 1958-59; Harlan Fiske Stone prof. constl. law, Columbia 1957—. Chief reporter Am. Law Inst. Model Penal Code, 1952-62; exec. dir., sec. Am. Law Inst., 1963—. Mem. Pres.'s Commn. on Law Enforcement and Adminstrn. Justice, 1965-67, N.Y. Temporary Commn. Rev. Penal Law and Criminal Code, 1961-69, Commn. Revision Fed. Ct. Appellate System, 1973-75. Fellow Am. Acad. Arts and Scis., Brit. Acad.; mem. Am. Bar Assn., Assn. Bar City of N.Y. (past v.p.). Democrat. Club: Century Assn. Author: Criminal Law and Its Administration (with J. Michael), 1940; The Federal Courts and the Federal System (with H. Hart, Jr.), 1953, 2d edit. (with others), 1973; Principles, Politics and Fundamental Law, 1961; The Nationalization of Civil Liberties and Civil Rights, 1969. Home: 179 E 70th St New York City NY 10021 Office: Box 36 435 W 116th St New York City NY 10027

WECKER, CHRISTOPH ULRICH, inst. exec.; b. Heilbronn, Germany, Dec. 9, 1921; s. Martin and Maria (Bartelmäs) W.; Dipl. rer. pol., U. Tübingen (Germany), 1953, Dr. rer. pol., 1954; m. Ingrid Paschmann, Sept. 7, 1951; 1 son, Thomas. Dir. German Cultural Inst., Damascus, Syria, 1956-61; dir. adminstrn., dep. sec. gen. Goethe-Inst., Munich, Germany, 1961-75; dir. Goethe House N.Y.-German Cultural Inst., 1975—. Contbr. articles to profl. jours. Home: 985 Fifth Ave New York NY 10028 Office: 1014 Fifth Ave New York NY 10028

WECKSTEIN, WILLIAM ARNOLD, educator; b. Irvington, N.J., June 25, 1947; s. Abraham M. and Helaine R. (Arnold) W.; B.A., Rutgers U., 1968, M.S. in Environ. Sci., 1971; m. Carole M. Hunter, June 24, 1972; 1 son, Michael Charles. Fellow in radiol. health Rutgers U., New Brunswick, N.J., 1968-70; tchr. Newark Bd. Edn., 1970-71; instr. Manhattan Coll., N.Y.C., 1972; middle sch. coordinator Germantown Acad., Fort Washington, Pa., 1971—. USPHS fellow, 1968-71. Mem. Nat. Sci. Tchrs. Assn. (life), Montgomery County Sci. Tchrs. Assn. Jewish. Home: 731 Falcon Dr Wyndmoor PA 19118 Office: Morris Rd Fort Washington PA 19034

WEDEEN, HARVEY DAVID, musician; b. Perth Amboy, N.J., Mar. 23, 1927; s. Nathan and Gertrude (Rappaport) W.; B.S. in French, Columbia U., 1951; M.S. in Piano, Juilliard Sch. Music, 1960; m. Helen Kwalwasser, Nov. 27, 1958; children—Lisa Judith, Laura Ruth. Piano debut Town Hall, N.Y.C., 1950, solo and chamber music recitals throughout U.S., 1950-70; asst. dir. Henry St. Sch. Music, N.Y.C., 1956-59; instr. piano Bowling Green (Ohio) State U., 1961-64; prof. piano, chmn. keyboard dept. Temple U., Phila., 1964—, dir. music inst. Ambler, Pa., 1971-75, artistic dir. music festival, Ambler, 1974; vis. prof. music Ecole Vincent d'Indy, Montreal, Que., Can., 1976—; owner, operator antique store, Bryn Mawr, Pa., 1976—; lectr., workshop clinician, judge nat. competitions. Music adv. panel Pa. Council on Arts, 1976—. Recipient Lindbach award, 1968. Mem. Music Tchrs. Nat. Assn. (certified)(v.p. coll. student activities Eastern div. 1966-69), Pa. Music Tchrs. Assn., Phi Mu Alpha. Home: 424 Owen Rd Wynnewood PA 19096 Office: Coll Music Temple U Philadelphia PA 19122

WEDEEN, SHIRLEY ULLMAN, curriculum coordinator, educator; b. N.Y.C., May 29, 1926; d. Hugo and Esther Ullman; B.A., Bklyn. Coll., 1946; M.A., N.Y. U., 1947, Ph.D., 1951; m. Peter Wedeen, Jan. 13, 1952; children—Van, Glenn. Substitute tchr. Bklyn. Coll., 1948-51, instr. edn., 1951-58, asst. prof., 1959-65, asso. prof., 1966-71, prof. edn., 1971—, asst. dean students, 1966-68, curriculum coordinator Sch. Edn., 1972—. Certified psychologist, N.Y. Mem. Am. Press Club, Internat. Reading Assn., N.Y. Acad. Pub. Edn., Am. Psychol. Assn., AAUP, AAAS, Coll. Reading Assn. Author: College Reader, 1958; Advanced College Reader, 1963; also articles. Home: 116 Buckingham Rd Brooklyn NY 11226 Office: Bklyn Coll Bedford Ave Brooklyn NY 11210

WEDEL, PAUL GEORGE, hosp. adminstr.; b. Elizabeth, N.J., Jan. 1, 1927; s. Paul John and Helen (Cleary) W.; grad. Peddie Sch., Hightstown, N.J., 1944; B.S. in Bus. Adminstrn., Am. U., 1952; M.S. in Hosp. Adminstrn., Northwestern U., 1955; m. Jean Marie Martin, June 18, 1949; children—Dana Lyn, Laurie Ann Wedel Musser, Paul John II, Kurt Frederick. Adminstrv. resident Harrisburg (Pa.) Polyclinic Hosp., 1953-54; asst. adminstr. Williamsport (Pa.) Hosp., 1954-59, adminstr., 1959-64; pres. Lancaster (Pa.) Gen. Hosp., 1964—. Bd. dirs. Inter-County Hospitalization Plan, Inc., 1966—, James Buchanan Found., Preservation Wheatland, 1968—; inc. trustee Episcopal Diocese of Central Pa., 1970-73, mem. diocesan council, 1973—. Served with USN. 1944-46, 50-51. Named Outstanding Young Man, Williamsport Jaycees, 1957. Fellow Am. Coll. Hosp. Adminstrs.; mem. Am. Hosp. Assn., Hosp. Assn. Pa. (bd. dirs. 1970-73), Lancaster C. of C. Clubs: Masons, Rotary (dir. Lancaster, pres. 1978-79), Hamilton. Home: 203 Riveredge Dr Rock Rimmon Ridges RD 1 Leola PA 17540 Office: 555 N Duke St Lancaster PA 17604

WEDIN, EDWARD JOHAN, chiropractor; b. Högsjö, Sweden, Oct. 5, 1904; s. Erik Johan and Matilda E. (Sjöström) W.; came to U.S., 1928, naturalized, 1934; student Columbia U.; grad. Chiropractic Inst. of N.Y., N.Y.C. Dir. clin. out patients Chiropractic Inst. of N.Y., 1938-64, also tchr. spinal mechanics and adjusting technique; pvt. practice chiropractic, N.Y.C., 1964—. Mem. Am. Chiropractic Assn., Swedish Soc., Am.-Scandinavian Soc. Lutheran. Home: 431 E 20th St New York City NY 10010 Office: 60 E 42d St New York City NY 10017

WEDZICHA, WALTER, educator; b. Jezor, Poland, June 5, 1920; s. Wladyslaw and Maria (Kruczek) W.; came to U.S., 1946, naturalized, 1953; A.B., U. Miami, 1965; M.A., U. Pitts., 1966; m. Sabina Purzynska, Nov. 28, 1945; children—John M., Christine S. Attaché, Consulate Gen. Poland in N.Y., N.Y.C., 1946-49; accountant, Miami, Fla., 1950-65; asst. prof. German and Russian, Clarkson Coll. Tech., Potsdam, N.Y., 1967—. NDEA fellow, 1965-66; Nat. Endowment for Humanities grantee, summers 1977, 78. Mem. Modern Lang. Assn. Author: Song of the City, 1957. Home: Route 1 Potsdam NY 13676 Office: Clarkson Coll Tech Potsdam NY 13676

WEEDEN, JAMES DENNIS, bank exec.; b. N.Y.C., Jan. 13, 1930; s. James Sumner and Mary Agnes (Kearon) W.; A.B., Adelphi U., 1957; M.B.A., N.Y.U., 1966; m. Justine Carolyn Klipp, Aug. 13, 1955; children—James, Christine, Robert, Gerard, David. Sr. trust adminstr. Bank of N.Y., N.Y.C., 1957-68; asst. v.p. Franklin Nat. Bank, N.Y.C., 1968-70; v.p., trust officer L.I. Trust Co., Garden City, N.Y., 1970—. Mem. advisory com. on edn. Garden City Community Fund, 1973—; sec. Central Garden City Property Owners Assn.; v.p., bd. dirs. Bank Fiduciary Funds. Served with AUS, 1951-53. Chartered fin. analyst. Mem. Garden City Hist. Soc., N.Y. Soc. Security Analysts, Fin. Analysts Assn. Am. Pension Conf. Republican. Roman Catholic. Home: 27 Hilton Ave Garden City NY 11530 Office: 82 7th St Garden City NY 11530

WEEKS, DAVID FRANK, found. exec.; b. Salt Lake City, Sept. 9, 1926; s. Frank Harold and Myrtle June (Larsen) W.; student So. Meth. U., 1945, U. Tex., 1946; B.S. (Union Pacific Carl Raymond Gray scholar), U. Idaho, 1949; m. Betty Alice Tellin, Aug. 14, 1949; children—David Rice, Clayton Frank. Announcer, Sta. KBIO, Burley, Idaho, 1949; Idaho rep. Nat. Found. for Infantile Paralysis, Boise, 1949-53, asst. to nat. dir. fund raising, N.Y.C., 1953-57; asst. nat. dir., March of Dimes, 1957-59; account exec. Kersting, Brown & Co., N.Y.C., 1959-61; exec. dir. Research to Prevent Blindness, Inc., N.Y.C., 1961-70, exec. v.p., 1970—; consumer rep. subcom. ophthalmic prostheses HEW-FDA, 1976—; cons. Bur. Med. Devices, FDA, 1977—. Mem. planning bd. City of Ho-Ho-Kus (N.J.), 1962-65, chmn., 1965, mem. city council, 1966-68, mayor, 1968-75, mem. zoning bd., 1975—; mem. Bergen County (N.J.) Ethics Bd., 1977—. Trustee, treas. Am. Tentative Soc., 1974—. Served with USN, 1944-46. Recipient Bronze Palm Eagle Scout award Boy Scouts Am., 1941; named Ky. Col., 1969; recipient Distinguished Pub. Service award Am. Acad. Ophthalmology and Otolaryngology, 1976. Mem. Am. Soc. Assn. Execs., Bergen County Mayors Assn. (v.p. 1973-74, pres. 1975-77), Soc. Valley Hosp. of Ridgewood (N.J.), Pan. Am. Ophthalmol. Assn. (asso.), Assn. for Research in Vision and Ophthalmology (hon.). Republican. Club: Metropolitan (N.Y.C.). Home: 8 Brookview Ct Ho-Ho-Kus NJ 07423 Office: 598 Madison Ave New York NY 10022

WEEKS, RICHARD RALPH, coll. dean; b. Champaign, Ill., Sept. 18, 1932; s. Frank Cook and Bertha Caroline (Pool) W.; B.S., U. Ill., 1955; M.B.A. (fellow), Washington U., 1960, D.B.A. (Am. Assn. Collegiate Schs. Bus. fellow), 1966; m. Sue Ann Grunwald, Aug. 29, 1953; children—Kimberly Sue, Bret William. Exec. sec. Am. Assn. Collegiate Schs. Bus., 1960-64, Beta Gamma Sigma, 1961-64; asst. dean, dir. M.B.A. program Coll. Bus. Adminstrn., Okla. State U., 1965-67; dean Walter E. Heller Coll. Bus. Adminstrn., Roosevelt U., 1967-70; dean Coll. Bus. Adminstrn., U. R.I., Kingston, 1970—, acting v.p. for bus. and fin., 1976-77. Dir. Bus. Opportunity Fair, 1969; mem. econ. devel. secretariat Econ. Renewal Council, State R.I., 1973-74. Bd. dirs. Friends Jamestown Philomenian Library, pres., 1974-76. Served to capt. USAF, 1955-58. Mem. Am. Assn. Collegiate Schs. Bus. (mem. standards com. 1972—, bd. dirs. 1976—), Nat. Assn. State Univs. and Land Grant Colls. (chmn. commn. on edn. for bus. professions 1976—), Eastern Fin. Assn. (dir. 1974-77), Am. Mkting. (dir. acad. placement 1966, 68), Council Profl. Edn. Bus. (sec.-treas. 1960-64), Beta Gamma Sigma (pres. 1978—). Club: Conanicut Yacht (Jamestown, R.I.). Editor: Faculty Personnel, 9th edit., 1965. Editor Am. Assn. Collegiate Schs. Bus. Bull., 1960-64, Beta Gamma Sigma Exchange, 1961-64; mem. editorial adv. bd. Bus. and Soc., 1968-70. Home: 76 Walcott Ave Jamestown RI 02835 Office: U RI Kingston RI 02881

WEGMAN, LEONARD S., cons. engr., mayor; b. N.Y.C., Mar. 7, 1911; s. Max and Nettie (Finkelstein) W.; B.S. Engring., City Coll. Sch. Tech., 1934; Columbia, 1938; m. Tilla Robinson, Mar. 27, 1936 (dec. June 1972); children—Richard Adam, Lydia Nan; m. 2d, Shirley Albert, June 20, 1975. Civil engr. N.Y.C. and related agencies on marine and hwy. constrn., 1935-40; civil engr. C.E., U.S. Army, N.Y. dist., 1941-44; chmn. Leonard S. Wegman Co., Inc., engrs., N.Y.C., 1945—, designers solid waste disposal systems, water systems, sewage treatment plants, hwys., bridges, other pub. works. Cons. U.S. govt., N.Y. State Comptroller, State Conn., cities Buffalo, N.Y.C., Miami, Jersey City, Atlanta, Westchester County, Phila., New Haven, Syracuse, N.Y., Memphis, ITT, others. Bd. dirs., past pres. United Community Fund of Great Neck, N.Y. Mayor of Kings Point, N.Y., 1974—. Recipient honor award Cons. Engrs. Council U.S., 1968; award for outstanding design pub. facility L.I. Assn., 1964; award Engring. News Record, 1971; Environmental award N.Y. State Soc. Profl. Engrs., 1970; Ecology award Bklyn. Engring. Club, 1974. Diplomate Am. Acad. Environ. Engrs. Fellow Am. Pub. Health Assn., ASCE; mem. Soc. Am. Mil. Engrs. (v.p. N.Y. post, Outstanding Engring. Achievement award 1978), Nat. Soc. Profl. Engrs., Am. Water Works Assn., Am. Pub. Works Assn., Air Pollution Control Assn., Water Pollution Control Fedn. Clubs: City (N.Y.C.); Muttontown Golf (v.p., gov. 1970-74). Contbr. articles to profl. jours. Office: 100 E 42d St New York City NY 10017

WEHBERG, DIRK ANTON, paper co. exec.; b. Groningen, Netherlands, May 12, 1947; s. Herman Frederik and Justine (Pessers) W.; came to U.S., 1971; License of Bus. Econ., Univ. St. Gall, Switzerland, 1970; M.B.A., N.Y. Univ., 1973; m. Carole Daisy Francois, Sept. 8, 1973. Buyer's asst., Bloomingdale's, N.Y.C., 1973-74; buyer Westvaco Corp., N.Y.C., 1974-76, asst. purchasing agt., 1976-78, mgr. paper and bd. scheduling and control, 1978—. Mem. Profl. Devel. Com., Purchasing Mgmt. Assn., Am. Mktg. Assn. Roman Catholic. Home: New York City NY

WEIANT, MONROE ALDEN, former investment co. exec.; b. Bklyn., Nov. 20, 1903; s. William Morrow and Maud Alden (Dunham) W.; B.L., Rutgers U., 1926; m. Lois May Dayer, July 18, 1931; children—Monroe Alden, William Morrow. Br. office mgr. Sutro & Kimbly Co. (after several mergers became T.L. Watson & Co.), N.Y.C.; partner T.L. Watson & Co., 1956-70; br. mgr., v.p. Hoppinatson, Inc., Perth Amboy, N.J., 1970-77; ret., 1978. Bd. dirs. Perth Amboy YMCA. Paul Harris fellow, 1974. Mem. Perth Amboy C. of C. (dir.), Zeta Psi. Episcopalian. Clubs: Echo Lake Country (Westfield, N.J.); Scarlet R (Rutgers U.); Rotary. Home: 11 Stoneleigh Park St Westfield NJ 07090

WEICKER, LOWELL P., JR., U.S. senator; b. Paris, France, May 16, 1931; B.A., Yale, 1953; LL.B., U. Va., 1958; m. Camille DiLorenzo Butler, Nov. 5, 1977. Commd. 1st lt. U.S. Army, 1953, advanced through grades to capt., 1959, resigned, 1964; admitted to Conn. bar; mem. Conn. Ho. of Reps., 1963-69; 1st selectman, Greenwich, Conn., 1964-68; mem. 91st Congress from 4th Conn. Dist., 1969-71; mem. U.S. Senate from Conn., 1971—, mem. Appropriations com., Select Com. on Small Bus., Energy and Natural Resources Com., Select Com. on Ethics. Republican. Office: 313 Russell Senate Office Bldg Washington DC 20510

WEIDA, LEWIS DIXON, credit co. exec.; b. Moran, Ind., Apr. 23, 1924; s. Charles R. and Luella M. (Dixon) W.; student Kenyon Coll., 1943, Purdue U., 1946; B.S., U. Ind., 1948; M.S., Columbia U., 1950. Mgr. statis. analysis, fin. rates unit Gen. Motors Acceptance Corp., N.Y.C., 1952-55; asst. to exec. v.p. Am. Express Co., N.Y.C., 1955—. Served with USAAF, 1943-46. Mem. Am. Mktg. Assn., Travel Research Assn. Democrat. Research in travel, fin. services and pub., 1958—. Home: 25 Tudor City Pl New York NY 10017 Office: 1350 Ave of Americas New York City NY 10004

WEIDEN, PAUL LUDWIG, lawyer; b. Frankfurt am Main, Germany, Jan. 28, 1908; s. Joseph and Selma (Mayer) Weiden-Baum; LL.D., U. Frankfurt, 1931; M.L., U. Eng., 1936; m. Gerda Kaufmann, July 12, 1937; 1 son, Paul Lincoln; m. 2d, Helga Zindel, Feb. 28, 1953 (div.); children—Peter Joseph, Michael David. Came to U.S., 1936, naturalized, 1942. Chief legal sect. Liberated Areas Br., Bd. Econ. Warfare, 1943-44; admitted to bar Eng., 1936, Oreg. bar, 1938, D.C. bar, 1943, N.Y. bar, 1947; practiced in Portland, Oreg., 1938-42; mem. firm Weiden, Grosswell & Gunnigle (name changed to Weiden & Gunnigle 1960), N.Y.C., 1947-76; mem. firm Zucker Weiden & Shapiro; atty. SEC, 1944-45; chmn. bd. dirs. various European and Am. corps., also Steinberg & Vorsaenger Corp., Wilag Corp (Wiesbaden) Ltd., Internat. Mortgage Corp., N.Y.C. Contbr. to European and Am. legal publs. Home: 920 Park Ave New York City NY 10028 Office: 200 Park Ave New York City NY 10017 also 38 Bockenheimer Anlage Frankfurt Germany

WEIDENBACHER, PETER, electronics co. exec.; b. N.Y.C., Feb. 19, 1925; s. Richard L. and Ethel A. Weidenbacher; B.S. in Econs. and Fin., Bucknell U., 1950; m. Alice S. Sandford, Sept. 22, 1974; children—Sally, Sam, Drew, Hugh, Nancy, Richie. With Scott Paper Co., Phila., 1950-51; with Henry G. Richter, Inc., Mountainside, N.J., 1951—, pres., 1968—; dir., v.p. Mountainside Profl. Bldg., Mountainside Village Mall. Served with USN, 1943-46. Recipient Outstanding Alumni award Bucknell U., 1970. Mem. Electronic Reps. Assn. (exec. com.), Bucknell U. Alumni Assn. (past chpt. pres.), Kappa Sigma. Republican. Clubs: Lions (Warrentownship pres. 1967), Bucknell Bison (exec. com.). Home: 802 North Dr Bricktown NJ 08723 Office: 608 Sherwood Pkwy Mountainside NJ 07092

WEIDENFELD, SHEILA RABB, TV producer, author; b. Cambridge, Mass., Sept. 7, 1943; d. Maxwell M. and Ruth (Cryden) Rabb; B.A., Brandeis U., 1965; m. Edward L. Weidenfeld, Aug. 11, 1968. Asso. producer With Mayor Lindsay, The New Yorkers and Alan Burke Show, Metromedia, Inc., WNEW-TV, N.Y.C., 1965-68; talent coordinator That Show with Joan Rivers, NBC, N.Y.C., 1968-71; coordinator NBC network game programs Who, What and Where and The Sale of the Century, N.Y.C., 1968-71; producer Panorama, Metromedia, Inc., WTTG-TV, Washington, 1971-73; creator/producer Take It From Here, NBC (WRC-TV), Washington, 1973-74; press sec. to first lady Betty Ford and spl. asst. to Pres. Gerald R. Ford 1974-77; mem. Pres.'s Adv. Commn. on Historic Preservation, 1977; TV producer, moderator On the Record, WRC-TV Channel 4, Washington, 1978—; mem. Sec. State's Adv. Commn. on Fgn. Service Inst., 1972. Corporator Dana Hall, Wellesley, Mass; bd. dirs. Wolf Trap Found., Women's Campaign Fund. Recipient awards for outstanding achievement in the media AAUW, 1973, 74. Mem. Washington Press Club, Am. Newspaper Women's Club, Am. Women in Radio and TV, Nat. Acad. TV Arts and Scis. (Emmy award 1972), Sigma Delta Chi. Author: First Lady's Lady, 1979. Home and office: 2903 Q St NW Washington DC 20017

WEIDENHEIMER, JOSEPH FRANCIS, pharm. co. exec.; b. N.Y.C., Mar. 4, 1918; s. Emil Francis and Anna Teresa (Egan) W.; B.S., Fordham U., 1939, M.S., 1941; m. Katherine Lamadore, June 13, 1942; children—Philip, Joanne, Christopher. Research biochemist Winthrop Chem. Co., Renssalaer, N.Y., 1942-46; biochemist, dept. head Lederle Labs. div. Am. Cyanamid Co., Pearl River, N.Y., 1946-67; dir. product devel. Miles Labs. Inc., West Haven, Conn., 1967—. Served to capt., inf., U.S. Army, 1942-44. Decorated D.S.C., Silver Star, Purple Heart. Fellow Am. Inst. Chemists; mem. Am. Chem. Soc., Am. Pharm. Assn., Acad. Pharm. Sci., AAAS. Roman Catholic. Contbr. articles to profl. jours. Patentee in field. Home: 360 Opening Hill Rd Madison CT 06443 Office: 400 Morgan Ln West Haven CT 06502

WEIDLER, MILTON JOSEPH, govt. ofcl.; b. Bklyn., June 13, 1923; s. Nathan and Fannie (Zucker) W.; B.S., N.Y. U., 1948, M.A., 1951; M.P.H., Columbia U., 1957; m. Irene Epstein, Nov. 11, 1942; children—Roy, Wendy, Susan. Interviewer N.Y. Div. Veterans Affairs, N.Y.C., 1948-50; editor, pub. Cliff Dweller Monthly Newspaper, N.Y.C., 1950-51; cons. in pub. health edn. N.Y.C. Dept. Health, 1951-57; chief media section Pa. Dept. Health, Harrisburg, 1957-64; chief, audiovisual and printing services div. D.C. Dept. Human Resources, Washington, 1964—. Served with U.S. Army, 1943-46. Fellow Am. Pub. Health Assn., Soc. Pub. Health Edn.; mem. Nat. Assn. Govt. Communicators. Democrat. Home: 2112 Ross Rd Silver Spring MD 20910 Office: Dept Human Resources 801 N Capitol St Washington DC 20002

WEIDNER, JAMES HENRY, editor, educator; b. Carlisle, Pa., Nov. 27, 1940; s. Chester Walter and Marion Bertha (Henry) W.; B.S. in Edn., U. Pa., 1962; children—James David, Jeffrey Walter, Timothy Allan. Tchr. English, No. Burlington County Regional Jr./Sr. High Sch., Columbus, N.J., 1962-66, chmn. dept., 1968—; editor W.B. Saunders & Co., Phila., 1966-68; pres. Weidner Assos., Inc., Cinnaminson, N.J., 1968—; owner Intercontinental Graphics, Dordrecht, Netherlands and Moorestown, N.J., 1973—; dir. TechType Graphics Corp., Moorestown. Recipient Community Service award Borough of Merchantville (N.J.), 1958; Quill and Scroll award, 1967; Am. Legion award. Mem. Assn. Secondary Sch. Suprs. and Dept. Heads N.J., Am. Med. Writers Assn., NEA, N.J., Burlington County edn. assns., Com. Book and Jour. Editors, Camden County Autopatch Repeater Assn. (sec.), Lang. Arts Assessment Com., Am. Radio Relay League, So. Counties Amateur Radio Assn., Alpha Sigma Phi. Club: Woodbine Swim. Office: 300 Chester Ave Moorestown NJ 08057

WEIERMAN, ROBERT JOSEPH, orthopedic surgeon; b. Neptune, N.J., July 31, 1942; s. Albert F. and Dorothy V. W.; B.A., St. Peter's Coll., 1964; M.D., Georgetown U., 1968; m. Claire A. Boyle, Apr. 12, 1969; children—Christine, Robert Joseph, Thomas. Intern, Jersey Shore Med. Center, Neptune, 1968-69, resident in gen. surgery, 1969-70; resident orthopedic surgery N.J. Coll. Medicine and Dentistry, Newark, 1970-73, N.J. Orthopedic Hosp., Orange, 1970-73; practice medicine specializing in orthopedic surgery, Irvington, N.J., 1973—; clin. asso. prof. surgery N.J. Coll. Medicine Dentistry, 1973—. Diplomate Am. Bd. Orthopedics. Fellow Am. Acad. Orthopedic Surgery, A.C.S.; mem. AMA, Essex County Med. Soc., N.J. Orthopedic Soc., Am. Acad. Cerebral Palsy and Developmental Medicine. Roman Catholic. Office: 986 Sanford Ave Irvington NJ 07111

WEIGAND, GENELLA SIMS, former county ofcl.; b. Sevierville, Tenn., Nov. 19, 1919; d. Walter and Texie Ethel (Teague) Sims; student Strayers Bus. Coll., Washington Sch. Secretaries; m. Bertrand G. McGinnis, July 15, 1953 (dec.); 1 dau., Anna Louise (Mrs. Richard N. Showalter); m. 2d, Walton W. Weigand. Engaged in real estate, 1968—; councilwoman Town of Seat Pleasant, Md., 1956-64, treas., 1961; mem. Prince George's County Bd. License Commrs., 1957-63; judge Orphans' Ct., Prince George's County, 1964-66; register of wills Prince George's County, Upper Marlboro, 1966-77; now ret. Mem. Prince George's Democratic Club, Sasscer Dem. Club, Chillum Dem. Club, Caravan Dem. Club, Prince George's Women's Dem. Club; del. Prince George's County Council Dem. Clubs, 1956—, United Dem. Women's Club, 1956—. Bd. dirs. Hist. and Cultural Trust Prince George's County. Mem. Am. Assn. Museums, English Speaking Union U.S., Md. Fedn. Women's Clubs, Heart Assn. So. Md., Md. Register Wills Assn., Bus. and Profl. Women's Club (cancer chmn.), Huntington Hist. Soc. Lioness. Club: Melwood. Home: 2 Snowball Dr Box 16 Huntington NY 11743

WEIGEL, ERNEST CHARLES, market research exec.; b. New Rochelle, N.Y., Aug. 17, 1917; s. Ernest Henry and Phyllis Barbara (Reitz) W.; B.S., Rutgers U., 1953, M.S., 1955; m. Ruth Ethel Lewis, Apr. 25, 1942; 1 son, Ernest Charles. Statis. cons. C.E.I.R., Inc., N.Y.C., 1961-65; mgr. research data process Grey Advt., Inc., 1965-68; mgmt. cons. Marcom, Inc., 1968-69; market research mgr. Sperry & Hutchinson Co., 1969—; dir. Curren Pfeiff Corp., Edison, N.J.; lectr. evening sch. Rutgers U., 1959-61. Served with AUS, 1942-45. Mem. Ops. Research Soc. Am., Am. Statis. Assn., Inst. Math. Statistics, Nat. Registry Sci. and Tech. Personnel, Matawan Hist. Soc. (treas. 1971-74), Rutgers U. Alumni Assn. Roman Catholic. Club: K.C. Contbr. articles to profl. publs. Home: 28 Beechwood Terr Matawan NJ 07747 Office: 330 Madison Ave New York City NY 10017

WEIGEL, WILLIAM FREDERICK, lawyer; b. N.Y.C., Sept. 26, 1923; s. Elmer Peter and Sara Madeline (Westerbeke) W.; student Princeton U., 1941-42; B.S. magna cum laude, Lehigh U., 1949; J.D., N.Y. U., 1951; m. Frances B. Perry, Feb. 14, 1952 (div.); children—Madeleine, Amy, Patricia, William Breck. Admitted to N.Y. bar, 1951; asso. firm Rogers Hoge & Hills, N.Y.C., 1951—, partner, 1959—, sr. partner, 1970—; asso. gen. counsel Proprietary Assn., 1960-71; sec., gen. counsel Am. Found. Pharm. Edn., 1971—; counsel Council Family Health, 1972—; atty. Village of Pelham (N.Y.), 1964-65, trustee, 1965-67, mayor, 1967-70; instr. law Bernard Baruch Sch., Coll. City N.Y.; lectr. N.Y. U. Grad. Sch. Law, Practising Law Inst. Served with USNR, 1942-46. Mem. Am., N.Y. (chmn. food, drug and cosmetic law sect. 1978—; ho. of dels. 1978—), N.Y.C. bar assns., Internat. Acad. Law Sci. Republican. Contbr. articles on trademark and food and drug law to profl. jours. Home: 201 E 66th St New York City NY 10021 Office: 90 Park Ave New York City NY 10016

WEIGRAU, TONI, personnel exec.; b. Phila., Apr. 29, 1937; d. Max H. and Violet B. W.; B.A., Rosemont Coll., 1959; M.A., U. Pa., 1964. Personnel asst. IRC, Inc., Phila., 1960-63; asst. to mng. dir. Island Block Corp., St. Thomas, V.I., 1963-65; customer service corr. IRC, Inc., div. TRW, Phila., 1977-78; sales asst. Naus & Newlyn, Inc., Paoli, Pa., 1968-69; personnel asst. Pa. Mfrs. Assn. Ins. Co., Phila., 1970-74, asst. dir. personnel, 1974-77, personnel dir., 1977—. Del. at large Nat. Women's Conf., Houston, 1977; mem. commn. to study governance of coll. Rosemont Coll., 1971-72, bd. dirs. alumnae assn., 1977—. Mem. Internat. Assn. Personnel Women (pres.), Am. Soc. Personnel Adminstrn., Del. Valley Ins. Personnel Group, Fedn. Orgns. for Profl. Women. Home: Apt WB514 The Greenhill in Lower Merion Philadelphia PA 19151 Office: 925 Chestnut St Philadelphia PA 19107

WEIHS, FRANK ALOIS, advt. exec.; b. N.Y.C., June 18, 1927; s. Frank I. and Florence (McGahan) W.; B.A. Cath. U. Am., 1950; m. Margaret Partee Weir, June 25, 1960; children—Randall F., Derek V., Dana C., April A. Advt. copywriter McGraw-Hill, 1951-53; copy chief Doubleday & Co. Inc., 1953-56; account exec. Schwab & Beatty, advt., 1956-62; mktg. dir. Crowell-Collier, Inc., 1962-64; advt. dir. RCA Record Club, 1964-68, creative dir. RCA In-house Advt. Agy., mem. RCA corp. advt. com., 1964-68; gen. mgr. Tatham & Weihs, dir. response advt. div. Tatham-Laird & Kudner, Inc., N.Y.C., 1968-71; pres. Weihs Advt., Inc., N.Y.C. and Sea Girt, N.J., 1971—; pres., creative dir. Intermark Advt., Sea Girt, N.J., also Miami, Fla., 1978—. Fgn. corr. for All Hands mag. at Bikini Atomic Bomb Tests, 1946. Served with USNR, 1944-46. Mem. C. of C. of Americas, Am. Assn. Advt. Agys. (mem. steering com. 1968—), Direct Mail Advt. Assn. Home: 623 Beacon Blvd Sea Girt NJ 08750 also Marco Island Fl 33937

WEIL, FRANK A., govt. ofcl.; b. Bedford, N.Y., Feb. 14, 1931; s. Sylvan and Ruth Alice (Norman) W.; B.A. cum laude, Harvard U., 1953, LL.B., 1956; m. Denie Sandison, Feb. 10, 1951; children—Deborah H. Weil Harrington, Amanda E., Sandison E., William S. Admitted to N.Y. bar; individual practice law, N.Y.C., 1957-60; gen. partner firm Loeb, Rhoades & Co., N.Y.C., 1960-71; pres. Abacus Fund, Inc., 1968-72; officer, dir. Paine, Webber, Jackson & Curtis, 1972-77; asst. sec. industry and trade Dept. Commerce, Washington, 1977—; dir. Dorr-Oliver, Inc., Stamford, Conn., 1968-77, Hamburg Savs. Bank, N.Y.C., 1975-77, J.B. Lippincott Co., Phila., 1975-77, Govt. Research Corp., 1975-77. Chmn. tax com., mem. N.Y. State Economic Devel. Bd., 1975-77; chmn. N.Y. State Bd. Equalization and Assessment, 1976-77; bd. dirs., pres. Norman Found., 1953-77, Hickrill Found., Inc., 1953-77; pres. Ednl. Alliance in N.Y., 1958-77; trustee Montefiore Hosp., 1960-77; trustee, sec. Fedn. Jewish Philanthropies, N.Y.C., 1965-77; trustee, chmn. Harvey Sch., 1969-76; trustee, vice. chmn. No. Westchester Hosp., 1971-77; trustee Hurricane Island Outward Bound Sch., 1975-77, Tchrs. Coll. Columbia U., 1976-77; mem. vis. com. Harvard U. Law Sch., Kennedy Sch. Govt. Clubs: Met., Fed. City (Washington); Economic, Harvard, Bond, City Midday, Board Room, Century Assn. (N.Y.C.). Author: The Securities Industry; Myth v. Reality, 1973. Office: Dept Commerce Room 3850 14th and Constitution Ave NW Washington DC 20230

WEILL, HAROLD, lawyer; b. N.Y.C., Apr. 30, 1908; s. Isaac and Fannie (Fogler) W.; student Columbia U., 1927-31; LL.D. (hon.), Beaver Coll., 1971; m. Lisbeth Goldmann, June 29, 1934; children—Patricia Rosenthal, Judith Levy, Victoria. Admitted to N.Y. bar, 1932, also D.C. bar, U.S. Circuit Ct. Appeals, Washington, U.S. Supreme Ct. bar; partner Leon, Weill & Mahony, N.Y.C., 1932—; mem. exec. com., dir. Helena Rubinstein, Inc., N.Y.C., 1955-73; pres., dir. Brit. Controlled Oil Fields, Inc., 1959-70; treas., dir. World Vets. Fund, 1957-70; dir. Ansbacher & Co., Ltd., Dublin. Chmn. bd. Children's Blood Fund, Inc., N.Y.C., 1955—; bd. dirs., pres. Talisman Found., Helena Rubenstein Found.; bd. govs., vice chmn. 3d Century fund, mem. exec. com., fin. com., investment com., budget com., chmn. subcom. obstetrics, mem. ops. com. N.Y. Hosp.; bd. govs. Weizmann Inst. Sci., 1975—; trustee Palm Springs Desert Mus. Decorated officer Ordre Nat. du Merite, chevalier Legion of Honor (France); Harold Weill Children's Blood Found. Clinic, N.Y. Hosp.-Cornell Med. Center dedicated in his honor, 1975. Fellow Weizmann Inst. Sci. (hon.); mem. N.Y. County Lawyers, Am., Fed. bar assns., Am. Soc. Internat. Law. Clubs: Hillcrest Country (Calif.); Town Tennis, City Athletic (N.Y.C.). Home: 1185 Park Ave New York City NY 10028 Office: 261 Madison Ave New York City NY 10016

WEIMAN, MARK BERNARD, writer/editor; b. Phila., Oct. 18, 1950; s. Jerome Saul and Hassie Isabel (Lasenky) W.; B.A., U. Pa., 1972. Editor, Norwood Edits., Darby, Pa., 1973-74; co-dir. Meml. Found. Redefinition Sanity, Amagansett, N.Y., 1974—; creator aluminum sculptures Tetragrammatron Series, 1975; co-author: Breaking Totem Taboos, 1974; Fragments of Delusional Systems, 1975; A Theater Key to Breaking Totem Taboos (folk opera), 1974; A Tribute to Jose Quintero, 1975; Goodbye My Cony Island Baby, 1978; co-author, dir. (with Claire Burch) film series The World's a Ward and Ward Enough, Paradoxes of Schizophrenia, Arrival of James Baldwin, Mysterious Circumstances; bibliographer: A Bibliography of Books in English on Sleep, Dreams, and Insomnia, 1978. Address: care General Delivery Amagansett NY 11930

WEIN, LOUIS PHILIP, business cons., civic worker; b. N.Y.C., Aug. 27, 1941; s. Louis Vincent and Rosita Cecilia (Mesqueue de La Guardia) W.; B.A. in Social Scis., Fordham U., 1970; postgrad. N.Y. U., 1974-76; m. Mary Ann Funicella, Oct. 8, 1966; children—Annemarie, Mary Diana, Joseph Louis. Group social worker Catholic Charities, N.Y.C., 1965-68; personnel specialist Brown Bros. Harriman & Co., N.Y.C., 1967-68; nat. mktg. dir. Mediterranean Importing Co., N.Y.C., 1970-73; cons. Exec. Office of Pres. of U.S., Washington, 1973—; pub. affairs cons. Detectives Endowment Assn., N.Y.C., 1973; dir. fed. relations Office of Mayor, N.Y.C., 1973-76, exec. dir. Mayor's Task Force for Emergency Preparedness, 1975-76; pres. The Wein Group, N.Y.C., 1976—; dir. Litus Corp., N.Y.C.; vis. prof. govt. relations N.Y. Chiropractic Coll., Westbury, 1973—; vis. lectr. Grad. Sch. Edn., L.I. U., Bklyn., 1974; guest lectr. Richmond Coll., S.I., N.Y., 1974-75. Active Boy Scouts Am., 1963-65; water safety instr. ARC, Washington, 1961-63; mem. citizens task force N.Y. State Assembly, 1967-73; mem. Community Planning Bd., S.I., 1968-73; mem. Regional Emergency Med. Service Council of N.Y.C., 1974-77; mem. Environ. Com. of N.Y.C. Health Systems Agy., 1975-77; mem. citizens adv. com. Law Enforcement Assistance Adminstrn., Washington, 1974-75; mem. bd. advisers Hassidic Corp. for Urban Concerns, 1973—; mem. steering com. N.Y.C. Community Devel. Agy., 1966; candidate for Mayor, City of N.Y., 1977; bd. dirs. Soc. for Prevention of Cruelty to Children, 1975-77; bd. dirs. Last Chance Pond and Wildlife Refuge Found., chmn., 1975—; trustee N.Y. Chiropractic Coll., 1971—. Served with USMC, 1959-63. Recipient numerous awards including: Highest Civilian award for Heroism, N.Y. Police Dept., 1976, Citizen's Citation, Nassau County, 1977, Honor award Hassidic Corp. for Urban Concerns, 1973, Citizen of the Month award Detectives Crime Clinic, 1976, Leadership award Boy Scouts Am., 1970. Mem. Am. Hist. Soc., Am. Legion, Marine Corps League, Honor Legion of N.Y. Police Dept. Republican. Roman Catholic. Clubs: Toastmasters Internat. (Pres.'s award 1975), K.C. Author of N.Y.C.'s 1st Social Service Directory, 1967; columnist S.I. Register, 1968-70; Lou Wein Day in Staten Island proclaimed in his honor. Home: 142 Townsend Ave Staten Island NY 10304 Office: 551 Fifth Ave New York NY 10017

WEINBAUM, MORRIS J., steel processing co. exec.; b. Sewickley, Pa., Dec. 20, 1924; B.S., Carnegie Inst. Tech. (now Carnegie Mellon U.), 1947, M.S., 1953; m. Claire M. Lebovitz, Jan. 11, 1948; children—David L., Stuart D., Judith S. Engr. NACA (now NASA), Cleve., 1947-50; 51-53; teaching asst. Carnegie Inst. Tech., Pitts., 1950-51; engr. Blaw Knox Co., Pitts., 1953-60; pres. Alon Processing Inc., Tarentum, Pa., 1960—; invited speaker UN Indsl. Devel. Orgn. meeting, Helsinki, Finland, 1974. Served with USNR, 1943-46. Mem. Am. Soc. Metals, Am. Petroleum Inst., Nat. Assn. Corrosion Engrs. Contbr. articles to tech. periodicals. Home: 124 Phillips Pl Pittsburgh PA 15217 Office: Alon Processing Inc Grantham St Tarentum PA 15084

WEINBERG, ALAN AARON, restaurant co. exec.; b. Bklyn., Sept. 9, 1931; s. Samuel Bernard and Sara Ruth (Gelberg) W.; Asso. Applied Arts and Scis., N.Y.C. Community Coll., 1953; B.S. in Econs., Bklyn. Coll., 1959; m. Sheila Rosenberg, Feb. 21, 1953; children—Eric, Mindy, Jay. Food and beverage control clk. Restaurant Assos. Industries, N.Y.C., 1955-56, asst. commissary mgr., 1956-57, buyer, 1957-59, asst. to purchasing agt., 1959-61, purchasing agt., 1961-65, dir. purchasing, 1965-75, v.p., dir. purchasing services and office services, 1975—; cons., lectr. in field. Served with U.S. Army, 1953-55. Certified purchasing agt. Nat. Assn. Purchasing Agts. Mem. Food Service Execs. Assn. (certified exec.), Am. Purchasing Assn. (certified purchasing profl.), Purchasing Mgmt. Assn N.Y., Nat. Restaurant Assn. Jewish. Home: 9 Hamlet Ct Somerset NJ 08873 Office: 1540 Broadway New York City NY 10036

WEINBERG, HAZEL JOAN, psychiatrist, psychoanalyst; b. N.Y.C., Apr. 28, 1934; d. Samuel Aaron and Harriet (Mahren) W.; A.B., Vassar Coll., 1953; M.D., Hahnemann Med. Coll., 1968. Intern Roosevelt Hosp., N.Y.C., 1968-69; resident in psychiatry Albert Einstein Coll. Medicine, Bronx Municipal Hosp. Center, N.Y.C., 1969-71, chief resident, 1971-72, asst. dir. psychiat. emergency services, clin. instr., 1972-72; candidate William Alanson White Inst., 1970-75, certificate, 1975; practice medicine specializing in psychiatry and psychoanalysis, N.Y.C., 1972—; asst. attending dept. psychiatry Roosevelt Hosp., also asso. attending outpatient dept.; attending psychiatrist N.Y. Hosp.; instr. clin. psychiatry U., Cornell U.; faculty William Alanson White Inst. Mem. Am. Psychiat. Assn., Am. Acad. Psychoanalysis, N.Y. County Med. Soc., William Alanson White Psychoanalytic Soc. Home and office: 500 E 77th St New York City NY 10021

WEINBERG, MARK HERMAN, mech. engr.; b. Elizabeth, N.J., Dec. 7, 1919; s. Louis and Esther (Satz) W.; M.E. with distinction, Stevens Inst. Tech., 1941; postgrad. N.Y. U., 1947-49; M.S., Newark Coll. Engring., 1964; m. Evelyne G. Turner, Feb. 11, 1945; children—William Martin, JoAnn Weinberg Taurog. Test engr. Universal Camera Corp., N.Y.C., 1941-44, head test div., 1946-49; instrument designer L.C. Eichner Instruments, Bloomfield, N.J., 1949; founder, chief engr., sec.-treas. Product Engring. Labs., Inc., Newark and Orange, N.J., 1950-61; chief engr. L.C. Eichner Instruments, Clifton, N.J., 1961-62; mech. engr. U.S. Army Picatinny Arsenal, Dover, N.J., 1962-66, supervisory gen. engr., 1966-77; chief instrumentation engring. br. arty./tank systems div., product assurance directorate, Armament Research and Devel. Command U.S. Army, 1977—; cons. in field. Pres. Men's Club Congregation B'nai Israel, Millburn, N.J., 1956-57, pres. congregation, 1968-72, life trustee, 1972—; pres. Brotherhood Council Millburn, Short Hills and Springfield, N.J., 1957-59; mem. Millburn-Short Hills Vol. 1st. Aid Squad, 1958-63. Served to 1st lt., U.S. Army, 1944-46. Registered profl. engr., N.J. Mem. Am. Soc. Nondestructive Testing. Patentee in field. Home: 184 White Oak Ridge Rd Short Hills NJ 07078 Office: DRDAR-QAR-I Bldg 62 US Army ARRADCOM Dover NJ 07801

WEINBERG, MILTON SOLOMON, physician; b. N.Y.C., Feb. 19, 1910; s. Joseph and Ida (Zupovich) W.; B.S., Pa. State Coll., 1930; M.D., Hahnemann Med. Coll., Phila., 1935; m. Ruth Rudick, Oct. 3, 1932 (dec.). Intern, Hahnemann Hosp., Scranton, Pa., 1935-36; resident house physician Park E. Hosp., N.Y.C., 1936-37; individual practice medicine, specializing in obstetrics and gynecology, Jackson Heights, N.Y., 1937—; clin. asso. to asst. clin. prof. obstetrics and gynecology N.Y. Med. Coll., 1958—; dir. gynecology Deepdale Gen. Hosp., Little Neck, N.Y., 1968—. Grievance com. N.Y. State Bd. Regents, 1962-71; mem. N.Y. State Bd. Medicine, 1971-73. Served from 1st. lt. to maj. U.S. Army, 1942-46; ETO. Decorated Purple Heart. Mem. Queens County, N.Y. State med. socs., Am. Coll. Obstetricians and Gynecologists, A.C.S., Internat. Coll. Surgeons. Republican. Jewish. Clubs: N. Hills Country, Physicians Sq., Masons. Home: 80-03 192d St Jamaica NY 11423 Office: 37-41 75th St Jackson Heights NY 11372

WEINBERGER, PHILIP MORRIS, clergyman; b. Sans, Poland, Sept. 1, 1926; s. Joshua and Esther (Birnbaum) W.; came to U.S., 1934, naturalized, 1944; Rabbinical degree Mesifta Theol. Sem., Bklyn., 1950; M.A. in Edn., U. Maine, 1958; Ph.D., N.Y. U., 1970; m. Hannah Slutsker, Apr. 15, 1954; children—Judah Zelig, Deborah Sarah, Samuel Aaron. Ordained rabbi, 1950; rabbi Congregation Beth Abraham, Bangor, Maine, 1956-59, Congregation Anshe Sholom, New Rochelle, N.Y., 1959—; prin. Anshe Sholom Religious Schs., 1959—; chaplain New Rochelle Police Dept., 1973—. City dir. Israel Bonds, Westchester County, 1959—; pres. Prins. Council Westchester Assn. Hebrew Schs. Bd. Jewish Edn. Recipient Humanitarian award Fedn. Jewish Philanthropies, 1972; named Man of Year, B'nai B'rith, 1966. Mem. Union Orthodox Rabbis (exec. bd.), Westchester Bd. Rabbis (pres.). Mem. B'nai B'rith. Home: 59A Locust Ave New Rochelle NY 10801 Office: 50 North Ave New Rochelle NY 10805

WEINER, CHARLES R., judge; b. Phila.; B.A., M.A., Ph.D., U. Pa.; LL.B., Temple U.; m., 3 children. Admitted to Pa. bar; practiced in Phila.; asst. dist. atty. Philadelphia County, 1952; judge U.S. Dist. Ct., Phila., 1967—; mem. U.S. Nat. Commn. for UNESCO, 1974—; faculty U. Pa., Temple U. Dir., chmn. program com. World Affairs Council; chmn. Sr. Adult Citizens Com.; chmn. com. on opportunities for higher edn. Fellowship Commn.; mem. speakers bur. Community Chest; active State Bd. Arts and Scis., Pub. Policy Com., Big Bros. Assn., Crime Prevention Assn., Planning Com. and Faculty for Conf. and Seminars for Dist. Ct. Judges, Thouron Scholarship Com., Vista; mem. Pa. Senate, 1952-66, minority floor leader, 1959-60, 63-64, majority floor leader, 1961-62; mem. Pres.'s Adv. Commn. on Inter-Govtl. Relations; bd. dirs. Jewish Exponent, Mental Health Assn. S.E. Pa., Berean Inst., Phila. Psychiat. Center, Phila. Tribune Charities, Phila. Wharton Center, Parkside YMCA, Jewish Y and Centers, Jewish Publ. Soc. Am., Lyric Opera; trustee, mem. exec. com. Fedn. Jewish Charities, Allied Jewish Appeal; trustee Baldwin Sch., Brith Sholom Found., John Marshall House; chmn. nat. council overseers, chmn. exec. com. Dropsie U.; bd. govs. Inst. Human Resources Devel., Hahnemann Med. Coll.; mem Roscoe Pound-Am. Trial Lawyers Found., Smithsonian Inst., Friends of Phila. Orch. Assn., Acad. Natural Scis. Phila, Pa. Hist. Soc., U. Pa. Mus.; grad. Barnes Inst. Served with USN, World War II; PTO. Recipient Phila. Fellowship award, Founders Day award Temple U., Alumni award U. Pa., Founders award Berean Inst.; fellow Harry S. Truman Library Inst. Mem. Am., Pa., Phila. (co-chmn., vice-chmn. various coms.) bar assns., County Bd. Law Examiners, Practising Law Inst. (dir.), Am. Law Inst. Club: Franklin Inn. Contbr. articles to legal jours. and newspapers. Address: 6613 S US Courthouse Independence Mall W Philadelphia PA 19106

WEINER, FRANK J., lawyer; b. Boston, Mar. 9, 1929; s. Benny and Anna (Braverman) W.; B.S., Boston U., 1950; M.B.A., Northeastern U., 1963; J.D., New Eng. Sch. Law, 1965; m. Helene Joyce Cabitt, Aug. 21, 1955; children—Richard Lawrence, Michael David. Traffic mgr. Murdoch & Hatch Motor Transport, Inc., Boston, 1953-55; gen. traffic mgr. Cargo-Imperial Freight Lines, Inc., Cambridge, Mass., 1955-58; asso. Barrett & Barrett, Boston and Milton, Mass., 1958-62; admitted to Mass. bar, 1965; partner Barrett & Weiner, Braintree, Mass., 1969; pvt. practice law, Boston, 1969—; sr. lectr. transp. law Northeastern U., Boston, 1956-75; faculty Transp. Law Inst., U. Denver Coll. Law, 1970-71, mem. ednl. com., 1970—; dir. dist. 1 Assn. ICC Practitioners, Boston. Chmn., Combined Jewish Philanthropies, Canton, Mass., 1966-68, Israel Emergency Fund, Canton, 1967-68; mem. lawyers com. Histradrut, Boston, 1967. Served with AUS, 1951-53. Mem. Motor Carrier Lawyers Assn. (exec. com. 1976-78), ICC Practitioners Assn., Am. Soc. Traffic and Transp., Am., Mass., Norfolk County, Boston bar assns., Mass. Trial Lawyers Assn., Tau Epsilon Phi. Jewish (v.p. temple 1960, 66-68, pres. 1968-69, dir.). Clubs: Masons, B'nai B'rith. Home: 44 Kings Rd Canton MA 02021 Office: 15 Court Sq Boston MA 02108

WEINER, MATEI, microbiologist; b. Bucharest, Rumania, Aug. 21, 1933; s. David and Rosalie (Dattel) W.; came to U.S., 1966, naturalized, 1971; B.Sc., U. Bucharest, 1957; M.S., Wagner Coll., 1970; postgrad. St. John's U., 1974—; m. Eva Braun, Mar. 19, 1964; children—Andrew, Robert. Technologist food inspection Dept. Health, Bucharest, 1958-66; microbiologist Maimonides Med. Center, Bklyn., 1967-70; supr. microbiology lab. Meth. Hosp. Bklyn., 1970—; instr. microbiology Sch. Med. Technology, 1970—. Grantee in aid Maimonides Med. Center, 1968. Specialist in med. microbiology and pub. health. Mem. Am. Soc. Microbiology, Med. Mycology Soc. N.Y.C., Am. Assn. Clin. Lab. Suprs. and Adminstrs. Contbr. articles to profl. jours. Home: 67-12 Harrow St Forest Hills NY 11375 Office: 506 6th St Brooklyn NY 11215

WEINER, MAX, psychologist, educator; b. Hartford, Conn., May 7, 1926; s. Harry Sam and Gertrude (Cohen) W.; B.A., U. Conn., 1950; M.A., Trinity Coll., 1953; Ph.D., Yale U., 1957; m. Gloria Sall, Feb. 24, 1960; children—William Ronald, Jennifer Sharon. Dir. guidance White Plains (N.Y.) Pub. Schs. 1956-59; asst. prof. edn. Bklyn. Coll., N.Y.C., 1959-64, asso. prof., 1964-68; prof. edn., exec. officer Ph.D. program in edn. Grad. Sch. of City U. N.Y., 1969-76, acting univ. dean for tchr. edn., 1973-74, dir. Ctr. for Advanced Study in Edn., 1970—; professorial lectr. Downstate Med. Center, Bklyn. 1967—; vis. prof., Japan Soc. for Promotion Sci. research fellow Nagoya U., 1978. Served with U.S. Army 1944-46. Certified psychologist, N.Y. Fellow Am. Psychol. Assn.; mem. Am. Ednl. Research Assn., Arthritis Found., N.Y. Acad. of Scis., AAAS. Contbr. numerous articles in field to profl. jours. Home: 24 Fenimore Rd New Rochelle NY 10804 Office: 33 W 42nd St New York NY 10036

WEINER, MELVIN MILTON, elec. engr.; b. Boston, Dec. 5, 1933; s. William Wolf and Kate (Berkowitz) W.; B.S., Mass. Inst. Tech., 1956, M.S., 1956; m. Sandra Roseman, Aug. 16, 1964; children—Steven William, Robert Jay. Coop. student Philco Corp., Phila., 1953-56; project engr. Chu Assos., Littleton, Mass., 1956-59; cons. elec. engr., Brookline, Mass., 1959-76; sr. engr. EG & G, Inc., Boston, 1963-65; sr. staff engr. Honeywell Radiation Center, Boston, 1965-67; staff engr. Am. Sci. & Engring., Inc., Cambridge, Mass., 1967-68; prin. research engr. Avco Everett Research Lab., Everett, Mass., 1971-78; mem. tech. staff The Mitre Corp., Bedford, Mass., 1978—. Founder, chmn. Motor Vehicle Safety Group, 1962—. Mem. IEEE, Am. Phys. Soc., Solar Energy Soc., Optical Soc. Am., Sigma Xi, Eta Kappa Nu (chpt. pres. 1965-68, nat. dir. 1969-71). Patentee in field. Home: 56 Marcellus Dr Newton Centre MA 02159

WEINER, PAUL IVAN, lawyer; b. Bklyn., Aug 4, 1942; s. Henry and Evelyn W.; B.A., Bklyn. Coll., 1964, LL.B., 1967; m. Ellen Schorr, July 25, 1976; children—Jason, Jill. Admitted to N.Y. State bar, 1968, Pa. bar, 1974; mem. firm. Katz & Wolchok, N.Y.C., 1968-70; labor counsel GAF Corp., N.Y.C., 1970-73, Certain-Teed Corp., Valley Forge, Pa., 1973-74, Nabisco, Inc., E. Hanover, N.J., 1974—; mem. faculty Practicing Law Inst. seminars on OSHA, chmn. seminar on employment discrimination litigation. Mem. Am. Bar Assn. (labor sect. equal employment com.), N.Y./N.J. Labor Counsel Assn. (chmn.). Author: Standard Setting under OSHA, 1977; contbr. articles on to Labor Law Jour., 1976-78. Office: Nabisco Inc East Hanover NJ 07936

WEINER, PETER RICHARD, financial analyst; b. Danbury, Conn., May 23, 1950; s. William and Marcia (Smith) W.; B.S. magna cum laude, Boston U., 1972; M.B.A., Cornell U., 1974. Ops. officer 1st Nat. City Bank, N.Y.C., 1974-75; account exec. Merrill Lynch, N.Y.C., 1975-76; fin. analyst F. & M. Schaefer, N.Y.C., 1976-78; mng. dir. Ashmont Arms Realty Trust, Milton, Mass., 1978—. Mem. Am. Mgmt. Assn., Assn. M.B.A. Execs., Beta Gamma Sigma. Home: 800 W Roxbury Pkwy Chestnut Hill MA 02167

WEINER, STEPHEN ARTHUR, lawyer; b. Bklyn., Nov. 20, 1933; s. Joseph Lee and Ruth (Lessall) W.; B.A. summa cum laude, Harvard U., 1954; J.D. cum laude, Yale U., 1957; m. Mina Rieur, Sept. 1, 1958; children—Karen, James. Admitted to N.Y. bar, 1958; asso. firm Winthrop, Stimson, Putnam & Roberts, N.Y.C., 1958-65, partner, 1968—; prof. law U. Calif. at Berkeley, 1965-68; lectr. Practising Law Inst., N.Y.C., 1970—, N.Y. Law Jour., N.Y.C., 1974. Asso. trustee N. Shore Hosp., Manhasset, N.Y. Mem. Assn. Bar City N.Y. (chmn. com. recruitment new lawyers; past mem. com. uniform state laws, com. state cts. superior jurisdiction, fed. cts. com., admissions com.), Phi Beta Kappa, Order of Coif. Contbr. articles to legal jours., chpts. to books. Home: 190 Harbor Rd Sands Point NY 11050 Office: 40 Wall St New York City NY 10005

WEINGAST, MARVIN, lab. dir.; b. Bklyn., Jan. 1, 1943; s. Abe and Rose (Altein) W.; B.S., L.I. U., 1967, M.S., 1971; postgrad. Poly. Inst., 1967-68. Analytic and pollution chemist Amerada Hess Corp., Port Reading, N.J., 1969-73; pollution chemist Chem. Constrn. Co., North Brunswick, N.J., 1973-74; dir. Indsl. Hygiene Lab., Nat. Starch and Chem. Corp., Plainfield, N.J., 1974—. Mem. Am. Chem. Soc., Am. Inst. Chemists, Am. Indsl. Hygiene Assn., AAAS, N.J. Acad. Scis., Mensa. Contbr. articles to profl. jours. Research in indsl. hygiene and pollution detection procedures. Home: 323 Gills Ln Iselin NJ 08830 Office: Nat Starch and Chem Corp 1735 W Front St Plainfield NJ 07063

WEINHOLD, J(ULIUS) FREDERICK, JR., govt. ofcl.; b. Oceanside, N.Y., Oct. 3, 1939; s. Julius Frederick and Dorothy Rita (Millard) W.; B.M.E., Cornell U., 1962; M.P.A., Princeton, U. 1968, M.S.E., 1968; m. Barbara Ann Bauer, Oct. 20, 1962; children—Susan Elizabeth, Robert Andrew. Tech. asst. energy policy staff Office Sci. and Tech., Exec. Office of Pres., Washington, 1968-72; sr. engr. Ford Found. Energy Policy Project, Washington, 1972-74; sr. engr. Fed. Energy Adminstrn., Washington, 1974-75; dir. evaluation ERDA, Washington, 1975-77; dir. tech. programs evaluation Dept. Energy, Washington, 1977—. Pres. ch. council Luth. Ch. of Redeemer, McLean, Va. Served with USN, 1962-66. Mem. Am. Nuclear Soc., ASME (chmn. exec. com. div. energetics). Contbr. to numerous govt. reports on energy policy, energy research and devel., 1968—. Home: 1309 Macbeth St McLean VA 22101 Office: Dept Energy Washington DC 20585

WEINMAN, JOEL B., optometrist; b. Bklyn., Jan. 8, 1937; s. Frank and Rose (Sobel) W.; student U. Pitts., 1954-56; B.S., O.D., Pa. Coll. Optometry, 1960; m. Gretchen FonDersmith, Sept. 20, 1970; children by previous marriage-Jay, Michael, Richard. Practice optometry, Kutztown, Pa., 1960—; instr. Reading Area Community Coll.; cons., lectr. rehab. of partially sighted children Kutztown State Coll. Mem. Gov.'s Council to Study Health Trend in State of Pa., 1970; mem. opticianary sci. adv. com. Reading Area Community Coll. Diplomate Nat. Bd. Optometric Examiners. Fellow Am. Acad. Optometry; mem. Am., Pa. (vision screening chmn. 1966-67, chmn. practice mgmt. 1967-68, 73—) optometric assns., Berks County Optometric Soc. (pres. 1968-69), Berkeleigh Optometric Profl. Assn. (pres. 1970—), Vision Conservation Inst., Am. Optometric Found., Am. Assn. Ethical Hypnosis, Beta Sigma Kappa. Jewish (dir. temple 1967-69). Clubs: Lions, Rotary. Home: 126 W Main St Kutztown PA 19530

WEINMANN, BERT MILLICENT LANDES (MRS. RICHARD A. WEINMANN), artist; b. N.Y.C., July 20, 1924; d. Harry and Esther (Lurie) Landes; student Hunter Coll., 1941-43, Queens Coll., 1958-59, Bklyn. Mus. Art Sch., 1959. New Sch. for Social Research, 1963; grad. Fashion Inst. Tech., 1943; also pvt. student art; m. Richard A. Weinmann, Dec. 26, 1944; children—Harriet, Elaine. Fashion illustrator, designer with Mainbocher, Maurice Rentner, Tabin Picker, others, 1942-50; exhibited one-woman shows Six Trees Gallery, Edgartown, Mass., 1971, Kron Gallery, Mattituck, N.Y., 1972, Firehouse Gallery, Garden City, N.Y., 1975, Unicorn Gallery, N.Y.C., 1974, Gallery 33, N.Y.C., 1976; exhibited in group shows at Palazzo Vecchio, Florence, Italy, 1972, Nat. Acad. Art, 1969, 72, 73. Hecksher Mus., Huntington, N.Y., 1971, Salvator Rosa, Naples, Italy, 1972, Port Washington (N.Y.) Pub. Library, 1972, Fairfield (Conn.) U., 1973, Royal Acad., Stockholm, 1978, also numerous art galleries; works represented in numerous pvt. collections; tchr. drawing and painting North Shore Community Arts Center, Great Neck, N.Y., 1973—. Mem. exec. bd. Great Neck Com. for Human Rights, 1962-76. Recipient awards from numerous juried art exhbns., purchase award Nassau Coll. Assn., 1973. Mem. Nat. Assn. Women Artists (co-chmn. fgn. exhbns. com. 1973-74, Ziuta G. and Joseph James Akston prize 1972), Women in Arts, Profl. Artists Guild, Artists in Am. Home and studio: 61 Franklin Pl Great Neck NY 11023

WEINROD, EMANUEL, apparel co. exec.; b. N.Y.C., Feb. 26, 1929; s. Edward and Bella (Bleustein) W.; B.S., N.Y. U., 1950; m. Barbara Gessler, Apr. 3, 1955; children—Hope, David, Amy. Sales mgr. Five Star Footwear Co., N.Y.C., 1950-65; v.p. mktg. Norwich Shoe Co., Inc., Norwich and N.Y.C., 1966—. Mem. Am. Footwear Industries Assn. (dir., mem. mktg. conf. planning com.), Assn. Fashion Service (men's and children's style com.), Jericho Jewish Center. Club: B'nai B'rith. Home: 17 Clinton Ln Jericho NY 11753 Office: 76 N Broadway Hicksville NY 11801

WEINSAFT, PAUL P., physician; b. Zbaraz, Austria, July 18, 1908; s. Lippe and Basia (Landsberg) W.; M.D., U. Paris, 1933; m. Claudia Carrel, Mar. 24, 1934. Intern, Edgewater Hosp., Chgo., 1941-42; resident VA Hosp., Martinsburg, W.Va., 1951-54; dir. Lab. Clin. Pathology, Paris, 1934-40; practice medicine, specializing in geriatric medicine, Winthrop, Mass., 1944-51, VA Hosp., N.Y.C., 1955-60, 61-65; med. dir. Bklyn. Hebrew Home and Hosp. for Aged, 1961-67; chief chronic disease Coney Island Hosp., 1967—; med. dir. Met. Jewish Geriatric Center, Bklyn., 1967—; cons. internal medicine Malmonides Med. Center, Bklyn., 1974—. Served with French Army, 1940-41. Diplomate Am. Bd. Internal Medicine. Fellow A.C.P., Am. Geriatric Soc., Am. Gerontol. Soc., N.Y. Acad. Medicine; mem. N.Y. Acad. Scis., N.Y. State, N.Y. County med. socs. Contbr. articles to profl. jours. Home: 205 W 54 St New York City NY 10019 Office: 4915 10th Ave Brooklyn NY 11212

WEINSTEIN, ALFRED BERNARD, psychotherapist; b. N.Y.C., Nov. 6, 1917; s. Morris and Mamie; B.A. in English, Bklyn. Coll., 1941; M.A. in Teaching English, Columbia U., 1947; Ed.D. in Secondary Sch. Adminstrn., 1951; postdoctoral in clin. psychology New Sch. for Social Research; certificate in psychotherapy Alfred Adler Inst., 1977; m. Muriel Band, Dec. 25, 1975; 1 son by previous marriage, Bruce. Asst. prin. Pub. Sch. 144, Bklyn., 1956-57; prin. Pub. Sch. 56, Bklyn., 1957-59, Pub. Sch. 144, Queens, 1959-64, Col. David Marcus Jr. High Sch., Bklyn., 1964-70; head unit 2 Bd. Examiners, N.Y.C. Bd. Edn., 1970-71; prin. Myra S. Barnes Intermediate Sch., S.I., N.Y., 1971-78; dir. edn. Maimonides Sch., Maimonides Inst., Far Rockaway, N.Y., 1978—; psychotherapist, instr. Alfred Adler Clinic, N.Y.C., 1977—; practice psychotherapy, hypnotherapy and marriage counseling, West Hempstead, N.Y., 1977—. Mem. exec. bd., former v.p. council suprs. and adminstrs. Local 1 AFL-CIO, N.Y.C., 1974-78. Served with USAAF, 1941-45. Decorated Air medal with 3 oak leaf clusters; licensed prin. day high schs. Mem. Doctorate Assn. of N.Y. Educators, Jr. High Sch. Prins. Assn. (pres. 1969-71), N.Y. Assn. Exptl. Study of Edn., N.Y. Acad. Pub. Edn., Assn. Supervision and Curriculum Devel., Bklyn. Coll. Alumni Assn. (dir.), Internat. Reading Assn., Phi Delta Kappa, Kappa Delta Phi. Clubs: Bnai Brith (pres. Schoolman's lodge 1969-71). Author: (with William Elfert) Achieving Reading Skills, 1958; (with Sidney Rauch) Mastery of College Reading Skills, 1968, World of Vocabulary series, 1976-77; editor (with Sidney Rauch and Muriel Weinstein) High Points, 1968-71; contbr. short story to New Voices-American Writing Today (C.I. Glicksberg), 1958. Home: 644 Pauley Dr West Hempstead NY 11552

WEINSTEIN, BERNARD M., hosp. adminstr.; b. Winthrop, Mass., Aug. 14, 1931; s. Morris and Bessie (Baron) W.; B.S., U. Mass., 1953; M.P.H., U. Pitts., 1959; m. Eileen Ellman, Mar. 5, 1961; children—Jeffery, Michelle Beth. Asst. adminstr. Albert Einstein Med. Center, Phila., 1959, then first asst. adminstr., 1962; asst. dir., adminstr. affiliation programs Mt. Sinai Hosp., N.Y.C., 1962-68; exec. dir. Bellevue Hosp. Center, N.Y.C., 1968—; clin. prof. dept. preventive medicine N.Y. U. Med. Sch. Cons. to Commr. Hosps. N.Y.C., HEW Task Force on Medicaid, City of Balt. Dept. Fin.; pres. council of exec. dirs. N.Y.C. Health and Hosps. Corp. Served to lt. USAF, 1954-56. Fellow Royal Soc. Health; mem. Am. Coll. Hosp. Adminstrs., Am. Pub. Health Assn., Am. Hosp. Assn. (chmn. program com. and mem. governing bd. pub.-gen. hosp. sect., mem. spl. com. on manpower, council manpower and edn.). Contbr. profl. jours. Office: Bellevue Hosp 27th St and 1st Ave New York City NY 10016

WEINSTEIN, CLEMENT, physician; b. Bklyn., Aprl. 11, 1926; s. Samuel and Sadie (Furman) W.; A.B., Columbia Coll., 1947; M.D., State U. N.Y., 1950; m. Gertrude Rindsberg, Sept. 23, 1950; children—Roslyn Sue, Fred David, Lawrence Mark, Barbara Joan. Intern Maimonides Hosp., N.Y.C., 1950-51; resident Montefiore Hosp., N.Y.C., 1954-55; Dazian fellow biochemistry Long Island Jewish Hosp., N.Y., 1955-56, Rosenstock fellow, 1956-59; practice medicine specializing in internal medicine and cardiology, Jamaica, N.Y., 1956—; staff physician Long Island Jewish Med. Center, New Hyde Park, N.Y., 1956—; attending physician Jamaica (N.Y.) Hosp., 1963—, dir. cardiology, 1963—; asst. prof. clin. medicine State U. N.Y., Stony Brook, 1973—. Chmn. Queens-Nassay chpt. Med. Commn. of Human rights, 1962-68; del. Dem. Nat. Conv., Miami Beach, Fla., 1972; mem. Health Profls. Against the War in Viet-nam, 1970-74. Served with USN, 1944-45; USPHS, 1951-53. Mem. Am. Heart Assn., A.C.P., N.Y. State Med. Soc., Queens County Med. Soc. Democrat. Jewish. Home: 69-18 179th St Flushing NY 11365 Office: 162-15 Highland Ave Jamaica NY 11432

WEINSTEIN, FRANCIS SAUL, physician, educator; b. Bridgeport, Conn., Mar. 12, 1910; s. Samuel and Anna (Turtz) W.; B.S., Rutgers U., 1931; M.D., N.Y. Med. Coll., 1935; m. Anna Posner, June 28, 1935; children—Stephen, Donald. Intern, Flower and Fifth Ave. Hosp., N.Y.C., 1935-36; resident Bellevue Hosp., N.Y.C., 1944-45, in otolaryngology U. Pa. Grad. Sch. Medicine, 1945-46; practice medicine specializing in otolaryngology, Newark, 1946-61, South Orange, N.J., 1961—; mem. staff St. Barnabas Hosp., Livingston, N.J., Newark Eye and Ear Infirmary; clin. asso. prof. surgery dept. otolaryngology Coll. Medicine and Dentistry N.J., Newark, 1976; clin. asst. Bellevue Hosp., 1946-52. Mem. exec. com. Newark Eye and Ear Infirmary, 1960-76, recipient award, 1976. Mem. AMA, N.J., Essex County med. assns., Acad. Medicine No. N.J., Am. Acad. Ophthalmology and Otolaryngology. Jewish. Home: 100 Stonehill Rd Apt R-3 Springfield NJ 07083 Office: 468 Irvington Ave South Orange NJ 07079

WEINSTEIN, GEORGE, accountant, mgmt. cons.; b. N.Y.C., Mar. 20, 1924; s. Morris J. and Sara (Broder) W.; B.S., U. Ill., 1944, student law sch., 1944-45; M.B.A., N.Y. U., 1947, student law sch., 1947-48; m. Shirley Beatrice Greenberg, Sept. 1, 1945; children—Stanley Howard, Jerrald, Sara Belle. Exec. sec. Illini Union Bldg., Champaign, Ill., 1944; with Homes & Davis, accountants, 1944; with Morris J. Weinstein, Groothuis & Co., 1944, partner, 1945-72; partner Weinstein Assos., fin. cons., N.Y.C. and Milw. 1973—; pres., dir. REIT Property Mgrs. Ltd., Milw.; pres., trustee Wis. Real Estate Investment Trust, Milw.; chmn. Ross Orgn., Orlando, Fla. Chmn. drives United Jewish Appeal, Fedn. Jewish Philanthropies. Bd. dirs., founder North Shore Hebrew Acad.; founder, past pres. Great Neck (N.Y.) Synagogue; treas. Sarah B. Weinstein Found.; trustee M. Rainville Trust; bd. dirs. Milw. Jewish Home, Jewish Nat. Fund, Milw. Mem. Am. Inst. Accountants, N.Y. Soc. C.P.A.'s, Hebrew Immigrant Soc., Tau Delta Phi (nat. treas.), Delta Sigma Phi. Jewish religion (pres. Synagogue, 1951-53, chmn. bd., 1955, hon. pres.). Mason (past master). Clubs: President's U. Ill.; Westmoreland, Ambassadors of Yeshiva U.; Milwaukee Athletic, Wisconsin. Home: 418 Central Park West New York City NY 10024 also 925 E Wells St Milwaukee WI 53233 Office: 418 Central Park West New York City NY 10023 also 925 Wells St Milwaukee WI 53233

WEINSTEIN, HOWARD, plumbing supply wholesale co. exec.; b. Phila., June 22, 1931; s. Jacob N. and Silvia (Goldstein) W.; B.S. in Econs., Wharton Sch., U. Pa., 1952; m. Lenore Sherman, June 27, 1954; children—J. Paul, Bruce, Lila, Ivan. Partner, pres., chmn. bd. Weinstein Supply Co., Phila., 1954—. Vice pres. parent advisory council Abington (Pa.) High Sch., 1976, treas., 1977; bd. dirs. Rydal Meadowbrook Civic Assn., 1978. Served to 1st lt. U.S. Army, 1952-54; Korea. Mem. Plumbing and Heating Supply House Employers Assn. (v.p. 1977), Middle Atlantic Wholesalers Assn., Am. Inst. Republican. Jewish. Clubs: Golden Slipper, Masons. Home: 1760 Cloverly Ln Rydal PA 19046

WEINSTEIN, IRVING, psychologist; b. N.Y.C., Jan. 25, 1928; s. Zesie and Celia (Schneider) W.; B.A., L.I. U., 1951; M.A., City U. N.Y., 1953. Supervising psychologist St. Vincent's Hosp. and Med. Center, N.Y.C., 1965-73; sr. staff and sr. psychologist Central Islip and Creedmoor State Hosps., 1956-60; staff psychologist Central State Hosp., Indpls., 1955-56; research asst. psychologist Bellevue Psychiat. Hosp.-N.Y. U. Med. Center, 1952-54; pvt. practice psychoanalytic psychotherapy, N.Y.C., 1960—; supr. psychotherapy Lincoln Inst. Psychotherapy, N.Y.C., 1970—. Served with U.S. Army, 1946-47. Certified psychologist, N.Y. State. Mem. N.Y. Soc. Clin. Psychologists, Am. Acad. Psychotherapists, Am., N.Y. State psychol. assns., Nat. Health Service Providers in Psychology. Office: 425 E 86th St New York City NY 10028

WEINSTEIN, MURRAY, physicist; b. N.Y.C., Jan. 21, 1930; s. Boris and Anna (Slavin) W.; B.S., City Coll. N.Y., 1951; M.A., Columbia U., 1954; m. Judith Katz, Mar. 17, 1951; children—Joseph Robert, Mark Jeffrey. Research asst. Pupin Cyclotron Lab., Columbia U., 1952-53; physicist Picatinny Arsenal, Dover, N.J., 1951-55, mem. air def. nuclear effects group, 1955-59, chief advanced research unit, 1959-60, chief nuclear warhead effects research unit, 1960-62, tech. asst. Feltman Research Lab., 1962-68, project officer nuclear weapon effects research, 1968-70, staff physicist Fuze div., 1970-72, asst. to tech. dir., 1972-74, staff physicist, engr. Plans Office, 1974-77, ops. research analyst Systems Evaluation Office, 1977—. Vice-pres. Dover Little Theatre, 1966; bd. govs. Dover Jewish Center, 1968—, pres., 1972-74. Mem. Am. Phys. Soc., Am. Def. Preparedness Assn. Home: 32 Taylor St Dover NJ 07801 Office: Bldg 151 HQARRADCOM Dover NJ 07801

WEINTRAUB, ARTHUR ELEAZER, research co. exec.; b. N.Y.C., July 18, 1935; s. Jacob and Sarah (Mauer) W.; B.A., Hunter Coll., 1956; M.Planning, N.Y. U., 1965; postgrad. (Nat. Endowment for Humanities fellow), Princeton U., 1977; m. Carole Buchwald, Apr. 14, 1962; children—Jill, David. Planner, U.S. Army Corps Engrs., N.Y.C., 1956-64; sr. urban planner Tri-State Regional Planning Commn., N.Y.C., 1964-67; lectr. in planning Vassar Coll., Poughkeepsie, N.Y., 1968-70; sr. v.p. Mid-Hudson Pattern, Inc., Poughkeepsie, 1967—; cons. N.Y. State Urban Devel. Corp., 1969-71, Hudson Valley Health Systems Agy., 1977-78, others. Vice pres. Newburgh (N.Y.) Bd. Edn., 1974—; mem. Orange County Charter Rev. Commn., 1977—, Orange County Fgn. Trade Zone Mgmt. Bd., 1976—; trustee St. Luke's Hosp., Newburgh, 1973—. Served with N.Y. N.G., 1952. Recipient Distinguished Community Service award Eastern Orange C. of C., 1968. Mem. Am. Inst. Planners, Am. Soc. for Pub. Adminstrn., Am. Soc. Planning Ofcls., Am. Pub. Health Assn. Contbr. articles to profl. jours. Home: 47 Susan Dr E Newburgh NY 12550

WEINTRAUB, DANIEL RALPH, health planner; b. N.Y.C., Apr. 23, 1939; s. Benjamin Zion and Ida (Barman) W.; B.A. in Biology, N.Y. U., 1959; D.D.S., Columbia U., 1963; certificate pub. health U. Wash., 1963; m. Sally Ann Franco, Mar. 16, 1968; children—David Arlo, Jeremy Michael. Rural community devel. adviser AID, Dominican Republic, 1966-68, population and pub. health adviser, 1968-69; asso. planning dir. Alan Guttmacher Inst. (formerly Center for Family Planning Program Devel.), N.Y.C., 1969-74; dep. dir. Family Planning Internat. Assistance, N.Y.C., 1974-76, chief operating officer, 1977—; v.p. internat. programs Planned Parenthood Fedn., Am., N.Y.C., 1978—; vol. leader, coordinator U.S. Peace Corps, Bolivia, 1964-65; cons. HEW, 1971-74, Nat. Center Health Statistics, 1974. Mem. Am. Mus. Natural History, Action for Child Transp. Safety. Recipient Certificate of Honor, Dominican Republic, 1969; commendation Dept. Interior, Cochabamba, Bolivia, 1965. Mem. Population Assn. Am., Nat. Geog. Soc. Author books on community devel. theory and practice, plans for area-wide family planning programs in met. areas, nat. studies including Need for Subsidized Family Planning Services: United States, Each State and County, 1971. Home: 8 Dock Ln Port Washington North NY 11050 Office: 810 7th Ave New York City NY 10019

WEINTRAUB, LOUIS, pub. relations exec.; b. Montreal, Que., Can., June 4, 1922; s. Samuel and Bella (Silverman) W.; student pub. schs., N.Y.C.; m. Renee Arum, Nov. 4, 1951; children—Toby, Joel, Judy. Came to U.S., 1923, naturalized, 1946. Washington bur. mgr. Pix, Inc., 1940-41; asst. to picture editor Washington Post, 1940-41; news photographer Office War Info., 1941-42; picture editor Keystone Pictures, Inc., N.Y.C., 1947-49; asst. to pub. N.Y. Age, 1949-50; dir. News Press Service, 1950-54; dir. pub. relations Pavelle Color and Pavelle Labs., Inc., 1951-57; pres. Weintraub & Fitz-Simons, Inc., pub. relations counsel, N.Y.C., 1958—, Photo Communications Co., Inc., visual cons., N.Y.C., 1958—. Pub. relations adviser Hon. W.Averell Harriman, 1954-60. N.Y. State Goodwill Ambassador, Brussels World's Fair, 1958; mem. Pres. Com. on Employment of Handicapped, 1958—; vice chmn., mem. bd. Citizen's Budget Commn., 1967—; v.p., mem. bd. Greater N.Y. Safety Council, 1969—. Served to cpl., Signal Corps, AUS, 1942-45. Decorated Croix de Guerre with Palms (France); recipient medal City of Orleans (France), 1948, Pub. Service award Philippines Lions Internat., 1959. Mem. Pub. Relations Soc. Am., Silurians, Nat. Press Club, Overseas Press Club, Fgn. Press Assn., Am. Legion, VFW, Nat. Press Photographers Assn. Club: B'nai B'rith. Home: 11 Maytime Dr Jericho NY 11753 Office: 488 Madison Ave New York City NY 10022

WEINTRAUB, SOL, educator; b. Luxembourg, July 3, 1937; s. Mordecai and Sarah (Patcas) W.; came to U.S., 1947, naturalized, 1955; B.S., Coll. City N.Y., 1958; M.A., Temple U., 1960, Ph.D., 1964; m. Rita T. Katz, Dec. 21, 1960; children—Lisa, Dina, Amy. Cons., Applied Data Research, Inc., Princeton, N.J., 1960-64; asst. prof. math. Queens Coll., City U. N.Y., 1964-72, asso. prof., 1972—. Mem. Am. Math. Soc., Assn. Computing Machinery. Author: Tables of the Cumulative Binomial Probability Distribution, 1963; (with A. Sard) Book of Splines, 1971; Introduction to Statistics, 1976. Office: 67-30 Kissena Blvd Queens Coll Flushing NY 11367

WEIR, MERRILL E., govt. ofcl.; b. Crawford County, Kans., June 24, 1909; s. George Elwood and Comorah Miranda (Landon) W.; B.S., Kan. State Coll., 1933; postgrad. Brookings Instn., 1960, Fgn. Ser. Inst., 1963; m. Ellen Hilda (Reichardt) Albert, Feb. 1944. Dir. Employment Security Agy., Alaska, 1956-63; AID adviser on employment ser. and manpower, Iran, 1963-65; with Internat. Tech. Assistance Corps, Labor Dept., 1965—, nampower devel. adviser, Venuzuela, 1965-66, Vietnam, 1966-70; dir. Internat. Manpower Inst., Washington, 1970-71; manpower adviser ILO, Colombo, Ceylon, 1971-72; unemployment ins. adviser OAS, Kingston, Jamaica, 1973; unemployment ins. cons. ILO, Tehran, Iran, 1974; manpower devel. adviser Bur. Internat. Labor Affairs, Labor Dept., Washington, 1976; project dir. U.S./Saudi Arabia Joint Econ. Commn., Riyadhi, Saudi Arabia, 1976-77. Served with AUS, 1941-42, USNR, 1942-45. Mem. Internat. Assn. Personnel in Employment. Am. Legion, VFW. (Distinguished Ser. award 1963). Home: 2016 Coleridge Dr Apt 303 Bldg 24 Silver Spring MD 20902

WEISBERG, GERARD MAXWELL, judge; b. Bklyn., Aug. 1, 1925; s. Reuben and Florence (Narder) W.; B.A. magna cum laude, St. John's U., 1946; J.D., Columbia, 1948; LL.M., Bklyn. Law Sch., 1966; m. Blanche Silber, Feb. 28, 1954; children—Bruce Adam, Andrea Ilene. Admitted to N.Y. State bar, 1948; gen. practice law specializing in labor relations, N.Y.C., 1948-62; dep. commr. Dept. Licenses City N.Y., 1962-66, commr. Dept. Markets, 1966-68, Dept. Consumer Affairs, 1968-69; judge Criminal Ct. City N.Y., 1969-77, Ct. of Claims of State of N.Y., 1977—. Guest lectr. various times Farmingdale State Community Coll., Manhattan Community Coll.; adj. lectr. law Kingsborough Community Coll., 1974—; lectr. labor relations N.Y. U., 1977—. Kings County chmn. Liberal party N.Y. State, 1962-65. Recipient citations U.S. Treasury Dept., 1943, 2d Spanish Evang. Ch., 1957, Presbyn. Ch. of Crossroads, 1961, United Hebrew Immigrant Aid Soc., Ch. St. Ignatius Loyola, 1964, Fedn. Jewish Philanthropies, 1967. Mem. N.Y. State, Bklyn. bar assns. Home: 2301 King's Hwy Brooklyn NY 11229 Office: 2 World Trade Center New York City NY 10047

WEISBERG, JOSEPH GOTLAND, editor, publisher; b. Boston, June 10, 1911; s. Abraham and Sarah (Brin) W.; A.B., Harvard U., 1933, J.D., 1936; m. Marjorie Mary Elbinger, May 8, 1939; children—Lawrenc, Helaine. Reporter, Boston Post, 1929-33; admitted to Mass. bar, 1936; individual practice law, Boston, 1936-44; asso. editor Jewish Advocate, Boston, 1944-52, editor, pub., 1952—; dir. Jewish Telegraphic Agy. Mem. Mass. Bd. Edn., 1965-73, Mass. Ednl. Communications Commn., 1968—; chmn. Brookline (Mass.) Com. on Town Reports; hon. trustee Temple Israel of Boston, Combined Jewish Philanthropies of Boston; trustee Beth Israel Hosp., New Eng. Sinai Hosp.; mem. exec. bd. Am. Jewish Hist. Soc.; mem. nat. council Jewish Joint Distbn. Com. Fellow Brandeis U.; recipient numerous citations, including Women's Am. ORT, Union Am. Hebrew Congregations, Zionist Orgn. Am., New Eng. Press Assn., B'nai B'rith. Mem. Am. Jewish Press Assn. (pres. 1961-63), New Eng. Press Assn., Overseas Press Club, World Assn. Jewish Journalists. Clubs: Harvard, Belmont Country. Home: 39 Chatham St Brookline MA 02146 Office: 251 Causeway St Boston MA 02114

WEISCHADLE, DAVID EMMANUEL, educator; b. Sayreville, N.J., Oct. 4, 1941; s. Richard George and Christina V. (Dailey) W.; B.S., Rutgers U., 1963, Ed.M., 1964, Ed.D., 1970; m. Mary Ann C. Piscopo, June 22, 1968; children—David Emmanuel, Douglas Eric. Tchr., Edison (N.J.) Pub. Schs., 1964-69; program devel. specialist N.J. Urban Schs. Devel. Council, 1969-70; project dir. Office Edn., dir. div. research planting and evaluation Trenton (N.J.) Pub. Schs., 1970-73; prof. ednl. adminstrn. Montclair State Coll., Upper Montclair, N.J., 1973—; ednl. cons. in ednl. planning and systems analysis fed., state and local edn., social and health agys., 1972—. Served from 2d lt. to capt. Signal Corps. AUS, 1965-67. Grantee Engelhard Found., 1963, U.S. Office Edn., N.J. Dept. Edn., 1970. Mem. Assn. Supervision and Curriculum Devel., Am. Ednl. Research Assn., Nat. Soc. for Study Edn., Internat. Soc. Ednl. Planners, Kappa Delta Pi. Club: K.C. Contbr. articles to profl. jours. Home: 6 Ribsam St Trenton NJ 08619 Office: Dept Ednl Leadership Montclair State Coll Upper Montclair NJ 07043

WEISE, WALLACE PLOSS, cons. engr.; b. Scotia, N.Y., Oct. 12, 1909; s. Albert Frederick and Ella Burhans (Ploss) W.; B.S. in Elec. Engring., Union Coll., Schenectady, N.Y., 1931; m. Frances Barker, Aug. 8, 1936; children—Kenneth, Frances, Janet. Test engr. Consol. Edison Co., N.Y.C., 1931-48; prin. engr. Ebasco Services Inc., 1948-70, Ralph M. Parsons Co., 1970-72; village cons. engr., Port Washington, N.Y., 1975—; ind. cons. engr., 1973—. Mem. sch. bd., New Hyde Park, N.Y., 1956-59. Registered profl. engr., N.Y. Mem. IEEE, N.Y. State Soc. Profl. Engrs., N.Y.C. Profl. Engring. Soc. (chmn. edn. com., dir. 1952-53). Address: 31 Carole Ave New Hyde Park NY 11040

WEISELBERG, NORMAN, physician; b. Bronx, N.Y., Mar. 16, 1915; s. Samuel and Ray W.; B.A., N.Y. U., 1936; D.D.S., U. Pa., 1943; M.D., St. Mungo's Med. Coll., Glasgow, Scotland, 1947; m. Ruth M. Pault, Aug. 21, 1938; children—Lora, Stanley. Intern, Jamaica (N.Y.) Hosp.; family practice medicine, Elmhurst, N.Y., 1948—; mem. staff, med. bd. Booth Meml. Med. Center, Flushing, N.Y., pres. med. staff, 1977—. Served as capt. U.S. Army, 1943-46. Diplomate Am. Bd. Family Practice (charter mem.). Fellow Am. Acad. Family Practice, AMA; mem. N.Y., Am. diabetes assns., Royal Coll. Physicians Edinburgh (licentiate), Royal Coll. Surgeons Edinburgh (licentiate), Royal Faculty Physicians and Surgeons Glasgow (licentiate). Office: 50-11 Junction Blvd Elmhurst NY 11373

WEISER, KENNETH DAVID, accountant; b. N.Y.C., Dec. 1, 1924; s. Maxwell R. and Rose (Kohlenberg) W.; B.A., Columbia, 1947; M.B.A., Harvard, 1949; m. Carol Ann Kane, June 6, 1950; children—Robert K., Betsy L., Edward S. C.P.A., M.R. Weiser & Co., N.Y.C., 1950—, sr. partner, 1967—. Bd. dirs., pres. Westchester Jewish Com. Service. Former mem. Republican Town Com. Scarsdale, N.Y. Trustee Fedn. Jewish Philanthropies N.Y., Assn., also mem. exec. com.; trustee YM-YWHA's N.Y. Served with AUS, 1943-45. C.P.A., N.Y. Mem. Am. Inst. C.P.A.'s, N.Y. State Soc. C.P.As, Am. Accounting Assn., Zeta Beta Tau. Clubs: Beach Point (Mamaroneck, N.Y. treas. 1962-67), Fairview Country (pres. 1977—) (Greenwich, Conn.); Harvard (N.Y.). Home: 41 Aspen Rd Scarsdale NY 10583 Office: 535 Fifth Ave New York City NY 10017

WEISER, NORMAN SIDNEY, publishing co. exec.; b. Mpls., Oct. 1, 1919; s. Simon and Rosa (Davidson) W.; B.A., Northwestern U., 1939; m. Ruth Miller, Mar. 23, 1943; children—Judith Ann, Richard Alan. Reporter, Radio Daily, N.Y.C., 1938-42; reporter, editor Billboard Mag., N.Y.C. and Chgo., 1947-52; pub. Down Beat Mag., Chgo., 1952-59; v.p. United Artists, N.Y.C., 1959-62, 64-68, Twentieth Century Fox, N.Y.C., 1962-64; v.p., dir. European ops., Music div. Paramount, London, 1968-69; v.p., gen. mgr. Chappell Music Co., 1969-73, pres., 1973-78; sr. v.p. Polygram Corp., 1974-78, cons., 1978—; pres. Weiser Music Complex, N.Y.C., 1978—, SESAC, Inc., 1978—. Served to capt. USAAF, 1942-47. Decorated Purple Heart, Commendation medal. Recipient Ben Gurion award Bonds for Israel, 1975. Mem. ASCAP (dir. 1974), Nat. Music Pubs. Assn. (v.p., dir. 1974), Country Music Assn. (chmn. bd. 1976-77). Club: B'nai B'rith. Author: Writers' Radio Theater, 1940; Writers' Radio-TV Theater, 1942; Under the Big Top, 1947; History AAF, World War II, 1947. Home: 58 W 58th St New York City NY 10019 Office: 15 E 48 St New York City NY 10019

WEISFOGEL, JERRY, psychiatrist; b. N.Y.C., May 27, 1928; s. Joseph and Rose (Fox) W.; B.S., Coll. City N.Y., 1952, M.A., 1953; M.D., N.Y. Med. Coll., 1957. Intern, Beth-El Hosp., Bklyn., 1957-58; resident psychiat. div. Kings County Hosp. Center, Bklyn., 1958-61; chief psychiatrist adult inpatient service Kings County Hosp., Bklyn., 1961-63, adult psychotherapy service, 1965-67, dir. emergency treatment service, 1967-68, supervising psychiatrist diagnostic service, 1968-70; psychiat. cons. Northport VA Hosp. (L.I.,N.Y.), 1968—, dept. rehab. medicine City Hosp., Elmhurst, N.Y., 1970—; instr. psychiatry State U. N.Y., Downstate Med. Center, 1961-68, clin. asst. prof. psychiatry, 1968-69, asst. prof., 1969-70; asst. clin. prof. psychiatry Mt. Sinai Sch. Medicine, N.Y.C., 1970—. NIMH grantee, 1963-65. Fellow Am. Psychiat. Assn., Am. Assn. Psychoanalytic Physicians, Am. Acad. Psychosomatic Medicine; mem. Bklyn. Psychiat. Soc. (pres. 1977-78, com. chmn.), Schilder Soc. Psychopathology of Psychotherapy (pres. 1974-76). Contbg. editor Ann. Survey Psychoanalysis, 1969; contbr. psychiat. articles to med. jours. Address: 7 E 85th St New York City NY 10028

WEISINGER, RICHARD HARRY, lawyer, metal mfg. co. exec.; b. Newark, Dec. 1, 1926; s. Albert I. and Esther (Karlin) W.; B.B.A., U. Miami, 1951; LL.B., N.Y. Law Sch., 1955; m. Gloria Lesser, July 3, 1955; children—Norman, Roberta, William, Janet. Accountant, Kabat, Groothuis & Co., C.P.A.'s, N.Y.C., 1951-53, David Koenig & Co., C.P.A.'s, N.Y.C., 1953-54; asst. to pres., controller Universal Pin Co., N.Y.C., 1954-58; admitted to N.Y. State bar, 1958, since practiced in N.Y.C.; mem. firm Jack N. Blinkoff, 1958-60; partner firm Blinkoff & Weisinger, 1960-68, Lowenthal, Landau, Fischer & Weisinger, 1968-71, Greenfield Stein & Weisinger, 1971—; pres., chmn. bd. Ultradynamics Corp., Englewood, N.J., 1968—; co-founder, v.p. Englewood Nat. Bank (merger Midland Bank & Trust Co.), Paramus, N.J., 1968, also dir.; dir., mem. exec. com. Midland Bank & Trust Co.; dir., mem. audit com. Vernitron Corp., 1976—. Served with USNR, 1944-46. Mem. Am. Bar Assn., Phi Delta Pi. Home: 41 Carol Dr Englewood Cliffs NJ 07632 Office: Greenfield Stein & Weisinger 380 Madison Ave New York City NY 10017

WEISMAN, IRVING, social worker, educator; b. N.Y.C., May 6, 1918; s. Max and Sadie (Berkowitz) W.; B.S., City Coll. N.Y., 1939; M.S., U. Buffalo, 1942; Ed.D., Columbia U., 1962; m. Cyrille Gold, May 1, 1941; children—Seth, Adam. Caseworker, Nat. Refugee Service, N.Y.C., 1941; warden's asst. Fed. Detention Hdqrs., Bur. Prisons, U.S. Dept. Justice, N.Y.C., 1942-43; psychiat. social worker to chief social worker VA, Camden and Union City, N.J., 1946-49; case supr. Altro Health and Rehab. Service, N.Y., 1949-50; field instr., lectr. Columbia U. Sch. Social Work, N.Y.C., 1950-57, asso. prof., 1957-62, prof., 1962—, acting dean, 1964-65, asso. dean, 1967-69; exec. officer doctoral program Hunter Coll. Sch. Social Work, City U. N.Y., 1975—; UN adviser on social welfare to Ceylon, Sri Lanka, 1963-64; sr. Simon research fellow U. Manchester (Eng.), 1970-71; cons. Office Juvenile Delinquency and Youth Devel., HEW, also Children's Bur.; cons. N.Y.C. Dept. Personnel, Westchester County (N.Y.) Dept. Mental Health. Served with USAAF, 1943-46. HEW grantee, 1968-71, 69-70, 71-74, 74, 77. Mem. AAUP, Am. Sociol. Assn., Council on Social Work Edn., Nat. Assn. Social Workers, Nat. Council on Crime and Delinquency, Soc. for Study of Addiction to Alcohol and Other Drugs (Eng.). Contbr. articles to profl. jours. Home: Alexander Ln Croton-on-Hudson NY 10520 Office: Hunter Coll Sch Social Work 129 E 79th St New York City NY 10021

WEISS, BRIAN, writer; b. Bklyn., Aug. 16, 1945; s. Morris and Ruth (Schimelman) W.; B.A. cum laude (N.Y. State Regents Coll. scholar), Coll. City N.Y., 1965; M.A., Hunter Coll., 1968; Ph.D. (NDEA Title IV fellow), City U. N.Y., 1974; J.D., Columbia U., 1978. Instr. English, Geneseo State Coll., State U. N.Y., 1968-72; adj. asst. prof. English, Baruch Coll., 1974-75; self-employed editorial cons., 1974—. Mem. Modern Lang. Assn. Am., Phi Beta Kappa, Mensa. Democrat. Home: 3424 Kingsbridge Ave Bronx NY 10463

WEISS, FLORENCE, telephone and telegraph co. exec.; b. N.Y.C., Nov. 8, 1938; d. Jules J. and Pearl (Finklestein) Weiss; student (Woodrow Wilson fellow), Columbia U., 1959-60; B.A. magna cum laude, Syracuse U., 1959. Econ. research asst. Nat. Econ. Research Assos., N.Y.C., 1960-63, econ. analyst, 1964-68, supr. research, 1968-71, asst. v.p., 1971-73, v.p., 1973-77; v.p. AT&T, N.Y.C., 1977—. Mem. Am. Econ. Assn. (mem. com. on status of women in econs. profession), Phi Beta Kappa, Phi Kappa Phi. Home: 101 W 12th St New York City NY 10011 Office: AT&T 195 Broadway New York City NY 10007

WEISS, GERSON, physician; b. N.Y.C., Aug. 1, 1939; s. Samuel and Lillian (Wolpe) W.; B.A., N.Y. U., 1960, M.D., 1964; m. Linda Gordon, Dec. 24, 1959; children—Jonathan, David, Michele, Andrew. Intern, fellow dept. medicine Johns Hopkins Sch. Medicine, 1964-65; resident obstetrics and gynecology N.Y. U. Med. Center, 1964-69; research fellow physiology U. Pitts. Sch. Medicine, 1971-73; asst. prof. obsetrics and gynecology N.Y. U. Med. Center, 1971-76, asso. prof., 1976—, dir. div. reproductive endocrinology, 1975—. Served to maj. MC, U.S. Army, 1969-71. Research grantee NIH, 1975-82, United Cerebral Palsy Found., 1977—; fellow John Polachek Found. for Med. Research. Mem. Am. Coll. Obstetrics and Gynecology, Endocrine Soc. Gynecologic Investigation, N.Y. Obstet. Soc., Soc. Study Reprodn., Phi Beta Kappa, Alpha Omega Alpha. Contbr. research articles reproductive endocrinology and gynecology to med. jours. Home: 390 1st Ave Apt 11D New York NY 10010 Office: 550 1st Ave New York NY 10016

WEISS, HENRY WALTER, lawyer; b. N.Y.C., Feb. 10, 1940; s. Harry H. and Henrietta (Weingarten) W.; A.B. summa cum laude (Rufus Choate scholar, Charles Downer Hazen fellow), Dartmouth Coll., 1960; B.A. (Reynolds fellow), Oxford U., 1962; LL.B. cum laude, Harvard U., 1965; m. Edith Richman, May 22, 1966 (div. 1976); children—Helen Petra, Alice Margery. Law sec. to judge Eastern Dist. N.Y., 1965-67; asso. firm Kaye, Scholer, Fierman, Hays & Handler, N.Y.C., 1967-73; partner firm Peck & Heller & Weiss, N.Y.C., 1973—; dir. 8th St Realty Corp. Mem. com. on state legis. Citizens Union, 1967-69; trustee Teaneck Polit. Assembly, 1973-74. Mem. Assn. Bar City N.Y., Fed. Bar Council, N.Y. State Bar Assn., Greater Gotham Bus. Council. Club: Dartmouth of Bergen County (trustee 1970—, sec. 1972-74, v.p. 1974-75, pres. 1975-76). Author corr. course manual: You and the Law, 1960; Deep Freeze, 1977; contbr. articles to profl. jours. Home: 305 E 40 St New York City NY 10016 Office: 5019 Lincoln Bldg 60 E 42d St New York City NY 10017

WEISS, JONATHAN ARTHUR, lawyer; b. Bryn Mawr, Pa., May 1, 1939; s. Paul and Victoria (Brodkin) W.; B.A. cum laude, Yale U., 1960, LL.B., 1963. Admitted to D.C. bar, 1964, N.Y. State bar, 1967, Supreme Ct. bar, 1967; with Solicitor's Gen. Office, Dept. Labor, 1963-65; mng. atty. Neighborhood Legal Services, Washington, 1965-66; guest lectr. Hebrew U., Jerusalem, 1966; atty. Center Social Welfare Policy and Law, Columbia U., 1967; mng. atty. Moblzn. for Youth Legal Services, Inc., N.Y.C., 1968-69; dir. Legal Services for Elderly Poor, N.Y.C., 1969—; vis. prof. law Tex. So. U. Law Sch., 1971; mem. Pres.'s Commn. on Civil Disorders, 1968. Recipient Distinguished Scholar medal Hofstra U., 1973; Fulbright research fellow, Italy, 1966. Mem. D.C. Bar Assn., Assn. Bar City N.Y. Clubs: Mory's, Elizabethan (Yale). Author: Right and Wrong: A Philosophical Dialogue between Father and Son, 1968; also papers, articles, revs.; editor: Law of the Elderly, 1977. Home: 142 W 87th St New York City NY 10024 Office: 2095 Broadway New York City NY 10023

WEISS, LAWRENCE CHARLES, hosp. adminstr.; b. Bklyn., Oct. 11, 1947; s. Daniel and Florence Francine (Wallach) W.; B.A., Hartwick Coll., 1969; M.A., U. Iowa, 1971; m. Harla Joy Musoff, Oct. 8, 1977. Asst. hosp. dir. Kings County Hosp. Center, Bklyn., 1971-73; asst. hosp. adminstr. Brookdale Hosp. Med. Center, Bklyn., 1973-76, Alexian Bros. Hosp., Elizabeth, N.J., 1977—; clin. instr. State U.N.Y., 1973—. Mem. Am. Coll. Hosp. Adminstrs., Am., N.J. hosp. assns., Nat. Assn. Health Care Adminstrs. Clubs: Masons, Hosp. Execs. Home: 1503 E 91st St Brooklyn NY 11236 Office: Alexian Brothers Hospital 655 E Jersey St Elizabeth NJ 07206

WEISS, NATHAN STRAUS, physician; b. Bklyn., Jan. 20, 1931; s. Max and Anna (Billet) W.; B.A., Ohio Wesleyan U., 1952; M.D., Chgo. Med. Sch., 1956; m. Helen Lois Bluhm, June 29, 1959; children—Lawrence Steven, Alan Stuart. Intern, Jewish Hosp. and Med. Center, Bklyn., 1956-57, resident, 1957-59, resident in allergy, 1965-66; private practice medicine specializing in pediatrics, 1961-65, in allergy, 1966—; dir. allergy dept. pediatrics Nassau County (N.Y.) Med. Center, also dir. allergy and immunology residency tng. program, 1976—; asst. prof. pediatrics State U. N.Y., Stonybrook. Served with USAF, 1959-61. Fellow Am. Acad. Allergy, Am. Coll. Allergists, Am. Assn. Certified Allergists. Author: (with James M. Rubin) Practical Points in Allergy, 1974. Home: 90 Tanyard Ln Huntington NY 11743 Office: 66 Commack Rd Commack NY 11725

WEISS, RITA LEONA, nurse; b. Bklyn., Jan. 18, 1928; d. Boris A. and Olga (Lutsky) Haykin; diploma Maimonides Hosp., Bklyn., 1948; m. Walter Morton Weiss, June 27, 1953; children—Lisa Ellen, Amy Beth, Jeffrey David. Head nurse Maimonides Hosp., Bklyn., 1948, 49-51, pvt. duty nurse, 1951; office nurse Dr. Morris Mindel, Bklyn., 1952-54; head nurse emergency dept. Mid-Island Hosp., Bethpage, N.Y., 1970-72, supr. central supply, 1972—. Mem. N.Y. State Nurses Assn. Jewish. Office: Mid Island Hosp 4295 Hempstead Turnpike Bethpage NY 11714

WEISS, TED, lawyer, Congressman; b. Hungary, Sept. 17, 1927; s. Joseph and Pearl W.; came to U.S., 1938, naturalized, 1953; B.A., Syracuse U., 1951, LL.B., 1952; m. Apr. 20, 1958; children—Thomas D., Stephen R. Admitted to N.Y. bar; asst. dist. atty., N.Y. County, 1955-59; mem. city council N.Y.C., 1962-76, chmn. com. on environ. protection, 1970—; partner firm Gaffin & Weiss, N.Y.C., 1962-70; counsel firm Fuchsberg & Fuchsberg, N.Y.C., 1970—; mem. 95th Congress from 20th N.Y. dist. Mem. N.Y. County Democratic Com., 1959—; mem. exec. council New Dem. Coalition N.Y. State., 196972; del. Dem. Nat. Conv., 1972. Served with AUS, 1946-47; PTO. Named Man of Year. Fedn. Jewish Philanthropies, 1962. Home: 320 W 87th St New York City NY 10024 Office: 37 W 65th St New York City NY 10007

WEISS, VLADIMIR STANLEY, engring. exec.; b. Zagreb, Yugoslavia, Aug. 23, 1931; s. Bogdan Michael and Gjurgjica Duda (Von Layer) W.; B.Sc. in Engring., U. Zagreb, 1954, M.Sc. in Engring., 1956; M.Sc. in Engring. U. Vienna, 1957; m. Branka-Marie Papa, Jan. 26, 1957; children—Theodore Daniel, Tamara Duda. Dept. head engring. Brueder Warchalowski, Vienna, Austria, 1956-57; research engr. Montreal Locomotive Works, Ltd. (Que., Can.), 1957-65; pres. Weiss & Assos., Montreal, 1965—, Con-Des Ltd., Montreal, 1966—, Weiss Engring., Ltd., Mississauga, Ont., Can., 1976—; tchr. evening classes McGill U., Montreal Inst. Tech. Mem. Instrument Soc. Am. (v.p. 1970-72, Distinguished Soc. Service award 1973), Engring. Joint Council, Order Engrs. of Que., Assn. Profl. Engrs. Ont., Nat., Mass. socs. profl. engrs., Am. Inst. Chem. Engrs., Canadian Soc. Mech. Engrs., Engring. Inst. Can., Fluid Power Soc., Canadian Pulp and Paper Assn., Que. C. of C., Canadian Fedn. Ind. Bus. Roman Catholic. Home: 69 Maplewood Rd Mississauga ON L5G 2M7 Canada Office: 5165 Sherbrooke St W Montreal PQ H4A 1T6 Canada also 2446 Cawthra Rd Mississauga ON L5A 3K6 Canada

WEISSBACH, HERBERT, biochemist; b. N.Y.C., Mar. 16, 1932; s. Louis and Vivian (Ruhalter) W.; B.S., Coll. City N.Y., 1953; M.S., George Washington U., 1955, Ph.D., 1957; m. Renee Kohl, Dec. 27, 1953; children—Larry, Nancy, Marjorie,Robert. Chemist, Nat. Heart Inst., Bethesda, Md., 1953-67, head sect. on enzymes and metabolism, lab. clin. biochemistry, 1967-68, acting chief lab. clin. biochemistry, 1968-69; asso. dir. Roche Inst. Molecular Biology, Nutley, N.J., 1969—; adj. prof. Columbia U., 1969—. Recipient Superior Service award HEW, 1968. Mem. Am. Chem. Soc. (recipient enzyme aard 1970), AAAS, Am. Soc. Biol. Chemists, Am. Soc. Pharmacology and Explt. Therapeutics, Am. Soc. Microbiology, Harvey Soc., Gerontological Soc.Editor: (with Sidney Pestka) Molecular Mechanism of Protein Biosynthesis, 1977; exec. editor Archives of Biochemistry and Bio- physics, 1972—; editor Internat. Jour. Neuropharmacology, 1969-76, Jour. Biol. Chemistry, 1972-77, Archives Biochemistry and Biophysics, 1967-72, Pharmacology and Experimental Therapeutics, 1967-72. Home: 333 Crestmont Dr Cedar Grove NJ 07009 Office: Roche Inst Molecular Biology Kingsland St Nutley NJ 07110

WEISSELBERG, EDWARD BERNARD, process equipment co. exec.; b. Jersey City, July 1, 1934; s. Arnold and Jeannette (Munz) W.; student Clark U., 1952-55; B.S. in Chem. Engring., Rensselaer Poly. Inst., 1958; m. Myrna Hope Greenwald, Oct. 31, 1959; children—Deborah Ruth, Michael Ward, Diane Arlene. With Wyssmont Co., Fort Lee, N.J., 1959—, chem. engr., 1960-61, purchasing agt., 1961-62, asst. to pres., 1962-63, sales mgr., 1963-64, pres., 1964-65, chmn. bd., pres., 1965—; officer Drying Services Corp., Fort Lee, 1970—; lectr. in field. Pres., Old Tappen (N.J.) Library Fund, 1971—; trustee, mem. sci. com. Bergen Community Mus., 1978—. Mem. Am. Inst. Chem. Engrs. (corr. sec. No. Jersey sect. 1972, rec. sec. 1973, treas. 1974-75, chmn. 1977). Jewish (trustee temple 1972-74, v.p. 1975-77, pres. 1978—). Mem. B'nai B'rith. Club: Chemists (N.Y.C.). Home: 1071 Washington Ave Old Tappan NJ 07675 Office: 1470 Bergen Blvd Fort Lee NJ 07024

WEISSMAN, ESTHER IRENE, psychologist; b. N.Y.C., June 27, 1946; d. Jacob and Clara (Unger) W.; B.A., Hunter Coll., 1967; Ed.M., Boston U., 1968, Ed.D., 1974. Tchr. Bronx (N.Y.) pub. schs., 1967; asst. vocational counselor placement service, Boston U., 1967-68; instr., counselor, 1969-70, psychotherapist, 1970-71; instr. Graham Jr. Coll., Boston, 1968-69, Garland Jr. Coll., Boston, 1971-72, Mass. Bay Community Coll., Watertown, Mass., 1971-73, Quincy (Mass.) Jr. Coll., 1972-74; psychotherapist Eastern Middlesex Guidance Center, Melrose, Mass., 1974-78; pvt. practice Psychology, Brighton, Mass., 1973—; prof. Boston State Coll., 1973—; psychologist Youth Activities Commn., State Mass., 1978—. Licensed Psychologist, Mass. Mem. Am. Psychol. Assn., Mass. Psychol. Assn., Adult Edn. Assn., Women Counselors and Psychologists Assn. Office: 1853 Commonwealth Ave Brighton MA 02135

WEISSMAN, JACK, accountant; b. N.Y.C., July 22, 1912; s. Louis and Ida (Lefkowitz) W.; grad. N.Y. U., 1934; m. Annette Betz, Apr. 30, 1938; children—Ivan M., Margaret I. Partner, Weissman, Taylor and Bildner, C.P.A.'s, Great Neck, N.Y., 1946—. Trustee Village of Great Neck, 1974-77, dep. mayor, 1977-78; mem. Temple Bethel, Great Neck. Mem. A.I.C.P.A.'s, N.Y. State C.P.A.'s. Clubs: Lions, Elks. Home: 25 Florence St Great Neck NY 11023 Office: 11 Middle Neck Rd Great Neck NY 11021

WEISSMAN, KENNETH BERNARD, banker; b. N.Y.C., May 22, 1906; s. Joseph and Celia Weissman; student Pace Coll., 1927; m. Rosalind Weissman, Mar. 12, 1932; 1 son, Alan. Engaged in pvt. banking, New Rochelle, N.Y., 1934—. Chmn. bd. Optometric Center N.Y., 1962—. N.Y.U. Dental Coll. named in his honor. Address: 225 Westchester Ave Portchester NY 10573

WEISSMAN, MORTON ARTHUR, real estate broker; b. Pitts., July 19, 1918; s. Felix A. and Radie W.; B.S., U. Pitts., 1940; m. Elaine R. Weissman, Oct. 12, 1968. Mgr. luggage dept. Rosenbaum Co.,

Pitts., 1952-59; real estate broker, v.p. indsl. dept. Arnheim & Neely, Inc., Pitts., 1960—; instr. real estate Allegheny Community Coll., Weaver Sch. Real Estate, U. Pitts. Formerly bd. dirs. United Cerebral Palsy, Pitts. Served with Med. Service Corps, AUS, 1941-46, also Korean War. Mem. Nat. Assn. Realtors, Greater Pitts. Bd. Realtors, Soc. Indsl. Realtors (nat. dir., past pres. Western Pa. chpt.), Pi Lambda Phi. Home: 128 N Craig St Apt 605 Pittsburgh PA 15213 Office: Arnheim & Neely Inc 820 Grant Bldg Pittsburgh PA 15219

WEISSMAN, WALTER, chem. engr.; b. Bronx, N.Y., Apr. 6, 1940; s. Edward and Frieda (Lewack) W.; B. Chem. Engring., Coll. City N.Y., 1961; M.S. in Chem. Engring., Newark Coll. Engring., 1966; m. Diane Zuckerman, June 21, 1964; 1 dau., Ellen Michelle. With Exxon Corp., 1961—; sect. head Florham Park, N.J., 1969-71, Baton Rouge, 1971-75, project mgr. petroleum and coal areas Corp. Research Feasibility Unit, Linden, N.J., 1975—, sr. engring. asso., 1978—; Exxon interviewer La. State U., 1974-75. Named outstanding young engring. alumni N.Y. Engring. Sch., Coll. City N.Y., 1969; Kirkpatrick Honor award Chem. Engring. mag., 1977. Mem. Am. Inst. Chem. Engrs., Am. Chem. Soc. Mem. B'nai B'rith. Patentee in field. Home: 271 Lorraine Dr Berkeley Heights NJ 07922 Office: Exxon Research and Engring Co PO Box 45 Linden NJ 07036

WEISSMAN, WILLIAM R., lawyer; b. N.Y.C., Aug. 16, 1940; s. Emanuel and Gertrude (Halpern) W.; B.A., Columbia U., 1962, J.D. cum laude, 1965; m. Barbra Phylis Gershman, Nov. 16, 1974; 1 son, Adam Jefferson; stepchildren—Eric, Jace, Julie. News dir., program dir. WKCR-FM, N.Y.C., 1960-62; admitted to N.Y. bar, 1965, D.C. bar, 1967, U.S. Supreme Ct. bar, 1968; law clk. U.S. Dist. Judge, Dallas, 1965-66; trial atty., antitrust div. Dept. Justice, Washington, 1966-69; spl. asst. U.S. atty., Washington, 1967; mem. firm Wald, Harkrader & Ross, Washington, 1969—. Mem. Arlington County Tenant-Landlord Commn., Arlington, Va., 1973-77, chmn., 1974-77. Parliamentarian, Arlington County Dem. Com., 1971-75. Mem. Am. Fed., Inter-Am. bar assns., Bar Assn. D.C. Club: Internat. Home: 3802 Lakeview Terr Falls Church VA 22041 Office: 1320 19th St NW Washington DC 20036

WEITBERG, MARTIN HARRY, physician; b. Phila., Jan. 9, 1926; s. Jacob and Rose Leah (Marmer) W.; B.A., U. Pa., 1950; M.D., Hahnemann Med. Coll., 1954; m. Ruth Grossman, June 18, 1950; children—Robin Lori, Jordan Steven. Intern, Phila. Gen. Hosp., 1954-55; fellow Cleve. Clinic Found., 1955-56; practice family medicine, Lindenwold, N.J., 1956—; mem. staff W. Jersey Hosps., Camden County; asst. instr. family medicine Hahnemann Med. Coll., 1966-72; sch. physician Laurel Springs (N.J.) Elementary Sch., 1957—. Served with USNR, 1944-46. Diplomate Am. Bd. Family Practice. Fellow Am. Acad. Family Physicians; mem. AMA (Physicians Recognition award 1973, 76), Am. Heart Assn., Am. Geriatrics Soc., Soc. Tchrs. of Family Medicine, N.J., Camden County med. socs., Phi Beta Kappa, Alpha Omega Alpha. Republican. Jewish. Home: 168 N Mansfield Blvd Cherry Hill NJ 08034 Office: 600 S White Horse Pike Lindenwold NJ 08021

WEITZENHOFFER, AARON MAX, JR., art dealer; b. Oklahoma City, Oct. 30, 1939; s. Aaron Max and Clara Irene (Rosenthal) W.; B.F.A., U. Okla., 1963. Co. mgr. La Jolla (Calif.) Playhouse, 1963-64; dir. David B. Findlay Gallery, N.Y., 1965-69; pres. Gimpel-Weitzenhoffer Gallery, N.Y.C.; dir. Seminole Mfg. Co., Columbus, Miss.; adj. prof. drama U. Okla. Chief pub. relations Okla. Health Dept., 1964-65. Recipient Tony award, 1978. Mem. The Players, Art Dealers Assn., N.Y. League Theatres and Producers, Delta Kappa Epsilon (trustee found.). Republican. Home: 70 E 77th St New York City NY 10021 Office: 1040 Madison Ave New York City NY 10021

WEITZMANN, ALBERT MICHAEL, lawyer, educator; b. Niagara Falls, N.Y., Dec. 28, 1912; s. Michael George and Mary Patricia (White) W.; student U. Vt., 1931-33; B.B.A., Niagara U., 1936; M.B.A., U. Pa., 1941; J.D., Temple U., 1949; m. Mary Cecilia Collins, Nov. 28, 1944; children—Michael Charles, Mary Patricia. Accountant, analyst Phila. Electric Co., 1941-49; asso. Shertz, Barnes & Shertz, 1949-54; asst. prof. accounting Villanova U., 1954-56, asst. prof. econs. and transp., 1956-57, asso. prof., 1957—; gen. practice law, 1950-74, econs., transp. and bus. law, 1974—; cons. in econs. and bus., 1951—. Mem. Am. Econ. Assn., AAUP, Am. Arbitration Assn., Am. Soc. Traffic and Transp., Am. Judicature Soc., Interstate Commerce Practitioners Assn., Am., Pa., Delaware County bar assns., Ret. Officer's Assn., Torch Soc. Delaware County, Lambda Iota, Phi Alpha Delta, Omega Delta Epsilon, Beta Gamma Sigma. Roman Catholic. Clubs: Lawyer's of Delaware County, MBA, Wharton Sch., Marple Newtown Swim. Contbr. articles to profl. jours. Home: 2405 W Chester Pike Broomall PA 19008 Office: Villanova U Villanova PA 19085

WELCH, MARY SCOTT STEWART, writer; b. Chgo., Dec. 14, 1919; d. William Scott and Myrtle (Ferrin) Stewart; A.B., U. Ill., 1940; m. Barrett Farley Welch, Mar. 23, 1943; children—Farley, Laurie, Margaret, Mary Barrett. West Coast editor Esquire, Hollywood, Calif., 1943-45; asso. editor Pageant Mag., N.Y.C., 1947-49; entertainment editor Look Mag., N.Y.C., 1949-52; food editor Glamour Mag., N.Y.C., 1953-55; columnist Seventeen, N.Y.C., 1960-63, Vogue Mag.; tchr. mag. writing Womanschool and Ethical Culture Soc., N.Y.C., 1975-77. Coordinator rape prevention com. NOW, N.Y.C., 1972-74. Served with USN, 1942-44. Mem. NOW (dir. 1973-75), Author's Guild, Author's League, Am. Soc. Journalists and Authors, Women in Communications, Nat. Women's Polit. Caucus, Nat. Women's Health Network, ACLU, Wilderness Soc., Sierra Club, Phi Beta Kappa. Author: The Family Wilderness Handbook, 1973; (with Ronnie Welch) Esquire Party Book, 1970; Seventeen Guide to Travel, 1970; Esquire Etiquette, 1958; What Every Young Man Should Know, 1970; Handbook for Hosts, 1950; Your First Hundred Meals, 1947, others; contbr. articles various mags. including Redbook, McCall's, Ladies Home Jour., Woman's Day, Cosmopolitan, Mademoiselle, Ms., Seventeen, Modern Maturity, Glamour, Vogue, others. Home: 30 Waterside Plaza New York City NY 10010 Office: 333 E 30 St New York City NY 10016

WELLER, JAC, mech. engr.; b. Lee County, Ga., Jan. 6, 1913; s. Allen Claude and Lillian McCamie (Yow) W.; B.S., Princeton U., 1936; m. Cornelia Richards Murray. Gen. foreman Gen. Motors Corp., Trenton, N.J., 1942-43; gen. supt. sales Johnson & Johnson, New Brunswick, N.J., 1943-45; treas. G.R. Murray Inc., Princeton, N.J., 1938—; farmer, 1971—. Nominated hon. curator U.S. Mil Acad. Mus., Brit. Army Sch. of Inf. Mus., Warminster. Served with Fla. N.G., 1928-31. Elected to Coll. Football Hall of Fame, 1957; named first string All Eastern guard for All Time team, 1969. Author 9 books, including: Wellington in India, Wellington in the Peninsula; contbr. articles to profl. publs., chpts. to books. Office: 349 Nassau St Princeton NJ 08540

WELLER, JAMES MANNIE, constrn. co. exec.; b. Glens Falls, N.Y., June 20, 1941; s. Hally Edwin and M. Angela (St. Onge) W.; B.S. in Civil Engring. cum laude, Norwich U., 1963; m. Mary Ann Cardinal, Nov. 28, 1963; children—Michael, Patti Lynn, Elisa. Project engr. Kamyr, Inc., Glens Falls, 1967-71; constrn. mgr. Unit Span Bldg. Systems, Albany, N.Y., 1971-72; cons. engr., v.p. Van

Amburgh Constrn. Co., Latham, N.Y., 1972-76; owner, gen. mgr. J.M. Weller Assos., Lake George, N.Y., 1976—. Registered profl. engr., Vt., N.Y., N.J., Calif., Pa., Conn. Mem. ASCE, Am. Inst. Steel Constrn. Roman Catholic (mem. parish council 1973-74, pres. 1974-75). Club: Lions. Home: RFD 1 Lake George NY 12845 Office: Box 403A RD1 Lake George NY 12845

WELLER, JOHN LOUIS, govt. ofcl.; b. Rexford, Mont., Apr. 24, 1910; s. Robert James and Theresa Bridget (McKaig) W.; B.S. Mont. State U., 1932; M.S., Yale U., 1933; m. Catherine Helen Craig, Aug. 29, 1942 (div. 1971); children—John Craig, Dennis Carroll. Various ry. ops. work, 1925-32; mech. engr. Fundacion Corp., Venezuela, 1934-36; asst. to trustees N.Y. N.H. & H. R.R. Co., New Haven, 1936-42; with Transworld Airlines, N.Y.C., 1945-57, v.p., 1952-57; pres. Seatrain Lines, Inc., Edgewater, N.J., 1957-64; v.p. Hayden Stone, Inc., N.Y.C., 1965-70; v.p. Paine, Webber, Jackson & Curtis, N.Y.C., 1970-73; cons. transp., New Haven, 1973-74; mem. staff Rail Services Planning Office, Washington, 1974—. Bd. cons. ENO Found. for Transp. Research, 1973-76. Served to lt. comdr. USNR, 1942-45. Recipient Gold medal Mont. Soc. Engrs., 1932; Strathcona Meml. fellow, 1932-33. Mem. ASME, Fin. Analysts Fedn., Aviation Writers Assn., Transp. Assn. Am. (dir. 1952-74). Clubs: Yale, Wings (N.Y.C.). Author: The New Haven Railroad, 1969; co-author: The Future of American Transportation, 1971; contbr. articles in field to profl. jours. Home: 6302 Wingate St Alexandria VA 22312 Office: Rail Services Planning Office 1900 L St NW Washington DC 20036

WELLER, JOHN WILLIAM, JR., fin. broker; b. Orange, N.J., Oct. 17, 1935; s. John William and Louise (Specht) W.; grad. Upsala Coll., 1957; m. Dorothy M. Meissner, Mar. 27, 1965; children—Jon William, Liesel Agatha. With Dreyfus Corp., 1957; pres. J. W. Weller & Co., Inc., Bloomfield, N.J.; trustee The Essex Troop; trustee Glendale Cemetery, Bloomfield, N.J., owner Dorroc Stables. Mem. Phila.-Balt.-Washington Stock Exchange. Served to capt. AUS, 1956-58. Recipient Draper award for Armor leadership, 1963. Mem. U.S. Trotting Assn. Kiwanian. Club: Glenridge Country. Home: Llewellyn Park West Orange NJ 07052

WELLER, PETER ANTHONY, automotive engr., automotive component mfg. co. exec.; b. Holland, Mich., Feb. 4, 1920; s. Peter and Huberdina Paulina Elizabeth (Susan) W.; B.S. in Aero. Engring., U. Mich., 1942; m. Evelyn Grace Mulder, Nov. 27, 1943; children—Susan Weller Kapp, Nancy Weller Black, John A., Frederick E., Sally Weller Martin. Devel. engr. Dow Chem. Co., Bay City, Mich., 1942-44; chief engr. Stalker Devel. Co., Bay City, 1946-50; research sect. head Carrier Corp., Syracuse, N.Y., 1950-59; mgr. engring. Am. Standard Corp., Detroit, 1959-68; pvt. practice engring., Detroit, 1968-70; dir. product engring. Davidson Rubber Co., Dover, N.H., 1970—. Elder Durham (N.H.) Evangelical Ch. Mem. Soc. Automotive Engrs., Engring. Soc. Detroit. Patentee refrigeration and automotive components. Home: 15 Woodridge Rd Durham NH 03824 Office: Davidson Rubber Co Indsl Park Dover NH 03820

WELLER, ROBERT, mktg. research co. exec.; b. N.Y.C., July 27, 1922; s. Ernest Otto and Amelia Louise (Strasser) W.; B.B.A., Baruch Sch. Bus., 1946; M.S., Columbia, 1948; m. Pearl Wasserman, Jan. 29, 1928; children—Steven, Janet, Nancy, Richard. Exec. v.p. Alfred Politz Research, N.Y.C., 1950-64; pres. Weller and Klein, N.Y.C., 1964-67; partner Nat. Mktg. Studies, N.Y.C., 1967—; lectr. statistics Baruch Coll., 1957-62, 71-74. Served with USAAF, 1943-45. Mem. Am. Statis. Assn., Am. Mktg. Assn., Beta Gamma Sigma. Lutheran. Contbr. articles to profl. jours. Home: 45 Cambridge Dr Allendale NJ 07401 Office: 501 Madison Ave New York NY 10022

WELLER, THOMAS HUCKLE, physician, educator; b. Ann Arbor, Mich., June 15, 1915; s. Carl V. and Elsie A. (Huckle) W.; A.B., U. Mich., 1936, M.S., 1937, LL.D., 1956; M.D., Harvard, 1940; Sc.D. (hon.), Gustavus Adolphus U., 1975; L.H.D. (hon.), Lowell U., 1977; m. Kathleen R. Fahey, Aug. 18, 1945; children—Peter Fahey, Nancy Kathleen, Robert Andrew, Janet Louise. Teaching fellow bacteriology Harvard Med. Sch., 1940-41, research fellow tropical medicine, pediatrics, 1947-48, instr. comparative pathology, tropical medicine, 1948-49, asst. prof. tropical pub. health Sch. Pub. Health, 1949-50, asso. prof., 1950-54, Richard Pearson Strong prof. tropical pub. health, head dept., 1954—; intern bacteriology and pathology Children's Hosp., Boston, 1941, intern medicine, 1942, asst. resident medicine, 1946, asst. dir. research div. infectious diseases, 1949-55; mem. commn. parasitic disease Armed Forces Epidemiol. Bd., 1953-72, dir., 1953-59. Served to maj. M.C., AUS, 1942-46; charge parasitology, bacteriology, virology sections Antilles Dept. Med. Lab., P.R. Recipient E. Mead Johnson award for devel. tissue culture procedures in study virus diseases, Am. Acad. Pediatrics, 1953; Kimble Methodology award, 1954; Nobel prize in physiology and medicine, 1954; George Ledlie prize, 1963; Weinstein Cerebral Palsy award, 1973. Diplomate Am. Bd. Pediatrics. Fellow Am. Acad. Arts and Scis.; mem. Harvey Soc., AMA, Am. Soc. Parasitologists, Am., Royal socs. tropical medicine and hygiene, Am. Pub. Health Assn., AAAS, Am. Epidemiological Soc., Nat. Acad. Scis., Am. Pediatric Soc., Assn. Am. Physicians, Soc. Exptl. Biology and Medicine, Am. Assn. Immunologists, Soc. Pediatric Research, Phi Beta Kappa. Sigma Xi, Alpha Omega Alpha. Author sci. papers. Home: 56 Winding River Rd Needham MA 02192 Office: 665 Huntington Ave Boston MA 02115

WELLES, ERNEST IRVING, chem. co. exec.; b. N.Y.C., Aug. 5, 1925; s. Henry and Lena (Halberg) W.; B.S. cum laude, Coll. City N.Y., 1946, B.S., Sch. Edn., 1949, M.S., 1953; Sc.D. (hon.), London Inst., 1973; m. Rita Zuckerman, Dec. 28, 1946; children—Neil S., Seth L. Chemist, Lucius Pitkin, Inc., N.Y.C., 1944-45; research chemist Nuodex Products Co., Elizabeth, N.J., 1946-50; group leader Foster D.Snell, Inc., N.Y.C., 1950-51; asst. tech. dir. Permatex, Inc., Bklyn., 1951-52; chief chemist Dexter Chem. Corp., N.Y.C., 1952-67; product mgr. textile chem. sales Quaker Chem. Corp., Conshohocken, Pa., 1967-74; dir. mktg., textile chem. sales Hart Products Corp., Jersey City, 1974; mktg. dir. Leatex Chem. Co., Phila., 1974—. Fellow Am. Inst. Chemists; mem. Am. Chem. Soc. (sr.), Am. Assn. Textile Chemists and Colorists, Am. Assn. Textile Technologists, Am. Oil Chemists Soc., Salesmen's Assn. Chem. Industries. Club: Masons. Patentee in field. Home: 1000 Conestoga Rd Rosemont PA 19010 Office: 2722 N Hancock St Philadelphia PA 19133

WELLINGTON, ALBERT PERRY, psychologist; b. Coimbra, Portugal, Jan. 19, 1918; s. Andre Pereira and Palmira de Oliveira (Gonsalves) De Figueiredo; came to U.S., 1945, naturalized, 1950; Diploma in Theology, Seventh-Day Adventist Sem., Portalegre, Portugal, 1944; Ph.D., Western U., San Diego, 1964; LL.B., La Salle U., Chgo., 1955; B.A. in Psychology, U. Calif., Riverside, 1962; M.A. in Psychology, Calif. State U., Sacramento, 1963; postgrad. (Univ. scholar), Dalhousie U., Halifax, N.S., Can., 1965; m. Ida Rudolfovna Zaft, Nov. 1, 1955; children—Oliver Andrei, Linda Ann, Michael Jerome; children by previous marriage—Ingrid, Harold. Apptd. to ministry Portuguese Union Seventh-day Adventists, 1944; minister asst. editor, adminstrv. asst. to pres. Portuguese Union, 1943-44; cons. in travel and immigration, 1945-50; psychiat. technician Patton (Calif.) State Hosp., 1951-62; probation officer San Bernardino County Probation Dept., 1963-64; grad. teaching asst. in psychology

Dalhousie U., 1965-66; sr. clin. psychologist Willard (N.Y.) Psychiat. Center, 1967—, acting head dept. psychology, 1968-70; psychol. cons. Auburn (N.Y.) Correctional Facility, 1969-77. Elder Seventh Day Adventist Ch., Ithaca, N.Y., 1973-74, head elder, 1975, supt. Sabbath sch., deacon, 1976-77, sch. bd. chmn. Seventh-Day Adventist Sch., Ithaca, 1977-78, ch. treas., 1978—. Licensed practicing psychologist, N.C. Fellow Royal Soc. Health; mem. Am. (asso.), Eastern, Brit. psychol. assns., Assn. Advancement of Behavior Therapy, AAAS. Contbr. articles to profl. and lit. jours. Home: PO Box 80 Interlaken NY 14847

WELLONS, KARYN SUE, govt. ofcl.; b. Chgo., Nov. 28, 1949; d. Clarence Peter and Edwina Marcia (Skibinski) Terenzi; student pvt. schs., Chgo.; m. Christopher Howe Wellons, Aug. 15, 1969. Traffic mgr. Bing Crosby Prodns., Chgo., 1968-69, J. Walter Thompson, Los Angeles and Chgo., 1969-71; asst. account exec. Henry J. Kaufman & Assoc., Washington, 1971-73; advt. specialist U.S. Postal Service, Washington, 1973—. Home: 8327 Bella Vista Ter Oxon Hill MD 20021

WELLS, DARLENE PENNY, marketing cons.; b. Peekskill, N.Y., Nov. 26, 1949; d. William R. and Ruth V. (Perosky) W.; B.S. in Geology, Knox Coll., 1971. Sec.-treas. Vicom Properties, Ltd., Latham, N.Y., 1973—; pres. Wells Assocs., Latham, 1975—. Vice pres. pub. relations Gov. Clinton council Boy Scouts Am., 1978—. Recipient Guardsman award Nat. Guard Bur., 1977. Mem. Albany Area C. of C. (exec. bd., v.p. 1978-79), Internat. Entrepreneurs Assn., Guilderland C. of C. Club: Zonta (exec. bd. 1978—, dist. chmn. pub. relations 1978). Home: PO Box 493 Latham NY 12110 Office: 848 New Loudon Rd Latham NY 12110

WELLS, DAVID ERNEST, geodesist; b. Montreal, Que., Can., June 29, 1939; s. Ernest Clarke and Dorothy Evelyn (Black) W.; B.Sci., Mt. Allison U., 1960; B. Applied Sci., U. B.C., 1965, M.Applied Sci., 1966; Ph.D., U. N.B., 1974; m. Solveig Waltl, June 20, 1964; children—Corey Dean, Tara Kim. Design engr. Bedford Inst. Oceanography, Dartmouth, N.S., 1965-74, research scientist, 1975—; lectr. U. N.B., 1971-72; cons. in field. Mem. Profl. Inst. Pub. Service Can., Assn. Profl. Engrs. N.S., Canadian Inst. Surveying, Canadian Geophys. Union, Geol. Assn. Can., Am. Geophys. Union, Inst. Nav. Contbr. articles to profl. jours. Home: 13 Garnett St Dartmouth NS B2W 2N9 Canada Office: PO Box 1006 Dartmouth NS B2Y 4A2 Canada

WELLS, ELIZABETH, mgmt. cons.; b. Atlanta, June 22, 1934; d. Samuel Alonzo and Martha (Steele) W.; B.S.H.E., U. Ga., 1955; M.S. (Grad. fellow), Cornell U., 1957; Ph.D., U. Cin., 1972; children—Sam Matthews, Mary Martha Matthews. Instr. child devel. Cornell U., Ithaca, N.Y., 1957-58; instr., asst. prof. dept. learning and devel. U. Cin., 1958-63, 66-74; founder Kaimosi Child Devel. Center, Kaimosi, Kenya, Africa, 1963-65; asst. prof. Center for Improving Teaching Effectiveness, Va. Commonwealth U., Richmond, 1974-76; exec. dir. Comprehensive Instl. Devel. Project, HEW, Washington, 1976-77; mgmt. cons., 1976—; cons. field human resources devel., faculty adminstrv. devel. in colls. and univs. Mem. Am. Assn. Higher Edn. (nat. coordinator women's caucus 1975-76, dir. 1977-80), AAUP, Organizational Devel. Network. Designer, developer mgmt. tng. programs; contbr. research in field. Address: 2727 29th St Washington DC 20008

WELLS, HAL MARION, psychologist, educator; b. Sioux City, Iowa, Apr. 11, 1920; s. Seth Marion and Josephine (Irvine) W.; B.A., State U. Iowa, 1940; S.T.B., Berkeley Div. Sch., 1946; M.A., Columbia, 1950; D.D., Mo., 1967; Ph.D., Sussex Coll., Eng., 1970; m. Beverley C. Adkins, Apr. 12, 1952; children—Laura I.; m. Madelene Harrison, 1967; 1 dau., Teo M. Cons. psychologist, 1947-56, 60—; asst. prof. psychology Dickinson Coll. 1957-60; asso. prof. psychology Elmira Coll., 1960-63; dir. research Coll. of Bus., Fairleigh Dickinson U.; asso. dir. Behavioral Sci. Lab., Carlisle, Pa., 1957-60; pvt. practice psychology 1947—. Serve with USCGR, 1942-43. Mem. Am. Sociol. Assn., Am. Personnel and Guidance Assn., InterAm. Psychol. Assn., Soc. for Projective Techniques, N.Y. Soc. Clin. Psychologists, N.Y. Acad. Scis. Home: 501 E 87th St New York City NY 10028 Office: 120 Central Park S New York City NY 10019

WELLS, JOSEPH PHILIP, educator; b. Pitts., Apr. 30, 1941; s. Richard Dow and Mary Elizabeth (Stevens) W.; B.S., Pa. State U., 1963, M.Ed., 1964; Ed.D., Columbia, 1973; children—Christopher J., Peter J. (dec.). Cons. to dir. office of univ. relations Office of Mayor of N.Y.C., 1969-70; asso. dir. Urban Corps Nat. Devel. Office, N.Y.C., 1969-70; exec. asst. to chancellor City U. N.Y., 1970-72, dir. fed. relations, 1972-73, dir. govt. relations, 1973-74, dir. community relations and acad. devel. Richmond Coll., City U. N.Y., 1974-76, dir. pub. and community relations Coll. S.I., 1976-78, cons. to chancellor City U. N.Y., 1978—. Mem. com. on state legislation Citizens Union N.Y.C., 1971—, com. on local candidates, 1973-74. Mem. Am. Polit. Sci. Assn., Am. Soc. Pub. Adminstrn., Inst. Internat. Edn., Phi Delta Kappa. Democrat. Club: City (N.Y.C.). Home: 310 W 47th St Apt 6E New York City NY 10036

WELLS, LIONELLE DUDLEY, psychiatrist, psychoanalyst; b. Winnsboro, S.C., Nov. 22, 1921; s. Lionelle Dudley and Mary Hunter (Hughey) W.; B.S., U. S.C., 1942; M.D., Med. U. S.C., 1945; m. Mildred Wohltmann, June 28, 1945; children—Lucia Linwood, Lionelle D., John Hunter, Diane Hughey. Intern, Met. Hosp., N.Y.C., 1945-46; resident VA Hosp., N. Little Rock, Ark., 1948-50; Graylyn Hosp., Winston-Salem, N.C., 1950-51; staff psychiatrist Vets. Oupatient Clinic, Boston, 1951-56, chief psychiatrist, 1956-59; asso. psychiatrist Mass. Gen. Hosp., Boston, 1956—; practice medicine specializing in psychiatry and psychoanalysis, Boston, 1959—; cons, VA Outpatient Clinic, Boston, 1959—, VA Hosp., Bedford, Mass., 1966—; asst. clin. prof. psychiatry Harvard Med. Sch., 1956—; lectr. psychiatry Boston U. med. Sch., 1977—; bd. dirs. Bay State Health Care Found., 1977—. Served to 1st lt. U.S. Army, 1946-47. Mem. Am. Psychoanalytic Assn., Am. Psychiat. Assn., AMA, Am. Geriatrics Soc., Am. Soc. Bariatric Physicians. Unitarian. Home: 73 Rolling Ln Weston MA 02193 Office: 82 Marlborough St Boston MA 02116

WELLS, MARY GEORGENE BERG (MRS. HARDING L. LAWRENCE), advt. agy. exec.; b. Youngstown, Ohio, May 25, 1928; d. Waldemar and Violet (Berg) Wells; ed. Carnegie Inst. Tech.; LL.D., Babson Coll., 1970, Carnegie-Mellon U., 1974; m. Harding L. Lawrence, Nov. 28, 1967; children by previous marriage—Kathryn, Pamela. With advt. dept. Macy's, N.Y.C., fashion advt. mgr., until 1951; copy group head McCann-Erickson, Inc., N.Y.C., 1952-57; with Doyle Dane Bernbach, N.Y.C., 1957-64, copy chief, v.p., 1963-64; sr. partner Jack Tinker & Partners, N.Y.C., 1964-66; chmn., chief exec. officer Wells, Rich, Greene, Inc., N.Y.C., 1966—. Mem. Commn. on Critical Choices for Ams., 1974—; speaker Econ. Summitt, Washington, 1974. Named to Copywriters Hall of Fame Copy Club, 1969, Mktg. Stateswoman of Year Sales Execs. Club N.Y., 1970, Advt. Woman of Year Am. Advt. Fedn., 1971. Home: 1 East End Ave New York City NY 10021 Office: 767 Fifth Ave New York City NY 10022

WELLS, OWEN WAYLAND, lawyer; b. Kittery, Maine, June 10, 1943; s. Flavius E. and Edna Cecil (Pettigrew) W.; B.A., U. Maine, 1965; J.D., George Washington U., 1968. Admitted to Maine bar, 1968; asso. firm Perkins, Thompson, Hinckley, Thaxter & Keddy, Portland, Maine, 1968-72; partner firm Perkins, Thompson, Hinckley & Keddy, Portland, 1973—; legal cons. U. Md., College Park, 1971—. Trustee, Alternative Theater, Portland, 1974—, Community Health Services, Inc., Portland, 1975—; pres. bd. overseers Berwick Acad., Portland, 1975—. Served to capt. Intelligence Corps, AUS, 1968-70. Decorated Bronze Star with oak leaf cluster. Mem. Am., Maine, Cumberland County bar assns., Portland Soc. Art (trustee 1975—, chmn. mus. com. 1975—). Republican. Methodist. Club: Portland Yacht (dir. 1975—). Home: Casco Fort Falmouth ME 04105 Office: 1 Canal Plaza Portland ME 04112

WELLS, PETER SCOVILLE, stock brokerage firm exec.; b. N.Y.C., Apr. 25, 1938; s. Jonathan Godfrey and Eleanore Shannon (Scoville) W.; student U. Va., 1956-58, Columbia U., 1959-61; m. Patricia Ann Trent, Dec. 8, 1973; 1 son by previous marriage, Peter Scoville. Asst. to controller Laird & Co., N.Y.C., 1961-63; asst. to partner charge ops. Goldman Sachs, N.Y.C., 1963-64; mgr. new bus. dept. B.J. Herkimer Co., N.Y.C., 1964-67; divisional policy and procedures adminstr. Paine, Webber, Jackson & Curtis, Inc., N.Y.C., 1967-70, asst. to exec. cashier, 1970-73, asst. v.p., mgr. employment services, adminstr. equal employment opportunity, 1973—. Cons. human affairs Gracie Sq. Hosp.; adv. bd. Mayor's Office for Handicapped. Served with AUS, 1958. Mem. Employment Mgmt. Assn., Securities Industries Assn., Wall St. Employment Mgrs., Uptown C. of C., N.Y.C. C. of C. (employers com.), N.Y. Community Council (employers com.), Phi Kappa Psi. Home: 449 E 78th St New York City NY 10021 Office: 25 Broad St New York City NY 10004

WELS, MARGUERITE SAMET, interior decorator; b. N.Y.C.; d. Max and Bertha (Levine) Samet; student N.Y. U., 1937, N.Y. Sch. Interior Design, 1938-41; m. Richard H. Wels, Dec. 12, 1954; children—Susan Rebecca, Amy Elizabeth. Interior decorator, Marguerite Samet, N.Y.C., 1946-60; interior decorator, head Marguerite Samet Assos., 1960—; co-ordinator U.S. Army Spl. Services, 1942-46; cons. United Bowling Centers, Inc., Interboro Gen. Hosp. Active in William Alanson White Inst. of Psychiatry, Psychoanalysis and Psychology, Am. Jewish Com., Islands Research Found.; program chmn. Jewish Mus. Mem. Am. Inst. Interior Designers, Am. Soc. Interior Designers (sec., mem. exec. bd. Met. N.Y. chpt.), Democratic Women's Workshop. Jewish. Clubs: Women's City, Woman Pays. Home: 911 Park Ave New York City NY 10021 Office: 75 E 55th St New York City NY 10021

WELS, PHILIP BERNARD, surgeon; b. N.Y.C., Mar. 24, 1916; s. Harry and Fannie (Weinstein) W.; B.A., U. Buffalo, 1937, M.A., 1939, M.D., 1941; m. Elayne Goldman, Nov. 25, 1948; children—Joan Carol, Robert Allan. Intern, Meyer Meml. Hosp., 1941-42, resident in surgery, 1946-48, now asso. attending staff; exchange teaching resident Millard Fillmore Hosp., 1948-49, chmn. dept. surgery, 1968—; exchange teaching resident Roswell Park Meml. Inst., 1949-50; practice medicine specializing in surgery, Buffalo, 1941—; asso. attending staff Children's Hosp., Buffalo; asst. clin. prof. surgery State U. N.Y. at Buffalo, 1957-68, asso. clin. prof., 1968-70, clin. prof., 1970—, asst. dean, 1964—. Served to capt. AUS, 1942-46. Named to U. Buffalo Athletic Hall of Fame. Diplomate Am. Bd. Surgery, Nat. Bd. Med. Examiners. Mem. ACS, Am. Burn Soc., Am. Trauma Soc., N.Y. State, Erie County, Maimonides med. socs., Buffalo, N.Y. State, Roswell Park surg. socs., Buffalo Acad. Medicine, N.Y. State Soc. Surgeons, Am. Coll. Gastroenterology, Sigma Xi. Clubs: Erie Downs Country (past pres.), Westwood Country, Buffalo. Contbr. articles to profl. jours. Home: 830 LeBrun Rd Eggertsville NY 14226 Office: 1275 Delaware Ave Buffalo NY 14209

WELS, RICHARD HOFFMAN, lawyer; b. N.Y.C., May 3, 1913; s. Isidor and Belle (Hoffman) W.; A.B., Cornell U., 1933; LL.B., Harvard U., 1936; student U. Ariz., 1944; m. Marguerite Samet, Dec. 12, 1954; children—Susan Rebecca, Amy Elizabeth. Admitted to N.Y. bar, 1936; spl. asst. dist. atty. N.Y. County, 1936-37; asso. law firm Handel and Panuch, 1937-38; mem. legal staff SEC, 1938-42; spl. asst. atty. gen. U.S., 1942; spl. counsel com. on naval affairs U.S. Ho. of Reps., 1943; mem. law firm Moss and Wels & Marcus, 1946-68, Sulzberger, Wels & Marcus, 1968-72, Moss, Wels & Marcus, 1972—; spl. counsel Sea-Air Com., Nat. Fedn. Am. Shipping, 1946; gen. counsel N.Y. State Bowling Proprs. Assn.; dir. H-R TV, Inc., Broadcast Data Base, Inc. Trustee, chmn. Bleuler Psychotherapy Center; counsel Am. Acad. Psychoanalysis; trustee, sec. William A. White Inst. Psychiatry, Psychoanalysis and Psychology, 1946—; trustee N.Y. State Sch. Psychiatry, Margaret Chase Smith Library, Skowhegan, Maine; commr. Interprofl. Commn. Marriage and Divorce Laws and Family Courts; chmn. bd. trustees Islands Research Found.; trustee, gov., chmn. Daytop Village, Daytop Village Found. Commd. ensign USNR 1942, advanced through grades to lt.; mem. staff Undersec. of Navy Forrestal, 1943-44, served PTO, 1944-46. Mem. Am. (chmn. ann. meeting planning com. of family law sect.), N.Y. State (vice-chmn. family law sect.), Fed., N.Y.C. (mem. spl. coms. broadcasting, mil. justice, chmn. improvement of family laws) bar assn., N.Y. County Lawyers Assn. (chmn. spl. com. on mil. justice, fed. cts., vice chmn. com. on pub. relations), Am. Judicature Soc., Inter-Am. Bar Assn., Mil. Orders World Wars, Naval Order U.S., Res. Officers Assn., Sphinx Head (Cornell U.), Am. Jewish Com. (chmn. com. pub. sch. affairs; vice chmn.; mem. nat. exec. council), Assn. ICC Practitioners, Am. Legion, Pi Lambda Phi. Jewish. Clubs: Harvard, Cornell (N.Y.C.); Nat. Lawyers (Washington); Harmonie, Sunningdale Country. Contbr. articles to profl. and lay periodicals, newspapers; editor in chief The Cornellian, 1933. Home: 911 Park Ave New York City NY 10021 Office: 18 E 48th St New York City NY 10017

WELTY, JAMES ALMAN, physician; b. Canton, Ohio, Aug. 9, 1897; s. Per Lee and Anna Belle (Hassler) W.; student Allegheny Coll., 1915-16, 17-18, 19; B.S., Pa. State Coll., 1922; M.D., U. Pa., 1927; m. Janice Elizabeth Conn, Oct. 10, 1931; children—Nancy Hassler Welty Shave, Martha Welty Minnicks. Intern, Allentown (Pa.) Gen. Hosp., 1927-28; gen. practice medicine, Oil City, Pa., 1928-76; mem. staff Oil City Hosp., 1928-75, pres. hosp. med. staff, 1948-49; mem. adv. bd. south side office N.W. Pa. Bank and Trust Co., 1962-70; dir. Citizens Banking Co., 1952-55; mem. adv. bd. south side office Oil City Nat. Bank, 1956-62. Mem. Venango County Cancer Soc., 1938-60, pres., 1956-57; active Venango County Tb Soc.; dir. Venango County br. Pa. Assn. for Blind; pres. South Side Bus. Men's Assn., 1954-56; chmn. Venango County Pub. Relations Com.; mem. commonwealth relations council U. Pa., 1976—, Pa. State U., 1976—. Served to 2d lt., pilot, AC, U.S. Army, 1918-19, to capt. Res., 1920-30. Mem. AMA, Pa. (v.p. 1954-56, com. med. econs. 1954-56, com. rural health and physician placement 1955-57, hosp. relations com. 1960-62), Venango County (ho. of dels.) med. socs., C. of C. Oil City (dir. 1966-67), Pa. State U. Drummers, Phi Delta Theta, Phi Alpha Sigma. Methodist (ofcl. bd. 1951-56, trustee 1956-62, 65-67). Clubs: Masons, K.T., Shriners. Address: 301 W 1st St Oil City PA 16301

WELTY, PATRICIA MARY, counselor, educator; b. Alexandria, Va., Oct. 27, 1946; d. William J. and Elizabeth Mary (Hayes) W.; B.S., U. Md., 1969; M.A., Trinity Coll., Washington, D.C., 1977. Tchr., Montgomery County Pub. Schs., Rockville, Md., 1969-78, guidance counselor, 1978—; exchange educator Dept. State, Singapore, 1974-75; counselor Commn. for Women. Advanced profl. certificate, Md. Mem. Am. Personnel and Guidance Assn., Nat., Montgomery County edn. assns. Home: 6820 Delaware St Chevy Chase MD 20015 Office: 850 Hungerford Dr Rockville MD 20850

WELZ, JOEY, music recording co. exec., musician, composer; b. Balt., Mar. 17, 1940; s. Joseph W. and Melba (Wilson) Welzant; grad. Harford Jr. Coll., 1976; children—Tina, Terry. Pres., Ursula Music Co., Belair, Md., 1963—; buyer Jacham Music Box Co., Balt., 1963; dir. Artist and Repertoir; gen. mgr. Monumental Records Co., Balt., 1965—; pres. Welz Music Co., Balt., 1965—; dist. supr. Handleman Co., 1966-76; pres. Dawn Prodns., Inc., Salisbury, Md., 1966-76; dist. supr., record buyer Zamoiski Record Distbg. Co., 1977—; gen. mgr. Canadian Am. Records Co., Salisbury, 1967-68; writer sound track (with Daniel Thompson) for film Green Woman, 1964; composer theme for film Rollerball, 1975, bicentennial song for State Md.; featured pianist with Bill Haley and the Comets band, 1956-65; recorded albums including: Vintage Ballads (Palmer record), 1969, Revival Fires (Palmer record), 1971; single Fire and Brimstone, 1977; leader Joey Welz Rock N Roll Revival band, 1968-71; appeared with numerous rock and roll musical groups; appeared TV programs including: Balt. At One, WBAL-TV, Larry Angelo Show, WJZ-TV, Buddy Deane Show, WJZ-TV; composer lyrics for numerous songs including: Forever, 1964, Baby, Let Your Hair Hang Down, 1965, Hey, Little Moonbeam, 1965, Just Because We're Young, 1960, Write to Me, Marie, 1960; author: Love in the Country, 1959, Turning on Love, 1962, Evolution of Rock, 1968. Served with U.S. Army, 1959-62. Named one of top Rock 'N' Roll Pianists, D.I.B., London, 1971; placed in top 25 all-time top rock pianists Keyboard Mag., 1976, 77. Mem. Am. Fedn. Musicians, Eastern Shore Police Assn. Home: PO Box 535 Belair MD 21014

WENDEL, PETER KENT, civil engr.; b. Lockport, N.Y., May 24, 1932; s. Leon Henry and Ethel Maude (Bundy) W.; B.S. in Civil Engring., U. Mich., 1955, postgrad., 1957-58; m. Marjorie Jane Harry, Apr. 2, 1955; children—Timothy Lee, Susan Medley, Christopher Kent, Eric Gordon (dec.), Bryan Taylor, Amy Lynn. Designer, Leon H. Wendel, cons. engr., Lockport, 1958-63; project engr. Wendel Assos., cons. engrs./planners, Lockport, 1964-69, partner, 1970—; pres. Wendel Engrs., Lockport and Buffalo, 1975—; dir. Olcott Yacht Harbor, Inc., Lockport Savings & Loan. Pres., fund drive chmn. Easter Niagara United Appeal, 1967-68; chmn. Eastern Niagara County chpt. A.R.C., 1966—. Bd. dirs., pres. Lockport (N.Y.) Sr. Citizens Center; v.p. Kenan Center, Lockport; chmn. Engring. Coll. capital campaign Western N.Y., U. Mich., 1977. Served to lt. (j.g.) USNR, 1955-57. Recipient Distinguished Service award Lockport Jr. C. of C., 1965, Grand Conceptor award-Engring. Excellence award Cons. Engrs. Council N.Y. State, 1973. Mem. ASCE (dir. Buffalo sect. 1970-72), Cons. Engrs. Council N.Y. State (treas. 1972-73, sec. 1973-74, pres. 1976-77), Am. Cons. Engrs. Council (dir.), Lockport Area C. of C. (dir. 1968-70, South Shore (pres. 1974-75) Lake (treas.) yacht racing assns., U.S. Power Squadron. Clubs: Yacht (comdr. Olcott, N.Y. 1967-69); Rotary (Lockport); Niagara on Lake (Ont., Can.) Sailing; U. Mich. (pres. 1978-79) (Buffalo). Home: 7400 Canal Rd Lockport NY 14094 Office: 7405 Canal Rd Lockport NY 14094

WENDEL, RICHARD FREDERICK, educator; b. Chgo., Apr. 29, 1930; s. Elmer Carl and Victoria Matilda (Jeffrey) W.; A.B., Augustana Coll., 1951; M.B.A., U. Pa., 1957, Ph.D. (fellow 1962-64), 1966; m. Leslie Jane Travis, June 15, 1957; children—John Travis, Andrew Stewart. Asst. to pres. Flexonics Corp., Maywood, Ill., 1957-59; sales rep., product mgr. dairy products Kordite Corp. div. Nat. Distillers Corp., Macedon, N.Y., 1959-62; instr. Wharton Sch. U. Pa., Phila., 1964-65; asst. prof. mktg. Grad. Sch. Adminstrn., Washington U., St. Louis, 1965-69; asso. prof. mktg. U. Conn. Sch. Bus. Adminstrn., Storrs, 1969-74, prof., 1974—; mem. U.S. Census Field Adv. Commn., 1967-69; mem. acad. adv. commn. Bur. Labor Statistics of Prices and Quality of Life, U.S. Bur. Census, 1971—; mem. Conn. Export Devel. Council, U.S. Dept. Commerce, 1972—. Bd. dirs. The Roper Center. Served with USAF, 1951-55. Center for Real Estate and Urban Econs. grantee, 1969-70. Mem. Am. Mktg. Assn., Am. Econs. Assn., N.Y. Acad. Scis., Am. Acad. Social and Polit. Sci. Republican. Episcopalian. Author: (with M.L. Bell) Economic Importance of Highway Advertising, 1966; editor: Readings in Marketing, 1973-74, 75-76, 76-77, 77-78; Add to Your Selling Know-How, 1968; editorial staff jour. Mktg., 1965-74. Home: Friendship Valley Brooklyn CT 06234 Office: Box U-41M Sch Bus Adminstrn U Conn Storrs CT 06268

WENDEL, THOMAS MICHAEL, airline co. exec.; b. Jamestown, N.D., July 15, 1936; s. Peter Thomas and Esther Marie (Jahnke) W.; B.S., Ursinus Coll., 1960; M.A. (NDEA fellow), San Jose State Coll., 1964; M.B.A., U. Santa Clara, 1969; m. Elise Ida Moennig, June 11, 1960; children—Gretchen, Heidi, Peter. Mem. data processing systems design staff Boeing Co., Seattle, 1960-62; data processing and systems, mgmt. staff Lockheed Corp., San Jose, Calif., 1962-68; dir. info. systems State N.J., Trenton, 1968-71; v.p. data processing Pan Am. World Airways, Inc., N.Y.C., 1971-75, v.p. corporate planning and info. services, 1975-77, sr. v.p. corporate planning, 1977—; adj. faculty San Jose State Coll., 1962-63; Lockheed Corp. rep. Codasyl Cobol Devel. Com., 1964-66; book reviewer McGraw Hill, 1969-71. Served with USMCR, 1954-56. Mem. Phi Kappa Phi. Author: (with W.H. Williams) Introduction to Data Processing and Cobol, 1969. Home: Cherry Brook Dr Princeton NJ 08540 Office: Pan Am Bldg 200 Park Ave New York City NY 10017

WENDLING, DONALD BRAND, constrn. materials co. exec.; b. Louisville, July 12, 1915; s. George Clifford and Annetta Ethel (Brand) W.; student Auburn U., 1940; m. Ann Marie Snedden, July 12, 1947; children—Donald Brand, Georganne. Asst. to v.p. sales Birmingham (Ala.) Slag Co., 1937-59; v.p. sales Vulcan Materials Co., Chgo., 1959-65; v.p. mktg. cement div. Martin Marietta Corp., N.Y.C., 1965-70, pres. Martin Marietta Aggregates, Bethesda, Md., 1970—, also v.p. Martin Marietta Corp. Mem. Am. Road Builders Assn. (dir.), Nat. Limestone Inst. (dir.), Am. Concrete Paving Assn. (dir.), Nat. Crushed Stone Assn. (dir.), Nat. Sand and Gravel Assn., Transp. Research Bd., Sigma Chi. Republican. Presbyterian. Clubs: Congressional Country, Bethesda Country (Bethesda, Md.); Vestavia Country (Birmingham, Ala.); Tamarack Country (Greenwich, Conn.). Home: 12701 Watertown Ct Potomac MD 20854 Office: 6801 Rockledge Dr Bethesda MD 20034

WENDROFF, EDWARD ROY, fin. co. exec.; b. Bklyn., Nov. 1, 1940; s. Charles and Etta (Goldstein) W.; A.A.S., Bklyn. Coll., 1962; B.S., N.Y. U., 1965; m. Joan Berkley, Jan. 30, 1965; children—Mary, Sheryl. Purchasing agt. Mitsui & Co. Inc., N.Y.C., 1965-68; asst. v.p. Merrill Lynch Pierce Fenner & Smith, Inc., Trenton, N.J., 1968—. Founder, treas. Congregation Beth Chaim, East Windsor, N.J., 1971, trustee, 1972-75. Mem. Chgo. Bd. Trade, N.Y. C. of C. Clubs: B'nai B'rith, K.P. Home: 4 Fern Dr East Windsor NJ 08520 Office: Merrill Lynch Lawrence Shopping Center Route 1 Trenton NJ 08648

WENGER, SAMUEL ESBENSHADE, environmentalist; b. Paradise, Pa., Apr. 20, 1938; s. Samuel Stoner and Ella Mae (Esbenshade) W.; B.A., Goshen Coll., 1960; M.Ed., Temple U., 1964; postgrad. Yale U., summer 1967; m. Ruth Arlene Derstine, June 13,

1965; children—Ann Elizabeth, Carla Mae, Tonya Lee. Tchr. sci. Twillingate (Nfld., Can.) Regional High Sch., 1960-62; tchr. sci., math Rockway High Sch., Kitchener, Ont., Can., 1962-63; tchr. chemistry and environ. edn. Manheim (Pa.) Central High Sch., 1964—; dir., coordinator river monitoring program Conestoga Valley Assn.; water quality cons. Chickies Creek Watershed Assn. Recipient Environ. Conservation Tchr. of Yr. award Nat. Assn. Conservation, 1975. Mem. Nat., Pa. sci. tchrs. assn., Pa. Edn. Assn., NEA, Manheim Central Edn. Assn. Republican. Mennonite. Author: A Watershed Becomes a Classroom, 1975. Home: 3 Fairview Dr Akron PA 17501 Office: Manheim Central High Sch Hershey Dr and Adele Ave Manheim PA 17545

WENIGER, SIDNEY N., real estate investor/developer; b. Bklyn., Apr. 20, 1920; s. Morris and Rose (Swerling) W.; B.C.E., Cooper Union Inst. Tech., 1941; M.M.E., Poly. Inst. Bklyn., 1949; L.H.D. (hon.) Graceland Coll., 1978; m. Leonore E. Sternick, Dec. 28, 1941; children—Earl Douglas, Bruce Gilbert, Cynthia Sue. Pres. various home bldg. corps. and pvt. utility cos., L.I., Fla., 1949-61; v.p. Kirkeby-Natus Corp., N.Y.C., 1962-65; v.p. Standard Fin. Corp., N.Y.C., 1965-67; owner, pres. Sidney N. Weniger Orgns., 1967—; pres. Gen. Resources Assos. Inc., 1967—. Nat. comml. panel arbiter Am. Arbitration Assn., 1958—. Mem. Internat. Council Shopping Centers, Nat. Assn. Real Estate Investment Funds. Trustee Optometric Center N.Y. Served to lt. USNR, 1944-46. Registered profl. engr., N.Y., N.J. Mem. Nat. Soc. Profl. Engrs., Am. Water Works Assn., Mortgage Bankers Assn. N.Y., Apt. Builder/Developer Conf. (adv. bd.), Assn. Navy Civil Engr. Corps Officers. Clubs: Little Rock, Marco Polo. Home: 40 E 80th St New York City NY 10021 Office: 745 Fifth Ave New York City NY 10022

WENNER, CLAUDE HENRY, elec. engr.; b. Merchantville, N.J., Sept. 10, 1922; s. Edwin Peter and Florence Hazel (Wiegand) W.; student Temple U., 1947-51; B.E.E., Drexel U., 1962; m. Carol Ann Bronson, Apr. 2, 1966. Asst. to comptroller Germantown Hosp., Phila., 1943-46; accountant Kramer Brothers, Inc., Phila., 1947-58; elec. engr. Jefferson Med. Coll., Phila., 1959-68, research asso. bioacoustics, 1968—. Mem. Am. Inst. Physics, Acoustical Soc. Am., Internat. Brotherhood Magicians, Soc. Am. Magicians. Republican. Methodist. Contbr. articles to profl. jours. Home: 95 Dayleview Rd Berwyn PA 19312 Office: Jefferson Med Coll 1025 Walnut St Philadelphia PA 19107

WENTWORTH, EDWIN CALVIN, letter carrier, union ofcl.; b. Rome, Maine, Apr. 22, 1940; s. Calvin Albion and Bertha Abbie (Gilpatrick) W.; ed. high sch.; m. Rosemary Elaine Parker, June 5, 1965; children—Michelle Elaine, Kimberly Ann. Apprentice machinist Bath Iron Works (Maine), 1964-66; sgt. City of Gardiner (Maine) Police Dept., 1966-69; radio dispatcher Maine State Police, Augusta, 1969-70; letter carrier, safety officer, license examiner U.S. Postal Service, Gardiner, 1970-78, injury compensation specialist, Auburn, Maine, 1978—; various positions br. 744 Nat. Assn. Letter Carriers, Gardiner, 1971—, sec.-treas., 1971—. Selectman, Town of Belgrade (Maine), 1975—. Served with U.S. Army, 1961-64. Mem. Nat. Assn. Identification Technicians, Kennebec County Municipal Officers Assn. (dir. 1975—), Am. Legion, Grange. Baptist. Clubs: Masons, Shriners, Odd Fellows. Home: Star Route Belgrade Lakes ME 04918 Office: Rodman Rd Auburn ME 04210

WENTWORTH, PAUL MESERVE, civil engr.; b. Washington, Dec. 12, 1903; s. Charles Austin and Pearl (Meserve) W.; B.S., Pa. State U., 1925; m. Eleanor Thompson, Nov. 14, 1929. Engr., Found. Co., N.Y.C., 1925-29, Santiago, Chile, 1929-31, Gibbs & Hill, Inc., N.Y.C., 1931-34; asst. forester Gt. Smokey Mountains Nat. Park, 1934-41; prin., asst. engr. Mueser, Rutledge, Wentworth & Johnston, and predecessor, N.Y.C., 1941-45, 45-51, Caracas, Venezuela, 1945-47, partner, 1951-76, cons., 1976—. Bd. dirs. Palisades Counselling Center, Rutherford, N.J.; elder 1st Presbyn. Ch., Rutherford. Fellow ASCE, Cons. Engrs. Council; mem. The Moles (emeritus), Xi Sigma Pi. Republican. Clubs: Upper Montclair Country, Pennington. Home: 84 Raymond Ave Rutherford NJ 07070 Office: 415 Madison Ave New York City NY 10017

WENTZ, HENRY STAUFFER, physician, clin. adminstr.; b. Leola, Pa., Mar. 14, 1921; s. Joseph Clair and Arline Marie (Stauffer) W.; A.B., Duke U., 1941; M.D., Thomas Jefferson U., 1944; m. Mary Louise Whitney, Apr. 24, 1945; children—William Henry, Louise Joanne. Intern, Lancaster (Pa.) Gen. Hosp., 1944-45, resident in internal medicine and pediatrics, 1945-46, asso. physician medicine, 1949-70, asso. dir. family and community medicine, coordinator teaching, 1970-74, chmn. dept. family and community medicine, 1974—; gen. practice family medicine, Strasburg, Pa., 1948-74; pres. Eastbrook Family Health Center, Ronks, Pa., 1974—; clin. lectr. dept. family and community medicine Milton S. Hershey Med. Center, Pa. State U., Hershey; clin. asst. prof. community medicine Temple U. Sch. Medicine. Served to capt., M.C., U.S. Army, 1946-48. Mem. AMA, Pa., Lancaster County med. socs., Am. Acad. Family Practice. Republican. Contbr. articles to med. jours. Home: 180 Hillcrest Ave Strasburg PA 17579 Office: RD 1 Ronks PA 17572

WENTZ, ROBERT JAMES, plumbing fixture and fittings engr.; b. Salem, Ohio, June 10, 1916; s. Archibald Hays and Olive Charlott (Bardo) W.; student Wittenberg Coll., 1935; grad. Salem Trade Sch., 1938; m. Kathryn Virginia Taylor, Oct. 8, 1938; children—Thomas N., Cheryl Kay Wentz Scheiderer, Draftsman, Deming Pump Co., Salem, 1937-39; product draftsman Eljer Co., Salem, 1939-41, chief insp. bomb line, 1942-44, quality control-foundry, 1945-46, product designer, Marysville, Ohio, 1947-48, product designer, 1949-57, chief product and process engr., 1958-64, maintenance supr., 1965-66, product design engr., 1967-69; chief design engr. Eljer Plumbingware, Pitts., 1969—. Dist. commr. Boy Scouts Am., 1940-60, dist. chmn., 1960; mem. Milford Center (Ohio) Town Council, 1952-60. Mem. ASTM. Republican. Presbyterian. Clubs: Masons, Lions (pres. 1966). Patentee anti-siphon float valve. Office: 3 Gateway Center Pittsburgh PA 15222

WENTZ, WILLIAM WESLEY, steel co. exec.; b. Palmerton, Pa., July 1, 1926; s. Howard Daniel and Mary Lavina W.; B.S. in Metallurgy, Pa. State U., 1951; m. Beatrice Louella Green Handwerk, Sept. 9, 1950; children—Howard Jeffrey, Jed Alan, Christopher Paul. Research and devel. metallurgist Rem-CRU Titanium Inc., 1951-58; mgr. product devel. Cricuble Steel Co., 1959-61, div. metallurgist, 1961-65, chief metallurgist, 1965-69; gen. supr. tech. services Sharon Steel Co. (Pa.), 1969-72, mgr. sales, alloy flat roll products, 1972-78, gen. mgr. mktg., 1978—. Mem. sch. bd. Western Beaver Sch. Dist., Beaver County, Pa., 1968-69. Served with USAF, 1945-47. Mem. Am. Soc. Metals, Am. Inst. Steel Engrs., Am. Inst. Mining, Metall. and Petroleum Engrs., Am. Ordnance Assn., Trout Unlimited. Republican. Contbr. articles to tech. jours. Home: 700 Woodlawn Dr Sharon PA 16146 Office: Sharon Steel Corp PO Box 291 Sharon PA 16146

WENTZEL, RICHARD CLAY, pub. relations cons.; b. Laureldale, Pa., June 19, 1922; s. Frederick DeHart and Miriam (Clay) W.; B.A., Ursinus Coll., Pa., 1949; m. Blanche Caroline Shirey, Aug. 24, 1946. Reporter, Phila. Record, 1940-41, and Norristown (Pa.) Times Herald, 1949-52; news editor Sta. WPAZ, Pottstown, Pa., 1953-54; dir. pub. and personnel relations Berkshire Internat. Corp., Reading, Pa., 1954-60; dir. pub. relations and advt. Textile Machine Works, Reading, 1960-61; owner Richard C. Wentzel Assos., Pub. Relations, Reading, 1961—; cons. Nat. Inst. Alcohol Abuse and Alcoholism, Indsl. Referral and Occupational Adv. Services, others. Bd. dirs. Berks County chpt. ARC, 1960-62, chmn. pub. relations com., 1960, nominating com., 1961; bd. dirs. Daniel Boone council Boy Scouts Am., 1960-63; bd. dirs. Berks County chpt. Nat. Council on Alcoholism, 1960-75, pres., 1965-67, chmn. labor-mgmt. com., 1968-75; bd. dirs. Berks chpt. Tb Assn., 1958-60; mem. pub. relations com. United Way Berks County, 1963-68; bd. dirs. YMCA Reading and Berks County, 1957-71, chmn. membership dr., 1964, chmn. pub. relations com., 1965-71; campaign pub. relations dir. Berks County chpt. Am. Cancer Soc., 1970—; elder St. Peter's United Ch. Christ, Wilshire, 1962—, v.p. consistory, 1963-65, 76-78, lay reader, 1970—; mem. salary com. Pa. SE conf. United Ch. Christ, 1974—. Served with USAF, 1943-46. Mem. Pub. Relations Soc. Am. (accredited), Internat. Assn. Bus. Communicators, Assn. Labor-Mgmt. Adminstrs. and Cons.'s on Alcoholism, Reading-Berks C. of C. (dir. 1957-59). Contbr. poems to mags. and anthologies. Lyricist: I Think She Winked at Me, One White Rose, She's Better Than Most, Why Didn't I Hear It from You?, Nine Little Kisses. Home: 73 Miller Dr Sinking Spring Reading PA 19608 Office: 3 E Lancaster Ave Reading PA 19607

WERBA, HENRY CARL, educator; b. Prague, Czechoslovakia, May 5, 1934; s. Othmar and Marina (Doroschkewitsch) W.; came to U.S., 1951, naturalized, 1967; B.A., U. Toledo, 1957, M.A., 1961; Ph.D., U. Conn., 1972; m. Rosemarie F. Amann, Aug. 23, 1957; children—Denise, Alexander, Roland. Instr. fgn. langs. Devilbiss High Sch., Toledo, 1961-66, Mary Manse Coll., Toledo, 1962-66, U. Toledo, 1962-65; Russian specialist, journalist, researcher Radio Liberty, Munich, Germany, 1967; asst. prof. fgn. langs. So. Conn. State Coll., New Haven, 1967-74, asso. prof., 1974—, coordinator Russian and German, 1967-72; violinist Toledo Symphony Orch., 1951-52. Mem. Modern Lang. Assn., Am. Assn. Tchrs. German, AAUP, Conn. State Employees Assn. Republican. Roman Catholic. Author lang. textbooks; contbr. articles to profl. jours. Home: 30 Fernwood Ln Cheshire CT 06410 Office: So Conn State Coll 501 Crescent St New Haven CT 06515

WERLY, JOHN MCINTYRE, historian, educator; b. Rochester, N.Y., Nov. 6, 1939; s. Berlyn McIntyre and Grace (Steinhauser) W.; B.A., Trinity Coll., Hartford, Conn., 1961, M.A., 1966; Ph.D. in U.S. History, Syracuse (N.Y.) U., 1972; m. Bonnie Windolf, July 8, 1961; children—Aric, Robyn, Scott. Instr. history Robinson Sch., W. Hartford, Conn., 1963-68; teaching asst. U.S. history Syracuse U., 1969-70; instr. U.S. history State U. N.Y., Cortland, 1970-72; asst. prof. history Southeastern Mass. U., N. Dartmouth, 1972—; community lectr. in field. Recipient Leo M. Sullivan Tchr. of Yr. award So. Mass. U. Faculty Fedn., 1976-77. Mem. Am. Hist. Assn., Orgn. Am. Historians. Contbr. hist. articles in field to profl. jours. Home: 20 Stillman St South Dartmouth MA 02748 Office: Southeastern Massachusetts Univ North Dartmouth MA 02747

WERMUTH, ANTHONY LEWIS, social scientist, writer; b. Phila., June 1, 1915; s. Paul Charles and Susan Aloysius (Manga) W.; B.S., U.S. Mil. Acad., 1940; postgrad. Army Command and Gen. Staff Coll., 1944, Army War Coll., 1958-59, Mass. Inst. Tech., 1966-67; M.A., Columbia, 1951, George Washington U., 1961; Ph.D., Boston U., 1971; m. Charlotte J. Malinowski, July 24, 1940; children—Philip (dec.), Anthony Lewis, Marianne N. Commd. 2d lt. inf., U.S. Army, 1940, advanced through grades to col.; asst. prof. English U.S. Mil. Acad., 1946-50; co. and bn. comdr. World War II; bn., regiment comdr., Korea, 1956-57; mem. faculty Army War Coll., 1959-62; brigade comdr., Germany, 1963-64; staff officer hdqrs. U.S. Army in Europe, Germany, Hdqrs, SHAPE, Paris; mil. asst. to chmn. Joint Chiefs of Staff; ret. 1966; dir. social sci. studies Center for Advanced Studies, Westinghouse Corp., 1966-73; polit. scientist Strategic Studies Inst., U.S. Army War Coll., 1974—. Decorated D.S.M. Mem. Internat. Inst. for Strategic Studies (London), Am. Polit. Sci. Assn., Am. Acad. Polit. and Social Sci., Acad. Polit. Sci., U.S. Naval Inst., Assn. U.S. Army, World Future Soc., Interuniv. Seminar on Armed Forces and Soc., Internat. Studies Assn., others. Home: 616 Sutton Dr Carlisle PA 17013 Office: Box 491 US Army War Coll Carlisle Barracks PA 17013

WERMUTH, WILLIAM CHARLES, IV, planner; b. Chgo., June 21, 1943; s. William Charles and Jeannette (Carling) W.; B.Arch., R.I. Sch. Design, 1967; m. Alice Leas, July 4, 1975; 1 son, William Charles. Planner, David M. Walker Assos., Inc., Phila., 1967-69; project dir. R.T.K.L., Inc., Balt., 1969-71; spl. projects dir. Kendree & Shephard Planning Cons., Phila., 1971-73; dir. planning Yerkes Assos., Inc., Bryn Mawr, Pa., 1973—. Mem. Am. Inst. Planning, Pa. Planning Assn., Phila. Econ. Council, Am. Assn. Coll. Newspaper Editors. Republican. Roman Catholic. Club: Optimist. Home: 326 Airdale Rd Rosemont PA 19010 Office: 101 Charles Dr Bryn Mawr PA 19010

WERNER, CHARLES ARTHUR, physician; b. Malverne, N.Y., Mar. 10, 1921; s. Charles Arthur and Gladys Rachel (Murrill) W.; B.S., U. Chgo., 1942; M.D., Cornell U. Med. Coll., N.Y.C., 1945; m. Dorothy Marie Pfretzschner, Sept. 18, 1971; children—Carol Anne, Catherine Alice, Charles Arthur, Christian Anton. Intern, N.Y. Hosp., 1945-46; NIH postdoctoral research fellow in medicine Cornell Med. Coll., 1948-50; asst. resident physician in medicine N.Y. Hosp.-Cornell Med. Center, N.Y.C., 1950-51; sr. resident in radiology Manhattan VA Hosp., N.Y.C., 1956-57; sr. research fellow Am. Tb Assn. at Bellevue Hosp., N.Y.C., 1957-58; med. dir. Pfizer Internat. Corp., N.Y.C., 1951-56, Robert E. Wilson, Inc., N.Y.C., 1957-59; asst. prof. medicine Cornell U., 1958-68; physician to outpatient dept. N.Y. Hosp., 1958-69; pvt. practice medicine specializing in internal medicine, Huntington, N.Y., 1956—; attending physician Huntington Hosp., 1956—; asst. attending physician Bellevue Hosp., 1958-69; U.S. del. All India Sci. Congress, Calcutta, 1951; resident fellow Explorers Club N.Y., 1974. Served to lt. j.g., USNR, 1942-45. Diplomate Am. Bd. Internal Medicine. Fellow A.C.P., Am. Coll. Chest Physicians, Am. Coll. Gastroenterologists; mem. AAAS, World Med. Assn., Am. Fedn. Clin. Research, N.Y. Acad. Medicine, AMA, Am. Thoracic Soc., Am. Soc. Tropical Medicine and Hygiene, Phi Beta Kappa. Home and Office: 3 Hamilton Ln Huntington NY 11743

WERNER, EDWIN ROBERT, ins. co. exec.; b. N.Y.C., Apr. 1, 1922; s. Edwin and Sidone Frances (Bruilotta) W.; student Pace U., 1940-42; children—Helen Werner Fuina, Paul J., Joyce Werner Bergman, Jane T., Karen L., Robert M. With Blue Cross/Blue Shield of Greater N.Y., 1961—, pres., 1972—, dir., 1977—; pres., dir. Health Services Improvement Fund, N.Y.C.; mem. adv. group health com. N.Y. State Senate, 1974—; mem. N.Y. State Hosp. Rev. and Planning Council, N.Y. State Council Health Care Financing, 1978—. Served with U.S. Army, 1942-45. Decorated D.S.M. Mem. Pub. Health Assn., Blue Cross Assn. (dir.), Blue Shield Assn. (dir. 1974—, chmn. 1978—), Hosp. Soc. Clubs: Westchester Hills Golf; Sky (N.Y.C.). Home: 51 Soundview Ave White Plains NY 10606 Office: 622 Third Ave New York City NY 10017

WERNICK, JACK HARRY, scientist; b. St. Paul, May 19, 1923; s. Joseph and Eva (Legan) W.; B.Met.E., U. Minn., 1947, M.S., 1948; Ph.D., Pa. State U., 1954; m. Sylvia Katz, Dec. 20, 1947; children—Phyllis Roberta Wernick Lauer, Rosanne Pauline. Staff, Manhattan Project, Los Alamos, 1944-46; mem. staff Bell Labs., Murray Hill, N.J., 1954—, head solid state chemistry research dept., 1963—; cons. U.S. Office Sci. and Tech., Nat. Bur. Standards, NSF; mem. steering com. div. nuclear fusion ERDA, 1977—. Served in U.S. Army, 1944-46. Fellow N.Y. Acad. Scis., Am. Phys. Soc.; mem. Am. Soc. Metals (McFarland award 1969), AAAS, IEEE, Am. Inst. Mining and Metall. Engrs., Am. Chem. Soc., Sigma Xi, Phi Lambda Upsilon. Jewish. Author: (with E.A. Nesbitt) Rare Earth Permanent Magnets, 1973; (with J.L. Shay) Chalcopyrite Crystals, 1975; editor: Materials and Energy: Selected Topics, 1977; contbr. articles to profl. jours. Home: 18 Stafford Dr Madison NJ 07940 Office: 600 Mountain Ave Murray Hill NJ 07974

WERNICK, RICHARD FRANK, composer, condr.; b. Boston, Jan. 16, 1934; s. Louis and Irene (Prince) W.; B.A., Brandeis U., 1955; M.A., Mills Coll., 1957; student Ernst Toch, Boris Blacher and Aaron Copland at Tanglewood, 1954-55; student with Irving Fine, Harold Shapero, Arthur Berger, Leon Kirchner; m. Beatrice Messina, July 15, 1956; children—Lewis, Adam, Peter. Mus. dir., composer-in-residence Royal Winnipeg (Man.) Ballet of Can., 1957-58; Ford Found. fellow Bay Shore (L.I.) Pub. Schs., 1962-64; instr. music U. Buffalo, 1964-65; asst. prof., mus. dir. symphony orch. U. Chgo., 1965-68; asso. prof., mus. dir. Pa. Contemporary Players, U. Pa., 1968—, chmn. dept. music, 1969-74, prof., 1977—; works include: Lyrics from IXI, 1967; Haiku of Basho, 1968; Moonsongs from the Japanese, 1969; A Prayer for Jerusalem (Walter W. Naumburg Found. Rec. award 1975), 1971; Kaddish-Requiem, 1972; Songs of Remembrance, 1973-74; String Quartet 2, 1973; Visions of Terror and Wonder, 1975-76 (Pulitzer award 1977); Comtemplations of the Tenth Muse, 1976; mus. dir. Community Youth Orch. of Delaware County (Pa.), 1973-74. Recipient Nat. Inst. Arts and Letters award 1976; Naumburg Rec. award, 1976; Pulitzer Prize, 1977; Nat. Endowment for Arts grantee, 1975; Guggenheim fellow, 1976—. Mem. ASCAP. Democrat. Jewish. Office: Dept Music U Pa 201 S 34th St Philadelphia PA 19174

WERSHAW, FREDERICK IRVING, mktg. co. exec.; b. New Haven, Mar. 17, 1928; s. Abraham and Henrietta (Lander) W.; B.S., Syracuse U., 1949, postgrad., 1949-50; m. Beverly Sondra Liskovsky, Nov. 25, 1950; children—Steven Lee, Lisa Beth. Vice-pres. mktg. and sales Tech. Tape Corp. and affiliates, 1950-54; partner Wershaw-Gould Co., 1954-66; owner Frederick I. Wershaw, Mgmt., 1966—, also pres.; v.p. sales Paper Novelty Mfg. Co., Stamford, Conn., 1966-70; pres. Synoptic Systems Corp., N.Y.C., 1970-71, Churchill Mktg. Corp., N.Y.C., 1970-76; mktg. cons. Scripto, Inc., Atlanta, 1973-74; v.p. mktg. Decor Noel Corp., Memphis, 1973—; pres. Dalon Industries, Inc., Stamford, 1975-77; corp. v.p. Baron Industries, Miami, Fla., also pres. Wettex div., 1976-77; v.p., dir. Specialized Travel & Tours, Inc., Stamford; dir. Think, Inc., 1975-77; mktg. cons. Random House Inc., N.Y.C., 1963-66, Nirvana div. Cleve Pak Corp., N.Y.C., 1972-74; dir. sales Litron div. L. & D. Inc., Scottsdale, Ariz. Legis. chmn. Muscular Dystrophy Assn., 1951-52; bd. dirs. Stamford Jewish Center, 1968-69. Served as officer USAAF, 1944-47. Mem. Zeta Beta Tau. Club: Roxbury Swim (com. chmn. Stamford 1967-69). Home: 24 Brodwood Dr Stamford CT 06902 Office: 25 3d St Stamford CT 06905

WESLAGER, CLINTON ALFRED, historian, author; b. Pitts., Apr. 30, 1909; s. Fred H. and Alice (Lowe) W.; B.A., U. Pitts., 1933; m. Ruth G. Hurst, June 9, 1934; children—Ruth Ann Weslager Tatnall, Clinton Alfred, Thomas. Sales promotion mgr. Life Savers Corp., Port Chester, N.Y., 1933-37; with E. I. du Pont de Nemours & Co., Inc., 1937-68, mgr. automotive spltys. div., Wilmington, Del., 1959-66, product mgr. automotive products div. consumer products, 1966-68. Vis. prof. U.S. history Wesley Coll., 1969, U. Del., 1970-73, Brandywine Coll., 1970-78. Pres. Richardson Park Bd. Sch. Trustees, 1953-57. Mem. Eastern States Archeol. Fedn. (pres. 1954-58), Archeol. Soc. Del. (pres. 1942-48, 50-53), AAUP, Sigma Delta Chi. Author: Delaware's Forgotten Folk, 1943; Delaware's Buried Past, 1944; Delaware's Forgotten River, 1947; The Nanticoke Indians, 1948; Brandywine Springs, 1949; Indian Place-Names in Delaware, 1950; Red Men on the Brandywine, 1953; The Richardsons of Delaware, 1957; Dutch Explorers, Traders, and Settlers, 1961; Garrett Snuff Fortune, 1965; English on the Delaware, 1967; The Log Cabin in America, 1969; History of the Delaware Indians, 1972; Magic Medicines of the Indians, 1974; The Stamp Act Congress, 1976; The Delaware Indian Westward Migration, 1978. Contbr. articles to profl. jours. Home: Old Public Rd Hockessin DE 19707

WESOLOW, ADAM, ADAM, thoracic-cardiovascular surgeon; b. Saugus, Mass., Feb. 6, 1923; s. Joseph and Adamina (Ploharska) W.; student Harvard U., 1941-44; M.D., Tufts U., 1948, M.S. in Surgery, 1951; Sc.D., Alliance Coll.; m. Wanda B. Kirbi, Oct. 7, 1945; children—Carl Adam, Paul David, Joan Marie, Adam John, Edward Alan. Surg. intern Johns Hopkins Hosp., Balt., 1948-49; Charleton research and teaching fellow Tufts Coll. Medicine, 1949-51; surg. resident Ziskind Surg. Research Lab., New Eng. Med. Center, Boston, 1949-52; surg. resident Kings County Hosp., 1954-56; sr. registrar thoracic surgery Guy's Hosp., London, 1956-58; 3d research scholar A.C.S., 1956-59; instr. surgery State U. N.Y. Downstate Med. Center, 1957-58, asst. prof., 1958-60, prof., 1960-64, clin. prof., 1964—; chmn. dept. surgery Meadowbrook Hosp., East Meadow, 1964-66; dir. cardiovascular research lab. Mercy Hosp., Rockville Centre, 1966—, chief thoracic-cardiovascular surgery, 1974—; chmn. dept. surgery Hosp. St. Raphael, New Haven, 1978—; pres. Nassau-Suffolk Regional Med. Program 1968-70; mem. U.S. Nat. Com. for Engring. in Medicine and Biology, 1967—; chmn. com. on device legis. Soc. Vascular Surgery and Internat. Cardiovascular Soc., 1966—; founding chmn., sec. U.S. Com. on Cardiovascular Devices Internat. Standards Orgn., 1972; chmn. Gordon Research Conf. on Biomaterials, 1973; chmn. subcom. 2 on cardiovascular implants U.S.A. tech. adv. group Internat. Standards Orgn., 1973. Served to capt. M.C., AUS, 1952-54. Elected to Wisdom Hall of Fame, 1970; recipient Man of Year Medicus award Polish-Am. Med. and Dental Assn., 1974. Mem. Royal Coll. Medicine, Royal Soc. Health, Am. Soc. Artificial Internal Organs (pres. 1966), Assn. Advancement Med. Instrumentation (chmn. subcom. on vascular prostheses), Cardiovascular Soc. Chile (hon.), Assn. Polish Surgeons (Warsaw; hon.), Polish-Am. Med. Soc. (Medicus) (hon.), Soc. Biomaterials (founding mem., exec. sec. 1974, pres. 1976), Nat. Acupuncture Research Soc., many nat., local surg., vascular socs. Author 2 books; contbr. numerous articles to profl. jours. Home: 44 Roosevelt Ave Lynbrook NY 11563 Office: Hosp St Raphael 1450 Chapel St New Haven CT 06511

WESSER, DAVID ROBERT, plastic surgeon; b. Newark, Sept. 29, 1933; s. Charles Samuel and Matilda (Kandler) W.; B.A. summa cum laude, Washington Sq. Coll., 1954; M.D., N.Y. U., 1958; children—Marius Charles Sebastian, Pavelle Garance Alethea. Resident in plastic surgery Mt. Sinai Hosp., N.Y.C., 1965, asst. prof. surgery, 1971—; practice medicine, specializing in plastic surgery, N.Y.C., 1965—; chief plastic surgery Elmhurst City Hosp., N.Y.C., 1971—; cons. plastic surgeon N.Y. State Rehab. Hosp., 1971—. Served to maj., US Army, 1967-69. Decorated Army Commendation

Medal; recipient Thomas Wolfe award N.Y. U., 1954, Caducean award, 1954; diplomate Am. Bd. Plastic and Reconstructive Surgeons. Fellow ACS; mem. Am. Soc. Plastic Surgeons, Soc. Mil. Plastic Surgeons, N.Y. Regional Soc. Plastic Surgeons, Phi Beta Kappa. Unitarian. Contbr. articles in field to med. jours. Home: 101 E 86 St New York City NY 10028 Office: 1045 Park Ave New York City NY 10028

WEST, ARTHUR JAMES, II, biologist; b. Boston, Dec. 14, 1927; s. Arthur James and Lillian (Laming) W.; B.S., Suffolk U., 1951, M.A. in Edn., 1956; M.S., U. N.H., 1962, Ph.D. in Zoology, 1964; m. Carolyn Barbara Ross, June 4, 1948 (div. May 1972); children—Arthur James, Gregory Thomas, Donald Robert. Faculty, Suffolk U., Boston, 1952-68, asso. prof. biology, 1964-65, prof., 1965-68, co-chmn. biology, 1964-68; dean, prof. div. natural sci. New Eng. Coll., Henniker, N.H., 1968-70; prof., chmn. dept. biology Suffolk U., 1970-72, 78—; asso. program dir. Pre-coll. Edn. in Scis., NSF, 1972-73; prof. dept. biology Suffolk U., 1973—; dir. R.S. Friedman Cobscook Bay Lab., 1975—; asst. prof., chmn. biology Mass. Coll. Optometry, 1957-60; instr., chmn. sci, Emerson Coll., 1956-59; staff Norwich U., 1960; cons. Ginn & Co. Sci. Publs., 1967—; civil service examiner Mass. Dept. Natural Resources, 1965—. Founding pres. Keltown Civic Assn., 1954; chmn. Woburn United Fund, 1958; mem. Woburn Sch. Com., 1955-60, chmn., 1957; chmn. Woburn YMCA, 1958, Woburn Republican City Com., 1959. Served with USN, 1946-47. NSF grantee, 1968-71, 70-71, 75—. Mem. AAAS, Am. Inst. Biol. Scis., Am. Soc. Parasitologists, Nat. Marine Edn. Assn. (dir. 1976—), Am. Soc. Zoologists, Boston Malacological Soc., Sigma Xi (Suffolk U. club pres. 1972), Sigma Zeta, Phi Beta Chi (pres. 1951), Beta Beta Beta, Phi Sigma. Clubs: Masons, Explorers. Research and publs. on Acanthocephala and undergrad. marine edn. Home: 29 Bradbury St Allston MA 02134

WEST, AUSTIN WARD, comml. printing co. exec.; b. Syracuse, N.Y., Dec. 27, 1915; s. Clarence Eugene and Sara Frances (Ward) W.; B.A., Williams Coll., 1938; m. Barbara Joy Cummings, June 22, 1940; children—Anne Butler West Russell, Sally Ford West Reilly, Austin Ward, David Cummings. Adjustor, Gen. Motors Co., Gen. Exchange Ins. Corp., Boston, 1939-42; chief mil. contracts Republic Aviation Corp., Farmingdale, N.Y., 1942-45; sec., dir. Vail-Ballou Press, Inc., Binghamton, N.Y., 1945-58; pres. Thomas J. Griffiths Sons, Inc., Utica, N.Y., 1958-74; pres., dir. Canterbury Press, Rome, N.Y., 1965—; dir. Columbian Mut. Life Ins. Co., Utica Fire Ins. Co., Marine Midland Bank-Central; trustee Oneida County Savs. Bank. Bd. dirs. Boys Scouts Am., Boys Club, Susquahanna Valley Home, Leukemia Soc. Am., Planned Parenthood. Mem. Internat. Printing Craftsmen (dir. Binghamton 1954-58, pres., 1955), Printing Industries Am. (dir. East-Central assn. 1962-71, pres. 1966), Rome C. of C. (dir.), Kappa Alpha Soc. Episcopalian (vestryman 1962-65, 76—). Clubs: Rotary; Fort Schuyler, Sadaquada Golf (Utica); Rome; Williams (N.Y.C.); Taconic Golf (Williamstown, Mass.). Home: RFD 1 Campus Rd Clinton NY 13323 Office: 301 Mill St Rome NY 13440

WEST, BOB, pharm. and chem. cons.; b. Ellenville, N.Y., Mar. 7, 1931; s. Harry and Elsie (May) Wicentowsky; B.S., Union U., Schenectady, 1952; M.S., Purdue U., 1954, Ph.D., 1956; grad. mgmt. seminar U. Chgo., 1972; m. Betty Parker, May 19, 1957 (div. 1973); children—Debra Ellen, Elizabeth Ann, Sharon Lynn. Chem. cons., research pharmacologist Am. Cyanamid Co., Stamford, Conn., 1958-60; v.p. Rosner-Hixson Labs., Chgo., 1960-68; dir. sci. and regulatory affairs Vick Chem. Co., Mt. Vernon, N.Y., 1968-75; pres. Bob West Assos., Greenwich, Conn., 1975—. Mem. bd. PTA, 1971. Mem. Drug Info. Assn. (chmn. com. dissemination of accurate info. 1972-74, program chmn. 1973-74, pres. 1974-75), Assn. Vitamin Chemists (dir., treas.), Am. Soc. Pharmacology and Exptl. Therapeutics, Soc. Toxicology, Acad. Pharm. Scis., Sigma Xi, Rho Chi, Phi Lambda Upsilon. Jewish (v.p. temple 1964-67). Home: PO Box 2001 Stamford CT 06906 Office: 289 Greenwich Ave Greenwich CT 06830

WEST, DANIEL JONES, JR., hosp. adminstr., rehab. counselor; b. Coaldale, Pa., Sept. 19, 1949; s. Daniel J. and Mildred Elizabeth (Kreiger) W.; B.S. cum laude, Pa. State U., 1971, Ed.M. summa cum laude, 1972, postgrad., from 1974; postgrad. Montgomery County Community Coll., Rutgers U., 1973; m. Linda Jean Werdt, Sept. 18, 1971; children—Jeffrey Bryan, Christopher Jones. Psychol. services asso. Commonwealth of Pa., Harrisburg State Hosp., 1972; adminstrv. dir. and counselor Good Samaritan Hosp. Alcoholism and Drug Counseling Center, Pottsville, Pa., 1972-74, adminstr., 1975—; cons. in drug abuse and alcoholism programming, 1974—; instr. dept. counselor edn. Pa. State U., University Park campus, 1974-75; instr. of continuing edn. Pa. State U., Schuylkill campus, 1973—, adviser to undergrad. rehab. edn. orgn., 1975; cons. to Temple U. Sch. of Social Adminstrn., 1974; moderator First Ann. Conf. on Drug and Alcohol Abuse, Bedford, Pa., 1977. Chmn. planning and implementation council of Schuylkill County, Gov.'s Council on Drug and Alcohol Abuse, State of Pa., 1973-74, mem. Drug Advisory Task Force, 1973-74; mem. Task Force of Child and Family Resource Devel. program of Schuylkill County, 1973—; mem. Schuylkill County Criminal Justice System Task Force, 1975—; mem. local advisory bd. Holy Family Home Health Care Agy. of Schuylkill County, 1977—, chairperson bd. edn. com., 1977—; bd. dirs. Health Systems Agy. of Northeast Pa., 1977—, St. David's Soc. of Schuylkill and Carbon Counties, 1976—. Certified Rehab. counselor. Mem. Am., Pa. psychol. assns., Am., Pa. personnel and guidance assns., Assn. for Advancement of Behavior Therapy, Nat., Pa. rehab. assns., Pa., N. Atlantic Regional assns. of counselor edn., Alcoholism Assn. of Pa., Assn. of Mental Health Adminstrs., Council of Rehab. Counselor Educators, Am. Ednl. Research Assn., Assn. for Advancement of Psychology, AAAS, Nat., Pa. vocat. guidance assns., Iota Alpha Delta, Keystone Hon. Soc., Pa. State Alumni Assn., Am. Pub. Health Assn. Clubs: Elks, Masons. Author of manuals on mgmt. and counseling and various tng. programs for rehab. counseling. Home: Dieters Development Elmer Ave RD 4 PO Box 4425 Pottsville PA 17901 Office: Alcoholism and Drug Counseling Center 727 E Norwegian St Pottsville PA 17901

WEST, EDWARD NASON, clergyman; b. Boston, Nov. 5, 1909; s. Edward Nason and Dora daVincente Bellizia (Willey) W.; B.S., Boston U., 1931, Litt.D., 1950; S.T.B., Gen. Theol. Sem., 1934, S.T.D., 1963; D.D., Ripon Coll., 1946; fellow Trinity Coll., London, 1948; Th.D., Russian Theol. Inst., Paris, 1953; D.D., U. King's Coll., Halifax, N.S., 1975. Ordained to ministry P.E. Ch. as deacon, 1934, priest, 1935; curate Ossining, N.Y., 1934-37, rector, 1937-41; sacrist Cathedral Ch. of St. John the Divine, N.Y., 1941-43, canon residentiary, 1943—, sub-dean of cathedral, 1966—; dep. to gen. conv., 1969—; lectr. liturgics Gen. Theol. Sem., 1957-60; Washburn lectr. Episcopal Theol. Sch., Cambridge, 1960; lectr. edn. N.Y. U., 1961-62; Purser Shortt lectr. U. Dublin, 1971; lectr. Anglican doctrine and worship Union Theol. Sem., 1965—; lectr. Diocesan Inst. Theology, 1973—; nat. chaplain Am. Guild Organists, 1944-49, 59-60, 68-70; vice chmn. Joint Commn. Ch. Architecture and Allied Arts, 1955—; chmn. Diocesan Commn. Ch. Bldg., 1942—; select preacher U. Dublin, 1952, 71; cons. Trinity Corp., U.S. Mil. Acad., West Point; warden Community of Holy Spirit; trustee St. Vladimir's Orthodox Theol. Sch. and Acad., Tolstoy Found., St. Peter's Sch. Served from capt. to maj., chaplain, U.S. Army Res. N.G., 1947-69; lt. col. N.Y. N.G., 1970—. Decorated officer Orange-Nassau (The Netherlands); officer Order Brit. Empire; chevalier Legion of Honor (France); State Conspicuous Service Cross, sub-prelate Order St. John Jerusalem (Gt. Britain); silver medal Red Cross of Japan; comdr. Order of Holy Sepulchre, Order of St. Gregory the Illuminator. Fellow Royal Soc. Arts; mem. P.E. Soc. for Promoting Religion and Learning in State N.Y., Pilgrims of U.S., St. Andrews Soc., St. George Soc., Soc. of Cincinnati. Clubs: Century, Univ., Columbia Faculty (N.Y.C.); Athenaeum (London). Author: Meditations on the Gospel of St. John, 1955; Things I Always Thought I Knew, 1957; A Glossary of Architectural and Liturgical Terms, 1958; (with Norman Laliberte) The History of the Cross, 1960; God's Image in Us, 1960; The Spent Night, 1960; also monographs; contbr. Ency. Americana, Funk & Wagnells Universal Standard Ency. Designer Emblem of Anglican Communion. Address: Cathedral Heights 1047 Amsterdam Ave New York City NY 10025

WEST, HARRY MILES, III, govt. ofcl.; b. Pitts., Oct. 14, 1939; s. Harry Miles and Margaret Mayme (DeRusha) W.; A.A., Montgomery Coll., 1959; B.S., U. Md., 1963; M.S., George Washington U., 1969, D.P.A., 1973; m. Theresa Tarnacki, Feb. 8, 1964; children—Kevin Miles, Gary Scott. Indsl. engr. A.C.F. Industries, Inc., Riverdale, Md., 1961-63; personnel research analyst/mgr. Navy Personnel Research Lab., Washington, 1963-69; asst. program mgr. Office Chief Naval Ops., Washington, 1969-73, program mgr., 1973-76, civilian manpower dir., 1976—; adj. prof. George Washington U., 1974-78. Recipient Navy Meritorious Civilian Service award, 1971; Navy fellow, 1969. Mem. George Washington U. Alumni Assn. (bd. dirs. 1977-78, program dir. 1977-78), George Washington U. Doctoral Assn. (pres. 1969-71), Am. Soc. for Pub. Adminstrn., Bliss Elec. Soc., Pi Alpha Alpha. Methodist. Home: 15004 Wellwood Rd Silver Spring MD 20904 Office: Office of Chief of Naval Operations (OP-120) Washington DC 20350

WEST, HARVEY GORDON, JR., librarian; b. Phila., June 11, 1945; s. Harvey Gordon and Helen Elaine (Eustace) W.; B.A., Trinity U., San Antonio, 1972; M.L.S., U. Tex., Austin, 1973; m. Jaton Louise Holder, Dec. 21, 1967; 1 son, Stephen MacPherian. Staff asst. to chief order div. Library of Congress, Washington, 1973—. Served with U.S. Army, 1968-69; Vietnam. Mem. Spl. Libraries Assn., D.C. Library Assn., Library of Congress Profl. Assn. Episcopalian. Home: 7608 Roanoke Ave Annandale VA 22003 Office: Library of Congress Order Div Washington DC 20540

WEST, JOHN PETTIT, surgeon; b. Clayton, Ala., Sept. 12, 1905; s. John Pettit and Alice (Floyd) W.; B.S., Ala. Poly. Inst., 1927; M.D., Cornell U., 1932; m. Mary Kyer, Sept. 6, 1939; children—John Pettit, William Kyer. Intern, St. Luke's Hosp., N.Y.C., 1933-35, resident, 1935; resident N.Y. Hosp., N.Y.C., 1935-39; asst. attending surgeon St. Luke's Hosp., 1939-42, cons. surgeon, 1971—; asst. attending surgeon N.Y. Hosp., 1939-42, cons. surgeon, 1971-76; acting dir. surgery St. Luke's Hosp., 1969-71; asst. prof. clin. surgery Cornell Med. Coll., N.Y.C., 1946-54, asso. prof. 1954-69; clin. prof. surgery Coll. Physicians and Surgeons, N.Y.C., 1969-76; cons. surgeon St. Luke's Hosp., N.Y.C., 1971—, St. Mary's Hosp., Passaic, N.J., 1973—, Rahway (N.J.) Hosp., 1966—; hon. staff N.Y. Hosp., N.Y.C., 1977—; mem. Sr. Med. Cons., N.Y.C., 1973—. Served with U.S. Army to lt. col., 1942-46. Decorated Bronze Star; recipient Soc. Alumni of St. Luke's Hosp. citation of Merit for distinguished service, 1976. Diplomate Am. Bd. Surgery. Mem. N.Y. Surg. Soc. (pres. 1961-63), AMA, Am. Surg. Assn., Pan-Pacific Surg. Assn., Internat. Soc. Surgery, N.Y. Soc. Relief of Widows and Orphans of Med. Men. Contbr. articles in field to med. jours.; author: Nursing Cave of the Surgical Patient, 5th edit., 1951, 6th edit., 1957. Home: 200 E 66th St New York City NY 10021 Office: 1107 Fifth Ave New York City NY 10028

WEST, ROBERT NELSON, SR., clergyman, religious assn. exec.; b. Lynchburg, Va., Jan. 28, 1929; s. Samuel Washington and Mary Evelyn (Wells) W.; B.A., Lynchburg Coll., 1950; postgrad. in law George Washington U., 1950-51; B.D., Starr King Sch. for Ministry, 1957; D.D. (hon.), Meadville/Lombard Theol. Sch., 1970; m. Nancy Kathryn Smith, May 5, 1951; children—Robert Nelson, Charles Hamilton, Thomas Parker, Mary Catherine. With ins. agy., Va., 1951-54; ordained to ministry Unitarian Universalist Ch.; minister Tennessee Valley Unitarian Ch., Knoxville, 1957-63, First Unitarian Ch., Rochester, N.Y., 1963-69; pres., chief exec. officer Unitarian Universalist Assn., Boston, 1969—. Served with USN, 1946-48. Democrat. Home: 33 Brimmer St Boston MA 02108 Office: 25 Beacon St Boston MA 02108

WEST, SUEANN JONETTA, sch. counselor; b. Uniontown, Pa., July 22, 1941; d. Jonathan Roland and Beatrice Lorraine (Spellman) W.; B.S., Calif. State Coll., 1963; M.A., W.Va. U., 1967. Elementary tchr. pub. schs., Butler, Pa., 1963-67; middle and sr. high counselor S.W. Butler County, Pa., 1967-68; elementary counselor pub. schs., Harford County, Md., 1968-76; middle sch. counselor Bel Air (Md.) Middle Sch., 1976—; career edn. cons. Md. State Dept. Edn., 1971-73; instr. continuing edn. Harford Community Coll.; lectr. in field. Sunday sch. supt. Grace Bible Ch., Fallston, Md., 1970-72. Named Outstanding Md. Counselor, Md. Personnel and Guidance Assn., 1976. Mem. AAUW (ednl. founds. chmn. 1977—), Md. Tchrs. Assn., Individual Psychol. Assn., NEA, Harford County Edn. Assn., Harford County Personnel and Guidance Assn. (pres. 1972-73), Am., Md., Harford County (pub. relations chmn.) personnel and guidance assns., Md., Am. sch. counselors assns., Am., Md. vocat. guidance assns., Delta Kappa Gamma. Republican. Baptist. Editor Compass Points, Jour. Md. Personnel and Guidance Assn., 1976-78. Home: 753 S Atwood Rd Bel Air MD 21014 Office: Moores Mill Rd Bel Air MD 21014

WESTERMANN, DAVID, lawyer, electronic co. exec.; b. N.Y.C., Mar. 2, 1920; s. John Jacob and Margaret (Maher) W.; A.B., Columbia U., 1941, LL.B., 1943; m. Edith E. West, Mar. 11, 1972; children by previous marriage—Nancy, John Jacob, David. Admitted to N.Y. bar, 1943; asso. firm Donald A. Gray, N.Y.C., 1947-48, William P. McCool, N.Y.C., 1948-50; lawyer Hazeltine Corp., Greenlawn, N.Y., 1950—, v.p., gen. counsel, 1961-66, pres., chief exec. officer, 1966-77, chmn., chief exec. officer, 1977—, also dir.; pres. Hazeltine Research, Inc., Chgo., 1963-66, dir., 1963—; Bannerman lectr. Naval Postgrad. Sch. Mem. bd. edn. S. Huntington Schs., Union Free Sch. Dist. 13, 1956-59, pres., 1959-60; trustee, fellow Polyclin. Inst. N.Y.; chmn. bd. dirs. Performing Arts Found. L.I.; trustee Urban League L.I., Inc., Electronic Industries Found.; bd. dirs. Action Com. for L.I. Served to 1st lt. AUS, 1942-46. Mem. Nat. Security Indsl. Assn. (trustee 1969—, chmn. 1975-76), L.I. Forum for Technology (chmn. 1977—), Nat. Contract Mgmt. Assn. (bd. advisors), L.I. Assn. Commerce and Industry (dir.), Am. Bar Assn., Am. Legion, Air Force Assn. Delta Psi, Phi Delta Phi. Clubs: Wings, Westhampton Country. Home: 15 Meadow Ln Westhampton Beach NY 11978 also 3050 Palm Aire Dr Pompano Beach FL 33060 Office: Hazeltine Corp Greenlawn NY 11740

WESTMEYER, TROY RUDOLPH, educator, govt. ofcl.; b. Toledo, Oct. 25, 1916; s. Rudolph C. and Eva (Westrup) W.; B.E., U. Toledo, 1940; M.S., Denver U., 1944; Ph.D., N.Y. U., 1963; m. Eleanor J. Dunham, Apr. 4, 1942; children—Wesley R., Lynne. Asso. prof. govt. mgmt. U. Denver, 1946-49; dir. fiscal survey commns. Commonwealth of Mass., Boston, 1949-56; sr. asso. Nat. Municipal League, N.Y.C., 1956-58, asso. dir., 1969; asso. dir. Ankara program N.Y. U. Grad. Sch. Pub. Adminstrn., N.Y.C., 1958-60, asso. dean, 1960-67, prof. pub. adminstrn., 1963—, acting dean, 1968-69; dir. N.Y. State Legis. Commn. on Expenditure Rev., Albany, 1970—. Served with USNR, 1943. Mem. Govtl. Research Assn. (sec.-treas. 1959-74), Am. Soc. Pub. Adminstrn. (pres. N.Y. met. chpt. 1968). Editor Govtl. Research Assn. Reporter, 1959-74; column editor Nat. Civic Rev., 1962—. Home: 60 Gary Rd Stamford CT 06903 Office: 111 Washington Ave Albany NY 12210 also 4 Washington Sq New York City NY 10003

WESTON, ALAN GEORGE, nurse; b. Carshalton, Eng., July 21, 1935; s. George James and Rose Helen (Dison) W.; came to U.S., 1967; grad. Darenth Park Sch. Nursing, 1963, Maidstone Sch. Nursing, 1966; B.S., St. Josephs, 1974; m. Rita Maud LeVine, June 7, 1958; children—Lynne Sandra, Andrew Martin, Sturat Christopher. Head nurse Darenth Park Hosp., Dartford, Kent, Eng., 1966-67; head nurse Quigley Meml. Hosp., Chelsea, Mass., 1967-71, instr., supr. W.E. Fernald State Sch., Waverley, Mass., 1971-75; dir. nursing services H.D. Goodall Hosp., Sanford, Maine, 1975—; nurse practitioner U. Mass., 1975; mem. Maine Council Nursing Adminstrs. Served with RAF, 1953-55. Mem. Am. Hosp. Assn., Nat. League for Nursing. Mem. Ch. of England. Home: 4 Stoney Brook Rd Sanford ME 04073 Office: 25 June St Sanford ME 04073

WESTON, JEROME LEE, engring. mgr.; b. Bklyn., Nov. 11, 1943; s. William and Mollie (Cohen) Weissbard; B.M.E., City Coll. N.Y., 1966; postgrad. in Bus. Adminstrn., Bernard Baruch Coll., 1968-71; m. Rosanne, Oct. 9, 1965; children—Gregory, Joseph. Sr. project engr. tech. research lab. Revere Copper and Brass Co., Bklyn., 1965-70; asst. chief engr. Park Nameplate Co., Flushing, N.Y., 1970-74; engring. mgr. Chemold Corp., Maspeth, N.Y., 1974-75; tech. dir. Park Nameplate Co., 1975—. Home: 3134 Eastern Pkwy Baldwin NY 11510 Office: 33-37 Farrington St Flushing NY 11354

WESTON, S(TEPHEN) BURNS, lawyer; b. Yellow Springs, Ohio, May 4, 1904; A.B., Antioch Coll., Yellow Springs, 1925; postgrad. Sorbonne Paris, France, 1925-26; LL.B., Yale U., 1929; LL.D., Cleve. Marshall Law Sch., 1969; m. Simonne Humphrey; children—Burns M., Monique W. Claque. Admitted to Ohio bar, 1930, N.Y. bar, 1976, U.S. Supreme Ct. bar, others; with firm Thompson, Hine & Flory, Cleve., until 1935; Ohio adminstr. Nat. Youth Adminstrn., 1935-40, exec. dir., acting chmn. nat. adv. com., Washington, 1940-42; exec. sec. U.S. sect. Anglo-Am. Caribbean Commn., Dept. of State, also acting chief Caribbean office, 1942-44; sr. partner firm Weston, Hurd, Fallon, Howley, Paisley, and predesessors, Cleve. Exec. dir. Postwar Planning Council, Met. Cleve. Devel. Council, 1944-46; mem. citizens adv. com. Justice Center, 1970—. Past trustee and chmn. bd. trustees Antioch Coll.; past trustee Cleve. Inst. Music; pres. Essex County Hist. Soc. Recipient award for outstanding pub. service League Young Democratic Clubs Ohio, 1936-38, George W. Yancey Meml. award Internat. Assn. Ins. Counsel, 1963, Brother's Keeper award Jewish Community Fedn. Cleve., 1968. Fellow Am., Ohio bar founds., Am. Coll. Trial Lawyers; mem. Am. Bar Assn. (past chmn. legis. council, sect. ins., Negligence and compensation law, mem. trial techniques com.), Bar Assn. Greater Cleve. (Common Pleas Ct. Docket Conf. 1951-53, coms. jud. candidates and campaign 1955-57, fed. cts. 1957-58, 65-66, trial coms. Disciplinary Matters 1956, 59, 60, chmn. spl. com. on sentencing procedures 1974-75, trustee 1961-64; pres. 1968-69), Am. Judicature Soc., Am. Law Inst., Internat. Assn. Ins. Counsel (mem. coms., past mem. exec. com.), Fedn. Ins. Counsel (mem. legislation com.), Cleve. Def. Attys. Group (past chmn.), Sixth Circuit Jud. Conf. (life). Clubs: Adirondack Mountain; Rowfant (council fellows, pres. 1973-74) (Cleve.). Contbr. to Trial Practice Manual of Ohio Legal Center, Ohio Bar Assn., 1965; also articles to profl. jours. Home and office: West-on-East Keene NY 12942

WETHERELL, ALBERT ANTHONY, educator; b. Long Island City, N.Y., Aug. 16, 1943; s. Albert M. and Hedwig D. W.; B.A., St. John's U., 1965; M.A., Fordham U., 1967. Tchr. history John D. Wells Jr. High Sch., Bklyn., 1967—, chmn. dept. history, 1969—, dir. student activities, 1969-77. Recipient Outstanding Tchr. award John D. Wells Jr. High Sch., 1972, 73, 74, 75, 76. Mem. Am. Hist. Soc., Nat. Geog. Soc., United Fedn. of Tchrs., Nat. Hist. Soc. Home: 193-12 47th Ave Flushing NY 11358 Office: 183 S 3d St Brooklyn NY 11211

WETLAUFER, DONALD BURTON, biochemist; b. New Berlin. N.Y., Apr. 4, 1925; s. George C. and Olga (Kirckhoff) W.; B.S. in Chemistry, U. Wis., Madison, 1946, M.S. in Biochemistry, 1952, Ph.D., 1954; m. Lucille O. Croce, May 5, 1950; children—Lise, Eric. Chemist, Argonne (Ill.) Nat. Lab., 1944, 46-47, Bjorksten Lab., Madison, 1948-50; Carlsberg Lab., Copenhagen, 1955-57; research asso. Harvard U., 1957-61, tutor biochem. sci., 1958-61; asso. prof., then prof. biochemistry U. Minn. Med. Sch., 1962-75; DuPont prof. chemistry, chmn. dept. U. Del., Newark, 1975—; vis. investigator Max Planck Inst. Ernahrungsphy., 1974-78; mem. fellowship rev. com. NATO, 1970; cons. Nat. Inst. Gen. Med. Sci., 1964—. NSF predoctoral fellow, 1952-54; Nat. Found. Infantile Paralysis postdoctoral fellow, 1955-56; Am. Heart Assn. postdoctoral fellow, 1956-58; grantee USPHS, 1961—, NATO, 1974-77, AEC, 1962; recipient Career Devel. award USPHS, 1961-62. Mem. Am. Chem. Soc., AAAS, Am. Soc. Biol. Chemists, Biophys. Soc., Phi Beta Kappa. Author research papers. Office: Dept Chemistry U Del Newark DE 19711

WETMORE, JAMES STUART, bishop; b. Hampton, N.B., Can., Oct. 22, 1915; s. Charles Talbot and Alberta Mae (McCordic) W.; Came to U.S., 1953. B.A., Kings Coll., Halifax, N.S., 1938, L.Th., 1939, B.S. Lit., 1949, D.D. (hon.), 1960; student Yale, 1947; m. Frances Howard Robinson, July 4, 1940; children—Nancy (Mrs. James L. Faulds), Charles E., Stuart Andrew, Mary, Robin. Ordained deacon 1938, priest, 1939; curate, then rector in N.B., 1939-47; Eastern field sec. Gen. Bd. Religious Edn., Ch. of England in Can., 1947-51, asst. gen. sec., 1951-53; dir. Christian edn. Episcopal Diocese N.Y., 1953-60, suffragan bishop, 1960—; sec. council Diocese N.Y., 1968—; hon. canon Cathedral St. John the Divine, N.Y.C., 1958—; pres. N.Y.C. Churchman's Clericus, 1960; chaplain Canadian Soc., N.Y.C., 1957—; mem. div. Christian edn. Nat. Council Chs., 1957-61, leadership tng. adv. com. div. Nat. Council P.E. Ch., 1956-62, mem. dept. Christian edn., 1961-65; chmn. Episcopal Ch. World Fair Com., 1963-66; dir. N.Y. State Council Chs., 1964—; mem. N.Am. adminstrv. com. World Council Christian Edn., 1953-65; bd. dirs. Council of Chs., City N.Y., 1960—; rep. N.Y. State to White House Conf., 1960; mem. dept. ch. renewal Nat. Council Chs., 1965-68; sec.-treas. Urban Christian Mission in N.Y.C., 1968-70; v.p. Ch. Plan Commn. for N.Y. Met. Region, 1966-70. Vice pres. P.E. City Mission Soc., N.Y.C., Youth Consultation Service; bd. dirs. Met. Urban Service Tng., St. Simeon Found., Westchester Council on Alcoholism, 1969-75; trustee St. Hilda's and St. Hugh's Sch., N.Y.C., Housing Devel. Corp.; bd. govs. King's Coll., Halifax; pres. St. Peter's Sch., Peekskill, 1970—, chmn. Episcopal Housing Corp., 1971—; pres. Friends of Kings Coll., Halifax, Inc., 1958—; sec. House of Bishop, 2d Province, 1961-65, pres., 1972—. Mem. Anglican Soc. (pres. 1970—), St. George's Soc. Pilgrims U.S. Author: Master,

What Shall We Do?, 1952; also chpts. in books. Home: 7 Fox Meadow Rd Scarsdale NY 10583 Office: 1047 Amsterdam Ave New York City NY 10025

WETTACH, CHARLES FRANK, writer; b. Montclair, N.J., Mar. 19, 1912; s. Archibald George and Carrie Adelaide (Stewart) W.; B.S. cum laude, Rutgers U., 1952; m. Virginia Holladay Van Nortwick, Dec. 31, 1936; children—Charles Edward, Nancy Wettach Rhodes, Thomas Stewart. Mgr., Stewart Travel Bur., Caldwell, N.J., 1933-35; contbr. numerous articles to popular publs., especially on travel or travel related subjects. Republican. Presbyterian. Club: Masons (Nutley, N.J.). Home and Office: 165 Rhoda Ave Nutley NJ 07110

WETTEREAU, RICHARD BRADWAY, newspaper editor; b. N.Y.C., Jan. 21, 1932; s. James Oswald and Elizabeth Saeger (Bradway) W.; B.A., Columbia U., 1954; m. Cynthia Fairhurst Parks, Oct. 1, 1972; 1 stepdaughter, Catherine Elston Parks. Reporter, asst. mng. editor L.I. Press, 1959-77; L.I. editor New York Post, 1977—. Active, Bayview Community Assn. Served as 2d lt. U.S. Army. Decorated Purple Heart. Mem. Nat. Ry. Hist. Soc., N. Hempstead Hist. Soc., N.Y. Press Club. Quaker. Editor: Homes of the Signers of the Declaration, 1976. Home: 195 Thompson Shore Rd Manhasset NY 11030 Office: 210 South St New York City NY 10002

WEXLER, DAVID JACOB, surgeon, gynecologist; b. Bklyn., Nov. 13, 1906; s. Jacob and Sarah (Wexler) W.; B.S., Coll. City N.Y., 1927; M.D., Tufts, 1931; m. Ida Schwartz, Apr. 15, 1934; children—Charles, Howard, Joan. Intern, Coney Island Hosp., Bklyn., 1931-33; resident Southside Hosp., Bayside, N.Y., 1933-34; sr. surgeon, chief gynecology Southside Hosp., 1934—, pres. med. bd., 1961-62; asso. attending gynecology Endocrine Clinic Jewish Hosp. Bklyn., 1942-68; cons. surgery Brookhaven Meml., Patchogue, N.Y.; sr. surgeon Good Samaritan Hosp., West Islip, N.Y.; attending surgeon Pilgrim State Hosp., West Brentwood, N.Y.; attending surgeon, dir. surgery Central Islip (N.Y.) State Hosp.; pvt. practice surgery, 1934—; asst. prof. clin. surgery Sch. Medicine, State U.N.Y. at Stony Brook. Exhibited one-man shows of sculpture. Dir. Group Health Ins. N.Y., 1958-74, now hon. councillor. Chmn. adv. bd. Islip Town Art Gallery. Recipient Art of Surg. Instrumentation award E. Weck Co. Fellow A.C.S. (mem. exec. council Eastern L.I. chpt.), Internat. Coll. Surgeons; mem. Suffolk County Med. Soc. (past pres.), Suffolk Acad. Medicine (pres. 1958-67), Southside Clin. Soc. (past pres.), Am., N.Y. State med. assns., Eastern L.I. chpt. A.C.S., Am. Fertility Soc., Pacific Sterility Soc., Internat. Fertility Assn. Lion. Author numerous articles in field. Inventor surg. instruments. Home: 161 W Bayberry Rd Islip NY 11751 Office: 111 Carleton Ave Islip Terrace NY 11752

WEXLER, HOWARD, toy and game designer; b. N.Y.C., Sept. 13, 1937; s. Ruby and Ann (Engelmyer) W.; B.S., Coll. City N.Y., 1960, M.S., 1962; Ph.D., Fordham U., 1970. Social worker Ednl. Alliance, N.Y.C., 1955-59; jr. high sch. sci. tchr., N.Y.C., 1959-63; sch. psychologist Commack Sch. Dist., L.I., N.Y., 1963-68; product mgr. mktg. Hasbro Industries, Providence, 1970-72; pres. Strongin & Wexler Assos., Toy Design, N.Y.C., 1973-75; prin. Howard Wexler, toy designer, N.Y.C., 1975—. Mem. Am. Psychol. Assn. Designer games Connect Four, Obsession and Touché. Home and Office: 300 E 40th St New York City NY 10016

WEXLER, JACQUELINE GRENNAN, coll. pres.; b. nr. Sterling, Ill., Aug. 2, 1926; B.A. cum laude, Webster Coll.; M.A., U. Notre Dame; postgrad. St. Louis U.; hon. degree Skidmore Coll., 1967; LL.D., Franklin and Marshall Coll., 1968, Temple U., 1970; Sc.D., Central Mich. U., 1970; D.H.L., Carnegie Inst. Tech., Brandeis U., Colo. Coll., 1967, Syracuse U., 1971; Hum.D., U. Mich.; m. 1969; 2 stepchildren. Joined Sisters of Loretto upon completion of undergrad. edn., left the order, 1967; formerly high sch. tchr., El Paso, Tex.; became asst. to pres. Webster Coll., Webster Groves, Mo., 1959, later exec. v.p., then pres., 1965-69; pres. Hunter Coll., N.Y.C., 1970—; corp. dir. Interpub. Group of Cos., 1974—; adv. com. to dir. NIH, 1978—; exec. panel chief naval ops. USN, 1978—; dir. United Tech. Corp., 1978—. Mem. Pres. Kennedy's Adv. Panel on Research and Devel. in Edn., N.Y.C. Mayor's Commn. City-State Relations; nat. steering com Project Head Start; v.p., dir., internat univ. studies Acad. Ednl. Devel., N.Y.C., 1969-70; mem. Commn. on City-State Relations, N.Y.C., 1971, Pres.'s Task Force on Urban Ednl. Opportunities, 1967. Trustee U. Pa., 1971; adv. bd. on regents univ. degrees State U. N.Y., 1971. Author: Where I Am Going, 1968. Office: Hunter Coll 695 Park Ave New York City NY 10021

WEXLER, JEFFREY, journalist; b. N.Y.C., May 25, 1947; B.A. in Econs. and Contemporary Civilization, Washington and Lee U., 1969; postgrad. Columbia U. Sch. Law, 1969-71. Mgr., Atlantic Beach Bridge, Nassau County, N.Y.; journalist in Va. and N.Y., 1965—; commentator Sta. WLUR, Lexington; editor Lynbrook (N.Y.) News, Meadowbrook (N.Y.) Times; columnist Nassau Herald; pub. affairs counsel to Congressman J.W. Wydler of N.Y.; mng. editor South Shore Record, Hewlett, N.Y., 1971—; editor, pub. Oceanside (N.Y.) Beacon, 1976—; pres. Shenandoah Valley Mag. Corp., 1978—; commr. pub. affairs Village of Cedarhurst (N.Y.), 1974—. Trustee Iron Mountain Inst.; historian Village of Cedarhurst; counsel Nassau County Village Ofcls. Assn.; commr. Nassau council Boy Scouts Am.; bd. dirs. Five Towns Community Council; mem. N.Y.C. Aux. Police, 1970-73; pres. South Shore Bicentennial Soc., 1975-77; bd. dirs. Cedarhust Bus. Assn., Oceanside Bd. Trade, Five Towns Community Center, 1979—. Robert E. Lee research scholar, 1968-69; recipient award Va. chpt. Soc. Cincinnati, 1968; named an Outstanding Young Man of Am., Jaycees, 1976. Mem. English Speaking Union, Am. Numismatic Assn. (life), Nat. Rifle Assn. (life), Am., S.Shore, Va. numismatic assns. Nassau County Press Assn. Washington and Lee U. Alumni (pres. L.I. chpt.), Token and Medal Soc., Soc. Paper Money Collectors, U.S. Naval Inst. (life), Sigma Delta Chi, Pi Sigma Alpha, Phi Epsilon Pi, Zeta Beta Tau. Author: Our Towns, A Bicentennial History, 1976; Stone Ground Poems, 1970; (novel) Wet Goods, 1973; also short stories. Clubs: Internat. House, Overseas Press, Deadline (N.Y.C.); Colonnade (Lexington, Va.); Peninsula Rifle and Pistol (exec. officer). Address: PO Box 292 Cedarhurst NY 11516

WEXLER, STEPHEN CHARLES, constrn. cons.; b. Newton, Mass., Sept. 9, 1942; s. Irving and Leona (Hurwitz) W.; B.S. cum laude in Civil Engring., U. Mass., 1964; M.B.A., U. Mich., 1967; postgrad. Babson U., 1965, Mass. Inst. Tech., 1973-74, Harvard U., 1977; children—Peter, Jeffrey. Engr., supt., purchasing agt. Wexler Constrn. Co., Inc., Newton, 1956-65; project mgr., estimator Jackson Constrn. Co., Needham, Mass., 1967-71; pres., co-founder Computrol Corp., Needham, 1969-71; v.p. for contract adminstrn. Walden Constrn., Inc., Acton, Mass., 1971-73; chief exec. officer, pres. SAI, Wellesley Hills, Mass., 1973—; chief exec. officer, pres. Wexco Internat., Wellesley Hills, 1978—; instr. U. N.H., 1976, Boston Soc. Architects, 1967-71; lectr. in field. Head coach Central Mass. Youth Athletic Assn. football program, Wayland, 1976-77; asst. coach Little League, Natick, Mass., 1977, Natick Soccer League, 1978; head coach Framingham Slo-Pitch League, 1970-76; constrn. supr. Creative Playground for Bennet Hemmenway Sch., Natick, 1977; active Rehab. Center for Aged, West Roxbury, Mass., 1975-78. Mem. Am. Arbitration Assn., Associated Gen. Contractors of Mass., Associated Builders and Contractors, Am. Mgmt. Assn., Am. Assn. Cost Engrs., ASCE, Nat. Assn. Network Scheduling Consultants (founder), Zeta Nu, Tau Beta Pi. Contbr. articles to profl. jours. Address: 26 Abbott Rd Wellesley Hills MA 02181

WEYBRIGHT, VICTOR, publisher; b. Keymar, Md., Mar. 16, 1903; s. Samuel Royer and Lillie Viola (Fogle) W.; student U. Pa., 1921-22, U. Chgo., 1924-26; m. Helen Talley. Feb. 28, 1950; stepchildren—Helen Sampson, Truman Talley. Asso. editor Butterick Pub. Co., N.Y. City, 1927-34; mng. editor Survey Asso., 1935-41, also cons. Reader's Digest; spl. asst. U.S. Ambassador to London, 1942-45; chmn. bd., editor in chief New Am. Library World Lit., Inc. 1945-66, chmn. exec. com., 1960-64; chmn. bd. Weybright and Talley, Inc., N.Y., 1966-70, Weybright and Talley, Ltd., London; dir. Times-Mirror Co., Los Angeles, 1961-65, The New English Library (Holdings), Ltd., London, 1961-66, Carroll County Times; founder New World Writing (lit. publ.), 1951. Mem. Am. Book Pubs. Council (mem. various coms. 1947-65, dir. 1954-57), Gypsy Lore Soc., P.E.N., Friends of the Land (founder, dir. 1940-62). Democrat. Episcopalian. Clubs: Century Assn., Players, Overseas Press, Nat. Beagle (N.Y.C.); Cosmos (Washington); Hamilton St., Timber Ridge Hunt (Md.); Savile (London). Author: Spangled Banner: A Biography of Francis Scott Key, 1935; The America's: South and North, 1940; Buffalo Bill and the Wild West (with Henry Blackman Sell) 1955; The Making of a Publisher, 1967; contbr. to tech. and popular publs. Home: 50 E 77th St New York City NY 10021 Office: 516 Fifth Ave New York City NY 10036

WEYMOUTH, ETHEL MARION, ret. educator, librarian; b. North Berwick, Maine, May 18, 1894; d. Woodbury Ellsworth and Winnette Evelyn (Hussey) W.; A.B., Bates Coll., 1920; M.S., Cornell U., 1930. Tchr. rural pub. schs., North Berwick, Maine, 1912-13, 15-17, Acton, Maine, 1914; tchr. math., phys. sci., librarian Wells (Maine) High Sch., 1920-64; Mem. NEA, AAAS, Cousteau Soc., Nat. Audubon Soc., Smithsonian Assos., ACLU, Sch. Sci. and Math. Assn., Wells Public Library, Am. Forestry Assn., Defenders of Wildlife. Congregationalist. Home: Wells ME 04090

WEYRICH, PAUL MICHAEL, polit. com. exec.; b. Racine, Wis., Oct. 7, 1942; s. Ignatius A. and Virginia M. (Wickstrom) W.; A.A., U. Wis., 1962; m. Joyce Anne Smigun, July 6, 1963; children—Dawn, Peter, Diana, Stephen, Andrew. News dir. Service Broadcasting, Kenosha, Wis., 1962-63; reporter Milw. Sentinel, 1963-64; polit. reporter, newscaster CBS, Milw., 1964-65; news dir. Sta. KQXI, Denver, 1966; asst. U.S. Sen. Gordon Allott of Colo., 1966-73; founder, pres. Heritage Found., 1973-74; dir. Com. for Survival of a Free Congress, Washington, 1974—; Washington editor The Wanderer, 1969-71; nat. editor Transport Central, 1968-73. Vice chmn., chmn. Racine County Young Republicans, 1960-62. Recipient Youth of Year award Racine Optimist Club, 1960, Excellence in Reporting citation Milw. Common Council, 1964, Documentary of Year award for Wis. TV, 1965. Mem. Central Electric Railroaders Assn. Greek Catholic. Author: The Role of Rails series, 1964; pub. Free Congress Polit. Reporter, 1975—. Home: 7053 Lanier St Annandale VA 22003 Office: 6 Library Ct Washington DC 20003

WHALEN, BRIAN BAYLES, govt. ofcl.; b. Sayre, Pa., June 17, 1940; s. Henry Joseph and Claire Degraw (Bayles) W.; B.A., Ohio Wesleyan U., 1961; M.A., Am. U., 1966; m. Carmen Enid Beauchamp, June 24, 1961 (separated); children—Marie Louise, Carmen Teresa, Brian Joseph. Mgmt. intern Navy Dept., Washington, 1964; budget analyst Naval Ship Systems Command, 1965-69, asst. br. chief maintenance br., 1969-70; dep. chief budget div. Econ. Devel. Adminstrn., U.S. Dept. Commerce, Washington, 1970-73, budget officer, 1973—. Bd. mgmt. Silver Spring (Md.) YMCA, 1973—, vice-chmn., 1974-76, chmn. fund raising, 1974-75, chmn. programs and membership, 1974-76, chmn. bd., 1976—. Nat. Inst. Pub. Affairs Career Edn. Awards fellow Cornell U., 1969-70. Mem. Am. Soc. Pub. Adminstrn., Am. Acad. Polit. and Social Scientists, Pi Sigma Alpha. Home: 30 Eastmoor Dr Silver Spring MD 20901 Office: Econ Devel Adminstrn US Dept Commerce Room 7322 14th and Constitution Ave Washington DC 20230

WHALEN, DAVID JOSEPH, space scientist; b. Providence, June 27, 1944; s. David Francis and Margaret Patricia (Conway) W.; B.A., Boston U., 1966; M.S., U. Mass., 1972; m. Mary Anne Pfeiffer, June 12, 1965; children—David Jeremiah, Mary Katherine. Staff astronomer U.S. Naval Observatory, 1972-73; systems analyst Honeywell, Inc., Newport News, Va., 1973-74; supr. orbital dynamics Western Union Westar ops., Vernon, N.J., 1974-75; mgr. spacecraft ops. support RCA Am. Communications, Vernon, N.J., 1975-77; systems engr. Space div. Gen. Electric Co., Valley Forge, Pa., 1977—. Served to lt. USN, 1966-71. Decorated Air medals (3). Mem. Am. Inst. Aeros. and Astronautics, Am. Astronautical Soc., AAAS. Home: Box 9 Vernon NJ 07462 Office: Space Div Gen Electric Co Valley Forge PA 19481

WHALEN, JOSEPH PHILIP, physician, educator; b. Troy, N.Y., June 18, 1933; s. Philip J. and Mary C. (Doyle) W.; A.B., Fordham U., 1955; M.D., State U. N.Y., 1959; m. Elizabeth Varga, July 28, 1972; children—Philip J., Joseph P., Mary P. Intern, State U. N.Y., Syracuse, 1959-60, resident in radiology, 1960-63; practice medicine specializing in radiology, N.Y.C., 1963—; instr. radiology Med. Coll., State U. N.Y., Syracuse, 1963-65, Albany (N.Y.) Med. Coll., 1965-66; asst. prof. radiology State U. N.Y., Syracuse, 1966-67, asso. prof., 1967-68; exec. officer dept. radiology N.Y. Hosp., N.Y.C., 1968—; asso. prof. radiology Cornell U. Med. Coll., N.Y.C., 1968-71, prof., 1971—, chmn. dept. radiology, 1976—; vis. investigator Royal Postgrad. Med. Sch., Hammersmith Hosp., Eng., 1972, Cornell Sch. Veterinary Medicine, 1974; cons. Meml. Hosp., Rockefeller U.; guest lectr. radiology to various univs. in U.S. and Eng., 1972—. Recipient Traveling fellow award Royal Soc. Medicine, 1972; NIH research grantee, 1974—, Winthrope Pharm. Co. grantee, 1973—, Ciba-Geigy Pharm. Co. grantee, 1974-75, NRC grantee, 19—; diplomate Am. Bd. Radiology (guest examiner). Fellow N.Y. Acad. Medicine, Faculty Radiologists of Royal Coll. Surgeons Ireland (hon.); mem. Radiol. Soc. N.Am., Assn. Univ. Radiologists, Am. Roentgen Ray Soc., Internat. Skeletal Soc., Harvey Soc., Soc. Gastrointestinal Radiologists (founding mem.) Caffey Soc. (hon.). Author: Radiology of the Abdomen, 1976; Radiologic Anatomy of the Colon, 1975. Contbr. chpts. to med. texts, articles to med. jours. Editorial bd. Am. Jour. Roentgenology, Cornell Veterinarian, Investigative Radiology, Skeletal Radiology. Office: New York Hosp 525 E 68th St New York City NY 10021

WHALEN, PAUL MICHAEL, computer scientist; b. Norwich, Conn., Sept. 8, 1946; s. Paul Michael and Madeline (Pedace) W.; Carnegie-Mellon U., 1969; M.S., U. Vt., 1970, Ph.D., 1977; m. Mary Lynn Kupcik, June 22, 1968; children—Kathleen Anne, Karen Nicole. Engring. analyst IBM, Essex Junction, Vt., 1970-71, Gen. Electric Corp., Burlington, Vt., 1971-72; sci. computation specialist U. Vt., Burlington, 1972-74, asso. dir. academic computing, 1974-78; pres. Interactive Computing Vt., Inc., S. Burlington, 1978—; lectr. computer sci., 1975—. Registered profl. engr., Vt. Mem. Assn. Computing Machinery, ASME, Nat., Vt. socs. profl. engrs. Roman Catholic. Home: Pamela Ct Williston VT 05495 Office: 100 Dorset St South Burlington VT 05401

WHAM, WILLIAM NEIL, publisher; b. N.Y.C., Dec. 28, 1934; s. William and Jessie (Neill) W.; B.S., Syracuse U., 1956; m. Lynn McCorvie, Mar. 6, 1966; children—Corvie, Avery. Salesman Mut. N.Y., N.Y.C., 1959-61; regional sales mgr. Doubleday Pub. Co., N.Y.C., 1961-64, Reinhold Pub. Co., N.Y.C., 1964-68; sales mgr. United Bus. Publs., N.Y.C., 1968; pres., pub. Internat. Scientific Communications, Inc., Fairfield, Conn., 1968—. Served with AUS, 1956-58. Founder Am. Lab. (scientific jour.); (with Kenneth S. Halaby) Internat. Lab. Home: 157 Pinewood Trail Trumbull CT 06611 Office: Internat Scientific Communications Inc 808 Kings Hwy Fairfield CT 06430

WHANG, BENJAMIN, civil engr.; b. Seoul, Korea, June 17, 1937; s. Andrew C.K. and Hyun Sook (Kim) W.; came to U.S., 1951, naturalized, 1957; B.C.E., Poly. Inst. Bklyn., 1959, M.C.E., 1961; Ph.D., M.I.T., 1968; m. Young Bo Kim, June 17, 1961; children—Suzi, Julie. Mem. staff David W. Taylor Naval Ship Research and Devel. Center, Bethesda, Md., 1961—, research structural engr., 1969-74, supervisory structural engr., head submarine group, 1974—; professorial lectr. engring. George Washington U., 1969—. Dept. Def. scholar, 1965-68; recipient Spl. Achievement award Navy Dept., 1972, 78. Mem. ASCE (Best Paper award 1969), Soc. Naval Architects and Marine Engrs., Sigma Xi, Tau Beta Pi, Chi Epsilon, Xi Epsilon. Presbyterian. Author research papers. Address: 11302 Fieldstone Ln Reston VA 22091

WHANG, JAMES SHIAPIN, environ. engr.; b. Peking, China, May 27, 1946; came to U.S., 1969, naturalized, 1976; M.S. in Environ. Engring., U. Md., 1971, Ph.D., 1974; m. Haibin E. Chen, Oct. 25, 1977. Environ. engr. DeLeuw, Cather & Co., Washington, 1974-75; environ. scientist, engr. Enviro Control, Inc., Rockville, Md., 1975-76; dir. environ. engring. Kamber Engring., Inc., Rockville, 1976—. NSF grantee, 1973-74; EPA grantee, 1977-78. Mem. ASCE, Nat. Water Pollution Control Fedn., Nat. Air Pollution Control Assn. Developed cost effective sewerage alternative facilities for rural communities.

WHARTON, BETTY ANN (MRS. JOHN FRANKLIN WHARTON), librarian; b. Pasadena, Calif., June 26, 1911; d. Edward Dyer and Leila Cunard (Von Ache) Jenks; student Pasadena Playhouse Coll. Theatre Arts, 1929-31, Columbia Sch. Library Service, 1961-63; m. Carl Edgar Fisher, Jan. 11, 1936 (div. 1947); 1 dau., Judith Kathleen Fisher Greenacre; m. 2d, John Franklin Wharton, Aug. 30, 1949 (dec. Nov. 1977). Actress, appearing as Mary Mason, 1928-49; motion picture actress R.K.O., Twentieth Century Fox, 1931-33; appeared in Broadway prodns., featured actress in Brother Rat, The Schoolhouse on the Lot, The Primrose Path, Charley's Aunt, Cafe Crown, others, 1934-42; radio actress, appeared on NBC, CBS, starred in Maudie's Diary, 1938-49; research librarian theatre collection N.Y. Pub. Library, N.Y.C., 1963—. Bd. dirs. Plays for Living, 1976—, Walter Hampden-Edwin Booth Theatre Collection and Library, 1977—, New Dramatists, 1978—; adv. council Sch. of Arts of N.Y. U., 1978—. Mem. Theatre Library Assn. (exec. bd.), Am. Soc. Theatre Research. Picture editor: Life Among the Playwrights, 1974. Home: 141 E 72d St New York City NY 10021 Office: Performing Arts Research Center 111 Amsterdam Ave New York City NY 10023

WHARTON, CLIFTON REGINALD, JR., univ. chancellor; b. Boston, Sept. 13, 1926; B.A., Harvard, 1947; M.A., Johns Hopkins U., 1948; M.A., U. Chgo., 1956, Ph.D. in Econs., 1958; LL.D., U. Mich., 1970, Johns Hopkins U., 1970, Wayne State U., 1970, Central Mich. U., 1970, Oakland U., 1971, No. Mich. U., 1975, Hahnemann Med Sch., 1975, Georgetown U., 1976, CCNY, 1978, Columbia U., 1978; m. 1950; two children. Exec. trainee Am. Internat. Assn. Econs. and Social Devel., 1948-49, program analyst, 1949-51, head reports and analysis, 1951-53; research asst. econs. U. Chgo., 1953-56, research asso., 1956-57; exec. asso. Agrl. Devel. Council, 1957-58, asso. Singapore region, 1958-64, dir. Am. univ. research program, 1964-67, v.p., 1967-70; pres. Mich. State U., 1970-78; chancellor SU NY, Albany, 1978—; vis. prof. U. Malaya (Singapore), 1958-60, U. Malaya, 1960-64, Stanford, 1964-65. Dir. Ford Motor Co., Equitable Life Assurance Soc. Mem. Presdl. Task Force Agr. in Vietnam, 1966; adv. panel E. Asia and pacific, State Dept., 1966-69; presdl. mission to Latin Am., 1969; chmn. food adv. panel OTA, U.S. Congress, 1974-76; chmn. bd. for internat. food and agr. devel. AID, 1976—; mem. Presdl. Commn. on World Hunger, 1978—. Trustee or dir. Rockefeller Found., 1970—, Asia Soc., 1969—, Overseas Devel. Council, 1969—, Carnegie Found., 1970—, Agrl. Devel. Council, 1973—. Mem. Agrl. Econs. Assn., Am. Econs. Assn., Asia Soci, Assn. Asian Studies, Nat. Acad. Edn., Council on Fgn. Relations, Internat. Assn. Agrl. Econs. Club: Univ. (N.Y.C.). Author articles. Editor: Subsistence Agriculture and Economic Growth, 1968. Office: Office of Chancellor State U NY State U Plaza Albany NY 12246

WHARTON, GEORGE CHRISTOPHER, educator; b. Nashville, Nov. 26, 1944; s. James Gilmer and Myrtle Amanda (Bledsoe) W.; B.A., William Penn Coll., 1967; M.A., U. S.D., 1969; Ph.D., La. State U., 1974. Chmn. dept. speech, dir. forensics, asst. prof. Okla. Bapt. U., Shawnee, 1972-73; communication area coordinator asst. prof. communication, dir. forensics, campus adviser WVAC-AM, gen. mgr. WMLN-AM-FM, Curry Coll., Milton, Mass., 1973—. Mem. Internat. Eastern communication assns., Speech Communication Assn., So., Mass. speech communication assns., ACLU, Common Cause, Wilderness Soc., Pub. Citizen, Nat. Trust Historic Preservation. Democrat. Author: Henry Watterson-A Study of Selected Speeches on Reconciliation in the Post-Bellum Period, 1974. Home: 149 Wheeler Circle Apt 232 Stoughton MA 02072 Office: Curry Coll Milton MA 02186

WHARTON, RALPH NATHANIEL, psychiatrist; b. Boston, June 15, 1932; s. Nathaniel Philip and Deeda (Levine) W.; A.B. cum laude, Harvard U., 1953; M.D., Columbia U., 1957, degree in psychoanalysis, 1970; m. Elinor R. Walden, Aug. 28, 1955; children—Naida, Philip, Laura. Intern, Cornell div. Bellevue Hosp., N.Y.C., 1957-58; resident Columbia-Presbyn. Med. Center, N.Y.C., 1961-64; practice medicine, specializing in psychiatry and neurology, N.Y.C., 1964—; asso. psychiatry Coll. Physicians and Surgeons, N.Y.C., 1964, asst. prof. clin. psychiatry, 1969, asso. prof., 1972; sr. research psychiatrist N.Y. State Psychiat. Inst., N.Y.C., 1964-70; asso. attending in psychiatry Columbia-Presbyn. Hosp., 1970—. Served with AUS, 1958-61. Fellow N.Y. Acad. Medicine, Am. Psychiat. Assn.; mem. Soc. Biol. Psychiatry. Author numerous publs. in field. Home: 68 Knickerbocker Rd Tenafly NJ 07670 Office: 1070 Park Ave New York City NY 10028

WHEALON, JOHN FRANCIS, bishop; b. Barberton, Ohio, Jan. 15, 1921; s. John J. and Mary (Zanders) W.; student St. Charles Coll., Catonsville, Md., 1940, St. Mary's Sem., Cleve., 1945; S.T.L., U. Ottawa (Can.), 1946; S.S.L., Pontifical Bibl. U., Rome, 1950; M.A. in Edn., John Carroll U., 1957. Ordained priest Roman Catholic Ch., 1945; asst. pastor Diocese Cleve., 1945-53; founding rector Borromeo Sem., Wickliffe, Ohio, 1953, tchr. Latin, Hebrew, Sacred Scripture, 1953-61; titular bishop Andrapa, 1961—; aux. bishop Cleve., 1961-66; bishop, Erie, Pa., 1966-69; archbishop Hartford, 1969—. Address: 134 Farmington Ave Hartford CT 06105

WHEAT, GORDON ALBERT, chiropractor; b. Granite, Md., Jan. 23, 1920; s. Mervin Edward and Carrie (Ironmonger) W.; Dr., Columbia Coll. Chiropractic, 1952; m. Betty Ann Fletcher, Aug. 1, 1943; children—Nancy Ellen, Gordon F. Gen. practice chiropractic medicine, Denton, Md., 1953—; asso. mem. Spears Chiropractic Sanitarium and Hosp. Served in USAAF, 1944-46. Mem. Am., Md., Eastern Shore chiropractic assns., Am. Legion, U.S. Power Squadron (past comdr. Miles River). Republican. Methodist. Club: Miles River Yacht Club. Home and Office: 200 S 7th St Denton MD 21629

WHEATLEY, CHARLES FELLOWS, JR., lawyer; b. Washington, Dec. 13, 1927; s. Charles Fellows and Marjorie (Meeker) W.; A.B. magna cum laude, Princeton, 1948; LL.B., cum laude, Harvard, 1951; m. Elaine A. Johnson, May 23, 1959; children—Charles F. III, Mark J. Admitted to D.C. bar, 1951; asso. firm Northcutt, Ely, 1951; partner Ely, McCarty & Duncan, 1957-61, McCarty & Wheatley, 1961-67; gen. counsel-gen. mgr. Am. Pub. Gas Assn., 1962—; sr. partner Wheatby & Miller, Washington, 1973—. Served to 1st lt. AUS, 1952-54. Contbr. articles to profl. jours. Home: 10713 Stanmore Dr Potomac MD 20854 Office: Watergate Office Bldg 2600 Virginia Ave NW Washington DC 20037

WHEATLEY, FRANK EDWARD, banker; b. Orange, N.J., Oct. 19, 1930; s. Frank Edward and Helen (Mulvihill) W.; grad. Am. Inst. Banking, 1960; m. Eileen Marie Donnelly, Apr. 11, 1959; children—Frank, Bill, Bob, Colleen, Karen, Jim. With Second Nat. Bank of Orange, 1954-61; with Heritage Bank N. (and predecessor banks), Morristown, N.J., 1961—, v.p., 1974—; investment officer Wharton (N.J.) Fire Dept., 1974—. Councilman, Wharton, 1965-68, mem. fire dept., 1965—, sec., 1968-69. Served with USNR, 1947-54. Certified consumer credit exec. Fellow Soc. Certified Consumer Credit Execs.; mem. N.J. Bankers Assn., Soc. Consumer Credit Execs., Internat. Consumer Credit Assn., Am. Inst. Banking, Am. Legion (life), N.J. Vol. Firemen's Exempt Assn., Wharton Firemen's Exempt Assn. (pres. 1975), Irish-Am. Assn. N.W. Jersey, Sigma Chi Epsilon. Home: 55 Columbia St Wharton NJ 07885 Office: 500 Route 10 Whippany NJ 07981

WHEATLEY, MAURICE EDWARD, hwy. constrn. co. exec.; b. Balt., Mar. 26, 1930; s. Morris Edward and Margaret (Collier) W.; grad. high sch.; m. June Virginia Dickey, May 26, 1951; children—Douglas Edward, Kenneth David. Engr. Md. Road Commn., 1949-63; estimator Crest Contracting Co., Baltimore County, 1963-68; exec. v.p. Ehrhardt & May, Inc., Balt., 1968-75; with Mohawk Constrn. Co., 1975—. Served with Md. N.G., 1948-56. Home: 4122 London Bridge Rd Sykesville MD 21784 Office: Mohawk Constrn Co 5500 Belle Grove Rd Baltimore MD 21225

WHEDON, GEORGE DONALD, med. investigator, physiologist; b. Geneva, N.Y., July 4, 1915; s. George Dunton and Elizabeth (Crockett) W.: A.B., Hobart Coll., 1936, Sc.D. (hon.), 1967; M.D., U. Rochester, 1941, Sc.D. (hon.), 1978; m. Margaret Brunssen, May 12, 1942; children—Karen Anne, David Marshall. Intern in medicine Mary Imogene Bassett Hosp., Cooperstown, N.Y., 1941-42; asst. in medicine U. Rochester Sch. Medicine, also asst. resident physician medicine Strong Meml. Hosp., Rochester, 1942-44; instr. medicine Cornell U. Med. Coll., 1944-50, asst. prof. medicine, 1950-52; chief metabolic diseases br. Nat. Inst. Arthritis, Metabolism and Digestive Diseases, NIH, Bethesda, Md., 1952-65, asst. dir., 1956-62, dir., 1962—. Mem. subcom. on calcium, com. dietary allowances Food and Nutrition Bd., NRC, 1959-64; cons. to office manned space flight NASA, 1963—; chmn. Am. Inst. Biol. Scis. med. program adv. panel to NASA, 1971-75; chmn. life scis. com. NASA, 1974-78, mem. space program adv. council, 1974-78; cons. Bur. Drugs, FDA, 1977—. Mem. med. alumni council U. Rochester Sch. Medicine, 1971-76; mem. trustees' council U. Rochester, 1971-76, vice chmn., 1973-74, chmn., 1974-75. Recipient Superior Service award USPHS, 1967, Alumni citation U. Rochester, 1971; Ayerst award Endocrine Soc., 1974; Exceptional Sci. Achievement medal NASA, 1974. Diplomate Am. Bd. Internal Medicine, Am. Bd. Nutrition. Mem. Am. Fedn. Clin. Research, Assn. Am. Physicians, Pan Am. Med. Assn., Aerospace Med. Assn. (Arnold D. Tuttle Meml. award 1978), Am. Rheumatism Assn., Md. Acad. Scis. (mem. sci. council 1964-70), Endocrine Soc., N.Y. Acad. Scis., AAAS, Am. Physiol. Soc., Am. Diabetes Assn., Am. Gasteroenterol. Assn., Gerontol. Soc., Am. Inst. Nutrition, Am. Acad. Orthopaedic Surgeons (hon.), Orthopaedic Research Soc., Dermatology Found. (trustee), Am. Soc. for Bone and Mineral Research (adv. bd.), Theta Delta Chi. Episcopalian. Editorial bd. Jour. Clin. Endocrlnology and Metabolism. 1960-67; adv. editor Calcified Tissue Research, 1967-76. Contbr. articles to profl. publs. Home: 5605 Sonoma Rd Bethesda MD 20034 Office: NIH Bethesda MD 20014

WHEELER, CHARLES MERVYN, JR., chemist; b. Moundsville, W.Va., Oct. 29, 1921; s. Charles Mervyn and Olive Ila (Powell) W.; student Kent State U., 1939-40; B.S., W.Va. U., 1947, M.S., 1948, Ph.D., 1950; m. May Kathleen Wickers, Dec. 18, 1943; children—Charles Mervyn, W. Randolph, Jennifer L., N. Kathleen, Timothy A., Anne O. Asst. prof. chemistry U. N.H., 1950-55, asso. of., 1955-75, prof., 1975—, dean students, 1960-61; cons. chemistry, Lima, Peru, 1957, 59, 60, India, 1965, 67, 68, 69; chmn. grad. chem. dept. Madurai U., 1968-69; panelist UNESCO Internat. Workshop Evaluation in Chemistry, U. Ceylon, 1968. Mem. Durham (N.H.) Zoning Bd. Adjustment, 1961-78, Durham Sch. Bd., 1962-66. Served with inf. AUS, 1942-46; PTO. John Barton Payne scholar, 1941-42; Research Corp. grantee, 1954; AEC grantee, 1955. Mem. Am. Chem. Soc., AAUP, Sigma Xi, Phi Lambda Upsilon, Phi Kappa Phi. Contbr. articles to profl. jours., 1952-76. Home: 47 Mill Rd Durham NH 03824 Office: Parsons Hall Durham NH 03824

WHEELER, FRANK MITCHELL, cons. engr.; b. Chgo., Nov. 25, 1935; s. George Shaw and Margaret Eleanor (Mitchell) W.; matriculation with honors Metall. Tech. Sch., Kladno, Czechoslovakia, 1957; M.S. with honors, Inst. Mining and Metallurgy, Ostrava, Czechoslovakia, 1962; postgrad., 1966-70; m. Jean Blacker Vafiades, June 21, 1960; children—Dennis, John, Sandra. Research asso. Inst. Mining and Metallurgy, Ostrava, Czechoslovakia, 1962-70; asso. Hatch Assos. Ltd., Cons. Engrs., Toronto, Ont., Can., 1970—. Mem. Assn. Profl. Engrs. Ont., Am. Inst. Mining and Metall. Engrs. Patentee in field. Contbr. articles to profl. jours. Home: 37 Tilson Rd Toronto ON M4S 1P3 Canada Office: Hatch Assos Ltd 21 St Clair Ave E Toronto ON M4T 1L9 Canada

WHEELER, JOHN STUART, urologist; b. Natick, Mass., Aug. 4, 1922; s. Henry Leslie and Anne (MacTaggart) W.; A.B., Dartmouth Coll., 1944; M.D., N.Y. Med. Coll., 1946; m. Virginia Smith, June 29, 1946; children—Joyce, John Stuart, Judith, James, Jane, Jeffrey. Intern, St. Albans (N.Y.) Naval Hosps., 1946; asst. resident gen. surgery Springfield (Mass.) Hosp., 1949-50; asst. resident urology Boston VA Hosp., 1950-51, resident, 1951-52; practice medicine, specializing in urology, Framingham, Mass., 1955—; clin. asso. Boston U., 1965—; urologist Leonard Morse Hosp., Natick, Mass., 1952—, Framingham Union Hosp., 1955—; courtesy staff Glover Meml. Hosp., Needham, Mass., 1960—; attending VA Hosp., Boston, 1955—; cons. Medfield State, Milford, Westborough State hosps. Served with USNR, 1946-49; ATO. Diplomate Am. Bd. Urology. Fellow A.C.S.; mem. Mass. (urol. sect. treas. 1973—), Middlesex W. Dist. (pres. 1979—), Thurber (pres. 1970) med. socs., Am. Urol. Assn. (sect. pres. 1976-77), Boston Surg. Soc., Am. Assn. Clin. Urologists. Congregationalist. Clubs: W. Dennis Yacht, Quechee, Masons, Rotary. Contbr. articles in field to med. jours. Home: 36 Great Rock Rd Sherborn MA 01770 Office: 167 Union Ave Framingham MA 01701

WHEELER, MARVIN DWAIN, psychologist; b. Smithfield, Pa., June 4, 1940: s. Ewing Mackroy and Blanche Olive (Humbert) W.; B.A., Waynesburg Coll., 1966; M.Ed., U. Pitts., 1967, Ph.D., 1976; m. Jean Ann Pasikowski, Aug. 2, 1969. Rehab. counselor Vocational Rehab. Center, Pitts., 1967-69, acting supr. counseling, 1969-71, coordinator mental health services, 1971-73; instr. adj. W.Va. U., Coll. Human Resources, Morgantown, W.Va., 1975, Community Coll., Allegheny County, West Mifflin, Pa., 1975—; asst. exec. dir. Mon-Yough Mental Health, McKeesport, Pa., 1973—; pvt. practice psychology, Pitts., 1977—; mem. staff depts. medicine and psychiatry Monongahela Valley Hosp., 1978—; co-chmn. com. on psychiat. aftercare United Mental Health, Pitts., 1969-70. Bd. dirs. Children's Council, McKeesport, Pa., 1974-77. Mem. Nat. Rehab. Assn., Am. Assn. Mental Deficiency, Am., Pa., Greater Pitts. psychol. assns., Phi Sigma Kappa. Home: 111 Weaver Dr Glenshaw PA 15116 Office: 1074 Greentree Rd Pittsburgh PA 15220

WHEELER, PHILIP CHARLES, educator; b. Bronx, N.Y., June 17, 1936; s. Harry C. and Constance J. (Spiegel) W.; A.A., Nassau Community Coll., 1968; B.A., Fairleigh Dickinson U., 1971; M.A., Kean Coll., 1974; m. Gail Layton, June 2, 1966; 1 dau., Caryn. Teller, platform asst., head teller Am. Savs. & Loan Assn., N.Y.C., 1959-63; adjuster, claims supr., personnel asst., sales rep. Sentry Ins. Co., Cedar Knolls, N.J., 1963-72; placement officer Essex County Coll., Newark, 1972-74; career counselor Bergen Community Coll., Paramus, N.J., 1974—. Mem. Nat. Vocat. Guidance Assn., Nat. Employment Counselors Assn., Am. Personnel and Guidance Assn., Am. Coll. Personnel Assn., Psi Chi. Home: 20 Devonshire Terr Flanders NJ 07836 Office: 400 Paramus Rd Paramus NJ 07652

WHEELER, THOMAS FRANCIS, JR., computer co. exec.; b. Norristown, Pa., Jan. 27, 1937; s. Thomas Francis and Dorothy Marie (Kane) W.; B.A., Villanova U., 1960; postgrad. Cath. U. Am., 1960-61; m. Margaret Raleigh, Apr. 4, 1964; children—Thomas, Michael, Marcy. Tchr. physics and math., Pottstown, Pa., 1962-63; programmer IBM, Armonk, N.Y., 1963-68, mgr. programming, 1968-74, asst. to v.p. systems devel., 1974-75, design mgr. communications and distributed systems, 1975-78, cons. corporate programming, engring. and tech., 1978—. Mem. exec. bd. Susquenango council Boy Scouts Am., also dist. chmn., Endicott, N.Y., 1969-74, dist. chmn. Dutchess County Council, 1976—, mem. nat. council, 1977—; mem.-at-large Adirondack Camp Commn., 1977—; mem. fin. com. campaign James Buckley U.S. Senate, 1976. Mem. Assn. Computing Machinery, IEEE Computer Soc. Republican. Roman Catholic. Home: Indian Hill Rd RD 3 Pound Ridge NY 10576 Office: IBM Old Orchard Rd Armonk NY 10504

WHEELOCK, KEITH WARD, cons. co. exec.; b. Phila., Oct. 17, 1933; s. Ward and Margot Trevor (Williams) W.; B.A., Yale, 1955; M.A., U. Pa., 1957; M.S. (Sloan fellow), Mass. Inst. Tech., 1972; m. Susan Bowen Kimball, June 15, 1956 (div. Nov. 1975); children—Helen Fraser, James Voorhees; m. 2d, Bente Lorentzen Ott, 1976. Fgn. service officer Dept. State, Washington, 1960-69; dir. programs and policy div. N.Y.C. Housing and Devel. Adminstrn., 1970-71; devel. officer Moody's Investors Service, Inc., N.Y.C., 1972-74, v.p. internat. ops., 1974-75, exec. v.p., 1975-76; pres. The Fantus Co., S. Orange, N.J., 1976—. Author: Nasser's New Egypt, A Critical Analysis, 1960; Political Risk Insurance and U.S. Investment in Spanish Speaking South America, 1972. Home: RD 1 Bedens Brook Rd Skillman NJ 08558 Office: 76 South Orange Ave South Orange NJ 07079

WHELAN, WILLIAM FRANCIS, JR., constrn. co. exec.; s. William Francis and Margaret S. (Smith) W.; student St. Joseph's Coll., 1951-55; m. M. Margaret Kenney, Aug. 25, 1962; children—Maureen, William, Margaret Ann, Andrew. News service dir. St. Joseph's Coll., Phila., 1959-65, pub. relations dir., 1966-70, communications instr., 1966—; consumer affairs dir. Korman Corp., Jenkintown, Pa., 1971-74, corporate v.p., 1975—; instr. journalism Montgomery County Community Coll., 1969-71; vis. lectr. pub. relations Temple U., 1976—. Pres., Morgandale Condominium Assn., 1972-75, trustee, 1972-75; v.p. Gypsy Lane Condominium Assn., 1972-74; bd. govs. St. Joseph's Coll., also mem. dean's adv. council, 1972-73. Served with AUS, 1955-58. Recipient Gold medal Am. Advt. Fedn. Dist., 1970. Mem. Am., Suburban (v.p. 1973-74), Phila. (exec. com. 1964-68) pub. relations assns., Home Builders Assn. (dir. 1975—), Am. Edn. Assn., Phila. Press Assn., Main Line C. of C. (dir. 1968-71), Delaware Valley Assn. Communicators (v.p. 1972), Am. Coll. Pub. Relations Assn. Club: City Line Optomists (dir. Bala Cynwyd, Pa. 1968-70, v.p. 1968-69). Editor St. Joseph's Alumni mag., 1965-70. Home: 850 Wright Dr Maple Glen PA 19002 Office: 101 Greenwood Ave Jenkintown PA 19046

WHETSTONE, ROY DOUGLAS, interior designer; b. Manns Choice, Pa., July 15, 1950; s. Lewis Eugene and Bessie Elizabeth (Hite) W.; B.S., U. Pitts., 1973. Interior designer, Dimling & Cable, Inc., Pitts., 1973-74, Park Interiors, Pitts., 1974-77, Jean O. Bugay & Assos., Pitts., after 1977, now Whetstone Environments, Pitts. Vol. St. Peters Sch. for Retarded, Pitts. Republican. Presbyterian. Author: A.B.C. Interior designer Cochran Hall Condominium models, Pitts. Home and Office: 6015 Walnut St Pittsburgh PA 15206

WHIPPLE, DEFOREST THOMPSON, nursing home adminstr.; b. Rochester, N.Y., May 4, 1916; s. Edward Gove Whipple and Delia King Thompson; A.B., Hamilton Coll., 1938; M.B.S. in Hosp. Adminstrn., Columbia U., 1947; m. Agnes H. Kennedy, July 20, 1946; children—William, Diane, Charles. Vet. postgrad. fellow in hosp. adminstrn. U. Rochester-Strong Meml. Hosp., 1947-49; adminstr. Columbia Meml. Hosp., Hudson, N.Y., 1949-65; exec. health adminstr. Monroe Community Hosp., Rochester, 1965-66; adminstr. Good Samaritan Nursing Home, Delmar, N.Y., 1976—. Pres. Hudson Community Chest, 1964. Served with Anti-Aircraft Arty., U.S. Army, 1941-45. Decorated Bronze Star medal. Mem. Am. Coll. Hosp. Adminstrs., Am. Hosp. Assn., Hosp. Assn. N.Y. State, C. of C. Republican. Presbyterian. Club: Tall Timbers Country. Home: Bethlehem Terr C-122 Slingerlands NY 12159 Office: 125 Rockefeller Rd Delmar NY 12054

WHIPPLE, LAWRENCE ALOYSIUS, fed. judge; b. N.Y.C., July 26, 1910; s. Earle and Mary E. (Flynn) W.; B.S., Columbia U., 1933; LL.B., John Marshall Law Sch., 1939; m. Virginia C. Golden, Apr. 20, 1940; children—Donald, Lawrence, Nancy, Virginia, John. Admitted to N.J. bar, 1941; acting magistrate, Jersey City, 1949-51; law enforcement dir. OPS, 1950; spl. asst. to U.S. atty. Justice Dept., 1951; exec. dir. Jersey City Housing Authority, 1953; dir. pub. safety, Jersey City, 1953-57; county counsel Judson County, 1958-62, prosecutor Hudson County, 1958-63; judge Superior Ct. of N.J., 1963-67; judge U.S. Dist. Ct., Dist. of N.J., Newark, 1967—, now chief judge. Mem. Fed., N.J., Hudson County (pres. 1957) bar assns., N.Y. Lawyers Assn., Am. Judicature Soc., Catholic Lawyers Guild, Nat. Assn. Pros. Attys., State Prosecutors Assn. N.J. Home: 217 Trenton Blvd Sea Girt NJ 08750 Office: US Post Office and Courthouse Bldg Newark NJ 07102

WHISNANT, JAMES EDWARD, mech. engr.; b. T oluca, N.C., Apr. 20, 1938; s. Perry Moore and Mary D. (Self) W.; B.S. in Indsl. Engring., B.S. in Mech. Engring., N.C. State U., 1961; m. Phyllis Elaine Greer, June 6, 1964; 1 dau., Jill Allison. Project engr. Armstrong Cork Co., Lancaster, Pa., 1961-68; sales engr. George J. Meyer Mfg. Co., Moorestown, N.J., 1968-71; sr. design engr. M&M Mars. Inc., Elizabethtown, Pa., 1971-73; project mgr. Am. Cyanamid Co., Wayne, N.J., 1973—. Mem. Nat. Right to Work Com. Republican. Methodist. Home: 3726 Nolt Rd Landisville PA 17538 Office: Am Cyanamid Co Berdan Ave Wayne NJ 07470

WHITAKER, EVELYN BERNICE, coll. adminstr., psychotherapist; b. N.Y.C., Sept. 27, 1935; d. Sam and Elizabeth (Simmons) Jenkins; B.A., Va. State Coll., 1956; M.S.W., Columbia U., 1965. Psychiat. social worker Rockland State Hosp., Orangeburg, N.Y., 1958-60; psychiat. social worker, asst. dir. social services Manhattan State Hosp., Wards Island, N.Y., 1960-70; asst. dean students, then dean students, dir. counseling N.Y.C. Community Coll., Bklyn., 1970—; pvt. practice psychotherapy, 1970—. Mem. Nat. Assn. Social Workers, Assn. Black Social Workers, Am. Orthopsychiat. Assn., Am. Personnel and Guidance Assn. Home: 21 St James Pl Brooklyn NY 11205 Office: 300 Jay St Brooklyn NY 11201

WHITCOMB, JAMES HOWARD, food co. exec.; b. Lewiston, Maine, June 12, 1927; s. Edwin H. and Alice (McLaughlin) W.; B.A., Bowdoin Coll., 1948; M.B.A., Harvard U., 1951; m. Eleanor Keady, June 7, 1952; children—Susan W., James H., Michael K., Andrew R. Field rep. Aetna Casualty and Surety Co., Boston, 1948-49; retail zone mgr. Time, Inc., N.Y.C., 1951-53; account exec. N. W. Ayer Co., Phila., 1953-57, account supr., N.Y.C., 1957-59; product mgr. Gen. Foods Corp., White Plains, N.Y., 1959-62, mktg. dir., Japan, 1962-64, gen. mgr., Australia, 1964-66, mng. dir., Eng., 1967-69, pres. Gen. Foods Europe, 1969-76, v.p. parent co., 1969-76, pres. Gen. Foods Latin Am., 1976—. Trustee, Council of the Ams., N.Y.C. Clubs: Harvard Bus. Sch. (N.Y.C.); Seaview Country (Absecon, N.J.); New Canaan (Conn.) Country. Home: 170 Bridle Path Ln New Canaan CT 06840 Office: General Foods Corp 250 North St White Plains NY 10625

WHITE, A. BURTON, surgeon; b. N.Y.C., June 2, 1927; s. Louis I. and Jessie (Levinson) W.; B.A., Cornell U., 1945; M.D., Hahnemann Med. Coll., 1949; m. Hannabelle Lee Shenkin, June 24, 1956; children—Jonathan Richard, Randolph Ellis, Liane Rachel. Intern, Beth-El Hosp., Bklyn., 1949-50, asst. resident internal medicine, 1950-51, asst. resident pathology, 1951; asst. resident surgery Rochester (N.Y.) Gen. Hosp., 1951; resident orthopedic surgery N.Y. U.-Bellevue Med. Center, N.Y.C., 1954-57; practice medicine specializing in orthopedic surgery, Great Neck and Franklin Square, N.Y., 1957—; attending orthopedic surgeon Nassau County Med. Center; sr. asst. attending orthopedic surgeon N. Shore U. Hosp., Manhasset, N.Y.; asst. attending orthopedic surgeon St. Francis Hosp., Nassau Hosp.; clin. instr. N.Y. U., 1959-67, Cornell Med. Coll., 1973—; dir. Med. Liability Mut. Ins. Co. Mem. Nassau County Bd. Health, 1966—, vice chmn., 1970, chmn., 1973-74. Regional chmn. Cornell Fund, 1966-67; pres. Gt. Neck Democratic Club, 1963-64; del. Dem. Nat. Conv., 1976; alt. del. N.Y. State Dem. Conv., 1962; bd. dirs. Great Neck United Community Fund; mem. profl. adv. com. Nassau Home Health Services Found., North Shore Vis. Nurse Assn., Nassau County br. Nat. Found. Served to capt. USAF, 1952-54. Diplomate Am. Bd. Orthopaedic Surgery. Fellow A.C.S., Am. Acad. Orthopaedic Surgeons (exams. and evaluations com., in tng. exam. com.), Nassau Acad. Medicine; mem. Med. Soc. State N.Y. (del. 1976), Nassau County Med. Soc. (chmn. med. legal com. 1965-67, chmn. legis. com. 1967-69, pres. 1976-77), Nassau Physicians Guild (dir.; 1st v.p. 1972, pres. 1973-76), N.Y. State Soc. Orthopaedic Surgeons (dir. 1972—), Eastern Orthopaedic Assn. Jewish (trustee temple 1968-69). Club: Masons. Home: 234 Lakeville Rd Lake Success NY 11020 Office: 1 Barstow Rd Great Neck NY 11021

WHITE, BARBARA LOUISE, banker; b. Coventry, R.I., Aug. 14, 1933; d. Francis Daley and Patricia Agnes (Maloney) Ford; grad. Cranston (R.I.) pub. schs., 1951; m. Charles E. White, Sept. 1, 1951; children—Charles E., Jr., Gerald A., Mary-Frances, Francis E. With Citizen Savs. Bank, Providence, 1957-61, 64—, asst. mgr., 1973-74, mgr., 1974-77, asst. ops. officer, 1977—. Active vol. with Catholic Charities and United Way fund drives, Cranston, R.I.; publicity chmn. Cranston League for Cranston's Future, 1974. Mem. Nat. Assn. Bank Women. Roman Catholic. Home: 3 Cedar St Cranston RI 02910 Office: Citizen Savings Bank 797 Westminster St Providence RI 02902

WHITE, BYRON R., asso. justice U.S. Supreme Ct.; b. Ft. Collins, Colo., June 8, 1917; graduated from U. Colo., 1938; Rhodes Scholar Oxford (Eng.) U.; grad. Yale Law Sch.; m. Marion Stearns; children—Charles, Nancy. Clk., Chief Justice U.S. Supreme Ct., 1946, 47; atty., Lewis, Grant and Davis, Denver, 1947-60; dep. atty. gen. U.S., 1961-62; asso. justice Supreme Ct. U.S., 1962—. Served with USN, World War II; PTO. Mem. Phi Beta Kappa, Phi Gamma Delta. Order of Coif. Address: Supreme Ct Bldg 1 First St NE Washington DC 20543

WHITE, CARL HARVEY, accountant; b. Garnett, Kans., May 30, 1918; s. Clifford Gibson and Susan Catherine (Baker) W.; B.S., U. Md., 1959; m. Osie Louise Sacks, Dec. 19, 1945; children—Catherine Virginia, Mark Steven. Enlisted pvt. U.S. Army, 1938, commd. 2d lt. A.C., 1943, advanced through grades to lt. col., 1959; statis. officer Hawaii, 1946-48; statistician, exec. comptroller Mil. Air Transport Service, Andrews AFB, 1949-53, data processing and statis. staff Air Force Systems Command 1959-61; comptroller, Alaska, 1953-58; ret., 1961; with Bur. Census, Washington, 1961—, asst. chief fin., 1967-68, chief gen. accounting, 1968—. Decorated Air medal with 3 oak leaf clusters. Mem. Assn. Govt. Accountants, Am. Accounting Assn., VFW. Episcopalian. Home: 7210 Kipling Pkwy District Heights MD 20028 Office: Bureau Census Washington DC 20233

WHITE, CHESTER FURMAN, mfg. co. exec.; b. Greenville, Ala., Sept. 1, 1940; s. Eugene Furman and Lena Mae (Barganier) W.; B.S., U. Ala., 1966, M.B.A. (grad. scholar), 1967; postgrad. N.Y. U., 1971—; m. Marla Nieva Calderon Sanchez, Jan. 26, 1973; children—Joel, Carlo. Examiner, State Ala. Revenue Dept., Montgomery, 1960-65; mgr. Internat. taxes Tex. Instruments, Inc., Dallas, 1967-71; supr. internat. tax adminstrn. Pfizer Internat., Inc., N.Y.C., 1972-74; dir. spl. tax projects Pfizer, Inc., N.Y.C., 1974—. Recipient John Burnis Allred award Tex. Soc. C.P.A.'s, 1969, Elijah Watts Sells certificate Am. Inst. C.P.A.'s, 1968, award Ala. Soc. C.P.A.'s, 1966, Austin Gold cup U. Ala., 1966, Mgmt. Com. award Tex. Instruments, 1970, Arthur Young & Co. Accounting award, 1965. Mem. Tax Execs. Inst., Assn. Internat. Students in Commerce and Econs., Tex. Soc. C.P.A.'s, Am. Inst. C.P.A.'s, N.Y. State Soc. C.P.A.'s, Beta Gamma Sigma, Beta Alpha Psi, Omicron Delta Kappa, Alpha Kappa Psi. Home: 153 Russet Rd Stamford CT 06903 Office: 235 E 42d St New York City NY 10017

WHITE, CLIFFORD DALE, bishop; b. Sac City, Iowa, Jan. 20, 1925; s. Daniel Columbus and Anna Frances (Holladay) W.; B.A., Morningside Coll., 1949; S.T.B., Boston U., 1951, Ph.D., 1961; m. Gwendolyn Ruth Horton, Aug. 25, 1946; children—Hazel, Jerry, Rebecca, David, Teresa, Lisa. Ordained to ministry United Methodist Ch., 1951; asso. gen. sec. Gen. Bd. Ch. and Society, Washington, 1961-68; pastor East Greenwich (R.I.) United Meth. Ch., 1968-71; dist. supr. So. New Eng. conf. United Meth. Ch., Providence, 1971-76; bishop N.J. area, Princeton, 1976—. Recipient Distinguished Alumnus award Boston U., 1970. Author column Teens in Together and United Meth. Today, 1963-70; editor: Dialogue in Medicine and Theology, 1967; contbr. articles to profl. publs. Office: Opinion Research Bldg N Harrison St Princeton NJ 08540*

WHITE, DEAN CASEY, pub. relations adminstr., assn. exec.; b. Chgo., June 13, 1917; s. John X. and Rose (Kelly) W.; Ph.D., 1st Nat. U., 1944; Litt.D., 1st National University, 1945; m. Hedy Keller, Mar. 31, 1942. Pub. relations cons. Inst. Human-Animal Relationship, Washington, 1940—, chief librarian, 1966; pub. relations cons. Belmar Constrn. Corp., 1943—; pres. Nat. Assn. Pet Industry, N.Y.C., 1962-65; editor in-chief Pet Digest, N.Y.C., pub. relations cons. Pet Health, Inc., 1955-65, Employ The Handicap League, 1940-64, League For Another Chance, 1967, Fraternity of Humanitarians, Washington, D.C., 1967; communication dir. U.S. Middle East Asia, Inc., 1975. Chmn. com. Pets in Housing, N.Y.C., 1958-64. Chmn. Humanitarians for Nixon-Lodge, 1960, Humanitarians for Goldwater-Miller, 1964; radio and TV dir. Bible Ch. for Saints and Sinners. Recipient citations U.S. Navy, 1947, Inst. for Human-Animal Relationship, 1956, Guiding Eyes for the Blind, 1960; medal Merit Employ. The Handicapped League, 1950; medal of service Nat. Pollsters and Factfinders, 1964; mayor's certificate of appreciation Mayor Robert Wagner, 1964; citation Nat. Assn. of Pet Industry, 1965; citation, U.S.O. 1966, and others. Mem. Mat. Better Bus. Bur., Pub. Relations Soc. Am., Overseas Press Club, Flag Wavers (pres.), Internat. Platform Assn. Presbyn. (chmn. finance com. 1967—; ruling elder). Odd Fellow. Clubs: Kiwanis; Publicity (N.Y.C.). Author: Diet or Die, 1953; Human-Animal Relationship, 1964; The Red Lining of America, 1978; contbr. stories to popular mags. Home: 92 Jackson Ave Rutherford NJ 07070 Office: Overseas Press Club New York City NY 10018

WHITE, DENIS NALDRETT, physician; b. Bristol, Eng., June 10, 1916; s. Percy Walter and Ethelind (Chambers) W.; B.A., Cambridge (Eng.) U., 1937; M.A., London (Eng.) Hosp. Med. Sch., 1940, M.D., 1955; m. Elizabeth Hogg Martin, Sept. 14, 1938; children—Dawn, Martin, Elizabeth, Denis. Came to Can., 1948, naturalized, 1951. Intern, London hosps. and affiliated hosps., 1939-42; resident Maida Vale Hosp., London, 1942-44, Maudsely Hosp., London, 1944-47; practice medicine specializing in neurology, London, 1944-48, Kingston, Ont., Can., 1948—; sr. register U. London, 1944-47; faculty medicine div. neurology Queens U. Sch. Medicine, Kingston, 1948—, prof., 1960—; mem. staff Kingston Gen. Hosp. Fellow Royal Coll. Physicians, A.C.P., Am. Inst. Ultrasound in Medicine; mem. Am. Neurol. Assn. Author: Ultrasonic Encephalography, 1970; Ultrasound in Medical Diagnosis, 1976; Ultrasound Encephalography II, 1976; editor Ultrasound in Medicine and Biology jour., 1972—, series editor procs. Ultrasound in Medicine, 1974—, Ultrasound in Biomedicine, 1976—. Office: Etherington Hall Queens Univ Kingston ON Canada

WHITE, F(REDERICK) CLIFTON, pub. affairs cons.; b. Leonardsville, N.Y., June 13, 1918; s. Frederick H. and Mary (Hicks) W.; A.B., Colgate U., 1940; postgrad. Cornell U., 1945-47; hon. degree Hillsdale Coll., 1974; m. Gladys Bunnell, June 22, 1940; children—F(rederick) Clifton, A. Carole White Green. Pres., F. Clifton White & Assos., Inc., Greenwich, Conn., 1961; pres. Pub. Affairs Analysts Inc., N.Y.C., 1970-77; pres. DirAction Services, Inc., Greenwich, 1966-70, chmn. bd., 1971—; pres. Pub. Affairs Counsellors, Inc., N.Y.C., 1957-60; instr. social sci. Cornell U., Ithaca, N.Y., 1945-50; lectr. polit. sci. Ithaca Coll., 1949-51; del. Pres.'s Hwy. Safety Council, 1953; exec. dep. commr. N.Y. State Bur. Motor Vehicles, 1952-55, acting commr., 1955; mem. adv. council on presdl. selection Brookings Instn., Washington, 1971—; mem. pub. membership inspection team USIA, 1972—; dir. Pub. Affairs Council, Washington, 1958-77. Del. Republican Nat. Conv., 1952, 56, 60, hon. del., 1972; del., chmn. Conv. Coms. Nat. Young Rep. Conv., 1949, 51, 53, 55; pres. N.Y. State Young Reps., 1950-52; spl. asst. N.Y. State Rep. State Chmn., 1950-52; dir. orgn. Nat. Nixon-Lodge Vols., 1960, Nat. Draft Goldwater Com., 1963; nat. dir. Goldwater for Pres. Com., 1963, 64, Citizens for Goldwater-Miller, 1964; campaign mgr. Buckley for Senate, N.Y., 1970; cons. to chmn. Com. to Reelect the Pres., 1972. Served to capt. USAAF, 1942-45. Decorated Air medal with 3 oak leaf clusters, D.F.C. Mem. Inst. Fiscal and Polit. Edn. (chmn.), Am. Assn. Polit. Cons. (pres. 1970-74), Internat. Assn. Polit. Cons. (dir. 1970-74, pres. 1978), Am. Polit. Sci. Assn., Am. Acad. Polit. and Sci. Assn., Acad. Polit. Sci., SAR, Am. Acad. Polit. and Social Sci. (adv. commn. intergovtl. relations 1976-78), Public Members Assn. Presbyterian. Club: Masons (32 deg.). Author: (with Joseph Eley) You Should Be a Politician, 1959; (with William J. Gill) Suite 3505, 1967; (with Charles Spiegler) Yes, We Can, 1972. Home: 8 Joshua Ln Greenwich CT 06830 Office: PO Box 1605 Greenwich CT 06830

WHITE, FRANK ANTHONY, JR., ins. co. exec.; b. Phila., Feb. 19, 1916; s. Frank Anthony and Gladys Southwell (Conway) W.; student St. Johns Coll., 1935-38, U. Ga., 1958; m. Mary Louise Martin, Apr. 18, 1953; 1 son, Frank A. Credit analyzer John Wanamaker Co., Phila., 1939-41; clk. Pa. Lumbermen's Mut. Ins. Co., Phila., 1941-46, fire insp., 1946-50, spl. agt., 1950-53, supr. spl. agts., 1953-56, resident v.p., So. div., 1957-71, v.p., 1971—, sec., 1978—; exec. com. N.C. Fire Ins. Rating Bur., 1953-59, 62-63, gov. bd., 1967-70; adv. bd. Rowan Tech. Inst., 1964-68; curriculum adv. bd. fire services N.C. Dept. Community Colls., 1968-71; bd. dirs. Mut. Ins. Ednl. Found. Pa., 1975—; chmn. bd. ins. placement facilities of Del. and Pa., 1977—. Served with AUS, 1943-46. Named hon. Ky. col. Mem. Nat. (chmn. coms.), Carolina, Ga., Tri-State assns. mut. ins. agts., Am. Mut. Ins. Alliance, Carolina Ins. Mgrs. Assn., Sigma Alpha Epsilon. Club: Optimist. Home: 554 Covered Bridge Rd Cherry Hill NJ 08034 Office: 211 S Broad St Philadelphia PA 19107

WHITE, FRANK JOSEPH, JR., constrn. industry assn. exec.; b. Worcester, Mass., Jan. 23, 1939; s. Frank Joseph and Celia (Carrigan) W.; B.S. with honors, Columbia U., 1964; M.A. in Econs., Trinity Coll., 1976; m. Flora V. Conte, June 17, 1962; children—Kristin Lynn, Alison Jennifer, Hilary Ellen. Asst. exec. dir. Gen. Bldg. Contractors N.Y. State, Inc., Albany, 1964-65; legis. dir., asst. dir. safety and tng. Asso. Gen. Contractors Am., Washington, 1965-66; exec. v.p. Asso. Gen. Contractors Conn., Inc., Woodbridge, 1966-78, pres., 1978—; dir. Conn. Bldg. Congress, 1969-72. Vice chmn. New Haven Equal Employment Opportunity Plan, 1971-75; pres., dir. Conn. Bldg. Congress Scholarship Fund, 1974—; mem. citizens adv. com. vocat. edn. Eli-Whitney Regional Vocat. and Tech. Sch., New Haven, 1969—; mem. Woodbridge Bd. Edn., 1975—, vice chmn., 1977—; mem. Conn. Assn. Bds. Edn., 1975—; mem. state commn. higher edn. evaluation team archtl. tech. program Hartford State Tech. Coll., 1976; bd. govs. Constrn. Inst., U. Hartford, 1976—; trustee Iron Workers locals 15 and 424 Pension Fund, Extended Benefit Fund, Vacation Fund, Apprenticeship and Tng. Fund, Meriden, Conn., Conn. State Bldg. Trades Hospitalization and Ins. Fund, West Haven, Conn., Conn. Laborers Legal Services Fund. Mem. Am. Soc. Assn. Execs., New Eng. Soc. Assn. Execs. Club: Quinnipiack (New Haven). Home: 7 Evergreen Dr Woodbridge CT 06525 Office: 6 Lunar Dr Woodbridge CT 06525

WHITE, GENERVA PRIDE, counselor; b. Jarratt, Va., Apr. 29, 1927; d. Charlie Boyd and Ollie Victoria (Drumgoole) Pride; B.S., Va. State Coll., 1949; M.A., Columbia U., 1958; m. Timothy Robert White, Apr. 8, 1972; 1 son, Thomas Dewey Moultrie. Tchr. pub. schs., Lynchburg, Va., 1949-61; tchr. pub. schs., Washington, 1961-69, guidance counselor, 1969—, chmn. sch. career edn., 1978—. Tchr., mem. religious edn. bd. 10th St. Baptist Ch., Washington. NSF grantee, 1964. Mem. Am., Nat. Capitol personnel, guidance assns., D.C. Sch. Counselor Assn. (chmn. speakers bur.), D.C. Elementary Sch. Counselor Assn., Chillum-Ray Citizens Assn., Voters in Contact Assn., Zeta Phi Beta. Home: 922 Ray Rd Hyattsville MD 20783

WHITE, GEORGE EDWARD, dentist; b. Jamestown, N.Y., July 31, 1941; s. Gordon Ennis and Margaret (Appleyard) W.; A.B., Colgate U., 1963; D.D.S., State U. N.Y., Buffalo, 1967; Ph.D., Mass. Inst. Tech., 1973; m. Oct. 21, 1972. Asso. prof., chmn. dept. oral pediatrics Tufts U. Sch. Dental Medicine, Boston, 1973—; chief dept. oral pediatrics New Eng. Med. Center Hosp., Boston, 1973—; practice pedodontics, Boston; lectr. Mass. Inst. Tech., 1975—; cons. Abcor, Inc. Nat. Inst. Dental Research grantee, 1973—. Fellow Am. Acad. Pedodontics; mem. Internat. Assn. Dental Research, Fedn. Dentaire Internationale, Acad. Gen. Dentistry, Am. Soc. Microbiology, AAAS. Author: Dental Caries: A Multifactorial Disease, 1975; founder, editor-in-chief Jour. Pedodontics; editor: Clin. Oral Pediatrics, 1979; contbr. articles to profl. jours. Home: 244 Kennedy Dr Malden MA 02148 Office: Dept Oral Pediatrics Tufts U Sch Dental Medicine 1 Kneeland St Boston MA 02111

WHITE, JAMES FRANCIS, Realtor, realty appraiser; b. Bayonne, N.J., Sept. 6, 1917; s. Michael and Mary (Duffy) W.; student Columbia, 1940-42, N.Y. U., 1941-42, New Sch. for Social Research, 1945; m. Ermalinda Russo, July 19, 1947; children—Janet Lynn, Judith Ann, Joan Ellen. Real estate appraiser Byrne, Bowman & Forshay, N.Y.C., 1941-42; officer in charge VA, Jersey City and New Brunswick, N.J., 1944-49; chief contact services VA Hosp., Lyons, N.J., 1949-52; owner, realtor, appraiser James F. White Realty Co., Union, N.J., 1950—; mem. Nat. Home Relocation Service. Bd. dirs. Boys Club of Union, 1969-76; mem. N.J. Developmental Disabilities Council, 1971-78; pres. Epilepsy Found. N.J., 1971-73, chmn. bd. dirs., 1973-74; mem. adv. bd. Child Study Inst., Kean Coll. of N.J., 1973-76. Served with Mil. Police, AUS, 1942-44. Recipient Nat. Citation plaque DAV, 1952; Realtor of Year award Eastern Union County Bd. Realtors, 1970, 72; Resolutions of commendation Twp. Union, 1970, 72, N.J. Legislature, 1972; Nat. Service award Epilepsy Found. Am., 1972, Leadership award, 1974. Mem. Columbia Soc. Real Estate Appraisers, Nat., N.J. assns. Realtors, Profl. Ins. Agts., Union C. of C., DAV of N.J. (state chmn. rehab. 1952), DAV of Jersey City (past comdr.), Vets. Alliance (past comdr.), Am. Legion (service officer 1967—). Episcopalian. Author fed., state programs aiding handicapped. Home: 9 Hayes Rd Union NJ 07083 Office: 1423 Stuyvesant Ave Union NJ 07083

WHITE, JAMES MATTOCKS, JR., lawyer; b. Brookline, Mass., Oct. 1, 1927; s. James Mattocks and Elizabeth Harrison (Gilman) W.; A.B., Yale, 1949; J.D., Harvard, 1952; m. Nita Micheilini, June 6, 1966; children—James M., Sarah K., Rebecca. Admitted to Mass. bar, 1953; asso. firm Bingham, Dana & Gould, Boston, 1953-61, partner, 1961—; dir. Fisons, Inc., Humphrey Browning MacDougal. Served with U.S. Army, 1951-52. Mem. Am., Mass., Boston bar assns., Am. Assn. Hosp. Attys. Republican. Episcopalian. Clubs: Somerset, Essex County; Yale of N.Y. Home: Beach St Manchester MA 01944 Office: 100 Federal St Boston MA 02110

WHITE, JOHN WILLIAM LOUD, utility co. exec.; b. Portland, Maine, Aug. 8, 1923; s. Ernest M. and Hilda C. (Loud) W.; student Dartmouth Coll., 1941-43; B.S. in Bus. and Engring. Adminstrn., Mass. Inst. Tech., 1944; m. Marian M. Morton, July 19, 1947; children—Martha White Nichols, Nathaniel, Marian, Benjamin. With Consumers Water Co., Portland, 1946—, v.p., 1962-66, pres., 1966—, also dir.; past corporator Portland Savs. Bank, Brunswick Savs. Instn.; corporator Maine Med. Center; dir. Canal Nat. Bank, Canal Corp.; trustee South Freeport (Maine) Water Dist., 1948-69, Freeport (Maine) Sewer Dist., 1973-77. Mem. Freeport Republican Town Com. Served with USN, 1941-45. Registered profl. engr., Maine, Pa., Mo., N.H. Mem. Am., New Eng. water works assns., Maine Water Utilities Assn., Nat. Assn. Water Cos. (pres. 1972-73, exec. com. 1969-76). Home: Harraseeket Rd South Freeport ME 04078 Office: Four Canal Plaza Portland ME 04112

WHITE, KEVIN HAGAN, mayor Boston, lawyer; b. Boston, Sept. 25, 1929; s. Joseph C. and Patricia (Hagan) W.; B.A., Williams Coll., 1952, D.Polit. Sci., 1968; LL.B., Boston Coll., 1955; student Harvard Grad. Sch. Pub. Adminstrn.; LL.D., Clark U., 1972; m. Kathryn Galvin, June 7, 1956; children—Mark, Caitlin, Elizabeth, Christopher, Patricia. Admitted to Mass. bar, 1955; asso. firm Cameron & White, Boston, 1955—; corporate counsel Standard Oil of Cal., 1955-56; legal asst. to dist. atty. Suffolk County, Mass., 1956-58; asst. dist. atty. Suffolk County, 1958-60; sec. State of Mass., Boston, 1960-68; mayor of Boston, 1968—. Trustee, mem. legis. action com. U.S. Conf. Mayors; mem. steering com. Nat. Urban Coalition; bd. dirs. Coalition for Human Needs and Budget Priorities. Chmn. Mass. Muscular Dystrophy Assn. Drive, 1963, 64, Mass. Heart Assn. Drive, 1965, 73. Mem. adv. council elected ofcls. Democratic Nat. Com. Named One of 10 Outstanding Young Men, Mass. C. of C., 1962; Man of Year, Histadrut, 1973, Service Employees Internat. Union AFL-CIO, 1971, Taxi Drivers Assn., 1973. Mem. Am., Mass., Boston bar assns., Nat. Assn. Secs. of State, Mass. Trial Lawyers Assn. Democrat. Roman Catholic. Home: 158 Mt Vernon St Boston MA 02108 Office: City Hall Boston MA 02201

WHITE, KRISTIN, med. journalist; b. Mineola, N.Y., Aug. 29, 1939; d. Eric W. and Cynthia Frances (Newman) Osterholm; A.B., Cornell U., 1959; m. Mark P. White, Oct. 7, 1959; 1 dau., Allison Kristin; m. 2d, George Nobbe, Jr., Aug. 10, 1974. Reporter, Syracuse (N.Y.) Herald Jour., 1959-60; pub. relations worker for M. Hohner Harmonicas, Leo Miller Assos., Westport, Conn., 1961-66; free-lance writer for mags. Billboard, Rolling Stone, Crawdaddy, 1964-70; editor pub. Country and Western Music Mag., 1968-69; pub. relations staff Atlantic Records, 1968-69; free-lance med. writer for Med. Tribune, Clin. Trends, Therapaeia, Frontiers in Psychiatry, Cosmopolitan, Nat. Enquirer, King Features Syndicate, Amsterdam News, Am. Cancer Soc., 1970—; med. writer cancer and allied diseases. Mem. Am. Med. Writers Assn. Home: 53 W 94th St New York City NY 10025

WHITE, MARGARET MARIE, psychologist; b. Cambridge, Mass., May 1, 1946; d. John Joseph and Rose Ceclia (Magee) W.; B.S. in Edn., Lowell U., 1967; M. in Guidance, Boston Coll., 1969; postgrad. Suffolk U., 1970, Tufts U., 1975, Boston State Coll., 1971. Tchr. and counselor, to 1972; sch. psychologist Everett (Mass.) Pub. Schs., 1972—. Vol. Pine St. Inn, Boston. Certified tchr., guidance counselor, sch. psychologist. Mem. Am. Assn. Clin. Counselors, Am., Mass., Boston personnel and guidance assns., Mass. Sch. Psychologists Assn., Nat. Alliance Family Life Assn., Mass., Everett, Nat. tchrs. assns. Democrat. Roman Catholic. Clubs: Boston Ski and Sport, Show of the Month, Internat., Jaycees. Home: 35 Kinsman St Everett MA 02149 Office: Supt's Office Nicholls Sch Vine St Everett MA 02149

WHITE, NEIL SPRAGUE, mfg. co. exec.; b. Oswego, N.Y., Nov. 4, 1917; s. Kirk Henry and Louise May (Petrie) W.; A.B., Harvard U., 1940; m. Kathryn Mary Heagerty, Nov. 25, 1943; children—Kathryn Louise, Virginia Ann. Project, then plant engr. Columbia Mills, Minetto, N.Y., 1941-55; with Eastman Kodak Co., Rochester, N.Y., 1955—, sr. asso. engr. tech., 1977—. Mem. Soc. Mfg. Engrs., Fluid Power Soc. Club: Harvard (Rochester). Patentee in field. Home: 826 Rumson Rd Rochester NY 14616 Office: Kodak Park Bldg 23 Area 7 Rochester NY 14650

WHITE, ROBERT CLARENCE, mfg. co. exec.; b. Jennings, Mo., June 2, 1918; s. Robert R and Eleanor V. (Moody) W.; B.S. in Chem. Engring., Washington U., 1939; m. Dorothy M. Weidle, May 11, 1946; children—Pamela J., Carolyn I., Robert R. Vice pres. mfg. Warner-Chilcott div. Warner-Lambert Co., Morris Plain, N.J., 1964-69; v.p. Warner-Lambert Co., Morris Plains, 1969—. Bd. dirs. Morristown (N.J.) YMCA, 1964-65, MORHELP, 1971-75; active fund-raising drive United Way. Served with USNR, 1943-46, 50-52. Mem. Am. Chem. Soc., Am. Pharm. Assn., Soc. Chem. Industry, Morris County C. of C. (dir. 1977—). Presbyterian. Clubs: Morris County (N.J.) Golf, Sea Pines. Home: 44 Blackberry Ln Morristown NJ 07960 Office: 201 Tabor Rd Morris NJ 07950

WHITE, RUTH MIRIAM WEIHS (MRS. PAUL WHITE), trade and finance co. exec.; b. Vienna, Austria; d. Hugo and Ilka (Herzog) Weihs; came to U.S., 1947, naturalized 1952; B.A. in Bus. Administrn., St. John's U., Shanghai, China, 1947; postgrad. N.Y. U., Coll. City N.Y.; m. Paul White, Sept. 18, 1949. Exec. sec. to chmn. bd. Pan Am. Trade Devel. Corp., N.Y.C., 1947-49, mgr., 1949-53, asst. v.p., 1953-58, v.p., 1958-74, sr. v.p., 1974—; pres. Indsl. Crystal Corp. Office: 2 Park Ave New York City NY 10016

WHITE, RUTH O'BRIEN (MRS. WALLACE B. WHITE), civic worker; b. N.Y.C., Dec. 20, 1909; d. Francis Athos and Caroline Rebecca (Young) O'Brien; student Packer Collegiate Inst., 1921-27, N.Y. Sch. Fine and Applied Art, 1927-30; m. Wallace Beasley White, June 5, 1931; 1 son, John Wallace. Dir.-at-large Nat. Tb and Respiratory Disease Assn., 1949-57, 60—, mem. exec. com., sec. bd., 1957-60, sec. pro tempore bd., 1961-62, mem. program and budget com., 1967-68; chmn. ann. meeting program com. Am. Lung Assn., 1973, 74; del. Nat. Social Welfare Assembly, 1957-67, mem. vol. com., 1962-68, program com., 1965-67; vice chmn. campaign women's div., 1961-63; del. Ramapo Conf., 1961; mem.-at-large women's com. Bklyn. Philharmonia, 1960-62, v.p., 1962; mem. Council Tb Assn. Greater N.Y., 1957-67, Community Council Greater N.Y., 1960—; chmn. med. social service com. United Hosp. Fund Bklyn., 1949-53, vice chmn. med. social service com. city wide orgn., 1959-62, chmn., 1962-66, mem. social service com., 1966-70, mem. pub. relations com., 1969—, vice chmn. legislation com. 1969—, mem. issues and social action com., 1967-70, sub-com. on nursing homes, 1967-70, vice chmn. campaign Bklyn. Women's div. 1961-63; bd. dirs. Bklyn. Tb and Health Assn., 1946—, v.p., 1957-60, pres., 1960-62, sec., 1966-72, mem. exec. com., 1946—, mem. legis. com., 1974—, vice chmn., 1975—; del. North Eastern Tb. Conf., 1960—, pres. 1962-63; mem. Bklyn. Action for Clean Air Com., 1965—; vice chmn. Council Lung Assns. N.Y. State, 1973-75, chmn., 1975—; mem. Nat. Tb Assn.-Nat. League Nurses Adv. Com., 1963; adv. com. N.Y. State Bd. Edn., div. vocat. rehab., 1954-57; mem. social services com. Cancer Care, Inc., 1966—, pub. relations com., 1969—, affiliate contbg. groups com., 1973—, bd. dirs., 1974—, chmn. nominating com., 1978—, mem. pub. affairs com., 1976—; bd. mgrs., exec. com. Bklyn. Thoracic Hosp., 1940-48, bd. trustees, 1948-57, pres. women's aux., 1956-57; women's exec. bd. Bklyn. Hosp., 1957—, v.p., 1967—, group leader, 1957-62, chmn. med. social service com., 1962-67, chmn. legis. com., 1971—, asst. treas., 1972—; mem. housing and community task force Met. Assn. Conglist. (deaconess). Club: Urban. Address: 651 Marlborough Rd Brooklyn NY 11230

WHITE, THOMAS, hosp. adminstr.; b. Farrell, Pa., May 30, 1943; s. Frank Paul and Elizabeth (Mattox) W.; B.S., Youngstown State U., 1970; M.S., U. Pitts., 1972; m. Rose Marie Taylor, June 28, 1968. With Sharon Gen. Hosp., 1961-70; preceptee Presbyn. U. Hosp., Pitts., 1971-72; resident Albany Med. Sch., 1971; asso. exec. dir. Jameson Meml. Hosp., New Castle, Pa., 1972-73, pres., 1973—; guest lectr. econs. dept. Duquesne U., 1975—. Mem. Human Services Bd., Mahoning and Shenango Health Edn. Network Bd.; mem. adv. com. Youngstown State U. Sch. Bus. Adminstrn.; mem. Sickle Cell Bd., Lawrence County Community Services; bd. dirs. ARC, Vis Nurse Assn., Bus. Coll., Assn. for Blind; mem. adv. bd. Lawrence County Vocat. Tech. High Sch.; mem. Civil Def. Adv. Bd., Blue Cross Rate Rev. Bd.; mem. project rev. com. Comprehensive Health Planning Agy.; mem. Mental Health/Mental Retardation Bd. Mem. Am. Coll. Hosp. Adminstrs., Am. Hosp. Assn., Am. Pub. Health Assn., Hosp. Assn. Pa. (mem. legis. key contact com., chmn. com. legis. affairs, mem. nominating com.), Hosp. Council Western Pa., Southwestern Pa. Hosp. Adminstrs. Assn. (chmn.), Youngstown State U., U. Pa., U. Pa. Grad. Sch. Pub. Health alumni assns. Home: 213 Mission Meade New Castle PA 16105 Office: W Leasure St New Castle PA 16105

WHITE, WILLIAM HENRY, educator; b. Norwich, Conn., Feb. 6, 1947; s. Alfred James and Claire Salome (Boucher) W.; B.A., Nasson Coll., 1969; M.Ed., U. N.H., 1973; m. Therese Louise Frechette, Aug. 28, 1976. Tchr. schs. in Griswold, Conn., 1969, Portsmouth (N.H.), 1973—; instr. psychology Nathaniel Hawthorne Coll., Rochester, N.H., 1976—. Served with USAF, 1969-73. Recipient Pres.'s Gold Key, Nasson Coll. Mem. NEA (del. 1974, 75, 77), N.H. Edn. Assn., Assn. Portsmouth Tchrs. (rec. sec. 1975-76), Nasson Coll. Alumni Assn. (treas. 1975-77, chmn. mktg. com. 1977—), Am. Personnel and Guidance Assn., Am. Sch. Couselor Assn., Assn. Humanistic Edn. and Devel., N.H. Sci. Tchrs. Assn. Democrat. Roman Cath. Home: 26 Whittier St Dover NH 03820 Office: Brackett Elementary Sch Rye St Portsmouth NH 03801

WHITE, WINIFRED DEMAREST (MRS. HERBERT A. WHITE), former assn. exec., editor; b. N.Y.C.; d. Peter Edward and Margaret (McLaughlin) Demarest; A.B., Coll. New Rochelle, 1914; postgrad. in journalism Columbia Extension, 1916-18; m. Joseph S. Gifford, Aug. 29, 1925 (dec. Feb. 1948); m. 2d, Herbert A. White, Nov. 14, 1964 (dec. Oct. 1972). Tchr. English, speech Bryant High Sch., N.Y.C., 1914-17; asst. to bursar Rockefeller Inst. for Med. Research, 1917-26; asst. editor, asst. to exec. sec. Am. Inst. Mining, Metall. and Petroleum Engrs., N.Y.C., 1947-59, editor, 1960—; exec. sec. Soc. Women Engrs., N.Y.C., 1961-73, asso. life mem., 1973—; freelance editor miscellaneous papers, 1959—. Recipient Ursula Laurus citation Coll. of New Rochelle, 1974. Editor: Ironmaking Proceedings, Open Hearth Proceedings, Honors Book, 1950-63, Proceedings Conf. on Women, 1971; editor Transactions Am. Soc. Heating, Refrigeration and Air-Conditioning Engrs., 1976, editorial proofreader, 1978. Home: 12 E 97th St New York City NY 10029

WHITEHEAD, ARLINE A., educator; b. Johnston, R.I., Aug. 20, 1921; s. Thomas J. and Eugenie (Bolduc) Duffy; Ed.B. in Elem. Edn., R.I. Coll., 1943, spl. edn. certificate in mental retardation, 1967; m. Ralph F. Whitehead; children—Susan A., Wendy J., Marcia E., William R. Tchr. 2d grade St. Mary's Sch., Lawton, Okla., 1959-61; tchr. kindergarten Dependents' Sch., Schwabisch Gmuend, Germany, 1962-64; pre-sch. tchr. mentally retarded Fogarty Center for Mentally Retarded, Providence, 1964-66; spl. edn. tchr. Providence Sch. Dept., 1966—. Specialist in handicapped, pre-sch. and primary levels. Home: 30 3d St Barrington RI 02806 Office: Pleasant View Sch Obediah Brown Rd Providence RI 02910

WHITEHOUSE, RAYMOND CHARLES, II, educator; b. Boston, Mar. 29, 1945; s. Raymond C. and Ruby Carolyn (Dobson) W.; B.S., Boston State U., 1967, M.S., 1973; postgrad. Boston U., 1975—; m. Gail Conti, Dec. 19, 1970. Sci. tchr. Quincy (Mass.) Pub. Schs., 1967—. Mem. Quincy Conservation Commn., 1968-69; campaign worker Boston Mayoral campaign, 1967-68; presentor nat. conv. Nat. Sci. Tchrs. Assn., 1975, 76, 78, steering com., 1977. NSF grantee, 1969, 70, 71. Mem. AAAS, Nat. Sci. Tchrs. Assn., Nat. Audubon Soc., Nat. Geographic Soc., Explorers Group. Author: Curriculum Activity Guide to Water Pollution and Environmental Studies, 1970. Home: 64 Washington Ct Quincy MA 02169 Office: 1012 Hancock St Quincy MA 02169

WHITEHURST, LOWELL EARL, mech. engr.; b. Greeneville, N.C., June 20, 1948; s. Booker T. and Eulah Bell (Jacobs) W.; student mech. engring. Evening Coll. Johns Hopkins U., 1972—; student bus. adminstrn. Morgan State U., 1978; m. Sandra Eileen Stokes, Apr. 12, 1969; children—Landis Eirin, Sherrod Elliot. Draftsman, designer Egli & Gompf, Inc., Balt., 1967-68; mech. designer, 1972-76; mech. designer Harold A. Schlenger Co., Balt., 1976, Henry Adams Inc., Balt., 1976-78; office engr. Robert J. Nash & Assos., Washington, 1978—; pres. Whitehurst Parekh Cons. Inc., engrs., Balt., 1977—. Treas. Hyman A. Blumberg Day Care Center, 1974-75; asst. track coach North Balt. Striders, 1978. Served with USAF, 1968-72. Mem. Am. Soc. Heating, Refrigeration and Air Conditioning Engrs., Am. Soc. Plumbing Engrs. Democrat. Mem. Pentecostal Evang. Ch. Home: 3702 The Alameda Baltimore MD 21218

WHITEHURST, WILLIAM WILFRED, JR., mgmt. cons.; b. Balt., Mar. 4, 1937; s. William Wilfred and Elizabeth (Hogg) W.; B.A., Princeton, 1958; M.S., Carnegie Inst. Tech., 1963; m. Linda Joan Potter, July 1, 1961; children—Catherine, William. Mathematician, Nat. Security Agy., Fort George G. Meade, Md., 1961-63; mgmt. cons. McKinsey & Co., Inc., Washington, 1963-66; partner L.E. Peabody & Asso., Washington, 1966-69, exec. v.p., dir. L.E. Peabody & Assos., Inc., 1970—. Served to lt. USNR, 1958-61. mem. Operations Research Soc. Am., Inst. Mgmt. Scis., Wash. Soc. Investment Analysts. Episcopalian. Clubs: University, Princeton (Washington); Princeton (N.J.) Quadrangle. Home: 12421 Happy Hollow Rd Cockeysville MD 21030 Office: 9300 Annapolis Rd Lanham MD 20801

WHITFIELD, EDWIN WYCLIFFE, elec. engr.; b. Perry, Fla., Feb. 17, 1925; s. Benjamin Wycliffe and Mary Estelle (Hendry) W.; B.E.E., Ga. Inst. Tech., 1951; m. Johanna Margaretha van Akelyen, Jan. 18, 1953. Tech. rep. Philco Corp., U.S. AFB, Okinawa, 1947-48; asst. engr. Sperry Gyroscope Co., Great Neck, N.Y., 1951-52, engr., 1952-59; sr. engr. Sperry Systems Mgmt., Sperry Rand Corp., Great Neck, 1959— Chief radiol. officer CD, Great Neck, 1957-58. Served with USN, 1943-46. Mem. IEEE, Eta Kappa Nu. Republican. Methodist. Holder 3 U.S. patents in field. Office: Sperry Rand Corp Marcus Ave Great Neck NY 11020

WHITHAM, SHARON ELIZABETH, nurse; b. Pitts., Oct. 22, 1950; d. Frank Anthony and Elizabeth Marie (Wojanis) Carlini; B.S.N., U. Pitts., 1972; m. Herbert Christopher Whitham, Apr. 29, 1972. Staff nurse Eye and Ear Hosp. U. Pitts., 1972, Albert Einstein Northern Hosp., Phila., 1972; staff nurse Friends Hosp., Phila., 1972-73, day nurse coordinator, 1973-75, head nurse, 1975-76, sr. nurse, 1976-77; staff devel. coordinator Sacred Heart Hosp., Allentown, Pa., 1977-78; head nurse devel. psychiatry Warren Hosp., Phillipsburg, N.J., 1978—. Roman Catholic. Home: 440 N 22d St Allentown PA 18104 Office: 1251 S Cedar Crest Blvd Suite 312C-D Allentown PA 18103

WHITING, HARRY ANDREW, JR., rehab. exec.; b. Albany, N.Y., Oct. 9, 1946; s. Harry Andrew and Maude Marian (Adams) W.; B.A., Gallaudet Coll., 1971; M.A., U. Wis., 1975; m. Margaret Louise Fast, Apr. 5, 1969; children—Daniel Balden, Timothy Alden. Counselor, Wis. Div. Vocat. Rehab., Milw., 1971-74; dir. Wis. Service Bur. for Deaf, Madison, 1974-76; exec. dir. Gov.'s Com. for People with Disabilities, 1976-77; asst. exec. dir. Nat. Assn. of Deaf, 1977-78; dir. handicapped services Rehab Group, Inc., 1978—; bd. dirs. Ser Vo Tel.; cons. adv. bd. deaf edn. Wis. Dept. Pub. Instrn. Mem. adv. council Cable TV, 1974-76. Mem. Profl. Rehab. Workers Adult Deaf. Home: 207 Dogwood Ave Takoma Park MD 20012 Office: 814 Thayer Ave Silver Spring MD

WHITLEY, MARK ROBERT, health and beauty aids co. exec.; b. Winchester, Mass., Aug. 4, 1948; s. Roberdell Smith and Muriel Ruth (Goudey) W.; A.B., Lafayette Coll., Easton, Pa., 1970; M.B.A., N.Y. U., 1978; m. Barbara McKinpey, June 5, 1971; 1 son, Matthew Robert. Brand asst. Procter & Gamble Co., Cin., 1972-74; bus. devel. asst. and asso., then product group mgr. Clairol Inc., div. Bristol-Myers Co., N.Y.C., 1974-78, product group supr., 1978—. Served with USNR, 1970-72. Address: Clairol 345 Park Ave New York NY 10022

WHITLOCK, EDWARD MADISON, JR., cons. civil engr.; b. Farmville, Va., Oct. 30, 1933; s. Edward M. and Mattie Leigh (Fretwell) W.; B.S. in Civil Engring., Va. Mil. Inst., 1955; m. Faith Wilson, June 14, 1975; children by previous marriage—Edward Madison III, Janis Loretta. Structural engr. Va. Steel Co., Richmond, 1957-60, head design div., 1959-60; transp. engr. Wilbur Smith & Assos., N.Y.C., 1960—, dir. transp. planning projects in U.S. and abroad, 1972—, adminstr. N.Y. and Phila. offices, 1966-72, adminstr. No. region, 1972—, v.p., 1968—; cons. to parking authorities, 1961—; guest lectr. Clemson U., 1974, Bklyn. Poly. Inst., 1971; participant Transp. Research Forum, 1972, Internat. Municipal Parking Congress, Miami, Fla., 1973; mem. Hwy. Research Bd. Com. on Transp. and Land Devel., Washington, 1965—. Active Aspetuck council Boy Scouts Am., 1966-70. Served from 2d lt. to 1st lt. inf. AUS, 1956-57. Registered profl. engr., N.Y., N.J., Conn., Md., Va., D.C., Del., Fla., Pa., S.C., Mich., Maine, R.I., Mass., Vt., N.H., Australia, Ont., Can. Fellow Am. Cons. Engrs. Council; mem. Am. Soc. C.E. (chmn. com. on planning and econs. of transp. facilities 1955—), Nat. Soc. Profl. Engrs., Inst. of Traffic Engrs. (research com. 1972-76), Nat. Parking Assn. (consultant's council 1974—), Internat. Downtown Execs. Assn., Am. Rd. Builders Assn. (airports adv. com. 1974-76), Met. Assn. of Urban Designers, Engrs. and Planners, N.Y. Engrs. Club, N.Y. Regional Plan Assn. Methodist. Contbr. articles on transp. to tech. jours. Home: 211 Greens Farm Rd Westport CT 06880 Office: PO Box 1809 New Haven CT 06507

WHITMAN, MARTIN J., financial cons.; b. N.Y.C., Sept. 30, 1924; s. Irving and Dora (Cukier) W.; B.S. magna cum laude, Syracuse U., 1949; M.A., New Sch. Social Research, 1956; postgrad. Princeton U., 1950; m. Lois M. Quick, Mar. 10, 1956; children—James Q., Barbara E., Thomas I. Research analyst Shearson Hammill & Co., N.Y.C., 1950-56, William Rosenwald, N.Y.C., 1956-58; head research Ladenburg, Thalmann & Co., N.Y.C., 1958-59; gen. partner Gerstley, Sunstein & Co., Phila., 1960-67; v.p., dir. Blair & Co., Inc., N.Y.C., 1967-69; chmn. bd. Alpha Group, Inc., N.Y.C., 1969—; pres. M.J. Whitman & Co., Inc., 1974—; vis. lectr. fin., investments Yale U., 1972—. Cons. SEC Study on Discloure, 1968. Served with USNR, 1942-46. Mem. Chartered Fin. Analysts, N.Y. Soc. Security Analysts. Contbr. numerous articles to profl. jours., also booklets. Home: 285 Central Park W New York City NY 10024 Office: 115 Broadway New York City NY 10006

WHITMAN, PHILIP MARTIN, mathematician; b. Pitts., Dec. 23, 1916; s. Edwin A. and Elsie (Van Duyne) W.; B.S., Haverford Coll., 1937; A.M., Harvard U., 1938, Ph.D., 1941. Instr. math. U. Pa., 1941-44; scientist Los Alamos Lab., 1944-46; asst. prof. math. Tuft U., 1946-48; mathematician Applied Physics Lab., Johns Hopkins U., 1948-61; prof. dept. math. R.I. Coll., Providence, chmn., 1961-67; cons. Weapons Systems Evaluation Group, Office Sec. Def., Ops. Evaluation Group, Office Chief Naval Ops., 1950-61. Fellow AAAS; mem. Am. Math. Soc., Math. Assn. Am., Ops. Research Soc. Am., Nat. Council Tchrs. Math., Phi Beta Kappa, Sigma Xi. Co-author: College Algebra, 5th edit., 1971; Essentials of College Algebra, 2d edit., 1958; Intermediate Algebra for College, 1960; College Algebra with Trigonometry, 1962; also jour. articles. Office: RI Coll Providence RI 02908

WHITMARSH, DAVID CAROTHERS, physicist; b. Barnesville, Ohio, Nov. 24, 1918; s. David Carothers and Mary (Parsons) W.; B.S. in Physics, Washington Jefferson Coll., 1940; M.S. in Physics, Syracuse U., 1942; m. Beatrice Dysart, Jan. 31, 1945; children—David C., Mary P., Anne C. Research asso. Underwater Sound Lab., Harvard U., 1942-45; research asso. in engring. research Applied Research Lab., Pa. State U., State College, 1945-47, asst. prof., 1947-52, asso. prof., 1952—; researcher under-water acoustics and oceanography. Mem. Am. Phys. Soc., Astron. Soc. Am., Marine Tech. Soc., Acoustical Soc. Am., N.Y. Acad. Sci. Republican. Contbr. articles to profl. jours. Patentee in field. Home: 219 E Irvin Ave State College PA 16801 Office: Applied Research Lab Pa State U PO Box 30 State College PA 16801

WHITMARSH, THEODORE FRANCIS, lawyer, investments; b. Englewood, N.J., Sept. 25, 1918; s. Karl Russell and Catherine (Clarke) W.; A.B., Harvard, 1942, LL.B., Fordham U., 1950; m. Mary Louise Ward, Feb. 19, 1944; children—Linda L., Carol P., Dorothy S. Admitted to N.Y. bar, 1950 since practiced in N.Y.C.; asst. sec., dir. Francis H. Leggett & Co., 1950-55, v.p., sec., dir., 1955-59; sec., dir. Thams & Hudson Pub. Co., N.Y.C., 1952-53; v.p., gen. mgr., asst. sec., dir. Hogan Faximile Corp., communications, N.Y.C., 1959-64; pres., dir. Hogan Faximile Corp. of Can., Ltd., Toronto, Ont., 1962-64, 103 E. 75th St. Apts., Inc., N.Y.C., 1957-70, Audley Clarke Co., 1968—. Served with AUS, 1942-46. Mem. Am., N.Y. State bar assns., Bar Assn. City N.Y., Huguenot Soc. Am. Clubs: River, Church, Union (N.Y.C.); Piping Rock. Home: 183 Linden Ln Glen Head NY 11545 Office: 103 Park Ave New York City NY 10017

WHITNEY, DONALD SANFORD, valve mfg. co. exec.; b. Springfield, Mass., Aug. 28, 1927; s. Perley and Alice W.; B.M.E., Western New Eng. Coll., 1962; postgrad. Mass. Inst. Tech.; m. Caroline Marano, Dec. 28, 1951; children—Sanford, Dawn. Design engr. Chapman Valve Mfg. Co., Springfield, 1950-62; dir. quality control Scovill Mfg. Co., Waterbury, Conn., 1962-68, ops. mgr., 1968-70; corporate dir. quality control Echlin Mfg. Co., Branford, Conn., 1970-74; U.S. dir. mgr. Worcester Controls Corp., West Boylston, Mass., 1974—; dir. Amcoin Corp. Served with USNR, 1945-47. Registered profl. engr., Mass. Mem. Am. Mgmt. Assn., Am. Soc. Quality Control. Clubs: Springfield County; N.Y. Athletic, Jockey. Home: 76 Northumberland St Springfield MA 01109 Office: 125 Hartwell St West Boylston MA 01583

WHITNEY, KENNETH JACK, navy officer; b. Prince Edward County, Ont., Can., Aug. 23, 1932; s. Jack Henry and Hazel Muriel (Rogers) W.; m. Heather Janette, Nov. 2, 1956; children—Geordie Jay, Kevin Jan, Tracey Janet, Patrick John. Enlisted in Royal Canadian Navy, 1951, advanced through grades to master warrant officer, 1976, now with bomb disposal sect. Mayor, Shearwater (N.S.). Mem. Maritime Locksmithing Assn., N.S. Black Belt Assn., Judo N.S. (pres.), Shearwater Granby Judo Club (pres.). Club: Odd Fellows. Home: PO Box 47/30 Martlet Pl Shearwater NS B0J 3A0 Canada Office: Fleet Diving Unit CFB Shearwater Shearwater NS B0J 3A0 Canada

WHITNEY, PHILIP MATHER, JR., mfg. co. exec.; b. Bridgeport, Conn., Dec. 20, 1941; s. Philip Mather and Eva Theresa (Trotter) W.; B.S. in Accounting magna cum laude, U. Bridgeport, 1963; m. Louise Hubbard. Sr. auditor Haskins & Sells, New Haven, 1963-67; cost accounting mgr. Bullard Co. subs. White Consol. Inds., Bridgeport, 1967-72, foundry controller, 1973; staff controller White Consol. Industries, Cleve., 1974-76; v.p. fin. ATF/Davidson Co., Whitinsville, Mass., 1976—. Served with U.S. Army, 1966. C.P.A., Conn. Mem. Am. Inst. C.P.A.'s, Conn. Soc. C.P.A.'s, Nat. Assn. Accountants, Beta Gamma Sigma. Home: Dudley Ln Sutton MA 01527 Office: Main St Whitinsville MA 01588

WHITNEY, RALPH ROYAL, JR., investment co. exec.; b. Phila., Dec. 10, 1934; s. Ralph Royal and Florence Elizabeth (Whitney) W.; B.A., U. Rochester, 1957, M.B.A., 1972; m. Fay Wadsworth, Apr. 4, 1959; children—Lynne Marie, Paula Sue, Brian Ralph. Spl. agt. Prudential Ins. Co., Rochester, N.Y., 1958-59, div. mgr., 1959-63; gen. agt. Nat. Life of Vt., Syracuse, N.Y., 1963-64; controller Wadsworth Mfg. Assos. Inc., Syracuse, 1946-65, v.p., 1965-68, pres., 1968-71; pres. Warren Components Corp., Warren, Pa., 1968—; partner Hammond Kennedy & Co., N.Y.C., 1972—, now also exec. v.p.; dir. Regency Electronics Inc., Energy Applications, Inc., AGP, Inc. Trustee Onondaga Community Coll., Syracuse Symphony. Served with AUS, 1958. Episcopalian (warden). Clubs: Lotos (N.Y.C.); Century (Syracuse). Home: 7099 Frank Long Rd RD 2 Jamesville NY 13078 Office: 230 Park Ave New York City NY 10017

WHITNEY, THOMAS PORTER, author; b. Toledo, Jan. 26, 1917; s. Herbert Porter and Louise (Metzger) W.; grad. Phillips Exeter Acad., 1934; A.B. summa cum laude Amherst Coll., 1937; M.A., Columbia U., 1940; m. Tryphena Gray, July 19, 1936 (div. Oct. 1949); children—John Herbert, Louise; m. 2d, Julia Zapolskaya, Aug. 3, 1953 (dec. Aug. 1965); m. 3d, Judith Forrestel, Oct. 14, 1966 (div. June 1973); 1 dau., Julia Forrestel W.; m. 4th, Marguerite Carusone, Sept. 21, 1974. Instr. social scis. Bennett Coll., 1940-41; social sci. analyst OSS, Washington, 1941-44; attache, chief econ. sect. U.S. Embassy, Moscow, USSR, 1944-47; staff corr. AP of Am., Moscow, USSR, 1947-53; fgn. news analyst AP of Am., N.Y.C., 1953-59; chmn. bd. Whitney Enterprises, Inc., N.Y.C., 1968-74; pres. Yulya Music, Inc.; propr. Whitney Book Shops Conn., 1975—; owner Thomas P. Whitney Racing Stable, 1975—. Trustee Julia A. Whitney Found., Washington (Conn.) Citizens Scholarship Found. Mem. Overseas Press Club Am. (pres. 1958-59, exofficio mem. bd. govs.), P.E.N., Washington Art Assn. (trustee), Phi Beta Kappa, Alpha Delta Phi. Clubs: Turf and Field, Thoroughbred of Am. Author: Has Russia Changed, 1960; Russia in My Life, 1962; contbr. articles to popular mags., Wall Street Jour., N.Y. Times Sunday mag. sect. Editor: The Communist Blueprint for the Future, 1962; Khrushchev Speaks, 1963; editor, translator The New Writing in Russia, 1964; In a Certain Kingdom, Twelve Russian Fairy Tales, 1972; The Young Russians, A Collection of Stories About Them, 1972. Translator: One Day in the Life of Ivan Denisovich, 1963; Scarlet Sails 1967; Prince Ivan, the Firebird and the Gray Wolf, 1968; The First Circle, 1968; Vasilisa the Beautiful, 1970; Forever Flowing, 1972; The Nobel Lecture on Literature (by Aleksandr Solzenitsyn), 1972; The Foundation Pit, 1973; The Gulag Archipelago (Solzenitsyn), Vol. 1, 1973, Vol. II, 1975. Address: Roxbury Rd Washington CT 06793

WHITTAKER, ALMA TEELE (MRS. VIRGIL G. WHITTAKER), former editor; b. Richmond, Va., Mar. 31, 1916; d. Joseph C. and Bessie L. (Scott) Teele; B.A., Va. Union U., 1935; postgrad. Temple U., 1944-45, Columbia U., 1954, N.Y. U., 1959, York Coll., 1971-73; m. Virgil G. Whittaker, Mar. 22, 1949; 1 son by previous marriage, Sylvester E. Dance. Tchr. nursery sch., Richmond, 1939-41; supr. statis. div. U.S. Signal Corps, Phila., 1942-49; supr. displaced persons div. Ch. World Service, N.Y.C., 1949-52; librarian Nat. Social Welfare Assembly, N.Y.C., 1952-62; mgmt. cons. Investors Planning Corp., N.Y.C., 1962-66; asso. dir. Jamaica (N.Y.) Community Corp., 1966-69; field rep. N.Y. State div. Human Rights, N.Y.C., 1969-70; exec. dir. Queens YWCA, Jamaica, 1970-75; asso. editor Queens Herald, 1975-77. Bd. dirs. Queens Child Guidance Corp., NCCJ, Queens Tb Assn. Sec., Queens County Republican Exec. Com., 1968-70. Recipient Community Service award United Democrats, 1970; Achievement award 26th Assembly Dist. Republican Club, 1970. Mem. Jamaica NAACP (edn. chmn. 1955-59, Achievement award 1970), Queens Urban League (housing chmn. 1961-62), Nat. Assn. Media Women (v.p. L.I. chpt.), Nat. Assn. Negro Bus. and Profl. Women's Clubs (Sojourner Truth award 1971), Va. Union U. Alumni Assn. Republican (sec. Queens county exec. com. 1968-70). Congregationalist. Home: 111-31 144th St Jamaica NY 11435

WHITTAKER, RICHARD PAWLING, orthopedic surgeon; b. Delaware County, Pa., June 12, 1940; s. Robert Lincoln and Helen (Rudolph) W.; M.D., U. Pa., 1966; m. Margaret Michael, June 27, 1964; children—Laura, Susan, Scott, Keith. Intern, Pa. Hosp., Phila., 1966-67; resident in orthopedic surgery Hosp. of U. Pa., Phila., 1968-71; practice medicine specializing in orthopedic surgery, Pottstown (Pa.) Orthopedic Assocs., 1974-77, pvt. practice, Pottstown, 1977—; mem. staff Pottstown Meml. Med. Center, 1974—. Mem. Pottsgrove Sch. Bd., 1977—. Served to maj. M.C., U.S. Army, 1971-74. Decorated Army Commendation medal. Mem. Eastern Orthopedic Assn., Am. Acad. Orthopedic Surgery, Orthopedics Overseas (dir. 1974), AMA, Am. Trauma Soc. (founding mem.), Pa. Orthopedic Soc., Dominican Orthopedic and Trauma Soc. (hon.). Presbyterian. Contbr. articles in field to med. jours.; author: (with Raymond Tronzo) Surgery of the Hip Joint, 1973. Home: 3017 Shire Dr Pottstown PA 19464 Office: 1603 E High St Pottstown PA 19464

WHITTEN, JAMES ROBERT, elec. engr.; b. Bartow, Fla., Dec. 12, 1927; s. Edward Earl and Hattie Donna (Crews) W.; B.E.E., U. Fla., 1951; M.E.E., Rensselaer Poly. Inst., 1955; m. Mary Jane Poorbaugh, June 2, 1950; children—Deborah Lee, Cynthia Jean, David Alan, Thomas Andrew. Electronic circuits engr. Gen. Engring. Lab., Gen. Electric Co., Schenectady, N.Y., 1951-61, project engr., Advanced Tech. Lab., 1961-66, mgr. communication circuits and studies program corporate research and devel., 1966—. Co-founder, pres. Citizens Involved in Govt. and Schs., 1968-69. Served with USN, 1946-48. Mem. IEEE, Sigma Xi. Republican. Episcopalian. Club: Condair Flyers (pres. 1976-77). Patentee in field. Home: 31 Sandalwood Ln Scotia NY 12302 Office: PO Box 43 Schenectady NY 12301

WHYTE, THOMAS JOSEPH, lawyer; b. Wheeling, W.Va., Dec. 31, 1932; s. Frank James and Katherine (Hack) W.; B.A., Ohio State U., 1954; LL.B., W.Va. U., 1960; m. Margaret Ann Brown, Aug. 31, 1954; children—Christopher, Lynn Ann, Kevin, Kathleen, Elizabeth. Admitted to W.Va. bar, 1960; law clk. U.S. Dist. Ct., Fairmont, W.Va., 1960; atty.-partner Furbee, Hardesty, Critchfield & Whyte, Fairmont, 1960-67; counsel Furbee, Amos, Webb & Critchfield, 1967-77; v.p. Consolidation Coal Co., Pitts., 1967-72, exec. v.p., 1972-77; partner Rose, Schmidt, Dixon, Hasley Whyte & Hardesty, Pitts., 1977—. Chmn. bd. dirs. Wheeling Coll.; chmn. vis. com. W.Va. U. Law Sch. Served to lt. comdr. USNR, 1954-57. Recipient Patrick Duffy Koontz award W.Va. U. Law Sch., 1960; W.Va. Law Sch. Assn. award, 1960. Mem. Am., Pa., W.Va., D.C., Allegheny County bar assns., Am. Judicature Soc., W.Va. Coal Assn. (past chmn. bd.), Western Pa. Coal Operators Assn. (past dir.), Bituminous Coal Operators Assn. (past pres., chmn.), Keystone Bituminous Coal Assn. (past pres., chmn.), Order of Coif, Phi Delta Phi (Outstanding Grad. award 1960), W.Va. U. Law Sch. Alumni Assn. (pres.). Clubs: Duquesne, St. Clair Country (Pitts.); Williams Country (Weirton, W.Va.). Editor-in-chief: W.Va. Law Rev., 1960. Home: 136 Warwick Dr Pittsburgh PA 15241 Office: 9th Floor Oliver Bldg Pittsburgh PA 15222

WIBBERLEY, HAROLD EVERS, JR., cons. engr.; b. Hagerstown, Md., July 17, 1921; s. Harold Evers and Myrtle Vivian (Bridendolph) W.; student U. Va., 1941-44; m. Amelia Lucille Baechtel, June 24, 1946; children—Murray, Bryan, Amelia. Design engr. City of Hagerstown, 1946-49; founder, pres. Baker-Wibberley & Assos., Inc., cons. engrs., Hagerstown, 1949—; mng. partner Baker-Wibberley-Coble & Assos., architects-engrs., Hagerstown, 1966—. Mem. Md. Game and Inland Fish Commn., 1967-68; vice-chmn. bd. rev. Md. Dept. Natural Resources, 1969—; mem. exec. bd. Mason-Dixon council Boy Scouts Am., 1965—. Served with USNR, 1944-46. Decorated Purple Heart. Named Distinguished Eagle Scout, Nat. council Boy Scouts Am., 1973. Registered profl. engr., Md., Pa., Mass., D.C. Mem. ARTBA, Am. Cons. Engrs. Council, Soc. Am. Mil. Engrs. (named Engr. of Distinction, Engrs. Joint Council 1973), Theta Tau. Democrat. Episcopalian. Club: Fountain Head Country (Hagerstown). Home: Route 8 Box 155 Hagerstown MD 21740 Office: 580 Northern Ave Hagerstown MD 21740

WICHMAN, ADOLPH R., gen. surgeon; b. Nuremberg, Germany, Feb. 7, 1918; s. Paul L. and Josephine (Ullman) W.; B.A., Cornell U., 1941; M.D., L.I. Coll., 1944; m. Ruby P. Clanahan, Feb. 8, 1947; children—Barbara Wichman Nowak, Beverly, Jeffrey. Intern Jersey City Med. Center, 1944-45; resident in surgery Bellevue Hosp., N.Y.C., 1947-48, Bklyn. Hosp., 1948-52; pvt. practice gen. surgery Morris County, N.J., 1952—; chief surgery St. Clare's Hosp., Denville, N.J., 1963-73, pres. med. staff, 1973-75. Hon. mem. bd. trustees Wilson Sch., Mountain Lakes, N.J., 1964—; founding mem., chmn. Morris County Drug Abuse Council, 1967—. Diplomate Am. Bd. Surgery. Fellow A.C.S. (pres. N.J. chpt. 1975-76, gov. 1977-80), Internat. Coll. Surgeons; mem. N.J. Soc. Surgeons, Morris County Med. Soc. (pres. 1966-67). Served to capt., M.C., U.S. Army, 1945-47.

Clubs: Rockaway River Country, Lackawanna Cornell. Home: 119 Lookout Rd Mountain Lakes NJ 07046

WICHMAN, SVEN HJALMAR, engr.; b. Tallinn, Estonia, June 24, 1924; s. Hendrik Mats and Aliide W.; came to U.S., 1950, naturalized, 1956; grad. Eng./Arch., Baltic U., Hamburg, Germany, 1949; B.C.E., Rensselaer Polytechnic Inst., 1951; M.C.E., Polytechnic Inst. Bklyn., 1957; m. Evi Pari, Dec. 16, 1951; children—Indrek, Mart, Hedy, Karl, Lia-Mai. Engr., M.W. Kellogg, 1951-56, Research-Cottrell, 1957-58, Brookhaven Nat. Lab., 1958-66; chief resident engr. project Turnkey U.S. Air Force, Tuy Hoa, Vietnam, 1966-67; chief engr., v.p. Preload Tech., Inc., Garden City, N.Y., 1967-74; pres. Sven Wichman Assos., Inc., Yaphank, N.Y., 1976—. Mem. ASCE, ASME, Nat. Soc. Profl. Engrs., Estonia Ednl. Soc. N.Y. v.p. 1972-76), Sigma Xi. Mem. Estonian Luth. Ch. N.Y. Patentee in cryogenics. Home: Raimond St Yaphank NY 11980 Office: 7 E 30th St New York City NY 10016

WICK, CAROL ANN MELLEN (MRS. LELAND HALL WICK), occupational therapist; b. Orange, N.J., Dec. 12, 1936; d. Earl Rufus and Isabel Pearl (Holloway) Mellen; B.S., Columbia, 1961; postgrad. N.Y. U., 1969—; m. Leland Hall Wick, May 25, 1974. Staff occupational therapist Meadowbrook Hosp., Hempstead, N.Y., 1961-62; sr. occupational therapist N.J. Orthopaedic Hosp., 1962-66, Easter Seal Center, Morris Plains, N.J., 1966-68; dir. occupational therapy John E. Runnells Hosp., Berkeley Heights, N.J., 1969-71; registered occupational therapist Robert E. Wood Johnson Meml. Hosp. of John F. Kennedy Community Hosp., Edison, N.J., 1971-74, sr. occupational therapist, 1974-75; occupational therapist Belleville (N.J.) Geriatric Hosp., 1975—. Mem. Am., N.J. occupational therapy assns. Home: 393 Wyoming Ave Millburn NJ 07041 Office: Belleville Geriatric Hosp Belleville NJ

WICKER, IREENE, writer, singer, entertainer radio and TV; b. Quincy, Ill.; d. Kenner and Margaret (Hunsaker) Seaton; student U. of Ill., 1 yr; student Goodman Theatre Sch., Art Inst. Chicago, 1927-30; m. Walter C. Wicker; children—Walter Charles, Nancy; m. 2d, Victor Hammer, Jan. 11, 1941. Began as actress in stock co. at 12; appeared at the Goodman Theatre, Chgo., 1929-30; dramatic staff CBS, 1930-31; played in Painted Dreams, Harold Teen, Today's Children, Song of the City, Judy and Jane, Great Plays, NBC; originated wrote and performed, Singing Lady radio program; Sunday dramatic program Ireene Wicker's Music Plays over N.B.C. and Mutual network; co-dir. Merry-Go-Round Children's Theatre; worked with profl. children on ABC-TV, 1951-54; with Shakespearean group American Theatre Wing and with Stella Adler and Joseph Kramm, 1955-56; ednl. mus. dramatizations children's classics WNYC, also WNYC-FM, 1959—, and syndicated by Broadcasting Found. Am., 1974—. Recipient highest honors 5 years in succession, for children's programs, by radio editors poll, conducted by New York World Telegram; award for distinguished service to radio, by poll of Radio Star Mag.; award Radio Guide Mag. for leading children's program, 4 yrs. in succession; Peabody award for children's radio programs, 1961, SAVE award, 1976. Mem. Broadcast Pioneers, Am. Women in Radio and TV, Authors Guild, Internat. Radio and Television Soc., Nat. Acad. TV Arts and Scis. Records for Record Guild Am. on Simon Sez label include Kipling's Just So Stories; Grimm's Fairy Tales; The Owl and the Pussycat and other stories; Anderson's Fairy Tales; song books and plays published by Irving Berlin, Inc. Author: The Little Hunchback Horse; Young Music Makers; Young Master Arts; also other books, plays and songs for children; 4 books and albums for Regal and De Luxe, Decca, Victor recs. Dir. Children's Radio for C.D.V.O. Presbyterian. Made 12 Golden Book Records, cassettes of mus. dramatization of childrens stories for N.Y. Pub. Library. Home: 781 Fifth Ave New York City NY 10022 Office: 667 Madison Ave New York City NY 10021

WICKHAM, DALE WALLACE, lawyer; b. Dayton, Ohio, Feb. 6, 1929; s. William Oscar and Hilda (Hauck) W.; A.B. cum laude, Harvard U., 1950, LL.B., 1953; children—Annette, Sarah, John. Admitted to D.C. bar, 1957, Ill. bar, 1972, Ohio bar, 1953, Va. bar, 1968, U.S. Supreme Ct. bar, 1956; practiced in Washington, 1956—, Chgo., 1971—; partner firm Mayer, Brown & Platt, Chgo. and Washington, 1971-77; sr. partner firm Wickham, Craft & Cihlar, Chgo. and Washington, 1977—; counsel on fed. tax policy to U.S. Congress Joint Commn. on IRS Taxation, 1959-62; spl. counsel 1969 Tax Reform Act, Senate Commn. on Fin., 1969-70; spl. tax counsel U.S. airline industry, other transp. cons., pub. cos. Co-founder, chmn. Mt. Vernon (Va.) Citizens for Better Govt. Served with USCG, 1953-56. Mem. Internat. Fiscal Assn., Am. Bar Assn. Author: A Topical Comparison of U.S. Income Tax Conventions, 1961; Legislative History of U.S. Tax Conventions, 1961. Home: 513 S Fairfax St Alexandria VA 22314 Office: Suite 1100 1050 17th St NW Washington DC 20036 also Suite 4700 One IBM Plaza Chicago IL 60611

WICKHAM, ROBERT DEAN, urologist; b. Pa., Aug. 11, 1923; s. Darley Jenkins and Ann Dell (Palmer) W.; A.B., Drew U., 1947; M.D., Albany (N.Y.) Med. Coll., 1952; m. Louise Jullien, Sept. 24, 1955; children—Louise, Lisa, Leslie, Robert D. Intern, then resident in urology Northwestern U. Hosp., Chgo., 1952-54; resident in urology Columbia U. Hosp., N.Y.C., 1955-57; practice medicine specializing in urology, N.Y.C., 1958—; attending surgeon Roosevelt Hosp., N.Y.C., 1958—, chief urology outpatient dept., 1978—; asst. clin. prof. urology Coll. Physicians and Surgeons, Columbia U., 1970—. Served with U.S. Army, 1943-46. Decorated Bronze Star with 2 oak leaf clusters. Diplomate Am. Bd. Urology. Fellow A.C.S.; mem. AMA, N.Y. State, N.Y. County med. socs., Am. Urol. Assn., N.Y. Acad. Medicine. Clubs: Met. Opera Men's, Knickerbocker Country. Office: 71 E 71st St New York City NY 10021

WIDLITZ, PAUL J., judge; b. Newark, Aug. 11, 1914; s. Meyer and Rose (Kaplan) W.; B.A., Pa. State Coll., 1936; LL.B., N.Y. U., 1939; m. Beatrice Landsman, July 20, 1944; children—Phyllis Widlitz Schwartz, Stephen. Admitted to N.Y. bar, 1941; judge Dist. Ct. Nassau County, N.Y., 1951-56, County Ct. Nassau County, 1957-61; justice Supreme Ct. State N.Y., Mineola, 1962—. Chmn. various drives Boy Scouts Am., Nassau County, 1955; del. N.Y. State Constl. Conv., 1907. Chmn., bd. dirs. Hebrew Acad. Nassau County, pres., 1958-63; trustee Israel Community Center, Levittown, N.Y. Served to lt. USAAF, 1943-46. Recipient Silver Beaver award Boy Scouts Am., 1959; gold medal V.F.W., 1959; medal of merit Jewish War Vets., 1961; Ann. award South Nassau County Lawyers Assn., 1960; Norman F. Lent Meml. award Criminal Cts. Bar Assn., 1966. Clubs: Masons, B'nai B'rith. Home: 36 Raspberry Ln Levittown NY 11756 Office: Nassau County Supreme Ct Bldg Supreme Ct Dr Mineola NY 11501

WIECZERZAK, JOSEPH WALTER, educator; b. Newark, Jan. 1, 1931; s. Joseph Stephen and Lottie (Grodzki) W.; B.A., Bklyn. Coll., 1952; M.A., N.Y. U., 1958, Ph.D., 1962; m. Dorothy Eleanor Kostecki, Nov. 20, 1966; children—Christopher, Barbara. Faculty, Bronx Community Coll., City U. N.Y., 1964—, prof. history, 1972—; prof. history and adj. prof. sociology Bronx Community Coll., 1975—. Served with U.S. Army, 1952-55. Kosciuszko Found. Exchange scholar to Poland, 1963; Internat. Research and Exchanges Bd. Sr. Exchange scholar to Poland, 1970-71. Mem. Polish Am. Hist. Assn. (pres. 1978), Am. Hist. Assn., Polish Inst. Arts and Scis. in Am. (dir. 1977—), Pilsudski Inst. Study of Modern History of Poland (dir. 1975—). Polish Nat. Catholic. Author: A Polish Chapter in Civil War America, 1967; contbg. editor: The Ethnic Dimension in American Society, 1974; asso. editor Polish Am. Studies, 1975; editorial bd. Polish Rev., 1970—. Address: 31 Hawthorne Ter Leonia NJ 07605

WIEDERHOLD, MICHAEL LEWIS, neurophysiologist; b. Milw., Aug. 2, 1939; s. Lewis Carl and Helene Rose (Lowitz) W.; S.B., Mass. Inst. Tech., 1961, S.M., 1963, Ph.D. (Nat. Inst. Gen. Med. Scis. fellow), 1967; m. Margaret Fisher Sayre, Feb. 27, 1971; 1 son, Theodore Lincoln. Asst. prof. elec. engring. Mass. Inst. Tech., 1967-69, also research asso. otolaryngology Mass. Eye and Ear Infirmary, Boston, 1967-69; staff fellow, sr. staff fellow Nat. Inst. Neurol. Diseases and Stroke, Bethesda, 1969-72; research physiologist, head neurol. scis. div., neurobiology dept. Armed Forces Radiobiology Research Inst., Bethesda, 1973—. Mem. Acoustical Soc. Am., Soc. Neuroscis., AAAS, Am. Physiol. Soc., Assn. Research in Otolaryngology (charter), Sigma Xi, Tau Beta Pi, Eta Kappa Nu. Contbr. articles to profl. jours. Home: 7214 Delfield St Chevy Chase MD 20015 Office: Armed Forces Radiology Research Inst Bethesda MD 20014

WIEGARTNER, PAUL JOHN, accountant; b. Jersey City, Jan. 5, 1939; s. John H. and Margaret (McGuinness) W.; B.S. in Accounting, St. Peters Coll., 1964; m. Rosemary Earl, Sept. 3, 1960; children—Arlene, Paul, Jr. Asst. tax mgr. Fedders Corp., Edison, N.J., 1965-66; supervising sr. accountant Peat Marwick Mitchell & Co., N.Y.C., 1966-71; asst. v.p., asst. sec. Engelhard Minerals and Chems. Corp., N.Y.C., 1971—. C.P.A., N.J. Mem. Inst. C.P.A.'s. Home: 129 Durie Ave Closter NJ 07624 Office: 1221 Ave of Americas New York City NY 10017

WIELAND, PEG DOODY MAST, economist, editor; b. Kattowitz, Germany; d. Paul and Lucy (Olbrich) Mast; dipl. rer. pol. Berlin (Germany) U.; M.A., New Sch. for Social Research, 1960, postgrad., 1964-68. Came to U.S., 1954, naturalized, 1959. Researcher, tng. officer U.S. Forces, Garmisch, Germany, 1948-54; research asst. Milbank Meml. Fund, N.Y.C., 1954-58; econ. analyst, editor Chase Manhattan Fgn. Trade Service publ. The Chase Manhattan Bank N.A., N.Y.C., 1958-68, research economist, editor Chase Manhattan Guide for Exporters publ., 1968-70, bank officer, 1970—. Mem. New Sch. Alumni Assn. (exec. com.), Fgn. Credit Interchange Bur. Office: Chase Manhattan Bank 1 Chase Manhattan Plaza New York City NY 10015

WIEMER-SUMNER, ANNE-MARIE, psychotherapist, coll. adminstr.; b. Königsberg, Germany, Mar. 3, 1938; d. Franz and Margarete (Neubacher) Wiemer; came to U.S., 1949, naturalized, 1956; B.A., Hunter Coll., 1963; M.S., N.Y. U., 1965; certificate psychoanalytic individual and group therapy Washington Sq. Inst. Psychotherapy, 1976; m. Eric Sumner, May 24, 1974; children—Erika, Trevor. Adminstrv. asst., counselor, asst. chmn. admissions N.Y. U., N.Y.C., 1956-69; asst. dean students Hunter Coll., N.Y.C., 1969-71; asso. dean students Cooper Union Advancement Art and Sci., N.Y.C., 1971—; supr. Washington Sq. Inst. Psychotherapy, 1977—; pvt. practice psychotherapy, N.Y.C., 1977—. Mem. Am. Group Psychotherapy Assn., Nat. Assn. Women Deans and Counselors, Coll. Placement Council, Eastern Coll. Personnel Officers, N.Y. State Financial Aid Adminstrv. Assn., Am. Personnel and Guidance Assn., Am. Psychol. Assn., Nat. Accreditation Assn. for Psychoanalysis. Home: 12 Washington Sq N New York City NY 10003 Office: Cooper Union Advancement Art and Sci 41 Cooper Sq New York City NY 10003

WIEN, STEPHEN SAUL, securities specialist; b. Bklyn., Dec. 27, 1936; s. Percy Joseph and Gertrude Sarah (Hutkin) W.; Diploma in Small Bus., Bklyn. Coll., 1961; grad. N.Y. Inst. Finance; m. Edith Dubers, May 10, 1959; children—Lawrence Scott, Brett Evan, Nicole Bari. With M.S. Wien & Co., Jersey City, 1954—, partner, 1956—, v.p., 1961-67, exec. v.p., 1968—; pres. Wien Group; pres. N.Y. Wholesale Candy House Corp., Newark. Mem. Jersey City Redevel. Bd. Served with AUS, 1958-61. Mem. Nat. Assn. Securities Dealers (mem. dist. bd., dist. bus. conduct com., dist. arbitration com., NASDAQ com.), Security Traders Assn. N.Y. (dir., mem. NASDAQ com., Nat. Securities Clearing Corp. com.), Cashiers Assn. Wall St. Clubs: Montammy Golf (bd. govs.) (Alpine, N.J.), Jockey, Crickett (Miami). Home: 18 Allison Dr Englewood Cliffs NJ 07632 Office: 1 Exchange Pl Jersey City NJ 07302 also 16 Belmont Ave Newark NJ

WIENER, HARRY, physician; b. Vienna, Austria, Oct. 29, 1924; s. Joseph and Beile Wiener; B.S., Bklyn. Coll., 1945; M.D., L.I. U., 1949. With Pfizer Inc., N.Y.C., 1958—, dir. profl. info., 1958—. Served with M.C., AUS, 1953-55; Korea. Mem. AMA, N.Y. Acad. Medicine, Am. Med. Writers Assn. Developer Wiener numbers for calculation of phys. properties of hydrocarbons, 1947, proposer theory of human pheromones, 1966, genetics-environment symmetry in schizophrenia, 1976. Home: 45 Tudor City Pl New York City NY 10017 Office: 235 E 42d St New York City NY 10017

WIENER, HOWARD EDWARD, ophthalmologist; b. N.Y.C., Oct. 30, 1918; s. Joseph D. and Ester (Solomon) W.; B.A., U. Va., 1940; M.D., N.Y.U., 1943; m. Marilyn Fenton, June 2, 1949; children—Benjamin R., John R., Patricia A. Intern, Cedars of Lebanon Hosp., Los Angeles, 1944; preceptor in ophthalmology Dr. Jack P. Cowen, Chgo., 1946-48; resident in ophthalmology Goldwater Meml. Hosp., N.Y.C., 1948-50; asst. attending surgeon Manhattan Eye, Ear and Throat Hosp., N.Y.C., 1952-55; staff ophthalmologist L.I.-Jewish-Hillside Med. Center, 1955—, dir. ophthalmology South Shore Div., 1973-76; chief ophthalmology S. Shore div. St. John's Episcopal Hosp., 1976—; attending ophthalmologist Peninsula Hosp. Center (Far Rockaway, N.Y.); mem. staff ophthalmology So. Nassau Community Hosp. (Oceanside, N.Y.). Mem. Hewlett Neck Bd. Appeals, 1973—. Served to 1st lt. M.C., AUS, 1944-46. Diplomate Am. Bd. Ophthalmology. Fellow Am. Acad. Ophthalmology and Otolaryngology, A.C.S.; mem. AMA, N.Y. Clin. Soc. Ophthalmology, Pan. Am. Ophthalmol. Assn., Assn. Research in Vision and Ophthalmology, Am. Soc. Contemporary Ophthalmology. Jewish. Club: Woodmere (N.Y.) Country. Home: 330 Dolphin Dr Hewlett Neck NY 11598 Office: 285 Central Ave Lawrence NY 11559

WIENER, MORRIS JAY, educator; b. Phila., Aug. 23, 1941; s. William V. and Sylvia L. (Bookbinder) W.; B.F.A., Phila. Coll. Art, 1967; M.Ed., Temple U., 1972, Ed.D., 1974; m. Diane Wiener, June 18, 1966; children—Ann Michael, Jennifer. Owner, operator Morris J. Wiener Photography, Cherry Hill, N.J., 1966-72; tchr. Woodbury (N.J.) Sch. Dist., 1967-72; asst. prof. Temple U., Phila., 1972-74; adj. faculty Camden County Community Coll.; dir. instructional resources Southeastern State Sch. and Hosp., Woodhaven, Pa., 1974—. Capt. Woodcrest Fire Co.; dep. chief Ashland Fire Co., Cherry Hill Fire Dept., 1977—; asst. fire marshal Fire Dist. 4, Cherry Hill, N.J.; mem. Ashland Ambulance and Rescue Squad, Cherry Hill, 1971—; mem. Camden County Pub. Safety Adv. Com. Recipient Bronze medal Carnegie Commn., 1966; Life Saving award of merit ARC, 1966. Mem. NEA, N.J. Edn. Assn., Mensa Soc. Am., Assn. Edn. Communications and Tech., Pa. Learning Resources Assn., Council Exceptional Children, Council Adminstrs. Spl. Edn., Assn. for Gifted. Home: 306 Pleasant Dr Cherry Hill NJ 08003 Office: Woodhaven Center 2900 Southampton Rd Philadelphia PA 19154

WIENER, NORMAN, export traffic exec.; b. N.Y.C., Jan. 28, 1923; s. George and Bessie (Faber) W.; student Coll. City N.Y., 1940-42; m. Marie Antoinette Hery, Mar. 7, 1946; children—George, Nicole, Herve, Bernard, Philippe. Clk., Whitehall Shipping Co., 1939-43, established Orbit Shipping Corp., (merged into Globe Shipping Co., Inc. 1969), N.Y.C., 1946—, v.p., 1969—; admitted to practice FMC; course chmn. World Trade Inst. Mem. Nat. Def. Exec. Res. of Dept. Transp.; mem. City of New Rochelle (N.Y.) Transit Commn. Bd. dirs. New Rochelle (N.Y.) Hosp. Served to lt. col. AUS, 1942-46. Mem. Nat. Def. Transp. Assn. (charter mem.), Res. Officers Assn. (chpt. pres. 1971—), Met. Traffic Assn., Am. Soc. Notaries, Mil. Order World Wars, Ret. Officers Assn., Order of Lafayette, Delta Nu Alpha (nat. essay contest winner). Clubs: Foreign Commerce (chmn. mil. affairs com. 1965—), Propeller, Rudder (all N.Y.C.). Home: 95 Elk Ave New Rochelle NY 10804 Office: 1 World Trade Center New York City NY 10048

WIENER, SOLOMON, author, former city ofcl.; b. N.Y.C., Mar. 5, 1915; s. Morris David and Anna (Pinchuk) W.; B.S., Cornell, 1936; M. Pub. Adminstrn., N.Y.U., 1946; m. Gertrude Klings, Feb. 24, 1946; children—Marjorie Diane, Willa Kay. Exam. asst. N.Y.C. Dept. Personnel, 1937-42, civil service examiner, 1946-55, asst. div. chief, 1955-59, div. chief, 1959-67, asst. dir. exams., 1967-70, dir. exams., 1970-72, asst. personnel dir. exams., 1972-75; author, 1975—. Tchr. Washington Irving Evening Adult Sch., N.Y.C., 1949-60, tchr.-in-charge, 1960-67. Served with AUS, 1942-46; PTO, col. Res. ret. Decorated Bronze Star medal. Mem. Am. Soc. Pub. Adminstrn., Internat. Personnel Mgmt. Assn., Profl. Assn. for Municipal Mgmt. (exec. v.p. 1969-75), Res. Officers Assn., Am. Def. Preparedness Assn. Author: A Handy Book of Commonly Used American Idioms, 1958; Manual de Modismos Americanos Más Comunes, 1959; A Handy Guide to Irregular Verbs and the Use and Formation of Tenses, 1959; Guía Completa de Los Verbos Irregulares en Inglés y el Uso y Formacion de los Tiempos, 1959; Questions and Answers on American Citizenship--An Americanization Manual and Naturalization Guide, 1960; Business Letter Writing, 1969; Mastering Business Letter Writing, 1978. Contbr. articles to personnel jours. Home: 523 E 14th St New York City NY 10009

WIENIK, PETER HARRIS, physician; b. Crocket, Tex., June 16, 1939; s. Harris and Molly (Emmerman) W.; B.A. with distinction, U. Va., 1961, M.D., 1965; m. Roberta Joan Fuller, Sept. 6, 1961; children—Julie Anne, Lisa Britt, Peter Harrison. Intern, Cleve. Met. Gen. Hosp., 1965-66, resident, 1969-70; resident Osler service Johns Hopkins Hosp., Balt., 1970-71; sr. asst. surgeon USPHS, 1966, advanced through grades to sr. surgeon, 1971; sr. staff asso. Balt. Cancer Research Center, div. cancer treatment Nat. Cancer Inst., 1966-71, chief sect. med. oncology, 1971-76, chief clin. oncology br., 1976—; acting dir., 1976—, asso. dir. div. cancer treatment, 1976—; asst. prof. medicine U. Md. Hosp., Balt., 1971-74, asso. prof. medicine, 1974-76, prof., 1976—; cons. hematology and med. oncology Union Meml. Hosp., Greater Balt. Med. Center, Franklin Sq. Hosp. Bd. dirs. Balt. City unit Am. Cancer Soc., 1971—, chmn. patient care com., 1972-75; mem. med. adv. com. Nat. Leukemia Assn., 1976—; chmn. adult leukemia com. Cancer and Leukemia Group B, 1976—. Recipient Z Soc. award U. Va., 1961, Byrd S. Leavell Hematology award U. Va. Sch. Medicine, 1965. Diplomate Am. Bd. Internal Medicine (med. oncology). Fellow AAAS, Am. Coll. Clin. Pharmacology, Internat. Soc. Hematology Royal Soc. Medicine (London), A.C.P.; mem. Am. Soc. Clin. Investigation, Phi Beta Kappa, Alpha Omega Alpha, Phi Sigma (award 1961). Mem. editorial bd. Cancer Treatment Reports, 1972-76, Leukemia Research, 1976—, Cancer Clin. Trials; co-editor Oncology Rounds, Am. Jour. Med. Scis., 1976—. Home: 5026 Round Tower Pl Columbia MD 21044 Office: U Md Hosp 22 S Greene St Baltimore MD 21201

WIENSHIENK, RALPH, lawyer, accountant; b. Kansas City, Mo., Sept. 27, 1919; s. Charles and Rebecca (Shultz) W.; B.S. in Econs., Northwestern U., 1940; LL.B. cum laude, Yale U., 1947; m. Valy Bloch, June 3, 1945 (div. Feb. 1960); children—Wendy Ann, Joan, Mark Ralph, John; m. 2d, Rita Cipes, 1966; children—Andrew, David, Nancy. Admitted to N.Y. bar, 1948, Ill. bar, 1948; vis. prof. law Yale U., 1947—; lawyer Gen. Counsel's Office, Sec. Air Force, also asso. gen. counsel Small Def. Plants Adminstrn., Washington, 1951-52; practiced in N.Y.C., 1952—; mem. firm Golden, Wienshienk & Mandel, 1952—; chmn. bd. McCall Pub. Corp., 1973—; dir., chmn. fin. com. Great Adventure Park, N.J. Chmn. urban affairs com., bd. dirs. YMCA Greater N.Y.; N.Y. bd. overseers Hebrew Union Coll. Served from pvt. to maj. USAAF, 1942-46. C.P.A. Mem. Bar Assn. City N.Y., Northwestern U., Yale alumni assns., Order of Coif, Phi Epsilon Pi. Jewish religion (pres. and trustee temple). Clubs: Yale (N.Y.C.); Fenway Golf (Scarsdale, N.Y.). Co-editor: Cases and Materials on Law and Accounting, 1949. Contbr. articles pub. in law jours. Home: 3 Kingston Rd Scarsdale NY 10583 Office: 10 E 40th St New York City NY 10016

WIER, JOSEPH RICHARD, petroleum engr.; b. Opelousas, La., Nov. 30, 1921; s. Harvey James and Hazel (Mornhinveg) M.; student U. Okla., 1940-41; B.S. in Petroleum Engring., La. State U., 1945; m. Nan Starr Stockton, Nov. 28, 1952; 1 son, Richard Harvey. Partner Harvey J. Wier & Sons, Opelousas, La., 1945-50; v.p. Harvey J. Wier & Sons, Inc., Houston, 1950-60; pres., dir. Huron Exploration Co., Inc., Gen. Exploration Co., Houston; pres. Equitable Petroleum Corp., N.Y.C., 1969-73, chmn. bd., 1973-75; dir. petroleum div. Amivest Corp., N.Y.C., 1975—; ind. petroleum exploration, 1976—. Served with USAAF, 1945-50. Registered profl. engr., La., Tex. Mem. Am. Inst. Mining, Metall. and Petroleum Engrs., Am. Assn. Petroleum Geologists, Soc. Exploration Geophysicists, Soc. Ind. Profl. Earth Scientists, Nat., N.Y. State socs. profl. engrs., Soc. Petroleum Evaluation Engrs., Assn. Profl. Geol. Scientists, Petroleum Exploration Soc. N.Y., Am. Petroleum Inst., Am. Arbitration Assn. (nat. panel arbitrators). Clubs: Masons (32 deg.), Shriners, Explorers (N.Y.). Home: 412 E 84th St New York City NY 10028 Office: Amivest Corp 505 Park Ave New York City NY 10022

WIER, RICHARD ROYAL, JR., lawyer, state ofcl.; b. Wilmington, Del., May 19, 1941; B.A. in English, Hamilton Coll., 1963; LL.B., U. Pa., 1966. Admitted to D.C. bar, 1967, Del. bar, 1967; asso. firm Connolly, Bove & Lodge, Wilmington, 1966-68; dep. atty. gen. State of Del., Wilmington, 1968-70, state prosecutor Del. Dept. Justice, 1970-74, atty. gen., 1975-79; mem. firm Prickett, Ward, Burt & Sanders, Wilmington, 1979—; lectr. in field, 1970-75. Active United Way Campaign Del., 1976. Mem. Nat. Dist. Attys. Assn. (Del. dir.), Council on Adminstrn. Justice, Del., D.C. bar assns., Nat. Assn. Democratic State-wide Elected Ofcls., Nat. Assn. Attys. Gen., Am., Del. trial lawyers assns., Am. Judicature Soc., Nat. Assn. Extradition Ofcls. (hon. life, regional v.p. 1968-75), Jud. Planning Commn. Recipient Law Enforcement award Newark (Del.) Police Dept., 1974, Outstanding Young Man award Claymont (Del.) Jaycees, 1975, Law Enforcement Commendation medal SAR, 1976, Ideal Citizen award Am. Found. for Sci. of Creative Intelligence, 1976, resolution commendation Del. Gen. Assembly Senate, 1976; named Hon. Citizen, Tenn., Ark., Fla., Nev. Home: 513 Brighton Rd North Hills

Wilmington DE 19809 Office: 1310 King St PO 1328 Wilmington DE 19899

WIERZALIS, EDWARD ALEXANDER, counseling psychologist; b. Shenandoah, Pa., May 3, 1947; s. Edward J. and Anna F. (Palubinsky) W.; B.A., Pa. State U., 1976; M.Ed., Temple U., 1977. Prof., chmn. social studies dept., athletic dir. Academia Santa Monica, Santurce, P.R., 1969-73; staff mem. Casa La Providencia, San Juan, P.R., 1969-71; mem. Diocesan Bd. Religious Edn., San Juan, 1970-71; prof. philosophy Colegio San Ignacio, Rio Piedras, P.R., 1973-74; tchr., center supr. Schuylkill County Child Devel. Program, Pottsville, Pa., 1974-75; acad. counselor Center for Continuing Edn. Temple U., Phila., 1976-77; counselor, career coordinator Shawnee High Sch., Medford, N.J., 1977—, asso. SECA (Ednl. Consultation Service), 1979—. Recipient Por Animo service award Associado de Padres y Estudiantes, 1973. Mem. Am., Burlington County, Greater Phila. personnel and guidance assns., Am., Pa. sch. counselors assns., Assn. Specialists in Group Work. Democrat. Roman Catholic. Clubs: K.C. Home: 16-B Madison Dr Maple Shade NJ 08052 Office: Shawnee High Sch Medford NJ 08055

WIESEN, JEREMY LESTER, lawyer, educator; b. N.Y.C., Feb. 27, 1942; s. Irving and Tobie (Mnuchin) W.; B.S. in Econs., Wharton Sch., U. Pa., 1963; J.D., Harvard, 1966; m. Belinda Brackenridge; 1 child, Gavin B. Admitted to N.Y. bar, 1969; asst. prof. Wharton Sch., U. Pa., 1966-69; vis. asst. prof. Grad. Sch. Bus. Adminstrn., Columbia, 1970-71; asso. prof. business law and accounting Grad. Sch. Bus. Adminstrn., N.Y. U., 1972—; of counsel O'Sullivan, Wolff, Karabell & Graev, 1974-77; spl. legal counsel SEC, 1968; counsel commn. auditors responsibilities, mem. com. on perpetration and detection of fraud Am. Inst. C.P.A.'s, 1976—; legal cons. U.S. Bankruptcy Laws, 1973; vis. asso. prof. Stanford Grad. Sch. Bus., 1977. Mem. Beta Gamma Sigma. Clubs: Harvard, Harmonie (N.Y.C.); Maidstone. Author: Legal Aspects of the Management Process, 1969, 76; Regulating Transactions in Securities, 1975. Home: 850 Park Av New York City NY 10021 Office: 100 Trinity Pl New York City NY 10006

WIESEN, MARVIN ARTHUR, pharmacist; b. Phila., Oct. 2, 1929; s. Harry and Esther Mary (Singer) W.; diploma med. tech., Franklin Sch. Sci. and Arts, 1948; B.S., Phila. Coll. Pharmacy and Sci., 1956; m. Barbara Refsin, June 19, 1954; children—Janice Faye, Karen Beryl, Scott Laurence. Mgr., Korvettes Pharmacy, Phila. 1959, Thrift Drug Store, Dover, Del., 1960; owner Dover Pharmacy Inc., 1961—; cons. in field, lectr. Pres. Dover Elementary Sch. PTA, 1965; Kent County (Del.) coordinator Boy Scouts Am., 1968; mem. Drug Abuse Clinic Dover, 1976; chmn. Consumer Affairs Council Dover, 1977; pres. Del. State Bd. Pharmacy, 1975-76, mem., 1974—; bd. dirs. Kent County Unit Am. Cancer Soc., 1968—, Kent County United Way, 1977—. Mem. Del. Pharm. Soc. (dir. 1972-75), Greater Dover-Smyrna C. of C. (dir. 1977—, v.p. for organizational affairs 1978—), Dover Found. Edn.; fellow Am. Coll. Apothecaries, Am. Coll. Med. Technologists. Registered pharmacist, Del., Pa., N.J., Ariz. Jewish. Clubs: Elks, Rotary, Masons, Shriners. Home: 931 Monroe Terr Dover DE 19901 Office: 805 S Governors Ave Dover DE 19901

WIESENBAUGH, JOSEPH MICHAEL, JR., oral surgeon; b. Phila., Oct. 19, 1939; s. Joseph M. and Claire Shirley (Doyle) W.; student Mt. St. Mary's Coll., 1957-59; D.D.S. magna cum laude, U. Md., 1963; M.S.D., U. Pacific, 1970; m. Kathleen Mary Wallace, Apr. 20, 1963; children—Stacie Marie, Michelle Ann, Kara Lynn, Joseph Michael II. Dental intern Wilford Hall USAF Hosp., San Antonio, 1964; practice dentistry, Balt., 1967; resident oral and maxillofacial surgery Fresno (Calif.) Gen. Hosp., 1967-69; practice oral and maxillofacial surgery, Hagerstown, Md., 1970—; drug research Upjohn Co., Kalamazoo, 1967—; staff Washington County Hosp., Waynesboro (Pa.) Hosp.; breeder angus cattle. Active Explorer Scouts, Hagerstown, Md., 1970—. Bd. dirs., pres. Am. Cancer Soc., Washington County, Md., Health Planning Council Appalachia, Md., 1972; council mem., exec. bd. dirs. Health Planning Council Appalachia, 1971—. Served to capt. USAF, 1963-67. Registered angus breeder. Diplomate Am. Bd. Oral and Maxillofacial Surgery. Fellow Internat. Soc. Oral Surgeons, Am. Dental Soc. Anesthesiology; mem. Am., Md. State, Washington County (sec. 1972-73, pres. elect 1974) dental assns., Am. Soc. Oral Surgery, Soc. Anesthesiology, Am., Md., Middle Atlantic socs. oral surgeons, Xi Psi. Rotarian. Contbr. articles, abstracts to dental jours. Home: Rocky Forge Farm Route 5 Box 260 Hagerstown MD 21740 Office: 1707 Potomac Ave Hagerstown MD 21740

WIESENBERG, JACQUELINE LEONARDI, lectr.; b. West Haven, Conn., May 4, 1928; d. Curzio and Filmenia Olga (Turriziana) Leonardi; B.A., State U. N.Y. at Buffalo, 1970, grad. student, 1970-73; m. Russel John Wiesenberg, Nov. 23: children—James Wynne, Deborann Donna. Interviewer, examiner Dept. Labor, New Haven, 1948-52; sec. W. I. Clark Co., Hamden, Conn., 1952-55: accountant VA Hosp., West Haven, 1956-60; accountant-commissary U.S. Air Force Missile Site, Niagara Falls, N.Y., 1961-62; tchr. Buffalo City Schs., 1970-73; accountant Erie County Social Services, Buffalo, 1971-73; lectr., 1973—. Capt., Nat. Found. March of Dimes, 1969—; chmn. Meals on Wheels, Town of Amherst, 1975-76; travel chmn. Girl Scouts Am., 1968-77. Mem. Internat. Platform Assn., Am. Astrol. Assn., Western N.Y. Conf. Aging, Epsilon Delta Chi, Alpha Iota. Contbr. articles to CAP, U.S. Air Force mag., 1955-60. Home: 14 Norman Pl Amherst NY 14226

WIESENBERG, RUSSEL JOHN, statistician; b. Kaukauna, Wis., Apr. 9, 1924; s. Emil Martin and Josephine (Appelbaker) W.; B.S., U. Wis., 1951; postgrad. Cornell U., 1960-61, U. Mich., 1969, George Washington U., 1976; m. Jacqueline Leonardi, Nov. 23, 1960; children—James Wynne, Deborann Donna. Analyst, Gen. Electric Co., West Lynn, Mass., 1951-56; specialist Internat. Gen. Electric Co., Rio de Janeiro, Brazil, 1956-59; statistician Gen. Motors Corp., Lockport, N.Y., 1959-65, sr. statistician, Harrison Radiator div., 1965—. Auditor, Community Chest Fund, 1952-55; umpire Little League Baseball, 1962-65; committeeman Buffalo Area council Boy Scouts Am., 1962—, Cub Scout committeeman, 1962-64, Webelos cubmaster, 1963-64; mem. Nat. Congress Parents and Tchrs., 1963—; heart fund Vol. Heart Assn., 1968; tournament dir. Am. Legion Baseball, 1975. Served with AUS, 1943-46. Decorated Bronze Star. Mem. AAAS, Am. Statis. Assn., Nat. Register Sci. and Tech. Personnel, U. Wis. Alumni Assn., Artus, Internat. Platform Assn., Phi Kappa Phi. Lutheran (capt. stewardship com.). Contbr. articles to profl. jours. Home: 14 Norman Pl Amherst NY 14226 Office: Harrison Radiator div Gen Motors Corp Lockport NY 14094

WIESENTHAL, MARVIN MEYER, psychoanalyst; b. Montreal, Que., Can., Jan. 25, 1943; s. Nathan and Molly (Feldman) W.; B.Sc., McGill U., 1965, M.D., 1967; D. Child Psychiatry, U. Toronto, 1972; grad. Can. Inst. Psychoanalysis, 1976; m. Ida Potashnik, Aug. 21, 1966; children—Stephanie, Melanie. Intern St. Mary's Hosp., Montreal, 1967-68; resident in psychiatry Inst. Living, Hartford, Conn., 1968-70, U. Toronto (Ont., Can.), 1970-72; pvt. practice medicine, specializing in psychiatry and psychoanalysis, Toronto, 1972—; cons. Chimo Youth Services. Mem. com. Jewish Family and Child Service, Toronto, Jewish Camp Council, Toronto. Mem. Can., Ont. med. assns., Ont. Psychiat. Assn., Canadian Psychoanalytic Soc. Office: 1739 Bathurst St Toronto ON M5P 3K5 Canada

WIESNER, JEROME BERT, univ. pres.; b. Detroit, May 30, 1915; s. Joseph and Ida (Friedman) W.; B.S., U. Mich., 1937, M.S., 1938; Ph.D., 1950; m. Laya Wainger, Sept. 1, 1940; children—Stepehn Jay, Zachary Kurt, Elizabeth Ann, Joshua A. Asso. dir. U. Mich. Broadcasting Service, 1937-40; chief engr. Acoustical Record Library, Library of Congress, 1940-42; staff Mass. Inst. Tech. Radiation Lab., 1942-45; staff U. Calif. Los Alamos Lab., 1945-46; mem. faculty Mass. Inst. Tech., 1946-71, dir. research lab. electronics, 1952-61, head dept. elec. engring., 1959-60, dean of sci., 1964-66, provost, 1966-71, pres., 1971—; spl. asst. Pres. on sci. and tech., 1961-64; mem. tech. assessment adv. council Office Tech. Assessment, U.S. Congress, 1976—; dir. Celanese Corp., Damon Engring., Schlumberger Ltd.; chmn. Pres.'s Sci. Adv. Com., 1961-64; mem. Army sci. adv. com., 1956-61. Bd. govs. Weizmann Inst. Sci.; trustee WGBH, Am. Found. for Blind; mem. corp. Mus. of Sci. in Boston. Fellow IEEE, Am. Acad. Arts and Scis.; mem. Am. Philos. Soc., AAUP, Am. Geophys. Union, Am. Soc. Engring Edn., Acoustical Soc. Am., Nat. Acad. Scis., Sigma Xi, Phi Kappa Phi, Eta Kappa Nu, Tau Beta Pi. Author: Where Science and Politics Meet, 1964. Home: 61 Shattuck Rd Watertown MA 02172 Office: Mass Inst Tech Cambridge MA 02139

WIETING, WILLIAM FRANK, physician; b. Boston, Oct. 21, 1938; s. Gilbert William and Katherine Nora (Peterson) W.; A.B., Hamilton Coll., 1959; M.D., Boston U., 1963; m. Amey Verna Pepin, Aug. 27, 1960; children—Geoffrey Scott Reid, Carl Philip. Intern, New Britain (Conn.) Gen. Hosp., 1963-64, resident, 1964-65; resident in internal medicine U.S. Naval Hosp., Chelsea, Mass., 1967-69; practice medicine specializing in internal medicine, Portsmouth, N.H., 1971—; cons. and courtesy staff internist York (Me.) Hosp., 1971—; dir. electrocardio graphy York Hosp., 1971—; cons. hyperbaric medicine U.S. Naval Regional Med. Clinic, Portsmouth, N.H., 1973—; lectr. in field; incorporator Portsmouth Hosp., 1977-78, trustee, 1979—; vice chief staff Portsmouth Hosp., 1976-78, chief staff, 1979—; chmn. profl. adv. com. Portsmouth Home Health Agy., Inc., 1975—; clin. instr. physiology and phys. medicine U. N.H., Durham, 1977—. Chmn. York Harbor (Me.) Planning Bd., 1972-74; mem. York Hist. and Improvement Soc., 1976—; bd. dirs. Seacoast Community Concert Assn., 1975—; trustee York United Meth. Ch., 1976—, York Art Assn., 1977—. Served to comdr. M.C. USNR, 1965-71. Recipient Am. Med. Assn. Physician Recognition award, 1976; diplomate Am. Bd. Med. Examiners, Am. Bd. Internal Medicine. Mem. Rockingham County Med. Soc., N.H. Med. Soc., Portsmouth Med. Soc. (pres. 1973-74), ACP, Undersea Med. Soc., Delta Phi. Methodist. Music dir., conductor The York Singers, 1973—. Home: PO Box 462 York Harbor ME 03911 Office: 402 State St Portsmouth NH 03801

WIGAND, ROBERT CHARLES, JR., civil engr.; b. S.I., N.Y., June 17, 1924; s. Robert Charles and Marion Carolyn (Waner) W.; student Colo. Sch. Mines, 1941-43; B.C.E., U. Colo., 1944; m. Wanda Constance Beelick, 1952; children—David Charles, Gwendolyn Mary, James Robert, John Theodore. Supt. trainee Callan Builders Inc., Manhasset, N.Y., 1946; jr. supt. and constrn. supt. Johns-Manville Corp., N.Y. and N.J., 1947-50; real estate supr. N.E. region Household Finance Corp., N.Y.C., 1953-55; engr. Franki Found. Co., N.Y.C., 1955, Worcester, Mass., 1956; engr. Burns & Roe, Inc., N.Y.C., 1957-58, siting engr. Project Mercury tracking stas., 1959-60, Indonesia, 1961, Europe, 1962; project mgr. Alaska tracking sta. NASA, Fairbanks, 1963-64, project mgr. Apollo tracking antennas, Greenbelt, Md., 1965-70, supr. tracking network facilities Greenbelt, 1971—. Served with USMCR, 1943-46, 50-52. Registered profl. engr., N.Y., Md.; registered land surveyor, N.Y., Md. Fellow ASCE, Am. Congress Surveying and Mapping; mem. Nat. Soc. Profl. Engrs., Soc. Am. Mil. Engrs., Assn. Energy Engrs., Marine Corps Res. Officers Assn., Alpha Tau Omega. Episcopalian. Club: Beltsville Garden. Author: The Earth-Moon Test Range, 1970; The Sun, the Moon and the San Fernando Earthquake, 1971; contbr. articles to tech. jours. Home: 4210 Sellman Rd Beltsville MD 20705 Office: Goodard Space Flight Center Greenbelt MD 20771

WIGGINS, CHARLES EDGAR, chemist; b. London, May 29, 1908; s. Arthur Edgar and Ellen (O'Connor) W.; student London U., 1926-29, Leeds U., 1938-39, Southampton U., 1959-60; came to U.S., 1974; m. Eileen Margaret Evans, Aug. 8, 1936; 1 dau., Jennifer Eileen Wiggins Brady. Tchr., lectr. schs., tech. colls. North London, Cambridge, U.K., 1929-41; sr. tech. rep. Central Council Phys. Edn., So. Region Eng., Reading, 1941-49; staff edn. dept. His Majesty's Colonial Service, Freetown, Sierra Leone, 1949-53; departmental head sci. Surrey (U.K.) Schs., 1953-72; analytical, research chemist Jaffrys' Labs. Inc., Ossining, N.Y., 1977—. Fellow Royal Hort. Soc.; mem. Royal Soc. Tchrs., Royal Inst. Pub. Health and Hygiene. Ch. Eng. Conservative. Club: Whippoorwill Country (Armonk, N.Y.). Home: 356 Quaker Rd Chappaqua NY 10514 Office: 109 Croton Ave Ossining NY 10562

WIGGINS, CHRIS, actor; b. Lancashire, Eng., Jan. 13, 1931; s. Walter and May (Ellor) W.; student pub. schs.; m. Erica Margaret Montesole, Mar. 25, 1968. Performer numerous TV plays for various TV networks U.S., Can., U.K. including title role Paul Bernard-Psychiatrist in U.S.A., Can., Australia; author radio, TV plays, documentaries, Children's theatre; creator TV series Angus; appeared as father TV series Swiss Family Robinson; most recent films: Two Solitudes, Highballin', Kavik. Recipient Henry Osborne trophy Dominion Drama Festival, 1955; Telegram Theatre award Toronto (Ont., Can.) Telegram, 1963-64; Etrog award Canadian Film Awards, 1969; Jessie deRivers award dramatic writing Canadian Authors Assn., 1974; Andrew Allan award for best acting performance in radio Assn. Canadian TV and Radio Artists, 1976. Address: Rural Route 1 18th Ave Unionville ON Canada

WIGGINS, JOSEPH JOHN, mfg. engr.; b. Irvington, N.J., June 7, 1925; s. Charles Thomas and Sarah Ann (Masterson) W.; diploma Stevens Inst., 1953; profl. certificates N.Y. U., 1957, Rutgers U., 1963; m. Margaret Coxey, Nov. 28, 1953; children—Eileen, Jean, Joseph, Anne. With Monroe Calculator Co., Orange, N.J., 1947-53; mfg. engr. A/M Varityper Div., East Hanover, N.J., 1960—. Past pres., treas., gen. mgr. Credit Union; active Boy Scouts Am., VITA. Served with U.S. Army, 1944-46. Decorated Combat Inf. Badge. Mem. IEEE, Soc. Mfg. Engrs. (zone capt., mem. edn. com., fin. com.), Armored Preparedness Soc. Democrat. Roman Catholic, Clubs: Computer, Rod and Gun. Home: 7 Merchant Pl Morris Plains NJ 07950

WIGMORE, DAVID, JR., pharm. co. exec.; b. Rotterdam, Netherlands, Mar. 18, 1937; s. David and Lena Cornelia (Van Den Bosch) W.; came to U.S., 1946, naturalized, 1949; B.S. (Gold scholarship medal), Seton Hall U., 1965; m. Marie E. Ippolito, Dec. 3, 1967; 1 son, David. Accountant, Gen. Foods Corp., Hoboken, N.J., 1956-62, auditor, 1962-69; cost engring. mgr. E.R. Squibb & Sons, Inc., New Brunswick, N.J., 1969-77, dir. cost ops. worldwide engring. and constrn., Princeton, N.J., 1978—, dir. and v.p. Mfg. Enterprises div. E.R. Squibb & Sons, Inc., 1978—. Mem. rent leveling bd. Twp. Highland Pk. (N.J.), 1977—. Certified cost engr. Mem. N.J. Soc. Profl. Engrs., Am. Assn. Cost Engrs., Nat. Assn. Accountants, Am. Mgmt. Assn., Jr. C. of C., Order of DeMolay. Republican. Club: Masons. Home: 18 Johnson St Highland Park NJ 08904 Office: PO Box 4000 Princeton NJ 08540

WIGNALL, ERNEST CARL, banker; b. Norwich, Conn., Jan. 22, 1927; s. Thomas John and Anna Margaret (Meyer) W.; grad. Wentworth Inst., Boston, 1950; postgrad. Grad. Sch. Savs. Banking, Brown U., 1960-62, Dartmouth and Amherst colls., 1966-67; m. Laura B. Saeger, June 24, 1959. Asst. sec. Norwich Savs. Soc., 1952-63; asst. v.p. Binghamton (N.Y.) Savs. Bank, 1963-71; v.p. Mechanics Savs. Bank, Hartford, Conn., 71-75, sr. v.p., 1975—; chmn. Binghamton City Planning Commn., 1966-71; dir., chmn. budget and fin. N.Y. Penn Health Planning Council, Inc., 1969-70; housing cons. Broome County Community Resources Found., Inc., 1970-71; adviser Broome County Housing Devel. Corp., 1970-71; housing adviser Found. of State U. N.Y. at Binghamton, 1970. Corporator, Inst. of Living, Hartford, 1972—, Hartford Hosp., 1972—; active United Way Greater Hartford, YMCA of Met. Hartford; trustee, mem. exec. com. Boys' Clubs of Hartford, 1973—; mem. adv. bd. and exec. com. Salvation Army, Hartford, 1973—. Served with USNR, 1945-46. Mem. Greater Hartford, Manchester bds. realtors, Nat. Assn. Mut. Savs. Banks, Savs. Banks Assn. Conn., Mortgage Bankers Assn. Am., Savs. Bank Housing Corp. of Conn. (dir.), Hartford County Home Builders Assn. (dir.), Greater Hartford C. of C. Republican. Lutheran. Clubs: Masons; Univ. (Hartford). Home: 8 Ranger Ln West Hartford CT 06117 Office: 80 Pearl St Hartford CT 06103

WIGNER, EUGENE PAUL, ret. educator; b. Budapest, Hungary, Nov. 17, 1902; s. Anthony and Elisabeth (Einhorn) W.; Chem. Engr. and Dr. Engring., Technische Hochschule, Berlin; hon. D.Sc., U. Wis., 1949, Washington U., 1950, Case Inst. Tech., 1956, U. Chgo., 1957, Colby Coll., 1959, U. Pa., 1961, Thiel Coll., 1964, U. Notre Dame, 1965, Technische Universität Berlin, 1966, Swarthmore Coll., 1966, Universite de Louvain (Belgium), 1967; Dr.Jr., U. Alta., 1967; L.H.D., Yeshiva U., 1963; hon. degrees U. Liege, 1967, U. Ill., 1968, Seton Hall U., 1969, Catholic U., 1969, Rockefeller U., 1970, Israel Inst. Tech., 1973, Lowell U., 1976, Princeton, 1976; m. Amelia Z. Frank, Dec. 23, 1936 (dec. 1937); m. 2d, Mary Annette Wheeler, June 4, 1941 (dec. 1977); children—David Wheeler, Martha Faith. Came to U.S., 1930, naturalized, 1937. Lectr. Princeton, 1930, halftime prof. math. physics, 1931-36, Thomas D. Jones prof. theoretical physics, 1938-71; prof. physics U. Wis., 1936-38; on leave of absence, 1942-45 at Metall. Lab., U. Chgo., 1946-47 as dir. research and devel. Clinton Labs.; dir. Civil Def. Research Project, Oak Ridge, 1964-65; Lorentz lectr. Inst. Lorentz, Leiden, 1957; cons. prof. La. State U., 1971—. Mem. gen. adv. com. AEC, 1952-57, 59-64; mem. math. panel NRC, 1952-54; physics panel NSF, 1953-64; vis. com. Nat. Bur. Standards, 1947-51. Decorated Medal of Merit, 1946; recipient Franklin medal Franklin Inst., 1950; citation N.J. Tchrs. Assn., 1951; Enrico Fermi award AEC, 1958; Atoms for Peace award, 1960; Max Planck medal German Phys. Soc., 1961; Nobel prize for physics, 1963; George Washington award Am. Hungarian Studies Found., 1964; Semmelweiss medal Am. Hungarian Med. Assn., 1965; Nat. Sci. medal, 1969; Pfizer award, 1971; Albert Einstein award, 1972. Fgn. mem. Royal Soc. Eng.; mem. Royal Netherlands Acad. Sci. and Letters, Am. Nuclear Soc. (dir. 1960-61), Am. Phys. Soc. (v.p. 1955, pres. 1956), Am. Math. Soc., Am. Acad. Arts and Scis., Am. Philos. Soc., Nat. Acad. Scis., Austrian Acad. Scis., German Phys. Soc., Franklin Inst., A.A.A.S., Sigma Xi; corr. mem. Acad. Sci., Gottingen, Germany. Address: 8 Ober Rd Princeton NJ 08540

WIKSTROM, NANCY SUE, accountant; b. West Plains, Mo., Feb. 12, 1942; d. Paul Evans and Marie Josephine (Callaway) Schwegman; student S.W. Mo. State Coll., 1960-61; B.S. in Bus. Adminstrn. cum laude, U. Mo., 1964; m. Donald John Wikstrom, Sept. 19, 1970; 1 son, Andrew John. Mem. audit staff Arthur Young & Co., N.Y.C., 1964-69, audit mgr., 1969-72; pvt. practice accounting, N.Y.C., Stamford, Conn., 1972—. C.P.A., N.Y. Mem. Arthur Young Businessperson's Assn. (v.p. 1976-77, treas. 1977—), Am. Inst. C.P.A.'s, N.Y. State Soc. C.P.A.'s, Am. Women's Soc. C.P.A.'s, Am. Soc. Women Accountants, Kappa Alpha Theta. Republican. Methodist. Home and office: 236 West Trail Stamford CT 06903

WILBER, MARGIE ROBINSON, editor; b. Florence, S.C., Apr. 13, 1920; d. Mack Donald and Bessie (Wright) Robinson; A.B., S.C. State Coll., 1942; student Am. U., 1954-55, George Washington U., 1955-58, Dept. Agr. Grad. Sch., 1961, 62, 65, 66; divorced; children—Norman L., Reginald G. Elementary sch. tchr., Marion, S.C., 1942-44; with State Dept., Washington, 1945—, editor, 1962—, asst. chief documentary editing sect., 1978—. Founder, exec. dir., pres. Crime Stoppers Club, Inc., 1967—. Mem. Woman's Nat. Democratic Club. Bd. dirs. D.C. Women's Commn. Crime Prevention; mem. Neighborhood Adv. Commn., Washington, 1976—. Recipient Community Service award Boys Club Greater Washington, 1968; commendation from President Nixon, 1970, Sigma Gamma Rho, 1971; Action Fed. Employee Distinguished Vol. Service award, 1973; award Iota Chi Lambda, 1973; UN Day award, 1974; Met. Washington Vol. Activist award, 1977; named Outstanding Citizen Capitol Hill Restoration Soc., 1974. Mem. Washington Urban League, D.C. Fedn. Bus. and Profl. Women's Clubs, Delta Sigma Theta. Composer: D.C.-Tribute to Nation's Capital, 1971; We Are Future America, 1972; Safe for the Children, 1972. Home: 1366 South Carolina Ave SE Washington DC 20003 Office: Dept State 21st and Virginia Ave NW Washington DC 20520

WILBUR, MARVIN CUMMINGS, clergyman; b. Sprague, Wash., July 12, 1914; s. George Henry and Harriet Starr (Nutter) W.; B.S. with honors, Oreg. State U., 1936; postgrad. George Washington U., 1937-38; B.D., Union Theol. Sem., 1943; D.D., Alma Coll., 1956; m. G. Marie Lacy, Nov. 1, 1945; children—Judy Marie, George Marvin, John Cummings. Ordained to ministry Presbyn. Ch., 1943; Presbyn. chaplain Yale U., 1946-49; dir. pub. info. Union Theol. Sem., 1949-51; sec. program materials United Presbyn. Ch. in U.S.A., N.Y.C., 1951-64; asst. dir. U.P. Found., N.Y.C., 1964—. Served as lt. comdr., chaplain, USNR, 1943-46. Recipient Outstanding Achievement award Nat. Visual Presentation Assn., 1954. Mem. Religious Pub. Relations Council (pres. 1955-57, 1st exec. sec. 1959—), Nat. Visual Communication Assn., Pub. Relations Soc. Am., Sigma Delta Chi, Phi Kappa Phi, Delta Phi Epsilon, Pi Kappa Phi. Editorial adv. bd. Pub. Relations News. Home: 32 Windsor Rd Tenafly NJ 07670 Office: 475 Riverside Dr New York City NY 10027

WILCHINS, SIDNEY ALFRED, physician; b. Paterson, N.J., Feb. 2, 1940; s. Philip A. and Esther (Blake) W.; B.A. in Biol. Scis., Rutgers Coll., 1961; M.D., Georgetown U., 1965; m. Carole Diane Brill, June 23, 1963; children—Joan Helen, Edward Victor. Intern St. Michael Med. Center, Newark, 1965, chief resident, 1966-69; practice medicine, specializing in obstetrics and gynecology, Roselle Park, N.J., 1970—; clin. asso. prof. N.J. Med. Sch., Newark, 1971—; adj. research prof. biomed. engring., dept. mech. engring. N.J. Inst. Tech.; attending physician St. Elizabeth Hosp.; asso. attending Alexian Bros. Hosp., Meml. Gen. Hosp.; asst. attending Elizabeth Gen. Hosp.; cons. obstetrics and gynecology Organon Pharms., Reed & Carnrick Drug Co., Planned Parenthood, Ortho Pharms., Block Drug Co. Bd. dirs. N.J. Fertility Found.; mem. med. assistance adv. council State of N.J., 1978—. Served to lt. comdr. M.C., USNR. Diplomate Am. Bd. Obstetrics and Gynecology. Fellow A.C.S., Am. Coll. Obstetrics and Gynecology, Internat. Coll. Surgeons, Royal Soc. Health, Am. Soc. Abdominal Surgeons, N.J. Obstet. and Gynec. Soc., Acad. Medicine N.J.; mem. Am. Fertility Soc., Med. Soc. N.J., Union County Med. Soc., Royal Soc. Medicine, ACLU, Common Cause, Soc. for Social

Responsibility in Sci., Phi Delta Epsilon, Tau Delta Phi. Contbr. articles to profl. jours. Home: 20 Denman Pl Elizabeth NJ 07208 Office: 14 E Westfield Ave Roselle Park NJ 07204

WILCOX, DAVID ERIC, cons.; b. Cortland, N.Y., Sept. 4, 1939; s. James A. and Lucille (Fiske) C.; B.S. in Elec. Engring., U. Buffalo, 1961; postgrad. Syracuse U., 1965, Marist Coll.; M.S., U. Bridgeport, 1977; m. Phyllipa Ann Wilcox, Jan. 23, 1977; children—Terri L., Cindy A. Research engring. mgr. input/output devices Rome (N.Y.) Air Devel. Center, 1966-70; dir. sales Mercon Inc., Winsooki, Vt., 1970-73, dir., 1972—; partner, exec. v.p. O'Neil & Wilcox Tng. Systems, Newburgh, N.Y., 1973—; instr. Dale Carnegie courses. Pres. N.Y. State Jaycees, 1972-73, chmn. bd., 1973-74; dir. U.S. Jaycees, 1970-71; bd. dirs., v.p. N.Y. State Spl. Olympics, 1972-73. Served to lt. USAF, 1961-65. Registered profl. engr., N.Y. Mem. Soc. Info. Display, IEEE, N.Y., State Soc. Profl. Engrs., Internat. Transactional Analysis Assn., Internat. Platform Assn. Methodist. Author: Information System Sciences, 1965; also articles. Patentee in field. Home: 110a Kridge Dr New Windsor NY 12550 Office: 9 Pacer Dr Newburgh NY 12550

WILCOX, EDWARD DONALD, JR., packaging machinery mfr.; b. Mpls., July 5, 1926; s. Edward Donald and Elsa (Hultgren) W.; B.S. in Mech. Engring., Worcester Poly. Inst., 1949; student Northeastern U., 1950-51; m. Arlene Silva, May 26, 1956; 1 dau., Allison Hadley. Mgr. mech. engring. Lever Bros. Co., 1952-56; mgr. corp. packaging engring. Union Camp Corp., Wayne, N.J., 1965-69, div. gen. mgr., 1969—; v.p., dir. Inglett & Co., Augusta, Ga. Served with USNR, 1944-46. Mem. Packaging Inst., Packaging Machinery Mfrs. Inst. (pres. 1978, dir.). Club: University (N.Y.C.). Home: 35 Sutton Pl New York City NY 10022 Office: 1600 Valley Rd Wayne NJ 07470

WILCOX, RICHARD LEON, pub. relations co. exec.; b. Windsor Locks, Conn., Nov. 6, 1918; s. Charles Leon and Julia Grace (FitzSimons) W.; B.A., Yale, 1940; m. Liliane M.A. Tokolsky-Lisfranc, July 25, 1963; children—Richard Leon, Peter, Paul, Taylor. Editor Life Mag., N.Y.C., 1940-44; pub. info. officer U.S. Coast Guard, 1944-46; free-lance writer, 1946-48; asso. Earl Newsom & Co., N.Y.C., 1948-50; head editorial dept. Exxon Corp., N.Y.C., 1950-63; exec. v.p. Infoplan, Internat., N.Y.C., 1964-69; owner, pres. Wilcox & Co., N.Y.C., 1969—, N.Y.C., 1969—; cons. to Yale Alumni Fund. Served with USCG, 1941-45. Decorated Navy Commendation medal; recipient Nat. Headliners Club award, 1942. Mem. Berzelius Soc. Republican. Episcopalian. Clubs: Elizabethan, Univ., Yale. Author: Literary England, 1943; Of Men and Battle, 1944; contbr. articles and fiction to U.S. and fgn. pubs. Home: 176 E 77th St New York City NY 10021 Office: 59 E 54th St New York City NY 10022

WILCOX, ROBERT LAWRENCE, fraternal assn. exec.; b. Rochester, N.Y., Oct. 19, 1941; s. Joseph Lawrence and Gladys Hazel (Birch) W.; A.A. in Sci., N.Y. State U., Alfred, 1961; B.S.A., U. Ga., 1964, postgrad., 1964-66. Horticulturist, Ga. State Hwy. Dept., Atlanta, 1966-68; asst. exec. dir. Phi Kappa Theta Internat., Worcester, Mass., 1968-70, exec. dir., 1970—, editor publs. Mem. Fraternity Execs. Assn. (treas.), Am., New Eng. socs. assn. execs., Am. Hort. Soc. Club: Univ. (Worcester). Office: 332 Main St Worcester MA 01608

WILDE, DANIEL UNDERWOOD, educator; b. Wilmington, Ohio, Dec. 27, 1937; s. Arthur John and Ruby Dale (Underwood) W.; B.S. in Elec. Engring., U. Ill., 1960; M.S., Mass. Inst. Tech., 1962, Ph.D., 1966. Research instr. medicine Boston U. Med. Sch., 1964-66; asst. prof. info. adminstrn. U. Conn., Storrs, 1966-69, asso. prof., 1970-75, prof., 1976—; asso. dir. New Eng. Research Application Center, Storrs, 1966-72, dir., 1973—; dir. Engring. Index, Inc. Cons., Am. Soc. for Metals, 1973—. Served with USAF. Recipient NASA Pub. Service award, 1975. Mem. Am. Soc. for Info. Sci., Assn. for Computing Machinery, IEEE, Assn. Info. and Dissemination Centers (sec.-treas. 1977—). Author: Introduction to Computing: Problem Solving, Algorithms and Data Structures, 1973; contbr. articles to profl. jours. Home: 188 Cedar Swamp Rd Storrs CT 06268 Office: NERAC Mansfield Profl Park Storrs CT 06268

WILDE, GEORGE HARVEY, assn. exec.; b. Jamaica, N.Y., Nov. 22, 1924; s. George Harvey and Irma (Bauman) W.; student pub. schs. Freeport, N.Y.; m. Mary Costas, May 7, 1949; children—Donna Marie Wilde Enfield, Dennis George. Receiving and shipping supr. Jamison Plastics, North Bellmore, N.Y., 1950-61; purchasing and expediting exec. Lerner Mfg., Melville, N.Y., 1961—; pres., founder Marine Environ. Council L.I. (formerly Save Our Bays Assn.), Seaford, 1971—; environ. adviser Seaford Planning Council, 1970—; coordinator L.I. Joint Action Network. Vice pres. Wantagh Preservation Soc., 1970-71. Served with USN, 1943-46. Recipient Appreciation certificate EPA, 1976. Mem. Am. Littoral Soc., Nat. Wildlife Fedn., Nature Conservancy, Nat. Geog. Soc., Smithsonian Assos. Editor, publisher L.I. Environ. Directory, 1976. Home: 2348 Maple St Seaford NY 11783

WILDEBUSH, JOSEPH FREDERICK, former trade assn. exec., economist; b. Bklyn., July 18, 1910; s. Harry Frederick and Elizabeth (Stolzenberg) W.; A.B., Columbia, 1931, postgrad. law sch., 1932; J.D., Bklyn. Law Sch., 1934; m. Martha Janssens, July 18, 1935; children—Diane Elaine (Mrs. Solon Finkelstein), Joan Marilyn (Mrs. Bobby Berry); m. 2d, Edith Sorensen, May 30, 1964. Admitted to N.Y. State bar, 1934, Fed. bar, 1935; practice law, N.Y.C., 1934-41; labor relations dir. Botany Mills, Passaic, N.J., 1945-48; exec. v.p. Silk and Rayon Printers and Dyers Assn. Am., Inc., Paterson, N.J., 1948-71; exec. v.p. Textile Printers and Dyers Labor Relations Inst., Paterson, 1954-72; mem. panel labor arbitrators Fed. Mediation and Conciliation Service, N.Y. State Mediation Bd., Am. Arbitration Assn., N.J. Mediation Bd., N.J. Pub. Employment Commn.; co-adj. faculty Rutgers U., 1948—; lectr. Pres., Pascack Valley Hosp., Westwood, N.J., 1950-64, chmn. bd., 1964-66, chmn. emeritus, 1967—; pres. Group Health Ins. N.J., 1962-66, chmn. dir., 1966—; dir. Group Health Ins. N.Y., 1950-75. Served as maj. C.E., AUS, 1941-43; Mem. N.Y. County Lawyers Assn., Am. Acad. Polit. and Social Sci., Indsl. Relations Research Assn., Ret. Officers Assn., Nat. Geog. Soc. Lutheran. Author articles profl. jours. Home and Office: 37 James Terr Pompton Lakes NJ 07442

WILDER, MARION BURT (MRS. RICHARD B. WILDER), civic worker; b. N.Y.C.; d. George Frederick and Grace (Knight) Burt; student pvt. schs.; m. John Williams Morgan; 1 son, George Frederick; m. Richard B. Wilder, Oct. 27, 1972. Bd. govs., v.p. Internat. Garden Club, Judson Health Center; hon. pres. women's com.; dir. N.Y. Women's Bible Soc.; mem. spl. fine arts com. State Dept. Mem. Inst. Social Scis., Army Relief Soc., Nat. Soc. Colonial Dames State N.Y., Soc. Daus. Holland Dames, Nat. Trust Historic Preservation, Huguenot Soc. Am., Met. Mus. Art (fellow), Am. Fedn. Arts, Soc. Four Arts Palm Beach, N.Y. Bible Soc. Episcopalian. Clubs: Colony; Regency Whist of New York; Everglades; Bath and Tennis (Palm Beach). Home: 200 E 66th St New York City NY 10021 also 389 S Lake Dr Palm Beach FL 33480 also Levin Brooks Kent CT

WILDES, WILLIAM HENRY, oil co. exec.; b. Boston, June 7, 1921; s. Clifford B. and Evelyn (Albano) W.; ed. Bentley Sch. Accounting and Finance, 1940-42, Northeastern U., 1950; m. Rita A. Benoit, Jan. 26, 1946; children—William H., Marie A. (Mrs. Richard J. Godart), Katherine E. (Mrs. Steven L. Bianchi), Nancy E. (Mrs. William B. Naughton). With Buckley & Scott Co., affiliate Atlantic Richfield, Watertown, Mass., 1939—, v.p., 1958—, sec.-treas., 1961—, adminstrv. v.p., 1961—, pres., treas., 1975—. Officer, dir. affiliated corps. Past chmn. Lexington Town 4-H Com., 1960-63; trustee various trust funds; ordained permanent deacon Archdiocese Boston, 1977. Served with AUS, 1942-45; ETO. Decorated Bronze Star medal. Mem. Mass. Oil Heat Assn. (past pres., dir.), Better Home Heat Council (dir., treas.), New Eng. Fuel Inst. (dir.), Northeastern U. Small Bus. Assos. (past dir.), Cath. Accountants Guild (past pres.). Club: K.C. Home: 3 Russell Sq Lexington MA 02173 Office: Riverside Park Weston MA 02193

WILDNAUER, RICHARD HARRY, pharm. co. exec.; b. New Kensington, Pa., Feb. 14, 1940; s. Richard Michael and Rosemary Elizabeth (Moore) W.; B.S. in Chemistry, St. Vincent Coll., 1962; Ph.D. in Biochemistry, W.Va. U., 1966; postgrad. biochemistry (NSF fellow) U. Kans., 1967; M.B.A. in Mgmt., Rider Coll., 1974; m. Sharon Ann Novick, Jan. 22, 1966; 1 dau., Tara Lynne. NIH trainee W.Va. U., 1963-66; with exploratory research div. Domestic Operating Co., Johnson & Johnson, New Brunswick, N.J., 1968-77, sr. research asso. in skin biology, 1975, asso. mgr. tech. planning, 1975-77; sr. project coordinator new products McNeil Pharm. Div. McNeil Labs., Ft. Washington, Pa., 1977—; mem. adj. faculty Center Profl. Devel., East Brunswick. Mem. N.Y. Acad. Scis., Soc. Investigative Dermatology, Sigma Xi. Roman Catholic. Contbr. articles to profl. jours.; reviewer Jour. Soc. Cosmetic Chemists, Jour. Investigative Dermatology. Home: 6 Pilgrim Run East Brunswick NJ 08816 Office: 500 Office Center Dr Fort Washington PA 19034

WILDRICK, KENYON JONES, clergyman; b. Rahway, N.J., June 14, 1933; s. Stanley B. and Adele (Jones) W.; B.A., Trinity Coll., Hartford, Conn., 1955; B.D., Princeton U., 1958, Th.M., 1962; m. Nancy Ruth Mersfelder, Aug. 23, 1958; children—Catherine Ruth, Margaret Jeanne, Kenyon Douglas. Ordained to ministry Presbyterian Ch., 1958; asst. minister Community Congregational Ch., Short Hills, N.J., 1958-61, asso. minister, 1961-67, sr. minister, 1967—; campus ministry Middle Atlantic Conf., 1962-65. Bd. dirs. Milburn-Short Hills chpt. ARC, 1963-64; ch. and ministry com. N.J. Assn., 1965—; bd. dirs. Gottscho Kidney Found., 1973-74, Humanity Community Center, Newark, 1973-76; pres. bd. trustees Overlook Protestant Chaplaincy Program, 1973—. Mem. Delta Phi. Club: Rotary (dir. Milburn Club 1973). Home: 79 Addison Dr Short Hills NJ 07078 Office: 200 Hartshorn Dr Short Hills NJ 07078

WILES, JOSEPH ST. CLAIR, pharmacologist; b. Bklyn., July 27, 1914; s. Joseph Emanuel and Lillian (Yearwood) W.; student evening div. Bklyn. Coll., 1933-39; A.B., Morris Brown Coll., 1941; postgrad. (Com. on Grad. Study-John Herndon scholar) Atlanta U., 1941-42, Columbia, 1950, Johns Hopkins U., 1962; m. Esther Louise Ogburn, June 30, 1945; children—Carmen (Mrs. Curtis Artis), Carole (Mrs. Curtis Gibson, Jr.). With Army Corps Engrs., various locations, 1942-43, biologist med. research lab., Edgewood Arsenal, Md., 1946-52, research pharmacologist Edgewood Arsenal biomed. lab., Aberdeen Proving Ground, Md., 1952—. Cons. in field. Pres. Rosemont Neighborhood Improvement Assn., 1962-68, 70-72; chmn. personnel com. Teen Centers div. Model Cities Agy., Balt., 1971—. Bd. dirs., v.p. St. James Community Service Ventures, Inc., Balt.; bd. mgrs. Center City br. YMCA, Balt. Served with AUS, 1943-46, 50-51; ETO, PTO. Recipient Sustained Superior Performance award Dept. Army, 1959, Quality Increase award Dept. Army, 1967; William A. Fountain and John H. Lewis Status Achievement award Morris Brown Coll., 1970. Mem. Research Soc. Am., AAAS, Am. Def. Assn., Soc. Toxicology, N.Y. Acad. Scis., Internat. Assn. Approved Basketball Ofcls. (dir.), Sigma Xi, Phi Beta Sigma. Episcopalian. Patentee in field. Contbr. articles to profl. jours. Home: 1423 N Ellamont St Baltimore MD 21216 Office: Toxicology Br Chem/Physiol Sect Chem Systems Lab Aberdeen Proving Ground MD 21010

WILES, MARGARET ISOBEL, violinist; b. Hamilton, Ohio, Dec. 25, 1911; d. Bertram Thompson and Dovie Mae (Osborne) Jones; Mus.B., DePauw U., Greencastle, Ind., 1935; student Royal Acad. Music, London, 1933-34; pupil of Arthur Catterall, Raphael Bronstein; m. Gordon Pitts Wiles, Jan. 6, 1937; children—John Christopher, Peter Thompson. Violinist, Durban (S. Africa) Broadcast Orch., 1940, Durban Symphony Orch., 1941-45; concertmaster Pietermaritzburg (S. Africa) Symphony Orch., 1945-51, Radio String Quartet, Durban, 1942-45; soloist throughout S. Africa, 1937-54; violinist Trenton, Princeton, N.J. and Little Colonial symphony orchs., 1951-57; asst. concertmaster Eastern Conn. Symphony Orch., 1957-71; instr. violin and viola Conn. Coll., 1957-75; condr. Conn. Coll. Symphony Orch., 1957-75, condr. emeritus, 1975—. Recipient Gold diploma in viola Natal (S. Africa) Eisteddfod, 1937. Mem. AAUP, Mu Phi Epsilon, Alpha Phi. Presbyn. Composer string quartets; editor viola instrn. book. Address: 30 Colony Rd East Lyme CT 06333

WILEY, BARRY HOLLAND, electronics co. exec.; b. Iola, Kans., Sept. 18, 1936; s. William G. and Kathryn (Holland) W.; B.A., U. Calif. at Berkeley, 1958; M.B.A., Harvard U., 1967; M.A., U. So. Calif., 1965; m. Leanna M. Hauder, June 15, 1963; children—Ann-Kristina, Timothy Holland, Michael Christian. Mem. physics group Solid State Radiations Inc., Los Angeles, 1961-63; project leader research and devel. TRW Semicondrs. Inc., Lawndale, Calif., 1963-65; mktg. project mgr. Air Reduction Co., Murray Hill, N.J., 1967-68; mgr. mktg. advanced tech. operation TRW Semicondrs. Inc., Lawndale, 1969-70, asst. plant mgr. TRW Lynn (Mass.) Facility, 1970-71; co-founder, pres. Tympanium Corp., Woburn, Mass., 1971—. Asso. dir. Chaplain's Discussion Group, Mass. Correctional Inst., Concord, Mass., 1975—. Served to capt. USMCR, 1958-61. Mem. Am. Phys. Soc., Lighter than Air Soc., Brit. Sch. Archaeology Iraq, Smaller Bus. Assn. NE, Harvard Bus. Sch. Alumni Assn.-Boston. Author: Nuclear Radiation Effects Manual, 1965; Introduction to Motorcycle Electrical Systems, 1975. Office: Tympanium Corp 116 Cummings Park Woburn MA 01801

WILEY, BERT CARLTON, physician; b. Covington, Ky., Mar. 7, 1908; s. Charles Herbert and Harriett Elizabeth (Hukill) W.; M.E., U. Cin., 1931; LL.B., LaSalle Extension U., Chgo., 1939; A.B., Ohio State U., 1940, M.D., 1943; m. Lucile Charlotte Kester, Oct. 21, 1944; 1 dau., Alice Constance. Materials handling engr. Alvey Ferguson Mfg. Co., Cin., 1930-38; vertical boring mill designer, King Machine Tool Co., Cin., 1935-36; with law office, Covington, 1934-35; intern Nashville Gen. Hosp., 1943: asst. dir. phys. med. dept. Miami Valley Hosp., Dayton, Ohio, 1944; dir. phys. medicine dept., Miami Valley Hosp., Dayton, Ohio, 1944-50; dir. phys. medicine and rehab. Acuff Clinic, Knoxville, Tenn., 1950-52; dir. phys. medicine dept., Conemaugh Valley Meml. Hosp., Johnstown, Pa., 1952-75; chief rehab. medicine service VA Hosp., Altoona, Pa., 1976—, pres. med. and dental staff. Served to capt. M.C. U.S. Army, 1953-54. Registered profl. engr., Ohio; lic. physician, Ohio, Tenn., Ky., Pa., Nebr., Calif. Mem. Blair County, Pa. Med. Socs., AMA, Am. Congress Rehab. Medicine, Am. Acad. Phys. Medicine and Rehab., Pitts. Inst. Legal Medicine. Baptist. Designer, maker phys. medicine equipment, early moist-heat unit displayed at Smithsonian Inst., 1973; contbr. articles in field to profl. publs. Home: Box 215 Route 4 Bedford PA 15522 Office: VA Hospital Altoona PA 16603

WILEY, TARLEY TARSON, cons. engr.; b. Champaign, Ill., May 17, 1908; s. Carroll Carson and Sina Belle (Adams) W.; B.S., U. Ill., 1930, M.S., 1931; m. Lyrrell Aline Sutton, Apr. 2, 1931; children—Carolyn (Mrs. Robert Millett), Cynthia (Mrs. Cynthia Kobarg), Catherine (Mrs. John Powers). Asst. engr. Ill. Div. Hwys., 1931-38; traffic control engr. Detroit, 1939-44, asst. city traffic engr., 1945-48; exec. dir. Dept. Traffic Engring., N.Y.C., 1949-50, commr. traffic, 1951-61; cons. traffic engr., pres. T.T. Wiley & Assos., Plainview, N.Y., 1962—. Adj. prof. civil engring., N.Y. U., N.Y.C., 1956-60; mem. Nat. Joint Com. on Uniform Traffic Control Devices, 1956-61. Recipient Engr. of Year award N.Y. Soc. Profl. Engrs., 1953, Distinguished Pub. Service award, Nat. Alpha Kappa Lambda, 1962, N.Y. Citizens Traffic Safety Bd. award, 1960, others; registered profl. engr., N.Y., N.J., Ohio, Mich., other states. Fellow ASCE, Inst. Transp. Engrs.; mem. Nat. Soc. Profl. Engrs., Transp. Research Bd. (asso.), Alpha Kappa Lambda, Chi Epsilon, Sigma Xi, Phi Eta Sigma. Methodist and Ref. Ch. Am. (deacon 1970—). Home: 315 Kenmore Rd Douglaston NY 11363 Office: 182 Fairchild Ave Plainview NY 11803

WILHELM, FREDERICK HENRY, physician; b. N.Y.C., July 7, 1930; s. Seymour Frederick and Doris (Fuld) W.; B.A., Columbia U., 1952; M.D., Jefferson Med. Coll., 1956; m. Alison Bradley, May 8, 1960; children—Barbara Ann, Frederick Henry, Pamela May, Scott David. Rotating intern Jefferson Med. Coll. Hosp., 1956-57; resident in medicine Beth Israel Hosp., N.Y.C., 1957-58, Hosp., N.Y.C., 1958, 60-62; med. officer Glenn Dale (Md.) Hosp., 1962-64; practice family Hyattsville, Md., 1964—; mem. staff Prince George Gen. Hosp., 1964—, vice chief family practice, 1973—; mem. staff Prince Georges Doctors Hosp., Providence Hosp.; clin. asst. prof. medicine Med. Sch., Georgetown U., Washington; preceptor family practice U. Md., Prince Georges Hosp. Served as lt. M.C., USNR, 1958-60. Diplomate Am. Bd. Family Practice. Fellow Am. Acad. Family Practice (charter); mem. AMA, Am. Heart Assn., Am. Soc. Internal Medicine, D.C. Thoracic Soc., Prince Georges County, (dir.), Md. (del. U.S. Pharmacopeal Conv.) med. socs. Democrat. Jewish. Clubs: Kenmont Swim, Cheverly Swim and Racquet. Office: 5807 Annapolis Rd Hyattsville MD 20784

WILHELM, JOSEPH LAWRENCE, archbishop; b. Walkerton, Ont. Can., Nov. 16, 1909; s. John and Magdalena (Uhrich) W.; J.C.L., Ottawa U., 1948. Ordained priest Roman Cath. Ch., 1934; asst. bishop's sec., Hamilton, Ont., 1934-40: chaplain Canadian Army, 1940-45; pastor St. Peter and Paul Ch., Hamilton, 1948-63; aux. bishop of Calgary, Alta., 1963-67; archbishop of Kingston, Ont., 1967—. Decorated Mil. Cross. Address: 279 Johnson St Kingston ON Canada

WILHELM, MICHAEL LEONARD, chiropractor; b. Uniontown, Pa., Sept. 5, 1945; s. Frank L. and Sue (Wyatt) W.; B.S., California (Pa.) State Coll., 1967; student Logan Coll. Chiropractic, 1969-71; D. Chiropractic, Palmer Coll. Chiropractic, 1973; postgra d. W.Va. U., 1968-69, Pa. State U., 1971. Tchr. elementary sch. Brownsville (Pa.) Area High Sch. Bd., 1968-69, Laurel Highlands Sch. Bd., Uniontown, 1969-70, Marietta (Ga.) pub. schs., 1967; individual practice chiropractic Brownsville, Pa., 1973—. Mem. Nat. Bd. Chiropractic Examiners, Cheyenne, Wyo.; del. White House Conf. on Children and Youth. Active Boy Scouts Am.; alumni bd. California State Coll.; trustee U. Pasadena Coll. Chiropractic, Found. for Advancement Chiropractic Research Inc. Certified in clin. nutrition Nat. Coll. Chiropractic. Mem. Am., Pa. chiropractic assns., W.Va., Ohio, Okla., Southwestern Pa. chiropractic socs., Internat. Arthritis Soc., Internat. Acad. Preventive Medicine, Internat. Coll. Applied Nutrition, Ohio Council Chiropractic Neurology. Mem. Christian Ch. Clubs: Elks, AMORC. Home: Old Mill Rd Chalk Hill PA 15421 Office: 109 Water St Brownsville PA 15417

WILHELMI, HENRY PAUL, landscape architect, community planning cons.; b. Syracuse, N.Y., Oct. 3, 1930; s. William and Caroline Albertine (Spingler) W.; B.S., Syracuse U., 1953, postgrad., 1956-63; m. Eleanor Guilfoyle Jerome, Aug. 4, 1973; children—Lauren, Eric, Lisa; stepchildren—Timothy, James, Kathleen, Karen. Landscape architect Nat. Park Service, Richmond, Va., 1955-56; planner Wheelwright Stevenson & Langran, Phila., 1957; prin. city planner Dept. Urban Improvement, City of Syracuse, 1958-64; partner Duryea and Wilhelmi, Syracuse, 1965-75; v.p. Duryea and Wilhelmi Profl. Corp., 1975—; pres. 1208 James Properties Ltd., 1971—. Occasional lectr., critic Syracuse U., 1959—; mem. Onondaga County Environ. Mgmt. Council, Onondaga County Planning Fedn. Served with AUS, 1953-55. Mem. Am. Soc. Landscape Architects, Nat. Assn. Housing and Redevel. Ofcls., Landmarks Assn. Central N.Y., Nat. Trust Historic Preservation. Episcopalian. Home: 7476 Elmcrest Rd Liverpool NY 13088 Office: 1208 James St Syracuse NY 13203

WILKERSON, WILLIAM GARFIELD, physician; b. Camden, N.J., June 16, 1916; s. Wyatt and Eva Gertrude (Dawson) W.; A.B., Lincoln U., 1941; postgrad., N.Y.U., 1945-46; M.D., U. Geneva (Switzerland), 1951; L.H.D., St. Peter's Coll., 1976; 1 dau., Iris Diane. Intern, Quincy (Mass.) City Hosp., 1952-53; resident in obstetrics Margaret Hague Hosp., Jersey City, 1953-54, Met. Hosp., N.Y.C., 1955-57; resident in surgery Kings County Hosp., Bklyn., 1954-55; spl. fellow in medicine Meml. Hosp. for Cancer and Allied Diseases, N.Y.C., 1957-59; mem. staff Margaret Hague Maternity Hosp., Jersey City, 1957-74; asst. med. dir. State Div. Disability Determination, 1974—; med. dir. Family Planning Program of Hudson County, 1970-74, N.J. State Drug Abuse Program, 1966-72; sr. med. examiner FAA; instr. N.Y.U. Mem. N.J. Assn. for Mental Health; pres. bd. dirs. Hudson County Mental Health Assn., 1966-71; active Am. Cancer Soc., ARC, YMCA, Goodwill Industries Am., NAACP, others; trustee, treas. Monumental Baptist Ch.; licensed minister Bapt. Ch.; chmn. Jersey City Human Rights Commn, 1975—. Served with USAF, 1941-46. Recipient Man of Achievement award Hudson County, 1966; 50th Anniversary Nat. Brotherhood award NCCJ, 1978. Fellow Am. Coll. Obstetricians and Gynecologists, Royal Coll. Surgeons (London); mem. Am. Soc. Abdominal Surgeons, Royal Acad. Med. (London), Christian Med. Soc., Flying Physicians Assn., Civil Aviation Med. Assn. Club: Lions. Office: 428 Bergen Ave Jersey City NJ 07304

WILKEY, MALCOLM RICHARD, judge; b. Murfreesboro, Tenn., Dec. 6, 1918; s. Malcolm Newton and Elizabeth (Gilbert) W., A.B., Harvard U., 1940, LL.B., 1948; m. Emma Secul Depolo, Dec. 21, 1959. Admitted to Tex. bar, 1948, N.Y. bar, 1963, U.S. Supreme Ct. bar, 1952, Ct. of Appeals, D.C. Circuit, 1958; partner firm Butler Binion Rice & Cook, 1948-54, 61-63; U.S. atty. So. Dist. Tex., 1954-58; asst. atty. gen. U.S., 1958-61; sec., asso. gen. counsel Kennecott Copper Corp. 1963-67, sec., gen. counsel, 1967-70; judge U.S. Ct. Appeals, D.C. Circuit, 1970—. Del. Republican Nat. Conv., 1960. Served from 2d lt. to lt. col. U.S. Army, 1941-45. Fellow Am. Bar Found.; mem. Am. Bar Assn. (commn. on a nat. inst. of justice), Assn. Bar City N.Y., Am. Law Inst., Phi Beta Kappa, Delta Sigma Rho. Club: Met. (Washington). Home: 540 N St SW Washington DC 20024 Office: US Ct Appeals Washington DC 20001

WILKINS, LEE GERTRUDE, psychologist; b. Mass.; d. David and Rae (Zweibelson) Abowitt; R.N., Bklyn. Jewish Hosp., 1936; R.L., St. Mary's Hosp., Bklyn., 1954; B.S., N.Y. U., 1956, M.A., 1958, Ph.D., 1964; certificate in psychoanalysis Postgrad. Center for Mental Health, N.Y.C., 1970, certificate in group psychoanalysis, 1974, certificate in family analytic therapy, 1976; diplomate in clin. hypnosis, 1976. married; children—Robert Stephen, Jane Leslie. Postdoctoral trainee Columbia, 1964-65; practice psychology specializing in psychoanalysis, hypnotherapy, behavioral therapy, N.Y.C., 1966—; asso. mem. staff Postgrad. Center for Mental Health, 1966—,supr., 1966-70, 73—; supr. Morton Prince Clinic, N.Y.C., 1972—; dir. Murray Hill Psychol. Group, N.Y.C., 1973—; condr. workshops. Bd. dirs. Inst. for Research in Hypnosis, N.Y.C. NIMH fellow, 1958-60; USPHS fellow, 1961-62; registered nurse, N.Y. State; certified psychologist, N.Y. State; registered record librarian, internat. Mem. Am., N.Y. State, Bklyn. psychol. assns., Assn. Advancement Behavior Therapy, Soc. Clin., Exptl. Hypnosis, Profl. Soc. Postgrad. Center for Mental Health, Sigma Theta Tau. Contbr. articles to profl. jours. Home: 280 Ocean Pkwy Brooklyn NY 11218 Office: 386 Park Ave S New York NY 10016

WILKINS, LLOYD HENDERSON, JR., elec. engr.; b. Norfolk, Va., July 5, 1929; s. Lloyd Henderson and Annie Bell (Porter) W.; B.E.E., Milw. Sch. Engring., 1958; m. Elois Angeles Smith, June 27, 1959; children—Karen Yvette, Lloyd Henderson. Elec. engr., automation AC Electronics div. Gen. Motors Corp., Milw., 1958-62, research labs. Westinghouse Elec. Corp., Pitts., 1962-64; adv. engr. systems products div. IBM, E. Fishkill, N.Y., 1964—. Bd. mgrs. N.Y.State, Am. Bapt. Chs., 1975-78, chmn. commn. Christian end., 1976-77. Mem. IEEE. Republican. Home: 18 Nassau Rd Poughkeepsie NY 12601 Office: IBM Dept 237A Bldg 300 East Fishkill NY 12533

WILKINSON, GEORGE SHOEMAKER, JR., accountant; b. Camden, N.J., July 25, 1940; s. George Shoemaker and Esther A. (Knaller) W.; B.S., Rutgers U., 1967, certificate in data processing, 1972; fin. courses Temple U., Rider Coll.; m. Josephine A. Murphy, Aug. 13, 1966; children—Jayne, Renee, Laura. Accounting clk. Garlock Inc., Camden, 1958-62; sr. accountant Robert C. Perina, C.P.A., Camden, 1962-67; fin. analyst RCA Service Co., Cherry Hill, N.J., 1967-68; accountant Arthur S. Kranley & Co., mgmt. cons., Cherry Hill, 1968-69; sr. staff accountant Main La Frentz & Co., C.P.A.'s, Phila., 1969-71; sec., treas. South Jersey Port Corp., Camden, 1971—; adj. faculty Camden County Coll., Blackwood, N.J., 1974—. Coach, dir. Merchantville (N.J.) Boys Baseball League; past pres. Merchantville Democratic Club; Camden County committeeman from Merchantville, 1976-77; councilman Borough of Merchantville, 1976—. C.P.A., N.J., Pa. Mem. Am., Pa. insts. C.P.A.'s, N.J. Soc. C.P.A.'s, Am., Nat. assns. accountants, Assn. Water Transp. Accounting Officers, Port of Phila. Maritime Soc., Rutgers U. Alumni Assn., Scarlet R Club. Democrat. Home: 127 Springfield Ave Merchantville NJ 08109 Office: PO Box 129 Broadway and Morgan Blvd Camden NJ 08101

WILKINSON, HARRY EDWARD, JR., bus. exec.; b. Richmond Heights, Mo., June 30, 1930; s. Harry Edward and Virginia (Shelton) W.; B.A. in Physics, Princeton U., 1952; M.B.A., Washington U., St. Louis, 1957; D.B.A., Harvard U., 1960; m. Sara Beth Kikendall, Aug. 30, 1958;children—Linda Beth, Cheryl Susan. Staff engr. Southwestern Bell Telephone Co., St. Louis, 1954-57., traffic engr. New Eng. Tel. & Tel. Co., Boston, 1957-60; sr. mgmt. cons. Harbridge House Inc., Boston, 1961-65; dean bus. adminstrn. Northeastern U., 1965-67, dir. Mgmt. Inst., 1965-67; pres., chmn. bd. Univ. Affiliates, Inc., 1967—; cons. to govt. and industry. Served to lt. (j.g.) USNR, 1952-54. Licensed psychologist, Mass. Mem. Soc. Advancement Mgmt. (nat. v.p. program devel. 1965-67), Acad. Mgmt., Am. Personnel and Guidance Assn., Am. Soc. Tng. and Devel., Greater Boston C. of C., Harvard Bus. Sch. Assn. Republican. Clubs: Executives, Harvard (Boston); Harvard Faculty (Cambridge, Mass.). Home: 8818 Cold Spring Rd Potomac MD 20854

WILKINSON, NANA MIRIAM SLATEN (MRS. WESLEY O. WILKINSON), realtor; b. Dahlgren, Ill., June 8, 1912; d. John R. and Fleta E. (Berry) Slaten; student Carthage Coll., 1930-32; grad. Real Estate Inst.; m. Wesley Owen Wilkinson, Feb. 14, 1945. Sec. pres.' office DePauw U., Greencastle, Ind., 1935-37; exec. sec. to v.p. Beach & Arthur Paper Co., Indiana Pa. and N.Y.C., 1937-45; realtor Henry B. Trachy Real Estate Agy., Franklin, N.H., 1970—; mem. 3d Dist. Belknap County N.H. Ho. of Reps., 1970-73. Mem. N.H. Fedn. Garden Clubs, 1957—, 1st v.p., 1966-67, state pres., 1967-69, legis. chmn., 1971-74, editor Lilac Letter, 1969-71; mem. Nat. Council State Garden Clubs, 1957—, treas. New Eng. region Symposium, 1969-71, chmn. New Eng. Regional Youth activities, 1969-71, mem. nominating com. New Eng. region 1971—, life mem., 1969—; pres. Tilton-Northfield Woman's Club, 1953-55; pres. Tilton Garden Club, 1959-61, now life mem.; mem. organizational study com., mem. nat. conv. com. Nat. Council State Garden Clubs, 1975—; mem. Tilton Park Commn., 1963—; mem. Tilton Planning Bd., 1969-70, Tilton Budget Com., 1976—; mem. Flood Plains Commn. N.H., 1972-74; treas. Tilton Republican Com., 1958—. Trustee Arthur S. Brown Found., 1973—. Recipient Presdl. citation N.H. Fedn. Garden Clubs, 1970, 73, Order Purple Finch for outstanding woman, 1970. Mem. Nat. Assn. Real Estate Brokers, Lakes Region Bd. Realtors, Nat. Wildlife Fedn., Audubon Soc. N.H., Nat. Resources Council N.H., Tilton Woman's Club, Nat. Assn. Parliamentarians, Mass. Horticulture Soc., Soc. for Protection N.H. Forests, Nat. Assn. Women Legislators. Congregationalist (pres. Ladies' Circle 1961-62, 70-71; chmn. music com. 1971—; trustee (1st woman 1965-70). Home: Mountain View Dr Tilton NH 03276 Office: 395 Central St Franklin NH 03235

WILKINSON, THOMAS ALLAN, engring. geologist; b. Fort Worth, Jan. 6, 1932; s. Joseph Ackinson and Grace (Wythe) W.; student Midwestern U., 1949-50; B.S. in Geology, Okla. U., 1954, M.S., 1956, postgrad., 1958-59; m. Rosalyn Sarah Schliz, Dec. 21, 1959; children—Kristin Allan, Nachelle Marie, Tedric Gordon. With Army Corps Engrs., various locations, 1959—, dist. geologist, Buffalo, 1965-71, chief foundations, materials br., 1971—. Lectr. Canisius Coll., Buffalo, 1971-72. Co-pres. Willow Ridge PTA, Amherst, N.Y., 1972-73. Served to 1st lt. C.E., 8th Army, AUS, 1955-57; Korea. Kansas City Assn. Trusts, Founds. scholar, 1960-61. Mem. Assn. Engring. Geologists, Soc. Am. Mil. Engrs., Geol. Soc. Am., Sigma Xi. Office: 1776 Niagara St Buffalo NY 14207

WILKS, PHILLIP HOWARD, sci. adminstr.; b. Dayton, Ohio, Apr. 13, 1934; s. Hyman Louis and Ida (Ganzer) W.; Chem. Engr., U. Cin., 1956; M.S., Northwestern U., 1957; Ph.D. (Westinghouse fellow 1965), U. Pitts., 1966; m. Geraldine Torf, Dec. 18, 1955; children—Andrew, David, Hugh. Engr., Gen. Electric Corp., Cin., 1957-62; adv. engr. Westinghouse Electric Co., Pitts., 1962-69; tech. dir. IONARC Indsl. Plasma Materials Co., Concord, N.H., 1969-75; pres. Plasma Materials Inc., Manchester, N.H., 1975—. Vice-chmn. Gordon Conf. Plasma Chemistry, Proctor Acad., Andover, N.H., 1974, chmn., 1976. Bd. dirs. Community Concerts Assn., Manchester, N.H., 1973—. Registered profl. engr., Ohio, N.H. Mem. Am. Chem. Soc., Sigma Xi, Tau Beta Pi. Jewish. Author: (with others) plasma chemistry sect. Chemical and Process Technology Ency., 1974. Developer 1st commercially successful indsl. scale plasma chemistry process, 1971. Home: 130 N Bend Dr Manchester NH 03104 Office: 75 W Hancock St Manchester NH 03102

WILL, CHARLES AUGUSTUS, ins. co. exec.; b. N.Y.C., Apr. 10, 1917; s. Charles and Gertrude (Zauner) W.; B.S., N.Y. U., 1951; m. Kathleen O'Donnell, Aug. 7, 1943; children—John Barry, Mary Kathleen, Peter Joseph. Chief underwriter Guardian Life Ins. Co. Am., 1948-50, asst. underwriting sec., 1950-60, underwriting sec., 1960-67; v.p. underwriting Cologne Life Reins. Co., Stamford, Conn., 1967-71, sr. v.p., 1971—. Served with USNR, 1944-46. Mem. Home Office Life Underwriters Assn., Inst. Home Office Underwriters (pres. 1957-58), Assurance Med. Soc. Gt. Britain, S. African Assn. Med. Underwriters. Club: Nyack Field. Home: 81 River Rd Grandview-on-Hudson NY 10960 Office: 1200 Bedford St Stamford CT 06905

WILLARD, HARRY LENTZ, research orgn. exec.; b. Fairfield, Ill., Jan. 16, 1914; s. Harry Dray and Bess Eleanor (Morris) W.; B.S. in Chem. Engring., U. Ill., 1935; postgrad. U. Pitts., 1935-36, Fordham U., 1937-39, George Washington U., 1946; m. Ann Duryea Kirk, June 17, 1944; children—Kirk Willard Thompson, Norman Lentz, John Morris. Research asst., organic synthesis fellow Mellon Inst., Pitts., 1935-36, from sr. fellow to adminstrv. fellow, Corn Products fellow, 1946-57; with tech. div. Carbide & Carbon Chems. Corp., N.Y.C., 1936-39; with tar and chems. div. Koppers Co., 1940-42; asst. mgr. research adminstrn. Union Carbide Corp., N.Y.C., 1957-65, asst. mgr. chems. and plastics div., 1965-69; dir. Chappaqua Research Assos., 1969-70; asst. to pres. N.Y. Ocean Sci. Lab., Montauk, N.Y., 1970—. Mgr. jobs placement Westchester-Rockland Met. area Nat. Alliance Businessmen, 1969-70; chmn. S. Fork-Shelter Island chpt. Nature Conservancy, 1974—, trustee, 1974—. Served to lt. col. U.S. Army, 1942-46; brig. gen. Res., 1946-73. Decorated Legion of Merit; named hon. alumnus Carnegie-Mellon U., 1968; registered profl. engr., Pa. Mem. AAAS, Am. Chem. Soc., Am. Inst. Chem. Engrs., N.Y. Acad. Scis. Republican. Episcopalian. Club: Army-Navy (Washington). Patentee rocket propulsion. Home: 50 Egypt Close East Hampton NY 11937 Office: NY Ocean Sci Lab Edgemere Rd Montauk NY 11954

WILLARD, JOHN GERARD, multi-nat. co. adminstr.; b. Pitts., Nov. 20, 1952; s. Cornelius Merle and May E. (Hinds) W.; B.A. in Journalism, Duquesne U., Pitts., 1974; m. Lorraine L. Franze, Sept. 2, 1978. Producer, dir. air talent Sta. WDUQ-FM, Pitts., 1971-73; master control tech. dir. Sta. KDKA-TV, Pitts., 1973; cons. communications Better Bus. Bur., Pitts., 1974; asst. account exec. Marc & Co., Advt., Pitts., 1975; adminstr. employee benefit adminstrn. Rockwell Internat. Inc., Pitts., 1975—. Mem. Am. Mensa Ltd., Smithsonian Nat. Instn., Nat. Rifle Assn. (marksmanship instr.), Stage 62 Kappa Tau Alpha, Alpha Tau Omega. Office: 600 Grant St Suite 5009A Pittsburgh PA 15219

WILLAUER, GEORGE JACOB, JR., educator; b. Phila., Oct. 30, 1935; s. George Jacob and Mary Catherine (Eshleman) W.; A.B., Wesleyan U., 1957; A.M., U. Pa., 1959, Ph.D., 1965; m. Cynthia Cameron Thun, June 11, 1966; children—George Jacob III, Elizabeth Christian. Asst. instr. U. Pa., Phila., 1958-62; instr. Conn. Coll., New London, 1962-66, asst. prof., 1966-72, asso. prof., 1972-78, prof., 1978—, chmn. dept. English, 1971-76. English-Speaking Union fellow in Eng., 1969, in Ireland, 1972. Mem. Modern Lang. Assn., Am. Studies Assn. Contbr. articles to profl. jours. Author: A Lyme Miscellany, 1776-1976, 1977. Home: RD 3 Lyme via Old Lyme CT 06371 Office: Connecticut Coll New London CT 06320

WILLCOX, FREDERICK PRESTON, inventor; b. Los Angeles, Aug. 1, 1910; s. Frederick William and Kate Lillian (Preston) W.; grad. high sch.; m. Velma Rose Gander, 1935; 1 dau., Ann Louise. Self-employed research and devel. engr. and cons., 1939-51; govt. cons., 1949-50, 61-65; tech. v.p. Fairchild Camera & Instrument Corp., 1951-60; self-employed inventor, 1960—. Served to maj. U.S. Army, 1940-45. Recipient Sherman Fairchild Photogrammetric award Am. Soc. Photogrammetry, 1951. Fellow AAAS; mem. Am. Soc. Photogrammetry, Soc. Photog. Scientists and Engrs., ASME, Am. Inst. Aeros. and Astronautics, Optical Soc. Am., Am. Def. Preparedness Assn. Episcopalian. Patentee photog., graphic arts and data communications equipment, high speed teleprinters and typewriters. Home and Office: 565 Oenoke Ridge New Canaan CT 06840

WILLE, CARROLL GERARD, lawyer; b. Balt., July 18, 1925; s. Raymond D. and Carolyn (Rettman) W.; student Mt. St. Mary's Coll., 1943, Muhlenberg Coll., 1944; B.A., U. Miami, 1947; J.D., Northwestern U., 1950; m. June Louise Biewald, Aug. 4, 1945; children—Diane, Carroll Alan, Nancy, Robin. Admitted to Pa. bar, 1951, since practiced in Phila.; asso. firm Goff and Rubin, Phila., 1954-62, partner, 1962-69; mng. partner Fell, Spalding, Goff & Rubin, Phila., 1969-75; sr. mem. Carroll G. Wille & Assos., West Chester, Pa., 1975—. Pres., Civic Assn. Rosemont, 1966-70. Served with USNR, 1943-46, 51-54; comdg. officer Naval Res. Law Co., Phila., 1969-70. Recipient citation Mayor Phila. for Civic Activities, 1963. Mem. Fed., Pa., Ill., Chgo., Phila., Chester County bar assns., Am. Trial Lawyers Assn., Am. Arbitration Assn., Northwestern Alumni Club Phila. (pres. 1966-68, 69-70, 71-74), Pa. Soc., Phi Delta Phi. Club: Union League (Phila.). Home: 722 Amherst Circle Ithan PA 19073

WILLETS, ELMORE ABRAM, JR., banker, oil producer; b. Sewickley, Pa., Sept. 19, 1919; s. Elmore A. and Lucy (Penn) W.; grad. Phillips Andover Acad., 1938; B.S., Yale, 1942; m. Mary Taylor, June 19, 1943 (div. 1977) children—Maxey Penn, Elmore Abram III, Sarah Ayres, Jefferson Dillard. Pres., dir. Willets & Paul Corp., oil producers, Belmont, N.Y., 1945—; pres., dir State Bank, Belmont, 1950—; partner Willets & Craig, oil producers, Midland, Tex; exec. v.p. Wichita Industries; dir. Craig Ltd., Citizens Nat. Bank, Wellsville, N.Y., Hotwork, Inc., Lexington, Ky. Trustee Pitts. Theol. Sem., Alfred U. Served as maj. F.A., AUS, 1944-45; ETO. Mem. Ind. Petroleum Assn. Am. (dir.), Phi Beta Kappa. Presbyn. Clubs: Allegheny Country, Edgeworth (Sewickley); Duquesne (Pitts.); University (N.Y.C.); Rolling Rock (Ligonier, Pa.); Crag Burn (East Aurora, N.Y.). Home: Brittany Apts Sewickley PA 15143 Office: Belmont NY also Investment Bdlg Pittsburgh PA 15222

WILLETS, SETH BARROWS, dentist; b. N.Y.C., Feb. 18, 1921; s. Robert Henry and Laura Georgia (Finney) W.; student U. Maine, 1939-40, Columbia U., 1940; D.D.S., Georgetown U., 1944; m. Elazabeth Leonori Rohland, Oct. 2, 1942 (div. 1955); children—Seth R., Pamela L. (Mrs. Adrian Gordon); m. 2d, Ruth Coles Donaldson Hayden, Mar. 24, 1955; children—William F., Thomas T., Clayton S. Pvt. practice dentistry, Glen Cove, N.Y., 1945-51, gen. practice, 1953-67; sr. dentist Mid Hudson Rehab. Center Narcotic Addiction Control Commn. State N.Y., Beacon, 1967-71; dentist Ray Brook (N.Y.) Rehab. Center, Dept. Correction, 1971-72, Green Havan Correctional Facility, Stormville, N.Y., 1972—; dentist III in charge Fishkill Correctional Facility, Beacon, N.Y., 1973—; extern Nassau County Tb San., Farmingdale, N.Y., 1945-46; asso. attending oral surgeon St. Luke's Hosp., 1954-66, Met. Hosp., N.Y.C., 1956-66; asst. attending oral surgeon Community Hosp., Glen Cove, N.Y., 1949-66. Instr. Jr. Rifle Glen Cove YMCA Center, 1964-66; troop committeeman troop 46 Boy Scouts Am., East Fishkill, N.Y., 1970-71, asst. scout master, 1971; sgt. East Fishkill Police Dept., 1970—. Served to lt. (j.g.) USNR, 1944-45; capt. Dental Corps USAF, 1951-53. Diplomate Bd. Oral Surgery State N.Y. Fellow L.I. Acad. Odontology; mem. ADA, Dental Soc. State N.Y., 9th Dist., Nassau County (v.p. 1951) dental socs., So. Dutchess and Putnam Sportsmens Assn. (pres. 1970-73), Dutchess County Fedn. Sportsmens Clubs (del. 1970—), Dutchess County Pistol Assn., Schroon Lake Fish and Game (hon.), Saranac Lake Fish and Game, Nat. Rifle Assn., U.S.C.G. Aux. (comdr. flotilla 1969), Kappa Sigma. Clubs: Hempstead Harbour Yacht; 336 Rifle and Pistol (Glen Head, N.Y.); WhortleKill Rod and Gun, Masons. Home: 47 Heaton Lane Wappingers Falls NY 12590 Office: Fishkill Correctional Facility Beacon NY 12508

WILLETTE, ROGER HENRY, molded pulp co. exec.; b. Millinocket, Maine, July 15, 1942; s. Rosaire Henry and Leona (Lemelin) W.; A.A., U. Maine, 1974, B.A. in Psychology, 1976; m. Geraldine F. Pare, Oct. 1, 1966; children—Laurie Ann, Traci Lynn, Kellie Marie. Asst. mgr. Laverdiere's Super Drug Store, Augusta, Maine, 1964-66; asst. personnel mgr. Bates Mfg. Co., Inc., Augusta, 1966-68, personnel mgr., 1968-73; mgr. of personnel and employee relations Lipman Bros., Inc., Augusta, 1973-74; asst. personnel mgr. Keyes Fibre Co., Waterville, Maine, 1974-76, personnel mgr., 1976—; bd. dirs. St. Augustine Fed. Credit Union, 1973-78, pres., 1978. Div. chmn. Kennebec Valley YMCA Bldg. Fund Com., 1971-74, chmn. pub. relations com., 1971-74; mem. Govs. Com. on Employment of the Handicapped, 1975-76, Gov.'s State Manpower Planning Council, 1975-76, Gov.'s Regional Manpower Planning Council, 1975-76, Gov.'s State Manpower Services Council, 1976-77, State Ednl. and Cultural Services Task Force on High Sch. Diploma Competencies, 1976; adv. bd. Kennebec Valley comprehensive alcoholism treatment program Mid Maine Med. Center, 1978; mem. St. Augustine Sch. Bd., 1978—; bd. dirs. Waterville chpt. ARC, 1978—, Kennebec Valley United Fund, 1969-75. Served to sgt. U.S. Army, 1961-64. Recipient U.S. Vice Presidential award Youth Opportunities Unlimited, 1968; Community Service award United Way of Kennebec Valley, 1974, Keyes Fibre Co., 1979; Top Brass Safety Shoe award Lehigh Safety Shoe Co., 1975; named Augusta's Outstanding Young Man, One of Maine's Thirteen Outstanding Young Men, Augusta Jaycees, 1968. Mem. Associated Industries of Maine Personnel Assn. Home: 27 Buena Vista Dr Augusta ME 04330 Office: Keyes Fibre Co Coll Ave Waterville ME 04901

WILLEY, RAYMOND CLYDE, dowser; b. Barton, Vt., Oct. 11, 1898; s. Clarence Henry and Elvira Sally (Farman) W.; student Middlebury Coll., 1917-18, Bowdoin Coll., 1919, U. Bordeaux (France), 1919; m. Elizabeth L. O'Bryan, Mar. 30, 1920; m. 2d, Sarah J. Hamilton, Mar. 13, 1926; children—Robert O., Elizabeth Willey Butler, Elvira Willey Tennant. With Butler Paper Co., Fresno, Calif., 1921, Standard Oil Co. N.Y., Albany, 1922-23, Gen. Electric Co., Schenectady, 1923-57; profl. dowser, 1952—; cons., lectr. in field. Served with M.C., U.S. Army, 1918-19. Mem. Am. Soc. Dowsers (founder and trustee 1961—, sec. 1967—, editor quar. 1967—), Brit. Soc. Dowsers. Republican. Mem. Reformed Ch. Am. Author: Modern Dowsing, 1976. Address: 957 Norwood Ave Schenectady NY 12303

WILLEY, WADE NORRIS, cookware products sales rep.; b. Milford, Del., Apr. 21, 1948; s. Norris Everett and Irene Betty W.; A.S., Harford Community Coll., 1969; B.S. in Bus., U. Balt., 1971. With Wear-Ever Aluminum Inc., Balt., 1969-71, asst. field counselor, 1969-70, field counselor, 1970-71; regional sales mgr. Thermo-Sentinel Corp., Dubois, Pa., 1972-74; regional sales mgr. for cookware cos., Ocean City, Md., 1974—. Recipient awards for sales records Thermo-Sentinel Corp., 1972. Mem. Direct Selling Assn., Single Christians Fellowship Internat. Methodist. Club: Kiwanis (treas. Ocean City club 1976-78). Home: 9103 Ocean Hwy PO Box 702 Ocean City MD 21842

WILLIAMS, ADOLPHUS LEVI, JR., coll. ofcl., lectr.; b. Wilminton, Del., Dec. 2, 1942; s. Adolphus L. and Eunice (Miles) W.; B.A. in Sociology, Va. Union U., 1968; postgrad. (fellow) Haverford Coll., 1968-69; J.D., U. Va., 1972. Dormitory dir. of Storer Hall, Va. Union U., Richmond, 1968, 69, instr. social studies, 1970; chief instr. Karate team, Haverford (Pa.) Coll., 1972-77, lectr. polit. sci., 1972-77, asst. dir. admissions, 1972-73; dir. pre-freshman summer program Haverford Coll., 1972-73, coach Haverford/Bryn Mawr Collegiate Karate team, 1974-76, dean student affairs, 1973—, pre-law adviser, 1974-77. Ofcl. registrar SSS, Haverford, 1975-76. Served with USMC, 1960-64. Woodrow Wilson Found. fellow, 1972-73; Andrew Mellon Found. grantee, 1974. Mem. Pa. Bar Assn., Am., Pa. assns. student personnel adminstrs., Am. Personnel and Guidance Assn., All America Karate Fedn., Northeast Assn. of Pre-Law Advisers, Alpha Phi Omega. Club: Rotary. Office: Haverford College Haverford PA 19041

WILLIAMS, ALBERT J., JR., engring. cons.; b. Media, Pa., Feb. 28, 1903; s. Albert J. and Rose (Cleeland) W.; A.B. in Elec. Engring., Swarthmore Coll., 1924; postgrad. U. Pa., evenings 1927-30, U. Calif. at Los Angeles, 1963; m. Phyllis Helen Zinke, Dec. 20, 1937; children—Albert J. III, Robert Ernest. Transformer engr. Bell Telephone Labs., N.Y.C., 1924-27; test engr. Leeds & Northrup Co., Phila., 1927-29, research engr., 1929-34, chief, elec. div. research dept., 1934-51, asso. dir. research, research and devel. dept., 1951-55, sci. adviser research and devel. dept., North Wales, Pa., 1955-67, sci. adviser corporate research dept., 1967-68, mem. devel. adv. com. co., 1959-68. Registered profl. engr., Pa. Fellow IEEE (recipient Morris E. Leeds award 1968), Franklin Inst. (Wetherill medal 1952), ASME (Rufus Oldenburger medal 1972); mem. Am. Phys. Soc., AAAS, Sigma Xi. Clubs: Old York Road Country (Spring House, Pa.); One Club Golf Association (Washington). Patents, publs. in field. Home and Office: 901 Llanfair Rd Ambler PA 19002

WILLIAMS, BRADFORD WARREN, biochemist; b. Meriden, Conn., Jan. 24, 1948; s. Daniel Norton and MaryLou (Siegfried) W.; B.S., Curry Coll., 1970; postgrad. Providence Coll., 1976—; m. Patricia Maryann Morosini, Aug. 30, 1969; 1 son, Daniel Wayne II. Chem. technologist New Eng. Nuclear Corp., Boston, 1971-72; clin. chemist Mass. Rehab. Hosp., Boston, 1972-74; radioimmuno assay specialist Clin. Chem. Labs., Boston, 1974-75; biochemist, neuroendocrine research labs. VA Med. Center, Providence, 1975—; instr. basic radioimmuno assay course New Eng. Clin. Radioassay Soc., 1977-78. Mem. Am. Chem. Soc., New Eng. Clin. Radioassay Soc., U.S. Coast Guard Aux., Riverside Sportsman's Assn. Congregationalist. Home: 168 Holland Ave Riverside RI 02915 Office: VA Med Center (151) Providence RI 02908

WILLIAMS, CECILIA LEE PURSEL, optometrist; b. Lewisburg, Pa., Nov. 15, 1948; d. Lee LaVerne and Geraldine May (Steininger) Pursel; student Lycoming Coll., 1966-68; B.S. (Women's Aux. of Pa. Optometrists scholar 1968-70, Pa. State grantee 1968-70), Pa. Coll. Optometry, 1970, O.D. (Women's Aux. of Pa. Optometrists scholar 1970-72, Pa. State grantee 1970-72), 1972; m. Richard Lee Williams, May 17, 1975. Research optometrist in soft lens materials Gumpelmayer Optik, Vienna, Austria, 1973; optometrist Sterling Optical Co. Contact Lens Center, Washington, 1974—. Recipient Clin. Efficiency award Pa. Coll. Optometry, 1972; lic. and/or certified optometrist, D.C., Pa., N.Y., N.J., Va. Mem. Optometric Center of Nation's Capital (dir.), Am. Optometric Soc. (sec. 1979), Optometric

Soc. D.C., Nat. Honor Soc. for Optometry, Omega Delta. Home: 2500 6th St S Arlington VA 22204 Office: 520 10th St NW Washington DC 20004

WILLIAMS, CLARENCE GEROME, coll. adminstr.; b. Goldsboro, N.C., Dec. 23, 1938; s. Lee Roy and Daisy W.; B.S., N.C. Central U., 1961; M.S., Hampton Inst., 1967; postgrad. Cornell U., 1965; Ph.D., U. Conn., 1972; m. Mildred Cogdell, Feb. 17, 1961; children—Clarence Gerome, Alton LeRoy. Tchr., coach Bruton High Sch., Williamsburg, Va., 1961-64; asst. to dean men Hampton (Va.) Inst., 1969-70; head counselor, summer program U. Conn., Storrs, 1969-72, counselor, counseling and testing center, 1969-72; asst. dean Grad. Sch. Mass. Inst. Tech., Cambridge, 1972-73, spl. asst. to pres., chancellor minority affairs, 1974—. Ford Found. fellow, 1971. Mem. Organizational Devel. Network, Am. Assn. Higher Edn., Am. Personnel and Guidnce Assn., Assn. Non White Concerns, Coll. Student Personnel Assn., Am. Coll. Personnel Assn., NAACP, N.C. Central U., Hampton Inst., U. Conn. alumni assns., Nat. Urban League, Alpha Phi Alpha, Phi Delta Kappa, Sigma Pi Phi. Home: 14 Cottonwood Rd Newton MA 02159 Office: 77 Mass Ave #10-211 Cambridge MA 02139

WILLIAMS, CLARENCE LEON, health planning, pub. policy exec.; b. Longview, Tex., Aug. 9, 1937; s. Ruby Marlene (McLemore) W.; B.A., Prarie View A. & M. Coll., 1959; M.A., Calif. State U., 1973; postgrad. U. Oreg., 1973-78; m. Kathleen Susan Robbins, June 7, 1975; 1 son, Clarence Leon. Exec. dir. Community Action Council, Galveston County, Tex., 1966-68, Economic Opportunity Commn., San Diego County, Calif., 1969-70; asso. dep. dir. program and contract dept., dir. planning budgeting evaluation dept. Economic and Youth Opportunities Agency, Los Angeles, 1970-71; dir. Rocky Mountain Forum Internat. Issues, Denver, 1976-77; cons. adminstr. Health Planning Regional Center, Phila., 1977-78; now with Albany (N.Y.) Interracial Council, Inc.; vis. asst. prof. Grad. Sch. Internat. Studies U. Denver, 1976-77; guest panelist and lectr., colls., univs.; cons. municipal county state govts., sch. dists.; cons. Pres.' Nat. Advisory Council OEO, 1971, White House Conf. on Hunger, 1969, White House Conf. on Aging, 1967. Served with USAF, 1961-64. Ford Found. fellow, 1974; Woodrow Wilson Nat. Found. fellow, 1973-74; U.S. State Dept. scholar-diplomat, 1977. Mem. Phi Kappa Phi, Alpha Kappa Delta. Home: 12 Woodshire Ct Ballston Lake NY 12019 Office: 50 N Lark Albany NY 12210

WILLIAMS, DANIEL EDWIN, psychologist, educator; b. Mobile, Ala., Nov. 24, 1933; s. Robert and Demaris (Lewis) W.; B.A., Seton Hall U., 1963; M.S., St. John's U., 1963, Ph.D., 1968; m. Mildred Elizabeth Onley, June 15, 1957; children—Denise, Michele, Melanie. Sch. psychologist Jersey City pub. schs., 1965-66, East Orange (N.J.) pub. schs., 1966-68; asso. prof. psychology Montclair State Coll., Upper Montclair, N.J., 1968—; pvt. practice clin. psychology, East Orange, 1974—. Mem. N.J. State Bd. Psychol. Examiners, 1975—. Mem. Plainfield Bd. Edn., 1974-75. Served with USAF, 1951-55. Diplomate in clin. psychology Am. Bd. Profl. Psychology. Mem. Am., N.J. psychol. assns., Nat., N.J. (founding chmn.) assns. Black psychologists Phi Delta Kappa. Club: Brookside Swim and Tennis (Union, N.J.). Home: 256 Geneva Pl Plainfield NJ 07062 office: 185 Central Ave East Orange NJ 07018

WILLIAMS, DANIEL EUGENE, educator; b. Wilkes-Barre, Pa., Aug. 28, 1924; s. Daniel P. and Jennie Ohlman (Tucker) W.; B.S., Wilkes Coll., 1948; M.S., Bucknell U., 1950. Tchr., counselor Dallas (Pa.) Twp., 1948-54; counselor U.S. Army Dependent Schs., Germany, 1954-56, Triton Regional High Sch., Runnemede, N.J., 1957-64; guidance dir. Blackhorse Pike Regional Sch. Dist., Blackwood, N.J., 1964—, dir. spl. services, 1972—. Condr. drug. edn. info. workshop Glassboro (N.J.) State Coll., summer 1970. Sec., Bicentennial Nat. Gymafa Ganu of U.S. and Can., Phila., 1976. Served with USNR, 1942-45. Mem. Am., N.J. personnel and guidance assns., Am. Sch. Counselor Assn., Camden County Guidance Assn., NEA, N.J., Camden edn. assns., Welsh Soc. (sec. 1968—), Cambrian Soc. Delaware Valley, Wilkes Coll. Alumni Assn. (pres. 1950-51). Presbyterian. (trustee, clk. session). Home: 450 Broadway Camden NJ 08103 also 367 S River St Wilkes-Barre PA 18702 Office: Highland Regional High Sch Erial Rd Blackwood NJ 08012

WILLIAMS, DAVID, ch. exec.; b. White Plains, N.Y., Oct. 30, 1904; s. David Louis and Alice Boyd (Johnston) W.; B.S., Princeton U., 1926; M.B.A., Harvard U., 1928; m. Parthenia D. Davis, June 12, 1928;children—Morton D., David L., R. Richardson. Syndicate dept. Kidder Peabody & Co., N.Y.C., 1928-31; security analyst Grayson M-P. Murphy & Co., N.Y.C., 1932-36; merchandiser Lord & Taylor, N.Y.C., 1936-47; divisional mgr. Cheney Bros., N.Y.C., 1947-53; mgmt. cons., N.Y.C., 1954-57; spl. asst. in mktg. Columbia Grad. Sch. Bus. Adminstrn., N.Y.C., 1957; prof. bus. adminstrn. Bates Coll., Lewiston, Maine, 1958-74, acting dean of men, 1968-70; acting adminstr. Episcopal Diocese of Maine, 1975-76. Incorporator, Central Maine Gen. Hosp.; treas., chmn. fin. com. Hendrick Hudson council Boy Scouts Am., 1945-47. Mem. Am. Accounting Assn., Am. Mktg. Assn., Am. Acad. Polit. and Social Scis. Episcopalian (sr. warden, vestryman 1944—). Clubs: Sleepy Hollow County (Scarborough, N.Y.); Martindale (Auburn, Maine). Home: 18 Mountain Ave Lewiston ME 04240

WILLIAMS, DAVID RUSSELL, educator; b. Indpls., Oct. 21, 1932; s. H. Russell and Mary Dean (Whitmer) W.; A.B. cum laude Columbia U., 1954, M.A., 1956; Ph.D., U. Rochester, 1965; m. Elsa Buehlmann, Jan. 30, 1960. Dir. music Windham Coll., Putney, Vt., 1959-62; opera coach Eastman Sch. Music, Rochester, N.Y., 1962-65, instr. theory, 1965-68, asst. prof., 1968-75, asso. prof., 1975—, adminstr. M.Music degree in performance and lit., 1972—, sec. faculty, 1972-77. Mem. Friends Rochester Pub. Library, 1970—. Mem. corporate bd. Hochstein Music Sch., Rochester, 1967—; v.p. bd. dirs. Rochester Chamber Orch., 1975—; bd. dirs. Rochester Philharmonic Orch., 1975-78, sec., 1976-78; mem. adv. bd. Opera Theatre Rochester, 1972—, pres. bd. dirs., 1973-74, v.p., 1974-76; bd. dirs. Rochester Community Players, 1969-74. Served with AUS, 1957-59. Mem. Coll. Music Soc. (mem. council 1972-74, sec. 1973—), ASCAP, Am. Music Center, Am. Musicological Soc., Nat. Assn. Schs. Music, N.Y. State Music Tchrs. Assn. (mem. exec. bd. 1970-74), Phi Beta Kappa, Phi Mu Alpha, Pi Kappa Lambda. Club: University. Author: Bibliography of the History of Music Theory, 1971. Editor opera vol. New Scribner Music Library, 1972. Composer: Five States of Mind, 1970. Home: 520 East Ave Rochester NY 14607

WILLIAMS, DOROTHY FRANCES, editor, educator; b. Brookline, Mass., Aug. 23, 1918; d. John Joseph and Gertrude (Riley) Williams; student Lasell Jr. Coll., 1938-39; B.S., Simmons Coll., 1941, hon. doctorate in Journalism, 1978; postgrad. Providence Coll., 1953-56; M.S., Boston U., 1967. Mem. personnel dept. Am. Optical Co., Boston, 1942-43; news editor Raytheon News, Raytheon Mfg. Co., Newton, Mass., 1943-45; editor Hammett Herald, J.L. Hammett Co., Cambridge, Mass., 1945-46; editor Your Home mag., Boston, 1946-50; prof. pub., editor Simmons Rev., Simmons Coll., Boston, from 1947, former chmn. dept. communications, now prof. pub. emeritus. Communications cons. labor, mgmt., alumni publs., writer-editor; dir. editorial graphic arts insts.; adviser Leadership Tng. Inst., U.S. Office Edn., 1972-75. Mem. corp. Editorial Projects for Edn., Washington. Recipient Am. Alumni Council and Council for Advancement and Support of Edn. awards for editorial achievement, 1948-76; awards for editorial excellence Internat. Council Indsl. Editors, Mass. Council Indsl. Editors, Am. Coll. Pub. Relations Assn.; award for excellence in graphic arts in Simmons Rev., Am. Graphic Arts Inst., Soc. Publ. Designers, Printing Industries Am., Lasell medallion Lasell Jr. Coll., 1972. Mem. Am. Assn. Higher Edn., New Eng. Bus. Communicators (treas. 1945-47), Nat. Conf. internat. Council Bus. Communicators (edn. coordinator 1967), Am. Alumni Council (mag. chmn. dist. 1 conf. 1964), Council Advancement and Support Edn. (dir. media workshops 1974-76, Sibley award for top mag. 1977, Eleanor Collier Meml. award 1978), Women in Communications, New Eng. Press Assn., Assn. Edn. in Journalism, Am. Film Assn., Advtg. Club Greater Boston, Am. Advt. Fedn. Author: The Labor Press in Profile, 1964; A Primer for the Graphically Illiterate, 1966; The Day A Lincoln Was Saved, 1963; Brave New World of Alumni Publications, 1971. Home: PO Box 1173 5 Wixon Rd Dennis Port MA 02639 Office: Simmons Coll 300 The Fenway Boston MA 02115

WILLIAMS, DOUGLAS, mgmt. cons.; b. Newburgh, N.Y., Oct. 13, 1912; s. Everett Frank and Marjorie (Tuthill) W.; A.B., Cornell U., 1934; M.B.A., Harvard Bus. Sch., 1936; m. Esther Jane Grant, Sept. 23, 1939; children—Penelope Grant (Mrs. Philip Winters), Grant Tuthill. With treasury dept. Air Reduction Co., 1936-37; asst. to pres. Compton Advt. Co., 1937-38; sales dept. Brown & Williamson Tobacco Co., 1938-39; statistician Am. Inst. Pub. Opinion, 1939; market research cons. Elmo Roper, 1939-41; asso. dir. Nat. Opinion Research Center (non-comml., non-profit orgn.), Denver, 1941; pres. Douglas Williams Assos., N.Y.C., 1947—. Pres., Larchmont Community Chest, 1959; bd. mgrs. West Side YMCA, N.Y.C. Served as lt. col. in Army Research Br., Information and Edn. Div., 1942-46. Conglist. Clubs: Larchmont Yacht, Winged Foot Golf; Cornell, Union League (N.Y.C.); Larchmont University; Desert Forest Fox. Co-author: New Era in Medical Research; Survey Among Small Business men for President's Conf. on Research; The Education of Employees. Home: 1060 Constable Dr Mamaroneck NY 10543 Office: 230 Park Ave New York City NY 10017

WILLIAMS, DUDLEY RIDAULT, lawyer; b. Martinsville, Va., June 19, 1939; s. Harry Pemberton and Ruth (Thomas) W.; B.A., Howard U., 1961; J.D., 1964; m. Katherine Ann Crowe, Oct. 25, 1969. Admitted to D.C. bar, 1966; partner firm Luck & Williams, Washington, 1966-67; exec. dir. D.C. br. NAACP, Washington, 1967-68; dep. dir. D.C. Law Students in Ct., Washington, 1969, dir., 1969-76; partner firm Cobb, Bradshaw & Borders, Washington, 1976—; legal adviser Pride, Inc., Washington, 1968—; cons. United Planning Orgn., Washington. Mem. S.E. Community Local Devel. Corp., Washington Urban League, Democratic State Com. Mem. Nat., D.C., Washington bar assns., Jud. Conf. D.C. Circuit. Home: 1209 33d Pl SE Washington DC 20019 Office: 1621 New Hampshire Ave NW Washington DC 20009

WILLIAMS, DWIGHT NELSON, health ins. co. exec.; b. Jonesville, Va., Sept. 8, 1936; s. Claude Clinton and Margaret Cornelius (Shumaker) W.; B.A. in Econs. and Bus. Adminstrn., Emory and Henry Coll., 1959; postgrad. Mgmt. Devel. Inst. U. Mich., 1967, Northwestern U., 1974; m. Janice Irene Ohman, Nov. 28, 1959; children—Melanie, Donna, Debbie, David. With Group Hospitalization, Inc., Blue Cross Plan, Washington, 1961—, personnel mgr., 1968-73, v.p. personnel and adinstrv. services, 1973—. Bd. dirs. ILDA Community Recreation Assn., Annandale, Va., 1972-73; v.p. Little Run Civic Assn., Annandale, 1969-70; active youth club activities Braddock Rd. Youth Club and Rutherford Swim Club, 1969—; mem. ch. adminstrv. bd. St. Matthew's Methodist Ch. Annandale, 1973—. Served with U.S. Army, 1960. Mem. Washington Personnel Assn., Am. Soc. Personnel Adminstrn. Home: 9029 Ashmeade Dr Fairfax VA 22030 Office: 550 12th St Sw Washington DC 20024

WILLIAMS, EDGAR, oil co. exec.; b. Learned, Miss., May 29, 1922; s. Robert Robinson and Mary (Johnson) W.; student Hinds Jr. Coll., 1948; B.A., Memphis Acad. Arts and Memphis State U., 1951; m. Doris A. Neidig, Aug. 2, 1952; children—Randall E., Crystal L. Supr. pubs. Fairchild Industries, Hagerstown, Md., 1951-60; mgr. presentations and pubs. Martin Marietta Corp., Balt., 1960-64; art dir. Fairchild Industries, Hagerstown, 1964-65; tech. writer Texaco Inc., Richmond, Va. and Beacon, N.Y., 1965-70, asst. mgr. media relations, N.Y.C., 1970-73, mgr. media relations, N.Y.C., White Plains, 1973—. Served with USNR, 1942-45. Mem. Pub. Relations Soc. Am., Assn. Petroleum Writers. Conservative Party. Office: 2000 Westchester Ave White Plains NY 10650

WILLIAMS, EDWARD BENNETT, lawyer; b. Hartford, Conn., May 31, 1920; s. Joseph Barnard and Mary (Bennett) W.; A.B. summa cum laude, Coll. Holy Cross, 1941, S.J.D., 1963; LL.B., Georgetown U., 1945, LL.D., 1968; LL.D., Loyola Coll., 1967, Fairfield U., 1968, Loyola U., Chgo., 1970, Albert Magnus Coll., 1971, St. Joseph's Coll., Phila., 1971, Lincoln (Ill.) Coll., 1972, Suffolk U., 1974, U. Detroit Sch. Law, 1976, Mt. St. Mary's Coll., 1977; m. Dorothy Adair Guider, May 3, 1946 (dec. 1959); children—Joseph Barnard, Ellen Adair, Peter Bennett; m. 2d, Agnes Anne Neill, June 11, 1960; children—Edward Neill, Dana Bennett, Anthony, Kimberly. Admitted to D.C. bar, 1944, since practiced in Washington; sr. partner firm Williams & Connolly, and predecessor firms, 1967—; prof. criminal law and evidence Georgetown U. Law Sch., 1946-58, gen. counsel univ., 1949—; guest prof. U. Frankfurt (Germany), 1954; vis. lectr. Yale Law Sch., 1971-72; pres., dir. Washington Redskins Football Club; pres. Williams Properties. Mem. U.S. Jud. Conf. Adv. Com. on Fed. Rules of Evidence, 1965-74, Chief Justice's Conf. on Court Facilities and Design, 1971-74; chmn. Md. Judicial Selection Commn. 6th Judicial Dist., 1971-78; mem. President's Fgn. Intelligence Adv. Bd., 1976-77. Treas. Dem. Nat. Com., 1974-77; trustee Coll. of Holy Cross, 1976—. Served with USAAF, 1941-43. Mem. Am. (chmn. spl. com. on crime prevention and control 1970), D.C. (v.p. 1950, 55-56, named Lawyer of Year 1966) bar assns., Am. Coll. Trial Lawyers (bd. regents 1968-72), Internat. Acad. Trial Lawyers (bd. dirs.). Democrat. Roman Catholic. Clubs: Univ., Federal City, Vinson, Nat. Lawyers, Met., Barristers, Alfalfa, Nat. Press (Washington). Author: One Man's Freedom, 1962. Contbr. articles to profl. pubs. Home: 8901 Durham Dr Potomac MD 20854 Office: Hill Bldg Washington DC 20006

WILLIAMS, EDWARD GEORGE, cardiologist; b. Passaic, N.J., Aug. 2, 1937; s. Edward George and Teresa Elizabeth (Mentes) W.; B.S. in Engring. Physics, Lehigh U., Bethlehem, Pa., 1960; M.D., Columbia U., 1964; m. Margaret Dena Mortland, June 30, 1962; children—Edward, Dena, Carolyn, Margaret, James, Jonathan, Lois, Catherine. Med. intern, resident, Nat. Heart, Lung and Cardiology fellow St. Luke's Hosp. Center, N.Y.C.; practice medicine specializing in cardiology, Elizabeth, N.J., 1971—; chief intensive care unit com. Elizabeth Gen. Hosp. Served with AUS, 1966-68; Vietnam. Decorated Bronze Star. Diplomate Am. Bd. Internal Medicine (cardiology). Mem. Christian, Union County med. socs. Address: 501 Hillcrest Ave Westfield NJ 07090

WILLIAMS, EDWARD T. H., clergyman; b. Bethlehem, Pa., Mar. 20, 1915; s. Edward H., III and Gladys E. (House) W.; student Thessalonica Agrl. and Indsl. Inst., Salonica, Greece, 1931; A.B., Williams Coll., 1938; S.T.B., Gen. Theol. Sem., 1942. Ordained to ministry Episcopal Ch. as deacon, 1942, priest, 1942; rector in Swanton, Vt., 1942-43, Bellows Falls, Vt., 1944-45, White River Junction, Vt., 1948-53; asso. rector in Burlington, Vt., 1946-48; canon All Saints Cathedral, Albany, N.Y., 1953-57, 61-65, hon. canon, 1957-61, 65—; asst. headmaster Hoosac Sch., Hoosick, N.Y., 1957-58; retreat master Albany Diocese Retreat House, 1959-61; chaplain Union U., Schenectady, 1961-65; mem. Order Holy Cross, West Park, N.Y., 1965-66; asso. rector St. Paul's Ch., Troy, N.Y., 1967; asst. dir. West campus Boston U., 1968-69, asso. dir., 1969-70; research asso., ministry studies bd. Nat. Council Chs. Christ, 1970-72; rector Holy Cross Ch., Troy N.Y., 1972-75; priest-in-charge Christ Ch., Bethel, Vt., 1975—; instr. Adirondack Community Coll., 1972. Asst. dir. Warren House, Troy, N.Y., 1972-75. Mem. exec. council Diocese of Vt., 1944-45, 46-53, spiritual advisor, 1976—; mem. exec. council Diocese of Albany, 1953-57, mem. bd. examining chaplains, 1961-65, mem. ecumenical commn., 1963-65; dir. youth New Eng. Province, 1949-52; dep. Gen. Conv. of Episcopal Ch., 1964. Bd. dirs., pres. Burlington Consumers Co-op, 1947-48; trustee Am. Farm Sch., 1955-74, East Hill Sch., Cornelia Bailey Pratt Trust Fund; bd. dirs. Faith Hope and Charity, Inc., 1976—, mem. exec. com., 1978—. Contbr. to Holy Cross Mag. Office: Parish House Christ Ch N Main St Bethel VT 05032

WILLIAMS, ELIOT PENFIELD, investment co. exec.; b. Winsted, Conn., July 4, 1942; s. Othneil Glanville and Janet Barbara (Sheldon) W.; B.A., Haverford Coll., 1964; M.B.A., U. Va., 1966; m. Susan Allen Rafferty, Aug. 14, 1965; children—Kirsten Avery, Brooksley Elizabeth. Sr. analyst Philco-Ford Corp., Phila., 1966; analyst Travelers Ins. Co., Hartford, Conn., 1969-73; asso. dir. research Travelers Corp., Hartford, 1973-75, dir. research, 1975—; instr. U. Conn. Sch. Ins. Head deacon First Ch. in Windsor (Conn.), 1973-74; bd. mgrs. Windsor-Bloomfield YMCA. Served to capt. U.S. Army, 1966-69. Chartered fin. analyst. Mem. Fin. Analysts Fedn., Hartford Soc. Fin. Analysts (v.p.). Republican. Home: 189 Palisado Ave Windsor CT 06095 Office: 1 Tower Sq Hartford CT 06115

WILLIAMS, GEORGE CHARLES, accountant; b. Buffalo, Jan. 19, 1897; s. Charles C. and Catherine (Vogt) W.; M.B.A., Am. U., 1923; B.Comml. Sci., Southeastern U., 1921, M.Comml. Sci., 1921, LL.D., 1961; m. Rosalie Elizabeth Titolo, Jan. 19, 1946; 1 son, George Charles. Asst. field auditor U.S. War Dept., Tex., La., 1917-19; auditor tech. and natural resources div. U.S. Internal Revenue, Washington, 1920-23; pvt. practice accounting, N.Y.C., 1923-35; tax adviser with John D. Rockefeller family, N.Y.C., 1935-62; co-executor Estate of Alta Rockefeller Prentice, 1962-72; com. mem. various trusts. Former trustee, mem. exec. com. Am. U. C.P.A., N.Y., N.C. Mem. Am. Inst. C.P.A.'s, N.Y. Soc. C.P.A.'s. Contbr. articles in profl. jours. Home and Office: 17 Roxbury Rd Rockville Centre NY 11570

WILLIAMS, GEORGE EARNEST, elevator co. exec.; b. Bartow, Fla., Nov. 27, 1923; s. Earnest Roscoe and Ruby Barnett (Mathews) W.; B.S. in Engring., U.S. Coast Guard Acad., 1944; postgrad. Harvard 1945-46; S.M. In Mgmt., Mass. Inst. Tech., 1949; m. Muriel Theodorsen, June 9, 1949. Asst. to pres. Indsl. Nucleonics Corp., Columbus, Ohio; project engr., bus. cons. Ebasco, N.Y.C.; design engr., prodn. supr. Minute Maid Corp., Orlando, Fla.; asst. controller, div. controller group controller, corp. dir. fin. planning and analysis United Technologies Corp., Hartford, 1957-76; sr. v.p. finance Otis Elevator Co., N.Y.C., 1976—. Mem. exec. com. Conn. Commn. Services and Expenditures, 1971. Served with USCG, 1941-47. Mem. Fin. Execs. Inst., Am. Inst. Aeros. and Astronautics, Am. Mgmt. Assn. Methodist. Originator pricing system purchase of Fla. oranges for concentrate mfg.; contbr. articles to financial jours. and handbooks. Home: 164 Mountain Spring Rd Farmington CT 06032 Office: 245 Park Ave New York City NY 10017

WILLIAMS, H. BRUCE, plastic and reconstructive surgeon; b. New Glasgow, N.S., Can., Sept. 20, 1929; s. Joseph Daniel Gaffney and Bessie Margaret (Bruce) W.; B.A., Acadia U., 1951; M.D., McGill U., 1955; m. Dorothy Howie Harris, June 20, 1958; children—Bruce, David. Intern, Montreal (Que.) Gen. Hosp., 1955-56, resident in surgery, 1956-58; resident in plastic surgery Montreal Gen. Hosp., Montreal Children's Hosp., 1958-60; practice medicine specializing in plastic surgery, 1958-60; dir. plastic surgery, Montreal Gen. Hosp., 1976—, Montreal Children's Hosp., 1976—; prof., dir. plastic surgery tng. program McGill U., Montreal, 1976—. Elder, Presbyterian Ch. Certified, Royal Coll. Surgeons Can., chmn. specialty com. in plastic surgery; diplomate Am. Bd. Plastic Surgeons. Fellow A.C.S.; mem. Que., Canadian (pres. 1975-76) socs. plastic surgeons, Am. Soc. Plastic and Reconstructive Surgeons (pres. ednl. found. 1976-77), Am. Soc. Surgery of the Hand, Am. Assn. Plastic Surgeons, Am. Burn Assn. Am. Assn. Surgery of Trauma. Contbr. articles to sci. jours. Home: 26 Edgehill Rd Montreal PQ H3Y 1E9 Canada Office: Montreal Gen Hosp 1650 Cedar Ave Montreal PQ 109 Canada

WILLIAMS, HAROLD THOMAS, ins. co. exec.; b. Liverpool, Eng., Mar. 4, 1926; s. Thomas and Doris (Jones) W.; B.A., Liverpool U., 1948; LL.B.; children—Gwen Ann, Grant Thomas. Came to U.S., 1945, naturalized, 1955. With U.S. Fidelity & Guaranty Co., Phila., 1948—, now mgr. Phila. br. Mem. Union League, Phila., 1972—. Bd. dirs. Syracuse YMCA. Served with Brit. Navy, 1943. C.L.U., C.P.C.U. Mem. Casualty Property Mgrs. Phila. (past pres.). Club: Siloam Lodge (Oklahoma City). Home: 528 Tory Hill Rd Devon PA 19333 Office: 2 Penn Center Plaza Philadelphia PA 19102

WILLIAMS, HARRISON ARLINGTON, JR., U.S. Senator; b. Plainfield, N.J., Dec. 10, 1919; s. Harrison A. and Isabel (Lamson) W.; A.B., Oberlin Coll., 1941; LL.B., Columbia U., 1948; student Georgetown U. Fgn. Service Sch.; m. Jeanette Smith, Aug. 24, 1974; children by previous marriage—Peter, Wendy, Jonathan, Nina. Admitted to N.H. and N.J. bars; mem. firm Pollis, Pappas and Williams, Elizabeth, N.J.; instr. law and fin. Rutgers U.; mem. 83d-84th Congress from 6th N.J. Dist.; U.S. Senator from N.J., 1958—, chmn. com. on human resources. Mem. Am., N.J. bar assns. Democrat. Presbyn. Home: Holland Rd Bedminster NJ 07921 Office: 970 Broad St Newark NJ 07102 also Russell Senate Office Bldg Washington DC 20510

WILLIAMS, HELEN ELIZABETH, clin. psychologist; b. Stantonsburg, N.C., Sept. 14, 1914; d. George Short and Helen (Heinzer) Williams; B.A., Randolph-Macon Woman's Coll., 1936; diploma Beacom Bus. Coll., 1938; M.A., Columbia, 1945, Ed.D., 1945. Tchr. English, Bridgeville (Del.) High Sch., 1936-37; congl. sec. U.S. Ho. of Reps., Washington, 1938-40; sec., asst. to dir. retail merchandising, asst. personnel mgr. in charge female personnel Am. Viscose Corp., N.Y.C., 1941-43; psychologist, psychotherapist Child Guidance Center, Westchester County Children's Assn., 1945-48; psychologist, psychotherapist Child Guidance Clinic of Pinellas County, Fla., 1948-50, acting dir., 1949-50; sr. clin. psychologist U.S. Naval Hosp., St. Albans, N.Y., 1952-55; guidance dir., sch. psychologist New Lincoln Sch., N.Y.C., 1955-56; chief psychologist out-patient dept. N.Y. Hosp., Westchester div., 1956-57; asst. dean, dir. counseling New Sch. for Social Research, N.Y.C., 1958-60;

psychologist Health and Guidance Center, Wilmington (Del.) Pub. Schs., 1960-61; part-time supervising clin. psychologist St. Vincent's Hosp., N.Y.C., 1961-77; pvt. practice psychol. counseling, 1961—. Fellow Am. Psychol. Assn.; mem. N.Y. State Psychol. Assn., Pi Lambda Theta, Kappa Delta Pi. Club: Congressional. Office: 37 W 70th St New York City NY 10023

WILLIAMS, HENRY, rehab. social service adminstr.; b. N.Y.C., Feb. 19, 1928; s. Richard Earl and Ellen (Yeadon) W.; B.S. in Exptl. Psychology, Columbia U., 1960; M.S. in Clin. Psychology, L.I. U., 1964; children—Henry, Patricia. Instr. spl. edn. Newark State Coll., Union, N.J., 1963-67; rehab. counselor N.Y. State Commn. for Blind and Visually Handicapped, 1964-66; asst. regional rep. for rehab. services HEW, N.Y.C., 1966-70; lectr. rehab. and community mental health N.Y. Sch. Psychiatry, N.Y.C., 1974-75; dir. rehab. service Manhattan Psychiat. Center, N.Y. State Dept. Mental Hygiene, N.Y.C., 1970-77, dep. dir. center, 1977—; cons. Social and Rehab. Service, HEW, 1970-72, White House Conf. Handicapped Individuals, 1976—; cons. non-white affairs N.Y. U. Sch. Pub. Adminstrn., N.Y.C., 1975—; mem. adv. com. Rehab. Service Adminstrn., HEW, 1975—; chmn. Commn. Standards and Accreditation Rehab. Counselor Edn., 1977—, Health Commn. 100 Black Men, 1977—; mem. steering com. Health Flak, Inc., 1972-73; chmn. mayor's Com. on Human Rights for Handicapped, N.Y.C., 1973—; mem. N.Y.C. Task Force on Community Residence and Rehab. Programs, 1974-76; mem. statewide com. on rehab. N.Y. State Dept. Mental Hygiene, 1971-74. Served with U.S. Army, 1953-55. Named Man of Year, Union County, N.J., 1963; recipient Meritorious Service award Union County Assn. Retarded Children, 1963, Distinguished Service award Nat. Assn. Non-white Rehab. Workers, 1975. Mem. Nat. Rehab. Assn. (dir. 1974—, chmn. council non-white mems. 1975—, commn. on profl. concerns 1976—), Am. Assn. Mental Deficiency (fin. com. 1971-74), Nat. Assn. Non-White Rehab. Workers (pres. 1969-73), Nat. Assn. Black Social Workers, Nat. Assn. Health Service Execs., Am. Soc. Pub. Adminstrs., Assn. Med. Rehab. Dirs., Nat. Urban League (adv. com. on rehab. 1972-75), Council Exceptional Children, NEA, Am. Arbitration Assn. Contbr. articles on rehab. to profl. publs. Home: 111 N 3rd Ave Mount Vernon NY 10550 Office: Manhattan Psychiatric Center Ward's Island NY 10035

WILLIAMS, HUBERT, city ofcl.; b. Savannah, Ga., Aug. 19, 1939; s. Charlie and Martha (Clark) W.; A.S., John Jay Coll. Criminal Justice, 1968, B.S., 1970; J.D., Rutgers U., 1974; grad. Nat. Inst., FBI Acad., 1978; m. Annette Williams, Dec. 9, 1962; children—Alexis, Susan, Hubert Carl. Police officer Newark Police Dept., 1962-73, dir. police, 1974—; exec. dir. Newark High-Impact Anti-Crime Program, 1973-74; adj. prof. Rutgers U. Sch. Criminal Justice; research fellow Harvard Law Sch. Center Criminal Justice, 1970-71. Mem. advisory bd. Nat. Inst. Law Enforcement and Criminal Justice. Recipient Achievement award Nat. Black Police Assn., 1975; Achievement award Police Acad. Assn., 1974. Mem. Nat. Orgn. Black Law Enforcement Execs. (pres.), Am., N.J. bar assns. Home: 520 Highland Ave Newark NJ 07104 Office: Newark Police Dept 22 Franklin St Newark NJ 07106

WILLIAMS, JAMES EDWARD, educator; b. Fayetteville, N.C.; s. Kernice and Jane (Smith) W.; B.S., N.C. Central U., 1958; M.A., U. D.C., 1974; postgrad. Johns Hopkins U., 1976-78. With IRS, Washington, 1958-63; tchr. Armstrong Adult Edn. Center, Washington, 1963—; cons. VA. Served with U.S. Army, 1950-53. HEW fellow, 1976-77; recipient Outstanding Service award Office Ednl. Programs and Services, Div. Adult and Continuing Edn., D.C. Pub. Schs., 1978. Mem. NEA, Am., Nat. Capitol personnel and guidance assns., Nat. Vocat. Guidance Assn., NAACP, Nat. Urban League. Methodist. Home: 5233 Lightning View Rd Columbia MD 21045

WILLIAMS, JAMES HENRY, JR., educator, mech. engr.; b. Newport News, Va., Apr. 4, 1941; s. James Henry Williams and Margaret Louise (Holt) Mitchell; S.B. (Homer L. Ferguson scholar), Mass. Inst. Tech., 1967, S.M., 1968; Ph.D., Trinity Coll., Cambridge (Eng.) U., 1970; 1 son, James Henry III. From apprentice to sr. design engr. Newport News Shipbldg. & Dry Dock Co., 1960-70; mem. faculty Mass. Inst. Engring., 1970—, Esther and Harold E. Edgerton asso. prof. mech. engring., 1974-75, housemaster New West Campus houses, 1975—; cons. in field. Recipient Charles F. Bailey Bronze medal Newport News Shipbldg. & Dry Dock Co. Apprentice Sch., 1961, Silver medal, 1962, Gold medal, 1963; So. Fellowships fellow, 1968-70; recipient Everett Moore Baker award for outstanding undergrad. teaching Mass. Inst. Tech., 1973, Ralph R. Teetor award, 1974, NSF Faculty Participation award, 1974. Creator world's largest yoyo, 1974. Contbr. articles to profl. jours. Home: 471 Memorial Dr Apt 100 Cambridge MA 02139 Office: Room 3-360 77 Massachusetts Ave Cambridge MA 02139

WILLIAMS, JAMES THOMAS, physician; b. Martinsville, Va., Nov. 10, 1933; s. Harry Pemberton and Ruth Ellen (Thomas) W.; B.S., Howard U., 1954, M.D., 1958; m. Jacqueline C. Shepard, Apr. 21, 1962; children—Lawrence D., Laurie C. Intern, Phila. Gen. Hosp., 1958-59; resident in medicine D.C. Gen. Hosp., 1959-60; resident in medicine Freedmen's Hosp., Washington, 1960-62, 64-65, mem. staff, 1969—; fellow in endocrinology Howard U. Coll. Medicine, Washington, 1965-67, asst. prof. medicine, 1967-74, asso. prof. medicine, 1974—, chief endocrine sect., dept. of medicine, 1973-76: practice medicine specializing in internal medicine, Washington, 1967—; mem. staffs Howard U. Hosp., D.C. Gen. Hosp. Served with M.C., U.S. Army, 1962-64. Diplomate Am. Bd. Internal Medicine, Am. Bd. Endocrinology and Metabolism. Fellow A.C.P.; mem. Endocrine Soc., Am. Diabetes Assn., Nat. Med. Assn. Democrat. Office: 2041 Georgia Ave NW Washington DC 20060

WILLIAMS, JOHN ALLEN, social worker; b. Wilton, Conn., Sept. 24, 1932; s. Chester S. and Elizabeth (Kemp) W.; B.A., Miami U., 1955; M.S.W., Adelphi U., 1960; m. Joyce Ellis, Jan. 31, 1959 (div.); children—Wendy Louse, Christopher Ellis, Sharon Elizabeth; m. 2d, Judith Brecher, Feb. 1, 1970. Clin. social worker Northport VA Hosp., 1960-64; dir. Stepping Stones, Huntington, N.Y., 1962-66; project dir. Montefiore Hosp., Bronx, N.Y., 1964-68, tng. dir. OEO Vista, 1966-67; dir. group treatment services Nassau County Drug Program, 1968-72; dir. community social service Northshore Hosp., Manhasset, N.Y., 1972—; dir. curriculum materials devel. center Sch. Social Welfare, SUNY, Stony Brook, 1979—; cons. in field. Served with U.S. Army, 1956-58. Recipient numerous awards. Mem. Nat. Assn. Social Workers, Social Workers Civil Rights Action, Acad. Cert. Social Workers, Internat. Snipe Class Assn. Democrat. Unitarian. Clubs: Sea Cliff Yacht; Internat. Yacht Racing Assn.; Contbr. numerous articles to profl. and yachting mags. Winner over 100 sailing awards and trophies. Home: 25 Orchard St Glen Head NY 11545 Office: Sch Social Welfare Health Sci Center SUNY Stony Brook NY 11794

WILLIAMS, JOHN CHAMBERLIN, radio systems engr.; b. Ridgway, Pa., Aug. 23, 1919; s. R.P. Dean and Wilma E. (Chamberlin) W.; B.E.E. (Evan Pugh scholar), Pa. State Coll., 1941; M.S. in Engring. Scis. and Applied Physics, Harvard, 1948, Ph.D. in Applied Physics, 1959; m. Gloria Bradley, Feb. 24, 1951; children—Douglas Bradley, Kathryn Joanne. Engr., AT&T Long Lines, Phila., 1941-42; staff Radiation Lab., Mass. Inst. Tech., Cambridge, 1942-45; research asst. Cruft Lab., Harvard, 1945-59; electronic instrumentation cons., 1945-55; asst. v.p. research Pickard & Burns Electronics, Waltham, Mass., 1959-63, dir. radio sci. dept., 1963-67, dir. research and systems, 1967-68; staff engr. RCA Govt. and Comml. Systems, Camden, N.J., 1968-74; mgr. advanced radiation systems RCA Missile & Surface Radar Div., Moorestown, N.J., 1974—; mem. long wave propagation discussion group U.S. Navy, 1961-69; alternate mem. submarine communications panel Nat. Security Indsl. Assn., 1969-70; asso. mem. sci. adv. com. Def. Intelligence Agy., 1974-77; mem. U.S. Commn. E on Interference Environment, Internat. Union Radio Sci., 1975—. Troop com. chmn. Boy Scouts Am., 1970-74. Mem. Am. Meteorol. Soc., Am. Geophys. Union, Am. Phys. Soc., AAAS, N.Y. Acad. Sci., Sigma Xi, Tau Beta Pi, Eta Kappa Nu. Republican. Presbyterian. Contbg. author: LORAN, 1948; Recent Advances in Atmospheric Electricity, 1959; Industrial Electronics, 1960. Patentee in field (3). Home: 19 Middleton Rd Moorestown NJ 08057 Office: RCA Marne Hwy Moorestown NJ 08057

WILLIAMS, JOSEPH WINSLOW, pathologist; b. Madras, India, Sept. 16, 1931; s. Joshua Robert and Helen (Tullah) W.; came to U.S., 1969; naturalized, 1976; student Voorhees Coll., Vellore, India, 1946-48; B. Medicine, B.S., Stanley Med. Coll., 1954; m. Jean Muir Whyte, May 20, 1967; children—Elizabeth, Helen, Fiona. House surgeon Govt. Stanley Hosp., Madras, 1955-56; sr. house officer Royal No. Infirmary, Inverness, Scotland, 1957, Perth (Scotland) Royal Infirmary, 1957-60; supt. Neyoor Hosp., India, 1965-66; resident pathology Marymount Hosp., Cleve., 1969-71, Mt. Sinai Hosp., N.Y.C., 1971-74; practice medicine specializing in pathology, 1974—; pathologist Bronx (N.Y.) VA Hosp., 1974—, asst. chief lab. service, 1977—; asst. prof. pathology Mt. Sinai Med. Center, N.Y.C., 1974—. Deacon Brick Presbyn. Ch., N.Y.C., 1976-79, v.p. bd. deacons, 1977-78, pres., 1978-79, pres. council, 1976—. Diplomate Am. Bd. Pathology. Fellow Royal Coll. Surgeons of Edinburgh. Contbr. articles in field to med. jours. Home: 1245 Park Ave Apt 5F New York City NY 10028 Office: Bronx VA Hosp 130 W Kingsbridge Rd Bronx NY 10468

WILLIAMS, KATHLEEN FRANCES, govt. adminstr.; b. Phila., Aug. 22, 1929; d. Gilbert Peter and Cynthia Amelia (Waters) W.; student Temple U., 1952-53; B.S., U. Pa., 1973. Keypunch operator U.S. Censor Bur., Phila., 1951; clk.-typist, U.S. Naval Shipyard, 1951-52, div. sec., 1952-58, inventory mgr., 1958-63, auditor, 1963-72, supply tech., 1972-76, supr. inventory div., 1976—; cons. to high sch. students for job placement. Bd. dirs. Heritage House, Phila., 1957—; pres. Continental Socs., Inc., 1969-71, sgt-at-arms, 1972-77, exec. com., Phila. chpt., 1967—, treas., 1975-78; active Big Sister, Big Sister Program, Phila., 1965—. Teen Aid, Inc., Phila., 1967—; vol. worker Marcy Douglas Hosp., Phila., 1955-68. Recipient Eugene Waymon Jones civic and cultural award, Com. of Councils, 1977, woman's achievement award Phila. Naval Shipyard, 1977, woman of yr. award Chapel Four Chaplains, 1963. Mem. Sub 'n Surface Club (sec. 1973—), Assn. Mgrs. and Bus. Adminstrs. Episcopalian. Clubs: Toastmasters, Chums. Home: 4323 Haverford Ave Philadelphia PA 19104 Office: US Naval Shipyard Naval Base Philadelphia PA 19112

WILLIAMS, KENNETH JOHN, nursing home adminstr.; b. Bancroft, Kans., Oct. 31, 1924; s. Clarence Aron and Veva Blanche (Holt) W.; diploma Newman Hosp. Sch. Nursing, 1954; B.S., Boston U., 1956; m. Shirley Ethel Bailey, Apr. 9, 1949; children—Sandra Kay, Kenneth John, Cheryl Ann. Staff nurse Newman Hosp., Emporia, Kans., 1954; head nurse, instr., supr. McLean Hosp., Belmont, Mass., 1954-56; supr. Togus (Maine) VA Center, 1956-62; partner, adminstr. Williams Health Care Facilities, Augusta, Maine, 1962—. Past v.p. Augusta area C. of C. Served with USN, 1943-45. Fellow Coll. Nursing Home Adminstrs.; mem. Maine State Nurses Assn., Nat. Assn. Bd. Examiners Nursing Home Adminstrs., Maine Health Care Assn. (past pres.) Republican. Clubs: Masons, Shriners, Lions (v.p.). Home: Box 84 Pond Rd Manchester ME 04531 Office: 303 State St Augusta ME 04330

WILLIAMS, LILLIAN BROWN, nurse; b. Ogden, Utah, July 27, 1935; d. Athon Elisha and Lucille Williams Brown; B.S., U. Utah, 1957; M.S., U. Wash., 1962; m. Edwin L. Williams, Nov., 1965; children—Landon Kemper, Vicki Estelle, Shawn Perry. Staff nurse, supr., head nurse Thomas Dee Meml. Hosp., Ogden, 1957-59; instr. Edison Tech. Sch., Seattle, 1963-64; supr., staff nurse Children's Hosp. Nat. Med. Center, Washington, 1959-62, asst. adminstr. for nursing, 1964—; faculty asso. Sch. Nursing, U. Md. Mem. Am., D.C. nurse assns., Am. Assn. Child Care in Hosps., Nat. League Nursing, Hosp. Council Nat. Capital Area, Am. Hosp. Soc., D.C. League Nursing, Sigma Theta Tau. Home: 3703 Bevan Dr Fairfax VA 22039 Office: 111 Michigan Ave Washington DC 20010

WILLIAMS, LON ALBERT, mech. engr.; b. Osceola, Iowa, Mar. 18, 1923; s. Alonzo Alva and Leona Frances (Rowe) W.; B.S. in M.E., Ill. Inst. Tech., 1952; M.S. in M.E., Northeastern U., 1966; m. Zella Elizabeth Torrey, Sept. 13, 1947; children—Alan Joseph. Devel. engr. Rheem Mfg. Co., Chgo., 1955-56; devel. engr. U.S. Steel Supply div., Chgo., 1956-58; dir. product devel. Craig Systems Corp., Lawrence, Mass., 1958-72; mgr. engring. Sippican Corp., Marion, Mass., 1972-74; sr. project engr. Crouse-Hinds Co., Syracuse, N.Y., 1974—; cons. in field. Judge, Onondaga County Mathematics Competition, 1975-77, Lowell Inst. Tech. Technorama, 1966-71. Served with Signal Corps, AUS, 1943-46. Registered profl. engr., Mass.; registered fallout shelter analyst. Mem. ASME, Soc. for Exptl. Stress Analysis, Illuminating Engring. Soc., Am. Radio Relay League, Sigma Phi Epsilon, Tau Beta Pi, Pi Tau Sigma. Republican. Methodist. Clubs: Lawrence Camera, Tech. Patentee in field. Home: PO Box 132 Liverpool NY 13088 Office: PO Box 4999 Syracuse NY 13221

WILLIAMS, MARY PIERCE, educator; b. Pitts., Dec. 27, 1925; d. William Torrence and Pearl (Anderson) P.; B.A., Allegheny Coll., 1944; M.Ed., Temple U., 1962, Ed.D., 1974; m. Andrew George Williams, Jr., May 21, 1945; children—H. Marjorie Williams Hotaling, Andrew George, Benjamin Ramage. Counselor, Schuylkill Valley High Sch., Leesport, Pa., 1960-64; counselor Gov. Mifflin High Sch., Shillington, Pa., 1965; asst. prof. Kutztown (Pa.) State Coll., 1966-73, prof., chmn. dept. psychology, 1973—. Mem. Am., Pa., Berks County psychol. assns., Am. Personnel and Guidance Assn., AAUW. Home: 312 Golf Rd Reading PA 19601 Office: Kutztown State Coll Kutztown PA 19530

WILLIAMS, MELVIN DONALD, anthropologist, educator; b. Pitts., Feb. 3, 1933; s. Aaron and Gladys Virginia (Barnes) W.; A.B., U. Pitts., 1955, M.A. (NDEA Title IV fellow), 1969, Ph.D., 1973; m. Faye Wanda Strawder, June 20, 1958; children—Aaron Ellsworth, Steven Rodney, Craig Haywood. Owner, operator Wholesale Periodical Distbn. Co., Pitts., 1955-66; instr. dept. sociology and anthropology Carlow Coll., 1969-71, asst. prof., 1971-75, chmn. dept. sociology and anthropology, 1973-75; asso. prof. anthropology U. Pitts., 1976—; Olie B. O'Connor prof. in Am. instns. Colgate U., 1976-77. Co-chmn. project area com. Urban Redevel. Authority, Pitts., 1972—; co-dir. interdisciplinary family community project Western Psychiat. Inst. and Clinic, Pitts., 1973-76; bd. dirs. Cath. Social Service of Allegheny County (Pa.), 1973-76. Served with U.S. Army, 1957-58. NSF field tng. fellow in anthropology, 1967, summer grantee, 1969-72; Community Action Pitts. grantee, 1969-71; Social Sci. Research Council grantee, 1974-75. Fellow Am. Anthrop. Assn.; mem. African Studies Assn., AAAS, AAUP, Am. Sociol. Assn., Assn. Study Afro-Am. Life and History, Soc. for Psychol. Anthropology. Author: Community in a Black Pentecostal Ch.; On the Street Where I Lived. Editor: Selected Readings in Afro-American Anthropology. Contbr. articles to profl. publs. Home: 7029 Apple St Pittsburgh PA 15206 Office: Dept of Anthropology U of Pitts Pittsburgh PA 15260

WILLIAMS, MONICA DONNELLY (MRS. BERNARD G. WILLIAMS), nursing adminstr.; b. N.Y.C., July 21, 1946; d. Francis Joseph and Monica Joan (McMahon) Donnelly; B.A. in French, Manhattanville Coll. of Sacred Heart, 1968; M.A. in French (Univ. fellow), Tufts U., 1969; B.S. in Nursing, Columbia, 1971; m. Bernard G. Williams, Aug. 19, 1972. Staff nurse, head nurse Vanderbilt Clinic, Columbia-Presbyn. Med. Centre, N.Y.C., 1971-72; dir. inservice edn. John T. Mather Meml. Hosp., Port Jefferson, N.Y., 1972-77, nursing care coordinator, 1977—. Attaché, Costa Rican Mission to UN, 1971-72. Mem. Modern Lang. Assn., Am. Nurses Assn., Suffolk County Inservice Council (sec. 1973-74), Nat. Soc. Lit. and Arts, Sigma Theta Tau. Roman Catholic. Home: 86 Soundview Dr Port Jefferson NY 11777 Office: Dept Nursing John T Mather Hosp North Country Rd Port Jefferson NY 11777

WILLIAMS, MORTIMER LEE, physician, surgeon; b. Roanoke, Va., June 12, 1924; s. Mortimer Harry and Frances (Lee) W.; B.A., U. Va., 1947, M.D., 1947; m. Katherine Ryland Brune; children—Jennifer Lee, David Lee, Howard Sawyer, Frances Lee, Phillip Lee. Intern, Union Meml. Hosp., Balt., 1947-48, asst. resident surgeon, 1948-49; asst. resident otolaryngology Johns Hopkins Hosp., Balt., 1949-50, chief resident, 1951-52; instr. otolaryngology Johns Hopkins Med. Sch., 1954-57, asst. prof., 1958-74, asso. prof., 1974—; chief otolaryngology Union Meml. Hosp., Balt., 1971—; chief otolaryngology Children's Hosp., Balt.; mem. staff Johns Hopkins Hosp. Cons., U.S. Vets. Hosp., 1954-64, USPHS Hosp., 1963—. Served as capt. M.C., AUS, 1950-54. Diplomate Am. Bd. Otolaryngology. Fellow A.C.S.; mem. Am. Acad. Ophthalmology and Otolaryngology, Am. Broncho-Esophagological Assn., Soc. Med. Cons. to Armed Forces, Med. and Chirurg. Faculty Md., Balt., Balt. City Med. Soc., AMA, I.M.P., Soc. Cincinnati, Soc. Colonial Wars, Phi Kappa Sigma, Pi Delta Epsilon. Republican. Clubs: Elkridge, Johns Hopkins (Balt.). Contbg. author: Tumors of the Head and Neck, 1957. Home: 111 Overhill Rd Baltimore MD 21210 Office: 201 E University Pkwy Baltimore MD 21218

WILLIAMS, NEAL THOMAS, mfg. co. pres.; b. East Orange, N.J., Mar. 16, 1921; s. Thomas John and Frieda (Apple) W.; A.B., Cornell U., 1948; postgrad. Columbia, 1948-50, Stevens Inst. Tech., 1950-52; m. Barbara Jeanette Hair, Aug. 28, 1948; children—Thomas John, Patricia Jean. Supr. magnetron engring. Westinghouse Electric Co., Fairmont, W.Va., 1942-44; research asso. Columbia U. Radiation Lab., N.Y.C., 1944-48, 52; mem. tech. staff Bell Tel. Labs., Murray Hill, N.J., 1951-52; research engr. T.A. Edison Research Labs., West Orange, N.J., 1953-60; chief engr. Seal A Metic Corp., Haledon, N.J., 1960-66; pres., chief engr. Platronics Seals, Clifton, N.J., 1966—. Mem. Am. Phys. Soc., N.Y. Acad. Scis., IEEE (sr.), Am. Electroplaters Soc. Clubs: Cornell of Essex Country; Lake Hopatcong Yacht (Hopatcong, N.J.). Patentee microwave magentrons, magnetic recording, ultra violet detectors, other devices. Home: PO Box 1002 5 Skyline Dr Hopatcong NJ 07843 Office: 320 Colfax Ave Clifton NJ 07013

WILLIAMS, RICHARD BLAND, JR., pathologist; b. Norfolk, Va., May 28, 1915; s. Richard Bland and Virginia Katherine (Heath) W.; M.D., U. Va., 1939; M.S., U. Pa., 1949; m. Thelma Katherine Cregger, June 8, 1939; children—Richard Bland, Robert Heath. Intern, Norfolk Naval Hosp., Portsmouth, Va., 1939-40; resident in pathology U. Pa., 1947-50; commd. lt. j.g., M.C., U.S. Navy, 1939, advanced through grades to capt., 1955; fellow in pathology U. Pa., 1947-50; head pathology div. Naval Med. Research Inst., Nat. Naval Med. Center, Bethesda, Md., 1950-62; sr. resident in pathology (hematology) George Washington U. Hosp., 1964-65; ret., 1962; dir. pathology lab. St. Mary's Hosp., Leonardtown, Md., 1964-69; co-dir. pathology Waynesboro (Pa.) Hosp., 1970—; dir. labs. Fulton County Med. Center, 1977—; head Hagerstown Med. Lab., 1977—. Decorated 2 Battle Stars; recipient letter from Pres. Truman. Fellow Am. Soc. Clin. Pathology; mem. Internat. Acad. Pathology, Franklin County Med. Soc., Pa. Assn. Clin. Pathology, AMA, Am. Assn. Pathology and Bacteriology, Radiation Research Soc. Democrat. Episcopalian. Home: Rt 4 Box 459 Hillcrest Heights Waynesboro PA 17268

WILLIAMS, ROBERT ALDEN, health physicist; b. Petrolia, Pa., Dec. 28, 1939; s. Harold Andrew and Celia Louise (Stewart) W.; B.S., Slippery Rock State Coll., 1965; postgrad. U. Tenn., 1965-66; m. Sandra Kay Lucas, Oct. 14, 1967; 1 son, Robert Forrest. Health physicist Armed Forces Radiobiology Research Inst., Bethesda, Md., 1966-69; environucleonics supr. Nuclear Materials and Equipment Corp., 1969-71; health and safety mgr. Babcock & Wilcox, Apollo, Pa., 1971-75, tech. control mgr., 1975-78; prin. engr. Westinghouse Electric Corp., 1978—. Served with USAF, 1957-60. AEC spl. fellow, 1965-66. Diplomate Am. Bd. Health Physics. Mem. Health Physics Soc., Inst. Nuclear Materials Mgmt., Nat. Mgmt. Assn., Franklin Mint Soc., Butler County Sportsmen's Conservation Council Alumni Assn. Club: Elks. Patentee in field. Home: 493 Longvue Dr New Kensington PA 15068 Office: Westinghouse Electric Corp Nuclear Fuel Div - Engring PO Box 355 Penn Center Bldg 5 Pittsburgh PA 15230

WILLIAMS, ROBERT ALEXANDER, assn. exec.; b. Wilkes-Barre, Pa., Jan. 27, 1915; s. William James and Jessie (Bryden) W.; A.B., Harvard U., 1937; m. Priscilla Nye, Sept. 8, 1939; children—Robert Alexander, Richard Taylor, David Michael, Anthony Owen. Commd. ensign U.S. Navy, 1937, advanced through grades to capt., 1967; staff supply officer Amphibious Forces, S.Pacific, 1942; supply officer U.S.S. Vincennes, 1943-45; comdg. officer Naval Supply Depot; Guontanamo Bay, Cuba, 1955-57; supply officer Polaris program, 1958-61; dep. controller Def. Supply Agy., 1962-64; treas.-controller Univs. Research Assn., Washington, 1967—. Mem. AAAS, Am. Geophys. Union, Am. Mineral Soc. Club: Army and Navy (Washington). Home: 2606 S Hayes St Arlington VA 22202 Office: 2100 Pennsylvania Ave NW Washington DC 20037

WILLIAMS, ROBERT CARL, architect, land devel. co. exec.; b. Chattanooga, May 21, 1931; s. Robert Carl and Ethel Beulah (Ortmeier) W.; grad. McCallie Sch., 1949; B.C.E., U. Tenn., 1954; B.A. in Architecture, Harvard Grad. Sch. Design, 1962; postgrad. spl. studies in planning Mass. Inst. Tech., 1963; children—Gregory Carl, Tanya Yolanda. Apprentice draftsman designer William Galvin, Cambridge, Mass., 1959-60, Drumney, Rosane, Anderson, Boston, 1960-62, Hugh Stubbins & Assos., Cambridge, 1962-63; partner Pan Design, Cambridge, 1963-64; prin. Robert C. Williams & Assos., Pittsfield, Vt., 1964—; pres., co-owner Hawk Mountain Corp. and Affiliates, 1964—. Chmn. Pittsfield Planning Commn., 1971-72. Served as capt. USAF, 1955-57. Mem. AIA, Boston Soc. Architects. Designer planned residential communities in Central Vt., Bolton

Valley (Vt.) resort ski lodge, various homes, indsl. bldgs., motels; 60-unit condominium community, Fayston, Vt. Home: Michigan Rd Pittsfield VT 05762 Office: Hawk Mountain Pittsfield VT 05762

WILLIAMS, ROGER, JR., chem. economist; b. Wilmington, Del., Feb. 19, 1920; s. Roger and Caddy W. (Jennings) W.; A.B., Amherst Coll., 1941; postgrad. Mass. Inst. Tech., 1946; m. Anna Marie Given, Feb. 11, 1950; children—Lynn Adair, Jan, Valerie, Roger III. Cost engr. ammonia dept. DuPont Co., Belle, W.Va., 1941-46, research staff asst. plastics dept. DuPont Co., Wilmington, Del., 1946-48; asso. editor Chem. Engring. mag. McGraw-Hill Pub. Co., N.Y.C., 1948-50; pres. Roger Williams Tech. & Econ. Services, Inc., cons. chem. economists, 1950-62, chmn., 1950—; mem. N.J. Council Research and Devel. Bd. dirs. Chemurgic Council. Fellow AAAS, Am. Inst. Chemists; mem. Am. Chem. Soc., Chem. Mktg. Research Assn., Soc. Chem. Industry, Chem. Splty. Mfrs. Assn., Synthetic Organic Chem. Mfrs. Assn., Am. C. of C. in France, Am. C. of C. (U.K.), Am. Assn. Cost Engrs., Indsl. Market Research Assn. (U.K.), European Chem. Market Research Assn., Internat. Trade Devel. Assn. (past pres.), Am. Phys. Soc., Am. Mktg. Assn., Soc. Plastics Industry, Comml. Chem. Devel. Assn., Am. Inst. Chem. Engrs., Assn. Cons. Chemists and Chem. Engrs. (past pres.), Buckingham Taxpayers Assn. (past pres.), Société de Chimie Industrielle (dir. Am. sect.), Phi Gamma Delta. Clubs: Chemists (N.Y.C.); Am. (London); Anglo-Belgian (London); Am. (Miami). Contbr. to books and periodicals on chem. engring. and econs. Home: Gladacres Mountain Rd Buckingham Valley PA Office: Washington RD PO Box 426 Princeton NJ 08540 also PO Box 487 New Canaan CT 08640 also 37/41 Bedford Row London WC1R 4JH England

WILLIAMS, ROLAND BARKSDALE, physician, educator; b. Balt., July 2, 1945; s. Roland Brown and Anethia Geraldine (Barksdale) W.; B.S., Howard U., Washington, 1966, M.S., 1972, M.D. (Lucy Moten Internat. Study fellow), 1971; M.P.H., Johns Hopkins, 1974, postgrad. in health edn., 1975-76. Commd. officer USPHS, 1970-76; intern USPHS Hosp., Balt., 1971-72; resident in preventive medicine Johns Hopkins, 1972—; asst. prof. community health Howard U.; health cons. HEW, NIH; med. dir. sickle cell anemia Provident Hosp.; prof., cons. Essex Community Coll.; physician Balt. Health Dept., Balt. Pub. Schs.; narrator weekly radio program Facts About Health The Public Should Know, 1973-75. Vestryman, St. James Episcopal Ch., 1974—; del. to Md. Council Episcopal Chs.; bd. dirs. Balt. Area Council on Alcoholism, Balt. Com. on Sickle Cell Anemia, Md. Conf. Social Concern, Boy Scouts Am. Troop 229, Md. Soc. for Med. Research; bd. dirs. United Fund Central Md., v.p., 1975; mem. exec. com. Community Chest Balt. Area. Recipient Research Achievement award Upjohn Co., 1971. Fellow Assn. Am. Med. Colls.; mem. AMA (Physician Recognition award 1976), Nat. Med. Assn., Balt. Med. Soc. (chmn. pub. med. info., 1975), Am. Pub. Health Assn., Soc. Pub. Health Educators, Commd. Officers Assn. USPHS, Am. Coll. Clin. Pharmacology, Smithsonian Nat. Assos., Howard U. Alumni Assn. (pres.). Author: Things You Should Know to Protect Your Health, 1974. Med. editor: Metropolitan mag., 1976. Home and Office: 3315 Dorchester Rd Baltimore MD 21215

WILLIAMS, ROLAND CHARLES, perfume corp. exec.; b. Portland, Oreg., May 29, 1928; s. Charles R. and Helen R. (Giesen) W.; B.B.A., U. Minn., 1952; m. Virginia M. Nicolaieff, June 19, 1948; children—Leslie T., Gary C., Marlies V. Asst. personnel mgr. Allstate Ins. Co., N.Y.C., 1954-60; corporate personnel mgr. Sandoz, Inc., East Hanover, N.J., 1960-71; v.p. indsl. relations Faberge, Inc., N.Y.C., 1971—. Served with AUS, 1946-49. Mem. Employers Assn. N.J. (dir.), Adminstrv. Mgmt. Soc., Am. Soc. Personnel Adminstrn., Chem. Personnel Assn., Am. Assn. Indsl. Mgmt., N.J. Pharm. and Fragrance Personnel Group. Home: 441 Lyncrest Rd Englewood NJ 07632 Office: 1345 Ave of the Americas New York City NY 10019

WILLIAMS, RONALD DAVID, chem. co. exec.; b. Marshall, Ark., Mar. 15, 1944; s. Noble Kentucky and Elizabeth (Karns) W.; B.A., Columbia U., 1966, B.S., 1967, M.B.A., 1973; m. Beth L. Process engr. DuPont, Deepwater, N.J., 1966; design engr. Combustion Engring. Co., Hartford, 1971; cons. Arthur Andersen & Co., N.Y.C., 1973-76; corp. planner Am. Metals Climax, Greenwich, Conn., 1976-77; project mgr. Olin Corp., Stamford, Conn., 1977—. Sec., Lawyers Com. on Tax Reform, 1972—. Served with USN, 1967-70; Vietnam. NASA traineeship, 1971; S.W. Mudd scholar, 1971. Mem. AAAS, Am. Mgmt. Assn., Am. Chem. Soc., Democrat. Home: 65 Glenbrook Rd Stamford CT 06902 Office: 120 Longridge Rd Stamford CT 06904

WILLIAMS, RUTHANN, mag. editor; b. New London, Conn., Dec. 16, 1942; d. Cecil Frederick and Eunice Margaret (Cardwell) W.; student George Peabody Coll., Nashville, 1960, Baylor U., Waco, Tex., 1961-62; M.A. candidate Drew U., 1977—. Mem. actuarial dept. Nat. Life & Accident Ins. Co., Nashville, 1961; mem. consumer relations staff Mountain States Telephone Co., Albuquerque, 1963-66; free-lance artist, writer, Chatham, N.J., 1966-70; exec. editor, art critic N.J. Music and Arts Mag., Chatham, 1970—; hostess arts-related program Sta. WMTR, Morristown, N.J., 1973; dir. Rubicon Graphics, Chatham, 1974—; faculty Caldwell (N.J.) Coll., 1976—. Bd. dirs. Arts Council of Morris Area, 1974—; mem. adv. panel N.J. State Council on the Arts, 1974—; bd. dirs. Friends of N.J. Pub. TV, 1976. Mem. Nat. Soc. Arts and Letters, Artists Equity of N.J. Exhibitor one-person art show Parthenon Mus., Nashville, 1971; winner numerous painting awards, 1965—. Home: 43 Floral Ave Murray Hill NJ 07974 Office: PO Box 567 Chatham NJ 07928

WILLIAMS, THEODORE HARVEY, air force officer; b. York, Pa., Jan. 26, 1944; s. Rodger and Kathryn Mae (Landis) W.; B.S., U. Nebr., 1970; M.Sc., Troy State Coll., 1976; M.Th., Marantha Bible Sem., 1976; D.Div., Neotarian Coll. Philosophy, 1976; m. Ruth Faye Rentzell, Jan. 22, 1977. Commd. airman U.S. Air Force, 1961, advanced through grades to capt., 1973; comdr. med. squadron sect., Griffiss AFB, N.Y., 1973-74; hosp. adminstr. Incirlik, Turkey, 1974-76; chief health professions recruiting team, Linthicum Heights, Md., 1976—. Mem. Am. Acad. Med. Adminstrs., Am. Pub. Health Assn., Am. Hosp. Assn., Am. Personnel and Guidance Assn., Am. Assn. Religious Couselors, Nat. Psychiat. Assn. Democrat. Home: 5207 Disney Ave Baltimore MD 21225 Office: 6700 Elkridge Landing Rd Suite D Linthicum Heights MD 21090

WILLIAMS, WARRENTON ARCHIBALD, realtor; b. Phila., June 9, 1911; s. Archibald W.J. and Mary J. (Creamer) W.; student Temple U., 1936-40; m. Claire Burdick, July 19, 1955; children—David W., Kristine A. Salesman C. Harry Heinz, Inc., Phila., 1936-41; sales mgr. Rowland & Banistor, Phila., 1941-47; self employed, Phila., 1947-52; self employed realtor Warrenton A. Williams Agy., Orleans, Mass., 1952—. Dir. Wajowa, Inc., Eastham, Mass.; pres. Brier Hill, Inc., Eastham, 1969-76; corporator Five Cents Savs. Bank. Chmn. Town Fin. Com., Eastham, 1957-60, Zoning and Bldg. By-Law Review Com., Eastham, 1957-60; chmn. Cape Cod Planning and Econ. Devel. Commn., 1969-72; bd. govs. Cape Cod Conservatory of Music; corporator Friendship Sch., Brewster, Mass; financial advisor Sea Pines Abroad, Falstenau, Austria, 1972-73. Mem. Cape Cod Bd. Realtors, NE Phila. Bd. Real Estate Brokers Assn. (co-founder 1947), Lower Cape Ins. Agts. Assn. (co-founder 1955), Brewster-Orleans-Eastham Ambulance Assn. (dir. 1957-66). Republican. Episcopalian. Home: South Pond Dr Brewster MA 02631 Office: US Route 6A Orleans MA 02642

WILLIAMS, WILEY HERBERT, constrn. and land devel. co. exec.; b. Brunswick, Ga., Mar. 4, 1929; s. Wiley Patrick and Era B. (Cain) W.; B.B.A. in Accounting, Lamar State Coll. Tech., 1957; children—Virginia, Sandra, Dolly. Accountant, Port Arthur (Tex.) News, 1952-57; sr. auditor Arthur Young & Co., Fort Worth, 1957-59; controller, sec.-treas. Ben Hogan Co., Fort Worth, 1959-63; controller, treas., v.p. Profl. Golf Co., Chattanooga, 1963-71; v.p. fin. Titan Group, Inc., Paramus, N.J., 1972—. Served with U.S. Army, 1950-52. C.P.A., Tex., Tenn. Mem. Am. Inst. C.P.A.'s., Tenn., Tex. Socs. C.P.A.'s. Clubs: Sertoma, Optimists. Home: 770 Anderson Ave Cliffside Park NJ 07010 Office: Titan Group Inc E 81 State Highway 4 Paramus NJ 07652

WILLIAMS, WILLIAM DAVID, analytical chemist; b. Pottstown, Pa., Jan. 28, 1940; s. Ernest Springer and Blanche Ida (Tyson) W.; B.S. in Chemistry, St. Joseph's Coll., 1966; M.S. in Chemistry, West Chester State Coll., 1974; m. Jane Lynn Bartleson, Aug. 25, 1973. With Quaker Chem. Corp., Conshohocken, Pa., 1962—, sr. technician metals lab., 1962-66, analytical chemist, analytical lab., 1966-71, group leader, analytical lab., 1971-76, mgr. analytical dept., 1977—. Mem. ofcl. bd., com. stewardship and fin. United Meth. Ch. Mem. Am. Chem. Soc., Soc. Applied Spectroscopy, Chromatography Forum Delaware Valley. Republican. Home: 967 Miller Rd Pottstown PA 19464 Office: Quaker Chem Corp Elm St Conshohocken PA 19428

WILLIAMS, WILLIAM GILBERT, III, newspaper editor; b. Salisbury, Md., Dec. 8, 1948; s. William Gilbert and Irene (Hickman) W.; A.A., Chesapeake Coll., 1969; B.S., U. Md., 1971; m. Betsy Ellen Mitchell, Jan. 12, 1969; 1 dau., Dawn Michelle. Reporter, Coastal Communications, Inc., Ocean City, Md., 1971-72, editor, 1973-74; editor Community Newspapers, Inc., Rehoboth Beach, Del., 1975. Eastern Shore Times, Beachcomber Newspapers, Atlantic Publs., Inc., Ocean City, 1976—; guest lectr. journalism U. Md., Salisbury State Coll. Mem. Worcester County Master Plan Study Com., 1974-75, Ocean City Economic Devel. Com., 1977—, Ocean City Museum Com. 1977—. Served to sgt. USAR, 1971-77. Mem. Md.-Del.-D.C. Press Assn. (5 editorial awards 1976-77). Democrat. Methodist. Club: Berlin Lions (sec. 1977). Home: Ocean City Blvd Berlin MD 21811

WILLIAMS, WILLIAM MAGAVERN, ednl. adminstr.; b. Niles, Mich., Dec. 22, 1931; s. Errol Edwin and Mary Elizabeth (Magavern) W.; B.A., Williams Coll., 1953; M.A., Columbia, 1966; m. Linda Carol Grush, June 15, 1958; children—Diana, William Magavern, Sarah. Tchr., McTernan Sch., Waterbury, Conn., 1953-54; tchr., adminstr., Riverdale Country Sch., N.Y.C., 1955-66; headmaster, Doane Acad., Burlington, N.J., 1966-70, Poly. Prep. Country Day Sch., Bklyn., 1970—. Bd. dirs. Bklyn. Central YMCA; bd. govs. Bklyn. Children's Mus.; trustee Bklyn. Inst. Arts and Scis., Plymouth Ch. of Pilgrims (Congregational), Profl. Children's Sch., N.Y.C. Mem. Nat. Assn. Secondary Sch. Prins., Guild Ind. Schs. N.Y.C. (sec.), Cum Laude Soc. (regent dist. III), Phi Gamma Delta. Office: Polytechnic Prep Country Day Sch 92nd St and 7th Ave Brooklyn NY 11201

WILLIAMS, WILLIE CLIFFORD, sch. adminstr.; b. Opp, Ala., Sept. 28, 1929; s. Wiley C. and Mattie Mae (Davis) W.; B.S. in Edn., Ala. State Coll., 1951; M.Ed., Boston State Coll., 1962; m. Dorothy Rae Reynolds, Apr. 7, 1956; children—Consuelo Yvette, Sherry Elaine, Jeffrey Clifford, Chriscinda. Sci., tchr. E. Boston High/Boston Trade High Sch., 1961-71; tchr., coordinator work study-drop out program Boston High Sch., 1971-76; asst. headmaster sci. Charlestown High Sch., 1976—; instr. phys. sci. Vet. instrn. program-counseling Boston State Coll. Served with M.C., U.S. Army, 1951-57. NSF grantee, 1971; Harvard U. Project Physics Course grantee, 1971. Mem. Boston Tchrs. Union, Am. Chem. Soc., Smith Inst., Alpha Phi Alpha. Democrat. Baptist. Clubs: Profl. Businessmen's of Boston, Playboy, Masons. Home: 124 Norwell St Dorchester MA 02121

WILLIAMSON, BETTY JAYNE HUGHES (MRS. JOSEPH ROBERT WILLIAMSON), systems design cons.; b. New Brunswick, N.J., May 29, 1941; d. Ronald Clyde and Esther (Wenzel) Hughes; B.S., Mich. State U., 1963; A.D.A., Duke U. Med. Center, 1964; m. Joseph Robert Williamson, June 3, 1972. Therapeutic dietitian Lankenau Hosp., Phila., 1964-65, asst. chief dietitian, 1965-66, chief dietitian, 1966-68; adminstrv. dietitian Hahnemann Med. Coll. and Hosp., Phila., 1968-72; asso.-facilities planning E.F. Johnson Co., Inc., Phila., 1972-75; v.p. Dynamic Systems, Inc., Phila., 1975—. Cons. Community Meml. Hosp., West Grove, Pa., The Larchwood Sch., Phila. Chmn. bicentennial com. United Ch. of Christ. Mem. Am., Pa. (adminstrn. chmn. 1974-75), Phila. (nominating chmn. 1973-74, sec., 1969-71, pres. 1972-73 spring meeting adv. bd.) dietetic assns., Pi Beta Phi Phi. Republican. Contbr. to Cyclopedia of Medicine, also jours. in field. Home: Foxgayte 26 Maryhill Rd Phoenixville PA 19460 Office: 613 W Cheltenham Ave Philadelphia PA 19126

WILLIAMSON, CHARLES JOSEPH, electronics co. exec.; b. Poughkeepsie, N.Y., Sept. 4, 1945; s. James Henry and Eleanore Constance (Devereaux) W.; B.S., SUNY, 1972; M.B.A., U. Conn., 1978. Systems asso. Travelers Ins. Co., Hartford, Conn., 1972-74; sr. programmer/analyst Hartford Nat. Corp., 1974-75; account mgr. NCR Corp., Hartford, 1976-78; sr. field sales engr. Tex. Instruments, Inc., Poughkeepsie, N.Y., 1978—; lectr. bus. programming Computer Processing Inst., 1976. Served with USAF, 1964-68. Mem. Am. Mgmt. Assn., The Futurists, Assn. MBA Execs. Home: 804 Cherry Hill Dr Poughkeepsie NY 12603 Office: 201 South Ave Poughkeepsie NY 12601

WILLIAMSON, FLETCHER PHILLIPS, real estate broker; b. Cambridge, Md., Dec. 16, 1923; s. William Fletcher and Florence M. (Phillips) W.; student U. Md., 1941, 42; m. Betty June (Stoker), Apr. 6, 1943; 1 son, Jeffrey Phillips; m. 2d, Helen M. Stumberg, Aug. 28, 1972. Test engr. Engring. Lab. Glen Martin Co., 1942-43; salesman Corkran Ice Cream Co., Cambridge, 1946-50; real estate broker, 1950—; chmn. bd. Williamson Real Estate, Dorchester Corp., 1963-72; v.p., dir. Cargo Handlers, Inc., WCEM, Inc., 1965-75; dir. Nat. Bank of Cambridge, Cam-Storage Inc., Dorchester Indsl. Devel. Corp.; co-receiver White & Nelson, Inc. Dir. Delmarva Council Boy Scouts Am. Past pres. Cambridge Hosp., United Fund of Dorchester County; bd. dirs. Del. Mus. Natural History, Dorchester County Pub. Library; bd. dirs., v.p. Game Conservation Internat. Served as ordnance tech. intelligence engr. AUS, 1943-46; ETO. Mem. Md. Real Estate Assn. (gov. 1956-66), Outdoor Writers Assn., Nat. Rifle Assn., Am. Ordnance Assn., Cambridge Dorchester C. of C. (dir. 1955—), Power Squadron (comdr. 1954-56), Dorchester County Bd. Realtors (pres.). Methodist. Clubs: Explorers, Shikar Safari, Chesapeake Bay Yacht, Camp Fire, Maryland, Masons, Shriners. Home: PO Box 715 Cambridge MD 21613 Office: The Point US 50 Cambridge MD 21613

WILLIAMSON, JEFFREY PHILLIPS, realtor; b. Cambridge, Md., Sept. 30, 1945; s. Fletcher Phillips and Betty June (Stoker) W.; B.A., Washington Coll., Chestertown, Md., 1967; m. Susan Elizabeth Polaski, May 9, 1975; 1 dau., Mary Elizabeth. Property mgr. Nat. Savs. & Trust Co., Washington, 1967-68; pub. sch. tchr., Dorchester, County, Md., 1968-72; appraiser, asso. broker Williamson Real Estate, Cambridge, 1962-72; ind. fee appraiser and broker, Cambridge, 1972—; pres. J.-J., Inc., Colonical Cons. Ltd. Certified rev. appraiser. Asso. Soc. Real Estate Appraisers; mem. N.E. Soc. Farm Mgrs. and Rural Appraisers, Nat. Assn. Realtors, Nat. Inst. Real Estate Brokers, Nat. Inst. Farm and Land Brokers, Dorchester County, Talbot County bds. realtors, Coastal Bd. Realtors Md., Coastal Multiple Listing Service, Cambridge Jaycees (past sec., treas., dir.; Keyman award 1971), Conseil Internat. de la Chasse. Republican. Episcopalian. Clubs: Md., Campfire of Am., Explorers, Phila. Gun. Engaged in restoration 17th century plantation, 1969—. Home: Eccleston's Hill Plantation Cambridge MD 21613 Office: Box 428 Cambridge MD 21613

WILLIAMSON-MICHAELS, SUE DODDS, antique dealer; b. Clarksburg, W.Va., Apr. 29, 1935; d. Okey Lee and Edna Elizabeth (Corder) Brown; B.S. cum laude, W.Va. U., 1957; postgrad. U. Md., 1960-63; m. Robert L. Michaels, Dec. 24, 1976; step-children—Lou, Lindy, Paul Michaels, Susan Quel. Tchr., Prince Georges Bd. Edn., 1957-64; owner Sue Williamson-Michaels, Antiques, New Market, Md., 1966—. Lectr., Hood Coll., Frederick (Md.) Community Coll., Carroll County Bd. Recreation. Sec., Williamsburg Village Civic Assn., 1965; co-chmn. Planned Parenthood Montgomery County, 1965-66. Town clk., New Market, 1969-74. Mem. Nat. Assn. Dealers in Antiques (state membership chmn. 1970-72), New Market Antique Dealers Assn. (pres. 1970), Early Am. Glass Club (pres. New Bremen chpt.), Mid-Am. Appraisers Assn., Olney C. of C., Mortar Bd. (editor 1957), Chi Omega. Methodist. Clubs: Mt. Airy Squares, New Market Garden. Contbr. articles to profl. jours. Address: PO Box 33 20 W Main St New Market MD 21774

WILLIG, WILLIAM PAUL, lawyer; b. Schenectady, Mar. 29, 1936; s. James Richard and Mildred Ann (Nock) W.; A.B., St. Michael's Coll., 1958; LL.B. J.D., Albany Law Sch., 1962. Admitted to N.Y. State bar, 1962; law ck.. Higgins Roberts Beyerl & Coan, Schenectady, 1962, asso., 1962-68, partner, 1968—, sec., 1973—; med. malpractice panelist 4th Jud. Dist., N.Y. Supreme Ct., 1975—; instr. law Am. Inst. Banking, 1965—, Union Coll., 1968-69. Mem. Ballston (N.Y.) Zoning Rev. Com., 1972-73; mem. Schenectady County Democratic Com., 1966-67; 1st ward pres. Schenectady County, 1967. Mem. Federated, N.Y. State, Schenectady County bar assns., Am. Trial Lawyers Assn., Antique and Classic Boat Soc. (pres., dir.), Inter-Club Golf Assn. (co-founder Capital dist. N.Y. State). Clubs: Edison (dir.), Lake George, Schenectady Racquet. Home: 194 West Side Dr Ballston Lake NY 12019 Office: 502 State St Schenectady NY 12305

WILLING, PEARL R. (MRS. STANLEY S. WILLING), economist; b. N.Y.C.; d. Elias and Anna (Zieger) Rushfield; M.A., N.Y. U., 1947, Ph.D., 1972; m. Stanley S. Willing, Feb. 7, 1942; children—Lynne Beth, Merritt Averell. Economist, U.S. Nat. War Labor Bd., N.Y.C., 1942-45; dir. N.Y. Sch. Fashion Design, N.Y.C., 1948, pres., 1948-54; v.p. Willing Assos., Inc., Indsl. Realtors, 1955—; v.p. Oaklawn Realty Corp., 1950—; pres. Warren Fifth Corp., 1963-73; formerly acting chief econs. br. planning div. N. Atlantic div. U.S. Army C.E., coordinator fed. womens program, 1972-73, 76, now regional economist N. Atlantic div., also counselor Equal Employment Opportunities program, 1972-76. Trustee Bridge Found.; bd. dirs., corr. sec. People for Animal Welfare, Inc. Mem. Am., Met. econ. assns., Humane Soc. U.S., Soc. Govt. Economists, Federally Employed Women (v.p. membership Met. N.Y. chpt. 1976-77), Omicron Delta Epsilon. Contbr. articles to profl. jours. Home: 4704 Delafield Ave Riverdale NY 10471 Office: 90 Church St New York NY 10007

WILLING, S. STANLEY, educator, cons.; b. N.Y.C., Oct. 28, 1919; s. Harry and Laura (Glickstein) W.; M.A., N.Y. U., 1941, Ed.D., 1958, Ph.D., 1969; m. Pearl Rushfield, Feb. 7, 1942; children—Lynne Beth, Merrit Averell. Research asst. USES, 1936-38; production mgr. Metro Textile Corp., 1941-42; mem. faculty N.Y. U., 1946-48, 56-63, L.I.U., 1956-66; dean, Pa. Coll. Optometry, Phila., 1966-68; chmn. dept. bus. St. Francis Coll., 1968—; pres. Willing Assos., Inc., indsl. consultants; dir. N.Y. Sch. of Fashion Design, 1948-54, N.Y. Corr. Sch., 1953-58; pres. Oaklawn Realty Corp., 1240 Realty Corp. Trustee Bridge Found. Mem. nat. panel of Am. Arbitration Assn.; mem. advisory council SBA, 1976—. Served in U.S. Army; dir. Adj.-Gen's Sch., 1943-45. Recipient award Outstanding Realty Deal. 1955, 56; Profl. Mgr. citation Soc. Advancement Mgmt., 1974. Fellow Am. Acad. Optometry; mem. Nat. Assn. Real Estate Editors, Nat. Assn. Real Estate Bds., N.Y. State Assn. Realty Boards, Bronx Real Estate Bd. (pres. 1966), Nat. Realty Club, Am. Psychol. Assn., Am. Personnel and Guidance Assn., AIM, Phi Delta Kappa, Delta Sigma Pi, Delta Mu Delta. Author series Fashion Tng. Manuals, Mag. articles. Editor Real Estate and Building News, 1959-66; cons. editor Dental Mgmt. mag., 1967—. Co-editor: 20th Anniversary Yearbook of Adult Education. Home: 4704 Delafield Ave Riverdale NY 10471 Office: 180 Remsen St Brooklyn NY 11201

WILLINGHAM, WARREN WILLCOX, psychologist, testing service exec.; b. Rome, Ga., Mar. 1, 1930; s. Calder Baynard and Eleanor (Willcox) W.; Ga. Inst. Tech. 1952; Ph.D., U. Tenn., 1955; m. Anna Michal, Mar. 17, 1954; children—Sherry, Judith, Daniel. Research asso. World Book Co., N.Y.C., 1959-60; dir. evaluation studies Ga. Inst. Tech., Atlanta, 1960-64; dir. research Coll. Bd., N.Y.C., 1964-68; dir. access research office Coll. Bd., Palo Alto, Calif., 1968-72; exec. dir. program research Ednl. Testing Service, Princeton, N.J., 1972—; mem. adv. bd. on ednl. requirements Sec. of Navy, 1968; cons. to numerous schs., colls., U.S. Office Edn. Served to lt. USNR, 1955-59. Recipient Am. award So. Soc. Philosophy and Psychology, 1958. Fellow Am. Psychol. Assn., AAAS; mem. Nat. Council on Measurement in Edn. (dir.), Am. Ednl. Research Assn., Sigma Xi. Author: Free Access Higher Education, 1970; the Source Book for Higher Education, 1973; College Placement and Exemption, 1974; also various monographs. Editor: Measurement in Education, 1969-72. Editorial bds. Jour. Ednl. Measurement, 1971—, Alternate Higher Education, 1976, Am. Ednl. Research Jour., 1968-71. Contbr. articles, tech. reports to profl. jours. Office: Educational Testing Service Princeton NJ 08540

WILLIS, DAVID PETER, pub. health planner, fund exec.; b. N.Y.C., Nov. 16, 1930; s. Nathan Aaron and Jeanette (Grant) W.; B.A., Haverford Coll., 1952; M.PH., U. Pitts., 1957. Planning analyst Phila. City Planning Commn., 1953-54; adminstrv. asst. Mass. Gen. Hosp., Boston, 1957-60; asst. dir. Hosp. Planning Assn., Pitts., 1960-63; asst. v.p. for health scis. Temple U., Phila., 1963-70; v.p. Milbank Meml. Fund, N.Y.C., 1970—; vis. prof. community medicine Dartmouth Med. Sch., Hanover, N.H., 1976—; asst. prof. pub. health Womans Med. Coll. Pa., 1963-69; asst. prof. Temple U. Med. Sch., 1963-70; prof. social policy Grad. Sch. Social Adminstrn., Temple U., 1969-70; adj. prof. N.Y. U., 1973-76; lectr. epidemiology Yale U., 1973-76; cons. USPHS, 1963—. Danforth fellow, 1952-53. Fellow Am. Pub. Health Assn.; mem. Am., Internat. hosp. assns., Phi Beta Kappa. Quaker. Editor Milbank Meml. Fund Quar., 1976—; series editor Milbank Resource Books, 1973-76; contbr. articles to profl. jours. Home: 929 Park Ave New York City NY 10028 Office: Milbank Meml Fund 1 E 75th St New York City NY 10021

WILLIS, JAMES LORNE, govt. ofcl.; b. Toronto, Ont., Can., July 28, 1926; s. John and Ethel (Chamberlain) W.; student in personnel adminstrn. U. Toronto Extension; m. Isabella Blackley, June 9, 1951; 1 dau., Janet Lynne. With City of Toronto, 1945—, chief clk. charge personnel dept. pub. works, 1956-65, gen. supt. dept., 1965-66, gen. services supr. dept., 1966-75, coordinator sanitation sect. dept. pub. works, 1975-76, coordinator resources dept., 1976—. Recipient Samuel A. Greeley Local Govt. Service award, 1975. Mem. Am. Pub. Works Assn., City of Toronto Adminstrv., Profl. and Supervisory Assn. Mem. Anglican Ch. Club: Sons of Scotland. Office: 505 Richmond St W Toronto ON M5V 1Y3 Canada

WILLIS, THORNTON WILSON, artist; b. Pensacola, Fla., May 25, 1936; s. Willard Wilson and Edna Mae (Hall) W.; B.S., U. So. Miss., 1962; M.A., U. Ala., 1966; m. Peggy Jean Whisenhant, June, 1960; 1 son, David Shaw. One-man exhibitions include: Henri Gallery, Washington, 1968, Paley and Lowe, N.Y.C., 1970, New Orleans Mus. Art, 1972; group exhibitions include: Phila. Civic Center, 1970, Whitney Mus., 1971; represented in permanent collections: Whitney Mus., N.Y.C., New Orleans Mus. Art, Rochester Meml. Gallery, Chase Manhattan Collection, William Paley Collection, CBS; vis. artist in residence La. State U., New Orleans, 1971-72. Served with U.S.M.C., 1954-57. John Simon Guggenheim fellow, 1978-79. Asso. editor Re-View, 1978—. Home: 85 Mercer St New York City NY 10012 Office: 87 Mercer St New York City NY 10012

WILLIS, WILLIAM ERVIN, lawyer; b. Huntington, W.Va., Oct. 11, 1926; s. Asa Hannon and Mae (Davis) W.; student Ind. U., 1944, N.Y. U., 1945; A.B., Marshall U., 1948; J.D., Harvard U., 1951; m. Joyce Litteral, Sept. 1, 1949; children—Kathryn, Anne, William. Admitted to N.Y. bar, 1952; practiced in N.Y.C., 1951—; mem. firm Sullivan & Cromwell, 1951—; lectr. Practising Law Inst., 1963—. Trustee Fed. Bar Council, 1968-72; mem. 2d Circuit Commn. on Reduction Burdens and Costs Civil Litigation, 1977—. Served with AUS, 1944-46. Fellow Am. Coll. Trial Lawyers, Am. Bar Found.; mem. Am., N.Y. State (chmn. antitrust sect. 1976-77, exec. com. 1976—) bar assns., Assn. Bar City N.Y., Am. Judicature Soc., Am. Arbitration Assn. (panel arbitrators), N.Y. Law Inst., N.Y. County Lawyers. Clubs: Broad Street; Internat. (Washington). Contbr. articles to legal jours. Home: Dogwood Ln Alpine NJ 07620 also Otterhole Rd West Milford NJ 07480 Office: 125 Broad St New York City NY 10004

WILLNER, ALLEN EUGENE, psychologist; b. N.Y.C., Dec. 24, 1928; s. Martin A. and Celia (Lindenauer) W.; B.A., N.Y. U., 1950; M.A., U. Mo., 1952; Ph.D., Mich. State U., 1956; m. Stella Catherine O'Rourke, Sept. 1, 1956; children—Sharon, Keith, Kenneth. Clin. psychologist Adams Newsom & Morrow Psychiat. Clinic, Wichita, Kans., 1956-57; asst. chief psychologist Winter VA Hosp., Topeka, 1957-62; sr. clin. psychologist, dir., assn. and abstraction research project Menninger Found., Topeka, 1962-67; asst. dir. psychol. services, dir. psychosomatic research, program dir. Sr. Citizen's Treatment Program, dir. abstraction research project L.I. Jewish-Hillside Med. Center, Glen Oaks, N.Y., 1967—; asso. prof. clin. Psychiatry State U. N.Y. at Stony Brook, 1973—; adj. prof. grad. psychology program L.I. U., 1974—; cons. med. staff Jewish Inst. Geriatric Care. Bd. dirs., mem. med. council, chmn. psychosocial com. Nassau chpt. Am. Heart Assn.; mem. profl. adv. bd. Nassau County chpt. Mended Hearts. Diplomate Am. Bd. Profl. Psychology. Mem. N.Y. Soc. Clin. Psychologists, Am., N.Y., Suffolk County psychol. assns., Am. Psychopath. Assn., Internat. Neuropsychol. Soc., Am. Psychosomatic Soc., Gerontol. Soc. Author: Willner Unusual Meanings Vocabulary Test, 1965; Willner Instance Similarities Test, 1971; Conceptual Level Analogies Test, 1971; co-author: Willner-Scheerer Analogy Test, 1965. Home: E Neck Rd Huntington Bay NY 11743 Office: Hillside Hosp Glen Oaks NY

WILLNER, JEFFREY STEVEN, radiologist; b. Newark, Dec. 21, 1944; s. Philip and Thelma (Kruman) W.; A.B., cum laude, Princeton U., 1966; postgrad. U. Va. Med. Sch., 1966-68; M.D., Mount Sinai Sch. Medicine, 1970; m. Suzanne Christina Hammond, Feb. 14, 1970; 1 dau., Viveka. Intern, Lenox Hill Hosp., N.Y.C., 1970-71; resident Mt. Sinai Hosp., N.Y.C., 1971-74; practice medicine specializing in radiology, 1974—; asst. attending radiologist Beekman Downtown Hosp., N.Y.C., 1974-75, Eastern L.I. Hosp., Greenport, N.Y., 1975—, Central Suffolk Hosp., Riverhead, N.Y., 1975—, Southampton (N.Y.) Hosp., 1976—. Diplomate Am. Bd. Radiology. Mem. Am. Coll. Radiology, L.I. Radiol. Soc., Sigma Xi. Contbr. chpt. to med. text. Home: Further Ln Amagansett NY 11930

WILLNER, MORRIS STEPHEN, mortgage banker; b. Stuttgart, Ger., Aug. 23, 1946; s. Charles and Sylvia (Kirschenblatt) W.; came to U.S., 1949, naturalized, 1954; B.S., U. Tampa, 1968; M.B.A., N.Y. U., 1970; m. J. Sherrie Corson, Mar. 29, 1969; children—Bruce, Michael Benjamin. Accountant, Arthur Young & Co., Phila., 1970-71; sr. v.p., chief fin. officer Fidelity Bond & Mortgage Co., 1971—; dir. Fidelity Bond & Mortgage Co. Legis. com. Apt. Council of Phila. Homebuilders, Pa. Homebuilders Assn.; bd. dirs., mem. budget com. Har Zion Temple. C.P.A., Pa. Mem. Pa. (adv. com. of mems. N.I.P.), Am. insts. C.P.A.'s, Cooperation with Bankers and Credit Execs. Jewish. Clubs: Locust, Green Valley Country, Golden Slipper. Home: 200 Oak Hill Rd Bala Cynwyd PA 19004 Office: S E 16th and Walnut Sts Philadelphia PA 19102

WILLOUGHBY, WILLIAM FRANKLIN, II, educator; b. Washington, Feb. 4, 1936; s. William Westel and Olive Patricia (De Zychlinska) W.; A.B., Johns Hopkins U., 1957, M.D., 1965, Ph.D., 1965; m. Judith Eleanor Barbaras, Oct. 25, 1975; children by previous marriage—Westel Woodbury, William Franklin, Laura, Mary Scott. Intern, Johns Hopkins Hosp., Balt., 1965-66, resident, 1966-67; Arthritis Found. fellow Scripps Clinic and Research Found., La Jolla, Calif., 1967-69; asst. prof. pathology and microbiology Case Western Res. U., Cleve., 1969-72; dir. Virginia Mason Research Center, Seattle, 1972-75; asso. prof. pathology and environ. health scis. Johns Hopkins Hosp. and U. Sch. Medicine, Balt., 1975—. Flight surgeon USAFR, 1975—. NIH fellow, 1959-63; Poncine scholar, 1972-75; NIH grantee, 1976—. Mem. N.Y. Acad. Scis., AAAS, Am. Thoracic Soc., Internat. Acad. Pathology, Coll. Am. Pathologists, Internat. Soc. Nephrology, Aerospace Med. Assn., Soc. USAF Flight Surgeons, Sigma Xi. Episcopalian. Contbr. articles to profl. jours. Home: 14 Gunpowder Rd Baltimore MD 21234 Office: Johns Hopkins Hosp Dept Pathology Baltimore MD 21205

WILLS, JAMES HENRY, educator; b. Richmond, Va., Aug. 7, 1912; s. James Henry and Sarah Macy (Baughman) W.; B.S., Va. Poly. Inst., 1934; M.S., Med. Coll. Va., 1936; Ph.D., U. Rochester, 1941; m. Ruth Elizabeth Cass, June 12, 1948. Asso. in pharmacology U. Rochester Sch. Medicine and Dentistry, 1941-46; asst. prof. pharmacology U. Tenn., 1946-47; asst. chief pharmacology br. Med. Research Lab., Edgewood Arsenal, Md., 1947-48, chief, 1948-57, asst. chief physiology div., 1957-61, chief, 1961-65; prof. pharmacology Albany (N.Y.) Med. Coll., 1965-75, prof. toxicology, 1969-75, asst. dir. Inst. Comparative and Human Toxicology, 1965-69, asso. dir., 1969-75; sr. research reviewer Nat. Inst. Occupational Safety and Health, 1975—. Exec. sec. N.Y. State Pesticide Control Bd., 1965-70; mem. toxicology subcom., food protection com., food and nutrition bd. NRC, 1952-70; mem. toxicology study sect. NIH, 1968-72; mem. med. adv. panel NASA, 1971-76. Recipient Decoration for Exceptional Civilian Service, Army Dept., 1965; Porter fellow Am. Physiol. Soc., 1940-41; Sec. of Army research and study fellow, 1958. Mem. Am. Chem. Soc., Am. Physiol. Soc., Am. Soc. Pharmacology and Exptl. Therapeutics, Soc. Exptl. Biology and Medicine, Soc. Toxicology, AAAS, N.Y. Acad. Scis., Sigma Xi. Contbr. to profl. jours. Home: 9706 Bellevue Dr Bethesda MD 20014 Office: 5600 Fishers Ln Rockville MD 20857

WILLS, LAWRENCE AUGUST, educator; b. N.Y.C., Feb. 24, 1938; s. August and Edna Clara (Davies) W.; B.S., L.I. U., 1960; M.S. in Bus., Hofstra U., 1965; m. S. Helen Hansen, Aug. 29, 1964; children—Michelle, Christopher, Sandra, Eric. Accountant, Peat, Marwick & Mitchell, 1961, Sperry Rand, 1962, Huntington, 1963, State U. N.Y., 1966, Research Assos., 1967; asst. prof. bus. adminstrn. State U. N.Y., Maritime Coll., Fort Schuyler, N.Y., 1974—; project dir. Research Found. L.I., 1972—; mem. faculty Center for Maritime Studies, Webb Inst. Naval Architecture, 1978; project researcher Maritime Adminstrn., 1978-79. Served with U.S. Army, 1960-61. Mem. World Trade Club L.I. (pres. 1972), Pa., Petroleum Assn. (mem. fuel com. 1976), Phi Sigma Kappa, Phi Delta Kappa, Delta Pi Epsilon. Home: PO Box 391 East Stroudsburg PA 18301 Office: Maritime Coll Ft Schuyler Bronx NY 10465

WILLS, ROBERT HENRY, JR., environ. engr.; b. Cortland, N.Y., Jan. 6, 1950; s. Robert Henry and Maxine (Russell) W.; student elec. tech. (Kiwanis scholar 1968-69), State U. N.Y., 1968-70, liberal arts Tompkins Cortland Community Coll., 1972, bus. adminstrn. Syracuse U., 1979; m. Martha Gay Resch, Dec. 29, 1973; children—Robert, James. Store mgr. Fay's Drug Co., New Hartford, N.Y., 1970-74; waste water treatment engr. Crucible Splty. Metals div. Colt Industries, Syracuse, N.Y., 1974—. Mem. Water Pollution Control Fedn., Fluid Power Soc., Am. Water Works Assn., N.Y. Water Pollution Control Assn. (vice chmn. indsl. waste com.). Home: 24 Bayberry Circle Liverpool NY 13088 Office: Crucible Inc PO Box 977 Syracuse NY 13201

WILLSIE, HARRY ALFORD, investor; b. Jacksonville, Mo., Dec. 20, 1928; s. James George and Lillian (Christianson) W.; came to Can., 1954, naturalized, 1962; student U. Mo., 1948-53; children—Billie Wayne, Alan Andre, Carol Dean, Debora Marie Suzanne. Sports editor, pub. relations ofcl. Quantico (Va.) Marine Post Newspaper, 1946-48; radio and TV nat. advt. sales rep. Horace N. Stovin Co., Toronto and Montreal, Que., 1953-57; founder, pres. All-Can. Gun Sales, Inc., Montreal, 1957-73, Coronet Guns and Gunsmitting Inc., Montreal, 1960-73, Montclair Fuel Oils Inc., Montreal, 1964-73; owner mgr. real estate (comml. and apt. properties), Montreal, Reno, Phoenix, P.R., 1974—. Served with USMC, 1946-48; ATO. Mem. Can. Skeet Shooting Assn. (pres. 1969-76), Shooting Fedn. Can. (dir. 1963-76), Que. Skeet Shooting Fedn. (dir. 1967—), Comité Conjoint (dir. 1974—), Nat. Skeet Shooting Assn. (exec. com. officer 1972—), Que. Provincial Trap Shooting Assn. (dir. 1959-67), Amateur Trap Shooting Assn. Am. (dir. 1959-68), Can. Trap Shooting Assn. (pres. 1963-67), Shooting Fedn. Can. (dir. Can. Olympic Assn. 1974-76). Editor Rod and Gun mag., 1965-74. Address: 447 Ave de Versailles Ville d'Esterel PQ J0T 1E0 Canada

WILLTON, CHARLES, right-of-way agt., appraiser; b. Centreton, Ont., Can., July 20, 1907; s. Wilbur Rufus and Violet (Thwaites) W.; certificate U. Toronto, 1947; m. Mary Edith Traver, Apr. 7, 1961. Chief officer Colonial Steamship Co., Port Colborne, Ont., 1948-53; property agt. Ont. Dept. Hwys., Willowdale, 1955-65, appraisal supr. No. region, N.Bay, Ont., 1965-67; pvt. practice right-of-way agt. and appraiser, Brantford, Ont., 1967—. Commr., Province of Ont. Served with Royal Canadian Navy, 1939-46. Mem. Brantford Regional Real Estate Assn., Am. Soc. Appraisers (past regional gov.), Am. Right of Way Assn., Am. Arbitration Assn. Clubs: Masons (32 deg.), Shriners, Order Eastern Star, Gentlemen of Creeks. Home: 115 Erie Ave Brantford ON N3S 2G3 Canada Office: PO Box 1282 Brantford ON N3T 5T3 Canada

WILMER, WILLIAM HOLLAND, II, lawyer; b. Birmingham, Ala., Feb. 28, 1931; s. William Holland and Frances (Arant) W.; B.A., Yale, 1952; LL.B., Harvard, 1955; m. Lucy Walcott Parrish, Dec. 28, 1964; children—William Holland III, Lucy Walcott Parrish. Admitted to Md. bar, 1958, D.C. bar, 1964; law clk. Md. Ct. of Appeals, 1959-60; partner Cross, Shriver, Bright & Washburne, Balt., 1966-68, Brune & Robertson, Balt., 1968-73; counsel Sun Life Ins. Co. Am., 1973—. Served with AUS, 1955-58. Mem. Am., Md., Balt. (chmn. com. probate, trusts and persons under disability 1973—) bar assns. Republican. Episcopalian. Clubs: Elkridge, Maryland, Merchants (Balt.); Yale (N.Y.C.). Home: Little Oxmead White Hall MD 21161 Office: 1100 Sun Life Bldg Baltimore MD 21201

WILMORE, VIOLET SMITH, counselor, social worker; b. Summit, N.J., Jan. 19, 1923; d. Herbert Samuel and Urselina Rebecca Smith; diploma N.Y. Bus. Sch., 1947; B.A., Kean Coll., 1974; m. Thomas Stanley Wilmore, Aug. 22, 1953; children—Pamela, Brenda. With RCA, Harrison, N.J., 1942-53; instr. piano pvt. studio, Boonton, N.J., 1951-53, Rathbun Conservatory Music, Plainfield, N.J., 1959-64; permanent substitute tchr. Abraham High Sch., Roselle, N.J. and Locust Sch., Roselle, 1962-64; library asst. Union (N.J.) Coll., 1964-65; teenage dir. YWCA, Elizabeth, N.J., 1965-67; instr. sociology Union Coll., 1976-78; counselor N.J. Manpower Council, 1967—, transfer coordinator, 1976—, acting dir. counseling, 1975-77; real estate saleswoman. Bd. dirs. Recreation Commn. City of Roselle, 1968—, Mt. Carmel (N.J.) Guild Mental Health Center, 1970-72, Central N.J. Lung Assn.; mem. N.J. Adv. Com. for Health. Certified sch. social worker/tchr., N.J. Mem. Union County (Pres. 1974) N.J. (exec. com. 1974-75) personnel and guidance assns., N.J., Am. coll. personnel assns., Am. Assn. Univ. Adminstrs., Nat. Council Negro Women, Nat. Vocat. Guidance Assn., Am. Sch. Counselors Assn., Humanistic Educators Assn., others. Democrat. Methodist. Club: Negro Bus./Profl. Women's (chairperson com. 1966-70). Home: 216 E 8th Ave Roselle NJ 07203 Office: Union Coll 1033 Springfield Ave Cranford NJ 07016

WILNER, MARIE, artist; b. Paris, July 24, 1910; d. Joseph and Helene Spring; B.A., Hunter Coll., 1927; student Art Students League 1929-32; m. Joseph Walter Wilner, Sept. 4, 1927; children—Harvey Ira, Helene Wilner Cornell, George D. One-woman shows: Galerie für Zeitgenossische Kunst, Hamburg, Germany, 1971, Galerie Renoir, Brussels, 1961, Galerie Raymond Duncan, 1962, Revel Gallery, N.Y.C., 1963, Evansville (Ind.) Mus. Art, 1963, Irving Gallery, Milw., 1964, Pietrantonio Westhampton Beach Gallery, 1964, Musée d'Art Moderne, Paris, Club Internat. Féminin, Paris, 1964, Sheldon Swope Mus., 1964, N.Y. U. Mus., 1965, Dickson Gallery, Washington, 1968, 69, LaSalle Coll, 1968, Bohman's Gallery, Stockholm, 1968, Rioboo Nueve Gallery, Buenos Aires, Argentina, 1969, Tweed Gallery, U. Minn., 1969, Galerie Diana de Renucy, N.Y., 1970, Bohman's Gallery, Stockholm, numerous others; exhibited in group shows: Knickerbocker Artists, Catherine Lorrilard Group, Irvington Mus., Ross Gallery, Newark, Pa. Acad. Fine Arts, Phila., Contemporary Arts Gallery, Barzansky Gallery, Collectors of Am., Village Art Center, Raymond Duncan Gallery, Paris, Athens, Brussels World Fair, Tokyo, Butler Art Inst., N.Y. U. Mus., Evansville (Ind.) Mus., Joe and Emily Mus., Fla., Birmingham Mus., Norfolk Mus., Ga. Mus., Nat. Mus. Art and Sport, Bronx Mus. Art, Deauville, France, Met. Mus. various galleries; traveling show Nat. Assn. Women Artists covering various museums U.S. and abroad; represented in permanent collections: museums of Angouleme and Cognac, France, Tweed Gallery U. Minn., Community Coll. N.Y., Sapad Obat Yam, Israel, Musée de Luxemberg, Paris. Recipient first prize N.J. Mus., 1957; Grumbacher-purchase award Nat. Assn. Women Artists, 1962; gold medal Am. Artists Profl. League, 1963; Talens prize Artist and Sculptors N.J., 1963; Bronze medal Internat. Art Exhbn., Charleroi, Belgium, 1972; chevalier 4th grade merit Queen Fabiola Belgium, 1974; numerous others. Work recorded in the Library of Congress, Washington. Mem. Nat. Assn. Women Artists (chmn. jury awards 1963; dir.), Am. Artists Profl. League, Soc. Am. Artists and Sculptors, League Present Day Artists (pres.), Royal Soc. Arts London (life), Arts Found. Caravan (chmn.), Internat. Arts Guild Monaco, Haute Academie Littéraire et Artistique de France, Internat. Platform Assn., Nat. Soc. Arts and Letters, Artists Equity (dir.), Alumni Assn. Hunter Coll., Internat. Arts Guild, Artists and Sculptors N.J., Kappa Pi. Address: 77 7th Ave New York City NY 10011

WILSON, CALVIN THOMAS, judge; b. Phila., Feb. 25, 1928; s. Ernest and Beatrice (Culbreth) W.; B.A., Lincoln U., 1949; LL.B., Howard U., 1952, J.D., 1952; m. Yvonne Garnett, Jan. 1, 1953; 1 son, Calvin T. II. Admitted to Pa. bar, 1956; asst. atty. gen. Commonwealth Pa., 1961-63; asst. city solicitor City of Phila., 1963-71; ct. adminstr. Phila. Municipal Ct., 1971; judge Pa. Ct. of Common Please Dist. One, Trial Div., 1971—; sec. Bd. Judges, 1976—; mem. Pres.'s Com. for Civil Rights Under Law, 1969-71; mem. Phila. Bd. City Trust, Taxes Rev., 1972—. Bd. dirs. Met. Hosp., Phila., 1976—. Recipient award for service above and beyond call of duty Phila. chpt. NAACP., 1963-64, Outstanding Service award Puerto Rican Citizens Com., 1976, Citizen Testimonial award Citizens Com. Phila., 1974, 77, award for services to Wissahickon Valley dist. Boy Scouts Am., 1977, 25th Silver Anniversary award Four Chaplins, 1977. Mem. Nat., Pa., Phila. bar assns., Barristers Club Phila., Am. Arbitration Assn., Pa. Guardsmen, Stenton Neighbors Com., Omega Psi Phi. Office: 236 City Hall Philadelphia PA 19107

WILSON, CARL BENOIT, ins. broker; b. Cleve., Oct. 11, 1930; s. Leelis Roscoe and Corrie Beatrice (Crawford) W.; student pub. schs., also specialized schs.; m. Gladys Hill, Feb. 22, 1959; children—Darryl, Michael, Carla. Sales rep. Moore Computer Forms, Inc., 1968-73; engaged in ins. bus., 1973—; dist. mgr. Am. Gen. Ins. Co., Mt. Vernon, N.Y., 1977—; notary pub. Active local Cub Scouts; choir dir. Grace Baptist Ch., Mt. Vernon, 1974—. Mem. Nat. Assn. Life Underwriters, Amalgamated Musicians Union. Address: 40 E Sidney Ave Mt Vernon NY 10550

WILSON, CHARLES FRANK, ednl. adminstr.; b. Drums, Pa., July 8, 1929; s. Lloyd and Mae (Callender) W.; 3 children. B.A. in Spanish and French, with honors, Pa. State U., State College, 1950, M.Ed. in Ednl. Adminstrn., 1958; Ed.D. in Secondary Adminstrn., Columbia U., N.Y.C., 1961; m. Joan Marie Decrio; children—Charles L., Philip M., James M. Tchr. Spanish, French Fort Lee (N.J.) High Sch., 1958-60, also basketball coach; prin. Wheatland-Chili Jr.-Sr. High Sch., Scottsville, N.Y., 1961-63; supervising prin. Kutztown (Pa.) Area Sch. Dist., 1963-70; supt. Allentown (Pa.) Sch. Dist., 1970—; vis. prof. Kutztown State Coll., 1968-69, Lehigh U., 1976-77. Exec. bd. United Way. Lehigh County, 1971-74; chmn. Allentown Youth Commn., 1975—; mem. pres.'s planning council United Wesleyan Coll. Mem. Am., Pa. assns. sch. adminstrs., Pa. State Alumni Assn., Urban Pa. Supts. (founder, chmn.), Phi Delta Kappa. Recipient Outstanding Lang. award Hazleton Penn State Center, 1948. Danforth fellow, 1975. Contbr. articles in field to profl. jours. Home: 828 N Arch St Allentown PA 18104 Office: 31 S Penn St Allentown PA 18105

WILSON, CHARLES PHILIP, psychiatrist; b. Scarsdale, N.Y., Dec. 15, 1920; s. Andrew and Edith Lydia (Rose) W.; B.A., Yale, 1942; M.D., Columbia, 1945, certificate in psychoanalytic medicine, 1952; m. Christine Bagaloff, Aug. 12, 1951; children—Cynthia, Scott Numo, Marc Numo. Intern, U.S. Naval Hosp., St. Albans, N.Y., 1945-46; resident psychiatry Manhattan State Hosp., N.Y.C., 1948-50; practice psychiatry and psychoanalysis, N.Y.C., 1949—; asst. clin. prof. psychiatry, mem. faculty, div. psychoanalytic edn. Downstate Med. Sch., State U. N.Y., Bklyn., 1965—; asso. psychiatrist in charge psychosomatic service Brookdale Hosp., Bklyn., 1969-71; lectr. psychosomatic liaison staff St. Luke's Hosp., N.Y.C., 1971—; collaborating psychoanalyst dept. psychiatry Columbia Coll. Phys. and Surg. Mem. med. bd. St. Luke's Hosp. Center, N.Y.C., 1959—. Served to lt. (j.g.) M.C., USNR, 1945-48. Fellow Am. Psychiat. Assn.; mem. Am. Psychoanalytic Assn. (exec. councillor), AMA, Psychoanalytic Assn. N.Y. (dir. 1971-74). Clubs: Barnard (N.Y.C.); Old Lyme (Conn.) Country. Editor Bull. Psychoanalytic Assn. N.Y., 1965—. Contbr. articles on dream symbols and psychosomatics to profl. jours. Address: 1148 Fifth Ave New York City NY 10028

WILSON, DONALD ALFRED, land boundary cons., surveyor; b. Greenville, Maine, Mar. 31, 1941; s. Donald Henry and Ada Robbins (Lawler) W.; B.S., U. Maine, 1965; M.S., U. N.H., 1967; m. Christine Marie Dalphin, Aug. 20, 1967; children—Richard David, Stephen James. Instr. forest resources U. N.H., 1967-68; instr. forest resources, surveying U. Maine, 1968-74; pres. Border Land Cons., Inc., Tamworth, N.H., 1974-76; land surveyor Parker Survey Assos., Inc., Seabrook, N.H., 1976-78; land boundary cons., 1977—. Registered land surveyor, profl. forester. Mem. Soc. Am. Foresters, Am. Forestry Assn., Am. Congress Surveying and Mapping, Can. Inst. Surveying, Maine Soc. Land Surveyors (past pres.), Vt. Soc. Surveyors, N.H. Land Surveyors Assn. (pres.), New Eng. Land Title Assn., Soc. Protection of N.H. Forests, Natural Resources Council Maine, Land Info. Inst. Republican. Congregationalist. Clubs: Masons, Shriners. Contbr. articles to profl. jours. Home and office: RFD Lamprey Rd East Kingston NH 03827

WILSON, EDMUND ALLENBY, JR., architect, planner, developer; b. Helena, Ark., Mar. 18, 1938; s. Edmund Allenby and Lillian Graham (Burke) W.; B.A., U. Ark., 1964, B.Arch., 1964; m. Darleen Jane Berkowicz, May 26, 1966; children—Artelia Lyn, Elise Courtney, Christopher Allenby. Designer, draftsman Alderman & Macneish, West Springfield, Mass., 1962-68; job capt. Diehl, Miller & Buselle, Princeton, N.J., 1968-69; prin., v.p. J. Robert Hillier, Architects/Planners, P.A., Princeton, 1969—; v.p. Design Interface, Inc.; guest design jurist Mercer County Community Coll. Served with Air N.G., 1962-68. Certified Nat. Council Archtl. Registration Bds.; licensed architect, N.J., Mass.; licensed planner, N.J. Mem. AIA, N.J. Soc. Architects. Roman Catholic. Home: 21 Bainbridge St Princeton NJ 08540 Office: 791 Alexander Rd Princeton NJ 08540

WILSON, EDWIN MARSHALL, JR., mfrs. rep.; b. Swedesboro, N.J., Mar. 28, 1940; s. E. Marshall and Kathryn L. Wilson; B.S. in Bus. Adminstrn., U. Southwestern La., 1964; m. Irene Faith Zappala, Sept. 16, 1968; children—Eric Marshall, Joseph John. Regional sales mgr. Bermilo div. Brown Co., North Stratford, N.H. and Mt. Holly, N.J., 1966-68; partner C.C. Lowry Co. Inc., Pennsville, N.J., 1968-74, pres., 1974—; pres. Apollo Enercon Co., 1978—. Chmn. Quinlan

Meml. Tournament, Pennsville, 1976-78. Mem. Pa. Mfrs. Reps. Assn. (v.p.), Middle Atlantic Wholesalers Assn., Am. Soc. San. Engrs., Quaker Tri-State Wholesalers Assn., Assn. Industry Mfrs. Reps., Del. Valley Trade Golf Assn. Republican. Roman Catholic. Clubs: Elks, Sakima Country (v.p.). Home: 25 K Dr Pennsville NJ 08070 Office: 2 S Hook Rd Pennsville NJ 08070

WILSON, FRANCES HELEN, occupational therapist; b. Pitts., Oct. 17, 1929; d. J. Vernon and Margaret Hassler (Prugh) Wilson; B.A., Conn. Coll., 1951; advanced standing certificate Columbia Sch. Occupational Therapy, 1953. Therapist, Washington County Soc. Crippled Children and Adults, Washington, Pa., 1953-54; staff therapist Oakland VA Hosp., U. Pitts., 1955-66; supr. occupational therapy Aspinwall VA Hosp., Pitts., 1966-74, Oakland VA Hosp., Pitts., 1974—. Active Jr. League Pitts., Inc. Mem. Western Pa. (treas. 1967-69), Am. occupational therapy assns. Republican. Presbyterian. Clubs: Conn. Coll. (treas. 1971—), Twentieth Century (Pitts.). Home: 14 Devon Ln Ben Avon Heights Pittsburgh PA 15202 Office: University Dr Pittsburgh PA 15240

WILSON, FRANK SINCLAIR, mfg. co. exec.; b. Ludlow, Mass., Apr. 20, 1923; s. David Weir and Alice (Tourville) W.; B.S. cum laude, U. Hartford, 1958; m. Joan Estelle Marshall, Sept. 18, 1948; children—Gail Estelle, Jeanne Celia, Peter Marshall. Prodn. control mgr. Cheney Bros., Inc., Manchester, Conn., 1956; prodn. control mgr. J.M. Ney Co., Bloomfield, Conn., 1956-58, prodn. mgr., 1958-61, dir. mfg., 1961-64, v.p., gen. mgr., 1964-72, chmn., pres., chief exec. officer, 1972—, dir., 1965—; dir. Crouse-Hinds, E.B. Industries, Hartford Nat. Bank, Spencer-Turbine, Stanadyne, Inc., Bristol Brass. Bd. regents U. Hartford; bd. dirs. Manchester Meml. Hosp., Inst. Living; corporator Hartford Hosp. Served with USNR, 1943-46, 51-52. Mem. Bloomfield C. of C., Soc. Mfg. Engrs., Am. Dental Trade Assn., Greater Hartford C. of C. (dir.), Hartford County Mfrs. Assn. (dir.), Am. Legion. Republican. Clubs: Masons, Rotary, Ellington Ridge Country (past pres.). Home: 34 Heritage Dr Glastonbury CT 06033 Office: Maplewood Ave Bloomfield CT 06002

WILSON, GEORGE LEWIS, painter; b. Windsor, N.C., Sept. 30, 1930; s. George Lee and Esther Queen (Harmon) W.; student Sch. Visual Arts, N.Y.C., 1957-59; grad. Art Inst. Pitts., 1955; student Nat. Acad. Sch. Fine Art, 1964; m. Frances Callender, Jan. 29, 1964; 1 dau., Carmen Josefa. Staff artist Martin Pollack Advt. Co., N.Y.C., 1957-59; operator comml. and fine art studio, 1959—; coordinator, arranger art exhbn. Harlem Studio Mus., 1968. Bd. dirs. Dennis Ln. Coop. Apts., Inc., 1976—. Served with AUS, 1950-53; Korea. Decorated Bronze Combat Star; Washington Sq. Outdoor Art Exhbn. travel grantee, 1971; recipient Emily Lowe competition award, 1963, 1st prize for traditional figure, Atlantic City, 1974, 76, West Hudson Art Festival, 1978. Mem. Bronx Council Arts. Baptist. Home: 665 E 181st St Bronx NY 10457 Office: 4197 Park Ave Bronx NY 10457

WILSON, HARVEY J., data processing co. exec.; b. Lousia, Ky., Jan. 7, 1939; s. Frederick Earl and Goldia Ellen (Workman) W.; B.S., Pa. State U., 1962; m. Marlynn A. Turki, June 9, 1962; children—Gregory Lawrence, Mitchell Grant. Civil engr. Dravo Corp., Pitts., 1955-62; mem. sales staff med. systems div. IBM, Phila., 1965-69; founder, v.p. Shared Med. Systems Corp., King of Prussia, Pa., 1969—; also dir. Served to lt. USNR, 1963-65; PTO. Office: 650 Park Ave King of Prussia PA 19406

WILSON, HOWARD HAZEN, internat. relations writer; b. La Salle, Ill., July 2, 1908; s. George Alexander and Florence Mellen (Hazen) W.; Ph.B. in History, U. Chgo., 1936, Ph.D. in Internat. Relations, 1941; m. Mary Louise Bennett, Dec. 6, 1933; 1 son, Howard Hazen. Asst. economist, internat. econs. U.S. Dept. Commerce, 1942-43; asso. economist U.S. Office Alien Property Custodian, 1943-44; divisional asst. Am. Republics affairs U.S. Dept. State, 1944-46; internat. relations intelligence research Hdqrs. U.S. Air Force, 1951-58, historian, 1958-66 (all Washington). Prof. Internat. relations Am. Inst. for Fgn. Trade, 1946-47; lectr. history Am. U., 1950; lectr. internat. law and orgn. Georgetown U., summer 1949; vis. prof. history Shephard Coll., summer 1950. Recipient Honor award Dept. Air Force, 1956. Mem. Am. Soc. Internat. Law, Am. Polit. Sci. Assn., Psi Upsilon. Author 9 books, numerous articles on internat. politics and history (under ofcl. anonymity or security restrictions), 1952-66; bibliography on enemy property control, 1943; contbr. Am. Jour. Internat. Law. Home: 2140 Wyoming Ave NW Washington DC 20008

WILSON, JAMES ADAMS, chem. co. exec.; b. Charleston, S.C., Dec. 19, 1913; s. Robert Lee and Katherine (Adams) W.; ed. Cornell U., 1931-34; B.S., N.Y. U., 1950, M.B.A., 1952; m. Marion Werhan, Aug. 27, 1938; children—Ron, Candy. Salesman, Dow Chem. Co., N.Y.C., 1934-39, asst. export mgr., 1939-43; prodn. mgr. Regal Chem. Corp., Bklyn., 1943-46; export mgr. Wilson Export & Import Corp., N.Y.C., 1946-49; v.p. Wilson Dye & Chem. Dist. Inc., N.Y.C., 1949-55, dir., pres., 1955—; pres. Argyle Chem. Co., Port Washington, N.Y., 1952—, also dir. Trustee Vil. Baxter Estates, 1954-58; chmn. bd. Chemists Bldg. Co., 1971-72. Mem. Synthetic Organic Chem. Mfrs. Assn., Am. Chem. Soc., AAAS, Am. Inst. Chemists, Soc. Am. Chem. Indsty, Société Chimie Industrielle, Sigma Chi. Republican. Episcopalian. Clubs: Chemists (pres., distinguished service award), N.Y. Pigment (pres.), Cornell of Nassau; North Hempstead Country (gov.). Home: 13 Hilltop Rd Port Washington NY 11050 Office: Wilson Dye Chem Dist Inc PO Box 925 Port Washington NY 11050

WILSON, JAMES JOSEPH, ednl. adminstr.; b. N.Y.C., Jan. 21, 1921; s. Francis James and Elizabeth S. (McCafferty) W.; B.S., L.I. U., 1942; M.A., Columbia U., 1944, advanced diploma ednl. adminstrn., 1952, advanced diploma supt. schs., 1953; LL.D., Portis Law Sch., Boston, 1956; Ed.D., Steed Coll., Johnson City, Tenn., 1960; m. Mary T. Kennedy, Oct. 30, 1948; 1 dau., Maureen Elizabeth. Tchr. high schs., also spl. lectr. Coll. City N.Y., 1942-44; pub. health specialist N.Y.C. Health Dept., 1944-47; edn. specialist N.Y.C. Bd. Edn., 1948-52; edn. asst. to Mayor N.Y.C., 1952-64; mem. chancellor's cabinet L.I. U., 1964; chmn. Urban Edn. Task Force, N.Y.C., 1973; edn. cons., urbanologist. Mem. nat. adv. bd. Center Study of the Presidency. Bd. dirs. chpt. ARC; vice chmn. bd. dirs. Orchestral Soc. Westchester; bd. sponsors St. Vincent's Home for Boys. Recipient N.Y.C. certificate of honor for work with youth, 1972, Outstanding Educator award L.I. U., Distinguished Educator award Bedford Park Acad., award Coll. City N.Y. Mem. NEA, Am. Assn. Sch. Adminstrs., St. Thomas Aquinas Assn. (life), Knights of Malta, Blue Key. Home: 4 Birch Brook Rd Bronxville NY 10708 Office: Stewart Porter Agy 75 Rockefeller Plaza New York City NY

WILSON, JAMES REID, JR., publishing co. exec.; b. Phila., Aug. 5, 1934; s. James Reid and Florence S. (Dunn) W.; B.S. in Econs., U. Pa., 1956; m. Eve-Ann Jones, Apr. 4, 1970; children—Suzanne Winters, Diantha Curtis. Asso. dir. Western Hemisphere promotion N.Y. Times, 1966-69; indsl. advt. mgr., 1969-74; corp. advt. mgr. U.S. News & World Report, N.Y.C., 1974—. Pres., Pa. Assn. Retarded Citizens, 1969-71; sr. v.p. Nat. Assn. Retarded Citizens, 1975-77, pres., 1977—. Recipient Humanitarian award Phila. Assn. Retarded Citizens, 1973. Mem. Pub. Relations Soc. Am., St. Nicholas Soc. N.Y. Republican. Presbyterian. Club: Union League (Phila.). Office: US News & World Report 45 Rockefeller Plaza New York City NY 10020

WILSON, JOHN FLETCHER, educator; b. Keyser, W.Va., June 1, 1923; s. James Vincent and Susan May (Patton) W.; B.A., Wayne State U., 1947, M.A., 1948; Ph.D., U. Wis., 1955. Instr. speech Monmouth (Ill.) Coll., 1948-50; instr. to asso. prof. Cornell U., Ithaca, N.Y., 1953-67; asso. prof. speech Herbert H. Lehman Coll., City U. N.Y., Bronx, 1967-71, prof., 1971—; cons. in field. Served with USAAF, 1943-46, USAF, 1950-51. Mem. AAUP, Speech Communication Assn., Internat. Communication Assn., Am. Forensic Assn., Eastern Communication Assn. (pres. 1977-78), N.Y. State Speech Assn. (pres. 1968-69), N.Y. State Forensic Assn. (pres. 1956-57), Rhetoric Soc. Am., Tau Kappa Epsilon. Republican. Presbyterian. Author: (with Carroll C. Arnold) Public Speaking as a Liberal Art, 1964, 4th edit., 1978; Dimensions of Public Communication, 1976. Home: 201 E 21st St Apt 3K New York City NY 10010

WILSON, JOHN FREDERICK, elec. engr., electronic mfg. co. exec.; b. Akron, Ohio, Mar. 16, 1932; s. Dawson Perry and Effie Pauline (Hanes) W.; B.Engring., Yale U., 1954, M.Engring., 1956; children—John Frederick, Kimberly C., Elesa S., Douglas P., Ann A. Design engr. Hughes Aircraft Corp., Culver City, Calif., 1956-58; engring. group leader Norden div. United Aircraft Co., Costa Mesa, Calif., 1958-60; design engr. Beckman Instruments, Fullerton, Calif., 1960-61, engring. group leader, 1961-63, engring. sect. head, 1963-64, sr. tech. staff mem., 1964-65; mgr. spl. products Astrodata, Inc., Anaheim, Calif., 1965-68, mgr. switching div., 1968-70, v.p. mktg., 1970-71; product line mgr. Frederick Electronics Corp. (Md.), subs. Plantronics, Inc., Santa Cruz, Calif., 1971, exec. v.p., 1971-72, pres., 1972—, also dir.; v.p. Plantronics, Inc., Cupertino, Calif., 1976—; dir. Plantronics Can., Montreal. Bd. dirs. Jeanne Bussard Workshop, Frederick, 1975—. Served with U.S. Army, 1956. Mem. IEEE (sr.). Contbr. articles on communication switching to tech. jours. Patentee in field. Home: Route 5 Box 241 Frederick MD 21701 Office: PO Box 502 Frederick MD 21701

WILSON, JOHN LENNOX, civil engr.; b. Morristown, N.J., Nov. 24, 1940; s. Robert Francis and Gladys Helen (Oliver) W.; B.S., Tufts U., 1963; M.S., Yale U., 1964; Ph.D., U. Pitts., 1972; m. Cheryl Jean Griffin, June 18, 1966; children—Hillary Robin, Robert Lennox. Planning engr. Jacob Feld, N.Y.C., 1964-65; design engr. Richardson Gordon Assos., Pitts., 1966-67; instr. civil engring. U. Pa., 1969-72, asst. prof., 1972-78, research asso. prof., 1978—; vis. lectr. Swarthmore Coll., 1977; pres. Suburban Home Inspection Service, 1977; cons. area legal and indsl. firms. Active, Deepdale Civic Assn. Yale fellow, 1964-65. Mem. Am. Acad. Mechanics, Am. Concrete Inst., Assn. Computing Machinery, Pa. Environ. Council, Am. Soc. Engring. Edn., ASCE, Chi Epsilon. Episcopalian. Author: (with H. Kunreuther) A Model for Flood Policy Analyses, 1978; contbr. articles to profl. jours. Home: 17 Princeton Rd Wayne PA 19087 Office: U Pa 220 S 33d St D3 Philadelphia PA 19104

WILSON, JOHN STERLING, lease underwriting and mgmt. co. exec.; b. Phila., Aug. 13, 1931; s. Walter Fulton and Pearl (Curry) W.; B.A., U. Pa., 1953, postgrad. Wharton Sch., 1953-54; postgrad. Drexel Inst. Tech., 1957-60; m. Jane Estelle Clark, June 19, 1954; children—Elizabeth Ann, Bryan Sterling. With Price Waterhouse & Co., Phila., 1957-64, audit mgr., 1962-64; sr. v.p., treas. Lease Financing Corp., Radnor, Pa., 1964—. Served as lt. (j.g.) USNR, 1954-57. C.P.A., Pa. Mem. Am., Pa. insts. C.P.A.'s, Nat. Assn. Accountants. Home: Glenside PA 19038 Office: Lease Financing Corp Radnor PA 19087

WILSON, KENNETH JAY, educator; b. Oklahoma City, Aug. 25, 1944; s. Kenneth J. and Betty Wallace (Bleakmore) W.; B.A. magna cum laude, Yale U., 1966, M. Phil. (Woodrow Wilson fellow), 1969, Ph.D., 1973. Instr. in English, U. Rochester, 1970-74, asst. prof. English, 1974—; sr. fellow Folger Shakespeare Library, 1976; Am. Council Learned Socs. fellow, asso. Clare Hall Cambridge (Eng.) U., 1977. Mem. Renaissance Soc. Am., Modern Lang. Assn., English-Speaking Union. Clubs: Elizabethan, Mory's. Contbr. articles on English Renaissance lit. to lit. jours.; editor: Letters of Sir Thomas Elyot, 1976. Home: 12 Arnold Park Rochester NY 14607 Office: Dept English U Rochester Rochester NY 14627

WILSON, LEONARD MUIR, JR., econ. cons.; b. N.Y.C., Mar. 14, 1926; s. Leonard Muir and Thelma (Bowman) W.; student Union Coll., 1944; A.B., Dartmouth Coll., 1946; M.S., Columbia U., 1951, postgrad., 1962-63; m. Nancy Hoyt Vail, June 30, 1951; children—Deborah Howe, Jody Hoyt, Lucinda Frost, Steven Vail. Lectr., research asst. Columbia U., N.Y.C., 1951-53; econ. analyst Shell Oil Co., N.Y.C., 1953-55; economist Gen. Motors Corp., N.Y.C., 1955-60, E.I. du Pont de Nemours & Co., Wilmington, Del. 1960-63; sr. economist United Fruit Co., Boston, 1963-64, dir. planning, 1964-67, asst. to pres., 1967-69, v.p. mgmt. info. and planning systems, 1969-71, sr. v.p., 1971; econ. cons. to agribus. 1971-75; sr. staff cons. Arthur D. Little, Inc., 1975-76; pres. Agribus. Assos., Inc., 1976—. Lectr., U. Del., 1960-62, Northeastern U., Boston, 1964-65. Served with USNR, 1946-47. Mem. Am. Econ. Assn., Beta Gamma Sigma, Zeta Psi. Home: 28 Hunting Ln Sherborn MA 01770 Office: 36 Washington St Wellesley Hills MA 02181

WILSON, MALCOLM, lawyer, banker, former gov. N.Y. State; b. N.Y.C., Feb. 26, 1914; s. Charles H. and Agnes (Egan) W.; B.A., Fordham U., 1933, LL.B., 1936, LL.D., 1959; LL.D., Siena Coll., 1959, Pace Coll., 1959, St. Bonaventure Coll., 1960, SUNY, 1978, Bklyn. Law Sch., 1962, Canisius Coll., 1963, Le Moyne Coll., 1964, St. John Fisher Coll., 1964, Manhattan Coll., 1964, Columbia U., 1974; L.H.D., Alfred U., 1961; m. Katharine McCloskey, Sept. 6, 1941; children—Kathy, Anne. Admitted to N.Y. bar, 1936, since practiced in White Plains; partner firm Kent, Hazzard, Jaeger, Wilson, Freeman & Greer, 1946-77; chmn. bd., chief exec. officer Manhattan Savs. Bank, 1977—; mem. N.Y. State Assembly from 1st Westchester Dist., 1939-58; lt. gov. N.Y. State, 1959-73, gov., 1974; dir. Carrier Corp., Shearson Hayden Stone, Inc., Colin Service Systems, Inc., Levin Fixture Corp.; trustee Manhattan Savs. Bank, Bd. dirs. Cath. Youth Orgn., Archdiocese N.Y., Farmers Mus., N.Y. State Hist. Assn.; trustee Nat. Conf. Christians and Jews. Served with USNR, 1943-45. Recipient John Peter Zenger award N.Y. State Soc. Newspaper Editors, 1957. Mem. Am., N.Y. State, Westchester County bar assns., Ancient Order Hibernians, Soc. Friendly Sons St. Patrick, N.Y. Farm Bur. K.C. Home: 24 Windsor Rd Scarsdale NY 10583 Office: 385 Madison Ave New York NY 10017

WILSON, MARTIN BERNARD, producer; b. Phila., Jan. 4, 1927; s. Bourse C. and Ida (Love) W.; student Va. Poly. Inst., 1944; m. Laura Brockman Dec. 8, 1957 (div. 1966); 1 son, Jeffrey Brad; m. 2d, Judith W. Mucha, Mar. 15, 1968 (div. 1975); 1 dau., Cyma Bethany. Pres. Mio Internat. Records, Inc., N.Y.C., 1968-73, Mio Music Co. Ltd., N.Y.C., 1968-73, Marty Wilson Prodns., Inc., 1973—, Marty Wilson Mus. Co., 1973—, Cyma Music Co., 1973—, Cyma Record Corp., 1978—, D & M Sound Corp., 1978—. Served with USAAF, 1944-46. Address: 185 West End Ave New York City NY 10023

WILSON, MYRON ALLEN, scientific cons.; b. Phila., Jan. 9, 1930; s. Alfred L. and Mamie A. (Heron) W.; B.S., Drexel U., 1962; m. Annalise S. Schaffroth, Dec. 30, 1961; children—David, Susan. Engr., missile and space div. Gen. Electric Co., Phila., 1959-61, engr., reentry systems div., 1964-73; engr. mil. systems dept. Burroughs Corp., Paoli, Pa., 1961-64; v.p. Evaluation Assos., Inc., Bala Cynwyd, Pa., 1973—. Mem. membership com. Ambler (Pa.) YMCA, 1973-74; coordinator major employee campaigns greater Phila. United Fund, 1970. Bd. dirs. North Penn Vis. Nurse Assn., Ambler, 1972-73; bd. dirs. Ambler Drug Abuse Program, 1972-74, sec., 1973. Registered profl. engr., Calif. Fellow AAAS; mem. IEEE (sr.), Ops. Research Soc. Am. Author textbooks in field of engring. Home: 1664 Miller Circle Center Square PA 19422 Office: GSB Bldg 1 Belmont Ave Bala Cynwyd PA 19004

WILSON, NED MONROE, educator; b. Columbus, Ga., July 19, 1938; s. Bruce Monroe and Anne Carolyn (Thompson) W.; B.A., Emory U., 1960; B.D., Drew U., 1963, Ph.D., 1968; 1 son, Andrew Elliott. Instr. religion Upsala Coll., East Orange, N.J., 1966-68; asst. prof. philosophy and religion Essex County Coll., Newark, N.J., 1968-72, asso. prof., 1972—, asst. dir. social sci. div., 1968-70, acting dir., summers 1970, 71, chmn. dept. philosophy, religion and edn., 1970-73. Fulbright-Hayes grantee, Poland, summer 1974. Mem. Am. Acad. Religion, Soc. Biblical Lit., N.Y. Area Patristics Seminar. Democrat. Methodist. Home: 8 Grove St Madison NJ 07940 Office: Essex County Coll 303 University Ave Newark NJ 07102

WILSON, REXFORD, fire protection engr.; b. Washington, Dec. 16, 1930; s. Eugene Smith and Louise Augustine (Rexford) W.; B.S. in Elec. Engring., U. Mass., 1957; children—Timothy, Christopher, Sarah Wells. Firefighter, Amherst (Mass.) Fire Dept., 1952-57; insp. Factory Ins. Assn., Phila., 1957; engr., editor fire record, field rep. Nat. Fire Protection Assn., Boston, 1958-66; exec. dir. Fire Marshals Assn. N. Am., Boston, 1965-66; dir. fire service extension U. Md., College Park, 1967-68; product developer Fenwal Inc., Ashland, Mass., 1968-70; pres. Firepro Inc., Wellesley, Mass., 1970—; lectr. various univs. Mem. town meeting Town of Amherst, 1954-57; mem. Wellesley Housing Authority, 1968-69. Served with USAF, 1950-52; Korea. Recipient Bldg. Research Inst. award, 1962. Mem. Soc. Fire Protection Engrs. (sec.-treas. 1972-77), Nat. Fire Protection Assn., Nat. Acad. Code Adminstrn., Internat. Municipal Signal Assn., Bldg. Ofcls. Conf. Am. Editor New Eng. Firebrand, 1973—. Contbr. articles to fire jours. Patentee portable fire-extinguishing system jumbo aircraft. Home: 32 Cunningham Rd Wellesley Hills MA 02181 Office: 3 Walnut Park Wellesley Hills MA 02181

WILSON, ROBERT ALFRED, rare book dealer, author, editor; b. Balt., Apr. 1, 1922; s. Robert Louis and Bessie May (Buchman) W.; A.B., Johns Hopkins, 1943. Third sec. embassy, vice-consul U.S. Diplomatic Corps, Warsaw, Poland, 1946-48, Pretoria, S. Africa, 1949; actor N.Y.C., 1949-52; various bus. positions, N.Y.C., 1953-62; pres. Phoenix Bookshop Inc., N.Y.C., 1962—; author: A Bibliography of Gregory Corso, 1966; Gertrude Stein: A Bibliography, 1974; A Bibliography of Denise Levertov, 1972; Auden's Library, 1975; Marianne Serves Lunch, 1976; Rider Haggard's "She", 1977; editor numerous books poetry, bibliography; contbr. articles to mags. Served with U.S. Army, 1943-46. Decorated Purple Heart, Bronze Star. Democrat. Anglican. Club: Grolier (N.Y.C.). Home: 452 W 25th St New York City NY 10001 Office: Phoenix Bookshop Inc 22 Jones St New York City NY 10014

WILSON, ROBERT JAMES, airline co. exec.; b. Grand Rapids, Mich., June 15, 1902; s. James Alexander and Annie Ellen (McAlpine) W.; A.B., U. Mich., 1925; J.D., 1929; m. Helen G., Aug. 22, 1959. Admitted to Mich. bar, 1929; partner firm Womer, Norcross & Judd, Grand Rapids, Mich., 1930-42; v.p., gen. counsel Capital Airlines, Washington, 1942-61, dir., 1961-67; partner firm Patterson Belkamp & Webb, N.Y.C. and Washington, 1967-69; chmn., pres. Universal Airlines, Inc., Washington, 1969—; exec. v.p., sec., treas. Nat. Alliance of Businessmen, 1969. City commr., E. Grand Rapids, Mich., 1935-42; sr. warden Ch. of Our Saviour, Oat - Lands, Va., 1973. Recipient Presdl. Citation, Pres. Gerald Ford, 1976; Presdl. Commendation, Pres. Richard M. Nixon, 1972. Mem. Am. Bar Assn., Mich., D.C. bar assns. Club: Internat. Home: Route 3 PO Box 394 Leesburg VA 22075 Office: 1730 K St Washington DC 20006

WILSON, ROBERT JOSEPH, farm supply and food mktg. co. exec.; b. Auburn, N.Y., Sept. 23, 1931; s. George E. and Mary A. (Barron) W.; B.B.A., LeMoyne Coll., 1953; m. Kay Reid, June 2, 1956; 1 son, David. Supervising sr. accountant, mgr. Hurdman and Cranstoun, C.P.A.'s, Syracuse, N.Y., 1953-67; mgr., prin. Haskins and Sells, C.P.A.'s, Liverpool, N.Y., 1967-68; successively sr. auditor, gen. auditor, group controller distbn. services Agway Inc., Syracuse, 1969—, past officer subs. Active Boy Scouts Am. Served with U.S. Army, 1953-55. Mem. Inst. Internal Auditors (certified, NE regional dir., internat. membership and admissions chmn., bd. regents), Fin. Execs. Inst. (chpt. pres., mem. NE area ops. com.), Nat. Soc. Accountants for Coops., Nat. Acctg. Assn. (past dir.), Am. Acctg. Assn., LeMoyne Coll. Golden Circle. Roman Catholic. Club: Optimists (pres. Marcellus, N.Y.; lt. gov. N.Y. zone; mem. dist. bd. N.Y. State). Home: 2 Beach Rd Marcellus NY 13108 Office: Agway Inc Box 4933 Syracuse NY 13221

WILSON, ROBERT LAWRENCE, author, antiquarian; b. St. James, Minn., June 24, 1939; s. John M. and Genevieve M. (Gustafson) W.; student Carleton Coll., 1957-61; m. Charlotte A. Breitmaier, Mar. 11, 1973; children—Heidi, Peter, Christopher. Researcher, Armouries, H.M. Tower, London, 1960; firearms curator Wadsworth Atheneum, Hartford, Conn., 1965; mus. trainee Corcoran Gallery of Art, Washington, 1959; hist. cons. Colt's Firearms Co., Hartford, 1966—, sales corr., 1964-65, asst. mgr. pub. relations, 1965; free lance author antique firearms and engraving, 1966—; cons. Winchester Mus. of Buffalo Bill Hist. Found., Cody, Wyo., 1977, Remington Arms Co. Mus., Ilion, N.Y., 1977—; hon. curator Kans. State Hist. Soc., 1977—; mem. adv. com. dept. arms and armor Met. Mus. Art, N.Y.C., 1977. Author: Samuel Colt Presents, 1961; The Arms Collection of Colonel Colt, 1964; The Evolution of the Colt, 1967; Colt Commemorative Firearms, 1968, rev. edit., 1974; The Rampant Colt, 1969; Theodore Roosevelt Outdoorsman, 1969; The Book of Colt Firearms, 1971; The Book of Winchester Engraving, 1975; (with R.E. Hable) Colt Pistols, 1976; (with P.R. Phillips) Paterson Colt Pistol Variations, 1979, The Colt Heritage, 1979; contbr. articles on firearms to profl. publs.; editor: Antique Arms Ann., 1971, Whales and Whalemen, Scrimshaw and Scrimshanders (E. Norman Flayderman), 1972. Fellow Co. Mil. Historians; mem. Conn. (life) N.Y. (life), Kans. (life) hist. socs., Am. Assn. Museums, Am. Soc. Arms Collectors, Conn. Gun Guild (hon. mem.), Ga. Arms Collectors Assn. (hon. mem.), Nat., Ky. rifle assns., Wadsworth Atheneum, Tex. Gun Collectors Assn. (hon. dir. 1971-72), Accademio di San Marciano. Presbyterian. Clubs: Campfire Am., African Safari N.Y.

WILSON, ROBERT WOODROW, radio astronomer; b. Houston, Jan. 10, 1936; s. Ralph Woodrow and Fannie May (Willis) W.; B.A., with honors in Physics, Rice U., 1957; Ph.D., Calif. Inst. Tech., 1962; m. Elizabeth Rhoads Sawin, Sept. 4, 1958; children—Philip Garrett, Suzanne Katherine, Randal Woodrow. Research fellow Calif. Inst. Tech., Pasadena, 1962-63; radio astronomer Bell Labs., Holmdel,

N.J., 1963—. Recipient Henry Draper medal Royal Astron. Soc., London, 1977, Herschel medal, 1977; Nobel prize for physics, 1978; NSF fellow, 1958-61; Cole fellow, 1957-58. Mem. Am. Astron. Soc., Internat. Astron. Union, Am. Phys. Soc., Internat. Sci. Radio Union, Phi Beta Kappa, Sigma Xi. Discovered of 3 deg. k Microwave Backgraound Radiation, 1965; discovered of CO and other molecules in interstellar space using their millimeter wavelength radiation. Home: 20 Spring Valley Dr Holmdel NJ 07733 Office: Bell Labs HOH L239 Holmdel NJ 07733*

WILSON, ROGER WINSLOW, steel co. exec.; b. N.Y.C., June 16, 1934; s. Louis Alexander and Winifred Isabel (Nellist) W.; B.S. in Bus. Adminstrn., N.Y. U., 1956; M.B.A., U. Pitts., 1961; m. Shirley Ann Tracy, Dec. 4, 1954; children—Nancy, Judy, Roger, Richard. Gen. mgr. tin mill products sales Nat. Steel Corp., Weirton, W.Va., 1969-72, asst. v.p., 1972-75, v.p. sales Weirton Steel div., 1975-76, v.p. mktg., Pitts., 1976-78, gen. mgr. sales Western region, 1978—; instr. coll. mgmt. course W.Va. No. Community Coll. Chmn. baseball park devel. Weirton Baseball Assn., City of Weirton Planning Commn.; pres. Sheltered Workshop Com. of Weirton; chmn. Master Plan Fund Drive. Recipient Founders Day award N.Y. U., 1956; named Weirton Man of Year, Jr. C. of C., 1959; named to Hall of Fame, Weirton Baseball Assn., 1971; named Outstanding Indsl. Salesman, Purchasing Mag., 1975. Mem. Am. Steel and Iron Inst., Am. Mktg. Assn. Clubs: Hon. Order of Ky. Cols., Adm. of Cherry River W.Va. Office: 2800 Grant Bldg Pittsburgh PA 15219

WILSON, SONJA MARIE ALSTON, nurse; b. Pittsboro, N.C., July 26, 1940; d. Julius Jerry and Nettie Mae (Stone) Alston; B.S. in Nursing, Winston-Salem State U., 1969; M.S., Hunter Coll., 1974; postgrad. N.Y. U., 1974—; m. Louis H. Wilson, Jr., Aug. 10, 1974. Staff nurse, head nurse, supr. Bronx (N.Y.) Municipal Hosp. Center, 1969-74; dir. ambulatory nursing Montefiore Hosp., Bronx, 1974—; adj. lectr. Lehman Coll. Sch. Nursing, 1974—; cons. Heighter Height Day Care Center, 1974—. Recipient award for outstanding contbn. to health fair Montefiore Hosp., 1975. Mem. N.Y. Assn. for Ambulatory Care, Nat. League for Nursing Forum, Soc. for Hosp. Nursing Service Adminstrs., Am. Nurses Assn., N.Y. State, New York County nurses assns., Concourse Village Group for Concerned Tenants. Democrat. Home: 779 Concourse Village E Apt 20C Bronx NY 10451 Office: Montefiore Hosp and Med Center 111 E 210th St Bronx NY 10467

WILSON, STEPHEN FREDERICK, psychotherapist, social worker; b. San Jose, Calif., June 10, 1941; s. Kenneth Frederick and Mildred Esther W.; B.S., U. Calif. at Santa Barbara, 1964; M.S.W., Rutgers-the-State U., 1971. Peace Crops vol., Somalia, 1964-66; group work cons. Bklyn. Bur. Community Service, 1971-74; dir. Michael's Farm, summer community for children, N.Y.C. and Liberty, N.Y., 1974-78; exec. dir. Am. Soc. Group Psychotherapy and Psychodrama, N.Y.C., 1976—, program coordinator, 1973—; adminstr., therapist, social worker Inst. for Sociotherapy, N.Y.C., 1973—. Certified in psychodrama, sociometry and group psychotherapy. Fellow Am. Soc. Group Psychotherapy and Psychodrama (head psychodramatic diet workshop ann. meeting 1973-77); mem. Nat. Assn. Social Workers, Am. Personnel and Guidance Assn. Office: 39 E 20th St New York City NY 10003

WILSON, VINCENT JOSEPH, JR., govt. ofcl., historian, editor; b. Cleve., Apr. 24, 1921; s. Vincent Joseph and Genevieve Margaret (Vleck) W.; student Georgetown U., 1939-41; A.B. with honors, Ariz. State U., 1948; M.A., Claremont Grad. Sch., 1949; postgrad. Harvard U., 1949-50; m. Mary Jo Cavender, Sept. 30, 1944; children—Nicholas Cavender, Liza Jane. Instr., English dept. Mitchell Coll., New London, Conn., 1950-53, chmn. dept., 1953-55; corr. New London Day, 1952-55; editor Nat. Security Agy., Fort Meade, Md., 1956-62, sr. staff writer, 1963-71, chief historian, sr. editor, 1972—; pub. Am. History Research Assn., 1962—; lectr. English, U. Md., 1959-67, George Washington U., 1963-65. Served to 1st lt. USAAF, 1943-46. Recipient Freedoms Found. at Valley Forge Washington medal, 1968, Honor award, 1974, Nat. Security Agy. Meritorious Service award, 1975. Mem. Am. Hist. Assn. Club: Cosmos (Washington). Author: The Book of the Presidents, 1962, 7th edit., 1977, The Book of Great American Documents, 1967, 76, The Book of the States, 1972, The Book of the Founding Fathers, 1974; contbr. articles in field to various publs. Home: 1711 Gold Mine Rd Brookeville MD 20729 Office: Nat Security Agy Fort Meade MD 20755

WILSON, WAYNE CLAIR, cosmetic co. exec.; b. Phila., Oct. 30, 1950; s. Harry Clair and Rosemary Roberta (McLaughlin) W.; B.A. in Econs. cum laude, Villanova U., 1974; M.B.A., Drexel U., 1978; m. Judith Ann Dodds, Aug. 19, 1972; 1 son, Graham Dodds. With Aloe Charm, Inc., West Conshohocken, Pa., 1976—, v.p., 1977—, also dir. Mem. Big Bros. Assn. Mem. Nat. Assn. Accountants, Assn. M.B.A. Execs., Am. Mgmt. Assn., Fin. Mgmt. Assn., Phi Theta Kappa, Phi Kappa Phi. Club: Villanova (Phila.). Home: 5156 Westley Dr Clifton Heights PA 19018 Office: 2 Union Hill Rd West Conshohocken PA 19428

WILSON, WILLIAM JAMES, market researcher; b. Mpls., May 8, 1936; s. Elmo C. and Harriett Ellis (Russo) W.; A.B., Yale, 1958; M.A., Corpus Christi Coll., Cambridge, Eng., 1964; postgrad. U. Vienna, Austria, 1964; m. Julie Steers, Sept. 24, 1960; children—Amanda Jane, Heather May. Internat. advt. devel. mgr. Reader's Digest, Europe, London, 1964-67; exec. v.p., dir. Internat. Research Assos., N.Y.C., 1968-71; pres., chief exec. officer Starch INRA Hooper, N.Y.C., 1971—; trustee Roper Pub. Opinion Research Center. Chmn. Old Greenwich (Conn.) Health Assn. Charity Drive, 1969. Served with U.S. Army, 1959. Mem. Am. Mktg. Assn., Internat. Advt. Assn., Am. Assn. Pub. Opinion Research, World Assn. Pub. Opinion Research, European Soc. Mktg. Research. Episcopalian. Clubs: Yale, Players (N.Y.C.); Am., Wentworth (Eng.). Home: Palmer's Island Old Greenwich CT 06870 Office: 566 E Boston Post Rd Mamaroneck NY 10543

WILSON, WILLIAM LANEY, state ofcl., lawyer; b. Cumberland, Md., May 9, 1914; s. William Laney and Rhea (Myers) W.; A.B., Washington and Lee U., 1936, LL.B., 1938; LL.D., Frostburg State U., 1975; m. Elizabeth Gracie, May 16, 1942; 1 dau., Amanda Lee. Admitted to Md. bar, 1938; gen. practice law, 1938-41, 45-52; partner firm Wilson & Sharer, 1968—; dir. Queen City Brewing Co., Cumberland, Md., 1952—, pres., 1957—; dir. 1st Nat. Bank & Trust Co., Cumberland, Md., 1955-71, 78—; dir., treas. U.S. Brewers Assn., 1972-75; bank commr. State of Md., 1971-78. Vice pres. Md. Bd. Edn., 1963-67; mem. Md. Roads Commn., 1970-71; bd. dirs. Cumberland Fair Assn., Inc., Meml. Hosp.; chmn. bd. trustees State Colls. Md., 1960-70; trustee So. Sem. Jer. Coll., 1972—. Fellow Md. Bar Found.; mem. Am., Md. (v.p. 1955) bar assns., Cumberland C. of C. (pres. 1962), Md. Hist. Soc. (trustee 1977—). Episcopalian (sr. warden 1960—). Clubs: Cumberland Country; Center, Maryland (Balt.). Home: 527 Washington St Cumberland MD 21502 Office: 100 S Liberty St Cumberland MD 21502

WILSON, ZANE ARTHUR, aviation cons.; b. Muncie, Ind., Dec. 26, 1942; s. Robert Theron and Frances Edna (Baker) W.; student Muncie pub. schs.; m. Shelvie Jean Croyle, Jan. 21, 1967; 1 son., Shane Jeoffrey. Free lance cons. aviation industry, Washington, 1969-74; pres. World Aviation Cons., Inc., Washington, 1977—; dir. Internat. Aviation Systems, Inc. Mem. nat. selection com. Hugh O'Brian Youth Found., 1978—. Served with USMC, 1960-69. Mem. Marine Corps. Combat Corrs. Assn., Nat. Aviation Club, Christian Pilots Assn. Republican. Mem. Ch. of Nazarene. Clubs: Montgomery Country, Capital Yacht, Internat. Yacht, Lincoln, Ocean Pines Country. Author: Quick Reference Aircraft Guide, 1977. Home: 1007 Trinity Gate St Herndon VA 22070 Office: 475 L'Enfant Plaza SW Suite 4110 Washington DC 20024

WILTON, MIRIAM MAE, psychologist; b. Mpls., Nov. 15, 1926; d. Andrew Oscar and Siiri Johanna (Kantonen) Kuusisto; A.B., Boston U., 1948, M.A., 1960, Ph.D., 1966; A.M., N.Y. U., 1952; children—Marilyn Wilton Hopkins, Richard Thomas, Melissa Miriam. Evaluator, Boston Childrens Services and South Shore Counseling, 1975-76; psychologist Human Resource Inst. Boston, Franklin, Mass., Fuller Meml. Hosp., South Attleboro, Mass.; faculty Framingham (Mass.) State Coll., prof. psychology, 1966—. Organist, choir dir. St. Joseph's Ch., Needham, Mass.; organist Temple Beth Avodah, Newton Center, Mass.; organist, choir dir. Grace Luth. Ch., Needham, Mass., 1978—. Mem. Am. Guild Organists, Am., Eastern, New Eng., Mass, psychol. assns. Home: 28 Sturbridge Rd Wellesley Hills MA 02181

WILTSE, JOHN HENRY, corporate sales and mktg. mgr.; b. Buffalo, July 10, 1929; s. Henry Floyd and Avis Loretta (Washburn) W.; student State U. N.Y., 1947-50, Chgo. Tech. Coll., 1951; m. Helen Marjorie Malone, Oct. 17, 1949; children—Jon Fredrick, David Henry, Peggy Ann, Mary Ellen. With Lamson Div. Diebold Inc., Syracuse, 1952—, distributor sales mgr., 1969-72, engring. mgr., 1973-74, sales mktg. mgr., 1975—; lectr. State U. N.Y., Oswego, and trade schs. Mem. Material Handling Inst. (edn. com.), Internat. Material Mgmt. Soc. (certified). Roman Catholic. Inventor conveyor controller. Home: 9 Jonquil Ln Liverpool NY 13088

WILTSE, PETER CHRISTIAN, lawyer; b. Buffalo, Jan. 13, 1936; s. Harry Hersey and Sally (Lutzhoff) W.; student Colgate U., 1953-56; J.D., U. Buffalo, 1960; m. Sandra M. McFarland, Aug. 14, 1976; 1 dau., Jessica; children by previous marriage—Lise Rene, Wende Liane, Heather Elizabeth. Admitted to N.Y. State bar, 1961, U.S. Supreme Ct. bar, 1967; asso. firm Saperston, McNaughtan & Saperston, Buffalo, 1960-63; asst. dist. atty. Erie County (N.Y.), 1963; partner Gross, Shuman & Wiltse, Buffalo, 1964-74; individual practice law Buffalo, 1974—. Republican com. mem. Town of Hamburg (N.Y.), 1965-75, exec. com., 1972-75. Mem. Am. Arbitration Assn., Erie County, N.Y. State bar assns., Am. Trial Lawyers Assn., Nat. Assn. Criminal Def. Lawyers. Club: Masons. Home: 202 Main St Hamburg NY 14075 Office: 17 Court St Suite 505 Buffalo NY 14202

WILTZ, HECTOR RAFAEL, psychiatrist; b. Havana, Cuba, Oct. 24, 1926; s. Hector Melchor and Maria (Asuncion) W.; M.D., Havana U., 1951; came to U.S., 1969, naturalized, 1975; m. Maria Dolores Corton, Aug. 15, 1951; children—Magdalena, Hector, Rafael. Resident in psychiatry Univ. Hosp., Havana, 1951-53, staff psychiatrist, 1953-55, prof. med. psychology, summers 1955-57; resident in psychiatry Rockland Psychiat. Center, N.Y.C., 1969-72, staff psychiatrist, 1972—; practice medicine specializing in psychiatry, Union City, N.J., 1973—. Diplomate Am. Bd. Psychiatry and Neurology. Mem. AMA, Am. Psychiat. Assn., Cuban Med. Assn. in Exile. Home: 7500 Park Ave North Bergen NJ 07047 Office: 3916 Bergen Line Ave Union City NJ 07084

WIMER, JAMES HAROLD, chem. co. exec.: b. Crawford, W.Va., Nov. 24, 1935; s. William Harold and Irene Mae (Mick) W.; B.S. in Bus. Adminstrn., W.Va. Wesleyan Coll., 1956; m. Imogene Ann Moss, Jan. 25, 1958; children—Ronald Eric, Brenda Ann. With Union Carbide Corp., 1956-61, 62—, asst. mgr. internat. accounting, N.Y.C., 1969-73, asst. mgr. domestic accounting, 1973-75, mgr. accounting, 1975—; tchr. seminars. Pres. Johnson Elementary Sch. PTA, 1967-68; leader Boy Scouts Am. Served with AUS, 1961-62. Mem. Am. Mgmt. Assn., Clarksburg C. of C. Methodist. Clubs: Rotary, K.P., Masons (32 deg.), Shriners. Home: 81 Easton Rd Westport CT 06880 Office: 270 Park Ave New York City NY 10017

WINBLAD, DOROTHY JEAN BROOKS (MRS. WILLIAM C. WINBLAD), theatre dir.; b. Cambridge, Md.; d. Harold Cleland and Fannie (Noble) Brooks; student St. Mary's Sem., 1942-43; B.A., Auburn U., 1964; postgrad. U. Md.; m. Roger Hugh Mullins, June 8, 1944 (dec. 1960); children—Nancy Eileen, Stephen Gregory; m. 2d, Wil liam Charles Winblad, Sept. 10, 1966. Dir. The Valiant, Auburn (Ala.) U., 1963, The Twelve Pound Look, 1964, The Farce of the Worthy Master Pierre Patelin, 1964; tech. dir. The Taming of th Shrew, Naval Acad., Annapolis, Md., 1966; dir. The Unwicked Witch, Children's Theatre of Annapolis, 1967, The Little Princess, 1969, Hansel and Gretel, 1970; costume designer, wardrobe mistress for Hartkee The Cat, 1968, v.p., 1968-70; stage and TV actress; awards judge Colonial Player's, Inc., Annapolis, 1967-68; stagecraft workshop dir. St. Mary's High Sch., Annapolis, 1971—; creative drama workshop chmn. Am. Theatre Assn., Friends Sch., Balt., 1971—; tchr., dir. Anne Arundel Coll., Severna Park, Md.; judge U.S. Army Internat. Festival for Performing Arts, 1976, 77. Recipient Gold Mask award Auburn Players of Auburn U., 1963. Mem. AAUW, Auburn Player's of Auburn U. (past pres.), Am. Ednl. Theatre Assn. (nat. conv. chmn. 1970, 75), Am. Theatre Assn. (treas. Mid-Atlantic chpt. 1972-74, v.p. 1974-75, pres. 1975-76), Mid-Atlantic Children's Theatre Conf. (rep.), Anne Arundel Arts Assn. (treas. 1967-69), Annapolis Fine Arts Festival Assn. (drama rep. 1968), Internat. Platform Assn., Kappa Alpha Theta (chpt. adviser 1962-65). Clubs: Newcomer's of Auburn U. (pres. 1958-59, ex-officio 1959-60), Kappa Alpha Theta Alumnae (1st pres. 1962-63). Editor: Cue Sheet. Address: 12 St Andrews Crossover Severna Park MD 21146

WINCHESTER, ALMA ELIZABETH TATSCH (MRS. CLARENCE FLOYD WINCHESTER), civic worker, radio writer and broadcaster; b. Fredericksburg, Tex.; d. Otto August and Meta (Hohenberger) Tatsch; spl. student Am. Conservatory Music (Chgo.), 1937-38; m. Clarence Floyd Winchester, Sept. 25, 1943. Singer Chgo. Civic Opera Jr. Chorus, 1937-38; writer radio script Evans Fur Co., Chgo., 1941-42; writer radio sta. KTSA, San Antonio, 1942-43; womens dir., writer, broadcaster radio sta. KNOE, Monroe, La., 1944-45; writer, msuic lead in Boyce Smtih Show, Sta. WGN, Chgo., 1944; womens dir., writer, broadcaster radio sta. WGGG, Gainesville, Fla., 1948-49; pub. relations Stokeley-Van Camp, Inc., Washington, 1954-55. Mem. Salvation Army Aux., Washington; mem. women's bd. Providence Hosp., Washington; Pan-Am. Liaison Com. Womens Orgns., Washington; mem. Womens Internat. Religious Fellowship in cooperation with UNESCO, UNICEF, Schs., embassies; past pres. City of Hope Med. Research chpt. 56, Washington. Mem. Internat. Platform Assn., Los Picaros (hon.), Howard University Faculty Wives. Mem. Christian Ch. Home: 2124 Sudbury Pl NW Washington DC 20012

WINCHESTER, CLARENCE FLOYD, nutrition cons.; b. Chgo., Oct. 14, 1901; s. Leon Alpheus and Nina Pearl (Thompson) W.; B.S., U. Calif. at Berkeley, 1924, M.S., 1935; Ph.D., U. Mo., 1939; m. Maxine Gertrude Kiefer, Sept. 15, 1924 (div. 1938); 1 dau., Maxine Claire (Mrs. Robert Cloon); m. 2d, Alma Elizabeth Tatsch, Sept. 25, 1943. Tchr. pub. schs., Los Angeles, 1924-28, Palo Verde, Calif., 1928-29, Fresno, Calif., 1929-31; research scientist U. N.H., 1931-32, U. Calif. at Davis, 1932-37, U. Mo., 1937-46; asso. prof. U. Fla., 1946-49; agrl. research scientist, Beltsville, Md., 1949-61; nutritionist U.S. Dept. Interior, 1961-66; lectr. Howard U., Washington, 1966-75; nutrition cons., 1975—. Served from 1st lt. to capt. U.S. Army, 1942-46. Fellow Intercontinental Biog. Assn., AAAS, Am. Inst. Chemists; mem. Am. Chem. Soc., Am. Inst. Nutrition, AAUP, Assn. Overseas Educators, Am. Soc. Animal Prodn., Sigma Xi, Gamma Sigma Delta, Alpha Chi Sigma, Gamma Alpha. Mason (32 deg.). Club: Cosmos (Washington). Home and office: 2124 Sudbury Pl NW Washington DC 20012

WINCKOWSKI, BRONISLAUS FRANK, elec. engr.; b. N.Y.C., Nov. 22, 1920; s. Frank and Rose (Zagrobelna) W.; B.S. in Elec. Engring., N.Y.U., 1942; m. Stella Piechota, Feb. 20, 1949. Project engr. in in design of lab. facilities for aero., elec. and structural testing facilities NACA, Langley AFB, Va., 1942-51; chief elec. engr. Haines Lundberg Waehler, N.Y.C., 1956-75, asst. chief engr., 1954-56, sr. engr., 1951-54, partner, chief elec. engr., 1975—. Served with Air Corps. Enlisted Res., 1944-47. Mem. Nat., N.Y. State socs. profl. engrs., Power Engring. Soc. and Industry Applications Soc., Illuminating Engring. Soc., Am. Arbitration Assn., IEEE (sr.), N.Y. U. Alumni Assn. Contbr. to Engring. Manual (R. Perry), 1st-3d edits. Home: 81-03 30th Ave Jackson Heights NY 11370 Office: 2 Park Ave New York City NY 10016

WINDAWI, HASSAN, research scientist; b. Shatrah, Iraq, Sept. 8, 1942; s. Mohammed and Kulthoom (Muhsim) W.; B.Sc., U. Wales, 1966; M.Sc., U. Sussex, 1967; Ph.D., U. Del., 1973; m. Elizabeth Joanne Scott, June 8, 1968; children—Anwar Jason, Sarah Elise. Research asso. Inst. Energy Conversion U. Del., 1973-75, postdoctoral research felow dept. chem. engring., 1975-78, research scientist, center for Catalytic Sci. and Technology, 1978—. Bd. dirs. Newark Day Nursery Assn., 1973-74. Mem. Am. Vacuum Soc., Catalysis Soc., Materials Research Soc., Sigma Xi, Sigma Pi Sigma. Contbr. articles to sci. and engring. jours. Home: 913 Rahway Dr Newark DE 19711 Office: Dept Chemical Engineering Univ Del Newark DE 19711

WINDEBANK, ROBERT WILLIAM, physicist; b. London, Feb. 22, 1929; s. Herbert William and Ellen Rose (Hayes) W.; S.E., London Tech. Coll., 1948; children—Steven, Leslie, Paul. Mem. staff Queen Mary Coll., U. London, 1945-52; co-founder G.V. Planer Ltd., Research & Devel., Eng., 1952-63; sr. devel. engr. Machlet Labs, Stamford, Conn., 1964-66; sr. physicist Gen. Time Research Labs., Stamford, 1967-70; mgr. new products Laser Optics, Inc., Danbury, Conn., 1970—; cons. electronics and optics. Mem. Optical Soc. Am., Soc. Photog. Scientists and Engrs. Contbr. articles to sci. jours.; patentee in field (18). Home: PO Box 131 Hawleyville CT 06440 Office: Laser Optics Inc Mill Plain Rd Danbury CT 06810

WINDELS, PAUL, JR., lawyer; b. Bklyn., Nov. 13, 1921; s. Paul and Louise E. (Gross) W.; A.B., Princeton, 1943; LL.B., Harvard, 1948; m. Patricia Ripley, Sept. 10, 1955; children—Paul III, Mary Hyde, James Hazen Ripley, Patrick Dillon. Admitted to N.Y. State bar, 1949; spl. asst. counsel N.Y. State Crime Comm., 1951; asst. U.S. atty. Eastern Dist. N.Y., 1953-56; N.Y. regional adminstr. SEC, 1956-61; spl. asst. U.S. atty. for prosecution securities frauds, 1956-58; lectr. law Am. Inst. Banking, 1950-57; partner firm Windels, Marx, Davies & Ives and predecessor firms, N.Y.C., 1961—; pres. Franklin Custodian Funds, 1962-67. Trustee, v.p. Bklyn. Law Sch.; chmn. Lycee Francais de N.Y.; trustee French Inst., Fedn. French Alliances. Served from pvt. to capt. F.A., AUS, 1943-46; ETO; maj. res. Decorated officer Nat. Order Merit, chevalier Order Academic Palms (France). Mem. Am., N.Y. State, N.Y. County bar assns., Security Traders Assn. N.Y. (dir.), Fed. Bar Council (trustee), Harvard Law Sch. Assn. (v.p.), Assn. Bar City of N.Y. Republican. Presbyterian. Clubs: Knickerbocker (N.Y.C.); Metropolitan (Washington). Author: Our Securities Markets-Some SEC Problems and Techniques, 1962. Home: 1220 Park Ave New York City NY 10028 Office: 51 W 51st St New York City NY 10019

WINDHAUSEN, JOHN DANIEL, educator; b. Syracuse, N.Y., Dec. 19, 1932; s. Charles Michael and Catherine Edna (Furlong) W.; A.B., LeMoyne Coll., 1955; M.A., Boston Coll., 1957; postgrad. U. Chgo., 1957-59, Harvard U., 1974; m. Janet Anne Flewelling, June 15, 1957; children—John, Charles, Thomas, Brenda, Lisa. Asso. prof. history, chmn. Soviet studies com. St. Anselm's Coll., Manchester, N.H., 1959—; teaching fellow Citizen Exchange Corps in USSR, 1966-75, academic council, 1972-75; research asso. Ill. Summer Lab. on Russia, 1974. Mem. NAACP, N.H. Council for Humanities, Manchester Inst. of Arts and Sci. (past dir.), AAUP, Internat. Faculty Assos., Am. Assn. for Advancement Slavic Studies, N.Am. Soc. Study of Sports History. Democrat. Roman Catholic. Editor, translator The Reign of Ivan the Great; Russian Society in the Age of Ivan the Great, 1978; contbr. articles on edn., athletics in Russia, history to profl. jours. Home: 211 Brickett Rd Manchester NH 03103 Office: St Anselm's College Manchester NH 03102

WINDLE, JOSEPH RAYMOND, bishop; b. Ashdad, Ont., Can., Aug. 28, 1917; s. James David and Bridget (Scollard) W.; student St. Alexander's Coll., Limbour, Que., 1936-39; D.D. Grand Sem., Montreal, 1943; D.C.L., Lateran U., Rome, 1953; LL.D., St. Leo, Fla., 1973. Ordained priest Roman Catholic Ch., 1943; asst. priest, later parish priest and vice-chancellor Pembroke Diocese, 1943-61; aux. bishop Ottawa, 1961-69; coadjutor bishop Pembroke, 1969-71, bishop, 1971—. K.C. Home: 188 Renfrew St Pembroke ON K8A 5R9 Canada

WINDLEY, CHARLES ELLIS, magician; b. Norfolk, Va., June 20, 1942; s. Irving Epps and Betty Ellis (Haddad) Jordan; student Am. U., 1960-61, Am. Acad. Dramatic Arts, 1962; student in mime Richard Morris, N.Y.C., 1959-60, in dance David Winters, N.Y.C., 1960-61, in acting Logan Ramsey, N.Y.C., 1959-60; m. Lisa Tagatac, Dec. 31, 1974. Apprentice to Earl Edwards, 1951-58, Dr. Neff, 1960-65, Chang, 1967, Volta Hull, 1972; appeared with circuses, 1964-67, amusement parks, 1964— designer, producer spl. magic show Nat. Park Service Summer in Parks, 1973; magician P.T. Barnum's Restaurant, Washington, 1973-74, Wonderful World of Fantasy, road co., Charlotte, N.C., 1973; magician Luzerne Hotel, Miami Beach, Fla., 1974, Wonderland of Magic, PTA fund-raising project, Va., Md., Pa., N.J., 1961-74, Suffolk County (N.Y.) Fair, 1969-74, Costa Line, Genoa, Italy, 1975-76, Shilling Prodns. Shopping Mall Promotion, 1969-77, Fantastic Wizard tour, 1977; ringmaster, magician Emmett Kelly Jr. Circus, N.Y.C., 1977: conv. entertainer; touring in The Fantastic Wizard show in civic auditoriums and dinner theaters; appeared in movies: Advise and Consent, 1960, Bridge to the Sun, 1961, Mondo Fraud, 1964; TV actor: Naked City, 1961-62, Car 54 Where are You?, 1962; appeared in plays, including: World of Suzi Wong, 1964, Fistful of Fire, 1960. Mem. Australian Soc. Magicians (hon. life). Author: Teaching and Learning with Magic, 1976; creator, builder Girl to Gorilla illusion for Reithoffer Carnival, 1966. Office: 1501 Broadway Suite 2907 New York City NY 10036

WINDSOR, JAMES MARCELLUS, assn. exec.; b. Annapolis, Md., Jan. 26, 1922; s. Marcellus and Lena (Schulz) W.; B.S. in Engring. U.S. Naval Acad., 1943; postgrad. U. Pitts., 1958; m. Betty Virginia Haselwood, Sept. 23, 1944; children—James Bradford, Robert Scott, Gail Suzanne (Mrs. Paul Strahan). Retired as comdr. Supply Corps, USN 1962; comptroller, asst. dir. Am. Home Econs. Assn., Washington, 1962-64; exec. v.p. Oil Heat Assn. of Greater Washington, 1964—. Dir. Ind. Heating Oil Dealers' Assn. of Md. Decorated Antarctic medal, Korean Service medal. Mem. Naval Acad. Alumni Assn., Am., Washington Soc. Assn. Execs., Ret. Officers Assn. Lutheran. Home and office: 1709 Tarrytown Ave Crofton MD 21114

WINDSOR, LAURENCE CHARLES, JR., communications and public affairs exec.; b. Bronxville, N.Y., July 4, 1935; s. Laurence Charles and Margaret (Phalen) W.; distinguished grad. St. John's Mil. Acad., 1953; student Grinnel Coll., 1953-55, U.S. Mil. Acad., 1957-58; m. Patricia Seelinger, Apr. 3, 1959 (div. 1976); children—Patience Wells, Laurence Edward; m. 2d, Ruth Ester Lindstrom, 1977. Circulation adminstrn. staff Hearst Mags., N.Y.C., 1959-62; promotion dir. Medalist Publs., Chgo., 1962-64, Mill & Factory Mag., N.Y.C., 1964-66, True Mag., N.Y.C., 1966-67, Purchasing Mag., N.Y.C., 1967-69; asso. promotion dir. Life Mag., N.Y.C., 1969-70, merchandising dir., 1970-72, v.p., dir. advt. and pub. relations Sterling Communications subs. Time-Life; spl. asst. to postmaster gen. U.S., Washington, 1972-74; exec. v.p. Calderhead, Jackson, Inc., 1974-75; v.p. ops. Tim David Mktg. Services, Inc., N.Y.C., 1976—; author, writer, pamphleteer, lectr. Pub. relations cons. Penobscot Charitable Trust, 1966; mem. pub. edn. com. N.Y. Gov's Conf. on Alcohol Problems. Served with USMC, 1955-57. Decorated Commemorative War Cross Royal Yugoslav Army; recipient Am. Spirit Honor medal as outstanding marine of year, 1955; Citation of Merit, Wis. Res. Officers Assn. Mem. U.S. Sales Promotion Exec. Assn. (dir.; Promotion Man of Year 1969), Am. Inst. Plant Engrs., Nat. Sci. Tchrs. Assn., Publicity Club Chgo., Nat. Darting Assn., Internat. Radio and TV Soc., Vet. Corps Arty. (distinguished-expert pistol award, 1st provisional regtl. medal, order of centennial legion), Marine Corps Combat Corr. Assn. (sec.), West Point Soc. N.Y. (gov. 1967—), Publicity Club N.Y., Nat. Acad. TV Arts and Scis., Marine Corps League, Nat. Rifle Assn., Met. Squash Racquets Assn., Road Runners Club, AAU (Conn. chpt.), New Eng. Soc., Alpha Phi Omega. Republican. Episcopalian. Clubs: Bedford Bicycle Polo; Bombay Bicycle; Union League, Manhattan (N.Y.C.). Address: RFD 1 Cantitoe Rd Katonah NY 10536 also Box 7 Union League Club 38 E 37th St New York City NY 10016

WINDSOR, PATRICIA FRANCES, novelist; b. N.Y.C., Sept. 21, 1938; d. Bernhard Edward and Antoinette (Gaus) Seelinger; student Bennington (Vt.) Coll., 1956-57; m. Laurence Charles Windsor Jr., Apr. 3, 1959 (separated 1978); children—Patience Wells, Laurence Edward. Vice-pres., Windsor-Morehead Assos., Advt., N.Y.C., 1960-63; tchr. modern dance Peekskill YWCA (N.Y.), 1967-68; author novels: The Summer Before, 1973; Something's Waiting for You, 1974; Home is Where Your Feet Are Standing, 1975; Diving for Roses, 1976; Mad Martin, 1976; contbr. short stories various anthologies; asst. dir. central inquiries Family Planning Assos., London, 1972-73, counselor, 1974-75; corr. Nat. Council Social Service London, 1974—; tchr. creative writing, Westchester, N.Y., 1975—; faculty Inst. Children's Lit., Redding Ridge, Conn., 1976—. Mem. Citizens Com. Employment, Chgo., 1963-64; active YWCA, No. Westchester Assn. Retarded Children. Recipient Honor Book of Book World Spring Book Festival, 1973, Best Book for Young Adults, ALA, 1973. Mem. PEN Am. Centre, Authors Guild. Home: PO Box 219 Katonah NY 10536 Office: care Internat Creative Mgmt 40 W 57th St New York City NY 10019

WINDSOR, ROBERT KENNEDY, corporate exec., inventor; b. Phila., Sept. 17, 1933; s. William Elmer and Margaret Kennedy (Wilson) W.; A.B., Bowdoin Coll., 1955; m. Mary Margaret Willis, June 25, 1955; (div. Mar. 1961); 1 son, David Kennedy. Traffic supr. Bell Telephone Co. Pa., Phila., 1955-64; gen. mgr. Soc. for Indsl. and Applied Maths., Phila., 1964-76; mng. partner Phoebus Co., 1973-76, pres., 1976—; partner Windsor & Knipe, Phila., 1968-76. Served with Signal Corps AUS, 1956-58. Mem. Chi Psi. Home: 216 Dupont Pkwy Apts New Castle DE 19720

WINEBAUM, SUMNER JOSEPH, publisher's rep.; b. Portsmouth, N.H., June 17, 1928; s. Harry and Mollie Rosemond (Shapiro) W.; A.B., U. Mich., 1950; m. Helen Auerbach; children—Samuel, Jacob. TV writer NBC and CBS, N.Y.C., 1950; mem. editorial staff Good Housekeeping mag., N.Y.C., 1951; asso. copy dir. Young & Rubicam, Inc., N.Y.C., 1952-62; pres. Young & Rubicam Ithalia, 1962-64, pres. Young & Rubicam France, 1964-67; pres. Dover (N.H.) News, Inc., 1967—; mktg. cons. Unilever Dunfey Family Hotels, N.Y.C., Boston, Atlanta, other locations, 1962-66. Adv. bd. Carter Gallery, U. N.H., Durham, 1975—. Recipient gold medals Art Dirs. Club, N.Y.C., 1961, 62; 1st prizes Advt. Age, 1957, 60; best advt. in France award, Palme d'Or, 1965. Mem. Atlantic Coast Periodicals Distbrs. Assn. (v.p. 1975-76), Council Periodical Distbrs. Am. (v.p. 1976—). Clubs: Portsmouth Country, Seacoast Indoor Tennis, B'nai B'rith. One man sculpture show Lamont Gallery Exeter, N.H., 1975. Home: Hampton Falls Rd Exeter NH 03833 Office: 35 4th St Dover NH 03820

WINELL, MARVIN, orthopaedic surgeon; b. N.Y.C., June 2, 1934; s. Irving D. and Frances W.; B.A., Columbia Coll., 1955; M.D., Downstate Med. Center State U. N.Y., 1961; m. Dale F. Lehmann, Nov. 2, 1968; children—Kenneth, Jonathan, Andrew, Jennifer, Rachel. Intern, surg. resident Kings County Hosp., Bklyn., 1961-63; researcher, resident orthopaedic surgery Columbia-Presbyn. Hosp., N.Y.C., 1963-67; practice medicine specializing in orthopaedic surgery, Plainfield, N.J., 1969—; mem. staff Muhlenberg Hosp., Plainfield, N.J., Kennedy Hosp., Edison, N.J., Raritan Valley Hosp., Green Brook, N.J.; asst. clin. prof. orthopaedic surgery Rutgers U., 1974—. Served to maj. U.S. Army, 1967-69. Diplomate Am. Bd. Orthopaedic Surgery. Fellow A.C.S., Am. Acad. Orthopaedic Surgery, N.J. Orthopaedic Soc. Office: 1038 Edgewood Ave Plainfield NJ 07060

WINER, JAMES PATRICK BENJAMIN, architect; b. N.Y.C., July 15, 1938; s. Abraham Raphael and Julia (Goodstein) W.; B.Arch., U. Pa., 1962; certificate urban design Archtl. Assn. Sch. Architecture, 1963; certificate Nat. Council Archtl. Registration Bds.; m. Margery F. Stein, Aug. 12, 1962; children—Alison Deborah, Sarah Ellen. Designer, Harbeson, Hough &Livingston & Larson, Architects, Phila., 1964; with Nolen-Swinburne & Assos., Architects, Phila., 1964-67; project and staff architect Vincent G. Kling & Partners, Phila., 1967-73; center City Planner, Phila. City Planning Commn., 1974-75; owner, prin. James P.B. Winer, Architecture-Planning, 1973—; corp. project engr. Witco Chem. Corp., 1976—. Vol. architect/planner Phila. Land Utlization Program, 1964-68. Asso. mem. devel. com. Phila. Orch. Assn., 1969—; 1962 class agt., adv. bd. U. Pa. Ann. Giving; vice chmn., bd. dirs. Friends of Chamounix Mansion, Phila.; bd. dirs. Citizens Adv. Com. for County Planning of Montgomery County, Pa.; trustee Friends Abington Pub. Library. Mem. AIA, N.J. Soc. Architects, Am. Soc. Planning Ofcls., Archtl. Assn. London (Eng.), Am. Arbitration Assn., Phila. Art Alliance, U. Pa. Alumni Club Met. N.J., Phila. Jr. C. of C. (v.p. 1967-68), Sigma Alpha Mu. Home: Necessity Corner 590 Ridgewood Rd Maplewood NJ 07040 Office: 100 Bauer Dr Oakland NJ 07436

WINFIELD, ARMAND GORDON, internat. plastics cons.; b. Chgo., Dec. 28, 1919; s. Benjamin Lionel and Helen (Oscar) W.; B.S., Franklin and Marshall Coll., 1941; postgrad. U. N.Mex., 1941, State U. Iowa, 1944, Washington U., St. Louis, 1948-50; m. Lillian Tsukea Kubota, June 8, 1951 (dec. Dec. 1965); m. 2d, Barbara Jane La Barge, July 23, 1966. Owner, Winfield Fine Art in Jewelry, N.Y.C., 1946-48; research dir. Hanley Plastics Co. div. Wallace Pencil Co., St. Louis, 1955-57; plastic cons. engr. DeBell & Richardson, Inc., Hazardville, Conn., 1957-64; pres. Armand G. Winfield Inc., 1964—; also lectr., writer; mem. faculty Washington U., 1956; guest lectr. Yale U., 1960-61; adviser USIA on plastics show to tour USSR, 1960-61; exec. v.p. Crystopal, Ltd., Hazardville, Conn., 1963; vis. critic in plastics Sch. Architecture, Coll. City N.Y., 1968-69; plastics cons. indsl. design dept., faculty Pratt Inst., Bklyn., 1964-70, instr. prodn. methods, 1968-70; lectr. U. Hartford, U. Kans., 1970, U. Ariz., 1978; adj. prof. plastics engring. U. Lowell (Mass.), 1978—. U.S. State Dept. grantee to USSR, 1961; UN grantee for study plastics in low cost housing for developing countries, 1968-69; UN grantee, Vienna, Austria, 1971; UNIDO expert in newer fibers and composites, India, 1977. Fellow Plastics and Rubber Inst. (Eng.); mem. Soc. Plastics Engrs. (pres. Western New Eng. sect. 1963-64, v.p. N.Y. sect. 1968-69, chmn. regional tech. conf. 1967, historian ann. tech. conf. 1968), Soc. Plastic Industry, Plastics Inst. Australia, Internat. Assn. Housing Sci. (charter), Internat. Assn. Amusement Parks and Attractions. Author: The Alexian Brothers, 1951; The Merchants Exchange of St. Louis, 1953; Plastics For Architects, Artists and Interior Designers, 1961; 100 Years You ng, 1968; also chpts. in books, monthly column in Display World Mag., 1965-68, Designer Mag., 1971-72, Museum Scope, 1976-77; numerous articles on plastics. Patentee in field. Office: 82 Dale St West Babylon NY 11704

WINHAM, GILBERT RATHBONE, educator; b. Flushing, N.Y., May 11, 1938; s. Alfred Rathbone and Margery Rankin (Post) W.; A.B., Bowdoin Coll., 1959; diploma in internat. law U. Manchester (Eng.), 1964; Ph.D., U. N.C., 1967; m. Linda Joyce Tanner, June 11, 1960; children—Nina Gail, Russell Post, Karla Joyce. Asst. prof. polit. sci. McMaster U., Hamilton, Ont., Can., 1967-72, asso. prof., 1972-75; dir. Centre Fgn. Policy Studies, asso. prof. polit. sci. Dalhousie U., Halifax, N.S., Can., 1975—; cons. Dept. External Affairs, Ottawa, Ont., 1974-75, Dept. State, 1974—; dir. Can.'s Future in New World Order program Donner Can. Found. Served with USNR, 1959-62. Can. Council Leave fellow, 1972-73. Mem. Can. Polit. Sci. Assn. (dir. 1974-76), Internat. Studies Assn. (dir. New Eng. region 1976-77). Contbr. articles to profl. jours. Home: 120 Shore Dr Bedford NS B0N 1B0 Canada Office: Centre Fgn Policy Studies Dalhousie U Halifax NS Canada

WINICK, ALBERT BERNARD, psychologist; b. N.Y.C., July 24, 1919; s. Jack and Mary (Rothberg) W.; B.S.S., Coll. City N.Y., 1941; M.A., N.Y. U., 1953; Ph.D., Walden U., 1974; m. Shirley Phillips, Dec. 7, 1946; 1 dau., Joyce L. Psychiat. social worker Bronx VA Hosp., 1946-48; chief personal consulation N.Y.C. Vets. Service Center, 1948-51; dir. psychol. testing N.Y. State Div. Vets Affairs, N.Y.C., 1951-62; rehab. psychologist N.Y. State Edn. Dept., N.Y.C., 1962-65; psychologist, Pub. Schs., Mt. Vernon, N.Y., 1965—; pvt. practice, Flushing, N.Y., 1959—. Served with AUS, 1942-45. Decorated Silver Star, Purple Heart. Mem. Am. Psychol. Assn., N.Y. State Assn. Sch. Psychologists, Doctorate Assn. N.Y. Educators, N.Y. U. Alumni Assn., VFW, DAV. Clubs: Masons, Odd Fellows. Home: 140-50 Ash Ave Flushing NY 11355

WINKLER, JOSEPH CONRAD, recreational products mfg. co. exec.; b. Newark, May 20, 1916; s. Charles and Mollie (Abrams) W.; B.S., N.Y. U., 1941; m. Geraldine M. Borok, Sept. 20, 1953; children—Charles H., David J. Gen. mgr. Indsl. Washing Machine Corp., New Brunswick, N.J., 1941-48; controller Mojud Corp., N.Y.C., 1948-52; controller, asst. treas. Barbizon Corp., N.Y.C., 1952-57; controller Ideal Toy Corp., N.Y.C., 1957-58, dir. fin. and adminstrn., 1960-62, v.p. finance, 1962-68, sr. v.p. finance, 1968-78, exec. v.p., chief operating officer, dir., 1978—; controller McGregor-Doniger, Inc., N.Y.C., 1958-59; dir. Ideal Toy Co. Ltd., Wokingham, Eng., Ideal Toy Corp. of Australia Ltd., Melbourne, ITC Industries Ltd., Hong Kong, Ideal Toy K.K., Tokyo, Ideal Toy Corp. of Can. Ltd., Toronto, Ont., Arxon Spiel & Freizeit, Rodgan W.Ger. Committeeman, troop treas. Boy Scouts Am., Tenafly, N.J., 1965-71. Served with Office Statis. Control, USAAF, 1945. Home: 96 Buckingham Rd Tenafly NJ 07670 Office: 184-10 Jamaica Ave Hollis NY 11423

WINN, HELEN HARTMANN (MRS. BURKHARD DANIEL WINN), librarian, educator; b. Houghton, N.Y., Aug. 21, 1916; d. Arthur and Claire Marie (Tucker) Hartmann; B.A., Barnard Coll., 1937; M.A., Columbia U., 1954, M.S., 1957; m. Burkhard Daniel Winn, July 2, 1938; children—Claire Marie (Mrs. Thomas Carlyle Marshall), Gregory Francis Tucker. Tchr. English, Oradell (N.J.) Jr. High Sch., 1954-56; librarian River Dell Jr. High Sch., 1956-58, River Dell Sr. High Sch., 1958-61; dir. River Dell Media Centers, 1961-72; dir. Center for Promotion of Humanities, 1966-69; chmn. River Dell Humanities Dept., 1967-71, 74-75, media specialist, 1974—. Trustee, River Dell Adult Edn. Center; mem. exec. com. Project Impact, N.J. Cultural Council. Recipient awards for excellence Rutgers Sch. Bd. Publs. Assn., 1960-63. Elementary and Secondary Edn. Act Title III fed. grantee, 1966-69; John Hay fellow Williams Coll., 1965. Mem. NEA, ALA, N.J. Edn. Assn., Bergen County Sch. Librarians Assn. (pres. 1960-62), Nat. Assn. for Humanities Edn., AAUW. Editor: Regional Bd. Edn. Newsletter, 1958-67. Contbr. articles to profl. jours. Home: 248 Country Club Dr Oradell NJ 07649 Office: Pyle St Oradell NJ 07649

WINNEY, JAMES RICHARD, packaging co. exec.; b. Ft. Erie, Ont., Can., Oct. 23, 1927; s. Harold Edgar and Ruth Eleanor (Barnhart) W.: m. Jean Borman, Sept. 22, 1948; children—Michael, Eileen, Richard, Jay, Patrick, Jeffrey. With Wagner Folding Box Corp., Buffalo, 1947—, v.p., 1969—, treas., 1974—. Active Boy Scouts Am.; past elder Alden (N.Y.) Presbyterian Ch., active ch. sponsored youth groups. Served with USNR, 1945-47. Mem. Purchasing Agts. Assn., Buffalo C. of C. Republican. Home: 1578 Crittenden St Alden NY 14004 Office: 1627 Broadway Buffalo NY 14212

WINOKUR, HERBERT SIMON, mgmt. cons.; b. Phila., July 29, 1919; s. Peter and Doll (Simon) W.; B.A. in Polit. Sci., U. Va., 1940; m. Marjorie Ann Lipman, July 12, 1942; children—Herbert Simon, Lisbeth (Mrs. Nigel S. Cload). Clk., partner Fed. Loan Co., Phila., 1938-74; partner Rettews Money Loan Co., Phila., 1958-74; pres. Exec. Consumer Discount Co., Phila., 1967-74; mgmt. cons., staff exec. George S. May Internat. Co., Park Ridge, Ill., 1974-75; pres. H.S. Winokur Assos., mgmt. cons., 1975—; partner Comml. Utility Cons., Wayne, Pa., 1976—. Bd. dirs. Jewish Employment Vocational Service, 1960-70. Served to maj. USAAF, 1942-45. Decorated Presdl. citation; Order Cloud (China). Mem. Assn. Pawnbrokers Pa. (treas.). Democrat. Jewish religion. Mem. B'nai B'rith. Club: Virginia (Phila.). Home: 266 Drummers Ln Wayne PA 19087

WINPISINGER, WILLIAM P., labor union ofcl.; b. Cleve., Dec. 10, 1924; student public schs., Cleve.; married; 5 children. Automotive mechanic, 1942-51; with Internat. Assn. Machinists and Aerospace Workers, 1947—, grand lodge rep., 1951-58, air transp. dept., 1958-64, automotive coordinator, 1965-67, gen. v.p., 1967, now pres., also co-chmn., union trustee pension fund; mem. Fed. Com. on Apprenticeship. Co-chmn. Machinists Non-Partison Polit. League; mem. council N.Y. State Sch. Indsl. and Labor Relations, Cornell U. Served with USNR, 1942-45. Mem. Nat. Planning Assn. (planning com.). Office: Internat Assn Machinists and Aerospace Workers 1300 Connecticut Ave NW Washington DC 20036*

WINSCHE, RICHARD ARNOLD, museum ofcl.; b. Jamaica, N.Y., July 10, 1934; s. John Hugo and Marie Agnes (O'Connor) W.; B.A., Adelphi U., 1957; M.A., L.I. U., 1969. Asst. curator Nassau County Mus., East Meadow, N.Y., 1960-65, asso. curator, 1965-67, historian, 1967—. Cons., towns of Hempstead, North Hempstead, Oyster Bay (all N.Y.), 1967—. Committeeman Republican party. Mem. Nat. Assn. Watch and Clock Collectors, U.S. Power Squadrons, U.S. Trotting Assn., Soc. Preservation L.I. Antiquities, N.Y. State, L.I., Nassau County hist. socs., Friends Nassau County Mus. (life). Contbr. articles to profl. jours. Home: 95-02 239th St Bellerose NY 11426 Office: Eisenhower Park East Meadow NY 11554

WINSOR, CURTIN, JR., banker; b. Phila., Apr. 28, 1939; s. Curtin and Elizabeth Browning (Donner) W.; B.A., Brown U., 1961; M.A., Sch. Internat. Service Am. U., 1964, Ph.D., 1971; m. Ann Hanbury, Nov. 18, 1962; children—Curtin III, Anita, Monica, Cristina. With U.S. Fgn. Service, 1967-71; spl. asst. to chmn. Republican Nat. Com., 1971-73; rep. Chase Manhattan Bank, Washington, 1973—. Pres. Arena Stage, Washington Drama Soc. Bd., 1974—; sec. bd. dirs. William H. Donner Found., 1976—; trustee Corcoran Gallery Art, 1976—; bd. govs. Donner Canadian Found., Toronto, 1966—; vice chmn. bd. Mainstream, Inc., Washington, 1975—; v.p., trustee Pan Am. Devel. Found., Washington, 1975-78; trustee Africare, Washington, 1974—. Named Alumni of Year, Sch. Fgn. Service, Am. U., 1977. Mem. Inst. Strategic Studies London. Episcopalian. Clubs: Met. of Washington, Univ.; Chevy Chase (Md.). Home: 4617 Hawthorne Ln NW Washington DC 20016 Office: Chase Manhattan Bank NA 900 17th St NW Washington DC 20006

WINSOR, WILLIAM TILLINGHAST, educator; b. Providence, Nov. 16, 1930; s. Edward Harrison and Hannah (More) W.; B.A., Brown U., 1952; M.A., Columbia U., 1957, Ph.D., 1963; m. Martha Elizabeth Muirhead, May 14, 1966; children—Julianna, Elizabeth, David, Andrew. English instr. Hunter Coll., N.Y.C., part-time, 1961-62; asst. prof. English, U. Bridgeport (Conn.), 1967-74, asso. prof. English, 1974—. Served with U.S. Army, 1952-54. Mem. AAUP (chpt. pres. 1973-75), Modern Lang. Assn. Home: Skilton Rd Watertown CT 06795 Office: English Dept Univ Bridgeport Bridgeport CT 06602

WINSTEAD, JACK ALAN, toxicologist, biochemist; b. Dixon, Ky., June 13, 1932; s. Roscoe Pyle and Venice (Gardner) W.; B.S., U. Ky., 1954; M.S., Okla. State U., 1959; Ph.D., U. Ill., 1964; M.A., Central Mich. U., 1975; m. Mary Anne Purdy, June 30, 1956; children—Karen, Katherine, Sheri. Commd. 2d lt. U.S. Air Force, 1954, advanced through grades to lt. col., 1975; dep. dir. Toxic Hazards div. Wright-Patterson AFB, Ohio, 1972-75, ret., 1975; profl. assos. Nat. Acad. Scis., Washington, 1975-78; dir. toxicol. rev. Cosmetic, Toiletry and Fragrance Assn., Washington, 1978—; research prof. chemistry St. Mary's U., San Antonio, 1965-68. Mem. Soc. Toxicology, Am. Soc. Biol. Chemists, Radiation Research Soc., Am. Chem. Soc., Am. Pub. Health Assn., AAAS, Sigma Xi. Baptist. Contbr. articles to profl. jours. Home: 1004 Kerge Ct Vienna VA 22180 Office: 1133 15th St Washington DC 20005

WINSTEN, SOL STEPHEN, psychiatrist; b. N.Y.C., July 24, 1909; s. Morris and Mollie (Nachmousky) W.; B.S., N.Y. U., 1932; M.D., U. Berne (Switzerland), 1939; m. May Chatzkelson, Aug. 15, 1940; children—Denise C., Brooke M., Patricia N. Intern, Jewish Meml. Hosp., N.Y.C., 1939-41; resident Lyons (N.J.) VA Hosp., 1949-52, chief psychiatrist, 1942-69; psychiatrist Mt. Carmel Guild Mental Health Center, Newark, 1969-75; dir. psychiat. outpatient service John E. Runnell's Hosp., Berkeley Heights, N.J., 1975—; asso. psychiatrist N.Y. Med. Coll., 1956-65; clin. asst. prof. psychiatry N.J. Med. Coll., 1973—, Rutgers Med. Sch., 1977—. Diplomate Am. Bd. Psychiatry and Neurology. Mem. AMA, Am., N.J. psychiat. assns., Essex County Med. Soc. Home and Office: 520 Phillip Lane Watchung NJ 07060

WINTER, GORDON ARNAUD, lt. gov. Nfld.; b. St. Johns, Nfld., Can., Oct. 6, 1912; s. Robert Gordon and Ethel Phyllis (Arnaud) W.; student Bishop Feild Coll., St. Johns, 1922-26, Loretto Sch., Musselburgh, Scotland, 1926-30; LL.D. (hon.), Meml. U., 1970; m. Millicent Anderson, Sept. 2, 1937; children—Linda Winter Barrett, Valda Winter Tiller. Pres., Nfld. Bd. Trade, 1946; chmn. St. John's Housing Corp., 1949-50; gov. CBC, 1952-58; mem. adv. bd. Nfld. Savs. Bank, 1959-62; mem. Nfld. adv. bd. Royal Trust Co., 1961-75; chmn. T & M Winter, Ltd., Standard Mfg. Co., Ltd.; lt. gov. Nfld., 1974—; mem. Nfld. del. to negotiated and signed terms of union between Nfld. and Can., 1948; minister of fin. 1st Provincial Govt. of Nfld., 1949. Chmn. bd. regents Meml. U., 1968-74. Decorated officer Order of Can., knight Order St. John of Jerusalem. Anglican. Club: Bally Haly Golf and Country. Home and Office: Govt House Saint John's NF Canada

WINTER, HERBERT REINHOLD, educator; b. Martinwaldau, Germany, June 25, 1928; s. Willi and Gertrud (Roehricht) W.; came to U.S., 1952, naturalized, 1954; A.A., North Park Coll., 1956; B.A., Augustana Coll., 1957; M.A., U. Ia., 1959, Ph.D., 1961; m. Ursula Jung, Mar. 26, 1959; children—John-Martin, Nadia. Asst. prof. polit. sci. Hartwick Coll., Oneonta, N.Y., 1961-63; asst. prof. polit. sci. R.I. Coll., Providence, 1963-67, asso. prof., 1967-72, prof., 1972—, acting chmn. dept., 1970-71, chmn. dept., 1971-75. R.I. dir. Senator Pell internship program, 1965-66; mem. adv. com. to Congressman Tiernan, 1968-72. Mem. exec. com. R.I. World Affairs Council, 1971—. Served with AUS, 1953-55. Mem. Am. Polit. Sci. Assn., Northeastern Polit. Sci. Assn., Internat. Studies Assn. (sec.-treas. New Eng. Region 1971-72, v.p. 1972-73, pres. 1973-75; mem. nat. governing council 1973-75), Am. Assn. U. Profs. (mem. exec. com. R.I. conf. 1968-72). Co-author: People and Politics: An Introduction to Political Science, 1977. Co-editor: Political Science: Introductory Essays and Readings, 1971. Home: 60 Belcourt Ave North Providence RI 02911 Office: RI Coll Providence RI 02908

WINTER, NATHAN HAROLD, educator; b. N.Y.C., Mar. 20, 1926; s. Sol and Fannie (Sachs) W.; A.B., N.Y. U., 1949, A.M., 1954, Ph.D., 1964; B.R.E., Jewish Theol. Sem. Am., 1951; J.D., Bklyn. Law Sch., 1956; hon. doctorate Jewish Theol. Sem. Am., 1977; m. Magda Markowitz, Feb. 5, 1949; children—Steven, Elaine P., Jonathan M. Ednl. dir. Oheb Shalom Religious Schs., South Orange, N.J., 1954-68; lectr. history Jewish Theol. Sem. Am., N.Y.C., 1964-68; prof. Hebrew culture and edn., N.Y. U., 1968—, head dept., Judge Abraham Lieberman prof. Hebraic studies, 1971—, also dir. Inst. for Hebrew and Judaic Studies. Cons. United Synagogues Am. Commn. on Edn., Melton Research Center, N.Y.C., Tchrs. Inst. Jewish Theol. Sem. Bd.

dirs. Cejwin Camps, Nat. Council Jewish Edn. Served with AUS, 1944-46; PTO. Recipient Founders Day award N.Y. U., 1964. Mem. AAUP, Nat. Assn. Profs. Hebrew, Assn. for Jewish Studies, Educators Assembly (pres. 1967-69). Author: Jewish Education in a Pluralist Society, 1966; Samson Benderly and Jewish Education in America, 1963. Contbr. articles to encys., maj. periodicals. Home: 46 Burroughs Way Maplewood NJ 07040 Office: NY U East Bldg Washington Sq New York City NY 10003

WINTERS, EDWARD WILLIAM, data systems co. exec.; b. Bronxville, N.Y., May 23, 1947; s. Edward and Caroline (Hanson) W.; B.S., Richmond Coll., City U. N.Y., 1970; M.S., N.Y. U., 1973; m. Ann Marie Eller, Jan. 25, 1969; 1 dau., Elizabeth. Computer applications engr. Norden div. United Aircraft, 1970; staff asst. AT&T Long Lines, White Plains, N.Y., 1970-72, mem. programming staff, 1972-74, data systems design supr., 1974—; system mgr. PSL System, 1974—; lectr. Assn. Computing Machinery Profl. Devel. Seminars, 1975, 76. Fellow Goodwin Watson Inst. Research and Program Devel. Mem. Am. Mgmt. Assn., Human Factors Soc., Soc. Mgmt. Info. Systems, Assn. Computing Machinery, IEEE. Contbr. articles to profl. jours.; reviewer SMIS Quar., 1977—. Home: 415 Windmill Way Somerville NJ 08876 Office: Bedminster NJ 07921

WINTERSTELLA, JOHN LIGE, publishing co. exec.; b. Long Branch, N.J., Oct. 14, 1941; s. Arthur S. and Evelyn (Schwarz) W.; B.S., Monmouth Coll., 1965; m. Judith Joy Oberg, Feb. 18, 1967; children—Judith Lynn, Kristen Dian. Advt. sales rep. Scranton Pub. Co., Chgo., 1965-69; account exec. Stuart Co. Advt. Inc., Newark, 1969-73; dir. mktg. Internat. Wastes Control Corp., N.Y.C., 1973; regional mgr. Am. City and County Mag., Municipal Index, Morgan-Grampian Pub. Co., N.Y.C., 1973—. Chmn., Manasquan Area Health Screening Program, 1973; vol. rescue mem. Manasquan 1st Aid Squad; mem. Manasquan Conservation Commn., So. Monmouth County Regional Drug Council; councilman Borough of Manasquan (N.J.), 1977-78; treas. alumni bd. trustees Monmouth Coll., 1972-73. Served with AUS, 1959-63. Mem. Bus. and Profl. Advt. Assn., Am. Littoral Soc., Am. Pub. Works Assn., Air Pollution Control Assn., Water Pollution Control Fedn., Internat. Game Fishing Assn., Water and Wastewater Equipment Mfrs. Assn. (del.). Clubs: Elks, Surf and Sea Fishing. Home: 436 Cedar Ave Manasquan NJ 08736 Office: 205 E 42d St New York City NY 10017

WINTHROP, AMORY, horse trainer, horse show rider; b. N.Y.C., Dec. 14, 1931; d. Robert and Theodora (Ayer) W.; student Bradford Jr. Coll., 1949-52, Columbia U., 1954-56. Tchr. hunt seat riding, Stockbridge, Mass., and Millbrook, N.Y., 1953-75; staff mem. Old Chatham Fox Hunt, 1953-54; pres. Morley Stables, 1965-67. Bd. dirs. Humane Soc. N.Y., 1958-60; bd. dirs. Fund for Animals, 1974—, Assistance Dogs Internat., 1978—, New Eng. Inst. Comparative Medicine, A Reform Fund; pres. Winley Found., 1967—. Mem. Am. Horse Show Assn. (judge 1966—), ASPCA, Animal Welfare Inst., Columbia-Greene Humane Soc., N.Y. Animal Adoption Soc. (dir.), Taconic Animal Protectors League (pres. 1976, 78—, 1st v.p. 1977-78), Wild Horse Organized Assistance (life), World Fedn. Protection Animals (life), Defenders Wildlife (life), N.Y. State Humane Assn. (insp. 1975—, chmn. horse adv. com.; dir.), Nat. Hunter and Jumper Assn. (pres. 1978—), Audubon Soc. Republican. Episcopalian. Club: River. Home: Little Rest Rd Millbrook NY 12545

WINTHROP, JOHN, brokerage and investment co. exec.; b. Boston, June 22, 1936; s. Nathaniel Thayer and Serita (Bartlett) W.; B.A., Harvard Coll., 1958; M.B.A., Columbia U., 1962; children—John, Henry Grenville, Bayard. Journalist, Atlantic Council U.S., Washington, 1962-63; chmn. Wood, Struthers & Winthrop Mgmt. Co., N.Y.C., 1974—; dir. Donaldson Lutkin & Jenrette; pres. deVegh Mut. Fund; dir. Green Bay & Western R.R., Ivanhoe Corp., Wood, Struthers & Winthrop Mgmt. Corp. Bd. dirs. Fresh Air Fund, Nat. Audubon Soc.; mem. corp. Greenwich Hosp. Served with USNR, 1958-60. Mem. N.Y. Soc. Security Analysts. Clubs: Bond, City Midday, Knickerbocker, Harvard (N.Y.); Porcellian (Cambridge, Mass.). Contbr. articles to Barrons, Wall St. Jour., Trusts and Estates, others. Home: 16 John St Greenwich CT 06830 Office: 14 Wall St New York City NY 10005

WISBEY, HERBERT ANDREW, JR., educator; b. Boston, Apr. 20, 1919; s. Herbert Andrew and Martha Marietta (Burgess) W.; B.S., U. R.I., 1941; M.A., U. Ariz., 1946; Ph.D., Columbia, 1951; m. Adelia May Wagner, Nov. 26, 1945; children—Thomas Burgess, Jane Catherine, Susan Marietta Wisbey Van Alst, Peter Andrew. Instr. Upsala Coll., East Orange, N.J., 1948-49, Monmouth Jr. Coll., Long Branch, N.J., 1949-52; asso. prof. dept. history, polit. sci. Keuka Coll., Keuka Park, N.Y., 1952-53, prof., 1953-62, also head dept., 1952-62; prof. history, program coordinator Corning (N.Y.) Community Coll., 1962-65; prof. history Elmira (N.Y.) Coll., 1965—, chmn. div. social scis., 1965-70, archivist, 1974—; cons. N.Y. State Hist. Trust, 1967-69. Served with AUS, 1942-45. Mem. Am. Studies Assn. N.Y. State (pres. 1967-68), Assn. Am. Archivists, Am. Folklore Assn., Orgn. Am. Historians, Am. Studies Assn., Am. Assn. State and Local History, Phi Gamma Delta. Author: Soldiers without Swords: A History of the Salvation Army in the United States, 1955; Pioneer Prophetess: Jemima Wilkinson, The Publick Universal Friend, 1964. Co-editor: Mark Twain in Elmira, 1977. Mem. editorial bd. New York Folklore Quar., 1957-72. Home: 4300 Fairway Ln Horseheads NY 14845 Office: Elmira Coll Elmira NY 14901

WISCH, NATHANIEL, physician; b. Bklyn., Dec. 28, 1933; s. Louis and Sarah (Rothenberg) W.; B.A. with distinction, U. Rochester, 1954; M.D., Northwestern U., 1958; m. Helen Slow, Apr. 7, 1956; children—Peter, Steven, Andrew, Karen. Intern, Kings County Hosp., Bklyn., 1958-59; resident in medicine Bklyn. VA Hosp., 1959-60; fellow in hematology Mt. Sinai Hosp., N.Y.C., 1960-61; sr. med. resident Montefiore Hosp., N.Y.C., 1961-62; clin. asst. medicine Mt. Sinai Hosp., N.Y.C., 1962-68, asso. attending, medicine/hematology, 1976—, asso. clin. prof. medicine sch. medicine, 1976—; practice medicine specializing in hematology-oncology, N.Y.C., 1962—; staff Lenox Hill Hosp., N.Y.C., 1969—, chief hematology, attending medicine, 1978—; founder, exec. v.p., sec. Med. Exam. Pub. Co. Inc., Garden City, 1960—. Adv. bd. United Leukemia Fund N.Y.C.; bd. dirs. Am. Assos. Ben Gurion U., Beer Sheba, Israel. Am. Cancer Soc. fellow, 1960. Diplomate Am. Bd. Internal Medicine. Fellow A.C.P.; mem. AMA, N.Y. State, N.Y. County med. socs., Am., Internat. hematology socs., N.Y. Acad. Medicine, Am., N.Y. State, N.Y. County socs. internal medicine. Jewish. Clubs: City Athletic, Shelter Rock Tennis. Office: 12 E 86th St New York City NY 10028

WISE, DONALD ALLEN, librarian; b. Mercedes, Tex., Jan. 25, 1930; s. Lawrence A. and Lucille A. (Crosswhite) W.; B.A., Okla. State U., 1953; M.A., St. Louis U., 1960, postgrad., 1961-63; postgrad. George Washington U., 1965-72; m. June E. Ruth, Sept. 2, 1961; 1 son, Kurt Geoffrey. Employed with U.S. Govt., 1955-60, 1963—, head acquisitions unit, geography and map div. Library of Congress, 1970—. Instr. geography St. Louis U., 1960-63; lectr. U.S. Dept. Agr. Grad. Sch., Washington, 1971—. Mem. Arlington County Bicentennial Com., 1972-76. Served with U.S. Army, 1953-55. Mem. Assn. Am. Geographers (treas. 1971-74), Spl. Libraries Assn., Am. Congress on Surveying and Mapping, Soc. for History of Discoveries, Am. Assn. State and Local History, Va. History Fedn. (pres. 1973-75), Va., Arlington (pres. 1969-70, archivist 1970—) hist. socs. Presbyn. (elder 1966-69, deacon 1976-78). Home: 5920 4th Rd N Arlington VA 22203 Office: Library of Congress Washington DC 20540

WISE, SAMUEL PAUL, III, psychiatrist; b. Plains, Ga., May 8, 1921; s. Burr Thaddeus and Lundie Louise (Lamar) W.; A.B., Emory U., 1941; M.D., Tulane U., 1946; m. Kathleen Ann Hughes, Nov. 25, 1966; children—Sarah Adrienne Wise Parker, Samuel Paul, Blake Burr, Frank Lamar, Melissa Marshall. Joined U.S. Army, 1943, advanced through grades to maj., 1952; rotating intern USPH Hosp., New Orleans, 1946-47, resident in internal medicine Letterman Army Hosp., San Francisco, 1948-49; resident in chest diseases Fitzsimons Army Hosp., Denver, 1950; researcher Walter Reed Army Hosp., Washington, 1951; chief medicine Ft. Jackson Army Hosp., Columbia, S.C., 1952-55; ret., 1955; practice medicine specializing in internal medicine, San Benito, Tex., 1955-59; clin. asst. prof. medicine Baylor U. Coll. Medicine, Houston, 1959-60; asso. chief of staff for research Parry Point (Md.) VA Hosp., 1960-63; psychoactive drug researcher Springfield Hosp. Center, Sykesville, Md., 1963-67, resident in psychiatry, 1964-67; psychiatrist-in-chief Dorchester County Mental Health Services, Cambridge, Md., 1967—; staff psychiatrist Eastern Shore Hosp. Center, Cambridge, 1967—; psychiat. cons. Dorchester Gen. Hosp., Cambridge, 1967—; cons. internal medicine Harlingen (Tex.) AFB, 1954-59; staff physician Jeff Davis Hosp., Houston, 1959-60; research asso. Psychiat. Inst., U. Md. Sch. Medicine, 1961-71, clin. instr. psychiatry, 1971—. Mem. Dorchester County (Md.) Human Resources Commn., 1973—; deacon 1st Baptist Ch., Cambridge, 1972-75, 76—. Recipient Convocation medal Acad. Psychosomatic Medicine, 1976. Diplomate Am. Bd. Internal Medicine. Fellow Royal Soc. Health Gt. Britain, Acad. Psychosomatic Medicine; mem. Am. Psychiat. Assn., Md. Psychiat. Soc., Dorchester County Med. Soc., Med.-Chiurg. Faculty Md., Am. Psychosomatic Soc., Christian Med. Soc. Democrat. Contbr. articles to profl. jours. Home: 103 High St Cambridge MD 21613 Office: Agnew Center Eastern Shore Hosp Center Cambridge MD 21613

WISEMAN, DOUGLAS CARL, educator; b. Nashua, N.H., Feb. 28, 1935; s. Howard W. and Ruth D. (Aiken) W.; B.E., Plymouth State Coll., 1961; M.S., Ph.D., Ind. U., 1970; m. Bonnie Lou Berry, Oct. 8, 1960; children—Mark, Lori, Kathleen. Tchr. high sch., Nashua, N.H., 1961, jr. high sch., 1963; teaching fellow Ind. U., 1962; tchr. high sch., Portage, Mich., 1964; instr. Plymouth (N.H.) State Coll., 1965, prof., dept. chmn., dir. athletics 1972-78; instr. Northeastern U., Boston, 1969-71. Mem. Ashland (N.H.) Sch. Bd., 1972-75, chmn., 1976—. Served with U.S. Army, 1953-56. Named Coach of Year, dist. 32N, Nat. Assn. Intercollegiate Athletics, 1973. Mem. AAHPER (v.p. phys. edn., sec.-treas. Eastern dist.), Am. Coll. Sports Medicine, Nat. Assn. Collegiate Dirs. Athletics, Assn. Phys. Edn. in Higher Edn., N.H. Assn. Health, Phys. Edn. and Recreation, Kappa Delta Pi. Republican. Contbr. articles to phys. edn. jours. Home: 80 Thompson St Ashland NH 03217 Office: Phys Edn Center Plymouth NH 03264

WISEMAN, JAMES RICHARD, archaeologist, classicist, educator; b. North Little Rock, Ark., Aug. 29, 1934; s. James Morgan and Bertie Lou (Sullivan) W.; A.B., U. Mo., 1957; M.A., U. Chgo., 1960, Ph.D., 1966; postgrad. Am. Sch. Classical Studies, Athens, 1959-60; m. Margaret Lucille Mayhue, Aug. 20, 1954; children—James Alexander, Stephen Michael. Instr., U. Tex., Austin, 1960-64, asst. prof., 1964-66, asso. prof., 1966-70, prof. classics, 1970-73; prof. classics Boston U., 1973—, prof. fine arts, 1975—, chmn. classical studies, 1974—; chmn. archeol. studies program, 1975-76; vis. asso. prof. classics U. Colo., 1970; vis. prof. Am. Sch. Classical Studies, Athens, 1978; dir. U. Tex. excavations, Ancient Corinth, Greece, 1965-72; co-dir. Yugoslavian-Am. archeol. excavations, Stobi, Yugoslavia, 1970—; project supr. Boston U. excavations 18th century glass factory, Temple, N.H., 1975-76. Served with USN, 1952-55. Am. Council Learned Socs. fellow, 1967-68, 78—; Ford Found. grantee, 1968-72; Smithsonian Instn. grantee, 1970-75; Guggenheim fellow, 1971-72, Nat. Endowment for Humanities grantee, 1968-69, 76—. Mem. Archeol. Inst. Am. (exec. com. 1973-75, 76-78), Am. Philol. Assn., Assn. for Field Archaeology (sec. 1970-73, nat. exec. com. 1970—), Am. Sch. of Classical Studies at Athens (exec. com. 1973-76), Soc. for Hist. Archaeology, Am. Acad. at Rome, Assn. of Ancient Historians, Internat. Inst. of Conservation. Author: Stobi, a Guide to the Excavations, 1973; The Land of the Ancient Corinthians, 1978; editor: Studies in the Antiquities of Stobi I, 1973, II, 1975; founding editor Jour. Field Archaeology, 1974—; contbr. articles to profl. jours. Home: 60 Browne St Brookline MA 02146 Office: Boston U Dept Classical Studies 745 Commonwealth Ave Boston MA 02215

WISER, VIVIAN DORIS, historian; b. Lyndonville, N.Y., June 17, 1915; d. Floyd J. and Alice Edith W.; A.B., U. Md., 1938, M.A., 1939, Ph.D., 1963. Archivist, Nat. Archives, Washington, D.C., 1943-46, 48-56; historian U.S. Dept. Agr., Washington, 1956—, in charge farm hist. research, 1970—; mem. Am. Archives Com. on Wider Use of Archives. Recipient certificate of merit U.S. Dept. Agr., 1962; Outstanding Woman Ph.D. award Phi Delta Gamma, 1963. Mem. Am. Hist. Assn., Orgn. Am. Historians, Md. Hist. Soc., Nat. Trust for Hist. Preservation, Internat. Personnel Mgmt. Assn., Agrl. Hist. Soc. (exec. com. 1976—). Baptist. Author: Century of Service, 1963; Protecting Am. Agriculture, 1974; editor: Two Centuries of American Agriculuture, 1976. Home: 9522 50th Pl College Park MD 20740 Office: 500 12th St SW Room 144 Washington DC 20250

WISHNER, JULIUS, psychologist; b. Poland, July 7, 1921; s. David and Pearl (Podbilevich) W.; A.B., Bklyn. Coll., 1946; A.M., Northwestern U., 1947, Ph.D., 1950; m. Dorothy Busker, Nov. 1, 1941; children—Karen Frances, Amy Rose. Mem. faculty dept. psychology U. Pa., 1949—, now prof.; chief psychologist Hosp. of U. Pa., 1951-59; vis. lectr. Harvard U., 1958-59; asso. prof. psychology Law Sch. U. Pa., 1959-63; vis. prof. Stanford U., 1967, Swarthmore Coll., 1968, Oxford U., 1972-73. Served with USAAF, 1943-45. Decorated D.F.C., Air medal. Fellow AAAS, Am. Psychol. Assn.; mem. AAUP (past mem. nat. council), Internat. Assn. Applied Psychology (past mem. exec. com.), Eastern Psychol. Assn., Psychonomic Soc. Contbr. articles to profl. jours. Office: 3815 Walnut St Philadelphia PA 19104

WISHON, GEORGE EDWIN, ofcl. USIA; b. Whitesboro, Okla., Dec. 17, 1929; s. L.C. and Eva Opal (Scott) W.; B.A., San Jose (Calif.) State U., 1951, M.A., 1952. Dir. binational centers USIA in Santo Domingo, Guatemala City, Turkey, Libya and Greece, 1953-55, 56-61; with USIA, State Dept., 1961—, cultural affairs officer, pub. affairs officer embassies, Egypt, Afghanistan, Lebanon, Kuwait, 1961-72, N. Africa desk officer, Washington, 1972-73, personnel officer N. Africa and Near East, 1973-75, cultural counselor embassy, Cairo, 1976—. Served with U.S. Army, 1955-56. Fulbright scholar, 1952-53. Mem. Am. Fgn. Service Assn., Middle East Inst. Home: 401 Ribier Ave Modesto CA 95350 Office: care USIA Washington DC 20547

WISNESKI, FRANK VINCENT, JR., investment co. exec.; b. Dorchester, Mass., Dec. 23, 1946; s. Frank Vincent and Gwendolyn Hudson (Tracy) W.; B.A., Yale U., 1968; m. Lynne Marie Briscoe, June 19, 1971; 1 dau., Corey Leslie. With Wellington Mgmt. Co., Boston, 1968—, v.p., 1973—. Home: 200 Powder Point Ave Duxbury MA 02332 Office: Wellington Mgmt Co 28 State St Boston MA 02109

WISSINGER, H. ANDREW, orthopaedic surgeon; b. Pitts., Sept. 14, 1930; s. Zonar A. and Marie K. (Knape) W.; B.S., U. Pitts., 1952, M.D., 1956; m. Patricia Bik; children by previous marriage—David F., Eric A. Intern, Western Pa. Hosp., Pitts., 1956-57, resident in gen. surgery, 1959-60; resident in orthopedic surgery U. Pitts. Med. Center, 1960-63; practice medicine specializing in orthopedic surgery, Pitts., 1963—; partner Oakland Orthopedic Associates, Pitts., 1965—; mem. active staff Presbyn.-U. Hosp. of Pitts., Childrens Hosp.; mem. sr. staff St. Margaret Meml. Hosp. of Pitts., chief dept. orthopedic surgery, 1973—; mem. sr. staff, chief dept. orthopedic surgery St. Francis Gen. Hosp., Pitts.; orthopedic cons. Indsl. Home for Crippled Children of Pitts., 1963—; clin. asso. prof. U. Pitts., dept. orthopedic surgery. Served to lt. USNR, 1957-59. Diplomate Am. Bd. Orthopedic Surgery. Mem. A.C.S., Am. Acad. Orthopedic Surgeons, (chmn. instructional course com. 1976-77), Pa., Allegheny County med. socs., Pitts. Acad. of Medicine, Am. Coll. Health Assn., AMA, Am. Soc. for Surgery of the Hand. Editor and chief Orthopedics, 1977-78; contbr. articles on orthopedic surgery to med. jours. Home: 4725 Bayard St Pittsburgh PA 15213 Office: 128 N Craig St Pittsburgh PA 15213

WIST, PAUL GABRIEL, accountant; b. Balt., July 25, 1929; s. George John and Regina Marie (Ward) W.; A.B.A., U. Balt. 1951; m. Mary Lee Vaeth, Oct. 23, 1954; children—Paul Gabriel, Timothy V., Matthew W., Ami A. Asso., C.W. Amos & Co., Balt., 1952-56, partner, 1956-69, mng. partner, 1969—. Bd. dirs. Md. Blue Cross, 1965-73; Associated Cath. Charities, 1976—; mem. adv. bd. St. Joseph Hosp., 1964—, Stella Maris Hospice, 1969-73; trustee Cardinal Shehan Center for Aging, 1977—, Am. Inst. Benevolent Fund, 1977—. Served with USNR, 1948-49. Recipient Cardinal Gibbons medal, 1973. Mem. Md. Assn. C.P.A.'s (pres. 1975-76), Am. Inst. C.P.A.'s (council 1974-75, 77—), Nat. Assn. Accountants. Roman Catholic. Clubs: Mchts. (Balt.), Towson (Md.) Golf and Country, Rotary. Home: 523 Saint Francis Rd Towson MD 21204 Office: 36 S Charles St Baltimore MD 21201

WISTER, WILLIAM DAVID, investment co. exec.; b. N.Y.C., Oct. 24, 1938; s. William Ducasse and Helen Francis (Albrecht) W.; B.A., Lafayette Coll., 1960; m. Carol Lynne Weeks, July 27, 1963; children—William David, Heather Lynne. Sr. portfolio mgr. U.S. Trust Co. of N.Y., N.Y.C., 1963-67; asst. sec./sr. portfolio mgr. Naess & Thomas, N.Y.C., 1967-69; sr. v.p., dir., mem. exec. com. Cyrus J. Lawrence, N.Y.C., 1967-69; sr. v.p., dir., mem. exec. com. Cyrus J. Lawrence, N.Y.C., 1969—. Chmn. bd. trustees 1st Congl. Ch., Old Greenwich, Conn., 1975—. Served to capt. USMCR, 1960-63. Mem. Fin. Analysts Fedn., Inst. Chartered Fin. Analysts, N.Y. Soc. Security Analysts. Clubs: Mchts. (N.Y.C.); Rocky Point Yacht (Old Greenwich, Conn.). Home: 19 Midbrook Ln Old Greenwich CT 06870 Office: 115 Broadway New York City NY 10006

WIT, HAROLD MAURICE, investment banker; b. Boston, Sept. 6, 1928; s. Maurice and Martha (Bassist) W.; A.B. magna cum laude (Harvard Prize scholar), Harvard, 1949; J.D., Yale, 1954; divorced; children—David Edmund, Hannah Edna. Admitted to N.Y. bar, 1954; asso. firm Cravath, Swaine & Moore, N.Y.C., 1954-58; asst. sec. One William St. Fund, Inc., N.Y.C., 1958-59, v.p., sec., 1959-60; asso. Allen & Co. Inc., 1960—, v.p., 1965-70, exec. v.p., 1970—; pub. Croton Press Ltd.; dir., mem. exec. com. Allen & Co., Inc.; pres., dir. Wit Securities Co.; dir. Grey Advt. Inc., Allegheny & Western Energy Corp., Toys RUs, Interstate Brands, Inc., MCI Communications Corp.; dir., mem. exec. com. DPF Inc.; mem. adv. bd. Nat. Taxpayers Union. Bd. dirs., co-founder Group for Ams. South Fork, Inc.; bd. dirs. Dolly Madison Fund, South Fork Land Found. Served as lt. (j.g.) USNR, 1951-53. Mem. Phi Beta Kappa, Phi Delta Phi. Clubs: Harvard (N.Y., Boston); Yale (N.Y.C.). Home: 160 E 65th St New York City NY 10021 also Cross Hwy East Hampton NY 11937 Office: 711 Fifth Ave New York City NY 10022

WITCHER, ROBERT CAMPBELL, bishop; b. New Orleans, Oct. 5, 1926; s. Charles Swanson and Lily Sebastian (Campbell) W.; B.A. Tulane U., 1949; B.D., Seabury-Western Theol. Sem., 1952; M.A., La. State U., 1960, Ph.D., 1968; m. Elisabeth Alice Cole, June 4, 1957; 2 children. Ordained priest Episcopal Ch., 1953, bishop, 1975; priest-in-charge St. Andrew Ch., Clinton, La. and St. Patrick Ch., Zachary, La., 1953-56; priest-in-charge St. Augustine Ch., Baton Rouge, La., 1953-54, rector, 1954-61; canon pastor Christ Ch. Cathedral, New Orleans, 1961-62; rector St. James Ch., Baton Rouge, 1962-75; coadjutor bishop L.I., 1975-77, bishop L.I., 1977—; pres. diocesan council; pres. Episcopal Found. Edn. L.I. Diocese; dir. numerous camps, confs. and retreats, 1953-75. Trustee U. of South, 1963-69, Seabury-Western Theol. Sem., 1963—; pres. trustees of estate Diocese of L.I.; pres. Ch. Charity Found., Mercer Sch. Theology; v.p. Anglican Soc. N.Am.; del. governing body Nat. Council Chs., 1978. Served to comdr. USNR. Author: The Founding of the Episcopal Church in Louisiana, 1805-38. Office: 36 Cathedral Ave Garden City NY 11530

WITEK, NICHOLAS JOSEPH, elec. engr.; b. Kingston, Pa., Dec. 23, 1945; s. Nicholas and Virginia (Dominick) W.; B.S., U. Scranton, 1967; M.S. in Elec. Engring. (NSF fellow), Cath. U. Am., 1971; m. Donna Hadley, Jan. 1, 1979. Instr. physics lab. U. Scranton, 1964; asst. prodn. engr. Solitron Devices Co., Riviera Beach, Fla., 1966; test engr. Sperry Gyroscope Co., Gt. Neck, N.Y., 1967; contract research engr. night vision lab. U.S. Army C.E. at Cath. U. Am., 1968; spacecraft integration and test mgr. Goddard Space Flight Center, NASA, Greenbelt, Md., 1969—. Recipient Project Recognition NASA, 1971, Project Outstanding Recognition award, 1973, Spl. Achievement award, 1975, Group Achievement award, 1975, Project Team Achievement award, 1978. Mem. AIAA, Sigma Xi. Home: 5613 Goucher Dr Collge Park MD 20740 Office: Goddard Space Flight Center Greenbelt Rd Greenbelt MD 20771

WITENBERG, EARL GEORGE, psychoanalyst, psychiatrist; b. Middletown, Conn., Aug. 30, 1917; s. Nathan and Goldie (Ruderman) W.; B.A., Wesleyan U., 1937, M.A., 1939; M.D., U. Rochester, 1943; m. Mary Jane Hoffman, Apr. 4, 1948 (dec.); children—William, Susan. Intern, Strong Meml. Hosp., Rochester, N.Y., 1943-44; resident in psychiatry Bellevue Hosp., N.Y.C., 1946-48; clin. dir. Postgrad. Center for Psychotherapy, N.Y.C., 1944-49, med. coordinator, 1949-51; chmn. exec. com., fellow W.A. White Inst., 1960-63, dir. inst., 1963—; practice medicine specializing in psychiatry and psychoanalysis, N.Y.C., 1948—; asso. clin. prof. Albert Einstein Coll. Medicine, 1974—. Served to lt. M.C., USNR, 1944-46. Fellow Am. Psychiat. Assn.; mem. Am. Acad. Psychoanalysis (pres. 1976-77, William Silverberg award 1977), Am. Coll. Psychoanalysts, AAAS, Sigma Xi, Phi Beta Kappa. Author: How Not to Succeed in Psychotherapy..., 1972; contbr. articles to med. jours., chpts. to books. Home: 215 E 68th St New York City NY 10021 Office: 20 W 74th St New York City NY 10023

WITHERSPOON, WILLIAM JAMES, guidance counselor; b. Richmond, Va., Aug. 9, 1916; s. William and Lelia (Carter) W.; student Winston-Salem Tchrs. Coll., 1935-40; M.S. in Recreation, Ind. U., 1956; postgrad. Temple U., U. Del., 1965-70; m. Gladys M.

Patterson, July 11, 1937; 1 son, William J. Dir. recreation Center, Winston-Salem, N.C., 1940-48; dir. Community Center, Ft. Wayne, Ind., 1948-52; exec. dir. Booker T. Washington Community Center, Altoona, Pa., 1952-57; asst. dir. Kingswood Community Center, Wilmington, Del., 1957-67; guidance counselor Wilmington Pub. Schs., 1967—. Sec.-treas. Del. dist. 2 Little League Baseball, 1964—; mem. Negro Coll. Fund Com., 1974-77. Recipient award for outstanding service Wilmington Athletic Boys Conf., 1968; certified in guidance and counseling Del. Dept. Pub. Instrn. Mem. Am., Del. personnel and guidance assns., Nat. Assn. Sch. Counselors, Wilmington Edn. Assn., Omega Psi Phi. Methodist. Clubs: Masons, Elks. Home: 107 S 25th St Wilmington DE 19802

WITHEY, ROBERT ARTHUR, state ofcl.; b. Long Branch, N.J., Dec. 21, 1929; s. Clarence Waldo and Mary Josephine (White) W.; B.A., Rutgers U., 1952, M.A., 1957, postgrad., 1957-59; m. Maria Ann Foderaro, Aug. 16, 1952; children—Robert J., Kimberly S., Theodore P. Tchr., counselor, coach, adminstr. pub. schs., Metuchen, N.J., 1952-59; cons. N.J. Dept. Edn., 1959-60, asst. dir., 1960-70, chief, 1970-72; dep. commr. Vt. Dept. Edn., Montpelier, 1972, commr., 1972—. Mem. Vt. Gov.'s Cabinet, Vt.-1202 Commn., Bicentennial Commn., Tchr. Retirement Commn., Ednl. TV Commn.; exec. sec. N.J. Assn. High Sch. Councils, 1961-68; mem. steering com. Ednl. Commn. of States. Mem. Nat., Vt. edn. assns., New Eng., Vt. supts. assns., Am. Assn. Sch. Adminstrs., Vt. Sch. Dirs. Assn. Clubs: Rotary, Exchange. Home: Mt Philo Rd Shelburne VT 05482 Office: Vermont Dept Edn State St Montpelier VT 05602

WITKIN, GEORGE JOSEPH, dentist, educator; b. N.Y.C., Dec. 22, 1915; s. William and Ida (Bloom) W.; B.A., N.Y. U., 1938, D.D.S., 1942; m. Mildred Hope Fisher, June 22, 1940; children—Georgia Hope, Roy Thomas. Pvt. practice dentistry specializing in peridontia and oral medicine, N.Y.C.; research fellow N.Y. U., 1942, asst., 1946-47, instr., 1947-49, asst. prof., 1949-59, asso. prof., 1959-65, prof., 1965—, chmn. dept. periodontia and oral medicine, 1966-69, asst. dean, 1966-72, asso. dean, 1972—, interim dean, 1975, also dir. tchr. tng. program; attending periodontist Univ. Hosp., N.Y. U., Med. Center, N.Y.C.; cons. USPHS, N.Y.C., 1960-65, VA Hosp., N.Y.C., 1965—, Goldwater Meml. Hosp., 1970—, Municipal Civil Service N.Y.C.; attending staff Meml. Hosp. Center, 1976—. Served from 1st lt. to maj. AUS, 1942-46. Recipient I. Hirschfeld Gold medal in periodontology, 1971. Diplomate Am. Bd. Peridontology, Am. Bd. Oral Medicine. Fellow Internat., Am. colls. dentists, N.Y. Acad. Dentists, Am. Acad. Oral Medicine; mem. Am. Acad. Periodontology, Northeastern Soc. Peridontists (past pres.), Associacao Paulista de Cirurgioes Dentistas, Am. Dental Assn., AAUP, AAAS, Yonkers (past pres.), 9th Dist. (past pres.) dental socs., Am. Soc. Periodontists, N.Y. Acad. Sci., Internat. Assn. Dental Research, Research Soc. Am., Omicron Kappa Upsilon, Alpha Omega Dental. Clubs: Saugatuck Harbor Yacht; Royal Yachting Assn. (Gt. Britain). Contbr. articles to profl. jours., textbooks. Home: 9 Sturges Commons Westport CT 06880 also 35 Park Ave New York City NY 10016 Office: 1 Rockefeller Plaza New York City NY 10020

WITKIN, LEE DANIEL, gallery owner, dir.; b. East Orange, N.J., Aug. 29, 1935; s. Alexander and Nannette (Hirsch) W.; B.A., N.Y.U., 1958. Editor, Constructioneer Mag., South Orange, N.J., 1959-68; asso. editor Popular Sci., N.Y.C., 1966; owner, dir. Witkin Gallery Inc., N.Y.C., 1969—; lectr. on photography and collecting; appraiser for museums, including Met. Mus. Art, Mus. Modern Art; pub. ltd. edit. print portfolios. Recipient Visual Dialogue Found. award, 1971. Author: (with Barbara London) The Photograp Collector's Guide, 1979. Office: 41 E 57th St New York City NY 10022

WITKIN, MILDRED HOPE FISHER (MRS. GEORGE JOSEPH WITKIN), psychologist, educator; b. N.Y.C.; d. Samuel and Sadie (Goldschmidt) Fisher; A.B., Hunter Coll., 1940; M.A., Columbia U., 1968; Ph.D., N.Y.U., 1973; m. George Joseph Witkin, June 22, 1940; children—Georgia Hope, Roy Thomas. Head counselor Camp White Lake, Camp Emanuel, Long Beach, N.J., 1938-40; tchr. econs., polit. sci. Hunter Coll. High Sch., 1940; dir., group leader follow-up program Jewish Vocation Assn., N.Y.C., 1940-42; investigator N.Y.C. Housing Authority, 1943-45; counselor Montclair State Coll., Upper Montclair, N.J., 1967-68; mem., lectr. Creative Problem-Solving Inst., U. Buffalo, 1968; psychol. counselor Fairleigh Dickinson U., Teaneck, N.J., 1968, dir. Counseling Center, 1969-74; pvt. practice psychotherapy, N.Y.C., also Westport, Conn.; family therapist and psychologist Payne Whitney Psychiat. Clinic, N.Y. Hosp., 1973—; clin. asst. prof. dept. psychiatry Cornell U. Med. Coll., 1974—; asso. dir. sex therapy and edn. program Cornell-N.Y. Hosp. Med. Center, 1974—; supr. master's and doctoral candidates, N.Y. U., 1975—; pvt. practice psychotherapy and sex therapy, N.Y.C., also Westport, Conn.; cons. counselor edn. tng. programs N.Y.C. Bd. Edn., 1971—; cons. Health Info. Systems, 1972—; vis. faculty numerous colls. and univs.; judge essays on good citizenship, Yonkers, N.Y., 1955; exhibited in group shows at Scarsdale (N.Y.) Art Show, 1959, Red Shutter Art Studio, Long Beach, 1968. Edn. legislation chmn. PTA, Yonkers, 1955; publicity chmn. United Jewish Appeal, Scarsdale, 1959-65; Scarsdale chmn. mothers com. Boy Scouts Am., 1961-64; mem. Morrow Assn. on Correction N.J., 1969—; bd. dirs. Girl Scouts U.S.A., Yonkers, 1954-56. Recipient Bronze pin for services Hunter Coll., 1940; United Jewish Appeal plaque, 1962; Founders Day award N.Y. U., 1973. Mem. Am. Psychol. Assn., AAUW, Women's Med. Assn. N.Y.C., Am. Coll. Personnel Assn. (nat. mem. commn. II 1973-76), Nat. Assn. Women Deans and Counselors, Am. Assn. Sex Educators, Counselors and Therapists (regional bd.), Soc. for Sci. Study Sex, Eastern Assn. Sex Therapists, Am. Assn. Marriage and Family Counselors, N.J. Assn. Marriage and Family Counselors, Ackerman Family Inst., Am. Personnel and Guidance Assn., Am., N.Y., N.J. psychol. assns., Creative Edn. Found., Am. Assn. for Higher Edn., Assn. for Counselor Supervision and Edn., Profl. Women's Caucus, League Women Voters, Pi Lambda Theta, Kappa Delta Pi, Alpha Chi Alpha. Contbr. articles to profl. jours. and textbooks; lectr. workshops. Home and office: 9 Sturges Commons Westport CT 06880 also 35 Park Ave New York City NY 10016

WITKOSKI, FRANCIS CLEMENT, cons. engr.; b. Scranton, Pa., Dec. 19, 1922; s. Harry I. and Pearl (Ritter) W.; B.S., U. Scranton, 1942; M.S., Bucknell U., 1950; m. Romayne F. Kapalski, Sept. 4, 1946; children—Michael, Susan, William, David, Amy. Asst. prof. chemistry U. Scranton, 1947-55; dir. research Pa. Dept. Hwys., Harrisburg, 1955-60; sec., tech. dir. Am. Testing Labs., Inc., Lancaster, Pa., 1960-63; pres. Materials Engring. & Service Co., Camp Hill, Pa., 1963—. Cons., Pa. Dept. Mines, Pa. State U., Dept. Mineral Industies, Prestressed Concrete Assn. Pa. Served to 1st lt. CWS, 1943-47. Registered profl. engr. Fellow Am. Inst. Chemists; mem. Nat. Soc. Profl. Engrs., Hwy. Research Bd., Alpha Chi Sigma. Home: 320 N 27th St Camp Hill PA 17011 Office: 21st and Chestnut Sts Box 621 Camp Hill PA 17011

WITLIN, JAMES ROYCE, meat packing co. exec.; b. San Antonio, July 2, 1944; s. Roy Victor and Joan (Robb) W.; student U. Pa., 1973-75; m. Elizabeth Ruth Rile, Aug. 30, 1965; children—Cathrine, Andrew. Quality assurance Oscar Mayer & Co., Phila., 1963-64, vacation relief, spl. projects supr., 1964-69, supt. night plant, 1969-71, prodn. supr. area I, 1971-77, area II, 1977—. Exec. bd. Abington (Pa.) YMCA, parent-child program, 1974—; active Boy Scouts Am. Mem. Am. Mgmt. Assn. Republican. Home: 697 Pembroke Rd Rydal PA 19046 Office: 3333 S Front St Philadelphia PA 19148

WITMER, CHARLES RUSSELL, borough cons.; b. Phila., June 26, 1898: s. William W. and Mable (Yatman) W.; student Muhlenberg Coll., 1916-17; certificate U. Pa., 1925; m. Sara M. Arnold, June 21, 1925; children—Charles Russell, William F. Clk. cashier Salomon Bros. & Hutzler, 1920-23, Wurts Dulles & Co., 1923-37; with Inter-County Hospitalization Plan, Inc., 1937-64. Chief burgess, Sellersville, 1930-32, borough sec., 1932-69, asst. borough sec., 1969-72; mem. Planning Commn., Bucks County, 1957-64, chmn., 1961-62; chmn. Sellersville Hist. and Achievement Authority. Mem. investment com. Commonwealth of Pa.-Municipal Employees Retirement Bd., 1961-74. Served as pvt. U.S. Army, 1917-19. Recipient service award Pa. Local Govtl. Secs. Assn., 1963, Pennridge Jaycees, 1966; Pres.'s award Pa. State Assn. Boroughs, 1970. Mem. Pa. Local Govtl. Secs. Assn. (pres. 1953-58), S.A.R. (pres. Valley Forge chpt. 1958-59, bd. mgrs. 1960-68). Republican. Mason (32 deg., Shriner). Home and office: 146 Lawn Ave Sellersville PA 18960

WITMER, KENNETH ISAIAH, city ofcl.; b. Lancaster, Pa., May 8, 1916; s. Isaiah Miller and Catherine Frances (Negley) W.; grad. Pa. State Police Acad., 1943; m. Helen Elizabeth Hersh, May 17, 1941. With Lancaster Police Dept., 1942-70, insp., 1962-70; dir. security Park City Center, Lancaster, 1970—; mem. City Council Lancaster, 1972—. Mem. Traffic Commn., Lancaster, 1972-76; chmn. Planning Commn., Lancaster, 1976—, Pub. Safety Commn., 1972-76; mem. Lancaster County Planning Commn., 1978—; trustee Lancaster Assn. Retarded Children, 1971-72. Mem. Fraternal Order Police (recipient distinguished service award 1962), Nat. League Cities, Am. Pub. Works Assn., Pa. League Cities. Republican. Presbyterian. Clubs: Masons, Shrine, Elks. Home: 804 Hilton Dr Lancaster PA 17603 Office: 146 Park City Center Lancaster PA 17601

WITORSCH, PHILIP, physician; b. N.Y.C., July 11, 1937; s. Benjamin and Sarah (Etkin) W.; A.B., Univ. Coll., N.Y. U., 1958, M.D., 1962; m. Joan Linda Pellman, June 7, 1959; children—Beth Joy, Jeffrey Lee. Intern and resident in internal medicine (Mead Johnson-A.C.P. residency scholar), Yale-New Haven Hosp., 1962-64; clin. asso., clin. investigator, Nat. Inst. Allergy and Infectious Diseases, NIH, Bethesda, 1964-67; resident, chief resident in internal medicine, fellow in pulmonary diseases, VA Hosp., Washington, 1967-69; chmn. pulmonary medicine, dir. med. intensive care unit, med. dir. respiratory therapy, sr. attending in medicine, Washington Hosp. Center, 1969—; asso. prof. medicine, George Washington U.; cons. in pulmonary diseases, VA Hosp., NIH, Dept. State, Andrews AFB. Served with USPHS, 1964-67. Diplomate Am. Bd. Internal Medicine. Fellow A.C.P., Am. Coll. Chest Physicians; mem. Soc. Critical Care Medicine, Am., D.C. Thoracic Socs., AMA (physicians recognition awards, 1972, 75, 78), Med. Soc. D.C., Am. Fedn. Clin. Research, So. Med. Assn., Am. Assn. Respiratory Therapy, Am. Heart Assn., Royal Soc. Medicine, Am. Soc. Internal Medicine, Phi Beta Kappa, Alpha Omega Alpha. Democrat. Jewish. Clubs: Inverness Recreation; Potomac Tennis. Contbr. articles to profl. med. jours. Home: 11033 Powder Horn Dr Potomac MD 20854 Office: 110 Irving St NW Washington DC 20010

WITT, DAVID HAMPTON, project engr.; b. Swansea, S.C., July 3, 1930; s. Lee Harold and Thelma (Crook) W.; B.S., Clemson U., 1951; M.S., George Washington U., 1973; m. Johnnie Lee Smith, June 7, 1952; children—Celia Jane, Richard David. Instr. textile engring. Clemson (S.C.) U., 1951-52; prodn. engr. J.P. Stevens Co., Clemson, 1954-55; partner Thelma C. Witt & Sons, Swansea, 1955—; ordnance engr. Aberdeen (Md.) Proving Ground, 1955-62, tech. asst., 1962-63, sr. test engr., group leader U.S. Army Test and Evaluation Command, 1966—; U.S. trials chmn. U.S., German, Brit. Tank Weapon Evaluation, 1975-77. Bus. mgr. boat regatta Havre de Grace, Md., 1970—; active Boy Scouts Am., 1971—; grants supr. Susquehanna Mus. Inc., 1976—. Served with ordnance U.S. Army, 1952-54. Recipient Meritorious Civilian Service award U.S. Army, 1976. Mem. Res. Officers Assn. (life), Am. Def. Preparedness Assn. (life). Republican. Methodist. Clubs: Chesapeake Swim (v.p. 1974), Lions (pres. Havre de Grace 1968-69, recognition and service award 1969). Home: 107 Brotherton Ct Havre de Grace MD 21078 Office: US Army Test and Evaluation Command Aberdeen Proving Ground MD 21005

WITT, JOHN JOSEPH, artist; b. Wilmington, Del., Jan. 30, 1940; s. Alex and Josephine (Glowiak) W.; B.F.A., Phila. Coll. Art, 1962; postgrad U. Md., 1964-65, Bklyn. Mus. Sch. Art, 1967-68; m. Constance Giumarro, Nov. 22, 1970. Sr. art dir. Western Union, N.Y.C., 1966-72; combat artist USMC Civilian Commn., Vietnam, 1968-69; freelance illustrator, designer, N.Y.C., 1972-74; courtroom trial artist ABC News, 1974; v.p., art dir. Druid Assos., Inc., N.Y.C., 1974—; exhbns.: Smithsonian Instn., 1969, Nat. Arts Club, N.Y.C., 1972, Hudson Valley Art Assn. Ann., White Plains, N.Y., 1972, Audubon Artists Ann., N.Y., 1973, Am. Artists Profl. League Ann., N.Y., 1973. Served with AUS, 1963-66. Recipient Gold medal Hudson Valley Art Assn., 1972, Louis E. Seley medal, Navy Combat Art award, 1978, Monaghan award Nat. Soc. Painters in Caseine and Acrylic, 1974. Mem. Soc. Illustrators (exec. com. 1975-78), Naval Art Lisaion and Coop. Com., USMC Combat Corr. Assn., Hudson Valley Art Assn., Audbuon Artists, Am. Artist Profl. League. Roman Catholic. Author, illustrator: Vietnam, 1972; illustrator: Portraits of Valor, USMC, 1974. Home: RD 1 Baptist Church Rd Yorktown Heights NY 10598 Office: 1114 Ave of Americas New York City NY 10036

WITT, LEONARD RAYMOND, psychologist, adminstr.; b. Jersey City, Aug. 31, 1923; s. John and Nellie W.; B.A., N.Y. U., 1950; M.A., U. Tex., 1951; M.P.A., State U. N.Y. at Albany, 1970; m. Betty Lou Christofferson, Feb. 4, 1950; children—Nancy Elizabeth, Stephan Neil. Parole employment officer N.Y. State Div. Parole, Albany, 1954-58, dir. project devel., N.Y.C., 1966-68, supr. parole placement, Albany, 1958-71; dir. community services N.Y. State Dept. Correctional Services, Albany, 1972—; lectr. Moran Inst. Delinquency and Crime, St. Lawrence U., Canton, N.Y., 1963; lectr. Tng. Inst. Parole Officers, Law-Medicine Inst. Boston U., Chickopee, Mass., 1964; lectr. N.Y. State Corrections Tng. Acad., 1974—. Served with USNR, 1942-46. Certified psychologist, N.Y. State. Mem. Am. Psychol. Assn., AAAS, Psychol. Assn. Northeastern N.Y., Pi Sigma Alpha. Office: State NY Dept Correctional Services State Office Bldg Campus Albany NY 12226

WITT, MARJORIE RUTH, nurse; b. Queens, N.Y., Feb. 16, 1943; d. Lester and Frances Vivian (Halperon) Hochman; R.N., Mt. Sinai Hosp. Sch. Nursing, 1963; B.A., Marymount Coll., 1975; M.A., Seton Hall U., 1978; m. John Witt, Feb. 12, 1965; 1 son, Eric. Staff nurse Mt. Sinai Hosp., N.Y.C., 1964-65, supr., 1970; dir. nursing Northfield Manor Nursing Home, West Orange, N.J., 1970-72; asst. dir. nursing Rahway (N.J.) Hosp., 1972-76; dir. nursing Helene Fuld Med. Center, Trenton, N.J., 1976—; mem. adv. com. Trenton State Coll. Continuing Edn. in Nursing, Guggenheim awardee, 1963. Mem. Am., N.J. assns. nursing adminstrs.

WITT, ROBERT, JR., steel co. exec.; b. Irvine, Ky., June 9, 1921; s. Robert and Lula Bell (Wilcox) W.; student Eastern Ky. State U., 1938-42; B.S., U. Ky., 1951; m. Mary Louise Hillis, Apr. 10, 1948; children—Roberta Louise, Ruth Ann. Lab. instr. mineral beneficiation U. Ky., Lexington, 1945-48; chief chemist, metallurgist Fluorspar dist. U.S. Steel Co., Mexico, Ky., 1951-54, preparation engr., coal div., Corbin, Ky., 1954-66; supt. coal preparation Frick dist. U.S. Steel Corp., Uniontown, Pa., 1968-74, dist. engr. Frick dist., 1974-77, chief engr. Frick dist., 1978—. Mem. Am. Inst. Mining, Metall. and Petroleum Engrs. (chmn. coal preparation subcom. 1971-72), Am. Mining Congress, Am. Forestry Assn., Internat. Platform Assn., Tau Beta Pi, Sigma Gamma Epsilon. Club: Masons. Home: 340 S Lombard St Uniontown PA 15401 Office: Fayette Bank Bldg Uniontown PA 15401

WITTEK, MARIE JOHNSON, educator; b. N.Y.C., Aug. 29, 1931; d. James M. and Mary H. (Sullivan) Johnson; B.A., St. Joseph's Coll., 1953; M.A., N.Y. U., 1955; Ph.D., 1968; m. Emil Wittek, Jan. 6, 1960; 1 dau., Orie. Tchr. speech N.Y.C. Bd. Edn., 1953-63, chmn. speech dept., 1967-69; asst. prof. speech St. Johns U., 1963-66; prof. edn. York Coll., City U. N.Y., 1966—; ednl. cons. to Irish Govt. Dir., N.Y.C. Bicentennial Corp., 1974-77; campaign coordinator for Carter, N.Y. State; mem. exec. bd. Loyola Sch. Recipient Founders Day award N.Y. U., 1968, medal City of N.Y., 1976. Mem. Speech Assn. Am., Folklore Soc., Am. Assn. Tchrs. Edn., Speech and Hearing Assn., N.Y.C. Archive Com. Roman Catholic. Club: N.Y. Univ. Home: 305 E 86th St New York City NY 10028 Office: York Coll 150-14 Jamaica Ave New York City NY 11234

WITTEN, LAURENCE CLAIBORNE, II, antiquarian bookseller; b. Cin., Apr. 3, 1926; s. Laurence Claiborne and Julia Eleanora (McLaren) W.; B.A., Williams Coll., 1948; Mus.B., Yale, 1951; m. Cora Nell Williams, Apr. 3, 1954; children—Julia, Patricia, Cecile. Owner, mgr. Laurence Witten Rare Books, Bethany, Conn., 1951-53, New Haven, 1953-66, Monroe, Conn., 1966-76, Southport, Conn., 1976—; lectr. on early mus. instruments; advisor, co-founder Yale U. Collection for Hist. Sound Recs.; mem. nat. adv. bd. Center for the Book, Library of Congress, 1978—. Mem. budget com. United Fund, 1960-65; bd. dirs. New Haven Symphony, 1962-65, Neighborhood Music Sch., New Haven, 1958-63; mem. Easton (Conn.) Planning and Zoning Commn., 1973-74. Served with AUS, 1944-46. Mem. Antiquarian Booksellers Assn. Am. (sec. 1975-78, pres. 1978—), Internat. League Antiquarian Booksellers, Medieval Soc. Am., Renaissance Soc. Am., Manuscript Soc., Am. Mus. Instruments Soc. (dir. 1975-77), Grolier Club, Old Book Table (pres. 1973-75). Republican. Contbr. articles to bibliog., discographical and mus. jours.; editor, pub. catalogues, including discoveries in early manuscripts and history of printing and learning. Office: PO Box 490 Southport CT 06490

WITTER, RICHARD EARL, retail book co. exec.; b. S.I., N.Y., Dec. 6, 1926; s. Earl William and Ida Irene (Reed) W.; A.B., Columbia, 1950; m. Dorothy Iris Nemser, Oct. 17, 1956; 1 dau., Dawn Carol. Owner, pres. F & S F Book Co., Inc., S.I., N.Y., 1950—. Address: 78 Ravenhurst Ave Staten Island NY 10310

WITTER, ROBERT WILLIAM, boat mfg. co. exec., naval architect; b. Dubuque, Iowa, July 27, 1929; s. Herbert Frank and Irma Marie (Herzog) W.; B.S., U.S. Coast Guard Acad., 1951; M.S. in Naval Arch., Mass. Inst. Tech., 1958; m. Janet Young, Dec. 29, 1951; children—Robert Y., Jonathan K., Sarah. Commd. ensign U.S. Coast Guard, 1951, advanced through grades to capt., 1972; dir. Field Testing and Devel. Center, Curtis Bay, Md., 1965-69, Nat. Data Buoy Devel. Project, Washington, 1969-70; comdg. officer Coast Guard Base, Portsmouth, Va., 1970-73, chief ocean engring. div. Hdqrs., Washington, 1973-74; ret., 1974; v.p.-engring. and comml. products Trojan Yacht Co., Lancaster, Pa., 1974—; del. Internat. Life-Boat Conf., 1963, 67, 71, Pan-Am. Congress Naval Arch. and Maritime Transport, 1966. Troop leader Boy Scouts Am., 1968-70. Recipient Sci. Achievement award USCG, 1968. Mem. Am. Soc. Naval Engrs., Am. Boat and Yacht Council, Royal Nat. Life-Boat Instn., U.S. Naval Inst., Pan-Am. Inst. Naval Engring. Republican. Contbr. articles in field to profl. jours. Home: 1309 Meadowbrook Rd Lancaster PA 17603 Office: PO Box 1571 Lancaster PA 17604

WITTER, WILLIAM DAVID, investment counselor; b. San Francisco, Sept. 2, 1929; s. Dean and Helen (Perkins) W.; grad. Hotchkiss Sch., 1947; B.A., Yale U., 1951; M.B.A., Stanford U., 1953; m. Susan Helen Rentschler, July 28, 1956 (div. 1970); children—Virginia Ann, Elizabeth Tacy, Sidney Waldon, William Perkins; m. 2d, Inger K. Kullberg, May 20, 1972; children—Michael David, Anna Christina. With Dean Witter & Co., investment bankers, N.Y.C., 1956-66, partner, 1959-66, mem. exec. com., 1964-66; pres. William D. Witter, Inc., N.Y.C., 1966—. Mem. adv. com. Stanford Bus. Sch., 1959-65, 71-77. Served to 1st lt. USAF, 1953-55. Clubs: Links, Boone and Crockett, Recess (N.Y.C.); Pacific Union, Bohemian (San Francisco). Home: 870 UN Plaza New York City NY 10017 Office: 280 Park Ave New York City NY 10017

WITTMER, FRANKLIN DONALD, chem. and food equipment mfg. co. exec.; b. Carlinville, Ill., Dec. 3, 1929; s. Franklin Benjamin and Eva Caroline (Zihlman) W.; B.S. in Chem. Engring. with honors, Mich. Technol. U., 1955, B.Sc. in Chemistry with honors, 1955; M.Sc. in Chem. Engring., U. Del., 1956; m. Nancy Genevieve McDonnell, Feb. 11, 1956; children—Bonita, Daniel. Various positions in aerospace industry, 1957-67; chem. engring. specialist Graham Mfg. Co., Batavia, N.Y., 1968-73; project mgr. process heat transfer systems Linde div. Union Carbide Corp., Buffalo, 1973-75; dir. engring. Bos-Hatten, Inc., Buffalo, 1975-77; mgr. engring. Blaw-Knox Food & Chem. Equipment Co., Buffalo, 1977—; process equipment design cons.; sponsor evening courses in mgmt. tng., 1972-75. Bd. dirs. Community Devel. Bd., Denver, 1960-63. Served with U.S. Army, 1951-53. Registered profl. engr., N.Y. Mem. Am. Inst. Chem. Engrs., ASME, Nat. Soc. Profl. Engrs., Am. Oil Chemist Assn., Tau Beta Pi, Phi Lambda Upsilon. Club: Fishing of Am. Contbr. articles to profl. jours. Patentee in fields of combustion, propulsion and thermodynamics. Home: 146 Culpepper Rd Williamsville NY 14221 Office: PO Box 1041 Buffalo NY 14240

WITTMER, PAUL WILLIAM, historian; b. Bklyn., Oct. 8, 1929; s. John Paul and Elsie Barbara (Brand) W.; A.B. in History cum laude with departmental honors, Hofstra U., 1950, certificate elementary and secondary prin., 1969; M.A. in History (Univ. scholar), Brown U., 1954; teaching certificate Adelphi U., 1956; Ph.D. in History of Edn., N.Y. U., 1967; m. Susan Margaret Coon, Feb. 20, 1965. Tchr. pub. schs., Westbury, N.Y., 1954-69; tchr.-in-charge Powell's Ln. Sch., Westbury, 1961-64; instr. in history of edn. N.Y. U., 1965-67; asst. prof. edn. Chgo. State Coll. 1967-68; asst. prof. med. edn. Mt. Sinai Sch. Medicine of City U. N.Y. and asst. to pres. Mt. Sinai Med. Center, 1969-70; asst. prof. history Tunxis Community Coll., Farmington, Conn., 1970-72, asso. prof., 1972-76, prof., 1976—, area coordinator arts, 1972-74, head dept. social scis., 1974-76; speaker, lectr. on Collins Co. to ednl., bus. orgns.; historian, dir. Canton (Conn.) Hist. Soc., 1974—, exec. sec., 1975—, pres., 1977—; chmn. Collins County exhibit Canton Hist. Mus., 1974—. Mem. choir Collinsville Congregational Ch., 1970—, deacon, 1977-78, chmn. parish life, 1978—; mem. Canton Am. Revolution Bicentennial

Commn., 1974—. Recipient Founders' Day award N.Y. U., 1968; named Hon. Sponsor, Mt. Sinai Sch. Medicine, 1970; certified elementary tchr., high sch. social studies tchr., elementary and secondary pub. sch. prin., N.Y. Mem. Am. Hist. Assn., NEA (life), Am. Acad. Polit. and Social Scis., History Edn. Soc., Am. Ednl. Studies Assn., New Eng. History Tchrs. Assn., New Eng. Assn. Oral History, Assn. Study Conn. History, Oral History Soc., Community Colls. Social Sci. Assn., Conn., Nat. hist. socs., Phi Alpha Theta, Pi Gamma Mu, Sigma Kappa Alpha, Phi Delta Kappa, Kappa Delta Pi. Republican. Club: Masons (Rockville Centre, N.Y.). Author: The Secularization of American Geology Textbooks in the Nineteenth Century, 1967; also articles. Home: 7 Overlook Dr Canton CT 06019 Office: Tunxis Community Coll Routes 6 and 177 Farmington CT 06032

WITTREICH, WARREN JAMES, cons. psychologist; b. Weehawken, N.J., Aug. 18, 1929; s. Andrew Otto and Muriel (Wilson) W.; A.B., Princeton U., 1951, M.A., 1953, Ph.D., 1954; m. Lois Vivian Llewellyn, Dec. 6, 1959; children—Michael, Benjamin, Peter, Debra, Susie (dec.), Andrea. Guest scientist Naval Med. Research Inst., Bethesda, Md., 1953-54; staff psychologist VA, East Orange, N.J., 1954-55; mgr. mktg. and consumer research Armstrong Cork Co., Lancaster, Pa., 1955-59; exec. v.p. Nat. Analysts, Inc., Phila., 1959-64; pres. Daniel Yankelovich, Inc. of Pa., Phila., 1964-67; pres. Wittreich Assos., Inc., Phila., 1967—; adj. prof. Pa. State U., 1956-58, U. Pitts., 1959-61, U. Pa., 1968-71; adviser U.S. sec. transp., 1968-72. Pres., Crossroads Found. for Research into Alcohol and Drug Abuse, 1975—. NSF fellow, 1952-53. Mem. Am., Eastern, Pa. psychol. assns., Internat. Assn. Applied Psychologists, Phila. Soc. Clin. Psychologists, Am. Mktg. Assn., Phi Beta Kappa, Sigma Xi. Episcopalian. Clubs: Princeton (N.Y.C. and Phila.). Home: 605 W Phil-Ellena St Philadelphia PA 19119 Office: Morgan House Box 27100 Philadelphia PA 19118

WIXOM, THEODORE MERSHON, linen rental co. exec.; b. Galesburg, Ill., June 15, 1937; s. Robert Nelson and Doris (Cox) W.; B.S. in Indsl. Mgmt., Miami U., Oxford, Ohio, 1960; m. Carolyn Sue Masson, Aug. 26, 1962; children—Elizabeth Kay, Margaret Marie. Plant mgr. F.W. Means & Co., Lexington, Ky., 1964-66, South Bend, Ind., 1966-68; staff plant mgr. Asso. Linen Services, Utica, N.Y., 1968-70, gen. mgr., 1970-74; v.p. ops. Community Linen Rental Services, Los Angeles, 1974-76; v.p., dir. Spalding's Services Ltd., Louisville, 1976-78; gen. mgr. N.Y. area Morgan Services, Inc., Buffalo, N.Y., 1978—. Instr. driving course Nat. Safety Council, Utica, 1972-73. Served to lt. (j.g.) USNR, 1960-62. Named engr. year Joint Engrs. Council Mohawk Valley, 1971. Certified Mfg. eng. Mem. Am. Inst. Indsl. Engrs. (v.p. region 5; sr. mem.; nat. bd. dirs.), Mohawk Valley Joint Engrs. Council (chmn. pub. relations com.), Soc. Mfg. Engrs., Linen Supply Assn. Am. (mem. nat. ops. com.), Alpha Kappa Psi, Theta Chi. Clubs: Masons, Rotary. Contbr. articles to profl. jours. Home: 91 Huntington Ct Williamsville NY 14221 Office: 325 Louisiana St Buffalo NY 14204

WIZNIA, PEARL PAULINE (MRS. BENJAMIN WIZNIA), artist, educator, social worker; b. N.Y.C., Oct. 17, 1914; d. Rubin Wolfe and Sophie (Richman) Guss; B.A., Hunter Coll., 1937; M.S.W., Columbia, 1949; M.A., Ariz. State Coll., 1953; m. Benjamin Wiznia, Oct. 13, 1940; 1 son, Robert Abraham. Social group worker, N.Y.C., 1934-38, 49; social worker, 1939-47; case-worker Community Service Soc., 1946-48, Child Guidance Clinic, N.Y. Juvenile Ct., 1948-50, psychiat.-out-patient clinic Phoenix-Ariz. VA Hosp., 1953-54, psychiat. and med. out-patient clinic, 1954-55; case worker psychiat. and med. in-patient West Haven VA Hosp., 1955-56; sr. psychiat. social worker child guidance clinic, Bridgeport, 1956-58; psychiat. social worker New Haven Bd. Edn., 1958—, Howard Ave. Counseling Service, 1973—; caseworker gen. practice, 1965-73; pvt. practice psychiat. social worker, 1973. Address: 516 Ellsworth Ave New Haven CT 06511

WOËL, RALPH, accountant; b. Jeremie, Haiti, Dec. 29, 1933; s. Gaston and Lina (Martineau) W.; came to U.S., 1956, naturalized, 1961; B.S., Coll. Port-au-Prince, Haiti, 1953; certified dental technician, N.Y. Sch. Mech. Dentistry, 1958; A.B.A., and B.C.S., Benjamin Franklin U., Washington, 1964; M.B.A., Calif. Nat. Open U., 1978; m. Hilda Esther Sotomayor, Sept. 5, 1959; children—Ralph, Brian Jacob. Staff accountant, firm Samuel H. Cohen, Washington, 1965-66, firm Regardie & Brooks, 1966-69; sr. accountant firm Herman Glazer, Silver Spring, Md., 1969-74; prin. Ralph Woël Mgmt. and Tax Cons., Silver Spring, 1974—; prof. advt., cost accounting and managerial accounting Gardner Sch. Bus., Washington, 1974-75; tchr., cons. Urban Bus. Edn. Assn., Washington, 1975, Inter Am. Research Assos., 1974-75; pres. Adminstrv. Technologists Assos., Inc., 1974—. Mem. Nat. Soc. Pub. Accountants, Am. Accounting Assn., Nat. Assn. Accountants, Nat. Soc. Tax Cons. Roman Catholic. Contbr. to preparation of Bus. Adminstrn. Manual in Spanish. Home and Office: 1002 Gabel St Silver Spring MD 20901

WOEPPEL, MARY ANITA CONFALONE, real estate broker; b. Bangor, Pa.; d. Nicholas and Rosa (Alterio) Confalone; student Fleichers Evening Coll., 1943-44; m. Charles William Woeppel, Apr. 27, 1946 (dec. Sept. 1976); children—Bill, Patricia. With U.S. Civil Service, to 1959; real estate salesman-broker Farrell & Knight, Haddonfield, N.J., 1959-69; real estate broker Fox & Lazo, Inc., Cherry Hill, N.J., 1969—. Pres. Cherry Hill (N.J.) Vol. Pearl Buck Assn. for Amerasian Children, 1965-67; active PTA. Licensed real estate broker, N.J.; designated Realtor; mem. Real Estate Million Dollar Sales Club, 1975-78. Mem. Camden County (N.J.) Bd. Realtors (Salesman of Year 1975), Nat., N.J. assns. Realtors, Realtors Nat. Mktg. Inst. (certified residential specialist). Roman Catholic. Home: 1143 W Valleybrook Rd Cherry Hill NJ 08034 Office: 80 Barclay Center Cherry Hill NJ 08034

WOGLOM, JAMES RUSSELL, environ. planner; b. Glen Ridge, N.J., May 17, 1926; s. Russell S. and Viola (Herslow) W.; student Shrivenham U., 1945; B.S. in Adminstrv. Engring., B.A. in Econs., Lafayette Coll., 1950; postgrad. Mass. Inst. Tech., 1955, Muhlenberg Coll., 1956; M.A. Polit. Sci., Lehigh U., 1960; Certificate in Advanced Mgmt., Northeastern U., 1971; m. Eleanor I. Crockett, June 7, 1952; children—David L., Russell C., George N., Mary Ellen. Asst. div. engr. Morris Knowles, Inc., Easton, Pa., 1950-55, asst. dir. city planning div., 1955-61; Metcalf & Eddy, dir. community planning and renewal, 1962-66, sr. asso., 1966-70, asst. v.p., 1970-72, div. v.p., 1972-75; v.p., prin. Camp Dresser & McKee, 1975-77, pres. environ. planning div., 1977—. Mem. Govs. Adv. Com. on Planning, Mass.; asso. trustee Lafayette Coll., 1978—. Served with AUS, 1944-46, ETO. Registered profl. engr., Nat. Engring. Council certificate, 30 states and D.C.; registered profl. planner N.J., Mich. Mem. Mass. Cons. Planners (pres. 1972-75), Nat. Soc. Profl. Engrs., Inst. Transp. Engrs., ASCE (sec. exec. com. city planning div., chmn. handbook com. city planning div.; sec. planning adminstrv. com., student chpt. adviser), Am. Inst. Planners (dir. Boston sect.), Am. Indsl. Devel. Council, Soc. Am. Mil. Engrs. (contact mem. 1976—), Am. Soc. Planning Ofcls., Nat. Recreation and Park Assn., Pi Gamma Mu, Alpha Phi Omega. Episcopalian. Author articles in field. Home: 9 Ledgetree Rd Medfield MA 02052 Office: One Center Plaza Boston MA 02108 also 1945 The Exchange NW Suite 290 Atlanta GA 30339 also 7105 Broadway Walnut Creek CA 94596 also One World Trade Center Suite 2637 New York City NY 10048

WOHL, HAROLD LEE, accounting exec.; b. Bklyn., June 2, 1935; s. Bernard E. and Mildred L. (Herzog) W.; student U. R.I., 1953-55; B.B.A., Coll. City N.Y., 1958, M.B.A., 1965; certificate continuing profl. edn.; m. Arlene Ruth Rosenberg, June 14, 1959; children—Leonard Alan, Karen Beth, Dana Ellen. Jr. accountant Eisner & Lubin, C.P.A.'s, N.Y.C., 1958; semi-sr. accountant Goldenberg & Goldenberg, C.P.A.'s, N.Y.C., 1958-62; partner Gold, Wohl & Gold, C.P.A.'s, N.Y.C., 1962-72, Goldenberg, Weisbrod & Wohl, C.P.A.'s, N.Y.C., 1972—; mem. faculty bank Found. Accounting Edn. C.P.A., N.Y. State. Mem. N.Y. Soc. C.P.A.'s (chmn. real estate accounting com. 1970-71), Am. Inst. C.P.A.'s. Club: K.P. (past chancellor). Editor Claremore Clarion, 1974-75, 75-76, 77-78. Address: Goldenberg Weisbrod Wohl CPA 654 Madison Ave New York City NY 10021

WOHL, MARTIN, educator; b. Greensboro, N.C., July 13, 1930; s. Stanley Siedenbach and Helen (Robertson) W.; student U.S. Mil. Acad., 1948-50; B.S., Mass. Inst. Tech., 1956, M.S., 1960; D.Eng., U. Calif., Berkeley, 1966; m. Ann Hedges Findley, Dec. 20, 1958 (div.); children—Charles Martin, Richard Thomas. Mem. staff, asst. prof. Mass. Inst. Tech., 1957-62; cons. to asst. sec. commerce, Washington, 1962-63; lectr. econs. Harvard, 1963-65; acting asso. prof. U. Calif., Berkeley, 1967; sr. staff mem. Rand Corp., 1967-68; mgr. transp. analysis dept., corporate planning staff Ford Motor Co., Dearborn, Mich., 1968-69; dir. transp. studies The Urban Inst., Washington, 1969-72; prof. Carnegie-Mellon U., Pitts., 1972—. Cons. to various govt. agys., cos. Bd. dirs. Cambridge (Mass.) Civic Assn., 1958-62. Served to 1st lt. AUS, 1953-55. Recipient Past Pres.'s award Inst. Traffic Engrs., 1958. NSF faculty fellow, 1965-66. Mem. Inst. Traffic Engrs., Regional Sci. Assn., Transp. Research Bd., Sigma Xi, Chi Epsilon. Author: (with John R. Meyer, John F. Kain) The Urban Transporation Problem, 1965; (with Brian Martin) Traffic System Analysis, 1967; Transportation Investment Planning, 1972; (with R. Kirby, K. Bhatt, M. Kemp and R. McGillivray) Para-Transit: Neglected Options for Urban Mobility, 1975. Home: 7520 Carriage Ln Pittsburgh PA 15221

WOHL, ROBERT ALLEN, aerospace co. exec.; b. Chgo., June 21, 1931; s. Max and Frieda (Friedmann) W.; student U. Wis., 1948-50; B.A., San Diego State U., 1952; postgrad. U. Calif. at Berkeley, 1954-56; J.D., U. San Diego, 1960; m. Christine Allison, 1974; children—Melissa, Suzanne. Admitted to Calif. bar, 1961; mgr. contracts Gen. Dynamics Corp., San Diego, 1956-62, mgr. program control, space programs, 1962-63, asst. to v.p., N.Y.C., 1963-68, corp. dir. contracts, 1968-70; v.p. adminstrn., sec. Canadair Ltd., Montreal, Que., Can., 1970—. Served with USAF, 1952-54; 1st lt. Res. Mem. Am. Bar Assn., Am. Soc. Internat. Law, Nat. Mgmt. Assn. (chpt. 1st v.p. 1962), Blue Key, Phi Alpha Delta (chpt. pres. 1956), Zeta Beta Tau. Club: Wings of New York. Home: 21 Pacific Ave Senneville PQ H9X 1A2 Canada Office: 1800 Laurentian Blvd St Laurent PQ H3C 3G9 Canada

WOHLER, JAMES RICHARD, II, brick mfg. co. exec.; b. Pitts., Sept. 9, 1940; s. James Richard and Anna Mary Walter (Bittner) W.; B.S., U. Pitts., 1963, M.S., 1966, Ph.D., 1969; m. Alison Jane Adams, Apr. 12, 1975; 1 dau., Elizabeth Jane; 1 son by previous marriage, James Richard III. Lab. asst. Mellon Inst., Pitts., 1958-63; asst. prof. biology Allegheny Coll., Meadville, Pa., 1968-72, asso. prof., chmn. biology dept., 1972-75; asst. v.p. Free-Col div. Freeport Brick Co., Meadville, 1974—. Indsl. and ednl. cons. Recipient grants NSF, IBM, Buhl Found. Mem. Am. Indsl. Hygiene Assn., Internat. Soc. Theoretical and Applied Limnology, Ecol. Soc. Am., Ohio, Pa. acads. sci., Sigma Xi. Author: Laboratory Manual of Limnology, 1974; Laboratory Manual of Experimental Botany, 1974. Contbr. to profl. jours. Home: RD 1 The Maples Saegertown PA 16433 Office: Free-Col div Freeport Brick Co Meadville PA 16335

WOHLTMAN, KEITH WILLIAM, educator; b. Rahway, N.J., Feb. 19, 1948; s. John William and Doris (Gibson) W.; B.A. in Chem. Edn., Montclair State Coll., 1970, M.A. in Chemistry, 1974. Tchr., Colonia (N.J.) Pub. Schs., 1970-78; research technician, laser physics/chem. research group Exxon Research & Engring. Co., Linden, N.J., 1978—. Mem. Internat. Oceanographic Found., Am. Chem. Soc., Costeau Soc. Episcopalian. Home: 98 Victor Ave Eatontown NJ 07724

WOITITZ, JANET GERINGER, counselor; b. N.Y.C., Mar. 27, 1938; d. Murray and Elizabeth (Beigel) Geringer; B.A., Antioch Coll., 1960; M.A., Montclair State Coll., 1971; Ed.D., Rutgers U., 1976; children—David, Lisa, Daniel. Counselor in pvt. practice, Montclair, N.J., 1975—; adj. prof. Montclair State Coll., 1972—; instr. Summer Sch. Alcohol Studies, Rutgers U. Mem. Am. Personnel and Guidance Assn., Orgn. Women for Legal Awareness, N.J. Assn. Alcoholism Counselors, N.J. Alcoholism Assn., N.J. Task Force on Women and Alcohol. Author: Marriage on the Rocks, 1979. Contbr. articles on alcoholism to profl. jours. Home and Office: 27 Marquette Rd Upper Montclair NJ 07043

WOJCIECHOWSKI, JERZY ANTONI, philosopher, educator; b. Brzesc, Poland, June 30, 1925; s. Roman and Antonina (Widawska) W.; came to Can., 1949, naturalized, 1955; student in mech. engring. Warsaw Tech. U., 1942-44; B.Ph. (Centre des Hautes Etudes Polonaises en Belgique scholar), Université de Louvain, 1949; Ph.L. (Ministère de la jeunesse du Québec scholar), Université Laval, 1951, Ph.D. magna cum laude, 1953; m. Cecile Cloutier, Dec. 27, 1966; children—Maria, Ewa. Tchr., Seminaire de Philosophie, Montreal, Que., Can., 1952-53; asst. prof. St. Francis Xavier U., Antigonish, N.S., Can., 1953-54; asst. prof. philosophy U. Ottawa (Ont., Can.), 1954-59, asso. prof., 1959-65, prof., 1965—; lectr. in field; cons. U. Victoria, Université de Moncton, Conf. of Rectors and Prins. of Que. Univs.; pres. planning com. 7th Inter-Am. Congress of Philosophy, 1964-67; chmn. organizing com. 1st Ottawa Conf. on Conceptual Basis of Classification of Knowledge, 1970-71. Served with Polish Underground Army, 1942-45. Humanities Research Council of Can., The Can. Council grantee, 1955, 60, 67-68, 73-74. Mem. Can. (1st hon. life mem.; v.p., acting pres. 1968-69, pres. 1969-70), Am., Am. Catholic (mem. exec. council 1966-69) philos. assns., Polish Soc. Arts and Scis. Abroad (London, Eng.), Polish Inst. Arts and Scis. in Am., Inter-Univ. Com. on Can. Slavs (pres. 1967-69), Polish Can. Congress (v.p. 1968-74, 76-78), Humanities Research Council of Can. (mem. exec. com. 1970-72, chmn. com. on external relations 1972-74), The Can. Council (mem. selection com. for spl. M.A. scholarships 1973), Metaphys. Soc. Am., Société Francaise de Philosophie. Author: Survey on the Status of Philosophy in Canada, 1970. Editor: Conceptual Basis of the Classification of Knowledge, 1974; co-editor: Polonia of Tomorrow, 1977. Contbr. numerous articles to profl. jours. Home: 80 Pleasant Park Rd Ottawa ON K1H 5L9 Canada Office: Dept Philosophy Univ of Ottawa Ottawa ON K1N 6N5 Canada

WOJTOWICZ, JOSEPH MARK, research and devel. exec.; b. Elizabeth, N.J., Feb. 13, 1945; s. Joseph and Claire (Boneski) W.; B.S. in Chemistry, Fairleigh Dickinson U., 1976, M.B.A. in Indsl. Mgmt., 1978; m. Lorraine Maul, July 17, 1971; children—Stacey, Lisa. Research tech. Diamond Shamrock Chem. Co., Harrison, N.J., 1963-65; research chemist plastics div. Allied Chem. Corp. Morristown, N.J., 1969-72; sr. sci. gen. diagnostics div. research. devel. Warner Lambert Co. Morris Plains, N.J., 1972—. Served with USAF, 1965-69. Recipient chemistry scholar award, 1975. Mem. Am. Assn. Clin. Chemists, Am. Mgmt. Assn., Am. Chem. Soc., Phi Omega Epsilon. Contbr. articles to profl. jours. Home: PO Box 258 Butternut Rd McAfee NJ 07428 Office: 170 Tabor Rd Morris Plains NJ 07950

WOLANIN, SOPHIE MAE, civic worker; b. Alton, Ill., June 11, 1915; d. Stephen and Mary (Fijalka) Wolanin; student Pa. State Coll., 1943-44; certificate secretarial sci. U. S.C., 1946, B.S. in Bus. Adminstrn. cum laude, 1948; Ph.D. honoris causa, Colo. State Christian Coll., 1972. Clk., stenographer, sec. Mercer County (Pa.) Tax Collector's Office, Sharon, 1932-34; receptionist, social sec., nurse-technician to doctor, N.Y.C., 1934-37; coil winder, assembler Westinghouse Electric Corp., Sharon, 1937-39, duplicator operator, typist, stenographer, 1939-44, confidential sec., Pitts., 1949-54; exec. sec., charter mem. Westinghouse Credit Corp., Pitts., 1954-72, hdqrs. sr. sec., 1972—, reporter WCC News, 1967-68, asst. editor, 1968-71, asso. editor, 1971—; student office sec. to dean U. S.C. Sch. Commerce, 1944-46, instr. math., bus. adminstrn., secretarial sci., 1946-48. Publicity and pub. relations chmn., corr. sec. South Oakland Rehab. Council, 1967-69; mem. nat. adv. bd. Am. Security Council; mem. Friends Winston Churchill Meml. and Library, Westminster Coll., Fulton, Mo. Fellow Ednl. Found., Intercontinental Biog. Assn. (life), Intercontinental Inst. Community Service (life); mem. Allegheny County Scholarship Assn. (life), Allegheny County League Women Voters, AAUW (life), Internat. Fedn. U. Women, N.E. Historic Geneal. Soc., U. S.C. Alumni Assn. Ednl. Found. (Pa. state fund chmn. 1967-68, pres.' council 1972—, ofcl. del., rep. inauguration Bethany Coll. pres.), Hypatian Lit. Soc., Acad. Polit. Sci. (Columbia) (life), Bus. and Profl. Women's Club Pitts. (bd. dirs. 1963—, editor Bull. 1963-65, treas. 1965-66, historian 1969-70, pub. relations 1971-76, Woman of Year 1972), Named to Woman's Hall of Fame; recipient numerous prizes Allegheny County Fair, 1952-67, citation Congl. Record, 1969, others. Liturgical Conf. N. Am. (life), Westinghouse Vet. Employees Assn., Nat. Soc. Lit. and Arts, Early Am. Soc., Am. Acad. Social and Polit. Sci., Societe Commemorative de Femmes Celebres, Nat. Trust Historic Preservation, Am. Judicature Soc., Am. Mus. Natural History (asso.), Nat. Hist. Soc. (founding mem.), Anglo-Am. Hist. Soc. (charter), Nat. Assn. Exec. Secs., Internat. Platform Assn., Smithsonian Assos., Asso. Nat. Archives, Nat., Pa., Fed. bus. and profl. women's clubs, Mercer County Hist. Soc. (life), Am. Bible Soc., UN Assn. U.S., Am. Counselors Soc., Am. Hort. Soc. Republican. Roman Catholic (mem. Cathedral Altar Soc., patron organ recitals). Clubs: Jonathan Maxcy of U. S.C. (charter); Univ. Catholic of Pitts.; Key of Pa., Fedn. Bus. and Profl. Women (hon.); Coll. (hon.) (Sharon). Contbr. articles to newspapers; Am. corr. Polish radio and TV. Home: 232 Meyran Ave Pittsburgh PA 15213 Office: 3 Gateway Center 23 S Pittsburgh PA 15222

WOLAVER, CARL LEROY, bus. exec.: b. Balt., Aug. 22, 1941: s. Walter E. and Harriett (Clark) W.; B.S. in Indsl. Engring., U. Cin., 1964; M.B.A., U. Fla., 1967; m. Marna J. Terry, Apr. 26, 1969; children—Nathan Edward, Alex Walter. Indsl. engr. Delco Div. Gen. Motors, Dayton, Ohio, 1964-65; sales supr., market analyst, mil. specialist Corning Glass Works (N.Y.), 1967-70: mktg. mgr., communications mgr., 76; dir. sales and mktg., Soundcoat, N.Y.C., 1976—; cons. GarDoc, Inc. Mem. Acoustical Soc. Am. Contbr. articles to profl. jours. Home: 35 Magnolia Ave Garden City NY 11530

WOLBACH, ALBERT BOGH, JR., physician; b. Allentown, Pa., Sept. 6, 1932; s. Albert Bogh and Gertrude Lillian (Mitchell) W.; A.B., U. pa., 1954: M.D., Jefferson Med. Coll., 1958; m. Shirley Ann Mentzer, Dec. 21, 1957; children—Sheryl Ann, Wendy Sue, Ann Mentzer. Intern, Lancaster Gen. Hosp., 1958-59; gen. practice medicine, Ephrata, Pa., 1961—; mem. med. staff Ephrata Community Hosp., 1961—, bd. dirs., 1969—. Mem. Ephrata Area Sch. Bd., 1971—, sec., 1974-77, v.p., 1977—. Served to lt. comdr. USPHS, 1959-61. Diplomate Am. Bd. Family Practice. Mem. AMA (certificate med. recognition 1972, 75, 78), Am. Acad. Family Practice, pa., Lancaster County med. socs., Am. Legion. Republican. Mem. Ch. of the Brethren. Clubs: Train Collectors Assn., Masons, Shriners, Elks. Home and Office: 923 W Main St Ephrata PA 17522

WOLDMAN, SHERMAN, pediatrician; b. Buffalo, Apr. 1, 1932; s. Joseph Harry and Sadie (Weinstein) W.; B.S. magna cum laude, U. Buffalo, 1953, M.D. with high honors, 1957; m. Fern Marlene Weinstein, Dec. 28, 1952; children—Deborah Janine, Scott Alan, Sabina Heide. Intern, Millard Fillmore Hosp., Buffalo, 1957-58; resident in pediatrics Children's Hosp., Buffalo, 1958-60; individual practice medicine, specializing in pediatrics, Buffalo, 1961-66, Cheektowaga, N.Y., 1962—; clin. asst. prof. pediatics State U. N.Y. at Buffalo, 1973—; attending pediatrician Buffalo Children's Hosp., 1977—; asso. attending pediatrician Millard Fillmore Hosp., 1974—. Preceptor PNA program State U. N.Y. Sch. Nursing, 1973—; chmn. physicians Williamsville (N.Y.) Central Schs., 1970—. Served with USAF, 1960-61. Diplomate Am. Bd. Pediatrics. Fellow Am. Acad. Pediatrics; mem. Leukemia Soc. Am. (pres. Western N.Y. chpt. 1977—, nat. trustee 1977—), N.Y. State, Erie County, Maimonides med. socs., Gibson Anat. Soc., Med. Student Aid Soc., Buffalo Pediatric Soc., Alpha Omega Alpha, Phi Lambda Kappa, Rho Chi. Home: 103 Dan-Troy Dr Williamsville NY 14221 Office: 4427 Union Rd Cheektowaga NY 14225

WOLF, ALEXANDER, psychoanalyst: b. N.Y.C., Apr. 16, 1907; s. Samuel and Rose (Held) W.; B.A., Columbia Coll., 1928; M.D., Cornell U., 1932; m. Florence Interrante, Mar. 17, 1973. Intern, Beth Israel Hosp., N.Y.C., 1932-33; resident in psychiatry St. Elizabeths Hosp., Washington, 1934-35; chief neurol. clinic Bellevue Hosp., N.Y.C., 1935-39, asst. vis. neurologist, 1935-39; practice psychoanalysis, N.Y.C., 1946—: chmn. faculty psychoanalysis N.Y. Med. Coll., 1960-61; mem. faculty, tng. analyst, sr. supr. Post-9rad. Center for Mental Health, N.Y.C., 1946—; mem. faculty N.Y. Center for Psychoanalytic Tng., 1975—; mem. advisory council Advanced Inst. for Psychotherapy, 1976—; prof. advisory com. Am. Psychotherapy Center Working with More Difficult Patient, 1974—; cons. in field. Served with U.S. Army, 1942-46. Recipient Wilfred c. Hulse Meml. award Eastern Group Psychotherapy Soc., 1963, Adolph Meyer award Assn. for Improvement Mental Health, 1957. Diplomate Am. Bd. psychiatry Neurology. Fellow Am. Soc. Group Psychotherapy and Psychodrama, Council for Psychoanalytic Psychotherapists, Am. Inst. for Psychotherapy and Psychoanalysis, Inst. for Practicing Psychotherapists and Allied professions, Am. Acad. Psychoanalysis, Am. Psychiat. Assn., AMA, N.Y. Acad. Medicine, Am. Group Psychotherapy Assn.; mem. Assn. Med. Group Psychoanalysis (past pres.); N.Y. Soc. for Clin. Psychiatry, Am. Acad. Nurology, Internat. Assn. Group Psychotherapy. Author: (with E. K. Schwartz) Psychoanalysis in Groups, 1962: (with others) Beyond the Couch: Dialogues on Teaching and Learning Psychoanalysis in Groups, 1970; Mem. editorial bd. Jour. Contemporary Psychotherapy, 1962—, Jour. Psychoanalysis in Groups, 1965—. Address: 11 E 68th St New York City NY 10021

WOLF, CARL THEODORE, market cons. co. exec.; b. Newark, July 7, 1943; s. Samuel and Irma (Wiener) W.; B.A., Rutgers, 1965; M.B.A., U. Pitts., 1966; m. Marion Frances Karp, Oct. 31, 1965; 1 dau., Karen. Sr. acquisitions analyst Sperry & Hutchinson Co., N.Y.C., 1966-69; pres. Sci. Restaurant Mgmt. Corp., Mountainside, N.J., 1969-71: v.p., gen. mgr. Brooke Bond Foods Inc., Lake Success, N.Y., 1971-77, Standard Brands, N.Y.C., 1977; pres. Market Finders, South Orange, N.J., 1978—; partner East/West Mktg. Co., South Orange, 1978—; dir. Cheez Co., Wisconsin Rapids, Wis.: instr. econs. Newark State Coll., Union, N.J., 1967-68. Served with N.J. Army N.G., 1966-72. Food Fair scholar, 1961-65; N.J. State scholar, 1961-65; U. Pitts. Tuition fellow, 1965-66; Henry Rutgers scholar, 1964-65. Mem. Assn. Corporate Growth, Nat. Food Distbrs. Assn., L.I. Assn. World Trade Club, Cheese Importers Am., Rutgers Alumni Assn., Eastern Dairy Deli Assn., Phi Beta Kappa, Beta Gamma Sigma. Home: 20 Collinwood Rd Maplewood NJ 07040 Office: 76 S Orange Ave South Orange NJ 07079

WOLF, FRANK JAMES, chemist; b. Xenia, Ohio, Nov. 7, 1916; s. Frank Andrew and Helen Sofronia (Hollingshead) W.; A.B., Miami U., Oxford, Ohio, 1938; Ph.D., U. Ill., 1942; postgrad. Cambridge (Eng.) U., 1954; m. Helen Estella Sellmyer, Feb. 5, 1942; children—Judith Anne (Mrs. Charles Arthur Judge), Frank Russell, Barbara Jane. With Merck & Co., Inc., Rahway, N.J., 1942—, dir. animal drug metabolism and radiochemistry, 1970—. Mem. N.Y. Acad. Scis., Am. Chem. Soc., Am. Soc. Exptl. Pharmacy and Therapeutics, Phi Beta Kappa, Phi Lambda Upsilon. Presbyterian (trustee). Club: Raritan (N.J.) Yacht. Author: Separation Methods in Organic Chemistry and Biochemistry, 1969. Contbr. to profl. jours. Patentee antibiotics, vitamins and other natural products. Home: 38 Genesee Trail Westfield NJ 07090 Office: 126 E Lincoln Ave Rahway NJ 07065

WOLF, FREDERICK BARTON, clergyman; b. Cedar Rapids, Ia., Apr. 12, 1922; s. Frederick Barton and Julietta (Reynolds) W.; B.A., Grinnell Coll., 1946; B.D., Seabury-Western Theol. Sem., 1945, D.D., 1969; LL.D., St. Frances Coll., 1969; J.U.D., Nasson Coll., 1969; S.T.D., Gen. Theol. Sem., 1974; m. Barbara Buckley, Oct. 5, 1946; children—Mary Julietta (Mrs. John de N. Wolf), Martha Clare, Jane Margaret. Ordained priest Episcopal Ch., 1946; priest-in-charge, then rector Trinity Ch., Belvidere, Ill., 1946-50; rector St. Christopher's Ch., Oak Park, Ill., 1950-54; dean Cathedral Ch. St. John, Quincy, Ill., 1954-58; asso. sec. dept. Christian edn. Nat. Council Episcopal Ch., 1958-59; rector St. Peter's Ch., Bennington, Vt., 1959-68; bishop of Me., 1968—. Dep., Episcopal Gen. Conv., 1964, 67; pres. standing com. Diocese Vt., 1964-68; chmn. gen. bd. examining chaplains Episcopal Ch., 1973-74; pres. Province New Eng., 1974—. Pres., Family Service Assn., Quincy, 1956-58, United Counselling Service, Bennington, 1966-68; vice-chmn. Vt. Housing Authority, 1968; chmn. bd. trustees Gen. Theol. Sem., N.Y.C., 1974—. Author: (with Barbara B. Wolf) Christian Forgiveness, 1957, Journey in Faith, 1959, Exploring Faith and Life, 1965. Home: 72 Applegate Ln Falmouth Foreside ME 04105 Office: 143 State St Portland ME 04101

WOLF, GARY WICKERT, lawyer; b. Slinger, Wis., Apr. 19, 1938; s. Leonard A. and Cleo C. (Wickert) W.; B.B.A., U. Minn., 1960, J.D. cum laude, 1963; m. Jacqueline J. Weltzin, Dec. 17, 1960; children—Gary Wickert II, Jonathan Leonard. Admitted to N.Y. bar, 1964; asso. Cahill, Gordon & Reindel, N.Y.C., 1963—, mem. firm, 1971—. Mem. Kappa Sigma, Phi Delta Phi. Club: Angler's (N.Y.C.). Home: 72 Fairfield Dr Short Hills NJ 07078 Office: 80 Pine St New York City NY 10005

WOLF, HERBERT LEONARD, elec. equipment mfg. co. exec.; b. Bklyn., Sept. 6, 1940; s. Arnold M. and Fanny (Lashkovitz) W.; B.S. in Mech. Engring., Bklyn. Poly. Inst., 1962; m. Maxine Wasserman, Mar. 22, 1964; children—Ellen, Barbara, Richard. Packaging engr. Western Union Telegraph, N.Y.C., 1962-63; ground support engr. Grumman Aircraft, Bethpage, N.Y., 1963-64; v.p. Pelham Sheet Metal Works, Inc., Bronx, N.Y., 1964-68; with Electrospace Corp., North Bergen, N.J., 1968-74, v.p., 1969-74, gen. mgr. Nanasi Co. div., 1968-74, corp. dir., 1972-74; div. mgr. Elec. Fittings Corp. div. ITE Imperial Corp., East Farmingdale, N.Y., 1975-77, gen. mgr. EFCOR Products div., 1976; v.p., gen. mgr. elec. components div. Gould Inc., East Farmingdale, 1976-77; gen. mgr. electronics mfg. Coleco Industries Inc., Amsterdam, N.Y., 1977-78, corp. v.p., dir. electronic ops., 1978—. Mem. Am. Mgmt. Assn., ASME, Am. Soc. Heating, Refrigeration and Air Conditioning Engrs. Home: 45 Kingsboro Ave Gloversville NY 12078 Office: 10 Park St Amsterdam NY 12010

WOLF, HOWARD JAY, city planner; b. Weehawkin, N.J., Sept. 16, 1935; s. Victor and Irene (Horowitz) W.; B.A. in Econs. and City Planning, Rutgers U., 1957; m. Judith Ann Greenwald, June 5, 1958; children—Lewis Charles, Marcia Lynn, Phyllis Kaye. Dep. adminstr. N.J. Green Acres Program, Trenton, 1961—. Chmn. Lawrence Twp., Mercer County, N.J., Parks and Recreation Council, 1967-69, Environ. Commn., 1967-68, Shade Tree Commn., 1967-69. Licensed planner, N.J. Mem. Am. Inst. Planners. Home: 287 Glenn Ave Lawrenceville NJ 08648 Office: PO Box 1390 Trenton NJ 08625

WOLF, PETER MICHAEL, planning cons., educator; b. New Orleans, Dec. 6, 1935; s. Morris and Ruth (New) W.; B.A., Yale U., 1957; M.A., Tulane U., 1963; Ph.D., Inst. Fine Arts, N.Y.U., 1968; m. Alessandra Cantey, July 3, 1967; children—Phelan Godchaux, Alexis Ambler. Partner, Wolf & Co., cotton brokers, New Orleans, 1958-62; asso. Wilbur Smith & Assos., transp. planners, N.Y.C., 1968-70; planning cons. Peter Wolf Assos., N.Y.C., 1968—; chmn. bd. of fellows, mem. faculty Inst. Architecture and Urban Studies, 1972—; mem. faculty N.Y.U., 1966-67, Pratt Inst., 1968-70; vis. prof. Cooper Union, 1971—; archtl. exhbns. include: Mus. Modern Art, N.Y.C., 1969, Whitney Mus. Am. Art, N.Y.C., 1970, Mus. Modern Art, 1973, Albany (N.Y.) Inst. Art, 1975. Fulbright fellow, Paris, 1965-66; Graham Found. fellow, 1967-68; Ford Found. and Am. Fedn. Arts grantee, 1969. Mem. N.Y. State Council on Arts (architecture and environ. panel 1974-77), Archtl. League N.Y. (exec. com. 1972—), N.Y. Cultural Council (visual arts com. 1971-74), Am. Inst. Planners, Am. Soc. Planning Ofcls., Internat. Fedn. Housing and Planning, Soc. Archtl. Historians, Archtl. League N.Y. Club: Yale (N.Y.C.). Author publs. in field. Home: 325 W End Ave New York City NY 10023 Office: 8 W 40th St New York City NY 10018

WOLF, ROBERT LAWRENCE, physician; b. N.Y.C., Aug. 7, 1928; s. Arthur Dewey and Rae (Goldberg) W.; B.S. in Medicine, Duke U., 1950, M.D., 1952; 1 son, Richard Hilary. Intern Mt. Sinai Hosp., N.Y.C., 1952-53, chief resident pathology, 1953-54, asst. resident in medicine, 1956-57, chief resident medicine, 1957-58, research fellow medicine, 1958-61, clin. asst. in medicine, 1960—, asst. attending physician in medicine, 1965—; practice medicine specializing in internal medicine, N.Y.C., 1960—; research fellow Arthritis and Rheumatism Found., N.Y.C., 1958-59. Syntex Research Found. research grantee, 1965—. Diplomate Am. Bd. Internal Medicine, Nat. Bd. Med. Examiners. Fellow A.C.P., Am. Coll. Chest Physicians, Am. Coll. Nuclear Medicine, Am. Coll. Nuclear Physicians; mem. Med. Soc. State N.Y., Med. Soc. County N.Y., AMA, Am., N.Y. heart assns., Am. Fedn. Clin. Research, Am. Nuclear Soc., N.Y. Acad. Scis., Met. Med. Soc., Soc. Nuclear Medicine, Soc. Exptl. Biology and Medicine, Am. Physiol. Soc., AAAS, Am. Inst. Biol. Scis., Am. Soc. Internal Medicine, Harvey Soc., Duke Med. Sch. Alumni Assn. (council 1965), Catecholamine Club. Contbr. articles to profl. jours. Patentee in radio immunoassay of angiotensin and renin activity. Home: 399 E 72d St New York City NY 10021 Office: 20 E 74th St New York City NY 10021

WOLF, WILLIAM MILTON, advt. exec.; b. N.Y.C., July 4, 1923; s. Saul and Bertha (Dryer) W.; B.A., City Coll. N.Y., 1942; postgrad. N.Y. U., 1946-48; m. Norma Miller, July 7, 1956; children—Adam Jason, Leonard Mark. Vice pres. Leonard Wolf & Assos., N.Y.C., 1950-60; advt. mgr. Barth's of L.I., Valley Stream, 1960-62; sr. copywriter Fairfax Advt., N.Y.C., 1962-63; with William Douglas McAdams Inc., N.Y.C., 1963—, exec. v.p., 1973—, also mem. exec. com. Served with USAAF, 1942-45. Mem. Pharm. Advt. Club, Jewish War Vets. Author short stories. Home: 489 Grenville Ave Teaneck NJ 07666 Office: 110 E 59th St New York City NY 10022

WOLFE, ANDREW DOUGHERTY, newspaper editor; b. Pitts., June 22, 1922; s. Charles Holmes and Madeleine (Dougherty) W.; grad. Milton (Mass.) Acad. Boy's Sch., 1940; A.B. magna cum laude, Harvard U., 1946, A.M., 1947; m. Carolyn Chace Sibley, July 17, 1943; children—Amy Wentworth, Madeleine Dougherty, Andrew Dougherty, John Sibley; m. 2d, Vivienne M. Tellier, Apr. 14, 1977. Reporter, editorial writer Rochester (N.Y.) Times-Union, 1947-52; dir. Univ. devel. U. Rochester, 1952-56; editor, pub. Wolfe Publs., Inc., Pittsford, N.Y., 1956—; pres. Xenia Corp., Pittsford, 1967—, Ski Advt., Pittsford, 1968—, Butternut Press, Inc., 1971—; dir. Marine Midland Trust of Rochester; trustee Rochester Savs. Bank. Chmn. Monroe County (N.Y.) Arts Resources Com., 1968-72; mem. N.Y. State Council on Arts, 1969—. Bd. dirs. George Eastman House, Margaret Strong Mus. Served with AUS, 1943-46, ETO. Recipient N.Y. State award N.Y. State Council on Arts, 1967, LeRoy Snyder award Rochester Jr. C. of C., Editorial Writing award Nat. Newspaper Assn., 1969. Author: Bold Century, 1968, Architecture Worth Saving in Pittsford, 1969, Views of Old Rochester and the Genesee Country, 1970; Saints, Sinners and Salesmen, 1971; Highways, By-Ways and Folkways of Monroe County, 1976. Home: 3635 Palmyra Rd Marion NY 14505 Office: 4 S Main St Pittsford NY 14534

WOLFE, ANTHONY LEE, architect: b. Pitts., June 5, 1926; s. Lawrence Logan and Mary Harper (Clark) W.; student Swarthmore Coll., 1946-48; B.Arch., Carnegie Inst. Tech., 1952; m. Marianne Leas, Aug. 19, 1950; children—Lawrence D., Sandra L. Draftsman, Ingham, Boyd & Pratt, Architects, Pitts., 1952-53; draftsman, designer Lawrence Wolfe, Architect, 1953-56; partner Lawrence and Anthony Wolfe, Architects, 1956-77; prin. architect Chester Engrs., Coraopolis, Pa., 1977—. Chmn., Ben Avon Borough Zoning Bd., 1969-75, Ben Avon Borough Planning Commn., 1972-75; bd. dirs. North Boros YMCA, Pitts., 1967. Served with AUS, 1944-46; ETO. Registered architect, Pa., N.J. Mem. AIA (past pres. Pitts. chpt., Sch. medal Carnegie Inst. Tech. 1952), Pa. Soc. Architects. Republican. Presbyterian. Important works include Manchester Elementary Sch., Pitts., Pitts. Aviary Addition, Butler Sewage Treatment Plant. Home: 7066 Woodland Ave Pittsburgh PA 15202 Office: 845 4th Ave Coraopolis PA 15108

WOLFE, CHARLES HENRY, accountant; b. Little Falls, N.Y., Nov. 14, 1918; s. Charles Lesley and Edna Hannah (Sibley) W.; grad. Albany Bus. Coll., 1939; m. Virginia Anne Croissant, May 29, 1941; children—Leslie Anne, Charles Henry. Accountant, Frank J. Wagner, Malone, N.Y., 1939-50; partner Gilmore, Edwards & Wolfe, Malone, 1950-54; owner Charles H. Wolfe, Malone, 1954-72; partner Wolfe & Dragon, Malone, 1972-76; with Dragon & Benware, 1977—; pres. Citizens Nat. Bank Malone, 1972-78, also dir.; dir. Covell Agy., Tierney Caron Agy., Hubbard Devel. Corp. Active N.Y. State Am. Legion Boy Scouts com.; bd. dirs., exec. com. Alice Hyde Meml. Hosp., 1961-76, sec., 1972-76, dir. emeritus, 1978—. Served with AUS, 1943-46. Mem. Empire State Assn. Pub. Accountants (past dir.), Nat. Assn. Pub. Accountants, Am. Legion (chmn. 4th dist. oratorical com.). Republican. Methodist. Club: Masons (Shriner). Home: 9 Third St Malone NY 12953 Office: PO Box 189 Malone NY 12953

WOLFE, FRANCIS JOSEPH, orgn. exec.; b. Bklyn., May 10, 1918; s. Francis J. and Loretta J. (Tyrrell) W.; m. Asta Thorbjornsen, Jan. 31, 1942; children—Robert, Kevin. Supr. records div. Central Hanover Bank and Trust Co., N.Y.C., 1938-41; mem. N.Y.C. Police Dept., 1941-68, capt., 1966-68, dep. insp., 1966-68; ret., 1968; spl. adviser on narcotics and organized crime Nassau County dist. atty., 1968-71; Eastern regional dir. Ins. Crime Prevention Inst., Westport, Conn., 1971-73, asst. dir., 1973—; dir. security Douglas Manor, N.Y., 1964-75; tchr., lectr. in field. Mem. publicity com. Udalls Cove Preservation, 1968-71; mem. Mayor N.Y.C. Narcotic Enforcement Rev. Bd., 1960-62. Recipient Mosler Scholar award. Mem. Patrolmen's Benevolent Assn., Sgts. Benevolent Assn., Police Honor Legion, Internat. Assn. Chiefs Police, Superior Officers Council, Holy Name Soc., Detectives Endowment Assn. Democrat. Roman Catholic. Author manuals. Home: 337 Kenmore Rd Queens NY 11363 Office: 15 Franklin St Westport NY 06880

WOLFE, JEAN ELIZABETH, med. artist; b. Newark, Oct. 3, 1925; d. Arthur Howard and Ethel (Harper) Wolfe; B.S., Russell Sage Coll., 1947; student Pratt Inst., 1949-50; diploma U. Rochester Sch. Medicine and Dentistry, 1955; postgrad. (W.B. Saunders fellow), U. Pa., 1955-56; M.F.A., U. Pa., 1973. Exhibitor, Pratt Inst. Galleries, Bklyn., 1958, N.Y. Med. Coll., 1958, Assn. Med. Illustrators, 1961-69, AMA, N.Y.C., 1965, Phila., 1965, A.C.S., Atlantic City, 1965, Research Study Club Los Angeles, 1966, Phila. Art Alliance, 1967, 73, U. Pa. Ophthal. Soc., 1967-68, N.J. Med. Soc., 1968, Cayuga Mus. History and Art, 1968, Pensacola Art Center, 1969, FAA Aero. Center, Oklahoma City, 1970, Scheie Eye Inst., 1972-75, Assn. Med. Illustrators Traveling Salon, 1978; contbg. illustrator Adler's Textbook Ophthalmology, 8th edit., 1969. Illustrations in med. books, jours., pharm. house pubs.; instr. Pembroke Coll. Brown U., 1947-49; mem. faculty Kimberley Sch., Upper Montclair, N.J., 1950-52; free lance med. illustration Studio N.Y. Med. Coll., 1956-60; instr. Pratt Inst., 1958-59; asso. in med. illustration U. Pa. Sch. Medicine, 1960-72, research asst. prof. med. art in ophthalmology, 1972—; guest lectr. Johns Hopkins Med. Sch., 1973, NIH; guest artist USAF, Air Force Acad. and NORAD, 1971. Recipient Merit certificate AMA; Appreciation certificate A.C.S.; 1st prize Pensacola Art Center, Am. Heart Assn., 1969. Mem. Phila. Art Alliance, Assn. Med. Illustrators (Ralph Sweet, Tom Jones awards, gov. 1970—, chmn. nominating com. 1972-73, vice chmn. bd. govs. 1973-74, chmn. bd. 1974-75), Soc. Illustrators, AAUP. Home: Colonial Towers B-9 27E Central Ave Paoli PA 19301

WOLFE, ROBERT RICHARD, educator; b. Chippewa Falls, Wis., Nov. 9, 1937; s. Lewis Samuel and Bernice (Quale) W.; B.S., U. Wis., 1960, M.S., 1961; Ph.D., Purdue U., 1964. Research engr. A.O. Smith Corp., Milw., 1961; asst. prof. agrl. engr. U. Wis., Madison, 1964-70; asso. prof. Rutgers U., New Brunswick, N.J., 1970-77, prof., 1977—. NSF grad. fellow, 1962. Mem. Am. Soc. for Engring. Edn., Am. Soc. Agrl. Engrs., Inst. Food Tech., Instrument Soc. Am., AAUP, Sigma Xi, Tau Beta Pi, Phi Kappa Phi, Alpha Epsilon, Alpha Zeta, Delta Theta Sigma. Office: Biol and Agrl Engring Dept Rutgers U New Brunswick NJ 08903

WOLFERT, REUBEN ROBERT, pharmacist; b. Phila., Dec. 26, 1935; s. Michael Albert and Rose Leah (Blavatt) W.: B.S., Phila. Coll. Pharmacy and Sci., 1957; certificate hosp. mgmt. Rutgers U., 1970; mgmt. certificate Pa. State U., 1973; m. Marian M. Budd, Oct. 10, 1957; children—Irwin, Joel, Allyse, Suzanne. Staff phamacist Einstein Med. Center Southern div., 1957-58; asst. dir. pharmacy, Northern div., 1958-61; dir. pharmacy service Inglis House (Phila. Home for Incurables), 1961-66; dir. pharmacy services Bryn Mawr (Pa.) Hosp., 1966—; adj. clin. instr. Temple U., Phila., 1972—. Bd. dirs. East Mount Airy Neighbors, 1961-65; pres. Congregation Beth Or, Spring House, Pa., 1975-77. Recipient Humanitarian award Chapel of the Four Chaplins, Phila., 1976, Quality Health Care award, Pfizer Co., 1974. Mem. Am., Pa., Delware Valley (pres. 1975-76) socs. hosp. pharmacists, Am., Pa. pharm. assns. Contbr. articles to profl. jours. Home: 618 Wayland Rd Plymouth Meeting PA 19462 Office: BrynMawr Hosp Bryn Mawr pA 19010

WOLFF, ALFRED R., educator; b. Far Rockaway, N.Y., Mar. 24, 1917; s. Herbert A. and Daisy (Kempner) W.; A.B., Dartmouth Coll., 1939; M.A., Tchrs. Coll., Columbia U., 1940, Ed.D., 1952; m. Adele Druss, Sept. 4, 1942; children—Nancy Wolff Woods, Edward F., Mary Wolff Bowles, Alfred R. Tchr. history The Park Sch., Balt., 1940-41, 1946; asst. dir. of student personnel U. Bridgeport (Conn.), 1946-48, dir. counseling, 1948-52, dir. of student personnel, 1952-61, dean of student personnel, 1961-75, prof. of edn., 1958—, coordinator of grad. program in counseling the aging 1975—; exec. sec. New Eng. Personnel and Guidance Conf., 1955-79. Bd. dirs. Milford Family and Child Guidance Clinic, 1973—, pres., 1974-76. Served with U.S. Army, 1941-46. Mem. Am., Conn. (Distinguished Service award 1973) personnel and guidance assns., Nat. Vocat. Guidance Assn., Nat. Assn. of Student Personnel Adminstrs. (regional Distinguished Service award 1977), Assn. for Counselor Edn. and Supervision, Am. Soc. of Group Psychotherapy, Am. Coll. Personnel Assn. Democrat. Contbr. article to profl. jour. Home: 133 Harkness Dr Milford CT 06460 Office: South Hall Univ of Bridgeport Bridgeport CT 06602

WOLFF, JAMES ALEXANDER, physician; b. N.Y.C., June 19, 1914; s. William Frederick and Blanche (Reitlinger) W.; B.A., Harvard U., 1935; M.D., N.Y. U., 1940; m. Janet Barbara Loeb, June 24, 1946; children—James Alexander, John Kendall, Barbara Ann, Timothy Grant. Intern Lenox Hill Hosp., N.Y.C., 1940-42; resident Boston Children's Hosp., 1945-48; practice and teaching medicine, specializing in pediatric hematology, N.Y.C., 1949—; attending pediatrician Babies Hosp., Columbia-Presbyn. Med. Center; prof. pediatrics Coll. Phys. and Surg., Columbia U., 1972—, dir. cancer control Columbia U. Cancer Center, 1978—; cons. Englewood Hosp., St. Lukes Hosp., Valley Hosp., Monticello Hosp. Served to capt. AUS, 1942-45. Decorated Silver Star. Mem. N.Y. Soc. for Study Blood (pres. 1964-65), Soc. for Pediatric Research, Am. Pediatric Soc., Internat. Soc. Pediatric Oncology. Home: 4439 Waldo Ave New York City NY 10471 Office: Babies Hosp 3975 Broadway New York City NY 10032

WOLFF, JOEL CHARLES, mgmt. cons. exec.; b. N.Y.C., Aug. 23, 1929; s. Samuel and Frances (Baruch) W.; B.S., Syracuse U., 1950, B.Indsl. Engring., 1951; postgrad. Coll. City N.Y., 1954-56; m. Mary Lillian Campbell, June 1, 1974; children by previous marriage—Steven, Melissa, Stacy. Methods engr. Radio Receptor Co., N.Y.C., 1951-52; quality control engr. Western Electric Co., Kearny, N.J., 1953-57; with Drake, Sheahan, Sweeney & Hupp, N.Y.C., 1957—, staff engr., 1957-61, asso., 1961-64, prin., 1964-67, partner, dir., 1967—; exec. v.p., dir. Drake, Sheahan, Stewart, Dougall, Inc., N.Y.C., 1973-75, pres., 1975—; lectr. indsl. engring., phys. distbn. Served as officer USAF, 1953. Mem. Am. Inst. Indsl. Engrs., Inst. Mgmt. Cons. (founding mem.), Nat. Council Phys. Distbn. Mgmt., Warehouse Edn. and Research Council (founding mem.). Office: 330 Madison Ave New York City NY 10017

WOLFF, LEO THOMAS, physician; b. Suffern, N.Y., Mar. 26, 1942; s. Leo E. and Ruth W.; B.S. cum laude, Siena Coll., 1964; M.D., Albany Med. Coll., 1968; m. Carol C. Corey, June 12, 1965; children—Kathleen, Deborah, Patricia, Kimberley. Intern St. Joseph Hosp. Health Center, Syracuse, N.Y., 1968-69, resident in family practice, 1969-71; clin. asst. instr. medicine, State U. N.Y. Upstate Med. Center, Syracuse, 1970-71; asst. dir. family practice, ambulatory care cons., Surgeon Gen.'s Office, Washington, 1971-73; instr. family medicine, Med. Coll. Va., Fairfax, 1972-73; chmn. dept. family practice Upstate Med. Center, Syracuse, 1973—, asso. prof., 1973-75, prof., 1975—; dir. med. edn., St. Joseph's Hosp. Health Center, 1973—; cons. in field. Bd. dirs. Vis. Nurse Assn. Central N.Y. State. Served to maj., M.C., U.S. Army, 1971-73. Recipient Mead Johnson award, 1970. Diplomate Am. Bd. Family Practice; Fellow Am. Acad. Family Physicians (charter); mem. Soc. Tchrs. Family Medicine (dir. 1976—), N.Y. Acad. Family Physicians (dir. research and edn. found. 1977—), N.Y. State Acad. Family Physicians, Assn. Am. Med. Colls., Assn. Chmn. Depts. Family Medicine, N.Y. State, Onondaga County med. socs. Home: 8033 Princess Path Liverpool NY 13088 Office: 301 Prospect Ave Syracuse NY 13203

WOLFF, LESTER LIONEL, congressman; b. N.Y.C., Jan. 4, 1919; s. Samuel and Hannah (Bartman) W.; student N.Y. U., 1935-39; m. Blanche Silver, Mar. 31, 1940; children—Bruce Stuart, Diane Hope Wolff Yorg. Lectr., N.Y. U., 1939-41; head mktg. dept. Collegiate Inst., N.Y.C., 1945-49; pres. Co-ordinated Mktg. Agy., N.Y.C., 1948-64; dir. Madison Life Ins. Co.; moderator, producer Between the Lines, weekly polit. affairs TV program, 1948-60; mem. 89th-96th Congress from 6th Dist. N.Y., mem. com. on fgn. affairs, chmn. subcom. on Asian and Pacific affairs chmn. select com. narcotics abuse and control, mem. com. on vets. affairs. Food industry chmn. Fedn. Jewish Philanthropies, 1954-63, United Jewish Appeal, 1958-63; food div. chmn. Boys Town Italy, 1955; mem. dinner bd. Italian Bd. Guardians dinner, 1962-63; speakers com. Fedn. Jewish Philanthropies, 1962-64; chmn. dinner com. Cath. Interracial Council, 1959; chmn. food div. NCCJ, 1960; chmn. Mayor N.Y.C. Com. Interfaith Day, 1950-51; comdr. congressional squadron CAP; chmn. bd. visitors U.S. Mcht. Marine Acad., Kings Point, N.Y. Served to maj. USAFA, World War II. Recipient Distinguished Service award Nat. Citizens Affairs Com., 1956; named Man of Year, Food Industry Sq. Club, 1962; Guest of Honor award United Jewish Appeal, 1961, Denver Jewish Hosp., 1962, Deborah Hosp., 1961; Great Neck (L.I.) Hadassah award, 1961; Golden Dozen award Printers Ink mag., 1962; Coronet medal St. Edwards U., 1964; recipient Captive Nations medal, 1965; Friend of the Irish award Internat. Gaelic Hall of Fame, 1974; decorated Eloy Alfaro Grand Cross, 1966. Mem. Sierra Club, Order Hibernians. Democrat. Jewish (trustee temple). Home: 5 North Dr Kensington NY 11021 Office: Rayburn House Office Bldg Washington DC 20515

WOLFF, PAUL MARTIN, lawyer; b. Kansas City, Mo., July 22, 1941; s. Joseph Lester and Eleanor Bess (Reitzes) W.; B.A., U. Wis., 1963; LL.B., Harvard U., 1966; m. Rhea S. Schwartz, Oct. 9, 1976. Admitted to D.C. bar, 1968, U.S. Supreme Ct. bar, 1973; clk. Hon. James R. Durfee, U.S. Ct. Claims, Washington, 1966-67; asso. Williams, Connolly & Califano, 1967-75, partner, 1975—; lectr. Cath. U. Law Sch., 1970-73; co-founder, mem. bd. dirs. Washington Council of Lawyers, 1970-74. Mem. Am., D.C. bar assns., Phi Beta Kappa, Phi Kappa Phi, Phi Eta Sig. Democrat. Jewish. Clubs: Fed. City, Harvard.

Home: 4770 Reservoir Rd NW Washington DC 20007 Office: 1000 Hill Bldg Washington DC 20006

WOLFF, THEODORE RALPH, elec. engr.; b. Plainfield, N.J., May 24, 1940; s. Ralph P. and Katherine (Dorwart) W.; student Franklin and Marshall Coll., 1959-60, Rutgers U., 1960-62; B.E.E., N.Y. U., 1968; Patricia Wodard, Oct. 24, 1969. Phys. chemist Celanese Research Co., Summit, N.J., 1960-63; phys. and organic chemist Allied Chem. Research Co., Morris Twp., N.J., 1963-69; sr. research asst. bioelectronics N.Y. U. Med. Center, N.Y.C., 1970—; lectr. and cons. in bioelectronics. Active Inwood Area Community Assn., Friends of Inwood Park. Mem. IEEE Computer Soc., Audio Engrng. Soc., N.Y. Audio Soc. (v.p.), Am. Def. Preparedness Assn., 6800 Computer Club. Libertarian. Unitarian. Invented Ambience Synthesizer. Home: 579 W 215th St New York City NY 10034 Office: 400 E 34th St New York City NY 10016

WOLFF, WALTER FERDINAND, plant and maintenance engr.; b. St. Paul, May 3, 1930; s. Ferdinand John and Irene Rose (Percy) W.; B.S., U. Md., 1966; m. Ethel Marie Bannister, July 16, 1955; children—Stephen V., Eric J., Christanne R., Katherine R. Enlisted U.S. Army, 1948, commd. 2d lt., M.I., 1959, advanced through grades to maj., 1969, ret., 1970; plant mgr. Our Lady of Angels Convent, Aston, Pa., 1971—. Committeeman, Rep. Pary, Concord Twp., Del. County, Pa., 1976-78. Decorated Bronze Star with oak leaf cluster. Lutheran. Mem. Am. Legion. Home: 107 Shavertown Rd Boothwyn PA 19061 Office: Convent Rd Aston PA 19014

WOLFLEY, ALAN, coal co. exec.; b. Rockford, Ill., Dec. 23, 1923; s. Chester E. and Lois K. (Karlson) W.; student Middlebury (Vt.) Coll., 1941-42; A.B. cum laude, Middlebury, 1947; M.B.A., Harvard Bus. Sch., 1949; m. Joanne Higgins, Jan. 6, 1945; children—C. Alan, Susan (Mrs. Peter Baumgartner), E. William. Budget supr. Merck & Co., Rahway, N.J., 1949-52; asst. to treas. Standard Vacuum Oil Co., White Plains, N.Y., Tokyo, Japan, 1952-59; asst. treas. Parke-Davis & Co., Detroit, 1959-64; v.p. finance Carborundum Co., Niagara Falls, N.Y., 1964-68; v.p. finance, dir. Scovill Mfg. Co., Waterbury, Conn., 1968-71; exec. v.p., dir., mem. exec. com. Cerro Corp., N.Y.C., 1971-76; chmn. Inconcoal Corp., Conn., 1976—, Incontrade Inc., Conn., 1973—; dir. Durable Wire, Inc., Colonial Bank & Trust Co., 1968-71, So. Peru Copper Co., N.Y.C., 1974-76, M.F. Fetterolf Coal Co., Marmon Group, Inc., 1976—, Am. Coal Industries Corp., 1978—. Served to capt. USAAF, 1942-45. Decorated Silver Star medal, D.F.C., Air medal, Purple Heart. Mem. Chi Psi. Republican. Methodist. Clubs: Harvard, Racquet and Tennis (N.Y.C.); Verbank (N.Y.) Hunt; Wee Burn Country (Darien, Conn.); Pine Valley Golf (Clementon, N.J.). Home: 22 Canaan Close New Canaan CT 06840 Office: 123 Main St New Canaan CT 06840

WOLFORT, FRANCIS GABRIEL, plastic surgeon; b. N.Y.C., Aug. 6, 1933; s. Francis G. and Margaret M. (Maher) W.; B.S., Mass. Inst. Tech., 1954; M.D., State U. N.Y., 1958; m. m. Floreen Fazendin, Nov. 28, 1959; children—Ramona, Sean, Maria. Intern, Boston City Hosp., 1961-66; resident in surgery Mass. Gen. Hosp., 1966-67; resident in plastic surgery Johns Hopkins Hosp., 1967-69, fellow in surgery, asst. prof. surgery, 1969-70; dir. plastic surgery Balt. City Hosp., 1970—; dir. plastic surgery Cambridge Hosp., Harvard U., 1970—, dir. surg. services, 1976—, program dir. plastic surg. residency, 1970—; asso. prof. surgery Harvard U. Served with USN, 1960-62. Diplomate Am. Bd. Surgery, Am. Bd. Plastic Surgery. Fellow A.C.S., Am. Assn. Plastic Surgeons, Am. Soc. Surgery of Hand, Am. Soc. Head and Neck Surgeons; mem. Am. Soc. Plastic and Reconstructive Surgery, Am. Burn Assn., Am. Assn. Surgery of Trauma, Plastic Surgery Research Council. Editor: Acute Hand Injuries-a Multi-specialty Approach, 1978. Contbr. articles med. jours. Home: 33 Monadnock Rd Wellesley Hills MA 02181 Office: Cambridge Hospital 1493 Cambridge St Cambridge MA 02139

WOLFSON, DEXTER, physician; b. Boston, June 8, 1907; s. Paul R. and Dora V. (Ragolsky) W.; B.S., Boston U., 1930, M.D., 1933; m. Hortense Lowenthal, Nov. 25, 1948; children—Marcia Sherry, James, Joan. Intern Danbury (Conn.) Hosp., 1936-37; practice of medicine, Bethel, Conn., 1938—; mem. med. staff Danbury Hosp. Served from lt. to capt. M.C., U.S. Army, 1934-36, 43-46; lectr. on race prejudice and discrimination to colored troops of 3d Air Force. World War II. Mem. AMA, Conn., Fairfield County med. socs. Clubs: Masons, Order Eastern Star. Home: 11 Grassy Plain Terr Bethel CT 06801 Office: 14 Grassy Plain St Bethel CT 06801

WOLFSON, ROBERT PRED, research engr.; b. Miami, Fla., May 29, 1926; s. O. Philip and Nora Jacqueline (Pred) W.; B.E., Tulane U., 1948; postgrad. Pa. State U., 1962-64, Poly. Inst. Bklyn., 1965; m. Helene Clare Abrahm, Nov. 12, 1949; s. Philip Michael, Robert P. Air conditioning engr. Equitable Equipment Co., New Orleans, 1948-49, Wood-Leppard Air Conditioning Co., Houston, 1949, Conditioned Air Corp., Miami, 1949-50, Lewco Co., Miami, 1950-54, Hill-York Corp., Miami, 1954-55; thermoelectric energy research engr. The Franklin Inst. Labs. Research and Devel., Phila., 1955-59; thermoelectric research and devel. mgr. Tenn. Products & Chem. Corp., Nashville, 1959-61; energy systems engr. Gen. Electric Co., 1961-71; sci. contamination specialist Bionetics Corp., Hampton, Va., 1972; Mars/Earth back contamination research, dir. energy programs Exotech Inc., Gaithersburg, Md., 1972—. Served with USNR, 1944-46. Mem. IEEE, Internat. Solar Energy Soc., Nat. Energy Research Orgn., Washington Acad. Scis. Contbr. reports, articles and chpts. to books on energy and planetary quarantine; speaker internat. symposium on planetary quarantine. Home: 10813 Larkmeade Ln Potomac MD 20854 Office: 1200 Quince Orchard Blvd Gaithersburg MD 20760

WOLHAR, ROBERT CHARLES, JR., lawyer; b. Wilmington, Del., Mar. 20, 1948; s. Robert Charles and Helen Ann W.; B.A., U. Del., 1970; J.D. cum laude (Alumni Assn. scholar), Detroit Coll. Law, 1973; LL.M. in Urban Affairs (John B. Gage fellow), U. Mo., Kansas City, 1974. Research teaching asst. U. Mo. at Kansas City Law Sch., 1973-74; admitted to Del., Mo. bar, 1974; asso. firm Paul R. Reed, Georgetown, Del., 1974-76; individual practice law, Georgetown, 1976-77; partner firm Wolhar & Moore, Georgetown, 1977—. Democratic committeeman for 3-37 Rep. Dist. of Del., 1977—; legal counsel Miss. Del. Pageant, Inc., 1977-78, pres., 1978—; legal counsel Del. chpt. Nat. Found./March of Dimes, 1976-78. Recipient Key Man award Del. Jaycees, 1976, 77; Presdl. award of Honor, Georgetown Jaycees, 1977. Mem. Am., Del., Mo., Sussex County bar assns., Am., Del. trial lawyers assns., Comml. Law League Am., ACLU. Democrat. Roman Catholic.

WOLIN, ROBERT HARVEY, mech. engr.; b. Bronx, Jan. 14, 1925; s. Abe and Rose (Rubenstein) W.; B.Engring., U. So. Calif., 1950; student Rutgers U., 1944-46; m. Miriam Lukacs, Nov. 5, 1950; children—Deborah Ann, Sandra Lynn. Engr., Hudson Refrigerating Co., Jersey City, 1950-51; estimator, engr. Richardson Engring. Co., New Brunswick, N.J., 1951-52; engr. Rayon Cons., Inc., N.Y.C., 1951-52; engr. Wigton-Abbott Corp., Plainfield, N.J., 1952-55; engr. Thermal Inc., Iselin, N.J., 1955-57; v.p., chief engr. Thermal Engring., Iselin, 1957-60; chief engr. Air Con, Inc., Mountainside, N.J., 1960—. Mem. E. Brunswick adv. bldg. safety com., 1972-77, Constrn. Bd. Appeals, 1977—; mem. S. County Hosp. Devel. Corp., 1971—, N.J. Mech. Sub-code Com., 1977—; pres. Jewish Center, E. Brunswick, 1961-62. Served with AUS, 1946-48. Mem. Am. Soc. Heating, Refrigerating and Air Conditioning Engrs., Profl. Engrs. in Constrn., Nat. Soc. Profl. Engrs. Address: 21 Patton Dr East Brunswick NJ 08816

WOLINSKY, IRA, nutrition scientist; b. N.Y.C., Mar. 30, 1938; s. Abraham and Rachel (Stupsky) W.; B.S., Coll. City N.Y., 1960; M.S., U. Kans., 1965, Ph.D., 1968; m. Mary Ann Leonardi, Jan. 9, 1965; children—Daniella, David. Lectr. nutrition Hebrew U., Jerusalem, 1968-74; vis. scientist U. Mo., Columbia, 1974; asso. prof. nutrition Pa. State U., University Park, 1974—. Mem. Am. Inst. Nutrition, Soc. Exptl. Biology and Medicine, N.Y. Acad. Scis., Nutrition Today Soc., Sigma Xi. Contbr. articles to biochem., nutritional publs. Home: 239 E Irvin Ave State College PA 16801 Office: Nutrition Program Coll Human Devel Pa State U University Park PA 16802

WOLK, ANTHONY EDWARD, govt. ofcl.; b. Whitney, Pa., Nov. 11, 1930; s. Anthony Joseph and Mary Cecelia (Hajduk) W.; B.S., Pa. State U., 1956; postgrad. George Washington U., 1968-69; m. Ida R. Blackburn, Jan. 28, 1956; children—Timothy A., John A. Design engr. Martin Co., Balt., 1956-57, Fairchild Aircraft Corp., Hagerstown, Md., 1957-60; research, devel. engr. U.S. Army, Ft. Detrick, Md., 1960-70; mech. engr. U.S. Naval Ship Engring. Center, Hyattsville, Md., 1971-72; mech. engr. U.S. FDA, Rockville, Md., 1972—; mem. engr. career devel. com. USPHS, 1977—. Chmn. troop advancement com. Boy Scouts Am., 1969-76; bd. dirs. Clover Hill Civic Assn., 1974-77; v.p. Frederick County Jr. Baseball League, 1977. Served with USAF, 1948-52. Recipient Engring. Achievement award Ft. Detrick br. Research Soc. Am., 1970. Mem. ASME (food, drug, beverage equipment com.), Sigma Xi. Club: Elks. Home: 800 Edgewood Farm Rd Frederick MD 21701 Office: 5600 Fishers Ln Rockville MD 20857

WOLK, HERMAN SHEPARD, historian; b. Springfield, Mass., May 30, 1931; s. Max and Jennie Libby (Robinson) W.; B.A., Am. Internat. Coll., 1954, M.A., 1956; postgrad. (Ford Found. fellow) U. Washington, 1958-59; m. Sandra Irene Goldman, May 31, 1953; children—Jill Lori, Traci Ann. History tchr. Tantasqua Regional High Sch., Mass., 1956-58; historian Hdqrs. Strategic Air Command, Offutt AFB, Nebr., 1959-66, Office Air Force History Hdqrs. USAF, Washington, 1966—, chief gen. histories br., 1976—; mem. Office of Sec. Def. Spl. Project on History Strategic Arms Competition, 1974-75. Served with AUS, 1954-55. Asia Found. teaching grantee Japan Soc., 1957. Mem. Air Force Assn., Am. Hist. Assn., Air Force Hist. Found., Am. Mil. Inst. Author: (with others) Evolution of the American Military Establishment Since World War II, 1978. Home: 2280 Georgian Woods Pl Silver Spring MD 20902 Office: Office Air Force History Hdqrs USAF Washington DC 20314

WOLK, NOLAN IRWIN, adminstrv. elec. engr.; b. N.Y.C., May 16, 1916; s. Harold and Molly (Miner) W.; B. Elec. Engring., City Coll. N.Y., 1938; diploma in communications engring. Brooklyn Poly. Inst., 1946. Civilian engr. hdqrs. staff eastern dist. U.S. Army Air Force, 1940-42; civilian electronic engr. U.S. Navy, N.Y., 1942-45; dir. pres. Interference Measurement Labs., N.Y.C., 1955—; engring. cons. in communications; researcher computer analysis of stochastic time series and systems, 1965. Mem. Inst. Radio Engrs. (sr.).

WOLLER, OLGA, author; b. Zidani Most, Yugoslavia; d. Ivan and Josephine V. (Stockel) Malgaj; student Acad. Fine Arts, Vienna, Austria; m. Rudolph Weigner, 1918; children—Raoul M., Madeleine R. (Mrs. John T. Taeni); m. 2d, Franz H. Woller, Apr. 14, 1934. Author: Sex Alarm, 1946; Strange Conflict, 1955; The Heartbeat of Rome (hist. novel). Composer songs: There Will Be Sunday; No, No Johnny, Let It Be; Foolish, But Oh So Sweet, Short Stories, 1963; The Eccentric Loves of Elagabal, 1964; The Affairs of an Empress: Poems, 1974. Home: 101 Greenway N Forest Hills NY 11375 also Pinehurst NC 28374

WOLLHEIM, DONALD ALLEN, author, publisher; b. N.Y.C., Oct. 1, 1914; s. Jacob Lewis and Rose (Grinnell) W.; B.A., N.Y. U., 1935; m. Elsie Balter, June 25, 1943; 1 dau., Elizabeth Rosalind. Editor, Ace Mags., N.Y.C., 1942-47, Avon Books, 1947-52, Ace Books, 1952-71; pres. DAW Books, 1971—; editor ann. best sci. fiction selections, 1965—; over 35 anthologies for mags., pocketbooks, etc., N.Y.C., 1942—; author 21 novels, 1 biography, 1 work lit. criticism The Universe Makers, 1971, including Mike Mars Series, 1960—. Mem. Sci. Fiction Writers Assn., Aviation Writers Assn., Western Writers Am., Mystery Writers Am., Miniature Figure Collectors Am., Sci. Fiction Research Assn., Order St. Fantony, Count Dracula Soc. (hon. nat. chmn. 1972). Clubs: Hydra; Overseas Press. Home: 66-17 Clyde St Rego Park NY 11374 Office: 1301 Ave of Americas New York City NY 10019

WOLLMAN, BARRY JAMES, textile co. exec.; b. Mt. Vernon, N.Y., May 25, 1939; s. David J. and Adele J. (Isaacs) W.; B.S., Rider Coll., 1961; m. Judith C. Rosen, Oct. 28, 1973; children (by previous marriage)—Robert C., John S., Susan L. With Men's Fabric Corp (became Wollman Industries, Inc. 1972), N.Y.C., 1961—, sec., 1965—; partner Hazleton Assos. (Pa.), 1965—. Mem. Textile Distbrs. Assn., Am. Arbitration Assn. Home: 17 Hewitt Ave White Plains NY 10605 Office: 110 W 40th St New York City NY 10018

WOLOZEN, JOHN JOSEPH, JR., hosp. exec.; b. Jersey City, June 22, 1952; s. John Joseph and Blanche Clara (Malinowski) W.; B.S. in Biology (Colgate-Palmolive scholar 1970, Polish Univ. Club N.J. scholar 1973), St. Peter's Coll., 1974; M.S. in Biology, Fairleigh-Dickinson U., 1976. Med. auditor div. profl. services St. Francis Community Health Center, Jersey City, 1975—, also mem. patient care evaluation com., fund raising com., 1977—; vol. emergency med. technician Jersey City Heights Vol. Ambulance Corps., 1976-77. Recipient Honorarium St. Peters Coll., 1970, Order of the Cross keys St. Peter's Coll., 1974. Mem. Am. Hosp. Assn., Am. Inst. Biol. Scis., Assn. Health Records, Nat. Assn. Health Service Execs., Lambda Delta Tau. Club: Fairleigh Dickinson U. Century. Home: 329 7th St Jersey City NJ 07302 Office: 25 McWilliams Pl Jersey City NJ 07302

WOLSKY, JACK, artist, educator; b. Rochester, N.Y., Aug. 5, 1930; s. Benjamin and Mary (Ditkofsky) W.; A.S., Rochester Inst. Tech., 1951; B.S., State Univ. Coll., Buffalo, 1955, M.S., 1957; m. Gladys Mindlin, Dec. 20, 1953; children—Bonnie, Sharon, Marsha. Prof. art State Univ. Coll., Brockport, N.Y., 1959—; instr. Rochester Inst. Tech., summers, 1961-63, Rochester Meml. Art Gallery, 1975—; one-man shows Rochester Inst. Tech., 1958, Meml. Art Gallery, Rochester, 1963, Galerie Internationale, N.Y.C., 1963, 65, Schuman & Oxford Gallery, Rochester, 1965, 67, 70, 73, 76, D.E. Kendall Galleries, Wellfleet, Mass., 1968, State U. N.Y., Cobleskill, 1976, Zenith Gallery, Washington, 1978; represented in permanent collections Rochester Meml. Art Gallery, New Britain (Conn.) Mus. Am. Art, Rochester Inst. Tech., Eastman Kodak Co., Gannett Co., Inc., Bausch & Lomb Optical Co., Marine Midland Trust Co., Lincoln 1st Bank of Rochester, State U. N.Y., Brockport. Recipient Kosciuszko Found. award, 1963; Distinguished Alumnus award State U. N.Y., Buffalo, 1971, Lillian Fairchild Meml. award U. Rochester, 1971; others. State U. N.Y. Faculty Research fellow, 1968, 70, 73; State U. N.Y. faculty exchange scholar, 1975. Home: 295 Washington St Spencerport NY 14559 Office: Art Dept State Univ Coll Brockport NY 14420

WOLTER, JOHN AMADEUS, librarian, govt. ofcl.; b. St. Paul, July 25, 1925; s. Amadeus Frank and Marjorie (Wears) W.; student Coll. St. Thomas, 1950; B.A., U. Minn., 1956, M.A., 1965, Ph.D., 1975; postgrad. Georgetown U., 1957; m. Joan Patricia Venard, July 6, 1956; children—Mark, Thomas, Matthew, David. Officer, seaman Isthmian Lines Inc., N.Y.C., 1943-50, 57-60; marine transp. officer Mil. Sea Transp. Ser., Washington, 1956-57; instr., map librarian U. Minn., 1961-64, asst. to dir. univ. libraries, 1964-65, research fellow, 1965-66; asst. prof. Wis. State U. at River Falls, 1966-68; asst. chief geography and map div. Library of Congress, Washington, 1968-78, chief, 1978—; mem. U.S. Bd. Geog. Names, 1969—. Mem. U.S. Nat. Com. Internat. Geog. Union, 1972—; dir. cartography div. Am. Congress Surveying and Mapping, 1972-74, U.S. mem. commn. on history of cartography Internat. Cartographic Assn., 1972-76. Served with U.S. Army, 1950-52. Mem. AAAS, Am. Geog. Soc., Assn. Am. Geographers, Spl. Libraries Assn. (sec.-treas. geog. and map div. 1965), Soc. History Discoveries (sec.-treas. 1972-75, council 1976-78), Soc. Social Studies Sci., Am. Congress Surveying and Mapping (chmn. publs. com. 1978—), N.Am. Soc. Oceanic History, Theta Delta Chi. Rev. editor cartography div. Surveying and Mapping, 1971-72. Editorial bd. Cartographica, 1971—, Am. Cartographer, 1974—, Terrae Incognitae, 1973-75, ACSM Bull., 1974—, Surveying and Mapping, 1972—. Contbr. articles to profl. jours. Home: 5404 Thunder Hill Rd Columbia MD 21043 Office: Geography and Map Div-Library of Congress Washington DC 20540

WOMER, ROBERT SYLVESTER, clergyman, editor; b. East Orange, N.J., Feb. 27, 1908; s. M. Wayne and Maybelle Baldwin (Ackerman) W.; LL.B., Detroit Coll. Law, 1932, J.D., 1972; D.D., Philathea Coll., 1950; m. Velma Marion Hutchinson, Aug. 27, 1929. Ordained to ministry United Ch. of Can., 1950; spl. preacher, cons. sec. Mich. Lord's Day Alliance, 1925-32; gen. sec. Sunday League, Inc., Newark, 1932—; editor Sunday Guardian, Newark, 1956—. Radio speaker, 1926—. Author religious study courses, contbr. to religious mags. in U.S., Can., Gt. Britain. Address: 279 Highland Ave Newark NJ 07104

WONG, DAVID C., physicist; Hong Kong, Sept. 26, 1941; s. Harry J. and Hang (Ngar) W.; came to U.S., 1962; Ph.D., U. Mass., Amherst, 1975; m. Kate Chan, Sept. 11, 1972. Research asso., instr. U. Mass., Amherst, 1975—; sr. scientist Machlett Lab., Stamford, Conn., 1976-77; tech. staff Tex. Instruments, Dallas, 1977—. Faculty research grantee U. Mass., 1975. Mem. Am. Phys. Soc., Northampton Fedn. Musicians. Contbr. articles to profl. jours. Home: 25 Weed Hill Ave Stamford CT 06907 Office: 13500 N Central Expressway Dallas TX 75222

WONG, PATRICK WAI-KWONG, chem. engr.; b. Canton, China, Jan. 15, 1952; s. Hen For and So Ping (Lee) W.; came to U.S., 1970; B.S. in Chem. Engring., Tri-State U., Angola, Ind., 1974; M.S. in Chem. Engring., Columbia U., 1978. Chem. engr. Pall Corp., Glen Cove, N.Y., 1974-76; deptl. chem. engr. Hoffmann La Roche, Nutley, N.J., 1977—, corr. devel. deptl. newspaper. NSF grantee, 1976-77, Office Water Research and Tech. grantee, 1976-77. Mem. Am. Inst. Chem. Engrs., Tau Sigma Eta, Tau Beta Pi, Phi Lambda Upsilon. Presbyterian. Home: 10 Cambridge St Glen Cove NY 11542 Office: Room 228 Bldg 71 Hoffmann La Roche 340 Kingsland Rd Nutley NJ 07110

WOO, GLENN FRANK, securities dealer, stock broker; b. Honolulu, June 8, 1945; s. Francis H.T. and Mabel S. (Lee) W.; student U. Hawaii, 1965; B.B.A., U. Notre Dame, 1967; M.B.A., Baruch Coll. of City U. N.Y., 1968, postgrad. (fellow), 1969; m. Linda Lew, June 21, 1969. With Pickard & Co., N.Y.C., 1967-68, Brod & Co., N.Y.C., 1968-69; pres., dir. Amswiss Internat. Corp., Jersey City, 1969—; mem. Boston Stock Exchange. Officer 6th St. Block Assn. Mem. Security Traders Assn. N.Y., Nat. Assn. Securities Dealers, U. Notre Dame Lacrosse Club Alumni Assn., L.I. and Raritan River Akita Clubs, Am. Stamp Dealers Assn. Office: 1 Exchange Pl Jersey City NJ 07302

WOO, SHIEN-BIAU, educator; b. Shanghai, Aug. 13, 1937; s. Chen-Kee and Kuo-Ing (Chang) W.; B.S. summa cum laude, Georgetown Coll., 1956; M.S., Washington U., St. Louis, 1962, Ph.D., 1964; m. Katy K.N. Wu, July 20, 1963; children—Chih-I, Chih-Lan. Came to U.S., 1956, naturalized, 1972. Research asso. U. Colo., Boulder, 1964-66; asst. prof. U. Del., Newark, 1966-70, asso. prof., 1970—. Officer, Chinese Community Assns., St. Louis, 1962-64, Denver, 1964-66, Wilmington, 1969-71. Trustee U. Del., Newark, 1976—. Mem. AAUP (pres. U. Del. chpt. 1971-73, nat. council 1974-77), Orgn. Chinese-Ams. (dir. 1977—), Sigma Xi. Democrat. Home: 55 Woodhill Ct Newark DE 19711 Office: Dept Physics U Del Newark DE 19711

WOO, THERESA TING, pediatrician; b. Peking, China, Oct. 15, 1911; d. Chinlin and Yee-new Woo; came to U.S., 1921, naturalized, 1944; B.A., U. Pacific, 1931; M.D., U. Mich., 1934; M.P.H., Harvard U., 1955. Intern, Hosp. Coll. Pa., Phila., 1934-35; resident in pediatrics Children's Meml. Hosp., Chgo., 1942, Babies Hosp., N.Y.C., 1943; physician U. Chgo. Student Health Service, 1955-56, U. Mich. Student Health Service, 1956-63; asst. prof. pub. health U. Mich., 1956-57; med. officer FDA, HEW, Washington, 1963—. Served to maj. M.C., USAR, 1950-53. Diplomate Am. Bd. Pediatrics. Fellow Am. Acad. Pediatrics; mem. Med. Soc. D.C., AMA, AAAS, Am. Med. Women's Assn., Montgomery-Prince Georges Pediatric Soc., U. Mich. Alumni Assn., Women's Med. Soc. D.C., Delta Omega, Iota Sigma Pi. Methodist. Home: 2939 Van Ness St NW Washington DC 20008

WOOD, BRIAN, financial corp. exec.; b. Stretford, U.K., Sept. 29, 1920 (came to U.S., 1947, naturalized, 1957); s. James William and Constance (Medcalf) W.; student Manchester U., 1935-38, Royal Coll. Tech., Manchester, 1946; m. Carolyn Elizabeth Wilber, May 31, 1945; children—Christine Elizabeth, Robin Ann Wood Pohlman. Salesman export div. J.P. Stevens & Co. Inc., 1947-54; v.p. Walker Bros. (N.Y.) Inc., 1954-62; export sales mgr. Warner Bros. Inc., 1962-63; exec. v.p., dir. Fenchurch Corp., N.Y.C., 1964-77; exec. v.p., dir. S.H. Lock, Inc., N.Y.C., 1964-74, pres., 1975—; exec. v.p., dir. Tozer Kemsley & Millbourn (Can.) Ltd., 1966-73, TKM Pacific Ltd., 1972-74; joint mng. dir. Fenchurch NV, Curacao, 1972-77. Mem. Nat. UN Day Com., 1978. Served to lt. comdr. Air br. Royal Navy, 1940-45. Mem. Trinidad and Tobago C. of C. N.Y. (dir., 1st v.p. 1970-73, pres. 1975—). Republican. Clubs: Patterson (Fairfield, Conn.); Jamaica (Kingston, Jamaica); Union (Port of Spain, Trinidad). Home: 109 Mill River Rd Fairfield CT 06430 Office: SH Lock Inc 535 Fifth Ave New York City NY 10017

WOOD, CLIFFORD HARLOW, educator; b. Boise, Idaho, Apr. 15, 1940; s. Paul Everett and Inez Ruth (Matter) W.; B.S. in Geography, U. Idaho, 1968, M.S., 1972; postgrad. U. Wis., 1972—; m. Alberta Gjertine Auringer, May 16, 1975; 1 dau., Jennifer Gjeneve. Cartographer, CIA, Washington, 1968-70; instr. U. Idaho, Moscow,

1970-72; project asst. geography dept. U. Wis., Madison, 1972-76; lectr. dept. geography U. Md., College Park, 1976—. Propr., Continental Cartographics, Madison, 1973—; cartographic cons. Idaho Bur. Mines and Geology, 1973—. Served with USAF, 1962-66. Mem. Am. Congress on Surveying and Mapping, Brit. Cartographic Soc., Internat. Cartographic Assn., Cam. Cartographic Assn., Am. Soc. Photogrammetry, Assn. Am. Geographers, Sigma Xi. Home: 6611 Wells Pkwy University Park MD 20782

WOOD, HARLESTON READ, steel co. exec.; b. Phila., Oct. 18, 1913; s. Alan and Elizabeth Frances (Read) W.; student Haverford Sch., 1929-31; A.B., Princeton, 1936; LL.D., Hobart and William Smith Coll., 1959; m. Emily Newbold Campbell, June 21, 1942; children—Harleston R., Alan, IV, Ross G., Morrow Campbell, Anthony B. With Alan Wood Steel Co., 1938-42, sales devel. engr., 1946-50, mgr. planning and devel., 1950-52, asst. v.p., v.p., 1952-55, pres., 1955-72, chmn. bd., 1962—, also dir.; dir. Fidelity Mut. Life Ins. Co., Fredericks Co., Penco Products Inc., Oaks, Pa., Alan Wood Coated Metals Co. Bd. dirs. Ursinus Coll. Mem. Am. Iron and Steel Inst., Council on Fgn. Relations. Episcopalian. Club: Philadelphia Country. Home: 641 Righters Mill Rd Narbeth PA 19072 Office: Conshohocken PA 19428

WOOD, HAROLD GRAY, marketing exec.; b. Jackson, Tenn., Aug. 6, 1926; s. Irby Gray and Lessie (Holland) W.; B.S., Union U., 1948; B.S. in Elec. Engring., U. Tenn., 1950; postgrad. Tex. Coll. Arts and Industries, 1956-59; m. Kaye Anne Lloyd, June 7, 1956; children—Lloyd Gray, Kenneth Martin. Commd. 2d lt. U.S. Army, Signal Corps, 1952, advanced through grades to capt., 1960; asst. to planning engr. Western Union Telegraph Co., N.Y.C., 1960; eastern regional mgr. Mil. Products div. Hoffman Electronics Corp., Los Angeles, 1960-64; Eastern sales mgr. Victory Electronics, Inc., Syosset, N.Y., 1964-65; mgr. Monmouth office Ling-Temco-Vought, Inc., 1965-69, mgr. Monmouth office LTV Electrosystems, Inc., 1969-71, mgr. Monmouth office E-Systems, Inc., 1971—. Mem. IEEE, Assn. U.S. Army, Armed Forces Communications and Electronics Assn., Am. Ordnance Assn., Assn. Old Crows, Army Aviation Assn. Am. Democrat. Baptist. Club: Masons. Home: 45 Sydney Ave Deal NJ 07723 Office: 776 Shrewsbury Ave Tinton Falls NJ 07724

WOOD, JAMES ARTHUR, JR., pub. relations exec., cartoonist, editor; b. Miami, Fla., June 6, 1927; s. James Arthur and Baldwin (Jennings) W.; B.A. cum laude, Washington and Lee U., 1950; m. Sallie Van Dyck, Nov. 10, 1951; children—Elizabeth Van Dyck, James Arthur, Baldwin Jennings. Editorial cartoonist Richmond (Va.) News Leader, 1950-56, Pitts. Press, 1956-63; dir. info. U.S. Ind. Telephone Assn., Washington, 1964—; cartoonist Farm Bur. News, 1978—; exhibited one-man show Pitts. Press Club, 1959; exhibited cartoons Nat. Collection of Cartoonists Soc., 1958-61, Brussels World Fair, 1958, Internat. Cartoon Exhibit The Great Challenge, 1959-60; permanent collections of all cartoons Alderman Library, Va. U.; represented in permanent collections: Akron U., William Allen White Found. Collection, Kans. U., drawings Library of Congress; dir. Nat. Center of Cartoon and Graphic Arts, 1964—. Served with USNR, World War II. Recipient Freedoms Found. awards, 1953, 54, 58, 59, 60, Christopher award, 1954, Gold Quill awards, 1960, 62, Patriotic Citation award, 1960, Huevos de Onix, Mexico City, 1977, Prin. Freedoms Found. award 1979. Mem. Nat. Cartoonists Soc., Assn. Am. Editorial Cartoonists (mem. bd., v.p. 1959-64, 1st v.p. 1974, pres. 1975), Advt. Artist of Pitts. (v.p. 1962-63), Phi Gamma Delta, Sigma Delta Chi, Omicron Delta Kappa. Democrat. Presbyterian. Clubs: Pitts. Press (dir. 1962-63), Nat. Press. Home: 7008 Tilden Ln Rockville MD 20852 Office: 1801 K St NW Suite 1201 Washington DC 20006

WOOD, JOHN SUMNER, lawyer, author; b. Milford, Mass., Mar. 2, 1902; s. Isaac Sumner and Octavia (Byrne) W.; S.B., Harvard U., 1925; J.D. with honors, George Washington U., 1933; m. Mary Leftwich Rawlings (dec. 1935); children—Sumner, Jr. (dec.), David, Judson; m. 2d, Peggy Angel, July 23, 1936; children—Wriley, Brooks, Octavia. Admitted to Washington, Md. bar, 1933; lawyer, trustee. Mem. Soc. Mayflower Descs. Democrat. Episcopalian. Clubs: Masons, Rotary, Farmington Country. Author: Malta, 1935; Laws Everyone Should Know, 1941; Cupid's Path in Ancient Plymouth, 1957; The Virginia Bishop, 1960; The Wood Family Index, 1966; The Horseshoe of the Potomac, 1973. Home: At Ye Wode Beallsville MD 20704 Office: The 1785 House Poolesville MD 20837

WOOD, LORING WAYLAND, physician, med. adminstr.; b. Worcester, Mass., Jan. 27, 1923; s. Abiel Wayland and Marion (Loring) W.; A.B., Dartmouth Coll., 1948; M.D., C.M., McGill U., 1951; m. Alice Marsha Spencer, Mar. 29, 1949; children—Karen Spencer, Eric Wayland. Intern, Ellis Hosp., Schenectady, 1951-52; resident in internal medicine Buffalo Gen. Hosp., 1952-53, 56-57, resident in cardiovascular disease, 1957-58; practice medicine specializing in internal medicine, Buffalo, 1958-67; med. dir. western area N.Y. Telephone Co., 1965-72, med. dir.-med. care, 1972-76, med. dir. research and devel., 1976—; asso. in medicine Buffalo Gen. Hosp., 1962-72, chief cardiac clinic, 1964-67; attending physician in medicine Buffalo VA Hosp., 1962-72; cons. cardiology Erie County (N.Y.) Health Dept., Buffalo Childrens Hosp., 1958-72; asst. clin. prof. medicine State U. of N.Y., Buffalo, 1963-72; coordinator undergrad. cardiovascular tng. grant, NIH, 1959-69; co-investigator Coronary Drug Project, NIH, 1966-72. Bd. dirs. Buffalo Area Council on Alcoholism, 1962-72, N.Y. State Heart Assembly, 1962-64; trustee United Fund of Buffalo. Served with U.S. Maritime Service, 1943-45, USNR, 1953-56. Fellow Soc. Advanced Med. Systems; mem. AMA (Physician Recognition award 1978—), Am. Occupational Med. Assn. (pres. Upstate N.Y. chpt. 1968), Med. Soc. N.Y. (chmn. sect. on occupational health 1974-76), Am. Coll. Preventive Medicine, N.Y. Heart Assn., Heart Assn. Western N.Y. (pres. 1965, dir. 1963-70). Presbyterian. Clubs: Dartmouth of New Canaan. Contbr. articles to med. jours. Home: 89 Llewellyn Dr New Canaan CT 06840 Office: 1095 Ave of Americas New York City NY 10036

WOOD, MARGARET BEATRICE, educator; b. Charleston, W.Va., Aug. 15, 1913; d. John Daniel and Ivory Bertha (Gardner) Morris; A.B. in Edn. cum laude, Howard U., 1934; M.Ed., U. Hartford (Conn.), 1960; postgrad. Bank St. Coll. Edn., N.Y.C., 1966-67; m. Alvin Bernard Wood, June 8, 1934; children—Alvin Bernard, Irene Beatrice Wood Llewellyn. Elementary sch. tchr. Hartford Bd. Edn., 1948-60, reading cons., 1960-66, coordinator reading instrn., dir. intensive reading instructional teams, 1966—; cons. in field. Mem. town council, dep. mayor, Bloomfield, Conn., 1969—. Recipient Nat. Sojourner Truth Meritorious Service award Nat. Council Negro Women, 1973. Mem. Internat., New Eng. reading assns., Conn. Assn. Reading Research (pres.), LWV, Urban League, NAACP, Links, Alpha Kappa Alpha, Delta Kappa Gamma. Democrat. Baptist. Home: 131 Wadhams Rd Bloomfield CT 06002 Office: 249 High St Hartford CT 06103

WOOD, MARY ANN FERNSLER, interior designer, design and decorator service co. exec.; b. Lebanon, Pa., July 10, 1938; d. Philip Adam and Helen Arlene (Jackson) Fernsler; student Drexel U., 1956-57, Boston U., 1958-59, N.Y. Sch. Interior Design, 1968-69; m. Harry Gildean, 1958; children—Michael, Anne; m. 2d, Frank D. Wood, Feb. 14, 1976; stepchildren—Steven, Cynthia. Seamstress, Heverling Decorators, Lebanon, Pa., 1969-72; dir. decoration service Westenberger, Maley and Myers, Lancaster, Pa., 1972-77; owner, operator Owl Hill Interiors, Lititz, Pa., 1977—; career guidance speaker Lititz Middle Sch. Vol. Office of Aging, Lancaster, 1976-78, Named Single Parent of Year in Lancaster County, Parents without Partners, 1975; decorator Lancaster Decorators House, 1975, 76. Mem. Pilot Club Lancaster (pres. 1978-79). Republican. Lutheran. Club: Lititz Woman's. Home and Office: 6 Karen Ct RD 3 Lititz PA 17543

WOOD, PATRICIA LYNNE, newspaper editor; b. San Francisco, Jan. 14, 1937; d. Robert John and Lynne Katherine (Wainwright) Valdaire; B.A., Radcliffe Coll., 1949; B.A., Acad. Dramatic Arts, 1952; m. Edward William Wood, Jr., Aug. 8, 1952. Freelance theatre and music artist, 1957-68; on-air personality Island Broadcasting System, Patchogue, N.Y., 1968-75; editor, co-pub. L.I. Traveler-Watchman, Southold, N.Y., 1978—. Address: Traveler St PO Box 725 Southold NY 11901

WOOD, PAUL MIX, operations researcher, state ofcl.; b. Carthage, N.Y., Dec. 28, 1930; s. LeRoy Alfred and Geneva (Adner) W.; student St. Lawrence U., 1950-51, Duke U., 1951-52; B.S., Syracuse U., 1956, M.S., 1958; M.S., Rensselaer Poly. Inst., 1971, M.B.A., 1975; m. Eloise Bess Hazard, Nov. 5, 1955; children—Michele, Susan. Chief systems analysis Hamilton Standard div. United Aircraft Corp., Windsor Locks, Conn., 1963-64; ops. analyst Tech. Ops., Inc., Fort Monroe, Va., 1964-65; research scientist Travelers Research Center, Inc., Hartford, Conn., 1965-68; asso. research scientist N.Y. State Dept. Health, Albany, 1968—. Served with USAF, 1952-54. Fellow AAAS, mem. Ops. Research Soc. Am. (consultative com. cost effectiveness sect. 1968-72), Am. Statis. Assn., Mensa. Home: 24 N Hill Dr Ballston Lake NY 12019 Office: Tower Bldg Empire State Plaza Albany NY 12237

WOOD, PAUL WINTHROP, artist; b. Kingsville, Ont., Can., Aug. 29, 1922; s. Albert Gardner and Louise (Moyer) W.; student Art Students League, 1939-41, NAD, 1946; m. Jacqueline Marie Stark, Sept. 4, 1953; children—Stephen, Gregory, Mark, Paul. Exhibited one-man show: Nassau Community Coll., Garden City, N.Y., 1966; group shows: Summit (N.J.) Art Center, 1974, Art U.S.A., N.Y.C., 1955, Silvermine, Conn., 1966; executed stained glass, tapestry designs, mosaics in numerous states; represented in permanent collections; owner, operator Paul Wood Studios, Port Washington, N.Y., 1948—; lectr. in field. Mem. Fine Arts Commn. Nassau County (N.Y.), 1969-70; chmn. art adv. council Port Washington Pub. Library, 1977—. Served with Coast Arty. Corps, U.S. Army, 1943-46. Decorated Army Commendation medal; recipient Emily Lowe award painting, 1960, Audubon Artists award, 1962, 71. Mem. Manhasset Art Assn. Profl. Artists Guild, Aquarelle Club. Democrat. Roman Catholic. Author: Stained Glass Crafting, 1967; Starting with Stained Glass, 1973; Artistry in Stained Glass, 1976; Painting Abstract Landscapes, 1971. Designer stained glass, tapestry, mosaic Temple Sinai, Roslyn, N.Y., 1964. Home: 6 Glamford Ave Port Washington NY 11050 Office: 3 Pleasant Ave Port Washington NY 11050

WOOD, PETER YORK, airport and hotel devel. co. exec.; b. Media, Pa., Apr. 12, 1928; s. Everett Jay and Ellen Marion (Peterson) W.; student Keystone Bus. Sch., 1948-49; m. Elizabeth Hoff Way, Nov. 14, 1970; children—Wenthy Joan, Terry York, Kristen Carlson. Founder, dir. Skytours, Inc., also Skytourist Club Internat., Swarthmore, Pa., 1946-51; pres. Skytours, Inc., also mgr. Delaware County Airport, Chester, Pa., 1952-58; adminstr., prop. Elnwood Nursing Home, Swarthmore, 1959-69; founder, prop. Skymaster Club Internat., Media, 1968—; pres., owner Skymaster Inns Internat., New Castle, Del., 1972—. Served as capt. CAP, 1941-56. Mem. Delaware County Aviation Assn. (co-founder, officer 1946—), Balloon Club Am. (co-founder 1951—), Aero Club Pa. (sec. 1960—), Am. Assn. Airport Execs., Am. Theatre Organ Soc. Club: Explorers (N.Y.C.). Home and Office: 700 N Middletown Rd Media PA 19063

WOOD, THOMAS FULLENWIDER, cons. chemist; b. Alton, Ind., Nov. 17, 1912; s. Charles Forest and Sallie Ellen (Fullenwider) W.; A.B., DePauw U., 1935; M.S., Washington U., 1940; m. Marie Kreiger, May 3, 1945; children—Thomas Charles, John Benton, Laurence Paul. Analytical chemist Guide Lamp div. Gen. Motors, Anderson, Ind., 1936-37; grad. asst. Washington U., St. Louis, 1938-40; prodn. chemist Givaudan-Delawanna, Inc., Clifton, N.J., 1940-42, 45-46; research chemist Givaudan Corp., Clifton, 1945-77, asso. research dir., 1975-77, cons., 1977—; chmn. lecture series N.J.-Passaic Valley subsect. Am. Chem. Soc., 1949. Mem. AAAS, Am. Inst. Chemists, Am. Chem. Soc., North Jersey Mineralogical Soc. Methodist. Inventor, lectr. and patentee in field. Home: 4 Hoover Pl Wayne NJ 07470 Office: 125 Delawanna Ave Clifton NJ 07014

WOODAMS, EDWARD ELLIS, food scientist; b. Brockport, N.Y., July 8, 1938; s. Elmer John and Lucretia F. (Kintz) W.; B. Agrl. Engring., Cornell U., 1961, M.S. in Food Sci., 1965; m. Andrea Burleigh, May 21, 1977. Mem. food sci. and tech. dept. N.Y. State Experiment Sta., Cornell U., Geneva, 1964—; house mgr. Geneva Concerts Inc., 1971—. Mem. phys. com. YMCA, 1976—. Mem. Inst. Food Technologists, Ch. Bowling League. Republican. Lutheran. Clubs: Station, St. Stephen's Mixed Bowling League, Sunset Golf League. Home: 323 Lyons Rd Geneva NY 14456 Office: Dept Food Sci and Tech NY Experiment Sta Geneva NY 14456

WOODARD, BRIAN TALCOTT, psychologist; b. Lewiston, Maine, Aug. 18, 1945; s. Harry Winchell and Janette (Talcott) W.; B.S., Springfield Coll., 1967, M.S., 1968; m. Susan Banks, Nov. 22, 1969; children—Thomas, Jeffrey. Instr. psychology Dutchess Community Coll., Poughkeepsie, N.Y., 1972-75; psychologist Multi-Media Center, Kingston, N.Y., 1970-76; sch. psychologist, Newburgh, N.Y., 1968-70, Kingston, N.Y., 1970—; cons. Gateway Industries, 1977, Assn. Retarded Children, 1974—. Served to capt. U.S. Army Res., 1968—, active duty, 1968-69. Mem. Assn. Children with Learning Disabilities, Am., Mid-Hudson psychol. assns., Sch. Psychologists Assn. N.Y. State. Clubs: Twaalfskill Country, Road Runners (N.Y.C.).

WOODARD, PAUL ESTY, med. librarian; b. Chico, Calif., Oct. 24, 1921; s. Herman Eugene and Cecile Ellen (Esty) W.; R.N., Wichita St. Joseph Hosp., 1950; B.A., Friends U., 1952; postgrad. Harvard U., summer 1952; Ph.D., Western U., 1955; certificate L.S., Mass. State Coll. at Framingham, 1973; m. Marion Kathryn Boyajian, July 28, 1962; children—Pamela, Geoffrey. Dir. student health Friends U., Wichita, 1950-52; nurse Mt. Auburn Hosp., Cambridge, Mass., 1952-53, Mass. Gen. Hosp., 1955-63; dir. inservice edn. New Eng. Bapt. Hosp., Boston, 1963-69; med. librarian, 1970—. Notary public, Mass., 1964—. Mem. phys. fitness council YMCA, Cambridge, 1961-63. Recipient Recognition awards ARC, 1955, 63, Am. Friends Service Com., 1946. Fellow Royal Numis. Soc. (London); mem. Med. Library Assn., Mediaeval Acad. Am. (life), New Eng. Historic Geneal. Soc., Nat. Geog. Soc., Alpha Kappa Tau. Mem. interdenominational Grace Chapel. Club: Men Librarians (Boston). Contbr. articles to profl. jours. Home: 46 Hickory Cliff Rd Newton Upper Falls MA 02164 Office: 91 Parker Hill Ave Boston MA 02120

WOODBURY, ALAN TENNEY, lawyer; b. Milw., July 7, 1943; s. Isaiah Tenney and Maxine Arvilla (Hooper) W.; B.A., Bowdoin Coll., 1965; J.D., Temple U., 1968; m. Deborah Carson Eayre, Jan. 27, 1968; children—Jeffrey Tenney, Alison Eayre. Admitted to Pa. bar, 1968; atty. Fidelity Mut. Life Ins. Co., Phila., 1968-71, asst. counsel, 1971-74, asso. counsel, 1974—, asst. v.p., 1976-78, 2d v.p., 1978—; v.p. Capital Analysts, Inc., 1970—, also dir.; asst. sec., treas., F.M.L. Growth Fund, Inc., F.M.L. Equity Income Fund, Combined Shares, Inc., 1970-75. Recipient Am. Jurisprudence Book prize, 1968. Mem. Am., Phila. bar assns., Assn. Life Ins. Counsel. Clubs: Bowdoin (Phila.), Martins Dam. Office: 15th St and S Penn Square Philadelphia PA 19101

WOODHAM, JEAN, sculptor; b. Midland City, Ala., Aug. 16, 1925; d. Marcus Morton and Alma (Clements) Woodham; B.A., Ala. Poly. Inst., 1946; student Sculpture Center, N.Y.C., 1946-49; (Kate Neal Kinley Meml. fellow), U. Ill., 1950; m. James Lee Caraway, Nov. 18, 1949 (div. 1968); children—Susan Melissa, Elizabeth Leigh. One-man shows Auburn U., 1950, U. Ill., 1952, Silvermine Guild of Artists, New Canaan, Conn., 1955, Davison Art Center Wesleyan U., Middletown, Conn., 1956, Stuttman Gallery, N.Y.C., 1959, Rive Gaucho Gallery, Darien, Conn., 1962, 1966, New Canaan (Conn.) Library, 1963, Wilton (Conn.) Library, 1963, Mattack Mus., 1968, Fairfield (Conn.) U., 1970; exhibited group shows museums, galleries U.S., Argentina, Belgium, Brazil, Chile, Eng., Mexico; exhibited Gen. Foods, N.Y. World's Fair, 1964-65; represented in permanent collections Massillon (Ohio) Mus., Norfolk (Va.) Mus. Arts, Westport (Conn.) Permanent Collection; instr. sculpture Stamford (Conn.) Mus.; asso. prof. Auburn (Ala.) U., 1974-75; participant Bd. Edn. Exhbns, N.Y.C.; slide lectures Ala. chpt. A.I.A., 1969, Fairfield U., 1970, Ga. Inst. Tech., 1971; chmn. Westport-Weston Arts Council Sculpture Exhbn., 1977. Bd. dirs. Rowayton Art Center. Recipient Naomi Lorne Meml. prize, Conn. Acad. Prize for Sculpture; Mr. and Mrs. Michael Salomone prize Nat. Assn. Women Artists, 1970, Medal of Honor for sculpture, 1974. Mem. Nat. Assn. Women Artists (chmn. sculpture 1965-66), Sculptors Guild (treas. 1960-65, exec. bd. N.Y.C. 1966-68, sec. 1972—, exec. bd. 1977-78), Audubon Artists (juror 1964), Artists Equity, Archtl. League N.Y. Archtl. commns. include welded bronze Menorah, Jewish Community Center, Harrison, N.Y.; welded bronze sculpture, Ala. State Coll., Montgomery; Menorah for Temple Israel, Westport, Conn., 1966-68; 3 sculptures for corporate hdqrs. Flintkote Co., White Plains, N.Y.; 3 welded bronze fountain sculptures Gen. Electric Credit Corp., Stamford, Conn., 1972; large oval sculpture in welded bronze Gen. Telephone Electronics, Stamford, 1973; Orbit bronze fountain sculpture Tex. Eastern Transmission of Houston Center, 1974-75; Scholar's Sphere Harry S. Truman High Sch., N.Y.C., 1976-78; Whirlwind bronze fountain sculpture for courtyd. Lewis Cooper Meml. Library and Art Center, Opelika, Ala., 1977. Home and studio: 26 Pin Oak Ln Westport CT 06880

WOODRICH, GLENN CARL, pencil mfg. co. exec.; b. Oak Harbor, Ohio, Sept. 4, 1926; s. Carl John and Alma Augusta W.; B.S., B.A., Bowling Green State U., 1950; m. Karis Elizabeth Baker, June 12, 1948; children—Kirk, Carol. Accountant, Acme Industries, Jackson, Mich., 1950-51; sales rep. Ditto, Inc., Denver, 1951-54; br. mgr. Duplicator Supply Co., Denver and Salt Lake City, 1954-57; from dist. sales mgr. to br. mgr. Bohn Bus. Machines, Inc., N.Y.C., 1958-64; mktg. team mgr. Xerox Corp., Stamford, Conn., 1964-68; corp. officer, v.p. mktg., writing products div. Joseph Dixon Crucible Co., Jersey City, 1968—. Mem. Planning and Zoning Commn., Weston, Conn., 1974—. Served with USAAF, 1945-46. Recipient 2 Leadership awards Xerox Corp., 1966; Merit award for community participation Sta. WICC, Bridgeport, Conn., 1968. Mem. Nat. Office Products Assn., Writing Instrument Mfrs. Assn. (dir. 1975—), Wholesale Stationers Assn. (mem. govt. relations com. 1973), Pencil Makers Assn., Nat. Sch. Supply Edn. Assn., Internat. Blueprint and Reprographics Assn., Research Inst. Am., Sales Execs. N.Y. (mem. speakers' bur. 1976—), Jersey City C. of C. Republican. Episcopalian. Clubs: Weston Field, Masons. Contbr. ann. econ. forecast to Jan. edits. So. Stationers' Mag., 1970—. Home: 33 High Acre Rd Weston CT 06883 Office: 167 Wayne St Jersey City NJ 07303

WOODRUFF, ARCHIBALD MULFORD, JR., former univ. pres.; b. Newark, July 30, 1912; s. Archibald M. and Eleanor B. (Van Etten) W.; B.A., Williams Coll., 1933; postgrad. U. Berlin, 1935; Ph.D., Princeton U., 1936; L.H.D. (hon.), Trinity Coll.; LL.D. (hon.), Tarkio Coll., Williams Coll.; m. Barbara Jane Bestor, July 13, 1940; children—Archibald Mulford III, Paul B., Nathan V. E., Timothy R. Mortgage dept. Prudential Ins. Co., 1936-42, 44-50; Kelly Meml. prof. ins. and urban land studies U. Pitts., 1950-59; dir. Bur. Bus. Research, 1954-59; dean Sch. Govt., George Washington U., Washington, 1959-64; provost U. Hartford (Conn.), 1964-67, chancellor 1967-70, pres., 1970-77; dir. Soc. for Savs., C.G. Fund, Inc., 1080 Corp., Hartford. Chmn. Nat. Capital Planning Commn. 1960-61, vice chmn., 1961-65; v.p., dir. Lincoln Found.; mem. Hartford Bd. Higher Edn.; chmn. research com. Urban Land Inst., 1966-71; trustee Tarkio (Mo.) Coll.; bd. dirs. Wadsworth Athenaeum, E.B. Found.; chmn. bd. Watkinson Sch.; bd. dirs. Land Reform Tng. Inst., Taiwan. Recipient Chinese Culture medal Ministry Edn. Republic China (Taiwan). Mem. Am. Econ. Assn., Nat. Council Devel. of Small Bus. Mgmt. (pres. 1957-58), Phi Beta Kappa. Universalist. Author books, monographs and articles on land econs. (chiefly taxation) and econs. of small bus. Home: PO Box 582 Simsbury CT 06070 Office: 1040 Prospect Ave Hartford CT 06117

WOODRUFF, MARIAN DAVIS, former state legislator, art gallery ofcl.; b. Boston, Dec. 15, 1922; d. Harvey Nathaniel and Alice Marion (Rohde) Davis; B.A., Smith Coll., 1945; m. Bliss Woodruff, Sept. 27, 1952; children—Nathaniel Rohde, William Watts, Davis Miller, Charlotte Bliss. Guide, Met. Mus. Art, N.Y.C., 1945-46; lectr. Mus. Art, R.I. Sch. Design, Providence, 1946-51; dir. edn. Currier Gallery Art, Manchester, N.H., 1962-66, 70—; program dir. Nashua (N.H.) Arts and Sci. Center, 1968-69; mem. N.H. Ho. of Reps. from 18th Dist., 1973-76. Mem. visual arts com. N.H. Commn. Arts; mem. White Mountain Environment Com., Nat. Alliance Arts Edn., Arts Advocacy Com., Nashua Conservation Commn., 1978—; bd. dirs. Daniel Clark Found., pres., 1977—; bd. dirs. United Health Services Agy., 1978—; mem. council Nashua League Craftsmen, League N.H. Craftsmen; founding mem. Nashua League Women Voters; bd. dirs. Nashua Headstart. Mem. Am. Assn. Museums, Order Women Legislators, N.H. Micological Soc. (pres. 1978—). Democrat. Unitarian-Universalist. Clubs: Appalachian Mountain, Randolph Mountain. Home: 40 Orange St Nashua NH 03060 Office: 192 Orange St Manchester NH 03104

WOODS, BEVERLY JO, counselor; b. Houston, Mar. 6, 1943; d. Alfred Joseph and Elizabeth Elaine Mims; student Tex. So. U., 1960-61; B.A., Howard U., 1964; M.A., Fordham U., 1973; m. Allie Woods, Dec. 20, 1969; 1 dau., Allyson Beverly. Caseworker, Cook County (Ill.) Dept. Social Services, 1964-67; pre-teen program dir. South Parkway YWCA, Chgo., 1967-68; psychiat. social work ast. N.Y. State Dept. Mental Hygiene, N.Y.C., 1970-71; advt. space sales rep. Metro Transit Schedules N.Y.C., 1977—; cons. Jewish Child Care Assn., 1976. asst. office vol. worker Democratic Nat. Conv., N.Y.C., 1976. Mem. Am. Personnel, Guidance Assn., Am. Coll. Personnel Assn., Alpha Kappa Alpha. Democrat. Methodist. Home:

255 W 108th St Apt 12C1 New York City NY 10025 Office: 2 Penn Plaza New York City NY 10001

WOODS, FREDERICK ELVERTON, realtor; b. New Bremen, N.Y., Feb. 10, 1927; s. Floyed Elliot and Iva (Rector) W.; B.A., Syracuse U., 1953, M.A., 1953; grad. Realtors Inst., 1972; m. Martha E. Hudson; children—Patricia Ann, Michael David, Sara Elizabeth. Tchr., Fayetteville (N.Y.)-Manlius Schs., 1954-56; salesman Kelley Real Estate, Dewitt, N.Y., 1956-58; treas. Kelley, Casey, Woods Real Estate, Dewitt, 1958-62; broker Longley-Jones Assos., Syracuse, N.Y., 1962-64; pres. Ludington-McMahon Assos., Realtors, Dewitt, 1964-74, Fred Woods Real Estate, Inc., Fayetteville, 1974—. Trustee, Fayetteville Village Bd., 1972—, Onondaga County Pub. Library, Syracuse, 1975—; commr. pub. works Fayetteville, 1973—. Served with AUS, 1944-48, 50-51. Mem. Nat. (dir.), N.Y. State (pres. 1978, dean Grad. Realtors Inst. 1975-76, dir. 1973—) assns. realtors, Greater Syracuse Bd. Realtors (pres. 1970; named Realtor of Year 1972), N.Y. State Soc. Real Estate Appraisers, Nat. Inst. Farm and Land Brokers, Realtors Nat. Mktg. Inst. Club: Shriners. Home: 413 Single Dr North Syracuse NY 13212 Office: PO Box 188 102 Limestone Plaza Fayetteville NY 13066

WOODS, JOHN FRANCIS, JR., lawyer, state ofcl.; b. Lyndhurst, N.J., Dec. 29, 1912; s. John Francis and Frances A. (Burke) W.; A.B., Princeton U., 1933; J.D., Harvard U., 1936. Admitted to N.J. bar, 1938; practiced in Lyndhurst, 1938-42; lawyer Govt. of N.J., 1946—, legal asst. to standing master Supreme Ct. N.J., Trenton, 1965-75; supr. mortgage foreclosure unit Superior Ct. N.J., 1975—. Served with USAAF, 1942-46; capt. USAF Res., ret. Mem. Phi Beta Kappa. Home: 315 Stuyvesant Ave Lyndhurst NJ 07071 Office: Room 305 State House Annex Trenton NJ 08625

WOODS, JOHN RUSSELL, minerals co. exec.; b. Ottawa, Ont., Can., May 10, 1930; s. Shirley Edwards and Catherine (Guthrie) W.; student pvt. schs.; m. Nancy Elizabeth Braden, Aug. 29, 1953; children—James, Jennifer. Vice pres. S.E. Woods Ltd., Hull, Que., Can., 1954-59; pres., gen. mgr. Holden Mfg. Co. Ltd., Hull, 1959-66; v.p. Lynx Can. Exploration Ltd., Toronto, Ont., 1970—; chmn. Eaglet Mines Ltd., Ottawa, 1971—, E.T.S. Tool Corp. Ltd.; pres. Scolopax Ltd.; v.p. Cogper Ltd., Ottawa, 1971—; chmn. Cancast Cement Co. Ltd., Canaba Korea Ventures Ltd. Nat. dir. fin. Liberal Party Can., Ottawa, 1968-72; chmn. Hull Red Cross, 1963, Can. Nat. Inst. Blind, Ottawa, 1968; chmn. bd. govs. Ashbury Coll. Served to lt., inf. Can. Army, 1950-53; Korea. Decorated knight comdr. Order Lazarus of Jerusalem. Mem. Can. Sport Fishing Inst. (pres. 1969—), Can. Horse Council (dir.). Clubs: Rideau, Country, Maganassippi Fish and Game, Shitepoke, Ottawa Valley Hunt (Ottawa); Cavalry and Guards (London). Home: Kildare Farm Route 1 Pakenham ON K0A 2X0 Canada Office: 140 Wellington St Ottawa ON K1P 5A2 Canada

WOODS, LOUIS RICHARD, JR., realtor; b. Pitts., Nov. 21, 1943; s. Louis Richard and Rose Mary (Schmitt) W.; student U. Md., 1967-68; grad. Realtors Inst., 1973; m. Susan Mary Bayer, May 14, 1966; children—Patrick Joseph, Melissa Ann. Sr. spacecraft controller RCA Service Co., Greenbelt, Md., 1965-71; sales asso. Pyramid Real Estate & Devel. Corp., Glen Burnie, Md., 1971-73, v.p., asso. broker, 1974-77; gen. sales mgr. H. James Azar Realty Co., Severna Park, Md., 1972-74; pres. Builder Sales Assn., Inc., 1977-78; pres. Century 21 Stuart Dietz & Co. Inc., 1978—. Vice pres. Anne Arundel County Young Democrats, 1974; lobbyist Md. Gen. Assembly, 1973-74; pres. Glen Burnie chpt. Am. Cancer Soc., 1978. Served with USAF, 1961-64. Mem. Nat., Md. assns. realtors, Anne Arundel County Bd. Realtors (v.p. 1973, pres. asso. div. 1972, Salesman of Year 1972), Anne Arundel County Million Dollar Sales Club (charter pres. 1975), Million Dollar Sales Assn. Democrat. Roman Catholic. Home: 506 Glenview Ave Glen Burnie MD 21061 Office: 420 Crain Hwy SW Glen Burnie MD 21061

WOODSIDE, ROBERT BRUCE, ofcl. Dept. Army; b. Wellsburg, W.Va., Nov. 24, 1913; s. Charles Sidman and Ida (Blakley) W.; student U. Md., 1956; m. Charlotte Melvina Murray, Dec. 29, 1940; children—Robert Bruce, Sandra Joan. Served with Signal Corps, U.S. Army, 1936-57, commd. 2d lt., 1942, advanced through grades to maj., 1950, advanced to lt. col. Res., 1959; chief Tng. Div., U.S. Army Signal Unit Survey, 1957-60; ret., 1960; electronic technician U.S. Army Signal Air Def. Engring. Agy., Ft. George G. Meade, Md., 1960-63; communication specialist Air Def., U.S. Army Strategic Communications Command, 1963-66; action officer dir. individual tng. dep. chief of staff for personnel, 1966-72; chief Army Mil. Affiliate Radio System, 1972-73; chief Telecommunications Automation Br., asst. chief of staff for communications electronics Automation Br., Fixed Communications Div., Communications System Directorate, Washington, 1973-75; dir. Eastern Area Army Mil. Affiliate Radio System, 1975—. Decorated Bronze Star medal; recipient Army Dept. Civilian Personnel Sustained Superior Performance award, 1961, Civilian Personnel Outstanding Achievement award, 1971; Outstanding Achievement award Nat. Sojourners, 1968. Mem. Nat. Sojourners (chpt. pres. 1962, comdr. 1963). Mason (K.T., Shriner). Home: 615 Carolyn Rd Glen Burnie MD 21061

WOOD-SMITH, DONALD, plastic surgeon; b. Sydney, Australia, June 30, 1931; s. William Frederick and Vera Mary; M.B., B.S., Sydney U., 1954; m. Lelia Christine, June 14, 1975; children—Christina Margaret, Donald William, Phillip Raynor. Surg. resident Lewisham Hosp., Sydney, 1954-56, Royal Marsden Hosp. and Royal Coll. Surgeons, Engl., 1957-58; resident plastic surgery N.Y. U. Hosp. Med. Center, 1960— 64, asst. and asso. attending surgeon, 1964—; vis. surgeon Bellevue Hosp., 1964—; chmn. plastic surgery Manhattan Eye Ear and Throat Hosp., 1975-77; asso. prof. plastic surgery N.Y. U., 1977—; surgeon, dir. plastic surgery Manhattan Eye Ear and Throat Hosp., 1977—; cons. plastic surgeon N.Y. Eye and Ear Infirmary. Diplomate Am. Bd. Plastic Surgery. Fellow A.C.S., Royal Coll. Surgeons of Edinburgh; mem. Am. Assn. Plastic Surgeons, Am. Soc. Plastic and Reconstructive Surgeons, Am. Soc. Maxillofacial Surgeons, Transplantation Soc., N.Y. Acad. Medicine, Brit. Assn. Plastic Surgeons. Republican. Clubs: N.Y. Athletic. Author: Nursing Care of the Plastic Surgery Patient, 1967; Cosmetic Facial Surgery, 1973; contbr. articles to med. jours. Office: 136 E 64th St New York City NY 10021

WOODWARD, JOHN THOMAS, elec. engr.; b. Balt., Feb. 7, 1939; s. Joseph Janiver and Amelie (DiPierron) W.; engring. certificate Johns Hopkins U., 1959, B.S. in Elec. Engring., 1964; m. Margaret Jean Zepp, Sept. 1, 1960; children—John Thomas, Mary Jennifer, Joseph Patrick (dec.), Margaret Joanne. Engr., Westinghouse Co., Balt., 1956-65; system engr. Vitro, Washington, 1965-66; project mgr. TRW Systems, Washington, 1966-69; program mgr. Gen. Electric Co., Syracuse, N.Y., 1969-71, mgr. advanced programs, Phila., 1971-73; sr. engr./scientist IBM, Gaithersburg, Md., 1973—. Mem. IEEE, Computer Soc. of IEEE, Am. Def. Preparedness Assn. Roman Catholic. Clubs: Lions. Patentee. Home: 28405 Honeysuckle Dr Damascus MD 20750 Office: 18100 Frederick Pike Gaithersburg MD 20760

WOODWARD, ROBERT BURNS, educator; b. Boston, Apr. 10, 1917; s. Arthur Chester and Margaret (Burns) W.; B.S., Mass. Inst. Tech., 1936, Ph.D., 1937; Sc.D. (hon.), Wesleyan U., Middletown, Conn., 1945, Victoria U., Manchester, Eng., 1954, Bucknell U., 1955., U. N.B. (Can.), 1956, Yale, 1956, Harvard, 1957, U. So. Calif., 1959, U. Chgo., 1961, New Eng. Coll. Pharmacy, 1961, Colby Coll., 1963, U. Cambridge (Eng.), 1964, Brandeis U., 1956, Stonehill Coll., 1966, U. Sheffield (Eng.), 1966; Israel Inst. Tech. (Haifa), 1966, Poly. Inst. Bklyn., 1967, U. Western Ont. (Can.), 1968, Columbia, 1969, U. Louvain (Belgium), 1970, U. Pierre and Marie Curie of Paris, 1975, U. St. Andrews (Scotland), 1976, U. London, 1976; LL.D., U. Glasgow, 1966; Dr. Tech. wiss., Eidg. Tech. Hochschule, Switzerland, 1967; A.M. (hon.), Harvard, 1946; m. Irja Pullman, July 30, 1938; children—Siiri Anne, Jean Kirsten; m. 2d, Eudoxia M. M. Muller, Sept. 14, 1946; children—Crystal Elizabeth, Eric Richard Arthur. Post doctoral fellow Harvard, 1937-38, mem. soc. fellows, 1938-40, from instr. to prof., 1941-50, Morris Loeb prof. chemistry, 1953-60, Donner prof. sci., 1960—; dir. Woodward Research Inst., Basel, Switzerland, 1963—; cons. chem. mfrs., also Polaroid Corp., 1942—, Chas. Pfizer & Co., Inc., 1951-70, also dir. Hon. lectr. many orgns.; Am. Swiss Found. lectr., 1948; Harrison Howe lectr., 1950; Centenary lectr. Chem. Soc. London, 1951; Stieglitz lectr., 1952; Edgar Fahs Smith Meml. lectr., 1959; Harvard lectr. at Yale, 1959; Morrell lectr. Cambridge U., 1959, Alexander Todd prof. Chemistry Christ's Coll., 1973-74, also fellow, 1973-74; lectr. Leermakers Symposium, Wesleyan U., 1972; synthesized quinine, 1944, patulin, 1950, cholesterol, 1951, cortisone, 1951, strychnine, 1954, lysergic acid, 1954, lanosterol, 1954, reserpine, 1956; deduced structure penicillin, 1945, strychnine, 1947, terramycin and aureomycin, 1952, ferrocene, 1952, cevine, 1954, magnamycin, 1956, synthesized chlorophyll, 1960, tetracycline, 1962, Colchicine, 1963, cephalosporin C, 1965, vitamin B12, 1972, Prostaglandins, 1972, streptonigrin, 1963, tetrodotoxin, 1964, oleandomycin, 1960. Mem. corp. Mass. Inst. Tech., 1966-71. Decorated Order of Rising Sun (Japan), 1970; recipient John Scott medal, 1946, Baekeland medal, 1955; Ledlie prize, 1955; Research Corp. award, 1955; Nichols medal, 1956; Theodore William Richards medal, 1956; Synthetic Organic Chemistry award, 1957, Roger Adams award, 1961 (both Am. Chem. Soc.), Davy medal, 1959; Willard Gibbs medal Chgo. sect. Am. Chem. Soc., 1957; Pius XI gold medal Pontifical Acad. Scis., 1961; Dickinson Coll. Priestley medallion, 1962; Synthetic Organic Chem. Mfrs. Assn. medal for creative research in synthetic organic chemistry, 1962; Nat. Medal of Sci., 1964; Nobel prize in chemistry, 1965; Lavoisier medal Société Chimique de France, 1968; Hanbury Meml. medal Pharm. Soc. Gt. Britain, 1970; Pierre Bruylant's medal U. Louvain, 1970; Sci. Achievement award A.M.A., 1971; Dr. B.C. Law Gold Medal Indian Assn. for Cultivation Sci., 1972; Arthur C. Cope award Am. Chem. Soc., 1973; Copley medal Royal Soc., 1978. Fellow The Chem. Soc. (hon.), Weizmann Inst. Sci. (hon.), Indian Nat. Sci. Acad. (fgn.), Royal Soc. Edinburgh (hon.), Indian Chem. Soc. (hon.), Indian Acad. Sci. (hon.), Am. Acad. Arts and Scis.; mem. German (hon.), Belgian (hon.), Swiss chem. socs., Royal Soc. (fgn.), Royal Irish Acad. (hon.), Austrian Acad. Scis. (corr.), Am. Philos. Soc., Nat., N.Y. (hon. life) acads. scis., Deutsche Akademie der Naturforscher (Leopoldina), Accademia Nazionale dei Lincei (fgn. mem.), Pharm. Soc., Japan (hon.), Pharm. Soc. Gt. Britain (hon.), Harvey Soc. N.Y. (hon.), Royal Instn. Gt. Britain (hon.), Yugoslav Acad. Scis. and Arts (fgn.), Acad. Scis. and Inst. France (fgn.), Spanish Royal Soc. Physics and Chemistry (hon.), Royal Acad. Scis. of Spain (fgn.), Acad. Scis. USSR (fgn.), Phi Lambda Upsilon (hon.). Office: Dept of Chemistry Harvard University 12 Oxford St Cambridge MA 02138

WOODWARD, RONALD EDWIN, architect; b. Bklyn., Jan. 22, 1926; s. John Edwin and Elizabeth (Sprigg) W.; B.S. in Mech.Engring., Rensselaer Poly. Inst., 1947, B.Arch., 1949, M.Arch., 1951; postgrad. U. Liverpool (Eng.), 1952-53; m. Adelaide Stephenson Doyle, May 29, 1954; children—Robin, Anne, John. Draftsman Eggers & Higgins, Architects, N.Y.C., 1954, R.C. Brugnoni, Architect, N.Y.C., 1955-56; asso. Holden Egan Wilson & Corser, Architects & Planners, N.Y.C., 1956-64; prin. Ronald Woodward, AIA, 1956—; supervising architect Burns & Roe, Inc., Woodbury, N.Y., 1964-73; asst. dir. Roe Assos., 1973-75, dir., 1975—. Served as lt. USNR, 1951-52; Korea. Fulbright fellow, Eng., 1952-53. Mem. AIA (tech. com., nat. council continuing edn. 1973—, chmn. N.Y. State continuing edn. com.), Am. Arbitration Assn. (nat. panel of arbitors), Sigma Xi, Pi Tau Sigma. Episcopalian (commn. on architecture diocese of L.I., warden). Prin. archtl. works include: Life Support Tech. Lab. for NASA, 1965; Parish Hall, Shelter Island, N.Y., 1968; Mercer Meml. Library, Garden City, N.Y., 1975. Home: 58 St James St S Garden City NY 11530 Office: 415 Crossways Park Dr Woodbury NY 11797

WOODWORTH, HUGH, JR., obstetrician, gynecologist; b. Syracuse, N.Y., July 16, 1931; s. Hugh and Jane (Baxter) W.; B.A., St. Lawrence U., 1953; M.D., State U. N.Y., Syracuse, 1962; M.S., Mayo Clinic, 1966; m. Karen Burgess, Oct. 20, 1962; children—Jeffrey, William, Jennifer, Melissa, Richard. Intern State U. N.Y. at Syracuse, 1962-63; resident Mayo Clinic, Rochester, Minn., 1963-66; practice medicine specializing in obstetrics and gynecology, Rochester, N.Y.; mem. staffs Rochester Gen., Highland hosps. Served with USN, 1954-56. Mem. Am. Coll. Obstetricians and Gynecologists, Med. Soc. N.Y., AMA, Monroe County Med. Soc. Mormon. Office: 625 Panorama Trail Rochester NY 14625

WOODWORTH, JAMES ANTHONY, civil engr.; b. Jamestown, N.Y., Mar. 31, 1952; s. Paul David and Christine R. Woodworth; B.S. in Civil Engring., Mich. Tech. U., Houghton, 1975. Civil engr. trainee Pa. Dept. Transp., 1971-74; project engr. Northwest Engring., Inc., Tidioute, Pa., 1975—. E.I.T. certificate. Mem. ASCE. Address: RD 6 Martin Rd Jamestown NY 14701

WOODYER, PETER JOHN, veterinarian; b. Bristol, Eng., July 31, 1938; s. William and Hilda Ellen (Brinton) W.; immigrated to Can., 1967, naturalized, 1976; W.; B.Vet. Med., Royal Vet. Coll., London, 1966; m. Patricia Anne A'Court, June 3, 1967; children—Peter Javier, Timothy Paul, Jennifer Margaret. Gen. vet. practice, Truro, N.S., 1966-67; large animal practice, Shubenacadie, N.S., 1967-69; small animal practice, Halifax, N.S., 1969-70, Dartmouth, N.S., 1970—; pres. Harbour Cities Vet. Hosp.; cons. in field. Mem. Royal Coll. Vet. Surgeons, Brit. Vet. Assn., Canadian, N.S. (sec. 1977) vet. med. assns., Brit. Small Animal Vet. Assn., Am. Animal Hosp. Assn. Mem. Ch. of Eng. Home: Compartment 12 Site 56 Bedford RR2 NS B0N 1B0 Canada Office: 32 Pelzant St Dartmouth NS B3A 3B3 Canada

WOOLF, HOWARD IRVIN, optometrist; b. Balt., Oct. 20, 1942; s. Gerson M. and Ina (Gray) W.; B.S., U. Md., 1963; Optometry D., Ill. Coll. Optometry, 1964-67; m. Barbara L. Etelson, Aug. 10, 1965; children—Michael Aaron, Brian Todd. Practice optometry, Pasadena, Md., 1967—; staff optometrist Comprehensive Child Care Clinic, Johns Hopkins Hosp., Balt., 1968—, Columbia (Md.) Hosp. and Clinics, 1969-71; clin. dir. Optometric Center Md., Balt., 1968-75; lectr. Sch. Nursing, Johns Hopkins Hosp., faculty Sch. for Health Services, 1976-78. Mem. Regional Planning Com. Comprehensive Health Planning, 1969—. Mem. Greater Balt. Optometric Soc. (sec. 1969-70), Am., Md. (treas. 1970-73, dir. 1971—), Anne Arundel (pres. 1973—) optometric assns., Ill. Coll. Optometry Alumni Assn. (dir. 1971—, pres. 1973—), Md. Zool. Soc., Phi Theta Upsilon. Lion (sight chmn. 1968—). Home: 2110 Carterdale Rd Baltimore MD 21209 Office: 2714 Mountain Rd Pasadena MD 21122

WOOLF, LEON M., social service adminstr., educator; b. Balt., Apr. 17, 1932; s. Israel H. and Ida B. (Sachs) W.; B.A., Yeshiva Coll., 1954, M.S.W., 1957; postgrad. Johns Hopkins U., 1973-74; m. Sara Lee Texer, Mar. 29, 1959; children—Marc A., Joel M., Jonathan S. Dir. sr. adult dept. Jewish Community Center, Balt., 1957-64, also dir. group work services, 1962-64; exec. dir. Met. Sr. Citizens Center, Balt., 1964-74; dep. dir. Balt. City Commn. on Aging and Retirement Edn., 1974—; dir. Waxter Center for Sr. Citizens, Balt., 1974—; asst. prof. therapeutic programming for aged U. Balt., 1975—; lectr. Community Coll. of Balt., 1970, Duke U., 1976—, U. Wis., 1974—; asst. prof. Morgan State U., 1978; retirement edn. seminars, Social Security Adminstrn., Washington, 1969; cons. to HEW, Am. Hosp. Assn.; Md. state del. to White House Conf. on Aging, 1971; mem. adv. com. to Office of Continuing Edn. of Coll. Notre Dame, Md., 1972-74. Staff dir. Citizens Com. for 1967 Waxter Center Bond Issue; mem. adv. com. Downtown Retail Dist. Study, 1976—; mem. mayor's Planning Com. on Nutrition Programs for the Elderly, 1972-74; mem. bd. advisers Model Cities Demonstration Project, Balt., 1968-70; bd. dirs. Foster Grandparents Program, Balt., 1974—; trustee Ret. Sr. Vol. Program, Balt., 1973—. Recipient Sommers award Yeshiva U., 1957. Mem. Nat. Inst. Sr. Centers (chmn. 1977—, regional del. 1971-75), Nat. Council on Aging (mem. bd.), Gerontol. Soc. Democrat. Jewish. Club: Advt. of Balt. Contbr. articles on gerontology and pub. welfare to profl. publs. Home: 3510 Labyrinth Rd Baltimore MD 21215 Office: 861 Park Ave Baltimore MD 21201

WOOLLEY, ALBAN EDWARD, JR., editor, photographer, author; b. ElDorado, Ark., Sept. 26, 1926; s. Alban Edward and Ira (Sawyer) W.; student La. State U., 1950-53; B.A., Goddard Coll., 1970, M.A., 1972; m. Dorothy C. McInnis, June 1952; m. 2d, Dorothy Ellen Riley, Nov. 1964 (div. 1977); children—Wynne, Michael, Jill, Amy, Alban Edward III, Daniel. Journalist, 1952-58, 61-67; adj. prof. dept. arts and scis. La. State U., 1954-58; asso. prof. State U. N.Y., New Paltz, 1958-61; asso. dir. spl. edn. New Paltz, 1967-68; photography editor Pageant Mag., N.Y.C., 1969-71; mng. editor Today's Health, Chgo., 1971-74; dir. pub. info. Mt. St. Mary Coll., Newburgh, N.Y., 1975-76; pres. Corsair Communications, New Paltz, N.Y., 1974—; editor Jour. Internat. Physicians, 1976-77; editorial dir. Lab. World Mag., Phila., 1977—; cons. N.Y. State Edn. Dept., 1967-69; exhibited 23 one-man photog. shows; photographs represented in permanent collections George Eastman House, Mus. Modern Art, Dartmouth Coll., La. Art Commn., State U. N.Y., La. State U. Democratic candidate N.Y. State Senate, 1968. Served with AUS, 1945-46. Recipient Jesse H. Neal editorial excellence award Am. Bus. Press, 1978. Mem. Soc. Photog. Educators, Nat. Press Photographers Assn., Am. Soc. Mag. Photographers, Photographers in Communication. Clubs: Explorers (N.Y.C.), Rotary Internat. Author 18 books on photography, 1963-75, including: Persia/Iran, Photography: A Practical and Creative Introduction; Creative 35mm Techniques, Photography. Editor at large Contemporary Photographer, 1959-61; contbg. editor PTN Publs., 1967-70. Home: 803 Edgemoor Rd Cherry Hill NJ 08034

WOOLWORTH, RICHARD GRISWOLD, recreational products mfg. co. exec.; b. Lancaster, Pa., Nov. 1, 1929; s. Chester McNutt and May (Gorton) W.; B.A., Dartmouth Coll., 1951; m. Helen Temple Baker, Dec. 29, 1950; children—Richard Griswold, Andrew B., Sally K., Louise G. Asst. to pres. Animal Trap Co. of Am. (Woodstream Corp. since 1966), Lititz, Pa., 1951-52, sec., 1954-64, v.p., 1958-64, pres., 1964—, chmn. bd., 1977—; chmn. bd. Hampden Color & Chem. Co., Springfield, Mass., 1974—; dir. Donsco, Inc., Wrightsville, Pa., 1973—, Fulton Bank, Lancaster, 1971—. Bd. dirs. Lancaster Gen. Hosp., 1966—, Windward Travel Center, Lancaster, 1975—, Greater Lancaster Corp., 1975—. Served with USAF, 1951-52. Mem. Young Pres. Orgn. Republican. Episcopalian. Clubs: Lancaster Country, Hamilton; Pine Valley (N.J.) Golf; Lyford Cay (Nassau); Metropolitan (Chgo.). Home: 1501 Clayton Rd Lancaster PA 17603 Office: 69 N Front St Lititz PA 17543

WOOTEN, RONALD LEE, lawyer; b. Bluefield, W.Va., Apr. 20, 1945; s. Jesse Willard and Beatrice (Boone) W.; B.A. in Economics, B.A. in History, Emory and Henry Coll., 1968; J.D., Memphis State U., 1972; m. Carol Ruth Campbell, June 22, 1968; children—Robert Lee, Caroline Campbell. Operating engr. U.S. Steel Corp., Uniontown, Pa., 1973-74, mine operating engr., 1974-75; asst. legis. counsel Am. Mining Congress, Washington, D.C., 1975-76, asst. gen. counsel, 1976-77, sr. counsel, / 1977—. Dir., Frick Dist. Fed. Employees Credit Union, 1974-75. Mem. Mine Inspectors Inst. of Am., Am. Inst. Mining Engrs., Delta Theta Phi. Home: 9358 Birchwood Ct Manassas VA 22110 Office: 1100 Ring Bldg Washington DC 20036

WORBOIS, ROBERT JOHN, mech. engr.; b. Chili, N.Y., Sept. 1, 1923; s. Wallace Edson and Grace Lenora (Smith) W.; B.S., U. Rochester, 1950; postgrad. Ill. Inst. Tech., 1950-52; m. Lois Evelyn Butler, Feb. 3, 1951; children—James Robert, Cheryl Ellen, John David, Susanne Grace, Allen Thomas. Pneumatic engr. Westinghouse Air Brake Co., Wilmerding, Pa., 1952, test engr., 1953-60, supervising test engr., 1960—. Served with USAAF, 1943-45. Decorated Air Medal with 5 oak leaf clusters, D.F.C. Mem. ASME, Rwy. Fuel and Operating Officers Assn. Republican. Methodist. Club: Gideons Internat. Patentee in field. Home: 269 Brownstown Rd North Huntingdon PA 15642 Office: Westinghouse Air Brake Co Wilmerding PA 15148

WORDEN, FREDERIC GARFIELD, neuroscientist, educator; b. Syracuse, N.Y., Mar. 22, 1918; s. Vivien S. and Alice Garfield (Davis) W.; A.B., Dartmouth Coll., 1939; M.D., U. Chgo., 1942; m. Katharine Cole, Jan. 8, 1944; children—Frederic, Dwight, Philip, Barbara, Katharine. Intern, Osler Med. Clinic, Johns Hopkins Hosp., Balt., 1942-43, house officer Henry Phipps Psychiat. Clinic, 1943, house officer to chief resident, 1946-50; asst. in psychiatry, Commonwealth Found. fellow Johns Hopkins Med. Sch., 1946-48, instr. psychiatry, 1949-52; tng. Balt. Psychoanalytic Inst., 1947-53; clin. dir. Sheppard and Enoch Pratt Hosp., Towson, Md., 1950-52, supr. therapy, 1952-53; research psychiatrist, prof. psychiatry Med. Sch., U. Calif. at Los Angeles, 1953-69, head div. adult psychiatry, 1968-69; prof. psychiatry, dir. neuroscis. research program Mass. Inst. Tech., 1969—. Mem. research scientist devel. rev. com. Nat. Inst. Mental Health; mem. com. on brain scis. NRC. Bd. dirs. Founds. Fund for Research in Psychiatry. Served to maj. AUS, 1943-46. Diplomate Am. Bd. Psychiatry and Neurology, Nat. Bd. Med. Examiners. Fellow Am. Acad. Arts and Scis.; mem. Am. Psychiat. Assn. (chmn. task force on research tng. council on med. edn. and devel.), Soc. for Neurosci. (chmn. program com. 1972), Acoustical Soc. Am., AAAS, Am. Psychoanalytic Assn., Brain Research Inst., Psychiat. Research Soc., N.Y. Acad. Scis., Los Angeles Psychoanalytic Inst., Los Angeles Psychoanalytic Soc. Clubs: St. Botolph (Boston). Author: (with R. Galambos) Auditory Processing of Biologically Significant Sounds, 1972; (with F.O. Schmitt) The Neurosciences: Third Study Program, 1974; also numerous research publs. in psychiatry, neurophysiology. Home: 45 Hilltop Rd Weston MA 02193 Office: 165 Allandale St Jamaica Plain Sta Boston MA 02130

WORDEN, KATHARINE COLE, sculptor; b. N.Y.C., May 4, 1925; d. Philip Gillette and Katharine (Pyle) Cole; student Potters Sch., Tucson, 1940-42, Sarah Lawrence Coll., 1942-44; m. Frederic G. Worden, Jan. 8, 1944; children—Rick, Dwight, Philip, Barbara,

Katharine. Sculptor, works exhibited Royce Galleries, Galerie Francoise Besnard (Paris), Cooling Gallery (London), Galerie Schumacher (Munich), Selected Artists Gallery, N.Y.C., Art Inst. Boston, Reid Gallery, Nashville, Weiner Gallery, N.Y.C.; works permanently exhibited Royce Galleries, Gilcrease Mus. (Tulsa), Galerie des Capucines (Paris), pvt. collections Grand Palais (Paris), Dakar and Bathurst, Africa. Occupational therapist psychopathic ward Los Angeles County Gen. Hosp., 1953-57; Headstart vol., Watts, Calif., 1965-67; tchr. sculpture Watts Towers Art Center, 1967-69; participant White House Women Doers Luncheon meeting, 1968; dir. Cambridgeport Problem Center, Cambridge, Mass., 1969-71; mem. Jud. Nominating Commn., 1976—; bd. overseers Boston Mus. Fine Arts, 1978; trustee Communication Research Inst., Miami, Fla., 1960-69, chmn. bd., 1966-69; bd. dirs. Boston Center for Arts. Mem. Common Cause (Mass. adv. bd. 1971-72, dir. 1974-75), Mass. Civil Liberties Union (exec. bd. 1973-74, dir. 1976-77). Home: 45 Hilltop Rd Weston MA 02193

WORKMAN, CLARK RAYMOND, mfg. co. exec.; b. Chgo., May 2, 1943; s. Raymond Arthur and Gertrude Kathrine (Beese) W.; B.S., Fairleigh Dickinson U., 1965, postgrad., 1965-70; m. Maria Bazaz, Nov. 25, 1965; children—Christine Ellen, Steven Clark. Br. mgr. Gen. Electric Credit Corp., Irvington, N.J., 1965-68; sales rep., Xerox Corp., N.Y.C., 1968-70, sales mgr., 1970-72, controller N.Y. br., 1972-74; br. mgr., regional mgr. east Saxon Bus. Products Co., N.Y.C., 1974-76; dir. br. ops. U.S.A., Toshiba Am. Inc., N.Y.C., Am. Mgmt. Assn. K.C. Home: 80 Prospect Ave Westwood NJ 07675 Office: Toshiba Am Inc 3 Park Ave New York City NY 10016

WORLEY, JOSEPH FRANCIS, plant pathologist; b. Washington, Oct. 10, 1928; s. Joseph Frank and Lottie Ema (Carson) W.; B.S., George Washington U., 1955, M.S., 1958, Ph.D., 1965; m. Anita Stouffer, June 6, 1958. Plant pathologist U.S. Dept. Agr., Beltsville, Md., 1956—. Served with AUS, 1950-51. Mem. Am. Phytopath. Soc., Bot. Soc. Am., Am. Soc. Plant Physiologists, Sigma Xi, Phi Beta Phi. Contbr. articles to profl. jours. Home: 10500 Rockville Pike Rockville MD 20852 Office: Beltsville Agrl Research Center West Beltsville MD 20705

WORLEY, ROBERT ELTON, engring. co. exec., environ. specialist; b. Dry Run, Pa., May 17, 1926; s. Thomas Elton and Grace C. W.; grad. in San. Engring., Internat. Corr. Sch., 1969; grad. microbiology HEW, Cin., 1974; m. Marion M. Sharp, Nov. 4, 1947; children—Ronald, Dianne Worley McNew, Roberta Worley Finley. Operator, Borough of Chambersburg (Pa.), 1948-59, lab. technician, 1959-66, water and wastewater supt., 1966-72; chief water-sewage ops. Arrowood Inc., Chambersburg, 1972—; condr. tng. sessions Pa. Dept. Community Affairs. Served with inf. U.S. Army, 1944-46; CIB, ETO. Mem. Water Pollution Control Assn. (certified), Am. Water Works Assn. (certified), Nat. Environ. Tng. Assn., Water Pollution Control Operators Assn. (chmn. certification central sect., pres. 1972) Democrat. Mem. Brethren Ch. Clubs: Am. Legion, V.F.W. Research in environment, especially water supply distbn. and wastewater plant discharge. Home: 11 E Orange St Shippensburg PA 17257 Office: Arrowood Inc 2400 Philadelphia Ave Chambersburg PA 17201

WORMER, DONALD ANDREW, surgeon; b. Olean, N.Y., Aug. 26, 1927; s. Duncan Lee and Catharine Anne W.; A.B., U. Rochester, 1950; M.D., U. Buffalo, 1955; m. Elinor Ann Bliss, July 11, 1953; children—Carol, Thomas, Susan, Julie. Intern, Millard Fillmore Hosp., Buffalo, 1955-56, resident surgery, 1956-59, chief resident surgery, 1959-60; chief surgery St. Francis Hosp., Olean, N.Y., 1975—. Served with U.S. Army, 1946-47. Diplomate Am. Bd. Surgery. Mem. AMA, N.Y. State Med. Assn., N.Y. State Soc. Surgeons, Cattaraugus County Med. Soc. Republican. Presbyterian. Home: 32 Maple Ave Portville NY 14770 Office: 9 Temple St Portville NY 14770

WORMSER, ALEX FRANCIS, engring. co. exec.; b. Frankfurt, Germany, July 25, 1932; s. Otto R. and Elizabeth F. (Boehm) W.; came to U.S., 1940, naturalized, 1944; B.E. in Mech. Engring., Yale U., 1954; m. Elizabeth V.S. Emerson, Dec. 26, 1964; children—Andrew, Matthew, Julia. Devel. engr. Gen. Electric Co., Lynn, Mass., 1957-64; founder, pres. Wingaersheek, Inc., Peabody, Mass., 1964-71, engring. mgr., 1971-74; founder, pres. Wormser Engring., Inc., Lynn, Mass., 1974—; chmn. bd. Wingaersheek, Inc. Served with USAF, 1954-56. Mem. Am. Inst. Chem. Engrs., Combustion Inst., Air Pollution Control Assn. Patentee field of combustion. Home: 24 High St Marblehead MA 01945 Office: 212 S Main St Middleton MA 01949

WORNE, HOWARD EDWARD, chem. co. exec.; b. Phila., Mar. 1, 1914; s. Edward H. and Lillian G. (Greene) W.; B.S., U. Mex., 1938; M.D., Universidad Libre Mexicana, 1940; Ph.D. in Biochemistry, Instituto Polytechnico Nacional, 1962; m. Phyllis Dolores Garofalo, Sept. 14, 1962; 1 dau., Elinor D. Pres., Nat. Solvents Corp., Elizabeth, N.J., 1942-45; v.p. Synthetic Resins, Inc., Toms River, N.J., 1943-47; v.p. Pentavir div. A.P. DeSanno & Sons, Phoenixville, Pa., 1947-48; sci. dir. Robinson Found., N.Y.C., 1950-55; pres. Pharm. Industries, Inc., Cherry Hill, N.J., 1955-62; pres. Enzymes, Inc., Cherry Hill, 1963-72, dir. Enzymes Japan, Inc., 1969-76; pres. Worne Biochems. Inc., Berlin, N.J., 1973—, chmn. bd., 1973—; chmn. bd. Worne Biochems., Europe, Ltd., 1976—, Bioferm Internat., Fermentation Industries, Biotech. de P.R. Nat. Grain Yeast Corp fellow, 1935-37. Mem. Am. Chem. Soc., N.J. Acad. Sci., N.Y. Acad. Sci., AAAS, Pan Am. Med. Assn., Soc. Cosmetic Chemists, Fed. Water Pollution Control Assn. Republican. Presbyterian. Author: Soil Microbiology, 1975; editor in chief Archives of Research, 1953-55; contbr. sci. papers in field to profl. jours.; patentee in field. Home: 205 Sunny Jim Dr Medford NJ 08055 Office: Lyon Industrial Park RTE 73 Berlin NJ 08009

WORONICK, SIMON ANTHONY, quality control technician; b. Meriden, Conn., Feb. 16, 1937; s. Simon Anthony and Stella (Bykowski) W.; ed. high sch.; m. Florence Kawecki, Dec. 28, 1963; children—Simon, Michael, David, Elizabeth Ann. Shipping supr. prodn. control Miller Co., 1962-71; staff receiving shipping Towle Mfg. Co., 1972-76; quality control technician clin. diagnostics Union Carbide Co., 1976—. Served with U.S. Army, 1960-62. Mem. Meriden Jaycees (life), Am. Def. Preparedness Assn. Roman Catholic. Home: 68 Pleasant St Meriden CT 06450

WORRAL, GORDON JAMES, publishing co. exec.; b. Toledo, Dec. 21, 1923; s. William and Ruth Irene (Tippett) W.; grad. high sch.; m. Mary Winona Winch, Oct. 16, 1948; children—Donald James, Douglas Walter, David William, Kevin Lewis, Bernard Martin. Printer apprentice William Worral Typesetting, Kenmore, N.Y., 1941-42; sec.-treas. West Side Pub. Co., Inc., 1946-62, pres., 1962-73; editor, pub. Riverside Rev., Buffalo, 1967—; pres. Worral Pub., Inc., Buffalo, 1973—. Pres., dir. Printing Industries Assn., Buffalo, 1969-70. Mem. Urban Waterfront Adv. Com. Western N.Y., 1975-76; pres., bd. dirs. River-Rock Resurgence Corp., 1977-78. Mem. Riverside Businessmen's Assn. (pres. 1972-74, Man of Year award 1974, Workhorse of Year award 1976). Served with AUS, 1943-45. Lutheran (pres. 1959-60; elder 1961-62, treas. 1975-76, del. Mo. Synod Eastern dist. conv. 1976). Kiwanian (pres. 1969-70). Home: 1371 Bowen Rd Elma NY 14059 Office: 946 Hertel Ave Buffalo NY 14216

WORRELL, RICHARD VERNON, physician; b. Bklyn., June 4, 1931; s. John Elmer and Elaine (Callender) W.; B.A., N.Y. U., 1952; M.D., Meharry Med. Coll., 1958; m. Audrey Frances Martiny, June 14, 1958; children—Philip Vernon, Amy Elizabeth. Intern Meharry Med. Coll., Nashville, 1958-59; resident gen. surgery Mercy-Douglass Hosp., Phila., 1960-61; resident orthopaedic surgery State U. N.Y. Buffalo Sch. Medicine Affiliated Hosps., 1961-64; resident in orthopaedic pathology Temple U. Med. Center, Phila., 1966-67; pvt. practice orthopaedic surgery, Phila., 1964-68; asst. prof. acting head div. orthopaedic surgery U. Conn. Sch. Medicine 1968-70; attending orthopaedic surgeon E.J. Meyer Meml. Hosp., Buffalo, Millard Fillmore Hosp., Buffalo, VA Hosp., Buffalo, Buffalo State Hosp.; clin. instr. orthopaedic surgery State U. N.Y. at Buffalo, 1970-74; chief orthopedic surgery VA Hosp., Newington, Conn., 1974—; asst. prof. surgery (orthopaedics) U. Conn. Sch. Medicine, 1974-77, asso. prof., 1977—; cons. in orthopaedic surgery Newington (Conn.) Children's Hosp., 1968-70. Bd. dirs. Big Bros. Greater Hartford. Served to capt. M.C., U.S. Army Res., 1962-69. Recipient certificate of merit for distinguished services to community and for betterment Black Ams., Dictionary Black Am. Biography, 1969. Diplomate Am. Bd. Orthopaedic Surgery, Nat. Bd. Med. Examiners. Fellow A.C.S., Am. Acad. Orthopaedic Surgeons; mem. Pan Am. Med. Assn., Orthopaedic Research Soc., Internat. Soc. Orthopaedic Surgery and Traumatology, Phila. Orthopaedic Soc., Erie County Med. Soc., Med. Soc. State N.Y., AMA, Royal Med Soc. (affiliate). Office: VA Hosp 555 Willard Ave Newington CT 06111

WORSHAM, BERTRAND RAY, psychiatrist; b. Atkins, Ark., Feb. 14, 1926; s. Lewis Henry and Emma Lavada (Burris) W.; B.A., U. Ark., 1951; M.D., 1955; m. Lynne Ellen Reynolds; children—Eric Dickson, Vicki Gayle, Richard Andrew. Intern, Hillcrest Med. Center, Tulsa, 1955-56; resident in psychiatry Menninger Sch. Psychiatry, Topeka, 1956-58; resident psychiatry and neurology U. Okla. Sch. Medicine, Oklahoma City, 1958-59, instr., 1959—; practice medicine specializing in psychiatry, Oklahoma City, 1959—; mem. staff Bapt. Med. Center, Coyne-Campbell, Deaconess, Doctors Gen., Presbyn., Mercy, Okla. U. Sch. Medicine, Children's Meml. hosps. (all Oklahoma City); dir. regional guidance center Okla. Dept. Pub. Health, 1966-70. Cons. Social Security Adminstrn., 1960—, Okla. Health Dept., 1960-73. Elector, Okla. Athletic Hall of Fame, 1969-70; mem. Okla. County Civil Def. Com., 1968-71, Oklahoma City Art Center. Served with USAAF, 1944-46; now comdr. USN Res. Menninger Found. fellow, 1976. Fellow Royal Soc. Health (Eng.), World Fedn. for Mental Helath; mem. AMA, So. Med. Assn., Am. Psychiat. Assn., Menninger Sch. Psychiatry Alumni Assn., U.S. Naval Inst., U.S. Navy League, Nat. Trust for Historic Preservation, Okla. Sci. and Arts Found., Okla. City Symphony Soc., Okla. Heritage Assn., Internat. Platform Assn., Res. Officers Assn. U.S., U.S. Naval Res. Assn., Am. Internat. biog. assns., Am. Security Council (nat. advisory bd., commemorative medal), Oklahoma City C. of C., Assn. Mil. Order of World Wars, Assn. Mil. Surgeons U.S. Home: 8068 Central Park Dr Alexandria VA 22309 Office: VA Hosp 50 Irving St NW Washington DC 20422

WORTHINGTON, ROBERT MELVIN, educator; b. Sask., Can., May 31, 1922; s. Charles Cleveland and Louesa Carolena (Gutman) W.; B.S. in Indsl. Arts, Eastern Ky. Coll., 1948, LL.D., 1972; M.A. in Indsl. Edn., U. Minn., 1949, Ph.D. in Edn., 1958; L.H.D., Lincoln U., 1973; m. Margaret E. Ward, Oct. 23, 1946; children—Robert W. (dec.), Charles F., Mary S., Steven L., Anne L. Instr. machine shop and drafting St. Paul High Schs., 1949-52; instr. mfg. processes Sch. Engring., Purdue U., 1952-53; teaching asst. U. Minn., 1953-54, instr. indsl. edn., 1954-56; indsl. edn. supr. Minn. Dept. Edn., 1956-58; prof., chmn. dept. indsl. edn. and tech. Trenton (N.J.) State Coll., 1958-65; asst. commr. edn., div. vocational edn. N.J. Dept. Edn., 1965-71; asso. commr. for adult, vocational and tech. edn. U.S. Office Edn., Washington, 1971-73; vis. prof. edn. Grad. Sch. Edn. Rutgers U., 1973—; chmn. Career Devel. Assos., Inc., Princeton, N.J. Vis. prof. vocat. edn. U. Mo., Columbia, 1975-76. Cons. St. Francis Vocational Sch. Curriculum and Facilities, Archdiocese of Phila., 1963-67, manpower devel. and tng. for sch. dropouts Bedford YMCA, Bklyn., 1964-66, Mass. Dept. Edn., 1976, Appalachian Regional Commn., 1976, Nat. Adv. Council on Career Edn. Instr., instr. trainer Minn. Firearms Safety Program, 1954-55; mem. Minn. Gov.'s Conf. on Children and Youth, 1956; mem. Pres.'s Com. Employment Handicapped; commr. Ewing Twp. Indsl. and Comml. Devel. Commn., 1963; chmn. Nat. Task Force Edn. and Tng. Minority Bus. Enterprise, 1972-74; mem. N.J. Adv. Council Vocational Edn., 1978. Served to 1st lt. USAAF, 1942-47. Recipient Outstanding Achievement award Regents of U. Minn., 1975; named Educator of Year, 1970, Outstanding Alumnus Eastern Ky. U., 1972. Mem. Am. Vocational Assn. (life, past com. chmn., past v.p. N.J. sect., sec., vice chmn. Council for Tchr. Edn.), Nat. Assn. Indsl. Tech. Tchr. Educators (past pres., hon. life mem.), Am. Ednl. Research Assn., Am. Assn. Sch. Adminstrs., Am. Indsl. Arts Assn. Epsilon Pi Tau, Phi Delta Kappa, Iota Lambda Sigma, Mu Iota Epsilon, Alpha Psi Omega. Sr. author: General Power Mechanics; Careers—An Overview, 1976; co-author: Protecting the Vision of Children. Toastmaster. Editor: Jour. of Indsl. Tchr. Edn., 1964-66. Editorial bd. Edn. Digest, 1970, 75, Sch. Shop Mag., 1966-69, Career Edn. Quar.; cons. editor Career Info. Center, 1976. Contbr. articles to profl. jours. Home: 2016 Scenic Dr West Trenton NJ 08628 Office: 1650 Pennington Rd West Trenton NJ 08618

WORTZEL, LAWRENCE HERBERT, educator; b. Newark, Sept. 28, 1932; s. Charles and Sadie (Bornstein) W.; B.S., Rutgers U., 1954; M.B.A. with distinction, Harvard U., 1963, D.B.A., 1967; m. Heidi Pamela Vernon, Dec. 23, 1956; children—Joshua Charles, Jennifer Rachel. Partner, owner 2 pharmacies, N.J., 1957-61; research asst., then research asso. Harvard U., 1963-65; mem. faculty Boston U., 1965—, prof. mktg., 1969—, chmn. dept., 1968-72, 73-75; vis. research prof. Mktg. Sci. Inst., 1976; cons. World Bank, 1978—. Served with AUS, 1956-57. Mem. Am. Mktg. Assn., Assn. Consumer Research, Am. Acad. Internat. Bus. Jewish. Co-author: The Development of Financial Managers, 1971. Contbr. profl. jours.; mem. editorial rev. bd. Jour. Mktg., 1976—. Home: 39 Stafford Rd Newton Centre MA 02159 Office: 226 Bay State Rd Boston MA 02215

WOSINSKI, JOHN FRANCIS, glass industry exec.; b. North Tonawanda, N.Y., Dec. 30, 1930; s. John Joseph and Helen Eve (Wojnicki) W.; B.S. in Geology, Denison U., 1953; M.S. in Geology, Brown U., 1958; m. Jean Adair Smith, June 9, 1956; children—John Smith, Wesley Winston. Geologist U.S. Geol. Survey, Boston, 1956-57; mineralogist Corning (N.Y.) Glass Works, 1958-60, supr. petrographic services, 1961-64, sr. engr. refractories, 1964-65, supr. refractory services, 1965-67, mgr. refractory services, 1967—. Instr. electronics U.S. Army Signal Corps, 1954-56; cons. glass tech. Corning (N.Y.) Mus., 1965-66, U. Mo., Rolla, 1965-66; prin. investigator Apollo 14-15 mission samples, 1971-72. Chmn. Town of Hornby Planning Bd., 1965-67. Served with AUS, 1954-56. Named Outstanding Young Man of Am., U.S. Jr. C. of C., 1969. Mem. Geol. Soc. Am., Am. Ceramic Soc., A.A.A.S., Am. Soc. Testing Materials, Soc. Glass Tech., Geochem. Soc., Internat. Pour L'Historie du Verre, Kappa Sigma, Sigma Xi. Home: POB 432 Corning NY 14830 Office: Corning Glass Works Corning NY 14830

WOZMAK, EUGENE HENRY, dentist; b. Haverhill, Mass., June 11, 1916; s. Frank T. and Mary (Chaplain) W.; Ph.G., Mass. Coll. Pharmacy, 1937; B.S., U. N.H., 1939; D.D.S., U. Pitts., 1944; m. Loretta Murphy, June 10, 1944; 1 son, Robert Francis. Individual practice dentistry Abington, Mass., 1947—. Pres. Health Care Products div. Help Internat., Atlanta; dir. Abington Nat. Bank, Living Sports Internat., Boston. Chmn. pres.'s council U. N.H. Served from pvt. to capt. Dental Corps, USAAF, 1944-47. Mem. ADA, Am. Dental Soc. Anesthesiology, Am. Acad. Implant Dentistry, Mass. Dental Soc. (del.), Am. Acad. Implant Dentistry (sec., pres.; editor newsletter), Am. Assn. Dental Editors, Internat. Platform Assn., N.E. Soc. Clin. Hypnosis, Kappa Psi. Club: Rotary. Mng. editor Jour. Implantology. Home: 98 Highfields Rd Abington MA 02351 Office: 469 Washington St Abington MA 02351

WRAY, EDWARD ORION, JR., nursing adminstr., educator; b. N.Y.C., June 11, 1931; s. Edward Orion and Charlotte Elizabeth (Dooley) W.; diploma Pa. Hosp., 1955; B.S., Columbia U., 1959, M.A., 1960; m. Diana Lonnquist, July 21, 1952; children—Pamela, Edward, Victoria, Gabriella, David. Staff nurse N.Y. Hosp., White Plains, 1955; asst. dir. High Point Hosp., Portchester, N.Y., 1955-56; dir. Milkbank Convalescent Home, Valhalla, N.Y., 1956-58; dir. nursing High Point Hosp., Portchester, N.Y., 1960-64; dir. nursing N.Y. Psychiat. Inst., N.Y.C., 1964-78; adminstr. Rockland Community Mental Health Center, Mt. Vernon, N.Y., 1978—; asst. prof. dept. nursing Columbia U., N.Y.C., 1964-78, asst. prof. dept. psychiatry, 1978—. Mem. Am. Nurses Assn., N.Y. State Nurses Assn., N.Y. County Registered Nurses Assn., Nat. League Nursing, Sigma Theta Tau, Phi Delta Kappa, Kappa Delta Phi. Democrat. Roman Catholic. Contbr. articles in field to profl. jours. Home: 30 Highridge Rd Mount Kisco NY 10549 Office: Rockland Community Mental Health Center Mount Vernon NY 10550

WRAY, HALTOM, textile co. exec.; b. Fort Worth, Jan. 23, 1931; s. Mabry and Lillian M. (Purser) W.; B.S., Rice U., 1954; M.A., Columbia U., 1971, M.Phil., 1976; m. Jacqueline Parker, May 25, 1956; children—Alicia, Anthony. Asst. tech. mgr. Shell Chem. Co., Houston, N.Y.C., 1954-70; sr. technologist Shell Oil Co., N.Y.C., 1970-71; capital planning analyst Springs Mills, N.Y.C., 1971—. Mem. Am. Inst. Chem. Engrs. Home: 310 W 91st St New York City NY 10024 Office: 104 W 40th St New York City NY 10018

WREN, JOHN BREEN, elec. engr.; b. Pitts., Dec. 9, 1917; s. John Breen and Margaret Elizabeth (Gannon) W.; B.S. in Elec. Engring., U. Pitts., 1938; m. Teresa Glanville, Nov. 28, 1940; children—Mary K., John B., Margaret J., Nora E., Sheila A., Anne C. Machinist to asst. foreman Hydril Co., Rochester, Pa., 1938-39; elec. tester Westinghouse Elec. Corp., E.Pitts., 1939-44, design engr., 1944-46, design engr., Buffalo, 1946-75, fellow engr., 1975—. Mem. IEEE (sr.), Soc. Mining Engrs. Patentee textile motors and mining motors. Home: 229 N Long St Williamsville NY 14221 Office: 4454 Genesee St Buffalo NY 14240

WRIGHT, BENJAMIN VAIDEN, JR., investment banker; b. Laurel, Miss., Apr. 10, 1910; s. Benjamin Vaiden and Bessie Elizabeth (Herring) W.; B.S., Oreg. State Coll., 1930; M.B.A., Harvard, 1932; m. Marjorie Elizabeth Eldredge, Apr. 6, 1940 (dec.); children—Benjamin Vaiden III, John Eldredge; m. 2d, Virginia Frankel, Oct. 19, 1974. With S.H. Kress Co., 1932-35; with Scudder, Stevens & Clark, Chgo. and N.Y., 1935-57; v.p. Champion Papers Co., Hamilton, O., 1957-62; v.p. Shields, Model, Roland & Co., Inc., N.Y.C., 1962—. Served to lt. col. USAAF, 1942-45. Home: 201 E 79th St New York City NY 10021

WRIGHT, DOUGLAS TYNDALL, govt. ofcl.; b. Toronto, Ont., Can., Oct. 4, 1927; S. George C. and Etta (Tyndall) W.; B.A.Sc. with honors in Civil Engring., U. Toronto, 1949; M.S. in Structural Engring., U. Ill., 1952; Ph.D. in Engring., U. Cambridge, 1954; D.Eng.(hon.), Carleton U., 1967; LL.D.(hon.), Brock U., 1967; D.Sc.(hon.), Meml. U. Nfld., 1969; m. Margaret Maxwell, May 21, 1955; children—William, Clyde, Robert, Sarah, Anna. Lectr. dept. civil engring. Queen's U., 1954-55, asst. prof., 1955-58, asso. prof., 1958; prof. civil engring. U. Waterloo, 1958-67, chmn. dept. civil engring., 1958-63, dean engring., 1959-66; chmn. Ont. Com. on Univ. Affairs Govt. of Ont., 1967-72, chmn. Ont. Commn. Post-Secondary Edn., Toronto, 1969-72, dep. provincial sec. for social devel., Toronto, 1972—; vis. prof. Universidad Nacional Autonoma de Mexico, 1964, 66, Universite de Sherbrooke, 1966-67; cons. engr. Netherlands and Mexican pavilions Expo 1967; Olympic Sports Palace, Mexico City, 1968, Ont. Place Dome and Forum, 1971. Bd. dirs. African Students Found., Toronto, Ont., 1961-66; bd. dirs. Ont. Curriculum Inst., 1964-67. Athlone fellow, 1952-54. Fellow Engring. Inst. Can. (delegate to Engrs. Council Profl. Devel. N.Y.C., 1961-70), ASCE; mem. Assn. Profl. Engrs. Province Ont., Internat. Assn. Bridge and Structural Engring., Internat. Assn. Shell Structures, Canadian Assn. Latin Am. Studies, Am. Acad. Mechanics, Canadian Inst. Internat. Affairs, Canadian Inst. Pub. Adminstrn. Clubs: Royal Canadian Yacht; University (Toronto). Contbr. articles to profl. jours. Home: 6B Wychwood Park Toronto ON M6G 2V5 Canada Office: Whitney Block Queen's Park Toronto ON M7A 1A2 Canada

WRIGHT, ESTELLA VIOLA HARRISON (MRS. WILLIAM M. WRIGHT), sculptor; b. Riceville, Ga.; d. Elijah and Elicia (Butler) Harrison; student Art Student's League, 1937, 48-50, (scholar) Newark Mus., 1961, summer 1962, Nat. Acad. Sch. Fine Arts, 1962, NAD, fall 1962; m. William M. Wright, Apr. 24, 1928 (dec. Feb. 1936). One-man shows at various banks, also Scott's Auditorium; exhibited in group shows at Artists of Am. at Master Inst., 1941, Audubon Artists Ann., 1942, NAD, 1962, Art Exhbn. Springfield (Mass.), 1962, Countee Cullen Pub. Library, 1963, Zynn-Kottler Gallery, N.Y.C., 1973, travelling exhbn. Ill. State U., 1978, others; life-size works various persons, including George Washington Carver, Noble Sissle, Booker T. Washington, Fredrick Douglas, Thomas Bethune, also portrait busts; executed trophy for Boy Scouts Am., Bklyn., 1977; represented in permanent collections including Mus. City of N.Y., Sch. Podiatry, Temple U. Gray Lady, Harlem Hosp., N.Y.C., 1951—; active ARC, John Brown Meml. Assn. Recipient certificate of pub. service State of N.Y., 1958, citation for meritorious service Bklyn. Women's Council, 1963. Mem. Art Student's League (life), John Brown Meml. Assn., Rosicrucian Anthrosophic League Sch. Philosophy. Address: 226 W 138th St New York City NY 10030

WRIGHT, HAROLD LOUIS, bishop; b. Boston, Oct. 25, 1929; s. Harold L. and Jeannette W. (Banks) W.; student New Eng. Conservatory Mus., 1946-52; A.A., Boston U., 1952, B.S., 1954; S.T.B., Gen. Theol. Sem., 1957; m. Edith Coralie Yancey, May 10, 1952; 4 children. Ordained priest Episcopal Ch., 1957, bishop, 1974; vicar Resurrection Ch., East Elmhurst, N.Y., 1957-62, rector, 1962-69; staff Diocese of N.Y., from 1970; now suffragan bishop N.Y.; mem. Ecclesiastical Ct., 1960-69; mem. Diocesan Exec. Council, 1965-66, sec., 1966-69; co-ordinator tng. and field edn. Exec. Council of Episcopal Chs., 1969-70, mem. standing com., 1969-70, sec., 1970—. Mem.-at-large Nat. Youth Commn., 1949-52; v.p. N.Y.C.

Sch. Bd., 1962-69. Office: 1047 Amsterdam St New York City NY 10025*

WRIGHT, JAMES SKELLY, circuit judge; b. New Orleans, Jan. 14, 1911; s. James Edward and Margaret (Skelly) W.; Ph.B., Loyola U., 1931, LL.B., 1934; LL.D., Yale U., 1961, U. Notre Dame, 1962, Howard U., 1964, U. So. Calif., 1975; m. Helen Mitchell Patton, Feb. 1, 1945; 1 son, James Skelly. High sch. tchr., 1931-35; lectr. English history Loyola U., 1936-37; admitted to U.S. Supreme Ct. bar; asst. U.S. atty., New Orleans, 1937-46; U.S. atty. E. Dist. La., 1948-49; U.S. dist. Judge, E. Dist. La., 1949-62; U.S. circuit judge, D.C., 1962-78, chief judge, 1978—; mem. faculty Loyola U. Sch. Law, 1950-62; James Madison lectr. N.Y. U., 1965; Robert L. Jackson lectr. Nat. Coll. State Trial Judges, 1966; lectr. U. Tex., 1967; Irvine lectr. Cornell U., 1968; Brainerd Currie lectr. Duke U., 1970; instr. contemporary civil rights Notre Dame in London, 1974; Meiklejohn lectr. Brown U., 1976. Served as lt. comdr. USCG, 1942-46. Observer U.S. State Dept. Internat. Fisheries Conf., London, 1943. Mem. La. (bd. govs.), Fed. (pres. New Orleans chpt.), D.C., Am., New Orleans bar assns., Am. Law Inst., Blue Key, Phi Delta Phi, Alpha Delta Gamma (nat. pres.). Roman Catholic. Democrat. Home: 5317 Blackistone Rd Westmoreland Hills Washington DC 20016 Office: US Courthouse Washington DC 20001

WRIGHT, JANE ELIZABETH, univ. librarian; b. Fulton, N.Y., Apr. 20, 1927; d. William Robertson and Genevieve Agnes (McCormick) Wright; B.E., State U. Coll. at Oswego, 1948, M.S., 1955; M.S. in L.S., Syracuse U., 1955. Tchr., Lowville Acad., 1948-49, Oswego (N.Y.) City Sch. Dist., 1949-54; childrens librarian Rochester Pub. Library, 1955-61; periodicals librarian State U. Coll. at Oswego, 1961-70, head tech. services, 1970-74, head periodicals dept., profl. studies area of collection devel. unit, 1974—. Mem. N.Y. State Govt. Documents Task Force. Mem. Am., N.Y. State library assns., State U. N.Y. Librarians Assn., Kappa Delta Pi, Phi Beta Mu, Delta Kappa Gamma. Club: Philomelian Alumnae. Home: 42 Lincoln Ave Oswego NY 13126

WRIGHT, JOHN HARRISON, JR., sch. adminstr.; b. Humboldt, Tenn., Apr. 25, 1930; s. John Harrison and Florence Sarah (Smith) W.; B.A., U. of South, 1954; Ed.M., Harvard U., 1966; postgrad. Stetson U., also U. Va., U. Perugia (Italy), Am. U.; m. Winston Case, Apr. 12, 1958; children—John Harrison, Catherine Isabel, Elizabeth Fullerton, Victoria Winston. Tchr., dir. admissions Sewanee (Tenn.) Mil. Acad., 1954-59; Fulbright tchr., Italy, 1959-61, Smith-Mundt tchr., Lebanon, 1960; tchr., dean of faculty Chatham (Va.) Hall, 1961-68; headmaster Gill Sch., Bernardsville, N.J., 1968-72; headmaster Gill/St. Bernard's Sch., Bernardsville, 1972—. Cons. intensive learning to various ind. schs. Trustee Matheny Sch. for Cerebral Palsied Children; chmn. Sch. Consortium N.J., Burlington Coll. (N.J.); bd. advisors Council for Advancement and Support Edn., D.C. Served with USAF, 1950-52. Mem. Sewanee Alumni of N.J. (pres.), Beta Theta Pi, Phi Delta Kappa. Democrat. Episcopalian (vestryman, lay reader, mem. dept. Christian edn. and chmn. commn. lay ministry Diocese of N.J.). Clubs: Adirondack League (Old Forge, N.Y.); Essex Hunt (Peapack, N.J.); Church, Harvard (N.Y.C.). Home: Claremont Rd Bernardsville NJ 07924 Office: Gill/St Bernard's Sch Box 239 Bernardsville NJ 07924

WRIGHT, LAURENCE CASTO, orthodontist; b. Cleve., Aug. 31, 1927; s. Laurence P. and Ruth A. (Casto) W.; student Westminster Coll., 1948-51; B.S., Western Res. U., 1952, D.D.S., 1955; certificate in orthodontics, U. Buffalo, 1957; m. Joan Finley, June 23, 1951; children—David, James, Douglas, Jonathan. Individual practice dentistry specializing in orthodontics, Buffalo, 1957—, asso. with Dr. Walter H. Ellis, 1957-59; mem. J. Sutton Regan Cleft Palate Clinic; staff mem. Children's Hosp., Buffalo. Club, dist. and state pres. Y's Men's Internat., 1958-64, internat. pres., 1966-67. Chmn. bd. mgrs. (N.E.) YMCA, 1971-72. Served with AUS, 1946-48. Fellow Internat. Coll. Dentists; mem. U. Buffalo Orthodontic Alumni Assn. (pres. 1968-70), 8th Dist. Orthodontic Soc. (pres. 1973-74), Erie County, N.Y. State dental socs., Western N.Y. Orthodontic Acad., Am. Dental Assn., Am. Assn. Orthodontics, Am. Cleft Palate Assn., Amherst C. of C., Delta Sigma Delta (treas., sec. 1962—). Rotarian. Home: 49 Colony Ct Buffalo NY 14226 Office: 3985 Main St Buffalo NY 14226

WRIGHT, LINDA SHICKEL, systems mgr.; b. Harrisonburg, Va., Sept. 4, 1947; d. Marcel Knicely and Helen Marie (Swestyn) Schickel; B.S. in Math., Coll. William and Mary, 1969; M.S. in Computer Sci., Rutgers U., 1973; m. John William Wright III, June 22, 1968. Programmer, U. Va. Computer Sci. Center, Charlottesville, 1969-70; systems analyst Western Electric Co., Naperville, Ill., 1970-72; mem. tech. staff Bell Telephone Labs., Murray Hill, N.J., 1972-74; computer resource specialist, supr. computer performance analysis, projects mgr., Sun Oil Co., Dallas, Phila., 1974-78; mgr. systems analysis and test Digital Equipment Corp., Tewksbury, Mass., 1978—; editor, v.p., dir. Computer Measurement Group, Inc. Author tech. articles in field. Home: 2108 Windsor Ridge Dr Westborough MA 01581 Office: Digital Equipment Corp 1925 Andover St Tewksbury MA 01876

WRIGHT, LYLE EARNEST, mortgage banker; b. Steel Tavern, Va., Sept. 2, 1919; s. Emmett Newton and Gladys Enola; student mech. engring. Columbia Tech. Sch., 1941-47; student Washington Trade Sch., 1941-47, Exec. Bus. and Mgmt. Inst., 1955-56, Nat. Sales Inst. N.Y., 1961-64; m. Margaret Pearl Stone, July 3, 1937. Pres., Wright Co., Hyattsville, Md., 1950-60, Universal Bldg. Products, Washington, 1964-68, Gen. Safety Corp., Forestville, Md., 1970-73, Check Data Control, Lanham, Md., 1973-77, Lyle E. Wright Assn., Lanham, 1977—. Served with paratroopers U.S. Army, 1943-46. Mem. Nat. Soc. of Inst. of Tech., Internat. Soc. Food Service Consultants, Nat. Retail Assn., Safety Engrs. Assn. Democrat. Roman Catholic. Club: Prince Geroge Country. Patentee plastic dome skylight, cement bldg. block, bank system, ceiling system, grease extractor, grass and vegetation barrier. Home: 9019 Spring Ave Lanham MD 20801 Office: PO Box 127 Lanham MD 20801

WRIGHT, MARK HEISLEY, assn. exec.; b. Albany, N.Y., May 19, 1948; s. Elmer Hawn and Betty Jane (Heisley) Wright Withington; B.S., N.H. Coll., 1971; M.S. in Psychology, City, U. N.Y., 1973; m. Linda A. Anderson, July 11, 1971; 1 son, Jason. Rehab. counselor Ridge Hill Rehab. Center, Yonkers, N.Y., 1971-73; psychologist Philbrook Center for Children and Youth, N.Y. State Hosp., Concord, 1973-75; sch. psychologist for spl. edn. emotionally disturbed children, Lakes Region, N.H., 1974-77; exec. dir. Lakes Region Family Counselling Services, Laconia, 1977—; condr. workshops, reading supr.; pvt. practice psychology, 1974-77; cons. Bd. dirs. Head Start Program Central N.H., 1973-76; pres. Big Bros. Assn., Manchester, N.H., 1970-71. Named Big Brother of Year, 1970; certified sch. psychologist, N.Y. Mem. Am. Assn. Clin. Counselors, Am. Personnel and Guidance Assn., N.H. Affiliation Psychol. Practitioners (chmn. 1976-77), N.H. Psychology Assn. (certified sch. psychologist), Kappa Delta Phi. Episcopalian. Home: Hazelnut Ln Gilford NH 03246 Office: 25 Beacon St E Laconia NH 03246

WRIGHT, PETER, labor relations specialist; b. N.Y.C., Jan. 21, 1934; s. Stuyvesant Bayard and Rebecca Addison (Holland) W.; student U. of South, 1952-53, George Washington U., 1953-56, 62-63, Washington Labor Studies Center, Fed. City Coll., 1974-76; m. Carolann Wright, 1956; children—Peter, Andrew S., Edward Stuyvesant. Air Force account Underwood Corp., CIA, Washington, 1953-56; with 1st Fed. Savs. & Loan Assn., Alexandria, Va., 1955; asst. exec. mgr. Truck Body & Equipment Assn., 1956-57; owner, operator Bayard's Bend Farm, 1957-61; pres., dir. Bayard's Bend Farms, Inc., 1960—; dir. supervisory tng. U.S. Dept. Agr., 1961-62, organizational and staffing analyst, 1963-66, personnel staffing specialist, chief tech. services sect. Far East personnel AID, Washington, 1966-68; supervisory personnel officer Office Personnel and Manpower, Washington, 1968; labor-mgmt. adviser Am. Fedn. Govt. Employees, 1968-69, asst. dir. labor mgmt. adviser, 1968-69, asst. dir. labor mgmt. dept., chief regulations rev., 1969-71; personnel mgmt., labor relations specialist U.S. Dept. Commerce, Rockville, Md., 1971-73; labor relations specialist Nat. Park Service, Dept. Interior, Washington, 1973-78; dir. labor and employee relations ACTION, Washington, 1978—; tchr. labor relations U.S. Dept. Agr. Grad. Sch., Washington, Albright Acad., Grand Canyon, Ariz., No. Va. Community Coll. Vice pres. Belmont Civic Assn., 1965-66; pres. Mason Neck Citizens' Assn., 1972-73; campaign mgr. City of Alexandria, 1956; city committeeman, 1955-57; v.p. No. Va. Young Republicans, 1956-57; del. state Rep. conv., 1956; Rep. co-committeeman, 1969-71. Mem. Soc. Fed. Labor Relations Profls., Indsl. Relations Research Assn., Am. Guernsey Breeders Assn., Phila. Assemblies, Old Gaffers Assn. Episcopalian. Club: Toastmasters (ednl. v.p. 1971-72). Home: 10904 Belmont Blvd Lorton VA 22079 Office: Bur Labor and Employee Relations ACTION 806 Connecticut Ave NW Washington DC 20525

WRIGHT, RICHARD DONALD, pharm. co. exec.; b. Chester, Pa., Mar. 18, 1936; s. Richard H. and Anita C. (Howery) W.; B.S. in Bus. Adminstrn., Pa. State U., 1963; m. Joan Cooke, Oct. 24, 1959; children—Richard, Paul, Susan. Trainee, corporate fin. mgmt., internal auditor, corporate staff auditor RCA, Cherry Hill, N.J., 1963-66; with Smith Kline French Labs. div. Smith Kline Corp., Phila., 1966—, mgr. budget, 1966-69, mgr. planning and control, 1969-70, mgr. fin. ops., 1970-72, controller mfg. ops., 1972-73, dir. fin. planning, 1973-74, controller pharm. ops., U.S., 1974—. Elder, mem. bd. Christian and Missionary Alliance. Mem. Fin. Execs. Inst. (certified), Planning Execs. Inst., Nat. Assn. Accountants, Sigma Tau Gamma. Lectr. and author in field. Home: 6 Timber Hill Ct Turnersville NJ 08012

WRIGHT, ROY THOMPSON, design engring. co. exec.; b. Catterick, Yorkshire, Eng., July 27, 1926; s. Harold Hercules and Elsie A. C. (Thompson) W.; came to U.S., 1965; student Oxford (Eng.) U., 1943-45; H.N.C., Nat. Inst. Engring., London, 1945; E.I.T., Pa. State U., 1973; D.D. (hon.), Mother Earth Ch., 1976; m. Carrice Faith Price, Aug. 2, 1947; children—Ruth Lavinia, Roy Peter. Ordained to ministry Nonconformist Protestant Ch., 1976; chief engr. W.T. Hills, Cardiff, Wales, 1962-65; project mgr. Hoare, Lea & Partners, Birmingham, Eng., 1956-62, Power Piping Co., Wednesbury, Eng., 1954-56; design engr. Babcock & Wilcox, Scotland, 1950-54, Bakelite, Birmingham, 1948-50; design engr. Catalytic Constrn. Co., Phila., 1965-66; chief engr. Utilities Engring. Assos., Phila., 1966-73; pres. Utility & Energy Systems, Inc., Willow Grove, Pa., 1973—; cons. to cons. engr. cos. Mem. Nat. Inst. Engring. (U.K.) (asso.), Inst. Heating, Ventilating Engrs. (U.K.), Am. Soc. Heating, Refrigeration and Air Conditioning Engrs. Club: Order Police (Phila.). Contbr. articles to profl. jours. Home: Blair Mill Vill E Apt 200B Horsham PA 19044 Office: PO Box 424 Willow Grove PA 19090

WRIGHT, STANLEY MARC, artist; b. Irvington, N.J., May 24, 1911; s. Harry and May (Wright) W.; grad. Pratt Inst., 1933; student (Tiffany Found. fellow) Jerry Fransworth Sch. Art, 1935; m. Carolyn Stiles Sterrett, Sept. 14, 1949. One man shows U.S. Capitol Bldg., Washington, Fleming Mus., Burlington, Vt., Wood Art Gallery, Montpelier, Vt., Montclair (N.J.) Mus., Paper Mill Gallery, Short Hills, N.J., Newark Art Club; exhibited in group shows Washington Congl. Galleries, Salmagundi Club, Met. Mus. Art, Bklyn. Mus., Phila. Mus., Newark Mus., Montclair Mus., Jersey City Mus., Fleming Mus., Nat. Acad., Grand Central Galleries, Audubon Artists, others; represented in permanent collections Fleming Mus., Burlington, Vt., Matijevic Galleries, Potsdam, N.Y., Wood Art Gallery, Montpelier, Ho. of Reps., Washington, State House, Montpelier, Golf Hall Fame, Med. Center U. Kans., Med. Center, Burlington, tchr. painting Newark Sch. Fine Art, 1945-49, South Orange Adult Sch., 1945-49, Wright Sch. Art, 1949—. Served to staff sgt., AUS, 1942-45. Decorated Bronze Star medal with 4 oak leaf clusters. Recipient many 1st prizes, 1933—. Fellow Internat. Inst. Arts and Letters; mem. Audubon Artists, Am. Artists Profl. League, Provincetown Art Assn., New Hope Art Assn., Am. Vets. Soc., Vt. Artists Assn. (bd. dirs. 1951—). Clubs: Salmagundi (N.Y.C.); Newark Art; Stowe (Vt.) Country, Rotary (pres. 1952-53). Address: RFD 2 Stowe VT 05672

WRIGHT, THEODORE PAUL, JR., educator; b. Port Washington, N.Y., Apr. 12, 1926; s. Theodore Paul and Margaret (McCarl) W.; B.A. magna cum laude, Swarthmore Coll., 1949; M.A., Yale U., 1951, Ph.D., 1957; m. Susan Jane Standfast, Feb. 18, 1967; children—Henry Sewall, Margaret Standfast, Catherine Berrian. Instr. govt. Bates Coll., Lewiston, Maine, 1955-57, asst. prof., 1957-64, asso. prof., 1964-65; asso. prof. polit. sci. Grad. Sch. Pub. Affairs, State U. N.Y. at Albany, 1965-71, prof., 1971—. Trustee, Am. Inst. Pakistan Studies, 1973—. Served with USNR, 1944-46. Carnegie intern Indian civilization, U. Chgo., 1961-62; Fulbright research prof. India, 1963-64; Nat. Def. Fgn. Lang. fellow, U. Calif. at Berkeley, 1967; Am. Inst. Indian Studies research fellow, India, 1969-70; Am. Council Learned Socs. grantee on South Asia, London, Eng., 1974-75. Mem. Am. Polit. Sci. Assn., Assn. Asian Studies, AAUP, Phi Delta Theta. Democrat. Clubs: Dutch Settlers of Albany; Adirondack Mountain. Author: American Support of Free Elections Abroad, 1964. Contbr. articles on Indian Muslims to profl. jours. Home: 27 Vandenburg Ln Latham NY 12110 Office: Grad Sch Pub Affairs ULB-96 State U NY Albany NY 12222

WRIGHT, THOMAS WESLEY, clergyman, educator; b. Xenia, Ohio, June 18, 1933; s. Joseph Raymond and Marian (Arnold) W.; B.A., Adrian Coll., 1955; D.M., Colgate-Rochester Div. Sch., 1961; M.A., Syracuse U., 1969; m. Ellen Udnes Christensen, June 26, 1953; children—David Alan, Ronald Erik, Brian Wesley. Ordained minister United Ch. Christ, 1962; minister edn. Park Ch., Elmira, N.Y., 1955-58; pastor in Hall, N.Y., 1958-61, Watertown, N.Y., 1961-66; co-pastor, team ministry Fairmount Community Ch., Syracuse, N.Y., 1966-68; tchr. West Genesee Schs., Syracuse, 1968-74; pastor-tchr. First Congl. Ch., Malone, N.Y., 1974—. Youth work coordinator N.Y. State, United Ch. Christ, 1959-66; youth edn., outdoor edn. and counseling specialist, curriculum cons.; lectr. philosophy of religion and edn. Hobart-Smith Coll., 1960-61, Jefferson Community Coll., 1965-66; instr. ednl. psychology North Country Community Coll., 1975—; mem. Inst. on Drug Edn. at Syracuse, 1972—; exec. sec. day tng. program Jefferson County Assn. for Retarded Children, 1965-66, pres. bd. dirs., 1964-65; chmn. Onondaga County Assn. Retarded Children ann. fund dr., 1969; mem. Franklin County Mental Health Bd., 1974-75; bd. dirs. Franklin County B.O.C. Ednl. Services, Mental Health Residencies; pres. Greater Malone Community Council, 1976—; community cons. N.Y. State Commn. Corrections, Franklin County Handicapped Screening and Services. Served with USCGR, 1951-52. Recipient Civic Service award Jefferson County chpt. ARC, 1966. Mem. Jefferson County, Franklin County ministerial assns., Onondaga Nature Centers, Nat. Wildlife Fedn. Clubs: Adirondack Mountain, Rotary. Contbr. articles to profl., conservation and religious jours. Home: 44 Washington St Malone NY 12953 Office: 3 Clay St Malone NY 12953

WRIGHT, WILLIAM ELLSWORTH, educator; b. Erie, Pa., May 3, 1928; s. Carl Goodrich and Lois Havens (Beckwith) W.; B.A., Allegheny Coll., 1950; M.A., Gannon Coll., 1966; postgrad. State U. N.Y. at Buffalo, 1965-67; m. Virginia Lois Dreger, May 16, 1954; children—Frederick, Russell, Michael. Partner Wright Agy., real estate and ins., Erie, 1950-55; office mgr., sales agt. Reg Little Builders, Erie, 1953-55; exec. asst., salesman Pyramid Industries, Erie, 1955-62; sec., bus. mgr. Zem Zem Hosp., Erie, 1962-63; prof., head dept. Bryant & Stratton Bus. Inst., Buffalo, 1965-68; asst. dean continuing edn. Erie Community Coll. (formerly Erie County Tech. Inst.), Buffalo, 1968-73, asst. dean bus. and pub. service, 1973-75, prof. econs., chmn. social sci. appts. com., 1975—. Lectr. various colls.; cons. Prudential Ins. Co., Kenworthy Ednl. Service; curriculum adviser Sheetmetal Workers Joint Apprentice Com.; real estate broker, N.Y., 1974—. Served with M.C., AUS, 1950-51. Project Concern grantee, 1971. Mem. Civil Service Employees Assn., Am. Assn. Jr. Colls., N.Y. Assn. Jr. Colls., Am. Inst. Banking (acad. council), Am. Econ. Assn., Greater Buffalo Bd. Realtors, Am. Mktg. Assn., Am. Statis. Assn. Mason (Shriner). Co-inventor outside plastic pipe coupling. Home: 4064 McKinley Pkwy Blasdell NY 14219 Office: 4140 Southwestern Blvd Orchard Park NY 14127

WRIGLEY, JOHN WARREN, film producer; b. Okmulgee, Okla., May 16, 1944; s. John Henry and Louise(Scott) W.; student Washington U., St. Louis, 1962-64. Audiovisual dir. No. Va. Community Coll., Annandale, 1967-69; media coordinator Area Manpower Insts. Devel. of Staff program Washington Tech. Inst., 1969-72; film instr. St. Albans Sch. for Boys, Washington, 1974-77; film instr. Smithsonian Assos., 1973; pres. Hermes Films, Ltd., Washington, 1975—. Served with U.S. Army, 1965-67. Mem. Washington Film Council, Nat. Trust for Historic Preservation. Mem. Reorganized Ch. of Jesus Christ of Latter-day Saints. Home and Office: 3218 39th St NW Washington DC 20016

WRISTON, WALTER BIGELOW, banker; b. Middletown, Conn., Aug. 3, 1919; s. Henry M. and Ruth (Bigelow) W.; B.A. with distinction, Wesleyan U., Middletown, Conn., 1941; postgrad. Ecole Francaise Middlebury, Vt., 1941, Am. Inst. Banking, 1946; M.A., Fletcher Sch. Internat. Law and Diplomacy, 1942; LL.D., Lawrence Coll., 1962, Tufts U., 1963, Brown U., 1969, Columbia, 1972, Fordham U., 1977; D.C.S., Pace U., 1974, St. John's U., 1974, N.Y. U., 1977; D.H.L., Lafayette Coll., 1975; m. Barbara Brengle, Oct. 24, 1942 (dec.); 1 dau., Catherine B.; m. 2d, Kathryn Ann Dineen, Mar. 14, 1968. Officer spl. div. Dept. State, Washington, 1941-42; jr. insp. comptrollers div. Citibank, N.A., 1946-50, asst. cashier, 1950-52, asst. v.p., 1952-54, v.p. 1954-58; sr. v.p. 1958-60, exec. v.p., 1960-67, pres., 1967-70, chmn., 1970—, also dir.; chmn., dir. Citicorp; dir. J.C. Penney Co., Gen. Electric Co., Chubb Corp.; trustee Rand Corp. Mem. Nat. Commn. on Productivity, 1970-74, Labor-Mgmt. Adv. Com., Nat. Commn. for Indsl. Peace, 1973-74, Adv. Com. on Reform Internat. Monetary System. Bd. govs. N.Y. Hosp.; trustee Am. Enterprise Inst.; bd. visitors Fletcher Sch. Law and Diplomacy; bd. dirs. Assos. Harvard Bus. Sch. Served with AUS, 1942-46. Mem. Council Fgn. Relations Bus. Council, Bus. Council. Club: Links, River, Sky (N.Y.C.); Metropolitan (Washington). Home: New York City Office: 399 Park Ave New York City NY 10043

WRUBLE, BRIAN FREDERICK, securities co. exec.; b. Kalamazoo, Apr. 18, 1943; s. Milton and Rose M. (Nathanson) W.; B.E.E., Cornell U., 1965, M.E.E., 1966; M.B.A., N.Y. U., 1976; m. Susan R. Shifrin, June 23, 1968; children—Amy Carolyn, Jordan Todd. Field engr. Sperry Systems Mgmt. div. Sperry Rand Corp., Lake Success, N.Y., 1966-69; v.p. Alliance One Instl. Service, N.Y.C., 1970-76; pres. Undershaft Corp., N.Y.C., 1973—; research analyst H.C. Wainwright & Co., N.Y.C., 1976-77; v.p. Wainwright Securities, Inc., N.Y.C., 1977—, Smith Barney, Harris Upham & Co., Inc., 1977—. Chartered fin. analyst. Mem. N.Y. Soc. Security Analysts, Fin. Analysts Fedn., IEEE, Beta Gamma Sigma, Phi Kappa Phi, Eta Kappa Nu. Home: 326 Dundee Rd Stamford CT 06903 Office: 1345 Ave of Americas New York City NY 10019

WU, CHENG-YI, chemist; b. Chia-Yi City, Taiwan, Jan. 1, 1941; s. Chih and Yu (Chang) W.; M.S., U. Fla., 1967; PH.D., U. Mass., 1972; m. Jane C. Tao, May 31, 1969; children—Winston C., Henry C. Supervisory analytical research chemist Merck, Rahway, N.J., 1972-75, sr. research chemist, 1975—; teaching asst. U. Mass., 1968-71. Mem. Am. Chem. Soc. Home: 1576 Rising Way Mountainside NJ 07092 Office: PO Box 2000 Rahway NJ 07065

WU, (JAMES) CHING, radiologist, ret. educator; b. Peking, May 12, 1907; s. Wu Tso Hai and Loo Sze Shih; came to U.S., 1959, naturalized, 1972; M.D., Nat. Peking U., 1926; M.S. in Radiology, U. Chgo., 1932; Ph.D. (hon.), U. Munich (Germany), 1933; m. Tang Shiu-jen; 1 son, Lin C.; 1 dau. Intern, Peking Union Med. Coll., 1927, resident in radiology, 1928-30, asst., instr., asst. prof., 1934-39; prof., chmn. dept. radiology Nat. Def. Med. Center, Taiwan, 1948-59; fellow Los Angeles Tumor Inst., 1955-56; research radiologist New Eng. Diakness Hosp., Boston, 1956-57; resident in radiology Newark Beth Israel Hosp., 1958-60, Newton Lower Falls (Mass.) Hosp., 1961; research radiologist Hosp. Joint Diseases and Med. Center, N.Y.C., 1961-67; asso. prof. radiology N.Y. U., N.Y.C., 1968-72, emeritus prof., 1972—; vis. prof. Tokyo U., 1952-53, U. So. Calif., 1959; chmn. del. Internat. Congress Radiology, 1953, 56, Internat. Mil. Medicine and Documentations Commn., 1958. Recipient Gold medal Republic of China, 1952, award AMA, 1970; NIH grantee, 1965. Mem. Am. Roentgen Ray Soc., Pan Am. (diplomate), Chinese (pres. 1952-54) med. assns., AAUP, Chinese Roentgen Ray Soc. (pres. 1949-58), N.Y. U. Alumni Assn., Am. Security Council (adv. bd.), N.Y. U. Med. Sch. Library Club. Mem. Christian Ch. Clubs: Met. Republic; Capitol Hill (Washington). Contbr. articles to med. jours. Home: 2 Birdseye Circle Stony Brook NY 11790

WU, JIN, oceanographer, engr., educator; b. Nanking, China, Apr. 9, 1934; s. Shiang-San and Aei-Feng (Chen) W.; came to U.S., 1959, naturalized, 1972; B.S., Nat. Cheng-Kung U., 1956; M.Sc., U. Iowa, 1961, Ph.D., 1964; m. Tzu-Chen Chang, Sept. 9, 1961; children—Victor Hua-Teh, Abraham Hua-Chung, Marvin Hua-Wei. Instr. physics Taitung Sr. High Sch., 1958-59; research asst., research asso. U. Iowa, 1959-63; research scientist Hydronautics, Inc., Laurel, Md., 1963-66, sr. research scientist, 1966-69, prin. research scientist, 1969-74, head geophys. fluid dynamics div., 1966-74, cons., 1974—; asso. prof. marine studies and civil engring. U. Del., Newark, 1974-75, prof., 1975—. Served with Chinese Navy, 1956-58. Mem. ASCE, Am. Geophys. Union. Contbr. numerous articles to profl. jours. Home: 1822 Greenplace Terr Rockville MD 20850 Office: Coll Marine Studies U Del Newark DE 19711

WU, JOHN NAICHI, mech. engr.; b. Soochow, China, Sept. 10, 1932; s. Shine Tze and Ven Lai (Shen) Wu; came to U.S., 1959, naturalized, 1972; Ph.D. (grad. sch. fellow), U. Fla., 1965; m. Mary Chan, July 15, 1961; children—Winthrop J., Jarvis C. Sr. research engr. Babcock & Wilcox Co., Alliance, Ohio, 1962-63, research specialist, 1965-66, group supr., 1966-77; mgr. material process lab. Erie (Pa.) plant Gen. Electric Co., 1977—. Mem. ASME, Acoustical Soc. Am. Club: Optimists (v.p. North Canton, Ohio chpt. 1977-78). Contbr. tech. papers to profl. jours. Home: 139 Putnam Dr Erie PA 16511 Office: Gen Electric Co 2901 E Lake Rd Erie PA 16511

WU, MAO-FOU, meteorologist; b. Nanking, China, July 28, 1932; s. Quang-Sung and Shiow-Jen (Chu) W.; came to U.S., 1963, naturalized, 1976; B.S., with honors, Naval Coll. Tech., 1955; M.S., U. Chgo., 1963, postgrad. 1963-65; Ph.D., Mass. Inst. Tech., 1970; m. Julia Liu, Dec. 16, 1966. Engr. Navy shipyard, Taiwan, 1956-58; ship surveyor Keelung Harbor Bur., Taiwan, 1958-60; instr. Naval Post Grad. Sch., 1960-62; research asso. Mass. Inst. Tech., 1969-72; staff scientist Environ. Research & Tech., Inc., Concord, Mass., 1972-77, sr. scientist systems and applied sci., 1977—; collaborator Jicamarca Radio Observatory Geophys. Inst. Peru. Chinese Ministry Edn. scholar, 1963-65; internat. fellow U.S. Nat. Acad. Sci.; NSF grantee, 1975—; recipient Best Performance Award, Environ. Research & Tech., Inc., 1975. Mem. Royal, Am. meteorol. socs., Am. Geophys. Union, Nat. Weather Assn., Meteorol. Soc. Japan, Sci. Research of Am., Sigma Xi. Club: Mass. Inst. Tech. Faculty. Author monographs for Dept. Transp.; contbr. articles to profl. jours. Office: 6811 Kenilworth Ave Riverdale MD 20840

WU, NING GAU, mech. engr.; b. Pookiang, China, July 24, 1922; s. Chi Chuen and Jean (Chu) W.; B.S., Chiao Tung U., 1944; M.S., U. Colo., 1948; Ph.D., U. Calif. at Berkeley, 1952; m. Shu-Wie Hsu Wu, July 14, 1950; children—Nora Wie, Eva Wie, Julie Wie. Came to U.S., 1947, naturalized, 1962. Engr., Jacuzzi Bros., Richmond, Calif., 1951-54, chief design engr., 1954-55, chief engr., 1955-63; devel. engr. IBM, Hopewell Junction, N.Y., 1963-65, sr. engr., 1965-71, mgr. engring., 1971—. Mem. ASME, Sigma Xi. Contbr. to profl. jours. Home: 8 Timberline Dr Poughkeepsie NY 12603 Office: IBM Corp Hopewell Junction NY 12533

WU, STEPHEN S., banker; b. Hong Kong, Mar. 22, 1922; s. K.W. and L.S. (Chan) W.; B.A., St. John's U., 1943; M.A., Stanford, 1948, Columbia, 1950; M.B.A., Boston U., 1957; C.F.A., U. Va., 1965; m. Grace W. Ing, June 23, 1951; children—Norman Nash, Charles Fairman. Mgmt. trainee Chase Nat. Bank, N.Y.C., 1948-50; with First Nat. Bank Boston, 1951—, v.p., 1969—; mem. exec. com. Petroleum Analysts Boston, 1964—. Lectr. Am. Inst. Banking, 1953—. Mem. commn. on ministry Episcopal Diocese Mass., 1970—; trustee Family Service Assn. Greater Boston, 1973—. Served with AUS, 1945. Recipient Award of Appreciation, U.S. Treasury, 1963. Mem. Financial Mgmt. Assn. (life). Episcopalian (chmn. com. 1970—). Home: 52 Ashton Ave Newton MA 02159 Office: 100 Federal St Boston MA 02106

WU, TSE CHENG, chemist; b. Hong Kong, Aug. 21, 1923; s. Shau Chuan and Shui (Chan) W.; B.S., Yenching U., 1946; M.S., U. Ill., 1948; Ph.D., Iowa State U., 1952; m. Janet Ling, June 14, 1963; children—Alan, Anna, Bernard. Came to U.S., 1947, naturalized, 1962. Prodn. chemist, Yungli Industries, Tangku, China, 1946-47; research asso. Iowa State U., Ames, 1952-53; research chemist duPont Co., Waynesboro, Va., 1953-60; research chemist Gen. Electric, Waterford, N.Y., 1960-71; sr. research chemist Abcor, Inc., Wilmington, Mass., 1971-77; research asso. Allied Chem. Corp., Morristown, N.J., 1977—. Mem. Troy Arts Guild, 1968-71. Recipient Gold medallion award for inventions Gen. Electric Co., 1967; Eastman Kodak Research fellow, 1951-52. Mem. Am. Chem. Soc., Sigma Xi, Phi Kappa Phi, Phi Lambda Upsilon, Alpha Chi Sigma. Contbr. profl. jours. Patentee in field of polymer chemistry. Home: 14-E Dorado Dr Morristown NJ 07960 Office: Allied Chemical Corp Morristown NJ 07960

WURF, JERRY, labor union ofcl.; b. N.Y.C., May 18, 1919; s. Sigmund and Lena (Tannenbaum) W.: A.B., N.Y. U., 1940; m. Mildred Kiefer, Nov. 26, 1960; children—Susan, Nicholas, Abigail. Worked in cafeteria, N.Y., 1940-43; an organizer local 448 Hotel and Restaurant Employees, 1943, organizer, adminstr. union's Welfare Fund, 1947; organizer in N.Y. for Am. Fedn. of State, County and Municipal Employees, 1947-58, exec. dir. dist. council 37, 1959-64, internat. pres., 1964—; v.p. exec. council AFL-CIO. Mem. exec. com. Com. for Nat. Health Ins., Leadership Conf. on Civil Rights; mem. exec. bd. Ams. for Democratic Action; mem. vis. com. Brookings Instn.; Mem. Am. Arbitration Assn. (dir.). Council on Fgn. Relations. Clubs: Nat. Democratic, Federal City. Home: 3846 Cathedral Ave NW Washington DC 20016 Office: 1625 L St NW Washington DC 20036

WURTS, CLARENCE ZANTZINGER, investment banker; b. Phila., Sept. 27, 1940; s. John Wister and Mary-Vaux Buckley (Zantzinger) W.; A.B. in History, Princeton U., 1962; m. Patricia Elizabeth Weaver, June 23, 1962; children—Charles Stewart V, Benjamin Weaver. Comml. credit analyst First Pa. Banking & Trust Co., Phila., 1962; securities analyst Drexel & Co., Phila., 1965-66; securities analyst Drexel Harriman Ripley, Phila., 1966-68, asst. v.p., dir., N.Y., 1968-69; partner Alex Brown & Sons (mem. N.Y. and Am. stock exchanges), N.Y.C., 1969—; gov. Phila. Stock Exchange, 1977—. Bd. dirs. Zool. Soc. Phila., 1977—. Served to 1st lt. arty. AUS, 1962-64. Clubs: The Brook (N.Y.); Philadelphia, Racquet (Phila.); Royal Nova Scotia Yacht Squadron (Halifax, N.S.). Home: Box 297 Plymouth Rd Blue Bell PA 19422 Office: Alex Brown & Sons Suite 1320 Three Girard Plaza Philadelphia PA 19102

WURZBURGER, WALTER SAMUEL, clergyman; b. Munich, Germany, Mar. 29, 1920; s. Adolf W. and Hedwig (Tannenwald) W.; B.A., Yeshiva U., 1944; M.A., Harvard U., 1946, Ph.D., 1951; m. Naomi C. Rabinovitz, Aug. 18, 1947; children—Benjamin W., Myron I., Joshua J. Rabbi, 1944; Rabbi Cong. Chai Odom, Boston, 1944-53, Shaarei Shomayim Congregation, Toronto, 1953-67, Shaaray Tefila Congregation, Far Rockaway, 1967—; editor Tradition, N.Y.C., 1961—; columnist Toronto Telegram, 1957-67; vis. asso. prof. philosophy Yeshiva U. Mem. exec. com. United Jewish Welfare Funds of Toronto, 1965-67; former chmn. commn. on adoptions, synagogue commn., now trustee Fedn. Jewish Philanthropies N.Y.; bd. dirs., chmn. com. on interreligious affairs Synagogue Council Am., 1973-75, now v.p. council; mem. interfaith com. United Community Funds of Toronto, 1960-67; v.p. synagogue commn. Fedn. Jewish Philanthropies, 1973-75; mem. nat. adv. com. United Jewish Appeal Am. Mem. Rabbinical Council Am. (pres.), Rabbinical Council Can. (past pres.), Inst. for Judaism and Contemporary Thought. Editor: A Treasury of Tradition. Contbr. articles to profl. jours., chpts. to books, Ency. Judaica. Home: 1152 Sage St Far Rockaway NY 11691 Office: 1250 Broadway New York City NY 10001

WYATT, DONALD EDGAR, physician; b. St. John's, Nfld., Can., June 7, 1926; s. Herbert Kitchener and Marion May (Soper) W.; student Ridley Coll., Ont., Can., 1942-43, Mt. Allison U., 1945-47, Meml. U. of Nfld., 1957-58; M.D., Dalhousie U., N.S., Can., 1963; m. Dorothy Mary Fanning, Sept. 8, 1953; children—George Robert Herbert, Lorelei Andrea. Mng. dir. Wyatt's Parts & Service, Ltd., St. John's, Nfld., 1951-56; underwriter Nat. Life Assurance Co. of Can., St. John's, 1956-57; intern Victoria Gen. Hosp., Camp Hill Hosp., Halifax Children's Hosp. (all Halifax, N.S., Can.), P.E.I. Hosp., Charlottetown, 1962-63; practice medicine specializing in family medicine, St. John's; med. officer Imperial Oil Ltd., St. John's, 1966—, Royal Bank of Can., St. John's, 1975—; physician (part-time) Student Health Services, Meml. U. of Nfld., St. John's, 1966-75, clin. asso. Faculty of Medicine, 1971—; provincial surgeon St. John Ambulance Assn. and Brigade, 1969—; sports physician Can. team to the World Student Games, Moscow, USSR, 1973, XXI Olympic Games, Montreal, Can., 1976; pres. Delta Ltd., 1976—; mgr. Candlelite Ltd., 1978—. Mem. nat. editorial adv. bd. Medifacts Ltd., Ottawa, Ont., Can., 1974—; mem. Can. Games Council, 1974—; mem. Can. Games nat. rev. com. of minister state for fitness and amateur sport, 1977-78; mem. St. John's Recreation Commn., 1975—; bd. dirs. Pub. Golf Assn., St. John's; chmn. bd. dirs. C.A. Pippy Park Campsite Com., 1976—. Served to lt. Royal Regt. of Can. Arty., Can. Army, 1956-63, capt. M.C., Can. Army, 1963—. Mem. Coll. Family Physicians Can. (certificant; sec. treas. Nfld. chpt. 1969-74, pres. Nfld. chpt. 1974-76, nat. dir. 1973-75, mem. com. on exams. 1973-76, nat. exec. com. 1974-75, chmn. com. on by-laws 1975—), Nfld. div. Can. Med. Assn. (chmn. com. on venereal diseases 1971-73, mem. exec. com. 1967-69), St. John's Gen. Practictioners Assn., Can. Acad. Sports Medicine, Sports Fedn. Can. (dir. 1974-75, 76—, v.p. 1975-76), Can. Games Soc. (dir. 1974—), Nfld. and Labrador Amateur Sports Fedn. (pres. 1973-76), St. John's Curling Assn., Canadian Council of Provincial Sport Fedns. (chmn. 1974-76). Mem. United Ch. of Can. Clubs: Bally Haly Golf and Curling; Rotary (group capt. 1975-77). Address: 207 Lemarchant Rd St John's NF A1C 2H5 Canada

WYATT, DOROTHY KATHARINE WOLF, chemist; b. Bklyn., Jan. 5, 1947; d. Warren Clemens and Dorothy Katharine (Wright) Wolf; B.S. cum laude with honors in chemistry (tuition scholar 1964-67, Regents scholar 1964-67), L.I. U., 1967; postgrad. U. Md., 1967-68, Am. U., 1978—; m. William Kermit Wyatt, May 9, 1970. Analytical research chemist/sci. asso. U.S. Pharmacopeia, Rockville, Md., 1968-77, supr. reference standards (lab. testing), 1977—. Mem. AAAS. Home: 15521 Wembrough St Colesville Silver Spring MD 20904 Office: US Pharmacopeia 12601 Twinbrook Pkwy Rockville MD 20852

WYATT, HERBERT, physician; b. Berlin, Germany, Feb. 7, 1910; s. Julius and Martha (Wilczewski) Kwiatkowski; M.D. summa cum laude, Friedrich Wilhelm U., Berlin, 1936; Ph.D., U. Coll. London, 1942; m. Marion Cusnir, Apr. 15, 1939; 1 son, Robert. Came to U.S., 1946, naturalized, 1953. Research asst. Pharm. Inst., U. Berlin, 1936; research fellow Rockefeller Found., U. Coll. London, 1937-40, Middlesex Hosp., London, 1940-41; research fellow, mem. clin. research unit and cardiology dept. Guy's Hosp., London, 1942-45; practice medicine specializing in internal medicine, New Haven, 1948—. Fellow Royal Soc. Health; mem. AMA, Am. Heart Assn., Am. Geriatric Soc., Conn., New Haven County med. socs. Clubs: Masons, Shriners, Order Eastern Star, Clinton Country (New Haven). Contbr. articles to profl. jours. Home: 135 Whitney Ave New Haven CT 06510

WYATT, ROBERT HARRY, gynecologist, obstetrician; b. Mahoning Valley, Pa., June 28, 1915; s. Raymond James and Agnes Linker (Stroh) W.; B.A., Brown U., 1939; M.D., Yale U., 1943; m. Mary Elizabeth Saunders, Aug. 19, 1943; children—Robert Saunders, Bradley Braton, Barbara Ann. Intern, U.S. Naval Hosp., Newport, R.I., 1943-44; resident obstetrics, gynecology Yale-New Haven Hosp., 1947-50: attending obstetrician, gynecologist St. Joseph's Hosp., Stamford, Conn., 1950-60, Stamford Hosp., 1950-65, Greenwich (Conn.) Hosp., 1950—; dir. dept. obstetrics gynecology Greenwich Hosp., 1969-75, alt. dir., 1975—. Diplomate Am. Bd. Obstetrics and Gynecology. Fellow Am. Coll. Obstetricians and Gynecologists (chmn. sect. Conn. 1967-70); mem. Conn. Soc. Am. Bd. Obstetricians Gynecologists (pres. 1963-64), Fairfield County, Greenwich (pres. 1977-78), Conn. (chmn. sect. obstetrics, gynecology 1963-64), Westchester Obstet. and Gynecol. Soc. (pres. 1975-76), AMA. Republican. Congregationalist. Club: Riverside (Conn.) Yacht. Home: 177 Indian Head Rd Riverside CT 06878 also 17 Seavers Rd Orleans MA 02653 Office: 1 Perryridge Rd Greenwich CT 06830

WYCHE, LA MONTE GEORGE, educator; b. Chgo., Sept. 16, 1941; s. George Dewey and Bernice (Thomas) W.; B.A., St. Augustine's Coll., 1963; M.A., Roosevelt U., 1968; Ph.D., U. Ill., 1973; m. Janise Marie Morgan, Aug. 23, 1964; children—La Monte George, Tracey Ndeonika, Marla Ebony. Tchr., Chgo. pub. schs., 1963-66; counselor clin. psychology U. Ill., Urbana, 1969-72; asst. prof. psychology U. Minn., Duluth, 1973-75; asst. supt. schs., chief psychologist Duluth Pub. Schs., 1973-75; asso. prof. sch. psychology Howard U., Washington, 1975—; detached group worker Juvenile Gang Groups, Chgo., 1963-67. Active St. George's Episcopal Ch. youth program, 1975—; coach youth basketball YMCA Met. Washington. Recipient Wilhelm Weinburg award NCCJ, 1973; Tchr. Corps award, 1968; So. fellow, 1970-71; John Hay Whitney fellow, 1971-72; Howard U. grantee, 1976-77. Mem. NAACP, Nat. Assn. Black Psychologists, Am. Psychol. Assn., Nat. Assn. Sch. Psychologists, Am. Ednl. Research Assn., Am. Soc. Psychologists in Pvt. Practice, St. Augustine's Coll., Roosevelt U., U. Ill. alumni assns., Phi Delta Kappa, Kappa Alpha Psi. Democrat. Episcopalian. Club: Wheaton Youth Hockey. Home: 7426 Carroll Ave Takoma Park MD 20012 Office: 2400 6th St NW Washington DC 20059

WYCHULIS, ADAM ROBERT, thoracic and cardiovascular surgeon; b. Shenandoah, Pa., Nov. 26, 1935; s. Adam J. and Lottie V. (Jurewicz) W.; B.S., Georgetown U., 1957, M.D., 1961: M.S. in Surgery, U. Minn., 1966; m. Mary Constance Fees, Apr. 30, 1960; children—Karlene, Laurie, Adam, Lisa, Marcy, Daniel, Amy. Intern, Geisinger Med. Center, Danville, Pa., 1961-62; fellow in gen. surgery Mayo Clinic, Rochester, Minn., 1962-66, fellow in thoracic and cardiovascular surgery, 1968-70; practice medicine, specializing in surgery, Newark, 1970-71; dir. surgery and chief thoracic surgery St. Michael's Med. Center, Newark, 1971—; asso. prof. surgery N.J. Med. Sch., Newark, 1978—; attending surgery Martland Hosp., Newark, 1971—; cons. cardiothoracic surgery VA Hosp., E. Orange, N.J., 1972—; cons. thoracic and cardiovascular surgery Paterson (N.J.) Gen. Hosp., 1970—, Newton (N.J.) Meml. Hosp., 1970—, Riverside Hosp., Boonton, N.J., 1971—; courtesy staff Mountainside Hosp., Montclair, N.J., 1970-71. Served to capt., U.S. Army, 1966-68. Diplomate Nat. Bd. Med. Examiners, Am. Bd. Surgery, Am. Bd. Thoracic Surgery. Fellow ACS, Am. Coll. Angiology, Internat. Coll. Angiology, Am. Coll. Chest Physicians, Am. Coll. Cardiology; mem. Assn. Acad. Surgeons, N.J. Soc. Thoracic Surgeons, Essex County Heart Assn., Am. Med. Assn., Med. Soc., N.J., N.Y. Soc. Thoracic Surgery, Soc. Surgeons of N.J., N.Y. Soc. Thoracic Surgery, Essex County Med. Soc., Royal Soc. Medicine, Mayo Alumni Soc., Mayo Alumni Soc. Thoracic Surgery, Priestly Soc., Am. Assn. Thoracic Surgery, Southeastern Surg. Congress, Sigma Xi. Contbr. articles in field to profl. jours. Home: 3 Timber Dr North Caldwell NJ 07006 Office: 306 High St Newark NJ 07102

WYCK, PETER HERBERT, producer; b. N.Y.C., Oct. 29, 1953; s. Werner A. and Ilka Lora (Newhaus) W.; student Ramapo Coll. N.J., 1971-73, Thomas A. Edison Coll., 1976. Instr., Creative Arts Center Teaneck (N.J.) Bd. Edn., 1968-69; producer Teaneck Recreation Dept., 1971; exec. producer Bergen Visual and Performing Arts Center, Teaneck, 1971—; media specialist for health, edn. welfare project Yeshiva U., N.Y.C., 1973; stage mgr. Cyrano Repertory Theatre, N.Y.C., 1973, Mahwan Small Town and Fancy Players, Mahwah, N.J., 1973; tech. dir., bd. dirs. North Jersey Regional Dance Co. (formerly Maywood Civic Ballet), Maywood, N.J., 1973—; founder, producer Ocean Theatre Co., Teaneck, Entertainment Producer Group, N.J., 1974; dir. mktg. services, gen. mgr. Valiant Instructional Materials Co., 1974—. Producer Cole—An Evening With Porter, 1976, Jerseyanna, 1976. Mem. Am., Am. Community theatre assns. Address: 41 Riverside Dr Oakland NJ 07436

WYCKOFF, DONALD DARYL, educator; b. Santa Moncia, Calif., Apr. 28, 1936; s. Donald K. and Mary Gladys (Hammer) W.; B.S., Mass. Inst. Tech., 1958; M.B.A., U. So. Calif., 1968; D.B.A., Harvard U., 1972; m. Valerie M. Abdou, Aug. 30, 1958; children—Michele, Abigail. Vice pres. Cosmodyne Corp., Torrance, Calif., 1959-68; dir. Logistics Systems, Inc., Cambridge, Mass., 1958-72; prof. Harvard Bus. Sch., Boston, 1972—; pres. D. Daryl Wyckoff Assos., Inc., Marblehead, Mass., 1973—; dir. Victoria Stations, Inc., Lex. Transp., London, Charles River Assos., MSI Data Inc.; cons. to Am. Trucking Assn., Assn. Am. Railroads, U.S. Govt. Mem. transp. com. New Eng. Council, 1976—. Mem. Transp. Research Forum (nat. v.p. 1974-75, pres. New Eng. chpt. 1975-76), Beta Gamma Sigma. Republican. Episcopalian. Author: Organizational Formality and Performance in the Motor Carrier Industry, 1974; Railroad Management, 1976; (with others) The Owner Operator: Independent Trucker, 1975, Operations Management: Text and Cases, 1975; The Motor Carrier Industry, 1977; The Domestic Airline Industry, 1977; The Chain Restaurant Industry, 1978; Management of Service Operations, 1978; contbr. articles to profl. jours. Home: 5 Shorewood Rd Marblehead MA 01945 Office: Morgan 7 Soldier Field Boston MA 02163

WYDLER, JOHN WALDEMAR, congressman; b. Bklyn., June 9, 1924; s. Waldemar and Ethel Z. (Roebuck) W.; student Brown U., 1941-42, 45-47; LL.B., Harvard, 1950; m. Brenda E. O'Sullivan, Oct. 25, 1959; children—Christopher, Kathleen, Elizabeth. Admitted to N.Y. State bar, 1950; pvt. practice law, 1950-53; with U.S. Atty.'s Office, Eastern Dist. N.Y., 1953-59; practiced in Mineola, N.Y., 1959-60; partner firm Wydler, Balin, Pares, Soloway, Seaton & Marglin, 1967—; mem. 88th-95th congresses from 5th Dist. N.Y., mem. com. on govt. ops., sci. and tech. com., ad hoc com. on energy; vice chmn. N.Y. bipartisan congressional delegation, 1976—; asst. minority floor leader, 1973, House Republican floor mgr., 1973-76, dean N.Y. Rep. Delegation. Mem. N.Y. State investigation commn. to probe N.Y.C. sch. constrn. irregularities, 1959-60; charter mem. Bishop's Mens Assn. of Cathedral Incarnation, Garden City, N.Y.; vice chmn. Nassau County Republican Exec. Com.; mem. Garden City Rep. Club; bd. visitors U.S. Mcht. Marine Acad., 1971—. Served with AUS, World War II; CBI; mem. USAF Res. Mem. Fed., Nassau County bar assns., Dist. Atty's Assn., Protestant Lawyers Assn., Am. Legion, VFW, U.S. Jr. C. of C., Phi Beta Kappa, Sigma Chi. Mason, Elk, Lion. Home: 63 1st St Garden City NY 11530 Office: 150 Old Country Rd Mineola NY 11501 also Rayburn House Office Bldg Washington DC 20515

WYGANT, JAMES PETER, food co. exec.; b. Montreal West, Que., Can., Oct. 31, 1926; s. Samuel Edwin and Louise (Biersach) W.; student McGill U., 1945-46, U. Syracuse, 1960-61; m. Ruth Evelyn Mitchell, June 11, 1948; children—Margaret, Patricia, Sally. Various assignments Campbell Sales Co. and Campbell Soup Co., 1949-61, gen. sales mgr. Campbell Soup Co., Toronto, Ont., Can., 1961-66; v.p. in charge grocery div. Standard Brands Ltd., Montreal, Que., 1966-69, v.p., dir., 1969-72; pres., chief exec. officer Gen. Bakeries Ltd., Don Mills, Ont., 1972—; dir. W.E. Long Co., Chgo. Served with Royal Can. Navy, 1944-45. Mem. Grocery Products Mfrs. Can. (dir. 1976—), Am. Bakery Assn. (gov. 1975—), Bakery Council Can. (dir. 1973—), Toronto Bd. Trade, Can. C. of C. Mem. United Ch. Can. Clubs: Thornhill Country, Bd. Trade. Home: 34 Elgin St Thornhill ON L3T 1W4 Canada Office: 75 Donway West Don Mills ON M3C 2E9 Canada

WYGLENDOWSKI, FRANK THOMAS, hosp. adminstr.; b. Orange, N.J., Jan. 12, 1949; s. Thaddeus Henry and Frances (Hanson) W.; A.Applied Sci., Paul Smiths Coll., 1971; m. Claire Ann Leimeux, Aug. 12, 1971; children—Frank Jason, Chantelle Marie. With Walt Disney World, Orlando, Fla., 1971-72; asst. dir. ARA, Jersey City, N.J., 1972-75; food service dir. Divine Providence Hosp., Williamsport, Pa., 1975—; faculty Williamsport Area Community Coll., 1977—. Mem. Am. Soc. Hosp. Food Service Adminstrs., Am. Mgmt. Assn., Alpha Phi Omega. Home: 1950 Garden View Plaza Williamsport PA 17701 Office: 1100 Grampian Blvd Williamsport PA 17701

WYMAN, FRANKLIN, JR., confection mfg. exec.; b. Boston, Mar. 27, 1921; s. Franklin and Madeleine (Cutter) W.; B.S., Harvard, 1943, M.B.A., 1946; m. Ruth Cheney, June 28, 1946; children—Franklin III, Janet (Mrs. William C. Coleman), Sylvia C., Charles C. Export mgr. Gen. Radio Co., Cambridge, Mass., 1947-50; gen. mgr. Boston Mailing Co., 1950-51; asst. controller State Mut. Life Ins. Co., Worcester, Mass., 1951-56; controller R.H. Stearns Co., Boston, 1956-64; pres., treas. Bailey's of Boston, Inc., 1964—, also dir.; dir. Bailey's of Boston, Inc., Donald Wyman, Inc., Henry and Frick, Inc., Falulah Paper Co., Automation Mgmt., Ft. Hill Mgmt. Co.; trustee, mem. real estate, auditing coms. Brookline Savs. Bank. Chmn., Dover-Sherborn Regional High Sch. Bldg. Com., 1962-63; chmn. personnel bd. Town of Brookline, 1972-77, mem. town retirement bd., 1978—; bd. dirs., v.p., exec. com. Hahnemann Hosp., 1969-77; trustee Boston Arts Festival, South Boston Neighborhood House, 1974—. Served to lt. USNR, 1943-46. Mem. Asso. Harvard Alumni (exec. com., dir.), Soc. Colonial Wars (lt. gov., mem. council). Republican. Episcopalian. Club: Country (gov.) (Brookline). Author: Profile Executive Greater Boston, 1958. Home: 83 Lee St Brookline MA 02146 Office: 26 Temple Pl Boston MA 02111

WYMAN, RACHEL, social worker, psychotherapist; b. N.Y.C., Jan. 7, 1920; d. Reuben and Liza (Bush) W.; B.S., Hunter Coll., 1939; M.S.W., G.W. Brown Sch. Social Work Washington U., 1942; Ph.D. in Human Relations, N.Y. U., 1969; m. Joseph H. Magdleno, Jan. 28, 1958 (div.); 1 son, Michael Linus. Case worker and supr. Montefiore Hosp. Social Service Dept., Pitts., 1942-45; supr., asst. dir. social service dept. Hosp. for Joint Diseases, N.Y.C., 1945-48; sr. counselor Jewish Family Service, N.Y.C., 1948-52; fellow in psychoanalytic psychotherapy Postgrad. Center Mental Health, 1974-77, supr. group therapy, 1977—; pvt. practice psychotherapy, faculty psychiat. div. N.Y. U., 1974-77; adj. prof. Union Grad. U. Certified psychologist, N.Y. State. Home and Office: 320 W 86th St New York City NY 10024

WYMAN, STANLEY MOORE, diagnostic roentgenologist; b. Cambridge, Mass., Aug. 3, 1913; s. John Palmer and Lelia Cummings (Moore) W.; A.B., Harvard U., 1935, M.D., 1939; m. Jessie Elinor Brooks, July 23, 1945 (dec. Apr. 1978); children—Stephen Brooks,

Jean Wyman Beebe, Martha, Barbara. Intern, Faulkner Hosp., Boston, 1939-40; resident in radiology Mass. Gen. Hosp., Boston, 1941-42, radiologist, 1946—; cons. Chelsea (Mass.) Naval Hosp., 1955-74, Tng. Com. NIH, 1965-68; asso. clin. prof. radiology Med. Sch., Harvard U., 1975—. Served to maj. M.C., U.S. Army, 1942-46. Decorated Bronze Star; diplomate Am. Bd. Radiology. Mem. AMA (del. 1974-77), Radiol. Soc. N.Am. (pres. 1968-69, Gold medal 1974), Am. Coll. Radiology (pres. 1970-71, Gold medal 1972, rep. to intersplty. com. AMA 1974-76), Am. Roentgen Ray Soc. (Silver medal 1952), New Eng. Roentgen Ray Soc. (pres. 1959-60; hon.), Mass. Radiol. Soc. (pres. 1969-70). Clubs: Aesculapian (Harvard); Economy (Cambridge). Contbr. articles to profl. jours.; licensed pilot, comml., single and multi-engine planes, instrument and glider ratings. Home: 295 Marsh St Belmont MA 02178 Office: 575 Mt Auburn St Cambridge MA 02138 also Zero Emerson Pl Boston MA 02114

WYNN, JOHN FOSTER, JR., govt. ofcl.; b. Petersburg, Va., Apr. 5, 1936; s. John Foster and Margaret (Harris) W.; B.S., Howard U., 1961, postgrad., 1961-64; postgrad. Cath. U., 1962-64; M.S., Am. U., 1976; m. Lynnette Kathleen Lacey, Dec. 2, 1961; children—Angela Karen, Melissa Elizabeth. With Bur. Ships, 1961-64, U.S. Army C.E., 1964-66, Naval Ship Engring. Center, 1966-73, 74, Naval Material Command, 1973-74; with Gen. Services Adminstrn., Arlington, Va., 1974—, asst. to asst. commr. office of standards and quality control, 1974—. Participant, Pres.'s Exec. Interchange Program, 1978-79. Mem. IEEE (sr.), Met. Joint Bd. Sci. Edn. Mem. ASME. Roman Catholic. Patentee brake locking device, submarine towing system, submarine mating system. Home: 3602 Tyrol Dr Landover MD 20785

WYNN, WILLIAM HARRISON, union exec.; b. South Bend, Ind., July 17, 1931; s. William and Effie (Welch) W.; student pub. schs., South Bend; m. Bonnie Day, Oct. 20, 1962; children—Mark and Brad (twins). Dept. head A & P Tea Co., South Bend, 1949-54; bus. rep. Retail Clks. Union Local 37, South Bend, 1954-59; rep. Retail Clks. Dist. Council 12, South Bend, 1959-61, sec.-treas., 1962-66; with Retail Clks. Internat. Union, Washington, 1961-62, 66—, internat. sec.-treas., 1976-77, internat. pres., 1977—; v.p. AFL-CIO, mem. exec. com. Internat. Fedn. Comml., Clerical, Tech. Employees; mem. exec. bd. Maritime Trades Dept. AFL-CIO; v.p. Food and Beverage Trades Dept. AFL-CIO; mem. labor policy adv. com. Multilateral Trade Negotiations; corp. mem. Muscular Dystrophy Assn.; mem. Pres's Com. on Employment Handicapped; mem. Com. Nat. Health Ins.; mem. exec. bd. A. Philip Randolph Inst.; dir. Union Labor Life Ins. Co.; mem. exec. com. Joint Labor Mgmt. Com. Retail Food Industry. Home: 7301 Admiral Dr Alexandria VA 22307 Office: 1775 K St NW Washington DC 20006

WYNNE, ARTHUR VINCENT, JR., press clipping bur. exec.; b. Orange, N.J., Oct. 4, 1933; s. Arthur Vincent and Marjorie E. (Stout) W.; B.A., U. Mich., 1955; M.B.A., U. Chgo., 1962; m. Patricia Ann Walters, Sept. 24, 1960; children—Arthur Vincent III, Bradley, Cathy. With Burrelle's, 1955—, midwest sales mgr., 1958-60, nat. sales mgr., N.Y.C., 1960—, partner, 1961—; pres. Internationale Fedn. Press Clipping Bureaux, Paris, France, 1965-72, N.J. Clipping Service, N.Y. State Clipping Service; partner New Eng. Newsclip Agy., Boston, 1970—; dir. Orange Savs. Bank. Chmn., past pres. Press Clipping Bur. Workshop, N.Y.C. Pres. Livingston Republican Club, 1966; councilman Livingston, 1967-71; mayor Livingston, 1968. Trustee Newark Acad. Served from 1st lt. USAAF, 1956-58. Mem. Pub. Relations Soc. Am., N.J. Press Assn., Livingston Jaycees, Publicity Club of N.Y., Employer's Assn. N.J. (pres. 1976-78), Sigma Chi. Presbyterian. Home: Sand Spring Rd Morristown NJ 07960 Office: 75 E Northfield Rd Livingston NJ 02039

WYNYARD, MARTIN, surgeon; b. Fulda, Germany, Apr. 1, 1924; s. Hanns and Lisa (Winkel) Weinberg; came to U.S., 1959, naturalized, 1966; M.B.B.S., Surgeon's Hall, Edinburgh, 1949; m. Ruth Reid, Feb. 20, 1946; children—David John, Douglas Michael, Peter Martin. Intern, St. James Hosp., London, resident in surgery, 1951-54, Queen Elizabeth Hosp., Birmingham, Eng., 1955-56; resident in thoracic surgery Brompton Hosp., London, 1956-57, Sully Hosp. Thoracic Centre, S. Wales, 1957-59; fellow Lahey Clinic, Boston, 1959-60; practice medicine, specializing in gen. and thoracic surgery, Syracuse, N.Y., 1963—; staff Community Gen. Hosp. Diplomate Am. Bd. Surgery, Am. Bd. Thoracic Surgery. Fellow Royal Coll. Surgeons (Eng.), Royal Soc. Medicine, Am. Coll. Chest Physicians, Am. Coll. Angiology; mem. Am. Soc. Gastrointestinal Endoscopy. Contbr. articles in field to med. jours. Home and Office: 4865 Broad Rd Syracuse NY 13215

WYON, JOHN BENJAMIN, med. educator; b. London, May 3, 1918; s. Guy Alfred and Emma Mildred (Hitchcock) W.; came to U.S., 1952; B.A., Cambridge U., 1940, M.B. Ch.B., 1942; M.P.H., Harvard U., 1953; m. Elizabeth Glynne Cranmer, July 10, 1946; children—Rachel Margaret, Thomas Cranmer. House surgeon, Halifax, Eng., 1942-43, Friends Ambulance Unit, Ethiopia, 1943-45; house physician Lewisham Hosp., London, 1945-48; physician Ch. Missionary Soc., India, 1949-52; field dir. Population Study, Harvard Sch. Pub. Health and Christian Med. Coll., Ludhiana, Punjab, India, 1953-60; instr. to sr. lectr. Harvard Sch. Pub. Health, 1960—. Mem. Am. Pub. Health Assn., Royal Soc. Medicine London, Population Assn. Am. Episcopalian. Author: (with John E. Gordon) The Khanna Study, 1971. Home: 73 Perry St Brookline MA 02146 Office: Dept Population Scis Harvard Sch Pub Health 665 Huntington Ave Boston MA 02115

WYRICK, CHARLES LLOYD, JR., museum adminstr.; b. Greensboro, N.C., May 5, 1939; s. Charles Lloyd and Edythe Ellen (Ellis) W.; B.A., Davidson Coll., 1961; M.F.A., U. N.C., 1964; m. Constance Michelle Hooper, Aug. 22, 1964; children—Charles Lloyd III, Christopher Conrad Hooper. Instr., Stephens Coll., Columbia, Mo., 1964-66; asst. head programs div. Va. Museum, Richmond, 1966-68; exec. dir. Assn. Preservation Va. Antiquities, Richmond, 1968-70; pres. Research & Restoration, Inc., Richmond, 1970-73; dir. Del. Art Mus., Wilmington, 1973—; cons. to gov. Va., 1972-73; mem. Richmond Commn. Archtl. Rev., 1969-72, New Castle County (Del.) Historic Rev. Bd., 1975—. Bd. visitors Davidson Coll., 1974—. Served to 1st lt. AUS, 1961-63. Recipient 1st award of Merit for Spl. Column Writing, Va. Press Assn., 1973. Mem. Am. Assn. Museums, Assn. Art Mus. Dirs., Internat. Council Museums. Club: Vicmead Hunt. Author: The 17th Street Market, 1972, also articles. Home: 2616 W 16th St Wilmington DE 19806 Office: 2301 Kentmere Pkwy Wilmington DE 19806

WYRTZEN, JAMES CHARLES, pastoral counselor; b. N.Y.C., Aug. 27, 1942; s. James and Malvina Wyrtzen; B.A., Moravian Coll. and Theol. Sem., 1964, M.Div., 1967; Pastoral Care Certificate, Insts. of Religion and Health, N.Y.C., 1970, Pastoral Counseling Certificate, 1973; m. Marcia Metz, Aug. 17, 1975; children—Andrew Mark, Christy. Ordained to ministry United Methodist Ch., 1966, pastor Westhampton Beach (N.Y.), United Meth. Ch., 1967-70, Whitestone (N.Y.) United Meth. Ch., 1970-73; dir. Whitestone Counseling Center, 1973-76, also staff therapist Yorkville (N.Y.) Counseling Center, South Nassau (N.Y.) Family Counseling Inst.; exec. dir. Center for Creative Living of Mental Health Assos., Allendale, N.J., 1976—, pres., 1976-77; pvt. practice psychotherapy, N.Y.C., 1973—. Pres. Hampton Council Chs., 1969-70. Recipient Cora Dosta Moses Homeltics prize Moravian Theol. Sem., 1967. Diplomate Am. Assn. Pastoral Counselors; mem. Am. Assn. Marriage and Family Counselors (clin. mem.). Democrat. Home: 2-20 34th St Fair Lawn NJ 07410 Office: Mental Health Assos Allendale Ave and Franklin Turnpike Allendale NJ 07401 also 16 E 79th St Suite 44 New York City NY 10021

WYSOCKI, BOLESLAW A(NTONI), psychologist, educator; b. Poland, June 10, 1912; s. Wladyslaw and Wiktoria (Mizia) Wysocki; student U. Cracow, U. Edinburgh (Scotland), Cambridge (Eng.) U., Oxford (Eng.) U., 1932-48; Ph.D., U. London (Eng.), 1954. Came to U.S., 1952, naturalized, 1958. Dir. edn. Ministry Edn., Gt. Britian, 1948-52; counselor, tchr. Marquette U., Milw., 1952-55; asso. prof. psychology Alliance (Pa.) Coll., 1955-57, Merrimack (Mass.) Coll., 1957-60, Regis (Mass.) Coll., 1960-62; prof. psychology Newton (Mass.) Coll., 1962—. Clin. work mental instns., 1952—. Served as mil. psychologist Polish Army, 1943-48. Mem. Am., Mass., Brit. psychol. socs., Polish Inst. Arts and Scis. in Am., AAUP. Contbr. articles to profl. jours. Home: 240 Brattle St Cambridge MA 02138 Office: 885 Centre St Newton MA 02159

WYSONG, EARL MARSHALL, JR., accountant, auditor; b. Washington, June 3, 1925; B.A., Eastern Wash. State Coll., 1961; M.B.A., George Washington U., 1964, D.B.A., 1972; m. Lois June Artz, Sept. 7, 1946. Accountant, Eastern Air Lines, Washington, 1946-49, 50; commd. 1st lt. USAF, 1950, advanced through grades to maj., 1962; with NATO Hdqrs., Izmir, Turkey, 1956-58; with SAC, Spokane, Wash., 1958-62; asst. dir. GAO, Washington, 1962—; adj. prof. U. Md., 1965-68, 74—, George Washington U., 1967-71, U. Calif. at Berkeley, 1971-73, Am. U., 1973, Golden Gate U., 1973. Served with AUS, 1943-46. C.P.A., Md.; certified mgr. Recipient Outstanding Service to Community award Citizens Assn., 1966; Career Devel. award GAO, 1967. Mem. Am. Inst. C.P.A.'s, Assn. Govt. Accountants (Nat. Achievement of Year award 1975), Assn. Systems Mgmt. (internat. distinguished service award 1978), Soc. Mgmt. Info. Systems, Am. Accounting Assn., Acad. of Mgmt. Contbr. articles to profl. jours. Home: 13014 Elkridge St Beltsville MD 20705 Office: 441 G St NW Washington DC 20548

WYSZKOWSKI, PAUL EDWARD, cons. engr.; b. E. Paterson, N.J., Mar. 10, 1932; s. Anthony Paul and Anna (Zayshla) W.; B.S.C.E., Newark Coll. Engring., 1954; m. Marilyn Joyce Bazydlo, June 20, 1959; children—Debra, Sandra, Bryan. Constrn. supr. N.Y. Dept. Pub. Works, N.Y.C., 1954; engr. Louis Berger Assos., Orange, N.J., 1956-59, Bur. Sanitary Engring. Calif. State Dept. Pub. Health, 1959-61, N.J. Dept. Health, 1961-63; v.p., dir. Charles J. Kupper Inc. Piscataway, N.J., 1963-71; private cons. environ. engr. Warren, N.J., 1971—. Served with U.S. Army, 1954-56. Lic. profl. engr., N.J., N.Y., Penn., Ohio, Calif., Ala. Diplomate Am. Acad. Environ. Engrs. Mem. Water Pollution Control Fedn., Am. Water Works Assn., Am., N.J. cons. engrs. council, ASCE, Nat., N.J. socs. profl. engrs. Roman Catholic. Author publs. in field. Home: 30 Skyline Dr Warren NJ 07060 Office: 55 Mountain Blvd Warren NJ 07060

YABLONSKY, HARVEY ALLEN, chemist, educator; b. Bklyn., Nov. 24, 1933; s. Samuel and Lillian (Pronsky) Y.; B.S., Bklyn. Coll., 1954, M.A., 1958; M.S., Stevens Inst. Tech., Hoboken, N.J., 1957, Ph.D., 1964; m. Ruth Marilyn Canstein, Aug. 23, 1964; children—Leedra Ross, Michael Robert. Research biochemist Messinger Research Found., Bklyn., 1956-58; research fellow Stevens Inst. Tech., 1959-63; lectr. chemistry Hunter Coll., N.Y.C., 1960-64; asst. prof. U.S. Mcht. Marine Acad., Kings Point, N.Y., 1963-64; lectr. phys. chemistry Rutgers U., 1967-69; head dept. phys. chemistry Bristol Myers Co., Hillside, N.J., 1964-69; prof. chemistry Kingsborough Coll., Bklyn., 1969—; cons. in field. Recipient Outstanding Educator Am. award, 1975. Crookes Stanley research fellow, 1960-63; accredited profl. chemist. Fellow Am. Inst. Chemists; mem. Am. Chem. Soc., Sigma Xi. Author: (textbook) Chemistry, 1975; also research papers. Home: 815 Springfield Ave Cranford NJ 07016 Office: Kingsborough Coll Oriental Blvd Brooklyn NY 11235

YACHTER, MORRIS, mathematics cons.; b. Poland, Mar. 15, 1912; s. Samuel and Dora Y.; came to U.S., 1929, naturalized, 1940; B.C.E., N.Y. U., 1940, M.A., 1943; Ph.D., Courant Inst. Math. Scis., N.Y. U., 1952. Aeronautical engr. Brewster Aeronautics, Johnsville, Pa., 1940-44; design engr. Republic Aviation Corp., Farmingdale, N.Y., 1944-46; sr. engr. M. W. Kellogg Co., N.Y.C., 1946-59; sr. engr. Ambac Industries, Garden City, N.Y., 1959-68; sr. staff engr. Lockheed Aircraft, Long Branch, N.J., 1970-71; cons. in applied mathematics, N.Y.C., 1952—. Mem. Am. Math. Soc., N.Y. Acad. Scis., Am. Inst. Aeronautics and Astronautics. Contbr. articles in field to profl. jours. Address: 278 Crosse Dr Cranbury NJ 08512

YAFFE, JOSEPH X., lawyer; b. Phila., May 6, 1913; s. Samuel and Rose (Schaffer) Y.; A.B., U. Pa., 1929-33; J.D., Temple U., 1936; m. Silvia F. Fishbein, July 21, 1940; children—Roy, Peter M., Lisa Jo. Admitted to Pa. bar, 1937; spl. dep. atty. gen. Commonwealth of Pa., 1937-54; partner Yaffe and Gould, Phila., 1954—; pres. Commonwealth Insular Devel., Inc. Counsel, dir. Police Athletic League, 1948—; counsel, dir. Elder Craftsmen Phila., 1959—, pres., 1965-66, chmn. bd. dirs., 1966-67; mem. exec. com. Nat. Community Relations Advisory Council, 1956-64, treas., 1960-64; pres. Jewish Community Relations Council Greater Phila., 1956-59, hon. pres., 1959—; commr. Pa. Fair Employment Practices Commn., 1960-61; commr. Phila. Fellowship Commn., 1956-76, v.p., 1960-63; commr. Pa. Human Relations Commn., 1961—, vice chmn., 1968-74, chmn., 1974—; counsel, dir. Soc. Crippled Children and Adults Phila. area, 1949—, pres., 1962-63, dir. Pa. Easter Seal Soc. for Crippled Children and Adults, 1969-72; nat. council Joint Distbn. Com., 1964-67; v.p. Internat. Assn. Ofcl. Human Rights Agys., 1967-68, counsel, 1973-76. Served as ensign USC-GR, 1942-45. Recipient Easter Seal Pres. medallion, 1965; Police Athletic League Founder's award, 1966, Distinguished Service award, 1970, Humanitarian award Salem Bapt. Ch., 1968; Pa. Ho. of Reps. Service award, 1971; Distinguished Merit award NCCJ, 1976. Mem. Am., Pa., Phila. bar assns., Pa. Soc. Clubs: Meadowlands Country (gov. 1963—, v.p. 1965-71, pres. 1971-73, hon. pres. 1973—), Masons, Shriners. Home: 1006 Arboretum Rd Wyncote PA 19095 Office: Two Penn Center Plaza Philadelphia PA 19102

YAGER, ROBERT LOUIS, internist; b. N.Y.C., June 15, 1931; s. Harry and Jeanette (Kahn) Y.; B.A., Harvard U., 1952; M.D., N.Y. U., 1956; m. J.A. Wheeler, Feb. 1, 1958; children—Lesley Claire, Erica Carlyn, Bryan Douglas. Intern, Charity Hosp. La., New Orleans, 1956-57, resident in internal medicine, 1960-62; practice medicine specializing in internal medicine, West New York, N.J., 1963—; mem. staff North Hudson/Palisade Gen. Hosp., 1963—, pres. med. staff, 1978-79: clin. asst. prof. medicine N.J. Coll. Medicine; dir. respiratory therapy Christ Hosp., Jersey City. Served with USNR, 1958-60. Elected to Hudson County Pub. Health Hall of Fame, 1975. Diplomate Am. Bd. Internal Medicine. Fellow Am. Acad. Chest Physicians. Office: 6600 Blvd E West West New York NJ 07093

YALOW, ROSALYN SUSSMAN, med. physicist; b. N.Y.C., July 19, 1921; d. Simon and Clara (Zipper) Sussman; A.B., Hunter Coll., 1941; M.S., U. Ill., 1942, Ph.D., 1945; D.Sc., U. Ill., 1974, Phila. Coll. Pharmacy and Sci., 1976, N.Y. Med. Coll., 1976, Med. Coll. Wis., 1977, Yeshiva U., 1977, Southampton Coll., 1978, Bucknell U., 1978, Princeton U., 1978, Jersey City State Coll., 1979, Med. Coll. Pa., 1979; D.Hum. Letters, Hunter Coll., CU NY, 1978, Sacred Heart U., 1978; m. A. Aaron Yalow, June 6, 1943; children—Benjamin, Elanna. Lectr., asst. prof. physics Hunter Coll., 1946-50; physicist, asst. chief radiosotope service VA Hosp., Bronx, N.Y., 1950-70, chief nuclear medicine, 1970—, acting chief radiosotope service, 1968-70, dir. Solomon A. Berson Research Lab., 1973; research prof. dept. medicine Mt. Sinai Sch. Medicine, CU NY, 1968-74; distinguished service prof., 1974; chief radioimmunoassay reference lab., VA, 1969, sr. med. investigator, 1972; cons. Lenox Hill Hosp., N.Y.C., 1956-62; sec. U.S. Nat. Com. on Med. Physics, 1963—; mem. nat. com. Radiation Protection, Subcom. 13, 1957—; mem. Pres.'s Study Group on Careers for Women, 1966—. Recipient William S. Middleton Med. Research award, 1960; Eli Lilly award Am. Diabetes Assn., 1961, Banting Med., 1978; Van Slyke award N.Y. med. sect. Am. Assn. Clin. Chemists, 1968; contbns. to sci. award A.C.P., 1971; Dickson prize U. Pitts., 1971; Howard Taylor Ricketts award U. Chgo., 1971; Gairdner Found. Internat. award, 1971; Commemorative medallion Am. Diabetes Assn., 1972; Nobel prize in Medicine and Physiology, 1977; Harvey lectr., 1966; Am. Gastroenterol. Assn. Meml. lectr., 1972; Joslyn lectr. New Eng. Diabetes Assn., 1972; Franklin I. Harris Meml. lectr., 1973; 1st Hagedorn Meml. lectr. Acta Endocrinologica Congress, 1973; Sustaining Membership award Assn. Mil. Surgeons, 1975; Albert Lasker Basic Med. Research award, 1976; La Madonnina Internat. prize of Milan, 1977; Gratum Genus Humanum Gold medal World Fedn. Nuclear Medicine and Biology, 1978; Virchow Gold medal Virchow-Pirquet Med. Soc., 1978; numerous others. Fellow N.Y. Acad. Sci. (A. Cressy Morrison natural scis. award 1975), Am. Bd. Radiology, Am. Coll. Radiology, Clin. Soc. N.Y. Diabetes Assn.; mem. Am. Acad. Arts and Scis., Nat. Acad. Scis., Am. Phys. Soc., Radiation Research Soc., Am. Assn. Physicists in Medicine, Biophys. Soc., Endocrine Soc. (Koch award 1972, pres. 1978—), Am. Physiol. Soc., Phi Beta Kappa, Sigma Xi, Sigma Pi Sigma, Pi Mu Epsilon, Sigma Delta Epsilon. Contbr. numerous articles to profl. jours. Home: 3242 Tibbett Ave Bronx NY 10463 Office: VA Med Center 130 W Kingsbridge Rd Bronx NY 10468

YANG, CHEN NING, physicist, educator; b. Hofei, Anhwei, China, Sept. 22, 1922; s. Ke Chuen Yang and Meng Hwa Lo; came to U.S., 1945, naturalized, 1964; B.Sc., Nat. S.W. Asso. U., China, 1942; Ph.D., U. Chgo., 1948; D.Sc., Princeton, 1958, Bklyn. Poly. Inst., 1965, U. Wroclaw (Poland), 1974, Gustavus Adolphus Coll., 1975; m. Chih Li Tu, Aug. 26, 1950; children—Franklin, Gilbert, Eulee. Instr. U. Chgo., 1948-49; mem. Inst. Advanced Study, Princeton, 1949-55, prof. 1955-66, Albert Einstein prof. State U. N.Y., Stony Brook, 1966—. Recipient Albert Einstein Commemorative award in sci., 1957; co-recipient (with Tsing-Dao Lee) Nobel prize for physics, 1957. Mem. Am. Phys. Soc., Nat. Acad. Sci., Am. Acad. Arts and Scis., Am. Philos. Soc., Sigma Xi. Home: 14 Woodhull Cove Setauket NY 11733 Office: Physics Dept State U NY Stony Brook NY 11794

YANG, DAVY TEH-WEI, elec. engr.; b. Nanking, China, Oct. 15, 1935; s. Shu-Cheng and Yeu-Chieh (Sung) Y.; arrived U.S., 1962, naturalized, 1972; B.S., U. Mo. at Rolla, 1965, M.S., 1965-66; m. Joanne L. Tao, Jan. 29, 1966; children—Ellen, Irene, Steven. Instr., Taipei Inst. Tech., 1958-62; research asst. U. of Mo. at Columbia, 1965-66; design engr. Haine, Landberg & Waehler Co., N.Y.C., 1966-67, Parsons-Jurden Co., N.Y.C., 1967-69; lead design engr. Gibbs & Hill, Inc., NYC 1969—, supr. nuclear power plant designing 1973—. Mem. IEEE, Eta Kappa Nu. Contbr. research in field. Home: 20 Darby Rd East Brunswick NJ 08816 Office: 393 7th Ave New York City NY 10001

YANG, JANN NAN, educator; b. Taiwan, China, Jan. 9, 1939; s. Ching-Shing and Ching-Ui (Yuan) Y.; came to U.S., 1963; B.S., Nat. Taiwan U., 1961; M.S., U. Hawaii, 1964; Sc.D. in Engring., Columbia U., 1967; m. Chuan C. Chen, Dec. 22, 1966; 1 dau., Cindy. NRC-NASA postdoctoral research asso. Jet Propulsion Lab., Pasadena, Calif., 1967-69, sr. research engr., 1969-73; NRC-AFSC vis. sr. research asso. USAF Materials Lab., Dayton, Ohio, 1973-74; asso. prof. engring. mechanics Va. Poly. Inst. and State U., Blacksburg, 1974-76; prof. engring. and applied sci. George Washington U., 1976—. Recipient certificates of recognition, monetary awards NASA, 1968-74; East-West Center scholar, 1963-65. Mem. ASCE, ASME, Am. Inst. Aeros. and Astronautics. Contbr. articles to profl. jours. Home: 6311 Torrence St Burke VA 20015 Office: Dept Civil Mech and Environ Engring George Washington Univ Washington DC 20052

YANG, JEN TAI, environ. engr.; b. Anhwei, China, Feb. 7, 1940; s. S. H. and Hsieh Yang; came to U.S., 1964, naturalized, 1976; B.S., Chengkung U., 1962; M.S., U. Tex., Austin, 1966, Ph.D., 1968; m. Julie Wang, Sept. 12, 1965; children—Newman, Kalen. Chief environ. engring. lab., Hittman Corp., Columbia Md., 1968-71; head water and sewerage ops. and enforcement State of Md. Health Dept., Balt., 1971-78; sr. environ. engr. U.S. EPA, 1978—; environ. cons., Data Tech. Industries. Registered profl. engr., Md. Mem. Am. Inst. Chemists, Water Pollution Control Fedn., Operators Assn. of Md., Am. Water Work Assn. Patentee waste water treatment process. Home: 6265 Cardinal Ln Columbia MD 21044 Office: 401 M St SW Washington DC 20460

YANG, KEI-HSIUNG, physicist; b. Yun-Lin Hsien, Taiwan, Dec. 10, 1940; s. P. C. Yang and C. C. Wu Yang; came to U.S., 1965, naturalized, 1975; B.S., Nat. Taiwan U., 1964; M.S., U. Notre Dame, 1967, Ph.D., U. Calif., Berkeley, 1974; m. Nancy L. T. Chen, June 12, 1971; children—Lawrence H., Andrew. Tching. asst. physics U. Calif., Berkeley, 1967-68; mem. tech. staff Bell Telephone Labs., Murry Hill, N.J., 1969; research asst. Lawrence Berkeley Lab. (Calif.), 1969-73; mem. research staff Gen. Electric Co. Research, Devel. Center, Schenectady, 1973—. Mem. Am. Phys. Soc. Contbr. articles in field to profl. jours. Home: 2001 Clifton Park Rd Schenectady NY 12309 Office: General Electric Co k-1 5C31 PO Box 8 Schenectady NY 12309

YANG, KER-CHIE, chem. engr.; b. Kwang-si, China, s. Peh-Lun and Wei-Hua (Tuan) Y.; came to U.S., naturalized, 1972; B.S. Ch.E., Cheng-Kung U.; M.S. Ch.E., Villanova U.; Ph.D., Pa. State U.; m. Catherine H.W. Lee, Jan. 15, 1966; 1 dau., Ruth. Chem. engr. Chinese Petroleum Corp., Kaohsiung, Taiwan; devel. engr. Matthey Bishop Inc., Malvern, Pa., 1965-68, supr. chem. devel., 1968-70, group leader, sr. research engr., 1973-75; mgr. chem. and refining devel. Handy & Harman, Fairfield, Conn., 1975—. Mem. Am. Inst. Chem. Engrs., Am. Chem. Soc., Am. Inst. Mining, Metall. and Petroleum Engrs., Chinese Inst. Chem. Engrs., Sigma Xi, Phi Kappa Phi. Author: (with R. Hogg) Recent Developments in Separation Science, Vol. IV, edited N. Li, 1978. Contbr. articles to profl. publs. Home: 15 Post Gate Rd Trumbull CT 06611 Office: 1770 Kings Hwy Fairfield CT 06430

YANG, MOSES D.K., clergyman, educator; b. Fukien, China, Mar. 19, 1940; s. Ling Siew and Ruth (Chandra) Y.; B.S., United Wesleyan Coll., Allentown, Pa., 1964; M.A., Columbia (S.C.) Bible Coll., 1966; m. Rose Aij Mei, Aug. 20, 1966; children—Elena, Victoria, Fay, Amos. Ordained to ministry Chinese Evang. Mission Am., 1966; asst. pastor Chinese Ch. N.Y.C., 1967; pastor Chinese Christian Ch., East Orange, N.J., 1967-74; founder, pastor Chinese Evang. Ch., N.Y.C.,

1969—, Pearl River, N.Y., 1973—, West Orange, N.J., 1975—, Highland Park, N.J., 1977—; founder, pres. N.Y. Inst. Bibl. Studies, 1975—; dir. Chinese Evang. Mission N.Am., 1976—; trustee Chinese Evang. Mission in Europe, 1973—; lectr. confs., retreats. Asso. mem. Am. Sci. Affiliation, Creation Research Soc. Home: 38 Bellows Ln Towaco NJ 07082 Office: 253 Centre St New York City NY 10013

YANG, WEN-CHING, chem. engr.; b. Taipei, Taiwan, Nov. 11, 1939; s. Ting-Lien and Ho (Lee) Y.; came to U.S., 1964, naturalized, 1972; B.S. in Chem. Engring., Nat. Taiwan U., 1962; M.S. in Chem. Engring., U. Calif., Berkeley, 1965; Ph.D. in Chem. Engring., Carnegie-Mellon U., 1968; m. Rae Tien, Aug. 24, 1968; children—Evonne R., Peter T. Sr. engr. Research and Devel. Center, Westinghouse Electric Corp., Pitts., 1968-76, fellow engr., 1976—. Served with Chinese Ordnance Corps, 1962-63. Mem. Am. Inst. Chem. Engr., Am. Chem. Soc. Contbr. articles in field to profl. jours. Patentee. Home: 46 Mount Vernon Ave Export PA 15632 Office: Westinghouse Electric Corp Beulah Rd Pittsburgh PA 15235

YANKAUER, MARY, gerontologist, social service adminstr.; b. Flushing, N.Y., Sept. 23, 1920; d. Sydney and Margaret Irene (Kerrins) Y.; B.S., Marymount Coll., 1941; certificate N.Y. U. Grad. Sch. Pub. Adminstrn., 1963. Spl. risk rep. Liberty Mut. Ins. Co., N.Y.C., 1943-62; exec. sec. N.Y.C. Mental Health Bd., 1962-66; asst. dir. govt. relations dept. Am. Nurses Assn., N.Y.C., 1966-67; adminstrv. asst. to dir. N.Y.C. Regional Med. Program, 1967-68; caseworker nursing home placement N.Y.C. Dept. Social Services, 1969; adminstrv. asst. N.Y.C. Narcotics Addiction Agy., 1969-71; exec. dir. The Burden Center for the Aging, Inc., N.Y.C., 1971—; lectr. and cons. gerontology to various colls. and profl. groups, 1970—; founder East Side Council on the Aging, N.Y.C., 1975, vice chmn., 1975—; chmn. com. on aging, Manhattan Community Bd. 8, 1974—. Vice pres. Democratic Jr. League of N.Y., 1948-49; mem. adv. com. N.Y. Citizens for Kennedy and Johnson, 1960; Democratic candidate for N.Y. State Assembly, 1965; campaign mgr. Municipal Ct. Judgeship, 9th Dist. Manhattan, N.Y., 1958; mem. community adv. bd. Jr. League Sr. Citizens Nespaper, 1976—; bd. dirs. Yorkville Civic Council. Recipient William Cushing and other awards for Outstanding Community Service. Mem. Am. Acad. Polit. and Social Scis., Acad. Polit. Sci., Nat. Assn. Social Workers, Gerontol. Soc., Pub. Health Assn. N.Y., Internat. Personnel Mgmt. Assn., AAUW, Profl. Assn. Municipal Mgmt., ACLU, Nat. Council Women of U.S., NAACP, Citizens Union, Council on Parks and Playgrounds. Club: Soroptomists Internat. Office: 445 E 85th St New York City NY 10028

YANOFF, JAY MYRON, educator; b. Louisville, Apr. 24, 1941; s. Max and Gertrude (Waldman) Y.; B.S., U. Louisville, 1963, M.A., 1966; Ed.D., Temple U., 1972; divorced; children—Brian, Neal. Prin., dir. Louisville Jewish Day Sch., 1968-70; instr. Temple U., 1970-72; coordinator staff tng. and evaluation Pa. Advancement Sch., Intensive Learning Center, Phila., 1972-75, coordinator tng. alternative programs, 1975-77; behavioral scientist U Pa. Sch. Dental Medicine, 1977—; cons. in field. Served with USCGR, 1963-69. Woodcock scholar, 1963; Crusade for Children scholar, 1964-66; grantee U.S. Office Edn., 1971-72. Mem. Am. Ednl. Research Assn., Assn. Children with Learning Disabilities, Assn. Supervision and Curriculum Devel., Am. Assn. Dental Schs. Contbr. articles to profl. jours. Co-author: The Psychology of Open Teaching and Learning, 1972; Real Learning: A Sourcebook for Teachers, 1976. Home: 7207 Lincoln Dr Philadelphia PA 19119

YANOFF, SEYMOUR L., TV exec.; b. Boston, Mar. 18, 1932; s. Victor and Jeanne (Chasen) Y.; ed. Harvard U., Boston State Coll., Williams Coll.; m. Judith Datz, Oct. 15, 1960; children—Donna, Michael. Account exec. Sta. WCOP, Boston, 1961-65; account exec. Sta. WBZ, Boston, 1965, gen. sales mgr., 1968-71, gen. mgr., 1971-73; sales mgr. Sta. KYW, Phila., 1966, Sta. WINS, N.Y.C., 1967; gen mgr., v.p. STa. WBZ-TV, Boston, 1973—. Trustee New Eng. Aquarium, 1976—. Served with U.S. Army, 1950-52. Recipient Other award Salvation Army, 1977, United Way award, 1977, Mass. Better Life award, 1977. Mem. New Eng. Broadcasters Assn., Advt. Club Boston, Nat. Assn. Broadcasters, Exec. Club Boston, Mass. Broadcasters Assn. (pres. 1976-77), Nat. Acad. TV Arts and Scis. (dir. 1977—). Clubs: Algonquin, Stadium. Home: 15 Emily Rd Framingham MA 01701 Office: WBZ-TV 1170 Soldiers Field Rd Boston MA 02134*

YANOW, RHODA MAE KORNFELD, artist; b. Newark; d. Sol and Bessie (Braun) Kornfeld; m. Alvin Yanow; children—Andy David, Mitchell Toby. Fashion illustrator; portrait artist; exhibited in one-woman shows including: Hait Gallery, 1977-78; group shows include: Springfield (Mass.) Mus. Fine Arts, 1976, NAD, 1976, 77, 78, Salmagundi Club, N.Y.C., 1976, 77, Nat. Arts Club, 1976, 77, 78; represented in permanent collections including: Town of W. Orange (N.J.), Newark Pub. Library. Recipient award Council of Am. Socs., 1975; Louis La Beaum Meml. award NAD, 1975; Dr. Ralph Weiler prize Nat. Acad., 1977, James A. Suydam bronze medal, 1975; Anna Hyatt Huntington gold medal, 1977; Catharine Lorillard Wolfe award for figure, 1979. Mem. Am. Artists Profl. League, Pastel Soc. Am., Allied Artists Am. (asso., award for pastel 1978), Catharine Lorillard Wolfe Art Club (gold medal 1975), Phila. Watercolor Club, Nat. Arts Club, Academic Artists. Club: Salmagundi. Home: 12 Korwel Circle West Orange NJ 07052

YANTA, WILLIAM JOSEPH, aerospace engr.; b. Runge, Tex., Nov. 20, 1939; s. Alex V. and Sophie R. (Dworaczyk) Y.; B.S., U. Tex., 1962, M.S., 1964; diploma Von Karman Inst. Fluid Dynamics, Brussels, 1965; Ph.D., Cath. U. Am., 1973; m. Margaret Jane Davis, June 6, 1964; children—Mark, Rachel. Research aerospace engr. Naval Surface Weapons Center (formerly Naval Ordnance Lab.), Aerodynamics br., White Oak, Silver Spring, Md., 1965—, specialist aerospace engr., 1970—. Mem. family life bur. Archdiocese of Washington. NATO fellow, 1964; recipient Meritorious Civilian Service award Dept. Navy, 1974. Mem. Am. Inst. Aeros. and Astronautics, Tau Beta Pi, Phi Kappa Phi, Sigma Gamma Tau. Contbr. articles to profl. publs. Office: Code K-8 White Oak Silver Spring MD 20910

YANUZZI, JOAN RUFF, psychologist, educator; b. Sayre, Pa., Aug. 3, 1923; d. Alfred and Regina Frances Ruff; A.B. with honors and distinction, U. Mich., 1945, M.A., 1947; Ph.D. in Counseling, Child Devel., Ednl. Psychology, Cornell U., 1967; 1 son, Christopher J. Instr. secondary edn. U. Hosp. Sch. U. Mich., Ann Arbor, 1945-48; dean of girls Friends Acad., Locust Valley, N.Y., 1948-53; Spanish tchr., jr. high guidance counselor pub. schs., Waverly, N.Y., 1953-62; grad. asst. ednl. psychology Cornell U., Ithaca, N.Y., 1964-65; dir. guidance Sayre (Pa.) area schs., 1962-70; prof. ednl. psychology Indiana U. Pa., 1970—; co-dir. Psychol. Services Assn., Indiana, Pa.; psychol. cons.; dir. communication, motivation workshops to mgmt., profl. groups; testing, evaluation cons. schs. practical nursing. Active Met. Opera Guild, Pitts. Symphony Soc. Profl. devel. grantee Indiana U. Pa., 1976-77; licensed psychologist, Pa.; certified in Spanish and guidance, N.Y.; certified sch. psychologist, guidance dir., secondary level tchr., Pa. Fellow Pa. Psychol. Assn.; mem. Am., Pa. personnel and guidance assns., Am., Pa. sch. counselors assns., Nat., Pa. edn. assns., Assn. Pa. State Coll. and U. Faculties, Alpha Omicron Pi, Phi Delta Kappa, Pi Lambda Theta, Delta Kappa Gamma, Phi Beta Kappa, Phi Kappa Phi. Co-author 1976 revision Am. Sch. Achievement Tests, Psychol. Services Bureau's PSB - Test for Practical Nursing. Home: 150 Dolores Circle Indiana PA 15701 Office: 252 Stouffer Hall Indiana U Pa Indiana PA 15701

YAO, JAMES KA-YING, surgeon, educator; b. Fukien, China, Mar. 6, 1933; s. Yao Yee Chun and Yu Poi Yee; came to Can., 1959, naturalized, 1969; student Mapua Inst. Tech., Manila, 1948-51; A.A., U. Southwestern Coll., Cebu, Philippines, 1953; M.D. cum laude, U. Philippines, Manila, 1958; B.Sc. in Medicine, U. Toronto (Ont., Can.), 1967; postgrad. U. Bristol (Eng.), 1966; m. Candace Anne Yao, June 28, 1969; children—James Andrew, Jennifer Anne, Emily Katherine, Christopher Donald, Sean Cameron, Sarah Margaret, Timothy Patrick, Gregory Leigh. Intern Toronto Gen. Hosp., 1959-60; resident U. Toronto Hosps., 1961-67; practice medicine, specializing in cardiovascular and thoracic surgery, Toronto, 1968—; mem. staffs St. Michael's Hosp., Scarborough Gen. Hosp.; St. John's Hosp.; asst. prof. surgery U. Toronto, 1975—. Recipient Pres's. Gold pin U. Philippines Coll. Medicine, 1958. Winthrop-Stearns scholar, 1957-58, Coll. scholar, 1953-57. Fellow Royal Coll. Surgeons of Can., A.C.S., Am. Coll. Chest Physicians; mem. Can., Ont. med. assns., Acad. Medicine Toronto, Phi Kappa Phi, Phi Sigma. Contbr. articles to profl. jours. Home: 139 Banbury Rd Toronto ON M3B 2L6 Canada Office: 30 Bond St Toronto ON M5B 1W8 Canada

YAO, SHANG JEONG, chemist; b. Canton, China, June 6, 1934; s. Wan Wien and Ly Yiu (Kong) Y.; came to U.S., 1958; naturalized, 1972; diploma chem. engring. Taipei Inst. Tech., 1955; M.A., U. Oreg., 1961; Ph.D., U. Minn., 1966; m. Huei-Ying Sun, Sept. 2, 1966; 1 son, Gene J. Robert A. Welch Found. postdoctoral fellow Tex. A. and M. U., 1966-67; postdoctoral fellow chemistry Northwestern U., 1967-68; asst. prof. chemistry Wilbur Wright Coll., Chgo., 1968-69; instr. U. Chgo. Med. Sch., 1969-71; research asso. N. Rothschild Lab. Surg. Research, Michael Reese Hosp. and Med. Center, Chgo., 1969-71; asst. prof. neurosurgery U. Pitts. Med. Sch., 1971-78, research asso. prof., 1978—; sr. scientist Montefiore Hosp., Pitts., 1971—; co-chmn. and co-editor biomed. session 7th Intersociety Energy Conversion Engring. Conf., San Diego, 1972; co-prin. investigator NIH grants, 1969-78; prin. investigator John A. Hartford Found. grant, 1977—. Mem. Am. Phys. Soc., Am. Soc. Artificial Internal Organs, Soc. Neurosci., Brit. Brain Research Assn. (hon.), Phi Lambda Upsilon. Roman Catholic. Author, patentee in field. Address: Dept Neurol Surgery Univ Pitts Pittsburgh PA 15261

YAP, RICARDO SAN JOSE, physician; b. Manila, Philippines, Apr. 3, 1940; s. Jose and Natividad (San Jose) Y.; M.D., U. Santo Tomas, 1964; m. Ellen B. Rosenberg, Jan. 24, 1971; children—Caryn Lisa, Beth Allyson. Resident in anesthesiology Jewish Hosp. and Med. Center, Bklyn., 1966-69; fellow in anesthesia Greenpoint Hosp., Bklyn., 1970-73; attending anesthesiologist, Franklin Gen. Hosp., Valley Stream, N.Y., 1973—. Diplomate Am. Bd. Anesthesiology. Fellow Am. Coll. Anesthesiologists; mem. N.Y. State Soc. Anesthesiologists, Am. Soc. Anesthesiologists, Nassau County, N.Y. State med. socs., Bonsai Soc. Greater N.Y. Roman Catholic. Home: 1117 Cedar Dr W New Hyde Park NY 11040 Office: 900 Franklin Ave Valley Stream NY

YARBOROUGH, ERNEST LYNWOOD, JR., ins. broker; b. Atlantic City, Nov. 13, 1944; s. Ernest Lynwood and Dolores (Stewart) Y.; B.A. in Social Sci., Moravian Coll., 1966; C.P.C.U., Wharton Sch., U. Pa., 1974; m. Carole Ann Gilliam, Sept. 3, 1964; children—Tracey Ann, Ernest Lynwood. Claim adjuster, underwriter Employers Liability Assurance Corp., Phila., 1967-68; office mgr. John H. Gilliam Agy., Bala Cynwyd, Pa., 1968-75; account rep. Cape Ins. Center, North Wildwood, N.J., 1975-76, gen. mgr., 1976-77, v.p., gen. mgr., 1977-. Bd. dirs. Cape May County United Way, 1978—. Mem. Ind. Ins. Agts. Am., Ind. Ins. Agts. Cape May County (pres. 1978), Profl. Ins. Agts. Am., Soc. C.P.C.U., Avalon C. of C. (dir. 1978). Republican. Roman Catholic. Clubs: Jersey Cape Racquet, Optimists (pres. 1969) (Bala-Cynwyd); Lions (v.p. 1977, 78)(Stone Harbor, N.J.). Contbr. articles in field to trade mags. Home: 21 E Inlet Dr Avalon NJ 08202 Office: 303 New Jersey Ave North Wildwood NJ 08260

YARBROUGH, CHARLES RICHARD, telephone co. exec.; b. Atlanta, Nov. 24, 1937; s. Robert Earl and Bessie Mae (Allison) Y.; A.B., U. Ga., 1959; m. Jane Wyatt Jones, June 7, 1958; children—Kenneth Charles, Maribeth. Account exec. WSB Radio, Atlanta, 1959-64; supr. So. Bell Telephone Co., Atlanta, 1964, pub. relations supr., 1965, pub. relations mgr., 1966-69, state pub. relations mgr., 1969-73, gen. pub. relations mgr., 1973-77; dir. pub. affairs AT & T, Washington, 1977—. Mem. Atlanta Advt. Club, Leadership Atlanta, Gridiron Soc., Ga. Assn. Broadcasters, Pub. Relations Soc. Am., Soc. Profl. Journalists, Sigma Delta Chi. Methodist. Home: 1209 Huntly Pl Alexandria VA 22307 Office: AT & T Room 710 2000 L St Washington DC 20036

YARDUMLEN, RICHARD, composer; b. Phila., Apr. 5, 1917; s. Haig Y. and Lucia (Atamian) Y.; student piano with George F. Boyle, conducting with Pierre Monteaux, harmony and counterpoint with William F. Happich, H. Alexander Matthews; D.Sacred Music, Maryville (Tenn.) Coll., 1972; Mus.D. (hon.), Widener Coll., 1978; m. Ruth Elsie Seckelman, Jan. 9, 1937; children—Vahaan, Vartan, (dec.), Miryam, Aram (dec.), Sarah (dec.), Nishan, Rebekah, Rachel, Esther Marie, Dara, Anahid, Mira-Estelle, Vera Renata. Tchr. advanced piano; pres. bd. dirs. The Lord's New Ch., Bryn Athyn, Pa., also music dir., 1939—; bd. dirs. Phila. Chamber Orch.; co-founder, bd. dirs. Chamber Symphony Phila., 1965; trustee Phila. Philharmonic Orch.; trustee, v.p. Grand Teton Music Festival; composer Three Preludes for Piano, 1936, 39, 44; Armenian Suite, 1937; Symphonic Suite, 1939; Three Pictographs for orch., 1941; Danse for piano, 1942; Desolate City, 1944; Prelude and Chorale for piano, 1944; Chromatic Sonata for piano, 1946; Psalm 30, 1947; Monologue for solo violin, 1947; Violin Concerto, 1949, middle movement, 1960; Epigram: William M. Kincaid for flute and strings (commd. by William Kincaid), 1951; String Quartet 1 (commd. by Phila. String Quartet), 1955; Cantus Animae et Cordis for string orch., 1955; Passacaglia, Recitatives and Fugue for piano and orch. (commd. for Rudolf Firkusny), 1957; Chorale-Prelude on Veni Sancte Spiritus for orch. (for Edward B. Benjamin Restful Music award), 1958; Symphony 1 (commd. Eugene Ormandy), 1961; Create in Me (anthem commd. Princeton Theol. Sem. for Sesquicentennial), 1962, Symphony 2 (Psalms), 1964; Magnificat for women's voice (commd. Hollins Coll.), 1965; Come, Creator Spirit (mass in English, commd. Fordham U. for 125th Anniversary), 1966; Abraham, oratorio (commd. Maryville Coll.), 1971; recs. on Collumbia, RCA, EMI, HNH records; chorales composed for The Lord's New Ch., 1940-77. Served with inf., U.S. Army, World War II. Recipient Composer award Lancaster (Pa.) Symphony, 1975; Gold medal Armenian Bicentennial Commemoration Com., 1976. Mem. ASCAP, Phila. Mus. Soc., Mus. Fund Soc. Address: Cold Spring Farm Bryn Athyn PA 19009

YAROSH, ROBERT THIEL, optometrist; b. Waterbury, Conn., Apr. 10, 1946; s. Nicholas and Edith Irene (Thiel) Y.; A.B., Transylvania Coll., 1968; M.S., Northeastern U., 1972; O.D., New Eng. Coll., 1975. Gen. practice optometry, Boston, 1975-77, Middlebury, Conn., 1977—. Mem. Nat. Eye Research Found., Am. Optometric Assn., Am. Acad. Optometry, Am. Optometric Found., Conn. Optometric Soc., Am. Pub. Health Assn., New Eng. Council Optometrists, AAAS, New Eng. Coll. Optometry Alumni Assn. Congregationalist. Home and office: 80 Yale Ave Middlebury CT 06762 Office: 9 Signor St East Hartford CT 06108

YAR-SHATER, EHSAN OLLAH, educator; b. Hamadan, Persia, Apr. 3, 1920 (came to U.S. 1958); s. Hashem and Rouhaniya Yar-S.; License in Persian Lit., U. Tehran (Iran), 1941, in Law, 1944, D.Litt., 1947; M.A. in Old and Middle Iranian, U. London (Eng.), 1951, Ph.D., 1960; m. Latifeh Alviya, Oct. 20, 1961. Asso. prof. Iranian philogy U. Tehran, 1953, prof. old Persian and Avestan, 1960; vis. asso. prof. Indo-Iranian, Columbia U., N.Y.C., 1958-60, Hagop Kevorkian prof. Iranian studies, 1961—, chmn. dept. Middle East langs. and cultures, 1968-73, dir. Iran Center, 1961—. Dir. Royal Inst. Publs., Tehran, 1954-61; gen. editor Persian Heritage Series, 1963—, Persian Text Series, 1951—, Persian Studies Series, 1971—; pres. Book Soc. Persia, 1957—; founder, gen. editor Rahnemay-e Ketab, lit. and bibliog. jour., 1957; gen. sec. Internat. Council Philosophy and Human Scis., Iran br., 1957-61. Trustee Am. Inst. Iranian Studies, 1968—. Mem. exec. com. Corpus Inscriptionum Iranicarum, 1954—, Bibliothèque des Oevres Classiques Persanes, 1967—, Ency. Persica, 1973—, Modern Persian Literature Series, 1977—. Author: Persian Poetry in the 15th Century, 1955; A Grammar of Southern Tati Dialects, 1969. Editor: (Avicenna) Theorems and Remarks, 1954; Iran Faces the Seventies, 1971; (with W.B. Henning) A Locust's Leg, 1964; (with David Bivar) Persian Inscriptions of East Mazandaran, 1978. Home: 450 Riverside Dr New York City NY 10027

YAS, SOLOMON M., broadcasting and retailing co. exec.; b. Montreal, Que., Can., Feb. 8, 1941; s. Julius and Anna Yas; came to U.S., 1944, naturalized, 1948; B.S., U. Mass., 1962; M.B.A., Boston Coll., 1971; m. Susan O'Neill, Mar. 19, 1966; children—David, Matthew, Adam. Dir. of personnel ARA Services, Phila., 1964-73; v.p. of personnel The Outlet Co., Providence, R.I., 1973—. Accredited exec. in personnel. Mem. Am. Mgmt. Assn., Am., New Eng. socs. for personnel adminstrn., Nat. Alliance of Bus. (mem. advisory bd. 1975—), Nat. Retail Mchts. Assn. (seminar leader 1977-78). Democrat. Jewish. Home: 15 Country Ln Sharon MA 02067 Office: 176 Weybosset St Providence RI 02902

YASIEJKO, WALTER GEORGE, chem. engr.; b. N.Y.C., May 6, 1951; s. George and Magdalena (Bojczuk) Y.; B.S. in Chem. Engring., Coll. City, of N.Y., 1974; m. Joann R. Leone, May 17, 1975; 1 son—Christopher George. Tech. engr. Commonwealth Edison Co., Chgo., 1973-74; process engr. E.I. DuPont De Nemours, Newark, Del., 1974-75, tech. engr., Memphis, 1975-77, supervisor prodn., Newark, 1977—. Mem. Am. Inst. Chem. Engrs. (dir., Memphis sect. 1977-78, chmn. pub. relations com. 1977-78), Omega Chi Epsilon. Republican. Ukrainian Catholic. Home: 10 Donna Dr Newark DE 19713 Office: DuPont Chambers Works Plant Deepwater NJ 08023

YASSKY, ALFRED DAVID, psychoanalyst; b. N.Y.C., Feb. 11, 1933; s. David and Rose (Giles) Y.; M.A., Columbia U., 1958. Intern, staff therapist Beth Israel Hosp., N.Y.C., 1960-61; psychologist Morristown (N.J.) Pub. Sch. System, 1961-62; research cons., group therapist Jewish Bd. Guardians, N.Y.C., 1963-64; counselor, psychotherapist, instr. Queens (N.Y.) Coll., 1964-65; sr. staff therapist Community Guidance Service, N.Y.C., 1963—; exec. dir. Am. Psychotherapy Seminar Center, N.Y.C., 1973—; dir. Center for Being and Becoming, 1975—; faculty New Sch. for Social Research, N.Y.C., 1976—, N.Y. U., 1977; coordinator profl. series Misericordia/Fordham Hosp., 1976—. Recipient Outstanding Profl. in Human Services award Acad. Human Services, 1974-75. Mem. Am. Psychol. Assn., Am. Group Psychotherapy Assn., Internat. Assn. Group Psychotherapy, Assn. for Humanistic Psychology, Am. Assn. Marriage and Family Counselors, Psychologist Interested in Study of Psychoanalysis, Am. Soc. Group Psychotherapy and Psychodrama. Office: 789 West End Ave New York City NY 10025

YATES, JAMES ARTHUR, plastic surgeon; b. Butler, Pa., June 5, 1935; s. Adolph Walter and Laura Marie (DeFoggie) Y.; A.B., Cornell U., 1956; M.D., U. Md., 1960; m. Kathleen Buffington, Jan. 16, 1975. Intern, Cleve. Clinic Hosp., 1960; resident in surgery, 1961; resident in surgery, U. Pitts., 1962-65, chief resident surgery, 1966; resident plastic surgery, R.I. Hosp., Providence, 1967, chief resident plastic surgery, 1967-68; practice medicine specializing in plastic surgery, Camp Hill and/Harrisburg, Pa., 1968—; asst. plastic surgeon, Harrisburg Polyclinic Hosp., Harrisburg Gen. Hosp.; cons. plastic surgeon, Carlisle (Pa.) Hosp., Community Gen. Osteo. Hosp., Harrisburg; chief plastic surgeon, Holy Spirit Hosp., Camp Hill, Pa.; clin. instr. in plastic surgery, Pa. State U., Hershey. Served to capt. M.C. U.S. Army, 1961-62. Diplomate Am. Bd. Plastic Surgery. Mem. AMA, Dauphin County, Pa. med. socs., Robert H. Ivy Plastic Surg. Soc., Am. Burn Assn., Am. Soc. Automotive Medicine, A.C.S., Am. Soc. Plastic and Reconstructive Surgeons, Am. Soc. Aesthetic Plastic Surgery, Am. Burn Victim Found., Vail Cosmetic Surgery Soc., West Shore C. of C. Roman Catholic. Clubs: West Shore Country, Raquet West. Research on burns; author, co-author articles in field to med. jours. Home: 833 Kiehl Dr Lemoyne PA 12043 Office: 797 Poplar Chruch Rd Camp Hill PA 17011

YATES, JANET LEE, coll. dean; b. Teaneck, N.J., Feb. 19, 1946; d. Ralph Hugh Cuthbert and Catherine Nicol (White) Yates; B.A., Montclair State Coll., 1968; M.S., U. Bridgeport, 1969; postgrad Pa. State U., 1970—. Asso. residence counselor U. Bridgeport (Conn.), 1968-69; asst. to dean student affairs Pa. State U., DuBois, 1969-74, asst. dean student affairs, 1974—. Sec. Clearfield Jefferson (Pa.) Mental Health Mental Retardation Bd., 1973-76, chmn., 1977. Mem. AAUW (pres. 1973-75), Am. Personnel and Guidance Assn., Am. Coll. Personnel Assn. Office: Pa State U DuBois PA 15801

YATES, JOHN ROBERT, JR., hosp. engr.; b. Boston, Feb. 9, 1930; s. John Robert and Rosemary Natalie (Logue) Y.; A.B., Northeastern U., 1954; m. Virginia Dianne Finocchio, July 3, 1954; children—Deborah A., John Robert, Thomas F., Catherine I. Commd. 2d lt. U.S. Marine Corps, 1954, advanced through grades to lt. col.; action officer, constrn. team, joint logistics rev. bd. Office Sec. Def., 1969-70; engr. III Marine Amphibious Force, Fleet Marine Force, Okinawa, 1970-71; comdg. officer, marine barracks U.S. Naval Base, Boston, 1971-74, ret., 1974; dir. engring. Soldiers' Home, Chelsea, Mass.; energy conservation coordinator Exec. Office of Human Services, Commonwealth of Mass. Mem. exec. bd. USO Council New Eng., 1971—; trustee Charlestown YMCA, 1974—, vice chmn., 1977-78. Decorated Joint Service Commendation medal, Navy Commendation medal, Army Commendation medal. Mem. Soc. Am. Mil. Engrs. (dir. Boston post), Am., New Eng. hosp. engrs. socs., Navy League U.S. (dir. Eastern Mass. council), VFW. Roman Catholic. Club: Wardroom (Boston). Home: 7 Boardman Ln Topsfield MA 01983 Office: Soldiers Home 91 Crest Ave Chelsea MA 02150

YATES, MICHAEL FRANCIS, mgmt. cons.; b. N.Y.C., Feb. 9, 1946; s. John Berchmans and Jane Ann (Gretz) Y.; student Canisius Coll., 1963-64; B.A., U. Buffalo, 1968; m. Christine Mary Dallos, Jan. 14, 1967; children—Erik Michael, Alison. Mgmt. trainee Sears, Roebuck & Co., Buffalo, 1968-69; cons. Rothman & D'Alessandro,

Inc., N.Y.C., 1969-71; sr. cons. Martin & Segal & Co., Inc., N.Y.C., 1971-75, A.S. Hansen, Inc., N.Y.C., 1975-78; exec. v.p. A.M. D'Alessandro & Co., Inc., North Haledon, N.J., 1978—. Pres. Lincoln Sch. PTA, 1975-77; asst. cub master Cub Scouts, 1977—. Mem. Am. Mgmt. Assn., Am. Compensation Assn., Am. Soc. Personnel Adminstrn., Adminstrv. Mgmt. Soc., Aircraft Owners and Pilots Assn., Pilots Internat. Assn. Home: RD 2 Lannon Ln Bethlehem NJ 08826 Office: High Mountain Plaza North Haledon NJ 07442

YATES, ROBERT JAMES, ins. broker; b. Pitts., Mar. 23, 1937; s. Donald Clarence and Helen (Anton) Y.; B.S., Grove City (Pa.) Coll., 1959; m. Nancy Diane Greiner, Aug. 13, 1960; children—Robert, Andrew, Karen. Owner Yates Ins. Agy., Pitts., 1960—; dir. N. Am. Fence Co., 1970-72. Bd. corporators North Hills Passavant Hosp., Pitts., 1974—; trustee First United Methodist Ch., Pitts., 1972—. Served with AUS, 1960-62. Recipient Leaders award Harleysville Ins. Co., 1973. Mem. Nat. Fedn. Ind. Bus., Harleysville Ins. Agts. Assn., Nat. Theater Organ Soc., Musical Box Soc. (internat v.p.). Internat. Republican. Home: 901 Glenshaw Ave Glenshaw PA 15116 Office: 708 South Ave Pittsburgh PA 15221

YATES, VANCE JOSEPH, veterinarian, animal pathologist, educator; b. Smithville, Ohio, Oct. 25, 1917; s. Albert E. and Edith M. (Plank) Y.; B.S., Ohio State U., 1940, D.V.M., 1949; Ph.D., U. Wis., 1960; m. Elisabeth Yoder, July 23, 1942; children—Rosemary, Peter, Jonathan, Christopher. Asst. prof. animal pathology U. R.I., Kingston, 1949-51, asso. prof., chmn. dept. animal pathology, 1951-55, prof., chmn., 1955—; vis. lectr. Rockefeller Found., Bogotá, Colombia, 1963-64, Baylor U. Med. Sch., Houston, 1971-72; cons. Plum Island Animal Disease Lab., U.S. Dept. Agr., Greenport, N.Y., 1978—. Served with USAAF, 1941-45. Mem. AVMA, Am. Assn. Avian Pathology, Sigma Xi, Alpha Zeta, Phi Kappa Phi, Common Cause. Republican. Methodist. Editorial bd. Avian Disease Jour., 1978; contbr. over 80 articles on infectious disease of animals to profl. jours. Home: 20 Springhill Rd Kingston RI 02881 Office: U RI Dept Animal Pathology Kingston RI 02881

YATES, WILLIAM FRANKLIN, JR., investment counselor; b. Berlin, N.H., Sept. 1, 1932; s. James Andrew and Harriet (Hall) Y.; A.B., Harvard 1955; M.B.A., Boston U., 1960; m. Mary C. J. Parker, Feb. 1, 1964; children—Rebecca L., William F., James A., Marie F. Investment analyst New Eng. Mut. Life Ins. Co., Boston, 1960-64, investment officer, 1964-72; portfolio mgr. Woodstock Corp., Boston, 1972-73, v.p., 1973—; officer, dir. Richmond Loan and Realty, Mo. Valley Farms, Progressive Enterprises, dir. Ameribanc, Inc., St. Joseph, Mo., Exchange Bank of Richmond (Mo.) Ray Land and Loan Co. Served with USAF, 1955-58. Mem. Boston Soc. Security Analysts. Clubs: Country (Brookline, Mass.), Harvard (Boston), Sakonnet Golf (Little Compton, R.I.). Home: 51 Chestnut St Boston MA 02108 Office: Woodstock Corp 100 Federal St Boston MA 02110

YATRON, GUS, congressman; b. Reading, Pa., Oct. 16, 1927; s. George H. and Theano (Lazos) Y.; student Kutztown State Tchrs. Coll., 1946-50; m. Mildred Menzies; children—George, Theana. With Yatron's Ice Cream Co., 1948—; formerly amateur and profl. boxer; mem. 91st-96th Congresses from 6th Pa. Dist. Mem. Reading Sch. Bd., 1955-61; mem. Pa. Ho. of Reps., 1956-60, Pa. Senate, 1960-68. Bd. dirs. Reading Pub. Mus. and Art Gallery. Mem. Reading Jr. C. of C. Democrat. Greek Orthodox. Club: Masons. Home: 1908 Hessian Rd Reading PA 19602

YATSEVITCH, GRATIAN MICHAEL, former army officer, diplomat, engr.; b. Kiev, Russia, Nov. 16, 1911; s. Michael Gratian and Margaret (Thomas) Y.; A.B., Harvard U., 1933, M.A., 1934, postgrad. (J.B. Woodworth fellow), 1935-40; m. Barbara Stewart Franks, July 2, 1973; children by previous marriage—Gael Yatsevitch McKibben, Peter, Kara, Gratian. Mining engr. Zlot Mines Ltd., also Beshina Gold Mines Ltd. of London in Yugoslavia, 1935-40, mgr. gold mine, 1936-40; commd. 2d lt. field arty.-U.S. Army, 1933, advanced through grades to col., 1951; chief cannon and aircraft armament br. devel. prodn. cannon, Office of Chief of Ordnance, 1940-45; mil. attache, Moscow, 1945-46; U.S. del. Allied Control Commn., Sofia, Bulgaria, 1946-47; mil. attache, Sofia, 1947-49; attache and spl. asst. to U.S. Ambassador, Turkey, 1952-57, Iran, 1957-63; sr. staff officer, Washington, 1950-52, 53-57; ret., 1969; hon. chmn. Star Trading and Marine Co., Washington; econ. cons. Middle E. Decorated Legion of Merit with oak leaf cluster. Clubs: Met. (Washington); Carlton, Lansdowne (London); Camden Yacht. Contbr. articles on arty. and mineral. subjects to mags. Home: Easterly Shermans Point Camden ME 04943 Office: Suite 450 1050 17th St NW Washington DC 20036

YAYAS, CHRISTY CALAVAS, cons. and data processing co. exec.; b. Bklyn., July 16, 1922; s. Nicholas Calavas and Anna (Savapouils) Y.; student St. John's U., 1940-41, N.Y. U., 1954-55; bus. mgmt. diploma Bklyn. Coll., 1959; m. Adele Helen Kirby, May 14, 1943; children—Sharon Lynn, Chris Kirby, Denise Darlene. Programming, methods mgr., mgmt. engring. dept. mgr., audit dept. mgr. U.S. Navy Ship's Stores Office, Bklyn., 1946-59; programming evaluation dept. mgr., product planning, programming rev. dept. mgr., Univac 1050 product mgr., regional dir. edn. Univac div. Sperry Rand Corp., N.Y.C., 1959-65; devel. control coordinator Sinclair Oil Corp., N.Y.C., 1965—, mgr. computer centers, mgmt. div., 1965-69; sr. v.p., dir. Astradyne Computer Industries, 1969—; tchr. computer systems course N.Y. Mgmt. Inst. Served with AUS, 1942-44. Recipient Arthur Neurod Sloan award for excellence in bus. mgmt., 1957. Mem. Assn. Computing Machinery, Data Processing Mgmt. Assn. Home: 4 Roxton Rd Plainview NY 11803 Office: 1122 Franklin Ave Garden City NY 11530

YEAGER, EDWARD JAMES, pharm. co. exec.; b. Phila., Nov. 1, 1919; s. W. Fiske and Euphemia Caroline (Wood) Y.; grad. Charles Morris Price Sch. Advt., 1951; certificate Pa. State U., 1963. With McNeil Labs., Inc., Ft. Washington, Pa., 1937—, exec. asst. advt., 1946-51, mgr. advt. promotion, 1951-60, mgr. sample advt. div., 1960-64, mgr. sample mfg., 1964-78, mgr. rep. service McNeil Consumer Products Co., 1978—. Publicity chmn. Ambler (Pa.) Adult Sch. Staff, 1975-79. Served with AUS, 1942-46; ETO. Mem. Am. Mgmt. Assn. Presbyterian. Home: 402 Welsh Rd Ambler PA 19002 Office: Camp Hill Rd Fort Washington PA 19034

YEAGER, JOHN GEORGE, criminologist, state ofcl.; b. Sewickley, Pa., Dec. 26, 1928; s. Samuel Blair and Margaret (Ingram) Y.; A.B. cum laude, Marietta Coll., 1950; M.S., U. Wis., 1951. Research asso. Psychol. Corp. of Pitts., 1951-52; analytical statistician Air Materiel Command; U.S. Air Force, 1952-53; dir. research and statistics, Bur. Correction, Dept. Justice, Commonwealth of Pa., 1954-68, dir. Bur. Criminal Justice Statistics, 1968-73; sr. statistician Bur. Research and Devel., Pa. State Police, Harrisburg, 1973—. Pvt. cons. in field. Treas. Human Relations Council Greater Harrisburg, 1964-68. Mem. Am. Sociol. Assn., Am. Statis. Assn. (chpt. pres. 1965-66; mem. nat. council dist. 4 1967-68), Nat. Council on Crime and Delinquency, Pa. Probation, Parole and Correctional Assn., Am. Correctional Assn., Pa. Wardens Assn., Nat. Jail Assn., Am. Soc. Pub. Adminstrn., Pa. Prison Soc., Am. Soc. Criminology, NAACP, Am. Civil Liberties Union. Internat. Assn. Chiefs Police, Adminstrv. Mgmt. Soc., Law and Soc. Assn., Pa. Chiefs Police Assn., Middle Atlantic Conf. Corrections, Nat. Assn. Trial Ct. Adminstrs., Am. Judicature Soc., Population Assn. Am., Assn. Correction Statistics and Research, Phi Beta Kappa, Alpha Kappa Delta. Elk. Unitarian. Author articles in field. Home: 5026 Locust Ln Harrisburg PA 17109 Office: Pa State Police Harrisburg PA 17120

YEAKEL, JOSEPH HUGHES, clergyman; b. Mahanoy City, Pa., Mar. 12, 1928; s. Claude Harrison and Florence Mae (Hughes) Y.; A.B., Lebanon Valley Coll., 1949, D.D. (hon.), 1968; M.Div., United Theol. Sem., 1952; LL.D., Otterbein Coll., 1976; S.T.D., Keuka Coll., 1978; m. Lois Josephine Shank, Mar. 26, 1948; children—Claudia Jo, Joseph Douglas, Joanna Irene, Mary Jo, Jody Lucile. Ordained to ministry United Methodist Ch., 1952; student asst. pastor Euclid Av. Evang. United Brethren Ch., Dayton, O., 1949-52; asst. pastor Otterbein Evang. United Brethren Ch., Hagerstown, Md., 1952-55; pastor Messiah Evang. United Brethren Ch., York, Pa., 1955-61, Meml. Evang. United Brethren Ch., Silver Spring, Md., 1961-63; asst. sec. Gen. Bd. Evangelism, Evang. United Brethren Ch., 1963-65, exec. sec., 1965-68; gen. sec., Gen. Bd. Evangelism, United Meth. Ch., Nashville, 1968-72; bishop Syracuse area United Methodist Ch., 1972—. Served with USNR, Seabees, 1945-46; PTO. Home: 220 Standish Dr Syracuse NY 13224 Office: 3049 E Genesee St Syracuse NY 13224

YEDLICKA, WILLIAM GEORGE, mfg. co. exec.; b. Apollo, Pa., Dec. 25, 1922; s. Joseph Frank and Katie (Cadina) Y.; B.S., U. Pitts., 1949, M.L., 1957; m. Theresa Unger, July 17, 1970; 1 son, Monte. Asst. sales mgr. Bowers Battery & Spark Plug Co. div. Gen. Battery, 1963-64, mgr. spl. applications batteries, 1964-65, central regional sales mgr., 1965-66, s. eastern regional sales mgr., 1966-67; spl. products mgr. E. Penn Mfg. Co., Inc., Lyon Station, Pa., 1967-74, sales mgr. indsl. railroad and mining, 1974—. Served with USAF, 1942-46. Decorated D.F.C., Air medal with 4 clusters. Mem. Material Handling Inst., Material Handling Equipment Dealers Assn., Nat. Elec. Mfrs. Assn. Republican. Presbyterian. Clubs: Berkshire Country, Pinehurst Country, Mason, Shriner. Home: 355 Lackawanna St Reading PA 19601 Office: Deka Rd Lyon Station PA 19536

YEH, CHUEN YUAN, chemist; b. Chiayi, Taiwan, Aug. 19, 1939; s. Huang Nan and Chen Yi (Yeh); came to U.S., 1963, naturalized, 1975; B.S., Nat. Taiwan U., 1962; M.S., Ga. Inst. Tech., 1965; Ph.D., Ohio State U., 1968; m. Chu Lin Yeh, Jan. 1, 1966; children—Cary, Kent, Shirley. Chemistry instr. Chinese Air Force Preparatory Sch., 1962-63; research asso. Ohio State U., Columbus, 1965-68; research chemist III, Allied Chem. Corp., 1968-77, sr. research chemist, 1977—. Scoutmaster Succasunna council Boy Scouts Am., 1977—. Recipient Invention awards Allied Chem. Corp., 1975, 77, 78. Mem. Am. Chem. Soc., Sigma Xi. Patentee in fields of chem. processes and catalysis. Home: 8 Avon Terr Succasunna NJ 07876 Office: PO Box 1087R Morristown NJ 07960

YELLOWITZ, IRWIN HERBERT, historian; b. N.Y.C., Mar. 7, 1933; s. Mitchell and Dora (Neuman) Y.; B.S.Ed., Coll. City N.Y., 1954, M.A., 1955; Ph.D., Brown U., 1961; m. Dec. 25, 1958; 1 dau., Michele. Instr., Coll. City N.Y., City U. N.Y., 1961-63, asst. prof. history, 1964-68, asso. prof., 1969-74, prof., 1975—. Mem. Am. Hist. Assn., Orgn. Am. Historians. Author: Labor and the Progressive Movement in New York State, 1897-1916, 1965; Industrialization and the American Labor Movement, 1850-1900, 1977; author, editor; The Position of the Worker in American Society, 1865-1896, 1969; editor, contbg. author: Essays in the History of New York City: A Memorial to Sidney Pomerantz, 1978; contbr. articles, revs. to profl. jours. Office: Dept History Coll City NY New York City NY 10031

YELTON, ROBERT HAROLD, architect, city planner, real estate developer; b. Cin., Nov. 8, 1940; s. Robert Harold and Florence Ida (Strathmann) Y.; B.S. in Architecture, U. Cin., 1964; M.City Planning, M.Urban Design (Richard King Mellon fellow), Harvard, 1969, M.B.A., 1977. Designer, Cellarius & Hilmer, Cin., 1963-64; sr. planner Bureau d'Etudes Lugli, Sfax, Tunisia, 1965-66; instr., researcher U. Cin., 1969; dir. planning Architects Collaborative, Cambridge, Mass., 1970-72; research prin. Mass. Inst. Tech., 1970; pres. Archplan, Inc., Boston, 1972-76; pres. Bay Devel. Co., constrn. and real estate devel., Boston, also N.Y.C., 1976—; developer, planner restoration and rehab. hist. bldgs. in Boston area. Legis. com. Ams. for Democratic Action, 1974-76. Grantee Community Projects Lab., Mass. Inst. Tech., 1969. Mem. AIA, Am. Inst. Planners, Am. Soc. Planning Ofcls., Boston Soc. Architects, Citizens Housing and Planning Assn., Nat. Assn. Housing and Redevel. Ofcls., Soc. Internat. Devel., Nat. Historic Trust. Democrat. Co-author: Tenant Cooperative Housing Rehabilitation, 1970; Town Plan for the Development of Selb, 1970. Contbr. to profl. jours. Chmn. editorial bd. Connection, 1966-69. Home: 152 W Concord St Boston MA 02118 Office: 184 High St Boston MA 02110

YEN, NAI-CHYUAN, physicist; b. Shaohsing, Chekiang, China, Apr. 12, 1936; s. Chia-hong and Ling-hsing (Wang) Y.; B.S., Cheng Kung U., 1957; M.S., U. R.I., 1962; Ph.D., Harvard U., 1971; m. Molly Mu-lan Kao, Sept. 2, 1967; children—Adelina Huey-ru, Beatrice Huey-ching, Clarette Huey-chuan. Came to U.S., 1960, naturalized, 1971. Design engr. Shihmen Devel. Commn., China, 1959; jr. engr.-project engr. Bendix Corp., Towson, Md., 1962-66; teaching fellow-research asst. physics Harvard U., Cambridge, Mass., 1966-71; sr. engr. Addressograph-Multigraph Co., Cleve., 1972; research physicist Naval Underwater Systems Center, New London, Conn., 1972—. Mem. Acoustical Soc. Am., IEEE, AAAS, Phi Kappa Phi, Sigma Xi, Tau Beta Pi. Researcher in field. Home: 9 Cross Dr Waterford CT 06385 Office: Naval Underwater Systems Center New London Lab New London CT 06320

YEN, SHERMAN, psychologist; b. Peking, China, Aug. 4, 1934; s. C.H. and Pei (Wong) Y.; came to U.S., 1956, naturalized, 1972; A.B., Bethel Coll., 1960; M.A., Wichita State U., 1962; Ph.D., Catholic U. Am., 1969; postgrad. Johns Hopkins U., 1972. Prof. psychology, dir. drug counselor tng. program Essex (Md.) Community Coll., 1976—; pres. Applied Research & Mgmt. Inc., 1970—. NIDA grantee, 1969. Mem. Am., Md. psychol. assns., Assn. Advancement Behavior Therapy, Am. Assn. Mental Deficiency. Author articles; editor: Teaching Behavior Modification, 1976. Address: PO Box 133 Owings Mills MD 21117

YEO, RICHARD SWEE-CHYE, polymer chemist, chem. engr.; b. Singapore, Aug. 18, 1945; s. Jwee Khiang and Chye Hong (Chia) Y.; came to U.S., 1976, naturalized, 1978; B.Sc., Ngee Ann Tech. Coll., Singapore, 1968; M.Sc., St. Francis Xavier U., Antigonish, N.S., Can., 1970; Ph.D., McGill U., Montreal, Que., Can., 1976; m. Mabel Yip-Bao Lee, June 29, 1977; 1 son, Jason Chia-Sim. Research asso. Brookhaven Nat. Lab., Upton, N.Y., 1976—. Mem. Am. Chem. Soc., Electrochem. Soc. Author govt. publs.; contbr. articles to profl. jours. Home: 65-16 Austin St Rego Park NY 11374 Office: DEE Bldg 815 Brookhaven Nat Lab Upton NY 11973

YERACARIS, CONSTANTINE ANTHONY, sociologist, educator; b. Rethymno, Crete, July 25, 1918; came to U.S., 1946, naturalized, 1957; s. Anthony Constantine and Polyxemi (Hourhourou) Y.; LL.B., U. Athens (Greece), 1944; M.A., U. Chgo., 1950, Ph.D., 1953; m. Bernice Levenfeld, Sept. 12, 1949; children—Flora Y. Putnam, Y. George, Peter M., Anthony M. Instr. sociology State U. N.Y. at Buffalo, 1949-53, asst. prof., 1953-57, asso. prof., 1957-62, prof., 1962—, chmn. dept. sociology, 1976—; cons. local govt. Acting dir. Center for Study of Aging, 1973-76. Served with Greek Army, 1940-41, 45-46. Grantee USPHS, 1960-66, HEW, 1972-75, State U. N.Y. Research Found., Ford Found. Mem. Am. Sociol. Assn., Am. Statis. Assn., AAAS, Gerontol. Soc., Population Assn. Am., Am. Pub. Health Assn., Soc. Study Social Problems, United Univ. Professions (chpt. pres. 1971-75, state exec. bd. 1972-76). Democrat. Greek Orthodox. Contbg. author books, contbr. articles to profl. publs. Home: 485 Norwood Ave Buffalo NY 14222 Office: Dept Sociology State U NY Buffalo Spaulding Quad Buffalo NY 14261

YERGER, CHARLES LLOYD, auto parts mfg. co. exec.; b. Buffalo, May 27, 1931; s. Lloyd Kratz and Dorothy Edna (Linick) Y.; student Erie Community Coll., 1974; m. Lynn Frederico, Apr. 14, 1956; children—Dorothy, Donald, Charles Lloyd. With Yerger Radio Service, Buffalo, 1944-47, Yerger Organ Co., Buffalo, 1954-58; own er Yerger Sales & Service Co., wholesale glass products, Western N.Y., 1956-60, Yerger Auto Glass Co., Depew, N.Y., 1961—, Yerger Glass Co., Depew, 1965—; pres., chmn. bd. Yerger Indust ries Inc., mfg. autoparts in kit form, Depew, 1967—. Served with AUS, 1947-51. Patentee in field. Office: Yerger Industries Inc 4990 Broadway Box 27 Depew NY 14043

YETTER, LAWRENCE ROBERT, chemist; b. Endicott, N.Y., Mar. 1, 1928; s. Walter Samuel and Gladys Wells (Custer) Y.; Chem. Tech., Broome Community Coll., 1947-49; m. Charlotte Lou Stokes, Sept. 9, 1950; children—Brian Lee, Gary Lynn, Renee Sue. With Gen. Electric Co., Schenectady, 1950-57; with IBM Corp., Owego, N.Y., 1957—, advisory phys. chemist, 1966—. Mem. Am. Soc. for Mass Spectrometry, Am. Vaccum Soc., Internat. Soc. Hybrid Microelectronics. Baptist. Home: 19 Barton Rd Apalachin NY 13732 Office: IBM Corp Route 17C Owego NY 13827

YINGLING, NATHANIEL DAVID, surgeon; b. Clearfield, Pa., Jan. 8, 1923; s. David Andrew and Besse (Neff) Y.; B.S., Dickinson Coll., 1943; M.D., Jefferson Med. Coll., 1947; m. Ada Ruth Howe, Feb. 11, 1950; children—Nathaniel David, Douglas B., Thomas H., John P., Michael G. Intern, Jefferson Med. Coll. Hosp., Phila., 1947-48; gen. practice medicine, Clearfield, Pa., 1948-51; gen. surg. resident Thayer VA Hosp.-Vanderbilt U., Nashville, 1953-56; practice medicine, specializing in gen. surgery, Clearfield, Pa., 1956—; chief Surg. Dept. Clearfield Hosp., 1958—. Sec., Clearfield-Lawrence Airport Authority, 1974—. Served with M.C., U.S. Army, 1951-53. Diplomate Am. Bd. Surgery, Am. Bd. Abdominal Surgery. Fellow ACS; mem. Pa., Clearfield County med. socs., Am. Med. Assn., Pan Am. Med. Assn. Republican. Methodist. Clubs: Elks, Masons (Shriner). Home: 201 Bigler Rd Clearfield PA 16830 Office: 1212 Turnpike Ave Clearfield PA 16830

YOCHUM, WILLIAM DAVID, architect; b. Harrisburg, Pa., June 12, 1922; s. Homer Elmont and Violet May (Metzger) Y.; B.S. in Architecture, Pa. State U., 1950; diploma Am. Command and Gen. Staff Coll., 1973, Indsl. Coll. of the Armed Forces, 1973; children by previous marriage—Harry A., William David. Architect, The General State Authority, Pa., 1950-55, U.S. Steel Corp., Shiremanstown, Pa., 1955-57; architect Dept. of Pub. Welfare, State of Pa., Harrisburg, 1957—; pvt. practice architecture, 1950—; cons. hosp. design, 1970—, Nat. Center for Barrier-Free Environment, 1978—. Civil Def. Fallout Shelter rep., 1962-78; mem. fin. com. Baughman Meml. Methodist Ch., 1978—. Served with inf. U.S. Army, 1943-46, with USAR, 1948-75. Decorated Army Commendation medal, Purple Heart, Bronze Star; Metz Medal (France). Mem. Pa. Assn. of Institutional Engrs., Assn. U.S. Army, Am. Rifle Assn., Res. Officers Assn. (state pres. 1968-69, nat. com. 1969-71), Am. Legion, DAV (state legis. rep. 1977-78), Mil. Order of the World Wars (chpt. v.p.), VFW, Nat. Trust Historic Preservation. Republican. Methodist. Maj. work Pa. Jr. Coll. Med. Arts. Home: 900 Brandt Ave New Cumberland PA 17070 Office: Dept of Public Welfare Commonwealth of Pennsylvania PO Box 2675 Harrisburg PA 17120

YOCOM, JOHN ERWIN, chem. engr.; b. Oberlin, Ohio, Nov. 20, 1922; s. Charles Herbert and Mary Inez (Willis) Y.; student Oberlin Coll., 1940-42; B.S., Mass. Inst. Tech., 1947; m. Elizabeth Clifford, Dec. 21, 1947; 1 dau., Judith Yocom Huling. Project leader, Battelle Meml. Inst., Columbus, Ohio, 1947-57; dir. tech. services Bay Area Air Pollution Control Dist., San Francisco, 1957-61; sr. staff mem. Arthur D. Little Inc., San Francisco, 1961-62; dir. engring. Travelers Research Corp., Hartford, 1965-70; v.p. chief engr. TRC-the Research Corp. of New Eng., Wethersfield, Conn., 1970—; lectr. Yale, City U. N.Y., U. Calif., Berkeley. Served with inf., AUS, 1943-46. Registered profl. engr., Calif., Conn., Fla., Ohio, S.C., Tex., Vt. Mem. Am. Inst. Chem. Engrs., Air Pollution Control Assn. Republican. Mem. United Ch. Christ. Club: Tennis. Contbr. to profl. jours. Home: 12 Fox Den Rd West Simsbury CT 06092 Office: 125 Silas Deane Hwy Wethersfield CT 06109

YODER, EDWARD WILLIAMS, elec. mfg. co. exec.; b. Hazleton, Pa., June 9, 1931; s. Edward Harrison and Beatrice Lloyd (Williams) Y.; Asso. in Tech., Temple U., 1953-55; A.A., Jacksonville U., 1960; J.D., U. Balt., 1966; m. Carolyn Ann Hill, Oct. 15, 1955; children—Karen Anne, Andrew David, John Edward. Admitted to Md. bar, 1967; field engr. Westinghouse Electric Corp., Balt., 1955-66, contract adminstr., 1966-69, sr. contract advisor, 1969-72, div. contract advisor, 1972-73, contracts mgr., 1973-76, bus. mgr., 1976—; asst. sec. Iran-Westinghouse Programs Service Co., 1977-79. Served with USN, 1949-53. Mem. Am., Md. bar assns., Temple U. Alumni Assn., Balt. U. Alumni Assn., Sigma Delta Kappa. Republican. Episcopalian. Home: 300 Hawthorne Rd Linthicum Heights MD 21090 Office: Iran-Westinghouse Programs Center PO Box 907 Tehran Iran

YODER, HILDA (MRS. ALBERT FRANCIS GARROU), ednl. adminstr.; b. Hickory, N.C., Jan. 1, 1903; d. Ellis Hampton and Elizabeth (Frye) Whitener; B.S., Lenoir Rhyne Coll., 1924, L.H.D., 1955; M.A., Tchrs. Coll., Columbia U., 1945; m. Luther Glenn Yoder, July 7, 1928 (dec. Oct. 1940); m. 2d, Albert Francis Garrou, Nov. 4, 1956. Tchr., supr. high sch., N.C., N.J., 1926-45; research anti-convulsive clinic psychiat. and neurol. dept. U. Va. Hosp., 1945-47; founder, pres. Yoder Sch., N.Y.C., 1949-77; lectr. postgrad. Sch. Ophthalmology, N.Y. U., Bellevue Med. Center, 1950-53; dir. reading clinic Inst. Ophthalmology, Columbia-Presbyn. Med. Center, 1950-56. Mem. Daus. Am. Colonists, D.A.R. Presbyn. Home: Valdese NC 28690

YODER, JAMES WILLARD, psychologist, clergyman; b. Shipshewana, Ind., May 19, 1902; s. James Michael and Sarah Ellen (Large) Y.; A.B., A.B. in Edn., Tri-State U., 1922, M.A., 1926; M.Div., U. South, 1956; postgrad. Ind. U., 1933-36, U. Chgo., summers 1927-33, U. Pa., 1930, N.Y. U., 1956-58; m. Elsie Mae Loertz, Oct. 2, 1932; children—J. James, James Willard, Felicia Yoder Pryor, Margaret Yoder Johnson, Sherida, Michael (dec.). Licensed to ministry Congregational Ch., 1922, ordained priest Episcopal Ch., 1938; minister Congl. chs., Ind., 1922-38, Episc. chs., Ind., 1938-48, including Indpls. Cathedral, 1943-45; dir. religious edn.

N.Y. Diocese, 1948-51; mem. staff Trinity Ch., N.Y.C., 1951-54; minister St. John's Parish, Montclair, N.J., 1954-58, St. Luke's Parish, Paterson, N.J., 1958-79; pastor St. John's Ch., Englewood, N.J., 1973—; psychologist Ind. U. Med. Sch., 1931-33, Eli Lilly & Co., Indpls., 1938-42, Hosp., Montclair, 1956-58, N.J. Addiction Program, Marlboro State Hosp., 1968—; dir. Evansville (Ind.) Guidance Clinic, 1933-37; mem. faculty Ind. U., 1930-34, Butler U., 1938-43, Purdue U., 1945-48, N.Y. U., 1950-51, Grad. Sch. Theology, U. South, 1951, William Paterson Coll., 1958-64; pres. Ind. Congl. Conf., 1935-36; chaplain Seton Tb Hosp., N.Y.C., 1950-54. Civilian chaplain U.S. Army, 1943-46. Recipient Distinguished Service award Tri-State U., 1976, certificate of appreciation Gov. N.J., 1964, Recognition of 50 Years in Ministry, Pres. U.S., 1972. Mem. Am. Psychol. Assn., AAUP, Kappa Delta Pi. Author Lenten series in Living Ch. mag., 1944; editor Indpls. Churchman, 1943-45, Newsletter Ind. Assn. Clin. Psychologists, 1943-46. Home: 137 Illinois Ave Paterson NJ 07503 Office: Discovery House Marlboro Hosp Marlboro NJ 07746

YOFFE, MORRIS, health care co. exec.; b. Mt. Carmel, Pa., Aug. 8, 1929; s. Max and Sarah (Wishkin) Y.; B.S., Drexel U., 1953; postgrad. Temple U., 1953-54; m. Chickee Esther Faith Margulis, June 25, 1955; children—Seth Michael, Eve Yoffe Natalo, Josh Aron and Lori Jo (twins). Self-employed C.P.A., 1958-63; pres., dir. Corporate Planners, Inc., Laverock, Pa., 1962—; founder, sr. partner Yoffe, Herman & Co., C.P.A.'s, Phila., 1963-70; founder, dir., pres. Am. Med. Affiliates, Inc., Jenkintown, Pa., 1968—; mem. Blue Cross Assn. Medicare Provider Appeals com., 1972, Batelle Research Nat. Nursing Home Costs Study, 1974-76; appeals hearing officer Social Security Adminstrn., HEW. Mem. Cheltenham Twp. Citizens Adv. Bd., 1975—, budget adv. com. Cheltenham Sch. Dist., 1976—, Phila. Citizens' Crime Commn., 1978—, Tay-Sachs Nat. Adv. Bd.; trustee Max and Sarah Wishkin Yoffe Ednl. Found.; bd. dirs. Met. Hosp., Phila., 1974—, fin. chmn., 1975-77; bd. dirs. Solomon Schecter Day Sch., 1975—. Recipient Alexander Van Renssalaer award Drexel U., 1952, Maimonides award State of Israel, 1978. Fellow Am. Coll. Nursing Home Adminstrs.; mem. Nat. Council Health Care Services (dir. 1969-70, treas., 1970), Am. Health Care Assn. (gov. council 1969-70, dir. 1970), Health Care Facilities Assn. Pa. (dir. 1969-70, 75-77), Am. Inst. C.P.A.'s, Pa. Inst. C.P.A.'s, Pa. Soc., Blue Key, Sigma Alpha Mu. Clubs: B'nai B'rith (dir. 1958-64, pres. 1960-61; nat. v.p. Soc. Fellows, Anti-defamation League); Ashbourne Country. Home: 7724 Morgan Ln Laverock PA 19118 Office: Foxcroft Square Jenkintown PA 19046

YOHO, BETTY EILEEN, librarian; b. Warren, Ohio; d. Chester Earl and Nora Vienna (Bell) Cavender; B.A. with high honors, Ohio Wesleyan U., 1945; postgrad. Katharine Gibbs Sch., N.Y., 1947; M.L.S., Drexel U., 1965. High sch. tchr., Ohio, 1945-47; sec. to pres. Warren Tool Corp., 1947-48; tchr. Drew Sch. for Girls, Carmel, N.Y., 1948-51; tchr., librarian Oakgrove Sch., Wilmington, Del., 1951-57; librarian Lombardy Sch., Wilmington, 1957—. Mem. ALA, Del. Sch. Library Assn. (pres.), Del. Library Assn. (treas.), NEA, Del. Edn. Assn., Phi Beta Kappa, Chi Omega, Kappa Delta Pi. Mem. Christian Ch. (past sec. bd.). Club: Racquets (former sec. bd.) (Wilmington). Home: 2300 Riddle Ave Wilmington DE 19806 Office: 412 Foulk Rd Wilmington DE 19803

YOKEN, MELVIN BARTON, educator; b. Fall River, Mass., June 25, 1939; s. Albert Benjamin and Sylvia Sarah (White) Y.; B.A., U. Mass., 1960, Ph.D., 1972; M.A.T., Brown U., 1961; m. Cynthia Stein, June 20, 1976; children—Andrew Brett, David Ryan. Instr. French, Southeastern Mass. U., North Dartmouth, 1966-71, asst. prof., 1972-75, asso. prof., 1976—. Pres., Friends of Fall River Pub. Library, 1972—, pres. bd. dirs., 1972—. Recipient Distinguished Service award City Fall River, 1974. Mem. Fall River C. of C., Modern Lang. Assn. (life), Am. Assn. Tchrs. French (life), Am. Council Tchrs. Fgn. Langs., Middlebury Amicale (life), New Eng. Fgn. Lang. Assn., Internat. Platform Assn., Francophone Club. Author: Claude Tillier, 1976; Speech is Plurality, 1978; Claude Tillier (1801-44): Fame and Fortune in His Novelistic Work, 1978. Home: 97 Delcar St Fall River MA 02720 Office: Dept French Southeastern Mass U North Dartmouth MA 02747

YOLTON, DAVID W., mass mdsg. entrepreneur; b. Normal, Ill., Mar. 15, 1934; s. Leroy W. and Helen M. (Norton) V.; B.Mus., Westminster Choir Coll., Princeton, N.J., 1956, M.Mus., 1957; certificate Paul Christiansen Choral Sch., Lamont Sch. Music, U. Denver, 1952; Williamson master classes, Austin, Tex., 1960; m. Shirlee Manlove, June 1, 1957; children—Mark, Kimberly. Minister of music chs. in Tex. and Pa., 1959-65; Amway direct distbr., 1965—; minister music Jenkintown (Pa.) United Methodist Ch., 1966-72; mus. dir., condr. Savoy Opera Co., Phila., 1974-77; guest condr. Pitts. Symphony Orch., 1976-77; pres. Volton Assos., Willow Grove, Pa., 1964—. Pres., chmn. CONTACT Phila., crisis intervention, 1976—; bd. dirs., regional rep. CONTACT Teleministries USA. Served with AUS, 1957-58. Recipient certificates of recognition CONTACT Teleministries U.S.A., awards Amway Corp. Mem. Del-Val Distbrs. Assn. (pres.), Amway Distbrs. Assn. U.S. Republican. Author: How to Improve the Church School, 1962. Composer works for English handbells. Home: 2250 Country Club Dr Huntingdon Valley PA 19006 Office: 306 N York Rd Willow Grove PA 19090

YONDA, ALFRED WILLIAM, mathematician; b. Cambridge, Mass., Aug. 10, 1919; s. Walter and Theophelia (Naruscewicz) Y.; B.S., U. Ala., 1952, M.A. in Math., 1954; m. Mary Jane McManus, Dec. 19, 1949 (dec.); children—Nancy, Kathryn, Elizabeth, John; m. 2d, Peggy A. Terrel, June 22, 1975. Mathematician rocket research Redstone Arsenal, Huntsville, Ala., 1953, U.S. Army Ballistic Research Labs., Aberdeen (Md.) Proving Grounds, 1954-56; instr. math. U. Ala., Tuscaloosa, 1954, Temple U., Phila., 1956-57; asso. scientist, research and devel. div. Avco Corp., Wilmington, Mass., 1957-59; sr. mem. tech. staff RCA, Camden, N.J., 1959-66; mgr. computer analysis and programming dept. Raytheon Co. space and information systems div., Sudbury, Mass., 1966-70, mgr. software systems lab., 1969-70, prin. engr. missiles systems div., 1970-73; mgr. systems analysis and programming GTE Sylvania, 1973—. Pres. Milford Area Assn. Retarded Children, 1970-74; vice-chmn. fin. com. Town of Medway, 1973-75; bd. dirs. Blackstone Valley Mental Health and Retardation Area Bd., 1970-76; trustee Medway Libraries, 1973—. Served with USAAF, 1943-46. Mem. AAAS, Math. Assn. Am., Assn. Computing Machinery, N.Y. Acad. Scis., Sigma Xi, Phi Eta Sigma, Pi Mu Epsilon (pres. Ala. chpt. 1953-54), Sigma Pi Sigma. Contbr. articles to profl. jours. Home: 12 Sunset Dr Medway MA 02053 Office: GTE Sylvania 140 1st Ave Waltham MA 02154

YOO, DAL, internist, hematologist, oncologist; b. Kwang Ju, Korea, Nov. 20, 1943; s. Bong Soo and Yang Hee (Kim) Y.; came to U.S., 1967, naturalized, 1972; B.Arts and Scis., Seoul Nat. U., 1963; M.D., Seoul Nat. U., 1967; m. Magnhild Gun Charlotte Nordanlycke, Apr. 14, 1974; 1 son, Derek Torgny. Rotating intern St. Luke's Hosp., Newburgh, N.Y., 1967-68, resident pathology, 1968-69; resident internal medicine Thomas Jefferson Hosp., Phila., 1969-70; resident internal medicine, fellow hematology and oncology George Washington U. Hosp., Washington, 1970-72, 74-75; practice medicine specializing in internal medicine, hematology and oncology, Washington, 1975—; asst. clin. prof. medicine George Washington U. Sch. Medicine, Washington, 1976—. Served to maj. M.C., U.S. Army, 1972-74. Diplomate Am. Bd. Internal Medicine. Fellow A.C.P.; mem. Am. Soc. Internal Medicine, Am. Soc. Hematology, Am. Soc. Clin. Oncology, Am. Heart Assn., Med. Soc. D.C., Washington Blood Club. Presbyterian. Home: 11229 Waycross Way Kensington MD 20795 Office: 2121 Pennsylvania Ave NW Washington DC 20037

YORK, JEROME BAILEY, truck body mfg. co. exec.; b. Memphis, June 22, 1938; s. Jerome Bailey and Rae Lolette (Irving) Y.; B.S., U.S. Mil. Acad., 1960; M.S., Mass. Inst. Tech., 1961; M.B.A., U. Mich., 1966; m. June 11, 1960 (div.); children—Lisa, Julie, Jerome Bailey III; m. 2d, 1977. Sr. project engr. Pontiac Motor div. Gen. Motors Corp., 1962-67; mgr. advanced bus. planning Ford Motor Co., Dearborn, Mich., 1967-70; staff v.p. bus. planning RCA Corp., N.Y.C., 1970-72, pres. Hertz Equipment Rental Corp. subs., 1972-75; group v.p. Baker Industries, Inc., Parsippany, N.J., 1976-78; pres. Delta Truck Body Co., Inc., Montgomeryville, Pa., 1978—. Served with U.S. Army, 1956-60. Registered profl. engr., Mich. Patentee carbureation and fuel injection. Office: PO Box 338 Montgomeryville PA 18936

YORK, SAMUEL, JR., digital equipment corp. exec.; b. St. Louis, Feb. 24, 1952; s. Samuel and Sallie Emma (Thomas) Y.; B.S.E.E., U. Mo., 1975; m. Karlah J. Ambrose, June 2, 1973; children—Eboni, Amber. Jr. engr. Southwestern Bell Telephone Co., Kansas City, Mo., 1976; engr. Digital Equipment Corp., Nashua, N.H., 1976-79, sales rep., 1979—; data processing, microprocessor instr. Daniel Webster Coll., summer 1977. Mem. IEEE. Baptist. Designer multiline communications processor for ACS System. Home: 21 Pearl St Dover NH 03820 Office: Digital Equipment Corp 55 Northeastern Blvd Nashua NH 03060

YOSHIKAWA, TAKATOSHI, beauty, barber and dental equipment mfg. co. exec.; b. Osaka, Japan, Apr. 23, 1930; s. Hidenobu and Shizue (Morita) Y.; B.A., Tokyo U., 1954; m. Akiko Inoue, May 29, 1957; children—Takaaki, Hirokazu. Shipbldg. engr. Osk Ltd., Osaka, 1954-55; products mgr. Takara Chukosho Co. Ltd., Osaka, 1955-56, market researcher, N.Y.C., 1956; founder Takara Co. N.Y. Inc., N.Y.C., 1956—; mng. dir. Takara Belmont Co. Ltd., Osaka, 1965—; pres. Takara Co. Can. Ltd., Mississauga, Ont., 1966—, Koken Mfg. Co. Inc., St. Louis, 1969; dir. Takara Standard Co. Ltd., Osaka, Takara Belmont London Ltd., subs.'s in France, W.Ger., Brazil. Mem. Nat. Beauty and Barber Mfrs. Assn., Japan Soc. Clubs: Fiddlers' Elbow Country, Nippon. Office: 1 Belmont Dr Somerset NJ 08873

YOST, FAYE FRANCES, mail order co. exec.; b. Belfast, Maine, Dec. 7, 1933; d. Herman D. and Frances E. Wood; student Atlantic Union Coll., S. Lancaster, Mass., 1955-56, Sch. Animal Sci., Newburyport Beach, Calif., 1974-75. Assembler, James Millen Mfg. Co., Malden, Mass., 1977-78; with parts dept. Automatic Radio Co., Malden, 1977; tester Computer Hardware Co., Malden, 1977-78; propr. Fayette Cosmetics, Malden, 1960—; tchr. animal grooming. Mem. Am. Legion Aux. (pres. 1952-53). Address: PO Box 356 Malden MA 02148

YOST, ROBERT CARSYL, marine corps officer; b. Buffalo, Apr. 4, 1941; s. Carsyl John and Kathleen Marion (Willis) Y.; B.A., Franklin Marshall U., 1963; M.Ed. in Counseling, U. Va., 1973; m. Margaret Anne Charrow, Apr. 15, 1967; children—Tracy Lynne, Erik Carsyl. Commd. 2d lt. U.S. Marine Corps, 1963, advanced through grades to maj., 1973; arty. officer, Okinawa, 1963-64; aerial observer, Vietnam, 1964-65; course writer, ceremonial officer Marine Barracks, Washington, 1965-67; comdr. arty. battery 1st Marine Div., Vietnam, 1968-69; task analyst Hdqrs., Washington, 1969-72; joint edn. drug alcohol officer, Camp Butler, Japan, 1973-76; bn. arty. ops. officer, Okinawa, Japan, 1976-77; adj. Hdqrs. 1st Marine Corps Dist., Garden City, N.Y., 1977—; participant summer sch. alcohol studies Rutgers U., 1975. Decorated Air medal; recipient letter appreciation Dept. Def. Schs. Pacific, 1976. Mem. Am. Personnel and Guidance Assn. Home: 239 Stockbridge Ave Buffalo NY 14215

YOST, ROBERT MORRIS, physician; b. Nevada, Iowa, Jan. 18, 1929; s. Hugh E. and Effie E. Y.; B.A., Gettysburg Coll., 1951; M.D., Temple U., 1955; m. Eleanore L. Gilfert, Dec. 28, 1951; children—Gretchen, David, Jacqueline, Valerie. Intern, Harrisburg (Pa.) Gen. Hosp., 1955-56; resident Sunbury Community Hosp., 1956, McDill AFB Hosp., 1956-58; practice family medicine, Ft. Washington, Pa., 1959—; mem. staff Chestnut Hill Hosp., Abington Meml. Hosp.; physician in charge Colonial Sch. Dist.; clin. instr. family medicine Jefferson Med. Sch., 1972—; asso. prof. dept. family medicine Temple Med. Sch., 1977—. Pres. Whitemarsh PTA; bd. dirs. Wissahickon chpt. ARC. Served to capt. USAF, 1956-58. Diplomate Am. Bd. Family Practice. Fellow Am. Acad. Family Practice (charter); mem. Am. Acad. Pediatrics, Pa., Montgomery County med. socs., Montgomery County Acad. Family Practice (pres.). Republican. Lutheran. Home: 7181 Lafayette Rd Fort Washington PA 19034 Office: 1244 Ft Washington Ave Fort Washington PA 19034

YOST, ZANE, architect; b. Zanesville, Ohio, May 3, 1930; s. Karl and Laverna (Imes) Y.; B.Arch., Mass. Inst. Tech., 1953; m. Megan Owen, Mar. 22, 1958; children—Owen, Deirdre, Jason, Molly. Asso., Victor Christ-Janer, New Canaan, Conn., 1957-63; pres. Zane Yost & Assos., Inc., Bridgeport, Conn., 1963—; pres. Bridge, Inc., Bridgeport, 1972—; tchr. Columbia U., 1967-69, Sacred Heart U., 1975-76; lectr. Yale U., 1968, U. Bridgeport, 1976. Mem. Conn. Gov's. Task Force on Housing, 1971-72. Served with U.S. Army, 1956-57. Mem. AIA, Am. Inst. Planners, Am. Soc. Planning Ofcls., Urban Land Inst. Democrat. Contbr. articles in field to profl. jours.; co-builder first wood geodesic dome, 1950. Home: 204 Briscoe Rd New Canaan CT 06840 Office: 144 Island Brook Ave Bridgeport CT 06606

YOUDELMAN, STANLEY ALAN, dentist; b. Oceanside, N.Y., Oct. 22, 1939; s. Jack and Marjorie (Baer) Y.; student State U. N.Y. at Buffalo, 1957-60, D.D.S. (Mosby Scholar 1964), 1964; student N.Y.U., 1966; m. Ronna Meryl Brock, Aug. 26, 1961; children—Jodi Linn, Michael David, Lonni Sue, Adam Kyle. Intern Morrisania City Hosp., Bronx, N.Y., 1964-65; oral surgery resident Mt. Sinai of Cleve. Hosp., 1966-67, resident anesthesia, 1967; pvt. practice dentistry, specializing in oral surgery, Brentwood, N.Y., 1968—; mem. emergency room com. St. John's Hosp., 1968-74, operating room com., 1976-78; attending in oral and maxillo-facial surgery dept., clin. instr. Nassau County Med. Center. Mem. Ann. Giving Commn. Southside Hosp., 1970-78, mem. audit com. 1970-76, surg. audit subcom., 1974-78; mem. cardio-pulmonary resuscitation com. Suffolk County Heart Assn., 1975-78, also mem. postgrad. edn. com., mem. bd. dirs. Diplomate Am. Bd. Oral Surgery. Fellow Suffolk Acad. Medicine; mem. Suffolk County Dental Soc. (editor Bull. 1970-71, mem. bd. dels. 1970-76, pres. 1977, chmn. bylaws com. 1976), 10th Dist. Dental Soc. (bd. dels. 1978-79), Am. Soc. Oral Surgeons, Am. Dental Soc. Anesthesiology, Am. Acad. Oral Pathology, Am. Heart Assn. (v.p. Suffolk County chpt., dir. 1977-78), N.Y. State Soc. Oral Surgeons (legis. com. 1975-78), Internat. Assn. Oral Surgeons, Ft. Salonga Assn., Action, Am. Motorcycle Assn. Club: Babylon Rod and Gun. Home: 8 Truxton Ln Fort Salonga NY 11769 Office: 601 Suffolk Ave Brentwood NY 11717 also 233 Union Ave Holbrook NY 11741

YOUNG, BILLIE, publishing co. exec., author; b. Bklyn., June 27, 1933; d. Albert and Reda (Bromberg) Y.; student Bklyn. Coll., 1949-51, New Sch. Social Research, 1953-54; m. Simeon Paget, Jan. 2, 1959; children—Bruce, Richard, Dana, Laurie, Leif, Kristie. Copywriter, Camp Chem. Co., Bklyn., 1950-53; reporter Cowles Communications, Deer Park, N.Y., 1968-69; pres. Ashley Books, Inc., Port Washington, N.Y., 1970—; treas. Born Blessed Publs., Los Angeles, 1973—; lectr., guest numerous TV talk shows; promoter books, cons. in field; free-lance writer. Dir. pub. relations Am. Repertory Theatre; active North Shore Community Arts Center, 1953-59, North Shore Hosp., 1958-63. Mem. ALA, Am. Booksellers Assn., Pubs. Ad Club, Cancer Care, Com. Small Mag. Editors and Pubs., Assn. Am. Pubs. Author: The Naked Chef, 1971; Vive La Difference, 1975; Viva La Difference, 1976; contbr. articles to newspapers, popular mags. Promoted Naked Came the Stranger as author, Penelope Ashe, 1969. Home: 14 Capi Ln Port Washington NY 11050 Office: 233 Main St Port Washington NY 11050

YOUNG, BRUCE KENNETH, obstetrician, gynecologist; b. N.Y.C., Aug. 11, 1938; s. Morton David and Cecele Barbara (Lebenson) Y.; B.A., Princeton U., 1959; M.D., N.Y. U., 1963; m. Phyllis Ann Lipsius, Dec. 16, 1962; children—Kathryn Rachel, Caroline Sue. Intern, Montefiore Hosp., N.Y.C., 1963-64; resident obstetrics, gynecology N.Y. U.-Bellevue Hosp., N.Y.C., 1964-68; asst. research scientist N.Y. U. Med. Center, 1968, asst. prof. Med. Sch., 1970-74, asso. prof., 1975—, asso. dir. obstetrics, gynecology, 1970—, dir. Med. Sch. div. maternal-fetal medicine, 1975—, dir. obstetrics, 1970—; individual practice medicine, specializing in fertility, obstetrics and gynecology, N.Y.C., 1970—; cons. in field. Obstetrics adv. com. N.Y.C. Dept. Health, 1971—; health profl. adv. com. Nat. Found., 1977—, Nat. Systemic Lupus Found., 1977—. Served to maj. USAF, 1968-70. Diplomate Nat. Bd. Med. Examiners, Am. Bd. Obstetrics and Gynecology, Am. Bd. Maternal-Fetal Medicine. Recipient Lyman Barton award, 1968, Hirsch Career Scientist award, 1972. Fellow Am. Coll. Obstetrics and Gynecology. Mem. Am. Fertility Soc., Soc. Study Reprodn., Harvey Soc., N.Y. Acad. Sci., N.Y. Acad. Medicine, N.Y. Perinatal Soc., N.Y. Obstet. Soc., AAAS. Contbr. articles to profl. publs. on obstetrics, gynecology, fertility; contbg. editor Perinatal Care, 1978. Office: 566 1st Ave Suite 2C New York City NY 10016

YOUNG, CHARLOTTE ALBISTON, educator, journalist; b. Rochester, N.Y., June 5, 1925; d. John A. and Florence E. (Zimmerman) Albiston; B.A., Alfred (N.Y.) U., 1947, M. M. Social Sci., 1948; m. Robert W. Young, Dec. 27, 1948 (dec.); 1 son, Douglas Bruce. Asst. athletic coach Alfred U., 1947-48; tchr. jr. high sch. social studies Spencerport (N.Y.) Sch., 1948-49; office accountant Neisner Bros., Rochester, 1949-50; adminstr. Las Vegas Hosp., 1950-51; adminstrv. sec.to chief of staff Children's Hosp., Columbus, Ohio, 1952-53; adminstrv. sec. tng. dept. Am. Optical Co., Southbridge, Mass., 1953-56; dir. pub. relations and devel. fund Day Kimball Hosp., Putnam, Conn., 1960-63; prof. social scis., chmn. history and polit. sci. dept. Annhurst Coll., Woodstock, Conn., 1964—; corr. Worcester (Mass.) Telegram and Evening Gazette. Interim dir. Home Health Aides and Homemaker Services, Putnam, summer 1972; tutor Bracken Library Bd., 1956-60; sec., chmn. supt. selection com. Woodstock Bd. Edn., 1966-71; Republican registrar of voters, 1960-64, 74; bd. dirs. Woodstock-Pomfret-Eastford Pub. Health Assn., finance dir., 1972-74; bd. trustees Conn. Library Service Center, 1966-71, chmn., 1968-71; pres. Bracken Meml. Library, 1960-64; mem. Woodstock Bicentennial Com., 1975-76. Mem. AAUP, Am. Judicature Soc., Am. Polit. Sci. Assn., Am., New Eng. hist. assns., Woodstock Hist. Assn. (life mem., founding mem., bd. dirs.), Woodstock Theft Detecting Soc., League Women Voters. Congregationalist. Home: Box 104 Rolling Acres Woodstock CT 06281 Office: Annhurst College Woodstock CT 06281

YOUNG, CHESLEY VIRGINIA BARNES (MRS. MORRIS N. YOUNG), author, civic worker; b. Hamburg, Ark., Sept. 7, 1919; d. Lewis Chesley and Winifred (Massey) Barnes; B.A., U. Ark., 1947; M.A., Columbia, 1951; m. Morris N. Young, Aug. 20, 1948; children—Cheryl Lesley Uiling, Charles Chesley. Statistician, U.S. Civil Service, Washington, Cin., 1942; tchr. pub. schs. N.Y.C. Dept. Edn. 1954-67; pres. Denton & Haskins Corp.; N.Y.C., v.p. Intercollegiate Syndicate, Inc. Pres. Women's Aux. N.Y. Polyclinic Hosp. and Med. Sch., 1967-68; mem. A.M.A. Aux., N.Y. State Med. Assn. Aux., New York County Med. Soc. Aux.; mem. pres.'s council Finch Coll., 1967-69. Served to capt. WAC, 1942-46. Mem. ASCAP, Nat., N.Y. State fedns. bus. and profl. women's clubs, Manhattan Bus. and Profl. Women's Club (pres. 1949-51), D.A.R. (regent N.Y.C. chpt., chmn. Regents Round Table Greater N.Y.), Mil. Order of World Wars, Nat. Women's Party, U. Ark. Alumni Assn. Greater N.Y. (charter), Nat. Huguenot Soc., Chester County (Pa.) Hist. Soc., Knights of Malta (dame comdr.), Order Lafayette, Pi Kappa, Zeta Tau Alpha, Kappa Delta Pi. Methodist. Clubs: Washington Square Business and Professional Women's, Women's Nat. Republican. Author: How to Read Faster and Remember More, 1965; Magic of a Mighty Memory, 1972; Amanda Gregg, 1979. Editor: Magic Tricks (Wilfred Johnson), 1952; Card Tricks (Wilfred Johnson), 1952. Composer songs: Have You, 1949; Come On, Come to the Fair, 1963. Contbr. articles to mags., newspapers. Donor (with husband) magic libraries to Library of Congress, U. Tex., U. Calif. at Berkeley. Home: 270 Riverside Dr New York City NY 10025 Office: 2 Fifth Ave New York City NY 10011

YOUNG, DANIEL HERBERT, III, mfrs. rep., cons.; b. Berwyn, Ill., June 1, 1929; s. Daniel Herbert and Eleonor Edith (Zelms) Y.; student Morton Jr. Coll., 1947-49; B.S. in Aero. Engring., Purdue U., 1952; M.B.A. in Mktg., U. Chgo., 1962; m. June Every-Clayton, Jan. 25, 1969; children—Daniel, Lisa, Lynn, Jonathan, Heather. Sr. aerodynamicist N.Am. Rockwell, Columbis, Ohio, 1952-56; manual writer Lytle Corp., Chgo., 1956-62; internat. account mgr. George J. Meyer Mfg., Chgo., N.Y.C., Australia, 1962-69; nat. account mgr. Hayssen Mfg. Co., Teaneck, N.J., 1969-72; gen. sales mgr. machinery Crown Cork & Seal Co., Balt., Phila., 1972-76; pres. Daniel H. Young Assos. Inc., Balt., 1976—. Pres., exec. bd. Mount Washington Country Sch. PTA. Served with U.S. Army, 1954-56. Mem. Master Brewers Assn. Am., Packaging Inst. (dir. Chesapeake chpt., profl. mem.), Purdue Alumni Assn., U. Chgo., Meyer alumni assns. Lutheran. Club: Circle Lodge Masons. Home and Office: 419 Dumbarton Rd Baltimore MD 21212

YOUNG, DOUGLAS F., judge; b., 1911; A.B., Rutgers U.; LL.B., St. John's U. Admitted to N.Y. State bar, 1937; justice N.Y. Supreme Ct., Nassau County, Mineola, N.Y. Mem. Am. Bar Assn. Office: NY Supreme Ct Mineola NY 11501

YOUNG, EARLE WILSON, JR., mech. engr.; b. Washington, Sept. 5, 1934; s. Earle Wilson and Florence (Stanford) Y.; B.M.E., George Washington U., 1960; M.S., Cath. U., 1970; m. Joan Regina Flaherty, Feb. 12, 1955; children—Deborah Anne, Kelly Jean, Stacey Lee, Stephen Earle. With NASA Goddard Space Flight Center, Greenbelt, Md., 1960—, supervisory engr., head simulation test sect., 1976—. Capt., sec. Woodland Beach Volunteer Fire Dept., 1958-61; pres. local P.T.A., 1973-75. Bd. dirs. Mayo Elementary Sch., 1967-75; chmn. bldg. com. Ch. Council, 1976-78. Mem. ASME, ASTM, Mayo Civic Assn., Mayo Athletic Assn. (coach), Sigma Tau. Elk. Club: Goddard

Engineers (pres. 1974-75). Home: 3925 Rhode Harbor Rd Edgewater MD 21037 Office: NASA/GSFC Greenbelt MD 20771

YOUNG, EDWIN PARSON, newspaper exec.; b. Pitts., July 19, 1908; s. Edwin Parson and Diana (Montanye) Y.; A.B., Cornell U., 1931; m. Elizabeth Miller Hoskins, Jan. 9, 1937 (dec. 1968); children—Diana Montanye (Mrs. David H. Carls), Edwin Parson III; m. 2d, Polly Brinton Meredith, Mar. 16, 1974. Editor-in-chief Cornell Daily Sun, 1930-31; reporter, columnist, critic Williamsport (Pa.) Sun, 1931-35; reporter, copy editor, rewrite Balt. Sun, 1935-38, asst. city editor, 1938-41, city editor, 1941-54; adminstrv. asst. Providence Jour. Co., 1954-57, gen. mgr. adminstrn., 1957-58, gen. mgr., 1958-69, v.p., asst. publisher, 1969-77, also dir.; Md. corr. Time, Life and Fortune, 1941-54; instr. English, Loyola Coll. Md., 1947-53; instr. bus. U. Balt., 1948-54; chmn. Providence Jour. Co. Retirement Commn.; dir. Providence Jour., Providence Gravure, Inc., Cable Vision of R.I., Seaport '76. Mem. Md. Hosp. Survey Com., 1947. Bd. dirs. R.I. Philharmonic Orch. Mem. Chesapeake Assn. of A.P. (chmn. continuing study com. on membership participation 1947-51, chmn. freedom information com. 1951-54), Md. Press Assn. (v.p. 1954), Greater Providence C. of C. (bd. dirs.), Newspaper Personnel Relations Assn. (pres. 1964-65, life), Am. Newspaper Pubs. Assn. (chmn. journalism edn. com. 1966-67), New Eng. Daily Newspaper Assn., Internat. Press Inst., Inter Am. Press Assn., A.I.M. (president's council), Am. Mgmt. Assn., R.I. Hist. Soc., Sigma Delta Chi, Alpha Delta Phi. Presbyn. Clubs: Hope, Turks Head, Agawam Hunt (Providence); Cornell of R.I. (pres., past bd. govs.); Leash (N.Y.C.); Newport Reading Room, Ida Lewis Yacht, Clambake, Bailey's Beach (Newport, R.I.); N. Am. Yacht Racing Union. Home: 40 School St Newport RI 02840 also Old Iron Point Cobbs Creek VA 23035

YOUNG, ESTHER CHRISTENSEN (MRS. CHARLES JACOB YOUNG), artist; b. Milw., May 10, 1895; d. Niels Anton and Mathilde (Thomesen) Christensen; student Layton Sch. Art, 1914, Art Student's League, N.Y.C., 1915, Milw. Downer Coll. and Sem., 1915-19; pvt. study; m. Charles Jacob Young, June 15, 1929; stepchildren—John Peter, David Whitman (dec. 1975); children—Niels Owen, Esther Van Horne Young Constable. Exhibited Layton Art Gallery (Milw.), Chgo. Art Inst., Pa. Acad. Fine Arts, Corcoran Art Gallery, Washington, Phila. Water Color Club, Women's Arts and Industries, N.Y.C., Nat. Assn. Women Artists, N.Y.C., Balt., Cleve. Museums Art, Balt. Water Color Club, Painters and Sculptors Soc. N.J., 1960; designer, craftsman, poet, free-lance fabric designer. Recipient numerous prizes in Jr. League Art and Poetry contests; medal for design of U.S. stamp for N.J. Tercentenary, 1964. Mem. Princeton Art Assn., Phila. Water Color Club Acad. Natural Sci. (life). Republican. Episcopalian. Clubs: Present Day; Garden, Nassau (Princeton); Acorn (Phila.); Contbr. poems, drawings to mags.; composer crossword puzzles. Home: 78 Stockton St Princeton NJ 08540 also Holiday House Van Hornesville NY 13475

YOUNG, FLORA DORSEY, sociologist, educator; b. Phila, July 3, 1928; d. Charles W. and Mary (Gaskins) Dorsey; B.A., Howard U., 1950, M.A., 1968; Ed.D., U. Pa., 1978; m. William P. Young, Sept. 2, 1950; children—Marie, William. Instr. sociology Glassboro (N.J.) State Coll., 1968-74, asst. prof., 1975—. Mem. Eastern, Am. sociol. assns., Ethnic Studies Soc., NAACP, Camden County Med. Soc. Aux., Nat. Med. Soc. Aux., Delta Sigma Theta, Pi Lambda Theta, Alpha Kappa Delta. Episcopalian. Club: S. Jersey Links (pres. 1978—). Home: 202 Warwick Rd Lawnside NJ 08045 Office: Glassboro State Coll Glassboro NJ 08028

YOUNG, FRANCIS ANTHONY, JR., printing co. exec.; b. Bklyn., Mar. 27, 1919; s. Francis Anthony and Alice Mary (McManus) Y.; B.S., Coll. Holy Cross, 1941; m. Jane Elizabeth Ahern, Feb. 14, 1943; 1 dau., Jane Young Loft. With Mail & Express Printing Co., N.Y.C., 1946—, v.p., after 1952, now pres., also dir.; v.p., dir. The Adams Group, Inc. Served to capt. USMCR, 1941-46, ret. as lt. col., 1958; PTO. Mem. Young Printing Execs. Club (pres. 1950-51). K.C. Home: 119 Canoe Brook Pkwy Summit NJ 07901 Office: 225 Varick St New York City NY 10014

YOUNG, GAIL THIBAULT, accountant, govt. ofcl.; b. Buffalo, Dec. 2, 1938; d. Charles Daniel and Addie Mae (Mongeon) Thibault; B.S., U. Md., 1961, M.B.A., 1969; postgrad. George Washington U., 1976—; m. Stewart Dotterer Young, Aug. 27, 1960. Accountant, ACF Industries, Inc. Riverdale, Md., 1961-62; price analyst Goddard Space Flight Center, NASA, Greenbelt, Md., 1962-64, fin. analyst, 1964-68, cost accountant, 1968-70, mgmt. researcher, 1970-71; systems accountant Nat. Oceanic and Atmospheric Adminstrn., Dept. Commerce, Rockville, Md., 1971-73, FAA and OST, Dept. Transp., Washington, 1973—; mem. faculty dept. accounting U. Md., College Park, 1973, George Washington U., 1978; founder, dir. Women's Nat. Bank, Washington, mem. exec. com., chmn. examining com., 1978—. C.P.A., Md. Mem. Am. Inst. C.P.A.'s, Assn. Govt. Accountants (award 1973), George Washington U. Doctoral Assn., Fed. Exec. Inst. Alumni Assn. Democrat. Roman Catholic. Home: 14653 Stonewall Dr Silver Spring MD 20904 Office: 400 7th St Washington DC 20590

YOUNG, JOAN ELAINE, microbiologist; b. Jersey City, Apr. 9, 1938; d. Edward and Eleanore Marie (Sossong) Johnson; student Jersey City Jr. Coll., 1957-58, Pasadena Jr. Coll., 1960; A.A., Upsala Coll., 1967-68; 1 son, John. Organic chemist Hoffman LaRoche, Nutley, N.J., 1958-60; microbiologist S.B. Penick Co., Jersey City, 1960-62, Hoffman LaRoche, Nutley, N.J., 1962-66; biochemist Warner Lambert Research Inst., Morris Plains, N.J., 1966-67; microbiologist M&M/Mars, Hackettstown, N.J., 1967-73, Airwick Industries, Teterboro, N.J., 1973—. Mem. Am. Soc. Microbiology, Research Soc. Am., ASTM. Clubs: Order of Eastern Star, Camelback Ski. Home: P-2 Apt 11B Panther Valley Hackettstown NJ 07840 Office: 380 North St Teterboro NJ 07608

YOUNG, JOHN ALBION, geologist; b. Newport, R.I., Aug. 29, 1909; s. John Albion and Ellen Spooner (Gladding) Y.; Ph.B., Brown U., 1932, Sc.M., 1934; Ph.D., Harvard, 1946; m. Helen Moseley Mackintosh, June 21, 1937. Instr. Mich. State U., East Lansing, 1939-44; geologist Sun Oil Co., McAllen, Tex., also Phila., 1944-46, 47-50, asst. dist. geologist, 1950, staff geologist, 1950-54, sr. staff geologist, 1955-70; asst. prof. geology Syracuse (N.Y.) U., 1946-47; dir. oil and gas div. Tax Shelter Adv. Service, Narberth, Pa., 1970-73; v.p., World Resources Corp., King of Prussia, Pa., 1973—; sr. v.p. exploration and prodn. Omni-Exploration, Inc., 1974—. Mem. com. on sci. and arts Franklin Inst., Phila., 1965—. Fellow Geol. Soc. Am.; mem. Am. Assn. Petroleum Geologists, Am. Assn. Petroleum Landmen. Clubs: St. Davids Golf (Wayne, Pa.); Explorers (N.Y.C.). Contbr. articles to profl. jours. Home: 142 Hunters Ln Devon PA 19333 Office: 100 Matsonford Rd Radnor PA 19087

YOUNG, JOHN WILLIAM, newspaper editor; b. New Haven, Oct. 23, 1929; s. William Edward and Florence Emma (Brown) Y.; student Tri-State Coll., Angola, Ind., 1950-51; m. Barbara Jean Lee, Jan. 5, 1958; children—Kimberlee, William, Kerri, Kaycee. Asst. mgr. advt., sales promotion Gen. Electric Supply Corp., Hartford, Conn., 1951-53; sales rep. Addressograph-Multigraph Corp., Hartford, 1953-54, Ralph C. Coxhead Corp., Hartford, 1954-55, A.S. Green Co., Pasadena, Calif., 1955-58; gen. mgr. P.J. O'Brien Co., Lancaster, Calif., 1958-60; founder Kimbill & Co., Inc., Shelton, Conn., 1960—, pres., pub. The Suburban News, 1963—. Served with USN, 1947-50. Recipient George Washington Outstanding Achievement award Freedoms Found. at Valley Forge, 1974; distinguished service citation Dept. Conn. Am. Legion, 1976-77. Mem. New Eng. Press Assn., Conn. Editorial Assn., Nat. Newspaper Assn., Am. Newspaper Reps., Tincan Sailors Assn. Clubs: Am. Legion, VFW. Home: 30 Fairmont Pl Shelton CT 06484 Office: 52 Center St Shelton CT 06484

YOUNG, JOSEPH WARREN, JR., dentist; b. Jersey City, Oct. 7, 1905; s. Joseph Warren and Anna Loretta (Donnellon) Y.; D.D.S., Temple U., 1930; m. Marguerite Bennett, June 15, 1932; children—Sally Ann (Mrs. James L. Howard), Joseph Warren III. Resident dental surgeon Hebrew Orphanage and Shelter Home, Germantown, Phila.; dental resident Philco Radio Corp., 1930; practice gen. dentistry, Jersey City, Nutley, N.J., attending dental surgeon Essex County (N.J.) County jail. Vice pres., dir. Glenwild Lake Co. Head football coach Lincoln High Sch., Jersey City, from 1925, head baseball coach, 1937; asst. head counselor Camp Merrimack, Contoocook, N.H., then head counselor. Pres. Nutley Health Council, now mem. adv. bd.; v.p. Nutley Vis. Nurse Assn., March Dimes; pres. Nutley Symphony Soc.; pres. Nutley Jr. High Sch. P.T.A.; chmn. Nutley Elks Crippled Children Com.; mem. N.J. Elks Crippled Children Com., mem. Bd. Edn. Essex County Vocational Schs. mem. adv. com. health dept. Town of Nutley, 1976—. Bd. dirs. United Dr.; pres. bd. trustees Nutley Pub. Library. Fellow Am. Acad. Medicine (hon.), Internat. Acad. Anesthesia (hon.); mem. N.J., Essex County, Hudson County dental socs., Am. Dental Assn., Essex County Fedn. Sportsmen's Clubs (pres.), Essex County Conservation Officers Assn. (pres.), Essex County Fish and Game Wardens' Assn., (pres.), Nutley C. of C. (dir.). Elk. Clubs: Cedar Grove Rod and Gun (pres.); Tuna (sec.) (Jersey City). Home: 259 Vreeland Ave Nutley NJ 07110

YOUNG, LARRY EMORY, structural engr.; b. Pitts., Sept. 17, 1941; s. Emory Louis and Marie V. (Wyatt) Y.; student U. Cin., 1965-67; m. Diane Marie Cowley, June 9, 1969; 1 dau., Christy Lynn. Chief bridge engr., dept. head Salvucci & Assos., Inc., 1972—. Served with USN, 1960-64. Mem. Assn. Bridge Constrn. and Design (dir., sec.), Am. Soc. Hwy. Engrs., Soc. Am. Mil. Engrs., Exptl. Aircraft Assn. Democrat. Home: 2538 Hunting Ridge Trail Bridgeville PA 15017 Office: 301 5th Ave Room 1800 Pittsburgh PA 15222

YOUNG, LEO, elec. engr.; b. Vienna, Aug. 18, 1926; s. Samuel and Marie Y.; came to U.S., 1953, naturalized, 1958; B.A., Cambridge U. (Eng.), 1946, M.A., 1950; M.S., Johns Hopkins U., 1956, D.Eng. (Westinghouse-B.G. Lamme grad. scholar), 1959; m. Fay Lilian, Jan. 4, 1953; children—Philip Michael, Sarah Anne, Joseph David. Lab. mgr. Decca Radar, Ltd., Surbiton, Surrey, Eng., 1951-53; adv. engr. Westinghouse Electric Corp., Balt., 1953-60; staff scientist, program mgr. Stanford Research Inst., Menlo Park, Calif., 1960-73; staff cons. Naval Research Lab., Washington, 1973—; pres. Pensions for Tech. Profls., 1975—. Fellow IEEE (Microwave prize 1963, nat. lectr. 1968, pres. Microwave Soc. 1969, dir. 1971-74, exec. v.p. 1979); mem. AAAS. Author: Microwave Filters, 1964; Systems of Units in Electricity and Magnetism, 1969; Advances in Microwaves, Vols. 1-8, 1966-74; Everything You Should Know About Pension Plans, 1976; others; contbr. articles to profl. jours. Patentee in field. Home: 6407 Maiden Ln Bethesda MD 20034

YOUNG, LIONEL WESLEY, radiologist; b. New Orleans, Mar. 14, 1932; s. Charles Henry and Ethel Elsie (Johnson) Y.; B.S., St. Benedict's Coll., 1953; M.D., Howard U., Washington, 1957; m. Florence Inez Brown, June 24, 1957; children—Tina Inez, Lionel Thomas, Owen Christopher. Rotating intern Detroit Receiving Hosp., 1957-58; resident radiology U. Rochester (N.Y.) Med. Center, 1958-61; radiologist U.S. Naval Hosp., Portsmouth, N.H., 1961-63; fellow pediatric radiology Children's Hosp. Cin., 1963-65; pediatric radiologist, asso. prof. radiology and pediatrics U. Rochester Med. Center, 1965-75; acting dir. radiology Children's Hosp. and prof. radiology and pediatrics U. Pitts., 1975—. Served to lt. comdr., M.C., USN, 1961-63. Fellow Am. Coll. Radiology; mem. Soc. Pediatric Radiology, AMA, Am. Roentgen Ray Soc., Radiol. Soc. N.Am. Democrat. Roman Catholic. Author: (with others) Pediatric Syllabus, 1974; contbr. articles in field to profl. jours. Home: 5425 Forbes Ave Pittsburgh PA 15217 Office: 125 De Soto St Pittsburgh PA 15213

YOUNG, LLOYD EMORY, coll. adminstr.; b. Aquasco, Md., Nov. 15, 1936; s. George C.L. and Lelia M. (Bullock) Y.; B.S., Morgan State Coll., 1959; M.A., Kean Coll., 1974; m. Juanita Dennis, June 25, 1971. Recorder, quality control officer Tri-State Transp. Commn., East Orange, N.J., 1962-63; mgr. men's dept. Orbach's Dept. Store, Newark, 1963-65; group leader, sr. group leader, sect. supr., counselor Kilmer Job Corps Center, Edison, N.J., 1965-68; coordinator student activities, dir. student activities, asst. dean student affairs Essex County Coll., Newark, 1968-74, asso. dean admissions, assessment and records, 1974—; lectr. in field. Served with U.S. Army, 1960-62. Mem. Century Assn. Excellence in Edn. (parliamentarian 1976—), Am. Personnel and Guidance Assn., Am. Assn. Higher Edn., Eastern Assn. Coll. Deans and Advisers Students, Am. Coll. Personnel Assn., N.J. Community Coll. Deans Assn., Phi Delta Kappa. Clubs: Masons, Shriners. Home: 603 Elizabeth Ave Newark NJ 07112 Office: 303 University Ave Newark NJ 07102

YOUNG, MAHONRI SHARP, writer, ret. museum dir.; b. N.Y.C., July 23, 1911; s. Mahonri Mackintosh and Cecilia (Sharp) Y.; A.B., Dartmouth, 1933; M.A., N.Y. U., 1951; m. Elizabeth Chamberlain, July 23, 1932 (div. 1940); m. 2d, Rhoda Satterthwaite, Dec. 7, 1940; 1 son, Mahonri Mackintosh II. Mem. art dept. Sarah Lawrence Coll., 1941-50; acting dir. community arts program Munson-Williams-Proctor Art Inst., Utica, N.Y., 1951-53; dir. Columbus (Ohio) Gallery Fine Arts, 1953-76; Am. corr. Apollo mag. Served with USAAF, 1942-46. Mem. Assn. Art Mus. Dirs., Phi Beta Kappa. Club: Century Assn. (N.Y.C.). Author: Old George, 1940; The Eight, The Paints of George Bellows, 1973; Early American Moderns, 1974. Contbr. articles to mags. Home: Bridgehampton NY 11932

YOUNG, MARGARET BUCKNER, civic worker, author; b. Campbellsville, Ky.; d. Frank W. and Eva (Carter) Buckner; B.A., Ky. State Coll., 1942; M.A., U. Minn., 1946; m. Whitney M. Young, Jr., Jan. 2, 1944 (dec. Mar. 1971); children—Marcia Elaine, Lauren Lee. Instr., Ky. State Coll., 1942-45; instr. edn. and psychology Spelman Coll., Atlanta, 1958-60. Dir. Philip Morris, Inc. Alternate del. UN Gen Assembly, 1973. Mem. pub. policy com. Advt. Council. Bd. dirs. Xavier U., Lincoln Center for Performing Arts, Lincoln Center Inst., UN Assn.; chmn. Whitney M. Young, Jr. Meml. Found.; trustee Blythedale Hosp. Children, Valhalla, N.Y., Met. Mus. Art; mem. Rockefeller U. Council; bd. govs. Off the Record luncheons Fgn. Policy Assn.; bd. govs. UN Assn.; bd. visitors U.S. Mil. Acad. Author: The First Book of American Negroes, 1966; The Picture Life of Martin Luther King, Jr., 1968; The Picture Life of Ralph J. Bunche, 1968; Black American Leaders-Watts, 1969; The Picture Life of Thurgood Marshall, 1970; pub. affairs phamphlet. Home: 330 Oxford Rd New Rochelle NY 10804

YOUNG, MAURICE ISAAC, mech. and aerospace engr.; b. Boston, Feb. 10, 1927; s. Joseph J. and Alice (Lifshitz) Y.; student Worcester Poly. Inst., 1944-45; Ph.B., U. Chgo., 1949, B.S., 1949; M.A., Boston U., 1950; Ph.D., U. Pa., 1960; m. Eleanor Cooper, Sept. 25, 1954; children—Rochelle, Gerald, Rosalind. Sr. dynamics engr. Bell Aircraft Corp., Buffalo, 1951-52, Ft. Worth, 1952-53; group engr. Jacobs Aircraft Engine Co., Pottstown, Pa., 1953-54; prin. tech. engr. Piasecki Helicopter and Aircraft Corp., Morton, Pa., 1954-56, Phila., 1956-58; sr. engring. specialist communications and weapons div. Philco Corp., Phila., 1958-61, mgr. applied mechs., 1958-61; mgr. helicopter research and advanced tech. Boeing Co., Vertol Div., Phila., 1961-68; prof. mech. and aerospace engring. U. Del., 1968—; cons. in field. Served with USAAF, 1946-47. duPont Faculty fellow, 1969-70; U.S. Army grantee, 1971-76. Fellow Am. Inst. Aeros., Astronautics (asso.); mem. Am. Helicopter Soc., Sigma Xi. Editorial bd. Internat. Jour. Rotorcraft, Powered Lift Aircraft, 1975—. Office: U Del Dept Mech and Aerospace Engring Newark DE 19711

YOUNG, MORRIS NATHAN, ophthalmologist, educator, author; b. Lawrence, Mass., July 20, 1909; s. Charles M. and Ida (Davis) Y.; B.S., Mass. Inst. Tech., 1930; M.A., Harvard, 1931; M.D., Columbia Coll. of Physicians and Surgeons, 1935; m. Chesley Virginia Barnes, Aug. 20, 1948; children—Cheryl Lesley Uiling, Charles Chesley. Intern, Queens Gen. Hosp., N.Y.C., 1935-37; resident Harlem Eye and Ear Hosp., N.Y.C., 1938-40; practice medicine specializing in ophthalmology, N.Y.C., 1945—; asst. attending ophthalmologist N.Y. Postgrad. Hosp. and Med. Sch., U. Hosp., N.Y. U., N.Y.C., 1947-61; cons. in ophthalmology Beth Israel Med. Center, N.Y.C., 1972—; prof. ophthalmology French and Polyclinic Med. Sch. and Health Center, N.Y.C., 1958-77, cons., 1969-77; cons. St. Vincent's Hosp. and Med. Center, N.Y.C., 1977—; med. adviser to N.Y.C. selective service dir., 1966—, N.Y.C. Dept. of Health, 1976—; dir. ophthalmology service Beekman Downtown Hosp., N.Y.C., 1970—; hon. cons. in lit. of magic to the Library of Congress, Washington, 1976—. Mem. pres.'s council Finch Coll., N.Y.C., 1968-75. Served with U.S. Army, 1941-45; ETO, MTO; col. Res. ret. Diplomate Am. Bd. Ophthalmology. Fellow Am. Acad. Ophthalmology and Otolaryngology, Soc. of Eye Surgeons; mem. Am. Acad. Compensation Medicine, Am. Assn. Ophthalmology, AMA, Assn. for Research in Vision and Ophthalmology, Nat. Soc. Prevention Blindness, N.Y. State, N.Y. County med. socs., N.Y. State Ophthal. Soc., N.Y. State Soc. Surgeons, Assn. Mil. Surgeons U.S. (mem. Manhattan exec. council 1968—), Contact Lens Assn. of Ophthalmologists, Pan Am. Glaucoma Soc., Res., Ret. officers assns., Soc. Mil. Ophthalmology, Assn. Harvard Chemists, N.Y. State Assn. of the Professions, Pan Am. Assn. Ophthalmologists, Pan Am. Med. Assn., Soc. of Mil. Ophthalmologists, Memory Research Center, Nat. Sojourners, Heroes of '76, Soc. of Am. Magicians, Magic Circle, Internat. Brotherhood of Magicians, Nat. Sheet Music Soc., Queens Gen. Hosp. Alumni Assn., Magic Collectors Assn., Order of Lafayette, Mil. Order World Wars, AMA. Clubs: Harvard, Masons, Lions, Knights of Malta (comdr. 1968—). Author: Hobby Magic, 1950; (with W.B. Gibson) Houdini on Magic, 1953; Bibliography of Memory, 1961, Houdini's Fabulous Magic, 1961, How to Develop an Exceptional Memory, 1962; (with C.V. Young) How to Read Faster and Remember More, 1965; (with J.C. Stoltzfus) A Complete Guide to Science Fair Competition, 1972; editor Magicol, 1949-52. Home: 2 Fifth Ave New York City NY 10011 Office: 170 Broadway New York City NY 10038

YOUNG, RICHARD ATLEE, pediatrician, clin. adminstr.; b. E. Liverpool, Ohio, Feb. 19, 1921; s. Edith Alice Potter; B.S., Gettysburg Coll., 1943; M.D., U. Md., 1946; m. Martha Lou Whipp, June 25, 1977; children—Marlene, Randall Atlee. Resident in pediatrics Mercy and Univ. Hosp., Balt., 1949-52; practice medicine specializing in pediatrics, Hagerstown, Md., 1951-77; dir. emergency dept. Washington County Hosp., Hagerstown, 1977—. Served with M.C., U.S. Army, 1947-49. Recipient Outstanding Physicians award State of Md., 1965; Bronze, Silver, Gold medals Md. Heart Assn., 1972. Home: 1420 The Terrace Hagerstown MD 21740 Office: Washington County Hospital King St Hagerstown MD 21740

YOUNG, ROBERT FRANCIS, publisher; b. N.Y.C., Dec. 14, 1919; s. Frank and Johanna Y. (Wecklein) Y.; B.B.A., Coll. City N.Y., 1941; m. Patricia Burrage, Mar. 31, 1950; children—Melinda, Julie, Steven, Christopher. Salesman, St. & Smith Pub. Co., N.Y.C., 1947-49, Look mag., N.Y.C., 1949-55, with Benton & Bowles, 1955-68, account supr., N.Y.C., 1959-63, sr. v.p., mgmt. supr., 1963-68; pub. Family Circle mag., N.Y.C., 1968—, dir., 1966—, pres., 1975—; dir. Australian Family Circle, Modern Medicine Australia, Better Homes & Gardens-Australia; dir. N.Y. Bd. Trade. Bd. dirs. Clear Pool Camp, Carmel, N.Y., 1976. Served to maj. USAAF, 1941-46. Decorated D.F.C., Air medal. Club: Gipsy Trail (Carmel). Home: 47 Warren St Hastings-on-Hudson NY 10706 Office: 488 Madison Ave New York City NY 10022

YOUNG, ROBERT MICHAEL, computer programmer; b. Charleston, W.Va., Nov. 5, 1947; s. Philip Clark and Mary Helen (Sheets) Y.; B.S. in Chemistry (NSF fellow), Georgetown U., 1969, postgrad., 1974—; postgrad. Ind. U., 1969-70; M.S. in Numerical Sci., Johns Hopkins U., 1973. Tchr., Mt. St. Josephs High Sch., Balt., 1970-71; research chemist Nat. Bur. Standards, Washington, 1971-73; research asst. Frederick (Md.) Cancer Research Center, Litton Bionetics, Inc., 1973-77, programmer analyst, 1977-78; account mgr. ADP Network Services, Washington, 1978-79, sr. tech. cons., 1979—. Mem. Am. Phys. Soc., AAAS, Laser Inst. Am., Am. Acad. Polit. and Social Sci. Democrat. Christian Scientist. Home: 815 Quince Orchard Blvd Apt 34 Gaithersburg MD 20760 Office: ADP Network Services 1333 New Hampshire Ave NW Washington DC 20036

YOUNG, ROD, puppeteer; b. Tehran, Iran, Apr. 16, 1933; s. Herrick Black and Charlotte Elizabeth (Young) Y.; came to U.S., 1935; student Atlanta Art Inst., 1951-52, Emory U., 1952-53, Miami U., 1954, U. Richmond, 1954; B.F.A., Coll. William and Mary, 1957. Puppeteer, WSB-TV, Atlanta, 1950-53; instr. puppetry U. Richmond (Va.), 1954-57; free lance puppeteer, N.Y.C., 1958-60; staff N.Y.C. Parks and Recreation Marionette Theatre, 1960-66, dir., 1967; dir., founder creative puppetry program N.Y.C. schs. and parks, 1967-71; free lance profl. puppeteer nationwide; puppeteer Joan Sutherland TV series Who's Afraid of Opera?, 1972-73; toured major cities with Raggedy Ann's Surprise, 1976-77; producer workshops for children Mus. City N.Y. with regular appearances there and at other maj. museums on East coast; also various TV appearances, programs for schs., libraries, clubs, pvt. parties. Served with U.S. Army, 1953. U.S. Virgin Islands Council of Arts grantee, 1971-72. Mem. Internat. Union Marionette Artists, Puppeteers of Am., Actors Equity, Puppetry Guild Greater N.Y. (pres. 1966-68, corr. sec. 1976—), Alpha Tau Omega. Presbyterian. News editor Nat. Puppetry Jour., 1953-59; puppet theatre editor Players Mag., 1956-58; editor, pub. Puppet Theatre Involvement newsletter, 1963, 67—. Address: 93 Perry St New York City NY 10014

YOUNG, ROYCE OLIVER, educator; b. Jamaica, W.I., June 6, 1920; s. Philip and Christine (Moosee) Y.; grad. RCA Insts., N.Y.C., 1946; B.Sc. in Elec. Engring., Bklyn. Poly. Inst., 1952; postgrad. Columbia, 1954-59; m. Arabella Hong, Aug. 7, 1949; children—Lisa Marie, Robin Keith. Came to U.S., 1944, naturalized, 1949. Electronic technician Winters Radio Labs., N.Y.C., 1947-49; from asst. dir. to dir. Electronics Lab., Pupin Physics Labs., Columbia, 1949-59; head electronics dept. Hudson Labs., Columbia, 1959-68; account exec.

C.B. Richard, Ellis & Co., N.Y.C., 1968-70; prof. math., physics Ramapo Coll. of N.J., Mahwah, 1972—. Mgr. field operations Bur. Noise Abatement, N.Y.C., 1970-72, cons., 1972—. Bd. dirs. Camerata di Musica. Served with AUS, 1946-47. Mem. IEEE, Acoustical Soc. Am., AAAS. Home: 45 White Birch Dr Pomona NY 10970 Office: Ramapo Coll NJ Mahwah NJ 07430

YOUNG, RUTH ANN, guidance counselor; b. Williamsport, Pa., Aug. 4, 1940; d. Oscar Franklin and Martha Alice (Young) Whidden; B.A., Lycoming Coll., Williamsport, 1962; M.S., Johns Hopkins U., Balt., 1974; m. William Robert Young, Aug. 4, 1962; 1 dau., Elizabeth Ann. Elementary tchr. Campbell (N.Y.) Central Sch., 1967-69; tchr. Oakington Elementary Sch., Havre-de-Grace, Md., 1969-74; guidance counselor Prospect Mill Elementary Sch., Bel Air, Md., 1974-78, Fallston (Md.) Sr. High, 1978—. Mem. NEA, Md., Harford County tchrs. assns., Am., Md., Harford County personnel and guidance assns., Am. Sch. Counselors Assn., Harford County Assn. for Children with Learning Disabilities (charter). Republican. Methodist. Office: Fallston Sr High Sch Fallston MD

YOUNG, WILLIAM EDMUND, machinery mfg. co. exec.; b. Ridgewood, N.J., Mar. 22, 1916; s. Walter and May Isabelle (Donahue) Junge; M.E., Stevens Inst. Tech., 1937; m. Barbara Shultz Stanford, Aug. 19, 1974; children—Paula Ann, David Walter. Instr. chemistry Stevens Inst. Tech., 1937-39; chief engr. Clay-Adams Co., N.Y.C., 1940-48; cons. mech. engring. N.Y.C., 1948-51; dir. engring. Standard Packaging Corp., N.Y.C., 1951-57; partner Mahaffy Engring. Co., Little Falls, N.J., 1957-62; pres. William E. Young & Co., Neptune, N.J., 1961—; dir. Research and Devel. Assos. Mil. and Food Packaging Inc., 1970—; expert witness patents, packaging machinery. Mem. Nat. Def. Exec. Res., U.S. Dept. Commerce, 1971—; trustee Freedoms Found., Valley Forge, Pa.; bd. dirs. Shore YMCA; bd. govs. Jersey Shore Med. Center. Served with N.J. NG, 1931-33. Registered profl. engr., N.J. Mem. Am. Chem. Soc., ASME, Packaging Inst. (profl. award 1969), Newcomen Soc., U.S. Navy League, Order of Lafayette. Republican. Episcopalian. Clubs: Stamford Yacht, Deal Golf and Country, Channel, U.S. Power Squadrons, Mason, Delta Tau Delta. Contbg. author: Modern Packaging Ency., 1957-76. Contbr. articles to profl. publs. Home: 60 W Concourse Neptune NJ 07753 Office: 600 Essex Rd Neptune NJ 07753

YOUNG, WILLIAM ROBINS, JR., aero. engr.; b. Phila., Feb. 6, 1925; s. William Robins and Evelyn Hester (Hutchins) Y.; B.S., Pa. State U., 1948, M.S., 1949; m. Jacqueline Muriel Barbeau, May 20, 1950; children—Carol Elizabeth, Jacqueline Ann, Barbara Elaine, Jennifer Louise. Propeller aerodynamicist Hamilton Standard div. United Aircraft Co., 1949-53; dynamic analyst Cornell Aero. Lab., Buffalo, 1953-57; engring. mgr. Sylvania Electric Products Co., Waltham, Mass., 1957-67; tech. staff Mitre Corp., Bedford, Mass., 1967—. Mem. Pa. State Alumni Council, 1949-57. Served with USAAF, 1943-45. Mem. Am. Inst. Aeros. and Astronautics (chmn. New Eng. sect. 1973-74), Air Force Assn., Am. Def. Preparedness Assn., Tau Beta Pi. Presbyterian. Home: 6 Oakmount Circle Lexington MA 02173 Office: Mitre Corp POB 208 Bedford MA 01730

YOUNGBLOOD, JOSEPH LEONARD, JR., lawyer; b. Orange, N.J., Mar. 18, 1946; s. Joseph Leonard and Maria Grace (DeCangi) Y.; B.A., Fordham U., 1968; J.D., Cornell U., 1971; m. Joetta Beebe, Aug. 23, 1969; children—Stacey Maria Louise, Joseph Leonard III. Admitted to N.J. bar, 1971; asso. firm Lloyd, Megargee & Steedle, Atlantic City, 1971-75; partner firm Lloyd, Megargee, Steedle & Connor, Atlantic City and Pleasantville, N.J., 1975—. Bd. dirs. Atlantic Mental Health Center, 1976—. Mem. Am., Atlantic County, N.J. bar assns., Am. Judicature Soc., Trial Attorneys N.J., N.J. Def. Assn. Republican. Methodist. Home: 1637 Franklin Blvd Linwood NJ 08244 Office: 600 Fire Rd PO Box 850 Pleasantville NJ 08232

YOUNGER, IRVING, lawyer, educator; b. N.Y.C., Nov. 30, 1932; s. Harry and Jean (Jossen) Yoskowitz; A.B. magna cum laude, Harvard U., 1953; LL.B., N.Y. U., 1958; m. Judith T. Weintraub, Jan. 21, 1955; children—Rebecca, Abigail M. Admitted to N.Y. State bar, 1958, U.S. Supreme Ct. bar, 1962; asso. firm Paul, Weiss, Rifkind, Wharton & Garrison, N.Y.C., 1958-60; asst. U.S. atty. So. Dist. N.Y., 1960-62; partner firm Younger & Younger and successors, N.Y.C., 1962-65; prof. law N.Y. U., 1965-68; judge Civil Ct. City N.Y., 1969-74; Samuel S. Leibowitz prof. trial techniques Cornell U., Law Sch., 1974—; vis. prof. law Harvard U. Sch. Law, 1978—. Served with U.S. Army, 1953-55. Mem. Am., N.Y. State bar assns., Am. Law Inst., Assn. Bar City N.Y., Assn. Am. Law Schs. (chmn. trial advocacy sect.). Home: 3 Fountain Pl Ithaca NY 14850 Office: Cornell U Law Sch Ithaca NY 14853

YOUNGMAN, JOHN CRAWFORD, lawyer; b. Williamsport, Pa., Jan. 25, 1903; s. Charles Worman and Margaret (Porter) Y.; B.S., U. Pa., 1924; LL.B., Harvard, 1927; m. Ruth Young Allen, Feb. 7, 1933 (dec. 1976); children—John Crawford, Charles Van Patten, Margaret Allen (Mrs. Margaret Y. Holman). Admitted to Pa. bar, 1927, U.S. Supreme Ct. bar; asso. Max L. Mitchell, Williamsport, 1927-37; practiced in Williamsport, 1937-43; partner firm Candor, Youngman, Gibson & Gault, Williamsport, 1943—. Dir., Williamsport Hotels Co. Mem. jud. conf. 3d Circuit Ct. of Appeals, Pa., Del., N.J., V.I., 1954—. Nat. asso. Boys Clubs Am., 1952—; chmn. Williamsport San. Authority, 1952—; mem. Williamsport Municipal Water Authority, 1966—. Trustee, Danville (Pa.) State Hosp., 1964—, pres., 1971. Recipient award for meritorious community service Grit Pub. Co., 1956. Mem. Am., Pa. (jud. ct. nominating commn.), bar assns., Kappa Sigma. Presbyterian. Mason. Research in use of French Vibert box trout egg stocking system, 1966—. Home: 54 Roderick Rd Williamsport PA 17701 Office: 23 W 3d St Williamsport PA 17701

YOUNGS, DAVID DALMER, obstetrician, gynecologist, psychiatrist; b. Dearborn, Mich., Nov. 19, 1937; s. Chalmer D. and Ruby C. (Kiteley) Y.; M.D., U. Mich., 1962; m. Margot V. Halpern, June 23, 1963; children—Peter Alexander, William Chalmer. Intern, Hartford (Conn.) Hosp., 1962-63; resident in obstetrics and gynecology Women's Hosp., U. Mich., Ann Arbor, 1963-66, 68-69; resident in psychiatry Univ. Hosp., Ann Arbor, 1969-72; mem. faculty dept. obstetrics and gynecology U. Mich. Med. Sch., Ann Arbor, 1972-73, Johns Hopkins U. Sch. Medicine, Balt., 1973-75, also dir. Center Social Studies in Human Reprodn.; practice medicine, specializing in obstetrics and gynecology and psychiatry, Portland, Maine, 1975—; cons. program for young mothers and infants Johns Hopkins Sch. Medicine; cons. Joseph P. Kennedy Jr. Found., 1976—. Served with AUS, 1966-68. Brush Fund of Cleve. grantee, 1973-75, Joseph P. Kennedy Jr. Found. grantee, 1975-78. Fellow Am. Coll. Obstetrics and Gynecology, Am. Psychiat. Assn.; mem. Norman F. Miller Gynecol. Soc., J. Donald Woodruff Soc. Contbr. articles to profl. jours. Home: 199 Middle Rd Falmouth ME 04105 Offie: 131 Chadwick St Portland ME 04102

YOUNGSON, JEANNE KEYES, film producer, author; b. Syracuse, N.Y., Dec. 20, 1924; d. Kenneth W. and Margaret E. (Gardiner) Keyes; student Maryville Coll., 1946, Tenn. Acad. Arts, 1952; postgrad. N.Y. U., 1953-55, New Sch. for Social Research, 1956-57, Inst. Tech., Mexico, 1958, Oxford U., 1977, Cambridge U., 1978; D.Litt., Sussex Coll., 1976, Ph.D. in Lang. Edn., 1978; m. Robert George Youngson, June 15, 1960 (dec. 1974). Pub. relations exec. Mus. of Modern Art, N.Y.C., 1952-58, Music Corp. of Am., N.Y.C., 1958-60; ind. film producer, 1960—; producer, dir. films including: Maude in Her Hat (1st prize Bklyn. Arts and Culture Assn. Film Festival), 1970; My Name is Debbie, 1973; Fred C. Boggs, The Unicorn (prize Assn. Internat du Film Animation), 1974; The Watercolor Lady, 1974; The Dracula Doll, 1977; The Horrible Dream of Eleanor Beem, 1977; Gleeps, 1978; organized internat. festival Films About, By and For Women, Balt., 1975. Served with USNR, 1945-46. Mem. Internat. Count Dracula Fan Club (pres., founder), Dracula Soc. (London), Soc. for Sci. Study of Sex, Assn. Internat. du Film Animation. Author: Dracula Made Easy, 1978; editor: Count Dracula Bi-Ann., 1978. Home: 29 Washington Square W New York City NY 10011 Office: 1 5th Ave New York City NY 10003

YOUNIS, ADELE LINDA, educator; b. N.Y.C.; d. Joseph and Sarah (Najjar) Younis; B.S., R.I. Coll., 1933; M.A., Boston U., 1943, Ph.D., 1961; student Brown U., 1948-49. Adult edn. tchr. Fall River (Mass.) pub. schs., 1934-42; tchr. social sci. Case High Sch., Swansea, Mass., 1942-47; prof. lit. and history Bryant Coll., 1947-52; faculty, dept. history Salem State Coll., 1956—, chmn. Grad. Sch. Hist. Studies, 1975-76, now prof. history; Cons. Inst. Higher Learning, Lima, Peru, Voice of Am., USIA; lectr. World Lebanese Union, 1968; lectr., radio commentator Fall River, New Bedford, Salem; leader archeol. expdns. to Near East, 1968-71. Mem. Fall River (Mass.) Civic Council, 1945-56; Am. Assn. for Middle East Studies fellowship for overseas study, summer 1963; lecture series on Arabic emigration. Mem. AAUW (corr. sec. Fall River br. 1950-52, 1st v.p. 1952-54, pres. 1954-56, chmn. higher edn. Mass. div. 1958-61), Nat. Archives, Am., New Eng. hist. assns., New Eng. Assn. Women Historians, Essex Inst. Hist. Collections, Am. Acad. Polit. and Social Scis., Boston Opera Assn., Boston Ballet Assn., Phi Alpha Theta, Pi Gamma Mu. Translator: Elias Moussly Journal, 1668-1683; Monseigneur Lucien Malouf of Boston; dir. Fall River Bicentennial on Near Easten in Culture and Social Intellectual Values, 1976; editor North Shore Ethnic Studies, 10 vols. Mem. editorial adv. bd. Bicentennial Research Assos. publs. Author: Prospects in Historical Studies and Opportunities, Salem, 1978; Conversations in History—1979, Salem: Immigration: Re-Evaluated, 1979. Contbr. articles to profl. jours. Home: 320 Lafayette St Apt 501 Salem MA 01970

YOUTCHEFF, JOHN SHELDON, physicist; b. Newark, Apr. 16, 1925; s. Slav Joseph and Florence Catherine (Davidson) Y.; A.B., Columbia, 1949, B.S., 1950; Ph.D., U. Calif. at Los Angeles, 1953; m. Elsie Marianne, June 17, 1950; children—Karen Janette, John Sheldon, Mark Allen, Heidi Mary Anne, Lisa Ellen. Ops. analyst Gen. Electric Co., Ithaca, N.Y., 1953-56, cons. engr. Missile & Space Div., Phila., 1956-64, mgr. advanced reliability programs, 1964-72; mgr. reliability and maintainability Litton Industries, College Pk., Md., 1972-73; program mgr. U.S. Postal Service Hdqrs., Washington, 1973—; instr. U. Pa., 1965-66, Villanova U., 1957—. Served to lt. USAAF, 1943-46; to comdr. USNR, 1946—. Registered profl. engr., Calif., D.C. Fellow AAAS, British Interplanetary Soc., Am. Inst. Aero. and Astronautics (asso.); mem. IEEE (sr.), Ops. Research Soc., Research Soc. Am., Am. Math. Soc., Am. Physics Soc., Am. Chem. Soc., Am. Astron. Soc., Am. Geol. Soc., Nat. Soc. Profl. Engrs., Engring. and Tech. Socs. Council Del. Valley (speakers bur.), Res. Officers Assn., Am. Legion. Roman Catholic. Clubs: Explorers (N.Y.C.), Optimists Internat. (pres. Valley Forge chpt. 1970-71). Holder 3 U.S. patents; contbr. articles to profl. jours. and proc. Home: 543 Midland Ave Berwyn PA 19312 Office: L'Enfant Plaza Washington DC 20260

YOUTT, JULIE WILSON, ednl. adminstr.; b. Detroit, Oct. 20, 1948; d. Donald Coyner and Barbara Hodges (Fitch) Wilson; B.A., Coll. Wooster, 1970; M.S., State U. N.Y., Plattsburgh, 1977; m. Robert William Youtt, Aug. 29, 1970; 1 son, Andrew Blanchard. Program coordinator career advancement program at Hanscom AFB, Mass., for Johnson & Wales Coll., 1977—. Mem. steering com. Women's Advisory Com. on Rape, Plattsburgh. Mem. Am. Personnel, Guidance Assn., Nat. Vocat. Guidance Assn. Presbyterian. Home: 284 Great Rd Acton MA 01720 Office: Edn Service Center DPT/31 Hanscom AFB MA 01731

YUILLE, ERNEST CLARKE, environ. exec.; b. Atlantic City, Sept. 7, 1932; s. Alexander Spencer and Annie Clarke (Williams) Y.; B.S., Hampton Inst., 1954; M.B.A., U. Louisville, 1969; m. Laura Louise McNeil, Dec. 23, 1954; children—Thomasina, Antonia, Eugenia, Ernestine. Research chemist Am. Cyanamid Co., Bound Brook, N.J., 1956-66; devel. chemist Celanese Coating Co., Louisville, 1967-69; sr. devel. engr. Am. Standard Co., Louisville, 1969-70; with Polaroid Corp., 1971—, now staff asst. environ. affairs. Mem. Plainfield (N.J.) City Council, 1967-68; bd. dirs. Merrimac Mission. Served with USAR, 1954-56. Mem. Am. Chem. Soc., New Eng. Water Pollution Control Fedn., Alpha Phi Alpha. Democrat. Patentee in field. Home: 5 Cedar Dr South Easton MA 02375 Office: Polaroid Corp 100 Duchaine Indsl Park New Bedford MA 02745

YULISH, CHARLES BARRY, internat. mgmt. and communications cons.; b. Cleve., Oct. 14, 1936; s. Isadore and Minna (Scott) Y.; B.A. in Govt., Kent State U., 1959; M.Pub. Adminstrn. (Maxwell fellow), Maxwell Sch. Citizenship and Pub. Affairs Syracuse U., 1961; postgrad. N.Y. U., 1963-64, New Sch. For Social Research, 1965-66; m. Barbara Pearlman, Aug. 22, 1973; 1 son, Aleksandr Jules-Nicholas. Spl. projects officer AEC, Washington, 1961-63; project mgr. Atomic Indsl. Forum, Inc., N.Y.C., 1963-66; pres. Charles Yulish Assos., Inc., mgmt. cons., N.Y.C., 1966—, now Internat. of Underwood Jordan Yulish Assos.; pres., chmn. bd. Energy Info. Service, Inc., N.Y.C., 1973—; mem. nat. adv. bd. Ams. for Energy Independence; dir. Inside Can. Pub. Relations Ltd.; lectr. on energy, govtl. affairs; speaker on energy-related topics. Bd. dirs. Koussevitsky Archives Soc. Recipient Spl. Act of Service award AEC, 1962. Mem. Am. Nuclear Soc., Atomic Indsl. Forum, Inc., AAAS. Contbr. articles on classical music to mus. and popular publs. Home: 2259 Edsall Ave Bronx NY 10463 Office: 230 Park Ave New York City NY 10011

YUNICH, DAVID LAWRENCE, tranps. co. exec.; b. Albany, N.Y., May 21, 1917; s. Max A. and Bessie (Feldman) Y.; A.B., Union Coll., 1939, LL.D., 1964; postgrad. Harvard Grad. Sch. Bus. Adminstrn., 1939-40; m. Beverly F. Blickman, June 11, 1941; children—Robert Hardle, Peter B. Mdse. councilor L. Bamberger & Co., Newark, 1947-48, pres., dir., 1955-62; v.p., Macy's N.Y., 1941-51, sr. v.p., 1951-62, pres., 1962-71; vice chmn. bd. R.H. Macy & Co. Inc., 1971-73, dir., 1958-73, now ret.; consumer cos. cons., 1973—; chmn., chief exec. officer N.Y.C. Transit. Dir. East River Savs. Bank, Prudential Ins. Co. Am., N.Y. Telephone Co., U.S. Industries, Inc., W.R. Grace & Co., Diners Club, Inc., J. Walter Thompson Co., Harwood Mfg. Co. Chmn. Met. Transp. Authority, 1974-75; mem. N.Y. State Banking Bd.; chmn. Gov.'s Commn. Financing Mass Transp.; chmn. Mayor's Council Econ. and Bus. Advisers, N.Y.C. Pres. Greater N.Y. council Boy Scouts Am. Bd. dirs. Nat. Jewish Hosp. Denver, Regional Plan Assn., Ednl. Broadcasting Corp.; trustee Carnegie Hall Corp., Saratoga Performing Arts, Albany Med. Coll., Union Coll., Schenectady, Skidmore Coll., Saratoga Springs, N.Y.; bd. govs., trustee Rutgers U., New Brunswick, N.J. Decorated chevalier Confrerie des Chevaliers du Tastevin. Mem. N.Y. Chamber of Commerce and Industry (chmn. bd.), Retail Dry Goods Assn. (pres. 1964-69), Nat. Retail Mchts. Assn. (dir.), Am. Mgmt. Assn. (dir.). Clubs: Harvard Bus. Sch., Harvard, Univ., Recess, Econ. (N.Y.C.); Blind Brook, Scarsdale (Westchester, N.Y.); Saratoga Golf and Polo (Saratoga Springs); Sandy Lane Golf (Barbados, W.I.). Home: Five Birches Cooper Rd Scarsdale NY 10583 Office: 1700 Broadway New York City NY 10019 also New York City Transit 370 Jay St Brooklyn NY 11201

YVONNE, poet, editor; b. Phila.; d. Vernon and Jacqueline Chism; B.A., Rosemont (Pa.) Coll., 1966; M.A., N.Y. U., 1968; postgrad. Bank St. Coll. Edn., N.Y.C., 1969-70. Tchr., N.Y.C. Bd. Edn., 1970-73; poetry editor Aphra Mag., 1972-74; contbg. editor Ms. Mag., 1973—. Nat. Endowment for the Arts fellow, 1974; Mary Roberts Rinehart fellow, 1974; recipient Anthology award III Puschart Press, 1978. Mem. Bronx Poets and Writers Alliance (pres. 1978—), Bronx Council on Arts, Bronx Hist. Soc., Authors Guild, Poetry Soc. Am. Republican. Roman Catholic. Office: care Ms Mag 370 Lexington Ave New York City NY 10030

ZACHARIASEWYCZ, EUGENE, veterinarian; b. Koblo, Ukraine, Jan. 4, 1926; s. Yaroslav and Helene (Wykowycz) Z.; came to U.S., 1961, naturalized, 1968; D.V.Sc., U. La Plata (Argentina), 1962; D.V.M., Veterinary Sch., Bern, Switzerland, 1965; m. Maria Komanowska, Aug. 30, 1964; 1 son, Adrian. Research instr. sect. of viral oncology, dept. clin. studies Sch. Veterinary Medicine, U. Pa. New Bolton Center, Kennett Square, 1966-71, part-time 1971-73; veterinarian in small animal practice. Mem. Am., Pa., Keystone veterinary med. assns., Providence Assn., Ukrainian Nat. Assn. Home: 1425 Donna Ave Woodlyn PA 19094 Office: 1408 Chester Pike Crum Lynne PA 19022

ZACHARIUS, MARTIN PHILIP, mech. engr.; b. N.Y.C., June 19, 1928; s. Herman Roy and Rebecca (Bengis) Z.; B.Mech. Engring., N.Y. U., 1951; m. Shirley Mofsovitz, Mar. 31, 1948; children—Wendy J. (Mrs. Howard W. Goldstein), Sherrie. Jr. designer Raisler Corp., N.Y.C., 1948; supervising engr. Bechtel Corp., 1952-53; sr. mech. engr. Krey & Hunt, N.Y.C., 1953-55; sr. mem. M.P. Zacharius & Assos., Cons. Mech. and Elec. Engrs., N.Y.C., 1955— pres. Tech. Installations, Inc., Mineola, 1973-77, N.Y.C., 1977—, Eng Zac Internat., Rio de Janeiro, 1977—; Instr., N.Y. U., N.Y.C., 1953-56. Active Am. Hosp. Assn.; mem. constrn. ind. panel Am. Arbitration Assn., N.Y.C. Mem. N.Y. Assn. Cons. Engrs. (recipient several awards), ASHRAE. Home: 30 Park Ave New York City NY 10016 Office: 99 Madison Ave New York City NY 10016

ZACK, EARL ROBERT, mgmt. cons., educator; b. Phila., June 5, 1913; s. Samuel Robert and Ida Alice (Sperling) Z.; B.A., City U. N.Y., 1934; M.A., N.Y. U., 1949, Ph.D., 1953; m. Nancy Elinor Matthews, Jan. 27, 1947; children—Melissa Susan, Jane Carol. Instr. speech, dir. speech clinic City Coll. N.Y., 1934-39; pres. Earl R. Zack Assos., N.Y.C., 1934-42; asst. dir. personnel RCA Communications, Inc., N.Y.C., 1946-55; dir. personnel devel. Sperry Gyroscope Corp., N.Y.C., 1955-62; prof. mgmt., dir. doctoral program Pace U. Grad. Sch., N.Y.C., 1962—; mgmt. cons., 1934-42, 62—. Mem. bd. advisers Hofstra U. Exptl. Coll., Hempstead, N.Y., 1957-60. Served to maj. AUS, 1942-45. Mem. Am. Psychol. Assn., AAAS, Acad. Mgmt. Republican. Presbyterian. Contbr. articles to profl. jours. Home: 161 Tullamore Rd Garden City NY 11530 Office: Pace Univ Grad Sch Pace Pl New York City NY 10038

ZACKRISON, HARRY BERTIL, JR., elec. engr.; b. Washington, Dec. 9, 1936; s. Harry Bertil and Ethel Clarieta (Barnes) Z.; A.A., Paul Smiths (N.Y.) Coll., 1962; student elec. engring. Clarkson Coll. Tech., Potsdam, N.Y., 1962-65; m. Eileen Philomena Dardis, July 24, 1965; children—Linda Mary, John Harry, Paul Anthony. Successively elec. draftsman, elec. designer, design elec. engr. H.D. Nottingham & Assos., architects and engrs., Arlington, Va., 1963-68; design elec. engr. Frank J. Sullivan & Assos., 1968-69; with Saunders, Pearson, Appleton & Partners, Washington, 1969-73, asso. and head elec. dept., 1970-73, Catelain, Samperton & Carcaterra Architects and Engrs., Washington, 1973-78; v.p., head elec. dept. The E/A Design Group, Washington, 1978—. Registered profl. engr., D.C., 7 other states. Mem. Nat., D.C. (chmn. program com. 1973-74, 77-78, pres.-elect 1979—), W.Va. socs. profl. engrs., Illuminating Engring. Soc. (sec. capitol sect. 1973-74, v.p. 1974-75, pres. 1975-77), IEEE, Profl. Engrs. in Pvt. Practice. Author numerous papers, guides in field. Home: 3802 Cobblestone Ct Alexandria VA 22306 Office: 1625 K Street NW Washington DC 20006

ZACKRISON, WALTER JOSEPH, mgmt. recruiting exec.; b. Bridgeport, Conn., May 5, 1932; s. Eric Walter and Loretta Gertrude (O'Hare) Z.; B.S., Fairfield U., 1954; postgrad. Bernard Baruch Coll., 1962-63; m. Marjorie Ann Goodwin, Apr. 27, 1957; children—Mary, Walter, Maura, Ann. Mktg. rep. Upjohn Co., N.Y.C., 1954-64; mem. pub. relations dept. Med. Soc. State N.Y., Albany, 1964-66; advt. mgr. Paper Industry Mgmt. Assn., N.Y.C., 1966-68; pres., chief exec. officer Zackrison Assos., Inc., Fairfield, New Haven, Hartford and Stamford, Conn., 1968—. Trustee Fairfield U., 1974—, Park City Hosp., Bridgeport, 1974—. Served with U.S. Army, 1956-58. Mem. Nat. Assn. Personnel Cons. (past pres. Conn. chpt., nat. dir.), Bridgeport C. of C. Republican. Roman Catholic. Clubs: Patterson Country (pres. 1977-78), Rotary, Landmark, Queechee Country. Home: 140 Winton Rd Fairfield CT 06430 Office: 88 Beach Rd Fairfield CT 06430

ZADEK, BEBE, advt. agy. exec.; b. N.Y.C.; d. Leo and Jeanne (seegall) Z.; B.A. magna cum laude, Syracuse U.; m. James L. Olsen, Apr. 2, 1977. Promotion dir. Kalb, Voorhis & Co., Washington, 1958-69; sales promotion dir. Piedmont Capital, Englewood, N.J., 1969-70; sr. account exec. Compton Jones Advt., Washington, 1970-72; pres. Advt. A La Carte, Washington, 1972—. Mem. Am. Soc. Assn. Execs., Am. Mktg. Assn., Washington Soc. Assn. Execs. Club: Advt. Office: 7315 Wisconsin Ave Washington DC 20014

ZADELL, HENRY JAMES, elec. engr.; b. Johnstown, Pa., July 28, 1936; s. Anthony and Frances (Schine) Z.; B.S. cum laude, U. Pitts., 1959; M.S., U. Pa., 1963. With RCA Corp., Camden, N.J., 1959—, sr. mem. staff, 1966—. Mem. Delaware Valley Citizens Council for Clean Air, Phila., 1972-74. Registered profl. engr., N.J., Pa. Mem. IEEE, Sigma Tau, Phi Theta Kappa, Eta Kappa Nu. Club: South Jersey Aero (treas. 1970-78) (Medford, N.J.). Contbr. articles in field to profl. jours.; patentee. Home: 114B Avon Rd Haddonfield NJ 08033 Office: RCA Corporation Bldg 10-8 Camden NJ 08102

ZADUNAISKY, JOSE ATILIO, physiologist, educator; b. Rosario, Argentina, July 15, 1932; s. Abraham and Juana (Lande) Z.; came to U.S., 1964, naturalized, 1972; M.D., U. Buenos Aires, Argentina, 1956; m. Maria F. Dabini, Apr. 12, 1954; children—Laura J., Edward P. Instr., Inst. of Physiology, U. Buenos Aires, 1952-56, research fellow, 1956-58, investigator Argentine Nat. Research Council, 1960-63; vis. research fellow dept. biochemistry U. Coll., Dublin, Ireland, 1958-59, Inst. Biol. Chemistry, U. Copenhagen, 1959-60; asso. prof. dept. ophthalmology U. Louisville, 1964-67, asso. in physiology, 1964-67, dir. research dept. ophthalmology, 1964-67; asso. prof. ophthalmology and physiology Yale U. Sch. Medicine, New Haven, 1967-73; prof. physiology and exptl. ophthalmology

N.Y. U. Sch. Medicine, N.Y.C., 1973; mem. Vision Study Sect. A, Nat. Eye Inst., 1976—; mem. organizing com. 1st Internat. Congresses of Eye Research, 1974, 76, 78. Recipient Nat. Eye Inst. award, 1961-1978, Seeing Eye, Inc. award, 1964-1976; Santamarina Found. fellow, 1957-58; NIH grantee, 1961-64. Fellow N.Y. Acad. Scis.; mem. Am. Physiol. Soc. (ednl. materials rev. bd. 1975), Assn. for Research in Vision and Ophthalmology (chmn. physiology and pharmacology, nat. meetings), Internat. Soc. Eye Research (sec. 1978—), Biophys. Soc., Soc. Gen. Physiologists, Am. Soc. Zoologists, AAAS, Membrane Transport Club N.Y. (founder), Sigma Xi. Democrat. Jewish. Contbr. articles on research in membrane physiology and ophthalmology to sci. publs.; editor Exptl. Eye Research, 1970—, Current Topics in Eye Research, 1978—. Home: 250 Trenor Dr New Rochelle NY 10804 Office: New York Univ Medical Center 550 1st Ave New York City NY 10016

ZADYLAK, STANLEY EDWARD, traffic mgr.; b. Mt. Pleasant, Pa., Nov. 6, 1943; s. Stanley B. and Ann D. Z.; student Durbin's Bus. Sch., 1961-62, Coll. Advance Traffic, 1969-71; m. Barbara Ann Ordelt, Aug. 26, 1972; children—Bryan Edward, Sheri Ann. Meat cutter Market Basket, Connellsville, Pa., 1961-62; steno Surgeon Gen.'s Office, USAF Hdqrs., Washington, 1962-65; file clk. Modulus Corp., Mt. Pleasant, 1965-70, traffic mgr., 1970—; cons. in field. Mem. Indsl. Fasteners Inst. Am., Traffic, Transp. Assn. Pitts., Laurel Mt. Traffic Assn. (past pres., chmn. bd.). Democrat. Roman Catholic. Clubs: Eagles, K.C. (3 deg.). Home: 201 Scottdale Ave Scottdale PA 15683 Office: 1000 Modulus Rd Mount Pleasant PA 15666

ZAFFARANO, RICHARD F., phys. scientist, govt. ofcl.; b. Bklyn., June 4, 1925; s. Nicholas and Amelia (Lagno) Z.; B.S. in Petroleum Engring., U. Okla., 1951; div.; children—Mark Alan, Michele Ann. Petroleum engr. Hudson-Eads, Inc., Wichita Falls, Tex., 1951-53; petroleum engr. U.S. Bur. Mines, Laramie, Wyo., 1953-60, phys. scientist, Washington, 1960-70, chief div. petroleum and natural gas, 1970-77; sr. staff advisor Energy Info. Adminstrn., Dept. Energy, Washington, 1977—. Served with USNR, 1943-46; PTO. Recipient spl. service awards for energy supply and demand study, planning U.S. Dept. Interior. Mem. Soc. Petroleum Engrs., Am. Inst. Chem. Engrs., Internat. Oil Scouts Assn., Soc. Plastics Industry. Roman Catholic. Author govt. publs. Home: 3101 S Manchester St Apt 908 Falls Church VA 22044 Office: 12th and Pennsylvania Ave NW Room 4426 Washington DC 20461

ZAFFINO, PATRICIA ANN, communications co. exec.; b. Warren, pa., Dec. 15, 1939; d. Michael and Rose Marie (pasquino) Z.; B.A., Hunter Coll., 1962. Med. copywriter/editor Pfizer Labs., N.Y.C., 1965-69: projects dir. Council for Interdisciplinary Communication in Medicine, N.Y.C., 1969-71; dir. creative services Health Learning Systems, W. Orange, N.J., 1971; v.p. Intramed Communications div. Sudler & Hennessey, Inc., N.Y.C., 1971-74; pres. Synthesis Communications, Inc., N.Y.C., 1974—, chmn. bd. dirs.; dir. Council for the Life Scis., Inc.; cons. Nat. High Blood Pressure Edn. Program, Bethesda, Md. Office: Synthesis Communications Inc 119 W 57 St New York City NY 10019

ZAFFUTO, STEPHEN FRED, ophthalmologist; b. Westfield, N.J., July 12, 1933; s. Federico Stefano and Catherine (Huzar) Z.; B.S., Coll. City N.Y., 1954; M.D., U. Pitts., 1964; m. Dolores Josephine Iannelli, Jan. 19, 1957; children—Celeste, Gerard. Intern, Lenox Hill Hosp., N.Y.C., 1964-65, resident in ophthalmology, 1965-68, asso. attending, 1968—; practice medicine, specializing in ophthalmology, Whitestone, N.Y., 1968—; adj. surgeon N.Y. Eye & Ear Infirmary, 1968; cons. Calvary Hosp., Bronx, 1969—; ophthalmologist N.Y. Foundling Hosp., Queen of Peace Residence, Hillcrest Gen. Hosp., Queens. Fellow Am. Acad. Ophthalmology and Otolaryngology; mem. AMA, Queens County Med. Soc. Home: 6 Blenheim Dr Manhasset NY 11030 Office: 16-20 157th St Whitestone NY 11357

ZAGAT, EUGENE HENRY, real estate operator; b. N.Y.C., Oct. 9, 1909; s. Paul Henry and Anna E. (Klatzkin) Z.; student Worcester Acad.; A.B. cum laude, Dartmouth Coll., 1930; student Harvard Law Sch., Columbia U., Oxford U. (Eng.), Sorbonne (France); m. Cornelia Pake Ernst, June 12, 1935 (div. 1964); children—Eugene Henry, Cornelia Ann (Mrs. Timothy Eland); m. 2d, Elizabeth Marie McNichol, Oct. 15, 1967. In circulation, ednl., subscription and nat. advt. depts. N.Y. Times, 1931-35; in real estate, 1935—; pres., treas. Algonquin Realty Corp., Paul H. Zagat & Co., Inc., Phoenix Realty Corp., Sunlight Realty Corp., Donmar Realty Corp., Progressive Income Corp.; past pres., treas. Devel. Revenue Corp., Cumulative Income Corp., Realty Revenue Corp., Cumulative Holding Corp., Intercontinental Realty Corp., 1935—. Lectr. real estate Coll. City N.Y. Former dir. Am. Council Nationalities Service; former v.p., dir. Ednl. Alliance; former dir. Edalia, Salomon, Surprise Lake camps; mem. real estate div. com. Nat. Found.; men's com. Planned Parenthood; past mem. men's com. Friends of Philharmonic; past mem. advance gifts com. U.S.O.; past jr. chmn. Manhattan United Jewish Appeal, One World award com.; mem. com. Assn. for Retarded Children; past chmn. West Side N.Y.C. Civil Def.; past asst. class agent Dartmouth Coll. Alumni Fund; mem. class exec. com. Dartmouth Coll. Mem. Broadway Assn., Inc. (dir.), 34th St. Midtown Assn. (past dir.), Real Estate Bd. N.Y., Pi Lambda Phi (past pres. Dartmouth), Alpha Delta Sigma (past pres. Dartmouth). Home: 799 Park Ave New York City NY 10021 Office: 600 Madison Ave New York City NY 10022

ZAHAVY, EDITH DORIS, educator; b. N.Y.C.; B.A., Hunter Coll., N.Y.C., 1940, M.S. in Reading, 1975; married; 3 children. Dir., Beth Hillel Kindergarten and Nursery, N.Y.C., 1945-50, Park E. Day Sch., N.Y.C., 1950-61; reading specialist N.Y.C. Bd. Edn., 1961—. Certified elementary and nursery edn. Mem. United Fedn. Tchrs., Internat. Reading Assn. Developed remedial reading techniques for N.Y.C. Schs. Home: 210 E 68th St New York City NY 10021 Office: 210 E 33d St New York City NY 10016

ZAHAVY, ZEV, clergyman, educator; b. N.Y.C., Sept. 8, 1920; s. I. David and Anna (Epstein) Z.; B.A., Yeshiva U., 1939, M.H.L., 1948, Ph.D., 1959; grad. Isaac Elchanan Theol. Sem., 1942; postgrad. Columbia, 1943-45; m. Edith Doris Medine, July 1, 1947; children—Tzvee, Reuvain, Miryam. Rabbi, 1942; asst. rabbi West Side Instl. Synagogue, N.Y.C., 1942-45; asso. rabbi Congregation Ohab Zedek, N.Y.C., 1945-52; rabbi Congregation Zichron Ephraim, N.Y.C., 1952-61; nat. dir. community consultation Am. Assn. Jewish Edn., 1961-62; instr. Yeshiva U., 1960-62; prof. City U. N.Y., 1964—; chaplain St. Vincent's Hosp. and Meml. Hosp., 1964-68. Cons. N.Y.C. Mayor's Commn. Human Relations, 1961-62; Jewish chmn. UN Appeal for Children, 1952-54; head Jewish chaplains N.Y. Civil Def., 1945-48; mem. Yorkville Welfare Council, 1954-60; mem. Lenox Hill Welfare Assn., 1954-60; instl. rep. Beth Hillel Inst. council Boy Scouts Am., 1945-50; v.p. N.Y. Region Rabbinical Council Am., 1954-56. Mem. bd. edn. Manhattan Day Sch., 1958-68; v.p. Gimel Found., 1973—. Mem. Am. Assn. U. Profs., N.E.A., Modern Lang. Assn., Nat. Council Hebrew Edn., Rabbinic Alumni Assn. (exec. bd. 1956-59), N.Y. Bd. Rabbis (exec. bd. 1950-55), Mizrachi Orgn., Assn. Childhood Edn. Author: The Oral Law in the Book of Jubilees, 1948; Independence and Modernity, 1953; Hearken Ye Heavens, 1963; Unraveling Dante's Gibberish, 1972; Earliest Recorded Theatre, 1973; Whitman as Guru, 1973; Idra Zuta Kadisha, 1977; Whence and Wherefore, 1978; A Space-Age Guide for the Perplexed, 1978; Heresy in the Atheist Church, 1976; Tannaitic Existentialism, 1976; The Remarkable KI TOV Factor, 1976. Editor: Library of Literary Classics, 1974. Home: 210 E 68th St New York City NY 10021

ZAHLER, HAROLD DAVID, fin. exec.; b. Newark, July 20, 1922; s. Max and May (Kopold) Z.; Weather Tech. Specialist, Weather Observer Sch., 1943; B.B.A., Rutgers U., 1947; M.A., Columbia U., 1949; m. Sondra Freedman, Nov. 24, 1949; children—Carol Fran (Mrs. James Christatos), Martin. Supervising auditor, div. local govt., State of N.J., Trenton, 1950-68; finance officer Town of Westfield, N.J., 1968-76; supervising auditor Suplee Clooney & Co., 1976—. Instr. Rutgers U., New Brunswick, N.J., 1973. Served with USAAF, 1943-46. Recipient Pi Mu Epsilon award for proficiency in math., 1940. Mem. Municipal Finance Officers of N.J. (trustee 1974-76), Municipal Finance Officers Assn. of the U.S. and Can., Registered Municipal Accountants Assn. N.J. Clubs: Kiwanis (treas. 1972-76), Westfield (N.J.) Stamp and Coins. Home: 719 Harding St Westfield NJ 07090 Office: 151 Jefferson Ave Elizabeth NJ 07201

ZAHN, FREDERICK ANTHONY, lawyer; b. Oklahoma City, Jan. 17, 1940; s. Fred H. and Betty (Anthony) Z.; B.A., Yale, 1962; J.D., Okla. U., 1965; LL.M., N.Y. U., 1970; m. Gwendolyne Reston, Sept. 3, 1966; children—Katherine, Heidi, Jennifer. Cons., Towers, Perrin, Forster & Crosby, Inc., Phila., N.Y.C., Chgo., 1965-67; admitted to Okla. bar, 1965; asst. gen. counsel Okla. State Ins. Commn., Oklahoma City, 1967-68; atty. Andrews, Mosburg, Davis, Elam, Legg & Kornfeld, Inc., Oklahoma City, 1968-71; pvt. practice law, Oklahoma City, 1971-77; v.p., gen. counsel Compass Group, Inc., Westport, Conn., 1977—; adviser Mcpl. Ct. Asso. prof. Oklahoma City U. Law Sch., 1972-77; lectr. Practising Law Inst. Chmn., Opera Guild, 1972-74; chmn. Central Okla. chpt. Multiple Sclerosis Soc., 1973-75. Mem. City Council, Ward 1, Oklahoma City, 1973-76. Bd. dirs. Oklahoma City Arts Council, Goodwill Industries, Muscular Dystrophy Group, YMCA; mem. exec. com. Oklahoma City Symphony Soc., 1973-74. Served with USAF Res., 1962-69. Named Outstanding Young Man of Oklahoma City, Jr. C. of C., 1971, Three Outstanding Young Oklahomans, Okla. Jr. C. of C., 1972. Mem. Am. (chmn. subcom. taxation U.S. citizens abroad internat. law sect.), Okla., Conn., Oklahoma County bar assns. Mem. Christian Ch. Securities editor Advocate mag., 1973-75. Home: Brae Haven 800 Verna Hill Rd Fairfield CT 06430 Office: 33 Riverside Ave Westport CT 06880

ZAKI, FOUAD GEORGE, biologist, educator; b. Cairo, Egypt, Dec. 20, 1915; s. George Ibrahim and Galila Zaki (Abdel-Sayed) Z.; came to U.S., 1960, naturalized. 1969; B.Sc., Cairo U., 1939, M.Sc., 1945, Ph.D., 1949; m. Pearl Iwinski, Nov. 23, 1957; 1 son, Nagi (Mark). Instr. biology Cairo (Egypt) U., 1939-45, asst. prof., 1945-56, asso. prof., 1956-58, prof., 1958-59; research asso. dept. medicine, also Children's Rehab. Center, U. Minn. Med. Sch., Mpls., 1960-65, asst. prof., 1965-67, asso. prof., 1967-69; sr. research fellow dept. pathology Squibb Inst. for Med. Research, New Brunswick, N.J., 1969—; asso. prof. N.J. Coll. Medicine & Dentistry, 1969—; cons. med. service VA Hosp., East Orange, N.J., 1969—. Recipient Minn. Med. Assn. medal, 1957. Mem. Acad. Medicine of N.J., Am. Assn. for Study Liver Diseases, Am. Soc. Cell Biology, Internat. Acad. Pathology, Am., German, Swiss philatelic socs. Contbr. numerous articles, book revs. to profl. jours. Home: 23 Eggers St East Brunswick NJ 08816 Office: Exptl Pathology Dept Squibb Inst for Med Research Princeton NJ 08540

ZAKI, MOUSTAFA ABDEL FATTAH, mech. engr., engring. co. exec.; b. Cairo, Egypt, Mar. 27, 1923; s. Abdel Fattah and Afkar (Alniklawi) Z.; came to U.S., 1968, naturalized, 1974; B.S., Cairo U., 1945; M.Sc., Alexandria U. (Egypt), 1950; Ph.D., Manchester U. (Eng.), 1953; m. Christiane Lindenau, Apr. 4, 1954; children—Fatima, Karima. Asst. lectr. U. Alexandria, 1946-50, lectr., 1953-54; lectr. Ain Shams U., Cairo, 1954-60; inspecting engr. Internat. Inspection Office, Dusseldorf, W. Ger., 1960-64; asso. prof. dept. mech. engring. Ain Shams U., Cairo, 1964-68; cons. UNESCO, 1969; research engr. Spence Engring. Co., Inc., Walden, N.Y., 1969-70, dir. engring. research and devel., 1970-73, dir. engring., 1974—; pres. Spence Controls Internat., 1977—; lectr. engring. and math. Orange County Community Coll., 1970-77. Mem. ASME, Am. Soc. Engring. Edn., Internat. Dist. Heating Assn., Fluid Controls Inst., Instrument Soc. Am., Am. Soc. Heating, Refrigerating and Air Conditioning Engrs., Inst. Engring. Inspection of London, Engrs. Syndicate of Cairo, Acoustical Soc. Am. Patentee in field. Home: 10 Westwood Dr Newburgh NY 12550 Office: 150 Coldenham Rd Walden NY 12586

ZAKRAYSEK, LOUIS, metall. engr.; b. Conemaugh Twp., Pa., Dec. 20, 1928; s. Louis and Matilda (Gasser) Z.; B.S., Pa. State U., 1952; m. Shirley Ann Hartman, Sept. 20, 1952; children—Mary Zakraysek Kenny, Nancy, Michelle Zakraysek Edwards. With Gen. Electric Co., Schenectady, 1952-53, Syracuse, 1953—, mgr. materials and processes, 1971—. Clk. vestry St. Thomas' Episcopal Ch., 1967-68; indsl. unit chmn. United Fund, 1967, federated unit chmn., 1969-70. Served with USNR, 1946-48. Fellow Am. Soc. Metals (pres.'s award 1968); mem. Inst. Printed Circuits (pres.'s award 1968), Soc. Automotive Engrs., Metall. Soc., Am. Inst. Mining and Metall. Engrs., Elfun Soc., Foremans Assn., GE Engrs. Assn. Contbr. to profl. jours. Republican. Home: 8432 Brewerton Rd Cicero NY 13039 Office: Gen Electric Co 3-24 Electronics Park Syracuse NY 13201

ZAKS, ELISABETH BROWN, credit union exec.; b. Phila., May 26, 1922; d. John B. and Mildred (Brown) Gehris; student Am. Savs. and Loan Inst., 1945; m. Henry C. Zaks, Mar. 4, 1944; children—Judith Ann Zaks Knipe, Phillip Henry. Office mgr., Hatboro Fed. Savs. & Loan Assn. (Pa.), 1941-46; teller, bookkeeper, office supr. NADC Fed. Credit Union, Naval Air Devel. Center, Warminster, Pa., 1962-67, mgr., 1967—. Named Pa. Credit Union Profl. of Year, 1977. Mem. Credit Union Execs. Soc. (treas. Delaware Valley council), Nat. Credit Union Mgmt. Assn., Cadillac Club. Methodist. Home: 36 Home Rd Hatboro PA 19040 Office: NADC Federal Credit Union Warminster PA 18974

ZALAR, CHARLES, govt. ofcl.; b. Franzdorf, Austria, Sept. 10, 1909; s. Joseph and Marianne (Oblak) Z.; B.S., Belgrade U., 1930; B.A., Ljubljana U., 1931, LL.M., 1935, Ph.D., 1936; postgrad. (scholar) Sorbonne, Paris, 1936-38, Rome U., 1941-43; Ph.D., Georgetown U., 1958: m. Minka Verbic, Aug. 16, 1936; 1 son, Gregory. Came to U.S., 1952, naturalized 1957. Fgn. service officer, Belgrade, Vatican, Paris, 1938-52; research analyst Library of Congress, 1952-62; sci. info. adminstr. NSF, Washington, 1962-71, asso. program dir., 1969-72, fgn. sci. adminstr., 1971—, program dir., 1972—. Cons. internat. law, 1946-52. Mem. French Soc. Comparative Legislation, Am. Polit., Sci. Assn., Am. Soc. Internat. Law, Internat. Polit. Sci. Assn., Am. Mil. Inst., A.A.A.S. Author: Yugoslav Communism, 1961. Home: 4545 Connecticut Ave NW Washington DC 20008 Office: 1800 G St NW Washington DC 20550

ZALDIVAR, NIEVES MARIA, physician, med. researcher; b. Camaguey, Cuba, Aug. 14, 1941; d. Armando Oscar and Luz Y. (Moran) Z.; came to U.S., 1966, naturalized, 1971; B.S., Inst. Havana, 1959; M.D., Mt. Sinai Sch. Medicine, 1971. Research asst. dept. hematology Mt. Sinai Hosp., N.Y.C., 1967-68, U. Miami (Fla.) dept. medicine, 1969; intern in pediatrics Mt. Sinai Hosp., 1971-72, fellow in pediatric infectious diseases, 1973-74; resident in pediatrics Jackson Meml. Hosp., Miami, 1972-73; practice medicine specializing in pediatrics, Miami, 1974-75, Bethesda, Md., 1975—; asst. prof. dept. pediatrics U. Miami Sch. Medicine, 1974-75; attending pediatrician Jackson Meml. Hosp., U. Miami, 1974-75: staff research physician Naval Med. Research Inst., Bethesda, 1975—. Herman Muehlstein scholar, 1970-71: Am. Cancer Soc. grantee, 1974, Am. Acad. Allergy grantee, 1974. Diplomate Am. Bd. Pediatrics. Mem. Am. Soc. Microbiology, Assn. Mil. Surgeons, AMA (Physician's Recognition award 1974-78), Alpha Omega Alpha. Contbr. articles on immunology and pediatrics to profl. jours. Office: Naval Medical Research Inst Bethesda MD 20014

ZALES, MICHAEL ROBERT, psychiatrist; b. N.Y.C., Apr. 26, 1937; s. Samuel and Gladys (Diamond) Z.; A.B., Princeton U., 1959; M.D., Albert Einstein Coll. Medicine, 1964; m. Ruth Elaine Aron, July 30, 1959; children—Melissa, Samuel. Intern, Greenwich (Conn.) Hosp., 1964-65; resident Coll. Medicine, U. Cin., 1967-70; Sol. W. Ginsburg fellow Group for the Advancement of Psychiatry, 1968-70; practice medicine specializing in psychiatry, Greenwich, 1970—; asst. attending psychiatrist Greenwich Hosp., 1970-71, asso. attending psychiatrist, 1971-77, sr. attending psychiatrist, 1977—; clin. instr. psychiatry Albert Einstein Coll. Medicine, N.Y.C., 1970-74, asst. clin. prof. psychiatry, 1974—; vis. lectr. Hebrew Union Coll.-Jewish Inst. Religion, 1974—; vis. lectr. in psychiatry Yale U., 1975—; cons. Greenwich Center for Child and Family Service, 1970—, Greenwich Dept. Health, 1973—, Dubois Day Treatment Center, 1972—, Jewish Home for Elderly, 1974—, Greenwich Hot Line, 1971-76, Leukemia Soc. Am., 1975-76, Drug Liberation Program, Community Centers Inc., 1972-75, The Heart Doctor's Heart Book, 1974. Mem. bd. assos. Bridgeport U., 1978—. Served with M.C., USNR, 1965-67. NSF fellow, 1961, Mayo Found. fellow, 1963, NIH fellow, 1963; recipient Israel Solidarity award, 1976; diplomate Am. Bd. Psychiatry and Neurology. Mem. Conn., Fairfield County, Greenwich med. socs., Am. Psychiat. Assn. (program com., Chmn. sub-com. for spl. lectures 1978—), Conn. Psychiat. Soc. (Fairfield/Litchfield chpt. program chmn. 1978—) Am. Group Psychotherapy Assn., Am. Coll. Psychiatrists (publs. com. 1978—), Group for Advancement Psychiatry (fin. com. 1973—, Sol. W. Ginsburg Fellowship com. 1974—, chmn., 1976—, mem. com. on psychiatry and religion 1972—), Am. Acad. Psychiatry and Law. Author: First Aid Handbook, 1967; mem. Am. editorial bd. Israel Annals of Psychiatry and Related Disciplines, 1974—; contbr. articles to publs. in field. Home: Edgewood Dr Greenwich CT 06830

ZALEZNAK, BERNARD DAVID, physician; b. Chgo., Nov. 11, 1924; s. Isadore and Fannie (Levine) Z.; A.B., U. Ill., 1945, B.S. in Medicine, 1945, M.D., 1947; m. Eleanor Inkles, Nov. 19, 1949; children—Howard Nelson, Robert R., Andrew S. Intern, Cumberland Hosp., Bklyn., 1947; resident Bethel Hosp., Bklyn., 1948, Kingston Ave. Hosp., 1949, N.Y.C. Hosp., 1950; practice medicine, specializing in pediatrics, Bklyn., 1951—; pres. med. staff Brookdale Hosp. Med. Center, Bklyn., 1977—, attending pediatrician, 1955—: asst. prof. clin. pediatrics N.Y. U., N.Y.C., 1975—. Served to lt., USNR, 1951-53. Mem. Am. Acad. Pediatrics, Am. Med. Assn., N.Y. State Med. Soc., Med. Soc. County of Kings (pres. 1972-73). Address: 988 Jerome St Brooklyn NY 11207

ZALL, ROBERT ROUBEN, food scientist, educator; b. Lowell, Mass., Dec. 6, 1925; s. Samuel and Sarah (Cohen) Z.; B.S., U. Mass., 1949, M.S., 1950; Ph.D., Cornell U., 1968; m. Mollie Leah Wiseblood, June 8, 1949; children—Linda, Judy Zall Kusek, Jonathan J. Gen. mgr. Grandview Dairies, Bklyn. and Arkport, N.Y., 1950-66; dairy industry cons., Ithaca, N.Y., 1966-68; dir. research, prodn. Crowley Foods Co., Binghamton, N.Y., 1968-71; prof. food sci. Cornell U., Ithaca, N.Y., 1971—; trustee Milk Industry Pension and Welfare Fund; dir. Friendship Food Co., Inc.; asso. Gurnham, Inc.; dairy industry cons., project dir. EPA-Industry demonstration whey processing plant. Served with AUS, 1944-46. Recipient Certificate of Appreciation, EPA, 1975. Mem. Internat. Assn. Milk, Food and Environ. Sanitarians, Inst. Food Technologists, Am. Soc. Agrl. Engrs., Phi Kappa Phi. Clubs: Sertoma, Masons. Author: (with Bela G. Liptak) Environmental Engineers Handbook, 1972. Contbr. numerous articles to profl. jours., popular mags. Home: 54 Woodcrest Ave Ithaca NY 14850 Office: Stocking Hall Dept Food Sci Cornell Univ Ithaca NY 14853

ZAMBITO, RAYMOND FRANCIS, oral surgeon, educator; b. N.Y.C., Nov. 9, 1926; s. John and Lucy (Mecca) Z.; student Bklyn. Coll., 1943-44; B.S., U. Scranton, 1948; D.D.S., N.Y. U. Coll. Dentistry, 1953, certificate in Oral Surgery, 1956; M.A. in Adminstrn. in Higher Edn., Tchrs. Coll., Columbia U., 1968, D.Ed. in Adminstrn. in Higher Edn., 1978; M.B.A. in Health Care Mgmt., Adelphi U., 1978; m. Dorothy M. Sikoryak, Apr. 23, 1960; children—Mary Lucille, Paul Michael, Christine Marie, John Raymond, Michael Sikoryak, Peter Ignatius. Intern in oral surgery Kings County Hosp. Center, Bklyn., 1956-57; resident in gen. anesthesiology Jewish Chronic Disease Hosp., Bklyn., 1957; resident in oral surgery and anesthesiology Cook County Hosp., Chgo., 1957-59; practice gen. dentistry, Kings Park, N.Y., 1953-55, Chgo., 1958-59, oral surgery, Bklyn., 1959-61, Williston Park, N.Y., 1961-66, N.Y.C., 1966-68, Jamaica, N.Y., 1968—; asst. dept. of oral and maxillo-facial surgery U. Ill. Coll. Dentistry, 1958-59; instr. Sch. of Dental and Oral Surgery, Columbia U., N.Y.C., 1961-66; chief of service in dept. dentistry St. Francis Hosp., Roslyn, N.Y., 1963-66, cons. in oral surgery and dental dept. adminstrn., 1975—; asst. attending oral surgeon Kings County Hosp. Center, Bklyn., 1959-62; attending oral surgeon L.I. Jewish Med. Center, New Hyde Park, N.Y., 1962-71; asst. attending oral surgeon Queens Hosp. Center, Jamaica, N.Y., 1964-65; asso. attending oral surgeon Elmhurst (N.Y.) Gen. Hosp., 1965-66; attending oral surgeon and dir. dentistry and oral surgery Lincoln Hosp., 1966-68: asst. prof. of dental surgery Albert Einstein Coll. of Medicine, Yeshiva U., 1966-68, asst. clin. prof., 1968-73; oral surgeon-in-charge Catholic Med. Center of Bklyn., 1968—; cons. in oral and maxillo-facial surgery St. Joseph's Hosp. and Med. Center, Paterson, N.J., 1976-77; asst. prof. dept. oral surgery and anesthesiology Fairleigh Dickinson U. Sch. of Dentistry, Hackensack, N.J., 1971-72, prof., 1972—, coordinator dir. hosp. dentistry, 1972—; adj. asso. prof. of clin. pharmacy and dentistry Bklyn. Coll. of Pharmacy, 1976-77; cons. oral surgeon Suffolk State Sch., Melville, N.Y., 1965-71; dir. Spl. Dental Clinic for the Handicapped, Bur. of the Handicapped, Cath. Charities, Bklyn., 1973-75. Lectr. for Christian Life Communities movement to secondary schs. and colls. in various states, 1962—; tchr. of confraternity religious classes, 1964—; mem. parish council St. Gertrude's Roman Cath. Ch., Bayville, N.Y., 1969-72, chmn., 1971-72; founder, chmn. Fedn. of Lay Orgns., Diocese of Rockville Centre, N.Y.C., 1968-72; pres. Davis Park Civic Assn., 1966-67; cons. Nat. Council of Cath. Men, Washington, 1967-72. Served with USN, 1944-46. Decorated Knight Order of Malta in U.S., 1976; HEW grantee, 1967-70; diplomate Am. Bd. Oral and Maxillofacial Surgery. Fellow Am. Coll. of Dentists, Internat. Coll. Dentists Am. Pub. Health Assn., Am. Dental Soc. of Anesthesiology, L.I. Acad. of Odontology; mem. Am. Soc. of Oral and Maxillofacial Surgeons, Am. Dental Assn. (mem. rev. com. council on hosp. and instnl. dental services 1975, cons. council on dental edn. 1973—), N.Y. State Soc. of Oral Surgeons (alternate del. to Am. Soc. Oral Surgeons 1975-77), Am. Acad. Oral Pathology, Am. Acad. of History of Dentistry, N.Y. State Dental Soc. of Anesthesiology, Am. Assn. of Hosp. Dentists, Cath. Dentists Guild (pres. 1955-56), Am. Hosp. Assn. (mem. council on profl. services 1976-78), Am. Coll. Oral and Maxillo Facial Surgeons (v.p. 1976-79), Christian Med. Soc., Internat. Assn. of Oral Surgeons, Nat. Fedn. of Christian Life Communities (pres. nat. fedn. 1971-73, del. to internat. gen. assembly in Dominican Republic 1970). Editor-in-chief Jour. Hosp. Dental Practice, 1973—. Contbr. numerous articles on oral surgery and dental edn. to profl. jours. Home: 603 Bayville Rd Locust Valley NY 11560 Office: Catholic Medical Center of Brooklyn and Queens 88-25 153rd St Jamaica NY 11432

ZAMORSKI, MARTIN THEODORE, non-ferrous metalcasting co. exec.; b. Belle Meade, N.J., Jan. 14, 1939; s. Michael and Blanche (Sledzewski) Z.; A.B. (Colin Kerr award 1961), Boston U., 1965. Pres. Somerville Casting Co. (N.J.), 1966—; owner Martin Investment Co. Committeeman, North Plainfield, N.J., 1971-72. Served with USAF, 1957-61. Mem. Am. Foundry Soc., Nat. Fedn. Ind. Bus., U.S. C. of C., Internat. Platform Assn., Jacques Costeau Soc., Am. Polish Heritage Soc. (chmn.). Club: Boston U. Home: 482 Watchung Rd Watchung NJ 07060 Office: 40 S Gaston Ave Somerville NJ 08876

ZANDER, DIETER WARREN, mfg. co. exec.; b. Cottbus, Germany, Dec. 16, 1915; s. Gustav Ernst and Edith D. (Dintelmann) Z.; Bacalaureat Degree, Ecole Superieure, Neuchatel, Switzerland, 1937; m. Jane Muriel Henley, Nov. 8, 1940. Divisional head Willis, Faber & Hubener, Hamburg, Germany, 1939-42; Joint venture partner Drake America Corp., N.Y.C., 1948-49; pres. Henley & Co., Inc., N.Y.C., 1949—; chmn. Hexagon Labs., Bronx, N.Y.; dir. Stauffer-Wacker Silicone Corp., Westport, Conn., Rutgers Nease Chem. Corp., State College, Pa., Ore and Chem. Corp., N.Y.C., Wacker Chem. Corp., N.Y.C. Mem. Mfg. Chemist Assn., Soc. Chem. Industries. Republican. Lutheran. Club: Sleepy Hollow Country (Scarborough, N.Y.). Home: 25 East End Ave New York City NY 10028 Office: 750 3d Ave New York City NY 10017

ZANFAGNA, PHILIP EDWARD, physician; b. Lawrence, Mass., Jan. 9, 1909; s. Alfredo and Anna (Riccio) Z.; student Boston U., 1927-29, M.D., 1934; m. Edna Edith Hill, Jan. 5, 1935; children—Philip Edward, James Alan. Intern Lawrence Gen. Hosp., 1934-35; resident Rutland State San., 1935-36; gen. practice medicine, Lawrence, 1936-42, specializing in allergy, 1942—; cons. in allergy Lawrence Gen. Hosp. Pres. Lawrence Tb and Health Assn., 1962-67, Greater Law Service Center, 1960-67, Mass. Citizens' Rights Assn., 1964—. Served from 1st lt. to maj. M.C., AUS, 1942-46. Fellow Am. Coll. Allergists, Internat. Corr. Soc. Allergists, Am. Bd. Clin. Immunology and Allergy; mem. Am. Acad. Allergy, N.E. Soc. Allergy, Nat. Soc. for Study of Headaches, A.M.A., Mass. Med. Soc., Internat. Soc. Fluoride Research (pres.). Democrat. Roman Catholic. Contbr. articles to profl. publs. Home: 7 Ingalls Ct Methuen MA 01844 Office: 163 Lawrence St Lawrence MA 01841

ZANG, JOSEPH ALBERT, JR., chem. engr.; b. Bklyn., July 26, 1926; s. Joseph Albert and Margaret (Louis) Z.; B.S.E., Princeton, 1950; m. Mabel Joy Bell, Nov. 13, 1965; children—Claire, Catherine. With AMF Inc., Stamford, Conn., 1950—, research specialist, 1966-70, lab. mgr., 1970-78, sr. research specialist, 1976-78, dir. chem. engring., 1978—. Served with USNR, 1944-46, 52-53. Mem. Am. Inst. Chem. Engrs., Am. Chem. Soc., Princeton Engring. Assn., Am. Soc. Bakery Engrs., Appalachian Trail Conf., Princeton Campus Club, U.S. Chess Fedn. Episcopalian. Patentee in field. Home: 104 Hillcrest Park Rd Cos Cob CT 06807 Office: 689 Hope St Stamford CT 06907

ZANGER, MARTIN HENRY, book, periodical wholesale exec.; b. Holyoke, Mass., July 22, 1925; s. Maurice Harry and Sarah (Pildescu) Z.; B.S., Carnegie Mellon U., 1947; A.B., Roosevelt U., 1947; m. Marilyn Kurtz, June 19, 1947; children—Mark Howard, Sally Rae, Abby Elizabeth. Pres., dir. Holyoke News Co., Inc., 1948-77, Bookland Inc., Holyoke, 1968-77, Holyoke Candy & Tobacco Co., 1950-53, Milmar Corp., real estate, Holyoke, 1957-61; trustee 526 Realty Trust, Holyoke, 1959—; pres. Martin Engring. Co., Holyoke, 1960-65, also dir.; dir. Datamann Inc., Hanover, N.H., 1975—. Bd. dirs. Congregation Rodphey Sholom, Holyoke, 1950—, pres., 1974-76; bd. dirs. Holyoke Hebrew Sch., 1955-72; gov. Forer Day Sch., 1952-56. Served with USNR, 1944-45. Mem. Atlantic Coast Ind. Distbrs. Assn. (dir. 1973-77), Ednl. Paperback Assn. (dir. 1975-77), Coll. Stores New Eng., Nat. Assn. Coll. Stores, Council of Periodical Distbrs., Am. Booksellers Assn., Atlantic Circulation Execs., Rolls Royce Owners Club, Tau Delta Phi, Theta Tau. Home: 40 Woodbine Ln Holyoke MA 01040 Office: 56 Suffolk St Holyoke MA 01040

ZANGWILL, ESTELLE PAULA RICHEST (MRS. DONALD P. ZANGWILL), speech pathologist; b. Pitts.; d. Joseph P. and Anne (Burckin) Richest; B.S., U. Pitts., 1950, M.S., 1963; m. Steven Osgood, June 7, 1948 (div. 1972); children—Linda Carole Johnston, Robert Alexander; m. 2d, Donald P. Zangwill, June 5, 1972. Speech pathologist Childrens Hosp., Pitts., 1960-76, coordinator mutidisciplinary diagnostic program for lang. disturbed children, 1966-68; mem. Browning Inst., Pitts. Psychoanalytic Center. Bd. dirs. Pitts. chpt. World Federalist. Mem. Am. Speech and Hearing Assn., Chartiers Mental Health and Mental Retardation Assn., Allegheny County Med. Soc. Aux., Womens Assn. Pitts. Symphony Soc., Arts and Crafts Center Pitts. Home: 109 Oak Park Pl Pittsburgh PA 15243

ZANI, FREDERICK CAESAR, guidance counselor; b. Medford, Mass., June 9, 1929; s. John and Catherine (Voluletti) Z.; B.S. in Edn. cum laude, Salem State Coll., 1954; M.Ed., Boston U., 1959, certificate in advanced grad. studies, 1967; m. Dorothy Ann Menezes, Feb. 20, 1960; children—Gregory Robert, Elizabeth Ruth. Tchr., 1954-60; tchr., pub. schs. Gloucester, Mass., 1960-65; guidance counselor, pub. schs., Attleboro, Mass., 1965—. Mem. Mass. Assn. Children with Learning Disabilities (v.p. Attleboro chpt. 1969-70), Attleboro, Mass. tchrs. assns., NEA, Attleboro Mental Health Center, Childrens Med. Center Parent Orgn. for Exceptional Children, Nat. Educators Fellowship. Mem. Christian and Missionary Alliance Ch. Contbr. articles to jours. Home: 709 Holmes Rd North Attleboro MA 02760

ZANJANIAN, MOHAMAD HOSSEIN, physician; b. Tehran, Iran, July 11, 1937; s. Mehdi and Narges Z.; came to U.S., 1968, naturalized, 1973; M.D., Tehran U. Sch. Medicine, 1965; m. Parvin Naghibi, July 25, 1964; children—Hooman, Sherwin, Donna. Intern, St. Joseph's Hosp. Med. Center, Paterson, N.J., 1968; resident pediatrics Brookdale Hosp. and Med. Center, Bklyn., 1969-70; allergy fellow St. Vincent's Hosp. and Med. Center of N.Y., N.Y.C., 1971-72; pvt. practice medicine, specializing in allergies, Passaic, N.J., 1973—; clin. asst. prof. dept. pediatrics N.J. Sch. Medicine, 1977—; cons. physician N.J. Dept. Labor and Industry, 1974—; dir. allergy and clin. immunology Beth Israel Hosp., Passaic, N.J. 1973—, chmn. infection com., 1975—. Diplomate Am. Bd. Allergy and Immunology, Am. Bd. Pediatrics. Fellow Am. Acad. Allergy, Am. Coll. Chest Physicians, Am. Coll. Allergists, Am. Acad. Pediatrics; mem. N.J. Med. Soc., N.J. Allergy Soc. Clubs: Montclair (N.J.) Beach; Totowa (N.J.) Raquet; N. Jersey Country, Willowbrook Raquet (Wayne, N.J.). Office: 186 Gregory Ave Passaic NJ 07055

ZANOTTI, DONALD JOHN, mech. engr.; b. Quincy, Mass., Aug. 11, 1939; s. Angelo Joseph and Caroline Mary (Tognazzi) Z.; Asso. in Mech. Engring., Northeastern U., 1962, B.S., 1966; m. Lorelei Elena Perry, June 5, 1960; children—Dawn Marie, Michelle Ann, Lisa Jean. Designer, NRC Equipment Corp., Newton, Mass., 1959-64; project engr. GCA Vacuum Industries, Somerville, Mass., 1964-70: with Internat. Vacuum Inc., Pembroke, Mass., 1970—, chief engr., 1970—. Mem. ASME, Am. Vacuum Soc., Am. Soc. for Metals, Sigma Epsilon Rho. Democrat. Roman Catholic. Home: 128 Cain Ave Braintree Highlands MA 02184 Office: International Vacuum Inc Oak St Pembroke MA 02359

ZANVETTOR, JORGE, physician; b. Buenos Aires, Argentina, July 31, 1935; s. Juan and Idelma Rosa (Veronesi) Z.; M.D., Buenos Aires Med. Sch., 1962. Intern, resident in obstetrics and gynecology Martland Hosp., Newark, 1970-74; practice medicine specializing in obstetrics and gynecology, Bayonne, N.J., 1974—; mem. staff Bayonne Hosp., 1974—. Fellow Am. Coll. Obstetricians and Gynecologists; mem. Internat. Coll. Surgeons, Am. Laparoscopist Soc. Roman Catholic. Home: 30 E 29th St Bayonne NJ 07002 Office: 738 Kennedy Blvd Bayonne NJ 07002

ZAPFFE, CARL ANDREW, cons. metallurgist; b. Brainerd, Minn., July 25, 1912; s. Carl and Ethel Marie (Moberg) Z.; student U. Minn., 1929-32; B.S., Mich. Technol. U., 1933, D.Eng. (hon.), 1960; M.S., Lehigh U., 1934; postgrad. (Gordon McKay scholar) Harvard, 1936-38, Sc.D., 1939; m. Adelaide Camille Denise duPont, May 22, 1937; children—Denise duPont Zapffe Digges, Carl Moberg, Jessie Gresham Ball Zapffe Morast, Carlotta Karen Zapffe Shelton, Barbara Ann, Augusta Camille Zapffe Kilgore, Elsie Isabel, Christina Ethel Zapffe Anderson. Metallurgist, Du Pont Co., Wilmington, Del., 1934-36; research asso., research engr. Battelle Meml. Inst., Columbus, Ohio, 1938-43; asst. tech. dir. Rustless Iron Steel Corp., Balt., 1943-45; owner C.A. Zapffe & Assos., Metall. Cons., Balt.. 1945—. Founder, historian Historic Heartland Assn., Inc., 1969—; scoutmaster Troop 35, Boy Scouts Am., 1955—. Recipient Silver Beaver award Boy Scouts Am., 1958; Proctor Meml. award Am. Electroplaters Soc., 1940, Silver medal award, 1951. Fellow Am. Soc. for Metals (charter), Am. Inst. Chemists; mem. Am. Chem. Soc., Am. Phys. Soc., Am. Geophys. Union, AAAS, ASTM, Am. Inst. Mining, Metall. and Petroleum Engrs., Am. Welding Soc., Nat. Assn. Corrosion Engrs., Brit. Iron and Steel Inst., Soc. History of Tech., Internat. Soc. Gen. Relativity and Gravitation, Brit. Inst. Metals, Astron. Soc. Pacific, Sigma Xi, various hist. socs. Clubs: Rotarian (pres. Balt. 1961-62), Gull Lake Yacht (commodore 1967-68). Author: Stainless Steel, 1949; 4 films on Stainless Steel— The Miracle Metal, 1960; Rotary!, 1962; The Archives of Troop 35, 1972; The Man Who Lived in Three Centuries, 1975; Seven Short Essays on (1-V2/C2)1/2, 1977. Founder fractographic analysis. Home and Office: 6410 Murray Hill Rd Baltimore MD 21212

ZAPPE, HANS HELMUT, research scientist; b. Hohenstadt, Sudetenland, Feb. 10, 1935; s. Hans Konrad and Marie (Puhr) Z.; came to U.S., 1964; B.S. (Equivalent), Institut d'Electromecanique de Paris, 1954, M.S. (Equivalent), 1963; m. Martha Ursula Schmidt, May 14, 1958; children—Hans Paul, Sabine Anne-Marie, Barbara Martha. Apprentice blacksmith, Ranstadt, Germany, 1950; racing car mechanic, Paris, 1950-51; designer Elektronenstrahl-Sichtgeräte PEK, Stuttgart, Germany, 1954-56; insp. IBM France, Paris, 1956-61; engr. Advanced Devel. Lab., Paris and La Gaude, France, 1961-64; staff engr. Devel. Lab., IBM Corp., Poughkeepsie, N.Y., 1964-66, research staff mem., Thomas J. Watson Research Center, Yorktown Heights, N.Y., 1966-73, mgr. research staff mems., 1973-78, 2d level mgr., 1978—. Recipient Invention Achievement awards IBM, 1968, 72, 73, 74, 75, 77, Outstanding Contbn. award, 1973, Outstanding Innovation awards, 1977, 78. Mem. Am. Phys. Soc., AAAS. Contbr. articles to profl. jours. Patentee in field. Home: Bonnie Brae Ave Granite Springs NY 10527 Office: IBM Thomas Watson Research Center POB 218 Yorktown Heights NY 10598

ZAPPONE, FRANCIS THOMAS, realtor, developer; b. Waterbury, Conn., Oct. 29, 1938; s. Nicholas C. and Marie E. Zappone; B.S. in Real Estate Mgmt., Quinnipiac Coll., Hamden, Conn., 1966; m. Carol A. Shea, Sept. 21, 1961; children—David F., Steven F., Susan Lynn. Gen. mgr., pres. Francis T. Zappone Co., Realtors, Waterbury, 1963—; pres. F.T. Zappone Constrn. Co., Inc., Gaslight Village, Inc.; sec., treas. Villa Solidor. Served with AUS, 1958. Mem. Waterbury Real Estate Bd. (past v.p., dir.), Multiple Listing Service Greater Waterbury (past dir.), Nat. Inst. Real Estate Brokers, Internat. Traders Club, Nat. Assn. Real Estate Bds., Urban Land Inst., Waterbury C. of C., Waterbury Home Builders Assn., Alpha Phi Omega. Clubs: Waterbury Rotary; Milford Yacht. Office: 37 Meriden Rd Waterbury CT 06705

ZAPRUDNIK, JAN, educator, historian, journalist; b. Byelorussia, Aug. 9, 1926; Licencié en sciences historiques Cath. U. Louvain, Belgium, 1954; Ph.D., N.Y. U., 1969; m. Olga Charytoncyk, Nov. 7, 1954; children—Nina, Vera. With Radio Liberty, N.Y.C., 1954—; supr. Byelorussian Service, N.Y.C., 1958—, asst. mgr. Byelorussian Ukrainian, Turco-Caucasian dept., 1963-75. Mem. exec. council Byelorussian Democratic Republic in Exile, 1958; sec. Byelorussian Inst. Arts and Scis., 1958; asst. prof. history Queens Coll., 1970-75; counselor Byelorussian Autocephalous Orthodox Ch., Byelorussian Am. Assn. Mem. Am. Assn. Advancement Slavic Studies, Assn. Study of the Nationalities. Co-editor: Napierad, 1948-53; Byelorussian Youth, N.Y.C., 1959-64; Bielarus, N.Y.C., 1970—; Annals of the Byelorussian Inst. of Arts and Scis., 1974—; editor: Naviny z Bielarusi, 1964-69; Facts on Byelorussia, 1972—. Contbr. articles to hist. jours. Home: 97 Vanderbilt Rd Manhasset NY 11030 Office: 30 E 42nd St New York City NY 10017

ZARATE, REMY ABELLAR, nurse; b. Sara, Iloilo, Philippines, Feb. 13, 1934; d. Bernardo D. and Carmen S. (Arban) Abellar; came to U.S., 1962; B.S. in Nursing, Central Philippine U., 1956; M.A. in Nursing Edn., N.Y. U., 1965; opthalmic nurse diploma, London, 1968; m. Juan M. Zarate, Sept. 16, 1972; children—JoAnn Mae, Jean Mary. Staff nurse Iloilo Mission Hosp., 1956-59; clin. instr. Luzon Colls. Sch. Nursing, Dagupan City, Philippines, 1959-62, dir. Sch. Nursing, 1969-72; intern, staff nurse James Ewing Hosp., N.Y.C., 1962-63; staff nurse Moorfields Eye Hosp., London, 1966-68; staff nurse N.Y. Eye and Ear Infirmary, N.Y.C., 1963-66, 72-74, dir. in-service edn., 1974—. Mem. In-service Edn. Dirs. N.Y.C. Home: 455 E 14 St New York City NY 10009 Office: NY Eye and Ear Infirmary 310 E 14th St New York City NY 10003

ZARELLA, MICHAEL PETER, mfg. co. exec.; b. Passaic, N.J., May 29, 1920; s. Michael and Mary (Griffin) Z.; student Rutgers U., Fordham U.; m. Dorothy R. Agnello, June 29, 1947; 1 dau., Darlene C. Zarella Rankin. Purchasing mgr. Curtiss Wright Corp., Woodridge, N.J., 1939-62; dir. purchasing Mack Trucks, Inc., Hagerstown, Md., 1962-66, v.p. purchasing, 1967-76, v.p. corp. material mgmt., Allentown, Pa., 1976-78, v.p. adminstrn., 1978—. Bd. dirs. Guiding Eyes for Blind, N.Y.C., 1972—, Allentown Hosp., 1978—; mem. adv. bd. Salvation Army, Allentown, 1977—. Served with USAF, 1943-46. Certified purchasing mgr. Mem. Am. Mgmt. Assn., Nat. Assn. Purchasing Mgmt. Home: 115 Heather Dr Rd 7 Allentown PA 18103 Office: PO Box M Allentown PA 18105

ZARET, SEYMOUR, dentist; b. Bridgeport, Conn., Jan. 12, 1939; s. Oscar and Julia (Mashewitz) Zaretsky; B.A. cum laude in Chemistry, Bklyn. Coll. City U. N.Y., 1960; D.D.S., N.Y. U., 1964; m. Anita Levy, Feb. 25, 1968; children—David Ian, Rebecca Ilyse. Practice gen. dentistry, Bklyn., 1966—; asst. operative dentist, div. dentistry, dept. surgery Maimonides Med. Center, Bklyn., 1974—; dental cons. Great Am. Ins. Co. Served with Dental Corps USAF, 1964-66. Recipient Founders Day award for outstanding scholarship N.Y. U. Coll. Dentistry, 1964; Certificate Honor Soc. for Dental Research, 1964. Mem. Am., N.Y. State dental assns., 2d Dist. Dental Soc. Bklyn., Acad. Gen. Dentistry, Omicron Kappa Upsilon, Alpha Omega, Sigma Epsilon Delta. K.P. Home: 1607 Hereford Rd Hewlett NY 11557 Office: 2520 Flatbush Ave Brooklyn NY 11234

ZARETSKY, GREGORY, trade cons.; b. Celinograd, Russia, Dec. 1, 1945; s. Joseph and Sophia (Zarecka) Z.; came to U.S., 1969, naturalized, 1975; M.A., U. Pa., 1972; children—Alexander, Lora. Faculty, U. Pa., Phila., 1970-73; with Pullman Swindel, Pitts., 1973—, cons. on East-West trade, 1978—. Address: 441 Smithfield St Pittsburgh PA 15222

ZARFES, MURRAY, pharm. services adminstr.; b. N.Y.C., June 29, 1929; s. Samuel and Sara (Weinstein) Z.; B.S., L.I. U., 1951, M.S., 1966; m. Audrey Elaine Cohen, Aug. 30, 1953; children—Marlene, Marc, David, Rene. Dir. pharmacy services Long Beach (N.Y.) Meml. Hosp., 1962-64, Harlem Hosp. Center, N.Y.C., 1965-72, Queens Hosp. Center, Jamaica, N.Y., 1972—; adj. clin. prof. Coll. Pharmacy and Allied Health Professions, St. John's U., Jamaica, 1972—. Com. chmn. Queens council Boy Scouts Am., 1966-68. Mem. Am. Pharm. Assn., Am. Soc. of Hosp. Pharmacists, Am. Bd. Diplomates in Pharmacy, Rho Chi. Republican. Jewish. Home: 158 Cowpens Dr Orangeburg NY 10962 Office: 82-68 164th St Queens Hospital Center Jamaica NY 11432

ZARGAJ, TOMISLAV, psychiatrist; b. Novomesto, Yugoslavia, June 19, 1933; s. Thomas and Maria (Okorn) Z.; came to U.S., 1964, naturalized, 1975; M.D., U. Ljubljana (Yugoslavia), 1956; m. Paula Maria Malesic, Nov. 1956; children—Paula, Thomas, Michael. Intern U. Hosp., Ljubljana, 1956-57, Celje Gen. Hosp., 1958-59, resident in psychiatry Inst. Mental Health, R.I. Med. Center, Howard 1964-66, Mass. Gen. Hosp., Boston, also Danvers (Mass.) State Hsop., 1967-68; practice medicine specializing in gen. medicine, Velenje, Yugoslavia, 1959-64, in psychiatry, Salem, Mass., 1970—; dir. clin. psychiatry Danvers State Hosp., 1968-70, asst. supt., 1970-73; asst. dir. Salem (Mass.) Hosp. Mental Health Center, 1973-74; asso. chief psychiat. service Salem Gen. Hosp., 1973—; teaching fellow Harvard Med. Sch., Cambridge, Mass., 1967-68, staff psychiatrist Mary Alley Hosp., Marblehead, Mass., Shoughnessey Hosp., Salem. Pres. North Shore Psychiat. Associates, Inc., 1973—; mem. Danvers-Salem Mental Health Area Bd. Served in Yugoslav Army, 1957-58. Diplomate Am. Bd. Psychiatry and Neurology. Fellow Mass. Med. Soc.; mem. AMA, Am. Psychiat. Assn., Mass. Psychiat. Soc., New Eng. Soc. of Psychiatry, New Eng. Soc. of Hypnosis, Am. Geriatrics Soc., The Soc. for Clin. and Exptl. Hypnosis, Menninger Found., Aircraft Owners and Pilots Assn. Roman Catholic. Clubs: Bass River Tennis. Home: 10 Fairview Rd Salem MA 01970 Office: 355 Essex St Salem MA 01970

ZARIN, JERRY, market research cons.; b. N.Y.C., June 23, 1934; s. George and Lillie Z.; B.S., N.Y. U., 1956; M.B.A., City U. N.Y., 1963; m. Mireille Erdman, May 7, 1958; children—Todd, Shari. Market researcher Ted Bates & Co. Advt., N.Y.C., 1956-59; market research mgr. new products Lever Bros. Co., N.Y.C., 1959-64; v.p. Smith Greenland Co. Advt., N.Y.C., 1964-66; v.p. Daniel & Charles Advt., N.Y.C., 1966-70; prin., v.p. mktg. Responsive Data Processing, Mt. Kisco, N.Y., 1970-72; pres. Zarin Research Assos., Inc., Roslyn, N.Y., 1972—; chmn. sensory testing panel Cosmo Expo, 1978. Bd. govs. Flower Hill Civic Assn., 1968-69. Mem. Am. Mktg. Assn. (co-chmn. new products conf. 1970). Office: 28 Woodland Rd Roslyn NY 11576

ZARINS, BERTRAM, surgeon; b. Tukums, Latvia, June 22, 1942; s. Richard Arthur and Maria Z.; came to U.S., 1946, naturalized, 1954; A.B. in Chemistry, Layfayette Coll., 1963; M.D. cum laude, State U. N.Y., 1967. Intern, Johns Hopkins Hosp., 1967-68, resident in gen. surgery, 1968-69; resident in orthopaedic Harvard U., 1970-73, instr. orthopaedic, 1976—; fellow in sports medicine and knee surgery Mass. Gen. Hosp., Boston, 1975, orthopaedic surgeon, 1976—; physician Boston Bruins Profl. Hockey Team, 1976—. Served with USNR, 1973-75. Edwin F. Cave Travelling fellow, 1975. Fellow A.C.S.; mem. AMA, Mass. Med. Soc., Am. Coll. Sports Medicine, Internat. Arthroscopy Assn., N.Am. Trauma Assn. (pres. 1978—), Nat. Athletic Trainers Assn. Club: Union Boat. Office: 275 Charles St Boston MA 02114

ZARWYN, BERTHOLD, phys. scientist; b. Vienna, Aug. 22, 1921; s. Joseph and Bronislava Regina (Unger) Z.; came to U.S., 1949, naturalized, 1955; M.E., Gliwice, Poland, 1946; Sc.D., Munich (W. Ger.) U., 1947; Ph.D., N.Y. U., 1954; Engring. Sc.D., Columbia, 1963. Project engr. Curtiss-Wright Corp., Woodridge, N.J., 1951-55; chief scientist Link Aviation Co., Binghamton, N.Y., 1957-58; head research staff Am. Bosch-Arma Corp., Garden City, N.Y., 1958-63; corporate cons. Cutler-Hammer Corp., Deer Park, N.Y., 1963-65; chief engr. Bell Aerosystems Corp., Niagara Falls, N.Y., 1965-66; sr. cons. Mitre Corp., Bedford, Mass., 1966-68; spl. asst. to commanding gen., acting chief engr. Hdqrs. U.S. Army Materiel Command, Arlington, Va., 1968-71, chief phys. scis. br., Washington, 1971-75, phys. scientist U.S. Army Harry Diamond Labs., Washington, 1975-78; chief system analysis br. U.S. Army Electronic Research and Devel. Command, Adelphi, Md., 1978—; adj. faculty, lectr., cons. in field; dir. Film Microelectronics Co. Inc., Burlington, Mass., 1965-67. Mem. IEEE, Am. Phys. Soc., N.Y. Acad. Scis., Sigma Xi. Editorial bd. Bavarian Soc. Engrs., 1947-49; translation panel Russian Jour. Applied Math. and Mechanics with Pergamon Inst., 1956-57. Inventor nuclear gyoscope, microwave holography, other items. Home: 9727 Mt Pisgah Rd Silver Spring MD 20903 Office: US Army Electronic Research and Devel Command Adelphi MD 20903

ZAUSNER, MARTIN, investor realtions cons.; b. N.Y.C., Aug. 9, 1929; s. Hy and Teddy (Rose) Z.; B.S., Syracuse U., 1950; M.S., Columbia, 1951; M.B.A., N.Y U., 1953; m. Adrienne Becker, Jan. 16, 1959. With Arthur Schmidt & Assos. Inc., N.Y.C., 1956—, chmn. bd., 1969—. Clubs: Bankers, Commanderie de Bordeaux, Confrerie des Chevaliers du Tastevin, Port Washington Tennis Acad., Princeton N.Y., Sky, W. Side Tennis. Author: Corporate Policy and the Investment Community, 1968; contbg. author: The Strategy of Corporate Financing, 1971; cons. editor: The Stock Market Handbook, 1970. Home: 923 Fifth Ave New York City NY 10021 Office: Arthur Schmidt & Assos Inc 342 Madison Ave New York City NY 10017

ZAVADA, MARY ROBERTA, editor; b. Passaic, N.J., Jan. 11, 1936; d. John Michael and Sophie Catherine (Majowicz) Zavada; A.B. magna cum laude (scholar), Coll. St. Elizabeth, 1957; M.A., DePaul

U., 1959; post-grad. (English-Speaking Union grant), U. London, 1962. Grad. asst. DePaul U., Chgo., 1957-58; feature writer United Press Internat., London, Eng., 1964; writer Honeywell, Inc., Newton Highlands, Mass., 1966-67; editor Sylvania Electronic Systems, Waltham, Mass., 1968-69; account exec. Anderson Assos., pub. relations and advt. Boston, 1969-70; editor Ednl. Testing Service, Princeton, N.J., 1971-74, dir. program editorial services, coll. bd. div., 1974—. Tchr. Pilot Adult Career evening program Mass. Bay Community Coll., 1969-70, Univ. Coll., Northeastern U., 1967-70; communications cons. div. retardation R.I. Dept. Health, 1971-72. Mem. Bus. and Profl. Women's Club, Kappa Gamma Pi (2d nat. v.p. 1969-71). Democrat. Roman Catholic. Contbr. articles and short stories to various mags. and newspapers. Home: 161 Franklin Corner Rd Lawrenceville NJ 08648 Office: Ednl Testing Service Rosedale Rd Princeton NJ 08541

ZAWAHIR, MEEYAPILLAI K. MADAR, surgeon; b. Kayamoli, Madras, India, Feb. 22, 1939; s. Kamsa Mohideen Madar and Ibrahimmal (Sickander) Z.; came to U.S., 1968; M.B., B.S., Madurai Med. Coll., India, 1964; m. Gani, Oct. 16, 1969; children—Fawzia, Nafeez, Parveen. Civil asst. surgeon Madras Med. Service, 1965-68; resident in surgery St. Clares Hosp., N.Y.C., 1968-73; pvt. practice medicine specializing in surgery, N.Y.C., 1973—; asso. attending surgeon St. Clares Hosp., N.Y.C.; attending in gen. and vascular surgery Kingsbrook J. Med. Center, Bklyn.; attending surgeon French and Polyclinic Med. and Health Center, N.Y.C.; asso. attending surgeon Victory Meml. Hosp., Bklyn., Doctors Hosp., N.Y.C. Served with Indian Cadet Corps. Diplomate Am. Bd. Surgery. Mem. N.Y. State, N.Y. County med. socs., John L. Madden Surg. Soc., Am., N.Y. socs. colon and rectal surgery. Office: 666 92d St Brooklyn NY 11228

ZAYAC, IVAN BOHDAN SIMON, architect; b. Lviv, Austria (now Ukrainian SSR), Oct. 6, 1910; s. Julian and Falina Knight Radwan (von Pawencki) Z.; came to U.S., 1948, naturalized, 1955; M.L., U. Jan. Kasimierz (Poland), 1932, M. Diplomatic Scis., 1934; diploma in music Lviv Conservatory of Music, 1933; postgrad. in law Sorbonne, U. Paris, 1946-48; postgrad. in architecture Ecole Superieure Nationale des Beaux Arts, Paris, 1947-48, Cooper Union, 1953; m. Elsa Schoenberg, May 3, 1947; 1 dau., Maria Falina. Judge, pres. of ct., asst. prof. law, Poland, 1935-44; law counselor Allgemeine Electrizität Gesellschaft, Bratislava, Czechoslovakia, 1944-45; with various archtl. firms, N.Y.C., 1950-53; with Eggers and Higgins Co., N.Y.C., 1953-57, Philip C. Johnson and Assos., N.Y.C., 1957-60, Edward Durell Stone and Assos., N.Y.C., 1963-70, I.M. Pei and Partners, N.Y.C., 1971-74; prin. Ivan Zayac, Architect, Forest Hills, N.Y., 1974—. Sec. Ukrainian Relief Com., 1940-43. Mem. Shevchenko Scientific Soc., Ukrainian Acad. Art and Scis., Ukrainian Engrs. Soc. Am. (past pres. N.Y. chpt.), Ukrainian Artists Assn., World Congress Free Ukrainians (past div. chmn.), Ukrainian Nat. Assn. (bd. dirs. 1977—), Selfreliance Assn. Am. Ukrainians (past dir.). Ukrainian Orthodox. Designer Ukrainian Cultural Center, Mus. Ukrainian Art, Hunter, N.Y. Home and Office: 68-49 Exeter St Forest Hills NY 11375

ZAYAC, PETER PAUL, physician; b. Johnson City, N.Y., July 21, 1932; s. Peter Paul and Thelma M. (Gallup) Z.; B.S., State U. N.Y., Binghamton, 1954; M.D., Northwestern U., 1958; m. Joan Kelly, Feb. 7, 1953; children—Peter, John, William, Mark, Kelly. Intern Mary Hitchcock Meml. Hosp., Hanover, N.H., 1958; resident in internal medicine Dartmouth Med. Sch., Hanover, 1962; practice medicine specializing in internal medicine, Binghamton, 1962—; pres. Assos. in Internal Medicine, P.C.; pres. elect med. staff Binghamton Gen. Hosp., 1978; adv. bd. Marine Midland Bank, Binghamton; dir. Columbian Mut. Ins. Co. Bd. dirs. State U. N.Y. Found. Forum. Mem. Broome County C. of C. (sec., dir.), Alpha Omega Alpha. Club: Binghamton City. Home: 8 Blackstone Ave Binghamton NY 13903 Office: 35 Grand Blvd Binghamton NY 13905

ZAYDON, JEMILLE ANN, educator; b. Peckville, Pa., Feb. 21, 1940; d. Joseph and Catherine Ann (Hazzouri) Zaydon; student Barry Coll. for Women, 1957-59; B.S., Marywood Coll., 1963, postgrad., 1964, 67; postgrad. Dade Jr. Coll., 1964, U. Scranton, 1964, Newark State Coll., 1965, Temple U., 1969, 73; M.S. in Edn., Wilkes Coll., 1978; L.H.D., Colo. Christian Coll., 1973. Tchr. St. Hugh Elementary Sch., Coconut Grove, Fla., 1963-64; Allapattah Elementary Sch., Miami, 1964-65, Columbus Elementary Sch., Westfield, N.J., 1965-66; communications instr. Keystone Job Corps, Drums, Pa., 1966-73; vol. instr. Keystone Rehab. Center, Scranton, Pa., 1970-71; curriculum cons. for mentally retarded, Vienna, Austria, 1974-75; instr. Northeastern ednl. intermediate unit Lackawanna County Area Vocat.-Tech. Sch., Scranton, 1974—; instr. English, Lackawanna Jr. Coll., Scranton, 1975—, chmn. dept. humanities for day, weekend and evening divs., 1977—; supr. recreation program, Hazleton, Pa., summer 1968; founder, adviser Keystone Kourier, 1967-69. Sec., Pa. Gov.'s Youth Fedn., 1963; supr. students Heart Fund campaign, 1968-71; developer program mentally retarded Allied Services for Handicapped Scranton, 1973; active ARC, March of Dimes, Heart Fund, Leukemia and United Fund drives, also Sickle Cell Anemia Found.; bd. dirs. Michael F. Harrity Meml. Fund, 1969-73. Recipient Staff Mem. of Year award Job Corps, 1969; Service scholarship Barry Coll., 1958; Educators award Dade County, 1973. Mem. Nat., Pa. State edn. assns., Beta Lambda Tau, Sigma Tau Delta, Theta Chi Beta (charter pres. 1961-63), Lambda Iota Tau (life). Democrat. Roman Catholic. Editor Lebanese Am. Jour., 1957-63. Home: 608 N Main Ave Scranton PA 18504 Office: Lackawanna Jr Coll Linden St and Jefferson Ave Scranton PA

ZDENEK, EDNA PRIZGINT, mech. engr.; b. S.I., N.Y., June 27, 1942; d. George A. and Helen (Lazicki) Prizgint; Asso. Sci., S.I. Community Coll., 1962; B.S.M.E., Newark Coll. Engring., 1965. Design engr. Picatinney Arsenal, Dover, N.J., 1965-66; application engr. Worthington Corp., Harrison, N.J., 1966-68; project engr. Uniplan, Princeton, N.J., 1968-70; prin., propr. Profl. Engrs. and Planners, Westfield, N.J., 1970—; bd. dirs. Conservacon, Inc., S.I., 1975—; tchr. math. Union Coll., 1971-73; profl. mem. N.J. State Adv. Bd. Dept. Labor and Industry, 1976—, Westfield Bd. Constrn. Appeals, 1977—. N.Y. State regents scholar, 1959-62; registered profl. planner, N.J.; registered profl. engr., N.Y., N.J., Pa., N.H. Mem. Nat. Soc. Profl. Engrs., Am. Soc. Heating, Refrigeration and Air Conditioning Engrs., Newark Coll. Engring. Alumni Assn. (trustee 1970-73). Home: 1121 Prospect St Westfield NJ 07090

ZDEP, STANLEY MICHAEL, psychologist; b. Hazleton, Pa., July 19, 1939; s. Stanley Joseph and Domicella (Stefanovich) Z.; A.B., Rutgers U., 1964; M.A., U. Hawaii, 1966, Ph.D. (NDEA fellow), 1967; m. Elizabeth Anne Gauz, Aug. 25, 1961. Project dir. Ednl. Testing Service, Princeton, N.J., 1967-69; nat. dir. research Girl Scouts USA, 1969-72; v.p. Opinion Research Corp., Princeton, 1972—; past mem. co-adj. faculty Rutgers U., Rider Coll., Trenton State Coll. Mem. Am. Psychol. Assn., Sigma Xi. Contbr. articles to profl. jours. Home: Rural Route 1 Box 251-H Pennington NJ 08534 Office: Opinion Research Corp N Harrison St Princeton NJ 08540

ZECH, JOHN RAYMOND, ins. co. exec.; b. Seattle, Dec. 4, 1927; s. Lando W. and Mae (Munro) Z.; B.A., U. Wash., 1949; LL.B., Harvard, 1955; m. Mary Ann Jacobson, July 23, 1949; children—John R., Ann E., William R., James L., Robert M. Underwriter, Prudential Ins. Co. Gt. Britain, N.Y.C., 1955-60, sec., 1960-61, v.p., 1961-63; underwriter Skandia Ins. Co., N.Y.C., 1955-60, sec., 1960-61, asst. mgr., 1961-63; underwriter Hudson Ins. Co., N.Y.C., 1955-60, sec., 1960-61, v.p., 1961-63; admitted to N.Y. State bar, 1956; v.p. Nat. Reins. Corp., N.Y.C., 1963-69, pres., dir., 1969—. Served to lt. (j.g.) USNR, 1949-52. Mem. Am., N.Y. bar assns., Am. Arbitration Assn. (dir.), Drug and Chem. Club (pres. 1976), Soc. C.P.C.U.'s, Phi Delta Theta. Clubs: Wee Burn Country (Darien, Conn.); Wall Street. Home: 67 St Nicholas Rd Darien CT 06820 Office: 123 William St New York City NY 10038

ZEDNOWICZ, JOSEPH BERNARD, clergyman; b. Mt. Carmel, Pa., Jan. 27, 1918; s. Joseph John and Mary Catherine (Venesky) Z.; B.A., St. Mary's Sem., 1942, B.D., M.S.T., 1944; M.A., Duquesne U., 1948; M.S., Shippensburg State Coll., 1972. Ordained priest Roman Catholic Ch., 1943; asst. supt. Holy Family Inst., Emsworth, Pa., 1944-45; lectr. in polit. sci. Duquesne U., 1945-48; asst. pastor St. Joseph's Ch., Mt. Carmel, 1948-57, pastor, 1957-68; teaching chaplain State Correctional Instn., Camp Hill, Pa., 1968—; tchr., supr. Prison Chaplaincy Tng. Program. Active Boy Scouts Am., 1950-65. Mem. Am. Cath. Correctional Chaplains Assn., Am. Correctional Assn., Am. Correctional Chaplains Assn., Am., Pa. personnel and guidance assns., Pa. Prison Chaplains Assn. (1st pres. 1975—). Clubs: K.C.; Fountain Springs Country (Ashland, Pa.); Elks. Home: 1 W Pine St Enola PA 17025 Office: PO Box 200 Camp Hill PA 17011

ZEEHANDELAAR, FREDERIK JULES, importer; b. Amsterdam, Netherlands, Dec. 22, 1917; s. Isadore and Sara (Vanderkous) Z.; student U. Amsterdam, 1935-38; came to U.S., 1946, naturalized, 1949; m. Geertruida Beffie, Aug. 10, 1947; children—Eric I., David N. Pres., North Atlantic Fertilizer & Chem. Co., Inc., N.Y.C., 1946-56; pres., treas. F.J. Zeehandelaar Inc., wild animal importers, New Rochelle, N.Y., 1957—; import adviser to pres. Am. Assn. Zool. Parks and Aquariums. Served to capt. Netherlands Free Forces, Brit. Army, 1942-46. Decorated Cross Merit, Queen Wilhelmina of Netherlands. Mem. N.Y. Zool. Soc., Am. Assn. Zool. Parks and Aquariums, Am. Assn. Zoo Keepers, Am. Assn. Lab. Animal Sci., Am. Assn. Zoo Veterinarians, Humane Soc. U.S., Am. Humane Assn. Democrat. Jewish. Clubs: Netherlands of N.Y., Mt. Kenya Safari, Rotary. Author: Zeebongo, The Wacky Wild Animal Business, 1971. Home: 1111 California Rd Eastchester NY 10709 Office: 6 Sickles Ave New Rochelle NY 10801

ZEEVELD, DAVID GORDON, planner; b. Washington, Oct. 9, 1945; s. William Gordon and Margaret Ford (Jewell) Z.; B.A. cum laude with honors in Sociology, Franklin Pierce Coll., 1970; M.A., Cath. U. Am., 1974; postgrad. Johns Hopkins U., 1977. Planning asst. Balt. Regional Planning Council, summer 1971; planning technician Howard County (Md.) Office Planning and Zoning, 1972—; ofcl. Howard County Zoning Enforcement and Land Devel. Adminstrn., 1977. Mem. Howard County Residential Services Com. for Retarded, 1973—, Howard County Com. for Farmland Preservation, 1975—. Mem. Am. Soc. Planning Ofcls. Republican. Episcopalian. Home: Deep Meadow 3173 Daisy Rd Woodbine MD 21797

ZEFERETTI, LEO C., congressman; b. Bklyn., July 15, 1927; s. Antonino and Catherine (D'Angelo) Z.; student N.Y. U., City U., City U. N.Y., m. Barbara L. Schiebel, Aug. 30, 1947; children—Linda (Mrs. Robert Gianfortune), Jan. Penologist, N.Y.C. Dept. Corrections, 1957-74, collective bargaining agt., N.Y.C.; mem. 94th-96th Congresses from 15th N.Y. Dist.; mem. Edn. and Labor Com., Mcht. Marine and Fisheries Com. Rep. to Pres.'s Conf. on Correction, also Conf. for Nat. Correction Acad., 1971; mem. Bay Ridge Civic Improvement Assn. Mem. N.Y. State Crime Control Planning Bd., 1973; bd. dirs. Health Inst. Plan of Greater N.Y., Internat. Found. Served with USNR, World War II; ETO. Decorated Order of St. Brigida (Italy); recipient Labor Relations award N.Y.C. Hispanic Soc. Grand Council, Law Enforcement medal S.A.R. Mem. Correction Officers Benevolent Assn. (pres. 1964-74), Correction Officers Columbia Assn. Democrat. Home: 9912 Fort Hamilton Pkwy Brooklyn NY 11209 Office: 1726 Longworth House Office Bldg Washington DC 20515

ZEHEL, WENDELL EVANS, surgeon; b. Brownsville, Pa., Mar. 6, 1934; s. Michael and Emma (Evans) Z.; B.A., Washington and Jefferson Coll., 1956; M.D., U. Pitts., 1960; m. Joan Leasure, Nov. 1, 1958; children—Lori Ann, Wendell Charles. Intern, Shadyside Hosp., Pitts., 1960-61; resident in surgery U. Pitts., VA Hosp., 1963-66, Wilmington (Del.) Med. Center, 1966-68; practice medicine, specializing in surgery, Pitts., 1968—; surgeon St. Clair Hosp., Pitts., 1968—. Served with USAF, 1961-63. Diplomate Am. Bd. Surgery. Fellow A.C.S.; mem. Assn. Advancement of Med. Instrumentation. Home: 553 Harrogate Dr Pittsburgh PA 15241 Office: 1000 Bower Hill Rd Pittsburgh PA 15243

ZEHRINGER, FRANCIS ALEXANDER, ret. law enforcement officer; b. Phila., Sept. 23, 1912; s. Augustus Oliver and Mary Cecilia (Stoltz); grad. FBI Nat. Police Acad., 1950; m. Ann S. Cluin, Sept. 27, 1933; children—Suzanne, Maryanne. Mgr., Warner Theatre, Atlantic City, 1929-41, Cojac Theatre, Ft. Myers, Fla., 1941-42; with Atlantic City Police Dept., 1942-73, sgt., 1948-58, capt., 1958-67, police adminstr., Boardwalk, 1962-69, insp. police, 1967-73; coordinator, prin. instr. S. Jersey Police Acad., 1954-71; comdr. municipal police Democratic Nat. Conv., 1964; part-time prof. law Atlantic Community Coll. and Glassboro State Coll., 1969-74. Active Boy Scouts, other civic activities; bd. dirs. Civil Def. Mem. Internat. Assn. Chiefs Police, Delaware Valley Profl. Police Officers Assn., N.Y. Met. Law Enforcement Conf., Internat. Conf. Police Assn., S. Jersey Suburban Police, AAU, All Sports Assn., Sages, Patrolmen's Benevolent Assn. Republican. Roman Catholic. Clubs: Old Timers, Bellevue Athletic. Home: 1420 Pitney Rd Absecon Highlands NJ 08201

ZEICHNER, BEN, psychiatrist; b. N.Y.C., May 22, 1938; s. George and Rose Zeichner; A.B., Hamilton Coll., 1959; M.D., N.Y. U., 1963; m. Christiane Keferstein, June 14, 1964; 1 son, Carl Gregory. Intern, Beth Israel Med. Center, N.Y.C., 1963-64; resident Topeka VA Hosp., 1964-67, Menninger Sch. Psychiatry, 1964-67; practice medicine specializing in psychiatry, Washington, 1968—; vis. physician Psychiat. Inst., 1970—; mem. staff Forensic Psychiat. Services of D.C., 1971—; asst. clin. prof. psychiatry Georgetown U., Washington, 1974—; teaching asst. Balt.-D.C. Psychoanalytic Inst., 1976—. Served with USPHS, 1965-70. Diplomate Am. Bd. Psychiatry and Neurology. Mem. Washington, No. Va., Am. psychiat. socs., Am. Group Psychotherapy Assn., D.C. Med. Soc., Balt., D.C. socs. for psychoanalysis, Am. Psychoanalytic Soc. Home: 7129 Helmsdale Rd Bethesda MD 20034 Office: 1545 18th St NW Washington DC 20036

ZEISS, CLIFFORD JOHN, psychiatrist; b. Bklyn., Apr. 24, 1920; s. John Philip Rudolph and Elizabeth (Monell) Z.; B.S., N.Y. U., 1941; M.D., N.Y. Med. Coll., 1944; postgrad. N.Y. Sch. Psychiatry, 1969-72; m. Ethel May Naughton, May 12, 1944; 1 dau., Holly Elizabeth Zeiss Bruce. Intern, Nassau Hosp., Mineola, N.Y., 1944-45, rotating resident, 1945-46; physician Republic Aviation Corp., Farmingdale, N.Y., 1948-50; practice medicine, specializing in family practice, Valley Stream, N.Y., 1949-69; resident in psychiatry Nassau County (N.Y.) Med. Center, 1969-72; practice medicine, specializing in psychiatry, Valley Stream, 1972—; mem. staff N.E. Nassau Psychiat. Center, Kings Park, N.Y. Vestryman, Holy Trinity Episcopal Ch., Valley Stream, 1954-60. Served to capt. M.C., AUS, 1943-44, 46-47. NIMH grantee, 1969-72. Mem. AMA (Physician's Recognition award 1969, 72), N.Y. State, Nassau County med. socs., Nassau Physicians Guild, Am., Nassau psychiat. socs. Republican. Club: Lions. Home and Office: 63 N Cottage St Valley Stream NY 11580

ZEITCHICK, ABRAHAM AARON, pvt. investigator; b. Russia, Dec. 6, 1902; s. Max and Lena Zeitchick; came to U.S., 1906, naturalized, 1906; m. Goldie Kober, May 20, 1930; children—Stanley, lMartin. Owner, pvt. investigator Security Guard and Investigation, Bklyn., 1975—; cons. in field. Bd. dirs. Bklyn. Jewish Community Council, 1972, treas. ambulatory com. Brookdale Hosp., 1972—; treas. Friends of Community Hosp., Bklyn., 1970—; mem. Legis. Com. on Mental Health, N.Y.C., 1977-78. Address: 1280 E 86th St Brooklyn NY 11236

ZEITLIN, BILL, wholesale co. exec.; b. N.Y.C., July 17, 1928; s. Max and Sarah Z.; student pub. schs., N.Y.C.; m. Dorothy Halpern, Mar. 20, 1949; children—Merryl, Edward, Randy. Founder, pres., chmn. bd. Edmer San. Supply Co., Inc., East Meadow, N.Y., 1959—. Pres., Cynron Civic Assn., 1958—. Served as sgt. USMC, 1944-48, 51-52. Mem. L.I. Distbrs. Assn. (pres.), N.Y. State San. Supply Assn. (pres. 1977—), Internat. San. Supply Assn. (dir. dist. 1 1977—), Am. Inst. Mgmt. Hebrew. Club: Old W stbury Golf and Country. Home: 1248 Julia Ln North Bellmore NY 11710 Office: 519 Newbridge Ave East Meadow NY 11554

ZEIZEL, LEO AARON, accountant; b. N.Y.C., Feb. 16, 1918; s. Morris and Ida (Gleicher) Z.; B.B.A., Coll. City N.Y., 1939; m. Thelma Rae Klinghoffer, Apr. 13, 1946; children—Carolyn Joan Zeizel Berfas, June Cora. Accountant, Samuel Heller & Co., 1939-40, Rochester Milk Mktg., 1942, N.Y. Met. Milk Market adminstr., N.Y.C., 1942; accountant Alfred Sperber & Co., 1945-46; partner Zeizel & Zeizel, 1946-73; prin. Leo A. Zeizel, C.P.A., N.Y.C., 1973—. Served to lt. USCGR, 1942-45. Mem. N.Y. State Soc. C.P.A.'s, Internat. Platform Assn. Author handbook and articles in field. Home: 219-19 Peck Ave Hollis Hills NY 11423 Office: 233 Broadway New York City NY 10007

ZELCER, ISAAC, neckwear mfg. co. exec.; b. Havana, Cuba, May 18, 1935; s. Kiwa and Sara (Horowitz) Z.; came to U.S., 1960, naturalized, 1966; ed. U. Havana; m. Loly Shaftal, Mar. 11, 1955; children—Alan, Elena, Robin. Asst. prodn. mgr. Spiegel Neckwear, N.Y.C., 1960-62; prodn. mgr. Fabil Mfg. Co., N.Y.C., 1962-63; prodn. mgr. Randa Neckwear Corp., Hackensack, N.J., 1963-65, asst. to pres., 1965-70, v.p., 1970-73, pres., 1973—; pres. Gino Pompeii Neckwear, Geoffrey Beene Neckwear; dir. Four Star Industries, P.R., GP Spa Formia, Italy. Mem. Neckwear Assn. Am. (dir.), N.J., Italian chambers commerce. Jewish. Clubs: Empire State (N.Y.C.); Cricket (Miami, Fla.). Home: 228-22 49th Rd Bayside NY 11364 Office: 21 E Lafayette St Hackensack NJ 07602

ZELENY, CAROLYN, sociologist, educator; b. Mpls., May 6, 1909; d. John and Carolyn (Rogers) Z.; A.B., Vassar Coll., 1930; M.A., Yale, 1939, Ph.D., 1944; postgrad. Columbia, 1939-40, N.Y.U., 1966-67. Tchr., Sandia Sch., Albuquerque, 1934-36; instr. sociology Skidmore Coll., Saratoga Springs, N.Y., 1941-43; research asso. Com. for Study Recent Immigration Europe, N.Y.C., 1944-47; research asso., asst. dir. Nat. Com. Immigration Policy, N.Y.C., 1947-50; research asso. med. research Yale/Russell Sage Found., Yale, N.Y.C. and New Haven, 1951-53; asso. prof. sociology and anthropology Wilson Coll., Chambersburg, Pa., 1953-61, prof., 1961-73, chmn. dept., 1953-73. prof. emeritus, 1974—; vis. prof. Dickinson Coll., summer 1973. Bd. sociol. sci. cons.'s NAACP Legal Def. and Edn. Fund, 1954-56, State Pa. desegregation schs., 1972-75. Univ. scholar Yale, 1938-39; recipient Lindback Distinguished Teaching award, 1969. Mem. Am. Sociol. Assn., Soc. Study Social Problems (sec. 1957-59), Pa. Sociol. Soc. (pres. 1962-63). Democrat. Episcopalian. Clubs: Soroptimist, Chambersburg Afternoon. Author: Relations Between Spanish Americans and Anglo-Americans in New Mexico, 1974; contbr. author: (with Maurice Davie) Refugees in America, 1947. Editor: (with Bernard and Miller) American Immigration Policy: A Reappraisal, 1950. Home: 266 N Main St Chambersburg PA 17201 Office: Wilson Coll Chambersburg PA 17201

ZELIK, BERNARD JOHN, psychologist, rehab. counselor; b. Pitts., Jan. 7, 1945; s. Andrew John and Marie Barbara (Moellar) Z.; B.A., Coll. of Steubenville (Ohio), 1967; M.Ed., U. Pitts., 1968; m. Josephine Ann Szczerba, Aug. 12, 1972. Psychologist, rehab. counselor Greater Pitts. Guild for Blind, 1969—; also pvt. practice; tchr. adjustment to blindness principle to select groups of profls. and grad. students. Bd. dirs. Cath. Com. for Blind in Diocese of Pitts. Licensed psychologist, Pa.; certified rehab. counselor. Mem. Am. Psychol. Assn., Greater Pitts. Psychol. Assn., Am. Assn. Mental Deficiency, Nat. Rehab. Assn., Am. Personnel and Guidance Assn., Am. Assn. Workers for Blind. Democrat. Roman Catholic. Home: 211 Delano Dr Pittsburgh PA 15236 Office: 4135 Brownsville Rd Suite 303-304 Whitehall PA 15227

ZELITCH, DAVID S., ins. co. exec.; b. Phila., May 7, 1924; s. Eli and Mollie (Cohen) Z.; student Wharton Sch., U. Pa., 1941-42, Bard Coll., Columbia, 1943-44, Drexel U., 1946-51; m. Lillian Elizabeth Goldman, Dec. 29, 1946; children—Steven, Susan, Dayle, Simone. Vice pres. Fidelity Interstate Life, Phila., 1950-60; exec. v.p., co-founder Union Fidelity Life, Phila., 1960-71, sr. v.p., 1971-78; cons. real estate Bernard C. Meltzer and Assos. Chmn. discriminations com. Anti-Defamation League, nat. vice chmn., regent Soc. Fellows; bd. dirs., chmn. pub. relations com. Phila. Geriatric Center; behavior modification weight loss control program vol. group leader dept. psychiatry U. Pa.; mem. pub. edn. and info. com. Jewish Family Service; nat. bd. dirs., mem. exec. com. Am. Assos., Ben Gurion U. of Negev, v.p., bd. dirs. Solomon Schechter Schs., Akiba Hebrew Acad.; v.p. Passover League Phila.; mem. Delaware Valley Regional Affairs Council; hon. pres. Bustleton-Somerton Synagogue. Served with AUS, 1942-45. Decorated Purple Heart. Mem. Nat. Assn. Life Ins. Cos., Life Ins. Mgmt. Assn. Jewish. Mason; mem. B'nai B'rith. Home: 803 Larkspur St Philadelphia PA 19116 Office: Union Fidelity Office Park Trevose PA 19047

ZELLER, DIANE LEINWAND, educator; b. Boston, June 21, 1940; d. Leo and Gusta (Rabinowicz) Leinwand; B.A., Barnard Coll., 1962; M.A., Columbia U., 1964, certificate in African studies, 1964, Ph.D., 1971; m. Jack A. Zeller, June 17, 1961; children—Susan Beth, Lisa Ariella. With overseas liaison com. Am. Council on Edn., Washington, 1971-77, program dir., 1976-77; asso. exec. dir. Soc. for Intercultural Edn., Tng. and Research, Georgetown U., Washington, 1977-78, exec. dir., 1978—; professorial lectr. Georgetown U., 1978—. Nat. Def. Fgn. Lang. fellow, 1966-68; Fgn. Area Fellowship Program fellow, 1966-67; Pub. Health Service fellow, 1968-69. Mem. African Studies Assn., Caribbean Studies Assn., Latin Am. Studies Assn., Soc. for Intercultural Edn., Tng. and Research, Am. Hist. Assn., others. Contbr. articles to profl. jours. Home: 11405 Rock

Bridge Rd Silver Spring MD 20902 Office: SIETAR Georgetown U Washington DC 20057

ZELLER, HOWARD ALFRED, justice N.Y. State supreme ct.; b. Syracuse, N.Y., Feb. 26, 1912; s. Alfred George and Katherine Emma (Miller) Z.; B.A., Hamilton Coll., Clinton, N.Y., 1933; LL.B., Syracuse U., 1936; m. Carmen L. Hickox, June 10, 1939; children—Robert, James, Richard, Jane Zeller Cleary. Admitted to N.Y. bar, 1936; pvt. practice, Oneida, 1936-44; dist. atty. Madison County, N.Y., 1946-50; justice 6th jud. dist. N.Y. State Supreme Ct., Oneida, 1950—, adminstrv. judge ct. within dist., 1962—. Bd. visitors Syracuse U. Coll. Law. Served with USNR, World War II. Mem. Am. Judicature Soc., Am., N.Y. State bar assns., Am. Legion, V.F.W. Home: South Main St Munnsville NY 13409 Office: Court House Oneida NY 13421

ZELLNER, CARL ALAN, urban planner; b. Oklahoma City, Oct. 4, 1935; s. August Louis and Gladys Gene (Gilstrap) Z.; B.A., Principia Coll., 1957; M. Urban Planning, U. Wash. at Seattle, 1964; postgrad. Harvard, 1965-67; m. Beverley Ann Holmes, Apr. 25, 1960; children—Charles, Carla, Danielle. Planning asso. U. Wash., Seattle, 1963-65; research asst. Joint Center for Urban Studies, Mass. Inst. Tech. and Harvard, Cambridge, 1965-67, Transp. Research Bd., Washington, 1967-69; planning dir. City of Gaithersburg (Md.), 1969-70; sr. asso. planner Alan M. Voorhees & Assos., Inc., Planning Cons., Boston, 1970-78; v.p. Zellner, Vanasse, Haugen & Assos., Inc., planning and engring. consultants, Boston, 1978—; lectr. transp. and environ. planning Boston State Coll., 1973—. Mem. Boston Landmarks Commn., 1976. Served with USCG, 1957-61. Wash. Fedn. Garden Clubs scholar, 1962-63. Mem. Am. Inst. Cert. Planners, Am. Planning Assn., Transp. Research Forum, Nat. Trust Historic Preservation, Soc. Preservation New Eng. Antiquities. Democrat. Author: (with E. Horwood and R. Ludwig) Community Consequences of Highway Improvement, 1965; (with R. Winfrey) Summary and Evaluation of Economic Consequences of Highway Improvements, 1971. Home: 7 Elm St Charlestown MA 02129 Office: 184 High St Boston MA 02110

ZELLNER, JOSEPH EDWARD, computer systems exec.; b. Dingolfing, Germany, Jan. 10, 1923; s. Eduard and Katharina (Parzl) Z.; came to U.S., 1951, naturalized, 1956; M.B.A., U. Chgo., 1963, postgrad., 1963-64; m. Nora Luschek, July 18, 1947; children—Katharina-Maria, Edward Joseph. Controller, treas. Goldenrod Creamery Co., Brodhead, Wis., 1953-58; asst. controller, exec. asst. for planning and control Pure Milk Assn., Chgo., 1958-65; asst. div. controller, mgr. tech. systems Standard Brands, Inc., N.Y.C., 1965-73; mgr. mgmt. infor. systems Standard Brands, Ltd., Montreal, Que., Can., 1973-76; dir. mgmt. info. systems Internat. Standard Brands, N.Y.C., 1976—. Instr. computers Loyola U., Chgo., 1965. C.P.A., Ill., Pa. Fellow AAAS; mem. Am. Inst. C.P.A.'s, Inst. Mgmt. Sci. Home: 135 E 54th St New York City NY 10022 Office: 625 Madison Ave New York City NY 10022

ZELT, ALBERT RALPH, indsl. engr.; b. Pitts., May 3, 1928; s. Albert Ralph and Irene (Kreamer) Z.; B.S., Carnegie Mellon U., 1950; M.B.A., U. Pitts., 1959; M.S., Duquesne U., 1976; m. Marilyn Weller Marks, Sept. 1, 1948; children—Albert Ralph, Roger Paul, Frederick Bruce. Student engr. Lorain (Ohio) Works, Nat. Tube div. U.S. Steel Corp., 1950-51, indsl. engr. Nat. Works, McKeesport, Pa., 1953-59, Pitts., 1960-63; indsl. engr. U.S. Steel Corp., Pitts., 1964, engr. facility plans, 1965—. Mem. Bd. Sch. Dirs. Bethel Park (Pa.), 1963-69; ruling elder Bethel Presbyn. Ch., 1959—. Served with C.E., U.S. Army, 1951-53. Mem. Assn. Iron and Steel Engrs., Am. Personnel and Guidance Assn. Home: 217 Navajo Rd Pittsburgh PA 15241 Office: 600 Grant St Pittsburgh PA 15230

ZEMAN, BARRY TILDEN, hosp. adminstr.; b. Pitts., Apr. 7, 1946; s. Clarence and Ann (Topel) Z.; B.B.A., U. Cin., 1969; M.P.H., U. Pitts., 1971; m. Carol Ann Briggs, June 14, 1969; 1 son, Joshua Benjamin. Coop. student and staff accountant Arthur Young & Co., Cin., 1966-69; asst. adminstr. L.I. Jewish Hillside Med. Center, New Hyde Park, N.Y., 1970-74, asso. adminstr. S. Shore div., Far Rockaway, N.Y., 1974-76; sr. asso. dir. S.I. Hosp., S.I., N.Y., 1976—; instr. health scis. Sch. Allied Health Professions, State U. N.Y., Stony Brook, 1973-76; adj. asst. prof. C.W. Post Center, L.I. U., 1975-76. Mem. Community Bd. 3, S.I., 1978; adv. com. Bd. Coop. Edn. Services Nassau County, 1974-77; mem. adv. com. Community Bd. 2, S.I., 1977—; mem. S.I., Council on Arts, 1977—; bd. dirs. Health Systems Agy. Dist. Bd., 1978. Served with Q.M.C., U.S. Army, 1972. Mem. Am. Coll. Hosp. Adminstrs., Am. Hosp. Assn., Am., N.Y.C. pub. health assns., Group Health Assn., Beta Alpha Psi. Office: Staten Island Hosp 101 Castleton Ave Staten Island NY 10301

ZEMAN, MILAN SAMUEL, chemist; b. Little Falls, N.Y., July 2, 1948; s. Steven Arnold and Elizabeth (Adasek) Z.; B.S. in Chemistry, Rochester Inst. Tech., 1971, also postgrad.; m. Sharon A. Mullaney, Feb. 19, 1972; children—Kristin, Elizabeth. Project mgr./chemist Paper Tech. Center, Xerox Corp., Webster, N.Y., 1971-74, project mgr./physicist, Transfer Tech. Center, 1974-76, chemist Spl. Materials Tech. Center, 1976—; cons. in field. N.Y. State Regents scholar, 1966-71. Mem. Penfield Jr. C. of C. (sec. 1977-78), Soc. Photographic Scientists and Engrs., Xerox Mgmt. Assn. Democrat. Lutheran. Contbr. articles to profl. jours. Home: 1831 Jackson Rd Penfield NY 14526 Office: Bldg 147 Joseph C Wilson Center for Tech Rochester NY 14644

ZENI, LEVIO EDWARD, state ofcl.; b. N.Y.C., Jan. 27, 1923; s. Joseph Francis and Sylvia (Flaim) Z.; B.S., U.S. Naval Acad., 1945; M.A. Law Diplomacy, Fletcher Sch. Law and Diplomacy, 1962; m. Geraldine Duston Lowell, Mar. 26, 1949; children—Constance Anne, Peter Ernst. Commd. ensign USN, 1945, advanced through grades to capt., 1965, ret. 1969; ocean sci. planner Smithsonian Inst., Washington, 1969-70; spl. projects engr. State of Md., Annapolis, 1970-71, dir. power plant siting program, 1972-75, adminstr. Energy and Coastal Zone Adminstrn., 1975—; mem. exec. com. So. States Energy Bd., 1977—. Chmn. adv. commn. Atomic Energy for Md., Annapolis, 1973-78; leader, com. chmn. Boy Scouts Am., Crofton, Md., 1966-70; v.p. Crofton Civic Assn., 1968-70, dir., 1970-72. Clubs: Naval Acad. Officers and Faculty, Naval Acad. Golf (Annapolis). Home: Box 117B Rutland Rd Davidsonville MD 21035 Office: Tawes State Office Bldg Annapolis MD 21401

ZENOWITZ, ALLAN RALPH, business cons.; b. Queens Village, L.I., N.Y., Apr. 18, 1928; s. Ralph and Ann Louise (Brickman) Z.; student Trinity Coll., 1947-49; spl. studies Harvard, 1948, Yale, 1947, U. Va., 1955; B.A. in Govt. and Internat. Relations, U. Conn., 1960; J.D., New Eng. Sch. Law, 1964. New Eng. area mgr. F. G. Ludwig, Inc., Hartford, Conn., 1953-54; dir. ARZ Pub. Relations and Devel., Hartford, 1955-56; mgmt. exec. Saks Fifth Ave., N.Y.C., 1956-57; dir. spl. situations Fred Gaertner, Jr. & Assos., mgmt. engrs., bus. consultants, N.Y.C., 1957-60. Aide to gov. Mass. as brig. gen., 1961-62; state dir. Mass. Civil Def. Agy., also Office Emergency Preparedness, 1965-71; mem. Mass. Emergency Communications Commn., Mass. Radiol. Advisory Protection Council; chmn. Mass. Gov.'s Water Emergency Advisory Com., 1965-71, Mass. Emergency Energy Com., 1970—; regional dir. U.S. Office of Civil Defense, 1971-72; regional dir. U.S. Def. Civil Preparedness Agy., 1972—; mem. exec. com. Christian A. Herter chair in internat. relations; mem. policy com. Boston Fed. Exec. Bd., 1971—; mem. U.S.-Can. Civil Emergency Advisory Com., 1971—; chmn. advisory council New Eng. Sch. Law, Law Enforcement Legal Edn. Program; del. NATO sr. civil engring. com., 1972. Cons., Republican Nat. Com., 1964-65; mem. Gt. Barrington Rep. Town Committee, 1964-65; Mass. Rep. State committeeman, 1964-65. Served as 1st lt. cav., U.S. Army, 1950-52; with NATO Forces, Germany; col. inf., Res.; past capt., 7th regt., N.Y.N.G. Recipient White House citation for oustanding pub. service, 1967; Distinguished Service citation Dept. Def., 1971, Meritorious Service medal, 1976, award Legion of Merit, 1977. Mem. Am. Acad. Polit. Sci., Am. Polit. Sci. Assn., Am. Soc. Internat. Law, Nat. Assn. State Dirs. Disaster Preparedness (pres. 1969-70, exec. com. 1968-71), Am. Soc. Pub. Adminstrn., Nat. Geog. Soc. Club: University (Boston). Home: 20 Berkshire Heights Rd Great Barrington MA 01230 Office: 37 Beacon St Boston MA 02108

ZENTNER, CHARLES RAYNARD, elec. engr.; b. Wilkinsburg, Pa., Feb. 1, 1941; s. Charles Raynard and Sarah Dorthea (Sloan) Z.; B.S., Pa. State U., 1963, M.S., 1968, Ph.D., 1975. Design engr. AC Spark Plug div. Gen. Motors Corp., 1963-65, design engr. Allison div., 1965-66; research asso. Applied Research Lab., State College, Pa., 1966-78; prin. engr. Raytheon Co., Portsmouth, R.I., 1978—. Mem. IEEE, Acoustical Soc. Am., Am. Soc. Engring. Educators, Sigma Xi. Home: 58 Arrowhead Ln Portsmouth RI 02871 Office: PO Box 360 Portsmouth RI 02871

ZEPKE, BRENT ERIC, lawyer; b. Mar. 28, 1943; B.S., U. N.C., 1967; M.S., Clemson U., 1969; J.D., U. Tenn., 1973; LL.M., Temple U., 1977; m.; 3 children. Customer engr. IBM, instr. applied math. Central Piedmont Community Coll., 1965-67; So. Edn. Bd. grantee, 1968; instr. indsl. engring. dept. Greenville Tech. Inst., 1968-69; instr. dept. statistics U. Tenn., 1969-71, instr. dept. indsl. and personnel mgmt., 1971-74, instr. bus. law, 1972-73; prin. Cons. Assos., Inc., Knoxville, Tenn., 1973-74; admitted to Tenn. bar, 1974, Pa. bar, 1975, D.C. bar, 1975, N.J. bar, 1976, corporate counsel, dir. research VICON, Inc., Knoxville, 1973-74; atty. Gulf Oil Corp., Phila., 1974—; participant Nat. Coll. of Advocacy, Harvard, 1975. Recipient Am. Jurisprudence award for outstanding achievement in estate planning, 1973. Mem. Am. Bar Assn., Am. Trial Lawyers Assn., Am. Inst. Indsl. Engrs., Phi Alpha Delta. Author: Mathematical Models for Managers, 1972, rev. edit., 1973; Industrial Management: A Numerical Approach, 1974; Products and the Consumer, 1975; Labor Law, 1977; Business Statistics, 1978. Features editor Gen. Issue, U. Tenn. Coll. Law, 1970-71. Home: 228 Burleigh Dr Somerdale NJ 08083 Office: 1 Presidential Blvd Bala-Cynwyd PA 19004

ZERR, JESSE BITLER, educator; b. Scarlets Mill, Pa., June 16, 1921; s. Levi Hoffman and Hazel (Bitler) Z; B.S. in Music Edn., West Chester State Coll., 1943; postgrad. music edn. Juilliard Sch. Music, 1946; M.A. in Music Edn., Columbia U., 1948; postgrad adminstrn. Temple U., 1950; Mus.D., Fremont Coll., 1952; m. Marjorie Cauthorn; children—Patricia, Craig Brad. Dir. music, Scott High Sch., Coatesville, Pa., 1944-45; dir. instrumental music LCC Regional High Sch., Clemonton, N.J., 1945-46; prof. music Harcum Jr. Coll., Bryn Mawr, Pa., 1965-69; dist. coordinator music Radnor Twp. Schs., Wyane, Pa., 1946-76; dir. Music, 1976—. Bd. dirs. Main Line Symphony Orch. Recipient Valley Forge Freedom Found. medal, 1969; W. Chester Coll. Distinguished Alumni award, 1975 Mem. NEA, Pa. Edn. Assn., Nat., Pa. music assns., Met. Opera Guild, Radnor Twp. Edn. Assn. Club: Shrine. Home: 6 Horse Shoe Ln Paoli PA 19301 Office: Radnor Twp Schs Wayne PA 19087

ZIEGELER, ANDREW, banker; b. N.Y.C., July 31, 1913; s. Carl and Jennie (Doty) Z.; student Am. Inst. Banking, 1949, grad. study certificate, 1960; grad. Stonier Grad. Sch. Banking, Rutgers U., 1953; B.S., N.Y.U., 1960; m. Irma Cunningham, Mar. 31, 1946; 1 dau., Barbara Ann (Mrs. Leroy Cubicciotti). Pres., chief exec. officer Mchts. Bank N.Y., N.Y.C., 1967—, also dir. Served with USAAF, 1944-45. Mem. East Side C. of C. (dir., past pres., chmn. bd.), Alumni Assn. Am. Inst. Banking (past pres.). Home: 301 E 69th St New York City NY 10021 Office: 434 Broadway New York City NY 10013

ZIEGENFUS, ROBERT CHARLES, educator; b. Palmerton, Pa., Feb. 1, 1944; s. Carl and Mildred Elsie (Ceban) Z.; B.S., Kutztown State Coll., 1965; M.S., Pa. State U., 1967; postgrad. Indiana U. (Pa.), 1973, Rutgers U., 1975-76. Faculty Northampton Community Coll., Bethlehem, Pa., 1967-77, co-dir. environ. studies program, 1973-76, dir., 1976-77, asso. prof. geography and environ. studies, 1974-77; faculty Rutgers U., 1977—. Chmn. Clean Air Council of Lehigh Valley, Pa., 1974-77. Mem. Assn. Am. Geographers (chmn. com. on two year colls. 1975-77), Nat. Council for Geogr. Edn., Population Reference Bureau, Population Assn. Am., Zero Population Growth, Pa. Council for Geographic Edn., Phi Delta Kappa. Club: Sierra. Book reviewer Houghton-Mifflin, N.Y.C., 1972-73, 76, McGraw-Hill, N.Y.C., 1972-73. Home: 1138-6 Easton Ave Somerset NJ 08903 Office: Rutgers Univ Dept Geography 185 College Ave New Brunswick NJ 08903

ZIEGLER, ALAN DENNIS, poet; b. Bklyn., Aug. 21, 1947; s. Matthew Irving and Pearl (Popowsky) Z.; B.S., Union Coll., Schenectady, 1970; M.A., Coll. City N.Y., 1974. Reporter, Binghamton (N.Y.) Evening Press, 1970; asso. editor Environment Info. Center, N.Y.C., 1972-74; adj. instr. English, Bronx Community Coll., 1974-76; tchr./coordinator Tchrs. and Writers Collaborative, 1974—, Poets-in-the-Schs., 1974—; works include Planning Escape, 1973; (with H. Greenberg and L. Zirlin) Sleeping Obsessions, 1976; (with Joseph Szabo) Almost Grown, 1978; contbr. poems and fiction and non-fiction to Paris Rev., Am. Poetry Rev., Poetry Now, The Village Voice, Unmuzzled Ox, The Falcon, Ardis Anthology New Am. Poetry, others. Co-editor Some lit. mag., 1972—; co-pub. Release Press, 1973—. Recipient award Am. Artists Exhbn., Inc., 1978. Dow Jones Newspaper Fund reporting intern, 1969. Home: 309 W 104th St New York City NY 10025

ZIEGLER, ARTHUR PAUL, JR., found. exec.; b. Pitts., June 20, 1937; s. Arthur Paul and Vinnie (DeWinter) Z.; M.A. in English, U. Pitts., 1959; postgrad. Union Theol. Sem., 1959-60, Western Res. U., 1960-61. Pub., dir. Van Trump, Ziegler & Shane, Pitts., 1964-72; pres. Ober Park Assos., Pitts., 1972—; pres. Pitts. History and Landmarks Found., 1964—, Landmarks Planning, Inc., Landmarks Design Services, Inc., Preservation Cons. Cons. Nat. Trust for Historic Preservation. Mem. Historic Resources of U.S., Pres.'s Adv. Panel on Historic Preservation, trustee Allegheny Found. Bd. dirs. Meadowcroft Village, Center for Preservation of Law, Soc. for Preservation of Duquesne Incline, Preservation Action, rev. panels Nat. Endowment for Arts, HUD, City of Pitts. Historic Landmarks Rev. Bd. Author: Lord of the Flies Casebook, 1964; Cora Street, 1965; (with James D. Van Trump) Landmark Architecture of Allegheny County, 1967; Historic Preservation in Inner City Areas, 1972; Revolving Funds for Historic Preservation, 1974; (with W.C. Kidney) Allegheny, 1976. Home: 904 Cedar Ave Pittsburgh PA 15212 Office: One Landmarks Sq Pittsburgh PA 15212

ZIEGLER, JOHN BENJAMIN, chemist; b. Rochester, N.Y., Jan. 2, 1917; s. John Benjamin and Sarah Jeanette (Murrell) Z.; B.S., U. Rochester, 1939; M.S., U. Ill., 1940, Ph.D., 1946; m. Dorothy Mary Zucker, June 29, 1946; children—Katherine Lois, Jeffrey Benjamin, Conrad Lawrence. Jr. chemist Merck and Co., Inc., Rahway, N.J., 1940-43; research chemist, U.S. OSRD, U. Ill., Urbana, 1943-46; chemist, J. T. Baker Chem. Co., Phillipsburg, N.J., 1946-48; asso. chemist, CIBA Pharm. Co., Summit, N.J., 1948-50, sr. chemist, 1950-52, supr. labs., 1952-65, mgr. process research, 1965-70; dir. chem. devel., pharms. div., Ciba-Geigy Corp., Summit, 1970-75, sr. staff scientist, 1975—; chmn. chem. advisory com. Union County Tech. Inst., 1964-69; mem. com. tech. tng., N.J. Council Research and Devel., 1969-70. Fellow Am. Inst. Chemists; mem. Am. Chem. Soc., Research Soc. Am., N.Y. Acad. Scis., Lepidopterists' Soc. (exec. council), Found. for Research on Lepidoptera, Alpha Chi Sigma. Republican. Contbr. chem., entomol. papers to sci. jours; patentee chem. technology. Home: 64 Canoe Brook Parkway Summit NJ 07901 Office: 556 Morris Ave Summit NJ 07901

ZIEGLER, TERRY L., newspaper editor; b. Williamsport, Pa., Apr. 5, 1931; s. Frank A. and Carmen D. (Lenker) Z.; B.A. magna cum laude, Lycoming Coll., 1963. Reporter Grit, Williamsport, 1949-51, 55-56, radio-TV editor, 1956-57, city editor, 1957-62, family sect. editor, 1962-68, feature editor, 1968-70, asst. to editor, 1970-71, mng. editor, 1971-72, asst. editor, 1972, editor, 1972—; dir. Grit Pub. Co., Williamsport, 1973—; adviser Lycoming Coll. Publs. Bd., 1971-74. Publicity chmn. Williamsport Community Concert Assn., 1949-51, dir., 1956-63, 3d v.p., 1963-68, pres., 1968—; dir. Lycoming Child Day Care Center, 1965, pres., 1966; mem. adv. bd. Susquehanna Valley Symphony Orch., 1972-75. Served from seaman to personnelman (2d class), USN, 1951-55. Mem. Pa. Soc. Newspaper Editors (dir. 1971-73), Williamsport-Lycoming C. of C. (dir. 1974-77). Club: Ross. Author: Eastward, Ho, 1955. Home: PO Box 1173 Williamsport PA 17701 Office: 208 W 3d St Williamsport PA 17701

ZIELONKA, ALFRED WALTER, educator; b. Buffalo, Feb. 15, 1930; s. Walter Edwin and Dorothy Elizabeth (Dissette) Z.; A.B. in French, Niagara U., 1952; M.S. in English Edn., Canisius Coll., 1959; Ed.D., State U. N.Y. at Buffalo, 1964; m. Joan Marie Cuddy, Feb. 19, 1955; children—Denise, Diane, Christine, Carole, Joanne. Tchr. English, Maryvale Sch. System, Cheektowaga, N.Y., 1957-61; teaching fellow, instr. edn. State U. N.Y., Buffalo, 1962-64; asso. prof. edn. Rosary Hill Coll., Buffalo, 1964—, chmn. dept. edn., 1964-69, asst. acad. dean, 1969-70, asso. acad. dean, 1970-71, exec. v.p., 1971-73, acting pres., 1973-74, prof. edn., 1976—. Bd. dirs. Traveler's Aid Buffalo; trustee WNED-TV, WNED-FM, WEBR-AM. Served with U.S. Army, 1952-56, 61-62. Mem. Am. Assn. for Higher Edn., Nat. Orgn. on Legal Problems in Edn., Buffalo Area C. of C. (vice chmn. sports devel. com. 1972-74), Phi Delta Kappa, Kappa Delta Pi. Club: University (Buffalo). Contbr. articles to profl. jours. Home: 266 Patrice Terr Williamsville NY 14221 Office: 4380 Main St Buffalo NY 14226

ZIEMNOWICZ, CHRISTOPHER HENRY, educator, mktg. exec.; b. Gdansk, Poland, Oct. 21, 1949; s. Stanley Anthony and Janina (Dabrowska) Z.; arrived U.S., 1958; B.B.A., George Mason Coll., U. Va., 1972; M.B.A., Am. U., 1974. lMem. hardware ops. staff Reston Hardware, Inc., Reston, Va., 1973-75; salesman summer and part-time Courtesy AMC-Jeep, Bethesda, Md., 1968-77; instr. mktg. and mgmt., dept. bus. adminstrn. Va. Poly. Inst. and State U., Blacksburg, Va., 1977—. Mem. research team Va. Poly Inst. and State U. and Warsaw Tech. U. Program, 1977—. Club: Univ. Office: Va Poly Inst Blacksburg VA 24061

ZIEN, TSE-FOU, mech. engr.; b. Shanghai, China, Aug. 9, 1937; s. Yih and Mon-Mei (Chang) Z.; came to U.S., 1960, naturalized, 1971; B.S., Nat. Taiwan U., 1958; M.S. (scholar), Brown U., 1963; Ph.D. in Aeros. (scholar), Calif. Inst. Tech., 1967; m. Suzy Shen, July 7, 1962; children—Livia Lea, Conroy Chi-Kan. Engr., 3d Shipyard Chinese Navy, 1959-60; grad. asst. Brown U., Providence, 1960-63, Calif. Inst. Tech., Pasadena, 1963-67; postdoctoral research asso. Case Western Res. U., Cleve., 1967-70; research aerospace engr. Naval Ordnance Lab., Silver Spring, Md., 1970-71, supervisory and research aerospace engr. Naval Surface Weapons Center, 1971—, mem. heat transfer panel Navy Aeroballistics com.; asso. professorial lectr. George Washington U., Washington, 1976—. Recipient Shu-Cheun award Nat. Taiwan U., 1955-58, Sir Lin's fellow, 1956-58; Outstanding Performance award Naval Ordnance Lab., Silver Spring, 1974. Fellow Am. Inst. Aeros. and Astronautics (asso., mem. fluid dynamics com.), Washington Acad. Scis. (ann. award for sci. achievement in engring. scis. 1977); mem. Am. Phys. Soc., Sigma Xi. Contbr. articles to profl. publs. Home: 3300 Beret Ln Wheaton MD 20906 Office: Naval Surface Weapons Center White Oak Silver Spring MD 20910

ZIER, ADOLFO, psychiatrist, neurologist; b. Havana, Cuba, Feb. 15, 1922; s. Bernard and Sara (Kastner) Z.; M.D., Havana U., 1946; m. Isabella Salvucci, Aug. 16, 1947. Came to U.S., 1947; naturalized, 1954. Attending psychiatrist Holy Name Hosp., Teaneck, N.J., 1963—, former chief dept. neuropsychiatry; asso. attending psychiatrist St. Lukes Hosp., N.Y.C., 1955-75; adj. attending neurologist Montefiore Hosp., Bronx, 1954-61; cons. psychiatrist N.Y.C. Youth Bd., 1955-65; cons. neuropsychiatrist Northside Center for Child Devel., N.Y.C., 1953—; sch. psychiatrist Bur. Child Guidance, Bd. Edn., N.Y.C., 1956—; attending psychiatrist Bergen Pines County Hosp., Paramus, N.J., 1963-68. Mem. AMA, Am. Psychiat. Assn., Am. Acad. Neurology, Bergen County Med. Soc., Assn. for Research Nervous and Mental Diseases. Home: 663 Queen Anne Rd Teaneck NJ 07666

ZIGLAR, WILLIAM LARRY, historian, educator; b. Yazoo City, Miss., Aug. 25, 1938; s. Willie Hubert and Freida Belle (Waaser) Z.; B.A., Miss. Coll., 1960, M.A., 1961; Ph.D., U. Maine, 1972, postdoctoral (NASA fellow), 1972-73; postdoctoral U. Pa., 1975-77; m. Brenda Joy Helms, June 25, 1960; children—Scott Lawrence, Heidi Lynn. Teaching fellow Miss. Coll., 1960-61; grad. asst. U. Maine, 1961-64, instr., summers 1961-64; instr. history Eastern Coll., St. Davids, Pa., 1964-66, asst. prof., 1966-72, asso. prof., 1972-75, prof., 1975—, chmn. social sci. div., 1976—, head history dept., 1974—, coordinator Am. studies program, 1968—; adj. prof. Ogontz campus Pa. State U., 1974—. Bd. dirs., mgr. Little League Baseball, Wayne, Pa., 1974-76; mgr. Little League Soccer, 1975-76, Radnor Girls Softball League, 1978; bd. dirs. Rowland Elementary Sch. PTA, 1975-77; bd. dirs. Wayne PTA, 1977-78, v.p., 1978. Named Prof. of Year, Eastern Coll., 1967, 73. Fellow Am. Studies Assn.; mem. Am., So. hist. assns., Orgn. Am. Historians, Soc. for History Tech., Assn. Caribbean Historians, Hist. Soc. Pa., Assn. State and Local History, Phi Alpha Theta, Pi Gamma Mu, Omicron Delta Kappa, Kappa Delta Pi, Pi Kappa Delta. Contbr. articles to profl. jours. Home: 408 Oak Ln Wayne PA 19087 Office: Eastern College Saint Davids PA 19087

ZIGO, PAUL EDWARD, coll. ofcl.; b. Newark, July 14, 1942; s. Edward and Jeannette Agnes (Fox) Z.; B.A. in History, Rutgers U., 1964; M.A. in Guidance, Rider Coll., 1973; m. Kim Irene Schmerler, Apr. 22, 1978. Asst. dir. community relations Monmouth Coll., West Long Branch, N.J., 1966-75, dir. community relations, 1975-77; dir. extension services and Weekend Coll., Brookdale Community Coll., Lincroft, N.J., 1977—; dir. Monmouth Jr. Sci. Symposium, 1975—. Mem. advisory council Monmouth County Office on Aging, 1975—; pres. Monmouth County Arts Council, 1976-78; mem. exec. bd.

Monmouth County United Way, 1977—; chmn. Monmouth County chpt. ARC, 1978—; bd. dirs. Monmouth County Community Services Council, 1977—. Served with U.S. Army, 1964-66. Mem. Nat. Council Community Services (charter), Am. Soc. Personnel Adminstrs., Am. Assn. Coll. and Univ. Adminstrs., Am. Council Arts, Tri-State TV Consortium (exec. bd.), Monmouth Ocean Devel. Council, Jersey Shore Pub. Relations Assn. (pres. 1974-75), Pi Kappa Delta (Outstanding Service award 1977), Alpha Phi Omega (outstanding service award 1974). Roman Catholic. Club: Belmar Kiwanis (pres. 1973-74). Home: 407 7th Ave Apt 4 Asbury Park NJ 07712 Office: Office Extension Services Brookdale Community College Lincroft NJ 07738

ZILKHA, PHYLLIS SIEGEL, psychologist; b. N.Y.C., Jan. 30, 1945; d. Barney and Ruth (Baer) Siegel; B.S., City Coll. N.Y., 1965; M.A., Columbia U., 1966; Ph.D., N.Y. U., 1977; m. Jalall Zilkha, Nov. 29, 1969. Research asst. City U. N.Y., 1966-70; research cons. Center for Urban Edn., 1971; research cons. Intelicor, Inc., N.Y.C., 1972; psychologist Sherut La'am, N.Y.C., 1973-74; adj. lectr. Hunter Coll., N.Y.C., 1972-77; indsl. psychologist Ins. Services Office, N.Y.C., 1977—; pvt. practice psychol. counseling, N.Y.C., 1977—. Mem. Jean Piaget Soc., Am. Psychol. Assn., Kappa Delta Pi. Home: 300 E 74th St New York City NY 10021

ZIMMER, ALAN EDWARD, neuroradiologist; b. N.Y.C., Feb. 10, 1929; s. Harry A. and Bess (Waldman) Z.; B.A., N.Y. U., 1949; M.D., U. Geneva, Switzerland, 1956; m. Harriet Lila Hochhauser, July 1, 1961; children—Michael A., David, Stuart. Intern, Garfield Meml. Hosp., Washington, 1956-57; resident in radiology Albert Einstein Coll. Medicine, 1957-60, fellow in neuroradiology, 1960-61; chief neuroradiology sect. Montefiore Hosp. Med. Center, N.Y.C., 1963-68; asst. prof. radiology Albert Einstein Coll., 1963-68, asst. clin. prof. radiology, 1968—; neuroradiologist, attending radiology Danbury (Conn.) Hosp., 1968—; asst. clin. prof. Yale U.; cons. in field. NIH fellow, 1961-63. Diplomate Am. Bd. Radiology. Mem. AMA, Am. Coll. Radiology, Radiol. Soc. N. Am., Am. Soc. Neuroradiology, N.Y. Roentgen Soc., Conn. State, Fairfield County med. socs. Jewish. Clubs: Neuroradiology Clubs N.Y. and Conn. Contbr. articles in field to profl. jours. Home: 75 Jordan Ln Stamford CT 06903 Office: Danbury Hospital Danbury CT 06810

ZIMMER, ALEX, cantor, religious educator; b. Bklyn., Aug. 21, 1922; s. Hyman and Hannah (Singer) Z.; B.S., N.Y. U., 1949, M.A., 1951; B.S. in Sacred Music, Hebrew Union Coll., 1954; m. Doris DuKaten, Dec. 8, 1945; children—William Howard, Michael Lance, Wendy Lee, Lisa Ann. Free lance profl. singer, 1937-52; chorister RCA, N.Y.C., 1945-49; choral soloist, mgr., asst. condr. Robert Shaw Chorale, N.Y.C., 1949-52; cantor, music dir. Central Synagogue Nassau County, Rockville Center, N.Y., 1953-55, dir. religious edn., 1954-55; cantor, music dir. Temple Ohabei Shalom, Brookline, Mass., 1955—. Lectr., recitalist on Jewish music, 1952—. Served with USAF, 1942-45. Decorated D.F.C., Air medal with 5 clusters. Recipient medalion of merit Israel Govt., 1973; citations merit Temple Ohabei Shalom Brotherhood, 1965, Am. Conf. Cantors, 1968. Mem. Am. Conf. Cantors (pres. 1965-67), New Eng. Jewish Music Forum (pres. 1956-66), Nat. Jewish Music Council, Nat. Assn. Tchrs. Singing (exec. bd. New Eng. region), Jewish Chataqua Soc. (life), Jewish War Vets. Home: 6 Valley Spring Rd Newton MA 02158 Office: Temple Ohabei Shalom 1187 Beacon St Brookline MA 02146

ZIMMER, DONALD WILLIAM, baseball club exec.; b. Cin., Jan. 17, 1931; s. Harold Lesley and Lorraine Bertha (Fiscus) Z.; student pub. schs., Cin.; m. Jean Carol Bauerle, Aug. 16, 1951; children—Thomas Jeffrey, Donna Jean. Baseball player Dodger Farm Clubs, 1949-54, Bklyn. Dodgers, 1954-57, Los Angeles Dodgers, 1958-59, Chgo. Cubs, 1960-61, N.Y. Mets, 1962, Cin. Reds, 1962, Los Angeles Dodgers, 1963, Wash. Senators, 1963-65. Toei Flyers, Tokyo, 1966; mgr. Reds Farms, Knoxville, Buffalo, Cin., 1967, Indpls., Cin., 1968, Padre Farms, Key West, Fla., 1969, San Diego Padres, 1971-72; coach Montreal (Que., Can.) Expos, 1970; coach Boston Red Sox, 1974-76, mgr., 1976—; mem. minor league All-Star Teams, Hornell, N.Y., 1950, Elmira, N.Y., 1951, Mobile, Ala., 1952, St. Paul, 1953; player World Series teams, 1955, 56, 59, coach, 1975. Recipient Bill Stern award NBC, 1949; named St. Paul Rookie of Year, 1953; mem. All Star Team, 1961. Mem. Profl. Baseball Players Am. (life), Old Time Ball Players Milw. Home: 10124 Yacht Club Dr Treasure Island FL 33706 Office: 24 Yawkey Way Boston MA 02215

ZIMMERMAN, BERNARD, investment banker; b. Bklyn., Dec. 7, 1932; s. Jacob and Pearl (Schechner) Z.; B.B.A., Coll. City N.Y., 1954; M.B.A., N.Y.U., 1957; m. Joyce M. Singer, Dec. 24, 1960; children—Wayne Jay, Ellen Holly. Financial exec. consumer products Spartans, Industries, Inc., N.Y.C., 1961-65; sr. v.p. Scheinman, Hochstin, and Trotta, Inc., N.Y.C., 1965-72; pres. Bernard Zimmerman and Co., Inc., 1972—; cons. Unity Buying Service Co., Inc., Hicksville, N.Y.; dir. Commonwealth Industries, Inc., Bryn Mawr, Pa., Steelmet, Inc., Pitts., cons. Olla Industries, Inc., Weehawken, N.J. Served with AUS, 1955-57. C.P.A., N.Y. Mem. N.Y. State Soc. C.P.A.'s, Am. Arbitration Assn. Home and Office: 18 High Meadow Rd Weston CT 06883

ZIMMERMAN, CLARENCE EDGAR, surgeon; b. Lancaster, Pa., Nov. 11, 1935; s. Simon Ralph and Martha Barbara (Weaver) Z.; B.A. magna cum laude, Yale U., 1957; M.D., Harvard U., 1961; m. Catherine Hill Herget, Dec. 30, 1959 (div. 1978); children—Catherine Weaver, Isabel Christie. Intern, Peter Bent Brigham Hosp., Boston, 1961-62, resident, 1962-68: NIH research fellow in transplantation, Harvard Med. Sch., 1966-67; instr. surgery Beth Israel Hosp., Harvard Med. Sch., Boston, 1968-72, asst. prof. surgery, 1972—; dir. Harvard Transplant Service, Beth Israel Hosp., Boston, 1972—; surgeon Harvard Community Health Plan, 1971—. Developer, implementor Mass. Organ Donor-Drivers license program, 1976. NIH grantee, 1969—; Milton Fund grantee, 1969-77. Fellow ACS; mem. Assn. for Acad. Surgery, Transplantation Soc., Assn. Am. Transplant Surgeons, Boston Surg. Soc. Republican. Clubs: The Country, Seminarians. Contbr. articles to profl. jours.; author: Techniques of Patient Care, 1977. Home: 192 Mather House Harvard U Cambridge MA 02138 Office: 330 Brookline Ave Boston MA 02215

ZIMMERMAN, DANIEL DAVID, physicist; b. Shiremanstown, Pa., Mar. 8, 1920; s. Walter Stone and Daysie Jane (Russell) Z.; B.S. in Physics, Muhlenberg Coll., 1943; m. Denby Smith, Nov. 2, 1946; children—Janice Elaine, Daniel David, Roxanne Faye. Physicist, Applied Physics Lab., Johns Hopkins U., Laurel, Md., 1943, 45—, now sr. staff physicst; physicist, radiation lab. Johns Hopkins U., 1943-45; staff instr. George Washington U. Sch. Engring. and Applied Sci.; spl. lectr. dept. elec. engring. Drexel U. Recipient Merit Service award OSRD, 1945; Outstanding Contbn. award Internat. Soc. Hybrid Microelectronics, 1971, Outstanding Service awards, 1975, 76. Mem. Internat. Soc. Hybrid Microelectronics (pres. 1975-76), Am. Vacuum Soc., ASTM, Am. Inst. Physics. Contbr. numerous articles to tech. publs. in field; patentee package sealer. Home: 10420 Brookmoor Dr Silver Spring MD 20901 Office: Johns Hopkins Univ Laurel MD 20810

ZIMMERMAN, GEORGE OGUREK, physicist, educator; b. Poland, Oct. 20, 1935; s. Charles and Carolin Olga (Fisher) Z.; B.S., Yale, 1958, M.S., 1959, Ph.D. (Univ. Wilson fellow 1959-60, D. N. Clark fellow 1959-61), 1963; m. Isa Kaftal, Oct. 4, 1964. Research asso. Yale, 1962-63; asst. prof. physics Boston U., 1963-68, asso. prof., 1968-74, prof., 1974—, asso. chmn. dept. physics, 1971-72, chmn. dept., 1973—; mem. staff Nat. Magnet Lab., Cambridge, Mass., 1964, vis. scientist, 1964—; asso. physicist U. Calif. at San Diego, 1973. Research Corp. grantee, 1964-65; Air Force Office Sci. Research grantee, 1966-72; NSF grantee, 1975—. Mem. Am. Phys. Soc., N.Y. Acad. Scis., AAAS, Phi Beta Kappa. Sigma Xi. Contbr. articles on low temperature physics, phase transitions to profl. jours. Home: 88 Blueberry Ln South Hamilton MA 01982 Office: 111 Cummington St Boston MA 02215

ZIMMERMAN, JOSEPH FRANCIS, polit. scientist, educator; b. Keene, N.H., June 29, 1928; s. John Joseph and May Veronica (Gallagher) Z.; B.A., U. N.H., 1950; M.A., Syracuse U., 1951, Ph.D., 1954; m. Margaret Bernadette Brennan, Aug. 2, 1958; one dau., Deirdre Ann. Instr. govt. Worcester (Mass.) Poly. Inst., 1954-55, asst. prof., 1955-57, asso. prof., 1957-62, prof., 1962-65; lectr. Clark U., Worcester, 1957-65; prof. polit. sci. State U. N.Y. at Albany, 1965—; staff dir. N.Y. State Joint Legis. Com. Mass Transp., 1967-68; research dir., 1968-73; research dir. N.Y. State Select Legis. Com. Transp., 1973-77, N.Y. State Senate Com. on Transp., 1977—. Pres. Citizens' Plan E Assn., Worcester, 1960-62, Citizens for Neighborhood Improvement Worcester, 1957-59. Served to capt. USAF, 1951-53. Named one of three outstanding young men Worcester Jr. C. of C., 1959, 61, Mass. Jr. C. of C., 1961. Mem. Am. Polit. Sci. Assn., Am. Soc. Pub. Adminstrn., Nat. Municipal League. Roman Catholic. Club: German-Am. Social. Author: State and Local Government, 1962; The Massachusetts Town Meeting: A Tenacious Institution, 1967; The Federated City: Community Control in Large Cities, 1972; Pragmatic Federalism, The Reassignment of Functional Responsibility, 1976. Contbr. articles to profl. publs. Home: 82 Greenock Rd Delmar NY 12054 Office: Grad Sch Pub Affairs State U NY Albany ULB-96 Albany NY 12222

ZIMMERMAN, MILTON A., food co. exec.; b. Indian Mills, N.J., June 8, 1921; s. Harry W. and Florence (Miller) Z.; student Temple U., 1948-49, Rutgers U., 1950-51; M.S., Mass. Inst. Tech., 1960; m. Marjorie P. Prickett, Dec. 24, 1941; children—M. Donald, Lois M., Robert H. With Campbell Soup Co., 1940—, dir. indsl. engring., 1953-60, asst. plant mgr., 1962-65, plant mgr., 1965-67, gen. mgr. canned food prodn., 1967-70, v.p. canned food prodn., 1970-76, v.p.-personnel, 1976—. Mem. N.J. State Econ. Devel. Council. Served with USAAF, 1942-45. Mem. Am. Mgmt. Assn., Soc. Sloan Fellows, N.J. C. of C. (dir.), Nat. Indsl. Conf. Bd. Home: 23 N Riding Dr Cherry Hill NJ 08003 Office: Campbell Pl Camden NJ 08101

ZIMMERMAN, MORTIMER FRED, financial exec.; b. Bklyn., July 17, 1922; s. Isaac and Esther (Goodman) Z.; B.B.A., Coll. City N.Y., 1947; postgrad. N.Y.U., 1964-67; m. Annette Furman, Oct. 19, 1947; children—John Mitchell, Robert Peter. Controller, L. Grossman Sons, Inc. (Mass.), 1958—; treas. ABC Consol. Corp., Long Island City, N.Y., 1963—; treas. Berlo Vending Co., Confection Cabinet Corp., ABC Gladieux Corp.; v.p. finance Nytronics, Inc., 1968-70; v.p., treas., chief financial Russ Togs, Inc., Long Island City, 1970—. Lectr. Am. Mgmt. Assn., N.Y.C. Served with AUS, 1943-45. C.P.A., N.Y. Mem. Financial Execs. Inst., Am. Inst. C.P.A.'s. Jewish religion (pres. temple). Home: 5 Vista Dr Great Neck NY 11021 Office: 27-11 49th Ave Long Island City NY 11101

ZIMMERMAN, RAE, urban planner, educator; b. N.Y.C., July 9, 1943; d. Max Herman and Lillian (Langberg) Liebelson; B.A. in Chemistry, U. Calif., Berkeley, 1965; M. City Planning, U. Pa., 1969; Ph.D., Columbia U., 1972; m. Michael Zimmerman, Jan. 29, 1967; children—Gabriel, Alexa. Research asso. rent control study for N.Y.C., U. Pa. Dept. City Planning, 1968-69; research analyst dept. city planning Inst. Urban Environment, Columbia U., N.Y.C., 1969-71; asst. chief tech. br. enforcement div. regional office EPA, N.Y.C., 1971-73, cons., 1973-77; asst. prof. planning Grad. Sch. Pub. Adminstrn. N.Y. U., N.Y.C., 1973-74, asso. prof., 1974—, dir. Pub. Policy Research Inst., 1976—; cons. environ. mgmt. and planning for pub. and pvt. orgns.; project dir. N.Y. U. outreach program of areawide water quality mgmt. program for N.Y.C., 1977-78; project dir. land mgmt. and water resources project and environ. permits project Dept. Interior, 1978-79. Editorial bd. Jour. Am. Inst. Planners, 1974—; reviewer Water Resources Planning Mgmt. Tech. Jour. ASCE, 1976—; author numerous publs. in field. Office: New York Univ Grad School Pub Adminstrn Washington Sq New York City NY 10003

ZIMMERMAN, STEVEN ERNEST, counselor; b. Hagerstown, Md., May 2, 1950; s. Bernard Carroll and Helen Louise (Bostetter) Z.; A.A., Hagerstown Jr. Coll., 1971; B.A., U. Md., 1972, M.A., 1975; postgrad Johns Hopkins U., 1976—; m. Leah Mary Whaley, Nov. 16, 1971; children—Kelly Leigh. Claims underwriting ins. investigator Equifax Inc., McLean, Va., 1973-75; dir. career planning and placement Loyola Coll., Balt., 1975—, instr. Grad. Sch. Edn., 1978—. Tchr. Youth Sch., United Methodist Ch., 1969. Mem. Am. Personnel and Guidance Assn., Am. Coll. Personnel Assn., Nat. Vocat. Guidance Assn., Coll. Placement Council, Assn. Sch., Coll. and Univ. Staffing, Mid Atlantic Placement Assn., Md./D.C. Assn. Career Devel in Higher Edn., U. Md. Alumni Assn., Hagerstown Jr. Coll. Alumni Assn., Phi Theta Kappa. Democrat. Home: 10561 Twin Rivers Rd Columbia MD 21044 Office: 4501 Charles St N Baltimore MD 21210

ZIMMERMANN, CAROLINE, direct marketing advt. exec.; b. Amityville, N.Y., Oct. 19, 1944; d. H. Paul and Frances (Short) Zimmermann; B.A. in English, Ga. State U., 1966. Fulfillment mgr. book club dept. Christian Herald Pub. Co., N.Y.C., 1966-68; v.p. William Steiner Assos., Inc., N.Y.C., 1968-72; pres. Zimmermann Mktg., Inc., N.Y.C., 1973—; partner Zimmermann & Tully Co., real estate holders, 1971—; speaker in field. Author: Laetrile—Hope Or Hoax, 1977; The Super Sneaker Book, 1978; Your Child Can Be a Model, 1979. Home: 34 W 88th St New York City NY 10024 Office: 35 W 88th St New York City NY 10024

ZIMPFER, WILLIAM EDWARD, librarian, educator; b. Columbus, Ohio, June 3, 1926; s. William Herman and Grace Belle (McCoy) Z.; B.A., Capital U., 1946; M.A. in Classics, U. Mich., 1948; B.D., Evang. Luth. Sem., Columbus, 1950; M.S. in L.S., Columbia, 1964. Instr., Capital U., Columbus, 1947-48; ordained to ministry Luth. Ch., 1950; pastor St. John Luth. Ch., Pitts., 1950-60; asso. pastor Zion Luth. Ch., Pitts., 1960-62; clerical librarian Columbia, 1962-64; librarian, asst. prof. Boston U. Sch. Theology, 1964—, mng. editor faculty publ. NEXUS, 1974-78, editor, 1978—. Bd. dirs. Gen. Theol. Library, Boston. Librarian, New Eng. Meth. Hist. Soc., Boston, 1964—. Mem. ALA, Am. Theol. Library Assn. Home: 151 Bittersweet Ln 218 Randolph MA 02368 Office: 745 Commonwealth Ave Boston MA 02215

ZINBERG, MILDRED, educator; b. Peekskill, N.Y., July 12; d. Irving and Rose (Einhorn) Flamenbaum; B.A., U. Wis., 1948; M.S. (fellow), U. Pitts., 1950; Ph.D. (Vocat. Rehab. grantee, NDEA fellow), City U. N.Y., 1969; m. Eugene Zinberg, Mar. 11, 1951; children—David, Helene, Adele. Speech and hearing pathologist, instr. speech Queens Coll., 1950-52; private practice speech and hearing therapy, N.Y.C., 1950—; prof. English and speech, dept. speech communication and theatre arts Queensborough Community Coll. of City U. N.Y., Bayside, 1962—, dir. speech clinic, 1974—. Lic. speech pathologist, N.Y. Mem. Am. Speech and Hearing Assn. (certified speech pathologist), Acoustical Soc. Am. (v.p. Met. N.Y. chpt.), Nat. Council Jewish Women, ACLU, LWV, AAUP, N.Y. State, L.I. speech and hearing assns. Home: 1071 Denton Ave New Hyde Park NY 11040

ZINK, LUBOR JAN, journalist, author; b. Klapy, Czechoslovakia, Sept. 20, 1920; s. Vilem and Bozena (Wohl) Z.; naturalized Brit. citizen, 1949, Canadian citizen, 1963; student Prague Sch. Econs., 1937-39, 1945-48; m. Zora Nechvile, Apr. 1, 1942; 1 son, Alec Guy. Info. Officer Ministry Fgn. Affairs, Prague, Czechoslovakia, 1945-48; monitor, broadcaster, BBC, Eng., 1948-51; polit. and econ. analyst Allied Authorities, W.Ger., 1951-57; editorial page editor Brandon (Man., Can.) Sun, 1958-62; polit. columnist Toronto (Ont., Can.) Telegram, 1962-71; polit. columnist Toronto Sun, 1971—; radio and TV commentaries. Progressive Conservative candidate Parliament, 1972, 74. Served to 1st lt. Czechoslovak Brigade, Brit. Army, 1940-45. Decorated Mil. Cross, medal for Bravery; recipient Canadian Nat. Newspaper award, 1961, Bowater award for Journalism, 1962. Mem. Parliamentary Press Gallery, Royal Canadian Legion. Author: The Uprooted, 1962; Under the Mushroom Cloud, 1962; Trudeaucracy, 1972; Viva Chairman Pierre, 1977; also novels (2) and books of poetry (4) in Czech. Home: 47 Queensline Dr Ottawa ON K2H 7J3 Canada Office: Parliamentary Press Gallery House of Commons Ottawa ON Canada

ZINKEVICH, FREDERICK NICHOLAS, metall. engr.; b. Brockton, Mass., Mar. 5, 1946; s. Fred C. and Helen (Douzanis) Z.; B.S. in Materials Sci. and Engring., Cornell U., 1968; m. Sandra Coughlin, Dec. 24, 1976; children—Frederick N., Jr., Heidi Lynn, Robert C. Metall. foreman U.S. Steel Corp., Gary, Ind., 1968-70, product metallurgist, 1970-72; sr. metallurgist ITT Grinnell Corp., Providence, R.I., 1972-75, mgr. standards, research, devel. and engring., 1975—, cons. to various divs. Recipient ITT quality citation, 1978. Mem. ASME, Am. Welding Soc., Am. Soc. Metals. Home: 53 N Main St Uxbridge MA 01569 Office: ITT Grinnell Corp 260 W Exchange St Providence RI 02901

ZINKHAM, RONALD LEE, ednl. adminstr.; b. Zelienople, Pa., Jan. 13, 1934; s. Benjamin Franklin and Iva Marie (Keefer) Z.; B.S., Slippery Rock State Coll., 1955; M.S. in Math., U. Pitts., 1960; m. Barbara Lee Brew, June 30, 1956; 1 dau., Lee Ann. Tchr. math. and sci. Shenango High Sch., New Castle, Pa., 1955-66; tchr. math. Seneca Valley Sr. High Sch., Harmony, Pa., 1966-67, prin., 1967—. NSF grantee, 1958. Mem. Nat., Pa. assns. secondary sch. prins. Club: Lions (pres. Zelienople chpt. 1966). Home: RD 2 Box 113 Harmony PA 16037 Office: RD 2 Harmony PA 16037

ZINMAN, JACQUES, ins. agy. exec.; b. Phila., Nov. 7, 1922; B.S., U. Va., 1943; postgrad. U. Pa., 1945-46. Pres. Zinman Group, ins. agy., 1950—; pres. Frankford Union Ins. Co. Presdl. elector Commonwealth of Pa., 1972. Bd. dirs., exec. com. Fedn. Jewish Charities. Mem. exec. com. Pa. Republican Finance Com. Served to ensign USNR, 1943-44. Recipient Outstanding Young Man Phila. award Jewish Nat. Fund, 1961. Mem. Ins. Soc. Phila., United Hunts Racing Assn. Club: Masons. Contbr. articles to profl. jours. Office: 309 Old York Rd Jenkintown PA 19046

ZINN, KEITH MARSHALL, surgeon, educator; b. Bklyn., Oct. 15, 1940; s. Victor and Eve (Lane) Z.; student N.Y. U., 1958-61; M.D. with honors in Pediatrics and Psychiatry, Downstate Med. Center, State U. N.Y., Bklyn., 1965. Intern, St. Luke's Hosp., N.Y.C., 1965-66; research asso. NIH, Bethesda, Md., 1966-68; research asso., NIH postdoctoral fellow dept. ophthalmology Harvard Med. Sch., 1968, Heed ophthalmic fellow, 1972-73; research asso., NIH postdoctoral fellow dept. corneal research Retina Found., Boston, 1968-69, research asso. dept. retina research, 1972-73; asst. resident to chief resident in ophthalmology Mt. Sinai Hosp., N.Y.C., 1969-71; Ednl. fellow dept. ophthalmology Mt. Sinai Sch. Medicine, 1971-72; chief clin. fellow retina service Mass. Eye & Ear Infirmary, Boston, 1972-73; dir. lab. for ocular fine structure dept. ophthalmology Mt. Sinai Sch. Medicine, N.Y.C., 1969—, instr., 1971-72, asst. prof., 1973-76, dir. resident edn., 1973-75, dir. ultrasonography lab., 1974, dir. retinal research unit, 1974—, asso. clin. prof., 1976—; clin. asst. ophthalmology Mt. Sinai Hosp., N.Y.C., 1969-72, asst. attending ophthalmologist, 1973-76, asso. attending ophthalmologist, 1976—; asst. attending ophthalmologist VA Hosp., Bronx, N.Y., 1974—, Elmhurst Gen. Hosp., N.Y.C., 1974—; cons. dept. ophthalmology Hosp. for Joint Diseases, N.Y.C., 1975—, career devel. program depts. medicine and surgery VA, Washington, 1976—; lectr. in field. Served with USPHS, 1966-68. Recipient George Schwartz prize in biology N.Y. U., 1961; licensed physician, N.Y., Calif. Diplomate Am. Bd. Ophthalmology. Fellow A.C.S., Internat. Coll. Surgeons, Pan.-Am. Assn. Ophthalmology, N.Y. Soc. Clin. Ophthalmology, Internat. Eye Found., Soc. Eye Surgeons, Am. Acad. Ophthalmology and Otolaryngology, N.Y. Acad. Medicine (William H. Hopper award 1971), Soc. for Heed Fellows; mem. Downstate Med. Coll. Alumni Assn., Mt. Sinai Hosp. Alumni Assn., Mass. Eye and Ear Infirmary Alumni Assn., N.Y. State Med. Soc., AMA (Physician's Recognition award 1971, 76), Assn. Research in Vision and Ophthalmology, Am. Assn. Ophthalmology, Research to Prevent Blindness (ophthal. asso.). Jewish. Author: The Pupil, 1972; contbr. numerous articles in field to med. jours.; editorial cons. Internat. Ophthalmology Clinics, 1971-73; reviewer Archives of Ophthalmology, 1972-75, Investigative Ophthalmology, 1975-76; contbg. editor, mem. editorial bd. Mt. Sinai Jour. Medicine, 1975—. Home: 125 E 87th St New York City NY 10028 Office: 1044 5th Ave New York City NY 10028

ZINN, WILLIAM, violinist, composer, bus. exec.; b. N.Y.C., Nov. 19, 1924; s. Philip and Anna (Miller) Z.; student State U. N.Y., 1952-54; m. Sophia Kalish, July 11, 1948; children—Karen Zinn Swaine, David Benjamin. Violinist, Balt. Symphony, 1944-45, Indpls. Symphony, 1945-46, Ft. Wayne Philharmonic, 1946-47, Pitts. Symphony, 1947-49, Mpls. Symphony, 1950-51; concertmaster New Britain (Conn.) Symphony, 1968—, Queens Symphony, 1969-71, Ridgefield (Conn.) Symphony, 1973—, Chappaqua (N.Y.) Symphony, 1976; soloist with orchs., on records, on radio and in recitals; founder Masterwork Piano Trio, Masterwork Piano Quartet, Classical String Quartet, Zinn's Ragtime String Quartet, Queens Festival Orch., Bayside, N.Y., 1965, Asociacion Musical William Zinn, Caracas, Venezuela, 1968, Vitametrics of Am., 1976, Internat. Symphony for World Peace, 1978; tchr. mech. drafting Mondell Inst., 1956; coach ensembles for Chamber Music Assos., 1973—; engr. N.Y.C. Bd. Edn. 1951-57, Bodin-Zinn Corp., 1957-58, Chem. Constrn. Corp., 1958-59; pres. Zinn Originals, Inc., 1959-68, Sparx, Inc., Trademark Hall of Fame, Inc., Nice Realty Corp., MFW Restaurant Corp.; sec.-treas. Spark Industries, Inc. Mem. ASCAP, Internat. Platform Assn., Am. Fedn. Musicians, Am. Humanist Assn. (N.Y. chpt.). Author: (with Edward Gordon) Themography, 1947; (with Dr. George S. Grosser) Vitametrics I, the Human Formula for Self-Evaluation, 1976, Vitametrics II, the Human Formula for

Self-Improvement, 1978. Composer: Chromatique (perpetual movement for woodwinds, strings and percussion), 1946, Piccolo Concerto, 1948, Violin Concerto, 1950, String Quartet, 1963, Chopinesque (piano solo), 1965, Ballet (night creatures), 1966 Andante for Strings, 1967, Concerto for Octahorn, 1976, The International Anthem For World Peace, 1977, String Symphony, 1977. Pioneer numerous products for home, personal, automobile and novelty use. Home: 35-19 215th Pl Bayside NY 11361

ZINNINGER, GEORGE FREDERICK, radiation oncologist: b. Cin., Aug. 26, 1933; s. Max Maser and Elizabeth Archer (Kennedy) Z.; A.B., Harvard U., 1955, M.S., 1970; M.D., U. Cin., 1959; m. Marie Daymon, Sept. 6, 1960; children—Elizabeth, George, Martha. Intern, State U. Iowa Hosps., Iowa City, 1959-60; resident in internal medicine Cin. Gen. Hosp., 1960-61; resident in radiology Mass. Gen. Hosp., 1963-66; asst. radiologist Mass. Gen. Hosp., Boston, 1966-71; asst. prof. radiation therapy Harvard Med. Sch., Boston, 1966-71; radiation therapist Thomas Jefferson U., Phila., 1971-75, asso. prof. radiation therapy, 1971—; chief radiation oncology Cooper Med. Center, Camden, N.J., 1975—. Bd. trustees Am. Cancer Soc., N.J. div., 1976. Served with USN, 1961-63. Recipient Physicians Recognition award, Am. Med. Assn., 1976; Nat. Cancer Inst. spl. fellow, 1970. Mem. Am. Med. Assn., Am. Soc. Therapeutic Radiologists, Radiol. Soc. N. Am., Radiation Research Soc., Alpha Omega Alpha. Club: Rotary. Editor: High Energy Photons and Electrons, 1976; contbr. Management of the Patient with Cancer, 1976. Home: 1016 Park Blvd Cherry Hill NJ 08002 Office: Cooper Med Center and Hosp Camden NJ 08103

ZINZ, DAVID ALBERT, photographer; b. Philipsburg, Pa., Nov. 2, 1952; s. Albert Calvin and Dolores Aleda (Helwig) Z.; student Pa. State U., 1970-72; diploma in profl. photography Sch. Modern Photography, 1976; student Winona Sch. Profl. Photography, 1974-75. Owner, mgr. David A. Zinz Photography, Winburne, Pa., 1973—; photog. lab. specialist Tallamy, Van Kuren, Gertis & Thielman, Engrs. and Surveyors, Orchard Park, N.Y. and Lanse Aerial Surveys, (Pa.); cons. West Branch Area High Sch. Yearbook Staff; photog. cons. to area rep. Taylor Pub. Co. Mem. Profl. Photographers Am., Wedding Photographers Am., Am. Film Inst., Nat. Small Bus. Assn., Smithsonian Assos., Cousteau Soc., Am. Motorcyclist Assn., U.S. CB Radio Assn. Home: PO Box 171 Winburne PA 16879 Office: 1 Trolley St Winburne PA 16879

ZIPP, ALAN STEVEN, accountant; b. Miami, Fla., Oct. 29, 1948; s. Monroe and Edith (Shier) Z.; B.S. in Accounting and Finance, U. Tenn., 1970; postgrad. (GAO fellow) systems info. program Wharton Sch. U. Pa., 1978; m. Paula Ann Mitchell, Aug. 19, 1971; 1 son, David Alan. Accountant, supervisory auditor U.S. GAO, Washington, 1971—; investigative auditor U.S. Office Fed. Elections, Washington, 1972; asso. Arthur Andersen & Co., Washington, 1972-73; partner Godbout and Zipp, Silver Spring, Md., 1973-74; teaching cons. Tulane U.; instr. accounting Prince George's Coll.; spl. cons., select com. on aging U.S. Ho. of Reps., 1976—; Bd. dirs. D.C. Grotto, 1975. Recipient Meritorious Service award Comptroller Gen. U.S., 1974, cash award U.S. GAO, 1975; C.P.A., Md. Mem. Am. Inst. C.P.A.'s, Nat. Assn. Accountants, Assn. Govt. Accountants, Md. Assn. C.P.A.'s, Nat. Soc. Pub. Accountants, Silver Spring Jaycees (dir. 1972-73), Nat. Speleological Soc. Republican. Author numerous reports to Congress; testified before congressional coms., 1974, 75, 76. Home: 2425 White Horse Ln Silver Spring MD 20906 Office: 441 G St NW Washington DC 20548

ZIPPEL, MARY-ELLA HOLST, ch. ofcl.; b. Detroit, Oct. 12, 1934; d. Spencer and Ruth Catherine (McCullough) Holst; B.A., U. Toledo, 1959; M.A., N.Y. U., 1970; m. Bert Zippel, Jan. 18, 1969; children—Patricia Hall, Darcy Hall. Sr. counselor, employment specialist N.Y. Dept. Labor, N.Y.C., 1962-75; religious edn. dir. Unitarian Ch. of All Souls, N.Y.C., 1976—. Mem. Nat. Vocat. Guidance Assn., Am. Personnel and Guidance Assn. Unitarian Universalist. Home: 150-74 Village Rd Jamaica NY 11432 Office: Unitarian Church of All Souls 1157 Lexington Ave New York City NY 10021

ZIPPER, HOWARD DAVID, physician; b. Oceanside, N.Y., Sept. 17, 1936; s. Joseph L. and Lillian (Ostroff) Z.; B.S., Phila. Coll. Pharmacy and Sci., 1957; student Columbia U., 1960; M.D., Downstate Med. Sch., State U. N.Y., 1964; m. Susan B. Glaser, May 15, 1959; children—Jeffrey Alan, Dale Beth. Intern, The N.Y. Hosp., Cornell Med. Center, 1964-65; resident surgery Kings County Hosp., Downstate Med. Center, N.Y., 1965-66; resident ENT, L.I. Coll. Hosp., 1966-68; chief resident ENT, Roosevelt Hosp., N.Y.C., 1968-69; asst. otolaryngologist Presbyn. Hosp., N.Y.C., 1969—; clin. instr. otolaryngology Coll. Physicians and Surgeons, Columbia U., 1969—; pvt. practice medicine specializing in otolaryngol. surgery, Lawrence, N.Y., 1969—; mem. staff S. Nassau Community Hosp., Peninsula Gen. Hosp., Rockaway, N.Y., St. John Hosp., Far Rockaway, N.Y., Long Beach (N.Y.) Meml. Hosp. Judge, Miss Long Island for Miss Am. Beauty Pageant, 1977. Mem. Nassau County Med. Soc., Nassau Otolaryngol. Soc., AMA, Am. Acad. Facial and Reconstructive Plastic Surgery, Am. Council Otolaryngology. Club: N.Y. Exchange (pres. state 1977-78). Office: 100 Barrett Rd Lawrence NY 11559

ZIPPER, MILTON, accountant; b. Oyster Bay, N.Y., Apr. 20, 1917; s. Samuel and Rose (Baker) Z.; B.S., Columbia, 1939; m. Bernice Horeis, Sept. 1, 1945; children—Carol Lee, Lorie Sue, Devie Lynn. Accountant, Leo T. Abbe, C.P.A.'s, N.Y.C., 1939-41; chief accountant Johnson, Drake & Piper Inc., Africa, 1941-43; asst. chief accountant Fgn. Econ. Adminstrn., N.Y.C., 1943-45; accountant Price Waterhouse & Co., N.Y.C., also Venezuela, 1945-49; pvt. practice accounting, Oyster Bay, 1949—; lectr. in field. C.P.A., N.Y. Mem. Oyster Bay C. of C., Am. Inst. C.P.A.'s, N.Y. State Soc. C.P.A.'s (pres. Nassau-Suffolk chpt. 1973-74), Nat. Assn. Accountants (pres. L.I. chpt. 1958-59). Clubs: Princeton, Rotary (dist. gov. 1961-62). Contbg. author Enc. Accounting Systems, 1976. Home: 2 Meudon Dr Locust Valley NY 11560 Office: 37 E Main St Oyster Bay NY 11771

ZITO, ROBERT JOSEPH, psychologist, educator; b. Newark, Feb. 28, 1937; s. James M. and Anna (Bilancia) Z.; B.A., Montclair State Coll.; M.A., George Peabody Coll.; Ed.D., Rutgers U.; m. Kathleen Carriere, Sept. 16, 1959; children—Allison, Michael, Marcella. Gen. practice psychology, 1963—; psychologist Elizabeth (N.J.) Schs., 1961-65; supr. counseling Kilmer (N.J.) Job Corps Center, 1965-66; dir. psychol. services Lawrence Twp. (N.J.) Schs., 1966-68; instr. Rutgers U., 1966-71; asso. prof. psychology Kean Coll. N.J., 1968—; pres. Smokers Control Centers; cons. Edison Nursing Home, Diet Control Centers, East Brunswick (N.J.) Police Dept., East Brunswick pub. schs., N.J. State Home for Girls, Mt. Carmel Guild, N.J. Civil Rights Commn. NIMH fellow, 1959; Phi Delta Kappa Research awardee, 1967; Am. Rehab. Counseling Research awardee, 1970. Mem. Am., N.J. psychol. assns., N.J. Soc. Clin. Hypnosis. Unitarian. Contbr. articles to profl. jours. Home: 71 Woodbridge Ave Highland Park NJ 08904 Office: 24 N 3d Ave Highland Park NJ 08904

ZITRON, BENJAMIN CHARLES, systems mgmt. co. exec.; b. Milw., Feb. 21, 1937; s. Arthur and Sarah (Brodsky) Z.; B.A., Yale U., 1960; postgrad. N.Y. U. Law Sch., 1962; m. Sharon Barr, June 19, 1960; children—Anne E., Jennifer. Systems analyst William S. Morris & Co., N.Y.C., 1962-64; systems engr. IBM Corp., N.Y.C., 1964-66; pres. Data Network Corp., N.Y.C., 1966-67; chmn. bd., pres. Allied Mgmt. & Systems Corp., N.Y.C., 1968—; former dir. Congressional Life Ins. Co., Sinnet Industries, Inc., South Chgo. Packing Co.; dir. Computer Methods Corp., Cassette Scis. Corp., Zitron Galleries Corp., Jeanskin Internat., Inc. Mem. Yale Com. on Enrollment and Scholarships, Wis., 1961-62; patron Lincoln Center Performing Arts, N.Y. Philharmonic Soc.; benefactor City Center N.Y. Recipient Commendation medal N.Y.C. Dept. Commerce, 1966. Mem. Assn. Systems Mgmt., Am. Mgmt. Assn. Jewish. Club: Yale (N.Y.C.). Patentee in field. Home: 211 E 70th St New York City NY 10021 Office: 114 E 32d St New York City NY 10016

ZLOTNICK, BERNARD, advt. agy. exec.; b. Bklyn., Nov. 23, 1935; s. Maurice and Sylvia (Levine) Z.; student Sch. Visual Art, 1953-56; m. Barbara Zickerman, Aug. 17, 1958; children—Steven, Michael. Art dir. Sudler & Hennessey, Advt., N.Y.C., 1957-66; creative dir. Young & Rubicam Internat., N.Y.C., 1966-71; exec. v.p. Barnett Zlotnick, Inc., N.Y.C., 1971-76; creative dir., sr. v.p. Leber Katz Partners, N.Y.C., 1976—; columnist trade publ. Art Direction mag., 1970—. Served with AUS, 1957-58. Mem. Art Dirs. Club N.Y. (numerous awards), Soc. Illustrators, Sch. Visual Arts Alumni Assn. (pres. 1976-77).

ZLOTOWITZ, BERNARD M., rabbi; b. N.Y.C., July 11, 1925; s. Aron and Fannie (Pasternak) Z.; B.A., Bklyn. Coll., 1948; M.A., Columbia U., 1965; B.H.L., Hebrew Union Coll.-Jewish Inst. Religion, N.Y.C., 1953, rabbi, M.H.L., 1955, D.H.L., 1974; m. Shirley Masef, June 12, 1949; children—Debra, Robin, Richard C., Alice R. Rabbi congregations in N.Y., N.C. and N.J., 1955-75; regional dir. Met. Council of Union Am. Hebrew Congregations, N.Y.C., 1975—; lectr. Bible, Hebrew Union Coll.-Jewish Inst. Religion, 1962-72; adj. asst. prof. religion C.W. Post Coll., 1968-72, U. N.C., Charlotte, 1973-74; lectr. Bibl. archaeology Jewish Museum, N.Y.C., 1972, Charlotte Mus., 1973; lectr: Hebrew Union Coll., 1977—. Bd. dirs. Nyack (N.Y.) Hosp., 1959-61. Mem. Internat. Orgn. Masoretic Studies (treas. 1972—), Central Conf. Am. Rabbis, N.J. Assn. Reform Rabbis, N.Y. Bd. Rabbis (exec. com. 1957-62), Am. Schs. Oriental Research, Am. Oriental Soc., AAUP, Asssn. Reform Rabbis N.Y.C. and Vicinity. Clubs: Masons, K.P., Rotary. Author: Folkways and Minhagim, 1970; Art in Judaism, 1975. Home: 15 Aberdeen Pl Fair Lawn NJ 07410 Office: 838 Fifth Ave New York City NY 10021

ZOHAR, URI, economist, educator; b. Haifa, Israel, Oct. 26, 1931; s. Amram and Ada (Kurash) Z.; B.Sc., Cal. Poly. U., 1964; M.A., Claremont Grad. Sch. and Univ. Center, 1965, Ph.D. (fellow), 1967; m. Shlomit Dital, Aug. 10, 1954; children—Asaf, Dawn Ayelet, Lilah Hiedy. Prof. econs. and adminstrv. studies York U., Toronto, Ont., Can., 1969—. Cons. on spl. projects of econ. planning UN Conf. Trade and Devel., N.Y.C., 1969-74; sr. cons. Can. Internat. Devel. Agy., Toronto, Nairobi, Kenya, 1969-73; chief cons. nat. transport planning Can. Transport Commn. and Can. Ministry Transport, Ottawa, Ont., 1973—; pres. Zohar Cons. Ltd., Willowdale, Ont., 1970—. Ford Found. research grantee York U., 1969-74; Mem. Am. Econ. Soc., Econometric Soc., Can., Eastern, Western econ. assns., Can. Profs. Assn., Alpha Zeta, Gamma Sigma Delta, Pi Gamma Mu. Author: Consumption and Saving in Developing Countries, 1968; Project Selection for National Plans, 1974; The Impact Approach to Project Selection, 1974; Economic Forecasting Model: Demand for Freight Transport in Canada, 1976; contbr. articles to profl. jours. Home: 15 Wembley Rd Toronto ON M6C 2E8 Canada Office: POB 375 Willowdale ON Canada

ZOMORRODIAN, SHAHNAZ ERFANI, pediatrician; b. Tehran, Iran, Oct. 25, 1944; s. Abdolhossain and Sedigheh (Hariri) Z.; M.D., Tehran U., 1970; m. Mohammad Hafez Erfani, June 6, 1969; children—Sadi, Seamae. Intern, Queens Gen. Hosp., N.Y.C., 1971-72; resident pediatrics N.Y. Polyclinic Hosp., N.Y.C., 1972-74; practice medicine specializing in pediatrics. Diplomate Am. Bd. Pediatrics. Fellow Am. Acad. Pediatrics (asso.). Home: 5 Tisdale Rd Scarsdale NY 10583

ZOPPO, JEROME JOE, marriage and family therapist; b. Caserta, Italy, July 7, 1928; s. Ralph Romualdo and Romilda (Veccia) Z.; A.B., Rutgers U., 1952, M.Ed., 1959; children—Darien Jay, Clifford Scott, Jennifer. Tchr. Midland Park (N.J.) Jr.-Sr. High Sch., 1957-59; counselor Youth Opportunity Center, Paterson, N.J., 1962-67; supervising psychologist Child Advancement Center, Watchung, N.J., 1969-76; clin. psychologist Cliffs Sch., Westwood, N.J., 1967-69; propr. Alpha Counseling Service, Leonia, N.J., 1959—; program devel. specialist Div. Mental Health and Hosps., Trenton, N.J., 1977—. Chmn. Waldwick Zoning Bd., 1954-60; exec. sec. Waldwick Planning Bd., 1955-60; chmn. Waldwick Assessment Com., 1956-58. Served with AUS, World War II. Licensed marriage and family counselor, sch. psychologist, ednl. and vocat. counselor, secondary sch. tchr.; licensed in group relations. Mem. Am. Psychol. Assn., Soc. Sci. Study Sex (pres. Eastern regional chpt.), Am. Assn. Sex Educators, Counselors and Therapists, Leonia C. of C., Rutgers U. Alumni Assn. Home: 244 Fort Lee Rd Leonia NJ 07605 Office: 244 Ft Lee Rd Leonia NJ 07605

ZOSA, ANGELO MARIO MERCADO, psychiatrist; b. Cebu City, Philippines, May 31, 1938; s. Manuel Alvarez and Amparo Sison (Mercado) Z.; A.A., U. St. Tomas, Manila, 1955, M.D. cum laude, 1960; m. Nancy Elizabeth Schadt, Apr. 29, 1967; children—Michael Angelo, Jennifer Ann, Christopher Francis, Kathryn Marie. Intern, USAF Hosp., Clark AFB, 1959-60; resident U. Kans. Med. Center, Kansas City, 1961-64, Phila. Gen. Hosp., 1964-66, Temple U. Hosp., Phila., 1966-67; dir. night partial hosp. program Temple U. Mental Health Center, Phila., 1967-72; dir. base service unit N.W. Center for Mental Helath, Phila., 1971-73; staff psychiatrist Abington Mental Health Center, Pa., 1973; med. dir. Montgomery County MH/MR Emergency Service, Norristown, Pa., 1973—; clin. asst. prof. psychiatry Temple U. Med. Sch.; bd. dirs. Hedwig House, Norristown, 1977—, Horsham Clinic, Ambler, Pa., 1978—; mem. Comm. on Drug and Alcohol Abuse, Montgomery County Med. Soc., 1974-77, Commn. on Mental Health, 1978—; mem. psychiat. com. Montgomery-Bucks PSRO, 1978—. Diplomate Am. Bd. Psychiatry and Neurology. Mem. Am., Pa. psychiat. socs., AMA, Assn. of Mental Health Adminstrs., Behavior Therapy and Research Soc., Pa. Med. Soc. Democrat. Roman Catholic. Contbr. articles to profl. jours. Home: 300 Bent Rd Wyncote PA 19095 Office: Wyncote House Twp Line and Washington Ln Wyncote PA 19095

ZOSS, ABRAHAM OSCAR, chem. co. exec.; b. South Bend, Ind., Feb. 17, 1917; s. Harry and Fannie (Friedman) Z.; B.S. in Chem. Engring., U. Notre Dame, 1938, M.S., 1939, Ph.D., 1941; m. Betty Jane Hurwich, Dec. 24, 1939; children—Roger, Joel, Hope Zoss Schladen; m. 2d, Magda Szanto, May 1978. With Gen. Aniline & Film Corp., Easton, Pa., 1941-54, tech. mgr., Linden, N.J., 1954-55, plant mgr., 1955-57; mgr. mfg. adminstrn., chem. div. MMinn. Mining and Mfg. Co., St. Paul, 1957-58, prodn. mgr. chem. div., 1958-60; v.p. Photek Inc., West Kingston, R.I., 1960-62; asst. corp. tech. dir. Celanese Corp., N.Y.C., 1962-65, corp. tech. dir., 1965-66, corp. dir. comml. devel., 1966-69; v.p. corp. devel. Tenneco Chems. Inc., N.Y.C., 1969-71, Universal Oil Products Co., Des Plaines, Ill., 1971-72; group v.p. Engelhard Industries div. Engelhard Minerals & Chem. Corp., Murray Hill, N.J., 1972-74, v.p. bus. devel., 1974-77; v.p. corp. devel. Chem. and Pollution Scis., Inc., Old Bridge, N.J., 1977—, dir., chief adminstrv. officer, 1978—; mem. field info. agy. Office Tech. Service, Commerce Dept., Europe, 1946. Recipient Centennial Sci. award U. Notre Dame, 1965. Fellow Am. Inst. Chemists (profl. chemist), AAAS; mem. Am. Chem. Soc., Am. Inst. Chem. Engring., N.Y. Acad. Scis., Comml. Devel. Assn., Soc. Chem. Industry, Catalysis Soc. N.Y., Assn. Corp. Growth, Nat. Planning Assn., Newcomen Soc. N.Am., Chemists Club N.Y.C., Met. Mus. Art N.Y.C., Mus. Modern Art N.Y.C. Club: B'nai B'rith. Contbr. articles to profl. jours. Patentee in field. Home: Claridge House I Apt 505 Verona NJ 07044 Office: PO Box 162 Old Bridge NJ 08857

ZOUARY, MAURICE H., film producer, TV producer; b. Bklyn., N.Y., July 17, 1921; s. Ellie Louis and Marie Louise Z.; student N.Y. Sch. of Indsl. Art and Design, 1937-39; m. Edith Brueckner, Feb. 3, 1959. Gen. asst. Randforce Amusement Theatre, N.Y.C., 1936-39, Translux Theatre, Circuit, N.Y.C., 1940-42; arts and media Buchanan Advt., N.Y.C., 1944-47; designer Egmont Arens Indsl. Design, N.Y.C., 1947-49; writer of film commercials Grey Advt. Agy., N.Y.C., N.Y., 1951-54; producer TV programs for various TV shows, N.Y. and Hollywood, 1949-51; founder Filmvideo Releasing Corp., N.Y.C., 1957, producer, 1957—; cons. to NBC and CBS, 1960—; pres. TV Nat. Releasing Corp., 1974—; lectr. on history of motion picture sound to various colls., 1968—. Served with USNR, 1942-43, C.E., U.S. Army, 1942-44. Mem. Internat. Radio and TV Soc., Nat. Assn. of TV Program Execs., Nat. Acad. of TV Arts and Scis., The DeForest Pioneers (award 1976), The Motion Picture Pioneers. Republican. Contbr. articles on pioneering of DeForest's synchronized sound on film, on history of entertainment as relates to communication media. Home: 56 Marlborough Rd Brooklyn NY 11226 Office: 37 W 57th St New York City NY 10019

ZSOLDOS, FRANK, chemist; b. N.Y.C., Jan. 14, 1925; s. Frank and Elizabeth (Schimpf) Z.; B.A., City U. N.Y., 1949; m. Eileen W. Kinsley, Aug. 29, 1959 (dec. 1971); children—Frank Joseph, Eileen Marie. Chemist, Ciba Pharms. Inc., N.Y.C., 1951, Heliogen Products Inc., L.I. City, N.Y., 1952-56, S.B. Penick & Co., N.Y.C., 1956-59, Voldale Inc., L.I. City, 1959-63, Hydrosan Inc., Ho-Ho-Kus, N.J., 1963-64, Robert Clare Inc., Denville, N.J., 1964-67; chief chemist Marotta Sci. Controls Inc., Boonton, N.J., 1967—; dir. research Eco Scis. Inc., Boonton, 1972—. Mem. Nat. Sanitation Found. (adv. com. swimming pool water chems. and processes 1968). Republican. Contbr. articles to sci. jours. and books; patentee procedure for water treatment. Home: 73 Florence Ave Denville NJ 07834 Office: 1500 Boonton Ave Boonton NJ 07005

ZUCCARELLI, FRANK EDWARD, artist; b. Olyphant, Pa., Oct. 23, 1921; s. Louis Ferdinand and Maria Jasimine (Fazzone) Z.; student Newark Sch. Fine and Indsl. Art, 1948, Art Students League, 1961; B.A., Kean Coll.; m. Audrey A. Clifton, July 19, 1958. Free lance artist and illustrator, N.J. and N.Y. 1949—; exhibited in group shows Salmagundi Club, N.Y.C., Lever House, N.Y.C., Am. Artists Profl. League, Nat. Arts Club, Pastel Soc. Am., Newark Mus., Pentagon, Washington, Navy Art Gallery, Washington, Overseas Press Club, N.Y.C.; represented in permanent collections U.S. Navy, Abe Sharpe Found.; instr. pictorial illustration, oil painting and life drawing Spectrum Inst. for the Advt. Arts, Somerville, N.J.; mem. Navy Art Cooperation and Liaison, Salmagundi Club, 1970—; ofcl. artist U.S. Navy. Served with USMC, 1942-45. Recipient Salmagundi Club prize, 1977. Fellow Am. Artist Profl. League; mem. Pastel Soc. Am., Artists Fellowship Inc. Club: Salmagundi (N.Y.C.). Home: 61 Appleman Rd Somerset NJ 08873 Office: 61 Appleman Rd Somerset NJ 08873

ZUCHNIEWICZ, ALEXANDER JOSEPH, airport ofcl.; b. Bayonne, N.J., Apr. 12, 1944; s. Alexander Albert and Josephine (Szlasa) Z.; student Fairleigh Dickinson U., 1978—; m. Martina Deptula, Feb. 15, 1970; children—Dean, Randy. With Port Authority of N.Y. and N.J., 1963-70, airport ops. supr., Teterboro (N.J.) Airport, 1974—. Advisor aviation Explorers div. Bergen council Boy Scouts Am., 1973—; v.p. Linden (N.J.) Vol. Ambulance Corps, 1975-77. Mem. Air Force Assn., Smithsonian Assos., Am. Assn. Airport Execs. Home: 308 E Elm St Linden NJ 07036 Office: 399 Industrial Ave Teterboro NJ 07608

ZUCK, ALFRED CHRISTIAN, cons. mech. engr.; b. Ridgefield, N.J., Dec. 16, 1924; s. Fredrick William and Margaret Christine (Umland) Z.; M.E., Poly. Inst. Bklyn., 1960; m. Vilma B. Zuck, May 6, 1951; children—Allyson, Jon, Randall. Designer, Syska & Hennessy, Inc., N.Y.C., 1946-52, partner, 1952-66, v.p., 1966-73, sr. v.p., 1973-78; prin. Edwards & Zuck, P.C., 1978—; nat. panel Am. Arbitration Assn. Served with U.S. Army, 1943-46, to 1st lt. USAF, 1951-52, to capt. Air N.G., 1948-56. Decorated 2 Bronze Stars; registered profl. engr., Calif., Conn., Del., Fla., Ga., Ill., Maine, Mass., Mich., N.J., N.Mex., N.Y., N.C., Ohio, Pa., Tenn., Tex., Utah, Vt., Wis., Wash.; registered engr. Nat. Council Engring. Examiners; licensed profl. planner, N.J. Mem. Nat., N.Y. (past chmn.) socs. profl. engrs., Profl. Engrs. in Pvt. Practice, Am. Cons. Engrs. Council, N.Y. Assn. Cons. Engrs. (past v.p. and dir.), Am. Soc. Mil. Engrs., Am. Soc. Heating, Refrigeration and Air Conditioning Engrs., N.Y. Bldg. Congress. Lutheran. Club: N.Y. Athletic. Home: 444 Weymouth Dr Wyckoff NJ 07481 Office: 300 E 42d St New York NY 10017

ZUCKER, ARNOLD HARRIS, psychiatrist, psychoanalyst, educator; b. Bklyn., July 29, 1930; s. Charles Israel and Bertha (Leff) Z.; B.A., Bklyn. Coll., 1950; M.D., State U. N.Y. Downstate Med. Center, Bklyn., 1954; certificate in psychoanalysis, Columbia, 1971; m. Marilyn Pistreich, June 10, 1962; children—Harvey Alan, Deborah, Shoshanna, David Michael. Intern, USPHS, 1954-55; resident Kings County Hosp., Bklyn., 1955-56, Southwestern Med. Sch., Dallas, 1958-59, Albert Einstein Coll. Medicine, Bronx, N.Y., 1959-60; practice medicine, specializing in psychiatry and psychoanalysis, Mt. Vernon, N.Y., 1960—; asso. prof. pastoral counseling Iona Coll., 1968—; mem. staff Mt. Vernon Hosp.; asst. clin. prof. psychiatry Albert Einstein Coll. Medicine, 1968—. Served with USPHS, 1956-58. Diplomate Am. Bd. Psychiatry and Neurology. Fellow Am. Psychiat. Assn., Am. Acad. Psychoanalysis, Am. Psychoanalytic Assn.; mem. AMA, Am., Westchester psychoanalytic socs., Assn. Psychoanalytic Medicine. Contbr. articles to profl. jours. Home: 1005 Pelhamdale Ave Pelham Manor NY 10803 Office: 120 E Prospect Ave Mount Vernon NY 10550

ZUCKER, NORMAN LIVINGSTON, polit. scientist, author; b. N.Y.C., Aug. 1, 1933; s. George Meyer and Beatrice Lillian (Livingston) Z.; B.A., Rutgers U., 1954, M.A., 1956, Ph.D., 1960; m. Naomi Judith Flink, June 25, 1961; children—Sara, George. Asst. prof. polit. sci. Tufts U., Medford, Mass., 1962-66; asso. prof. polit. sci. U. R.I., Kingston, 1966-69, prof., 1969—; manuscript cons. to pubs. Wurzweiler Found. grantee, 1963; Am. Philos. Soc. grantee, 1964. Mem. Am., New Eng. polit. sci. assns., AAUP. Author: The Coming Crisis in Israel: Private Faith and Public Policy, 1973; The American

Party Process, 1968; George W. Norris, 1968. Home: 11 Locust Dr Kingston RI 02881 Office: Dept Polit Sci U RI Kingston RI 02881

ZUCKER, WILLIAM HENRY, computer applications engr.; b. Bronx, N.Y., Aug. 16, 1952; s. William and Grace Amelia (Weissert) Z.; B.A. in Econs., SUNY at Stony Brook, 1974; M.B.A. in Mgmt. Sci., Hofstra U., 1978. Coordinator, Grumman Aerospace Corp., Bethpage, N.Y., 1974-76, data mgr., 1976-77, computer applications engr., 1977—. Mem. Beta Gamma Sigma. Lutheran. Home: Westbury NY

ZUCKERMAN, ARTHUR EDWARD, life ins. broker; b. Newark, Oct. 4, 1923; s. David Zuckerman and Adele (Rapfogel) Z.; B.S. in Bus. Adminstrn., Lehigh U., 1947; m. Maria Caprio, Sept. 5, 1957; children—Eric, Lisa Ann. Pres. A.E. Zuckerman & Co., Newark, 1966—; Insad, Inc., Newark, 1975. Served with U.S. Army, 1943-46. C.P.A., C.L.U. Mem. Am. Soc. C.L.U.'s (v.p. Greater Newark chpt. 1978-79), Am. Inst. C.P.A.'s, N.J. Soc. C.P.A.'s, Am. Coll. C.L.U.'s, Assn. Advanced Life Underwriting, Life Underwriters Polit. Action Com., Nat. Assn. Life Underwriters, Million Dollar Round Table. Club: Essex County Country (West Orange, N.J.). Home: 9 Rand Dr West Orange NJ 07052 Office: 60 Park Pl Newark NJ 07102

ZUCKERMAN, PAUL HERBERT, lawyer; b. Bklyn., Mar. 7, 1935; s. Max Bernard and Minnie (Mendelson) Z.; B.S. in Economics, Wharton Sch. Finance Commerce U. Pa., 1957; M.B.A. in Corp. Finance, N.Y. U., 1964; J.D., Bklyn. Law Sch., 1967; m. Sara Shiffman, Aug. 25, 1963; children—David Isaac, Daniel Mark. Admitted to N.Y. bar, 1968, U.S. Supreme Ct. bar, 1973; security analyst U.S. Trust Co., N.Y.C., 1962-66; sr. security analyst CNA Mgmt. Corp., N.Y.C., 1966-71, mgr. research, 1971-73; individual practice law, N.Y.C., 1973—; vice chmn. bus. div. adv. bd. Borough Manhattan Community Coll. Served with Supply Corps U.S. Navy, 1957-60. Mem. Am., N.Y.C. bar assns., Fed. Bar Council, N.Y. Soc. Security Analysts, Bklyn. C. of C. (coordinating com. on econ. devel., vice chmn. mktg. subcom.). Jewish. Home: 1626 E 23rd St Brooklyn NY 11229 Office: Suite 3553 1 World Trade Center New York City NY 10048

ZUFALL, DOROTHY LUKASIK, educator; b. Passaic, N.J., Apr. 23, 1930; d. George and Mary Lukasik; B.S. in Biol. Scis., Rutgers U., 1952; M.A., Rider Coll., 1975; M.A., in Mgmt., Central Mich. U., 1976; 1 son, Robert E. Staff med. technologist Presbyn. Hosp., Newark, 1952-54; supervisory med. technologist Prudential Ins. Co. Am., Newark, 1954-57; ednl. coordinator Sch. Med. Tech., Somerset (N.J.) Hosp., 1970-77; ednl. coordinator, head dept. edn. Somerset Med. Center, Somerville, N.J., 1977—. BPW Found. scholar, 1973. Mem. Am. Chem. Soc., Am. Pub. Health Assn., Am. Soc. Allied Health Professions, Am. Soc. Health Manpower Edn. and Tng., Am. Soc. Med. Technologists, Consumer Health Educators Assn. N.J., AAUW. Republican. Methodist. Book reviewer Am. Jour. Med. Tech., 1974—; contbr. Allied Abstracts and Book Revs.; asso. editor Am. Jour. Med. Tech., 1978—; contbr. articles to profl. jours. Home: 297 S Finley Ave Basking Ridge NJ 07920 Office: Somerset Med Center Somerville NJ 08876

ZUG, CHARLES KELLER, III, surgeon; b. Youngstown, O., July 17, 1931; s. Charles Keller and Jeanette (Barres) Z.; B.A., Lehigh U., 1952; M.D., Temple U., 1956; m. Dorothy Kathryn Mayor, Apr. 13, 1957; children—Charles Keller IV, Kathryn A., Martin M. Intern, St. Lukes Hosp., Bethlehem, Pa., 1956-57; resident Pa. Hosp., Phila., 1957-61; practice medicine specializing in surgery, Bethlehem, Pa., 1963—; mem. staff St. Luke's Hosp., 1963—, chief dept. surgery, 1976—; asso. prof. surgery Sch. Medicine, Temple U., 1978—; dir. Pa. Blue Shield, 1977—, 1st Valley Bank, 1978—; cons. Consol. Rail Corp., 1977—; chmn. Pa. Med. Polit. Action Com., 1976—. Pres. Family Counseling Service Northampton County, 1969-70; chmn. prof. div. United Fund, 1967-68; chmn. bldg. com. Bethlehem Parking Authority, 1976—. Served as capt. U.S. Army, 1961-63. Diplomate Am. Bd. Surgery. Fellow A.C.S.; mem. AMA, Pa., Northampton County (past pres.) med. socs., Alpha Omega Alpha. Democrat. Mem. Moravian Ch. Club: Rotary (Bethlehem). Home: 418 N New St Bethlehem PA 18018 Office: 801 Ostrum St Bethlehem PA 18015

ZUHL, DONALD EUGENE, EDP co. exec.; b. St. Joseph, Mich., Apr. 20, 1935; s. Robert Carl and Martha Amelia (Adler) Z.; B.A., Johns Hopkins U., 1961; M.A., Am. U., 1970. Programmer/analyst Social Security Adminstrn., Balt., 1963-65; sr. programmer Bunker-Ramo Corp., Silver Spring, Md., 1966-67; sr. analyst Documentation Inc., Bethesda, Md., 1966-67; project mgr. Informatics Inc., Rockville, Md., 1969-72, Gen. Telephone & Electronics Info. Systems, Silver Spring, 1972-77, Sigma Data Services Corp., Silver Spring, 1977—. Served with Signal Corps, U.S. Army, 1957-60. Mem. Assn. Computing Machinery. Republican. Lutheran. Club: Kiwanis. Home: 8503 Irvington Ave Bethesda MD 20034 Office: 962 Wayne Ave Silver Spring MD 20910

ZUIDERHOF, BARBARA M., data services exec.; b. Ponce de Leon, Fla., July 21, 1939; d. J. P. and Alvesta (Simmons) Paul; student Santa Monica City Coll., 1958-60, U. Calif. at Los Angeles, 1961-63; m. B.S. Zuiderhof, (dec.); children—Matthew, Noah, Heather. Vice-pres. Mgmt. Scis. Corp., Santa Monica, Calif., 1967-69; v.p. Profl. Computer Services, Anaheim, Calif., 1970-73; cons. Data Services, 1974; pres. Postal Data Corp., La Plata, Md., 1976—. Pres. local PTA, 1978—; co-chairperson Accountability Reporting Citizens Com., 1977-78. Mem. Mail Advt. Services Assn., Direct Mail Mktg. Assn. Office: 400 7 Hwy 301 La Plata MD 20646

ZUKOTYNSKI, STEFAN, elec. engr.; b. Warsaw, Poland, Feb. 26, 1939; s. Julian and Krystyna (Stasinska) Z.; came to Can., 1966, naturalized, 1973; Ph.D., U. Warsaw, 1966; m. Susan Zofia Nirenberski, Jan. 2, 1968; 1 dau., Katherine Anne. Postdoctoral fellow physics U. Alta. (Can.), 1966-68; mem. faculty U. Toronto, 1968—, asso. prof. elec. engring., 1972—; cons. Elec. Engring. Consociated Ltd., Toronto, 1968—. Registered profl. engr., Ont. Mem. Assn. Profl. Engrs. Ont., Canadian Assn. Physicists, Am. Phys. Soc., IEEE. Contbr. articles to profl. jours. Home: 32 Maryvale Crescent Thornhill ON L4J 2H4 Canada Office: Dept Elec Engring Univ Toronto Toronto ON M5S 1A4 Canada

ZUMOFF, BARNETT, physician, med. researcher; b. Bklyn., June 1, 1926; s. Abraham and Stella (Zumoff) Z.; A.B., Columbia, 1945; M.D., L.I. Coll. Medicine, 1949; m. Selma Silver, Nov. 11, 1951; children—Janine, Francine, Linda. Rotating intern Bklyn. Jewish Hosp., 1949-50; med. intern Mass. Meml. Hosp., Boston, 1950-51; resident in medicine Bklyn. Jewish Hosp., 1951; resident in pathology Bklyn. VA Hosp., 1953-54; resident in medicine Univ. Service, Kings County Hosp., 1954-55, clin. asst. medicine, 1957-62; spl. fellow medicine Meml. Center, N.Y.C., 1955-57, clin. asst. medicine, 1958-62; research fellow medicine Columbia Research Service, Goldwater Meml. Hosp., N.Y.C., 1957-60; asst. medicine James Ewing Hosp., N.Y.C., 1959-62; asso. attending physician div. neoplastic medicine Montefiore Hosp., N.Y.C., 1961-63, attending physician dept. oncology, 1963—, attending physician dept. medicine, 1977—, asst. dir. Clin. Research Center, 1961-76, dir. Clin. Research Center, 1976—, dir. cancer endocrinology, 1976—, sr. investigator Inst. Steroid Research, 1963—; USPHS research fellow Sloan-Kettering Inst., N.Y.C., 1955-57, asst., then asso., 1957-62; clin. instr. medicine Downstate Med. Center, Bklyn., 1957-62; instr. medicine Cornell U. Med. Coll., 1958-62; mem. faculty Albert Einstein Coll. Medicine, 1965—, asso. prof. medicine, 1971-77, prof. medicine, 1978—; vis. physicians Rockefeller U. Hosp., 1978—. Served to capt. M.C., USAF, 1951-53, now brig. gen. Res. Decorated Meritorious Service medal, Air Force Commendation medal, Nat. Def. Service medal, Armed Forces Res. medal; Cross of Gallantry with palm (Vietnam). Diplomate Am. Bd. Internal Medicine. Fellow A.C.P.; mem. Am. Soc. Clin. Investigation, Endocrine Soc., Am. Fedn. Clin. Research, Am. Phys. Soc., Am. Heart Assn. (fellow council on arteriosclerosis), Soc. Armed Forces Med. Consultants, Am. Coll. Clin. Pharmacology, N.Y. Acad. Sci., AAAS, Assn. Mil. Surgeons (pres. N.Y. chpt. 1971-72), Aerospace Med. Assn., Soc. USAF Flight Surgeons, Res. Officers Assn. (nat. surgeon 1964-65, chmn. nat. conv. 1978, N.Y. State surgeon 1974-75, exec. com. N.Y. State dept. 1975-78, v.p. for air 1978—, pres. Nassau chpt. 1976-77), Air Force Assn. (med. adv. council 1965-72), Mil. Order World Wars (surgeon N.Y. chpt. 1976—), Mensa, Workmen's Circle (nat. exec. bd. 1978—). Jewish. Contbr. numerous articles to profl. jours. Home: 3710 Bedford Ave Brooklyn NY 11229 Office: 111 E 210th St Bronx NY 10467

ZUPANEC, RALPH, surgeon; b. Joliet, Ill., Aug. 18, 1913; s. Ralph and Anna (Ogulin) Z.; B.S., U. Kans., 1932, M.D., 1934; m. Marjorie Hirst, Apr. 19, 1941; children—Donald Merrill, Nancy. Intern U. Kans. Med. Center, Kansas City, 1934-35; fellow surgery Cleve. Clinic, 1935-39; resident U. Hosp., Boston, 1939-41; practice medicine specializing in gen. surgery, Pittsfield, Mass., 1946—; chief med. staff Berkshire Med. Center, Pittsfield, 1960-65; mem. staffs Berkshire Med. Center, Hillcrest Hosp. (both Pittsfield); clin. instr. Albany (N.Y.) Med. Coll., 1961—; asst. prof. surgery U. Mass., Worcester, 1976—; chief med. div. Civil Def., Pittsfield, 1951-56. Served with USNR, 1941-46. Diplomate Am. Bd. Surgery, Nat. Bd. Med. Examiners. Mem. Mass., Berkshire Dist. med. socs., AMA, A.C.S., New England Surg. Soc. Club: Lions. Contbr. sect. to med. texts. Home: 616 Pomeroy Ave Pittsfield MA 01201 Office: East St Profl Bldg 4 2d St Pittsfield MA 01201

ZURAV, DAVID BERNARD, lawyer; b. N.Y.C., Apr. 21, 1926; s. Irwin and Ida (Levine) Z.; B.S. in Econs., U. Pa., 1950; LL.B., Rutgers U., 1953; m. Frances Stalford, Mar. 18, 1951; children—Ilene, Edward. Admitted to N.J. bar, 1953, U.S. Supreme Ct. bar, 1957; practiced in Union, N.J., 1953-70, 71—; partner firm Zurav & Myers, Union, 1970-71; atty. Springfield Twp. Planning Bd., 1961—, Union Twp. Planning Bd., 1975—; spl. counsel N.J. Dept. Transp., 1970; dir., gen. counsel Brunswick Capital Corp., Hillside, N.J., 1966-70. Mem. adv. bd. 1st N.J. Bank Union, 1966—. Union County freeholder, 1968-71. Served with USNR, 1944-46. Republican municipal chmn., Springfield, N.J., 1967-68. Mem. Am., N.J., Union County, Essex County bar assns., N.J. Inst. Municipal Attys., Nat. Panel Arbitrators, Am. Arbitration Assn., Lawyers Club of Union (past pres.). Home: 1 Archbridge Ln Springfield NJ 07081 Office: 1460 Morris Ave Union NJ 07083

ZUTZ, HARRY DAVID, ins. exec.; b. Wilmington, Del., Dec. 12, 1917; s. David and Mary (Willis) Z.; B.A., U. Del., 1940; m. Gladys Rich, Mar. 7, 1943; children—Marsha Zutz Borin, Lawrence I. Founder, Harry David Zutz Ins. Inc., Wilmington, 1940, pres., 1940—; pres. Zutz and Co. Ltd., Zutz and Co. (U.K.) Ltd.; partner H.D. Zutz and Co.; pres. H.B. Swirz; dir. Spanel Internat. Active Jewish Fedn. of Del., Inc.; past pres., life mem. Jewish Community Center; mem. Del. Bd. Edn., 1960-67; co-chmn. div. United Community Fund; pres. The 200 Block W. 9th St. Corp.; mem. Del. Safety Council; bd. dirs. Grand Opera House, Wilmington, Arthritis Found. Recipient numerous citations State of Israel, 1975. Mem. Nat., Del. assns. ind. ins. agts., Nat. Assn. Casualty and Surety Agts., Am. Mgmt. Assn., Better Bus. Bur., Com. of '39 (founding), Del. C. of C. Democrat. Jewish religion. Clubs: Brandywine Country (past pres., dir.), B'nai B'rith (past pres.) (Wilmington); Holly Hills Country (Alloway, N.J.). Home: 4005 Lakeview Dr Hillside Farms Greenville Wilmington DE 19807 Office: PO Box 2287 Suite 1700 300 Delaware Ave Wilmington DE 19899

ZWAHLEN, JOHN, retail exec.; b. N.H., Sept. 27, 1932; s. Hans and Santina (Floria) Z.; student pub. schs., N.Y.C.; m. Sylvia Schoenfeld, Sept. 15, 1955; children—Bruce, Bryan, Keith. Asst. v.p. Hermans World of Sporting Goods, Carteret, N.J., 1954—. Served with USAAF, 1950-52. Mem. Nat. Sporting Goods Assn. Home: 345 Skyline Lake Dr Ringwood NJ 07456 Office: 2 Germak Dr Carteret NJ 07008

ZWANGER, JEROME, physician; b. N.Y.C., Apr. 4, 1923; s. Benjamin and Evelyn Z.; A.B., U. Pa., 1943; M.D., Chgo. Med. Sch., 1947; m. Bernice E. Lomazov, May 22, 1955; children—Susan, Roberta, Melissa, Betsy. Intern, Wyckoff Heights Hosp., Bklyn., 1947-49; resident L.I. Coll. Hosp., Bklyn., 1949-52; practice medicine specializing in radiology; asst. dir. dept. radiology L.I. Coll. Hosp., N.Y., 1953-54; radiologist L.I. Jewish Hosp., 1955-60; dir. radiology Central Gen. Hosp., Plainview, N.Y., 1961—; asst. prof. clin. radiology State U. N.Y., Stony Brook, 1974—. Diplomate Am. Bd. Radiology. Fellow Am. Coll. Radiology (councilor 1975—); mem. Radiol. Soc. N.Am., Nassau County Med. Soc. (v.p. 1978—), Med. Soc. N.Y., AMA, U. Pa. Alumni Assn. (trustee 1977—). Office: 126 Hicksville Rd Massapequa NY 11758

ZWASS, VLADIMIR, computer scientist; b. Lvov, USSR, Feb. 3, 1946; s. Adam and Friderike (Getzler) Z.; came to U.S., 1970; M.S., Moscow Inst. Energetics, 1969; M.Ph., Columbia U., 1974, Ph.D., 1975; m. Alicia Kogut, Apr. 24, 1977. Mem. profl. staff Internat. Atomic Energy Agy., Vienna, Austria, 1970; asst. prof. computer sci. Fairleigh Dickinson U., 1975—, chmn. com. computer sci., 1976—; cons. Met. Life Ins. Co., Citibank. Columbia U. fellow, 1970-71; Helena Rubinstein Found. scholar, 1971-75. Mem. Assn. Computer Machinery, IEEE, Sigma Xi, Eta Kappa Nu. Author: Introduction to Computer Science, 1978; contbr. articles to profl. jours.; guest editor Soviet E. European Fgn. Trade, 1976. Home: 538 Churchill Rd Teaneck NJ 07666 Office: Fairleigh Dickinson U Teaneck NJ 07666

ZWERLING, LILLIAN, interior designer; b. N.Y.C., Feb. 24, 1917; d. Morris and Sarah (Dupkin) Schochet; student N.Y. Sch. Interior Design, 1968, Finch Coll., 1970-75, N.Y. U., 1976; m. Robert Zwerling, Oct. 23, 1938; children—Linda Ellen, Diane Judith, Barbara Nan. Asst. estimator J. Kessler Painting Contractor, 1934, Triangle Sheet Metal, Inc., Bklyn., 1935-38; owner, mgr. Lillian Zwerling Interiors, N.Y.C., 1970—.

ZWICK, RICHARD FRANCIS, elec. mfg. co. exec.; b. Teaneck, N.J., Apr. 21, 1935; s. John George and Barbara Madeline (Ulrich) Z.; B.S.I.E., Fairleigh Dickinson U., 1959; m. Barbara Francine Paterno, Mar. 29, 1959. Engr. time standards and methods Bendix Corp., Teterboro, N.J., 1959-69; indsl. engr. Singer-Kearfott Co., Little Falls, N.J., 1969-73; sr. indsl. engr., mgr. prodn. control Philips Broadcast Equipment Corp., Montvale and Mahwah, N.J., 1973-76; mgr. prodn. planning/material control Electro-Optical Systems div. Magnavox Govt. & Indsl. Electric Co., Mahwah, 1976—. Mem. Franklin Lakes (N.J.) Bd. Health, 1978—, pres., 1979. Mem. No. N.J. Police Revolver League (pres. 1977—). Republican. Roman Catholic. Home: 225 Lincoln St Franklin Lakes NJ 07417 Office: 46 Industrial Ave Mahwah NJ 07430

ZWICKER, CHARLES HARRISON, coll. dean; b. N.Y.C., Apr. 13, 1912; s. Harry and Sarah (Goldstein) Z.; B.S., N.Y. U., 1933, M.B.A., 1950; m. Mildred Waldman, Oct. 25, 1941; children—Peter A., Robert P. With Charles H. Zwicker & Co., C.P.A.'s, N.Y.C., 1935-40; partner Samuel Shedler & Co., C.P.A.'s, N.Y.C., 1940-44, Zwicker, Sturmer & Co., C.P.A.'s, 1944-46, Rosenblum, Zwicker & Co., 1946-49, Zwicker & Simon, Garden City, N.Y., 1949—; mem. faculty C.W. Post Center L.I. U., Greenvale, 1957—, prof., 1965—, dean Sch. Profl. Accountancy, 1974—; dir. 1st Nat. Bank Glen Head, J. Ramsey Reese, Inc. C.P.A., N.Y. James F. Bender Endowed profl. accounting and money mgmt. Mem. Am. Inst. C.P.A.'s, N.Y. State Soc. C.P.A.'s, Am. Accounting Assn., Nat. Assn. Accountants, Inst. Internal Auditors. Jewish religion. Club: N.Y. U. Contbr. articles to profl. jours. Home: 56 Arbor Rd Roslyn Heights NY 11577 Office: CW Post Center Long Island Univ Greenvale NY 11548

ZWIRN, DAVID BERNARD, univ. counselor and adminstr.; b. Auburn, N.Y., Jan. 20, 1942; s. Irving and Pola Frances (Lewin) Z.; A.B., U. Pa., 1964, J.D., 1967; M.Ed., U. Va., 1976. Spl. agt. FBI, Birmingham, Ala., Detroit, N.Y.C., 1967-71; mem. legal staff New York County (Manhattan) Dist. Atty.'s Office, N.Y.C., 1971-74; asst. to dean students St. Bonaventure (N.Y.) U., 1976-77; coordinator jurisdiction and procedures, resident hall dir., counselor U. Tampa, Fla., 1977—. Mem. Am. Personnel and Guidance Assn., Am. Coll. Personnel Assn., Nat. Assn. Student Personnel Adminstrs., Dewy-Hogan-Morgenthau Assn. Home: 14 Keeler Ave Moravia NY 13118 Office: Box 2743 401 W Kennedy Blvd Tampa FL 33606

ZYGMONT, FRANK JOHN, JR., fgn. mktg. adminstr.; b. White Plains, N.Y., May 7, 1945; s. Frank John and Leslie L. (Lovelett) Z.; A.A.S., State U. N.Y., Cobleskill, 1965; m. Maureen Granfield, June 27, 1970. Field service mgr. Cognitronics Corp., Stamford, Conn., 1968-74; mktg. tech. service mgr. Qwip Systems, N.Y.C., 1974-77, fgn. mktg. mgr., 1977-78; program mgr. Exxon Enterprises Inc., N.Y.C., 1978—. Served with U.S. Army, 1965-68. Mem. Am. Mgmt. Assn. Roman Catholic. Home: Harmony Rd Brewster NY 10509 Office: 1251 Ave of Americas Room 1952 New York City NY 10020

ZYSMAN, SIMON ASHER, psychologist; b. Tel Aviv, Israel, Oct. 6, 1949; s. Majer and Rachel (Shraga) Z.; came to U.S., 1958, naturalized, 1963; B.A., Queens Coll., 1972; M.S., Bklyn. Coll., 1974; Ph.D., Fla. Inst. Tech., 1978. Research asst. Bklyn. Coll., 1973-74; tchr. Bd. Edn., N.Y.C., 1973-74; psychologist-in-tng. Bur. Child Guidance, Bklyn., 1974-75; grad. asst. Fla. Inst. Tech., Melbourne, 1975; cons. psychologist Morton Prince Center for Hypnotherapy, N.Y.C., 1975-77; psychologist Willowbrook Devel. Center, Staten Island, N.Y., 1975-77; psychologist Kings Park (N.Y.) Psychiat. Center, 1977—. Inst. Research in Hypnosis fellow, 1974-76. Mem. Profl. Assn. Developmental Disabilities (pres. 1977), Assn. Sch. Psychologists, Am. Psychol. Assn., Psi Chi. Home: 152-18 Union Turnpike Flushing NY 11367

ZYTARUK, GEORGE JOHN, univ. adminstr.; b. Edwand, Alta., Can., May 6, 1927; s. John and Doris (Winnick) Z.; B.Ed., U. Alta., 1949, B.A., 1953, M.A., 1958; Ph.D. (Can. fellow), U. Wash., Seattle, 1965; m. JoAnn Korenda, July 12, 1958; children—Carolyn Anne, John Andrew, Maria Catharine. Tchr. secondary schs., Alta., 1949-51, 54-58; prin. secondary sch., Athabasca, Edmonton, Alta., 1958-63; prof. U. Alta., 1965-67; prof. Nipissing U. Coll., North Bay, Ont., Can., 1967—, pres., 1967—, ex-officio mem. bd. govs. Imperial Order Daus. Empire postgrad. overseas fellow U. London, 1953-54. Mem. Modern Lang. Assn., Nat., Canadian councils tchrs. English, D.H. Lawrence Soc. Am. (pres. 1978—). Mem. Ukrainian Orthodox Ch. Club: Rotary. Author: D.H. Lawrence's Response to Russian Literature, 1971. Editor: Quest for Rananim: D.H. Lawrence's Letters to S.S. Koteliansky, 1970. Home: Rural Route 3 Silver Lady Ln North Bay ON Canada

Who's Who in America

Biographees of the East

The following biographees of the Eastern region have sketches appearing in the 40th edition of *Who's Who in America*.

Aach, Herbert
Aaron, Daniel
Aaron, Harold Robert
Aaron, Henry
Aarons, Stuart Harry
Aaronson, Robert Jay
Abashian, Alexander
Abato, Anthony Albert, Jr.
Abbe, Elfriede Martha
Abbe, George Bancroft
Abberley, John J.
Abbett, Robert William
Abbey, Arthur Newton
Abbey, Richard Sargent
Abbot, William Wright
Abbott, Alvin Arthur
Abbott, Charles Cortez
Abbott, Charles Homer
Abbott, Edward Leroy
Abbott, George
Abbott, Lawrence
Abbott, Loretta
Abbott, Lynn DeForrest, Jr.
Abbott, Robert Tucker
Abbott, Roy Twining, Jr.
Abdnor, James
Abel, DeForest Williams, Jr.
Abel, Elie
Abel, I(orwith) W(ilbur)
Abel, Reuben
Abel, Walter Charles
Abeles, James David
Abeles, Joseph Charles
Abeles, Robert Heinz
Abeles, Sigmund M.
Abell, Paul Irving
Abeloff, Abram Joseph
Abelow, Robert
Abelson, Alan
Abelson, Philip Hauge
Abelson, Raziel Alter
Abelson, Robert Paul
Abercrombie, Alexander Vaughan, III
Abernathy, Frederick Henry
Abernathy, Maurine Howard
Abernethy, Robert Gordon
Abersfeller, Heinz Andrew
Abhau, William Conrad
Abkowitz, Martin Aaron
Ablon, Ralph E.
Abood, Leo George
Abourezk, James G.
Abouzeid, George Aziz
Abplanalp, Glen Harold
Abraham, Henry Julian
Abrahams, Doris Cole
Abrahams, Robert David
Abrahamsen, David
Abrahamsen, Samuel
Abrahamson, Albert
Abram, Morris Berthold
Abramovitz, Max
Abramowitz, Morton I.
Abrams, Carl Victor
Abrams, David N.
Abrams, Earl Bernard
Abrams, George Joseph
Abrams, Harry Nathan
Abrams, Herbert LeRoy
Abrams, Meyer Howard
Abrams, Monroe Robert
Abrams, Richard
Abramson, Arnold Ernest
Abramson, Arthur Seymour
Abramson, Arthur Simon
Abramson, Harold Alexander
Abramson, Robert J.
Abshire, David Manker
Abt, Clark Claus
Abzug, Bella Savitzky (Mrs. Martin M. Abzug)
Accettura, Guy
Acconci, Vito (Hannibal)
Achenbaum, Alvin Allen
Acheson, David Campion
Acheson, George Hawkins
Achhammer, Bernard George
Achilles, Theodore Carter
Achinstein, Asher
Achinstein, Peter Jacob
Achorn, Robert Comey
Acker, Charles Roy
Acker, Nathaniel Hull
Ackerman, James Sloss
Ackerman, Robert Kilgo
Ackerman, Sanford Selig
Ackermann, Robert John
Ackley, Roger Kurth
Ackoff, Russell Lincoln

Acomb-Walker, Evelyn Martha
Acree, Vernon Darrell
Acton, David
Acton, Norman
Adair, Robert Kemp
Adam, Claus
Adam, John, Jr.
Adam, Malcolm
Adam, Ray Charles
Adamec, Donald Arthur
Adamian, Gregory H.
Adams, Alice Patricia
Adams, Alton George
Adams, Alvin Philip
Adams, Andrew Joseph
Adams, Andrew Stanford
Adams, Arlin Marvin
Adams, Arthur Harvey
Adams, Arthur Merrihew
Adams, Arthur Stanton
Adams, Bruce Leonard
Adams, Carolyn Ethel
Adams, Charles Francis
Adams, Charles J.
Adams, Charles Jairus
Adams, Daniel Putnam
Adams, David, IV
Adams, David Charles
Adams, Earl William, Jr.
Adams, Edward James
Adams, Edward Thomas
Adams, Edwin Melville
Adams, Elijah
Adams, Francis L(ee)
Adams, Harriet Stratemeyer (Carolyn Keene)
Adams, James Luther
Adams, James Troy
Adams, Joey
Adams, John Clinton
Adams, John Gibbons
Adams, John Hanly
Adams, John Quincy
Adams, John Wesley, Jr.
Adams, John Weston
Adams, John Willard, Jr.
Adams, Joseph Peter
Adams, Lane Webster
Adams, Léonie
Adams, Lewis Greenleaf
Adams, Mac Carter
Adams, Morton
Adams, Park, III
Adams, Paul Winfrey
Adams, Phoebe-Lou
Adams, Ranald Trever, Jr.
Adams, Raymond Curtis, Jr.
Adams, Raymond Del
Adams, Richard Towsley
Adams, Richard Varian
Adams, Rob Lee
Adams, Roy Stilz
Adams, Russell Baird
Adams, Samuel Clifford, Jr.
Adams, Sherman
Adams, Stanley
Adams, Theadore Lionel
Adams, Theodore Floyd
Adams, Thomas Boylston
Adams, Thomas Hinckley, Jr.
Adams, Ware
Adams, William Henry
Adams, William Hensley
Adamson, Robert Edward, Jr.
Addabbo, Joseph Patrick
Addams, Charles Samuel
Adderley, Nathaniel
Addison, Anne Simone Pomex
Addison, Francis Girault, III
Addison, Walter John
Adduci, Vincent James
Ade, Erwin Jerome
Adel, Judith
Adelman, Irma Glicman (Mrs. Frank L. Adelman)
Adelmann, Frederick Joseph
Adelmann, Howard Bernhardt
Adelson, Howard Laurence
Aderente, Henry John
Aders, Robert O.
Adikes, Park Thomas
Adkerson, J(oseph) Carson
Adkins, John Nathaniel
Adkins, William Hughlett, II
Adkinson, Burton Wilbur
Adler, Benjamin
Adler, Charles
Adler, David
Adler, Francis Heed
Adler, Frank Kurt

Adler, Gerald
Adler, Howard, Jr.
Adler, James Barron
Adler, John Hans
Adler, Larry
Adler, Lee
Adler, Luther
Adler, Michael H.B.
Adler, Peter Herman
Adler, Renata
Adler, Richard
Adler, Richard Brooks
Adler, Robert Philip
Adler, Samuel Marcus
Adler, Selig
Adler, Stephen Louis
Adolfo (Sardina, Adolfo)
Adreon, Harry Barnes
Adrian, Barbara (Mrs. Franklin C. Tramutola)
Aegerter, Ernest
Affinito, Lilyan Helen
Affleck, James G.
Affronti, Lewis Francis
Agard, Frederick Browning
Agassi, Joseph
Agee, Darrell Lee
Agee, Sam Wilkerson
Agger, Donald George
Aggrey, Orison Rudolph
Agha, Mehemed Fehmy
Aghajanian, George Kevork
Agle, Charles Klemm
Agnew, Allen Francis
Agnew, Bruce Andras
Agnew, Franklin Ernest, III
Agnew, James Blanchard
Agopoff, Agop Minass
Agosta, Karin Engstrom
Agosta, Vito Dante
Agronsky, Martin Zama
Aguilar, Francis Joseph
Agus, Jacob Bernard
Ahern, James Francis
Ahern, James Richard
Ahern, John Irenaeus
Ahern, Timothy Ignatius
Aherne, John Robert
Ahlberg, John Harold
Ahlbrandt, Roger Sheridan
Ahlert, Robert Christian
Ahlfors, Lars Valerian
Ahlquist, Harold E., Jr.
Ahlstrom, Bjorn
Ahlstrom, Sydney Eckman
Ahmann, Mathew Hall
Ahr, George William
Ahrens, Edward Hamblin, Jr.
Ahrens, Thomas H.
Ahrensfeld, Thomas Frederick
Aibel, Howard James
Aidekman, Alex
Aiken, Henry David
Aiken, Thomas Worthen
Aiken, William
Aikman, Frank, Jr.
Aikman, John Edgar
Ailes, Roger Eugene
Ailes, Stephen
Ailey, Alvin
Ailloni-Charas, Dan
Ainsworth, Dorothy Sears
Ainsworth, Mary Dinsmore Salter
Airis, Thomas Fergrieve
Aissen, Michael Israel
Aitken, Hugh George Jeffrey
Aitken, Webster
Aitkens, Alfred Thomas
Ajello, Carl Richard
Ajl, Samuel Jacob
Ajzenberg-Selove, Fay
Akaishi, Tadashi
Akaka, Daniel Kahikina
Aki, Keiiti
Alajalov, Constantin
Albanese, Licia
Albaugh, Kenneth Clocker, Jr.
Albee, Edward Franklin
Albee, George Wilson
Albee, Grace Arnold
Albers, Anni
Albers, Henry
Albert, Alfred Gerhardt
Albert, Calvin
Albert, Edward
Albert, John
Albert, Leo N.
Albert, Robert Bertrand
Albert, Robert Hartman

Alberts, Robert C.
Albertson, Jack
Alberty, Robert Arnold
Albig, Reed Harrison
Albion, Robert Greenhalgh
Albosta, Richard Francis
Albrand, Martha (Mrs. Sydney J. Lamon)
Albrecht, Arthur John
Albrecht, Harold L.
Albrecht, Ralph Gerhart
Albrecht-Carrié, René
Albright, Archie Earl, Jr.
Albright, Burl
Albright, George Franklin
Albright, Harry Wesley, Jr.
Albright, Hugh Norton
Albright, Ivan Le Lorraine
Albright, Joseph Medill Patterson
Albright, Penrose Lucas
Albright, Raymond Jacob
Albus, James Sacra
Alcalay, Albert S.
Alcopley, L.
Alcorn, Howard Wells
Alcorn, Hugh Meade, Jr.
Alcott, James Arthur
Alden, Douglas William
Alden, Vernon Roger
Alderfer, Arthur Alderfer
Alderfer, Harold Freed
Alderman, Bissell
Aldewereld, Simon
Aldisert, Ruggero John
Aldredge, Theoni Vachliotis
Aldrich, Alexander
Aldrich, Charles Duane
Aldrich, Clarence Knight
Aldrich, Frank Nathan
Aldrich, George Davenport
Aldrich, George Hoover
Aldrich, Hulbert
Aldrich, Malcolm Pratt
Aldrich, Nelson Wilmarth
Aldrich, Nelson Wilmarth, Jr.
Aldrich, Richard Orth
Aldridge, Mary Hennen Dellinger
Aleo, Joseph John
Alessandroni, Venan Joseph
Alevizos, Susan Bamberger
Alevizos, Theodore George
Alexander, Benjamin
Alexander, Brooke
Alexander, Charles Haynes
Alexander, Charles Thomas
Alexander, Clifford L., Jr.
Alexander, Donald Crichton
Alexander, Edward Lawson
Alexander, Edward Porter
Alexander, Gilbert Henry
Alexander, Herbert E.
Alexander, Holmes
Alexander, James Eckert
Alexander, James Radcliffe
Alexander, Jane
Alexander, John Davis
Alexander, John Frank
Alexander, John Gordon
Alexander, John Heald
Alexander, John Macmillan, Jr.
Alexander, Judd Harris
Alexander, Lawrence Dennis
Alexander, Lee
Alexander, Lewis McElwain
Alexander, Lloyd Chudley
Alexander, Maurice Myron
Alexander, Norman E.
Alexander, Ralph William
Alexander, Rosemary Elizabeth
Alexander, Rowland Bernard
Alexander, Roy
Alexander, Ruth Wilbur
Alexander, Shana
Alexander, Theodore Martin
Alexander, Vincent Arthur
Alexander, William Valentine, Jr.
Alexander, William Vollie, Jr.
Alexander, Willis Walter
Alexandre, D. L.
Alfange, Dean
Alfange, Dean, Jr.
Alfano, Charles Thomas
Alfoldi, Andrew
Alford, Joe Benge
Alford, John Morris
Alford, Neill Herbert, Jr.

Alfred, William
Algren, Nelson
Al-Hafeez, Humza (Leonard 12X Weir)
Alker, Hayward Rose, Jr.
Allaby, Stanley Reynolds
Allain, Emery Edgar
Allam, Mark Whittier
Allan, Frank Nathaniel
Allan, Harry Thain
Allan, Virginia Rachel
Allan, Walter Scott
Allan, William
Allan, William Alexander
Alland, Alexander, Jr.
Allansmith, Mathea Reuter
Allard, David Henry
Allard, Joseph
Allard, William Albert
Allaway, Howard
Allaway, William Hubert
Allee, John Percy
Allen, Anita Ford
Allen, Anna Foster
Allen, Aris Tee
Allen, Arthur Wright, Jr.
Allen, Betty Lou (Mrs. Ritten Edward Lee, III)
Allen, Brooke Empie
Allen, Catherine Louise
Allen, Charles, Jr.
Allen, Charles William
Allen, C(laxton) Edmonds
Allen, Clifford Robertson
Allen, Courtney Keith
Allen, Donald Clinton
Allen, Donald Gilson
Allen, Dwight William
Allen, Edward Lawrence
Allen, Ernest Mason
Allen, Eugene Murray
Allen, Frances Elizabeth
Allen, Fred Cary
Allen, Fred Harold, Jr.
Allen, Fred Tirrell
Allen, Gay Wilson
Allen, George Howard
Allen, Gordon E.
Allen, Harry Clay, Jr.
Allen, Henry Freeman
Allen, Howard Dyer
Allen, James Browning
Allen, James Caldwell
Allen, James Elbert
Allen, James Patrick, Jr.
Allen, James R.
Allen, Jerry Leeman
Allen, John Leo
Allen, Joseph Henry
Allen, Joseph Percival
Allen, Lafe Franklin
Allen, Lew, Jr.
Allen, Maryon Pittman (Mrs. James Browning Allen)
Allen, Mel
Allen, Michael Glynne
Allen, Milton Burke
Allen, Nicholas Eugene
Allen, Raymond Bernard
Allen, Reginald
Allen, Robert Day
Allen, Robert Fay
Allen, Robert Sharon
Allen, Samuel Washington
Allen, Victor Harvey
Allen, Wells Preston, Jr.
Allen, Wilbur James
Allen, Willard Myron
Allen, Woody
Allers, Franz
Alley, Edward Lee
Allfrey, Vincent George
Allin, John Maury
Alling, Norman Larrabee
Allis, William Phelps
Allison, Dwight Leonard, Jr.
Allison, Graham Tillett, Jr.
Allison, John R.
Allison, Mary Lucille
Allison, Richard Clark
Allison, Royal Bertram
Allman, Conrad Scott
Allner, Walter Heinz
Alloway, Lawrence
Allport, Peter Ward
Allshouse, Merle Frederick
Allshouse, Thomas James
Allsopp, Thomas
Allyn, Henry Gregory, Jr.
Alm, Alvin L.

Almgren, Edward S.
Almgren, Frederick Justin, Jr.
Almgren, Herbert Philip
Almirall, Lloyd Vincent
Almon, Edward Francis
Almond, James Lindsay, Jr.
Almquist, Elmer Hugo, Jr.
Almy, Thomas Pattison
Alper, Allen Myron
Alper, Jerome Milton
Alper, Thelma Gorfinkle
Alperovitz, Gar
Alpert, Hollis
Alpert, Warren
Alpher, Ralph Asher
Alsop, Joseph Wright
Alspach, Russell King
Alston, Charles Henry
Altabe, Joan Augusta Berg
Altbach, Philip G.
Alter, David Emmet, Jr.
Alter, Gerald Milton
Alter, Jean Victor
Althouse, Ernest E.
Altizer, Thomas Jonathan Jackson
Altman, David Ronald
Altman, Peter Alexander
Altman, Roger Charles
Altmann, Alexander
Altmann, Andrew Taylor
Altschul, Arthur Goodhart
Altschul, Frank
Altschul, Selig
Altschule, Mark David
Altshul, Harold Milton
Altshuler, Alan Anthony
Altshuler, Nathan
Alvey, Edward, Jr.
Alvis, John Hubbard
Alyea, Ethan Davidson
Alyea, Hubert Newcombe
Amado, Ralph David
Amar, Henri
Amara, Lucine
Amarel, Saul
Amato, Vincent Vito
Amaya, Mario Anthony
Amazeen, Edward Sutherland
Amber, Eugene Lewis
Amberg, William Joseph
Ambler, Ernest
Ambro, Jerome A.
Ambros, Dieter Hans
Ambrose, Myles Joseph
Ambrus, Clara Marie
Ambrus, Julian L.
Amburn, Ellis Edward
Amen, Irving
Ament, Richard
Ames, Amyas
Ames, Charles Oakes
Ames, George Joseph
Ames, John Lewis
Ames, Joseph Lynn
Ames, Louise Bates
Ames, Milton Benjamin, Jr.
Ames, Morgan P.
Ames, Oakes
Ames, Robert Barbour
Ames, Robert San
Amidon, Ellsworth Lyman
Amino, Leo
Amirikian, Arsham
Amling, Frederick
Ammarell, Raymond Robert, Jr.
Ammerman, Albert Merlin
Ammerman, Joseph Scofield
Ammidon, Hoyt
Ammons, Archie Randolph
Amory, Cleveland
Amory, Robert, Jr.
Amos, Franklyn Boothroyd
Amos, Harold
Amos, James Lysle
Amper, Alan
Amram, David Werner, III
Amram, Philip Werner
Amsterdam, Gustave Gerald
Amundsen, Lawrence Hardin
Amussen, Theodore Smith
Anastasi, Anne (Mrs. John Porter Foley, Jr.)
Anastasio, James
Anastos, George
Ancell, Nathan S.
Ancharoff, Maurice
Ancona, Barry
Ancona, George Ephraim

Baldwin, William Russell
Baldyga, Donald Arthur
Bales, Richard Henry Horner
Bales, Robert Freed
Balgooyen, Henry Warren
Balis, Moses Earl
Balk, Alfred William
Ball, David George
Ball, Eric Glendinning
Ball, George Wildman
Ball, Herbert Morton
Ball, John Fleming
Ball, John H(anstein)
Ball, Mary Margaret
Ball, Robert Hamilton
Ball, Robert M.
Ballak, Leopold
Ballam, Samuel Humes, Jr.
Ballantine, Ian
Ballantyne, Robert Jadwin
Ballard, Allen Butler, Jr.
Ballard, Edward Brooks
Ballard, Eugene Henry
Ballard, Frederic Lyman
Ballard, Frederick Armstrong
Ballard, John Henry
Ballard, Lucinda (Mrs. Howard Dietz)
Ballengee, James McMorrow
Balliett, Gene (Howard Eugene)
Balliett, Whitney
Ballin, William Christopher
Ballinger, Harry Russell
Balloch, Anthony Edward
Balluffi, Robert Weierter
Balogh, Karoly Charles
Balsam, Arthur
Balsam, Martin Henry
Balsley, James Robinson
Balsley, Philip Elwood
Baltake, Joseph John, Jr.
Baltay, Charles
Balter, Robert Brandon
Balthrop, Carmen Arlene
Baltimore, David
Baltzell, E(dward) Digby
Bam, Foster
Bamberger, Bernard Jacob
Bamberger, Edward Clinton, Jr.
Bamberger, Fritz
Bambury, Joseph Anthony, Jr.
Bampton, James William
Bancroft, Harding Foster
Bandeen, William Reid
Bane, Frank
Banerji, Ranan Bihari
Banes, Daniel
Banfield, Edward Christie
Bang, Frederik Barry
Bangs, John Kendrick
Bank, Merrill Lee
Banker, Brooks
Banker, Paul Albert
Banks, Ephraim
Banks, Harlan Parker
Banks, Henry H.
Banks, J(oseph) Eugene
Banks, Louis Layton
Banks, Otis Gordon
Banks, Robert Sherwood
Banks, Russell
Banks, Samuel Alston
Banks, Talcott Miner
Bankson, Ellis Edwin
Bankston, Archie Moore, Jr.
Bannard, Walter Darby
Banner, William Augustus
Bannerman, Robin Mowat
Bannister, Constance
Bannister, Dan Wesley
Bannister, Thomas Turpin
Bannon, Barbara Anne
Banthin, John Frederick
Bantle, Louis Francis
Banyard, Alfred Lothian
Banzhaf, John F., III
Banzhaf, Max
Barab, Seymour
Barabba, Vincent Pasquale
Barach, Alvan Leroy
Barach, Arnold Bauer
Baragwanath, Albert Kingsmill
Barahal, Hyman Samuel
Baraka, Imamu (LeRoi Jones)
Barall, Milton
Baranik, Rudolf
Baranowski, Frank Paul
Baranski, Joan Sullivan
Barasch, Clarence Sylvan
Baratz, Morton Sachs
Barbe, Walter Burke
Barber, Arthur Whiting
Barber, Bernard
Barber, Charles Finch
Barber, Edward John
Barber, Everett McMullin
Barber, John Merrell
Barber, Joseph
Barber, Joseph Thomas
Barber, Samuel
Barber, Saul Benjamin
Barber, Sherburne F.
Barber, William Joseph
Barbieri, Christopher George
Barbour, Hugh Revell
Barbour, William Albert
Barbour, William Ernest, Jr.
Barbour, William Rinehart, Jr.
Barchoff, Herbert
Barclay, Hartley Wade
Barclay, Ronald David
Bardon, Marcel
Bardos, Thomas Joseph
Barefoot, John Roy, Jr.
Bares, Rudolph, Jr.
Baretski, Charles Allan
Barg, Herbert
Barger, A. Clifford
Barger, Harold
Barger, Richard Wilson
Barghoorn, Elso Sterrenberg
Bargmann, Valentine
Barish, Norman Norton
Baritz, Loren
Barka, Tibor
Barkan, Alexander Elias
Barkell, Howard
Barker, Cecile deLisle
Barker, Charles Albro
Barker, C(larence) Austin
Barker, Harold Grant
Barker, James Rex
Barker, Leslie Paxton
Barker, Robert Whitney
Barker, Robinson Franklin
Barker, Stephen Francis
Barker, W. Gardner
Barkhorn, Henry Charles
Barkhorn, Jean Cook (Mrs. Henry C. Barkhorn)
Barkhuus, Arne
Barkin, Solomon
Barksdale, Phillip Dunlap, Jr.
Barksdale, Walter Lane
Barley, Frank Jay
Barlow, Charles Franklin
Barlow, George Herbert
Barlow, Klara (born Alma Claire Williams)
Barlow, Mark, Jr.
Barlow, Robert Francis
Barlow, Walter Greenwood
Barlow, Wayne Brewster
Barmack, Joseph Ephraim
Barnard, Charles Nelson
Barnard, Druie Douglas, Jr.
Barnard, George Bosler
Barnard, John, Jr.
Barnard, John Darrell
Barnard, Kurt
Barnathan, Julius
Barndt, William Henry
Barneby, Malcolm Richard
Barnes, Allan Campbell
Barnes, Bernard
Barnes, Carl Belton
Barnes, Carlyle Fuller
Barnes, Charles Benjamin
Barnes, Clive Alexander
Barnes, Djuna
Barnes, Edward Larrabee
Barnes, Frank Plummer
Barnes, Frederick Walter, Jr.
Barnes, Harry George, Jr.
Barnes, Howard Clarence
Barnes, Howard G.
Barnes, Irston Roberts
Barnes, Jack Whittier
Barnes, John David
Barnes, Lawson
Barnes, Leo
Barnes, Melvin Wallace
Barnes, Robert Gaylord
Barnes, Robert Goodwin
Barnes, Robert Merton
Barnes, Thomas Joseph
Barnes, Wallace
Barnes, William Oliver, Jr.
Barnes, Willis Clifford
Barnes, Wilson King
Barnet, Ann Birnbaum
Barnet, Sylvan
Barnet, Will
Barnett, Arthur Doak
Barnett, Charles Ebbert, III
Barnett, David
Barnett, David Leon
Barnett, Frank Eugene
Barnett, Henry Lewis
Barnett, Herbert
Barnett, Jonathan
Barnett, Proctor Hawthorne
Barnett, Robert P(ray)
Barnett, Robert Warren
Barnette, Curtis Handley
Barney, Albert Wilkins, Jr.
Barney, William Joshua, Jr.
Barnhart, Clarence Lewis
Barnouw, Erik
Barnum, John Wallace
Barnwell, David Kitzmiller
Baron, Carolyn
Baron, Hans
Baron, Harry
Baron, Judson Richard
Baron, Melvin Leon
Baron, Richard Warren
Baron, Salo W.
Baron, Samuel
Baron, Sydney Stuart
Barondess, Jeremiah Abraham
Barone, John Anthony
Baroni, Geno C.
Baroody, William Joseph
Barr, Alfred Hamilton, Jr.
Barr, Irwin Robert
Barr, Joseph Moran
Barr, Joseph Walker
Barr, Richard David
Barr, Robert Alfred, Jr.
Barr, Stringfellow
Barr, Thomas Delbert
Barrack, William Sample, Jr.
Barraclough, Geoffrey
Barraclough, Solon Lovett
Barrand, Harry Percival, Jr.
Barrett, Alan Hildreth
Barrett, Clifton Waller
Barrett, Edmund Stanislaus
Barrett, Edward Mitchell
Barrett, Edward Ware
Barrett, Herbert
Barrett, James Emmett
Barrett, J(ohn) Patrick
Barrett, Loretta Anne
Barrett, Raymond James
Barrett, Richard David
Barrett, Richard Henry
Barrett, Wayne Thomas
Barrie, Erwin Seaver
Barrie, George
Barringer, Brandon
Barringer, Philip E.
Barrington, Thomas M.
Barron, Alexander Johnston
Barron, Dean James
Barron, Norman Macdonald
Barron, Roger L.
Barron, Tilton Marshall
Barrow, John Curtis
Barrow, Thomas Davies
Barry, Allen Gifford
Barry, David Joseph
Barry, David W.
Barry, Edward William
Barry, Herbert, III
Barry, Mary Alice
Barry, Robert Thomas
Barsky, Arthur Joseph
Barstow, Richard
Bartch, Carl Edward
Bartel, Benjamin
Bartels, John Ries
Bartels, Millard
Bartels, Stanley Leonard
Bartenstein, Frederick, Jr.
Barter, Robert Henry
Barth, Alan
Barth, Edna Smith (Mrs. George Francis Barth)
Barth, Elmer Ernest
Barth, John Simmons
Barth, Max
Barth, Richard
Bartha, Dennis Richard
Barthelme, Donald
Bartholdson, John Robert
Bartholomew, Arthur Peck, Jr.
Barth-Wehrenalp, Gerhard
Bartilucci, Andrew Joseph
Bartlett, Charles Leffingwell
Bartlett, Charles William
Bartlett, Claude Jackson
Bartlett, Dewey Follett
Bartlett, Edmund
Bartlett, Ford
Bartlett, Gene Ebert
Bartlett, Irving Henry
Bartlett, Jennifer Losch
Bartlett, Lynn Conant
Bartlett, Marshall Kinne
Bartlett, Robert Merrill
Bartlett, Thomas Alva
Bartley, Robert LeRoy
Bartling, Martin Luther, Jr.
Bartocha, Bodo
Bartolacci, Guido James
Bartolacci, Raymond Anthony
Barton, Blayney Jones
Barton, Carl P.
Barton, Carlyle, Jr.
Barton, Donald Wilber
Barton, James Don, Jr.
Barton, Leon Samuel Clay, Jr.
Barton, Robert A.
Barton, Robert Thomas, Jr.
Barton, Russell William
Barton, Walter Earl
Barton, William Blackburn
Barton, William Louis
Bartoo, James Breese
Bartos, Armand Phillip
Bartram, John Bowman
Bartram, Maynard Cleveland, Jr.
Baruch, Eduard
Baruch, Jordan Jay
Baryshnikov, Mikhail
Barzelay, Ross
Barzun, Jacques
Bascom, Perry Bagnall
Basel, Louis
Baserga, Renato Luigi
Bashkow, Theodore Robert
Basie, William (Count)
Baskerville, Charles Alexander
Bass, Bernard Morris
Bass, George Henry, II
Bass, Hyman
Bass, Mary Carson
Bass, Mary Popkin
Bass, Robert Ness
Basset, Gene
Bassett, Charles Andrew Loockerman
Bassett, Glenn Cottrell, Jr.
Bassett, John Edwin
Bassett, John Jewett
Bassett, William Akers
Bassin, Jules
Bassin, Milton G.
Bassin, Robert Harris
Bastable, Charles William, Jr.
Bastedo, Philip
Bastian, James Harold
Bastian, Walter Maximillian, Jr.
Basu, Samarendra
Batchelder, Earle Clayton
Batchelder, Laurence
Batchelder, Ronald Lee
Bate, Walter Jackson
Bateman, Dupuy, Jr.
Bateman, Durward Franklin
Bateman, Fred Willom
Bateman, William Bailey
Bates, Charles Carpenter
Bates, Charles Turner
Bates, Edward Brill
Bates, G(eorge) Wallace
Bates, Grace Elizabeth
Bates, Henry George
Bates, James Earl
Bates, Maurice Edward
Bates, Robert Caldwell
Bates, Thomas Fulcher
Bates, William, Jr.
Bateson, Richard G.
Batley, Harry A.
Bator, Francis Michel
Bator, Paul Michael
Battelle, Kenneth Everette
Battelle, Phyllis Marie
Batten, Frank
Batten, Fred William
Batten, Roger Lyman
Batten, William Milfred
Batterman, Boris William
Battey, Bryan M.
Battin, Richard Horace
Battle, Hyman Llewellyn, Jr.
Battle, Lucius Durham
Battle, Mark Garvey
Battle, Solomon Oden
Battle, Warren Rich
Batzer, R. Kirk
Bauchat, James L.
Baucus, Max S.
Bauder, Ward W.
Baue, Arthur Edward
Bauer, Benjamin Baumzweiger
Bauer, Edward Greb, Jr.
Bauer, George William
Bauer, Harry Charles
Bauer, Paul David
Bauer, Raymond Augustine
Bauer, Simon Harvey
Bauer, Theodore James
Bauer, Walter Herman
Bauersfeld, Carl F.
Baugh, Albert Croll
Baughman, Fred Hubbard
Bauke, Joseph Padur
Baukhages, Frederick Edwin
Bauknight, William Cooper
Baum, Joseph H.
Baum, Richard Theodore
Baum, Stanley
Baum, Stefan Helmuth
Baum, Warren C.
Baum, Cardinal William
Bauman, Arnold
Bauman, Helen Wood
Bauman, Robert Edmund
Baumer, Franklin L.
Baumgarten, Herbert Joseph
Baumgartner, Leona (Mrs. Alexander D. Langmuir)
Baumm, Norman Howard
Baumol, William Jack
Baumwoll, Joel Philip
Baur, John Ireland Howe
Baur, Philip John, Jr.
Bautz, Edward, Jr.
Baxley, Marvin Owen (Max)
Baxter, John Lincoln
Baxter, Richard Reeve
Baxter, Samuel Serson
Baxter, Willard Ellis
Baxter, William MacNeil
Bay, Eugene Albert, Jr.
Bay, Howard
Bayard, Alexis Irenee duPont
Bayer, Mildred V. N. Brant
Bayerschmidt, Carl Frank
Bayh, Birch Evans, Jr.
Bayles, Rogers
Bayles, Samuel Heagan
Baylis, Arthur Eugene
Baylis, Chester, Jr.
Bayne, Marmaduke Gresham
Baynes, Harold Losey
Bazelon, David Lionel
Beach, Morrison H.
Beach, Norman Frederick
Beach, Robert Marion
Beachboard, Walter William
Beachem, Cedric Duane
Beacher, Lawrence Lester
Beagle, Charles Wellington
Beal, Dallas Knight
Beal, W(alter) H(enry) Jack
Beale, Betty (Mrs. George K. Graeber)
Beall, John Glenn, Jr.
Beals, Carleton
Beals, John David, Jr.
Beals, Lawrence Wilson
Beals, Loren Alan
Beals, Ralph Everett
Beam, Philip Conway
Beam, Walter Raleigh
Beaman, Chester Earl
Beaman, Richard Bancroft
Beame, Abraham David
Beams, Jesse Wakefield
Bean, Charles Palmer
Bean, Jacob
Bean, John Malcolm William
Beane, Alpheus C.
Beane, Frank Eastman
Bear, Charles Benson
Beard, Anson McCook, Jr.
Beard, Edward Peter
Beard, Frank
Beard, Geoffrey G.
Beard, James Andrews
Beard, John Robert
Beard, Richard Leonard
Beard, Robin
Bearden, Joyce Alvin
Bearden, Romare Howard
Beardsley, James Hartness
Beardsley, Monroe Curtis
Beardsley, Robert Eugene
Beardsley, Theodore S(terling), Jr.
Bearn, Alexander Gordon
Beasley, Cecil Ackmond, Jr.
Beason, Robert Gayle
Beatley, Charles Earle, Jr.
Beattie, Diana Scott
Beattie, Donald Sherman
Beattie, Edward James
Beattie, James Monroe
Beatty, David Dee
Beatty, George Edward
Beatty, John Matthew
Beaty, Orren, Jr.
Beauchamp, William Ellsworth
Beaudet, Eugene Charles
Beaudouin, John Tyrell
Beaufort, John David
Beaumont, Richard Austin
Beaver, Howard Oscar, Jr.
Beaver, Lucile Elizabeth
Beavers, Ellington McHenry
Beazley, Bernard Joseph
Bechill, William Daniel
Bechtel, William Russell
Beck, Audrey Phillips (Mrs. Curt Frederick Beck)
Beck, Charles Elmore
Beck, Clifford Keith
Beck, Curt Werner
Beck, Glenn Hans
Beck, Julian
Beck, Lewis White
Beck, Margit
Beck, Martin Luther
Beck, Robert Alfred
Beck, Robert Arthur
Beck, Robert Nelson
Beck, Rosemarie
Becken, Eugene Duane
Becker, Arthur Bernard
Becker, Donald Raymond
Becker, Edward Roy
Becker, Eleanor Holden
Becker, Ernest I.
Becker, Ernest Lovell
Becker, George Henry, Jr.
Becker, Isidore A.
Becker, Mortimer
Becker, Nathan Maurice
Becker, Otto August
Becker, Ralph Elihu
Becker, Richard Stanley
Becker, Robert A.
Becker, Stephen
Becker, William Watters
Beckerman, Bernard
Beckers, William Kurt
Beckett, John Angus
Beckett, Wheeler Martin Alfred
Beckett, William Wade
Beckham, Edgar Frederick
Beckham, William J., Jr.
Beckhard, Herbert
Beckley, Donald K.
Beckman, Aldo Bruce
Beckman, Ben
Beckman, Harry
Beckman, Norman
Beckmann, Robert Bader
Beckstead, Dan John
Beckwith, Charles Gates
Beckwith, Edmund Ruffin, Jr.
Beckwith, Herbert Lynes
Beckwith, Jonathan Roger
Beckwith, Warren Irving
Becton, Julius Wesley, Jr.
Bedar, Rudolph
Bedard, Patrick Joseph
Bedau, Hugo Adam
Beddall, Thomas Henry
Beddow, Thomas John
Bedell, Berkley Warren
Bedford, Brian
Bedini, Silvio A.
Bednar, Charles Sokol
Bedwell, Theodore Cleveland, Jr.
Beebe, Leo Clair
Beebe, Richard Townsend
Beebe, William Andrews
Beebe, William Bovell
Beech, Keyes
Beecham, Clayton Tremain
Beedle, Lynn Simpson
Beeler, Thomas Taylor, III
Beeman, Alice Lee
Beene, Geoffrey
Beer, Irving
Beér, János Miklós
Beer, Michael
Beer, Samuel Hutchison
Beer, Walter Eugene, Jr.
Beer, Warren Frederick
Beerits, Henry Christopher
Beerman, Herman
Beers, David Monroe
Beers, Henry Samuel
Beers, Lewis Franklin, Jr.
Beers, Roland Frank
Beesley, Joseph L.
Beeson, Jack Hamilton
Beeson, Richard Calvin
Beeton, Ralph Albert
Beg, Mirza Abdul Baqi
Begell, William
Begg, John Murray
Beggs, Harry George
Beggs, Thomas Montague
Beghe, Renato
Beghian, Leon Edward
Begleiter, Alvin Leon
Beha, James Joseph
Behan, Edmund Joseph
Behan, Robert F.
Behr, Robert McLean
Behre, Charles Henry, Jr.
Behrends, Ralph Eugene
Behrman, Jere Richard
Beidler, John Kaufman
Beik, Paul Harold
Beilenson, Anthony Charles
Beilenson, Edna
Beim, David Odell
Beimfohr, Edward George
Beinecke, Edwin John
Beinecke, William S.
Beisel, William Robert
Beiser, Gerald J.
Beith, Robert Bruce
Bekefi, George
Belafonte, Harry
Belanger, Mark Henry
Belcher, Benjamin Moore
Belcher, Donald Jenks
Belcher, Taylor Garrison
Belden, Clark
Belden, Frederick Hesley
Beldock, Howard Norton
Beldock, Myron
Belen, Frederick Christopher
Belenson, Allen George
Belfer, Arthur B.
Belfer, Robert Alexander
Belfield, John Cotton
Belford, Lee Archer
Bel Geddes, Barbara
Bel Geddes, Joan
BeLieu, Kenneth Eugene
Belin, Gaspard d'Andelot
Belinger, Harry Robert
Belitt, Ben
Belknap, Chauncey
Belknap, Norton
Bell, Albert Laverne
Bell, Bernard R.
Bell, Carolyn Shaw
Bell, Charles Anderson
Bell, Daniel
Bell, David Bonar
Bell, Davitt Stranahan
Bell, Derrick Albert
Bell, Drummond Crilley
Bell, Harrison Bancroft
Bell, Howard Hughes
Bell, James Adrian
Bell, James Frederick
Bell, James Frederick
Bell, Julius Arthur
Bell, Maurice Evan
Bell, Robert Kinsloe
Bell, Victor Altmark, Jr.
Bell, Vincent Gruber, Jr.
Bell, Walter Douglas
Bell, Wendell
Bell, Whitfield Jenks, Jr.
Bell, William Henry, Jr.
Bell, Wilson B.
Bellagamba, Laurence
Belling, Susan
Bellino, Carmine Salvatore
Bellis, Benjamin Neil
Belliveau, Fred
Bellm, Charles Newton, Sr.
Bellotti, Francis Xavier
Bellows, Everett Hollis
Bellows, Kendrick Fitzroy, Jr.
Belmont, August
Belmont, Herman Samuel
Belser, Jess Lawrence
Belsley, Gilbert Lyle
Belting, Robert Henry
Belury, Nicholas George
Belushi, John
Beman, Deane Randolph
Benacerraf, Baruj
Benacerraf, Paul
Benade, Leo Edward
Benbow, Terence Howard
Bencher, Walter Seaman
Benchley, Nathaniel Goddard
Benchley, Peter Bradford
Benchoff, James Martin
Bender, James Frederick
Bender, Louis
Bender, Max
Bender, Morris B.
Bender, Morton Alvin
Bendetsen, Karl Robin
Bendheim, Robert Austin
Bendiner, Robert Marvin
Bendixen, Henrik Holt
Benedict, Donald Lee
Benedict, Joseph Targonski
Benedict, Manson
Benedict, Robert Clyde
Benedikt, Michael
Benenson, David Maurice
Benenson, Edward Hartley
Benenson, Mark Keith
Benetar, David L.
Benezet, Louis Tomlinson
Bengtz, Ture
Beni, John Joseph
Benincasa, Pius A.
Beningson, Robert Matthew
Benington, Herbert Davidson
Benjamin, Adam, Jr.
Benjamin, Albert, III
Benjamin, Burton Richard
Benjamin, Mary Avezzana (Mrs. Harold G. Henderson)
Benjamin, Richard
Benjamin, Robert S.
Benjamin, Seward I.
Benjamin, Theodore Simon
Benke, Paul Arthur
Benko, Paul Charles

Benkovic. Stephen James
Benn, Nathan Herman
Benn, Ralph Philip
Bennack, Frank Anthony, Jr.
Benne, Kenneth Dean
Benner, Nolan Paul
Bennet, Douglas Joseph, Jr.
Bennett, Alvin LeRoy
Bennett, Carl
Bennett, Charles Dana
Bennett, Clarence Edwin
Bennett, Edward Nevill
Bennett, Elmer Frank
Bennett, Elmer James
Bennett, George Frederick
Bennett, Harry Louis
Bennett, Harve (Harve Fischman)
Bennett, Irving
Bennett, Ivan Loveridge, Jr.
Bennett, Jack Franklin
Bennett, James Edgar
Bennett, Jay
Bennett, Joan
Bennett, Josiah Whitney
Bennett, Marion Tinsley
Bennett, Michael
Bennett, Miriam Frances
Bennett, Norman E.
Bennett, Reynold
Bennett, Richard Earle
Bennett, Richard Gordon
Bennett, Richard Joseph
Bennett, Richard Kistler
Bennett, Robert Eugene
Bennett, Robert Martin
Bennett, Robert Russell
Bennett, Thomas Peter
Bennett, Walter Edward
Bennett, William Lauriston
Bennett, William Ralph
Bennett, William Ralph, Jr.
Bennett, William Tapley, Jr.
Bennink, Richard Ellis
Bennsky, George Michael
Benoit, Emile
Benoit, John James
Benoit, Leroy James
Benoliel, Peter Andre
Bensinger, Peter Benjamin
Bensley, Robert Russell
Benson, Bruce Buzzell
Benson, Dean Stodder
Benson, Ezra Taft
Benson, John Edward
Benson, Larry Dean
Benson, Lois Mary
Benson, Lucy Peters Wilson
Benson, Mary Sumner
Benson, Morton
Benson, Robert Dale
Benson, Robert Elliott
Benson, Roy Stanley
Benson, Stanton Floyd
Benson, William Edward Barnes
Bent, Bruce Roger
Bent, Donn Newberry
Bent, James Edward
Bent, John Peale, Jr.
Bent, Robert Dunlop
Bent, Willard Osborn
Bentel, Maria-Luise Ramona Azzarone (Mrs. Frederick R. Bentel)
Bentinck-Smith, William
Bentley, Eric
Bentley, Gerald Eades
Bentley, Helen Delich (Mrs. William Roy Bentley)
Bentley, William Harris
Benton, George Stock
Benton, Joseph George
Benton, Joseph Nelson, Jr.
Benton, Raymond Stetson
Benton, Robert Douglas
Benton, William Joseph
Bentsen, Lloyd Millard, Jr.
Ben-Veniste, Richard
Benz, John Stephen
Ben-Zion
Beplat, Tristan E.
Berall, Frank Stewart
Beranek, Leo Leroy
Berchtold, William Edward
Berdolt, John Philip
Bereday, George Zygmunt Fijalkowski
Berelson, Bernard R.
Berend, Robert William
Berendzen, Richard Earl
Berengarten, Sidney
Berenson, Marisa
Beres, David
Beresford, John P.
Beresford, Spencer Moxon
Bereston, Eugene Sydney
Beretta, David
Berfield, Morton Lang
Berg, Harvey Allen
Berg, Jean Horton
Berg, John Edward
Berg, Joseph Wilbur, Jr.
Berg, Mildred Marie
Berg, Norman Alf
Berg, Robert Lewis
Berg, Stephen Walter
Berg, Warren Stanley
Bergelin, Olaf Preysz
Bergen, John Vanderveer
Bergen, Stanley Silvers, Jr.
Bergenfield, Bert Kevin
Bergenheim, Robert Carlton
Berger, Arthur Victor
Berger, David
Berger, Eric
Berger, Frank Milan
Berger, Harold
Berger, Harold
Berger, Jason
Berger, Marilyn
Berger, Morris Isaiah
Berger, Morroe
Berger, Murry P.
Berger, Oscar
Berger, Patricia Wilson
Berger, Raoul
Berger, Thomas Louis
Bergerac, Michel C.
Bergeron, Urban Leo
Bergethon, Kaare Roald
Bergey, William Earl
Berggren, Willard Paul
Berghof, Herbert
Bergin, Daniel Edward
Bergin, Edward Daniel
Bergin, John Francis
Bergin, Robert P.
Bergin, Thomas Goddard
Bergin, William Francis
Bergleitner, George Charles, Jr.
Bergman, Bernard Aaron
Bergman, Charles Cabe
Bergman, Harry
Bergman, Paul Maximilian
Bergmann, Fred Heinz
Bergmann, Otto
Bergmann, Peter Gabriel
Bergold, Harry Earl, Jr.
Bergsma, Daniel
Bergson, Abram
Bergson, Herbert Augustus
Bergson, Maria
Bergsten, C. Fred
Bergstrand, Wilton Everet
Beringer, E. Robert
Beringer, Frederick Marshall
Berk, Alan S.
Berke, Jules
Berkeley, Austin West
Berkeley, Norborne, Jr.
Berkelman, Karl
Berkman, Jack Neville
Berko, Stephan
Berkowitz, Bernard Solomon
Berkowitz, David Sandler
Berkowitz, Leon
Berkowitz, Monroe
Berkowitz, Robert Howard
Berkowitz, William
Berkowitz, William
Berkwitt, George Joseph
Berl, Walter George
Berland, Kenneth K.
Berle, Milton
Berle, Peter Adolf Augustus
Berlin, Ira
Berlin, Irving
Berlin, Seymour Sanford
Berlind, Bruce Peter
Berlind, Roger Stuart
Berliner, Ernst
Berliner, Hans Jack
Berliner, Henry Adler, Jr.
Berliner, Joseph Scholom
Berliner, Robert William
Berliner, William Michael
Berlitz, Charles Frambach
Berman, Alan
Berman, Ariane R.
Berman, Bernard Alvin
Berman, Byron
Berman, Edgar Frank
Berman, Harold Joseph
Berman, Harry Louis
Berman, Herbert
Berman, Joshua Mordecai
Berman, Lawrence
Berman, Mira
Berman, Morton
Berman, Myron Philip
Berman, Philip I.
Berman, Ronald Stanley
Berman, Stuart Saul
Berman, Tony
Bern, Howard Leonard
Bernabo, Raymond Andrew
Bernard, Hugh Yancey, Jr.
Bernard, Kenneth
Bernard, Kenneth A.
Bernard, Michael Mark
Bernard, Viola Wertheim
Bernardo, Charles Michael
Bernat, William Albert
Bernays, Edward L.
Bernbach, William
Bernd, Joseph Laurence
Berndt, Alvin Harold
Berne, Robert Matthew
Bernegger, E. Lloyd
Berner, Robert Frank
Berner, Stephen Paul
Berner, T. Roland
Bernhard, Arnold
Bernhard, Berl
Bernhard, Henry Paul
Bernhard, Robert Arthur
Bernhard, Russell Sherman
Bernhard, William Francis
Bernhardt, John Bowman
Bernheim, Elinor Kridel (Mrs. Leonard H. Bernheim)
Bernier, Joseph Leroy
Bernlohr, Robert William
Bernson, James Allan
Bernstein, Alvin P.
Bernstein, Bernard
Bernstein, Carl
Bernstein, David
Bernstein, David W.
Bernstein, George Kaskel
Bernstein, Irving
Bernstein, Jeremy
Bernstein, Joel
Bernstein, Lawson Frederick
Bernstein, Leonard
Bernstein, Lester
Bernstein, Louis
Bernstein, Marshall Menline
Bernstein, Martin
Bernstein, Marver Hillel
Bernstein, Paul
Bernstein, Philip
Bernstein, Philip Sidney
Bernstein, Richard Barry
Bernstein, Richard Jacob
Bernstein, Robert
Bernstein, Robert Louis
Bernstein, Theodore Menline
Bernstein, Theresa
Bernstein, Victor Heine
Bernt, Benno Anthony
Berol, Kenneth Rossin
Berra, Lawrence Peter (Yogi)
Berridge, George Bradford
Berrigan, Daniel J.
Berrigan, Philip Francis
Berriman, W. Thomas
Berry, Betty Blaisdell
Berry, Brian Joe Lobley
Berry, Charles Horace
Berry, Charles Oscar
Berry, Donald Cadmus, Jr.
Berry, George Packer
Berry, Harold James
Berry, James Dufer, Jr.
Berry, J(ames) Raymond
Berry, John Nichols, III
Berry, Margaret Ethel
Berry, Mary Frances
Berry, Max Nathan
Berry, Richard Emerson
Bers, Lipman
Bersch, George Morton
Bersi, Robert Marion
Berson, Jerome Abraham
Berson, Robert Chambliss
Berstein, Ira Borah
Berstein, Israel
Berthel, John Hallock
Berthoff, Warner Bement
Berthold, Fred, Jr.
Bertino, Joseph Rocco
Bertocci, Peter Anthony
Bertoia, Harry
Bertolet, John Herbine
Berton, Lee
Beruh, Joseph
Besbekos, George Angelo
Beshany, Philip Arthur
Beshar, Robert Peter
Besley, Lowell
Bess, Jerome
Bessie, Simon Michael
Bessman, Maurice Jules
Bessom, Malcolm Eugene
Best, Allen Charles
Best, Marshall Ayres
Best, Richard Warner
Best, Robert Mulvane
Bestor, Charles Lemon
Betcher, Albert Maxwell
Betchkal, James Joseph
Beth, Richard Alexander
Bethe, Hans Albrecht
Bethell, John Torrey
Bethke, Robert Harder
Bethune, John Lemuel
Betkowski, Walter Christopher
Betterley, George Morgan
Bettis, Valerie
Bettoney, Wilfred Estey
Betts, Charles Dudley Ames
Betts, Ernest Claire, Jr.
Betts, James Franklin
Betts, John Frederick, Jr.
Betz, Barbara Jean
Betz, John Frederick
Betzig, Edward
Beutel, William Charles
Bevan, Wendell Lowell, Jr.
Bever, Michael Berliner
Beveridge, George David, Jr.
Beveridge, Norwood Pierson, Jr.
Bevilacqua, Joseph A.
Beville, Hugh Malcolm, Jr.
Bewkes, Eugene Garrett
Bewkes, Eugene Garrett, Jr.
Beychok, Sherman
Beyer, Eugene Edward, Jr.
Beyer, John Regan
Beyer, Karl Henry, Jr.
Beyer, Robert Carlyle
Beyer, Robert Thomas
Bhagwati, Jagdish Natwarlal
Bharati, Agehananda
Bhaskar, Surindar Nath
Biaggi, Mario
Biancolli, Louis
Bibring, Grete Lehner
Bich, Marcel (Baron)
Bichy, Charles Edward, Jr.
Bickel, Bertram Watkins
Bickel, Robert John
Bickerman, Elias Joseph
Bickerton, Robert Keith
Bickford, Edward Davidson
Bickford, John Howe
Bicking, John Francis
Bickley, William Elbert
Bickmore, Lee Smith
Bicksler, James Lazaroff
Biddinger, Clyde Marion
Biddle, Eric Harbeson
Biddle, James
Biddle, John Hunter
Biddle, Livingston Ludlow, Jr.
Biddle, Theodore William
Biden, Joseph Robinette, Jr.
Bieber, Samuel
Biebuyck, Daniel Prosper
Biederman, Barron Zachary
Biegel, Herman Charles
Biegler, John Charles
Bielenstein, Hans Henrik August
Biemann, Klaus
Biemiller, Andrew John
Bien, Peter Adolph
Bienen, Henry Samuel
Bienstock, Abraham Lawrence
Bier, William Christian
Bierer, William E.
Bieri, John Genther
Bieringer, Leroy J.
Bieringer, Walter H.
Bierman, Arthur
Bierman, Harold, Jr.
Biernat, Joseph Anthony
Bierstedt, Robert
Bierwirth, John Cocks
Bierwirth, John E.
Biester, Edward George, Jr.
Bigart, Homer
Bigeleisen, Jacob
Bigelow, Donald Nevius
Bigelow, Karl Worth
Biggar, Charles Patrick
Biggers, John Dennis
Biggs, John, Jr.
Biggs, John Melvin
Biggs, Wellington Allen
Bigham, James John
Bigham, Milton Robert
Bighinatti, Enso Victor
Bijur, Herbert Isaac
Bikel, Theodore
Bilaniuk, Olexa Myron
Bilby, Kenneth W.
Bildersee, Barnett
Bilger, Donald Earle
Bilhorn, William Wilson
Biller, Hugh Frederick
Biller, Joel Wilson
Billera, I. John
Billings, Edward Robert
Billings, Franklin Swift, Jr.
Billings, Marland Pratt
Billingsley, James Ray
Billington, Clyde M., Jr.
Billington, James Hadley
Billman, John Henry
Billmeyer, Fred Wallace, Jr.
Billock, William Byron
Binder, Frederick Moore
Binder, Leonard James
Binford, Chapman Hunter
Bing, Kurt
Bing, Sir Rudolf
Bingay, James Sclater
Bingeman, Jonas Byron
Binger, Wilson Valentine
Bingham, Charles Marvin
Bingham, Eula
Bingham, Jonathan Brewster
Bingham, Sidney Hedley
Binion, Rudolph
Binkley, Luther John
Binns, James Hazlett
Biondi, Manfred Anthony
Birch, Albert Francis
Birch, Jack Willard
Birch, Norman Anton
Birchby, Kenneth Lee
Birchenall, Charles Ernest
Bird, Caroline
Bird, George Lloyd
Bird, George Richmond
Bird, John Alexander
Bird, Robert James
Bird, Robert Montgomery
Birdwhistell, Ray L.
Birely, William Cramer
Birenbaum, William M.
Birk, Roger Emil
Birkenhead, Thomas Bruce
Birkhead, Guthrie Sweeney, Jr.
Birkhead, Kenneth Milton
Birkhoff, Garrett
Birkimer, Donald Leo
Birman, Joseph Leon
Birmingham, Martin F.
Birmingham, Matthew Thomas, Jr.
Birmingham, Patrick Joseph
Birmingham, Stephen
Birnbaum, Asher J.
Birnbaum, Henry
Birnbaum, Norman
Birnbaum, Robert Jack
Birnbaum, Stephen Norman
Birney, Robert Charles
Birnie, William Alfred Hart
Birrell, George Andrew
Birsh, Arthur Thomas
Bisbee, Royal Daniel
Biscardi, Chester
Bischoff, Kenneth Bruce
Bischoff, Ralph Frederic
Bisguier, Arthur Bernard
Bishop, Barbara Janet
Bishop, Carolyn Benkert
Bishop, Elizabeth
Bishop, Gordon Bruce
Bishop, Hewlett Ryder
Bishop, Isabel (Mrs. Harold G. Wolff)
Bishop, Joseph Warren, Jr.
Bishop, Robert Lyle
Bishop, Robert Milton
Bishton, Robert Arthur
Bissell, George Seymour
Bissell, Marshall Philip
Bissell, Pelham St. George, III
Bissell, Phil (Charles P. Bissell)
Bissell, Richard Mervin, Jr.
Bissell, Thomas Ashley
Bisselle, Morgan Fitch
Bisset, Andrew Walzer
Bisset, John Thomas
Bissinger, Frederick Lewis
Bissonnette, Georges Louis
Bistline, James Adams
Bitner, Harry
Bittinger, Donald S.
Bittman, William Omar
Bittner, Egon
Biunno, Vincent P.
Bixby, Allan Barton
Bixby, Paul Warren
Bixby, R. Burdell
Bjorhus, Robert Einar
Bjork, Richard Emil
Black, Charles Lund, Jr.
Black, Cyril Edwin
Black, Daniel James
Black, David
Black, David Statler
Black, Emilie Annabelle
Black, Eugene Robert
Black, George
Black, Harold Stephen
Black, Joseph E.
Black, Leonard J.
Black, Max
Black, Peter
Black, Robert Bruce
Black, Robert Duncan
Black, Robert Foster
Black, Robert Perry
Black, Roe Coddington
Black, Theodore Michael
Black, Walter Evan, Jr.
Black, William
Blackadar, Alfred Kimball
Blackall, Eric Albert
Blackburn, Douglas Bryan
Blackburn, Morris Atkinson
Blackburn, Thomas Harold
Blackett, Donald Watson
Blackiston, Henry Curtis
Blackler, Antonie William Charles
Blackman, Alfred Churchill
Blackman, Charles Franklin
Blackman, Robert Irwin
Blackman, Robert Lyle
Blackmar, Dana, III
Blackmer, Donald Laurence Morton
Blackmon, Lawrence George
Blackmon, Rosemary Barnsdall
Blackmore, Robert Long
Blackmun, Harry Andrew
Blackstone, Henry
Blackwell, Cecil
Blackwell, David Jefferson
Blackwell, Earl
Blackwell, John Davenport
Blackwell, William Allen
Blackwood, George William
Blackwood, Russell Thorn, III
Bladen, Ronald
Blades, Brian Brewer
Blades, Herbert William
Blady, John Valentine
Blagowidow, George
Blain, Daniel
Blaine, Charles Gillespie
Blaine, Nell Walden
Blair, Benjamin Franklin
Blair, Charles Stanley
Blair, Clay Drewry, Jr.
Blair, Forbes Wesley
Blair, James Walter, Jr.
Blair, John Louis
Blair, Robert Noel
Blair, Thomas S.
Blair, William Draper, Jr.
Blair, William Granger
Blair, William McCormick, Jr.
Blair, William Mellville
Blair, William Richards, Jr.
Blair, William Sutherland
Blake, Alfred Greene
Blake, Bud (Julian Watson)
Blake, Eugene Carson
Blake, Harlan Morse
Blake, James Hubert (Eubie Blake)
Blake, James J.
Blake, John Ballard
Blake, John Lewis
Blake, Ran
Blake, Stewart Prestley
Blake, Vincent Patrick
Blake, Whitney
Blake, William Dewey
Blakely, Susan
Blakeman, Royal E.
Blakemore, William Stephen
Blakeslee, Alton Lauren
Blakeslee, Arthur Leopold, III
Blakeslee, Edward Eaton
Blakinger, Richard Jerome
Blalock, Joseph Rogers
Blanc, Peter (William Peters Blanc)
Blanc, William Andre
Blanchard, Carl Richard
Blanchard, George Samuel
Blanchard, James J.
Blanchard, Lawrence Eley, Jr.
Blanchard, Richard Frank
Blanchard, Roger Wilson
Blanchet, George Arthur
Blanchette, Robert Wilfred
Bland, Chester
Bland, Edward Franklin
Bland, Guy Emery
Blandford, John Russell
Blandin, Amos Noyes, Jr.
Blank, Albert Abraham
Blank, Blanche Davis
Blank, David
Blank, David M.
Blank, Samuel Allan
Blankenheimer, Bernard
Blankertz, Donald Frederic
Blanshard, Brand
Blanton, Edward Lee, Jr.
Blasier, Cole
Blasier, Robert Dalton
Blasingame, Ralph Upshaw
Blass, Bill
Blatchford, Nicholas
Blatman, Saul
Blatsos, John
Blatt, Burton
Blatt, Genevieve
Blatz, Durand Barrett
Blatz, George Joseph
Blau, Abram
Blau, Harvey Ronald
Blau, Joseph Leon
Blau, Peter Michael
Blaustein, Albert Paul
Blauvelt, Howard W.
Blazes, Bernard Benjamin
Blecher, Melvin
Blechman, Harry
Bleck, Max Emil
Blegen, Judith Eyer
Bleiberg, Robert Marvin
Bleibtreu, Jacob
Bleich, Hans Heinrich
Bleicken, Gerhard David
Bleier, Richard M.
Bleier, Robert Patrick (Rocky)
Bleiler, Everett Franklin
Bleiweiss, Herbert Irving
Blendon, Robert Jay
Blenko, Walter John
Blesh, Rudi (Rudolph Pickett Blesh)
Blesser, William Benjamin
Blevins, Herbert Harner
Bley, Carla Borg (Mrs. Michael Mantler)
Bley, Paul
Blickwede, Donald Johnson
Blinder, Abe Lionel
Blinken, Donald Mayer
Blinken, Robert James
Bliss, Anthony Addison
Bliss, Chester Ittner
Bliss, Dorothy Elizabeth
Bliss, Francis Walter
Bliss, Richard Mitchell
Bliss, Robert Landers
Bliss, Sally Brayley
Blistein, Elmer Milton
Blitman, Charles H.
Blitman, Howard Norton
Blitzer, Charles
Bliven, Bruce, Jr.
Bliven, Naomi
Blizzard, Robert M.
Bloch, Henry Simon
Bloch, Herbert
Bloch, Konrad
Bloch, Martin B.
Bloch, William Albert
Block, Adolph
Block, Edward Martel
Block, Frank Emmanuel
Block, Haskell Mayer
Block, Henry David
Block, Herbert Lawrence (Herblock)
Block, James Alexander
Block, Joseph Douglas
Block, Jules Richard
Block, Leonard Nathan
Block, Marvin Avram
Block, Murray Harold
Block, Robert Charles
Block, S. Lester
Block, William
Block, Zenas
Blodgett, John Quigg
Bloede, Victor Gustav
Bloembergen, Nicolaas
Bloetjes, Mary Kiefer
Blomquist, John Emil
Blomquist, Robert Oscar
Blomster, Ralph Norman
Blondell, Joan
Bloom, Claire
Bloom, Edward Alan
Bloom, Frederick Stuart
Bloom, Harold
Bloom, James Richard
Bloom, Joel N.
Bloom, Julius
Bloom, Lee Hurley
Bloom, Pauline
Bloomer, Robert Asa
Bloomfield, Arthur Irving
Bloomfield, Lincoln Palmer
Bloomfield, Morton Wilfred
Bloomquist, Howard Richard
Bloss, Meredith
Blough, Carman George
Blough, Donald S.
Blough, Glenn Orlando
Blough, Herbert Allen
Blough, Roger M.
Blough, Roy
Blouin, Michael Thomas
Blount, Clarence William
Blount, Jonathan
Blount, Melvin (Mel) Cornell
Blount, Robert Haddock

Blount, Stanley Freeman
Bloustein, Edward J.
Blout, Elkan Rogers
Blow, George
Bludman, Sidney Arnold
Blue, William L(acy)
Bluemle, Lewis William, Jr.
Bluhdorn, Charles G.
Bluhm, Heinz
Blum, Harold F.
Blum, Jerome
Blum, John Curtis
Blum, John Morton
Blum, John Robert Halsey
Blum, Lester
Blum, Robert Edward
Blum, Walter Ellery
Blumberg, Baruch Samuel
Blumberg, Gerald
Blumberg, Herbert Kurt
Blumberg, Joe Morris
Blumberg, Phillip Irvin
Blume, Albert Max Karl
Blume, Jack Paul
Blume, Judy Sussman
Blume, Martin
Blume, Peter
Blumenauer, Thomas William, Jr.
Blumenfeld, Alfred Morton
Blumenfeld, M. Joseph
Blumenkranz, Joseph
Blumenstock, David Albert
Blumenthal, Andre
Blumenthal, Henry
Blumenthal, Herman Bertram
Blumenthal, John
Blumenthal, Richard
Blumenthal, Richard Alan
Blumenthal, W. Michael
Blumer, Frederick Elwin
Blunck, Herbert Christopher
Blunt, William Williams, Jr.
Blyth, John William
Blythe, James Edwin
Boal, Arthur McClure
Board, Joseph Breckinridge, Jr.
Boardman, Arthur Goddard, Jr.
Boardman, Richard Stanton
Boas, Herbert Allan, Jr.
Boas, Robert Sanford
Boatwright, H(erbert) Lee, III
Bobbitt, James McCue
Bobbitt, Oliver Beirne, Jr.
Bobeck, Andrew H.
Bober, John D.
Bober, Lawrence Harold
Bober, Phyllis Pray
Bobinski, George Sylvan
Bobker, Lee Robert
Bobroff, Harold
Bobrow, Davis Bernard
Bock, Alexander Pershing
Bock, Harry H.
Bock, Jerry (Jerrold Lewis)
Bockelman, Charles Kincaid
Bockman, Marilyn Modern
Bockus, Henry L.
Bodansky, Oscar
Bodden, William Michael
Boddiger, George Cyrus
Bode, Carl
Bode, Hendrik Wade
Bode, Robert W.
Bodell, Gerald Edward
Bodenstein, Dietrich H. F. A.
Bodian, David
Bodine, James Forney
Bodine, William Warden, Jr.
Bodman, Richard Stockwell
Boe, Nils Andreas
Boe, Roy Lars Magnus
Boegehold, Alan Lindley
Boehm, Charles Harold
Boehm, David Alfred
Boehm, Werner William
Boeker, Paul Harold
Boell, Edgar John
Boenning, Henry Dorr, Jr.
Boerrigter, Glenn Charles
Boesky, Ivan Frederick
Boettger, Thomas Edward
Bogardus, John Arthur, Jr.
Bogash, Richard
Bogdan, Victor Michael
Bogdanoff, Leonard
Bogdonoff, Morton David
Bogdonoff, Seymour Moses
Bogen, Samuel Adams
Bogert, Henry Lawrence
Bogert, Ivan Lathrop
Bogert, Jonathan
Boggs, Corinne C. (Lindy)
Boggs, Dane Ruffner
Boggs, Elizabeth Monroe (Mrs. Fitzhugh W. Boggs)
Boggs, J. Caleb
Boggs, Jean Sutherland
Boggs, Robert Newell
Boggs, Thomas Hale, Jr.
Boghosian, Varujan Yegan
Bogin, Benjamin
Bogle, Hugh Andrew
Bogle, John Clifton
Bogorad, Lawrence
Bogorad, Samuel Nathaniel
Bogren, George Gustave
Boguslavsky, George William
Bohen, Patrick James
Bohle, Bruce William
Bohlen, Nina
Bohm, Magnus Richard
Bohnen, Eli Aaron
Bohner, Charles Henry
Bois, Maurice Paul
Boisi, James O.
Bok, Derek Curtis
Bolan, James Thomas
Bolan, Thomas Anthony
Boland, Christopher Thomas, II
Boland, Edward P.
Boland, Lawrence
Boland, Thomas Aloysius
Boldosser, Kenneth Edgar
Boldt, Elihu Aaron
Bolduc, Ernest Joseph
Bolen, David B.
Bolen, Lin L.
Bolender, Carroll Herdus
Bolenius, William C.
Boles, Russell Sage
Boley, Forrest Irving
Bolis, John Miervaldis
Böll, Heinrich
Bolle, Donald Martin
Bolles, Edmund Blair
Bollman, Mark Brooks, Jr.
Bollum, Frederick James
Bolotowsky, Ilya
Bolster, Arthur Stanley, Jr.
Bolt, Richard Henry
Bolte, Charles Guy
Bolwell, Edwin Barry
Bolz, Ray Emil
Bomgardner, William Earl
Bonafede, Vincent Ignatius
Bonan, Seon Pierre
Bonansea, Bernardino Maria
Bonawitz, Irving Maurice
Bonazzi, Elaine Claire
Bonbright, James Cummings
Bond, Arthur Chalmer
Bond, Calhoun
Bond, Cornelius Combs, Jr.
Bond, Horatio Lockerby
Bond, Langhorne McCook
Bond, Niles Woodbridge
Bond, Richard P.
Bond, William Henry
Bondurant, Stuart
Bondy, Philip Kramer
Bondy, Philip Lederer
Bondy, Robert Earl
Bone, Arthur Ellsworth
Bonebrake, Roy Conrad
Bongartz, Roy
Bonham, George Wolfgang
Boni, Albert
Bonilla, Charles Francis
Bonini, William Emory
Bonior, David Edward
Bonker, Don L.
Bonn, Robert Thomas
Bonnefous, Jean-Pierre
Bonnell, Allen Thomas
Bonnell, John Sutherland
Bonner, Charles William, III
Bonner, Francis Truesdale
Bonner, John Tyler
Bonner, Thomas Neville
Bonner, Walter Joseph
Bonner, Willard Hallam
Bonney, Weston Leonard
Bonomi, John Gurnee
Bonomo, Victor A.
Bonosaro, Carol Alessandra
Bonsack, Samuel Elliott, III
Bonsal, Dudley Baldwin
Bonsal, Philip Wilson
Bonsignore, Joseph John
Bontoyan, Warren Roberts
Boochever, Louis Charles
Boocock, Sarane Spence (Mrs. C. Brett Boocock, Jr.)
Booher, Edward E.
Book, John Alph
Booker, James Edward
Bookhammer, Eugene Donald
Bookman, George B.
Bookman, Ronald Westmoreland, Jr.
Bookspan, Michael Lloyd
Bookstaver, David Richard
Boomsliter, Paul Colgan
Boone, Robert Raymond
Boone, Walter Fredrick
Boonisar, Richard
Boorsch, Jean
Boorse, Henry A.
Boorstin, Daniel J.
Booth, Charles Loomis
Booth, Edgar Hirsch
Booth, George
Booth, John Avery
Booth, John Edward
Booth, John Thomas
Booth, Mitchell B.
Booth, Philip
Booth, Richard Earl
Booth, Robert Gray
Booth, Theodore Harrington
Booth, Wallace Wray
Booth, William Wallace
Booth, Windsor Peyton
Boothby, Willard Sands, Jr.
Boothe, Armistead Lloyd
Boothe, Leon Estel
Booty, John Everitt
Boozer, Emerson, Jr.
Bopp, Walter Steneck
Borah, Richard Thomas
Borders, William D.
Bordogna, Joseph
Bordt, Frederick John, Jr.
Borei, Hans Georg
Borel, Armand
Boretz, Benjamin Aaron
Borg, Alfred Francis
Borg, Bjorn
Borg, Dorothy
Borg, Malcolm Austin
Borg, Sidney Fred
Borgatta, Edgar F.
Borge, Victor
Borgstedt, Douglas
Borisewitsch, Kiprian
Borison, Herbert Leon
Bork, Robert Heron
Borkland, Ernest Waldermar, Jr.
Borklund, Carl Wilbur
Borland, Hal
Borland, John Nelson
Borle, André Bernard
Borne, Mortimer
Bornemann, Alfred Henry
Bornstein, Lester Milton
Borofsky, Ruth Braverman
Borowitz, Sidney
Borowsky, Irvin J.
Borroff, Marie
Borsari, George Robert, Jr.
Borsher, Harry Nathan
Borst, Lyle Benjamin
Bortner, Doyle McClean
Borton, Hugh
Borum, Wylie Griffin
Bosch, Allan Whitworth
Bose, Amar Gopal
Boshkov, Stefan Hristov
Bosland, Paul Cullen
Boslow, Harold Meyer
Boss, Kenneth Jay
Boss, Richard Woodruff
Bosserman, Joseph Norwood
Bossidy, Lawrence Arthur
Bost, Raymond Morris
Boster, Davis Eugene
Bostert, Russell Henry
Bostick, Winston Harper
Boswell, Marion Lillard
Boswell, Victor Rickman
Bosworth, Raymond Francis
Bothmer, Bernard V.
Bothmer, Dietrich Felix von
Bothner-By, Aksel Arnold
Bothwell, Lawrence L.
Botkin, Henry
Botstein, Leon
Bott, Raoul
Bottiglia, William Filbert
Bottkol, Joseph McGrath
Bottler, Edgar O.
Botts, Truman Arthur
Botwinick, Michael
Boucher, (Charles) Gene
Boucher, Louis Jack
Boucher, Thomas O'Neil
Boucot, Katharine Rosenbaum (Mrs. Samuel Booth Sturgis)
Boudin, Leonard B.
Bougas, Stanley John
Boughton, Walter Leroy
Boughton, Welby Edward
Bouhuys, Arend
Boulanger, Robert Norman
Boulden, Kenneth Webster
Boulos, Sami Ibrahim
Boultinghouse, Marion Craig Bettinger
Boulton, Charles Vincent
Bourdon, David Joseph, Jr.
Bourgault, Roy Francis
Bourgeois, Louise
Bourjaily, Monte Ferris
Bourland, James Fagan
Bourne, Frank Card
Bourne, Henry Clark, Jr.
Bourne, Peter Geoffry
Bourne, Philip Walley
Bourneuf, Henri J.
Bourquin, Rene Mark
Bousfield, Weston Ashmore
Boutell, Clarence Burley (Clip)
Boutin, Bernard Louis
Bouton, James Alan
Bova, Benjamin William
Bovard, James Moorhead
Bovasso, Julia (Julie) Anne
Bove, Januar D., Jr.
Bovey, Frank Alden
Bowden, Burnham
Bowden, Robert John
Bowden, William Paul, Jr.
Bowden, William Robert, Jr.
Bowditch, Nathaniel Rantoul
Bowdler, William G.
Bowen, Charles Parnell, Jr.
Bowen, Douglas Malcomsom
Bowen, Harold Gardiner, Jr.
Bowen, Harvey Kent
Bowen, John Sheets
Bowen, Murray
Bowen, Orlando Moore
Bowen, William Gordon
Bower, John Arnold, Jr.
Bower, Marvin
Bower, Richard Stuart
Bowerman, Richard H.
Bowers, Francis Robert
Bowers, Fredson Thayer
Bowers, John Z.
Bowers, Raymond
Bowers, Roy Anderson
Bowersock, Donald Curtis
Bowersock, Glen Warren
Bowersock, Justin Dewitt, III
Bowery, Thomas Glenn
Bowie, David (David Robert Jones)
Bowie, Morris A.
Bowie, Norman Ernest
Bowie, Robert Richardson
Bowie, Thomas Donald
Bowker, John Gerald
Bowles, Aubrey Russell, Jr.
Bowles, Chester
Bowles, Edward Lindley
Bowles, Paul
Bowles, Walter Donald
Bowling, James Chandler
Bowman, A. Smith
Bowman, Ben Cook
Bowman, Frank Paul
Bowman, James Kinsey
Bowman, Linn Bruce
Bowman, Peter William
Bowman, Richard Carl
Bowman, Robert Gibson
Bowman, Victor
Bowman, Ward Simon, Jr.
Bownes, Hugh Henry
Bowser, James William
Bowsher, Charles Arthur
Boxer, Stanley Robert
Boyce, Carroll Wilson
Boyce, Frank Gordon
Boyce, Joseph Canon
Boyce, William Edward
Boychuk, Joseph Michael
Boyd, Aquilino Edgardo
Boyd, Charles Alexander
Boyd, David Preston
Boyd, Earl Neal
Boyd, Gordon
Boyd, Hugh Newell
Boyd, James
Boyd, J(esse) Cookman, Jr.
Boyd, John Dominic
Boyd, Julian Parks
Boyd, Linn John
Boyd, Malcolm
Boyd, Maurice Oswald
Boyd, Robert
Boyd, Robert Osborn
Boyd, Robert Stewart
Boyd, Robert Wright, Jr.
Boyd, Samuel Matthew
Boyd, Thomas Munford
Boyd, William, Jr.
Boyden, Alan Arthur
Boyden, Sidney Millard
Boyer, David Creighton
Boyer, Ernest LeRoy
Boyer, Robert Allen
Boyer, Vincent Saull
Boyes, Jon L.
Boykan, Martin
Boykin, Lykes M.
Boylan, George Sylvester, Jr.
Boylan, J. Richard
Boylan, William Alvin
Boyle, Kay
Boyle, Richard John
Boyle, Robert Patrick
Boyle, Willard Sterling
Boyle, William Leo, Jr.
Boynton, Robert Paul
Boynton, Willard Harold
Bozeman, Adda Bruemmer
Bozone, Billie Rae
Bozorth, Richard Milton
Bozzuto, Adam John
Brace, Gerald Warner
Brace, John Wells
Brace, Robert DeWitt
Brace, William Francis
Braceland, Francis James
Brach, Paul Henry
Brack, William Dennis
Bracken, Charles Herbert
Bracken, John Paul
Bracken, John Robert
Brackman, Robert
Bracy, Terrence Lester
Bradburn, James Rupert
Bradbury, Charles William, Jr.
Bradbury, Robert Milton, Jr.
Brademas, John
Braden, Spruille
Braden, Thomas Wardell
Braderman, Eugene Maur
Bradford, Barbara Taylor
Bradford, David Holland, Jr.
Bradford, Hilary Phariss
Bradford, John Carroll
Bradford, Robert Ernest
Bradford, Robert Fiske
Bradford, William Leslie
Bradlee, Benjamin Crowninshield
Bradley, Earl Halliday
Bradley, Edward Sculley
Bradley, Emmett Hughes
Bradley, Francis Xavier
Bradley, Gene Elliott
Bradley, Patricia Ellen
Bradley, Paul Lincoln
Bradley, Stanley Edward
Bradley, Sterling Gaylen
Bradley, Wilmot Hyde
Bradshaw, Eugene Barry
Bradshaw, Robert Walker
Bradshaw, Thomas Alexander
Bradsher, Henry St. Amant
Bradway, Joseph Fowler, Jr.
Brady, Frank Robert
Brady, James Winston
Brady, John Paul
Brady, Joseph John
Brady, Joseph Vincent
Brady, Nicholas Frederick
Brady, Roscoe O.
Brady, Rupert Joseph
Brady, William Patrick
Brady, Wray Grayson
Bragarnick, Robert
Braham, William Walter
Brainard, Alexander Nash
Brainard, Paul Henry
Brainard, William Crittenden
Brainerd, John G.
Brainerd, Stanford Howard
Braislin, Gordon Stuart
Braisted, Paul Judson
Brakeley, George Archibald, Jr.
Bralley, James Alexander, Jr.
Bramble, James Henry
Brameld, Theodore
Brammer, Noah Grover
Bramson, Leon
Bramwell, Henry
Branch, Claude Raymond
Branch, William Blackwell
Brand, Edward Cabell
Brand, Joseph Lyon
Brand, Oscar
Brand, Robert Allyn
Brandborg, Stewart Monroe
Brandenburg, David John
Brandenburg, John Nelson
Brandenburg, Richard George
Brandon, Alfred Northrup
Brandon, Arthur Leon
Brandon, Brumsic, Jr.
Brandon, (Oscar) Henry
Brandow, George Elmer
Brandow, Theodore
Brandt, Carol
Brandt, Mortimer Stirling
Brandt, Nathan Henry, Jr.
Brandt, Richard Martin
Brandt, Richard Paul
Brandt, Warren
Brandwein, Naftali Chaim
Brandwen, Maxwell
Branin, M(anlif) Lelyn
Branley, Franklyn Mansfield
Brannan, Robert Russel
Branscomb, Lewis McAdory
Branson, Herman Russell
Brant, Henry
Branton, Daniel
Branton, Wiley Austin
Brasfield, Evans Booker
Brashares, William Charles
Brashich, Deyan Ranko
Brass, Philip
Brassler, Norman
Braswell, Arnold Webb
Bratt, Floyd Clarence
Bratton, Joseph Key
Braucher, Robert
Brault, Gerard Joseph
Braun, Armin Charles John
Braun, Daniel Carl
Braun, George August
Braun, Kurt
Braun, Ludwig
Braun, Walter Gustav
Braunwald, Eugene
Braunwald, Nina Starr
Brautigan, Richard
Braver, Rita Lynn
Braverman, Robert Jay
Braxton, Anthony
Braxton, Wilbert Leo
Bray, Leslie William, Jr.
Bray, Michael Dennis
Bray, Oscar S.
Bray, Philip James
Brayman, Harold
Brazell, Karen Woodard
Brazelton, Thomas Berry
Bream, Julian
Breathitt, Edward Thompson
Breaux, John B.
Brebbia, John Henry
Brecher, Edward Moritz
Brecher, Melvin
Brecher, Samuel
Brecht, Warren Frederick
Breck, Luther Adams
Brecker, Manfred
Bredemeier, Harry Charles
Bredo, William
Bredon, Glen Eugene
Breecher, Charles Herman
Breed, Nathaniel Preston
Breeden, Edward Lebbaeus, Jr.
Breedis, Charles
Breedlove, Howell Adams, Jr.
Breen, F. Glenn
Breese, Gerald William
Breeskin, Adelyn Dohme
Breger, William N.
Breggin, Peter Roger
Bregman, Benjamin Bernard
Bregman, Jacob Israel
Brehm, William Keith
Breines, Simon
Breinin, Goodwin M.
Breinin, Raymond
Breit, Gregory
Breitbach, Harry Franklin
Breitbarth, S. Robert
Breitel, Charles D.
Breitenfeld, Frederick, Jr.
Breitkreuz, George William
Brement, Marshall
Bremermann, Herbert John, Jr.
Bremser, George, Jr.
Brendler, Herbert
Brennan, Daniel Joseph
Brennan, Donald George
Brennan, Francis Patrick
Brennan, Harold James
Brennan, James G.
Brennan, James Thomas
Brennan, Joseph Cantwell
Brennan, Joseph Edward
Brennan, Joseph Gerard
Brennan, Michael Joseph
Brennan, Paul Joseph
Brennan, William Joseph, Jr.
Brennan, William Robert, Jr.
Brennen, William Stuart
Brenner, Charles
Brenner, David
Brenner, Edward John
Brenner, Egon
Brenner, Erma
Brenner, Frank
Brenner, Joseph Donald
Brenner, Theodore Engelbert
Brent, Andrew Jackson
Brent, Robert Leonard
Brent, Walter Rudolf
Brereton, Harmar
Bresee, James Collins
Bresin, Millard
Breslin, Jimmy
Breslin, John Pershing
Breslow, Ronald Charles
Bresnahan, William Alman
Bresnick, Edward
Bressler, Bernard
Bressler, Charles
Bressler, Marvin
Brett, Barbara Jeanne Zink
Brettholle, Frank Marsh
Brettschneider, Bertram Donald
Brett-Smith, John Ralph Brett
Bretz, Frank Henry
Breunig, LeRoy Clinton
Breuninger, Tyrone
Breverman, Harvey
Brevig, Per Andreas
Brew, John Otis
Brewer, Helene Maxwell
Brewer, John Withrow
Brewer, Marion Carey
Brewer, Melvin Duane
Brewer, Oliver Gordon, Jr.
Brewer, Ronald Junior
Brewer, William Conant, Jr.
Brewer, William Dodd
Brewster, Carroll Worcester
Brewster, Herbert Stevens, Jr.
Brewster, Robert Charles
Brewster, Seward Blanchard
Brewster, William Souther
Bria, George Emil
Brian, Harry Findley
Brice, Neil Mather
Brickbauer, Charles Gustav
Brickell, Edward Ernest, Jr.
Bricker, George W(alter), Jr.
Bricker, William Rudolph
Brickfield, Cyril Francis
Bricklin, Mark Harris
Bricklin, Patricia Ellen
Brickman, Morrie
Brickman, William Wolfgang
Brickwedde, Ferdinand Graft
Bridegam, Willis Edward, Jr.
Bridenbaugh, Carl
Bridge, John Frost
Bridges, Samuel Willard, Jr.
Bridges, William Andrew
Brieant, Charles La Monte, Jr.
Brief, Henry
Briggs, Charles Christian
Briggs, David Garrison
Briggs, Edward Samuel
Briggs, Ernest
Briggs, F. Norman
Briggs, Harold Melvin
Briggs, Herbert Spencer
Briggs, Herbert Whittaker
Briggs, John Gurney, Jr.
Briggs, Kenneth Arthur
Briggs, Morton Winfield
Briggs, Philip
Briggs, Shirley Ann
Briggs, W. Bradford
Bright, Harold Elias
Bright, Harold Frederick
Bright, John
Bright, Margaret
Bright, Willard Mead
Brightman, Emerson Eliot
Brightman, Henry S.
Brightman, Robert Lloyd
Brighton, Carl Theodore
Briles, Nelson Kelley
Brill, Curt Kenneth
Brill, Daniel Herbert
Brill, Henry
Brilliant, Richard
Brim, Orville Gilbert, Jr.
Brimmer, Andrew Felton
Brinberg, Herbert Raphael
Brinckerhoff, Charles M.
Brinckerhoff, Drew Quackenbush
Brink, Frank, Jr.
Brink, William Joseph, Jr.
Brinkley, David
Brinkley, Homer Lee
Brinkley, Joseph Willard
Brinkman, Richard Gene
Brinkmann, Heinrich Wilhelm
Brinnin, John Malcolm
Brinton, Samuel Jervis, Jr.
Briscoe, John Hanson
Brisson, Frederick
Bristol, Benjamin Hiel
Bristol, Lee Hastings, Jr.
Bristol, Rexford Allyn
Britt, Rolland W.
Brittain, Alfred, III
Brittenham, Raymond Lee
Broadbent, Thomas Valentine
Broadhead, James Lowell
Broadman, Arthur R.
Brobeck, John Raymond
Broches, Aron
Brochin, Murry David
Brock, Alice May
Brock, James Sidney
Brock, Karena Diane

Byrne, Margery Eleanor Little (Mrs. Thomas E. Byrne)
Byrne, Robert Eugene
Byrne, Thomas Ryan
Byrnes, Arthur F.
Byrnes, Edward T.
Byrnes, John W.
Byroade, Henry Alfred
Byrod, Fred Jacob
Byrom, Fletcher Lauman
Byron, Goodloe Edgar
Bysiewicz, Shirley Raissi
Cabeen, Samuel Kirkland
Cabell, Richard Aylett
Cabell, William Daniel
Cabot, John G. L.
Cabot, Louis Wellington
Cabot, Paul Codman
Cabot, Thomas Dudley
Cadbury, William Edward, Jr.
Caddy, Edmund Harrington Homer, Jr.
Cades, Stewart Russell
Cadge, William Fleming
Cadigan, George Leslie
Cadigan, Robert James
Cadigan, William Joseph
Cadmus, Paul
Cady, Howard Stevenson
Caesar, Henry A., II
Caesar, Irving
Caffrey, Andrew Augustine
Caffrey, Francis David
Cage, John
Cahan, William George
Cahill, George Francis, Jr.
Cahill, Joseph T.
Cahn, Charles, II
Cahn, Jean Camper
Cahn, John Werner
Cahn, Joshua Binion
Cahn, Robert
Cahners, Walter James
Cain, Elizabeth D. McCall (Mrs. Walker O. Cain)
Cain, George Harvey
Cain, James Mallahan
Cain, Walker O.
Caine, Lynn
Cairns, Gordon Mann
Cairns, Robert William
Cairns, Theodore LeSueur
Cajori, Charles Florian
Cakmak, Ahmet Sefik
Calabi, Eugenio
Calabresi, Guido
Calabro, Louis
Calame, Gerald Paul
Calcagno, Lawrence
Calder, Alexander
Calder, Alexander, Jr.
Calder, Cameron H.
Calder, Kenneth Thomas
Calder, Robert George, Jr.
Calderone, Frank Anthony
Calderone, Mary Steichen (Mrs. Frank A. Calderone)
Calderwood, Stanford Matson
Caldwell, Carlyle G.
Caldwell, Charles Gambill
Caldwell, Janet Taylor (Mrs. William E. Stancell)
Caldwell, Joseph Morton
Caldwell, Sarah
Caldwell, William Anthony
Caldwell, William Edward, Jr.
Calfee, William Howard
Calhoon, Jesse Mayo
Calhoun, Jose Machado
Calhoun, Joseph Dukes
Califano, Joseph Anthony, Jr.
Caliguiri, Richard S.
Caliquiri, Lawrence Anthony
Calisher, Hortense (Mrs. Curtis Harnack)
Calisti, Louis J. P.
Calkins, Carroll Cecil
Calkins, Charles Richard
Calkins, Evan
Calkins, Gary Nathan
Calkins, Robert De Blois
Callaham, John Robert
Callahan, Daniel John
Callahan, Daniel Joseph, III
Callahan, Harry Morey
Callahan, Joseph Patrick
Callan, John Henry
Callander, Bruce Douglas
Callaway, Ben Anderson
Callaway, David Henry, Jr.
Callaway, James Thorpe
Callaway, Paul Smith
Callaway, William Howard
Callen, Earl Robert
Callen, Herbert Bernard
Callender, John Hancock
Calligar, Dee Martin
Callmer, James Peter
Callo, Joseph Francis
Callow, Allan Dana
Callum, Myles
Calman, Robert Frederick
Calmer, Ned
Calver, James Lewis
Calvert, Gordon Lee
Calvert, James Francis
Cambel, Ali B.
Cambere, Ara Angele
Cameron, Allen
Cameron, Barney George
Cameron, Donald Angus
Cameron, Duncan Hume
Cameron, John Lansing
Cameron, Thomas William Lane
Camicia, Nicholas Thomas
Caminos, Horacio
Caminos, Ricardo Augusto
Camm, Frank Ambler
Cammarosano, Joseph Raphael
Camp, James Leonidas, Jr.
Camp, Katherine Merrill Lindsley
Camp, Lawrence Hicks
Camp, Wesley Douglass
Camp, William Perrine
Campana, Richard John
Campanella, Roy
Campbell, Alan Keith
Campbell, Ashley Sawyer
Campbell, Byron Adams
Campbell, Catherine Hartshorn (Mrs. Crawford Campbell)
Campbell, Colin Dearborn
Campbell, Colin Goetze
Campbell, Donald Alfred
Campbell, Douglass
Campbell, Edmund Douglas
Campbell, Edwin Denton
Campbell, Frank Carter
Campbell, George Stuart
Campbell, H. Stuart
Campbell, Herbert Peterkin
Campbell, Hugh Stewart
Campbell, James Fromhart
Campbell, John Coert
Campbell, John Palmer
Campbell, Joseph
Campbell, Kenneth
Campbell, Levin Hicks
Campbell, Linzy Leon
Campbell, Loraine Leeson (Mrs. Walter E. Campbell)
Campbell, Marion (Mrs. Douglass Campbell)
Campbell, Mary Eastman
Campbell, Nicholas Joseph, Jr.
Campbell, Norman Lloyd
Campbell, Robert Charles
Campbell, Robert Craig
Campbell, Robert Duff
Campbell, Robert Emmett
Campbell, Robert Gordon
Campbell, Ronald Neil
Campbell, Stewart Fred
Campbell, Van Clyde
Campbell, Walter Edward
Campbell, Walter Eugene
Campbell, William Durant
Campbell, William Steen
Campioli, Mario Ettore
Campion, Donald Richard
Canaday, John E.
Canal, Carlos M., Jr.
Canapary, Herbert Carton
Canavan, John Joseph
Canby, Vincent
Cancelliere, Marion A.
Cancro, Robert
Cane, Melville Henry
Canellakis, Evangelo Stamatios
Canfield, Cass
Canfield, Edward Francis
Canfield, William Newton
Canham, Erwin Dain
Canham, Robert Allen
Caniff, Milton Arthur
Cannell, Peter Best
Cannella, John Matthew
Canning, Jessie Marie
Cannon, Bradford
Cannon, Herbert Seth
Cannon, Howard Henry
Cannon, Howard Walter
Cannon, John
Cannon, Joseph Edward
Cannon, LeGrand, Jr.
Cannon, Mark Wilcox
Cannon, Norman Lawrence
Cannon, William John
Cansler, Leslie Ervin
Cant, Gilbert
Cantarella, Michele Francesco
Cantarow, Abraham
Cantella, Vincent Michele
Canter, Milton Ernest
Canter, Stanley D.
Cantini, Virgil D.
Cantlay, George Gordon
Cantor, B. Gerald
Cantor, Charles Robert
Cantor, Edward Allen
Cantor, Samuel Charles
Cantrell, Lana
Cantwell, James Francis
Cantwell, John Dalzell, Jr.
Cantwell, John Walsh
Cantwell, Mary
Cantwell, Raymond Joseph
Cantwell, Robert
Cantwell, Robert Emmett
Canty, Donald James
Canup, William Caleb
Capalbo, Carmen Charles
Caparn, Rhys (Mrs. Herbert Johannes Steel)
Capasso, Henry F.
Capek, Milic
Caplan, Albert Joseph
Caplan, Gerald
Caplan, Louis
Caples, James Stephen
Caples, John
Caplin, Mortimer Maxwell
Caplow, Theodore
Capone, Alphonse William
Capone, Lucien, Jr.
Capote, Truman
Capouya, Emile
Capp, Al
Cappiello, Tony
Cappon, Rene Jacques
Capra, Jack Remo
Capranica, Robert Rudy
Capron, William Mosher
Caputo, Bruce F.
Caras, Roger Andrew
Caravatt, Paul Joseph, Jr.
Carb, Stephen Ames
Carbine, John Dugan
Carbine, Patricia Theresa
Carbone, Peter Philip
Carbone, Robert Frank
Card, Annon Melton
Cardenas, Blandina
Cardinali, Albert John
Cardoni, Horace Robert
Cardozo, Benjamin Mordecai
Cardozo, Manoel
Cardozo, Michael Hart
Cardwell, James Bruce
Carelli, Gabor Paul
Caretto, Albert Alexander
Carewe, Sylvia
Carey, Charles Jeremiah
Carey, Edward John
Carey, Francis E.
Carey, Francis James
Carey, Gerard V.
Carey, Hugh Leo
Carey, J. Edwin
Carey, James Henry
Carey, Jane Perry Clark
Carey, John
Carey, Raymond Bernard, Jr.
Carey, Richard Fremont
Carey, Robert Williams
Carey, William Nelson, Jr.
Carey, William Polk
Cargill, Ian Peter M.
Cargill, James Nelson
Cargo, William Ira
Caris, Theodore
Carleton, John Walker
Carlhian, Jean Paul
Carlin, Robert Burnell
Carliner, David
Carlisle, Richard F.
Carlisle, Robert Bruce
Carlock, John K.
Carlos, James Paul
Carlough, Edward F.
Carlson, Bruce Robbins
Carlson, Charles Arthur, Jr.
Carlson, Earland Irving
Carlson, Henning Maurice
Carlson, John Swink
Carlson, Lenus Jesse
Carlson, Marvin Albert
Carlson, Norman A.
Carlson, Norman Eugene
Carlson, Reynold Erland
Carlson, Robert Oscar
Carlson, Suzanne Olive
Carlson, Theodore Joshua
Carlsson, Percy Allan
Carlton, Steven Norman
Carlton, Winslow
Carlton-Jones, Dennis
Carlucci, Frank Charles, III
Carmichael, Alexander Douglas
Carmichael, Allan Russell
Carmichael, Donald Scott
Carmichael, Douglas
Carmichael, James H.
Carmichael, William Daniel
Carmody, Martin Doan
Carnahan, Frances Morris
Carnahan, Ralph Herbert
Carnell, Paul Herbert
Carnes, James Robert
Carnes, Wilson Woodrow
Carnese, Paul Joseph, Jr.
Carney, Dennis Joseph
Carney, John Owen
Carnicero, Jorge
Carolan, Vincent Lydon
Carovano, John Martin
Carp, George
Carp, Richard Irvin
Carpender, James Wood Johnson
Carpenter, Charles Irving
Carpenter, Clifford Earl
Carpenter, Delma Rae, Jr.
Carpenter, Donald DuBois
Carpenter, Frank Morton
Carpenter, Gene Blakely
Carpenter, Helen McCracken
Carpenter, James Morton
Carpenter, John Elliott
Carpenter, John Marshall
Carpenter, Malcolm Breckenridge
Carpenter, Monte Cutler
Carpenter, Robert R. M.
Carpenter, Stanley Sherman
Carpino, Louis A.
Carr, Arthur Charles
Carr, Arthur Japheth
Carr, Bernadette Patricia (Carrozza)
Carr, Charles Jelleff
Carr, Edward Albert, Jr.
Carr, Francis Thomas
Carr, Hubert Franklin
Carr, Kenneth Monroe
Carr, Lawrence Edward, Jr.
Carr, M. Robert
Carr, Malcolm Wallace
Carr, Martin Douglas
Carr, Milton L.
Carr, Oscar Clark, Jr.
Carr, William George
Carra, Andrew Joseph
Carreiro, Joseph Alvarez
Carret, Philip Lord
Carretta, Albert Aloysius
Carrico, Harry Lee
Carrier, Ronald Edwin
Carrington, John Claiborne
Carrington, Malcolm, Jr.
Carroll, Albert
Carroll, Donald Cary
Carroll, Edward Gonzalez
Carroll, Elisabeth
Carroll, Sister Elizabeth
Carroll, Francis Brian
Carroll, George Joseph
Carroll, Gladys Hasty
Carroll, Gordon
Carroll, Holbert Nicholson
Carroll, James Matthew
Carroll, J(efferson) Roy, Jr.
Carroll, Lewis Andrew
Carroll, Loren
Carroll, Mark Sullivan
Carroll, Marshall Elliott
Carroll, Mitchell Benedict
Carroll, Robert Joseph
Carroll, Robert W.
Carroll, Thomas Sylvester
Carroll, Vinnette Justine
Carrow, Milton Michael
Carruth, Charles Weldon
Carruth, Gorton Veeder
Carruth, Hayden
Carson, Charles William, Jr.
Carson, Gerald Hewes
Carson, Lettie Gay (Mrs. Gerald H. Carson)
Carson, Ralph Moore
Carstens, Harold Henry
Carstensen, Hans Louis, Jr.
Carswell, Robert
Carter, Alan
Carter, Clarence Holbrook
Carter, David Giles
Carter, David Vernon
Carter, Edward Walter, III
Carter, Elliott Cook, Jr.
Carter, Everett Charlie
Carter, Forest Charles
Carter, Granville Wellington
Carter, Harlon Bronson
Carter, Harry Tyson
Carter, Hugh Alton, Jr.
Carter, James Earl, Jr. (Jimmy)
Carter, James R.
Carter, John Bernard
Carter, John Mack
Carter, Joseph Ray
Carter, Richard
Carter, Robert Lee
Carter, Ronald
Carter, Rosalynn Smith
Carter, Samuel Thomson, III
Carter, Sidney
Carter, Theresa Howard
Carter, Wilfred Wilson
Carter, William Alvin
Carter, William Beverly, Jr.
Carter, William Gilbert
Carter, William Hodding, III
Carter, William Minor
Carter, William Walton
Carthy, Margaret
Cartmell, Peter
Cartmell, Vinton Aikins
Carton, John Victor
Carton, Marvyn
Carucci, Samuel Anthony
Carusi, Eugene Cassin
Caruso, Richard Vincent
Carvel, Elbert Nostrand
Carver, George Allen
Carver, Stanley Lloyd
Carwile, Atwood Smith
Cary, Charles
Cary, Charles Oswald
Cary, Frank Taylor
Cary, Freeman Hamilton
Cary, James Donald
Cary, Sturges Flagler
Cary, William Lucius
Casals-Ariet, Jordi
Casarett, George William
Casazza, Alfred John
Cascieri, Arcangelo
Case, Charles Carroll
Case, Clifford Philip
Case, Eugene Lawrence
Case, Everett Needham
Case, Hadley
Case, John Crowther
Case, Josephine Young (Mrs. Everett Case)
Case, Lynn Marshall
Case, Manning Eugene, Jr.
Case, Richard Werber
Casei, Nedda
Casey, Albert Vincent
Casey, Claude C., Jr.
Casey, Edward Dennis
Casey, Eugene Bernard
Casey, James J.
Casey, Maurice Francis
Casey, Ralph Edward
Casey, Samuel Alexander
Casey, Thomas F.
Cash, Frank Errette, Jr.
Cash, James Barrett, Jr.
Cash, Rowley Vincent
Cashen, Henry Christopher, II
Cashin, Bonnie
Cashin, Richard Marshall
Casner, Andrew James
Cason, Robert Benjamin
Caspar, Donald Louis Dvorak
Caspar, George John
Caspari, Max Edward
Caspary, Vera
Casper, Leonard Ralph
Caspersen, Finn Michael Westby
Cass, A. Carl
Cass, Millard
Cass, Rosemary Higgins
Cassavetes, John
Cassell, Eric Jonathan
Cassell, George Louis
Cassella, William Nathan, Jr.
Casselman, William E., II
Cassels-Brown, Alastair Kennedy
Cassidy, James Joseph
Cassill, Ronald Verlin
Cassimatis, Peter John
Cassini, Oleg Lolewski
Castagna, Edwin
Castagnetta, Grace Sharp
Castaldo, Vincent Richard
Castano, Giovanni
Castel, Nico
Castellan, Gilbert William
Castelli, Alexander Gerard
Caster, Richard C. (Rich)
Castle, Emery Neal
Castle, Jerome
Castle, Joseph Lanktree
Castle, Wendell Keith
Castle, William Bosworth
Castle, William Eugene
Castleman, Benjamin
Castleman, (Esther) Riva
Castleman, Louis Samuel
Casty, David
Caswell, John Beveridge
Cataldo, Bernard Francis
Catania, Anthony Charles
Catanzaro, Joseph Anthony
Catanzaro, Tony
Catapano, Joseph John
Cates, John Martin, Jr.
Catharine, Sister Marie
Cathcart, Harold Robert
Cathcart, Robert Stephen
Catherman, Byron King
Catherwood, Cummins
Catlin, Sara Huntington
Catravas, George Nicholas
Catterson, Walter Paul
Cattier, Jean
Catto, Henry Edward, Jr.
Catton, Bruce
Catton, William Bruce
Cauna, Nikolajs
Causey, Beverley Douglas, Jr.
Cauthen, Baker James
Cauthen, Irby Bruce, Jr.
Cauthen, Steve
Cava, Michael Patrick
Cavaglieri, Giorgio
Cavallo, Diana
Cavallon, Giorgio
Cavanagh, Edward Francis, Jr.
Cavanaugh, Gordon
Cavanaugh, John Joseph
Cave, Jere Shunk
Cave, John Barnhardt
Cave, Vernal Gordon
Cavell, Stanley Louis
Caverly, Gardner A.
Cavers, David Farquhar
Cavert, Twila Lytton (Mrs. Samuel McCrea Cavert)
Caves, Richard Earl
Cavett, Dick
Cavin, Patty (Mrs. F. Edward Cavin)
Cavior, Warren Joseph
Cawl, Franklin Robert, Jr.
Cawley, Edward Philip
Cawley, Francis Riggs
Caws, Peter James
Cayne, Bernard Stanley
Cebra, John Joseph
Cecere, Ada Rasario
Cecere, Gaetano
Cedarbaum, Bernard
Cedrone, Louis Robert, Jr.
Cefola, Michael
Cella, Phyllis Ann
Celler, Emanuel
Celli, Mario C.
Celli, Vittorio
Ceravolo, Joseph
Cerminaro, John
Cervenka, Arthur Frank
Cesarani, Salvatore Joseph
Cesario, Virginia Naill
Cetta, Lewis Thomas
Chabon, Steve
Chabrier, Jacques Rene
Chadenet, Bernard
Chadwick, George Albert, Jr.
Chadwick, William G.
Chaet, Bernard Robert
Chafee, John Hubbard
Chafetz, Morris Edward
Chaikin, Sol Chick
Chait, Arnold
Chait, Frederick
Chait, Lawrence G.
Chako, Nicholas
Chakrabarty, Ananda Mohan
Chalabi, A. Fattah
Chalek, Sol
Chalker, William Rogers
Chalkley, Donald Thomas
Chall, Jeanne Sternlicht
Challinor, David
Chalmers, Gordon Hall
Chalmers, Thomas Clark
Chamberlain, Betty
Chamberlain, Charles Ernest
Chamberlain, John
Chamberlain, John Rensselaer
Chamberlain, Lloyd Baxter
Chamberlain, Mark Munroe
Chamberlain, Neil Cornelius Wolverton
Chamberlain, Ross Edwin
Chamberlain, Thomas Gassner
Chamberlain, Willard Thomas
Chamberlain, William E.
Chamberlin, George Leonard
Chamberlin, John Stephen
Chamberlin, Ward Bryan, Jr.
Chambers, Arthur Woodburne, Jr.
Chambers, Earl Denton
Chambers, Justice Marion
Chambers, Melber
Chambers, Robert Warner
Chambers, S. James
Chambliss, Rollin
Chamlin, Max
Champion, (Charles) Hale
Chan, Lo-Yi Cheung Yuen
Chance, Britton
Chance, Henry Martyn, II
Chancellor, John William
Chandler, Alfred Dupont, Jr.
Chandler, Caroline A.
Chandler, Edgar Hugh Storer
Chandler, George Alfred
Chandler, James E.
Chandler, John, Jr.
Chandler, John Wesley
Chandler, Kenneth Ashton
Chandler, Margaret Kueffner
Chandler, Robert Flint, Jr.
Chandler, Wallace Lee
Chaney, William R.
Chang, David Ping-Chung
Chang, Kwang-Chih
Chang, Min Chueh
Chang, Nai Yong
Chang, Sheldon Shou Lien
Channell, Donald Everett
Channing, Mark Gunther
Chapanis, Alphonse
Chapin, Frederic Lincoln
Chapin, Harry Forster
Chapin, Hugh A.
Chapin, Richard
Chapin, Schuyler Garrison
Chaplin, James Crossan, IV
Chapman, Albert L.
Chapman, Alger Baldwin
Chapman, Alger Baldwin, Jr.
Chapman, Carleton Burke
Chapman, Christian Addison
Chapman, Donald D.
Chapman, Gilbert W.
Chapman, Grosvenor
Chapman, Harry Moulton
Chapman, Janet Carter Goodrich (Mrs. John William Chapman)
Chapman, John William, Jr.
Chapman, Leonard Fielding, Jr.
Chapman, Richard Palmer
Chapman, Robert B., III
Chapman, Robert DeWitt
Chapman, Thomas William
Chappell, James Wilbert
Chappell, Robert Harvey, Jr.
Chappell, Vere Claiborne
Chappell, Warren
Chappell, William Venroe, Jr.
Charanis, Peter
Charbonnet, Pierre Numa, Jr.
Chard, Roland Turner
Chargaff, Erwin
Charlap, E. Paul
Charlap, Guy Jose
Charles, Carl Francis
Charles, Raymond Alanson
Charman, Frederick Montague
Charney, Jule Gregory
Charney, Nicolas Herman
Charnin, Martin Jay
Charpentier, Arthur Aldrich
Charpie, Robert Alan
Charren, Peggy
Charters, Alexander Nathaniel
Charton, Marvin
Chartrand, Robert Lee
Charyk, Joseph Vincent
Charyn, Jerome
Chase, Aurin Moody, Jr.
Chase, Doris Totten
Chase, Edward Fuller
Chase, Edward Payson
Chase, Goodwin
Chase, Herman Burleigh
Chase, Ilka
Chase, Irving Hanson
Chase, John David
Chase, John Peirce
Chase, Lucia
Chase, Mary Coyle
Chase, Merrill Wallace
Chase, Nicholas Joseph
Chase, Norman Eli
Chase, Robert Arthur
Chase, Robert Willard
Chase, Stuart
Chase, William Howard
Chase, William Thomas, III
Chaseman, Joel
Chasen, Robert E.
Chasins, Edward A.
Chassler, Seymour Murray
Chatelain, Leon, Jr.
Chatlos, William Edward
Chatterjee, Malaya
Chaudhry, Anand
Chauncey, Henry
Chaut, Robert
Chaves, Jose Maria
Chavez, Edward A.

Condon, John Peter
Condon, Joseph Francis
Condon, Lester Patrick
Condon, Richard
Condon, Verner Holmes, Jr.
Cone, Edward Toner
Conese, Eugene Paul
Congdon, Thomas B., Jr.
Conger, Clement Ellis
Conger, Kyril B.
Conigliaro, Salvatore Alfred
Conklin, Everett Lawson
Conklin, George Melville
Conklin, George Taylor, Jr.
Conklin, Gordon Leroy
Conklin, Harold Colyer
Conklin, Kenneth Edward
Conlan, John B.
Conlan, Richard John
Conland, Stephen
Conley, Carroll Lockard
Conley, Clare Dean
Conley, Howard Harry, Jr.
Conley, Patrick
Conlon, James A.
Conlon, James Joseph
Conn, Harold O.
Connare, William Graham
Connell, Elizabeth Bishop (Mrs. John T. Connell)
Connell, Grover
Connell, Hugh Paul
Connell, John Gibbs, Jr.
Connell, Lawrence
Connell, William Francis
Connelly, Albert Ray
Connelly, John Edward, Jr.
Connelly, John Francis
Connelly, Marc
Connelly, William Howard
Conner, James Elwood
Conner, John Davis
Conner, Lewis Philip, Jr.
Conner, Richard H.
Conner, Troy Blaine, Jr.
Conner, William Curtis
Conners, William James, III
Conners, William Patrick
Connery, Paul Joseph
Connery, Robert Howe
Connolly, Paul Raymond
Connolly, Vincent James Patrick
Connor, Frances Partridge
Connor, J. Robert
Connor, John Thomas
Connor, Ralph
Connor, Thomas Byrne
Connor, Walter Robert
Connors, Edward Michael
Connors, John Michael, Jr.
Conomikes, John Gus
Conover, Harry
Conover, Harvey
Conrad, Anthony Lee
Consoli, Marc-Antonio
Constance, Thomas Ernest
Constant, Frank Woodbridge
Constant, George Zachary
Conta, Bart Joseph
Conta, Lewis Dalcin
Conte, Silvio O.
Conti, James Joseph
Converse, Gordon Noble
Converse, John Marquis
Conway, Alvin James
Conway, Edmund Virgil
Conway, Gerald Richard
Conway, Harry Donald
Conway, James Francis, Jr.
Conway, Jill Kathryn Ker
Conway, Martha Bell
Conway, Patrick Joseph
Conway, William Gaylord
Conwill, Allan Franklin
Cony, Edward Roger
Conyers, John, Jr.
Conze, Peter H.
Conzen, Willibald Hermann
Coogle, Joseph Moore, Jr.
Cook, Benjamin Hopson
Cook, Charles Davenport
Cook, Charles David
Cook, Charles Robert
Cook, Christopher Capen
Cook, Donald C.
Cook, Fred James
Cook, Gladys Emerson
Cook, Howard Alexander
Cook, John Alfred
Cook, Langdon Pingry
Cook, LeRoy Franklin, Jr.
Cook, Murray Clifton
Cook, Nathan Henry
Cook, Paul Wentworth
Cook, Peter Geoffrey
Cook, Ramona Graham
Cook, Richard Kaufman
Cook, Robert Andrew
Cook, Walter Blackwell
Cook, William Sutton
Cooke, Alfred Alistair
Cooke, Edward William
Cooke, Eileen Delores
Cooke, Jacob Ernest
Cooke, James Negley, Jr.
Cooke, Lawrence Henry
Cooke, Lloyd Miller
Cooke, Merritt Todd
Cooke, Paul Denvir
Cooke, Richard Dickson, Jr.
Cooke, Robert Edmond
Cooke, Robert John
Cooke, Roy Francis
Cooke, Terence Cardinal
Cooke, William Donald
Cooksey, Howard Harrison
Cookson, Albert Ernest
Cool, Rodney Lee
Cooley, David William
Cooley, Thomas McIntyre, II
Coolidge, Harold Jefferson
Coolidge, John Washburn
Coolidge, Rita
Coombes, James Arthur
Coombs, Charles Anthony
Coombs, Philip Hall
Coon, Carleton Stevens
Coon, Carleton Stevens, Jr.
Coon, Julius Mosher
Cooney, Barbara
Cooney, David Martin
Cooney, Joan Ganz
Cooney, John Gordon
Cooney, Joseph Patrick
Coons, Albert Hewett
Coons, Sheldon R.
Coontz, Gustaf
Cooper, David Shearer
Cooper, Edward Brooks
Cooper, Edwin Lavern
Cooper, Francis Loren
Cooper, Franklin Seaney
Cooper, George Brinton
Cooper, Gustav Arthur
Cooper, Irving Ben
Cooper, James Wayne
Cooper, John Allen Dicks
Cooper, John Crossan, Jr.
Cooper, John Lewis
Cooper, John N.
Cooper, Kenneth Banks
Cooper, Leon N.
Cooper, Lester Irving
Cooper, Louise Field
Cooper, Mario
Cooper, Milton
Cooper, Norman
Cooper, Richard Foss
Cooper, Richard Lee
Cooper, Richard Newell
Cooper, Robert Arthur, Jr.
Cooper, Robert Shanklin
Cooper, Susan Mary
Cooper, Theodore
Cooper, Thomas A.
Cooper, Warren Stanley
Cooper, Weldon
Cooper, William Eugene
Cooper, William Marion
Cooper, William Wager
Cooperman, James
Cooperman, Philip
Cooperstein, Sherwin Jerome
Coor, Lattie Finch
Coover, Robert Lowell
Cope, Oliver
Cope, William Henry
Copeland, Arthur Herbert, Jr.
Copeland, Donald Eugene
Copeland, Frederick Cleveland
Copeland, Jo
Copeland, John Alexander, III
Copeland, John Wilson
Copeland, Lammot du Pont
Copeland, Norman Arland
Copeland, Randall E.
Copeland, William John
Copenhaver, Charles Leonard
Copenhaver, John Harrison, Jr.
Coplan, Norman Allan
Copland, Aaron
Coplans, John Rivers
Coppenbarger, Howard Lee
Coppens, Philip
Coppersmith, Jerome
Coppersmith, S. James
Coppoc, William Joseph
Coppock, Joseph David
Coppola, Andrew Joseph
Coquillette, Robert McTavish
Corbató, Fernando José
Corbett, Winfield Scott
Corbin, Albert Charles
Corbin, Arnold
Corbin, Claire (Mrs. Arnold Corbin)
Corbin, Ralph Arthur
Corbin, Sol Neil
Corcoran, Ambrose Leslie
Corcoran, Howard Francis
Corcoran, John Joseph
Corcoran, John William
Corcoran, Thomas Gardiner
Corcoran, Thomas John
Corcoran, Walter George
Cordasco, Francesco
Cordes, Alexander Charles
Cordes, John Henry
Cordier, Ralph Waldo
Cordrey, Richard Stephen
Corea, (Armando) Chick
Corea, Luis Felipe
Corell, Robert Walden
Corelli, Franco
Corelli, John Charles
Corey, Edwin Raymond
Corey, Elias James
Cori, Carl Ferdinand
Cori, Gregory Salvatore
Coriden, Guy Edward
Coriell, Lewis Lemon
Corinaldi, Austin
Corish, Joseph Ryan
Corkle, Francesca Therese
Corley, Frank Winston, Jr.
Corliss, John Ozro
Corman, James Charles
Corn, Joseph Edward, Jr.
Corn, Leslie Joan
Corn, Merton
Corn, Morton
Cornblath, Marvin
Cornelio, Albert Carmen
Cornelison, Floyd Shovington, Jr.
Cornelius, Marty
Cornell, Corwin David
Cornell, David M.
Cornell, George Wade
Cornell, George Washington, II
Cornell, John Paul
Cornell, Samuel Douglas
Cornell, William Ainsworth
Cornelsen, Rufus
Cornely, Paul Bertau
Corner, George Washington
Cornett, Richard Orin
Cornfield, Melvin
Corning, Erastus, 2d
Cornman, James Welton
Cornwall, Joseph Clift
Cornwall, Richard S.
Cornwell, David Lance
Cornwell, Elmer Eckert, Jr.
Corr, John Patrick
Corrada, Baltasar
Correa, Gustavo
Correa, Henry A.
Corrick, Ann Marjorie
Corrigan, Frank William
Corrigan, Robert Foster
Corrigan, William Thomas
Corrin, Brownlee Sands
Corroon, Richard Francis
Corrsin, Stanley
Corry, Martha Lucille
Corsa, Helen Storm
Corsaro, Frank Andrew
Corson, Dale Raymond
Corson, Fred Pierce
Corson, John Jay
Corson, Robert William
Cort, David
Cort, David Allison
Cortada, James N.
Cortelyou, Robert Voorhees
Cortissoz, Paul
Cortlandt, Lyn
Cortner, Jean Alexander
Corwin, Virginia
Corwin, William Gaub
Coryell, Glynn Heath
Cosell, Howard (Howard William Cohen)
Coser, Lewis Alfred
Cosgrove, John Edward
Cosgrove, John Patrick
Cosmopulos, Stavros
Cossutta, Araldo Alfred
Costa, Ernest Fiorenzzo
Costa, Mary
Costanza, Angelo Anthony
Costanza, Margaret
Costanzo, Gesualdo
Costanzo, Henry John
Costello, Joseph A.
Costello, Patricia Ann
Costello, Russell Hill
Costello, Timothy William
Costle, Douglas M.
Cotellessa, Robert Francis
Cotlow, Lewis Nathaniel
Cotner, Thomas Ewing
Cott, Betty (Mrs. Ted Cott)
Cottam, Howard Rex
Cotter, Francis Patrick
Cotter, John Patrick
Cotter, Joseph Francis
Cotter, William Donald
Cotter, William Joseph
Cotter, William Ross
Cotterman, Myron Lee
Cotting, James Charles
Cotton, Dana Meserve
Cottone, Benedict Peter
Cotts, Robert Milo
Cotzias, George C.
Couch, Jack Vernon
Couch, Virgil Lee
Coudert, Alexis Carrel
Coudert, Ferdinand Wilmerding
Coughanowr, Donald Ray
Coughlan, John Appleby
Coughlan, (John) Robert
Coughlin, Howard
Coughlin, John Thomas
Coughlin, Leo Daniel, Jr.
Coughlin, Paul Joseph, Jr.
Coughlin, Richard James
Coughlin, Richard John
Coughlin, Robert Lawrence, Jr.
Coughran, Tom Bristol
Coulling, Sidney Baxter
Coulson, Robert
Coulter, James Bennett
Coulter, Kirkley Schley
Coulter, Roger Brooke
Countryman, Vern
Counts, James Curtis
Coupal, Joseph Richard, Jr.
Coupe, John Donald
Couper, Louise Pettigrew
Couper, Richard Watrous
Courant, Ernest David
Cournand, Andre F.
Courtney, Charles Edward
Courtright, Harry Richard
Cousineau, Melvin E.
Cousins, Norman
Coval, Naomi Miller
Covalt, Donald A.
Covatta, Nicholas Joseph, Jr.
Covert, Eugene Edzards
Covey, Charles William
Coville, Cabot
Cowan, Dwaine Oliver
Cowan, Edward
Cowan, Fairman Chaffee
Cowan, Frank
Cowan, J Milton
Cowan, Kenneth James
Cowan, Louis G.
Cowan, Richard Alan
Cowan, Richard Summer
Cowan, Robert George
Cowan, Stuart DuBois
Cowan, Thomas Anthony
Cowan, Wallace Edgar
Cowan, Wayne Harper
Cowart, Elgin Courtland, Jr.
Cowart, William Slater, Jr.
Cowden, Thomas Kyle
Cowen, David
Cowen, Wilson
Cowen, Wilson Walker
Cowens, David William
Cowgill, Ursula Moser
Cowherd, Raymond Gibson
Cowles, Arthur Woodruff
Cowles, Gardner
Cowles, John Todd
Cowley, Malcolm
Cowling, Vincent Frederick
Cox, Allyn
Cox, Alvin Earl
Cox, Archibald
Cox, Charles Donald
Cox, Charles Kennedy
Cox, Claire
Cox, Donald Morgan
Cox, Edwin
Cox, Gardner
Cox, George Walter, Jr.
Cox, Harvey Gallagher
Cox, John Roger
Cox, John William
Cox, Kenneth Allen
Cox, Louis Anthony
Cox, Rachel Dunaway (Mrs. Reavis Cox)
Cox, Reavis
Cox, Richard Joseph
Cox, Sally
Cox, Thomas Riggs, Jr.
Cox, Warren Jacob
Cox, William Meredith
Cox, William Walter
Coxe, George Harmon
Coxe, Louis Osborne
Coyle, Donald Walton
Cozzolino, Salvatore J.
Crabbe, Buster Clarence L.
Craft, Robert Homan
Cragwall, Joseph Samuel, Jr.
Craig, Albert Morton
Craig, Andrew Billings, III
Craig, David W.
Craig, Douglas Broward
Craig, James Barkley
Craig, John Merrill
Craig, Nancy Ellen
Craig, Paul Max, Jr.
Craig, Wilmot Russell
Craighill, Francis Hopkinson, III
Craighill, George Bowdoin, Jr.
Craigie, Walter Williams, Sr.
Craigmyle, Ronald M.
Crain, C. William
Crain, J. Wendell
Crain, James Francis
Cram, Reginald Maurice
Cramer, Edward M.
Cramer, Harold
Cramer, Morgan Joseph, Jr.
Cramer, Shannon Davenport, Jr.
Cramer, William Cato
Cramer, William Smith
Crampton, Scott Paul
Cramton, Roger Conant
Cranch, Edmund Titus
Crandall, Robert Lloyd
Crandell, Walter Bain
Crandon, Albert Seabury
Crane, Bruce
Crane, Edward Matthews, Jr.
Crane, Irving Donald
Crane, John Bever
Crane, Keith
Crane, Leo Stanley
Crane, Philip Miller
Crane, Robert Kellogg
Crane, Royston Campbell
Crane, William Joseph
Cranefield, Paul Frederic
Cranmer, H. Jerome
Cranston, Alan
Crary, Albert Paddock
Crary, Calvert Horton
Crass, Maurice Frederick, Jr.
Crater, Robert Winfield
Cratsley, Edward Kneeland
Craven, Clifford John
Crawford, Albert Benjamin, Jr.
Crawford, Bruce Edgar
Crawford, Cheryl
Crawford, Clare Wootten-Mason
Crawford, David Mackay
Crawford, Earl Boyd
Crawford, Eugene Benson, Jr.
Crawford, Frances Miriam
Crawford, Franklin David
Crawford, H(azle) R(eid)
Crawford, Kenneth Charles
Crawford, Kenneth Gale
Crawford, Meredith Pullen
Crawford, Morris DeCamp, Jr.
Crawford, Olga Elvera Anderson (Mrs. William John Crawford)
Crawford, Ralston
Crawford, William Avery
Crawford, William Hulfish
Crawford, William Rex, Jr.
Crawley, Thomas Edward
Creamer, George Bernard
Creamer, Thomas Fishback
Creamer, William Henry, III
Creasman, Ralph Dedrick
Crecine, John Patrick
Creech, Fulton Hunter
Creech, Hugh John
Creech, Wilbur Lyman
Creedon, John Joseph
Creegan, Robert Francis
Creeger, George Raymond
Creel, Dana Shannon
Creighton, Harriet Baldwin
Creighton, William Forman
Creitz, Walter Marsby
Crelin, Edmund Slocum
Cremin, Lawrence Arthur
Crenna, Richard
Crenner, James Joseph
Crenshaw, Ben
Crenshaw, Craig Moffett
Crenshaw, Francis Nelson
Crenshaw, Gordon Lee
Crenshaw, Willis Clarence, Jr.
Crepet, William Louis
Creskoff, Jacob Joshua
Crespi, Irving
Crespin, Regine (Mrs. Lou Bruder)
Cressman, George Parmley
Creutz, Edward Chester
Creviston, Richard LeRoy
Crichton, John Henderson
Crilly, William Michael
Crimmins, Alfred Stephen, Jr.
Crimmins, John Hugh
Crimmins, John Michael
Crinkley, Richmond Dillard
Criqui, William Edmund
Crisley, Francis Daniel
Crisona, James Joseph
Crispe, A. Luke
Crispell, Kenneth Raymond
Crist, Frederic Eugene
Crist, Judith (Klein)
Cristofer, Michael
Crites, Stephen Decatur
Crittenberger, Willis Dale, Jr.
Crittenden, Gazaway Lamar
Critz, Richard Laurens
Crizer, Pat William
Crocker, Lester Gilbert
Crockett, Gibson M.
Croft, Luther Gordon
Croll, Philip Dengler
Crom, James Oliver
Crombie, David Joseph
Cromley, Allan Wray
Cromley, Raymond Avolon
Crompton, Alfred W.
Cromwell, Richard P.
Cromwell, William Kennedy, III
Cronan, Calvin Shaw
Cronbach, Robert M.
Cronheim, Charles A.
Cronin, Bonnie Kathryn Lamb
Cronin, Daniel Anthony
Cronin, Joseph
Cronin, Neil Reynolds
Cronin, Paul William
Cronin, Philip Mark
Cronin, Raymond Valentine
Cronkite, Walter
Cronquist, Arthur John (Franklin Arthur Beers)
Cronyn, Hume
Crook, Dorothy
Crook, Robert Wayne
Crooks, Kathleen Morphew
Crosby, Gordon Eugene, Jr.
Crosby, Harry Herbert
Crosby, John Campbell
Crosby, Joseph Patrick
Crosby, Kenneth McCorkle
Crosby, Philip Bayard
Crosby, Sumner McKnight
Crosland, Edward Burton
Cross, Charles Tenney
Cross, Eason, Jr.
Cross, Frank Moore, Jr.
Cross, George R.
Cross, Harold Dick
Cross, Hershner
Cross, Irv
Cross, John Henry Aaron
Cross, Lenora Routon
Cross, Richard James
Cross, Robert Dougherty
Cross, Sam Young, Jr.
Cross, Theodore Lamont
Cross, William Redmond, Jr.
Crossette, George
Crossfield, Albert Scott
Crossman, William Whittard
Crouse, Farrell Rondall
Crout, John Richard
Crow, Duward Lowery
Crow, William Langstaff
Crowe, Philip Kingsland
Crowe, William James, Jr.
Crowell, Albert Dary
Crowell, Alfred Augustus
Crowell, Richard Henry
Crowell, Robert Leland
Crowell, Thomas Irving
Crowl, Philip Axtell
Crowley, Daniel Francis
Crowley, Francis Edward
Crowley, John Joseph, Jr.
Crowley, John Schaft
Crown, David Allan
Croxton, Frederick Emory
Croxton, Fred(erick) E(mory), (Jr.)
Crozier, William Marshall, Jr.
Cruickshank, Alexander Middleton
Cruikshank, Nelson Hale
Cruikshank, Warren Lott
Crum, John Kistler
Crum, Morrison Colyer
Crumb, George Henry
Crumb, Owen Joseph
Crumley, James Robert, Jr.
Cruz-Romo, Gilda
Cserr, Robert
Csoka, Stephen
Csonka, Larry Richard
Cua, Antonio S.
Cubeta, Paul Marsden
Cueman, Robert Ramsden
Cueto, Manuel Richard
Culbertson, David J.
Culbertson, Horace Coe
Culbertson, Janet Lynn
Culbertson, John Harrison
Culbertson, Robert Elmore
Cullen, Austin I.
Cullen, Bill
Cullen, George
Culler, Arthur Dwight
Culley, Perry Hager
Culligan, Glendy (Mrs. William R. Pabst, Jr.)
Culligan, John William
Cullina, William Michael
Cullinan, Elizabeth
Cullins, Peter Kendall
Cullman, Edgar Meyer
Cullman, Hugh
Cullman, Joseph Frederick, 3d
Culver, Edward Holland
Culver, John C.
Cumming, Hugh Evershed
Cumming, Hugh Smith, Jr.
Cumming, Robert Emil
Cummings, Barton A.
Cummings, John Joseph, Jr.
Cummings, Martin Marc
Cummings, Melbourne Wesley
Cummings, Milton Curtis, Jr.
Cummings, Nathan
Cummings, Parke
Cummings, Virginia Lisette
Cummins, Herman Zachary
Cundey, Paul Edward
Cuneo, Ernest
Cuneo, Gilbert Anthony
Cuneo, Paul Kleist
Cunerd, Earl H.
Cunningham, Charles Crehore
Cunningham, George Woody
Cunningham, Jack
Cunningham, James Vincent
Cunningham, Keith Allen
Cunningham, Merce
Cunningham, Morris
Cunningham, Richard Greenlaw
Cunningham, Robert Morton
Cunningham, Rosemary
Cunningham, Thomas William
Cunningham, Walter Jack
Cunningham, William Alexander, III
Cuomo, Mario Matthew
Curie, Eve
Curley, John Francis, Jr.
Curley, John Joseph, Jr.
Curnen, Edward Charles, Jr.
Curpier, Orison Bodo
Curran, Donald Frederick
Curran, Jean Alonzo
Curran, John J.
Currie, Bruce
Currier, Albert Eldred
Currier, Ruth
Curry, Abram Stauffer
Curry, Andrew Gibson
Curry, Bernard Francis
Curry, Bryce Quention
Curry, Haskell Brooks
Curry, Stowers Leigh, Jr.
Curson, Theodore
Curtin, Jane Therese
Curtin, John T.
Curtin, Philip De Armond
Curtin, Phyllis
Curtin, Sharon Rose
Curtis, Carl Thomas
Curtis, Charlotte Murray
Curtis, Christopher Michael
Curtis, Edward Peck
Curtis, James Michael
Curtis, Joseph
Curtis, Kenneth Merwin
Curtis, Laurence
Curtis, Roger William
Curtis, Staton Russell
Curtis, Walter W.
Curtis, William Edgar
Curtiss, Willis David
Cusack, Michael Joseph
Cusack, William Joseph
Cushing, Frederic Sanford
Cushing, Harry Cooke, IV
Cushman, David Wayne
Cushman, Helen Merle Baker
Cushman, Robert
Cushmore, Charles Laurence, Jr.
Cusson, Annette Forest
Custer, Raymond Thomas
Custin, Mildred
Custis, Donald L.
Cutchins, Clifford Armstrong, III

Devine, James Brendan
Devine, John Francis
Devine, Richard Joseph
Devine, Samuel Leeper
Devine, Thomas John
Devino, William Stanley
Devins, Thomas Vincent
De Vita, Vincent Theodore, Jr.
Devitt, James E.
Devlin, Albert Thomas
Devlin, Rick
Devlin, Walter John
DeVoe, Arthur Gerard
Devons, Samuel
DeVoss, James Thomas
deVries, Henry P.
De Vries, Peter
DeWeese, James Arville
de Weldon, Felix Weihs
Dewey, Bradley, Jr.
Dewey, Clarence Forbes, Jr.
Dewey, Edward Russell
Dewey, Lawrence R.
Dewhurst, Colleen
De Wind, Adrian William Andrews
De Witt, Eugene A.
DeWitt, Lew Calvin
DeWitt, Paul Burton
DeWitt, Robert Lionne
Dews, Peter Booth
Dexter, David Lawrence
Dexter, John
Dexter, John Bondy
Dexter, Lewis
Dexter, Robert Reginald
Dey, Charles Frederick
d'Harnoncourt, Anne
Dial, Morse Grant, Jr.
Diamandopoulos, Peter
Diamond, David Leo
Diamond, Freda
Diamond, Leo Aaron
Diamond, M. Jerome
Diamond, Sigmund
Diamond, William
Diamonstein, Barbaralee Dworkin
Dianis, Walter Joseph
Diassi, Patrick Andrew
Diaz, Joaquin Basilio
Diaz, Justino
Dibner, Bern
Dibner, David
Dibner, David Robert
diBonaventura, Mario
DiCarlo, Louis Michael
Dichter, Ernest
Dichter, Misha
Dicke, Robert Henry
Dickerman, Marion
Dickerson, George William
Dickerson, Nancy Hanschman
Dickey, Charles Denston, Jr.
Dickey, Charles Richard
Dickey, Ervin John, Jr.
Dickey, Francis George
Dickey, John Sloan
Dickey, Raymond Roosevelt
Dickey, Robert, III
Dickinson, Alfred James
Dickinson, Alice Braunlich
Dickinson, Charles Bruce
Dickinson, Edwin Walter
Dickinson, Elmer Newton, Jr.
Dickinson, Fairleigh Stanton, Jr.
Dickinson, Frank Herman
Dickinson, Sidney Edward
Dickinson, William Boyd
Dickinson, William Boyd, Jr.
Dickinson, William Louis
Dickler, Gerald
Dicks, Norman De Valois
Dickson, Carroll J.
Dickson, David Watson Daly
Dickson, Evelyn Wight (Mrs. Carroll J. Dickson)
Dickson, Sally Isabelle
Dickson, William Petty, Jr.
Dickstein, Sidney
Didion, Joan
Di Domenica, Robert Anthony
Diebold, Albert Richard
Diebold, Charles Robert
Diebold, John
Diefenderfer, A(lfred) James
Diehl, Val Burl
Diehl, Walter Francis
Diehm, Victor Christian
Diener, Bert
Diener, Theodor Otto
Dienstfrey, Harris David
Diercks, Frederick Otto
Dierdorff, John Ainsworth
Dies, Douglas Hilton
Dies, Edward Jerome
Dietel, William Moore
Dieter, George E., Jr.
Dietrich, Joseph Robert
Dietrich, Robert Lee
Dietsch, Robert William
Dietz, Albert George Henry
Dietz, Earl Daniel
Dietz, Frank Tobias
Dietz, Howard
Dietz, William Stephens
Dietze, Gottfried
Dievler, David Harold
Di Falco, Saverio Samuel
di Genova, Mario Henry
Digges, Sam Cook
Diggins, Peter Sheehan
Diggs, Charles C., Jr.
DiGia, Robert M.
Di Gioia, Anthony Michael, Jr.
Di Giovanni, Anthony
Dike, Kenneth Onwuka
Dikov, Joseph
Dill, Ellis Harold
Dill, William Rankin
Dillard, Dudley
Dillard, Hardy Cross
Dillard, Joseph King
Dillard, Oliver Williams
Dillavou, George Jackson
Dille, Guy
Dillenbeck, Douglas DeWitt
Dillenberger, John
Diller, Phyllis
Diller, William F.
Dilley, Frank Brown
Dilling, Mildred
Dillman, Grant
Dillon, Mrs. C. Douglas
Dillon, Clarence Douglas
Dillon, Conley Hall
Dillon, Diane Claire Sorber
Dillon, Donald
Dillon, Lionel (Leo) John
Dillon, Robert E.
Dillon, Robert Morton
Dillon, Thomas Church
Dils, Robert Earl
Di Luglio, Thomas Ross
Dilworth, Joseph Richardson
Dilworth, Richard Hanson
DiMaggio, Frank Louis
Diman, William Alexander
Dimendberg, David Charles
DiMichael, Salvatore George
Dimitri, Piero
Dimitry, John Randolph
Dimock, Marshall Edward
Dinbergs, Anatol
Dince, Robert Reuben
Dine, Jim
Dinerstein, Robert Charles
Dingell, John David, Jr.
Dingle, Raymond
Dingledy, Paul George
Dingman, Michael David
Dinicola, Albert James
Dinin, Benjamin George
Dinkeloo, John Gerard
Dinneen, Gerald Paul
Dinneen, James Francis
Dinsmore, Gordon Griffith
Dinwiddie, Donal
Dionne, Joseph Lewis
DiPalma, Joseph Rupert
DiPrima, Richard Clyde
Dirlam, Arland Augustus
DiSalle, Michael Vincent
di Sant'Angelo, Giorgio
Disbrow, Richard Edwin
Dische, Zacharias
Di Sciullo, John
Disharoon, Leslie Benjamin
Disher, John Howard
Dispeker, Thea
Di Stefano, Joseph Robert
Ditte, Andre Jacques
Dittes, James Edward
Ditzen, Lowell Russell
Ditzler, John William
Diver, William
Divers, William Keeveny
Divine, William Robinson
Dix, William Shepherd
Dixon, Fitz Eugene, Jr.
Dixon, George Francis, Jr.
Dixon, Jeane L.
Dixon, John Morris
Dixon, John Robert
Dixon, Joseph Ardiff
Dixon, Paul Rand
Dixon, Robert James
Dixon, Robert Livingston
Dixon, Roger Coit
Dixon, William James
Dizard, Wilson Paul, Jr.
Djerassi, Isaac
Djilas, Milovan
Doar, John
Dobbins, Charles Gordon
Dobbins, James Joseph
Dobbins, Richard Andrew
Dobell, Byron Maxwell
Dobelle, Evan Samuel
Dobriansky, Lev Eugene
Dobson, Alan
Dobson, Douglas Richard
Dobson, Gwen Armstrong
Dobyns, Lloyd (Allen), Jr.
Dockstader, Frederick J.
Docter, Charles Alfred
Doctorow, Edgar Lawrence
Dodd, Charles Gardner
Dodd, Christopher J.
Dodd, Edward Howard, Jr.
Dodds, Robert James, Jr.
Doder, Dusko
Dodge, Charles Granville
Dodge, Charles Malcolm
Dodge, Cleveland E.
Dodge, Cleveland Earl, Jr.
Dodge, Ernest Stanley
Dodson, Daryl Theodore
Dodson, Edward Griffith, Jr.
Dodson, Glenn Arthur
Dodson, Owen Vincent
Dodson, Richard Wolford
Doebele, William August
Doenges, Byron Frederick
Doenges, Norman Arthur
Doerfler, Leo G.
Doering, Otto Charles, Jr.
Doering, William von Eggers
Doerschuk, Ernest Edwin, Jr.
Doescher, N. Gregory
Doft, Floyd Shelton
Dohanian, Diran Kavork
Doherty, Edmond John
Doherty, Josephine Kristan
Doherty, Richard P.
Doherty, Robert Cunningham
Doherty, Robert John
Doherty, William Oliver
Dohl, Paul Raymond
Dohlman, Claes Henrik
Doi, James Isao
Doig, Jameson Wallace
Doku, Hristo Chris
Dolan, John Ralph
Dolan, Raymond Bernard
Dolan, Thomas Paul
Dolan, William David, Jr.
Doland, Dilman John
Dolbeare, Kenneth Marsh
Dolbier, Maurice (Wyman)
Dole, Elizabeth Hanford
Dole, Hollis Mathews
Dole, Robert J.
Dole, Vincent Paul
Dolger, Jonathan
Dolin, Anton
Dollard, Elizabeth
Dolmatch, Theodore Bieley
Dolmetsch, Carl Richard, Jr.
Dolven, Richard Joel
Doman, Glenn Joseph
Doman, Nicholas R.
Domanska, Janina
Domar, Evsey David
Domareki, Joseph Theodore
Domenicali, Charles Angelo
Domenici, Pete V(ichi)
Domingo, Placido
Domino, Antoine (Fats)
Domokos, Gabor
Domonkos, Anthony Nicholas
Doms, Keith
Donahue, Donald Jordan
Donahue, Jack Clifford
Donahue, John Francis
Donahue, Robert William
Donahue, Thomas Reilly
Donald, David Herbert
Donald, David Richard
Donaldson, Coleman duPont
Donaldson, Gordon
Donaldson, James Bowie
Donaldson, Jeff Richardson
Donaldson, Samuel Andrew
Donaldson, William Henry
Donati, Enrico
Donegan, Charles Edward
Donegan, E. Cary, Jr.
Donelan, Joseph Francis, Jr.
Doner, Dean Benton
Doney, Willis Frederick
Donlan, Charles Joseph
Donlan, James Emmett
Donlan, John F.
Donley, Edward
Donlon, William Joseph
Donnahoe, Alan Stanley
Donnahoo, Robert W.
Donnelley, Dixon
Donnelly, Brendan Paul
Donnelly, John
Donnelly, Robert Leo
Donnelly, Robert Oliver
Donnelly, Thomas Andrew
Donnelly, Thomas Joseph
Donner, Martin Walter
Donoghue, John Daniel
Donohoo, Horrie Van Waldo
Donohue, Albert F.
Donohue, Eugene James
Donohue, Jerry
Donohue, Mark Neary
Donough, Robert John
Donovan, Charles Francis
Donovan, David Gerard
Donovan, Egbert Herbert
Donovan, Gerald Alton
Donovan, Hedley Williams
Donovan, James Alport, Jr.
Donovan, Jerome Francis
Donovan, John Chauncey
Donovan, John Dennis
Donovan, Leitch (Donovan P. Leitch)
Donovan, Paul F.
Donovan, Richard Arthur
Donovan, Robert John
Donovan, Thomas Francis
Doob, Leonard William
Dooher, M(uredach) Joseph
Doole, George Arntzen
Dooley, Arch Richard
Dooley, Delmer John
Dooley, Paul
Dooley, William Edward
Dooling, John Francis, Jr.
Dooling, (John) Stuart
Doolittle, Arthur King
Doolittle, Duane Smith
Doolittle, Jesse William, Jr.
Dorain, Paul Brendel
Doran, Ambrose Benedict
Doran, Charles Edward
Doran, William Michael
Dorati, Antal
Dore, Stephen Edward, Jr.
Dore, Vincent Cyril
Doremus, Robert Heward
Dorf, Erling
Dorfman, Allen Bernard
Dorfman, Joseph
Dorhoffer, Alan Miles
Doria, Anthony Notarnicola
Doris, John Francis
Dorkin, Frederic Eugene
Dorman, Gerald Dale
Dormann, Henry O.
Dornan, Robert Kenneth
Dornfeld, Isaac Joseph
Dorr, Goldthwaite Higginson
Dorrance, George Morris, Jr.
Dorrance, John Thompson, Jr.
Dorris, Michael Anthony
Dorritie, John Francis
Dorsen, Norman
Dorsett, Burt
Dorsey, Eugene Carroll
Dorsey, John Russell
Dorsey, Rhoda Mary
Dorst, John Phillips
Dorsz, Edmund John
Dorton, Joseph La Drue
Doten, George William
Doub, William Offutt
Doubleday, Nelson
Doud, Robert Skinner
Douds, Charles Tucker
Dougherty, George Wighton
Dougherty, James Douglas
Dougherty, James Thomas
Dougherty, John Joseph
Dougherty, John L.
Dougherty, Jude Patrick
Dougherty, Richard
Dougherty, Russell Elliott
Douglas, Bodie Eugene
Douglas, Bryce
Douglas, Cathleen Curran Heffernan (Mrs. William O. Douglas)
Douglas, Clarence James, Jr.
Douglas, Fred Robert
Douglas, Helen Gahagan (Mrs. Melvyn Douglas)
Douglas, Herbert Paul, Jr.
Douglas, John Jay
Douglas, John Waldo
Douglas, Melvyn
Douglas, Mike
Douglas, Paul Wolff
Douglas, Scott
Douglas, Walter Spalding
Douglass, John William
Douglass, Lathrop
Douglass, Paul F.
Douglass, Raymond Donald
Dove, Ulysses
Dow, Charles William
Dow, Sterling
Dow, Wilbur Egerton, Jr.
Dowd, David Joseph
Dowd, James Edward
Dowd, Thomas Nathan
Dowden, Carroll Vincent
Dowden, Raymond Baxter
Dowdey, Clifford Shirley, Jr.
Dowds, John Joseph
Dowe, Thomas Whitfield
Dowell, Earl Hugh
Dowell, John Carson
Dowling, Harry Filmore
Dowling, John E.
Dowling, John Elliott
Dowling, Joseph Albert
Dowling, Robert Joseph
Downe, Edward R., Jr.
Downes, Edmund William
Downes, Edward Olin Davenport
Downey, Fairfax Davis
Downey, John Alexander
Downey, John Owens
Downey, Juan Antonio
Downey, Mortimer Leo, III
Downey, Morton
Downey, Thomas Joseph
Downing, Thomas Nelms
Downs, Harry
Downs, Wilbur George
Downs, William Randall, Jr.
Doyle, Charlotte Lackner (Mrs. James J. Doyle)
Doyle, Donald Earl
Doyle, James Aloysius
Doyle, James Edwin (Ned)
Doyle, James Henry, Jr.
Doyle, James Marion, Jr.
Doyle, Joseph
Doyle, Marion Wade (Mrs. Henry Grattan Doyle)
Doyle, Mathias Francis
Doyle, Robert Bates
Doyle, Robert Edward
Doyle, Robert Emmett
Doyle, William Thomas
Doyle, Wilson Keyser
Dozier, Ollin Kemp
Dozoretz, Louis
Draddy, Vincent de Paul
Drake, Alfred Capurro
Drake, Charles Lum
Drake, Clifford Barnes
Drake, Francis Edward, Jr.
Drake, Frank Donald
Drake, Harrington
Drake, Richard Matthews
Drake, William Frank, Jr.
Drake, William Plummer
Draper, Theodore
Draper, Verden Rolland
Draper, William Franklin
Draus, Frank John
Drayton, William
Drazek, Stanley Joseph
Dreben, Burton Spencer
Dreier, John C.
Drennan, Merrill William
Drennen, William Miller
Drescher, John Mummau
Dresselhaus, Mildred Spiewak
Dressner, Howard Roy
Drew, Elizabeth
Drew, Elizabeth Heineman
Drew, James Mulcro
Drew, Russell Cooper
Drew, Thomas Bradford
Drewes, Werner
Drewry, Cecelia Belle Hodges (Mrs. Henry N. Drewry)
Drewry, Elizabeth Belle
Drewry, Guy Carleton
Drexler, Arthur Justin
Drexler, Michael David
Drexler, Rosalyn
Dreyfus, Alfred Stanley
Dreyfus, George Joseph
Dreyfuss, Ralph Franklyn
Drickamer, Jewel Annette
Driggs, Adrian Paul
Drinan, Robert Frederick
Drinkwater, Robert Edward
Drinnon, Richard
Driscoll, Edward Joseph
Driscoll, Frederick Joseph
Driscoll, John Gerard
Driscoll, Lee Francis, Jr.
Driscoll, Robert Swanton
Driscoll, William Michael
Driver, Albert Westcott
Driver, Donald
Driver, Lottie Elizabeth
Driver, Tom Faw
Driver, William Joseph
Driver, William Raymond, Jr.
Drobile, James Albert
Dropkin, John Joseph
Drorbaugh, Wells, Jr.
Drosdoff, Matthew
Druck, Kalman Breschel
Drucker, Darrell Irving, Jr.
Drucker, William Richard
Druckman, Jacob Raphael
Drummond, Roscoe
Drummond, Sally Hazelet
Drumwright, James Robert
Drury, Allen Stuart
Dry, John Marion
Dryden, Franklin Bridges
Drye, John Wilson, Jr.
Drysdale, Douglas D.
Duane, Harry Brewerton, III
Duane, Morris
Duane, Thomas David
Duba, John Gorman
Dubas, Danielle Marie
Dube, John
Duberman, Martin
Dubin, Fred Stanley
Dubin, Isadore Nathan
Dubin, Seth Harris
Dublin, Thomas David
Duboff, Samuel J.
Du Bois, Cora
DuBois, John Harry
DuBois, Josiah Ellis, Jr.
Dubos, Rene Jules
DuBose, Charles
DuBrul, Stephen McKenzie, Jr.
Dubs, Adolph
Duchac, Kenneth Farnham
Duchin, Harold
Duchin, Peter Oelrichs
Duckert, Audrey Rosalind
du Cret, Dudley Vaughan
Dudan, Peter
Dudden, Arthur Power
Dudick, Michael Joseph
Dudley, Albert Henry, Jr.
Dudley, Eastham Waller
Dudley, Edward Richard
Dudley, George Austin
Dudley, Jonathan Ellwood
Dudley, Tilford E.
Dudman, Richard Beebe
Dudrow, Louis Albert
Duell, Daniel Paul
Duff, Daniel Vincent
Duff, James Henry
Duff, John Bernard
Duff, John Carr
Duff, Stewart Mills
Duffey, Joseph Daniel
Duffin, Richard James
Duffy, Brian Francis
Duffy, Edward C.
Duffy, Francis Ramon
Duffy, Jacques Wayne
Duffy, James Edward
Duffy, John Paul
Duffy, Kevin Thomas
Duffy, Michael Peter
Duffy, William
Dufresne, Armand Alphee, Jr.
Dufton, Charles Henry
Dugan, George
Dugan, James Patrick
Dugan, John Leslie, Jr.
Dugan, Joseph Harry
Dugan, Ruth Roberta
Dugdale, Grant
Dugdale, William Morris
Duggan, Stephen Pierce
Duggan, Timothy John
Dugger, Gordon Leslie
Duhamel, Pierre Albert
Duin, Robert Alan
Dukakis, Michael Stanley
Duke, Angier Biddle
Duke, Emanuel
Duke, James Alan
Duke, Paul Robert
Duke, Paul Welden
Duke, Robert Dominick
Duke, Steven Barry
Duker, Abraham Gordon
Dukes, Thaddeus Anthony
Dulles, Avery
Dulles, Eleanor Lansing
Dumaine, Frederic C.
Duman, Maximilian George
Dumaresq, John Edward
Dumbauld, Edward
Dumont, Allan Eliot
Dunbar, Alexander Hamilton
Dunbar, Charles Elmer
Dunbar, John Burton
Dunbar, Lemuel Cotton
Dunbar, Leslie Wallace
Duncan, Charles Tignor
Duncan, Charles William, Jr.
Duncan, David Beattie
Duncan, Donald Stuart
Duncan, Francis
Duncan, Frederick Geller
Duncan, George
Duncan, John Bonner
Duncan, John C.
Duncan, John James
Duncan, John Vernon
Duncan, Laurence Ilsley
Duncan, Robert Blackford
Duncan, Sheldon Forbes
Duncan, Thomas Clark
Duncan, William H.
Duncan-Peters, Stephen James
Dunfey, John Philip
Dungan, Ralph Anthony
Dunham, Corydon Bushnell
Dunham, Donald Carl
Dunham, Richard Lind
Dunham, Robert
Dunham, Stuart A.
Dunham, William Barrett
Dunham, William Henry
Dunham, William Huse, Jr.
Dunhill, Robert
Dunkel, Wilbur Dwight
Dunkelberger, Harold Aberly
Dunker, Henry Traugott, Jr.
Dunlap, George Wesley
Dunlap, Richard Freeman
Dunlap, William Crawford
Dunleavy, Francis J.
Dunlop, Douglas Morton
Dunlop, George Rodgers
Dunlop, John Thomas
Dunlop, Robert Galbraith
Dunn, Carroll Hilton
Dunn, Charles T.
Dunn, Charles William
Dunn, Edward K.
Dunn, Ellen Catherine
Dunn, Frederick Wallace
Dunn, James Joseph
Dunn, James Michael, Jr.
Dunn, James Robert
Dunn, John Michael
Dunn, Joseph Willcox, Jr.
Dunn, Justin Stephen
Dunn, Mignon
Dunn, Oscar Lewis, Jr.
Dunn, Richard Byam
Dunn, Richard Slator
Dunn, Robert Thomas
Dunn, Stannard
Dunn, Theodore Franklin
Dunn, Thomas G.
Dunne, James Joseph
Dunne, Thomas Leo
Dunner, Joseph
Dunnigan, Frank Joseph
Dunning, James Dorr
Dunning, James Henry Fitzgerald
Dunning, James Morse
Dunnington, John Hughes
Dunphy, Edwin Blakeslee
Dunst, Laurence David
Dunston, Alfred Gilbert, Jr.
Dunton, Edward Albert
Du Pont, Edmond
duPont, Eleuthere Irenee
du Pont, John Eleuthere
duPont, Pierre Samuel
Du Pont, Pierre Samuel, IV
DuPont, Robert L., Jr.
Dupré, Louis
Dupree, Anderson Hunter
Dupree, Thomas Henderson
Duprey, John Paul
DuPuis, Robert Newell
Dupuy, Frank Russell, Jr.
Dupuy, Trevor Nevitt
Duran, S. Jerold
Durand, John Donald
Durant, Frederick Clark, III
Durant, Thomas Morton
Durbin, Howard Border
Durbin, James E.
Durbin, James Harold
Durbin, William Anthony
Durdin, Frank Tillman
Duren, William Larkin, Jr.
Durfee, Harold Allen
Durfee, James Randall
Durgin, Don
Durgin, Eugene J.
Durham, John Hendrick
Durkee, William Porter
Durkin, John A.
Durland, Lewis Hudson
Durrell, Donald DeWitt
Duryee, A. Wilbur
Duscha, Julius Carl
Dusenberry, William Howard
Dusseau, John LaFontaine
Dute, Richard Earl
Dutro, John Thomas, Jr.
Dutton, Frederick Gary
Dutton, John Altnow
Dutton, Wilmer Coffman, Jr.
Duval, Albert Frank
DuVal, Miles P., Jr.
Du Val, Philip Livingston Rollin

du Vigneaud, Vincent
Duvoisin, Roger Antoine
Dwight, Edward Harold
Dwight, James Scutt, Jr.
Dwight, William
Dwight, William, Jr.
Dwinell, Lane
Dworetzky, Murray
Dworkin, Ronald Myles
Dwyer, Albert Hayden
Dwyer, Edward James
Dwyer, John L.
Dwyer, John Philip
Dwyer, Joseph Gerald
Dybeck, Alfred Charles
Dyck, Arthur James
Dyck, Martin
Dyckman, William Tompkins
Dyen, Isidore
Dyer, Eldon
Dyer, Frank Reynolds, Jr.
Dyer, George Bell
Dyer, Ira
Dyer, Richard Morgan
Dykes, Jefferson Chenowth
Dykstra, Vergil Homer
Dykstra, William Henry
Dylan, Bob (Robert Allen Zimmerman)
Dymsza, William Alexander
Dynes, Russell Rowe
Dyson, Charles Henry
Dyson, Freeman John
Dyson, Robert Harris, Jr.
Dystel, Oscar
Dziewanowski, Marian Kamil
Eacker, Edward Wilcox
Eades, James Beverly, Jr.
Eagen, Michael John
Eager, John Howard, III
Eagle, Harry
Eagleburger, Lawrence Sidney
Eagles, Eldon Lewis
Eagles, William McCoy
Eagleson, Halson Vashon
Eagleson, Peter Sturges
Eagleson, William Boal, Jr.
Eagleton, Thomas Francis
Eaker, Ira
Ealy, Lawrence Orr
Eames, Earl Ward, Jr.
Eames, Herbert Howell, Jr.
Eames, John Heagan
Earle, Clifford John, Jr.
Earle, Kenneth Martin
Earll, Jerry Miller
Early, Joseph Daniel
Early, William James
Earnshaw, Virginia Watson
Eason, John Walter
Eastburn, David Plumb
Easterlin, Richard Ainley
Easterly, Harry Watkey, Jr.
Eastham, Thomas
Eastland, James O.
Eastman, Harland Horace
Eastman, William Don
Easton, Charles Clement, Jr.
Easton, Glenn Hanson, Jr.
Easum, Donald B.
Eaton, Allen Ober
Eaton, Charles Edward
Eaton, Conrad Paul
Eaton, Edward Hough
Eaton, Fredrick M.
Eaton, James Edmonds
Eaton, Joseph W.
Eaton, Robert Edward Lee
Eaton, William James
Eaton, William Mellon
Eaves, Elsie
Eaves, Robert Wendell
Ebbitt, Kenneth Cooper
Eberhard, John Paul
Eberhart, Mignon Good
Eberhart, Richard
Eberle, Edward Radcliffe
Eberle, Irmengarde
Eberle, William Denman
Eberman, Paul Wilmot
Ebersole, Mark Chester
Eberstadt, Rudolph, Jr.
Ebert, Charles H.V.
Ebert, James David
Ebert, Joyce Anne
Ebert, Robert Higgins
Eccleston, Archibald, III
Echelman, Shirley T.
Echols, John Minor
Eckardt, Arthur Roy
Eckaus, Richard Samuel
Eckel, Paul Edward
Eckelberry, Don Richard
Ecker, Allan Benjamin
Eckert, Charles
Eckert, William Henry
Eckman, Fern Marja
Eckman, John Whiley
Eckstein, Harry
Eckstein, Jerome
Eckstein, Otto
Economaki, Chris (Christopher) Constantine
Economos, George Themistocles
Economos, Michael Emmanuel
Eddison, John Corbin
Eddy, Bob
Eddy, Charles Russell
Eddy, Edward Danforth
Eddy, Elizabeth Schlamm (Mrs. Scott Eddy)
Edel, Abraham
Edelman, Arthur Jay
Edelman, Gerald Maurice
Edelman, Harold
Edelman, Isidore Samuel
Edelman, Judith Hochberg
Edelman, Marian Wright (Mrs. Peter B. Edelman)
Edelman, Peter Benjamin
Edelson, Alan Martin
Edelson, Edward
Eden, Charles Henry
Eden, Murray
Edens, Donald Keith
Eder, Howard Abram
Eder, Richard Gray
Edersheim, Maurits Ernst
Edes, Nik Bruce
Edgar, Robert William
Edge, Robert Laneer
Edgell, Robert Louis
Edgerly, William Skelton
Edgerton, Harold Eugene
Edgerton, Mills Fox, Jr.
Edgerton, Milton Thomas, Jr.
Edgerton, Samuel Youngs, Jr.
Edgett, William Maloy
Edick, Glenn Ellis
Edidin, Michael Aaron
Edison, Robert Donald
Edlund, Milton Carl
Edlund, Sidney Wendell
Edly, Alan John
Edman, John Richard
Edminster, Talcott W.
Edmonds, Anne Carey
Edmonds, George P.
Edmonds, John Kirkpatrick
Edmonds, Walter Dumaux
Edmondson, John Preston
Edmondson, John Richard
Edmondson, William Brockway
Edmonston, William Edward, Jr.
Edsall, John Tileston
Edson, Peter
Edstrom, John Warren
Edwards, Alfred Conway
Edwards, Arthur Anderson
Edwards, Charles Mundy, Jr.
Edwards, Corwin D.
Edwards, Don
Edwards, Douglas
Edwards, Edmund Barber
Edwards, George Allen, Jr.
Edwards, Gilbert Franklin
Edwards, Gordon
Edwards, Jack
Edwards, James Cook
Edwards, Julia Spalding
Edwards, Lena Frances
Edwards, Lester Richard
Edwards, Marvin H. Mickey
Edwards, Max Nixon
Edwards, Richard Ambrose
Edwards, Robert Lomas
Edwards, Russell
Edwards, Ryan Hayes
Edwards, Sherman
Edwards, Thomas Cunningham
Edwards, Thomas Robert, Jr.
Edwards, Willard
Eells, Richard
Effler, Donald Brian
Eforo, John Francis
Efron, Samuel
Egan, Daniel
Egan, Frank T.
Egan, John Taylor
Egan, Michael Joseph
Egan, Robert Francis
Egan, Roger Edward
Egbert, Lawrence Deems
Egbert, Richard Cook
Egdahl, Richard Harrison
Egeberg, Roger Olaf
Eger, Joseph
Eger, Milton Jerome
Egeth, Howard Elliott
Egger, Rowland Andrews
Eggers, Alfred John, Jr.
Eggers, Ernest Russell
Eggers, Melvin Arnold
Eggert, Franklin Paul
Eggleston, Arthur Francois
Egleson, Jim (James Downey)
Eglevsky, Andre
Ehinger, Charles E.
Ehinger, Robert Francis
Ehlers, Joseph Henry
Ehlers, Kathryn Hawes (Mrs. James D. Gabler)
Ehrbar, Al Frederick
Ehre, Victor Tyndall
Ehrenkranz, Joel Stanley
Ehrenpreis, Irvin
Ehrenpreis, Leon
Ehrenreich, Henry
Ehrensberger, Ray
Ehrhardt, George, Jr.
Ehrhart, Carl Yarkers
Ehrich, Manfred William, III (Terry)
Ehrich, Robert William
Ehrlich, Alvin Q.
Ehrlich, Arnold
Ehrlich, George Edward
Ehrlich, Gertrude
Ehrlich, Ira Robert
Ehrlich, Paul
Ehrlich, Thomas
Ehrling, Sixten
Ehrmann, Henry Walter
Eiberson, Harold
Eichelberger, Clark Mell
Eichenberg, Fritz
Eichhorn, Gunther Louis
Eichorn, John Frederick Gerard, Jr.
Eidson, William Whelan
Eidt, Clarence Martin, Jr.
Eiges, Sydney Hirsh
Eikenberg, John H.
Eikerenkoetter, Frederick Joseph, II (Reverend Ike)
Eilts, Hermann Frederick
Eimbinder, Jerry
Eimicke, Victor W(illiam)
Einhorn, Arthur
Einhorn, Edward Martin
Einhorn, Herbert Arthur
Eirich, Frederick Roland
Eisch, John Joseph
Eisele, Albert Alois
Eisele, Donn Fulton
Eiseley, Loren Corey
Eiseman, Myron Joseph
Eiseman, Philip
Eisen, Henry
Eisen, Herman N.
Eisenberg, Jerome Cecil
Eisenberg, Kenneth Sawyer
Eisenberg, Lee B.
Eisenberg, Leon
Eisenberg, Norman
Eisenberg, Ruth
Eisenberg, Walter Leo
Eisenbud, Merril
Eisenhart, Charles Robert
Eisenhauer, Robert Stoll
Eisenhower, John Sheldon Doud
Eisenhower, Mamie Geneva Doud
Eisenhower, Milton Stover
Eisenman, Alvin
Eisenmenger, Robert Waltz
Eisenpreis, Alfred
Eisenstaedt, Alfred
Eisenstein, Ira
Eisenstein, Julian Calvert
Eisert, Sandra Lee
Eisner, Will
Eister, Allan Wardell
Eiszner, James Richard
Eizenstat, Stuart
Ekas, Claude Philip, Jr.
Ekblom, Harry Edward
Ekeblad, Frederick Alfred
Ekeblad, Raymond Edwin
Ekelund, John Joseph
Ekin, Kenneth Huntley
Eklund, Coy Glenwood
Eklund, Donald Arthur
Elam, Leslie Albert
Elberg, Darryl Gerald
Elder, Fred Kingsley, Jr.
Elder, Robert Lee
Elder, Samuel Adams
Eldredge, Hanford Wentworth
Eldredge, Joseph Lippincott
Eldridge, John Cole
Eldridge, John William
Eldridge, Larry (William Lawrence Eldridge)
Eldridge, Paul
Eldridge, Roy
Eleftheriou, Basil Eleftherios
Elegant, Lawrence
Eley, Lemuel Leslie, Jr.
Elfenbein, Julien
Elfers, William
Elfin, Mel
Elfvin, John Thomas
Elgart, Larry
Elgin, Joseph Clifton
Elias, Albert Jay, II
Elias, Robert Henry
Elias, Rosalind
Elicker, Paul H.
Eliot, Alexander
Eliot, Charles William, II
Eliot, Theodore Lyman, Jr.
Eliot, Thomas Hopkinson
Elisburg, Donald Earl
Eliscu, Edward
Elkes, Terrence Allen
Elkin, Eleanor Scott
Elkin, Milton
Elkind, David
Elkins, Hillard
Elkins, Stanley Maurice
Elkins, Wilson Homer
Elks, Hazel Hulbert (Mrs. David Elks)
Ellberg, Joshua
Elledge, Scott Bowen
Ellenberger, Jack Stuart
Ellenbogen, Henry
Ellenbogen, Milt
Ellentuck, Erik
Ellin, Marvin
Ellinghaus, William M.
Ellington, Mercer Kennedy
Elliot, Robert Sherrard, Jr.
Elliott, Albert Randle
Elliott, Benjamin Paul
Elliott, Byron Kauffman
Elliott, Donald Harrison
Elliott, Edward Procter
Elliott, Eleanor Thomas
Elliott, Frank Abercrombie
Elliott, Frank Nelson
Elliott, George Paul
Elliott, Joanne
Elliott, John, Jr.
Elliott, John Frank
Elliott, Lloyd Hartman
Elliott, Osborn
Elliott, Philip Clarkson
Elliott, Raymond Henry
Elliott, Robert B.
Elliott, Robert Raymond
Elliott, Ronnie (Mrs. John Paul Knapp)
Elliott, Warren G.
Elliott, Willard Buford
Elliott-Smith, Paul Henry
Ellis, Albert
Ellis, Anthony Thornton
Ellis, Billy Joe
Ellis, Calvert N.
Ellis, Charles Calvert
Ellis, David Maldwyn
Ellis, Frank Hale
Ellis, Franklin Henry, Jr.
Ellis, George Hathaway
Ellis, Harry Bearse
Ellis, James Thornton
Ellis, John
Ellis, John Taylor
Ellis, John Tracy
Ellis, Kent
Ellis, Laurence Brewster
Ellis, Brother Patrick (H. J. Ellis)
Ellis, Ralph Edgar
Ellis, Richard Akers
Ellis, Richard Emanuel
Ellis, Robert Leslie
Ellis, Rudolph Lawrence
Ellis, Vincent Henry
Ellis, William Ben
Ellis, William Leigh
Ellis, Winifred Elizabeth
Ellison, Bruce
Ellison, Cyril Lee
Ellison, Jerome
Ellison, Newell Windom
Ellison, Ralph (Waldo)
Ellison, Rose Ruth
Ellison, Solon Arthur
Ellman, Lawrence
Ells, Jonathan Fairbanks
Ellsworth, Arthur Whitney
Ellsworth, John Edwards
Ellsworth, Robert Fred
Ellwanger, James Warren
Elman, Philip
Elmlark, Harry Eugene
Elmo, John Sebastian
Elmslie, Kenward Gray
Elsasser, Theodore Herman
Elsasser, Walter Maurice
Elsberg, Milton Leonard
Elsberg, Stuart Michael
Elsbree, John Francis
Elsey, George McKee
Elson, Charles
Elson, Edward Lee Roy
Elston, Charles William
Elston, Lloyd Warren
Elton, Roger Dilworth
Elton, Wallace Wesley
Elwood, Hugh McJunkin
Ely, Atwood Collins
Ely, James Wallace
Ely, Northcutt
Ely, Roy Addison
Ely, Thomas Sharpless
Embry, Lloyd Bowers
Embry, Robert Campbell, Jr.
Emeny, Brooks
Emerson, Alice Frey
Emerson, Charles Dunlap
Emerson, Daniel Everett
Emerson, David Frederick
Emerson, Edward Everett
Emerson, Paul Carlton
Emerson, Rupert
Emerson, Thomas Irwin
Emerson, William Keith
Emerson, William Richard
Emery, Albert Waldron, Jr.
Emery, Clifton Woodford, Jr.
Emery, David Farnham
Emery, John Colvin, Jr.
Emery, Kenneth Orris
Emery, Sherman Raymond
Emil, Sister Mary (Sister Mary Emil Penet)
Emken, Robert Allan
Emma, Arthur Jerome
Emme, Eugene Morlock
Emmett, Martin Frederick Cheere
Emmons, Alton Thomas
Emmons, Howard Wilson
Emo, Vincent Albert
Empie, Paul Chauncey
Emrey, Richard Clay
Emrich, Raymond Jay
Emshwiller, Ed
Enders, John Franklin
Enders, Richard Warren
Endicott, Kenneth Milo
Endicott, Robert Rantoul
Endleman, Robert
Endress, Henry
Enell, John Warren
Eney, Harry Vernon
Enfield, Clifton Willis
Engebretsen, Arden Bernt
Engel, Eva Johanna
Engel, Gilson Colby
Engel, Irving M.
Engel, John Hurd
Engel, Lehman
Engel, Lewis Libman
Engel, Louis Henry, Jr.
Engel, Paul Bernard
Engel, Paul Huber
Engel, Peter H.
Engel, Ralph
Engel, William King
Engelberg, Edward
Engelbrecht, Robert Martin
Engelder, Theodore Carl
Engelhardt, Nickolaus Louis, Jr.
Engelhardt, Sara Lawrence
Engelman, Melvin Alkon
Engelmann, Lothar Klaus
Engelson, Joyce
Engen, Donald Davenport
Engen, Trygg
Enger, Walter Melvin
Engerman, Stanley Lewis
Engert, Cornelius Van H.
England, Anthony W.
England, Bayard L(anning)
Englander, Roger
Engle, James Bruce
Engle, Mary Allen English
Engle, Ralph Landis, Jr.
Englehardt, David Meyer
Engler, David
Engler, Jean Evans
Engler, John George, II
Engler, Robert
Englert, Roy Theodore
Engley, Donald Brown
English, E(ugene) Schuyler
English, Glenn
English, James Andrew
English, James Fairfield, Jr.
English, John Earle
English, Joseph T.
English, Maurice
English, Nicholas Conover
English, O. Spurgeon
English, Robert Joseph
English, Spofford Grady
English, Van Harvey
English, Woodruff Jones
Englund, John Emil
Engman, Lewis August
Engram, William Carl
Enloe, M. Neil
Ennis, Thomas Allen
Ennis, Thomas Elmer, Jr.
Enochs, Rodney Lee
Enquist, Irving Fridtjof
Ensign, Chester Oscar, Jr.
Ensign, William Lloyd
Ensley, Grover William
Enslin, Morton Scott
Enslin, Theodore Vernon
Enslow, Ridley Madison, Jr.
Entremont, Philippe
Entwisle, George
Ephraim, Charles
Ephron, Nora
Epp, Edward Rudolph
Epperly, William Robert
Eppinger, Eugene
Eppinger, Josua, III
Epps, Augustus Charles
Epstein, Barbara (Mrs. Jason Epstein)
Epstein, Benjamin Robert
Epstein, Daniel Mark
Epstein, David Mayer
Epstein, Eleni Sakes (Mrs. Sidney Epstein)
Epstein, Franklin Harold
Epstein, Henry David
Epstein, Howard Michael
Epstein, Jason
Epstein, Joseph
Epstein, Lionel Charles
Epstein, Nathan Bernard
Epstein, Sidney
Epstine, Harry M.
Epting, Lawrence
Erb, Lillian Edgar (Mrs. David Charles Erb)
Erb, Paul
Erb, Robert Allan
Erber, Robert
Erdman, Carl L. N.
Erdman, William James, II
Erfft, Kenneth Reynders
Erhardt, Warren Richard
Erhart, Charles Huntington, Jr.
Ericksen, Ephraim Gordon
Ericksen, Jerald Laverne
Erickson, Don
Erickson, Florence Henrietta
Erickson, James Huston
Erickson, Ralph O.
Erickson, Raymond Leroy
Erickson, Roland Axel
Erickson, William Clarence
Ericson, Richard Ferdinand
Erikson, George Emil
Erikson, Kai Theodor
Erim, Kenan Tevfik
Eringen, Ahmed Cemal
Erk, Frank Chris
Erlanger, Bernard Ferdinand
Erlenborn, John Neal
Erlich, Alvin Lewis
Erlich, Victor
Erlick, Everett Howard
Ermenc, Joseph John
Ermolaev, Herman Sergei
Ernst, Frederic
Ernst, Jimmy
Ernst, John Louis
Ernst, Richard James
Ernst, Roger
Errichetti, Angelo Joseph
Erskine, Albert Russel, Jr.
Erskine, George Bernard
Erslev, Allan Jacob
Ertegun, Ahmet
Ertel, Allen Edward
Ertell, Merton William
Ervin, Ralph William, Jr.
Erving, Julius Winfield
Erwin, David Williams
Erwin, Frank William
Erwin, James Shrewsbury
Erwin, Robert Gillespie
Erwin, William James
Esaki, Leo
Esch, Marvin L.
Esch, Robin Ernest
Eschallier, Adrien Reid
Eshbach, William Wallace
Eshelman, William Robert
Eshleman, Edwin D.
Eskandarian, Edward
Eskin, Jules Louis
Esman, Milton Jacob
Espie, Robert Grant
Esposito, Michael John
Esposito, Philip Anthony
Espy, Ridgway Bowers, Jr.
Espy, Robert Hamilton Edwin
Espy, Willard R.
Esselen, William Brigham
Essigmann, Martin White
Estabrook, Robert Harley
Esterhai, John Louis
Estern, Neil
Esterow, Milton
Estes, Eleanor
Estes, Howell Marion, Jr.
Estes, Rice
Estes, Robert Mason
Estes, Thomas Stuart
Estes, William Kaye
Estin, Hans Howard
Estner, Charthel Arthur
Estrup, Peder Jan Zwergius
Esty, David Cameron
Esty, Frederick Russell
Esty, John Cushing, Jr.
Etherington, Edwin Deacon
Etherington, Roger Bennett
Ethridge, Samuel Broughton
Etnier, Stephen Morgan
Etra, Max Jacob
Etris, Samuel Franklin
Ets, Marie Hall (Mrs. Harold Ets)
Etting, Emlen
Ettinger, Austen Arnold
Ettinghausen, Elizabeth Sgalitzer
Ettinghausen, Richard
Etzel, Edward
Etzioni, Amitai Werner
Eubank, Alvah Hovey, Jr.
Eurich, Alvin Christian
Eurich, Nell
Eusden, John Dykstra
Eustace, Robert Joseph
Eva, William Duncan
Evan, William Martin
Evans, Abbie Huston
Evans, Alfred Spring
Evans, Alona Elizabeth
Evans, Audrey Elizabeth
Evans, Billy Lee
Evans, Bob Overton
Evans, Clifford
Evans, David Walter
Evans, Edward Gordon, Jr.
Evans, Edward Steptoe, Jr.
Evans, Edwin Charles
Evans, Emory Gibbons
Evans, Frank Edward
Evans, Frederick John
Evans, George Heberton, Jr.
Evans, George Russell
Evans, Gordon Goodwin
Evans, Grose
Evans, Gwynne Blakemore
Evans, Hugh E.
Evans, James Carmichael
Evans, James Hurlburt
Evans, Jerry Norman
Evans, John Harvey
Evans, John James
Evans, Joni
Evans, Joseph Henry
Evans, Lawrence Boyd
Evans, Maurice
Evans, Nolly Seymour
Evans, Ormond Keister, Jr.
Evans, Philip Morgan
Evans, Richard Bates
Evans, Robert
Evans, Robert, Jr.
Evans, Robert Van Orman
Evans, Rowland, Jr.
Evans, Samuel London
Evans, Theodore Schlosser
Evans, Thomas Beverley, Jr.
Evans, Thomas Mellon
Evans, Walter Fontaine
Evans, William John
Evarts, Charles McCollister
Evarts, Edward Vaughan
Evarts, Harry Franklin
Evelyn, Douglas Everett
Evenden, Frederick George
Everbach, Otto George
Everett, Houston Spencer, Jr.
Everett, James LeGrand, III
Everett, John Rutherford
Everett, Robert Rivers
Everett, Roberts
Evers, Herbert
Evers, William Louis
Evons, Harry
Ewalt, Jack Richard
Ewart, Donald Linsley
Ewell, Albert Hunter, Jr.
Ewell, Raymond Henry
Ewell, Tom (Yewell Tompkins)
Ewen, Harold Irving
Ewers, John Canfield
Ewing, Bayard
Ewing, David Walkley
Ewing, Frank Marion
Ewing, Galen Wood
Ewing, John Isaac
Ewing, Richard Tucker
Ewing, Robert Edward

Flynn, William James
Flynt, John James, Jr.
Foa, Joseph Victor
Foa, Uriel Gaston
Foard, Susan Lee
Fobes, Donald Edwards
Focke, Arthur Bernard
Focke, Theodore Brown
Fodor, Eugene
Fodor, Eugene Nicholas
Foelber, Charles Hepburn
Foell, Earl William
Fogarty, Anne
Fogarty, Charles Franklin
Fogarty, John Thomas
Fogel, Herbert Allan
Fogel, Lawrence
Fogel, Robert William
Fogel, Seymour
Foisie, Philip Manning
Folch-Pi, Jordi
Foldi, Andrew Harry
Foley, Adrian M., Jr.
Foley, Alice Loretta
Foley, Henry Elliott
Foley, James Bernard
Foley, James Thomas
Foley, Joan Coleman
Foley, Patrick Martin
Foley, Paul
Foley, Theodore Thomas
Foley, Thomas Stephen
Foley, William Edward
Foley, William Thomas
Folger, John Clifford
Folk, John William
Folkman, Moses Judah
Folley, Jarrett Harter
Folmar, Laurie Worth
Folsom, James Cannon
Foltz, Edwin Joseph
Foltz, Richard Harry
Foner, Philip S.
Fontaine, Edward Paul
Fontaine, Joan
Foose, Richard Martin
Fooshee, Malcolm
Foote, Emerson
Foote, Franklin Manley
Foote, Freeman
Foote, Nelson Northrup
Foote, Timothy Gilson
Foott, Roger
Forbath, Thomas Paul
Forbes, Edward Coyle
Forbes, Elliot
Forbes, Francis Murray, Jr.
Forbes, Gilbert Burnett
Forbes, James Wendell
Forbes, John Douglas
Forbes, John George
Forbes, Malcolm Stevenson
Forbes, Murray
Forbes, Thomas Rogers
Force, Roland Wynfield
Forchheimer, Rudolph
Ford, Dexter
Ford, Donald Herbert
Ford, Eileen Otte (Mrs. Gerard W. Ford)
Ford, Franklin Lewis
Ford, Frederick Wayne
Ford, George Harry
Ford, Harold Eugene
Ford, James Wade
Ford, Jesse Hill
Ford, John Bailey
Ford, John Gilmore
Ford, John Joseph
Ford, John William
Ford, Joseph Francis
Ford, Loretta C.
Ford, Morgan
Ford, Nevil
Ford, T. Mitchell
Ford, Wendell Hampton
Ford, Whitey (Edward Charles Ford)
Ford, William David
Ford, William Dudley
Forehand, Jack Marion
Forelle, Conrad
Foreman, Carl
Foreman, Carol Lee Tucker
Foreman, James Davis
Forer, Raymond
Forese, James John
Forest, Herbert Leon
Forester, John Gordon, Jr.
Forge, Andrew Murray
Forger, Robert Durkin
Fork, Richard Lynn
Forker, Olan Dean
Forlano, Anthony
Forlenza, Gerard A.
Forman, Charles William
Forman, Harrison
Forman, H(arry) N(orris)
Forman, H(enry) Chandlee
Forman, Milos
Forman, Phillip
Forman, Stanley Joseph
Fornara, Charles William
Fornes, Maria Irene
Forrest, Edward John
Forrest, Frederick August
Forrest, Herbert Emerson
Forrestal, Michael Vincent
Forrester, Bruce Millar
Forrester, Jay Wright
Forrester, Maureen Katherine Stewart
Forrester, William Ray
Forrow, Brian Derek
Forsberg, Franklin S.
Forson, Norman Ray
Forst, Donald
Forstall, Walton
Forster, Arnold
Forster, Robert
Forster, Robert Elder, II
Forster, Roy Philip
Forster, William Hall
Forsyth, Frederick
Forsythe, Carl Stanford
Forsythe, Edwin B.
Forsythe, Richard Hamilton
Fort, David Bayard
Fortas, Abe
Fortenbaugh, Samuel Byrod, Jr.
Fortess, Karl Eugene
Forth, Stuart
Fortin, Luis Horacio
Fortune, Philip Robert
Fortune, Robert Russell
Foshay, Arthur Wellesley
Foss, Lukas
Foss, Richard Westley
Fosse, Bob
Foster, Archibald McGhee
Foster, Arthur Rowe
Foster, Charles Alvin
Foster, Charles Howell
Foster, David Ramsey
Foster, Dean
Foster, Edson L.
Foster, Elizabeth Read
Foster, John Horace
Foster, Margery Somers
Foster, Mark Gardner
Foster, Norman Ross
Foster, Paul
Foster, Paul Lowe
Foster, Paul Marvel
Foster, Robert Francis
Foster, William Chapman
Foubert, Eugene F.
Foulis, Ronald Jamieson
Foulke, William Green
Foulkes, William Wilkinson, Jr.
Fouraker, Lawrence Edward
Foust, Alan Shivers
Fouts, John David
Fouty, William Joseph
Fowkes, Robert Allen
Fowle, William Cowper
Fowler, Charles Albert
Fowler, Conrad John
Fowler, Earl Bealle, Jr.
Fowler, Harry Winthrop
Fowler, Henry Hamill
Fowler, James Alexander, Jr.
Fowler, James Edward
Fowler, James Randlett
Fowler, Robert Howard
Fowler, William Wyche, Jr.
Fox, Abljah Upson
Fox, Arthur Joseph, Jr.
Fox, Bertrand
Fox, Edward Alexander
Fox, Eldon E.
Fox, Francis Henry
Fox, Frank
Fox, Gordon Albert
Fox, Henry Jackson
Fox, Irwin Sonny
Fox, Jack Jay
Fox, James Frederick
Fox, Jean Ann
Fox, John French
Fox, John Gaston
Fox, John George
Fox, John Michael
Fox, Joseph P.
Fox, Kenneth Russell
Fox, Lawrence Aaron
Fox, Louis Joseph
Fox, Marvin
Fox, Matthew Ignatius
Fox, Michael Wilson
Fox, Mortimer Joseph, Jr.
Fox, Paul Harris
Fox, Paula (Mrs. Martin Greenberg)
Fox, Renée Claire
Fox, Robert Alan
Fox, Robert John
Fox, Samuel Mickle, III
Fox, Sidney Albert
Fox, Siv Cedering (Mrs. David Lawrence Fox)
Fox, Terry J.
Fox, Thomas G., Jr.
Fox, Thomas Walton
Fox, Virgil (Keel)
Fox, William Thornton Rickert
Foy, Fred Calvert
Foy, Lewis Wilson
Foye, Morris Cotton, III
Fradley, Frederick Macdonell
Fraenkel, George Kessler
Fraenkel, Osmond Kessler
Frager, Albert S.
Frager, Malcolm
Fragomen, Austin Thomas
Fraiberg, Lawrence Phillip
Frame, Donald Murdoch
Frampton, Hollis
Frampton, Peter
France, Robert Rinehart
Frances, Evan Barbara (Mrs. Alexander Frances)
Francescatti, Zino Rene
Francis, Arlene (Mrs. Martin Gabel)
Francis, Charles Driver, Jr.
Francis, Edwin Augustus
Francis, Henry Sayles
Francis, John Joseph
Francis, Muriel Bultman
Francis, Richard Louis
Francis, Robert
Francis, Winthrop Nelson
Franck, Frederick Sigfred
Franck, Thomas Martin
Franck, William Francis
Francke, Donald Eugene
Francke, Linda Bird
Franco, Johan (Henri Gustave)
Franco, John Martin
Frangos, James George
Frank, Albert Eugene
Frank, Charles Raphael, Jr.
Frank, Curtiss E.
Frank, David D.
Frank, Eli, Jr.
Frank, Elke
Frank, F. Alexander
Frank, Gerold
Frank, Isaiah
Frank, Jerome David
Frank, Joseph
Frank, Lloyd
Frank, Morton
Frank, Reuven
Frank, Richard Asher
Frank, Robert Stephen
Frank, Ronald Edward
Frank, Stanley Donald
Franke, Frederick Rahde
Frankel, Andrew John
Frankel, Charles
Frankel, Larry
Frankel, Marvin E.
Frankel, Max
Frankel, Robert James
Frankel, Sandor
Frankel, Stanley Arthur
Frankenheim, Samuel
Frankenthaler, Helen
Frankfurt, Harry Gordon
Frankfurt, Stephen Owen
Frankhauser, Mahlon Mundell
Frankl, Daniel Richard
Frankl, Spencer Nelson
Frankl, William Stewart
Franklin, Alan Douglas
Franklin, Edward Ward
Franklin, George S.
Franklin, Hardy R.
Franklin, Kenneth L(inn)
Franklin, Mitchell
Franklin, Richard Ewell
Franklin, Robert Dumont
Franks, Lucinda Laura
Frankum, James Edward
Franta, William Alfred
Frantz, Charles
Frantz, Ray William, Jr.
Franzblau, Abraham Norman
Franzen, Ulrich
Frasconi, Antonio
Fraser, Donald MacKay
Fraser, Henry S.
Fraser, James Howard
Fraser, Joseph T., Jr.
Frawley, Ernest David
Frazer, Alfred Knox
Frazer, Arthur Watson
Frazer, John Ronald
Frazetta, Frank
Frazier, Joe
Frazier, John Earl
Frazier, Lee Rene
Frazier, Shervert Hughes, Jr.
Fread, Danny Lee
Freas, Frank Kelly
Frechette, Van Derck
Frederick, Pauline
Frederick, Stanley
Fredericks, Wayne
Fredine, Clarence Gordon
Fredland, John Roger
Fredrick, Laurence William
Fredricksen, Cleve John
Fredrickson, Donald Sharp
Fredrickson, William Russell
Freed, Dean Winslow
Freed, Murray Monroe
Freed, Stanley Arthur
Freedberg, A. Stone
Freedberg, Irwin Mark
Freedberg, Sydney Joseph
Freedman, Abraham E.
Freedman, Alfred Mordecai
Freedman, Elisha Chaim
Freedman, Frank Harlan
Freedman, Guy Linder
Freedman, Henry Hillel
Freedman, Monroe Henry
Freedman, Solomon
Freedman, Walter
Freedman, Walter S.
Freehafer, Edward Geier
Freehling, William Wilhartz
Freeland, T. Paul
Freelander, Israel Robert
Freeman, Albert Cornelius, Jr.
Freeman, Arnold Irving
Freeman, David Forgan
Freeman, David Hugh
Freeman, Douglas Haig
Freeman, Elsa S.
Freeman, George Clemon, Jr.
Freeman, Graydon LaVerne
Freeman, Hal MacKenzie
Freeman, Harrop Arthur
Freeman, Harry
Freeman, Harry Boit, Jr.
Freeman, Herbert
Freeman, Ira Henry
Freeman, Jack E.
Freeman, James Leo
Freeman, Linton Clarke
Freeman, Lucy
Freeman, Mark
Freeman, Maurice Tracy
Freeman, Max Herbert
Freeman, Milton Victor
Freeman, Neal Blackwell
Freeman, Orville Lothrop
Freeman, Raymond Lee
Freeman, Richard Francis
Freeman, Robert Schofield
Freeman, Robert Turner, Jr.
Freeman, Roger Morse, Jr.
Freeman, Rowland Godfrey, III
Freeman, Ruth Benson
Freese, Robert Gerard
Frei, Emil, III
Freiberg, Albert Daniel
Freid, Jacob
Freidberg, Sidney
Freidel, Frank Burt, Jr.
Freidson, Eliot Lazarus
Freiman, David Galland
Freis, Edward David
Freitag, Robert Frederick
Freizer, Louis A.
Frelinghuysen, Peter H.B.
Fremont, Rudolph Eric
French, Anthony Philip
French, Bevan Meredith
French, Bruce Hartung
French, Charles Ezra
French, Herbert Eliot
French, Isabelle Frances
French, Raymond
French, Richard Frederic
French, S. Roy, Jr.
French, William Daniel
French, William Taylor
Frenkil, Victor
Frenzel, Bill
Freret, Julian Payne
Frerichs, Ernest Sunley
Fresco, Jacques Robert
Frese, Walter Frederick
Frese, Walter Wenzel
Fretwell, Elbert Kirtley, Jr.
Freudenheim, Tom Lippmann
Freudenstein, Ferdinand
Freudenthal, Alfred Martin
Freund, Ernest Hans
Freund, Gerald
Freund, Paul Abraham
Freund, Richard Alan
Freund, Tibor
Freund, William Curt
Freundlich, August Ludwig
Freundlich, Lawrence Stewart
Frey, Alexander Hamilton
Frey, Carl
Frey, Frederick Ward
Frey, James McKnight
Frey, Robert Ketterman
Freyd, Peter John
Freyhan, Fritz Adolf
Fri, Robert Wheeler
Frick, Ford Christopher
Frick, Philip William
Frick, Sidney Wanning
Fricke, Howard Rudolph
Fricke, Richard Irvin
Fridge, Benjamin Wall
Fried, Albert, Jr.
Fried, Charles
Fried, Charles Arnold
Fried, Edward R.
Fried, Herbert Daniel
Fried, Lawrence
Fried, Louis
Fried, Morton Herbert
Fried, Walter Jay
Friedan, Betty
Friedberg, M. Paul
Friedberg, Simeon Adlow
Friede, Eleanor Kask
Frieden, Bernard Joel
Friedenberg, Richard Myron
Friedheim, Jerry Warden
Friedhoff, Arnold
Friedlander, David
Friedlander, Gerhart
Friedlander, Paul Josef Crost
Friedlich, Bruce
Friedman, Alvin
Friedman, Alvin E.
Friedman, Arnold D'Arcy
Friedman, B(ernard) H(arper)
Friedman, Bruce Jay
Friedman, Edward Alan
Friedman, Edward Macy
Friedman, Emanuel A.
Friedman, Ephraim
Friedman, Gerald Manfred
Friedman, Herbert
Friedman, Howard W.
Friedman, Irving Sigmund
Friedman, Izchak
Friedman, Jay Bentley
Friedman, Jerome Isaac
Friedman, Joseph Bivens
Friedman, Louis Frank
Friedman, Ralph
Friedman, Robert Sidney
Friedman, Sidney
Friedman, Wilbur Harvey
Friedrich, Lawrence William
Friedrich, Otto Alva
Friedrichs, Robert Winslow
Frieman, Edward Allan
Friend, Charlotte
Friend, Irwin
Friend, Rodney
Friend, Theodore Wood, III
Friend, Walter William, Jr.
Friendly, Alfred
Friendly, Fred W.
Friendly, Henry Jacob
Friis, Erik Johan
Frings, Ketti
Frisbee, John Lee
Frisch, Harry Lloyd
Frischknecht, Lee Conrad
Fritchey, Clayton
Fritchman, Harry Vernon
Frith, James Robert
Frith, Margaret
Fritsch, Charles Theodore
Fritschler, A(llen) Lee
Fritts, Harry Washington, Jr.
Fritts, Robert Eugene
Fritz, Charles Andrew, Jr.
Frock, Edmond Burnell
Frodin, Reuben
Froehlich, S. Charles
Froehlke, Robert Frederick
Froessel, Charles William
Frohock, Wilbur Merrill
Fromkes, Saul
Frondel, Clifford
Frosch, Aaron R.
Frosch, Robert Alan
Frost, Douglas Van Anden
Frost, Frederick George, Jr.
Frost, Frederick William
Frost, James Arthur
Frost, Robert Edwin
Frothingham, A. Michael
Frudakis, Evangelos William
Frudden, Mark Perrin
Frumer, Louis Reshin
Fruton, Joseph Stewart
Fry, C. Herbert
Fry, Guy
Fry, John
Frye, Richard Nelson
Frye, Royal Merrill
Frye, Theodore Raymond
Frye, William Ruggles
Fryer, Malcolm Forrest, Jr.
Fryling, George Richard
Fubini, Eugene Ghiron
Fuchs, Fritz
Fuchs, Hanno
Fuchs, Joseph Louis
Fuchs, Lawrence Howard
Fuchsberg, Jacob David
Fucillo, Edward A.
Fuerbringer, Otto
Fugazy, William Denis
Fuhrman, Ralph Edward
Fujita, Shigeji
Fukagawa, Tetsuya
Fulbright, Freeman
Fulbright, James William
Fuld, Stanley H.
Fulham, Gerard Aquinas
Fulham, Thomas Anthony
Fullagar, William Alfred
Fullam, John P.
Fuller, Dudley Dean
Fuller, Edwin Keith
Fuller, Frances Leonore (Mrs. Worthington C. Miner)
Fuller, Jack Glendon, Jr.
Fuller, John Garsed Campbell
Fuller, John Grant
Fuller, John Langworthy
Fuller, Lawrence Joseph
Fuller, Lon Luvois
Fuller, Margaret Hartwell (Mrs. Francis A. Fuller)
Fuller, Reginald Horace
Fuller, Richard Buckminster
Fuller, Robert Arthur
Fuller, Robert Ferrey
Fuller, Stephen Dow
Fuller, Theodore
Fulmer, Hugh Scott
Fulmer, Vincent Anthony
Fulrath, Logan
Fulton, Eileen
Fulton, James Franklin
Fulton, James Murdock
Fulton, Marshall Nairne
Fulton, Richard
Fulton, Richard Alsina
Fulton, Thomas
Funari, John H.
Funaro, George Joseph
Funk, Carl William
Funk, Charles Earle, Jr.
Funk, Frank E.
Funk, Max Otto
Funk, Paul Eugene
Funke, Lewis B.
Funkhouser, Elmer Newton, Jr.
Funkhouser, Richard Nelson
Fuoss, Raymond Matthew
Fuqua, Charles John
Fuqua, Don
Furash, Edward Elliott
Furgurson, Ernest Baker, Jr.
Furlaud, Richard Mortimer
Furley, David John
Furman, David Dickson
Furman, John Rockwell
Furman, Roy Lance
Furnas, Howard Earl
Furnas, Joseph Chamberlain
Furness, Betty
Furniss, Warren Todd
Furry, Wendell Hinkle
Furst, Milton
Furstenberg, Egon Edvard
Furth, Hans Gerhard
Furth, Harold Paul
Furth, Jacob
Fusee, Frederick George
Fusfeld, Herbert Irving
Fussell, Paul
Futia, Leo Richard
Fye, Paul McDonald
Fye, Robert Wallace
Gabelman, Irving Jacob
Gable, Fred Burnard
Gabo, Naum
Gabriel, Earl A.
Gabriel, Mordecai Lionel
Gabriel, Peter Paul
Gabrielli, Domenick L.
Gabrilove, Jacques Lester
Gaby, Daniel Manual
Gaccione, Anthony Salvatore
Gaddis, William
Gaden, Elmer Lewis, Jr.
Gadsden, Henry White
Gaebelein, Frank Ely
Gaertner, Johannes Alexander
Gaffney, Paul Cotter
Gagarin, Andrew
Gagge, Adolf Pharo
Gagliardi, Lee Parsons
Gaglio, Sam Peter
Gagnebin, Albert Paul
Gagnon, John Henry
Gagnon, Paul Adelard
Gaguine, Benito
Gahman, Floyd
Gailius, Gilbert Keistutis
Gaines, Alan McCulloch
Gaines, Ernest J.
Gaines, William Maxwell
Gaither, William Samuel
Gajdusek, Daniel Carleton
Galamian, Ivan Alexander
Galand, Rene Marie
Galanter, Eugene
Galbraith, Francis Joseph
Galbraith, John Kenneth
Galbraith, Ralph Arthur
Galbraith, Virginia Lee
Gale, Herbert Morrison
Gale, William Henry
Galella, Ronald Edward
Galenson, Walter
Galimir, Felix
Galin, Miles A.
Galkin, Elliott Washington
Gall, Joseph Grafton
Gallagher, Anne Timlin
Gallagher, Bernard Patrick
Gallagher, Buell Gordon
Gallagher, Charles E.
Gallagher, D. Nora
Gallagher, Eugene Bernard
Gallagher, Harold John
Gallagher, Helen
Gallagher, Hubert R.
Gallagher, James Roswell
Gallagher, Robert Francis
Gallagher, Terrence Vincent
Gallagher, Thomas Anthony
Gallagher, Vernon Francis
Gallagher, Walter Edward
Gallahger, Matthew Peter, Jr.
Galler, Sidney Roland
Galletti, Pierre Marie
Galli, Robert George
Gallie, Walston Chubb
Galligan, Clarence Joseph
Galligan, Thomas Joseph, Jr.
Gallo, Robert Charles
Gallo, William Victor
Gallop, Myer Robert
Galloway, James Vance
Galloway, William Jefferson
Gallup, Donald Clifford
Gallup, George Horace
Gallup, George Horace, III
Galluzzi, Nicholas Joseph
Galston, Arthur William
Galston, Clarence Elkus
Galvin, Ruth Mehrtens
Galvin, Thomas John
Gam, Rita Elenore
Gamache, Joseph Hector
Gamble, Kathryn Elizabeth
Gamble, Philip Lyle
Gambrell, Charles Glenn
Gambuti, Gary
Gamer, Saul Richard
Gammon, Roland Irvine
Gammons, Robert Franklin
Gamser, Howard G.
Gamso, Rafael Robert
Gamsu, Richard Castle
Gan, Chester Anthony
Gane, John Frederick
Gange, Joseph George
Gangel, Richard Merrill
Gangemi, Marie Elaina
Ganley, Oswald Harold
Gann, Donald Stuart
Ganner, Thomas Alan
Gannon, Donald Albert
Gannon, John Deane
Ganoe, Charles Stratford
Gans, Herbert J.
Gans, Hiram Selig
Gantt, Paul Hawkins
Gantz, Marvin Everett, Jr.
Ganz, Erwin M.
Ganz, Michael Joseph
Ganz, Samuel
Ganzel, Charles William
Ganzi, Richard Louis
Garagiola, Joe
Garance, Dominick (D.G. Garan)
Garavaglia, Brother Abdon Lewis
Garba, Edward Aloysius
Garbacz, Gerald George
Garbarini, Robert Frank
Garber, Harry Douglas
Garber, John Augustus
Garber, Paul Edward
Garbis, Marvin Joseph
Garbo, Norman
Garceau, Oliver

García, Celso-Ramón
Garcia, Julio Hernan
Garcia, Robert
Gardiner, Robert Hallowell
Gardiner, Robert McPherson
Gardner, Alvin Frederick
Gardner, Austin Thayer
Gardner, Burdett Harmon
Gardner, Ellis Benjamin, Jr.
Gardner, Eric Freeman
Gardner, Frederick Calkin
Gardner, George Edward
Gardner, George Peabody, Jr.
Gardner, John Champlin, Jr.
Gardner, John William
Gardner, Joseph Lawrence
Gardner, Keith
Gardner, Marshall C.
Gardner, R. H. (Rufus Hallette III)
Gardner, Ralph David
Gardner, Randolph Scott
Gardner, Richard Alan
Gardner, Richard Hartwell
Gardner, Stephen Symmes
Gardner, Walter
Gardner, Warner Winslow
Gardner, William Michael
Gardner, William Ullman
Gardner, Wofford Gordon
Garfield, Bernard Howard
Garfield, Brian Wynne
Garfield, David Crosby
Garfield, Eugene
Garfin, Alvin
Garfinkel, Marvin
Garfunkel, Art
Gargana, John Joseph, Jr.
Garland, Carl Wesley
Garland, Phyllis Twyla Jean (Phyl)
Garlinghouse, F. Mark
Garman, Wilford Olden Higgett
Garman, Willard Hershel
Garment, Leonard
Garn, Edwin Jacob
Garner, Harvey Louis
Garner, Wendell Richard
Garnsey, Leon Leslie
Garrahy, John Joseph
Garratt, George Alfred
Garraty, John Arthur
Garretson, Albert Henry
Garrett, Arthur Sellers
Garrett, Bernard Robert
Garrett, Ethel Shields
Garrett, George Palmer, Jr.
Garrett, George William
Garrett, Gilda Deloris Jones
Garrett, Johnson
Garrett, Robert Young, Jr.
Garrett, Sylvester
Garrett, Wilbur Eugene
Garrick, Nathan Henry, Jr.
Garrison, Charles William, Jr.
Garrison, Guy Grady
Garrison, John Dorsey
Garrison, Lloyd Kirkham
Garrison, Mortimer, Jr.
Garrison, Walter R.
Garrity, Devin Adair
Garrity, James Franklin
Garrity, W. Arthur, Jr.
Garroway, Dave
Garside, Bettis Alston
Garside, John Rushforth, II
Garsoïan, Nina Guéorguiévna
Gart, Murray Joseph
Gartenberg, Seymour Lee
Garth, Leonard I.
Garthoff, Raymond Leonard
Gartland, William Joseph, Jr.
Gartley, Markham Ligion
Gartner, Arthur Edward
Gartner, Lawrence Mitchel
Gartner, Murray
Garver, Robert Wright
Garvey, Edward Robert
Garvey, Richard Conrad
Garvey, Robert Robey, Jr.
Garvin, Clifton Canter, Jr.
Gary, Charles Lester
Gary, Wyndham Lewis
Gasch, Oliver
Gaskill, William John
Gaspari, George Robert
Gasparro, Frank
Gass, Manus M.
Gassaway, Franklin Drennan
Gassenheimer, Earl Cadden
Gasser, Henry Martin
Gasser, William Daniel
Gaston, Don F.
Gates, Dillard Herbert
Gates, Edward Dwight
Gates, Edwin Wilder
Gates, Howard Perry, Jr.
Gates, James David
Gates, Marshall DeMotte, Jr.
Gates, Moore, Jr.
Gates, Olcott
Gates, Paul Wallace
Gates, Samuel Eugene
Gates, Theodore Ross
Gates, William Lewis
Gatje, Robert Frederick
Gatos, Harry Constantine
Gatski, Robert Lawrence
Gatzke, Hans Wilhelm
Gaud, William Steen
Gaudion, Donald Alfred
Gaudrault, Robert Joseph
Gauer, Charlotte Edwina
Gaulke, Ramon George
Gault, Stanley Carleton
Gault, Thomas Gower
Gault, Willis Manning
Gaultney, John Orton
Gausman, Edith Marie
Gauthier, Joseph Delphis
Gauthier, Victor Arthur, Jr.
Gavazzi, Aladino A.
Gavenus, Edward Richard
Gaver, Mary Virginia
Gavin, Austin
Gavin, James M.
Gavin, Joseph Gleason, Jr.
Gavoor, Richard Haig
Gay, Eustace, Sr.
Gay, Peter
Gay, William Ingalls
Gay, Zhenya
Gaydos, Joseph Matthew
Gaylin, Willard
Gaylor, Donald Hughes
Gaylord, Charles Nelson
Gayner, Esther K.
Gazin, Charles Lewis
Gazzara, Ben
Gazzolo, Dorothy Haven
Geanakoplos, Deno John
Gearing, Frederick Osmond
Geber, Anthony
Gecker, Edith Fishman
Geddes, Robert Louis
Geddes, William Worth
Gee, Edwin Austin
Geer, James Hamilton
Geer, John Farr
Geer, Will
Geerdes, James (Divine)
Geerlings, Gerald Kenneth
Geertsma, Robert Henry
Geertz, Clifford James
Geffen, Maxwell Myles
Gefter, William Irvin
Gehman, Jesse Mercer
Gehrig, Leo Joseph
Gehron, William Jules
Geib, Philip Oldham
Geiberger, Allen L.
Geier, George
Geiger, George
Geiger, Robert Keith
Geis, Bernard
Geiser, Elizabeth Able
Geisert, Wayne Frederick
Geismar, Maxwell David
Geismar, Richard Lee
Geissinger, John Blank
Geist, Jacob Myer
Geitz, William Daniel
Gelatt, Roland
Gelb, Arthur
Gelb, Bruce S.
Gelb, Harold Seymour
Gelb, Leslie Howard
Gelb, Richard Lee
Gelbach, Myron Schenck, Jr.
Gelband, Stephen Laurence
Gelbart, Abe
Gelbart, Larry
Gelbaum, Bernard Russell
Gelber, Jack
Gelboin, Harry Victor
Geldard, Frank Arthur
Geldmacher, Robert Carl
Geldzahler, Henry
Gelfan, Lewis David
Gelfand, Meyer
Gelfand, Morris Arthur
Gelfman, Robert William
Gelineau, Louis Edward
Gellert, George Geza
Gellhorn, Alfred
Gellhorn, Walter
Gellis, Sydney Saul
Gellman, Aaron Jacob
Gelman, David Graham
Gelman, Frank Herman
Gelmis, Joseph Stephan
Gelsanliter, John David
Gemmell, Joseph P.
Gemmill, Chalmers Laughlin
Gemmill, Elizabeth H.
Gemmill, Henry
Gemmill, Kenneth Wilfred
Genauer, Emily
Gendron, Odore Joseph
Geneen, Harold Sydney
Geng, Edward Joseph
Genge, William Harrison
Genin, Roland
Gennaro, Peter
Genné, Elizabeth Steel
Gennis, Joseph
Genovese, Eugene Dominick
Gentile, Gloria Irene
Gentry, Grant Claybourne
Gentzler, W(aldo) Emerson
Geoghegan, John Joseph
Geoghegan, William Davidson
George, Austin Herbert
George, Charles
George, Charles William
George, Clarke Maranville
George, Morris Ferguson
George, Phyllis
George, Scott
George, Thomas
George, W. H. Krome
George, William Arthur
Georges, George Harry
Georges, Paul
Geraghty, James
Gerard, Emanuel
Gerardia, Helen
Gerathy, E. Carroll
Gerber, David
Gerber, Ella
Gerber, John Christian
Gerber, Lewis Franklin, Jr.
Gerber, Thomas William
Gerber, William
Gerbner, George
Gerety, Peter Leo
Gerety, Pierce Joseph
Gergen, Kenneth Jay
Gerhardt, Harrison Alan
Gerhardt, Lillian Noreen
Gerhart, Eugene Clifton
Gerjuoy, Edward
Germain, Jean-Paul
German, Edward Cecil
Germani, Gino
Gernert, Robert Eugene
Gernsback, Marcellus Harvey
Gerold, Nicolas John
Gerra, Ralph Alexander
Gerrard, Forrest J.
Gerrity, Edward Joseph, Jr.
Gerrity, John Love
Gerry, Elbridge Thomas
Gerschenkron, Alexander
Gershenfeld, Louis
Gershinowitz, Harold
Gershon, Elliot Sheldon
Gershon, Michael David
Gerson, Irwin Conrad
Gerson, Louis Lieb
Gerson, Nathaniel Charles
Gerson, Noel Bertram
Gerst, Irving
Gerst, Paul Howard
Gert, Gerard Martin
Gertler, Menard M.
Geschwind, Norman
Gesell, Gerhard Alden
Getchell, John Stirling
Getlein, Frank
Getler, Michael
Gette, Warren Andrews
Getts, Clark H.
Getz, Stan
Gevantman, Lewis Herman
Gewirtz, Gerry
Geyelin, Philip Laussat
Geyer, Alan
Geyer, Georgie Anne
Geyer, John Charles
Gezork, Herbert
Ghandhi, Sorab Khushro
Ghents, John Henry
Ghiardi, John Felix Linus
Ghiglia, Oscar Alberto
Ghormley, Ralph McDougall
Ghormley, William Kerr
Giacco, Alexander Fortunatus
Giacconi, Riccardo
Giacomantonio, Archimedes Aristides Michael
Giaever, Ivar
Giaimo, Robert Nicholas
Giamatti, Angelo Bartlett
Giancarlo, Gene
Gianelly, Anthony Alfred
Gianturco, Delio E.
Giardino, Alfred A.
Gibb, Thomas Robinson Pirie, Jr.
Gibbens, Alfred Morton
Gibbons, Arthur Stephen
Gibbons, Edward F.
Gibbons, Eugene Francis
Gibbons, John Joseph
Gibbs, Alan John
Gibbs, Hubert Smith
Gibbs, Julian Howard
Gibbs, Martin
Gibbs, Richard Burpee
Gibbs, Richard Leslie
Gibbs, William Eugene
Gibian, Thomas George
Giblin, Edmund Burke
Gibran, Kahlil
Gibson, Althea
Gibson, Charles Merritt, Jr.
Gibson, Daniel Parke
Gibson, Eleanor Jack (Mrs. James J. Gibson)
Gibson, George Dandridge
Gibson, James
Gibson, James J.
Gibson, John Egan
Gibson, Kenneth Allen
Gibson, Ralph Edward
Gibson, Raymond Eugene
Gibson, Richard Cushing
Gibson, Robert Fisher
Gibson, Robert McKenzie
Gibson, Sam Thompson
Gibson, William
Giddings, Horace Alpheus
Giddins, Gary Mitchell
Giddon, Donald Bernard
Gideon, Miriam
Gideonse, Harry David
Gidney, Dean Robert
Gienger, Edwin B., Jr.
Gifford, Don Creighton
Gifford, Frank Newton
Gifford, Harry Cortland Frey
Gifford, John Archer
Gifford, Nelson Sage
Gifford, Prosser
Gifford, William Leo
Gignoux, Edward Thaxter
Gikow, Ruth
Gilbane, Jean Ann (Mrs. Thomas F. Gilbane)
Gilbane, Thomas Freeman
Gilbane, William James
Gilbart, Arthur William
Gilbert, Ben William
Gilbert, Charles Edward
Gilbert, Charles Richard Alsop
Gilbert, Creighton Eddy
Gilbert, Felix
Gilbert, Gerald Frederick, Jr.
Gilbert, Harry Ephraim, Jr.
Gilbert, Henry Boas
Gilbert, Joseph
Gilbert, Lewis Dusenbery
Gilbert, Lou
Gilbert, Phil Edward, Jr.
Gilbert, Robert Pertsch
Gilbert, Rod Gabriel
Gilbert, Walter
Gilbert, William Kent
Gilbertson, William LeRoy
Gilbride, John Thomas
Gildea, Joseph James
Gildenhorn, Joseph Bernard
Gilder, Rosamond
Gildston, Phyllis Sylvia
Giles, Richard Alden
Giles, Robert Hartmann
Giles, Terry Duncan
Giles, William Clement, Jr.
Giles, William Yale
Gilhooley, John J.
Gilinsky, Stanley Ellis
Gilkeson, Robert Fairbairn
Gill, Ardian C.
Gill, Brendan
Gill, Howard Read, Jr.
Gill, Raymond Joseph
Gill, Thomas James, III
Gill, William Albert, Jr.
Gill, William Nelson
Gilleland, Brady Blackford
Gillen, James Frederick John
Gillen, Robert Leonard
Gillenson, Lewis William
Gillenwater, Jay Young
Giller, Edward Bonfoy
Gilles, Nicholas Chester
Gillespie, Alexander Joseph, Jr.
Gillespie, Daniel Curtis, Sr.
Gillespie, George Joseph, III
Gillespie, Gregory
Gillespie, John Birks (Dizzy)
Gillespie, Kingsley
Gillespie, McDonald
Gillett, Allen Lewis
Gillett, Charles
Gillett, Jonathan Newell
Gillette, Hyde
Gillette, Robert Stone
Gilliam, Carroll Lewis
Gilliam, James Howard, Sr.
Gilliand, Merle Ellsworth
Gilliatt, Neal
Gilliatt, Penelope Ann Douglass
Gillilan, William J.
Gilliland, William Nathan
Gillilland, Whitney
Gillin, Donald George
Gilliom, Judith Carr
Gillis, Bernard Thomas
Gillispie, Charles Coulston
Gilman, Alfred
Gilman, Benjamin Arthur
Gilman, Charles, Jr.
Gilman, Donald Lawrence
Gilman, Dorothy (Dorothy Gilman Butters)
Gilman, Herbert
Gilman, John Joseph
Gilman, Martin John
Gilman, Richard
Gilman, Sander Lawrence
Gilman, Stanley Francis
Gilmer, B. von Haller
Gilmont, Ernest Rich
Gilmore, Clarence Percy
Gilmore, Grant
Gilmore, Myron Piper
Gilmour, Lloyd Straube
Gilpatric, Roswell Leavitt
Gilpin, Robert George, Jr.
Gilreath, Esmarch Senn
Gilroy, Frank Daniel
Gimbel, Bruce A.
Gimbel, Peter Robin
Gimma, Joseph A.
Ginader, George Hall
Gingerich, Owen Jay
Gingold, Hermione Ferdinanda
Giniger, Kenneth Seeman
Ginn, Ronald (Bo)
Ginn, William Henry, Jr.
Ginsberg, Allen
Ginsberg, Harold Louis
Ginsberg, Harold Samuel
Ginsberg, Milton
Ginsberg, Mitchell I.
Ginsburg, Charles David
Ginsburg, Martin David
Ginsburg, Nathan
Ginsburg, Ruth Bader
Ginsburgh, Robert Neville
Gintell, Burton
Ginzberg, Eli
Ginzburg, Ralph
Ginzburg, Yankel Jacob
Giobbi, Edward Giacchino
Giordano, Anthony Bruno
Giordano, Richard Vincent
Giordmaine, Joseph Anthony
Giovanni, Nikki
Giovannitti, Len
Gips, Walter Fuld, Jr.
Gipson, Francis Elmo
Girard, René Noel
Giroux, Robert
Gisel, William George
Gish, Lillian
Gitlow, Abraham Leo
Gittelsohn, Roland Bertram
Gittelson, Bernard
Gittelson, Natalie Leavy
Gittler, Joseph Bertram
Gittlin, A. Sam
Giudice, Sal John
Giuffrida, Joseph Gilbert
Giuggio, John Peter
Giuliano, Samuel John
Giulini, Carlo Maria
Giurgola, Romaldo
Giusti, George
Givan, Walker
Givens, Austin Lawrence
Givens, Joseph Edwin
Gkonos, James William
Gladfelter, Millard E.
Gladieux, Bernard Louis
Gladstone, Herbert Jack
Gladstone, Milton
Gladstone, Richard Bennett
Glancey, Thomas Francis
Glanville-Hicks, Peggy
Glasberg, Paula Drillman
Glaser, Gilbert Herbert
Glaser, Joseph Bernard
Glaser, Julius Simson
Glaser, Michael Lance
Glaser, Paul Michael
Glaser, Renee
Glaser, Robert
Glaser, Robert Leonard
Glaser, Vera Romans
Glasgow, Jesse Edward
Glashow, Sheldon Lee
Glass, Carson McElyea
Glass, Frederick Marion
Glass, Henry Edward
Glass, M. Milton
Glass, Milton Louis
Glass, Philip
Glass, William Everett
Glasser, Frances Paul
Glasser, Joseph
Glasser, Leo George
Glasser, Otto John
Glasser, Robert Gene
Glassgold, Alfred Emanuel
Glassick, Charles Etzweiler
Glassie, Henry Haywood
Glassman, Herbert Haskel
Glassman, Irvin
Glassmeyer, Edward
Glatfelter, Charles Henry
Glatfelter, Philip Henry, III
Glatzer, Nahum Norbert
Glaubman, Michael Juda
Glazer, David
Glazer, Frank
Glazer, Nathan
Glazier, Lyle Edward
Gleason, Andrew Mattei
Gleason, Francis Joseph
Gleason, James Marne
Gleason, Jean Berko
Gleason, John F.
Gleason, John Martin
Gleason, Thomas
Gleazer, Edmund John, Jr.
Glekel, Newton
Glenn, Benjamin Duke, Jr.
Glenn, Charles Melancthon, Jr.
Glenn, Morton Bernard
Glenn, William Wallace Lumpkin
Glennan, Thomas Keith
Glennon, Harrison Randolph, Jr.
Glenville, Peter
Gleysteen, Culver
Gleysteen, William Henry, Jr.
Glibert, Joseph Francis
Glick, Garland Wayne
Glick, Jacob Ezra
Glick, Paul Charles
Glick, Philip Milton
Glickman, Carl K.
Glickman, Daniel Robert
Glickman, Maurice
Glicksman, Arvin S(igmund)
Glicksman, Maurice
Gliedman, Marvin L.
Glier, Ingeborg Johanna
Glikes, Erwin Arno
Glimcher, Melvin Jacob
Glimp, Fred Lee
Glines, Carroll Vane, Jr.
Glixon, David M(orris)
Glock, Marvin David
Glover, Charles Carroll, III
Glover, John Desmond
Glover, William
Gluck, Herman Randolph
Gluck, Louise Elisabeth
Glucksberg, Sam
Gluckstern, Robert Leonard
Glueck, Bernard Charles
Glueck, Sheldon
Glushien, Morris P.
Glynn, Arthur Lawrence
Gobel, George
Goble, Alfred Theodore
Goddard, David Rockwell
Goddard, James Lee
Goddard, Robert Hale Ives
Godding, George Arthur
Godenne, Ghislaine Dudley
Godfrey, Arthur
Godfrey, Edward Settle, III
Godfrey, Edwin Drexel, Jr.
Godfrey, James Brown
Godfrey, Kneeland Allen, Jr.
Godfrey, Wilfred
Godine, David Richard
Godley, Gene Edwin
Godwin, Charles William
Godwin, Frank Joseph, Jr.
Godwin, Mills Edwin, Jr.
Goeb, Roger
Goebel, Walther Frederick
Goeden, James Peter
Goedicke, Hans
Goeglein, Myrwil L.
Goeke, Leo Francis
Goelet, Robert G.
Goellner, Jack Gordon
Goeltz, Richard Karl
Goers, Melvin Armand
Goeschel, Arthur L.
Goetchius, Eugene Van Ness
Goettel, Gerard Louis
Goetzinger, Charles Stephen, Jr.
Goewey, Gordon Ira
Goff, Regina Mary
Goffio, Frank Louis
Goffman, Erving
Goggi, Pio Paul
Goggin, Myron DeWight
Gogick, Kathleen Christine
Goglia, Gennaro Louis
Goheen, Robert Francis
Goin, Lauren Jackson
Gokhale, Narayan Ramchandra
Golany, Gideon Solomon
Golay, Frank Hindman
Gold, Albert
Gold, Bill (William Emil)
Gold, Edward Bernard
Gold, Milton Jacob
Gold, Thomas
Goldberg, Arthur Joseph
Goldberg, Avram Jacob
Goldberg, Carney
Goldberg, David Alan
Goldberg, Harold
Goldberg, Harold Seymour
Goldberg, Herman Raphael
Goldberg, Icchok Ignacy
Goldberg, Irving Hyman
Goldberg, Martin
Goldberg, Melvin Arthur
Goldberg, Michael
Goldberg, Morrell
Goldberg, Ray Allan
Goldberg, Rita Maria
Goldberg, Seymour
Goldberg, Sid
Goldberg, Stanley Robert
Goldberger, Edward
Goldberger, Marvin L.
Goldblith, Samuel Abraham
Golden, Daniel Lewis
Golden, Jerome Benjamin
Golden, Sidney
Golden, Soma Suzanne
Golden, William Theodore
Goldenberg, Louis
Goldenson, Leonard Harry
Goldenson, Robert Myar
Goldfarb, Ronald Lawrence
Goldfeder, Anna
Goldfeld, Stephen Michael
Goldfield, Edwin David
Goldfrank, Esther S.
Goldhaber, Alfred Scharff
Goldhaber, Gertrude Scharff
Goldhaber, Jacob Kopel
Goldhaber, Maurice
Goldhaber, Paul
Goldhammer, Robert Frederick
Goldhirsh, Bernard Allan
Goldin, Judah
Goldin, Leon
Goldin, Milton
Golding, Elizabeth Bass
Goldman, Aaron
Goldman, Arthur Sworn
Goldman, Donald Howard
Goldman, Eric Frederick
Goldman, Henry Maurice
Goldman, Irving
Goldman, Jacob E.
Goldman, James
Goldman, Joseph Bernard
Goldman, Joseph Elias
Goldman, Leo
Goldman, Marshall Irwin
Goldman, Martin Raymond Rubin
Goldman, Melvin
Goldman, Michael Paul
Goldman, Oscar
Goldman, Ralph
Goldman, Richard Franko
Goldman, Robert Irving
Goldman, Simon
Goldman, William
Goldmann, Sidney
Goldmark, Peter Carl
Goldovsky, Boris
Goldring, Pat Mayer
Goldring, William
Goldschlager, Morris
Goldschmidt, Arthur Eduard
Goldschmidt, Charles
Goldsmith, Barbara
Goldsmith, Clifford Henry
Goldsmith, Edward Ira
Goldsmith, Jerry
Goldsmith, John Alan
Goldsmith, Lee Selig
Goldsmith, Samuel Lunt, Jr.
Goldsmith, Sidney
Goldstein, Abraham Samuel
Goldstein, Alvin
Goldstein, Arnold Leonard
Goldstein, Bernard Herbert
Goldstein, David Henry
Goldstein, Elliott
Goldstein, George
Goldstein, Jack Stanley
Goldstein, Jerome

Goldstein, Joan
Goldstein, Joseph
Goldstein, Lewis Charles
Goldstein, Mark E.
Goldstein, Martin
Goldstein, Sidney
Goldstein, Sidney
Goldstein, Stanley Philip
Goldstein, Sydney
Goldstine, Herman Heine
Goldston, Robert Conroy
Goldstone, Harmon Hendricks
Goldstone, Sanford
Goldthwait, John Turner
Goldwater, Barry Morris, Jr.
Golembeski, Jerome John
Golffing, Francis
Golinkin, Joseph Webster
Golino, Carlo Luigi
Gollob, Herman Cohen
Golodner, Jack
Golub, Leon Albert
Goluskin, Norman Lewis
Gomberg, Harold
Gomberg, William
Gomezplata, Albert
Gomez-Quiroz, Juan
Gompf, Arthur Milton
Gonzales, Carlotta (Mrs. Richard Lahey)
Gonzalez, Efren William
Gonzalez, Emilio
Gonzalez, Eugene Robert
Gonzalez, Nancie Loudon
Gonzalez-Muela, Joaquin
Gooch, Horace, Jr.
Good, Dale Edward
Good, Robert Alan
Good, Roland Hamilton, Jr.
Goodale, James Campbell
Goodale, Robert Lincoln
Goodall, William, Jr.
Goodbody, John Collett
Goodby, James Eugene
Goodchild, Anthony Albert
Goode, James Arthur
Goode, Lewis Bouldin, Jr.
Goode, Marian Elizabeth
Goode, Richard Benjamin
Goode, Stephen Hogue
Goodell, Charles Ellsworth
Goodell, Warren Franklin
Goodenough, Ward Hunt
Goodfriend, James Herman
Goodgold, Joseph
Goodhart, Robert Stanley
Gooding, Judson
Goodkind, Louis William
Goodling, George A.
Goodling, William F.
Goodloe, Robert Douglas
Goodman, Andrew
Goodman, Benny
Goodman, Bernard Maurice
Goodman, Bertram
Goodman, Charles Morton
Goodman, Charles Schaffner
Goodman, DeWitt Stetten
Goodman, Donald C.
Goodman, Edward
Goodman, Ellen Holtz
Goodman, George Jerome Waldo
Goodman, Henry Atlas
Goodman, Henry Maurice
Goodman, Irving
Goodman, Julian
Goodman, Leo Magill
Goodman, Leon
Goodman, Maurice
Goodman, Nelson
Goodman, Percival
Goodman, Roy Matz
Goodman, Sam Richard
Goodman, Stanley Leonard
Goodman, Walter
Goodner, John Ross, Jr.
Goodnough, Robert Arthur
Goodpaster, Andrew Jackson
Goodrich, Frances
Goodrich, Kenneth Paul
Goodrich, Leland Matthew
Goodrich, Lloyd
Goodrich, Nathaniel Herman
Goodrich, Richard Lane
Goodrich, William Dennett
Goodsill, Stanley Chase
Goodson, Louie Aubrey, Jr.
Goodson, Mark
Goodspeed, Norwick Royall Givens
Goodwillie, John
Goodwin, Bernard
Goodwin, Donald Leslie
Goodwin, George, Jr.
Goodwin, Harry Eugene
Goodwin, Karl Perley
Goodwin, Merrill Harry
Goodwin, Richard Hale
Goodwin, Robert Delmege
Goodwin, Sidney Siler
Goodwyn, Kendall Wirt
Goody, Richard Mead
Goodyear, Austin
Goodyear, Frank Henry, Jr.
Goodyear, George Forman
Goodykoontz, Charles Alfred
Googins, Robert Reville
Gookin, Ralph Burton
Goott, Daniel
Goralski, Robert
Goran, Michael J.
Gorbey, James Henry
Gordenker, Leon
Gordh, George Rudolph
Gordis, Robert
Gordon, Albert Hamilton
Gordon, Alvin Joseph
Gordon, Angus Neal, Jr.
Gordon, Bernard
Gordon, Charles
Gordon, Cyrus Herzl
Gordon, Dexter Keith
Gordon, Donald Edward
Gordon, Edmund Wyatt
Gordon, Elliott Morton
Gordon, Ernest
Gordon, Eugene Irving
Gordon, George Selbie
Gordon, George Stanley
Gordon, Harold
Gordon, Harry Haskin
Gordon, Howard Frederick
Gordon, James Braund
Gordon, Joseph Keller
Gordon, Kenneth Thornton
Gordon, Lincoln
Gordon, Lyle Joseph
Gordon, Melvin Jay
Gordon, Milton A.
Gordon, Mortimor S.
Gordon, Nicholas
Gordon, Paul Curtis
Gordon, Robert Boyd
Gordon, Robert Sirkosky, Jr.
Gordon, Roy Gerald
Gordon, Ruth
Gordon, S. Stewart
Gordon, Samuel
Gordon, Sanford Daniel
Gordon, Thomas Christian, Jr.
Gordon, William Richard
Gordon, William Talbott
Gordone, Charles
Gore, Chester A.
Gore, Fred Cordon
Gore, Willis Carroll
Gores, Harold Bismark
Gores, Landis
Gorey, Edward St. John
Gorham, Donald R.
Gorham, William
Gorin, William
Gorkin, Jess
Gorlin, Richard
Gorman, Cliff
Gorman, Frank David
Gorman, John Leonard
Gormley, Robert John
Gornick, Joseph Louis
Gorovitz, Samuel
Gorsline, George William
Gortner, Ross Aiken, Jr.
Gortner, Willis Alway
Gorton, James Allen
Gorwitz, Bertram Kall
Gosnell, Charles Francis
Goss, James Hassell
Goss, Richard Johnson
Gossard, Arthur Charles
Gosselin, Richard Pettengill
Gosselin, Robert Edmond
Gossett, Louis
Gossett, Oscar Milton
Gossick, Lee Van
Gotfryd, Alexander
Gothelf, Sy Paul
Goto, Kanji
Gott, Edwin Hays
Gott, Rodney Cleveland
Gott, Vincent Lynn
Gottesman, Callman
Gottesman, Frederick Irving
Gottfried, Kurt
Gottfried, Martin
Gotthilf, Daniel Lawrence
Gottlieb, Bertram
Gottlieb, Leo
Gottlieb, Morton Edgar
Gottlieb, Paul
Gottlieb, Philip Morris
Gottlieb, Robert Adams
Gottschalk, Charles Max
Gottschalk, Hans W.
Gottschalk, John Simison
Gottschalk, Walter Helbig
Gottschall, Edward Maurice
Gottshall, Ralph Kerr
Gottwald, Bruce Cobb
Gottwald, Floyd Dewey
Gottwald, Floyd Dewey, Jr.
Gotwals, Vernon Detwiler, Jr.
Gouger, Matthew M.
Goulard, Everett Maurice
Gould, Bernard Albert
Gould, Bernard Sidney
Gould, Dirk Samuel
Gould, Elliott
Gould, George Jean
Gould, Harry Edward, Jr.
Gould, Jay Reid
Gould, Jean Rosalind
Gould, John Thomas
Gould, Kenneth Lawrence
Gould, Milton Samuel
Gould, Morton
Gould, Stephen Jay
Goulden, Joseph Chesley
Goulding, Phil G.
Goulding, Raymond Walter
Gouldner, Helen
Gourdine, Simon Peter
Gourley, Desmond Robert Hugh
Gouse, S. William, Jr.
Gousseland, Pierre Leopold
Gove, Harry Edmund
Govoni, Albert Peter
Gowdy, Curtis
Gowetz, Irene
Goyen, Charles William
Grabach, John Robert
Grabar, Oleg
Grabino, Harold
Grabois, Neil Robert
Grace, J. Peter
Grace, Jason Roy
Grace, Oliver Russell
Grace, Walter Law
Grad, Harold
Gradwell, John David
Grady, John Francis
Grady, John Henry
Grady, Joseph Harold
Graebner, Herbert Conrad
Graebner, Norman Arthur
Graese, Clifford Ernest
Graetzer, John Stephen, Jr.
Graf, Edward Louis, Jr.
Graf, Rudolf F.
Graf, Uta
Graff, Henry Franklin
Graff, William
Graffman, Gary
Grafly, Dorothy
Grafton, Martha Stackhouse (Mrs. Thomas H. Grafton)
Grafton, Samuel
Grafton, Thurman Stanford
Gragan, Philip A.
Gragg, Williford
Graham, Annie Laurie
Graham, Denver Hawkins
Graham, Dunstan
Graham, Erwin Montgomery, Jr.
Graham, Fred Patterson
Graham, George Gordon
Graham, Gordon Marion
Graham, Harry Thompson
Graham, Howard Barret
Graham, Hugh Davis
Graham, John Robert, Jr.
Graham, Katharine
Graham, Martha
Graham, Mortimer Elliott
Graham, Otto Everett, Jr.
Graham, Patricia Albjerg (Mrs. Loren R. Graham)
Graham, Thomas Carlisle
Graham, Virginia
Grahame, Orville Francis
Grainger, William Saville
Gralley, Robert Emory
Gram, Harvey B., Jr.
Grambs, Jean Dresden
Gramley, Lyle Elden
Gramm, Donald
Granbery, E(dwin) Carleton, Jr.
Grandmaison, J. Joseph
Grandy, Cyrus Wiley
Granger, Carl Victor
Granger, David
Granger, Jeffrey Solon
Granger, Shelton B.
Graning, Harald Martin
Grannis, Chandler Brinkerhoff
Granstrom, Marvin Leroy
Grant, Brooke
Grant, Cary
Grant, Frances Ruth
Grant, James Deneale
Grant, James Pineo
Grant, John Benjamin
Grant, John Francis
Grant, John L.
Grant, Lindsey
Grant, Merrill Theodore
Grant, Murray
Grant, Nicholas John
Grant, Robert England
Grant, Stephen Walkley
Grant, Walter Randolph
Grant, William Chase, Jr.
Grant, William Robert
Granville, Maurice Frederick
Grape, Finn
Grapski, Ladislaus F.
Grass, Alexander
Grassi, Joseph Gerald
Grassley, Charles E.
Grasso, Ella T. (Mrs. Thomas A. Grasso)
Grau, Shirley Ann (Mrs. James Kern Feibleman)
Graubard, Seymour
Graubard, Stephen Richards
Graulty, William Willard
Gravagno, Emilio Anthony
Graves, Earl Gilbert
Graves, Edward S.
Graves, Ernest, Jr.
Graves, Fred Hill
Graves, Harold Nathan, Jr.
Graves, John Earl
Graves, Michael
Graves, Morris Cole
Graves, Nancy Stevenson
Graves, Nelson Montgomery
Graves, Ralph
Graves, Thomas Ashley, Jr.
Graves, Walter Albert
Gray, Ann Maynard
Gray, Arthur
Gray, Arthur, Jr.
Gray, Barry Sherman
Gray, C. Vernon
Gray, Carl Albert
Gray, Charles Montgomery
Gray, Clarke Thomas
Gray, Cleve
Gray, Edward
Gray, Edward Zigmund
Gray, Elizabeth Stuart
Gray, Francine du Plessix
Gray, George
Gray, Gordon
Gray, Gordon L.
Gray, Hanna Holborn
Gray, Harry Jack
Gray, Herbert Walter
Gray, Jerome Bethel
Gray, John Davis
Gray, John Edmund
Gray, Louis Patrick, III
Gray, Paul Edward
Gray, Peter
Gray, Robert Loren
Gray, Truman Stretcher
Gray, Wallace Allison
Gray, William Barton
Graybeal, Sidney Norman
Grayson, Cary Travers, Jr.
Grayson, Gene
Grayson, Gerald Herbert
Grayson, James McDonald
Grayson, Richard Steven
Grayson, Robert Allen
Graziani, Sante
Graziano, Anthony Walter, Jr.
Graziano, Frank Joseph
Greaser, Maylin H.
Greason, Arthur LeRoy, Jr.
Greaves, Clive Walter
Greaves, William
Grebanier, Bernard
Grebin, Burton
Grech, Anthony Paul
Greco, Jose
Greeley, Arthur White
Greeley, Dana McLean
Green, Adolph
Green, Alvin
Green, Ashbel
Green, Bert Franklin, Jr.
Green, Clifford Scott
Green, David
Green, David Henry
Green, Earl Leroy
Green, Ernest Gideon
Green, Fitzhugh
Green, Frank William
Green, Gareth Montraville
Green, Gerald
Green, Hubert
Green, Jack Peter
Green, James Weston
Green, James Wilder
Green, James Wyche
Green, Jerome George
Green, John Cawley
Green, John Orne
Green, Joseph
Green, June Lazenby
Green, Leon, Jr.
Green, Louis Craig
Green, M. Edwin
Green, Marcus Herbert
Green, Marshall
Green, Mayer Albert
Green, Melville Saul
Green, Paula
Green, Raymond S(ilvernail)
Green, Robert Edward, Jr.
Green, Robert Holt
Green, Robert Lamar
Green, S. William
Green, Samuel Magee, II
Green, Thomas George
Green, Wayne Sanger, II
Green, William John
Green, William Thomas
Greenacre, Phyllis
Greenawalt, David Franklin
Greenawalt, Kenneth William
Greenawalt, Robert Kent
Greenaway, Emerson
Greenbacker, John Everett
Greenbaum, Dorothea Schwarcz
Greenberg, Alfred Henry
Greenberg, Allan
Greenberg, Byron Stanley
Greenberg, Charles
Greenberg, Gerald Lewis
Greenberg, Howard
Greenberg, Irwin Morton
Greenberg, Jack
Greenberg, Maurice Raymond
Greenberg, Milton
Greenberg, Nathan
Greenberg, Oscar Wallace
Greenberg, Sanford David
Greenberg, Simon
Greenberger, Martin
Greenburg, Dan
Greene, Arthur Albert, Jr.
Greene, Balcomb
Greene, Bette
Greene, Bradford Marson
Greene, Burton
Greene, Carla
Greene, Charles Edward
Greene, Francis Thornton
Greene, Fred
Greene, Frederick Davis, II
Greene, Harold H.
Greene, Harris Carl
Greene, Irving Lewis
Greene, Jack Phillip
Greene, Jeffrey Alden
Greene, Joseph Nathaniel, Jr.
Greene, Luther Ward
Greene, Michael Joseph Lenihan
Greene, Nathan Ira
Greene, Nicholas Misplee
Greene, Richard Leighton
Greene, Richard Thaddeus
Greene, Robert William
Greene, Robert Zemon
Greene, Stephen
Greene, Stephen
Greene, Stewart
Greene, Thomas McLernon
Greene, William Daniel
Greenewalt, Crawford Hallock
Greenfeld, Alexander
Greenfield, Bruce Harold
Greenfield, Eloise Little
Greenfield, Gordon Kraus
Greenfield, Irving H.
Greenfield, Irwin Gilbert
Greenfield, James Lloyd
Greenfield, James Robert
Greenfield, Lazar John
Greenfield, Meg
Greenfield, Robert Kauffman
Greenfield, Seymour Stephen
Greengard, Paul
Greenhaus, Lawrence Roy
Greenhill, Maurice H.
Greenland, Leo
Greenlaw, Robert Piper
Greenleaf, Jonathan Whitman
Greenleaf, Robert Kiefner
Greenleaf, Thomas Raymond
Greenlee, Howard Scott
Greenlief, Francis Stevens
Greenough, William Croan
Greenspan, Alan
Greenspan, Bernard
Greenspan, Bud
Greenspan, Harvey Philip
Greenspan, Martin
Greenspan, Richard Henry
Greenstein, Fred Irwin
Greenstein, Julius Sidney
Greenwall, Frank Koehler
Greenwalt, Tibor Jack
Greenwood, Walter Bart
Greenwood, William Warren
Greep, Roy Orval
Greer, Howard Earl
Greer, Joseph Moss
Greer, Lionel W.
Greer, Roger Clement
Greer, Thomas Vernon
Gregg, Davis Weinert
Gregg, Donald Crowther
Gregg, Hugh
Gregg, James Calvin
Gregg, Richard Alexander
Gregg, Richard Nelson
Gregg, Walter Emmor
Gregor, Arthur
Gregorian, Vartan
Gregory, Anne Elizabeth
Gregory, Charles Oscar
Gregory, Cynthia Kathleen (Mrs. Terrence S. Orr)
Gregory, Dick
Gregory, Edward Wadsworth, Jr.
Gregory, Horace Victor
Gregory, James
Gregory, Jules
Gregory, Vincent Lewis, Jr.
Greidinger, B. Bernard
Greif, Herbert
Greitzer, Herman S.
Grenander, Ulf
Grenquist, Peter Carl
Gresham, Robert Coleman
Gresov, Boris Vladimir
Gressle, Lloyd Edward
Gretsch, Fred, Jr.
Grey, Jerry
Grey, Joel Stanley
Gribbel, John, II
Gribbins, Joseph Patrick
Gribble, William Charles, Jr.
Gridley, William Gill
Grieb, John Richard
Griebel, Richard Herman
Grier, Paul Livingston
Gries, Konrad
Griesa, Thomas Poole
Griess, Thomas Everett
Griffenhagen, George Bernard
Griffin, Carleton Hadlock
Griffin, George Wortham, Jr.
Griffin, Gilroye Alfred, Jr.
Griffin, Henry Ludwig
Griffin, Herschel Emmett
Griffin, James Edward
Griffin, John Henry
Griffin, John I.
Griffin, Martin Ignatius Joseph, Jr.
Griffin, Richard George
Griffin, Robert P.
Griffin, Robert Thomas
Griffin, Stephen James
Griffin, William Marvin
Griffin, William Thomas
Griffis, John William, Jr.
Griffith, Edwin Claybrook
Griffith, Ernest Stacey
Griffith, Robert Frederick
Griffith, Robert Kenaston
Griffith, Samuel Blair, II
Griffith, Thomas
Griffith, William Edgar
Griffiths, Charles Henry
Griffiths, Daniel Edward
Griffiths, Robert Budington
Griffo, James Vincent, Jr.
Grigg, Austin Earnest
Grigg, Milton LaTour
Griggs, Marc Michael
Grigsby, Henry Jefferson, Jr.
Grigsby, Margaret Elizabeth
Grika, Larry Arnold
Griliches, Zvi
Grill, Howard
Grim, Samuel Oram
Grimaldi, Anthony Eugene
Grimaldi, John Vincent
Grimes, Howard Ray
Grimes, Tammy
Grimes, William Alexander
Grimes, William Alvan
Grimm, Goetz
Grimm, Peter
Grimm, Roland DuBois
Grimsley, Will Henry
Grin, S. Spencer
Grindel, Carl William
Grinstead, Eugene Andrews
Grippe, Peter
Grippi, Salvatore William
Grisanti, Eugene Philip
Grist, Reri
Griswold, Edward Mansfield
Griswold, Erwin Nathaniel
Griswold, Gordon Cox
Griswold, John Carroll
Grizzard, George
Groden, John Francis
Grody, Donald
Grodzins, Lee
Groeger, Joseph Herman
Groenfeldt, John Samuel
Groeschel, August Herman
Grombach, John V.
Gromer, Frank Joseph, Jr.
Gronert, Bernard George
Gronowicz, Antoni
Gronquist, Carl Harry
Gronseth, James Bernhardt
Grooms, Red
Gropp, Louis Oliver
Grose, Clarence Herman
Grose, William Rush
Groseclose, Elgin
Groshans, Werner
Gross, Abraham
Gross, Ben S.
Gross, Bertram Myron
Gross, Courtlandt Sherrington
Gross, Dean Cochran
Gross, Eric Taras Benjamin
Gross, Ernest Arnold
Gross, Franz Bruno
Gross, Fritz A.
Gross, Harold Bancroft
Gross, John Hammes
Gross, Lambert John
Gross, Leroy
Gross, Llewellyn Zwicker
Gross, Ludwik
Gross, Martin Louis
Gross, Mason Welch
Gross, Neal
Gross, Robert Alfred
Gross, Robert Russell
Gross, Ronald Martin
Gross, Sidney
Gross, Spencer
Gross, Stephen Mark
Gross, Theodore Lawrence
Gross, William Anthony
Grosschmid-Zsogod, Geza Benjamin
Grosse, Aristid V.
Grossi, Olindo
Grossinger, Paul
Grossman, Abner Jesse
Grossman, Gordon William
Grossman, Jacob
Grossman, Karl H.
Grossman, Lawrence
Grossman, Lawrence Kugelmass
Grossman, Maurice
Grossmann, Walter
Grosvenor, Gilbert Melville
Grosvenor, Melville Bell
Grosvenor, Robert Strawbridge
Groth, John
Grotz, William Arthur
Grout, Donald Jay
Grove, Brandon Hambright, Jr.
Grove, David Lawrence
Grover, Norman LaMotte
Groves, Earl Wilson
Groves, George L., Jr.
Groves, Richard Hulbert
Grub, Phillip Donald
Grubb, H. Dale
Grubb, Herbert John
Grubb, Wilson Lyon
Grube, Lewis Blaine
Gruberg, Cy
Gruchacz, Robert S.
Gruen, David Henry
Gruenberg, Ernest Matsner
Gruenberg, Robert
Gruenther, Homer H.
Grum, Clifford J.
Grumbach, Doris
Grumm, John Grant
Grunauer, Mortimer
Grunbaum, Adolf
Grundmann, Christoph Johann
Grunebaum, Ernest Michael
Grunebaum, Kurt H.
Gruner, Heinz Ernst Reinhard
Grunewald, Donald
Grunow, John E. D.
Grunwald, Ernest Max
Grunwald, Henry Anatole
Grunwald, Joseph
Gruppe, Karl Heinrick
Gruskin, Mary J. (Mrs. Alan D. Gruskin)
Gruzen, Jordan Lee
Gryder, John William
Grymes, Douglas
Gstalder, Herbert William
Gualtierotti, Torquato
Guandolo, John
Guare, John
Guarini, Frank J., Jr.

Guarrera, Frank
Gubanich, John A.
Gude, Gilbert
Gue, Ronald Lee
Guenther, George Carpenter
Guenther, Robert Wallace
Guerlac, Henry Edward
Guernsey, Janet Brown (Mrs. William Guernsey)
Guernsey, Otis Love, Jr.
Guerra, Emilio Louis
Guerrant, David Edward
Guerrero, Jose
Guertin, Alfred N.
Guest, Barbara
Guest, James Alfred
Guest, Robert Henry
Guettel, Henry Arthur
Gugelot, Piet Cornelis
Guggenheim, Malvina Halberstram
Guggenheimer, Heinrich Walter
Guidotti, Guido
Guidry, Frederick Hollies
Guiher, James Morford, Jr.
Guild, Alden
Guild, Henry Rice
Guild, Nelson Prescott
Guilden, Ira
Guiler, Leonard Kent
Guilfoyle, George H.
Guilfoyle, John W.
Guiney, Samuel Benton, Jr.
Guinier, Ewart
Guinzburg, Thomas
Gulick, Clarence Swift
Gulick, Luther Halsey
Gulick, Walter Lawrence
Gull, Cloyd Dake
Gullander, Werner Paul
Gulledge, Charles Glenn
Gullett, Donald Edward
Gulley, Warren L.
Gulliksen, Harold (Oliver)
Gullion, Edmund Asbury
Gulliver, Adelaide Cromwell
Gumbart, William Barnum
Gummere, John
Gummo, Blanchard Stanley
Gumpel, Hugh
Gumpert, Gunther
Gunckel, James Eugene
Gundersen, Sven Martin
Gunderson, Norman Gustav
Gunkel, Wesley Winnfred
Gunn, Hartford Nelson, Jr.
Gunn, William George
Gunning, Francis Patrick
Gunning, Robert Clifford
Gunsberg, Sheldon
Gunson, Leo Joseph
Gunter, John Brown, Jr.
Gunther, Jane Perry (Mrs. John Gunther)
Gupta, Om Prakash
Guptill, Leighton
Gureck, William Alexander
Gurfein, Murray Irwin
Gurin, Arnold
Gurney, Albert Ramsdell, Jr.
Gurr, Lena
Gursky, Herbert
Gurtin, Morton Edward
Gurwitch, Arnold Andrew
Gury, Jeremy
Gusberg, Saul Bernard
Gussman, Lawrence
Gussow, Alan
Gussow, Burton Walter
Gussow, Don
Gussow, Roy
Gustafson, John Alfred
Gustin, Ralph Livingston, Jr.
Guston, Philip
Gutermuth, Clinton Raymond
Guth, Raymond Charles
Guth, William Donald
Gutheim, Frederick
Gutheim, Robert Julius
Guthke, Karl Siegfried
Guthman, Edwin O.
Guthridge, Richard Clay
Guthrie, Arlo
Guthrie, Eugene Harding
Guthrie, Harvey Henry, Jr.
Guthrie, Henry Blandy
Guthrie, Janet
Guthrie, John Reiley
Gutman, Robert
Gutmann, James
Gutoff, Reuben
Guttay, Andrew John Robert
Guttenplan, Harold Esau
Guttentag, Jack Mark
Guttentag, Marcia
Gutter, Robert Harold
Guttman, Helene Nathan
Gutwirth, Marcel Marc
Guyer, David Leigh
Guyer, Tennyson
Guzzetti, Louis Adolph, Jr.
Guzzi, Paul H.
Gwathmey, Charles
Gwathmey, Robert
Gwiazda, Stanley John
Haak, Robert Arnold
Haar, Charles Monroe
Haas, F. Otto
Haas, Harold
Haas, John Charles
Haas, Marc
Haas, Vinton Benjamin, Jr.
Haas, Warren James
Haas, William Paul
Haase, Gunter Roland
Haase, Richard Henry
Haase, Walter
Habeeb, Virginia Thabet
Habel, Robert Earl
Haber, Edgar
Haber, Francis Colin
Haber, Jack N.
Haber, Ralph Norman
Haberern, John Franklin
Haberman, Alan L.
Habermann, Helen Margaret
Habib, Philip Charles
Habif, David V.
Hack, John Tilton
Hackel, Allan Richard
Hackel, Stella Bloomberg
Hacker, Andrew
Hacker, Harold Schworm
Hacker, Marilyn
Hackes, Peter Sidney
Hackett, Albert
Hackett, John Francis
Hackl, Alphons J.
Hackmyer, Arnold A(bner)
Hadden, Alexander Hawthorne
Haddon, Gerard Vincent
Haddon, William, Jr.
Haddy, Francis John
Hadidian, Dikran Yenovk
Hadley, Herbert Motter
Hadley, John Michael
Hadley, Katherine Blodgett
Hadley, Morris
Hadley, Rollin van Nostrand
Hadley, Susan Jane
Hadlock, Wendell Stanwood
Hadsel, Fred Latimer
Haehl, John George, Jr.
Hafer, Frederick Douglass
Haffer, Louis Paul
Haffner, Alden Norman
Haffner, Alfred Loveland, Jr.
Hafstad, Lawrence Randolph
Hagan, Charles Francis
Hagan, Thomas William
Hagan, Ward Stanley
Hagedorn, Thomas Michael
Hagel, Raymond Charles
Hagelstein, Robert Philip
Hageman, Howard Garberich
Hagen, John P.
Hagen, Uta
Hagendorn, William
Hagerty, James C.
Hagerty, William Walsh
Haggerty, Bernard Joseph
Haggerty, Dan
Haggerty, Robert Johns
Hagin, Rosa Anita
Hagis, Peter, Jr.
Hagmann, John Shugart
Hagner, Arthur Feodor
Hagopian, Louis Thomas
Hagopian, Peter B.
Hagstrum, Homer Dupre
Hague, Raoul
Hahm, Charles
Hahn, Emily
Hahn, Gilbert, Jr.
Hahn, James Maglorie
Haidt, Harold
Haight, Gordon Sherman
Haight, J. Rothery
Haigney, John Eustace
Haigwood, Paul Bentley
Hails, Robert Emmet
Haimes, Yacov Yosseph
Haines, Charles S., II
Haines, Walter Wells
Hainfeld, Frederick, Jr.
Haire, John Russell
Hairston, Guy Edward, Jr.
Hairston, William Russell, Jr.
Hajian, Arshag Berge
Hakala, Neil Victor
Hakimoglu, Ayhan
Halaby, Najeeb E.
Halasi-Kun, George Joseph
Halasz, Laszlo
Halberstam, David
Halberstam, Michael Joseph
Haldeman, Harry R. (Bob)
Haldeman, Jack Carroll
Hale, Ezra Andrews
Hale, Gerald Albert
Hale, Judson Drake
Hale, Laurence Swart
Hale, Lucius Melvin
Hale, Mason Ellsworth, Jr.
Hale, Nancy
Hale, Oron James
Hale, Richard Ernest
Hale, Robert Beverly
Haley, Alex Palmer
Haley, Roger Kendall
Halford, Ralph Stanley
Halio, Jay Leon
Hall, A. James
Hall, Albert Carruthers
Hall, Andrew Douglass
Hall, Arthur Raymond, Jr.
Hall, Brinley Morgan
Hall, Cameron Parker
Hall, Daniel Ray Acomb
Hall, Delores
Hall, Donald
Hall, Donald Perry
Hall, Donald S.
Hall, Eben Clarke
Hall, Edward Byron
Hall, Elizabeth
Hall, Ernest E.
Hall, Frederick Wilson
Hall, George Atwater
Hall, George E(lisha)
Hall, George Everett
Hall, Gus (Arvo Kusta Halberg)
Hall, Hal Ogden
Hall, Homer James
Hall, James Curtis
Hall, James Fay, Jr.
Hall, James Nolan
Hall, James Stanley
Hall, Jay Gordon
Hall, John Fry
Hall, John Goodale
Hall, John Gordon
Hall, Joseph Edgar
Hall, Lawrence Carl
Hall, Lawrence Sargent
Hall, Lee
Hall, Leonard Wood
Hall, Louis Harrison, Jr.
Hall, Lyle Gillis
Hall, Newman A.
Hall, Paul
Hall, Robert Anderson, Jr.
Hall, Robert Bruce
Hall, Robert Burnett, Jr.
Hall, Robert Carlton
Hall, Robert Noel
Hall, Robert Stanton
Hall, Robert Thallon
Hall, Robert William
Hall, Spencer Gilbert
Hall, Susan
Hall, Thomas Oscar, Jr.
Hall, Thomas William
Hall, Wilfred McGregor
Hall, William Charles
Hall, William Darlington
Hall, William Jackson
Hall, Wilson Dudley
Hallam, Beverly Linney
Halle, Katherine Murphy
Halle, Morris
Halleck, Charles White
Hallen, Philip Burgh
Haller, Calvin John
Haller, Charles E.
Haller, Ellis Metcalf
Haller, Henry Edwin, Jr.
Haller, John
Halliday, Walter John
Hallie, Philip Paul
Hallinan, Nancy
Hallinan, Richard James
Hallingby, Paul, Jr.
Hallman, H. Theodore, Jr.
Hallo, William Wolfgang
Halloran, Leo Augustine
Hallowell, Burton Crosby
Hallowell, Henry Richardson
Hallowell, Howard Thomas, Jr.
Hallowell, Roger Haydock
Hallwachs, Robert Gordon
Halper, Albert
Halperin, Daniel Israel
Halpern, Benjamin
Halpern, Bruce Peter
Halpern, Harry
Halpern, Manfred
Halpern, Martin
Halpern, Nathan Loren
Halpern, Seymour
Halpin, William Curtis
Halpine, Stuart Francis
Halprin, Rose L.
Halsema, James J(ulius)
Halsey, Ashley
Halsey, James H.
Halsey, Stephen Simmons
Halsey, William Darrach
Halsman, Philippe
Halstead, Dirck S.
Halstead, George Chappell
Halsted, John Burt
Halston (Roy Halston Frowick)
Halvorson, Harlyn Odell
Ham, John Raphael (Jack)
Hamarneh, Sami Khalaf
Hamberg, Daniel
Hamblen, James Ernest
Hamblet, Julia Estelle
Hamblet, Newman
Hambleton, Thomas Edward
Hamblin, Francis Newell
Hamburg, David A.
Hamburg, Marian Virginia
Hamburger, Philip (Paul)
Hamburger, Robert Arthur
Hamcke, William Robert
Hameka, Hendrik Frederik
Hamel, Dana Bertrand
Hamel, Rodolphe
Hamel, William Rogers
Hamill, Dorothy Stuart
Hamill, William (Pete)
Hamilton, Allan Corning
Hamilton, Ann Ruth Frances
Hamilton, Charles Henry
Hamilton, Charles Stuart, Jr.
Hamilton, Charles Vernon
Hamilton, David Peter
Hamilton, Douglas Leland
Hamilton, Fowler
Hamilton, George E., Jr.
Hamilton, George Heard
Hamilton, H(orace) George
Hamilton, Howard Britton
Hamilton, Hughbert Clayton
Hamilton, Iain Ellis
Hamilton, James Bruce
Hamilton, John Ross
Hamilton, Lee Herbert
Hamilton, Lyman Critchfield, Jr.
Hamilton, Robert Morrison
Hamilton, Robert Smith
Hamilton, Thomas Stewart
Hamilton, Virginia (Mrs. Arnold Adoff)
Hamilton, William Cowles
Hamlet, James Frank
Hamlin, Arthur Tenney
Hamlin, Robert Henry
Hamlisch, Marvin
Hamm, Charles
Hamm, Edward Frederick, Jr.
Hamm, Frank Coleman
Hammaker, Paul M.
Hamme, Donald George
Hammer, Carl
Hammer, Harold Harlan
Hammer, Philip Gibbon
Hammer, Ruth
Hammerschmidt, Andrew Lewis
Hammerschmidt, John Paul
Hammerschmidt, William Warner
Hammes, Gordon G.
Hammill, Leroy Richard
Hammond, Benjamin Franklin
Hammond, Caleb Dean
Hammond, Charles Philip
Hammond, George
Hammond, Guyton Bowers
Hammond, Harold Earl
Hammond, Harold Francis
Hammond, Jane Laura
Hammond, John
Hammond, Lewis Machen
Hammond, Mason
Hammond, Paul Young
Hammond, Robert Morris
Hammond, William Churchill, Jr.
Hamovitch, William
Hampel, Alvin
Hampton, Benjamin Bertram
Hampton, Colin Campbell
Hampton, Lionel Leo
Hampton, Robert Edward
Hampton, Willard Gardinier
Hamrick, Earle Anthony, Jr.
Hanbury, George Lafayette, II
Hance, William Adams
Hancock, Gerre Edward
Hancock, John Shonk
Hancock, Walker Kirtland
Hand, Judson Larrabee
Handelman, George Herman
Hander, O. Benjamin
Handler, Milton
Handler, Philip
Handlin, Oscar
Hands, William Arthur
Handsaker, Morrison
Handy, Carleton Thomas
Handy, John Abner, Jr.
Handy, Robert Theodore
Handy, Rollo Leroy
Handyside, Holsey Gates
Hanes, John Wesley, Jr.
Hanfmann, George Maxim Anossov
Hanford, William Edward
Hanga, Fred, Jr.
Hanham, Harold John
Hanke, Byron Reidt
Hanke, Lewis Ulysses
Hanke, Peter Stevenson
Hankey, William Campbell
Hankin, Leonard J.
Hankins, Richard Poole
Hankinson, Clyce Leroy
Hanks, John Harold
Hanks, Lenore Durkee
Hanks, Nancy
Hanks, Robert Jack
Hanley, Dexter L.
Hanley, Edward James
Hanley, James Michael
Hanley, William
Hanna, Archibald, Jr.
Hanna, Edward Arnold
Hanna, Paul Johnston
Hanna, Roland Pembrook
Hannah, Archibald Douglas
Hannah, Paul Francis
Hannan, Joseph Anthony
Hannan, Nancy Hughes
Hannay, N(orman) Bruce
Hannifin, Patrick J.
Hanning, Robert William
Hannon, John William, Jr.
Hannum, Erwin Charles
Hannum, John Berne
Hanrahan, Donald Eugene
Hanrahan, John Vincent (Jack)
Hanscom, Leslie Rutherford
Hansen, Chris Anthony
Hansen, Clifford Peter
Hansen, Eric Richard
Hansen, George Vernon
Hansen, Harry
Hansen, Harry Louis
Hansen, Herbert Edwin
Hansen, Hobart Garfield
Hansen, Jorgen Hartmann
Hansen, Kent Forrest
Hansen, Morris Howard
Hansen, Orval
Hansen, Robert Joseph
Hanser, Richard Frederick
Hansmann, Ralph Emil
Hanson, Angus Alexander
Hanson, Anne Coffin
Hanson, Arthur Briggs
Hanson, Carl Arnold
Hanson, Carl Thor
Hanson, Earl Dorchester
Hanson, George Fulford
Hanson, Harold Palmer
Hanson, Howard
Hanson, John Conrad
Hanson, Joseph J.
Hanson, Kitty
Hanson, Maurice Francis (Maury)
Hanson, Pauline
Hanson, Richard Arthur
Hanson, Walter Edward
Hanson, Wesley Turnell, Jr.
Hanway, John, II
Hanzalek, Frederick Joseph
Hapala, Milan Ernest
Happ, Harvey Heinz
Happel, Henry William
Happel, John
Happer, William, Jr.
Harari, Hananiah
Harbaugh, William Henry
Harber, Leonard Coleman
Harbeson, John Frederick
Harburg, Edgar Y.
Harby, Jack DeLaMotte
Harchar, Harry A.
Hardee, William Covington
Hardeen, Theodore, Jr.
Harden, Richard Martin
Harder, F. William
Harder, Frederick Eugene John
Harder, Kelsie Brown
Harder, Lewis Bradley
Harder, William Hartman
Hardesty, Charles Howard, Jr.
Hardesty, Egbert Railey
Hardiman, Joseph Raymond
Hardin, Adlai Stevenson
Hardin, Charles Roe, Jr.
Hardin, John Alexander
Hardin, Lowell Stewart
Hardin, Paul
Hardin, William Downer
Harding, Fann
Harding, James Gordon
Harding, Ralph L., Jr.
Harding, Robert LeGrande
Harding, Vincent
Hardinge, Harlowe
Hardis, Stephen Roger
Hardison, Osborne Bennett, Jr.
Hardison, Ruth Inge
Hardon, John Anthony
Hardt, Chester R.
Hardwick, Elizabeth
Hardy, George
Hardy, Gordon Alfred
Hardy, James Daniel
Hardy, Jerome Spilman
Hardy, Jerry Frank
Hardy, Joseph
Hare, Raymond Arthur
Hargrave, Alexander Davidson
Hargroves, Vernon Carney
Hari, Kenneth Stephen
Haring, Howard Jack
Harkarvy, Benjamin
Harkavy, Oscar
Harkaway, William Irving
Harken, Dwight Emary
Harker, Robert Ian
Harkey, Ira Brown, Jr.
Harkin, Thomas R.
Harkins, George Frederick
Harkins, William Edward
Harkness, Albert
Harkness, Albert, Jr.
Harkness, Earl
Harkness, John Cheesman
Harkness, Rebekah West
Harkness, Richard Long
Harkness, Sarah Pillsbury
Harkrader, Carleton Allen
Harlan, James Clarke
Harlan, John Frederick, Jr.
Harlan, Robert Warren
Harlan, Roma Christine
Harleman, Donald Robert Fergusson
Harleston, Bernard Warren
Harley, Philip Baker
Harley, Robison Dooling
Harley, William Gardner
Harllee, John
Harman, Alexander M(arrs)
Harman, Sidney
Harmon, John Henry
Harmon, John Matney
Harmon, Lily
Harmon, Lindsey Richard
Harmon, Reginald Carl
Harnack, Robert Spencer
Harned, David Baily
Harnedy, Edmund Richard
Harner, Paul B.
Harness, William Edward
Harnest, Grant Hopkins
Harnick, Sheldon Mayer
Harnwell, Gaylord P.
Harootian, Khoren Der
Harp, Elmer, Jr.
Harp, Reno Sheffer, Jr.
Harp, Sybil Chance
Harper, Heather Mary
Harper, John Dickson
Harper, John Leslie
Harper, Laura Jane
Harper, Paul Church, Jr.
Harper, Ralph Champlin
Harper, Robert Alexander
Harper, Robert Allan
Harpham, Virginia Ruth
Harr, Karl Gottlieb, Jr.
Harr, Luther Armstrong
Harrar, Helen Joanne
Harrar, J. George
Harrell, George Thomas, Jr.
Harrell, Lynn Morris
Harrigan, Arthur Washington
Harriman, Edward Eugene
Harriman, William Averell
Harrington, Chester David, Jr.
Harrington, Donald Szantho
Harrington, Edward Francis
Harrington, Frank Leighton, Jr.
Harrington, George William
Harrington, Hollis E.
Harrington, John Joseph Edward
Harrington, John Vincent
Harrington, Michael
Harrington, Michael Joseph
Harrington, Paul Francis
Harrington, William Fields
Harriott, Peter
Harris, Alfred
Harris, Arthur Brooks
Harris, Charles David
Harris, Charles Frederick
Harris, Charles Upchurch
Harris, Christopher
Harris, Cyril Manton
Harris, Dale Benner
Harris, David Henry
Harris, David Taylor
Harris, Donald
Harris, Eddie
Harris, Edward
Harris, Edward Monroe, Jr.
Harris, Forest Klaire
Harris, Franco
Harris, Fred R.
Harris, Frederick George
Harris, Gordon McLeod
Harris, Henry Ellis
Harris, Henry Hiter, Jr.
Harris, Henry Upham, Jr.
Harris, Henry William
Harris, Herbert E., III
Harris, Huntington
Harris, James Robert, II
Harris, Joseph David
Harris, Julie
Harris, Leonard R.
Harris, Louis
Harris, Malcolm Edward
Harris, Marguerite
Harris, Mark
Harris, Marvin
Harris, Michael Marcus-Myers
Harris, Milton
Harris, Nelson George
Harris, Patricia Roberts
Harris, Paul Stewart
Harris, Reed
Harris, Reese Harvey, Jr.
Harris, Robert Harry
Harris, Robert Jennings
Harris, Robert Taylor
Harris, Ruth Bates
Harris, Sam
Harris, Sanford Arnold
Harris, T. George
Harris, Thomas Everett
Harris, William Gibson
Harris, William James, Jr.
Harris, William Robert
Harris, Zellig Sabbetai
Harrison, Albertis Sydney, Jr.
Harrison, Anna Jane
Harrison, Arthur Dudley
Harrison, Brian Granville
Harrison, Charles Henry
Harrison, Dean Willard
Harrison, Edward Robert
Harrison, Evelyn Byrd
Harrison, Gilbert A.
Harrison, Harold Edward
Harrison, Horace Hawes
Harrison, James Joshua, Jr.
Harrison, John Hartwell
Harrison, John Robert
Harrison, John Sidney
Harrison, Joseph Graham
Harrison, Lawrence Elliot
Harrison, Marion Edwyn
Harrison, Robert Drew
Harrison, S. David
Harrison, Selig Seidenman
Harrison, W. Spencer
Harrison, Wallace Kirkman
Harrison, William Henry
Harrison, William Wright
Harriss, Lynn Merriam Froebel
Harriton, Abraham
Harrop, William Caldwell
Harrower, Norman, Jr.
Harry, Robert Lee
Harsch, Joseph C.
Harshaw, David Hare
Harshbarger, Boyd
Hart, Constance Gray
Hart, Cyril Spearing
Hart, Eric Mullins
Hart, Frederick Donald
Hart, Gary
Hart, George Luzerne, Jr.
Hart, Jack
Hart, James Wirth
Hart, Jeffrey
Hart, Kitty Carlisle
Hart, Loring Edward
Hart, Orson H.
Hart, Parker Thompson
Hart, Ralph Albert Millet
Hart, Samuel Leo
Hart, Stanley Robert
Hart, William Forris
Hart, William S.
Hart, William Sebastian
Harte, Robert Adolph
Harteck, Paul
Harter, Donald Robert

Hartford, Huntington
Hartgen, Vincent Andrew
Hartigan, Grace
Hartland-Thunberg, Penelope
Hartle, Robert Wyman
Hartley, Edward Neal
Hartline, Haldan Keffer
Hartman, David Downs
Hartman, Geoffrey H.
Hartman, George Eitel
Hartman, Howard Carl
Hartman, Philip
Hartman, William Ralph
Hartmanis, Juris
Hartmann, Edward George
Hartmann, Frederick Howard
Hartmann, Frederick William
Hartmann, Gregory Kemenyi
Hartmann, Robert Elliott
Hartmann, Robert Trowbridge
Hartranft, Joseph Beckwith, Jr.
Hartshorn, John Elden
Hartshorn, Joseph Harold
Hartshorne, Marion Holmes
Hartstein, Jacob I.
Hartt, Frederick
Hartt, Julian Norris
Hartung, Walter Magnus
Hartwell, Stephen
Hartwig, Cleo
Hartz, Paul Ferdinand
Hartzell, N. Russell, Jr.
Hartzog, George Benjamin, Jr.
Harvey, Abner McGehee
Harvey, Alexander, II
Harvey, Curran Whitthorne, Jr.
Harvey, Donald Joseph
Harvey, Donald Phillips
Harvey, Douglass Coate
Harvey, Edmund Huxley, Jr. (Tad)
Harvey, James Neal
Harvey, Jasper Elliott
Harvey, John Collins
Harvey, John Frederick
Harvey, Lawrence Elliot
Harvey, Paul Henry
Harvey, Rejane Marcelle
Harvey, Robert Dixon Hopkins
Harvey, Robert Wilson
Harvey, Thomas William
Harvey, Virginia Lee
Harvey, Watkins Proctor
Harvey, William Burnett
Harvey, Zola Emile
Harwit, Martin Otto
Harwood, Douglas Amend
Harwood, Edward Crosby
Harwood, Jerry
Harwood, Richard Lee
Harwood, Richard Roberts, Jr.
Haselden, Clyde LeRoy
Haselton, Wallace Meredith
Haselton, William Raymond
Hasen, Irwin Hanan
Haskell, Barbara
Haskell, Blanton Winship
Haskell, Douglas
Haskell, Joseph Farrell
Haskell, Robert Nelson
Haskins, Arthur Lyman
Haskins, Caryl Parker
Haskins, George Lee
Haslam, Charles Linn
Hasse, William Frederick
Hassenfeld, Merrill Lloyd
Hassialis, Menelaos Dimitri
Hassinger, Harold Bertram
Hassler, Howard E.
Hasso, Signe Eleonora Cecilia
Hastings, Alice Turner
Hastings, Donald Francis
Hastings, Glenn Arthur
Hastings, John Woodland
Hastings, Philip Kay
Hastings, Robert Haven
Hastings, Wilmot Reed
Hatch, George Brien
Hatch, John Davis
Hatch, Orrin Grant
Hatch, Robert Littlefield
Hatch, Robert McConnell
Hatch, Robert Norris
Hatch, Sinclair
Hatcher, Jack
Hatcher, Robert Douglas
Hatfield, Henry Caraway
Hatfield, Mark
Hatfield, Robert Sherman
Hatfield, Zadie
Hathaway, Baxter Levering
Hathaway, Carl Emil
Hathaway, Dale Ernest
Hathaway, William Dodd
Hatheway, John Harris
Hathorn, Richmond Yancey
Hatzfeld, Helmut Anthony
Hauck, Charles Francis
Hauck, John Joseph
Hauck, William Francis
Hauer, Charles Robert
Haufler, George Joseph
Haugaard, Niels
Hauge, Gabriel
Haugen, Einar Ingvald
Haugerud, Howard Edward
Haughey, Carlos Harold
Hauptfleisch, Louis Alois
Haus, Hermann Anton
Hauschka, Theodore Spaeth
Hauser, Charles Newland McCorkle
Hauser, Harry Raymond
Hauser, Norbert
Hauser, Rita Eleanore Abrams
Hauser, Walter
Hausman, Jack
Hausman, Samuel
Hausmann, Emil John
Hausner, Henry H.
Hauspurg, Arthur
Hausrath, Jill Anne
Havard, William Clyde, Jr.
Havas, Peter
Haveliwala, Yoosuf Abdulkaiyum
Havens, Leston Laycock
Havens, Richard Woodruff
Havens, William Westerfield, Jr.
Haviland, Henry Field
Haviland, John Kenneth
Haviland, Peter Robbins
Haviland, Virginia
Hawe, Thomas Philip
Hawkanson, Robert Oscar
Hawkes, John
Hawkins, Edler Garnett
Hawkins, Howard Robert
Hawkins, Roger Everett
Hawkins, Walter Lincoln
Hawkins, William Lycett
Hawks, Thomas Harris
Hawley, Alexander
Hawley, Samuel Waller
Haworth, Donald Robert
Haworth, Leland John
Hawthorne, Carlton McCarthy
Hawthorne, William Rede
Hawver, Carl Fullerton
Hay, Elizabeth Dexter
Hay, James Donald
Hay, John
Hayakawa, Samuel Ichiye
Hayashi, Teruo Terry
Haycraft, Howard
Hayde, Joan Cora
Hayden, Ralph Frederick
Hayden, Richard Hamilton
Hayden, Tom
Haydon, Alvah Edison, Jr.
Hayes, Alfred
Hayes, Arthur Michael
Hayes, Bartlett Harding, Jr.
Hayes, David Vincent
Hayes, Earl Thomas
Hayes, Elvin
Hayes, Harold Thomas Pace
Hayes, Helen
Hayes, James Joseph
Hayes, James Leslie
Hayes, James Louis
Hayes, Mark Allan
Hayes, Richard Lloyd
Hayes, Robert Samuel
Hayes, Samuel Linton, III
Hayes, Samuel Perkins
Hayford, Warren J.
Haymaker, George Tomer, Jr.
Hayman, Harry
Hayman, Seymour
Haymes, Harmon Hayden
Haynes, Donald
Haynes, Hilda Mocile Lashley
Haynes, James Marvin, Jr.
Haynes, John Mabin
Haynes, Kenneth George
Haynes, Michael James
Haynes, Moses Alfred
Haynes, Sophy Pellegrini-Quaranbotti
Haynes, Thomas Morris
Hays, Brooks
Hays, David Arthur
Hays, David Glenn
Hays, Donald C.
Hays, Donald Osborne
Hays, James Douglas
Hays, Lewis W.
Hays, Paul R.
Hays, Ronald Jackson
Haythornthwaite, Robert Morphet
Hayward, John Tucker
Haywood, Charles
Hayworth, Don
Hazard, Geoffrey Cornell, Jr.
Hazard, John Newbold
Hazard, John Wharton
Hazard, Leland
Hazard, Rowland Keough
Hazard, William Tedford
Hazel, James Frederic
Hazel, Lewis Frederick
Hazeltine, James Ezra, Jr.
Hazelton, Paul Vernon
Hazelton, Roger
Hazelton, Ruth Ardelle
Hazen, Allen Tracy
Hazen, David Comstock
Hazen, Edward Gates
Hazen, Joseph Chalmers, Jr.
Hazen, Richard
Hazen, William Harris
Hazlehurst, Robert Purviance, Jr.
Hazlett, McCrea
Hazlitt, Henry
Hazo, Samuel John
Hazzard, George William
Hazzard, Shirley
Heacock, Burtis Emerson
Heacock, Walter Judson
Head, Edward Dennis
Head, James Dean
Head, Mary Johnston
Heagy, Henry Cyrus
Heald, Mark Aiken
Healey, Frank Henry, Jr.
Healey, Joseph Peter
Healey, Robert Joseph
Healy, Arthur Kelly David
Healy, George Robert
Healy, Harold Harris, Jr.
Healy, Nicholas Joseph
Healy, Patrick, III
Healy, Paul Francis
Healy, Robert William
Healy, Timothy Stafford
Heaps, Alvin Eugene
Heaps, Marvin Dale
Heard, Edwin Anthony
Heard, Harold
Heard, Jerry Michael
Hearn, George Henry
Hearne, Joseph Frederic
Hearst, Austine McDonnell
Hearst, Catherine Campbell (Mrs. Randolph A. Hearst)
Hearst, William Randolph, Jr.
Hearth, Donald Payne
Heath, Douglas Hamilton
Heath, Dwight Braley
Heath, Gloria Whitton
Heath, James Edward
Heath, Peter Lauchlan
Heath, William Webster
Heatwole, Marion Grove
Hebb, Furman Helveston
Hebbard, William Lawrence
Hebbeler, James Arthur
Hebert, Bliss Edmund
Hechinger, Fred Michael
Hecht, Alan Dannenberg
Hecht, Anthony Evan
Hecht, George Anthony
Hecht, George Joseph
Hecht, Jaime Selig
Hecht, Max Knobler
Hecht, Robert Earl, Sr.
Hechtman, Robert Aaron
Heck, L. Douglas
Heck, Martin Henry
Heckart, Eileen
Hecker, Arthur Orr
Heckler, Margaret Mary
Heckman, John Dries
Heckscher, William Sebastian
Hedberg, Hollis Dow
Hedberg, Robert Daniel
Hedges, Donald W.
Hedges, Ralph Richard
Hedges, William Leonard
Hedley-Whyte, John
Hedlund, Charles John
Hedlund, Floyd Frederick
Hedrick, Floyd Dudley
Hedrick, Frederic Cleveland, Jr.
Hedrick, Ira Grant
Hedrick, Jay Eldred
Heebner, Albert Gilbert
Heefner, William Frederick
Heelan, Bernard Francis
Heelan, Patrick Aidan
Heeschen, David Sutphin
Heezen, Bruce Charles
Heffelfinger, Thomas Browning
Heffelfinger, William Stewart
Heffernan, John William
Heffernan, Joseph Victor
Heffernan, Phillip Thomas, Jr.
Heffner, Richard Douglas
Hefner, Frank Karl
Hefner, Thomas Reeder
Hefner, W. G. (Bill)
Heft, Arnold Abraham
Heftel, Cecil
Hegelmann, Julius
Hegner, Casper Forman
Hegsted, David Mark
Hegyi, Julius
Heidelberger, Michael
Heidt, Lawrence Joseph
Heiges, Donald Russel
Heiges, Jesse Gibson
Heiges, Richard Fickes
Heikoff, Joseph Meyer
Heilbroner, Robert L.
Heilbronner, Walter Leo
Heilig, William Wright
Heilman, Earl Bruce
Heilman, Horace Richard
Heilmeier, George Harry
Heiloms, May (Mrs. Samuel Helloms)
Heilpern, George Seymour
Heilprin, Laurence Bedford
Heilshorn, John William
Heiman, Frederick Douglas
Heimann, John Gaines
Heimann, Robert Karl
Heimbaugh, James Ross
Heimberger, Charles J.
Heimert, Alan Edward
Hein, John William
Heindel, Richard Heathcote
Heine, Edward Joseph, Jr.
Heine, Harold Warren
Heineman, William Arthur
Heinemann, George Alfred
Heiner, Robert Graham
Heinfelden, Curt H.G.
Heinl, Robert Debs, Jr.
Heins, Maurice Haskell
Heinsius, Howard
Heinsohn, Thomas William
Heinz, Edward Ralph
Heinz, Hans Joachim
Heinz, Henry John, II
Heinz, Henry John, III
Heinze, Robert Harold
Heinze, Walter O.
Heir, Milton
Heires, John Hopkins
Heiser, Rolland V.
Heiskell, Andrew
Heiskell, Marian Sulzberger (Mrs. Andrew Heiskell)
Heisler, Clifford Budd
Heisler, Philip Samuel
Heisman, Ursula Melita Hirschfeld
Hejduk, John Quentin
Hekman, Edward John
Helck, Clarence Peter
Held, Julius Samuel
Held, Richard Marx
Held, Warren Howard, Jr.
Heldring, Frederick
Helfer, Herman Lawrence
Helfferich, Donald Lawrence
Helfgott, Roy B.
Heliker, John
Hellawell, Robert
Hellenbrand, Samuel Henry
Hellendale, Robert
Heller, Ann Williams
Heller, Arthur
Heller, Charles Kaye
Heller, Jack Isaac
Heller, James John
Heller, John Herbert
Heller, John Roderick, Jr.
Heller, Joseph
Heller, Louis Benjamin
Heller, Peter
Heller, Philip
Heller, Richard H.
Heller, Robert Clarence
Heller, William Mohn
Hellerich, Mahlon Howard
Hellerman, Fred
Hellerson, Charles Benedict
Hellman, F(rederick) Warren
Hellman, Geoffrey Theodore
Hellman, Henry Martin
Hellman, Joseph S.
Hellman, Lillian
Hellman, Louis M.
Hellman, Morton J.
Hellman, Samuel
Hellmuth, Paul Francis
Hellmuth, William Frederick, Jr.
Helly, Walter Sigmund
Helm, Harold Holmes
Helm, Lewis Marshall
Helmetag, Carl, Jr.
Helmick, Louis Gaston, Jr.
Helmreich, Jonathan Ernst
Helms, Charles Brumm, Jr.
Helms, J. Lynn
Helms, Richard McGarrah
Helmstetter, Charles Edward
Helpern, Milton
Helrich, Martin
Helsing, John Eric
Helwig, Elson Bowman
Hemenway, Curtis Leland
Hemming, Roy G.
Hempel, Carl Gustav
Hempstone, Smith, Jr.
Hemry, Leslie Plumb
Hencken, Hugh O'Neill
Hendel, Charles William
Hendel, Samuel
Henderson, Albert
Henderson, Arthur Pearce
Henderson, Bruce Doolin
Henderson, Charles, Jr.
Henderson, David
Henderson, Donald Ainslie
Henderson, Douglas Boyd
Henderson, Edward Shelton
Henderson, Ernest, III
Henderson, Harry Brinton, Jr.
Henderson, Horace Edward
Henderson, Ian Hamilton
Henderson, James Alexander
Henderson, James McInnes
Henderson, John Batty
Henderson, John Brown
Henderson, Lenneal Joseph, Jr.
Henderson, Loy Wesley
Henderson, Madeline Mary Berry
Henderson, Oscar Warren
Henderson, Ralph Ernest
Henderson, Skitch Cedric
Henderson, William Charles
Hendin, David Bruce
Hendin, Herbert Martin
Hendl, Walter
Hendley, Coit Taylor, Jr.
Hendon, Robert Randall
Hendricks, Barbara
Hendricks, Ernest L.
Hendricks, Sterling B.
Hendricks, Walter
Hendrickson, James Briggs
Hendrickson, Robert Frederick
Hendrickson, Robert Meland
Hendrickson, Warren Edwin
Hendrie, Joseph Mallam
Hendrix, Thomas Russell
Hendry, George Stuart
Henel, Heinrich Edmund Karl
Heney, Joseph Edward
Heney, Thomas Tracy
Henke, Robert Henry
Henkelman, Willard Max
Henkin, Daniel Zwie
Henkin, Louis
Henle, Gertrude
Henle, Guy
Henley, Arthur
Henley, Earle Burr, Jr.
Henley, Henry Howard, Jr.
Henley, Vernard William
Henn, Harry George
Henne, Frances Elizabeth
Hennebach, Ralph L.
Henneman, Dorothy Hughes
Henneman, Elwood
Hennes, Robert Taft
Hennessey, Edward Francis
Hennessey, John William, Jr.
Hennessy, Augustine Paul
Hennessy, Carroll Ambrose
Hennessy, Edward Lawrence, Jr.
Hennessy, John Francis, Jr.
Hennessy, Wesley Joseph
Henney, Richard Bernard
Henning, Edward Ira
Henning, George Thomas, Jr.
Hennings, Arthur George
Hennings, Josephine Silva (Halpin)
Henningsen, Peter, Jr.
Henrichs, Albert Maximinus
Henricks, Arthur Philip, Jr.
Henry, Anthony Ray
Henry, Camille Wilfrid
Henry, Carl Ferdinand Howard
Henry, David Howe, II
Henry, Donald Wallace
Henry, Edward LeRoy
Henry, Gene Patrick
Henry, James Buchanan
Henry, James Fredrick
Henry, John Bernard
Henry, John Case
Henry, John Joseph
Henry, J(ohn) Porter, Jr.
Henry, Joseph Louis
Henry, Marion Lucas
Henry, Ralph Seth
Henry, Richard Charles
Henry, Richard Warfield
Henry, Ryder
Henry, Stuart Compton
Henry, Walter Lester, Jr.
Henry, William Lawrence
Hensel, H. Struve
Henshaw, Edmund Lee, Jr.
Henshaw, Francis Harold
Henshaw, Jonathan Cook
Henshel, Harry Bulova
Henske, John M.
Hensley, Robert Thornton
Hensley, Russell Duane
Henson, James Maury
Hentoff, Margot
Hentoff, Nathan Irving
Henze, Paul Bernard
Hepburn, James Gordon
Hepburn, Katharine
Hepfer, Frank Frederick
Heppel, Leon Alma
Herber, Elmer Charles
Herberg, John Clifford
Herberick, Bernard Felix
Herbert, Albert Edward, Jr.
Herbert, Charles Jerome
Herbert, James Paul
Herbert, James S.
Herbert, John Ruggles
Herbert, Robert Louis
Herbrandson, Harry Fred
Herbst, Robert LeRoy
Herd, John Victor
Hereford, Frank Loucks, Jr.
Herer, Jerome Bernard
Herge, Henry Curtis, Sr.
Herge, J. Curtis
Hering, Anthony Joseph, Jr.
Herlihy, David Joseph
Herlihy, Francis Bond
Herlihy, James Leo
Herling, John
Herling, John Phillip
Hermach, Francis Lewis
Herman, Beaumont Alexander
Herman, George Edward
Herman, Jerry
Herman, Kenneth
Herman, Morris
Herman, Robert Dixon
Herman, Robert S.
Herman, Sanford Meyer
Herman, Stan
Herman, Theodore
Herman, Theodore Lee
Herman, Woodrow Charles
Hermann, William Henry
Hermanovski, Egils P.
Hermanowicz, Henry Joseph
Hermanowski, Charles C.
Hermes, Julius
Herndon, James Francis
Herndon, Terry Eugene
Hernstadt, Judith Filenbaum
Hero, Alfred Olivier, Jr.
Herold, Edward William
Herold, John William, Jr.
Herpel, George Lloyd
Herr, Frederick John, Jr.
Herr, Kenneth Julian
Herrick, George Q.
Herrick, H.T.
Herrick, Robert Ford
Herridge, Frances
Herring, (Edward) Pendleton
Herring, William Conyers
Herrington, John David, III
Herrmann, Benjamin Edward
Herrmann, Daniel Lionel
Herrmann, Donald Joseph
Herrnstein, Richard Julius
Herrold, Kenneth Frederick
Herron, Lowell William
Hersberger, Arthur Bucher
Herschbach, Dudley Robert
Herschensohn, Bruce
Herscher, Irenaeus Joseph
Hersey, George Leonard
Hersey, John
Hersh, Seymour M.
Hershberger, Ervin N.
Hershenson, David Bert
Hershey, Alfred Day
Hershey, Lenore (Mrs. Solomon G. Hershey)
Hershey, Nathan
Hershman, Jacob Earl
Hershman, Mendes
Hertig, Arthur Tremain
Hertz, Barbara Valentine (Mrs. David Bendel Hertz)
Hertz, David Bendel
Hertz, Roy
Hertzberg, Arthur
Hertzfeld, Kurt Maximilian
Hertzog, Donald Paul
Herwitz, David Richard
Herz, Leonard
Herz, Martin Florian
Herzberg, Ben
Herzberg, Donald Gabriel
Herzenberg, Arvid
Herzfeld, Charles Maria
Herzog, Arthur, III
Herzog, Chaim
Herzog, Harold Kenneth
Herzog, Lester William, Jr.
Herzog, Paul M.
Heskett, James Lee
Heslin, James J.
Hess, Arthur
Hess, Arthur E.
Hess, Donald K.
Hess, Eugene Lyle
Hess, George Kellogg, Jr.
Hess, Hans Ober
Hess, Leon
Hess, Raymond Leonard, Jr.
Hess, Stephen
Hess, Thomas B.
Hesse, William R.
Hesselberg, Arthur Kenneth
Hesser, Leon Francis
Hession, Charles Henry
Hessman, James David
Hester, E. Elizabeth
Heston, William May
Heth, Donald Gerdes
Hetherington, James Alexander, II
Hetsko, Cyril Francis
Hettich, Arthur Matthias
Hettinger, Albert John, Jr.
Hettrick, John Lord
Hetzel, Frederick Armstrong
Hetzel, Frederick Joseph
Heuberger, Oscar
Heuer, Kenneth John
Heuer, Scott, Jr.
Heumann, Karl Fredrich
Heussler, Robert William
Heutchy, Alvin Earl
Hewes, Henry
Hewes, Laurence Ilsley, Jr.
Hewes, Laurence Ilsley, III
Hewett, John Brand
Hewitt, Don S.
Hewitt, John G.
Hewitt, Vivian Ann Davidson (Mrs. John Hamilton Hewitt)
Hewitt, William Patrick
Hewlett, Frank West
Hewlett, Horace Wilson
Hewlett, Richard Greening
Hexner, Peter Eugen
Hexter, David Benjamin
Hexter, Jack H.
Hexter, Maurice Beck
Hexter, Richard Martin
Heying, Theodore Louis
Heyman, Charles B.
Heyman, David John
Heyman, George Harrison, Jr.
Heyman, Ken
Heyn, Arno Harry Albert
Heyn, Ernest V.
Heyssel, Robert Morris
Hiatt, Howard H.
Hibbard, George A.
Hibbard, Robert
Hibbard, Walter Rollo, Jr.
Hibbett, Howard Scott
Hibbitt, Peyton Molyneaux
Hichar, Joseph Kenneth
Hickcox, Curtiss Bronson
Hicken, Philip Burnham
Hickey, Edward Joseph, Jr.
Hickey, Walter B.D.
Hickey, William Mace
Hickman, Cleveland Pendleton, Jr.
Hickman, J. Kenneth
Hickman, John Hampton, III
Hickman, Lauren Craig
Hickman, Leon Edward
Hickman, Robert Emmett
Hickok, Richard Sanford
Hickok, Robert Blair
Hicks, Beatrice Alice
Hicks, Byron Adna
Hicks, Granville
Hicks, Harry Leslie
Hicks, Leslie Hubert
Hicks, Orton Havergal
Hicks, Paul B., Jr.
Hicks, Virginia Sybil Drake
Hidalgo, Edward
Hidy, Ralph Willard
Hiebert, Erwin Nicholas
Hiebert, Ray Eldon
Higbee, Arthur Lloyd, Jr.
Higbee, Edward
Higginbotham, Aloyisus Leon, Jr.
Higginbottom, Samuel Logan
Higgins, Dick

Higgins, George Edward
Higgins, George Vincent
Higgins, Howard David
Higgins, James Henry
Higgins, Milton P.
Higgins, Paul Vincent
Higgins, Robert Louis
Higgins, Theodore Rundlett
Higgins, William Henry Clay, III
Higginson, James Jackson
Higginson, Thomas Lee
High, Rebecca Stickney
Higham, John
Highet, Gilbert
Highland, John Norbert, Jr.
Highsaw, James Leonard, Jr.
Hight, Joseph William
Hightower, John Brantley
Higinbotham, William Alfred
Higonnet, Patrice Louis-René
Hilal, Sadek Kamil
Hilberg, Raul
Hilburn, Earl Drayton
Hildebrand, Francis Begnaud
Hildebrand, Richard Allen
Hildebrand, Ruth Moorhead (Mrs. Francis E. Hildebrand)
Hildreth, Eugene A.
Hile, E.T.
Hill, Albert Gordon
Hill, Alfred
Hill, Andrew William
Hill, Calvin
Hill, Carl McClellan
Hill, Carol Dechellis
Hill, Charles Strunk
Hill, Derek Leonard
Hill, Dorothy Kent
Hill, Dumond Peck
Hill, Fentress, II
Hill, George Jackson, III
Hill, George Roy
Hill, Henry
Hill, Henry Parker
Hill, Herman Riddick, Jr.
Hill, Ira D.
Hill, Isaac William
Hill, James Daniel
Hill, James Scott
Hill, James Tomilson, Jr.
Hill, Karl Allen
Hill, Kermit Eugene
Hill, Lucius Gordon, Jr.
Hill, Martha
Hill, Norman
Hill, Richard Devereux
Hill, Robert C.
Hill, Robert Leland
Hill, Robert Mason
Hill, Robert White
Hill, Samuel Dennis
Hill, Terrell Leslie
Hill, Thomas Donald, Jr.
Hill, Thomas Mason, Jr.
Hill, Thomas William, Jr.
Hill, William Calvin
Hill, William Charles
Hill, William Edwin
Hill, William Plummer
Hill, Wilmer Bailey
Hillcourt, William
Hillebrecht, Robert R.
Hilleman, Maurice Ralph
Hillenkoetter, Roscoe Henry
Hiller, Kermit
Hiller, Lejaren Arthur, Jr.
Hillerbrand, Hans Joachim
Hillhouse, Gordon Emerson
Hillier, James
Hilliker, Grant Gilbert
Hillis, Elwood Haynes
Hillis, Mary Olive
Hillman, Henry L.
Hillman, Herman David
Hillman, Robert Sandor
Hills, Carla Anderson
Hills, Frederic Wheeler
Hills, George Strough
Hills, Patricia Gorton Schulze
Hills, Ralph Gorman
Hillyer, Kazuko Tatsumura
Hilsman, Roger
Hiltner, Seward
Hilton, Alice Mary
Hilton, Andrew Carson
Hilton, George J.
Hilton, Mary Nelson
Hilton, Ordway
Hilton, Robert Parker
Himes, Chester Bomar
Himmelfarb, Gertrude (Mrs. Irving Kristol)
Himmelfarb, Milton
Hinchman, William Rossiter, Jr.
Hinckley, G(eorge) F(ox) Steedman
Hinden, Stanley Jay
Hinderas, Natalie L.
Hindle, Brooke
Hindus, Milton
Hiner, Louis Chase
Hinerfeld, Norman Martin
Hines, Earl Kenneth Fatha
Hines, Howard Harry
Hines, Jerome
Hines, Lawrence Gregory
Hines, William Eugene
Hines, William Meredith, Jr.
Hingle, Pat
Hingson, Robert Andrew
Hinich, Melvin Jay
Hinkelman, Harold Irvin
Hinkle, Barton Leslie
Hinkley, Leo Thomas, Jr.
Hinman, Charles B.
Hinman, George Lyon
Hinsey, Joseph Clarence
Hinshaw, William Russell
Hinton, William Miller
Hinz, Carl Frederick, Jr.
Hippeau, Claude Jean Charles
Hippel, John F. E.
Hipple, Walter John, Jr.
Hiro, (Yasuhiro Wakabayashi)
Hironaka, Heisuke
Hirsch, Barry
Hirsch, Charles Bronislaw
Hirsch, Eric Donald, Jr.
Hirsch, Felix Edward
Hirsch, George Aaron
Hirsch, James Gerald
Hirsch, Joseph
Hirsch, Judd
Hirsch, Jules
Hirsch, Leo Henry, Jr.
Hirsch, Nathaniel David M'ttron
Hirsch, Richard Lewis
Hirsch, Robert Louis
Hirschfeld, Albert
Hirschfeld, Tomas Beno
Hirschfield, Alan J.
Hirschfield, Robert Sidney
Hirschhorn, Kurt
Hirschman, Albert Otto
Hirschmann, Ira
Hirsh, Allan Thurman, Jr.
Hirshson, Stanley Philip
Hirst, George Keble
Hirst, Julian Fravel
Hirst, William, Jr.
Hitch, Charles Johnston
Hitchcock, Ethan Allen
Hitchcock, Henry Russell
Hitchcock, Robert M.
Hitchcock, William Kenneth
Hitchner, Stephen Ballinger
Hite, Garth E.
Hite, Shere D.
Hitesman, Walter Wood, Jr.
Hitt, Russell Trovillo
Hitti, Philip Khuri
Hittinger, William Charles
Hittle, James D.
Hitzig, William Maxwell
Hixon, Lawrence Betts
Hixon, Robert Charles
Hlavaty, Julius Hayman
Ho, Monto
Ho, Yu-Chi
Hoag, David Garratt
Hoagland, Hudson
Hoagland, Jimmie Lee
Hoagland, Mahlon Bush
Hoagland, Sister Mary Arthur
Hoagland, Robert A.
Hoard, James Lynn
Hobbs, Gerald Stephen
Hobbs, Herman Hedberg
Hobbs, Horton Holcombe, Jr.
Hobbs, Ranald Purcell
Hobbs, Richard Lewis
Hoberman, Henry Don
Hoberman, Morton
Hoblin, Philip J., Jr.
Hobson, Burton Harold
Hobson, Katherine Thayer
Hobson, Mrs. Laura Zametkin
Hobstetter, John Norman
Hoch, Frank William
Hochberg, Bayard Zabdial
Hochman, Stanley Richard
Hochmann, John Leonard
Hochstadt, Harry
Hochstadt, Joy
Hochuli, Paul Richard
Hock, Nicholas George
Hockensmith, Roy Douglas
Hockett, Charles Francis
Hocking, James Robert
Hoctor, Thomas Francis
Hodes, Horace Louis
Hodge, Edwin, Jr.
Hodge, John Dennis
Hodge, Raymond Joseph
Hodges, Fletcher, Jr.
Hodges, John Hendricks
Hodges, Margaret Moore
Hodges, Walter Paul
Hodgkin, John Pease
Hodgkins, Edward Ruggles
Hodgson, Charles Clark
Hodgson, Richard
Hodgson, Robert James
Hodkinson, Sydney Phillip
Hodnett, Edward
Hodous, Robert Power
Hodson, Kenneth Joe
Hoebel, Bartley Gore
Hoeber, Paul B.
Hoefer, Paul Frederick Adam
Hoefling, John Alan
Hoehler, Fred Kenneth, Jr.
Hoehn, Elmer L.
Hoel, Lester A.
Hoelker, Rudolf Franz
Hoenack, August Frederick
Hoenemeyer, Frank Joseph
Hoenig, Sidney B.
Hoenigswald, Henry Max
Hoey, Joseph Patrick
Hoff, Ebbe Curtis
Hoff, Gerhardt Michael
Hoff, Margo
Hoff, William Jay
Hoffa, Harlan Edward
Hoffberger, Jerold Charles
Hoffberger, LeRoy Edward
Hoffberger, Stanley Alan
Hoffleit, (Ellen) Dorrit
Hoffman, Abbie
Hoffman, Arthur Samuel
Hoffman, Carter Osburn
Hoffman, Daniel
Hoffman, David Dale
Hoffman, Dustin
Hoffman, Edwin Karl
Hoffman, Elliot Lee
Hoffman, Howard Stanley
Hoffman, Irwin D.
Hoffman, James Williams
Hoffman, Joseph Frederick
Hoffman, Kenneth Myron
Hoffman, Leslie Arthur
Hoffman, Michael Lindsay
Hoffman, Philip Eisinger
Hoffman, S. Joseph
Hoffman, Walter Edward
Hoffman, William M.
Hoffmann, Henry Acker
Hoffmann, Léon-François
Hoffmann, Ludwig Carl
Hoffmann, Malcolm Arthur
Hoffmann, Roald
Hoffmann, Sal B.
Hoffmann, Stanley
Hofheinz, Roy Mark, Jr.
Hofmann, Hans
Hofmeyer, George August
Hofstadter, Albert
Hogan, Alice Hamilton
Hogan, Ernest Lynn, Jr.
Hogan, James Charles
Hogan, James John
Hogan, John Arthur
Hogan, Joseph Lloyd
Hogan, Thomas Bernard
Hogan, William Joseph
Hogard, Earl L., Jr.
Hoge, Warren McClamroch
Hogeland, Richard Wright
Hogeman, George L.
Hogin, Philip Edward
Hogrogian, Nonny
Hoguet, Robert Louis
Hohenberg, John
Hohenrath, William Edward
Hohler, George Robert
Hohn, Harry George
Hohn, Richard Gregory
Hoie, Claus
Holahan, Richard Vincent
Holbert, Theodore Frank
Holbik, Karel
Holbrook, George Edward
Holbrook, Luther Gardner
Holbrooke, Richard Charles Albert
Holcomb, Donald Frank
Holden, Arthur Cort
Holden, Donald
Holden, James Stuart
Holden, John Bernard
Holden, Raymond Thomas
Holden, Richard E.
Holden, William P.
Holder, Geoffrey
Holdheim, William Wolfgang
Holdridge, Barbara
Holladay, Harlan
Hollaender, Alexander
Holland, Arthur John
Holland, Clarence Adrian
Holland, Daniel Mark
Holland, Heinrich Dieter
Holland, Hubert Brian
Holland, James Frederick
Holland, Kenn
Holland, Kenneth George
Holland, Laurence Bedwell
Holland, Leonard
Holland, Norman Norwood
Holland, Richard G., Jr.
Holland, Robert Carl
Holland, Robert Debnam
Holland, Robert Lee
Hollander, Edwin Paul
Hollander, John
Hollander, Joseph Lee
Hollander, Lorin
Hollander, Milton Bernard
Hollander, Morton Joseph
Hollander, Richard Allen
Hollander, Richard Isaac
Holldobler, Berthold Karl
Holleb, Arthur Irving
Hollenbeck, Harold Capistran
Hollenbeck, Ralph Anthony
Hollender, Alfred Leo
Hollenshead, David Smith
Hollerbach, Serge
Holley, Frank Edward
Hollings, Ernest Frederick
Hollingshead, August de Belmont
Hollingsworth, Cecil Michael
Hollingsworth, Jack Waring
Hollingsworth, Samuel Hawkins, Jr.
Hollinshead, Byron S., Jr.
Hollister, Barrett
Hollister, Solomon Cady
Holloman, John Lawrence Sullivan, Jr.
Hollomon, John Herbert
Hollos, Paul Edmond
Holloway, Frederic Ancrum Lord
Holloway, James Lemuel, III
Holloway, Jerome Knight
Holloway, John Thomas
Holloway, Robert Ross
Holls, William Martin, Jr.
Holm, Celeste
Holm, Hanya
Holm, Jeanne Marjorie
Holm, Melvin Carl
Holman, Benjamin F.
Holman, Bud George
Holman, Charles Richardson
Holman, Cranston William
Holman, M. Carl
Holman, Wayne James, Jr.
Holme, Thomas Timings
Holmer, Paul LeRoy
Holmes, Alan Robert
Holmes, Charles Harvey
Holmes, Darrell
Holmes, Dyer Brainerd
Holmes, Edward Warren
Holmes, Ernest Lee
Holmes, George Washington, III
Holmes, Henry Hazelton
Holmes, John Clellon
Holmes, Larry
Holmes, Lyle Anderson
Holmes, Marjorie Rose
Holmes, Max Jacob
Holmes, Melvin Almont
Holmes, Oliver Wendell
Holmes, Preston Turner
Holmes, Richard Turner
Holmes, Roger Wellington
Holmes, Thomas A.
Holmes, Walter Stephen, Jr.
Holmgren, Harry D.
Holmgren, Laton Earle
Holmgren, Patricia Kern
Holmgren, Theodore J.
Holmquest, P.S.
Holstein, Edwin Joseph
Holstein, William Kurt
Holt, Donald Dale
Holt, Edwin Graves
Holt, Leon Conrad, Jr.
Holt, Marjorie Sewell
Holt, Nancy Louise
Holt, Robert Rutherford
Holt, Victoria
Holtermann, E. Louis, Jr.
Holtfreter, Johannes Friedrich Karl
Holt-Harris, John Evan, Jr.
Holton, A. Linwood, Jr.
Holton, Gerald
Holtz, Sidney
Holtzclaw, Benjamin Clark
Holtzman, Elizabeth
Holtzman, Kenneth Dale
Holtzman, M. Jay
Holtzman, Richard Edward
Holway, Frederick S.
Holz, Harold A.
Holzer, Hans
Holzman, Franklyn Dunn
Holzman, Philip Seidman
Holzman, Robert Stuart
Holzman, William
Holzner, Burkart
Homans, George Caspar
Homburger, Freddy
Homer, Porter Wyman
Homer, William Innes
Homme, Herbert Gordon
Homrighausen, Elmer George
Homsey, Samuel
Homsey, Victorine (Mrs. Samuel E. Homsey)
Honaman, R(ichard) Karl
Honan, Elliot Francis
Honemann, Daniel Henry
Honey, James Kuhn
Honig, Edwin
Honig, Marvin Ira
Honig, Mervin
Honigberg, Bronislaw Mark
Honkala, Fred Saul
Honnold, John Otis, Jr.
Honsinger, Leroy Vernon
Hood, Charles Harvey
Hood, Edward Exum, Jr.
Hood, Gilbert Henry, Jr.
Hood, Harvey Perley
Hood, Robert Eric
Hoof, Wayne
Hoogenboom, Ari Arthur
Hook, Edward Watson, Jr.
Hooker, John Lee
Hooker, R(oger) Wolcott
Hooks, Benjamin Lawson
Hoon, Paul Waitman
Hooper, Edith Ferry
Hooper, Edwin Bickford
Hooper, John Allen
Hooper, Lucien Obed
Hoopes, Janet Louise
Hoopes, John Eugene
Hoopes, Townsend Walter
Hoot, William John
Hoover, Charles William
Hoover, John Elwood
Hoover, John Page
Hoover, Joseph Samuel
Hoover, Linn
Hoover, Roland Armitage
Hoover, Theressa
Hope, Norman Victor
Hope, Samuel Howard
Hopfield, John Joseph
Hopkins, Albert Lafayette, Jr.
Hopkins, Bert Earl
Hopkins, Charles Howard
Hopkins, Edward J.
Hopkins, Frank Albert
Hopkins, Frank Snowden
Hopkins, George Edgar
Hopkins, Joseph Gerard Edward
Hopkins, Samuel
Hopkins, Shirley Knight
Hopper, Clarence Heller
Hopper, Grace Brewster Murray
Hopper, Henry George
Hopper, Stanley Romaine
Hopper, Thomas Washburn
Hopper, Walter Everett
Hopper, William David
Hopps, Hope Elizabeth Byrne
Hopwood, George Richard
Horan, Francis Harding
Horan, James D.
Horan, John J.
Horan, Justin Thomas
Horecker, Bernard Leonard
Horgan, John Joseph, Jr.
Horgan, Paul
Horn, Andre Raphael
Horn, Carol Ellen
Horn, Daniel
Horn, Gerald Anthony
Horn, Martin Louis, Jr.
Horn, Roger Alan
Hornbake, Ralph Lee
Hornbeck, David Wallace
Hornbeck, John Austin
Hornblower, Ralph, Jr.
Hornbostel, Charles Christian
Hornbostel, Peter Anthony
Horne, David Hamilton
Horne, John E.
Horne, Lena
Horne, Marilyn
Horne, Ralph Warren
Horne, Walter Batcheller
Horner, Charles Thompson, Jr.
Horner, Matina Souretis
Hornig, Donald Frederick
Hornig, James Frederick
Hornor, Frank Berkshire
Hornsby, Marvin Jackson
Hornung, Lenora Virginia
Horovitz, Israel Arthur
Horovitz, Samuel Bertram
Horowitz, Daniel L.
Horowitz, David H.
Horowitz, Don Roy
Horowitz, Harold
Horowitz, Irving Louis
Horowitz, Morris A.
Horowitz, Paul
Horowitz, Raymond Jack
Horowitz, Sidney
Horowitz, Stanley
Horowitz, Stanley Harris
Horowitz, Vladimir
Horowitz, William
Horrigan, Edward A., Jr.
Horseman, Roy Mertzell
Horsfall, James Gordon
Horsky, Charles Antone
Horsman, John Gordon, Jr.
Horstmann, Dorothy Millicent
Horton, Alan Williams
Horton, Charles Crosley
Horton, Charles Robert
Horton, Donald Paul
Horton, Frank
Horton, Howard Leavitt
Horton, Jared C.
Horton, John Alden
Horvitz, Harold
Horvitz, Wayne Louis
Horwitt, Will
Horwitz, Karl
Horwitz, Martin
Horwitz, Paul
Hosenball, S. Neil
Hosking, Robert Leroy
Hosler, Charles Luther, Jr.
Hosmer, Craig
Hosner, John Frank
Hossack, Alexander
Hotchkiss, Gerald Godfrey
Hotchkiss, Robert Sherman
Hotchkiss, Rollin Douglas
Hotchkiss, Wesley Akin
Hotchkiss, Winchester Fitch
Hotchner, Aaron Edward
Hott, Louis Randell
Hottel, Hoyt Clarke
Hottelet, Richard Curt
Hotz, Robert Bergmann
Hou, Chi Ming
Houbolt, John Cornelius
Houbrick, Richard Stephen
Hough, Henry Beetle
Hough, Richard Ralston
Houghtaling, Earle Hannum, Jr.
Houghton, Alan Nourse
Houghton, Amory
Houghton, Amory, Jr.
Houghton, Arthur Amory, Jr.
Houghton, Charles Norris
Houghton, Henry Garrett
Houghton, James Richardson
Houghton, Katharine
Houghton, Walter Edwards
Houghton, Woodson Plyer
Houle, Joseph E.
Hourani, George Fadlo
Hourigan, Andrew, Jr.
Hourtoule, Gilbert Otto
House, Arthur Stephen
House, Charles Staver
House, Jeffrey Wheeler
Houseman, John
Houser, John W.
Houser, William Douglas
Housewright, Riley Dee
Houska, Charles Robert
Housman, Kenneth Alfred
Houston, Charles Snead
Houston, Howard Edwin
Houston, Peyton Hoge
Houston, Ray Bertholf
Hovde, Carl Frederick
Hovey, Justus Allan, Jr.
Hovey, Richard Bennett
Hovey, Walter Read
Hoving, Thomas
Hoving, Walter
Hovnanian, H. Philip
Howar, Barbara Dearing
Howard, August
Howard, Charles Frank
Howard, Daggett Horton
Howard, David
Howard, Donald Searcy
Howard, Edward Douglas, II
Howard, Elston Gene
Howard, Harry Nicholas
Howard, Humbert Lincoln
Howard, J. Woodford, Jr.
Howard, Jack
Howard, Jack Rohe
Howard, James J.
Howard, James Merriam, Jr.
Howard, James Stephen, III
Howard, Jane Temple
Howard, John Arnold
Howard, John Brigham
Howard, John Eager
Howard, John Stuart
Howard, John Tasker
Howard, Joseph Harvey
Howard, Katherine Graham (Mrs. Charles P. Howard)
Howard, Kingston Lee
Howard, Lawrence Cabot
Howard, Lee Milton
Howard, Richard Alden
Howard, Richard (Joseph)
Howard, Robert Thornton
Howard, William Allen
Howard, Willie Thomas, Jr.
Howard-Flanders, Paul
Howarth, Thomas
Howat, John Keith
Howe, Albert Spaulding, Jr.
Howe, Buddy
Howe, Ernest Joseph
Howe, Fisher
Howe, Gordon
Howe, Irving
Howe, James Tarsicius
Howe, John Strother
Howe, Roger Evans
Howe, Wesley Jackson
Howell, Albert Charles
Howell, Alfred Hunt
Howell, Alvin Harold
Howell, Barbara Thompson
Howell, Benjamin Franklin, Jr.
Howell, Elsworth Seaman
Howell, Hannah Johnson
Howell, Henry Wardwell
Howell, James Theodore
Howell, Janet K. Gregg
Howell, John I.
Howell, Roger, Jr.
Howell, Wilbur Samuel
Howells, William White
Hower, John
Howes, Barbara
Howes, Thomas Prince
Howie, George Williamson
Howland, Harold Edward
Howland, Murray Shipley, Jr.
Howland, Richard Hubbard
Howland, Wilfred Glenroy
Howland, William Stapleton
Howlett, Carolyn Chance
Howlett, Duncan
Howlett, Philip Gerad
Howley, Frank Leo
Howley, Roger
Howorth, M. Beckett
Howrey, Edward F.
Howse, Robert Davis
Howse, W.L., Jr.
Hoxie, Ralph Gordon
Hoy, Cyrus Henry
Hoyer, Vincent Edgar
Hoyt, Austin
Hoyt, Henry Hamilton
Hoyt, Henry Hamilton, Jr.
Hoyt, Homer
Hoyt, Kenneth Boyd
Hoyt, Mary Finch
Hoyt, Nelly Schargo (Mrs. N. Deming Hoyt)
Hoyt, William Vernor
Hromadko, George
Hrycak, Peter
Hsieh, Jui Sheng
Hsu, Ching-yu
Hsu, John Tseng Hsin
Hsueh, Chun-tu
Hubbard, Allen Skinner
Hubbard, Carroll, Jr.
Hubbard, Cortlandt Van Dyke
Hubbard, Elizabeth
Hubbard, Frederic George
Hubbard, Howard James
Hubbard, John Perry
Hubbard, Lafayette Ronald
Hubbard, Robert Merrill
Hubbell, John William
Hubbell, Lester Earle
Hubbell, Richard Whittaker
Hubbert, Marion King
Hubel, David Hunter
Huber, Albert John
Huber, August
Huber, Don Lawrence
Huber, Edward Frederick
Huber, Howard R.
Huber, John Franklin
Hubley, Faith Elliott
Hubley, George Wilbur, Jr.
Hubley, John

Hubley, Reginald Allen
Hubner, Robert Wilmore
Huck, John Lloyd
Huckaba, Charles Edwin
Huckaby, Thomas Gerald
Hudelson, George David
Hudnut, William Herbert, Jr.
Hudon, Edward Gerard
Hudson, Anthony Webster
Hudson, Harold Jordon, Jr.
Hudson, Harriet Dufresne
Hudson, Jack William, Jr.
Hudson, Ralph Percy
Hudson, Rock (Roy Fitzgerald)
Hudson, William Noel
Hudson, William Thomas
Hudson, Winthrop Still
Huebner, John Mudie
Huebner, Robert Joseph
Huettner, Richard Alfred
Hufnagel, Charles Anthony
Hug, Arthur, Jr.
Huggins, Charles Edward
Huggins, Lawrence Patrick
Huggins, Nathan Irvin
Huggins, William Herbert
Hughes, Albert Raymond, Jr.
Hughes, Allen
Hughes, Andrew Wesley
Hughes, Blake
Hughes, Carl Wilson
Hughes, Elinor Lambert
Hughes, Emmet John
Hughes, Everett Cherrington
Hughes, Harold Kenneth
Hughes, H(arry) Herbert
Hughes, John
Hughes, John Edward
Hughes, John Lawrence
Hughes, Joseph D.
Hughes, Leo Aloysius, Jr.
Hughes, Lloyd Lynnell
Hughes, Marija Matich
Hughes, Michaela Kelly
Hughes, Phillip Samuel
Hughes, Richard Joseph
Hughes, Richard Michael
Hughes, Robert Edward
Hughes, Robert Joseph
Hughes, Royston Charles
Hughes, Thomas Joseph
Hughes, Thomas Lowe
Hughes, William Frank
Hughes, William John
Hughs, Robert Nathaniel
Huitt, Ralph Kinsloe
Huizenga, John Robert
Hull, Harry
Hull, Norman James, Jr.
Hull, Treat Clark
Hulm, John Kenneth
Hulse, Stewart Harding, Jr.
Hulsizer, Robert Inslee, Jr.
Hultberg, John
Humann, Christian
Hume, David DesJardins
Hume, David Lang
Hume, David Newton
Hume, John Chandler
Hume, John E.N., Jr.
Hume, Patrick Henry
Hume, Paul Chandler
Hume, Robert Ibelle
Hume, Warren Charles
Humelsine, Carlisle Hubbard
Humes, Bernard James
Humes, James Calhoun
Humes, John P.
Humeston, Edward Judson, Jr.
Hummel, Arthur William, Jr.
Hummel, Charles Frederick
Humperdinck, Engelbert (Arnold George Dorsey)
Humphrey, Arthur Earl
Humphrey, Edward
Humphrey, Hubert Horatio, Jr.
Humphrey, Joseph Harrison
Humphrey, Muriel Fay Buck (Mrs. Hubert Horatio Humphrey)
Humphrey, Richard Sears, Jr.
Humphreys, George Hoppin, II
Humphreys, James W.
Humphreys, Mabel Gweneth
Humphreys, Robert Russell
Humphries, John O'Neal
Humphries, Kenneth B.
Humphry, James, III
Humphry, John Ames
Hundley, John Walker
Hungerford, Cyrus Cotton
Hunneman, Robert Ingle
Hunsberger, Isaac Moyer
Hunt, Alfred Mortimer
Hunt, Howard Francis
Hunt, John David
Hunt, John Wesley
Hunt, Leamon Ray
Hunt, Pearson
Hunt, Richard Howard
Hunt, William Dudley, Jr.
Hunter, Barbara Way
Hunter, Clarence E.
Hunter, David Robert
Hunter, David Romeyn
Hunter, David Wittmer
Hunter, Edward
Hunter, Evan
Hunter, Frank Herbert
Hunter, Henry Hamilton
Hunter, James, III
Hunter, James Augustus (Catfish)
Hunter, (James) Graham
Hunter, James Megargee
Hunter, John, Jr.
Hunter, J(ohn) Robert
Hunter, John Stuart
Hunter, Kim (Janet Cole)
Hunter, Kristin Elaine Eggleston (Mrs. John I. Lattany)
Hunter, Ralph William
Hunter, Sam
Hunter, Thomas Harrison
Hunter, William Carroll
Hunting, Constance Coulter
Huntington, Charles Ellsworth
Huntington, David Hans
Huntington, Earl Lloyd
Huntington, Hillard Bell
Huntington, Samuel Phillips
Huntington, Thomas Foster
Huntley, Charles William
Huntley, Robert Edward Royall
Hunton, Eppa, IV
Hunziker, Robert McKee
Hupper, John Roscoe
Hurd, Frederick William
Hurlbert, Donald Earl
Hurlburt, Wilbur Franklyn, Jr.
Hurlbut, Cornelius Searle, Jr.
Hurley, Daniel Francis
Hurley, Donald Joseph
Hurley, James Edward
Hurley, Kenneth Duane
Hurley, Marie V.
Hurley, Patrick Mason
Hurley, Robert Emmet
Hurson, Daniel L.
Hurst, Kenneth Thurston
Hurst, Robert Philip
Hurvich, Leo Maurice
Hurwich, Robert Allan
Hurwitz, David
Hurwitz, Henry, Jr.
Hurwitz, Jerard
Husa, Karel
Husby, Donald Evans
Hushing, William Collins
Husmann, Ronald Hugh
Hussar, Daniel Alexander
Hussey, George Frederick, Jr.
Hussey, Ward MacLean
Husted, Walter
Huston, Harris Hyde
Huston, James Alvin
Huston, John Albert
Huston, John Wilson
Hutchens, John Kennedy
Hutchens, Joseph Warren
Hutcheson, John A.
Hutcheson, Thomas Barksdale, Jr.
Hutchin, Claire Elwood, Jr.
Hutchings, Imri J.
Hutchins, Curtis Marshall
Hutchins, Frank McAllister
Hutchins, John Richard, III
Hutchins, Maude Phelps McVeigh
Hutchins, Robert Senger
Hutchinson, Charles Smith, Jr.
Hutchinson, Edmond Carlton
Hutchinson, Edward Prince
Hutchinson, Everett
Hutchinson, Franklin
Hutchinson, Frederick Edward
Hutchinson, John Joseph
Hutchinson, Pemberton
Hutchinson, Warner Alton, Jr.
Hutchison, Dorris Jeannette
Hutchison, Stuart Nye, Jr.
Hutchison, William Robert
Huth, Donald Earl
Huth, Edward Janavel
Huth, William Edward
Huthmacher, J. Joseph
Hutner, Seymour Herbert
Hutson, Frank Alfred, Jr.
Hutson, Jean Blackwell (Mrs. John O. Hutson)
Hutt, Peter Barton
Hutter, Donald Stephen
Hutter, Robert Victor Paul
Hutter, Rudolf Gustav Emil
Hutton, Ann Hawkes
Hutton, James
Hutton, James Franklin
Hutton, James Morgan, III
Hutton, Robert Franklin
Hutton, Robert William
Hutton, William Edward
Huxtable, Ada Louise
Huyett, Daniel Henry, 3d
Huygens, Remmert William
Huyser, Robert Ernest
Hyatt, David
Hyatt, Donald Bishop
Hyde, Edward W.
Hyde, Edwin
Hyde, Fritz Carleton, Jr.
Hyde, Harold Eldred
Hyde, Henry van Zile
Hyde, James Nevins
Hyde, Laurin Eber
Hyde, Mary Morley Crapo (Mrs. Donald F. Hyde)
Hyde, Walter Lewis
Hyde, William Truslow, Jr.
Hyland, Edward William
Hyland, Richard Francis, Jr.
Hyland, William Francis
Hyland, William George
Hyle, John F.
Hyman, Arthur
Hyman, Herbert Hiram
Hyman, Milton
Hyman, Morton Peter
Hyman, Ralph Alan
Hyman, Seymour
Hymes, Dell Hathaway
Hymoff, Edward
Hynes, Samuel
Hyson, Charles David
Hytche, William Percy
Iakovos, Archbishop (Demetrios A. Coucouzis)
Ian, Janis
Ianni, Francis Alphonse
I'Anson, Lawrence Warren
Iavicoli, Mario Anthony
Ibranyi, Francis Joseph
Ice, Lewis Melvin
Ichniowski, Casimir Thaddeus
Idema, James Mead
Idzerda, Stanley John
Ignatius, Paul Robert
Ignatow, David
Igusa, Jun-Ichi
Ihara, Michio
Ihrke, Walter Rudolph
Ijams, Maitland Tabb
Ikard, Frank Neville
Ikeler, Harold Edwin, Jr.
Ikenberry, Henry Cephas, Jr.
Ikenberry, Stanley Oliver
Ikle, Fred Charles
Ilchman, Alice Stone
Ilchman, Warren Frederick
Iliescu, Nicolae
Illick, John Rowland
Illig, James Michael
Imbrie, John
Imlach, George (Punch)
Immergut, Edmund Heinz
Impellizzeri, Irene Helen
Ince, Eugene St. Clair, Jr.
Indiana, Robert
Inez, Colette
Ingalls, Daniel Henry Holmes
Ingalls, James Warren, Jr.
Ingbar, Sidney Harold
Ingelfinger, Franz Joseph
Ingersoll, Charles Edward
Ingersoll, John E.
Ingersoll, Paul Mills
Ingersoll, Ralph McAllister
Ingham, Charles S.
Ingle, John Ide
Inglis, David Rittenhouse
Ingraham, H. Gardner
Ingraham, Harold Gillette, Jr.
Ingraham, Hollis Steadman
Ingram, George, Jr.
Ingram, William Truitt
Ink, Gary Louis
Inman, Bobby Ray
Innis, Donald Quayle
Innis, Roy Emile Alfredo
Inoue, Shinya
Insley, Will
Intriligator, Melvin
Ioanes, Raymond Andrew
Iorio, John Anthony
Ippolito, Angelo
Irby, Mildred
Irby, Richard Logan
Ireland, William Dunning, Jr.
Irenay, Metropolitan (John Bekish)
Ireton, John Francis, Jr.
Irish, Marian Doris
Irvin, John Blake
Irvine, John Withers, Jr.
Irvine, Louva Elizabeth
Irvine, Ralstone Robert
Irvine, Thomas Francis, Jr.
Irvine, William Michael
Irving, Flora Miller
Irving, Frederick
Irving, George W., Jr.
Irving, James Tutin
Irving, Michael Henry
Irving, Robert Augustine
Irvis, K. Leroy
Irwin, Arthur Samuel
Irwin, Francis William
Irwin, George Rankin
Irwin, Graham Wilkie
Irwin, Helen Trathen
Irwin, Howard Samuel, Jr.
Irwin, John Nichol, II
Irwin, Leo Howard
Irwin, Robert James Armstrong, Jr.
Irwin, Theodore
Irwin, Wayne
Isaac, William H.
Isaacman, Daniel
Isaacman, Irwin Theodore
Isaacs, Edgar E.
Isaacs, Harold Robert
Isaacs, Kenneth L.
Isaacs, Norman Ellis
Isaacs, Reginald Roderic
Isaacs, Rufus Philip
Isaacson, Bernard Benjamin
Isaacson, Gerald Sidney
Isaacson, Walter Francis
Isaacson, William Joseph
Isard, Walter
Isbell, Horace Smith
Isbell, John Rolfe
Isbister, James David
Iselin, Donald Grote
Iselin, John Jay
Iselin, Philip H.
Iseman, Joseph Seeman
Isenberg, Bruce Kenneth
Isenberg, Henry David
Isenbergh, Max
Isenburger, Eric
Isenburger, Herbert Rudolf
Isensee, Allan Robert
Isidore, Anthony
Israel, Adrian Cremieux
Israel, Richard Jerome
Israeli, Nathan
Israelson, Max Roth
Issackedes, Jordan
Issawi, Charles Philip
Isselbacher, Kurt Julius
Istel, Jacques Andre
Istomin, Eugene
Ito, Susumu
Ittleson, Henry Anthony
Itzler, Ronald Stephen
Ivanetic, Mirjan
Iversen, John Donald
Iverson, Marvin Alvin
Ives, Burl (Icle Ivanhoe)
Ives, Charles Pomeroy, 2d
Ives, David Otis
Ives, Dermod
Ives, George Skinner
Ives, Philip
Ives, Stephen Bradshaw, Jr.
Ivey, John Courtney
Ivins, James Elbert
Ivison, Maynard C.
Iwasawa, Kenkichi
Izard, Carroll Ellis
Izenour, George Charles
Jablonski, Edward
Jablonski, Wanda Mary
Jack, Harold Harry
Jack, Homer Alexander
Jackel, Lawrence
Jackendoff, Nathaniel
Jackman, Lloyd Miles
Jackson, Anne (Anna June Jackson)
Jackson, Arnold William
Jackson, D. Brooks
Jackson, David Munro
Jackson, David Pingree
Jackson, Denise Suzanne
Jackson, Dudley Pennington
Jackson, Elmer Martin, Jr.
Jackson, Elmore
Jackson, Eugene Delaney
Jackson, Eugene Wesley
Jackson, Francis Xavier
Jackson, Frederick Andrew
Jackson, Frederick Way, III
Jackson, George Lyman
Jackson, Hazel Brill
Jackson, J. Harry
Jackson, Jack B.
Jackson, John Burton
Jackson, John Jay
Jackson, John Tillson
Jackson, Joseph Gray
Jackson, Kate
Jackson, Kenneth Arthur
Jackson, Lee
Jackson, Lionel Stewart
Jackson, Nyle M.
Jackson, Philip Chappell, Jr.
Jackson, Reginald Martinez
Jackson, Richard George
Jackson, Richard Montgomery
Jackson, Robert Tilden
Jackson, Samuel Charles
Jackson, Stanley Bartlett
Jackson, Thomas Searing
Jackson, Timothy Edward
Jackson, Walter Harry
Jackson, Ward
Jackson, William Brown
Jackson, William David
Jackson, William MacLeod
Jackson, William Richard
Jackson, William Thomas Hobdell
Jackson, William Ward
Jacob, Charles Elmer
Jacob, Emerson Donald
Jacob, Harry Myles
Jacob, Henry George
Jacobi, Herbert John
Jacobi, John Edward
Jacobi, Lou
Jacobs, Alan Martin
Jacobs, Andrew, Jr.
Jacobs, Arthur Theodore
Jacobs, Bradford McElderry
Jacobs, David
Jacobs, Frederick L.
Jacobs, Harry Allan, Jr.
Jacobs, Helen Hull
Jacobs, James Albert
Jacobs, Jane
Jacobs, Jay
Jacobs, Jim
Jacobs, Klaus Karl Ewald
Jacobs, Lawrence Pierce
Jacobs, Milton
Jacobs, Robert Allan
Jacobs, Sophia Yarnall
Jacobs, Walter William
Jacobs, William Ketchum, Jr.
Jacobs, William Paul
Jacobs, Woodrow Cooper
Jacobsen, Arthur
Jacobsen, Edward Hastings
Jacobsen, Josephine Winder Boylan
Jacobsohn, Peter M.W.S.
Jacobson, Albert Sigfried
Jacobson, Alf Edgar
Jacobson, Alfred Thurl
Jacobson, Avrohm
Jacobson, Charlotte Stone
Jacobson, Dorothy Houston
Jacobson, Edwin
Jacobson, Gaynor I.
Jacobson, Harold Gordon
Jacobson, Ira
Jacobson, Ishier
Jacobson, Joel Ross
Jacobson, Leslie Sari
Jacobson, Melvin Joseph
Jacobson, Robert
Jacobus, John M., Jr.
Jacoby, Jay Joshua
Jacoby, Robert Bird
Jacoby, Robert Eakin, Jr.
Jacoby, William Jerome, Jr.
Jacolow, Jerald Joshua
Jacovides, George
Jacox, Harold William
Jacquet, Jean Baptiste Illinois
Jadot, Jean Lambert Octave
Jaeckle, Edwin F.
Jaffe, Anthony Robert
Jaffe, Arthur Michael
Jaffe, Harold
Jaffe, Jan Paynter
Jaffe, Julian Joseph
Jaffe, Leo
Jaffe, Paul Lawrence
Jaffee, Michael
Jaffin, Charles Leonard
Jaffrey, Harold
Jagendorf, Moritz Adolph
Jagger, Mick (Michael Philip Jagger)
Jagiello, Georgiana Mary
Jagoda, Barry Lionel
Jahn, Charles Richard
Jahn, Edwin Cornelius
Jahn, Laurence Roy
Jahn, Robert George
Jahoda, Fritz
Jahoda, Kurt
Jain, Piyare Lal
Jakab, Irene
Jakes, John William
Jaklitsch, Joseph John, Jr.
Jakobson, Roman
Jambor, Agi
James, Allix Bledsoe
James, Benjamin David
James, Charles Franklin, Jr.
James, Clifford Cyril
James, Daniel, Jr.
James, Daniel J.
James, Eric
James, Forrest Donald
James, Herbert Isidor
James, Howard Anthony, Jr.
James, Howard P.
James, Jack Milton
James, Robert Leo
James, Sidney Lorraine
James, Wilbur Albert
James, Winfield Henry
Jameson, Dorothea
Jamieson, David Donald
Jamieson, Edward Leo
Jamieson, Graham A.
Jamison, John Ambler
Jamison, Judith
Jamison, Philip Duane, Jr.
Jamouneau, Walter Corey
Jampolis, Neil Peter
Janaske, Paul Carlyle
Jandl, Henry Anthony
Jandl, James Harriman
Jane, John Anthony
Janeway, Carol Janet Brown (Mrs. William Hall Janeway)
Janeway, Charles Alderson
Janeway, Eliot
Janeway, Elizabeth Hall
Janeway, Michael Charles
Janis, Allen Ira
Janis, Byron
Janis, Donald Leon
Janis, Irving Lester
Janis, Jay
Janis, Sidney
Janklow, Morton Lloyd
Jankowski, Gene F.
Jannarone, John Robert
Jannetta, Peter Joseph
Janney, Stuart Symington, Jr.
Janos, John William
Janosik, Edward Gabriel
Janowitz, Dorris
Janowitz, Henry David
Jansen, Marius Berthus
Janson, Horst Woldemar
Janson, Joseph Bror, II
Janssen, Werner
Jantzen, William J.
January, Don
Jaquith, Richard Herbert
Jaramillo, Mari-Luci
Jaray, Cornell
Jareckie, Stephen Barlow
Jarman, William Jackson
Jarmolow, Kenneth
Jarrard, Jerald Osborne
Jarrard, Leonard Everett
Jarriel, Thomas Edwin
Jarvis, Lucy Howard (Mrs. Serge Jarvis)
Jarvis, Marshall Houston
Jasen, Matthew Joseph
Jasinowski, Jerry Joseph
Jaskiewicz, Leonard Albert
Jaskilka, Samuel
Jaskot, John Joseph
Jaslow, Robert Irwin
Jasper, David Westwater
Jastrow, Robert
Jaszi, George
Jauchem, Clarence Ralph
Jaus, William Currie
Javan, Ali
Javert, Carl Theodore
Javits, Eric Moses
Javits, Jacob Koppel
Jay, Herbert Lloyd
Jaynes, Lawrence C.
Jayson, Lester Samuel
Jeanloz, Roger William
Jedlicka, Judith Ann
Jeffers, Michael Bogue
Jefferson, Edward Graham
Jefferson, Howard B.
Jeffords, James Merrill
Jeffrey, George Alan
Jeffrey, Louis Paul
Jeffrey, Richard Carl
Jeffrey, Robert George, Jr.
Jeffrey, Thomas Stanley, Jr.
Jeffrey, William Hartley
Jeffries, Robert Joseph
Jeghers, Harold Joseph
Jehlik, Paul Joseph
Jekeli, Walter
Jelinek, Hans
Jelinek, Robert Alan
Jelliffe, Charles Gordon
Jellinek, Roger
Jellinghaus, Carl Frederic
Jen, Frank Chifeng
Jenckes, Ernest Ashley
Jencks, Christopher Sandys
Jencks, Francis Haynes
Jencks, William Platt
Jenkins, Alfred le Sesne
Jenkins, Edward C.
Jenkins, Ferguson Arthur
Jenkins, George Pollock
Jenkins, Paul
Jenkins, Robert Ellsworth, Jr.
Jenkins, William Ambrose
Jenkins, Wilmer Atkinson, II
Jenks, George Merritt
Jenks, Homer (Simeon)
Jenks, Thomas Elijah
Jenks, William Alexander
Jennewein, Carl Paul
Jenney, Melvin Richard
Jennings, Bojan Hamlin
Jennings, Edward Morton, Jr.
Jennings, Frank Gerard
Jennings, James Monroe, II
Jennings, John Melville
Jennings, Joseph Ashby
Jennings, Lewellyn A.
Jennings, Manson Van Buren
Jennings, Peter Charles
Jennings, Stuart Yatman
Jennings, Waylon
Jennings, William Mitchell
Jennison, Marshall Walker
Jenrette, John Wilson, Jr.
Jenrette, Richard Hampton
Jensen, Alfred Julius
Jensen, Eric Finn
Jensen, Finn Bjorn
Jensen, Harry Arthur
Jensen, Henry Edward
Jensen, Oliver Ormerod
Jensen, Robert P.
Jensen, Vernon Hortin
Jenson, Paul Gerhard
Jeppesen, Myron Alton
Jeppson, Gabriella De Ferrari
Jeppson, John, 2d
Jerge, Charles
Jernigan, Homer Large
Jesse, Mary Jane
Jessen, George Eli
Jesseramsing, Chitmansing
Jessup, Claude Ambrose
Jessup, John Knox
Jester, Roberts Charles, Jr.
Jestin, Heimwarth B.
Jette, Ellerton Marcel
Jewell, William MacIntyre
Jewett, Frank Baldwin, Jr.
Jewett, Hugh Judge
Jewett, John Gibson
Jewitt, David Willard Pennock
Jex, Victor Bird
Jochum, Veronica
Jockers, Harold William
Joelson, Charles S.
Joffe, Joseph
Joffrey, Robert (Abdullah Jaffa Bey Khan)
Johann, Robert Oliver
Johanos, Donald
Johansen, Eivind Herbert
Johansen, Erling
Johanson, Patricia Maureen
John, DeWitt
John, Erwin Roy
John, Fritz
John, Ralph Candler
Johnpoll, Alexander Cecil
Johns, Don Herbert
Johns, Glenn Franklyn
Johns, Jasper
Johns, Richard James
Johnsen, John Herbert
Johnson, A. Dexter
Johnson, Albert Edward
Johnson, Albert Pemberton
Johnson, Albert Walter
Johnson, Allan Raymond
Johnson, Andrew Emerson, III
Johnson, Archibald DeBaun
Johnson, Arne Robert
Johnson, Arthur Menzies
Johnson, Aubrey Kenneth
Johnson, Avery Fischer
Johnson, Bert Willard
Johnson, Boine Theodore, Jr.
Johnson, Briard Poland
Johnson, Bruce Alfred
Johnson, Charles Christopher, Jr.
Johnson, Charles Kobler
Johnson, Charlotte Buel
Johnson, David Simonds
Johnson, Davis Gilman

Kelmenson, Leo Arthur
Kelne, Nathan
Kelsey, Frances Oldham, (Mrs. Fremont Ellis Kelsey)
Kelsey, John Forsyth, Jr.
Kelso, David James
Kelso, James Leon
Kelso, John Hodgson
Kelton, John T.
Keltz, Joel Sammel
Kemelman, Harry
Kemeny, John George
Kemmer, Richard Julius
Kemmerer, John L., Jr.
Kemmerling, John David
Kemp, Frank Burrill
Kemp, Jack F.
Kemp, Robert
Kemper, Russell Nay
Kempner, Joseph
Kempner, Robert Max Wasilii
Kempster, Norman Roy
Kempton, James Murray
Kendall, Donald McIntosh
Kendall, John Plimpton
Kendall, Katherine Anne
Kende, Andrew Steven
Kendig, Edwin Lawrence, Jr.
Kendig, Perry Fridy
Kendler, Bernhard
Kendrick, Caldwell Chappelear
Kenen, Peter Bain
Kenison, Frank Rowe
Keniston, Kenneth
Kenley, James Bunting
Kenly, F. Corning, Jr.
Kenna, Edgar Douglas, Jr.
Kennan, George Frost
Kennedy, Adrienne Lita
Kennedy, Berenice Connor (Mrs. Jefferson Kennedy, Jr.)
Kennedy, Bernard Joseph
Kennedy, Charles Francis
Kennedy, Charles Joseph
Kennedy, Clement
Kennedy, Davis Lee
Kennedy, Donald
Kennedy, Donald Davidson, Jr.
Kennedy, Edward Eugene
Kennedy, Edward Moore
Kennedy, Edwin L.
Kennedy, Ethel Skaker
Kennedy, Eugene Francis, Jr.
Kennedy, Eugene Patrick
Kennedy, Frances Midlam (Mrs. Joseph Conrad Kennedy)
Kennedy, Frank Brittain
Kennedy, George D.
Kennedy, James Ross
Kennedy, James Walter
Kennedy, Joan Bennett (Mrs. Edward Moore Kennedy)
Kennedy, John Henry
Kennedy, John Raymond
Kennedy, Keith Furnival
Kennedy, Quentin James
Kennedy, Roger George
Kennedy, Rose Fitzgerald (Mrs. Joseph P. Kennedy);
Kennedy, Sargent
Kennedy, Thomas James, Jr.
Kennedy, Thomas Leo
Kennedy, Wilbert Keith
Kennedy, William Blair
Kennedy, William Fritz
Kennedy, William James
Kennedy, X.J. (Joseph)
Kennelty, John Earl
Kenner, William Hugh
Kennerly, David Hume
Kenney, Howard Washington
Kenney, James Francis
Kenney, John Andrew, Jr.
Kenney, Richard Lawrence
Kenney, W. John
Kenney, William Richardson
Kennick, William Elmer
Kennison, Hugh Foster
Kenny, Herbert Andrew
Kenny, Thomas Henry
Kensil, James Lewis
Kensing, Henry Vincent
Kent, Allegra
Kent, Allen
Kent, Amos Eugene
Kent, George Clarence
Kent, Richard Travis
Kentera, Chris William
Kentera, George Richard
Kenworthy, Carroll H.
Kenyon, Carleton Weller
Kenyon, Charles Moir
Kenyon, Hewitt
Kenyon, Richard Albert
Kenyon, Robert Edwin, Jr.
Kenyon, William Houston, Jr.
Keogh, Eugene James
Keogh, James
Keosian, John
Keough, Francis Paul
Kepes, Gyorgy
Kephart, A. Evans
Keppel, Francis
Keppel, John
Keppler, Herbert
Kerby, William Frederick
Kerker, Milton
Kern, Alfred M.
Kern, Charles J.
Kern, Edith
Kern, Harry Frederick
Kern, Irving John
Kern, John Staige
Kern, Richard Arminius
Kernan, Alvin Bernard
Kerney, James, Jr.
Kernodle, Rigdon Wayne
Kerr, Chester Brooks
Kerr, Dorothy Marie Burmeister
Kerr, Graham
Kerr, Hugh Thomson
Kerr, James Allen
Kerr, Jean
Kerr, Paul Sidney
Kerr, Walter F.
Kerr, William Keister
Kerrebrock, Jack Leo
Kerridge, Robert Louis
Kershaw, Andrew
Kershaw, Joseph Alexander
Kerst, Richard Nevin
Kerstetter, William Edward
Kertesz, Andre
Kertz, Hubert Leonard
Kerwin, Walter Thomas, Jr.
Kerxton, Alan Smith
Kessel, Lawrence Reefer
Kesselhaut, Arthur Melvyn
Kessen, William
Kessler, Irving Kenneth
Kessler, Karl Gunther
Kessler, Milton
Kessler, Robert Clarence
Kester, John Gordon
Kesting, Theodore
Kestnbaum, Albert S.
Ketcham, Charles Brown
Ketchledge, Raymond Waibel
Ketchum, Alton Harrington
Ketchum, Carlton Griswold
Ketchum, David Storey
Ketchum, Gardner Mason
Ketchum, Harry Wilbur
Ketchum, Milo Smith
Ketchum, Richard Malcolm
Ketchum, William M.
Ketter, Robert Lewis
Kettle, James William
Kety, Seymour S(olomon)
Key, Bruce
Key, David McKendree
Key, Milton Eugene
Key, Ted
Keyes, Baldwin Longstreth
Keyes, Fenton
Keyfitz, Nathan
Keys, Samuel Robert
Keyser, Frank Ray, Jr.
Keyserling, Leon H.
Keyserling, Mary Dublin
Khachadurian, Avedis
Khadduri, Majid
Kharasch, Robert Nelson
Khayatt, Shaker Albert
Kheel, Theodore Woodrow
Khorana, Har Gobind
Khuri, Nicola Najib
Kiam, Victor Kermit, II
Kibbe, Milton Homer
Kibbee, Robert Joseph
Kibbey, Donald Eugene
Kibre, Pearl
Kibrick, Anne
Kidd, Aubrey Vivian
Kidd, Charles Vincent
Kidd, Michael
Kidd, Robert Charles, II
Kidde, John Frederick
Kidder, George Howell
Kidder, James Hugh
Kideney, James Williams
Kieb, Ormonde Anton
Kiefer, Charles Frederick
Kiefer, Frank Xavier
Kiefer, Jack Carl
Kiefer, Norvin Charles
Kieffer, James Milton
Kieffer, Jarold Alan
Kieft, Lester
Kiely, Robert James
Kienbusch, William
Kier, Porter Martin
Kieran, John Francis
Kiernan, Edwin A., Jr.
Kiernan, Owen Burns
Kiernan, Peter DeLacy
Kiernan, Richard Francis
Kiernan, Richard Rowen
Kiesel, Charles Arthur
Kiesewetter, William Burns
Kiev, Isaac Edward
Kight, Alonzo Barnard
Kiker, Ralph Douglas, Jr.
Kilberg, Barbara (Bobbie) Greene
Kilberg, William Jeffrey
Kilborne, Robert Stewart
Kilbourne, Edwin Dennis
Kilbridge, James Xavier
Kilbridge, Maurice D.
Kilcarr, J. Kenneth
Kiley, Daniel Urban
Kiley, Richard Paul
Kilgore, Ann Hitch
Kilham, Walter H., Jr.
Kill, Lawrence
Killebrew, Gwendolyn
Killefer, Tom
Killelea, Joseph Richard
Killian, Lewis Martin
Killian, Robert Kenneth
Killpack, Larry Movell
Kilmer, Billy (William Orland, Jr.)
Kilpatrick, James Jackson, Jr.
Kilpatrick, Robert Donald
Kilpatrick, Samuel James, Jr.
Kilty, Jerome Timothy
Kim, Jai Soo
Kim, Richard E.
Kim, Wan Hee
Kimatian, Stephen H.
Kimball, Allyn Winthrop
Kimball, David Tenney
Kimball, Lindsley Fiske
Kimball, Penn Townsend, II
Kimball, Robert Eric
Kimball, Roland Baldwin
Kimball, Thomas Lloyd
Kimball, Yeffe
Kimberg, Daniel Victor
Kimberly, John Robbins
Kimble, Kenneth Leroy
Kimbrough, Emily (Emily Kimbrough Wrench)
Kimbrough, Emory Calloway Landon, Jr.
Kimmel, Caesar Paul
Kimpel, Benjamin Franklin
Kincaid, John Franklin
Kindleberger, Charles P., II
Kinerson, Kendall Scott
King, Alan
King, Allen Lewis
King, August Allen
King, Benton Davis
King, Billie Jean Moffitt
King, Carleton James
King, Charles Glen
King, Chester Harding
King, Cyril Bernard
King, Edward Beverly, Jr.
King, Elmer Richard
King, Francis Walter
King, George Joseph
King, Glen Doyle
King, Harry O.
King, James Barton
King, James M., Jr.
King, John Francis
King, John Gordon
King, John Harry, Jr.
King, John William
King, Kendall Willard
King, Kerryn
King, Louis Delwin
King, Marian
King, Norman Chancis
King, Paul Hamilton
King, Peter
King, Preston Cloud, Jr.
King, Robert Doan
King, Robert Leroy
King, Ronold Wyeth Percival
King, Rufus
King, Stephen Edwin
King, Theodore Matthew
King, Thomas Burness
King, Thomas Creighton
King, Warren Thomas
King, Willard Fahrenkamp (Mrs. Edmund Ludwig King)
King, William Dickey
King, William Haven
King, William Joseph
King, William Richard
King, Woodie, Jr.
Kingery, William David
Kingman, Dong
Kingman, Edward Rockwell
Kingman, William Lockwood
Kingrey, Joseph Peter
Kingsbury, Frederick Hutchinson, Jr.
Kingsbury, James Merwin
Kingsbury-Smith, Joseph
Kingslake, Rudolf
Kingsley, Daniel Thain
Kingsley, John McCall, Jr.
Kingsley, Sidney
Kingsley, Thomas Drowne
Kingsnorth, Neil George
Kingston, Joseph Paul
Kinigstein, Jonah
Kinnaird, Clark
Kinnard, William James, Jr.
Kinnear, George Espy Ridgeway, II
Kinnear, James Wesley, III
Kinnell, Galway
Kinney, Douglas Merrill
Kinney, Francis Lawrence
Kinney, Samuel Marks, Jr.
Kinney, Sheldon Hoard
Kinney, William Sloane, Jr.
Kinoshita, Jin Harold
Kinoshita, Toichiro
Kinsella, Thomas J.
Kinslow, Jon Pare
Kinsolving, Charles Lester
Kinstler, Everett Raymond
Kintner, Earl Wilson
Kintner, William Roscoe
Kiplinger, Austin Huntington
Kipnis, Claude
Kipnis, Igor
Kipp, Donald Bogart
Kirby, Allan Price, Jr.
Kirby, Fred Morgan, II
Kirby, James Cordell, Jr.
Kirby, James Edmund, Jr.
Kirby, John Pendy
Kirby, Robert Emory
Kirch, Max Samuel
Kircher, Donald Peter
Kirchhofer, Alfred Henry
Kirchner, Isabelle Loretta
Kirchner, John Albert
Kirchner, Leon
Kirchner, Walther
Kiriacon, Arthur Jack
Kirjassoff, Gordon Louis
Kirk, Alan Goodrich, II
Kirk, Alexis Vemian
Kirk, Daniel Lee
Kirk, Donald
Kirk, Grayson Louis
Kirk, Roger
Kirk, Ronald T.
Kirk, William Johnson
Kirkbride, Chalmer Gatlin
Kirkendall, Ernest Oliver
Kirkland, Bryant Mays
Kirkland, Gelsey
Kirkland, Joseph Lane
Kirkley, Terry Allen
Kirkman, Elwood F.
Kirkpatrick, Charles Lincoln
Kirkpatrick, Evron Maurice
Kirkpatrick, Jeane Duane Jordan
Kirkpatrick, Lyman Bickford, Jr.
Kirkpatrick, Ralph
Kirkpatrick, Richard Bogue
Kirkpatrick, Robert Lewis
Kirkpatrick, William Alexander
Kirksey, Robert Edward
Kirkwood, James
Kirschstein, Ruth Lillian
Kirshen, Philip Howard
Kirshner, Don
Kirstein, George Garland
Kirstein, Lincoln
Kirsten, Dorothy
Kirtland, Lynn
Kirwan, Thomas M.
Kiselewski, Joseph
Kislik, Louis A.
Kislik, Richard William
Kisner, Ronald Harris
Kissel, Lester
Kissick, William Lee
Kissiloff, William
Kissinger, Henry Alfred
Kissinger, Walter Bernhard
Kisslinger, Leonard Sol
Kissner, Franklin H.
Kitamura, Toshi
Kitchen, Herbert Nord
Kitchen, Robert Wilson, Jr.
Kiteley, Murray James
Kitman, Marvin
Kitt, Loren Wayne
Kitto, Richard Charles Jackson
Kittredge, Charles James
Kittredge, John Kendall
Kittredge, Robert Briggs
Kittrell, Flemmie Pansy
Kittrie, Nicholas N(orbert Nehemiah)
Kitzinger, Ernst
Kivitt, Theodore Tobias
KixMiller, Richard Wood
Kjeldaas, Terje, Jr.
Kjellstrom, John Alfred
Klaerner, Curtis Maurice
Klages, Roy Arthur
Klagsbrunn, Hans Alexander
Klaman, Saul B.
Klapinsky, Raymond Joseph
Klapper, Joseph Thomas
Klappert, Peter
Klarman, Herbert Elias
Klatell, Jack
Klatskin, Gerald
Klauder, Norman
Klaus, Elmer Erwin
Klavan, Israel
Klaw, Barbara Van Doren
Klay, Andor C.
Kleban, Edward Lawrence
Kleberg, Jack Carl
Kleiman, Alan Boyd
Klein, Arthur Luce
Klein, Calvin Richard
Klein, Charles
Klein, Charlotte Conrad
Klein, David
Klein, Edward Elkan
Klein, Isaac
Klein, Joseph
Klein, Lawrence Robert
Klein, Marcus
Klein, Martin Jesse
Klein, Robert
Klein, Robert
Klein, Seymour Miller
Klein, Stanley
Klein, William Kenneth
Kleindienst, Richard Gordon
Kleine, Herman
Kleinert, Robert William
Kleinholz, Frank
Kleinman, Abraham Morris
Kleinoder, Jack
Kleinrock, Lewis James
Kleinschrod, Walter Andrew
Kleinzeller, Arnost
Kleisner, George Harry
Klema, Ernest Donald
Klemens, Roney Walter
Klement, Jerome Joseph
Klemm, Frederick Alvin
Klemme, Carl William
Klemperer, William
Kleppe, Thomas S.
Klerman, Gerald Lawrence
Kleyle, Helen Murray
Kligler, Milton Richard
Kligler, Seymour H.
Kligman, Albert Montgomery
Klima, Otto
Klimpl, Emanuel S.
Klinck, Patricia Ewasco
Kline, Charles Talcott
Kline, Ernest P.
Kline, George Louis
Kline, L(eonard) Patton
Kline, Morris
Kline, Nathan Schellenberg
Kline, Oral Lee
Kline, Reamer
Kline, Robert Parks
Kline, Robert Reeves
Kline, Sidney DeLong
Kling, Vincent George
Kling, William
Klingensmith, M(erle) Joseph
Klingenstein, Frederick Adler
Klion, Stanley Ring
Klitgaard, Georgina
Klitzke, Theodore Elmer
Klock, Charles Gleason
Klonis, Stewart
Klopfer, Donald Simon
Klopp, Richard Packard
Klosner, Jerome Martin
Kloss, John Anthony
Klosson, Boris Hansen
Klots, Allen Trafford
Klotz, Herbert Werner
Klotz, John Wesley
Klotzbach, Robert James
Klotzman, Dorothy Ann
Kluge, John Werner
Kluger, Richard
Klugman, Jack
Klumpp, Theodore George
Knaplund, Paul William
Knapp, Daniel C.
Knapp, David Curtis
Knapp, Edward Donald
Knapp, George Francis
Knapp, John Merrill
Knapp, J(oseph) Burke
Knapp, Joseph Grant
Knapp, Peter Hobart
Knapp, Whitman
Knauer, Georg Nicolaus
Knauer, Virginia Harrington Wright (Mrs. Wilhelm F. Knauer)
Knauss, John Atkinson
Knebel, Fletcher
Kneeland, George J.
Kneisel, Frank
Kneitel, Thomas Stephen
Kneller, John William
Knepper, John Albert
Knickerbocker, Daniel Candee, Jr.
Knies, Paul Henry
Knieter, Gerard Leonard
Knigge, Karl Maximillian
Knight, Douglas Maitland
Knight, Frances Gladys
Knight, Fred Barrows
Knight, Frederick Hawley
Knight, Gladys (Gladys Maria)
Knight, H. Stuart
Knight, Harry W.
Knight, John Lowden
Knight, Norman
Knight, Robert Huntington
Knight, Walter Early
Knight, William Edwards
Knigin, Michael Jay
Knipe, James Launcelot
Knipp, Julian Knause
Knisel, Russell H.
Knobel, Franklin E.
Knobil, Ernst
Knoblauch, Harold Carl
Knobler, Alfred Everett
Knobler, Peter Stephen
Knobloch, William Richard
Knoedler, Elmer L.
Knoell, W.H.
Knoff, Gerald Everett
Knoll, Jerry
Knopf, Alfred, Jr.
Knopf, Alfred A.
Knopp, Marvin Isadore
Knoppers, Antonie Theodoor
Knorr, Klaus Eugene
Knorr, Norman John
Knortz, Herbert Charles
Knortz, Walter Robert
Knott, Henry Joseph
Knott, James
Knowles, Alison
Knowles, Asa Smallidge
Knowles, Edward F.
Knowles, Jeremy Randall
Knowles, John
Knowles, John Hilton
Knowles, William Townsend
Knowlton, Hugh, Jr.
Knowlton, Perry Hosmer
Knowlton, William Allen
Knowlton, Winthrop
Knox, Bernard MacGregor Walker
Knox, Charles Robert
Knox, John
Knox, Northrup Rand
Knox, Robert Seiple
Knox, Seymour Horace, III
Knox, Walter Eugene, III
Knox, William Edward
Knox, William Wallace
Knudsen, Raymond Barnett
Knudsen, Rudolph Edgar, Jr.
Knudson, Harry Edward, Jr.
Knudten, Edwin Herman
Knutson, David Harry
Knutti, Ralph Eddy
Kobak, James Benedict
Koblenzer, Peter Johann
Kobler, John
Koblitz, David Randall
Kobrick, A. Morris
Koch, Carl
Koch, Edward I.
Koch, George William
Koch, H. William
Koch, John
Koch, Kenneth
Koch, Richard Henry
Koch, Robert Alan
Koch, Robert Bruce
Kochen, Simon Bernard
Kocher, Edward Mitchell
Kocher, Eric
Kocisko, Stephen John
Kocivar, Ben
Kockelmans, Joseph J.
Koedel, John Gilbert, Jr.
Koehler, George Applegate
Koehler, John Theodore
Koehler, Robert Earl
Koehler, Robert Earl
Koehlinger, James Frederick
Koehnlein, John Frederick
Koelle, George Brampton
Koenig, Karl Fred
Koenig, Robert P.
Koerner, Henry
Koerner, James David
Koerner, Victor Frederick
Koester, Helmut Heinrich
Kogel, Marcus David
Kogstad, Arthur Woodrow
Kohák, Erazim Václav
Kohl, Benedict M.
Kohl, John Clayton
Kohlbrenner, Bernard John
Kohler, Charlotte
Kohler, Heinz
Kohlmeier, Louis Martin, Jr.
Kohn, Harold Elias
Kohn, Henry
Kohn, Henry Irving
Kohn, Joseph John
Koisch, Francis Paul
Kojian, Miran Haig
Kok, Bessel
Koke, Richard Joseph
Kolasa, Blair John
Kolatch, Alfred Jacob
Kolatch, Myron
Kolb, Lawrence Coleman
Kolbe, Henry Walter
Kole, John William
Kolibachuk, John Filimon
Kolin, Oscar
Koller, Herbert Richard
Koller, Noemie Benczer (Mrs. Earl L. Koller)
Kollmorgen, Leland Stanford
Kolodin, Irving
Kolodner, Ignace Izaak
Kolody, John Theodore
Kolodzie, Ronald A.
Kolsky, Herbert
Koltnow, Peter Gregory
Kolton, Paul
Komar, Arthur B.
Komarovsky, Mirra (Mrs. Marcus A. Heyman)
Komer, Robert William
Komidar, Joseph Stanley
Komisar, David Daniel
Komoski, Paul Kenneth
Kone, Elliott H.
Kone, Eugene Harold
Koner, Pauline
Konigsburg, Elaine Lobl
Koning, Hans (Koningsberger)
Konner, Joan Weiner
Konski, James Louis
Kontos, Constantine William
Konvitz, Milton Ridvas
Koons, Donaldson
Koop, Charles Everett
Koop, Theodore Frederick
Koopmans, Tjalling Charles
Kopelman, Arie
Kopelman, Leonard
Kopenhaver, Patricia Ellsworth
Kopit, Arthur
Kopp, George William
Kopp, W. Brewster
Koppelman, Chaim
Koppes, Wayne Farland
Kopple, Robert
Koprowski, Hilary
Koranyi, Adam
Korbel, John Joseph
Korchnoy, Emanuel Allen
Korda, Michael Vincent
Korda, Reva (Mrs. William Korda)
Korff, Serge Alexander
Korle, Sinan Arif
Korn, Bertram Wallace
Korn, David
Korn, Gerald Edward
Korn, Philip A.
Korn, Richard
Kornberg, Warren Stanley
Kornegay, Horace Robinson
Korologos, Tom Chris
Korper, Hazel Priest
Korry, Edward Malcolm
Korson, Jay Henry
Korsyn, Irene Hahne
Korth, Fred
Kortmann, Louis William
Kortz, Edwin Wunderly
Korzenik, Armand Alexander
Kosheff, Martin Joel
Koshland, Stephen Abraham
Kosinski, Antoni Albert
Kosinski, Jerzy Nikodem
Koski, Walter S.
Koskoff, Theodore I.
Kosloff, Irving S.
Kosner, Edward A(lan)
Koso, Dusan Alexander
Kosovich, Dushan Radovan
Kosowsky, David Israel

Koss, Leopold G.
Kossar, Arnold Franklyn
Kossiakoff, Alexander
Kostant, Bertram
Kostelanetz, Andre
Kostelanetz, Boris
Kostelanetz, Richard (Cory)
Koster, John Peter, Jr.
Kostmayer, Peter Houston
Kotker, Norman Richard
Kotlowitz, Robert
Kotrady, John
Kotschnig, Walter Maria
Kott, Jan
Kotz, Nathan Kallison (Nick)
Kotz, Samuel
Kotzky, Alex Sylvester
Kountz, John R.
Kourides, Peter Theologos
Kourkene, Jacques, II
Kousoulas, Dimitrios George
Koutoukas, H. M.
Kouwenhoven, John Atlee
Kovach, Eugene George
Kovach, George Paul
Kovasznay, Leslie Stephen George
Kowalski, Stephen Wesley
Kozelka, Robert Marvin
Kozin, Frank
Kozinski, Andrzej Wladyslaw
Kozloff, Max
Kozlowski, Henry Joseph
Kozol, Jonathan
Kraft, C. William, Jr.
Kraft, Charles Henry
Kraft, Erwin Otto
Kraft, John Christian
Kraft, Joseph
Kraft, Leo
Kraft, Ralph Wayne
Kraft, Tim
Krahl, Maurice Edward
Krakowski, Adam Joseph
Krall, Anders Albert Walter
Kramer, Aaron
Kramer, Alan Sharfsin
Kramer, Amihud
Kramer, Arthur Bennett
Kramer, Bernard
Kramer, Charles Russell
Kramer, Eric Max
Kramer, Francis Ronald
Kramer, George M.
Kramer, George P.
Kramer, Henry Theodore
Kramer, James Joseph
Kramer, Lawrence F., Jr.
Kramer, Martin S.
Kramer, Maurice
Kramer, Milton Joseph
Kramer, Morton
Kramer, Norman M.
Kramer, Philip
Kramer, Reuben Robert
Kramer, Robert
Kramer, Russell Arnold
Kramer, Samual Noah
Kramer, Sidney
Kramer, Simon Paul
Kramish, Arnold
Kramrisch, Stella
Krane, Stephen Martin
Kranepool, Edward Emil, III
Krank, Donald Francis
Krantz, John Christian, Jr.
Kranyik, Robert Donald
Kranzdorf, Norman Melvin
Krasna, Alvin Isaac
Krasner, Lee
Krasner, Louis
Krathwohl, David Reading
Kratzer, Guy Livingston
Kraus, Alfredo (Alfredo Kraus Trujillo)
Kraus, Hans Peter
Kraus, Sister Irene
Kraus, Lili
Kraus, Robert
Krause, Charles Frederick
Krause, Harry Norman
Krause, Richard Michael
Krause, Robert Frederick
Kraushaar, Otto Frederick
Krauss, Ruth Ida (Mrs. Crockett Johnson)
Krauss, Samuel George
Krauter, Thomas F.
Kravis, Irving Bernard
Kravitz, Edward Arthur
Kravitz, Sanford Lawrence
Krebs, Rockne
Kreeger, David Lloyd
Kreger, William Castles
Krehbiel, Peter W.
Kreider, Donald Lester
Kreidler, Robert Neil
Kreindler, Lee Stanley
Krementz, Jill
Kremer, Fred, Jr.
Kremer, Merle William
Krendel, Ezra Simon
Krensky, Harold
Krents, Milton Ellis
Krenz, Donald A.
Kreps, Juanita Morris (Mrs. Clifton H. Kreps, Jr.)
Kresh, Paul
Kreshover, Seymour Jacob
Kress, Roy Alfred
Kressler, James Phillip
Kretchmer, Norman
Kretzmann, Norman John Karl
Kreuzer, Barton
Kreyling, Edward George, Jr.
Kridel, Norman Thomas
Krieg, Arthur Frederick
Krieg, William Laurence
Krieger, Dorothy Terrace
Krieger, Robert Edward
Krieger, Robert Lyman
Krieghbaum, (Hiram) Hillier
Krim, Arthur B.
Krim, Seymour
Krims, Leslie Robert
Krimsky, Emanuel
Kring, Walter Donald
Krinsky, Norman Irving
Krinsly, Stuart Z.
Krisch, Adolph Oscar
Krisch, Joel
Krisher, William K.
Kristeller, Paul Oskar
Kristofferson, Kris
Kritchevsky, David
Krizay, John
Kroeber, Karl
Kroeger, Hal A.
Kroesen, Frederick James, Jr.
Kroger, William Meers
Krogman, Wilton Marion
Krol, John Cardinal
Kroll, Boris
Kroll, Fred J.
Kroll, Milton Paul
Kroll, William
Krombein, Karl vonVorse
Kron, Arthur Adam
Kronauer, Clifford John, Jr.
Krone, Gerald Sidney
Krone, Helmut
Kronen, Leif Christian
Kronenberger, Louis
Kroner, Lawrence Roy
Kronke, Walter Christian
Kronman, Joseph Henry
Kronstadt, Arnold Mayo
Krooth, David Louis
Krooth, Robert Schild
Kropf, Allen
Kropf, Richard Thomas
Kropotkin, Igor Nicholas
Krosby, H. Peter
Krout, John Edward
Krout, W. Vincent
Krowe, Allen Julian
Kruegel, James Henry
Krueger, Robert Charles
Kruener, Harry Howard
Kruger, Arthur Newman
Kruger, Gustav Otto, Jr.
Kruger, Jerome
Kruger, Joseph
Krugman, Saul
Krukowski, Nancy Harrow (Mrs. Jan Krukowski)
Krulitz, Leo Morrion
Krumhansl, James Arthur
Krumme, Robert Darrell
Krumrine, Charles Sidney
Krupsak, Mary Anne
Krupska, Danya (Mrs. Ted Thurston)
Kruse, Cornelius Wolfram
Kruse, James Joseph
Krusen, Leslie Conard
Krushenick, Nicholas
Kruskal, Martin David
Kryza, Elmer Gregory
Krzywicki, Paul Matthew
Krzyzanowski, Richard Lucien
Ku, Y. H.
Kubiak, Teresa Wojtaszek
Kubie, John Samuel
Kubler, George Alexander
Kubzansky, Philip Eugene
Kucera, Henry
Kuczynski, Pedro-Pablo
Kuebler, Ernest William
Kuehne, Martin Eric
Kuenne, Robert Eugene
Kuesel, Thomas Robert
Kufeld, William Manuel
Kuffler, Stephen William
Kugel, Kenneth
Kugel, Robert Benjamin
Kugelmass, Isaac Newton
Kugler, Arthur Noble
Kuh, Edwin
Kuh, Katharine
Kuhbach, Arend Gerdes
Kuhlenbeck, Hartwig
Kuhlman, Kertis Paul
Kuhlthau, Alden Robert
Kuhlthau, Conrad William, III
Kuhn, Albin Owings
Kuhn, Bowie
Kuhn, Ferdinand
Kuhn, John Lucien
Kuhn, Lloyd Wilson
Kuhn, Margaret (Maggie)
Kuhn, Reinhard
Kuhn, Thomas Samuel
Kuhnen, S. Marie
Kuhnheim, Earl James
Kuhns, Richard Francis, Jr.
Kuhns, William George
Kuhrt, Wesley Amos
Kuivila, Henry Gabriel
Kulczycki, Lucas L.
Kulik, Edward Joseph
Kulkosky, Edward
Kullback, Solomon
Kullen, Sol
Kullman, Charles
Kumin, Maxine Winokur
Kunitz, Stanley Jasspon
Kunsberg, Stanley Harris
Kunsela, William Rudolph
Kunstler, William Moses
Kunz, George James
Kunzig, Robert Lowe
Kupchick, Alan Charles
Kuper, J. B. Horner
Kupersmith, Harry
Kupfer, Carl
Kupfer, Robert Donald
Kupferman, Lawrence Edward
Kupferman, Meyer
Kupferman, Theodore R.
Kupperian, James Edward, Jr.
Kuralt, Charles Bishop
Kurnit, Shepard
Kurnow, Ernest
Kurth, Lester D.
Kurtz, Donald Julian
Kurtz, Donald Richardson
Kurtz, Jerome
Kurtz, Paul
Kurtz, Robert Benton
Kurtz, Stephen Guild
Kurtz, Thomas Eugene
Kurucz, John
Kurzman, Stephen
Kuschner, Marvin
Kushen, Allan Stanford
Kushner, Harold Joseph
Kushner, Harvey
Kushner, Lawrence Maurice
Kushner, Robert Arnold
Kushnerick, John Peter
Kuslan, Louis Isaac
Kuss, Henry John, Jr.
Kutner, David Haas
Kutner, Maurice Breger
Kuttas, George
Kuusisto, Allan Andrew
Kuykendall, Jerome Kenneth
Kuznets, Simon Smith
Kvernland, Jack Theodore
Kwalwasser, Jacob
Kwasnick, Paul
Kyburg, Henry Guy Ely, Jr.
Kyhl, Robert Louis
Kyl, John Henry
Kyle, Peter Edward
Kyros, Peter N.
Labatut, Jean
LaBerge, Walter Barber
Labes, Leon Martin
LaBlanc, Charles Wesley, Jr.
Labouisse, Henry Richardson
Labrecque, Thomas Goulet
Labunski, Stephen Bronislaw
LaCasce, Elroy Osborne, Jr.
Lacey, Frederick Bernard
Lacheman, Ernest René
Lachenbruch, David
Lachman, Lawrence
Lackas, John Christopher
Lacks, Stanley Bernard
Lacy, Bill N.
Lacy, Dan Mabry
Lacy, Jerry (Gerald LeRoy)
Ladd, Charles Cushing, III
Ladd, Delano Wood, Jr.
Ladd, John
Ladd, Joseph Carroll
Laden, Karl
Lader, Joan Summers
Lader, Lawrence
Laderman, Ezra
Laderman, Gabriel
Ladin, Eugene
Lado, Robert
La Dow, Clyde Stuart
Ladson, Thomas Alvin
La Due, John Samuel
Laeri, John Howard
La Falce, John Joseph
LaFarge, Louis Bancel
LaFauci, Horatio Michael
LaFeber, Walter Frederick
Laferriere, Roland Paul
Lafferty, James Martin
Lafferty, Ralph Fredrick
Lafley, Alan Frederick
LaForce, Arnold Robertson
LaFrance, Francis X.
Lagano, Santo Rocco
Lagassé, Henry Albert
Lagather, Robert B.
Lagnese, Joseph Francis, Jr.
Lahey, Edward Vincent, Jr.
Lahey, Richard Francis
Lahlou, Michel B.
LaHood, Charles George, Jr.
Lahr, John
Laidlaw, Robert W.
Laing, Charles Burnett
Laing, Ronald David
Laing, William Scott
Laingen, Lowell Bruce
Laird, Campbell
Laird, Melvin R.
Laird, William Frederick
Laise, Carol Clendening
Laise, Frederic Stevens
Laitin, Joseph
Lake, Richard Harrington
Lake, William Thomas
Lala, Dominick J.
LaLande, William Alfred, Jr.
Lall, Arthur Samuel
Lally, Francis Joseph
Lam, Sau-Hai
Lamarr, Hedy (born Hedwig Keisler)
Lamarsh, John Raymond
Lamb, Floyd Alvin
Lambdin, Thomas Oden
Lambe, Thomas William
Lambert, Byron Cecil
Lambert, Eleanor
Lambert, Jay Wilfred
Lambert, Jean
Lambert, John Harold (Jack)
Lambert, Sam M.
Lambert, William G.
Lambert, William Wilson
Lamberton, James Kirkland, Jr.
Lambertsen, Christian James
Lambing, Malcolm Elwyn, Jr.
Lambooy, John Peter
Lamborn, Robert Louis
Lambros, Lambros John
Lami, Albert
Lamm, Donald Stephen
LaMond, Gaylord Marvin
Lamone, Rudolph Philip
LaMont, Barbara Gibson
Lamont, Corliss
Lamont, Elizabeth Carrington Brown
Lamont, Lansing
Lamont, Rosette Clementine
Lamont-Havers, Ronald William
La Motte, Clyde Wilson
Lampard, Eric Edwin
Lampert, James Benjamin
Lamperti, John Williams
Lamphere, Robert Joseph
Lamport, Felicia (Mrs. Benjamin Kaplan)
Lan, Donald
Lana, Robert Edward
Lancaster, Bruce Morgan
Lancaster, Edwin Beattie
Lancaster, Kelvin John
Lancaster, Otis Ewing
Lancefield, Rebecca Craighill
Lancour, Adlore Harold
Land, Edwin Herbert
Land, Francis LaVerne
Land, George Thomas Lock
Landau, Genevieve Millet (Mrs. Sidney Landau)
Landau, George Walter
Landau, Jacob
Landau, Peter Edward
Landau, Robert
Landau, Siegfried
Landauer, Jerry Gerd
Landeck, Armin
Landegger, Carl Clement
Lander, Edward Clark
Landers, Matthew Patrick
Landes, David Saul
Landes, Robert Nathan
Landis, Frederick
Landis, Lewis Rex
Lando, Robert Nathan
Landon, Edward August
Landon, Harold Ransom
Landon, Sealand Whitney
Landor, John Henry
Landovitz, Leon Fred
Landrum, Thomas Walter
Landry, Lionel
Landsiedel, Henry Clay
Landstrom, Karl Sigurd
Landy, David
Lane, Alvin Seymour
Lane, Arthur Stephen
Lane, Burton
Lane, David Oliver
Lane, Donald Edward
Lane, Harold M.
Lane, James McConkey
Lane, John Dennis
Lane, Kenneth Jay
Lane, Lyle Franklin
Lane, Mark
Lane, Nancy
Lane, Newton Alexander
Lane, Richard N.
Lane, Robert Edwards
Lane, Thomas Henry
Lane, Warren C., Jr.
Lanford, Oscar Erasmus, Jr.
Lang, Cecil Yelverton
Lang, Daniel
Lang, George
Lang, John Sanford
Lang, Mabel Louise
Lang, Norton David
Lang, Pearl
Lang, Robert Todd
Lang, William Charles
Lang, William Henry
Langbaum, Robert Woodrow
Langbein, Walter B.
Langdon, Jervis, Jr.
Lange, Barbara Pearson (Mrs. Gordon Lange)
Lange, Frederick
Lange, Hans William
Lange, Phil C.
Lange, Roland H.
Lange, Victor
Langella, Frank
Langenberg, Donald Newton
Langenberg, Frederick Charles
Langenfeld, Nicholas Joseph
Langer, William Leonard
Langerman, Harold A.
Langfitt, Thomas William
Langhoff, Severin Peter, Jr.
Langie, Louis Antoine, Jr.
Langlais, Bernard
Langland, Joseph Thomas
Langley, Jane Pickens
Langmuir, Alexander Duncan
Langstaff, Elliot Kennedy
Langstaff, John Meredith
Langton, Basil Cedric
Langworthy, David Collie
Lanham, Edwin Moultrie
Lanin, Lester
Laning, Edward
Laning, Robert Comegys
Lank, William Albert
Lankford, Francis Greenfield, Jr.
Lanouette, William John
Lansbury, Angela Brigid
Lansbury, Edgar George
Lansdale, Robert Tucker
Lansner, Kermit Irvin
Lantz, Michael
Lantzsch, Guenther Christian
Lantzy, Anamary Bobal
Lanyon, Wesley Edwin
Lanz, John Robert
Lanzetta, John Thomas
Lanzl, George Frank
Lanzoni, Vincent
LaPalombara, Joseph
Lapham, Lewis Henry
Lapham, Lewis Jay
Lapham, Robert J.
Lapolla, Paul McCormick
Laporte, Cloyd, Jr.
Laporte, William Frederic
Laqueur, Walter
Laragh, John Henry
Laraja, Frank Donato
Lardner, Ring Wilmer, Jr.
Laredo, Ruth
Larese, Edward John
Lariar, Lawrence
Larkin, Brian James
Larkin, Felix Edward
Larkin, June Noble
Larkin, Roger Allen
Larned, William Edmund, Jr.
Larner, Joseph
Larochelle, Donald Raymond
LaRocque, Gene Robert
Larrabee, Carroll Burton
Larrabee, Donald Richard
Larrabee, Eric
Larrabee, Martin Glover
Larrow, Robert William
Larsen, Elmer Conrad
Larsen, Harry Irgens
Larsen, John Walter
Larsen, Jonathan Zerbe
Larsen, Louis Royter
Larson, Clarence Edward
Larson, Eric Gustav
Larson, Fritz Henry
Larson, Godfrey Edward
Larson, Harold Vernon
Larson, Jess
Larson, John Hyde
Larson, Roberts Browning
Larson, Russell Edward
Larson, Thomas Bryan
LaRue, (Adrian) Jan (Pieters)
Larus, Charles Taft
LaRussa, Joseph Anthony
Lasagna, Louis Cesare
LaSalle, Joseph Pierre
Lascara, Vincent Alfred
Lasdon, Lloyd I.
Lash, Joseph P.
Lashinsky, Herbert
Lashof, Joyce R. Cohen
Lashof, Richard Kenneth
Laske, Arthur Charles
Lasker, Joseph L.
Lasker, Mary (Mrs. Albert D. Lasker)
Laski, Frank Joseph
Laskowski, Matthew Ludwig
Lasky, Burton S.
Lasky, David
Lasky, Victor
Lassaw, Ibram
Lassettre, Edwin Nichols
Lassner, Franz George
Lasswell, Harold Dwight
Laster, Leonard
Laster, Richard
Latane, James Wilson
Latch, Edward Gardiner
Latchum, James Levin
Lateef, Yusef
Lateiner, Jacob
Latham, Allen, Jr.
Latham, A(rthur) Russell
Latham, Earl
Latham, Willard
Lathem, Edward Connery
Lathrop, Gertrude K.
Laties, Alan Malev
Latimer, John Francis
Latimer, Murray Webb
Latimer, Peyton Randolph
Latour, Wallace Charles
LaTourrette, James Thomas
Latta, Delbert L.
Latta, Gordon Eric
Latta, William Charlton
Lattes, Raffaele
Lattimer, John Kingsley
Latz, Murray Jesse
Laub, David James
Laubach, Gerald David
Lauber, Joel David
Lauber, Thornton Stuart
Lauck, Daniel Wayne
Lauder, Estee
Lauer, Dolor John
Lauerman, Harold William
Laufer, Hans
Lauffer, Max Augustus, Jr.
Laughlin, Charles Vaill
Laughlin, James
Laughlin, John Seth
Laughlin, Robert Newton
Laurent, Lawrence Bell
Laurents, Arthur
Laurrell, Robert William
Lauson, Henry Dumke
Lautenberg, Frank R.
Lautenberg, Frank R.
Lauterbach, Robert Emil
Laux, Peter John
Lavalle, Paul
Lavarnway, Henry George, Jr.
La Varre, William
LaVeck, Gerald DeLoss
Lavely, John Hillman
Lavender, David Charles
Laventhol, David Abram
LaVenture, William Burrows
Laverge, Jan
Lavery, Charles Joseph
Lavery, William Edward
Lavey, Kenneth Henry
Lavin, John Halley
Lavine, Samuel Phillips
Law, Harold Bell
Law, Lloyd William
Law, Lloyd William, Jr.
Law, Warren Aubrey
Laware, John Patrick
Lawi, David Steven
Lawler, Beverley Rhea
Lawler, Bruce Gibbs
Lawler, Joseph Christopher
Lawler, Thomas Newman
Lawless, William Josselyn, Jr.
Lawley, Alan
Lawrason, F. Douglas
Lawrence, Charles Barnes, Jr.
Lawrence, Charles Radford, II
Lawrence, George Hill Mathewson
Lawrence, Harold
Lawrence, Henry Sherwood
Lawrence, James Fugate
Lawrence, Jerome
Lawrence, John Howard
Lawrence, Josephine
Lawrence, Justus Baldwin
Lawrence, Mary Georgene Wells (Mrs. Harding Lawrence)
Lawrence, Merloyd Ludington
Lawrence, Nathaniel Morris
Lawrence, Paul Roger
Lawrence, Philip Signor
Lawrence, Richard Wesley, Jr.
Lawrence, Robert
Lawrence, Robert Theodore
Lawrence, Ruddick Carpenter
Lawrence, Seymour
Lawrence, Vera Brodsky
Lawrence, Walter, Jr.
Lawrence, William Porter
Lawry, Sylvia (Mrs. Stanley Englander)
Laws, Hubert
Lawson, Fred Alexander
Lawson, James Dean
Lawson, James Raymond
Lawson, John Shults
Lawson, Thomas Elsworth
Lawson, Thomas Sawyer
Lawson-Johnston, Peter Orman
Lawton, Eugene Alfred
Lax, Benjamin
Lax, Peter David
Lax, Philip
Lay, Chris Andrew
Laylin, John Gallup
Layng, Edwin Tower
Layton, Billy Jim
Layton, Caleb Rodney, III
Layton, Irving
Layton, J. R.
Layton, LeRoy
Lazarus, Gustav
Lazarus, Herbert Benedict
Lazarus, Herman
Lazarus, Maurice
Lazerowitz, Alice Ambrose (Mrs. Morris Lazerowitz)
Lazrus, Benjamin
Lazrus, Oscar M.
Lazzari, Pietro
Lea, Robert Martin
Leach, David Miles
Leach, George Myron
Leach, Ralph F.
Leach, Reginald (Reggie) Joseph
Leach, Robert Ellis
Leach, Wilford
Leachman, Robert Briggs
Leacock, Eleanor Burke
Leader, Albert Harry
Leader, Solomon
Leaf, Alexander
Leaf, Boris
League, Archie William
Leahy, Osmund Alfred
Leahy, Patrick Joseph
Leahy, Thomas Francis
Leahy, William F.
Lear, Evelyn
Lear, Robert William
Leard, John Earnshaw
Leary, Frederick John
Leary, John Charles
Leary, William James
Leatham, John Tonkin
Leather, Richard Brenk
Leaverton, Paul Emmett, Jr.
Leavitt, Ithaman Martin
Leavitt, Joseph
Leavitt, Lloyd Richardson, Jr.
Leavitt, Milo David, Jr.
Leavitt, Thomas Whittlesey
Leavy, Herbert Theodore
Lebed, Hartzel Zangwill
Lebensohn, Zigmond Meyer
Leblanc, Hugues
Le Blanc, Moreland Paul, Jr.
LeBlond, Richard Knight, II
LeBoutillier, Martin
Lebow, Sylvan

Long, Donlin Martin
Long, Franklin A.
Long, Gillis William
Long, Howard Charles
Long, J. Emery
Long, John Herbert
Long, Kenneth Robert
Long, Morton
Long, Norton E.
Long, Robert Lyman John
Long, Robert Radcliffe
Long, Rowland Hornshaw
Long, Russell Billiu
Longaker, Richard Pancoast
Longfield, James Edgar
Longini, Richard Leon
Longley, James Bernard
Longmoore, John Thomas
Longo, Joseph Stephen
Longo, Vincent
Longstreth, William Thacher
Longworth, Alice Lee Roosevelt
Longyear, John Munro, III
Loo, Beverly Jane
Looker, Charles
Lookstein, Joseph Hyman
Loomba, Narendra Paul
Loomer, Fenwick Dane
Loomis, Henry
Loomis, John Edward
Loomis, Philip Albert, Jr.
Loomis, Worth (Alfred Worthington)
Looney, William Boyd
Loos, A(mandus) William
Loos, Karl Dickson
Loper, Ben Hubert
Lopez, Andrew
Lopez, Robert Sabatino
Lopez-Rey, José
Lorant, Stefan
Lorber, Stanley H.
Lorch, Edgar R.
Lorch, Maristella De Panizza (Mrs. Edgar R. Lorch)
Lord, Albert Bates
Lord, Charles Edwin
Lord, Clifford Lee
Lord, George deForest
Lord, Glenn Richard
Lord, Jere Williams, Jr.
Lord, John Wesley
Lord, Joseph Simon, III
Lord, Mary Pillsbury (Mrs. Oswald Bates Lord)
Lord, Milton Edward
Lord, Richard Collins
Lord, Walter
Lord, Winston
Lorde, Audre Geraldin
Lore, Henry Edgar
Lore, Martin Maxwell
Lorenson, Edward Paul
Lorenz, John George
Lorenz, John Robbins
Lorenz, Lee Sharp
Lorian, Victor
Lorimer, Frank
Lorimer, Graeme
Lorinczi, George Gabriel
Loring, Augustus Peabody
Loring, John Robbins
Lorish, Robert Eugene
Lorry, Wilfred Fleet
Lorsung, Thomas Nicholas
Losee, Thomas Penny, Jr.
Loss, Louis
Losten, Basil Harry
Lothrop, Gilbert M.
Lothrop, Kristin Curtis
Lott, Bernice
Lott, Trent
Lotz, Walter Edward, Jr.
Loubet, Nathaniel Rothschild
Louchheim, Donald Harry
Louchheim, Katie Scofield
Loucks, Charles Ernest
Loucks, Daniel Peter
Loud, Nelson Montgomery
Louden, James Keith
Loudon, Dorothy
Lougee, Laurence Wheeler
Lougee, Robert Wayne
Lough, Frederick Charles
Loughery, Kevin Michael
Loughery, Richard Miller
Loughlin, Francis Anthony
Loughran, John L.
Louis, Jean Francois
Louis, Murray
Lounsbury, Robert Hastings
Lourie, Norman Victor
Lourie, Reginald Spencer
Louttit, James Russell
Louttit, Richard Talcott
Louttit, Thomas Robley
Louviere, Vernon Ray
Loux, Norman Landis
Lovass-Nagy, Victor
Love, Howard McClintic
Love, John Burke
Love, Nancy
Love, Philip Hampton
Love, Richard Harvey
Love, Robert Alonzo
Love, Warner Edwards
Lovejoy, Thomas Eugene, Jr.
Loveless, Herschel Cellel
Lovell, James C., Jr.
Lovell, Malcolm Read, Jr.
Lovell, Michael C.
Lovell, Ralph Marston
Lovelle, Susan Edith
Loveman, Charles Edward
Lovesky, Jerome
Lovestone, Jay
Lovett, Laurence Dow
Lovett, Robert Abercrombie
Lovitt, George Harold
Low, Emmet Francis, Jr.
Low, Francis Eugene
Low, George Michael
Low, George Prescott
Low, James Patterson
Low, Lawrence David
Low, Stephen
Low, V. Theodore
Lowance, Carter O.
Lowe, Adolph
Lowe, Dewey Kwoc Kung
Lowe, E. (Edwin) Nobles
Lowe, Harry
Lowe, Jack Warren
Lowe, John, III
Lowe, Victor (Augustus)
Lowell, John
Lowell, Juliet
Lowen, Theodore Whitney
Lowen, Walter
Lowen, Warren Kealoha
Lowens, Irving
Lowenstein, Alan Victor
Lowenstein, Allard Kenneth
Lowenstein, James Gordon
Lowenstein, Louis
Lower, Elmer Wilson
Lower, Katherine Dorothy
Lowi, Theodore J(ay)
Lowman, George Frederick
Lowman, Robert Morris
Lowry, A. Robert
Lowry, Alfred
Lowry, Bates
Lowry, James David
Lowry, Joseph Marvin
Lowry, Ralph Addison
Lowry, Walter Rea
Lowry, Wilson McNeil
Loy, Frank Ernest
Loy, John Robert
Loynd, Richard Birkett
Loynes, John Hamilton
Lozyniak, Andrew
Lu, David John
Lubalin, Herbert Frederick
Lubanko, Walter Alexander
Lubar, Jeffrey Stuart
Lubar, Robert
Lubell, Samuel
Lubensky, Earl Henry
Lubic, Ruth Watson
Lubin, Isador
Lubin, Laurence Vernon
Lubin, Martin
Lubkin, Gloria Becker
Luboff, Norman
Lubovitch, Lar
Lucas, Darrell Blaine
Lucas, J. Richard
Lucas, James Edward
Lucas, Jean Marie Conley
Lucas, Vane Basil, Jr.
Lucas, William Blair
Lucas, William Lipscomb
Lucca, John James
Lucchesi, Bruno
Luce, Charles Franklin
Luce, Henry, III
Luce, Robert Bonner
Lucey, Charles Emmet
Lucey, Charles Timothy
Lucey, Robert Francis
Lucht, Allan Power
Lucht, John Charles
Lucht, Robert August
Lucido, Chester Charles, Jr.
Lucier, Francis Paul
Lucioni, Luigi
Luck, David Jonathan Lewis
Luck, Georg Hans Bhawani
Lucker, Jay K.
Luckett, Hubert Pearson
Luckett, Robert A.
Luckey, E. Hugh
Luckhardt, Virginia Ethel
Luckinbill, Laurence George
Lucking, Walter Theodore
Lucky, Robert Wendell
Ludeman, Douglas Henry
Ludford, Geoffrey Stuart Stephen
Ludington, Francis Henry, Jr.
Ludlow, John Alfred
Ludlum, Robert
Ludlum, Robert Phillips
Ludtke, James Buren
Ludwig, Daniel K.
Ludwig, George Harry
Ludwig, John McKay
Ludwig, Kenneth John
Ludwig, Richard Milton
Ludwigson, John Ormont
Luening, Otto
Luetkemeyer, John Alexander
Lufkin, Dan W.
Lugar, Richard Green
Lugenbeel, Edward Elmer
Luginbuhl, William Hossfeld
Luhrs, Albert Weigand
Lührs, Britta Bauer
Luikart, Fordyce Whitney
Luisi, Hector
Lujan, Manuel, Jr.
Lukacs, John Adalbert
Lukas, J. Anthony
Lukash, William Matthew
Luke, David Lincoln, III
Luke, John Anderson
Luke, Robert Alfred
Luke, Stanley
Luken, Thomas A.
Lukens, Alan Wood
Lukens, Paul Bourne
Luker, James Allison
Lukoff, Herman
Luksus, Tzaims
Lumbard, Joseph Edward, Jr.
Lumiansky, Robert Mayer
Lumley, John Leask
Lumley, John Morris
Lumpkin, George Thomas, Jr.
Lumsden, Arthur James
Lund, David Harrison
Lund, Joseph Wheelock
Lund, Peter Anthony
Lund, Richard H.
Lundberg, Ferdinand Edgar
Lundberg, John Kessander
Lundberg, Robert Saunier
Lundeberg, Philip Karl
Lundgren, Lawrence William
Lundine, Stanley Nelson
Lundquist, Clarence Theodore
Lundquist, James H.
Lundvall, Bruce Gilbert
Lundy, Daniel Francis
Lundy, Victor Alfred
Lunghino, Donald Joseph
Lunin, Martin
Lunn, John Aleck
Luongo, Alfred L.
Luongo, C. Paul
Luria, Salvador Edward
Luria, Sydney Aaron
Lurie, Alison
Lurie, Harold
Lurie, Ranan Raymond
Lurie, William L.
Lusby, Ralston Newell
Lush, Gerson Harrison
Lusky, Louis
Luster, George Orchard
Lustig, Harry
Lustig, Robert T.
Lustman, Benjamin
Luther, Frank (Francis Luther Crow)
Lutkins, LaRue Robbins
Lutnicki, Victor A.
Luton, Johnston Edward
Luttinger, Joaquin Mazdak
Luttrell, A. Lothrop
Lutz, Wilbur Masser
Lux, John H.
Lydecker, Richard Ackerman
Lydman, Jack Wilson
Lye, Len
Lyet, Jean Paul
Lyle, Joseph Melvin, Jr.
Lyman, Henry
Lynch, Charles Allen
Lynch, Charles McKenna, Jr.
Lynch, Daniel Francis
Lynch, Edmund Elliott
Lynch, John Francis
Lynch, Kevin Andrew
Lynch, Robert Merrill
Lynch, Thomas Francis
Lynch, Vincent de Paul
Lynch, Warren
Lyne, Austin Francis
Lynes, (Joseph) Russell, (Jr.)
Lynett, Lawrence Wilson
Lyng, Richard Edmund
Lynn, Kenneth Schuyler
Lynn, Laurence Edwin, Jr.
Lynn, Robert P.
Lynn, Walter Royal
Lynton, Ernest Albert
Lynton, Harold S.
Lyon, Bryce Dale
Lyon, Cecil Burton
Lyon, Charles Stuart
Lyon, Eugene Davisson
Lyon, Frank Randolph, Jr.
Lyon, Fred William
Lyon, George Robert
Lyon, Richard Harold
Lyon, Scott Calvin
Lyons, Edward P.
Lyons, Eugene
Lyons, Francis Joseph
Lyons, Gene Martin
Lyons, J(ames) Austin, Jr.
Lyons, John Bartholomew
Lyons, John H.
Lyons, Joseph Norman
Lyons, Paul Robert
Lyons, Richard Joseph
Lyons, Thomas William
Lyons, William Aloysius
Lystad, Mary Hanemann (Mrs. Robert Lystad)
Lystad, Robert Arthur
Lytle, Richard
Lytle, William Eben
Maas, Michael
Maas, Peter
Maas, Werner Karl
Maass, Arthur
Maass, William George
Mabbs, Edward Carl
Mabee, Carleton
Mabon, John Scott
Mabon, Prescott Cliffton
MacAdam, Walter Kavanagh
MacArthur, Donald Malcolm
Macauley, Robie Mayhew
MacAusland, Earle Rutherford
MacAvoy, Paul Webster
Mac Avoy, Thomas Coleman
MacBain, Gavin Keith
Macbeth, Norman
MacCallan, W(illiam) David
MacCampbell, James Curtis
MacCamy, Richard Carlton
Mac Cowatt, Haskell Pawling
MacCracken, James
MacDermot, Galt
Macdonald, Cynthia Lee
Macdonald, Donald Arthur
Macdonald, Dwight
MacDonald, Frank Aborn
MacDonald, Gordon James Fraser
MacDonald, Herbert Stanley
Mac Donald, James Gordon
MacDonald, John Winchester
MacDonald, Margaret Mary
MacDonald, Nestor Joseph
MacDonald, Richard Annis
Macdonald, Robert Munro
MacDonald, Robert Taylor
MacDonald, Ronald Gordon
MacDonald, William Francis
MacDonald, William Lloyd
MacDonald, William McCullough
MacDonnell, Robert George
MacDonough, Thomas F.
Macdougall, Iver Cameron
MacDougall, Malcolm Douglas
MacDougall, Roderick Martin
Mace, Dean Tolle
Macera, Salvatore
MacFadyen, John A., Jr.
MacFadyen, John Hayter
Macfarlan, Duncan
MacGinitie, Walter Harold
MacGowan, Charles Frederic
MacGregor, Clark
Machacek, John W.
Machado, Luis
Machlin, Milton Robert
Machlup, Fritz
MacInnes, Helen (Mrs. Gilbert Highet)
MacIntosh, William James
MacIntyre, Alasdair Chalmers
MacIntyre, A(lfonso) Everette
MacIntyre, Malcolm Ames
Macioce, Thomas Matthew
MacIver, Loren
Mack, James Decker
Mack, John Edward
Mack, Julia Cooper
Mack, Raymond Francis
Mack, Ruth P.
Mack, Walter Staunton
Mack, William Paden
Mackay, Albert George
Mackay, John Alexander
MacKay, William Erskine
MacKaye, William Ross
MacKendrick, Lilian
MacKenzie, Charles Sherrard
Mackenzie, James William
MacKenzie, John Pettibone
MacKenzie, Ossian
MacKenzie, Ransom Gillet
Mackerodt, Fred
MacKethan, Edwin Robeson
Mackey, George Whitelaw
Mackey, Howard Hamilton, Sr.
Mackey, Sheldon Elias
Mackey, Willard Clyde, Jr.
MacKimm, J(ames) Bradley
Mackin, Catherine
MacKinnon, Aleck MacDonald
MacKinnon, Alexander Donald
MacKinnon, George E.
Mackinnon, Robert Neale
Mackler, Tina
Macklin, Gordon Stanley, Jr.
MacKowski, John Joseph
Macksey, Richard Alan
MacLaine, Allan Hugh
MacLaughlin, Robert Stacy
MacLaury, Bruce King
Maclean, Daniel Crawford, III
MacLean, Donald Isidore
Macleay, Donald
MacLeish, Archibald
Mac Leod, Arthur C.
Macleod, Donald
MacLeod, Gavin
MacLeod, William John
MacMahon, Brian
MacMahon, Harold Edward
MacMahon, Lloyd Francis
MacManus, Yvonne Cristina
MacMaster, Robert Ellsworth
MacMillan, Douglas Clark
MacMillan, Gary Duane
MacMillan, James Murdock
MacMillan, O. Townsend
MacMillan, William Leedom, Jr.
MacMillen, William Charles, Jr.
MacMullen, Ramsay
MacNamara, Donal Eoin Joseph
Macnamara, Thomas Edward
MacNaughton, Donald Sinclair
MacNaughton, James Robert
MacNeil, Cornell Hill
MacNeill, Arthur Edson
MacNelly, Jeffrey Kenneth
MacNichol, Edward Ford, Jr.
Macnutt, Glenn Gordon
Macomber, Allison Rufus
Macomber, John D.
MacPhail, Leland Stanford, Jr.
MacQueen, Kenneth H.
MacRae, Cameron Farquhar
Macrae, Donald Pollard
Mac Rae, George Winsor
MacRae, Gordon
Macrae, John, III
Macridis, Roy Constantine
MacRury, King
MacTaggart, Barry
Macurdy, John Edward
MacVane, John Franklin
MacVicar, Margaret Love Agnes
MacVittie, Robert William
MacWilliams, Donald Gribble
MacWilliams, John J.
Macy, Bill (William Macy Garber)
Macy, John Williams, Jr.
Madansky, Leon
Madden, Carl Halford
Madden, Edward Harry
Madden, Frank Augustus, Jr.
Madden, John Beckwith
Madden, Kenneth Cromwell
Madden, Murdaugh Stuart
Maddin, Robert
Maddock, Charles Sanford
Maddox, Dan Waite
Maddox, Elliott
Maddox, Garry Lee
Madeira, Francis King Carey
Madigan, Edward R.
Madigan, Joseph Edward
Madigan, Michael J.
Madison, Charles A(llan)
Madow, Leo
Madtes, Richard Eastman
Maechling, Charles, Jr.
Maeck, John Van Sicklen
Maedel, George Frederick
Maeder, Paul Fritz
Maeroff, Gene Irving
Maes, Robert Adamson
Maffry, August
Magafan, Ethel
Magasanik, Boris
Magaw, Elden Samuel
Magaziner, Henry Jonas
Magee, John Francis
Magee, Peter Noel
Magee, Warren Egbert
Mager, Ezra Pascal
Magill, J(ames) Marion
Magill, Robert Nathaniel
Magill, Samuel Hays
Maginn, Edward Joseph
Maginn, Wallace Allton
Maglich, Bogdan C.
Maglione, Ralph John, Jr.
Magnus, Wilhelm
Magnuson, Warren Grant
Magoun, Francis Peabody, Jr.
Magovern, Frederick John
Magrane, John Scott
Magraw, Richard Mueller
Maguire, Andrew
Maguire, Bassett
Maguire, John David
Maguire, John Joseph
Maguire, John MacArthur
Maguire, Robert Edward
Mahan, Archie Irvin
Maher, Adrian William
Maher, Brendan Arnold
Maher, Frank Barry
Maher, Patrick Joseph
Mahey, John Andrew
Mahl, George Franklin
Mahler, Harry Bez
Mahlmann, John James
Mahlstedt, Walter
Mahon, George Herman
Mahon, James Joseph
Mahon, Malachy Thomas
Mahoney, Carl Francis
Mahoney, Sister Colette
Mahoney, David Joseph, Jr.
Mahoney, George Perry
Mahoney, Gerard Michael
Mahoney, J. Daniel
Mahoney, James Owen
Mahoney, John F.
Mahoney, Margaret Ellerbe
Mahoney, Michael Robert Taylor
Mahoney, Thomas Henry Donald
Mahoney, Tom (John Thomas)
Mahoney, William Grattan
Mahony, Walter Butler, Jr.
Mahrous, Haroun
Maidenberg, Hyman Jonah
Maier, Herbert Caille
Maier, William Morris
Mailer, Norman
Mailliard, William Somers
Mailman, Lloyd Stanley
Main, Jackson Turner
Mair, George F(isk)
Mairhuber, John Carl
Maisano, Franklin
Maislin, Isidore
Maisonrouge, Jacques Gaston
Maitin, Samuel Calman
Majewski, Lawrence James
Majno, Guido
Major, Clarence
Major, Winfield Watson
Majthenyi, Ladislaus D.
Mak, Dayton Seymour
Makarova, Natalia
Makdisi, George
Makela, Benjamin R.
Makosky, John Donald
Makowski, Stanley Matthew
Maktos, John
Malafronte, Donald
Malamed, Seymour H.
Malamud, Bernard
Malanga, Gerard Joseph
Malarkey, Martin Francis, Jr.
Malas, Spiro
Malcolm, Norman Adrian
Malcolm, Walter David
Malek, Frederic Vincent
Malenbaum, Wilfred
Malenka, Bertram Julian
Maletz, Herbert Naaman
Maley, Donald
Malfitano, Joseph John
Malik, Charles Habib
Malin, Irving
Malin, Robert Abernethy
Malina, Judith
Malis, Leonard Irving
Malkiel, Burton Gordon
Malkin, Myron Samuel
Malkin, Peter Laurence
Malkus, Willem Van Rensselaer
Mallary, Raymond DeWitt
Mallary, Richard Walker
Mallary, Robert
Maller, Robert Russell
Mallette, Malcolm Francis
Malley, Francis John
Malley, John Wallace
Malley, Robert Joseph
Mallick, Earl William
Mallory, Elizabeth Grinstead (Mrs. John Mallory)
Mallory, Frank Bryant
Mallory, George Barron
Mallory, George Kenneth
Malm, James Royal
Maloff, Saul
Malone, Dennis Philip
Malone, Dumas
Malone, Edward H.
Malone, Joseph Lawrence
Malone, Thomas Logan, Jr.
Maloney, Barry Charles
Maloney, Edward Francis
Maloney, Sister Elizabeth Ann
Maloney, George Thomas
Maloney, John Alexander
Maloney, John Frederick
Maloney, Kenneth Morgan
Maloney, Thomas James
Maloney, Thomas Joseph
Maloney, Walter E.
Maloy, Richard Joseph
Maloy, Robert Michael
Malozemoff, Plato
Malsin, Arthur
Maltby, George Langford
Maltz, Albert
Maltz, Maxwell
Manasco, Carter
Manassero, Henri J.P.
Manatos, Andrew Emanuel
Manatos, Mike
Manch, Joseph
Mancheski, Frederick John
Manchester, William
Mancill, Frank H.
Mandac, Evelyn Lorenzana
Mandan, Robert
Mandanici, John C.
Mandel, H(arold) George
Mandel, Irwin Daniel
Mandel, Robert D.
Mandelbaum, Bernard
Mandelbaum, Maurice H.
Mandell, Abe
Mandell, Samuel Philip
Mandell, Stephen Arnold
Mandelstam, Robert Stanley
Manderino, Louis Lawrence
Mandeville, Robert Clark, Jr.
Mandil, I. Harry
Maneker, Deanna Marie
Manell, Abram E.
Manes, Nella Cellini
Manes, Stephen Gabriel
Maness, Irving
Manfull, Melvin Lawrence
Mangan, Margaret Mary J.
Mangan, Robert Martin
Manger, Julius, Jr.
Manges, Horace S.
Mangione, Charles Frank (Chuck)
Mangione, Jerre Gerlando
Mangone, Gerard J.
Mangouni, Norman
Manhard, Philip Wallace
Manheim, Paul Ernest
Manilow, Barry
Manion, John Joseph, Jr.
Manion, Thomas Anthony
Manischewitz, Bernard
Mankiewicz, Don M(artin)
Mankiewicz, Frank Fabian
Mankiewicz, Joseph Leo
Mankin, Henry Jay
Mankowski, Bruno
Manley, Albert Edward
Manley, Joan A. Daniels
Manley, Robert Russell
Manley, William Tanner
Mann, Abby
Mann, Charles August
Mann, David Emerson
Mann, Eugene Thomas
Mann, Forbes
Mann, Frank Eugene
Mann, Herbert Frederick
Mann, Herbie
Mann, James Harold
Mann, John H.
Mann, Kenneth Walker
Mann, Lyle Eugene
Mann, Marion
Mann, Martin
Mann, Marty
Mann, Robert Henry
Mann, Robert Wellesley
Mann, Seymour Zalmon
Mann, Theodore

Mann, Theodore Ralph
Mann, Wallace Harper
Manners, Robert Alan
Manning, Bayless Andrew
Manning, Burt
Manning, Charles Frederick
Manning, Edward Peter
Manning, Elizabeth MacDonald
Manning, Farley
Manning, Gordon
Manning, Margaret Raymond
Manning, Robert Joseph
Manning, William Frederick
Manning, William Raymond
Mano, D. Keith
Manoff, Richard Kalman
Manoli, Dominick L.
Manoogian, Torkom
Manor, LeRoy Joseph
Mansell, Frank Luther
Mansell, Irving Lawson
Mansell, Thomas Norman
Mansfield, Harvey Claflin, Jr.
Mansfield, Harvey Claflin, Sr.
Mansfield, James Ray
Mansfield, John Howard
Mansfield, John Kenneth
Mansfield, Walter Roe
Manski, Wladyslaw Julian
Manson, Julius Joel
Mantell, Charles L.
Manthorne, Mary Elizabeth Arnold
Manton, Edwin Alfred Grenville
Manton, Ruth McCarthy
Manuel, Frank Edward
Manuel, Ralph Nixon
Manwell, Reginald Dickinson
Mapel, William
Mapel, William Marlen Raines
Mapes, Charles Maynard
Mapp, Alf Johnson, Jr.
Mara, Richard Thomas
Maramorosch, Karl
Maran, Stephen Paul
Marandon, Andrew
Marantis, Zachary
Marbury, William Luke
Marcase, Michael Paul
Marceau, J. Edward
Marceau, Marcel
Marcello, Amedeo Alfred
Marcellus, John Robert, III
March, Eugene Airey
March, George Patrick
Marcham, Frederick George
Marchesi, Vincent Thomas
Marco, Guy Anthony
Marcuccio, Phyllis Rose
Marcus, Edward
Marcus, Hyman
Marcus, Leonard Marshall
Marcus, Philip Irving
Marcus, Ruth Barcan
Marcus, Sheldon
Marcus, Steven
Marcuse, James Edgar
Marcuvitz, Nathan
Marcy, Carl Milton
Mardaga, Thomas Joseph
Marden, Brice
Marden, Philip Ayer
Marden, Virginia McAvoy (Mrs. Orison Swett Marden)
Marder, John G.
Marek, George Richard
Marek, Richard William
Marella, Philip Daniel
Margenau, Henry
Margetts, Walter Thomas, Jr.
Margileth, Andrew Menges
Margolin, Edward
Margolis, Daniel Herbert
Margolis, David I.
Margolis, George
Margolis, Henry Melville
Margolis, Joseph
Margulies, Harold
Margulies, Joseph
Marichal, Juan
Mariella, Raymond P.
Maril, Herman
Marinatos, Anthony
Marini, Robert Charles
Marino, Anthony Wayne Martin
Marion, Jerry Baskerville
Marion, John Francis
Marion, John Louis
Marion, Loretta Hunt
Maris, Albert Branson
Marisol (Marisol Escobar)
Mark, Bernard
Mark, Hans Michael
Mark, Herman F(rancis)
Mark, Lester Charles
Mark, Louis, Jr.
Mark, Melvin
Mark, Peter Herman
Mark, Shelley M.
Mark, Vernon Herschel
Marke, Julius Jay
Markell, Robert Joseph
Marker, Robert Sydney
Markert, Clement Lawrence
Markey, Edward John
Markey, Howard Thomas
Markey, Winston Roscoe
Markham, Jesse William
Markley, Rodney Weir
Markoe, Frank, Jr.
Markovitz, Hershel
Marks, Barry Alan
Marks, Claude
Marks, Dorothy Louise Ames (Mrs. Leonard H. Marks)
Marks, Edwin S.
Marks, Johnny (John D.)
Marks, Joseph
Marks, J(oseph) David
Marks, Leonard Harold
Marks, Marc Lincoln
Marks, Paul Alan
Marks, Rachel Bryant
Marks, Raymond H.
Marks, Roberta Grace
Marks, Sidney
Markun, Patricia Maloney (Mrs. David Joseph Markun)
Markward, John Oliver
Marland, Sidney Percy, Jr.
Marlas, James Constantine
Marlenee, Ronald Charles
Marler, James Emmett
Marler, Peter Robert
Marlowe, Donald E.
Marlowe, Sylvia (Mrs. Leonid Berman)
Marmion, Harry Alphonsus
Marmion, William Henry
Maroney, Daniel Vincent, Jr.
Marple, Dorothy Jane
Marquis, Vernon Maley
Marriott, Alice Sheets (Mrs. John Willard Marriott)
Marriott, John Willard
Marriott, John Willard, Jr.
Marron, Donald Baird
Marschalk, Harry Robert
Marschall, Albert Rhoades
Marsching, Ronald
Marsden, Donald Dearborn
Marsh, Burton Wallace
Marsh, Dean Mitchell
Marsh, John O., Jr.
Marsh, Joseph Franklin, Jr.
Marsh, Julian Bunsick
Marsh, Pamela Olive
Marsh, Quinton Neely
Marsh, Rabe Ferguson, Jr.
Marsh, Robert Mortimer
Marshak, Robert Eugene
Marshak, Robert Reuben
Marshall, Carter Lee, Jr.
Marshall, Charles Burton
Marshall, Clarence Taylor
Marshall, Clifford Wallace
Marshall, Colin Marsh
Marshall, Dorothy Nepper
Marshall, E. G.
Marshall, George Nichols
Marshall, Henrietta Harrison
Marshall, James
Marshall, James Edward
Marshall, Jean McElroy
Marshall, John Aloysius
Marshall, Lawrence Marcellus
Marshall, Lois
Marshall, Martin Vivan
Marshall, Nelson
Marshall, Ray
Marshall, Robert Gerald
Marshall, Robert James
Marshall, Robert Pearson, Jr.
Marshall, Stanley Charles
Marshall, Thomas Oliver, Jr.
Marshall, Thurgood
Marshall, Victor Fray
Marshall, William, Jr.
Marshall, William Jefferson
Marshall, William Joseph
Marston, Robert Andrew
Marteka, Vincent James, Jr.
Martens, Robert John
Marticelli, Joseph John
Martin, Abner Broadwater
Martin, Alastair Bradley
Martin, Albert C.
Martin, Albert Sidney, Jr.
Martin, Albro
Martin, Alfred Manuel (Billy)
Martin, Alvin Charles
Martin, Anthony Alphonse
Martin, Armour Emerson
Martin, Bernard Lee
Martin, Bruce Douglas
Martin, Charles
Martin, Charles E.
Martin, David Allan
Martin, David Nathan
Martin, Dwight
Martin, Edward Dana
Martin, Edwin McCammon
Martin, Edwin Wilson, Jr.
Martin, Ethelbert Cowley
Martin, Francis David
Martin, George (Whitney)
Martin, Guy
Martin, Guy Richard
Martin, Harold Clark
Martin, Henry H.
Martin, James Alfred, Jr.
Martin, James Mordecai
Martin, James Russell
Martin, John Arthur
Martin, John Butlin
Martin, John Joseph
Martin, John Joseph
Martin, John L.
Martin, John McKenzie
Martin, John Rupert
Martin, Julian S. (Julian Sienkiewicz)
Martin, Lee Gwynne
Martin, Louis Edward
Martin, Lowell A.
Martin, Marie Young
Martin, Monroe Harnish
Martin, Morgan Graham
Martin, Paul Cecil
Martin, Paul Logan
Martin, Paul Simeon
Martin, Ralph Guy
Martin, Ralph Harding
Martin, Richard
Martin, Robert Bruce
Martin, Roblee Boettcher
Martin, Samuel Preston, III
Martin, Townsend Bradley
Martin, Vincent George
Martin, Wilbur Forrest
Martin, William Harris
Martin, William McChesney, Jr.
Martin, William Oliver
Martin, William Read Harper
Martin, William Ted
Martindale, James Vaughan
Martinelli, Ezio
Martinet, Marjorie Dorsey
Martinez, Arabella
Martino, Donald
Martino, Giovanni
Martins, Peter
Martinuzzi, Leo Sergio, Jr.
Marton, Emery
Marton, Ladislaus Laszlo
Martorana, Sebastian Vincent
Martyn, James Louis
Martz, Louis Lohr
Martz, Walter Atlee
Marusi, Augustine Raymond
Marvel, William
Marvel, William Worthington
Marvin, Burton Wright
Marvin, Eleanor D. (Mrs. Earl Marvin)
Marx, Anne (Mrs. Frederick E. Marx)
Marx, Frank
Marx, George L.
Marx, Gertie Florentine
Marx, Henry Mosler
Marx, Leo
Marx, Otto, Jr.
Masani, Pesi Rustom
Masey, Jack
Mashikian, Hagop Serop
Masland, Frank Elmer, III
Masland, Richard Lambert
Maslow, Will
Masnick, George Stephan
Mason, Alpheus Thomas
Mason, Austin Blake
Mason, Birny, Jr.
Mason, Brian Harold
Mason, Charles Ellis, III
Mason, Earl Henry
Mason, Edward Allen
Mason, Edward Sagendorph
Mason, Frank Earl
Mason, Frank Herbert
Mason, Harold Jesse
Mason, Herbert Warren, Jr.
Mason, Jerry
Mason, Jimilu
Mason, John Clarke
Mason, John Russell
Mason, Jonathan
Mason, Lowell Blake
Mason, Lucius Randolph
Mason, Madeline
Mason, Martin Alexander
Mason, Ralph Schweizer
Mason, Raymond Adams
Mason, Robert
Mason, Ronald Lawrence
Mason, Thomas Boyd
Mason, Warren Perry
Masoner, Paul Henry
Masotta, Robert Edward
Masotti, Lewis Richard
Massalski, Tadeusz Bronislaw
Massel, Mark S.
Massengale, John Edward, 3d
Massey, Harold
Massey, Robert Unruh
Massey, Walter Eugene
Massey, William S.
Massi, Frank
Massie, Reginald David
Massie, Robert Kinloch
Massie, Suzanne
Massimino, Sal Thomas
Massow, Rosalind (Mrs. Norton Luger)
Masten, John E.
Masteroff, Joe
Masters, Charles Day
Masters, Jon Joseph
Masters, Richard E.
Masters, Roger Davis
Masterson, Charles Francis
Masterson, Kleber Sandlin
Masterton, William Lewis
Mastey, Anthony Daniel
Mastroianni, Luigi, Jr.
Mataxis, Theodore Christopher
Mateer, Frank Marlon
Mater, Gene P.
Materna, Ted
Matheke, Otto George, Jr.
Mather, Austin Wheeler
Mather, John Russell
Mather, Norman Wells
Mathers, William Harris
Mathews, Carmen Sylva
Mathews, Edward James
Mathews, Elmer Clarence
Mathews, Forrest David
Mathews, James Kenneth
Mathews, Max Vernon
Mathews, Richard Albert
Mathias, Charles McCurdy, Jr.
Mathias, James Herman
Mathias, Joseph Simon
Mathieson, Andrew Wray
Mathieu, Robert P.
Mathis, John Harris
Mathis, Robert Couth
Mathis, Sharon Bell (Mrs. Leroy F. Mathis)
Mathis, William Lowrey
Mathur, Vishnu Sahai
Matlock, Jack Foust, Jr.
Matloff, Maurice
Matricciani, Joseph Stephen
Matson, Frederick Rognald
Matson, George Donald
Matson, Greta
Matsumoto, Teruo
Matsunaga, Spark Masayuki
Matsushima, Satoshi
Matt, Thelma Lee
Mattern, Donald Eugene
Matteson, Robert Johnson Montgomery
Mattfeld, Jacquelyn Phillips Anderson
Matthews, A(lan) Bruce
Matthews, Benjamin Alfonzo
Matthews, Edward Joseph, Jr.
Matthews, Gareth Blanc
Matthews, George Bostert
Matthews, Herbert Lionel
Matthews, Howard Bierly
Matthews, Jack
Matthews, John Bowers, Jr.
Matthews, Leonard Sarver
Matthews, Mary Jean O'Leary
Matthews, Samuel Arthur
Matthias, Willard C.
Matthiessen, Peter
Mattingly, John Robert
Mattoon, Henry Amasa, Jr.
Mattson, Joe Oliver Philip
Mattson, Walter Edward
Matuszak, Stephen Anthony
Matz, John Edwin
Matzkin, Rose Ellis (Mrs. Max N. Matzkin)
Matzner, Milton John
Mauchly, John William
Mauck, Elwyn Arthur
Maude, Edward Joseph
Mauldon, James Grenfell
Maule, Hamilton Bee
Maull, Flora Davis (Mrs. Baldwin Maull)
Maumenee, Alfred Edward
Maunsbach, Eric
Maurer, Gilbert Charles
Maurer, Joseph Abele
Maurer, Paul Herbert
Maurin, Mario Leon
Maury, Reuben
Mautner, Henry George
Mavrinac, Albert Anthony
Maw, Carlyle Elwood
Mawhinney, Eugene Alberto
Max, Peter
Maxa, Rudolph Joseph, Jr.
Maxey, David Roy
Maxon, Robert George
Maxwell, Arthur Eugene
Maxwell, Bryce
Maxwell, Carla Lena
Maxwell, Roberta
Maxwell, Vera Huppe
Maxwell, W. Richard
Maxwell, William
Maxwell, William Joseph
May, Donald
May, Edgar
May, Elaine
May, Elizabeth Stoffregen (Mrs. Geoffrey May)
May, Ernest Max
May, Ernest Richard
May, Georges Claude
May, Gita
May, Peter William
May, Timothy James
May, William Frederic
Maybury-Lewis, David Henry Peter
Mayer, Albert
Mayer, Arno Joseph
Mayer, Arthur L.
Mayer, J. Gerald
Mayer, Jean
Mayer, John Anton
Mayer, Klaus
Mayer, Manfred Martin
Mayer, Martin Prager
Mayer, Richard Dean
Mayer, Robert George
Mayer, William Dixon
Mayerson, Philip
Mayes, Charles Ray
Mayes, Herbert Raymond
Mayfield, Richard Heverin
Mayhew, David Raymond
Mayhew, Richard
Maynard, A. Rogers
Maynard, Aubre de Lambert
Maynard, Frederick Charles, Jr.
Maynard, Joseph Alfred
Mayne, William
Maynes, Charles William
Maynes, E. Scott
Maynor, Dorothy
Mayo, Charles George
Mayo, Dana Walker
Mayo, Louis Harkey
Mayo, Maurice George
Mayo, Thomas Tabb, IV
Mayor, John Roberts
Mayo-Smith, Richmond
Mayr, Ernst (Walter)
Mays, Marshall Trammell
Mays, Morley Josiah
Mays, Willie Howard, Jr.
Mazan, Walter Lawrence
Maze, Clarence, Jr.
Mazer, William
Mazlish, Bruce
Mazlish, Elaine
Mazo, Earl
Mazur, Abraham
Mazur, Allan Carl
Mazur, Michael
Mazur, Paul Myer
Mazuy, Cordelia Kay Knight
Mazzeo, Joseph Anthony
Mazzo, Kay
Mazzola, Anthony Thomas
Mazzola, John William
Mazzola, Vincent Pontorno
Mazzoli, Romano L.
McAdams, Andrew Jack
McAdams, Brian
Mc Adams, William Alfred
McAdoo, Bob
McAdoo, Richard Budd
McAfee, Jerry
McAfee, John G.
McAfee, Ralph LaVerne
McAfee, William
McAleer, Edward Cornelius
McAllester, David Park
McAllister, Donald
McAllister, James M.
McAnulty, Henry Joseph
McArdle, Paul Francis
McArdle, Richard Edwin
McArthur, Janet Ward
McArthur, John Hector
McAulay, Archibald Hendrie
McAuliffe, Dennis Philip
McBean, Alan Johnston
McBean, Alexander Marshall
McBeath, William Henninger
McBee, James Leonard, Jr.
McBratney, Robert Bruce
McBride, H. T.
McBride, John Alexander
McBride, Lloyd
McBride, Patricia
McBride, Raymond Andrew
McBride, Thomas Frederick
McBride, William Bernard
McBrier, C. Robert
McBurney, Andrew Marvell
Mc Burney, Lane Fordyce
McCabe, Cynthia Jaffee
McCabe, Edward Aeneas
McCabe, Edward James, Jr.
McCabe, Eugene Joseph
McCabe, Frank John
McCabe, Frank Wells
Mc Cabe, Gerard Benedict
McCabe, Gerard Francis
McCabe, Gibson
Mc Cabe, Marshall Edward
McCabe, Thomas Bayard
McCabe, Thomas Bayard, Jr.
McCaffery, William Arthur
McCaffrey, Joseph Francis
McCaffrey, Neil
McCaffrey, Robert Henry, Jr.
McCaffrey, William Joseph
McCahan, Walter K.
McCall, Charlie Campbell
McCall, David Bruce
McCallion, Harry John
Mc Callister, Charles E.
McCallum, David
McCally, Charles Thomas
McCampbell, Donald H.
McCance, Thomas
McCandless, Robert Cecil
McCandlish, Fairfax Sheild
McCandlish, Robert John, Jr.
McCann, Frances Veronica
Mc Cann, Joseph James
McCann, William Edward
McCardell, Adrian LeRoy, Jr.
McCardell, Archie Richard
McCardle, Dorothy Bartlett (Mrs. Carl Wesley McCardle)
Mc Carn, Grace Hayden
McCarrick, Theodore Edgar
Mc Carroll, Michael Arthur
McCarter, Francis E.P.
McCarthy, Barbara Philippa
McCarthy, Charles Joseph
McCarthy, Cornelius Stephen
McCarthy, D. Justin
McCarthy, Daniel Christopher Jr.
McCarthy, Denis Michael
McCarthy, Edward Francis
McCarthy, Edward James
McCarthy, Edward James (Ed)
McCarthy, Eugene Joseph
McCarthy, George Denis
McCarthy, Gerald T.
McCarthy, John Joseph
Mc Carthy, John Michael
McCarthy, John Robert
McCarthy, Joseph John
McCarthy, Joseph Weston
McCarthy, Kathryn Agnes
McCarthy, Mary
McCarthy, Mary Frances
Mc Carthy, Patrick Edward
McCarthy, Robert Vincent
McCarthy, Stephen Anthony
Mc Carthy, Thomas Patrick
Mc Carthy, Timothy Patrick
McCartney, Kenneth Hall
Mc Cartney, Robert Charles
McCarty, A. Cleve
McCarty, Maclyn
McCarty, Robert Lee
McCarty, Stuart
McCauley, Alfred Robert
McCauley, Bruce Gordon
McCauley, William Andrew
McCausland, Thomas Gerome
Mc Chesney, Russell James
McClafferty, John Joseph
McClain, Austin Vail
McClain, William Harold
McClary, Terence E.
McCleary, Charles David
Mc Cleary, Joel West
McCleery, William Thomas
McClellan, Bruce
McClellan, Edwin
McClellan, James Edward
McClellan, James Edward, Jr.
McClellan, Stan Leon
McClelland, Clyde Lloyd
McClelland, David Clarence
McClelland, John Finley
Mc Clendon, Sarah Newcomb
McClester, John Richard
McClintock, David William
McClintock, Frank Ambrose
McClinton, Katharine Morrison
McCloskey, Paul N., Jr.
McCloskey, Peter Francis
McCloskey, Robert
McCloskey, Robert James
McCloy, John Jay
McCloy, William Ashby
McClung, Richard Goehring
McClure, Brooks
McClure, Donald Stuart
McClure, James A.
McClure, James Warren
McClure, Richard Fowler
McClure, William Pendleton
McCluskey, Ellen L.
McCluskey, Robert Timmons
McCollough, Clair R.
McCollum, Robert Wayne
McColough, Charles Peter
McComas, Donald Earl
McComb, James Newell
McCombe, Leonard
McCombs, Philip Algie
McCombs, Robert Pratt
McConagha, Alan
McCone, Alan
McConnachie, Brian John
McConnaughy, John Edward, Jr.
McConnell, J(ames) H(oge) Tyler
McConnell, John Wilkinson
McConnell, John William, Jr.
McConnon, James Charles
McCord, David (Thompson Watson)
McCord, James Iley
McCord, Kenneth Armstrong
McCord, Marshal
McCord, William Maxwell
McCorison, Marcus Allen
McCorkindale, Douglas Hamilton
McCormack, Donald Paul
McCormack, Edward Joseph
McCormack, Elizabeth Jane
McCormack, Fred Allen
McCormack, John W.
McCormack, Mike
McCormack, Patricia Seger
McCormack, Robert Morris
McCormack, Thomas Joseph
McCormick, Barnes Warnock
McCormick, Donald Bruce
McCormick, Edward Allen
McCormick, Henry J.
Mc Cormick, James Charles
McCormick, James Harold
McCormick, John Owen
McCormick, John Patrick
McCormick, Joseph Carroll
McCormick, Joseph Raymond
McCormick, Kenneth Dale
Mc Cormick, Richard Patrick
McCormick, Thomas Francis
McCormick, Thomas Julian
McCormick, Willard F.
McCormick, William Martin
McCormick, William Morgan
McCormick, William Thomas
McCoy, Charles Allan
McCoy, Clarence John, Jr.
McCoy, Ralph Richard
McCoy, Richard Hugh
McCoy, Seth
McCracken, Daniel Delbert
McCracken, Guy F.
Mc Cracken, James
McCree, Wade Hampton, Jr.
McCron, Raymond Charles
McCrone, Harold Warfield, Jr.
McCrory, Wallace Willard
McCrumm, John Doench
McCubbin, Melvin A.
McCue, Carolyn Moore
McCue, Gerald Mallon
McCullen, Joseph Thomas, Jr.
McCulloch, Frank W.
McCulloch, James Aloysius
McCulloch, John Irvin Beggs
McCulloch, Robert Manning
McCullough, Donald Frederick
Mc Cullough, John Price
McCullough, John Thompson
McCullough, Robert Willis
McCullough, Roland Alexander
McCune, Barron Patterson
McCune, Charles L.
McCune, James Elliot

McCune, John Francis, III
McCune, William James, Jr.
McCurdy, Alexander, Jr.
McCurdy, Gilbert Geier
McCurdy, Gilbert James Cathcart
McCurdy, Patrick Pierre
McCurdy, Richard Clark
McDade, Herbert Hardinge, Jr.
McDade, Joseph Michael
McDaniel, Boyce Dawkins
McDaniel, Joseph Milton, Jr.
McDaniel, William Earl
McDarrah, Fred William
McDermott, Albert Leo
McDermott, Edward Aloysious
McDermott, Gerald Edward
McDermott, John Joseph
McDermott, Robert Emmet
McDermott, Thomas Joseph
McDermott, Walsh
McDermott, William C(offman)
McDermott, William Vincent, Jr.
McDevitt, Gerald Vincent
McDevitt, John William
McDevitt, Vincent Paul
McDonald, Alonzo Lowry
McDonald, Edwin Anderson
McDonald, Frank Bethune
McDonald, John Peter
McDonald, Joseph Anthony
Mc Donald, Lawrence P.
McDonald, Miles Francis
McDonald, Robert Emmett
McDonald, William James
McDonell, Horace George, Jr.
McDonnell, Michael Thomas, Jr.
Mc Donough, Joseph Corbett
McDonough, Mathias John
McDonough, Robert Paul
McDonough, Roger Henry
McDowall, Roddy
McDowell, Edwin Stewart
McDowell, Fletcher Hughes
McDowell, John Herbert
McDowell, John Nelson
McDowell, Putnam Ballou
McDuffie, George Eaddy, Jr.
McElhanney, Robert Gordon
McElhannon, Raymond Jackson
McElhinny, Wilson Dunbar
McElrath, Damian Edmund
McElrath, Richard Elsworth
McElroy, Dennis Lee
McElroy, Joseph L.
McElroy, Joseph Prince
McElroy, Randolph Williams
McElroy, William Theodore
McElwaine, Robert Marshall
Mc Elwee, John Gerard
McEntee, Kenneth
McEnteer, Ben
McEvilla, Joseph David
McEwen, James Leonard
McEwen, Robert Cameron
McEwen, William Edwin
McEwen, William Peter
McFadden, James Patrick
Mc Fadden, Mary Josephine
McFadden, Peter William
McFadden, Thomas Joseph
McFall, Russell Whitney
McFarlan, Ronald Lyman
McFarland, Alex Jonathan
McFarland, Carl
McFarland, James Henry, Jr.
McFarland, Marvin Wilks
McFeatters, Dale Stitt
McFeely, William Shield
McGann, John Raymond
McGannon, Donald Henry
McGarrah, Robert Eynon
McGarry, Frederick Jerome
McGarry, Patrick Stephen
McGarvey, Elsie Siratz (Mrs. James P. McGarvey)
McGary, Carroll Rodney
McGaughan, Alexander Stanley
Mc Gaughy, John Bell
McGavern, John Howard
McGeady, Leon Joseph
McGeary, Martin Nelson
McGeary, Robert William
McGee, Gale
McGee, Thomas W.
McGehee, Benjamin Harris
McGehee, Carden Coleman
McGhee, George Crews
McGhee, Nancy Bullock (Mrs. Samuel C. McGhee)
McGhee, Robert Earl
McGiffert, David Eliot
Mc Giffert, John Rutherford
McGill, Arthur Chute
McGill, Dan Mays
McGill, Frank
McGill, Raymond Bruce
McGill, William James
McGillicuddy, John Francis
McGinley, Edward Francis
McGinley, Phyllis
McGinness, Arthur Francis, Jr.
McGinnis, Arthur Joseph
McGinnis, George S.
McGinnis, James Douglas
McGinnis, Thomas Charles
McGlinn, Frank Cresson Potts
McGlothlin, James Harrison
McGlynn, Joseph Leo, Jr.
McGoldrick, John Gardiner
McGovern, George Stanley
McGovern, John Joseph
McGovern, Joseph W.
McGovern, R. Gordon
McGowan, Carl
McGowan, Harold
McGowan, Harold Paul
McGrail, Richard P.
McGrath, Francis Joseph
McGrath, John Joseph
McGrath, Kyran Murray
McGrath, Lee Parr
McGrath, William Restore
McGraw, Donald Cushing, Jr.
McGraw, Harold Whittlesey, Jr.
McGraw, James Duane
McGraw, John Louis
McGraw, Walter John
McGraw, William Corbin
McGregor, Frank Rutherford
McGrillies, Mary Campbell
McGrory, Mary
Mc Gruder, Stephen Jones
McGuckin, James Frederick
McGuiness, William F.
McGuinness, Aims Chamberlain
McGuinness, William James
McGuire, Chester Crawford
McGuire, Dorothy Hackett
McGuire, Edward Perkins
McGuire, Harold Frederick
McGuire, John Richard
McGuire, Leslie Sarah
McGuire, Mrs. Marie C.
McGuire, William
McGuire, William
McGuire, William James
Mc Guire, William Lawrence
McGurn, Barrett
McGurn, John Martin
McHarg, Ian Lennox
McHenry, William Barnabas
McHose, Allen Irvine
McHugh, John Laurence
Mc Hugh, Matthew
Mc Hugh, Paul (Rodney)
McHugh, Simon Francis, Jr.
McIlhany, Sterling Fisher
McIlhenny, Henry Plumer
McIlhenny, James Harrison
McIlvaine, John Harmon, Jr.
McIlvaine, Robinson
McIlwain, William Franklin
McInerney, James Eugene, Jr.
McIninch, Ralph Aubrey
McInnes, William Charles
McIntire, Sumner Harmon
McIntosh, James Alexander
McIntyre, James Talmadge, Jr.
McIntyre, Jane O'Neill Mahady
McIntyre, Joseph George, Jr.
McIntyre, Oswald Ross
McIntyre, Thomas James
McIsaac, George Scott
McKain, Walter Cecil
McKay, Arthur Raymond
McKay, Dean Raymond
McKay, Jim
McKay, Kenneth Gardiner
McKay, Robert Budge
McKay, Robert James, Jr.
McKay, Vernon
McKeachie, William Eugene
McKean, Gordon William
McKean, Roland Neely
Mc Kechnie, Donna Ruth
McKee, Frank Wray
McKee, Gordon Norfolk, Jr.
McKee, Henry Hunt
McKee, James, Jr.
McKee, James Wilson, Jr.
McKee, Joseph Vincent, Jr.
McKee, Kinnaird Rowe
McKee, Madison Dryden, Jr.
McKee, William F.
McKeefery, William J.
McKeel, Sam Stewart
McKeever, Porter
McKelvey, Jean Trepp
McKelvey, John Jay, Jr.
McKelvey, Vincent Ellis
McKenna, Alex George
Mc Kenna, F(rancis) E(ugene)
McKenna, Hugh Franklin
McKenna, James Aloysius, Jr.
McKenna, James Edward
McKenna, Malcolm Carnegie
McKennan, Robert Addison
McKenney, David Dearborn
McKenney, Walter Gibbs, Jr.
McKenzie, George Kenneth
McKenzie, John Fitzgerald
McKenzie, Lionel Wilfred
McKeon, Newton Felch
McKeough, Richard Blair
McKeown, William Taylor
McKersie, Robert Bruce
McKhann, Charles Fremont
McKhann, Guy Mead
McKiernan, John Sammon
McKillop, David Holmes
McKillop, Lucille
McKim, Paul Arthur
McKinley, David Hopwood
McKinley, Douglas Webster
McKinley, Gordon Wells
McKinley, John Key
McKinley, Theodore David
McKinley, William A.
McKinney, Donald Lee
McKinney, George Wesley, Jr.
McKinney, Peter Starkweather
McKinney, Robert Hurley
McKinney, Robert Moody
McKinney, Stewart B.
McKinney, Theophilus Elisha, Jr.
McKinnon, Alan Leo
McKitrick, Eric Louis
McKnew, Thomas Willson
McKnight, John Lacy
McKusick, Victor Almon
McKusick, Vincent Lee
McLafferty, Fred Warren
McLain, John Howard
Mc Lain, Joseph Howard
McLanathan, Richard Barton Kennedy
McLane, John Roy, Jr.
McLaren, Malcolm Grant, IV
McLaughlin, Edward Francis, Jr.
McLaughlin, Emily
McLaughlin, Francis
McLaughlin, John D.
McLaughlin, John Patrick, Jr.
McLaughlin, Kathleen
McLaughlin, Peter Joseph
McLaughlin, Robert Allen
McLaughlin, Robert William
Mc Laughlin, William Henry, Jr.
McLean, Don
McLean, Vincent Ronald
McLean, William Henry
Mc Lean, William L., III
McLendon, John Aycock
McLennan, James Alan, Jr.
McLennan, William Edward
McLeod, John Wishart
McLoughlin, Ellen Veronica
McLoughlin, William G.
McLucas, John Luther
McLure, Charles E., Jr.
Mc Mahon, Charles Joseph, Jr.
McMahon, Ernest Edward
McMahon, George Joseph
McMahon, Gerald J.
McMahon, John Francis
McManaway, James Gilmer
McMann, Renville Hupfel, Jr.
McManus, Charles Anthony, Jr.
McManus, Charles Edward, Jr.
McManus, John Francis, III
Mc Manus, William J.
Mc Menamy, Edward L.
McMennamin, George Barry
McMillan, Brockway
McMillan, Charles William
McMillan, Daniel Alexander, III
McMillan, Kenneth
McMillen, Alan Bourne
McMillen, Eleanor Eva
McMillen, Louis Albert
McMillen, Russell Gross
McMillen, Wheeler
McMullan, Dorothy
McMullen, Albert J.
McMullen, John Joseph
McMurray, Joseph Patrick Brendan
McMurray, Kay
Mc Murray, Robert
Mc Nab, Maxwell Douglas
McNabb, Frederick William, Jr.
McNair, Malcolm Perrine
McNally, Arthur Jerome
McNally, Frank J.
McNally, James Ferguson
McNally, Terrence
Mc Namara, Francis Joseph, Jr.
McNamara, Francis Terry
McNamara, J(ohn) Donald
McNamara, Joseph Patrick
McNamara, Paul James
McNamara, Rieman, Jr.
McNamara, Robert Strange
McNamee, Bernard Joseph
McNamee, Daniel V., Jr.
McNaughton, Robert Forbes, Jr.
McNaughton, William Hugh
McNeice, John Ambrose, Jr.
McNeil, Clarid F.
McNeil, Claudia Mae
McNeil, George Joseph
McNeil, Gomer Thomas
McNeil, Henry Slack
McNeil, Marshall
McNeil, Neil Venable
McNeil, Robert Lincoln, Jr.
McNeill, Andrew John
McNeill, Charles James
McNeill, Corbin Asahel
McNeill, Robert Eugene
McNeill, Robert L.
McNeily, Peter William G.
McNerney, Chester Thomas
McNew, George Lee
McNicol, Donald Edward
McNiff, Phillip James
McNulty, Albert Joseph
Mc Nulty, Carrell Stewart, Jr.
McNulty, James Joseph
McNulty, John Bard
McNulty, Kneeland
McPeake, Thomas Everett
McPhee, Henry Roemer
McPhee, John Angus
McPherson, Harry Cummings, Jr.
McPherson, James Munro
McPherson, John Barkley
McPherson, William Alexander
McQuade, Henry Ford
Mc Quade, Walter
McQuary, Joan Susan
Mc Queen, Robert Charles
Mc Queeney, Henry Martin, Sr.
McQuilkin, William Winters
Mc Quillan, Margaret Mary
McQuinn, William Patrick
McRae, Dee (Dorothy Sue)
McRae, Thomas Kenneth
McRoberts, Robert Arthur
McShea, Joseph
McSorley, Arthur
McSpadden, Peter Ford
McSurdy, Elmer Brazier
McSweeney, Edward
McSweeney, John Daniel
McTaggart, Lynne Ann
McVay, Donald C., Jr.
McVicker, Charles Taggart
McVie, Thomas Ballantyne
McVoy, James David
McWhorter, Alan Louis
McWilliams, Carey
McWilliams, John Wesley
McWilliams, William James
Meacham, William Shands
Mead, Edward Jairus
Mead, Frank Spencer
Mead, Jeremiah
Mead, John Milton
Mead, Margaret
Mead, Wayland McCon
Meade, Edwin Baylies
Meade, Everard Kidder, Jr.
Meade, Gordon Montgomery
Meade, Henry Joseph
Meade, Julia
Meade, Richard Andrew
Meade, Robert Heber
Meade, Walter Wathen
Meader, Ralph Gibson
Meader, Stephen Warren
Meadmore, Clement Lyon
Meador, Daniel John
Meadow, Lynne (Carolyn) Elizabeth
Meadows, Audrey
Meadows, Clyde W.
Meadows, Paul
Meads, Donald Edward
Meagher, Brendan John
Meagher, Mark Joseph
Meagher, William R.
Meakin, John David
Meanor, H. Curtis
Means, David Hammond
Means, Marianne Hansen
Meany, Edmond Stephen, Jr.
Meany, George
Meara, Anne
Mears, Walter Robert
Mebane, William Black
Meck, John Foster
Meckling, William Howard
Medalie, Richard James
Medearis, Donald Norman, Jr.
Medeiros, Humberto Sousa
Meder, Albert Eugene, Jr.
Medhus, Sigurd Duane
Medici, Paul Thomas
Medina, Harold R.
Medina, Kathryn Bach
Medina, William A.
Meditz, Walter Joseph
Medley, Kenneth Wayne
Mednis, Edmar John
Medvecky, Robert Stephen
Meehan, Thomas Edward
Meek, Frederick Mayer
Meek, Peter Gray
Meek, Samuel Williams
Meeker, David Olan, Jr.
Meeker, Leonard Carpenter
Meeker, Thomas George
Meell, Edward Joseph
Meem, James Lawrence, Jr.
Meerkamper, Beat
Megan, Thomas Ignatius
Meggers, Betty J(ane)
Meggitt, Mervyn John
Mehegan, John Francis
Mehle, Roger William
Mehlman, Frederick Gordon
Mehos, Charles Arthur
Mehring, Howard William
Mehrtens, Paul Henry
Mehta, Zubin
Meier, David Edward
Meier, Gerhard J.
Meier, Johann Hans
Meier, John Henry
Meier, Richard Alan
Meijer, Paul Herman Ernst
Meikle, Thomas Harry, Jr.
Meiklejohn, David Shirra
Meiklejohn, Donald
Meinecke, Willard Henry
Meinkoth, Norman August
Meinwald, Jerrold
Meirovitch, Leonard
Meisch, Adrien Ferdinand Joseph
Meiselman, David Israel
Meisels, Joseph Frederick
Meiser, Sister Mary Adele
Meiser, Robert Newman
Meislich, Herbert
Meislin, Bernard Joshua
Meissner, Herman Paul
Meissner, William Walter
Meister, Alton
Meites, Louis
Mekeel, Herbert Surface
Melady, Thomas Patrick
Melaugh, Edward Gerard
Melby, Edward Carlos, Jr.
Melcher, Daniel
Melcher, George W., Jr.
Melcher, James Russell
Melcher, John
Melchert, James Frederick
Melervey, Arthur Charles
Melfe, Thomas Andrew
Melfi, Leonard Anthony
Melis, Francis Kenneth
Melissinos, Adrian Constantin
Mellam, Leo Leslie
Mellink, Machteld Johanna
Mellis, Joel Paul
Mellman, William Jules
Mellon, Paul
Mellon, Richard Prosser
Mellon, Seward Prosser
Mellor, George Lincoln
Mellors, Robert Charles
Mellow, James Robert
Melman, Seymour
Melniker, Benjamin
Melone, Joseph James
Meloy, John Calvin, III
Melrose, Alice Gunhild
Melson, Robert Henry
Meltzer, Allan Harold
Meltzer, Donald Richard
Meltzer, Doris
Meltzer, Jay H.
Meltzer, Leon
Meltzer, Milton
Melville, Donald Burton
Melville, Donald Robert
Melville, Robert Seaman
Melville, William Robert
Melvin, Mael Avramy
Melvin, Norman Cecil
Menard, Henry William, Jr.
Menard, Wilfred Charles, Jr.
Mencher, Bruce Stephan
Mencher, Ely
Mencher, Melvin
Mencke, John Bernhard
Mende, Robert Graham
Mendeloff, Albert Irwin
Mendels, Joseph
Mendelsohn, Everett Irwin
Mendelsohn, Robert H.
Mendelsohn, Walter
Mendelson, Burton Gershon
Mendelson, Elliott
Mendelson, Michael
Menees, Timothy Ryan
Menegus, Alfred Aurelius
Menen, Aubrey (Salvator Aubrey Clarence Menon)
Meng, John Joseph
Menger, Carl S.
Menguy, Rene
Menihan, John Conway
Menkart, John
Menke, George Herman
Menkes, Joshua
Menkes, Sigmund Josef
Mennin, Peter
Menotti, Gian Carlo
Menter, Sanford
Menzies, Ian Stuart
Merahn, Lawrence Wilburn
Mercer, Charles
Mercer, Marian
Mercer, Samuel, Jr.
Mercer, William Crawford
Mercouri, Melina (Maria Amalia)
Mercure, Alex P.
Meredith, Charles Eymard
Meredith, Hugh Stockdell
Meredith, Lewis Douglas
Meredith, Morley
Meredith, Scott
Meredith, William (Morris)
Mereness, Dorothy Ann
Mergen, Francois
Mergentime, Bernard Charles
Merhige, Robert Reynold, Jr.
Meriwether, W. Delano
Merk, Frederick
Merker, Frank Ferdinand
Merkl, Neil Matthew
Merkle, Edward Arrol
Merkling, Frank
Merman, Ethel
Mermel, Thaddeus Walter
Mermelstein, Milton E.
Merriam, Eve
Merriam, William Rush
Merrick, David (David Margulies)
Merrick, Robert Graff
Merrifield, Philip Ralph
Merrifield, Robert Bruce
Merrill, Ambrose Pond, Jr.
Merrill, Arthur Alexander
Merrill, Bob
Merrill, Dina (Mrs. Cliff Robertson)
Merrill, Edward Clifton, Jr.
Merrill, Edward Wilson
Merrill, Ezra
Merrill, James
Merrill, James Mercer
Merrill, Jean Fairbanks
Merrill, Joseph Hartwell
Merrill, Leland Gilbert, Jr.
Merrill, Oliver Boutwell
Merrill, Philip
Merrill, Robert
Merrill, Walter McIntosh
Merriman, Daniel
Merritt, Hiram Houston
Merritt, James Harmer
Merritt, Paul Eugene
Merritt, Schuyler, II
Merritt, Stanley S.
Merriwether, Duncan
Merry, Eugene Webster
Mersheimer, Walter Lyon
Merskey, Clarence
Merton, Robert K.
Merwin, Charles Lewis
Merwin, Horace
Merwin, William Stanley
Mescon, Herbert
Meselson, Matthew Stanley
Meserve, Robert William
Mesirov, Leon I.
Meskill, Thomas J.
Meskill, Victor Peter
Mesrobian, Arpena Sachaklian
Messemer, George J.
Messenkopf, Eugene John
Messer, Thomas M.
Messerli, Jonathan Carl
Messing, Gordon Myron
Messner, Robert Thomas
Mesthene, Emmanuel George
Mestres, Ricardo Angelo
Metcalf, Arthur George Bradford
Metcalf, Charles William
Metcalf, George Forrest
Metcalf, Keyes DeWitt
Metcalf, Lee
Metcalf, Michael Pierce
Metcalf, Stanley Warren
Metcalf, William Henry, Jr.
Metcalfe, Ralph H.
Metrakos, Robert Arthur
Metraux, Rhoda
Metter, Bertram Milton
Mettler, Frederick Albert
Metz, George Harold
Metz, George William
Metz, John A.
Metz, Robert Roy
Metzger, Bruce Manning
Metzger, Samuel
Metzger, Walter Paul
Metzler, Owen Eugene
Metzner, A.W. Kenneth
Metzner, Arthur Berthold
Metzner, Charles Miller
Meyer, Albert Julius
Meyer, Andre
Meyer, Armin Henry
Meyer, Arthur B.
Meyer, Ben Franklin
Meyer, Carl Edwin, Jr.
Meyer, Cyril F.
Meyer, Donald Burton
Meyer, Edward Henry
Meyer, Eugene Bown
Meyer, Harry M., Jr.
Meyer, Helen (Mrs. Abraham J. Meyer)
Meyer, Hugo Bardill
Meyer, John M., Jr.
Meyer, John Robert
Meyer, Karl
Meyer, Leonard B.
Meyer, Malcolm
Meyer, Maurice, Jr.
Meyer, Rabban
Meyer, Robert Haldeman
Meyer, Sheldon
Meyer, Susan E.
Meyer, Ursula
Meyer, Walter Frederick
Meyer, Wayne Eugene
Meyerhoff, Joseph
Meyerowitz, William
Meyers, Dale (Mrs. Mario Cooper)
Meyers, Edward
Meyers, Howard
Meyers, John Allen
Meyers, Marvin
Meyers, Michael (Ozzie)
Meyerson, Martin
Meyner, Helen Stevenson
Meyner, Robert Baumle
Meyvaert, Paul Jeffrey
Michael, Henry N.
Michael, Sherwood Albert
Michael, William Herbert, Jr.
Michaelis, Frederick Hayes
Michaelis, Michael
Michaelis, Paul Charles
Michaels, David Dory
Michaels, James Walker
Michaels, Lorne
Michaelsen, Edward Hugo
Michaelson, Charles Donald
Michaelson, Julius C.
Michalis, Clarence Fahnestock
Michalos, James
Michals, Duane Steven
Michanowsky, George
Michejda, Oskar
Michel, Aloys Arthur
Michel, Kenneth George
Michelman, Herbert
Michels, Eugene
Michelson, Edward J.
Michelson, Max, Jr.
Michener, Charles Thomson
Michener, James Albert
Michtom, Benjamin Franklin
Mickel, Ernest Preston
Mickelson, Sig
Mickle, David Grant
Mickley, Harold Somers
Middendorf, John Harlan
Middlebrook, Robert Ward
Middlebrook, Stephen Beach
Middlebrooks, Evann, Jr.
Middleton, Donald Earl
Middleton, Drew
Middleton, John Tylor
Middleton, Robert

Mider, George Burroughs
Midgley, Leslie
Miele, Alfonse Ralph
Miele, Ralph, Jr.
Migeon, Claude Jean
Miklozek, Frank Louis
Mikulka, Charles
Mikulski, Barbara Ann
Mikulsky, Joan Marilyn
Milano, Robert John
Milbank, Jeremiah
Milbrath, Robert Henry
Milburn, Richard Henry
Milch, Harold Carlton
Miles, Jeanne Patterson
Miles, Kenneth (Penie)
Miles, Leland Weber
Miles, Rufus Edward, Jr.
Miles, Virginia
Milgrom, Felix
Milhorat, Ade Thomas
Milhorat, Thomas Herrick
Millar, Jack William
Millard, Charles E. F.
Millard, George Richard
Millard, Mark Jacob
Miller, A. Edward
Miller, Alan B.
Miller, Albert Howard
Miller, Albert Jay
Miller, Andrew Pickens
Miller, Angela Jean
Miller, Arnold Ray
Miller, Arthur
Miller, Arthur Raphael
Miller, Carroll Lee Liverpool
Miller, Charles Leslie
Miller, Charles O.
Miller, Clarence E.
Miller, Clemmy Olin
Miller, David
Miller, David Philip
Miller, D(avid) Thomas
Miller, David Vern
Miller, DeWitt L.
Miller, Donald Baldwin
Miller, Donald Herbert, Jr.
Miller, Donald Lang
Miller, Donald Peter
Miller, Donald Spencer
Miller, E. Willard
Miller, Edward August
Miller, Edward Kirkbride
Miller, Edward Stanley
Miller, Emanuel
Miller, Foil Allan
Miller, Francena Lounsbery Nolan
Miller, Francis Don
Miller, Frederick Robeson
Miller, George Armitage
Miller, G(eorge) William
Miller, Glen Barkalow, Jr.
Miller, Harbaugh
Miller, Harold
Miller, Harold Blaine
Miller, Harold Joseph
Miller, Harold T.
Miller, Harriet Evelyn
Miller, Hasbrouck Bailey
Miller, Helena Agnes
Miller, Henry Knight
Miller, Henry Louis
Miller, Herbert John
Miller, Herbert John, Jr.
Miller, Hope Ridings Miller
Miller, Irma Ganz
Miller, Israel
Miller, Jack Richard
Miller, James Albert, Jr.
Miller, James Elwood
Miller, James Francis
Miller, J(ames) Gormly
Miller, James Jay
Miller, James Lowry
Miller, James Monroe
Miller, James Rogers, Jr.
Miller, James Roland
Miller, James Wilkinson
Miller, Jane Beachy
Miller, Jason
Miller, Joan Vita
Miller, John Adalbert
Miller, John Albert
Miller, John Francis
Miller, John George
Miller, John Harrison
Miller, John Haynes
Miller, John Homer
Miller, John L.
Miller, John Perry
Miller, John Richard
Miller, John Robinson, Jr.
Miller, John Wade, Jr.
Miller, Jordan Yale
Miller, Joseph Frank
Miller, Joseph Hillis
Miller, Lambert H.
Miller, Lester Frederick
Miller, Linda B.
Miller, Linda Kay
Miller, Loye Wheat, Jr.
Miller, Marvin Julian
Miller, Mary Owings
Miller, Merle
Miller, Michael Shaffer
Miller, Mildred
Miller, Mitch(ell William)
Miller, Morton David
Miller, Nathan
Miller, Neal Elgar
Miller, Newton Edd, Jr.
Miller, Norman Charles, Jr.
Miller, Norman Richard
Miller, Orlando Jack
Miller, Paul

Miller, Paul A.
Miller, Paul Ausborn
Miller, Paul Fetterolf, Jr.
Miller, Paul George
Miller, Paul Lukens
Miller, Philip Lieson
Miller, Philip R.
Miller, Randolph Crump
Miller, Raymond Louis
Miller, Raymond Wiley
Miller, Rene Harcourt
Miller, Reuben George
Miller, Richard Irwin
Miller, Richard McDermott
Miller, Robert
Miller, Robert
Miller, Robert Demorest
Miller, Robert Harvey
Miller, Robert Martin
Miller, Robert Wiley
Miller, Ruby Sills (Mrs. Glenn K. Miller)
Miller, Samuel Clifford
Miller, Saul
Miller, S(eymour) M(ichael)
Miller, Sidney
Miller, Stanley R.
Miller, Stewart Edward
Miller, Theodore Robert
Miller, Thomas Hulbert, Jr.
Miller, Thomas Robert
Miller, Vernon Xavier
Miller, Walter Neal
Miller, Walter Richard
Miller, William Christian
Miller, William Robert
Miller, William Taylor
Millett, John David
Millett, Katherine Murray (Kate)
Millhiser, Ross R.
Milligan, Glenn Ellis
Milliken, Frank Roscoe
Millikin, John Harriman
Millimet, Joseph Allen
Millman, Herbert
Millman, Jacob
Millon, Henry Armand
Millon, René
Millonzi, Robert I.
Mills, Bradford
Mills, David Harlow
Mills, Edwin Smith
Mills, Eugene Sumner
Mills, Gordon T.
Mills, Hawthorne Quinn
Mills, James Spencer
Mills, Paul Swinton
Mills, Raymond Edwin
Mills, Robert Hugh
Mills, Theodore Mason
Mills, Willis Nathaniel, Jr.
Milman, Doris Hope
Milne, Lorus Johnson
Milnes, Arthur George
Milnes, Sherrill Eustace
Milsom, Robert Cortlandt
Milstein, Milton
Milstein, Nathan
Miltimore, Louis Demarest
Milton, Arthur Gregory
Milton, Peter Winslow
Minahan, Daniel Francis
Minch, John Joseph
Mindlin, Raymond David
Miner, Harold Sheldon
Miner, Robert Gordon
Miner, Robert Graham
Miner, Ward Lester
Miner, Worthington C. (Tony)
Mineta, Norman Y.
Mingle, Frank Albright
Mingus, Charles
Minicus, Robert George
Minish, Joseph George
Mink, Louis Otto, Jr.
Mink, Patsy Takemoto
Minkoff, Jack
Minnelli, Liza
Minnich, John Harvey
Minor, Charles Venable
Minsky, Marvin Lee
Mintener, James Bradshaw
Minter, Philip Clayton
Minton, Dwight Church
Minton, Paul Dixon
Minton, Walter Joseph
Mintz, Bernard
Mintz, Morton Abner
Mintz, Sidney Wilfred
Mintz, Walter
Mintzes, Joseph
Mirabal, George Molina
Mirabella, Grace
Mirand, Edwin Albert
Mires, Maynard Harold, Jr.
Mirick, Henry Dustin
Mirken, Alan Bennett
Mirkin, Abraham Jonathan
Mirman, Irving R.
Mirsky, Jeannette
Mish, Charles Carroll
Mishler, Jacob
Mishoe, Luna Isaac
Mishtowt, George Illarion
Mislow, Kurt Martin
Misner, Charles William
Mitchell, Allan Gillette
Mitchell, Arthur
Mitchell, Broadus
Mitchell, Charles
Mitchell, Charles Stuart, Jr.
Mitchell, Clarence M., Jr.
Mitchell, David Ira
Mitchell, David W.
Mitchell, Donald J.

Mitchell, Ehrman Burkman, Jr.
Mitchell, Ellsworth Douglas
Mitchell, George John
Mitchell, George Washington, Jr.
Mitchell, George Wilder
Mitchell, Hamilton Barnes
Mitchell, Herbert Hall
Mitchell, Howard
Mitchell, James Free, Jr.
Mitchell, James Lowry, II
Mitchell, James Matlack
Mitchell, John Blair
Mitchell, John Fulton Berrien
Mitchell, John Murray, Jr.
Mitchell, John Newton
Mitchell, Joseph (Quincy)
Mitchell, Josephine Margaret (Mrs. Lowell Schoenfeld)
Mitchell, Loften
Mitchell, Lydell Douglas
Mitchell, Martha M.
Mitchell, Ormond Glenn
Mitchell, Parren James
Mitchell, Robert Dale
Mitchell, Robert Lynne
Mitchell, Robert Watson
Mitchell, William
Mitgang, Herbert
Mitnick, Samuel Alexander
Mitovich, John
Mittelman, Norman
Mittelstadt, Charles Anthony
Mittleman, Ann
Mittleman, Marvin Harold
Mitze, Clark H.
Mixon, Alan
Mixter, David Mason
Miyares, Benjamin David
Mizener, Arthur Moore
Mizrahi, Abraham Mordechay
Mizuki, Tai
Moakley, John Joseph
Mobraaten, William Lawrence
Moccia, Alfred John
Mock, Jesse Alexander, Jr.
Mock, Lawrence Edward
Mock, Robert Claude
Mockler, Colman Michael, Jr.
Modell, Stephen Irving
Modigliani, Franco
Modlin, George Matthews
Modlin, Philip Hodgin
Moe, Gordon Kenneth
Moe, Henry Allen
Moe, Richard
Moede, Austin Lyn
Moeller, Charles, Jr.
Moeller, Dade William
Moeller, Karl Dieter
Moeller, Robert Charles, III
Moevs, Robert Walter
Moffat, Jay P.
Moffett, Alfred Robert
Moffett, Anthony Toby
Moffett, Harry Lee
Moffett, James Davis
Moffett, Kenworth William
Moffett, William Earl
Moffitt, Charles William
Moffitt, George, Jr.
Moffo, Anna
Mogel, Leonard Henry
Mogey, John McFarland
Mohan, Robert Paul
Mohler, Daniel Nathan
Mohler, Harold Sheaffer
Mohler, Stanley Ross
Mohlie, Raymond Eugene
Mohn, Paul Eugene
Mohr, Henry
Mohr, Mel
Mohrhardt, Foster Edward
Mohun, Cecil Peabody
Moir, George Russell
Moise, Edwin Evariste
Moise, William Sidney
Molden, Herbert George
Molho, Emanuel
Molinaro, Albert Philip, Jr.
Moll, Clarence Russel
Moll, Lloyd Henry
Mollenhoff, Clark Raymond
Moller, Hans
Molleur, Richard Raymond
Mollison, Richard Devol
Mollman, John Peter
Mollo-Christensen, Erik Leonard
Molloy, Robert Thomas
Molnar, Thomas
Molowa, Albert Long
Molter, Nelson Joseph
Moltz, James Edward
Moment, Gairdner B(ostwick)
Monagan, John Stephen
Monaghan, Charles Andrew
Monaghan, Hugh Joseph, II
Monan, James Donald
Monasch, Burton I.
Monath, Norman
Mondale, Joan Adams
Mondale, Walter Frederick
Mondello, Anthony Louis
Money, John William
Mongan, Agnes
Mongerson, Paul Almon
Monk, Ivan
Monk, Julius Withers
Monk, Thelonious Sphere
Monks, Robert Augustus Gardner
Monrian, William Henry, Jr.
Monroe, Brooks
Monroe, James Harrison
Monroe, Robert Allan

Monroe, Robert Rawson
Monroe, Vernon Earl, Jr.
Monroney, Michael
Monsarrat, John
Monsen, George Richard
Montagu, Ashley
Montana, Patrick Joseph
Montean, John Joseph
Monteux, Claude
Montgomery, Charles William
Montgomery, David Campbell
Montgomery, Deane
Montgomery, Earl Edward
Montgomery, Edgar Roger
Montgomery, Harry Thomas
Montgomery, James Alan, Jr.
Montgomery, John Dickey
Montgomery, Merle Aline
Montgomery, Raymond Braislin
Montgomery, Robert
Montgomery, Ruth Shick
Montgomery, William Wayne
Montias, John Michael
Montoya, Carlos
Montroll, Elliott Waters
Montrone, Paul Michael
Moody, Raymond Avery, Jr.
Moody, Robert Earle
Moody, Roland Herbert
Moody, Tom Rush, Jr.
Moody, Whitson Jarvis
Moog, Robert Arthur
Moon, Eric Edward
Mooney, George Austin
Mooney, James Russell
Mooney, Robert Knapp
Moonie, Clyde Wickliffe
Moore, Acel
Moore, Albert Cunningham
Moore, Arthur Cotton
Moore, Arthur James
Moore, Asher
Moore, Barrington, Jr.
Moore, Bob Stahly
Moore, Brian
Moore, Bruce
Moore, Carman Leroy
Moore, Charles Ellet, Jr.
Moore, David Graham
Moore, Donald Banford
Moore, Dongan Reynolds
Moore, Edward Frederick
Moore, Elisabeth Luce
Moore, Ellis Oglesby
Moore, Eugene Bedford, Jr.
Moore, Francis Daniels
Moore, Frank
Moore, Frank Stanley
Moore, Garry
Moore, Gene Gabriel
Moore, Geoffrey Hoyt
Moore, George Bacon
Moore, George Mansfield
Moore, George Stevens
Moore, Harold Emery, Jr.
Moore, Harold R.
Moore, Howard Kimball
Moore, Howard Roswald, Jr.
Moore, James Mendon
Moore, James William
Moore, John Coleman
Moore, John Denis Joseph
Moore, John Joseph
Moore, John Lovell, Jr.
Moore, Jonathan
Moore, Leonard Page
Moore, Leslie
Moore, Maurice Thompson
Moore, Melba
Moore, Nonnie Eilers
Moore, Norman Slawson
Moore, Omar Khayyam
Moore, Paul, Jr.
Moore, Richard Allan
Moore, Richard Anthony
Moore, Richmond, Jr.
Moore, Robert Condit
Moore, Robert Edward
Moore, Robert Lowell, Jr. (Robin Moore)
Moore, Robert Stuart
Moore, Robert William
Moore, Roderick Dunn
Moore, Ronnie Malcolm
Moore, Stanford
Moore, Stephen Gates
Moore, Terris
Moore, Thomas Holmes
Moore, Thomas Justin, Jr.
Moore, Thomas Ronald
Moore, Thomas Waldrop
Moore, Warner Richard
Moore, William Henson, III
Moore, Withers McAlister
Moorefield, James Lee
Moores, Edward Harrison
Moorhead, Carlos J.
Moorhead, Paul Sidney
Moorhead, William Singer
Moorman, James W.
Moos, Eugene
Moose, Richard M.
Moot, Robert Clinton
Mora, Rafael Alberto
Morabito, Bruno Paul
Morales, Pablo Adriano
Moran, George Bernard
Moran, James D.
Moran, John Joseph
Moran, Joseph E.
Moran, Joseph Milbert
Moran, Joseph William
Moran, Juliette M.
Moran, Robert Daniel
Morani, Alma Dea

Morant, Ricardo Bernardino
Morath, Max Edward
Moraud, Marcel Ian
Morawetz, Herbert
Morck, Roland Anton
Mordell, Donald Louis
Mordwin, William
More, Douglas McLochlan
Morefield, Frederick Lawrence
Morehouse, Edward Lyman
Moreland, Allen Barwick
Moreland, Jesse Earl
Morell, William Nelson, Jr.
Moreno, Rita
Morey, James Newman
Morgan, Alfred Y.
Morgan, Bruce Ray
Morgan, Charles Hill
Morgan, Charles Sumner
Morgan, Donald Grant
Morgan, Edmund Sears
Morgan, Edward P.
Morgan, Edward Pierpont
Morgan, George Jefferson
Morgan, Herbert Roy
Morgan, John Davis, Jr.
Morgan, Joseph
Morgan, Joy Elmer
Morgan, Leon Alford
Morgan, Millett Granger
Morgan, Norma Gloria
Morgan, Perry Eugene
Morgan, Robert Arthur
Morgan, Robert Burren
Morgan, Roy Edward
Morgan, Russell Hedley
Morgan, Thomas Ellsworth
Morgan, William Francis
Morgello, Clemente Frank
Morgenstern, Marvin
Morgenthaler, Frederic Richard
Morgenthau, Hans Joachim
Morgenthau, Robert Morris
Morgenthau, Ruth Schachter
Moriarty, James William
Moriarty, Michael
Morice, Joseph Richard
Morie, Thomas Albert
Morin, Alexander Joseph
Morin, James Brendon
Morin, Patrick Joyce
Morini, Erica
Morison, Elting Elmore
Morison, Robert Swain
Moritz, Charles Fredric
Moritz, Charles Worthington
Moritz, Donald Irwin
Morley, Felix Muskett
Morley, Henry Barclay
Morley, Michael Darwin
Morley, Roger Hubert
Morone, James Anthony
Moroney, William Martin
Moross, Jerome
Morowitz, Harold Joseph
Morrell, Sydney
Morrill, Bernard
Morrill, William Ashley
Morris, Alvin Leonard
Morris, Andrew Jackson
Morris, Donald Richard
Morris, Edward Karrick
Morris, Edwin Thaddeus
Morris, Ernest Brougham
Morris, Eugene Jerome
Morris, Frank Eugene
Morris, Garrett
Morris, George Edmund
Morris, Grinnell
Morris, James Peppler
Morris, Janet Patricia
Morris, Jesse Carr, Jr.
Morris, John Albert
Morris, John Barton
Morris, John Milton
Morris, John Woodland
Morris, Kelso Bronson
Morris, Kenneth Baker
Morris, Kyle Randolph
Morris, Logan
Morris, Mac Glenn
Morris, Mary Elizabeth
Morris, Max King
Morris, Raymond Philip
Morris, Richard Brandon
Morris, Robert
Morris, Robert
Morris, Robert Eastin
Morris, Walter A., Jr.
Morris, William
Morris, Willie
Morrisett, Lloyd N.
Morrison, Ashton Byrom
Morrison, Bayard Hunter, III
Morrison, Chloe Anthony (Aka Toni Morrison)
Morrison, George Harold
Morrison, George Leroy, Jr.
Morrison, Hugh Sinclair
Morrison, Jack Sherman
Morrison, James Carleton
Morrison, Joseph Paul Eldred
Morrison, M. Jan
Morrison, Manley Glenn
Morrison, Martin Earl
Morrison, Orville C.
Morrison, Theodore
Morrison, Thomas Watson
Morrissey, Charles David
Morrissey, Leonard Eugene, Jr.
Morrissey, Thomas Leo
Morrow, Andrew Glenn
Morrow, David Warren
Morrow, Donald Anthony
Morrow, E. Frederic

Morrow, Hugh
Morrow, John Howard
Morrow, Joyce Knoedler
Morrow, Paul Edward
Morrow, Winston Vaughan
Morse, David A.
Morse, Edmond Northrop
Morse, Ellsworth Harry, Jr.
Morse, F. Bradford
Morse, Harold Marston
Morse, John Harleigh
Morse, Joseph
Morse, Philip McCord
Morse, Richard Hart
Morse, Richard McGee
Morse, Richard Stetson
Morse, Robert Alan
Morse, Robert Warren
Morss, Sherman
Mortensen, James E.
Mortensen, William Henry
Mortenson, Kenneth Ernest
Mortimer, John H.
Mortola, Edward Joseph
Morton, Azie Taylor
Morton, Charles Bruce, II
Morton, Donald John
Morton, Edward James
Morton, Frederic
Morton, Harry Edward
Morton, Herbert Charles
Morton, Jay Robert
Morton, John Henderson
Morton, Marcus
Morton, Richard Freeman
Morton, Rogers Clark Ballard
Morton, William Gilbert
Morton, William Hanson
Mosbacher, Emil, Jr.
Mosby, Henry Sackett
Mosconi, Willie (William Joseph)
Moscow, Warren
Mosel, Tad
Moseley, Carlos DuPre
Moseley, Clark Irving
Moseley, Edwin M.
Moseley, Frederick Strong, III
Moseley, Herbert Clifton
Moseley, William Brewster
Moser, Hugo Wolfgang
Moser, Marvin
Moser, Richard Goodwin
Moser, Robert Harlan
Moses, Harlan Taft
Moses, Robert
Moses, Robert Davis
Moses, William Bryan, Jr.
Mosettig, Michael David
Mosher, Frederick Camp
Mosher, Giles Edmund, Jr.
Mosher, Sol
Moskin, John Robert
Moskovitz, Irving
Moskowitz, Sam (Sam Martin)
Mosler, John
Mosley, John Brooke, Jr.
Mosmiller, Joseph William
Moss, Arnold
Moss, Charles
Moss, Geoffrey
Moss, Howard
Moss, Ira Lloyd
Moss, Joe Francis
Moss, John Hall
Moss, Lawrence Kenneth
Moss, Melvin Lionel
Moss, N. Henry
Moss, Robert Adams
Moss, Ronald Jay
Mosso, David Lyle
Most, Harry
Most, Nathan
Mostad, William
Mostel, Zero
Mosteller, Frederick
Mostow, George Daniel
Moszynski, Jerzy Robert
Motherway, Joseph Edward
Motherwell, Robert
Mott, Gilbert Culver
Mott, Stewart Rawlings
Mott, Thomas Hezekiah, Jr.
Mott, William Chamberlain
Motta, John Richard
Motter, David Calvin
Mottl, Ronald Milton
Motz, Lloyd
Moulton, Barbara
Moulton, Horace Platt
Moulton, James Malcolm
Moulton, William Gamwell
Moultrie, Fred
Moultrie, H. Carl
Mount, Ward
Mountain, Worrall Frederick
Mountcastle, Katharine Babcock
Mountcastle, Vernon Benjamin, Jr.
Mower, Lyman
Mowitz, Robert James
Moxon, John
Moy, Seong
Moyer, Gordon Van Zandt
Moyer, Ira
Moyer, Kenneth Evan
Moyers, Bill D.
Moyles, William Philip
Moynahan, Julian Lane
Moynihan, Daniel Patrick
Moynihan, James Francis
Moynihan, William Trumbull
Mozdzer, Henry Anthony
Mrdeza, George Edward
Mrowka, Stanislaw Grzegorz

Muan, Arnulf
Muckenhoupt, Benjamin
Mudd, Emily Hartshorne
Mudd, Roger Harrison
Mudd, Sidney P.
Muddle, Frank Lord
Muehl, Ernest William
Muelder, Walter George
Mueller, Carl Muth
Mueller, Gerhard Otto Walter
Mueller, Hugo Johannes
Mueller, Paul Henry
Mueller, Robert Kirk
Mueller, Ronald A.H.
Mueller, William Randolph
Muench, John
Mues, Edward Frederick, Jr.
Mueser, William Henry
Mugar, John Martin
Mugavero, Francis J.
Muhlenberg, Frederick Augustus
Muhlfeld, Frank Bearss
Muir, Emily Lansingh (Mrs. William H. Muir)
Muir, Gloria Ludwig
Muir, John Dapray
Muir, Malcolm
Muir, Warren R.
Muirhead, Peter Parker
Mulcahy, Edward William
Mulcahy, Robert Edward
Muldowney, Joseph John
Mulhearn, John Robert
Mulhern, Francis James
Mulholland, James Sylvester, Jr.
Mulholland, Robert E.
Mull, Martin
Mullan, James Boyd
Mullane, Denis Francis
Mullaney, Joseph E.
Mullen, Buell (Mrs. J. Bernard Mullen)
Mullen, James Hanna
Mullen, Maralin Niska
Mullen, Richard Leslie
Muller, Frank B.
Muller, John H.
Muller, Julian Pershing
Muller, Leonard Arthur
Muller, Robert Sielke
Müller, Ronald Ernst
Muller, Steven
Muller, William Henry, Jr.
Mullestein, William Ernest
Mulligan, Gerald Joseph (Gerry)
Mulligan, James Kenneth
Mulligan, John Joseph
Mulligan, Joseph Francis
Mulligan, Richard
Mulligan, William G.
Mulligan, William Hughes
Mullin, Charles Samuel
Mullin, Mark Joseph
Mullin, Roger William, Jr.
Mullinix, Edward Wingate
Mullins, John Madison
Mullins, Lorin John
Mullins, William Wilson
Mulreany, Robert H.
Mulrooney, Charles Richard
Mulroy, Joseph William
Multer, Abraham J.
Multhauf, Robert Phillip
Mulvey, William W.
Mumaw, John Rudy
Mumford, David Bryant
Mumford, George Saltonstall, Jr.
Mumford, L. Quincy
Mumford, Lewis
Mumford, Milton Christopher
Mumford, William Walden
Mumma, Albert G.
Mumma, Richard Allen
Munck, Allan Ulf
Muncy, Lysbeth Walker
Mund, Vernon Arthur
Mundell, Robert Alexander
Mundheim, Robert Harry
Mundt, Ray B.
Mundy, Edwin Francis
Mundy, John Hine
Munford, Howard McCoy
Munger, Martin Darwin
Munitz, Milton Karl
Munkenbeck, Alfred Hedges, Jr.
Munn, Bruce Watson
Munn, Stephen P.
Munro, Hamish Nisbet
Munro, Joseph Alfred
Munroe, George Barber
Munroe, John Andrew
Munroe, Marshall Evans
Munroe, Pat
Munsat, Theodore Leon
Munsell, Albert Lowell
Munson, Frank William
Munson, Halsey James, IV
Munson, Harold Lewis
Munson, Howard G.
Munson, Lawrence Shipley
Munson, Thurman Lee
Munson, Townsend
Munsterberg, Hugo
Munte, Hans Herbert
Munves, William
Mur, Raphael
Murayama, Makio
Murbach, J. Frederick
Murchie, Guy
Murchison, David Claudius
Murden, Forrest Dozier
Murdoch, Joseph Bert
Murdoch, Keith Rupert
Murdoch, Wallace Pierce
Murdock, William Orrice
Murnane, George, Jr.
Murphy, Albert Thomas, Jr.
Murphy, Anne Marie
Murphy, Arthur Richard, Jr.
Murphy, Arthur William
Murphy, Austin de la Salle
Murphy, Austin John
Murphy, Betty Jane Southard (Mrs. Cornelius F. Murphy)
Murphy, C. Gordon
Murphy, Charles S.
Murphy, Daniel Joseph
Murphy, Edward Francis
Murphy, Eugene Francis
Murphy, Francis
Murphy, Gardner
Murphy, George Arthur
Murphy, George Edward
Murphy, Geraldine Joanne
Murphy, Grayson Mallet-Prevost
Murphy, Hugh Cornelius
Murphy, J. Hugh
Murphy, James Russell
Murphy, James Sherman
Murphy, John Damian
Murphy, John Francis
Murphy, John Henry, III
Murphy, John Joseph
Murphy, John Joseph
Murphy, John Michael
Murphy, Joseph F.
Murphy, Joseph S.
Murphy, Joseph Stephen
Murphy, Morgan Francis
Murphy, Patrick Vincent
Murphy, Raymond John
Murphy, Robert Daniel
Murphy, Robert Francis
Murphy, Robert Francis
Murphy, Rosemary
Murphy, Royse Peak
Murphy, Thomas Austin
Murphy, Thomas Francis
Murphy, Thomas Francis
Murphy, Thomas John
Murphy, Thomas S.
Murphy, Tom
Murphy, Walter Francis
Murphy, William Beverly
Murphy, William Joseph
Murphy, William Parry
Murr, Brown Lewis, Jr.
Murra, John Victor
Murray, Albert L.
Murray, Allen Edward
Murray, Andrew Evans
Murray, David
Murray, Donald M.
Murray, Edward Stevenson
Murray, Francis Wisner, III
Murray, Frank Jerome
Murray, George Francis
Murray, Gordon Louis
Murray, Henry Alexander
Murray, Herbert Frazier
Murray, J. Elliston
Murray, J. Ralph
Murray, James Joseph, III
Murray, James Patrick
Murray, James Walker
Murray, Joan Elizabeth
Murray, John Einar
Murray, Joseph Edward
Murray, Martin Leo
Murray, Paul Brady
Murray, Pauli
Murray, Peg
Murray, Peter Ross
Murray, Raymond Carl
Murray, Richard Maximilian
Murray, Robert Bruce
Murray, Robert Fulton, Jr.
Murray, Robert Gray
Murray, Robert Keith
Murray, Roger Franklin
Murray, Russell, II
Murray, Thomas Francis
Murray, Thomas Joseph
Murray, Wallace Shordon
Murrin, Thomas Edward
Murrin, Thomas Joseph
Murtagh, Frederick, Jr.
Murtha, John Patrick
Murtha, John Stephen
Musburger, Brent Woody
Muscarelle, Joseph Louis, Jr.
Muschel, Louis Henry
Muschenheim, Carl
Muscio, Umberto Vincent
Muse, Leonard Gaston
Muse, Martha Twitchell
Muse, Thomas Calvert
Musgrave, Richard Abel
Musgrave, Ross Howard
Musgrave, Stanley Dean
Musham, William Charles
Mushett, Charles W.
Mushlin, Harry Ralph
Muskie, Edmund Sixtus
Muss, Joshua Alan
Mussenden, William Frederick
Musser, Warren VanDyke
Mustille, Anthony Nicholas
Mutch, Thomas Andrew
Muth, George Edward
Muth, John Francis
Muus, Jytte Marie
Muuss, Rolf Eduard
Myer, Elizabeth Gallup
Myer, John Randolph
Myers, Alan Louis
Myers, Albert Ray
Myers, Alice Christine
Myers, Arthur B.
Myers, Bernard Samuel
Myers, Charles Andrew
Myers, Charles Frank
Myers, Charles Vincent
Myers, Dale DeHaven
Myers, Gary Arthur
Myers, Gerald E.
Myers, Harold Mathews
Myers, Israel
Myers, J. Barry
Myers, Jack Duane
Myers, Jacob Martin
Myers, Jerome Keeley
Myers, Joel Norman
Myers, John Henry, III
Myers, Joseph Harriman
Myers, Michael (Ozzie)
Myers, Robert John
Myers, Robert Julius
Myers, Robert Lee, Jr.
Myers, Robert Manson
Myers, Ronald Elwood
Myers, Samuel Lloyd
Myers, Thomas Kromer
Myers, Vernon C.
Myers, Warren Powers Laird
Myerson, Bernard
Myerson, Bess
Myerson, David Joel
Myerson, Paul Graves
Myhill, John
Myles, Jack Carroll
Myren, Richard Albert
Myrer, Anton Olmstead
Myskowski, Walter Joseph
Naber, Walter Jerome, Jr.
Nabokov, Nicolas
Nabokov, Vladimir
Nabrit, James Madison, Jr.
Nace, Barry John
Nace, Harold Russ
Nachman, Gerald Weil
Nachmias, Jacob
Nachtigall, Richard Henry
Nader, Ralph
Nadich, Judah
Nadien, David
Nadler, Arch
Nadler, Sigmond Harold
Nadler, William Hicks
Naef, Weston John
Naeser, Charles Rudolph
Naetzker, Louis
Nafe, John Elliott
Naftalin, Micah Harry
Nagel, Carl Edward
Nagel, Edward McCaul
Nagel, Ernest
Nagel, Thomas
Nagler, Alois Maria
Nagler, Benedict
Nagourney, Herbert
Nagy, Alexander Charles
Nagy, Gregory
Nagy, Ivan Akos
Nagy, Robert David
Nahas, Gabriel Georges
Nahavandi, Amir Nezameddin
Nahm, Milton Charles
Naimoli, Vincent J.
Naka, Fumio Robert
Nakashima, George Katsutoshi
Nalle, Beauveau Borie
Nalle, Richard Tilghman, Jr.
Namath, Joseph William
Namuth, Hans
Nance, Allan Taylor
Nance, James Wilson
Nance, Walter Elmore
Nannes, Caspar Harold
Nardo, Sebastian Vincent
Narin, Stephen B.
Naroll, Raoul
Narva, Martin Henry
Narva, Morton I.
Nasca, John Joseph
Nash, Bernard Elbert
Nash, Johnny
Nash, Leonard Kollender
Nash, Paul
Nash, Peter Gillette
Nash, Philleo
Nash, Ray
Nash, Robert Johnson
Nash, Robert Lewis
Nashed, M. Zuhair
Nashman, Alvin E.
Nason, John William
Nassikas, John Nicholas
Nastase, Ilie
Nastuk, William Leo
Natanson, Maurice Alexander
Nathan, Helmuth Max
Nathan, Paul S.
Nathan, Peter E.
Nathan, Richard Perle
Nathan, Robert Roy
Nathan, Shepherd
Nathan, Theodore Reade
Nathans, Daniel
Nathans, Robert
Nathanson, Neal
Natsios, Nicholas Andrew
Nattans, Roger Howard
Naughton, John Patrick
Naugle, John Earl
Nauheim, Ferdinand Alan
Naumann, Oscar Edward
Naumann, Robert Alexander
Nave, Henry John
Navin, John J.
Navin, Robert Francis
Nawy, Edward George
Nazzaro, James Russell
Neagley, Ross Linn
Neaher, Edward Raymond
Neal, Alfred Clarence
Neal, Frank Getchell, Jr.
Neal, Harold L., Jr.
Neal, Harry Edward
Neal, Julian Spencer
Neal, Marcus Pinson, Jr.
Neal, Minor Avon
Neale, Daniel Christopher
Neale, J. Henry
Neale, Russell Frederick
Neale, William F.
Nealon, William Joseph
Neaman, Milton R.
Nearing, Dudley Woodruff, Jr.
Nearing, Scott
Neary, Colleen
Neathery, Robert Walter, Jr.
Neblett, Carol
Necarsulmer, Henry
Nedzi, Lucien Norbert
Nee, Joseph Francis
Nee, Sister Mary Coleman
Needham, James Joseph
Needham, Richard Lee
Neel, Alice
Neel, Samuel Ellison
Neely, Mildred Sola (Mrs. Bruce W. Neely)
Nees, Bernard Joseph
Nef, Evelyn Stefansson
Nef, John Ulric
Neff, Robert Arthur
Neff, Russell Bowden
Neff, Walter Perry
Negherbon, Vincent Robert
Negroponte, John Dimitri
Nehari, Zeev
Nehmer, Stanley
Neier, Aryeh
Neikirk, Joseph Randolph
Neil, LaVerne
Neill, Richard Robert
Neilly, Andrew Hutchinson, Jr.
Neilson, Elizabeth Anastasia
Neilson, Winthrop Cunningham, III
Neiman, Fraser
Neiman, LeRoy
Neiman, Walter
Neimark, Sheridan
Neimeyer, Richard Dawe
Neisner, Melvin Bauer
Nelkin, Mark
Nelson, Bruce Warren
Nelson, Carl Roger
Nelson, Carl Truman
Nelson, Clifford Roy
Nelson, Curtis Andrew
Nelson, David
Nelson, David Lewis
Nelson, Erland Randall
Nelson, Gaylord Anton
Nelson, George
Nelson, George Francis
Nelson, George Laurence
Nelson, Gerald Kenneth
Nelson, Ivan
Nelson, James Clifford
Nelson, James Hissom, Jr.
Nelson, James Rodney
Nelson, John Charles
Nelson, John Howard
Nelson, John Marbury, III
Nelson, John Oliver
Nelson, John Robert
Nelson, Joseph Nathan
Nelson, Kottom Ray
Nelson, Lawrence Ernest
Nelson, Leonard Martin
Nelson, Lewis Clair
Nelson, Lindsey
Nelson, Nels Robert
Nelson, Norton
Nelson, Philip Francis
Nelson, Robert Louis
Nelson, Ron
Nelson, Theodore Wirt
Nelson, Waldo Emerson
Nelson, Walter Henry
Nelson, William
Nelson, William Henry, III
Nelson, William Linton
Nelson, William Richard
Nelson, Willie
Nelsova, Zara
Nemecek, Albert Duncan, Jr.
Nemiah, John Case
Nemir, Rosa Lee (Mrs. Elias J. Audi)
Nemshick, Andrew James
Nemtzow, Bernard
Nenneman, Richard Arthur
Neppl, Walter Joseph
Nero, Peter
Nerode, Anil
Nes, David Gulick
Nesbitt, George Lyman
Nesbitt, James Colin
Nesbitt, Lowell
Nesbitt, Robert Edward Lee, Jr.
Nesbitt, Rosemary Sinnett (Mrs. George R. Nesbitt)
Ness, Frederic William
Ness, Norman Frederick
Nessen, Ronald Harold
Nesson, Charles Rothwell
Netanyahu, Benzion
Nettels, Curtis Putnam
Netter, Eric Max
Netzer, Dick
Neubauer, Joseph A.
Neubauer, Walter Kenneth
Neuberger, Katherine (Mrs. Harry H. Neuberger)
Neuberger, Roy R.
Neufeld, Maurice Frank
Neuhoff, Roger Alan
Neumaier, John Joseph
Neuman, Robert Sterling
Neuman, William Frederick
Neumann, Ellsworth Traver
Neumann, Emanuel
Neumann, Harry, Jr.
Neumann, Robert Gerhard
Neumann, Vera Salaff
Neumann, Wencel Alexander, Jr.
Neuschel, Richard Frederick
Neustadt, Barbara Mae
Neustadt, Richard Elliott
Neuthaler, Paul David
Neuts, Marcel F.
Neva, Franklin Allen
Nevelson, Louise
Neviaser, Robert Jon
Neville, Emily Cheney
Neville, Howard Ralph
Neville, James Francis
Nevin, Crocker
Nevin, John Anthony
New, John Calhoun
New, John Gabriel
New, Noah Carroll
Newbauer, John Arthur
Newberne, Paul Medford
Newbold, Herbert Leon, Jr.
Newburger, Frank L., Jr.
Newburger, Howard Martin
Newbury, George Adelbert
Newby, Hayes Augustus
Newcomb, David Royal
Newcomb, Richard Fairchild
Newcomb, Robinson
Newcomb, Thomas Finley
Newcomer, Clarence Charles
Newell, Allen
Newell, Barbara Warne
Newell, Eric James
Newell, George Sealy
Newell, Guy Rene
Newell, Norman Dennis
Newell, Paul Haynes, Jr.
Newell, Reginald Edward
Newell, Robert Lincoln
Newhall, John Breed
Newhouse, Edward
Newhouse, Robert Joyce, Jr.
Newhouse, Samuel I.
Newland, Chester Albert
Newlin, Albert Chauncey
Newman, Andrew Joseph, Jr.
Newman, Arnold Abner
Newman, Bernard
Newman, Charles
Newman, Cynthia Stair
Newman, Edward
Newman, Edwin Harold
Newman, Elias
Newman, Frank
Newman, Harry Rudolph
Newman, Herbert Ellis
Newman, Howard Arthur
Newman, James Blakey
Newman, James Wilson
Newman, John Nicholas
Newman, Jon Ormond
Newman, Joseph H.
Newman, Joseph Herbert
Newman, Laraine
Newman, Monroe
Newman, Peter Kenneth
Newman, Philip E.
Newman, Philip Freedman
Newman, Rachel
Newman, Richard Alan
Newman, Richard Joseph
Newman, Samuel O.
Newman, Samuel Raphael
Newman, Theodore R., Jr.
Newman, Thomas Daniel
Newman, William Kincaid
Newman, William Louis
Newquist, Lester John
Newsom, Carroll Vincent
Newsome, John Charles
Newton, Blake Tyler, Jr.
Newton, Carl Elbridge
Newton, Derek Arnold
Newton, Earle Williams
Newton, George Cheney, Jr.
Newton, James Quigg, Jr.
Newton, Norman Thomas
Newton, Warren Childs
Ney, Edward Noonan
Neyer, Joseph
Nezelek, Edward Lewis
Ngai, Shih Hsun
Nicarry, Wayne A.
Nicastro, Louis Joseph
Nichinson, David Bernard
Nichol, Henry Ferris
Nicholas, Nancy
Nicholas, Robert Bates
Nicholas, Thomas Andrew
Nicholl, Louise Townsend
Nicholls, John Hamilton
Nichols, Alexander Lowber
Nichols, Carl Wheeler
Nichols, Charles Walter, Jr.
Nichols, David Arthur
Nichols, Edwin James
Nichols, Frederick Doveton
Nichols, James Hastings
Nichols, James Robbs
Nichols, Jeannette Paddock
Nichols, John Henry, Jr.
Nichols, Kenneth David
Nichols, Leonard Francis
Nichols, Philip, Jr.
Nichols, Richard Maurice
Nichols, Robert Lee
Nichols, Roger Loyd
Nichols, Roy Calvin
Nichols, Stephen George, Jr.
Nichols, Thomas S.
Nichols, Wade Hampton, Jr.
Nichols, William
Nicholson, Ben
Nicholson, Douglas Robert
Nicholson, Gunnar Walfrid Enander
Nicholson, Howard White
Nicholson, James John
Nicholson, Jesse Thompson
Nicholson, John Burton, Jr.
Nicholson, John Harris
Nicholson, Richard Earl
Nicholson, Thomas Dominic
Nicholson, William B.
Nichtern, Claire Joseph (Mrs. Sol Nichtern)
Nickel, Hans Erich
Nickerson, Albert Lindsay
Nickerson, Dorothy
Nickerson, Eugene H.
Nickerson, Herman, Jr.
Nickerson, James Findley
Nickerson, Ruth
Nickerson, Walter John
Nicklin, George Leslie, Jr.
Nicklis, John Osborne
Nickon, Alex
Nicolai, William
Nida, Eugene Albert
Nida, Jane Bolster (Mrs. Dow Hughes Nida)
Nidecker, John E.
Niden, George
Niebel, Benjamin Willard
Niebell, Paul Milton, Sr.
Niederlehner, Leonard
Niedermair, John Charles
Niehans, Jurg Max
Niehaus, Myron Stanley, Jr.
Nielsen, Aldon Dale
Nielsen, Charles Lester, Jr.
Nielsen, John Phillip
Niemi, Taisto John
Nightingale, Fred John
Nightingale, Stephen Edwards
Nigrelli, Ross Franco
Nijenhuis, Albert
Nikolais, Alwin
Niles, Henry Edward
Nill, Kenneth Wellman
Nilsen, Clifford Theodore
Nimetz, Matthew
Nimitz, Chester William, Jr.
Nin, Anais
Nippes, Ernest Frederick
Nirenberg, Louis
Nirenberg, Marshall Warren
Nisbet, Robert A.
Nisonoff, Alfred
Nissen, Clyde Theodore
Nissim, Rudolf
Niswander, Melvin Carter
Nitowsky, Harold Martin
Nitze, Paul Henry
Nivison, William
Nix, Robert N. C.
Nix, Robert Nelson Cornelius, Jr.
Nix, William Hawley
Nixon, Agnes Eckhardt
Nixon, Eugene Ray
Nixon, Frank Leslie
Nixon, Jack Lowell
Nizel, Abraham Edward
Nizer, Louis
Noah, Harold Julius
Noall, Roger
Noback, Charles Robert
Nobile, Arthur
Noble, Charles Carmin
Noble, Ernest Pascal
Noble, John Alexander
Noble, Joseph Veach
Noble, Marshall Hays
Noble, Merrill Emmett
Noble, Ransom Elwood, Jr.
Noble, Robert Warren
Nodtvedt, Magnus
Noel, Don Obert, Jr.
Noël Hume, Ivor
Noether, Emiliana Pasca
Noether, Gottfried Emanuel
Noguchi, Isamu
Nolan, Helen Dorothy
Nolan, James Parker
Nolan, John Francis
Nolan, John Lester
Nolan, Thomas Brennan
Noland, Kenneth Clifton
Noland, Lloyd U., Jr.
Noll, Chuck
Noll, Walter
Nolte, Judith Ann
Nolte, Richard Henry
Noon, Theodore Woods, Jr.
Noonan, John Thomas
Noonan, Patrick Francis
Noordergraaf, Abraham
Nooter, Robert Harry
Norcott, Alfred A.
Norcross, Carl Hafey
Nordell, Hans Roderick
Norden, Carl William
Norden, Robert B.
Nordhausen, August Henry
Nordlinger, Stephen Edward
Nordmeyer, George
Nordquest, Richard Edward
Norfleet, Norwood

Norman, Andrew Edward
Norman, Dorothy Stecker
Norman, Lewis Sheppard, Jr.
Norman, Richard Arthur
Norris, Arthur Hughes
Norris, Charles Morgan
Norris, Ernest Eden
Norris, Louis William
Norris, Martin Joseph
Norris, Robert Bayless
Norris, Robert Fogg
Norris, Robert Frank
Norris, Robert James
Norris, Robert Manning
Norstad, Lauris
North, Eleanor Beryl
North, Harper Qua
North, Helen Florence
North, James Weir
North, Nelson Luther
North, Robert Hugh
North, Thomas
North, William Haven
Northart, Leo Joseph
Northrop, Edward Skottowe
Northrop, Eugene Stanley
Northrop, Filmer Stuart Cuckow
Northrup, Herbert Roof
Northup, Robert Edgar
Norton, Adelbert James
Norton, Eleanor Holmes
Norton, Eunice Marie
Norton, Howard Melvin
Norton, John
Norton, Paul Allen
Norton, Paul Foote
Norton, Victor Thane
Norton, (William) Elliot
Norton-Taylor, Duncan
Norwood, Bernard
Norwood, George McIntosh, Jr.
Noss, John Boyer
Nossen, Robert Joseph
Nosworthy, John Marshall
Notestein, Frank Wallace
Notman, Donald Douglas
Nova, Saul Harry
Novack, George
Novak, Anthony
Novak, Eugene Francis
Novak, Michael (John), (Jr.)
Novak, Robert David Sanders
Novak, William Joseph
Novarr, David
Novello, Frederick Charles
Nover, Naomi (Goll)
Novick, Robert
Novick, Sheldon Mark
Novik, Ylda Farkas (Mrs. David Novik)
Novikoff, Alex Benjamin
Novotny, Rudolph Francis
Nowak, Henry James
Nowell, Peter Carey
Noyes, Blancke
Noyes, Crosby Stuart
Noyes, Donald Partelow
Noyes, Edward Roland, Jr.
Noyes, Eliot Fette
Noyes, Guy Emerson
Noyes, Jansen, Jr.
Noyes, Newbold
Noyes, Pierrepont T.
Noyes, Robert Edwin
Noyes, Thomas Ewing
Noyes-Kane, Dorothy
Nozick, Martin
Nozick, Robert
Noznesky, Harry Joseph
Nuckolls, Robert Theodore
Nuesse, Celestine Joseph
Nugent, Daniel Paul
Nugent, Brother Gregory
Nugent, Joseph C.
Nugent, Vincent Joseph
Nulty, Lawrence Frederick
Nunn, Donald G.
Nunn, John Allen
Nunneley, Emory Trufant
Nunnemacher, Rudolph Fink
Nurick, Gilbert
Nurnberger, Thomas Salisbury, Jr.
Nutter, Charles Armel
Nutter, G(ilbert) Warren
Nutting, Albert Deane
Nuzzo, Salvatore Joseph
Nyborg, Wesley Lemars
Nyce, Vincent Wasser
Nye, Edwin Packard
Nye, Joseph Samuel, Jr.
Nye, Thomas Russell
Nyere, Robert Alan
Nyhus, Paul Luther
Nyquist, Ewald B(erger)
Nyro, Laura
Nystrom, Harold Charles
Nystrom, John Warren
Oakar, Mary Rose
Oakes, Howard Edward
Oakes, James L.
Oakes, John Bertram
Oakes, John Cogswell
Oakes, Stewart Francis
Oakley, Bert Tuttle
Oakley, Cletus Odia
Oakley, Owen Horace
Oakley, Richard Putney
Oakley, Walter Thurston
Oakley, Wilbur Riley
Oaks, James Howard
Oates, Stephen Baery
Oatis, William Nathan
Obenshain, Richard Dudley
Ober, Bernard H.
Ober, Frank Benedict
Ober, Stuart Alan
Ober, William B.
Oberdorfer, Louis F.
Oberg, Albin Harold
Oberg, James L.
Oberkoetter, Frank Frederick
Oberlin, David Wright
Obermayer, Leon Jacob
Obermeyer, Ernest David
Obermeyer, Jack Arthur
Obolensky, Marilyn Wall
Obolensky, Serge
O'Brasky, David Morton
O'Brian, Jack
O'Brien, Brian
O'Brien, Edward Ignatius
O'Brien, Edward William
O'Brien, George Dennis
O'Brien, Henry Xavier
O'Brien, Hubert Francis
O'Brien, James Jerome
O'Brien, Jeanne Dufour
O'Brien, Joseph Michael
O'Brien, Lawrence Francis
O'Brien, Mary Elizabeth
O'Brien, Neal Ray
O'Brien, Ralph Hawley
O'Brien, Raymond Vincent, Jr.
O'Brien, Richard Desmond
O'Brien, Richard Duncan
O'Brien, Robert Brownell, Jr.
O'Brien, Thomas Stanton
O'Brien, William Howard
O'Brien, William John
O'Bryan, James William
O'Byrne, John Coates
O'Callaghan, Jerry Alexander
Ochoa, Severo
Ochojski, Paul Maximillian
Ochs, Martin Shelby
Ockenga, Harold John
Ockershausen, Andrew Martin
O'Connell, Brian
O'Connell, Denis Joseph
O'Connell, Donald William
O'Connell, George Danthine
O'Connell, John James, III
O'Connell, Joseph Cleophas
O'Connell, Lenahan
O'Connell, Paul Edmund
O'Connell, Philip Raymond
O'Connell, Quinn
O'Connell, Raymond Griffin
O'Connell, Richard Henry
O'Connor, Albert Dennis
O'Connor, Elizabeth
O'Connor, Francis X.
O'Connor, Sister George Aquin (Margaret M.)
O'Connor, George E.
O'Connor, Harvey
O'Connor, James Joseph
O'Connor, James Joseph
O'Connor, James Patrick
O'Connor, John Andrew, Jr.
O'Connor, John Joseph
O'Connor, John Joseph
O'Connor, John Joseph, Jr.
O'Connor, John Martin
O'Connor, Leonard Albert
O'Connor, Mary Consolata
O'Connor, Neal William
O'Connor, Norman
O'Connor, Robert Barnard
O'Connor, Robert Brendan
O'Connor, Robert Emmet
O'Connor, (Robert) Patrick
O'Connor, Roderic Ladew
O'Connor, Stanley James
O'Connor, William Francis
O'Connor, William Francis
O'Connor, William Joseph
O'Connor, William P.
O'Daniel, Glenn Lowell
O'Day, Royal Lewis
Oddis, Joseph Anthony
O'Dea, Thomas Emmett
Odell, Frank Harold
Odell, Harry Irvine
O'Dell, Scott
Odenkirchen, Carl Josef
Odiorne, George Stanley
O'Donnell, Alice Louise
O'Donnell, Charles Robert
O'Donnell, James Francis
O'Donnell, John Joseph
O'Donnell, John Logan
O'Donnell, Sister Miriam Teresa
O'Dwyer, John Joseph
Odyniec, Francis Anthony, Jr.
Oechsli, Leonard Paul
Oehser, Paul Henry
Oelbaum, Harold
Oelgeschlager, Guenther Karl
Oettinger, Anthony Gervin
Oettinger, Katherine Brownell
Offenbacher, Elmer Lazard
Offit, Sidney
Offner, Elliot Melville
Offner, Eric Delmonte
Offutt, Harry Andrew, Jr.
O'Friel, Zachary Michael
Oganesoff, Igor Michael
O'Gara, James Vincent, Jr.
Ogburn, Charlton
Ogden, Alfred
Ogden, Michael Joseph
Ogden, William Sterling
Ogdon, Thomas Hammer
Ogilby, Lyman Cunningham
Ogilvie, Robert Edward
Ogilvy, Stewart Marks
Ogle, Jane Hutchinson
O'Gorman, Ned
Ogren, William W.
Ohanian, John David
O'Hara, Alfred Peck
O'Hara, James Grant
O'Hara, John Brangs
O'Hara, Mary
O'Hara, Paul Franklin, Jr.
O'Hara, William James
O'Hare, Sister Jeanne d'Arc
O'Hearn, Robert Raymond
O'Herron, Jonathan
Ohlin, Lloyd Edgar
Ohlke, Clarence Carl
Ohlson, Douglas Dean
Ohlsson, Garrick Olof
Ohmann, Richard Malin
Ohsol, Ernest Osborne
Oishi, Satoshi
O'Kane, Daniel Joseph, Jr.
O'Keefe, Bernard Joseph
O'Keefe, Robert James
O'Keeffe, Adrian Francis
Okin, Franklin Jay
Okin, Robert Laurence
Okpaku, Joseph Ohiomogben
Okress, Ernest Carl
Okun, Arthur M.
Okun, Herbert Stuart
Okun, Milton Theodore
Olah-de-Garab, Gabor
Olcott, William Alfred
Old, Lloyd John
Oldenburg, Claes Thure
Oldenburg, Richard Erik
Older, Jack Stanley
Oldershaw, Louis Frederick
Oldman, Oliver
O'Leary, Brian Todd
O'Leary, Daniel Hugh
O'Leary, Denis Joseph
O'Leary, Edward Cornelius
O'Leary, James John
O'Leary, John Francis
O'Leary, Richard A.
O'Leary, Wilfred Leo
Oleksiw, Daniel Philip
Olevsky, Julian
Olick, Arthur Seymour
Olick, Philip Stewart
Oliner, Arthur Aaron
Olinsky, Tosca (Mrs. Charles F. Barteau)
Oliphant, Patrick
Olitski, Jules
Oliver, Alexander Roger
Oliver, Alvin E.
Oliver, Andrew
Oliver, Covey Thomas
Oliver, Edith
Oliver, Jack Ertle
Oliver, James Arthur
Oliver, James Henry
Oliver, Mary
Oliver, Robert Bruce
Oliver, Thomas Keyser, Jr.
Oliver, William Albert, Jr.
Oller, Anna Kathryn
Ollom, John Frederick
Olmstead, Cecil Jay
Olmsted, George Hamden
Olmsted, Mildred Scott (Mrs. Allen Seymour Olmsted, II)
Olmsted, Robert Groves
Olsen, Charles Nicholas
Olsen, Donald James
Olsen, Einar Arthur
Olsen, Herluf Vagn, Jr.
Olsen, Kenneth Harry
Olsen, Leif Henry
Olshan, Kenneth S.
Olson, Clinton Louis
Olson, Frank Albert
Olson, Harry Andrew, Jr.
Olson, Harry F.
Olson, James Chester
Olson, Jane Virginia
Olson, Jay Raymond, Jr.
Olson, Lawrence
Olson, Loren Keith
Olson, Robert Goodwin
Olson, Robert Leslie
Olson, Wallace Earl
Olsson, Nils William
Olsson, Sture Gordon
Olsten, William
Olzman, Saul
O'Mahoney, Robert M.
O'Malley, James, Jr.
O'Malley, Thomas Patrick
Oman, Clifford Edward
Oman, William Morse
Omang, Joanne Brenda
O'Mara, Fred Bates
O'Mara, John Mowbray
O'Mara, Joseph George
Omata, Robert Rokuro
O'Meara, Andrew Pick
O'Meara, Edward Thomas
Omer, Daniel Oliver
Omlor, John Joseph
Onassis, Jacqueline Bouvier Kennedy (Mrs. Aristotle Onassis)
Ondetti, Miguel Angel
O'Neal, Arthur Daniel, Jr.
O'Neal, Frederick
O'Neal, Ryan
O'Neil, James Francis
O'Neil, Stephen Edward
O'Neil, Thomas Francis
O'Neill, Eugene Francis
O'Neill, Francis Aloysius, Jr.
O'Neill, Gerard Kitchen
O'Neill, Grover, Jr.
O'Neill, James Edward
O'Neill, James Patrick
O'Neill, James Ward
O'Neill, John Joseph, Jr.
O'Neill, Michael James
O'Neill, Michael Joyce
O'Neill, Patrick Henry
O'Neill, Paul Henry
O'Neill, Reginald Finbarr
O'Neill, Richard Winslow
O'Neill, Robert Charles
O'Neill, Robert Edward
O'Neill, Thomas P.
O'Neill, Thomas P., III
Oneto, George J.
Ongley, Patrick Augustine
Onken, George Marcellus
Onorato, Nicholas Louis
Opel, John Roberts
Openshaw, Albert
Openshaw, Richard Alfred
Ophuls, Marcel
Opler, Marvin Kaufmann
Oppenheim, Alfred
Oppenheim, Dennis Allen
Oppenheim, Irwin
Oppenheim, Saul Chesterfield
Oppenheimer, Franz Martin
Oppenheimer, Jane Marion
Oppenheimer, Joel Lester
Oppenheimer, Monroe
Oppenheimer, Reuben
Opper, Franz Frederick
Oppermann, Paul
Oppold, William Andrew
Orbach, Jerry
Orban, Kurt
Orbison, James Lowell
Orcutt, Guy Henderson
Ordassy, Carlotta
Ording, James Henry
Orear, Jay
O'Reilly, Anthony John Francis
O'Reilly, Richard Thomas
Oren, John Birdsell
Orfila, Alejandro
Orgel, Stephen Kitay
Oriscak, Joseph John
Orkin, Lazarus Allerton
Orkin, Louis Richard
Orloff, Jack
Orman, Leonard Arnold
Ormandy, Eugene
Ormes, Robert Verner
Ormsby, Charles Alfred
Ornauer, Richard Lewis
Orne, Martin Theodore
Orner, Frederick Judd
Ornstein, Franklin H.
O'Roark, Sarah Ann (Mrs. Thomas L. O'Roark)
O'Rorke, Edward Arthur
O'Rourke, Andrew Terence
O'Rourke, Lawrence Michael
O'Rourke, Lawrence Stephen
O'Rourke, Patrick Jake
O'Rourke, William Andrew
Orowan, Egon
Orr, Dudley Wainright
Orr, James Hunter
Orr, Terry
Orr, Warren Gregg, II
Orr, William Campbell
Orr, William Pratt
Orrick, Norwood Bentley
Orsy, Ladislas
Ortiz, Francis Vincent, Jr.
Ortiz Mena, Antonio
Ortlip, Paul Daniel
Ortner, James Louis
Orton, Don Alfred
Orton, Vrest
Ortwein, Mathias Joseph
Orville, Philip Moore
Orwen, Gifford Phillips
Orze, Joseph John
Osborn, Edward Bartley
Osborn, Elburt Franklin
Osborn, Paul
Osborn, Robert Chesley
Osborn, Robert Elim
Osborne, David Paul
Osborne, John
Osborne, Richard de Jongh
Osborne, Stanley de Jongh
Osenenko, John
Oser, Bernard Levussove
Osgood, Cornelius
Osgood, Robert Endicott
Osius, Larry Clark
Oski, Frank Aram
Osler, Howard Lloyd
Osmalov, Robert
Osmer, Margaret
Osmond, James Robert
Osnos, Peter Lionel Winston
Osol, Arthur
Osserman, Elliott Frederick
Ossorio, Alfonso Angel
Osta, Frank Mark
Ostar, Allan William
Osterberg, Robert Charles
Ostergard, Paul Michael
Osterhaus, Joseph Cyril
Osterweis, Steven Levy
Ostfeld, Adrian Michael
Ostriker, Jeremiah Paul
Ostrom, John H.
Ostrow, Joseph W.
Ostrow, Philip Bernard
Ostrow, Stuart
Ostrum, Dean Gardner
Ostwald, Martin
O'Sullivan, Emmet Patrick
O'Sullivan, John Edward
O'Sullivan, Kevin Patrick
O'Sullivan, Patrick Brett
Oswald, Frederick William
Oswald, George Charles
Oswald, John Wieland
Oswald, Robert Leon
Oteri, Joseph Santo
Othmer, Donald Frederick
Otis, Elizabeth Richards (Mrs. Otis Kiser)
O'Toole, Dermott Patrick
O'Toole, John E.
O'Toole, Thomas Joseph
Ott, Charles Adam, Jr.
Ott, David Ewing
Ottaway, David Blackburne
Ottaway, James H.
Ottenberg, James Simon
Ottenheimer, Edwin
Ottenstein, David Lewis
Otterbourg, Robert Kenneth
Otth, Edward John, Jr.
Ottina, John Renaldo
Ottinger, Richard Lawrence
Ottmar, Jerome
Otto, Robert Henry
Oulahan, George McCall Courts
Ould, Edward Hatcher, Jr.
Ourednik, Rudolph Frank
Oursler, Fulton, Jr.
Oursler, William Charles (Will Oursler)
Outerbridge, David Eugene
Outhwaite, Leonard
Outlaw, Edward Groves
Outwater, John Ogden
Ove, Peter
Overbeck, Gene Edward
Overbeck, Henry West
Overby, Andrew Norris
Overman, Melvin Mac
Overmyer, William Edward
Overstreet, Bonaro Wilkinson
Overton, Edward Franklin
Overton, Joseph Allen, Jr.
Overton, Richard Cleghorn
Overton, Spencer Milton
Owen, Brian Thomas
Owen, David Rogers
Owen, George E.
Owen, Harry Goddard
Owen, Henry
Owen, John Atkinson, Jr.
Owen, Nathan Richard
Owen, Richard
Owen, Stephen Cooke, Jr.
Owen, Thomas Barron
Owen, Thomas John
Owen, Walter Shepherd
Owens, Charles Richard
Owens, Hugh Franklin
Owens, Robert Hunter
Owens, Rochelle
Owens, William A.
Owsley, David Thomas
Oxarart, Frank Joseph, Jr.
Oxenburg, Allen Sven
Oxenfeldt, Alfred Richard
Oxtoby, John Corning
Oyler, Thomas T(anian)
Ozawa, Seiji
Ozick, Cynthia
Ozment, Steven E.
Ozmon, Howard
Paar, Jack
Pabst, William Richard, Jr.
Pacala, Leon
Pace, Eric Dwight
Pace, Frank, Jr.
Pace, Norma
Pace, Stephen Shell
Pace, Warren M.
Pach, Stewart Warner
Pacino, Al (Alfred)
Pack, Howard M.
Pack, Richard Morris
Pack, Robert M.
Packard, George Randolph
Packard, Sidney R.
Packard, Vance Oakley
Packel, Israel
Packer, Arnold Herman
Packer, Leo S.
Packer, Richard William
Pacun, Norman
Padgett, George Arthur
Padovano, Anthony John
Padovano, Anthony Thomas
Padover, Saul K.
Paeff, Bashka
Paganelli, Robert Peter
Paganucci, Paul Donnelly
Page, Charles Greenleaf
Page, Charles Hunt
Page, Chester Hall
Page, Cornelius Albert
Page, Ellis Batten
Page, Frederick West
Page, Geraldine
Page, Harry Robert
Page, John Boyd
Page, Lorne Albert
Page, Richard S.
Page, Robert Eugene
Page, Robert Gaston
Page, Robert Griffith
Page, Robert Henry
Page, Robert Jeffress
Page, Shelby H.
Page, Walter Hines
Paget, Richard Moscrop
Pagliaro, Harold Emil
Paglio, Lydia Elizabeth
Pahlman, William Carroll
Paier, Adolf Arthur, Jr.
Paige, Hilliard Wegner
Paine, Gaylord Lord
Paine, Ralph Delahaye, Jr.
Paine, Stephen William
Painter, Mary Ella
Painton, Joseph Frederick
Pais, Abraham
Paisner, Bruce Lawrence
Pak, Hyung Woong
Pakenham, (Edward) Michael
Palade, George Emil
Palamara, Francis Joseph
Palamountain, Joseph Cornwall, Jr.
Palay, Sanford Louis
Palermo, Joseph
Paley, David
Paley, Grace
Paley, Louis J.
Paley, William S.
Palfrey, John Gorham
Palisca, Claude Victor
Palitz, Clarence Yale, Jr.
Pall, David B.
Palladino, Nunzio Joseph
Pallone, Nathanial John
Palmer, Archie M(acInnes)
Palmer, Arnold Daniel
Palmer, Charles Douglas
Palmer, Donald Ferguson
Palmer, Donald Kaye
Palmer, Edward Everett
Palmer, Edward Lewis
Palmer, Erwin George
Palmer, Forrest Charles
Palmer, Francis Henry
Palmer, Frederick Fraser
Palmer, James Alvin
Palmer, James Edward
Palmer, John James Ellis
Palmer, Katherine E.H. Van Winkle
Palmer, Lane Morris
Palmer, Milton Meade
Palmer, Norman Dunbar
Palmer, Richard Bradbury
Palmer, Richard Creighton
Palmer, Richard Emery
Palmer, Richard Francis
Palmer, Robert Baylis
Palmer, Robert Bolling
Palmer, Robert Everett Allen
Palmer, Robert Joseph
Palmer, Robert Moffett
Palmer, Robert Roswell
Palmer, Russell E.
Palmer, Stephen Eugene
Palmer, Stephen Eugene, Jr.
Palmer, William Bailey
Palmer, William Charles
Palmer, William James
Palmer, William Preston
Palmieri, Edmund Louis
Pan, Elizabeth Lim
Pan, Huo-Hsi
Pancoast, Charles Edward, III
Pancoast, Edwin Caleb
Pane, Remigio Ugo
Panes, Jack Samuel
Panichas, George Andrew
Panitt, Merrill
Panitz, Murray Wolfe
Pannill, Fitzhugh Carter, Jr.
Panoff, Robert
Panofsky, Hans Arnold
Panshin, Alexei
Panson, Gilbert Stephen
Pantages, Louis James
Pantaleoni, Helenka
Pantas, Leo James
Pao, Yih-Hsing
Paolino, Thomas Joseph
Paone, Peter
Papaliolios, Costas Demetrios
Paparello, Frank Nicholas
Pape, Harry, Jr.
Papert, Frederic Stuart
Papitto, Ralph Raymond
Papone, Aldo
Papoulis, Athanasios
Papp, Joseph
Pappagianis, George Spiros
Pappas, Thomas Anthony
Pappenheimer, Alwin Max, Jr.
Pappenheimer, John Richard
Paradiso, Louis John
Parcell, Malcolm Stevens
Pardee, Arthur Beck
Pardee, Arthur E., Jr.
Pardee, John (Jack) Perry
Pardue, Austin
Parelman, Samuel Theodore
Parente, William Joseph
Paris, Dorothy
Paris, Leonard Alton
Parish, Betty Waldo
Parish, James Robert
Park, Colin
Park, David Allen
Park, Douglas Bradford
Park, Gilman
Park, James Theodore
Park, John Robinson
Park, Lawrence
Park, Lee I.
Park, Robert Duane
Park, Robert Hiram
Park, Roy Hampton
Park, William Edgar
Park, William John
Parke, Robert Beatty
Parkening, Christopher William
Parker, Albert
Parker, Alfred
Parker, Brant Julian
Parker, Bruce Covell
Parker, Claude Atlas

Rodgers, Richard
Rodimer, Frank Joseph
Rodino, Peter Wallace, Jr.
Rodman, Charles Gilbert
Rodman, Harry Eugene
Rodman, Leroy Eli
Rodman, Morton Joseph
Rodman, Selden
Rodman, Sumner
Rodnan, Gerald Paul
Rodwin, Lloyd
Roe, Albert Sutherland
Roe, Kenneth Andrew
Roe, Robert A.
Roe, William Price
Roebling, Mary G.
Roedel, Paul Robert
Roedel, Philip Morgan
Roeder, George Albert, Jr.
Roeder, Kenneth David
Roedig, John B.
Roehm, Luther Schechinger
Roehm, Perry Reinhardt
Roen, Sheldon R.
Roeper, Albert Peter
Roerick, William (George)
Roesch, Clarence Henry
Roesch, Kurt Ferdinand
Roesner, Larry August
Roessler, Ronald James
Roessner, Gilbert George
Roever, Luis Conrad
Rogers, Archibald Coleman
Rogers, Bernard William
Rogers, Charles Everett, Jr.
Rogers, Charles H.
Rogers, David Elliott
Rogers, Elmer Gillis
Rogers, Eric Malcolm
Rogers, Eugene Charles
Rogers, Francis Day
Rogers, Francis Millet
Rogers, Frank Waters
Rogers, Fred Baker
Rogers, Fred McFeely
Rogers, Hartley, Jr.
Rogers, Irving Emerson
Rogers, James Frederick
Rogers, Jordan Thomas
Rogers, Joseph Patrick
Rogers, Kenneth Cannicott
Rogers, Kenneth Dyer
Rogers, Lewis Henry
Rogers, Peter
Rogers, Peter Philip
Rogers, Rutherford David
Rogers, Stephen
Rogers, Thomas Francis
Rogers, Thomas Hunton
Rogers, Virgil Madison
Rogers, Warren Joseph, Jr.
Rogers, William Dill
Rogers, William Pierce
Rogers, William Raymond, Jr.
Rogerson, James Russell
Rogerson, John Bernard, Jr.
Roget, Einar Leonard
Rogg, Nathaniel H.
Rogge, O(etje) John
Rogin, Gilbert Leslie
Rogin, Lawrence Morris
Rogliano, Aldo Thomas
Rogoff, Julian
Rogoff, Kenneth Saul
Rogovin, Mitchell
Rohatyn, Felix George
Rohm, Robert Hermann
Rohmann, Charles Peter
Rohr, Donald Gerard
Rohrbaugh, Lewis Henry
Rohrer, Don Hathaway
Rohrer, Paul Walter
Rohsenow, Warren Max
Roiphe, Anne
Rokaw, Daniel Roy
Roland, Johnny Earl
Rolander, Carl Arthur, Jr.
Roll, Edgar A.
Roll, George Arthur
Roll, Irwin Clifford
Rollins, Alfred Brooks, Jr.
Rollins, Calvin Dwight
Rollins, J. Donald
Rollins, Reed Clark
Rollins, Theodore Sonny
Rollinson, Carl Linden
Roloff, Michael
Rolontz, Robert
Romaine, Henry Simmons
Roman, Nancy Grace
Romano, John
Romano, Umberto
Romanoff, Alexis Lawrence
Romansky, Monroe James
Romanyshyn, John Mike
Rome, Donald Lee
Rome, Harold Jacob
Rome, Morton Phillips
Romer, Alfred
Romer, Robert Horton
Romey, William Dowden
Rommel, Wilfred H.
Romney, Carl F.
Romney, Henry John
Romney, Seymour Leonard
Romoser, George Kenneth
Romualdi, James Philip
Ronan, William John
Roncalio, Teno
Roncallo, Angelo Dominic
Roncarelli, Edward Alexander
Rondileau, Adrian
Roney, Jay Louis
Rongione, Louis Anthony
Ronne, Finn
Rooney, Andrew Aitken
Rooney, Arthur Joseph
Rooney, Francis Charles, Jr.
Rooney, Fred B.
Rooney, Kevin Davitt
Rooney, Miriam Theresa
Rooney, Paul Monroe
Rooney, William Richard
Roop, John Wesley
Roos, Lloyd Irving
Roosa, Robert Vincent
Roosa, Stuart
Roosevelt, Archibald Bulloch, Jr.
Roosevelt, John A.
Roosevelt, Julian Kean
Roosevelt, Theodore, III
Roosevelt, W. Emlen
Roosevelt, William Donner
Root, Nina J.
Root, Oren
Root, William Alden
Roper, Clyde Forrest Eugene
Roper, Laura Wood (pen name Laura N. Wood)
Ropp, Clarence Daniel Luther
Rorem, Ned
Rorer, William Herbert, III
Rorke, Lucy Balian
Rorty, Richard McKay
Rosa, Raymond Ulric
Rosan, Richard Adams
Rosand, Aaron
Rosati, James
Rosato, Francis Ernest
Rose, Albert
Rose, Daniel
Rose, David John
Rose, David Shepherd
Rose, Frederick Phineas
Rose, Harry Melvin
Rose, Herman
Rose, Hugh
Rose, Israel Harold
Rose, James McKinley, Jr.
Rose, John Charles
Rose, Leonard
Rose, Mary Carman (Mrs. Alexander Grant Rose)
Rose, Merle Richard
Rose, Milton Curtiss
Rose, Peter Isaac
Rose, Philip
Rose, Reginald
Rose, Richard Loomis
Rose, Stephen Jay
Rose, Thornton Turner
Rose, Wilford Allen
Rose, William Palen
Rose, Willie Lee
Roseberg, Carl Andersson
Roseman, Saul
Rosemberg, Eugenia
Rosemond, George P.
Rosen, Alex
Rosen, Bernard
Rosen, Charles Welles
Rosen, Fred
Rosen, Fred Saul
Rosen, George
Rosen, Gerald Harris
Rosen, Leo
Rosen, Martin M.
Rosen, Milton William
Rosen, Philip
Rosen, Richard
Rosen, Robert Arnold
Rosen, Ruben Paul
Rosen, Saul David
Rosen, Stanley Howard
Rosenbaum, Irving M.
Rosenbaum, Robert Abraham
Rosenberg, Alex
Rosenberg, Alexandre Paul
Rosenberg, Charles Ernest
Rosenberg, Gilbert
Rosenberg, Harold
Rosenberg, Henry A., Jr.
Rosenberg, Jakob
Rosenberg, James LeRoy
Rosenberg, Jerome Laib
Rosenberg, Jerry Martin
Rosenberg, John David
Rosenberg, Maurice
Rosenberg, Nancy Sherman (Mrs. Lawrence C. Rosenberg)
Rosenberg, Norman
Rosenberg, Paul
Rosenberg, Paul Bayard
Rosenberg, Robert Michael
Rosenberg, Ruth Yalowich (Mrs. Arthur Earl Rosenberg)
Rosenberg, Steven Aaron
Rosenberg, William
Rosenberger, Donald Markley
Rosenberger, Homer Tope
Rosenberger, Russell Edward
Rosenberger, Walter Emerson
Rosenblatt, Arthur Isaac
Rosenblatt, Louis
Rosenblatt, Peter Ronald
Rosenblatt, Roger
Rosenblith, Walter Alter
Rosenbloom, Daniel
Rosenbloom, Morris Victor
Rosenblum, Harold Arthur
Rosenblum, Marvin
Rosenblum, Myron
Rosenblum, Samuel
Rosenbluth, Marshall Nicholas
Rosenfeld, Ronald Marvin
Rosenfeld, Seymour
Rosenfield, Isadore
Rosenfield, James Harold
Rosenfield, John Max
Rosengarten, Adolph George, Jr.
Rosengarten, Martin
Rosengren, William Rudolph
Rosenhaupt, Hans
Rosenhaus, Matthew Bernard
Rosenhouse, Irwin
Rosenman, Dorothy (Mrs. Samuel I. Rosenman)
Rosenn, Max
Rosenow, Edward Carl, Jr.
Rosenquist, James Albert
Rosenquit, Bernard
Rosenshine, Allen Gilbert
Rosenstein, Howard
Rosensweig, Robert Lawrence
Rosensweig, Stanley Harold
Rosenthal, Aaron
Rosenthal, Abraham Michael
Rosenthal, Arthur Jesse
Rosenthal, Benjamin Stanley
Rosenthal, Franz
Rosenthal, Gerald David
Rosenthal, Gilbert
Rosenthal, Jacob (Jack)
Rosenthal, Lawrence Michael
Rosenthal, Lucy Gabrielle
Rosenthal, Macha Louis
Rosenthal, Michael Jay
Rosenthal, Milton Frederick
Rosenthal, Robert
Rosenthal, Tony (Bernard)
Rosenthal, William J.
Rosenthal, William Sanford
Rosenwald, Julius, II
Rosenwald, William
Rosier, James Louis
Rosin, Axel G.
Rosky, Theodore Samuel
Rosler, Lee
Rosner, Fred
Rosoff, Arnold Z.
Rosovsky, Henry
Rosow, Jerome Morris
Ross, Alan
Ross, Alexander
Ross, Arthur
Ross, Beatrice Brook
Ross, Bradford
Ross, Charles Robert
Ross, Claude Gordon Anthony
Ross, Donald Keith
Ross, Frederick Arthur
Ross, Frederick James, Jr.
Ross, Gilbert Irving
Ross, Griff Terry
Ross, Howard
Ross, Ian Munro
Ross, Jacob John, Jr.
Ross, James Barrett
Ross, James Brent
Ross, James Francis
Ross, Jerrold
Ross, John
Ross, John Harold
Ross, John Michael
Ross, John Theodore
Ross, Leon
Ross, Lillian
Ross, Margaret Louise
Ross, Marion Collier
Ross, Matthew Harold
Ross, Nancy Wilson (Mrs. Stanley P. Young)
Ross, Richard Morrow, Jr.
Ross, Richard Starr
Ross, Roderic Henry
Ross, Sheldon Jules
Ross, Sherman
Ross, Stanley
Ross, Steven J.
Ross, Steven Sander
Ross, Stuart Tennent
Ross, Sydney
Ross, Thomas Bernard
Ross, Warren Reinhard
Rossant, James Stephan
Rossbach, Jay Harry, Jr.
Rosset, Barnet Lee, Jr.
Rossey, Paul William
Rossi, Alice Schaerr (Mrs. Peter H. Rossi)
Rossi, Bruno
Rossi, Frank Paul
Rossi, Peter Henry
Rossner, Judith
Rosten, Leo Calvin (pseudonym Leonard Q. Ross)
Rostky, George Harold
Roston, Arnold
Rostow, Eugene Victor
Rostropovich, Mstislav
Roszak, Theodore
Rota, Gian Carlo
Rotenberg, Sheldon
Roth, Arthur Thomas
Roth, Charles
Roth, David James
Roth, George Leith, Jr.
Roth, Harold Leonard
Roth, Harvey Paul
Roth, Herbert, Jr.
Roth, James Luther Aumont
Roth, Philip
Roth, Robert
Roth, Russell Burton
Roth, Stanley
Roth, Stephen Alan
Roth, William V., Jr.
Rothballer, Alan Burns
Rothberg, Abraham
Rothe, G. H. Riedel
Rothenberg, Allen W.
Rothenberg, Jerome (Dennis)
Rothenberg, Robert Edward
Rothenberg, Robert Philip
Rothermel, Daniel Krott
Rothfield, Lawrence I.
Rothholz, Peter Lutz
Rothman, David J.
Rothman, Donald Nahum
Rothrauff, Guido Anthony, Jr.
Rothschild, Ernest Leo
Rothschild, Joseph
Rothschild, Louis Samuel
Rothschild, Stanford Zadoc, Jr.
Rothschild, V. Henry, II
Rothschild, Walter
Rothschild, Walter N., Jr.
Rothstein, Jesse
Rothwell, Bernard Joseph, II
Rotter, Paul Talbott
Rottman, Ellis
Rotunno, Noreda Anthony
Roubos, Gary Lynn
Roudiez, Leon Samuel, Jr.
Roueché, Berton
Rough, Gaylord Earl
Rouland, Jay Thomas
Rounds, Joseph Bradford
Rouner, Leroy Stephens
Rounes, Aristides K.
Rourke, Francis Edward
Rouse, Irving
Rouse, Merl L.
Rouse, Richard Oliver, Jr.
Rouse, Robert Sumner
Roush, James Lee
Roussakis, Nicolas
Rousseas, Stephen William
Rousseau, Viateur
Rousseau, William Caubu
Rousselot, Harold Anthony
Rousso, Eli Louis
Routien, John Broderick
Routtenberg, Max Jonah
Rovelstad, Howard
Rovensky, William Richard
Rover, Harold Vincent
Rovere, Richard Halworth
Rovin, Sheldon
Rowan, Carl Thomas
Rowan, Jan Christopher
Rowan, Keith Patterson
Rowan, Robert Bellarmine
Rowden, Marcus Aubrey
Rowe, Charles Spurgeon
Rowe, David Nelson
Rowe, Elizabeth (Mrs. James Henry Rowe, Jr.)
Rowe, Harrison Edward
Rowe, Henry Stuart Payson
Rowe, Herbert Joseph
Rowe, James Henry, Jr.
Rowe, Thomas Joseph
Rowe, Wallace Prescott
Rowell, George Barker
Rowen, Hobart
Rowland, Benjamin Allen
Rowland, Charles Sherman
Rowland, Herbert Leslie
Rowland, John Carter
Rowland, Lewis Phillip
Rowland, Richard Creswell
Rowland, Thomas Mifflin
Rowlands, David Thomas
Rowlands, Marvin Lloyd, Jr.
Rowlingson, Donald Taggart
Rowny, Edward Leon
Rowson, Richard Cavanagh
Roy, Philip H.
Roy, Robert Hall
Roy, Rustum
Roybal, Edward R.
Roylance, D.C.
Rozeboom, Lloyd Eugene
Rozel, Samuel Joseph
Rozelle, Alvin Ray (Pete)
Rozen, Jerome George, Jr.
Ruark, Arthur Edward
Rub, Louis John
Rubbia, Carlo
Rubel, Donald Clarke
Ruben, Lawrence
Ruben, Robert Joseph
Rubenstein, Albert
Rubenstein, Bernard Wolf
Rubenstein, Herbert
Rubenstein, Howard Joseph
Rubenstein, Jerry G.
Rubenstein, Lewis W.
Rubin, Albert Louis
Rubin, Benjamin Norman
Rubin, Bernard
Rubin, Edwin Manning
Rubin, Emanuel
Rubin, Irving
Rubin, Jerome S.
Rubin, Joan Alleman
Rubin, Mel
Rubin, Samuel
Rubin, Samuel Harold
Rubin, Seymour Jeffrey
Rubin, Theodore Isaac
Rubin, William
Rubinstein, Alvin Zachary
Rubinstein, Hyman Solomon
Ruccius, Frederick Edward, Jr.
Rucker, Ronald Eugene
Ruda, Edwin
Rudd, Eldon
Rudd, Hughes Day
Rudd, Paul Ryan
Ruddle, Francis Hugh
Ruddley, John
Ruddock, Andrew Emerson
Rudel, Julius
Rudel, Thomas Ryder
Rudenstine, Neil Leon
Ruder, William
Ruderman, Malvin Avram
Rudin, Jacob Philip
Rudman, Jack
Rudofker, Samuel
Rudolf, Max
Rudolph, Frederick
Rudolph, Paul Marvin
Rudow, David Barry
Rudy, Charles
Rudy, Raymond Bruce, Jr.
Rudy, Willis
Ruebhausen, Oscar Melick
Rueger, William Frederick
Ruellan, Andree
Rueppel, Merrill Clement
Ruff, Charles F. C.
Ruffer, David Gray
Ruffi, Stephen Joseph
Ruffin, Albert Leslie, Jr.
Ruffle, John Frederick
Rugger, Gerald K.
Ruggieri, George Daniel
Ruggiero, John Salvator
Ruggles, Eleanor
Ruggles, Richard
Rugoff, Milton
Ruina, Jack Philip
Ruinsky, Sam
Ruitenbeek, Hendrik M.
Ruiz, Aldelmo
Ruiz-de-Conde, Justina Malaxechevarria
Rukeyser, Merryle Stanley
Rukeyser, Merryle Stanley, Jr.
Rukeyser, Muriel
Rukeyser, William Simon
Rule, Elton H.
Rumbaugh, Ronald Roland
Rumble, Richard Edwards
Rumford, Beatrix Tyson
Rumler, Robert Hoke
Rummel, F.C.
Rumrill, Charles Lewis
Runals, Clarence Rider
Runes, Dagobert David
Runge, Albert Louis
Runk, Benjamin Franklin Dewees
Runnels, Harold Lowell
Rupp, William John
Ruppe, Philip E.
Ruppel, George Robert
Rusch, Hugh Leonard
Rusch, William George
Ruscha, Edward
Rush, Alvin
Rush, Kenneth
Rush, Richard Henry
Rusher, William Allen
Rusk, Howard A.
Rusk, William Sener
Russell, Allan David
Russell, Donald Frank
Russell, Edwin F.
Russell, Elizabeth Buckley Shull
Russell, Francis
Russell, Franklin Alexander
Russell, Frederick Arthur
Russell, George Allen
Russell, Harvey Clarence
Russell, Helen Louise
Russell, James Agar
Russell, James Alvin, Jr.
Russell, John
Russell, John Carl
Russell, John Clifford
Russell, John Jewett
Russell, Joseph William
Russell, Joyce Anne Rogers
Russell, Ken
Russell, Lao (Mrs. Walter Russell)
Russell, Nipsey
Russell, Paul Farr
Russell, Paul Snowden
Russell, Percy Hickling
Russell, Peter Byrom
Russell, Peter Gardiner
Russell, Robert Hilton
Russell, Stephen
Russell, Thomas Wright, Jr.
Russell, William Henry
Russell, William Kable
Russo, James Ralph
Russo, Martin A.
Rust, Stirling Murray, Jr.
Rust, William Fitzhugh, Jr.
Rust, William James
Rusterholz, Kenneth George
Rustgi, Moti Lal
Rustici, Charles John
Rustin, Bayard
Rutenber, Culbert Gerow
Rutenber, Ralph Dudley, Jr.
Ruth, Alpheus Landis
Ruth, Franklin William, Jr.
Rutherford, Paul Harding
Rutherford, Richard James
Rutkin, Seymour
Rutland, Robert Allen
Rutledge, John William
Rutledge, Philip Casteen
Rutsch, Alexander
Rutstein, David Davis
Ruttenberg, Derald H.
Ruttenberg, Stanley Harvey
Rutter, Frances Tompson
Ruzicka, Rudolph
Ryan, Alvan Sherman
Ryan, Cornelius Thomas
Ryan, Donald Francis
Ryan, Gerard Spencer
Ryan, Hewson Anthony
Ryan, John Donald
Ryan, John T., Jr.
Ryan, John William
Ryan, Kenneth John
Ryan, Leo Joseph
Ryan, Leonard Eames
Ryan, Michael E.
Ryan, Michael Patrick
Ryan, Patrick James
Ryan, Raymond D.
Ryan, Regina Claire (Mrs. Paul Deutschman)
Ryan, Robert John
Ryan, Stephen Pintard
Ryan, Thomas Patrick, Jr.
Ryan, William Lawrence
Ryder, Frank Glessner
Ryder, Kenneth Gilmore
Ryder, Norman Burston
Ryerson, Joseph Leslie
Ryerson, Margery Austen
Ryerson, William Newton
Ryker, Charles Edwin
Rylance, George Austin
Ryle, Joseph Donald
Ryor, John
Ryskamp, Charles Andrew
Saal, Hubert Daniel
Saalfrank, Charles Weaks
Saam, Frank Emile
Sabatella, Raymond Francis, Jr.
Sabatini, David Domingo
Sabel, Robert Hunter
Sabin, Arnold Leonard
Sabine, Gordon Arthur
Sabrosky, Curtis Williams
Sabsevitz, Irving
Sabshin, Melvin
Saccio, Leonard John
Sacco, Ignatius Joseph
Sachar, Abram Leon
Sachar, Edward Joel
Sachs, Alan Richard
Sachs, Allan Maxwell
Sachs, Benjamin K.
Sachs, Murray
Sachs, Raymond Joseph, Jr.
Sachs, Robert
Sachs, Sidney Stanley
Sachse, Harry Rubenstein
Sachse, William Lewis
Sack, Sylvan Hanan
Sackett, Arthur Johnson
Sackett, Leland Russell, Jr.
Sackler, Arthur Mitchell
Sackler, Howard
Sacks, Albert Martin
Sacks, Gerald Enoch
Sacks, Henry
Sacks, Howard Raymond
Sadao, Shoji
Saddler, Donald Edward
Sadek, George
Sadik, Marvin Sherwood
Sadik-Khan, Orhan Idris
Sadove, Aaron Solomon
Safar, Peter
Safer, John
Safer, Morley
Saffiotti, Umberto
Safford, Arthur Raymond
Safiol, George E.
Safire, William
Safran, Claire
Safran, Nadav
Sagan, Carl Edward
Sage, Andrew Gregg Curtin, II
Sage, Andrew Patrick, Jr.
Sage, Leslie William
Sagendorf, Forrest Cowles (Bud)
Sager, Merel Seaman
Sagerholm, James Alvin
Sagle, Robert Franklin
Sagorsky, Irving Saul
Sagurton, Edwin Connell
Sahakian, Mabel Marie Lewis (Mrs. William S. Sahakian)
Sahakian, William S(ahak)
Saidenberg, Daniel
Saidy, Anthony Fred
Saikowski, Charlotte
Saini, TejBhan Singh
St. Clair, James Draper
St. Clair, Jesse Walton, Jr.
St. Clair, John Wilson
St. Clair, Nelson Lewis, Jr.
St. Germain, Fernand Joseph
St John, Adrian, II
St. John, Robert
St. John, Seymour
St. Johns, Adela Rogers
Saint-Subber, Arnold
Sajkovic, Vladimir
Saker, John E.
Saker, Joseph J.
Salant, Richard S.
Salant, Robert Stephen
Salant, Walter S.
Salatich, William George
Salhanick, Hilton Aaron
Saliba, Jacob
Saliba, Philip E.
Salik, Julian Oswald
Salinger, Jerome David
Salisbury, Harrison Evans
Salisbury, John Francis
Salisbury, Kevin Mahon
Salizzoni, Frank Louis
Salkever, Louis Romov
Salkind, Alvin J.
Salley, John Jones
Salmen, Stanley
Salmon, John Hearsey McMillan
Salmon, Larry
Salmon, Paul Blair
Salmon, Walter Jay

Salomon, Isidore Lawrence
Salomon, Mardoqueo Isaac
Salomon, Robert Stephen, Jr.
Salomon, William Roger
Salomone, Arcangelo William
Salpeter, Edwin Ernest
Salsberg, Arthur Philip
Salsbury, Jason Melvin
Salton, Gerard
Saltonstall, Leverett
Saltsburg, Howard Mortimer
Saltzer, Paul
Saltzman, Arnold Asa
Saltzman, Barry
Saltzman, Charles Eskridge
Saltzman, Harry
Salvadori, Massimo (Max William)
Salyard, Robert Russel
Salzarulo, Leonard Michael
Salzer, Felix
Salzman, Herbert
Salzman, Sheldon Robert
Salzman, Stanley
Samios, Nicholas Peter
Sammartino, Peter
Sammet, George, Jr.
Sammons, Jeffrey Leonard
Sammons, Robert Lee
Sample, Frederick Palmer
Sampson, Arthur Francis
Sampson, Harold Ray
Samson, John Gadsden
Samton, Peter
Samuel, Athanasius Yeshue
Samuel, Donald Carol
Samuel, Howard David
Samuels, Abram
Samuels, Alta Grant (Mrs. Warren S. Samuels)
Samuels, John Stockwell, III
Samuels, Nathaniel
Samuels, Sheldon Wilfred
Samuels, Stanley Arnold
Samuelson, Derrick William
Samuelson, Paul Anthony
Sanasardo, Paul Saviour
Sanchez, Adel
Sanchez, Leon
Sanchez, Phillip Victor
Sand, Edward Austin
Sand, Leonard B.
Sandbank, Henry
Sandel, Ardis
Sander, Frank Ernest Arnold
Sanders, Andrew Dominick
Sanders, Benjamin Elbert
Sanders, Charles Addison
Sanders, Charles Lionel
Sanders, Charles Loy
Sanders, Irwin Taylor
Sanders, Ronald
Sanders, Terry Bentley, Jr.
Sanders, William Joseph
Sanderson, Bennett
Sanderson, Francis Thayer
Sanderson, Fred Hugo
Sanderson, Walton White
Sandground, Mark B.
Sandifer, Durward Valdamir
Sandler, Charles Ross
Sandler, Elisabeth Krabisch (Mrs. Howard R. Sandler)
Sandler, Elisabeth Krabisch (Mrs. Howard R. Sandler)
Sandmaier, Philip James, Jr.
Sandman, Edgar Augustus
Sandoe, Nichol Main
Sandonato, Barbara Lee
Sands, Edith Sylvia Abeloff (Mrs. Abraham M. Sands)
Sands, Thomas Jahn
Sandson, John Ivan
Sanfelici, Arthur Hugo
Sanford, Charles Steadman, Jr.
Sanford, George Foster, Jr.
Sanford, Leda
Sanger, Richard Paulett
Sangree, Walter Hinchman
Sanik, John, Jr.
Sann, Paul
Sannwald, Wolfgang
San Soucie, Robert Louis
Santini, James David
Santini, John Amedeo
Santora, Phillip Joseph
Santos, George Wesley
Santry, Arthur Joseph, Jr.
Santulli, Thomas Vincent
Sapers, Carl Martin
Saperston, Alfred Morton
Saperston, Howard Truman, Sr.
Saphier, Michael
Sapinsky, Joseph Charles
Sapir, Philip
Sapolsky, Harvey Morton
Sappington, Lee Edward
Sarasin, Ronald A.
Sarason, Seymour Bernard
Sarbanes, Paul Spyros
Sarber, Raymond William
Sarbin, Hershel Benjamin
Sard, Arthur
Sardi, Vincent, Jr.
Sarett, Lewis Hastings
Sarett, Morton Rueben
Sargeant, Howland H.
Sargeant, Winthrop
Sargent, Cyril Garbutt
Sargent, Daniel I.
Sargent, Francis W.
Sargent, James Cunningham
Sargent, John Turner
Sargent, Joseph Denny
Sargent, Leon Frank
Sargent, Ralph Millard
Sargoy, Edward Abraham
Sarkissian, Karekin
Sarlat, Noah
Sarles, Harvey Julian
Sarles, Peter Mason
Sarna, Nahum Mattathias
Sarnoff, Albert
Sarnoff, Stanley Jay
Sarnoff, William
Sarosdy, Aurel Francis
Sarris, Andrew George
Sarro, Ronald Armand
Sarry, Christine
Sarton, May
Sartorelli, Alan Clayton
Sartori, K. J.
Sartwell, Philip Earl
Sarvella, Patricia Ann
Sasaki, Hideo
Saso, Charles Frederick
Sass, Daniel Benjamin
Sass, Louis DeWald
Sasser, James Ralph
Sasson, Michel
Sassoon, Vidal
Sassower, Doris Lipson (Mrs. George Sassower)
Sassower, Philip Sheldon
Satenstein, Frank
Sater, Alex Joel
Satterfield, Charles Nelson
Satterfield, David Edward, III
Satterfield, John Roberts, Jr.
Satterthwaite, Joseph Charles
Satterthwaite, Willis Hibbs
Satterwhite, Henry Allen
Satz, David Meyer, Jr.
Sauer, Louis
Sauer, Robert Arthur
Saul, George Brandon
Saul, George Brandon, II
Saul, Leon Joseph
Saul, Ralph Southey
Saunders, Byron Winthrop
Saunders, Charles Baskerville, Jr.
Saunders, Dero Ames
Saunders, Donald Kilbourne
Saunders, Edward A.
Saunders, Harold Henry
Saunders, Jason Lewis
Saunders, John Warren, Jr.
Saunders, Joseph Francis
Saunders, R. Duane
Saunders, Richard Henry, Jr.
Saunders, Rubie Agnes
Saunders, Sally Love
Saunders, Wilbour Eddy
Saunders, William Hundley, Jr.
Sause, George Gabriel
Savacool, John Kenneth
Savage, Robert H.
Savage, Warren Fairbank
Savedoff, Malcolm Paul
Saville, Thorndike, Jr.
Savin, Robert Shevryn
Savinelli, Emilio Alfred
Savoca, Carmen Salvatore
Savrin, Louis
Sawabini, Wadi Issa
Saward, Ernest Welton
Sawin, Alton, Jr.
Sawin, Nancy Churchman
Sawyer, Alan Frederick
Sawyer, Edwin Albert
Sawyer, Harold Samuel
Sawyer, Henry Washington, III
Sawyer, Horace Adali, Jr.
Sawyer, John Edward
Sawyer, Robert Scott
Sawyer, William Ballard Hoyt
Sax, Herbert
Saxe, Edward Lawrence
Saxe, Emanuel
Saxena, Brij B.
Saxon, Charles David
Saxon, James Joseph
Saxon, Philip Dunham
Saxton, Mark
Sayles, Leonard Robert
Sayles, Thomas Dyke, Jr.
Saypol, Ronald Dietz
Sayre, Edward Vale
Sayre, Eleanor Axson
Sayre, Francis Bowes, Jr.
Sayre, Robert Marion
Scaasi, Arnold Martin
Scaff, Jack Hall
Scaggs, Howard Irwin
Scaife, Richard Mellon
Scalera, Ralph Francis
Scammon, Richard Montgomery
Scanga, Italo
Scanlan, Eugene Richard
Scanlon, Charles Joseph
Scanlon, George Francis, Jr.
Scanlon, Jane Cronin (Mrs. Joseph C. Scanlon)
Scanlon, John J.
Scanlon, Peter Redmond
Scanlon, Robert Gilbert
Scarbrough, W. Carl
Scarf, Herbert Ely
Scarff, Donald Douglas
Scarff, John Edwin
Scarne, John
Scarola, John Anthony
Scarpitti, Frank Roland
Scarton, Bennie, Jr.
Scavullo, Francesco
Schaaf, C(arl) Hart
Schachtel, Irving I.
Schachter, Oscar
Schachter, Stanley
Schack, Mario Lawrence
Schaeberle, Robert Martin
Schaefer, Adolph (Oscar), Jr.
Schaefer, Donald A.
Schaefer, Herman Albert
Schaefer, Raymond Herman
Schaefer, Robert Joseph
Schaefer, Robert Wayne
Schaefer, Rudolph J.
Schaefer, Vincent Joseph
Schaefer, William David
Schaefer, William Donald
Schaefer, William Goerman, Jr.
Schaeffer, Bobb
Schaeffer, Henri Bella (Mrs. Themis De Vitis)
Schaeffer, Oliver Adam
Schaefler, Leon
Schafer, Alice Turner
Schafer, George Ezra
Schafer, Richard Donald
Schaffer, David Irving
Schaffer, Edmund John
Schaffer, Franklin Edwin
Schaffer, Gloria Wilinski
Schaffer, Robert Henry
Schaffer, Rose Nussbaum
Schaffer, Stanley G.
Schaffner, Charles Etzel
Schaffner, Robert Michael
Schaffter, Dorothy
Schafler, Norman I.
Schanberg, Sydney Hillel
Schannen, Richard Harold
Schantz, William R., Jr.
Schapiro, Donald
Schapiro, Meyer
Schapiro, Morris A.
Scharper, Philip Jenkins
Scharrer, Berta Vogel
Schary, Dore
Schary, Saul
Schatz, Arthur Herschel
Schatz, Edward Ralph
Schatz, S. Michael
Schaufele, William Everett, Jr.
Schaufuss, Peter
Schaut, Quentin Lemar
Schechner, Richard
Schechner, Sheridan
Schechter, Abel Alan
Schechter, Edmund
Schechter, Martin
Schecter, Harry
Scheeler, James Arthur
Scheer, Alan Austin
Scheer, Julian Weisel
Scheer, Stuart Charles
Scheffler, Israel
Scheibe, Fred Karl
Scheibel, Kenneth Maynard
Scheid, Francis
Scheide, William Hurd
Scheie, Harold Glendon
Schein, Edgar Henry
Schein, Harvey L.
Schein, Jerome Daniel
Schein, Julius Bernard
Scheinberg, Labe Charles
Scheiner, Samuel
Schell, John Le Roy
Schell, Orville Hickok, Jr.
Schellenger, James Knox Polk
Schelling, John Paul
Schelling, Thomas Crombie
Schenck, Harry Paul
Schene, Arthur V.
Schenk, Faye L. (Mrs. Max Schenk)
Schenk, Peter Joseph
Schenk, Worthington George, Jr.
Schenkel, James Milton
Schenker, Alexander Marian
Schenkman, Alfred Seymour
Schepens, Charles Louis
Scheraga, Harold Abraham
Scherer, Otto Ernest
Scherer, Raymond Lewis
Scherer, William Franklin
Scherick, Edgar Jay
Scherman, Thomas
Scherman, William Harris
Scherr, Lawrence
Schetz, Joseph Alfred
Scheu, Edward Magnus, Jr.
Scheu, William Edward
Scheuer, James Haas
Scheuer, Lucile Magdalin
Scheuer, Sidney Henry
Scheuerman, Leroy J.
Schevill, James Erwin
Schewel, Stanford
Schick, George
Schickel, Richard
Schickele, Peter
Schieder, Joseph Eugene
Schieffelin, William Jay, III
Schier, Richard Francis
Schiessler, Robert Walter
Schiff, Frank
Schiff, Jerome Arnold
Schiff, John M(ortimer)
Schiff, Saul Ben
Schiffman, Irving Israel
Schiffrin, Andre
Schild, Albert
Schildkraut, Joseph Jacob
Schiller, Arthur Adam
Schiller, Everett Lyle
Schiller, Milton S.
Schiller, Pieter Jon
Schilling, Charles Henry
Schilling, Richard Robert, Jr.
Schilling, Sylvester Paul
Schilling, Warner Roller
Schimmel, Annemarie Brigitte
Schimmel, Caroline Fearey
Schimmel, Caroline Fearey
Schimmel, Paul Reinhard
Schimmel, Stuart Barr
Schindler, Aaron Isador
Schindler, Alexander Moshe
Schindler, Clayton Moss
Schindler, James Schwartz
Schineller, Richard John
Schinkel, Kenneth Calvin
Schipper, James Howard
Schippers, Thomas
Schisgal, Murray
Schlafly, Hubert Joseph, Jr.
Schlagel, Richard Harold
Schlageter, Robert
Schlaifer, Charles
Schlaikjer, Jes (Wilhelm)
Schlang, Joseph
Schlanger, Arnold Geoffrey
Schlanser, Lawrence Edward
Schlaretzki, Walter Ernest
Schlatter, Richard
Schlesinger, Arthur (Meier), Jr.
Schlesinger, Edward Bruce
Schlesinger, James Rodney
Schlesinger, Robert Walter
Schlesinger, Stephen Lyons
Schleyer, Paul von Ragué
Schlezinger, Julius
Schlink, Frederick John
Schloss, Ezekiel
Schlosser, Herbert S.
Schlotterbeck, Walter Albert
Schluter, Fredric Edward
Schmalz, William Herbert
Schmalzer, Victor David
Schmalzried, Marvin Eugene
Schmeisser, Gerhard
Schmeller, Kurt Richard
Schmeltzer, Edward
Schmelzer, Menahem H.
Schmertz, Mildred Floyd
Schmick, William Frederick, Jr.
Schmid, Bernard Francis
Schmid, John Henry
Schmid, John Samuel
Schmid, Wilfried
Schmidt, Adolph William
Schmidt, Benno Charles
Schmidt, Blaine Galen
Schmidt, Charles Wilson
Schmidt, Cyril James
Schmidt, Harold Robert
Schmidt, Harvey Lester
Schmidt, Helen Laubach
Schmidt, Herman J.
Schmidt, J. Paul
Schmidt, Klaus Franz
Schmidt, Louis Edward
Schmidt, Michael Jack
Schmidt, (Orval) (Frederick) Fred
Schmidt, Paul Felix
Schmidt, Richard Marten, Jr.
Schmidt, Richard Penrose
Schmidt, Robert Louis
Schmidt, Terry Lane
Schmidt, Thomas Carson
Schmidt, William Alvin
Schmidt, Wilson Emerson
Schmidt-Nielsen, Bodil Mimi (Mrs. Roger G. Chagnon)
Schmieder, Frank Joseph
Schmiedeshoff, Frederick William
Schmitt, Arthur Joseph
Schmitt, Francis Otto
Schmitt, George Herbert
Schmitt, Harrison Hagan
Schmitt, Waldo LaSalle
Schmitter, Charles Harry
Schmittlein, Albert Edward
Schmuller, Aaron
Schmults, Edward Charles
Schnabel, Karl Ulrich
Schnader, Donald Dixon
Schnaitman, William Kenneth
Schnall, Herbert Kenneth
Schneewind, Jerome Borges
Schneider, Alan
Schneider, Alexander
Schneider, Alfred Reuben
Schneider, Donald Frederic
Schneider, F. Russell
Schneider, Frederick H.
Schneider, George Joseph
Schneider, Howard
Schneider, John Arnold
Schneider, John Hoke
Schneider, Marius George
Schneider, Ralph Frederick
Schneider, Ronald Milton
Schneider, William Charles
Schneiderman, Irwin
Schneiders, Gregory Stephen
Schneierson, Sol Stanley
Schnell, George Adam
Schneps, Jack
Schnering, Philip Blessed
Schnittker, John Alvin
Schnitzer, Howard Joel
Schnitzer, Robert C.
Schober, Marshall
Schoberl, Anthony Denis
Schoen, Herbert Paul
Schoen, William Jack
Schoenbach, Sol Israel
Schoenbaum, Samuel
Schoenborn, Edwin August
Schoener, Edgar Chapman
Schoening, Roger Warren
Scholes, Samuel Ray, Jr.
Scholtz, Elizabeth
Schomer, Howard
Schonberg, Harold C.
Schonfeld, Fabian
Schonk, Robert Martin
Schonwald, Gary Alan
Schooley, Allen Heaten
Schooley, Charles Earl
Schoon, Owen Harry
Schoonover, Jean Way
Schor, Stanley Sidney
Schork, John Edward
Schork, Rudolph Joseph, Jr.
Schorr, Alvin Louis
Schorr, Daniel Louis
Schorr, Lisbeth Bamberger
Schorr, Marvin Gerald
Schorske, Carl Emil
Schott, Elihu
Schott, Francis Helmut
Schottland, Charles Irwin
Schoultz, Robert Francis
Schowalter, William Raymond
Schrader, George Alfred, Jr.
Schrader, Martin Harry
Schrag, Adele Frisbie
Schrag, Karl
Schram, Martin Jay
Schramm, George Joseph
Schramm, John Clarendon
Schreiber, Flora Rheta
Schreiber, Richard William
Schreiber, William Matthew
Schrieffer, John Robert
Schrier, Allan Martin
Schrier, Morris Martin
Schriesheim, Alan
Schroder, Andrew J., III
Schroder, Walter Lynus
Schroeder, Aaron Harold
Schroeder, Alfred Christian
Schroeder, Frederick H.
Schroeder, Henry John, Jr.
Schroeder, Herman Elbert
Schroeder, John Louis
Schroeder, John Power
Schroth, Thomas Nolan
Schruben, John Henry
Schrumpf, Susan Spinelli
Schubart, Mark Allen
Schubert, John Edward
Schubert, Leo
Schubert, Richard Francis
Schuck, Victoria
Schucker, Charles
Schudel, Hansjoerg
Schudt, William Arthur, Jr.
Schuerch, Conrad
Schuknecht, Harold Frederick
Schulberg, Budd
Schuller, Gordon Joseph
Schuller, Grete
Schuller, Gunther
Schullian, Dorothy May
Schulman, Robert Arnold
Schulte, Henry Frank
Schulte, William Frederick
Schultes, Richard Evans
Schultz, Andrew Schultz, Jr.
Schultz, Claire Kelly (Mrs. Wallace L. Schultz)
Schultz, Erwin Gilbert
Schultz, George La Vie
Schultz, James Clement
Schultz, Leonard Peter
Schultz, Leslie P.
Schultz, Maxwell I.
Schultz, Richard Dale
Schultz, Sigrid (Lillian)
Schultz, Stanley George
Schultz, Theodore John
Schultze, Charles Louis
Schultze, Helmuth Willi
Schulz, Juergen
Schulz, Robert L(udwig)
Schulze, Richard Taylor
Schumacher, Elmer Weldon
Schumacher, George Adam
Schuman, Daniel Gerald
Schuman, William Howard
Schumm, Joseph James, Jr.
Schupack, Mark Barry
Schure, Alexander
Schussheim, Morton Joel
Schut, Harold John
Schutta, Henry Szczesny
Schutte, Giles W.
Schutte, Thomas Frederick
Schutz, Herbert Dietrich
Schuyler, William Earl, Jr.
Schwab, Hermann Caspar
Schwab, Martin Jay
Schwacha, George
Schwait, Allen Louis
Schwalje, Joseph Louis
Schwan, Herman Paul
Schwann, William
Schwarting, Arthur Ernest
Schwartz, Abba Philip
Schwartz, Abraham
Schwartz, Alfred Lowin
Schwartz, Anna Jacobson
Schwartz, Arthur Harry
Schwartz, Bernard
Schwartz, Bernard
Schwartz, Bernard Leon
Schwartz, Bertram
Schwartz, Carl Herbert, Jr.
Schwartz, Charles Frederick
Schwartz, David
Schwartz, Edward Arthur
Schwartz, Frederic N.
Schwartz, Harold
Schwartz, Harry
Schwartz, Harry Kane
Schwartz, Harry Sweitcher
Schwartz, Howard Arthur
Schwartz, Irving Leon
Schwartz, Jack Theodore
Schwartz, Jules Jacob
Schwartz, Lillian Feldman
Schwartz, Louis Brown
Schwartz, Lynne Sharon
Schwartz, Michael Averill
Schwartz, Mischa
Schwartz, Richard Derecktor
Schwartz, Richard Jay
Schwartz, Robert
Schwartz, Robert George
Schwartz, Robert Nash
Schwartz, Seymour I.
Schwartz, Stephen Lawrence
Schwartz, Stuart Carl
Schwartz, William Benjamin
Schwartzman, Alan
Schwartzman, David
Schwarz, Daniel
Schwarz, Daniel Tracy
Schwarz, Frederic George
Schwarz, Gerard Ralph
Schwarz, Gerhart Steven
Schwarz, Helmut Julius
Schwarz, Henry Marshall
Schwarz, Michael Jay
Schwarz, Ralph Jacques
Schwarz, Sanford
Schwarzschild, Martin
Schwarzschild, William Harry, Jr.
Schwebel, Milton
Schwebel, Stephen Myron
Schweber, Silvan Samuel
Schwed, Peter
Schweickart, Russell L.
Schweickert, William Peter
Schweiker, Malcolm Alderfer
Schweiker, Richard Schultz
Schweikle, Carl Frederick
Schweitz, Robert Edwin
Schweitzer, Gertrude
Schweitzer, H. George
Schweitzer, Paul Henry
Schwengel, Fred Delbert
Schwenk, Adolph Glaser
Schwenke, Thomas Glenn
Schwenn, Lee William
Schwerin, Horace S.
Schwiebert, Leslie Nordean
Schwieger, John Henry
Schwimmer, David
Schwoebel, William Sylvester
Scofield, Henry Harland
Scofield, John
Scofield, Milton N.
Scoll, David E.
Scollard, Patrick John
Scotes, Thomas James
Scotese, Peter G.
Scott, Alexander Robinson
Scott, Andrew Gregg
Scott, Arnold Duane
Scott, Charles Waldo
Scott, David Bytovetzski
Scott, Donald Albert
Scott, Donald Hunt
Scott, Edgar
Scott, Edward William, Jr.
Scott, Frederick Isadore, Jr.
Scott, George Campbell
Scott, Hugh
Scott, Ira Oscar, Jr.
Scott, Irene Feagin
Scott, James Campbell
Scott, James Hernandez
Scott, Jessie M.
Scott, John Walker
Scott, Jonathan LaVon
Scott, Joseph Welch
Scott, Kenneth Elsner
Scott, Michael
Scott, Nathan Alexander, Jr.
Scott, Rachel Ann
Scott, Ralph Mason
Scott, Robert Charles Lewis
Scott, Robert Montgomery
Scott, Robert Vernon
Scott, Roderic MacDonald
Scott, Roland Boyd
Scott, Stanley Southall
Scott, Tasso Harold
Scott, Thomas Frederick McNair
Scott, William Campbell
Scott, William Clement, III
Scott, William Lloyd
Scott, William Reese
Scott, William Wallace
Scotto, Renata
Scoville, Herbert, Jr.
Scoville, William Beecher
Scowcroft, Brent
Scranton, William Maxwell
Scranton, William Warren
Screvane, Paul Rogers
Scribner, Charles, Jr.
Scribner, Fred Clark, Jr.
Scribner, Joseph M.
Scribner, Louie Lorraine
Scrimenti, Adolph Robert
Scrimshaw, Nevin Stewart
Scudder, Richard B.
Scudder, Thayer
Scudder, Townsend, III
Sculfort, Maurice Charles
Scullion, William Joseph
Scully, David Williams
Scully, Francis Joseph
Scully, James Arnold
Scully, John Carroll
Scully, Vincent Edward
Scurlock, Arch Chilton
Scuro, Joseph Eugene
Seabrook, John Martin

Seal, John Ridley
Sealock, Richard Burl
Seaman, Alfred Jarvis
Seaman, Barbara (Ann Rosner)
Seaman, William Bernard
Seamans, Frank L.
Seamans, Robert Channing, Jr.
Searles, Dewitt Richard
Searls, David Churchill
Searls, Frederick Taylor
Sears, Arthur, Jr.
Sears, Bradford George
Sears, Gordon Mortimer
Sears, James Patrick
Sears, John Patrick
Sears, John Raymond, Jr.
Sears, Robert Needham
Seasonwein, Milton Bernstein
Seath, John
Seaver, Philip Henry
Seawell, Leon T., Jr.
Seawell, William Thomas
Sebold, Russell Perry, III
Sebrell, William Henry, Jr.
Sechrist, Elizabeth Hough
Seckler, Stanley George
Secondari, Helen Jean Rogers
Secter, David Irving
Sedaka, Neil
Sedlin, Elias David
See, Harold Wentz
Seegal, Herbert Leonard
Seegal, Samuel Melbourne
Seeger, Charles Louis
Seeger, Michael
Seeger, Pete
Seegraber, Frank Joseph
Seeley, Harry Wilbur, Jr.
Seeley, John George
Seeley, Robert Thomas
Seelig, Gerard Leo
Seelig, Richard Paul
Seelye, Talcott Williams
Seevers, Gary Leonard
Segal, Bernard Gerard
Segal, Charles Paul
Segal, Erich
Segal, George
Segal, George
Segal, Harry Louis
Segal, Irving Ezra
Segal, Jonathan Bruce
Segal, Lore
Segal, Martin
Segal, Maurice Sidney
Segal, Sheldon Jerome
Segal, William Charles
Segall, Arthur A.
Segall, Harold Abraham
Segall, John Louis
Segall, Maurice
Seggel, Richard Louis
Seggerman, Harry Gurney Atha
Segovia, Andres
Seib, Charles Bach
Seiberlich, Carl Joseph
Seibert, Donald Vincent
Seibert, Russell Jacob
Seibert, Wilson Adriance, Jr.
Seibold, Frederick Carl, Jr.
Seid, Herman
Seid, Ruth (Jo Sinclair, pseudonym)
Seiden, Henry
Seidensticker, Edward George
Seidler, I. Marshall
Seidlin, Joseph
Seidman, Bert
Seidman, Harold
Seidman, Jacob Stewart
Seifert, William Walther
Seifried, Dean Bardon
Seitz, Collins Jacques
Seitz, Frederick
Seitz, Howard Alexander
Seitz, Nicholas Joseph
Seitz, Peter
Seixas, Frank Archibald
Sekler, Eduard Franz
Selby, Cecily Cannan (Mrs. Henry M. Selby)
Selby, John Edward
Selby, John Rodney
Selden, Albert W.
Selden, David Seeley
Selden, Richard Thomas
Selden, William Kirkpatrick
Seldes, George
Seldes, Marian
Selesky, Harold F.
Seley, Jason
Self, Margaret Cabell
Selig, Karl-Ludwig
Seliger, Charles
Seliger, Howard H.
Seligman, Daniel
Seligman, Germain
Seligmann, James Frederick
Seligmann, Werner
Selikoff, Irving John
Sell, William Edward
Sellars, Lee Tecumseh
Selle, Elaine Louise Babcock
Sellers, Mark Ashley
Sellew, Francis Bernard
Sellin, (Johan) Thorsten
Sellinger, Joseph Anthony
Sellon, John A.
Sells, Leonard Little
Sells, Robert Lee
Selove, Walter
Selsam, Milicent Ellis
Seltzer, Ronald
Seltzer, Ruth
Selwyn, Donald
Selznick, Irene Mayer
Semans, Truman Thomas
Semmes, Benedict Joseph, Jr.
Semon, Warren Lloyd
Semple, T. Darrington, Jr.
Sen, Samar Ranjan
Sencer, David Judson
Sendak, Maurice Bernard
Senecal, Vance Evan
Sener, Joseph Ward
Senkier, Robert Joseph
Senn, Milton John Edward
Sennett, William Clifford
Senseman, Ronald Sylvester
Senter, William Joseph
Serban, Andrei George
Serenbetz, Warren Lewis
Sergel, Christopher Roger
Sergievsky, Orest
Serkin, Peter
Serkin, Rudolf
Serpa, Thomas Rose
Serra-Badue, Daniel Francisco
Serraino, Charles
Sert, Jose Luis
Seslowsky, Harvey Michael
Sessa, Frank Bowman
Sessions, Cliff
Sessions, Robert Evans
Sessions, Roger Huntington
Setchkarev, Vsevolod
Sethness, Charles Olin
Setlow, Jane Kellock
Setlow, Richard Burton
Seton, Anya
Seton, Charles B.
Setterberg, Carl
Setton, Kenneth M.
Setzer, Gene Willis
Setzler, William Edward
Seuffert, Charles Francis
Sevareid, Arnold Eric
Sevcenko, Ihor
Sevel, Bernard Jerome
Severance, Craig
Severinghaus, John Walter
Severo, Richard
Severs, Jonathan Burke
Sevik, Maurice
Sevy, Roger Warren
Sewall, Richard Benson
Seward, Doris Marie
Seward, George Chester
Seward, Harold Aloysius
Seward, Ralph Theodore
Sewell, Winifred
Sexton, Burton Hathaway
Sexton, Richard
Sexton, William Cottrell
Seybolt, George Crossan
Seyferth, Dietmar
Seymour, Charles, Jr.
Seymour, Ernest Richard
Seymour, Robert Edward
Seymour, Walton
Seymour, Whitney North
Seymour, Whitney North, Jr.
Seznec, Alain
Sferra, Amedeo Gennaro
Sgarro, Louis
Shackford, Roland Herbert
Shackleton, Polly (Mrs. Robert W. Shackleton)
Shad, John Sigsbee Rees
Shaefer, Richard Francis
Shaeffer, Charles Wayne
Shafer, Eldon Eugene
Shafer, Guy Carlton
Shafer, Raymond Philip
Shaffer, Charles Norman
Shaffer, Jerome Arthur
Shaffer, John Hixon
Shaffer, Kenneth Raymond
Shaffer, Mary L.
Shaffer, Russell K.
Shafroth, Will
Shafto, Robert Austin
Shagass, Charles
Shah, Idries
Shaheen, John Michael
Shaheen, William Henry
Shaifer, Norman
Shain, Charles Edward
Shainman, Irwin
Shaker, Theodore Frederick
Shakespeare, Frank Joseph
Shakno, Robert Julian
Shakow, David
Shalala, Donna Edna
Shalleck, Milton
Shallenberger, Robert Urson
Shalowitz, Erwin Emmanuel
Shamos, Morris Herbert
Shanahan, Eileen
Shanahan, Robert Bart
Shands, Harley Cecil
Shands, William Ridley, Jr.
Shane, Rita
Shane, Sheldon Richard
Shanet, Howard Stephen
Shanken, Edward Dean
Shanker, Albert
Shankman, Florence Vogel
Shankman, Jacob Kestin
Shanks, Ann Zane
Shanks, Hershel
Shanley, Bernard Michael
Shanley, Paul Joseph
Shannon, Claude Elwood
Shannon, David Allen
Shannon, Donald Hawkins
Shannon, Edgar Finley, Jr.
Shannon, James A.
Shannon, Thomas Francis
Shantzer, Louis
Shapere, Dudley
Shapero, Harold Samuel
Shapiro, Albert
Shapiro, Alvin Philip
Shapiro, Arthur Kyle
Shapiro, Ascher Herman
Shapiro, David Israel
Shapiro, David Joel
Shapiro, David Louis
Shapiro, E. Donald
Shapiro, Eli
Shapiro, George M.
Shapiro, Harry
Shapiro, Harry Lionel
Shapiro, Harvey
Shapiro, Irving Meyer
Shapiro, Irving Saul
Shapiro, Irwin Ira
Shapiro, Jerome Herbert
Shapiro, Joel Elias
Shapiro, Leon Nathan
Shapiro, Louis
Shapiro, Marvin Lincoln
Shapiro, Maurice Mandel
Shapiro, Nils Allen
Shapiro, Norman Richard
Shapiro, Philip
Shapiro, Richard Gerald
Shapiro, Robert Frank
Shapiro, Ronald Maurice
Shapiro, Sam
Shapiro, Seymour
Shapiro, Sidney
Shapp, Martha Glauber
Shapp, Milton J.
Shapshak, Rene
Sharaff, Irene
Sharbaugh, Harry Robert
Sharify, Nasser
Sharits, Paul Jeffrey
Sharp, Daniel Asher
Sharp, Eliot Hall
Sharp, Lauriston
Sharp, Lewis Inman
Sharp, Marion Leale (Mrs. James Riddle Sharp)
Sharp, Morris Louis
Sharp, Philip R.
Sharpe, Carleton Fordham
Sharpe, Henry Dexter, Jr.
Sharpe, Myron Emanuel
Sharpley, John Miles
Sharrah, Marion Lester
Sharrow, Leonard
Sharwell, William Gay
Shatin, Harry
Shattuck, Roger Whitney
Shatzkin, Leonard
Shaub, Harold Arthur
Shaughnessy, Daniel Robert, Jr.
Shaull, Richard
Shaver, George Jacob, Jr.
Shaw, Arnold Franklin
Shaw, Brackley
Shaw, Bruno
Shaw, Dickson Courtney, III
Shaw, Edward Pease
Shaw, (Francis) Harold
Shaw, Harry Lee, Jr.
Shaw, Herbert Weller, Jr.
Shaw, Joseph Thompson, Jr.
Shaw, Luther Gardner
Shaw, Milton Herbert
Shaw, Oscar Moore
Shaw, Reid Lonsdale
Shaw, Russell Burnham
Shaw, Spencer
Shaw, Walter Burns
Shaw, William Frederick
Shay, Donald Emerson
Shayne, Neil T.
Shayon, Robert Lewis
Shea, Dion Warren Joseph
Shea, Donald James
Shea, Edward Emmet
Shea, Francis Michael
Shea, George William
Shea, Hamilton
Shea, James J., Jr.
Shea, Jeremiah Patrick
Shea, Joseph Francis
Shea, Robert Francis
Shea, Robert McConnell
Shea, Timothy Edward
Shea, William A.
Sheaffer, Louis
Sheahan, John Bernard
Shear, Harold Edson
Sheard, William James
Shearer, Jesse Lowen
Shearer, Ross Sterling
Shearer, Thaddeus Errington
Sheckels, G. Dale
Shedd, William Edgar, III
Sheed, Wilfrid John Joseph
Sheehan, Donald Thomas
Sheehan, Harold William
Sheehan, Helen Lee
Sheehan, John C(lark)
Sheehan, John Joseph
Sheehan, John Joseph
Sheehan, John M.
Sheehan, Louis James
Sheehan, Mark Thomas
Sheehan, Neil
Sheehan, Walter Francis
Sheehy, Eugene Paul
Sheehy, Gail Henion
Sheeline, Paul Cushing
Sheen, Fulton John
Sheets, Donald Guy
Sheets, Herman Ernest
Sheffey, Fred Clifton, Jr.
Shehan, Lawrence Joseph
Sheib, Simon
Sheinberg, George Charles
Sheingold, Leonard Sumner
Sheldon, Courtney Roswell
Sheldon, David Frederick
Sheldon, Eleanor Harriet Bernert
Sheldon, Eric
Sheldon, Georgiana Hortense
Sheldon, Sidney
Sheldon, Walter Herman
Sheldon, William Herbert
Shelesnyak, Moses Chaim
Shelhoss, Emmett Clayton
Shelley, Walter Brown
Shelly, Warner S.
Shelton, Harriette Woodward
Shelton, Reid LeRoy
Shen, Benjamin Shih-Ping
Shen, Chia Theng
Shen, Shan-Fu
Shenefield, John Hale
Shenstone, Allen Goodrich
Shenton, James Patrick
Shepack, Lawrence Frederick
Shepard, Elaine Elizabeth
Shepard, John Carroll
Shepard, Robert Andrews
Shepard, Sam
Shepard, Tazewell Taylor
Shepard, Thomas Rockwell, Jr.
Shepard, Thomas Zachary
Shepardson, Edwin Stanley
Shepardson, Wallace Lloyd
Shepherd, Dennis Granville
Shepherd, Henry Longdon
Shepherd, Herman Robert
Shepherd, Richard Jennings
Shepley, Hugh
Shepley, James Robinson
Shepp, Archie
Sheppard, Charles Stewart
Sheppard, Eugenia
Sheppard, Posy (Mrs. John Wade Sheppard)
Sher, David
Sher, Stanley Owen
Sherbell, Rhoda
Sherbourne, Everett Christian
Sherer, Albert William, Jr.
Sherf, Arden Frederick
Sheridan, John Edward
Sherif, Carolyn Wood
Sheriff, Seymour
Sherk, Robert Kenneth
Sherman, Charles Daniel, Jr.
Sherman, Frederick George
Sherman, Irving Harold
Sherman, John Foord
Sherman, Jonathan Goodhue
Sherman, Louis
Sherman, Malcolm Lee
Sherman, Merritt
Sherman, Robert Arthur
Sherman, Roger James
Sherman, Ronald King
Sherman, Saul Lawrence
Sherman, Stuart Capen
Sherman, William Courtney
Sherman, William Samuel
Shero, Fred Alexander
Sherockman, Andrew Antolcik
Sherr, Rubby
Sherrer, Charles David
Sherrick, Ronald Paul
Sherrill, Hugh Virgil
Sherrod, Robert Lee
Sherry, Joseph A.
Sherry, Sol
Shertzer, George Edwin
Sherwin, James Terry
Sherwin, Judith Johnson
Sherwood, Aaron Wiley
Sherwood, Arthur Murray
Sherwood, Sidney
Sherwood, Thorne
Shestack, Alan
Shestack, Jerome Joseph
Shestack, Melvin Bernard
Shetland, Margaret Louise
Shettles, Landrum Brewer
Shevelov, George Yury
Shewmaker, Russell Newton
Shick, George Barton, Jr.
Shields, Alexander
Shields, Richard Tyner
Shields, Robert Campbell
Shields, Robert Hazen
Shiely, Albert Raymond, Jr.
Shientag, Florence Perlow
Shiere, Frederic Roland
Shiffler, Neil Frederick
Shifley, Ralph Louis
Shifrin, Seymour
Shih, Chung-wen
Shikler, Aaron
Shilensky, Morris
Shillito, Barry J.
Shils, Edward B.
Shimamoto, George Gentoku
Shimkin, Leon
Shimura, Goro
Shineman, Edward William, Jr.
Shinn, Allen Mayhew
Shinn, George Latimer
Shinn, Richard Randolph
Shinn, Roger Lincoln
Shinozuka, Masanobu
Shipler, David Karr
Shipley, Joseph T.
Shipley, L(inwood) Parks
Shipley, Samuel Lynn
Shipman, Charles William
Shipman, Peter Herbert
Shipman, William Davis
Shippee, Nathan Mathewson
Shippen, Edward
Shire, Donald Thomas
Shirer, William Lawrence
Shires, George Thomas, II
Shirk, Frank Charles
Shirkey, Albert Patterson
Shirley, George Irving
Shirley, Hardy Lomax
Shiskin, Julius
Shister, Joseph
Shively, Donald Howard
Shiya, George Gilbert
Shlaudeman, Harry Walter
Shmoys, Jerry
Shnayerson, Robert Beahan
Shneiderov, Anatol James
Shober, Edward Wharton, Jr.
Shobert, Erle Irwin, II
Shock, Nathan Wetherill
Shockley, Loren Colson
Shoemaker, Frank Crawford
Shoemaker, Louise Proehl
Shoemaker, P. Kenneth
Shoemaker, Robert John
Shon, Frederick John
Shoniker, Fintan Raymond
Shook, Karel Francis Antony
Shooman, Martin Lawrence
Shor, Edgar Leroy
Shore, Ferdinand John
Shore, Nathan Allen
Shore, Sidney
Short, Robert Louis
Short, Robert Waltrip (Bobby)
Short, Walter Joseph
Short, Winthrop Allen
Shortlidge, Joseph Bacon
Shortway, Richard Anthony
Shoulberg, Harry
Shoup, Carl Sumner
Shoupp, William Earl
Shovlin, John P.
Showalter, English
Showers, Donald McCollister
Showers, Ralph Morris
Shrady, Frederick Charles
Shreeve, Charles Alfred, Jr.
Shriver, Eunice Mary Kennedy (Mrs. Robert Sargent Shriver, Jr.)
Shriver, Harry Clair
Shriver, Robert Sargent, Jr.
Shrock, Robert Rakes
Shrontz, Frank Anderson
Shropshire, Walter, Jr.
Shuart, James M.
Shubert, Joseph Francis
Shuchter, Claude F.
Shuff, Lily
Shugart, Kenneth Laverne, Jr.
Shuker, Gregory Brown
Shulevitz, Uri
Shull, Clifford G.
Shull, Leo
Shull, Leon
Shulman, Arthur
Shulman, Edward M.
Shulman, Herman L.
Shulman, Marcy Lee
Shulman, Marshall Darrow
Shulman, Martin
Shulman, Max
Shulman, Max L.
Shulman, Robert Gerson
Shulman, Stephen Neal
Shulman, Steven
Shultz, Richard Carl
Shumaker, John Jeffries
Shuman, Charles Ross
Shuman, Frederick Gale
Shuman, Stanley Saxe
Shumate, Stuart
Shumlin, Herman
Shumway, Frank Ritter
Shur, Barnett Israel
Shur, Walter
Shurcliff, Sidney Nichols
Shurcliff, William Asahel
Shure, Ralph Deane
Shurick, Edward Palmes
Shuster, Bud
Shuster, William Weymann
Shutler, Philip Dickinson
Shutt, Merrill Moran
Shuttleworth, Harry Benson
Shuttleworth, Herbert Lewis, II
Shuttleworth, Ronald Gordon
Shyer, Herbert Paul
Sibal, Abner Woodruff
Sibigtroth, Joseph Clarence
Sibilia, P.E.
Sibley, Alden Kingsland
Sibley, Charles Gald
Sibley, Frederic Grant
Sica, Albert Joseph
Sickle, Norbert Howard
Sidamon-Eristoff, Anne Phipps
Sidbury, James Buren
Sidebottom, John Herbert
Sidell, William
Sidey, Hugh Swanson
Sidney, Sylvia (Koskow, Sophia)
Sieben, Horst Otto
Siebens, Arthur A.
Siebert, Muriel
Siebert, William McConway
Sieder, Violet Marot
Siegal, Jacob J.
Siegel, Alan Michael
Siegel, Benjamin M.
Siegel, Eli
Siegel, Herbert Bernard
Siegel, Herbert Jay
Siegel, Irving Herbert
Siegel, Leo Harold
Siegel, Nathaniel Harold
Siegel, Paul Noah
Siegel, Seymour
Siegel, Seymour Nathaniel
Siegel, Simon B.
Siegel, Stuart Samuel
Siegel, Thomas Louis
Siegel, William M.
Siegfried, Robert Edwin
Siegman, Henry
Siegmeister, Elie
Siekevitz, Philip
Sieling, Dale Harold
Siemer, Deanne C.
Siems, Leonard A.A.
Sienko, Michell J.
Siesel, Alfred J.
Siever, Raymond
Sievering, Nelson Frederick, Jr.
Sievers, Albert John, III
Sievers, Harry Joseph
Sievers, Robert H.
Sieverts, Frank Arne
Siffert, Robert Spencer
Sifton, Charles Proctor
Sifton, David Whittier
Sigel, Stanley Jordan
Sigety, Charles Edward
Siggelkow, Richard Albert
Sigler, Andrew Clark
Sigmon, Richard Roland
Sigmond, Robert M.
Sigmund, Paul Eugene
Sihler, William Wooding
Siipola, Elsa Margareeta (Mrs. Harold E. Israel)
Siker, Ephraim S.
Sikes, Robert L.F.
Silagi, Selma (Mrs. Robert Silagi)
Silas (Koskinas) of Amphipolis
Silber, Gordon Rutledge
Silber, John Robert
Silberman, Charles Eliot
Silberman, H. Lee
Silberman, James Henry
Silberman, Laurence Hirsch
Silberstein, Norman Ronald
Silbert, Earl J.
Silbert, Theodore H.
Silen, William
Silipigni, Alfredo
Silk, George
Silk, Leonard Solomon
Sillars, Robert N., Jr.
Sillcocks, Henry Jackson
Sillcox, Lewis Ketcham
Sillesky, John Darrison
Sillin, Lelan Flor, Jr.
Silloway, Charles Thompson
Sills, Arthur Jack
Sills, Beverly (Mrs. Peter B. Greenough)
Sills, David Lawrence
Sills, Stanley S.
Silsby, William Sands
Siltzbach, Louis Elliott
Silva, Ruth Caridad
Silveira, Augustine, Jr.
Silver, Charles Hal
Silver, Charles Morton
Silver, Horace Ward Martin Tavares
Silver, Joe
Silver, Julius
Silver, Stuart Martin
Silverberg, Lorence A.
Silverblatt, Arthur
Silverman, Abner David
Silverman, Al
Silverman, Alvin Michaels
Silverman, Burton Philip
Silverman, Fred
Silverman, Herbert R.
Silverman, Hirsch Lazaar
Silverman, Joseph
Silverman, Matthew
Silverman, Oscar Ansell
Silverman, Paul Hyman
Silverman, Robert Eugene
Silverman, Samuel
Silverman, Samuel Joshua
Silverman, Syd
Silverman, William Maurice
Silvers, Earl Reed, Jr.
Silvers, Robert B.
Silvers, Willys Kent
Silverstein, Joseph Harry
Silverstein, Leonard Lewis
Silverstone, Harris Julian
Silvert, Kalman Hirsch
Silvestro, Clement Mario
Simches, Seymour Oliver
Simeone, Fiorindo Anthony
Simes, Frank James
Simic, Charles
Simis, Theodore Luckey
Simmel, Marianne Lenore
Simmermon, James Everett
Simmonds, Geoffrey Roy
Simmonds, James Henry
Simmons, Charles
Simmons, David Arthur
Simmons, Edward Joseph
Simmons, Edwin Howard
Simmons, Howard Ensign, Jr.
Simmons, Joseph Jacob, III
Simmons, Kenneth Dale
Simmons, Lawrence Whitley
Simmons, Marvin Gene
Simmons, Matty
Simmons, Ozzie Gordon
Simmons, Richard D.
Simmons, Richard Morgan, Jr.
Simmons, Richard Sheridan
Simmons, Samuel Lee
Simmons, Warren Hathaway, Jr.

Simon, Abbey
Simon, Albert
Simon, Carl Julian
Simon, Caroline Klein
Simon, Charles Jacob
Simon, David
Simon, Dorothy Martin
Simon, Eckehard (Peter)
Simon, Eric Jacob
Simon, Ernest Robert
Simon, George Thomas
Simon, Henry
Simon, Herbert Alexander
Simon, John Gerald
Simon, John Ivan
Simon, John Jacob
Simon, John Kenneth
Simon, Joseph Patrick
Simon, Max Michael
Simon, Neil
Simon, Paul
Simon, Ralph Emanuel
Simon, Sheldon
Simon, Sidney
Simon, Stanley
Simon, William Edward
Simonds, John Ormsbee
Simonds, Philip Douglas
Simone, Nina
Simonelli, Charles Francis
Simonpietri, Andre C.
Simons, Howard
Simons, Lawrence B.
Simons, Lewis Martin
Simons, Samuel Stoney
Simons, Thomas Cunningham
Simonson, Roy Walter
Simont, Marc
Simpich, William Morris
Simpkins, Gilbert Arnott
Simpson, Adele
Simpson, Alan
Simpson, Carole Estelle
Simpson, Cary Hatcher
Simpson, Charles Hammond
Simpson, Charles Reagan
Simpson, Geddes Wilson
Simpson, Howard Russell
Simpson, James Richardson
Simpson, James Shores
Simpson, John Wistar
Simpson, Louis Aston Marantz
Simpson, Robert Edward
Simpson, R(obert) Smith
Simpson, Seymour David
Simpson, William Kelly
Sims, Everett Martin
Sims, Ivor Donald
Sims, John Haley (Zoot)
Sims, John Rogers, Jr.
Sims, Naomi Ruth
Sims, Peter (LaRoca)
Sinai, Isaac Robert
Sinanoglu, Oktay
Sinclair, Joseph Samuels
Sinclair, Keith Val
Sinclair, Rolf Malcolm
Sinden, Harry
Sindermann, Carl James
Sinex, Francis Marott
Sinfelt, John Henry
Singer, Arthur Louis, Jr.
Singer, Esther Forman (Mrs. Sidney Singer)
Singer, Henry A.
Singer, Isaac Bashevis
Singer, Isadore Manual
Singer, Jacques
Singer, Leon
Singer, Martin Melvin
Singer, Maxine Frank
Singer, Norman
Singer, Samuel Loewenberg
Singer, Sarah Beth
Singer, S(iegfried) Fred
Singer, Stephen Lee
Singer, Thomas Eric
Singer-Magdoff, Laura Joan Silver (Mrs. Samuel Magdoff)
Singleton, Charles Southward
Singleton, Donald Edward
Singleton, Fred G.
Singleton, George Monroe
Singleton, John Paul
Singleton, Philip Arthur
Singley, Mark Eldridge
Singsen, Antone Gerhardt
Sinkford, Jeanne Craig
Sinks, Lucius Frederick
Sinness, Lester Snowdon
Sinsheimer, Warren Jack
Sinzer, Joseph Francis
Siple, Walter Helck
Sippel, John Parker
Sirica, John J.
Sirignano, William Alfonso
Sirkin, Abraham M.
Sirna, Anthony Alfred, III
Sirovich, Lawrence
Sirowitz, Leonard
Sisco, Joseph John
Sisk, Philip Laurence
Siskind, William Leigh
Sitkin, Irwin Jay
Sitterley, Eugene Fletcher
Sitterly, Charlotte Moore
Siu, Ralph Gun-Hoy
Sivard, Robert Paul
Sive, David
Sizer, Irwin Whiting
Sizer, Theodore Ryland
Skala, Martin
Skalafuris, Angelo James
Skalak, Richard
Skallerup, Walter Thorwald, Jr.
Skantze, Lawrence Albert
Skardon, James Altick
Skehan, James William
Skehan, Patrick William
Skell, Philip S.
Skelly, Thomas Francis
Skillin, Edward Simeon
Skillin, Glenn Barrie
Skillman, Hope
Skillman, John Frosch, Jr.
Skillman, Thomas J., Jr.
Skinner, Brian John
Skinner, Burrhus Frederic
Skinner, Cornelia Otis
Skinner, Frederick James
Skinner, Ralph Harold, Jr.
Skinner, Richard Stephen, Jr.
Skinner, Walter Jay
Skinner, Wickham
Skipper, James Everett
Sklar, Richard J. (Rick)
Sklar, Robert Anthony
Sklare, Marshall
Skolnikoff, Eugene Bertram
Skolovsky, Zadel
Skoog, Charles Vernon, Jr.
Skouras, Spyros Solon
Skrable, Kenneth William
Skromme, Lawrence Hilmer
Skrypynk, Mstyslav Stephan
Skubitz, Joseph
Skurla, George Martin
Slacik, Karl Francis
Slack, John M., Jr.
Slack, Lewis
Slade, Jarvis James
Slade, John Hans
Sladen, William Joseph Lambart
Slais, Louis Joseph
Slanetz, Lawrence William
Slappey, Sterling Greene
Slater, John Edmund
Slater, Joseph Elliott
Slater, Joseph Locke
Slater, Robert James
Slatoff, Walter Jacob
Slattery, Kenneth F.
Slaughter, Adolph James
Slaughter, Harrison T.
Slavin, Simon
Slawsky, Zaka Israel
Slawson, John
Slayton, Mariette Elizabeth Paine (Mrs. Ronald Alfred Slayton)
Slayton, William Larew
Slechta, Robert Frank
Sleeper, Sherwin James
Slenczynska, Ruth
Slepian, David
Slepian, Paul
Slesinger, Reuben Emanuel
Slesnick, William Ellis
Sligh, Frederick Henry
Slingerland, Donald McDonald
Slingluff, Thomas Rowland, Jr.
Slitor, Richard Eaton
Slive, Seymour
Sloan, Grace McCalmont
Sloan, Raymond Paton
Sloane, Eric
Sloane, Madeleine Edison
Sloane, Patricia Hermine
Sloat, Frederick Parmalee
Slobodin, Alex
Slobody, Lawrence Boris
Slocum, John Howard
Slocum, Wilber James
Slone, Dennis
Slosberg, Samuel Louis
Sloshberg, Leah Phyfer (Mrs. Willard Sloshberg)
Slotkin, Richard Sidney
Slotnick, Herbert Norman
Sloves, Marvin
Sloviter, Henry Allan
Slowey, Jack William
Slowinski, Walter Aloysius
Sloyan, Gerard Stephen
Sloyan, Sister Mary Stephanie
Smagorinsky, Joseph
Small, S(aul) Mouchly
Small, William Andrew
Small, William Edwin, Jr.
Small, William Newell
Smalls, Charlie
Smallwood, Franklin
Smart, George Norman Russell
Smart, L(ouis) Edwin, Jr.
Smart, Stephen Bruce, Jr.
Smeal, Eleanor Cutri
Smeal, Frank Paul
Smeltzer, Norman Harold
Smerling, Julian Melvin
Smiddy, Joseph Charles
Smiley, Donald Burdette
Smiley, Malcolm Finlay
Smiley, Pril
Smit, Jacobus Wilhelmus
Smith, A. Robert
Smith, Ada Beatrice Queen Victoria Louisa Virginia (Bricktop)
Smith, Albert
Smith, Albert Barnes, Jr.
Smith, Allan Kellogg
Smith, Anne Mollegen
Smith, Anthony Wayne
Smith, Austin
Smith, Bailey
Smith, Barbara Herrnstein
Smith, Barry Vincent
Smith, Bromley Keables
Smith, Bulkeley, Jr.
Smith, Byron Capleese
Smith, Charles Alphonso
Smith, C(harles) Carney
Smith, Charles Curtis
Smith, Charles Llewellyn, Jr.
Smith, Charles Whitley
Smith, Claude Carroll
Smith, Clement Andrew
Smith, Curtis Griffin
Smith, Cyrus Rowlett
Smith, Dale Edwin
Smith, Datus Clifford, Jr.
Smith, David Beach
Smith, David English
Smith, David Gilbert
Smith, David Lee
Smith, David Martyn
Smith, David Shiverick
Smith, DeWitt Clinton, Jr.
Smith, Donald Eugene
Smith, Donald Kaye
Smith, Donald Lloyd
Smith, Douglas
Smith, Douglas LaRue
Smith, Douglas Rathbone
Smith, Edgar Pichard
Smith, Edith Lucile
Smith, Edward Holman
Smith, Elden Theodore
Smith, Ellis Wendle
Smith, Eugene Lewis
Smith, Foster Lee
Smith, Frank MacGregor, Jr.
Smith, Frederick Adair, Jr.
Smith, F(rederick) Dow(swell)
Smith, Frederick Edward
Smith, Frederick Plimpton
Smith, Frederick Rutledge
Smith, G. E. Kidder
Smith, Gardner Watkins
Smith, George Elwood
Smith, George Franklin, Jr.
Smith, George Patrick, II
Smith, George Thomas
Smith, Gerald Wayne
Smith, Gerard Coad
Smith, Gordon Hunt
Smith, Gordon Mackintosh
Smith, G(ordon) Roysce, Jr.
Smith, Grant W(arren)
Smith, Gregg
Smith, H. Sheldon
Smith, Halsey
Smith, Harlan William
Smith, Harold Hill
Smith, Harold Lee
Smith, Harrison Venture
Smith, Hedrick Laurence
Smith, Henrietta Tamar
Smith, Henry Oliver
Smith, Herbert Livingston, III
Smith, Howard Godwin
Smith, Howard Kingsbury
Smith, Howard McQueen
Smith, J. Joseph
Smith, J. Stanford
Smith, Jaclyn
Smith, James David Blackhall
Smith, James Gerald
Smith, J(ames) Henry
Smith, James Oscar
Smith, James Roswell
Smith, Jeffrey Bordeaux
Smith, Jeffrey Greenwood
Smith, Jesse Morgan, Jr.
Smith, Jessica
Smith, John Brewster
Smith, John Edwin
Smith, John Henry
Smith, John Lewis, Jr.
Smith, Jonathan Leslie
Smith, Joseph Edward
Smith, Joseph Henry
Smith, Joseph LeConte, Jr.
Smith, Josephine Woolley
Smith, Julian Cleveland, Jr.
Smith, Kendrick
Smith, Kenneth Acton
Smith, Kenneth Alan
Smith, Kenneth Danforth
Smith, Lester Wickham
Smith, Levering
Smith, Lewis Motter, Jr.
Smith, Lillian May
Smith, Liz
Smith, Lloyd
Smith, Malcolm Bernard
Smith, Malcolm Sommerville
Smith, Margaret Chase
Smith, Mark Kern, Jr.
Smith, Marshall Francis
Smith, Marvin Hugh
Smith, Maureen Margaret
Smith, Maurice Frederik
Smith, Merlin Gale
Smith, Michael Brackett
Smith, Michael Francis
Smith, Morgan Kinmonth
Smith, Mortimer Brewster
Smith, Myron George
Smith, Nate
Smith, Neal Edward
Smith, Norman Clark
Smith, Norman Obed
Smith, Olcott Damon
Smith, Oliver
Smith, Paul Davis
Smith, Paul Frederick
Smith, Peter Walker
Smith, Philip Alan
Smith, Philip Cleary
Smith, Phillip Hartley
Smith, Ralph Lee
Smith, Raymond D(aniel)
Smith, Raymond William
Smith, Red (Walter Wellesley)
Smith, Rhoten Alexander
Smith, Richard Austin
Smith, Richard B.
Smith, Richard Emerson (Dick Smith)
Smith, Richard Frederick
Smith, Richard Jay
Smith, Richard Joyce
Smith, Richard Miller
Smith, Richard Schiedt
Smith, Robert E. (Buffalo Bob)
Smith, Robert Gillen
Smith, Robert Harold
Smith, Robert I.
Smith, Robert John
Smith, Robert Louis
Smith, Robert Moors
Smith, Robert Rutherford
Smith, Robert Virgil
Smith, Robert William
Smith, Robyn Caroline
Smith, Roger Carlyle
Smith, Roger Haskell
Smith, Russell Jack
Smith, Ruth Lillian Schluchter
Smith, Samuel Kreis
Smith, Sidney Butler
Smith, Stanford
Smith, Stanley Roger
Smith, Stuart Seaborne
Smith, Sylvester Comstock, Jr.
Smith, Terence Fitzgerald
Smith, Timothy Lawrence
Smith, Tony
Smith, W. Mason
Smith, Walter Joseph, Jr.
Smith, Walter Tilford
Smith, Warner Taliaferro
Smith, Warren Brierley, Jr.
Smith, Wayne Augustus
Smith, Wendell Ross
Smith, Wesley Sanford
Smith, William Arthur
Smith, William Harold
Smith, William Henry Preston
Smith, William Jay
Smith, William Leigh
Smith, William Martin
Smith, William Stanford
Smith, William Vick
Smith, William Young
Smith, Willis Allen
Smithberg, Eugene Herbert
Smithdeal, William Fralin
Smithies, Arthur
Smithson, John Royston
Smithwick, Reginald Hammerick
Smits, Theodore Richard
Smoker, Edward Heise
Smokler, Jerold
Smolanoff, Michael Louis
Smolar, Boris (Ber)
Smolin, Ronald Philip
Smothers, William Joseph
Smotrich, David Isadore
Smullyan, Arthur Francis
Smyly, Susan Vanderbilt
Smyser, Hamilton Martin
Smyth, Henry Field, Jr.
Smyth, Joel Douglas
Smyth, Peter Richard
Smythe, Hugh Heyne
Snapp, Roy Baker
Snapper, Ernst
Snavely, Tipton Ray
Snavely, William Pennington
Snead, George Murrell, Jr.
Snead, Jesse Carlyle
Sneath, William Scott
Sneider, Richard Lee
Snell, Fred Manget
Snell, George Davis
Snelling, Richard Arkwright
Snelson, Kenneth Duane
Snibbe, Richard Wilson
Snider, Edward Malcolm
Snider, Edwin Wallace
Snider, Ray Solomon
Snoddy, John Martin
Snodgrass, William DeWitt
Snoke, Albert Waldo
Snoke, Harry Conwell
Snow, George Abraham
Snow, Herman Bernard
Snow, James Byron, Jr.
Snow, Phoebe
Snowden, Frank Martin, Jr.
Snowden, Lawrence Fontaine
Snowdon, John Colin
Snyder, Arthur
Snyder, Arthur Fenimore French
Snyder, Asa Edward
Snyder, Edward Pheatt
Snyder, Edwin Knowlson
Snyder, Elmer Andrew
Snyder, Jacob Rowland
Snyder, Joan
Snyder, John Crayton
Snyder, John Joseph
Snyder, John Stewart
Snyder, John Wesley
Snyder, Joseph Harry
Snyder, Joseph Julien
Snyder, Louis Irving, Jr.
Snyder, Louis L.
Snyder, Nathan
Snyder, Paul L.
Snyder, Richard Elliot
Snyder, Richard Lynne
Snyder, Roy Dietrich, Jr.
Snyder, Solomon Halbert
Snyder, Tom
Snyder, William Cordes, Jr.
Snyder, William Penn, III
Snyder, William Russell
Snyderman, Reuven Kenneth
Soars, Harold Marshall, Jr.
Sobel, Edna H.
Sobel, Lester Albert
Sobel, Raymond
Sober, Sidney
Sobiloff, Myer Nathaniel
Sobin, Julian Melvin
Sobin, Morris
Sobol, Donald J.
Soby, James Thrall
Socolow, Arthur Abraham
Socransky, Sigmund Sydney
Soderberg, Carl Richard
Soderholm, Lars Gustav
Soderlind, Sterling Eugene
Soffen, Gerald Alan
Soffer, Milton David
Soffer, Sheldon
Softness, Donald Gabriel
Softness, John
Sohl, Walter Wood, Jr.
Sohlin, Donnelly Allen
Sohmer, Bernard
Sohn, Louis Bruno
Sokal, Joseph Emanuel
Sokol, Herman
Sokol, Sidney S.
Sokolow, Anna
Solari, Joseph G.
Solarz, Stephen Joshua
Solaun, Mauricio
Solbert, Peter Omar Abernathy
Solbrig, Otto Thomas
Soldow, James Joseph
Solecki, R. Stefan
Solender, Sanford
Soliman, Patricia Kathleen Brehaut (Mrs. Anwar El Sayed I. Soliman)
Solinger, David Morris
Solino, Louis
Soll, David Benjamin
Sollberger, Harvey Dene
Sollenberger, Howard Edwin
Solnit, Albert Jay
Soloff, Louis Alexander
Solomon, Anthony Morton
Solomon, Arthur Kaskel
Solomon, Henry
Solomon, Joel W.
Solomon, Joseph
Solomon, Maynard Elliott
Solomon, Neil
Solomon, Richard Allan
Solomon, Richard Lester
Solomon, Robert
Solomon, Samuel Joseph
Solomon, Vita Petrosky
Solomons, David
Solov, Zachary
Solow, Martin
Solow, Robert Merton
Soltan, Jerzy Wladyslaw
Soltis, Andrew Eden, Jr.
Solverud, Truman
Solzbacher, William Aloysius
Solzhenitsyn, Alexander
Somers, Anne Ramsay
Somers, George Fredrick
Somers, Herman Miles
Somers, Suzanne (Suzanne Mahoney)
Somerset, Joseph Bernard
Somerville, William B.
Somit, Albert
Sommer, Alphonse Adam, Jr.
Sommer, Nolan Ben
Sommerburg, Miriam
Sommerfeld, Raynard Matthias
Sommerfield, Charles Michael
Sommers, Davidson
Somogi, Judith
Sondak, Norman Edward
Sondheim, Stephen Joshua
Sonenberg, Martin
Sonfist, Alan
Songer, Wesley Ansel
Sonnabend, Paul
Sonnabend, Roger Philip
Sonne, Clarence Melvin, Jr.
Sonneborn, Henry, III
Sonnekalb, William Frederick, Jr.
Sonnemann, Harry
Sonnemann, Roger Christopher
Sonnenberg, Benjamin
Sonnenblick, Benjamin Paul
Sonnenfeldt, Helmut
Sontag, Frederick H.
Sontag, James Mitchell
Sontag, Susan
Sontheimer, Morton
Soong, Tsu-Teh
Soper, Alexander Coburn
Sorel, Claudette
Sorel, Edward
Sorensen, Erik Per
Sorensen, Raymond Andrew
Sorensen, Theodore Chaikin
Sorensen, Thomas Chaikin
Sorenson, Ralph Zellar, II
Sorg, Herbert Peter
Soria, Dario
Sorkin, Martin
Sorokin, Peter Pitirimovich
Sorrel, William Edwin
Soschin, Ethel U(man)
Sosnik, Harry
Sosnow, Lawrence Ira
Soter, George Nicholas
Soubry, Emile Edmund
Soubry, Kenneth William Stephen
Soudder, Edward Wallace, Jr.
Souders, William Franklin
Soule, Arthur Bradley
Soule, Gardner Bosworth
Sour, Robert Bandler
Sousa, John Philip, III
Souter, David Hackett
Southam, Chester Milton
Southard, Frank Allan, Jr.
Southard, Shelby Edward
Southern, Eileen (Mrs. Joseph Southern)
Southern, Terry
Southgate, Donald Frederic
Southwick, Charles Henry
Southwick, Paul
Southwick, Philip Lee
Southwick, Wayne Orin
Southworth, Hamilton
Southworth, Herman McDowell
Southworth, William Dixon
Soutter, Lamar
Soutter, Thomas D.
Souzzo, Frank Vincent
Sovern, Michael Ira
Sowers, William Armand
Soyer, David
Soyer, Isaac
Soyer, Raphael
Spacek, Sissy (Mary Elizabeth)
Spadaro, Louis Michael
Spaid, Joseph Snyder
Spain, James William
Spain, Jayne Baker
Spalek, John M.
Spanbock, Maurice Samuel
Spanel, Abram Nathaniel
Spanfeller, James John
Spanier, Maury L.
Spaniol, Joseph Frederick, Jr.
Spanovich, Milan
Sparer, Paul
Sparks, David Stanley
Sparks, Henry Alvy
Sparling, Robert John
Spatz, Sidney S.
Spaulding, Earle Henry
Spaventa, George
Speakes, Larry Melvin
Speakman, Edwin Aaron
Speaks, Ruben Lee
Spear, Harvey Milton
Speare, Elizabeth George
Spears, Robert Rae
Speas, Robert Dixon
Specht, Heinz
Speck, Robert Hursey
Spector, Johanna Lichtenberg
Spector, Joseph Robert
Spector, Lawrence
Spector, Louis
Spector, Melbourne Louis
Spector, Robert Donald
Speer, Edgar B.
Speer, Talbot Taylor
Speidel, David Harold
Speidel, John Joseph
Speiser, Marvin M.
Speiser, Stuart Marshall
Speizman, Milton David
Spellman, Gladys Noon
Spellman, Mitchell Wright
Spence, Arthur Mearns
Spence, Hartzell
Spence, Jonathan Dermot
Spence, Richard Dee
Spencer, Daniel Lloyd
Spencer, Edgar Winston
Spencer, Frank Cole
Spencer, F(rederick) Gilman
Spencer, Harry Irving, Jr.
Spencer, Ivan Carlton
Spencer, James Jacob
Spencer, Mildred Dolores
Spencer, Ralph Lee
Spencer, Richard Paul
Spencer, Samuel
Spencer, Thaxter Parks
Spencer, Thomas Ancrum
Spencer, William Hobson
Spencer, William Ira
Spengler, Kenneth Clifford
Sperakis, Nicholas George
Sperling, Godfrey, Jr.
Speth, James Gustave
Speziale, John Albert
Spicer, George Washington
Spiegel, Ernest Adolf
Spiegel, Herbert
Spiegel, Jacob J.
Spiegel, James Irving
Spiegel, Melvin
Spiegel, Sam
Spiegel, Walter F.
Spiegelberg, George Alfred
Spiegelman, Sol
Spiegler, Gerhard Ernst
Spieler, Francis Joseph
Spielvogel, Carl
Spier, Peter Edward
Spiers, Ronald Ian
Spies, Claudio
Spies, Emerson George
Spilhaus, Athelstan
Spilka, Mark
Spillane, Mickey (Frank Morrison)
Spiller, David Henry
Spiller, Eberhard Adolf
Spiller, Robert Ernest
Spiller, Robert James
Spilman, Raymond
Spilman, Robert Henkel
Spindel, Benjamin
Spindel, William
Spindler, Francis Edward
Spingarn, Jerome H.

Spingarn, Stephen J.
Spinks, Leon
Spiro, Herbert John
Spiro, Howard Marget
Spiro, Walter Anselm
Spitz, Charles Thomas, Jr.
Spitz, Seymour James, Jr.
Spitzer, Frank Ludwig
Spitzer, Lyman, Jr.
Spitzler, Robert Theodore
Spivack, Herbert Daniel
Spivacke, Harold
Spivak, Alvin A.
Spivak, Jonathan Martin
Spivak, Lawrence Edmund
Spoehr, Alexander
Spong, William Belser, Jr.
Sponsler, George Curtis, III
Spoor, Thomas Richard
Sporer, Max Frank
Sporn, Michael Benjamin
Sporn, Philip
Spragg, Howard Eugene
Sprague, Everett Russell
Sprague, Howard Bennett
Sprague, Irvine Henry
Sprague, James Mather
Sprague, John Louis
Sprague, L(loyd) Dean
Sprague, Milton Alan
Sprague, Peter Julian
Sprague, Robert Chapman
Sprague, Wallace Arthur
Sprague, William Wallace
Spreen, Roger Elmore
Sprinchorn, Evert Manfred
Spring, Bernard Polmer
Spring, David
Spring, William Charles, Jr.
Springer, Douglas Hyde
Springer, John Kelley
Springer, John Shipman
Springer, Ursula
Springsteen, George Stoney, Jr.
Spritzer, Ralph Simon
Sprole, Frank Arnott
Sproull, Robert Lamb
Sprout, Harold
Sprout, William Bradford, Jr.
Sprow, Howard Thomas
Sprung, Arnold
Spungin, Gardner Mawney
Spurlock, Estelle Elizabeth
Spurlock, Jeanne
Spurrier, William Atwell
Squibb, Robert Leslie
Squire, James Robert
Squires, Donald Fleming
Squires, James Duane
Srb, Adrian Morris
Sreebny, Leo M.
Srere, Benson M.
Srinivasan, Parithychery Rengaswamy
Srole, Leo
Staab, Walter Edward
Staas, Howard Walter
Staats, Elmer Boyd
Stabenau, James Raymond
Stabler, Donald Billman
Stabler, Wells
Stabler, W(inder) Laird, Jr.
Stack, J. William, Jr.
Stack, Maurice Daniel
Stacy, Thomas Jefferson, Jr.
Stadtler, John Walmsley
Stadtman, Earl Reece
Staebler, Neil
Staff, George Leon
Stafford, Edward Stephen
Stafford, George Millard
Stafford, Jean
Stafford, Martin Douglas
Stafford, Paul Gordon
Stafford, Paul Tutt
Stafford, Robert Theodore
Stage, Thomas Benton
Stahl, Charles Drew
Stahl, Frederick Andrew
Stahl, Frederick Arthur
Stahl, Lesley R.
Stahl, O(scar) Glenn
Stahr, Elvis Jacob, Jr.
Stainback, Thomas Nathaniel
Stair, Frederick Rogers, Jr.
Stair, Gobin
Stakgold, Ivar
Staley, Austin L.
Stalling, Bettin
Stallman, Robert Wooster
Stam, David Harry
Stamas, Stephen
Stambaugh, Armstrong A., Jr.
Stamp, Neal Roger
Stampfl, Rudolf Alois
Stanbury, John Bruton
Standish, John Spencer
Stanford, Alfred Boller
Stanford, Dennis Joe
Stanford, George Alonzo
Stange, George Robert
Stanger, Ila
Stanger, John William
Stanger, Russell
Stanger, Wesley Allen, Jr.
Stankard, Francis Xavier
Stankiewicz, Edward
Stankiewicz, Richard Peter
Stanley, Bob
Stanley, Edmund Allport, Jr.
Stanley, Edward Lane
Stanley, Frederick Austin
Stanley, Julian Cecil, Jr.
Stanley, Oran Bert
Stanley, Thomas Bahnson, Jr.
Stanley, Timothy Wadsworth
Stanton, Bernard Freeland
Stanton, Elizabeth Ann
Stanton, Frank (Nicholas)
Stanton, Phoebe Baroody
Stanton, Thomas Joseph
Stanton, Thomas Joyce, Jr.
Stanwick, Tad
Stanwix-Hay, Allen Thomas
Stanwyck, Edmund
Stapleford, Frederick Hamilton
Staples, O. Sherwin
Staples, Robert Innes
Stapleton, Katharine Laurence
Stapleton, Walter King
Starbuck, George Edwin
Starch, Daniel
Stare, Fredrick John
Starer, Robert
Stark, Bruce Gunsten
Stark, Dennis Edwin
Stark, Fortney Hillman, Jr.
Stark, Karen
Stark, Leland William Frederick
Stark, Nathan Julius
Stark, Richard Boies
Stark, Robert Edward
Stark, Robert William Corey
Starkey, Robert Lyman
Starkweather, David Walter
Starling, James Holt
Starnes, Richard
Starr, Arnold
Starr, Benjamin Fred, Jr.
Starr, David
Starr, Edward
Starr, Irving Sumner
Starr, Manya Garbat
Starr, Marjorie
Starr, Mark
Starr, Martin Kenneth
Starr, Wilmarth Holt
Starry, Donn Albert
Startup, Charles Harry
Starzinger, Vincent Evans
Stashower, Michael David
Stassen, Harold Edward
Staszesky, Francis Myron
Statland, Edward Morris
Staub, Marshal Gerald
Stauderman, Albert Philip
Stauffer, Charles Henry
Stauffer, Glenn Floyd
Stauffer, Hans
Stauffer, Robert Allen
Stauffer, Sarah Ann
Stead, Eugene Anson, Jr.
Steadman, Charles Walters
Steadman, John Montague
Steadman, Richard Cooke
Steamer, Robert Julius
Stearns, Charles Edward
Stearns, George L., II
Stearns, Milton Sprague, Jr.
Stearns, Peter Nathaniel
Stearns, Richard Byron, Jr.
Stearns, Robert Leo
Stearns, Russell Bangs
Stearns, Stephen Russell
Steber, Eleanor
Stec, Annette
Stecker, Russell Lee
Steckler, Larry
Stedman, Murray Salisbury, Jr.
Steefel, Robert David
Steeger, Henry
Steegmuller, Francis
Steele, Charles Glen
Steele, George
Steele, Hoyt Post
Steele, Jack
Steele, James Bruce, Jr.
Steele, John Hyslop
Steele, John Lawrence
Steele, Lendell Eugene
Steele, Margaret Therese
Steele, Richard Charles
Steele, Robert Hampton
Steele, William Taylor, Jr.
Steelman, Alan Watson
Steen, Frederick Henry
Steen, Melvin Clifford
Steer, Charles Melvin
Steere, Douglas Van
Steere, William Campbell
Steers, Newton Ivan, Jr.
Steese, Edward
Steeves, Harrison Ross
Stefan, Joseph
Stefanelli, Joseph James
Steffens, Dorothy R.
Stefl, Charles Arthur
Steg, Leo
Steger, Meritt Homer
Stegmaier, Charles Roger
Steibel, Leonard Harold
Steig, William
Steiger, Chauncey Allen
Steiger, William A.
Steigman, Alex J.
Steim, Joseph Matson
Steimle, Douglas Bruning
Steimle, Edmund Augustus
Stein, Bernard
Stein, Calvin Warren
Stein, Claire Alpern
Stein, Edwin Eugene
Stein, Emanuel
Stein, Frances Patiky
Stein, George Nathan
Stein, Herbert
Stein, Howard
Stein, Howard
Stein, Howard S.
Stein, Irvin
Stein, Jerome Leon
Stein, Jess
Stein, Leon
Stein, Marvin
Stein, Maurice Robert
Stein, Melvin
Stein, Otto Ludwig
Stein, Richard George
Stein, Richard Stephen
Stein, Robert
Stein, Sol
Stein, Stanley
Stein, William Howard
Steinbach, Henry Burr
Steinberg, Eric Joseph
Steinberg, Erwin Ray
Steinberg, Jacob
Steinberg, Malcolm Saul
Steinberg, Martin Remez
Steinberg, Michael
Steinberg, Paul Martin
Steinberg, Rafael Mark
Steinberg, Saul
Steinberg, Saul Phillip
Steinbreder, Harry John, Jr.
Steinbrink, Stuart Henry
Steinem, Gloria
Steiner, Alfred
Steiner, Gilbert Yale
Steiner, Gitta Hana
Steiner, John Marcus
Steiner, Lee Rabinowitz
Steiner, Michael
Steiner, Paul
Steiner, Richard Lewis
Steiner, Robert Lisle
Steinert, Alan, Jr.
Steinfeld, Jesse Leonard
Steinfeld, Thomas Albert
Steingut, Stanley
Steinhardt, Arnold
Steinhardt, Martin
Steinhardt, Ralph Gustav, Jr.
Steinhart, Albert B.
Steinheimer, Roy Lee, Jr.
Steinkraus, Warren Edward
Steinman, John Frederick
Steinman, Robert Cleeton
Steinmann, Anne (Mrs. Herbert R. Steinmann)
Steinmetz, Richard Bird, Jr.
Steinruck, Charles Francis, Jr.
Steinway, Henry Ziegler
Steirman, Hy
Steiwer, Frederick Herbert
Stella, Frank
Stella, John Anthony
Stellar, Eliot
Stellar, Raymond Frank
Stelling, Henry Barthold, Jr.
Stelzer, Irwin Mark
Stemmler, Edward Joseph
Stempel, Irving Robert
Stempler, Jack Leon
Stendahl, Krister
Stender, John Henry
Stengel, Louis C., Jr.
Stengle, James Marshall
Stennis, John Cornelius
Stepanchev, Stephen
Stephan, Gary
Stephan, Ralph William, Jr.
Stephans, William Jacob, Jr.
Stephansky, Ben Solomon
Stephens, Clarence Francis
Stephens, Claude Odell
Stephens, Jack Edward
Stephens, Olin James, II
Stephens, Roy Malcolm
Stephens, William Edwards
Stephens, William Theodore
Stephenson, Charles Eugene
Stephenson, Marion
Stephenson, Revis Lindsay
Stepp, Howard Wellington
Sterenbuch, Martin
Sterling, Elwyn Franklin
Sterling, Lionel N.
Sterling, Richard Whitney
Stern, Alfred R.
Stern, Arthur Lewis
Stern, Burton Sidney
Stern, Charles
Stern, Frank
Stern, Fritz Richard
Stern, Guy
Stern, Harold P.
Stern, Herbert Jay
Stern, Isaac
Stern, Laurence Marcus
Stern, Laurent
Stern, Leah Gordon (Mrs. Mordecai A. Stern)
Stern, Leon Thomas (LeFevre)
Stern, Leonard Norman
Stern, Martin
Stern, Philip Maurice
Stern, Richard Martin
Stern, Robert A. M.
Stern, Thomas Noel
Stern, Walter Phillips
Stern, William Louis
Sternbach, Leo Henryk
Sterne, Joseph Robert Livingston
Sterner, Michael Edmund
Sternik, Hans Gregory
Sternlicht, Sanford
Sternlight, Peter Donn
Sterns, Sydney S.
Sternstein, Joseph Philip
Sternstein, Sanford Samuel
Sterrett, Samuel Black
Sterzing, Carl Bruce
Stetin, Sol
Stetler, C. Joseph
Stetson, John Charles
Stetson, Richard Pratt
Stetten, DeWitt, Jr.
Stettner, Walter Fritz
Stevens, Albert John
Stevens, Bartholomew Martin
Stevens, Charles Edward
Stevens, George, Jr.
Stevens, Holly
Stevens, John Bradford
Stevens, John Paul
Stevens, John Richard
Stevens, Kenneth Noble
Stevens, May
Stevens, Raymond Donald, Jr.
Stevens, Richard Kingsbury
Stevens, Risë
Stevens, Robert Bradley
Stevens, Robert David
Stevens, Robert Edwin
Stevens, Robert Ten Broeck
Stevens, Roger L.
Stevens, Russell Bradford
Stevens, Theodore Fulton
Stevens, Whitney
Stevens, William Dollard
Stevenson, Adlai Ewing, III
Stevenson, Dean T.
Stevenson, Eric Van Cortlandt
Stevenson, Harvey
Stevenson, John
Stevenson, Langdon Riddle
Stevenson, Lloyd Grenfell
Stevenson, Robert Ayer
Stever, Horton Guyford
Steward, Donn Horatio
Stewart, Alexander Coutts
Stewart, Alexander Doig
Stewart, Andrew
Stewart, Charles David
Stewart, Charles Edward, Jr.
Stewart, Charles Thorp
Stewart, Edward William
Stewart, Ellen
Stewart, Forrest Jeremiah
Stewart, Franklin Randolph
Stewart, Harold Leroy
Stewart, Herbert Rowland
Stewart, Irvin
Stewart, James
Stewart, James Pentland
Stewart, James William, Jr.
Stewart, John Daugherty
Stewart, John David
Stewart, John Harger
Stewart, Joseph Lester
Stewart, Leroy Elliott (Slam)
Stewart, Margaret McBride
Stewart, Mary Florence Elinor
Stewart, Potter
Stewart, Richard Edwin
Stewart, Richard More
Stewart, Robert Burgess
Stewart, Robert Fletcher
Stewart, Robert Gordon
Stewart, Robert L.
Stewart, Robert McLean
Stewart, Thomas Dale
Stewart, Thomas Penney
Stewart, Ward
Stewart, William Charles
Stewart, Zeph
Stibolt, Hans Peter, Jr.
Stiefel, Herbert Julius
Stier, Howard Livingston
Stifel, Laurence Davis
Stiff, Robert Henry
Stiles, Everett Love
Stiles, Phillip John
Still, Bayrd
Still, Clyfford
Stiller, Jerry
Stillman, Chauncey (Devereux)
Stillman, Karl Greene
Stillman, Richard Noyes
Stillwell, Hamilton
Stillwell, Margaret Bingham
Stillwell, Richard
Stilo, Anthony Joseph
Stilwell, James Joseph
Stilwell, Richard Dale
Stilwell, Richard Giles
Stimmel, Barry
Stimpson, John H.
Stinebring, Warren Richard
Stingel, Donald Eugene
Stinnett, Caskie
Stinson, George Arthur
Stinson, Richard James
Stires, David Warfield
Stirling, Marion
Stith, Marion Crawley
Stitt, Edward Sonny
Stivers, Robert Winthrop
Stix, Thomas Howard
Stock, Charles Chester
Stockdale, James Bond
Stocker, Arthur Frederick
Stocker, Jule E(lias)
Stocker, Philip W.
Stocking, Collis
Stockman, David Allen
Stockmayer, Walter Hugo
Stockwell, Ernest Farnham, Jr.
Stoddard, George Dinsmore
Stoddard, Philip Arnold
Stoddard, Robert Waring
Stoddart, John B., Jr.
Stoecker, Karl A.
Stoessel, Walter John, Jr.
Stohl, Ralph N.
Stohn, Mary
Stoia, Alexander Patrick
Stoker, Warren Cady
Stokes, Arnold Paul
Stokes, Carl Burton
Stokes, Charles Junius
Stokes, Donald Elkinton
Stokes, J. Tyson
Stokes, Katharine Martin
Stokes, Louis
Stokley, Robert Willson
Stokoe, William Clarence
Stokowski, Leopold (Boleslawawicz Stanislaw Antoni)
Stoll, Norman Rudolph
Stoller, Ezra
Stolley, Richard Brockway
Stolp, Lauren Elbert
Stoltz, Merton Philip
Stoltzfus, William Alfred, Jr.
Stolz, Mary Slattery
Stone, Alan Abraham
Stone, Charles Bragdon
Stone, David Barnes
Stone, Desmond
Stone, Dewey David
Stone, Donald Crawford
Stone, Dorothy Maharam
Stone, Edward Durell
Stone, Elizabeth Wenger
Stone, Elliot J.
Stone, Franz Theodore
Stone, Frederick Logan
Stone, Gerald Paul
Stone, I. F. (Isidor Feinstein)
Stone, Jacob Chauncey
Stone, Jeremy Judah
Stone, Joseph
Stone, Lawrence
Stone, Marshall Harvey
Stone, Martin
Stone, Martin Lawrence
Stone, Marvin Lawrence
Stone, Mead Wilmer, Jr.
Stone, Peter H.
Stone, Philip James, III
Stone, Richard Bernard
Stone, Robert Anthony
Stone, Robert Granville
Stone, Robert L.
Stone, Robert Winthrop
Stone, Roger David
Stone, Scott Clinton Stuart
Stone, Thomas Jefferson
Stone, William
Stonesifer, Richard James
Stoodley, Bartlett Hicks
Stookey, John Hoyt
Stookey, Noel Paul
Stoops, John
Storey, Charles Moorfield
Stork, Gilbert Josse
Storms, Clifford Beekman
Storrow, James J., Jr.
Storrs, Richard S.
Stott, Alexander Law
Stotter, Harry Shelton
Stottlemyer, David Lee
Stotz, Elmer Henry
Stouffer, George Andrew Washington, Jr., univ. dean; b. Mechanicsburg, Pa., Oct. 11
Stout, Arthur Wendel, Jr.
Stout, Juanita Kidd
Stout, Myron Stedman
Stout, Robert Daniel
Stover, Carl Frederick
Stowe, David Henry
Stowe, David Metz
Strachan, John Rupert
Stracher, Alfred
Strack, Harold Arthur
Strader, Thomas Edward
Straetz, Robert P.
Straight, Beatrice Whitney
Straka, Laszlo Richard
Stralem, Pierre
Strand, Curt Robert
Strand, Kaj Aage Gunnar
Strand, Mark
Strang, Charles Graham
Strang, William Gilbert
Strange, Robert Henry
Strasberg, Lee
Strasfogel, Ian
Strasfogel, Ignace
Strassburger, Eugene Bonn
Strassenburg, Arnold Adolph
Strasser, Gabor
Strasser, Michael William
Strasser, William Carl, Jr.
Strater, Henry (Mike)
Straton, John Charles, Jr.
Strattner, Lawrence Wenz, Jr.
Stratton, Henry Maurice
Stratton, Julius Adams
Stratton, Samuel Studdiford
Stratton, Walter Love
Straub, Carl Benton
Straub, Peter Thornton
Straubel, James Henderson
Strauch, Karl
Straus, Donald Blun
Straus, Elizabeth Allen (Mrs. Donald Blun Straus)
Straus, Gladys Guggenheim (Mrs. Roger W. Straus)
Straus, Joseph Pennington
Straus, Kenneth Hollister
Straus, Lewis Brown
Straus, Murray Arnold
Straus, Oscar S., II
Straus, R. Peter
Straus, Roger W., Jr.
Strausberg, Marc
Strauss, Anna Lord
Strauss, Elliott Bowman
Strauss, Harold L.
Strauss, Peter
Strauss, Peter Edward
Strauss, Robert Schwarz
Strauss, Simon David
Strauss, Ulrich Paul
Strausz-Hupe, Robert
Straw, H. Thompson
Strawbridge, Francis Reeves, III
Strawbridge, G. Stockton
Strawser, Neil Edward
Strayer, Joseph Reese
Stream, Arnold Crager
Strean, Bernard M.
Streibert, Theodore Cuyler
Streibig, Kenneth Carl
Streisand, Barbra Joan
Streit, Clarence Kirshman
Strichman, George A.
Strickland, Bonnie Ruth
Strickland, Harold Allison, Jr.
Strickland, Nellie B.
Strickler, James Calvin
Strider, Robert Edward Lee, II
Strieder, John William
Striner, Herbert Edward
Stringham, Luther Winters
Strisik, Paul
Strobos, Robert Julius
Strogoff, Alfred
Strohmeier, Gustav Hans
Strohmeier, William Dengler
Strohmeyer, John
Stroke, George Wilhelm
Stroke, Hinko Henry
Strome, Charles Bowman, Jr.
Strong, Earl Poe
Strong, Everett Milton
Strong, Henry
Strong, John Donovan
Strong, Robert Lyman
Stronski, Victor
Stroock, Alan Maxwell
Strosahl, William
Stroud, Peter Anthony
Stroup, Herbert Hewitt
Stroup, Russell Cartwright
Strouse, Charles
Strout, Richard Lee
Struble, Louis Price, Jr.
Struchtemeyer, Roland August
Strum, Gary Jerome
Strunk, Orlo Christopher, Jr.
Strype, Frederick Culver, Jr.
Stuart, Constance Cornell (Mrs. Charles E. Stuart)
Stuart, Douglas Bailey
Stuart, Edward Bernard
Stuart, George Rogers Clark
Stuart, James Alexander
Stuart, Johannes
Stuart, John McHugh, Jr.
Stuart, Kenneth James
Stuart, Lyle
Stuart, Mary
Stuart, Neil Wade
Stuart, Roger Winship
Stubbins, Hugh A., Jr.
Stubblefield, Robert Lee
Stubbs, Harold LeRoy
Stuber, Stanley Irving
Stuckeman, Herman Campbell
Studds, Gerry Eastman
Stuhr, Edward Phillip
Stulman, Julius
Stump, John Sutton
Stumpf, Joseph George
Stunkard, Albert James
Stupar, Branko
Sturc, Ernest
Sturgeon, Theodore Hamilton
Sturgis, Robert Shaw
Sturgis, Somers Hayes
Sturm, Albert Lee
Sturm, Douglas Earl
Sturm, Frederick Charles, III
Sturtevant, Brereton
Sturtevant, Julian Munson
Sturtevant, William Curtis
Stutz, Geraldine (Mrs. David Gibbs)
Stutz, Herbert Walter
Stutzman, Leroy Franklin
Stuver, Francis Edward
Stycos, Joseph Mayone
Styne, Jule
Styron, William
Suarez-Murias, Marguerite C.
Subak, John Thomas
Suck, Richard Lewis
Sudan, Ravindra Nath
Suenholz, Herman Harry
Suer, Marvin David
Sugar, Bert Randolph
Sugarman, Alan William
Sugarman, Jule M.
Sugarman, Norman Alfred
Suhler, John Stuart
Suiter, Grant
Suits, Chauncey Guy
Sulcer, Frederick Durham
Sulkin, Sidney
Sullivan, Adèle Woodhouse
Sullivan, Barry Francis
Sullivan, Charles Andrew
Sullivan, Daniel George
Sullivan, Donald
Sullivan, Edward Daniel
Sullivan, Eugene John Joseph
Sullivan, Fred R.
Sullivan, George Edmund
Sullivan, Henry Paul
Sullivan, James H.
Sullivan, Brother Jeremiah Stephen
Sullivan, John Daniel
Sullivan, John Edward
Sullivan, John Francis, Jr.

Sullivan, John Lawrence
Sullivan, John McGrath
Sullivan, John Patrick
Sullivan, John Stephen
Sullivan, John Vincent
Sullivan, Joseph Charles
Sullivan, Joseph Timothy Patrick
Sullivan, Kevin Irving
Sullivan, Leon Howard
Sullivan, Leonard, Jr.
Sullivan, Mark, Jr.
Sullivan, Mark A.
Sullivan, Mortimer Allen
Sullivan, Patrick Joseph
Sullivan, Richard Howard
Sullivan, Richard Paul
Sullivan, Timothy John
Sullivan, Walter Francis
Sullivan, Walter Seagar
Sullivan, Warren
Sullivan, William Christopher
Sullivan, William Daniel
Sullivan, William Francis
Sullivan, William Hallisey, Jr.
Sullivan, William Healy
Sulzberger, Arthur Ochs
Summerfield, Martin
Summerford, Ben Long
Summerlin, Sam
Summers, Alden Bernard, Jr.
Summers, Clyde Wilson
Summers, James Irvin
Summers, Joseph Holmes
Summers, Robert
Sumter, John Eliot, Jr.
Sundberg, Clifford Stanley
Sunderland, Ray, Jr.
Sunderlin, Charles Eugene
Sunderman, Frederick William
Sundlun, Bruce George
Sundquist, James Lloyd
Sundstrom, Frank Leander
Sunkin, Irving Burton
Sunshine, Donald Raymond
Surface, Thomas James
Surgenor, Douglas MacNevin
Surrency, Erwin Campbell
Surrey, Milt
Surrey, Stanley Sterling
Surrey, Walter Sterling
Surut, Lee Eli
Suslak, Howard Robinson
Suss, Fredric Thomas
Susser, Mervyn Wilfred
Sussex, Ian Mitchell
Susskind, David Howard
Susskind, Leonard
Susskind, Walter
Sussman, Aaron
Sussman, Barry
Sussman, Bernard Jules
Sussman, Gerald
Sussman, Leonard Richard
Sussman, Martin Victor
Sussna, Edward
Suter, Cary Grayson
Suter, Emanuel
Sutherland, Edwin Van Valkenburg
Sutherland, Joan
Sutherland, Malcolm Read, Jr.
Sutherland, William Anderson
Sutherlund, David Arvid
Sutman, Francis Xavier
Sutnick, Alton Ivan
Sutphen, Duncan Dunbar, Jr.
Sutphen, Harold Amerman, Jr.
Sutton, Charles William
Sutton, George Walter
Sutton, Horace Ashley
Sutton, Jonathan Stone
Sutton, Percy E.
Sutton, Robert George
Sutton, Roger Beatty
Sutton, Thomas Carl
Sutton, Walter
Suydam, Frederick Henry
Suzy (Aileen Mehle)
Sveda, Michael
Svendsen, Louise Averill (Mrs. Thoralf Svendsen)
Svetlova, Marina
Svikhart, Clifford Miles
Swados, Elizabeth A.
Swain, Robert Cuthbertson
Swalin, Richard Arthur
Swan, Clara Lincoln
Swan, Dana Merrill
Swan, Marshall
Swan, Roy Craig
Swanberg, William Andrew
Swankin, David Arnold
Swann, Frederick Lewis
Swann, Lynn Curtis
Swanson, August George
Swanson, Carl Pontius
Swanson, David Heath
Swanson, Gloria (Gloria May Josephine Swanson)
Swanson, Gordon Merle
Swanson, Howard Paul
Swanson, John William
Swanson, Lawrence Wilbur
Swanson, William Fredin, Jr.
Swanstrom, Edward Ernest
Swantz, Alexander
Swartz, Howard Marshall
Swartz, Stephen Arthur
Swarz, Sahl
Swarztrauber, Sayre Archie
Swayze, John Cameron, Sr.
Swearer, Howard Robert
Swearingen, Lawson Lewis
Sweat, Herbert J.
Sweazey, George Edgar
Sweeney, Francis Joseph, Jr.
Sweeney, James Francis, Jr.
Sweeney, James Johnson
Sweeny, Henry Ware Allen
Sweet, Herman Royden
Sweet, John Howard
Sweet, Norman Leland
Sweet, William Herbert
Sweetser, Albert Gibby
Sweetser, Edward Horatio
Sweger, Harry John, Jr.
Sweigart, John Winfield, Jr.
Swenson, Eric Pierson
Swenson, John William
Swenson, Karen
Swenson, May
Swenson, Orvar
Swern, Daniel
Swets, John Arthur
Swezey, Robert Dwight
Swid, Stephen Claar
Swidler, Joseph Charles
Swift, David Everett
Swift, John Francis
Swigert, John Leonard, Jr.
Swihart, James Wilbur
Swinarton, Robert Wallace
Swinburne, Herbert Hillhouse
Swindler, William Finley
Swinehart, James Stephen
Swing, John Temple
Swing, Peter Gram
Swink, Earl Thomas
Swink, John Lewis
Swinton, Stanley Mitchell
Switzer, George Shirley
Swope, Gerard, Jr.
Swords, Raymond Joseph
Swords, Vincent Thomas
Sykes, Gresham M'Cready
Sykes, James Andrews
Sykes, Lynn Ray
Sykes, Melvin Julius
Sykes, Walter Henry
Sylk, Harry Stanley
Sylvander, Nels Elmer
Sylvester, Richard Standish
Symington, James Wadsworth
Symington, Lloyd
Symmers, William Garth
Symmes, Harrison Matthews
Symmons-Symonolewicz, Konstantin
Symon, James Gordon
Symons, George Edgar
Synan, Joseph Alexander, Sr.
Sypher, Wylie
Syrett, Harold Coffin
Szabad, George Michael
Szabo, Albert
Szabo, Daniel
Szasz, Thomas Stephen
Sze, Tsung Wei
Szekely, Julian
Szenberg, Michael
Szent-Gyorgyi, Albert
Szep, Paul Michael
Szmant, Alina Margarita (Mrs. Philip N. Froelich, Jr.)
Szulc, Tad
Szymanski, Herman Alowisious
Tabatznik, Bernard
Tabell, Anthony
Taber, Gladys
Taber, Robert Clinton
Tabler, Levi Earl, Jr.
Tabler, William Benjamin
Tabor, Herbert
Tabor, John Kaye
Tabor, Neil
Taeni, John Ignatius
Taeni, Madeleine Renata Weigner (Mrs. John Taeni)
Taeuber, Conrad
Tafel, Edgar
Taff, Charles A.
Taff, Paul Kenneth
Taft, Charles Kirkland
Taft, Henry Waters
Taft, Horace Dwight
Taft, Julia Vadala
Taft, William Howard, III
Taggart, Kenneth Dale
Taggart, Leslie Davidson
Tagiuri, Renato
Tagliacozzo, Daisy Margot
Tague, Barry Elwert
Tague, Charles Francis
Taishoff, Lawrence Bruce
Taishoff, Sol Joseph
Tait, Edward Thomas
Talalay, Paul
Talbot, Gerald Edgerton
Talbot, John Mayo
Talbot, Phillips
Talbot, Richard Burritt
Talbot, Richard Joseph
Talbot, Timothy Ralph
Talbot, William Howe McElwain
Talbott, Francis Leo
Talbott, Frank, Jr.
Talbott, Frank, III
Talbott, Malcolm Daily
Talbott, Orwin Clark
Talbott, Strobe
Talcott, Burt Lacklen
Talese, Gay
Taliaferro, Francis Tournier
Talkov, Leo
Talley, Carol Lee
Talley, Charles Richmond
Talley, George Clyde, Jr.
Talley, Truman Macdonald
Tallman, William Chester
Talma, Louise J.
Tam, Reuben
Tamir, Theodor
Tamm, Edward Allen
Tampas, John Peter
Tan, Chor Weng
Tandy, Jessica
Tanenbaum, Elias
Tanenbaum, Marc Herman
Tangney, Eugene Michael
Tanguy, Charles Reed
Tanimoto, Taffee Tadashi
Tanis, James Robert
Tank, Martin Marcus
Tankersley, George Jackson
Tannenbaum, Samuel William
Tannenbaum, Sidney Alan
Tannenwald, Theodore, Jr.
Tanner, Charles William
Tanner, Henry
Tanselle, George Thomas
Tansill, Frederick Riker
Tanzer, Radford Chapple
Tape, Gerald Frederick
Tapley, Donald Fraser
Taplin, Frank E.
Taplinger, Terry Lent
Tappan, John Rudolph
Tappé, Albert Anthony
Tapply, Horace Gardner
Taquey, Charles Henri
Taran, Leonardo
Taras, Anthony F.
Taras, John
Tarbell, George Schuyler, Jr.
Tarbox, Frank Kolbe
Tarbutton, Lloyd Tilghman
Targ, William
Tarn, Nathaniel
Tarnow, Robert Laurence
Tarrants, William Eugene
Tart, Stephen M., Jr.
Tarter, Fred Barry
Tarzwell, Clarence Matthew
Tash, Martin Elias
Tassell, Gustave
Tassie, John M.
Tate, James
Tate, James Hugh Joseph
Tate, Merze
Tatel, David Stephen
Tatem, John William, Jr.
Tatlow, Richard Henry, III
Tatum, George Bishop
Taub, Henry
Taub, James Monroe
Tauber, Maurice Falcolm
Taubes, Frederick
Taubman, Martin Arnold
Tauc, Jan
Taulbee, John Earl
Taulbee, Orrin Edison
Tauro, G. Joseph
Taussig, Helen Brooke
Taussig, Richard S.
Tavel, Ronald
Taveras, Juan Manuel
Tavitian, Henry Ohanes
Tavoulareas, William Peter
Tawil, Joseph
Tawney, Lenore
Taylor, Arthur Canning, Jr.
Taylor, Arthur Robert
Taylor, Benjamin Franklin
Taylor, Bernard J., II
Taylor, Billy (William Edward)
Taylor, C. Bruce
Taylor, Carl Ernest
Taylor, Charles
Taylor, Charles Forbes
Taylor, Charles Henry Jr.
Taylor, Charles Lincoln, Jr.
Taylor, Charles Richard
Taylor, Clyde Calvin, Jr.
Taylor, David Peter
Taylor, Edward Curtis
Taylor, Eldon Donivan
Taylor, Elizabeth
Taylor, Eugene Charles
Taylor, Eugene Jackson
Taylor, Francis Charles
Taylor, Frank Eugene
Taylor, Gene
Taylor, George Albert
Taylor, George Frederick
Taylor, Gerald L.
Taylor, Glenn Erwin, Jr.
Taylor, Gray
Taylor, Harold
Taylor, Harold Ralph
Taylor, Henry Junior
Taylor, Hobart, Jr.
Taylor, Howard M., Jr.
Taylor, Jack Duffy
Taylor, James Allwood
Taylor, James Davidson
Taylor, James Watson
Taylor, John Alan
Taylor, John Dwayne
Taylor, John Joseph
Taylor, John Whitfield
Taylor, John Williams
Taylor, Joshua Charles
Taylor, Lane
Taylor, Lauriston Sale
Taylor, Lisa Suter
Taylor, Lloyd F.
Taylor, Lynnette Dobbins
Taylor, Maxwell Davenport
Taylor, Millard Benjamin
Taylor, Nettie Barcroft
Taylor, Norman William
Taylor, Paul
Taylor, Peter Hillsman
Taylor, Prentiss Hottel
Taylor, Richard
Taylor, Richard Ray
Taylor, Richard William
Taylor, Robert E. Lee, Jr.
Taylor, Robert Edward
Taylor, Robert Edward
Taylor, Robert Lee
Taylor, Robert Lewis
Taylor, Robert Saxton
Taylor, Robert Stevens
Taylor, Roger Conant
Taylor, Samuel Albert
Taylor, Sherril Wightman
Taylor, Telford
Taylor, Theodore Brewster
Taylor, Theodore Walter
Taylor, Theophilus Mills
Taylor, Thomas Kauffman
Taylor, Wallace Gingell
Taylor, William Davis
Taylor, William O.
Taylor, Winifred Elizabeth
Tcherkassky, Marianna Alexsavena
Teaf, Howard Morris, Jr.
Teague, Sam Fuller
Teale, Edwin Way
Tear, Robert
Tebaldi, Renata
Tebbel, John
Tedeschi, Henry
Tedesko, Anton
Tedrow, John Charles Fremont
Teegen, Otto John
Teevan, Richard Collier
Teich, Barnett
Teicher, Louis
Teichert, Curt
Teiger, David Alan
Teitelbaum, David
Teitelbaum, Hubert
Teitell, Conrad Laurence
Teitler, Samuel L.
Teitz, Richard Stuart
Telford, Ira Rockwood
Teller, Aaron Joseph
Teller, Walter Magnes
Telles, Raymond L., Jr.
Teltsch, Kathleen
Temin, Peter
Temple, Wick
Templeton, David L.
Templeton, Robert James
Tennant, John Selden
Tenney, Charles Henry
Tenney, Daniel Gleason, Jr.
Tenney, Stephen Marsh
Tenny, Francis Briggs
Teper, Lazare
Ter-Arutunian, Rouben
Terenzio, Joseph Vincent
Terenzio, Peter Bernard
Tereshko, Daniel William
ter Horst, Jerald Franklin
Terhorst, Paul Byrne
Terner, Emanuel M.
Ternes, Alan Paul
Terracciano, Anthony Patrick
Terrace, Herbert S(ydney)
Terrel, Charles Lynn
Terrell, Huntington
Terrell, Roy Alfred, Jr.
Terres, John Kenneth
Terretta, Paul
Terrie, Henry Larkin, Jr.
Terrien, Samuel Lucien
Terrill, Clair Elman
Terrill, Robert Carl
Terrill, Ross Gladwin
Terris, Milton
Terry, Benjamin Pellington
Terry, Clark
Terry, John Hart
Terry, Kenton Frederick
Terry, Luther Leonidas
Terry, Megan
Terry, Nathan Maxson
Terry, Richard Allan
Terry, Robert Davis
Terry, Walter
Terzick, Peter Edward
Tesarik, David Breese
Tesoro, George Alfred
Tessieri, John Edward
Tetlow, Edwin
Thackray, Arnold Wilfrid
Thaddeus, Patrick
Thaler, William John
Thalhimer, William B., Jr.
Thalken, Margaret Mary
Thane, Elswyth (Mrs. William Beebe)
Tharp, Louise Marshall Hall
Tharp, Twyla
Tharrington, Robert William
Thaxter, Sidney Warren
Thayer, Edwin Cabot
Thayer, H. Standish
Thayer, Jack Glover
Thayer, Lee
Thayer, Robert Helyer
Thayer, Russell, III
Thayer, Walter Nelson
Theberge, James Daniel
Theis, John William
Thelin, Valfred Pierre
Theobald, George John, Jr.
Theriault, George French
Thernstrom, Stephan Albert
Theroux, Alexander Louis
Thieblot, Robert Jean
Thiele, Albert E.
Thielens, Alexis Ollier
Thieme, Theodore Louis
Thier, Samuel Osiah
Thimmesch, Nicholas Palen
Thom, Joseph M.
Thomas, Alexander
Thomas, Brother Alexander F.
Thomas, Alfred
Thomas, Brooks
Thomas, Byron
Thomas, Calvert
Thomas, Carol Monroe
Thomas, Charles Allen, Jr.
Thomas, Charles Carl Wilson
Thomas, Charles Columbus
Thomas, Charles Davis
Thomas, David Ansell
Thomas, David Duval
Thomas, David Lloyd
Thomas, Deroy C.
Thomas, Donald Llewellyn
Thomas, Donald Roff
Thomas, Edmond George
Thomas, Edwin Russell
Thomas, Evan Welling, II
Thomas, Franklin Augustine
Thomas, Garth Johnson
Thomas, George Brinton
Thomas, George Rixse
Thomas, Gerald Eustis
Thomas, Gordon Alexander
Thomas, Gordon Walter
Thomas, Harold Allen, Jr.
Thomas, Harold B.
Thomas, Helen A. (Mrs. Douglas B. Cornell)
Thomas, H(enry) Grant
Thomas, Howard Emery
Thomas, Jack Eugene
Thomas, James William
Thomas, Jess
Thomas, Jimmy Lynn
Thomas, John Bowman
Thomas, John Henry, Jr.
Thomas, John M.
Thomas, Lewis
Thomas, Louis Godfrey Lee
Thomas, Lowell
Thomas, Michael Tilson
Thomas, Minor Wine, Jr.
Thomas, Norman Edwin
Thomas, Owen Clark
Thomas, Raleigh Haywood, Jr.
Thomas, Ralph Stephens
Thomas, Richard
Thomas, Richard Edward
Thomas, Ross Elmore
Thomas, W. Bruce
Thomas, Walter Ivan
Thomas, William Ross
Thomas, William S.
Thomas, William Stephen
Thomason, Alan Mims
Thomason, James R.
Thomopoulos, Anthony D.
Thompson, Bard Thompson
Thompson, Benjamin
Thompson, Brian John
Thompson, Carol Lewis
Thompson, Clive Dunavon
Thompson, Craig Ringwalt
Thompson, David Duvall
Thompson, Edward Kramer
Thompson, Edward Thorwald
Thompson, Frank, Jr.
Thompson, Frederick Roeck
Thompson, George Clifford
Thompson, George Lee
Thompson, George Robert
Thompson, Gerald Luther
Thompson, Graves Haydon
Thompson, Harry Charles
Thompson, Hartwell Greene
Thompson, Herbert Burton
Thompson, Jack Edward
Thompson, James Burleigh, Jr.
Thompson, John Irvin
Thompson, John Matthew, Jr.
Thompson, John Murray
Thompson, John Theodore
Thompson, Kenneth W(infred)
Thompson, LaRoy Bernard
Thompson, Loring Moore
Thompson, Lovell
Thompson, Mack Eugene
Thompson, Margaret Myrtle
Thompson, N. David
Thompson, Page
Thompson, Paul Williams
Thompson, Porter
Thompson, Randall
Thompson, Robert Calvin
Thompson, Robert McBroom
Thompson, Sada Carolyn
Thompson, Thomas Edward
Thompson, Thomas Kirkland
Thompson, W. Blake
Thompson, Walter Andrew Lewis
Thompson, Willard Spencer
Thompson, William Cannon, Jr.
Thompson, William David
Thompson, William Irwin
Thompson, William Page
Thompson, William Phelps
Thompson, William Reid
Thompson, William Taliaferro, Jr.
Thompson, Winifred Grace
Thomsen, Donald Laurence, Jr.
Thomsen, Roszel C.
Thomsen, Wells Hamlen
Thomson, Clifton Samuel
Thomson, Douglas
Thomson, James Claude, Jr.
Thomson, Lewis Clark
Thomson, Meldrim
Thomson, Robert William
Thomson, Vernon Wallace
Thomson, Virgil
Thon, Robert William, Jr.
Thon, William
Thone, Charles
Thorbecke, Erik
Thornburgh, Richard Lewis
Thorndike, Joseph Jacobs, Jr.
Thorndike, Richard King
Thorndike, Robert Ladd
Thorne, Francis
Thorne, Oakleigh Blakeman
Thorne, Samuel Edmund
Thornhill, Arthur Horace, Jr.
Thorning, Joseph Francis
Thornsjo, Douglas Fredric
Thornton, Edward Ralph
Thornton, Henry Moser
Thornton, John Vincent
Thornton, John William
Thornton, Richard Stanley
Thornton, Robert Donald
Thornton, William Norman, Jr.
Thoron, Gray
Thorp, Almus Morse
Thorp, Willard Long
Thorpe, Merle, Jr.
Thorsen, Robert Mitchel
Thorson, Phillip Thorwald
Thorup, Oscar Andreas
Thrall, Donald Stuart
Thrasher, James Parker
Throop, Allen Eaton
Thrun, Robert
Thumm, Garold Wesley
Thurber, David Lawerence
Thurber, Davis Peabody
Thurber, James Perry, Jr.
Thurlow, Elwin Wilbur
Thurston, Carl Givens
Thurston, John L.
Thurston, Philip Hale
Thursz, Daniel
Tiant, Luis Clemente (Vega)
Tibbetts, Hubert M.
Tibbitts, Clark
Tibbs, DeLloyd Orville
Tibby, John Knox Milligan, Jr.
Tice, Linwood Franklin
Tice, William Russell
Ticktin, Richard Mayer
Tidball, M(ary) Elizabeth Peters (Mrs. Charles S. Tidball)
Tidyman, Ernest
Tieckelmann, Howard
Tiede, Tom Robert
Tiedemann, Arthur Everett
Tiedemann, Carl Hans
Tiegs, Cheryl
Tiemann, Norbert Theodore
Tien, Ping King
Tierney, Brian
Tierney, Howard Sherwood
Tierney, Paul James
Tietjen, August Carl
Tietjen, Paul Lindhorst
Tietjens, Norman Orwig
Tiffeau, Jacques Emile
Tiffin, Pamela Kimberley
Tiger, Lionel
Tilden, Elwyn Earle
Tiller, Carl William
Tilley, Robert James
Tillinghast, Charles Carpenter, Jr.
Tillinghast, John Avery
Tillinghast, Pardon Elisha
Tillman, Rodney
Tilson, John Quillin
Timasheff, Serge Nicholas
Timberg, Sigmund
Timbers, William Homer
Timby, Elmer Knowles
Timlen, Thomas Michael
Timmons, Bascom N.
Timmons, Benson Ellison Lane, III
Timmons, William Evan
Timms, Peter Rowland
Timon, William Edward, Jr.
Timpson, Carl William, Jr.
Tindale, Thomas Keith
Ting, Samuel Chao Chung
Ting, Walasse
Tinghitella, Stephen
Tingley, Henry Francis, Jr.
Tinkcom, Harry Marlin
Tinkham, Michael
Tinsley, Samuel Weaver
Tinsley, Thomas A.
Tippet, Algernon Clark
Tippett, James Russell
Tippo, Oswald
Tipton, Jennifer
Tipton, Russell D.
Tipton, Stuart Guy
Tisch, Laurence Alan
Tisch, Preston Robert
Tishler, Max
Tishman, Robert V.
Tisza, Laszlo
Titelman, J. Richard
Tkach, Walter Robert
Tober, Barbara D. (Mrs. Donald Gibbs Tober)
Tobey, Alton
Tobey, Joel Nye
Tobias, Abraham Joel
Tobias, Julius
Tobin, James
Tobin, Richard Lardner
Tobler, John Henry
Tobriner, Walter Nathan
Toby, Jackson
Todaro, George Joseph
Todd, David Fenton Michie

Todd, Robert Emerson
Todd, Samuel Richard, Jr.
Todd, Webster Bray
Todman, Terence A.
Todman, William Selden
Todrank, Gustave Herman
Tofany, Vincent Leon
Toffler, Alvin
Toksöz, Mehmet Nafi
Toland, John Willard
Toledano, Ralph de
Tolentino, Shirley Ann
Toll, John Sampson
Tolles, Walter Edwin
Tolley, William Pearson
Tolman, Leland Locke
Tolor, Alexander
Tolson, Hillory Alfred
Tolson, Jay Henry
Tolson, Julius Henry
Tolstoy, Alexandra Leo
Tomaselli, Julius Louis
Tomasson, Helgi
Tomb, Paul David
Tomchin, Julian
Tomkins, Silvan Solomon
Tomkowit, Thaddeus Walter
Tomlinson, Alexander Cooper
Tomlinson, J. Richard
Tomlinson, James Francis
Tomlinson, John Doren
Tomlinson, Joseph Robert
Tomlinson, Mel Alexander
Tomlinson, William D. (Frank)
Tomlinson, William West
Tommaney, James Joseph
Tompa, Robert James
Tompkins, Harvey John
Tompkins, James McLane
Tompkins, Pauline
Tompkins, William F.
Tomson, Bernard
Tondel, Lyman M., Jr.
Toner, Joseph Stanley
Toney, Anthony
Tong, Hing
Tonkin, Leo Sampson
Tonndorf, Juergen
Tontz, Robert L.
Tooker, George
Toolan, John Peter
Toole, Wycliffe David, Jr.
Tooman, H. Kenneth
Toomre, Alar
Toon, M. Spalding
Toon, Malcolm
Toone, Elam Cooksey, Jr.
Toong, Tau-Yi
Toor, Herbert Lawrence
Toote, Gloria E.A.
Topp, Lee Jay
Topping, Seymour
Torbet, Robert George
Torborg, Jeffrey Allen
Torell, Bruce Norris
Torell, John Raymond, III
Torgersen, Paul Ernest
Toribara, Taft Yutaka
Torn, Rip (Elmore Torn, Jr.)
Torras, Joseph Hill
Torre, Douglas Paul
Torre, Joseph Paul (Joe)
Torrence, (John) Richard
Torrey, Henry Cutler
Torrey, John Gordon
Torrey, William Arthur
Tose, Leonard H.
Tosteson, Daniel Charles
Totenberg, Roman
Toth, Robert Charles
Toulmin, Priestley, III
Toumey, Hubert (Hugh) John
Tousey, Richard
Touster, Ben
Touster, Saul
Tovish, Harold
Towbin, Belmont
Towe, George Coffin
Towe, Kenneth Crawford
Towe, Peter M.
Towell, William Earnest
Tower, Bertram B.
Tower, Donald Bayley
Tower, Ensley Anthony
Tower, Horace Linwood, III
Towers, Constance Mary
Towers, John
Towey, James Fischer
Towi, Thea
Towle, Sidney Norwood
Townend, Frank
Townes, Philip Leonard
Townley, Hugh
Towns, Charles Henry
Townsend, Charles Coe
Townsend, Charles Cooper
Townsend, Charles Edward
Townsend, Edward
Townsend, Edward Thomas
Townsend, James Benjamin
Townsend, John Robert
Townsend, John William, Jr.
Townsend, M. Wilbur
Townsend, Robert (Chase)
Townsend, Stanley Russell
Townsend, Thomas Perkins
Tozzi, Giorgio
Trabant, Edward Arthur
Trachtenberg, Stephen Joel
Trachtman, Paul
Tracy, Berry Bryson
Tracy, Osgood Vose
Tracy, Robert Allen
Tracy, Robert M.
Traendly, Wallace Francis
Trafford, William Bradford
Trager, Frank Newton
Trager, William
Train, Harry Depue, II
Train, Russell Errol
Transue, William Reagle
Trapp, Frank Anderson
Trapp, Gerald Bernard
Trapp, Maria Augusta von
Traschen, Isadore
Trask, David Frederic
Trask, Harry Albert
Traub, J(oseph) F(rederick)
Traub, Marvin Stuart
Traube, Shepard
Traum, Jerome S.
Trautman, Donald Theodore
Trautman, Ray L.
Trautmann, Les Raymond
Travers, Edward Patrick
Traversi, Derek Antona
Traviesas, Herminio
Travis, Irven
Travis, Martin Bice
Travis, Stephen Michael
Traylor, Lawrence Milton
Traylor, Orba Forest
Treadwell, Carleton Raymond
Treadwell, Mary
Treadwell, Mary
Trebilcock, Paul
Trebus, Robert Stanley
Tredinnick, George Donald
Tree, Marietta Peabody
Tree, Michael
Treen, David Conner
Trefethen, Lloyd MacGregor
Trefflich, Henry
Tregre, Louis Severin
Tregurtha, Paul Richard
Treiber, William Frederick
Treiman, Sam Bard
Treleaven, Phillips Albert
Trelfa, Richard Thomas
Trelogan, Harry Chester
Tremain, Alan
Tremaine, Frank
Treman, Arthur Bott, Jr.
Tremmel, Ernest Bernard
Trenbath, Phillips Stockton
Trench, William Frederick
Trent, Mary Vance
Trent, Richard Darrell
Trescher, Robert Lincoln
Tressler, Josef Snyder
Tretick, Stanley
Treusch, Paul Ellsworth
Trevas, Simon Harrison
Trezise, Philip Harold
Trezza, Alphonse Fiore
Tribbitt, Sherman Willard
Tribble, Hugh Wallace
Trible, Paul Seward, Jr.
Tribus, Myron
Trice, William Henry
Triffin, Robert
Trigere, Pauline
Trigg, D. Thomas
Triggiani, Leonard Vincent
Triggle, David John
Trilling, Leon
Trimble, Henry Weeks, Jr.
Trimble, I. Ridgeway
Trimble, Lester Albert
Trimble, William Cattell, Jr.
Trimmer, Harold Sharp, Jr.
Tripp, Hulbert Willis
Tripp, Louis Reed
Tripp, Ralph Harry
Trippe, Kenneth Alvin Battershill
Trist, Eric Lansdown
Tritsch, Robert Grant
Trivus, Robert Howard
Trizzino, Victor Francis
Troan, John
Trobe, Jacob Louis
Troen, Philip
Troester, Carl Augustus, Jr.
Trogdon, Floyd Harrison
Trohan, Walter
Troilo, Joseph Carmen
Trombley, Kenneth Edward
Trosk, George
Trost, Carlisle Albert Herman
Trotta, Elizabeth (Liz Ann)
Trottenberg, Arthur Donald
Trotter, Herbert, Jr.
Trotti, John Boone
Troupe, Ralph Anderson
Trout, Arthur Roger
Trout, John Francis
Trout, Maurice Elmore
Trout, Monroe Eugene
Troutman, E. Mac
Trowbridge, Alexander Buel, Jr.
Trowbridge, C. Robertson
Troy, Agnes Virginia
Troy, Anthony Francis
Trubin, John
True, Edward Keene
Trueblood, Alan Stubbs
Trueschler, Bernard Charles
Truesdell, Clifford Ambrose, III
Trueswell, Richard William
Trueworthy, Orson William
Truitt, Anne Dean
Truman, David Bicknell
Truman, Jock Curtis
Truman, Margaret (Daniel)
Trumbull, Richard
Trumbull, Robert
Trump, Benjamin Franlin
Trump, Guy Winston
Trumpler, Paul Robert
Truslow, John Bacchus
Trussell, Charles Tait
Trussell, Ray Elbert
Trustman, Benjamin Arthur
Truxal, John Groff
Trynin, Nathan Kalman
Tsai Wen-Ying
Tsantes, John James
Tsapogas, Makis Joakim
Tschacbasov, Nahum
Tschebotarioff, Gregory P.
Tso, Tien Chioh
Tsongas, Paul Efthemios
Tsu, John B.
Tubby, Roger Wellington
Tuch, Hans Nathan
Tuchman, Barbara Wertheim
Tuck, Grayson Edwin
Tuck, William Munford
Tucker, Albert William
Tucker, Cynthia Delores Nottage (Mrs. William M. Tucker)
Tucker, Frank Mayer, Jr.
Tucker, James Guy
Tucker, Lem (Lemuel)
Tucker, Marcia
Tucker, Richard Frank
Tucker, Robert Charles
Tucker, Ronald Dwain
Tucker, Sterling
Tucker, William Ellsworth, Jr.
Tucker, Woodie
Tuckson, Coleman Reed
Tudor, Antony
Tudor, David
Tuholski, James M.
Tuite, James Joseph
Tuite, Joseph Patrick
Tukey, John Wilder
Tulin, Marshall
Tulley, Harry Arthur
Tullio, Louis Joseph
Tullis, Robert Haas, Jr.
Tulloch, George Sherlock, Jr.
Tullock, Gordon
Tully, Andrew Frederick, Jr.
Tully, Charles R.
Tumin, Melvin Marvin
Tumulty, Philip Anthony
Tung, David Hsi Hsin
Tunis, William David
Tunison, Eileen Feretic
Tunley, Roul
Tunnard, Christopher
Tunnell, James Miller, Jr.
Tuohy, John Joseph
Tupper, Eleanor (Mrs. George O. Bierkoe)
Turano, Emanuel Nicolas
Turbyfill, John Ray
Turci, George Primo
Turcotte, Henry Joseph
Tureck, Rosalyn
Turekian, Karl Karekin
Turini, Ronald Walter
Turk, James Clinton
Turkes, Walter Robert
Turlington, Edgar Lawrence, Jr.
Turnbull, Agnes Sligh (Mrs. James Lyall Turnbull)
Turnbull, Benjamin Walton
Turnbull, David
Turnbull, Harrison Freeman
Turnbull, William Watson
Turndorf, Herman
Turner, Alice Kennedy
Turner, David Reuben
Turner, Donald Frank
Turner, Edward Felix, Jr.
Turner, Floyd
Turner, Francis Cutler
Turner, Frederick Charles
Turner, George Pearce
Turner, Halcott Mebane
Turner, Henry Brown
Turner, Herbert David
Turner, Howard Sinclair
Turner, James Castle
Turner, James Steven
Turner, Michael Dowling
Turner, Morris Nolten
Turner, Pete
Turner, Richard Weimer
Turner, Ruth Dixon
Turner, Stansfield
Turner, Victor Witter
Turner, William Homer Heyward
Turnheim, Palmer
Turnure, James Harvey
Turro, Nicholas John
Tusiani, Joseph
Tuten, John Cole
Tuthill, John Wills
Tuttle, Charles Egbert
Tuttle, Edwin Ellsworth
Tuve, Merle Antony
Twardowicz, Stanley Jan
Tweedy, Gordon Bradford
Tweedy, Harold Lathrop
Twiggs, James Glenn
Twinam, Joseph Wright
Twiname, John Dean
Twitty, James Watson
Twomey, Jerome Denis
Tworkov, Jack
Tydings, Joseph Davies
Tye, Norwood Burl
Tyler, Anne (Mrs. Taghi M. Modarressi)
Tyler, Edward Royall
Tyler, Harold Russell, Jr.
Tyler, Morris
Tyler, Roger Browne
Tyndall, Albert Forbes, Jr.
Tyner, Alfred McCoy Sulaimon Saud
Tyng, Anne Griswold
Tynion, James T.
Tyree, David Merrill
Tyree, John Augustine, Jr.
Tyree, Sheppard Young, Jr.
Tyson, Charles Roebling
Tyson, Charles Roebling
Tyson, Irwin Wood
Tyson, Ralph Robert
Tyvoniuk, Bishop Job (Dmitri Yakovlevich)
Tzimas, Nicholas Achilles
Ubell, Earl
Ubell, Robert Neil
Uberall, Herbert Michael Stefan
Uccello, Antonina Phyllis
Ucelay, Margarita
Ucko, Kurt
Udall, Morris King
Udall, Stewart Lee
Udenfriend, Sidney
Udovitch, Abraham Labe
Ufford, Charles Wilbur
Ughetta, William C.
Uhl, Edward George
Uhl, Wilfred Otto
Uhlig, Herbert H.
Uhrich, Richard Lee
Uitti, Karl David
Ulam, Adam Bruno
Uldrick, John Paul
Ulerich, William Keener
Ulfelder, Howard
Ulinski, John Anthony, Jr.
Ullman, Albert Conrad
Ullman, Richard Henry
Ulman, Lewis Holmes
Ulmer, Bernhard
Ulmer, Gordon Irvine, Jr.
Ulmer, Melville Jack
Ulrich, Max Marsh
Ulrich, Robert Gardner
Umbreit, Wayne William
Umstead, William Lee
Underhill, Jacob Berry, III
Underweiser, Irwin Philip
Underwood, Don
Underwood, James Martin
Underwood, Lamar
Underwood, Wilson McMaster
Ungar, Frederick
Ungaro, Joseph Michael
Unger, Ferdinand Thomas
Unger, Irwin
Unger, Stephen Herbert
Ungerer, Jean Tomi
Ungers, Oswald M.
Unitas, John Constantine
Unna, Warren W.
Unsell, Lloyd Neal
Unsworth, Richard Preston
Unterberg, Thomas Israel
Unwin, Nora Spicer
Upbin, Hal Jay
Updike, John Hoyer
Upjohn, Everard Miller
Uplinger, Robert Jaqua
Uppman, Theodor
Upson, Howard Edwin
Upson, James Julian
Upson, Robert William
Upson, Stuart Barnard
Upston, John Edwin
Upton, Arthur Canfield
Upton, Arvin Edward
Upton, John Davis
Upton, Richard F.
Urbach, Frederick
Urbahn, Maximilian Otto
Urban, Henry Zeller
Urban, Joseph
Urbanowski, Frank
Urbina, Ricardo Manuel
Urbon, Victor Andrew
Uricchio, William Andrew
Uris, Leon
Urofsky, Melvin Irving
Urquhart, John Alexander
Urry, Grant Wayne
Ursano, James Joseph
Usdane, William Miller
Usery, Willie J., Jr.
Usher, Elizabeth Reuter (Mrs. Harry T. Usher)
Utermohle, Charles Edward, Jr.
Uthoff, Michael
Utz, John Philip
Utz, Lois Marie
Uyterhoeven, Hugo Emil Robert
Vachon, Brian Peter
Vaeth, Joseph Gordon
Vafakos, William Paul
Vagelos, Pindaros Roy
Vagliano, Alexander Marino
Vaglio-Laurin, Roberto
Vagts, Detlev Frederick
Vague, Harold Raymond
Vahanian, Gabriel
Vail, George Raymond
Vaill, Peter Brown
Vaillant, Geroge Eman
Vaky, Viron Peter
Valbuena-Briones, Angel Julian
Valency, Maurice
Valenstein, Lawrence
Valente, Benita
Valente, Michael Feeney
Valenti, Jack Joseph
Valentine, Herman Edward
Valeo, Francis Ralph
Valeriani, Richard Gerard
Valicenti, Mitchel Joseph
Valk, John Garry
Vallee, Bert Lester
Valley, George Edward, Jr.
Valli, Frankie (Frank Castelluccio)
Valtin, Heinz
Valtin, Rolf
Van Alen, William Laurens
van Altena, William Foster
Van Antwerpen, Franklin John
Vanaria, Louis Michael
Van Artsdalen, Donald West
Van Bortel, Francis John
Van Brunt, Albert Daniel
Van Brunt, Edwin David
Van Brunt, John, Jr.
Van Buren, Clayton H.
van Buren, Paul Matthews
Van Buren, Raeburn
Van Burkalow, Anastasia
Van Buskirk, Alden Lothrop
Vance, Cyrus Roberts
Vance, Forrest Leslie
Vance, John F.
Vance, John Thomas
Vance, Sheldon Baird
Vancil, Richard Franklin
Van Cleve, Ruth Gill
Van Coetsem, Frans Camille Cornelis
Van Cott, Harold Porter
van Croonenburg, E.J.
Vandam, Leroy David
Van Deerlin, Lionel
van de Kamp, Peter
Vandell, Robert Frank
Van de Maele, Albert Camille Louis
VanDemark, Noland Leroy
Vandemark, Robert Goodyear
Vandenberg, Hoyt Sanford, Jr.
van den Haag, Ernest
van den Heuvel, Stanley
vanden Heuvel, William J.
Vanderbilt, Oliver DeGray
Van der Heuvel, Gerry Burch (Mrs. Kenneth Van der Heuvel)
Vander Jagt, Guy
Van der Kloot, William George
van der Kroef, Justus Maria
Vandermark, Robert Earl
Vanderryn, Jack
Vandersall, John Henry
Van der Slice, Austin
Vanderslice, George F.
Vanderslice, Joseph Thomas
Vanderslice, Thomas Aquinas
Vander Velde, Wallace Earl
van der Ven, Arnold Francis Marie
Vander Voort, Dale Gilbert
Van Der Waag, Walter E.
Van DerZee, James
Vanderzell, John Howard
Van Deusen, Glyndon Garlock
van de Velde, Robert Whitsett
Vandeventer, Braden
VanDeventer, John Francis
Vande Wiele, Raymond Laurent
Vandivert, William Wilson
Van Doren, Dorothy Graffe (Mrs. Mark Van Doren)
Vandow, Eva Shribman (Mrs. Jules Vandow)
Van Dusen, Albert Clarence
Van Dusen, Henry Hugh
Van Dusen, Lewis Harlow, Jr.
Van Duzer, Albert Wiencke
Van Dyke, Willard Ames
Vanek, Jaroslav
van Ekris, Anthonie Cornelis
VanFossan, Robert Virgil
Van Fossan, Robert Virgil
Van Gaasbeck, Harry Robert
Van Gelder, Richard George
Van Gelderen, Barbara
VanGraafeiland, Ellsworth Alfred
Van Gundy, Gregory Frank
vanHaeften, Carl Frederick
Van Hamel, Martine
van Hengel, Maarten
Van Hollen, Christopher
Van Horn, Kent Robertson
Van Houten, Franklyn Bosworth
Van Houten, Leonard Erskine
Van Houten, Robert Wallace
Van Houweling, Cornelius Donald
van Itallie, Jean-Claude
Van Itallie, Theodore Bertus
Van Meter, Herbert Ensign
Van Ness, Hendrick Charles
Van Nest, Dean Gillette
Van Norden, Langdon
Van Norden, William E.
Van Nostrand, Morris Abbott, Jr.
Vannoy, Walter Monroe, Jr.
Van Nuys, Francis
Vanocur, Sander
VanPoole, Thomas Bennett, Jr.
Van Rensselaer, Stephen
Van Sant, Gus Greene
Vansant, Nicholas
Van Scott, Eugene Joseph
Van Sinderen, Alfred White
Van Soest, Bert Edward
Van Tassel, Roger Carleton
Van Til, Cornelius
van Urk, J. Blan
Van Veen, Henry George
Van Veen, Stuyvesant
Van Vleck, John Hasbrouck
Van Voorhis, John
Van Voorhis, Steven Coerte
Van Voorhis, Walter Roe
Van Vunakis, Helen
Van Wagenen, Harold William, Jr.
Van Wagenen, Richard Whitmore
Van Wagner, James R.
Van Wormer, Benjamin Francis
Varma, Ranbir
Varrone, Angelo Robert
Vartan, Vartanig Garabed
Vartanian, Vahan
Vasington, Frank Daniel
Vassallo, Thomas Charles
Vassil, Pamela
Vassos, John
Vasta, Bruno Morreale
Vaughan, James Roland
Vaughan, John George, Jr.
Vaughan, Joseph Lee
Vaughan, Samuel Snell
Vaughan, Sarah Lou
Vaughan, Victor Clarence, III
Vaughan, Woodrow Wilson
Vaughn, Jack Hood
Vaughn, Thomas Hunt
Vaupen, Burton
Vavala, Domenic Anthony
Vayda, Andrew Peter
Vayna, Ladislas
Vazquez, Alberto M.
Vazquez, Siro
Veach, Carson Ward
Veals, Ralph Langdon
Vear, Judd Gray
Veatch, Henry Babcock
Vedam, Kuppuswamy
Veenema, Ralph James
Velder, Eli
Velie, Lester
Velikovsky, Immanuel
Velmans, Loet Abraham
Vendler, Helen Hennessy
Venezian, Angelo Ralph
Venezky, Richard Lawrence
Vennard, Edwin
Vento, Bruce Frank
Venturi, Robert
Venza, Jac
Verano, Anthony Frank
Verblaauw, Tunis
Verdery, John Duane
Verdisco, George Michael
Verdon, Gwen (Gwyneth Evelyn)
Verdy, Violette
Vereen, Ben
Verheyen, Egon
Vermeule, Cornelius Clarkson, III
Vermeule, Emily Townsend (Mrs. Cornelius C. Vermeule III)
Vermilye, Dyckman Ware
Vermilyea, David Augustus
Verner, James Melton
Verney, Gilbert
Vernon, Leo
Vernon, Raymond
Vernon, Weston (Wes), III
Veronis, George
Veronis, John James
Veronis, Peter
Verrecchia, Alfred Joseph
Verrett, Shirley
Verrill, Charles Owen, Jr.
Ver Standig, Helen
Very, Donald Leroy
Vest, George Southall
Vestner, Eliot Noble, Jr.
Vette, James Ira
Vetter, Edward Oswald
Vevier, Charles
Vezeau, Sister Jeannette Eva
Vickers, Jon
Vickery, William McCall
Vickrey, Robert Remsen
Vickrey, William Spencer
Victory, Antony Michael
Vidal, Gore
Vidich, Arthur Joseph
Viebranz, Alfred Colville
Vielehr, Jerome Edward
Viener, John David
Viereck, Peter
Vierling, Bernard Julius
Vieser, Milford August
Vieser, Richard William
Vieth, Wolf Randolph
Vigdor, Justin Leonard
Vigier, Francois Claude Denis
Vigilante, Joseph Louis
Vila, George Raymond
Villa, Joseph Emil
Villarreal, Carlos Castaneda
Villars, Felix Marc Hermann
Villee, Claude Alvin, Jr.
Villella, Edward Joseph
Villers, Philippe
Villers, Raymond
Vincent, Donald Edward Perry
Vincent, Helen
Vincent, Lewis Adam
Vincent, William Shafer
Vinci, Piero
Vincow, Gershon
Vine, Allyn Collins
Vine, Richard David
Viner, Arthur William
Vineyard, George Hoagland

Vinick, Bernard Sidney	Wadsworth, Dyer Seymour	Wall, Howard Elden	Wang, Hao	Wasserman, Jack	Weber, J. Sherwood
Vining, Daniel Rutledge	Wadsworth, Francis Thomas	Wall, Kelvin A.	Wang, Hsien Chung	Wasserman, Louis Robert	Weber, Samuel
Vining, Elizabeth Gray	Wadsworth, Frank Whittemore	Wall, Nathan Sanders	Wang, Jui Hsin	Wasserman, Paul	Webster, Bethuel Matthew
Vink, Pieter Carel	Wadsworth, Joseph	Wall, Shannon Jerome	Wang, Ping Chun	Wasserman, Robert Harold	Webster, Dwight Albert
Vinson, Fred Moore, Jr.	Wadsworth, Robert Haigh	Wallace, Andrew Hugh	Wang, Shih Chun	Wasson, Houston Hutchinson	Webster, Eleanor Rudd
Vinson, Jack Roger	Waehler, Frank James	Wallace, Anthony Edward	Wang, Shih Yi	Waterbury, Lester Elba	Webster, Frederick Seth
Viola, Alfred	Wagenknecht, Edward	Wallace, Anthony Francis Clarke	Wangeman, Frank G.	Waterhouse, Keith	Webster, George Drury
Viola, Herman Joseph	Wager, Walter Herman	Wallace, Bruce	Wapiennik, Carl Francis	Waterman, Bernard Eugene	Webster, Henry deForest
Viorst, Milton	Waggoner, Leland Tate	Wallace, Carl S.	Wapner, Seymour	Waters, David Rogers	Webster, Larry Russell
Vipond, David Spruks	Waggoner, Margaret Ann	Wallace, Clayton Morey	Ward, Albert Timothy	Waters, Edward Neighbor	Webster, Maurie
Viscardi, Henry, Jr.	Waggoner, Paul Edward	Wallace, David Alexander	Ward, Alfred Dudley	Waters, Eugene Paul	Webster, Ronald Lee
Viscuglia, Felix Alfred	Waggonner, Joe David, Jr.	Wallace, David William	Ward, Arthur George	Waters, George Wilbur	Webster, Stokely
Visich, Marian, Jr.	Wagman, Nicholas Emory	Wallace, DeWitt	Ward, Brien Dale	Waters, Herbert Ogden	Webster, Vera Rouse
Vitale, Alberto Aldo	Wagner, Alan Cyril	Wallace, Edward Bruce	Ward, Carl Small	Waters, William Henry, Jr.	Webster, William Merle, Jr.
Vitale, Michael Anthony	Wagner, Charles Abraham	Wallace, Felix Anthony	Ward, Charles	Waters, William Wadsworth	Wechsberg, Joseph
Vitt, Sam B.	Wagner, Edmund Francis	Wallace, George Edward	Ward, David Harris	Watkin, William Ward, Jr.	Wechsler, Henry
Vivian, Johnson Edward	Wagner, Edward Harrison	Wallace, George Egbert	Ward, Douglas Turner	Watkins, David Roy	Wechsler, Herbert
Viviano, Bartholomew Joseph	Wagner, Edward Kurt	Wallace, J. Brougham	Ward, Frederick Champion	Watkins, Frederick Davis	Wecht, Cyril Harrison
Vivona, Stefano	Wagner, Herman Block	Wallace, Joan Edaire Scott	Ward, Hiley Henry	Watkins, James David	Wechter, Vivienne Thaul
Vizza, Robert Francis	Wagner, Norman Otto	Wallace, John	Ward, Howard Hoffman	Watkins, John Chester Anderson	Weckesser, Ernest Prosper, Jr. (E. C. Lane)
Vlahakos, Viola James	Wagner, Peter Ewing	Wallace, John Clements	Ward, Howard Leon	Watkins, Ralph James	Weddington, Sarah Ragle
Vodicka, Ruth Kessler (Chai)	Wagner, Philip Marshall	Wallace, Kenneth Donald	Ward, John Milton	Watkins, Robert Dorsey	Weddle, Stephen Shields
Vogel, Charles A., Jr.	Wagner, Robert Earl	Wallace, Lila Acheson	Ward, John William	Watkins, Thomas Prescott	Wedel, Cynthia Clark
Vogel, Ezra F.	Wagner, Robert F.	Wallace, Malcolm Vincent Timothy	Ward, Joseph Simeon	Watkins, Wesley Wade	Wedel, Paul George
Vogel, Henry James	Wagner, Robert Roderick	Wallace, Mike	Ward, Lynd Kendall	Watson, Alfred Michael	Wedel, Waldo Rudolph
Vogel, Herbert Davis	Wagner, Robert Wanner	Wallace, Mimi	Ward, Paul Langdon	Watson, Alfred Nelson	Wedemeyer, Albert Coady
Vogel, John H.	Wagner, Walter Frederick, Jr.	Wallace, Phyllis Ann	Ward, Philip Henry, III	Watson, Arthur Richard	Wee, Paul Allen
Vogelstein, John L.	Wagner, William L.	Wallace, Robert Ash	Ward, Ralph E., Jr.	Watson, Barbara M.	Weed, William Henry
Vogt, Evon Zartman, Jr.	Wagoner, Harold Eugene	Wallace, Spencer Miller, Jr.	Ward, Robert George	Watson, Charles Flagler	Weeden, Alan Norman
Vohs, Thomas Raymond	Wahl, Milton Heins	Wallace, Thomas C(hristopher)	Ward, Robert Joseph	Watson, Donald Clarke	Weedon, William Stone
Voigt, Garth K.	Wahl, Paul	Wallace, Thomas P.	Ward, Robert Lyle	Watson, Douglas Fleming	Weeks, Alice Mary (Mrs. Albert W. Weeks)
Volcker, Paul A.	Wahrsager, Sigmund	Wallace, Walter L.	Ward, Rodman, Jr.	Watson, Geoffrey Stuart	Weeks, David Frank
Volkman, (Rosalyn) Elizabeth	Wainio, Walter	Wallace, Willard Mosher	Ward, Roger Coursen	Watson, George Henry	Weeks, Edward Augustus
Volkmer, Harold L.	Wainwright, Carroll Livingston, Jr.	Wallace, William, III	Ward, Thomas Greydon	Watson, Jack H., Jr.	Weeks, John Wingate
Volle, Robert Leon	Wainwright, Nicholas Biddle	Wallace, William Edward	Ward, Virgil Scott	Watson, James Dewey	Weeks, Lewis George
Vollmar, John Raymond	Wainwright, Stuyvesant, II	Wallace, William Huston	Ward, William Binnington	Watson, James Lopez	Weeks, Richard Ralph
Vollmer, William Elwell	Waite, Charles Morrison	Wallach, Allan Henry	Ward, William Francis, Jr.	Watson, James S., Jr.	Weems, Katharine Lane
Volner, Jill Wine	Waite, Robert George Leeson	Wallach, Anne Jackson	Ward, William Frazee	Watson, Joseph John	Wegener, Peter Paul
Volpe, Edmond Loris	Waite, Robert Montrose	Wallach, Edward Eliot	Ward, William Ralph, Jr.	Watson, Neale Wheeler	Wegman, Harold Hugh
Volpe, Raymond France	Waite, Stephen Holden	Wallach, Eli	Warde, George Andres	Watson, Robert Fletcher	Wehle, John Louis
vom Baur, Francis Trowbridge	Waite, William Wiley	Wallach, Hans	Wardeberg, Helen L.	Watson, Robert Tanner	Wei, James
von Arx, William Stelling	Waith, Eugene Mersereau	Wallach, Ira	Warden, Clarence Arthur, Jr.	Watson, Roy Garrett	Weicker, Lowell Palmer, Jr.
von Auw, Alvin	Wakefield, Dan	Wallach, Ira David	Warden, Richard Dana	Watson, Stuart Dade	Weidner, Richard Tilghman
von Beckh, Harald J.	Wakefield, Walter Leggett	Wallach, Morton Bertram	Wardlow, Elwood M.	Watson, Thomas J., Jr.	Weidner, Roswell Theodore
Vonberg, William George	Wakeham, Helmut Richard Rae	Wallach, Sidney	Wardwell, Allen	Watson, Winsor Hays, Jr.	Weigand, Richard Stuart
von der Heyden, Ingolf Mueller	Wakeland, Henry H.	Wallechinsky, David	Ware, Harris Oliver	Watt, Douglas (Benjamin)	Weiger, John George
Von Eckardt, Wolf	Wakelin, James Henry, Jr.	Walleigh, Robert Shuler	Ware, John Haines, III	Watt, Graham Wend	Weiger, Ralph James
Von Erffa, Helmut Hartmann	Wakeman, Rick	Wallendorf, Paul E.	Ware, John Rosswork	Watt, James	Weigl, Henry
von Euler, Leo Hans	Waksman, Byron Halsted	Wallenstein, Alfred Franz	Ware, Thaddeus Van	Watt, William Joseph	Weigle, Richard Daniel
Von Feldt, Elmer	Walbesser, Henry Herman, Jr.	Waller, Edward Carson, III	Warfel, Ruth Elizabeth	Watt, William Whyte	Weil, Frank Alan
von Furstenberg, Betsy	Walbridge, Smith Starr	Waller, John Henry	Warfield, George	Wattel, Harold Louis	Weil, Gilbert Harry
Von Furstenberg, Diane Simone Michelle	Walch, John Weston	Waller, Theodore	Warga, Jack	Wattenberg, Ben J.	Weil, Kurt Hermann
von Gronicka, André	Wald, George	Waller, Wilhelmine Kirby (Mrs. Thomas Mercer Waller)	Warga, Mary Elizabeth	Watters, Frank Carleton	Weil, Lisl
von Groschwitz, Gustave	Wald, Haskell Philip	Wallhauser, George Marvin	Warhol, Andy	Watts, André	Weil, Stephen Edward
von Hoffman, Nicholas	Wald, Niel	Wallich, Henry Christopher	Waring, Fred M.	Watts, Charles Henry, II	Weilbacher, William Manning
Von Kann, Clifton Ferdinand	Wald, Palmer Bernard	Wallis, Charles Langworthy	Warlick, Robert Patterson	Watts, Daniel Thomas	Weill, Claudia
Von Klemperer, Alfred Herbert	Wald, Patricia McGowan	Wallis, Frank Brower	Warman, John Boyle	Watts, David A., Jr.	Weill, Georges Gustave
von Klemperer, Klemens	Wald, Richard C.	Wallis, George Edward	Warne, Colston Estey	Watts, Edward Everett, Jr.	Weill, Harold
Von Kutzleben, Siegfried Edwin	Wald, Robert Lewis	Wallis, Gordon Todd	Warneke, Heinz	Watts, Franklin Mowry	Weill, Robert Julian
Von Laue, Theodore Herman	Wald, Samuel Stanley	Wallis, Wilson Allen	Warner, Aaron W.	Watts, Glenn Ellis	Weill, Sanford I.
von Lehmden-Maslin, Alys Augusta	Wald, Sylvia	Wallop, Malcolm	Warner, Beverly Walden	Watts, Henry Miller, Jr.	Weimar, Karl Siegfried
von Mehren, Arthur Taylor	Waldau, Walter F.	Wallwork, Gealy Weston	Warner, Bradford Arnold	Watts, James Winston	Wein, George Theodore
von Moltke, Wilhelm Viggo	Walden, Amelia Elizabeth (Mrs. John William Harmon)	Walrath, John Frederick	Warner, Charles Arthur	Waugh, James Corwin	Weinberg, Chester
Vonnegut, Kurt, Jr.	Walden, Stanley	Walser, Mackenzie	Warner, Francis James	Waugh, John Stewart	Weinberg, Edward
von Ringelheim, Paul Helmut	Waldheim, Kurt	Walsh, Cornelius Robert	Warner, Helene Bliss	Wax, Bernard	Weinberg, Herschel Mayer
Von Stade, Frederica	Waldhorn, Herbert Francis	Walsh, Ethel Bent	Warner, John Christian	Waxman, Henry Arnold	Weinberg, John Livingston
von Summer, Alexander Carl, Jr.	Waldman, Anne Lesley	Walsh, George William	Warner, John Edward	Way, Alva Otis	Weinberg, Martin Herbert
Voorde, Frances	Waldman, Diane	Walsh, Grace Jayne Kelleher (Mrs. John Edward Walsh)	Warner, John William	Wayland, Russell Gibson, Jr.	Weinberg, Robert Leonard
Voorhees, Arthur Bostwick, Jr.	Waldo, (Clifford) Dwight	Walsh, Grace Jayne Kelleher (Mrs. John Edward Walsh)	Warner, Kenneth Wilson, Jr.	Wayland, Sloan Rigdon	Weinberg, Sidney James, Jr.
Voorhees, Enders McClumpha	Waldron, Hicks Benjamin, Jr.	Walsh, James Aloysius	Warner, Rawleigh, Jr.	Wayne, Joel Robert	Weinberg, Steven
Vooys, Daniel William	Waldron, William Augustus	Walsh, James Edward	Warner, Robert Cadman	Waynick, Arthur Henry	Weinberger, Harold
Vore, Kenneth Lanning	Waldrop, Frank Campbell	Walsh, James Jerome	Warner, Sam Bass, Jr.	Ways, Max	Weinblatt, Myron Benjamin
Vorenberg, James	Waldrop, Gideon William	Walsh, James Joseph	Warner, Theodore Kugler, Jr.	Wean, Raymond John, Jr.	Weiner, Arnold Murray
Vorspan, Albert	Wales, Walter D.	Walsh, James Paul	Warner, Brother Thomas William	Wear, James Smith	Weiner, Charles
Vos, Frank	Walfred, Hugo Anderson	Walsh, John Walter	Warner, Walter Edwards, Jr.	Wearly, William Levi	Weiner, Charles R.
Vosbeck, William Frederick, Jr.	Walgren, Doug	Walsh, Julia Margaret Curry (Mrs. Thomas M. Walsh)	Warner, Wellman Joel	Weatherbee, Artemus Edwin	Weiner, Jerome Harris
Vosburgh, Frederick George	Walker, Alice	Walsh, Lawrence Edward	Warner, William Whitesides	Weathersby, William Henry	Weiner, John Clarence, Jr.
Vose, Clement Ellery	Walker, Angus Lightfoot	Walsh, Margaret Ellen Walsh (Mrs. James Thomas Walsh)	Warnke, Paul Culliton	Weaver, A. Vernon	Weiner, Myron
Vose, Robert Churchill, Jr.	Walker, B.J.	Walsh, Patrick Craig	Warntz, William	Weaver, Charles Henry	Weiner, Walter Herman
Voss, Charlotte Elizabeth	Walker, Beth Bready	Walsh, Peter Joseph	Warren, Albert	Weaver, Charles Steele	Weiner, Warren
Voss, James Frederick	Walker, Charles Allen	Walsh, Ulysses (Jim)	Warren, Austin	Weaver, Earl Sidney	Weinfeld, Edward
Voss, James Milton	Walker, Charles Arthur, Jr.	Walsh, Warren Bartlett	Warren, Charles	Weaver, Edwin Snell	Weingarten, Hilde (Mrs. Arthur Kevess)
Voth, Robert Clayton	Walker, Charles Leland	Walsh, William Bertalan	Warren, Edus Houston, Jr.	Weaver, Frederick S.	Weingarten, Murray
Voultsos-Vourtzis, Pericles Count	Walker, Charls Edward	Walsh, William Francis	Warren, Frederick Hayes	Weaver, Fritz William	Weinhouse, Sidney
Vreeland, Diana Dalziel	Walker, Clinton W.	Walsh, William Raymond, Jr.	Warren, Harold Hubbard	Weaver, James	Weinig, Robert Walter
Vrenios, Anastasios	Walker, Cora T.	Walske, M(ax) Carl, Jr.	Warren, Jack Hamilton	Weaver, John Borland	Weinman, Robert Alexander
Vroom, Victor Harold	Walker, David Allen Hatch	Walt, Sherman Abbott	Warren, John Cushman	Weaver, John Boyd	Weinreb, Lloyd Lobell
Vrooman, Warren Terry	Walker, Donald Anthony	Waltemade, Henry George	Warren, Louis Bancel	Weaver, Kenneth Newcomer	Weinrich, Carl
Waage, John Arthur	Walker, Donald Ezzell	Walter, C. Richard	Warren, Lucian Crissey	Weaver, Narvin Blake	Weins, Leo Matthew
Waage, Karl Mensch	Walker, Donald Gregory	Walter, F. Austin	Warren, Matthew	Weaver, Paul Raymond	Weinstein, Alvin Seymour
Waalkes, T. Phillip	Walker, Eric Arthur	Walter, Henry Glendon, Jr.	Warren, Richard	Weaver, Robert Clifton	Weinstein, Bernard M.
Wachenfeld, William Thomas	Walker, Everett	Walter, James Elias	Warren, Richard Kearney	Weaver, Warren	Weinstein, Frederic Daniel
Wachman, Harold Yehuda	Walker, George Gholson	Walters, Barbara	Warren, Robert Penn	Weaver, Warren, Jr.	Weinstein, George
Wachman, Marvin	Walker, Gordon Arlon	Walters, George Merle	Warren, S. Reid, Jr.	Weaver, Warren Eldred	Weinstein, Herbert
Wachob, Robert Milton	Walker, Herman, Jr.	Walters, Johnnie McKeiver	Warren, Shields	Weaver, William Merritt, Jr.	Weinstein, I. Bernard
Wachs, Moses	Walker, James Calvin	Walters, Leonard Moore	Warriner, David Dortch	Weaver, Winston Odell	Weinstein, Jack B.
Wachsler, Robert Alan	Walker, James Carter	Walters, Raymond, Jr.	Warring, Frederick Chauncey, Jr.	Webb, Charles	Weinstein, Leo
Wachtel, Harry H.	Walker, James Herron	Walters, Richard J.	Warrington, Howard Moody	Webb, Charles Albert	Weinstein, Lewis H.
Wachtell, Richard Lloyd	Walker, John Luther	Walters, Robert Leo	Warschauer, Murray H.	Webb, Charles Richard, Jr.	Weinstein, Louis
Wachtler, Sol	Walker, John T.	Walters, Walter Henry	Warshaw, Jules J.	Webb, George Arthur	Weinstein, Peter David
Wacker, Louis Henry Bud	Walker, Joseph	Walther, Charles Rolland	Warshaw, Leon J.	Webb, Hamilton Brookholding	Weinstein, Roy
Wacker, Peter Oscar	Walker, Luther Loneith	Walther, John Henry	Warshaw, Saul Leon	Webb, James Edwin	Weinstein, Steve
Wacker, Warren Ernest Clyde	Walker, Mallory Elton	Walton, Clarence	Warthen, Harry Justice, Jr.	Webb, James Lewis Adrian	Weintraub, Lionel
Waddell, Alfred Moore, Jr.	Walker, Mort	Walton, James M.	Warthin, Aldred Scott, Jr.	Webb, James Prevost	Weintraub, Michael Ira
Waddell, C(harles) Eugene	Walker, Norma Elizabeth Peden	Walton, John	Warthin, Thomas Angell	Webb, Kempton Evans	Weintraub, Monroe Joseph
Waddell, James	Walker, Oliver Mallory	Walton, Richard Eugene	Wartik, Thomas	Webb, Ralph Junior	Weintraub, Stanley
Wadden, Robert Vincent	Walker, Peter Cuyler	Walton, William Griffin	Wartofsky, Marx William	Webb, Richard Pierce	Weintraub, Wiktor
Wade, James O'Shea	Walker, Philip Leroy, Jr.	Waltz, Joseph McKendree	Warwick, John Petersen	Webb, Robert Kiefer	Weir, John Marshall
Wade, Melvin Rogers	Walker, Richard David	Walworth, Arthur	Wasby, Milton Charles	Webb, Thomas Crawford	Weis, Joseph Francis, Jr.
Wade, Richard Clement	Walker, Robert Smith	Walworth, Edward Henry, Jr.	Washburn, Abbott McConnell	Webb, Watt Wetmore	Weis, Konrad Max
Wade, Robert Hirsch Beard	Walker, Russell Wagner	Walworth, Theodore Holton, Jr.	Washburn, Henry Bradford, Jr.	Webb, William Hess	Weisberger, Barbara
Wadelton, Francis Bacon	Walker, Samuel Sloan, Jr.	Walzer, Michael Laban	Washburn, John Henry	Webb, William Loyd, Jr.	Weisburger, John Hans
Wadleigh, John Remey	Walker, Vincent Henry	Walzer, William Charles	Washburn, Wilcomb Edward	Webber, Christopher A.	Weiser, Norman Sidney
Wadleigh, Kenneth R.	Walker, Wilbert Alden	Wampler, William Creed	Washington, Bennetta Bullock	Webber, Donald Wedgwood	Weisgall, Hugo David
Wadleigh, Winthrop	Walker, Wilbur Gordon	Wandycz, Piotr Stefan	Washington, Walter E.	Webber, Gordon	Weisinger, Herbert
Wadley, Ellen Pearl	Walker, William Nickerson	Wang, An	Wasiele, Harry W., Jr.	Webber, Payson Rex	Weisl, Edwin L., Jr.
Wadlington, Walter James	Walker, Winthrop Brooks	Wang, Arthur Woods	Wasilewski, Vincent Thomas	Webber, William R. (Bill)	Weismiller, Edward Ronald
Wadmond, Lowell Curtis	Walker, Wyatt Tee		Waskow, Arthur Irwin	Weber, Alfons	Weiss, Andrew
Wadsworth, Christopher	Walkley, Lawrence E.		Wasser, Henry	Weber, Alfred	Weiss, Bernard
	Wall, Alexander James		Wasserman, Albert	Weber, Annemarie	Weiss, David
	Wall, Donald Reed		Wasserman, Dale	Weber, Arnold R.	Weiss, Edwin
			Wasserman, Edel	Weber, Ben Brian	Weiss, Egon Arthur
			Wasserman, Harry H.	Weber, Eugene William	Weiss, Harry
				Weber, Gerald Joseph	
				Weber, Gustave Walter	